Elizabeth Mortimer ("Kate") m. Henry Percy ("Hotspur") 1364–1403 — Henry, Earl of Northumberland 1394–1455

EDWARD IV 1442–1483 (1461–83) m. Elizabeth Woodville d. 1492 — EDWARD V 1470–1483 (1483)

Richard, Duke of York 1472–1483

Elizabeth of York 1465–1503 m. HENRY VII (below)

Edmund, Earl of Rutland 1443–1460

Edmund Mortimer†

George, Duke of Clarence 1449–1478 m. Isabel Neville (below)

D0026130

Anne Mortimer m. Richard, Earl of Cambridge (below) — Richard Plantagenet, Duke of York 1411–1460 m. Cicely Neville (below)

RICHARD III 1452–1485 (1483–85) m. Anne Neville (below)

Edward, Prince of Wales

HENRY V 1387–1422 (1413–22) m. Catherine 1401–1437

HENRY VI 1421–1471 (1422–61) m. Margaret of Anjou d. 1482

Edward, Prince of Wales 1453–1471 m. Anne Neville (below)

Arthur m. Catherine of Aragon (below)

Margaret m. James IV of Scotland — James V of Scotland

Mary, Queen of Scots

JAMES I 1566–1625 (1603–25)

Thomas, Duke of Clarence d. 1421

John of Lancaster, Duke of Bedford 1389–1435

Humphrey, Duke of Gloucester 1391–1447 m. Eleanor Cobham d. 1454

Margaret Beaufort m. Edmund Tudor, Earl of Richmond — HENRY VII 1457–1509 (1485–1509) m. Elizabeth of York (above)

HENRY VIII 1491–1547 (1509–47) m. Catherine of Aragon

John Beaufort, Duke of Somerset 1403–1444

MARY I 1516–1558 (1553–58) m. Philip of Spain

m. Anne Boleyn

Edmund Beaufort, Duke of Somerset 1406–1455 — Henry Beaufort, Duke of Somerset 1436–1464‡

ELIZABETH I 1533–1603 (1558–1603)

Isabel Neville d. 1476 m. George, Duke of Clarence (above)

m. Jane Seymour

EDWARD VI 1537–1553 (1547–53)

Richard Neville, Earl of Salisbury 1400–1460 — Richard Neville, Earl of Warwick 1428–1471

John Neville, Marquess of Montague d. 1471

Anne Neville d. 1485 m. Edward, Prince of Wales (above)

m. RICHARD III (above)

m. Anne of Cleves

m. Katherine Howard

m. Katherine Parr

Cicely Neville m. Richard Plantagenet, Duke of York (above)

Mary m. Charles Brandon — Frances

Jane Grey 1537–1554

Humphrey, Duke of Buckingham 1402–1460 — Humphrey Stafford d. 1455 — Henry, Duke of Buckingham 1454?–1483 — Edward, Duke of Buckingham 1478–1521

RICHARD II, 1377–99   RICHARD was the eldest son of EDWARD THE BLACK PRINCE, himself the eldest son of KING EDWARD III, who ruled England from 1327 to 1377. When the BLACK PRINCE died in battle in France in 1376, RICHARD became the legitimate heir to the throne. He ruled from EDWARD's death in 1377 until he was deposed in 1399 by HENRY BOLINGBROKE, the eldest son of JOHN OF GAUNT, DUKE OF LANCASTER. Because he was the fourth son of EDWARD III, GAUNT and his Lancastrian descendants had weaker hereditary claims to the throne than did RICHARD. When deposed, RICHARD had no children to succeed him, but he recognized EDMUND MORTIMER, FIFTH EARL OF MARCH, as his heir presumptive. This MORTIMER was descended from LIONEL, DUKE OF CLARENCE, the third son of EDWARD III, and therefore also had stronger hereditary claims to the throne than did BOLINGBROKE. SHAKESPEARE combined this MORTIMER with his uncle EDMUND MORTIMER, who married OWAIN GLYNDŴR'S DAUGHTER.

HENRY IV, 1399–1413   HENRY BOLINGBROKE, eldest son of JOHN OF GAUNT, seized the throne from RICHARD II in 1399. When HENRY died in 1413, he was succeeded by his eldest son, PRINCE HAL, who became HENRY V.

HENRY V, 1413–22   HENRY V became king in 1413 and reigned until his death in 1422. He was succeeded by his son, HENRY VI.

HENRY VI, 1422–61   HENRY VI was less than one year old when he succeeded his father, HENRY V. In the young king's minority, his uncle HUMPHREY, DUKE OF GLOUCESTER, was named Lord Protector, and the kingdom was ruled by an aristocratic council. HENRY VI assumed personal authority in 1437. He was deposed in 1461 by his third cousin, who was crowned EDWARD IV. HENRY was murdered in 1471.

EDWARD IV, 1461–83   EDWARD, the eldest son of RICHARD, DUKE OF YORK, seized the throne from HENRY VI in 1461. His Yorkist claim to the throne derived from his grandmother, ANNE MORTIMER, who was descended from LIONEL, third son of EDWARD III, and was sister to that EDMUND MORTIMER recognized by RICHARD II as his heir presumptive; EDWARD IV's grandfather, RICHARD, EARL OF CAMBRIDGE, was the son of EDMUND OF LANGLEY, fifth son of EDWARD III. EDWARD IV reigned until his death in 1483. His heir was his eldest son (EDWARD), but the throne was usurped by his brother RICHARD, DUKE OF GLOUCESTER.

RICHARD III, 1483–85   RICHARD III was the youngeer brother of EDWARD IV. After the death of EDWARD IV in 1483, RICHARD prevented the coronation of EDWARD V with a claim of illegitimacy and succeeded to the throne himself. EDWARD and his younger brother, RICHARD, DUKE OF YORK, were murdered in the Tower of London. RICHARD III was killed at the Battle of Bosworth Field in 1485, and the kingdom fell to the victor, HENRY TUDOR, EARL OF RICHMOND.

HENRY VII, 1485–1509   HENRY TUDOR seized the throne from RICHARD III in 1485. He was descended from JOHN OF GAUNT by JOHN's third marriage, with CATHERINE SWYNFORD. He married ELIZABETH, daughter of EDWARD IV, uniting the houses of Lancaster and York. He died in 1509 and was succeeded by his son, HENRY VIII.

HENRY VIII, 1509–47   HENRY was the second son of HENRY VII. His older brother, ARTHUR, died in 1502. HENRY VIII's first wife was CATHERINE OF ARAGON, who bore his daughter MARY. His second wife, ANNE BOLEYN, was the mother of ELIZABETH. His third wife, JANE SEYMOUR, bore him a son, who succeeded to the throne as EDWARD VI after HENRY VIII died in 1547.

EDWARD VI, 1547–53   EDWARD VI was nine years old when he became king. From 1547 to 1549, the realm was governed by a Lord Protector, the DUKE OF SOMERSET; power then passed to JOHN DUDLEY, DUKE OF NORTHUMBERLAND. When EDWARD VI died in 1553, NORTHUMBERLAND attempted unsuccessfully to prevent the succession of MARY TUDOR by installing as queen his daughter-in-law, LADY JANE GREY, a great-granddaughter of HENRY VII.

MARY I, 1553–58   MARY, daughter of HENRY VIII and his first wife, CATHERINE OF ARAGON, came to the throne in 1553. She married KING PHILIP OF SPAIN but died childless. She was succeeded by her half sister, ELIZABETH.

ELIZABETH I, 1558–1603   ELIZABETH, the daughter of HENRY VIII and his second wife, ANNE BOLEYN, became queen after the death of her half sister, MARY, in 1558. She ruled until her death in 1603. She was succeeded by her cousin JAMES.

JAMES I, 1603–1625   JAMES VI OF SCOTLAND became JAMES I OF ENGLAND in 1603. His claim to the throne of England derived from his great-grandmother, MARGARET TUDOR, a daughter of HENRY VII who married JAMES IV OF SCOTLAND. JAMES ruled England and Scotland until his death in 1625; he was succeeded by his son, CHARLES I.

God — Creator
monarch — state,

THE NORTON
SHAKESPEARE

BASED ON THE OXFORD EDITION

SECOND EDITION

3214

*The original Oxford Text on which this
edition is based was prepared by*

Stanley Wells
Gary Taylor
General Editors

John Jowett
William Montgomery

The Norton Shakespeare, Second Edition, is based on *William Shakespeare: The Complete Works*,
Second Edition, and is published by arrangement with Oxford University Press,
with additional material from W. W. Norton & Company, Inc.

THE NORTON SHAKESPEARE

Based on the Oxford Edition

SECOND EDITION

Stephen Greenblatt, *General Editor*
HARVARD UNIVERSITY

Walter Cohen
CORNELL UNIVERSITY

Jean E. Howard
COLUMBIA UNIVERSITY

Katharine Eisaman Maus
UNIVERSITY OF VIRGINIA

With an Essay on the Shakespearean stage
by Andrew Gurr

W·W·NORTON & COMPANY · NEW YORK · LONDON

W. W. Norton & Company has been independent since its founding in 1923, when William Warder Norton and Mary D. Herter Norton first published lectures delivered at the People's Institute, the adult education division of New York City's Cooper Union. The Nortons soon expanded their program beyond the Institute, publishing books by celebrated academics from America and abroad. By mid-century, the two major pillars of Norton's publishing program—trade books and college texts—were firmly established. In the 1950s, the Norton family transferred control of the company to its employees, and today—with a staff of four hundred and a comparable number of trade, college, and professional titles published each year—W. W. Norton & Company stands as the largest and oldest publishing house owned wholly by its employees.

Editor: Julia Reidhead
Manuscript editor: Carol Flechner
Electronic media editor: Eileen Connell
Editorial assistant: Rivka Genesen
Production manager: Diane O'Connor
Photo research: Rivka Genesen
Interior design: Antonina Krass
Managing editor, College: Marian Johnson

Copyright © 2008, 1997 by W. W. Norton & Company, Inc.
Text and some commentaries copyright © 1986, 2005 by Oxford University Press

Composition by Binghamton Valley Composition.
Manufacturing by R. R. Donnelley.

Library of Congress Cataloging-in-Publication Data

Shakespeare, William, 1564–1616.
The Norton Shakespeare / Stephen Greenblatt, general editor ; Walter Cohen, Jean E. Howard, Katharine Eisaman Maus [editors] ; with an essay on the Shakespearean stage by Andrew Gurr. — 2nd ed.
p. cm.
"Based on the Oxford edition."
Includes bibliographical references and index.
ISBN: 978-0-393-92991-1
I. Greenblatt, Stephen, 1943– II. Cohen, Walter, 1949– III. Howard, Jean E. (Jean Elizabeth), 1948– IV. Maus, Katharine Eisaman, 1955– V. Gurr, Andrew.
VI. Title.
PR2754.G74 2008
822.3'3—dc22
2007046599

W. W. Norton & Company, Inc., 500 Fifth Avenue, New York, NY 10110
www.wwnorton.com

W. W. Norton & Company Ltd., Castle House, 75/76 Wells Street, London W1T 3QT

3 4 5 6 7 8 9 0

Contents

GENERAL INTRODUCTION   1
Stephen Greenblatt

THE COMPLETE WORKS   101

Appendices   3287

DOCUMENTS 3299

TIMELINE 3322

Contents by Genre

Comedies

Histories

Tragedies

Romances

Poetry

Lost Plays

Illustrations

Preface

Shakespeare's principal medium, the drama, was thoroughly collaborative, and it involved as well continual efforts at revision and renewal. It seems appropriate, then, that this edition of his works is itself the result of sustained collaboration and revision. Two lists of editors' names on the title-page spread hint at the collaboration that has brought to fruition the *Norton Shakespeare*. But the title page does not tell the full history of this project. The text on which the *Norton Shakespeare* is based was published in both modern-spelling and original-spelling versions by Oxford University Press, in 1986. Under the general editorship of Stanley Wells and Gary Taylor, the Oxford text was a thorough rethinking of the entire body of Shakespeare's works, the most far-reaching and innovative revision of the traditional canon in centuries. When many classroom instructors who wanted to introduce their students to the works of Shakespeare through a modern text expressed a need for the pedagogical apparatus they have come to expect in an edition oriented toward students, Norton negotiated with Oxford to assemble an editorial team of its own to prepare the necessary teaching materials around the existing Oxford text. Hence ensued a collaboration of two publishers and two editorial teams.

To what extent is this the *Norton Shakespeare* and to what extent the Oxford text? Introductions (both the General Introduction and those to individual plays and poems), footnotes, glosses, bibliographies, genealogies, annals, maps, documents, and illustrations have all been the responsibility of the Norton team. Andrew Gurr's much-admired essay on the London theater in Shakespeare's time, specially commissioned for the *Norton Shakespeare*, has been moved in this second edition to the front matter.

The textual notes and variants derive for the most part from the work of the Oxford team, especially as represented in *William Shakespeare: A Textual Companion* (Oxford University Press, 1987), a remarkably comprehensive explanation of editorial decisions that is herewith strongly recommended to instructors as a valuable companion to this volume. Several of the textual notes—those to *The First Part of Henry the Sixth*, Various Poems, *The Two Noble Kinsmen*, *The Merry Wives of Windsor*, *Troilus and Cressida*, The Sonnets and "A Lover's Complaint"—have been substantially updated in the current edition, and all Textual Variants are now gathered in an appendix.

The Oxford text is widely available and already well known to scholars. A few words here may help clarify the extent of our fidelity to that text and the nature of the collaboration that has brought about this volume. The Oxford editors have profited from the massive and sustained attention accorded their edition by Shakespeare scholars across the globe, and of course they have continued to participate actively in the ongoing scholarly discussion about the nature of Shakespeare's text. In the reprintings of the Oxford volumes and in various articles over the past years, the Oxford editors have made a number of refinements of the edition they originally published. Such changes have been incorporated silently here. A small number of other changes made by the Norton team, however, were not part of the Oxford editors' design and were only accepted by them after we reached, through lengthy consultation, a mutual understanding about the nature, purpose, and intended audience of this volume. In all such changes, our main concern was for the classroom; we wished to make fully and clearly available the scholarly innovation and freshness of the Oxford text, while at the same time making certain that this was a superbly useful teaching text. It is a pleasure here to record, on behalf of the Norton team, our gratitude for the personal and professional generosity of the Oxford editors in offering advice and entertaining arguments in our common goal of providing the best student Shakespeare for our times. The Norton changes to the Oxford text are various, but in only a few instances are they major. The following brief notes are sufficient to summarize all of these changes, which are also indicated in appropriate play introductions, footnotes, or textual notes.

1. The Oxford editors, along with other scholars, have strenuously argued—in both the Oxford text and elsewhere—that the now-familiar text of *King Lear*, so nearly omnipresent in our classrooms as to seem unquestionably authoritative but in reality dating from the work of Alexander Pope (1723) and Lewis Theobald (1733), represents a wrongheaded conflation of two distinct versions of the play: Shakespeare's original creation as printed in the 1608 Quarto and his substantial revision as printed in the First Folio (1623). The Oxford text, therefore, prints both *The History of King Lear* and *The Tragedy of King Lear*. Norton follows suit, but where Oxford presents these two texts sequentially, we print them on facing pages. While each version may be read independently, and to ensure this we have provided glosses and footnotes for each, the substantial points of difference between the two are immediately apparent and available for comparison. But even many who agree with the scholarly argument for the two texts of *Lear* nevertheless favor making available a conflated text, the text on which innumerable performances of the play have been based and on which a huge body of literary criticism has been written. With the reluctant acquiescence, therefore, of the Oxford editors, we have included a conflated *Lear*, a text that has no part in the Oxford canon and that has been edited by Barbara K. Lewalski of Harvard University rather than by Gary Taylor, the editor of the Oxford *Lears*.

The Norton Shakespeare, then, includes three separate texts of *King Lear*. The reader can compare them, understand the role of editors in constructing the texts we now call Shakespeare's, explore in considerable detail the kinds of decisions that playwrights, editors, and printers make and remake, witness firsthand the historical transformation of what might at first glance seem fixed and unchanging. The *Norton Shakespeare* offers extraordinary access to this supremely brilliant, difficult, compelling play.

2. Among several other plays, *Hamlet* offers similar grounds for objections to the traditional conflation, but both the economics of publishing and the realities of bookbinding—not to mention our recognition of the limited time in the typical undergraduate syllabus—preclude our offering three (or even four) *Hamlets* to match three *Lears*. What we have provided in this edition is a convenient selection of parallel passages that will enable teachers to convey some of the complex, often enigmatic issues, at once stylistic and conceptual, raised by the different texts of the play.

The Oxford text of *Hamlet* was based upon the Folio text, with an appended list of Additional Passages from the Second Quarto (Q2). These additional readings total more than two hundred lines, a significant number, among which are lines that have come to seem very much part of the play as widely received, even if we may doubt that they belong with all the others in any single one of Shakespeare's *Hamlets*. The Norton team, while following the Oxford text, has moved the Q2 passages from the appendix to the body of the play. But in doing so, we have not wanted once again to produce a conflated text. We have therefore indented the Q2 passages, printed them in a different typeface, and numbered them in such a way as to make clear their provenance. Those who wish to read the Folio version of *Hamlet* can thus simply skip over the indented Q2 passages, while at the same time it is possible for readers to see clearly the place that the Q2 passages occupy. We have adopted a similar strategy with several other plays: passages printed in Oxford in appendices are generally printed here in the play texts, though clearly demarcated and not conflated. In the case of *The Taming of the Shrew* and the related quarto text, *The Taming of a Shrew*, however, we have followed Oxford's procedure and left the quarto passages in an appendix, since we believe the texts reflect two distinct plays rather than a revision of one. We have similarly reproduced Oxford's brief appendices to A *Midsummer Night's Dream* and *Henry V,* enabling readers to consider alternative revisions of certain passages.

3. For reasons understood by every Shakespearean (and rehearsed at some length in this volume), the Oxford editors chose to restore the name "Sir John Oldcastle" to the character much better known as Falstaff in *1 Henry IV.* (They made comparable changes in the names of the characters known as Bardolph and Peto.) But for reasons understood by everyone who has presented this play to undergraduates or sampled the centuries of enthusiastic criticism, the Norton editors, with the Oxford editors' gracious agreement, have for this classroom edition opted for the familiar name "Falstaff" (and those of his boon companions), properly noting the change and its significance in the play's introduction.

4. The Oxford editors chose not to differentiate between those stage directions that appeared in the early editions up to and including the Folio and those that have been added by subsequent editors. Instead, in *A Textual Companion* they include separate lists of the original stage directions. These lists are not readily available to readers of the Norton text, whose editors opted instead to bracket all stage directions that derive from editions published after the Folio. Readers can thus easily see which stage directions derive from texts that may bear at least some relation to performances in Shakespeare's time, if not to Shakespeare's own authorship. The Norton policy is more fully explained in the General Introduction.

5. The Oxford editors have newly prepared complete texts of the multiauthored *King Edward III* and *Sir Thomas More,* in which Shakespeare may have had a hand as collaborator. The texts are available online at wwnorton.com/shakespeare. In addition, the *Norton Shakespeare,* Second Edition, continues to print, with a revised introduction, notes, and glosses, passages from *Sir Thomas More* that appear in the surviving manuscript to be in Shakespeare's own handwriting, and we include for the first time an introduction and bibliography to *King Edward III.*

The collaboration with Oxford was obviously essential to the creation of the *Norton Shakespeare.* But in preparing this Second Edition and making it something fresh and engaging, the critically important collaboration has been with the thousands of people who have used the book. Many of these, teachers and students alike, have generously offered helpful suggestions along with praise. Guided by their responses, as well as by recent developments in Shakespeare scholarship, we determined to look afresh at every detail and to make a wide range of changes. The General Introduction and the individual play introductions have been substantially revised, in some cases wholly rewritten, to make them clearer and more accessible. Textual notes throughout have been updated in response to new findings, and there are hundreds of new and fine-tuned notes and glosses, designed to make this edition an even better tool for learning and pleasure. The General Bibliography has been reorganized and extensively updated, with 7 new sections and over 350 new entries. The Selected Bibliographies, too, have been updated as well as newly annotated. A new introduction provides an illuminating guide to the array of maps, three of them archival and three new, showing places important to Shakespeare's plays. The genealogies have been revised, as has been the text/contexts Timeline. New annotated film lists, including over 50 films, now follow the play introductions. Instructors who emphasize films in their courses may wish to assign *Shakespeare and Film: A Norton Guide* by Samuel Crowl, available packaged with the *Norton Shakespeare.* Finally, in response to many requests, we are making the *Norton Shakespeare* available in three different formats: the familiar one-volume clothbound edition, new two-volume chronological splits (*Early Plays and Poems* and *Later Plays*), and four genre paperbacks, each with a new introduction.

    With the Second Edition of the *Norton Shakespeare,* the publisher expands its extensive online resource, Norton Literature Online (wwnorton.com/literature). Students who activate the free password in each new copy of the book gain access to an array of general resources, among them a glossary of literary terms, advice on writing about literature and using MLA documentation style, an author portrait gallery, more than 100 maps, and over 90 minutes of recorded readings and musical selections, among them 80 songs by Shakespeare. With their passwords, students also gain access to a site specifically developed to support the *Norton Shakespeare* (wwnorton.com/shakespeare). Based on content prepared by Mark Rose, University of California, Santa Barbara, this Web site invites students to explore six of the most widely taught plays—*The Merchant of Venice, 1 Henry IV, Hamlet, Othello, King Lear,* and *The Tempest*—through different contextual lenses. For each of these plays, the Web site provides materials on the elements of theater, sources, stage history, and critical receptions, as well as the complete Oxford text. Audio clips and stills from classic productions, etchings, photographs, and costume-design illustrations help students appreciate performance aspects of the plays. The student Web site also includes the redesigned "Shakespearean Chronicle, 1558–1616," an illustrated timeline that interweaves three kinds of chronologies illuminating Shakespeare's life and times. As noted above, a password-protected section of the Web site also includes the complete texts of *The Book of Sir Thomas More* and *The Reign of King Edward the Third,* prepared by the editors of the *Oxford Shakespeare.*

The creation of this edition has drawn heavily on the resources, experience, and skill of its remarkable publisher, the independent, employee-owned company W. W. Norton. Our principal guide has been our brilliant editor Julia Reidhead, whose calm intelligence, common sense, and steady focus have been essential in enabling us to reach our goal. With this Second Edition, we were blessed with the characteristically thoughtful oversight of Marian Johnson, managing editor, college department; scrupulous manuscript editing by Carol Flechner; and the assistance of an extraordinary group of Norton staffers: editorial assistant Rivka Genesen, who, among many other things, coordinated the art program; production manager Diane O'Connor; designer Antonina Krass; editor of the *Norton Shakespeare* Web site Eileen Connell; and proofreaders Paula Noonan and Ann Warren.

The *Norton Shakespeare* editors have, in addition, had the valuable—indeed, indispensable—support of a host of undergraduate and graduate research assistants, colleagues, friends, and family. Even a partial listing of those to whom we owe our heartfelt thanks is very long, but we are all fortunate enough to live in congenial and supportive environments, and the edition has been part of our lives for a long time. We owe special thanks for sustained dedication and learning to our principal assistants: Tiffany Alkan, Lianne Habinek, and Emily Peterson. Particular thanks are due to Noah Heringman for his work on the texts assembled in the documents section and for the prefatory notes and comments on those texts; to Philip Schwyzer for preparing the genealogies and the glossary and for conceiving and preparing the (now online) "Shakespearean Chronicle"; and to Holger Schott Syme for reconceiving and extensively updating the General Bibliography. In addition, we are deeply grateful to Ezra Feldman, Francesca Mari, Douglas McQueen-Thomson, Jeffrey Patterson, and Benjamin Woodring. All of these companions, and many more besides, have helped us find in this long collective enterprise what the "Dedicatorie Epistle" to the First Folio promises to its readers: delight. We make the same promise to the readers of our edition and invite them to continue the great Shakespearean collaboration.

STEPHEN GREENBLATT
WALTER COHEN
JEAN E. HOWARD
KATHARINE EISAMAN MAUS

Acknowledgments

Among our many critics, advisers, and friends, the following were of special help in providing critiques for particular plays or of the project as a whole: Janet Adelman (University of California, Berkeley), Joel Altman (University of California, Berkeley), Rebecca Bach (University of Alabama at Birmingham), John Baxter (Dalhousie University), Edward I. Berry (University of Victoria), Timothy Billings (Middlebury College), Bruce Boehrer (Florida State University), Barbara Bono (University at Buffalo, SUNY), Gordon M. Braden (University of Virginia), Douglas Brooks (Texas A&M University), Stephen Buhler (University of Nebraska—Lincoln), Richard Burt (University of Florida), Joseph F. Ceccio (University of Akron), Julie Crawford (Columbia University), Christy Desmet (University of Georgia), Heather Dubrow (University of Wisconsin—Madison), Laurie Ellinghausen (University of Missouri—Kansas City), Chris Fitter (Rutgers, State University of New Jersey), Susan Fraiman (University of Virginia), Daniel Gil (University of Oregon), Miriam Gilbert (University of Iowa), Suzanne Gossett (Loyola University), Elizabeth Hanson (Queen's University), Jim Harner (Texas A&M University), Jonathan Gil Harris (George Washington University), Don Hedrick (Kansas State University), Roze Hentschell (Colorado State University), Clifford Huffman (Stony Brook University, SUNY), John Huntington (University of Illinois at Chicago), Sujata Iyengar (University of Georgia), Kimberly Johnson (Brigham Young University), Coppélia Kahn (Brown University), Sean Keilen (University of Pennsylvania), Theodore B. Leinwand (University of Maryland), Zachary Lesser (University of Pennsylvania), Naomi Liebler (Montclair State University), Joyce MacDonald (University of Kentucky), Leah Marcus (Vanderbilt University), Mark Matheson (University of Utah), Robert Matz (George Mason University), Kristen McDermott (Central Michigan University), Ted McGee (University of Waterloo), Scott McMillin (late of Cornell University), Gordon McMullan (King's College London), John Moore (Pennsylvania State University), Carol Neely (University of Illinois at Urbana-Champaign), Lori Newcomb (University of Illinois at Urbana-Champaign), Karen Newman (New York University), Hillary Nunn (University of Akron), Thomas G. Olsen (SUNY at New Paltz), Jim O'Rourke (Florida State University), Paul Parrish (Texas A&M University), Michael Payne (Bucknell University), Rebecca J. Perederin (University of Virginia), Curtis Perry (Arizona State University), Susan Phillips (Northwestern University), Tanya Pollard (Brooklyn College, CUNY), Kristen Poole (University of Delaware), Arnold Preussner (Truman State University), Phyllis Rackin (University of Pennsylvania), Peter L. Rudnytsky (University of Florida), Benjamin Saunders (University of Oregon), Barbara Sebek (Colorado State University), Tracey Sedinger (University of Northern Colorado), Jyotsna Singh (Michigan State University), Andrew Stott (University at Buffalo, SUNY), Garrett Sullivan (Pennsylvania State University), Ramie Targoff (Brandeis University), Henry Turner (University of Wisconsin—Madison), Martine van Elk (California State University, Long Beach), William N. West (University of Colorado at Boulder), Linda Woodbridge (Pennsylvania State University), Lingui Yang (Texas A&M University).

General Introduction
by
STEPHEN GREENBLATT

"He was not of an age, but for all time!"

The celebration of Shakespeare's genius, eloquently initiated by his friend and rival Ben Jonson, has over the centuries become an institutionalized rite of civility. The person who does not love Shakespeare has made, the rite implies, an incomplete adjustment not simply to a particular culture—English culture of the late sixteenth and early seventeenth centuries—but to "culture" as a whole, the dense network of constraints and entitlements, dreams and practices that links us to nature. Indeed, so absolute is Shakespeare's achievement that he has himself come to seem like great creating nature: the common bond of humankind, the principle of hope, the symbol of the imagination's power to transcend time-bound beliefs and assumptions, peculiar historical circumstances, and specific artistic conventions.

The near-worship that Shakespeare inspires is one of the salient facts about his art. But we must at the same time acknowledge that this art is the product of peculiar historical circumstances and specific conventions, four centuries distant from our own. The acknowledgment is important because Shakespeare the working dramatist did not typically lay claim to the transcendent, visionary truths attributed to him by his most fervent admirers; his characters more modestly say, in the words of the magician Prospero, that their project was "to please" (*The Tempest,* Epilogue, line 13). The starting point, and perhaps the ending point as well, in any encounter with Shakespeare is simply to enjoy him, to savor his imaginative richness, to take pleasure in his infinite delight in language.

"If then you do not like him," Shakespeare's first editors wrote in 1623, "surely you are in some manifest danger not to understand him." Over the years, accommodations have been devised to make liking Shakespeare easier for everyone. When the stage sank to melodrama and light opera, Shakespeare—in suitably revised texts—was there. When the populace had a craving for hippodrama, plays performed entirely on horseback, *Hamlet* was dutifully rewritten and mounted. When audiences went mad for realism, live frogs croaked in productions of *A Midsummer Night's Dream.* When the stage was stripped bare and given over to stark exhibitions of sadistic cruelty, Shakespeare was our contemporary. And when the theater itself had lost some of its cultural centrality, Shakespeare moved effortlessly to Hollywood and the soundstages of the BBC.

This virtually universal appeal is one of the most astonishing features of the Shakespeare phenomenon: plays that were performed before glittering courts thrive in junior-high-school auditoriums; enemies set on destroying one another laugh at the same jokes and weep at the same catastrophes; some of the richest and most complex English verse ever written migrates with spectacular success into German and Italian, Hindi, Swahili, and Japanese. Is there a single, stable, continuous object that underlies all of these migrations and metamorphoses? Certainly not. The global diffusion and long life of Shakespeare's works depend on their extraordinary malleability, their protean capacity to elude definition and escape secure possession. At the same time, they are not without identifiable shared features: across centuries and continents, family resemblances link many of the wildly diverse manifestations of plays such as *Romeo and Juliet, Hamlet,* and *Twelfth Night.* And if there is no clear limit or end point, there is a reasonably clear beginning: the

1

England of the late sixteenth and early seventeenth centuries, when the plays and poems collected in this volume made their first appearance.

An art virtually without end or limit but with an identifiable, localized, historical origin: Shakespeare's achievement defies the facile opposition between transcendent and time-bound. It is not necessary to choose between an account of Shakespeare as the scion of a particular culture and an account of him as a universal genius who created works that continually renew themselves across national and generational boundaries. On the contrary: crucial clues to understanding his art's remarkable power to soar beyond its originary time and place lie in the very soil from which that art sprang.

Shakespeare's World

Life and Death

Life expectancy at birth in early modern England was exceedingly low by our standards: under thirty years old, compared with over seventy today. Infant mortality rates were extraordinarily high, and it is estimated that in the poorer parishes of London only about half the children survived to the age of fifteen, while the children of aristocrats fared only a little better. In such circumstances, some parents must have developed a certain detachment—one of Shakespeare's contemporaries writes of losing "some three or four children"—but there are many expressions of intense grief, so that we cannot assume that the frequency of death hardened people to loss or made it routine.

Still, the spectacle of death, along with that other great threshold experience, birth, must have been far more familiar to Shakespeare and his contemporaries than to ourselves. There was no equivalent in early modern England to our hospitals, and most births and deaths occurred at home. Physical means for the alleviation of pain and suffering were extremely limited—alcohol might dull the terror, but it was hardly an effective anesthetic—and medical treatment was generally both expensive and worthless, more likely to intensify suffering than to lead to a cure. This was a world without a concept of antiseptics, with little actual understanding of disease, with few effective ways of treating earaches or venereal disease, let alone the more terrible instances of what Shakespeare calls "the thousand natural shocks that flesh is heir to."

The worst of these shocks was the bubonic plague, which repeatedly ravaged England, and particularly English towns, until the third quarter of the seventeenth century. The plague was terrifyingly sudden in its onset, rapid in its spread, and almost invariably lethal. Physicians were helpless in the face of the epidemic, though they prescribed amulets,

Bill recording plague deaths in London, 1609.

preservatives, and sweet-smelling substances (on the theory that the plague was carried by noxious vapors). In the plague-ridden year of 1564, the year of Shakespeare's birth, some 254 people died in Stratford-upon-Avon, out of a total population of 800. The year before, some 20,000 Londoners are thought to have died; in 1593, almost 15,000; in 1603, 36,000, or over a sixth of the city's inhabitants. The social effects of these horrible visitations were severe: looting, violence, and despair, along with an intensification of the age's perennial poverty, unemployment, and food shortages. The London plague regulations of 1583, reissued with modifications in later epidemics, ordered that the infected and their households be locked in their homes for a month; that the streets be kept clean; that vagrants be expelled; and that funerals and plays be restricted or banned entirely.

The plague, then, had a direct and immediate impact on Shakespeare's own profession. City officials kept records of the weekly number of plague deaths; when these surpassed a certain number, the theaters were peremptorily closed. The basic idea was not only to prevent contagion but also to avoid making an angry God still angrier with the spectacle of idleness. While restricting public assemblies may in fact have slowed the epidemic, other public policies in times of plague, such as killing the cats and dogs, may have made matters worse (since the disease, as we now know, was spread not by these animals but by the fleas that bred on the black rats that infested the poorer neighborhoods). Moreover, the playing companies, driven out of London by the closing of the theaters, may have carried plague to the provincial towns.

Even in good times, when the plague was dormant and the weather favorable for farming, the food supply in England was precarious. A few successive bad harvests, such as occurred in the mid-1590s, could cause serious hardship, even starvation. Not surprisingly, the poor bore the brunt of the burden: inflation, low wages, and rent increases left large numbers of people with very little cushion against disaster. Further, at its best, the diet of most people seems to have been seriously deficient. The lower classes then, as throughout most of history, subsisted on one or two foodstuffs, usually low in protein. The upper classes disdained green vegetables and milk and gorged themselves on meat. Illnesses that we now trace to vitamin deficiencies were rampant. Some, but not much, relief from pain was provided by the beer that Elizabethans, including children, drank almost incessantly. (Home brewing aside, enough beer was sold in England for every man, woman, and child to have consumed 40 gallons a year.)

Wealth

Despite rampant disease, the population of England in Shakespeare's lifetime was steadily growing, from approximately 3,060,000 in 1564 to 4,060,000 in 1600 and 4,510,000 in 1616. Though the death rate was more than twice what it is in England today, the birthrate was almost three times the current figure. London's population in particular soared, from 60,000 in 1520 to 120,000 in 1550, 200,000 in 1600, and 375,000 half a century later, making it the largest and fastest-growing city not only in England but in all of Europe. Every year in the first half of the seventeenth century, about 10,000 people migrated to London from other parts of England—wages in London tended to be around 50 percent higher than in the rest of the country—and it is estimated that one in eight English people lived in London at some point in their lives. The economic viability of Shakespeare's profession was closely linked to this extraordinary demographic boom: between 1567 and 1642, a theater historian has calculated, the London playhouses were paid close to 50 million visits.

As these visits to the theater indicate, in the capital city and elsewhere a substantial number of English men and women, despite hardships that were never very distant, had money to spend. After the disorder and dynastic wars of the fifteenth century, England in the sixteenth and early seventeenth centuries was for the most part a nation at peace, and with peace came a measure of enterprise and prosperity: the landowning classes busied themselves building great houses, planting orchards and hop gardens, draining marshlands, bringing untilled "wastes" under cultivation. The artisans and laborers who actually accomplished these tasks, although they were generally paid very little, often managed to accumulate something, as did the small freeholding farmers, the yeomen, who are repeatedly celebrated in the period as the backbone of English national independence and well-being. William Harrison's *Description of England* (1577) lovingly itemizes the yeoman's precious possessions: "fair garnish of pewter on his cupboard, with so much more odd vessel going about the house, three or four featherbeds, so many coverlets and carpets of tapestry, a silver salt[cellar], a bowl for wine (if not a whole nest) and a dozen of spoons." There are comparable accounts of the hard-earned acquisitions of the city dwellers—masters and apprentices in small workshops, shipbuilders, wool merchants, clothmakers, chandlers, tradesmen, shopkeepers, along with lawyers, apothecaries, schoolteachers, scriveners, and the like—whose pennies from time to time enriched the coffers of the players.

The chief source of England's wealth in the sixteenth century was its textile industry, an industry that depended on a steady supply of wool. In *The Winter's Tale*, Shakespeare provides a warm, richly comic portrayal of a rural sheepshearing festival, but the increasingly intensive production of wool had in reality its grim side. When a character in Thomas More's *Utopia* (1516) complains that "the sheep are eating the people," he is referring to the practice of enclosure: throughout the sixteenth and early seventeenth centuries, many acres of croplands once farmed in common by rural communities were enclosed with fences by wealthy landowners and turned into pasturage. The ensuing misery, displacement, and food shortages led to repeated riots, some of them violent and bloody, along with a series of government proclamations, but the process of enclosure was not reversed.

The economic stakes were high, and not only for the domestic market. In 1565, woolen cloth alone made up more than three-fourths of England's exports. (The remainder consisted mostly of other textiles and raw wool, with some trade in lead, tin, grain, and skins.) The Company of Merchant Adventurers carried cloth to distant ports on the Baltic and Mediterranean, establishing links with Russia and Morocco (each took about 2 percent of London's cloth in 1597–98). English lead and tin, as well as fabrics, were sold in Tuscany and Turkey, and merchants found a market for Newcastle coal on the island of Malta. In the latter half of the century, London, which handled more than 85 percent of all exports, regularly shipped abroad more than 100,000 woolen cloths a year at a value of at least £750,000. This figure does not include the increasingly important and profitable trade in so-called New Draperies, including textiles that went by such exotic names as bombazines, calamancoes, damazellas, damizes, mockadoes, and virgenatoes. When the Earl of Kent in *King Lear* insults Oswald as a "filthy worsted-stocking knave" (2.2.14–15) or when the aristocratic Biron in *Love's Labour's Lost* declares that he will give up "taffeta phrases, silken terms precise, / Three-piled hyperboles" and woo henceforth "in russet yeas, and honest kersey noes" (5.2.406–07, 413), Shakespeare is assuming that a substantial portion of his audience will be alert to the social significance of fabric.

There is amusing confirmation of this alertness from an unexpected source: the report of a visit made to the Fortune playhouse in London in 1614 by a foreigner, Father Orazio Busino, the chaplain of the Venetian embassy. Father Busino neglected to mention the name of the play he saw, but like many foreigners, he was powerfully struck by the presence of gorgeously dressed women in the audience. In Venice, there was a special gallery for courtesans, but socially respectable women would not have been permitted to attend plays, as they could in England. In London, not only could middle- and upper-class women go to the theater, but they could also wear masks and mingle freely with male spectators and women of ill repute. The bemused cleric was uncertain about the ambiguous social situation in which he found himself:

These theatres are frequented by a number of respectable and handsome ladies, who come freely and seat themselves among the men without the slightest hesitation. On the evening in question his Excellency and the Secretary were pleased to play me a trick by placing me amongst a bevy of young women. Scarcely was I seated ere a very elegant dame, but in a mask, came and placed herself beside me. . . . She asked me for my address both in French and English; and, on my turning a deaf ear, she determined to honour me by showing me some fine diamonds on her fingers, repeatedly taking off not fewer than three gloves, which were worn one over the other. . . . This lady's bodice was of yellow satin richly embroidered, her petticoat of gold tissue with stripes, her robe of red velvet with a raised pile, lined with yellow muslin with broad stripes of pure gold. She wore an apron of point lace of various patterns: her head-tire was highly perfumed, and the collar of white satin beneath the delicately-wrought ruff struck me as extremely pretty.

Father Busino may have turned a deaf ear on this "elegant dame" but not a blind eye: his description of her dress is worthy of a fashion designer and conveys something of the virtual clothes cult that prevailed in England in the late sixteenth and early seventeenth centuries, a cult whose major shrine, outside the royal court, was the theater.

Imports, Patents, and Monopolies

England produced some luxury goods, but the clothing on the backs of the most fashionable theatergoers was likely to have come from abroad. By the late sixteenth century, the English were importing substantial quantities of silks, satins, velvets, embroidery, gold and silver lace, and other costly items to satisfy the extravagant tastes of the elite and of those who aspired to dress like the elite. The government tried to put a check on the sartorial ambitions of the upwardly mobile by passing sumptuary laws—that is, laws restricting to the ranks of the aristocracy the right to wear certain of the most precious fabrics. But the very existence of these laws, in practice almost impossible to enforce, only reveals the scope and significance of the perceived problem.

Sumptuary laws were in part a conservative attempt to protect the existing social order from upstarts. Social mobility was not widely viewed as a positive virtue, and moralists repeatedly urged people to stay in their place. Conspicuous consumption that was tolerated, even admired, in the aristocratic elite was denounced as sinful and monstrous in less exalted social circles. English authorities were also deeply concerned throughout the period about the effects of a taste for luxury goods on the balance of trade. One of the principal English imports was wine: the "sherris" whose virtues Falstaff extols in 2 Henry IV came from Xeres in Spain; the malmsey in which poor Clarence is drowned in Richard III was probably made in Greece or in the Canary Islands (from whence came Sir Toby Belch's "cup of canary" in Twelfth Night); and the "flagon of rhenish" that Yorick in Hamlet had once poured on the Gravedigger's head came from the Rhine region of Germany. Other imports included canvas, linen, fish, olive oil, sugar, molasses, dates, oranges and lemons, figs, raisins, almonds, capers, indigo, ostrich feathers, and that increasingly popular drug from the New World, tobacco.

Joint-stock companies were established to import goods for the burgeoning English market. The Merchant Venturers of the city of Bristol (established in 1552) handled great shipments of Spanish sack, the light, dry wine that largely displaced the vintages of Bordeaux and Burgundy when trade with France was disrupted by war. The Muscovy Company (established in 1555) traded English cloth and manufactured goods for Russian furs, oil, and beeswax. The Venice Company and the Turkey Company—uniting in 1593 to form the wealthy Levant Company—brought silk and spices home from Aleppo and carpets from Istanbul. The East India Company (founded in 1600), with its agent at Bantam in Java, brought pepper, cloves, nutmeg, and other spices from east Asia, along with indigo, cotton textiles, sugar, and saltpeter from India. English privateers "imported" American products, especially sugar, fish, and hides, in huge quantities, along with more precious cargoes. In 1592, a privateering expedition principally funded by Sir Walter Ralegh captured a huge Portuguese carrack (sailing ship), the Madre de Dios, in the Azores and brought it back to Dartmouth. The ship, the largest that had ever entered any English port, held 536 tons of pepper, cloves, cinnamon, cochineal, mace, civet, musk, ambergris,

Cannoneer. From *Edward Webbe, . . . His Travailes* (1590).

and nutmeg, as well as jewels, gold, ebony, carpets, and silks. Before order could be established, the English seamen began to pillage this immensely rich prize, and witnesses said they could smell the spices on all the streets around the harbor. Such piratical expeditions were rarely officially sanctioned by the state, but the queen had in fact privately invested £1,800, for which she received about £80,000.

In the years of war with Spain, 1586–1604, the goods captured by the privateers annually amounted to 10 to 15 percent of the total value of England's imports. But organized theft alone could not solve England's balance-of-trade problems. Statesmen were particularly worried that the nation's natural wealth was slipping away in exchange for unnecessary things. In his *Discourse of the Commonweal* (1549), the prominent humanist Sir Thomas Smith exclaims against the importation of such trifles as mirrors, paper, laces, gloves, pins, inkhorns, tennis balls, puppets, and playing cards. And more than a century later, the same fear that England was trading its riches for trifles and wasting away in idleness was expressed by the Bristol merchant John Cary. The solution, Cary argues in "An Essay on the State of England in Relation to Its Trade" (1695), is to expand productive domestic employment. "People are or may be the Wealth of a Nation," he writes, "yet it must be where you find Employment for them, else they are a Burden to it, as the Idle Drone is maintained by the Industry of the laborious Bee, so are all those who live by their Dependence on others, as Players, Ale-House Keepers, Common Fiddlers, and such like, but more particularly Beggars, who never set themselves to work."

Stage players, all too typically associated here with vagabonds and other idle drones, could have replied in their defense that they not only labored in their vocation but also exported their skills abroad: English acting companies routinely traveled overseas and performed as far away as Bohemia. But their labor was not regarded as a productive contribution to the national wealth, and plays were in truth no solution to the trade imbalances that worried authorities.

The government attempted to stem the flow of gold overseas by establishing a patent system initially designed to encourage skilled foreigners to settle in England by granting them exclusive rights to produce particular wares by a patented method. Patents were granted for such things as the making of hard white soap (1561), ovens and furnaces (1563), window glass (1567), sailcloths (1574), drinking glasses (1574), sulphur, brimstone, and oil (1577), armor and horse harness (1587), starch (1588), white writing paper made from rags (1589), aqua vitae and vinegar (1594), playing cards (1598), and mathematical instruments (1598).

Although their ostensible purpose was to increase the wealth of England, encourage technical innovation, and provide employment for the poor, the effect of patents was often the enrichment of a few and the hounding of poor competitors by wealthy monopolists, a group that soon extended well beyond foreign-born entrepreneurs to the favorites of the monarch who vied for the huge profits to be made. "If I had a monopoly out" on folly, the Fool in *King Lear* protests, glancing at the "lords and great men" around him, "they would have part on't." The passage appears only in the quarto version of the play (*History of King Lear* 4.135–36); it may have been cut for political reasons from the Folio. For the issue of monopolies provoked bitter criticism and parliamentary debate for decades. In 1601, Elizabeth was prevailed upon to revoke a number of the most hated monopolies, including aqua vitae and vinegar, bottles, brushes, fish livers, the coarse sailcloth known as poldavis and mildernix, pots, salt, and starch. The whole system was revoked during the reign of James I by an act of Parliament.

Haves and Have-Nots

When in the 1560s Elizabeth's ambassador to France, the humanist Sir Thomas Smith, wrote a description of England, he saw the commonwealth as divided into four sorts of people: "gentlemen, citizens, yeomen artificers, and laborers." At the forefront of the class of gentlemen was the monarch, followed by a very small group of nobles—dukes, marquesses, earls, viscounts, and barons—who either inherited their exalted titles, as the eldest male heirs of their families, or were granted them by the monarch. Under Elizabeth, this aristocratic peerage numbered between 50 and 60 individuals; James's promotions increased the number to nearer 130. Strictly speaking, Smith notes, the younger sons of the nobility were only entitled to be called "esquires," but in common speech they were also called "lords."

Below this tiny cadre of aristocrats in the social hierarchy of gentry were the knights, a title of honor conferred by the monarch, and below them were the "simple gentlemen." Who was a gentleman? According to Smith, "whoever studieth the laws of the realm, who studieth in the universities, who professeth liberal sciences, and to be short, who can live idly and without manual labor, and will bear the port, charge and countenance of a gentleman, he shall be called master . . . and shall be taken for a gentleman." To "live idly and without manual labor": where in Spain, for example, the crucial mark of a gentleman was "blood," in England it was "idleness," in the sense of sufficient income to afford an education and to maintain a social position without having to work with one's hands.

For Smith, the class of gentlemen was far and away the most important in the kingdom. Below were two groups that had at least some social standing and claim to authority: the citizens, or burgesses, those who held positions of importance and responsibility in their cities, and yeomen, farmers with land and a measure of economic independence. At the bottom of the social order was what Smith calls "the fourth sort of men which do not rule." The great mass of ordinary people have, Smith writes, "no voice nor authority in our commonwealth, and no account is made of them but only to be ruled." Still, even they can bear some responsibility, he notes, since they serve on juries and are named to such positions as churchwarden and constable.

In everyday practice, as modern social historians have observed, the English tended to divide the population not into four distinct classes but into two: a very small empowered group—the "richer" or "wiser" or "better" sort—and all the rest who were without much social standing or power, the "poorer" or "ruder" or "meaner" sort. References to the "middle sort of people" remain relatively rare until after Shakespeare's lifetime; these people are absorbed into the rulers or the ruled, depending on speaker and context.

The source of wealth for most of the ruling class, and the essential measure of social status, was landownership, and changes to the social structure in the sixteenth and seventeenth centuries were largely driven by the land market. The property that passed into private hands as the Tudors and early Stuarts sold off confiscated monastic estates and then their own crown lands for ready cash amounted to nearly a quarter of all the land in England. At the same time, the buying and selling of private estates was on the rise throughout the period. Land was bought up not only by established landowners seeking to enlarge their estates but by successful merchants, manufacturers, and urban professionals; even if the taint of vulgar moneymaking lingered around such figures, their heirs would be taken for true gentlemen. The rate of turnover in landownership was great; in many counties, well over half the gentle families in 1640 had appeared since the end of the fifteenth century. The class that Smith called "simple gentlemen" was expanding rapidly: in the fifteenth century, they had held no more than a quarter of the land in the country; but by the later seventeenth century, they controlled almost half. Over the same period, the land held by the great aristocratic magnates held steady at 15 to 20 percent of the total.

Riot and Disorder

London was a violent place in the first half of Shakespeare's career. There were thirty-five riots in the city in the years 1581–1602, twelve of them in the volatile month of June 1595. These included protests against the deeply unpopular lord mayor Sir John Spencer, attempts to release prisoners, anti-alien riots, and incidents of "popular market regulation." There is an unforgettable depiction of a popular uprising in *Coriolanus*, along with many other glimpses in Shakespeare's works, including John Cade's grotesque rebellion in *The First Part of the Contention (2 Henry VI)*, the plebeian violence in *Julius Caesar*, and Laertes' "riotous head" in *Hamlet*.

The London rioters were mostly drawn from the large mass of poor and discontented apprentices who typically chose as their scapegoats foreigners, prostitutes, and gentlemen's servingmen. Theaters were very often the site of the social confrontations that sparked disorder. For two days running in June 1584, disputes between apprentices and gentlemen triggered riots outside the Curtain Theatre involving up to a thousand participants. On one occasion, a gentleman was said to have exclaimed that "the apprentice was but a rascal, and some there were little better than rogues that took upon them the name of gentlemen, and said the prentices were but the scum of the world." These occasions culminated in attacks by the apprentices on London's law schools, the Inns of Court.

The most notorious and predictable incidents of disorder came on Shrove Tuesday (the Tuesday before the beginning of Lent), a traditional day of misrule when apprentices ran riot. Shrove Tuesday disturbances involved attacks by mobs of young men on the brothels of the South Bank, in the vicinity of the Globe and other public theaters. The city authorities took precautions to keep these disturbances from getting completely out of control but evidently did not regard them as serious threats to public order.

Of much greater concern throughout the Tudor and early Stuart years were the frequent incidents of rural rioting against the enclosure of commons and wasteland by local landlords (and, in the royal forests, by the crown). This form of popular protest was at its height during Shakespeare's career: in the years 1590–1610, the frequency of anti-enclosure rioting doubled from what it had been earlier in Elizabeth's reign.

Although they often became violent, anti-enclosure riots were usually directed not against individuals but against property. Villagers—sometimes several hundred, often

fewer than a dozen—gathered to tear down newly planted hedges. The event often took place in a carnival atmosphere, with songs and drinking, that did not prevent the participants from acting with a good deal of political canniness and forethought. Especially in the Jacobean period, it was common for participants to establish a common fund for legal defense before commencing their assault on the hedges. Women were frequently involved, and on a number of occasions wives alone participated in the destruction of the enclosure, since there was a widespread, though erroneous, belief that married women acting without the knowledge of their husbands were immune from prosecution. In fact, the powerful Court of Star Chamber consistently ruled that both the wives and their husbands should be punished.

Peddler. From Jost Amman, *The Book of Trades* (1568).

Although Stratford was never the scene of serious rioting, enclosure controversies there turned violent more than once in Shakespeare's lifetime. In January 1601, Shakespeare's friend Richard Quiney and others leveled the hedges of Sir Edward Greville, lord of Stratford manor. Quiney was elected bailiff of Stratford in September of that year but did not live to enjoy the office for long. He died from a blow to the head struck by one of Greville's men in a tavern brawl. Greville, responsible for the administration of justice, neglected to punish the murderer.

There was further violence in January 1615, when William Combe's men threw to the ground two local aldermen who were filling in a ditch by which Combe was enclosing common fields near Stratford. The task of filling in the offending ditch was completed the next day by the women and children of Stratford. Combe's enclosure scheme was eventually stopped in the courts. Although he owned land whose value would have been affected by this controversy, Shakespeare took no active role in it, since he had previously come to a private settlement with the enclosers insuring him against personal loss.

Most incidents of rural rioting were small, localized affairs, and with good reason: when confined to the village community, riot was a misdemeanor; when it spread outward to include multiple communities, it became treason, punishable by death. The greatest of the anti-enclosure riots, those in which hundreds of individuals from a large area participated, commonly took place on the eve of full-scale regional rebellions. The largest of these disturbances, Kett's Rebellion, involved some 16,000 peasants, artisans, and townspeople who rose up in 1549 under the leadership of a Norfolk tanner and landowner, Robert Kett, to protest economic exploitation. The agrarian revolts in Shakespeare's lifetime were on a much smaller scale. In the abortive Oxfordshire Rebellion of 1596, a carpenter named Bartholomew Steere attempted to organize a rising against enclosing gentlemen. The optimistic Steere promised his followers that "it was but a month's work to overrun England" and informed them "that the commons long since in Spain did rise and kill all gentlemen . . . and since that time have lived merrily there." Steere expected several hundred men to join him on Enslow Hill on November 21, 1596, for the start of the rising; no more than twenty showed up. They were captured, imprisoned, and tortured. Several were executed, but Steere apparently cheated the hangman by dying in prison.

Rebellions, most often triggered by hunger and oppression, continued into the reign of James I. The Midland Revolt of 1607, which may be reflected in *Coriolanus,* consisted of a string of agrarian risings in the counties of Northamptonshire, Warwickshire, and Leicestershire, involving assemblies of up to 5,000 rebels in various places. The best known of their leaders was John Reynolds, called "Captain Powch" because of the pouch he wore, whose magical contents were supposed to defend the rebels from harm. (According to the chronicler Edmund Howes, when Reynolds was captured and the pouch opened, it contained "only a piece of green cheese.") The rebels, who were called by themselves and others both "Levelers" and "Diggers," insisted that they had no quarrel with the king but only sought an end to injurious enclosures. But Robert Wilkinson, who preached a sermon against the leaders at their trial, credited them with the intention to "level all states as they leveled banks and ditches." Most of the rebels got off relatively lightly, but, along with other ringleaders, Captain Powch was executed.

The Legal Status of Women

Even though England was ruled for over forty years by a powerful woman, the great majority of women in the kingdom had very restricted social, economic, and legal standing. To be sure, a tiny number of influential aristocratic women, such as the formidable Countess of Shrewsbury, Bess of Hardwick, wielded considerable power. But, these rare exceptions aside, women were denied any rightful claim to institutional authority or personal autonomy. When Sir Thomas Smith thinks of how he should describe his country's social order, he declares that "we do reject women, as those whom nature hath made to keep home and to nourish their family and children, and not to meddle with matters abroad, nor to bear office in a city or commonwealth."

Then, with a kind of glance over his shoulder, he makes an exception of those few for whom "the blood is respected, not the age nor the sex": for example, the queen.

English women were not under the full range of crushing constraints that afflicted women in some countries in Europe. Foreign visitors were struck by their relative freedom, as shown, for example, by the fact that respectable women could venture unchaperoned into the streets and attend the theater. Single women, whether widowed or unmarried, could, if they were of full age, inherit and administer land, make a will, sign a contract, possess property, sue and be sued, without a male guardian or proxy. But married women had no such rights under the common law.

Early modern writings about women and the family constantly return to a political model of domination and submission, in which the father justly rules over wife and children as the monarch rules over the state. This conception of a woman's role conveniently ignores the fact that a *majority* of the adult women at any time in Shakespeare's England were not married. They were either widows or spinsters (a term that was not yet pejorative), and thus for the most part managing their own affairs. Even within marriage, women typically had more control over certain spheres than moralizing writers on the family cared to admit. For example, village wives oversaw the production of eggs, cheese, and beer, and sold these goods in the market. As seamstresses, pawnbrokers, secondhand clothing dealers, peddlers, and the like—activities not controlled by the all-male guilds—women managed to acquire some economic power of their own, and, of course, they participated as well in the unregulated, black-market economy of the age and in the underworld of thievery and prostitution.

Women were not in practice as bereft of property as, according to English common law, they should have been. Demographic studies indicate that the inheritance system called primogeniture, the orderly transmission of property from father to eldest male heir, was more often an unfulfilled wish than a reality. Some 40 percent of marriages failed to produce a son, and in such circumstances fathers often left their land to their daughters, rather than to brothers, nephews, or male cousins. In many families, the father died before his male heir was old enough to inherit property, leaving the land, at least temporarily, in the hands of the mother. And while they were less likely than their brothers to inherit land ("real property"), daughters normally inherited a substantial share of their father's personal property (cash and movables).

In fact, the legal restrictions upon women, though severe in Shakespeare's time, actually worsened in subsequent decades. The English common law, the system of law based on court decisions rather than on codified written laws, was significantly less egalitarian in its approach to wives and daughters than were alternative legal codes (manorial, civil, and ecclesiastical) still in place in the late sixteenth century. The eventual triumph of common law stripped women of many traditional rights, slowly driving them out of economically productive trades and businesses.

Limited though it was, the economic freedom of Elizabethan and Jacobean women far exceeded their political and social freedom—the opportunity to receive a grammar-school or university education, to hold office in church or state, to have a voice in public debates, or even simply to speak their mind fully and openly in ordinary conversation. Women who asserted their views too vigorously risked being perceived as shrewish and labeled "scolds." Both urban and rural communities had a horror of scolds. In the Elizabethan period, such women came to be regarded as a threat to public order, to be dealt with by the local authorities. The preferred methods of correction included public humiliation—of the sort Katherine endures in *The Taming of the Shrew*—and such physical abuse as slapping, bridling, and soaking by means of a contraption called the "cucking stool" (or "ducking stool"). This latter punishment originated in the Middle Ages, but its use spread in the sixteenth century, when it became almost exclusively a punishment for women. From 1560 onward, cucking stools were built or renovated in many English provincial towns; between 1560 and 1600, the contraptions were installed by rivers or ponds in Norwich, Bridport, Shrewsbury, Kingston-upon-Thames, Marlborough, Devizes, Clitheroe, Thornbury, and Great Yarmouth.

Such punishment was usually intensified by a procession through the town to the sound of "rough music," the banging together of pots and pans. The same cruel festivity accompanied the "carting" or "riding" of those accused of being whores. In some parts of the country, villagers also took the law into their own hands, publicly shaming women who married men much younger than themselves or who beat or otherwise domineered over their husbands. One characteristic form of these charivaris, or rituals of shaming, was known in the West Country as the Skimmington Ride. Villagers would rouse the offending couple from bed with rough music and stage a raucous pageant in which a man, holding a distaff, would ride backward on a donkey, while his "wife" (another man dressed as a woman) struck him with a ladle. In these cases, the collective ridicule and indignation was evidently directed at least as much at the henpecked husband as at his transgressive wife.

Women and Print

Books published for a female audience surged in popularity in the late sixteenth century, reflecting an increase in female literacy. (It is striking how many of Shakespeare's women are shown reading.) This increase is probably linked to a Protestant longing for direct access to the Scriptures, and the new books marketed specifically for women included devotional manuals and works of religious instruction. But there were also practical guides to such subjects as female education (for example, Giovanni Bruto's *Necessarie, Fit, and Convenient Education of a Young Gentlewoman*, 1598), midwifery (James Guillemeau's *Child-birth; or, The Happy Delivery of Women*, 1612), needlework (Federico di Vinciolo's *New and Singular Patternes and Workes of Linnen*, 1591), cooking (Thomas Dawson's *The Good Husewifes Jewell*, 1587), gardening (Pierre Erondelle's *The French Garden for English Ladyes and Gentlewomen to Walke In*, 1605), and married life (Patrick Hannay's *A Happy Husband; or, Directions for a Maide to Choose Her Mate*, 1619). As the authors' names suggest, many of these works were translations, and almost all were written by men.

Starting in the 1570s, writers and their publishers increasingly addressed works of recreational literature (romance, fiction, and poetry) partially or even exclusively to women. Some books, such as Robert Greene's *Mamillia, a Mirrour or Looking-Glasse for the Ladies of Englande* (1583), directly specified in the title their desired audience. Others, such as Sir Philip Sidney's influential and popular romance *Arcadia* (1590–93), solicited female readership in their dedicatory epistles. The ranks of Sidney's followers eventually included his own niece, Mary Wroth, whose romance *Urania* was published in 1621.

In the literature of Shakespeare's time, women readers were not only wooed but also frequently railed at, in a continuation of a popular polemical genre that had long inspired heated charges and countercharges. Both sides in the polemic generally agreed that it was the duty of women to be chaste, dutiful, shamefast, and silent; the argument was whether women fulfilled or fell short of this proper role. Ironically, then, a modern reader is more likely to find inspiring accounts of courageous women not in the books written in defense of female virtue but in attacks on those who refused to be silent and obedient.

The most famous English skirmish in this controversy took place in a rash of pamphlets at the end of Shakespeare's life. Joseph Swetnam's crude *Araignment of Lewd, Idle, Froward, and Unconstant Women* (1615) provoked three fierce responses attributed to women: Rachel Speght's *A Mouzell [Muzzle] for Melastomus*, Ester Sowernam's *Ester Hath Hang'd Haman*, and Constantia Munda's *Worming of a Mad Dogge*, all 1617. There was also an anonymous play, *Swetnam, the Woman-hater, Arraigned by Women* (1618), in which Swetnam, depicted as a braggart and a lecher, is put on trial by women and made to recant his misogynistic lies.

Prior to the Swetnam controversy, only one English woman, "Jane Anger," had published a defense of women (*Jane Anger, Her Protection for Women*, 1589). Learned women writers in the sixteenth century tended not to become involved in public debate but rather to undertake a project to which it was difficult for even obdurately chauvinistic

SWETNAM,
THE
VVoman-hater,
ARRAIGNED BY
WOMEN.

A new Comedie,
Acted at the *Red Bull*, by the late
Queenes Seruants.

LONDON,
Printed for *Richard Meighen*, and are to be sold at his Shops
at Saint *Clements* Church, ouer-against *Essex* House, and
at *Westminster* Hall. 1 6 2 o.

Title page of *Swetnam, the Woman-hater, Arraigned by Women* (1620), a play written in response to Joseph Swetnam's *The Araignment of Lewd, Idle, Froward and Unconstant Women* (1615); the woodcut depicts the trial of Swetnam in Act 4.

males to object: the translation of devotional literature into English. Thomas More's daughter Margaret More Roper translated Erasmus (*A Devout Treatise upon the Pater Noster*, 1524); Francis Bacon's mother, Anne Cooke Bacon, translated Bishop John Jewel (*An Apologie or Answere in Defence of the Churche of Englande*, 1564); Anne Locke Prowse, a friend of John Knox, translated the *Sermons of John Calvin* in 1560; and Mary Sidney, Countess of Pembroke, completed the metrical version of the Psalms that her brother Sir Philip Sidney had begun. Elizabeth Tudor (the future queen) herself translated, at the age of eleven, Marguerite de Navarre's *Miroir de l'âme pécheresse* (*The Glass of the Sinful Soul*, 1544). The translation was dedicated to her stepmother, Catherine Parr, herself the author of a frequently reprinted book of prayers.

There was in the sixteenth and early seventeenth centuries a social stigma attached to print. Far from celebrating publication, authors, and particularly female authors, often apologized for exposing themselves to the public gaze. Nonetheless, a number of women ventured beyond pious translations circulated in manuscript. Some, including Elizabeth Tyrwhitt, Anne Dowriche, Isabella Whitney, Mary Sidney, and Aemilia Lanyer, composed and published their own poems. Aemilia Lanyer's *Salve Deus Rex Judaeorum*, published in 1611, is a poem in praise of virtuous women, from Eve and the Virgin Mary to her noble patron, the Countess of Cumberland. "A Description of Cookeham," appended to the poem, may be the first English-country-house poem.

The first Tudor woman to translate a play was the learned Jane Lumley, who composed an English version of Euripides' *Iphigenia at Aulis* (c. 1550). The first known original play in English by a woman was by Elizabeth Cary, Viscountess Falkland, whose *Tragedie of Mariam, the Faire Queene of Jewry* was published in 1613. This remarkable play, which was not intended to be performed, includes speeches in defense of women's equality, though the most powerful of these is spoken by the villainous Salome, who schemes to divorce her husband and marry her lover. Cary, who bore eleven children, herself had a deeply troubled marriage, which effectively came to an end in 1625, when, defying her husband's staunchly Protestant family, she openly converted to Catholicism. Her biography was written by one of her four daughters, all of whom became nuns.

Henry VIII and the English Reformation

There had long been serious ideological and institutional tensions in the religious life of England, but officially, at least, England in the early sixteenth century had a single religion, Catholicism, whose acknowledged head was the pope in Rome. In 1517, drawing upon long-standing currents of dissent, Martin Luther, an Augustinian monk and professor of theology at the University of Wittenberg, challenged the authority of the pope and attacked several key doctrines of the Catholic Church. According to Luther, the Church, with its elaborate hierarchical structure centered in Rome, its rich monasteries and convents, and its enormous political influence, had become hopelessly corrupt, a conspiracy of venal priests who manipulated popular superstitions to enrich themselves and amass worldly power. Luther began by vehemently attacking the sale of indulgences—certificates promising the remission of punishments to be suffered in the afterlife by souls sent to purgatory to expiate their sins. These indulgences were a fraud, he argued; purgatory itself had no foundation in the Bible, which in his view was the only legitimate source of religious truth. Christians would be saved not by scrupulously following the ritual practices fostered by the Catholic Church—observing fast days, reciting the ancient Latin prayers, endowing chantries to say prayers for the dead, and so on—but by faith and faith alone.

This challenge, which came to be known as the Reformation, spread and gathered force, especially in northern Europe, where major leaders like the Swiss pastor Huldrych Zwingli and the French theologian John Calvin established institutional structures and elaborated various and sometimes conflicting doctrinal principles. Calvin, whose thought came to be particularly influential in England, emphasized the obligation of governments to implement God's will in the world. He advanced too the doctrine of predestination, by which, as he put it, "God adopts some to hope of life and sentences others to eternal death." God's "secret election" of the saved made Calvin uncomfortable, but his study of the Scriptures had led him to conclude that "only a small number, out of an incalculable multitude, should obtain salvation." It might seem that such a conclusion would lead to passivity or even despair, but for Calvin predestination was a mystery bound up with faith, confidence, and an active engagement in the fashioning of a Christian community.

The Reformation had a direct and powerful impact on those territories, especially in northern Europe, where it gained control. Monasteries were sacked, their possessions seized by princes or sold off to the highest bidder; the monks and nuns, expelled from their cloisters, were encouraged to break their vows of chastity and find spouses, as Luther and his wife, a former nun, had done. In the great cathedrals and in hundreds of smaller churches and chapels, the elaborate altarpieces, bejeweled crucifixes, crystal reliquaries holding the bones of saints, and venerated statues and paintings were attacked as "idols" and often defaced or destroyed. Protestant congregations continued, for the most part, to celebrate the most sacred Christian ritual, the Eucharist, or Lord's Supper, but they did so in a profoundly different spirit from that of the Catholic Church—more as commemoration than as miracle—and they now prayed not in the ancient liturgical Latin but in the vernacular.

"The Pope as Antichrist riding the Beast of the Apocalypse." From *Fierie Tryall of God's Saints* (1611; author unknown).

The Reformation was at first vigorously resisted in England. Indeed, with the support of his ardently Catholic chancellor, Thomas More, Henry VIII personally wrote (or at least lent his name to) a vehement, often scatological attack on Luther's character and views, an attack for which the pope granted him the honorific title "Defender of the Faith." Protestant writings, including translations of the Scriptures into English, were seized by officials of the church and state and burned. Protestants who made their views known were persecuted, driven to flee the country, or arrested, put on trial, and burned at the stake. But the situation changed drastically and decisively when in 1527 Henry decided to seek a divorce from his first wife, Catherine of Aragon, in order to marry Anne Boleyn.

Catherine had given birth to six children, but since only a daughter, Mary, survived infancy, Henry did not have the son he craved. Then as now, the Catholic Church did not ordinarily grant divorce, but Henry's lawyers argued on technical grounds that the marriage was invalid (and, therefore, by extension, that Mary was illegitimate and hence unable to inherit the throne). Matters of this kind were far less doctrinal than diplomatic: Catherine, the daughter of Ferdinand of Aragon and Isabella of Castile, had powerful allies in Rome, and the pope ruled against Henry's petition for a divorce. A series of momentous events followed, as England lurched away from the Church of Rome. In 1531, Henry charged the entire clergy of England with having usurped royal authority in the administration of canon law (the ecclesiastical law that governed faith, discipline, and morals, including such matters as divorce). Under extreme pressure, including the threat of mass confiscations and imprisonment, the Convocation of the English Clergy begged for pardon, made a donation to the royal coffers of over £100,000, and admitted that the king was "supreme head of the English Church and clergy" (modified by the rider "as far as the law of Christ allows"). On May 15 of the next year, the convocation submitted to the demand that the king be the final arbiter of canon law; on the next day, Thomas More resigned his post.

In 1533, Henry's marriage to Catherine was officially declared null and void, and on June 1 Anne Boleyn was crowned queen (a coronation Shakespeare depicts in his late play *All Is True*). The king was promptly excommunicated by the pope, Clement VII. In the following year, the parliamentary Act of Succession confirmed the effects of the divorce and required an oath from all adult male subjects confirming the new dynastic settlement. Thomas More and John Fisher, Bishop of Rochester, were among the small number who refused. The Act of Supremacy, passed later in the year, formally declared the king to be "Supreme Head of the Church in England" and again required an oath to this effect. In 1535 and 1536, further acts made it treasonous to refuse the oath of royal supremacy or, as More had tried to do, to remain silent. The first victims were three Carthusian monks who rejected the oath—"How could the king, a layman," said one of them, "be Head of the Church of England?"—and in May 1535, they were duly hanged, drawn, and quartered. A few weeks later, Fisher and More were convicted and beheaded. Between 1536 and 1539, the monasteries were suppressed and their vast wealth seized by the crown.

Royal defiance of the authority of Rome was a key element in the Reformation but did not by itself constitute the establishment of Protestantism in England. On the contrary, in the same year that Fisher and More were martyred for their adherence to Roman Catholicism, twenty-five Protestants, members of a sect known as Anabaptists, were burned for heresy on a single day. Through most of his reign, Henry remained an equal-opportunity persecutor, ruthless to Catholics loyal to Rome and hostile to some of those who espoused Reformation ideas, though many of these ideas gradually established themselves on English soil.

Even when Henry was eager to do so, it proved impossible to eradicate Protestantism, as it would later prove impossible for his successors to eradicate Catholicism. In large part this tenacity arose from the passionate, often suicidal heroism of men and women who felt that their souls' salvation depended on the precise character of their Christianity. It arose, too, from a mid-fifteenth-century technological innovation that made it almost impossible to suppress unwelcome ideas: the printing press. Early Protestants quickly grasped that with a few clandestine presses they could defy the Catholic authorities and flood the country with their texts. "How many printing presses there be in the world," wrote the Protestant polemicist John Foxe, "so many block-houses there be against the high castle" of the pope in Rome, "so that either the pope must abolish knowledge and printing or printing at length will root him out." By the century's end, it was the Catholics who were using the clandestine press to propagate their beliefs in the face of Protestant persecution.

The greatest insurrection of the Tudor age was not over food, taxation, or land but over religion. On Sunday, October 1, 1536, stirred up by their vicar, the traditionalist parishioners of Louth in Lincolnshire, in the north of England, rose up in defiance of the ecclesiastical visitation sent to enforce royal supremacy. The rapidly spreading rebellion, which became known as the Pilgrimage of Grace, was led by the lawyer Robert Aske. The city of Lincoln fell to the rebels on October 6, and though it was soon retaken by royal forces, the rebels seized cities and fortifications throughout Yorkshire, Durham, Northumberland, Cumberland, Westmoreland, and northern Lancashire. Carlisle, Newcastle, and a few castles were all that were left to the king in the north. The Pilgrims soon numbered 40,000, led by some of the region's leading noblemen. The Duke of Norfolk, representing the crown, was forced to negotiate a truce, with a promise to support the rebels' demands that the king restore the monasteries, shore up the regional economy, suppress heresy, and dismiss his evil advisers.

The Pilgrims kept the peace for the rest of 1536, on the naive assumption that their demands would be met. But Henry moved suddenly early in 1537 to impose order and capture the ringleaders; 130 people, including lords, knights, heads of religious houses, and, of course, Robert Aske, were executed.

In 1549, two years after the death of Henry VIII, the west and the north of England were the sites of further unsuccessful risings for the restoration of Catholicism. The Western Rising is striking for its blend of Catholic universalism and intense regionalism among people who did not yet regard themselves as English. One of the rebels' articles, protesting against the imposition of the English Bible and religious service, declares, "We the Cornish men (whereof certain of us understand no English) utterly refuse this new English." The rebels besieged but failed to take the city of Exeter. As with almost all Tudor rebellions, the number of those executed in the aftermath of the failed rising was far greater than those killed in actual hostilities.

Henry VIII's Children: Edward, Mary, and Elizabeth

Upon Henry's death in 1547, his ten-year-old son, Edward VI, came to the throne, with his maternal uncle Edward Seymour named as Lord Protector and Duke of Somerset. Both Edward and his uncle were staunch Protestants, and reformers hastened to transform the English Church accordingly. During Edward's reign, Archbishop Thomas Cranmer formulated the forty-two articles of religion that became the core of Anglican orthodoxy and wrote the first Book of Common Prayer, which was officially adopted in 1549 as the basis of English worship services.

Somerset fell from power in 1549 and was replaced as Lord Protector by John Dudley, later Duke of Northumberland. When Edward fell seriously ill, probably of tuberculosis, Northumberland persuaded him to sign a will depriving his half sisters, Mary (the daughter of Catherine of Aragon) and Elizabeth (the daughter of Anne Boleyn), of their claim to royal succession. The Lord Protector was scheming to have his daughter-in-law, the Protestant Lady Jane Grey, a granddaughter of Henry VII, ascend to the throne. But when Edward died in 1553, Mary marshaled support, quickly secured the crown from Lady Jane (who had been titular queen for nine days), and had Lady Jane executed, along with her husband and Northumberland.

Queen Mary immediately took steps to return her kingdom to Roman Catholicism. Even though she was unable to get Parliament to agree to restore church lands seized under Henry VIII, she restored the Catholic Mass, once again affirmed the authority of the pope, and put down a rebellion that sought to depose her. Seconded by her ardently Catholic husband, Philip II, King of Spain, she initiated a series of religious persecutions that earned her (from her enemies) the name "Bloody Mary." Hundreds of Protestants took refuge abroad in cities such as Calvin's Geneva; almost three hundred less fortunate Protestants were condemned as heretics and burned at the stake.

The Family of Henry VIII: An Allegory of the Tudor Succession. By Lucas de Heere (c. 1572). Henry, in the middle, is flanked by Mary to his right, and Edward and Elizabeth to his left.

Mary died childless in 1558, and her younger half sister Elizabeth became queen. Elizabeth's succession had been by no means assured. For if Protestants regarded Henry VIII's marriage to Catherine as invalid and hence deemed Mary illegitimate, so Catholics regarded his marriage to Anne Boleyn as invalid and deemed Elizabeth illegitimate. Henry VIII himself seemed to support both views, since only three years after divorcing Catherine, he beheaded Anne Boleyn on charges of treason and adultery, and urged Parliament to invalidate the marriage. Moreover, though during her sister's reign Elizabeth outwardly complied with the official Catholic religious observance, Mary and her advisers were deeply suspicious, and the young princess's life was in grave danger. Poised and circumspect, Elizabeth warily evaded the traps that were set for her. As she ascended the throne, her actions were scrutinized for some indication of the country's future course. During her coronation procession, when a girl in an allegorical pageant presented her with a Bible in English translation—banned under Mary's reign—Elizabeth kissed the book, held it up reverently, and laid it to her breast; when the abbot and monks of Westminster Abbey came to greet her in broad daylight with candles (a symbol of Catholic devotion) in their hands, she briskly dismissed them with the telling words "Away with those torches! we can see well enough." England had returned to the Reformation.

Many English men and women, of all classes, remained loyal to the old Catholic faith, but English authorities under Elizabeth moved steadily, if cautiously, toward ensuring at least an outward conformity to the official Protestant settlement. Recusants, those who refused to attend regular Sunday services in their parish churches, were fined heavily. Anyone who wished to receive a university degree, to be ordained as a priest in the Church of England, or to be named as an officer of the state had to swear an oath to the royal supremacy. Commissioners were sent throughout the land to confirm that religious services were following the officially approved liturgy and to investigate any reported backsliding into Catholic practice or, alternatively, any attempts to introduce more radical reforms than the queen and her bishops had chosen to embrace. For the Protestant exiles who streamed back were eager not only to undo the damage Mary had done but to carry the Reformation much further. They sought to dismantle the church hierarchy, to purge the calendar of folk customs deemed pagan and the church service of ritual practices deemed superstitious, to dress the clergy in simple garb, and, at the extreme edge, to smash "idolatrous" statues, crucifixes, and altarpieces. Throughout her long reign, however, Elizabeth herself remained cautiously conservative and determined to hold in check what she regarded as the religious zealotry of Catholics, on the one side, and Puritans, on the other.

Shakespeare's plays tap into the ongoing confessional tensions: "Sometimes," Maria in *Twelfth Night* says of the sober, festivity-hating steward Malvolio, "he is a kind of puritan" (2.3.125). But they tend to avoid the risks of direct engagement: "The dev'l a puritan that he is, or anything constantly," Maria adds a moment later, "but a timepleaser, an affectioned ass" (2.3.131–32). *The Winter's Tale* features a statue that comes to life—exactly the kind of magical image that Protestant polemicists excoriated as Catholic superstition and idolatry—but the play is set in pre-Christian world of the Delphic oracle. And as if this careful distancing might not be enough, the play's ruler goes out of his way to pronounce the wonder legitimate: "If this be magic, let it be an art / Lawful as eating" (5.3.110–11).

In the space of a single lifetime, England had gone officially from Roman Catholicism, to Catholicism under the supreme headship of the English king, to a guarded Protestantism, to a more radical Protestantism, to a renewed and aggressive Roman Catholicism, and finally to Protestantism again. Each of these shifts was accompanied by danger, persecution, and death. It was enough to make some people wary. Or skeptical. Or extremely agile.

The English Bible

Luther had undertaken a fundamental critique of the Catholic Church's sacramental system, a critique founded on the twin principles of salvation by faith alone (*sola fide*) and the absolute primacy of the Bible (*sola scriptura*). *Sola fide* contrasted faith with "works," by which was meant primarily the whole elaborate system of rituals sanctified, conducted, or directed by the priests. Protestants proposed to modify or reinterpret many of these rituals or, as with the rituals associated with purgatory, to abolish them altogether. *Sola scriptura* required direct lay access to the Bible, which meant in practice the widespread availability of vernacular translations. The Roman Catholic Church had not always and everywhere opposed such translations, but it generally preferred that the populace encounter the Scriptures through the interpretations of the priests, trained to read the Latin translation known as the Vulgate. In times of great conflict, this preference for clerical mediation hardened into outright prohibition of vernacular translation and into persecution and book burning.

Zealous Protestants set out, in the teeth of fierce opposition, to put the Bible into the hands of the laity. A remarkable translation of the New Testament, by an English Lutheran named William Tyndale, was printed on the Continent and smuggled into England in 1525; Tyndale's translation of the Pentateuch, the first five books of the Hebrew Bible, followed in 1530. Many copies of these translations were seized and burned, as was the translator himself, but the printing press made it extremely difficult for authorities to eradicate books for which there was a passionate demand. The English Bible was a force that could not be suppressed, and it became, in its various forms, the single most important book of the sixteenth century.

Tyndale's translation was completed by an associate, Miles Coverdale, whose rendering of the Psalms proved to be particularly influential. Their joint labor was the basis for the Great Bible (1539), the first authorized version of the Bible in English, a copy of which was ordered to be placed in every church in the kingdom. With the accession of Edward VI, many editions of the Bible followed, but the process was sharply reversed when Mary came to the throne in 1553. Along with people condemned as heretics, English Bibles were burned in great bonfires.

Marian persecution was indirectly responsible for what would become the most popular as well as most scholarly English Bible, the translation known as the Geneva Bible, prepared, with extensive, learned, and often fiercely polemical marginal notes, by English exiles in Calvin's Geneva and widely diffused in England after Elizabeth came to the throne. In addition, Elizabethan church authorities ordered a careful revision of the Great Bible, and this version, known as the Bishops' Bible, was the one read in the churches. The success of the Geneva Bible in particular prompted those Elizabethan Catholics who now in turn found themselves in exile to bring out a vernacular translation of their own in order to counter the Protestant readings and glosses. This Catholic translation, known as the Rheims Bible, may have been known to Shakespeare, but he seems to have been far better acquainted with the Geneva Bible, and he would also have repeatedly heard the Bishops' Bible read aloud. Scholars have identified over three hundred references to the Bible in Shakespeare's work; in one version or another, the Scriptures had a powerful impact on his imagination.

A Female Monarch in a Male World

In the last year of Mary's reign, 1558, the Scottish Calvinist minister John Knox thundered against what he called "the monstrous regiment of women." When the Protestant Elizabeth came to the throne the following year, Knox and his religious brethren were less inclined to denounce female rulers, but in England as elsewhere in Europe there remained a widespread conviction that women were unsuited to wield power over men. Many men seem to have regarded the capacity for rational thought as exclusively male; women, they assumed, were led only by their passions. While gentlemen mastered the arts of rhetoric and warfare, gentlewomen were expected to display the virtues of silence and good housekeeping. Among upper-class males, the will to dominate others was acceptable and, indeed, admired; the same will in women was condemned as a grotesque and dangerous aberration.

One of the Armada portraits (c. 1588). Note Elizabeth's hand on the globe.

Apologists for the queen countered these prejudices by appealing to historical precedent and legal theory. History offered inspiring examples of just female rulers, notably Deborah, the biblical prophetess who judged Israel. In the legal sphere, crown lawyers advanced the theory of "the king's two bodies." As England's crowned head, Elizabeth's person was mystically divided between her mortal "body natural" and the immortal "body politic." While the queen's natural body was inevitably subject to the failings of human flesh, the body politic was timeless and perfect. In political terms, therefore, Elizabeth's sex was a matter of no consequence, a thing indifferent.

Elizabeth, who had received a fine humanist education and an extended, dangerous lesson in the art of survival, made it immediately clear that she intended to rule in more than name only. She assembled a group of trustworthy advisers, foremost among them William Cecil (later named Lord Burghley, also known as Burleigh), but she insisted on making many of the crucial decisions herself. Like many Renaissance monarchs, Elizabeth was drawn to the idea of royal absolutism, the theory that ultimate power was properly concentrated in her person and, indeed, that God had appointed her to be His deputy in the kingdom. Opposition to her rule, in this view, was not only a political act but also a kind of impiety, a blasphemous grudging against the will of God. Apologists for absolutism contended that God commands obedience even to manifestly wicked rulers whom He has sent to punish the sinfulness of humankind. Such arguments were routinely made in speeches and political tracts and from the pulpits of churches, where they were incorporated into the *First* and *Second Book of Homilies*, which clergymen were required to read out to their congregations.

In reality, Elizabeth's power was not absolute. The government had a network of spies, informers, and agents provocateurs, but it lacked a standing army, a national police force, an efficient system of communication, and an extensive bureaucracy. Above all, the queen had limited financial resources and needed to turn periodically to an independent and often recalcitrant Parliament, which by long tradition had the sole right to levy taxes and to grant subsidies. Members of the House of Commons were elected from their boroughs, not appointed by the monarch, and although the queen had considerable influence over their decisions, she could by no means dictate policy. Under these constraints, Elizabeth ruled through a combination of adroit political maneuvering and imperious command, all the while enhancing her authority in the eyes of both court and country by means of an extraordinary cult of love.

"We all loved her," Elizabeth's godson Sir John Harington wrote, with just a touch of irony, a few years after the queen's death, "for she said she loved us." Ambassadors, courtiers, and parliamentarians all submitted to Elizabeth's cult of love, in which the queen's gender was transformed from a potential liability into a significant asset. Those who approached her generally did so on their knees and were expected to address her with extravagant compliments fashioned from the period's most passionate love poetry; she in turn spoke, when it suited her to do so, in the language of love poetry. The court moved in an atmosphere of romance, with music, dancing, plays, and the elaborate, fancy-dress entertainments called masques. The queen adorned herself in gorgeous clothes and rich jewels. When she went on one of her summer "progresses," ceremonial journeys through her land, she looked like an exotic, sacred image in a religious cult of love, and her noble hosts virtually bankrupted themselves to lavish upon her the costliest pleasures. England's leading artists, such as the poet Edmund Spenser and the painter Nicholas Hilliard, enlisted themselves in the celebration of Elizabeth's mystery, likening her to the goddesses and queens of mythology: Diana, Astraea, Gloriana. Her cult drew its power from cultural discourses that ranged from the secular (her courtiers could pine for her as a cruel Petrarchan mistress) to the sacred (the veneration that under Catholicism had been due to the Virgin Mary could now be directed toward England's semidivine queen).

There was a sober, even grim, aspect to these poetical fantasies: Elizabeth was brilliant at playing one dangerous faction off another, now turning her gracious smiles on one favorite, now honoring his hated rival, now suddenly looking elsewhere and raising an obscure upstart to royal favor. And when she was disobeyed or when she felt that her prerogatives had been challenged, she was capable of an anger that, as Harington put it, "left no doubtings whose daughter she was." Thus, when Sir Walter Ralegh, one of the queen's glittering favorites, married without her knowledge or consent, he found himself promptly imprisoned in the Tower of London. And when the Protestant polemicist John Stubbs ventured to publish a pamphlet stridently denouncing the queen's proposed marriage to the French Catholic Duke of Alençon, Stubbs and his publisher were arrested and had their right hands chopped off. (After receiving the blow, the now prudent Stubbs lifted his hat with his remaining hand and cried, "God save the Queen!")

The queen's marriage negotiations were a particularly fraught issue. When she came to the throne at twenty-five years old, speculation about a suitable match, already widespread, intensified and remained for decades at a fever pitch, for the stakes were high. If Elizabeth died childless, the Tudor line would come to an end. The nearest heir was her cousin Mary, Queen of Scots, a Catholic whose claim was supported by France and by the papacy, and whose penchant for sexual and political intrigue confirmed the worst fears of English Protestants. The obvious way to avert the nightmare was for Elizabeth to marry and produce an heir, and the pressure upon her to do so was intense.

More than the royal succession hinged on the question of the queen's marriage; Elizabeth's perceived eligibility was a vital factor in the complex machinations of international diplomacy. A dynastic marriage between the Queen of England and a foreign ruler would forge an alliance powerful enough to alter the balance of power in Europe. The English court hosted a steady stream of ambassadors from kings and princes eager to win the hand of the royal maiden, and Elizabeth, who prided herself on speaking fluent French and Italian (and on reading Latin and Greek), played her romantic part with exemplary skill, sighing and spinning the negotiations out for months and even years.

Most probably, she never meant to marry any of her numerous foreign (and domestic) suitors. Such a decisive act would have meant the end of her independence, as well as the end of the marriage game by which she played one power off against another. One day she would seem to be on the verge of accepting a proposal; the next, she would vow never to forsake her virginity. "She is a Princess," the French ambassador remarked, "who can act any part she pleases."

The Kingdom in Danger

Beset by Catholic and Protestant extremists, Elizabeth contrived to forge a moderate compromise that enabled her realm to avert the massacres and civil wars that poisoned France and other countries on the Continent. But menace was never far off, and there were constant fears of conspiracy, rebellion, and assassination. Many of the fears swirled around Mary, Queen of Scots, who had been driven from her own kingdom in 1568 by a powerful faction of rebellious nobles and had taken refuge in England. Her presence, under a kind of house arrest, was the source of intense anxiety and helped generate continual rumors of plots. Some of these plots were real enough, others imaginary, still others traps set in motion by the secret agents of the government's intelligence service under the direction of Sir Francis Walsingham. The situation worsened greatly after the St. Bartholomew's Day Massacre of Protestants (Huguenots) in France (August 24, 1572), after Spanish imperial armies invaded the Netherlands in order to stamp out Protestant rebels, and after the assassination there of Europe's other major Protestant leader, William of Orange (1584).

The queen's life seemed to be in even greater danger after Pope Gregory XIII's proclamation in 1580 that the assassination of the great heretic Elizabeth (who had been excommunicated a decade before) would not constitute a mortal sin. The immediate effect of the proclamation was to make existence more difficult for English Catholics, most of whom were loyal to the queen but who fell under grave suspicion. Suspicion was intensified by the clandestine presence of English Jesuits, trained at seminaries abroad and smuggled back into England to serve the Roman Catholic cause. When Elizabeth's spymaster Walsingham unearthed an assassination plot in the correspondence between the Queen of Scots and the Catholic Anthony Babington, the wretched Mary's fate was sealed. After vacillating, a very reluctant Elizabeth signed the death warrant in February 1587, and her cousin was beheaded.

The long-anticipated military confrontation with Catholic Spain was now unavoidable. Elizabeth learned that Philip II, her former brother-in-law and onetime suitor, was preparing to send an enormous fleet against her island realm. It was to sail to the Netherlands, where a Spanish army would be waiting to embark and invade England. Barring its way was England's small fleet of well-armed and highly maneuverable fighting vessels, backed up by ships from the merchant navy. The Invincible Armada reached English waters in July 1588, only to be routed in one of the most famous and decisive naval battles in European history. Then, in what many viewed as an act of God on behalf of Protestant England, the Spanish fleet was dispersed and all but destroyed by violent storms.

As England braced itself to withstand the invasion that never came, Elizabeth appeared in person to review a detachment of soldiers assembled at Tilbury. Dressed in a white gown and a silver breastplate, she declared that though some among her councillors had urged her not to appear before a large crowd of armed men, she would never fail to trust the loyalty of her faithful and loving subjects. Nor did she fear the Spanish armies. "I know I have the body of a weak and feeble woman," Elizabeth declared, "but I have the heart and stomach of a king, and of England too." In this celebrated speech, Elizabeth displayed many of her most memorable qualities: her self-consciously histrionic command of grand public occasion, her subtle blending of magniloquent rhetoric and the language of love, her strategic appropriation of traditionally masculine qualities, and her great personal courage. "We princes," she once remarked, "are set on stages in the sight and view of all the world."

The English and Otherness

Shakespeare's London had a large population of resident aliens, mainly artisans and merchants and their families, from Portugal, Italy, Spain, Germany, and, above all, France and the Netherlands. Many of these people were Protestant refugees, and they were accorded some legal and economic protection by the government. But they were not always welcome by the local populace. Throughout the sixteenth century, London was the site of repeated demonstrations and, on occasion, bloody riots against the communities of foreign artisans, who were accused of taking jobs away from Englishmen. There was widespread hostility as well toward the Welsh, the Scots, and especially the Irish, whom the English had for centuries been struggling unsuccessfully to subdue. The kings of England claimed to be rulers of Ireland, but in reality they effectively controlled only a small area known as the Pale, extending north from Dublin. The great majority of the Irish people remained stubbornly Catholic and, despite endlessly reiterated English repression, burning of villages, destruction of crops, and massacres, incorrigibly independent.

Shakespeare's *Henry V* (1598–99) seems to invite the audience to celebrate the conjoined heroism of English, Welsh, Scots, and Irish soldiers all fighting together as a "band of brothers" against the French. But such a way of imagining the national community must be set against the tensions and conflicting interests that often set these brothers at each other's throats. As Shakespeare's King Henry realizes, a feared or hated foreign enemy helps at least to mask these tensions, and, indeed, in the face of the Spanish Armada, even the bitter gulf between Catholic and Protestant Englishmen seemed to narrow significantly. But the patriotic alliance was only temporary.

Another way of partially masking the sharp differences in language, belief, and custom among the peoples of the British Isles was to group these people together in contrast to the Jews. Medieval England's Jewish population, the recurrent object of persecution, extortion, and massacre, had been officially expelled by King Edward I in 1290, but Elizabethan England harbored a tiny number of Jews or Jewish converts to

A Jewish man poisoning a well. From Pierre Boaistuau, *Certaine Secrete Wonders of Nature* (1569).

Christianity who were treated with suspicion and hostility. One of these was Elizabeth's own physician, Roderigo Lopez, who was tried in 1594 for an alleged plot to poison the queen. Convicted and condemned to the hideous execution reserved for traitors, Lopez went to his death, in the words of the Elizabethan historian William Camden, "affirming that he loved the Queen as well as he loved Jesus Christ; which coming from a man of the Jewish profession moved no small laughter in the standers-by." It is difficult to gauge the meaning here of the phrase "the Jewish profession," used to describe a man who never, as far as we know, professed Judaism, just as it is difficult to gauge the meaning of the crowd's cruel laughter.

Elizabethans appear to have been fascinated by Jews and Judaism but uncertain whether the terms referred to a people, a foreign nation, a set of strange practices, a living faith, a defunct religion, a villainous conspiracy, or a messianic inheritance. Protestant Reformers brooded deeply on the Hebraic origins of Christianity; government officials ordered the arrest of those "suspected to be Jews"; villagers paid pennies to itinerant fortune-tellers who claimed to be descended from Abraham or masters of cabalistic mysteries; and London playgoers, perhaps including some who laughed at Lopez on the scaffold, enjoyed the spectacle of the downfall of the wicked Barabas in Christopher Marlowe's *Jew of Malta* (c. 1592) and the forced conversion of Shylock in Shakespeare's *Merchant of Venice* (1596–97). Few if any of Shakespeare's contemporaries would have encountered on English soil Jews who openly practiced their religion, though England probably harbored a small number of so-called Marranos, Spanish or Portuguese Jews who had officially converted to Christianity but secretly continued to observe Jewish practices. Jews were not officially permitted to resettle in England until the middle of the seventeenth century, and even then their legal status was ambiguous.

Shakespeare's England also had a small African population whose skin color was the subject of pseudoscientific speculation and theological debate. Some Elizabethans believed that Africans' blackness resulted from the climate of the regions in which they lived, where, as one traveler put it, they were "so scorched and vexed with the heat of the sun, that in many places they curse it when it riseth." Others held that blackness was a curse inherited from their forefather Chus, the son of Ham, who had, according to Genesis, wickedly exposed the nakedness of the drunken Noah. George Best, a proponent of this theory of inherited skin color, reported that "I myself have seen an Ethiopian as black as coal brought into England, who taking a fair English woman to wife, begat a son in all respects as black as the father was, although England were his native country, and an English woman his mother: whereby it seemeth this blackness proceedeth rather of some natural infection of that man."

As the word "infection" suggests, Elizabethans frequently regarded blackness as a physical defect, though the blacks who lived in England and Scotland throughout the sixteenth century were also treated as exotic curiosities. At his marriage to Anne of Denmark, James I entertained his bride and her family by commanding four naked black youths to dance before him in the snow. (The youths died of exposure shortly afterward.) In 1594, in the festivities celebrating the baptism of James's son, a "Black-Moor" entered pulling an elaborately decorated chariot that was, in the original plan, supposed to be drawn in by a lion. There was a black trumpeter in the courts of Henry VII and Henry VIII, while Elizabeth had at least two black servants, one an entertainer and the other a page. Africans became increasingly popular as servants in aristocratic and gentle households in the last decades of the sixteenth century.

Man with head beneath his shoulders. From a Spanish edition of Sir John Mandeville's *Travels*. See *Othello* 1.3.144–45: "and men whose heads / Do grow beneath their shoulders." Such men were occasionally reported by medieval travelers to the East.

An Indian dance. From Thomas Hariot, *A Briefe and True Report of the New Found Land of Virginia* (1590 ed.).

Some of these Africans were almost certainly slaves, though the legal status of slavery in England was ambiguous. In Cartwright's case (1569), the court ruled "that England was too Pure an Air for Slaves to breathe in," but there is evidence that black slaves were owned in Elizabethan and Jacobean England. Moreover, by the mid-sixteenth century, the English had become involved in the profitable trade that carried African slaves to the New World. In 1562, John Hawkins embarked on his first slaving voyage, transporting some three hundred blacks from the Guinea coast to Hispaniola, where they were sold for £10,000. Elizabeth is reported to have said of this venture that it was "detestable, and would call down the Vengeance of Heaven upon the Undertakers." Nevertheless, she invested in Hawkins's subsequent voyages and loaned him ships.

English men and women of the sixteenth century experienced an unprecedented increase in knowledge of the world beyond their island, for a number of reasons. Religious persecution compelled both Catholics and Protestants to live abroad; wealthy gentlemen (and, in at least a few cases, ladies) traveled in France and Italy to view the famous cultural monuments; merchants published accounts of distant lands such as Turkey, Morocco, and Russia; and military and trading ventures took English ships to still more distant shores. In 1496, a Venetian tradesman living in Bristol, John Cabot, was granted a license by Henry VII to sail on a voyage of exploration; with his son Sebastian, he discovered Newfoundland and Nova Scotia. Remarkable feats of seamanship and reconnaissance soon followed: on his ship the *Golden Hind,* Sir Francis Drake circumnavigated the globe in 1579 and laid claim to California on behalf of the queen; a few years later, a ship commanded by Thomas Cavendish also completed a circumnavigation. Sir Martin Frobisher explored bleak Baffin Island in search of a Northwest Passage to the Orient; Sir John Davis explored the west coast of Greenland and discovered the Falkland Islands off the coast of Argentina; Sir Walter Ralegh ventured up the Orinoco Delta, in what is now Venezuela, in search of the mythical land of El Dorado. Accounts of these and other exploits were collected by a clergyman and promoter of empire, Richard Hakluyt, and published as *The Principal Navigations* (1589; expanded edition 1599).

"To seek new worlds for gold, for praise, for glory," as Ralegh characterized such enterprises, was not for the faint of heart: Drake, Cavendish, Frobisher, and Hawkins all died at sea, as did huge numbers of those who sailed under their command. Elizabethans sensible enough to stay at home could do more than read written accounts of their fellow countrymen's far-reaching voyages. Expeditions brought back native plants (including, most famously, tobacco), animals, cultural artifacts, and, on occasion, samples of the native peoples themselves, most often seized against their will. There were exhibitions in London of a kidnapped Eskimo with his kayak and of Virginians with their canoes. Most of these miserable captives, violently uprooted and vulnerable to European diseases, quickly perished, but even in death they were evidently valuable property: when the English will not give one small coin "to relieve a lame beggar," one of the characters in *The Tempest* wryly remarks, "they will lay out ten to see a dead Indian" (2.2.30–31).

Perhaps most nations learn to define what they are by defining what they are not. This negative self-definition is, in any case, what Elizabethans seemed constantly to be doing, in travel books, sermons, political speeches, civic pageants, public exhibitions, and theatrical spectacles of otherness. The extraordinary variety of these exercises (which include public executions and urban riots, as well as more benign forms of curiosity) suggests that the boundaries of national identity were by no means clear and unequivocal. Even peoples whom English writers routinely, viciously stigmatize as irreducibly alien—Italians, Indians, Turks, and Jews—have a surprising instability in the Elizabethan imagination and may appear for brief, intense moments as powerful models to be admired and emulated before they resume their place as emblems of despised otherness.

James I and the Union of the Crowns

Though under great pressure to do so, the aging Elizabeth steadfastly refused to name her successor. It became increasingly apparent, however, that it would be James Stuart, the son of Mary, Queen of Scots, and by the time Elizabeth's health began to fail, several of her principal advisers, including her chief minister, Robert Cecil, had been for several years in secret correspondence with him in Edinburgh. Crowned King James VI of Scotland in 1567 when he was but one year old, Mary's son had been raised as a Protestant by his powerful guardians, and in 1589 he married a Protestant princess, Anne of Denmark. When Elizabeth died on March 24, 1603, English officials reported that on her deathbed the queen had named James to succeed her.

Upon his accession, James—now styled James VI of Scotland and James I of England—made plain his intention to unite his two kingdoms. As he told Parliament in 1604, "What God hath conjoined then, let no man separate. I am the husband, and all of the whole isle is my lawful wife; I am the head and it is my body; I am the shepherd and it is my flock." But the flock was less perfectly united than James optimistically envisioned: English and Scottish were sharply distinct identities, as were Welsh and Cornish and other peoples who were incorporated, with varying degrees of willingness, into the realm.

Fearing that to change the name of the kingdom would invalidate all laws and institutions established under the name of England, a fear that was partly real and partly a cover for anti-Scots prejudice, Parliament balked at James's desire to be called "King of

Funeral procession of Queen Elizabeth. From a watercolor sketch by an unknown artist (1603).

Great Britain" and resisted the unionist legislation that would have made Great Britain a legal reality. Although the English initially rejoiced at the peaceful transition from Elizabeth to her successor, there was a rising tide of resentment against James's advancement of Scots friends and his creation of new knighthoods. Lower down the social ladder, English and Scots occasionally clashed violently on the streets: in July 1603, James issued a proclamation against Scottish "insolencies," and in April 1604, he ordered the arrest of "swaggerers" waylaying Scots in London. The ensuing years did not bring the amity and docile obedience for which James hoped, and, though the navy now flew the Union Jack, combining the Scottish cross of St. Andrew and the English cross of St. George, the unification of the kingdoms remained throughout his reign an unfulfilled ambition.

Unfulfilled as well were James's lifelong dreams of ruling as an absolute monarch. Crown lawyers throughout Europe had long argued that a King, by virtue of his power to make law, must necessarily be above law. But in England, sovereignty was identified not with the King alone or with the people alone but with the "King in Parliament." Against his absolutist ambitions, James faced the crucial power to raise taxes that was vested not in the monarch but in the elected members of the Parliament. He faced as well a theory of republicanism that traced it roots back to ancient Rome and that prided itself on its steadfast and, if necessary, violent resistance to tyranny. Shakespeare's fascination with monarchy is apparent throughout his work, but in his Roman plays in particular, as well as in his long poem *The Rape of Lucrece*, he manifests an intense imaginative interest in the idea of a republic.

The Jacobean Court

With James as with Elizabeth, the royal court was the center of diplomacy, ambition, intrigue, and an intense jockeying for social position. As always in monarchies, proximity to the king's person was a central mark of favor, so that access to the royal bedchamber was one of the highest aims of the powerful, scheming lords who followed James from his sprawling London palace at Whitehall to the hunting lodges and country estates to which he loved to retreat. A coveted office, in the Jacobean as in the Tudor court, was the Groom of the Stool, the person who supervised the disposal of the king's wastes. The officeholder was close to the king at one of his most exposed and vulnerable moments, and enjoyed the further privilege of sleeping on a pallet at the foot of the royal bed and putting on the royal undershirt. Another, slightly less privileged official, the Gentleman of the Robes, dressed the king in his doublet and outer garments.

The royal lifestyle was increasingly expensive. Unlike Elizabeth, James had to maintain separate households for his queen and for the heir apparent, Prince Henry. (Upon Henry's death at the age of eighteen in 1612, his younger brother, Prince Charles, became heir, eventually succeeding his father in 1625.) James was also extremely generous to his friends, amassing his own huge debts in the course of paying off theirs. As early as 1605, he told his principal adviser that "it is a horror to me to think of the height of my place, the greatness of my debts, and the smallness of my means." This smallness notwithstanding, James continued to lavish gifts upon handsome favorites such as the Earl of Somerset, Robert Carr, and the Duke of Buckingham, George Villiers.

The attachment James formed for these favorites was highly romantic. "God so love me," the king wrote to Buckingham, "as I desire only to live in the world for your sake, and that I had rather live banished in any part of the earth with you than live a sorrowful widow's life without you." Such sentiments, not surprisingly, gave rise to widespread rumors of homosexual activities at court. The rumors are certainly plausible, even though the surviving evidence of same-sex relationships, at court or elsewhere, is extremely difficult to interpret. A statute of 1533 made "the detestable and abominable vice of buggery committed with mankind or beast" a felony punishable by death. (English law declined to recognize or criminalize lesbian acts.) The effect of the draconian laws against buggery and

sodomy seems to have been to reduce actual prosecutions to the barest minimum: for the next hundred years, there are no known cases of trials resulting in a death sentence for homosexual activity alone. If the legal record is, therefore, unreliable as an index of the extent of homosexual relations, the literary record (including, most famously, the majority of Shakespeare's sonnets) is equally opaque. Any poetic avowal of male-male love may simply be a formal expression of affection based on classical models, or, alternatively, it may be an expression of passionate physical and spiritual love. The interpretive difficulty is compounded by the absence in the period of any clear reference to a homosexual "identity," even though there are many references to same-sex acts and feelings. What is clear is that male friendships at the court of James and elsewhere were suffused with a potential eroticism, at once delightful and threatening, that subsequent periods policed more anxiously.

In addition to the extravagant expenditures on his favorites, James was also the patron of ever more

James I. By John De Critz the Elder (c. 1606).

Two Young Men. By Crispin van den Broeck (c. 1590).

elaborate feasts and masques. Shakespeare's work provides a small glimpse of these in *The Tempest,* with its exotic banquet and its "majestic vision" of mythological goddesses and dancing nymphs and reapers. The actual Jacobean court masques, designed by the great architect, painter, and engineer Inigo Jones, were spectacular, fantastic, technically ingenious, and staggeringly costly celebrations of regal magnificence. With their exquisite costumes and their elegant blend of music, dancing, and poetry, the masques, generally performed by the noble lords and ladies of the court, were deliberately ephemeral exercises in conspicuous expenditure and consumption: by tradition, at the end of the performance, the private audience would rush forward and tear to pieces the gorgeous scenery. And although masques were enormously sophisticated entertainments, often on rather esoteric allegorical themes, they could on occasion collapse into grotesque excess. In a letter of 1606, Sir John Harington describes a masque in honor of the visiting Danish king in which the participants, no doubt toasting their royal majesties, had had too much to drink. A lady playing the part of the Queen of Sheba attempted to present precious gifts, "but, forgetting the steps arising to the canopy, overset her caskets into his Danish Majesty's lap. . . . His Majesty then got up and would dance with the Queen of Sheba; but he fell down and humbled himself before her, and was carried to an inner chamber and laid on a bed." Meanwhile, Harington writes, the masque continued with a pageant of Faith, Hope, and Charity, but Charity could barely keep her balance, while Hope and Faith "were both sick and spewing in the lower hall." This was, we can hope, not a typical occasion.

While the English seem initially to have welcomed James's free-spending ways as a change from the relative parsimoniousness of Queen Elizabeth, they were dismayed by its consequences. Elizabeth had died owing £400,000. In 1608, the royal debt had risen to £1,400,000 and was increasing by £140,000 a year. The money to pay off this debt, or at least to keep it under control, was raised by various means. These included customs farming (leasing the right to collect customs duties to private individuals); the highly unpopular impositions (duties on the import of nonnecessities, such as spices, silks, and currants); the sale of crown lands; the sale of baronetcies; and appeals to an increasingly grudging and recalcitrant Parliament. In 1614, Parliament demanded an end to impositions before it would relieve the king and was angrily dissolved without completing its business.

James's Religious Policy and the Persecution of Witches

Before his accession to the English throne, the king had made known his view of Puritans, the general name for a variety of Protestant sects that were agitating for a radical reform of the Church, the overthrow of its conservative hierarchy of bishops, and the rejection of a large number of traditional rituals and practices. In a book he wrote, *Basilikon Doron* (1599), James denounced "brainsick and heady preachers" who were prepared "to let King, people, law and all be trod underfoot." Yet he was not entirely unwilling to consider religious reforms. In religion, as in foreign policy, he was above all concerned to maintain peace.

On his way south to claim the throne of England in 1603, James was presented with the Millenary Petition (signed by 1,000 ministers), which urged him as "our physician" to heal the disease of lingering "popish" ceremonies. He responded by calling a conference on the ceremonies of the Church of England, which duly took place at Hampton Court Palace in January 1604. The delegates who spoke for reform were moderates, and there was little in the outcome to satisfy Puritans. Nevertheless, while the Church of England continued to cling to such remnants of the Catholic past as wedding rings, square caps, bishops, and Christmas, the conference did produce some reform in the area of ecclesiastical discipline. It also authorized a new English translation of the Bible, known as the King James Bible, which was printed in 1611, too late to have been extensively used by Shakespeare. Along with Shakespeare's works, the King James Bible has probably had the profoundest influence on the subsequent history of English literature.

Having arranged this compromise, James saw his main task as ensuring conformity. He promulgated the 1604 Canons (the first definitive code of canon law since the Reformation), which required all ministers to subscribe to three articles. The first affirmed royal supremacy; the second confirmed that there was nothing in the Book of Common Prayer "contrary to the Word of God" and required ministers to use only the authorized

The "swimming" of a suspected witch (1615).

services; the third asserted that the central tenets of the Church of England were "agree-able to the Word of God." There were strong objections to the second and third articles from those of Puritan leanings inside and outside the House of Commons. In the end, many ministers refused to conform or subscribe to the articles, but only about 90 of them, or 1 percent of the clergy, were deprived of their livings. In its theology and composition, the Church of England was little changed from what it had been under Elizabeth. In hindsight, what is most striking are the ominous signs of growing religious divisions that would by the 1640s burst forth in civil war and the execution of James's son Charles.

James seems to have taken seriously the official claims to the sacredness of king-ship, and he certainly took seriously his own theories of religion and politics, which he had printed for the edification of his people. He was convinced that Satan, perpetually warring against God and His representatives on earth, was continually plotting against him. James thought, moreover, that he possessed special insight into Satan's wicked agents, the witches, and in 1597, while King of Scotland, he published his *Dae-monology*, a learned exposition of their malign threat to his godly rule. Hundreds of witches, he believed, were involved in a 1590 conspiracy to kill him by raising storms at sea when he was sailing home from Denmark with his new bride.

In the 1590s, Scotland embarked on a virulent witch craze of the kind that had since the fifteenth century repeatedly afflicted France, Switzerland, and Germany, where many thousands of women (and a much smaller number of men) were caught in a nightmar-ish web of wild accusations. Tortured into lurid confessions of infant cannibalism, night flying, and sexual intercourse with the devil at huge, orgiastic "witches' Sabbaths," the vic-tims had little chance to defend themselves and were routinely burned at the stake.

In England, too, there were witchcraft prosecutions, but on a much smaller scale and with significant differences in the nature of the accusations and the judicial procedures. Witch trials began in England in the 1540s; statutes against witchcraft were enacted in 1542, 1563, and 1604. English law did not allow judicial torture, stipulated lesser pun-ishments in cases of "white magic," and mandated jury trials. Juries acquitted more than half of the defendants in witchcraft trials; in Essex, where the judicial records are partic-ularly extensive, some 24 percent of those accused were executed, while the remainder of those convicted were pilloried and imprisoned or sentenced and reprieved. The accused were generally charged with *maleficium*, an evil deed—usually harming neighbors, caus-ing destructive storms, or killing farm animals—but not with worshipping Satan.

After 1603, when James came to the English throne, he somewhat moderated his enthusiasm for the judicial murder of witches, for the most part defenseless, poor women resented by their neighbors. Although he did nothing to mitigate the ferocity of the ongoing witch hunts in his native Scotland, he did not try to institute Scottish-style per-secutions and trials in his new realm. This relative waning of persecutorial eagerness prin-cipally reflects the differences between England and Scotland, but it may also bespeak some small, nascent skepticism on James's part about the quality of evidence brought against the accused and about the reliability of the "confessions" extracted from them. It is sobering to reflect that plays like Shakespeare's *Macbeth* (1606), Thomas Middleton's *Witch* (before 1616), and Thomas Dekker, John Ford, and William Rowley's *Witch of Edmonton* (1621) seem to be less the allies of skepticism than the exploiters of fear.

The Playing Field

Cosmic Spectacles

The first permanent, freestanding public theaters in England date only from Shakespeare's own lifetime: a London playhouse, the Red Lion, is mentioned in 1567, and James Burbage's playhouse, The Theatre, was built in 1576. (The innovative use of these new stages, crucial to a full understanding of Shakespeare's achievement, is, in this volume, the subject of a separate essay by the theater historian Andrew Gurr, pages 79–99.) But it is misleading to identify English drama exclusively with these specially constructed playhouses, for in fact there was a rich and vital theatrical tradition in England stretching back for centuries. Many towns in late medieval England were the sites of annual festivals that mounted elaborate cycles of plays depicting the great biblical stories, from the creation of the world to Christ's Passion and its miraculous aftermath. Most of these plays have been lost, but the surviving cycles, such as those from York, are magnificent and complex works of art. They are sometimes called "mystery plays," either because they were performed by the guilds of various crafts (known as "mysteries") or, more likely, because they represented the mysteries of the faith. The cycles were most often performed on the annual feast day instituted in the early fourteenth century in honor of the Corpus Christi, the sacrament of the Lord's Supper, which is perhaps the greatest of these religious mysteries.

The Feast of Corpus Christi, celebrated on the Thursday following Trinity Sunday, helped give the play cycles their extraordinary cultural resonance, but it also contributed to their downfall. For along with the specifically liturgical plays traditionally performed by religious confraternities and the "saints' plays," which depicted miraculous events in the lives of individual holy men and women, the mystery cycles were closely identified with the Catholic Church. Protestant authorities in the sixteenth century, eager to eradicate all remnants of popular Catholic piety, moved to suppress the annual procession of the Host, with its gorgeous banners, pageant carts, and cycle of visionary plays. In 1548, the Feast of Corpus Christi was abolished. Towns that continued to perform the mysteries were under increasing pressure to abandon them. It is sometimes said that the cycles were already dying out from neglect, but recent research has shown that many towns and their guilds were extremely reluctant to give them up. Desperate offers to strip away any traces of Catholic doctrine and to submit the play scripts to the authorities for their approval met with unbending opposition from the government. In 1576, the courts gave York permission to perform its cycle but only if

> in the said play no pageant be used or set forth wherein the Majesty of God the Father, God the Son, or God the Holy Ghost or the administration of either the Sacraments of baptism or of the Lord's Supper be counterfeited or represented, or anything played which tend to the maintenance of superstition and idolatry or which be contrary to the laws of God . . . or of the realm.

Such "permission" was tantamount to an outright ban. The local officials in the city of Norwich, proud of their St. George and the Dragon play, asked if they could at least parade the dragon costume through the streets, but even this modest request was refused. It is likely that as a young man Shakespeare had seen some of these plays: when Hamlet says of a noisy, strutting theatrical performance that it "out-Herods Herod," he is alluding to the famously bombastic role of Herod of Jewry in the mystery plays. But by the century's end, the cycles were no longer performed.

Early English theater was by no means restricted to these civic and religious festivals. Payments to professional and amateur performers appear in early records of towns and aristocratic households, although the terms—"ministralli," "histriones," "mimi," "lusores," and so forth—are not used with great consistency and make it difficult to distinguish among minstrels, jugglers, stage players, and other entertainers. Performers acted in town halls and the halls of guilds and aristocratic mansions, on scaffolds erected in town squares and marketplaces, on pageant wagons in the streets, and in inn yards. By the fifteenth century and probably earlier, there were organized companies of players traveling under noble patronage. Such companies earned a living providing amusement, while enhancing the prestige of the patron.

A description of a provincial performance in the late sixteenth century, written by one R. Willis, provides a glimpse of what seems to have been the usual procedure:

> In the City of Gloucester the manner is (as I think it is in other like corporations) that when the Players of Interludes come to town, they first attend the Mayor to

Panorama of London, showing two theaters, both round and both flying flags: a flying flag indicated that a performance was in progress. The Globe is in the foreground, and the Beargarden or Hope is to the left.

inform him what nobleman's servant they are, and so to get licence for their public playing; and if the Mayor like the Actors, or would show respect to their Lord and Master, he appoints them to play their first play before himself and the Aldermen and common Council of the City and that is called the Mayor's play, where every-one that will come in without money, the Mayor giving the players a reward as he thinks fit to show respect unto them.

In addition to their take from this "first play," the players would almost certainly have supplemented their income by performing in halls and inn yards, where they could pass the hat after the performance or even on some occasions charge an admission fee. It was no doubt a precarious existence.

The "Interludes" mentioned in Willis's description of the Gloucester performances are likely plays that were, in effect, staged dialogues on religious, moral, and political themes. Such works could, like the mysteries, be associated with Catholicism, but they were also used in the sixteenth century to convey polemical Protestant messages, and they reached outside the religious sphere to address secular concerns as well. Henry Medwall's *Fulgens and Lucrece* (c. 1490–1501), for example, pits a wealthy but dis-solute nobleman against a virtuous public servant of humble origins, while John Hey-wood's *Play of the Weather* (c. 1525–33) stages a debate among social rivals, including a gentleman, a merchant, a forest ranger, and two millers. The structure of such plays reflects the training in argumentation that students received in Tudor schools and, in particular, the sustained practice in examining all sides of a difficult question. Some of Shakespeare's amazing ability to look at critical issues from multiple perspectives may be traced back to this practice and the dramatic interludes it helped to inspire.

Another major form of theater that flourished in England in the fifteenth century and continued on into the sixteenth was the morality play. Like the mysteries, morali-ties addressed questions of the ultimate fate of the soul. They did so, however, not by rehearsing scriptural stories but by dramatizing allegories of spiritual struggle. Typically, a person named Human or Mankind or Youth is faced with a choice between a pious life in the company of such associates as Mercy, Discretion, and Good Deeds and a dis-solute life among riotous companions like Lust or Mischief. Plays like *Mankind* (c. 1465–70) and *Everyman* (c. 1495) show how powerful these unpromising-sounding dramas could be, in part because of the extraordinary comic vitality of the evil charac-ter, or Vice, and in part because of the poignancy and terror of an individual's encounter with death. Shakespeare clearly grasped this power. The hunchbacked Duke of Gloucester in *Richard III* gleefully likens himself to "the formal Vice, Iniquity." And when Othello wavers between Desdemona and Iago (himself a Vice figure), his anguished dilemma echoes the fateful choice repeatedly faced by the troubled, vulnerable protagonists of the moralities.

If such plays sound a bit like sermons, it is because they were. Clerics and actors shared some of the same rhetorical skills. It would be misleading to regard churchgoing and playgoing as comparable entertainments, but in attacking the stage, ministers often seemed to regard the professional players as dangerous rivals. The players themselves were generally too discreet to rise to the challenge; it would have been foolhardy to present the theater as the Church's direct competitor. Yet in its moral intensity and its command of impassioned language, the stage frequently emulates and outdoes the pulpit.

Music and Dance

Playacting took its place alongside other forms of public expression and entertainment as well. Perhaps the most important, from the perspective of the theater, were music and dance, since these were directly and repeatedly incorporated into plays. Many plays, comedies and tragedies alike, include occasions that call upon the characters to dance: hence Beatrice and Benedick join the other masked guests at the dance in *Much Ado About Nothing;* in *Twelfth Night,* the befuddled Sir Andrew, at the instigation of the drunken Sir Toby Belch, displays his skill, such as it is, in capering; Romeo and Juliet first see each other at the Capulet ball; the witches dance in a ring around the hideous caldron and perform an "antic round" to cheer Macbeth's spirits; and, in one of Shakespeare's strangest and most wonderful scenes, the drunken Antony in *Antony and Cleopatra* joins hands with Caesar, Enobarbus, Pompey, and others to dance "the Egyptian Bacchanals."

Moreover, virtually all plays in the period, including Shakespeare's, apparently ended with a dance. Brushing off the theatrical gore and changing their expressions from woe to pleasure, the actors in plays like *Hamlet* and *King Lear* would presumably have received the audience's applause and then bid for a second round of applause by performing a stately pavane or a lively jig. Indeed, jigs, with their comical leaping dance steps often accompanied by scurrilous ballads, became so popular that they drew not only large crowds but also official disapproval. A court order of 1612 complained about the "cutpurses and other lewd and ill-disposed persons" who flocked to the theater at the end of every play to be entertained by "lewd jigs, songs, and dances." The players were warned to suppress these disreputable entertainments on pain of imprisonment.

The displays of dancing onstage clearly reflected a widespread popular interest in dancing outside the walls of the playhouse as well. Renaissance intellectuals conjured up visions of the universe as a great cosmic dance, poets figured relations between men and women in terms of popular dance steps, stern moralists denounced dancing as an incitement to filthy lewdness, and, perhaps as significant, men of all classes evidently spent a great deal of time worrying about how shapely their legs looked in tights and how gracefully they could leap. Shakespeare assumes that his audience will be quite familiar with a variety of dances. "For hear me, Hero," Beatrice tells her friend, "wooing, wedding, and repenting is as a Scotch jig, a measure, and a cinquepace" (2.1.60–61). Her speech dwells on the comparison a bit, teasing out its implications, but it still does not make much sense if you do not already know something about the dances and perhaps occasionally venture to perform them yourself.

Closely linked to dancing and even more central to the stage was music, both instrumental and vocal. In the early sixteenth century, the Reformation had been disastrous for sacred music: many church organs were destroyed, choir schools were closed, the glorious polyphonal liturgies sung in the monasteries were suppressed. But by the latter part of the century, new perspectives were reinvigorating English music. Latin Masses were reset in English, and tunes were written for newly translated, metrical psalms. More important for the theater, styles of secular music were developed that emphasized music's link to humanist eloquence, its ability to heighten and to rival rhetorically powerful texts.

Richard Tarlton. Tarlton was the lead comedian of the Queen's Company from 1583, the year of its founding, until 1588, when he died.

This link is particularly evident in vocal music, at which Elizabethan composers excelled. Renowned composers William Byrd, Thomas Morley, John Dowland, and others wrote a rich profusion of madrigals (part songs for two to eight voices unaccompanied) and ayres (songs for solo voice, generally accompanied by the lute). These works, along with hymns, popular ballads, rounds, catches, and other forms of song, enjoyed immense popularity, not only in the royal court, where musical skill was regarded as an important accomplishment, and in aristocratic households, where professional musicians were employed as entertainers, but also in less exalted social circles. In his *Plaine and Easie Introduction to Practicall Musicke* (1597), Morley tells a story of social humiliation at a failure to perform that suggests that a well-educated Elizabethan was expected to be able to sing at sight. Even if this is an exaggeration in the interest of book sales, there is evidence of impressively widespread musical literacy, reflected in a splendid array of music for the lute, viol, recorder, harp, and virginal, as well as the marvelous vocal music.

Whether it is the aristocratic Orsino luxuriating in the dying fall of an exquisite melody or bully Bottom craving "the tongs and the bones," Shakespeare's characters frequently call for music. They also repeatedly give voice to the age's conviction that there was a deep relation between musical harmony and the harmonies of the well-ordered individual and state. "The man that hath no music in himself," warns Lorenzo in *The Merchant of Venice*, "nor is not moved with concord of sweet sounds, / Is fit for treasons, stratagems, and spoils" (5.1.82–84). This conviction, in turn, reflects a still deeper link between musical harmony and the divinely created harmony of the cosmos. When Ulysses, in *Troilus and Cressida*, wishes to convey the image of universal chaos, he speaks of the untuning of a string (1.3.109).

The playing companies must have regularly employed trained musicians, and many actors (like the actor who in playing Pandarus in *Troilus and Cressida* is supposed to accompany himself on the lute) must have possessed musical skill. Unfortunately, we possess the original settings for very few of Shakespeare's songs, possibly because many of them may have been set to popular tunes of the time that everyone knew and no one bothered to write down.

Alternative Entertainments

Plays, music, and dancing were by no means the only shows in town. There were jousts, tournaments, royal entries, religious processions, pageants in honor of newly installed civic officials or ambassadors arriving from abroad; wedding masques, court masques, and costumed entertainments known as "disguisings" or "mummings"; juggling acts, fortune-tellers, exhibitions of swordsmanship, mountebanks, folk healers, storytellers, magic shows; bearbaiting, bullbaiting, cockfighting, and other blood sports; folk festivals such as Maying, the Feast of Fools, Carnival, and Whitsun Ales. For several years, Elizabethan Londoners were delighted by a trained animal— Banks's Horse—that could, it was thought, do arithmetic and answer questions. And there was always the grim but compelling spectacle of public shaming, mutilation, and execution.

Most English towns had stocks and whipping posts. Drunks, fraudulent merchants, adulterers, and quarrelers could be placed in carts or mounted backward on asses and paraded through the streets for crowds to jeer and throw refuse at. Women accused of being scolds could be publicly muzzled by an iron device called a "brank" or tied to a cucking stool and dunked in the river. Convicted criminals could have their ears cut off, their noses slit, their foreheads branded. Public beheadings (generally reserved for the elite) and hangings were common. In the worst cases, felons were sentenced to be "hanged by the neck, and being alive cut down, and your privy members to be cut off, and your bowels to be taken out of your belly and there burned, you being alive."

Shakespeare occasionally takes note of these alternative entertainments: at the end of *Macbeth*, for example, with his enemies closing in on him, the doomed tyrant declares, "They have tied me to a stake. I cannot fly, / But bear-like I must fight the course" (5.7.1–2). The audience is reminded then that it is witnessing the human equivalent of a popular spectacle—a bear chained to a stake and attacked by fierce dogs—that they could have paid to watch at an arena near the Globe. And when, a few moments later, Macduff enters carrying Macbeth's head, the audience is seeing the theatrical equivalent of the execution of criminals and traitors that they could have also watched in the flesh, as it were, nearby. In a different key, the audiences who paid to see *A Midsummer Night's Dream* or *The Winter's Tale* got to enjoy the comic spectacle of a Maying and a Whitsun Pastoral, while the spectators of *The Tempest* could gawk at what the Folio list of characters calls a "salvage and deformed slave" and to enjoy an aristocratic magician's wedding masque in honor of his daughter.

An Elizabethan hanging.

The Enemies of the Stage

In 1624, a touring company of players arrived in Norwich and requested permission to perform. Permission was denied, but the municipal authorities, "in regard of the honorable respect which this City beareth to the right honorable the Lord Chamberlain," gave the players 20 shillings to get out of town. Throughout the sixteenth and early seventeenth centuries, there are many similar records of civic officials prohibiting performances and then, to appease a powerful patron, paying the actors to take their skills elsewhere. As early as the 1570s, there is evidence that the London authorities, while mindful of the players' influential protectors, were energetically trying to drive the theater out of the city.

Why should what we now regard as one of the undisputed glories of the age have aroused so much hostility? One answer, curiously enough, is traffic: plays drew large audiences—the public theaters could accommodate thousands—and residents objected to the crowds, the noise, and the crush of carriages. Other, more serious concerns were public health and crime. It was thought that numerous diseases, including the dreaded bubonic plague, were spread by noxious odors, and the packed playhouses were obvious breeding grounds for infection. (Patrons often tried to protect themselves by sniffing nosegays or stuffing cloves into their nostrils.) The large crowds drew pickpockets and other scoundrels. On one memorable afternoon, a pickpocket was caught in the act and tied for the duration of the play to one of the posts that held up the canopy above the stage.

Syphilis victim in a tub. Frontispiece to the play *Cornelianum Dolium* (1638), possibly authored by Thomas Randolph. The tub inscription translates as "I sit on the throne of love, I suffer in the tub," and the banner as "Farewell O sexual pleasures and lusts."

The theater was, moreover, a well-known haunt of prostitutes and, it was alleged, a place where innocent maids were seduced and respectable matrons corrupted. It was darkly rumored that "chambers and secret places" adjoined the theater galleries, and in any case, taverns, disreputable inns, and whorehouses were close at hand.

There were other charges as well. Plays were performed in the afternoon and, therefore, drew people, especially the young, away from their work. They were schools of idleness, luring apprentices from their trades, law students from their studies, housewives from their kitchens, and potentially pious souls from the sober meditations to which they might otherwise devote themselves. Wasting their time and money on disreputable shows, citizens exposed themselves to sexual provocation and outright political sedition. Even when the content of plays was morally exemplary—and, of course, few plays were so gratifyingly high-minded—the theater itself, in the eyes of most mayors and aldermen, was inherently disorderly.

The attack on the stage by civic officials was echoed and intensified by many of the age's moralists and religious leaders, especially those associated with Puritanism. While English Protestants earlier in the sixteenth century had attempted to counter the Catholic mystery cycles and saints' plays by mounting their own doctrinally correct dramas, by the century's end a fairly widespread consensus, even among those mildly sympathetic toward the theater, held that the stage and the pulpit were in tension with one another. After 1591, a ban on Sunday performances was strictly enforced, and in 1606, Parliament passed an act imposing a fine of £10 on any person who shall "in any stage-play, interlude, show, May-game, or pageant, jestingly or profanely speak or use the holy name of God, or of Christ Jesus, or of the Holy Ghost, or of the Trinity (which are not to be spoken but with fear and reverence)." If changes in the printed texts are a reliable indication, the players seem to have complied at least to some degree with the ruling. The Folio (1623) text of *Richard III*, for example, omits the Quarto's (1597) four uses of "zounds" (for "God's wounds"), along with a mention of "Christ's dear blood shed for our grievous sins"; "God's my judge" in *The Merchant of Venice* becomes "well I know"; "By Jesu" in *Henry V* becomes a very proper "I say"; and in all the plays, "God" from time to time metamorphoses to "Jove."

But for some of the theater's more extreme critics, these modest expurgations were tiny bandages on a gaping wound. In his huge book *Histriomastix* (1633), William Prynne regurgitates half a century of frenzied attacks on the "sinful, heathenish, lewd, ungodly Spectacles." In the eyes of Prynne and his fellow antitheatricalists, stage plays were part of a demonic tangle of obscene practices proliferating like a cancer in the body of society. It is "manifest to all men's judgments," he writes, that

effeminate mixed dancing, dicing, stage-plays, lascivious pictures, wanton fashions, face-painting, health-drinking, long hair, love-locks, periwigs, women's curling, powdering and cutting of their hair, bonfires, New-year's gifts, May-games, amorous pastorals, lascivious effeminate music, excessive laughter, luxurious disorderly Christmas-keeping, mummeries . . . [are] wicked, unchristian pastimes.

Given the anxious emphasis on effeminacy, it is not surprising that denunciations of this kind obsessively focused on the use of boy actors to play the female parts. The enemies of the stage charged that theatrical transvestism excited illicit sexual desires, both heterosexual and homosexual.

Since cross-dressing violated a biblical prohibition (Deuteronomy 22:5), religious antitheatricalists attacked it as wicked regardless of its erotic charge; indeed, they often seemed to consider any act of impersonation as inherently wicked. In their view, the theater itself was Satan's domain. Thus a Cambridge scholar, John Greene, reports the sad fate of "a Christian woman" who went to the theater to see a play: "She entered in well and sound, but she returned and came forth possessed of the devil. Whereupon certain godly brethren demanded Satan how he durst be so bold, as to enter into her a Christian. Whereto he answered, that *he found her in his own house,* and therefore took possession of her as his own" (italic in original). When the "godly brethren" came to power in the mid-seventeenth century, with the overthrow of Charles I, they saw to it that the playhouses, temporarily shut down in 1642 at the onset of the Civil War, remained closed. The theater did not resume until the restoration of the monarchy in 1660.

Faced with enemies among civic officials and religious leaders, Elizabethan and Jacobean playing companies relied on the protection of their powerful patrons. As the liveried servants of aristocrats or of the monarch, the players could refute the charge that they were mere vagabonds, and they claimed, as a convenient legal fiction, that their public performances were necessary rehearsals in anticipation of those occasions when they would be called upon to entertain their noble masters. But harassment by the mayor and aldermen continued unabated, and the players were forced to build their theaters outside the immediate jurisdiction of the city authorities, either in the suburbs or in the areas known as the "liberties." A liberty was a piece of land within the City of London itself that was not directly subject to the authority of the lord mayor. The most significant of these from the point of view of the theater was the area near St. Paul's Cathedral called "the Blackfriars," where, until the dissolution of the monasteries in 1538, there had been a

Dominican monastery. It was here that in 1608 Shakespeare's company, then called the King's Men, built the indoor playhouse in which they performed during the winter months, reserving the open-air Globe in the suburb of Southwark for their summer performances.

Censorship and Regulation

In addition to those authorities who campaigned to shut down the theater, there were others whose task was to oversee, regulate, and censor it. Given the outright hostility of the former, the latter may have seemed to the London players equivocal allies rather than enemies. After all, plays that passed the censor were at least licensed to be performed and hence conceded to have some limited legitimacy. In April 1559, at the very start of her reign, Queen Elizabeth drafted a proposal that for the first time envisaged a system for the prior review and regulation of plays throughout her kingdom:

> The Queen's Majesty doth straightly forbid all manner interludes to be played either openly or privately, except the same be notified beforehand, and licensed within any city or town corporate, by the mayor or other chief officers of the same, and within any shire, by such as shall be lieutenants for the Queen's Majesty in the same shire, or by two of the Justices of Peace inhabiting within that part of the shire where any shall be played. . . . And for instruction to every of the said officers, her Majesty doth likewise charge every of them, as they will answer: that they permit none to be played wherein either matters of religion or of the governance of the estate of the commonweal shall be handled or treated upon, but by men of authority, learning and wisdom, nor to be handled before any audience, but of grave and discreet persons.

This proposal, which may not have been formally enacted, makes an important distinction between those who are entitled to address sensitive issues of religion and politics—authors "of authority, learning and wisdom" addressing audiences "of grave and discreet persons"—and those who are forbidden to do so.

The London public theater, with its playwrights who were the sons of glovers, shoemakers, and bricklayers and its audiences in which the privileged classes mingled with rowdy apprentices, masked women, and servants, was clearly not a place to which the government wished to grant freedom of expression. In 1581, the Master of the Revels, an official in the lord chamberlain's department whose role had hitherto been to provide entertainment at court, was given an expanded commission. Sir Edmund Tilney, the functionary who held the office, was authorized

> to warn, command, and appoint in all places within this our Realm of England, as well within franchises and liberties as without, all and every player or players with their playmakers, either belonging to any nobleman or otherwise . . . to appear before him with all such plays, tragedies, comedies, or shows as they shall in readiness or mean to set forth, and them to recite before our said Servant or his sufficient deputy, whom we ordain, appoint, and authorize by these presents of all such shows, plays, players, and playmakers, together with their playing places, to order and reform, authorize and put down, as shall be thought meet or unmeet unto himself or his said deputy in that behalf.

What emerged from this commission was in effect a national system of regulation and censorship. One of its consequences was to restrict virtually all licensed theater to the handful of authorized London-based playing companies. These companies would have to submit their plays for official scrutiny, but in return they received implicit, and on occasion explicit, protection against the continued fierce opposition of the local authorities. Plays reviewed and allowed by the Master of the Revels had been deemed fit to be performed before the monarch; how could mere aldermen legitimately claim that such plays should be banned as seditious?

The key question, of course, is how carefully the Master of the Revels scrutinized the plays brought before him either to hear or, more often from the 1590s onward, to peruse. What was Tilney, who served in the office until his death in 1610, or his successor, Sir George Buc, who served from 1610 to 1621, looking for? What did they insist be cut before they would release what was known as the "allowed copy," the only version licensed for performance? Unfortunately, the office books of the Master of the Revels in Shakespeare's time have been lost; what survives is a handful of scripts on which Tilney, Buc, and their assistants jotted their instructions. These suggest that the readings were rather painstaking, with careful attention paid to possible religious, political, and diplomatic repercussions. References, directly or strongly implied, to any living Christian prince or any important English nobleman, gentleman, or government official were particularly sensitive and likely to be struck. Renaissance political life was highly personalized; people in power were exceptionally alert to insult and zealously patrolled the boundaries of their prestige and reputation.

Moreover, the censors knew that audiences and readers were quite adept at applying theatrical representations distanced in time and space to their own world. At a time of riots against resident foreigners, Tilney read *Sir Thomas More,* a play in which Shakespeare probably had a hand, and instructed the players to cut scenes that, even though they were set in 1517, might have had an uncomfortable contemporary resonance. "Leave out the insurrection wholly," Tilney's note reads, "and the cause thereof and begin with Sir Thomas More at the Mayor's sessions, with a report afterwards of his good service done being sheriff of London upon a mutiny against the Lombards only by a short report and not otherwise at your own perils. E. Tilney." Of course, as Tilney knew perfectly well, most plays succeed precisely by mirroring, if only obliquely, their own times, but this particular reflection evidently seemed to him too dangerous or provocative.

The topical significance of a play depends in large measure on the particular moment in which it is performed and on certain features of the performance—for example, a striking resemblance between one of the characters and a well-known public figure—that the script itself will not necessarily disclose to us at this great distance or even to the censor at the time. Hence the Master of the Revels noted angrily of one play performed in 1632 that "there were diverse personated so naturally, both of lords and others of the court, that I took it ill." Hence, too, a play that was deemed allowable when it was first written and performed could return, like a nightmare, to haunt a different place and time. The most famous instance of such a return involves Shakespeare, for on the day before the Earl of Essex's attempted coup against Queen Elizabeth in 1601, someone paid the Lord Chamberlain's Men (the name of Shakespeare's company at the time) 40 shillings to revive their old play about the deposition and murder of Richard II. "I am Richard II," the queen declared. "Know ye not that?" However distressed she was by this performance, the queen significantly did not take out her wrath on the players: neither the playwright nor his company was punished, nor was the Master of the Revels criticized for allowing the play in the first place. It was Essex and several of his key supporters who lost their heads.

Evidence suggests that the Master of the Revels often regarded himself not as the strict censor of the theater but as its friendly guardian, charged with averting catastrophes. He was a bureaucrat concerned less with subversive ideas per se than with potential trouble. That is, there is no record of a dramatist being called to account for his heterodox beliefs; rather, plays were censored if they risked offending influential people, including important foreign allies, or if they threatened to cause public disorder by exacerbating religious or other controversies. The distinction is not a stable one, but it helps to explain the intellectual boldness, power, and freedom of a censored theater in a society in which the perceived enemies of the state were treated mercilessly. Shakespeare could have Lear articulate a searing indictment of social injustice—

> Robes and furred gowns hide all. Plate sin with gold,
>   And the strong lance of justice hurtless breaks;
>   Arm it in rags, a pygmy's straw does pierce it.
>   (4.5.155–57)

—and evidently neither the Master of the Revels nor the courtiers in their robes and furred gowns protested. But when the Spanish ambassador complained about Thomas Middleton's anti-Spanish allegory *A Game at Chess*, performed at the Globe in 1624, the whole theater was shut down, the players were arrested, and the king professed to be furious at his official for licensing the play in the first place and allowing it to be performed for nine consecutive days.

In addition to the system for the licensing of plays for performance, there was also a system for the licensing of plays for publication. At the start of Shakespeare's career, such press licensing was the responsibility of the Court of High Commission, headed by the Archbishop of Canterbury and the Bishop of London. Their deputies, a panel of junior clerics, were supposed to review the manuscripts, granting licenses to those worthy of publication and rejecting any they deemed "heretical, seditious, or unseemly for Christian ears." Without a license, the Stationers' Company, the guild of the book trade, was not supposed to register a manuscript for publication. In practice, as various complaints and attempts to close loopholes attest, some playbooks were printed without a license. In 1607, the system was significantly revised when Sir George Buc began to license plays for the press. When Buc succeeded to the post of Master of the Revels in 1610, the powers to license plays for the stage and the page were vested in one man.

Theatrical Innovations

The theater continued to flourish under this system of regulation after Shakespeare's death; by the 1630s, as many as five playhouses were operating daily in London. When the theater reemerged after the eighteen-year hiatus imposed by Puritan rule, it quickly resumed its cultural importance, but not without a number of significant changes. Major innovations in staging resulted principally from Continental influences on the English artists who accompanied the court of Charles II into exile in France, where they supplied it with masques and other theatrical entertainments.

The institutional conditions and business practices of the two companies chartered by Charles after the Restoration in 1660 also differed from those of Shakespeare's theater. In place of the more collective practice of Shakespeare's company, the Restoration theaters were controlled by celebrated actor-managers who not only assigned themselves starring roles, in both comedy and tragedy, but also assumed sole responsibility for many business decisions, including the setting of their colleagues' salaries. At the same time, the power of the actor-manager, great as it was, was limited by the new importance of outside capital. No longer was the theater, with all of its properties from script to costumes, owned by the "sharers"—that is, by those actors who held shares in the joint-stock company. Instead, entrepreneurs would raise capital for increasingly fantastic sets and stage machinery that could cost as much as £3,000, an astronomical sum, for a single production. This investment, in turn, not only influenced the kinds of new plays written for the theater but helped to transform old plays that were revived, including Shakespeare's.

In his diary entry for August 24, 1661, Samuel Pepys notes that he has been "to the Opera, and there saw Hamlet, Prince of Denmark, done with scenes very well, but above all, Betterton did the prince's part beyond imagination." This is Thomas Betterton's first review, as it were, and it is typical of the enthusiasm he would inspire throughout his fifty-year career on the London stage. Pepys's brief and scattered remarks on the plays he voraciously attended in the 1660s are precious because they are among the few records from the period of concrete and immediate responses to theatrical performances. Modern readers might miss the significance of Pepys's phrase "done with scenes": this production of *Hamlet* was only the third play to use the movable sets first introduced to England by its producer, William Davenant. The central historical fact that makes the productions of this period so exciting is that public theater had been banned altogether for eighteen years until the Restoration of Charles II.

A brief discussion of theatrical developments in the Restoration period will enable us at least to glance longingly at a vast subject that lies outside the scope of this introduction: the rich performance history that extends from Shakespeare's time to our own, involving tens of thousands of productions and adaptations for theater, opera, Broadway musicals, and, of course, films. The scale of this history is vast in space as well as time: as early as 1607, there is a record of a *Hamlet* performed on board an English ship, HMS *Dragon,* off the coast of Sierra Leone, and troupes of English actors performed in the late sixteenth and early seventeenth centuries as far afield as Poland and Bohemia.

William Davenant, who claimed to be Shakespeare's bastard son, had become an expert on stage scenery while producing masques at the court of Charles I, and when the theaters reopened, he set to work on converting an indoor tennis court into a new kind of theater. He designed a broad open platform like that of the Elizabethan stage, but he replaced the relatively shallow space for "discoveries" (tableaux set up in an opening at the center of the stage, revealed by drawing back a curtain) and the "tiring-house" (the players' dressing room) behind this space with one expanded interior, framed by a proscenium arch, in which scenes could be displayed. These elaborately painted scenes could be moved on and off, using grooves on the floor. The perspecti-val effect for a spectator of one central painted panel with two "wings" on either side was that of three sides of a room. This effect anticipated that of the familiar "picture frame" stage, developed fully in the nineteenth century, and began a subtle shift in the-ater away from the elaborate verbal descriptions that are so central to Shakespeare and toward the evocative visual poetry of the set designer's art.

Another convention of Shakespeare's stage, the use of boy actors for female roles, gave way to the more complete illusion of women playing women's parts. The king issued a decree in 1662 forcefully permitting, if not requiring, the use of actresses. The royal decree is couched in the language of social and moral reform: the introduction of actresses will require the "reformation" of scurrilous and profane passages in plays, and this, in turn, will help forestall some of the objections that shut the theaters down in 1642. In reality, male theater audiences, composed of a narrower range of courtiers and aristocrats than in Shakespeare's time, met this intended reform with the assumption that the new actresses were fair game sexually; most actresses (with the partial excep-tion of those who married male members of their troupes) were regarded as, or actu-ally became, whores. But despite the social stigma and the fact that their salaries were predictably lower than those of their male counterparts, the stage saw some formidable female stars by the 1680s.

The first recorded appearance of an actress was that of a Desdemona in December 1660. Betterton's Ophelia in 1661 was Mary Saunderson (c. 1637–1712), who became Mrs. Betterton a year later. The most famous Ophelia of the period was Susanna Mount-fort, who appeared in that role for the first time at the age of fifteen in 1705. The per-formance by Mountfort that became legendary occurred in 1720, after a disappointment in love, or so it was said, had driven her mad. Hearing that *Hamlet* was being performed, Mountfort escaped from her keepers and reached the theater, where she concealed her-self until the scene in which Ophelia enters in her state of insanity. At this point, Mount-fort rushed onto the stage and, in the words of a contemporary, "was in truth Ophelia herself, to the amazement of the performers and the astonishment of the audience."

That the character Ophelia became increasingly and decisively identified with the mad scene owes something to this occurrence, but it is also a consequence of the text used for Restoration performances of *Hamlet.* Having received the performance rights to a good number of Shakespeare's plays, Davenant altered them for the stage in the 1660s, and many of these acting versions remained in use for generations. In the case of *Hamlet,* neither Davenant nor his successors did what they so often did with other plays by Shakespeare—that is, alter the plot radically and interpolate other material. But many of the lines were cut or "improved." The cuts included most of Ophelia's sane speeches, such as her spirited retort to Laertes' moralizing; what remained made her part almost entirely an emblem of "female love melancholy."

Thomas Betterton (1635–1710), the prototype of the actor-manager, who would be the dominant figure in Shakespeare interpretation and in the theater generally through

The Spanish Tragedie:

OR,

Hieronimo is mad againe.

Containing the lamentable end of *Don Horatio*, and
Belimperia; with the pittifull death of *Hieronimo*.

Newly corrected, amended, and enlarged with new
Additions of the *Painters* part, and others, as
it hath of late been diuers times acted.

LONDON,

Printed by W. White, for I. White and T. Langley,
and are to be fold at their Shop ouer againft the
Sarazens head without New-gate. 1615.

Title page of Thomas Kyd's *Spanish Tragedie*
(1615). The first known edition dates from 1592.

the nineteenth century, made Hamlet his premier role. A contemporary who saw his last performance in the part (at the age of seventy-four, a rather old Prince of Denmark) wrote that to *read* Shakespeare's play was to encounter "dry, incoherent, & broken sentences," but that to see Betterton was to "prove" that the play was written "correctly." Spectators especially admired his reaction to the Ghost's appearance in the Queen's bedchamber: "his Countenance . . . thro' the violent and sudden Emotions of Amazement and Horror, turn[ed] instantly on the Sight of his fathers Spirit, as pale as his Neckcloath, when every Article of his Body seem's affected with a Tremor inexpressible." A piece of stage business in this scene, Betterton's upsetting his chair on the Ghost's entrance, became so thoroughly identified with the part that later productions were censured if the actor left it out. This business could very well have been handed down from Richard Burbage, the star of Shakespeare's original production, for Davenant, who had coached Betterton in the role, had known the performances of Joseph Taylor, who had succeeded Burbage in it. It is strangely gratifying to notice that Hamlets on stage and screen still occasionally upset their chairs.

Shakespeare's Life and Art

Playwrights, even hugely successful playwrights, were not ordinarily the objects of popular curiosity in early modern England, and few personal documents survive from Shakespeare's life of the kind that usually give the biographies of artists their appeal: no diary, no letters, private or public, no accounts of his childhood, almost no contemporary gossip, no scandals. Shakespeare's exact contemporary, the great playwright Christopher Marlowe, lived a mere twenty-nine years—he was murdered in 1593—but he left behind tantalizing glimpses of himself in police documents, the memos of high-ranking government officials, and detailed denunciations by sinister double agents. Ben Jonson recorded his opinions and his reading in a remarkable published notebook, *Timber; or, Discoveries Made upon Men and Matter,* and he also shared his views of the world (including some criticisms of his fellow playwright Shakespeare) with a Scottish poet, William Drummond of Hawthornden, who had the wit to jot them down for posterity. From Shakespeare, there is nothing comparable, not even a book with his name scribbled on the cover and a few marginal notes such as we have for Jonson, let alone working notebooks.

Yet Elizabethan England was a record-keeping society, and centuries of archival labor have turned up a substantial number of traces of its greatest playwright and his family. By themselves the traces would have relatively little interest, but in the light of Shakespeare's plays and poems, they have come to seem like precious relics and manage to achieve a considerable resonance.

Shakespeare's Family

William Shakespeare's grandfather Richard farmed land by the village of Snitterfield, near the small, pleasant market town of Stratford-upon-Avon, about 96 miles northwest of London. The playwright's father, John, moved in the mid-sixteenth century to Stratford, where he became a successful glover, landowner, moneylender, and dealer in wool and other agricultural goods. In or about 1557, he married Mary Arden, the daughter of a prosperous and well-connected farmer from the same area, Robert Arden of Wilmcote.

John Shakespeare was evidently highly esteemed by his fellow townspeople, for he held a series of important posts in local government. In 1556, he was appointed ale taster, an office reserved for "able persons and discreet," in 1558 was sworn in as a constable, and in 1561 was elected as one of the town's fourteen burgesses. As burgess, John served as one of the two chamberlains, responsible for administering borough property and revenues. In 1567, he was elected bailiff, Stratford's highest elective office and the equivalent of mayor. Although John Shakespeare signed all official documents with a cross or other sign, it is likely, but not certain, that he knew how to read and write. Mary, who also signed documents only with her mark, is less likely to have been literate.

According to the parish registers, which recorded baptisms and burials, the Shakespeares had eight children, four daughters and four sons, beginning with a daughter Joan born in 1558. A second daughter, Margaret, was born in December 1562 and died a few months later. William Shakespeare ("Gulielmus, filius Johannes Shakespeare"), their first son, was baptized on April 26, 1564. Since there was usually a few days' lapse between birth and baptism, it is conventional to celebrate Shakespeare's birthday on April 23, which happens to coincide with the feast of St. George, England's patron saint, and with the day of Shakespeare's death fifty-two years later.

William Shakespeare had three younger brothers, Gilbert, Richard, and Edmund, and two younger sisters, Joan and Anne. (It was often the custom to recycle a name, so the firstborn Joan must have died before the birth in 1569 of another daughter

"Southeast Prospect of Stratford-upon-Avon, 1746." From *The Gentleman's Magazine* (December 1792).

christened Joan, the only one of the girls to survive childhood.) Gilbert, who died in his forty-fifth year in 1612, is described in legal records as a Stratford haberdasher; Edmund followed William to London and became a professional actor, but evidently of no particular repute. He was only twenty-eight when he died in 1607 and was given an expensive funeral, perhaps paid for by his successful older brother.

At the high point of his public career, John Shakespeare, the father of this substantial family, applied to the Herald's College for a coat of arms, which would have marked his (and his family's) elevation from the ranks of substantial middle-class citizenry to that of the gentry. But the application went nowhere, for soon after he initiated what would have been a costly petitioning process, John apparently fell on hard times. The decline must have begun when William was still living at home, a boy of twelve or thirteen. From 1576 onward, John Shakespeare stopped attending council meetings. He became caught up in costly lawsuits, started mortgaging his land, and incurred substantial debts. In 1586, he was finally replaced on the council; in 1592, he was one of nine Stratford men listed as absenting themselves from church out of fear of being arrested for debt.

The reason for the reversal in John Shakespeare's fortunes is unknown. Some have speculated that it may have stemmed from adherence to Catholicism, since those who remained loyal to the old faith were subject to increasingly vigorous and costly discrimination. But if John Shakespeare was a Catholic, as seems quite possible, it would not necessarily explain his decline, since other Catholics (and Puritans) in Elizabethan Stratford and elsewhere managed to hold on to their offices. In any case, his fall from prosperity and local power, whatever its cause, was not absolute. In 1601, the last year of his life, his name was included among those qualified to speak on behalf of Stratford's rights. And he was by that time entitled to bear a coat of arms, for in 1596, some twenty years after the application to the Herald's office had been initiated, it was successfully renewed. There is no record of who paid for the bureaucratic procedures that made the grant possible, but it is likely to have been John's oldest son William, by that time a highly successful London playwright.

Education

Stratford was a small provincial town, but it had long been the site of an excellent free school, originally established by the Church in the thirteenth century. The main purpose of such schools in the Middle Ages had been to train prospective clerics; since many aristocrats could neither read nor write, literacy by itself conferred no special distinction and was not routinely viewed as desirable. But the situation began to change markedly in the sixteenth century. Protestantism placed a far greater emphasis upon lay literacy: for the sake of salvation, it was crucially important to be intimately acquainted with the Holy Book, and printing made that book readily available. Schools became less strictly bound up with training for the Church and more linked to the general acquisition of "literature," in the sense both of literacy and of cultural knowledge. In keeping with this new emphasis on reading and with humanist educational reform, the school was reorganized during the reign of Edward VI (1547–53). School records from the period have not survived, but it is almost certain that William Shakespeare attended the King's New School, as it was renamed in Edward's honor.

Scholars have painstakingly reconstructed the curriculum of schools of this kind and have even turned up the names and rather impressive credentials of the schoolmasters who taught there when Shakespeare was a student. (Shakespeare's principal teacher was Thomas Jenkins, an Oxford graduate, who received £20 a year and a rent-free house.) A child's education in Elizabethan England began at age four or five with two years at what was called the "petty school," attached to the main grammar school. The little scholars carried a "hornbook," a sheet of paper or parchment framed in wood and covered, for protection, with a transparent layer of horn. On the paper was written

The Cholmondeley sisters, c. 1600–10. This striking image brings to mind Shakespeare's fascination with twinship, both identical (notably in *The Comedy of Errors*) and fraternal (in *Twelfth Night*).

the alphabet and the Lord's Prayer, which were reproduced as well in the slightly more advanced *ABC with the Catechism,* a combination primer and rudimentary religious guide.

After students demonstrated some ability to read, the boys could go on, at about age seven, to the grammar school. Shakespeare's images of the experience are not particularly cheerful. In his famous account of the Seven Ages of Man, Jaques in *As You Like It* describes

> the whining schoolboy with his satchel
> And shining morning face, creeping like snail
> Unwillingly to school.
>
> (2.7.144–46)

The schoolboy would have crept quite early: the day began at 6:00 A.M. in summer and 7:00 A.M. in winter and continued until 5:00 P.M., with very few breaks or holidays.

At the core of the curriculum was the study of Latin, the mastery of which was in effect a prolonged male puberty rite involving much discipline and pain as well as pleasure. A late sixteenth-century Dutchman (whose name fittingly was Batty) proposed that God had created the human buttocks so that they could be severely beaten without risking permanent injury. Such thoughts dominated the pedagogy of the age, so that even an able young scholar, as we might imagine Shakespeare to have been, could scarcely have escaped recurrent flogging.

Shakespeare evidently reaped some rewards for the miseries he probably endured: his works are laced with echoes of many of the great Latin texts taught in grammar schools. One of his earliest comedies, *The Comedy of Errors,* is a brilliant variation on a theme by the Roman playwright Plautus, whom Elizabethan schoolchildren often performed as well as read; and one of his earliest tragedies, *Titus Andronicus,* is heavily indebted to Seneca. These are among the most visible of the classical influences that are often more subtly and pervasively interfused in Shakespeare's works. He seems to have had a particular fondness for *Aesop's Fables,* Apuleius's *Golden Ass,* and above all Ovid's *Metamorphoses.* His learned contemporary Ben Jonson remarked that Shakespeare had "small Latin and less Greek," but from this distance what is striking is not the limits of Shakespeare's learning but rather the unpretentious ease, intelligence, and gusto with which he draws upon what he must have first encountered as laborious study.

Traces of a Life

In November 1582, William Shakespeare, at the age of eighteen, married twenty-six-year-old Anne Hathaway, who came from the village of Shottery, near Stratford. Their first daughter, Susanna, was baptized six months later. This circumstance, along with the fact that Anne was eight years Will's senior, has given rise to a mountain of speculation, all the more lurid precisely because there is no further evidence. Shakespeare depicts in several plays situations in which marriage is precipitated by a pregnancy, but he also registers, in *Measure for Measure* (1.2.125ff.), the Elizabethan belief that a "true contract" of marriage could be legitimately made and then consummated simply by the mutual vows of the couple in the presence of witnesses.

On February 2, 1585, the twins Hamnet and Judith Shakespeare were baptized in Stratford. Hamnet died at the age of eleven, when his father was already living for much of the year in London as a successful playwright. These are Shakespeare's only known children, although the playwright and impressario William Davenant in the mid-seventeenth century claimed to be his bastard son. Since people did not ordinarily advertise their illegitimacy, the claim, though impossible to verify, at least suggests the unusual strength of the Shakespeare's posthumous reputation.

William Shakespeare's father, John, died in 1601; his mother died seven years later. They would have had the satisfaction of witnessing their eldest son's prosperity, and not only from a distance, for in 1597 William purchased New Place, the second largest house in Stratford. In 1607, the playwright's daughter Susanna married a successful and well-known physician, John Hall. The next year, the Halls had a daughter, Elizabeth, Shakespeare's first grandchild. In 1616, the year of Shakespeare's death, his daughter Judith married a vintner, Thomas Quiney, with whom she had three children. Shakespeare's widow, Anne, died in 1623, at the age of sixty-seven. His first-born, Susanna, died at the age of sixty-six in 1649, the year that King Charles I was beheaded by the parliamentary army. Judith lived through Cromwell's Protectorate and on to the Restoration of the monarchy; she died in February 1662, at the age of seventy-seven. By the end of the century, the line of Shakespeare's direct heirs was extinct.

Patient digging in the archives has turned up other traces of Shakespeare's life as a family man and a man of means: assessments, small fines, real-estate deeds, minor actions in court to collect debts. In addition to his fine Stratford house and a large garden and cottage facing it, Shakespeare bought substantial parcels of land in the vicinity. When in *The Tempest* the wedding celebration conjures up a vision of "barns and garners never empty," Shakespeare could have been glancing at what the legal documents record as his own "tithes of corn, grain, blade, and hay" in the fields near Stratford. At some point after 1610, Shakespeare seems to have begun to shift his attention from the London stage to his Stratford properties, although the term "retirement" implies a more decisive and definitive break than appears to have been the case. By 1613, when the Globe Theatre burned down during a performance of *All Is True* (*Henry VIII*), Shakespeare was probably residing for the most part in Stratford, but he retained his financial interest in the rebuilt playhouse and probably continued to have some links to his theatrical colleagues. Still, by this point, his career as a playwright was substantially over. Legal documents from his last years show his main concern to be the protection of his real-estate interests in Stratford.

Half a century after Shakespeare's death, a Stratford vicar and physician, John Ward, noted in his diary that Shakespeare and his fellow poets Michael Drayton and Ben Jonson "had a merry meeting, and it seems drank too hard, for Shakespeare died of a fever there contracted." It is not inconceivable that Shakespeare's last illness was somehow linked, if only coincidentally, to the festivities on the occasion of the wedding in February 1616 of his daughter Judith (who was still alive when Ward made his diary entry). In any case, on March 25, 1616, Shakespeare revised his will, and on April 23 he died. Two days later, he was buried in the chancel of Holy Trinity Church beneath a stone bearing an epitaph he is said to have devised:

> Good friend for Jesus' sake forbear,
> To dig the dust enclosed here:
> Blest be the man that spares these stones,
> And curst be he that moves my bones.

The verses are hardly among Shakespeare's finest, but they seem to have been effective: though bones were routinely dug up to make room for others—a fate imagined with unforgettable intensity in the graveyard scene in *Hamlet*—his own remains were undisturbed. Like other vestiges of sixteenth- and early seventeenth-century Stratford, Shakespeare's grave has for centuries been the object of a tourist industry that borders on a religious cult.

Shakespeare's will has been examined with an intensity befitting this cult; every provision and formulaic phrase, no matter how minor or conventional, has borne a heavy weight of interpretation, none more so than the bequest to his wife, Anne, of only "my second-best bed." Scholars have pointed out that Anne would in any case have been provided for by custom and that the terms are not necessarily a deliberate slight, but the absence of the customary words "my loving wife" or "my well-beloved wife" is difficult to ignore.

Portrait of the Playwright as Young Provincial

The great problem with the surviving traces of Shakespeare's life is not that they are few but that they are dull. Christopher Marlowe was a double or triple agent, accused of brawling, sodomy, and atheism. Ben Jonson, who somehow clambered up from bricklayer's apprentice to classical scholar, served in the army in Flanders, killed a fellow actor in a duel, converted to Catholicism in prison in 1598, and returned to the Church of England in 1610. Provincial real-estate investments and the second-best bed cannot compete with such adventurous lives. Indeed, the relative ordinariness of Shakespeare's social background and life has contributed to a persistent current of speculation that the glover's son from Stratford-upon-Avon was not in fact the author of the plays attributed to him.

The anti-Stratfordians, as those who deny Shakespeare's authorship are sometimes called, almost always propose as the real author someone who came from a higher social class and received a more prestigious education. Francis Bacon, the Earl of Oxford, the Earl of Southampton, even Queen Elizabeth, have been advanced, among many others, as glamorous candidates for the role of clandestine playwright. Several famous people, including Mark Twain and Sigmund Freud, have espoused these theories, though very few scholars have joined them. Since Shakespeare was quite well-known in his own time as the author of the plays that bear his name, there would need to have been an extraordinary conspiracy to conceal the identity of the real master who (the theory goes) disdained to appear in the vulgarity of print or on the public stage. Like many conspiracy theories, the extreme implausibility of this one only seems to increase the fervent conviction of its advocates.

To the charge that a middle-class author from a small town could not have imagined the lives of kings and nobles, one can respond by citing the exceptional qualities that Ben Jonson praised in Shakespeare: "excellent *Phantsie*; brave notions, and gentle expressions." Even in ordinary mortals, the human imagination is a strange faculty; in Shakespeare, it seems to have been uncannily powerful, working its mysterious, transforming effects on everything it touched. His imagination was intensely engaged by what he found in books. He seems throughout his life to have been an intense, voracious reader, and it is fascinating to witness his creative encounters with Raphael Holinshed's *Chronicles of England, Scotlande, and Irelande*, Plutarch's *Lives of the Noble Grecians and Romans*, Ovid's *Metamorphoses*, Montaigne's *Essays*, and the Bible, to name only some of his favorite books. But books were clearly not the only objects of Shakespeare's attention; like most artists, he drew upon the whole range of his life experiences.

To integrate some of the probable circumstances of Shakespeare's early years with the particular shape of the theatrical imagination associated with his name, let us indulge briefly in the biographical daydreams that modern scholarship is supposed to have rendered forever obsolete. The vignettes that follow are conjectural, but they may suggest ways in which his life as we know it found its way into his art.

1. THE GOWN OF OFFICE

Shakespeare was a very young boy—not quite four years old—when the Stratford council elected his father, John, to a year's term as bailiff (the equivalent of mayor). The office, the town's highest, was attended with considerable ceremony. The bailiff and his deputy were entitled to appear in public in furred gowns, attended by leather-clad sergeants bearing maces before them. On Rogation Days (three days of prayer for the harvest, before Ascension Day), they would solemnly pace out the parish boundaries, and they would similarly walk in processions on market and fair days. On Sundays, the sergeants would accompany the bailiff to church, where he would sit with his wife in a front pew, and he would have a comparable seat of honor at sermons in the Guild Chapel.

Public deference was a matter of law as well as custom: any inhabitant who spoke disrespectfully to the bailiff or other town officer was subject to the penalty of three days and three nights in the stocks. Newcomers who sought employment—notably including traveling players who hoped to stage performances—were obliged to obtain the bailiff's permission. In the year that John Shakespeare held office, two such professional playing companies arrived in Stratford. They must have proceeded to the bailiff's house on Henley Street and presented the letters of recommendation, with wax seals, that showed that they were not vagabonds. They would have spoken with more than ordinary deference, since it was the bailiff who would decide whether they would be sent packing or—as was the case—allowed to post their bills announcing the performances. The first of these performances was usually free to all comers. The bailiff would have been expected to attend, for it was his privilege to determine the level of the reward to be paid out of the city coffers; he would, presumably, have been given one of the best seats in the guildhall, where a special stage had been erected. It is impossible to know whether John Shakespeare took his family to these plays, but his little boy would certainly have been aware of what was happening.

On a precocious child (or even, for that matter, on an ordinary child), the effect of his father's office and the elaborate rituals that attended it would be at least threefold. First, the ceremony would convey irresistibly the power of clothes (the gown of office) and of symbols (the mace) to transform identity as if by magic. Second, it would invest the father with immense power, distinction, and importance, awakening what we may call a lifelong dream of high station. And third, pulling slightly against this dream, it would provoke an odd feeling that the father's clothes do not fit, a perception that the office is not the same as the man, and an intimate, firsthand knowledge that when the robes are put off, their wearer is inevitably glimpsed in a far different, less exalted light.

2. PROGRESSES AND ELECTIONS

This second biographical fantasy, slightly less plausible than the first but still quite likely, involves a somewhat older child witnessing two characteristic forms of Elizabethan political ceremony, both of which were well known in the provinces. Queen Elizabeth was fond of going on what were known as "progresses," triumphant ceremonial journeys around her kingdom. Let us imagine that the young Shakespeare—say, in 1574, when he was ten years old—went with his kinsfolk or friends to Warwick, some 8 miles distant, to witness a progress. He would thus have participated as a spectator in an elaborate celebration of charismatic power: the courtiers in their gorgeous clothes, the nervous local officials bedecked in velvets and silks, and at the center, carried in a special litter like a painted idol, the bejeweled queen. Let us imagine further that in addition to being struck by the overwhelming force of this charisma, the boy was struck, too, by the way this force depended paradoxically on a sense that the queen was after all quite human. Elizabeth was in fact fond of calling attention to this peculiar tension between near-divinization and human ordinariness. For example, on this occasion at Warwick (and what follows really happened), after the trembling Recorder, presumably a local civil official of high standing, had made his official welcoming speech, Elizabeth offered her hand to him to be kissed: "Come hither, little Recorder," she said. "It was told me that you would be afraid to look upon me or to speak boldly; but you were not so afraid of me as I was of you; and I now thank you for putting me in mind of my duty." Of course, the charm of this royal "confession" of nervousness depends on its manifest implausibility: it is, in effect, a theatrical performance of humility by someone with immense confidence in her own histrionic power.

A royal progress was not the only form of spectacular political activity that Shakespeare might well have seen in the 1570s; it is still more likely that he would have witnessed parliamentary elections, particularly since his father was qualified to vote. In 1571, 1572, 1575, and 1578, there were shire elections conducted in nearby Warwick, elections that would certainly have attracted well over a thousand voters. These were often memorable events: large crowds came together; there was usually heavy drinking and carnivalesque festivity; and, at the same time, there was enacted, in a very different register from that of the monarchy, a ritual of empowerment. The people, those entitled to vote by virtue of meeting the property and residence requirements, chose their own representatives by giving their votes—their voices—to candidates for office. Here, legislative sovereignty was conferred not by God but by the consent of the community, a consent marked by shouts and applause.

Recent cultural historians have been so fascinated by the evident links between the spectacles of the absolutist monarchy and the theater that they have largely ignored the significance of this alternative public arena, one that generated intense excitement throughout the country. A child who was a spectator at a parliamentary election in the 1570s might well have found the occasion enormously compelling. It is striking, in any case, how often the adult Shakespeare returns to scenes of acclamation and mass consent, and striking, too, how much the theater depends on the soliciting of popular voices.

3. EXORCISMS

A third and final fantasy is even more speculative than the second and involves a controversial claim, which has long been hotly debated— that Shakespeare either was a secret Catholic or was at least raised in a Roman Catholic household in a time of official suspicion and persecution of recusancy. A late seventeenth-century Anglican clergyman, Richard Davies, jotted down in some notes on Shakespeare that "he died a papist." In a modern biographical study, E. A. J. Honigmann convincingly linked several of the schoolmasters who taught in Stratford at the time that Shakespeare would have been a pupil to a network of Catholic families in Lancashire with whom one "William Shakeshafte," possibly a young schoolmaster or player, was connected in the late 1570s or early 1580s.

Exorcism: Nicole Aubry in the cathedral at Laon, 1566.

Catholics in Elizabethan England were not free to practice their religion—any more than Protestants, in Catholic countries, were free to practice theirs—and the beleaguered faithful, beset with spies, came together only at great risk to confess and receive Communion from clandestine priests. Under the circumstances, although a substantial portion of the population may have retained a residual inward loyalty to the traditional faith, the vast majority fell away from outward Catholic practice. After all, the churches, great and small, were now the places of Protestant worship; the innumerable local saints' shrines and pilgrimage sites had been systematically destroyed; the monasteries and convents had been abolished, their property bestowed on royal favorites or sold at bargain prices to local magnates. Seeking a spectacular way to demonstrate the enduring spiritual power and authenticity of the Roman Church, the embattled Counter-Reformers turned to an ancient ritual: exorcism. Devils who possessed the souls of troubled men and women had once been exorcised in public, but now the healing rite had to be conducted in secret, in a barn in a remote village, perhaps, or in the attic of the secluded house of a Catholic loyalist. The danger for those who presided was enormous—brutal interrogation, torture, and an unspeakably horrible execution was the usual fate of the missionary priests who were caught—but the vivid demonstration of the Church's triumph over evil was sufficiently compelling to warrant the risk. For despite the lynx-eyed alertness of the Protestant authorities, Catholics staged a surprising number of clandestine exorcisms, many of which drew substantial crowds.

Accepting for the moment that William Shakespeare was raised in the recusant faith of his father and mother, let us imagine that one day in the early 1580s the young man attended an exorcism of which he had learned through the secret network of the faithful. Here, based on an eyewitness account of such an occasion recently transcribed by Gerard Kilroy, is what he is likely to have seen. At the center of a large room, emptied of other furniture in order to accommodate the many observers, stood a bed. A young woman sat on the bed, and a priest, in clerical vestments, stood over her, preaching a sermon. As he spoke, the woman began to writhe and scream. At first the screams, uttered by a deep voice that could not have been the woman's although it came from her mouth, were not intelligible. Gradually, the bystanders began to make out some of the words, blasphemous oaths—"God's wounds! God's nails!"—followed by menaces, spoken as if by a rabid Protestant: "Popish priests, popish priests, to prison with them and hang them, hang them, hang them." The exorcist held up the Eucharist over the writhing woman, and the screams intensified. "Who are you?" he demanded. "I am Modu," the voice replied. "Depart, Modu!" shouted the priest, bringing the consecrated wafer closer to the demoniac. When that did not succeed in driving the devil out, the priest advanced a chafing dish of fire and brimstone, provoking more shouting and cursing, and then displayed a painting of the Blessed Virgin. "I will not behold or see her," screamed the demonic voice.

The longer the scene continued, the more there was confirmation of the contested tenets of the Catholic faith. The devil admitted that the Virgin Mary was a particularly efficacious intercessor, that purgatory existed, that the wafer, consecrated by the priest, actually was the body and blood of Christ. The devil also revealed that all Protestants were his followers. Finally, under the irresistible force of spiritual compulsion, he agreed to depart forever from the body of the possessed. The departure was difficult: again and again the tormented young woman gaped, as if her mouth were being torn open. She screamed in pain, rose up only to be cast down violently by invisible hands, cried out that she was being drowned, and called upon Jesus and his mother to save her. Only when a sacred relic was placed directly on her flesh did the devil finally leave her.

There is no way to know if William Shakespeare actually witnessed such a scene, but if he did, he would have carried away several indelible impressions: an awareness that strange, alien voices may speak from within ordinary, familiar bodies; an intimation of the immense, cosmic forces that may impinge upon human life; a belief in the possibility of making contact with these forces and compelling them to speak. These are, after all, the foundation stones of great tragedy.

Many years later, Shakespeare brooded about demonic possession when he was writing his greatest tragedy about the presence of evil in the world, *King Lear*. "This is the foul fiend Flibbertigibbet," shouts the madman, Poor Tom; "The Prince of Darkness is a gentleman. Modo he's called, and Mahu" (3.4.103, 127–28). But Poor Tom in that play is faking it; he is actually the noble Edgar, who has disguised himself as a madman in order to escape persecution. Did Shakespeare as a teenager already think that the whole compelling event, in all of its metaphysical weirdness, was a powerful theatrical fraud, a piece of pious propaganda? Perhaps. But if so, he also clearly understood that evil exists, that persecution is real, and that illusion has an irresistible force.

These imaginary portraits of the playwright as a young provincial introduce us to several of the root conditions of the Elizabethan theater. Biographical fantasies, though entirely speculative and playful, are useful in part because some people have found it difficult to conceive how Shakespeare, with his provincial roots and his restricted range of experience, could have so rapidly and completely mastered the central imaginative themes of his times. Moreover, it is sometimes difficult to grasp how seeming abstractions such as market society, monarchical state, and theological doctrine were actually experienced directly by peculiar, distinct individuals. Shakespeare's plays were social and collective events, but they also bore the stamp of a particular artist, one endowed with a remarkable capacity to craft lifelike illusions (what Jonson called "excellent *Phantsie*"), a daring willingness to articulate an original vision ("brave notions"), and a loving command, at once precise and generous, of language ("gentle expressions"). These plays are stitched together from shared cultural experiences, inherited dramatic devices, and the pungent vernacular of the day, but we should not lose sight of the extent to which they articulate an intensely personal vision, a bold shaping of the available materials. Four centuries of feverish biographical speculation, much of it foolish, bears witness to a basic intuition: the richness of these plays, their inexhaustible openness, is the consequence not only of the auspicious collective conditions of the culture but also of someone's exceptional skill, inventiveness, and courage at taking those conditions and making of them something rich and strange.

The Theater of the Nation

What precisely are the collective conditions highlighted by these vignettes? First, the growth of Stratford-upon-Avon, the bustling market town of which John Shakespeare was bailiff, is a small version of a momentous sixteenth-century development that made Shakespeare's career possible: the making of an urban "public." That development obviously depended on adequate numbers; the period experienced a rapid and still unexplained growth in population. With it came an expansion and elaboration of market relations: markets became less periodic, more continuous, and more abstract—centered, that is, not on the familiar materiality of goods but on the liquidity of capital and goods. In practical terms, this meant that it was possible to conceive of the theater not only as festive entertainment for special events—lord mayor's pageants, visiting princes, seasonal festivals, and the like—but as a permanent, year-round business venture. The venture relied on ticket sales—it was an innovation of this period to have money advanced in the expectation of pleasure rather than offered to servants afterward as a reward—and counted on habitual playgoing with a concomitant demand for new plays from competing theater companies: "But that's all one, our play is done," sings Feste at the end of *Twelfth Night* and adds a glance toward the next afternoon's proceeds: "And we'll strive to please you every day" (5.1.394–95).

Second, the royal progress is an instance of what the anthropologist Clifford Geertz has called the Theater State, a state that manifests its power and meaning in exemplary public performances. Professional companies of players, like the one Shakespeare belonged to, understood well that they existed in relation to this Theater State and would, if they were fortunate, be called upon to serve it. Unlike Ben Jonson, Shakespeare did not, as far as we know, write royal entertainments on commission, but his plays were frequently performed before Queen Elizabeth and then before King James and Queen Anne, along with their courtiers and privileged guests. There are many fascinating glimpses of these performances, including a letter from Walter Cope to Robert Cecil, early in James's reign. "Burbage is come," Cope writes, referring to the leading actor of Shakespeare's company, "and says there is no new play that the queen hath not seen, but they have revived an old one, called *Love's Labours Lost,* which for wit and mirth he says will please her exceedingly. And this is appointed to be played tomorrow night at my Lord of Southampton's." Not only would such theatrical performances have given great pleasure—evidently, the queen had already exhausted the company's new offerings—but they conferred prestige upon those who commanded them and those in whose honor they were mounted.

Monarchical power in the period was deeply allied to spectacular manifestations of the ruler's glory and disciplinary authority. The symbology of power depended on regal magnificence, reward, punishment, and pardon, all of which were heavily theatricalized. Indeed, the conspicuous public display does not simply serve the interests of power; on many occasions in the period, power seemed to exist in order to make pageantry possible, as if the nation's identity were only fully realized in theatrical performance. It would be easy to exaggerate this perception: the subjects of Queen Elizabeth and King James were acutely aware of the distinction between shadow and substance. But they were fascinated by the political magic through which shadows could be taken for substantial realities, and the ruling elite was largely complicit in the formation and celebration of a charismatic absolutism. At the same time, the claims of the monarch who professes herself or himself to be not the representative of the nation but its embodiment were set against the counterclaims of the House of Commons. And this institution, too, as we have glimpsed, had its own theatrical rituals, centered on the crowd whose shouts of approval, in heavily stage-managed elections, chose the individuals who would stand for the polity and participate in deliberations held in a hall whose resemblance to a theater did not escape contemporary notice.

Third, illicit exorcism points both to the theatricality of much religious ritual in the late Middle Ages and the Renaissance and to the heightened possibility of secularization. English Protestant authorities banned the medieval mystery plays, along with pilgrimages and other rituals associated with holy shrines and sacred images, but playing companies could satisfy at least some of the popular longings and appropriate aspects of the social energy no longer allowed a theological outlet. That is, official attacks on certain Catholic practices made it more possible for the public theater to appropriate and exploit their allure. Hence, for example, the plays that celebrated the solemn miracle of the Catholic Mass were banned, along with the most elaborate church vestments, but in *The Winter's Tale* Dion can speak in awe of what he witnessed at Apollo's temple:

> I shall report,
> For most it caught me, the celestial habits—
> Methinks I so should term them—and the reverence
> Of the grave wearers. O, the sacrifice—
> How ceremonious, solemn, and unearthly
> It was i'th' off'ring!

(3.1.3–8)

And at the play's end, the statue of the innocent mother breathes, comes to life, and embraces her child.

The theater in Shakespeare's time, then, is intimately bound up with all three crucial cultural formations: the market society, the theater state, and the Church. But it is important to note that the institution is not *identified* with any of them. The theater may be a market phenomenon, but it is repeatedly and bitterly attacked as the enemy of diligent, sober, productive economic activity. Civic authorities generally regarded the theater as a pestilential nuisance, a parasite on the body of the commonwealth, a temptation to students, apprentices, housewives, even respectable merchants to leave their serious business and lapse into idleness and waste. That waste, it might be argued, could be partially recuperated if it went for the glorification of a guild or the entertainment of an important dignitary, but the only group regularly profiting from the theater were the players and their disreputable associates.

For his part, Shakespeare made a handsome profit from the commodification of theatrical entertainment, but he seems never to have written "city comedy"—plays set in London and more or less explicitly concerned with market relations—and his characters express deep reservations about the power of money and commerce: "That smooth-faced gentleman, tickling commodity," Philip the Bastard observes in *King John*, "wins of all, / Of kings, of beggars, old men, young men, maids" (2.1.574, 570–71). We could argue that the smooth-faced gentleman is none other than Shakespeare himself, for his drama famously mingles kings and clowns, princesses and panderers. But the mingling is set against a romantic current of social conservatism: in *Twelfth Night*, the aristocratic heiress Olivia falls in love with someone who appears far beneath her in wealth and social station, but it is revealed that he (and his sister Viola) are of noble blood; in *The Winter's Tale*, Leontes' daughter Perdita is raised as a shepherdess, but her noble nature shines through her humble upbringing, and she marries the Prince of Bohemia; the strange island maiden with whom Ferdinand, son of the King of Naples, falls madly in love in *The Tempest* turns out to be the daughter of the rightful Duke of Milan. Shakespeare pushes against this conservative logic in *All's Well That Ends Well*, but the noble young Bertram violently resists the unequal match thrust upon him by the King, and the play's mood is notoriously uneasy.

Similarly, Shakespeare's theater may have been patronized and protected by the monarchy—after 1603, his company received a royal patent and was known as the King's Men—but it was by no means identical in its interests or its ethos. To be sure, *Richard III* and *Macbeth* incorporate aspects of royal propaganda, but given the realities of censorship, Shakespeare's plays, and the period's drama as a whole, are surprisingly independent and complex in their political vision. There is, in any case, a certain inherent tension between kings and player kings: Elizabeth and James may both have likened themselves to actors onstage, but they were loath to admit their dependence on the applause and money, freely given or freely withheld, of the audience. The charismatic monarch insists that the sacredness of authority resides in the body of the ruler, not in a costume that may be worn and then discarded by an actor. Kings are not *representations* of power—or do not admit that they are—but claim to be the thing itself. The government institution that was actually based on the idea of representation, Parliament, had theatrical elements, as we have seen, but it significantly excluded any audience from its deliberations. And Shakespeare's oblique portraits of parliamentary representatives, the tribunes Sicinius Velutus and Junius Brutus in *Coriolanus*, are anything but flattering.

Finally, the theater drew significant energy from the liturgy and rituals of the late medieval Church, but as Shakespeare's contemporaries widely remarked, the playhouse and the Church were scarcely natural allies. Not only did the theater represent a potential competitor to worship services, and not only did ministers rail against prostitution and other vices associated with playgoing, but theatrical representation itself, even when ostensibly pious, seemed to many to empty out whatever it presented, turning substance into mere show. The theater could and did use the period's deep currents of religious feeling, but it had to do so carefully and with an awareness of conflicting interests.

Shakespeare Comes to London

How did Shakespeare decide to turn his prodigious talents to the stage? When did he make his way to London? How did he get his start? To these and similar questions we have a mountain of speculation but no secure answers. There is not a single surviving record of Shakespeare's existence from 1585, when his twins were baptized in Stratford church, until 1592, when a rival London playwright made an envious remark about him. In the late seventeenth century, the delightfully eccentric collector of gossip John Aubrey was informed that prior to moving to London the young Shakespeare had been a schoolteacher in the country. Aubrey also recorded a story that Shakespeare had been a rather unusual apprentice butcher: "When he killed a calf, he would do it in a high style, and make a speech."

These and other legends, including one that has Shakespeare whipped for poaching game, fill the void until the unmistakable reference in Robert Greene's *Groats-Worth of Witte, Bought with a Million of Repentance* (1592). An inspired hack writer with a university education, a penchant for self-dramatization, a taste for wild living, and a strong streak of resentment, Greene, in his early thirties, was dying in poverty when he penned his last farewell, piously urging his fellow dramatists Christopher Marlowe, Thomas Nashe, and George Peele to abandon the wicked stage before they were brought low, as he had been, by a new arrival: "For there is an upstart crow, beautified with our feathers, that with his 'Tiger's heart wrapped in player's hide' supposes he is as well able to bombast out a blank verse as the best of you, and, being an absolute *Johannes Factotum,* is in his own conceit the only Shake-scene in a country." If "Shake-scene" is not enough to identify the object of his attack, Greene parodies a line from Shakespeare's early play *Richard Duke of York (3 Henry VI):* "O tiger's heart wrapped in a woman's hide!" (1.4.138). Greene is accusing Shakespeare of being an upstart, a plagiarist, an egomaniacal jack-of-all-trades—and, above all perhaps, a popular success.

By 1592, then, Shakespeare had already arrived on the highly competitive London theatrical scene. He was successful enough to be attacked by Greene and, a few months later, defended by Henry Chettle, another hack writer who had seen Greene's manuscript through the press (or, some scholars speculate, had written the attack himself and passed it off as the dying Greene's). Chettle expresses his regret that he did not suppress Greene's diatribe and spare Shakespeare "because myself have seen his demeanor no less civil than he excellent in the quality he professes." Besides, Chettle adds, "divers of worship have reported his uprightness of dealing, which argues his honesty and his facetious [polished] grace in writing that approves his art." "Divers of worship": not only was Shakespeare established as an accomplished writer and actor, but he evidently had aroused the attention and the approbation of several socially prominent people. In Elizabethan England, aristocratic patronage, with the money, protection, and prestige it alone could provide, was probably a professional writer's most important asset.

This patronage, or at least Shakespeare's quest for it, is most visible in the dedications in 1593 and 1594 of his narrative poems *Venus and Adonis* and *The Rape of Lucrece* to the young nobleman Henry Wriothesley, Earl of Southampton. It may be glimpsed as well, perhaps, in the sonnets, with their extraordinary adoration of the fair youth, though the identity of that youth has never been determined. What return Shakespeare got for his exquisite offerings is likewise unknown. We do know that among wits and gallants, the narrative poems won Shakespeare a fine reputation as an immensely stylish and accomplished poet. An amateur play performed at Cambridge University at the end of the sixteenth century, *The Return from Parnassus,* makes fun of this vogue, as a foolish character effusively declares, "I'll worship sweet Mr. Shakespeare, and to honour him will lay his *Venus and Adonis* under my pillow." Many readers at the time may have done so: the poem went through sixteen editions before 1640, more than any other work by Shakespeare.

Patronage was crucially important not only for individual artists but also for the actors, playwrights, and investors who pooled their resources to form professional theater companies. The public playhouses had enemies, especially among civic and religious authorities, who wished greatly to curb performances or to ban them altogether. An act of 1572 included players among those classified as vagabonds, threatening them, therefore, with the horrible punishments meted out to those regarded as economic parasites. The players' escape route was to be nominally enrolled as the servants of high-ranking noblemen. The legal fiction was that their public performances were a kind of rehearsal for the command performances before the patron or the monarch.

When Shakespeare came to London, presumably in the late 1580s, there were more than a dozen of these companies operating under the patronage of various aristocrats.

We do not know for which of these companies, several of which had toured in Stratford, he originally worked, nor whether he began, as legend has it, as a prompter's assistant and then graduated to acting and playwriting. Shakespeare is listed among the actors in Ben Jonson's *Every Man in His Humour* (performed in 1598) and *Sejanus* (performed in 1603), but we do not know for certain what roles he played, nor are there records of any of his other performances. Tradition has it that he played Adam in *As You Like It* and the Ghost in *Hamlet,* but he was clearly not one of the leading actors of the day.

By the 1590s, the number of playing companies in London had been considerably reduced, in part through competition and in part through legislative restriction. (In 1572, knights and gentry lost the privilege of patronizing a troupe of actors; in 1598, justices of the peace lost the power to authorize performances.) By the early years of the seventeenth century, there were usually only three companies competing against one another in any season, along with two children's companies, which were often successful at drawing audiences away from the public playhouses. Shakespeare may initially have been associated with the Earl of Leicester's company or with the company of Ferdinando Stanley, Lord Strange; both groups included actors with whom Shakespeare was later linked. Or he may have belonged to the Earl of Pembroke's Men, since there is evidence that they performed *The Taming of a Shrew* and a version of *Richard Duke of York (3 Henry VI)*. At any event, by 1594, Shakespeare was a member of the Lord Chamberlain's Men, for his name, along with those of Will Kemp (or Kempe) and Richard Burbage, appears on a record of those "servants to the Lord Chamberlain" paid for performance at the royal palace at Greenwich on December 26 and 28. Shakespeare stayed with this company, which during the reign of King James received royal patronage and became the King's Men, for the rest of his career.

Many playwrights in Shakespeare's time worked freelance, moving from company to company as opportunities arose, collaborating on projects, adding scenes to old plays, scrambling from one enterprise to another. But certain playwrights, among them the most successful, wrote for a single company, often agreeing contractually to give that company exclusive rights to their theatrical works. Shakespeare seems to have followed such a pattern. For the Lord Chamberlain's Men, he wrote an average of two plays per year. His company initially performed in The Theatre, a playhouse built in 1576 by an entrepreneurial carpenter, James Burbage, the father of the actor Richard, who was to perform many of

Edward Alleyn (1566–1626). Artist unknown. Alleyn was the great tragic actor of the Lord Admiral's Men (the principal rival to Shakespeare's company). He was famous especially for playing the great Marlovian heroes.

Shakespeare's greatest roles. When in 1597 their lease on this playhouse expired, the Lord Chamberlain's Men passed through a difficult and legally perilous time, but they formed a joint-stock company, raising sufficient capital to lease a site and put up a splendid new playhouse in the suburb of Southwark, on the south bank of the Thames. This playhouse, the Globe, opened in 1599. Shakespeare is listed in the legal agreement as one of the principal investors; and when the company began to use Blackfriars as their indoor playhouse around 1609, he was a major shareholder in that theater as well. The Lord Chamberlain's Men, later the King's Men, dominated the theater scene, and the shares were quite valuable. Then as now, the theater was an extremely risky enterprise—most of those who wrote plays and performed in them made pathetically little money—but Shakespeare was a notable exception. The fine house in Stratford and the coat of arms he succeeded in acquiring were among the fruits of his multiple mastery, as actor, playwright, and investor in the London stage.

The Shakespearean Trajectory

Even though Shakespeare's England was in many ways a record-keeping society, no reliable record survives that details the performances, year by year, in the London theaters. Every play had to be licensed by a government official, the Master of the Revels, but the records kept by the relevant officials from 1579 to 1621, Sir Edmund Tilney and Sir George Buc, have not survived. A major theatrical entrepreneur, Philip Henslowe, kept a careful account of his expenditures, including what he paid for the scripts he commissioned, but unfortunately Henslowe's main business was with the Rose and the Fortune theaters and not with the playhouses at which Shakespeare's company performed. A comparable ledger must have been kept by the shareholders of the Lord Chamberlain's Men, but it has not survived. Shakespeare himself apparently did not undertake to preserve for posterity the sum of his writings, let alone to clarify the chronology of his works or specify which plays he wrote alone and which with collaborators.

The principal source for Shakespeare's works is the 1623 Folio volume of *Mr. William Shakespeares Comedies, Histories, & Tragedies*. Most scholars believe that the editors were careful to include only those plays for which they knew Shakespeare to be the main author. Their edition does not, however, include any of Shakespeare's nondramatic poems, and it omits two plays in which Shakespeare is now thought to have had a significant hand, *Pericles, Prince of Tyre* and *The Two Noble Kinsmen*, along with his probable contribution to the multiauthored *Sir Thomas More*. (A number of other plays were attributed to Shakespeare, both before and after his death, but scholars have not generally accepted any of these into the established canon.) Moreover, the Folio edition does not print the plays in chronological order, nor does it attempt to establish a chronology. We do not know how much time would normally have elapsed between the writing of a play and its first performance, nor with

Title page of Thomas Heywood's *If You Know Not Me, You Know No Body; or, The Troubles of Queene Elizabeth* (1632 ed.).

a few exceptions, do we know with any certainty the month or even the year of the first performance of any of Shakespeare's plays. The quarto editions of those plays that were published during Shakespeare's lifetime obviously establish a date by which we know a given play had been written, but they give us little more than an end point, because there was likely to be a substantial though indeterminate gap between the first performance of a play and its publication.

With enormous patience and ingenuity, however, scholars have gradually assembled a considerable archive of evidence, both external and internal, for dating the composition of the plays. Besides actual publication, the external evidence includes explicit reference to a play, a record of its performance, or (as in the case of Greene's attack on the "upstart crow") the quoting of a line, though all of these can be maddeningly ambiguous. The most important single piece of external evidence appears in 1598 in *Palladis Tamia,* a long book of jumbled reflections by Francis Meres that includes a survey of the contemporary literary scene. Meres finds that "the sweet, witty soul of Ovid lives in melliflous and honey-tongued Shakespeare, witness his *Venus and Adonis,* his *Lucrece,* his sugered Sonnets among his private friends, etc." Meres goes on to list Shakespeare's accomplishments as a playwright as well:

> As Plautus and Seneca are accounted the best for Comedy and Tragedy among the Latins: so Shakespeare among the English is the most excellent in both kinds for the stage; for Comedy, witness his *Gentlemen of Verona,* his *Errors,* his *Love labors lost,* his *Love labours won,* his *Midsummers night dream,* & his *Merchant of Venice:* for Tragedy his *Richard the 2, Richard the 3, Henry the 4, King John, Titus Andronicus* and his *Romeo and Juliet.*

Meres thus provides a date by which twelve of Shakespeare's plays had definitely appeared (including one, *Love's Labour's Won,* that appears to have been lost or that we know by a different title). Unfortunately, Meres provides no clues about the order of appearance of these plays, and there are no other comparable lists.

Faced with the limitations of the external evidence, scholars have turned to a bewildering array of internal evidence, ranging from datable sources and topical allusions on the one hand to evolving stylistic features (ratio of verse to prose, percentage of rhyme to blank verse, colloquialisms, use of extended similes, and the like) on the other. Thus, for example, a cluster of plays with a high percentage of rhymed verse may follow closely upon Shakespeare's writing of the rhymed poems *Venus and Adonis* and *The Rape of Lucrece* and, therefore, be datable to 1594–95. Similarly, vocabulary overlap probably indicates proximity in composition, so if four or five plays share relatively "rare" vocabulary, it is likely that they were written in roughly the same period. Again, there seems to be a pattern in Shakespeare's use of colloquialisms, with a steady increase from *As You Like It* (1599–1600) to *Coriolanus* (1608), followed in the late romances by a retreat from the colloquial.

More sophisticated computer analysis should provide further guidance in the future, even though the precise order of the plays, still very much in dispute, is never likely to be settled to universal satisfaction. Still, certain broad patterns are now widely accepted. These patterns can be readily grasped in the *Norton Shakespeare,* which presents the plays in the chronological order proposed by the Oxford editors.

Shakespeare began his career, probably in the early 1590s, by writing both comedies and history plays. The attack by Greene suggests that he made his mark with the series of theatrically vital but rather crude plays based on the foreign and domestic broils that erupted during the unhappy reign of the Lancastrian Henry VI. Modern readers and audiences are more likely to find the first sustained evidence of unusual power in *Richard III* (c. 1592), a play that combines a brilliantly conceived central character, a dazzling command of histrionic rhetoric, and an overarching moral vision of English history.

At virtually the same time that he was setting his stamp on the genre of the history play, Shakespeare was writing his first—or first surviving—comedies. Here, there are even fewer signs than in the histories of an apprenticeship: *The Comedy of Errors*, one of his early efforts in this genre, already displays a rare command of the resources of comedy: mistaken identity, madcap confusion, and the threat of disaster, giving way in the end to reconciliation, recovery, and love. Shakespeare's other comedies from the early 1590s, *The Taming of the Shrew, The Two Gentlemen of Verona*, and *Love's Labour's Lost*, are no less remarkable for their sophisticated variations on familiar comic themes, their inexhaustible rhetorical inventiveness, and their poignant intimation, in the midst of festive celebration, of loss.

Successful as are these early histories and comedies, and indicative of an extraordinary theatrical talent, Shakespeare's achievement in the later 1590s would still have been all but impossible to foresee. Starting with *A Midsummer Night's Dream* (c. 1595), Shakespeare wrote an unprecedented series of romantic comedies—*The Merchant of Venice, The Merry Wives of Windsor, Much Ado About Nothing, As You Like It*, and *Twelfth Night* (c. 1602)—whose poetic richness and emotional complexity remain unmatched. In the same period, he wrote a sequence of profoundly searching and ambitious history plays—*Richard II, 1* and *2 Henry IV*, and *Henry V*—which together explore the death throes of feudal England and the birth of the modern nation-state ruled by a charismatic monarch. Both the comedies and histories of this period are marked by their capaciousness, their ability to absorb characters who press up against the outermost boundaries of the genre: the comedy *Merchant of Venice* somehow contains the figure, at once nightmarish and poignant, of Shylock, while the *Henry IV* plays, with their somber vision of crisis in the family and the state, bring to the stage one of England's greatest comic characters, Falstaff.

If in the mid to late 1590s Shakespeare reached the summit of his art in two major genres, he also manifested a lively interest in a third. As early as 1593, he wrote the crudely violent tragedy *Titus Andronicus*, the first of several plays on themes from Roman history, and a year or two later, in *Richard II*, he created in the protagonist a figure who achieves by the play's close the stature of a tragic hero. In the same year that Shakespeare wrote the wonderfully farcical "Pyramus and Thisbe" scene in *A Midsummer Night's Dream*, he probably also wrote the deeply tragic realization of the same story in *Romeo and Juliet*. But once again, the lyric anguish of *Romeo and Juliet* and the tormented self-revelation of *Richard II*, extraordinary as they are, could not have led anyone to predict the next phase of Shakespeare's career, the great tragic dramas that poured forth in the early years of the seventeenth century: *Hamlet, Othello, King Lear, Macbeth, Antony and Cleopatra*, and *Coriolanus*. These plays, written from 1601 to 1607, seem to mark a major shift in sensibility, an existential and metaphysical darkening that many readers think must have originated in a deep personal anguish, perhaps caused by the death of Shakespeare's father, John, in 1601.

Whatever the truth of these speculations—and we have no direct, personal testimony either to support or to undermine them—there appears to have occurred in the same period a shift as well in Shakespeare's comic sensibility. The comedies written between 1601 and 1604, *Troilus and Cressida, All's Well That Ends Well*, and *Measure for Measure*, are sufficiently different from the earlier comedies—more biting in tone, more uneasy with comic conventions, more ruthlessly questioning of the values of the characters and the resolutions of the plots—to have led many twentieth-century scholars to classify them as "problem plays" or "dark comedies." This category has recently begun to fall out of favor, since Shakespeare criticism is perfectly happy to demonstrate that *all* of the plays are "problem plays." But there is another group of plays, among the last Shakespeare wrote, that continue to constitute a distinct category. *Pericles, Cymbeline, The Winter's Tale*, and *The Tempest*, written between 1608 and 1611, when the playwright had developed a remarkably fluid, dreamlike sense of plot and a poetic style that could veer, apparently effortlessly, from the tortured to the ineffably sweet, are known as the "romances." These plays share an interest in the moral and emotional life less of the adolescents who dominate the earlier comedies than of their parents. The romances are deeply concerned with patterns of loss and recovery, suffering and redemption, despair and renewal. They have seemed to many critics to constitute a deliberate con-clusion to a career that began in histories and comedies and passed through the dark and tormented tragedies.

One effect of the practice of printing Shakespeare's plays in a reconstructed chronological order, as this edition does, is to produce a kind of authorial plot, a progress from youthful exuberance and a heroic grappling with history, through psy-chological anguish and radical doubt, to a mature serenity built upon an understand-ing of loss. The ordering of Shakespeare's "complete works" in this way reconstitutes the figure of the author as the beloved hero of his own, lived romance. There are numerous reasons to treat this romance with considerable skepticism: the precise order of the plays remains in dispute, the obsessions of the earliest plays crisscross with those of the last, the drama is a collaborative art form, and the relation between authorial consciousness and theatrical representation is murky. Yet a longing to identify Shake-speare's personal trajectory, to chart his psychic and spiritual as well as professional progress, is all but irresistible.

The Fetishism of Dress

Whatever the personal resonance of Shakespeare's own life, his art is deeply enmeshed in the collective hopes, fears, and fantasies of his time. For example, through-out his plays, Shakespeare draws heavily upon his culture's investment in costume, sym-bols of authority, visible signs of status—the fetishism of dress he must have witnessed from early childhood. Disguise in his drama is often assumed to be incredibly effective: when Henry V borrows a cloak, when Portia dresses in a jurist's robes, when Viola puts on a young man's suit, it is as if each has become unrecognizable, as if identity resided in clothing. At the end of *Twelfth Night,* even though Viola's true identity has been dis-closed, Orsino continues to call her Cesario; he will do so, he says, until she resumes her maid's garments, for only then will she be transformed into a woman:

Cesario, come—
For so you shall be while you are a man;
But when in other habits you are seen,
Orsino's mistress, and his fancy's queen.
(5.1.372–75)

The pinnacle of this fetishism of costume is the royal crown, for whose identity-conferring power men are willing to die, but the principle is everywhere from the filthy blanket that transforms Edgar into Poor Tom to the coxcomb that is the badge of the licensed fool. Antonio, wishing to express his utter contempt, spits on Shylocks' "Jew-ish gaberdine," as if the clothing were the essence of the man; Kent, pouring insults on the loathsome Oswald, calls him a "filthy worsted-stocking knave"; and innocent Inno-gen, learning that her husband has ordered her murder, thinks of herself as an expen-sive cast-off dress, destined to be ripped at the seams:

Poor I am stale, a garment out of fashion,
And for I am richer than to hang by th' walls
I must be ripped. To pieces with me!
(*Cymbeline* 3.4.50–52)

What can be said, thought, felt, in this culture seems deeply dependent on the clothes one wears—clothes that one is, in effect, *permitted* or *compelled* to wear, since there is little freedom in dress. Shakespearean drama occasionally represents some-thing like such freedom: after all, Viola in *Twelfth Night* chooses to put off her "maiden weeds," as does Rosalind, who declares, "We'll have a swashing and a martial outside" (*As You Like It* 1.3.114). But these choices are characteristically made under the pres-sure of desperate circumstances, here shipwreck and exile. Part of the charm of Shake-speare's heroines is their ability to transform distress into an opportunity for self-fashioning, but the plays often suggest that there is less autonomy than meets the eye. What looks like an escape from cultural determinism may be only a deeper form of constraint. We may take, as an allegorical emblem of this constraint, the transformation of the beggar Christopher Sly into a nobleman in the playful Induction to *The Taming of the Shrew*. The transformation seems to suggest that you are free to make of yourself whatever you choose to be—the play begins with the drunken Sly indignantly claiming the dignity of his pedigree ("Look in the Chronicles" [Induction 1.3–4])—but in fact he is only the subject of the mischievous lord's experiment, designed to demonstrate the interwovenness of clothing and identity. "What think you," the lord asks his huntsman,

> if he were conveyed to bed,
> Wrapped in sweet clothes, rings put upon his fingers,
> A most delicious banquet by his bed,
> And brave attendants near him when he wakes—
> Would not the beggar then forget himself?

To which the huntsman replies, in words that underscore the powerlessness of the drunken beggar, "Believe me, lord, I think he cannot choose" (Induction 1.33–38).

Petruccio's taming of Katherine is similarly constructed around an imposition of identity, an imposition closely bound up with the right to wear certain articles of clothing. When the haberdasher arrives with a fashionable lady's hat, Petruccio refuses it over his wife's vehement objections: "This doth fit the time, / And gentlewomen wear such caps as these." "When you are gentle," Petruccio replies, "you shall have one, too, / And not till then" (4.3.69–72). At the play's close, Petruccio demonstrates his authority by commanding his tamed wife to throw down her cap: "Off with that bauble, throw it underfoot" (5.2.126). Here as elsewhere in Shakespeare, acts of robing and disrobing are intensely charged, a charge that culminates in the trappings of monarchy. When Richard II, in a scene that was probably censored from the stage as well as the printed text during the reign of Elizabeth, is divested of his crown and scepter, he experiences the loss as the eradication of his name, the symbolic melting away of his identity:

> Alack the heavy day,
> That I have worn so many winters out
> And know not now what name to call myself!
> O, that I were a mockery king of snow,
> Standing before the sun of Bolingbroke
> To melt myself away in water-drops!
>
> (4.1.247–52)

When Lear tears off his regal "lendings" in order to reduce himself to the nakedness of the Bedlam beggar, he is expressing not only his radical loss of social identity but the breakdown of his psychic order as well, expressing, therefore, his reduction to the condition of the "poor bare forked animal" that is the primal condition of undifferentiated existence. And when Cleopatra determines to kill herself in order to escape public humiliation in Rome, she magnificently affirms her essential being by arraying herself as she had once done to encounter Antony:

> Show me, my women, like a queen. Go fetch
> My best attires. I am again for Cydnus
> To meet Mark Antony.
>
> (5.2.223–25)

Such scenes are a remarkable intensification of the everyday symbolic practice of Renaissance English culture, its characteristically deep and knowing commitment to illusion: "I know perfectly well that the woman in her crown and jewels and gorgeous gown is an aging, irascible, and fallible mortal—she herself virtually admits as much—yet I profess that she is the Virgin Queen, timelessly beautiful, wise, and just." Shakespeare understood how close this willed illusion was to the spirit of the theater, to the actors' ability to work on what the chorus in *Henry V* calls the "imaginary forces" of the audience. But there is throughout Shakespeare's works a counterintuition that, while it does not exactly overturn this illusion, renders it poignant, vulnerable, fraught. The "masculine usurp'd attire" that is donned by Viola, Rosalind, Portia, Jessica, and other Shakespeare heroines alters what they can say and do, reveals important aspects of their character, and changes their destiny, but it is, all the same, not theirs and not all of who they are. They have, the plays insist, natures that are neither transformed nor altogether concealed by their dress: "Pray God defend me," exclaims the frightened Viola. "A little thing would make me tell them how much I lack of a man" (*Twelfth Night* 3.4.268–69).

The Paradoxes of Identity

The gap between costume and identity is not simply a matter of what women supposedly lack; virtually all of Shakespeare's major characters, men and women, convey the sense of both a *self-division* and an *inward expansion*. The belief in a complex inward realm beyond costumes and status is a striking inversion of the clothes cult: we know perfectly well that the characters have no inner lives apart from what we see on the stage, and yet we believe that they continue to exist when we do not see them, that they exist apart from their represented words and actions, that they have hidden dimensions. How is this conviction aroused and sustained? In part, it is the effect of what the characters themselves say: "My grief lies all within," Richard II tells Bolingbroke,

> And these external manner of laments
> Are merely shadows to the unseen grief
> That swells with silence in the tortured soul.
> (4.1.285–88)

Similarly, Hamlet, dismissing the significance of his outward garments, declares, "I have that within which passeth show— / These but the trappings and the suits of woe" (1.2.85–86). And the distinction between inward and outward is reinforced throughout this play and elsewhere by an unprecedented use of the aside and the soliloquy.

The soliloquy is a continual reminder in Shakespeare that the inner life is by no means transparent to one's surrounding world. Prince Hal seems open and easy with his mates in Eastcheap, but he has a hidden reservoir of disgust:

> I know you all, and will a while uphold
> The unyoked humour of your idleness.
> Yet herein will I imitate the sun,
> Who doth permit the base contagious clouds
> To smother up his beauty from the world,
> That when he please again to be himself,
> Being wanted he may be more wondered at
> By breaking through the foul and ugly mists
> Of vapours that did seem to strangle him.
> (*1 Henry IV* 1.2.173–81)

"When he please again to be himself": the line implies that identity is a matter of free choice—you decide how much of yourself you wish to disclose—but Shakespeare employs other devices that suggest more elusive and intractable layers of inwardness. There is a peculiar, recurrent lack of fit between costume and character, in fools as in princes, that is not simply a matter of disguise and disclosure. If Hal's true identity is partially "smothered" in the tavern, it is not completely revealed either in his soldier's armor or in his royal robes, nor do his asides reach the bedrock of unimpeachable self-understanding.

Identity in Shakespeare repeatedly slips away from the characters themselves, as it does from Richard II after the deposition scene and from Lear after he has given away his land and from Macbeth after he has gained the crown. The slippage does not mean that they retreat into silence; rather, they embark on an experimental, difficult fashioning of themselves and the world, most often through role-playing. "I cannot do it," says the deposed and imprisoned Richard II. "Yet I'll hammer it out" (5.5.5). This could serve as the motto for many Shakespearean characters: Viola becomes Cesario, Rosalind calls herself Ganymede, Kent becomes Caius, Edgar presents himself as Poor Tom, Hamlet plays the madman that he has partly become, Hal pretends that he is his father and a highwayman and Hotspur and even himself. Even in comedy, these ventures into alternate identities are rarely matters of choice; in tragedy, they are always undertaken under pressure and compulsion. And often enough it is not a matter of role-playing at all, but of a drastic transformation whose extreme emblem is the harrowing madness of Lear and of Leontes.

There is a moment in *Richard II* in which the deposed King asks for a mirror and then, after musing on his reflection, throws it to the ground. The shattering of the glass serves to remind us not only of the fragility of identity in Shakespeare but of its characteristic appearance in fragmentary mirror images. The plays continually generate alternative reflections, identities that intersect with, underscore, echo, or otherwise set off that of the principal character. Hence, Desdemona and Iago are not only important figures in Othello's world, they also seem to embody partially realized aspects of himself; Falstaff and Hotspur play a comparable role in relation to Prince Hal, Fortinbras and Horatio in relation to Hamlet, Gloucester and the Fool in relation to Lear, and so forth. In many of these plays, the complementary and contrasting characters figure in subplots, subtly interwoven with the play's main plot and illuminating its concerns. The note so conspicuously sounded by Fortinbras at the close of *Hamlet*—what the hero might have been, "had he been put on"—is heard repeatedly in Shakespeare and contributes to the overwhelming intensity, poignancy, and complexity of the characters. This is a world in which outward appearance is everything and nothing, in which individuation is at once sharply etched and continually blurred, in which the victims of fate are haunted by the ghosts of the possible, in which everything is simultaneously as it must be and as it need not have been.

Are these antinomies signs of a struggle between contradictory and irreconcilable perspectives in Shakespeare? In certain plays—notably, *Measure for Measure, All's Well That Ends Well, Coriolanus,* and *Troilus and Cressida*—the tension seems both high and entirely unresolved. But Shakespearean contradictions are more often reminiscent of the capacious spirit of Montaigne, who refused any systematic order that would betray his sense of reality. Thus, individual characters are immensely important in Shakespeare—he is justly celebrated for his unmatched skill in the invention of particular dramatic identities, marked with distinct speech patterns, manifested in social status, and confirmed by costume and gesture—but the principle of individuation is not the rock on which his theatrical art is founded. After the masks are stripped away, the pretenses exposed, the claims of the ego shattered, there is a mysterious remainder; as the shamed but irrepressible Paroles declares in *All's Well That Ends Well,* "Simply the thing I am / Shall make me live" (4.3.310–11). Again and again, the audience is made to sense a deeper energy, a source of power that at once discharges itself in individual characters and seems to sweep right through them.

The Poet of Nature

In *The Birth of Tragedy,* Nietzsche called a comparable source of energy that he found in Greek tragedy "Dionysos." But the god's name, conjuring up Bacchic frenzy, does not seem appropriate to Shakespeare. In the late seventeenth and eighteenth centuries, it was more plausibly called Nature: "The world must be peopled," says the delightful Benedick in *Much Ado About Nothing* (2.3.213–14), and there are frequent invocations elsewhere of the happy, generative power that brings couples together—

> Jack shall have Jill,
> Naught shall go ill,
> the man shall have his mare again, and all shall be well.
> (*A Midsummer Night's Dream* 3.3.45–47)

—and the melancholy, destructive power that brings all living things to the grave: "Golden lads and girls all must, / As chimney-sweepers, come to dust" (*Cymbeline* 4.2.263–64).

But the celebration of Shakespeare as a poet of nature—often coupled with an inane celebration of his supposedly "natural" (that is, untutored) genius—has its distinct limitations. For Shakespearean art brilliantly interrogates the "natural," refusing to take for granted precisely what the celebrants think is most secure. His comedies are endlessly inventive in showing that love is not simply natural: the playful hint of bestiality in the line quoted above, "the man shall have his mare again" (from a play in which the Queen of the Fairies falls in love with an ass-headed laborer), lightly unsettles the boundaries between the natural and the perverse. These boundaries are called into question throughout Shakespeare's work, from the cross-dressing and erotic crosscurrents that deliciously complicate the lives of the characters in *Twelfth Night* and *As You Like It* to the terrifying violence that wells up from the heart of the family in *King Lear* or from the sweet intimacy of sexual desire in *Othello*. Even the boundary between life and death is not secure, as the ghosts in *Julius Caesar, Hamlet,* and *Macbeth* attest, while the principle of natural death (given its most eloquent articulation by old Hamlet's murderer, Claudius!) is repeatedly tainted and disrupted.

Disrupted, too, is the idea of order that constantly makes its claim, most insistently in the history plays. Scholars have observed the presence in Shakespeare's works of the so-called Tudor myth—the ideological justification of the ruling dynasty as a restoration of national order after a cycle of tragic violence. The violence, Tudor apologists claimed, was divine punishment unleashed after the deposition of the anointed king, Richard II, for God will not tolerate violations of the sanctified order. Traces of this propaganda certainly exist in the histories—Shakespeare may, for all we know, have personally subscribed to its premises—but a closer scrutiny of his plays has disclosed so many ironic reservations and qualifications and subversions as to call into question any straightforward adherence to a political line. The plays manifest a profound fascination with the monarchy and with the ambitions of the aristocracy, but the fascination is never simply endorsement. There is always at least the hint of a slippage between the great figures, whether admirable or monstrous, who stand at the pinnacle of authority and the vast, miscellaneous mass of soldiers, scriveners, ostlers, poets, whores, gardeners, thieves, weavers, shepherds, country gentlemen, sturdy beggars, and the like who make up the commonwealth. And the idea of order, though eloquently articulated (most memorably by Ulysses in *Troilus and Cressida*), is always shadowed by a relentless spirit of irony.

The Play of Language

If neither the individual nor nature nor order will serve, can we find a single comprehensive name for the underlying force in Shakespeare's work? Certainly not. The work is too protean and capacious. But much of the energy that surges through this astonishing body of plays and poems is closely linked to the power of language. Shakespeare was the supreme product of a rhetorical culture, a culture steeped in the arts of persuasion and verbal expressiveness. In 1512, the great Dutch humanist Erasmus published a work called *De copia verborum* that taught its readers how to cultivate "copiousness," verbal richness, in discourse. (Erasmus obligingly provides, as a sample, a list of 144 different ways of saying "Thank you for your letter.") Recommended modes of variation include putting the subject of an argument into fictional form, as well as the use of synonym, substitution, paraphrase, metaphor, metonymy, synecdoche, hyperbole, diminution, and a host of other figures of speech. To change emotional tone, he suggests trying *ironia, interrogatio, admiratio, dubitatio, abominatio*—the possibilities seem infinite.

In Renaissance England, certain syntactic forms or patterns of words known as "figures" (also called "schemes") were shaped and repeated in order to confer beauty or heighten expressive power. Figures were usually known by their Greek and Latin names, though in an Elizabethan rhetorical manual, *The Arte of English Poesie*, George Puttenham made a valiant if short-lived attempt to give them English equivalents, such as "*Hyperbole*, or the Overreacher," "*Ironia*, or the Dry Mock," and "*Ploce*, or the Doubler." Those who received a grammar-school education throughout Europe at almost any point between the Roman Empire and the eighteenth century probably knew by heart the names of up to one hundred such figures, just as they knew by heart their multiplication tables. According to one scholar's count, Shakespeare knew and made use of about two hundred.

As certain grotesquely inflated Renaissance texts attest, lessons from *De copia verborum* and similar rhetorical guides could encourage mere prolixity and verbal self-display. But even though he shared his culture's delight in rhetorical complexity, Shakespeare always understood how to swoop from baroque sophistication to breathtaking simplicity. Moreover, he grasped early in his career how to use figures of speech, tone, and rhythm not only to provide emphasis and elegant variety but also to articulate the inner lives of his characters. Take, for example, these lines from *Othello*, where, as scholars have noted, Shakespeare deftly combines four common rhetorical figures—*anaphora, parison, isocolon,* and *epistrophe*—to depict with painful vividness Othello's psychological torment:

> By the world,
> I think my wife be honest, and think she is not.
> I think that thou art just, and think thou art not.
> I'll have some proof.
>
> (3.3.388–91)

Anaphora is simply the repetition of a word at the beginning of a sequence of sentences or clauses ("I/I"). *Parison* is the correspondence of word to word within adjacent sentences or clauses, either by direct repetition ("think/think") or by the matching of noun with noun, verb with verb ("wife/thou"; "be/art"). *Isocolon* gives exactly the same length to corresponding clauses ("and think she is not/and think thou art not"), and *epistrophe* is the mirror image of *anaphora* in that it is the repetition of a word at the end of a sequence of sentences or clauses ("not/not"). Do we need to know the Greek names for these figures in order to grasp the effectiveness of Othello's lines? Of course not. But Shakespeare and his contemporaries, convinced that rhetoric provided the most natural and powerful means by which feelings could be conveyed to readers and listeners, were trained in an analytical language that helped at once to promote and to account for this effectiveness. In his 1593 edition of *The Garden of Eloquence*, Henry Peacham remarks that *epistrophe* "serveth to leave a word of importance in the end of a sentence, that it may the longer hold the sound in the mind of the hearer," and in *Directions for Speech and Style* (c. 1599), John Hoskins notes that *anaphora* "beats upon one thing to cause the quicker feeling in the audience."

Shakespeare also shared with his contemporaries a keen understanding of the ways that rhetorical devices could be used not only to express powerful feelings but to hide them: after all, the artist who created Othello also created Iago, Richard III, and Lady Macbeth. He could deftly skewer the rhetorical affectations of Polonius in *Hamlet* or the pedant Holophernes in *Love's Labour's Lost*. He could deploy stylistic variations to mark the boundaries not of different individuals but of different social realms; in *A Midsummer Night's Dream*, for example, the blank verse of Duke Theseus is played off against the rhymed couplets of the well-born young lovers, and both in turn contrast with the prose spoken by the artisans. At the same time that he thus marks boundaries between both individuals and groups, Shakespeare shows a remarkable ability to establish unifying patterns of imagery that knit together the diverse strands of his plot and suggest subtle links among characters who may be scarcely aware of how much they share with one another.

One of the hidden links in Shakespeare's own works is the frequent use he makes of a somewhat unusual rhetorical figure called *hendiadys*. An example from the Roman poet Virgil is the phrase *pateris libamus et auro*, "we drink from cups and gold" (*Georgics* 2.192). Rather than serving as an adjective or a dependent noun, as in "golden cups" or "cups of gold," the word "gold" serves as a substantive joined to another substantive, "cups," by a conjunction, "and." Shakespeare uses the figure over three hundred times in all, and since it does not appear in ancient or medieval lists of tropes and schemes and is treated only briefly by English rhetoricians, he may have come upon it directly in Virgil. *Hendiadys* literally means "one through two," though Shakespeare's versions often make us quickly, perhaps only subliminally, aware of the complexity of what ordinarily passes for straightforward perceptions. When Othello, in his suicide speech, invokes the memory of "a malignant and a turbaned Turk," the figure of speech at once associates enmity with cultural difference and keeps them slightly apart. And when Macbeth speaks of his "strange and self-abuse," the *hendiadys* seems briefly to hold both "strange" and "self" up for scrutiny. It would be foolish to make too much of any single feature in Shakespeare's varied and diverse creative achievement, and yet this curious rhetorical scheme has something of the quality of a fingerprint.

But all of his immense rhetorical gifts, though rich, beautiful, and supremely useful, do not adequately convey Shakespeare's relation to language, which is less strictly functional than a total immersion in the arts of persuasion may imply. An Erasmian admiration for copiousness cannot fully explain Shakespeare's astonishing vocabulary of some 25,000 words. (His closest rival among the great English poets of the period was John Milton, with about 12,000 words, and most major writers, let alone ordinary people, have much smaller vocabularies.) This immense word hoard, it is worth noting, was not the result of scanning a dictionary; in the late sixteenth century, there were no English dictionaries of the kind to which we are now accustomed. Shakespeare seems to have absorbed new words from virtually every discursive realm he ever encountered, and he experimented boldly and tirelessly with them. These experiments were facilitated by the very fact that dictionaries as we know them did not exist and by a flexibility in grammar, orthography, and diction that the more orderly, regularized English of the later seventeenth and eighteenth centuries suppressed.

Owing in part to the number of dialects in London, pronunciation was variable, and there were many opportunities for phonetic association between words: the words "bear," "barn," "bier," "bourne," "born," and "barne" could all sound like one another. Homonyms were given greater scope by the fact that the same word could be spelled so many different ways—Christopher Marlowe's name appears in the records as Marlowe, Marloe, Marlen, Marlyne, Merlin, Marley, Marlye, Morley, and Morle—and by the fact that a word's grammatical function could easily shift, from noun to verb, verb to adjective, and so forth. Since grammar and punctuation did not insist on relations of coordination and subordination, loose, nonsyntactic sentences were common, and etymologies were used to forge surprising or playful relations between distant words.

It would seem inherently risky for a popular playwright to employ a vocabulary so far in excess of what most mortals could possibly possess, but Shakespeare evidently counted on his audience's linguistic curiosity and adventurousness, just as he counted on its general and broad-based rhetorical competence. He was also usually careful to provide a context that in effect explained or translated his more arcane terms. For example, when Macbeth reflects with horror on his murderous hands, he shudderingly imagines that even the sea could not wash away the blood; on the contrary, his bloodstained hand, he says, "will rather / The multitudinous seas incarnadine." The meaning of the unfamiliar word "incarnadine" is explained by the next line: "Making the green one red" (2.2.59–61).

What is most striking is not the abstruseness or novelty of Shakespeare's language but its extraordinary vitality, a quality that the playwright seemed to pursue with a kind of passionate recklessness. Perhaps Samuel Johnson was looking in the right direction when he complained that the "quibble," or pun, was "the fatal Cleopatra for which

[Shakespeare] lost the world, and was content to lose it." For the power that continually discharges itself throughout the plays, at once constituting and unsettling everything it touches, is the polymorphous power of language, language that seems both costume and that which lies beneath the costume, personal identity and that which challenges the merely personal, nature and that which enables us to name nature and thereby distance ourselves from it.

Shakespeare's language has an overpowering exuberance and generosity that often resembles the experience of love. Consider, for example, Oberon's description in *A Midsummer Night's Dream* of the moment when he saw Cupid shoot his arrow at the fair vestal: "Thou rememb'rest," he asks Puck,

> Since once I sat upon a promontory
> And heard a mermaid on a dolphin's back
> Uttering such dulcet and harmonious breath
> That the rude sea grew civil at her song
> And certain stars shot madly from their spheres
> To hear the sea-maid's music?
>
> (2.1.148–54)

Here, Oberon's composition of place, lightly alluding to a classical emblem, is infused with a fantastically lush verbal brilliance. This brilliance, the result of masterful alliterative and rhythmical technique, seems gratuitous—that is, it does not advance the plot, but rather exhibits a capacity for display and self-delight that extends from the fairies to the playwright who has created them. The rich music of Oberon's words imitates the "dulcet and harmonious breath" he is intent on recalling, breath that has, in his account, an oddly contradictory effect: it is at once a principle of order, so that the rude sea is becalmed like a lower-class mob made civil by a skilled orator, and a principle of disorder, so that celestial bodies in their fixed spheres are thrown into mad confusion. And this contradictory effect, so intimately bound up with an inexplicable, supererogatory, and intensely erotic verbal magic, is a key to *A Midsummer Night's Dream*, with its exquisite blend of confusion and discipline, lunacy and hierarchical ceremony.

The fairies in this comedy seem to embody a pervasive sense found throughout Shakespeare's work that there is something uncanny about language, something that is not quite human, at least in the conventional and circumscribed sense of the human that dominates waking experience. In the comedies, this intuition is alarming but ultimately benign: Oberon and his followers trip through the great house at the play's close, blessing the bridebeds and warding off the nightmares that lurk in marriage and parenthood. But there is in Shakespeare an alternative, darker vision of the uncanniness of language, a vision also embodied in creatures that test the limits of the human—not the fairies of *A Midsummer Night's Dream* but the weird sisters of *Macbeth*. When in the tragedy's opening scene the witches chant "Fair is foul, and foul is fair" (1.1.10), they unsettle through the simplest and most radical act of linguistic equation (x is y) the fundamental antinomies through which a moral order is established. And when Macbeth appears onstage a few minutes later, his first words unconsciously echo what we have just heard from the witches' mouths: "So foul and fair a day I have not seen" (1.3.36). What is the meaning of this linguistic "unconscious"? On the face of things, Macbeth presumably means only that the day of fair victory is also a day of foul weather, but the fact that he echoes the witches (something that we hear but that he cannot know) intimates an occult link between them, even before their direct encounter. It is difficult, perhaps impossible, to specify exactly what this link signifies—generations of emboldened critics have tried without notable success—but we can at least affirm that its secret lair is in the play's language, like a half-buried pun whose full articulation will entail the murder of Duncan, the ravaging of his kingdom, and Macbeth's own destruction.

Macbeth is haunted by half-buried puns, equivocations, and ambiguous grammatical constructions known as amphibologies. They manifest themselves most obviously in the words of the witches, from the opening exchanges to the fraudulent assurances that deceive Macbeth at the close, but they are also present in his most intimate and private reflections, as in his tortured broodings about his proposed act of treason:

> If it were done when 'tis done, then 'twere well
> It were done quickly. If th'assassination
> Could trammel up the consequence, and catch
> With his surcease success: that but this blow
> Might be the be-all and the end-all, here,
> But here upon this bank and shoal of time,
> We'd jump the life to come.
>
> (1.7.1–7)

The dream is to reach a secure and decisive end, to catch as in a net (hence "trammel up") all of the slippery, unforeseen, and uncontrollable consequences of regicide, to hobble time as one might hobble a horse (another sense of "trammel up"), to stop the flow ("success") of events, to be, as Macbeth later puts it, "settled." But Macbeth's words themselves slip away from the closure he seeks; they slide into one another, trip over themselves, twist and double back and swerve into precisely the sickening uncertainties their speaker most wishes to avoid. And if we sense a barely discernible note of comedy in Macbeth's tortured language, a discordant playing with the senses of the word "done" and the hint of a childish tongue twister in the phrase "catch / With his surcease success," we are in touch with a dark pleasure to which Shakespeare was all his life addicted.

Look again at the couplet from *Cymbeline*: "Golden lads and girls all must, / As chimney-sweepers, come to dust."

The playwright who insinuated a pun into the solemn dirge is the same playwright whose tragic heroine in *Antony and Cleopatra*, pulling the bleeding body of her dying lover into the pyramid, says, "Our strength is all gone into heaviness" (4.16.34). He is the playwright whose Juliet, finding herself alone on the stage, says, "My dismal scene I needs must act alone" (*Romeo and Juliet* 4.3.19), and the playwright who can follow the long, wrenching periodic sentence that Othello speaks, just before he stabs himself, with the remark "O bloody period!" (5.2.366). The point is not merely the presence of puns in the midst of tragedy (as there are stabs of pain in the midst of Shakespearean comedy); it is rather the streak of wildness that they so deliberately disclose, the sublimely indecorous linguistic energy of which Shakespeare was at once the towering master and the most obedient, worshipful servant.

The Dream of the Master Text

Shakespeare and the Printed Book

Ben Jonson's famous tribute to Shakespeare—"He was not of an age, but for all time!"—comes in one of the dedicatory poems to the 1623 First Folio of *Mr. William Shakespeares Comedies, Histories, & Tragedies*. This large, handsome volume, the first collection of Shakespeare's plays, was not, as far as we know, the product of the playwright's own design. We do not even know if he would have approved of the Folio's division of each play into five acts or its organization of the plays into three loose generic categories. Several of the plays grouped among the histories—*Richard Duke of York* (3 *Henry VI*), *Richard II,* and *Richard III*—had been printed separately during Shakespeare's lifetime as tragedies; one of the most famous of his tragedies had appeared as *The History of King Lear*. The Folio editors evidently decided to group together as "histories" only those plays which dealt with English history after the Norman Conquest; hence, *King Lear,* set in ancient Britain, appears with the "tragedies," and so, too, despite its happy ending, does *Cymbeline, King of Britain*. One play, *Troilus and Cressida,* was printed first as a "history," then printed in a second version with a preface that describes it as a "comedy," and then printed in the Folio as a "tragedy." As a fitting

Sixteenth-century printing shop. Engraving by Jan van der Straet. From *Nova Reperta* (1580).

emblem of the confusion, *Troilus and Cressida* does not appear in the Folio title page: apparently included only at the last minute, it was placed, unpaginated, after the last of the histories and the first of the tragedies. Modern readers, who remain perplexed by its genre, may take some consolation from the fact that for Shakespeare and his contemporaries generic boundaries were not hard and fast.

Published seven years after the playwright's death, the Folio was printed by the London printers William and Isaac Jaggard, who were joined in this expensive venture by Edward Blount, John Smethwicke, and William Aspley. It was edited by two of Shakespeare's old friends and fellow actors, John Heminges and Henry Condell, who claimed to be using "True Originall Copies" in the author's own hand. (None of these copies has survived, or, more cautiously, none has to date been found.) Eighteen plays included in the First Folio had already appeared individually in print in the small-format and relatively inexpensive texts called "Quartos" (or, in one case, the still smaller format called "Octavo"); to these, Heminges and Condell added eighteen others never before published: *All's Well That Ends Well, Antony and Cleopatra, As You Like It, The Comedy of Errors, Coriolanus, Cymbeline, All Is True* (*Henry VIII*), *Julius Caesar, King John, Macbeth, Measure for Measure, The Taming of the Shrew, The Tempest, Timon of Athens, Twelfth Night, The Two Gentlemen of Verona, The Winter's Tale,* and *1 Henry VI.** None of the

*This sketch simplifies several complex questions such as the status of the 1594 Quarto called *The Taming of a Shrew,* sufficiently distinct from the similarly titled Folio text as to constitute for many editors a different play.

plays included in the Folio has dropped out of the generally accepted canon of Shake-speare's works, and only two plays not included in the volume (*Pericles* and *The Two Noble Kinsmen*) have been allowed to join this select company, along with the nondramatic poems. Of the latter, *Venus and Adonis* (1593) and *The Rape of Lucrece* (1594) first appeared during Shakespeare's lifetime in Quartos with dedications from the author to the Earl of Southampton. *Shakespeare's Sonnets* (1609) were apparently printed without his authorization, as were his poems in a collection called *The Passionate Pilgrim* (1599).

Over the centuries, there have been many attempts to discover and authenticate additional works partly or entirely written by Shakespeare. An interesting case has been made for sections of a history play entitled *King Edward the Third* and for some small traces in the eighteenth-century tragicomedy *The Double Falsehood,* allegedly based on a manuscript of the lost Shakespearean play *Cardenio. The Norton Shakespeare* includes a poem, "Shall I die?" whose original inclusion in the 1988 *Oxford Shakespeare* provoked vigorous debate and much skepticism. Still more skepticism greeted the attri-bution to Shakespeare of a long poem called "A Funeral Elegy," printed in an appendix to *The Norton Shakespeare's* first edition and now dropped in the wake of widespread consensus that the attribution was false. In the future, other claimants will no doubt come forward, but, with the very few additions already noted, the Folio will always remain the foundation of Shakespeare's dramatic canon.

The plays were the property of the theatrical company in which Shakespeare was a shareholder. It was not normally in the interest of such companies to have their scripts circulating in print, at least while the plays were actively in repertory: players evidently feared competition from rival companies and thought that reading might dampen play-going. Plays were generally sold only when the theaters were temporarily closed by plague, or when the company was in need of capital (four of Shakespeare's plays were published in 1600, presumably to raise money to pay the debts incurred in building the new Globe), or when a play had grown too old to revive profitably. There is no evidence that Shakespeare himself disagreed with this professional caution, no sign that he wished to see his plays in print. Unlike Ben Jonson, who took the radical step of rewrit-ing his own plays for publication in the 1616 folio of his *Works*, Shakespeare evidently was not interested in constituting his plays as a canon. If in the sonnets he imagines his verse achieving a symbolic immortality, this dream apparently did not extend to his plays, at least through the medium of print.

Moreover, there is no evidence that Shakespeare had an interest in asserting autho-rial rights over his scripts or that he or any other working English playwright had a pub-lic "standing," legal or otherwise, from which to do so. (Jonson was ridiculed for his presumption.) There is no indication whatever that he could, for example, veto changes in his scripts or block interpolated scenes or withdraw a play from production if a par-ticular interpretation, addition, or revision did not please him. To be sure, in his advice to the players, Hamlet urges that those who play the clowns "speak no more than is set down for them," but—apart from the question of whether the Prince speaks for the playwright—the play within the play in *Hamlet* is precisely an instance of a script altered to suit a particular occasion. It seems likely that Shakespeare would have rou-tinely accepted the possibility of such alterations. Moreover, he would of necessity have routinely accepted the possibility, and in certain cases the virtual inevitability, of cuts in order to stage his plays in the two to two and one-half hours that was the normal per-forming time. There is an imaginative generosity in many of Shakespeare's scripts, as if he were deliberately offering his fellow actors more than they could use on any one occasion and, hence, giving them abundant materials with which to reconceive and revivify each play again and again as they or their audiences liked it. The Elizabethan theater, like most theater in our own time, was a collaborative enterprise, and the col-laboration almost certainly extended to decisions about selection, trimming, shifts of emphasis, and minor or major revision.

For many years, it was thought that Shakespeare himself did little or no revising. Some recent editors—above all the editors of the *Oxford Shakespeare*, whose texts the

Norton presents—have argued persuasively that there are many signs of authorial revision, even wholesale rewriting. But there is no sign that Shakespeare sought through such revision to bring each of his plays to its "perfect," "final" form. On the contrary, many of the revisions seem to indicate that the scripts remained open texts, that the playwright and his company expected to add, cut, and rewrite as the occasion demanded.

Ralph Waldo Emerson once compared Shakespeare and his contemporary Francis Bacon in terms of the relative "finish" of their work. All of Bacon's work, wrote Emerson, "lies along the ground, a vast unfinished city." Each of Shakespeare's dramas, by contrast, "is perfect, hath an immortal integrity. To make Bacon's work complete, he must live to the end of the world." Recent scholarship suggests that Shakespeare was more like Bacon than Emerson thought. Neither the Folio nor the quarto texts of Shakespeare's plays bear the seal of final authorial intention, the mark of decisive closure that has served, at least ideally, as the guarantee of textual authenticity. We want to believe, as we read the text, "This is the play as Shakespeare himself wanted it read," but there is no license for such a reassuring sentiment. To be "not of an age, but for all time" means in Shakespeare's case not that the plays have achieved a static perfection, but that they are creatively, inexhaustibly unfinished.

That we have been so eager to link certain admired scripts to a single known playwright is closely related to changes in the status of artists in the Renaissance, changes that led to a heightened interest in the hand of the individual creator. Like medieval painting, medieval drama gives us few clues as to the particular individuals who fashioned the objects we admire. We know something about the places in which these objects were made, the circumstances that enabled their creation, the spaces in which they were placed, but relatively little about the particular artists themselves. It is easy to imagine a wealthy patron or a civic authority in the late Middle Ages commissioning a play on a particular subject (appropriate, for example, to a seasonal ritual, a religious observance, or a political festivity) and specifying the date, place, and length of the performance, the number of actors, even the costumes to be used, but it is more difficult to imagine him specifying a particular playwright and still less insisting that the entire play be written by this dramatist alone. Only with the Renaissance do we find a growing insistence on the name of the maker, the signature that heightens the value and even the meaning of the work by implying that it is the emanation of a single, distinct shaping consciousness.

In the case of Renaissance painting, we know that this signature does not necessarily mean that every stroke was made by the master. Some of the work, possibly the greater part of it, may have been done by assistants, with only the faces and a few finishing touches from the hand of the illustrious artist to whom the work is confidently attributed. As the skill of individual masters became more explicitly valued, contracts began to specify how much was to come from the brush of the principal painter. Consider, for example, the Italian painter Luca Signorelli's contract of 1499 for frescoes in Orvieto Cathedral:

> The said master Luca is bound and promises to paint [1] all the figures to be done on the said vault, and [2] especially the faces and all the parts of the figures from the middle of each figure upwards, and [3] that no painting should be done on it without Luca himself being present. . . . And it is agreed [4] that all the mixing of colours should be done by the said master Luca himself.

Such a contract at once reflects a serious cash interest in the characteristic achievement of a particular artist and a conviction that this achievement is compatible with the presence of other hands, provided those hands are subordinate, in the finished work. For paintings on a smaller scale, it was more possible to commission an exclusive performance. Thus, the contract for a small altarpiece by Signorelli's great teacher, Piero della Francesca, specifies that "no painter may put his hand to the brush other than Piero himself."

There is no record of any comparable concern for exclusivity in the English theater. Unfortunately, the contracts that Shakespeare and his fellow dramatists almost certainly signed have not, with one significant exception, survived. But plays written for the professional theater are by their nature an even more explicitly collective art form than paintings; they depend for their full realization on the collaboration of others, and that collaboration may well extend to the fashioning of the script. It seems that some authors may simply have been responsible for providing plots that others then dramatized; still others were hired to "mend" old plays or to supply prologues, epilogues, or songs. A particular playwright's name came to be attached to a certain identifiable style—a characteristic set of plot devices, a marked rhetorical range, a tonality of character—but this name may refer in effect more to a certain product associated with a particular playing company than to the individual artist who may or may not have written most of the script. The one contract whose details do survive, that entered into by Richard Brome and the actors and owners of the Salisbury Court Theatre in 1635, does not stipulate that Brome's plays must be written by him alone or even that he must be responsible for a certain specifiable proportion of each script. Rather, it specifies that the playwright "should not nor would write any play or any part of a play to any other players or playhouse, but apply all his study and endeavors therein for the benefit of the said company of the said playhouse." The Salisbury Court players want rights to everything Brome writes for the stage; the issue is not that the plays associated with his name be exclusively *his* but rather that he be exclusively *theirs*.

Recent textual scholarship, then, has been moving steadily away from a conception of Shakespeare's plays as direct, unmediated emanations from the mind of the author and toward a conception of them as working scripts, composed and continually reshaped as part of a collaborative commercial enterprise in competition with other, similar enterprises. One consequence has been the progressive weakening of the idea of the solitary, inspired genius, in the sense fashioned by Romanticism and figured splendidly in the statue of Shakespeare in the public gardens in Germany's Weimar, the city of Goethe and Schiller: the poet, with his sensitive, expressive face and high domed forehead sitting alone and brooding, a skull at his feet, a long-stemmed rose in his crotch. In place of this projection of German Romanticism, we have now a playwright and sometime actor who is also (to his considerable financial advantage) a major shareholder in the company—the Lord Chamberlain's Men, later the King's Men—to which he loyally supplies for most of his career an average of two plays per year.

These developments are salutary insofar as they direct attention to the actual conditions in which the textual traces that the Folio calls Shakespeare's "Comedies, Histories, & Tragedies" came to be produced, reproduced, consumed, revised, and transmitted to future generations. They highlight elements that Shakespeare shared with his contemporaries, and they insistently remind us that we are encountering scripts written primarily for the stage and not for the study. They make us more attentive to such matters as business cycles, plague rolls, the cost of costumes, government censorship, and urban topography and less concerned with the elusive and enigmatic details of the poet's biography—his supposed youthful escapades and erotic yearnings and psychological crises.

All well and good. But the fact remains that in 1623, seven years after the playwright's death, Heminges and Condell thought they could sell copies of their expensive collection of Shakespeare's plays—"What euer you do," they urge their readers, "buy"—by insisting that their texts were "as he conceiued them." This means that potential readers in the early seventeenth century were already interested in Shakespeare's "conceits"—his "wit," his imagination, and his creative power—and were willing to assign a high value to the products of his particular, identifiable skill, one distinguishable from that of his company and of his rival playwrights. After all, Jonson's tribute praises Shakespeare not as the playwright of the incomparable King's Men but as the equal of Aeschylus, Sophocles, and Euripides. And if we now see Shakespeare's dramaturgy in the context of his contemporaries and of a collective artistic practice, readers continue to have little difficulty recognizing that most of the plays attached to his name tower over those of his rivals.

From Foul to Fair: The Making of the Printed Play

What exactly is a printed play by Shakespeare? Is it like a novel or a poem? Is it like the libretto or the score of an opera? Is it the trace of an absent event? Is it the blueprint of an imaginary structure that will never be completed? Is it a record of what transpired in the mind of a man long dead? We might say cautiously that it is a mechanically reproduced version of what Shakespeare wrote, but unfortunately, with the possible (and disputed) exception of a small fragment from a collaboratively written play called *Sir Thomas More*, virtually nothing Shakespeare actually wrote in his own hand survives. We might propose that it is a printed version of the script that an Elizabethan actor would have held in his hands during rehearsals, but here, too, no such script of a Shakespeare play survives; and besides, Elizabethan actors were evidently not given the whole play to read. To reduce the expense of copying and the risk of unauthorized reproduction, each actor received only his own part, along with the cue lines. (Shakespeare uses this fact to delicious comic effect in *A Midsummer Night's Dream* 3.1.80–88.) Nonetheless, the play certainly existed as a whole, either in the author's original manuscript or in the copy prepared for the government censor or for the company's prompter or stage manager, so we might imagine the text we hold in our hands as a printed copy of one of these manuscripts. But since no contemporary manuscript survives of any of Shakespeare's plays, we cannot verify this hypothesis. And even if we could, we would not have resolved the question of the precise relation of the printed text either to the playwright's imagination or to the theatrical performance by the company to which he belonged.

All of Shakespeare's plays must have begun their textual careers in the form of "foul papers," drafts presumably covered with revisions, crossings-out, and general "blotting." To be sure, Heminges and Condell remark that so great was the playwright's facility that they "have scarce received from him a blot in his papers." This was, however, a routine and conventional compliment in the period. The same claim, made for the playwright John Fletcher in an edition published in 1647, is clearly contradicted by the survival of Fletcher's far-from-unblotted manuscripts. It is safe to assume that, since Shakespeare was human, his manuscripts contained their share of second and third thoughts scribbled in the margins and between the lines. Once complete, this authorial draft would usually have to be written out again, either by the playwright or by a professional scribe employed by the theater company, as "fair copy."

In the hands of the theater company, the fair copy (or sometimes, it seems, the foul papers themselves) would be annotated and transformed into "the book of the play" or the "playbook" (what we would now call a "promptbook"). Shakespeare's authorial draft presumably contained a certain number of stage directions, though these may have been sketchy and inconsistent. The promptbook clarified these and added others, noted theatrical properties and sound effects, and on occasion cut the full text to meet the necessities of performance. The promptbook was presented to the Master of the Revels for licensing, and it incorporated any changes upon which the master insisted. As the editors of the *Oxford Shakespeare* put it, the difference between foul papers and promptbook is the difference between "the text in an as yet individual, private form" and "a socialized text."

But the fact remains that for Shakespeare's plays, we have neither foul papers nor fair copies nor promptbooks. We have only the earliest printed editions of these texts in numerous individual quartos and in the First Folio. (Quartos are so called because each sheet of paper was folded twice, making four leaves or eight pages front and back; folio sheets were folded once, making two leaves or four pages front and back.) From clues embedded in these "substantive" texts—substantive because (with the exception of *The Two Noble Kinsmen*) they date from Shakespeare's own lifetime or from the collected works edited by his associates using, or claiming to use, his own manuscripts—editors attempt to reconstruct each play's journey from manuscript to print. Different plays took very different journeys.

Of the thirty-six plays included in the First Folio, eighteen had previously appeared in quarto editions, some of these in more than one printing. Generations of editors have distinguished between "good Quartos," presumably prepared from the author's own draft or from a scribal transcript of the play (fair copy), and "bad Quartos." The latter category, first formulated as such by A. W. Pollard in 1909, includes, by widespread but not universal agreement, the 1594 version of *The First Part of the Contention* (2 *Henry VI*), the 1595 *Richard Duke of York* (3 *Henry VI*), the 1597 *Richard the Third*, the 1597 *Romeo and Juliet*, the 1600 *Henry the Fifth*, the 1602 *Merry Wives of Windsor*, the 1603 *Hamlet*, and *Pericles* (1609). Some editors also regard the 1591 *Troublesome Reign of King John*, the 1594 *Taming of a Shrew*, and the 1608 *King Lear* as bad Quartos, but others have strenuously argued that these are distinct rather than faulty texts, and the whole concept of the bad Quarto has come under increasingly critical scrutiny. The criteria for distinguishing between "good" and "bad" texts are imprecise, and the evaluative terms seem to raise as many questions as they answer. Nevertheless, the striking mistakes, omissions, repetitions, and anomalies in a number of the Quartos require some explanation beyond the ordinary fallibility of scribes and printers.

The explanation most often proposed for suspect Quartos is that they are the products of "memorial reconstruction." The hypothesis, first advanced in 1910 by W. W. Greg, is that a series of features found in what seem to be particularly flawed texts may be traced to the derivation of the copy from the memory of one or more of the actors. Elizabethan actors, Greg observed, often found themselves away from the London theaters—for example, on tour in the provinces during plague periods—and may not on those occasions have had access to the promptbooks they would ordinarily have used. In such circumstances, those in the company who remembered a play may have written down or dictated the text, as best they could, perhaps adapting it for provincial performance. Moreover, unscrupulous actors may have sold such texts to enterprising printers eager to turn a quick profit.

Memorially reconstructed texts tend to be much shorter than those prepared from foul papers or fair copy; they frequently paraphrase or garble lines, drop or misplace speeches and whole scenes, and on occasion fill in the gaps with scraps from other plays. In several cases, scholars think they can detect which roles the rogue actors played, since these parts (and the scenes in which they appear) are reproduced with greater accuracy than the rest of the play. Typically, these roles are minor ones, since the leading parts would be played by actors with a greater stake in the overall financial interest of the company and, hence, less inclination to violate its policy. Thus, for example, editors speculate that the bad Quarto of *Hamlet* (Q1) was provided by the actor playing Marcellus (and doubling as Lucianus). What is often impossible to determine is whether particular differences between a bad Quarto and a good Quarto or Folio text result from the actor's faulty memory or from changes introduced in performance, possibly with the playwright's own consent, or from both. Shakespearean bad Quartos ceased to appear after 1609, perhaps as a result of greater scrutiny by the Master of the Revels, who after 1606 was responsible for licensing plays for publication as well as performance.

The syndicate that prepared the Folio had access to the manuscripts of the King's Men. In addition to the previously published editions of eighteen plays, they made use of scribal transcripts (fair copies), promptbooks, and (more rarely) foul papers. The indefatigable labors of generations of bibliographers, antiquaries, and textual scholars have recovered an extraordinary fund of information about the personnel, finances, organizational structure, and material practices of Elizabethan and Jacobean printing houses, including the names and idiosyncrasies of particular compositors who calculated the page length, set the type, and printed the sheets of the Folio. This impressive scholarship has for the most part intensified respect for the seriousness with which the Folio was prepared and printed, and where the Folio is defective, it has provided plausible readings from the Quartos or proposed emendations to approximate what Shakespeare is likely to have written. But it has not succeeded, despite all its heroic efforts, in transforming the Folio, or any other text, into an unobstructed, clear window into Shakespeare's mind.

The dream of the master text is a dream of transparency. The words on the page should ideally give the reader unmediated access to the astonishing forge of imaginative power that was the mind of the dramatist. Those words welled up from the genius of the great artist, and if the world were not an imperfect place, they would have been set down exactly as he conceived them and transmitted to each of us as a precious inheritance. Such is the vision—at its core closely related to the preservation of the holy text in the great scriptural religions—that has driven many of the great editors who have for centuries produced successive editions of Shakespeare's works. The vision was not yet fully formed in the First Folio, for Heminges and Condell still felt obliged to apologize to their noble patrons for dedicating to them a collection of mere "trifles." But by the eighteenth century, there were no longer any ritual apologies for Shakespeare; instead, there was a growing recognition not only of the supreme artistic importance of his works but also of the uncertain, conflicting, and in some cases corrupt state of the surviving texts. Every conceivable step, it was thought, must be undertaken to correct mistakes, strip away corruptions, return the texts to their pure and unsullied form, and make this form perfectly accessible to readers.

Paradoxically, this feverishly renewed, demanding, and passionate editorial project has produced the very opposite of the transparency that was the dream of the master text. The careful weighing of alternative readings, the production of a textual apparatus, the writing of notes and glosses, the modernizing and regularizing of spelling and punctuation, the insertion of scene divisions, the complex calculation of the process of textual transmission from foul papers to print, the equally complex calculation of the effects that censorship, government regulation, and, above all, theatrical performance had on the surviving documents all make inescapably apparent the fact that we do not have and never will have any direct, unmediated access to Shakespeare's imagination. Every Shakespeare text, from the first that was published to the most recent, has been edited: it has come into print by means of a tangled social process and inevitably exists at some remove from the author.

Heminges and Condell, who knew the author and had access to at least some of his manuscripts, lament the fact that Shakespeare did not live "to have set forth and overseen his own writings." And even had he done so—or, alternatively, even if a cache of his manuscripts were discovered in a Warwickshire attic tomorrow—all of the editorial problems would not be solved, nor would all of the levels of mediation be swept away. Certainly, the entire textual landscape would change. But the written word has strange powers: it seems to hold on to something of the very life of the person who has written it, but it also seems to pry that life loose from the writer, exposing it to vagaries of history and chance independent of those to which the writer was personally subject. Moreover, with the passing of centuries, the language itself and the whole frame of reference within which language and symbols are understood have decisively changed. The most learned modern scholar still lives at a huge experiential remove from Shakespeare's world and, even holding a precious copy of the First Folio in hand, cannot escape having to read across a vast chasm of time what is, after all, an edited text. The rest of us cannot so much as indulge in the fantasy of direct access: our eyes inevitably wander to the glosses and the explanatory notes.

The Oxford Shakespeare

The shattering of the dream of the master text is no cause for despair, nor should it lead us to throw our hands up and declare that one text is as good as another. What it does is to encourage the reader to be actively interested in the editorial principles that underlie the particular edition that he or she is using. It is said that the great artist Brueghel once told a nosy connoisseur who had come to his studio, "Keep your nose out of my paintings; the smell of the paint will poison you." In the case of Shakespeare, it is increasingly important to bring one's nose close to the page, as it were, and sniff the ink. More precisely, it is important to understand the rationale for the choices that the editors have made.

The text of the *Norton Shakespeare* is, with very few changes, that published by the Oxford University Press in 1988 and, in a second edition, in 2005. The *Oxford Shakespeare* was the extraordinary achievement of a team of editors, Stanley Wells, Gary Taylor, John Jowett, and William Montgomery, with Wells and Taylor serving as the general editors. The Oxford editors approached their task with a clear understanding that, as we have seen, all previous texts have been mediated by agents other than Shakespeare; however, they regard this mediation not as a melancholy obstacle intervening between the reader and the "true" Shakespearean text but rather as a constitutive element of this text. The art of the playwright is thoroughly dependent on the craft of go-betweens.

Shakespeare's plays were not written to be circulated in manuscript or printed form among readers. They were written to be performed by the players and, as the preface to the Quarto *Troilus and Cressida* indelicately puts it, "clapper-clawed with the palms of the vulgar." The public was, thus, never meant to be in a direct relationship with the author but in a "triangular relationship" in which the players gave voice and gesture to the author's words. As we have seen, Shakespeare was the master of the unfinished, the perpetually open. And even if we narrow our gaze and try to find only what Shakespeare himself might have regarded as a textual resting point, a place to stop and go on to another play, we have, the Oxford editors point out, a complex task. For whatever Shakespeare wrote was meant from the start to be supplemented by an invisible "paratext" consisting of words spoken by Shakespeare to the actors and by the actors to each other concerning emphasis, stage business, tone, pacing, possible cuts, and so forth. To the extent that this paratext was ever written down, it was recorded in the promptbook. Therefore, in contrast to standard editorial practice, the Oxford editors prefer, when there is a choice, copy based on the promptbook to copy based on the author's own draft. They choose the text immersed in history—that is, in the theatrical embodiment for which it was intended by its author—over the text unstained by the messy, collaborative demands of the playhouse. The closest we can get to Shakespeare's "final" version of a play—understanding that for him as for us there is no true "finality" in a theatrical text—is the latest version of that play performed by his company during his professional life—that is, during the time in which he could still oversee and participate in any cuts and revisions.

This choice does not mean that the Oxford editors are turning away from the very idea of Shakespeare as author. On the contrary, Wells and Taylor are deeply committed to establishing a text that comes as close as possible to the plays as Shakespeare wrote them, but they are profoundly attentive to the fact that he wrote them as a member of a company of players, a company in which he was a shareholder and an actor as well as a writer. "Writing" for the theater, at least for Shakespeare, is not simply a matter of setting words to paper and letting the pages drift away; it is a social process as well as an individual act. The Oxford editors acknowledge that some aspects of this social process may have been frustrating to Shakespeare: he may, for example, have been forced on occasion to cut lines and even whole scenes to which he was attached, or his fellow players may have insisted that they could not successfully perform what he had written, compelling him to make changes he did not welcome. But compromise and collaboration are part of what it means to be in the theater, and Wells and Taylor return again and again to the recognition that Shakespeare was, supremely, a man of the theater.

Is there a tension between the Oxford editors' preference for the performed, fully socialized text and their continued commitment to recovering the text as Shakespeare himself intended it? Yes. The tension is most visible in their determination to strip away textual changes arising from circumstances, such as government censorship, over which Shakespeare had no control. ("We have, wherever possible," they write, put "profanities back in Shakespeare's mouth.") It can be glimpsed as well in the editors' belief, almost a leap of faith, that there was little revision of Shakespeare's plays in his company's revivals between the time of his death and the publication of the Folio. But the tension is mainly a creative one, for it forces them (and, therefore, us) to attend to the playwright's unique imaginative power as well as his social and historical entanglements.

The Oxford editors took a radical stance on a second major issue: the question of authorial revision. Previous editors had generally accepted the fact that Shakespeare practiced revision within individual manuscripts—that is, while he was still in the act of writing a particular play—but they generally rejected the notion that he undertook substantial revisions from one version of a play to another (and, hence, from one manuscript to another). Wells and Taylor point out that six major works (*Hamlet, Othello, 2 Henry IV, King Lear, Richard II,* and *Troilus and Cressida*) survive in two independent substantive sources, both apparently authoritative, with hundreds of significant variant readings. Previous editors have generally sought to deny authority to one edition or another ("faced with two sheep," the Oxford editors observe wryly, "it is all too easy to insist that one *must* be a goat") or have conflated the two versions into a single text in an attempt to reconstruct the ideal, definitive, complete, and perfect version that they imagine Shakespeare must have reached for each of his plays. But if one doubts that Shakespeare ever conceived of his plays as closed, finished entities, if one recalls that he wrote them for the living repertory of the commercial playing company to which he belonged, then the whole concept of the single, authoritative text of each play loses its force. In a startling departure from the editorial tradition, the *Oxford Shakespeare* printed two distinct versions of *King Lear,* quarto and Folio, and the editors glanced longingly at the impractical but alluring possibility of including two texts of *Hamlet, Othello,* and *Troilus.*

The *Oxford Shakespeare* was published in both old-spelling and modern-spelling editions. The former, the first of its kind ever published, raised some reviewers' eyebrows because the project, a critical edition rather than a facsimile, required the modern editors to invent plausible Elizabethan spellings for their emendations and to add stage directions. The modern-spelling edition, which is the basis for Norton's text, is noteworthy for taking the principles of modernization further than they had generally been taken. Gone are such words as "murther," "mushrump," "vild," and "porpentine," which confer on many modern-spelling editions a certain cozy, Olde-English quaintness; Oxford replaces them with "murder," "mushroom," "vile," and "porcupine."

The inclusion of two texts of *King Lear* aroused considerable controversy when the *Oxford Shakespeare* first appeared, although by now the arguments for doing so have received widespread, though not unanimous, scholarly support. Other features remain controversial: "Ancients" Pistol and Iago have been modernized to "Ensigns"; *Henry VIII* has reverted to its performance title *All Is True;* demonic spirits in *Macbeth* sing lyrics written by Thomas Middleton. The white-hot intensity of the debates triggered by the *Oxford Shakespeare*'s editorial choices casts an interesting light on the place of Shakespeare not only in the culture at large but in the psyches of millions of individuals: any alteration, however minor, in a deeply familiar and beloved text, even an alteration based on thoughtful and highly plausible scholarly principles, arouses genuine anxiety. The anxiety in this case was intensified not only by the boldness of certain crucial emendations but also by the fact that the editors' explanations, arguments, and justifications for all their decisions were printed in a separate, massive volume, *William Shakespeare: A Textual Companion.* This formidable, dense volume is an astonishing monument to the seriousness, scholarly rigor, and immense labor of the Oxford editors. Anyone who is interested in pursuing why Shakespeare's words appear as they do in the current edition, anyone who wishes insight into the editors' detailed reasons for making the thousands of decisions required by a project of this kind, should consult the *Textual Companion.*

The Norton Shakespeare

The primary task that the editors of the *Norton Shakespeare* set themselves was to present the modern-spelling Oxford *Complete Works* in a way that would make the text more accessible to modern readers. The *Oxford Shakespeare* prints little more than the text itself: along with one-page introductions to the individual works, it contains a short general introduction, a list of contemporary allusions to Shakespeare, and a brief glossary. But while it is possible to enjoy a Shakespeare play on stage or screen without any assistance beyond the actors' own art, many readers at least since the eighteenth century have found it far more difficult to understand and to savor the texts without some more substantial commentary.

In addition to writing introductions, textual notes, and brief bibliographies for each of the works, the Norton editors provide glosses and footnotes designed to facilitate comprehension. Such is the staggering richness of Shakespeare's language that it is tempting to gloss everything. But there is a law of diminishing returns: too much explanatory whispering at the margins makes it difficult to enjoy what the reader has come for in the first place. Our general policy is to gloss only those words that cannot be found in an ordinary dictionary or whose meanings have altered out of recognition. The glosses attempt to be simple and straightforward, giving multiple meanings for words only when the meanings are essential for making sense of the passages in which they appear. We try not to gloss the same word over and over—it becomes distracting to be told three times on a single page that "an" means "if"—but we also assume that the reader does not have a perfect memory, so after an interval we will gloss the same word again.

Marginal glosses generally refer to a single word or a short phrase. The footnotes paraphrase longer units or provide other kinds of information, such as complex plays on words, significant allusions, textual cruxes, historical and cultural contexts. Here, too, however, we have tried to check the impulse to annotate so heavily that the reader is distracted from the pleasure of the text, and we have avoided notes that provide interpretation, as distinct from information.

Following the works, the Norton editors have provided lists of textual variants. These are variants from the control text only—that is, they do not record all of the variants in all of the substantive texts, nor do they record all of the myriad shifts of meaning that may arise from modernization of spelling and repunctuation. Readers who wish to pursue these interesting, if complex, topics are encouraged to consult the *Textual Companion,* along with the old-spelling *Oxford Shakespeare,* the Norton facsimile of the First Folio, and the quarto facsimiles published by the University of California Press. The *Norton Shakespeare* does provide a convenient list for each play of the different ways the same characters are designated in the speech prefixes in the substantive texts. These variants (for example, Lady Capulet in *Romeo and Juliet* is called, variously, "Lady," "Mother," "Wife," "Old Woman," etc.) often cast an interesting light on the ways a particular character is conceived. Variants as they appear in this edition, as well as their line numbers, are printed in boldface; each is followed by the corresponding reading in the control text, and sometimes the source from which the variant is taken. Further information on readings in substantive texts is given in brackets.

Stage directions pose a complex set of problems for the editors of a one-volume Shakespeare. The printing conventions for the stage directions in sixteenth- and seventeenth-century plays were different from those of our own time. Often all of the entrances for a particular scene are grouped together at the beginning, even though some of the characters clearly do not enter until later; placement in any case seems at times haphazard or simply incorrect. There are moments when the stage directions seem to provide stunning insight into the staging of the plays in Shakespeare's time, other moments when they are absent or misleading. It is difficult to gauge how much the stage directions in the substantive editions reflect Shakespeare's own words or at least decisions. It would seem that he was often relatively careless about them, understanding perhaps that these decisions in any precise sense would be the first to be made and unmade by different productions.

The Oxford editors, like virtually all modern editors, necessarily altered and supplemented the stage directions in their control texts. They decided to mark certain of the stage directions with a special sign to indicate a dubious action or placement, but they did not distinguish between the stage directions that came from the substantive texts and those added in later texts, from the seventeenth century to the present. They referred readers instead to the *Textual Companion,* which provides lists of the exact wording of the stage directions in the substantive texts.

The editors of the *Norton Shakespeare* share a sense of the limitations of the early stage directions and share as well some skepticism about how many of these should be attributed even indirectly to Shakespeare. Hence, we do not routinely differentiate between quarto and Folio stage directions; we do so only when we think it is a significant point. But there is, it seems to us, a real interest in knowing which stage directions come from those editions of the plays published up to the 1623 Folio (and including *The Two Noble Kinsmen,* published shortly thereafter) and which were added when the editors were no longer in contact with Shakespeare's presence or his manuscripts. Therefore, we have placed brackets around all stage directions that were added after the First Folio. Unbracketed stage directions, then, all derive from editions up through the Folio.

The *Norton Shakespeare* has made several other significant departures from the Oxford text. The Oxford editors note that when *1 Henry IV* was first performed, probably in 1596, the character we know as Sir John Falstaff was called Sir John Oldcastle. But in the wake of protests from Oldcastle's descendants, one of whom, William Brooke, tenth Baron Cobham, was Elizabeth I's lord chamberlain, Shakespeare changed the name to "Falstaff" (and probably for similar reasons changed the names of Falstaff's companions, Russell and Harvey, to "Bardolph" and "Peto"). Consistent with their decision not to honor changes that Shakespeare was *compelled* to make by censorship or other forms of pressure, the Oxford editors changed the names back to their initial form. But this decision is a problem for several reasons. It draws perhaps too sharp a distinction between those things that Shakespeare did under social pressure and those he did of his own accord. More seriously, it pulls against the principle of a text that represents the latest performance version of a play during Shakespeare's lifetime: after all, even the earliest quarto title page advertises "the humorous conceits of Sir John Falstaff." And, of course, it asks the reader to ignore completely and radically centuries of response—elaboration, fascination, and love—all focused passionately on Sir John Falstaff. The response is not a modern phenomenon: it began with Shakespeare, who developed the character as Sir John Falstaff in *2 Henry IV* and *The Merry Wives of Windsor.* Norton thus restores the more familiar names.

Another major departure from the Oxford text is Norton's printing of the so-called Additional Passages, especially in *Hamlet.* Consistent with their decision not to conflate quarto and Folio texts, the Oxford editors adhere to their control text for *Hamlet,* the Folio, and print those passages that appear only in the Second Quarto in an appendix at the end of the play. As explained at length in the Textual Note to the play, the Norton editors decided not to follow this course, but instead chose a different way of demarcating the quarto and Folio texts (inserting the quarto passages, indented, in the body of the text), one that makes it easier to see how the quarto passages functioned in a version of the play that Shakespeare also authored.

The *Norton Shakespeare* follows Oxford in printing separate quarto and Folio texts of *King Lear,* to which we have added a conflated version of the play so that readers will have the opportunity to assess for themselves the effects of the traditional editorial practice. Moreover, we have departed from Oxford in printing the quarto and Folio texts of the plays on facing pages, so that their differences can be readily weighed. In the hundreds of changes, some trivial and other momentous, it is possible to glimpse, across what Prospero calls "the dark backward and abysm of time," a thrilling sight: Shakespeare at work.

The Shakespearean Stage

by

ANDREW GURR

Publication by Performance

The curt exchange between the sentries in the first six lines of *Hamlet* tells us that it is very late at night (" 'Tis now struck twelve") and that " 'tis bitter cold." This opening was staged originally at the Globe in London in broad daylight, at 2 o'clock probably on a hot summer's afternoon. The words required the audience, half of them standing on three sides of the stage platform and all of them as visible to one another as the players were, to imagine themselves watching a scene quite the opposite of what they could see and feel around them. The original mode of staging for a Shakespearean play was utterly different from the cinematic realism we are used to now, where the screen gives us close-ups on a simulacrum of reality, an even more privileged view of the actors' facial twitches than we get in ordinary life. Eloquence then was in words, not facial expressions.

The playgoers of Shakespeare's time knew the plays in forms at which we can only now guess. It is a severe loss. Shakespeare's own primary concept of his plays was as stories "personated" onstage, not as words on a page. He himself never bothered to get his playscripts into print, and more than half of them were not published until seven years after his death, in the First Folio of his plays published as a memorial to him in 1623. His fellow playwright Francis Beaumont called the printing of plays "a second publication"; the first was their showing onstage. Print recorded a set of scripts, written for the original players to teach them what they should speak in the ensemble of the play in production. The only technology then available to record the performances was the written word. If video recordings had existed at that time, our understanding of Shakespeare would be vastly different from what it is today.

Since the texts were composed only to be a record of the words the players were to memorize, we now have to infer how the plays were originally staged largely by guesswork. Shakespeare was himself a player and shareholder in his acting company, and he expected to be present at rehearsals. Consequently, the stage directions in his scripts are distinctly skimpy compared with some of those provided by his fellow playwrights. He was cursory even in noting entrances and exits, let alone how he expected his company to stage the more complex spectacles, such as heaving Antony up to Cleopatra on her monument. There are sometimes hints in the stage directions and more frequently in the words used to describe some of the actions, and knowing what the design of the theater was like is a help as well. Knowing more about how Shakespeare expected his plays to be staged can transform how we think about them. But gaining such knowledge is no easy matter. One of the few certainties is that Shakespeare's plays in modern performance are even more different from the originals than modern printed editions are from the first much-thumbed manuscripts.

The Shakespearean Mindset

The general mindset of the original playgoers, the patterns of thinking and expectation that Tudor culture imposed on Shakespeare's audiences, is not really difficult to identify.

It is less easy, though, to pin it down in the sort of detail that tells us what the original concept of staging the plays would have been like. We know that all the original playgoers paid for the privilege of attending the plays and committed themselves willingly to suspend their disbelief in what they were to see. They knew as we do that they were paying to be entertained by fictions. Beyond that, we need reminding today that going to open-air performances in daylight in Shakespeare's time meant being constantly aware that one was in a theater, a place designed to offer illusions. On the one hand, this consciousness of oneself and where one was meant that the players had to do more to hold attention than is needed now, when audiences have nothing but the stage to look at and armchairs to sit in. On the other hand, it made everyone more receptive to extratheatrical tricks, such as Hamlet's reference to "this distracted globe," or Polonius's claim in the same play to have taken the part of Julius Caesar at the university and been killed by Brutus. The regular playgoers at the Globe who recognized Polonius as the man who had played Caesar in Shakespeare's play of the year before, and who recognized Hamlet as the man who had played Brutus, would laugh at this theatrical in-joke. But two scenes later, when Hamlet kills Polonius, they would think of it again, in a different light.

Features of the original mindset such as these are readily identifiable. For others, though, we need to look further, into the design of the theaters and into the staging traditions that they housed and that Shakespeare exploited. Invisibility has a part to play in *A Midsummer Night's Dream* that we can easily underrate, for instance. Invisibility onstage is a theatrical in-joke, an obvious privileging of the audience, which is allowed to see what the characters onstage can't. The impresario Philip Henslowe's inventory of costumes used at the Rose theater in 1597, which lists "a robe for to go invisible," indicates a fictional device that openly expects the willing suspension of the audience's disbelief. In *A Midsummer Night's Dream,* the ostensible invisibility of all the visible fairies emphasizes the theatricality of the whole presentation while pandering to the audience's self-indulgent superiority, the feeling that it knows what is going on better than any character, whether he be Bottom or even Duke Theseus. That prepares us for the mockery of stage realism we get later, in the mechanicals' play in Act 5, and even for the doubt we as willing audience might feel over Theseus's own skepticism about the dangers of imagination that he voices in his speech at the beginning of Act 5.

More to the point, though, it throws into question our readiness to be an audience, since we have ourselves been indulging in just the games of suspending disbelief that the play staged by the mechanicals enters into so unsuccessfully. When Theseus disputes with Hippolyta about the credibility of the lovers' story, he voices the very skepticism—about the lover, the lunatic, and the poet—that any sensible realist in the audience would have been feeling for most of the previous three acts in the forest. The play starts and ends at the court in broad daylight, while the scenes of midsummer madness take place at night in a forest. At the early amphitheaters, all the plays were staged in broad daylight, between 2 and 5 o'clock in the afternoon, and without any persuasive scenery: the two stage posts served as trees onstage. So the play, moving as it does from daylight realism to nocturnal fantasy and back again, with a last challenge to credulity in the mechanicals' burlesque of how to stage a play, has already thoroughly challenged the willing suspension of the viewers' disbelief. *A Midsummer Night's Dream* is a play about nocturnal dreams and fictions that are accepted as truths in broad daylight. It was only a small extension of this game to have the women's parts played by boys, as well as plots in which the girls dressed as boys, to the point where in *As You Like It* Rosalind was played by a boy playing a girl pretending to be a boy playing a girl.

The Shakespeare plays were written for a new and unique kind of playhouse, the Elizabethan amphitheater, which had a distinctive design quite different from modern theaters. Elizabethans knew what the standard features in their theaters stood for, and Shakespeare drew on that knowledge for the staging of his plays. The physical features of the playhouses were a potent element in the ways that the plays were designed for the Elizabethan mindset. When Richard III, the archdeceiver and playactor, appears "aloft between two Bishops" to claim the crown in *Richard III* 3.7, his placing on the stage balcony literally above the crowd on the stage would, even without the accompanying priests, have signified his ironic claim to a social and moral superiority that ought to have matched his elevation. When Richard II comes down from the wall of Flint Castle to the "base court" in *Richard II* 3.3, Elizabethans would have seen his descent as a withdrawal from power and status. These theaters were still new when Shakespeare started to write for them, and their novelty meant that the plays were written more tightly to fit their specific design than the plays of later years, when theatergoing had become a more routine social activity and different kinds of theater were available.

London Playgoing and the Law

This heightened sense of theatricality, or "metatheater," in Shakespearean audiences was far from the only difference in their mindset from that of all modern audiences. Regular playgoing in London only started in the 1570s, and through Shakespeare's earlier years it was always a perilous and precarious activity. The Lord Mayor of London and the mayors of most of England's larger towns hated playgoing and tried to suppress it whenever and wherever it appeared. Playgoing was exciting not only because it was new but because it was dangerous. The hostility of so many authorities to plays meant that they were seen almost automatically as subversive of authority. Paradoxically, the first London companies were only able to establish themselves in London through the active support of Queen Elizabeth and her Privy Council, which tried hard, in the face of constant complaints from the Lord Mayor, to ensure that the best companies would be on hand every Christmas to entertain the Queen's leisure hours. Popular support for playgoing depended on royal protection for the leading companies.

London was by far the largest city in England. Within a few years of Shakespeare's death, it became the largest in Europe. It was generally an orderly place to live, especially in the city itself. Even in the suburbs, where the poorer people had to live, there were not many of the riots and other disorders that preachers always associated with the brothels, animal-baiting arenas, and playhouses clustering there. The reputation that the playhouses gained for promoting riots was not well justified. Any crowd of people was seen by the authorities as a potential riot, and playhouses regularly drew some of the largest crowds that London had yet seen. The city's government was not designed to control large crowds of people. There was no paid police force, and the Lord Mayor was held responsible by the Privy Council, the Queen's governing committee, for any disorders that did occur. So the city authorities found that playgoing challenged their control over their people.

The rapid growth of London did not help the situation. Officially, the city was governed by the Lord Mayor and his council. But he had authority only inside the city, and London now spread through a large suburban area in the adjacent counties of Middlesex to the north and Surrey across the river to the south. Because the court and the national government were housed in London, the Privy Council often intervened in city affairs in its own interests, as well as when orders were needed that covered broader zones than the city itself. The periodic outbreaks of bubonic plague were one clear instance of such a need, because the plague took no notice of parish or city boundaries. The intrusion of the professional companies to play in London provided another. In the early years, they were chronic travelers, and London was simply one of many stopovers. But the Queen enjoyed seeing plays at Christmas, and her council accordingly supported the best companies so that they could perform for her. It protected the playing companies against the hatred of successive Lord Mayors, except when a national emergency such as a plague epidemic erupted. The Privy Council took control then by ordering the 126 parishes in and around London to list all deaths from plague separately from ordinary deaths. Each Thursday, the parish totals were added together. When the total number of deaths from plague in these lists rose above 30 in any one week, the Privy Council closed all places of public assembly. This meant especially the playhouses, which created by far the largest gatherings. When the theaters were closed, the playing companies had to revert to their traditional practice of going on tour to play in the towns through the country, provided that the news of plague did not precede them.

Plague was not the only reason for the government to lay its controlling hand on the companies. From the time the post was inaugurated in 1578, the Master of the Revels controlled all playing. He was executive officer to the Lord Chamberlain, the Privy Council officer responsible for the annual season of royal entertainment and thus, by extension, for the professional playing companies. The Master of the Revels licensed each company and censored its plays. He was expected to cut out any references to religion or affairs of state, and he tried to prevent other offenses by banning the depiction of any living person onstage. After 1594, he issued licenses to the approved London playhouses, too. Later still, the printing of any playbook was allowed only if he gave authority for it. The companies had to accept this tight control because the government was its only protector against the hostile municipal authorities, who included not only the Lord Mayor of London but also the mayors of most of the major towns in the country.

Most mayors had the commercial interest of keeping local employees at work to justify their hostility to playgoing. But across the country, the hostility went much deeper. A large proportion of the population disliked the very idea of playacting. Their reasons, ostensibly religious, were that for actors to pretend to be characters they were unlike in life was a deception and that for boys to dress as women was contrary to what the Bible said. Somewhere beneath this was a more basic fear of pretense and deceit, of people not acting honestly. It put actors into the same category as con men, cheats, and thieves. That was probably one reason why companies of boys acting men's parts were thought rather more tolerable than men pretending to be other kinds of men. The deception involved in boys playing men was more transparent than when men played characters other than themselves. There was also a strong Puritan suspicion about shows of any kind, which looked too much like the Catholic ceremonial that the new Church of England had renounced. Playgoing found much better favor on the Catholic side of English society than on the Puritan side. Different preachers took different positions over the new phenomenon of playgoing. But few would speak in its favor, and most of them openly disapproved of it. Playgoing was an idle pastime, and the devil finds work for idle hands.

In the 1590s, when *Romeo and Juliet* and Shakespeare's histories and early comedies were exciting audiences, only two playhouses and two companies were officially approved by the Queen's Privy Council for the entertainment of London's citizens. The other main forms of paid entertainment were bear- and bullbaiting, which were much harder on the performers than was playing and so could be staged less frequently. The hostility to plays meant that the right to perform was confined to only a few of the most outstanding companies. These few companies were in competition with one another, and this led to a rapid growth in the quality of their offerings. But playacting was always a marginal activity. Paying to enter a specially built theater in order to see professional companies perform plays was still a new phenomenon, and it still met with great opposition from the London authorities. The open-air theaters like the Globe were built out in the suburbs. London as a city had no centrally located playhouses until after the civil war and the restoration of the monarchy, in 1661. And even playing in the city's suburbs, where they were free from the Lord Mayor's control, the companies had to work under the control of the Privy Council. All the great amphitheaters were built either in Middlesex or in Surrey. At the height of their success, in the years after Shakespeare's death, the Privy Council never licensed more than four or five playhouses in London.

Playgoing in London was viewed even by the playgoers as an idle occupation. The largest numbers who went to the Globe were apprentices and artisans taking time off from work, often surreptitiously, and law students from the Inns of Court doing the same. These fugitives were linked with the wealthier kind of idler, "gallants" or rich gentlemen and other men of property, along with soldiers and sailors on leave from the wars, people visiting London from the country on business or pleasure (usually both), and above all the women of London. Women were not expected to be literate, but one did not need to be able to read and write to enjoy hearing and seeing a play. A respectable woman had to make sure she was escorted by a man. He might be a husband or a friend, or her page if she was rich, or her husband's apprentice if she was a middle-class citizen. She might have a mask on, part of standard women's wear outdoors to protect the face against the weather and to assert modesty—and perhaps anonymity. Market women (applewives and fishwives) went to plays in groups. Whores were expected to be there looking for business, especially from the gallants, but they usually had male escorts, too.

The social range of playgoers at the two playhouses approved for use in 1594 was almost complete, stretching from the aristocracy to the poorest workmen and boys. Many people disapproved of plays, but at peak times up to 25,000 a week flocked to see the variety of plays being offered. Prices for playgoing remained much the same throughout the decades up to 1642, when the parliamentary government that was fighting the King closed all the theaters for eighteen years. Until then, one could get standing room at an amphitheater for 1 penny ($\frac{1}{240}$th of a modern pound, roughly 1 cent),

The city of London and its suburbs in 1572.

or a seat on a bench in the roofed galleries for twopence. A seat in a lord's room cost sixpence, which was not much less than a day's wage for a skilled artisan in 1600. The smaller roofed theaters that opened in 1599 were much more expensive. They were called "private" theaters to distinguish them from the "public" open-air amphitheaters, although the claim to privacy was mainly a convenient fiction to escape the controls imposed on the "public" theaters. At the Blackfriars hall theater, sixpence only gained you a seat in the topmost gallery, while a seat in the pit near the stage cost three times that amount and a seat in a box five times, or half a skilled worker's weekly wage.

It was not only the plays and players that were the sights at the playhouses. The richest lords and gallants went to be seen as much as they went to see. At the Globe, the costliest rooms were positioned alongside the balcony "above," over the stage. They were called "lords' rooms," and the playgoers who chose to sit there had a limited view of what went on beneath them. They saw no "discoveries," for instance, such as Portia's three caskets in *The Merchant of Venice,* which were uncovered underneath them inside the alcove in the center of the *frons scenae* (the wall at the back of the stage), or anything other than the backs of the players when they entered. But as audience, they were themselves highly visible, and that was what they paid for. In the hall, or "private," playhouses, with much higher admission prices than at the Globe, there were boxes flanking the stage for the gentry, which gave them a better view of the "discoveries." But at these "select" (because costlier) hall playhouses, where, unlike the Globe, everyone had a seat, some of the most colorful and exhibitionistic gallants could go one better. Up to fifteen gallants could pay for a stool to sit and watch the play on the stage itself, sitting in front of the boxes that flanked the stage. Each would enter from the players' dressing room (the "tiring-house") with his stool in hand before the play started. This gave them the best possible view of the play and easily the most conspicuous place in the audience's eye. Playgoing was a public occasion in which the visibility of audience members allowed them to play almost as large a part as the players.

Through the 1590s, the only permanent and custom-made playhouses were the large open-air theaters. Paying sixpence for a ferry across the river, as the richer playgoers did, or walking across London Bridge to the Rose or the Globe, or else trudging north through the mud of Shoreditch and Finsbury Fields or Clerkenwell to the Theatre or the Fortune in order to see a play, did not have great appeal when it was raining. Consequently, the companies were always trying to secure roofed halls nearer the city center. Up to 1594, they could use city inns, especially in winter, but the Lord Mayor's hostility to playing never made them reliable places for performing. Two constant problems troubled the players throughout these first years of professional theater in London: the city officials' chronic hatred of plays and the periodic visitations of the plague, which always led the government to close the theaters as soon as the number of plague deaths rose to dangerously high levels.

Playgoing was not firmly established in London until the Privy Council chose to protect it in 1594 and to approve specific playhouses for the two companies that it officially sanctioned. By then, Shakespeare had already made his mark. He became a player, a shareholder, and the resident playwright for one of these two companies. That status gained him a privileged place in the rapidly growing new world of playgoing. From then on, although his theater was still located only in the suburbs of the city, his work had the law behind it. That status was amply confirmed in 1603, when the new King made himself the company's patron. The King's Men held their status until the King himself lost power in 1642.

The Design of the Globe

The Globe was Shakespeare's principal playhouse. He put up part of the money for its construction and designed his best plays for it. It was built on the south side of the Thames in 1599, fashioned out of the framing timbers of an older theater. Essentially, it was a polygonal scaffold of twenty bays or sections, nearly 100 feet in outside diameter, making a circle of three levels of galleries that rose to more than 30 feet high, with wooden bench seating and cushions for those who could afford them. This surrounded an open "yard," into which the stage projected.

The yard was over 70 feet in diameter. Nearly half the audience stood on their feet to watch the play from inside this yard, closest to the stage platform. The stage extended out nearly to the middle of the yard, so the actors could stand in the center of the crowd. The uncertain privilege of having standing room in the open air around the stage platform could be bought with the minimal price for admission, 1 penny (about a cent). It had the advantage of proximity to the stage and the players; its disadvantage was keeping you on your feet for the two or three hours of the play, as well as leaving you subject to the weather. If you wanted a seat, or if it rained and you wanted shelter, you paid twice as much to sit in the three ranks of roofed galleries that circled behind the crowd standing in the yard. With some squeezing, the theater could hold over 3,000 people. It was an open-air theater because that gave it a larger capacity than a roofed hall. The drawback of its being open to the weather was more than outweighed by the gain in daylight that shone on stage and spectators alike.

The stage was a great square platform as much as 40 feet wide. It had over it a canopied roof, or "heavens," to protect the players and their expensive costumes from rain. This canopy was held up by two pillars rising through the stage. The stage platform was about 5 feet high and without any protective rails, so that the eyes of the audience in the yard were at the level of the players' feet. At the back of the stage, a wall—the *frons scenae*—stretched across the front of the players' tiring-house, the attiring or dressing room. It had a door on each flank and a wider curtained space in the center, which was used for major entrances and occasionally for set-piece scenes. Above these entry doors was a gallery or balcony, most of which was partitioned into rooms for the wealthiest spectators. A central room "above" was sometimes used in staging: for example, as Juliet's balcony, as the place for Richard III to stand between the bish-

The second Globe, from Wenceslaus Hollar's engraving of the "Long View" of London (1647). The two captions saying "The Globe" and "Beere bayting h." were accidentally transposed in the original. The Globe is the round structure in the center of the picture.

A photograph of the interior framework of the "new" Globe, on the south bank of the Thames in London, showing the general dimensions of the yard and the surrounding galleries.

ops, as the wall of Flint Castle in *Richard II,* and as the wall over the city gates of Harfleur in *Henry V.* After 1608, when Shakespeare's company acquired the Blackfriars consort of musicians, this central gallery room was turned into a curtained-off music room that could double as an "above" when required. Fewer than half of Shakespeare's plays need an "above."

The Original Staging Techniques

Shakespearean staging was emblematic. The "heavens" that covered the stage was the colorful feature from which gods descended to the earth of the stage platform. When Jupiter made his appearance in *Cymbeline,* in clouds of "sulphurous breath" provided by fireworks, he was mounted on an eagle being lowered through a trapdoor in the heavens. The other trapdoor, set in the stage platform itself, symbolized the opposite, a gateway to hell. The large stage trap was the place where the Gravedigger came to work at the beginning of Act 5 of *Hamlet.* It was the cell where Malvolio was imprisoned in *Twelfth Night.* The Shakespearean mindset accepted such conventions automatically.

Shakespeare inherited from Marlowe a tradition of using the stage trap as the dreaded hell's mouth. Barabbas plunges into it in *The Jew of Malta,* and the demons drag the screaming Faustus down it at the end of *Dr. Faustus.* Hell was not a fiction taken lightly by Elizabethans. Edward Alleyn, by far the most famous player of Faustus in the 1590s, wore a cross on his breast while he played the part, as insurance—just in case the fiction turned serious. Tracking the Elizabethan mindset about the stage trapdoor can give us a few warnings of what we might overlook when we come fresh to the plays today.

In the original staging of *Hamlet* at the Globe, the stage trap had two functions. Besides serving as Ophelia's grave, it was the distinctive entry point, not used by any other character, for the Ghost in Act 1. When he tells his son that he is "for the day confined to fast in fires," the first audiences would have already taken the point that he

The Globe as reconstructed in Southwark near the original site in London.

had come up from the underworld. His voice comes from under the stage, telling the soldiers to swear the oath of secrecy that Hamlet lays upon them. The connection between that original entry by the Ghost through the trap and the trap's later use for Ophelia is one we might easily miss. At the start of Act 5, the macabre discussion between the Gravediggers about whether she committed suicide and is, therefore, con-

The *frons scenae* of the new Globe.

A gesture using the language of hats, as shown by the man attending the brothers Browne.

signed to hell gets its sharpest edge from the association of the trap, here the grave being dug for her, with the Ghost's purgatorial fires. More to the point, though, Hamlet, as he eavesdrops on the curtailed burial ceremony, makes the same connection when he discovers that it is the body of Ophelia being so neglectfully interred. He remembers the other apparition that came up through the trap and springs forward in a grotesque parody of the Ghost, crying, "This is I, Hamlet the Dane!" It is a melodramatic claim to be acting a new role, that of his father the dead King. The first audiences would have remembered the ghost of dead King Hamlet using the stage trap at this point more readily than we do now. Hamlet's private knowledge of the Ghost and the trapdoor sets him, as so often happens in the play, at odds with his audience. Consequently, centuries of editors, like the characters onstage, have misread this claim as a declaration that young Hamlet ought to be King.

Since his own name is Hamlet, and since he alone could have made the connection between the Ghost and the trapdoor, he was all too likely to be misunderstood. In the next scene, Osric certainly shows that he understands Hamlet's graveside claim that he is his father's ghost to be a claim that he should now be King of Denmark. That explains why Osric insists on keeping his hat in his hand when he comes to invite Hamlet to duel with Laertes. With equals, an Elizabethan gentleman would doff his hat in greeting and then put it back on. Only in the presence of your master, or as a courtier in the presence of the King, did you keep it in your hand. Osric is trying tactfully to acknowledge what he thinks is Hamlet's lunatic claim to be King. He missed the private connection that Hamlet had made with the trapdoor and his father's ghost. Tudor body language, with its wordless gestures and signals that defined human relations, was an aspect of social life so widely understood that it needed no stage direction. The language of hats was a part of the Shakespearean mindset that we now have to register in footnotes.

Other signifiers are necessarily more elusive. We might take heart from the range of the comments made in *Much Ado About Nothing* 4.1 when Hero is accused and is seen to go red. Each of the viewers—Claudio, Leonato, and Friar Francis—gives a different reading (or "noting") of her blush. Different mindsets lead to visual indicators being read in different ways. Each reading tells as much about the observer as about the thing observed. We might add that since the blush is commented on so extensively, Shakespeare must have been concerned to save the boy playing Hero from the necessity of holding his breath long enough to produce the right visual effect.

Costume was a vital element in the plays, a mute and instant signifier of the scene. If a character entered carrying a candle and dressed in a gown with a nightcap on his head, he had evidently just been roused from bed. Characters who entered wearing cloaks and riding boots and possibly holding a whip had just ended a long journey. York,

A sketch by Henry Peacham of an early staging of *Titus Andronicus* by Shakespeare's company (1595). Note the attempt at a Roman costume for Titus but not for his soldiers, who carry Tudor halberds, and note Aaron's makeup and wig.

entering in *Richard II* with a gorget (a metal neck plate, the "signs of war about his agèd neck" [2.2.74]), was preparing for battle. Even the women's wigs that the boys wore could be used to indicate the wearer's state of mind. Hair worn loose and unbound meant madness, whether in *Hamlet*'s Ophelia or *Troilus*'s Cassandra.

Comparable audience expectations could be roused by other visual features. Characters with faces blackened and wigs of curly black wool were recognized as Moors,

Johannes de Witt's drawing of the Swan Theatre in 1596, showing two boys playing women greeted by a chamberlain.

alien and dangerous non-Christians. Aaron the Moor in *Titus Andronicus* and the Prince of Morocco in *The Merchant of Venice* acquire that character as soon as they come in view. Othello, by Iago's report and by his own first appearance, takes on the same stereotype. By contrast, Iago is dressed like a simple and honest soldier. Only in the course of Act 1 does it become apparent that it is Othello who is the honest soldier, Iago the un-Christian alien. The play neatly reverses the visual stereotypes of Elizabethan staging. Twentieth-century playgoers miss most of these signals and the ways that the original players used them to show the discrepancy between outward appearance and inner person. As King Lear said, robes and furred gowns hide all.

For *The Merchant of Venice,* Shylock wore his "Jewish gabardine" and may also have put on a false nose, as Alleyn was said to have done for the title role in *The Jew of Malta.* Other national characteristics were noted by features of dress, such as the Irish "strait strossers" (tight trousers) that Macmorris would have worn in *Henry V.* The dress of the women in the plays, who were usually played by boys with unbroken voices, was always a special expense. The records kept by Philip Henslowe, owner of the Rose playhouse and impresario for the rival company to Shakespeare's, show that he paid the author less for the script of *A Woman Killed with Kindness* than he paid the costumer for the heroine's gown.

Women's clothing and the decorums and signals that women's costume contained were very different from those of men and men's clothing. Men frequently used their hats, doffing them to signal friendship and holding them in their hands while speaking to anyone in authority over them. Women's hats were fixed to their heads and were rarely if ever taken off in public. The forms and the language of women's clothes reflected the silent modesty and the quiet voices that men thought proper for women. Women had other devices to signal with, including handkerchiefs, fans, and face masks, and the boys playing the women's parts in the theaters exploited such accessories to the full. A lady out of doors commonly wore a mask to protect her complexion. When Othello is quizzing Emilia in 4.2 about his wife's behavior while she spoke to Cassio, he asks Emilia, who should have been chaperoning her mistress, whether Desdemona had not sent her away "to fetch her fan, her gloves, her mask, nor nothing?" There is little doubt that the boys would have routinely worn masks when they played gentlewomen onstage, and not just at the masked balls in *Romeo and Juliet, Love's Labour's Lost,* and *Much Ado About Nothing.*

Other features of the original staging stemmed from the actor–audience relationship, which differs radically in daylight, when both parties can see one another, from what we are used to in modern, darkened, theaters. An eavesdropping scene onstage, for instance, works rather on the same basis as the "invisible" fairies in *A Midsummer Night's Dream,* where the audience agrees to share the pretense. At the Globe, it also entailed adopting the eavesdropper's perspective. In *Much Ado,* the two games of eavesdropping played on Benedick and Beatrice are chiefly done around the two stage posts. In these scenes, the posts that held up the stage cover, or "heavens," near what we now think of as the front of the stage were round, like the whole auditorium, and their function was to allow things to be seen equally by all of the audience, wherever people might be standing or sitting. Members of the audience, sitting in the surrounding galleries or standing around the stage itself at the Globe or its predecessors, had the two tall painted pillars in their sight all the time, wherever they were in the playhouse. And since the audience was in a complete circle all around the stage, if the stage posts were used for concealment there was always a large proportion of the audience who could see the player trying to hide behind a post. It was a three-dimensional game in which the audience might find itself behind any of the game players, victims or eavesdroppers, complicit in either role.

The first of *Much Ado's* eavesdropping scenes, 2.3, starts as usual in Shakespeare with a verbal indication of the locality. Benedick tells his boy, "Bring it hither to me in the orchard." So we don't need stage trees to tell us where we are supposed to be. He later hides "in the arbour" to listen to what Don Pedro and the others have set for him; this means concealing himself behind a stage post, closer to the audience than the playactors who are talking about him. Don Pedro asks, "See you where Benedick hath hid himself?" a self-contradiction that confirms the game. When it is Beatrice's turn in her arbor scene, 3.1, she slips into a "bower" behind "this alley," which again signals a retreat behind the prominent stage post. These games are played with both of the eavesdroppers hiding behind the post at the stage edge, while the others do their talking at center stage between the two posts.

Such games of eavesdropping, using the same bits of the stage structure, make a strong visual contrast with all that goes on at what we two-dimensional thinkers, used to the pictorial staging of the cinema, call the "back" of the stage, or upstage—where, for instance, the Friar starts the broken-off wedding and where Claudio and Don Pedro later figure at Leonato's monument. These events are more distant from the audience, less obviously comic and intimate. The close proximity of players to audience in such activities as eavesdropping strongly influenced the audience's feeling of kinship with the different groupings of players.

A multitude of other staging differences can be identified. Quite apart from the fact that the language idioms were more familiar to the playgoers at the original Globe than they are now, all playgoers in 1600, many of them illiterate, were practiced listeners. The speed of speech, even in blank verse, was markedly higher then than the recitation of Shakespeare is today. The original performances of *Hamlet,* if the Folio version reflects what was usually acted, would have run for not much more than two and a half hours (the time quoted by Ben Jonson for a play as long as *Hamlet*), compared with the more than four hours that the full Folio or 1605 quarto text with at least one intermission would take today. Quicker speaking, quicker stage action, no intermissions, and the audience's ability to grasp the language more quickly meant that the plays galloped along. The story, not the verse, carried the thrust of the action. Occasional set speeches, like Hamlet's soliloquies or Gaunt's "sceptred isle" speech in *Richard II,* would be heard, familiar as they already were to many in the audience, like a solo aria in a modern opera. In theory if not in practice, the business of hearing, as "audience" (from the Latin *audire,* "to hear"), was more important than the business of seeing, as "spectators" (from the Latin *spectare,* "to see"). The visual aspects of acting, like scenic staging, are inherently two-dimensional and do not work well when the audience completely surrounds the actors. Most of Shakespeare's fellow writers, notably Jonson, understandably set a higher priority on the audience's hearing their verse than on their seeing what the players did with the lines. The poets wanted listeners, although the players did try to cater to the viewers. Yet for all the games with magic tricks and devils spouting fireworks that were part of the Shakespearean staging tradition, spectacle was a limited resource on the scene-free Elizabethan stage. Shakespeare in this was a poet more than a player. Even in his last and most richly staged plays—*Cymbeline, The Winter's Tale,* and *The Tempest*—he made notably less use of such "spectacles" than did his contemporaries.

One piece of internal evidence about the original staging is Hamlet's advice to the visiting players. In 3.2, before they stage the *Mousetrap* play that he has rewritten for them, he lectures them on what a noble student of the theater then considered to be good acting. He objects first to overacting and second to the clown who ad libs with his own jokes and does not keep to the script. How far this may have been Shakespeare's own view it is impossible to say. Hamlet is an amateur lecturing professionals about how they should do their job. His views are what we would expect an amateur playwright with a liking for plays that are "caviar to the general" to hold. His objections to the clown are noteworthy, because once the original performances ended, the clown would conclude the afternoon's entertainment with a comic song-and-dance jig. Thomas Platter, a young German-speaking Swiss student, went to the Globe in 1599 to see *Julius Caesar.* He reported back home that

> on 21 September after lunch I and my party crossed the river, and there in the playhouse with the thatched roof witnessed an excellent performance of the tragedy of the first emperor Julius Caesar with a cast of about fifteen people. When the play

The hall screen in the Middle Temple Hall, built in 1574. Shakespeare's company staged *Twelfth Night* in this hall in February 1602.

was over they danced marvellously and gracefully together as their custom is, two dressed as men and two as women.[1]

The script for one jig survives, probably played by Will Kemp, who was the Shakespeare company clown until he left just before *Hamlet* came to the Globe. Its story is a bawdy knockabout tale of different men trying to seduce a shopkeeper's wife in rhyming couplets, hiding in a chest from her husband, and beating one another up. There is nothing to say what the audience reaction to such a jig might have been after they had seen a performance of *Julius Caesar* or *Hamlet*. It is possible that the Globe players stopped offering that kind of coda when they acquired the clown who played Feste in *Twelfth Night* in 1601. The song with which Feste ends that play might have become an alternative form of closure, replacing the traditional bawdy jig.

Vigorous and rapid staging was inevitable when the half of the audience closest to the stage had to stand throughout the performance. Shakespeare's plays were distinctive among the other plays of the time for their reliance on verbal sparkle over scenes of battle and physical movement, but even the soliloquies raced along. There was little occasion for long pauses and emoting. Dumb shows, like the players' prelude to the *Mousetrap* play in *Hamlet*, were the nearest that the players came to silent acting. There were no intermissions—apples, nuts, and drink were peddled in the auditorium throughout the performance—and the only "comfort stations" were, for the men, the nearest blank wall; for the women, whatever convenient pots or bottles they might be carrying under their long skirts.

Nor were there any pauses to change scenes. There was no static scenery apart from an emblematic candle to signify a night scene, a bed "thrust out" onto the stage, or the canopied chair of state on which the ruler or judge sat for court scenes. Usually any special locality would be signaled in the first words of a new scene, but unlocalized scenes were routine. Each scene ended when all the characters left the stage and another set entered. No act breaks appear in the plays before *The Tempest*. *Henry V* marked each act with a Chorus, but even he entered on the heels of the characters from the previous scene. Blue-coated stagehands were a visibly invisible presence onstage. They would draw back the central hangings on the *frons scenae* for a discovery scene, carry on the chair of state on its dais for courtroom scenes, or push out the bed with Desdemona on it for the last act of *Othello*. They served the stage like the house servants with whom the nobility peopled every room in their great houses, silent machines ready to spring into action when needed.

There has been a great deal of speculation about the tiring-house front at the rear of the stage platform: did it look more like an indoor set or an outdoor one, like the hall screen of a great house or palace or like a housefront exterior? In fact, it could easily be either. The upper level of the *frons*, the balconied "above," might equally represent a musicians' gallery, like those in the main hall of a great house, or a city wall under which the central discovery space served as the city gates, as it did for York in *Richard Duke of York* (*3 Henry VI*) 4.8, or *Henry V*'s Harfleur (3.3.78). The "above" could equally be an indoor gallery or an outdoor balcony. The appearance of the stage was everything and nothing, depending on what the play required. Players and playwrights expected the audience members to use their imagination, as they had to with the opening lines of *Hamlet*, or, as the Prologue to *Henry V* put it, to "piece out our imperfections with your thoughts."

Shakespeare's Companies and Their Playhouses

Shakespeare's plays were written for a variety of staging conditions. Until 1594, when he joined a new company under the patronage of the Lord Chamberlain, the Queen's officer responsible for licensing playing companies, poets had written their plays for any kind of playhouse. The Queen's Men, the largest and best company of the 1580s, is on record as playing at the Bell, the Bel Savage, and the Bull inns inside the city, and at the Theatre and the Curtain playhouses in the suburbs. Early in 1594, it completed this sweep of all the available London venues by playing at the Rose. But in that year, the system of playing changed. The Lord Mayor had always objected to players using the city's inns, and in May 1594 he succeeded in securing the Lord Chamberlain's agreement to a total ban. From then on, only the specially built playhouses in the suburbs were available for plays.

The Queen's Men had been set up in 1583, drawn from all the then-existing major companies with the best players. This larger and favored group at first monopolized playing in London. But it was in decline by the early 1590s, and the shortage of companies to perform for the Queen at Christmas led the Lord Chamberlain and his son-in-law, the Lord Admiral, to set up two new companies in its place as a duopoly in May 1594. Shakespeare became a "sharer," or partner, in one of these companies. As part of the same new establishment, his company, the Lord Chamberlain's Men, was allocated the Theatre to perform in, while its partner company in the duopoly, the Lord Admiral's Men, was assigned to the Rose. This was the first time any playing company secured a playhouse officially authorized for its use alone.

The Theatre, originally built in 1576 by James Burbage, father of the leading player of the Lord Chamberlain's company, was in Shoreditch, a suburb to the north of the city. The Rose, built in 1587 by Philip Henslowe, father-in-law of the Lord Admiral's leading player, Edward Alleyn, was in the suburb of Southwark, on the south bank of the Thames. Henslowe's business papers, his accounts, some lists of costumes and other resources, and his "diary," a day-by-day listing of each day's takings and the plays that brought the money in, have survived for the period from 1592 until well into the next decade. Together they provide an invaluable record of how one of the two major companies of the later 1590s, the only rival to Shakespeare's company, operated through these years.[2] Some of Shakespeare's earlier plays, written before he joined the Lord Chamberlain's Men, including *1 Henry VI* and *Titus Andronicus,* were performed at the Rose. After May 1594, the new company acquired all of his early plays; every Shakespeare play through the next three years was written for the Theatre. Its familiarity supplied one sort of resource to the playwright. But the repertory system laid heavy demands on the company.

Henslowe's papers give a remarkable record of the company repertory for these years. Each afternoon, the same team of fifteen or so players would stage a different play. With only two companies operating in London, the demand was for constant change. No play at the Rose was staged more than four or five times in any month, and it was normal to stage a different play on each of the six afternoons of each week that they performed. A new play would be introduced roughly every three weeks—after three weeks of transcribing and learning the new parts; preparing the promptbook, costumes, and properties; and rehearsing in the mornings—while each afternoon, whichever of the established plays had been advertised around town on the playbills would be put on. The leading players had to memorize on average as many as eight hundred lines for each afternoon. Richard Burbage, who played the first Hamlet in 1601, probably had to play Richard III, Orlando in *As You Like It,* and Hamlet on successive afternoons while at the same time learning the part of Duke Orsino and rehearsing the new *Twelfth Night*—and still holding at least a dozen other parts in his head for the rest of the month's program. In the evenings, he might be called on to take the company to perform a different play at court or at a nobleman's house in the Strand. The best companies made a lot of money, but not without constant effort.

The companies were formed rather like guilds, controlled by their leading "sharers." Each senior player shared the company's profits and losses equally with his fellows. Most of the plays have seven or eight major speaking parts for the men, plus two for the boys playing the women. A normal London company had eight or ten sharers, who collectively chose the repertory of plays to be performed, bought the playbooks from the poets, and put up the money for the main company resource of playbooks and costumes (not to mention the wagon and horses for touring when plague forced the London theaters to close). Shakespeare made most of his fortune from his "share," first in his company and later in its two playhouses.

As a playhouse landlord, Henslowe took half of the takings from the galleries each afternoon for his rent, while the players shared all the yard takings and the other half of the gallery money. From their takings, the sharers paid hired hands to take the walk-on parts and to work as stagehands, musicians, bookkeeper or prompter, and "gatherers" at the different entry gates. The leading players also kept the boys who played the women's parts, housing and feeding them as "apprentices" in an imitation of the London livery companies and trades, which ran apprenticeships to train boys to become skilled artisans, or "journeymen." City apprenticeships ran for seven years from the age of seventeen, but the boy players began much younger, because unbroken voices were needed. They graduated to become adult players at an age when the city apprentices were only beginning their training. Most of the "extras," apart from the playing boys, would be left in London whenever the company had to go on tour.

Because the professional companies of the kind that Shakespeare joined all started as traveling groups rather than as companies settled at a single playhouse in London, the years up to 1594 yielded plays that could be staged anywhere. The company might be summoned to play at court, at private houses, or at the halls of the Inns of Court as readily as at inns or innyards or the custom-built theaters themselves. They traveled the country with their plays, using the great halls of country houses, or town guildhalls and local inns, wherever the town they visited allowed them. Consequently, the plays could not demand elaborate resources for staging. In this highly mobile tradition of traveling

2. See *Henslowe's Diary,* ed. R. A. Foakes (Cambridge, Eng.: Cambridge University Press, 1961).

companies, they were written in the expectation of the same basic but minimal features being available at each venue. Besides the stage platform itself, the basic features appear to have been two entry doors, usually a trap in the stage floor, a pair of stage pillars, sometimes a discovery space, and very occasionally a heavens with descent machinery. Apart from these fixtures, properties such as chairs and a table, a canopied throne on a dais, and sometimes a bed were also in regular use, though in a pinch these could be as mobile as the players themselves. The only essential traveling properties were players, playbooks, and costumes.

Once the two authorized companies settled permanently at the Theatre and the Rose in 1594, they slowly lost some of this mobility. The demands of versatility and readiness to make rapid changes now had to be switched from the venues to the plays themselves. A traveling company needed very few plays, since the locations and audiences were always changing. When the venues became fixed, it was the plays that had to keep changing. The Henslowe papers record that the Lord Admiral's Men staged an amazingly varied repertory of plays at the Rose. Shakespeare's company must have been equally versatile. The practice of giving popular plays long runs did not begin until the 1630s, by which time the number of London playhouses had grown to as many as five, all offering their plays each afternoon. Shakespeare's company in London had only the one peer from 1594 until 1600; and only two from then until 1608, aside from the once-weekly plays by the two boy companies, the "little eyases" mentioned in *Hamlet*, that started with the new century.

From May 1594 to April 1597 at the Theatre, in addition to all his earlier plays that he brought to his new company, Shakespeare gave them possibly *Romeo and Juliet* and *King John,* and certainly *Richard II, A Midsummer Night's Dream, 1 Henry IV,* and *The Merchant of Venice.* But then they ran into deep trouble, because they lost the Theatre. In April 1597, its original twenty-one-year lease expired, and the landlord, who disliked plays, refused to let them renew it. Anticipating this, the company's impresario, James Burbage, had built a new theater for them, a roofed place in the Blackfriars near St. Paul's Cathedral. The Blackfriars precinct was a "liberty," free from the Lord Mayor's jurisdiction. But the plan proved a disaster. The rich residents of Blackfriars objected, and the Privy Council stopped the theater from opening. From April 1597, Shakespeare's company had to rent the Curtain, an old neighbor of their now-silent Theatre, and it was there that the next four of Shakespeare's plays—*2 Henry IV, Much Ado About Nothing, The Merry Wives of Windsor,* and probably *Henry V*—were first staged.

In December 1598, losing hope of a new lease for the old Theatre, the Burbage sons had it pulled down and quietly transported its massive framing timbers across the Thames to make the scaffold for the Globe on the river's south bank, near the Rose. Most of their capital was sunk irretrievably into the Blackfriars theater, and they could afford only half the cost of rebuilding. So they raised money as best they could. Some of the company's more popular playbooks were sold to printers, including *Romeo and Juliet, Richard III, Richard II,* and *1 Henry IV.* More to the point, the Burbage brothers raised capital for the building by cutting in five of the leading players, including Shakespeare, and asking them to put up the other half of its cost. The Globe, its skeleton taken from the old Theatre, thus became the first playhouse to be owned by its players, and, within the limits set by the old frame, the first one built to their own design.

For this theater, one-eighth of which he personally owned, Shakespeare wrote his greatest plays: *Julius Caesar, As You Like It, Hamlet, Twelfth Night, Othello, All's Well That Ends Well, Measure for Measure, King Lear, Macbeth, Pericles, Antony and Cleopatra, Coriolanus, Cymbeline, The Winter's Tale,* and most likely *Troilus and Cressida* and *Timon of Athens.* As the first playhouse to be owned by the players who expected to use it, its fittings must have satisfied all the basic needs of Shakespearean staging. At one time or another, the company staged every one of Shakespeare's plays there.

In 1600, a company consisting entirely of boys started using the Blackfriars playhouse that Richard Burbage's father had tried to open four years before. Companies of boy players had a higher social status than the adult professionals, and, playing only in halls, they commanded a more affluent clientele. The boys performed only once a week, and the relative infrequency of their crowds, plus their skills as trained singers (they were choir-school children turned to making money for their choirmasters), proved less offensive to the local residents than a noisy adult company with its drums and trumpets. Leasing the Blackfriars to the boy company made a minor profit for the Burbages, who took the rent for eight years.

In the longer run, though, this arrangement provided a different means for the Burbage–Shakespeare company to advance its career. The boys' eight years of playing in their rented hall playhouse eventually made it possible for the company of adult players to renew Burbage's old plan of 1596. Shakespeare's company had been made the King's Men when James came to the throne in 1603, and their new patron gave them a status that made it impossible for the residents of Blackfriars to prevent them from implementing the original plan. During a lengthy closure of all the theaters because of a plague epidemic in 1608, the boys' manager surrendered his lease of the hall playhouse to the Burbages. They then took possession for their own company of the playhouse that their father had built for them twelve years before. They divided the new playhouse property among the leading players as they had done in 1599 with the Globe.

A section from Wenceslaus Hollar's "Long View" of London, printed in 1644. Drawn from a standpoint on the tower of the church that is now Southwark Cathedral, Hollar's view shows the roof of the great hall in which the Blackfriars playhouse was built. It can be seen as the long angled roof with two central chimneys, below and to the east of St. Bride's Church.

They were the King's Men, the leading company in the country, and their status after ten years of playing at the Globe was matched by their wealth. By the time theaters reopened late in 1609, the company had established a new system of playing.

The King's Men now had two playhouses, a large open amphitheater and a much smaller roofed hall. Instead of selling or renting one out and using the other for themselves, they decided to use both in turn, for half of each year. It was a reversion to the old system with the city inns, where through the summer they played in the large open yards and in the winter played at inns with big indoor rooms. This time, though, the company owned both playhouses. Their affluence and their high status are signaled by the fact that they chose to keep one of their playhouses idle while they used the other, despite there now being a shortage of playhouses in London. That affluence was needed in 1613, when the Globe burned down at a performance of *All Is True (Henry VIII)* and the company chose the much more expensive option of rebuilding it instead of reverting to the Blackfriars for both winter and summer. That decision, in its way, was the ultimate gesture of affection for their original playhouse. It was a costly gesture, but it meant that the Globe continued in use by the company until all the theaters were closed down by Parliament in 1642.

In 1609, when they reopened after the closure for plague, Shakespeare's company had made several changes in their procedures. The restart was at the Blackfriars, and although they offered the same kind of plays, they began to alter their style of staging. Along with the Blackfriars playhouse, they acquired a famous consort of musicians who played on strings and woodwinds in a music room set over the stage. The new consort was a distinct enhancement of the company's musical resources, which until then had been confined to song, the occasional use of recorders or hautboys, and military drums and trumpets for the scenes with soldiery. In 1608, a central room on the Globe's stage balcony was taken over to serve as a music room like the one at the Blackfriars. From this time on, the King's Men's performances began with a lengthy overture or concert of music before the play.

With that change, the plays themselves now had music to back their singers and provide other sorts of atmospheric effects. Some of the songs and music that appear in the plays not printed until the First Folio of 1623, such as the song that Mariana hears in *Measure for Measure* 4.1, may have been added after Shakespeare's time to make use of this new resource. Shakespeare did use songs, sometimes with string accompaniment, quite regularly in the early plays, but instrumental music hardly ever appears. The last play that he wrote alone, *The Tempest*, was the only one in which he made full use of this new resource.

All the plays containing soldiers and battles used the military drums that in war conveyed signals to infantry formations, as well as the trumpets that were used for signaling to cavalry. These were usually employed for offstage noises, sound effects made from "within" (inside the dressing room or tiring-house behind the stage). Soldiers marching in procession, as in the dead march at the close of *Hamlet,* would have the time marked by an onstage drum. Shakespeare never calls for guns to be fired onstage, even though other writers did, but he did have other noises at his command. A small cannon or "chamber" might be used, fired from the gable-fronted heavens over the stage, as Claudius demands in *Hamlet* and as the Chorus to Act 3 of *Henry V* notes. It was wadding from a ceremonial cannon shot that set the gallery thatch alight at a performance of *All Is True* in July 1613 and burned the Globe to the ground. Stage battles such as Shrewsbury at the end of *1 Henry IV,* written for the Theatre, were accompanied by sword fights that were not the duels of *Hamlet*'s finale but exchanges with broadswords or "foxes" slammed against metal shields or "targets." That action guaranteed emphatic sound effects. The drums and trumpets, with clashes of swords and a great deal of to-ing and fro-ing onto and off the stage, were highlighted in between the shouted dialogue by some hard fighting between the protagonists. The leading players were practiced swordsmen, who knew they were being watched by experts. These were the scenes of "four or five most vile and ragged foils" that the fourth Chorus self-consciously derided in *Henry V* at the Curtain.

The second great reason for noise in the amphitheaters was to mark storm and tempest. Stagehands used the kind of device that Jonson mocked in the Prologue to *Every Man in His Humour*, written for its 1616 publication. His play, wrote Jonson, was free from choruses that wafted you over the seas, "nor rolled bullet heard / To say, it thunders; nor tempestuous drum / Rumbles, to tell you when the storm doth come." For centuries, lead balls rolling down a tin trough were a standard way of making thunder noises in English theaters. The tempest in Act 3 of *King Lear* is heralded several times in the text before a stage direction, "Storm and tempest" (Folio 2.2.450), tells us that it has at last arrived. In 2.2, Cornwall notes its coming twice (Folio 2.2.452, 473). Kent comments on the "Foul weather" in his first line in Act 3, prefaced by the entry stage direction for Act 3, "Storm still," which is repeated for 3.2. Such stage directions appear in both texts (Q has "Storm" for the equivalent Scenes 8, 9, and also at 11, F's 3.4, where F omits any further reference to these noises). These explicit signals indicate that the stagehands provided offstage noises, for all that Lear himself outstorms them with his violent speeches in 3.2.

The main question about the storm scenes in *King Lear* is this: with such consistent emphasis on storm in the language, what was the design behind the stage directions? In the centuries that *Lear* has been restaged, the tempest has been made to roar offstage in a wide variety of ways, often with so much effect that, in the face of complaints that the storm noises made it difficult for the audience to hear the words, some modern productions reduced the storm to solely visual effects, or even left Lear's own raging language to express it unsupported. But the two stage directions indicate that in the original performances the "storm in nature" was not left to Lear himself to convey. The two "Storm still" directions in the Folio suggest a constant rumbling, not the intermittent crashes that might allow Lear to conduct a dialogue with the occasional outbursts of storm noises, as some modern productions have done.

Shakespeare left regrettably few stage directions to indicate the special tricks or properties that he wanted. Curtained beds are called for in *Othello* 5.2 and *Cymbeline* 2.2, and there is the specification "Stocks brought out" in *King Lear* 2.2.132. Small and portable things like papers were a much more common device, from the letters in *The Two Gentlemen of Verona* 1.2.46, 1.3.44, and 2.1.95 to Lear's map at 1.1.35. Across the whole thirty-eight plays, though, there are very few such directions. Shakespeare's economy in preparing his scripts is a major impediment to the modern reader. He hardly ever bothered to note the standard physical gestures, such as kneeling or doffing a hat, and did little more to specify any special effects. Nonetheless, it is important not to imagine elaborate devices or actions where the text does not call for them. On the whole, the demands Shakespeare made of his fellows for staging his plays appear to have been remarkably modest. Since he was a company shareholder, his parsimony may have had a simple commercial motive. Stage properties cost the company money, and one had to be confident of a new play's popularity before investing much in its staging.

There may have been other reasons for avoiding extravagant staging spectacles. Shakespeare made little use of the discovery space until the last plays, for instance, for reasons that we can only guess at. The few definite discoveries in the plays include Portia's caskets in *The Merchant of Venice*, Falstaff sleeping off his sack in *1 Henry IV* 2.5.482, the body of Polonius in *Hamlet*, Hermione's statue in *The Winter's Tale* 5.3.20, and the lovers in *The Tempest* 5.1.173, who are found when discovered to be playing chess. The audience's shock when Hermione moves and comes out of the discovery space onto the main stage is rare in Shakespeare: in every other play, whether comedy or tragedy, the audience knows far more than the characters onstage about what is going on. Shakespeare matched this late innovation in *The Winter's Tale* with his last play, *The Tempest*. After the preliminary and soothing concert by the resident Blackfriars musicians, it opens with a storm at sea so realistic that it includes that peculiarly distinctive stage direction "Enter Mariners, wet" (1.1.46). That startling piece of stage realism turns out straightaway to be not real at all but a piece of stage magic.

THE COMPLETE WORKS

THE COMPLETE WORKS

The Two Gentlemen of Verona

Readers and playgoers have often found both startling and disconcerting the events that conclude *The Two Gentlemen of Verona*. Proteus, a young man thwarted in his love for Silvia, who loves Proteus's friend Valentine, says that since wooing her with words has not worked, he will follow the soldier's path and "love you 'gainst the nature of love: force ye" (5.4.58). At that moment, Valentine steps out of hiding and stops the attempted rape by denouncing Proteus as a treacherous friend. Overcome with remorse for the betrayal of Valentine, though not explicitly for his attempted sexual violence, Proteus begs forgiveness. Generously, Valentine says he is content. He then announces that he will give Silvia to Proteus as a sign of the renewal of the friendship between the two men. A near rape and the blatant offer of a woman as an object of exchange between men—is this the stuff of comedy?

Apparently a number of directors, actors, and critics have thought not. In the mid-eighteenth century, it became common to cut Valentine's offer to give Silvia to his friend, a stage tradition that largely held until William Charles Macready, the famous actor and producer of Shakespeare's plays, reintroduced the lines in 1841. As late as 1952, however, Denis Carey's production at the Bristol Old Vic again deleted Valentine's offer. Some critics have been so certain Shakespeare could not have written the scene as it stands that they argued that it was altered in the playhouse. How is it that Shakespeare concluded his comedy with events that have seemed to many so distasteful and so disconcerting?

One answer might be that Shakespeare was simply a young dramatist not fully in control of his craft. *The Two Gentlemen of Verona* is, after all, one of his earliest plays, perhaps *the* earliest. It bears marks of its early date of composition. It has, for example, the smallest cast of any of the plays. Many scenes contain only two or three speakers, as if Shakespeare had not yet mastered the skill of orchestrating a full complement of stage voices and bodies. It is marked as well by a number of plot inconsistencies and confusing details. Valentine and Proteus leave Verona to go to the Emperor's court, for example, but end up attaching themselves to the Duke of Milan—an important nobleman, certainly, but not the Emperor. Likewise, the geographical placement of some scenes is vague. Verona, Milan, Mantua, and Padua are places of which characters speak, but the names often are used interchangeably and seem collectively to be Shakespeare's shorthand for "Italy" rather than distinct places.

In other ways, however, the play is both an accomplished theatrical piece and a genuine precursor of many aspects of Shakespeare's later comic techniques and structures. The contemporary film *Shakespeare in Love* takes this view, using scenes and speeches from *The Two Gentlemen of Verona* to indicate Shakespeare's youthful promise as a writer of romantic comedy and as a rival to Christopher Marlowe, the premier London dramatist of the early 1590s. The play features lovers whose fickle or thwarted passions lead them into all sorts of difficulties: treachery to friends, banishment, disguise. Strikingly, these difficulties get sorted out only after most of the drama's significant players decamp to a forest somewhere outside Milan. There, in a green world complete with a band of outlaws, the fickle Proteus reverts to his original love for Julia, Silvia's disapproving father forgoes his objections to Valentine, friendship is renewed between the two young men, the outlaws are pardoned and unworthy lovers dismissed. The utopian possibilities for social renewal in a world beyond the walls and customs of the city are celebrated in this play as they are later to be in *A Midsummer Night's Dream, As You Like It*, and other Shakespearean romantic comedies of the 1590s. *Two Gentlemen* also contains the first of Shakespeare's cross-dressed heroines, the faithful Julia, who follows her fickle lover from Verona to Milan and then, as his page, accompanies him into the woods in his pursuit of Silvia. Male disguise allows Julia a freedom of action and movement not normally granted to early modern women, but, as was often to be the case in later Shakespearean comedies, this freedom has as its ultimate goal the heroine's embrace of a mate and of marriage.

The excellence of much of the play, then, suggests that its disturbing ending may not be due to Shakespeare's relative inexperience as a playwright; rather, it may stem from the subject matter of the play itself—that is, from Shakespeare's ambitious attempt to probe the relationship between two kinds of human bonds: friendship between men and romantic love between a man and a woman. In the Renaissance, each of these was a privileged relationship, but their relative worth was a matter for debate and disagreement. In staging his exploration of the competing claims of love and friendship, Shakespeare drew on two different sources. The first was a Spanish prose romance published in 1542, Jorge de Montemayor's *Diana Enamorada*. Translated into French in 1578 and into English in the 1580s, it was published in English in 1598. Shakespeare, then, could have read the story in French or in the unpublished English version. He could also have learned of it from an anonymous court play of 1585, *The History of Felix and Philiomena,* now lost.

The Montemayor romance focuses on a man's unfaithfulness in love. Don Felix leaves Felismena for Celia; Felismena pursues him in the guise of a page; Celia falls in love with the page and conveniently dies when the page rejects her. Shakespeare retains much of this material in the Proteus-Silvia-Julia triangle but adds the Valentine plot, probably drawn from the story of two friends, Titus and Gisippus, told by Boccaccio and then recounted in Book 2, Chapter 12, of Thomas Elyot's *Book of the Governor* (1531). In this story, Titus falls in love with the woman Gisippus is to marry, and Gisippus gives the woman to his friend. Later, Gisippus takes upon himself the blame for a murder Titus is wrongly accused of committing. The story unabashedly advances the claims of heroic male friendship over other ties, including those of male-female love. Shakespeare's achievement in *The Two Gentlemen of Verona* is to join together aspects of these two stories. In his play, there are two pairs of lovers, not just a fickle Proteus figure moving between two women, and the close friendship between Valentine and Proteus is given a prominence equal to that of the male-female love stories.

In foregrounding the importance of male friendship, Shakespeare joined a long tradition of writers who celebrated such friendships, sometimes comparing them favorably with the presumably more dangerous relationships men could have with women. In *The Governor,* for example, Elyot praised male friendship in terms

Male friendship ("Steadfast is the love based on inclination"). From Richard Brathwaite, *The English Gentleman,* 2nd ed. (1633).

that would be echoed in other early modern texts: "Verily it is a blessed and stable connection of sundry wills, making of two persons one in having and suffering. And therefore a friend is properly named of philosophers the other I. For that in them is but one
mind and one possession and that which more is, a man more rejoiceth at his friend's
good fortune than at his own" (Book 2, Chapter 11). By contrast, Sir Francis Bacon
(who also wrote an essay in praise of friendship) in his essay "Of Love" captures the fear
and disdain with which passionate love between men and women was often regarded:
"In life it doth much mischief, sometimes like a siren, sometimes like a fury. You may
observe that amongst all the great and worthy persons (whereof the memory
remaineth, either ancient or recent) there is not one that hath been transported to the
mad degree of love; which shows that great spirits and great business do keep out this
weak passion."

    The Two Gentlemen of Verona participates both in the celebration of male friend-
ship and to some extent in the comic deflation of male-female love. Several times male
characters speak of the strange transformations of the self that passion for a woman can
induce. Proteus, choosing to stay in Verona with Julia rather than follow his friend to
Milan for an education in courtiership, speaks of his own choice disdainfully. Of Valentine he says:

> He after honour hunts, I after love.
> He leaves his friends to dignify them more,
> I leave myself, my friends, and all, for love.
> Thou, Julia, thou hast metamorphosed me,
> Made me neglect my studies, lose my time,
> War with good counsel, set the world at naught;
> Made wit with musing weak, heart sick with thought.
>   (1.1.63–69)

The play is one of Shakespeare's first explorations of what it means to be transformed,
or "metamorphosed," by love of a woman. Perhaps Shakespeare was taking his cue from
the Roman poet Ovid's vastly popular book the *Metamorphoses,* which contained numerous tales of people transformed by love. In Ovid, gods sometimes assume the shapes of
mortals or of animals to pursue their beloved; or women turn into trees or flowers in
their flight from unwanted amorous advances. In *The Two Gentlemen of Verona,* Proteus's name echoes that of the sea god who could change shape at will and who was thus
often associated with a fickle nature. It is Proteus who in the above passage first mentions being metamorphosed by love, but the play rings many changes on this idea. Sometimes the transformations wrought by love seem comic to others. Speed, for example,
has excellent fun laughing at the strange transformations of his master, Valentine, who,
in love with Silvia, begins to act like a perfect malcontent, "metamorphosed with a mistress" (2.1.26–27). A malcontent, here meaning someone made melancholy by love, was
a stock figure in Renaissance literature and the visual arts, sometimes rendered comic
by his disordered attire or his moody alienation from his fellow men.

    Often, however, in this play, love is shown to have more positive consequences. It
leads to heroic feats such as Julia's daring cross-dressed journey in pursuit of Proteus
and to the outpouring of poetry and songs. However fickle Proteus's passion for Silvia
shows him to be, it also moves him to offer her the gorgeous song "Who is Silvia? What
is she, / That all our swains commend her?" (4.2.37–38). In *Shakespeare in Love,* this
lyricism is what compels Viola De Lesseps, the aristocratic heroine, to fall in love with
the youthful Shakespeare who wrote those verses. Valentine, under the influence of
love, is prepared to scale the walls of Silvia's tower to bear her, willingly, away. Clearly,
however, not all the metamorphoses wrought by love are either comic or admirable.
Love also makes men dangerous and hurtful. Under the influence of his fickle passions,
Proteus abandons one woman for another, betrays Valentine's marriage plans to Silvia's
father, and threatens to rape the woman he supposedly adores. As moralists warned, the
passion of man for woman can turn a man into a beast.

By contrast, friendship between men, though much compromised in this text, holds the promise of an ennobling intimacy. When Proteus and Valentine must part in the first scene, Proteus's language betrays the depth of his love for and dependence on his friend:

> Wilt thou be gone? Sweet Valentine, adieu.
> Think on thy Proteus when thou haply seest
> Some rare noteworthy object in thy travel.
> Wish me partaker in thy happiness
> When thou dost meet good hap; and in thy danger—
> If ever danger do environ thee—
> Commend thy grievance to my holy prayers;
> For I will be thy beadsman, Valentine.
>
> (1.1.11–18)

Here, the friend is imagined as "the other I," sharer of every joy, intimate of every thought. The delight with which Valentine later welcomes Proteus to the Duke's court and even his eventual offer of Silvia to his friend are signs of the potential depth of male bonds in the play.

But at what cost to women are the bonds between men to be privileged? By the way he creates the characters of Julia and Silvia, Shakespeare invites his audience to take them and their emotions seriously and makes it difficult to overlook the men's irresponsible and callous treatment of them. If Proteus can be faithful neither to his male friend nor to his female beloved, the women are models of constant affection. Each, moreover, risks a good deal for her beloved, and each is respectful of her female rival. Julia courts public scandal by dressing as a boy and following Proteus to Milan; Silvia flees her father's court to follow the banished Valentine into the forest. These are both bold and attractive women.

Julia, in particular, is a complex figure, proud and silly in the scene in which she pretends not to want to read the letter her maid has brought her from Proteus (1.2), but

The love melancholic. Isaac Oliver, *Edward, First Lord Herbert of Cherbury* (1617).

impressively dignified when, disguised as a male page, she is faced with the task of being Proteus's messenger to Silvia (4.4). Asked by Silvia to describe Julia, the disguised woman says that Julia is of her color and height. She knows this, she claims, because once she wore Julia's clothes "to play the woman's part" (4.4.152) in a holiday pageant. Moreover, the part she played

> 'twas Ariadne, passioning
> For Theseus' perjury and unjust flight;
> Which I so lively acted with my tears
> That my poor mistress, movèd therewithal,
> Wept bitterly; and would I might be dead
> If I in thought felt not her very sorrow.
> (4.4.159–64)

Ariadne, of course, is an archetype of the betrayed woman. She helped her lover, Theseus, escape the man-eating Minotaur in the labyrinth on Crete, but then was abandoned by him on the island of Naxos. The abandoned Julia, so transformed by love and grief that she no longer can lay claim to her own name, finds a point of identification in Ariadne's grief and in imagining what "Julia" would have felt to see the enactment of Ariadne's story. This is a wonderfully complicated moment, a representation of a woman's grief and self-alienation and also her empathetic engagement with the story of *another* woman's grief. It at once reveals the cost, to women, of men's inconstancy and makes it difficult to accept that women should simply become the objects of exchange between male friends.

The nearly tragic consciousness here granted to Julia is countered in this play by the boisterous comic voices of Speed and Lance, two of Shakespeare's earliest and liveliest clowns. Their presence helps suggest that however complicated Shakespeare's exploration of the tension between love and friendship becomes, the outcome will not be fully tragic. Speed is a clever clown, excellent at puns and wordplay, devastatingly accurate in his parodic imitation of Valentine's lovesick behavior and clever enough to see, when his master cannot, that Silvia has induced Valentine to write a love letter to himself. Lance, who may have been added to the play in the later stages of composition, is a doltish clown whose command of the English language is remarkable mainly for its deficiencies. If Speed specializes in puns, the witty play on the double meaning of words, Lance specializes in malapropisms, the linguistic blunders by which one word is mistaken for another. He can, for example, when leaving home to follow his master to Milan, say that he has received his "proportion, like the prodigious son" (2.3.3), by which he means that he has received his portion, or inheritance, like the prodigal son in the biblical story who received his inheritance and squandered it. In Lance's fractured English, nothing is communicated straightforwardly. He blunders into meaning, his linguistic mistakes turning the language of the learned and the witty on its head. In Lance's mouth, words become unfamiliar and unpredictable, always ready to yield up an obscene innuendo or to forge unlikely connections between different domains of meaning.

Lance's larger role in the play is as comically unsettling as his language. As was to be increasingly true of many of Shakespeare's low-life characters and subplots, his behavior mirrors and comments on the behavior of his "betters," but in a deflationary and unpredictable way. Lance's great love is for his dog, Crab. When he must leave for Milan, he is in an agony of grief because his dog, like a hard-hearted mistress, sheds no tears for his departure. "I think Crab, my dog, be the sourest-natured dog that lives. My mother weeping, my father wailing, my sister crying, our maid howling, our cat wringing her hands, and all our house in a great perplexity, yet did not this cruel-hearted cur shed one tear" (2.3.4–8). So deep is Lance's affection for his dog that when Crab, who in the end does accompany his master to Milan, disgraces himself by pissing under the Duke's table at a banquet, Lance takes the blame—and the subsequent punishment—upon himself. It is "the bit with the dog" that in *Shakespeare in Love* particularly wins the approval of Queen Elizabeth.

"I'll be sworn I have sat in the stocks for puddings he hath stolen" (4.4.25–26). From Geffrey Whitney, *A Choice of Emblemes* (1586).

The highborn lovers, Proteus and Valentine, do not always show an equal devotion to their human mistresses. Lance's attachment threatens to expose both the element of absurdity lurking inside every grand passion and also the falsity of the assumption that only the well-born are capable of self-sacrifice. Moreover, when Lance contemplates marriage, he is not very romantic. As Lance and Speed read a catalog of the qualities of Lance's beloved (3.1.269–351), Lance focuses on the practical: the woman's ability to fetch and carry, to sew and to milk. And her faults, which are manifold, pale in his eyes beside her wealth. Set against the rarified courtship rituals of his masters, Lance's pragmatism underscores the mundane aspects of the institution of marriage to which courtship will lead.

Together the two clowns do much to increase the hilarity and confusion that permeate this early comedy: a play in which letters are only with great difficulty delivered to their receivers, love tokens given to one mistress are rerouted to another, and masculine affection proves remarkably fickle and unsteady. When something like order descends on this society, it does so in a locale where Lance does not go—the forest outside Milan. The initial scenes in the forest are striking in that they have the fairy-tale quality of a Robin Hood story come to life. Banished from Milan, Valentine and Speed are beset by robbers in the forest; but these outlaws are so impressed with Valentine's bearing and his skill in languages that they make him captain of their forest band (4.1.61–64). Outside the town, living apart from women, the outlaws establish an alternative community where Valentine, despite his grief at being separated from Silvia, finds a measure of contentment. Several of Shakespeare's later comedies will depend on the contrast between the flawed life of town or court and the less fettered existence of rural spaces. *The Two Gentlemen of Verona* tries out this juxtaposition, contrasting to the betrayals and confusions of urban life and male-female courtship the straightforward male camaraderie of the forest.

The arrival of women and of Proteus, Valentine's friend-turned-rival, disrupts this harmonious male community as first Silvia appears, escorted by the timid Eglamour, and then Proteus, attended by Julia, disguised as his page. Suddenly, the potential for violence escalates as the frustrated Proteus threatens Silvia with rape, and the two men both lay claim to her affections. The disguised Julia can only watch. Just moments before Proteus, Silvia, and Julia had arrived, Valentine had made a speech that obliquely suggests one way their encounter might end. Alone in the woods, Valentine describes how he can

> sit alone, unseen of any,
> And to the nightingale's complaining notes
> Tune my distresses and record my woes.
> (5.4.4–6)

By mentioning the nightingale, Valentine evokes a horrific tale of sexual violence. In a story made famous by Ovid in the *Metamorphoses*, the beautiful Philomela was raped by her brother-in-law, Tereus, and eventually transformed into a nightingale. The bird's song is so melancholy because it is a perpetual lament for Philomela's lost chastity.

As it turns out, no one undergoes Philomela's fate in *The Two Gentlemen of Verona*. Silvia escapes rape, just as Julia avoids Ariadne's fate when the fickle Proteus returns his affections to her. But the close of this early comedy, through its mythic allusions and flirtation with sexual violence, hints at the tragic endings that have narrowly been averted. In this regard, the play is not unlike *A Midsummer Night's Dream,* in which there is a properly comic ending with lover wedded to lover. However, the last act of that play includes an unintentionally comic enactment of the tragic story of Pyramus and Thisbe, lovers whose passion ended in death, not marriage. Though *Two Gentlemen* ends comically, with two couples reunited and male friendship restored, the violent and unexpected turnabouts in the play's concluding moments indicate the difficulty of joining a tale of heroic male friendship to a tale of romantic love between men and women. Especially for the women, the "happy" ending comes at a cost. The two marriages are arranged only *after* male friendship has been renewed and Valentine has offered—without consulting Silvia—to give his beloved to his friend. Moreover, once that offer has been made, Silvia never speaks again in the play. Her response to all that has happened remains cloaked in silence, while Julia's male disguise, which she never removes, continues to remind the audience of the dangers she has faced because of Proteus's fickleness. As we have seen, this is an ending that since at least the eighteenth century has bothered readers and actors, perhaps because dominant culture has come to value love between men and women over other kinds of emotional bonds. In the Renaissance, the matter was not so settled, a reminder of the different ways in which Shakespeare both is and is not our contemporary.

JEAN E. HOWARD

TEXTUAL NOTE

The Two Gentlemen of Verona was first published in the 1623 First Folio (F), though it may have been written as early as 1590–91, making it perhaps the first of Shakespeare's theatrical compositions. F includes some unusual features, such as the listing at the beginning of each scene of all the characters in the scene no matter when they come onstage. This may have been done partly to imitate classical practice. The text also lacks any other stage directions except exits. These and other features lead editors to believe the play was transcribed by Ralph Crane, a professional scribe who seems to have been employed by Shakespeare's company to prepare several of his playscripts, including *The Two Gentlemen of Verona,* for publication in F.

The Folio text contains a number of confusing plot details and frequent inconsistencies as to the exact Italian setting in which various scenes occur. This suggests that Crane may have been working from Shakespeare's unrevised working papers. On the other hand, there is unusual consistency in regard to speech prefixes for characters' names, indicating that he may have worked from a script prepared for the playhouse or that he was unusually careful in attending to such detail. It is unclear whether the act and scene divisions in the text are Crane's additions or represent playhouse practice.

SELECTED BIBLIOGRAPHY

Brooks, Harold F. "Two Clowns in a Comedy (to Say Nothing of the Dog): Speed, Launce (and Crab) in 'The Two Gentlemen of Verona.'" *Essays and Studies: Collected for the English Association.* London: John Murray, 1963. 91–100. Examines how the clowns, Lance and Speed, contribute to the play's thematic unity by paralleling events and ideas involving the main characters.

Carroll, William C. "'And love you 'gainst the nature of love': Ovid, Rape, and *The Two Gentlemen of Verona.*" *Shakespeare's Ovid: "The Metamorphoses" in the Plays and Poems.* Ed. A. B. Taylor. Cambridge: Cambridge University Press, 2000. 49–65.

Argues that this seemingly genial comedy is darkened by an Ovidian view of male desire entailing possession and control of women.

Kiefer, Frederick. "Love Letters in *The Two Gentlemen of Verona.*" *Shakespeare Studies* 18 (1986): 65–85. Explores the role of letters in the negotiation of love in *Two Gentlemen,* which contains more letters than any of Shakespeare's other comedies.

Lindenbaum, Peter. "Education in *The Two Gentlemen of Verona.*" *Studies in English Literature 1500–1800* 15 (1975): 229–44. Discusses how the play achieves unity by its focus on the education of the protagonists, especially Proteus.

Masten, Jeffrey. "*The Two Gentlemen of Verona.*" Vol. 3 of *A Companion to Shakespeare's Works: The Comedies.* Ed. Richard Dutton and Jean E. Howard. 4 vols. Oxford: Blackwells, 2003. 266–88. Argues against the idea that *Two Gentlemen* is an immature play because of its focus on male friendship rather than heterosexual love and notes the persistence of intense male friendship throughout Shakespeare's writing career.

Rivlen, Elizabeth. "Mimetic Service in *The Two Gentlemen of Verona.*" *English Literary History* 72 (2005): 105–28. Focuses on the large number of servants in *Two Gentlemen* and the capacity of servants not just to mirror but to alter elite identities.

Sargent, Ralph M. "Sir Thomas Elyot and the Integrity of *The Two Gentlemen of Verona.*" *PMLA* 65 (1950): 1166–80. Explores Jorge de Montemayor's *Diana Enamorada* and Thomas Elyot's *The Book of the Governor* as sources for Shakespeare's investigation of the conflict between heterosexual love and male friendship.

Schlueter, June, ed. *"The Two Gentlemen of Verona": Critical Essays.* New York: Garland, 1996. Gathers together eighteenth- and nineteenth-century comments on the play along with essays by twentieth-century critics and reviews of notable theater and television productions.

Slights, Camille Wells. "*The Two Gentlemen of Verona* and the Courtesy Book Tradition." *Shakespeare Studies* 16 (1983): 13–31. Argues that the play explores the fashioning of a Renaissance gentleman.

Weimann, Robert. "Laughing with the Audience: 'The Two Gentlemen of Verona' and the Popular Tradition of Comedy." *Shakespeare Survey* 22 (1969): 35–42. Discusses the use of the play's two clowns to structure the audience's comic responses.

FILMS

The Two Gentlemen of Verona. 1983. Dir. Don Taylor. UK. 137 min. This BBC-TV version, in color, employs period music and elegant Italian settings in a performance that foregrounds the heterosexual love plot.

Shakespeare in Love. 1998. Dir. John Madden. UK. 123 min. Starring Gwyneth Paltrow and Joseph Fiennes. Includes scenes and speeches from *The Two Gentlemen of Verona* as examples of Shakespeare's early success with comedy and love lyric.

The Two Gentlemen of Verona

DUKE of Milan
SILVIA, his daughter
PROTEUS, a gentleman of Verona
LANCE, his clownish servant
VALENTINE, a gentleman of Verona
SPEED, his clownish servant
THURIO, a foolish rival to Valentine
ANTONIO, father of Proteus
PANTHINO, his servant
JULIA, beloved of Proteus
LUCETTA, her waiting-woman
HOST, where Julia lodges
EGLAMOUR, agent for Silvia in her escape
OUTLAWS
Servants, musicians

1.1

[*Enter*] VALENTINE[1] *and* PROTEUS[2]

VALENTINE   Cease to persuade, my loving Proteus.
    Home-keeping youth have ever homely° wits.   *dull*
    Were't not affection° chains thy tender° days   *love / young*
    To the sweet glances of thy honoured love,
5   I rather would entreat thy company
    To see the wonders of the world abroad
    Than, living dully sluggardized° at home,   *made very lazy*
    Wear out thy youth with shapeless° idleness.   *aimless*
    But since thou lov'st, love still,° and thrive therein—   *constantly*
10   Even as I would, when I to love begin.
PROTEUS   Wilt thou be gone? Sweet Valentine, adieu.
    Think on thy Proteus when thou haply° seest   *by chance*
    Some rare noteworthy object in thy travel.
    Wish me partaker in thy happiness
15   When thou dost meet good hap;° and in thy danger—   *fortune*
    If ever danger do environ° thee—   *surround*
    Commend° thy grievance to my holy prayers;   *Entrust*
    For I will be thy beadsman,[3] Valentine.
VALENTINE   And on a love-book[4] pray for my success?

1.1 Location: Presumably Verona, though we learn
this only from the title.
1. St. Valentine is the patron saint of lovers. Valentine's
name may thus indicate his role as faithful lover.
2. In classical mythology, a sea god who could change
shape at will. The name suggests a fickle nature. In 1.1,
it is pronounced with three syllables; elsewhere in the
play, often with two. In F, the names of all the characters who appear in a given scene are listed as it opens,

even if they enter at a later point. This edition marks
entrances when characters actually appear onstage. In
this scene, Speed enters at line 70, though in F his
entrance is not marked and his name is listed with that
of Proteus and Valentine at the beginning of the scene.
3. One who prays (counts the beads of a rosary) for
another's spiritual welfare.
4. A book about love (instead of a prayer book). Valentine is twitting Proteus for making love his religion.

20 PROTEUS   Upon some book I love I'll pray for thee.
   VALENTINE   That's on some shallow story of deep love—
      How young Leander crossed the Hellespont.[5]
   PROTEUS   That's a deep story of a deeper love,
      For he was more than over-shoes[6] in love.
25 VALENTINE   'Tis true, for you are over-boots in love,
      And yet you never swam the Hellespont.
   PROTEUS   Over the boots? Nay, give me not the boots.°   *do not mock me*
   VALENTINE   No, I will not; for it boots° thee not.   *profits*
   PROTEUS   What?
   VALENTINE   To be in love, where scorn is bought with groans,
30   Coy looks with heart-sore sighs, one fading moment's mirth
      With twenty watchful,° weary, tedious nights.   *wakeful*
      If haply won, perhaps a hapless° gain;   *an unlucky*
      If lost, why then a grievous labour won;
      However,° but a folly bought with wit,   *Either way*
35   Or else a wit by folly vanquishèd.
   PROTEUS   So by your circumstance° you call me fool.   *lengthy discourse*
   VALENTINE   So by your circumstance° I fear you'll prove.   *situation*
   PROTEUS   'Tis love you cavil at. I am not love.
   VALENTINE   Love is your master, for he masters you,
40   And he that is so yokèd by a fool
      Methinks should not be chronicled for wise.
   PROTEUS   Yet writers say 'As in the sweetest bud
      The eating canker° dwells, so doting love   *harmful caterpillar*
      Inhabits in the finest wits of all.'
45 VALENTINE   And writers say 'As the most forward bud
      Is eaten by the canker ere it blow,°   *blossom*
      Even so by love the young and tender wit
      Is turned to folly, blasting° in the bud,   *withering*
      Losing his verdure° even in the prime,°   *greenness / spring*
50   And all the fair effects of future hopes.'
      But wherefore waste I time to counsel thee
      That art a votary[7] to fond° desire?   *foolish*
      Once more adieu. My father at the road°   *harbor*
      Expects my coming, there to see me shipped.[8]
55 PROTEUS   And thither will I bring thee, Valentine.
   VALENTINE   Sweet Proteus, no. Now let us take our leave.
      To Milan let me hear from thee by letters
      Of thy success° in love, and what news else   *fortune (good or bad)*
      Betideth° here in absence of thy friend;   *Happens*
60   And I likewise will visit thee with mine.
   PROTEUS   All happiness bechance to thee in Milan.
   VALENTINE   As much to you at home; and so farewell.   *Exit*
   PROTEUS   He after honour hunts, I after love.
      He leaves his friends to dignify° them more,   *bring honor to*
65   I leave° myself, my friends, and all, for love.   *neglect*
      Thou, Julia, thou hast metamorphosed° me,   *transformed*
      Made me neglect my studies, lose° my time,   *waste*

5. In classical mythology, Leander drowned while swimming the Hellespont to visit his love, Hero. Shakespeare probably had read in manuscript Christopher Marlowe's poem "Hero and Leander."
6. So deep as to cover the shoes (or boots); recklessly or excessively.

7. One devoted to a particular pursuit; one bound by vows to a religious life.
8. Although Verona and Milan are inland, Shakespeare writes of Verona as if it were located, like London, on a tidal river leading to the sea.

War with good counsel, set the world at naught;
Made wit with musing weak, heart sick with thought.°   *melancholy ideas*
     [*Enter* SPEED]

70   SPEED   Sir Proteus, save° you. Saw you my master?   *God save (a greeting)*
      PROTEUS   But now he parted hence to embark for Milan.
      SPEED   Twenty to one, then, he is shipped already,
      And I have played the sheep[9] in losing him.
      PROTEUS   Indeed, a sheep doth very often stray,
75   An if° the shepherd be a while away.   *An if = If*
      SPEED   You conclude that my master is a shepherd, then, and
        I a sheep?
      PROTEUS   I do.
      SPEED   Why then, my horns are his horns,[1] whether I wake or
        sleep.
      PROTEUS   A silly answer, and fitting well a sheep.
80   SPEED   This proves me still a sheep.
      PROTEUS   True, and thy master a shepherd.
      SPEED   Nay, that I can deny by a circumstance.°   *argument*
      PROTEUS   It shall go hard but I'll prove it by another.[2]
      SPEED   The shepherd seeks the sheep, and not the sheep the
85   shepherd. But I seek my master, and my master seeks not me.
      Therefore I am no sheep.
      PROTEUS   The sheep for fodder follow the shepherd, the shepherd
        for food follows not the sheep. Thou for wages followest
        thy master, thy master for wages follows not thee. Therefore
90   thou art a sheep.
      SPEED   Such another proof will make me cry 'baa'.
      PROTEUS   But dost thou hear: gav'st thou my letter to Julia?
      SPEED   Ay, sir. I, a lost mutton,° gave your letter to her, a laced   *sheep*
        mutton,° and she, a laced mutton, gave me, a lost mutton,   *prostitute (slang)*
95   nothing for my labour.
      PROTEUS   Here's too small a pasture for such store° of muttons.   *abundance*
      SPEED   If the ground be overcharged,° you were best stick[3] her.   *overburdened*
      PROTEUS   Nay, in that you are astray. 'Twere best pound° you.   *empound; beat*
      SPEED   Nay sir, less than a pound shall serve me for carrying
100   your letter.
      PROTEUS   You mistake. I mean the pound, a pinfold.°   *pen for stray animals*
      SPEED   From a pound to a pin?[4] Fold it° over and over   *Multiply*
      'Tis threefold too little for carrying a letter to your lover.
      PROTEUS   But what said she?
105   SPEED [*nods, then says*]   Ay.°   *Yes*
      PROTEUS   Nod-ay? Why, that's 'noddy'.°   *a fool*
      SPEED   You mistook, sir. I say she did nod, and you ask me if she
        did nod, and I say 'Ay'.
      PROTEUS   And that set together is 'noddy'.
110   SPEED   Now you have taken the pains to set it together, take it
        for your pains.
      PROTEUS   No, no. You shall have it for bearing the letter.
      SPEED   Well, I perceive I must be fain° to bear with you.   *willing*
      PROTEUS   Why, sir, how do you bear with me?

---

9. Been foolish, with a pun on "ship." "Ship" and "sheep" were pronounced similarly.
1. As Speed's master, Valentine owns Speed's horns. Traditionally, the horns signified the cuckold and were attributed to men whose wives were unfaithful.
2. It shall fare ill with me unless I prove my claim by using another argument.
3. Stab or slaughter the extra sheep, with a pun on "stick" as meaning "have sexual intercourse with."
4. Proverbially, pins have little value (e.g., "not worth a pin"). Speed fears he is going to be paid too little for carrying the letter to Julia.

115 SPEED   Marry,[5] sir, the letter very orderly,° having nothing but the   *dutifully*
        word 'noddy' for my pains.

PROTEUS   Beshrew me° but you have a quick wit.   *Curse me (a mild oath)*

SPEED   And yet it cannot overtake your slow purse.

PROTEUS   Come, come, open the matter in brief. What said she?

120 SPEED   Open your purse, that the money and the matter may
        be both at once delivered.

PROTEUS [*giving money*]   Well, sir, here is for your pains. What
        said she?

SPEED   Truly, sir, I think you'll hardly win her.[6]

125 PROTEUS   Why? Couldst thou perceive so much from her?

SPEED   Sir, I could perceive[7] nothing at all from her, no, not so
        much as a ducat[8] for delivering your letter. And being so hard°   *stingy; cold*
        to me, that brought your mind,° I fear she'll prove as hard to   *wishes*
        you in telling° your mind. Give her no token but stones,[9] for   *when you tell her*

130   she's as hard as steel.

PROTEUS   What said she? Nothing?

SPEED   No, not so much as 'Take this for thy pains'. To testify°   *attest to*
        your bounty, I thank you, you have testerned me;[1] in requital
        whereof, henceforth carry your letters yourself. And so, sir, I'll

135   commend you to my master.   [*Exit*]

PROTEUS   Go, go, be gone, to save your ship from wreck,
        Which cannot perish having thee aboard,
        Being destined to a drier death on shore.[2]
        I must go send some better messenger.

140   I fear my Julia would not deign° my lines,   *graciously accept*
        Receiving them from such a worthless post.°   *Exit*   *messenger; blockhead*

1.2

Enter JULIA *and* LUCETTA

JULIA   But say, Lucetta, now we are alone—
        Wouldst thou then counsel me to fall in love?

LUCETTA   Ay, madam, so you stumble not unheedfully.°   *carelessly*

JULIA   Of all the fair resort° of gentlemen   *company*

5   That every day with parle° encounter me,   *talk*
        In thy opinion which is worthiest love?

LUCETTA   Please you° repeat their names, I'll show my mind   *If you will*
        According to my shallow simple skill.

JULIA   What think'st thou of the fair Sir Eglamour?[1]

10 LUCETTA   As of a knight well spoken, neat,° and fine,   *elegant*
        But were I you, he never should be mine.

JULIA   What think'st thou of the rich Mercatio?

LUCETTA   Well of his wealth, but of himself, so-so.

JULIA   What think'st thou of the gentle Proteus?

15 LUCETTA   Lord, lord, to see what folly reigns in us!

JULIA   How now? What means this passion° at his name?   *outburst of emotion*

LUCETTA   Pardon, dear madam, 'tis a passing° shame   *great*

---

5. A mild oath suggesting surprise, from the Virgin
Mary's name.
6. You'll have a hard time winning her.
7. Punning on an obsolete meaning of "perceive" as
"receive."
8. A coin worth about three shillings sixpence, a generous tip.
9. Precious stones; pebbles; perhaps also, testicles.
token: love gift.

1. Given me a testern, a coin worth much less than the
ducat Speed wanted.
2. *Which . . . shore*: alluding to the proverb "He that is
born to be hanged shall never be drowned."
1.2 Location: Out of doors, maybe in Julia's garden.
1. Not the same Eglamour who assists Silvia in 4.3.
The name is found in medieval romances and by the
1590s seems to have acquired comic associations.

That I, unworthy body as I am,
Should censure° thus on lovely gentlemen.   *pass judgment*
20   JULIA   Why not on Proteus, as of all the rest?
LUCETTA   Then thus: of many good, I think him best.
JULIA   Your reason?
LUCETTA   I have no other but a woman's reason:
I think him so because I think him so.
25   JULIA   And wouldst thou have me cast my love on him?
LUCETTA   Ay, if you thought your love not cast away.
JULIA   Why, he of all the rest hath never moved° me.   *proposed marriage to*
LUCETTA   Yet he of all the rest I think best loves ye.
JULIA   His little speaking shows his love but small.
30   LUCETTA   Fire that's closest kept° burns most of all.   *most enclosed*
JULIA   They do not love that do not show their love.
LUCETTA   O, they love least that let men know their love.
JULIA   I would I knew his mind.
LUCETTA   [*giving Proteus' letter*]   Peruse this paper, madam.
35   JULIA   'To Julia'—say, from whom?
LUCETTA   That the contents will show.
JULIA   Say, say—who gave it thee?
LUCETTA   Sir Valentine's page; and sent, I think, from Proteus.
He would have given it you, but I being in the way
40   Did in your name receive it.[2] Pardon the fault, I pray.
JULIA   Now, by my modesty, a goodly broker.°   *go-between*
Dare you presume to harbour wanton lines?°   *receive love letters*
To whisper, and conspire against my youth?
Now trust me, 'tis an office of great worth,
45   And you an officer fit for the place.
There. Take the paper.
     [*She gives* LUCETTA *the letter*]
                              See it be returned,
Or else return no more into my sight.
LUCETTA   To plead for love deserves more fee than hate.
JULIA   Will ye be gone?
LUCETTA   That you may ruminate.°   *Exit*   *meditate*
50   JULIA   And yet I would I had o'erlooked° the letter.   *examined*
It were a shame to call her back again
And pray her to° a fault for which I chid her.   *ask her to commit*
What fool is she, that knows I am a maid
And would not force the letter to my view,
55   Since maids in modesty say 'No' to that
Which they would have the profferer° construe 'Ay'.   *giver*
Fie, fie, how wayward is this foolish love
That like a testy° babe will scratch the nurse   *cranky*
And presently,° all humbled, kiss the rod.[3]   *immediately after*
60   How churlishly I chid Lucetta hence
When willingly I would have had her here.
How angerly I taught my brow to frown
When inward joy enforced my heart to smile.
My penance is to call Lucetta back
65   And ask remission for my folly past.

---

2. An inconsistency in the text. In 1.1, Speed said he
delivered the letter to Julia. He may have mistaken
Lucetta for Julia or may have lied to Proteus.

3. Children sometimes had to kiss the stick with which
they were beaten.

What ho! Lucetta!
        [*Enter* LUCETTA]
LUCETTA   What would your ladyship?
JULIA   Is't near dinner-time?
LUCETTA   I would it were,
  That you might kill° your stomach° on your meat   *expend / hunger; rage*
  And not upon your maid.
        [*She drops and picks up the letter*][4]
JULIA   What is't that you
70 Took up so gingerly?°   *cautiously*
LUCETTA   Nothing.
JULIA   Why didst thou stoop then?
LUCETTA   To take a paper up that I let fall.
JULIA   And is that paper nothing?
75 LUCETTA   Nothing concerning me.
JULIA   Then let it lie for those that it concerns.
LUCETTA   Madam, it will not lie where it concerns,
  Unless it have a false interpreter.
JULIA   Some love of yours hath writ to you in rhyme.
80 LUCETTA   That I might sing it, madam, to a tune,
  Give me a note. Your ladyship can set.[5]
JULIA   As little by such toys° as may be possible.   *trifles*
  Best sing it to the tune of 'Light o' love'.[6]
LUCETTA   It is too heavy° for so light a tune.   *serious*
85 JULIA   Heavy? Belike it hath some burden,[7] then?
LUCETTA   Ay, and melodious were it, would you sing it.
JULIA   And why not you?
LUCETTA   I cannot reach so high.[8]
JULIA   Let's see your song.
        [*She tries to take the letter*][9]
        How now, minion![1]
LUCETTA   Keep tune° there still. So you will sing it out.[2]   *in tune; in good humor*
90 And yet methinks I do not like this tune.[3]
JULIA   You do not?
LUCETTA   No, madam, 'tis too sharp.°   *high-pitched; bitter*
JULIA   You, minion, are too saucy.
LUCETTA   Nay, now you are too flat,°   *low-pitched; blunt*
95 And mar the concord° with too harsh a descant.°   *harmony / melody*
  There wanteth but a mean to fill your song.[4]
JULIA   The mean is drowned with your unruly bass.°   *low notes; bad conduct*
LUCETTA   Indeed, I bid the base for[5] Proteus.
JULIA   This bauble° shall not henceforth trouble me.   *trifle (the letter)*
100 Here is a coil with protestation.°   *fuss about a love vow*
        [*She tears the letter and drops the pieces*]

---

4. There is no indication in F of when Lucetta drops the letter that she here picks up. Some directors and editors assume that she drops it, either advisedly or inadvertently, before leaving the stage at line 49. To have her drop and immediately retrieve the letter, as here, may suggest that Lucetta is trying once more to call her mistress's attention to this missive.
5. Set to music. Julia takes it to mean "set store by," or "give value to."
6. A popular song in Shakespeare's time.
7. Refrain; heavy load; perhaps punningly referring to the weight of a body during intercourse.
8. Sing so high a note, hope to win so high-ranking a lover.

9. Some editors and directors believe that Lucetta yields the letter at this point, but her refusal to do so seems to be what motivates Julia's anger in the ensuing lines. At some point before line 100, Julia must wrest the letter from her maid.
1. Hussy; with a possible pun on "minim," a musical term for a half note.
2. Finish singing it; come to the end of your anger.
3. Julia may have struck or threatened to strike Lucetta.
4. There lacks but a tenor to complete your song. Her implication is that Julia lacks a man to fulfill her desires.
5. I sang the bass part for; I acted in the interests of (a phrase from the game called prisoner's base).

Go, get you gone, and let the papers lie.
You would be fing'ring them to anger me.

LUCETTA [*aside*]   She makes it strange,° but she would be best   *pretends not to care*
    pleased
To be so angered with another letter.   [*Exit*]

105 JULIA   Nay, would I were so angered with the same.
O hateful hands, to tear such loving words;
Injurious wasps,[6] to feed on such sweet honey
And kill the bees that yield it with your stings.
I'll kiss each several° paper for amends.   *separate*
    [*She picks up some of the pieces of paper*]

110 Look, here is writ 'Kind Julia'—unkind Julia,
As° in revenge of thy ingratitude   *As if*
I throw thy name against the bruising stones,
Trampling contemptuously on thy disdain.
And here is writ 'Love-wounded Proteus'.

115 Poor wounded name, my bosom as a bed
Shall lodge thee till thy wound be throughly° healed;   *completely*
And thus I search° it with a sovereign° kiss.   *probe; cleanse / healing*
But twice or thrice was 'Proteus' written down.
Be calm, good wind, blow not a word away

120 Till I have found each letter in the letter
Except mine own name. That, some whirlwind bear
Unto a ragged, fearful, hanging° rock   *overhanging*
And throw it thence into the raging sea.
Lo, here in one line is his name twice writ:

125 'Poor forlorn Proteus', 'passionate Proteus',
'To the sweet Julia'—that I'll tear away.
And yet I will not, sith° so prettily   *since*
He couples it to his complaining names.
Thus will I fold them, one upon another.

130 Now kiss, embrace, contend, do what you will.
    [*Enter* LUCETTA]

LUCETTA   Madam, dinner is ready, and your father stays.°   *waits*
JULIA   Well, let us go.
LUCETTA   What, shall these papers lie like telltales here?
JULIA   If you respect° them, best to take them up.   *value*

135 LUCETTA   Nay, I was taken up° for laying them down.   *scolded*
Yet here they shall not lie, for° catching cold.   *for fear of*
JULIA   I see you have a month's mind° to them.   *strong desire*
LUCETTA   Ay, madam, you may say what sights you see.
I see things too, although you judge I wink.°   *close my eyes*

140 JULIA   Come, come, will't please you go?   *Exeunt*

1.3

Enter ANTONIO *and* PANTHINO

ANTONIO   Tell me, Panthino, what sad° talk was that   *serious*
Wherewith my brother held you in the cloister?°   *covered walk*
PANTHINO   'Twas of his nephew Proteus, your son.
ANTONIO   Why, what of him?
PANTHINO   He wondered that your lordship

5 Would suffer him to spend his youth at home
While other men, of slender° reputation,   *insignificant*

---

6. Referring to her hurtful fingers.   1.3 Location: Antonio's house in Verona.

Put forth° their sons to seek preferment° out—   *Send / advancement*
Some to the wars, to try their fortune there,
Some to discover islands far away,
10   Some to the studious universities.
For any or for all these exercises
He said that Proteus your son was meet,°   *fit*
And did request me to importune° you   *beg*
To let him spend his time no more at home,
15   Which would be great impeachment to his age°   *reproach in his old age*
In having known no travel in his youth.

ANTONIO   Nor need'st thou much importune me to that
Whereon this month I have been hammering.°   *thinking hard*
I have considered well his loss of time,
20   And how he cannot be a perfect° man,   *complete*
Not being tried and tutored in the world.
Experience is by industry achieved,
And perfected by the swift course of time.
Then tell me, whither were I best to send him?

25   PANTHINO   I think your lordship is not ignorant
How his companion, youthful Valentine,
Attends° the Emperor[1] in his royal court.   *Waits upon*

ANTONIO   I know it well.

PANTHINO   'Twere good, I think, your lordship sent him thither.
30   There shall he practise° tilts and tournaments,   *take part in*
Hear sweet discourse, converse with noblemen,
And be in eye of° every exercise   *witness*
Worthy his youth and nobleness of birth.

ANTONIO   I like thy counsel. Well hast thou advised,
35   And that thou mayst perceive how well I like it,
The execution of it shall make known.
Even with the speediest expedition°   *swiftness*
I will dispatch him to the Emperor's court.

PANTHINO   Tomorrow, may it please you, Don Alfonso,
40   With other gentlemen of good esteem,
Are journeying to salute the Emperor
And to commend their service to his will.

ANTONIO   Good company. With them shall Proteus go.
    [*Enter* PROTEUS *with a letter. He does not see* ANTONIO
    and PANTHINO]
And in good time.° Now will we break with him.[2]   *at the right moment*

45   PROTEUS   Sweet love, sweet lines, sweet life!
Here is her hand, the agent of her heart.
Here is her oath for love, her honour's pawn.°   *pledge*
O that our fathers would applaud our loves
To seal our happiness with their consents.
50   O heavenly Julia!

ANTONIO   How now, what letter are you reading there?

PROTEUS   May't please your lordship, 'tis a word or two
Of commendations° sent from Valentine,   *greetings*
Delivered by a friend that came from him.

55   ANTONIO   Lend me the letter. Let me see what news.

PROTEUS   There is no news, my lord, but that he writes
How happily he lives, how well beloved

---

1. One of several inconsistencies in the plot. Proteus   of Milan, not at the Emperor's court.
and Valentine are later shown at the court of the Duke   2. Reveal the plan to him.

And daily gracèd° by the Emperor,   *honored*
Wishing me with him, partner of his fortune.
60 ANTONIO And how stand you affected° to his wish?   *disposed*
PROTEUS As one relying on your lordship's will,
And not depending on his friendly wish.
ANTONIO My will is something sorted with° his wish.   *in agreement with*
Muse° not that I thus suddenly proceed,   *Wonder*
65 For what I will, I will, and there an end.
I am resolved that thou shalt spend some time
With Valentinus in the Emperor's court.
What maintenance° he from his friends° receives,   *money / family*
Like exhibition° thou shalt have from me.   *The same allowance*
70 Tomorrow be in readiness to go.
Excuse it not,³ for I am peremptory.°   *resolved*
PROTEUS My lord, I cannot be so soon provided.°   *equipped*
Please you deliberate a day or two.
ANTONIO Look what° thou want'st shall be sent after thee.   *Whatever*
75 No more of stay. Tomorrow thou must go.
Come on, Panthino. You shall be employed
To hasten on his expedition. [*Exeunt* ANTONIO *and* PANTHINO]
PROTEUS Thus have I shunned the fire for fear of burning
And drenched me in the sea where I am drowned.
80 I feared to show my father Julia's letter
Lest he should take exceptions° to my love,   *object*
And with the vantage of mine own excuse⁴
Hath he excepted most° against my love.   *raised most obstacles*
O, how this spring of love resembleth
85 The uncertain glory of an April day,
Which now shows all the beauty of the sun,
And by and by a cloud takes all away.
      [*Enter* PANTHINO]
PANTHINO Sir Proteus, your father calls for you.
He is in haste, therefore I pray you go.
90 PROTEUS Why, this it is. My heart accords thereto,°   *agrees to it*
And yet a thousand times it answers 'No'.⁵   *Exeunt*

2.1

Enter VALENTINE [*and*] SPEED
SPEED [*offering* VALENTINE *a glove*] Sir, your glove.
VALENTINE   Not mine.
My gloves are on.
SPEED Why then, this may be yours, for this is but one.¹
VALENTINE Ha, let me see. Ay, give it me, it's mine—
Sweet ornament, that decks a thing divine.
5 Ah, Silvia, Silvia!
SPEED Madam Silvia, Madam Silvia!
VALENTINE How now, sirrah?²
SPEED She is not within hearing, sir.
VALENTINE Why, sir, who bade you call her?
10 SPEED Your worship, sir, or else I mistook.

---

3. Do not offer reasons why you should be excused
from this.
4. And by taking advantage of my lie (that the letter
came from Valentine).
5. *My* . . . *'No'*: Suggesting that he is divided between

desire to go and desire to stay.
2.1 Location: Milan.
1. Punning on "one," which could be pronounced like
"on."
2. Fellow; a form of address to social inferiors.

VALENTINE Well, you'll still be° too forward.   *persist in being*
SPEED And yet I was last chidden for being too slow.
VALENTINE Go to,[3] sir. Tell me, do you know Madam Silvia?
SPEED She that your worship loves?
15 VALENTINE Why, how know you that I am in love?
SPEED Marry, by these special marks: first, you have learned,
  like Sir Proteus, to wreath° your arms, like a malcontent;[4] to   *fold*
  relish° a love-song, like a robin redbreast; to walk alone, like   *sing*
  one that had the pestilence;° to sigh, like a schoolboy that   *plague*
20 had lost his ABC;° to weep, like a young wench that had buried   *primer; spelling book*
  her grandam; to fast, like one that takes° diet; to watch,° like   *keeps to a / lie awake*
  one that fears robbing; to speak puling,° like a beggar at Hal-   *whiningly*
  lowmas.[5] You were wont, when you laughed, to crow like a
  cock; when you walked, to walk like one of the lions. When
25 you fasted, it was presently° after dinner; when you looked   *immediately*
  sadly, it was for want of money. And now you are metamor-
  phosed with a mistress, that when I look on you I can hardly
  think you my master.
VALENTINE Are all these things perceived in me?
30 SPEED They are all perceived without ye.°   *in your appearance*
VALENTINE Without me?[6] They cannot.
SPEED Without you? Nay, that's certain, for without° you were   *unless*
  so simple, none else would.° But you are so without these fol-   *(perceive them)*
  lies[7] that these follies are within you, and shine through you
35 like the water in an urinal,° that not an eye that sees you but   *glass jar for urine*
  is a physician to comment on your malady.
VALENTINE But tell me, dost thou know my lady Silvia?
SPEED She that you gaze on so as she sits at supper?
VALENTINE Hast thou observed that? Even she I mean.
40 SPEED Why sir, I know[8] her not.
VALENTINE Dost thou know her by my gazing on her, and yet
  know'st her not?
SPEED Is she not hard-favoured,° sir?   *ugly*
VALENTINE Not so fair, boy, as well favoured.°   *gracious; esteemed*
45 SPEED Sir, I know that well enough.
VALENTINE What dost thou know?
SPEED That she is not so fair as of you well favoured.°   *looked on with favor*
VALENTINE I mean that her beauty is exquisite but her favour°   *graciousness*
  infinite.
50 SPEED That's because the one is painted° and the other out of   *wearing cosmetics*
  all count.°   *unable to be counted*
VALENTINE How painted? And how out of count?
SPEED Marry, sir, so painted to make her fair that no man
  counts° of her beauty.   *takes account; values*
55 VALENTINE How esteem'st thou me? I account of her beauty.
SPEED You never saw her since she was deformed.[9]
VALENTINE How long hath she been deformed?
SPEED Ever since you loved her.
VALENTINE I have loved her ever since I saw her, and still I see
60 her beautiful.

3. Expression of impatience.
4. A person made melancholy and discontented by
love. Such people were often depicted with folded arms.
5. All Saints' Day, November 1, when it was customary
to give charity to beggars.
6. Valentine has taken Speed to mean "They are all

perceived when you are absent."
7. But you are so outwardly marked by these follies.
8. Punning on "know" as meaning "to be sexually
familiar with."
9. Altered (Speed implies that Valentine's love for Silvia distorts his view of her).

SPEED   If you love her you cannot see her.

VALENTINE   Why?

SPEED   Because love is blind. O that you had mine eyes, or your
own eyes had the lights° they were wont to have when you   *power to see clearly*
65   chid at Sir Proteus for going ungartered.[1]

VALENTINE   What should I see then?

SPEED   Your own present folly and her passing° deformity; for he   *excessive*
being in love could not see to garter his hose, and you being in
love cannot see to put on your hose.

70   VALENTINE   Belike, boy, then you are in love, for last morning you
could not see to wipe my shoes.

SPEED   True, sir. I was in love with my bed. I thank you, you
swinged° me for my love, which makes me the bolder to chide   *beat*
you for yours.

75   VALENTINE   In conclusion, I stand affected to° her.   *in love with*

SPEED   I would you were set.[2] So your affection would cease.

VALENTINE   Last night she enjoined me to write some lines to one
she loves.

SPEED   And have you?

80   VALENTINE   I have.

SPEED   Are they not lamely writ?

VALENTINE   No, boy, but as well as I can do them. Peace, here she
comes.

         [*Enter* SILVIA]

SPEED [*aside*]   O excellent motion!° O exceeding puppet!° Now   *puppet show* / *(Silvia)*
85   will he interpret[3] to her.

VALENTINE   Madam and mistress, a thousand good-morrows.

SPEED [*aside*]   O, give° ye good e'en!° Here's a million of   *God give* / *evening*
manners.

SILVIA   Sir Valentine and servant,[4] to you two thousand.

90   SPEED [*aside*]   He should give her interest, and she gives it him.[5]

VALENTINE   As you enjoined me, I have writ your letter
Unto the secret, nameless friend of yours;
Which I was much unwilling to proceed in
But for my duty to your ladyship.

         [*He gives her a letter*]

95   SILVIA   I thank you, gentle servant. 'Tis very clerkly° done.   *like a scholar*

VALENTINE   Now trust me, madam, it came hardly off;°   *was not done easily*
For being ignorant to whom it goes
I writ at random, very doubtfully.

SILVIA   Perchance you think too much of so much pains?

100   VALENTINE   No, madam. So it stead° you I will write—   *help*
Please you command—a thousand times as much.
And yet . . .

SILVIA   A pretty period.° Well, I guess the sequel.°   *pause* / *what is next*
And yet I will not name it. And yet I care not.
And yet, take this again.

         [*She offers him the letter*]

105   And yet I thank you,
Meaning henceforth to trouble you no more.

---

1. Garters kept stockings from falling down. Going
"ungartered" was a traditional sign of love melancholy.
2. Seated; satisfied. Speed has interpreted "stand" as
carrying its bawdy connotation of "having an erection."
3. Provide commentary (as if in a puppet show).

4. In courtly love literature, a man devoted to a lady is
called her servant.
5. He should surpass her in compliments, but she surpasses him.

SPEED [*aside*]   And yet you will, and yet another yet.

VALENTINE   What means your ladyship? Do you not like it?

SILVIA   Yes, yes. The lines are very quaintly° writ,   *skillfully*

110   But since unwillingly, take them again.

    [*She presses the letter upon him*]

    Nay, take them.

VALENTINE   Madam, they are for you.

SILVIA   Ay, ay. You writ them, sir, at my request,

    But I will none of them. They are for you.

    I would have had them writ more movingly.

115   VALENTINE   Please you, I'll write your ladyship another.

SILVIA   And when it's writ, for my sake read it over,

    And if it please you, so. If not, why, so.

VALENTINE   If it please me, madam? What then?

SILVIA   Why, if it please you, take it for your labour.

120   And so good morrow, servant.   *Exit*

SPEED [*aside*]   O jest unseen, inscrutable, invisible

    As a nose on a man's face or a weathercock on a steeple.

    My master sues to her, and she hath taught her suitor,

    He being her pupil, to become her tutor.

125   O excellent device!° Was there ever heard a better?—   *trick*

    That my master, being scribe, to himself should write the letter.

VALENTINE   How now, sir—what, are you reasoning with your self?

SPEED   Nay, I was rhyming. 'Tis you that have the reason.

VALENTINE   To do what?

130   SPEED   To be a spokesman from Madam Silvia.

VALENTINE   To whom?

SPEED   To yourself. Why, she woos you by a figure.°   *device; indirect means*

VALENTINE   What figure?

SPEED   By a letter, I should say.

135   VALENTINE   Why, she hath not writ to me.

SPEED   What need she, when she hath made you write to
    yourself? Why, do you not perceive the jest?

VALENTINE   No, believe me.

SPEED   No believing you indeed, sir. But did you perceive her

140   earnest?[6]

VALENTINE   She gave me none, except an angry word.

SPEED   Why, she hath given you a letter.

VALENTINE   That's the letter I writ to her friend.

SPEED   And that letter hath she delivered, and there an end.

145   VALENTINE   I would it were no worse.

SPEED   I'll warrant you, 'tis as well.

    For often have you writ to her, and she in modesty

    Or else for want of idle time could not again reply,

    Or fearing else some messenger that might her mind discover,

150   Herself hath taught her love himself to write unto her lover.

    —All this I speak in print,° for in print I found it.[7] Why muse   *very precisely*
    you, sir? 'Tis dinner-time.

VALENTINE   I have dined.°   *(on love)*

SPEED   Ay, but hearken, sir. Though the chameleon[8] love can

---

6. To be serious. Valentine takes "perceive" to mean "receive," and takes "earnest" to mean "pledge" or "money given to seal a bargain."
7. Speed's reference to a printed speech probably shouldn't be taken literally. More likely, he is making fun of Valentine's inability to understand Silvia's trick by stressing his own care with language.
8. A small lizard that can exist for long periods without food and was thought to feed on air.

155   feed on the air, I am one that am nourished by my victuals,
    and would fain° have meat. O, be not like your mistress—be   *be eager to*
    moved, be moved![9]   *Exeunt*

2.2

Enter PROTEUS [*and*] JULIA

PROTEUS   Have patience, gentle Julia.

JULIA   I must where is no remedy.

PROTEUS   When possibly I can I will return.

JULIA   If you turn not,° you will return the sooner.   *are not unfaithful*
    [*She gives him a ring*][1]

5   Keep this remembrance for thy Julia's sake.

PROTEUS   Why then, we'll make exchange. Here, take you this.
    [*He gives her a ring*]

JULIA   And seal the bargain with a holy kiss.
    [*They kiss*]

PROTEUS   Here is my hand for my true constancy.
    And when that hour o'erslips° me in the day   *passes by*

10   Wherein I sigh not, Julia, for thy sake,
    The next ensuing hour some foul mischance
    Torment me for my love's forgetfulness.
    My father stays° my coming. Answer not.   *awaits*
    The tide is now. [JULIA *weeps*] Nay, not thy tide of tears,

15   That tide will stay° me longer than I should.   *delay*
    Julia, farewell.   [*Exit* JULIA]
             What, gone without a word?
    Ay, so true love should do. It cannot speak,
    For truth hath better deeds than words to grace° it.   *adorn*
    [*Enter* PANTHINO]

PANTHINO   Sir Proteus, you are stayed for.

PROTEUS   Go, I come, I come.—

20   Alas, this parting strikes poor lovers dumb.   *Exeunt*

2.3

Enter LANCE[1] [*with his dog Crab*][2]

LANCE [*to the audience*]   Nay, 'twill be this hour ere I have done
    weeping. All the kind° of the Lances have this very fault. I have   *family; kin*
    received my proportion,° like the prodigious[3] son, and am   *portion*
    going with Sir Proteus to the Imperial's° court. I think Crab, my   *(for "Emperor's")*

5   dog, be the sourest-natured dog that lives. My mother weeping,
    my father wailing, my sister crying, our maid howling, our cat
    wringing her hands, and all our house in a great perplexity, yet
    did not this cruel-hearted cur shed one tear. He is a stone, a
    very pebble-stone, and has no more pity in him than a dog.

10   A Jew would have wept to have seen our parting.[4] Why, my
    grandam, having no eyes,° look you, wept herself blind at   *being blind*
    my parting. Nay, I'll show you the manner of it.[5] This shoe is my
    father. No, this left shoe is my father. No, no, this left shoe is

---

9. Be kind; be induced (to eat).
2.2 Location: probably Julia's house or garden.
1. The action in this scene resembles a betrothal ceremony, and thus in the Elizabethan period a legally binding agreement to marry.
2.3 Location: A street in Verona.
1. A shortened form of "Lancelot."
2. "Crab" may mean "crab apple" or a "crabbed, ill-

tempered person."
3. Lance frequently confuses one word with another.
His reference here is to the biblical parable of the
prodigal son, who wastes his inheritance but is welcomed home again (Luke 15:11–32).
4. Alluding to proverbs claiming that Jews and dogs
lack pity.
5. Taking off his shoes for demonstration.

my mother. Nay, that cannot be so, neither. Yes, it is so, it is so,
it hath the worser sole.[6] This shoe with the hole[7] in it is my
mother, and this my father. A vengeance on't, there 'tis.[8] Now,
sir, this staff is my sister, for, look you, she is as white as a lily
and as small° as a wand.° This hat is Nan our maid. I am the   *slender / small stick*
dog. No, the dog is himself, and I am the dog. O, the dog is me,
and I am myself. Ay, so, so. Now come I to my father. 'Father,
your blessing.' Now should not the shoe speak a word for weeping. Now should I kiss my father. Well, he weeps on. Now come
I to my mother. O that she could speak now, like a moved°   *full of emotion*
woman. Well, I kiss her. Why, there 'tis. Here's my mother's
breath[9] up and down.° Now come I to my sister. Mark the moan   *exactly*
she makes.[1]—Now the dog all this while sheds not a tear nor
speaks a word. But see how I lay the dust with my tears.

[*Enter* PANTHINO]

PANTHINO   Lance, away, away, aboard. Thy master is shipped,
and thou art to post° after with oars.° What's the matter? Why   *hurry / in a rowboat*
weep'st thou, man? Away, ass, you'll lose° the tide if you tarry   *miss*
any longer.

LANCE   It is no matter if the tied[2] were lost, for it is the unkindest tied that ever any man tied.

PANTHINO   What's the unkindest tide?

LANCE   Why, he that's tied here, Crab my dog.

PANTHINO   Tut, man, I mean thou'lt lose the flood,° and in los-   *miss the tide*
ing the flood, lose thy voyage, and in losing thy voyage, lose
thy master, and in losing thy master, lose thy service, and in
losing thy service—

[LANCE *puts his hand over Panthino's mouth*]

Why dost thou stop my mouth?

LANCE   For fear thou shouldst lose thy tongue.

PANTHINO   Where should I lose my tongue?

LANCE   In thy tale.

PANTHINO   In thy tail!°   *rear end*

LANCE   Lose the tide, and the voyage, and the master, and the
service, and the tied? Why, man, if the river were dry, I am
able to fill it with my tears. If the wind were down, I could
drive the boat with my sighs.

PANTHINO   Come, come away, man. I was sent to call° thee.   *summon*

LANCE   Sir, call me what thou darest.

PANTHINO   Wilt thou go?

LANCE   Well, I will go.   *Exeunt*

2.4

Enter VALENTINE, SILVIA, THURIO, [*and*] SPEED

SILVIA   Servant!

VALENTINE   Mistress?

SPEED [*to* VALENTINE]   Master, Sir Thurio frowns on you.

VALENTINE   Ay, boy, it's for love.

SPEED   Not of you.

---

6. Punning on "soul" and alluding to medieval debates
about whether women had souls.
7. Punning on "hole" as "female genitalia."
8. Presumably Lance is now satisfied with his positioning of the shoes.
9. Comparing the smelly shoe to his mother's breath.

1. Perhaps Lance makes his staff "moan" by swishing
it in the air.
2. Taking "tide" for "tied," or one who is tied up, meaning Crab.
2.4 Location: The Duke's court in Milan.

VALENTINE   Of my mistress, then.

SPEED   'Twere good you knocked° him.   *struck*

SILVIA [*to* VALENTINE]   Servant, you are sad.

VALENTINE   Indeed, madam, I seem so.

10   THURIO   Seem you that you are not?

VALENTINE   Haply° I do.   *Perhaps*

THURIO   So do counterfeits.

VALENTINE   So do you.

THURIO   What seem I that I am not?

15   VALENTINE   Wise.

THURIO   What instance° of the contrary?   *evidence*

VALENTINE   Your folly.

THURIO   And how quote° you my folly?   *detect; observe*

VALENTINE   I quote it in your jerkin.°   *short coat*

20   THURIO   My 'jerkin' is a doublet.°   *jacket; couple or pair*

VALENTINE   Well then, I'll double your folly.

THURIO   How!

SILVIA   What, angry, Sir Thurio? Do you change colour?

VALENTINE   Give him leave, madam, he is a kind of chameleon.[1]

25   THURIO   That hath more mind to feed on your blood than live
in your air.[2]

VALENTINE   You have said, sir.

THURIO   Ay, sir, and done too, for this time.

VALENTINE   I know it well, sir, you always end ere you begin.

30   SILVIA   A fine volley of words, gentlemen, and quickly shot off.

VALENTINE   'Tis indeed, madam, we thank the giver.

SILVIA   Who is that, servant?

VALENTINE   Yourself, sweet lady, for you gave the fire.°   *spark*
rio borrows his wit from your ladyship's looks, and spends what

35   he borrows kindly° in your company.   *properly; naturally*

THURIO   Sir, if you spend word for word with me, I shall make
your wit bankrupt.

VALENTINE   I know it well, sir. You have an exchequer° of words,   *treasury*
and, I think, no other treasure to give your followers. For it

40   appears by their bare liveries[3] that they live by your bare° words.   *worthless*

SILVIA   No more, gentlemen, no more. Here comes my father.

[*Enter the* DUKE]

DUKE   Now, daughter Silvia, you are hard beset.°   *set upon (by man)*
Sir Valentine, your father is in good health,
What say you to a letter from your friends
Of much good news?

45   VALENTINE   My lord, I will be thankful
To any happy messenger° from thence.   *bringer of happy news*

DUKE   Know ye Don Antonio, your countryman?

VALENTINE   Ay, my good lord, I know the gentleman
To be of worth, and worthy estimation,

50   And not without desert so well reputed.

DUKE   Hath he not a son?

VALENTINE   Ay, my good lord, a son that well deserves
The honour and regard of such a father.

DUKE   You know him well?

---

1. Chameleons can change color, perhaps suggesting
that Thurio is fickle in love.
2. Chameleons were supposed to live on air (see note

to 2.1.154), but Thurio would rather drink Valentine's
blood.
3. By their threadbare clothing.

55	VALENTINE I knew him as myself, for from our infancy	
	We have conversed,° and spent our hours together.	*kept company*
	And though myself have been an idle truant,	
	Omitting° the sweet benefit of time	*Neglecting*
	To clothe mine age° with angel-like perfection,	*adorn my years*
60	Yet hath Sir Proteus—for that's his name—	
	Made use and fair advantage of his days:	
	His years but young, but his experience old;	
	His head unmellowed,° but his judgement ripe.	*without gray hair*
	And in a word—for far behind his worth	
65	Comes all the praises that I now bestow—	
	He is complete,° in feature° and in mind,	*perfect / appearance*
	With all good grace to grace a gentleman.	
	DUKE Beshrew me, sir, but if he make this good°	*proves this to be true*
	He is as worthy for an empress' love	
70	As meet° to be an emperor's counsellor.	*fit*
	Well, sir, this gentleman is come to me	
	With commendation from great potentates,°	*rulers; men of power*
	And here he means to spend his time awhile.	
	I think 'tis no unwelcome news to you.	
75	VALENTINE Should I have wished a thing° it had been he.	*anything*
	DUKE Welcome him then according to his worth.	
	Silvia, I speak to you, and you, Sir Thurio;	
	For Valentine, I need not cite° him to it.	*urge*
	I will send him hither to you presently.	[*Exit*]
80	VALENTINE This is the gentleman I told your ladyship	
	Had come along with me, but that his mistress	
	Did hold his eyes locked in her crystal looks.	
	SILVIA Belike that° now she hath enfranchised° them	*Perhaps / freed*
	Upon some other pawn for fealty.⁴	
85	VALENTINE Nay, sure, I think she holds them prisoners still.	
	SILVIA Nay, then he should be blind, and being blind	
	How could he see his way to seek out you?	
	VALENTINE Why, lady, love hath twenty pair of eyes.	
	THURIO They say that love hath not an eye at all.⁵	
90	VALENTINE To see such lovers, Thurio, as yourself.	
	Upon a homely object love can wink.°	*close its eyes*
	SILVIA Have done, have done. Here comes the gentleman.	
	[*Enter* PROTEUS]	
	VALENTINE Welcome, dear Proteus. Mistress, I beseech you	
	Confirm his welcome with some special favour.	
95	SILVIA His worth is warrant for his welcome hither,	
	If this be he you oft have wished to hear from.	
	VALENTINE Mistress, it is. Sweet lady, entertain him⁶	
	To be my fellow-servant to your ladyship.	
	SILVIA Too low a mistress for so high° a servant.	*tall; distinguished*
100	PROTEUS Not so, sweet lady, but too mean° a servant	*lowly*
	To have a look of° such a worthy mistress.	*from*
	VALENTINE Leave off discourse of disability.°	*unworthiness*
	Sweet lady, entertain him for your servant.	
	PROTEUS My duty will I boast of, nothing else.	
105	SILVIA And duty never yet did want his meed.°	*lack his reward*

4. *Upon . . . fealty:* Because of some other lover's pledge of faithful service.

5. Referring to the blindness of Cupid.

6. Take him into your service.

Servant, you are welcome to a worthless mistress.

PROTEUS   I'll die on° him that says so but yourself.   *die fighting*

SILVIA   That you are welcome?

PROTEUS   That you are worthless.

[*Enter a* SERVANT]⁷

SERVANT   Madam, my lord your father would speak with you.

SILVIA   I wait upon his pleasure.   [*Exit the* SERVANT]

110   Come, Sir Thurio,
Go with me. Once more, new servant, welcome.
I'll leave you to confer of° home affairs.   *talk about*
When you have done, we look to hear from you.

PROTEUS   We'll both attend upon your ladyship.

[*Exeunt* SILVIA *and* THURIO]

115 VALENTINE   Now tell me, how do all from whence you came?

PROTEUS   Your friends are well, and have them much com-
mended.°   *sent their regards*

VALENTINE   And how do yours?

PROTEUS   I left them all in health.

VALENTINE   How does your lady, and how thrives your love?

PROTEUS   My tales of love were wont to weary you.

120 I know you joy not in a love-discourse.

VALENTINE   Ay, Proteus, but that life is altered now.
I have done penance for contemning° love,   *despising*
Whose high imperious thoughts have punished me
With bitter fasts, with penitential groans,

125 With nightly tears and daily heart-sore sighs.
For in revenge of my contempt of love
Love hath chased sleep from my enthrallèd° eyes,   *enslaved*
And made them watchers of mine own heart's sorrow.
O gentle Proteus, love's a mighty lord,

130 And hath so humbled me as° I confess   *that*
There is no woe to° his correction,°   *equal to / punishment*
Nor to his service no such joy on earth.
Now, no discourse except it be of love.
Now can I break my fast, dine, sup, and sleep

135 Upon the very naked name of love.

PROTEUS   Enough. I read your fortune in your eye.
Was this the idol that you worship so?

VALENTINE   Even she; and is she not a heavenly saint?

PROTEUS   No, but she is an earthly paragon.

VALENTINE   Call her divine.

140 PROTEUS   I will not flatter her.

VALENTINE   O flatter me; for love delights in praises.

PROTEUS   When I was sick you gave me bitter pills,
And I must minister the like to you.

VALENTINE   Then speak the truth by° her; if not divine,   *about*

145 Yet let her be a principality,°   *angel*
Sovereign° to all the creatures on the earth.   *Superior*

PROTEUS   Except my mistress.

VALENTINE   Sweet, except not any,°   *make no exceptions*
Except° thou wilt except against° my love.   *Unless / insult*

PROTEUS   Have I not reason to prefer° mine own?   *advance*

---

7. Even though F does not indicate the entrance of a
servant at this point and assigns the following line to
Thurio, many editors have assumed that a servant must
enter here to bring the message that Silvia's father
would speak with her.

150 VALENTINE   And I will help thee to prefer her, too.
        She shall be dignified with this high honour,
        To bear my lady's train, lest the base earth
        Should from her vesture° chance to steal a kiss   *garments*
        And, of so great a favour growing proud,
155   Disdain to root° the summer-swelling flower,   *receive the roots of*
        And make rough winter everlastingly.
    PROTEUS   Why, Valentine, what braggartism° is this?   *excessive boasting*
    VALENTINE   Pardon me, Proteus, all I can is nothing
        To her⁸ whose worth makes other worthies nothing.
        She is alone.°   *unique*
160 PROTEUS   Then let her alone.
    VALENTINE   Not for the world. Why man, she is mine own,
        And I as rich in having such a jewel
        As twenty seas, if all their sand were pearl,
        The water nectar, and the rocks pure gold.
165   Forgive me that I do not dream on thee°   *pay attention to you*
        Because thou seest me dote upon my love.
        My foolish rival, that her father likes
        Only for° his possessions are so huge,   *because*
        Is gone with her along, and I must after;
170   For love, thou know'st, is full of jealousy.
    PROTEUS   But she loves you?
    VALENTINE   Ay, and we are betrothed. Nay more, our marriage hour,
        With all the cunning manner of our flight,
        Determined of:° how I must climb her window,   *Decided upon*
175   The ladder made of cords, and all the means
        Plotted and 'greed on for my happiness.
        Good Proteus, go with me to my chamber
        In these affairs to aid me with thy counsel.
    PROTEUS   Go on before. I shall enquire you forth.°   *seek you out*
180   I must unto the road,° to disembark   *harbor*
        Some necessaries that I needs must use,
        And then I'll presently° attend you.   *at once*
    VALENTINE   Will you make haste?
    PROTEUS   I will.   *Exit* [VALENTINE]
185   Even as one heat another heat expels,⁹
        Or as one nail by strength drives out another,
        So the remembrance of my former love
        Is by° a newer object quite forgotten.   *because of*
        Is it mine eye, or Valentine's praise,
190   Her true perfection, or my false transgression
        That makes me, reasonless,° to reason thus?   *wrongly; without cause*
        She is fair, and so is Julia that I love—
        That I did love, for now my love is thawed,
        Which like a waxen image 'gainst a fire
195   Bears no impression of the thing it was.
        Methinks my zeal° to Valentine is cold,   *affection*
        And that I love him not as I was wont.
        O, but I love his lady too-too much,
        And that's the reason I love him so little.

---

8. *all . . . her:* all I can say is nothing in comparison   9. Referring to a popular belief that the application of
with her.   heat takes away the pain of a burn.

200 How shall I dote on her with more advice,°   *upon more deliberation*
    That thus without advice begin to love her?
    'Tis but her picture° I have yet beheld,   *outer appearance*
    And that hath dazzled my reason's light.
    But when I look on her perfections
205 There is no reason but° I shall be blind.   *doubt that*
    If I can check my erring love I will,
    If not, to compass° her I'll use my skill.   *Exit*   *win*

2.5

Enter SPEED *and* LANCE [*with his dog Crab*]

SPEED   Lance, by mine honesty, welcome to Milan.[1]

LANCE   Forswear° not thyself, sweet youth, for I am not wel-   *Perjure*
come. I reckon this always, that a man is never undone° till he   *ruined*
be hanged, nor never welcome to a place till some certain shot°   *tavern bill*
5   be paid and the hostess say 'Welcome'.

SPEED   Come on, you madcap. I'll to the alehouse with you
presently, where, for one shot of five pence, thou shalt have
five thousand welcomes. But sirrah, how did thy master part
with Madam Julia?

10 LANCE   Marry, after they closed[2] in earnest they parted very
fairly in jest.

SPEED   But shall she marry him?

LANCE   No.

SPEED   How then, shall he marry her?

15 LANCE   No, neither.

SPEED   What, are they broken?°   *no longer engaged*

LANCE   No, they are both as whole as a fish.[3]

SPEED   Why then, how stands the matter with them?

LANCE   Marry, thus: when it stands well with him[4] it stands well
20   with her.

SPEED   What an ass art thou! I understand thee not.

LANCE   What a block° art thou, that thou canst not! My staff[5]   *stupid person*
understands° me.   *comprehends; supports*

SPEED   What thou sayst?

25 LANCE   Ay, and what I do too. Look thee, I'll but lean, and my
staff under-stands me.

SPEED   It stands under thee indeed.

LANCE   Why, stand-under and under-stand is all one.

SPEED   But tell me true, will't be a match?

30 LANCE   Ask my dog. If he say 'Ay', it will. If he say 'No', it will.
If he shake his tail and say nothing, it will.

SPEED   The conclusion is, then, that it will.

LANCE   Thou shalt never get such a secret from me but by a
parable.°   *an indirect speech*

35 SPEED   'Tis well that I get it so. But Lance, how sayst thou[6] that
my master is become a notable lover?

LANCE   I never knew him otherwise.

SPEED   Than how?

2.5 Location: A street in Milan.
1. F reads "Padua," probably a first thought rejected
but not canceled.
2. Came to an agreement; embraced.
3. Lance takes "broken" to mean "in pieces" and replies
with a proverb.

4. When it goes well with him; when he has an erection.
5. A stick used when walking; also a euphemism for
"penis." Lance may play with his staff during this dialogue.
6. What can you say about the fact.

LANCE   A notable lubber,° as thou reportest him to be.   *clumsy, stupid person*
40 SPEED   Why, thou whoreson[7] ass, thou mistak'st° me.   *misunderstand*
LANCE   Why, fool, I meant not thee, I meant thy master.[8]
SPEED   I tell thee my master is become a hot lover.
LANCE   Why, I tell thee I care not, though he burn himself in
love. If thou wilt, go with me to the alehouse. If not, thou art
45 an Hebrew, a Jew, and not worth° the name of a Christian.   *worthy*
SPEED   Why?
LANCE   Because thou hast not so much charity in thee as to go
to the ale[9] with a Christian. Wilt thou go?
SPEED   At thy service.   *Exeunt*

2.6

Enter PROTEUS

PROTEUS   To leave my Julia shall I be forsworn;°   *guilty of vow-breaking*
To love fair Silvia shall I be forsworn;
To wrong my friend I shall be much forsworn.
And e'en that power° which gave me first my oath   *(love)*
5   Provokes me to this three-fold perjury.
Love bade me swear, and love bids me forswear.
O sweet-suggesting° love, if thou hast sinned   *sweetly seductive*
Teach me, thy tempted subject, to excuse it.
At first I did adore a twinkling star,
10 But now I worship a celestial sun.
Unheedful° vows may heedfully° be broken,   *Careless / advisedly*
And he wants° wit that wants resolvèd will°   *lacks / determination*
To learn° his wit t'exchange the bad for better.   *teach*
Fie, fie, unreverent tongue, to call her bad
15 Whose sovereignty so oft thou hast preferred°   *recommended*
With twenty thousand soul-confirming° oaths.   *soul-confirmed; devout*
I cannot leave° to love, and yet I do.   *cease*
But there I leave to love where I should love.
Julia I lose, and Valentine I lose.
20 If I keep them I needs must lose myself.
If I lose them, thus find I by their loss
For Valentine, myself, for Julia, Silvia.[1]
I to myself am dearer than a friend,
For love is still° most precious in itself,   *always*
25 And Silvia—witness heaven that made her fair—
Shows Julia but° a swarthy Ethiope.[2]   *to be merely*
I will forget that Julia is alive,
Rememb'ring that my love to her is dead,
And Valentine I'll hold an enemy,
30 Aiming at Silvia as a sweeter friend.
I cannot now prove constant to myself
Without some treachery used to Valentine.
This night he meaneth with a corded° ladder   *rope*
To climb celestial Silvia's chamber-window,
35 Myself in counsel his competitor.[3]

---

7. Literally, "son of a whore." A term of abuse frequently used in jest.
8. Punning on "mistake." Lance understood Speed to
mean "you misjudge me" or "you confuse me with
someone else."
9. Referring to a church-ale, a charitable festival at which
ale was sold in aid of the church or to relieve the poor.

2.6 Location: The Duke's court in Milan.
1. Proteus claims that to hold on to his selfhood and
his love (Silvia), he must give up Julia and Valentine.
2. Ethiopian, or black African. The comparison rests
on a European idealization of female fairness or whiteness.
3. Myself in on the secret as his partner.

Now presently I'll give her father notice
Of their disguising and pretended° flight,   *intended*
Who, all enraged, will banish Valentine;
For Thurio he intends shall wed his daughter.
40   But Valentine being gone, I'll quickly cross°   *thwart*
By some sly trick blunt Thurio's dull proceeding.
Love, lend me wings to make my purpose swift,
As thou hast lent me wit to plot this drift.°   *Exit*   *scheme*

2.7

Enter JULIA *and* LUCETTA

JULIA   Counsel, Lucetta. Gentle girl, assist me,
And e'en in kind love I do conjure° thee,   *entreat*
Who art the table° wherein all my thoughts   *notebook; tablet*
Are visibly charactered° and engraved,   *written*
5   To lesson° me, and tell me some good mean°   *teach / way*
How with my honour I may undertake
A journey to my loving Proteus.
LUCETTA   Alas, the way is wearisome and long.
JULIA   A true-devoted pilgrim is not weary
10   To measure° kingdoms with his feeble steps.   *make his way through*
Much less shall she that hath love's wings to fly,
And when the flight is made to one so dear,
Of such divine perfection as Sir Proteus.
LUCETTA   Better forbear till Proteus make return.
15   JULIA   O, know'st thou not his looks are my soul's food?
Pity the dearth that I have pinèd in
By longing for that food so long a time.
Didst thou but know the inly° touch of love   *inward*
Thou wouldst as soon go kindle fire with snow
20   As seek to quench the fire of love with words.
LUCETTA   I do not seek to quench your love's hot fire,
But qualify° the fire's extreme rage,   *lessen*
Lest it should burn above the bounds of reason.
JULIA   The more thou damm'st it up, the more it burns.
25   The current that with gentle murmur glides,
Thou know'st, being stopped, impatiently doth rage.
But when his fair course is not hinderèd
He makes sweet music with th'enamelled° stones,   *shiny*
Giving a gentle kiss to every sedge°   *plant*
30   He overtaketh in his pilgrimage.
And so by many winding nooks he strays
With willing sport to the wild ocean.
Then let me go, and hinder not my course.
I'll be as patient as a gentle stream,
35   And make a pastime of each weary step
Till the last step have brought me to my love.
And there I'll rest as after much turmoil
A blessèd soul doth in Elysium.[1]
LUCETTA   But in what habit° will you go along?   *clothing*
40   JULIA   Not like a woman, for I would prevent°   *forestall*
The loose encounters of lascivious men.

2.7 Location: Julia's house.   1. In Greek mythology, the final abode, after death, of
                                     blessed souls.

Gentle Lucetta, fit° me with such weeds°   *equip / clothing*
As may beseem some well-reputed page.
LUCETTA Why then, your ladyship must cut your hair.
45 JULIA No, girl, I'll knit° it up in silken strings   *bind*
With twenty odd-conceited° true-love knots.[2]   *strangely devised*
To be fantastic° may become a youth   *fanciful*
Of greater time° than I shall show° to be.   *age / appear*
LUCETTA What fashion, madam, shall I make your breeches?
50 JULIA That fits as well as 'Tell me, good my lord,
What compass° will you wear your farthingale?'[3]   *fullness*
Why, e'en what fashion thou best likes, Lucetta.
LUCETTA You must needs have them with a codpiece,[4] madam.
JULIA Out, out,° Lucetta. That will be ill-favoured.°   *Not so / unbecoming*
55 LUCETTA A round hose,[5] madam, now's not worth a pin
Unless you have a codpiece to stick pins on.
JULIA Lucetta, as thou lov'st me let me have
What thou think'st meet and is most mannerly.°   *seemly; modest*
But tell me, wench, how will the world repute me
60 For undertaking so unstaid° a journey?   *reckless*
I fear me it will make me scandalized.°   *disgraced*
LUCETTA If you think so, then stay at home, and go not.
JULIA Nay, that I will not.
LUCETTA Then never dream on infamy, but go.
65 If Proteus like your journey when you come,
No matter who's displeased when you are gone.
I fear me he will scarce be pleased withal.°   *with it*
JULIA That is the least, Lucetta, of my fear.
A thousand oaths, an ocean of his tears,
70 And instances of infinite° of love   *an infinity*
Warrant me° welcome to my Proteus.   *Assure me I will be*
LUCETTA All these are servants to deceitful men.
JULIA Base men, that use them to so base effect.
But truer stars did govern Proteus' birth.[6]
75 His words are bonds, his oaths are oracles,
His love sincere, his thoughts immaculate,
His tears pure messengers sent from his heart,
His heart as far from fraud as heaven from earth.
LUCETTA Pray heaven he prove so when you come to him.
80 JULIA Now, as thou lov'st me, do him not that wrong
To bear a hard opinion of his truth.
Only deserve my love by loving him,
And presently° go with me to my chamber   *at once*
To take a note of what I stand in need of
85 To furnish me upon my longing° journey.   *love-prompted*
All that is mine I leave at thy dispose,°   *in your care*
My goods, my lands, my reputation;
Only in lieu thereof dispatch me hence.°   *help me hurry away*
Come, answer not, but to it presently.
90 I am impatient of my tarriance.°   *Exeunt*   *delay*

2. Ornamental ribbons supposed to symbolize love.   (line 56).
3. Hooped petticoat.   5. Breeches fitting the legs and thighs tightly and
4. A pouch attached to the front of men's breeches,   puffed out at the hips.
covering the genital area. In the Elizabethan period, 6. The stars' position at one's birth supposedly deter-
codpieces could be elaborately decorated, as with pins mined one's character.

3.1

Enter DUKE, THURIO, [*and*] PROTEUS

DUKE   Sir Thurio, give us leave,° I pray, awhile.   *leave us alone*
    We have some secrets to confer about.   [*Exit* THURIO]
    Now tell me, Proteus, what's your will with me?
PROTEUS   My gracious lord, that which I would discover°   *reveal*
5   The law of friendship bids me to conceal.
    But when I call to mind your gracious favours
    Done to me, undeserving as I am,
    My duty pricks° me on to utter that   *urges*
    Which else no worldly good should draw from me.
10   Know, worthy prince, Sir Valentine my friend
    This night intends to steal away your daughter.
    Myself am one made privy to the plot.
    I know you have determined to bestow her
    On Thurio, whom your gentle daughter hates,
15   And should she thus be stol'n away from you
    It would be much vexation to your age.
    Thus, for my duty's sake, I rather chose
    To cross° my friend in his intended drift°   *thwart / plan*
    Than by concealing it heap on your head
20   A pack of sorrows which would press you down,
    Being unprevented,° to your timeless° grave.   *unstopped / early*
DUKE   Proteus, I thank thee for thine honest care,
    Which to requite° command me¹ while I live.   *repay*
    This love of theirs myself have often seen,
25   Haply,° when they have judged me fast asleep,   *Perchance*
    And oftentimes have purposed to forbid
    Sir Valentine her company and my court.
    But fearing lest my jealous aim might err,
    And so unworthily disgrace the man—
30   A rashness that I ever yet have shunned—
    I gave him gentle looks, thereby to find
    That which thyself hast now disclosed to me.
    And that thou mayst perceive my fear of this,
    Knowing that tender youth is soon suggested,°   *tempted*
35   I nightly lodge her in an upper tower,
    The key whereof myself have ever kept;
    And thence she cannot be conveyed away.
PROTEUS   Know, noble lord, they have devised a mean°   *plan*
    How he her chamber-window will ascend,
40   And with a corded ladder fetch her down,
    For which the youthful lover now is gone,
    And this way comes he with it presently,
    Where, if it please you, you may intercept him.
    But, good my lord, do it so cunningly
45   That my discovery° be not aimèd° at;   *disclosure / guessed*
    For love of you, not hate unto my friend,
    Hath made me publisher of this pretence.²
DUKE   Upon mine honour, he shall never know
    That I had any light° from thee of this.   *information*
50 PROTEUS   Adieu, my lord. Sir Valentine is coming.   [*Exit*]

3.1 Location: The Duke's court in Milan.   2. Has caused me to make this plan public.
1. Ask anything of me.

[*Enter* VALENTINE]

DUKE Sir Valentine, whither away so fast?[3]

VALENTINE Please it° your grace, there is a messenger   *If it please*
That stays° to bear my letters to my friends,   *waits*
And I am going to deliver them.

55 DUKE Be they of much import?

VALENTINE The tenor° of them doth but signify   *general sense*
My health and happy being at your court.

DUKE Nay then, no matter. Stay with me awhile.
I am to break with thee of° some affairs   *disclose to you*
60 That touch me near, wherein thou must be secret.
'Tis not unknown to thee that I have sought
To match my friend Sir Thurio to my daughter.

VALENTINE I know it well, my lord; and sure the match
Were° rich and honourable. Besides, the gentleman   *Would be*
65 Is full of virtue, bounty, worth, and qualities
Beseeming° such a wife as your fair daughter.   *Suited to*
Cannot your grace win her to fancy him?

DUKE No, trust me. She is peevish, sullen, froward,°   *perverse*
Proud, disobedient, stubborn, lacking duty,
70 Neither regarding° that she is my child   *taking into account*
Nor fearing me as if I were her father.[4]
And may I say to thee, this pride of hers
Upon advice° hath drawn my love from her,   *After consideration*
And where° I thought the remnant° of mine age   *whereas / remainder*
75 Should have been cherished by her child-like duty,
I now am full resolved to take a wife,
And turn her out to who will take her in.
Then let her beauty be her wedding dower,
For me and my possessions she esteems not.

80 VALENTINE What would your grace have me to do in this?

DUKE There is a lady of Verona[5] here
Whom I affect,° but she is nice,° and coy,   *love / hard to please*
And naught esteems° my agèd eloquence.   *does not value*
Now therefore would I have thee to my tutor—
85 For long agone° I have forgot° to court,   *ago / forgotten how*
Besides, the fashion of the time is changed—
How and which way I may bestow° myself   *conduct*
To be regarded in her sun-bright eye.

VALENTINE Win her with gifts if she respect° not words.   *heeds*
90 Dumb jewels often in their silent kind°   *nature*
More than quick words do move a woman's mind.

DUKE But she did scorn a present that I sent her.

VALENTINE A woman sometime scorns what best contents her.
Send her another. Never give her o'er,
95 For scorn at first makes after-love the more.
If she do frown, 'tis not in hate of you,
But rather to beget more love in you.
If she do chide, 'tis not to have you gone,
Forwhy° the fools° are mad if left alone.   *Because / (women)*
100 Take no repulse, whatever she doth say:

---

3. Valentine may be crossing the stage without noticing
the Duke or starting to retreat on seeing him.
4. Nor respecting me as a father should be respected.

5. F reads "in Verona," another sign of inconsistency in
regard to the play's setting.

For° 'Get you gone' she doth not mean 'Away'.   *By*
Flatter and praise, commend, extol their graces;
Though ne'er so black,° say they have angels' faces.   *dark-complexioned*
That man that hath a tongue I say is no man
105 If with his tongue he cannot win a woman.
DUKE   But she I mean is promised by her friends
Unto a youthful gentleman of worth,
And kept severely from resort of men,
That no man hath access by day to her.
110 VALENTINE   Why then I would resort to her by night.
DUKE   Ay, but the doors be locked and keys kept safe,
That no man hath recourse to her by night.
VALENTINE   What lets° but one may enter at her window?   *hinders*
DUKE   Her chamber is aloft, far from the ground,
115 And built so shelving° that one cannot climb it   *projecting so far out*
Without apparent hazard of his life.
VALENTINE   Why then, a ladder quaintly° made of cords   *skillfully*
To cast up, with a pair of anchoring hooks,
Would serve to scale another Hero's[6] tower,
120 So° bold Leander would adventure it.   *Provided*
DUKE   Now as thou art a gentleman of blood,°   *well-born; passionate*
Advise me where I may have such a ladder.
VALENTINE   When would you use it? Pray sir, tell me that.
DUKE   This very night; for love is like a child
125 That longs for everything that he can come by.
VALENTINE   By seven o'clock I'll get you such a ladder.
DUKE   But hark thee: I will go to her alone.
How shall I best convey the ladder thither?
VALENTINE   It will be light, my lord, that you may bear it
130 Under a cloak that is of any length.
DUKE   A cloak as long as thine will serve the turn?
VALENTINE   Ay, my good lord.
DUKE   Then let me see thy cloak,
I'll get me one of such another length,
VALENTINE   Why, any cloak will serve the turn, my lord.
135 DUKE   How shall I fashion me to wear° a cloak?   *get used to wearing*
I pray thee let me feel thy cloak upon me.
      [*He lifts Valentine's cloak and finds a letter and a rope-ladder*]
What letter is this same? What's here? 'To Silvia'?
And here an engine° fit for my proceeding.   *instrument (the ladder)*
I'll be so bold to break the seal for once.
      [*Reads*]
140 'My thoughts do harbour° with my Silvia nightly,   *dwell*
And slaves they are to me, that send them flying.
O, could their master come and go as lightly,
Himself would lodge where, senseless,° they are lying.   *without feeling*
My herald° thoughts in thy pure bosom rest them,   *message-bearing*
145 While I, their king, that thither them importune,°   *command*
Do curse the grace° that with such grace° hath blessed them,   *good fortune / favor*
Because myself do want° my servants' fortune.   *lack*
I curse myself for° they are sent by me,   *because*
That they should harbour where their lord should be.'
150 What's here?

---

6. See note to 1.1.22. Hero, Leander's beloved, lived in a tower.

'Silvia, this night I will enfranchise thee'?
'Tis so, and here's the ladder for the purpose.
Why, Phaëton,[7] for° thou art Merops' son   *since*
Wilt thou aspire to guide the heavenly car,
155   And with thy daring folly burn the world?
Wilt thou reach° stars because they shine on thee?   *grasp at*
Go, base intruder, over-weening° slave,   *presumptuous*
Bestow thy fawning smiles on equal mates,°   *mates of your own rank*
And think my patience, more than thy desert,
160   Is privilege for° thy departure hence.   *Allows*
Thank me for this more than for all the favours
Which, all too much, I have bestowed on thee.
But if thou linger in my territories
Longer than swiftest expedition°   *speed*
165   Will give thee time to leave our royal court,
By heaven, my wrath shall far exceed the love
I ever bore my daughter or thyself.
Be gone. I will not hear thy vain excuse,
But as thou lov'st thy life, make speed from hence.   *Exit*
170   VALENTINE   And why not death, rather than living torment?
To die is to be banished from myself,
And Silvia is my self. Banished from her
Is self from self, a deadly banishment.
What light is light, if Silvia be not seen?
175   What joy is joy, if Silvia be not by—
Unless it be to think that she is by,
And feed upon the shadow° of perfection.   *image; memory*
Except I be by Silvia in the night
There is no music in the nightingale.
180   Unless I look on Silvia in the day
There is no day for me to look upon.
She is my essence, and I leave° to be   *cease*
If I be not by her fair influence[8]
Fostered, illumined, cherished, kept alive.
185   I fly not death to fly his deadly doom.[9]
Tarry I here I but attend on° death,   *wait for*
But fly I hence, I fly away from life.
            [*Enter* PROTEUS *and* LANCE]
    PROTEUS   Run, boy, run, run, and seek him out.
    LANCE   So-ho, so-ho![1]
190   PROTEUS   What seest thou?
    LANCE   Him we go to find. There's not a hair on's head but 'tis
        a Valentine.[2]
    PROTEUS   Valentine?
    VALENTINE   No.
195   PROTEUS   Who then—his spirit?
    VALENTINE   Neither.

7. Famous in Greek mythology for his reckless ambition, Phaëton set the world on fire when he tried to drive the chariot of his father, Helios, the sun god. Phaëton's mother, Clymene, was married to Merops, not Helios, making Phaëton illegitimate. The rest of the line, naming Merops as Phaëton's father, may question Phaëton's status as the son of Helios (and so his ability to drive the sun god's chariot) or may be an ironic means of calling attention to his illegitimacy.

8. Alluding to the popular belief that the stars exert power, or "influence," over individuals.
9. I cannot escape death by fleeing the Duke's death sentence.
1. A cry in hare hunting and hawking.
2. Punning on "hare" and on Valentine's name. Every part, down to the "hair," of the creature he sees suggests a "valentine," or stereotypical lover.

PROTEUS   What then?

VALENTINE   Nothing.

LANCE   Can nothing speak?

[*He threatens* VALENTINE]

200 Master, shall I strike?

PROTEUS   Who wouldst thóu strike?

LANCE   Nothing.

PROTEUS   Villain, forbear.

LANCE   Why, sir, I'll strike nothing. I pray you—

205 PROTEUS   Sirrah, I say forbear. Friend Valentine, a word.

VALENTINE   My ears are stopped, and cannot hear good news,
  So much of bad already hath possessed them.

PROTEUS   Then in dumb silence will I bury mine,°   (*my news*)
  For they are harsh, untuneable,° and bad.   *out of tune*

VALENTINE   Is Silvia dead?

210 PROTEUS   No, Valentine.

VALENTINE   No Valentine indeed, for sacred Silvia.
  Hath she forsworn me?

PROTEUS   No, Valentine.

VALENTINE   No Valentine, if Silvia have forsworn me.
  What is your news?

215 LANCE   Sir, there is a proclamation that you are vanished.°   (*for "banished"*)

PROTEUS   That thou art banished. O that's the news:
  From hence, from Silvia, and from me thy friend.

VALENTINE   O, I have fed upon this woe already,
  And now excess of it will make me surfeit.°   *sicken*

220 Doth Silvia know that I am banishèd?

PROTEUS   Ay, ay; and she hath offered to the doom,°   *sentence*
  Which unreversed stands in effectual force,[3]
  A sea of melting pearl, which some call tears.
  Those at her father's churlish feet she tendered,°   *offered*

225 With them, upon her knees, her humble self,
  Wringing her hands, whose whiteness so became them
  As if but now they waxèd° pale, for woe.   *turned*
  But neither bended knees, pure hands held up,
  Sad sighs, deep groans, nor silver-shedding tears[4]

230 Could penetrate her uncompassionate sire,
  But Valentine, if he be ta'en, must die.
  Besides, her intercession chafed him so
  When she for thy repeal° was suppliant   *recall from exile*
  That to close° prison he commanded her,   *tightly enclosed*

235 With many bitter threats of biding° there.   *staying permanently*

VALENTINE   No more, unless the next word that thou speak'st
  Have some malignant power upon my life.
  If so I pray thee breathe it in mine ear,
  As ending anthem° of my endless dolour.°   *final hymn / grief*

240 PROTEUS   Cease to lament for that° thou canst not help,   *what*
  And study° help for that which thou lament'st.   *devise*
  Time is the nurse and breeder of all good.
  Here if thou stay thou canst not see thy love.
  Besides, thy staying will abridge thy life.

245 Hope is a lover's staff. Walk hence with that,
  And manage it° against despairing thoughts.   *use it as a weapon*

---

3. Which, unless reversed, will be enforced.   4. Tears that flow like silver streams.

Thy letters may be here, though thou art hence,
Which, being writ to me, shall be delivered
Even in the milk-white bosom of thy love.

250 The time now serves not to expostulate.°　　　　　　　*complain; argue*
Come, I'll convey thee through the city gate,
And ere I part with thee confer at large°　　　　　　　*discuss at length*
Of all that may concern thy love affairs.
As thou lov'st Silvia, though not for thyself,

255 Regard thy danger, and along with me.

VALENTINE I pray thee, Lance, an if° thou seest my boy　　*an if = if*
Bid him make haste, and meet him at the North Gate.

PROTEUS Go, sirrah, find him out. Come, Valentine.

VALENTINE O my dear Silvia! Hapless Valentine.

　　　　　　　[*Exeunt* PROTEUS *and* VALENTINE]

260 LANCE I am but a fool, look you, and yet I have the wit to think
my master is a kind of a knave. But that's all one,° if he be but　*all right*
one knave.⁵ He lives not now that knows me to be in love, yet
I am in love, but a team of horse shall not pluck that from me,
nor who 'tis I love; and yet 'tis a woman, but what woman

265 I will not tell myself; and yet 'tis a milkmaid; yet 'tis not a
maid,° for she hath had gossips;⁶ yet 'tis a maid, for she is her　*virgin*
master's maid, and serves for wages. She hath more qualities°　*abilities*
than a water-spaniel,⁷ which is much in a bare° Christian.　　*mere*

　　　　　　　[*He takes out a paper*]

Here is the catalogue of her conditions. '*Imprimis*,⁸ she can

270 fetch and carry'—why, a horse can do no more. Nay, a horse
cannot fetch, but only carry, therefore is she better than a
jade.° '*Item*, she can milk.' Look you, a sweet virtue in a maid　*an inferior horse*
with clean hands.

　　　　　　　[*Enter* SPEED]

SPEED How now, Signor Lance, what news with your master-

275 ship?

LANCE With my master's ship? Why, it is at sea.

SPEED Well, your old vice still, mistake the word.⁹ What news
then in your paper?

LANCE The blackest news that ever thou heard'st.

280 SPEED Why, man, how 'black'?

LANCE Why, as black as ink.

SPEED Let me read them.

LANCE Fie on thee, jolt-head,° thou canst not read.　　　*blockhead*

SPEED Thou liest. I can.

285 LANCE I will try thee. Tell me this: who begot thee?

SPEED Marry, the son of my grandfather.

LANCE O illiterate loiterer, it was the son of thy grandmother.
This proves that thou canst not read.

SPEED Come, fool, come. Try me in thy paper.

290 LANCE [*giving* SPEED *the paper*] There: and Saint Nicholas¹ be
thy speed.°　　　　　　　　　　　　　　　　　　　　*protection*

SPEED '*Imprimis*, she can milk.'

---

5. If he is only moderately a rascal; only a knave in one area (love).
6. Women who attended at childbirth; people who served as sponsors at the baptism of a newborn child.
7. A dog used for hunting waterfowl.
8. The paper employs the language of official docu-

ments. "*Imprimis*," Latin for "in the first place," was used to begin inventories. "*Item*" (line 272), meaning "also," was used to introduce subsequent articles in a list.
9. *your . . . word*: your customary fault of making blunders with language.
1. The patron saint of schoolchildren and scholars.

LANCE	Ay, that she can.	
SPEED	'*Item*, she brews good ale.'	
295 LANCE	And thereof comes the proverb 'Blessing of your heart, you brew good ale'.	
SPEED	'*Item*, she can sew.'	
LANCE	That's as much as to say 'Can she so?'	
SPEED	'*Item*, she can knit.'	
300 LANCE	What need a man care for a stock° with a wench when she can knit him a stock?°	dowry stocking
SPEED	'*Item*, she can wash and scour.'	
LANCE	A special virtue, for then she need not be washed and scoured.²	
305 SPEED	'*Item*, she can spin.'	
LANCE	Then may I set the world on wheels,° when she can spin for her living.	take life easy
SPEED	'*Item*, she hath many nameless° virtues.'	inexpressible
LANCE	That's as much as to say 'bastard virtues', that indeed	
310	know not their fathers, and therefore have no names.	
SPEED	Here follows her vices.	
LANCE	Close at the heels of her virtues.	
SPEED	'*Item*, she is not to be broken° with fasting, in respect of° her breath.'	tamed on account of
315 LANCE	Well, that fault may be mended with a breakfast. Read on.	
SPEED	'*Item*, she hath a sweet mouth.'³	
LANCE	That makes amends for her sour breath.	
SPEED	'*Item*, she doth talk in her sleep.'	
LANCE	It's no matter for that, so she sleep not in her talk.	
320 SPEED	'*Item*, she is slow in words.'	
LANCE	O villain, that set this down among her vices! To be slow in words is a woman's only virtue. I pray thee out with't, and place it for her chief virtue.	
SPEED	'*Item*, she is proud.'°	haughty; lascivious
325 LANCE	Out with that, too. It was Eve's legacy,⁴ and cannot be ta'en from her.	
SPEED	'*Item*, she hath no teeth.'	
LANCE	I care not for that, neither, because I love crusts.	
SPEED	'*Item*, she is curst.'°	shrewish
330 LANCE	Well, the best is, she hath no teeth to bite.	
SPEED	'*Item*, she will often praise° her liquor.'	appraise (by tasting)
LANCE	If her liquor be good, she shall. If she will not, I will; for good things should be praised.	
SPEED	'*Item*, she is too liberal.'°	bold; wanton
335 LANCE	Of her tongue she cannot, for that's writ down she is slow of. Of her purse she shall not, for that I'll keep shut. Now of another thing⁵ she may, and that cannot I help. Well, proceed.	
SPEED	'*Item*, she hath more hair than wit, and more faults than hairs, and more wealth than faults.'	
340 LANCE	Stop there. I'll have her. She was mine and not mine twice or thrice in that last article. Rehearse° that once more.	Repeat

2. *washed and scoured*: slang for "knocked down and beaten."
3. A sweet tooth; a wanton nature.
4. In the Garden of Eden, Satan, in the form of a serpent, tempted Eve, wife of the first man, Adam, to eat fruit from the tree of Knowledge of good and evil, which God had forbidden humans to taste. Eve was thus guilty of the sin of pride for disobeying God and putting her will before his command. See Genesis 2:15–3:24.
5. "Purse" (line 336) and "another thing" (line 337) were colloquial terms for "female genitalia."

SPEED   '*Item*, she hath more hair than wit'—

LANCE   'More hair than wit.' It may be. I'll prove it: the cover of
the salt° hides the salt, and therefore it is more° than the salt.   saltcellar / greater

345   The hair that covers the wit is more than the wit, for the
greater hides the less. What's next?

SPEED   'And more faults than hairs'—

LANCE   That's monstrous. O that that were out!

SPEED   'And more wealth than faults.'

350   LANCE   Why, that word makes the faults gracious.° Well, I'll   pleasing
have her, and if it be a match—as nothing is impossible—

SPEED   What then?

LANCE   Why then will I tell thee that thy master stays° for thee   waits
at the North Gate.

355   SPEED   For me?

LANCE   For thee? Ay, who art thou? He hath stayed for a better
man than thee.

SPEED   And must I go to him?

LANCE   Thou must run to him, for thou hast stayed so long that

360   going° will scarce serve the turn.   walking

SPEED   Why didst not tell me sooner? Pox of⁶ your love letters!
[*Exit*]

LANCE   Now will he be swinged° for reading my letter. An   beaten
unmannerly slave, that will thrust himself into secrets. I'll
after, to rejoice in the boy's correction.   *Exit*

3.2

Enter [*the*] DUKE [*and*] THURIO

DUKE   Sir Thurio, fear not but that she will love you
Now Valentine is banished from her sight.

THURIO   Since his exile she hath despised me most,
Forsworn my company, and railed at me,

5   That° I am desperate° of obtaining her.   So that / hopeless

DUKE   This weak impress° of love is as a figure   impression
Trenchèd° in ice, which with an hour's heat   Cut
Dissolves to water and doth lose his form.
A little time will melt her frozen thoughts,

10   And worthless Valentine shall be forgot.

[*Enter* PROTEUS]

How now, Sir Proteus, is your countryman,
According to our proclamation, gone?

PROTEUS   Gone, my good lord.

DUKE   My daughter takes his going grievously?

15   PROTEUS   A little time, my lord, will kill that grief.

DUKE   So I believe, but Thurio thinks not so.
Proteus, the good conceit° I hold of thee—   opinion
For thou hast shown some sign of good desert—
Makes me the better° to confer with thee.   the more willing

20   PROTEUS   Longer than I prove loyal to your grace
Let me not live to look upon your grace.

DUKE   Thou know'st how willingly I would effect
The match between Sir Thurio and my daughter?

PROTEUS   I do, my lord.

---

6. May disease take (a curse).   3.2 Location: The Duke's court in Milan.

25 DUKE And also, I think, thou art not ignorant
　　　　How she opposes her° against my will?　　　　　　　　*herself*
　　PROTEUS She did, my lord, when Valentine was here.
　　DUKE Ay, and perversely she persevers so.
　　　　What might we do to make the girl forget
30　　　The love of Valentine, and love Sir Thurio?
　　PROTEUS The best way is to slander Valentine
　　　　With falsehood, cowardice, and poor descent,
　　　　Three things that women highly hold in hate.
　　DUKE Ay, but she'll think that it is spoke in hate.
35　PROTEUS Ay, if his enemy deliver° it.　　　　　　　　　*report*
　　　　Therefore it must with circumstance° be spoken　　*supporting detail*
　　　　By one whom she esteemeth as his friend.
　　DUKE Then you must undertake to slander him.
　　PROTEUS And that, my lord, I shall be loath to do.
40　　　'Tis an ill office for a gentleman,
　　　　Especially against his very° friend.　　　　　　　　*true*
　　DUKE Where your good word cannot advantage° him　　*profit*
　　　　Your slander never can endamage° him.　　　　　　*harm*
　　　　Therefore the office is indifferent,°　　　　　　　　*neutral*
45　　　Being entreated to it by your friend.[1]
　　PROTEUS You have prevailed, my lord. If I can do it
　　　　By aught that I can speak in his dispraise
　　　　She shall not long continue love to him.
　　　　But say this weed° her love from Valentine,　　　　*uproot*
50　　　It follows not that she will love Sir Thurio.
　　THURIO Therefore, as you unwind her love from him,
　　　　Lest it should ravel and be good to none
　　　　You must provide to bottom it on me;[2]
　　　　Which must be done by praising me as much
55　　　As you in worth dispraise Sir Valentine.
　　DUKE And Proteus, we dare trust you in this kind
　　　　Because we know, on Valentine's report,
　　　　You are already love's firm votary,°　　　　　　　*disciple*
　　　　And cannot soon revolt, and change your mind.
60　　　Upon this warrant shall you have access
　　　　Where you with Silvia may confer at large.
　　　　For she is lumpish,° heavy, melancholy,　　　　　*low-spirited*
　　　　And for your friend's sake will be glad of you;
　　　　Where you may temper° her, by your persuasion,　*mold*
65　　　To hate young Valentine and love my friend.
　　PROTEUS As much as I can do, I will effect.
　　　　But you, Sir Thurio, are not sharp enough.
　　　　You must lay lime[3] to tangle° her desires　　　　*capture*
　　　　By wailful sonnets, whose composèd° rhymes　　　*well-crafted*
70　　　Should be full-fraught° with serviceable vows.[4]　*laden*
　　DUKE Ay, much is the force of heaven-bred poesy.
　　PROTEUS Say that upon the altar of her beauty
　　　　You sacrifice your tears, your sighs, your heart.
　　　　Write till your ink be dry, and with your tears
75　　　Moist it again; and frame some feeling line
　　　　That may discover° such integrity;°　　　　　　　*reveal / sincerity*
　　　　For Orpheus'[5] lute was strung with poets' sinews,°　*nerves*

1. Being asked to do it by a friend like me.
2. To wind it like a skein of thread upon me.
3. Birdlime, a sticky substance used to trap birds.
4. Promises to be of service.
5. A figure in Greek mythology famous for his entranc-
ing music.

Whose golden touch could soften steel and stones,
Make tigers tame, and huge leviathans°   *whales*
80   Forsake unsounded deeps to dance on sands.
After your dire-lamenting elegies,°   *love poems*
Visit by night your lady's chamber-window
With some sweet consort.° To their instruments   *band of musicians*
Tune° a deploring dump.° The night's dead silence   *Sing / sad melody*
85   Will well become such sweet-complaining grievance.
This, or else nothing, will inherit° her.   *win*
DUKE   This discipline° shows thou hast been in love.   *instruction*
THURIO   And thy advice this night I'll put in practice.
Therefore, sweet Proteus, my direction-giver,
90   Let us into the city presently
To sort° some gentlemen well skilled in music.   *select*
I have a sonnet that will serve the turn
To give the onset° to thy good advice.   *start*
DUKE   About it, gentlemen.
95   PROTEUS   We'll wait upon your grace till after supper,
And afterward determine our proceedings.
DUKE   Even now about it. I will pardon you.°   *excuse you from service*
Exeunt [THURIO *and* PROTEUS *at one door, and the* DUKE *at another*]

4.1

Enter [*the*] OUTLAWS
FIRST OUTLAW   Fellows, stand fast. I see a passenger.°   *traveler*
SECOND OUTLAW   If there be ten, shrink not, but down with 'em.
[*Enter* VALENTINE *and* SPEED]
THIRD OUTLAW   Stand,° sir, and throw us that° you have about ye.   *Halt / that which*
If not, we'll make you sit, and rifle° you.   *search*
SPEED [*to* VALENTINE]   Sir, we are undone. These are the villains
5   That all the travellers do fear so much.
VALENTINE [*to the* OUTLAWS]   My friends.
FIRST OUTLAW   That's not so, sir. We are your enemies.
SECOND OUTLAW   Peace. We'll hear him.
THIRD OUTLAW   Ay, by my beard will we. For he is a proper° man.   *handsome*
10   VALENTINE   Then know that I have little wealth to lose.
A man I am, crossed with adversity.
My riches are these poor habiliments,°   *clothes*
Of which if you should here disfurnish° me   *deprive*
You take the sum and substance that I have.
15   SECOND OUTLAW   Whither travel you?
VALENTINE   To Verona.
FIRST OUTLAW   Whence came you?
VALENTINE   From Milan.
THIRD OUTLAW   Have you long sojourned there?
20   VALENTINE   Some sixteen months,[1] and longer might have stayed
If crooked° fortune had not thwarted me.   *evil*
FIRST OUTLAW   What, were you banished thence?
VALENTINE   I was.
SECOND OUTLAW   For what offence?
VALENTINE   For that which now torments me to rehearse.°   *tell*

4.1 Location: A forest between Mantua and Milan.
1. A claim not consonant with the play's overall time scheme. Either this is a textual inconsistency or Valentine is lying.

25 I killed a man,[2] whose death I much repent,
But yet I slew him manfully, in fight,
Without false vantage or base treachery.°   *unfair advantage*
FIRST OUTLAW   Why, ne'er repent it, if it were done so.
But were you banished for so small a fault?
30 VALENTINE   I was, and held me glad of such a doom.°   *sentence*
SECOND OUTLAW   Have you the tongues?°   *skill in languages*
VALENTINE   My youthful travel therein made me happy,°   *fortunate; skilled*
Or else I had been often miserable.
THIRD OUTLAW   By the bare scalp of Robin Hood's fat friar,°   *(Friar Tuck)*
35 This fellow were a king for our wild faction.°   *band*
FIRST OUTLAW   We'll have him. Sirs, a word.
          [*The* OUTLAWS *confer*]
SPEED [*to* VALENTINE]   Master, be one of them.
It's an honourable kind of thievery.
VALENTINE   Peace, villain.
SECOND OUTLAW   Tell us this: have you anything to take to?[3]
40 VALENTINE   Nothing but my fortune.°   *luck*
THIRD OUTLAW   Know, then, that some of us are gentlemen
Such as the fury of ungoverned youth
Thrust from the company of aweful° men.   *respectable*
Myself was from Verona banishèd
45 For practising° to steal away a lady,   *plotting*
An heir, and near allied unto the Duke.
SECOND OUTLAW   And I from Mantua, for a gentleman
Who, in my mood,° I stabbed unto the heart.   *anger*
FIRST OUTLAW   And I, for suchlike petty crimes as these.
50 But to the purpose, for we cite our faults
That they may hold excused our lawless lives.
And partly seeing you are beautified
With goodly shape, and by your own report
A linguist, and a man of such perfection
55 As we do in our quality° much want—   *profession*
SECOND OUTLAW   Indeed because you are a banished man,
Therefore above the rest[4] we parley° to you.   *talk*
Are you content to be our general,
To make a virtue of necessity
60 And live as we do in this wilderness?
THIRD OUTLAW   What sayst thou? Wilt thou be of our consort?°   *company*
Say 'Ay', and be the captain of us all.
We'll do thee homage, and be ruled by thee,
Love thee as our commander and our king.
65 FIRST OUTLAW   But if thou scorn our courtesy, thou diest.
SECOND OUTLAW   Thou shalt not live to brag what we have
offered.
VALENTINE   I take your offer, and will live with you,
Provided that you do no outrages
On silly° women or poor passengers.   *defenseless*
70 THIRD OUTLAW   No, we detest such vile, base practices.
Come, go with us. We'll bring thee to our crews°   *bands of men*
And show thee all the treasure we have got,
Which, with ourselves, all rest at thy dispose.°   *Exeunt*   *disposal*

2. Why Valentine lies here is much debated. He may be protecting Silvia's reputation or trying to impress the outlaws.
3. Any way to support yourself.
4. For that above all other reasons.

4.2

Enter PROTEUS

PROTEUS Already have I been false to Valentine,
And now I must be as unjust to Thurio.
Under the colour° of commending him   pretext
I have access my own love to prefer.°   advance
5 But Silvia is too fair, too true, too holy
To be corrupted with my worthless gifts.
When I protest true loyalty to her
She twits me with my falsehood to my friend.
When to her beauty I commend my vows
10 She bids me think how I have been forsworn
In breaking faith with Julia, whom I loved.
And notwithstanding all her sudden quips,°   sharp rebukes
The least whereof would quell a lover's hope,
Yet, spaniel-like, the more she spurns my love,
15 The more it grows and fawneth on her still.
But here comes Thurio. Now must we to her window,
And give some evening music to her ear.

[Enter THURIO *with Musicians]*

THURIO How now, Sir Proteus, are you crept before us?
PROTEUS Ay, gentle Thurio, for you know that love
20 Will creep° in service where it cannot go.°   crawl / walk
THURIO Ay, but I hope, sir, that you love not here.
PROTEUS Sir, but I do, or else I would be hence.
THURIO Who, Silvia?
PROTEUS   Ay, Silvia—for your sake.
THURIO I thank you for your own.° Now, gentlemen,   own sake
25 Let's tune, and to it lustily awhile.

[Enter the HOST, *and* JULIA *dressed as a page-boy. They
talk apart]*

HOST Now, my young guest, methinks you're allycholly.° I pray   melancholy
you, why is it?
JULIA Marry, mine host, because I cannot be merry.
HOST Come, we'll have you merry. I'll bring you where you
30 shall hear music, and see the gentleman that you asked for.
JULIA But shall I hear him speak?
HOST Ay, that you shall.
JULIA That will be music.
HOST Hark, hark.[1]
35 JULIA Is he among these?
HOST Ay. But peace, let's hear 'em.

Song[2]

Who is Silvia? What is she,
    That all our swains° commend her?   lovers
Holy, fair, and wise is she.
40   The heaven such grace did lend her
That she might admirèd be.

4.2 Location: Outside the Duke's palace under Silvia's
window by moonlight.
1. Probably music plays.

2. Not ascribed to anyone in F. Julia's later comments
suggest that Proteus sings while playing a stringed
instrument.

Is she kind as she is fair?
  For beauty lives with kindness.
Love° doth to her eyes repair°   *(Cupid) / pay a visit*
45   To help° him of his blindness,   *cure*
  And, being helped, inhabits there.

Then to Silvia let us sing
  That Silvia is excelling.
She excels each mortal thing
50   Upon the dull earth dwelling.
  To her let us garlands bring.

HOST   How now, are you sadder than you were before? How do
     you, man? The music likes° you not.   *pleases*
JULIA   You mistake. The musician likes me not.
55 HOST   Why, my pretty youth?
JULIA   He plays false,[3] father.
HOST   How, out of tune on the strings?
JULIA   Not so, but yet so false that he grieves my very heart-strings.
HOST   You have a quick° ear.   *perceptive*
60 JULIA   Ay, I would I were deaf. It makes me have a slow° heart.   *heavy*
HOST   I perceive you delight not in music.
JULIA   Not a whit when it jars so.°   *is so discordant*
HOST   Hark what fine change° is in the music.   *modulation*
JULIA   Ay, that 'change' is the spite.
65 HOST   You would have them always play but one thing?
JULIA   I would always have one play but one thing. But host,
     doth this Sir Proteus that we talk on often resort unto this
     gentlewoman?
HOST   I tell you what Lance his man told me, he loved her out
70   of all nick.°   *excessively*
JULIA   Where is Lance?
HOST   Gone to seek his dog, which tomorrow, by his master's
     command, he must carry for a present to his lady.
JULIA   Peace, stand aside. The company parts.
75 PROTEUS   Sir Thurio, fear not you. I will so plead
     That you shall say my cunning drift° excels.   *scheme*
THURIO   Where meet we?
PROTEUS   At Saint Gregory's[4] well.
THURIO   Farewell.
       [Exeunt THURIO *and the Musicians]*
      [Enter SILVIA, *above]*°   *(at her window)*
PROTEUS   Madam, good even to your ladyship.
SILVIA   I thank you for your music, gentlemen.
80 Who is that that spake?
PROTEUS   One, lady, if you knew his pure heart's truth
     You would quickly learn to know him by his voice.
SILVIA   Sir Proteus, as I take it.
PROTEUS   Sir Proteus, gentle lady, and your servant.
85 SILVIA   What's your will?
PROTEUS   That I may compass yours.[5]

---

3. Is unfaithful; plays out of tune.
4. Patron saint of musicians and singers.

5. *compass:* win. Punning on "will." That I may win
your good will; that I may conquer your sexual desire.

SILVIA   You have your wish. My will is even this,
    That presently you hie you home to bed.
    Thou subtle, perjured, false, disloyal man,
    Think'st thou I am so shallow, so conceitless°   *witless*
90   To be seducèd by thy flattery,
    That hast deceived so many with thy vows?
    Return, return, and make thy love amends.
    For me—by this pale queen of night[6] I swear—
    I am so far from granting thy request
95   That I despise thee for thy wrongful suit,
    And by and by intend to chide myself
    Even for this time I spend in talking to thee.
PROTEUS   I grant, sweet love, that I did love a lady,
    But she is dead.
JULIA [*aside*]   'Twere false if° I should speak it,   *even if*
100   For I am sure she is not burièd.
SILVIA   Say that she be, yet Valentine, thy friend,
    Survives, to whom, thyself art witness,
    I am betrothed. And art thou not ashamed
    To wrong him with thy importunacy?°   *improper requests*
105 PROTEUS   I likewise hear that Valentine is dead.
SILVIA   And so suppose am I, for in his grave,
    Assure thyself, my love is burièd.
PROTEUS   Sweet lady, let me rake it from the earth.
SILVIA   Go to thy lady's grave and call hers thence,
110   Or at the least, in hers sepulchre° thine.   *bury*
JULIA [*aside*]   He heard not that.
PROTEUS   Madam, if your heart be so obdurate,
    Vouchsafe me yet your picture for my love,
    The picture that is hanging in your chamber.
115   To that I'll speak, to that I'll sigh and weep;
    For since the substance of your perfect self
    Is else devoted,[7] I am but a shadow,°   *mere nothing*
    And to your shadow° will I make true love.   *image*
JULIA [*aside*]   If 'twere a substance, you would sure deceive it
120   And make it but a shadow, as I am.
SILVIA   I am very loath to be your idol, sir,
    But since your falsehood shall become you well°   *make you fit*
    To worship shadows and adore false shapes,
    Send to me in the morning, and I'll send it.°   *(the picture)*
    And so, good rest.   [*Exit*]
125 PROTEUS   As wretches have o'ernight,
    That wait for execution in the morn.   [*Exit*]
JULIA   Host, will you go?
HOST   By my halidom,° I was fast asleep.   *holy relic (an oath)*
JULIA   Pray you, where lies° Sir Proteus?   *lodges*
130 HOST   Marry, at my house. Trust me, I think 'tis almost day.
JULIA   Not so; but it hath been the longest night
    That e'er I watched, and the most heaviest.°   [*Exeunt*]   *saddest*

---

6. The moon, imagined as Diana, goddess of chastity.   7. Is devoted to someone else.

4.3

Enter [*Sir*] EGLAMOUR

EGLAMOUR   This is the hour that Madam Silvia
Entreated me to call, and know her mind.
There's some great matter she'd employ me in.
Madam, madam!
     [*Enter* SILVIA *above*]

SILVIA   Who calls?

EGLAMOUR   Your servant, and your friend.

5   One that attends your ladyship's command.

SILVIA   Sir Eglamour, a thousand times good morrow!

EGLAMOUR   As many, worthy lady, to yourself.
According to your ladyship's impose°   *command*
I am thus early come, to know what service
10   It is your pleasure to command me in.

SILVIA   O Eglamour, thou art a gentleman—
Think not I flatter, for I swear I do not—
Valiant, wise, remorseful,° well accomplished.   *compassionate*
Thou art not ignorant what dear good will
15   I bear unto the banished Valentine,
Nor how my father would enforce me marry
Vain Thurio, whom my very soul abhors.
Thyself hast loved, and I have heard thee say
No grief did ever come so near thy heart
20   As when thy lady and thy true love died,
Upon whose grave thou vowed'st pure chastity.
Sir Eglamour, I would° to Valentine,   *would go*
To Mantua, where I hear he makes abode;
And for° the ways are dangerous to pass   *because*
25   I do desire thy worthy company,
Upon whose faith and honour I repose.°   *rely*
Urge not¹ my father's anger, Eglamour,
But think upon my grief, a lady's grief,
And on the justice of my flying hence
30   To keep me from a most unholy match,
Which heaven and fortune still° rewards with plagues.   *always*
I do desire thee, even from a heart
As full of sorrows as the sea of sands,
To bear me company and go with me.
35   If not, to hide what I have said to thee
That I may venture to depart alone.

EGLAMOUR   Madam, I pity much your grievances,
Which, since I know they virtuously are placed,
I give consent to go along with you,
40   Recking° as little what betideth° me   *Caring / happens to*
As much I wish all good befortune° you.   *befall*
When will you go?

SILVIA   This evening coming.

EGLAMOUR   Where shall I meet you?

SILVIA   At Friar Patrick's cell,
Where I intend holy confession.
45   EGLAMOUR   I will not fail your ladyship.

4.3 Location: The same place, the next morning.   1. Do not offer as an excuse.

Good morrow, gentle lady.
SILVIA   Good morrow, kind Sir Eglamour.   *Exeunt*

4.4

Enter LANCE *[and his dog Crab]*

LANCE *[to the audience]*   When a man's servant shall play the
cur° with him, look you, it goes hard. One that I brought up   act like a stupid dog
of° a puppy, one that I saved from drowning when three or four   from
of his blind brothers and sisters went to it.° I have taught him,   met their death
5   even as one would say precisely 'Thus I would teach a dog'.
I was sent to deliver him as a present to Mistress Silvia from
my master, and I came no sooner into the dining-chamber but
he steps me to[1] her trencher° and steals her capon's leg. O, 'tis   wooden plate
a foul thing when a cur cannot keep° himself in all compa-   behave
10   nies. I would have, as one should say, one that takes upon him
to be a dog indeed, to be, as it were, a dog at° all things. If I had   adept at
not had more wit than he, to take a fault upon me that he did,
I think verily he had been hanged for't. Sure as I live, he had
suffered for't. You shall judge. He thrusts me himself into the
15   company of three or four gentleman-like dogs under the
Duke's table. He had not been there—bless the mark[2]—a
pissing-while[3] but all the chamber smelled him. 'Out with the
dog,' says one. 'What cur is that?' says another. 'Whip him out,'
says the third. 'Hang him up,' says the Duke. I, having been
20   acquainted with the smell before, knew it was Crab, and goes
me to the fellow that whips the dogs. 'Friend,' quoth I, 'you
mean to whip the dog.' 'Ay, marry do I,' quoth he. 'You do him
the more wrong,' quoth I, "twas I did the thing you wot° of.' He   know
makes me no more ado, but whips me out of the chamber.
25   How many masters would do this for his servant? Nay, I'll be
sworn I have sat in the stocks[4] for puddings[5] he hath stolen,
otherwise he had been executed. I have stood on the pillory[6]
for geese he hath killed, otherwise he had suffered for't. (*To
Crab*) Thou think'st not of this now. Nay, I remember the trick
30   you served me when I took my leave of Madam Silvia. Did not
I bid thee still mark° me, and do as I do? When didst thou see   watch
me heave up my leg and make water against a gentlewoman's
farthingale?° Didst thou ever see me do such a trick?   hooped petticoat
   [Enter PROTEUS, *with* JULIA *dressed as a page-boy]*
PROTEUS *[to* JULIA]   Sebastian[7] is thy name? I like thee well,
35   And will employ thee in some service° presently.   work; sexual business
JULIA   In what you please. I'll do what I can.
PROTEUS   I hope thou wilt.—How now, you whoreson peasant,
   Where have you been these two days loitering?
LANCE   Marry, sir, I carried Mistress Silvia the dog you bade me.
40   PROTEUS   And what says she to my little jewel?

4.4 Location: The same place, somewhat later.
1. *he steps me to:* he (the dog) steps forward to Lance's
embarrassment or to his detriment. Here and in line
14, "thrusts me," Lance is describing the dog's actions
and their negative effect on himself.
2. An apology for offensive language.
3. Slang for "a very short time." Lance here employs it
literally.
4. An instrument of punishment in which the offender

sat with feet clamped between two wooden planks into
which ankle holes had been cut.
5. Dishes made of animal intestines or stomachs
stuffed with meat and spices.
6. An instrument of punishment similar to the stocks.
One stood with head and hands clamped between
wooden planks.
7. A name sometimes associated with male homoeroticism and the arrow-pierced body of St. Sebastian.

LANCE   Marry, she says your dog was a cur, and tells you currish thanks is good enough for such a present.

PROTEUS   But she received my dog?

LANCE   No indeed did she not. Here have I brought him back
45   again.

PROTEUS   What, didst thou offer her this from me?

LANCE   Ay, sir. The other squirrel⁸ was stolen from me by the
hangman° boys in the market place, and then I offered her   *fit for the hangman*
mine own, who is a dog as big as ten of yours, and therefore
50   the gift the greater.

PROTEUS   Go, get thee hence, and find my dog again,
Or ne'er return again into my sight.
Away, I say. Stay'st thou to vex me here?
                                        [*Exit* LANCE *with Crab*]
A slave, that still on end° turns me to shame.   *always*
55   Sebastian, I have entertainèd thee
Partly that I have need of such a youth
That can with some discretion do my business,
For 'tis no trusting to yon foolish lout,
But chiefly for thy face and thy behaviour,
60   Which, if my augury° deceive me not,   *fortune-telling skills*
Witness good bringing up, fortune, and truth.
Therefore know thou, for this I entertain thee.
Go presently, and take this ring with thee.
Deliver it to Madam Silvia.
65   She loved me well delivered° it to me.   *who gave*

JULIA   It seems you loved not her, to leave° her token.   *part with*
She is dead belike?°   *perchance*

PROTEUS   Not so. I think she lives.

JULIA   Alas.

PROTEUS   Why dost thou cry 'Alas'?

70   JULIA   I cannot choose but pity her.

PROTEUS   Wherefore shouldst thou pity her?

JULIA   Because methinks that she loved you as well
As you do love your lady Silvia.
She dreams on him that has forgot her love;
75   You dote on her that cares not for your love.
'Tis pity love should be so contrary,
And thinking on it makes me cry 'Alas'.

PROTEUS   Well, give her that ring, and therewithal°   *along with it*
This letter. [*Pointing*] That's her chamber. Tell my lady
80   I claim the promise for her heavenly picture.
Your message done, hie home unto my chamber,
Where thou shalt find me sad and solitary.   [*Exit*]

JULIA   How many women would do such a message?
Alas, poor Proteus, thou hast entertained
85   A fox to be the shepherd of thy lambs.
Alas, poor fool,⁹ why do I pity him
That with his very heart despiseth me?
Because he loves her, he despiseth me.
Because I love him, I must pity him.
90   This ring I gave him when he parted from me,

8. A disparaging reference to the small dog Proteus   9. Julia is referring to herself.
intended to give Silvia.

To bind him to remember my good will.
And now am I, unhappy messenger,
To plead for that which I would not obtain;
To carry that which I would have refused;
95   To praise his faith, which I would have dispraised.
I am my master's true-confirmèd love,
But cannot be true servant to my master
Unless I prove false traitor to myself.
Yet will I woo for him, but yet so coldly
100   As, heaven it knows, I would not have him speed.°   *succeed*
        [*Enter* SILVIA]
Gentlewoman, good day. I pray you be my mean°   *agent, means*
To bring me where to speak with Madam Silvia.
SILVIA   What would you with her, if that I be she?
JULIA   If you be she, I do entreat your patience
105   To hear me speak the message I am sent on.
SILVIA   From whom?
JULIA   From my master, Sir Proteus, madam.
SILVIA   O, he sends you for a picture?
JULIA   Ay, madam.
110   SILVIA   Ursula, bring my picture there.
        [*An attendant brings a picture*]
Go, give your master this. Tell him from me
One Julia, that his changing thoughts forget,
Would better fit his chamber than this shadow.°   *portrait*
JULIA   Madam, please you peruse this letter.
        [*She gives* SILVIA *a letter*]¹
115   Pardon me, madam, I have unadvised°   *inadvertently*
Delivered you a paper that I should not.
        [*She takes back the letter and gives* SILVIA *another letter*]
This is the letter to your ladyship.
SILVIA   I pray thee, let me look on that again.
JULIA   It may not be. Good madam, pardon me.
120   SILVIA   There, hold. I will not look upon your master's lines.
I know they are stuffed with protestations,
And full of new-found° oaths, which he will break   *newly made*
As easily as I do tear his paper.
        [*She tears the letter*]
JULIA   Madam, he sends your ladyship this ring.
        [*She offers* SILVIA *a ring*]
125   SILVIA   The more shame for him, that he sends it me;
For I have heard him say a thousand times
His Julia gave it him at his departure.
Though his false finger have profaned the ring,
Mine shall not do his Julia so much wrong.
130   JULIA   She thanks you.
SILVIA   What sayst thou?
JULIA   I thank you, madam, that you tender° her.   *show concern for*
Poor gentlewoman, my master wrongs her much.
SILVIA   Dost thou know her?
135   JULIA   Almost as well as I do know myself.
To think upon her woes I do protest

---

1. Possibly the first letter is from Proteus to Julia. Whether Julia offers it to Silvia by mistake or deliberately (as she later seems deliberately to mistake two rings) is open to question.

That I have wept a hundred several times.

SILVIA   Belike she thinks that Proteus hath forsook her?

JULIA   I think she doth; and that's her cause of sorrow.

140 SILVIA   Is she not passing° fair?   *exceedingly*

JULIA   She hath been fairer, madam, than she is.
When she did think my master loved her well
She, in my judgement, was as fair as you.
But since she did neglect her looking-glass,

145 And threw her sun-expelling mask[2] away,
The air hath starved° the roses in her cheeks   *withered*
And pinched the lily tincture° of her face,   *white color*
That now she is become as black as I.

SILVIA   How tall was she?

150 JULIA   About my stature; for at Pentecost,[3]
When all our pageants of delight° were played,   *pleasing performances*
Our youth got me to play the woman's part,[4]
And I was trimmed° in Madam Julia's gown,   *dressed*
Which servèd me as fit, by all men's judgements,

155 As if the garment had been made for me;
Therefore I know she is about my height.
And at that time I made her weep agood,°   *in earnest*
For I did play a lamentable° part.   *pitiable*
Madam, 'twas Ariadne, passioning

160 For Theseus' perjury and unjust flight;[5]
Which I so lively° acted with my tears   *convincingly*
That my poor mistress, movèd therewithal,
Wept bitterly; and would I might be dead
If I in thought felt not her very sorrow.

165 SILVIA   She is beholden to thee, gentle youth.
Alas, poor lady, desolate and left.
I weep myself to think upon thy words.
Here, youth. There is my purse. I give thee this
For thy sweet mistress' sake, because thou lov'st her.

170 Farewell.   [*Exit*]

JULIA   And she shall thank you for't, if e'er you know her.—
A virtuous gentlewoman, mild, and beautiful.
I hope my master's suit will be but cold,°   *unsuccessful*
Since she respects 'my mistress'' love so much.

175 Alas, how love can trifle with itself.
Here is her picture. Let me see, I think
If I had such a tire,° this face of mine   *headdress*
Were full as lovely as is this of hers.
And yet the painter flattered her a little,

180 Unless I flatter with myself too much.
Her hair is auburn, mine is perfect yellow.
If that be all the difference in his love,
I'll get me such a coloured periwig.
Her eyes are grey as glass, and so are mine.

185 Ay, but her forehead's low, and mine's as high.[6]

---

2. A mask to block the sun worn by upper-class Englishwomen to preserve their light complexions.
3. Religious days seven weeks after Easter, when plays and theatrical pageants were staged in many English towns.
4. Act the female role, as boys conventionally did in the Elizabethan theater.
5. In Greek mythology, Ariadne hanged herself after she was abandoned by her lover, Theseus. *passioning:* sorrowing.
6. Mine's as high as hers is low. High foreheads were considered a sign of beauty.

What should it be that he respects° in her   *esteems*
But I can make respective° in myself,   *worthy of esteem*
If this fond love were not a blinded god?
Come, shadow, come, and take this shadow up,[7]
For 'tis thy rival.
              [*She picks up the portrait*]
190   O thou senseless form,
Thou shalt be worshipped, kissed, loved, and adored;
And were there sense° in his idolatry   *reason*
My substance should be statue in thy stead.[8]
I'll use thee kindly, for thy mistress' sake,
195   That used me so; or else, by Jove I vow,
I should have scratched out your unseeing eyes,
To make my master out of love with thee.   *Exit*

5.1

              Enter [Sir] EGLAMOUR
EGLAMOUR   The sun begins to gild the western sky,
And now it is about the very hour
That Silvia at Friar Patrick's cell should meet me.
She will not fail; for lovers break not hours,°   *appointments*
5   Unless it be to come before their time,
So much they spur their expedition.°   *hasten their progress*
              [*Enter* SILVIA]
See where she comes. Lady, a happy evening!
SILVIA   Amen, amen. Go on, good Eglamour,
Out at the postern° by the abbey wall.   *back door or side door*
10   I fear I am attended° by some spies.   *followed*
EGLAMOUR   Fear not. The forest is not three leagues off.
If we recover° that, we are sure° enough.   *Exeunt*   *reach / safe*

5.2

              Enter THURIO, PROTEUS, [*and*] JULIA [*dressed as a page-boy*]
THURIO   Sir Proteus, what says Silvia to my suit?
PROTEUS   O sir, I find her milder than she was,
And yet she takes exceptions at° your person.   *objects to*
THURIO   What? That my leg is too long?
5   PROTEUS   No, that it is too little.
THURIO   I'll wear a boot, to make it somewhat rounder.
JULIA [*aside*]   But love will not be spurred to what it loathes.[1]
THURIO   What says she to my face?
PROTEUS   She says it is a fair one.
10   THURIO   Nay, then, the wanton lies. My face is black.
PROTEUS   But pearls are fair; and the old saying is,
      'Black men are pearls in beauteous ladies' eyes'.
JULIA [*aside*]   'Tis true, such pearls[2] as put out ladies' eyes,
      For I had rather wink° than look on them.   *shut my eyes*
15   THURIO   How likes she my discourse?
PROTEUS   Ill, when you talk of war.

---

7. Probably addressing herself as a "shadow," or mere
nothing, Julia means "pick up Silvia's portrait" or "take
up the challenge posed by this woman."
8. My person ("substance") should be an idol ("statue")
to Proteus rather than Silvia's picture.
5.1 Location: An abbey in Milan.
5.2 Location: The Duke's court in Milan.

1. F assigns this line to Proteus and lines 13 and 14 to
Thurio, but it makes more sense to assign them to the
disguised Julia, whose covert comments on the words of
Proteus and Thurio provide the scene with much of its
humor.
2. Punning on the medical meaning of "pearl" as a thin
film or cataract growing over the eye.

THURIO   But well when I discourse of love and peace.

JULIA [*aside*]   But better indeed when you hold your peace.

THURIO   What says she to my valour?

20   PROTEUS   O sir, she makes no doubt of that.

JULIA [*aside*]   She needs not, when she knows it cowardice.

THURIO   What says she to my birth?

PROTEUS   That you are well derived.°   *descended*

JULIA [*aside*]   True: from a gentleman to a fool.

25   THURIO   Considers she my possessions?

PROTEUS   O ay, and pities them.

THURIO   Wherefore?

JULIA [*aside*]   That such an ass should owe° them.   *own*

PROTEUS   That they are out by lease.°   *rented out*

JULIA   Here comes the Duke.

      [*Enter the* DUKE]

30   DUKE   How now, Sir Proteus. How now, Thurio.
      Which of you saw Eglamour of late?

THURIO   Not I.

PROTEUS   Nor I.

DUKE   Saw you my daughter?

PROTEUS   Neither.

DUKE   Why then, she's fled unto that peasant° Valentine,   *rascal*
      And Eglamour is in her company.

35   'Tis true, for Friar Laurence[3] met them both
      As he in penance wandered through the forest.
      Him he knew well, and guessed that it was she,
      But being masked, he was not sure of it.
      Besides, she did intend confession

40   At Patrick's cell this even, and there she was not.
      These likelihoods confirm her flight from hence;
      Therefore I pray you stand not to discourse,
      But mount you presently, and meet with me
      Upon the rising of the mountain foot

45   That leads toward Mantua, whither they are fled.
      Dispatch,° sweet gentlemen, and follow me.   [*Exit*]   *Hurry*

THURIO   Why, this it is to be a peevish° girl,   *silly; perverse*
      That flies her fortune when it follows her.
      I'll after, more to be revenged on Eglamour

50   Than for the love of reckless Silvia.   [*Exit*]

PROTEUS   And I will follow, more for Silvia's love
      Than hate of Eglamour that goes with her.   [*Exit*]

JULIA   And I will follow, more to cross that love
      Than hate for Silvia, that is gone for love.   *Exit*

5.3

      [*Enter the*] OUTLAWS [*with*] SILVIA [*captive*]

FIRST OUTLAW   Come, come, be patient. We must bring you to
      our captain.

SILVIA   A thousand more mischances than this one
      Have learned° me how to brook° this patiently.   *taught / endure*

5   SECOND OUTLAW   Come, bring her away.

FIRST OUTLAW   Where is the gentleman that was with her?°   *(Eglamour)*

---

3. Possibly a slip for "Friar Patrick," mentioned in the   friar in the forest.
preceding scene, although there may be more than one   **5.3** Location: At the frontiers of the Mantua forest.

THIRD OUTLAW   Being nimble-footed he hath outrun us;
But Moses and Valerius follow him.
Go thou with her to the west end of the wood.
10   There is our captain. We'll follow him that's fled.
The thicket is beset,° he cannot scape.   surrounded
          [*Exeunt the* SECOND *and* THIRD OUTLAWS]
FIRST OUTLAW [*to* SILVIA]   Come, I must bring you to our captain's cave.
Fear not. He bears an honourable mind,
And will not use a woman lawlessly.
15   SILVIA [*aside*]   O Valentine! This I endure for thee.   *Exeunt*

                          5.4
          Enter VALENTINE
VALENTINE   How use° doth breed a habit in a man!   custom
This shadowy desert,° unfrequented woods   uninhabited spot
I better brook° than flourishing peopled towns.   endure
Here can I sit alone, unseen of any,
5   And to the nightingale's[1] complaining notes
Tune my distresses and record my woes.
O thou° that dost inhabit in my breast,   (addressing Silvia)
Leave not the mansion[2] so long tenantless
Lest, growing ruinous, the building fall
10   And leave no memory of what it was.
Repair me with thy presence, Silvia.
Thou gentle nymph, cherish thy forlorn swain.
What hallooing and what stir is this today?
These are my mates, that make their wills their law,
15   Have° some unhappy passenger° in chase.   Who have / traveler
They love me well, yet I have much to do
To keep them from uncivil outrages.
Withdraw thee, Valentine. Who's this comes here?
          [*He stands aside.*
          Enter PROTEUS, SILVIA, *and* JULIA *dressed as a page-boy*]
PROTEUS   Madam, this service I have done for you—
20   Though you respect not aught your servant doth—
To hazard life, and rescue you from him
That would have forced your honour° and your love.   violated your chastity
Vouchsafe me for my meed° but one fair look.   reward
A smaller boon than this I cannot beg,
25   And less than this I am sure you cannot give.
VALENTINE [*aside*]   How like a dream is this I see and hear!
Love lend me patience to forbear awhile.
SILVIA   O miserable, unhappy that I am!
PROTEUS   Unhappy were you, madam, ere I came.
30   But by my coming I have made you happy.
SILVIA   By thy approach° thou mak'st me most unhappy.   amorous advances
JULIA [*aside*]   And me, when he approacheth to your presence.
SILVIA   Had I been seizèd by a hungry lion
I would have been a breakfast to the beast
35   Rather than have false Proteus rescue me.
O heaven be judge how I love Valentine,

5.4 Location: Another part of the forest.   a nightingale after Tereus raped her; her song is a lament.
1. In the classical mythology, Philomela was turned into   2. Referring to his body as Silvia's home.

Whose life's as tender° to me as my soul.   *precious*
And full as much, for more there cannot be,
I do detest false perjured Proteus.

40   Therefore be gone, solicit me no more.

PROTEUS   What dangerous action, stood it next to death,
Would I not undergo for one calm° look!   *gentle*
O, 'tis the curse in love, and still approved,°   *always confirmed*
When women cannot love where they're beloved.

45 SILVIA   When Proteus cannot love where he's beloved.
Read over Julia's heart, thy first, best love,
For whose dear sake thou didst then rend thy faith
Into a thousand oaths, and all those oaths
Descended into perjury° to love me.   *were forsworn*

50   Thou hast no faith left now, unless thou'dst two,[3]
And that's far worse than none. Better have none
Than plural faith, which is too much by one,
Thou counterfeit° to thy true friend.   *deceiver; false friend*

PROTEUS   In love
Who respects friend?

SILVIA   All men but Proteus.

55 PROTEUS   Nay, if the gentle spirit of moving words
Can no way change you to a milder form
I'll woo you like a soldier, at arm's end,°   *at swordpoint*
And love you 'gainst the nature of love: force ye.

SILVIA   O heaven!

PROTEUS *[assailing her]*   I'll force thee yield to my desire.

60 VALENTINE *[coming forward]*   Ruffian, let go that rude uncivil touch,
Thou friend of an ill fashion.

PROTEUS   Valentine!

VALENTINE   Thou common° friend, that's without faith or love,   *superficial*
For such is a friend now. Treacherous man,
Thou hast beguiled my hopes. Naught but mine eye

65   Could have persuaded me. Now I dare not say
I have one friend alive. Thou wouldst disprove me.
Who should be trusted, when one's right hand
Is perjured to the bosom?° Proteus,   *false to the heart*
I am sorry I must never trust thee more,

70   But count the world a stranger for thy sake.[4]
The private wound is deepest. O time most accursed,
'Mongst all foes that a friend should be the worst!

PROTEUS   My shame and guilt confounds me.
Forgive me, Valentine. If hearty sorrow

75   Be a sufficient ransom for offence,
I tender't° here. I do as truly suffer   *offer it*
As e'er I did commit.

VALENTINE   Then I am paid,
And once again I do receive thee° honest.   *accept you as*
Who by repentance is not satisfied

80   Is nor of heaven nor earth. For these are pleased;
By penitence th' Eternal's wrath's appeased.
And that my love may appear plain and free,

---

3. You have no faithfulness left now, unless you were to have two lovers (Julia and Silvia).

4. But cut myself off from the world (in disillusionment) because of your treachery.

All that was mine in Silvia[5] I give thee.

JULIA   O me unhappy!
    [*She faints*]

PROTEUS   Look to the boy.

VALENTINE   Why, boy!

85   Why wag,° how now? What's the matter? Look up. Speak.   *sweet boy*

JULIA   O good sir, my master charged me to deliver a ring to
    Madam Silvia, which out of my neglect was never done.

PROTEUS   Where is that ring, boy?

JULIA   Here 'tis. This is it.
    [*She gives* PROTEUS *the ring*]

90   PROTEUS   How, let me see!
    Why, this is the ring I gave to Julia.

JULIA   O, cry you mercy, sir, I have mistook.
    [*She offers* PROTEUS *another ring*]
    This is the ring you sent to Silvia.

PROTEUS   But how cam'st thou by this ring? At my depart

95   I gave this unto Julia.

JULIA   And Julia herself did give it me,
    And Julia herself hath brought it hither.

PROTEUS   How? Julia?

JULIA   Behold her that gave aim to° all thy oaths   *was the object of*
100   And entertained 'em deeply in her heart.
    How oft hast thou with perjury cleft the root?°   *bottom of her heart*
    O Proteus, let this habit° make thee blush.   *disguise*
    Be thou ashamed that I have took upon me
    Such an immodest raiment, if shame live
105   In a disguise of love.[6]
    It is the lesser blot, modesty finds,
    Women to change their shapes° than men their minds.   *appearances; clothes*

PROTEUS   Than men their minds! 'Tis true. O heaven, were man
    But constant, he were perfect. That one error
110   Fills him with faults, makes him run through all th' sins;
    Inconstancy falls off ere it begins.[7]
    What is in Silvia's face but I may spy
    More fresh in Julia's, with a constant° eye?   *faithful*

VALENTINE   Come, come, a hand from either.
115   Let me be blessed to make this happy close.°   *ending; union*
    'Twere pity two such friends should be long foes.
    [JULIA *and* PROTEUS *join hands*]

PROTEUS   Bear witness, heaven, I have my wish for ever.

JULIA   And I mine.
    [*Enter the* OUTLAWS *with the* DUKE *and* THURIO *as captives*]

OUTLAWS   A prize, a prize, a prize!

VALENTINE   Forbear, forbear, I say. It is my lord the Duke.
    [*The* OUTLAWS *release the* DUKE *and* THURIO]
120   [*To the* DUKE]   Your grace is welcome to a man disgraced,
    Banishèd Valentine.

DUKE   Sir Valentine!

THURIO   Yonder is Silvia, and Silvia's mine.

---

5. All my claims to Silvia; all that was mine, in the person of Silvia; all the love I gave to Silvia.
6. *if . . . love*: if a disguise one wears for the sake of love can be considered shameful; if one who pretends to feel love is capable of feeling shame.
7. The inconstant man begins to deceive, or "fall off," even before he swears constancy.

VALENTINE   Thurio, give back,° or else embrace thy death.   *stand back*
    Come not within the measure° of my wrath.   *reach*
125 Do not name Silvia thine. If once again,
    Verona[8] shall not hold thee. Here she stands.
    Take but possession of her with a touch—
    I dare thee but to breathe upon my love.
  THURIO   Sir Valentine, I care not for her, I.
130 I hold him but a fool that will endanger
    His body for a girl that loves him not.
    I claim her not, and therefore she is thine.
  DUKE   The more degenerate and base art thou
    To make such means° for her as thou hast done,   *efforts*
135 And leave her on such slight conditions.°   *trivial reasons*
    Now by the honour of my ancestry
    I do applaud thy spirit, Valentine,
    And think thee worthy of an empress' love.
    Know then I here forget all former griefs,°   *grievances*
140 Cancel all grudge, repeal° thee home again,   *recall*
    Plead a new state in thy unrivalled merit,[9]
    To which I thus subscribe:° Sir Valentine,   *bear witness*
    Thou art a gentleman, and well derived.
    Take thou thy Silvia, for thou hast deserved her.
145 VALENTINE   I thank your grace. The gift hath made me happy.
    I now beseech you, for your daughter's sake,
    To grant one boon° that I shall ask of you.   *favor*
  DUKE   I grant it, for thine own, whate'er it be.
  VALENTINE   These banished men that I have kept withal°   *lived with*
150 Are men endowed with worthy qualities.
    Forgive them what they have committed here,
    And let them be recalled from their exile.
    They are reformèd, civil, full of good,
    And fit for great employment, worthy lord.
155 DUKE   Thou hast prevailed. I pardon them and thee.
    Dispose of them as thou know'st their deserts.
    Come, let us go. We will include all jars°   *end all discord*
    With triumphs,° mirth, and rare solemnity.°   *pageants / festivity*
  VALENTINE   And as we walk along I dare be bold
160 With our discourse to make your grace to smile.
    What think you of this page, my lord?
  DUKE   I think the boy hath grace in him. He blushes.
  VALENTINE   I warrant you, my lord, more grace than boy.[1]
  DUKE   What mean you by that saying?
165 VALENTINE   Please you, I'll tell you as we pass along,
    That you will wonder° what hath fortunèd.°   *marvel at / happened*
    Come, Proteus, 'tis your penance but to hear
    The story of your loves discoverèd.°   *revealed*
    That done, our day of marriage shall be yours,
170 One feast, one house, one mutual happiness.   *Exeunt*

---

8. Probably another slip for "Milan."
9. Argue (that there is) a new situation created by your
unparalleled merit.

1. He has more feminine charm ("grace") than male
gender (that is, "he" is really a girl).

The Taming of the Shrew

One of Shakespeare's first comedies—probably written in 1592 or earlier—*The Taming of the Shrew* is also one of his most controversial, focusing as it does on the battle between the sexes and on the process by which a strong-willed woman is made to submit to the control of her husband. In actuality, the play is more complex than such a bald description indicates. An early example of Shakespeare's extraordinary theatrical craftsmanship, it consists of two interwoven plots and a frame tale. This complex structure allows for contrasts and parallels in the development of the play's main themes, complicating how the audience thinks about the drama's examination of the relationship between the sexes and the possibility that people can change their social identities either as a result of choice or of coercion. Perhaps not surprisingly, the play has elicited wildly varying reactions from generations of readers, audiences, and theater practitioners.

In the frame story, a poor tinker, Christopher Sly, is made to believe that he is a nobleman with servants, a wife, fine food, and even erotic artwork at his command. This hoax, shown in the play's first two scenes (called Inductions), is engineered by a real Lord who has found Sly drunk and asleep outside a tavern. The Lord's trick leads to many jokes at Sly's expense. While the tinker likes playing the part of a nobleman, he doesn't do it very well. His language, especially, betrays him. For example, Sly doesn't know how to address a lady, anxiously inquiring of his servants what to call his elegant spouse and settling on the absurd title "Madam wife." The hilarity of this scene is compounded by the fact that Sly's "wife" is really the Lord's page, Bartholomew, dressed up to impersonate a woman. Sly thus mistakes the sex of the person he would take to bed. He is also ignorant of the tastes and customs of the nobility, asking for cheap ale when he should call for sack, the sweet wine favored by gentlemen.

While these blunders make Sly an object of humor, he is also the figure for whose viewing pleasure the main play's two central plots unroll. As a temporary lord, Sly has a troupe of actors to entertain him. At least until he falls asleep, Sly watches them enact a comedy about courtship and marriage in which the primary plot involves a strong-willed woman, Katherine Minola, who is "tamed" by a fortune-seeking suitor named Petruccio. In the other plot, Kate's seemingly demure sister, Bianca, is pursued by three adoring suitors and eventually elopes with one of them without her father's knowledge or consent. All three actions are united by themes of disguise and transformation. Snatched from the mud and given the clothes and the privileges of a lord, Sly is temporarily translated from one social class and identity to another, even though his behavior and the snickers of his "attendants" repeatedly remind the audience that he is not *really* a nobleman. In their pursuit of Bianca, several of her suitors also don disguises. One, Hortensio, poses as a teacher of music and mathematics; another, Lucentio, pretends to be Cambio, a language instructor; meanwhile, Lucentio's servant, Tranio, assumes his master's identity and in that disguise poses as yet another of Bianca's many admirers. Love makes men willing to transform themselves, although in this plot these changes are volitional and reversible. When the disguised gentlemen tire of acting as scholars-for-hire, they simply reclaim their houses, fortunes, and social positions and demote their servants.

In the main plot, more subtle questions of disguise arise. Petruccio, to teach Katherine that she must obey him, acts the part of "shrew tamer," a role in which he appears at his own wedding in outlandish and ragged clothes and, during a sojourn at his country house, turns the world on its head by denying Kate sleep, food, and any exercise of her own will. But if his servant Grumio is to be believed, this may not simply be a one-time disguise. Hearing of his master's plan to wed the rich and shrewish Katherine, Grumio says:

> O' my word, an she knew him as well as I do she would think scolding would do little good upon him. She may perhaps call him half a score knaves or so. Why, that's nothing; an he begin once he'll rail in his rope-tricks. I'll tell you what, sir, an she stand him but a little he will throw a figure in her face and so disfigure her with it that she shall have no more eyes to see withal than a cat. You know him not, sir.
> (1.2.104–10)

Grumio's words raise doubts about Petruccio's "real" nature. Is he temporarily adopting the role of a shrew tamer and verbal bully, or is that his customary mode of being or a role that he has previously adopted in dealing with servants and other social inferiors? And as Petruccio attempts to transform Kate from shrew to obedient spouse, new questions arise: is he forcing her to deform her nature or helping her experiment with a role that might bring out untapped aspects of her personality or lead to greater control of her social environment? Is there, in fact, anything like a "real self," or is personhood a succession of social roles adopted because of coercion, social expectations, material circumstances, or the drive for social mastery?

The multiple instances of disguise and transformation in the three plots certainly invite reflection on the sources of and possibilities for change both in people's behavior and in their social circumstances. From the play one might, for example, conclude that lords and gentlemen can play with their social roles with more success and less risk than can tinkers. Sly's transformation is thrust upon him; but his lack of wealth and education would in any case make it impossible for him to "pass" as nobility without the complicity of the Lord who found him asleep outside the tavern. His transformation is precarious, a mere dream from which he will have to awaken, no matter how much he might want to live on in his new circumstances. But for Lucentio, his role as a Latin master is nothing *but* a temporary stratagem, a part that his education allows him to play to perfection but that his social rank permits him to cast aside when he has won his bride. Similarly, the social fact of gender sets different limits on possible presentations and transformations of self. Petruccio's outrageous behavior—striking his servants and starving his wife—makes him admired by other men. Hortensio, for example, one of Bianca's suitors who eventually marries a wealthy widow, decides to model himself after Petruccio and to take lessons from him on how to tame a wife. But what is deemed to be Kate's outrageous behavior—striking a sister and defying a father and would-be husband—elicits only scorn and condemnation. Like class, gender limits one's permissible or possible range of action and the transformations of self one can effect. Unless she is willing to endure severe privation and penalties, Kate can only undergo one kind of transformation—toward greater docility and subservience to her husband. In such circumstances, it is difficult to determine—as many critics wish to do—whether Katherine finds her "real" self through her encounters with Petruccio. Like many characters in the play, she can only improvise a self in relation to the social constraints and possibilities available to her, and the constraints operating upon a tinker or a woman are very different from those affecting a university-educated gentleman or a lord.

The social hierarchies that shape the possibilities for personal transformations are, in the Sly frame tale, given a peculiarly English inflection. The Sly episodes refer repeatedly to the Warwickshire countryside that was Shakespeare's own birthplace. Sly mentions Greet, an actual village near Stratford, and Burton Heath (possibly Barton-on-the-Heath, another village close to Stratford), and the men enumerated as his tavern companions—Stephen Sly, John Naps, Peter Turf, and Henry Pimpernel—for the most part have homely English names. Moreover, the contrast between Sly and the Lord who carries him to his house mirrors the gap in sixteenth-century rural England between poor laborers, barely making a living at a succession of marginal jobs, and wealthy landowners. As arable and common land was fenced in or enclosed to increase the opportunities for grazing sheep, many landowners made huge profits, wool being one of England's most important exports. But enclosures, a number of which occurred in the Stratford region, also caused hardship for small tenant farmers forced off the enclosed land and, in some cases, driven into vagrancy.

Sly, simply called "Beggar" in the speech prefixes in the First Folio, is a poor man with a checkered employment history. He describes himself as "old Sly's son of Burton Heath, by birth a pedlar, by education a cardmaker, by transmutation a bearherd, and now by present profession a tinker" (Induction 2.17–19). A cardmaker makes the metal combs used to prepare wool for spinning; thus Sly has had some tangential involvement with the wool industry, although he seems primarily to have led an itinerant life mending pots, selling cheap goods from a pedlar's pack, and running up whatever tab he could at the local tavern. The Induction reveals the enormous gap in wealth and education separating this man from the leisured aristocrats who pick him up on the way home from hunting and use him for their evening's sport. The trick they play upon him is a fantastic one, but the details of the Lord's privilege and Sly's drunken poverty are evoked with vivid realism. For such a man as Sly, what hope is there of becoming a Lord?

By contrast, Bianca and her suitors exist in an Italian setting at many removes from Sly's English-countryside milieu. The events in this story line are drawn directly from George Gascoigne's *Supposes* (1566), itself an adaption of a work by Ariosto, *I Suppositi,* which employs the disguised identities, clever servants, and gullible fathers found in classical comedy. Wealth is also a crucial factor in this plot, for despite his speeches about the necessity for suitors to gain his daughters' love, Baptista is willing to give them to their wealthiest wooers. The suitors' money comes mostly from trade. Bianca's suitors testify to the number of ships they have at sea and to the luxury goods and property they have acquired through their ventures. In this world of prosperous urban merchants, Baptista can indulge his daughters with some training in the arts and languages, but he still expects to control their marriage choices. Kate he delivers to the frankly fortune-hunting Petruccio, but he ultimately has less luck with his supposedly compliant daughter, Bianca, whose name, meaning "white," implies her virtue and purity. Bianca not only elopes, but, in the play's final banquet scene, she refuses to come when her new husband summons her, suggesting that her earlier docility may have been a calculated pose. If her sister is gradually tamed, Bianca ultimately reveals her own considerable capacity to play the shrew, her education and social position having given her the wherewithal to manipulate the courtship process to her own advantage.

It is against this backdrop that the particular features of the main plot become apparent. The relationship between Kate and Petruccio has long been regarded as the play's most riveting story line. In fact, in the eighteenth century, the famous actor David Garrick produced a shortened version of the play simply called *Catharine and Petruchio,* which cut the Bianca plot and held the stage for nearly one hundred years. The interest in Kate and Petruccio is understandable, for Shakespeare created for them a story of taming at once enjoyable and deeply troubling. Though set in Italy, this plot line feels English, connected in subterranean ways to the world of Christopher Sly. For one thing, Petruccio is not just a creature of the city; he has a farmhouse that serves as this play's "green world," or place of transformations. Moreover, Petruccio is distinguished in many ways from the other Italian suitors. He has, for example, a sullen and quarrelsome servant, Grumio, in every respect the antithesis of the clever attendants, Tranio and Biondello, who help Lucentio win Bianca and, in fact, seem to do most of their master's thinking and plotting for him. This may be a kind of affectionate joke made at the expense of English domestic servants, who, despite their crude ways, at least aren't shown as mastering their masters. Moreover, while Hortensio, Gremio, and Lucentio woo Bianca with song and poetry, Petruccio woos Kate by contradicting her every word and taming her, like a hawk, by making her go hungry and sleepless. The language of

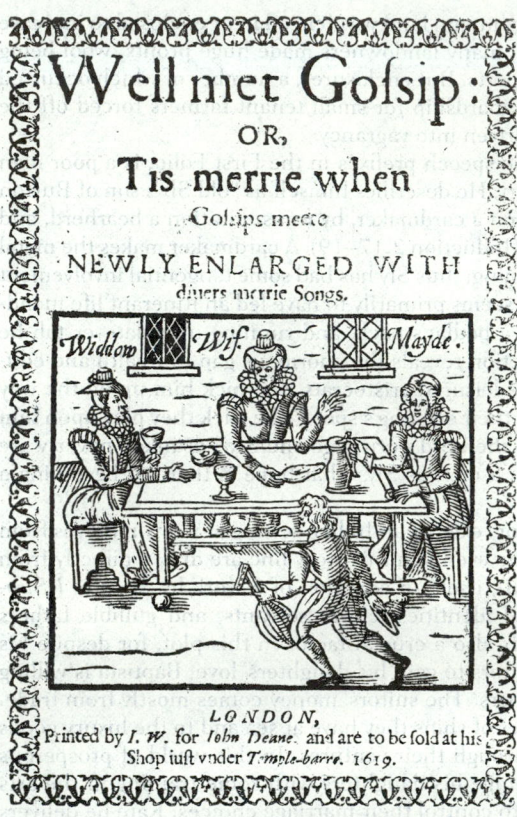

"Gadding." Title page of Samuel Rowlands, *Tis Merrie When Gossips Meete* (1619).

blood sport permeates both the Induction and the Petruccio scenes. The Lord who picks up Sly has just returned from hunting and speaks knowledgeably about the abilities of each of his hounds; Petruccio repeatedly compares the taming of a wife to the transformation of a wild hawk into a docile hunting falcon, aligning wife taming with other manly English sports.

Finally, of course, the source for the Petruccio-Kate plot is not an Italian comedy, as in the Bianca-Lucentio plot, but a folk story about taming a difficult wife, variants of which circulated throughout northern Europe in Shakespeare's day, including the vicious English ballad entitled "A Merry Jest of a Shrewd and Curst Wife Lapped in Morel's Skin for Her Good Behavior." In this ballad, a strong-willed wife is beaten bloody by her husband and then wrapped inside the salted skin of a dead horse named Morel. This mode of taming is more physically brutal than that employed by Petruccio, but both the play and the ballad assume that a husband can use extreme means to curb the will of a forward wife.

Despite his Italian name, then, Petruccio is in many ways an Englishman; and the play implicitly suggests that unlike his Italian counterpart, the true Englishman defines his manhood through the firm and, if necessary, cruel mastery of wife and servant. By contrast, the less assertive Lucentio takes direction from his servant, supplicates his betrothed on bended knee, and ends up with a wife he cannot master. Petruccio's bluff manliness constituted one of the period's privileged versions of English masculinity. In some respects he resembles the English military hero Talbot in *1 Henry VI,* a history play that Shakespeare had a hand in writing probably sometime not long after he composed *The Taming of the Shrew.* Petruccio also anticipates Shakespeare's portrait of England's great warrior king Henry V, the protagonist in a series of history plays that Shakespeare penned in the second half of the 1590s. Outspoken, commanding in battle or brawl, and adept at the blunt rhetorical and physical mastery of women, each of these male heroes in his own way helped define what distinguished a proper Englishman from what was French, Italian, or simply foreign.

This subtle Englishing of Kate and Petruccio may have heightened the original audience's interest in and even identification with them, as the play implicitly pits virile English wooing and wedding against the sophisticated ineffectiveness of Italian practices. Men and women, however, may not have been equally drawn to what they witnessed. In the wake of the modern women's movement, certainly, the very idea of "taming" a woman and curbing her tongue have seemed offensive to many readers and viewers. In *Taming of the Shrew,* language is a vehicle for domination. Sly cannot effectively play

Cucking stool, used to discipline scolds, shrews, and witches. From T. N. Brushfield, *Chester Archaeological and Historic Society Journal* (1855–62).

a lord because he has not mastered the language of the elite. Kate can be eloquent, but because of her gender her verbal independence is read by her father and suitors as a sign of shrewishness. In part, Petruccio tames Kate's tart tongue by aggressive use of his own. A clear sign that he has succeeded occurs in 4.6, when, at her husband's behest, Kate calls the sun the moon and an old man a budding virgin. Her words at this point no longer express her own perceptions but her husband's blatantly willful reading of reality. In the play's last scene, she also makes a lengthy speech about a wife's duty to obey her husband that conforms to the patriarchal ideology of the day and her husband's wishes but is disturbingly far from her earlier expression of women's right to independent speech and thought. Some directors have found this curbing of the female tongue and will so intolerable that they have made production choices that downplay the extent of Kate's submission to Petruccio or that mitigate the linguistic coercion and physical cruelty that are part of his taming methods. For example, in many productions, Kate delivers her last speech about wifely duty while signaling, by winks and gestures, that she does not really believe it, or the director omits the lines in which Kate offers to put her hand beneath her husband's foot as a token of submission. Such choices signal a desire to "save" Shakespeare from accusations that his play celebrates a crude form of male dominance.

Even in Shakespeare's own day, it is not clear that everyone, including men, would have found Petruccio's behavior entirely laudable. The proper relationship between husband and wife was a matter of discussion and debate. Many Protestant preachers enjoined husbands to use no violence against their wives and to treat them as spiritual equals and domestic helpmeets. They lauded marriage not merely as an economic arrangement but as a union demanding mutual affection and respect from both parties. At the same time, few disputed that in the last analysis husbands were masters of their wives and that the household was "a little commonwealth," a realm in which the husband's supremacy over wife and children mirrored the supremacy of the monarch over his subjects. Disorder in the domestic realm was treated as a serious matter, intimating the possibility of a breakdown of order and hierarchy in the culture at large.

Strong-willed women were particularly apt to be labeled as disorderly in early modern towns and villages, even if their "crimes" involved nothing more than talkativeness.

Husband dominator. From a German playing card by Peter Flötner (1520).

A shrew, in fact, was commonly defined as a woman with a wagging tongue who, partly because of her garrulousness, was not properly submissive to her husband. The ideal wife, by contrast, was chaste, silent, and obedient. The talkativeness that could mark a woman as a shrew could also be interpreted as a sign of her sexual promiscuity, on the theory that one kind of looseness leads to another. Women deemed unruly were subject to various kinds of punishment. These could include being "cucked"—ducked into water on a "cucking stool"—or being fitted with a scold's bridle, a torturous harness that fitted around a woman's head with a metal bit that went into her mouth and prevented her from speaking and sometimes caused her to gag and her mouth to bleed or her teeth to be knocked loose. The husbands of disorderly and aggressive women could also be punished for failure to control their wives. Charivaris, or "rough ridings," were shaming rituals in which neighbors came to the house of a disorderly woman and made her or her husband ride backward through the town on a horse while bystanders shouted and played cacophonous music. This signaled that the world had been turned upside down and rendered inharmonious by her disorderliness and his inability to control his wife.

In *The Taming of the Shrew,* no man is submitted to a "rough riding" even though at the end of the play both Lucentio and Hortensio seem to have lost control of their wives. Instead, all the attention focuses on the taming of Kate and on the strategies employed by Petruccio to make her compliant with his will. On the eighteenth- and nineteenth-century stage, Petruccio often carried a whip, symbol of his power to control his wife and servants with physical force. Whether or not he *literally* carries a whip, Petruccio employs coercion—verbal, psychological, and physical—to control his wife, subjecting her to public humiliation and private deprivation in order to teach her proper submissiveness to the authority of her husband. In so doing, he reinforces the hierarchical principle upon which the entire Elizabethan social order was premised, warning not only unruly men but also servants and beggars that, except in jest, they cannot usurp the places of their masters. But is this account of *The Taming of the Shrew* adequate? Is the play as fiercely repressive as some critics assume? It is precisely on this point that readers, critics, and actors differ.

Some critics, for example, emphasize how Shakespeare mitigates the violence of many versions of the folktale on which the main plot is modeled. Kate is not, for example, beaten and wrapped in a salted horsehide, nor does Petruccio force her to sleep with him before their return to Padua. In his farmhouse, he keeps her awake by disordering the bed and talking at her, but only after their return to the relative safety and familiarity of her father's house does he speak of his intention to "bed" her. In short, sexual conquest does not seem to be part of his taming practices. Perhaps more importantly, many actors, audiences, and critics have seen in Kate and Petruccio's relationship an attractive mutuality and vitality they find difficult to reconcile with the idea that the play is simply a lesson in how to subordinate a woman. For example, when Petruccio first woos Kate in 2.1, the two of them engage in a verbal sparring match dazzling in its complexity and speed. Puns and insults fly back and forth, with Kate giving as good as she gets. The following exchange is typical:

PETRUCCIO   Come, come, you wasp, i'faith you are too angry.
KATHERINE   If I be waspish, best beware my sting.
PETRUCCIO   My remedy is then to pluck it out.
KATHERINE   Ay, if the fool could find it where it lies.
PETRUCCIO   Who knows not where a wasp does wear his sting?
        In his tail.
KATHERINE   In his tongue.
PETRUCCIO   Whose tongue?
KATHERINE   Yours, if you talk of tales, and so farewell.
PETRUCCIO   What, with my tongue in your tail? Nay, come again,
        Good Kate, I am a gentleman.
KATHERINE   That I'll try.
        She strikes him
PETRUCCIO   I swear I'll cuff you if you strike again.

(2.1.207–16)

This is a beautifully orchestrated encounter, with Kate and Petruccio trading rapid-fire, one-line insults and deftly topping one another's puns. Their exchange has erotic intensity. These two are taking one another's measure, listening intently, struggling for advantage. Petruccio is not above talking dirty, and Katherine is not above making physical contact, albeit with a blow and not a caress. This is light years away from the vapid wooing of Lucentio and Bianca, hiding behind the screen of school Latin. On the stage, something vital and alive goes on between Katherine and Petruccio, and they have often been compared with Shakespeare's other witty couples, such as Benedick and Beatrice in *Much Ado About Nothing*, iconoclasts who seem more real and finally better and more equally matched than the more conventional couples with whom they are contrasted. Many critics, in fact, have argued that the real love story of the play belongs to Kate and Petruccio, and that his taming of her is merely a way of showing her the advantages of outwardly conforming to society's expectations so that she can have the husband, the home, and the social approval she surely must crave. Many argue that it is Kate's spirit that attracts Petruccio and that her spirit is never broken, just redirected, as in the final scene when Kate takes out her aggressions not against her husband but against the other wives, whom she lectures on their marriage duties.

The debate about how to interpret *The Taming of the Shrew* will surely continue. In performance, directors and actors sometimes emphasize the drama's playful and farcical elements, sometimes its dark, violent, and repressive potential. Critics and readers remain similarly divided as to what they see in this tale of woman tamed. Most agree, however, that *The Taming of the Shrew* deals with issues that deserve the thoughtful and sometimes heated critical debate the play has engendered. For example, while Kate's taming does not involve the kinds of physical brutality in the "Merry Jest" ballad, it is nonetheless true that in Petruccio's farmhouse Kate is deprived of sleep, food, and the protection of family and female companionship—techniques akin to modern methods of torture and brainwashing. As Kate says, she is "starved for meat, giddy for lack of sleep, / With oaths kept waking and with brawling fed" (4.3.9–10). This is horrifying, even if the horror is mitigated by the laughter-inducing techniques of knockabout farce. Grumio makes the audience laugh as he tantalizes Kate with one kind of food and then another, while ultimately withholding them all, but this does not erase the fact that Kate is hungry and that her hunger is used to starve her into complying with Petruccio's wishes. There is similar cruelty lurking behind the trick played on Sly in the Induction. The beggar is tantalized with the prospect of riches he can never retain. *The Taming of the Shrew* makes a joke out of the enormous gap between the poverty of a tinker and the privilege of a lord, comedy from the physical and psychic trials that lie in wait for a strong-willed woman.

It is perhaps appropriate to conclude by focusing again on the role of Sly. As he watches the play the actors perform for him, he at first makes comments on the action, but these stop after the first act, and he presumably falls asleep on stage. In another contemporary play, however, called *The Taming of a Shrew*, Sly makes interjections throughout, including a brief speech in which he vows to go home and tame his own wife, having learned from Petruccio how it is done. Scholars disagree about the relationship of *The Taming of the Shrew* and *The Taming of a Shrew*: they dispute which came first and whether Shakespeare had a hand in both (for a fuller discussion, see the Textual Note). Among the many differences between the two texts, however, is Sly's continuing stage prominence right to the end of *The Taming of a Shrew* and his final assertion that

> I'll to my
> Wife presently and tame her too,
> An if she anger me.
> (Additional Passages E.19–21)

No one knows for certain if Shakespeare wrote these lines or why they don't appear in *The Taming of the Shrew*. Like almost everything else connected to this play, they are subject to various interpretations. Perhaps because they are put in Sly's mouth they are discredited, taken as another example of the reductiveness of his responses to the pastimes of the cultural elite—in this case, to the play staged in the Lord's house by the traveling players. Maybe *only* a tinker would take this as the "message" of the play. On the other hand, perhaps Sly's response to what he has just watched indicates why this vital and attractive play seems to many readers to traffic in dangerous matters and to be easily used to justify the crudest kinds of male tyranny. It is a little disconcerting that *even* a downtrodden tinker can find comfort in the thought that while he is neither a lord nor a gentleman, he shares with them the same right to tame his wife "an if she anger me." Impoverished and ridiculed, Sly nonetheless feels entitled by virtue of his gender to dominate his spouse, perhaps thereby compensating for his powerlessness in other areas. In short, there is always something lower than a beggar—a beggar's wife. The play published in the First Folio omits Sly's speech, but in our day *The Taming of the Shrew* nonetheless remains, along with *The Merchant of Venice*, one of Shakespeare's most controversial plays: a spur to thought and to debate, a reminder of the serious matters that often lie at the heart of Shakespeare's "festive" comedies.

JEAN E. HOWARD

TEXTUAL NOTE

The Taming of the Shrew was first printed in the 1623 First Folio (F), the control text for this edition. Certain features of the text indicate that it was set from Shakespeare's "foul papers," or perhaps a scribal copy of them, rather than from a theatrical promptbook. Stage directions, exits, and entrances are not handled with the precision customary for a text that would have been used as the basis for an actual performance.

The greatest mystery surrounding the text is its relationship to another play, *The Taming of a Shrew*, entered in the Stationers' Register on May 2, 1594, and published the same year. This play bears many resemblances to Shakespeare's, and for years scholars have debated which preceded the other or whether, in fact, they both derived from a common original, now lost. Many editors have assumed that Shakespeare's play was the source for *The Taming of a Shrew*, though the subplots, in particular, differ substantially; and an interesting argument has been advanced by Leah Marcus that *A Shrew* is earlier than *The Shrew*, that it is at least partly by Shakespeare, and that, in her view, it inscribes an older version of patriarchy than that evident in *The Shrew*. Whatever one decides about order of composition, it is significant that *A Shrew* contains a number of passages involving Christopher Sly not found in *The Shrew*, passages in which Sly continues to comment on the play he watches and finally wakes from his "dream" announcing his intention to go home and tame his own wife. No one knows why these passages appear in one play and not the other. One possibility is that they were written by Shakespeare but for some reason deleted by him or by someone else from the manuscript that served as the basis for the Folio edition of the play, or were added by him at a date later than the composition of that manuscript. For their intrinsic interest, and because of their possible Shakespearean origin, these materials concerning Sly are printed at the end of this edition of *The Shrew* as Additional Passages.

The Oxford editors believe, on balance, that *A Shrew* imitates and is later than *The Shrew*, and this assumption affects their dating of Shakespeare's play, which would have to have been written before 1594, when *A Shrew* was published and designated as belonging to Pembroke's Men, a company that went bankrupt in 1593 and so must have had the play in their repertoire before that time. In addition, a stage direction in *A Shrew* refers to "Simon," who has been plausibly identified as Simon Jewell, an actor who was buried on August 21, 1592. This circumstantial evidence, along with stylistic features that mark the play as an early example of Shakespeare's art, suggests a date of composition of 1592 or earlier.

The Folio text of *The Taming of the Shrew* bears some marks of confusion or incomplete revision in the subplot, particularly in the handling of the character of Hortensio. Shakespeare may have decided rather late to make him one of Bianca's wooers. He is, for example, not included in the "bidding" for Bianca in which Tranio (disguised as Lucentio) and Gremio engage in 2.1. Other anomalies regarding his part are mentioned in the notes to this text, but in performance these issues seldom bother audiences.

In two instances, the present edition marks new scenes where most contemporary editions do not. The first is 3.3, which follows Petruccio's arrival in disheveled dress for his wedding. During this prenuptial scene, Lucentio has no speaking part, and there is no requirement that he be onstage. Consequently, the Oxford editors mark a new scene, 3.3, after everyone exits to attend the wedding and Lucentio comes onstage speaking with Tranio about Bianca before Gremio returns at 3.3.21 to describe the offstage wedding. Another new scene is marked after 4.4—that is, after the episode in which the Pedant, posing as Lucentio's father, meets Baptista and negotiates the marriage of Bianca and Lucentio. This edition makes a separate scene of the ensuing conversation between Biondello and Lucentio in which Biondello explains how Lucentio can elope with Bianca. This change is justified both because the stage has just been cleared before Lucentio's and Biondello's entry and also because there is plausibly a time gap between the two events. In addition, 4.4 shows signs of revision on Shakespeare's part, including indecision about whether or not to include Lucentio in that scene. Making Lucentio and Biondello's conversation a separate scene clarifies the different foci of the two episodes: the first concentrating on Tranio and the Pedant's tricking of Baptista, the second on Biondello's plans for Lucentio to elope.

SELECTED BIBLIOGRAPHY

Aspinall, Dana E., ed. *The Taming of the Shrew: Critical Essays*. New York: Routledge, 2002. A broad selection of twentieth-century critical essays about the play plus reviews of notable film, television, and stage versions.

Boose, Lynda. "Scolding Brides and Bridling Scolds: Taming the Woman's Unruly Member." *Shakespeare Quarterly* 42 (1991): 179–213. Draws on the research of nineteenth-century scholars to recover the early modern punishments, including iron gags and ducking stools, used against women accused of being shrews or scolds.

Haring-Smith, Tori. *From Farce to Metadrama: A Stage History of "The Taming of the Shrew," 1594–1983*. Westport, Conn.: Greenwood Press, 1985. A comprehensive stage history of the play and of some major adaptations from the late 1590s to the early 1980s.

Huston, J. Dennis. "Enter the Hero: The Power of Play in *The Taming of the Shrew.*" *Shakespeare's Comedies of Play.* New York: Columbia University Press, 1981. 58–93. Argues that Shakespeare playfully experiments with comic form in *The Taming of the Shrew* and creates a hero, Petruccio, who teaches Kate how to play with social roles in order to gain control over her environment.

Korda, Natasha. "Household Kates: Domesticating Commodities in *The Taming of the Shrew.*" *Shakespeare's Domestic Economies: Gender and Property in Early Modern England.* Philadelphia: University of Pennsylvania Press, 2002. 52–75. Explores the play as part of an historical shift that made women managers of domestic property and suggests that in taming Kate, Petruccio educates her about the proper management and consumption of household goods.

Marcus, Leah. "The Shakespearean Editor as Shrew-Tamer." *English Literary Renaissance* 22 (1992): 177–200. Examines and queries the historical process by which *The Taming of a Shrew* came to be regarded, not as a source for Shakespeare's *The Taming of the Shrew*, but as a debased derivative of it.

Newman, Karen. "Renaissance Family Politics and Shakespeare's *Taming of the Shrew.*" *Fashioning Femininity and English Renaissance Drama.* Chicago: University of Chicago Press, 1991. 33–50. Argues that Kate's linguistic freedom constitutes her main threat to male authority and that that freedom is never completely curtailed.

Orlin, Lena Cowen. "The Performance of Things in *The Taming of the Shrew.*" *Yearbook of English Studies* 23 (1993): 167–88. Notes the abundance of objects, especially household objects, in *The Taming of the Shrew* and analyzes their functions.

Smith, Amy L. "Performing Marriage with a Difference: Wooing, Wedding, and Bedding in *The Taming of the Shrew.*" *Comparative Drama* 36 (2002): 289–320. Uses Judith Butler's theories of performativity to argue that within Kate and Petruccio's self-conscious performance of courtship and marriage lies the potential for a critical reworking of gender norms, rather than outright submission to or resistance of them.

Walker, Kim. "Wrangling Pedantry: Education in *The Taming of the Shrew.*" *Shakespeare Matters: History, Teaching, Performance.* Ed. Lloyd Davis. Newark: University of Delaware Press, 2003. 191–208. Examines the importance of women's education in the play and in several adaptations of it and suggests that humanist education plays a role in Bianca's transformation into a shrew.

FILMS

The Taming of the Shrew. 1929. Dir. Samuel Taylor. USA. 63 min. One of the first "talkies," this black-and-white film, starring Douglas Fairbanks as Petruccio and Mary Pickford as Katherine, ends with Pickford's famous "wink" at the conclusion of her speech of submission.

Kiss Me Kate. 1953. Dir. George Sidney. USA. 109 min. Film version of the Cole Porter musical starring Howard Keel and Kathryn Grayson in which a group of actors is shown performing Shakespeare's play, the events of which mirror their own circumstances. Songs include "Brush Up Your Shakespeare" and "Where Is the Life That Late I Led?"

The Taming of the Shrew. 1967. Dir. Franco Zeffirelli. Italy/USA. 122 min. Broad-comedy performance starring the real-life couple of Elizabeth Taylor and Richard Burton as Katherine and Petruccio.

The Taming of the Shrew. 1980. Dir. Jonathan Miller. UK. 127 min. Intelligent BBC-TV version starring John Cleese as Petruccio and Sarah Badel as Katherine with sets modeled on Vermeer interiors.

10 Things I Hate About You. 1999. Dir. Gil Juner. USA. 97 min. Loose adaptation of Shakespeare's plot in which Julia Stiles plays a headstrong character, Kat Stratford, who comes to an accommodation with bad boy Heath Ledger as Patrick Verona.

The Taming of the Shrew

THE PERSONS OF THE PLAY

In the Induction

CHRISTOPHER SLY, beggar and tinker
A HOSTESS
A LORD
BARTHOLOMEW, his page
HUNTSMEN
SERVANTS
PLAYERS

In the play-within-the-play

BAPTISTA Minola, a gentleman of Padua
KATHERINE, his elder daughter
BIANCA, his younger daughter
PETRUCCIO, a gentleman of Verona, suitor of Katherine
GRUMIO $\Big\}$ his servants
CURTIS
GREMIO, a rich old man of Padua, suitor of Bianca
HORTENSIO, another suitor, who disguises himself as Licio, a teacher
LUCENTIO, from Pisa, who disguises himself as Cambio, a teacher
TRANIO $\Big\}$ his servants
BIONDELLO
VINCENTIO, Lucentio's father
A PEDANT (schoolmaster), from Mantua
A WIDOW
A TAILOR
A HABERDASHER
An OFFICER
SERVINGMEN, including NATHANIEL, PHILIP, JOSEPH, and PETER
Other servants of Baptista and Petruccio

Induction 1

Enter CHRISTOPHER SLY *[the] beggar, and [the]* HOSTESS

SLY   I'll feeze you,° in faith.   *fix you; beat you*

HOSTESS   A pair of stocks,[1] you rogue.

SLY   You're a baggage.° The Slys are no rogues. Look in the   *whore*
Chronicles[2]—we came in with Richard Conqueror,[3] therefore
5   *paucas palabras*,[4] let the world slide.° Sessa![5]   *go by*

Induction 1 Location: In front of a country tavern.
1. A threat to have him put in the stocks (an instrument of public punishment consisting of two wooden planks with semicircles carved into them; the criminal sat with his or her feet clamped between the planks).
2. Histories, especially histories of England such as

Raphael Holinshed's *Chronicles of England, Scotland, and Ireland* (2nd ed., 1587).
3. A blunder for "William the Conqueror," who took the English throne in 1066.
4. Misquoting *pocas palabras*, Spanish for "few words," a phrase from Thomas Kyd's *Spanish Tragedy* (c. 1587).
5. Probably equivalent to "Be quiet."

HOSTESS You will not pay for the glasses you have burst?

SLY No, not a denier. Go by, Saint Jeronimy![6] Go to thy cold
bed and warm thee.

HOSTESS I know my remedy, I must go fetch the headborough.°   *constable*
[*Exit*]

10 SLY Third or fourth or fifth borough, I'll answer him by law. I'll
not budge an inch, boy.[7] Let him come, and kindly.°   *and welcome! (ironic)*
[*He*] *falls asleep.*
Wind horns.° *Enter a* LORD *from hunting, with his train*   *Horns sound*

LORD Huntsman, I charge thee, tender well° my hounds.   *care well for*
Breathe Merriman[8]—the poor cur is embossed°—   *exhausted*
And couple Clowder with the deep-mouthed brach.[9]

15 Saw'st thou not, boy, how Silver made it good
At the hedge corner, in the coldest fault?[1]
I would not lose the dog for twenty pound.

FIRST HUNTSMAN Why, Belman is as good as he, my lord.
He cried upon it at the merest loss,[2]

20 And twice today picked out the dullest scent.
Trust me, I take him for the better dog.

LORD Thou art a fool. If Echo were as fleet
I would esteem him worth a dozen such.
But sup° them well, and look unto them all.   *feed*

25 Tomorrow I intend to hunt again.

FIRST HUNTSMAN I will, my lord.

LORD [*seeing* SLY] What's here? One dead, or drunk? See, doth he breathe?

SECOND HUNTSMAN He breathes, my lord. Were he not warmed with ale
This were a bed but cold to sleep so soundly.

30 LORD O monstrous beast! How like a swine he lies.
Grim death, how foul and loathsome is thine image.[3]
Sirs, I will practise° on this drunken man.   *play a trick on*
What think you: if he were conveyed to bed,
Wrapped in sweet° clothes, rings put upon his fingers,   *scented*

35 A most delicious banquet by his bed,
And brave° attendants near him when he wakes—   *finely dressed*
Would not the beggar then forget himself?

FIRST HUNTSMAN Believe me, lord, I think he cannot choose.°   *do otherwise*

SECOND HUNTSMAN It would seem strange unto him when he waked.

40 LORD Even as a flatt'ring° dream or worthless fancy.   *pleasing*
Then take him up, and manage well the jest.
Carry him gently to my fairest chamber,
And hang it round with all my wanton pictures.°   *erotic artworks*
Balm° his foul head in warm distillèd waters,   *Anoint*

45 And burn sweet wood to make the lodging sweet.[4]

---

6. Misquoting a popular line—"Hieronimo, beware! go by, go by!"—from Kyd's *Spanish Tragedy* and confusing Hieronimo, Kyd's hero, with Saint Jerome. *denier*: French coin of little value.
7. Term of abuse applicable to either sex.
8. Give Merriman time to recover his breath.
9. And put Clowder on a leash with the female hound ("brach") who bays deeply.
1. When the scent was faintest.
2. When the scent had been completely lost.
3. Your likeness (invoking the common comparison between sleep and death).
4. Aromatic woods like juniper were often burned to make a room smell fragrant.

Procure me music ready when he wakes
To make a dulcet° and a heavenly sound,   *melodious*
And if he chance to speak be ready straight,°   *at once*
And with a low submissive reverence°   *deep bow*
50   Say 'What is it your honour will command?'
Let one attend him with a silver basin
Full of rose-water and bestrewed with flowers;
Another bear the ewer,° the third a diaper,°   *water jug / towel*
And say 'Will't please your lordship cool your hands?'
55   Someone be ready with a costly suit,
And ask him what apparel he will wear.
Another tell him of his hounds and horse,
And that his lady mourns at his disease.
Persuade him that he hath been lunatic,
60   And when he says he is,° say that he dreams,   *is indeed mad*
For he is nothing but a mighty lord.
This do, and do it kindly,° gentle sirs.   *naturally; fittingly*
It will be pastime passing° excellent,   *exceedingly*
If it be husbanded with modesty.°   *prudently managed*
65 FIRST HUNTSMAN   My lord, I warrant you we will play our part
As he shall think by our true diligence
He is no less than what we say he is.
  LORD   Take him up gently, and to bed with him;
And each one to his office° when he wakes.   *assigned role*

                     [SERVINGMEN *carry* SLY *out*]

      Trumpets sound
70   Sirrah,[5] go see what trumpet 'tis that sounds.

                               [*Exit a* SERVINGMAN]

Belike° some noble gentleman that means,   *Perhaps*
Travelling some journey, to repose him here.

      Enter [*a*] SERVINGMAN
How now? Who is it?
  SERVINGMAN   An't° please your honour, players   *If it*
That offer service to your lordship.

      Enter PLAYERS
75 LORD   Bid them come near. Now fellows, you are welcome.
  PLAYERS   We thank your honour.
  LORD   Do you intend to stay with me tonight?
  A PLAYER   So please your lordship to accept our duty.°   *services; respect*
  LORD   With all my heart. This fellow I remember
80   Since once he played a farmer's eldest son.
'Twas where you wooed the gentlewoman so well.
I have forgot your name, but sure that part
Was aptly fitted° and naturally performed.   *well suited (to you)*
  ANOTHER PLAYER   I think 'twas Soto[6] that your honour means.
85 LORD   'Tis very true. Thou didst it excellent.
Well, you are come to me in happy time,°   *at the right time*
The rather for° I have some sport in hand   *Especially since*
Wherein your cunning° can assist me much.   *skill*

---

5. A form of address to social inferiors.
6. Possibly a reference to a character of this name in John Fletcher's *Women Pleased*. Since that play was first acted around 1620, the reference must be a late addition to Shakespeare's text or else refer to a character in an earlier play, now lost.

There is a lord will hear you play tonight;
90 But I am doubtful of your modesties°   *self-control*
Lest, over-eyeing of° his odd behaviour—   *noticing; staring at*
For yet his honour never heard a play—
You break into some merry passion,°   *fit of laughter*
And so offend him; for I tell you, sirs,
95 If you should smile he grows impatient.
A PLAYER   Fear not, my lord, we can contain ourselves
Were he the veriest antic° in the world.   *most eccentric fellow*
LORD [*to a* SERVINGMAN]   Go, sirrah, take them to the buttery[7]
And give them friendly welcome every one.
100 Let them want° nothing that my house affords.   *lack*

                    Exit one with the PLAYERS

[*To a* SERVINGMAN] Sirrah, go you to Barthol'mew, my page,
And see him dressed in all suits° like a lady.   *in every detail*
That done, conduct him to the drunkard's chamber
And call him 'madam', do him obeisance.°   *pay him respects*
105 Tell him° from me, as he will win my love,   *(Bartholomew, the page)*
He bear himself with honourable° action   *becoming*
Such as he hath observed in noble ladies
Unto their lords by them accomplishèd.°   *performed*
Such duty to the drunkard let him do
110 With soft low tongue° and lowly courtesy,   *voice*
And say 'What is't your honour will command
Wherein your lady and your humble wife
May show her duty and make known her love?'
And then with kind embracements, tempting kisses,
115 And with declining head into his bosom[8]
Bid him shed tears, as being overjoyed
To see her noble lord restored to health,
Who for this seven years hath esteemèd him°   *thought himself to be*
No better than a poor and loathsome beggar.
120 And if the boy have not a woman's gift
To rain a shower of commanded° tears,   *produced on demand*
An onion will do well for such a shift,°   *purpose*
Which, in a napkin being close conveyed,°   *secretly carried*
Shall in despite[9] enforce a watery eye.
125 See this dispatched with all the haste thou canst.
Anon° I'll give thee more instructions.   *Soon*

                    Exit a SERVINGMAN

I know the boy will well usurp° the grace,   *assume*
Voice, gait, and action of a gentlewoman.
I long to hear him call the drunkard husband,
130 And how my men will stay themselves from laughter
When they do homage to this simple peasant.
I'll in to counsel them. Haply° my presence   *Perhaps*
May well abate the over-merry spleen[1]
Which otherwise would grow into extremes.   [*Exeunt*]

---

7. Pantry, often used to store liquor as well as food.
8. And with his head bowing down into his chest.
9. In spite of an inability to cry.

1. May well lessen the impulse to laugh. Emotional outbursts, including laughter, were thought to originate in the spleen.

Induction 2

Enter aloft[1] [SLY,] the drunkard, with attendants, some
with apparel, basin, and ewer, and other appurte-
nances; and LORD

SLY   For God's sake, a pot of small ale!°   *weak, cheap ale*

FIRST SERVINGMAN   Will't please your lordship drink a cup of
    sack?°   *costly imported wine*

SECOND SERVINGMAN   Will't please your honour taste of these
    conserves?°   *candied fruits*

THIRD SERVINGMAN   What raiment will your honour wear today?

5 SLY   I am Christophero Sly. Call not me 'honour' nor 'lordship'.
    I ne'er drank sack in my life, and if you give me any conserves,
    give me conserves of beef.° Ne'er ask me what raiment I'll   *salted beef*
    wear, for I have no more doublets° than backs, no more stock-   *jackets*
    ings than legs, nor no more shoes than feet—nay, sometime
10 more feet than shoes, or such shoes as my toes look through
    the over-leather.

LORD   Heaven cease this idle humour[2] in your honour.
    O that a mighty man of such descent,
    Of such possessions and so high esteem,
15 Should be infusèd with so foul a spirit.

SLY   What, would you make me mad? Am not I Christopher
    Sly—old Sly's son of Burton Heath,[3] by birth a pedlar, by
    education a cardmaker,[4] by transmutation a bearherd,° and   *keeper of a tame bear*
    now by present profession a tinker?° Ask Marian Hacket, the   *pot mender*
20 fat alewife[5] of Wincot, if she know me not. If she say I am
    not fourteen pence on the score[6] for sheer° ale, score me up   *for nothing but*
    for the lying'st knave in Christendom. What, I am not
    bestraught;° here's—   *crazy*

THIRD SERVINGMAN   O, this it is that makes your lady mourn.

25 SECOND SERVINGMAN   O, this is it that makes your servants droop.

LORD   Hence comes it that your kindred shuns your house,
    As beaten hence by your strange lunacy.
    O noble lord, bethink thee of thy birth.
    Call home thy ancient° thoughts from banishment,   *former*
30 And banish hence these abject lowly dreams.
    Look how thy servants do attend on thee,
    Each in his office, ready at thy beck.°   *command*
    Wilt thou have music?   *Music*
               Hark, Apollo[7] plays,
    And twenty cagèd nightingales do sing.
35 Or wilt thou sleep? We'll have thee to a couch
    Softer and sweeter than the lustful bed

Induction 2 Location: A bedroom in the Lord's house.
1. Upon the gallery above the stage. Whether this long
and complex scene was in fact performed "aloft" is open
to question. At a later point (1.1.242–47), F has Sly
commenting from above on the play presented by the
traveling actors who arrive in Induction 1. If Induction 2
is played on the main stage, Sly must at some point
ascend to the gallery, or he must observe the entire play
from the side of the main stage.
2. Heaven put an end to this foolish fantasy. According
to Renaissance medical theory, humors, or bodily fluids,

determined one's disposition.
3. Possibly Barton-on-the-Heath, a village not far from
Stratford-upon-Avon.
4. Maker of metal combs used to prepare wool for
spinning.
5. Female proprietor of a tavern. Wincot is a small village near Stratford; individuals named Hacket were living there in 1591.
6. In debt. Accounts were originally kept by notching, or
"scoring," a stick, later by making marks on a wall or door.
7. Greek god of music, who played the lyre.

On purpose trimmed up for Semiramis.[8]
Say thou wilt walk, we will bestrew the ground.
Or wilt thou ride, thy horses shall be trapped,°   *fitted with adornments*
40   Their harness studded all with gold and pearl.
Dost thou love hawking? Thou hast hawks will soar
Above the morning lark. Or wilt thou hunt,
Thy hounds shall make the welkin° answer them   *sky*
And fetch shrill echoes from the hollow earth.
45   FIRST SERVINGMAN   Say thou wilt course,° thy greyhounds are as swift   *hunt hares*
As breathèd° stags, ay, fleeter than the roe.[9]   *well-exercised*
SECOND SERVINGMAN   Dost thou love pictures?[1] We will fetch thee straight
Adonis[2] painted by a running brook,
And Cytherea all in sedges° hid,   *water rushes*
50   Which seem to move and wanton° with her breath   *play amorously*
Even as the waving sedges play wi'th' wind.
LORD   We'll show thee Io[3] as she was a maid,
And how she was beguilèd and surprised,
As lively° painted as the deed was done.   *realistically*
55   THIRD SERVINGMAN   Or Daphne[4] roaming through a thorny wood,
Scratching her legs that one shall swear she bleeds,
And at that sight shall sad Apollo weep,
So workmanly° the blood and tears are drawn.   *skillfully*
LORD   Thou art a lord, and nothing but a lord.
60   Thou hast a lady far more beautiful
Than any woman in this waning age.[5]
FIRST SERVINGMAN   And till the tears that she hath shed for thee
Like envious° floods o'errun her lovely face   *spiteful*
She was the fairest creature in the world;
65   And yet° she is inferior to none.   *still*
SLY   Am I a lord, and have I such a lady?
Or do I dream? Or have I dreamed till now?
I do not sleep. I see, I hear, I speak.
I smell sweet savours,° and I feel soft things.   *odors*
70   Upon my life, I am a lord indeed,
And not a tinker, nor Christopher Sly.
Well, bring our lady hither to our sight,
And once again a pot o'th' smallest° ale.   *weakest*
SECOND SERVINGMAN   Will't please your mightiness to wash your hands?
75   O, how we joy to see your wit restored!
O that once more you knew but what you are!
These fifteen years you have been in a dream,
Or when you waked, so waked as if you slept.
SLY   These fifteen years—by my fay,° a goodly nap.   *faith*
80   But did I never speak of° all that time?   *during*

---

8. Legendary Queen of Assyria, known for her great beauty and many sexual adventures.
9. Small deer proverbial for its swiftness.
1. Probably the "wanton pictures" referred to earlier (Induction 1.43). As described in the following lines, they are conventional erotic scenes, mostly derived from Ovid's *Metamorphoses*.
2. In classical mythology, a beautiful boy whom Aphrodite (Cytherea) loved. This scene shows Aphrodite

spying on Adonis while he bathes in the brook.
3. Raped by Zeus, who concealed himself in a cloud or thick mist, she was then turned into a cow by Hera.
4. A nymph who was turned into a laurel tree as she fled from Apollo.
5. Alluding to the popular belief that the world had steadily degenerated from the perfection of paradise or the classical Golden Age.

FIRST SERVINGMAN   O yes, my lord, but very idle words,
 For though you lay here in this goodly chamber
 Yet would you say ye were beaten out of door,
 And rail upon the hostess of the house,°   *tavern*
85 And say you would present° her at the leet°   *accuse / local court*
 Because she brought stone jugs and no sealed quarts.[6]
 Sometimes you would call out for Cicely Hacket.
SLY   Ay, the woman's maid of the house.
THIRD SERVINGMAN   Why, sir, you know no house, nor no such maid,
90 Nor no such men as you have reckoned up,
 As Stephen Sly, and old John Naps of Greet,[7]
 And Peter Turf, and Henry Pimpernel,
 And twenty more such names and men as these,
 Which never were, nor no man ever saw.
95 SLY   Now Lord be thankèd for my good amends.°   *recovery*
ALL   Amen.
SLY   I thank thee. Thou shalt not lose by it.
   Enter [BARTHOLOMEW *the Page, as*] *Lady, with attendants*
BARTHOLOMEW   How fares my noble lord?
SLY   Marry,[8] I fare° well,   *get on; feed*
 For here is cheer° enough. Where is my wife?   *food*
100 BARTHOLOMEW   Here, noble lord. What is thy will with her?
SLY   Are you my wife, and will not call me husband?
 My men should call me lord. I am your goodman.[9]
BARTHOLOMEW   My husband and my lord, my lord and husband;
 I am your wife in all obedience.
SLY   I know it well. [*To the* LORD] What must I call her?
105 LORD   Madam.
SLY   Al'ce Madam or Joan Madam?[1]
LORD   Madam, and nothing else. So lords call ladies.
SLY   Madam wife, they say that I have dreamed,
 And slept above some fifteen year or more.
110 BARTHOLOMEW   Ay, and the time seems thirty unto me,
 Being all this time abandoned° from your bed.   *banned*
SLY   'Tis much. Servants, leave me and her alone.
          [*Exeunt* LORD *and attendants*][2]
 Madam, undress you and come now to bed.
BARTHOLOMEW   Thrice-noble lord, let me entreat of you
115 To pardon me yet for a night or two,
 Or if not so, until the sun be set,
 For your physicians have expressly charged,
 In peril to incur[3] your former malady,
 That I should yet absent me from your bed.
120 I hope this reason stands for my excuse.
SLY   Ay, it stands[4] so that I may hardly tarry° so long. But I would   *delay*

---

6. She served from unmarked stone jugs rather than from the officially measured and stamped ("sealed") quarts.
7. Greet is a small village not far from Stratford. The names may be those of Stratford citizens.
8. Mild oath, derived from the Virgin Mary's name.
9. Husband: a term normally not used by lords.
1. Misusing the usual title for a noblewoman. "Alice"

and "Joan" are names rarely associated with the upper classes in Elizabethan texts.
2. F has no stage direction here, but those attending on Sly probably obey his command and leave the stage. It is unclear, however, whether the Lord leaves the stage with the other attendants at this point.
3. *In peril to incur:* Because of the risk of bringing on.
4. Punning on "stand" as meaning "to have an erection."

be loath to fall into my dreams again. I will therefore tarry in
despite of the flesh and the blood.

    Enter A MESSENGER

MESSENGER Your honour's players, hearing your amendment,
125   Are come to play a pleasant comedy,
    For so your doctors hold it very meet,°   *suitable*
    Seeing too much sadness hath congealed your blood,
    And melancholy is the nurse of frenzy.[5]
    Therefore they thought it good you hear a play
130   And frame your mind to mirth and merriment,
    Which bars° a thousand harms and lengthens life.   *prevents*
SLY Marry, I will let them play it. Is not a comonty°   *(for "comedy")*
    A Christmas gambol, or a tumbling trick?
BARTHOLOMEW No, my good lord, it is more pleasing stuff.
SLY What, household stuff?°   *furnishings; events*
135 BARTHOLOMEW   It is a kind of history.°   *story*
SLY Well, we'll see't. Come, madam wife, sit by my side
    And let the world slip. We shall ne'er be younger.

    [BARTHOLOMEW *sits*]

1.1

    Flourish.° Enter LUCENTIO *and his man,* TRANIO   *Fanfare of trumpets*
LUCENTIO Tranio, since for° the great desire I had   *because of*
    To see fair Padua, nursery of arts,[1]
    I am arrived fore° fruitful Lombardy,   *before*
    The pleasant garden of great Italy,
5   And by my father's love and leave am armed
    With his good will and thy good company,
    My trusty servant, well approved° in all,   *reliable*
    Here let us breathe,° and haply institute   *pause; rest*
    A course of learning and ingenious° studies.   *liberal; intellectual*
10   Pisa, renownèd for grave citizens,
    Gave me my being, and my father first°—   *before me*
    A merchant of great traffic° through the world,   *business*
    Vincentio, come of the Bentivolii.[2]
    Vincentio's son, brought up in Florence,
15   It shall become° to serve° all hopes conceived[3] *befit / fulfill*
    To deck° his fortune with his virtuous deeds.   *adorn*
    And therefore, Tranio, for the time I study,
    Virtue and that part of philosophy
    Will I apply° that treats of happiness   *pursue; study*
20   By virtue specially to be achieved.
    Tell me thy mind, for I have Pisa left
    And am to Padua come as he that leaves
    A shallow plash° to plunge him in the deep,   *pool*
    And with satiety seeks to quench his thirst.
25 TRANIO *Mi perdonate,°* gentle master mine.   *Pardon me*
    I am in all affected° as yourself,   *inclined*
    Glad that you thus continue your resolve

---

5. According to Renaissance humoral theory, excessive
sadness could cause thickening of the blood and thus
delirium, or "frenzy." *nurse:* nourisher.
1.1 Location: A street in Padua.
1. A center for learning ("arts"). Padua's famous univer-

sity attracted many English students in Shakespeare's
time.
2. Descended from the Bentivolii (perhaps a reference
to the famous Bentivoglio family of Bologna).
3. That is, by relatives and friends.

To suck the sweets of sweet philosophy.
Only, good master, while we do admire
30   This virtue and this moral discipline,
Let's be no stoics nor no stocks,[4] I pray,
Or so devote to Aristotle's checks[5]
As Ovid be an outcast quite abjured.[6]
Balk logic° with acquaintance that you have,   *Bandy words*
35   And practise rhetoric in your common talk.
Music and poesy use to quicken° you;   *revive; animate*
The mathematics and the metaphysics,
Fall to them as you find your stomach° serves you.   *appetite*
No profit grows where is no pleasure ta'en.
40   In brief, sir, study what you most affect.°   *like*
LUCENTIO   Gramercies,° Tranio, well dost thou advise.   *Thank you*
If, Biondello, thou wert come ashore,[7]
We could at once put us in readiness
And take a lodging fit to entertain
45   Such friends as time in Padua shall beget.
But stay a while, what company is this?
TRANIO   Master, some show to welcome us to town.
          Enter BAPTISTA *with his two daughters,* KATHERINE
          and BIANCA; GREMIO, *a pantaloon,*[8] HORTENSIO, *suitor*
          to Bianca. LUCENTIO, [*and*] TRANIO *stand by*
BAPTISTA   Gentlemen, importune me no farther,
For how I firmly am resolved you know:
50   That is, not to bestow° my youngest daughter   *give in marriage*
Before I have a husband for the elder.
If either of you both love Katherina,
Because I know you well and love you well
Leave shall you have to court her at your pleasure.
55   GREMIO   To cart her[9] rather. She's too rough for me.
There, there, Hortensio. Will you° any wife?   *Do you want*
KATHERINE [*to* BAPTISTA]   I pray you, sir, is it your will
To make a stale of me amongst these mates?[1]
HORTENSIO   'Mates', maid? How mean you that? No mates° for you *husbands*
60   Unless you were of gentler, milder mould.°   *nature*
KATHERINE   I'faith, sir, you shall never need to fear.
Iwis it is not half-way to her heart,[2]
But if it were, doubt not her care should be
To comb your noddle° with a three-legged stool,   *hit your head*
65   And paint° your face, and use you like a fool.   *(with blood)*
HORTENSIO   From all such devils, good Lord deliver us.
GREMIO   And me too, good Lord.
TRANIO [*aside to* LUCENTIO]   Husht, master, here's some good
          pastime toward.°   *in view*

4. Wooden posts devoid of feeling. Punning on "stoics," the Greek philosophers who advocated both indifference to pleasure or pain and patient endurance.
5. Restraints. Aristotle defined virtue as a mean, the avoiding of excess (or deficiency).
6. *As . . . abjured:* That Ovid be renounced. Ovid was a Roman poet whose erotic writings were popular in the Renaissance. (His *Ars Amatoria* is mentioned by Lucentio at 4.2.8.)
7. Padua, an inland city, did not have a port. Shake-

speare's knowledge of Italian geography seems to have been shaky.
8. Foolish old man: a stock character from the Italian commedia dell'arte whose usual role was to hinder young lovers.
9. To carry her though the street in, or tied to, a cart. This was a common punishment for disorderly women.
1. To make me a laughingstock or a prostitute or a decoy (for Bianca) among these crude fellows.
2. Certainly, marriage does not even half interest her. (Kate speaks of herself in the third person here.)

That wench is stark mad or wonderful froward.°   *incredibly willful*

70 LUCENTIO [*aside to* TRANIO]   But in the other's silence do I see
    Maid's mild behaviour and sobriety.
    Peace, Tranio.

TRANIO [*aside to* LUCENTIO]   Well said, master. Mum, and gaze your fill.

BAPTISTA   Gentlemen, that I may soon make good

75   What I have said—Bianca, get you in.
    And let it not displease thee, good Bianca,
    For I will love thee ne'er the less, my girl.

KATHERINE   A pretty peat!° It is best   *pet; spoiled child*
    Put finger in the eye,° an° she knew why.   *(to weep) / if*

80 BIANCA   Sister, content you° in my discontent.   *satisfy yourself*
    [*To* BAPTISTA] Sir, to your pleasure° humbly I subscribe.°   *will / submit*
    My books and instruments shall be my company,
    On them to look and practise by myself.

LUCENTIO [*aside to* TRANIO]   Hark, Tranio, thou mayst hear
      Minerva[3] speak.

85 HORTENSIO   Signor Baptista, will you be so strange?°   *unnatural; cruel*
    Sorry am I that our good will effects°   *causes*
    Bianca's grief.

GREMIO   Why will you mew° her up,   *confine (like a falcon)*
    Signor Baptista, for° this fiend of hell,   *because of*
    And make her bear the penance° of her tongue?   *punishment*

90 BAPTISTA   Gentlemen, content ye. I am resolved.
    Go in, Bianca.   [*Exit* BIANCA]
    And for I know she taketh most delight
    In music, instruments, and poetry,
    Schoolmasters will I keep within my house

95   Fit to instruct her youth. If you, Hortensio,
    Or, Signor Gremio, you know any such,
    Prefer° them hither; for to cunning° men   *Recommend / skillful*
    I will be very kind, and liberal
    To mine own children in good bringing up.

100   And so farewell. Katherina, you may stay,
    For I have more to commune with Bianca.   *Exit*

KATHERINE   Why, and I trust I may go too, may I not? What,
    shall I be appointed hours, as though belike I knew not what
    to take and what to leave? Ha!   *Exit*

105 GREMIO   You may go to the devil's dam.[4] Your gifts are so good
    here's none will hold° you. Their love[5] is not so great, Horten-   *tolerate*
    sio, but we may blow our nails° together and fast it fairly out.[6]   *wait patiently*
    Our cake's dough on both sides.[7] Farewell. Yet for the love I
    bear my sweet Bianca, if I can by any means light on a fit man

110   to teach her that wherein she delights, I will wish° him to her   *recommend*
    father.

HORTENSIO   So will I, Signor Gremio. But a word, I pray.
    Though the nature of our quarrel yet never brooked parle,°   *permitted discussion*
    know now, upon advice,° it toucheth° us both—that we may   *reflection / concerns*

115   yet again have access to our fair mistress and be happy rivals
    in Bianca's love—to labour and effect one thing specially.

---

3. Roman goddess of wisdom.   5. Love of them (that is, of women).
4. The devil's mother, imagined as the stereotypical   6. And abstain as best we can.
shrew and said to be worse than the devil himself.   7. Proverbial expression of failure.

GREMIO What's that, I pray?

HORTENSIO Marry, sir, to get a husband for her sister.

GREMIO A husband?—a devil!

120 HORTENSIO I say a husband.

GREMIO I say a devil. Think'st thou, Hortensio, though her
father be very rich, any man is so very° a fool to be married to   *completely*
hell?

HORTENSIO Tush, Gremio. Though it pass° your patience and   *exceeds*
125 mine to endure her loud alarums,° why, man, there be good   *calls to arms; scoldings*
fellows in the world, an a man could light on them, would take
her with all faults, and money enough.

GREMIO I cannot tell, but I had as lief° take her dowry with this   *would as willingly*
condition: to be whipped at the high cross⁸ every morning.

130 HORTENSIO Faith, as you say, there's small choice in rotten
apples. But come, since this bar in law° makes us friends, it   *legal obstacle*
shall be so far forth friendly maintained⁹ till by helping Bap-
tista's eldest daughter to a husband we set his youngest free for
a husband, and then have to't° afresh. Sweet Bianca! Happy   *begin the fight*
135 man be his dole.¹ He that runs fastest gets the ring.² How say
you, Signor Gremio?

GREMIO I am agreed, and would I had given him the best horse
in Padua to begin his wooing that would thoroughly woo her,
wed her, and bed her, and rid the house of her. Come on.

Exeunt [HORTENSIO *and* GREMIO]. *Manent°*   *Remain*
TRANIO *and* LUCENTIO

140 TRANIO I pray, sir, tell me: is it possible
That love should of a sudden take such hold?

LUCENTIO O Tranio, till I found it to be true
I never thought it possible or likely.
But see, while idly I stood looking on
145 I found the effect of love in idleness,³
And now in plainness do confess to thee,
That art to me as secret° and as dear   *intimate*
As Anna⁴ to the Queen of Carthage was,
Tranio, I burn, I pine, I perish, Tranio,
150 If I achieve not this young modest girl.
Counsel me, Tranio, for I know thou canst.
Assist me, Tranio, for I know thou wilt.

TRANIO Master, it is no time to chide you now.
Affection is not rated° from the heart.   *driven out by scolding*
155 If love have touched you, naught remains but so—
*Redime te captum quam queas minimo.*⁵

LUCENTIO Gramercies,° lad. Go forward, this contents.   *Thanks*
The rest will comfort, for thy counsel's sound.

TRANIO Master, you looked so longly° on the maid   *persistently*
160 Perhaps you marked not what's the pith° of all.   *main point*

---

8. Cross set on a pedestal in the town center, the normal site for punishment in an English village.
9. *it . . . maintained*: we'll pursue the matter as
friends.
1. May the winner's fate be that of a happy man.
2. A proverb alluding to the ring that riders in a jousting match try to catch on their lances. Also punning on
"ring" as referring to both "wedding ring" and female
genitalia.
3. Punning on a flower known as "love-in-idleness,"

whose juice was thought to induce love. (See *A Midsummer Night's Dream* 2.1.166–68.)
4. Sister to Dido, Queen of Carthage. In both Virgil's
Aeneid and Christopher Marlowe's *Dido, Queen of
Carthage* (1594), Dido tells Anna of her secret love for
Aeneas.
5. Latin: Ransom yourself from captivity at the lowest
possible price. A phrase from Terence, quoted as it
appears in Lily's Latin grammar, a standard Elizabethan
school text.

LUCENTIO   O yes, I saw sweet beauty in her face,
    Such as the daughter of Agenor[6] had,
    That made great Jove to humble him to her hand
    When with his knees he kissed the Cretan strand.
165 TRANIO   Saw you no more? Marked you not how her sister
    Began to scold and raise up such a storm
    That mortal ears might hardly endure the din?
    LUCENTIO   Tranio, I saw her coral lips to move,
    And with her breath she did perfume the air.
170   Sacred and sweet was all I saw in her.
    TRANIO [aside]   Nay, then 'tis time to stir him from his trance.
    [To LUCENTIO] I pray, awake, sir. If you love the maid,
    Bend thoughts and wits to achieve her. Thus it stands:
    Her elder sister is so curst° and shrewd°   *quarrelsome / shrewish*
175   That till the father rid his hands of her,
    Master, your love must live a maid at home,
    And therefore has he closely mewed her up
    Because° she will not be annoyed with° suitors.   *So that / troubled with*
    LUCENTIO   Ah, Tranio, what a cruel father's he!
180   But art thou not advised° he took some care   *aware*
    To get her cunning schoolmasters to instruct her?
    TRANIO   Ay, marry am I, sir, and now 'tis plotted.
    LUCENTIO   I have it, Tranio.
    TRANIO   Master, for° my hand,   *by*
    Both our inventions° meet and jump° in one.   *schemes / agree*
    LUCENTIO   Tell me thine first.
185 TRANIO   You will be schoolmaster
    And undertake the teaching of the maid.
    That's your device.°   *plan*
    LUCENTIO   It is. May it be done?
    TRANIO   Not possible; for who shall bear your part,
    And be in Padua here Vincentio's son,
190   Keep house, and ply his book,° welcome his friends,   *study*
    Visit his countrymen, and banquet them?
    LUCENTIO   Basta,° content thee, for I have it full.°   *Enough / fully planned*
    We have not yet been seen in any house,
    Nor can we be distinguished by our faces
195   For man or master. Then it follows thus:
    Thou shalt be master, Tranio, in my stead;
    Keep house, and port,° and servants, as I should.   *social position*
    I will some other be, some Florentine,
    Some Neapolitan, or meaner° man of Pisa.   *poorer*
200   'Tis hatched, and shall be so. Tranio, at once
    Uncase° thee. Take my coloured hat and cloak.[7]   *Undress*
    When Biondello comes he waits on thee,
    But I will charm° him first to keep his tongue.   *persuade; use magic on*
    TRANIO   So had you need.
            [They exchange clothes][8]
205   In brief, sir, sith° it your pleasure is,   *since*

6. Europa. Jove transformed himself into a bull and carried her across the sea to Crete to rape her.
7. The outfit of an Elizabethan gentleman. Servants usually wore uniforms, like the "blue coats" of Petruccio's servants (4.1.74).
8. F does not indicate at what point in this exchange

Lucentio and Tranio trade clothes; perhaps they begin during Lucentio's previous speech. This exchange of clothes, emphasizing the ease with which social identity is shifted, is an important visual enactment of one of the play's main preoccupations.

    And I am tied to be obedient—
    For so your father charged me at our parting,
    'Be serviceable° to my son,' quoth he,   *diligent in service*
    Although I think 'twas in another sense—
210   I am content to be Lucentio
    Because so well I love Lucentio.
LUCENTIO   Tranio, be so, because Lucentio loves,
    And let me be a slave t'achieve that maid
    Whose sudden sight hath thralled° my wounded⁹ eye.   *enslaved*
        Enter BIONDELLO
215   Here comes the rogue. Sirrah, where have you been?
BIONDELLO   Where have *I* been? Nay, how now, where are *you*?
    Master, has my fellow Tranio stolen your clothes, or you
    stolen his, or both? Pray, what's the news?
LUCENTIO   Sirrah, come hither. 'Tis no time to jest,
220   And therefore frame your manners to the time.
    Your fellow Tranio here, to save my life
    Puts my apparel and my count'nance on,
    And I for my escape have put on his,
    For in a quarrel since I came ashore
225   I killed a man, and fear I was descried.°   *observed*
    Wait you on him, I charge you, as becomes,°   *is fitting*
    While I make way from hence to save my life.
    You understand me?
BIONDELLO   I sir? Ne'er a whit.°   *Not at all*
LUCENTIO   And not a jot of Tranio in your mouth.
230   Tranio is changed into Lucentio.
BIONDELLO   The better for him. Would I were so too.
TRANIO   So could I, faith, boy, to have the next wish after—
    That Lucentio indeed had Baptista's youngest daughter.
    But sirrah, not for my sake but your master's I advise
235   You use your manners discreetly in all kind of companies.
    When I am alone, why then I am Tranio,
    But in all places else your master, Lucentio.
LUCENTIO   Tranio, let's go.
    One thing more rests° that thyself execute°—   *remains / must do*
240   To make one among these wooers. If thou ask me why,
    Sufficeth my reasons are both good and weighty.   *Exeunt*
        The presenters¹ above speak
FIRST SERVINGMAN   My lord, you nod. You do not mind° the play.   *pay attention to*
SLY   Yes, by Saint Anne² do I. A good matter, surely. Comes
    there any more of it?
245   BARTHOLOMEW   My lord, 'tis but begun.
SLY   'Tis a very excellent piece of work, madam lady. Would
    'twere done.
        They sit and mark°   *observe*

1.2

Enter PETRUCCIO *and his man,* GRUMIO

PETRUCCIO   Verona, for a while I take my leave
    To see my friends in Padua; but of all

---

9. Wounded by Cupid's arrow.
1. Figures who introduce and comment on the action
of a play for the audience.

2. A common oath. St. Anne was the mother of the Virgin Mary and the patron saint of married women.
1.2 Location: In front of Hortensio's house in Padua.

My best-belovèd and approvèd friend
Hortensio, and I trow° this is his house.   *believe*
5   Here, sirrah Grumio, knock, I say.
GRUMIO   Knock, sir? Whom should I knock? Is there any man
has rebused[1] your worship?
PETRUCCIO   Villain, I say, knock me here[2] soundly.
GRUMIO   Knock you here, sir? Why, sir, what am I, sir, that I
10   should knock you here, sir?
PETRUCCIO   Villain, I say, knock me at this gate,
And rap me well or I'll knock your knave's pate.
GRUMIO   My master is grown quarrelsome. I should knock you first,
And then I know after who comes by the worst.[3]
15   PETRUCCIO   Will it not be?
Faith, sirrah, an° you'll not knock, I'll ring it.[4]   *if*
I'll try how you can sol-fa° and sing it.   *sing a scale*
He wrings him by the ears. [GRUMIO *kneels*][5]
GRUMIO   Help, masters, help! My master is mad.
PETRUCCIO   Now knock when I bid you, sirrah villain.
Enter HORTENSIO
20   HORTENSIO   How now, what's the matter? My old friend Grumio
and my good friend Petruccio? How do you all at Verona?
PETRUCCIO   Signor Hortensio, come you to part the fray?
Con tutto il cuore ben trovato,[6] may I say.
HORTENSIO   *Alla nostra casa ben venuto, molto onorato signor*
25   *mio Petruccio.*[7]
Rise, Grumio, rise. We will compound° this quarrel.   *settle*
[GRUMIO *rises*]
GRUMIO   Nay, 'tis no matter, sir, what he 'leges° in Latin. If this   *alleges*
be not a lawful cause for me to leave his service—look you, sir:
he bid me knock him and rap him soundly, sir. Well, was it fit
30   for a servant to use his master so, being perhaps, for aught
I see, two-and-thirty, a pip out?[8]
Whom would to God I had well knocked at first,
Then had not Grumio come by the worst.
PETRUCCIO   A senseless villain. Good Hortensio,
35   I bade the rascal knock upon your gate,
And could not get him for my heart to do it.
GRUMIO   Knock at the gate? O heavens, spake you not these
words plain? 'Sirrah, knock me here, rap me here, knock me
well, and knock me soundly'? And come you now with
40   knocking at the gate?
PETRUCCIO   Sirrah, be gone, or talk not, I advise you.
HORTENSIO   Petruccio, patience. I am Grumio's pledge.°   *guarantor*
Why this' a heavy chance[9] 'twixt him and you,

---

1. Grumio regularly blunders and puns. Here he
means "abused" or "rebuked," or perhaps both.
2. Knock here for me: a conventional usage that Grumio misunderstands or pretends to understand as
"strike me." *Villain*: low-born man (often a contemptuous term of address).
3. *I should . . . worst*: You want me to give the first
blow, but then I know I'd have the worse of it.
4. I'll ring the bell; with a pun on "wring."
5. While F gives no stage direction indicating that
Grumio kneels at this point, at line 26 Hortensio
orders him to "rise." This may mean that he has been

brought to his knees when Petruccio wrings his ears at
line 17.
6. With all my heart, welcome (Italian).
7. Welcome to our house, my most honored Signor
Petruccio.
8. Drunk; a bit crazy. Probably alluding to the card
game one-and-thirty, in which the aim is to accumulate
exactly thirty-one points. To collect thirty-two means
the player has overshot or been excessive. A "pip" is a
spot on a card; hence "a pip out" means "off by one."
9. *Why . . . chance*: This is a sad occurrence.

Your ancient,° trusty, pleasant servant Grumio.   *long-standing*

45 And tell me now, sweet friend, what happy gale
Blows you to Padua here from old Verona?

PETRUCCIO   Such wind as scatters young men through the world
To seek their fortunes farther than at home,
Where small experience grows. But in a few,°   *in short*

50 Signor Hortensio, thus it stands with me:
Antonio, my father, is deceased,
And I have thrust myself into this maze[1]
Happily to wive and thrive as best I may.
Crowns° in my purse I have, and goods at home,   *Five-shilling coins*

55 And so am come abroad to see the world.

HORTENSIO   Petruccio, shall I then come roundly° to thee   *speak plainly*
And wish thee to a shrewd, ill-favoured wife?
Thou'dst thank me but a little for my counsel,
And yet I'll promise thee she shall be rich,

60 And very rich. But thou'rt too much my friend,
And I'll not wish thee to her.

PETRUCCIO   Signor Hortensio, 'twixt such friends as we
Few words suffice; and therefore, if thou know
One rich enough to be Petruccio's wife—

65 As wealth is burden° of my wooing dance—   *refrain; chief theme*
Be she as foul° as was Florentius' love,[2]   *ugly*
As old as Sibyl,[3] and as curst and shrewd
As Socrates' Xanthippe[4] or a worse,
She moves° me not—or not° removes at least°   *annoys / nor / at all*

70 Affection's edge° in me, were she as rough   *intensity*
As are the swelling Adriatic seas.
I come to wive it wealthily in Padua;
If wealthily, then happily in Padua.

GRUMIO [*to* HORTENSIO]   Nay, look you, sir, he tells you flatly

75 what his mind is. Why, give him gold enough and marry him
to a puppet or an aglet-baby,[5] or an old trot° with ne'er a tooth   *hag*
in her head, though she have as many diseases as two-and-fifty
horses. Why, nothing comes amiss so money comes withal.°   *with it*

HORTENSIO   Petruccio, since we are stepped thus far in,

80 I will continue that° I broached in jest.   *what*
I can, Petruccio, help thee to a wife
With wealth enough, and young and beauteous,
Brought up as best becomes a gentlewoman.
Her only fault—and that is faults enough—

85 Is that she is intolerable curst,°   *shrewish*
And shrewd and froward° so beyond all measure   *willful*
That, were my state° far worser than it is,   *fortune*
I would not wed her for a mine of gold.

PETRUCCIO   Hortensio, peace. Thou know'st not gold's effect.

90 Tell me her father's name and 'tis enough,

---

1. This uncertain world; this unpredictable business of "wiving and thriving."
2. Florent, the knight in John Gower's *Confessio Amantis*, who had to marry the ugly old woman who had saved his life by answering a riddle he had been commanded to solve. On their wedding night, as a reward for his compliance, she became young and beautiful.

A version of this story also appears in Chaucer's *Wife of Bath's Tale*.
3. The Cumaean Sibyl, a prophetess in classical mythology, had immortality without eternal youth.
4. The philosopher's notoriously shrewish wife.
5. Small figure used as a tag or ornament on dresses, laces, and other goods.

For I will board⁶ her though she chide as loud
As thunder when the clouds in autumn crack.
HORTENSIO   Her father is Baptista Minola,
An affable and courteous gentleman.
95   Her name is Katherina Minola,
Renowned in Padua for her scolding tongue.
PETRUCCIO   I know her father, though I know not her,
And he knew my deceasèd father well.
I will not sleep, Hortensio, till I see her,
100   And therefore let me be thus bold with you
To give you over° at this first encounter,   leave you
Unless you will accompany me thither.
GRUMIO   I pray you, sir, let him go while the humour° lasts.   mood
O' my word, an she knew him as well as I do she would think
105   scolding would do little good upon him. She may perhaps call
him half a score knaves or so. Why, that's nothing; an he begin
once he'll rail in his rope-tricks.⁷ I'll tell you what, sir, an she
stand° him but a little he will throw a figure⁸ in her face and   withstand; arouse
so disfigure her with it that she shall have no more eyes to see
110   withal than a cat. You know him not, sir.
HORTENSIO   Tarry, Petruccio, I must go with thee,
For in Baptista's keep° my treasure is.   custody; stronghold
He hath the jewel of my life in hold,
His youngest daughter, beautiful Bianca,
115   And her withholds from me and other more,°   others besides
Suitors to her and rivals in my love,
Supposing it a thing impossible,
For those defects I have before rehearsed,
That ever Katherina will be wooed.
120   Therefore this order hath Baptista ta'en:
That none shall have access unto Bianca
Till Katherine the curst have got a husband.
GRUMIO   Katherine the curst—
A title for a maid of all titles the worst.
125 HORTENSIO   Now shall my friend Petruccio do me grace,°   a favor
And offer me disguised in sober robes
To old Baptista as a schoolmaster
Well seen° in music, to instruct Bianca,   skilled
That so I may by this device at least
130   Have leave and leisure to make love to her,
And unsuspected court her by herself.
          Enter GREMIO [*with a paper,*]⁹ *and* LUCENTIO *disguised*
          [*as a schoolmaster*]
GRUMIO   Here's no knavery.¹ See, to beguile the old folks, how
the young folks lay their heads together. Master, master, look
about you. Who goes there, ha?
135 HORTENSIO   Peace, Grumio, it is the rival of my love.
Petruccio, stand by a while.

---

6. Woo aggressively; go aboard, as in a sea battle; have
sexual intercourse with.
7. An obscure phrase: "rope-tricks" may refer to rhetorical or sexual feats. Grumio's point seems to be that
when Petruccio "rails," he will be more aggressive than
Katherine.

8. A figure of speech.
9. Presumably Lucentio's list of books for Bianca's
studies.
1. Spoken sarcastically; perhaps referring to the plotting
of Petruccio and Hortensio rather than to that of Gremio
and Lucentio, whom Grumio may not yet have seen.

GRUMIO   A proper stripling,° and an amorous!   *handsome youth (ironic)*
      [PETRUCCIO, HORTENSIO, *and* GRUMIO *stand aside*]
GREMIO [*to* LUCENTIO]   O, very well—I have perused the note.°   *listing of books*
    Hark you, sir, I'll have them° very fairly bound—   *(the books)*
140   All books of love, see that at any hand°—   *in any case*
    And see you read no other lectures to her.
    You understand me. Over and beside
    Signor Baptista's liberality,
    I'll mend° it with a largess.° Take your paper, too,   *increase / gift*
145   And let me have them very well perfumed,
    For she is sweeter than perfume itself
    To whom they go to. What will you read to her?
LUCENTIO   Whate'er I read to her, I'll plead for you
    As for my patron, stand you so assured,
150   As firmly as yourself were still in place°—   *always present*
    Yea, and perhaps with more successful words
    Than you, unless you were a scholar, sir.
GREMIO   O this learning, what a thing it is!
GRUMIO [*aside*]   O this woodcock,[2] what an ass it is!
155 PETRUCCIO   Peace, sirrah.
HORTENSIO   Grumio, mum. [*Coming forward*] God save you, Signor Gremio.
GREMIO   And you are well met, Signor Hortensio.
    Trow° you whither I am going?   *Know*
    To Baptista Minola.
160   I promised to enquire carefully
    About a schoolmaster for the fair Bianca,
    And by good fortune I have lighted well
    On this young man, for learning and behaviour
    Fit for her turn,° well read in poetry   *use*
165   And other books—good ones, I warrant ye.
HORTENSIO   'Tis well, and I have met a gentleman
    Hath promised me to help me to another,
    A fine musician, to instruct our mistress.
    So shall I no whit be behind in duty
170   To fair Bianca, so beloved of me.
GREMIO   Beloved of me, and that my deeds shall prove.
GRUMIO [*aside*]   And that his bags° shall prove.   *money bags*
HORTENSIO   Gremio, 'tis now no time to vent° our love.   *express*
    Listen to me, and if you speak me fair°   *courteously*
175   I'll tell you news indifferent° good for either.   *equally*
    Here is a gentleman whom by chance I met,
    Upon agreement from us to his liking°   *If we accept his terms*
    Will undertake to woo curst Katherine,
    Yea, and to marry her, if her dowry please.
180 GREMIO   So said, so done, is well.
    Hortensio, have you told him all her faults?
PETRUCCIO   I know she is an irksome brawling scold.
    If that be all, masters, I hear no harm.
GREMIO   No, sayst me so, friend? What countryman?
185 PETRUCCIO   Born in Verona, old Antonio's son.
    My father dead, his fortune lives for me,°   *is mine*

---

2. Wild bird easily caught and so thought to be stupid.

And I do hope good days and long to see.
GREMIO   O sir, such a life with such a wife were strange.
But if you have a stomach, to't, a'° God's name.   in
190   You shall have me assisting you in all.
But will you woo this wildcat?
PETRUCCIO   Will I live!
GRUMIO   Will he woo her? Ay, or I'll hang her.
PETRUCCIO   Why came I hither but to that intent?
Think you a little din can daunt mine ears?
195   Have I not in my time heard lions roar?
Have I not heard the sea, puffed up with winds,
Rage like an angry boar chafèd with sweat?
Have I not heard great ordnance° in the field,   cannon
And heaven's artillery thunder in the skies?
200   Have I not in a pitchèd battle heard
Loud 'larums,° neighing steeds, and trumpets' clang?   calls to arms
And do you tell me of a woman's tongue,
That gives not half so great a blow° to hear   loud noise
As will a chestnut in a farmer's fire?
205   Tush, tush—fear° boys with bugs.°   frighten / bogeymen
GRUMIO   For he fears none.
GREMIO   Hortensio, hark.
This gentleman is happily° arrived,   fortunately
My mind presumes, for his own good and ours.
210   HORTENSIO   I promised we would be contributors,
And bear his charge° of wooing, whatsoe'er.   expense
GREMIO   And so we will, provided that he win her.
GRUMIO   I would I were as sure of a good dinner.

   Enter TRANIO, *brave,*° [*as Lucentio,*] *and* BIONDELLO   richly dressed

TRANIO   Gentlemen, God save you. If I may be bold, tell me, I
215   beseech you, which is the readiest way to the house of Signor
Baptista Minola?
BIONDELLO   He that has the two fair daughters—is't he you
mean?
TRANIO   Even he, Biondello.
220   GREMIO   Hark you, sir, you mean not her to—
TRANIO   Perhaps him and her, sir. What have you to do?³
PETRUCCIO   Not her that chides, sir, at any hand, I pray.
TRANIO   I love no chiders, sir. Biondello, let's away.
LUCENTIO [*aside*]   Well begun, Tranio.
HORTENSIO   Sir, a word ere you go.
225   Are you a suitor to the maid you talk of—yea or no?
TRANIO   And if I be, sir, is it any offence?
GREMIO   No, if without more words you will get you hence.
TRANIO   Why, sir, I pray, are not the streets as free
For me as for you?
GREMIO   But so is not she.
230   TRANIO   For what reason, I beseech you?
GREMIO   For this reason, if you'll know—
That she's the choice° love of Signor Gremio.   chosen; excellent
HORTENSIO   That she's the chosen of Signor Hortensio.
TRANIO   Softly, my masters. If you be gentlemen,

---

3. What business is it of yours?

235   Do me this right,° hear me with patience.   *justice*
        Baptista is a noble gentleman
        To whom my father is not all unknown,
        And were his daughter fairer than she is
        She may more suitors have, and me for one.
240   Fair Leda's daughter⁴ had a thousand wooers;
        Then well one more may fair Bianca have,
        And so she shall. Lucentio shall make one,
        Though Paris came,⁵ in hope to speed° alone.   *succeed*
    GREMIO   What, this gentleman will out-talk us all!
245 LUCENTIO   Sir, give him head, I know he'll prove a jade.°   *worn-out horse*
    PETRUCCIO   Hortensio, to what end are all these words?
    HORTENSIO   Sir, let me be so bold as ask you,
        Did you yet ever see Baptista's daughter?
    TRANIO   No, sir, but hear I do that he hath two,
250   The one as famous for a scolding tongue
        As is the other for beauteous modesty.
    PETRUCCIO   Sir, sir, the first's for me. Let her go by.
    GREMIO   Yea, leave that labour to great Hercules,
        And let it be more than Alcides' twelve.⁶
255 PETRUCCIO   Sir, understand you this of me in sooth,°   *truth*
        The youngest daughter whom you hearken° for   *lie in wait; yearn*
        Her father keeps from all access of suitors,
        And will not promise her to any man
        Until the elder sister first be wed.
260   The younger then is free, and not before.
    TRANIO   If it be so, sir, that you are the man
        Must stead° us all, and me amongst the rest,   *help*
        And if you break the ice and do this feat,
        Achieve° the elder, set the younger free   *Win*
265 For our access, whose hap shall be° to have her   *he who is lucky enough*
        Will not so graceless be to be ingrate.
    HORTENSIO   Sir, you say well, and well you do conceive;°   *understand*
        And since you do profess to be a suitor
        You must, as we do, gratify° this gentleman,   *reward*
270   To whom we all rest generally beholden.
    TRANIO   Sir, I shall not be slack. In sign whereof,
        Please ye we may contrive° this afternoon,   *pass, spend (time)*
        And quaff carouses° to our mistress' health,   *toasts*
        And do as adversaries do in law—
275   Strive mightily, but eat and drink as friends.
    GRUMIO *and* BIONDELLO   O excellent motion!° Fellows, let's be gone.   *proposal*
    HORTENSIO   The motion's good indeed, and be it so.
    Petruccio, I shall be your *ben venuto*.°   *Exeunt*   *welcome (your host)*

2.1

Enter KATHERINE *and* BIANCA [*her hands bound*]
    BIANCA   Good sister, wrong me not, nor wrong yourself
        To make a bondmaid and a slave of me.

---

4. Helen of Troy. In Marlowe's *Doctor Faustus,* her face
is said to have "launched a thousand ships."
5. Even if Paris (who stole Helen of Troy from her husband) were to come.
6. Hercules, the hero of classical mythology who suc-

cessfully performed twelve seemingly impossible tasks
("labours"), was also called Alcides (descendant of
Alcaeus).
2.1 Location: Baptista's house in Padua.

That I disdain, but for these other goods,°   possessions
Unbind my hands, I'll pull them off myself,
5 Yea, all my raiment to my petticoat,
Or what you will command me will I do,
So well I know my duty to my elders.

KATHERINE Of all thy suitors here I charge thee tell
Whom thou lov'st best. See thou dissemble not.

10 BIANCA Believe me, sister, of all the men alive
I never yet beheld that special face
Which I could fancy more than any other.

KATHERINE Minion,° thou liest. Is't not Hortensio?   Hussy

BIANCA If you affect° him, sister, here I swear   love
15 I'll plead for you myself but you shall have him.

KATHERINE O then, belike you fancy riches more.
You will have Gremio to keep you fair.

BIANCA Is it for him you do envy me so?
Nay, then, you jest, and now I well perceive
20 You have but jested with me all this while.
I prithee, sister Kate, untie my hands.

KATHERINE If that be jest, then all the rest was so. *Strikes her*
                    Enter BAPTISTA

BAPTISTA Why, how now, dame, whence grows this insolence?
Bianca, stand aside.— Poor girl, she weeps.—
25 Go ply thy needle, meddle not with her.
[*To* KATHERINE] For shame, thou hilding° of a devilish spirit,   worthless creature
Why dost thou wrong her that did ne'er wrong thee?
When did she cross thee with a bitter word?

KATHERINE Her silence flouts° me, and I'll be revenged.   mocks
                    [*She*] *flies after* BIANCA

30 BAPTISTA What, in my sight? Bianca, get thee in. *Exit* [BIANCA]

KATHERINE What, will you not suffer me?° Nay, now I see   let me have my way
She is your treasure, she must have a husband.
I must dance barefoot on her wedding day,[1]
And for your love to her lead apes in hell.[2]
35 Talk not to me. I will go sit and weep
Till I can find occasion of revenge.   [*Exit*]

BAPTISTA Was ever gentleman thus grieved as I?
But who comes here?
                    Enter GREMIO, LUCENTIO [*as a schoolmaster*] *in the*
                    habit of a mean man,° PETRUCCIO *with* [HORTENSIO *as*   man of low social rank
                    a musician,] TRANIO [*as Lucentio*], *with* [BIONDELLO]
                    his boy bearing a lute and books

GREMIO Good morrow, neighbour Baptista.

40 BAPTISTA Good morrow, neighbour Gremio. God save you,
gentlemen.

PETRUCCIO And you, good sir. Pray, have you not a daughter
Called Katherina, fair and virtuous?

BAPTISTA I have a daughter, sir, called Katherina.

45 GREMIO You are too blunt. Go to it orderly.°   properly

PETRUCCIO You wrong me, Signor Gremio. Give me leave.
[*To* BAPTISTA] I am a gentleman of Verona, sir,

---

1. Proverbially expected of older unmarried sisters.   2. *lead apes in hell:* the proverbial destiny of unmarried
women.

That hearing of her beauty and her wit,
Her affability and bashful modesty,
50   Her wondrous qualities and mild behaviour,
Am bold to show myself a forward° guest   *eager*
Within your house to make mine eye the witness
Of that report which I so oft have heard,
And for an entrance to my entertainment[3]
55   I do present you with a man of mine [*presenting* HORTENSIO]
Cunning in music and the mathematics
To instruct her fully in those sciences,
Whereof I know she is not ignorant.
Accept of him, or else you do me wrong.
60   His name is Licio, born in Mantua.
BAPTISTA   You're welcome, sir, and he for your good sake.
But for my daughter, Katherine, this I know:
She is not for your turn,° the more my grief.   *will not suit you*
PETRUCCIO   I see you do not mean to part with her,
65   Or else you like not of my company.
BAPTISTA   Mistake me not, I speak but as I find.°   *as the facts stand*
Whence are you, sir? What may I call your name?
PETRUCCIO   Petruccio is my name, Antonio's son,
A man well known throughout all Italy.
70   BAPTISTA   I know him well.[4] You are welcome for his sake.
GREMIO   Saving° your tale, Petruccio, I pray   *With all respect to*
Let us that are poor petitioners speak too.
Baccare,° you are marvellous forward.   *Stand back (mock Latin)*
PETRUCCIO   O pardon me, Signor Gremio, I would fain be doing.[5]
75   GREMIO   I doubt it not, sir. But you will curse your wooing.
[*To* BAPTISTA] Neighbour, this is a gift[6] very grateful,° I am sure   *pleasing*
of it. To express the like kindness, myself, that have been more
kindly beholden to you than any, freely give unto you this
young scholar [*presenting* LUCENTIO] that hath been long
80   studying at Rheims,[7] as cunning in Greek, Latin, and other
languages as the other in music and mathematics. His name
is Cambio.[8] Pray accept his service.
BAPTISTA   A thousand thanks, Signor Gremio. Welcome, good
Cambio. [*To* TRANIO] But, gentle sir, methinks you walk like a
85   stranger. May I be so bold to know the cause of your coming?
TRANIO   Pardon me, sir, the boldness is mine own
That, being a stranger in this city here,
Do make myself a suitor to your daughter,
Unto Bianca, fair and virtuous.
90   Nor is your firm resolve unknown to me
In the preferment of the eldest sister.
This liberty is all that I request:
That upon knowledge of my parentage
I may have welcome 'mongst the rest that woo,
95   And free access and favour as the rest.
And toward the education of your daughters

---

3. And as an entrance fee for my reception ("enter-   as meaning "have sexual intercourse").
tainment") as a suitor.   6. That is, Petruccio's gift of Hortensio/Licio.
4. Probably, I know him by reputation.   7. French city famous for its university.
5. I am eager to get on with it (with a pun on "doing" 8. Italian for "exchange"

I here bestow a simple instrument,
And this small packet of Greek and Latin books.
If you accept them, then their worth is great.

100 BAPTISTA Lucentio is your name[9]—of whence, I pray?

TRANIO Of Pisa, sir, son to Vincentio.

BAPTISTA A mighty man of Pisa. By report
I know him well. You are very welcome, sir.
[*To* HORTENSIO] Take you the lute, [*to* LUCENTIO] and you the
set of books.

105 You shall go see your pupils presently.°   *immediately*
Holla, within!

      Enter a Servant

          Sirrah, lead these gentlemen
To my daughters, and tell them both
These are their tutors. Bid them use them well.

      [*Exit Servant with* LUCENTIO *and* HORTENSIO,
                       BIONDELLO *following*]

[*To* PETRUCCIO] We will go walk a little in the orchard,°   *garden*

110 And then to dinner. You are passing° welcome—   *extremely*
And so I pray you all to think yourselves.

PETRUCCIO Signor Baptista, my business asketh haste,
And every day I cannot come to woo.
You knew my father well, and in him me,

115 Left solely heir to all his lands and goods,
Which I have bettered rather than decreased.
Then tell me, if I get your daughter's love,
What dowry shall I have with her to wife?

BAPTISTA After my death the one half of my lands,

120 And in possession° twenty thousand crowns.   *immediately*

PETRUCCIO And for that dowry I'll assure her of
Her widowhood,[1] be it that she survive me,
In all my lands and leases whatsoever.
Let specialties° be therefore drawn between us,   *explicit contracts*

125 That covenants may be kept on either hand.

BAPTISTA Ay, when the special thing is well obtained—
That is her love, for that is all in all.

PETRUCCIO Why, that is nothing, for I tell you, father,
I am as peremptory as she proud-minded,

130 And where two raging fires meet together
They do consume the thing that feeds their fury.
Though little fire grows great with little wind,
Yet extreme gusts will blow out fire and all.[2]
So I to her, and so she yields to me,

135 For I am rough, and woo not like a babe.

BAPTISTA Well mayst thou woo, and happy be thy speed.°   *fortune*
But be thou armed for some unhappy words.

PETRUCCIO Ay, to the proof,[3] as mountains are for winds,
That shakes not though they blow perpetually.

      Enter HORTENSIO *with his head broke*

140 BAPTISTA How now, my friend, why dost thou look so pale?

---

9. How Baptista knows this is unclear. He may read the name in one of the schoolbooks.
1. Widow's share of the estate.
2. Implying that those who have opposed Katherine so far have been too weak ("little wind") and that he will subdue her with his "extreme gusts."
3. In impenetrable armor. Proof armor was tested for its strength.

HORTENSIO   For fear, I promise you, if I look pale.

BAPTISTA   What, will my daughter prove a good musician?

HORTENSIO   I think she'll sooner prove a soldier.

Iron may hold with° her, but never lutes.   *withstand*

145   BAPTISTA   Why then, thou canst not break° her to the lute?   *train*

HORTENSIO   Why no, for she hath broke the lute to me.

I did but tell her she mistook her frets,[4]

And bowed° her hand to teach her fingering,   *bent*

When, with a most impatient devilish spirit,

150   'Frets,[5] call you these?' quoth she, 'I'll fume° with them,'   *be in a rage*

And with that word she struck me on the head,

And through the instrument my pate made way,

And there I stood amazèd for a while,

As on a pillory,[6] looking through the lute,

155   While she did call me rascal, fiddler,

And twangling jack,° with twenty such vile terms,   *knave*

As° had she studied to misuse me so.   *As if*

PETRUCCIO   Now, by the world, it is a lusty° wench!   *lively*

I love her ten times more than e'er I did.

160   O, how I long to have some chat with her!

BAPTISTA [*to* HORTENSIO]   Well, go with me, and be not so
        discomfited.

Proceed in practice° with my younger daughter.   *Continue your lessons*

She's apt to learn, and thankful for good turns.

Signor Petruccio, will you go with us,

165   Or shall I send my daughter Kate to you?

PETRUCCIO   I pray you, do.   *Exeunt. Manet°* PETRUCCIO   *Remains*

        I'll attend° her here,   *await*

And woo her with some spirit when she comes.

Say that she rail, why then I'll tell her plain

She sings as sweetly as a nightingale.

170   Say that she frown, I'll say she looks as clear

As morning roses newly washed with dew.

Say she be mute and will not speak a word,

Then I'll commend her volubility,

And say she uttereth piercing° eloquence.   *moving*

175   If she do bid me pack,° I'll give her thanks   *go away*

As though she bid me stay by her a week.

If she deny to wed, I'll crave° the day   *beg to know*

When I shall ask the banns,[7] and when be married.

But here she comes, and now, Petruccio, speak.

        Enter KATHERINE

180   Good morrow, Kate, for that's your name, I hear.

KATHERINE   Well have you heard, but something° hard of hearing.   *somewhat*

They call me Katherine that do talk of me.

PETRUCCIO   You lie, in faith, for you are called plain Kate,

And bonny Kate, and sometimes Kate the curst,

185   But Kate, the prettiest Kate in Christendom,

---

4. Placed her fingers upon the wrong bars ("frets") on the lute's fingerboard.

5. Kate plays on "frets" as also meaning "annoyances" or "vexations."

6. An instrument of public punishment in which the offender's head and hands were fastened in wooden clamps.

7. Have the banns read. Banns were required announcements in church of a forthcoming wedding.

Kate of Kate Hall,[8] my super-dainty Kate—
For dainties are all cates,[9] and therefore 'Kate'—
Take this of me, Kate of my consolation:
Hearing thy mildness praised in every town,
190   Thy virtues spoke of, and thy beauty sounded[1]—
Yet not so deeply as to thee belongs—
Myself am moved to woo thee for my wife.

KATHERINE   Moved? In good time.° Let him that moved you hither   *Indeed*
Re-move you hence. I knew you at the first
You were a movable.[2]

195 PETRUCCIO   Why, what's a movable?
KATHERINE   A joint-stool.[3]
PETRUCCIO   Thou hast hit it. Come, sit on me.
KATHERINE   Asses are made to bear,° and so are you.   *carry loads*
PETRUCCIO   Women are made to bear,[4] and so are you.
KATHERINE   No such jade° as you, if me you mean.   *worn-out horse*
200 PETRUCCIO   Alas, good Kate, I will not burden[5] thee,
For knowing° thee to be but young and light.[6]   *Because I know*
KATHERINE   Too light° for such a swain° as you to catch,   *quick / bumpkin*
And yet as heavy as my weight should be.[7]
PETRUCCIO   Should be?—should buzz.[8]
KATHERINE   Well ta'en, and like a buzzard.[9]
205 PETRUCCIO   O slow-winged turtle,° shall a buzzard take thee?   *turtledove*
KATHERINE   Ay, for a turtle, as he takes a buzzard.[1]
PETRUCCIO   Come, come, you wasp, i'faith you are too angry.
KATHERINE   If I be waspish, best beware my sting.
PETRUCCIO   My remedy is then to pluck it out.
210 KATHERINE   Ay, if the fool could find it where it lies.
PETRUCCIO   Who knows not where a wasp does wear his sting?
In his tail.
KATHERINE   In his tongue.
PETRUCCIO   Whose tongue?
KATHERINE   Yours, if you talk of tales,° and so farewell.   *gossip; genitals*
PETRUCCIO   What, with my tongue in your tail? Nay, come again,
Good Kate, I am a gentleman.
215 KATHERINE   That I'll try.°   *test*

She strikes him

PETRUCCIO   I swear I'll cuff you if you strike again.
KATHERINE   So may you lose your arms.[2]
If you strike me you are no gentleman,
And if no gentleman, why then, no arms.

---

8. Either an obscure allusion or an ironic reference to Kate's home as a place famous because she lives there.
9. For delicacies ("dainties") are called "cates."
1. Proclaimed; tested for depth.
2. Piece of furniture; changeable person.
3. Wooden stool made by a joiner.
4. Bear children; bear the weight of a lover.
5. Lie on you in sexual intercourse; make you pregnant; make accusations against you; accompany you with a musical refrain, or "burden."
6. Not heavy; wanton; lacking a musical accompaniment.
7. She is claiming social prominence ("weight") and

refusing the implication that she is wanton ("light") or like a coin that has been clipped so that it is lighter than it should be.
8. Punning on "be" and "bee," Petruccio suggests Kate should make a buzzing sound.
9. A hawk that cannot be trained to "take," or capture, prey; a fool.
1. Obscure line probably meaning that if a fool ("buzzard") mistakes me for a faithful love ("turtledove"), he'll be making as big a mistake as the turtledove makes when it captures a buzzing insect (another meaning of "buzzard").
2. Lose your claim to a coat of arms (sign of noble status); loosen your grip on me.

220	PETRUCCIO	A herald,° Kate? O, put me in thy books.[3]	*An authority on heraldry*
	KATHERINE	What is your crest[4]—a coxcomb?[5]	
	PETRUCCIO	A combless cock,[6] so Kate will be my hen.	
	KATHERINE	No cock of mine. You crow too like a craven.°	*cock that won't fight*
	PETRUCCIO	Nay, come, Kate, come. You must not look so sour.	
225	KATHERINE	It is my fashion when I see a crab.°	*crab apple; sour person*
	PETRUCCIO	Why, here's no crab, and therefore look not sour.	
	KATHERINE	There is, there is.	
	PETRUCCIO	Then show it me.	
	KATHERINE	Had I a glass° I would.	*mirror*
	PETRUCCIO	What, you mean my face?	
230	KATHERINE	Well aimed,° of such a young one.	*A good guess*
	PETRUCCIO	Now, by Saint George,° I am too young for you.	*England's patron saint*
	KATHERINE	Yet you are withered.	
	PETRUCCIO	'Tis with cares.	
	KATHERINE	I care not.	
	PETRUCCIO	Nay, hear you, Kate. In sooth, you scape° not so.	*escape*
	KATHERINE	I chafe° you if I tarry. Let me go.	*annoy; inflame*
235	PETRUCCIO	No, not a whit. I find you passing gentle.	

'Twas told me you were rough, and coy,° and sullen,   *disdainful*
And now I find report a very liar,
For thou art pleasant, gamesome,° passing° courteous,   *playful / very*
But slow in speech, yet sweet as springtime flowers.

240   Thou canst not frown. Thou canst not look askance,°   *scornfully*
Nor bite the lip, as angry wenches will,
Nor hast thou pleasure to be cross in talk,
But thou with mildness entertain'st thy wooers,
With gentle conference,° soft, and affable.   *conversation*

245   Why does the world report that Kate doth limp?
O sland'rous world! Kate like the hazel twig
Is straight and slender, and as brown in hue
As hazelnuts, and sweeter than the kernels.
O let me see thee walk. Thou dost not halt.°   *limp*

250	KATHERINE	Go, fool, and whom thou keep'st command.[7]	
	PETRUCCIO	Did ever Dian[8] so become a grove	

As Kate this chamber with her princely gait?
O, be thou Dian, and let her be Kate,
And then let Kate be chaste and Dian sportful.°   *playful; amorous*

255	KATHERINE	Where did you study all this goodly speech?	
	PETRUCCIO	It is extempore, from my mother-wit.°	*native intelligence*
	KATHERINE	A witty mother, witless else° her son.	*otherwise*
	PETRUCCIO	Am I not wise?	
	KATHERINE	Yes, keep you warm.[9]	
	PETRUCCIO	Marry, so I mean, sweet Katherine, in thy bed.	

260   And therefore setting all this chat aside,
Thus in plain terms: your father hath consented
That you shall be my wife, your dowry 'greed on,

---

3. Heralds kept books listing gentlemen and their coats of arms.
4. Image on a coat of arms; a fleshy ridge or comb on a rooster's head.
5. Court fool's cap (resembling a cock's comb or crest).
6. A cock with its comb cut down (and thought, there-

fore, to be gentle), with a pun on "cock" as "penis."
7. And command your servants (not me).
8. Goddess of the hunt and of chastity.
9. Alluding to the proverbial phrase "enough wit to keep oneself warm," implying that the person has few brains.

And will you, nill you,° I will marry you.   *if you will or not*
Now, Kate, I am a husband for your turn,°   *needs*
265   For by this light, whereby I see thy beauty—
Thy beauty that doth make me like thee well—
Thou must be married to no man but me,

      Enter BAPTISTA, GREMIO, [*and*] TRANIO [*as Lucentio*]

For I am he am born to tame you, Kate,
And bring you from a wild Kate° to a Kate   *(punning on "wildcat")*
270   Conformable° as other household Kates.   *Submissive*
Here comes your father. Never make denial.
I must and will have Katherine to my wife.
BAPTISTA   Now, Signor Petruccio, how speed you with my daughter?
PETRUCCIO   How but well, sir, how but well?
275   It were impossible I should speed amiss.
BAPTISTA   Why, how now, daughter Katherine—in your dumps?°   *dejected*
KATHERINE   Call you me daughter? Now I promise you
You have showed a tender fatherly regard,
To wish me wed to one half-lunatic,
280   A madcap ruffian and a swearing Jack,
That thinks with oaths to face the matter out.°   *get his way brazenly*
PETRUCCIO   Father, 'tis thus: yourself and all the world
That talked of her have talked amiss of her.
If she be curst, it is for policy,°   *part of a scheme*
285   For she's not froward,° but modest as the dove.   *willful*
She is not hot, but temperate as the morn.
For patience she will prove a second Grissel,[1]
And Roman Lucrece[2] for her chastity.
And to conclude, we have 'greed so well together
290   That upon Sunday is the wedding day.
KATHERINE   I'll see thee hanged on Sunday first.
GREMIO   Hark, Petruccio, she says she'll see thee hanged first.
TRANIO   Is this your speeding?° Nay then, goodnight our part.[3]   *progress*
PETRUCCIO   Be patient, gentlemen. I choose her for myself.
295   If she and I be pleased, what's that to you?
'Tis bargained 'twixt us twain, being alone,
That she shall still be curst in company.
I tell you, 'tis incredible to believe
How much she loves me. O, the kindest Kate!
300   She hung about my neck, and kiss on kiss
She vied° so fast, protesting oath on oath,   *went me one better*
That in a twink° she won me to her love.   *instant*
O, you are novices. 'Tis a world° to see   *worth a world*
How tame, when men and women are alone,
305   A meacock° wretch can make the curstest shrew.   *timid*
Give me thy hand, Kate. I will unto Venice,
To buy apparel 'gainst° the wedding day.   *in preparation for*
Provide the feast, father, and bid the guests.
I will be sure my Katherine shall be fine.°   *richly dressed*
310   BAPTISTA   I know not what to say, but give me your hands.
God send you joy, Petruccio! 'Tis a match.

---

1. Griselda, proverbial for "wifely patience." Chaucer's *Clerk's Tale* offers one version of her story.
2. In Roman legend, a married woman who killed herself after being raped by Tarquin. Shakespeare's *Rape of Lucrece* recounts the story.
3. Good-bye to our chances (of gaining Bianca).

GREMIO *and* TRANIO   Amen, say we. We will be witnesses.

PETRUCCIO   Father, and wife, and gentlemen, adieu.
　　I will to Venice. Sunday comes apace.
315　We will have rings, and things, and fine array;
　　And kiss me, Kate. We will be married o' Sunday.
　　　　　　　　Exeunt PETRUCCIO *and* KATHERINE [*severally*]°　　*separately*

GREMIO   Was ever match clapped up° so suddenly?　　*settled*

BAPTISTA   Faith, gentlemen, now I play a merchant's part,
　　And venture madly on a desperate mart.°　　*risky bargain*

320 TRANIO   'Twas a commodity lay fretting by you.⁴
　　'Twill bring you gain, or perish on the seas.

BAPTISTA   The gain I seek is quiet in the match.

GREMIO   No doubt but he hath got a quiet catch.
　　But now, Baptista, to your younger daughter.
325　Now is the day we long have looked for.
　　I am your neighbour, and was suitor first.

TRANIO   And I am one that love Bianca more
　　Than words can witness, or your thoughts can guess.

GREMIO   Youngling, thou canst not love so dear° as I.　　*deeply; expensively*

TRANIO   Greybeard, thy love doth freeze.

330 GREMIO　　　　　　　　　　　　　But thine doth fry.
　　Skipper,° stand back. 'Tis age that nourisheth.　　*Irresponsible youth*

TRANIO   But youth in ladies' eyes that flourisheth.

BAPTISTA   Content you, gentlemen. I will compound° this strife.　　*settle*
　　'Tis deeds must win the prize, and he of both°　　*whichever of you*
335　That can assure my daughter greatest dower
　　Shall have my Bianca's love.
　　Say, Signor Gremio, what can you assure her?

GREMIO   First, as you know, my house within the city
　　Is richly furnishèd with plate and gold,
340　Basins and ewers to lave° her dainty hands;　　*wash*
　　My hangings all of Tyrian⁵ tapestry.
　　In ivory coffers I have stuffed my crowns,°　　*coins*
　　In cypress chests my arras counterpoints,°　　*tapestry bedcovers*
　　Costly apparel, tents° and canopies,　　*bed curtains*
345　Fine linen, Turkey cushions bossed° with pearl,　　*embossed*
　　Valance° of Venice gold in needlework,　　*Fringe on bed drapery*
　　Pewter, and brass, and all things that belongs
　　To house or housekeeping. Then at my farm
　　I have a hundred milch-kine° to the pail,　　*dairy cows*
350　Six score fat oxen standing in my stalls,
　　And all things answerable to° this portion.　　*on the same scale as*
　　Myself am struck° in years, I must confess,　　*advanced*
　　And if I die tomorrow this is hers,
　　If whilst I live she will be only mine.

355 TRANIO   That 'only' came well in. Sir, list to me.
　　I am my father's heir and only son.
　　If I may have your daughter to my wife
　　I'll leave her houses three or four as good,
　　Within rich Pisa walls, as any one
360　Old Signor Gremio has in Padua,

---

4. It (that is, Katherine) was a piece of merchandise deteriorating in value or a sexually available woman fretting with irritation while in your possession.

5. Crimson or purple. (The Mediterranean city of Tyre was famous for dye of this color.)

Besides two thousand ducats by the year
Of fruitful land,[6] all which shall be her jointure.°   *marriage settlement*
What, have I pinched° you, Signor Gremio?   *distressed*

GREMIO   Two thousand ducats by the year of land—

365   My land amounts not to so much in all.
That she shall have; besides, an argosy°   *a merchant ship*
That now is lying in Marseilles road.°   *harbor*
What, have I choked you with an argosy?

TRANIO   Gremio, 'tis known my father hath no less

370   Than three great argosies, besides two galliasses°   *large cargo ships*
And twelve tight° galleys. These I will assure her,   *watertight*
And twice as much whate'er thou off 'rest next.

GREMIO   Nay, I have offered all. I have no more,
And she can have no more than all I have.

375   If you like me, she shall have me and mine.

TRANIO   Why then, the maid is mine from all the world.
By your firm promise Gremio is out-vied.°   *outbid*

BAPTISTA   I must confess your offer is the best,
And let° your father make her the assurance,   *provided*

380   She is your own. Else, you must pardon me,
If you should die before him, where's her dower?

TRANIO   That's but a cavil. He is old, I young.

GREMIO   And may not young men die as well as old?

BAPTISTA   Well, gentlemen,

385   I am thus resolved. On Sunday next, you know,
My daughter Katherine is to be married.
[*To* TRANIO] Now, on the Sunday following shall Bianca
Be bride to you, if you make this assurance;
If not, to Signor Gremio.

390   And so I take my leave, and thank you both.

GREMIO   Adieu, good neighbour.   *Exit* [BAPTISTA]
                                                   Now I fear thee not.
Sirrah, young gamester, your father were a fool
To give thee all, and in his waning age
Set foot under thy table.[7] Tut, a toy!°   *nonsense*

395   An old Italian fox is not so kind, my boy.   *Exit*

TRANIO   A vengeance on your crafty withered hide!
Yet I have faced it with a card of ten.[8]
'Tis in my head to do my master good.
I see no reason° but supposed Lucentio   *possible action*

400   Must get° a father called supposed Vincentio—   *beget; obtain*
And that's a wonder; fathers commonly
Do get their children, but in this case of wooing
A child shall get a sire, if I fail not of my cunning.   *Exit*

3.1

Enter LUCENTIO [*with books, as Cambio*], HORTENSIO
[*with a lute, as Licio*], *and* BIANCA

LUCENTIO   Fiddler, forbear. You grow too forward, sir.
Have you so soon forgot the entertainment

---

6. *Besides . . . land:* As well as fertile land that brings in an income of 2,000 ducats (Venetian gold coins) each year.
7. Become your dependent.

8. I have bluffed and won with a card of little value (a ten spot).
3.1 Location: Baptista's house in Padua.

Her sister Katherine welcomed you withal?°   *with*

HORTENSIO   But, wrangling pedant, this Bianca is,

5   The patroness of heavenly harmony.

Then give me leave to have prerogative,°   *precedence*

And when in music we have spent an hour

Your lecture° shall have leisure for as much.   *lesson*

LUCENTIO   Preposterous[1] ass, that never read so far

10   To know the cause why music was ordained!

Was it not to refresh the mind of man

After his studies or his usual pain?°   *labor*

Then give me leave to read philosophy,

And while I pause, serve in° your harmony.   *serve up (contemptuous)*

15 HORTENSIO   Sirrah, I will not bear these braves° of thine.   *insults*

BIANCA   Why, gentlemen, you do me double wrong

To strive for that which resteth in my choice.

I am no breeching[2] scholar in the schools.

I'll not be tied to hours nor 'pointed times,

20   But learn my lessons as I please myself;

And to cut off all strife, here sit we down.

[*To* HORTENSIO] Take you your instrument, play you the whiles.°   *in the meantime*

His lecture will be done ere you have tuned.

HORTENSIO   You'll leave his lecture when I am in tune?[3]

25 LUCENTIO   That will be never. Tune your instrument.

     [HORTENSIO *tunes his lute.* LUCENTIO *opens a book*]

BIANCA   Where left we last?

LUCENTIO   Here, madam.

     [*Reads*] 'Hic ibat Simois, hic est Sigeia tellus,

         Hic steterat Priami regia celsa senis.'[4]

30 BIANCA   Construe them.°   *Translate the lines*

LUCENTIO   'Hic ibat', as I told you before—'Simois', I am

Lucentio—'hic est', son unto Vincentio of Pisa—'Sigeia tellus',

disguised thus to get your love—'hic steterat', and that Lucen-

tio that comes a-wooing—'Priami', is my man Tranio—'regia',

35   bearing my port°—'celsa senis', that we might beguile the old   *taking my social position*

pantaloon.°   *foolish old man*

HORTENSIO   Madam, my instrument's in tune.

BIANCA   Let's hear. [HORTENSIO *plays*] O fie, the treble jars.°   *is discordant*

LUCENTIO   Spit in the hole,[5] man, and tune again.

     [HORTENSIO *tunes his lute again*]

40 BIANCA   Now let me see if I can construe it. 'Hic ibat Simois',

I know you not—'hic est Sigeia tellus', I trust you not—

'hic steterat Priami', take heed he hear us not—'regia', presume

not—'celsa senis', despair not.

HORTENSIO   Madam, 'tis now in tune.

LUCENTIO   All but the bass.

45 HORTENSIO   The bass is right, 'tis the base knave that jars.

     [*Aside*] How fiery and forward our pedant is!

---

1. Literally, putting last what should come first; reversing the natural order of things.
2. Youthful (in breeches); liable to be whipped (breeched).
3. When my lute is in the proper pitch. Lucentio responds with a pun on "in tune" as meaning "in harmony" with Bianca.
4. Latin lines from Penelope's letter to her husband Ulysses in Ovid's *Heroides*: "Here flowed the Simois; here is the Sigeian land; here stood old Priam's lofty palace."
5. Moisten the lute's peg hole (to aid tuning). Lucentio speaks contemptuously and may not be giving serious advice.

Now, for my life, the knave doth court my love.
Pedascule,° I'll watch you better yet.   *Little pedant*
BIANCA [*to* LUCENTIO]   In time I may believe; yet, I mistrust.
50   LUCENTIO   Mistrust it not, for sure Aeacides[6]
    Was Ajax, called so from his grandfather.
    BIANCA   I must believe my master, else, I promise you,
    I should be arguing still upon that doubt.
    But let it rest. Now Licio, to you.
55   Good master, take it not unkindly, pray,
    That I have been thus pleasant with you both.
    HORTENSIO [*to* LUCENTIO]   You may go walk and give me leave°   *allow me leisure*
    awhile.
    My lessons make no music in three parts.°   *for three voices*
    LUCENTIO   Are you so formal,° sir? Well, I must wait.   *precise*
60   [*Aside*] And watch withal, for but° I be deceived   *unless*
    Our fine musician groweth amorous.
    HORTENSIO   Madam, before you touch the instrument
    To learn the order of my fingering,
    I must begin with rudiments of art,
65   To teach you gamut[7] in a briefer sort,°   *quicker way*
    More pleasant, pithy, and effectual
    Than hath been taught by any of my trade;
    And there it is in writing, fairly drawn.
             [*He gives a paper*]
    BIANCA   Why, I am past my gamut long ago.
70   HORTENSIO   Yet read the gamut of Hortensio.
    BIANCA [*reads*]
       'Gam-ut I am, the ground° of all accord,   *lowest note; basis*
         A—re—to plead Hortensio's passion.
         B—mi—Bianca, take him for thy lord,
           C—fa, ut—that loves with all affection.
75   D—sol, re—one clef, two notes[8] have I,
         E—la, mi—show pity, or I die.'
    Call you this gamut? Tut, I like it not.
    Old fashions please me best. I am not so nice°   *capricious*
    To change true rules for odd inventions.
         Enter a MESSENGER
80   MESSENGER   Mistress, your father prays you leave your books
    And help to dress your sister's chamber up.
    You know tomorrow is the wedding day.
    BIANCA   Farewell, sweet masters both. I must be gone.
    LUCENTIO   Faith, mistress, then I have no cause to stay.
         [*Exeunt* BIANCA, MESSENGER, *and* LUCENTIO]
85   HORTENSIO   But I have cause to pry into this pedant.
    Methinks he looks as though he were in love.
    Yet if thy thoughts, Bianca, be so humble°   *low*
    To cast thy wand'ring eyes on every stale,°   *bait; lure*
    Seize thee that list.[9] If once I find thee ranging,°   *unfaithful*
90   Hortensio will be quit with thee by changing.[1]   *Exit*

---

6. Aeacides, or Ajax, was named after his grandfather
Aeacus. Lucentio pretends to continue the lesson.
7. A musical scale, named after its lowest note,
"gamma-ut."

8. Referring perhaps to his one love and two identities.
9. Let anyone who wants you take you.
1. Will get even with you or get rid of you by finding
another love.

3.2

Enter BAPTISTA, GREMIO, TRANIO [AS LUCENTIO],
KATHERINE, BIANCA, AND OTHERS, ATTENDANTS[1]

BAPTISTA [*to* TRANIO] Signor Lucentio, this is the 'pointed day
    That Katherine and Petruccio should be married,
    And yet we hear not of our son-in-law.
    What will be said, what mockery will it be,
5   To want° the bridegroom when the priest attends   *lack*
    To speak the ceremonial rites of marriage?
    What says Lucentio to this shame of ours?
KATHERINE   No shame but mine. I must forsooth be forced
    To give my hand opposed against my heart
10 Unto a mad-brain rudesby° full of spleen,[2]   *unmannerly fellow*
    Who wooed in haste and means to wed at leisure.
    I told you, I, he was a frantic° fool,   *mad*
    Hiding his bitter jests in blunt behaviour,
    And to be noted for a merry man
15 He'll woo a thousand, 'point the day of marriage,
    Make friends, invite them, and proclaim the banns,
    Yet never means to wed where he hath wooed.
    Now must the world point at poor Katherine
    And say 'Lo, there is mad Petruccio's wife,
20 If it would please him come and marry her.'
TRANIO   Patience, good Katherine, and Baptista, too.
    Upon my life, Petruccio means but well.
    Whatever fortune stays° him from his word,   *incident keeps*
    Though he be blunt, I know him passing wise;
25 Though he be merry, yet withal he's honest.[3]
KATHERINE   Would Katherine had never seen him, though.

                                                    Exit weeping

BAPTISTA   Go, girl. I cannot blame thee now to weep.
    For such an injury would vex a very saint,
    Much more a shrew of thy impatient humour.

                  Enter BIONDELLO

30 BIONDELLO   Master, master, news—old news, and such news as
    you never heard of.
BAPTISTA   Is it new and old too? How may that be?
BIONDELLO   Why, is it not news to hear of Petruccio's coming?
BAPTISTA   Is he come?
35 BIONDELLO   Why, no, sir.
BAPTISTA   What then?
BIONDELLO   He is coming.
BAPTISTA   When will he be here?
BIONDELLO   When he stands where I am and sees you there.
40 TRANIO   But say, what to thine old news?
BIONDELLO   Why, Petruccio is coming in a new hat and an old
    jerkin,° a pair of old breeches thrice-turned,[4] a pair of boots   *jacket*

3.2 Location: In front of Baptista's house.
1. Many editors include Lucentio, disguised as Cambio, among the characters who enter at this point, though he speaks no lines in the events leading up to and including Petruccio's arrival for his wedding. The Oxford editors feel that Lucentio only comes onstage when all the characters who enter at 3.2 to attend Katherine and Petruccio's wedding (3.2.116–20) leave. They then mark a new scene, 3.3, when Lucentio enters with Tranio.

2. Caprice; impulsiveness. Contemporary medical theorists claimed that high and low spirits originated in the spleen.
3. Some critics find Tranio's familiarity with Petruccio improbable. Possibly these lines were originally meant to be spoken by Hortensio.
4. Turned inside out three times (to make them last longer).

that have been candle-cases,[5] one buckled, another laced, an
old rusty sword ta'en out of the town armoury with a broken
45 hilt, and chapeless,[6] with two broken points,[7] his horse hipped,°   *lame in the hips*
with an old mothy saddle and stirrups of no kindred,° besides,   *unmatched*
possessed with the glanders[8] and like to mose in the chine,[9]
troubled with the lampass,[1] infected with the fashions,° full   *farcins (small tumors)*
of windgalls,[2] sped with spavins,[3] rayed with the yellows,°   *disfigured by jaundice*
50 past cure of the fives,[4] stark spoiled with the staggers,[5] be-
gnawn with the bots,[6] weighed in the back° and shoulder-   *swaybacked*
shotten,[7] near-legged before[8] and with a half-cheeked° bit and   *improperly attached*
a headstall[9] of sheep's leather which, being restrained° to   *tightened*
keep him from stumbling, hath been often burst and now
55 repaired with knots, one girth° six times pieced,° and a woman's   *saddle strap / mended*
crupper of velour[1] which hath two letters for her name fairly set
down in studs, and here and there pieced with packthread.°   *twine*

BAPTISTA   Who comes with him?

BIONDELLO   O sir, his lackey, for all the world caparisoned° like   *outfitted*
60 the horse, with a linen stock° on one leg and a kersey boot-   *stocking*
hose[2] on the other, gartered with a red and blue list;° an old   *strip of cloth*
hat, and the humour of forty fancies pricked in't for a
feather[3]—a monster, a very monster in apparel, and not like a
Christian footboy or a gentleman's lackey.

65 TRANIO   'Tis some odd humour pricks° him to this fashion;   *incites, urges*
Yet oftentimes he goes but mean-apparelled.

BAPTISTA   I am glad he's come, howsoe'er he comes.

BIONDELLO   Why, sir, he comes not.

BAPTISTA   Didst thou not say he comes?

70 BIONDELLO   Who? That Petruccio came?

BAPTISTA   Ay, that Petruccio came.

BIONDELLO   No, sir. I say his horse comes with him on his back.

BAPTISTA   Why, that's all one.°   *the same thing*

BIONDELLO   Nay, by Saint Jamy,
75   I hold° you a penny,   *bet*
         A horse and a man
         Is more than one,
         And yet not many.

Enter PETRUCCIO *and* GRUMIO[*fantastically dressed*]

PETRUCCIO   Come, where be these gallants? Who's at home?

80 BAPTISTA   You are welcome, sir.

PETRUCCIO   And yet I come not well.

BAPTISTA   And yet you halt° not.   *limp*

---

5. In other words, discarded and used to store old candle ends.
6. Without the metal tip that protects the sword's point.
7. With two laces that don't hold up his hose; with two points (instead of one) on his broken sword.
8. The first in a catalogue of horse diseases, most of which are described in Gervase Markham's *Discourse of Horsemanship* (1593). The glanders caused swellings and nasal discharge.
9. Obscure phrase, probably meaning the horse was apt to suffer discharge from the nostrils, indicating the last stage of glanders.
1. A disease characterized by swellings in the mouth.
2. Soft tumors usually appearing on the fetlock, so

called because they were thought to contain air.
3. Rendered useless by swelling of the leg joints.
4. Swelling of glands below the ears.
5. A disease causing loss of balance.
6. Eaten by intestinal worms.
7. With sprained shoulders.
8. With knock-kneed forelegs.
9. The part of the bridle that fits around the horse's head. Sheepskin would be inferior to the animal skins normally used.
1. *crupper*: strap that passes under a horse's tail to keep the saddle straight, *velour*: velvet.
2. A coarse wool stocking.
3. Possibly an absurdly fanciful decoration attached to the hat instead of a feather.

TRANIO   Not so well apparelled as I wish you were.

PETRUCCIO   Were it not better I should rush in thus—

85   But where is Kate? Where is my lovely bride?
How does my father? Gentles,[4] methinks you frown.
And wherefore gaze this goodly company
As if they saw some wondrous monument,
Some comet or unusual prodigy?

90   BAPTISTA   Why, sir, you know this is your wedding day.
First were we sad, fearing you would not come;
Now sadder that you come so unprovided.°   unprepared
Fie, doff this habit,° shame to your estate,°   outfit / social place
An eyesore to our solemn festival.

95   TRANIO   And tell us what occasion of import
Hath all so long detained you from your wife
And sent you hither so unlike yourself?

PETRUCCIO   Tedious it were to tell, and harsh to hear.
Sufficeth I am come to keep my word,

100   Though in some part enforcèd to digress,°   deviate from my plan
Which at more leisure I will so excuse
As you shall well be satisfied withal.
But where is Kate? I stay too long from her.
The morning wears, 'tis time we were at church.

105   TRANIO   See not your bride in these unreverent° robes.   disrespectful
Go to my chamber, put on clothes of mine.

PETRUCCIO   Not I, believe me. Thus I'll visit her.

BAPTISTA   But thus, I trust, you will not marry her.

PETRUCCIO   Good sooth,° even thus. Therefore ha' done with words.   Yes indeed

110   To me she's married, not unto my clothes.
Could I repair what she will wear° in me   wear out (in sex)
As I can change these poor accoutrements,
'Twere well for Kate and better for myself.
But what a fool am I to chat with you

115   When I should bid good morrow to my bride,
And seal the title with a lovely° kiss!   Exit [with GRUMIO]   loving

TRANIO   He hath some meaning in his mad attire.
We will persuade him, be it possible,
To put on better ere he go to church.   [Exit with GREMIO]

120   BAPTISTA   I'll after him, and see the event° of this.   Exeunt   outcome

3.3

[Enter LUCENTIO as Cambio, and TRANIO as Lucentio]

TRANIO   But, sir, to love concerneth us to add[1]
Her father's liking, which to bring to pass,
As I before imparted to your worship,
I am to get a man—whate'er he be

5   It skills° not much, we'll fit him to our turn—   matters
And he shall be Vincentio of Pisa,
And make assurance here in Padua
Of greater sums than I have promisèd.

---

4. The polite term of address to men and women of the gentry.
3.3 Location: Scene continues.

1. To the love between Bianca and Lucentio it is necessary for us to add.

So shall you quietly enjoy your hope,°   *what you hope for*

10   And marry sweet Bianca with consent.

LUCENTIO   Were it not that my fellow schoolmaster

    Doth watch Bianca's steps so narrowly,

    'Twere good, methinks, to steal our marriage,°   *elope*

    Which once performed, let all the world say no,

15   I'll keep mine own, despite of all the world.

TRANIO   That by degrees we mean to look into,

    And watch our vantage° in this business.   *opportunity*

    We'll overreach the greybeard Gremio,

    The narrow-prying° father Minola,   *overly suspicious*

20   The quaint° musician, amorous Licio,   *skillful; crafty*

    All for my master's sake, Lucentio.

      Enter GREMIO

    Signor Gremio, came you from the church?

GREMIO   As willingly as e'er I came from school.

TRANIO   And is the bride and bridegroom coming home?

25   GREMIO   A bridegroom, say you? 'Tis a groom° indeed—   *crude, lower-class man*

    A grumbling groom, and that the girl shall find.

TRANIO   Curster° than she? Why, 'tis impossible.   *More cantankerous*

GREMIO   Why, he's a devil, a devil, a very fiend.

TRANIO   Why, she's a devil, a devil, the devil's dam.°   *mother*

30   GREMIO   Tut, she's a lamb, a dove, a fool to him.²

    I'll tell you, Sir Lucentio: when the priest

    Should ask if Katherine should be his wife,

    'Ay, by Gog's woun's,'³ quoth he, and swore so loud

    That all amazed the priest let fall the book,

35   And as he stooped again to take it up

    This mad-brained bridegroom took° him such a cuff   *gave*

    That down fell priest, and book, and book, and priest.

    'Now take them up,' quoth he, 'if any list.'°   *choose*

TRANIO   What said the vicar when he rose again?

40   GREMIO   Trembled and shook, forwhy° he° stamped and swore   *because* / (Petruccio)

    As if the vicar meant to cozen⁴ him.

    But after many ceremonies done

    He calls for wine. 'A health,' quoth he, as if

    He had been aboard,° carousing to his mates   *(a ship)*

45   After a storm; quaffed off the muscatel⁵

    And threw the sops all in the sexton's face,

    Having no other reason

    But that his beard grew thin and hungerly°   *sparsely; as if hungry*

    And seemed to ask him sops as he was drinking.

50   This done, he took the bride about the neck

    And kissed her lips with such a clamorous smack

    That at the parting all the church did echo,

    And I seeing this came thence for very shame,

    And after me, I know, the rout° is coming.   *crowd*

55   Such a mad marriage never was before.

      Music plays

    Hark, hark, I hear the minstrels play.

---

2. A good-natured innocent compared with him.
3. By God's (Christ's) wounds (a common oath).
4. Cheat (by not performing a legally binding ceremony).

5. Wine with small cakes, or "sops," soaked in it, traditionally drunk by the newly married couple and their guests.

Enter PETRUCCIO, KATHERINE, BIANCA, HORTENSIO
[*as Licio*], BAPTISTA, [GRUMIO, *and others*, attendants]

PETRUCCIO   Gentlemen and friends, I thank you for your pains.
I know you think to dine with me today,
And have prepared great store of wedding cheer.°   *food and drink*
60   But so it is my haste doth call me hence,
And therefore here I mean to take my leave.
BAPTISTA   Is't possible you will away tonight?
PETRUCCIO   I must away today, before night come.
Make° it no wonder. If you knew my business,   *Consider*
65   You would entreat me rather go than stay.
And, honest° company, I thank you all   *worthy*
That have beheld me give away myself
To this most patient, sweet, and virtuous wife.
Dine with my father, drink a health to me,
70   For I must hence; and farewell to you all.
TRANIO   Let us entreat you stay till after dinner.
PETRUCCIO   It may not be.
GREMIO   Let me entreat you.
PETRUCCIO   It cannot be.
KATHERINE   Let me entreat you.
PETRUCCIO   I am content.
KATHERINE   Are you content to stay?
75   PETRUCCIO   I am content you shall entreat me stay,
But yet not stay, entreat me how you can.
KATHERINE   Now, if you love me, stay.
PETRUCCIO   Grumio, my horse.
GRUMIO   Ay, sir, they be ready. The oats have eaten the horses.[6]
KATHERINE   Nay, then, do what thou canst, I will not go today,
80   No, nor tomorrow—not till I please myself.
The door is open, sir, there lies your way.
You may be jogging whiles your boots are green.[7]
For me, I'll not be gone till I please myself.
'Tis like you'll prove a jolly,° surly groom,   *an arrogant*
85   That take it on you at the first so roundly.[8]
PETRUCCIO   O Kate, content thee. Prithee, be not angry.
KATHERINE   I will be angry. What hast thou to do?[9]
Father, be quiet. He shall stay° my leisure.   *await*
GREMIO   Ay, marry, sir. Now it begins to work.
90   KATHERINE   Gentlemen, forward to the bridal dinner.
I see a woman may be made a fool
If she had not a spirit to resist.
PETRUCCIO   They shall go forward, Kate, at thy command.
Obey the bride, you that attend on her.
95   Go to the feast, revel and domineer,°   *feast sumptuously*
Carouse full measure to her maidenhead.
Be mad and merry, or go hang yourselves.
But for my bonny Kate, she must with me.
Nay, look not big,° nor stamp, nor stare, nor fret.   *defiant*

6. Either Grumio gets it the wrong way around, or he is joking about the great quantity of oats the horses have eaten.
7. You can be off now while your boots are new ("green"). Proverbial expression for getting an early start or getting rid of an unwelcome guest.
8. That takes charge at the outset so outspokenly.
9. What business is it of yours?

100   I will be master of what is mine own.
              She is my goods, my chattels. She is my house,
              My household-stuff, my field, my barn,
              My horse, my ox, my ass, my anything,
              And here she stands, touch her whoever dare.[1]
105   I'll bring mine action on° the proudest he   *attack; sue (in court)*
              That stops my way in Padua. Grumio,
              Draw forth thy weapon, we are beset with thieves.
              Rescue thy mistress if thou be a man.
              Fear not, sweet wench. They shall not touch thee, Kate.
110   I'll buckler° thee against a million.   *shield*

                 Exeunt PETRUCCIO, KATHERINE [*and* GRUMIO]

BAPTISTA   Nay, let them go—a couple of quiet ones!
GREMIO   Went they not quickly I should die with laughing.
TRANIO   Of all mad matches never was the like.
LUCENTIO   Mistress, what's your opinion of your sister?
115 BIANCA   That being mad herself she's madly mated.
GREMIO   I warrant him, Petruccio is Kated.[2]
BAPTISTA   Neighbours and friends, though bride and bridegroom wants° *are missing*
              For to supply° the places at the table,   *To fill*
              You know there wants no junkets° at the feast.   *sweetmeats*
120   Lucentio, you shall supply the bridegroom's place,
              And let Bianca take her sister's room.
TRANIO   Shall sweet Bianca practise how to bride it?
BAPTISTA   She shall, Lucentio. Come, gentlemen, let's go.

                                        Exeunt

4.1

        Enter GRUMIO

GRUMIO   Fie, fie on all tired jades,° on all mad masters, and all   *worn-out horses*
    foul° ways. Was ever man so beaten? Was ever man so rayed?°   *muddy / dirtied*
    Was ever man so weary? I am sent before to make a fire, and
    they are coming after to warm them. Now were not I a little
5   pot and soon hot,[1] my very lips might freeze to my teeth, my
    tongue to the roof of my mouth, my heart in my belly ere
    I should come by a fire to thaw me. But I with blowing the fire
    shall warm myself, for considering the weather, a taller[2] man
    than I will take cold. Holla! Hoa, Curtis!

        Enter CURTIS

10 CURTIS   Who is that calls so coldly?
GRUMIO   A piece of ice. If thou doubt it, thou mayst slide from
    my shoulder to my heel with no greater a run but my head and
    my neck. A fire, good Curtis!
CURTIS   Is my master and his wife coming, Grumio?
15 GRUMIO   O ay, Curtis, ay, and therefore fire, fire! Cast on no
    water.[3]
CURTIS   Is she so hot a shrew as she's reported?

---

1. Petruccio warns others to leave Kate alone. In cata-
loguing the ways she is one of his possessions, he
alludes to the Tenth Commandment, which forbids
coveting a neighbor's wife or property.
2. Mated with a "Kate"; afflicted with Kate (imagined
as a disease).
4.1 Location: Petruccio's country house.

1. Proverbial for a small person who quickly becomes
angry.
2. Punning on "taller" as meaning "sturdier."
3. Alluding to the popular song "Scotland's Burning,"
in which the words "Fire, fire" are followed by "Cast on
water, cast on water."

GRUMIO She was, good Curtis, before this frost; but thou
know'st, winter tames man, woman, and beast, for it hath
20 tamed my old master, and my new mistress, and myself, fellow Curtis.

CURTIS Away, you three-inch° fool. I am no beast.   *short*

GRUMIO Am I but three inches? Why, thy horn[4] is a foot, and
so long am I, at the least. But wilt thou make a fire, or shall I
25 complain on thee to our mistress, whose hand—she being
now at hand—thou shalt soon feel to thy cold comfort, for
being slow in thy hot office.°   *fire-making duties*

CURTIS I prithee, good Grumio, tell me—how goes the world?

GRUMIO A cold world, Curtis, in every office but thine. And
30 therefore fire, do thy duty, and have thy duty,° for my master   *take your reward*
and mistress are almost frozen to death.

CURTIS There's fire ready, and therefore, good Grumio, the
news.

GRUMIO Why, 'Jack boy, ho boy!',[5] and as much news as wilt thou.

35 CURTIS Come, you are so full of cony-catching.[6]

GRUMIO Why, therefore fire, for I have caught extreme cold.
Where's the cook? Is supper ready, the house trimmed, rushes
strewed,[7] cobwebs swept, the servingmen in their new fustian,°   *coarse cloth*
the white stockings, and every officer° his wedding garment   *servant*
40 on? Be the Jacks fair within, the Jills fair without,[8] the carpets° *table coverings*
laid, and everything in order?

CURTIS All ready, and therefore, I pray thee, news.

GRUMIO First, know my horse is tired, my master and mistress
fallen out.

45 CURTIS How?

GRUMIO Out of their saddles into the dirt, and thereby hangs a
tale.

CURTIS Let's ha't, good Grumio.

GRUMIO Lend thine ear.

50 CURTIS Here.

GRUMIO [*cuffing him*] There.

CURTIS This 'tis to feel a tale, not to hear a tale.

GRUMIO And therefore 'tis called a sensible tale,[9] and this cuff
was but to knock at your ear and beseech listening. Now I
55 begin. *Inprimis*,° we came down a foul° hill, my master riding   *First / muddy*
behind my mistress.

CURTIS Both of° one horse?   *on*

GRUMIO What's that to thee?

CURTIS Why, a horse.

60 GRUMIO Tell thou the tale. But hadst thou not crossed° me   *interrupted*
thou shouldst have heard how her horse fell and she under
her horse; thou shouldst have heard in how miry a place, how
she was bemoiled,° how he left her with the horse upon her,   *covered with mud*
how he beat me because her horse stumbled, how she waded
65 through the dirt to pluck him off me, how he swore, how she
prayed that never prayed before, how I cried, how the horses
ran away, how her bridle was burst, how I lost my crupper,

---

4. The proverbial sign of a cuckold; an erect penis.
Grumio implies that he is "long" enough to cuckold
Curtis.
5. A line from another popular song.
6. Trickery, with a play on the "catches," or songs, of

which Grumio is fond. A cony is a rabbit.
7. Scattered on the floor.
8. Jacks and Jills were manservants and maidservants;
also leather drinking vessels and metal drinking vessels.
9. Reasonable; capable of being felt.

with many things of worthy memory which now shall die in
oblivion, and thou return unexperienced° to thy grave.   *ignorant; unknowing*

70   CURTIS   By this reckoning he is more shrew than she.

GRUMIO   Ay, and that thou and the proudest of you all shall find
when he comes home. But what° talk I of this? Call forth   *why*
Nathaniel, Joseph, Nicholas, Philip, Walter, Sugarsop, and
the rest. Let their heads be sleekly combed, their blue coats[1]

75   brushed, and their garters of an indifferent° knit. Let them   *ordinary; a matching*
curtsy with their left legs and not presume to touch a hair of
my master's horse-tail till they kiss their hands.[2] Are they all
ready?

CURTIS   They are.

80   GRUMIO   Call them forth.

CURTIS [*calling*]   Do you hear, ho? You must meet my master to
countenance[3] my mistress.

GRUMIO   Why, she hath a face of her own.

CURTIS   Who knows not that?

85   GRUMIO   Thou, it seems, that calls for company to countenance
her.

CURTIS   I call them forth to credit[4] her.

Enter four or five servingmen

GRUMIO   Why, she comes to borrow nothing of them.

NATHANIEL   Welcome home, Grumio!

90   PHILIP   How now, Grumio?

JOSEPH   What, Grumio?

NICHOLAS   Fellow Grumio!

NATHANIEL   How now, old lad!

GRUMIO   Welcome you, how now you, what you, fellow you, and

95   thus much for greeting. Now, my spruce° companions, is all   *smartly dressed*
ready and all things neat?

NATHANIEL   All things is ready. How near is our master?

GRUMIO   E'en at hand, alighted by this, and therefore be not—
Cock's° passion, silence! I hear my master.   *God's (a common oath)*

Enter PETRUCCIO *and* KATHERINE

100   PETRUCCIO   Where be these knaves? What, no man at door
To hold my stirrup nor to take my horse?
Where is Nathaniel, Gregory, Philip?

ALL SERVANTS   Here, here sir, here sir.

PETRUCCIO   Here sir, here sir, here sir, here sir!

105   You logger-headed° and unpolished grooms,   *stupid*
What! No attendance! No regard! No duty!
Where is the foolish knave I sent before?

GRUMIO   Here, sir, as foolish as I was before.

PETRUCCIO   You peasant swain,° you whoreson,° malthorse   *farm laborer / bastard*
drudge,[5]

110   Did I not bid thee meet me in the park[6]
And bring along these rascal knaves with thee?

GRUMIO   Nathaniel's coat, sir, was not fully made,
And Gabriel's pumps° were all unpinked° i'th' heel.   *shoes / not ornamented*
There was no link[7] to colour Peter's hat,

---

1. The usual servant uniform.
2. A greeting signifying inordinate submissiveness.
3. Greet, pay respects to; with a pun in the next line on "countenance" as meaning "face."
4. Honor, with pun in next line on "credit" as meaning "offer financial assistance."

5. Stupid, menial worker. The slow, heavy malt horse was used to grind malt by turning a treadmill.
6. A piece of ground comprising woodland and pasture attached to a country house and used for recreation.
7. Torch, the smoke of which was used to blacken shoes.

115   And Walter's dagger was not come from sheathing.°   *having a sheath fixed*
      There were none fine but Adam, Ralph, and Gregory.
      The rest were ragged, old, and beggarly.
      Yet as they are, here are they come to meet you.
PETRUCCIO   Go, rascals, go and fetch my supper in.

                                       Exeunt servants

120   [*Sings*]   'Where is the life that late I led?
                Where are those—'8
      Sit down, Kate, and welcome. Soud, soud, soud, soud.9

           Enter servants with supper

      Why, when, I say?—Nay, good sweet Kate, be merry.—
      Off with my boots, you rogues, you villains. When?
125   [*Sings*]   'It was the friar of orders gray,
                As he forth walkèd on his way.'1
      Out, you rogue, you pluck my foot awry.
      [*Kicking a servant*] Take that, and mend the plucking of the other.
      Be merry, Kate. [*Calling*] Some water, here. What, hoa!

          Enter one with water

130   Where's my spaniel Troilus? Sirrah, get you hence,
      And bid my cousin Ferdinand come hither—
      One, Kate, that you must kiss and be acquainted with.
      [*Calling*] Where are my slippers? Shall I have some water?
      Come, Kate, and wash, and welcome heartily.

           [*A servant drops water*]

135   You whoreson villain, will you let it fall?
KATHERINE   Patience, I pray you, 'twas a fault unwilling.
PETRUCCIO   A whoreson, beetle-headed,° flap-eared knave.   *thick-headed*
      Come, Kate, sit down, I know you have a stomach.°   *an appetite; temper*
      Will you give thanks, sweet Kate, or else shall I?
      What's this—mutton?
FIRST SERVINGMAN   Ay.
PETRUCCIO   Who brought it?
140 PETER   I.
PETRUCCIO   'Tis burnt, and so is all the meat.
      What dogs are these? Where is the rascal cook?
      How durst you villains bring it from the dresser°   *cook; sideboard*
      And serve it thus to me that love it not?
145   There, [*throwing food*] take it to you, trenchers,° cups, and all,   *plates*
      You heedless jolt-heads° and unmannered slaves.   *careless blockheads*
      What, do you grumble? I'll be with you straight.

          [*He chases the servants away*]

KATHERINE   I pray you, husband, be not so disquiet.
      The meat was well, if you were so contented.
150 PETRUCCIO   I tell thee, Kate, 'twas burnt and dried away,
      And I expressly am forbid to touch it,
      For it engenders choler,2 planteth anger,
      And better 'twere that both of us did fast,
      Since of ourselves° ourselves are choleric,   *by our natures*
155   Than feed it with such overroasted flesh.

---

8. Probably a fragment of a ballad, now lost, lamenting a newlywed's loss of freedom.
9. An expression of impatience.
1. Another fragment of a lost song, perhaps one of the many songs about a friar's seduction of a nun.
2. It causes anger. An excess of the choleric humor was believed to provoke anger.

Be patient, tomorrow't shall be mended,
And for this night we'll fast for company.°   *together*
Come, I will bring thee to thy bridal chamber.   *Exeunt*
          Enter servants severally
NATHANIEL   Peter, didst ever see the like?
160 PETER   He kills her in her own humour.³
          Enter CURTIS, *a servant*
GRUMIO   Where is he?
CURTIS   In her chamber,
Making a sermon of continency° to her,   *on self-control*
And rails, and swears, and rates,° that she, poor soul,   *scolds*
165 Knows not which way to stand, to look, to speak,
And sits as one new risen from a dream.
Away, away, for he is coming hither.   [*Exeunt*]
          Enter PETRUCCIO
PETRUCCIO   Thus have I politicly° begun my reign,   *cunningly*
And 'tis my hope to end successfully.
170 My falcon⁴ now is sharp° and passing° empty,   *hungry / extremely*
And till she stoop⁵ she must not be full-gorged,°   *fully fed*
For then she never looks upon her lure.°   *falconer's bait*
Another way I have to man my haggard,°   *tame my female hawk*
To make her come and know her keeper's call—
175 That is, to watch her° as we watch these kites°   *keep her awake / hawks*
That bate and beat,⁶ and will not be obedient.
She ate no meat today, nor none shall eat.
Last night she slept not, nor tonight she shall not.
As with the meat, some undeservèd fault
180 I'll find about the making of the bed,
And here I'll fling the pillow, there the bolster,
This way the coverlet, another way the sheets,
Ay, and amid this hurly I intend°   *will pretend*
That all is done in reverent care of her,
185 And in conclusion she shall watch° all night,   *stay awake*
And if she chance to nod I'll rail and brawl
And with the clamour keep her still awake.
This is a way to kill a wife with kindness,
And thus I'll curb her mad and headstrong humour.
190 He that knows better how to tame a shrew,
Now let him speak. 'Tis charity to show.°   *Exit*   (*his methods*)

4.2
          Enter TRANIO [*as Lucentio,*] *and* HORTENSIO [*as Licio*]
TRANIO   Is't possible, friend Licio, that Mistress Bianca
Doth fancy any other but Lucentio?
I tell you, sir, she bears me fair in hand.°   *leads me on*
HORTENSIO   Sir, to satisfy you in what I have said,
5   Stand by, and mark the manner of his teaching.
          [*They stand aside.*]
          Enter BIANCA [*and* LUCENTIO *as Cambio*]
LUCENTIO   Now, mistress, profit you in what you read?
BIANCA   What, master, read you? First resolve° me that.   *answer*

---

3. He subdues her choleric humor by outdoing her in
bad temper.
4. In what follows, Petruccio likens his methods of dis-
ciplining Katherine to the training of a wild hawk.

5. Fly to the bait; submit to my authority.
6. That flutter and flap their wings (instead of settling
on the falconer's fist).
4.2 Location: Padua, in front of Baptista's house.

LUCENTIO   I read that I profess,° *The Art to Love.*[1]   *what I practice*
BIANCA   And may you prove, sir, master of your art.
10   LUCENTIO   While you, sweet dear, prove mistress of my heart.
          [*They stand aside*]
HORTENSIO   Quick proceeders,[2] marry! Now tell me, I pray,
     You that durst swear that your mistress Bianca
     Loved none in the world so well as Lucentio.
TRANIO   O despiteful° love, unconstant womankind!   *cruel*
15   I tell thee, Licio, this is wonderful.°   *astonishing*
HORTENSIO   Mistake no more, I am not Licio,
     Nor a musician as I seem to be,
     But one that scorn to live in this disguise
     For such a one° as leaves a gentleman   *(Bianca)*
20   And makes a god of such a cullion.°   *base fellow*
     Know, sir, that I am called Hortensio.
TRANIO   Signor Hortensio, I have often heard
     Of your entire° affection to Bianca,   *sincere*
     And since mine eyes are witness of her lightness°   *sexual infidelity*
25   I will with you, if you be so contented,
     Forswear Bianca and her love for ever.
HORTENSIO   See how they kiss and court. Signor Lucentio,
     Here is my hand, and here I firmly vow
     Never to woo her more, but do forswear her
30   As one unworthy all the former favours
     That I have fondly° flattered her withal.   *foolishly*
TRANIO   And here I take the like unfeignèd oath
     Never to marry with her, though she would entreat.
     Fie on her, see how beastly° she doth court him!   *lewdly*
35   HORTENSIO   Would all the world but he had quite forsworn.[3]
     For me, that I may surely keep mine oath
     I will be married to a wealthy widow
     Ere three days pass, which hath as long loved me
     As I have loved this proud disdainful haggard.°   *intractable woman; hawk*
40   And so farewell, Signor Lucentio.
     Kindness in women, not their beauteous looks,
     Shall win my love; and so I take my leave,
     In resolution as I swore before.   [*Exit*]
TRANIO   Mistress Bianca, bless you with such grace
45   As 'longeth° to a lover's blessèd case.°   *belongs / state*
     Nay, I have ta'en you napping, gentle love,
     And have forsworn you with Hortensio.
BIANCA   Tranio, you jest. But have you both forsworn me?
TRANIO   Mistress, we have.
LUCENTIO   Then we are rid of Licio.
50   TRANIO   I'faith, he'll have a lusty° widow now,   *lively; lustful*
     That shall be wooed and wedded in a day.
BIANCA   God give him joy.
TRANIO   Ay, and he'll tame her.
BIANCA   He says so, Tranio.
55   TRANIO   Faith, he is gone unto the taming-school.

---

1. Ovid's *Ars Amatoria*, in which the poet calls himself the "Professor of Love" and treats erotic love as a science.
2. Taking up the allusion to a university degree implicit in Bianca's "master of your art," Hortensio puns on

"proceeding" from a bachelor's to a master's degree.
3. I wish that everyone but Cambio had given her over (so that she will be left an old maid as she deserves; Hortensio apparently assumes that Bianca would never marry a poor musician).

BIANCA The taming-school—what, is there such a place?
TRANIO Ay, mistress, and Petruccio is the master,
    That teacheth tricks eleven-and-twenty long[4]
    To tame a shrew and charm her chattering tongue.[5]

Enter BIONDELLO

60 BIONDELLO O, master, master, I have watched so long
    That I am dog-weary, but at last I spied
    An ancient angel[6] coming down the hill
    Will serve the turn.
TRANIO   What is he, Biondello?
BIONDELLO Master, a marcantant[7] or a pedant,°   *schoolmaster*
65   I know not what, but formal in apparel,
    In gait and countenance surely like a father.
LUCENTIO And what of him, Tranio?
TRANIO If he be credulous and trust my tale,
    I'll make him glad to seem° Vincentio   *pretend to be*
70 And give assurance to Baptista Minola
    As if he were the right Vincentio.
    Take in your love, and then let me alone.

[*Exeunt* LUCENTIO *and* BIANCA]

Enter a PEDANT[8]

PEDANT God save you, sir.
TRANIO   And you, sir. You are welcome.
    Travel you farre on, or are you at the farthest?
75 PEDANT Sir, at the farthest for a week or two,
    But then up farther and as far as Rome,
    And so to Tripoli,[9] if God lend me life.
TRANIO What countryman, I pray?
PEDANT   Of Mantua.
TRANIO Of Mantua, sir? Marry, God forbid,
80 And come to Padua careless of your life!
PEDANT My life, sir? How, I pray? For that goes hard.°   *is difficult to deal with*
TRANIO 'Tis death for anyone in Mantua
    To come to Padua. Know you not the cause?
    Your ships are stayed° at Venice, and the Duke,   *detained*
85 For private quarrel 'twixt your Duke and him,
    Hath published and proclaimed it openly.
    'Tis marvel, but that you are but newly come,
    You might have heard it else proclaimed about.[1]
PEDANT Alas, sir, it is worse for me than so,°   *my plight is even worse*
90 For I have bills for money by exchange[2]
    From Florence, and must here deliver them.
TRANIO Well, sir, to do you courtesy
    This will I do, and this I will advise you.
    First tell me, have you ever been at Pisa?
95 PEDANT Ay, sir, in Pisa have I often been,

4. Who teaches tricks that are exactly appropriate or of just the right number. An allusion to the card game one-and-thirty, in which the object is to accumulate exactly thirty-one points. See note to 1.2.31.
5. Tranio's apparent knowledge of Hortensio's plans is puzzling and may be an indication that some text has been lost.
6. Worthy old man. Punning on "angel" as meaning both "valuable gold coin" and "divine messenger." The coin had a picture of the archangel Michael on it.

7. Biondello's version of *mercatante,* the Italian word for "merchant."
8. Because this character is said (at line 90) to have "bills for money," some editors have designated him a "merchant" like the corresponding character in George Gascoigne's comedy *Supposes* (1566).
9. The north African trading center or the city in Syria.
1. *but that . . . about:* if you hadn't just arrived, you would have heard it announced everywhere.
2. Promissory notes that the bearer could exchange for cash.

Pisa renownèd for grave citizens.

TRANIO   Among them know you one Vincentio?

PEDANT   I know him not, but I have heard of him,
A merchant of incomparable wealth.

100 TRANIO   He is my father, sir, and sooth to say,
In count'nance somewhat doth resemble you.

BIONDELLO [*aside*]   As much as an apple doth an oyster, and all
one.°   *but no matter*

TRANIO   To save your life in this extremity

105 This favour will I do you for his sake,
And think it not the worst of all your fortunes
That you are like to Sir Vincentio.
His name and credit° shall you undertake,°   *social status / assume*
And in my house you shall be friendly lodged.

110 Look that you take upon you° as you should.   *act your part*
You understand me, sir? So shall you stay
Till you have done your business in the city.
If this be courtesy, sir, accept of it.

PEDANT   O sir, I do, and will repute° you ever   *consider*

115 The patron of my life and liberty.

TRANIO   Then go with me to make the matter good.
This, by the way, I let you understand—
My father is here looked for every day
To pass assurance° of a dower in marriage   *convey legal guarantee*

120 'Twixt me and one Baptista's daughter here.
In all these circumstances I'll instruct you.
Go with me to clothe you as becomes you.   *Exeunt*

4.3

Enter KATHERINE *and* GRUMIO

GRUMIO   No, no, forsooth. I dare not, for my life.

KATHERINE   The more my wrong, the more his spite appears.[1]
What, did he marry me to famish me?
Beggars that come unto my father's door

5   Upon entreaty have a present° alms,   *immediate*
If not, elsewhere they meet with charity.
But I, who never knew how to entreat,
Nor never needed that I should entreat,
Am starved for meat, giddy for lack of sleep,

10   With oaths kept waking and with brawling fed,
And that which spites° me more than all these wants,   *vexes*
He does it under name of perfect love,
As who should say° if I should sleep or eat   *As if to say*
'Twere deadly sickness, or else present° death.   *instant*

15   I prithee, go and get me some repast.
I care not what, so it be wholesome food.

GRUMIO   What say you to a neat's foot?°   *ox foot or calf's foot*

KATHERINE   'Tis passing good. I prithee, let me have it.

GRUMIO   I fear it is too choleric° a meat.   *conducive to anger*

20   How say you to a fat tripe finely broiled?

KATHERINE   I like it well. Good Grumio, fetch it me.

GRUMIO   I cannot tell, I fear 'tis choleric.

4.3 Location: Petruccio's country house.
1. The more injustice I suffer, the more he seems to want me to suffer.

What say you to a piece of beef, and mustard?

KATHERINE A dish that I do love to feed upon.

25 GRUMIO Ay, but the mustard is too hot a little.

KATHERINE Why then, the beef, and let the mustard rest.

GRUMIO Nay, then I will not. You shall have the mustard,
Or else you get no beef of Grumio.

KATHERINE Then both, or one, or anything thou wilt.

30 GRUMIO Why then, the mustard without the beef.

KATHERINE Go, get thee gone, thou false, deluding slave,
    Beats him
That feed'st me with the very name° of meat.   *only the name*
Sorrow on thee and all the pack of you,
That triumph thus upon my misery.

35 Go, get thee gone, I say.
    Enter PETRUCCIO *and* HORTENSIO, *with meat*

PETRUCCIO How fares my Kate? What, sweeting,° all amort?°   *sweetheart / dejected*

HORTENSIO Mistress, what cheer?

KATHERINE   Faith, as cold as can be.

PETRUCCIO Pluck up thy spirits, look cheerfully upon me.
Here, love, thou seest how diligent I am

40 To dress° thy meat myself and bring it thee.   *prepare*
I am sure, sweet Kate, this kindness merits thanks.
What, not a word? Nay then, thou lov'st it not,
And all my pains is sorted to no proof.°   *are to no purpose*
Here, take away this dish.

KATHERINE   I pray you, let it stand.

45 PETRUCCIO The poorest service is repaid with thanks,
And so shall mine before you touch the meat.

KATHERINE I thank you, sir.

HORTENSIO Signor Petruccio, fie, you are to blame.
Come, Mistress Kate, I'll bear you company.

50 PETRUCCIO [*aside*] Eat it up all, Hortensio, if thou lov'st me.
[*To* KATHERINE] Much good do it unto thy gentle heart.
Kate, eat apace; and now, my honey love,
Will we return unto thy father's house,
And revel it as bravely as the best,

55 With silken coats, and caps, and golden rings,
With ruffs, and cuffs, and farthingales,² and things,
With scarves, and fans, and double change of bravery,°   *finery*
With amber bracelets, beads, and all this knavery.°   *tricks of dress*
What, hast thou dined? The tailor stays thy leisure,

60 To deck thy body with his ruffling° treasure.   *ornate (with ruffles)*
    Enter TAILOR [*with a gown*]
Come, tailor, let us see these ornaments.
Lay forth the gown.
    Enter HABERDASHER [*with a cap*]
                What news with you, sir?

HABERDASHER Here is the cap your worship did bespeak.

PETRUCCIO Why, this was moulded on a porringer°—   *porridge bowl*

65 A velvet dish.³ Fie, fie, 'tis lewd and filthy.
Why, 'tis a cockle° or a walnut-shell,   *mollusk shell*

---

2. *ruffs:* fashionable high collars made of starched linen or lace. *cuffs:* bands, often made of lace, sewn onto sleeves for ornament. *farthingales:* hooped petticoats.

3. It's merely a dish made of velvet. Velvet caps were often associated with prostitutes.

A knack,° a toy, a trick,° a baby's cap.   *knickknack / trifle*
Away with it! Come, let me have a bigger.
KATHERINE   I'll have no bigger. This doth fit the time,°   *suit current fashion*
70   And gentlewomen wear such caps as these.
PETRUCCIO   When you are gentle you shall have one, too,
And not till then.
HORTENSIO [*aside*]   That will not be in haste.
KATHERINE   Why, sir, I trust I may have leave to speak,
And speak I will. I am no child, no babe.
75   Your betters have endured me say my mind,
And if you cannot, best you stop your ears.
My tongue will tell the anger of my heart,
Or else my heart concealing it will break,
And rather than it shall I will be free
80   Even to the uttermost as I please in words.
PETRUCCIO   Why, thou sayst true. It is a paltry cap,
A custard-coffin,[4] a bauble, a silken pie.
I love thee well in that thou lik'st it not.
KATHERINE   Love me or love me not, I like the cap
85   And it I will have, or I will have none.   [*Exit* HABERDASHER]
PETRUCCIO   Thy gown? Why, ay. Come, tailor, let us see't.
O mercy, God, what masquing stuff[5] is here?
What's this—a sleeve? 'Tis like a demi-cannon.°   *large cannon*
What, up and down carved like an apple-tart?[6]
90   Here's snip, and nip, and cut, and slish and slash,
Like to a scissor in a barber's shop.
Why, what i'° devil's name, tailor, call'st thou this?   *in the*
HORTENSIO [*aside*]   I see she's like° to have nor cap nor gown.   *likely*
TAILOR   You bid me make it orderly and well,
95   According to the fashion and the time.
PETRUCCIO   Marry, and did,° but if you be remembered   *Indeed I did*
I did not bid you mar it to the time.
Go hop me[7] over every kennel° home,   *gutter*
For you shall hop without my custom,° sir.   *patronage; business*
100   I'll none of it. Hence, make your best of it.
KATHERINE   I never saw a better fashioned gown,
More quaint,° more pleasing, nor more commendable.   *elegant*
Belike° you mean to make a puppet of me.   *It seems*
PETRUCCIO   Why true, he means to make a puppet of thee.
105 TAILOR   She says your worship means to make a puppet of her.
PETRUCCIO   O monstrous arrogance! Thou liest, thou thread,
    thou thimble,
Thou yard, three-quarters, half-yard, quarter, nail,[8]
Thou flea, thou nit,° thou winter-cricket, thou.   *egg of a louse*
Braved° in mine own house with° a skein of thread!   *Defied; adorned / by*
110   Away, thou rag, thou quantity,° thou remnant,   *fragment*
Or I shall so bemete° thee with thy yard°   *measure; beat / ruler*
As thou shalt think on prating[9] whilst thou liv'st.
I tell thee, I, that thou hast marred her gown.

4. Pastry crust around a custard or open pie (perhaps with a pun on "costard," slang for "head").
5. Extravagant clothing suitable for theatrical masques.
6. With slits like the top of an apple pie. The gown's sleeves may have been designed so as to reveal fabric of another color underneath.
7. You can go hopping.
8. Measure of cloth, a sixteenth of a yard; Petruccio is literally belittling the tailor. "Yard" is slang for "penis."
9. You will think twice before you talk idly, with a pun on "prat" as slang for "beat on the buttocks."

TAILOR   Your worship is deceived. The gown is made
115   Just as my master had direction.
        Grumio gave order how it should be done.
    GRUMIO   I gave him no order, I gave him the stuff.°   *material*
    TAILOR   But how did you desire it should be made?
    GRUMIO   Marry, sir, with needle and thread.
120   TAILOR   But did you not request to have it cut?
    GRUMIO   Thou hast faced° many things.   *trimmed; defied*
    TAILOR   I have.
    GRUMIO   Face not me. Thou hast braved° many men. Brave°   *dressed finely / Defy*
        not me. I will neither be faced nor braved. I say unto thee
125   I bid thy master cut out the gown, but I did not bid him cut it
        to pieces. Ergo° thou liest.   *Therefore*
    TAILOR [showing a paper]   Why, here is the note of the fashion,
        to testify.
    PETRUCCIO   Read it.
130   GRUMIO   The note lies in's throat if he° say I said so.   *it*
    TAILOR [reads]   'Imprimis,° a loose-bodied gown.'[1]   *First*
    GRUMIO   Master, if ever I said loose-bodied gown, sew me in the
        skirts of it and beat me to death with a bottom° of brown   *spool*
        thread. I said a gown.
135   PETRUCCIO   Proceed.
    TAILOR [reads]   'With a small compassed° cape.'   *flared*
    GRUMIO   I confess the cape.
    TAILOR [reads]   'With a trunk° sleeve.'   *wide*
    GRUMIO   I confess two sleeves.
140   TAILOR [reads]   'The sleeves curiously° cut.'   *carefully; elaborately*
    PETRUCCIO   Ay, there's the villany.
    GRUMIO   Error i'th' bill,° sir, error i'th' bill. I commanded the   *order (for the dress)*
        sleeves should be cut out and sewed up again, and that I'll
        prove upon thee though thy little finger be armed in a thimble.
145   TAILOR   This is true that I say. An° I had thee in place where,°   *If / in a suitable place*
        thou shouldst know it.
    GRUMIO   I am for thee straight. Take thou the bill,[2] give me thy
        mete-yard,° and spare not me.   *yardstick*
    HORTENSIO   Godamercy, Grumio, then he shall have no odds.°   *advantage*
150   PETRUCCIO   Well, sir, in brief, the gown is not for me.
    GRUMIO   You are i'th' right, sir. 'Tis for my mistress.
    PETRUCCIO [to the TAILOR]   Go, take it up unto° thy master's use.   *take it away for*
    GRUMIO [to the TAILOR]   Villain, not for thy life. Take up my
        mistress' gown for thy master's use!°   *sexual purposes*
155   PETRUCCIO   Why, sir, what's your conceit° in that?   *meaning*
    GRUMIO   O, sir, the conceit is deeper than you think for. 'Take
        up my mistress' gown to his master's use'—O fie, fie, fie!
    PETRUCCIO [aside]   Hortensio, say thou wilt see the tailor paid.
        [To the TAILOR] Go, take it hence. Be gone, and say no more.
    HORTENSIO [aside to the TAILOR]   Tailor, I'll pay thee for thy
160   gown tomorrow.
        Take no unkindness of his hasty words.
        Away, I say. Commend me to thy master.   *Exit* TAILOR
    PETRUCCIO   Well, come, my Kate. We will unto your father's
        Even in these honest, mean habiliments.

---

1. A loose-fitting dress. In the next line, Grumio takes this to mean a dress suitable for a wanton, or loose, woman.   2. Grumio puns on "bill" as also meaning a "weapon" or "halberd," a staff with a blade attached.

165   Our purses shall be proud, our garments poor,
      For 'tis the mind that makes the body rich,
      And as the sun breaks through the darkest clouds,
      So honour peereth° in the meanest habit.   *can be seen*
      What, is the jay more precious than the lark
170   Because his feathers are more beautiful?
      Or is the adder better than the eel
      Because his painted skin contents the eye?
      O no, good Kate, neither art thou the worse
      For this poor furniture° and mean array.   *clothing; attire*
175   If thou account'st it shame, lay it on me,°   *blame me*
      And therefore frolic; we will hence forthwith
      To feast and sport us° at thy father's house.   *amuse ourselves*
      Go call my men, and let us straight to him,
      And bring our horses unto Long Lane end.
180   There will we mount, and thither walk on foot.
      Let's see, I think 'tis now some seven o'clock,
      And well we may come there by dinner-time.°   *about noon*
    KATHERINE   I dare assure you, sir, 'tis almost two,
      And 'twill be supper-time° ere you come there.   *about 6 P.M.*
185   PETRUCCIO   It shall be seven ere I go to horse.
      Look what I speak, or do, or think to do,
      You are still crossing° it. Sirs, let't alone.   *contradicting*
      I will not go today, and ere I do
      It shall be what o'clock I say it is.
190   HORTENSIO [*aside*]   Why, so this gallant will command the sun.

                                   [*Exeunt*]

4.4

Enter TRANIO [*as Lucentio,*] *and the* PEDANT *dressed*
like Vincentio, booted and bare-headed[1]

    TRANIO   Sir, this is the house. Please it you that I call?
    PEDANT   Ay, what else. And but[2] I be deceived,
      Signor Baptista may remember me
      Near twenty years ago in Genoa—
5   TRANIO   Where we were lodgers at the Pegasus.[3]—
      'Tis well, and hold your own° in any case   *keep to your role*
      With such austerity as 'longeth° to a father.   *belongs*
      Enter BIONDELLO
    PEDANT   I warrant you. But sir, here comes your boy.
      'Twere good he were schooled.
10   TRANIO   Fear you not him. Sirrah Biondello,
      Now do your duty throughly,° I advise you.   *thoroughly*
      Imagine 'twere the right Vincentio.
    BIONDELLO   Tut, fear not me.
    TRANIO   But hast thou done thy errand to Baptista?
15   BIONDELLO   I told him that your father was at Venice
      And that you looked for him this day in Padua.

4.4 Location: Padua. In front of Baptista's house.
1. In F, the Pedant is mistakenly given a second entry at line 18, where he is described as "booted and bare-headed," indicating that he is dressed for travel but has taken off his hat, perhaps in deference to Baptista, whom he is about to meet. The present stage direction conflates F's two stage directions regarding the Pedant's entrance.
2. Unless (the Pedant is rehearsing his speech to Baptista).
3. Common name for an inn (marked by a sign of the flying horse of classical mythology).

TRANIO [*giving money*] Thou'rt a tall° fellow. Hold thee° that   *worthy / Take*
     to° drink.   *for*
     Here comes Baptista. Set your countenance, sir.
     Enter BAPTISTA, *and* LUCENTIO [*as Cambio*]
TRANIO   Signor Baptista, you are happily met.
20   [*To the* PEDANT] Sir, this is the gentleman I told you of.
     I pray you stand good father to me now.
     Give me Bianca for my patrimony.
PEDANT   Soft,° son. [*To* BAPTISTA] Sir, by your leave, having   *Just a moment*
     come to Padua
     To gather in some debts, my son Lucentio
25   Made me acquainted with a weighty cause
     Of love between your daughter and himself,
     And for the good report I hear of you,
     And for the love he beareth to your daughter,
     And she to him, to stay him° not too long   *keep him waiting*
30   I am content in a good father's care[4]
     To have him matched, and if you please to like
     No worse than I, upon some agreement
     Me shall you find ready and willing
     With one consent to have her so bestowed,
35   For curious° I cannot be with you,   *overly particular*
     Signor Baptista, of whom I hear so well.
BAPTISTA   Sir, pardon me in what I have to say.
     Your plainness and your shortness please me well.
     Right true it is your son Lucentio here
40   Doth love my daughter, and she loveth him,
     Or both dissemble deeply their affections.
     And therefore if you say no more than this,
     That like a father you will deal with him
     And pass° my daughter a sufficient dower,   *grant*
45   The match is made, and all is done.
     Your son shall have my daughter with consent.
TRANIO   I thank you, sir. Where then do you know best
     We be affied,° and such assurance ta'en   *betrothed*
     As shall with either part's agreement stand?[5]
50 BAPTISTA   Not in my house, Lucentio, for you know
     Pitchers have ears,[6] and I have many servants.
     Besides, old Gremio is heark'ning still,°   *always listening*
     And happily° we might be interrupted.   *perhaps*
TRANIO   Then at my lodging, an it like you.°   *if it please you*
55   There doth my father lie,° and there this night   *lodge*
     We'll pass° the business privately and well.   *settle*
     Send for your daughter by your servant here.
     My boy shall fetch the scrivener° presently.   *scribe; notary*
     The worst is this, that at so slender warning
60   You are like to have a thin and slender pittance.°   *scanty meal*
BAPTISTA   It likes me well. Cambio, hie° you home   *hurry*
     And bid Bianca make her ready straight,
     And if you will, tell what hath happened—
     Lucentio's father is arrived in Padua—

---

4. Content with the care that should be shown by a good father.
5. As shall confirm the agreements of both parties.
6. Proverbial for "Someone may be eavesdropping." The handles of a pitcher are its "ears."

65 And how she's like to be Lucentio's wife.   [*Exit* LUCENTIO][7]
BIONDELLO   I pray the gods she may with all my heart.
TRANIO   Dally not with the gods, but get thee gone.

                                   Exit [BIONDELLO][8]

Signor Baptista, shall I lead the way?
Welcome. One mess° is like to be your cheer.°   *dish / entertainment*
70 Come, sir, we will better it in Pisa.
BAPTISTA   I follow you.   *Exeunt*

4.5

Enter LUCENTIO *and* BIONDELLO

BIONDELLO   Cambio.
LUCENTIO   What sayst thou, Biondello?
BIONDELLO   You saw my master wink and laugh upon you?
LUCENTIO   Biondello, what of that?
5 BIONDELLO   Faith, nothing, but he's left me here behind to
expound the meaning or moral of his signs and tokens.
LUCENTIO   I pray thee, moralize° them.   *interpret*
BIONDELLO   Then thus: Baptista is safe, talking with the deceiving father of a deceitful son.
10 LUCENTIO   And what of him?
BIONDELLO   His daughter is to be brought by you to the supper.
LUCENTIO   And then?
BIONDELLO   The old priest at Saint Luke's church is at your
command at all hours.
15 LUCENTIO   And what of all this?
BIONDELLO   I cannot tell, except they are busied about a coun-
terfeit assurance.° Take you assurance[1] of her *cum privilegio*   *betrothal agreement*
ad imprimendum solum[2]—to th' church take the priest, clerk,
and some sufficient honest witnesses.
20 If this be not that you look for, I have no more to say,
But bid Bianca farewell for ever and a day.
LUCENTIO   Hear'st thou, Biondello?
BIONDELLO   I cannot tarry, I knew a wench married in an afternoon as she went to the garden for parsley to stuff a rabbit,
25 and so may you, sir, and so adieu, sir. My master hath
appointed me to go to Saint Luke's to bid the priest be ready
t'attend against° you come with your appendix.[3]   *Exit*   *by the time*
LUCENTIO   I may and will, if she be so contented.
She will be pleased, then wherefore should I doubt?
30 Hap what hap may, I'll roundly go about her.[4]
It shall go hard° if Cambio go without her.   *Exit*[5]   *be unfortunate*

---

7. F does not mark an exit for Lucentio/Cambio here, but it makes sense that he would follow Baptista's order. If Lucentio exits here and Biondello at line 66 as in F, or at line 67 as in this text, then their *reentry* a few lines later can mark a new scene (see Textual Note). Some editors assume Biondello and perhaps Lucentio never leave the stage since Biondello says (at 4.5.5–6) that he has been left behind by Tranio to explain things to Lucentio. In that case, no scene break would be introduced after Baptista exits.
8. F here has a mysterious stage direction: "Enter Peter." Some editors have argued that this is the name of an actor inadvertently introduced into the stage directions. Others assume it is the name of one of Lucentio's servants, who enters to tell the disguised Tranio and Baptista that their meal is ready; this possibility is not

entirely satisfactory, especially since Baptista and Tranio still have to *proceed* to Lucentio's house for their meal. Perhaps something has been lost or garbled in this portion of the scene.
4.5 Location: Scene continues.
1. Make yourself sure.
2. With the exclusive right to print (a Latin phrase used by printers on the title pages of their books). Biondello urges Lucentio to confirm his "exclusive right" to Bianca and may be punning on "print" as meaning "to father a child."
3. Appendage (the bride).
4. Come what may, I'll pursue her eagerly.
5. At the corresponding point in *A Shrew*, Sly, still on-stage, comments on the action. See Additional Passages B.

4.6

Enter PETRUCCIO, KATHERINE, HORTENSIO [*and servants*]

PETRUCCIO   Come on, i' God's name. Once more toward our father's.
　Good Lord, how bright and goodly shines the moon!

KATHERINE   The moon?—the sun. It is not moonlight now.

PETRUCCIO   I say it is the moon that shines so bright.

5　KATHERINE   I know it is the sun that shines so bright.

PETRUCCIO   Now, by my mother's son—and that's myself—
　It shall be moon, or star, or what I list°　　　　　　　　　*please*
　Or ere° I journey to your father's house.　　　　　　　　*Before*
　Go on, and fetch our horses back again.

10　Evermore crossed° and crossed, nothing but crossed.　*contradicted*

HORTENSIO [TO KATHERINE]   Say as he says or we shall never go.

KATHERINE   Forward, I pray, since we have come so far,
　And be it moon or sun or what you please,
　And if you please to call it a rush-candle,[1]

15　Henceforth I vow it shall be so for me.

PETRUCCIO   I say it is the moon.

KATHERINE   I know it is the moon.

PETRUCCIO   Nay then you lie, it is the blessèd sun.

KATHERINE   Then God be blessed, it is the blessèd sun,

20　But sun it is not when you say it is not,
　And the moon changes even as your mind.[2]
　What you will have it named, even that it is,
　And so it shall be still for Katherine.

HORTENSIO   Petruccio, go thy ways.° The field is won.　　*do as you wish*

25　PETRUCCIO   Well, forward, forward. Thus the bowl should run,
　And not unluckily against the bias.[3]
　But soft, company is coming here.

　　　Enter [*old*] VINCENTIO

　[*To* VINCENTIO] Good morrow, gentle mistress, where away?
　Tell me, sweet Kate, and tell me truly too,

30　Hast thou beheld a fresher gentlewoman,
　Such war of white and red within her cheeks?
　What stars do spangle heaven with such beauty
　As those two eyes become that heavenly face?
　Fair lovely maid, once more good day to thee.

35　Sweet Kate, embrace her for her beauty's sake.

HORTENSIO   A° will make the man mad to make the woman of　*He*
　him.°　　　　　　　　　　　　　　　　　　　*call him a woman*

KATHERINE   Young budding virgin, fair, and fresh, and sweet,
　Whither away, or where is thy abode?

40　Happy the parents of so fair a child,
　Happier the man whom° favourable stars　　　　　　　　*to whom*
　Allots thee for his lovely bedfellow.

PETRUCCIO   Why, how now, Kate, I hope thou art not mad.
　This is a man, old, wrinkled, faded, withered,

45　And not a maiden as thou sayst he is.

KATHERINE   Pardon, old father, my mistaking eyes

4.6 Location: A road somewhere between Petruccio's
house and Padua.
1. Candle made from rush dripped in grease, thus giving poor light.
2. Implying that Petruccio is mad as well as fickle.

Lunatics and women were imagined to be governed by
the moon.
3. A metaphor from the game of bowls in which the
ball, or bowl, was weighted so that it ran along a "bias,"
or curving path.

That have been so bedazzled with the sun
That everything I look on seemeth green.°   *youthful*
Now I perceive thou art a reverend father.
50   Pardon, I pray thee, for my mad mistaking.
PETRUCCIO   Do, good old grandsire, and withal° make known   *in addition*
Which way thou travell'st. If along with us,
We shall be joyful of thy company.
VINCENTIO   Fair sir, and you, my merry mistress,
55   That with your strange encounter° much amazed me,   *greeting*
My name is called Vincentio, my dwelling Pisa,
And bound I am to Padua, there to visit
A son of mine which long I have not seen.
PETRUCCIO   What is his name?
VINCENTIO   Lucentio, gentle sir.
60   PETRUCCIO   Happily met, the happier for thy son.
And now by law as well as reverend age
I may entitle thee my loving father.
The sister to my wife, this gentlewoman,
Thy son by this hath married.[4] Wonder not,
65   Nor be not grieved. She is of good esteem,
Her dowry wealthy, and of worthy birth,
Beside, so qualified° as may beseem   *with such qualities*
The spouse of any noble gentleman.
Let me embrace with old Vincentio,
70   And wander we to see thy honest son,
Who will of thy arrival be full joyous.
          [*He embraces* VINCENTIO]
VINCENTIO   But is this true, or is it else your pleasure
Like pleasant travellers to break a jest°   *crack a joke*
Upon the company you overtake?
75   HORTENSIO   I do assure thee, father, so it is.
PETRUCCIO   Come, go along, and see the truth hereof,
For our first merriment hath made thee jealous.°   *suspicious*
          Exeunt [*all but* HORTENSIO]
HORTENSIO   Well, Petruccio, this has put me in heart.
Have to my widow, and if she be froward,°   *difficult*
80   Then hast thou taught Hortensio to be untoward.°   *Exit*   *unmannerly*

5.1

Enter BIONDELLO, LUCENTIO, *and* BIANCA. GREMIO
    is out before°   *Gremio enters first*
BIONDELLO   Softly and swiftly, sir, for the priest is ready.
LUCENTIO   I fly, Biondello; but they may chance to need thee at
   home, therefore leave us.
BIONDELLO   Nay, faith, I'll see the church a' your back[1] and then
5   come back to my master's as soon as I can.
        Exeunt [LUCENTIO, BIANCA, *and* BIONDELLO][2]
GREMIO   I marvel Cambio comes not all this while.

---

4. By now has married. It is unclear how Petruccio and Hortensio know this, especially since Hortensio has heard "Lucentio" (Tranio) forswear Bianca (in 4.2). The inconsistency may suggest textual alteration in the role of Hortensio.
5.1 Location: Padua, in front of Lucentio's house.
1. At your back. Probably, I'll see the church as you

leave it after the wedding.
2. In F, Lucentio and Bianca exit first (after line 3) and Biondello presumably follows after line 5, though no exit is explicitly marked for him. Gremio, onstage before this trio, apparently does not see them stealing away to the church.

Enter PETRUCCIO, KATHERINE, VINCENTIO, GRUMIO,
with attendants

PETRUCCIO Sir, here's the door. This is Lucentio's house.
My father's bears° more toward the market-place.   *lies*
Thither must I, and here I leave you, sir.

10 VINCENTIO You shall not choose but drink before you go.
I think I shall command your welcome here,
And by all likelihood some cheer is toward.°   *food is being prepared*
    [He] knocks

GREMIO They're busy within. You were best knock louder.
    *[*VINCENTIO *knocks again. The]* PEDANT *looks out
    of the window*

PEDANT What's he that knocks as he would beat down the gate?

15 VINCENTIO Is Signor Lucentio within, sir?

PEDANT He's within, sir, but not to be spoken withal.

VINCENTIO What if a man bring him a hundred pound or two
to make merry withal?

PEDANT Keep your hundred pounds to yourself. He shall need

20 none so long as I live.

PETRUCCIO *[to* VINCENTIO*]* Nay, I told you your son was well
beloved in Padua. *[To the* PEDANT*]* Do you hear, sir, to leave
frivolous circumstances,° I pray you tell Signor Lucentio that   *matters*
his father is come from Pisa and is here at the door to speak

25 with him.

PEDANT Thou liest. His father is come from Padua and here
looking out at the window.

VINCENTIO Art thou his father?

PEDANT Ay, sir, so his mother says, if I may believe her.

30 PETRUCCIO *[to* VINCENTIO*]* Why, how now, gentleman? Why,
this is flat knavery, to take upon you another man's name.

PEDANT Lay hands on the villain. I believe a° means to cozen°   *he / cheat*
somebody in this city under my countenance.°   *name; person*
    Enter BIONDELLO

BIONDELLO *[aside]* I have seen them in the church together,

35 God send 'em good shipping.° But who is here? Mine old mas-   *fair sailing*
ter, Vincentio—now we are undone and brought to nothing.

VINCENTIO *[to* BIONDELLO*]* Come hither, crackhemp.[3]

BIONDELLO I hope I may choose, sir.

VINCENTIO Come hither, you rogue. What, have you forgot me?

40 BIONDELLO Forgot you? No, sir, I could not forget you, for
I never saw you before in all my life.

VINCENTIO What, you notorious villain, didst thou never see
thy master's father, Vincentio?

BIONDELLO What, my old worshipful old master? Yes, marry,

45 sir, see where he looks out of the window.

VINCENTIO Is't so indeed?
    He beats BIONDELLO

BIONDELLO Help, help, help! Here's a madman will murder me.
                                                            [Exit]

PEDANT Help, son! Help, Signor Baptista!   *[Exit above]*

PETRUCCIO Prithee, Kate, let's stand aside and see the end of

50 this controversy.
    [They stand aside.]

---

3. Rogue (deserving to stretch the hangman's hemp rope).

Enter PEDANT *with servants,* BAPTISTA, TRANIO [*as*
      Lucentio]

TRANIO [*to* VINCENTIO] Sir, what are you that offer° to beat my   presume
      servant?

VINCENTIO What am I, sir? Nay, what are you, sir? O immortal
      gods, O fine villain, a silken doublet, a velvet hose, a scarlet
55   cloak, and a copintank° hat—O, I am undone, I am undone!   high-crowned
      While I play the good husband at home, my son and my ser-
      vant spend all at the university.

TRANIO How now, what's the matter?

BAPTISTA What, is the man lunatic?

60   TRANIO Sir, you seem a sober, ancient gentleman by your habit,
      but your words show you a madman. Why sir, what 'cerns° it   concerns
      you if I wear pearl and gold? I thank my good father, I am able
      to maintain it.

VINCENTIO Thy father! O villain, he is a sailmaker in Bergamo.[4]

65   BAPTISTA You mistake, sir, you mistake, sir. Pray what do you
      think is his name?

VINCENTIO His name? As if I knew not his name—I have
      brought him up ever since he was three years old, and his
      name is Tranio.

70   PEDANT Away, away, mad ass. His name is Lucentio, and he is
      mine only son, and heir to the lands of me, Signor Vincentio.

VINCENTIO Lucentio? O, he hath murdered his master! Lay
      hold on him, I charge you, in the Duke's name. O my son, my
      son! Tell me, thou villain, where is my son Lucentio?

75   TRANIO Call forth an officer.
            [*Enter an* OFFICER]
      Carry this mad knave to the jail. Father Baptista, I charge you
      see that he be forthcoming.°   available when needed

VINCENTIO Carry me to the jail?

GREMIO Stay, officer, he shall not go to prison.

80   BAPTISTA Talk not, Signor Gremio. I say he shall go to prison.

GREMIO Take heed, Signor Baptista, lest you be cony-catched°   duped
      in this business. I dare swear this is the right Vincentio.

PEDANT Swear if thou dar'st.

GREMIO Nay, I dare not swear it.

85   TRANIO Then thou wert best say that I am not Lucentio.

GREMIO Yes, I know thee to be Signor Lucentio.

BAPTISTA Away with the dotard. To the jail with him.
            Enter BIONDELLO, LUCENTIO, *and* BIANCA

VINCENTIO Thus strangers may be haled° and abused. O mon-   dragged about
      strous villain!

90   BIONDELLO O, we are spoiled and—yonder he is. Deny him,
      forswear him, or else we are all undone.
            Exeunt BIONDELLO, TRANIO, *and* PEDANT, *as fast as may be*

LUCENTIO [*to* VINCENTIO] Pardon, sweet father.
            [*He*] *kneels*

VINCENTIO Lives my sweet son?

BIANCA [*to* BAPTISTA] Pardon, dear father.

95   BAPTISTA How hast thou offended? Where is Lucentio?

LUCENTIO Here's Lucentio, right son to the right Vincentio,
      That have by marriage made thy daughter mine,

---

4. An Italian town associated with Harlequin, the witty, resourceful servant of the Italian commedia dell'arte.

While counterfeit supposes[5] bleared thine eyne.°   *deceived your eyes*

GREMIO   Here's packing° with a witness,[6] to deceive us all.   *plotting*

100 VINCENTIO   Where is that damnèd villain Tranio,
That faced and braved° me in this matter so?   *defied*

BAPTISTA   Why, tell me, is not this my Cambio?

BIANCA   Cambio is changed into Lucentio.

LUCENTIO   Love wrought these miracles. Bianca's love
105 Made me exchange my state° with Tranio   *social position*
While he did bear my countenance in the town,
And happily I have arrived at the last
Unto the wishèd haven of my bliss.
What Tranio did, myself enforced him to.
110 Then pardon him, sweet father, for my sake.

VINCENTIO   I'll slit the villain's nose that would have sent me to
the jail.

BAPTISTA   But do you hear, sir, have you married my daughter
without asking my good will?

115 VINCENTIO   Fear not, Baptista. We will content you. Go to, but
I will in to be revenged for this villainy.   *Exit*

BAPTISTA   And I to sound the depth° of this knavery.   *Exit*   *discover the extent*

LUCENTIO   Look not pale, Bianca. Thy father will not frown.

Exeunt [LUCENTIO *and* BIANCA]

GREMIO   My cake is dough,[7] but I'll in among the rest, Out of
120 hope of all° but my share of the feast.   [*Exit*]   *With hope of nothing*

KATHERINE [*coming forward*]   Husband, let's follow to see the
end of this ado.

PETRUCCIO   First kiss me, Kate, and we will.

KATHERINE   What, in the midst of the street?

125 PETRUCCIO   What, art thou ashamed of me?

KATHERINE   No, sir, God forbid; but ashamed to kiss.

PETRUCCIO   Why then, let's home again. Come sirrah, let's away.

KATHERINE   Nay, I will give thee a kiss. Now pray thee love, stay.

[*They kiss*]

PETRUCCIO   Is not this well? Come, my sweet Kate.
130 Better once than never, for never too late.[8]   *Exeunt*

5.2

Enter BAPTISTA, VINCENTIO, GREMIO, *the* PEDANT,
LUCENTIO *and* BIANCA, [PETRUCCIO, KATHERINE,
and HORTENSIO,] TRANIO, BIONDELLO, GRUMIO, *and*
[*the*] WIDOW, *the servingmen with* TRANIO *bringing
in a banquet*[1]

LUCENTIO   At last, though long,° our jarring notes agree,   *after a long time*
And time it is when raging war is done
To smile at scapes° and perils overblown.   *escapes*
My fair Bianca, bid my father welcome,
While I with selfsame kindness welcome thine.
5 Brother Petruccio, sister Katherina,
And thou, Hortensio, with thy loving widow,
Feast with the best, and welcome to my house.

---

5. False ideas. Possibly an illusion to Gascoigne's *Supposes* (1566), which was Shakespeare's main source for
the Bianca and Lucentio plot.
6. With clear evidence; without any doubt.
7. Proverbial expression for a failed project.

8. Two proverbs combined: "Better late than never"
and "It is never too late to mend."
5.2 Location: Lucentio's house in Padua.
1. Light meal of fruit, sweetmeats, and wine following
the main meal.

My banquet is to close our stomachs up
10 After our great good cheer.° Pray you, sit down,   *feast; happiness*
For now we sit to chat as well as eat.
   [*They sit*]
PETRUCCIO   Nothing but sit, and sit, and eat, and eat.
BAPTISTA   Padua affords this kindness, son Petruccio.
PETRUCCIO   Padua affords nothing but what is kind.
15 HORTENSIO   For both our sakes I would that word were true.
PETRUCCIO   Now, for my life, Hortensio fears² his widow.
WIDOW   Then never trust me if I be afeard.°   *afraid*
PETRUCCIO   You are very sensible, and yet you miss my sense.
I mean Hortensio is afeard of you.
20 WIDOW   He that is giddy thinks the world turns round.³
PETRUCCIO   Roundly° replied.   *Boldly*
KATHERINE   Mistress, how mean you that?
WIDOW   Thus I conceive by him.⁴
PETRUCCIO   Conceives° by me! How likes Hortensio that?   *Becomes pregnant*
25 HORTENSIO   My widow says thus she conceives her tale.⁵
PETRUCCIO   Very well mended. Kiss him for that, good widow.
KATHERINE   'He that is giddy thinks the world turns round'—
I pray you tell me what you meant by that.
WIDOW   Your husband, being troubled with a shrew,
30 Measures my husband's sorrow by his woe.
And now you know my meaning.
KATHERINE   A very mean meaning.
WIDOW   Right, I mean you.
KATHERINE   And I am mean indeed respecting you.⁶
PETRUCCIO   To her, Kate!
35 HORTENSIO   To her, widow!
PETRUCCIO   A hundred marks⁷ my Kate does put her down.°   *defeat her*
HORTENSIO   That's my office.⁸
PETRUCCIO   Spoke like an officer!⁹ Ha' to thee,° lad.   *Here's to you*
   [*He*] *drinks to* HORTENSIO
BAPTISTA   How likes Gremio these quick-witted folks?
40 GREMIO   Believe me, sir, they butt together¹ well.
BIANCA   Head and butt? An hasty-witted body
Would say your head and butt were head and horn.²
VINCENTIO   Ay, mistress bride, hath that awakened you?
BIANCA   Ay, but not frighted me, therefore I'll sleep again.
45 PETRUCCIO   Nay, that you shall not. Since you have begun,
Have at° you for a better jest or two.   *I shall come at*
BIANCA   Am I your bird? I mean to shift my bush,³
And then pursue me as you draw your bow.
You are welcome all.
                        Exit BIANCA [*with* KATHERINE *and the* WIDOW]

---

2. Is afraid of. The widow takes it to mean "frightens."
3. That is, people judge everything by their own experience, implying that Petruccio is afraid of his wife.
4. Thus I understand him.
5. Thus she understands or intends her remark, with a
pun on "tail" as meaning "genitalia."
6. I am moderate (like the mathematical "mean" compared with you; I demean myself in dealing with you.
7. A substantial wager, since 1 mark was equivalent to
13 shillings and 4 pence, or two-thirds of a pound. An
unskilled laborer might earn £6 to £8 in a year.

8. That's my job, with a pun on "put her down" as
meaning "force or lay her down in sexual intercourse."
9. Like one who knows his duty.
1. They thrust their heads or horns together, with a
pun on "butt" as meaning "buttocks."
2. Would say your butting head was a cuckold's horned
head.
3. Alluding to the Elizabethan sport of shooting sitting
birds with a bow and arrow. There may also be a bawdy
pun on "bush" as meaning "pubic area" and the target
of Petruccio's (phallic) arrow.

50 PETRUCCIO   She hath prevented° me here, Signor Tranio.   *stopped; anticipated*
    This bird you aimed at, though you hit her not.
    Therefore a health to all that shot and missed.
    TRANIO   O sir, Lucentio slipped° me like his greyhound,   *unleashed*
    Which runs himself and catches for his master.
55 PETRUCCIO   A good swift° simile, but something currish.°   *witty / base; doglike*
    TRANIO   'Tis well, sir, that you hunted for yourself.
    'Tis thought your deer does hold you at a bay.⁴
    BAPTISTA   O, O, Petruccio, Tranio hits you now.
    LUCENTIO   I thank thee for that gird,° good Tranio.   *taunt*
60 HORTENSIO   Confess, confess, hath he not hit you here?
    PETRUCCIO   A° has a little galled° me, I confess,   *He / wounded*
    And as the jest did glance away from me,
    'Tis ten to one it maimed you two outright.
    BAPTISTA   Now in good sadness,° son Petruccio,   *in all seriousness*
65 I think thou hast the veriest shrew of all.
    PETRUCCIO   Well, I say no.—And therefore, Sir Assurance,
    Let's each one send unto° his wife,   *summon*
    And he whose wife is most obedient
    To come at first when he doth send for her
70 Shall win the wager which we will propose.
    HORTENSIO   Content.° What's the wager?   *Agreed*
    LUCENTIO   Twenty crowns.°   *coin worth 5 shillings*
    PETRUCCIO   Twenty crowns!
    I'll venture so much of° my hawk or hound,   *on*
75 But twenty times so much upon my wife.
    LUCENTIO   A hundred, then.
    HORTENSIO   Content.
    PETRUCCIO   A match,° 'tis done.   *Agreed*
    HORTENSIO   Who shall begin?
80 LUCENTIO   That will I.
    Go, Biondello, bid your mistress come to me.
    BIONDELLO   I go.   *Exit*
    BAPTISTA   Son, I'll be your half Bianca comes.⁵
    LUCENTIO   I'll have no halves, I'll bear it all myself.
    Enter BIONDELLO
    How now, what news?
85 BIONDELLO   Sir, my mistress sends you word
    That she is busy and she cannot come.
    PETRUCCIO   How? She's busy and she cannot come?
    Is that an answer?
    GREMIO   Ay, and a kind one, too.
    Pray God, sir, your wife send you not a worse.
    PETRUCCIO   I hope, better.
90 HORTENSIO   Sirrah Biondello,
    Go and entreat my wife to come to me forthwith.
    Exit BIONDELLO
    PETRUCCIO   O ho, 'entreat' her—nay, then she must needs come.
    HORTENSIO   I am afraid, sir, do what you can,
    Enter BIONDELLO
    Yours will not be entreated. Now, where's my wife?

---

4. Your deer turns on you and holds you at a distance. Punning on "deer" and "dear."

5. I'll put up half the stake (and therefore collect half of any winnings) in wagering that Bianca will come first.

95 BIONDELLO   She says you have some goodly jest in hand.
       She will not come. She bids you come to her.
    PETRUCCIO   Worse and worse! She will not come—O vile,
       Intolerable, not to be endured!
       Sirrah Grumio, go to your mistress.
100   Say I command her come to me.   *Exit* [GRUMIO]
    HORTENSIO   I know her answer.
    PETRUCCIO   What?
    HORTENSIO   She will not.
    PETRUCCIO   The fouler fortune mine, and there an end.[6]
           Enter KATHERINE
    BAPTISTA   Now by my halidom,° here comes Katherina.   *by all I hold sacred*
    KATHERINE [*to* PETRUCCIO]   What is your will, sir, that you send
       for me?
105 PETRUCCIO   Where is your sister and Hortensio's wife?
    KATHERINE   They sit conferring by the parlour fire.
    PETRUCCIO   Go, fetch them hither. If they deny° to come,   *refuse*
       Swinge me them soundly forth[7] unto their husbands.
       Away, I say, and bring them hither straight.   [*Exit* KATHERINE]
110 LUCENTIO   Here is a wonder, if you talk of wonders.
    HORTENSIO   And so it is. I wonder what it bodes.
    PETRUCCIO   Marry, peace it bodes, and love, and quiet life;
       An aweful° rule and right supremacy,   *inspiring awe*
       And, to be short, what not° that's sweet and happy.   *everything*
115 BAPTISTA   Now fair befall thee, good Petruccio,
       The wager thou hast won, and I will add
       Unto their losses twenty thousand crowns,
       Another dowry to another daughter,
       For she is changed as she had never been.[8]
120 PETRUCCIO   Nay, I will win my wager better yet,
       And show more sign of her obedience,
       Her new-built virtue and obedience.
           Enter KATHERINE, BIANCA, *and* [*the*] WIDOW
       See where she comes, and brings your froward° wives   *willful*
       As prisoners to her womanly persuasion.
125   Katherine, that cap of yours becomes you not.
       Off with that bauble, throw it underfoot.
           [KATHERINE *throws down her cap*]
    WIDOW   Lord, let me never have a cause to sigh
       Till I be brought to such a silly pass.
    BIANCA   Fie, what a foolish duty call you this?
130 LUCENTIO   I would your duty were as foolish, too.
       The wisdom of your duty, fair Bianca,
       Hath cost me a hundred crowns since supper-time.
    BIANCA   The more fool you for laying° on my duty.   *gambling*
    PETRUCCIO   Katherine, I charge thee tell these headstrong women
135   What duty they do owe their lords and husbands.
    WIDOW   Come, come, you're mocking. We will have no telling.
    PETRUCCIO   Come on, I say, and first begin with her.
    WIDOW   She shall not.

---

6. Worse luck for me (if you're right), and that's that.   8. As if she had never existed before; as if she had never
7. Beat them soundly for me, and bring them out.   been what she was before (a shrew).

PETRUCCIO   I say she shall: and first begin with her.
140   KATHERINE   Fie, fie, unknit that threat'ning, unkind brow,
And dart not scornful glances from those eyes
To wound thy lord, thy king, thy governor.
It blots° thy beauty as frosts do bite the meads,°   *disfigures / meadows*
Confounds thy fame° as whirlwinds shake fair buds,   *Ruins your reputation*
145   And in no sense is meet° or amiable.   *fitting*
A woman moved° is like a fountain troubled,   *angry*
Muddy, ill-seeming,° thick, bereft of beauty,   *ugly*
And while it is so, none so dry or thirsty
Will deign to sip or touch one drop of it.
150   Thy husband is thy lord, thy life, thy keeper,
Thy head, thy sovereign, one that cares for thee,
And for thy maintenance commits his body
To painful labour both by sea and land,
To watch the night in storms, the day in cold,
155   Whilst thou liest warm at home, secure and safe,
And craves no other tribute at thy hands
But love, fair looks, and true obedience,
Too little payment for so great a debt.
Such duty as the subject owes the prince,
160   Even such a woman oweth to her husband,
And when she is froward, peevish,° sullen, sour,   *obstinate*
And not obedient to his honest will,
What is she but a foul contending rebel,
And graceless traitor to her loving lord?
165   I am ashamed that women are so simple°   *foolish*
To offer war where they should kneel for peace,
Or seek for rule, supremacy, and sway
When they are bound to serve, love, and obey.
Why are our bodies soft, and weak, and smooth,
170   Unapt to° toil and trouble in the world,   *Unfitted for*
But that our soft conditions° and our hearts   *dispositions*
Should well agree with our external parts?
Come, come, you froward and unable worms,°   *weak creatures*
My mind hath been as big° as one of yours,   *proud*
175   My heart° as great, my reason haply more,   *spirit*
To bandy word for word and frown for frown;
But now I see our lances are but straws,
Our strength as weak,° our weakness past compare,   *(as straws)*
That seeming to be most which we indeed least are.
180   Then vail your stomachs, for it is no boot,[9]
And place your hands below your husband's foot,
In token of which duty, if he please,
My hand is ready, may it do him ease.°   *give him comfort*
PETRUCCIO   Why, there's a wench! Come on, and kiss me, Kate.
[*They kiss*]
185   LUCENTIO   Well, go thy ways, old lad, for thou shalt ha't.[1]
VINCENTIO   'Tis a good hearing° when children are toward.[2]   *thing to hear*
LUCENTIO   But a harsh hearing when women are froward.
PETRUCCIO   Come, Kate, we'll to bed.

9. Then lower your pride, for it is of no profit.   2. Obedient (the opposite of "froward," line 187).
1. You shall have the prize.

We three are married, but you two are sped.°   *defeated*
190   'Twas I won the wager, though [*to* LUCENTIO] you hit the white,[3]
And being a winner,° God give you good night.   *since I am a winner*
                Exit PETRUCCIO [*with* KATHERINE]
HORTENSIO   Now go thy ways, thou hast tamed a curst shrew.
LUCENTIO   'Tis a wonder, by your leave, she will be tamed so.
                       [*Exeunt*][4]

Additional Passages

The Taming of a Shrew, printed in 1594 and believed to derive from Shakespeare's play as performed, contains episodes continuing and rounding off the Christopher Sly framework that may echo passages written by Shakespeare but not printed in the Folio. They are given below.

A. The following exchange occurs at a point for which there is no exact equivalent in Shakespeare's play. It could come before 2.1. The "two fine gentlewomen" to whom Sly refers in line 8 would thus be Katherine and Bianca. The "fool" of the first line is Sander, the counterpart of Grumio. "Sim" is short for Simon, the name of the Lord with whom Sly converses.

      Then SLY *speaks*
SLY   Sim, when will the fool come again?
LORD   He'll come again, my lord, anon.
SLY   Gi's° some more drink here. Zounds,[1] where's the tapster?°   *Give us / tavern keeper*
  Here, Sim, eat some of these things.
5   LORD   So I do, my lord.
SLY   Here, Sim, I drink to thee.
LORD   My lord, here comes the players again.
SLY   O brave, here's two fine gentlewomen.

B. This passage comes between 4.5 and 4.6. If it originates with Shakespeare, it implies that Grumio accompanies Petruccio at the beginning of 4.6. Ferando is the name of Petruccio's counterpart in *A Shrew*.

SLY   Sim, must they be married now?
LORD   Ay, my lord.
      Enter FERANDO *and* KATE *and* SANDER
SLY   Look, Sim, the fool is come again now.

C. Sly interrupts the action of the play-within-the-play. This could be inserted at 5.1.92 of Shakespeare's play, when Biondello, Tranio, and the Pedant all run away from the angry Vincentio. In *A Shrew*, the Duke (Vincentio's counterpart) has threatened to send to prison the people (Phylotus and Valeria) who have impersonated him and his son.

      PHYLOTUS *and* VALERIA *runs away*.
      Then SLY *speaks*
SLY   I say we'll have no sending to prison.
LORD   My lord, this is but the play. They're but in jest.
SLY   I tell thee, Sim, we'll have no sending to prison, that's flat.°   *final*

---

3. Hit the target (with a pun on "Bianca," which means "white" in Italian).
4. In *A Shrew*, the Christopher Sly story concludes the

play. See Additional Passages E.
1. By God's wounds (a strong oath).

Why, Sim, am not I Don Christo Vary? Therefore I say they
5   shall not go to prison.
LORD   No more they shall not, my lord. They be run away.
SLY   Are they run away, Sim? That's well. Then gi's some more
      drink, and let them play again.
LORD   Here, my lord.
          SLY   *drinks and then falls asleep*

D. Sly is carried off. This could be placed between 5.1 and 5.2 in Shakespeare's play.

                                    Exeunt omnes°   *They all exit*
          SLY *sleeps*
LORD   Who's within there? Come hither, sirs, my lord's
      Asleep again. Go take him easily° up   *gently*
      And put him in his own apparel again,
      And lay him in the place where we did find him
5   Just underneath the alehouse side below.
      But see you wake him not in any case.
BOY   It shall be done, my lord. Come help to bear him hence.
                                    Exit

E. *The Taming of a Shrew* ends with the following episode.

          Then enter two bearing of SLY *in his own apparel again*
          and leaves him where they found him and then goes out.
          Then enter the TAPSTER
TAPSTER   Now that the darksome night is overpast
      And dawning day appears in crystal sky,
      Now must I haste abroad. But soft, who's this?
      What, Sly! O wondrous, hath he lain here all night?
5   I'll wake him. I think he's starved[1] by this,°   *this time*
      But° that his belly was so stuffed with ale.   *Except*
      What ho, Sly, awake, for shame!
SLY   Sim, gi's some more wine. What, 's all the players gone?
      Am not I a lord?
10 TAPSTER   A lord with a murrain![2] Come, art thou drunken still?
SLY   Who's this? Tapster? O Lord, sirrah, I have had
      The bravest° dream tonight that ever thou   *finest*
      Heardest in all thy life.
TAPSTER   Ay, marry, but you had best get you home,
15   For your wife will course° you for dreaming here tonight.   *trounce*
SLY   Will she? I know now how to tame a shrew.
      I dreamt upon it all this night till now,
      And thou hast waked me out of the best dream
      That ever I had in my life. But I'll to my
20   Wife presently and tame her too,
      An if° she anger me.   *An if = If*
TAPSTER   Nay, Tarry, Sly, for I'll go home with thee
      And hear the rest that thou hast dreamt tonight.
                                    Exeunt omnes

---

1. He'd have died from cold.
2. Pestilence or plague. "With a murrain" was often used as an oath or expression of anger. The tapster probably means "A plague on that" (Sly's dream of being a lord).

The First Part of the Contention
of the Two Famous Houses
# of York and Lancaster
(The Second Part of Henry VI)

What happens to a kingdom when the sitting monarch is too weak to rule effectively? Shakespeare explores this difficult problem in *The First Part of the Contention of the Two Famous Houses of York and Lancaster,* in which Henry VI, crowned when he was nine months old, has never been able to establish control over his realm. As his assertive French wife, Margaret of Anjou, exclaims in exasperation to the Duke of Suffolk, who had wooed her for Henry:

> when in the city Tours
> Thou rann'st a-tilt in honour of my love
> And stol'st away the ladies' hearts of France,
> I thought King Henry had resembled thee
> In courage, courtship, and proportion.
> But all his mind is bent to holiness,
> To number Ave-Maries on his beads.
>
> (1.3.54–60)

Margaret thought she would be marrying a chivalric hero, one adept at the arts of love and war; instead, she finds herself wed to an ineffective, pious man who elsewhere openly expresses his desire to live as a private person rather than as his country's King. Partly as a result of Henry's deficiencies, Margaret grows increasingly independent, conducting a love intrigue with Suffolk and openly defying her husband's wishes. Presented as a sexualized figure of gender disorder, Margaret is as powerful as her husband is weak. Margaret, however, represents but one of the threats to Henry's authority and the well-being of the country. Lacking the strong hand of a powerful monarch to rein them in, Henry's nobles quarrel and threaten civil war, and eventually a group of rebellious commoners storm London, killing all who oppose them. The kingdom slides into chaos.

In the early modern period, the king stood at the top of the social order and was invested with enormous responsibilities. The symbolic head and heart of the body politic, the monarch was enjoined to rule wisely, to care for the welfare of his subjects, and to take counsel from and exert control over the nobility. Some theories of kingship argued that monarchs had their authority from God; rebellion against a sitting monarch was a form of treason punishable by death. Given the centrality of the king to the health of the kingdom and its subjects, an evil or a weak king could have a disastrous impact on the realm. Tyrants—that is, kings who followed their passions, refused to take counsel, and ignored the welfare of their subjects—were anxiously discussed by the political thinkers of the period. Could they ever be overthrown? Must their tyranny be endured? In plays such as *Richard III* and *Macbeth*, Shakespeare dramatized such tyrant kings and in each case showed their deaths at the hands of high-placed subjects. Henry VI poses a different kind of danger. Rather than an evil or personally ambitious monarch, he is simply ineffectual and weak, unable to control the ambition and selfish desires of his nobles or to see to the welfare of his subjects. In effect, *The First Part of the Contention* explores what happens when a kingdom is left rudderless, graphically depicting the brutality let loose when the King is unable to assert his authority, commoners are set against nobles, and nobles begin to destroy one another.

The First Part of the Contention may well be the first English history play Shakespeare wrote (for a fuller discussion of the genre of the history play and Shakespeare's work in that genre, see the introduction to *1 Henry VI*). It has been dated as early as 1591 and exists in two distinct versions: a quarto edition printed in 1594 and a longer version printed in the First Folio in 1623 (for the differences between these two texts, see the Textual Note). Historically, the protracted broils depicted in this and the following play were known as the Wars of the Roses (1455–85) because the House of York, which staked its claim to England's throne through Lionel, Duke of Clarence, third son of Edward III, took a white rose for its emblem, while the House of Lancaster, which claimed the throne through John of Gaunt, fourth son of Edward III, became identified with the red rose. While giving a war the name of a flower might suggest a trivial or symbolic struggle, Shakespeare's plays decisively refute such an idea. Collectively they explore the horror of a kingdom divided against itself.

When read, the play can seem chaotic, a series of violent acts carried out by a bewildering array of characters who rise to the forefront of attention only to disappear quickly from view. But the play is more carefully structured than may at first be apparent. For the first two acts, Henry's weakness is counterbalanced by the strength of Humphrey, Duke of Gloucester, a man who since the King's youth has served as Lord Protector of the realm and who attempts to see that the common people are fairly treated and the quarrelling nobles kept in check. The play reaches a decisive turning point in Act 3 when Gloucester is driven from office by the Queen, Suffolk, York, and the Cardinal Beaufort (who is also the Bishop of Winchester). Once Gloucester is gone, no one can protect the King or the kingdom from the ambition of Richard, Duke of York, the most powerful of the nobles who would supplant Henry. From Act 3 on, York and his minions dominate the action, countered primarily by the equally strong-willed Margaret. In the brutal struggles that follow upon Gloucester's death, one powerful figure after another suffers disgrace or death, including Cardinal Beaufort, Suffolk, and Somerset. York, however, does not fall but, like Margaret, moves with unnerving single-mindedness into the power vacuum created by the King's passivity.

Henry VI, depicted as a child, carried by the Earl of Warwick.

To register the disaster that has overtaken England, Shakespeare relentlessly focuses on the actual human bodies maimed, brutalized, and destroyed by the play's contending forces. The death of Gloucester is exemplary. In *The First Part of the Contention*, he is strangled onstage in his bed; in the Folio version of the play his death occurs offstage. But in both texts, the corpse is eventually displayed to the audience while Warwick recites a grisly description of the state of the body. In contrast to the paleness of a man who has died peacefully, the good Duke's

> face is black and full of blood;
> His eyeballs further out than when he lived,
> Staring full ghastly like a strangled man;
> His hair upreared; his nostrils stretched with struggling;
> His hands abroad displayed, as one that grasped
> And tugged for life and was by strength subdued.
> Look on the sheets. His hair, you see, is sticking;
> His well-proportioned beard made rough and rugged,
> Like to the summer's corn by tempest lodged.
> It cannot be but he was murdered here.
> The least of all these signs were probable.
>
> (3.2.168–78)

This terrible inventory of the unnatural state of Gloucester's dead body highlights the marks of his futile struggle for life—the bulging eyes, the disordered hair and beard, the outstretched hands. Warwick's point is that these are *not* the signs of a soul weighed down by sin and unprepared for death, as is true of Cardinal Beaufort, whose death occurs in the next scene; rather, Gloucester's disordered corpse testifies to the horrific and untimely circumstances in which he died.

In this extremely violent play, many other bodies suffer indignity, pain, and death. In Act 4, Suffolk, captured on his flight to France, is beheaded offstage by his captors. His body is then taken to England, where Queen Margaret, in one of the most macabre scenes in Shakespeare, carries his severed head around the court, lamenting her dead lover. Later, the rebels attacking London capture Lord Saye, a supporter of King Henry. After enumerating a catalog of his crimes, including the "crime" of literacy, the followers of Jack Cade, the chief rebel, behead Saye along with his son-in-law. Cade's followers then stick the severed heads on poles and carry them through the streets, grotesquely making them "kiss" at every corner. After five days of living in the woods without food have rendered him too famished to fight effectively, Jack Cade is himself beheaded and his head taken to the King. This is hardly an exhaustive list of the forms of violence depicted in the play. It does not, for example, take account of those slain in battle, such as Somerset, or of the shameful treatment Cade visits upon defeated enemies such as Sir Humphrey Stafford and his brother, whose armor he strips from their corpses before he drags their bodies behind his horse toward London.

Some small portion of this violence displays the monarch's sanctioned power to punish unruly or disobedient subjects. In Elizabethan England, traitors' heads were regularly displayed on London Bridge, and public executions were popular spectacles, showing the King's power over traitors and criminals. In *The First Part of the Contention*, the most spectacular scene of public correction involves Eleanor Cobham, Gloucester's wife. A proud and ambitious woman who hopes to see her husband displace Henry as King of England, Cobham dabbles in the forbidden arts of witchcraft and conjuration, soliciting prophecies about the fate of the King and two of his nobles, Suffolk and Somerset. Such prophecies were considered politically dangerous because they caused uncertainty and unrest among the common people and could be used to foment sedition. They had been specifically banned by Henry VIII, Edward VI, and Elizabeth. Like many famous prophecies, those delivered to Eleanor Cobham are ambiguous. For example, "The Duke yet lives that Henry shall depose, / But him outlive, and die a violent death" (1.4.29–30) can mean either that Henry shall depose a duke or that a duke shall depose Henry. Nor is it entirely clear who shall outlive whom and die a violent death. The ambiguity of such statements was exactly what rulers feared, since under the cover of a benign interpretation they could be used to predict and promote rebellion. For engaging in witchcraft and conjuration as well as for circulating such prophecies, Eleanor Cobham is first shamed—she must walk through London carrying a candle and wearing only a sheet, her crimes listed on a piece of paper pinned to her back—and then banished, and her confederates hanged and burned. The King here appears to be using sanctioned violence to punish dangerously seditious subjects.

Yet in much of the play, the state either fails to control violence or else uses it with questionable justice. Even Eleanor's case is more ambiguous than the above account suggests. She did undeniably dabble in witchcraft, yet she was urged on by people in the employ of Suffolk and the Cardinal, who wished through her acts to disgrace her innocent husband and dislodge him from power. Legally, Eleanor's punishment is just, yet it occurs in a context of chicanery and treachery that the King either does not or will not see until Gloucester, the chief prop of royal justice, has been removed. Between the discovery of Eleanor's witchcraft and her public shaming, the play shows the audience another troubling example of a ritual of justice. Earlier Peter Thump, an apprentice, had accused his master, Horner, of saying that the Duke of York—not Henry—was the rightful ruler of England. Thump had no proof but his own word, and Horner had no defense but denial. To resolve the issue, Gloucester orders a day of combat for the man and master: whoever wins the duel would be assumed to have spoken the truth. Such trials by combat were customary in adjudicating disputes among nobles. But the apprentice is terrified, having no experience with such contests or with the weapons commonly used in them: the sword or lance. As it is dramatized, the trial by combat becomes a parody of justice. Rather than fighting with swords, the two contestants appear with sandbags attached to poles, and Horner is roaring drunk. It is under these conditions that the apprentice kills his master, and the King, who has now taken Gloucester's staff of office from him as the result of Eleanor's treason, seems satisfied that justice has prevailed. But the ludicrous nature of the drunken encounter threatens to empty such traditional rituals of their meaning and legitimacy.

With Gloucester's death, the King's fair and effective control of the machinery of justice and of violence is further compromised. Under the pressure of an enraged commons, Henry *does* banish Suffolk for his role in Gloucester's death, but the King cannot begin to contain the escalating stage violence. In the second half of the play, his loss of control is demonstrated by the spectacular rise to power of the lower-class rebel Jack Cade, one of York's minions. As he marches toward London, Cade boasts that the laws of England are to come from his mouth, and he arrogates to himself the right to kill whom he chooses. The murder of Lord Saye, the death of the clerk of Chartham, the desecration of Stafford's body—these are a mere sampling of events in a brutal career, and the play does not shrink from showing what is cruel and arbitrary in Cade's brief reign of terror. Critics often take Shakespeare's representation of Cade as confirming Elizabethan fears about the dangers of popular rule.

Yet interpreting Cade and his actions is a complicated business. Does Shakespeare create this character simply to discredit popular rebellion, or does he use Cade to articulate the legitimate grievances of the common people and employ Cade's brutality as a disquieting mirror of the brutality of the ruling classes? It is important to remember that Cade is not synonymous with "the commons" in this play. In the opening acts, while he is still in power, Gloucester is presented as a champion of the people and promotes a commonwealth in which the king and nobles care for the needs of the commoners and are responsive to their petitions. The people, in turn, seem confident that their views will be heard by those near the King. For example, in 1.3, three commoners wait with petitions for Gloucester: Peter Thump wishes to report his master's treasonous words about the Duke of York; another man complains that Cardinal Beaufort's man has unlawfully seized his land, house, and wife; a third protests that the Duke of Suffolk has enclosed the commons of Melford. (Enclosures—fencing in land once shared by many for growing food and grazing cattle—were a main cause of rural protest in the sixteenth and seventeenth centuries.) How these commoners behave as political agents registering grievances with those in power is revealing. First, the petitioners believe that they can get redress from the Lord Protector, the figure nearest the King himself. Second, they use peaceful means to obtain their desires. Third, they act from a position of loyalty to their King and his Lord Protector. Thump, in particular, puts himself at personal risk to report an act of treason against Henry. These figures hardly constitute a mob or many-headed monster. Even when they become enraged by Gloucester's murder and demand the banishment of Suffolk, they couch their protest as a desire to protect the King rather than to seize power for themselves.

It is crucial to note, however, that in 1.3 the petitioners are largely thwarted in their appeal for justice because they mistake Suffolk for Gloucester. Suffolk and the Queen are interested in dealing with York's supposed treason because they can use that accusation to prevent York from becoming Regent of France. They ignore the other petitions, one of which details a complaint against Suffolk himself. It is the nobles and not the commoners who fail to exercise their political duties responsibly. Timid and gullible and surrounded by selfish nobles like Suffolk, the King disregards the welfare and the needs of the common people, who are presented in this scene as loyal and orderly actors in a hierarchical commonwealth.

Cade enters the picture only when the one noble—Gloucester—who cares about maintaining this paternal relationship between the commons and the King is about to be killed. At the end of 3.1, York, in soliloquy, reveals his intention to use the army levied against Ireland to further his own political ends; in addition, he will employ the Kentishman Jack Cade as his stalking horse in his move to seize the crown. Cade will pretend to be John Mortimer, a claimant to the throne through the Yorkist line, in order to test the waters for York's own bid for power. Cade is thus never an entirely independent agent of the people; rather, he is at least in part the tool of an ambitious nobleman who employs him because he is stubborn, strong, and impervious to pain. York reports that in battle against the Irish, Cade

> fought so long till that his thighs with darts
> Were almost like a sharp-quilled porcupine;
> And in the end, being rescued, I have seen
> Him caper upright like a wild Morisco,
> Shaking the bloody darts as he his bells.
>
> (3.1.362–66)

Will Kemp doing his morris dance. From Kemp's *Nine Days' Wonder* (1600).

Morris dancers tied bells to their legs, and these shook and jangled as they danced. The powerful image of the wounded Cade dancing depicts a man endowed with enormous spirit and physical strength. It is worth recalling that one of the most famous clowns of the 1590s, Will Kemp, who may have played the part of Cade, was himself a noted acrobat and dancer; in 1599, he left Shakespeare's company and did a celebrated morris dance from London to Norwich. Skilled and strong, Cade and Kemp suggest both what was feared and what was admired about hardhanded men, some of whom were employed in the London theater industry and some of whom would have been in the audience. In fact, the Cade scenes must have been powerfully charged, because out of this rebel's mouth—along with arbitrary brutality and pompous self-aggrandizement— issues a critique of social and economic inequality that, endowed with a long history, also spoke to living issues in the London of the 1590s.

Historically, Cade's rebellion occurred in 1450, but in portraying it, Shakespeare draws on accounts of many instances of popular social protest. For example, he takes from Raphael Holinshed's *Chronicles of England, Scotland, and Ireland* (1587) details from the Peasants' Revolt of 1381, in which rebels such as Wat Tyler burned London Bridge and attacked the Savoy (John of Gaunt's house) and the Inns of Court, both places of privilege that became a focus for lower-class anger. Other popular uprisings occurred in 1517, when apprentices on Ill May Day attacked foreign workers in the City of London; in 1549 (Kett's Rebellion); and in London itself throughout the decade of the 1590s. Between 1581 and 1602, there were numerous outbreaks of disorder in London directed against various forms of economic hardship, some of which stemmed from disruptions and changes in the English cloth trade that disadvantaged English weavers. Protests also occurred against the high price of commodities such as butter and fish and against the granting of monopolies that put the sale of key goods, such as starch, in the hands of a small group. Apprentices were often involved in and blamed for these riots. Many of Cade's followers in *The First Part of the Contention* are artisans: weavers and butchers. Through Cade, their economic grievances find expression, along with the articulation of an alternative model of social and economic organization much more radically utopian than that implied in Gloucester's hierarchical paternalism.

This tradition of popular radicalism, whose roots went back at least to the fourteenth century, stressed that all men had been equally redeemed by Christ's blood and that there was as much nobility in the labor of an honest man as in the fine silks and the educated speech of a gentleman. A riddle common throughout Europe from the fourteenth century on—"When Adam delved and Eve span, who then was the gentleman?"—suggests the egalitarian purposes for which the Bible could be appropriated. The first man and woman, digging in the earth and spinning cloth, knew no distinctions of rank, simply the dignity of labor. Often, popular protest stressed the value of manual labor, as opposed to the idleness of the rich, and claimed the clouted shoe or hobnailed boot of the rural peasant and the leather apron of the urban laborer as valued emblems of their working lives.

The Cade scenes are filled with references to this egalitarian tradition. In 4.2, when the rebels first describe how Cade means to reform the commonwealth, they make clear that in their view working men, and only working men, should be magistrates and rulers. Referring to Scripture, the second rebel says: "Yet it is said 'Labour in thy vocation'; which is as much to say as 'Let the magistrates be labouring men'; and therefore should we be magistrates" (4.2.14–16). By contrast, the present nobility "scorn to go in leather aprons" (4.2.10–11) and have no respect for handicraftsmen. Part of Cade's success is that he is able to mobilize such artisan anger against the privileges of gentlemen, whether those be conferred by literacy or by inherited wealth. Much of Cade's violence is directed against those who can read and write, like the clerk of Chartham or Lord Saye. Literacy, whether defined as the ability to read or to read and write, was not nearly so widespread as it has since become. These skills were acquired by only a small part of the population, who thereby had certain advantages wherever the reading or writing of documents had importance, such as in courts of law. Cade would not only kill all the lawyers, but he would also punish all those who wrote on parchment, that is, those in control of written documents. He also promises that when he is in charge, bread will be cheap, beer of the highest quality, all material goods enjoyed in common, and all men dressed in a common livery.

It is hardly necessary to point out how often Cade contradicts himself in articulating his vision of a commonwealth of equals and how he undermines the utopian aspirations of the tradition of popular radicalism to which his words repeatedly refer. In his egalitarian commonwealth, Cade, of course, would be King, and from his mouth would come all the laws by which others would live. Women would have no rights in his commonwealth but would be fair game for rape. When a Sergeant complains to Cade that his wife has been ravished by one of Cade's men, Cade authorizes his man to cut out the Sergeant's tongue, cripple him, and then knock out his brains. Cade then invites his followers to enter London, where they will "lustily stand to it" and "take up these commodities following—item, a gown, a kirtle, a petticoat, and a smock" (4.7.134–36). The violence and arbitrary cruelty repeatedly displayed make Cade a frightening figure and one whom even his followers often recognize as a charlatan and a hypocrite.

Yet Cade's personal viciousness does not simply wipe away the power of the social critique to which he intermittently gives voice and which had a history extending far beyond this play. When Cade learns that Lord Saye has his horse covered with an elaborate cloth, he bluntly states a point of view that must have resonated with some in Shakespeare's audience: "Marry, thou ought'st not to let thy horse wear a cloak when honester men than thou go in their hose and doublets" (4.7.42–43). Moreover, Shakespeare gives plenty of evidence in the play that if many commoners feel anger and resentment toward the nobility, many nobility are in their turn full of contempt for the lower classes. Act 4, which is dominated by Cade, opens with the scene in which Suffolk is captured and questioned by the Captain of a ship. Furious that when he reveals himself as the Duke of Suffolk his captors do not free him immediately, Suffolk contemptuously attacks the Captain:

> Obscure and lousy swain, King Henry's blood,
> The honourable blood of Lancaster,
> Must not be shed by such a jady groom.
> (4.1.51–53)

The speech goes on in a similar vein for twelve more lines, making clear the truth of the second rebel's claim that the gentlemen of England do not have much respect for hardhanded men. Nor, after the grisly murder of Gloucester, can it be thought that only the common people have the capacity for lawless violence. In short, the play dramatizes many instances of class-based antagonisms rooted in the unequal distribution of wealth and cultural capital.

This complicated political drama seems unequivocally to confirm only one principle: the absence of a strong and just king leaves the commonwealth at risk, but at risk not solely from its most disenfranchised members. Cade, who offers the most radical critique of social inequality, is personally vilified and discredited within the play; but it is arguable that the larger context for his grim saturnalia of violence is the unspeakable selfishness of the English nobles. Many of them—York, Suffolk, Winchester—are everything Cade accuses the nobility of being. Moreover, though Cade is killed in this play, civil war does not vanish with his death, because the ambition and selfishness of these English nobles have not been contained. York still lives, and it will take Shakespeare another two plays to trace the destructive legacy of his ambition.

Some critics have suggested that given the venality of many of the nobles and the cruelty and hypocrisy of Cade, the play privileges the point of view of Alexander Iden, the landowning gentleman who kills Cade. Iden is well worth scrutiny. A property holder, a man who has built a brick wall around his garden, Iden also has charitable impulses. He "sends the poor well pleasèd from [his] gate" and at first does not want to fight with Cade, a "poor famished man" (4.9.21, 41). Does Iden's garden represent an

The houses of York and Lancaster depicted as two parts of a rosebush conjoined,
by the marriage of Henry VII and Elizabeth of York, to form the Tudor dynasty.
Title page to Edward Halle's (or Hall's) *Union of the Two Noble and Illustre Famelies
of Lancastre & Yorke* (1550 ed.).

English Eden? Shakespeare sounds several evocative notes through the creation of
this figure. Iden conjures up the virtues of rural England as opposed to the values of
the corrupt court or the rampaging urban artisans. And he anticipates the emergence
of the bourgeois property holder as the backbone of the nation. But Iden is not the

dominant force in the political landscape of the play, nor, despite his seeming independence, are his loyalties in doubt. When he learns who the poor famished man really is, Iden is glad to have killed Cade; and when he delivers the rebel's head to King Henry, he receives a knighthood in return. The independent property holder is certainly the King's man and no friend to those who would level the social order and make property common. How deeply Shakespeare—the man from rural Stratford who eventually became a major property holder in that town—idealized Iden, or replicated his political stance, is a matter for debate.

JEAN E. HOWARD

TEXTUAL NOTE

The play commonly known as *2 Henry VI* existed in two versions in the early modern period. In 1594, a quarto version (Q) entitled *The First Part of the Contention of the Two Famous Houses of York and Lancaster* was published; it was followed in 1600 and 1619 by two other quartos based on the first. In 1623, a version of the play about a third longer than Q was included in the First Folio (F), where it was entitled *The Second Part of Henry VI*. The relationship between these two texts is one of the vexed issues in Shakespearean scholarship. In the 1920s, several scholars proposed that Q had been prepared by several actors who had performed in a London production of the play and had reconstructed as much of the script as they could remember. The stage directions in Q are unusually full, indicating the quarto's probable theatrical origins. It may derive, indirectly, from the promptbook prepared for either a London performance or a provincial tour.

Recently, some scholars have questioned whether memorial reconstruction (actors piecing together scripts from memory) provides an adequate explanation for the differences so often found among variant texts that survive for many early modern plays. In particular, Steven Urkowitz has argued that the 1594 Quarto of this play is not a product of memorial reconstruction but is Shakespeare's early version, which he later revised. Urkowitz maintains that both the 1594 and the 1623 texts were prepared by Shakespeare, even though they differ from one another in important ways. He argues, for example, that Queen Margaret is a fiercer and more assertive figure in F than in Q. Urkowitz urges that each version of the play be studied on its own. Other textual editors argue that many people—actors, compositors, censors, scribes—may have had a hand in altering a play as it moved onto the stage or into print. Shakespeare may not himself have been responsible for all the differences we now perceive between quarto and Folio texts; nonetheless, the existing texts are distinct entities and should be examined separately rather than conflated into one amalgamated version.

The Oxford edition of the play adheres to the view, dominant since the 1920s, that the quarto is, indeed, a memorial reconstruction of some version of the Folio text, probably a version that had been abridged and otherwise revised on its way from the authorial "foul papers" on which F is based to the promptbook that lies behind Q. Therefore, while F serves as the primary control text, the Oxford edition, like most others, uses many of Q's stage directions to clarify playhouse practice. More controversially, the Oxford edition also assumes that in preparing the Folio text, the compositors who set type drew on the printed quarto versions in some places, probably because the manuscript serving as the basis of F was occasionally illegible or hard to use. At five points (indicated in the Textual Variants), the Oxford editors use Q rather than F as control text. At other points, they follow the quarto placement of particular events, interpolate material found only in Q, or replace Folio material with quarto material when they believe that the changes represent authorial revisions to the version of the Folio text on which Q was based. The Oxford editors also retain the title used for the 1594 Quarto on the grounds that it is more descriptive of the play's content than the blander

Second Part of Henry VI, and because it is the title by which the play was probably known during Shakespeare's own lifetime.

The Oxford text differs, then, in many ways from modern texts based more exclusively on F. One striking change occurs at the beginning of 3.2: the Oxford edition follows Q in showing the actual murder of Gloucester onstage; F only shows the murderers running from the scene of the crime. The Oxford text also incorporates some quarto material about the Cade rebellion not found in F. These additions, lines 116–31 and 134–36 of 4.7, report the burning of London Bridge, the rape of a Sergeant's wife by one of Cade's men, and Cade's own boast that he will lead his men in sexual assaults upon the women of the city. Together, they darken further F's depiction of Cade's lawlessness. Another substantive change involves the Oxford editors' choice to print the quarto version of the final fight between York and Clifford (5.3.20–30) rather than the Folio version. The two differ markedly in tone; Q stresses the enmity of York and Clifford, F their mutual respect and chivalric honor. This edition prints both, providing the Folio version as an inset passage, and this juxtaposition affords an excellent opportunity to examine one of the important places where F and Q diverge.

The Oxford text in two places follows Q's ordering of particular incidents. In 1.4, a scene involving conjuration, F has a spirit deliver prophecies concerning the fate of several characters—the King, Suffolk, Somerset. York then breaks in upon the scene, seizes the written transcription of the prophecies, and reads them out a second time. The Oxford editors, however, follow Q: when York breaks into the scene of conjuration, he does *not* read the prophecies aloud, an act that seems theatrically redundant. Rather, they are read aloud by King Henry in the next scene (2.1.177–87), when the conjuring episode is reported to him. Similarly, in Act 5, the Oxford edition follows Q in having the final fight between Richard and Somerset occur as 5.2, right before Clifford's battle with York, rather than placing Somerset's death later as young Clifford is bearing off the body of his dead father. The quarto arrangement thus puts maximum emphasis on York's triumph over old Clifford, King Henry's champion.

The Oxford edition differs from most modern texts in one other interesting way. At the beginning of 4.2 in F, two minor characters are listed as Bevis and John Holland. Most editors assume that these are the names of actual players, George Bevis and John Holland, who at some time acted in the play, rather than of fictional characters, yet they use these names as speech prefixes. In the Oxford text, Bevis and Holland are designated, as in Q, simply as "rebels."

Scene numbers follow most modern editions, except that the Oxford edition makes one continuous scene of what are traditionally Scenes 7 and 8 of Act 4, Cade's attack on London and his encounter with Buckingham and Clifford. Oxford also divides Act 5 into five scenes rather than the usual three. Placing the fight between Richard and Somerset after Scene 1 requires setting that fight off as 5.2. In addition, the Oxford editors believe that the stage is cleared after the encounter in which York kills old Clifford, whose body is carried off by his son. Henry and Margaret's enusing flight from the battlefield is thus set off as a separate scene, 5.4.

SELECTED BIBLIOGRAPHY

Carroll, William. "Theories of Kingship in Shakespeare's England." *A Companion to Shakespeare's Works.* Vol. II: *The Histories.* Ed. Richard Dutton and Jean E. Howard. Malden, Mass.: Blackwell, 2003. 125–45. Lays out the main ideas circulating in early modern England and Scotland about the powers and duties of the king as well as limits to his power.

Cartelli, Thomas. "Jack Cade in the Garden: Class Consciousness and Class Conflict in *2 Henry VI.*" *Enclosure Acts: Sexuality, Property, and Culture in Early Modern England.* Ed. Richard Burt and John Michael Archer. Ithaca, N. Y.: Cornell University Press, 1994. 48–64. Explores the class-based antagonism between Jack Cade and members of the propertied elite, including Alexander Iden, into whose garden the starving Cade intrudes.

Fitter, Chris. "Emergent Shakespeare and the Politics of Protest: 2 *Henry VI* in Historical Contexts." *English Literary History* 72 (2005): 129–58. Discusses the connections between the play and political events in Shakespeare's own lifetime and argues for Shakespeare's radical political leanings.

Greenblatt, Stephen. "Murdering Peasants: Status, Genre, and the Representation of Rebellion." *Representations* no. 1 (1983): 1–29. Explores the difficulties of representing early modern popular insurrection and the ideological instability of such representations.

Helgerson, Richard. "Staging Exclusion." *Forms of Nationhood: The Elizabethan Writing of England.* Chicago: University of Chicago Press, 1992. 195–245. Argues that through a predominantly negative representation of Cade and through a focus on the consolidation of monarchical rule, Shakespeare was instrumental in disrupting the traditional link between the theater and popular revolt.

Howard, Jean E., and Phyllis Rackin. "*Henry VI, Part II.*" *Engendering a Nation: A Feminist Account of Shakespeare's English Histories.* London: Routledge, 1997. 65–82. Examines the relationship between political disorder and gender disorder with special attention paid to Queen Margaret, King Henry, Eleanor Cobham, and Jack Cade.

Knowles, Ronald. "The Farce of History: Miracle, Combat, and Rebellion in 2 *Henry VI.*" *The Yearbook of English Studies* 21 (1991): 168–86. Examines the dramatic techniques of ironic juxtaposition, mirroring, and parody through which Shakespeare staged historical events and processes.

Manley, Lawrence. "From Strange's Men to Pembroke's Men: 2 *Henry VI* and *The First Part of the Contention.*" *Shakespeare Quarterly* 54 (2003): 253–87. Argues that the Quarto is a revision of some version of the longer Folio text and that this revision, which includes a harsher treatment of Eleanor Cobham, sprang from the play's transfer from Lord Strange's Men to Pembroke's Men.

Patterson, Annabel. "The Peasant's Toe: Popular Culture and Popular Pressure." *Shakespeare and the Popular Voice.* Cambridge, Mass.: Blackwell, 1989. 32–51. Argues that there was a cultural tradition of popular protest in Shakespeare's England to which his representation of Jack Cade is indebted.

Urkowitz, Steven. "'If I Mistake in These Foundations Which I Build Upon': Peter Alexander's Textual Analysis of *Henry VI Parts 2 and 3.*" *English Literary Renaissance* 18 (1988): 230–56. Refutes the idea of memorial reconstruction—that is, that the Quarto is a text derived from actors' memories of performance—and, instead, sees the Folio text as Shakespeare's purposeful revision of the Quarto.

FILM

Henry VI, Part Two. 1983. Dir. Jane Howell. UK/USA. Sumptuously costumed but tepid BBC-TV production with Julia Foster as Margaret, David Burke as Gloucester, Peter Benson as Henry VI, and Trevor Peacock as Cade.

The First Part of the Contention
of the Two Famous Houses
# of York and Lancaster
(The Second Part of Henry VI)

THE PERSONS OF THE PLAY

Of the King's Party

KING HENRY VI
QUEEN MARGARET
William de la Pole, Marquis, later Duke, of SUFFOLK, the Queen's lover
Duke Humphrey of GLOUCESTER, the Lord Protector, the King's uncle
Dame Eleanor Cobham, the DUCHESS of Gloucester
CARDINAL BEAUFORT, Bishop of Winchester, Gloucester's uncle
   and the King's great-uncle
Duke of BUCKINGHAM
Duke of SOMERSET
Old Lord CLIFFORD
YOUNG CLIFFORD, his son

Of the Duke of York's Party

Duke of YORK
EDWARD, Earl of March ⎫ his sons
Crookback RICHARD ⎭
Earl of SALISBURY
Earl of WARWICK, his son

The petitions and the combat

Two or three PETITIONERS
Thomas HORNER, an armourer
PETER Thump, his man
Three NEIGHBOURS, who drink to Horner
Three PRENTICES, who drink to Peter

The conjuration

Sir John HUME ⎫ priests
John SOUTHWELL ⎭
Margery Jordan, a WITCH
Roger BOLINGBROKE, a conjurer
ASNATH, a spirit

The false miracle

Simon SIMPCOX
SIMPCOX'S WIFE
The MAYOR of Saint Albans
Aldermen of Saint Albans
A BEADLE of Saint Albans
Townsmen of Saint Albans

Eleanor's penance

Gloucester's SERVANTS
Two SHERIFFS of London
Sir John STANLEY
HERALD

The murder of Gloucester

Two MURDERERS
COMMONS

The murder of Suffolk

CAPTAIN of a ship
MASTER of that ship
The Master's MATE
Walter WHITMORE
Two GENTLEMEN

The Cade Rebellion

Jack CADE, a Kentishman suborned by the Duke of York
Dick the BUTCHER
Smith the WEAVER
A Sawyer   Cade's followers
JOHN
REBELS
Emmanuel, the CLERK of Chatham
Sir Humphrey STAFFORD
STAFFORD'S BROTHER
Lord SAYE   those who die at the rebels' hands
Lord SCALES
Matthew Gough
A SERGEANT
Three or four CITIZENS of London
Alexander IDEN, an esquire of Kent, who kills Cade

Others

VAUX, a messenger
A POST
MESSENGERS
A SOLDIER
Attendants, guards, servants, soldiers, falconers

1.1

Flourish° of trumpets, then hautboys.° Enter, at one   Fanfare / oboes
door, KING HENRY and Humphrey Duke of GLOUCESTER,
the Duke of SOMERSET, the Duke of BUCKINGHAM, CAR-
DINAL BEAUFORT, and others. Enter, at the other door,
the Duke of YORK, and the Marquis of SUFFOLK, and
QUEEN MARGARET, and the Earl[s] of SALISBURY and
WARWICK[1]

1.1 Location: The palace, London.
1. This stage direction, like many others, is modeled primarily upon that in Q. Many editors believe Q is based
indirectly on a promptbook and closely reflects play-

house practice. In F, Salisbury, Warwick, Gloucester, and
Beaufort enter with the King, while Somerset and Buckingham enter with the Queen, Suffolk, and York.

SUFFOLK [*kneeling before* KING HENRY] As by your high imperial majesty
    I had in charge° at my depart° for France,   *was charged / departure*
    As Procurator° to your excellence,   *deputy*
    To marry Princess Margaret for your grace,°   *on your behalf*
5   So, in the famous ancient city Tours,
    In presence of the Kings of France and Sicil,[2]
    The Dukes of Orléans, Calaber,° Bretagne, and Alençon,   *Calabria*
    Seven earls, twelve barons, and twenty reverend bishops,
    I have performed my task and was espoused,
10   And humbly now upon my bended knee,
    In sight of England and her lordly peers,
    Deliver up my title in the Queen
    To your most gracious hands, that are the substance
    Of that great shadow° I did represent—   *image (of royalty)*
15   The happiest° gift that ever marquis[3] gave,   *most fortunate; best*
    The fairest queen that ever king received.
KING HENRY Suffolk, arise. Welcome, Queen Margaret.
    I can express no kinder° sign of love   *more natural*
    Than this kind° kiss.   *affectionate*
               [*He kisses her*]
               O Lord that lends me life,
20   Lend me a heart replete with thankfulness!
    For thou hast given me in this beauteous face
    A world of earthly blessings to my soul,
    If sympathy° of love unite our thoughts.   *mutual feeling*
QUEEN MARGARET Th'excess of love I bear unto your grace
25   Forbids me to be lavish of my tongue
    Lest I should speak more than beseems a woman.
    Let this suffice: my bliss is in your liking,°   *your affection for me*
    And naught can make poor Margaret miserable
    Unless the frown of mighty England's King.[4]
29.1   QUEEN MARGARET *Great King of England, and my gracious lord,*
       The mutual conference° that my mind hath had—   *intimate talk*
       By day, by night; waking, and in my dreams;
       In courtly company, or at my beads°—   *while praying*
29.5   *With you, mine alder liefest° sovereign,*   *entirely most precious*
       Makes me the bolder to salute my king
       With ruder terms, such as my wit affords
       And overjoy of heart doth minister.°   *suggest*
30   KING HENRY Her sight did ravish, but her grace in speech,
    Her words yclad° with wisdom's majesty,   *clad*
    Makes me from wond'ring° fall to weeping joys,   *admiring*
    Such is the fullness of my heart's content.
    Lords, with one cheerful voice, welcome my love.

---

2. Sicily. Queen Margaret's father, René, the Duke of Anjou, was Sicily's king in name only.
3. A nobleman ranking below a duke and above an earl. In *1 Henry VI*, Suffolk holds the rank of earl; here he appears as a marquis; later in this scene, Henry will make him a duke for his service as royal marriage broker.
4. Oxford adopts the 1594 Quarto version of the Queen's initial speech, lines 24–29; the Folio version, which follows as an indented passage (lines 29.1–29.8), may be the author's original draft.

35 LORDS *kneel*[*ing*] Long live Queen Margaret, England's happiness.
    QUEEN MARGARET We thank you all.
                Flourish. [*They all rise*]
    SUFFOLK [*to* GLOUCESTER] My Lord Protector, so it please your grace,
        Here are the articles of contracted peace
        Between our sovereign and the French King Charles,
40   For eighteen months concluded by consent.
    GLOUCESTER (*reads*) Imprimis:° it is agreed between the French   *First*
        King Charles and William de la Pole, Marquis of Suffolk,
        ambassador for Henry, King of England, that the said Henry
        shall espouse the Lady Margaret, daughter unto René, King
45   of Naples, Sicilia, and Jerusalem, and crown her Queen of
        England, ere the thirtieth of May next ensuing.
            Item:° it is further agreed between them that the duchy of   *Likewise*
        Anjou and the county of Maine shall be released and delivered
        to the King her fa—
                Duke Humphrey [GLOUCESTER] *lets* [*the paper*] *fall*[5]
    KING HENRY Uncle, how now?
50 GLOUCESTER   Pardon me, gracious lord.
        Some sudden qualm° hath struck me at the heart   *illness; fear*
        And dimmed mine eyes that I can read no further.
    KING HENRY [*to* CARDINAL BEAUFORT] Uncle of Winchester,
        I pray read on.
    CARDINAL BEAUFORT [*reads*] Item: it is further agreed between
55   them that the duchy of Anjou and the county of Maine shall
        be released and delivered to the King her father, and she sent
        over of° the King of England's own proper° cost and charges,   *at / personal*
        without dowry.
    KING HENRY They please us well. [*To* SUFFOLK] Lord Marquis,
        kneel down.
                [SUFFOLK *kneels*]
60   We here create thee first Duke of Suffolk,
        And gird thee with the sword.
                [SUFFOLK *rises*]
                                Cousin[6] of York,
        We here discharge your grace from being regent
        I'th' parts° of France till term of eighteen months   *(English) regions*
        Be full° expired. Thanks uncle Winchester,   *fully*
65   Gloucester, York, and Buckingham, Somerset,
        Salisbury, and Warwick.
        We thank you all for this great favour done
        In entertainment° to my princely Queen.   *welcome*
        Come, let us in, and with all speed provide
70   To see her coronation be performed.
                Exeunt KING [HENRY], QUEEN [MARGARET],
                and Suffolk. GLOUCESTER *stays all the rest*
    GLOUCESTER Brave peers of England, pillars of the state,
        To you Duke Humphrey must unload his grief,

---

5. In subsequent stage directions, "Humphrey" will often be silently changed to "Gloucester." As with many directions, this one appears only in Q, not in F.

6. A form of address customarily used by English monarchs to nobles.

Your grief, the common grief of all the land.
What—did my brother Henry° spend his youth,   *Henry V*
His valour, coin, and people in the wars?   75
Did he so often lodge in open field
In winter's cold and summer's parching heat
To conquer France, his true inheritance?[7]
And did my brother Bedford toil his wits
To keep by policy° what Henry got?   80   *political skill*
Have you yourselves, Somerset, Buckingham,
Brave York, Salisbury, and victorious Warwick,
Received deep scars in France and Normandy?
Or hath mine uncle Beaufort and myself,
With all the learnèd Council of the realm,   85
Studied so long, sat in the Council House
Early and late, debating to and fro,
How France and Frenchmen might be kept in awe,°   *obedience*
And had his highness in his infancy
Crownèd in Paris in despite of foes?   90
And shall these labours and these honours die?
Shall Henry's conquest, Bedford's vigilance,
Your deeds of war, and all our counsel die?
O peers of England, shameful is this league,
Fatal this marriage, cancelling your fame,   95
Blotting your names from books of memory,
Razing the characters° of your renown,   *Erasing the records*
Defacing monuments of conquered France,
Undoing all, as° all had never been!   *as though*

CARDINAL BEAUFORT   Nephew, what means this passionate discourse,   100
This peroration° with such circumstance?[8]   *rhetorical speech*
For France, 'tis ours; and we will keep it still.°   *always*

GLOUCESTER   Ay, uncle, we will keep it if we can—
But now it is impossible we should.
Suffolk, the new-made duke that rules the roast,°   105   *roost*
Hath given the duchy of Anjou and Maine
Unto the poor King René, whose large style°   *exalted title*
Agrees not with the leanness of his purse.

SALISBURY   Now by the death of Him that died for all,[9]
These counties were the keys of Normandy—   110
But wherefore weeps Warwick, my valiant son?

WARWICK   For grief that they are past recovery.
For were there hope to conquer them again
My sword should shed hot blood, mine eyes no tears.
Anjou and Maine? Myself did win them both!   115
Those provinces these arms of mine did conquer—
And are the cities that I got with wounds
Delivered up again with peaceful words?
Mort Dieu![1]

YORK   For Suffolk's duke, may he be suffocate,°   120   *choked (a pun)*
That dims the honour of this warlike isle!

---

7. England laid claim to France throughout the four-teenth century, and Henry V won the title "heir of France" with the Treaty of Troyes in 1420. See *Henry V* 1.1.85–90.

8. Such long-winded formality; so many details.
9. An oath equivalent to "by Christ's death."
1. God's death (French oath).

France should have torn and rent my very heart
Before I would have yielded to this league.
I never read but° England's kings have had   *I have always read that*
125   Large sums of gold and dowries with their wives—
And our King Henry gives away his own,
To match with° her that brings no vantages.°   *wed / profits (dowry)*

GLOUCESTER   A proper jest, and never heard before,
That Suffolk should demand a whole fifteenth²
130   For costs and charges in transporting her!
She should have stayed in France and starved in France
Before—

CARDINAL BEAUFORT   My lord of Gloucester, now ye grow too hot!
It was the pleasure of my lord the King.

135 GLOUCESTER   My lord of Winchester, I know your mind.
'Tis not my speeches that you do mislike,
But 'tis my presence that doth trouble ye.
Rancour will out. Proud prelate, in thy face
I see thy fury. If I longer stay
140   We shall begin our ancient bickerings—
But I'll be gone, and give thee leave to speak.
Lordings,° farewell, and say when I am gone,   *My lords*
I prophesied France will be lost ere long.   *Exit*

CARDINAL BEAUFORT   So, there goes our Protector in a rage.
145   'Tis known to you he is mine enemy;
Nay more, an enemy unto you all,
And no great friend, I fear me, to the King.
Consider, lords, he is the next of blood³
And heir apparent to the English crown.
150   Had Henry got an empire by his marriage,
And all the wealthy kingdoms of the west,⁴
There's reason he° should be displeased at it.   *(Gloucester)*
Look to it, lords—let not his smoothing° words   *flattering*
Bewitch your hearts. Be wise and circumspect.
155   What though the common people favour him,
Calling him 'Humphrey, the good Duke of Gloucester',
Clapping their hands and crying with loud voice
'Jesu maintain your royal excellence!'
With 'God preserve the good Duke Humphrey!'
160   I fear me, lords, for all this flattering gloss,°   *fair appearance*
He will be found a dangerous Protector.

BUCKINGHAM   Why should he then protect our sovereign,
He being of age⁵ to govern of himself?
Cousin of Somerset, join you with me,
165   And all together, with the Duke of Suffolk,
We'll quickly hoist° Duke Humphrey from his seat.   *remove*

CARDINAL BEAUFORT   This weighty business will not brook° delay—   *permit*
I'll to the Duke of Suffolk presently.°   *Exit*   *immediately*

2. A tax of one-fifteenth of the value of personal property.
3. Because Henry VI did not yet have children, the heir to the throne was Gloucester, his father's brother.
4. An anachronistic reference to the European conquest of the Americas.

5. Henry VI being old enough. At the time represented in this scene, the historical King was twenty-four and Gloucester was no longer Protector. Shakespeare here as elsewhere alters his sources.

SOMERSET   Cousin of Buckingham, though Humphrey's pride
170   And greatness of his place be grief to us,
       Yet let us watch the haughty Cardinal;
       His insolence is more intolerable
       Than all the princes in the land beside.
       If Gloucester be displaced, he'll be Protector.
175 BUCKINGHAM   Or° thou or I, Somerset, will be Protector,   *Either*
       Despite Duke Humphrey or the Cardinal.

Exeunt BUCKINGHAM *and* SOMERSET

SALISBURY   Pride went before, ambition follows him.[6]
       While these do labour for their own preferment,°   *advancement*
       Behoves it us to labour for the realm.
180   I never saw but Humphrey Duke of Gloucester
       Did bear him like a noble gentleman.
       Oft have I seen the haughty Cardinal,
       More like a soldier than a man o'th' church,
       As stout° and proud as° he were lord of all,   *arrogant / as if*
185   Swear like a ruffian, and demean° himself   *conduct*
       Unlike the ruler of a commonweal.
       Warwick, my son, the comfort of my age,
       Thy deeds, thy plainness,° and thy housekeeping°   *honesty / hospitality*
       Hath won thee greatest favour of the commons,
190   Excepting none but good Duke Humphrey.
       And, brother York,[7] thy acts in Ireland,
       In bringing them to civil discipline,°   *civilized order*
       Thy late exploits done in the heart of France,
       When thou wert Regent for our sovereign,
195   Have made thee feared and honoured of the people.
       The reverence of° mine age and Neville's name[8]   *respect for*
       Is of no little force if I command.
       Join we together for the public good,
       In what we can to bridle° and suppress   *restrain*
200   The pride of Suffolk and the Cardinal
       With Somerset's and Buckingham's ambition;
       And, as we may, cherish° Duke Humphrey's deeds   *encourage*
       While they do tend° the profit of the land.   *promote*
WARWICK   So God help Warwick, as he loves the land,
205   And common profit of his country!
YORK   And so says York, [*aside*] for he hath greatest cause.
SALISBURY   Then let's away, and look unto the main.[9]
WARWICK   Unto the main? O, father, Maine is lost!
       That Maine which by main° force Warwick did win,   *overwhelming*
210   And would have kept so long as breath did last!
       Main chance, father, you meant—but I meant Maine,
       Which I will win from France or else be slain.

Exeunt WARWICK *and* SALISBURY. *Manet°* YORK   *Remains*

YORK   Anjou and Maine are given to the French;
       Paris is lost, the state of Normandy
215   Stands on a tickle° point now they are gone;   *an unstable*
       Suffolk concluded on the articles,

6. A variation on the proverb "Pride goes before and shame comes after." Salisbury seems to refer to the Cardinal, who exited first, as "pride" and to Buckingham and Somerset as "ambition."
7. York was actually Salisbury's brother-in-law, having married Salisbury's sister Cicely.
8. Neville was the family name of the Earl of Salisbury and of his son, Warwick.
9. And consider the principal matter at stake. A gambling term, with subsequent puns on the several meanings of "main," including wordplay on "Maine," a French province lost in Suffolk's treaty.

The peers agreed, and Henry was well pleased
To change two dukedoms for a duke's fair daughter.
I cannot blame them all—what is't to them?
220 'Tis thine[1] they give away and not their own!
Pirates may make cheap pennyworths of° their pillage,   *sell at a low price*
And purchase friends, and give to courtesans,
Still° revelling like lords till all be gone,   *Continually*
Whileas the seely° owner of the goods   *While the helpless*
225 Weeps over them, and wrings his hapless° hands,   *unlucky*
And shakes his head, and, trembling, stands aloof,
While all is shared and all is borne away,
Ready to starve and dare not touch his own.
So York must sit and fret and bite his tongue,
230 While his own lands are bargained for and sold.
Methinks the realms of England, France, and Ireland
Bear that proportion° to my flesh and blood   *relation*
As did the fatal brand Althaea burnt
Unto the prince's heart of Calydon.[2]
235 Anjou and Maine both given unto the French!
Cold° news for me—for I had hope of France,   *Unwelcome*
Even as I have of fertile England's soil.
A day will come when York shall claim his own,
And therefore I will take the Nevilles' parts,[3]
240 And make a show of love to proud Duke Humphrey,
And, when I spy advantage,° claim the crown,   *opportunity*
For that's the golden mark° I seek to hit.   *target*
Nor shall proud Lancaster[4] usurp my right,
Nor hold the sceptre in his childish fist,
245 Nor wear the diadem upon his head
Whose church-like humours° fits not for a crown.   *pious temperament*
Then, York, be still a while till time do serve.
Watch° thou, and wake when others be asleep,   *Stay awake*
To pry into the secrets of the state—
250 Till Henry, surfeit° in the joys of love   *sickened from excess*
With his new bride and England's dear-bought queen,
And Humphrey with the peers be fall'n at jars.°   *into contention*
Then will I raise aloft the milk-white rose,[5]
With whose sweet smell the air shall be perfumed,
255 And in my standard° bear the arms of York,   *military flag*
To grapple with the house of Lancaster;
And force perforce° I'll make him yield the crown,   *by violent coercion*
Whose bookish rule hath pulled fair England down.   *Exit*

1.2

Enter Duke Humphrey [of GLOUCESTER] *and his wife*
Eleanor [the DUCHESS]

DUCHESS   Why droops my lord, like over-ripened corn°   *grain*
         Hanging the head at Ceres' plenteous load?[1]

1. It is your own (York is addressing himself and referring to his claim to the throne).
2. Althaea, mother of Meleager, Prince of Calydon,
was told by the Fates that her son would live only as
long as a log burning in the fire at his birth. She
snatched the log from the flames, but later, when
Meleager killed her brothers, Althaea returned the log
to the fire and Meleager's heart stopped beating. See
Ovid, *Metamorphoses* 8.

3. And therefore will I ally myself with Salisbury and
Warwick.
4. Henry VI was also Duke of Lancaster.
5. The emblem of the Yorkists; the red rose was the
Lancastrian emblem.
1.2 Location: The Duke of Gloucester's house, London.
1. At the rich harvest of Ceres (the Roman goddess of
agriculture and the harvest).

Why doth the great Duke Humphrey knit his brows,
As frowning at the favours of the world?
5 Why are thine eyes fixed to the sullen earth,
Gazing on that which seems to dim thy sight?
What seest thou there? King Henry's diadem,
Enchased° with all the honours of the world?   *Adorned*
If so, gaze on, and grovel on thy face²
10 Until thy head be circled with the same.
Put forth thy hand, reach at the glorious gold.
What, is't too short? I'll lengthen it with mine;
And having both together heaved° it up,   *raised*
We'll both together lift our heads to heaven
15 And never more abase our sight so low
As to vouchsafe one glance unto the ground.
GLOUCESTER   O Nell, sweet Nell, if thou dost love thy lord,
Banish the canker° of ambitious thoughts!   *ulcer*
And may that hour when I imagine ill
20 Against my king and nephew, virtuous Henry,
Be my last breathing in this mortal world!
My troublous dream this night° doth make me sad.   *this past night*
DUCHESS   What dreamed my lord? Tell me and I'll requite it
With sweet rehearsal° of my morning's dream.³   *recital*
25 GLOUCESTER   Methought this staff, mine office-badge° in court,   *symbol of my position*
Was broke in twain—by whom I have forgot,
But, as I think, it was by th' Cardinal—
And on the pieces of the broken wand
Were placed the heads of Edmund, Duke of Somerset,
30 And William de la Pole, first Duke of Suffolk.
This was my dream—what it doth bode, God knows.
DUCHESS   Tut, this was nothing but an argument°   *a proof*
That he that breaks a stick of Gloucester's grove
Shall lose his head for his presumption.
35 But list° to me, my Humphrey, my sweet duke: *listen*
Methought I sat in seat of majesty
In the cathedral church of Westminster,
And in that chair° where kings and queens are crowned,   *throne*
Where Henry and Dame Margaret kneeled to me,
40 And on my head did set the diadem.
GLOUCESTER   Nay, Eleanor, then must I chide outright.
Presumptuous dame! Ill-nurtured° Eleanor!   *Ill-bred*
Art thou not second woman in the realm,
And the Protector's wife beloved of him?
45 Hast thou not worldly pleasure at command
Above the reach or compass of thy thought?
And wilt thou still be hammering° treachery   *devising*
To tumble down thy husband and thyself
From top of honour to disgrace's feet?
50 Away from me, and let me hear no more!
DUCHESS   What, what, my lord? Are you so choleric°   *hot-tempered*
With Eleanor for telling but her dream?
Next time I'll keep my dreams unto myself
And not be checked.°   *rebuked*

---

2. Crawl on the ground (perhaps to seek supernatural aid).   3. Morning dreams were popularly believed to be true.

55   GLOCESTER   Nay, be not angry; I am pleased again.

                  Enter a MESSENGER

    MESSENGER   My Lord Protector, 'tis his highness' pleasure

        You do prepare to ride unto Saint Albans,

        Whereas° the King and Queen do mean to hawk.   *Where*

    GLOCESTER   I go. Come, Nell, thou wilt ride with us?

60   DUCHESS   Yes, my good lord, I'll follow presently.°   *immediately*

            Exeunt GLOCESTER [*and the* MESSENGER]

        Follow I must; I cannot go before

        While Gloucester bears this base° and humble mind.   *servile*

        Were I a man, a duke, and next of blood,

        I would remove these tedious stumbling blocks

65   And smooth my way upon their headless necks.

        And, being a woman, I will not be slack

        To play my part in fortune's pageant.[4]

        [*Calling within*]   Where are you there? Sir John![5] Nay, fear not man.

        We are alone. Here's none but thee and I.

           Enter Sir John HUME

70   HUME   Jesus preserve your royal majesty.

    DUCHESS   What sayst thou? 'Majesty'? I am but 'grace'.[6]

    HUME   But by the grace of God and Hume's advice

        Your grace's title shall be multiplied.

    DUCHESS   What sayst thou, man? Hast thou as yet conferred

75   With Margery Jordan, the cunning witch[7] of Eye,

        With Roger Bolingbroke, the conjuror?

        And will they undertake to do me good?

    HUME   This they have promisèd: to show your highness

        A spirit raised from depth of underground

80   That shall make answer to such questions

        As by your Grace shall be propounded him.

    DUCHESS   It is enough. I'll think upon the questions.

        When from Saint Albans we do make return,

        We'll see these things effected to the full.

85   Here, Hume [*giving him money*], take this reward. Make merry, man,

        With thy confederates in this weighty cause.   *Exit*

    HUME   Hume must make merry with the Duchess' gold;

        Marry,[8] and shall. But how now, Sir John Hume?

        Seal up your lips, and give no words but mum;

90   The business asketh silent secrecy.

        Dame Eleanor gives gold to bring the witch.

        Gold cannot come amiss were she a devil.

        Yet have I gold flies from another coast[9]—

        I dare not say from the rich Cardinal

95   And from the great and new-made Duke of Suffolk,

        Yet I do find it so; for, to be plain,

        They, knowing Dame Eleanor's aspiring humour,°   *ambitious nature*

        Have hired me to undermine the Duchess,

---

4. In Roman mythology, the goddess Fortune symbolized the element of chance in human life and was often depicted with a rudder (as the pilot of destiny), wings, or a wheel. Here Fortune is imagined as directing a medieval play ("pageant") or leading a ceremonial procession.

5. Priests were commonly addressed as "sir."

6. The appropriate title for a duchess.

7. Cunning women, sometimes prosecuted for witchcraft, were familiar village figures who made a living by telling fortunes, healing sicknesses, making love potions, and finding lost objects.

8. By the Virgin Mary (a mild oath).

9. I have gold that comes from another quarter.

And buzz° these conjurations in her brain.   *whisper*
100 They say 'A crafty knave does need no broker',°   *middleman; agent*
Yet am I Suffolk and the Cardinal's broker.
Hume, if you take not heed you shall go near
To call them both a pair of crafty knaves.
Well, so it stands; and thus, I fear, at last
105 Hume's knavery will be the Duchess' wrack,°   *ruin*
And her attainture° will be Humphrey's fall.   *conviction*
Sort° how it will, I shall have gold for all.   *Exit*   *Turn out*

1.3

Enter PETER, *the armourer's man*,° [*with*] *two or three*   *apprentice*
[*other*] PETITIONERS

FIRST PETITIONER   My masters, let's stand close. My Lord Pro-
tector will come this way by and by and then we may deliver
our supplications in the quill.°   *as a group*
SECOND PETITIONER   Marry, the Lord protect him, for he's a
5   good man, Jesu bless him.
Enter the Duke of SUFFOLK *and* QUEEN [MARGARET]
FIRST PETITIONER   Here a° comes, methinks, and the Queen   *he*
with him. I'll be the first, sure.[1]
[*He goes to meet* SUFFOLK *and the* QUEEN]
SECOND PETITIONER   Come back, fool—this is the Duke of Suf-
folk and not my Lord Protector.
10 SUFFOLK [*to the* FIRST PETITIONER]   How now, fellow[2]—wouldst
anything with me?
FIRST PETITIONER   I pray, my lord, pardon me—I took ye for my
Lord Protector.
QUEEN MARGARET [*seeing his supplication, she reads*]   'To my
15   Lord Protector'—are your supplications to his lordship? Let
me see them.
[*She takes First Petitioner's supplication*]
What is thine?
FIRST PETITIONER   Mine is, an't° please your grace, against   *if it*
John Goodman, my lord Cardinal's man, for keeping my
20   house and lands and wife and all from me.
SUFFOLK   Thy wife too? That's some wrong indeed. [*To the* SEC-
OND PETITIONER] What's yours?
[*He takes the supplication*]
What's here? [*Reads*] 'Against the Duke of Suffolk for enclos-
ing the commons[3] of Melford'! [*To the* SECOND PETITIONER]
25   How now, Sir Knave?
SECOND PETITIONER   Alas, sir, I am but a poor petitioner of our
whole township.
PETER [*offering his petition*]   Against my master, Thomas
Horner, for saying that the Duke of York was rightful heir to
30   the crown.

1.3 Location: The palace, London.
1. In F, these lines are assigned to Peter, but lines
12–13 suggest they are spoken by the First Petitioner,
who here pushes himself forward to get the attention of
the Queen and Suffolk (whom he believes to be
Gloucester).

2. A common form of address to a social inferior.
3. Fencing in for private use land once used by the entire
community. The practice of enclosure, which benefited
landowners while forcing into poverty the lower classes
who had farmed the land, was a chronic source of unrest
in many regions in early modern England.

QUEEN MARGARET   What sayst thou? Did the Duke of York say
   he was rightful heir to the crown?
PETER   That my master was? No, forsooth, my master said that
   he was and that the King was an usurer.
35 QUEEN MARGARET   An usurper thou wouldst say.
PETER   Ay, forsooth—an usurper.
SUFFOLK [*calling within*]   Who is there?
        Enter [a] servant
   Take this fellow in and send for his master with a pursuivant°   *an officer*
   presently. [*To* PETER] We'll hear more of your matter before
40   the King.   *Exit [the servant] with [*PETER] *the armourer's man*
QUEEN MARGARET [*to the* PETITIONERS]   And as for you that love to be protected
   Under the wings of our Protector's grace,
   Begin your suits anew and sue to him.
       [*She*] *tears the supplication*[4]
   Away, base cullions![5] Suffolk, let them go.
45 ALL PETITIONERS   Come, let's be gone.   *Exeunt* PETITIONERS
QUEEN MARGARET   My lord of Suffolk, say, is this the guise?°   *custom*
   Is this the fashions in the court of England?
   Is this the government of Britain's isle,
   And this the royalty of Albion's° king?   *England's*
50   What, shall King Henry be a pupil still
   Under the surly Gloucester's governance?
   Am I a queen in title and in style,°   *form of address*
   And must be made a subject to a duke?
   I tell thee, Pole, when in the city Tours
55   Thou rann'st a-tilt[6] in honour of my love
   And stol'st away the ladies' hearts of France,
   I thought King Henry had resembled thee
   In courage, courtship,° and proportion.[7]   *courtly manners*
   But all his mind is bent to holiness,
60   To number Ave-Maries on his beads.[8]
   His champions are the prophets and apostles,[9]
   His weapons holy saws° of sacred writ,   *sayings*
   His study is his tilt-yard,° and his loves   *jousting arena*
   Are brazen images of canonizèd saints.
65   I would the college of the cardinals
   Would choose him Pope, and carry him to Rome,
   And set the triple crown° upon his head—   *papal crown*
   That were a state fit for his holiness.
SUFFOLK   Madam, be patient—as I was cause
70   Your highness came to England, so will I
   In England work your grace's full content.
QUEEN MARGARET   Beside the haught° Protector have we Beaufort   *arrogant*
   The imperious churchman, Somerset, Buckingham,
   And grumbling York; and not the least of these
75   But can do more in England than the King.

---

4. In Q, Suffolk is the one who "tears the papers." This
is one of the places where F gives more initiative to
Margaret than does Q.
5. Lowborn rascals. "Cullion" comes from the Italian
word *coglioni,* meaning "testicles."
6. You took part in a jousting tournament.
7. Physical grace; physique.

8. Referring to a Roman Catholic devotion in which a
string of beads (a rosary) is used to keep track of prayers
said in a particular sequence. Among the prayers are "Ave
Maria," or "Hail Mary," addressed to the Virgin Mary.
9. A champion stood in for the King at jousts and tournaments. Margaret scornfully suggests that Henry VI
makes holy men rather than real warriors his champions.

SUFFOLK   And he of these that can do most of all
Cannot do more in England than the Nevilles:
Salisbury and Warwick are no simple peers.
QUEEN MARGARET   Not all these lords do vex me half so much
80   As that proud dame, the Lord Protector's wife.
She sweeps it through the court with troops of ladies
More like an empress than Duke Humphrey's wife.
Strangers in court do take her for the queen.
She bears a duke's revenues on her back,°   *wears costly clothing*
85   And in her heart she scorns our poverty.
Shall I not live to be avenged on her?
Contemptuous° base-born callet° as she is,   *Despicable / whore*
She vaunted 'mongst her minions° t'other day   *followers*
The very train of her worst-wearing° gown   *poorest*
90   Was better worth° than all my father's lands,   *worth more*
Till Suffolk gave two dukedoms° for his daughter.   *(Maine and Anjou)*
SUFFOLK   Madam, myself have limed a bush[1] for her,
And placed a choir of such enticing birds
That she will light° to listen to their lays,°   *perch / songs*
95   And never mount to trouble you again.
So let her rest; and, madam, list to me,
For I am bold to counsel you in this:
Although we fancy not the Cardinal,
Yet must we join with him and with the lords
100   Till we have brought Duke Humphrey in disgrace.
As for the Duke of York, this late complaint[2]
Will make but little for his benefit.
So one by one we'll weed them all at last,
And you yourself shall steer the happy helm.
          Sound a sennet.° Enter KING HENRY, *[with] the Duke*   *trumpet call*
          of YORK *and the Duke of* SOMERSET *on both sides,*
          whispering with him. [Also] enter Duke Humphrey
          [of GLOUCESTER*], Dame Eleanor the* DUCHESS
          [of Gloucester], the Duke of BUCKINGHAM,
          the Earl[s] of SALISBURY *and* WARWICK, *and* CARDINAL
          *[*BEAUFORT *Bishop] of Winchester*
105   KING HENRY   For my part, noble lords, I care not which:
Or° Somerset or York, all's one to me.   *Either*
YORK   If York have ill demeaned° himself in France   *conducted*
Then let him be denied the regentship.
SOMERSET   If Somerset be unworthy of the place,
110   Let York be regent—I will yield to him.
WARWICK   Whether your grace be worthy, yea or no,
Dispute not that: York is the worthier.
CARDINAL BEAUFORT   Ambitious Warwick, let thy betters speak.
WARWICK   The Cardinal's not my better in the field.°   *in battle*
115   BUCKINGHAM   All in this presence are thy betters, Warwick.
WARWICK   Warwick may live to be the best of all.
SALISBURY   Peace, son; [*to* BUCKINGHAM] and show some reason,
          Buckingham,
Why Somerset should be preferred in this.

---

1. Have set a trap. Elizabethans caught birds by smearing bushes and twigs with a sticky substance known as
birdlime.

2. This recent complaint. Suffolk means that Peter's
claim against his master casts doubt on York's loyalty to
the King.

QUEEN MARGARET   Because the King, forsooth, will have it so.

120 GLOUCESTER   Madam, the King is old enough himself
To give his censure.° These are no women's matters.   *judgment*

QUEEN MARGARET   If he be old enough, what needs your grace
To be Protector of his excellence?

GLOUCESTER   Madam, I am Protector of the realm,

125 And at his pleasure will resign my place.

SUFFOLK   Resign it then, and leave thine insolence.
Since thou wert king—as who is king but thou?—
The commonwealth hath daily run to wrack,
The Dauphin³ hath prevailed beyond the seas,

130 And all the peers and nobles of the realm
Have been as bondmen to thy sovereignty.

CARDINAL BEAUFORT [*to* GLOUCESTER]   The commons hast thou
racked,° the clergy's bags   *overtaxed*
Are lank and lean with thy extortions.

SOMERSET [*to* GLOUCESTER]   Thy sumptuous buildings⁴ and thy wife's attire

135 Have cost a mass of public treasury.

BUCKINGHAM [*to* GLOUCESTER]   Thy cruelty in execution
Upon offenders hath exceeded law
And left thee to the mercy of the law.

QUEEN MARGARET [*to* GLOUCESTER]   Thy sale of offices and
towns in France—

140 If they were known, as the suspect° is great—   *suspicion*
Would make thee quickly hop without thy head.⁵

Exit GLOUCESTER

QUEEN [MARGARET] *lets fall her fan*⁶
[*To the* DUCHESS] Give me my fan—what, minion,° can ye not?   *hussy*

She gives the DUCHESS *a box on the ear*

I cry you mercy,° madam! Was it you?   *beg your pardon*

DUCHESS   Was't I? Yea, I it was, proud Frenchwoman!

145 Could I come near your beauty with my nails,
I'd set my ten commandments° in your face.   *(ten fingers)*

KING HENRY   Sweet aunt, be quiet—'twas against her will.°   *unintentional*

DUCHESS   Against her will? Good King, look to't in time!
She'll pamper thee and dandle thee like a baby.

150 Though in this place most master⁷ wear no breeches,
She shall not strike Dame Eleanor unrevenged!   *Exit*

BUCKINGHAM [*aside to* CARDINAL BEAUFORT]   Lord Cardinal, I
will follow Eleanor
And listen after Humphrey how he proceeds.
She's tickled° now, her fury needs no spurs—   *vexed*

155 She'll gallop far enough to her destruction.   *Exit*

Enter Duke Humphrey [*of* GLOUCESTER]

GLOUCESTER   Now, lords, my choler being overblown°   *dispelled*
With walking once about the quadrangle,
I come to talk of commonwealth affairs.
As for your spiteful false objections,

---

3. "Dauphin" was the title of the oldest son of the French King, but here it refers to the French King himself, Charles VII, and bears witness to the fact that England did not acknowledge Charles's right to the throne.
4. Probably a reference to Greenwich Palace. In 1437,

Gloucester obtained a grant to expand the old manor, which he lent to Henry VI and Margaret for their honeymoon.
5. Proverbial expression meaning to be beheaded.
6. In Q, the Queen lets fall a glove, not a fan.
7. The one most in control (the Queen).

160 Prove them, and I lie open to the law.
But God in mercy so deal with my soul
As I in duty love my King and country.
But to the matter that we have in hand—
I say, my sovereign, York is meetest° man   *the most suitable*
165 To be your regent in the realm of France.

SUFFOLK Before we make election,° give me leave   *a choice*
To show some reason of no little force
That York is most unmeet of any man.

YORK I'll tell thee, Suffolk, why I am unmeet:
170 First, for° I cannot flatter thee in pride;   *because*
Next, if I be appointed for the place,
My lord of Somerset will keep me here
Without discharge,° money, or furniture,°   *payment / equipment*
Till France be won into the Dauphin's hands.
175 Last time I danced attendance on his will[8]
Till Paris was besieged, famished, and lost.

WARWICK That can I witness, and a fouler fact°   *deed*
Did never traitor in the land commit.

SUFFOLK Peace, headstrong Warwick.

180 WARWICK Image of pride, why should I hold my peace?

Enter [guarded, HORNER *the*] *armourer and* [PETER] *his
man*

SUFFOLK Because here is a man accused of treason—
Pray God the Duke of York excuse himself!

YORK Doth anyone accuse York for a traitor?

KING HENRY What mean'st thou, Suffolk? Tell me, what are these?

185 SUFFOLK Please it your majesty, this is the man
[*He indicates* PETER]
That doth accuse his master [*indicating* HORNER] of high treason.
His words were these: that Richard Duke of York
Was rightful heir unto the English crown,
And that your majesty was an usurper.

190 KING HENRY [*to* HORNER] Say, man, were these thy words?

HORNER An't shall please your majesty, I never said nor
thought any such matter. God is my witness, I am falsely
accused by the villain.

PETER [*raising his hands*] By these ten bones,° my lords, he did   *(ten fingers)*
195 speak them to me in the garret one night as we were scouring
my lord of York's armour.

YORK Base dunghill villain and mechanical,°   *manual laborer*
I'll have thy head for this thy traitor's speech!
[*To* KING HENRY] I do beseech your royal majesty,
200 Let him have all the rigour of the law.

HORNER Alas, my lord, hang me if ever I spake the words. My
accuser is my prentice, and when I did correct him for his
fault the other day, he did vow upon his knees he would be
even with me. I have good witness of this, therefore, I beseech
205 your majesty, do not cast away° an honest man for a villain's   *destroy*
accusation.

---

8. I did as he wished. York refers to events depicted in *1 Henry VI,* specifically to Somerset's failure to supply him with reinforcements during the wars in France. See *1 Henry VI* 4.3.9–11.

KING HENRY [*to* GLOUCESTER]   Uncle, what shall we say to this in law?

GLOUCESTER   This doom,° my lord, if I may judge by case: *judgment*
    Let Somerset be regent o'er the French,
210   Because in York this breeds suspicion.⁹
    [*Indicating* HORNER *and* PETER] And let these have a day
       appointed them
    For single combat in convenient place,
    For he [*indicating* HORNER] hath witness of his servant's malice.
    This is the law, and this Duke Humphrey's doom.

215 KING HENRY   Then be it so. [*To* SOMERSET] My lord of Somerset,
    We make you regent o'er the realm of France
    There to defend our rights 'gainst foreign foes.

SOMERSET   I humbly thank your royal majesty.

HORNER   And I accept the combat willingly.

220 PETER [*to* GLOUCESTER]   Alas, my lord, I cannot fight; for God's
    sake, pity my case! The spite of man prevaileth against me.
    O Lord, have mercy upon me—I shall never be able to fight a
    blow! O Lord, my heart!

GLOUCESTER   Sirrah,¹ or° you must fight or else be hanged.   *either*

225 KING HENRY   Away with them to prison, and the day
    Of combat be the last of the next month.
    Come, Somerset, we'll see thee sent away.   *Flourish. Exeunt*

1.4

Enter Margery Jordan, a WITCH; *Sir John* HUME
[*and John* SOUTHWELL, *two priests*]; *and Roger*
    BOLINGBROKE, *a conjuror*¹

HUME   Come, my masters, the Duchess, I tell you, expects per-
    formance of your promises.

BOLINGBROKE   Master Hume, we are therefore° provided. Will   *for that purpose*
    her ladyship behold and hear our exorcisms?°   *conjuring of spirits*

5 HUME   Ay, what else? Fear you not her courage.

BOLINGBROKE   I have heard her reported to be a woman of an
    invincible spirit. But it shall be convenient, Master Hume,
    that you be by her, aloft, while we be busy below. And so, I
    pray you, go in God's name and leave us.   *Exit* HUME

10   Mother Jordan, be you prostrate and grovel on the earth.
       She lies down upon her face.
       Enter Eleanor [the DUCHESS *of Gloucester] aloft*
    John Southwell, read you and let us to our work.

DUCHESS   Well said, my masters, and welcome all. To this gear°   *business*
    the sooner the better.
       [*Enter* HUME *aloft*]

BOLINGBROKE   Patience, good lady—wizards know their times.
15   Deep night, dark night, the silent of the night,
    The time of night when Troy was set on fire,²
    The time when screech-owls cry and bandogs° howl,   *chained watchdogs*

---

9. Because this matter casts doubt on York's loyalty.
1. A common form of address to a social inferior.
1.4 Location: Gloucester's garden, London.
1. Neither Q nor F names John Southwell as one of the two priests in this scene, but he is named in dialogue at line 11. Q has Eleanor enter at the beginning of the scene; F, as here, has her enter aloft a few lines into the scene. After Hume's exit at line 9, he must reenter aloft

at some point to attend Eleanor. This entry is not marked, but having Hume reenter after line 13 leaves enough time for him to exit the stage at line 9 and make an entrance above.
2. Virgil's *Aeneid*, Book 2, describes how the Greeks, having entered Troy through treachery, set fire to the ancient city.

And spirits walk, and ghosts break up° their graves—   *burst open*
That time best fits the work we have in hand.
20   Madam, sit you, and fear not. Whom we raise
We will make fast within a hallowed verge.°   *magic circle*
Here do the ceremonies belonging,[3] *and make the*
circle. SOUTHWELL *reads 'Coniuro te',*[4] *&c. It thunders*
and lightens terribly, then the spirit [ASNATH][5] *riseth*
ASNATH   Adsum.°   *I am here*
WITCH   Asnath,
By the eternal God whose name and power
25   Thou tremblest at, answer that° I shall ask,   *what*
For till thou speak, thou shalt not pass from hence.
ASNATH   Ask what thou wilt, that° I had said and done.   *would that*
BOLINGBROKE [*reads*]   'First, of the King: what shall of him
      become?'
ASNATH   The Duke yet lives that Henry shall depose,
30   But him outlive, and die a violent death.[6]
      [*As the spirit speaks,* SOUTHWELL *writes the answer*]
BOLINGBROKE [*reads*]   'Tell me what fate awaits the Duke of Suffolk.'
ASNATH   By water shall he die, and take his end.
BOLINGBROKE [*reads*]   'What shall betide the Duke of Somerset?'
ASNATH   Let him shun castles. Safer shall he be
35   Upon the sandy plains than where castles mounted° stand.   *on mountains*
Have done—for more I hardly can endure.
BOLINGBROKE   Descend to darkness and the burning lake!
False° fiend, avoid!°   *Treacherous / be gone*
      Thunder and lightning. [*The spirit*] *sinks down again*[7]
38.1   BOLINGBROKE   *Then down, I say, unto the damnèd pool*
            Where Pluto[8] *in his fiery wagon° sits*   *chariot*
            Riding, amidst the singed and parchèd smokes,
            The roads of Ditis by the River Styx.[9]
38.5   *There howl and burn for ever in those flames.*
            Rise, Jordan, rise and stay° thy charming spells—   *halt*
            Zounds,° we are betrayed!   *By God's wounds (oath)*
      Enter the Duke[s] *of* YORK *and* BUCKINGHAM *with their guard,* [*among them*
      Sir Humphrey STAFFORD] *and break in*
YORK   Lay hands upon these traitors and their trash.
      [BOLINGBROKE, SOUTHWELL, *and Jordan are taken pris-*
      oner. BUCKINGHAM *takes the writings from*
      BOLINGBROKE *and* SOUTHWELL]
40   [*To Jordan*] Beldam,° I think we watched you at an inch.°   *Witch / closely*
[*To the* DUCHESS] What, madam, are you there? The King
      and common weal
Are deep indebted for this piece of pains.°   *your trouble*

---

3. The rituals necessary (for conjuring spirits).
4. I conjure you (Latin), the beginning of a spell.
5. An anagram of "Sathan," a variant form of "Satan." Demons were supposed to be invoked by anagrams.
6. *The . . . death:* Like many prophecies, this one is ambiguous. The syntax of the first line can mean that there lives a duke whom Henry shall depose or who shall depose Henry. The duke is probably York, who in *Richard Duke of York* (*3 Henry VI*) forces Henry to entail the crown to York rather than to Henry's own son, thus symbolically deposing him. York, however, dies a

violent death after the Battle of Wakefield, and Henry outlives him. But Henry also dies a violent death, murdered in the Tower of London by the Duke of York's son, Richard, Duke of Gloucester, who eventually becomes King Richard III.
7. For lines 37–38, Q substitutes the following indented passage (lines 38.1–38.7); it may record a revision made in rehearsal to cover the spirit's descent.
8. In classical mythology, the god of the infernal regions.
9. The river of Hades over which Charon ferried the dead.

My lord Protector will, I doubt it not,
See you well guerdoned° for these good deserts.   *rewarded*
DUCHESS   Not half so bad as thine to England's king,
45   Injurious° Duke, that threatest where's no cause.   *Abusive*
BUCKINGHAM   True, madam, none at all—
    [*He raises the writings*]
                        what call you this?
    [*To his men*] Away with them. Let them be clapped up close°   *imprisoned securely*
    And kept asunder. [*To the* DUCHESS] You, madam, shall with us.
50   Stafford, take her to thee.
                [*Exeunt* STAFFORD *and others to the* DUCHESS
                          and HUME *above*]
    We'll see your trinkets here all forthcoming.[1]
    All away!
                Exeunt [*below, Jordan,* SOUTHWELL, *and*
              BOLINGBROKE, *guarded, and, above,* HUME *and*
              the DUCHESS *guarded by* STAFFORD *and others.*
                    YORK *and* BUCKINGHAM *remain*]
YORK   Lord Buckingham, methinks you watched her well.
    A pretty plot,° well chosen to build upon.   *trick; plot of ground*
55   Now pray, my lord, let's see the devil's writ.
    [BUCKINGHAM *gives him the writings*]
    What have we here?
    [*He*] *reads* [*the writings*]
                Why, this is just°   *precisely*
    Aio Aeacidam, Romanos vincere posse.[2]
    These oracles are hardily° attained   *with difficulty*
    And hardly understood. Come, come, my lord,
60   The King is now in progress towards Saint Albans;
    With him the husband of this lovely lady.
    Thither goes these news as fast as horse can carry them—
    A sorry breakfast for my lord Protector.
BUCKINGHAM   Your grace shall give me leave, my lord of York,
65   To be the post° in hope of his reward.   *messenger*
YORK [*returning the writings to* BUCKINGHAM]   At your pleasure,
    my good lord.   *Exit* BUCKINGHAM
    [*Calling within*] Who's within there, ho!
    Enter a SERVINGMAN
    Invite my lords of Salisbury and Warwick
    To sup with me tomorrow night. Away.   *Exeunt* [*severally*]°   *separately*

2.1

    Enter KING [HENRY], QUEEN [MARGARET] *with her hawk*
    on her fist, Duke Humphrey [*of* GLOUCESTER],
    CARDINAL [BEAUFORT], *and* [*the Duke of*] SUFFOLK, *with*
    falconers hollering
QUEEN MARGARET   Believe me, lords, for flying at the brook°   *hawking for waterfowl*
    I saw not better sport these seven years' day;
    Yet, by your leave, the wind was very high,
    And, ten to one, old Joan had not gone out.[1]

---

1. We'll see that your worthless goods (the conjuring paraphernalia) are produced as evidence against you.
2. I say that you, descendant of Aeacus, the Romans can conquer. A famously ambiguous response by an oracle to King Pyrrhus's question about whether he
would conquer Rome.
2.1 Location: St. Albans.
1. The hawk named "Old Joan" would probably not have flown because of the high wind.

KING HENRY [*to* GLOUCESTER]   But what a point,² my lord, your falcon made,
5   And what a pitch° she flew above the rest!   *height*
     To see how God in all his creatures works!
     Yea, man and birds are fain° of climbing high.   *fond*
SUFFOLK   No marvel, an it like° your majesty,   *if it please*
     My Lord Protector's hawks do tower so well;
10   They know their master loves to be aloft,°   *to rule over others*
     And bears his thoughts above his falcon's pitch.³
GLOUCESTER   My lord, 'tis but a base ignoble mind
     That mounts no higher than a bird can soar.
CARDINAL BEAUFORT   I thought as much; he would be above the clouds.
15   GLOUCESTER   Ay, my lord Cardinal, how think you by that?
     Were it not good your grace could fly to heaven?
KING HENRY   The treasury of everlasting joy.
CARDINAL BEAUFORT [*to* GLOUCESTER]   Thy heaven is on earth;
          thine eyes and thoughts
20   Beat on° a crown, the treasure of thy heart,   *Think obsessively about*
     Pernicious Protector, dangerous peer,
     That smooth'st it so with° King and common weal!   *Who so flatters*
GLOUCESTER   What, Cardinal? Is your priesthood grown peremptory?
     *Tantaene animis caelestibus irae?*⁴
25   Churchmen so hot? Good uncle, hide such malice
     With some holiness—can you do it?
SUFFOLK   No malice, sir, no more than well becomes°   *is appropriate to*
     So good° a quarrel and so bad a peer.   *just*
GLOUCESTER   As who, my lord?
SUFFOLK   Why, as you, my lord—
30   An't like your lordly Lord's Protectorship.
GLOUCESTER   Why, Suffolk, England knows thine insolence.
QUEEN MARGARET   And thy ambition, Gloucester.
KING HENRY   I prithee peace,
     Good Queen, and whet not on° these furious peers—   *do not encourage*
     For blessèd are the peacemakers on earth.⁵
35   CARDINAL BEAUFORT   Let me be blessèd for the peace I make
     Against this proud Protector with my sword.
          [GLOUCESTER *and* CARDINAL BEAUFORT *speak privately to*
          one another]
GLOUCESTER   Faith, holy uncle, would't were come to that.
CARDINAL BEAUFORT   Marry, when thou dar'st.
GLOUCESTER   Dare? I tell thee, priest,
     Plantagenets⁶ could never brook° the dare!   *tolerate*
40   CARDINAL BEAUFORT   I am Plantagenet as well as thou,
     And son to John of Gaunt.

---

2. High position to which hawks fly to await prey.
3. Alluding to Gloucester's heraldic crest, which consisted of a falcon with a maiden's head. Suffolk is accusing Gloucester of overweening ambition.
4. Quoting Virgil's *Aeneid* 1.11, "Can there be such anger in heavenly minds?"
5. Quoting Jesus' Sermon on the Mount (Matthew 5:9).
6. "Plantagenet" was a name given the kings descended from Geoffrey, Count of Anjou, and Matilda, daughter of Henry I, thought to derive from the Latin words for

"a sprig of broom," which Geoffrey wore in his cap. Gloucester, a grandson of John of Gaunt, was a Plantagenet. John of Gaunt was Beaufort's father, but Beaufort's mother, Catherine Swynford, gave birth to him and his brothers before she married Gaunt; this explains why Gloucester calls Beaufort a bastard (line 42). Historically, the Beauforts, though eventually legitimated, were barred from any claim to the throne. The lines referring to Beaufort's bastardy, 38–43, appear only in Q and not in F.

GLOUCESTER   In bastardy.

CARDINAL BEAUFORT   I scorn thy words.

GLOUCESTER   Make up no factious numbers for the matter,[7]

45 In thine own person answer thy abuse.°   *insult; offense*

CARDINAL BEAUFORT   Ay, where thou dar'st not peep; an if° thou dar'st,   *an if = if*
This evening on the east side of the grove.

KING HENRY   How now, my lords?

CARDINAL BEAUFORT [*aloud*]   Believe me, cousin Gloucester,
Had not your man put up° the fowl so suddenly,   *raised; startled*
We had had more sport. [*Aside to* GLOUCESTER] Come with thy
50   two-hand sword.

GLOUCESTER [*aloud*]   True, uncle.
[*Aside to* CARDINAL BEAUFORT] Are ye advised?° The east side   *agreed*
of the grove.

CARDINAL BEAUFORT [*aside to* GLOUCESTER]
I am with you.

KING HENRY   Why, how now, uncle Gloucester?

GLOUCESTER   Talking of hawking, nothing else, my lord.
[*Aside to the* CARDINAL] Now, by God's mother, priest, I'll shave
55   your crown[8] for this,
Or all my fence° shall fail.   *skill in fencing*

CARDINAL BEAUFORT [*aside to* GLOUCESTER]
                     Medice, teipsum[9]—
Protector, see to't well; protect yourself.

KING HENRY   The winds grow high; so do your stomachs,° lords.   *tempers*
How irksome is this music to my heart!
60 When such strings jar,[1] what hope of harmony?
I pray, my lords, let me compound° this strife.   *settle*
              Enter one crying 'a miracle'

GLOUCESTER   What means this noise?
Fellow, what miracle dost thou proclaim?

ONE   A miracle, a miracle!

65 SUFFOLK   Come to the King—tell him what miracle.

ONE [*to* KING HENRY]   Forsooth, a blind man at Saint Alban's shrine[2]
Within this half-hour hath received his sight—
A man that ne'er saw in his life before.

KING HENRY   Now God be praised, that to believing souls
70 Gives light in darkness, comfort in despair!
              Enter the MAYOR *of Saint Albans and his brethren*
              [*aldermen*] *with music, bearing the man* [SIMPCOX]
              between two in a chair. [*Enter* SIMPCOX'S WIFE
              and other townsmen with them]

CARDINAL BEAUFORT   Here comes the townsmen on° procession   *in*
To present your highness with the man.
              [*The townsmen kneel*]

KING HENRY   Great is his comfort in this earthly vale,
Although by sight his sin be multiplied.[3]

GLOUCESTER [*to the townsmen*]   Stand by, my masters, bring
75   him near the King.

---

7. Call in no supporters for this quarrel.
8. Alluding to a tonsure, or a shaved circular patch, often seen on the heads of religious men.
9. Physician, (heal) thyself (see Luke 4:23).

1. When instruments such as these grow discordant.
2. A shrine to the first British martyr, who was beheaded by the Romans for giving sanctuary to Christians.
3. Although his sight will lead him into more temptation.

His highness' pleasure is to talk with him.
       [*They rise and bear* SIMPCOX *before the* KING]
KING HENRY [*to* SIMPCOX]   Good fellow, tell us here the circumstance,
       That we for thee may glorify the Lord.
       What, hast thou been long blind and now restored?
SIMPCOX   Born blind, an't please your grace.
80 SIMPCOX'S WIFE   Ay, indeed, was he.
SUFFOLK   What woman is this?
SIMPCOX'S WIFE   His wife, an't like your worship.
GLOUCESTER   Hadst thou been his mother
       Thou couldst have better told.
KING HENRY [*to* SIMPCOX]   Where wert thou born?
85 SIMPCOX   At Berwick,⁴ in the north, an't like your grace.
KING HENRY   Poor soul, God's goodness hath been great to thee.
       Let never day nor night unhallowed° pass,   *unblessed*
       But still° remember what the Lord hath done.   *continually*
QUEEN MARGARET [*to* SIMPCOX]   Tell me, good fellow, cam'st
             thou here by chance,
90   Or of devotion to this holy shrine?
SIMPCOX   God knows, of pure devotion, being called
       A hundred times and oftener, in my sleep,
       By good Saint Alban, who said, 'Simon, come;
       Come offer° at my shrine and I will help thee.'   *make an offering*
95 SIMPCOX'S WIFE   Most true, forsooth, and many time and oft
       Myself have heard a voice to call him so.
CARDINAL BEAUFORT [*to* SIMPCOX]
       What, art thou lame?
SIMPCOX   Ay, God almighty help me.
SUFFOLK   How cam'st thou so?
SIMPCOX   A fall off of a tree.
SIMPCOX'S WIFE [*to* SUFFOLK]
       A plum tree,⁵ master.
GLOUCESTER   How long hast thou been blind?
SIMPCOX   O, born so, master.
100 GLOUCESTER   What, and wouldst climb a tree?
SIMPCOX   But that° in all my life, when I was a youth.   *Only that once*
SIMPCOX'S WIFE [*to* GLOUCESTER]   Too true—and bought his
             climbing very dear.
GLOUCESTER [*to* SIMPCOX]   Mass,° thou loved'st plums well   *By the Mass (an oath)*
       that wouldst venture so.
SIMPCOX   Alas, good master, my wife desired some damsons,°   *tiny plums; testicles*
105   And made me climb with danger of my life.
GLOUCESTER [*aside*]   A subtle knave, but yet it shall not serve.
       [*To* SIMPCOX] Let me see thine eyes: wink° now, now open   *close your eyes*
       them. In my opinion yet thou seest not well.
SIMPCOX   Yes, master, clear as day, I thank God and Saint Alban.
110 GLOUCESTER   Sayst thou me so? [*Pointing*] What colour is this cloak of?
SIMPCOX   Red, master; red as blood.
GLOUCESTER   Why, that's well said.
       [*Pointing*] And his cloak?
SIMPCOX   Why, that's green.

---

4. Town on the Scottish border, far from St. Albans.   5. Slang for "female thighs and genitals."

GLOUCESTER [*pointing*]   And what colour's
    His hose?
SIMPCOX   Yellow, master; yellow as gold.
GLOUCESTER   And what colour's my gown?
SIMPCOX   Black, sir; coal-black, as jet.°   *glossy black stone*
115   KING HENRY   Why, then, thou know'st what colour jet is of?
    SUFFOLK   And yet I think jet did he never see.
    GLOUCESTER   But cloaks and gowns before this day, a many.°   *a multitude*
    SIMPCOX'S WIFE   Never before this day in all his life.
    GLOUCESTER   Tell me, sirrah, what's my name?
120   SIMPCOX   Alas, master, I know not.
    GLOUCESTER [*pointing*]   What's his name?
    SIMPCOX   I know not.
    GLOUCESTER [*pointing*]   Nor his?
    SIMPCOX   No, truly, sir.
125   GLOUCESTER [*pointing*]   Nor his name?
    SIMPCOX   No indeed, master.
    GLOUCESTER   What's thine own name?
    SIMPCOX   Simon[6] Simpcox, an it please you, master.
    GLOUCESTER   Then, Simon, sit thou there the lying'st knave
130   In Christendom. If thou hadst been born blind
     Thou mightst as well have known our names as thus
     To name the several colours we do wear.
     Sight may distinguish colours, but suddenly
     To nominate° them all—it is impossible.   *name*
135   Saint Alban here hath done a miracle.
     Would you not think his cunning° to be great   *skill*
     That could restore this cripple to his legs again?
    SIMPCOX   O master, that you could!
    GLOUCESTER [*to the* MAYOR *and aldermen*]   My masters of Saint
    Albans, have you not
140   Beadles[7] in your town, and things called whips?
    MAYOR   We have, my lord, an if it please your grace.
    GLOUCESTER   Then send for one presently.°   *immediately*
    MAYOR [*to a townsman*]   Sirrah, go fetch the beadle hither
    straight.   *Exit one*
    GLOUCESTER   Bring me a stool.
             [*A stool is brought*]
     [*To* SIMPCOX]   Now, sirrah, if you mean
145   To save yourself from whipping, leap me° o'er   *for me*
     This stool and run away.
    SIMPCOX   Alas, master,
     I am not able even to stand alone.
     You go about to torture me in vain.
         Enter a BEADLE *with whips*
    GLOUCESTER   Well, sirrah, we must have you find your legs.
150   [*To the* BEADLE] Whip him till he leap over that same stool.
    BEADLE   I will, my lord.
     [*To* SIMPCOX] Come on, sirrah, off with your doublet quickly.

---

6. Q and F both call the character "Sander Simpcox" at this point. At line 93 of F, however, Simpcox refers to himself as "Simon." It has been proposed that "Sander" was the name of an actor who played the part of

Simpcox, that his name entered Q at this point, and that this portion of F derives from Q.
7. Minor parish officials who administered punishment to vagabonds and those guilty of petty offenses.

SIMPCOX   Alas, master, what shall I do? I am not able to stand.
     After the BEADLE *hath hit him once, he leaps over the*
     stool and runs away. [Some of the townsmen] follow
     and cry, 'A miracle! A miracle!'
KING HENRY   O God, seest thou this and bear'st so long?
155 QUEEN MARGARET   It made me laugh to see the villain run!
GLOUCESTER [*to the* BEADLE]   Follow the knave, and take this
     drab° away.   slut
SIMPCOX'S WIFE   Alas, sir, we did it for pure need.°   out of utter poverty
     [*Exit the* BEADLE *with the* WIFE]
GLOUCESTER [*to the* MAYOR]   Let them be whipped through
     every market-town
     Till they come to Berwick, from whence they came.
     Exeunt [the] MAYOR *[and any remaining townsmen]*
160 CARDINAL BEAUFORT   Duke Humphrey has done a miracle today.
SUFFOLK   True: made the lame to leap and fly away.
GLOUCESTER   But you have done more miracles than I—
     You made, in a day, my lord, whole towns to fly.[8]
     Enter the Duke of BUCKINGHAM
KING HENRY   What tidings with our cousin Buckingham?
165 BUCKINGHAM   Such as my heart doth tremble to unfold.
     A sort of naughty persons, lewdly bent,[9]
     Under the countenance and confederacy°   protection and complicity
     Of Lady Eleanor, the Protector's wife,
     The ringleader and head of all this rout,
170 Have practised° dangerously against your state,   plotted
     Dealing with witches and with conjurors,
     Whom we have apprehended in the fact,°   in the very act
     Raising up wicked spirits from under ground,
     Demanding of King Henry's life and death
175 And other° of your highness' Privy Council.   other members
     And here's the answer the devil did make to them.
     [BUCKINGHAM *gives* KING HENRY *the writings*][1]
KING HENRY [*reads*]   'First of the King: what shall of him become?
     The Duke yet lives that Henry shall depose,
     But him outlive and die a violent death.'
180 God's will be done in all. Well, to the rest.
     [*Reads*] 'Tell me what fate awaits the Duke of Suffolk?
     By water shall he die, and take his end.'
SUFFOLK [*aside*]   By water must the Duke of Suffolk die?
     It must be so, or else the devil doth lie.
185 KING HENRY [*reads*]   'What shall betide the Duke of Somerset?
     Let him shun castles. Safer shall he be
     Upon the sandy plains than where castles mounted stand.'
CARDINAL BEAUFORT [*to* GLOUCESTER]   And so, my Lord
     Protector, by this means
     Your lady is forthcoming° yet at London.   in custody
190 [*Aside to* GLOUCESTER] This news, I think, hath turned your
     weapon's edge.°   blunted your sword

---

8. Referring to the French towns Suffolk gave away
when he arranged Henry's marriage to Margaret.
9. A gang of evil people, wickedly inclined.
1. Neither Q nor F directs Buckingham to hand Henry
the prophecies, but he clearly must do so if, as in Q,

Henry is to read them out at this point. Lines 177–87
follow the substance of York's reading of the prophecies
in F's 1.4, but they have been reconstructed by the
Oxford editors to fit their quarto placement here. For
details, see the Textual Variants.

'Tis like, my lord, you will not keep your hour.[2]

GLOUCESTER Ambitious churchman, leave° to afflict my heart.   *cease*

Sorrow and grief have vanquished all my powers,

And, vanquished as I am, I yield to thee

195 Or to the meanest groom.°   *poorest servant*

KING HENRY O God, what mischiefs work the wicked ones,

Heaping confusion on their own heads thereby!

QUEEN MARGARET Gloucester, see here the tainture° of thy nest,   *defilement*

And look thyself be faultless, thou wert best.

200 GLOUCESTER Madam, for myself, to heaven I do appeal,

How I have loved my King and common weal;

And for my wife, I know not how it stands.

Sorry I am to hear what I have heard.

Noble she is, but if she have forgot

205 Honour and virtue and conversed° with such   *consulted*

As, like to pitch, defile nobility,

I banish her my bed and company,[3]

And give her as a prey to law and shame

That hath dishonoured Gloucester's honest name.

210 KING HENRY Well, for this night we will repose us here;

Tomorrow toward London back again,

To look into this business thoroughly,

And call these foul offenders to their answers,

And poise° the cause in justice' equal scales,   *weigh*

215 Whose beam stands sure,[4] whose rightful cause prevails.

Flourish. Exeunt

2.2

Enter the Duke of YORK *and the Earls of* SALISBURY
and WARWICK

YORK Now, my good lords of Salisbury and Warwick,

Our simple supper ended, give me leave

In this close walk° to satisfy myself   *secluded path*

In craving your opinion of my title,

5 Which is infallible, to England's crown.

SALISBURY My lord, I long to hear it out at full.

WARWICK Sweet York, begin, and if thy claim be good,

The Nevilles are thy subjects to command.

YORK Then thus:

10 Edward the Third, my lords, had seven sons:

The first, Edward the Black Prince, Prince of Wales;

The second, William of Hatfield; and the third,

Lionel Duke of Clarence; next to whom

Was John of Gaunt, the Duke of Lancaster;

15 The fifth was Edmund Langley, Duke of York;

The sixth was Thomas of Woodstock, Duke of Gloucester;

William of Windsor was the seventh and last.

Edward the Black Prince died before his father

And left behind him Richard, his only son,

---

2. Appointment (for the duel previously arranged between Gloucester and Cardinal Beaufort).
3. Echoing the language of church law, which permitted marital separation "from bed and board" in cases of adultery, heresy, and cruelty.

4. Whose bar (from which the two scales are suspended) is perfectly balanced and therefore allows accurate measurements.
2.2 Location: The Duke of York's garden, London.

20   Who, after Edward the Third's death, reigned as king
    Till Henry Bolingbroke, Duke of Lancaster,
    The eldest son and heir of John of Gaunt,
    Crowned by the name of Henry the Fourth,
    Seized on the realm, deposed the rightful king,
25   Sent his poor queen to France from whence she came,
    And him to Pomfret; where, as well you know,
    Harmless Richard was murdered traitorously.
  WARWICK [*to* SALISBURY]   Father, the Duke of York hath told the truth;
    Thus got the house of Lancaster the crown.
30 YORK   Which now they hold by force and not by right;
    For Richard, the first son's heir, being dead,
    The issue of the next son should have reigned.
  SALISBURY   But William of Hatfield died without an heir.
  YORK   The third son, Duke of Clarence, from whose line
35   I claim the crown, had issue Phillipe, a daughter,
    Who married Edmund Mortimer, Earl of March;[1]
    Edmund had issue, Roger, Earl of March;
    Roger had issue, Edmund, Anne and Eleanor.
  SALISBURY   This Edmund, in the reign of Bolingbroke,
40   As I have read, laid claim unto the crown,
    And, but for Owain Glyndŵr, had been king,
    Who kept him in captivity till he died.
    But to the rest.
  YORK   His eldest sister, Anne,
    My mother, being heir unto the crown,
45   Married Richard, Earl of Cambridge, who was son
    To Edmund Langley, Edward the Third's fifth son.
    By her I claim the kingdom: she was heir
    To Roger, Earl of March, who was the son
    Of Edmund Mortimer, who married Phillipe,
50   Sole daughter unto Lionel, Duke of Clarence.
    So if the issue of the elder son
    Succeed before the younger, I am king.
  WARWICK   What plain proceedings is more plain than this?
    Henry doth claim the crown from John of Gaunt,
55   The fourth son; York claims it from the third:
    Till Lionel's issue fails, John's should not reign.
    It fails not yet, but flourishes in thee
    And in thy sons, fair slips of such a stock.[2]
    Then, father Salisbury, kneel we together,
60   And in this private plot° be we the first   *plot of ground*
    That shall salute our rightful sovereign
    With honour of his birthright to the crown.
  SALISBURY *and* WARWICK [*kneeling*]   Long live our sovereign
      Richard, England's king!
  YORK   We thank you, lords;

1. Like Raphael Holinshed and Edward Hall, whose chronicles Shakespeare used as sources for this play, Shakespeare conflates Edmund Mortimer, the fifth Earl of March, who was named heir to the throne by Richard II, with his uncle of the same name who was captured by Glyndŵr, a Welsh lord Shakespeare was later to depict in *1 Henry IV* as a rebel against the King. Although Shakespeare here says Glyndŵr kept Mortimer imprisoned until he died, in *1 Henry IV* he follows the chronicles in having Mortimer eventually marry Glyndŵr's daughter.
2. Fair cuttings of such a tree.

[SALISBURY *and* WARWICK *rise*]

            but I am not your king

65   Till I be crowned, and that° my sword be stained   *until*

      With heart-blood of the house of Lancaster—

      And that's not suddenly to be performed,

      But with advice° and silent secrecy.   *deliberation*

      Do you, as I do, in these dangerous days,

70   Wink at° the Duke of Suffolk's insolence,   *Ignore*

      At Beaufort's pride, at Somerset's ambition,

      At Buckingham, and all the crew of them,

      Till they have snared the shepherd of the flock,

      That virtuous prince, the good Duke Humphrey.

75   'Tis that they seek, and they, in seeking that,

      Shall find their deaths, if York can prophesy.

SALISBURY   My lord, break off—we know your mind at full.

WARWICK   My heart assures me that the Earl of Warwick

      Shall one day make the Duke of York a king.

80 YORK   And Neville, this I do assure myself—

      Richard shall live to make the Earl of Warwick

      The greatest man in England but the King.   *Exeunt*

2.3

Sound trumpets. Enter KING HENRY *and state,*° *with*   *persons of rank*
guard, to banish the DUCHESS: KING HENRY *and* QUEEN
[MARGARET], *Duke Humphrey* [*of* GLOUCESTER], *the*
Duke of SUFFOLK *and the Duke of* BUCKINGHAM,
CARDINAL [BEAUFORT], *and, led with officers, Dame*
Eleanor Cobham [*the* DUCHESS, *Margery Jordan the*
WITCH, *John* SOUTHWELL *and Sir John* HUME *the two*
priests, and Roger BOLINGBROKE *the conjuror*]; *then*
enter to them the Duke of YORK *and the Earls of*
SALISBURY *and* WARWICK[1]

KING HENRY [*to the* DUCHESS]   Stand forth, Dame Eleanor
    Cobham, Gloucester's wife.

        [*She comes forward*]

    In sight of God and us your guilt is great;

    Receive the sentence of the law for sins

    Such as by God's book are adjudged to death.[2]

[*To the* WITCH, SOUTHWELL, HUME, *and* BOLINGBROKE] You

5   four, from hence to prison back again;

    From thence, unto the place of execution.

    The witch in Smithfield[3] shall be burned to ashes,

    And you three shall be strangled° on the gallows.   *hanged*

              [*Exeunt* WITCH, SOUTHWELL, HUME, *and*
                      BOLINGBROKE, *guarded*]

[*To the* DUCHESS] You, madam, for° you are more nobly born,   *because*

10   Despoilèd° of your honour in your life,   *Deprived*

    Shall, after three days' open penance done,

    Live in your country here in banishment

2.3 Location: A London hall of justice.
1. F's stage direction simply reads "Sound Trumpets. Enter the King and State, with Guard to banish the Duchess." Q does not mention Jordan, the two priests, or Bolingbroke, but F clearly requires them.
2. *Receive . . . death:* alluding to Exodus 22:18: "Thou

shalt not suffer a witch to live." At times throughout Elizabeth's reign, witch hunts were conducted and laws against witchcraft strictly enforced.
3. Famous as the site in London where heretics were burned.

With Sir John Stanley in the Isle of Man.⁴
DUCHESS   Welcome is banishment; welcome were my death.
15   GLOUCESTER   Eleanor, the law, thou seest, hath judgèd thee;
I cannot justify° whom the law condemns.   excuse
                                                Exit [*the* DUCHESS, *guarded*]
Mine eyes are full of tears, my heart of grief.
Ah, Humphrey, this dishonour in thine age
Will bring thy head with sorrow to the grave.
20   [*To* KING HENRY] I beseech your majesty, give me leave to go.
Sorrow would° solace, and mine age would ease.   desires
KING HENRY   Stay, Humphrey Duke of Gloucester. Ere thou go,
Give up thy staff.⁵ Henry will to himself
Protector be; and God shall be my hope,
25   My stay, my guide, and lantern to my feet.
And go in peace, Humphrey, no less beloved
Than when thou wert Protector to thy King.
QUEEN MARGARET   I see no reason why a king of years°   who is of age
Should be to be° protected like a child.   need to be
30   God and King Henry govern England's helm!
Give up your staff, sir, and the King his° realm.   the king's
GLOUCESTER   My staff? Here, noble Henry, is my staff.
As willingly do I the same resign
As erst° thy father Henry made it mine;   formerly
35   And even as willing at thy feet I leave it
As others would ambitiously receive it.
        [*He lays the staff at King Henry's feet*]
Farewell, good King. When I am dead and gone,
May honourable peace attend thy throne.   *Exit*
QUEEN MARGARET   Why, now is Henry King and Margaret Queen,
40   And Humphrey Duke of Gloucester scarce himself,
That bears so shrewd a maim;⁶ two pulls° at once—   pluckings; tugs
His lady banished and a limb° lopped off.   (his staff)
        [*She picks up the staff*]
This staff of honour raught,° there let it stand   seized
Where it best fits to be, in Henry's hand.
        [*She gives the staff to* KING HENRY]
45   SUFFOLK   Thus droops this lofty pine and hangs his sprays;°   branches
Thus Eleanor's pride dies in her youngest days.°   in its youth
YORK   Lords, let him go. Please it your majesty,
This is the day appointed for the combat,
And ready are the appellant° and defendant—   challenger
50   The armourer and his man—to enter the lists,°   dueling area
So please your highness to behold the fight.
QUEEN MARGARET   Ay, good my lord, for purposely therefor
Left I the court to see this quarrel tried.
KING HENRY   A° God's name, see the lists and all things fit;   In
55   Here let them end it, and God defend the right.
YORK   I never saw a fellow worse bestead,°   prepared
Or more afraid to fight, than is the appellant,
The servant of this armourer, my lords.

---

4. An island off England's northwest coast.
5. Emblem of his office as Protector.
6. Who endures so painful a mutilation.

Enter at one door [HORNER] *the armourer and his*
NEIGHBOURS, *drinking to him so much that he is*
drunken; and he enters with a drum[mer] before him
and [carrying] his staff with a sandbag fastened to it.
[Enter] at the other door [PETER] *his man, [also] with*
a drum[mer] and [a staff with] sandbag, and PRENTICES
drinking to him

60 FIRST NEIGHBOUR [*offering drink to* HORNER] Here, neighbour
Horner, I drink to you in a cup of sack,° and fear not, neigh-   *sherry*
bour, you shall do well enough.

SECOND NEIGHBOUR [*offering drink to* HORNER] And here,
neighbour, here's a cup of charneco.°   *port*

THIRD NEIGHBOUR [*offering drink to* HORNER] Here's a pot of
65 good double° beer, neighbour, drink and be merry, and fear   *extra-strong*
not your man.

HORNER [*accepting the offers of drink*] Let it come,° i'faith I'll   *Pass it around*
pledge you all, and a fig⁷ for Peter.

FIRST PRENTICE [*offering drink to* PETER] Here, Peter, I drink to
70 thee, and be not afeard.

SECOND PRENTICE [*offering drink to* PETER] Here, Peter, here's
a pint of claret wine for thee.

THIRD PRENTICE [*offering drink to* PETER] And here's a quart for
me, and be merry, Peter, and fear not thy master. Fight for
75 credit° of the prentices!   *the honor*

PETER [*refusing the offers of drink*] I thank you all. Drink and
pray for me, I pray you, for I think I have taken my last
draught in this world. Here, Robin, an if° I die, I give thee my   *an if = if*
apron; and, Will, thou shalt have my hammer; and here, Tom,
80 take all the money that I have. O Lord bless me, I pray God,
for I am never able to deal with my master, he hath learned so
much fence° already.   *fencing skill*

SALISBURY Come, leave your drinking, and fall to blows.
[*To* PETER] Sirrah, what's thy name?

85 PETER Peter, forsooth.

SALISBURY Peter? What more?

PETER Thump.

SALISBURY Thump! Then see that thou thump thy master well.

HORNER Masters, I am come hither, as it were, upon my man's
90 instigation, to prove him a knave and myself an honest man;
and touching the Duke of York, I will take my death° I never   *stake my life on it*
meant him any ill, nor the King, nor the Queen; and therefore,
Peter, have at thee° with a downright° blow.   *I come at thee / vertical*

YORK Dispatch; this knave's tongue begins to double.°   *to slur his words*
*Sound trumpets [an] alarum to the combatants.*⁸
They fight and PETER *hits* [HORNER] *on the head and*
strikes him down

95 HORNER Hold, Peter, hold—I confess, I confess treason.
                                                    He dies

YORK [*to an attendant, pointing to* HORNER] Take away his
weapon. [*To* PETER] Fellow, thank God and the good wine in
thy master's wame.°   *belly*

---

7. Slang for "vulva"; hence, an obscene insult. It was
typically accompanied by a gesture in which the thumb
was thrust between two closed fingers or into the
mouth.

8. In F, the line "Sound Trumpets, Alarum to the Combatants" is spoken by York as part of his prior speech.

PETER *He kneels down*° O God, have I overcome mine enemy
100   in this presence? O, Peter, thou hast prevailed in right.
    KING HENRY [*to attendants, pointing to* HORNER] Go, take hence
        that traitor from our sight,
    For by his death we do perceive his guilt.
    And God in justice hath revealed to us
    The truth and innocence of this poor fellow,
105   Which he° had thought to have murdered wrongfully.   *Whom he (Horner)*
    [*To* PETER] Come, fellow, follow us for thy reward.
        Sound a flourish. Exeunt [some carrying HORNER'*s body]*

<h3 style="text-align:center">2.4</h3>

Enter Duke Humphrey [of GLOUCESTER] *and his men
in mourning cloaks*[1]

    GLOUCESTER   Thus sometimes hath the brightest day a cloud;
    And after summer evermore succeeds°   *follows*
    Barren winter, with his wrathful nipping° cold;   *biting*
    So cares and joys abound as seasons fleet.°   *fly by*
5   Sirs, what's o'clock?
    SERVANT   Ten, my lord.
    GLOUCESTER   Ten is the hour that was appointed me
    To watch the coming of my punished Duchess;
    Uneath° may she endure the flinty streets,   *Scarcely*
10   To tread them with her tender-feeling feet.
    Sweet Nell, ill can thy noble mind abrook°   *endure*
    The abject° people gazing on thy face   *lowly born*
    With envious° looks, laughing at thy shame,   *spiteful*
    That erst did follow thy proud chariot wheels
15   When thou didst ride in triumph through the streets.
    But soft, I think she comes; and I'll prepare
    My tear-stained eyes to see her miseries.
        Enter the DUCHESS, *Dame Eleanor Cobham, barefoot,
        [with] a white sheet about her, written verses pinned
        on her back*[2] *[and carrying a] wax candle in her hand;
        [she is] accompanied with the [two]* SHERIFFS
        of London, and Sir John STANLEY, *and officers with
        bills and halberds*[3]
    SERVANT [*to* GLOUCESTER]   So please your grace, we'll take her°   *rescue her by force*
    from the sheriffs.
    GLOUCESTER   No, stir not for your lives, let her pass by.
20   DUCHESS   Come you, my lord, to see my open shame?
    Now thou dost penance too. Look how they gaze,
    See how the giddy multitude do point
    And nod their heads, and throw their eyes on thee.
    Ah, Gloucester, hide thee from their hateful° looks,   *full of hate*
25   And, in thy closet° pent up, rue my shame,   *private chamber*
    And ban° thine enemies—both mine and thine.   *curse*
    GLOUCESTER   Be patient, gentle Nell; forget this grief.
    DUCHESS   Ah, Gloucester, teach me to forget myself;
    For whilst I think I am thy married wife,

---

9. Only Q records, "He [Peter] kneels down," just as Q,
and not F, indicates, "He [Horner] dies" (line 95).
2.4 Location: A London street.
1. Hooded black garments worn to funerals to express
sorrow.

2. Eleanor's offenses were presumably detailed in
these verses.
3. Both bills and halberds were long-handled weapons.
Bills had a curved blade, halberds an axlike blade with
a spike at the back.

30   And thou a prince, Protector of this land,
     Methinks I should not thus be led along,
     Mailed up⁴ in shame, with papers on my back,
     And followed with a rabble that rejoice
     To see my tears and hear my deep-fet groans.⁵
35   The ruthless flint doth cut my tender feet,
     And when I start,° the envious people laugh,   *flinch*
     And bid me be advisèd how I tread.
     Ah, Humphrey, can I bear this shameful yoke?
     Trowest° thou that e'er I'll look upon the world,   *Believeth*
40   Or count them happy that° enjoys the sun?   *who*
     No, dark shall be my light, and night my day;
     To think upon my pomp shall be my hell.
     Sometime I'll say I am Duke Humphrey's wife,
     And he a prince and ruler of the land;
45   Yet so he ruled, and such a prince he was,
     As he stood by whilst I, his forlorn Duchess,
     Was made a wonder and a pointing stock°   *an object of scorn*
     To every idle rascal° follower.   *lowborn*
     But be thou mild and blush not at my shame,
50   Nor stir at nothing till the axe of death
     Hang over thee, as sure it shortly will.
     For Suffolk, he that can do all in all
     With her° that hateth thee and hates us all,   *(Margaret)*
     And York, and impious Beaufort that false priest,
55   Have all limed bushes⁶ to betray thy wings,
     And fly thou how thou canst, they'll tangle thee.
     But fear not thou until thy foot be snared,
     Nor never seek prevention of° thy foes.   *safeguards against*
     GLOUCESTER   Ah, Nell, forbear; thou aimest all awry.
60   I must offend before I be attainted,°   *condemned for treason*
     And had I twenty times so many foes,
     And each of them had twenty times their power,
     All these could not procure me any scathe°   *harm*
     So long as I am loyal, true, and crimeless.
65   Wouldst have me rescue thee from this reproach?
     Why, yet thy scandal were not wiped away,
     But I in danger for the breach of law.
     Thy greatest help is quiet, gentle Nell.
     I pray thee sort° thy heart to patience.   *adapt*
70   These few days' wonder will be quickly worn.⁷
          Enter a HERALD
     HERALD   I summon your grace to his majesty's parliament
     holden° at Bury⁸ the first of this next month.   *to be held*
     GLOUCESTER   And my consent ne'er asked herein before?
     This is close° dealing. Well, I will be there.   *Exit* HERALD   *secret*
75   My Nell, I take my leave; and, Master Sheriff,
     Let not her penance exceed the King's commission.
     FIRST SHERIFF   An't please your grace, here my commission stays,°   *ends*

---

4. Enveloped: a term from falconry that describes the condition of a hawk wrapped in cloth so as to prevent its flying away.
5. Moans fetched from deep within me.
6. Coated bushes with birdlime (see note to 1.3.92).
7. What was marveled at for a few days will soon be forgotten.
8. Bury St. Edmunds, a town in Suffolk.

And Sir John Stanley is appointed now
To take her with him to the Isle of Man.
80 GLOUCESTER   Must you, Sir John, protect° my lady here?   *keep in custody*
STANLEY   So am I given in charge, may't please your grace.
GLOUCESTER   Entreat° her not the worse in that° I pray   *Treat / just because*
You use her well. The world may laugh again,
And I may live to do you kindness if
85 You do it her. And so, Sir John, farewell.
          [GLOUCESTER *begins to leave*]
DUCHESS   What, gone, my lord, and bid me not farewell?
GLOUCESTER   Witness my tears—I cannot stay to speak.
          Exeunt GLOUCESTER *and his men*
DUCHESS   Art thou gone too? All comfort go with thee,
For none abides with me. My joy is death—
90 Death, at whose name I oft have been afeard,
Because I wished this world's eternity.°   *immortality on earth*
Stanley, I prithee go and take me hence.
I care not whither, for I beg no favour,
Only convey me where thou art commanded.
95 STANLEY   Why, madam, that is to the Isle of Man,
There to be used according to your state.°   *rank; condition*
DUCHESS   That's bad enough, for I am but reproach;°   *in a state of shame*
And shall I then be used reproachfully?
STANLEY   Like to a duchess and Duke Humphrey's lady,
100 According to that state you shall be used.
DUCHESS   Sheriff, farewell, and better than I fare,
Although thou hast been conduct° of my shame.   *conductor*
FIRST SHERIFF   It is my office, and, madam, pardon me.
DUCHESS   Ay, ay, farewell—thy office is discharged.
          [*Exeunt* SHERIFFS]
105 Come, Stanley, shall we go?
STANLEY   Madam, your penance done, throw off this sheet,
And go we to attire you for our journey.
DUCHESS   My shame will not be shifted⁹ with my sheet—
No, it will hang upon my richest robes
110 And show itself, attire me how I can.
Go, lead the way, I long to see my prison.   *Exeunt*

3.1

Sound a sennet. Enter to the parliament: enter two
heralds before, then the Duke[s] of BUCKINGHAM *and*
SUFFOLK, *and then the Duke of* YORK *and* CARDINAL
[BEAUFORT], *and then* KING [HENRY] *and* QUEEN [MAR-
GARET,] *and then the Earl[s] of* SALISBURY *and* WAR-
WICK [*with attendants*]

KING HENRY   I muse° my lord of Gloucester is not come   *am surprised*
'Tis not his wont° to be the hindmost man,   *habit*
Whate'er occasion keeps him from us now.
QUEEN MARGARET   Can you not see, or will ye not observe,
5 The strangeness of his altered countenance?
With what a majesty he bears himself?

---

9. Changed, with a pun on "shifted" as meaning "put   3.1 Location: A great hall, Bury St. Edmunds.
on new undergarments."

How insolent of late he is become?
How proud, how peremptory, and unlike himself?
We know the time since° he was mild and affable,   *We remember when*
10 And if we did but glance a far-off look,
Immediately he was upon his knee,
That all the court admired him for° submission.   *was amazed at his*
But meet him now, and be it in the morn
When everyone will give the time of day,°   *say good morning*
15 He knits his brow, and shows an angry eye,
And passeth by with stiff unbowèd knee,
Disdaining° duty that to us belongs.   *Not paying*
Small curs are not regarded when they grin,°   *snarl; show the teeth*
But great men tremble when the lion roars—
20 And Humphrey is no little man in England.
First, note that he is near you in descent,
And, should you fall, he is the next will mount.°   *mount the throne*
Meseemeth then it is no policy,°   *not prudent*
Respecting° what a rancorous mind he bears   *Considering*
25 And his advantage following your decease,
That he should come about your royal person,
Or be admitted to your highness' Council.
By flattery hath he won the commons' hearts,
And when he please to make commotion,°   *incite rebellion*
30 'Tis to be feared they all will follow him.
Now 'tis the spring, and weeds are shallow-rooted;
Suffer° them now, and they'll o'ergrow the garden,   *Tolerate*
And choke the herbs for want of husbandry.
The reverent care I bear unto my lord
35 Made me collect° these dangers in the Duke.   *deduce*
If it be fond,° call it a woman's fear;   *foolish*
Which fear, if better reasons can supplant,
I will subscribe° and say I wronged the Duke.   *concur*
My lord of Suffolk, Buckingham, and York,
40 Reprove° my allegation if you can,   *Refute*
Or else conclude my words effectual.°   *decisive*
SUFFOLK   Well hath your highness seen into this Duke,
And had I first been put to speak my mind,
I think I should have told your grace's tale.
45 The Duchess by his subornation,°   *instigation*
Upon my life, began her devilish practices;
Or if he were not privy to those faults,°   *crimes*
Yet by reputing° of his high descent,   *boasting*
As next the King he was successive heir,
50 And such high vaunts° of his nobility,   *boasts*
Did instigate the bedlam¹ brainsick Duchess
By wicked means to frame° our sovereign's fall.   *devise*
Smooth runs the water where the brook is deep,
And in his simple show° he harbours treason.   *outward appearance*
55 The fox barks not when he would steal the lamb.
[*To* KING HENRY] No, no, my sovereign, Gloucester is a man
Unsounded° yet, and full of deep deceit.   *Unfathomed*

---

1. Insane (a shortened form of "Bethlehem Hospital," a notorious asylum maintained by the City of London).

CARDINAL BEAUFORT [*to* KING HENRY]   Did he not, contrary to
    form of law,
  Devise strange° deaths for small offences done?   *cruel; illegal*
60 YORK [*to* KING HENRY]   And did he not, in his Protectorship,
    Levy great sums of money through the realm
    For soldiers' pay in France, and never sent it,
    By means whereof the towns each day revolted?
  BUCKINGHAM [*to* KING HENRY]   Tut, these are petty faults to°   *compared to*
    faults unknown,
65   Which time will bring to light in smooth Duke Humphrey.
  KING HENRY   My lords, at once:° the care you have of us   *once and for all*
    To mow down thorns that would annoy our foot
    Is worthy praise, but shall I speak my conscience?
    Our kinsman Gloucester is as innocent
70   From meaning treason to our royal person
    As is the sucking lamb or harmless dove.
    The Duke is virtuous, mild, and too well given
    To dream on evil or to work my downfall.
  QUEEN MARGARET   Ah, what's more dangerous than this fond
    affiance?°   *foolish confidence*
75   Seems he a dove? His feathers are but borrowed,
    For he's disposèd as the hateful raven.
    Is he a lamb? His skin is surely lent him,
    For he's inclined as is the ravenous wolf.[2]
    Who cannot steal a shape that means deceit?[3]
80   Take heed, my lord, the welfare of us all
    Hangs on the cutting short that fraudful° man.   *treacherous*
    Enter the Duke of SOMERSET
  SOMERSET [*kneeling before* KING HENRY]   All health unto my
    gracious sovereign.
  KING HENRY   Welcome, Lord Somerset. What news from France?
  SOMERSET   That all your interest in those territories
85 Is utterly bereft you—all is lost.
  KING HENRY   Cold news, Lord Somerset; but God's will be done.
    [SOMERSET *rises*]
  YORK [*aside*]   Cold news for me, for I had hope of France,
    As firmly as I hope for fertile England.
    Thus are my blossoms blasted° in the bud,   *withered*
90   And caterpillars eat my leaves away.
    But I will remedy this gear° ere long,   *business*
    Or sell my title for a glorious grave.
    Enter Duke Humphrey [of] GLOUCESTER
  GLOUCESTER [*kneeling before* KING HENRY]   All happiness unto
    my lord the King.
    Pardon, my liege, that I have stayed° so long.   *delayed*
95 SUFFOLK   Nay, Gloucester, know that thou art come too soon
    Unless thou wert more loyal than thou art.
    I do arrest thee of high treason here.
  GLOUCESTER [*rising*]   Well, Suffolk's Duke, thou shalt not see me blush,
    Nor change my countenance for this arrest.

---

2. *Is he . . . wolf*: alluding to the Sermon on the Mount, which warns of "false prophets, which come to you in sheep's clothing, but inwardly they are ravening wolves" (Matthew 7:15).
3. Who that intends to deceive cannot assume an appropriate disguise?

100 A heart unspotted is not easily daunted.
The purest spring is not so free from mud
As I am clear from treason to my sovereign.
Who can accuse me? Wherein am I guilty?

YORK 'Tis thought, my lord, that you took bribes of France,
105 And, being Protector, stayed° the soldiers' pay,   *withheld*
By means whereof his highness hath lost France.

GLOUCESTER Is it but thought so? What are they that think it?
I never robbed the soldiers of their pay,
Nor ever had one penny bribe from France.
110 So help me God, as I have watched the night,°   *stayed up all night*
Ay, night by night, in studying good for England,
That doit° that e'er I wrested from the King,   *a coin of little value*
Or any groat° I hoarded to my use,   *a coin worth 4 pence*
Be brought against me at my trial day!
115 No: many a pound of mine own proper store,°   *personal fortune*
Because I would not tax the needy commons,
Have I dispursèd° to the garrisons,   *paid*
And never asked for restitution.

CARDINAL BEAUFORT It serves you well, my lord, to say so much.
120 GLOUCESTER I say no more than truth, so help me God.

YORK In your Protectorship you did devise
Strange tortures for offenders, never heard of,
That° England was defamed by° tyranny.   *So that / was infamous for*

GLOUCESTER Why, 'tis well known that whiles I was Protector
125 Pity was all the fault that was in me,
For I should° melt at an offender's tears,   *would*
And lowly words were ransom for their fault.
Unless it were a bloody murderer,
Or foul felonious thief that fleeced poor passengers,°   *travelers*
130 I never gave them condign° punishment.   *well-deserved*
Murder, indeed—that bloody sin—I tortured
Above the felon or what trespass else.[4]

SUFFOLK My lord, these faults are easy,° quickly answerèd,   *slight*
But mightier crimes are laid unto your charge
135 Whereof you cannot easily purge yourself.
I do arrest you in his highness' name,
And here commit you to my good lord Cardinal
To keep until your further time of trial.

KING HENRY My lord of Gloucester, 'tis my special hope
140 That you will clear yourself from all suspense.°   *suspicion*
My conscience tells me you are innocent.

GLOUCESTER Ah, gracious lord, these days are dangerous.
Virtue is choked with foul ambition,
And charity chased hence by rancour's hand.
145 Foul subornation[5] is predominant,
And equity exiled° your highness' land.   *exiled from*
I know their complot° is to have my life,   *plot*
And if my death might make this island happy
And prove the period° of their tyranny,   *mark the end*
150 I would expend it with all willingness.
But mine is made the prologue to their play,

---

4. More than any other kind of crime.   5. Instigating others to commit crimes, including perjury.

For thousands more that yet suspect no peril
Will not conclude their plotted tragedy.
Beaufort's red sparkling eyes blab his heart's malice,
155 And Suffolk's cloudy brow his stormy hate;
Sharp Buckingham unburdens with his tongue
The envious load that lies upon his heart;
And doggèd° York that reaches at the moon,   *currish; determined*
Whose overweening arm I have plucked back,
160 By false accuse° doth level° at my life.   *accusation / aim*
[*To* QUEEN MARGARET] And you, my sovereign lady, with the rest,
Causeless have laid disgraces on my head,
And with your best endeavour have stirred up
My liefest liege° to be mine enemy.   *dearest sovereign*
165 Ay, all of you have laid your heads together—
Myself had notice of your conventicles°—   *secret meetings*
And all to make away my guiltless life.
I shall not want° false witness to condemn me,   *lack*
Nor store of treasons to augment my guilt.
170 The ancient proverb will be well effected:
'A staff is quickly found to beat a dog'.
CARDINAL BEAUFORT [*to* KING HENRY]   My liege, his railing is intolerable.
If those that care to keep your royal person
From treason's secret knife and traitor's rage
175 Be thus upbraided, chid, and rated at,°   *berated; scolded*
And the offender granted scope of speech,
'Twill make them cool in zeal unto your grace.
SUFFOLK [*to* KING HENRY]   Hath he not twit° our sovereign lady here   *upbraided*
With ignominious words, though clerkly couched,°   *cleverly phrased*
180 As if she had subornèd some to swear
False allegations to o'erthrow his state?°   *high position*
QUEEN MARGARET   But I can give the loser leave to chide.
GLOUCESTER   Far truer spoke than meant. I lose indeed;
Beshrew° the winners, for they played me false!   *Curse*
185 And well such losers may have leave to speak.
BUCKINGHAM [*to* KING HENRY]   He'll wrest the sense,° and hold   *distort the meaning*
us here all day.
Lord Cardinal, he is your prisoner.
CARDINAL BEAUFORT [*to some of his attendants*]   Sirs, take
away the Duke and guard him sure.
GLOUCESTER   Ah, thus King Henry throws away his crutch
190 Before his legs be firm to bear his body.
Thus is the shepherd beaten from thy side,
And wolves are gnarling° who shall gnaw thee first.   *snarling*
Ah, that my fear were false; ah, that it were!
For, good King Henry, thy decay° I fear.   *ruin*
        Exit GLOUCESTER, [*guarded by*] *the Cardinal's men*
195 KING HENRY   My lords, what to your wisdoms seemeth best
Do or undo, as if ourself were here.
QUEEN MARGARET   What, will your highness leave the Parliament?
KING HENRY   Ay, Margaret, my heart is drowned with grief,
Whose flood begins to flow within mine eyes,
200 My body round engirt with misery;
For what's more miserable than discontent?
Ah, uncle Humphrey, in thy face I see

The map of honour, truth, and loyalty;
And yet, good Humphrey, is the hour to come
205 That e'er I proved thee false, or feared thy faith.°   *doubted your loyalty*
What louring° star now envies thy estate,   *gloomy*
That these great lords and Margaret our Queen
Do seek subversion of thy harmless life?
Thou never didst them wrong, nor no man wrong.
210 And as the butcher takes away the calf,
And binds the wretch, and beats it when it strains,
Bearing it to the bloody slaughterhouse,
Even so remorseless have they borne him hence;
And as the dam° runs lowing up and down,   *mother*
215 Looking the way her harmless young one went,
And can do naught but wail her darling's loss;
Even so myself bewails good Gloucester's case
With sad unhelpful tears, and with dimmed eyes
Look after him, and cannot do him good,°   *give him help*
220 So mighty are his vowèd enemies.
His fortunes I will weep, and 'twixt each groan,
Say 'Who's a traitor? Gloucester, he is none'.
                    Exeunt KING, SALISBURY, *and* WARWICK
QUEEN MARGARET Free° lords, cold snow melts with the sun's hot beams.   *Noble*
Henry my lord is cold in great affairs,
225 Too full of foolish pity; and Gloucester's show
Beguiles him as the mournful crocodile
With sorrow snares relenting passengers,⁶
Or as the snake rolled in a flow'ring bank
With shining chequered slough° doth sting a child   *skin*
230 That for the beauty thinks it excellent.
Believe me, lords, were none more wise than I—
And yet herein I judge mine own wit good—
This Gloucester should be quickly rid the world
To rid us from the fear we have of him.
235 CARDINAL BEAUFORT That he should die is worthy policy;
But yet we want a colour° for his death.   *pretext*
'Tis meet he be condemned by course of law.
SUFFOLK But, in my mind, that were no policy.
The King will labour still° to save his life,   *continually*
240 The commons haply° rise to save his life;   *perhaps*
And yet we have but trivial argument°   *evidence*
More than mistrust° that shows him worthy death.   *Other than suspicion*
YORK So that, by this, you would not have him die?
SUFFOLK Ah, York, no man alive so fain as I.
245 YORK [*aside*] 'Tis York that hath more reason for his death.
[*Aloud*] But my lord Cardinal, and you my lord of Suffolk,
Say as you think, and speak it from your souls.
Were't not all one an empty° eagle were set   *a hungry*
To guard the chicken from a hungry kite,°   *bird of prey*
250 As place Duke Humphrey for the King's Protector?

---

6. Compassionate travelers. Sixteenth-century natural historians claimed that crocodiles moaned and wept in order to lure sympathetic humans to their death.

QUEEN MARGARET   So the poor chicken should be sure of death.

SUFFOLK   Madam, 'tis true; and were't not madness then
    To make the fox surveyor° of the fold,   *guardian*
    Who being accused a crafty murderer,
255   His guilt should be but idly posted over°   *foolishly ignored*
    Because his purpose is not executed?
    No—let him die in that he is a fox,
    By nature proved an enemy to the flock,
    Before his chaps° be stained with crimson blood,   *jaws*
260   As Humphrey, proved by reasons, to my liege.[7]
    And do not stand on quillets° how to slay him;   *subtle distinctions*
    Be it by gins,° by snares, by subtlety,   *traps*
    Sleeping or waking, 'tis no matter how,
    So he be dead; for that is good conceit°   *a good idea*
265   Which mates° him first that first intends deceit. *checkmates; kills*

QUEEN MARGARET   Thrice-noble Suffolk, 'tis resolutely spoke.

SUFFOLK   Not resolute, except° so much were done;   *unless*
    For things are often spoke and seldom meant;
    But that° my heart accordeth with my tongue,   *to show that*
270   Seeing the deed is meritorious,
    And to preserve my sovereign from his foe,
    Say but the word and I will be his priest.[8]

CARDINAL BEAUFORT   But I would have him dead, my lord of Suffolk,
    Ere you can take due orders for a priest.[9]
275   Say you consent and censure° well the deed,   *approve*
    And I'll provide his executioner;
    I tender so the safety of my liege.

SUFFOLK   Here is my hand; the deed is worthy doing.

QUEEN MARGARET   And so say I.

280 YORK   And I. And now we three have spoke it,
    It skills not greatly who impugns our doom.[1]

            Enter a POST

POST   Great lord, from Ireland am I come amain°   *in haste*
    To signify that rebels there are up°   *up in arms*
    And put the Englishmen unto the sword.
285   Send succours, lords, and stop the rage betime,°   *promptly*
    Before the wound do grow uncurable;
    For, being green,° there is great hope of help.   *[Exit]*   *fresh*

CARDINAL BEAUFORT   A breach that craves a quick expedient stop!
    What counsel give you in this weighty cause?

290 YORK   That Somerset be sent as regent thither.
    'Tis meet° that lucky ruler be employed—   *fit (said scornfully)*
    Witness the fortune he hath had in France.

SOMERSET   If York, with all his far-fet° policy,   *cunning*
    Had been the regent there instead of me,
295   He never would have stayed in France so long.

YORK   No, not to lose it all as thou hast done.
    I rather would have lost my life betimes

---

7. Just as Humphrey proved (to be a fox or enemy) to
Henry.
8. I will kill him. Suffolk alludes to the priest's role
in administering the sacrament of last rites to dying

Christians.
9. Can become a priest; can arrange to have a priest
there.
1. It doesn't matter who questions our decision.

Than bring a burden of dishonour home
By staying there so long till all were lost.
300 Show me one scar charactered° on thy skin. _inscribed_
Men's flesh preserved so whole do seldom win.
QUEEN MARGARET Nay, then, this spark will prove a raging fire
If wind and fuel be brought to feed it with.
No more, good York; sweet Somerset, be still.
305 Thy fortune, York, hadst thou been regent there,
Might happily° have proved far worse than his. _perhaps_
YORK What, worse than naught? Nay, then a shame take all!
SOMERSET And, in the number,° thee that wishest shame. _among them_
CARDINAL BEAUFORT My lord of York, try what your fortune is.
310 Th'uncivil kerns of Ireland² are in arms
And temper clay° with blood of Englishmen. _moisten the earth_
To Ireland will you lead a band of men
Collected choicely, from each county some,
And try your hap° against the Irishmen? _luck_
315 YORK I will, my lord, so please his majesty.
SUFFOLK Why, our authority is his consent,
And what we do establish he confirms.
Then, noble York, take thou this task in hand.
YORK I am content. Provide me soldiers, lords,
320 Whiles I take order° for mine own affairs. _arrange_
SUFFOLK A charge, Lord York, that I will see performed.
But now return we to the false Duke Humphrey.
CARDINAL BEAUFORT No more of him—for I will deal with him
That henceforth he shall trouble us no more.
325 And so, break off; the day is almost spent.
Lord Suffolk, you and I must talk of that event.
YORK My lord of Suffolk, within fourteen days
At Bristol I expect my soldiers;
For there I'll ship them all for Ireland.
330 SUFFOLK I'll see it truly done, my lord of York.

Exeunt. Manet YORK³

330.1 YORK _Let me have some bands of chosen soldiers,_
And York shall try his fortune 'gainst those kerns.
QUEEN MARGARET _York, thou shalt. My lord of Buckingham,_
Let it be your charge to muster up such soldiers
330.5 _As shall suffice him in these needful wars._
BUCKINGHAM _Madam, I will, and levy such a band_
As soon shall overcome those Irish rebels.
But, York, where shall those soliders stay° for thee _wait_
YORK _At Bristol I will expect them ten days hence._
330.10 BUCKINGHAM _Then thither shall they come, and_
so farewell. _Exit_
YORK _Adieu, my lord of Buckingham._
QUEEN MARGARET _Suffolk, remember what you have to do—_
And you, Lord Cardinal—concerning Duke Humphrey.

---

2. Barbaric Irish foot soldiers or rebels. Kerns were the most numerous, poorest, and most lightly armed of the Irish soldiers who fought against the English during Elizabeth's reign. Many Elizabethan writers described the Irish as an inferior, uncivilized "race" and used the term "kern" to signify all Irish opponents of England.

3. The entire debate on Duke Humphrey's death in 3.1 is handled differently by Q and F. Oxford retains F's version of the debate, but Q may represent authorial revision. The following indented Q lines (330.1–330.15), roughly corresponding to lines 310–30, are of particular interest because they supply Buckingham with speeches for this latter part of the scene.

'Twere good that you did see to it in time.
330.15   Come, let us go, that it may be performed.

Exeunt all. Manet YORK

YORK   Now, York, or never, steel thy fearful thoughts,
    And change misdoubt° to resolution.   *fear*
    Be that thou hop'st to be, or what thou art
    Resign to death; it is not worth th'enjoying.
335   Let pale-faced fear keep° with the mean-born° man   *dwell / lowborn*
    And find no harbour in a royal heart.
    Faster than springtime showers comes thought on thought,
    And not a thought but thinks on dignity.°   *high estate (kingship)*
    My brain, more busy than the labouring spider,
340   Weaves tedious° snares to trap mine enemies.   *laborious*
    Well, nobles, well: 'tis politicly done
    To send me packing with an host of men.
    I fear me° you but warm the starvèd° snake,   *I am afraid / frozen*
    Who, cherished in your breasts, will sting your hearts.
345   'Twas men I lacked, and you will give them me.
    I take it kindly. Yet be well assured
    You put sharp weapons in a madman's hands.
    Whiles I in Ireland nurse a mighty band,
    I will stir up in England some black storm
350   Shall blow ten thousand souls to heaven or hell,
    And this fell° tempest shall not cease to rage   *ferocious*
    Until the golden circuit° on my head   *crown*
    Like to the glorious sun's transparent beams
    Do calm the fury of this mad-bred flaw.[4]
355   And for a minister° of my intent,   *an agent*
    I have seduced a headstrong Kentishman,
    John Cade of Ashford,
    To make commotion,° as full well he can,   *rebellion*
    Under the title of John Mortimer.[5]
360   In Ireland have I seen this stubborn Cade
    Oppose himself against a troop of kerns,
    And fought so long till that his thighs with darts[6]
    Were almost like a sharp-quilled porcupine;
    And in the end, being rescued, I have seen
365   Him caper° upright like a wild Morisco,[7]   *leap*
    Shaking the bloody darts as he° his bells.   *as would the dancer*
    Full often like a shag-haired[8] crafty kern
    Hath he conversèd with the enemy
    And, undiscovered, come to me again
370   And given me notice of their villainies.
    This devil here shall be my substitute,
    For that° John Mortimer, which now is dead,   *Because*
    In face, in gait, in speech, he doth resemble.
    By this I shall perceive the commons' mind,

---

4. This storm ("flaw") created by madness.
5. The Mortimers are the family line by which York claims the crown. See York's account of his claim in 2.2.10–52.
6. Light spears or arrows, the weapons for which kerns were known.
7. A Moor who converted to Christianity; a morris dancer. Deriving from the Spanish word for "Moor," the morris dance was originally a Spanish dance that

reenacted Christian battles with Moors. From the fifteenth century, it was associated with English popular festivals and was usually performed by men with bells attached to their legs who carried sticks and wore costumes from English folklore.
8. Alluding to the popular notion that the Irish grew "glibs," or long, thick bangs, in order to disguise themselves and escape punishment for their crimes.

375 How they affect° the house and claim of York. *like*
Say he be taken, racked,[9] and torturèd—
I know no pain they can inflict upon him
Will make him say I moved him to those arms.
Say that he thrive, as 'tis great like° he will— *very likely*
380 Why then from Ireland come I with my strength
And reap the harvest which that coistrel° sowed. *base fellow*
For Humphrey being dead, as he shall be,
And Henry put apart, the next for me. *Exit*

3.2

The curtains [are] drawn [apart, revealing] Duke
Humphrey [of GLOUCESTER] in his bed [with] two men
lying on his breast, smothering him in his bed[1]

FIRST MURDERER [*to the* SECOND MURDERER] Run to my lord
of Suffolk—let him know
We have dispatched the Duke as he commanded.

SECOND MURDERER O that it were to do![2] What have we done?
Didst ever hear a man so penitent?
Enter the Duke of SUFFOLK

5 FIRST MURDERER Here comes my lord.

SUFFOLK Now, sirs, have you dispatched this thing?

FIRST MURDERER Ay, my good lord, he's dead.

SUFFOLK Why, that's well said. Go, get you to my house.
I will reward you for this venturous° deed. *dangerous*
10 The King and all the peers are here at hand.
Have you laid fair° the bed? Is all things well, *rearranged*
According as I gave directions?

FIRST MURDERER 'Tis, my good lord.

SUFFOLK Then draw the curtains close; away, be gone!
Exeunt [the] MURDERERS [*drawing the curtains as they leave*]
Sound trumpets, then enter KING [HENRY] *and* QUEEN
[MARGARET], CARDINAL [BEAUFORT], *the Duke of* SOM-
ERSET, [*and*] *attendants*

15 KING HENRY [*to* SUFFOLK] Go call our uncle to our presence straight.° *immediately*
Say we intend to try his grace today
If° he be guilty, as 'tis publishèd. *To find whether*

SUFFOLK I'll call him presently,° my noble lord. *Exit* *at once*

KING HENRY Lords, take your places; and, I pray you all,
20 Proceed no straiter° 'gainst our uncle Gloucester *more severely*
Than from true evidence, of good esteem,° *worthy of belief*
He be approved in practice culpable.° *determined guilty*

QUEEN MARGARET God forbid any malice should prevail
That faultless may condemn a noble man![3]
25 Pray God he may acquit him° of suspicion! *himself*

KING HENRY I thank thee, Meg. These words content me much.
Enter SUFFOLK
How now? Why look'st thou pale? Why tremblest thou?
Where is our uncle? What's the matter, Suffolk?

---

9. Tortured by having one's limbs fastened to a frame that stretched the body.
3.2 Location: Gloucester's bedchamber and an adjoining room of state, Bury St. Edmunds.
1. F's stage direction reads, "Enter two or three running over the Stage, from the Murder of Duke Humfrey." Q, by contrast, indicates that the actual smothering of Gloucester is shown onstage.
2. Would that it were still to be done (so that it could remain undone).
3. That may condemn a noble man who is blameless.

SUFFOLK   Dead in his bed, my lord—Gloucester is dead.

30   QUEEN MARGARET   Marry, God forfend!°   *forbid*

CARDINAL BEAUFORT   God's secret judgement. I did dream tonight°   *last night*
   The Duke was dumb and could not speak a word.

      KING HENRY *falls* [*to the ground*]⁴

QUEEN MARGARET   How fares my lord? Help, lords—the King is
   dead!

SOMERSET   Rear° up his body; wring him by the nose.⁵   *Raise*

35   QUEEN MARGARET   Run, go, help, help! O Henry, ope thine eyes!

SUFFOLK   He doth revive again. Madam, be patient.

KING HENRY   O heavenly God!

QUEEN MARGARET   How fares my gracious lord?

SUFFOLK   Comfort, my sovereign; gracious Henry, comfort.

KING HENRY   What, doth my lord of Suffolk comfort me?

40   Came he right now° to sing a raven's note⁶   *a moment ago*
   Whose dismal tune bereft° my vital powers;   *robbed me of*
   And thinks he that the chirping of a wren,
   By crying comfort from a hollow° breast   *an insincere*
   Can chase away the first-conceivèd° sound?   *previously perceived*

45   Hide not thy poison with such sugared words.

      [*He begins to rise.* SUFFOLK *offers to assist him*]

   Lay not thy hands on me—forbear, I say!
   Their touch affrights me as a serpent's sting.
   Thou baleful messenger, out of my sight!
   Upon thy eyeballs murderous tyranny

50   Sits in grim majesty to fright the world.
   Look not upon me, for thine eyes are wounding—
   Yet do not go away. Come, basilisk,⁷
   And kill the innocent gazer with thy sight.
   For in the shade° of death I shall find joy;   *shadow*

55   In life, but double death, now Gloucester's dead.

QUEEN MARGARET   Why do you rate° my lord of Suffolk thus?   *chide*
   Although the Duke was enemy to him,
   Yet he most Christian-like laments his death.
   And for myself, foe as he was to me,

60   Might liquid tears, or heart-offending° groans,   *heart-wounding*
   Or blood-consuming⁸ sighs recall his life,
   I would be blind with weeping, sick with groans,
   Look pale as primrose with blood-drinking sighs,
   And all to have the noble Duke alive.

65   What know I how the world may deem° of me?   *judge*
   For it is known we were but hollow friends,
   It may be judged I made the Duke away.
   So shall my name with slander's tongue be wounded
   And princes' courts be filled with my reproach.

70   This get I by his death. Ay me, unhappy,
   To be a queen, and crowned with infamy.

KING HENRY   Ah, woe is me for Gloucester, wretched man!

---

4. In Q, the stage direction reads, "The King falls in a sound" (swoon). F reads, "King sounds."
5. This was thought to revive circulation and restore consciousness.
6. According to popular superstition, an omen of death.

7. A mythical reptile, hatched from a cock's egg, whose look was supposed to be fatal.
8. It was popularly believed that each sigh or groan drew a drop of blood from the heart.

QUEEN MARGARET Be woe° for me, more wretched than he is.   *woeful; sorry*
    What, dost thou turn away and hide thy face?
75 I am no loathsome leper—look on me!
    What, art thou, like the adder, waxen deaf?⁹
    Be poisonous too and kill thy forlorn queen.
    Is all thy comfort shut in Gloucester's tomb?
    Why, then Queen Margaret was ne'er thy joy.
80 Erect his statuë and worship it,
    And make my image but an alehouse sign.¹
    Was I for this nigh wrecked upon the sea,
    And twice by awkward° winds from England's bank°   *unfavorable / shore*
    Drove back again unto my native clime?
85 What boded this, but° well forewarning winds   *but that*
    Did seem to say, 'Seek not a scorpion's nest,
    Nor set no footing on this unkind shore'.
    What did I then, but cursed the gentle gusts
    And he that loosed them forth their brazen caves,²
90 And bid them blow towards England's blessèd shore,
    Or turn our stern upon a dreadful rock.
    Yet Aeolus would not be a murderer,
    But left that hateful office unto thee.
    The pretty vaulting° sea refused to drown me,   *bounding*
95 Knowing that thou wouldst have me drowned on shore
    With tears as salt as sea through thy unkindness.
    The splitting rocks cow'red in the sinking sands,³
    And would not dash me with their ragged sides,
    Because thy flinty heart, more hard than they,
100 Might in thy palace perish° Margaret.   *destroy*
    As far as I could ken° thy chalky cliffs,   *see*
    When from thy shore the tempest beat us back,
    I stood upon the hatches° in the storm,   *deck*
    And when the dusky sky began to rob
105 My earnest-gaping° sight of thy land's view,   *earnestly peering*
    I took a costly jewel from my neck—
    A heart it was, bound in with diamonds—
    And threw it towards thy land. The sea received it,
    And so I wished thy body might my heart.
110 And even with this I lost fair England's view,
    And bid mine eyes be packing° with my heart,   *be gone*
    And called them blind and dusky spectacles°   *instruments of sight*
    For losing ken of Albion's° wishèd coast.   *England's*
    How often have I tempted Suffolk's tongue—
115 The agent of thy foul inconstancy—
    To sit and witch° me, as Ascanius⁴ did,   *bewitch*
    When he to madding° Dido would unfold   *going mad (with love)*
    His father's acts, commenced in burning Troy!
    Am I not witched like her? Or thou not false like him?
120 Ay me, I can no more.° Die, Margaret,   *my strength fails*

---

9. Alluding to the belief that adders stopped up their ears to resist attempts to charm them.
1. Inns and shops in Elizabethan London were usually distinguished by signs bearing images rather than words.
2. Referring to Aeolus, whom Zeus appointed ruler of the winds, which he kept in caves. *brazen:* strong (as brass).

3. Rocks that ordinarily break ships into pieces crouched down fearfully in the sands where ships usually sink.
4. In Book 1 of the *Aeneid*, Venus sends Cupid in the form of Ascanius, son of Aeneas, to bewitch Dido, Queen of Carthage, and inflame her with love for Aeneas.

For Henry weeps that thou dost live so long.
    Noise within. Enter the Earls of WARWICK *and*
      SALISBURY, [with] *many* COMMONS
WARWICK [*to* KING HENRY]   It is reported, mighty sovereign,
    That good Duke Humphrey traitorously is murdered
    By Suffolk and the Cardinal Beaufort's means.
125   The commons, like an angry hive of bees
    That want° their leader, scatter up and down   *lack*
    And care not who they sting in his revenge.
    Myself have calmed their spleenful° mutiny,   *angry*
    Until they hear the order° of his death.   *manner*
130 KING HENRY   That he is dead, good Warwick, 'tis too true.
    But how he died God knows, not Henry.
    Enter his chamber, view his breathless corpse,
    And comment then upon° his sudden death.   *And then explain*
WARWICK   That shall I do, my liege.—Stay, Salisbury,
135   With the rude multitude till I return.
      Exeunt [WARWICK *at one door,*] SALISBURY [*and*
            COMMONS *at another*][5]
KING HENRY   O thou that judgest all things, stay° my thoughts,   *restrain*
    My thoughts that labour to persuade my soul
    Some violent hands were laid on Humphrey's life.
    If my suspect° be false, forgive me God,   *suspicion*
140   For judgement only doth belong to thee.
    Fain would I go to chafe his paly° lips   *pale*
    With twenty thousand kisses, and to drain°   *rain; let fall*
    Upon his face an ocean of salt tears,
    To tell my love unto his dumb, deaf trunk,°   *body*
145   And with my fingers feel his hand unfeeling.° *which lacks feeling*
    But all in vain are these mean obsequies,°   *funeral rites*
    [*Enter*] WARWICK [*who*] *draws* [*apart*] *the curtains and*
      shows GLOUCESTER [*dead*] *in his bed. Bed put forth*
    And to survey his dead and earthy image,
    What were it but to make my sorrow greater?
WARWICK   Come hither, gracious sovereign, view this body.
150 KING HENRY   That is to see how deep my grave is made:
    For with his soul fled all my worldly solace,
    For seeing him I see my life° in death.   *that my life will end*
WARWICK   As surely as my soul intends to live
    With that dread King° that took our state° upon Him *(Christ)/condition*
155   To free us from his Father's wrathful curse,
    I do believe that violent hands were laid
    Upon the life of this thrice-famèd° Duke.   *very famous*
SUFFOLK   A dreadful oath, sworn with a solemn tongue!
    What instance° gives Lord Warwick for his vow?   *evidence*
160 WARWICK   See how the blood is settled in his face.
    Oft have I seen a timely-parted ghost[6]
    Of ashy semblance, meagre, pale, and bloodless,

---

5. Q has Salisbury exit at this point, while the dialogue in F and Q indicates that Warwick also leaves the stage. He must return to reveal Gloucester's corpse at line 146. Some editors have suggested that Salisbury stays onstage with the Commons here, but at line 243 he is directed to enter, and it appears that the Commons are also then offstage. Both must have exited at some point.
6. The corpse of someone who died a natural death.

Being all descended to the labouring heart;[7]
Who, in the conflict that it holds with death,
165 Attracts the same° for aidance° 'gainst the enemy;   *(the blood)/aid*
Which, with the heart, there cools, and ne'er returneth
To blush and beautify the cheek again.
But see, his face is black and full of blood;
His eyeballs further out than when he lived,
170 Staring full ghastly like a strangled man;
His hair upreared; his nostrils stretched with struggling;
His hands abroad displayed,° as one that grasped   *spread wide*
And tugged for life and was by strength subdued.
Look on the sheets. His hair, you see, is sticking;
175 His well-proportioned beard made rough and rugged,
Like to the summer's corn by tempest lodged.°   *beaten down*
It cannot be but he was murdered here.
The least of all these signs were probable.°   *sufficient proof*
SUFFOLK Why, Warwick, who should do the Duke to death?
180 Myself and Beaufort had him in protection,
And we, I hope, sir, are no murderers.
WARWICK But both of you were vowed Duke Humphrey's foes,
[*To* CARDINAL BEAUFORT] And you, forsooth, had the good
    Duke to keep.°   *guard*
'Tis like you would not feast him like a friend;
185 And 'tis well seen he found an enemy.
QUEEN MARGARET Then you, belike,° suspect these noblemen   *perchance*
As guilty of Duke Humphrey's timeless° death?   *untimely*
WARWICK Who finds the heifer dead and bleeding fresh,
And sees fast° by a butcher with an axe,   *near*
190 But will suspect 'twas he that made the slaughter?
Who finds the partridge in the puttock's° nest   *kite's (bird of prey)*
But may imagine how the bird was dead,°   *killed*
Although the kite soar with unbloodied beak?
Even so suspicious is this tragedy.
195 QUEEN MARGARET Are you the butcher, Suffolk? Where's your knife?
Is Beaufort termed a kite? Where are his talons?
SUFFOLK I wear no knife to slaughter sleeping men.
But here's a vengeful sword, rusted with ease,°   *lack of use*
That shall be scourèd in his rancorous heart
200 That° slanders me with murder's crimson badge.   *Who*
Say, if thou dar'st, proud Lord of Warwickshire,
That I am faulty in Duke Humphrey's death.
       Exit CARDINAL [BEAUFORT *assisted by* SOMERSET]
WARWICK What dares not Warwick, if false Suffolk dare him?
QUEEN MARGARET He dares not calm his contumelious° spirit,   *insolent*
205 Nor cease to be an arrogant controller,°   *critic; slanderer*
Though Suffolk dare him twenty thousand times.
WARWICK Madam, be still, with reverence may I say,
For every word you speak in his behalf
Is slander to your royal dignity.
210 SUFFOLK Blunt-witted lord, ignoble in demeanour!
If ever lady wronged her lord so much,
Thy mother took into her blameful bed
Some stern° untutored churl, and noble stock   *rough*

---

7. The blood having all drained into the palpitating heart.

Was graffed with crabtree slip, whose fruit thou art,[8]
215 And never of the Nevilles' noble race.
WARWICK   But that the guilt of murder bucklers° thee   shields
And I should rob the deathsman° of his fee,   executioner
Quitting° thee thereby of ten thousand shames,   Freeing
And that my sovereign's presence makes me mild,[9]
220 I would, false murd'rous coward, on thy knee
Make thee beg pardon for thy passèd° speech,   just uttered
And say it was thy mother that thou meant'st—
That thou thyself wast born in bastardy!
And after all this fearful homage° done,   cowardly submission
225 Give thee thy hire° and send thy soul to hell,   reward
Pernicious blood-sucker of sleeping men!
SUFFOLK   Thou shalt be waking while I shed thy blood,
If from this presence° thou dar'st go with me.   the King's presence
WARWICK   Away, even now, or I will drag thee hence.
230 Unworthy though thou art, I'll cope° with thee,   fight
And do some service to Duke Humphrey's ghost.
                    Exeunt SUFFOLK and WARWICK
KING HENRY   What stronger breastplate than a heart untainted?
Thrice is he armed that hath his quarrel just;
And he but naked, though locked up in steel,°   armored
235 Whose conscience with injustice is corrupted.
COMMONS (within)   Down with Suffolk! Down with Suffolk![1]
QUEEN MARGARET   What noise is this?
        Enter SUFFOLK and WARWICK with their weapons drawn
KING HENRY   Why, how now, lords? Your wrathful weapons drawn
Here in our presence? Dare you be so bold?
240 Why, what tumultuous clamour have we here?
SUFFOLK   The trait'rous Warwick with the men of Bury
Set all upon me, mighty sovereign!
COMMONS [within]   Down with Suffolk! Down with Suffolk!
        Enter from [the COMMONS] the Earl of SALISBURY
SALISBURY [to the COMMONS, within]   Sirs, stand apart. The
        King shall know your mind.
[To KING HENRY] Dread lord, the commons send you word
245   by me
Unless Lord Suffolk straight be done to death,
Or banishèd° fair England's territories,   banished from
They will by violence tear him from your palace
And torture him with grievous ling'ring death.
250 They say, by him the good Duke Humphrey died;
They say, in him they fear your highness' death;
And mere° instinct of love and loyalty,   pure
Free from a stubborn opposite° intent,   antagonistic
As being thought to contradict your liking,[2]
255 Makes them thus forward in° his banishment.   insistent upon

8. *noble . . . art*: into the trunk of a great tree was inserted a cutting, or "slip," from an inferior, wild one, and you are the result. The analogy puns on "stock" as meaning "an aristocratic line of descent" and implies that the pedigree has been tainted. "Noble stock" may also refer to the trunk of a noblewoman's body into which a worthless "slip," such as the penis of a lowborn man, has been inserted.

9. It was illegal to draw weapons in the King's presence.
1. In Q, this line is printed inside a longer stage direction: "Exit Warwick and Suffolk, and then all the Commons within, cries, down with Suffolk, down with Suffolk. And then enter again, the Duke of Suffolk and Warwick, with their weapons drawn."
2. That might be thought to contradict your wishes.

They say, in care of your most royal person,
That if your highness should intend to sleep,
And charge that no man should disturb your rest
In pain of your dislike, or pain of death,
260 Yet, notwithstanding such a strait° edict,   strict
Were there a serpent seen with forkèd tongue,
That slily glided towards your majesty,
It were but necessary you were waked,
Lest, being suffered° in that harmful slumber,   permitted to remain
265 The mortal worm° might make the sleep eternal.   deadly serpent
And therefore do they cry, though you forbid,
That they will guard you, whe'er° you will or no,   whether
From such fell° serpents as false Suffolk is,   cruel
With whose envenomèd and fatal sting
270 Your loving uncle, twenty times his worth,
They say, is shamefully bereft of life.
COMMONS (within)   An answer from the King, my lord of Salisbury!
SUFFOLK   'Tis like° the commons, rude unpolished hinds,°   probable / boors
Could send such message to their sovereign.
275 But you, my lord, were glad to be employed,
To show how quaint° an orator you are.   skilled
But all the honour Salisbury hath won
Is that he was the Lord Ambassador
Sent from a sort° of tinkers³ to the King.   gang
280 COMMONS (within)   An answer from the King, or we will all break in!
KING HENRY   Go, Salisbury, and tell them all from me
I thank them for their tender loving care,
And had I not been 'cited° so by them,   urged
Yet did I purpose as they do entreat;
285 For sure my thoughts do hourly prophesy
Mischance unto my state by Suffolk's means.
And therefore by His° majesty I swear,   (God's)
Whose far unworthy deputy I am,
He shall not breathe° infection in this air   breathe out; spread
290 But three days longer, on the pain of death.   Exit SALISBURY
QUEEN MARGARET [kneeling]   O Henry, let me plead for gentle°   noble
    Suffolk.
KING HENRY   Ungentle Queen, to call him gentle Suffolk.
No more, I say! If thou dost plead for him
Thou wilt but add increase unto my wrath.
295 Had I but said, I would have kept my word;
But when I swear, it is irrevocable.
[To SUFFOLK] If after three days' space thou here beest found
On any ground that I am ruler of,
The world shall not be ransom for thy life.
300 Come, Warwick; come, good Warwick, go with me.
I have great matters to impart to thee.
        Exeunt KING [HENRY] and WARWICK [with attendants
            who draw the curtains as they leave]. Manent°   Remain
                QUEEN [MARGARET] and SUFFOLK

---

3. Tinkers were usually itinerant pot menders and were synonymous with vagrants and gypsies.

QUEEN MARGARET [*rising*]   Mischance and sorrow go along with you!
    Heart's discontent and sour affliction
    Be playfellows to keep you company!
305   There's two of you, the devil make a third,
    And threefold vengeance tend upon your steps!
SUFFOLK   Cease, gentle Queen, these execrations,
    And let thy Suffolk take his heavy° leave.   *sorrowful*
QUEEN MARGARET   Fie, coward woman[4] and soft-hearted wretch!
310   Hast thou not spirit to curse thine enemies?
SUFFOLK   A plague upon them! Wherefore° should I curse them?   *Why*
    Could curses kill, as doth the mandrake's groan,[5]
    I would invent as bitter searching° terms,   *piercing*
    As curst, as harsh, and horrible to hear,
315   Delivered strongly through my fixèd° teeth,   *clenched*
    With full as many signs of deadly hate,
    As lean-faced envy[6] in her loathsome cave.
    My tongue should stumble in mine earnest words;
    Mine eyes should sparkle like the beaten flint;
320   My hair be fixed on end, as one distraught;
    Ay, every joint should seem to curse and ban.°   *curse*
    And, even now, my burdened heart would break
    Should I not curse them. Poison be their drink!
    Gall,° worse than gall, the daintiest that they taste![7]   *Bile (a bitter fluid)*
325   Their sweetest shade a grove of cypress trees![7]
    Their chiefest prospect° murd'ring basilisks![8]   *view*
    Their softest touch as smart° as lizards' stings!   *sharp*
    Their music frightful as the serpent's hiss,
    And boding screech-owls[9] make the consort° full!   *group of musicians*
330   All the foul terrors in dark-seated hell—
QUEEN MARGARET   Enough, sweet Suffolk, thou torment'st thyself,
    And these dread curses, like the sun 'gainst glass,
    Or like an overchargèd gun, recoil
    And turn the force of them upon thyself.
335 SUFFOLK   You bade me ban, and will you bid me leave?°   *stop*
    Now by this ground that I am banished from,
    Well could I curse away a winter's night,
    Though standing naked on a mountain top,
    Where biting cold would never let grass grow,
340   And think it but a minute spent in sport.
QUEEN MARGARET   O let me entreat thee cease. Give me thy hand,
    That I may dew it with my mournful tears;
    Nor let the rain of heaven wet this place
    To wash away my woeful monuments.°   *signs of grief (tears)*
    [*She kisses his palm*]
345   O, could this kiss be printed in thy hand
    That thou mightst think upon these lips by the seal,°   *imprint*

---

4. In calling Suffolk a woman, Margaret questions his manhood. The pun in the next line on "spirit" as meaning "semen" as well as "courage" continues Margaret's assault on Suffolk's masculinity.
5. It was popularly believed that the mandrake—an herb whose root was thought to resemble a man and to grow wherever the semen of a man executed for murder had fallen—killed humans with its dreadful scream when it was uprooted.
6. Envy was traditionally described as an emaciated woman. See Ovid, *Metamorphoses* 2.949ff.
7. From ancient times, trees associated with death. Frequently planted in graveyards, their wood was used for coffins.
8. See note to line 52 above.
9. Thought to be harbingers of death.

Through whom° a thousand sighs are breathed for thee! *which (her lips)*
So get thee gone, that I may know my grief.
'Tis but surmised whiles thou art standing by,
350 As one that surfeits° thinking on a want.° *gorges / famine*
I will repeal thee,° or, be well assured, *win your recall*
Adventure to be banishèd° myself. *Risk banishment*
And banishèd I am, if but from thee.
Go, speak not to me; even now be gone!
355 O, go not yet. Even thus two friends condemned
Embrace, and kiss, and take ten thousand leaves,
Loather a hundred times to part than die.
Yet now farewell, and farewell life with thee.
SUFFOLK Thus is poor Suffolk ten times banishèd—
360 Once by the King, and three times thrice by thee.
'Tis not the land I care for, wert thou thence,
A wilderness is populous enough,
So Suffolk had thy heavenly company.
For where thou art, there is the world itself,
365 With every several° pleasure in the world; *distinct*
And where thou art not, desolation.
I can no more. Live thou to joy° thy life; *enjoy*
Myself no joy in naught but that thou liv'st.
          Enter VAUX
QUEEN MARGARET Whither goes Vaux so fast? What news, I prithee?
370 VAUX To signify unto his majesty
That Cardinal Beaufort is at point of death.
For suddenly a grievous sickness took him
That makes him gasp, and stare, and catch the air,
Blaspheming God and cursing men on earth.
375 Sometime he talks as if Duke Humphrey's ghost
Were by his side; sometime he calls the King,
And whispers to his pillow as to him
The secrets of his over-chargèd° soul; *overburdened*
And I am sent to tell his majesty
380 That even now he cries aloud for him.
QUEEN MARGARET Go tell this heavy message to the King.
          Exit VAUX
Ay me! What is this world? What news are these?
But wherefore grieve I at an hour's poor loss[1]
Omitting° Suffolk's exile, my soul's treasure? *Ignoring*
385 Why only, Suffolk, mourn I not for thee,
And with the southern clouds[2] contend in tears—
Theirs for the earth's increase, mine for my sorrow's?
Now get thee hence. The King, thou know'st, is coming.
If thou be found by° me, thou art but dead. *near*
390 SUFFOLK If I depart from thee, I cannot live.
And in thy sight to die, what were it else
But like a pleasant slumber in thy lap?[3]
Here could I breathe my soul into the air,

---

1. Alluding to the Cardinal's old age and suggesting that
he has in any case but a short time (an hour) to live.
2. It was generally thought that rain came from the
south.
3. Punning on "die in thy lap" as meaning "have an
orgasm while in your embrace."

As mild and gentle as the cradle babe
395   Dying with mother's dug° between his lips;   *nipple*
Where, from° thy sight, I should be raging mad,   *out of*
And cry out for thee to close up mine eyes,
To have thee with thy lips to stop my mouth,
So shouldst thou either turn° my flying soul   *return to me*
400   Or I should breathe it, so, into thy body—
    [*He kisseth her*]
And then it lived in sweet Elysium.[4]
By thee to die were but to die in jest;[5]
From thee to die were torture more than death.
O, let me stay, befall what may befall!
405   QUEEN MARGARET Away. Though parting be a fretful corrosive,°   *painful remedy*
It is applièd to a deathful° wound.   *deadly*
To France, sweet Suffolk. Let me hear from thee.
For wheresoe'er thou art in this world's Globe
I'll have an Iris[6] that shall find thee out.
410   SUFFOLK I go.
QUEEN MARGARET And take my heart with thee.
    She kisseth him
SUFFOLK A jewel, locked into the woefull'st cask°   *casket*
That ever did contain a thing of worth.
Even as a splitted barque,° so sunder° we—   *boat / part*
This way fall I to death.
415   QUEEN MARGARET   This way for me.   *Exeunt* [*severally*]

3.3

Enter KING [HENRY *and the Earls of*] SALISBURY
and WARWICK. *Then the curtains be drawn* [*revealing*]
CARDINAL [BEAUFORT] *in his bed raving and staring as
if he were mad*

KING HENRY [*to* CARDINAL BEAUFORT] How fares my lord? Speak, Beaufort,
    to thy sovereign.
CARDINAL BEAUFORT If thou beest death, I'll give thee England's treasure
Enough to purchase such another island,
So° thou wilt let me live and feel no pain.   *If*
5   KING HENRY Ah, what a sign it is of evil life
Where death's approach is seen so terrible.
WARWICK Beaufort, it is thy sovereign speaks to thee.
CARDINAL BEAUFORT Bring me unto my trial when you will.
Died he° not in his bed? Where should he die?   (*Gloucester*)
10   Can I make men live whe'er° they will or no?   *whether*
O, torture me no more—I will confess.
Alive again? Then show me where he is.
I'll give a thousand pound to look upon him.
He hath no eyes! The dust hath blinded them.
15   Comb down his hair—look, look: it stands upright,
Like lime twigs[1] set to catch my wingèd soul.

---

4. In classical mythology, the paradise where blessed
souls dwelled.
5. To die near you or by means of you is not really to die
(with a continuing pun on "die" as meaning "attain
orgasm").

6. In Greek mythology, Iris was a messenger of the
gods, particularly of Hera.
3.3 Location: The Cardinal's bedchamber, London.
1. Twigs smeared with birdlime. See note to 1.3.92.

Give me some drink, and bid the apothecary
Bring the strong poison that I bought of him.

KING HENRY   O Thou eternal mover of the heavens,°   *(God)*
20   Look with a gentle eye upon this wretch.
O, beat away the busy meddling fiend
That lays strong siege unto this wretch's soul,
And from his bosom purge this black despair.

WARWICK   See how the pangs of death do make him grin.°   *bare his teeth*

25   SALISBURY   Disturb him not; let him pass peaceably.

KING HENRY   Peace to his soul, if God's good pleasure be.
Lord Card'nal, if thou think'st on heaven's bliss,
Hold up thy hand, make signal of thy hope.

          CARDINAL [BEAUFORT] *dies*

He dies and makes no sign. O God, forgive him.

30   WARWICK   So bad a death argues a monstrous life.

KING HENRY   Forbear to judge, for we are sinners all.
Close up his eyes and draw the curtain close,
And let us all to meditation.°   *prayer*

          Exeunt [drawing the curtains. The bed is removed]

4.1

Alarums within, and the chambers° be discharged like as   *small cannon*
it were a fight at sea. And then enter the CAPTAIN *of the*
ship, the MASTER, *the Master's* MATE, *Walter* WHITMORE[1]
and others. [With them, as their prisoners,] the Duke of
SUFFOLK, *disguised [and two* GENTLEMEN]

CAPTAIN   The gaudy, blabbing, and remorseful day[2]
Is crept into the bosom of the sea;
And now loud-howling wolves arouse the jades[3]
That drag the tragic melancholy night;
Who, with their drowsy, slow, and flagging wings
5   Clip° dead men's graves, and from their misty jaws   *Embrace*
Breathe foul contagious darkness in the air.
Therefore bring forth the soldiers of our prize,°   *captured ship*
For whilst our pinnace° anchors in the downs,°   *small ship/anchorage*
Here shall they make their ransom on the sand,
10   Or with their blood stain this discoloured shore.[4]
Master, [*pointing to the* FIRST GENTLEMAN] this prisoner freely give I thee,
[*To the* MATE] And thou, that art his mate, make boot of this.[5]
          [*He points to the* SECOND GENTLEMAN]
[*To Walter* WHITMORE] The other [*pointing to* SUFFOLK],
          Walter Whitmore, is thy share.

FIRST GENTLEMAN [*to the* MASTER]   What is my ransom, Master,
15   let me know.

MASTER   A thousand crowns, or else lay down your head.

MATE [*to the* SECOND GENTLEMAN] And so much shall you give,
          or off goes yours.

4.1 Location: At sea off the Kentish coast.
1. Q's stage direction reads, "Water Whickmore," anticipating the later play on "Walter" and "Water."
2. The garish, telltale (revealing secrets of the dark), and guilty day.
3. Usually worn-out cart horses, here an allusion to the

dragons of Hecate that, according to classical mythology, drew Night's chariot.
4. Or discolor this shore with their blood.
5. Make a profit from (the ransom of) this second prisoner.

CAPTAIN [*to both the* GENTLEMEN]   What, think you much to
        pay two thousand crowns,
    And bear the name and port° of gentlemen?   *demeanor*
20 WHITMORE   Cut both the villains' throats! [*To* SUFFOLK] For die you shall.
    The lives of those which we have lost in fight
    [   ]⁶
    Be counterpoised° with such a petty sum.   *Be compensated*
    FIRST GENTLEMAN [*to the* MASTER]   I'll give it, sir, and therefore
        spare my life.
    SECOND GENTLEMAN [*to the* MATE]   And so will I, and write
25   home for it straight.
    WHITMORE [*to* SUFFOLK]   I lost mine eye in laying the prize aboard,°   *boarding the ship*
    And therefore to revenge it, shalt thou die—
    And so should these, if I might have my will.
    CAPTAIN   Be not so rash; take ransom; let him live.
30 SUFFOLK   Look on my George⁷—I am a gentleman.
    Rate° me at what thou wilt, thou shalt be paid.   *Value*
    WHITMORE   And so am I; my name is Walter⁸ Whitmore.
            [SUFFOLK] *starteth*
    How now—why starts thou? What doth thee affright?
    SUFFOLK   Thy name affrights me, in whose sound is death.
35   A cunning man did calculate my birth,⁹
    And told me that by 'water' I should die.
    Yet let not this make thee be bloody-minded;
    Thy name is Gualtier,¹ being rightly sounded.
    WHITMORE   Gualtier or Walter—which it is I care not.
40   Never yet did base dishonour blur our name
    But with our sword we wiped away the blot.
    Therefore, when merchant-like I sell revenge,
    Broke be my sword, my arms° torn and defaced,   *coat of arms*
    And I proclaimed a coward through the world.
45 SUFFOLK   Stay, Whitmore; for thy prisoner is a prince,
    The Duke of Suffolk, William de la Pole.
    WHITMORE   The Duke of Suffolk muffled up in rags?
    SUFFOLK   Ay, but these rags are no part of the Duke.
    Jove sometime went disguised, and why not I?
50 CAPTAIN   But Jove was never slain as thou shalt be.
    SUFFOLK   Obscure and lousy° swain, King Henry's blood,²   *lice-infested*
    The honourable blood of Lancaster,
    Must not be shed by such a jady groom.³
    Hast thou not kissed thy hand° and held my stirrup?   *(a gesture of servility)*
55 Bare-headed plodded by my foot-cloth mule⁴
    And thought thee happy when I shook° my head?   *nodded*
    How often hast thou waited at my cup,
    Fed from my trencher,° kneeled down at the board°   *platter / table*
    When I have feasted with Queen Margaret?

---

6. A line appears to be missing from F at this point,
probably one indicating that the ransom demanded can
never compensate for the lives lost in battle.
7. Alluding to the image of St. George and the dragon
on the insignia of the Order of the Garter, the highest
order of English knighthood.
8. "Walter" was usually pronounced "water." The spirit
Asnath, conjured by Roger Bolingbroke, had predicted

that Suffolk should die by "water" (see 1.4.32).
9. An astrologer cast my horoscope.
1. French for "Walter."
2. A dubious claim: Suffolk's mother was a distant
cousin to Henry VI.
3. Servant in charge of horses; contemptible fellow.
4. The animal used to bear the large, richly ornamented cloth displayed in royal processions.

60   Remember it, and let it make thee crestfall'n,[5]
     Ay, and allay this thy abortive° pride,   *monstrous*
     How in our voiding lobby° hast thou stood   *antechamber*
     And duly waited for my coming forth?
     This hand of mine hath writ° in thy behalf,   *written testimonials*
65   And therefore shall it charm° thy riotous tongue.   *silence*
WHITMORE   Speak, Captain—shall I stab the forlorn swain?°   *wretched peasant*
CAPTAIN   First let my words stab him as he hath me.
SUFFOLK   Base slave, thy words are blunt° and so art thou.   *harmless*
CAPTAIN   Convey him hence and, on our longboat's side,
     Strike off his head.
70   SUFFOLK   Thou dar'st not for thy own.
CAPTAIN Pole—
SUFFOLK   Pole?[6]
CAPTAIN   Ay, kennel,° puddle, sink,° whose filth   *open gutter / cesspool*
     and dirt
     Troubles the silver spring where England drinks,
     Now will I dam up this thy yawning mouth
     For swallowing the treasure of the realm.
75   Thy lips that kissed the Queen shall sweep the ground,
     And thou that smiledst at good Duke Humphrey's death
     Against the senseless° winds shalt grin in vain,   *unfeeling*
     Who in contempt shall hiss at thee again.
     And wedded be thou to the hags of hell,
80   For daring to affy° a mighty lord   *betroth*
     Unto the daughter of a worthless king,
     Having neither subject, wealth, nor diadem.
     By devilish policy art thou grown great,
     And like ambitious Sylla,[7] overgorged
85   With gobbets° of thy mother's° bleeding heart.   *chunks / (England's)*
     By thee Anjou and Maine were sold to France,
     The false revolting° Normans, thorough° thee,   *rebellious / because of*
     Disdain to call us lord, and Picardy
     Hath slain their governors, surprised our forts,
90   And sent the ragged soldiers, wounded, home.
     The princely Warwick, and the Nevilles all,
     Whose dreadful swords were never drawn in vain,
     As hating thee, are rising up in arms;
     And now the house of York, thrust from the crown,
95   By shameful murder of a guiltless king[8]
     And lofty, proud, encroaching tyranny,
     Burns with revenging fire, whose hopeful colours
     Advance° our half-faced sun,[9] striving to shine,   *Display*
     Under the which is writ, '*Invitis nubibus*'.°   *In spite of clouds*
100 The commons here in Kent are up in arms,
     And, to conclude, reproach and beggary
     Is crept into the palace of our King,

---

5. Humble; deprived of a "crest" (coat of arms).
6. The fact that Suffolk's family name could be pro-
nounced "pool" leads to the punning insults that follow.
Lines 71–72 are garbled in F (see Textual Variants).
Oxford's reconstruction assumes that abbreviations for
"Suffolk" and "Lieutenant" were misread as "Sir" and
"Lord" by those who set type from the Folio manuscript.
7. The Roman dictator Lucius Cornelius Sulla (138–78

B.C.E.), notorious for drawing up lists of enemies whom
he executed or banished.
8. Alluding to the deposition and murder of Richard II,
which allowed the Lancastrian branch of the royal family to seize the throne. Shakespeare dramatizes these
events in *Richard II*.
9. A sun emerging above clouds was the badge of
Edward III and his successor, Richard II.

And all by thee. [*To* WHITMORE] Away, convey him hence.

SUFFOLK O that I were a god, to shoot forth thunder
105 Upon these paltry, servile, abject drudges.
Small things make base men proud. This villain here,
Being captain of a pinnace, threatens more
Than Bargulus, the strong Illyrian pirate.[1]
Drones° suck not eagles' blood, but rob beehives.   *Beetles; parasites*
110 It is impossible that I should die
By such a lowly vassal as thyself.
Thy words move rage, and not remorse in me.

CAPTAIN But my deeds, Suffolk, soon shall stay thy rage.

SUFFOLK I go of message° from the Queen to France—   *as messenger*
115 I charge thee, waft° me safely cross the Channel!   *convey*

CAPTAIN Walter—

WHITMORE Come, Suffolk, I must waft thee to thy death.

SUFFOLK *Paene gelidus timor occupat artus*[2]—
It is thee I fear.

120 WHITMORE Thou shalt have cause to fear before I leave thee.
What, are ye daunted now? Now will ye stoop?

FIRST GENTLEMAN [*to* SUFFOLK] My gracious lord, entreat
him—speak him fair.

SUFFOLK Suffolk's imperial tongue is stern and rough,
Used to command, untaught to plead for favour.
125 Far be it we should honour such as these
With humble suit. No, rather let my head
Stoop to the block than these knees bow to any
Save to the God of heaven and to my king;
And sooner dance upon a bloody pole[3]
130 Than stand uncovered to the vulgar groom.
True nobility is exempt from fear;
More can I bear than you dare execute.

CAPTAIN Hale° him away, and let him talk no more.   *Drag*

SUFFOLK Come, 'soldiers', show what cruelty ye can,
135 That this my death may never be forgot.
Great men oft die by vile Besonians;[4]
A Roman sworder and banditto° slave   *cutthroat and lawless*
Murdered sweet Tully; Brutus' bastard hand[5]
Stabbed Julius Caesar; savage islanders
140 Pompey the Great;[6] and Suffolk dies by pirates.

Exit WHITMORE *with* SUFFOLK

CAPTAIN And as for these whose ransom we have set,
It is our pleasure one of them depart.
[*To the* SECOND GENTLEMAN] Therefore, come you with us and
[*to his men, pointing to the* FIRST GENTLEMAN] let him go.

Exeunt. Manet the FIRST GENTLEMAN

---

1. An ancient pirate alluded to in Ciero's *De Officiis* (*On Public Duties*), a text much used in Elizabethan schools.
2. Cold fear seizes my limbs almost entirely (perhaps alluding to Virgil, *Aeneid* 7.446; Lucan, *Pharsalia* 1.246; or both).
3. Punning on his name ("Pole") and on Elizabethan slang for "head" ("poll"), Suffolk alludes to the fact that heads of executed criminals were set upon poles in public places. Londoners would often pass by such poles as they crossed the bridge on their way to the theaters in Southwark.

4. Base fellows. From the Spanish word *bisoño*, meaning "recruit": foot soldiers were usually poor commoners.
5. Brutus, who helped murder Caesar, was rumored to have been his illegitimate son. *Tully*: the Roman orator Cicero, who was in fact murdered by Roman soldiers.
6. Alluding either to Plutarch's claim that the Egyptians who murdered this Roman general were led by one born on the island of Chios or to the tradition that Pompey was murdered on the island of Lesbos.

Enter WHITMORE *with* [*Suffolk's head and*] *body*

WHITMORE   There let his head and lifeless body lie,

145   Until the Queen his mistress bury it.   *Exit*

FIRST GENTLEMAN   O barbarous and bloody spectacle!

His body will I bear unto the King.

If he revenge it not, yet will his friends;

So will the Queen, that living held him dear.

[*Exit with Suffolk's head and body*]

4.2

Enter two REBELS *with long staves*[1]

FIRST REBEL   Come and get thee a sword, though made of a

lath;[2] they have been up° these two days.   in revolt

SECOND REBEL   They have the more need to sleep now then.

FIRST REBEL   I tell thee, Jack Cade the clothier[3] means to dress

5   the commonwealth, and turn it,[4] and set a new nap upon it.[5]

SECOND REBEL   So he had need, for 'tis threadbare. Well, I say it

was never merry world in England since gentlemen came up.°   came into fashion

FIRST REBEL   O, miserable age! Virtue is not regarded in handi-

craftsmen.°   artisans

10   SECOND REBEL   The nobility think scorn to go in leather

aprons.°   (workers' attire)

FIRST REBEL   Nay more, the King's Council are no good

workmen.

SECOND REBEL   True; and yet it is said 'Labour in thy vocation';

15   which is as much to say as 'Let the magistrates be labouring

men'; and therefore should we be magistrates.

FIRST REBEL   Thou hast hit it; for there's no better sign of a

brave° mind than a hard° hand.   fine / calloused

SECOND REBEL   I see them! I see them! There's Best's son, the

20   tanner of Wingham—

FIRST REBEL   He shall have the skins of our enemies to make

dog's leather[6] of.

SECOND REBEL   And Dick the butcher—

FIRST REBEL   Then is sin struck down like an ox, and iniquity's

25   throat cut like a calf.

SECOND REBEL   And Smith the weaver—

FIRST REBEL   Argo,[7] their thread of life is spun.

SECOND REBEL   Come, come, let's fall in with them.

Enter Jack CADE, *Dick* [*the*] BUTCHER, *Smith the*

WEAVER, *a sawyer,* [*and a drummer,*] *with infinite num-*

bers, [*all*] *with long staves*

CADE   We, John Cade, so termed of° our supposed father—   named for

30   BUTCHER [*to his fellows*]   Or rather of stealing a cade° of   barrel

herrings.

CADE   For our enemies shall fall before us,[8] inspired with the

spirit of putting down kings and princes—command silence!

4.2 Location: Blackheath, Kent.
1. Staves are mentioned only in the Q stage directions
and dialogue, and may reflect performance.
2. A strip of wood commonly used as a sword or dagger
by the Vice figure in English morality plays.
3. Clothiers, or textile workers, were involved in
a number of uprisings throughout the sixteenth
century.

4. Turn it inside out (as a way of renewing old cloth),
with a secondary sense of inverting the social hierarchy.
5. Improve its surface texture, probably by brushing
the outer fibers ("nap") of the cloth; reform it.
6. Inferior leather used in glove making.
7. A variant form of *ergo*, Latin for "therefore."
8. Borrowing biblical language and punning on the
Latin *cadere*, meaning "fall."

BUTCHER   Silence!

35   CADE   My father was a Mortimer—

BUTCHER   [*to his fellows*]   He was an honest man and a good bricklayer.[9]

CADE   My mother a Plantagenet—

BUTCHER   [*to his fellows*]   I knew her well, she was a midwife.

40   CADE   My wife descended of the Lacys[1]—

BUTCHER   [*to his fellows*]   She was indeed a pedlar's daughter and sold many laces.

WEAVER   [*to his fellows*]   But now of late, not able to travel with her furred pack,[2] she washes bucks[3] here at home.

45   CADE   Therefore am I of an honourable house.

BUTCHER   [*to his fellows*]   Ay, by my faith, the field is honourable, and there was he born, under a hedge; for his father had never a house but the cage.°   prison

CADE   Valiant I am—

50   WEAVER   [*to his fellows*]   A° must needs, for beggary is valiant.[4]   He

CADE   I am able to endure much—

BUTCHER   [*to his fellows*]   No question of that, for I have seen him whipped[5] three market days together.

CADE   I fear neither sword nor fire.

55   WEAVER   [*to his fellows*]   He need not fear the sword, for his coat is of proof.[6]

BUTCHER   [*to his fellows*]   But methinks he should stand in fear of fire, being burned i'th' hand for stealing of sheep.[7]

CADE   Be brave, then, for your captain is brave and vows refor-

60   mation. There shall be in England seven halfpenny loaves sold for a penny, the three-hooped pot shall have ten hoops,[8] and I will make it felony to drink small° beer. All the realm shall   weak
be in° common, and in Cheapside[9] shall my palfrey° go to   held in / saddle horse
grass. And when I am king, as king I will be—

65   ALL CADE'S FOLLOWERS   God save your majesty!

CADE   I thank you good people!—there shall be no money. All shall eat and drink on my score,° and I will apparel them all   at my expense
in one livery that they may agree like brothers, and worship me their lord.

70   BUTCHER   The first thing we do let's kill all the lawyers.

CADE   Nay, that I mean to do. Is not this a lamentable thing that of the skin of an innocent lamb should be made parchment? That parchment, being scribbled o'er, should undo a man? Some say the bee stings, but I say 'tis the bee's wax.° For   sealing wax
75   I did but seal[1] once to a thing, and I was never mine own man since. How now? Who's there?

Enter [*some bringing forth*] *the* CLERK *of Chatham*

WEAVER   The Clerk of Chatham—he can write and read and cast account.°   do arithmetic

---

9. Punning on "Mortimer" and "mortarer" (meaning "builder").
1. The family name of the earls of Lincoln.
2. Not able to travel with her peddler's pack made of skins with the hair turned outward; not able to make a living ("travail") with her sexual organs.
3. She washes laundry; she absolves ("washes") cuckolds (husbands with horns, like bucks) of their shame by helping them get even with their unfaithful wives.
4. Worthy of praise; sturdy. The Weaver is referring ironically to the fact that Elizabethan poor laws made it

illegal to give alms to able-bodied, or "valiant," beggars.
5. The usual punishment for vagabonds.
6. Impenetrable (from dirt?); well worn.
7. Thieves were branded on one hand with a "T" for "thief."
8. "Hoops," or regularly spaced bands on pots, were used for measuring. Cade means that for the price of a three-hooped pot (about a quart), one will receive over three times that amount.
9. Elizabethan London's chief commercial district.
1. Sign and seal (a legal document).

CADE O, monstrous!

80 WEAVER We took him setting of boys' copies.[2]

CADE Here's a villain.

WEAVER He's a book in his pocket with red letters[3] in't.

CADE Nay, then he is a conjuror!

BUTCHER Nay, he can make obligations° and write court hand.[4]   *bonds*

85 CADE I am sorry for't. The man is a proper° man, of mine   *handsome*
honour. Unless I find him guilty, he shall not die. Come
hither, sirrah, I must examine thee. What is thy name?

CLERK Emmanuel.

BUTCHER They use to write that on the top of letters[5]—'twill go
90 hard with you.

CADE Let me alone. [*To the* CLERK] Dost thou use to write thy
name? Or hast thou a mark[6] to thyself like an honest plain-
dealing man?

CLERK Sir, I thank God I have been so well brought up that I
95 can write my name.

ALL CADE'S FOLLOWERS He hath confessed—away with him!
He's a villain and a traitor.

CADE Away with him, I say, hang him with his pen and inkhorn
about his neck.   *Exit one with the* CLERK

Enter [a MESSENGER]*[7]

100 MESSENGER Where's our general?

CADE Here I am, thou particular[8] fellow.

MESSENGER Fly, fly, fly! Sir Humphrey Stafford and his brother
are hard by with the King's forces.

CADE Stand, villain, stand—or I'll fell thee down. He shall be
105 encountered with a man as good as himself. He is but a
knight, is a?

MESSENGER No.[9]

CADE To equal him I will make myself a knight presently.
[*He kneels and knights himself*]
Rise up, Sir John Mortimer.
[*He rises*]
110 Now have at him!

Enter Sir Humphrey STAFFORD *and his brother,*
with [a] drum[mer] and soldiers

STAFFORD [*to Cade's followers*] Rebellious hinds,° the filth and   *peasants*
scum of Kent,
Marked for the gallows, lay your weapons down;
Home to your cottages, forsake this groom.
The King is merciful, if you revolt.°   *turn against Cade*

STAFFORD'S BROTHER [*to Cade's followers*] But angry, wrathful,
115 and inclined to blood,
If you go forward. Therefore, yield or die.

CADE [*to his followers*] As for these silken-coated slaves, I pass° not.   *care*
It is to you, good people, that I speak,

---

2. Preparing writing exercises for schoolboys. Village clerks often doubled as schoolmasters.
3. Alluding to the red printing in almanacs and primers.
4. The script used for legal documents.
5. The name, which means "God is with us," commonly appeared on legal documents.

6. Those who were illiterate often "signed" documents by using distinctive marks.
7. Q calls this figure "Tom," F "Michael."
8. Private (as opposed to "general" in the previous line).
9. No, nothing but a knight. The Messenger is replying to the negative implied in the prior sentence: "He is nothing but a knight, is he?"

Over whom, in time to come, I hope to reign—
120   For I am rightful heir unto the crown.
STAFFORD   Villain, thy father was a plasterer
And thou thyself a shearman,[1] art thou not?
CADE   And Adam was a gardener.
STAFFORD'S BROTHER   And what of that?
CADE   Marry, this: Edmund Mortimer, Earl of March,
125   Married the Duke of Clarence' daughter, did he not?
STAFFORD   Ay, sir.
CADE   By her he had two children at one birth.
STAFFORD'S BROTHER   That's false.
CADE   Ay, there's the question—but I say 'tis true.
130   The elder of them, being put to nurse,
Was by a beggar-woman stol'n away,
And, ignorant of his birth and parentage,
Became a bricklayer when he came to age.
His son am I—deny it an° you can.   *if*
135 BUTCHER   Nay, 'tis too true—therefore he shall be king.
WEAVER   Sir, he made a chimney in my father's house, and the
bricks are alive at this day to testify. Therefore deny it not.
STAFFORD [*to Cade's followers*]   And will you credit this base drudge's words
That speaks he knows not what?
140 ALL CADE'S FOLLOWERS   Ay, marry, will we—therefore get ye gone.
STAFFORD'S BROTHER   Jack Cade, the Duke of York hath taught you this.
CADE [*aside*]   He lies, for I invented it myself.
[*Aloud*] Go to, sirrah[2]—tell the King from me that for his
father's sake, Henry the Fifth, in whose time boys went to
145   span-counter° for French crowns,[3] I am content he shall   *played a game of toss*
reign; but I'll be Protector over him.
BUTCHER   And, furthermore, we'll have the Lord Saye's[4] head
for selling the dukedom of Maine.
CADE   And good reason, for thereby is England maimed, and
150   fain to go with a staff, but that my puissance° holds it up.   *power*
Fellow-kings, I tell you that that Lord Saye hath gelded the
commonwealth, and made it an eunuch, and, more than that,
he can speak French, and therefore he is a traitor!
STAFFORD   O gross and miserable ignorance!
155 CADE   Nay, answer if you can: the Frenchmen are our enemies;
go to, then, I ask but this—can he that speaks with the tongue
of an enemy be a good counsellor or no?
ALL CADE'S FOLLOWERS   No, no—and therefore we'll have his
head!
STAFFORD'S BROTHER [*to* STAFFORD]   Well, seeing gentle words
160   will not prevail,
Assail them with the army of the King.
STAFFORD   Herald, away, and throughout every town
Proclaim them traitors that are up with Cade;

---

1. One who cuts the nap from cloth during its manufacture.
2. Term used to address inferiors.
3. Alluding to Henry V's conquest of France. "French
crowns" might refer to French coins, kings, kingdoms,

or the bald heads that were symptomatic of the venereal
diseases blamed on the French.
4. *Lord Saye*: James Fiennes, Treasurer of England,
was associated with Suffolk in the loss of Anjou and
Maine.

That those which fly before the battle ends
165   May, even in their wives' and children's sight,
    Be hanged up for° example at their doors.   *to make an*
    And you that be the King's friends, follow me!
           Exeunt [the] STAFFORD[s] *and his men [their soldiers]*
CADE   And you that love the commons, follow me!
    Now show yourselves men—'tis for liberty.
170   We will not leave one lord, one gentleman—
    Spare none but such as go in clouted shoon,°   *hobnailed shoes*
    For they are thrifty honest men, and such
    As would, but that they dare not, take our parts.
BUTCHER   They are all in order, and march toward us.
175 CADE   But then are we in order when we are
    Most out of order.° Come, march forward!   *rebellious*
                             Exeunt

4.3

Alarums to the fight; [excursions,]° wherein both the   *skirmishes*
STAFFORDS *are slain. Enter Jack* CADE, [*Dick the*
BUTCHER,] *and the rest*
CADE   Where's Dick, the butcher of Ashford?
BUTCHER   Here, sir.
CADE   They fell before thee like sheep and oxen, and thou
    behaved'st thyself as if thou hadst been in thine own slaughter-
5   house. Therefore, thus will I reward thee—the Lent shall be
    as long again as it is. Thou shalt have licence to kill for a hun-
    dred, lacking one.[1]
BUTCHER   I desire no more.
CADE   And to speak truth, thou deserv'st no less.
        [*He appareis himself in the Staffords' armour*]
10   This monument of the victory will I bear, and the bodies shall
    be dragged at my horse heels till I do come to London, where
    we will have the Mayor's sword borne before us.
BUTCHER   If we mean to thrive and do good, break open the
    jails and let out the prisoners.
15 CADE   Fear not° that, I warrant thee. Come, let's march towards   *Don't worry about*
    London.   *Exeunt [dragging the Staffords' bodies]*

4.4

Enter KING [HENRY] *reading a supplication,* QUEEN
[MARGARET] *with Suffolk's head, the Duke of*
BUCKINGHAM, *and the Lord* SAYE, *with others*
QUEEN MARGARET [*aside*]   Oft have I heard that grief softens the mind,
    And makes it fearful and degenerate;
    Think, therefore, on revenge, and cease to weep.
    But who can cease to weep and look on this?
5   Here may his head lie on my throbbing breast,
    But where's the body that I should embrace?

4.3 Location: Scene continues.
1. Butchers were not permitted to slaughter meat during Lent (the forty-day period before Easter during
which Christians were to avoid eating flesh) except by
special license to provide food for the ill. Cade promises

the Butcher that he will have such a license and that
Lent will be twice as long as it is now. *Thou . . . one:*
You can kill ninety-nine animals, or serve ninety-nine
customers.
4.4 Location: The palace, London.

BUCKINGHAM [*to* KING HENRY] What answer makes your grace
    to the rebels' supplication?
KING HENRY I'll send some holy bishop to entreat,
    For God forbid so many simple souls
10   Should perish by the sword. And I myself,
    Rather than bloody war shall cut them short,
    Will parley° with Jack Cade their general.   *speak*
    But stay, I'll read it over once again.
        [*He*] *read*[*s*]
QUEEN MARGARET [*to* Suffolk's head] Ah, barbarous villains!
    Hath this lovely face
15   Ruled like a wandering planet over me,[1]
    And could it not enforce them to relent,
    That were unworthy to behold the same?
KING HENRY Lord Saye, Jack Cade hath sworn to have thy head.
SAYE Ay, but I hope your highness shall have his.
KING HENRY [*to* QUEEN MARGARET] How now, madam? Still
20   lamenting and mourning
    Suffolk's death?
    I fear me, love, if that I had been dead,
    Thou wouldest not have mourned so much for me.
QUEEN MARGARET No, my love, I should not mourn, but die for thee.
        Enter a MESSENGER [*in haste*]
25 KING HENRY How now? What news? Why com'st thou in such haste?
MESSENGER The rebels are in Southwark[2]—fly, my lord!
    Jack Cade proclaims himself Lord Mortimer,
    Descended from the Duke of Clarence' house,
    And calls your grace usurper, openly,
30   And vows to crown himself in Westminster.
    His army is a ragged multitude
    Of hinds and peasants, rude and merciless.
    Sir Humphrey Stafford and his brother's death
    Hath given them heart and courage to proceed.
35   All scholars, lawyers, courtiers, gentlemen,
    They call false caterpillars° and intend their death.   *treacherous parasites*
KING HENRY O, graceless° men; they know not what they do.[3]   *sinful*
BUCKINGHAM My gracious lord, retire to Kenilworth°   *(a royal castle)*
    Until a power be raised to put them down.
40 QUEEN MARGARET Ah, were the Duke of Suffolk now alive
    These Kentish rebels would be soon appeased!°   *made peaceful*
KING HENRY Lord Saye, the trait'rous rabble hateth thee—
    Therefore away with us to Kenilworth.
SAYE So might your grace's person be in danger.
45   The sight of me is odious in their eyes,
    And therefore in this city will I stay
    And live alone as secret as I may.
        Enter another MESSENGER
SECOND MESSENGER [*to* KING HENRY] Jack Cade hath almost gotten
    London Bridge;

---

1. It was popularly believed that influences from the
stars ("wandering planets") determined the fate of
those born under them.
2. A suburb of London (in Shakespeare's time, the site

of brothels and theaters).
3. An echo of Jesus' words on the cross to those who
crucified and mocked him. See Luke 23:34.

The citizens fly and forsake their houses;
50   The rascal people, thirsting after prey,
Join with the traitor; and they jointly swear
To spoil° the city and your royal court.   plunder
BUCKINGHAM [*to* KING HENRY]   Then linger not, my lord; away,
take horse!
KING HENRY   Come, Margaret. God, our hope, will succour us.
QUEEN MARGARET [*aside*]   My hope is gone, now Suffolk is
55   deceased.
KING HENRY [*to* SAYE]   Farewell, my lord. Trust not the Kentish
rebels.
BUCKINGHAM [*to* SAYE]   Trust nobody, for fear you be betrayed.
SAYE   The trust I have is in mine innocence,
And therefore am I bold and resolute.
Exeunt [SAYE *at one door, the rest at another*]

4.5

Enter the Lord SCALES *upon the Tower, walking.*
Enter three or four CITIZENS *below*
SCALES   How now? Is Jack Cade slain?
FIRST CITIZEN   No, my lord Scales,[1] nor likely to be slain, for he
and his men have won the bridge, killing all those that did
withstand them. The Lord Mayor craveth aid of your honour
5   from the Tower to defend the city from the rebels.
SCALES   Such aid as I can spare you shall command,
But I am troubled here with them myself.
The rebels have essayed° to win the Tower.   attempted
Get you to Smithfield,[2] there to gather head,°   raise forces
10   And thither will I send you Matthew Gough.
Fight for your king, your country, and your lives!
And so, farewell, for I must hence again.
Exeunt [SCALES *above, the* CITIZENS *below*]

4.6

Enter Jack Cade, [the WEAVER, *the* BUTCHER,] *and the
rest.* [CADE] *strikes his sword on London Stone*[1]
CADE   Now is Mortimer lord of this city. And, here sitting upon
London Stone, I charge and command that, of the city's cost,
the Pissing Conduit[2] run nothing but claret wine this first
year of our reign. And now henceforward it shall be treason
5   for any that calls me otherwise than Lord Mortimer.
Enter a SOLDIER, *running*
SOLDIER   Jack Cade, Jack Cade!
CADE   Zounds,° knock him down there!   God's wounds (an oath)
They kill him
BUTCHER   If this fellow be wise, he'll never call ye Jack Cade
more; I think he hath a very fair warning.
[*He takes a paper from the soldier's body and reads it*]
10   My lord, there's an army gathered together in Smithfield.

4.5 Location: The Tower, London.
1. Thomas de Scales fought with Talbot in France and
was charged by the King with the defense of the Tower.
2. Area just outside London's walls and to the northwest.
4.6 Location: Cannon Street, London.

1. An ancient stone found in Cannon Street and
famous as a London landmark.
2. The nickname for Little Conduit, a fountain used by
lower-class Londoners as a water supply.

CADE   Come then, let's go fight with them—but first, go on and
set London Bridge afire, and, if you can, burn down the Tower
too. Come, let's away.   *Exeunt*

4.7

Alarums. [Excursions, wherein] Matthew GOUGH *is
slain, and all the rest [of his men] with him. Then enter
Jack* CADE *with his company [among them the* BUTCHER,
the WEAVER, *and* JOHN, *a rebel]*

CADE   So, sirs, now go some and pull down the Savoy;¹ others
to th' Inns of Court²—down with them all.

BUTCHER   I have a suit unto your lordship.

CADE   Be it a lordship, thou shalt have it for that word.

5   BUTCHER   Only that the laws of England may come out of your
mouth.

JOHN [*aside to his fellows*]   Mass, 'twill be sore° law then, for he   harsh
was thrust in the mouth with a spear, and 'tis not whole yet.

WEAVER [*aside to* JOHN]   Nay, John, it will be stinking law, for his
10   breath stinks with eating toasted cheese.

CADE   I have thought upon it—it shall be so. Away! Burn all
the records of the realm. My mouth shall be the Parliament
of England.

JOHN [*aside to his fellows*]   Then we are like to have biting°   severe
15   statutes unless his teeth be pulled out.

CADE   And henceforward all things shall be in common.

Enter a MESSENGER

MESSENGER   My lord, a prize, a prize! Here's the Lord Saye
which sold the towns in France. He that made us pay one-and-
twenty fifteens and one shilling to the pound the last subsidy.³

Enter a rebel with the Lord SAYE⁴

20   CADE   Well, he shall be beheaded for it ten times. [*To* SAYE] Ah,
thou say, thou serge—nay, thou buckram lord!⁵ Now art thou
within point-blank° of our jurisdiction regal. What canst thou   within reach
answer to my majesty for giving up of Normandy unto Moun-
sieur Basimecu,⁶ the Dauphin of France? Be it known unto
25   thee by these presence,⁷ even the presence of Lord Mortimer,
that I am the besom° that must sweep the court clean of such   broom
filth as thou art. Thou hast most traitorously corrupted the
youth of the realm in erecting a grammar school; and,
whereas before, our forefathers had no other books but the
30   score and the tally,⁸ thou hast caused printing to be used and,
contrary to the King his° crown and dignity, thou hast built a   the King's
paper-mill.⁹ It will be proved to thy face that thou hast men

---

4.7 Location: Smithfield; London.
1. An anachronistic reference to the London residence
of the Duke of Lancaster, which was burned down during a 1381 uprising and not rebuilt until 1505.
2. The buildings where London's lawyers were trained
and lived.
3. He who made us pay very high personal property taxes
in the last tax assessment. A "fifteen" was a levy of one-
fifteenth of the property value; "twenty-one fifteens"
would be a tax in excess of the value of the property itself.
4. F and Q both read, "Enter George." As elsewhere,
the Oxford editors change what is assumed to be an
actor's name to the generic "a rebel."
5. Say was an expensive silk fabric, serge a durable

woolen fabric often worn by the lower classes, and
buckram a coarse linen also worn by the poor.
6. Punning on *baise mon cul*, French for "kiss my ass."
7. "These presents" was a legal term meaning "the
present document," a phrase that begins many legal
writings of the period. Cade, however, means "in the
presence of the King, who declares the law."
8. A rudimentary device for keeping track of financial
transactions. Sticks were marked, or "scored," split into
two pieces, and then divided between the debtor and
creditor. Each half was called a "tally."
9. Printing presses and paper mills were not in fact established in England until late in the fifteenth century.
Under Elizabeth, they were subject to strict regulation.

about thee that usually talk of a noun and a verb and such
abominable words as no Christian ear can endure to hear.
35   Thou hast appointed justices of peace to call poor men before
them about matters they were not able to answer. Moreover,
thou hast put them in prison, and, because they could not
read,[1] thou hast hanged them when indeed only for that
cause° they have been most worthy to live. Thou dost ride on   *for that reason alone*
40   a foot-cloth,[2] dost thou not?
SAYE   What of that?
CADE   Marry, thou ought'st not to let thy horse wear a cloak
when honester men than thou go in° their hose and doublets.   *wear only*
BUTCHER   And work in their shirts, too; as myself, for example,
45   that am a butcher.
SAYE   You men of Kent.
BUTCHER   What say you of Kent?
SAYE   Nothing but this—'tis *bona terra, mala gens.*[3]
CADE   *Bonum terrum*—zounds, what's that?
50   BUTCHER   He speaks French.
FIRST REBEL   No, 'tis Dutch.
SECOND REBEL   No, 'tis Out-talian, I know it well enough.
SAYE   Hear me but speak, and bear me where you will.
Kent, in the commentaries Caesar writ,
55   Is termed the civil'st° place of all this isle;   *most civilized*
Sweet is the country, because full of riches;
The people liberal,° valiant, active, wealthy;   *generous*
Which makes me hope you are not void of pity.
I sold not Maine, I lost not Normandy;
60   Yet to recover them would lose my life.
Justice with favour° have I always done,   *leniency*
Prayers and tears have moved me—gifts could never.
When have I aught° exacted at your hands,   *anything*
But to maintain the King, the realm, and you?
65   Large gifts have I bestowed on learnèd clerks°   *scholars*
Because my book preferred me to[4] the King,
And seeing ignorance is the curse of God,
Knowledge the wing wherewith we fly to heaven.
Unless you be possessed with devilish spirits,
70   You cannot but forbear to murder me.
This tongue hath parleyed unto° foreign kings   *negotiated with*
For your behoof°—   *behalf*
CADE   Tut, when struck'st thou one blow in the field?°   *battlefield*
SAYE   Great men have reaching hands.[5] Oft have I struck
75   Those that I never saw, and struck them dead.
REBEL   O monstrous coward! What, to come behind folks?
SAYE   These cheeks are pale for watching for your good—
CADE   Give him a box o'th' ear, and that will make 'em red again.
       [*One of the rebels strikes* SAYE]
SAYE   Long sitting° to determine poor men's causes   *(as a judge)*
80   Hath made me full of sickness and diseases.

1. Read Latin. By demonstrating reading knowledge of Latin, a person charged with a crime in early modern England could plead "benefit of clergy" and thereby be excused from hanging.
2. An ornamented cloth hung over the back of a horse and reaching to the ground on each side.
3. A good land, a bad people.

4. Because my own education brought me to the attention of the King (and improved my social position).
5. A variation on the classical proverb "Kings have long hands," suggesting that monarchs and influential people such as lord Saye have influence that causes much to happen even when they are not present.

CADE Ye shall have a hempen caudle,[6] then, and the health
o'th' hatchet.°   *executioner's ax*

BUTCHER [*to* SAYE] Why dost thou quiver, man?

SAYE The palsy, and not fear, provokes me.

85 CADE Nay, he nods at us as who should say 'I'll be even with
you'. I'll see if his head will stand steadier on a pole or no.
Take him away, and behead him.

SAYE Tell me wherein have I offended most?
Have I affected wealth or honour? Speak.

90 Are my chests filled up with extorted gold?
Is my apparel sumptuous to behold?
Whom have I injured, that ye seek my death?
These hands are free from guiltless bloodshedding,
This breast from harbouring foul deceitful thoughts.

95 O let me live!

CADE [*aside*] I feel remorse in myself with his words, but I'll bridle it. He shall die an it be but for pleading so well for his life.
[*Aloud*] Away with him—he has a familiar° under his tongue;   *demon*
he speaks not a God's name. Go, take him away, I say, to the

100 Standard[7] in Cheapside, and strike off his head presently;° and   *immediately*
then go to Mile End Green—break into his son-in-law's house,
Sir James Cromer, and strike off his head, and bring them both
upon two poles hither.

ALL CADE'S FOLLOWERS It shall be done!

105 SAYE Ah, countrymen, if, when you make your prayers,
God should be so obdurate as yourselves,
How would it fare with your departed souls?
And therefore yet relent and save my life!

CADE Away with him, and do as I command ye!
Exeunt [*the* BUTCHER *and*] *one or two*
with the Lord SAYE

110 The proudest peer in the realm shall not wear a head on his
shoulders unless he pay me tribute. There shall not a maid be
married but she shall pay to me her maidenhead,[8] ere they
have it. Married men shall hold of me *in capite*.[9] And we
charge and command that their wives be as free° as heart can   *sexually available*

115 wish or tongue can tell.
Enter a REBEL

REBEL O captain, London Bridge is afire!

CADE Run to Billingsgate and fetch pitch and flax and
quench it.
Enter the BUTCHER *and a* SERGEANT

SERGEANT Justice, justice, I pray you, sir, let me have justice of

120 this fellow here.

CADE Why, what has he done?

SERGEANT Alas, sir, he has ravished° my wife.   *raped*

BUTCHER [*to* CADE] Why, my lord, he would have 'rested° me   *arrested*
and I went and entered my action in his wife's proper house.[1]

---

6. Caudel was a warm gruel, but "a hempen caudel"
was a slang term for "hangman's noose."
7. A water conduit in Cheapside often used as a place
of execution.
8. Alluding to a supposed feudal practice by which a
lord had the right to sleep with the bride of any of his

vassals on the night of her wedding.
9. A Latin phrase indicating property held by grant
directly from the king, with a pun on *caput* (Latin for
"head") as slang for "maidenhead."
1. Stated my case in his wife's own house; had sex in
his wife's own body.

125   CADE   Dick, follow thy suit in her common place.² [*To the*   *bastard*
      SERGEANT] You whoreson° villain, you are a sergeant—you'll
      take any man by the throat for twelve pence, and 'rest a man
      when he's at dinner, and have him to prison ere the meat be
      out of his mouth. [*To the* BUTCHER] Go, Dick, take him hence:
130   cut out his tongue for cogging,° hough° him for running, and,   *deception / cripple*
      to conclude, brain him with his own mace.°   *staff of office*

                    Exit [the BUTCHER] *with the* SERGEANT

  REBEL   My lord, when shall we go to Cheapside and take up
      commodities upon our bills?³
  CADE   Marry, presently. He that will lustily stand to it⁴ shall go
135   with me and take up these commodities following—item, a
      gown, a kirtle, a petticoat, and a smock.⁵
  ALL CADE'S FOLLOWERS   O brave!

          Enter two with the Lord Saye's head and Sir James
          Cromer's upon two poles

  CADE   But is not this braver? Let them kiss one another, for they
      loved well when they were alive.

          [*The two heads are made to kiss*]

140   Now part them again, lest they consult about the giving up
      of some more towns in France. Soldiers, defer the spoil°   *destruction; plunder*
      of the city until night. For with these borne before us
      instead of maces will we ride through the streets, and at
      every corner have them kiss. Away!

          Exeunt [two with the heads. The others begin to follow]

145   Up Fish Street! Down Saint Magnus' Corner!⁶ Kill and
      knock down! Throw them into Thames!

          Sound a parley

      What noise is this? Dare any be so bold to sound retreat or
      parley when I command them kill?

          Enter the Duke of BUCKINGHAM *and old Lord* CLIFFORD

  BUCKINGHAM   Ay, here they be that dare and will disturb thee!
150   Know, Cade, we come ambassadors from the King
      Unto the commons, whom thou hast misled,
      And here pronounce free pardon to them all
      That will forsake thee and go home in peace.
  CLIFFORD   What say ye, countrymen, will ye relent
155   And yield to mercy whilst 'tis offered you,
      Or let a rebel lead you to your deaths?
      Who loves the King and will embrace his pardon,
      Fling up his cap and say 'God save his majesty'.
      Who hateth him and honours not his father,
160   Henry the Fifth, that made all France to quake,
      Shake he his weapon at us,° and pass by.   *Defy us*

          They [fling up their caps and] forsake CADE

  ALL CADE'S FOLLOWERS   God save the King! God save the King!
  CADE   What, Buckingham and Clifford, are ye so brave?° [*To*   *arrogant*
      the rabble] And you, base peasants, do ye believe him? Will
165   you needs be hanged with your pardons about your necks?

---

2. Pursue your sexual desire in her vagina; pursue your
legal suit in her meetinghouse.
3. And acquire goods on credit or by means of our
weapons ("bills"); and rape women, punning on "commodity" as meaning "female sexual organs" and "bills"
as meaning "penises."
4. Apply himself manfully; have an erection.
5. Slang terms for "female sexual organs."
6. Place at the north end of London Bridge opposite
Southwark.

Hath my sword, therefore, broke through London gates that
you should leave me at the White Hart[7] in Southwark?
I thought ye would never have given out° these arms till you   *abandoned*
had recovered your ancient freedom. But you are all recreants
170   and dastards,° and delight to live in slavery to the nobility. Let   *traitors and cowards*
them break your backs with burdens, take your houses over
your heads, ravish your wives and daughters before your
faces. For me, I will make shift for one,° and so God's curse   *take care of myself*
light upon you all.
175   ALL CADE'S FOLLOWERS   We'll follow Cade! We'll follow Cade!
        They run to CADE *again*
     CLIFFORD   Is Cade the son of Henry the Fifth
That thus you do exclaim you'll go with him?
Will he conduct you through the heart of France
And make the meanest° of you earls and dukes?   *lowest born*
180   Alas, he hath no home, no place to fly to,
Nor knows he how to live but by the spoil—
Unless by robbing of your friends and us.
Were't not a shame that whilst you live at jar°   *at odds*
The fearful° French, whom you late vanquishèd,   *timid*
185   Should make a start° o'er seas and vanquish you?   *rouse themselves*
Methinks already in this civil broil
I see them lording it in London streets,
Crying '*Villiago!*'[8] unto all they meet.
Better ten thousand base-born Cades miscarry°   *meet disaster*
190   Than you should stoop unto a Frenchman's mercy.
To France! To France! And get what you have lost!
Spare England, for it is your native coast.
Henry hath money; you are strong and manly;
God on our side, doubt not of victory.
195   ALL CADE'S FOLLOWERS   A Clifford!° A Clifford! We'll follow   *To Clifford*
the King and Clifford!
        [*They forsake* CADE]
     CADE [*aside*]   Was ever feather so lightly blown to and fro as this
multitude? The name of Henry the Fifth hales° them to   *draws*
an hundred mischiefs, and makes them leave me desolate.
200   I see them lay their heads together to surprise° me. My sword   *capture*
make way for me, for here is no staying. [*Aloud*] In despite of
the devils and hell, have through° the very middest of you!   *here I come through*
And heavens and honour be witness that no want of resolu-
tion in me, but only my followers' base and ignominious trea-
205   sons, makes me betake me to my heels.
        He runs through them with his staff, and flies away
     BUCKINGHAM   What, is he fled? Go, some, and follow him,
And he that brings his head unto the King
Shall have a thousand crowns for his reward.
        Exeunt some of them [*after* CADE]
     [*To the remaining rebels*] Follow me, soldiers, we'll devise a mean°   *way*
210   To reconcile you all unto the King.   *Exeunt*

---

7. An inn, with a pun on the coward's "white heart"   8. A variation on the Italian word for "coward."
(because drained of its blood or spirit).

4.8

Sound trumpets. Enter KING HENRY, QUEEN
[MARGARET], *and* [*the Duke of*] SOMERSET
on the terrace

KING HENRY   Was ever King that joyed° an earthly throne   enjoyed
And could command no more content than I?
No sooner was I crept out of my cradle
But I was made a king at nine months old.
5 Was never subject longed to be a king
As I do long and wish to be a subject.

Enter the Duke of BUCKINGHAM *and* [*Lord*] CLIFFORD
[*on the terrace*]

BUCKINGHAM [*to* KING HENRY]   Health and glad tidings to your majesty.
KING HENRY   Why, Buckingham, is the traitor Cade surprised?
Or is he but retired to make him strong?

Enter [*below*] *multitudes with halters¹ about their
necks*

10 CLIFFORD   He is fled, my lord, and all his powers do yield,
And humbly thus with halters on their necks
Expect° your highness' doom° of life or death.   Await / sentence
KING HENRY   Then, heaven, set ope° thy everlasting gates   open
To entertain my vows of thanks and praise.
15 [*To the multitudes below*] Soldiers, this day have you redeemed your lives,
And showed how well you love your prince and country.
Continue still° in this so good a mind,   always
And Henry, though he be infortunate,°   unlucky
Assure yourselves will never be unkind.
20 And so, with thanks and pardon to you all,
I do dismiss you to your several countries.°   different regions
ALL CADE'S FORMER FOLLOWERS   God save the King! God save
the King!   [*Exeunt multitudes below*]

Enter a MESSENGER [*on the terrace*]

MESSENGER [*to* KING HENRY]   Please it your grace to be advertisèd°   informed
25 The Duke of York is newly come from Ireland,
And with a puissant and a mighty power
Of galloglasses and stout Irish kerns²
Is marching hitherward in proud array,
And still proclaimeth, as he comes along,
30 His arms are only to remove from thee
The Duke of Somerset, whom he terms a traitor.
KING HENRY   Thus stands my state,° 'twixt Cade and York distressed,   condition
Like to a ship that, having scaped a tempest,
Is straightway calmed° and boarded with a pirate.   becalmed
35 But now is Cade driven back, his men dispersed,
And now is York in arms to second° him.   support
I pray thee, Buckingham, go and meet him,
And ask him what's the reason of these arms.

4.8 Location: Kenilworth Castle.
1. Cade's followers wore nooses as a sign of their
submission.

2. See note to 3.1.310. *galloglasses*: professional Irish
mercenary soldiers who were usually armed with axes
and rode on horseback.

Tell him I'll send Duke Edmund° to the Tower;   *Somerset*
40   And, Somerset, we will commit thee thither,
      Until his army be dismissed from him.
SOMERSET   My lord, I'll yield myself to prison willingly,
      Or unto death, to do my country good.
KING HENRY [*to* BUCKINGHAM]   In any case, be not too rough in terms,°   *language*
45   For he is fierce and cannot brook° hard language.   *endure*
BUCKINGHAM   I will, my lord, and doubt not so to deal
      As all things shall redound unto your good.
KING HENRY   Come, wife, let's in and learn to govern better;
      For yet° may England curse my wretched reign.   *up until now*

                              Flourish. Exeunt

                              4.9

      Enter Jack CADE[1]
CADE   Fie on ambitions; fie on myself that have a sword and yet
      am ready to famish. These five days have I hid me in these
      woods and durst not peep out, for all the country is laid° for   *set with traps*
      me. But now am I so hungry that if I might have a lease of my
5   life for a thousand years, I could stay° no longer. Wherefore   *delay*
      o'er a brick wall have I climbed into this garden to see if I can
      eat grass or pick a sallet° another while, which is not amiss to   *salad*
      cool a man's stomach° this hot weather. And I think this word   *hunger; anger*
      'sallet' was born to do me good; for many a time, but for a
10   sallet,° my brain-pan had been cleft with a brown bill;[2] and   *helmet*
      many a time, when I have been dry, and bravely marching, it
      hath served me instead of a quart pot to drink in; and now the
      word 'sallet' must serve me to feed on.
            [*He*] *lies down picking of herbs and eating them.*
            Enter [*Sir*] *Alexander* IDEN *and* [*five of*] *his men*
IDEN   Lord, who would live turmoilèd° in the court   *harried*
15   And may enjoy such quiet walks as these?
      This small inheritance my father left me
      Contenteth me, and worth a monarchy.
      I seek not to wax great by others' waning,
      Or gather wealth I care not with what envy;
20   Sufficeth that° I have maintains my state,   *that what*
      And sends the poor well pleasèd° from my gate.   *(with their alms)*
            [CADE *rises to his knees*]
CADE [*aside*]   Zounds, here's the lord of the soil come to seize
      me for a stray° for entering his fee-simple[3] without leave. [*To*   *trespasser*
      IDEN] A villain, thou wilt betray me and get a thousand crowns
25   of the king by carrying my head to him; but I'll make thee eat
      iron like an ostrich[4] and swallow my sword like a great pin, ere
      thou and I part.

4.9 Location: Alexander Iden's garden, in Kent.
1. Q's stage direction indicates that Jack Cade enters at one door and Alexander Iden and his men at another. Q's version of this scene is shorter than F's and makes clear what F only implies: that Iden is accompanied by attendants. The presence of these figures makes Cade's offer to fight Iden seem the more courageous. In Q, Iden enters unarmed, orders one of his men to fetch his sword, and chivalrously orders them to stand aside while he fights Cade. In F, Iden presumably enters armed.
2. A long-handled weapon with an axlike blade. The brown color is from blood or varnish.
3. Property that belonged forever to its owner and his or her heirs; on it, stray animals could legally be seized.
4. It was popularly believed that ostriches ate iron.

IDEN　Why, rude companion,° whatsoe'er thou be,　　　*lowborn fellow*
I know thee not. Why then should I betray thee?
30 Is't not enough to break into my garden,
And, like a thief, to come to rob my grounds,
Climbing my walls in spite of me the owner,
But thou wilt brave° me with these saucy terms?　　　*taunt*
CADE　Brave thee? Ay, by the best blood that ever was
35 broached°—and beard° thee too! Look on me well—I have eat　　*shed / defy*
no meat these five days, yet come thou and thy five men, an
if I do not leave you all as dead as a doornail I pray God I may
never eat grass more.
IDEN　Nay, it shall ne'er be said while England stands
40 That Alexander Iden, an esquire of Kent,
Took odds° to combat a poor famished man.　　　*advantage*
Oppose thy steadfast gazing eyes to mine—
See if thou canst outface me with thy looks.
Set limb to limb, and thou art far the lesser—
45 Thy hand is but a finger to my fist,
Thy leg a stick comparèd with this truncheon.°　　　*thick staff (his leg)*
My foot shall fight with all the strength thou hast,
And if mine arm be heavèd in the air,
Thy grave is digged already in the earth.
50 As for words, whose greatness answers words,[5]
Let this my sword report what speech forbears.
[*To his men*] Stand you all aside.
CADE　By my valour, the most complete° champion that ever I　　*accomplished*
heard. [*To his sword*] Steel, if thou turn the edge° or cut not　　*fail to cut*
55 out the burly-boned clown in chines° of beef ere thou sleep in　　*roasts*
thy sheath, I beseech God on my knees thou mayst be turned
to hobnails.
　　　[CADE *stands.*] *Here they fight, and* CADE *falls down*
O, I am slain! Famine and no other hath slain me! Let ten
thousand devils come against me, and give me but the ten
60 meals I have lost, and I'd defy them all. Wither, garden, and
be henceforth a burying place to all that do dwell in this
house, because the unconquered soul of Cade is fled.
IDEN　Is't Cade that I have slain, that monstrous traitor?
Sword, I will hallow thee for this thy deed
65 And hang thee o'er my tomb when I am dead.
Ne'er shall this blood be wipèd from thy point
But thou shalt wear it as a herald's coat
To emblaze the honour that thy master got.[6]
CADE　Iden, farewell, and be proud of thy victory. Tell Kent
70 from me she hath lost her best man, and exhort all the world
to be cowards. For I, that never feared any, am vanquished by
famine, not by valour.　　　*He dies*
IDEN　How much thou wrong'st me, heaven be my judge.
Die, damnèd wretch, the curse of her that bore thee!
75 And [*stabbing him again*] as I thrust thy body in with my sword,[7]
So wish I I might thrust thy soul to hell.

5. This line may be corrupt. It may mean "As for words, I whose might more than matches your words." 6. *But ... got:* Just as a device on a herald's coat proclaims his lord's identity and status, so the blood on Iden's sword proclaims the fame he has won for killing Cade. 7. As I thrust my sword into your body.

Hence will I drag thee headlong° by the heels   *head downward*
Unto a dunghill, which shall be thy grave,
And there cut off thy most ungracious head,
80   Which I will bear in triumph to the King,
Leaving thy trunk for crows to feed upon.

Exeunt [with the body]

5.1

Enter the Duke of YORK *and his army of Irish*
with [a] drum[mer] and soldiers [bearing] colours

YORK   From Ireland thus comes York to claim his right,
And pluck the crown from feeble Henry's head.
Ring, bells, aloud; burn, bonfires, clear and bright,
To entertain° great England's lawful king.   *welcome*
5   Ah, *sancta maiestas!*° Who would not buy thee dear?   *sacred majesty*
Let them obey that knows not how to rule;
This hand was made to handle naught but gold.
I cannot give due action to my words,
Except° a sword or sceptre balance it.   *Unless*
10   A sceptre shall it have, have I° a sword,   *as sure as I have*
On which I'll toss the fleur-de-lis of France.[1]

Enter the Duke of BUCKINGHAM

[*Aside*] Whom have we here? Buckingham to disturb me?
The King hath sent him sure—I must dissemble.
BUCKINGHAM   York, if thou meanest well, I greet thee well.
15   YORK   Humphrey of Buckingham, I accept thy greeting.
Art thou a messenger, or come of pleasure?
BUCKINGHAM   A messenger from Henry, our dread liege,
To know the reason of these arms° in peace;   *armed men*
Or why thou, being a subject as I am,
20   Against thy oath and true allegiance sworn,
Should raise so great a power without his leave,
Or dare to bring thy force so near the court?
YORK [*aside*]   Scarce can I speak, my choler is so great.
O, I could hew up rocks and fight with flint,
25   I am so angry at these abject terms;°   *insulting words*
And now, like Ajax Telamonius,[2]
On sheep or oxen could I spend my fury.
I am far better born than is the King,
More like a king, more kingly in my thoughts;
30   But I must make fair weather° yet a while,   *pretend to be mild*
Till Henry be more weak and I more strong.
[*Aloud*] Buckingham, I prithee pardon me,
That I have given no answer all this while;
My mind was troubled with deep melancholy.
35   The cause why I have brought this army hither
Is to remove proud Somerset from the King,
Seditious to his grace and to the state.
BUCKINGHAM   That is too much presumption on thy part;
But if thy arms be to no other end,

5.1 Location: The remainder of the play takes place in an open field between St. Albans and London.
1. On which I'll impale the national emblem of France, the lily flower.

2. A Greek hero of the Trojan War who went mad and slaughtered a flock of sheep, taking them to be his Greek enemies.

40   The King hath yielded unto thy demand:
         The Duke of Somerset is in the Tower.
     YORK   Upon thine honour, is he prisoner?
     BUCKINGHAM   Upon mine honour, he is prisoner.
     YORK   Then, Buckingham, I do dismiss my powers.
45   Soldiers, I thank you all; disperse yourselves;
         Meet me tomorrow in Saint George's field[3]
         You shall have pay and everything you wish.   *Exeunt soldiers*
         [*To* BUCKINGHAM] And let my sovereign, virtuous Henry,
         Command° my eldest son—nay, all my sons—   *Demand*
50   As pledges of my fealty and love.
         I'll send them all as willing as I live.
         Lands, goods, horse, armour, anything I have
         Is his to use, so° Somerset may die.   *provided that*
     BUCKINGHAM   York, I commend this kind° submission.   *natural; proper*
55   We twain will go into his highness' tent.
               Enter KING HENRY *and attendants*
     KING HENRY   Buckingham, doth York intend no harm to us,
         That thus he marcheth with thee arm in arm?
     YORK   In all submission and humility
         York doth present himself unto your highness.
60   KING HENRY   Then what intends these forces thou dost bring?
     YORK   To heave the traitor Somerset from hence,
         And fight against that monstrous rebel Cade,
         Who since I heard to be discomfited.°   *defeated*
               Enter IDEN *with Cade's head*
     IDEN   If one so rude° and of so mean condition°   *uncultivated / low rank*
65   May pass into the presence of a king,
         [*Kneeling*] Lo, I present your grace a traitor's head,
         The head of Cade, whom I in combat slew.
     KING HENRY   The head of Cade? Great God, how just art thou!
         O let me view his visage, being dead,
70   That living wrought me such exceeding trouble.
         Tell me, my friend, art thou the man that slew him?
     IDEN [*rising*]   Iwis,° an't like° your majesty.   *Truly / if it please*
     KING HENRY   How art thou called? And what is thy degree?°   *rank*
     IDEN   Alexander Iden, that's my name;
75   A poor esquire[4] of Kent that loves his king.
     BUCKINGHAM [*to* KING HENRY]   So please it you, my lord, 'twere not amiss
         He were created knight for his good service.
     KING HENRY   Iden, kneel down.
              [IDEN *kneels and* KING HENRY *knights him*]
                  Rise up a knight.
         [IDEN *rises*]
         We give thee for reward a thousand marks,
80   And will° that thou henceforth attend on us.   *command*
     IDEN   May Iden live to merit such a bounty,
         And never live but true unto his liege.   *Exit*
           Enter Queen [MARGARET] *and the Duke of* SOMERSET
     KING HENRY   See, Buckingham, Somerset comes wi'th' Queen.
         Go bid her hide him quickly from the Duke.

---

3. One of the main drill grounds for Elizabethan militia, located south of the Thames.   4. A member of the gentry ranking just below a knight.

85   QUEEN MARGARET   For thousand Yorks he shall not hide his head,
      But boldly stand and front° him to his face.   *confront*
      YORK   How now? Is Somerset at liberty?
      Then, York, unloose thy long imprisoned thoughts,
      And let thy tongue be equal with thy heart.
90   Shall I endure the sight of Somerset?
      False King, why hast thou broken faith with me,
      Knowing how hardly I can brook abuse?⁵
      'King' did I call thee? No, thou art not king;
      Not fit to govern and rule multitudes,
95   Which dar'st not—no, nor canst not—rule a traitor.
      That head of thine doth not become a crown;
      Thy hand is made to grasp a palmer's° staff,   *pilgrim's*
      And not to grace an aweful° princely sceptre.   *awe-inspiring*
      That gold must round engird these brows of mine,
100   Whose smile and frown, like to Achilles' spear,
      Is able with the change to kill and cure.⁶
      Here is a hand to hold a sceptre up,
      And with the same to act° controlling laws.   *enact*
      Give place! By heaven, thou shalt rule no more
105   O'er him whom heaven created for thy ruler.
      SOMERSET   O monstrous traitor! I arrest thee, York,
      Of capital treason 'gainst the King and crown.
      Obey, audacious traitor; kneel for grace.
      YORK [*to an attendant*]   Sirrah, call in my sons to be my bail.
                                       [*Exit attendant*]
110   I know, ere they will have me go to ward,°   *into custody*
      They'll pawn° their swords for my enfranchisement.°   *pledge / freedom*
      QUEEN MARGARET [*to* BUCKINGHAM]   Call hither Clifford; bid
            him come amain,°   *at once*
      To say if that the bastard boys of York
      Shall be the surety for their traitor father.   [*Exit* BUCKINGHAM]
115   YORK   O blood-bespotted Neapolitan,⁷
      Outcast of Naples, England's bloody scourge!
      The sons of York, thy betters in their birth,
      Shall be their father's bail, and bane° to those   *destruction*
      That for my surety will refuse the boys.
          Enter at one door York's sons EDWARD *and crookback*
          RICHARD *with* [*a*] *drum*[*mer*] *and soldiers*⁸
120   See where they come. I'll warrant they'll make it good.
          Enter at the other door CLIFFORD *and his son, with* [*a*]
          drum[*mer*] *and soldiers*
      QUEEN MARGARET   And here comes Clifford to deny their bail.
      CLIFFORD [*kneeling before* KING HENRY]   Health and all happi-
            ness to my lord the King.
            [*He rises*]
      YORK   I thank thee, Clifford. Say, what news with thee?
      Nay, do not fright us with an angry look—

---

5. Knowing with what difficulty I can tolerate deception.
6. Telephus, wounded by Achilles' spear, was cured by rust from that same spear.
7. Margaret's father claimed the throne of Naples. Elizabethan writers typically associated Italy with sexual vice, criminality, and the evils of Roman Catholicism.

8. This spectacular double entry of York's sons, followed by Clifford and his son, each accompanied by drummer and soldiers, is indicated only in Q. F's stage directions read, "Enter Edward and Richard" and "Enter Clifford."

125 We are thy sovereign, Clifford; kneel again.
For thy mistaking so, we pardon thee.
CLIFFORD This is my king, York; I do not mistake.
But thou mistakes me much to think I do.
[*To* KING HENRY] To Bedlam[9] with him! Is the man grown mad?

130 KING HENRY Ay, Clifford, a bedlam° and ambitious humour°   *mad / disposition*
Makes him oppose himself against his king.
CLIFFORD He is a traitor; let him to the Tower,
And chop away that factious pate° of his.   *rebellious head*
QUEEN MARGARET He is arrested, but will not obey.

135 His sons, he says, shall give their words for him.
YORK [*to* EDWARD *and* RICHARD] Will you not, sons?
EDWARD Ay, noble father, if our words will serve.
RICHARD And if words will not, then our weapons shall.
CLIFFORD Why, what a brood of traitors have we here!

140 YORK Look in a glass,° and call thy image so.   *mirror*
I am thy king, and thou a false-heart traitor.
Call hither to the stake my two brave bears,
That with the very shaking of their chains,
They may astonish these fell-lurking° curs.[1]   *savagely waiting*

145 [*To an attendant*] Bid Salisbury and Warwick come to me.
[*Exit attendant*]
Enter the Earls of WARWICK *and* SALISBURY *with* [*a*]
drum[*mer*] *and soldiers*
CLIFFORD Are these thy bears? We'll bait thy bears to death,
And manacle the bearherd° in their chains,   *bear keeper (York)*
If thou dar'st bring them to the baiting place.°   *bear pit*
RICHARD Oft have I seen a hot o'erweening° cur   *overconfident*

150 Run back and bite,° because he was withheld;   (*his keeper*)
Who, being suffered with° the bear's fell° paw,   *injured by / savage*
Hath clapped his tail between his legs and cried;
And such a piece of service will you do,
If you oppose yourselves° to match Lord Warwick.   *undertake*

155 CLIFFORD Hence, heap of wrath, foul indigested lump,
As crooked in thy manners as thy shape![2]
YORK Nay, we shall heat you thoroughly anon.°   *soon*
CLIFFORD Take heed, lest by your heat you burn yourselves.
KING HENRY Why, Warwick, hath thy knee forgot to bow?

160 Old Salisbury, shame to thy silver hair,
Thou mad misleader of thy brainsick son!
What, wilt thou on thy deathbed play the ruffian,
And seek for sorrow with thy spectacles?°   *eyes; eyeglasses*
O, where is faith? O, where is loyalty?

165 If it be banished from the frosty head,
Where shall it find a harbour in the earth?
Wilt thou go dig a grave to find out° war,   *in seeking out*
And shame thine honourable age with blood?

---

9. The shortened name of a London lunatic asylum. See note to 3.1.51.
1. York refers to the Elizabethan sport of bearbaiting, in which a tame bear was chained to a stake and set upon with dogs. Warwick's family crest depicted a bear chained to a staff. See below, lines 200–1.

2. *foul . . . shape:* alluding to the fact that Richard of Gloucester was deformed from birth (he was a hunchback) and to the notion that bears are born as formless lumps and licked into shape by their mothers. *indigested:* ill-formed.

Why, art thou old and want'st° experience?   *lack*
170   Or wherefore dost abuse it if thou hast it?
      For shame in duty bend thy knee to me,
      That bows unto the grave with mickle° age.   *much*
SALISBURY   My lord, I have considered with myself
      The title of this most renownèd Duke,
175   And in my conscience do repute his grace
      The rightful heir to England's royal seat.
KING HENRY   Hast thou not sworn allegiance unto me?
SALISBURY   I have.
KING HENRY   Canst thou dispense with heaven for[3] such an oath?
180   SALISBURY   It is great sin to swear unto a sin,
      But greater sin to keep a sinful oath.
      Who can be bound by any solemn vow
      To do a murd'rous deed, to rob a man,
      To force a spotless virgin's chastity,
185   To reave° the orphan of his patrimony,   *bereave*
      To wring the widow from her customed right,[4]
      And have no other reason for this wrong
      But that he was bound by a solemn oath?
QUEEN MARGARET   A subtle traitor needs no sophister.°   *expert in false reasoning*
KING HENRY [*to an attendant*]   Call Buckingham, and bid him
190   arm himself.   [*Exit attendant*]
YORK [*to* KING HENRY]   Call Buckingham and all the friends thou hast,
      I am resolved for death or dignity.°   *(the crown)*
CLIFFORD   The first, I warrant thee, if dreams prove true.
WARWICK   You were best to go to bed and dream again,
195   To keep you from the tempest of the field.
CLIFFORD   I am resolved to bear a greater storm
      Than any thou canst conjure up today—
      And that I'll write upon thy burgonet°   *helmet*
      Might I but know thee by thy household badge.°   *family crest*
200   WARWICK   Now by my father's badge, old Neville's crest,[5]
      The rampant bear chained to the ragged° staff,   *jagged*
      This day I'll wear aloft° my burgonet,   *on top of*
      As on a mountain top the cedar shows
      That keeps his leaves in spite of any storm,
205   Even to affright thee with the view thereof.
CLIFFORD   And from thy burgonet I'll rend thy bear,
      And tread it under foot with all contempt,
      Despite the bearherd that protects the bear.
YOUNG CLIFFORD   And so to arms, victorious father,
210   To quell the rebels and their complices.°   *accomplices*
RICHARD   Fie, charity, for shame! Speak not in spite—
      For you shall sup with Jesu Christ tonight.
YOUNG CLIFFORD   Foul stigmatic,[6] that's more than thou canst tell.
RICHARD   If not in heaven, you'll surely sup in hell.

                                              Exeunt [*severally*]

---

3. Can you win dispensation from heaven for breaking.
4. Her traditional right to a portion of her husband's estate.
5. The Neville badge was actually a bull. Warwick inherited the badge of a bear from his father-in-law, Richard Beauchamp.
6. One branded with the mark of crime, as Richard is "branded" with deformity.

5.2

[*An alehouse sign: a castle.*] *Alarums to the battle. Then
enter the Duke of* SOMERSET *and* RICHARD *fighting.*
RICHARD *kills* [SOMERSET] *under the sign*

RICHARD   So lie thou there—
  For underneath an alehouse' paltry sign,
  The Castle in Saint Albans, Somerset
  Hath made the wizard famous in his death.[1]
5 Sword, hold thy temper;[2] heart, be wrathfull still—
  Priests pray for enemies, but princes kill.
        Exit [*with Somerset's body. The sign is removed*]

5.3

Alarum again. Enter the Earl of WARWICK

WARWICK   Clifford of Cumberland, 'tis Warwick calls!
  An if thou dost not hide thee from the bear,
  Now, when the angry trumpet sounds alarum,
  And dead° men's cries do fill the empty air,   *dying*
5 Clifford I say, come forth and fight with me!
  Proud northern lord, Clifford of Cumberland,
  Warwick is hoarse with calling thee to arms!
CLIFFORD [*within*]   Warwick, stand still; and stir not till I come.
        Enter [*the Duke of*] YORK
WARWICK   How now, my noble lord? What, all afoot?°   *not on horseback*
10 YORK   The deadly-handed Clifford slew my steed.
  But match to match I have encountered him,
  And made a prey for carrion kites and crows
  Even of the bonny beast he loved so well.
        Enter [*Lord*] CLIFFORD
WARWICK [*to* CLIFFORD]   Of one or both of us the time is come.
15 YORK   Hold, Warwick—seek thee out some other chase,°   *game*
  For I myself must hunt this deer to death.
WARWICK   Then nobly, York; 'tis for a crown thou fight'st.
  [*To* CLIFFORD] As I intend, Clifford, to thrive today,
  It grieves my soul to leave thee unassailed.   *Exit*
20 YORK   Clifford, since we are singled here alone,
  Be this the day of doom to one of us.
  For know my heart hath sworn immortal hate
  To thee and all the house of Lancaster.
CLIFFORD   And here I stand and pitch my foot to thine,
25 Vowing not to stir till thou or I be slain.
  For never shall my heart be safe at rest
  Till I have spoiled° the hateful house of York.   *stripped of honor*
        Alarums. They fight. YORK *kills* CLIFFORD
YORK   Now, Lancaster, sit sure—thy sinews shrink.°   *powers fail*
  Come, fearful° Henry, grovelling on thy face—   *timid*
30 Yield up thy crown unto the prince of York.[1]   *Exit*
30.1   CLIFFORD   *What seest thou in me, York? Why dost thou pause?*
    YORK   *With thy brave bearing° should I be in love,*   *fine appearance*

5.2 Location: Scene continues.
1. Somerset's death under the sign of the Castle Inn
confirms the spirit's warning that he shun castles (see
1.4.34–36). *in his:* by his (Somerset's).
2. Retain the resiliency of steel.

5.3 Location: Scene continues.
1. Oxford adopts Q's version of the confrontation
between Clifford and York at lines 20–30; the F version,
an edited text of which follows in the indented passage
(lines 30.1–30.12), may be the author's original draft.

But that thou art so fast mine enemy.

CLIFFORD   *Nor should thy prowess want° praise and esteem,*   lack

30.5   *But that 'tis shown ignobly and in treason.*

YORK   *So let it help me now against thy sword,*

As I in justice and true right express it.

CLIFFORD   *My soul and body on the action both.*[2]

YORK   *A dreadful lay.° Address° thee instantly.*   wager / Prepare

30.10   CLIFFORD   *La fin couronne les oeuvres.*[3]

Alarums. They fight. YORK *kills* CLIFFORD

YORK   *Thus war hath given thee peace, for thou art still.*

Peace with his soul, heaven, if it be thy will.   *Exit*

Alarums, then enter YOUNG CLIFFORD

YOUNG CLIFFORD   Shame and confusion, all is on the rout!°   in disorderly retreat

Fear frames° disorder, and disorder wounds   gives rise to

Where it should guard. O, war, thou son of hell,

Whom angry heavens do make their minister,

35   Throw in the frozen° bosoms of our part°   cowardly / faction

Hot coals of vengeance! Let no soldier fly!

He that is truly dedicate° to war   dedicated

Hath no self-love; nor he that loves himself

Hath not essentially, but by circumstance,°   merely by accident

The name of valour.

[*He sees his father's body*]

40   O, let the vile world end,

And the premisèd° flames of the last day   foreordained

Knit earth and heaven together.

Now let the general trumpet blow his blast,[4]

Particularities° and petty sounds   Individual affairs

45   To cease! Wast thou ordainèd, dear father,

To lose thy youth in peace, and to achieve

The silver livery of advisèd° age,   wise

And in thy reverence and thy chair-days,° thus   old age

To die in ruffian battle? Even at this sight

50   My heart is turned to stone, and while 'tis mine

It shall be stony. York not our old men spares;

No more will I their babes. Tears virginal

Shall be to me even as the dew to fire,[5]

And beauty that the tyrant oft reclaims°   calms the tyrant

55   Shall to my flaming wrath be oil and flax.

Henceforth I will not have to do with pity.

Meet I an infant of the house of York,

Into as many gobbets° will I cut it   lumps of flesh

As wild Medea young Absyrtus did.[6]

60   In cruelty will I seek out my fame.

Come, thou new ruin of old Clifford's house,

He takes [*his father's body*] *up on his back*

As did Aeneas old Anchises bear,[7]

2. I wager both my soul and body on the outcome of this fight (action).
3. The end crowns the works (French).
4. Young Clifford is evoking doomsday, when a trumpet will summon everyone to judgment (see 1 Corinthians 15:52).
5. Dew was popularly believed to make fire burn more fiercely.

6. According to classical mythology, as Medea fled over the sea with her lover, Jason, she murdered her brother Absyrtus and scattered bits of his body on the waves so that her father would stop to collect the fragments and be delayed in his pursuit of her.
7. In Virgil's *Aeneid* 2.707–29, Aeneas carries his aged father, Anchises, on his back in their escape from the burning city of Troy.

So bear I thee upon my manly shoulders.
But then Aeneas bare a living load,
65 Nothing so heavy as these woes of mine.   [*Exit with the body*]

5.4

*Alarums again. Then enter three or four bearing the
Duke of* BUCKINGHAM *wounded to his tent. Alarums
still. Enter* KING [HENRY], QUEEN [MARGARET], *and
others*

QUEEN MARGARET   Away, my lord! You are slow. For shame, away!
KING HENRY   Can we outrun the heavens?° Good Margaret, stay.   *escape our fate*
QUEEN MARGARET   What are you made of? You'll nor° fight nor fly.   *neither*
Now is it manhood, wisdom, and defence,
5 To give the enemy way, and to secure us°   *save ourselves*
By what° we can, which° can no more but fly.   *whatever means / who*
    Alarum afar off
If you be ta'en, we then should see the bottom
Of all our fortunes; but if we haply scape°—   *by chance escape*
As well we may if not° through your neglect—   *if we don't fail*
10 We shall to London get where you are loved,
And where this breach now in our fortunes made
May readily be stopped.
    Enter [YOUNG] CLIFFORD
YOUNG CLIFFORD [*to* KING HENRY]   But that my heart's on future
    mischief set,
I would speak blasphemy ere° bid you fly;   *before I would*
15 But fly you must; uncurable discomfit°   *irreversible defeat*
Reigns in the hearts of all our present parts.°   *remaining forces*
Away for your relief, and we will live
To see their day and them our fortune give.[1]
Away, my lord, away!   *Exeunt*

5.5

Alarum. Retreat. Enter the Duke of YORK, [*his sons*
EDWARD *and*] RICHARD, *and soldiers,* [*including a*]
drum[*mer*] *and* [*some bearing*] *colours*

YORK [*to* EDWARD *and* RICHARD]   How now, boys! Fortunate this
    fight hath been,
I hope, to us and ours for England's good
And our great honour, that so long we lost
Whilst faint-heart Henry did usurp our rights.
5 Of Salisbury, who can report of him?
That winter° lion who in rage forgets   *aged*
Agèd contusions and all brush of time,[1]
And, like a gallant in the brow° of youth,   *prime*
Repairs° him with occasion.° This happy day   *Revives / action*
10 Is not itself, nor have we won one foot
If Salisbury be lost.
RICHARD   My noble father,

5.4 Location: Scene continues.
1. *we . . . give*: we will survive to see a day of victory like
theirs and to make them suffer misfortunes like ours.

5.5 Location: Scene continues.
1. Bruises of old age and all assaults of time.

Three times today I holp° him to his horse;   helped
Three times bestrid him;[2] thrice I led him off,
Persuaded him from any further act;
15 But still° where danger was, still there I met him,   always
And like rich hangings in a homely° house,   humble
So was his will in his old feeble body.
     Enter [the Earls of] SALISBURY *and* [WARWICK]
EDWARD [*to* YORK] See, noble father, where they both do come—
The only props unto the house of York!
20 SALISBURY Now, by my sword, well hast thou fought today;
By th' mass, so did we all. I thank you, Richard.
God knows how long it is I have to live,
And it hath pleased him that three times today
You have defended me from imminent death.
25 Well, lords, we have not got that which we have[3]—
'Tis not enough our foes are this time fled,
Being opposites of such repairing nature.[4]
YORK I know our safety is to follow them,
For, as I hear, the King is fled to London,
30 To call a present court of Parliament.
Let us pursue him ere the writs° go forth.   summons to Parliament
What says Lord Warwick, shall we after them?
WARWICK After them? Nay, before them if we can!
Now by my hand, lords, 'twas a glorious day!
35 Saint Albans battle won by famous York
Shall be eternized° in all age to come.   immortalized
Sound drums and trumpets, and to London all,
And more such days as these to us befall! [*Flourish.*] *Exeunt*

---

2. Stood over the fallen Salisbury to protect him.
3. We have not secured what we have won.

4. Since they are enemies who can quickly recover
what they have lost.

Richard Duke of York
(3 Henry VI)

There are two Richards in the play known in its octavo version as *The True Tragedy of Richard Duke of York and the Good King Henry the Sixth* (3 Henry VI). As the play begins, the title character, Richard of York, is leading an attempt to seize the English throne from Henry VI, the Lancastrian King. This Richard is killed at the end of the first act, and it is his tragic death to which the play's title refers. He, however, has four sons: Edward, Edmund (known as the Earl of Rutland), George, and Richard. This second Richard, who eventually acquires the title Duke of Gloucester, is a hunchback; and much of the play chronicles his attempts to continue his father's efforts to seize the English throne. Near the end of the play, this second Richard meditates on his condition:

> Then, since the heavens have shaped my body so,
> Let hell make crooked my mind to answer it.
> I had no father, I am like no father;
> I have no brother, I am like no brother;
> And this word, 'love', which greybeards call divine,
> Be resident in other men like one another
> And not in me—I am myself alone.
>
> (5.6.78–84)

This chilling pronouncement places Richard outside kinship networks, even though his two older brothers, Edward and George, are very much alive; and it exempts him from ordinary bonds of human affection.

Claiming to know nothing of love, Richard blames his isolation on his deformity. He is not "like" other men, not like his brothers, because heaven has shaped his body crookedly. This is a convenient explanation for villainy and alienation. But the play's exploration of deformity and its relationship to the breakdown of social order and emotional bonds is more complex than Richard here allows. Is Richard's hunchback the cause of his villainy or merely its outward sign? Are his villainy and deformity unique or simply the most tangible manifestation of a social deformity that reaches far beyond this single character? Richard's hump invites such questions, but the answers must be sought by broadly surveying the dramatic world in which Richard is placed.

Richard Duke of York is one of the most ambitious of Shakespeare's history plays simply in terms of the historical matter it covers. It is in part a continuation of *The First Part of the Contention of the Two Famous Houses of York and Lancaster* (2 Henry VI), the play in which Shakespeare began to dramatize the Wars of the Roses between the Lancastrian descendants of Edward III, who took the red rose for their symbol, and his Yorkist descendants, who claimed the white. In the struggles between these two branches of the family, the Yorkists asserted that Henry VI's grandfather, Henry IV, had illegitimately usurped the throne from Richard II, the son of Edward III's oldest male offspring, Edward, the Black Prince. Even though the Lancastrians could claim the throne through John of Gaunt, Edward III's fourth son, the Yorkists felt that they had a superior claim as descendants of the third son, Lionel, Duke of Clarence, and his daughter Philippa. In *Richard Duke of York*, Shakespeare depicts many of the most significant military encounters stemming from the struggle between the two branches of the family, stretching from the Battle of Wakefield (1460), in which the Duke of York

317

was captured and killed by the Lancastrian forces of Henry VI, to the Battle of Tewkesbury in 1471, in which Edward, the eldest son of Richard Duke of York, decisively defeated the Lancastrian army. It is after the latter battle, and Richard Duke of Gloucester's subsequent murder of Henry VI in the Tower of London, that the hunchbacked Richard speaks his chilling lines about having no father and no brother.

As with all his history plays, Shakespeare's *Richard Duke of York* takes many liberties with its historical sources, in this case Raphael Holinshed's *Chronicles of England, Scotland, and Ireland* (1587 edition) and Edward Hall's *Union of the Two Noble and Illustre [Illustrious] Famelies of Lancastre & Yorke* (1548). Many historical events are simply omitted or conflated with other events, and aspects of the historical record are altered for dramatic or thematic purposes. For example, at the time of the Battle of Wakefield, at which Richard Duke of York was killed, his son Richard was only seven years old. But in Shakespeare's play, he is a grown man who himself participates in the battle and after it vows revenge for his father's death. Moreover, that death is handled with grim originality. In Hall, Clifford decapitates York, then puts a paper crown on his severed head and presents it on a pole to Margaret, Henry VI's warlike queen. In Holinshed, Clifford verbally torments York before beheading him. But in none of the sources does Margaret dominate the scene as she does in Shakespeare's play. In *Richard Duke of York*, she taunts York ferociously and—a detail found in none of the sources—to wipe his tears gives him a handkerchief that has been dipped in the blood of Rutland, York's twelve-year-old son, who had been butchered by Clifford earlier in the same battle. Eventually both Margaret and Clifford stab York, and Margaret orders his head displayed on the gates of the city of York. This act is typical of Margaret's audacity throughout the play. The only character to appear in all four of Shakespeare's first histories (*The First Part of the Contention [2 Henry VI]*, *Richard Duke of York [3 Henry VI]*, *1 Henry VI*, and *Richard III*), Margaret dominates much of the action of this one. Fiercely protective of her son's rights and skilled as both general and diplomat, she is unmatched as a publicly powerful figure by any of the female characters in Shakespeare's later histories.

The scene in which Margaret tortures York and he excoriates her as an Amazonian whore must have been riveting theater. In September of 1592, Robert Greene, a rival playwright, published *Greene's Groats-worth of Wit*, in which he makes fun of Shakespeare by parodying a line from this scene. Richard at one point exclaims of Margaret, "O tiger's heart wrapped in a woman's hide!" (1.4.138). Greene writes of Shakespeare that "there is an upstart Crow, beautified with our feathers, that with his *Tiger's heart wrapt in a Player's hide*, supposes he is as well able to bombast out a blank verse as the best of you: and being an absolute *Johannes fac totum* [jack-of-all-trades], is in his own conceit the onely Shakes-scene in a country." Greene, who had a university education, clearly resented Shakespeare, who did not but who was

Seventeenth-century ornamental halberd from southern Germany.

nonetheless having considerable theatrical success. Greene accuses Shakespeare either of appropriating his work or of acting in his dramas ("beautified with our feathers") and of thinking too well of himself and his many theatrical skills. Particularly striking is Greene's own appropriation of Richard's line about Margaret to apply to Shakespeare. Implicitly, Greene suggests that there is something as unnatural and presumptuous in Shakespeare's theatrical ambition as in the cruelty and ambition of Henry's manlike Queen. At the same time, this appropriative gesture pays tribute, however grudging, to Shakespeare's skill as a writer of memorable dialogue. Affronted by Shakespeare's success, Greene nonetheless grants his rival the homage of parody. The lines have another value as well. Although *Richard Duke of York* was first printed in a shortened octavo version in 1595, Greene's comments suggest that some version of the play had been staged or was circulating in manuscript by late summer of 1592 (see Textual Note).

This early play, then, may have brought Shakespeare contemporary notoriety. It certainly shows his boldness in adopting chronicle history to fit the requirements of the theater. And while some critics have seen *Richard Duke of York* as flawed, evidencing Shakespeare's weariness with his dramatization of the Wars of the Roses or his inability to shape so much matter into coherent form, theatrical productions of this play attest to its viability on the stage. The vicious energies of hate and ambition that propel the play make its enactment an intense and exhausting experience. The vigorous stage battles, the soaring rhetorical duels between the contending factions, the centrality of the ruthless Margaret, the emergence of the alienated Richard, Duke of Gloucester as the brooding antihero—these are elements that, particularly in the post–World War II period, have led to many memorable productions, productions that emphasize a once-civil world spiraling vertiginously toward chaos.

But the play is also more than the sum of its memorable parts. When Richard asserts, "I am myself alone," his chosen isolation follows from the play's carefully orchestrated dramatization of the breakdown of social order, particularly as epitomized in the breakdown of family ties. From its inception, the Wars of the Roses, a continuing civil war, was also a family feud in that it pitted the Lancastrian and Yorkist descendants of Edward III against one another. But in the prior play, *The First Part of the Contention,* members of each family line and their followers typically remained loyal to their faction. Family lineage was a source of pride and identity. One sees this also in *1 Henry VI* in the idealized relationship between the English hero Lord Talbot and his son John. John aspires in all respects to emulate his father, and the two of them die together in battle defending England and the honor of their family name. In *Richard Duke of York,* by contrast, family bonds are hideously fragile; and when they break, chaos ensues. Unflinching in its depiction of emotional and physical violence, the play examines the forms of monstrous individualism that emerge when the social identities provided by networks of kinship and feudal loyalty no longer exert their hold. In effect, *Richard Duke of York* depicts the radical separation of self from defining social networks as a species of monstrosity.

The signal event in the play's treatment of the sundering of family bonds is King Henry's startling offer, at the beginning of Act 1, to entail the crown to Richard, Duke of York in exchange for Henry's right to hold the throne during his lifetime. Henry has a son, Prince Edward, and his act negates his son's right to the throne. It also transforms the crown of England from a symbol of lineal succession into an alienable property. The immediate consequence is that Henry's supporters turn from him in disgust and his wife, Queen Margaret, proclaims:

> I here divorce myself
> Both from thy table, Henry, and thy bed,
> Until that act of Parliament be repealed
> Whereby my son is disinherited.

> (1.1.248–51)

Suddenly, Edward is *her* son, not Henry's; and soon thereafter she is raising an army to lead against the Yorkists. Many in the play describe Margaret's acts as unnatural, yet they

Edward IV (1442–1483). Probably painted during his reign; artist unknown.

follow from Henry's feckless negation of his role as guarantor of his son's succession. It was a truism of the early modern gender system that unmanly men, unnatural in their weakness, opened the door to a corresponding anomaly, the manlike woman. Margaret is represented as such a figure, taking Henry's place both at the head of his army and also as champion of young Edward's lineal rights. In both roles, the Queen is highly effective for much of the play. Though demonized, Margaret embodies strengths that contradict the patriarchal view that women are inherently weaker than men and therefore less suited to have dominion either in the state or in the household.

Occasionally, especially in his early plays, Shakespeare wrote what Hereward T. Price called "mirror scenes," that is, scenes that are separate from the main line of plot development but that symbolically encapsulate, or mirror, some of the play's chief thematic concerns. In *Richard Duke of York,* 2.5 is such a scene. Having given command of his army to Clifford and Margaret, Henry sits contemplatively upon a molehill while the Battle of Towton proceeds without him. Voicing his longing for the simplicity of a pastoral life, Henry suddenly sees a soldier carry onstage a man he has killed. It turns out to be the soldier's father, who was forced to serve with the Yorkist forces, while the son had been impressed into King Henry's service. The King then observes a second soldier carry onstage a man *he* has killed. It turns out to be the soldier's son. The scene schematically underscores one of the play's primary emblems of social disintegration: namely, the severing of bonds between father and son, son and father, leaving nothing to replace these bonds but individual rapaciousness. In both instances, the killers of the dead men have brought the bodies onstage to search them for money—"some store of crowns" (2.5.57) and "gold" (80). The ironic power of the scene is heightened, of course, because its central events are witnessed and lamented by King Henry, who has already disinherited his own son and as King is the symbolic fountainhead from which the familial disorder before him flows.

But the most interesting variation on the theme of disseevered families is embodied in the persons of Richard, Duke of York and his four sons: Edward, George, Richard, and Rutland. At the beginning of the play, the Yorks constitute an unusually integrated unit. Richard's sons support their father and urge him to seize the crown. Before he is captured at the Battle of Wakefield, Richard praises his offspring, assuming that in the battle "they have demeaned themselves / Like men born to renown by life or death" (1.4.7–8). At Wakefield, one of Richard's sons, the young Rutland, is killed. Just before the remaining three sons learn that their father has also died as a consequence of that battle, they praise him, as he has praised them. No one is more gracious than young Richard, who says, "Methinks 'tis prize enough to be his son" (2.1.20). At that moment, three suns appear in the heavens, each distinct, and then these suns join together.

The pun on "suns/sons" seems to lead Edward to interpret this odd spectacle to mean that the three sons of Richard,

> Each one already blazing by our meeds,
> Should notwithstanding join our lights together
> And over-shine the earth as this the world.
>
> (2.1.36–38)

He then pledges to have three suns emblazoned on his shield.

Like all portents, the exact significance of this one is unclear. To Edward, it seems to imply the unwavering unity of the three sons of York. Yet Richard, who is to be as devastated as any of them by the news of their father's death, treats Edward's assertion that he will wear three suns on his shields as the occasion for a joke that distances him from his brother. "Nay, bear three daughters—by your leave I speak it— / You love the breeder better than the male" (2.1.41–42). With the death of the powerful patriarch, Richard, Duke of York, fraternal rivalry quickly replaces fraternal unity, and broken allegiances multiply. When Edward insists on marrying a commoner, the widow Lady Elizabeth Gray, War-

"My ashes, as the phoenix, may bring forth / A bird that will revenge upon you all" (1.4.36–37). From Geffrey Whitney, *A Choice of Emblemes* (1586).

wick, who is Edward's strongest supporter and who has been sent to France to secure a French bride for Edward, turns against him in disgust. George temporarily abandons his brother, marries Warwick's daughter, and joins the Lancastrian cause. Richard, always outwardly loyal, privately vows to hack his way to the throne and displace both of his brothers in the process.

With ties of kinship and loyalty broken, nothing remains but the sheer exertion of individual will. Richard emerges as both the most fascinating and the most horrific character in the second half of the play because his will is indomitable and his desires unchecked by any moral constraints. The audience probably registers this fact most decisively during the bravura soliloquy that Richard speaks after he and George have watched—and obscenely commented upon—Edward's wooing of Lady Gray. Soliloquies, in which a character speaks to himself but is overheard by the theater audience, help create the illusion of interiority and inner subjectivity. Perhaps goaded by jealousy at the sight of Edward's successful wooing of Lady Gray, Richard in his soliloquy both reveals his frustrations and desires and hardheadedly maps a future course. In quick succession, he contemplates the number of people who before him have claims on the throne; resigns himself to seek instead the pleasures of courtship and love; despairs, since his deformed body prevents him from being loved; resolves therefore to seek the crown at any cost; and vows to change himself into any imaginable persona necessary to achieve his end. The soliloquy is long (3.2.124–95) and relentless. Richard tracks his argument like a bloodhound, registering his predicament with memorably vivid language.

> And yet I know not how to get the crown,
> For many lives stand between me and home.
> And I—like one lost in a thorny wood,

> That rends the thorns and is rent with the thorns,
> Seeking a way and straying from the way,
> Not knowing how to find the open air,
> But toiling desperately to find it out—
> Torment myself to catch the English crown.
>   (3.2.172–79)

Struggle and frustration are evident in the repetitions of this passage. Seeking, straying, toiling, Richard is in constant motion, throwing himself against impossible barriers. The crown eludes him, yet he goes on. He is by turns attractive and frightening.

Many prototypes are drawn upon to create this distinctive character. His "individuality" does not emerge from nowhere but depends on Shakespeare's skillful appropriation of prior dramatic resources. Richard's characterization owes much, for example, to the striving, overreaching stage heroes created by Shakespeare's early rival Christopher Marlowe. Like Marlowe's Tamburlaine, Richard makes his heaven "to dream upon the crown" (3.2.168) and stops at nothing to achieve that goal. In part, he is also fashioned after the Vice figure from the medieval religious drama. The Vice was the character—often witty and quite disconcertingly entertaining—who embodied the principle of evil and tried to compel others to sin. Richard's witty asides, as much as his aggression and lack of scruple, reveal his kinship to the Vice. Perhaps this character's strongest association, however, is with the figure of the stage Machiavel, whom Richard himself evokes at the end of his soliloquy. The historical Niccolò Machiavelli was an Italian political philosopher whose influential book *The Prince* pragmatically rather than moralistically detailed the tactics and principles that made for successful government in the modern world. In the popular imagination, he came to stand for the hypocrisy and political cunning associated with Protestant England's symbolic enemy, Catholic Italy.

Sharing affinities with each of these figures but not fully modeled on any of them, Richard functions in Shakespeare's play to suggest what emerges when one no longer acknowledges the primacy of the identities constructed by the words "son" and "brother." In a society that defined people in terms of their place within family structures and social hierarchies, to separate oneself from those structures and hierarchies risked being read as monstrous and unnatural. Richard is riveting precisely because he seems so autonomous and so indifferent to the bonds and loyalties—to family and to king—that supposedly hold his society together and constrain the actions of its members. Though not the only one in the play whose ambition corrodes ties of blood and allegiance, Richard most fully epitomizes ambition's deforming effects. One way to read Richard's crooked back is as a physical sign of his unnatural inner being. Yet it is also true that to Richard his crooked body is the cause of (or at least the excuse for) his behavior. In modern psychological terms, he is compensating for a handicap in the only way he can. But it is a measure of Shakespeare's distance from us that such a reading of Richard's deformity is countered by another that emphasizes the moral significance of physical signs and is deeply ambivalent about the very idea of the socially autonomous individual.

Marriage is one way to incorporate individuals into social structures, but in *Richard Duke of York* the breakdown of social bonds is both caused and symbolized by its disorderly marriages. In the feudal world depicted in most of Shakespeare's early history plays, marriages in noble or monarchical families were primarily premised not on love but on dynastic convenience. Wives were to be chosen for the dowry or the territory or the alliances they brought with them. To marry for love was viewed as dangerous because it introduced irrational passion into what was supposed to be a rational choice and threatened the husband's control of himself and of his spouse. In marrying the widow Lady Gray, Edward makes such a passion-driven marriage and thereby nearly loses control of the kingdom. By his actions, he forfeits Warwick's loyalty and temporarily that of his brother George. King Henry had also made an irrational match in marrying the dowerless Margaret (see *The First Part of the Contention* 1.1). In *Richard Duke of York,* this initial lack of control finds its consequence in Henry's inability to govern Margaret and in the increasingly topsy-turvy nature of their marriage.

The end of the play, however, refocuses on the marriage of Edward and Lady Gray to bring a tenuous and highly ironized sense of resolution to the play's action. In the final scene, King Edward admires the son to which his wife, now Queen Elizabeth, has given birth and invites his brothers Richard and Clarence to do the same. The ambience is domestic in a modern way. This is a marriage of affection more than utility. Edward calls the babe "Ned" (5.7.16) and his wife "Bess" (15), the nicknames suggesting intimacy. But if Edward thinks this cozy domesticity, so pleasing to him but so politically ill advised, can reestablish the Yorkist dynasty and center it on him and his descendants, the presence of Richard signals otherwise. Leaning down to kiss the babe, Richard says, "And that I love the tree from whence thou sprang'st, / Witness the loving kiss I give the fruit" (31–32). The tree he refers to is, of course, the family of York, the family tree from which he himself springs. But then, in an aside, he adds: "To say the truth, so Judas kissed his master, / And cried 'All hail!' whenas he meant all harm" (33–34). For Richard to cast himself as the betrayer of Christ bodes badly for the happy family: Edward, Ned, and Bess. To late twentieth-century audiences and theatergoers, the King's doting attention to his wife and son may make him seem quite modern and quite human. Yet viewed historically and in its dramatic context, the King's behavior also signals his weakness, his propensity to let his affections overrule his reason. Fixated on his Ned and his Bess, he seems oblivious to the threat posed by his alienated, thoroughly undomestic brother.

Richard Duke of York ends, then, with a scene that underscores the tenuousness of Edward's purchase on power and threatens a renewal of civil war and family strife. The play's imaginative landscape is dominated by those willful, monstrous individuals such as Richard and Margaret who thrive amid the chaos of a disintegrating society. Few can oppose them, most especially not "the good King Henry," a man disastrously unsuited to play a monarch's part. Hovering on the periphery of this play's action and killed before its final scene, Henry is gradually transformed into a mere observer of the public world around him. Saintly and detached, he comes to represent the antithesis of Richard's surging, self-centered ambition, finally serving almost as choric commentator and as prophet. He predicts, for example, that Henry, Earl of Richmond (later Henry VII) will be England's savior (4.7.68–76), and he predicts (5.6.37–43) that many will come to curse the hunchbacked Richard (later Richard III). But hope for release from Richard's evil lies far in the future, and Henry's increasing saintliness neither erases his responsibility for civil war nor solves the immediate problem of secular rule. Neither saints nor monsters are particularly suited to govern other men. Edward is neither and so seems more fit to rule; yet he is unable to control, or even to recognize, his brother's villainy. *Richard Duke of York* feels so grim because its compelling depiction of the unraveling of England's social fabric suggests little about how that fabric can once again be rewoven.

JEAN E. HOWARD

TEXTUAL NOTE

In 1595, *The True Tragedy of Richard Duke of York and the Good King Henry the Sixth* was published in an octavo volume, and the same text appeared in quarto format in 1600. In 1602, control of the play fell to Thomas Pavier, who in 1619 issued another, edited, quarto version. Both of these quartos are based on the Octavo of 1595 (O) and have no independent textual authority. In 1623, a play approximately one thousand lines longer than any of these early texts appeared in Shakespeare's First Folio (F) under the title *The third part of Henry the Sixt*. While some scholars believe that the 1595 Octavo text is an early draft of the play included in the First Folio, the Oxford editors follow the majority of editors since the 1920s in assuming that the Octavo is a memorial reconstruction of an abridged and revised version of the Folio text. (For a discussion of theories of memorial reconstruction, see the Textual Note to *The First Part of the Contention [2 Henry VI].*) Consequently, the control text for *Richard Duke of York* is F, though the Oxford editors have retained the title used in the Octavo text on the theory that that was the title by which the play was probably known during Shakespeare's lifetime. They assume that the manuscript used for setting the Folio copy was the author's "foul papers," which had not been marked up for theatrical performance, because F contains a number of vague and unspecific stage directions as well as a high proportion of musical cues. Interestingly, several speeches bear actor's names (Gabriel, Sinklo, Humfrey) rather than characters' (Messenger [1.2.49] and First Gamekeeper and Second Gamekeeper [3.1]). The Octavo text, however, is believed to have been based on the promptbook for a theatrical production and contains important stage directions and perhaps some authorial revisions that occurred between the play's foul-papers stage and the promptbook. In some cases, when Octavo staging seems preferable to that suggested in F, this edition has rearranged dialogue or speech assignments to accord with such staging. These changes are marked in the notes and Textual Variants.

The Oxford text employs the standard act and scene divisions into which the play was divided in the eighteenth century, with two exceptions. A new scene is marked at 4.3.27, indicating that the stage is cleared between the time Edward's guards fly from his tent and Edward is subsequently brought onstage as a captive. And at the very end of Act 4, Scene 10 is introduced to separate Henry's conversation with Warwick about Edward's return from the Low Countries from his subsequent conversation with Exeter before he is surprised and seized by Edward and Richard, Duke of Gloucester.

SELECTED BIBLIOGRAPHY

Bergeron, David. "The Play-Within-the-Play in 3 *Henry VI*." *Tennessee Studies in Literature* 22 (1977): 37–47. Examines four instances of Shakespeare's early use of the play within the play in 3 *Henry VI*.

Berman, Ronald. "Fathers and Sons in the *Henry VI* Plays." *Shakespeare Quarterly* 13 (1962): 487–97. Explores the disruption of relations between fathers and sons, kings and subjects under conditions of war and unstable monarchy.

Carroll, D. Allen. "Greene's 'Upstart Crow' Passage: A Survey of Commentary." *Research Opportunities in Renaissance Drama* 28 (1985): 111–27. Explores the possible meanings of Robert Greene's attack on Shakespeare as an "upstart Crow," a phrase used in Shakespeare's play to describe Queen Margaret.

Champion, Larry. "Developmental Structure in Shakespeare's Early Histories: The Perspective of 3 *Henry VI*." *Studies in Philology* 76 (1979): 218–38. Argues that the play reveals Shakespeare's increasing technical sophistication and mastery of dramatic structure.

Hunt, Maurice. "Unnaturalness in Shakespeare's 3 *Henry VI*." *English Studies: A Journal of English Language and Literature* 80 (1999): 146–67. Links Shakespeare's play to Thomas Sackville and Thomas Norton's earlier tragedy, *Gorboduc*, as each explores the motif of unnatural behavior and its political consequences.

Kahn, Coppélia. " 'The Shadow of the Male': Masculine Identity in the History Plays." *Man's Estate: Masculine Identity in Shakespeare*. Berkeley: University of California Press, 1981. 47–81. Argues that in the early history plays masculine identity emerges primarily from emulation of or rivalry with the father.

Leggatt, Alexander. "Henry VI." *Shakespeare's Political Drama: The History Plays and the Roman Plays*. London: Routledge, 1988. 1–31. Explores the undermining of heroism and the breakdown of social order in the three plays featuring Henry VI.

Levine, Nina S. "Ruling Women and the Politics of Gender in 2 and 3 *Henry VI.*" *Women's Matters: Politics, Gender, and Nation in Shakespeare's Early History Plays.* Newark: University of Delaware Press, 1998. 68–96. Argues that in 3 *Henry VI* the misogyny surrounding Margaret's representation is tempered by her role in fighting for her son's succession to the throne and her defense of the English national interest.

Loehlin, James N. "Brecht and the Rediscovery of 1 *Henry VI.*" *Shakespeare's History Plays: Performance, Translation and Adaptation in Britain and Abroad.* Ed. Ton Hoenselaars. Cambridge: Cambridge University Press, 2004. 133–50. Examines the role of Bertolt Brecht's dramatic theory on the resurgence of interest in performing the Henry VI plays after 1960.

Williamson, Marilyn L. " 'When Men Are Rul'd by Women': Shakespeare's First Tetralogy." *Shakespeare Studies* 19 (1987): 41–59. Explores how strong female characters such as Margaret become scapegoats for the chaos of civil war.

FILM

The Tragedy of Richard the Third. 1983. Dir. Jane Howell. UK/USA. 112 min. A BBC-TV production with Julia Foster as Margaret and Peter Benson as a bookish and ineffectual Henry VI. (Released as *Richard III* in the United Kingdom.)

The True Tragedy of Richard Duke of York and the Good King Henry the Sixth

THE PERSONS OF THE PLAY

Of the King's Party

KING HENRY VI
QUEEN MARGARET
PRINCE EDWARD, their son
Duke of SOMERSET
Duke of EXETER
Earl of NORTHUMBERLAND
Earl of WESTMORLAND
Lord CLIFFORD
Lord Stafford
SOMERVILLE
Henry, young Earl of Richmond
A SOLDIER who has killed his father
A HUNTSMAN who guards King Edward

The Divided House of Neville

Earl of WARWICK, first of York's party, later of Lancaster's
Marquis of MONTAGUE, his brother, of York's party
Earl of OXFORD, their brother-in-law, of Lancaster's party
Lord HASTINGS, their brother-in-law, of York's party

Of the Duke of York's Party

Richard Plantagenet, Duke of YORK
EDWARD, Earl of March, his son, later Duke of York and KING EDWARD IV
LADY GRAY, a widow, later Edward's wife and queen
Earl RIVERS, her brother
GEORGE, Edward's brother, later Duke OF CLARENCE
RICHARD, Edward's brother, later Duke OF GLOUCESTER
Earl of RUTLAND, Edward's brother
Rutland's TUTOR, a chaplain
SIR JOHN Mortimer, York's uncle
Sir Hugh Mortimer, his brother
Duke of NORFOLK
Sir William Stanley
Earl of Pembroke
Sir John MONTGOMERY
A NOBLEMAN
Two GAMEKEEPERS
Three WATCHMEN, who guard King Edward's tent
LIEUTENANT of the Tower

The French

KING LOUIS
LADY BONA, his sister-in-law
Lord Bourbon, the French High Admiral

Others

A SOLDIER who has killed his son
A SECOND SOLDIER who has killed his father
Mayor of Coventry
MAYOR of York
Aldermen of York
Soldiers, messengers, and attendants

1.1

[*A chair of state.*][1] *Alarum.° Enter Richard Plantagenet,*   Call to arms
Duke of YORK, [*his two sons*] EDWARD, *Earl of March,*
[*and*] *Crookback°* RICHARD, *the Duke of* NORFOLK,   hunchback
[*the*] *Marquis* [*of*] MONTAGUE, [*and*] *the Earl of*
WARWICK, *with drum*[*mers*] *and soldiers.* [*They all*
wear] *white roses*[2] *in their hats*

WARWICK   I wonder how the King escaped our hands?
YORK   While we pursued the horsemen of the north,
He slyly stole away and left his men;
Whereat the great lord of Northumberland,
5   Whose warlike ears could never brook retreat,[3]
Cheered up the drooping army; and himself,
Lord Clifford, and Lord Stafford, all abreast,
Charged our main battle's° front, and, breaking in,   army's
Were by the swords of common soldiers slain.[4]
10   EDWARD   Lord Stafford's father, Duke of Buckingham,
Is either slain or wounded dangerous.°   dangerously
I cleft his beaver° with a downright° blow.   helmet visor / vertical
That this is true, father, behold his blood.
        [*He shows a bloody sword*]
MONTAGUE [*to* YORK]   And, brother,[5] here's the Earl of Wiltshire's blood,
        [*He shows a bloody sword*]
15   Whom I encountered as the battles joined.
RICHARD [*to Somerset's head, which he shows*]
Speak thou for me, and tell them what I did.
YORK   Richard hath best deserved of all my sons.
[*To the head*] But is your grace dead, my lord of Somerset?

1.1 Location: The Parliament House, London.
1. Although neither O nor F indicates a chair or a raised platform ("a state"), Warwick's lines at 22–27, King Henry's at 50–51, and the stage direction at 32 ("They go up") all suggest that both stage properties are required here. Since the play focuses on the struggle for the English throne, it is fitting that it open with a vacant chair of state.
2. Emblem of the Yorkists. This play depicts part of what is called the Wars of the Roses between the Yorkists, who wore the white rose, and the Lancastrians, who wore the red rose. For Shakespeare's dramatization of the origin of this convention, see *1 Henry VI* 2.4. In O, when the Lancastrian faction enters at line 49, below,

they wear red roses. Both here and at line 49, F's stage directions make no mention of roses. O concludes this direction "with Drum and Soldiers, with white Roses in their hats," leaving ambiguous whether the roses are worn by the soldiers alone or by the entire party.
3. Could never endure hearing the trumpet call signaling retreat.
4. Shakespeare names York (rather than a common soldier) as the person who killed Clifford at several points later in the play. *The First Part of the Contention* (2 *Henry VI*) dramatizes this death in 5.3.
5. The historical Montague was York's nephew. He was also, as Shakespeare suggests elsewhere in this play, Warwick's brother.

NORFOLK   Such hap have all the line of John of Gaunt.[6]

20   RICHARD   Thus do I hope to shake King Henry's head.
    [*He holds aloft the head, then throws it down*]

WARWICK   And so do I, victorious prince of York.
    Before I see thee seated in that throne
    Which now the house of Lancaster usurps,
    I vow by heaven these eyes shall never close.

25   This is the palace of the fearful° King,   frightened
    And this [*pointing to the chair of state*], the regal seat—possess it, York,
    For this is thine, and not King Henry's heirs'.

YORK   Assist me then, sweet Warwick, and I will,
    For hither we have broken in by force.

30   NORFOLK   We'll all assist you—he that flies shall die.

YORK   Thanks, gentle° Norfolk. Stay by me, my lords   noble
    And soldiers—stay, and lodge by me this night.
    They go up [*upon the state*]

WARWICK   And when the King comes, offer him no violence
    Unless he seek to thrust you out perforce.°   by force
    [*The soldiers withdraw*][7]

35   YORK   The Queen this day here holds her Parliament,
    But little thinks we shall be of her council;
    By words or blows here let us win our right.

RICHARD   Armed as we are, let's stay within this house.

WARWICK   'The Bloody Parliament' shall this be called,

40   Unless Plantagenet, Duke of York, be king,
    And bashful Henry deposed, whose cowardice
    Hath made us bywords° to our enemies.   objects of scorn

YORK   Then leave me not, my lords. Be resolute—
    I mean to take possession of my right.

45   WARWICK   Neither the King nor he that loves him best—
    The proudest he that holds up° Lancaster—   supports
    Dares stir a wing if Warwick shake his bells.[8]
    I'll plant Plantagenet,[9] root him up who dares.
    Resolve thee, Richard—claim the English crown.
    [YORK *sits in the chair.*]
    Flourish.° *Enter* KING HENRY, [*Lord*] CLIFFORD,   Trumpet fanfare
    the Earl of NORTHUMBERLAND, *the Earl of*
    WESTMORLAND, *the Duke of* EXETER, *and the rest.*
    [*They all wear*] *red roses in their hats*

50   KING HENRY   My lords, look where the sturdy° rebel sits—   stubborn
    Even in the chair of state! Belike he means,
    Backed by the power of Warwick, that false peer,
    To aspire unto the crown and reign as king.
    Earl of Northumberland, he slew thy father—

---

6. **May all the descendants of John of Gaunt have the same fate.** John of Gaunt held the title Duke of Lancaster; Somerset was his grandson, and Henry VI his great-grandson. The Yorkists contended that John of Gaunt's son Henry IV had usurped Richard II's crown.
7. Neither F nor O indicates when the soldiers leave the stage, but we can assume that they do leave since they are given a reentrance at line 170.

8. **If Warwick makes a move.** Elizabethans attached bells to the legs of falcons in order to further frighten the falcon's prey; Warwick is comparing himself to such a threatening bird.
9. **Richard, Duke of York was also called Richard Plantagenet.** The Plantagenets were the medieval dynasty that began to rule England in 1154, when Henry II assumed the throne. The Yorkist and Lancastrian families were both descended from this dynasty.

55   And thine, Lord Clifford—and you both have vowed revenge
      On him, his sons, his favourites, and his friends.
NORTHUMBERLAND   If I be not, heavens be revenged on me.
CLIFFORD   The hope thereof makes Clifford mourn in steel.¹
WESTMORLAND   What, shall we suffer this? Let's pluck him down.
60   My heart for anger burns—I cannot brook it.
KING HENRY   Be patient, gentle Earl of Westmorland.
CLIFFORD   Patience is for poltroons,° such as he [indicating YORK].   cowards
      He durst not sit there had your father lived.
      My gracious lord, here in the Parliament
65   Let us assail the family of York.
NORTHUMBERLAND   Well hast thou spoken, cousin,° be it so.   kinsman
KING HENRY   Ah, know you not the city° favours them,   (London)
      And they have troops of soldiers at their beck?°   absolute command
EXETER   But when the Duke is slain, they'll quickly fly.
70 KING HENRY   Far be the thought of this from Henry's heart,
      To make a shambles° of the Parliament House.   slaughterhouse
      Cousin of Exeter, frowns, words, and threats
      Shall be the war that Henry means to use.
      [To YORK] Thou factious° Duke of York, descend my throne   rebellious
75   And kneel for grace and mercy at my feet.
      I am thy sovereign.
YORK   I am thine.
EXETER   For shame, come down—he made thee Duke of York.
YORK   It was mine inheritance, as the earldom² was.
EXETER   Thy father was a traitor to the crown.³
80 WARWICK   Exeter, thou art a traitor to the crown
      In following this usurping Henry.
CLIFFORD   Whom should he follow but his natural king?
WARWICK   True, Clifford, and that's Richard Duke of York.
KING HENRY [to YORK]   And shall I stand and thou sit in my throne?
85 YORK   It must and shall be so—content thyself.
WARWICK [to KING HENRY]   Be Duke of Lancaster, let him be king.
WESTMORLAND   He is both king and Duke of Lancaster—
      And that, the Lord of Westmorland shall maintain.
WARWICK   And Warwick shall disprove it. You forget
90   That we are those which chased you from the field,
      And slew your fathers, and, with colours° spread,   flags
      Marched through the city to the palace gates.
NORTHUMBERLAND   Yes, Warwick, I remember it to my grief,
      And, by his soul, thou and thy house shall rue it.
95 WESTMORLAND [to YORK]   Plantagenet, of thee, and these thy sons,
      Thy kinsmen, and thy friends, I'll have more lives
      Than drops of blood were in my father's veins.
CLIFFORD [to WARWICK]   Urge it no more, lest that, instead of words,
      I send thee, Warwick, such a messenger
100   As shall revenge his death before I stir.

---

1. In armor (rather than the black cloaks that were
conventionally worn by mourners).
2. The earldom of March, which York inherited from

his mother and through which he claimed the throne.
3. York's father, the Earl of Cambridge, was executed
for treason (see *Henry V* 2.2).

WARWICK [*to* YORK]   Poor Clifford, how I scorn his worthless threats.

YORK [*to* KING HENRY]   Will you we° show our title to the crown?   *Do you wish us to*
    If not, our swords shall plead it in the field.

KING HENRY   What title hast thou, traitor, to the crown?
105   Thy father was, as thou art, Duke of York;[4]
    Thy grandfather, Roger Mortimer, Earl of March.
    I am the son of Henry the Fifth,
    Who made the Dauphin[5] and the French to stoop
    And seized upon their towns and provinces.

110 WARWICK   Talk not of France, sith° thou hast lost it all.   *since*

KING HENRY   The Lord Protector[6] lost it, and not I.
    When I was crowned, I was but nine months old.

RICHARD   You are old enough now, and yet,° methinks, you lose.   *and even now*
    [*To* YORK] Father, tear the crown from the usurper's head.

115 EDWARD [*to* YORK]   Sweet father, do so—set it on your head.

MONTAGUE [*to* YORK]   Good brother, as thou lov'st and honour'st arms,
    Let's fight it out and not stand cavilling thus.

RICHARD   Sound drums and trumpets, and the King will fly.

YORK   Sons, peace!

NORTHUMBERLAND[7]   Peace, thou—and give King Henry leave°   *permission*
120   to speak.

KING HENRY   Ah, York, why seekest thou to depose me?
    Are we not both Plantagenets by birth,
    And from two brothers lineally descent?
    Suppose by right and equity thou be king—

        KING HENRY   *Peace, thou—and give King Henry leave to*
124.1   *speak.*

        WARWICK   *Plantagenet shall speak first—hear him, lords,*
           And be you silent and attentive too,
           For he that interrrupts him shall not live.

        KING HENRY [*to* YORK]   *Think'st thou that I will leave my*
124.5   *kingly throne,*

125 Think'st thou that I will leave my Kingly throne,
    Wherein my grandsire and my father sat?
    No—first shall war unpeople this my realm;
    Ay, and their colours, often borne in France,
    And now in England to our heart's great sorrow,
130   Shall be my winding-sheet.° Why faint you,[8] lords?   *burial shroud*
    My title's good, and better far than his.

WARWICK   Prove it, Henry, and thou shalt be king.

KING HENRY   Henry the Fourth by conquest got the crown.

YORK   'Twas by rebellion against his king.°   *(Richard II)*

135 KING HENRY [*aside*] I know not what to say—my title's weak.

---

4. In fact, the historical York's father was not the Duke of York. York inherited that title from his uncle (Edward).

5. Title of the oldest son of the French King.

6. Humphrey, Duke of Gloucester, was Lord Protector during Henry VI's youth and, as such, had oversight of the King and kingdom. His downfall is dramatized in *The First Part of the Contention* (*2 Henry VI*).

7. For lines 120–25, Oxford follows O. F assigns line 120 to King Henry, then gives three lines to Warwick and has Henry begin again at 125, omitting the Octavo

passage here printed as 121–24. For the F version, see the inset passage that follows (lines 124.1–124.5). Critics such as Steven Urkowitz have argued that the difference here between O and F indicates two different views of Henry's character, and they treat O and F as completely separate texts, with O composed first. Here as elsewhere, Oxford takes these Octavo lines as an authorial revision that occurred sometime between the play's foul-paper stage and the subsequent promptbook.

8. Why do you lose heart?

[*To* YORK] Tell me, may not a king adopt an heir?
YORK What then?
KING HENRY An if° he may, then am I lawful king—   *An if=If*
    For Richard, in the view of many lords,
140   Resigned the crown to Henry the Fourth,
    Whose heir my father was, and I am his.
YORK He rose against him,° being° his sovereign,   *(Richard) / who was*
    And made him to resign his crown perforce.
WARWICK Suppose, my lords, he did it unconstrained—
145   Think you 'twere prejudicial to his crown?°   *his claim to the throne*
EXETER No, for he could not so resign his crown
    But° that the next heir should succeed and reign.   *Without ensuring*
KING HENRY Art thou against us, Duke of Exeter?
EXETER His° is the right, and therefore pardon me.   *(York's)*
150 YORK Why whisper you, my lords, and answer not?
EXETER [*to* KING HENRY] My conscience tells me he is lawful king.
KING HENRY [*aside*] All will revolt from me and turn to him.
NORTHUMBERLAND [*to* YORK] Plantagenet, for all the claim thou lay'st,
    Think not that Henry shall be so deposed.
155 WARWICK Deposed he shall be, in despite° of all.   *spite*
NORTHUMBERLAND Thou art deceived— 'tis not thy southern power
    Of Essex, Norfolk, Suffolk, nor of Kent,
    Which makes thee thus presumptuous and proud,
    Can set the Duke up° in despite of me.   *(on the throne)*
160 CLIFFORD King Henry, be thy title right or wrong,
    Lord Clifford vows to fight in thy defence.
    May that ground gape and swallow me alive
    Where I shall kneel to him that slew my father.
KING HENRY O, Clifford, how thy words revive my heart!
165 YORK Henry of Lancaster, resign thy crown.
    What mutter you, or what conspire you, lords?
WARWICK Do right unto this princely Duke of York,
    Or I will fill the house with armèd men
    And over the chair of state, where now he sits,
170   Write up his title with usurping blood.[9]
        He stamps with his foot and the soldiers
        show themselves
KING HENRY My lord of Warwick, hear me but one word—
    Let me for this my lifetime reign as king.
YORK Confirm the crown to me and to mine heirs,
    And thou shalt reign in quiet while thou liv'st.
175 KING HENRY I am content. Richard Plantagenet,
    Enjoy the kingdom after my decease.
CLIFFORD What wrong is this unto the prince your son?
WARWICK What good is this to England and himself?
WESTMORLAND Base, fearful, and despairing Henry.
180 CLIFFORD How hast thou injured both thyself and us?
WESTMORLAND I cannot stay to hear these articles.°   *terms of agreement*
NORTHUMBERLAND Nor I.
CLIFFORD Come, cousin, let us tell the Queen these news.

---

9. With the blood of Henry, whom Warwick considers a usurper.

WESTMORLAND [*to* KING HENRY]   Farewell, faint-hearted and
 degenerate king,
185 In whose cold blood no spark of honour bides.°   *lives*
          Exit [with his soldiers][1]

NORTHUMBERLAND [*to* KING HENRY]   Be thou a prey unto the
 house of York,
 And die in bands° for this unmanly deed.   *fetters*
           Exit [with his soldiers]

CLIFFORD [*to* KING HENRY]   In dreadful war mayst thou be overcome,
 Or live in peace, abandoned and despised.
           Exit [with his soldiers]

190 WARWICK [*to* KING HENRY]   Turn this way, Henry, and regard them not.

EXETER [*to* KING HENRY]   They seek revenge and therefore will not yield.

KING HENRY   Ah, Exeter.

WARWICK   Why should you sigh, my lord?

KING HENRY   Not for myself, Lord Warwick, but my son,
 Whom I unnaturally shall disinherit.
195 But be it as it may. [*To* YORK] I here entail°   *bequeath*
 The crown to thee and to thine heirs for ever,
 Conditionally, that here thou take thine oath
 To cease this civil war, and whilst I live
 To honour me as thy king and sovereign,
200 And nor by treason nor hostility
 To seek to put me down and reign thyself.

YORK   This oath I willingly take and will perform.

WARWICK   Long live King Henry. [*To* YORK] Plantagenet, embrace him.
   [YORK *descends.* HENRY *and* YORK *embrace*]

KING HENRY [*to* YORK]   And long live thou, and these thy forward° sons. *precocious*
205 YORK   Now York and Lancaster are reconciled.

EXETER   Accursed be he that seeks to make them foes.
   Sennet.[2] *Here [York's train] comes down [from the state]*[3]

YORK [*to* KING HENRY]   Farewell, my gracious lord, I'll to my castle.[4]
    Exeunt YORK *and his sons* [EDWARD *and*
        RICHARD, *with soldiers*]

WARWICK   And I'll keep London with my soldiers.
           Exit [with soldiers]

NORFOLK   And I to Norfolk with my followers.
           Exit [with soldiers]

210 MONTAGUE   And I unto the sea from whence I came.
           Exit [with soldiers]

KING HENRY   And I with grief and sorrow to the court.
   [KING HENRY *and* EXETER *turn to leave.*]
   Enter QUEEN [MARGARET] *and* PRINCE [EDWARD]

EXETER   Here comes the Queen, whose looks bewray° her anger. *reveal*
 I'll steal away.

---

1. F gives no exit for Westmorland, Northumberland,
or Clifford; O marks a separate exit for each, as here.
Each man is probably followed out by his soldiers.
2. Trumpet notes signaling a procession.

3. F's "Here they come down" again indicates that a
state is required for the scene.
4. Sandal, located near Wakefield in Yorkshire.

KING HENRY Exeter, so will I.

QUEEN MARGARET Nay, go not from me—I will follow thee.

215 KING HENRY Be patient, gentle Queen, and I will stay.

QUEEN MARGARET Who can be patient in such extremes?
Ah, wretched man, would I had died a maid
And never seen thee, never borne thee son,
Seeing thou hast proved so unnatural a father.
220 Hath he deserved to lose his birthright thus?
Hadst thou but loved him half so well as I,
Or felt that pain° which I did for him once,   (labor pains)
Or nourished him as I did with my blood,
Thou wouldst have left thy dearest heart-blood there
225 Rather than have made that savage Duke thine heir
And disinherited thine only son.

PRINCE EDWARD Father, you cannot disinherit me.
If you be king, why should not I succeed?

KING HENRY Pardon me, Margaret; pardon me, sweet son—
230 The Earl of Warwick and the Duke enforced me.

QUEEN MARGARET Enforced thee? Art thou king, and wilt be forced?
I shame° to hear thee speak! Ah, timorous wretch,   *am ashamed*
Thou hast undone thyself, thy son, and me,
And giv'n unto the house of York such head[5]
235 As thou shalt reign but by their sufferance.
To entail him and his heirs unto the crown—
What is it, but to make thy sepulchre
And creep into it far before thy time?
Warwick is Chancellor and the Lord of Calais;
240 Stern Falconbridge commands the narrow seas;°   *(Straits of Dover)*
The Duke° is made Protector of the Realm;   *(York)*
And yet shalt thou be safe? Such safety finds
The trembling lamb environèd° with wolves.   *surrounded*
Had I been there, which am a seely° woman,   *helpless*
245 The soldiers should have tossed me on their pikes°   *axlike weapons*
Before I would have granted° to that act.   *assented*
But thou preferr'st thy life before thine honour.
And seeing thou dost, I here divorce myself
Both from thy table, Henry, and thy bed,[6]
250 Until that act of Parliament be repealed
Whereby my son is disinherited.
The northern lords that have forsworn thy colours
Will follow mine, if once they see them spread—
And spread they shall be, to thy foul disgrace
255 And the utter ruin of the house of York.
Thus do I leave thee. [*To* PRINCE EDWARD] Come, son, let's away.
Our army is ready—come, we'll after them.

KING HENRY Stay, gentle Margaret, and hear me speak.

QUEEN MARGARET Thou hast spoke too much already.
[*To* PRINCE EDWARD]   Get thee gone.

---

5. Such freedom to act. To give a horse its head means
to loosen its reins and let it go where it will.
6. *I here . . . bed:* echoing the language of church law,
which permitted marital separation "from bed and
board" in cases of adultery, heresy, and cruelty.

260 KING HENRY   Gentle son Edward, thou wilt stay with me?
QUEEN MARGARET   Ay, to be murdered by his enemies.
PRINCE EDWARD [*to* KING HENRY]   When I return with victory
     from the field,
   I'll see your grace. Till then, I'll follow her.
QUEEN MARGARET   Come, son, away—we may not linger thus.
                                        [*Exit with* PRINCE EDWARD][7]
265 KING HENRY   Poor Queen, how love to me and to her son
   Hath made her break out into terms of rage.
   Revenged may she be on that hateful Duke,
   Whose haughty spirit, wingèd with desire,
   Will coast° my crown, and, like an empty° eagle,   *attack / a hungry*
270   Tire° on the flesh of me and of my son.   *Feed ravenously*
   The loss of those three lords torments my heart.
   I'll write unto them and entreat them fair.°   *courteously*
   Come, cousin, you shall be the messenger.
EXETER   And I, I hope, shall reconcile them all.
                                        Flourish. Exeunt[8]

1.2

Enter RICHARD, EDWARD [*Earl of March*],
and [*the Marquis of*] MONTAGUE

RICHARD   Brother, though I be youngest give me leave.°   *allow me (to speak)*
EDWARD   No, I can better play the orator.
MONTAGUE   But I have reasons strong and forcible.
          Enter the Duke of YORK
YORK   Why, how now, sons and brother—at a strife?
5   What is your quarrel? How began it first?
EDWARD   No quarrel, but a slight contention.
YORK   About what?
RICHARD   About that which concerns your grace and us—
   The crown of England, father, which is yours.
10 YORK   Mine, boy? Not till King Henry be dead.
RICHARD   Your right depends not on his life or death.
EDWARD   Now you are heir—therefore enjoy it now.
   By giving the house of Lancaster leave to breathe,°   *permission to rest*
   It will outrun you, father, in the end.
15 YORK   I took an oath that he should quietly reign.
EDWARD   But for a kingdom any oath may be broken.
   I would break a thousand oaths to reign one year.
RICHARD [*to* YORK]   No—God forbid your grace should be forsworn.
YORK   I shall be if I claim by open war.
20 RICHARD   I'll prove the contrary, if you'll hear me speak.
YORK   Thou canst not, son—it is impossible.
RICHARD   An oath is of no moment° being not took   *consequence*
   Before a true and lawful magistrate
   That hath authority over him that swears.
25   Henry had none, but did usurp the place.
   Then, seeing 'twas he that made you to depose,°   *swear an oath*

---

7. O omits the Queen's last line and has her exit at line   "Flourish" before Richard's entrance in the next line.
261, Prince Edward at 263.   **1.2** Location: York's castle, Sandal (in Yorkshire).
8. F marks a single exit for Exeter here and places the

Your oath, my lord, is vain and frivolous.
Therefore to arms—and, father, do but think
How sweet a thing it is to wear a crown,
30 Within whose circuit° is Elysium[1]   circumference
And all that poets feign° of bliss and joy.   imagine
Why do we linger thus? I cannot rest
Until the white rose that I wear be dyed
Even in the luke-warm blood of Henry's heart.
35 YORK   Richard, enough! I will be king or die.
    [*To* MONTAGUE] Brother, thou shalt to London presently°   at once
    And whet on Warwick to this enterprise.
    Thou, Richard, shalt to the Duke of Norfolk
    And tell him privily° of our intent.   secretly
40 You, Edward, shall to Edmund Brook, Lord Cobham,
    With whom the Kentishmen will willingly rise.°   rebel; take arms
    In them I trust, for they are soldiers
    Witty, courteous, liberal, full of spirit.
    While you are thus employed, what resteth more°   what else remains
45 But that I seek occasion how to rise,
    And yet the King not privy to my drift,°   aware of my intent
    Nor any of the house of Lancaster.
               Enter a MESSENGER
    But stay, what news? Why com'st thou in such post?°   haste
MESSENGER   The Queen, with all the northern earls and lords,
50 Intend here to besiege you in your castle.
    She is hard by with twenty thousand men,
    And therefore fortify your hold,° my lord.   castle
YORK   Ay, with my sword. What—think'st thou that we fear them?
    Edward and Richard, you shall stay with me;
55 My brother Montague shall post to London.
    Let noble Warwick, Cobham, and the rest,
    Whom we have left protectors of the King,
    With powerful policy° strengthen themselves,   cunning
    And trust not simple Henry nor his oaths.
60 MONTAGUE   Brother, I go—I'll win them, fear it not.
    And thus most humbly I do take my leave.   *Exit*
               Enter SIR JOHN *Mortimer and his brother Sir Hugh*
YORK   Sir John and Sir Hugh Mortimer, mine uncles,
    You are come to Sandal in a happy° hour.   fortunate
    The army of the Queen mean to besiege us.
65 SIR JOHN   She shall not need, we'll meet her in the field.
YORK   What, with five thousand men?
RICHARD   Ay, with five hundred, father, for a need.°   if necessary
    A woman's general—what should we fear?
               A march [*sounds*] *afar off*
EDWARD   I hear their drums. Let's set our men in order,
70 And issue forth and bid them battle straight.°   at once
YORK [*to* SIR JOHN *and Sir Hugh*]   Five men to twenty—though
               the odds be great,
    I doubt not, uncles, of our victory.
    Many a battle have I won in France

---

1. In classical mythology, the paradise where blessed souls dwelled.

Whenas° the enemy hath been ten to one—   *When*
75   Why should I not now have the like success?   *Exeunt*

1.3

Alarums, and then enter the young Earl of RUTLAND
and his TUTOR [*a chaplain*]

RUTLAND   Ah, whither shall I fly to scape° their hands?   *escape*
    Enter [*Lord*] CLIFFORD [*with soldiers*]
Ah, tutor, look where bloody Clifford comes.
CLIFFORD [*to the* TUTOR]   Chaplain, away—thy priesthood saves thy life.
    As for the brat of this accursèd duke,
5   Whose father slew my father—he shall die.
TUTOR   And I, my lord, will bear him company.
CLIFFORD   Soldiers, away with him.
TUTOR   Ah, Clifford, murder not this innocent child
    Lest thou be hated both of° God and man.   *Exit* [*guarded*]   *by*
    [RUTLAND *falls to the ground*]
10   CLIFFORD   How now—is he dead already?
    Or is it fear that makes him close his eyes?
    I'll open them.
RUTLAND [*reviving*]   So looks the pent-up° lion o'er the wretch   *caged*
    That trembles under his devouring paws,
15   And so he walks, insulting° o'er his prey,   *scornfully triumphing*
    And so he comes to rend his limbs asunder.
    Ah, gentle Clifford, kill me with thy sword
    And not with such a cruel threat'ning look.
    Sweet Clifford, hear me speak before I die.
20   I am too mean° a subject for thy wrath.   *lowly*
    Be thou revenged on men, and let me live.
CLIFFORD   In vain thou speak'st, poor boy. My father's blood
    Hath stopped the passage where thy words should enter.
RUTLAND   Then let my father's blood open it again.
25   He is a man, and, Clifford, cope° with him.   *fight*
CLIFFORD   Had I thy brethren here, their lives and thine
    Were not revenge sufficient for me.
    No—if I digged up thy forefathers' graves,
    And hung their rotten coffins up in chains,
30   It could not slake° mine ire nor ease my heart.   *lessen*
    The sight of any of the house of York
    Is as a fury to torment my soul.
    And till I root out their accursèd line,
    And leave not one alive, I live in hell.
35   Therefore—
RUTLAND   O, let me pray before I take my death.
    [*Kneeling*] To thee I pray: sweet Clifford, pity me.
CLIFFORD   Such pity as my rapier's point affords.
RUTLAND   I never did thee harm—why wilt thou slay me?
CLIFFORD   Thy father hath.
40   RUTLAND   But 'twas ere I was born.
    Thou hast one son—for his sake pity me,
    Lest in revenge thereof, sith° God is just,   *since*

1.3 Location: A battlefield between Sandal and Wakefield.

He be as miserably slain as I.
Ah, let me live in prison all my days,
45 And when I give occasion of offence,
Then let me die, for now thou hast no cause.
CLIFFORD   No cause? Thy father slew my father, therefore die.

[*He stabs him*]

RUTLAND   *Dii faciant laudis summa sit ista tuae.*[1]   [*He dies*]
CLIFFORD   Plantagenet—I come, Plantagenet!
50 And this thy son's blood cleaving to my blade
Shall rust upon my weapon till thy blood,
Congealed with this, do make me wipe off both.

Exit [with Rutland's body and soldiers][2]

1.4

Alarum. Enter Richard Duke of YORK

YORK   The army of the Queen hath got° the field;   *won*
My uncles[1] both are slain in rescuing me;
And all my followers to the eager foe
Turn back,° and fly like ships before the wind,   *Turn their backs*
5 Or lambs pursued by hunger-starvèd wolves.
My sons—God knows what hath bechancèd° them.   *happened to*
But this I know—they have demeaned° themselves   *conducted*
Like men born to renown by life or death.
Three times did Richard make a lane to me,
10 And thrice cried, 'Courage, father, fight it out!'
And full as oft came Edward to my side,
With purple falchion° painted to the hilt   *curved sword*
In blood of those that had encountered him.
And when the hardiest warriors did retire,
15 Richard cried, 'Charge and give no foot of ground!'
[   ][2]
And cried 'A crown or else a glorious tomb!
A sceptre or an earthly sepulchre!'
With this, we charged again—but out, alas—
20 We bodged° again, as I have seen a swan   *gave way*
With bootless° labour swim against the tide   *fruitless*
And spend her strength with over-matching° waves.   *against too powerful*

A short alarum within

Ah, hark—the fatal followers do pursue,
And I am faint and cannot fly their fury;
25 And were I strong, I would not shun their fury.
The sands° are numbered that makes up my life.   *(of the hourglass)*
Here must I stay, and here my life must end.

Enter QUEEN [MARGARET, *Lord*] CLIFFORD, [*the Earl of*]
NORTHUMBERLAND, [*and*] *the young* PRINCE [EDWARD,
with] soldiers

Come bloody Clifford, rough Northumberland—
I dare your quenchless fury to more rage!

---

1. "The gods grant that this may be the height of your glory" (Ovid, *Heroides* 2.66).
2. Although no Folio or Octavo stage direction indicates whether any soldiers are present during this scene, Clifford's command at line 7 makes it clear that some, at least, escort the tutor offstage. Some may remain to exit here. Oxford notes that "the question, unresolvable, is an important one, for it asks, essentially, whether Clifford's murder of Rutland is witnessed by anyone."
1.4 Location: Scene continues.
1. Sir John and Sir Hugh Mortimer.
2. It has been conjectured that this missing line referred to Edward, who, like his brother Richard, may have cried out encouragement to York's forces.

30   I am your butt,° and I abide your shot.   *target (in archery)*
    NORTHUMBERLAND   Yield to our mercy, proud Plantagenet.
    CLIFFORD   Ay, to such mercy as his ruthless arm,
    With downright payment,³ showed unto my father.
    Now Phaëton hath tumbled from his car,⁴
35   And made an evening at the noontide prick.⁵
    YORK   My ashes, as the phoenix,⁶ may bring forth
    A bird° that will revenge upon you all,   *child*
    And in that hope I throw mine eyes to heaven,
    Scorning whate'er you can afflict me with.
40   Why come you not? What—multitudes, and fear?
    CLIFFORD   So cowards fight when they can fly no further;
    So doves do peck the falcon's piercing talons;
    So desperate thieves, all hopeless of their lives,
    Breathe out invectives 'gainst the officers.
45   YORK   O, Clifford, but bethink thee once again,
    And in thy thought o'errun° my former time,   *review*
    And, if thou canst for blushing, view this face
    And bite thy tongue, that slanders him with cowardice
    Whose frown hath made thee faint and fly ere this.
50   CLIFFORD   I will not bandy with thee word for word,
    But buckle° with thee blows twice two for one.   *join in close combat*
    [*He draws his sword*]
    QUEEN MARGARET   Hold, valiant Clifford: for a thousand causes
    I would prolong a while the traitor's life.
    Wrath makes him deaf—speak thou, Northumberland.
55   NORTHUMBERLAND   Hold, Clifford—do not honour him so much
    To prick thy finger though to wound his heart.
    What valour were it when a cur doth grin°   *show its teeth*
    For one to thrust his hand between his teeth
    When he might spurn° him with his foot away?   *kick*
60   It is war's prize to take all vantages,°   *opportunities*
    And ten to one is no impeach of valour.⁷
    [*They*] *fight and take* [YORK]
    CLIFFORD   Ay, ay, so strives the woodcock with the gin.⁸
    NORTHUMBERLAND   So doth the cony° struggle in the net.   *rabbit*
    YORK   So triumph thieves upon their conquered booty,
65   So true° men yield, with robbers so o'ermatched.   *honest*
    NORTHUMBERLAND [*to the* QUEEN]   What would your grace have
         done unto him now?
    QUEEN MARGARET   Brave warriors, Clifford and Northumberland,
    Come make him stand upon this molehill here,
    That wrought° at mountains with outstretchèd arms   *reached*
70   Yet parted but° the shadow with his hand.   *only*
    [*To* YORK] What—was it you that would be England's king?
    Was't you that revelled in our Parliament,

---

3. Alluding to the "downright," or vertical, sword stroke that York used to kill Clifford's father in *The First Part of the Contention*.
4. Phaeton, in classical mythology, was the son of Phoebus (the sun god) and nearly set the world on fire when he attempted to drive his father's chariot ("car," the sun). Zeus hurled a thunderbolt, and Phaeton fell blazing to his death. This is one of the play's many allusions to the fact that the sun was an emblem of the

house of York. See note to 2.1.40.
5. The noon mark on a sundial.
6. A mythological bird that periodically built an elaborate funeral pyre, set itself on fire, and was reborn from its own ashes.
7. And for ten to fight with one does not call our bravery into question.
8. Trap. *woodcock:* a bird reputed to lack brains and thus easily caught in traps.

And made a preachment° of your high descent?   *sermon*
Where are your mess of° sons to back you now?   *group of four*
75 The wanton Edward and the lusty George?
And where's that valiant crookback prodigy,°   *marvel; monster*
Dickie, your boy, that with his grumbling voice
Was wont to cheer his dad in mutinies?
Or with the rest where is your darling Rutland?
80 Look, York, I stained this napkin° with the blood   *handkerchief*
That valiant Clifford with his rapier's point
Made issue from the bosom of thy boy.
And if thine eyes can water for his death,
I give thee this to dry thy cheeks withal.°   *with*
85 Alas, poor York, but that I hate thee deadly
I should lament thy miserable state.
I prithee, grieve, to make me merry, York.
What—hath thy fiery heart so parched thine entrails°   *inner organs*
That not a tear can fall for Rutland's death?
90 Why art thou patient, man? Thou shouldst be mad,
And I, to make thee mad, do mock thee thus.
Stamp, rave, and fret, that I may sing and dance.
Thou wouldst be fee'd,° I see, to make me sport.   *paid*
York cannot speak unless he wear a crown.
95 [*To her men*] A crown for York, and, lords, bow low to him.
Hold you his hands whilst I do set it on.
       [*She puts a paper crown on York's head*]
Ay, marry, sir, now looks he like a king,
Ay, this is he that took King Henry's chair,
And this is he was his adopted heir.
100 But how is it that great Plantagenet
Is crowned so soon and broke his solemn oath?
As I bethink me, you should not be king
Till our King Henry had shook hands with death.
And will you pale° your head in Henry's glory,   *enclose*
105 And rob his temples of the diadem
Now, in his life, against your holy oath?
O 'tis a fault too, too, unpardonable.
Off with the crown,
      [*She knocks it from his head*]
           and with the crown his head,
And whilst we breathe,° take time to do him dead.°   *rest / kill him*
110 CLIFFORD   That is my office for my father's sake.
QUEEN MARGARET   Nay, stay—let's hear the orisons° he makes.   *prayers*
YORK   She-wolf of France, but worse than wolves of France,
Whose tongue more poisons than the adder's tooth—
How ill-beseeming° is it in thy sex   *unbecoming*
115 To triumph like an Amazonian trull[9]
Upon their woes whom fortune captivates!°   *subdues*
But that° thy face is visor-like,[1] unchanging,   *Were it not that*
Made impudent with use of evil deeds,
I would essay,° proud Queen, to make thee blush.   *attempt*

9. In the manner of an Amazonian whore. Amazons were a tribe of mythical warrior women who governed themselves and lived separate from men. Sometimes they were accused of sexual impropriety because to beget offspring they would mate with men they had conquered but did not marry.
1. Masklike; fixed in expression like the frontpiece of a helmet. Perhaps alluding to the practice of prostitutes who wore masks.

120   To tell thee whence thou cam'st, of whom derived,
         Were shame enough to shame thee— wert thou not shameless.
         Thy father bears the type° of King of Naples,   *title*
         Of both the Sicils,² and Jerusalem—
         Yet not so wealthy as an English yeoman.³
125   Hath that poor monarch taught thee to insult?
         It needs not, nor it boots° thee not, proud Queen,   *profits*
         Unless the adage must be verified
         That beggars mounted run their horse to death.
         'Tis beauty that doth oft make women proud—
130   But, God he knows, thy share thereof is small;
         'Tis virtue that doth make them most admired—
         The contrary doth make thee wondered at;
         'Tis government° that makes them seem divine—   *self-control*
         The want thereof makes thee abominable.
135   Thou art as opposite to every good
         As the antipodes⁴ are unto us,
         Or as the south to the septentrion.⁵
         O tiger's heart wrapped in a woman's hide!
         How couldst thou drain the life-blood of the child
140   To bid the father wipe his eyes withal,
         And yet be seen to bear a woman's face?
         Women are soft, mild, pitiful,° and flexible—   *full of pity*
         Thou stern, obdurate, flinty, rough, remorseless.
         Bidd'st thou me rage? Why, now thou hast thy wish.
145   Wouldst have me weep? Why, now thou hast thy will.
         For raging wind blows up incessant showers,
         And when the rage allays° the rain begins.   *abates*
         These tears are my sweet Rutland's obsequies,
         And every drop cries vengeance for his death
150   'Gainst thee, fell° Clifford, and thee, false Frenchwoman.   *cruel*
     NORTHUMBERLAND   Beshrew° me, but his passions move me so   *Curse*
         That hardly can I check my eyes from tears.
     YORK   That face of his the hungry cannibals
         Would not have touched, would not have stained with blood—
155   But you are more inhuman, more inexorable,
         O, ten times more than tigers of Hyrcania.⁶
         See, ruthless Queen, a hapless° father's tears.   *an unlucky*
         This cloth thou dipped'st in blood of my sweet boy,
         And I with tears do wash the blood away.
160   Keep thou the napkin and go boast of this,
         And if thou tell'st the heavy° story right,   *sorrowful*
         Upon my soul the hearers will shed tears,
         Yea, even my foes will shed fast-falling tears
         And say, 'Alas, it was a piteous deed'.
165   There, take the crown—and with the crown, my curse:
         And in thy need such comfort come to thee
         As now I reap at thy too cruel hand.
         Hard-hearted Clifford, take me from the world.
         My soul to heaven, my blood upon your heads.

---

2. Naples and Sicily (known as the Kingdom of the Two Sicilies).
3. Landowner below the rank of gentleman.
4. People living on the opposite side of the world.

5. North. The word refers to the seven stars that make up the Great Bear constellation.
6. Region in ancient Persia known for the cruelty of its tigers (see *Aeneid* 4.366–67).

170   NORTHUMBERLAND   Had he been slaughter-man to all my kin,
     I should not, for my life, but weep with him,
     To see how inly° sorrow gripes his soul.   *inward*
   QUEEN MARGARET   What—weeping-ripe,° my lord Northumberland?   *ready to weep*
     Think but upon the wrong he did us all,
175   And that will quickly dry thy melting tears.
   CLIFFORD   Here's for my oath, here's for my father's death.
         [*He stabs* YORK]
   QUEEN MARGARET   And here's to right our gentle-hearted King.
         [*She stabs* YORK]
   YORK   Open thy gate of mercy, gracious God—
     My soul flies through these wounds to seek out thee.
                           [*He dies*]
180   QUEEN MARGARET   Off with his head and set it on York gates,
     So York may overlook the town of York.
                Flourish. Exeunt [*with York's body*]

2.1

     [A] *march. Enter* EDWARD [*Earl of March*]
     and RICHARD, *with* [*a*] *drum*[*mer*] *and soldiers*
   EDWARD   I wonder how our princely father scaped,
     Or whether he be scaped away or no
     From Clifford's and Northumberland's pursuit.
     Had he been ta'en we should have heard the news;
5   Had he been slain we should have heard the news;
     Or had he scaped, methinks we should have heard
     The happy tidings of his good escape.
     How fares my brother? Why is he so sad?
   RICHARD   I cannot joy until I be resolved
10   Where our right valiant father is become.°   *has betaken himself*
     I saw him in the battle range about,
     And watched him how he singled Clifford forth.
     Methought he bore him in the thickest troop,
     As doth a lion in a herd of neat;°   *cattle*
15   Or as a bear encompassed round with dogs,
     Who having pinched° a few and made them cry,   *bitten*
     The rest stand all aloof and bark at him.
     So fared our father with his enemies;
     So fled his enemies my warlike father.
20   Methinks 'tis prize enough to be his son.
         Three suns appear in the air[1]
     See how the morning opes her golden gates
     And takes her farewell of the glorious sun.
     How well resembles it the prime of youth,
     Trimmed° like a younker° prancing to his love!   *Dressed up / young man*
25   EDWARD   Dazzle mine eyes, or do I see three suns?
   RICHARD   Three glorious suns, each one a perfect sun;
     Not separated with the racking° clouds,   *drifting*
     But severed in a pale clear-shining sky.
         [*The three suns begin to join*]

2.1. Location: Fields near the border, or marches, between Wales and England.
1. This stage direction appears in O, which may have been based on a theatrical promptbook (see Textual Note). It suggests that the acting company who performed the play had some kind of artificial "suns" they used as properties for this scene.

See, see—they join, embrace, and seem to kiss,
30 As if they vowed some league inviolable.
Now are they but one lamp, one light, one sun.
In this the heaven figures° some event.   *prefigures*
EDWARD 'Tis wondrous strange, the like yet never heard of.
I think it cites° us, brother, to the field,   *urges*
35 That we, the sons of brave Plantagenet,
Each one already blazing by our meeds,°   *merits*
Should notwithstanding join our lights together
And over-shine the earth as this° the world.   *this phenomenon*
Whate'er it bodes, henceforward will I bear
40 Upon my target three fair-shining suns.²
RICHARD Nay, bear three daughters—by your leave I speak it—
You love the breeder° better than the male.   *childbearer; woman*
        *Enter one blowing*³
But what art thou whose heavy looks foretell
Some dreadful story hanging on thy tongue?
45 MESSENGER Ah, one that was a woeful looker-on
Whenas° the noble Duke of York was slain—   *When*
Your princely father and my loving lord.
EDWARD O, speak no more, for I have heard too much.
RICHARD Say how he died, for I will hear it all.
50 MESSENGER Environèd° he was with many foes,   *Surrounded*
And stood against them as the hope of Troy⁴
Against the Greeks that would have entered Troy.
But Hercules⁵ himself must yield to odds;
And many strokes, though with a little axe,
55 Hews down and fells the hardest-timbered oak.
By many hands your father was subdued,
But only slaughtered by the ireful arm
Of unrelenting Clifford and the Queen,
Who crowned the gracious Duke in high despite,°   *in great contempt*
60 Laughed in his face, and when with grief he wept,
The ruthless Queen gave him to dry his cheeks
A napkin steepèd in the harmless blood
Of sweet young Rutland, by rough Clifford slain;
And after many scorns, many foul taunts,
65 They took his head, and on the gates of York
They set the same; and there it doth remain,
The saddest spectacle that e'er I viewed.
EDWARD Sweet Duke of York, our prop to lean upon,
Now thou art gone, we have no staff, no stay.°   *support*
70 O Clifford, boist'rous° Clifford—thou hast slain   *savage*
The flower of Europe for his chivalry,
And treacherously hast thou vanquished him—
For hand to hand he would have vanquished thee.
Now my soul's palace° is become a prison.   *(my body)*
75 Ah, would she° break from hence that this my body   *(my soul)*
Might in the ground be closèd up in rest.

---

2. As elsewhere, Shakespeare here slightly changes his sources. In Holinshed's *Chronicles*, Edward chose the sun as his badge because he had seen three suns join in one before the Battle of Mortimer's Cross, which he won. *target:* shield.
3. Blowing a horn as messengers did to announce themselves.
4. *hope of Troy:* Hector, a mighty warrior in Homer's *Iliad*, who defended the city of Troy against Greek invaders.
5. A mythic hero of enormous physical strength and courage.

For never henceforth shall I joy again—
Never, O never, shall I see more joy.

RICHARD   I cannot weep, for all my body's moisture
80 Scarce serves to quench my furnace-burning heart;
Nor can my tongue unload my heart's great burden,
For selfsame wind° that I should speak withal   *breath*
Is kindling coals that fires all my breast,
And burns me up with flames that tears would quench.
85 To weep is to make less the depth of grief;
Tears, then, for babes—blows and revenge for me!
Richard, I bear thy name; I'll venge° thy death   *revenge*
Or die renownèd by attempting it.

EDWARD   His name that valiant Duke hath left with thee,
90 His dukedom and his chair⁶ with me is left.

RICHARD   Nay, if thou be that princely eagle's bird,
Show thy descent by gazing 'gainst the sun:⁷
For 'chair and dukedom', 'throne and kingdom' say—
Either that is thine or else thou wert not his.

> *March. Enter the Earl of* WARWICK *[and the] Marquis*
> *[of]* MONTAGUE, *with drum[mers], [an] ensign,*
> *and soldiers*

95 WARWICK   How now, fair lords? What fare?° What news abroad?   *success*

RICHARD   Great lord of Warwick, if we should recount
Our baleful° news, and at each word's deliverance   *deadly*
Stab poniards° in our flesh till all were told,   *daggers*
The words would add more anguish than the wounds.
100 O valiant lord, the Duke of York is slain.

EDWARD   O Warwick, Warwick! That Plantagenet,
Which held thee dearly as his soul's redemption,
Is by the stern Lord Clifford done to death.

WARWICK   Ten days ago I drowned these news in tears.
105 And now, to add more measure to your woes,
I come to tell you things sith° then befall'n.   *since*
After the bloody fray at Wakefield fought,
Where your brave father breathed his latest° gasp,   *last*
Tidings, as swiftly as the posts° could run,   *messengers*
110 Were brought me of your loss and his depart.°   *death*
I then in London, keeper of the King,
Mustered my soldiers, gathered flocks of friends,
And, very well appointed° as I thought,   *equipped*
Marched toward Saint Albans to intercept the Queen,
115 Bearing the King in my behalf along—
For by my scouts I was advertisèd°   *informed*
That she was coming with a full intent
To dash our late° decree in Parliament   *recent*
Touching King Henry's oath and your succession.
120 Short tale to make, we at Saint Albans met,
Our battles° joined, and both sides fiercely fought;   *armies*
But whether 'twas the coldness of the King,
Who looked full gently on his warlike queen,
That robbed my soldiers of their heated spleen,°   *fiery passion*
125 Or whether 'twas report of her success,

---

6. Seat of his authority as Duke.
7. Eagles, described by Elizabethans as the king of

birds, were supposed to be able to gaze unblinkingly at
the sun.

Or more than common fear of Clifford's rigour—
Who thunders to his captains blood and death—
I cannot judge; but, to conclude with truth,
Their weapons like to lightning came and went;
130 Our soldiers', like the night-owl's lazy flight,
Or like an idle thresher with a flail,[8]
Fell gently down, as if they struck their friends.
I cheered them up with justice of our cause,
With promise of high pay, and great rewards.
135 But all in vain. They had no heart to fight,
And we in them no hope to win the day.
So that we fled—the King unto the Queen,
Lord George your brother, Norfolk, and myself
In haste, post-haste, are come to join with you.
140 For in the Marches° here we heard you were,   Welsh borders
Making another head° to fight again.   Raising another army
EDWARD Where is the Duke of Norfolk, gentle Warwick?
And when came George from Burgundy to England?
WARWICK Some six miles off the Duke is with his soldiers;
145 And for your brother—he was lately sent
From your kind aunt, Duchess of Burgundy,[9]
With aid of soldiers to this needful war.
RICHARD 'Twas odd belike[1] when valiant Warwick fled.
Oft have I heard his praises in pursuit,°   (of enemies)
150 But ne'er till now his scandal of retire.[2]
WARWICK Nor now my scandal, Richard, dost thou hear—
For thou shalt know this strong right hand of mine
Can pluck the diadem from faint° Henry's head   weak
And wring the aweful° sceptre from his fist,   awe-inspiring
155 Were he as famous and as bold in war
As he is famed for mildness, peace, and prayer.
RICHARD I know it well, Lord Warwick—blame me not.
'Tis love I bear thy glories make me speak.
But in this troublous time what's to be done?
160 Shall we go throw away our coats of steel,
And wrap our bodies in black mourning gowns,
Numb'ring our Ave-Maries with our beads?[3]
Or shall we on the helmets of our foes
Tell our devotion[4] with revengeful arms?
165 If for the last, say 'ay', and to it, lords.
WARWICK Why, therefore Warwick came to seek you out,
And therefore comes my brother Montague.
Attend me, lords. The proud insulting Queen,
With Clifford and the haught° Northumberland,   haughty
170 And of their feather many more proud birds,
Have wrought° the easy-melting King like wax.   worked on
[To EDWARD] He swore consent to your succession,

---

8. Threshers beat grain from wheat with specially
designed sticks, or "flails."
9. According to the chronicles, both George and Richard
were sent for safety to the court of Philip of Burgundy;
his wife, the Duchess of Burgundy, whom Warwick mentions, was a granddaughter of John of Gaunt.
1. The odds must have been much against him.
2. Defamation or condemnation of him for retreating

(from his enemies).
3. Rosary beads are used in Roman Catholic devotion
for keeping track of the prayers one has said, including
"Ave Marias" ("Hail Marys"), prayers addressed to the
Virgin Mary.
4. Proclaim the object of our devotion (York), with a
pun on "telling" as meaning "counting," which is what
one does when saying the rosary.

His oath enrollèd° in the Parliament.   *officially recorded*
And now to London all the crew are gone,
175   To frustrate both his oath and what beside
May make against° the house of Lancaster.   *be unfavorable to*
Their power, I think, is thirty thousand strong.
Now, if the help of Norfolk and myself,
With all the friends that thou, brave Earl of March,⁵
180   Amongst the loving Welshmen canst procure,
Will but amount to five-and-twenty thousand,
Why, *via,*° to London will we march,   *onward*
And once again bestride our foaming steeds,
And once again cry 'Charge!' upon our foes—
185   But never once again turn back and fly.
RICHARD   Ay, now methinks I hear great Warwick speak.
Ne'er may he live to see a sunshine day
That cries 'Retire!' if Warwick bid him stay.
EDWARD   Lord Warwick, on thy shoulder will I lean,
190   And when thou fail'st—as God forbid the hour—
Must Edward fall, which peril heaven forfend!°   *forbid*
WARWICK   No longer Earl of March, but Duke of York;
The next degree° is England's royal throne—   *step*
For King of England shalt thou be proclaimed
195   In every borough as we pass along,
And he that throws not up his cap for joy,
Shall for the fault make forfeit of his head.
King Edward, valiant Richard, Montague—
Stay we no longer dreaming of renown,
200   But sound the trumpets and about our task.
RICHARD   Then, Clifford, were thy heart as hard as steel,
As thou hast shown it flinty by thy deeds,
I come to pierce it or to give thee mine.
EDWARD   Then strike up drums—God and Saint George°   *patron saint of England*
for us!
        Enter a MESSENGER
205   WARWICK   How now? What news?
MESSENGER   The Duke of Norfolk sends you word by me
The Queen is coming with a puissant° host,   *powerful*
And craves your company for speedy counsel.
WARWICK   Why then it sorts.° Brave warriors, let's away.   *is fitting*
                        [*March.*] *Exeunt*

2.2

[*York's head is thrust out, above.*]¹
Flourish. Enter KING [HENRY], QUEEN [MARGARET],
[*Lord*] CLIFFORD, [*the Earl of*] NORTHUMBERLAND,
and young PRINCE EDWARD, *with* [*a*] *drum*[*mer*]
and trumpet[*er*]s
QUEEN MARGARET   Welcome, my lord, to this brave town of York.
Yonder's the head of that arch-enemy
That sought to be encompassed with your crown.

---

5. The title by which Edward and his father before him laid claim to the throne of England. See line 192 and note to 1.1.78.
2.2. Location: Before the walls of York.
1. Neither F nor O indicates in stage directions that York's head is displayed above the stage, but Queen Margaret's words in lines 2–4 and King Henry's response suggest that it remains visible, perhaps (as Oxford proposes) until 2.6.110.

Doth not the object cheer your heart, my lord?

5   KING HENRY   Ay, as the rocks cheer them that fear their wreck.
To see this sight, it irks my very soul.
Withhold revenge, dear God—'tis not my fault,
Nor wittingly have I infringed my vow.

CLIFFORD   My gracious liege,° this too much lenity   sovereign
10   And harmful pity must be laid aside.
To whom do lions cast their gentle looks?
Not to the beast that would usurp their den.
Whose hand is that the forest bear doth lick?
Not his that spoils° her young before her face.   takes as prey
15   Who scapes the lurking serpent's mortal sting?
Not he that sets his foot upon her back.
The smallest worm will turn, being trodden on,
And doves will peck in safeguard of their brood.
Ambitious York did level° at thy crown,   aim
20   Thou smiling while he knit his angry brows.
He, but a duke, would have his son a king,
And raise° his issue° like a loving sire;   raise in rank / offspring
Thou, being a king, blest with a goodly son,
Didst yield consent to disinherit him,
25   Which argued thee a most unloving father.
Unreasonable creatures° feed their young,   Animals
And though man's face be fearful to their eyes,
Yet, in protection of their tender ones,
Who hath not seen them, even with those wings
30   Which sometime they have used with fearful flight,
Make war with him that climbed unto their nest,
Offering their own lives in their young's defence?
For shame, my liege, make them your precedent!
Were it not pity that this goodly boy
35   Should lose his birthright by his father's fault,
And long hereafter say unto his child
'What my great-grandfather and grandsire got
My careless father fondly° gave away'?   foolishly
Ah, what a shame were this! Look on the boy,
40   And let his manly face, which promiseth
Successful fortune, steel thy melting heart
To hold thine own and leave thine own with him.

KING HENRY   Full well hath Clifford played the orator,
Inferring° arguments of mighty force.   Offering
45   But, Clifford, tell me—didst thou never hear
That things ill got had ever bad success?°   outcome
And happy always was it for that son
Whose father for his hoarding went to hell?
I'll leave my son my virtuous deeds behind,
50   And would my father had left me no more.
For all the rest is held at such a rate°   cost
As brings a thousandfold more care to keep
Than in possession any jot of pleasure.
Ah, cousin York, would thy best friends did know
55   How it doth grieve me that thy head is here.

QUEEN MARGARET   My lord, cheer up your spirits—our foes are nigh,
And this soft courage makes your followers faint.°   lose heart
You promised knighthood to our forward° son.   precocious

Unsheathe your sword and dub[2] him presently.°   *at once*
60   Edward, kneel down.
      [PRINCE EDWARD *kneels*]
    KING HENRY   Edward Plantagenet, arise a knight—
    And learn this lesson: draw thy sword in right.
    PRINCE EDWARD [*rising*]   My gracious father, by your kingly leave,
    I'll draw it as apparent° to the crown,   *heir*
65   And in that quarrel° use it to the death.   *cause*
    CLIFFORD   Why, that is spoken like a toward° prince.   *bold*
      Enter a MESSENGER
    MESSENGER   Royal commanders, be in readiness—
    For with a band of thirty thousand men
    Comes Warwick backing of° the Duke of York;[3]   *supporting*
70   And in the towns, as they do march along,
    Proclaims him king, and many fly to him.
    Darraign your battle,° for they are at hand.   *Deploy your troops*
    CLIFFORD [*to* KING HENRY]   I would your highness would depart
      the field—
    The Queen hath best success when you are absent.
    QUEEN MARGARET [*to* KING HENRY]   Ay, good my lord, and leave
75   us to our fortune.
    KING HENRY   Why, that's my fortune too—therefore I'll stay.
    NORTHUMBERLAND   Be it with resolution then to fight.
    PRINCE EDWARD [*to* KING HENRY]   My royal father, cheer these
      noble lords
    And hearten those that fight in your defence.
80   Unsheathe your sword, good father; cry 'Saint George!'°   *England's patron saint*
      March. Enter EDWARD [*Duke of York, the Earl of*] WAR-
      WICK, RICHARD, [GEORGE,[4] *the Duke of*]
      NORFOLK, [*the Marquis of*] MONTAGUE, *and soldiers*
    EDWARD   Now, perjured Henry, wilt thou kneel for grace,
    And set thy diadem upon my head—
    Or bide° the mortal° fortune of the field?   *wait for / fatal*
    QUEEN MARGARET   Go rate° thy minions,° proud insulting boy!   *chide / favorites*
85   Becomes it thee to be thus bold in terms
    Before thy sovereign and thy lawful king?
    EDWARD   I am his king, and he should bow his knee.
    I was adopted heir by his consent.
    GEORGE [*to* QUEEN MARGARET]   Since when his oath is broke—
      for, as I hear,
90   You that are king, though he do wear the crown,
    Have caused him by new act of Parliament
    To blot our brother out, and put his own son in.
    CLIFFORD   And reason too—
    Who should succeed the father but the son?
95   RICHARD   Are you there, butcher? O, I cannot speak!
    CLIFFORD   Ay, crookback, here I stand to answer thee,
    Or any he the proudest of thy sort.°   *gang*
    RICHARD   'Twas you that killed young Rutland, was it not?
    CLIFFORD   Ay, and old York, and yet not satisfied.

---

2. Confer the rank of knight by the ceremony of striking the shoulder with a sword.
3. Edward has now assumed the title Duke of York
after the death of his father at Margaret's hands.

4. Here and elsewhere, F's stage directions read
"Clarence" rather than "George." The Duke of Clarence
is the title he eventually assumes.

100   RICHARD   For God's sake, lords, give signal to the fight.

     WARWICK   What sayst thou, Henry, wilt thou yield the crown?

     QUEEN MARGARET   Why, how now, long-tongued Warwick, dare
          you speak?

     When you and I met at Saint Albans last,

     Your legs did better service than your hands.

105   WARWICK   Then 'twas my turn to fly—and now 'tis thine.

     CLIFFORD   You said so much before, and yet you fled.

     WARWICK   'Twas not your valour, Clifford, drove me thence.

     NORTHUMBERLAND   No, nor your manhood that durst make you stay.

     RICHARD   Northumberland, I hold thee reverently.°   *in respect*

110   Break off the parley, for scarce I can refrain

     The execution of my big-swoll'n heart[5]

     Upon that Clifford, that cruel child-killer.

     CLIFFORD   I slew thy father—call'st thou him a child?

     RICHARD   Ay, like a dastard° and a treacherous coward,   *base coward*

115   As thou didst kill our tender brother Rutland.

     But ere sun set I'll make thee curse the deed.

     KING HENRY   Have done with words, my lords, and hear me speak.

     QUEEN MARGARET   Defy them, then, or else hold close thy lips.

     KING HENRY   I prithee give no limits to my tongue—

120   I am a king, and privileged to speak.

     CLIFFORD   My liege, the wound that bred this meeting here

     Cannot be cured by words—therefore be still.

     RICHARD   Then, executioner, unsheathe thy sword.

     By him that made us all, I am resolved

125   That Clifford's manhood lies upon his tongue.°   *exists only in words*

     EDWARD   Say, Henry, shall I have my right or no?

     A thousand men have broke their fasts today

     That ne'er shall dine unless thou yield the crown.

     WARWICK [*to* KING HENRY] If thou deny,° their blood upon thy head;   *refuse*

130   For York in justice puts his armour on.

     PRINCE EDWARD   If that be right which Warwick says is right,

     There is no wrong, but everything is right.

     RICHARD   Whoever got° thee, there thy mother stands—   *sired*

     For, well I wot,° thou hast thy mother's tongue.   *know*

135   QUEEN MARGARET   But thou art neither like thy sire nor dam,

     But like a foul misshapen stigmatic,[6]

     Marked by the destinies[7] to be avoided,

     As venom° toads or lizards' dreadful stings.   *poisonous*

     RICHARD   Iron of Naples, hid with English gilt,[8]

140   Whose father bears the title of a king—

     As if a channel° should be called the sea—   *gutter*

     Sham'st thou not, knowing whence thou art extraught,°   *descended*

     To let thy tongue detect° thy base-born heart?   *reveal*

---

5. From acting passionately. Passions were supposed to cause the heart to swell.

6. A deformed person; a criminal marked by means of an iron brand for his or her crime.

7. The Fates, three goddesses in classical mythology thought to determine the course of a person's life.

8. You cheap product of Naples, hiding under the gold veneer of an English marriage. Since Naples is synonymous in many Elizabethan texts with prostitution and venereal disease, "iron" may also refer to the metal noses allegedly worn by wealthy people to disguise the disfiguring effects of syphilis.

EDWARD   A wisp of straw⁹ were° worth a thousand crowns   *would be*

145   To make this shameless callet° know herself.   *whore*

Helen of Greece was fairer far than thou,

Although thy husband may be Menelaus;¹

And ne'er was Agamemnon's brother° wronged   *(Menelaus)*

By that false woman, as this king by thee.

150   His father° revelled in the heart of France,   *(Henry V)*

And tamed the King, and made the Dauphin² stoop;

And had he matched° according to his state,°   *(Henry VI) wed / rank*

He might have kept that glory to this day.

But when he took a beggar to his bed,

155   And graced thy poor sire with his bridal day,³

Even then that sunshine brewed a shower for him

That washed his father's fortunes forth of° France,   *out of*

And heaped sedition on his crown at home.

For what hath broached this tumult but thy pride?

160   Hadst thou been meek, our title° still had slept,   *claim to the throne*

And we, in pity of the gentle King,

Had slipped° our claim until another age.   *postponed*

GEORGE [*to* QUEEN MARGARET]   But when we saw our sunshine

      made thy spring,

And that thy summer bred us no increase,°   *harvest*

165   We set the axe to thy usurping root.

And though the edge hath something° hit ourselves,   *to some extent*

Yet know thou, since we have begun to strike,

We'll never leave till we have hewn thee down,

Or bathed thy growing with our heated bloods.

170   EDWARD [*to* QUEEN MARGARET]   And in this resolution I defy thee,

Not willing any longer conference

Since thou deniest the gentle King to speak.

Sound trumpets—let our bloody colours wave!

And either victory, or else a grave!

175   QUEEN MARGARET   Stay, Edward.

EDWARD   No, wrangling woman, we'll no longer stay—

These words will cost ten thousand lives this day.

    [*Flourish. March.*] *Exeunt* [EDWARD *and his men*

    at one door and QUEEN MARGARET *and her men*

    at another door]⁴

2.3

Alarum. Excursions.° Enter [*the Earl of*] WARWICK¹   *Skirmishes*

WARWICK   Forespent° with toil, as runners with a race,   *Exhausted*

I lay me down a little while to breathe;°   *rest*

For strokes received, and many blows repaid,

---

9. Being made to wear or hold straw was a practice by which women were marked as scolds in public shaming rituals.

1. The Trojan War was said to have begun because the Greek Helen, the most beautiful woman in the world, betrayed her husband, Menelaus, and eloped with the Trojan warrior Paris.

2. The French King's oldest son, later Charles VII of France.

3. And brought honor to your impoverished father by marrying you.

4. Oxford proposes that Edward and Margaret and their men exit at separate stage doors to indicate symbolically their enmity. F and O read simply "Exeunt omnes."

2.3 Location: The remaining scenes in Act 2 take place in the fields near York.

1. While Shakespeare does not specify the locale, the events in this and the following three scenes resemble those associated with a battle waged at Towton in Yorkshire in 1461.

Have robbed my strong-knit° sinews of their strength,   *powerful*
5   And, spite of spite,° needs must I rest a while.   *come what may*
        Enter EDWARD [*the Duke of York*] *running*
    EDWARD Smile, gentle heaven, or strike, ungentle° death!   *ignoble*
    For this world frowns, and Edward's sun² is clouded.
    WARWICK How now, my lord, what hap?° What hope of good?   *fortune*
        Enter GEORGE [*running*]
    GEORGE Our hap is loss, our hope but sad despair;
10 Our ranks are broke, and ruin follows us.
    What counsel give you? Whither shall we fly?
    EDWARD Bootless° is flight—they follow us with wings,   *Useless*
    And weak we are, and cannot shun pursuit.
        Enter RICHARD, *running*
    RICHARD Ah, Warwick, why hast thou withdrawn thyself?
15 Thy brother's³ blood the thirsty earth hath drunk,
    Broached° with the steely point of Clifford's lance.   *Set flowing*
    And in the very pangs of death he cried,
    Like to a dismal clangour heard from far,
    'Warwick, revenge—brother, revenge my death!'
20 So, underneath the belly of their steeds
    That stained their fetlocks in his smoking° blood,   *steaming*
    The noble gentleman gave up the ghost.
    WARWICK Then let the earth be drunken with our blood.
    I'll kill my horse, because I will not fly.
25 Why stand we like soft-hearted women here,
    Wailing our losses, whiles the foe doth rage;
    And look upon,° as if the tragedy   *on*
    Were played in jest by counterfeiting actors?
    [*Kneeling*] Here, on my knee, I vow to God above
30 I'll never pause again, never stand still,
    Till either death hath closed these eyes of mine
    Or fortune given me measure of revenge.
    EDWARD [*kneeling*] O, Warwick, I do bend my knee with thine,
    And in this vow do chain my soul to thine.
35 And, ere my knee rise from the earth's cold face,
    I throw my hands, mine eyes, my heart to Thee,°   *(God)*
    Thou setter up and plucker down of kings,⁴
    Beseeching Thee, if with Thy will it stands°   *agrees*
    That to my foes this body must be prey,
40 Yet that Thy brazen gates of heaven may ope
    And give sweet passage to my sinful soul.
        [*They rise*]
    Now, lords, take leave until we meet again,
    Where'er it be, in heaven or in earth.
    RICHARD Brother, give me thy hand; and, gentle° Warwick,   *noble*
45 Let me embrace thee in my weary arms.
    I, that did never weep, now melt with woe
    That winter should cut off our springtime so.
    WARWICK Away, away! Once more, sweet lords, farewell.
    GEORGE Yet let us all together to our troops,
50 And give them leave° to fly that will not stay;   *permission*

2. Good fortune, alluding to the sun as Edward's   4. Echoing a biblical description of God in Daniel 2:21
emblem.   See also 3.3.157, where Margaret calls Warwick the
3. Warwick's half brother, the Bastard of Salisbury. "setter-up and puller-down of kings."

And call them pillars that will stand to° us;   *by*
And, if we thrive, promise them such rewards
As victors wear at the Olympian games.⁵
This may plant courage in their quailing breasts,
55   For yet is hope of life and victory.
Forslow° no longer—make we hence amain.°   *Exeunt*   *Delay / speedily*

2.4
Alarums. Excursions. Enter RICHARD *at one door
and [Lord]* CLIFFORD *at the other*

RICHARD   Now, Clifford, I have singled thee alone¹
Suppose this arm is for the Duke of York,
And this for Rutland, both bound to revenge,
Wert thou environed° with a brazen wall.   *surrounded*
5   CLIFFORD   Now, Richard, I am with thee here alone.
This is the hand that stabbed thy father York,
And this the hand that slew thy brother Rutland,
And here's the heart that triumphs in their death
And cheers these hands that slew thy sire and brother
10   To execute the like upon thyself—
And so, have at thee!
They fight. [The Earl of] WARWICK *comes and rescues*
RICHARD. *[Lord]* CLIFFORD *flies*
RICHARD   Nay, Warwick, single out some other chase°—   *prey*
For I myself will hunt this wolf to death.   *Exeunt*

2.5
Alarum. Enter KING HENRY

KING HENRY   This battle fares like to the morning's war,¹
When dying clouds contend with growing light,
What time° the shepherd, blowing of° his nails,   *When / on*
Can neither call it perfect day nor night.
5   Now sways it this way like a mighty sea
Forced by the tide to combat with the wind,
Now sways it that way like the selfsame sea
Forced to retire by fury of the wind.
Sometime the flood prevails, and then the wind;
10   Now one the better, then another best—
Both tugging to be victors, breast to breast,
Yet neither conqueror nor conquerèd.
So is the equal poise° of this fell° war.   *balance / deadly*
Here on this molehill² will I sit me down.
15   To whom God will, there be the victory.
For Margaret my queen, and Clifford, too,
Have chid me from the battle, swearing both
They prosper best of all when I am thence.
Would I were dead, if God's good will were so—
20   For what is in this world but grief and woe?

---

5. The Olympian Games in ancient Greece were festivals that included athletic contests. Victors were presented with garlands of olive leaves.
2.4
1. I have isolated you from the herd (a hunting
term).

2.5
1. In O, King Henry's ensuing fifty-four-line soliloquy
as found in F is reduced to thirteen lines, perhaps
shortened for performance.
2. See 1.4.68, where Richard, Duke of York is made to
stand on a molehill before his death.

O God! Methinks it were a happy life
To be no better than a homely swain.°   *simple shepherd*
To sit upon a hill, as I do now;
To carve out dials quaintly,° point by point,   *sundials artfully*
25   Thereby to see the minutes how they run:
How many makes the hour full complete,
How many hours brings about° the day,   *completes*
How many days will finish up the year,
How many years a mortal man may live.
30   When this is known, then to divide the times:
So many hours must I tend my flock,
So many hours must I take my rest,
So many hours must I contemplate,
So many hours must I sport myself,
35   So many days my ewes have been with young,
So many weeks ere the poor fools will ean,°   *give birth*
So many years ere I shall shear the fleece.
So minutes, hours, days, weeks, months, and years,
Passed over to the end they° were created,   *for which they*
40   Would bring white hairs unto a quiet grave.
Ah, what a life were this! How sweet! How lovely!
Gives not the hawthorn bush a sweeter shade
To shepherds looking on their seely° sheep   *innocent*
Than doth a rich embroidered canopy
45   To kings that fear their subjects' treachery?
O yes, it doth—a thousandfold it doth.
And to conclude, the shepherd's homely curds,
His cold thin drink out of his leather bottle,
His wonted° sleep under a fresh tree's shade,   *customary*
50   All which secure and sweetly he enjoys,
Is far beyond a prince's delicates,°   *delicacies*
His viands° sparkling in a golden cup,   *food*
His body couchèd in a curious° bed,   *an ornate*
When care, mistrust, and treason waits on him.
    Alarum. Enter at one door a SOLDIER *with a dead man*
    in his arms. [KING HENRY *stands apart*][3]
55 SOLDIER   Ill blows the wind that profits nobody.
This man, whom hand to hand I slew in fight,
May be possessèd with some store of crowns;°   *coins*
And I, that haply° take them from him now,   *by chance*
May yet ere night yield both my life and them
60   To some man else, as this dead man doth me.
    [*He removes the dead man's helmet*]
Who's this? O God! It is my father's face
Whom in this conflict I, unwares, have killed.
O, heavy times, begetting such events!
From London by the King was I pressed forth;[4]
65   My father, being the Earl of Warwick's man,°   *servant*

---

3. Here Oxford adopts a combination of Folio and Octavo staging. F indicates a simultaneous entrance, at two different doors, of a "Son that hath kill'd his Father" and a "Father that hath kill'd his Son." O, as here, designates both figures as simply "a soldier with a dead man in his arms" and "another soldier with a dead man," and gives them entrances at lines 54 and 78,

respectively, but without mention of two doors. In O, the relationship between the living and the dead is revealed through the dialogue only.
4. Forcibly enlisted. Because England had no standing army until the latter half of the seventeenth century, many soldiers in Elizabethan England were conscripts.

Came on the part° of York, pressed by his master;   side
And I, who at his hands received my life,
Have by my hands of life bereavèd him.
Pardon me, God, I knew not what I did;
70   And pardon, father, for I knew not thee.
My tears shall wipe away these bloody marks,
And no more words till they have flowed their fill.
        [*He weeps*]
KING HENRY   O piteous spectacle! O bloody times!
Whiles lions war and battle for their dens,
75   Poor harmless lambs abide their enmity.
Weep, wretched man, I'll aid thee tear for tear;
And let our hearts and eyes, like civil war,
Be blind with tears, and break, o'ercharged° with grief.   overburdened
        Enter at another door another SOLDIER *with a dead*
        man [*in his arms*]
SECOND SOLDIER   Thou that so stoutly hath resisted me,
80   Give me thy gold, if thou hast any gold—
For I have bought it with an hundred blows.
        [*He removes the dead man's helmet*]
But let me see: is this our foeman's° face?   enemy's
Ah, no, no, no—it is mine only son!
Ah, boy, if any life be left in thee,
85   Throw up thine eye! [*Weeping*] See, see, what showers arise,
Blown with the windy tempest of my heart,
Upon thy wounds, that kills mine eye and heart!
O, pity, God, this miserable age!
What stratagems,° how fell,° how butcherly,   violent acts / cruel
90   Erroneous,° mutinous, and unnatural,   Criminal
This deadly quarrel daily doth beget!
O boy, thy father gave thee life too soon,
And hath bereft thee of thy life too late!°   recently
KING HENRY   Woe above woe! Grief more than common grief!
95   O that my death would stay° these ruthful° deeds!   stop / pitiful
O, pity, pity, gentle heaven, pity!
The red rose and the white are on his face,
The fatal colours of our striving houses;
The one his purple blood right well resembles,
100   The other his pale cheeks, methinks, presenteth.
Wither one rose, and let the other flourish—
If you contend, a thousand lives must wither.
FIRST SOLDIER   How will my mother for a father's death
Take on with° me, and ne'er be satisfied!   Rage against
105   SECOND SOLDIER   How will my wife for slaughter of my son
Shed seas of tears, and ne'er be satisfied!
KING HENRY   How will the country for these woeful chances°   events
Misthink° the King, and not be satisfied!   Think ill of
FIRST SOLDIER   Was ever son so rued a father's death?
110   SECOND SOLDIER   Was ever father so bemoaned his son?
KING HENRY   Was ever king so grieved for subjects' woe?
Much is your sorrow, mine ten times so much.
FIRST SOLDIER [*to his father's body*]   I'll bear thee hence where
        I may weep my fill.
        Exit [*at one door*] *with* [*the body of*] *his father*

SECOND SOLDIER [*to his son's body*] These arms of mine shall be
     thy winding sheet;°   *shroud*
115   My heart, sweet boy, shall be thy sepulchre,
     For from my heart thine image ne'er shall go.
     My sighing breast shall be thy funeral bell,
     And so obsequious° will thy father be,   *dutiful in mourning*
     E'en for the loss of thee, having no more,
120   As Priam[5] was for all his valiant sons.
     I'll bear thee hence, and let them fight that will—
     For I have murdered where I should not kill.
                  Exit [*at another door*] *with* [*the body of*] *his son*

KING HENRY Sad-hearted men, much overgone° with care,   *overcome*
     Here sits a king more woeful than you are.
              Alarums. Excursions. Enter PRINCE EDWARD[6]
125 PRINCE EDWARD Fly, father, fly—for all your friends are fled,
     And Warwick rages like a chafèd° bull!   *an angered*
     Away—for death doth hold us in pursuit!
              Enter QUEEN [MARGARET]
QUEEN MARGARET Mount you, my lord—towards Berwick[7] post
     amain.°   *ride speedily*
     Edward and Richard, like a brace° of greyhounds   *pair*
130   Having the fearful flying hare in sight,
     With fiery eyes sparkling for very wrath,
     And bloody steel grasped in their ireful hands,
     Are at our backs—and therefore hence amain.°   *at full speed*
              Enter EXETER
EXETER Away—for vengeance comes along with them!
135   Nay—stay not to expostulate°—make speed—   *argue*
     Or else come after. I'll away before.
KING HENRY Nay, take me with thee, good sweet Exeter.
     Not that I fear to stay, but love to go
     Whither the Queen intends. Forward, away.   *Exeunt*

2.6

A loud alarum. Enter [*Lord*] CLIFFORD, *wounded with
an arrow in his neck*

CLIFFORD Here burns my candle out—ay, here it dies,
     Which, whiles it lasted, gave King Henry light.
     O Lancaster, I fear thy overthrow
     More than my body's parting with my soul!
5   My love and fear° glued many friends to thee—   *Love and fear of me*
     And, now I fall, thy tough commixture[1] melts,
     Impairing Henry, strength'ning misproud° York.   *arrogant*
     The common people swarm like summer flies,
     And whither fly the gnats but to the sun?[2]
10   And who shines now but Henry's enemies?
     O Phoebus, hadst thou never given consent
     That Phaëton[3] should check° thy fiery steeds,   *manage*

---

5. King of Troy during the Trojan War. His fifty sons, of whom Hector was one, were killed defending the city.
6. F indicates a single entrance for "the Queen, the Prince, and Exeter" at line 124, and they speak in the order Prince-Queen-Exeter; O has Margaret enter first, then Prince Edward, and finally Exeter. Oxford follows O and divides the entrances, but places them in F's order of speech.

7. Berwick-upon-Tweed, a village near Scotland in Northumberland.
2.6
1. The compound of love and fear that I commanded.
2. Alluding to the sun as Edward's emblem. See note to 2.1.40.
3. The son of Phoebus, god of the sun. See note to 1.4.34.

Thy burning car° never had scorched the earth!   *chariot*
And, Henry, hadst thou swayed° as kings should do,   *ruled*
15 Or as thy father and his father did,
Giving no ground unto the house of York,
They never then had sprung like summer flies;
I and ten thousand in this luckless realm
Had left no mourning widows for our death;
20 And thou this day hadst kept thy chair° in peace.   *throne*
For what doth cherish° weeds, but gentle air?   *nurture*
And what makes robbers bold, but too much lenity?
Bootless are plaints,° and cureless are my wounds;   *Useless are pleas*
No way to fly, nor strength to hold out flight;
25 The foe is merciless and will not pity,
For at their hands I have deserved no pity.
The air hath got into my deadly wounds,
And much effuse° of blood doth make me faint.   *effusion*
Come York and Richard, Warwick and the rest—
30 I stabbed your fathers' bosoms; split my breast.
> [*He faints.*]
> *Alarum and retreat. Enter* EDWARD [*Duke of York, his*
> *brothers*] GEORGE *and* RICHARD, [*the Earl of*] WARWICK,
> [*the Marquis of*] MONTAGUE, *and soldiers*[4]

EDWARD   Now breathe we, lords—good fortune bids us pause,
And smooth the frowns of war with peaceful looks.
Some troops pursue the bloody-minded Queen,
That led calm Henry, though he were a king,
35 As doth a sail filled with a fretting° gust   *blowing fitfully*
Command an argosy° to stem° the waves.   *a merchant ship / resist*
But think you, lords, that Clifford fled with them?

WARWICK   No—'tis impossible he should escape;
For, though before his face I speak the words,
40 Your brother Richard marked him for the grave.
And whereso'er he is, he's surely dead.
> CLIFFORD *groans*

EDWARD   Whose soul is that which takes her heavy leave?[5]

RICHARD   A deadly groan, like life and death's departing.

EDWARD [*to* RICHARD]   See who it is.
> [RICHARD *goes to* CLIFFORD]
             And now the battle's ended,
45 If friend or foe, let him be gently used.

RICHARD   Revoke that doom° of mercy, for 'tis Clifford;   *sentence*
Who not contented that he lopped the branch
In hewing Rutland when his leaves put forth,
But set his murd'ring knife unto the root
50 From whence that tender spray° did sweetly spring—   *shoot*
I mean our princely father, Duke of York.

WARWICK   From off the gates of York fetch down the head,
Your father's head, which Clifford placèd there.
Instead whereof let this supply the room[6]—

---

4. In F, the order of names in the stage direction ends with "Montague and Clarence" (George) placed after "Soldiers." The peculiarity of listing these noble figures last may suggest that they were added as an afterthought. Montague does not speak during the scene. Neither he nor George is indicated in O's stage directions, in which George speaks the same lines as in F.
5. In F, lines 42 and 43 and half of line 44 are assigned to Richard. O divides them as here. Oxford, as elsewhere, argues that this is an instance of authorial revision between foul papers and promptbook.
6. Let Clifford's head take its place.

55   Measure for measure[7] must be answerèd.°   *given in return*

    EDWARD   Bring forth that fatal screech-owl to our house,[8]

       That nothing sung but death to us and ours.

       [CLIFFORD is *dragged forward*]

       Now death shall stop his dismal threat'ning sound

       And his ill-boding° tongue no more shall speak.   *doom-promising*

60   WARWICK   I think his understanding is bereft.°   *destroyed*

       Speak, Clifford, dost thou know who speaks to thee?

       Dark cloudy death o'ershades his beams of life,

       And he nor° sees nor hears us what we say.   *neither*

    RICHARD   O, would he did—and so perhaps he doth.

65   'Tis but his policy to counterfeit,

       Because he would avoid such bitter taunts

       Which in the time of death he gave our father.

    GEORGE   If so thou think'st, vex him with eager° words.   *bitter*

    RICHARD   Clifford, ask mercy and obtain no grace.

70   EDWARD   Clifford, repent in bootless penitence.

    WARWICK   Clifford, devise excuses for thy faults.

    GEORGE   While we devise fell° tortures for thy faults.   *cruel*

    RICHARD   Thou didst love York, and I am son to York.

    EDWARD   Thou pitied'st Rutland—I will pity thee.

75   GEORGE   Where's Captain Margaret to fence° you now?   *protect*

    WARWICK   They mock thee, Clifford—swear as thou wast wont.

    RICHARD   What, not an oath? Nay, then, the world goes hard

       When Clifford cannot spare his friends an oath.

       I know by that he's dead—and, by my soul,

80   If this right hand would buy but two hours' life

       That I, in all despite, might rail at him,

       This hand° should chop it off, and with the issuing blood   *(his left hand)*

       Stifle° the villain whose unstanchèd° thirst   *Choke / insatiable*

       York and young Rutland could not satisfy.

85   WARWICK   Ay, but he's dead. Off with the traitor's head,

       And rear it in the place your father's stands.

       And now to London with triumphant march,

       There to be crownèd England's royal king;

       From whence shall Warwick cut the sea to France,

90   And ask the Lady Bona[9] for thy queen.

       So shalt thou sinew° both these lands together.   *tie firmly*

       And, having France thy friend, thou shalt not dread

       The scattered foe that hopes to rise again,

       For though they cannot greatly sting to hurt,

95   Yet look to have them buzz to offend thine ears.

       First will I see the coronation,

       And then to Brittany I'll cross the sea

       To effect this marriage, so it please my lord.

    EDWARD   Even as thou wilt, sweet Warwick, let it be.

100   For in thy shoulder° do I build my seat,   *with your support*

       And never will I undertake the thing

       Wherein thy counsel and consent is wanting.

       Richard, I will create thee Duke of Gloucester,

---

7. Alluding to the strict rule of justice described in Mark 4:24: "With what measure ye mete, it shall be measured unto you."
8. Bring forth that creature ominous to our house.

Screech owls were traditionally thought to be harbingers of death.
9. The sister-in-law of King Louis XI of France and daughter of Louis, Duke of Savoy.

And George, of Clarence; Warwick, as ourself,
105 Shall do and undo as him pleaseth best.
RICHARD Let me be Duke of Clarence, George of Gloucester—
For Gloucester's dukedom is too ominous.[1]
WARWICK Tut, that's a foolish observation—
Richard, be Duke of Gloucester. Now to London
110 To see these honours in possession.

Exeunt. [*York's head is removed*]

3.1

Enter two [GAME]KEEPERS, *with crossbows in their hands*

FIRST GAMEKEEPER Under this thick-grown brake° we'll shroud   thicket
    ourselves,
For through this laund° anon the deer will come,   clearing
And in this covert will we make our stand,
Culling the principal° of all the deer.   Selecting the best
5 SECOND GAMEKEEPER I'll stay above the hill, so both may shoot.
FIRST GAMEKEEPER That cannot be—the noise of thy crossbow
Will scare the herd, and so my shoot is lost.
Here stand we both, and aim we at the best.°   as well as we can
And, for° the time shall not seem tedious,   so that
10 I'll tell thee what befell me on a day
In this self place where now we mean to stand.
FIRST GAMEKEEPER Here comes a man—let's stay till he be past.
    [*They stand apart.*]

Enter KING HENRY, *disguised, with a prayer-book*

KING HENRY From Scotland am I stolen, even of° pure love,   out of
To greet mine own land with my wishful° sight.   longing
15 No, Harry, Harry—'tis no land of thine.
Thy place is filled, thy sceptre wrung from thee,
Thy balm washed off wherewith thou wast anointed.
No bending knee will call thee Caesar° now,   emperor
No humble suitors press to speak for right,°   beg for justice
20 No, not a man comes for redress of° thee—   from
For how can I help them and not myself?
FIRST GAMEKEEPER [*to the* SECOND GAMEKEEPER] Ay, here's a
    deer whose skin's a keeper's fee.[1]
This is the quondam° king—let's seize upon him.   former
KING HENRY Let me embrace thee, sour adversity,
25 For wise men say it is the wisest course.
SECOND GAMEKEEPER [*to the* FIRST GAMEKEEPER] Why linger
    we? Let us lay hands upon him.
FIRST GAMEKEEPER [*to the* SECOND GAMEKEEPER] Forbear
    awhile—we'll hear a little more.
KING HENRY My queen and son are gone to France for aid,
And, as I hear, the great commanding Warwick
30 Is thither gone to crave the French King's sister
To wife for Edward. If this news be true,
Poor Queen and son, your labour is but lost—
For Warwick is a subtle orator,
And Louis a prince soon won with moving words.

---

1. Referring to the fact that three previous Dukes of
Gloucester had suffered violent deaths.
3.1 Location: A forest in northern England near the

Scottish border.
1. Traditionally, hunters presented the horns and skin
of a captured deer to the park's gamekeeper.

35 By this account, then, Margaret may win him—
For she's a woman to be pitied much.
Her sighs will make a batt'ry° in his breast,   *a breach*
Her tears will pierce into a marble heart,
The tiger will be mild whiles she doth mourn,
40 And Nero² will be tainted° with remorse   *touched*
To hear and see her plaints,° her brinish° tears.   *pleas / salty*
Ay, but she's come to beg; Warwick to give.
She on his left side, craving aid for Henry;
He on his right, asking a wife for Edward.
45 She weeps and says her Henry is deposed,
He smiles and says his Edward is installed;
That she, poor wretch, for grief can speak no more,
Whiles Warwick tells his title,³ smooths the wrong,
Inferreth° arguments of mighty strength,   *Presents*
50 And in conclusion wins the King from her
With promise of his sister and what else
To strengthen and support King Edward's place.
O, Margaret, thus 'twill be; and thou, poor soul,
Art then forsaken, as thou went'st forlorn.
SECOND GAMEKEEPER [*coming forward*] Say, what art thou that
55   talk'st of kings and queens?
KING HENRY More than I seem, and less than I was born to:
A man at least, for less I should not be;
And men may talk of kings, and why not I?
SECOND GAMEKEEPER Ay, but thou talk'st as if thou wert a king.
60 KING HENRY Why, so I am, in mind—and that's enough.
SECOND GAMEKEEPER But if thou be a king, where is thy crown?
KING HENRY My crown is in my heart, not on my head;
Not decked with diamonds and Indian stones,°   *pearls*
Nor to be seen. My crown is called content—
65 A crown it is that seldom kings enjoy.
SECOND GAMEKEEPER Well, if you be a king crowned with content,
Your crown content and you must be contented
To go along with us—for, as we think,
You are the king King Edward hath deposed,
70 And we his subjects sworn in all allegiance
Will apprehend you as his enemy.
KING HENRY But did you never swear and break an oath?
SECOND GAMEKEEPER No—never such an oath, nor will not now.
KING HENRY Where did you dwell when I was King of England?
75 SECOND GAMEKEEPER Here in this country, where we now remain.
KING HENRY I was anointed king at nine months old,
My father and my grandfather were kings,
And you were sworn true subjects unto me—
And tell me, then, have you not broke your oaths?
80 FIRST GAMEKEEPER No, for we were subjects but° while you were king.   *only*
KING HENRY Why, am I dead? Do I not breathe a man?
Ah, simple men, you know not what you swear.
Look as I blow this feather from my face,

2. A notoriously cruel Roman Emperor.   3. While Warwick asserts Edward's claim to the throne.

And as the air blows it to me again,
85 Obeying with° my wind when I do blow,   *Submitting to*
And yielding to another when it blows,
Commanded always by the greater gust—
Such is the lightness° of you common men.   *fickleness*
But do not break your oaths, for of that sin
90 My mild entreaty shall not make you guilty.
Go where you will, the King shall be commanded;
And be you kings, command, and I'll obey.
FIRST GAMEKEEPER   We are true subjects to the King, King Edward.
KING HENRY   So would you be again to Henry,
95 If he were seated as King Edward is.
FIRST GAMEKEEPER   We charge you, in God's name and in the King's,
To go with us unto the officers.
KING HENRY   In God's name, lead; your king's name be obeyed;
And what God will, that let your king perform;
100 And what he will I humbly yield unto.   *Exeunt*

3.2

Enter KING EDWARD, [RICHARD *Duke* OF] GLOUCESTER,
[GEORGE *Duke* OF] CLARENCE, *and the* LADY GRAY

KING EDWARD   Brother of Gloucester, at Saint Albans field
This lady's husband, Sir Richard Gray, was slain,
His lands then seized on by the conqueror.
Her suit is now to repossess those lands,
5 Which we in justice cannot well deny,
Because in quarrel of the house of York
The worthy gentleman did lose his life.
RICHARD OF GLOUCESTER   Your highness shall do well to grant her suit—
It were dishonour to deny it her.
10 KING EDWARD   It were no less; but yet I'll make a pause.
RICHARD OF GLOUCESTER [*aside to* GEORGE]   Yea, is it so?
I see the lady hath a thing° to grant   *(sexual) favor*
Before the King will grant her humble suit.
GEORGE OF CLARENCE [*aside to* RICHARD] He knows the game;
    how true he keeps the wind![1]
15 RICHARD OF GLOUCESTER [*aside to* GEORGE]   Silence.
KING EDWARD [*to* LADY GRAY]   Widow, we will consider of your suit;
And come some other time to know our mind.
LADY GRAY   Right gracious lord, I cannot brook° delay.   *tolerate*
May it please your highness to resolve me now,
20 And what your pleasure° is shall satisfy me.   *will; sexual desire*
RICHARD OF GLOUCESTER [*aside to* GEORGE]   Ay, widow? Then
    I'll warrant° you all your lands   *guarantee*
An if° what pleases him shall pleasure you.   *An if = If*

3.2 Location: The palace, London.
1. "The game" suggests the "sport" of hunting animals or of pursuing sex partners, as well as the objects of both pursuits. Hounds "keep the wind" by keeping the prey against the wind so that it does not catch the scent of the hunter and run away. Clarence implies that Edward pursues Lady Gray with similar skill. The following lines are full of sexual wordplay that Clarence and Richard clearly intend, but that Lady Gray probably does not.

Fight closer, or, good faith, you'll catch a blow.[2]

GEORGE OF CLARENCE [*aside to* RICHARD]   I fear° her not unless   *fear for*
    she chance to fall.[3]

RICHARD OF GLOUCESTER [*aside to* GEORGE]   God forbid that!
25   For he'll take vantages.°   *opportunities*

KING EDWARD [*to* LADY GRAY]   How many children hast thou,
    widow? Tell me.

GEORGE OF CLARENCE [*aside to* RICHARD]   I think he means to
    beg a child of her.[4]

RICHARD OF GLOUCESTER [*aside to* GEORGE]   Nay, whip me
    then—he'll rather give her two.

LADY GRAY [*to* KING EDWARD]   Three, my most gracious lord.

RICHARD OF GLOUCESTER [*aside*]   You shall have four, an° you'll   *if*
30   be ruled by him.

KING EDWARD [*to* LADY GRAY]   'Twere pity they should lose their
    father's lands.

LADY GRAY   Be pitiful, dread lord, and grant it them.

KING EDWARD [*to* RICHARD *and* GEORGE]   Lords, give us leave°—   *leave us alone*
    I'll try this widow's wit.

RICHARD OF GLOUCESTER [*aside to* GEORGE]   Ay, good leave
    have you; for you will have leave,
35   Till youth take leave and leave you to the crutch.[5]
    [RICHARD *and* GEORGE *stand apart*]

KING EDWARD [*to* LADY GRAY]   Now tell me, madam, do you love
    your children?

LADY GRAY   Ay, full as dearly as I love myself.

KING EDWARD   And would you not do much to do them good?

LADY GRAY   To do them good I would sustain some harm.

40 KING EDWARD   Then get your husband's lands, to do them good.

LADY GRAY   Therefore I came unto your majesty.

KING EDWARD   I'll tell you how these lands are to be got.

LADY GRAY   So shall you bind me to your highness' service.

KING EDWARD   What service wilt thou do me, if I give them?

45 LADY GRAY   What you command, that rests in me to do.

KING EDWARD   But you will take exceptions to my boon.°   *request*

LADY GRAY   No, gracious lord, except° I cannot do it.   *unless*

KING EDWARD   Ay, but thou canst do what I mean to ask.

LADY GRAY   Why, then, I will do what your grace commands.

RICHARD OF GLOUCESTER [*to* GEORGE]   He plies her hard, and
50   much rain wears the marble.

GEORGE OF CLARENCE   As red as fire! Nay, then her wax must
    melt.

LADY GRAY [*to* KING EDWARD]   Why stops my lord? Shall I not
    hear my task?

KING EDWARD   An easy task—'tis but to love a king.

LADY GRAY   That's soon performed, because I am a subject.

---

2. Fight nearer to avoid his thrusts. Conflating sexual slang and the language of dueling, Richard puns on "blow" as meaning both "hit" and "sexual thrust."
3. Stumble; submit to sex.
4. To ask her to bear him a child; to petition for guardianship of one of her children. English monarchs generated income by gaining control of wealthy orphans

from the Court of Wards and Liveries and arranging their marriages in ways profitable to the monarch.
5. *Ay . . . crutch:* Yes, we will leave you alone, for you will take liberties (with Lady Gray) until your youth departs and leaves you walking on crutches (too old for love). The multiple puns in these lines include "crutch" as a play on "crotch."

55   KING EDWARD   Why, then, thy husband's lands I freely give thee.

LADY GRAY [*curtsies*]   I take my leave, with many thousand thanks.

RICHARD OF GLOUCESTER [*to* GEORGE]   The match is made—she
    seals it with a curtsy.

KING EDWARD [*to* LADY GRAY]   But stay thee—'tis the fruits of
    love I mean.

LADY GRAY   The fruits of love I mean, my loving liege.

60   KING EDWARD   Ay, but I fear me in another sense.
    What love think'st thou I sue so much to get?

LADY GRAY   My love till death, my humble thanks, my prayers—
    That love which virtue begs and virtue grants.

KING EDWARD   No, by my troth, I did not mean such love.

65   LADY GRAY   Why, then, you mean not as I thought you did.

KING EDWARD   But now you partly may perceive my mind.

LADY GRAY   My mind will never grant what I perceive
    Your highness aims at, if I aim aright.°   *guess correctly*

KING EDWARD   To tell thee plain, I aim to lie with thee.

70   LADY GRAY   To tell *you* plain, I had rather lie in prison.

KING EDWARD   Why, then, thou shalt not have thy husband's
    lands.

LADY GRAY   Why, then, mine honesty° shall be my dower;   *chastity*
    For by that loss I will not purchase them.

KING EDWARD   Therein thou wrong'st thy children mightily.

75   LADY GRAY   Herein your highness wrongs both them and me.
    But, mighty lord, this merry inclination
    Accords not with the sadness° of my suit.   *seriousness*
    Please you dismiss me either with ay or no.

KING EDWARD   Ay, if thou wilt say 'ay' to my request;

80   No, if thou dost say 'no' to my demand.

LADY GRAY   Then, no, my lord—my suit is at an end.

RICHARD OF GLOUCESTER [*to* GEORGE]   The widow likes him
    not—she knits her brows.

GEORGE OF CLARENCE   He is the bluntest wooer in Christendom.

KING EDWARD [*aside*]   Her looks doth argue° her replete with modesty;   *prove*

85   Her words doth show her wit incomparable;
    All her perfections challenge° sovereignty.   *lay claim to*
    One way or other, she is for a king;
    And she shall be my love or else my queen.
    [*To* LADY GRAY] Say that King Edward take thee for his queen?

90   LADY GRAY   'Tis better said than done, my gracious lord.
    I am a subject fit to jest withal,
    But far unfit to be a sovereign.

KING EDWARD   Sweet widow, by my state° I swear to thee   *kingship*
    I speak no more than what my soul intends,

95   And that is to enjoy thee for my love.

LADY GRAY   And that is more than I will yield unto.
    I know I am too mean to be your queen,
    And yet too good to be your concubine.

KING EDWARD   You cavil,° widow—I did mean my queen.   *object frivolously*

100   LADY GRAY   'Twill grieve your grace my sons should call you father.

KING EDWARD   No more than when my daughters call thee mother.
    Thou art a widow and thou hast some children;
    And, by God's mother, I, being but a bachelor,
    Have other some.° Why, 'tis a happy thing   *some others*

105   To be the father unto many sons.
       Answer no more, for thou shalt be my queen.
RICHARD OF GLOUCESTER [to GEORGE]   The ghostly father°   priest
       now hath done his shrift.[6]
GEORGE OF CLARENCE   When he was made a shriver, 'twas for
       shift.[7]
KING EDWARD [to RICHARD and GEORGE]   Brothers, you muse°   wonder
       what chat we two have had.
              [RICHARD and GEORGE come forward]
RICHARD OF GLOUCESTER   The widow likes it not, for she looks
110   very sad.
KING EDWARD   You'd think it strange if I should marry her.
GEORGE OF CLARENCE   To who, my lord?
KING EDWARD   Why, Clarence, to myself.
RICHARD OF GLOUCESTER   That would be ten days' wonder at
       the least.
GEORGE OF CLARENCE   That's a day longer than a wonder lasts.[8]
115 RICHARD OF GLOUCESTER   By so much is the wonder in extremes.°   exceedingly great
KING EDWARD   Well, jest on, brothers—I can tell you both
       Her suit is granted for her husband's lands.
                          Enter a NOBLEMAN
NOBLEMAN   My gracious lord, Henry your foe is taken
       And brought as prisoner to your palace gate.
120 KING EDWARD   See that he be conveyed unto the Tower—
       [To RICHARD and GEORGE] And go we, brothers, to the man
              that took him,
       To question of his apprehension.
       [To LADY GRAY] Widow, go you along. [To RICHARD and GEORGE]
              Lords, use her honourably.
                          Exeunt. Manet° RICHARD   Remains
RICHARD OF GLOUCESTER   Ay, Edward will use women honourably.
125 Would he were wasted, marrow, bones, and all,[9]
       That from his loins no hopeful branch may spring
       To cross° me from the golden time I look for.   keep
       And yet, between my soul's desire and me—
       The lustful Edward's title burièd°—   eliminated
130 Is Clarence, Henry, and his son young Edward,
       And all the unlooked-for° issue of their bodies,   unforeseen
       To take their rooms° ere I can place myself.   places
       A cold premeditation° for my purpose.   A discouraging prospect
       Why, then, I do but dream on sovereignty
135 Like one that stands upon a promontory
       And spies a far-off shore where he would tread,
       Wishing his foot were equal with his eye,[1]
       And chides the sea that sunders him from thence,
       Saying he'll lade° it dry to have his way—   empty
140 So do I wish° the crown being so far off,   wish for
       And so I chide the means that keeps me from it,

---

6. Has heard her confession and given absolution.
7. It was for a purpose; it was in order to gain access to her undergarments ("shift").
8. Referring to the proverbial expression "nine day's wonder," something that for a short while causes a sensation.

9. Would he were destroyed by disease. Elizabethan medical theory held that syphilis attacked the bones, affected male "mettle," or semen, and caused sterility.
1. Wishing he were able to attain what his eye sees.

And so I say I'll cut the causes off,
Flattering me with impossibilities.
My eye's too quick, my heart o'erweens° too much,   *presumes*
145   Unless my hand and strength could equal them.
Well, say there is no kingdom then for Richard—
What other pleasure can the world afford?
I'll make my heaven in a lady's lap,
And deck my body in gay ornaments,
150   And 'witch° sweet ladies with my words and looks.   *bewitch*
O, miserable thought! And more unlikely
Than to accomplish° twenty golden crowns.   *obtain*
Why, love forswore° me in my mother's womb,   *abandoned*
And, for° I should not deal in her soft laws,   *so that*
155   She did corrupt frail nature with some bribe
To shrink mine arm up like a withered shrub,
To make an envious° mountain on my back—   *a detested*
Where sits deformity to mock my body—
To shape my legs of an unequal size,
160   To disproportion me in every part,
Like to a chaos,° or an unlicked bear whelp[2]   *formless mass*
That carries no impression like the dam.[3]
And am I then a man to be beloved?
O, monstrous fault, to harbour such a thought!
165   Then, since this earth affords no joy to me
But to command, to check,° to o'erbear° such   *rebuke / dominate*
As are of better person° than myself,   *appearance*
I'll make my heaven to dream upon the crown,
And whiles I live, t'account this world but hell,
170   Until my misshaped trunk that bears this head
Be round impalèd° with a glorious crown.   *enclosed*
And yet I know not how to get the crown,
For many lives stand between me and home.°   *(my goal)*
And I—like one lost in a thorny wood,
175   That rends the thorns and is rent with the thorns,
Seeking a way and straying from the way,
Not knowing how to find the open air,
But toiling desperately to find it out—
Torment myself to catch the English crown.
180   And from that torment I will free myself,
Or hew my way out with a bloody axe.
Why, I can smile, and murder whiles I smile,
And cry 'Content!' to that which grieves my heart,
And wet my cheeks with artificial tears,
185   And frame my face to all occasions.
I'll drown more sailors than the mermaid[4] shall;
I'll slay more gazers than the basilisk;[5]
I'll play the orator as well as Nestor,[6]
Deceive more slyly than Ulysses[7] could,

2. Alluding to the popular belief that bears were born as formless lumps and licked into shape by their mothers.
3. That does not resemble its mother.
4. A fabulous marine monster, resembling a woman, who sang sweet songs to lure sailors onto the rocks and to their death.
5. A mythical reptile, hatched from a cock's egg, whose look was supposed to be fatal.
6. The Greek King and aged counselor present at the siege of Troy, famous for his skill in speech.
7. The Greek warrior famous for his cunning, hero of Homer's *Odyssey*.

190　　　And, like a Sinon,[8] take another Troy.
　　　　I can add colours to the chameleon,[9]
　　　　Change shapes with Proteus[1] for advantages,
　　　　And set the murderous Machiavel[2] to school.
　　　　Can I do this, and cannot get a crown?
195　　　Tut, were it farther off, I'll pluck it down.　　　　　　　　　　*Exit*

3.3

　　　[*Two chairs of state.*][1] *Flourish. Enter* KING LOUIS
　　　[*of France*]*, his sister the* LADY BONA, [*Lord*] *Bourbon*
　　　his admiral, PRINCE EDWARD, QUEEN MARGARET,
　　　and the Earl of OXFORD. LOUIS [*goes up upon the*
　　　state,] *sits, and riseth up again*

KING LOUIS　Fair Queen of England, worthy Margaret,
　　　　Sit down with us. It ill befits thy state
　　　　And birth that thou shouldst stand while Louis doth sit.
QUEEN MARGARET　No, mighty King of France, now Margaret
5　　　Must strike her sail° and learn a while to serve　　　*humble herself*
　　　　Where kings command. I was, I must confess,
　　　　Great Albion's° queen in former golden days,　　　　*England's*
　　　　But now mischance hath trod my title down,
　　　　And with dishonour laid me on the ground,
10　　　Where I must take like seat unto my fortune[2]
　　　　And to my humble state conform myself.
KING LOUIS　Why, say, fair Queen, whence springs this deep despair?
QUEEN MARGARET　From such a cause as fills mine eyes with tears
　　　　And stops my tongue, while heart is drowned in cares.
15　KING LOUIS　Whate'er it be, be thou still like thyself,
　　　　And sit thee by our side.
　　　　　　　Seats her by him
　　　　　　　　　　　Yield not thy neck
　　　To fortune's yoke, but let thy dauntless mind
　　　Still ride in triumph over all mischance.
　　　Be plain, Queen Margaret, and tell thy grief.
20　　　It shall be eased if France° can yield relief.　　　*the King of France*
QUEEN MARGARET　Those gracious words revive my drooping
　　　　　　　thoughts,
　　　　And give my tongue-tied sorrows leave to speak.
　　　　Now, therefore, be it known to noble Louis
　　　　That Henry, sole possessor of my love,
25　　　Is of° a king become a banished man,　　　　　　　*Instead of*

---

8. Like a treacherous man. According to Virgil, Sinon's lies convinced the Trojans to accept as a gift the wooden horse in which the Greek soldiers who later sacked Troy were concealed.
9. A reptile able to change the color of its skin in order to blend into its surroundings.
1. A Greek sea god who was able to assume different shapes at will.
2. Niccolò Machiavelli (1469–1527), an Italian political philosopher popularly known in England as a depraved advocate of political cunning and ruthlessness.
3.3 Location: The King's palace, France.
1. Louis's request for Margaret to "sit down with us" at line 2 suggests that at least two chairs of state are required, possibly three (including one for Lady Bona).
2. Where I must take a position in keeping with my fortune.

And forced to live in Scotland a forlorn,°   *an outcast*
While proud ambitious Edward, Duke of York,
Usurps the regal title and the seat
Of England's true-anointed lawful King.
30 This is the cause that I, poor Margaret,
With this my son, Prince Edward, Henry's heir,
Am come to crave thy just and lawful aid.
An if thou fail us all our hope is done.
Scotland hath will to help, but cannot help;
35 Our people and our peers are both misled,
Our treasure seized, our soldiers put to flight,
And, as thou seest, ourselves in heavy plight.
KING LOUIS   Renownèd Queen, with patience calm the storm,
While we bethink a means to break it off.
40 QUEEN MARGARET   The more we stay,° the stronger grows our foe.   *delay*
KING LOUIS   The more I stay, the more I'll succour thee.
QUEEN MARGARET   O, but impatience waiteth on° true sorrow.   *attends*
        Enter [the Earl of] WARWICK
And see where comes the breeder of my sorrow.
KING LOUIS   What's he approacheth boldly to our presence?
45 QUEEN MARGARET   Our Earl of Warwick, Edward's greatest friend.
KING LOUIS   Welcome, brave Warwick. What brings thee to France?
        He descends. She ariseth
QUEEN MARGARET [*aside*]   Ay, now begins a second storm to rise,
For this is he that moves both wind and tide.
WARWICK [*to* KING LOUIS]   From worthy Edward, King of Albion,
50 My lord and sovereign, and thy vowèd friend,
I come in kindness and unfeignèd love,
First, to do greetings to thy royal person,
And then, to crave a league of amity,°   *friendship*
And lastly, to confirm that amity
55 With nuptial knot, if thou vouchsafe to grant
That virtuous Lady Bona, thy fair sister,
To England's King in lawful marriage.
QUEEN MARGARET [*aside*]   If that go forward, Henry's hope is done.
WARWICK (*to* [LADY] BONA)   And, gracious madam, in our King's behalf
60 I am commanded, with your leave and favour,
Humbly to kiss your hand, and with my tongue
To tell the passion of my sovereign's heart,
Where fame, late ent'ring at his heedful ears,
Hath placed thy beauty's image and thy virtue.
65 QUEEN MARGARET   King Louis and Lady Bona, hear me speak
Before you answer Warwick. His demand
Springs not from Edward's well-meant honest love,
But from deceit, bred by necessity.
For how can tyrants safely govern home
70 Unless abroad they purchase° great alliance?   *obtain*
To prove him tyrant this reason may suffice—
That Henry liveth still; but were he dead,
Yet here Prince Edward stands, King Henry's son.
Look, therefore, Louis, that by this league and marriage
75 Thou draw not on thy danger and dishonour,
For though usurpers sway the rule° a while,   *wield power*
Yet heav'ns are just and time suppresseth wrongs.

WARWICK Injurious° Margaret.   *Insulting*

PRINCE EDWARD   And why not 'Queen'?

WARWICK Because thy father Henry did usurp,

80   And thou no more art prince than she is queen.

OXFORD Then Warwick disannuls° great John of Gaunt,   *cancels*
     Which did subdue the greatest part of Spain;
     And, after John of Gaunt, Henry the Fourth,
     Whose wisdom was a mirror to the wisest;

85   And, after that wise prince, Henry the Fifth,
     Who by his prowess conquerèd all France.
     From these our Henry lineally descends.

WARWICK Oxford, how haps it in this smooth discourse
     You told not how Henry the Sixth hath lost

90   All that which Henry the Fifth had gotten?
     Methinks these peers of France should smile at that.
     But for the rest, you tell a pedigree
     Of threescore and two years³—a silly° time   *trifling*
     To make prescription for a kingdom's worth.⁴

95   OXFORD Why, Warwick, canst thou speak against thy liege,
     Whom thou obeyedest thirty and six years,
     And not bewray° thy treason with a blush?   *reveal*

WARWICK Can Oxford, that did ever fence the right,°   *defend justice*
     Now buckler° falsehood with a pedigree?   *shield*

100 For shame—leave Henry, and call Edward king.

OXFORD Call him my king by whose injurious doom°   *insulting judgment*
     My elder brother, the Lord Aubrey Vere,⁵
     Was done to death? And more than so, my father,
     Even in the downfall° of his mellowed years,   *decline*

105 When nature brought him to the door of death?
     No, Warwick, no—while life upholds this arm,
     This arm upholds the house of Lancaster.

WARWICK And I the house of York.

KING LOUIS Queen Margaret, Prince Edward, and Oxford,

110 Vouchsafe, at our request, to stand aside
     While I use further conference° with Warwick.   *talk further*

          [QUEEN MARGARET *comes down from the state and,*
               with PRINCE EDWARD *and* OXFORD, *stands apart*]⁶

QUEEN MARGARET Heavens grant that Warwick's words bewitch him not.

KING LOUIS Now, Warwick, tell me even upon thy conscience,
     Is Edward your true king? For I were loath

115 To link with him that were not lawful chosen.

WARWICK Thereon I pawn my credit and mine honour.

KING LOUIS But is he gracious in the people's eye?

WARWICK The more that⁷ Henry was unfortunate.

KING LOUIS Then further, all dissembling set aside,

120 Tell me for truth the measure of his love
     Unto our sister Bona.

---

3. Meaning the sixty-two years between 1399, when
Henry IV deposed Richard II, and 1461, when Henry
VI was deposed by Edward.
4. To make a claim based on custom for something as
valuable as a kingdom.

5. Eldest son of the twelfth Earl of Oxford, John de
Vere. Both were executed for treason by the Yorkists in
1462.
6. F's stage direction reads "They stand aloof."
7. The more (gracious) because.

WARWICK   Such it seems
    As may beseem° a monarch like himself.   *befit*
    Myself have often heard him say and swear
    That this his love was an eternal plant,
125 Whereof the root was fixed in virtue's ground,
    The leaves and fruit maintained with beauty's sun,
    Exempt from envy, but not from disdain,[8]
    Unless the Lady Bona quit° his pain.°   *end / (by loving him)*
KING LOUIS [*to* LADY BONA]   Now, sister, let us hear your firm resolve.
130 LADY BONA   Your grant, or your denial, shall be mine.
    (*To* WARWICK) Yet I confess that often ere this day,
    When I have heard your king's desert° recounted,   *merit*
    Mine ear hath tempted judgement to desire.
KING LOUIS [*to* WARWICK]   Then, Warwick, thus—our sister
        shall be Edward's.
135 And now, forthwith, shall articles be drawn
    Touching the jointure° that your king must make,   *marriage settlement*
    Which with her dowry shall be counterpoised.°   *equally balanced*
    [*To* QUEEN MARGARET] Draw near, Queen Margaret, and be a
        witness
    That Bona shall be wife to the English king.
        [QUEEN MARGARET, PRINCE EDWARD, *and* OXFORD *come
        forward*]
140 PRINCE EDWARD   To Edward, but not to the English king.
    QUEEN MARGARET   Deceitful Warwick—it was thy device
    By this alliance to make void my suit!
    Before thy coming Louis was Henry's friend.
    KING LOUIS   And still is friend to him and Margaret.
145 But if your title to the crown be weak,
    As may appear by Edward's good success,
    Then 'tis but reason that I be released
    From giving aid which late° I promised.   *recently*
    Yet shall you have all kindness at my hand
150 That your estate requires and mine can yield.
    WARWICK [*to* QUEEN MARGARET]   Henry now lives in Scotland at his ease,
    Where having nothing, nothing can he lose.
    And as for you yourself, our quondam° queen,   *former*
    You have a father able to maintain you,
155 And better 'twere you troubled him than France.
    QUEEN MARGARET   Peace, impudent and shameless Warwick, peace!
    Proud setter-up and puller-down of kings!
    I will not hence till, with my talk and tears,
    Both full of truth, I make King Louis behold
160 Thy sly conveyance° and thy lord's false love,   *deceit*
        POST° *blowing a horn within*   *Messenger*
    For both of you are birds of selfsame feather.
    KING LOUIS   Warwick, this is some post to us or thee.
        Enter the POST
    POST (*to* WARWICK)   My lord ambassador, these letters are for you,

---

8. Exempt from malice, but not exempt from (being hurt by) her disdain for him.

Sent from your brother Marquis Montague;

165 (*To* LOUIS) These from our King unto your majesty;
    (*To* [QUEEN] MARGARET) And, madam, these for you, from
        whom I know not.
        They all read their letters
OXFORD [*to* PRINCE EDWARD] I like it well that our fair Queen and mistress
    Smiles at her news, while Warwick frowns at his.
PRINCE EDWARD Nay, mark how Louis stamps° as he were   (*his foot*)
    nettled.°   *angry*
170 I hope all's for the best.
KING LOUIS Warwick, what are thy news? And yours, fair Queen?
QUEEN MARGARET Mine, such as fill my heart with unhoped joys.
WARWICK Mine, full of sorrow and heart's discontent.
KING LOUIS What! Has your king married the Lady Gray?
175 And now to soothe° your forgery° and his,   *smooth over / deceit*
    Sends me a paper to persuade me patience?
    Is this th'alliance that he seeks with France?
    Dare he presume to scorn us in this manner?
QUEEN MARGARET I told your majesty as much before—
180 This proveth Edward's love and Warwick's honesty.
WARWICK King Louis, I here protest in sight of heaven
    And by the hope I have of heavenly bliss,
    That I am clear from this misdeed of Edward's,
    No more my king, for he dishonours me,
185 But most himself, if he could see his shame.
    Did I forget that by the house of York
    My father came untimely to his death?⁹
    Did I let pass th'abuse done to my niece?¹
    Did I impale him° with the regal crown?   *encircle his head*
190 Did I put Henry from his native right?
    And am I guerdoned° at the last with shame?   *rewarded*
    Shame on himself, for my desert is honour.
    And to repair my honour, lost for him,
    I here renounce him and return to Henry.
195 [*To* QUEEN MARGARET] My noble Queen, let former grudges pass,
    And henceforth I am thy true servitor.°   *servant*
    I will revenge his wrong to Lady Bona
    And replant Henry in his former state.
QUEEN MARGARET Warwick, these words have turned my hate to love,
200 And I forgive and quite forget old faults,
    And joy that thou becom'st King Henry's friend.
WARWICK So much his friend, ay, his unfeignèd friend,
    That if King Louis vouchsafe to furnish us
    With some few bands of chosen soldiers,
205 I'll undertake to land them on our coast
    And force the tyrant from his seat by war.

9. Actually, Warwick's father, the Earl of Salisbury of *The First Part of the Contention*, was executed by the Lancastrians. Perhaps Warwick means that his father would not have died in the Yorkist cause had the Yorkists never tried to seize the throne.
1. Holinshed's *Chronicles* reports that while visiting Warwick's house, Edward attempted to sexually assault his host's daughter or niece.

'Tis not his new-made bride shall succour him.
And as for Clarence, as my letters tell me,
He's very likely now to fall from° him   *desert*
210 For matching° more for wanton lust than honour,   *marrying*
Or than for strength and safety of our country.
LADY BONA [*to* KING LOUIS]   Dear brother, how shall Bona be revenged,
But by thy help to this distressèd Queen?
QUEEN MARGARET [*to* KING LOUIS]   Renownèd Prince, how shall
    poor Henry live
215 Unless thou rescue him from foul despair?
LADY BONA [*to* KING LOUIS]   My quarrel and this English
    Queen's are one.
WARWICK   And mine, fair Lady Bona, joins with yours.
KING LOUIS   And mine with hers, and thine, and Margaret's.
Therefore at last I firmly am resolved:
220 You shall have aid.
QUEEN MARGARET   Let me give humble thanks for all at once.
KING LOUIS [*to the* POST]   Then, England's messenger, return in post°   *haste*
And tell false Edward, thy supposèd king,
That Louis of France is sending over masquers[2]
225 To revel it with him and his new bride.
Thou seest what's passed, go fear° thy king withal.°   *frighten / with it*
LADY BONA [*to the* POST]   Tell him, in hope he'll prove a widower shortly,
I'll wear the willow garland[3] for his sake.
QUEEN MARGARET [*to the* POST]   Tell him my mourning weeds°   *apparel*
    are laid aside,
230 And I am ready to put armour on.
WARWICK [*to the* POST]   Tell him from me that he hath done me wrong,
And therefore I'll uncrown him ere't be long.
[*Giving money*] There's thy reward—be gone.   *Exit* POST
KING LOUIS   But, Warwick, thou and Oxford, with five thousand men,
235 Shall cross the seas and bid false Edward battle;
And, as occasion serves, this noble Queen
And Prince shall follow with a fresh supply.
Yet, ere thou go, but answer me one doubt:
What pledge have we of thy firm loyalty?
240 WARWICK   This shall assure my constant loyalty:
That if our Queen and this young Prince agree,
I'll join mine eldest daughter[4] and my joy
To him forthwith in holy wedlock bands.
QUEEN MARGARET   Yes, I agree, and thank you for your motion.°   *proposal*
245 [*To* PRINCE EDWARD] Son Edward, she is fair and virtuous,
Therefore delay not. Give thy hand to Warwick,
And with thy hand thy faith irrevocable
That only Warwick's daughter shall be thine.
PRINCE EDWARD   Yes, I accept her, for she well deserves it,

---

2. The actors in courtly revels and entertainments that were often staged to celebrate the marriages of members of the Elizabethan aristocracy.
3. Token of a forsaken lover.
4. The historical Edward was betrothed (but never married) to Warwick's second daughter, Anne. She eventually married Richard Duke of York (later Richard III). Warwick's eldest daughter married George of Clarence.

250 And here to pledge my vow I give my hand.
　　　　　He gives his hand to WARWICK
KING LOUIS　Why stay we now? These soldiers shall be levied,
　　And thou, Lord Bourbon, our high admiral,
　　Shall waft° them over with our royal fleet.　　　　　*convey by water*
　　I long till Edward fall by war's mischance
255　For mocking marriage with a dame of France.
　　　　　　　　　　　　　　　Exeunt. Manet WARWICK
WARWICK　I came from Edward as ambassador,
　　But I return his sworn and mortal foe.
　　Matter of marriage was the charge he gave me,
　　But dreadful war shall answer his demand.
260　Had he none else to make a stale° but me?　　　　　*laughingstock*
　　Then none but I shall turn his jest to sorrow.
　　I was the chief that raised him to the crown,
　　And I'll be chief to bring him down again.
　　Not that I pity Henry's misery,
265　But seek revenge on Edward's mockery.　　　　　*Exit*

4.1

Enter RICHARD [*Duke* OF GLOUCESTER, GEORGE
Duke of] CLARENCE, [*the Duke of*] SOMERSET, *and*
[*the Marquis of*] MONTAGUE

RICHARD OF GLOUCESTER　Now tell me, brother Clarence, what think you
　　Of this new marriage with the Lady Gray?
　　Hath not our brother made a worthy choice?
GEORGE OF CLARENCE　Alas, you know 'tis far from hence to France;
5　How could he stay° till Warwick made return?　　　　　*wait*
SOMERSET　My lords, forbear this talk—here comes the King.
　　　　　Flourish. Enter KING EDWARD, *the* LADY GRAY [*his*]
　　　　　Queen, [*the Earl of*] Pembroke, [*and the Lords*]
　　　　　Stafford [*and*] HASTINGS. *Four stand on one side* [*of*
　　　　　the King], *and four on the other*
RICHARD OF GLOUCESTER　And his well-chosen bride.
GEORGE OF CLARENCE　I mind° to tell him plainly what I think.　　　　　*intend*
KING EDWARD　Now, brother of Clarence, how like you our choice,
10　That you stand pensive, as half-malcontent?°　　　　　*partly discontented*
GEORGE OF CLARENCE　As well as Louis of France, or the Earl
　　of Warwick,
　　Which° are so weak of courage and in judgement　　　　　*Who*
　　That they'll take no offence at our abuse.°　　　　　*insult*
KING EDWARD　Suppose they take offence without a cause—
15　They are but Louis and Warwick; I am Edward,
　　Your king and Warwick's, and must have my will.°　　　　　*way; sexual desire*
RICHARD OF GLOUCESTER　And you shall have your will,
　　　　because our king.
　　Yet hasty marriage seldom proveth well.
KING EDWARD　Yea, brother Richard, are you offended too?
RICHARD OF GLOUCESTER　Not I, no—God forbid that I should
20　　　wish them severed

4.1 Location: The palace, London.

Whom God hath joined together. Ay, and 'twere pity
To sunder them that yoke° so well together.   *who are coupled*

KING EDWARD   Setting your scorns and your mislike° aside,   *displeasure*
Tell me some reason why the Lady Gray
25   Should not become my wife and England's queen.
And you too, Somerset and Montague,
Speak freely what you think.

GEORGE OF CLARENCE   Then this is my opinion: that King Louis
Becomes your enemy for mocking him
30   About the marriage of the Lady Bona.

RICHARD OF GLOUCESTER   And Warwick, doing what you gave in charge,
Is now dishonourèd by this new marriage.

KING EDWARD   What if both Louis and Warwick be appeased
By such invention° as I can devise?   *scheme*

35   MONTAGUE   Yet, to have joined with France in such alliance
Would more have strengthened this our commonwealth
'Gainst foreign storms than any home-bred marriage.

HASTINGS   Why, knows not Montague that of itself
England is safe, if true within itself?

40   MONTAGUE   But the safer when 'tis backed with France.

HASTINGS   'Tis better using France than trusting France.
Let us be backed with God and with the seas
Which he hath giv'n for fence impregnable,
And with their helps only° defend ourselves.   *alone*
45   In them and in ourselves our safety lies.

GEORGE OF CLARENCE   For this one speech Lord Hastings well deserves
To have the heir of the Lord Hungerford.[1]

KING EDWARD   Ay, what of that? It was my will and grant—
And for this once my will shall stand for law.

RICHARD OF GLOUCESTER   And yet, methinks, your grace hath
50   not done well
To give the heir and daughter of Lord Scales
Unto the brother[2] of your loving bride.
She better would have fitted me or Clarence,
But in° your bride you bury° brotherhood.   *because of / forget*

GEORGE OF CLARENCE   Or else you would not have bestowed
55   the heir
Of the Lord Bonville on your new wife's son,°   *(Sir Thomas Gray)*
And leave your brothers to go speed elsewhere.

KING EDWARD   Alas, poor Clarence, is it for a wife
That thou art malcontent? I will provide thee.

GEORGE OF CLARENCE   In choosing for yourself you showed
60   your judgement,
Which being shallow, you shall give me leave
To play the broker° in mine own behalf,   *marriage broker*
And to that end I shortly mind to leave you.

KING EDWARD   Leave me, or tarry. Edward will be king,
65   And not be tied unto his brother's will.

1. To marry a rich heiress. Clarence is objecting to the   wealthy marriage partners.
Queen's upstart relatives, such as Hastings, being given   2. That is, Anthony Woodville, second Earl Rivers.

LADY GRAY   My lords, before it pleased his majesty
        To raise my state to title of a queen,
        Do me but right, and you must all confess
        That I was not ignoble of descent—
70   And meaner° than myself have had like fortune.³   *people of lower rank*
        But as this title honours me and mine,
        So your dislikes, to whom I would be pleasing,
        Doth cloud my joys with danger° and with sorrow.   *apprehension*
KING EDWARD   My love, forbear to fawn upon° their frowns.   *be abject before*
75   What danger or what sorrow can befall thee
        So long as Edward is thy constant friend,
        And their true sovereign, whom they must obey?
        Nay, whom they shall obey, and love thee too—
        Unless they seek for hatred at my hands,
80   Which if they do, yet will I keep thee safe,
        And they shall feel the vengeance of my wrath.
RICHARD OF GLOUCESTER [*aside*]   I hear, yet say not much, but
        think the more.
                Enter [the] POST [*from France*]
KING EDWARD   Now, messenger, what letters or what news from France?
POST   My sovereign liege, no letters and few words,
85   But such as I, without your special pardon,
        Dare not relate.
KING EDWARD   Go to, we pardon thee. Therefore, in brief,
        Tell me their words as near as thou canst guess° them.   *approximate*
        What answer makes King Louis unto our letters?
90 POST   At my depart these were his very words:
        'Go tell false Edward, thy supposèd king,
        That Louis of France is sending over masquers
        To revel it with him and his new bride.'
KING EDWARD   Is Louis so brave? Belike° he thinks me Henry.   *Perhaps*
95   But what said Lady Bona to my marriage?
POST   These were her words, uttered with mild disdain:
        'Tell him in hope he'll prove a widower shortly,
        I'll wear the willow garland for his sake.'
KING EDWARD   I blame not her, she could say little less;
100   She had the wrong. But what said Henry's queen?
        For I have heard that she was there in place.
POST   'Tell him', quoth she, 'my mourning weeds are done,
        And I am ready to put armour on.'
KING EDWARD   Belike she minds to play the Amazon.⁴
105   But what said Warwick to these injuries?
POST   He, more incensed against your majesty
        Than all the rest, discharged me with these words:
        'Tell him from me that he hath done me wrong,
        And therefore I'll uncrown him ere't be long.'
110 KING EDWARD   Ha! Durst the traitor breathe out so proud words?
        Well, I will arm me, being thus forewarned.
        They shall have wars and pay for their presumption.
        But say, is Warwick friends with Margaret?

3. In fact, the historical Lady Gray was the first com-   4. Legendary warrior woman. See note to 1.4.115.
moner to become Queen of England.

POST   Ay, gracious sovereign, they are so linked in friendship
115   That young Prince Edward marries Warwick's daughter.
GEORGE OF CLARENCE   Belike the elder; Clarence will have the younger.
Now, brother King, farewell, and sit you fast,
For I will hence to Warwick's other daughter,
That, though I want° a kingdom, yet in marriage   lack
120   I may not prove inferior to yourself.
You that love me and Warwick, follow me.

Exit CLARENCE, *and* SOMERSET *follows*

RICHARD OF GLOUCESTER   Not I—[*aside*] my thoughts aim at a
further matter.
I stay not for the love of Edward, but the crown.
KING EDWARD   Clarence and Somerset both gone to Warwick?
125   Yet am I armed against the worst can happen,
And haste is needful in this desp'rate case.
Pembroke and Stafford, you in our behalf
Go levy men and make prepare° for war.   preparation
They are already, or quickly will be, landed.
130   Myself in person will straight follow you.

Exeunt Pembroke and Stafford

But ere I go, Hastings and Montague,
Resolve my doubt. You twain, of all the rest,
Are near'st to Warwick by blood and by alliance.
Tell me if you love Warwick more than me.
135   If it be so, then both depart to him—
I rather wish you foes than hollow° friends.   false
But if you mind to hold your true obedience,
Give me assurance with some friendly vow
That I may never have you in suspect.°   under suspicion
140   MONTAGUE   So God help Montague as he proves true.
HASTINGS   And Hastings as he favours Edward's cause.
KING EDWARD   Now, brother Richard, will you stand by us?
RICHARD OF GLOUCESTER   Ay, in despite of all that shall withstand you.
KING EDWARD   Why, so. Then am I sure of victory.
145   Now, therefore, let us hence and lose no hour
Till we meet Warwick with his foreign power.°   *Exeunt*   army

4.2

Enter [the Earls of] WARWICK *and* OXFORD *in England,
with French soldiers*

WARWICK   Trust me, my lord, all hitherto° goes well.   thus far
The common sort by numbers swarm to us.

Enter [the Dukes of] CLARENCE *and* SOMERSET

But see where Somerset and Clarence comes.
Speak suddenly, my lords, are we all friends?
5   GEORGE OF CLARENCE   Fear not that, my lord.
WARWICK   Then, gentle Clarence, welcome unto Warwick—
And welcome, Somerset. I hold it cowardice
To rest mistrustful where a noble heart
Hath pawned° an open hand in sign of love,   pledged

4.2 Location: Fields near Warwick.

10   Else might I think that Clarence, Edward's brother,
        Were but a feignèd friend to our proceedings.
        But come, sweet Clarence, my daughter shall be thine.
        And now what rests° but, in night's coverture,°   *remains / shadow*
        Thy brother being carelessly encamped,
15   His soldiers lurking° in the towns about,   *idling*
        And but attended by a simple guard,
        We may surprise and take him at our pleasure?
        Our scouts have found the adventure very easy;
        That, as Ulysses and stout Diomed
20   With sleight° and manhood° stole to Rhesus' tents   *stealth / bravery*
        And brought from thence the Thracian fatal steeds,[1]
        So we, well covered with the night's black mantle,
        At unawares° may beat down Edward's guard   *Suddenly*
        And seize himself—I say not 'slaughter him',
25   For I intend but only to surprise° him.   *capture*
        You that will follow me to this attempt,
        Applaud the name of Henry with your leader.
                They all cry 'Henry'
        Why, then, let's on our way in silent sort,°   *manner*
        For Warwick and his friends, God and Saint George!°   *patron saint of England*
                                                        Exeunt

                        4.3
        Enter three WATCHMEN, *to guard the King's*
        [*Edward's*] *tent*

FIRST WATCHMAN   Come on, my masters, each man take his stand.°   *post*
        The King by this is set him down° to sleep.   *settled (in a chair)*
SECOND WATCHMAN   What, will he not to bed?
FIRST WATCHMAN   Why, no—for he hath made a solemn vow
5   Never to lie and take his natural rest
        Till Warwick or himself be quite suppressed.°   *vanquished*
SECOND WATCHMAN   Tomorrow then belike shall be the day,
        If Warwick be so near as men report.
THIRD WATCHMAN   But say, I pray, what nobleman is that
10   That with the King here resteth in his tent?
FIRST WATCHMAN   'Tis the Lord Hastings, the King's chiefest friend.
THIRD WATCHMAN   O, is it so? But why commands the King
        That his chief followers lodge in towns about him,
        While he himself keeps° in the cold field?   *lodges*
15   SECOND WATCHMAN   'Tis the more honour, because more dangerous.
THIRD WATCHMAN   Ay, but give me worship° and quietness—   *dignity*
        I like it better than a dangerous honour.
        If Warwick knew in what estate° he° stands,   *condition / (Edward)*
        'Tis to be doubted° he would waken him.   *feared*
20   FIRST WATCHMAN   Unless our halberds[1] did shut up° his passage.   *bar*
SECOND WATCHMAN   Ay, wherefore else guard we his royal tent

---

1. The Greek warriors Ulysses and Diomedes captured the horses of the Thracian prince Rhesus in a night raid, after an oracle predicted that Troy would not fall to the Greeks as long as the horses of Rhesus grazed on the plains of Troy (see *The Iliad*, Book 10). *fatal*: fateful.
4.3 Location: King Edward's camp near Warwick.
1. Long-handled weapons with axlike blades.

But to defend his person from night-foes?
    Enter [the Earl of] WARWICK, [GEORGE *Duke of*]
    CLARENCE, [*the Earl of*] OXFORD, [*and the Duke of*]
    SOMERSET, *and French soldiers. Silent all*

WARWICK   This is his tent—and see where stand his guard.
    Courage, my masters—honour now or never!
25   But follow me, and Edward shall be ours.
FIRST WATCHMAN   Who goes there?
SECOND WATCHMAN   Stay or thou diest.
    WARWICK *and the rest all cry 'Warwick, Warwick!'*
    and set upon the guard, who fly, crying 'Arm, arm!' WAR-
    WICK *and the rest follow them*

4.4

    [*With*] *the drum*[*mer*] *playing and trumpet*[*er*] *sound-*
    ing, enter [*the Earl of*] WARWICK, [*the Duke of*]
    SOMERSET, *and the rest bringing the* KING [EDWARD]
    out in his gown, sitting in a chair. RICHARD [*Duke of*
    GLOUCESTER] *and* [*Lord*] HASTINGS *flies over the stage*

SOMERSET   What are they that fly there?
WARWICK   Richard and Hastings—let them go. Here is the Duke.
KING EDWARD   'The Duke'! Why, Warwick, when we parted,
    Thou calledst me king.
WARWICK   Ay, but the case is altered.[1]
5   When you disgraced me in my embassade,°   *diplomatic mission*
    Then I degraded you from being king,
    And come now to create you Duke of York.
    Alas, how should you govern any kingdom
    That know not how to use ambassadors,
10   Nor how to be contented with one wife,
    Nor how to use your brothers brotherly,
    Nor how to study for the people's welfare,
    Nor how to shroud° yourself from enemies?   *conceal*
KING EDWARD [*seeing* GEORGE]   Yea, brother of Clarence, art
        thou here too?
15   Nay, then, I see that Edward needs must down.°   *must fall*
    Yet, Warwick, in despite of all mischance,
    Of thee thyself and all thy complices,
    Edward will always bear himself as king.
    Though fortune's malice overthrow my state,°   *sovereignty*
20   My mind exceeds the compass of her wheel.[2]
WARWICK   Then, for his° mind, be Edward England's king.   *in his (Edward's)*
    [WARWICK] *takes off* [*Edward's*] *crown*
    But Henry now shall wear the English crown,
    And be true king indeed, thou but the shadow.
    My lord of Somerset, at my request,
25   See that, forthwith, Duke Edward be conveyed
    Unto my brother, Archbishop of York.
    When I have fought with Pembroke and his fellows,
    I'll follow you, and tell what answer
    Louis and the Lady Bona send to him.

4.4 Location: Scene continues.
1. Proverbial for "things have changed."
2. My thoughts escape the control of fortune. The

goddess Fortune was often depicted turning a wheel on which human destinies both rose and fell, sometimes coming full circle.

30 Now for a while farewell, good Duke of York.
They [begin to] lead [EDWARD] *out forcibly*
KING EDWARD What fates impose, that men must needs abide.°   *endure*
It boots not to resist both wind and tide.³
Exeunt some with EDWARD
OXFORD What now remains, my lords, for us to do
But march to London with our soldiers?
35 WARWICK Ay, that's the first thing that we have to do—
To free King Henry from imprisonment
And see him seated in the regal throne.   *Exeunt*

4.5

Enter [Earl] RIVERS *and* [his sister,] LADY GRAY
[Edward's queen]
RIVERS Madam, what makes you in this sudden change?¹
LADY GRAY Why, brother Rivers, are you yet to learn
What late misfortune is befall'n King Edward?
RIVERS What? Loss of some pitched battle against Warwick?
5 LADY GRAY No, but the loss of his own royal person.
RIVERS Then is my sovereign slain?
LADY GRAY Ay, almost slain—for he is taken prisoner,
Either betrayed by falsehood of his guard
Or by his foe surprised at unawares,
10 And, as I further have to understand,
Is new committed to the Bishop of York,
Fell° Warwick's brother, and by that° our foe.   *Cruel / therefore*
RIVERS These news, I must confess, are full of grief.
Yet, gracious madam, bear it as you may.
15 Warwick may lose, that now hath won the day.
LADY GRAY Till then fair hope must hinder life's decay,
And I the rather° wean me from despair   *I am the more obliged to*
For love of Edward's offspring in my womb.
This is it that makes me bridle° passion   *control*
20 And bear with mildness my misfortune's cross.
Ay, ay, for this I draw in many a tear
And stop the rising of blood-sucking² sighs,
Lest with my sighs or tears I blast° or drown   *blight*
King Edward's fruit, true heir to th'English crown.
25 RIVERS But, madam, where is Warwick then become?°   *gone*
LADY GRAY I am informèd that he comes towards London
To set the crown once more on Henry's head.
Guess thou the rest—King Edward's friends must down.
But to prevent the tyrant's violence—
30 For trust not him that hath once broken faith—
I'll hence forthwith unto the sanctuary,³
To save at least the heir of Edward's right.
There shall I rest secure from force and fraud.
Come, therefore, let us fly while we may fly.
35 If Warwick take us, we are sure to die.   *Exeunt*

3. Compare with 3.3.48, where Margaret says that
Warwick "moves both wind and tide." *boots*: profits.
4.5 Location: The palace, London.
1. What is the reason for this sudden change of mind?

2. It was popularly believed that each sigh consumed
a drop of blood from the heart.
3. Place that by law conferred immunity from arrest.

4.6

Enter RICHARD [*Duke of* GLOUCESTER], *Lord*
HASTINGS, *and Sir William Stanley* [*with soldiers*]

RICHARD OF GLOUCESTER   Now my lord Hastings and Sir
    William Stanley,
    Leave off to wonder why I drew you hither
    Into this chiefest thicket of the park.°   *hunting grounds*
    Thus stands the case: you know our King, my brother,
5   Is prisoner to the Bishop here, at whose hands
    He hath good usage and great liberty,
    And, often but attended with weak guard,
    Comes hunting this way to disport° himself.   *amuse*
    I have advertised° him by secret means   *informed*
10   That if about this hour he make this way
    Under the colour° of his usual game,°   *pretext / hunting*
    He shall here find his friends with horse and men
    To set him free from his captivity.

Enter KING EDWARD *and a* HUNTSMAN *with him*

HUNTSMAN   This way, my lord—for this way lies the game.
15 KING EDWARD   Nay, this way, man—see where the huntsmen stand.
    Now, brother of Gloucester, Lord Hastings, and the rest,
    Stand you thus close° to steal the Bishop's deer?   *concealed*
RICHARD OF GLOUCESTER   Brother, the time and case requireth haste.
    Your horse stands ready at the park corner.
20 KING EDWARD   But whither shall we then?
HASTINGS   To Lynn,[1] my lord,
    And shipped from thence to Flanders.
RICHARD OF GLOUCESTER [*aside*]   Well guessed, believe me—for
    that was my meaning.
KING EDWARD   Stanley, I will requite thy forwardness.°   *reward your zeal*
RICHARD OF GLOUCESTER   But wherefore stay we? 'Tis no time
25   to talk.
KING EDWARD   Huntsman, what sayst thou? Wilt thou go along?
HUNTSMAN   Better do so than tarry and be hanged.
RICHARD OF GLOUCESTER   Come then, away—let's have no more ado.
KING EDWARD   Bishop, farewell—shield thee from Warwick's frown,
30   And pray that I may repossess the crown.   *Exeunt*

4.7

Flourish. Enter [*the Earl of*] WARWICK *and* [GEORGE
Duke of] CLARENCE *with the crown. Then* [*enter*] KING
HENRY, [*the Earl of*] OXFORD, [*the Duke of*] SOMERSET,
[*with*] *young Henry Earl of Richmond,* [*the Marquis of*]
MONTAGUE, *and* [*the*] LIEUTENANT [*of the Tower*]

KING HENRY   Master Lieutenant, now that God and friends
    Have shaken Edward from the regal seat
    And turned my captive state to liberty,

4.6 Location; The Archbishop of York's park or hunting
ground, Yorkshire.

1. King's Lynn, a town on the Norfolk coast.
4.7 Location: The Tower, London.

My fear to hope, my sorrows unto joys,
5   At our enlargement° what are thy due fees?[1]   *release*
    LIEUTENANT   Subjects may challenge° nothing of their sovereigns—   *demand*
    But if an humble prayer may prevail,
    I then crave pardon of your majesty.
    KING HENRY   For what, Lieutenant? For well using me?
10   Nay, be thou sure I'll well requite thy kindness,
    For that it made my prisonment a pleasure—
    Ay, such a pleasure as encagèd birds
    Conceive when, after many moody thoughts,
    At last by notes of household harmony
15   They quite forget their loss of liberty.
    But, Warwick, after God, thou sett'st me free,
    And chiefly therefore I thank God and thee.
    He was the author, thou the instrument.
    Therefore, that I may conquer fortune's spite
20   By living low,° where fortune cannot hurt me,   *humbly*
    And that the people of this blessèd land
    May not be punished with my thwarting stars,[2]
    Warwick, although my head still wear the crown,
    I here resign my government to thee,
25   For thou art fortunate in all thy deeds.
    WARWICK   Your grace hath still° been famed for virtuous,   *always*
    And now may seem as wise as virtuous
    By spying and avoiding fortune's malice,
    For few men rightly temper with the stars.[3]
30   Yet in this one thing let me blame your grace:
    For choosing me when Clarence is in place.
    GEORGE OF CLARENCE   No, Warwick, thou art worthy of the sway,°   *rule*
    To whom the heav'ns in thy nativity[4]
    Adjudged an olive branch and laurel crown,[5]
35   As likely to be blest in peace and war.
    And therefore I yield thee my free consent.
    WARWICK   And I choose Clarence only° for Protector.[6]   *alone*
    KING HENRY   Warwick and Clarence, give me both your hands.
    Now join your hands, and with your hands your hearts,
40   That no dissension hinder government.
    I make you both Protectors of this land,
    While I myself will lead a private life
    And in devotion spend my latter days,
    To sin's rebuke and my creator's praise.
45   WARWICK   What answers Clarence to his sovereign's will?
    GEORGE OF CLARENCE   That he consents, if Warwick yield consent,
    For on thy fortune I repose myself.
    WARWICK   Why, then, though loath, yet must I be content.

---

1. Wealthy prisoners paid fees for special food and services.
2. My bad luck. Stars were believed to emit influences that might either favor or thwart the actions of individuals.
3. Because not many men correctly conform to or come to terms with their fate.

4. The precise position of the stars at one's birth was held to determine the course of one's life.
5. Symbols of peace and victory, respectively.
6. The title of an individual given charge of the kingdom while the monarch is absent, incapacitated, or a youth.

We'll yoke together, like a double shadow
50 To Henry's body, and supply° his place—   take
I mean in bearing weight of government—
While he enjoys the honour and his ease.
And, Clarence, now then it is more than needful
Forthwith that Edward be pronounced a traitor,
55 And all his lands and goods be confiscate.
GEORGE OF CLARENCE   What else? And that succession be
    determined.
WARWICK   Ay, therein Clarence shall not want his part.[7]
KING HENRY   But with the first of all your chief affairs,
Let me entreat—for I command no more—
60 That Margaret your queen and my son Edward
Be sent for, to return from France with speed.
For, till I see them here, by doubtful fear
My joy of liberty is half eclipsed.
GEORGE OF CLARENCE   It shall be done, my sovereign, with all speed.
65 KING HENRY   My lord of Somerset, what youth is that
Of whom you seem to have so tender care?
SOMERSET   My liege, it is young Henry, Earl of Richmond.[8]
KING HENRY   Come hither, England's hope.
    [KING HENRY] *lays his hand on [Richmond's] head*
                                        If secret powers
Suggest but truth to my divining° thoughts,   *prophesying*
70 This pretty lad will prove our country's bliss.
His looks are full of peaceful majesty,
His head by nature framed to wear a crown,
His hand to wield a sceptre, and himself
Likely in time to bless a regal throne.
75 Make much of him, my lords, for this is he
Must help you more than you are hurt by me.
            Enter a POST
WARWICK   What news, my friend?
POST   That Edward is escapèd from your brother°   *(the Archbishop of York)*
And fled, as he hears since, to Burgundy.
80 WARWICK   Unsavoury news—but how made he escape?
POST   He was conveyed by Richard Duke of Gloucester
And the Lord Hastings, who attended him
In secret ambush on the forest side
And from the Bishop's huntsmen rescued him—
85 For hunting was his daily exercise.
WARWICK   My brother was too careless of his charge.
    [*To* KING HENRY]   But let us hence, my sovereign, to provide
A salve for any sore that may betide.°   *occur*
        Exeunt. Manent° SOMERSET, RICHMOND, *and* OXFORD   *Remain*
SOMERSET [*to* OXFORD]   My lord, I like not of this flight of Edward's,

---

7. George of Clarence would be next in line to the throne if the Lancastrian claim were dismissed and Edward pronounced a traitor. *want*: lack.
8. Somerset's nephew was the future Henry VII, the founder of the Tudor dynasty. The Wars of the Roses, represented in this play and in *The First Part of the Contention*, ended upon his accession to the throne, depicted at the end of *Richard III*.

90   For doubtless Burgundy will yield him help,
        And we shall have more wars before't be long.
        As Henry's late presaging prophecy
        Did glad my heart with hope of this young Richmond,
        So doth my heart misgive me, in these conflicts,
95   What may befall him, to his harm and ours.
        Therefore, Lord Oxford, to prevent the worst,
        Forthwith we'll send him hence to Brittany,
        Till storms be past of civil enmity.
    OXFORD   Ay, for if Edward repossess the crown,
100   'Tis like that Richmond with the rest shall down.°   fall
    SOMERSET   It shall be so—he shall to Brittany.
        Come, therefore, let's about it speedily.   *Exeunt*

                                4.8
        Flourish. Enter [KING] EDWARD, RICHARD [*Duke* OF
        GLOUCESTER], *and* [*Lord*] HASTINGS, *with a troop of*
        Hollanders
    KING EDWARD   Now, brother Richard, Lord Hastings, and the rest,
        Yet thus far fortune maketh us amends,
        And says that once more I shall interchange
        My wanèd° state for Henry's regal crown.   diminished
5   Well have we passed and now repassed the seas
        And brought desirèd help from Burgundy.
        What then remains, we being thus arrived
        From Ravenspurgh¹ haven before the gates of York,
        But that we enter, as into our dukedom?
        [HASTINGS *knocks at the gates of York*]
10 RICHARD OF GLOUCESTER   The gates made fast? Brother, I like not this.
        For many men that stumble at the threshold
        Are well foretold that danger lurks within.
    KING EDWARD   Tush, man, abodements° must not now affright us.   omens
        By fair or foul means we must enter in,
15   For hither will our friends repair to us.
    HASTINGS   My liege, I'll knock once more to summon them.
        [*He knocks.*]
        Enter, on the walls, the MAYOR *of York, and his Brethren*
        [*aldermen*]
    MAYOR   My lords, we were forewarnèd of your coming,
        And shut the gates for safety of ourselves—
        For now we owe allegiance unto Henry.
20 KING EDWARD   But, Master Mayor, if Henry be your king,
        Yet Edward at the least is Duke of York.
    MAYOR   True, my good lord, I know you for no less.
    KING EDWARD   Why, and I challenge nothing but my dukedom,
        As being well content with that alone.
    RICHARD OF GLOUCESTER [*aside*]   But when the fox hath once
25   got in his nose,

─────────────────────────────

4.8 Location: Outside the walls of York.   1. Town on the coast of Yorkshire.

He'll soon find means to make the body follow.

HASTINGS Why, Master Mayor, why stand you in a doubt?
Open the gates—we are King Henry's friends.

MAYOR Ay, say you so? The gates shall then be opened.
    [They] descend²

RICHARD OF GLOUCESTER A wise stout° captain, and soon   *valiant*
30   persuaded.

HASTINGS The good old man would fain° that all were well,   *wish*
So 'twere not long of him;³ but being entered,
I doubt not, I, but we shall soon persuade
Both him and all his brothers unto reason.
    Enter [below] the MAYOR *and two aldermen*

35 KING EDWARD So, Master Mayor, these gates must not be shut
But in the night or in the time of war.
What—fear not, man, but yield me up the keys,
    *[*KING EDWARD*] takes [some] keys [from the* MAYOR*]*
For Edward will defend the town and thee,
And all those friends that deign° to follow me.   *are willing*
    March. Enter Sir John MONTGOMERY *with [a]*
    drum[mer] and soldiers

40 RICHARD OF GLOUCESTER Brother, this is Sir John Montgomery,
Our trusty friend, unless I be deceived.

KING EDWARD Welcome, Sir John—but why come you in arms?

MONTGOMERY To help King Edward in his time of storm,
As every loyal subject ought to do.

45 KING EDWARD Thanks, good Montgomery, but we now forget
Our title to the crown, and only claim
Our dukedom till God please to send the rest.

MONTGOMERY Then fare you well, for I will hence again.
I came to serve a king and not a duke.

50 Drummer, strike up, and let us march away.
    The drum[mer] begins to [sound a] march

KING EDWARD Nay, stay, Sir John, a while, and we'll debate
By what safe means the crown may be recovered.

MONTGOMERY What talk you of debating? In few words,
If you'll not here proclaim yourself our king

55 I'll leave you to your fortune and be gone
To keep them back that come to succour you.
Why shall we fight, if you pretend° no title?   *claim*

RICHARD OF GLOUCESTER *[to* KING EDWARD*]* Why, brother,
    wherefore stand you on nice points?⁴

KING EDWARD When we grow stronger, then we'll make our claim.

60 Till then 'tis wisdom to conceal our meaning.

HASTINGS Away with scrupulous wit!° Now arms must rule.   *reasoning*

RICHARD OF GLOUCESTER And fearless minds climb soonest unto crowns.
Brother, we will proclaim you out of hand,
The bruit° thereof will bring you many friends.   *news*

65 KING EDWARD Then be it as you will, for 'tis my right,

---

2. F's stage direction reads "He descends," as if only the Mayor comes down from the walls.

3. So long as he is not held responsible.

4. Why do you dwell on such overly precise distinctions?

And Henry but usurps the diadem.

MONTGOMERY   Ay, now my sovereign speaketh like himself,
And now will I be Edward's champion.

HASTINGS   Sound trumpet, Edward shall be here proclaimed.
                    [*To* MONTGOMERY]⁵

70   Come, fellow soldier, make thou proclamation.
                    Flourish

MONTGOMERY   Edward the Fourth, by the grace of God King of
England and France, and Lord of Ireland—
And whosoe'er gainsays° King Edward's right,   *denies*
By this I challenge him to single fight.
                    [*He*] *throws down his gauntlet*⁶

75   ALL   Long live Edward the Fourth!

KING EDWARD   Thanks, brave Montgomery, and thanks unto you all.
If fortune serve me I'll requite° this kindness.   *repay*
Now, for this night, let's harbour here in York;
And when the morning sun shall raise his car°   *chariot*
80   Above the border of this horizon,
We'll forward towards Warwick and his mates.
For well I wot° that Henry is no soldier.   *know*
Ah, froward° Clarence, how evil it beseems thee   *perverse*
To flatter Henry and forsake thy brother!
85   Yet, as we may, we'll meet both thee and Warwick.
Come on, brave soldiers—doubt not of the day
And, that once gotten, doubt not of large pay.   *Exeunt*

4.9

Flourish. Enter KING [HENRY, *the Earl of*] WARWICK,
[*the Marquis of*] MONTAGUE, [GEORGE *Duke of*]
CLARENCE, *and* [*the Earl of*] OXFORD¹

WARWICK   What counsel, lords? Edward from Belgia,°   *the Low Countries*
With hasty° Germans and blunt° Hollanders,   *rash / merciless*
Hath passed in safety through the narrow seas,
And with his troops doth march amain° to London,   *at full speed*
5   And many giddy people flock to him.

KING HENRY   Let's levy men and beat him back again.

GEORGE OF CLARENCE   A little fire is quickly trodden out,
Which, being suffered, rivers cannot quench.

WARWICK   In Warwickshire I have true-hearted friends,
10   Not mutinous in peace, yet bold in war.
Those will I muster up. And thou, son° Clarence,   *son-in-law*
Shalt stir in Suffolk, Norfolk, and in Kent,
The knights and gentlemen to come with thee.
Thou, brother Montague, in Buckingham,
15   Northampton, and in Leicestershire shalt find
Men well inclined to hear what thou command'st.
And thou, brave Oxford, wondrous well beloved

---

5. F assigns lines 71–72 to a "Soul⟨dier⟩" and 73–74 to
Montgomery; O omits line 70 and the following stage
direction and assigns all the lines to Montgomery.
6. Throwing down a gauntlet, or glove, was a medieval
rite of chivalry. To pick it up was to accept a challenge
to duel.

4.9 Location: The Bishop of London's palace.
1. F includes Somerset at this entrance and does not
mark a scene division here or at line 32. Somerset has
no lines in this scene. Oxford omits him until the stage
direction at 5.1.71, begins a new scene (4.10) after
4.9.32, and places Exeter's entrance there.

In Oxfordshire, shalt muster up thy friends.
My sovereign, with the loving citizens,
20 Like to his island girt in with the ocean,
Or modest Dian² circled with her nymphs,
Shall rest in London till we come to him.
Fair lords, take leave and stand not to reply.
Farewell, my sovereign.
25 KING HENRY   Farewell, my Hector,³ and my Troy's true hope.
GEORGE OF CLARENCE   In sign of truth, I kiss your highness'
    hand.
        [*He kisses King Henry's hand*]
KING HENRY   Well-minded Clarence, be thou fortunate.
MONTAGUE   Comfort, my lord, and so I take my leave.
        [*He kisses King Henry's hand*]
OXFORD   And thus I seal my truth° and bid adieu.   ° affirm my loyalty
        [*He kisses King Henry's hand*]
30 KING HENRY   Sweet Oxford, and my loving Montague,
And all at once,° once more a happy farewell.   [*Exit*]   ° together
WARWICK   Farewell, sweet lords—let's meet at Coventry.
                        Exeunt [*severally*]°   ° separately

4.10

[*Enter* KING HENRY *and the Duke of* EXETER]
KING HENRY   Here at the palace will I rest a while.
Cousin of Exeter, what thinks your lordship?
Methinks the power that Edward hath in field
Should not be able to encounter mine.
5 EXETER   The doubt° is that he will seduce the rest.   ° fear
KING HENRY   That's not my fear. My meed° hath got° me fame.   ° merit / won
I have not stopped mine ears to their demands,
Nor posted off° their suits with slow delays.   ° postponed
My pity hath been balm to heal their wounds,
10 My mildness hath allayed their swelling griefs,
My mercy dried their water-flowing tears.
I have not been desirous of their wealth,
Nor much oppressed them with great subsidies,°   ° taxes
Nor forward of° revenge, though they much erred.   ° eager for
15 Then why should they love Edward more than me?
No, Exeter, these graces challenge grace;°   ° claim favor
And when the lion fawns upon the lamb,
The lamb will never cease to follow him.
        Shout within 'A Lancaster'[*, 'A York'*]¹
EXETER   Hark, hark, my lord—what shouts are these?
        Enter [KING] EDWARD *and* [RICHARD *Duke of*
        GLOUCESTER, *with*] *soldiers*
20 KING EDWARD   Seize on the shame-faced° Henry—bear him hence, ° timid
And once again proclaim us King of England.

---

2. The goddess of the moon, of hunting, and of chastity,
often depicted presiding over a circle of virginal nymphs
in the forest. Queen Elizabeth was sometimes represented as Diana.
3. The greatest warrior of Troy, killed when the Greeks
conquered the city (see note to 2.1.51). By one legendary account, London was founded as a second Troy by

Brutus (or Brute), a Trojan who conquered Albion and
renamed it Britain.
4.10 Location: Scene continues.
1. F indicates "A Lancaster, A Lancaster"; Oxford's
emendation suggests offstage conflict between the two
armies.

You are the fount that makes small brooks to flow.
Now stops thy spring—my sea shall suck them dry,
And swell so much the higher by their ebb.
25 Hence with him to the Tower—let him not speak.

        Exeunt [some] with KING HENRY *[and* EXETER]

And lords, towards Coventry bend we our course,
Where peremptory° Warwick now remains.   *overbearing*
The sun shines hot, and, if we use delay,
Cold biting winter mars our hoped-for hay.°   *expected harvest*
30 RICHARD OF GLOUCESTER   Away betimes,° before his forces join,   *quickly*
And take the great-grown traitor unawares.
Brave warriors, march amain towards Coventry.   *Exeunt*

5.1

Enter [the Earl of] WARWICK, *the Mayor of Coventry,*
two MESSENGERS, *and others upon the walls*[1]

WARWICK   Where is the post that came from valiant Oxford?
    [*The* FIRST MESSENGER *steps forward*]
  How far hence is thy lord, mine honest fellow?
FIRST MESSENGER   By this° at Dunsmore,[2] marching hitherward.   *By now*
WARWICK   How far off is our brother Montague?
5   Where is the post that came from Montague?
    [*The* SECOND MESSENGER *steps forward*]
SECOND MESSENGER   By this at Da'ntry,[3] with a puissant° troop.   *powerful*
    Enter SOMERVILLE [*to them, above*]
WARWICK   Say, Somerville—what says my loving son?
  And, by thy guess, how nigh is Clarence now?
SOMERVILLE   At Southam[4] I did leave him with his forces,
10   And do expect him here some two hours hence.
    [*A march afar off*]
WARWICK   Then Clarence is at hand—I hear his drum.
SOMERVILLE   It is not his, my lord. Here Southam lies.[5]
  The drum your honour hears marcheth from Warwick.
WARWICK   Who should that be? Belike,° unlooked-for friends.   *Perhaps*
15 SOMERVILLE   They are at hand, and you shall quickly know.
    Flourish. Enter [below KING] EDWARD, [*and*] RICHARD
    [*Duke* OF GLOUCESTER, *with*] *soldiers*
KING EDWARD   Go, trumpet, to the walls, and sound a parley.[6]
    [*Sound a parley*]
RICHARD OF GLOUCESTER   See how the surly Warwick mans the wall.
WARWICK   O, unbid° spite—is sportful° Edward come?   *unwelcome / lecherous*
  Where slept our scouts, or how are they seduced,
20   That we could hear no news of his repair?°   *approach*

5.1 Location: Before the walls of Coventry.
1. This entire scene was probably played with Warwick's party in the gallery above the main stage and King Edward and Richard of Gloucester below, looking upward in lines 16–17 and throughout. In stage directions following lines 59, 67, and 72, first Oxford, then the Marquis of Montague, and then the Duke of Somerset enter. They may enter above to Warwick or, more probably, enter below, cross the stage, and then exit through a stage door as if "into the city" and thus out of

view. F gives each an entrance but no exit; O marks both an entrance and an exit for each.
2. Dunsmore Heath, between Coventry and Daventry.
3. Daventry, a Northamptonshire town about 20 miles southeast of Coventry.
4. A town about 10 miles southeast of Coventry.
5. Southam is in this direction.
6. A trumpet signal requesting a conference between warring troops.

KING EDWARD   Now, Warwick, wilt thou ope the city gates,
    Speak gentle words, and humbly bend thy knee,
    Call Edward king, and at his hands beg mercy?
    And he shall pardon thee these outrages.
25 WARWICK   Nay, rather, wilt thou draw thy forces hence,
    Confess who set thee up and plucked thee down,
    Call Warwick patron, and be penitent?
    And thou shalt still remain the Duke of York.
RICHARD OF GLOUCESTER   I thought at least he would have said 'the King'.
30   Or did he make the jest against his will?
WARWICK   Is not a dukedom, sir, a goodly gift?
RICHARD OF GLOUCESTER   Ay, by my faith, for a poor earl[7] to give.
    I'll do thee service for so good a gift.
WARWICK   'Twas I that gave the kingdom to thy brother.
35 KING EDWARD   Why then, 'tis mine, if but by Warwick's gift.
WARWICK   Thou art no Atlas[8] for so great a weight;
    And, weakling, Warwick takes his gift again;
    And Henry is my king, Warwick his subject.
KING EDWARD   But Warwick's king is Edward's prisoner,
40   And, gallant Warwick, do but answer this:
    What is the body when the head is off?
RICHARD OF GLOUCESTER   Alas, that Warwick had no more forecast,°   anticipated
    But whiles he thought to steal the single ten,[9]
    The king was slyly fingered° from the deck.   stolen
45 [To WARWICK]   You left poor Henry at the Bishop's palace,
    And ten to one you'll meet him in the Tower.
KING EDWARD   'Tis even so—[to WARWICK] yet you are Warwick still.
RICHARD OF GLOUCESTER   Come, Warwick, take the time°—   seize the moment
    kneel down, kneel down.
    Nay, when? Strike now, or else the iron cools.[1]
50 WARWICK   I had rather chop this hand off at a blow,
    And with the other fling it at thy face,
    Than bear so low a sail° to strike to thee.   be so humble as
KING EDWARD   Sail how thou canst, have wind and tide thy friend,
    This hand, fast wound about thy coal-black hair,
55   Shall, whiles thy head is warm and new cut off,
    Write in the dust this sentence with thy blood:
    'Wind-changing° Warwick now can change no more'.   Fickle
    Enter [the Earl of] OXFORD, with [a] drum[mer]
    and soldiers [bearing] colours°   flags
WARWICK   O cheerful colours! See where Oxford comes.
OXFORD   Oxford, Oxford, for Lancaster!
    [OXFORD *and his men pass over the stage and*
    exeunt into the city]
RICHARD OF GLOUCESTER [to KING EDWARD]   The gates are
60   open—let us enter too.
KING EDWARD   So other foes may set upon our backs?
    Stand we in good array, for they no doubt

---

7. Dukes are higher in rank than earls.
8. In Greek mythology, a giant who bore the weight of the heavens on his shoulders.
9. Alluding to the conventions of card games in which

the ten is valuable, but less so than the king. *single*: mere.
1. Referring to the proverb "Strike while the iron is hot," with a pun on "strike" as meaning "to lower a sail" or "to yield."

Will issue out again and bid us battle.
If not, the city being but of small defence,
65 We'll quickly rouse[2] the traitors in the same.
WARWICK [*to* OXFORD, *within*]   O, welcome, Oxford—for we want° thy help.   *need*

Enter [the Marquis of] MONTAGUE *with [a]*
drum[mer] and soldiers [bearing] colours

MONTAGUE   Montague, Montague, for Lancaster!
[MONTAGUE *and his men pass over the stage and*
exeunt into the city]
RICHARD OF GLOUCESTER   Thou and thy brother both shall
bye° this treason   *atone for*
Even with the dearest blood your bodies bear.
70 KING EDWARD   The harder matched, the greater victory.
My mind presageth happy gain and conquest.

Enter [the Duke of] SOMERSET *with [a] drum[mer]*
and soldiers [bearing] colours

SOMERSET   Somerset, Somerset, for Lancaster!
[SOMERSET *and his men pass over the stage*
and exeunt into the city]
RICHARD OF GLOUCESTER   Two of thy name, both dukes of Somerset,
Have sold their lives unto the house of York—
75 And thou shalt be the third, an° this sword hold.[3]   *if*

*Enter [*GEORGE *Duke of]* CLARENCE *with [a]*
drum[mer] and soldiers [bearing] colours

WARWICK   And lo, where George of Clarence sweeps along,
Of force enough to bid his brother battle;
With whom an upright zeal to right° prevails   *for justice*
More than the nature of a brother's love.
80 GEORGE OF CLARENCE   Clarence, Clarence, for Lancaster!
KING EDWARD   *Et tu, Brute*[4]—wilt thou stab Caesar too?
[*To a trumpeter*] A parley, sirra,[5] to George of Clarence.
Sound a parley. RICHARD [OF GLOUCESTER] *and*
[GEORGE OF] CLARENCE *whisper together*
WARWICK   Come, Clarence, come—thou wilt if Warwick call.
GEORGE OF CLARENCE   Father of Warwick, know you what this means?
[*He*] *takes his red rose out of his hat and throws*
it at WARWICK
85 Look—here I throw my infamy at thee!
I will not ruinate my father's house,
Who gave his blood to lime° the stones together,   *cement*
And set up Lancaster. Why, trowest thou,° Warwick,   *do you believe*
That Clarence is so harsh, so blunt,° unnatural,   *uncivilized*
90 To bend the fatal instruments of war
Against his brother and his lawful king?
Perhaps thou wilt object° my holy oath.   *invoke*

---

2. A hunting term meaning "to surprise creatures in their lair."
3. Richard addresses Edmund, the fourth Duke of Somerset. The defection of his older brother Henry, the third Duke, from Edward's cause is described in 4.1 and 4.2. Richard threw the head of their father, the sec-

ond Duke, across the stage in the play's first scene.
4. "You, too, Brutus": Julius Caesar's exclamation when he realized that his friend was one of the conspirators to his murder.
5. Fellow: a customary form of address to a social inferior.

To keep that oath were more impiety
Than Jephthah, when he sacrificed his daughter.[6]
95   I am so sorry for my trespass made
That, to deserve well at my brothers' hands,
I here proclaim myself thy mortal foe,
With resolution, wheresoe'er I meet thee—
As I will meet thee, if thou stir abroad°—   *(outside Coventry)*
100   To plague thee for thy foul misleading me.
And so, proud-hearted Warwick, I defy thee,
And to my brothers turn my blushing cheeks.
[*To* KING EDWARD] Pardon me, Edward—I will make amends.
[*To* RICHARD] And, Richard, do not frown upon my faults,
105   For I will henceforth be no more unconstant.
KING EDWARD   Now welcome more, and ten times more beloved,
Than if thou never hadst deserved our hate.
RICHARD OF GLOUCESTER [*to* GEORGE] Welcome, good
      Clarence—this is brother-like.
WARWICK [*to* GEORGE]   O, passing° traitor—perjured and unjust!   *unsurpassed*
110   KING EDWARD   What, Warwick, wilt thou leave the town and fight?
Or shall we beat the stones about thine ears?
WARWICK [*aside*]   Alas, I am not cooped° here for defence.   *shut up*
[*To* KING EDWARD] I will away towards Barnet[7] presently,
And bid thee battle, Edward, if thou dar'st.
115   KING EDWARD   Yes, Warwick—Edward dares, and leads the way.
Lords, to the field—Saint George and victory!
            Exeunt [*below* KING EDWARD *and his company*].
            March. [*The Earl of*] WARWICK *and his company*
                       [*descend and*] *follow*

5.2

Alarum and excursions. Enter [KING] EDWARD
bringing forth [*the Earl of*] WARWICK, *wounded*
KING EDWARD   So lie thou there. Die thou, and die our fear—
For Warwick was a bug° that feared° us all.   *goblin / frightened*
Now, Montague, sit fast°—I seek for thee   *be on guard*
That Warwick's bones may keep thine company.   *Exit*
5   WARWICK   Ah, who is nigh? Come to me, friend or foe,
And tell me who is victor, York or Warwick?
Why ask I that? My mangled body shows,
My blood, my want of strength, my sick heart shows,
That I must yield my body to the earth
10   And by my fall the conquest to my foe.
Thus yields the cedar[1] to the axe's edge,
Whose arms gave shelter to the princely eagle,[2]
Under whose shade the ramping lion[3] slept,

---

6. Alluding to the biblical story in which Jephthah, an Israelite leader, kills his daughter in fulfillment of a vow. He swore that if he were victorious in battle, he would sacrifice to God whoever first met him from his house when he returned from the battlefield (see Judges 11).
7. Shakespeare treats this town, which is about 10 miles north of London and 75 miles southeast of Coventry, as though it were near Coventry.
5.2 Location: Near Barnet.
1. Often regarded as the king of evergreens and thus a

symbol of sovereignty.
2. Probably referring to Richard, Duke of York. In 2.1.91, his son Richard refers to the Duke of York as a "princely eagle." The eagle was often described as the king of birds.
3. Under whose protection Henry VI rested. A reference both to the lion as king of the animal world and to the Lancastrian coat of arms, which showed three lions rampant or reared on their hind legs.

Whose top-branch over-peered° Jove's spreading tree⁴   rose above
15   And kept low shrubs from winter's powerful wind.
These eyes, that now are dimmed with death's black veil,
Have been as piercing as the midday sun
To search the secret treasons of the world.
The wrinkles in my brows, now filled with blood,
20   Were likened oft to kingly sepulchres—
For who lived king, but I could dig his grave?
And who durst smile when Warwick bent his brow?
Lo now my glory smeared in dust and blood.
My parks,° my walks, my manors that I had,   hunting grounds
25   Even now forsake me, and of all my lands
Is nothing left me but my body's length.
Why, what is pomp, rule, reign, but earth and dust?
And, live we how we can, yet die we must.
              Enter [the Earl of] OXFORD and [the Duke of] SOMERSET
SOMERSET   Ah, Warwick, Warwick—wert thou as we are,
30   We might recover all our loss again.
The Queen from France hath brought a puissant power.°   powerful army
Even now we heard the news. Ah, couldst thou fly!
WARWICK   Why, then I would not fly. Ah, Montague,
If thou be there, sweet brother, take my hand,
35   And with thy lips keep in my soul a while.⁵
Thou lov'st me not—for, brother, if thou didst,
Thy tears would wash this cold congealèd blood
That glues my lips and will not let me speak.
Come quickly, Montague, or I am dead.
40   SOMERSET   Ah, Warwick—Montague hath breathed his last,
And to the latest gasp cried out for Warwick,
And said 'Commend me to my valiant brother.'
And more he would have said, and more he spoke,
Which sounded like a canon in a vault,
45   That mote° not be distinguished; but at last   might
I well might hear, delivered with a groan,
'O, farewell, Warwick.'
WARWICK   Sweet rest his soul. Fly, lords, and save yourselves—
For Warwick bids you all farewell, to meet in heaven. *He dies*
50   OXFORD   Away, away—to meet the Queen's great power!
              Here they bear away [Warwick's] body. Exeunt

                                  5.3
              Flourish. Enter KING EDWARD *in triumph, with*
              RICHARD [*Duke* OF GLOUCESTER, GEORGE *Duke of*]
              CLARENCE, *and soldiers*
KING EDWARD   Thus far our fortune keeps an upward course,
And we are graced with wreaths of victory.
But in the midst of this bright-shining day
I spy a black suspicious threatening cloud
5   That will encounter with our glorious sun
Ere he attain his easeful western bed.
I mean, my lords, those powers that the Queen

4. Jove's tree, according to Virgil, was the oak, the king   escaped through the mouth at death.
of deciduous trees.   5.3 Location: Scene continues.
5. Kiss me. Many Elizabethans believed the soul

Hath raised in Gallia° have arrived our coast,   *France*
  And, as we hear, march on to fight with us.
10 GEORGE OF CLARENCE A little gale will soon disperse that cloud,
  And blow it to the source from whence it came.
  Thy very beams will dry those vapours up,
  For every cloud engenders not a storm.
  RICHARD OF GLOUCESTER The Queen is valued° thirty thousand   *estimated to be*
      strong,
15 And Somerset, with Oxford, fled to her.
  If she have time to breathe,° be well assured,   *gather her strength*
  Her faction will be full as strong as ours.
  KING EDWARD We are advertised° by our loving friends   *informed*
  That they do hold their course toward Tewkesbury.[1]
20 We, having now the best at Barnet field,
  Will thither straight, for willingness rids way[2]—
  And, as we march, our strength will be augmented
  In every county as we go along.
  Strike up the drum, cry 'Courage!'; and away.
                        [*Flourish. March.*] *Exeunt*

5.4

Flourish. March. Enter QUEEN [MARGARET], PRINCE
EDWARD, [*the Duke of*] SOMERSET, [*the Earl of*]
OXFORD, *and soldiers*

QUEEN MARGARET Great lords, wise men ne'er sit and wail their loss,
  But cheerly° seek how to redress their harms.   *cheerfully*
  What though the mast be now blown overboard,
  The cable broke, the holding-anchor[1] lost,
5 And half our sailors swallowed in the flood?
  Yet lives our pilot° still. Is't meet that he   *(Henry)*
  Should leave the helm and, like a fearful lad,
  With tearful eyes add water to the sea,
  And give more strength to that which hath too much,
10 Whiles, in his moan,° the ship splits on the rock   *state of grief*
  Which industry and courage might have saved?
  Ah, what a shame; ah, what a fault were this.
  Say Warwick was our anchor—what of that?
  And Montague our top-mast—what of him?
15 Our slaughtered friends the tackles[2]—what of these?
  Why, is not Oxford here another anchor?
  And Somerset another goodly mast?
  The friends of France our shrouds[3] and tacklings?
  And, though unskilful, why not Ned° and I   *(her son Edward)*
20 For once allowed the skilful pilot's charge?°   *responsibility*
  We will not from the helm to sit and weep,
  But keep our course, though the rough wind say no,
  From shelves° and rocks that threaten us with wreck.   *sandbanks*
  As good to chide the waves as speak them fair.

1. A town in Gloucestershire.
2. For eagerness to travel makes the journey seem
shorter.
5.4 Location: Fields near Tewkesbury.
1. The anchor meant to stabilize the ship by taking

hold of the sea bottom.
2. Ropes and pulleys used for raising and lowering
sails.
3. Ropes that brace and support the mast.

25   And what is Edward but a ruthless sea?
      What Clarence but a quicksand of deceit?
      And Richard but a raggèd° fatal rock?   *jagged*
      All these the enemies to our poor barque.°   *ship*
      Say you can swim—alas, 'tis but a while;
30   Tread on the sand—why, there you quickly sink;
      Bestride the rock—the tide will wash you off,
      Or else you famish. That's a threefold death.
      This speak I, lords, to let you understand,
      If° case some one of you would fly from us,   *In*
35   That there's no hoped-for mercy with the brothers York
      More than with ruthless waves, with sands, and rocks.
      Why, courage then—what cannot be avoided
      'Twere childish weakness to lament or fear.
PRINCE EDWARD   Methinks a woman of this valiant spirit
40   Should, if a coward heard her speak these words,
      Infuse his breast with magnanimity°   *great courage*
      And make him, naked,° foil° a man at arms.   *unarmed / defeat*
      I speak not this as doubting any here—
      For did I but suspect a fearful man,
45   He should have leave to go away betimes,°   *at once*
      Lest in our need he might infect another
      And make him of like spirit to himself.
      If any such be here—as God forbid—
      Let him depart before we need his help.
50 OXFORD   Women and children of so high a courage,
      And warriors faint°—why, 'twere perpetual shame!   *fainthearted*
      O brave young Prince, thy famous grandfather°   *(Henry V)*
      Doth live again in thee! Long mayst thou live
      To bear his image and renew his glories!
55 SOMERSET   And he that will not fight for such a hope,
      Go home to bed, and like the owl by day,
      If he arise, be mocked and wondered at.
QUEEN MARGARET   Thanks, gentle Somerset; sweet Oxford, thanks.
PRINCE EDWARD   And take his thanks that yet° hath nothing else.   *who as yet*
      Enter a MESSENGER
60 MESSENGER   Prepare you, lords, for Edward is at hand
      Ready to fight—therefore be resolute.
OXFORD   I thought no less. It is his policy
      To haste thus fast to find us unprovided.°   *unprepared*
SOMERSET   But he's deceived; we are in readiness.
65 QUEEN MARGARET   This cheers my heart, to see your forwardness.
OXFORD   Here pitch our battle°—hence we will not budge.   *deploy our army*
      Flourish and march. Enter KING EDWARD, RICHARD
      [*Duke* OF GLOUCESTER], *and* [GEORGE *Duke* OF]
      CLARENCE, [*with*] *soldiers*
KING EDWARD [*to his followers*]   Brave followers, yonder stands
          the thorny wood
      Which, by the heavens' assistance and your strength,
      Must by the roots be hewn up yet ere night.
70   I need not add more fuel to your fire,
      For well I wot° ye blaze to burn them out.   *know*
      Give signal to the fight, and to it, lords.

QUEEN MARGARET [*to her followers*]   Lords, knights, and
      gentlemen—what I should say
      My tears gainsay;° for every word I speak   *hinder*
75   Ye see I drink the water of my eye.
      Therefore, no more but this: Henry your sovereign
      Is prisoner to the foe, his state usurped,
      His realm a slaughter-house, his subjects slain,
      His statutes cancelled, and his treasure spent—
80   And yonder is the wolf that makes this spoil.
      You fight in justice; then in God's name, lords,
      Be valiant, and give signal to the fight.
          Alarum, retreat, excursions. Exeunt

5.5

      Flourish. Enter [KING] EDWARD, RICHARD [DUKE OF
      GLOUCESTER, *and* GEORGE *Duke* OF] CLARENCE, [*with*]
      QUEEN [MARGARET, *the Earl of*] OXFORD, [*and the Duke
      of*] SOMERSET [*guarded*]

KING EDWARD   Now here a period of° tumultuous broils.   *an end to*
      Away with Oxford to Hames Castle¹ straight;
      For Somerset, off with his guilty head.
      Go bear them hence—I will not hear them speak.
5 OXFORD   For my part, I'll not trouble thee with words.
                              Exit [*guarded*]
SOMERSET   Nor I, but stoop with patience to my fortune.
                              Exit [*guarded*]
QUEEN MARGARET   So part we sadly in this troublous world
      To meet with joy in sweet Jerusalem.²
KING EDWARD   Is proclamation made that who finds Edward
10   Shall have a high reward and he his life?
RICHARD OF GLOUCESTER   It is, and lo where youthful Edward
      comes.
      Enter PRINCE [EDWARD, *guarded*]
KING EDWARD   Bring forth the gallant—let us hear him speak.
      What, can so young a thorn begin to prick?
      Edward, what satisfaction° canst thou make   *amends*
15   For bearing arms, for stirring up my subjects,
      And all the trouble thou hast turned me to?
PRINCE EDWARD   Speak like a subject, proud ambitious York.³
17.1   ALL THE LANCASTER PARTY   *Saint George for Lancaster!*
      Alarums to the battle. [*The house of*] *York flies, then
      the chambers*° [*are*] *discharged. Then enter* KING   *small cannon*
      [EDWARD, GEORGE OF] CLARENCE, *and* [RICHARD OF]
      GLOUCESTER, *and* [*their followers; they*] *make a great
      shout, and cry 'For York! For York!' Then* QUEEN [MAR-
      GARET], PRINCE [EDWARD], OXFORD *and* SOMERSET
      [*are all*] *taken* [*prisoner. Flourish,*] *and enter all
      again*

5.5 Location: Scene continues.
1. Hammes Castle, near Calais.
2. Referring to heaven, which is described as the new
Jerusalem in Revelation 21:2.

3. O abridges 5.4.82–5.5.17 and may reflect authorial
revision. An edited text of the abridged passage is given
as the inset passage that follows (lines 17.1–17.10).

KING EDWARD   *Now here a period of*° *tumultuous broils*   an end to
            Away with Oxford to Hames Castle straight;
            For Somerset, off with his guilty head.
17.5   *Go, bear them hence—I will not hear them speak.*
OXFORD   *For my part, I'll not trouble thee with words.*
                                          Exit [*guarded*]
SOMERSET   *Nor I, but stoop with patience to my death.*
                                          Exit [*guarded*]
KING EDWARD [*to* PRINCE EDWARD]   *Edward, what*
            satisfaction° *canst thou make*   amends
            For stirring up my subjects to rebellion?
17.10   PRINCE EDWARD   *Speak like a subject, proud ambitious York.*
        Suppose that I am now my father's mouth—
        Resign thy chair, and where I stand, kneel thou,
20   Whilst I propose the self-same words to thee,
        Which, traitor, thou wouldst have me answer to.
QUEEN MARGARET   Ah, that thy father had been so resolved.
RICHARD OF GLOUCESTER   That you might still have worn the petticoat
        And ne'er have stolen the breech° from Lancaster.   trousers
25 PRINCE EDWARD   Let Aesop[4] fable in a winter's night—
        His currish riddles sorts not with this place.[5]
RICHARD OF GLOUCESTER   By heaven, brat, I'll plague ye for that word.
QUEEN MARGARET   Ay, thou wast born to be a plague to men.
RICHARD OF GLOUCESTER   For God's sake take away this captive scold.
30 PRINCE EDWARD   Nay, take away this scolding crookback° rather.   hunchback
KING EDWARD   Peace, wilful boy, or I will charm° your tongue.   silence with a spell
GEORGE OF CLARENCE [*to* PRINCE EDWARD]   Untutored lad,
        thou art too malapert.°   saucy
PRINCE EDWARD   I know my duty—you are all undutiful.
        Lascivious Edward, and thou, perjured George,
35   And thou, misshapen Dick—I tell ye all
        I am your better, traitors as ye are,
        And thou usurp'st my father's right and mine.
KING EDWARD   Take that, the likeness of this railer° here.   scold (Margaret)
            [KING EDWARD] *stabs* [PRINCE EDWARD]
RICHARD OF GLOUCESTER   Sprawl'st thou?[6] Take that, to end thy agony.
            RICHARD *stabs* [PRINCE EDWARD]
40 GEORGE OF CLARENCE   And there's for twitting me with perjury.
            [GEORGE] *stabs* [PRINCE EDWARD, *who dies*]
QUEEN MARGARET   O, kill me too!
RICHARD OF GLOUCESTER   Marry,[7] and shall.
            [*He*] *offers to kill her*
KING EDWARD   Hold, Richard, hold—for we have done too much.
RICHARD OF GLOUCESTER   Why should she live to fill the world
        with words?
            [QUEEN MARGARET *faints*]

4. An ancient storyteller famous for his fables about
animals. Like Richard, he reputedly was physically
deformed. *fable*: tell tales.
5. His mean and cynical comments are not welcome
here.
6. Do you convulse in the agonies of death?
7. A mild oath invoking the name of the Virgin Mary.

KING EDWARD   What—doth she swoon? Use means for her recovery.
RICHARD OF GLOUCESTER [*aside to* GEORGE]   Clarence, excuse
45   me to the King my brother.
    I'll hence to London on a serious matter.
    Ere ye come there, be sure° to hear some news.   *expect*
GEORGE OF CLARENCE [*aside to* RICHARD]   What? What?
50   RICHARD OF GLOUCESTER [*aside to* GEORGE]   The Tower, the Tower.
                                                                Exit
QUEEN MARGARET   O Ned, sweet Ned—speak to thy mother, boy.
    Canst thou not speak? O traitors, murderers!
    They that stabbed Caesar shed no blood at all,
    Did not offend, nor were not worthy blame,
55   If this foul deed were by to equal it.°   *to compare with it*
    He was a man—this, in respect,° a child;   *in comparison*
    And men ne'er spend their fury on a child.
    What's worse than murderer that I may name it?
    No, no, my heart will burst an if I speak;
60   And I will speak that so my heart may burst.
    Butchers and villains! Bloody cannibals!
    How sweet a plant have you untimely cropped!
    You have no children, butchers; if you had,
    The thought of them would have stirred up remorse.
65   But if you ever chance to have a child,
    Look in his youth to have him so cut off
    As, deathsmen, you have rid° this sweet young Prince!   *killed*
KING EDWARD   Away with her—go, bear her hence perforce.
QUEEN MARGARET   Nay, never bear me hence—dispatch° me here.   *kill*
70   Here sheathe thy sword—I'll pardon thee my death.
    What? Wilt thou not? Then, Clarence, do it thou.
GEORGE OF CLARENCE   By heaven, I will not do thee so much ease.
QUEEN MARGARET   Good Clarence, do; sweet Clarence, do thou do it.
GEORGE OF CLARENCE   Didst thou not hear me swear I would not do it?
75   QUEEN MARGARET   Ay, but thou usest° to forswear thyself.   *are accustomed*
    'Twas sin before, but now 'tis charity.
    What, wilt thou not? Where is that devil's butcher,
    Hard-favoured° Richard? Richard, where art thou?   *Ugly*
    Thou art not here. Murder is thy alms-deed°—   *act of charity*
80   Petitioners for blood thou ne'er putt'st back.°   *you never turn away*
KING EDWARD   Away, I say—I charge ye, bear her hence.
QUEEN MARGARET   So come to you and yours as to this Prince!
                                                        Exit [*guarded*]
KING EDWARD   Where's Richard gone?
GEORGE OF CLARENCE   To London all in post° [—*aside*] and as I guess,   *haste*
85   To make a bloody supper in the Tower.
KING EDWARD   He's sudden if a thing comes in his head.
    Now march we hence. Discharge the common sort°   *ordinary soldiers*
    With pay and thanks, and let's away to London,
    And see our gentle Queen how well she fares.
90   By this° I hope she hath a son for me.   *Exeunt*   *By now*

5.6

*Enter on the walls [*KING*] HENRY VI, [*reading a book,*]*
RICHARD [*Duke of GLOUCESTER, and] the* LIEUTENANT
[*of the Tower*][1]

RICHARD OF GLOUCESTER   Good day, my lord. What, at your
    book so hard?

KING HENRY   Ay, my good lord—'my lord', I should say, rather.
    'Tis sin to flatter; 'good' was little better.°   *(than flattery)*
    'Good Gloucester' and 'good devil' were alike,
5   And both preposterous°—therefore not 'good lord'.   *unnatural*

RICHARD OF GLOUCESTER [*to the* LIEUTENANT]   Sirrah,° leave us   *Fellow*
    to ourselves. We must confer.   [*Exit* LIEUTENANT]

KING HENRY   So flies the reckless° shepherd from the wolf;   *careless*
    So first the harmless sheep doth yield his fleece,
    And next his throat unto the butcher's knife.
10   What scene of death hath Roscius[2] now to act?

RICHARD OF GLOUCESTER   Suspicion always haunts the guilty mind;
    The thief doth fear each bush an officer.

KING HENRY   The bird that hath been limèd[3] in a bush
    With trembling wings misdoubteth° every bush.   *fears*
15   And I, the hapless male° to one sweet bird,°   *father / child*
    Have now the fatal object in my eye
    Where my poor young was limed, was caught and killed.

RICHARD OF GLOUCESTER   Why, what a peevish° fool was that of Crete,   *silly*
    That taught his son the office of a fowl![4]
20   And yet, for all his wings, the fool was drowned.

KING HENRY   I, Daedalus; my poor boy, Icarus;
    Thy father, Minos,[5] that denied our course;
    The sun that seared the wings of my sweet boy,
    Thy brother Edward;[6] and thyself, the sea,
25   Whose envious gulf did swallow up his life.
    Ah, kill me with thy weapon, not with words!
    My breast can better brook° thy dagger's point   *tolerate*
    Than can my ears that tragic history.
    But wherefore dost thou come? Is't for my life?
30 RICHARD OF GLOUCESTER   Think'st thou I am an executioner?

KING HENRY   A persecutor I am sure thou art;
    If murdering innocents be executing,
    Why, then thou art an executioner.

RICHARD OF GLOUCESTER   Thy son I killed for his presumption.

35 KING HENRY   Hadst thou been killed when first thou didst presume,
    Thou hadst not lived to kill a son of mine.

5.6 Location: The Tower, London.
1. The precise setting is ambiguous. F's stage directions indicate that the scene takes place "on the Walls," O's that it occurs "in the Tower." Richard's first line makes clear that Henry is reading, which may mean he is in an inner chamber. His murder could be staged in a small alcove at the back of the main stage, on the walls (up in the gallery), or in full view on the main stage.
2. An ancient Roman actor (actually best known as a comedian) whom many Elizabethans cited as the archetype of a great tragedian.

3. Caught with birdlime, a sticky substance smeared on twigs.
4. Alluding to the myth of Daedalus, who, in order to escape imprisonment in Crete, designed wings made of wax and feathers for himself and his son Icarus. When Icarus flew too near the sun, the wax melted, and he fell to his death in the sea.
5. The King of Crete who imprisoned Daedalus and Icarus.
6. Referring to the sun insignia associated with Edward.

And thus I prophesy: that many a thousand
Which now mistrust no parcel of my fear,[7]
And many an old man's sigh, and many a widow's,
40 And many an orphan's water-standing° eye—   *flooded with tears*
Men for their sons', wives for their husbands',
Orphans for their parents' timeless° death—   *untimely*
Shall rue the hour that ever thou wast born.
The owl shrieked at thy birth—an evil sign;
45 The night-crow[8] cried, aboding° luckless time;   *foretelling*
Dogs howled, and hideous tempests shook down trees;
The raven rooked her° on the chimney's top;   *crouched*
And chatt'ring pies° in dismal discords sung.   *magpies*
Thy mother felt more than a mother's pain,
50 And yet brought forth less than a mother's hope—
To wit, an indigested° and deformèd lump,   *a shapeless*
Not like the fruit of such a goodly tree.
Teeth hadst thou in thy head when thou wast born,[9]
To signify thou cam'st to bite the world;
55 And if the rest be true which I have heard
Thou cam'st—

RICHARD   I'll hear no more. Die, prophet, in thy speech,
          He stabs him
For this, amongst the rest, was I ordained.

KING HENRY   Ay, and for much more slaughter after this.
60 O, God forgive my sins, and pardon thee.   *He dies*

RICHARD OF GLOUCESTER   What—will the aspiring blood of
          Lancaster
Sink in the ground? I thought it would have mounted.
See how my sword weeps for the poor King's death.
O, may such purple° tears be alway shed   *blood-red*
65 From those that wish the downfall of our house!
If any spark of life be yet remaining,
Down, down to hell, and say I sent thee thither—
          [*He*] *stabs him again*
I that have neither pity, love, nor fear.
Indeed, 'tis true that Henry told me of,
70 For I have often heard my mother say
I came into the world with my legs forward.
Had I not reason, think ye, to make haste,
And seek their ruin that usurped our right?
The midwife wondered and the women cried
75 'O, Jesus bless us, he is born with teeth!'—
And so I was, which plainly signified
That I should snarl and bite and play the dog.
Then, since the heavens have shaped my body so,
Let hell make crooked my mind to answer° it.   *match*
80 I had no father, I am like no father;
I have no brother, I am like no brother;
And this word, 'love', which greybeards call divine,
Be resident in men like one another
And not in me—I am myself alone.

7. Who do not share any of my fears.
8. A mythical bird supposed to be an evil omen.

9. Richard III was popularly believed to have been born
with teeth, a physical sign of his monstrous character.

85 Clarence, beware; thou kept'st me from the light—
But I will sort° a pitchy° day for thee.   *arrange / dark*
For I will buzz° abroad such prophecies   *whisper*
That Edward shall be fearful of his life,
And then, to purge his fear, I'll be thy death.
90 Henry and his son are gone; thou, Clarence, art next;
And by one and one I will dispatch the rest,
Counting myself but bad till I be best.
I'll throw thy body in another room
And triumph, Henry, in thy day of doom. *Exit [with the body]*

5.7

[*A chair of state.*] *Flourish. Enter* KING EDWARD, [LADY
GRAY *his*] *Queen,* [GEORGE *Duke* OF] CLARENCE, RICH-
ARD [*Duke* OF GLOUCESTER, *the Lord*] HASTINGS, *a
nurse,* [*carrying the infant*] *Prince* [*Edward*], *and
attendants*

KING EDWARD   Once more we sit in England's royal throne,
Repurchased with the blood of enemies.
What valiant foemen, like to autumn's corn,
Have we mowed down in tops° of all their pride!   *at the peak*
5 Three dukes of Somerset, threefold renowned
For hardy and undoubted° champions;   *fearless*
Two Cliffords, as the father and the son;
And two Northumberlands—two braver men
Ne'er spurred their coursers° at the trumpet's sound.   *warhorses*
10 With them, the two brave bears, Warwick and Montague,[1]
That in their chains fettered the kingly lion
And made the forest tremble when they roared.
Thus have we swept suspicion° from our seat°   *worry / throne*
And made our footstool of security.
15 [*To* LADY GRAY] Come hither, Bess, and let me kiss my boy.
[*The nurse brings forth the infant prince.* KING
EDWARD *kisses him*]
Young Ned, for thee, thine uncles and myself
Have in our armours watched° the winter's night,   *stayed awake during*
Went all afoot in summer's scalding heat,
That thou mightst repossess the crown in peace;
20 And of our labours thou shalt reap the gain.
RICHARD OF GLOUCESTER [*aside*]   I'll blast° his harvest, an your   *wither*
head were laid;[2]
For yet I am not looked on° in the world.   *noticed*
This shoulder was ordained so thick to heave;
And heave it shall some weight or break my back.
25 Work thou the way, and thou shalt execute.[3]
KING EDWARD   Clarence and Gloucester, love my lovely queen;
And kiss your princely nephew, brothers, both.
GEORGE OF CLARENCE   The duty that I owe unto your majesty
I seal upon the lips of this sweet babe.
[*He kisses the infant prince*]
30 LADY GRAY   Thanks, noble Clarence—worthy brother, thanks.

5.7 Location: The Palace, London.
1. The coat of arms of these brothers included the
image of a bear chained to a staff.

2. Once your head is laid in the grave.
3. Devise a way, (my head), and you, (shoulder and
hand), shall carry it out.

RICHARD OF GLOUCESTER   And that I love the tree° from whence   *(family of York)*
    thou sprang'st,
Witness the loving kiss I give the fruit.
    [*He kisses the infant prince*]
[*Aside*] To say the truth, so Judas kissed his master,
And cried 'All hail!' whenas he meant all harm.[4]

35 KING EDWARD   Now am I seated as my soul delights,
Having my country's peace and brothers' loves.
GEORGE OF CLARENCE   What will your grace have done with
    Margaret?
René her father, to the King of France
Hath pawned the Sicils° and Jerusalem,   *Naples and Sicily*
40 And hither have they sent it° for her ransom.   *(the money raised)*
KING EDWARD   Away with her, and waft her° hence to France. *convey her by water*
And now what rests° but that we spend the time   *remains*
With stately triumphs,° mirthful comic shows,   *festivals*
Such as befits the pleasure of the court?
45 Sound drums and trumpets—farewell, sour annoy!°   *bitter troubles*
For here, I hope, begins our lasting joy.   [*Flourish.*] *Exeunt*

---

4. Judas, identifying Jesus to the officers eager to arrest him, greeted him with a kiss and the salutation "All hail."
whenas: when.

Titus Andronicus

Human sacrifice. Gang rape. Mutilation. Ritual butchery. Mother-son cannibalism. *Titus Andronicus* delighted audiences of the 1590s, and the memory of its enormous popular success was still alive more than twenty years later, when Shakespeare's contemporary, Ben Jonson, referred to it as a famous old crowd-pleaser in his comedy *Bartholomew Fair.* Several centuries of critics since then, however, have deplored the play's gratuitous violence. The late-seventeenth-century playwright Edward Ravenscroft considered *Titus Andronicus* "a heap of rubbish"; the twentieth-century poet and critic T. S. Eliot called it "one of the stupidest and most uninspired plays ever written." Some have even claimed that Shakespeare could not have written *Titus Andronicus*, even though contemporaries testify to his authorship and it inaugurates themes that will interest him again: he returns to the Machiavellian villain in *Richard III,* to the urgency of revenge in *Hamlet,* to the old man unwisely relinquishing power in *Lear,* to questions of race and intermarriage in *Othello* and *The Tempest,* to important moments in Roman history in *The Rape of Lucrece, Julius Caesar, Coriolanus,* and *Antony and Cleopatra.*

Of course, Shakespeare himself, writing his first tragedy in 1592 (with, some scholars argue, the help of George Peele), could not have anticipated the reasons for which he would eventually be canonized. Moreover, the distinction between "high art" and "low entertainment" that often underlies complaints about *Titus Andronicus* would have been unfamiliar to Shakespeare and to his audience: the contrast between popular and elite culture was drawn differently in early modern England than it has been in later centuries. Even by the standards of Shakespeare's contemporaries, however, *Titus Andronicus* is an extravagantly bloody play, often deliberately shocking or grotesque. It seems worth asking how it fits into an oeuvre in which many have been reluctant to grant it a place.

Generically speaking, *Titus Andronicus* is a tragedy of revenge, a very old form that originated in ancient Greece, flourished in ancient Rome, and was revived in the 1580s in England by Shakespeare's predecessor Thomas Kyd. English Renaissance revenge tragedies typically feature a man whose family members have been raped or murdered by a king, duke, or emperor. Because the administration of justice rests in the hands of the very person who has committed the outrage, no redress is obtainable through established institutions. As a result, the hero takes matters into his own hands. Ironically, as he struggles to impose a just order upon his world, he loses his own moral bearings and even his sanity: the commonsensical standards of "justice" upon which he has initially relied often come to seem either flawed or unreachable. In the final scenes, the revenger wreaks some appalling vengeance upon his enemies and then is killed or commits suicide himself. By staging the spectacle of a subject exterminating his "betters," Renaissance revenge tragedy taps into frustrations and ambivalences that must have accumulated in the hierarchical, deliberately inequitable social arrangements of early modern England. Spectators could experience a vicarious thrill of sympathy with the revenger and relish the atrocities represented onstage, even while, at the end of the play, acknowledging the moral unacceptability of revenge and the necessity for the revenger's death.

Titus Andronicus differs from roughly contemporary revenge tragedies in degree rather than in kind. Revengers typically begin as conscientious, law-abiding types: otherwise their eventual descent into illegality would furnish little dramatic interest. In Titus's case, these traits are highly exaggerated: when offered the imperial diadem, his sense of propriety induces him to defer to Saturninus, the eldest son of the last emperor, even though in Rome the office of emperor was not necessarily an inherited one. Of course, the obligation that Saturninus thus incurs makes Titus's later suffering at the hands of the imperial family seem all the more galling. At the same time, Shakespeare complicates the action by giving Saturninus's wife, Tamora, an excellent reason for hating Titus: in the first scene, he has ignored her desperate pleas and sacrificed her eldest son. So, in fact, Titus's revenge is a response to Tamora's own vengeance. The doubling of reprisals in *Titus Andronicus* gives some pretext for the play's relentless bloodiness; but it is worth remembering too that bloodiness is an earmark of revenge tragedy then and now. One modern corollary to a play like *Titus Andronicus* is the movie thriller in which a rogue cop or ex-military officer brutally retaliates against those who have murdered his partners or loved ones: the kind of film, in other words, that is likely to attract a vast audience even while provoking condemnation of "media violence." *Titus* seems considerably less grotesque when it is compared with other plays of its kind rather than, say, with *Romeo and Juliet*.

In its elaborately detailed antique setting, however, *Titus Andronicus* differs strikingly from most Renaissance revenge tragedies. The play is an early manifestation of Shakespeare's enduring interest in classical culture, a "Roman" play akin to *Julius Caesar, Coriolanus*, and *Antony and Cleopatra*. But in contrast to the later Roman plays, which are based on history and biography, the plot of *Titus Andronicus* is pure fiction. Unfettered by fact, Shakespeare is free to fabricate an extravagant nightmare universe that presses against the frontiers of plausibility. At the same time, he puts a great deal of emphasis on the play's "Roman-ness," making constant reference to classical myths, to legendary and historical figures, to imperial institutions, to the places and customs of ancient Rome.

Shakespeare creates what might be called a "Rome effect" by an eclectic process of extracting and combining motifs from a wide variety of classical stories. Titus as he appears in the opening scene, for instance—in his austere patriotism, his intolerance of dissent, his acute sense of personal and family honor, his traditional piety, and his ferocious commitment to patriarchal hierarchy—is a recurrent Roman personality type. Shakespeare could have found precedents for these traits in numerous figures from Roman history. After a victory in battle, Horatius killed his sister for lamenting her betrothed, a man of the enemy nation whom he himself had slain in combat; Gaius Mucius Scaevola deliberately burned off his right hand in the presence of an enemy king to demonstrate the resolution of the Romans; Titus Manlius Torquatus was a general so severe that he had his own son executed for eagerly anticipating an order to engage the enemy; Marcus Portius Cato's contempt for "softness" made him both an extraordinary military leader and an eloquent misogynist; Appius Claudius killed his daughter after her sexual honor was compromised. Most likely, Shakespeare had all these exemplary figures in mind, and probably more. Likewise the career of Titus's son Lucius, a soldier who defends Rome bravely against external enemies but who finds himself persecuted by his own countrymen, recalls the experience of several historic figures: the brothers Publius Scipio Africanus and Lucius Scipio Asiaticus, who subdued much of North Africa and Asia only to be falsely accused of embezzlement; or Caius Marcius Coriolanus, who after his exile joined Rome's enemies and marched on his native city.

Similarly, Titus's daughter Lavinia has a number of classical precursors. The story of her rape and mutilation is loosely based on a story that, as retold in Ovid's *Metamorphoses*, was commonly assigned to Elizabethan boys in school. In this ancient legend, King Tereus rapes his sister-in-law Philomela and cuts out her tongue in order to prevent her from revealing his identity. Philomela, however, imparts the truth to her sister Progne (or Procne), Tereus's wife, by weaving a tapestry that illustrates the crime. In revenge, Progne butchers her own son by Tereus and serves him to her husband as part of a feast. The similarities between Lavinia's plight and Philomela's are often noted in *Titus Andronicus*, and Lavinia herself reveals the truth about the crime when she gets her stumps on a copy of the *Metamorphoses*.

Progne serving Itys to Tereus. From Antonio Tempesta, *Ovid's "Metamorphoses"* (1606).

But Philomela is not the only model for Lavinia. Shakespeare draws upon the story of the rape of Lucretia, an ancient Roman matron violated by Tarquin, the king's son; she committed suicide after revealing the crime to her male relatives. She was revenged by a group of men who, like Lucius in *Titus Andronicus,* used the outrage as a pretext for overthrowing tyrannical power and setting up a new government. Shakespeare also incorporates into *Titus Andronicus* some features of the story of Appius and Virginia. Virginia was a young Roman woman who was sexually threatened by a powerful judge and killed by her father to prevent her rape; like Lucretia, she became the pretext for a revolutionary uprising. Lavinia's story, then, is an amalgam of classical rape narratives. Her terribly mutilated body condenses a long history of sporadic violence against women into a single, intensely imagined brutalization. Like Titus, Lavinia seems to sum up a whole tradition, one highly prestigious in an age that venerated the classics, and at the same time deeply disturbing.

This particular way of imagining "Rome," as an anthology of stories, reflects Shakespeare's education in Renaissance England. England had, of course, been a Roman territory, and marks of the Roman occupation persisted. Romans had built the road system still in use in Shakespeare's time; the remains of their fortifications were (and are) still visible in many locations. But England had been a remote outpost of the empire, not a place where the treasures of antiquity were commonly to be found. While Renaissance Italians could ground their knowledge of antiquity upon great architecture and statuary all around them, the English, few of whom traveled to Italy in the sixteenth century, imbibed the classical past through books, through a grammar-school curriculum that emphasized a firm grounding in Latin literature and history. For Shakespeare and his compatriots, in other words, the Roman past had less to do with places or artifacts than with texts.

The influence of these texts echoes through *Titus Andronicus*: Ovid's *Metamorphoses,* a fantastic compilation of pagan myths; Virgil's *Aeneid,* which recounts the epic voyage of the Trojan prince Aeneas to Carthage and then Italy; the gory legends of vengeance dramatized by the tragedian Seneca; the histories of the Roman Republic and Empire, written by Livy, Plutarch, Tacitus, Sallust, and Suetonius. In *Titus Andronicus,* the sign of Rome's dominion often seems less a moral or political superiority than a kind of narrative ascendancy. Shakespeare's Goths and Africans apparently have no history, no myths, of their own: instead, they invoke and mimic examples provided by their conquerors, just as Renaissance Europeans revived the classical literary inheritance, testifying to its importance in the very acts of reading and imitating it.

In *Titus Andronicus,* all the characters in the play are acutely conscious of the glorious Roman past as it is enshrined in narrative. Their dependence on old stories means that their lives have a curiously derivative quality. The characters not only model their behavior on these stories, but they consistently exceed the prototype. Whereas in the *Metamorphoses* one man rapes Philomela and cuts out her tongue afterward, in *Titus Andronicus* two men rape Lavinia, and they cut off her hands as well. Whereas Progne cooks one child, Titus bakes two. "For worse than Philomel you used my daughter," Titus declares, "And worse than Progne I will be revenged" (5.2.193–94). He both invokes and goes beyond his original example, intensifying the original crime in a way characteristic of revengers ancient and modern: "An act is not revenged," writes the ancient tragedian Seneca, "unless it is surpassed." Thus there is an interesting corollary between the spiraling ferocity typical of the revenge plot and the competitive way in which the characters in Shakespeare's revenge play fit themselves into a Roman tradition by exceeding its paradigms, enacting its stories "with a vengeance," as one says.

Triumphal arch and its collapse. From Jan van der Noot, *A Theatre for Worldlings* (1569).

Of course, the oppressive weight of the past is a problem not merely for the characters of *Titus Andronicus* but also for its playwright. Like his characters, Shakespeare recycles the old stories with a difference, "surpassing" them just as the revenger surpasses the original crime. From our point of view, Shakespeare seems the world's preeminent dramatist, secure in the greatness that was already beginning to be accorded him at the time of his death. But in the early years of his career, Shakespeare might well have wondered whether and how it was possible to use, even while surpassing, the examples earlier writers had set for him. The notorious excesses of *Titus Andronicus* are one way of employing, even while going beyond, the examples he inherited.

If, in fact, Shakespeare worried about how he would measure up against his predecessors, and about whether the present and future would be able to compete with the past, it is interesting that he sets *Titus Andronicus* in the late fourth century C.E. At this point in history, Rome had dominated Europe, North Africa, and the Middle East for almost five hundred years: in both extent and duration, its empire was historically unprecedented and has never been achieved again. The Roman ritual that embodies and celebrates that rule is the "triumph" with which *Titus Andronicus* begins: a victory procession accorded, from time immemorial, to conquering Roman generals when they returned from the perimeters of the empire with barbarian chieftains in tow. By the fourth century, however, the long Roman dominion was drawing to a close. Shakespeare's sixteenth-century audience knows that although Titus may still be winning battles against the Goths, the time is near when the boundaries of the empire will crumble and invaders will sweep down from the north, annihilating Rome's power and bringing the era of classical civilization to an end.

In *Titus Andronicus*, then, Shakespeare portrays a society teetering on the verge of obsolescence: it has a long, long history but not much of a future. The signs of decadence, corruption, and loss of cultural confidence are everywhere. For instance, the difference between Roman and barbarian initially seems clearly, even absolutely, marked: Tamora and her sons are in chains, Titus and his sons conquering heroes. "Thou art a Roman, be not barbarous," Marcus advises Titus, as if the two terms were necessarily incompatible. Even in the first scene, however, the Roman sense of superiority seems unwarranted. The quarrel over the imperial throne precedes Titus's victory celebration, suggesting the institutional instability that will ultimately subvert Rome from within even as uncouth armies threaten to overwhelm it from without. Moreover, the climax of Titus's victory celebration is his insistence on sacrificing Alarbus despite Tamora's maternal pleas: a case in which the traditional forms of piety that underlie Roman civilization seem to require the barbaric practice of human sacrifice. If Rome's conviction of racial and cultural supremacy—of *deserving* to rule the world—was once a workable notion, it is so no longer. The obsession with the past that pervades *Titus Andronicus* thus seems oddly empty. Even as inherited stories provide the only paradigms for action, they fail to nourish a fertile sense of tradition that might help Rome renew itself.

As traditional distinctions lose their prestige and their plausibility, the social procedures that depend on such distinctions likewise begin to collapse. The play's first scene neatly exemplifies the problem. The brothers Saturninus and Bassianus quarrel first over the possession of the imperial throne and then over the possession of Lavinia, whom both wish to marry. In Shakespeare's England, the first dispute would have been settled according to the principle of "primogeniture," which gave priority in inheritance to the elder brother; the second would have been settled in favor of the younger brother, on the grounds of his preexisting betrothal to Lavinia. In Rome, however, it seems impossible to settle competing claims in an orderly way. In fact, Saturninus does eventually get the throne and Bassianus the woman, but not without a good deal of confusion and some lethal violence. The suggestion is that established methods of allocating property or privilege to one or another person may be quite arbitrary, but that the alternative to such methods is chaos.

In case the point is not sufficiently clear, Shakespeare immediately follows the quarrel between the two Roman brothers with another scene of sibling rivalry, this time between Tamora's sons, once again over sexual access to Lavinia. Unlike their Roman counterparts, these men are seeking not marriage but an adulterous relationship, and their villainous confidant Aaron has little difficulty massaging their illicit ambitions into plans for a rape. Adultery and rape seem the "opposites" of the marriage desired by the Roman men; and certainly the ferocity of the Gothic brothers' attack on Lavinia makes abundantly clear why such behavior is intolerable. At the same time, Shakespeare's juxtaposition of scenes suggests, subversively, the *similarities* between Roman marriage and rape. In neither case is Lavinia's consent at issue: she becomes the property of whoever happens to carry her off by force. Once again the distinction between legitimate and illegitimate behavior seems indispensable and at the same time remarkably indistinct.

The characters apparently best equipped to function in this world of collapsing distinctions are Aaron and Tamora, whose interracial adultery is perceived as particularly scandalous by both Romans and Goths. Their relationship is perhaps the most obvious example of the play's tendency to juxtapose opposites that turn out to have a great deal in common. Both Tamora and Aaron are outsiders who recognize from the outset the artificiality of the precepts by which Rome pretends to govern itself and the world. Neither character has much to gain by endorsing Rome's view of itself, which has relegated them to positions of servitude and powerlessness. In a world in which women are treated as the sexual property of their male relatives, "good" women like Lavinia seem destined for passivity and victimization. One acquires power in such circumstances by refusing to play by the rules. In a few lines, Tamora—manipulative, ruthless, and cunning—transfers herself from the extreme of subjugation, as Titus's captive, to the apex of power as empress of Rome.

Aaron is Tamora's natural counterpart. He is a stage descendant of the "black men" of the medieval morality plays, which conflated traditional depictions of the devil with racist conceptions of "Moors" and "Africans." But at the same time that Shakespeare exploits to the full Aaron's capacity for gleeful villainy, he makes Aaron's point of view comprehensible, even at some points attractive, to the audience. Roman hierarchies would consign Aaron permanently to a subordinate position, for racial rather than sexual reasons; and like Tamora, he sees no reason to accept the validity of that assignment. Why should he collaborate in his own oppression? It is no coincidence that Shakespeare's verse seems at its best in this play when Aaron is delivering a soliloquy. His view of the world is very close to what the play as a whole seems to endorse: that the assumptions upon which ethical behavior and social institutions depend represent fictions rather than facts.

For the dramatic technique of *Titus Andronicus*, like its villains, seems to insist that the "normal" or the "proper" is a mere construct, that apparently vivid distinctions are not as clear-cut as they seem, that moral opposites have a way of turning into one another. We have already seen Shakespeare setting the behavior of Bassianus and Saturninus beside the behavior of Chiron and Demetrius, as well as associating his white empress with his black slave. Such juxtapositions seem to be designed to induce a sort of evaluative vertigo, an effect that becomes most intense, perhaps, in the figure of the unnamed infant who results from Tamora's adultery with Aaron. In the view of most of the play's characters, this child physically embodies, and thus serves as both proof and symbol of, its parents' utter depravity. At the same time, Aaron's unexpectedly fierce solicitude for the child—which contrasts attractively with Titus's casual willingness to slaughter his own son—prevents the audience from taking at face value the rhetoric of disgust and fear discharged upon the little unfortunate from everyone else in the play. This is, after all, a baby. Every time it is brought onstage, the function it seems designed to serve in the play's symbolic economy powerfully conflicts with its intrinsic infant appeal.

In other cases, Shakespeare produces jarringly appropriate incongruities not by juxtaposing characters but by evoking apparently inappropriate dramatic genres.

Ethiopian soldier. From Cesare Vecellio, *De gli habiti antichi et moderni* (1590).

For instance, when Quintus and Martius find Bassianus's body, the audience knows they are being framed for murder, and one might expect a playwright to exploit the pathos of the situation, encouraging the audience to pity and sympathize with the innocent characters. Instead, the scene is played for laughs, as Titus's sons struggle farcically to pull one another out of a hole. Another jarring technique in *Titus Andronicus* is the deliberately awful play on words: "Mark, Marcus, mark" (3.1.143), cries Titus as they behold the ravished and mutilated Lavinia. In such cases, Shakespeare's humor shatters the norms of dramatic and moral suitability, implying the artificiality of what is conventionally considered "normal" or "proper."

If the moral and social problem of *Titus* is that eventually nothing is taboo, the aesthetic problem of the play is that literary convention too comes to seem entirely artificial. Shakespeare's deliberate rule breaking in *Titus Andronicus* risks looking like, or simply being the equivalent of, tasteless incompetence. This is especially true when terrible suffering is at stake. Marcus's long, garishly metaphorical speech at the sight of his niece's bleeding body, for instance, seems grossly beside the point. Is Shakespeare merely being inept here—is he as out of control as Marcus seems to be? Or is he deliberately exploring the limits of his medium by unexpectedly violating its usual rules, in the manner of modern surrealists, absurdists, or postmodernists? The critical debate about *Titus Andronicus* has largely involved quarrels between those who would claim the former and those who would claim the latter.

Even if Shakespeare sometimes seems to share the heartlessness of Aaron and Tamora, he does not represent the Goth and the African as admirable characters. Rebelling against the principles of "civilization" puts them outside any moral community. At the end of the play, Lucius orders Aaron starved to death and Tamora's body thrown over the city walls, as if it were mere garbage. Their treatment indicates his conviction that their behavior has put themselves outside the classification of the human, so that when they are starving, no one has an obligation to relieve them, and when they are dead, no one need respect their remains. The final scene reasserts the difference between human society and what Titus calls "a wilderness of tigers," a difference that the revenge plot has come close to erasing. And despite the abundant evidence that Roman social organization is fundamentally flawed and soon to be toppled, it is not surprising that both Goths and Romans should greet Lucius's restoration of order at the end of the play with profound relief.

Titus Andronicus, then, suggests that the principles of Roman order are patently false and often arbitrarily oppressive; but it also suggests that acknowledging this arbitrariness or rebelling against this falsity and oppression will have disastrous consequences. What produces Roman "virtue" seems to be a delusion; but being undeluded, as Tamora and Aaron are and Titus becomes, is even more terrible. In Shakespeare's later tragedies, the alternative to normality is often a visionary possibility that seems, if only it could be lived out, to improve upon the status quo: the loves of Romeo and Juliet, Antony and Cleopatra, Othello and Desdemona are examples of such "constructive rule breaking." In *Titus Andronicus*, however, traditional taboos, however cruel, brittle, or despotic they seem, are the sole guarantors of order. Once they are shattered, nothing can take their place, and sheer chaos ensues.

The pessimism, even nihilism, of this vision, combined with Shakespeare's almost playful emphasis on what most writers prefer to skirt or play down, is doubtless what has made *Titus* seem merely bad to so many readers since the late seventeenth century. From another point of view, however, *Titus Andronicus* is a daring experiment, one that Shakespeare did not repeat but that nonetheless provides fascinating insight into his development as a dramatist.

KATHARINE EISAMAN MAUS

TEXTUAL NOTE

There are three extant quarto editions of *Titus Andronicus*. The First Quarto (Q1) was printed in 1594 and seems to derive directly from Shakespeare's manuscript. Only one copy of Q1 now survives. Q2, published in 1600, was prepared from a copy of Q1 whose last few pages had been damaged; the printer invented several lines to fill in text missing from the final scene of the play. In most cases, Q2's deviations from Q1 have no authority, but in several instances, it seems to have preserved corrected readings not found in the single copy of Q1 now extant. (Since proofreading in Elizabethan times was done while the text was in the process of being printed instead of beforehand, it is often the case that copies printed late in a press run will rectify errors present in earlier copies.) The most notable of Q2's corrections is the omission of three and a half lines from 1.1. These lines seem inappropriate to their context: they suggest that Alarbus has already been sacrificed, an act portrayed later in the scene. Q3 reprints Q2 with some minor corrections and corruptions.

The First Folio of 1623 (F) was prepared from Q3, apparently a copy annotated by comparison with the playhouse promptbook. It includes one entire scene missing from the quartos, the "fly-killing scene" at the end of Act 3, probably written by Shakespeare for a revival of the play in 1594. It also includes more stage directions than the quarto texts, as well as one complete and one fragmentary line that are probably authentic.

In general, Q1 is the most authoritative text, but the Oxford editors accept eight substantive readings from Q2 and resort to F for the fly-killing scene and some stage directions. The three and a half lines omitted from 1.1 and two other passages from Q1 probably intended for deletion are to be found, indented, after 1.1.35, 1.1.283, and 4.3.91, respectively.

SELECTED BIBLIOGRAPHY

Barker, Francis. "A Wilderness of Tigers: *Titus Andronicus*, Anthropology, and the Occlusion of Violence." *The Culture of Violence: Tragedy and History*. Chicago: University of Chicago Press, 1993. 143–206. Cultural anthropology and the history of criminal prosecution in early modern England illuminate *Titus Andronicus*, particularly the "Clown scene."

Bartels, Emily. "Making More of the Moor: Aaron, Othello, and Renaissance Refashionings of Race." *Shakespeare Quarterly* 41 (1990): 433–54. Aaron in the context of other sixteenth-century English depictions of black Africans.

James, Heather. "Cultural Disintegration in *Titus Andronicus*: Mutilating Titus, Virgil, and Rome." *Violence in Drama*. Ed. James Redmond. New York: Cambridge University Press, 1991. 123–40. Shakespeare's debt to Virgil's *Aeneid*.

Kahn, Coppélia. "The Daughter's Seduction in *Titus Andronicus;* or, Writing Is the Best Revenge." *The Roman Shakespeare: Warriors, Wounds, and Women.* New York: Routledge, 1997. 46–76. Discussion of the play, focusing primarily on Lavinia.

Loomba, Ania. "Wilderness and Civilization in *Titus Andronicus.*" *Shakespeare, Race, and Colonialism.* New York: Oxford University Press, 2002. 75–90. Focuses on the alliance between Aaron and Tamora.

Palmer, D. J. "The Unspeakable in Pursuit of the Uneatable: Language and Action in *Titus Andronicus.*" *Critical Quarterly* 14 (1972): 320–39. The representation of suffering.

Vickers, Brian. "*Titus Andronicus* with George Peele." *Shakespeare, Co-Author: A Historical Study of Five Collaborative Plays.* New York: Oxford University Press, 2002. 148–243. Discusses the likelihood that Shakespeare and George Peele collaborated on *Titus Andronicus.*

Waith, Eugene. "The Metamorphosis of Violence in *Titus Andronicus.*" *Shakespeare Survey* 10 (1957): 39–59. Shakespeare's debt to Ovid's *Metamorphoses.*

FILMS

Titus Andronicus. 1985. Dir. Jane Howell. UK. 120 min. This production, stylized and self-consciously theatrical, is often considered one of the best of the BBC series and a major influence on Taymor's bigger-budget film (1999).

Titus. 1999. Dir. Julie Taymor. USA. 162 min. A visually stunning adaptation of Shakespeare's play, emphasizing its stomach-churning violence. The fine cast includes Anthony Hopkins as Titus and Jessica Lange as Tamora.

Titus Andronicus

THE PERSONS OF THE PLAY

SATURNINUS, eldest son of the late Emperor of Rome; later
    Emperor
BASSIANUS, his brother
TITUS ANDRONICUS, a Roman nobleman, general against the
    Goths
LUCIUS ⎫
QUINTUS ⎬ sons of Titus
MARTIUS ⎪
MUTIUS ⎭
LAVINIA, daughter of Titus
YOUNG LUCIUS, a boy, son of Lucius
MARCUS ANDRONICUS, a tribune of the people, Titus' brother
PUBLIUS, his son
SEMPRONIUS ⎫
CAIUS ⎬ kinsmen of Titus
VALENTINE ⎭
A CAPTAIN
AEMILIUS
TAMORA, Queen of the Goths, later wife of Saturninus
ALARBUS ⎫
DEMETRIUS ⎬ her sons
CHIRON ⎭
AARON, a Moor, her lover
A NURSE
A CLOWN
Senators, tribunes, Romans, Goths, soldiers, and attendants

1.1

*Flourish. Enter the Tribunes and Senators[1] aloft, and
then enter [below]* SATURNINUS *and his followers at one
door and* BASSIANUS *and his followers at the other, with
drum° and colours°*   *drummer / standard-bearer*

SATURNINUS Noble patricians, patrons° of my right,   *supporters*
  Defend the justice of my cause with arms.
  And countrymen, my loving followers,
  Plead my successive title° with your swords.   *right to succeed*
5 I am his first-born son that was the last
  That ware° the imperial diadem of Rome.   *wore*
  Then let my father's honours live in me,
  Nor wrong mine age° with this indignity.   *seniority*
BASSIANUS Romans, friends, followers, favourers of my right,

1.1 Location: Before the Roman Capitol, represented
by the upper stage ("aloft"). The tomb of the Andronicus family, a stage structure or a trapdoor, is accessible
onstage.

1. Respectively the representatives of the common
people (plebeians) and the upper classes (patricians).

10 If ever Bassianus, Caesar's[2] son,

Were gracious° in the eyes of royal Rome,   *Found favor*

Keep° then this passage° to the Capitol,   *Defend / path*

And suffer not dishonour to approach

The imperial seat, to virtue consecrate,°   *consecrated*

15 To justice, continence, and nobility;

But let desert[3] in pure election[4] shine,

And, Romans, fight for freedom in your choice.

Enter MARCUS ANDRONICUS *aloft with the crown*

MARCUS   Princes that strive by factions and by friends

Ambitiously for rule and empery,°   *imperial rule*

20 Know that the people of Rome, for whom we stand

A special party,[5] have by common voice

In election for the Roman empery

Chosen Andronicus, surnamèd *Pius*[6]

For many good and great deserts to Rome.

25 A nobler man, a braver warrior,

Lives not this day within the city walls.

He by the Senate is accited° home   *summoned*

From weary wars against the barbarous Goths,

That with his sons, a terror to our foes,

30 Hath yoked° a nation strong, trained up in arms.   *subdued*

Ten years are spent since first he undertook

This cause of Rome, and chastisèd with arms

Our enemies' pride. Five times he hath returned

Bleeding to Rome, bearing his valiant sons

35 In coffins from the field;[7]

35.1   *and at this day*

To the monument of the Andronici

Done sacrifice of expiation,

And slain the noblest prisoner of the Goths.

And now at last, laden with honour's spoils,

Returns the good Andronicus to Rome,

Renownèd Titus, flourishing in arms.

Let us entreat by honour of his° name   *(the late Emperor's)*

40 Whom worthily you would have now succeeded,[8]

And in the Capitol and Senate's right,[9]

Whom you pretend° to honour and adore,   *claim*

That you withdraw you and abate your strength,

Dismiss your followers, and, as suitors should,

45 Plead your deserts in peace and humbleness.

SATURNINUS   How fair the Tribune speaks to calm my thoughts.

BASSIANUS   Marcus Andronicus, so I do affy°   *trust*

In thy uprightness and integrity,

And so I love and honour thee and thine,

50 Thy noble brother Titus and his sons,

And her to whom my thoughts are humbled all,

---

2. The previous Emperor (Bassianus is Saturninus's younger brother).

3. Merit (as opposed to birth order).

4. Free choice of the citizens.

5. A representative elected for a particular purpose.

6. He has been given the honorary title of "Dutiful."

7. The following indented passage (lines 35.1–35.4),

found in Q1 following a comma after "field" but not included in Q2 or Q3 or F, conflicts with the subsequent action and presumably should have been deleted. (In the second line, Q1 reads "of that" for "of the.")

8. Whose place you want a worthy candidate to fill.

9. To choose a new emperor, traditionally an elected and not an inherited office.

Gracious Lavinia, Rome's rich ornament,
That I will here dismiss my loving friends
And to my fortunes and the people's favour
55 Commit my cause in balance to be weighed.
                        Exeunt [his] soldiers [and followers]
SATURNINUS Friends that have been thus forward in my right,
I thank you all, and here dismiss you all,
And to the love and favour of my country
Commit myself, my person, and the cause.
                        [Exeunt his soldiers and followers]
         [To the Tribunes and Senators]
60 Rome, be as just and gracious unto me
As I am confident° and kind to thee.   *trusting*
Open the gates and let me in.
BASSIANUS Tribunes, and me, a poor competitor.°   *co-petitioner*
        Flourish.° They go up into the Senate House.   *Trumpet fanfare*
        Enter a CAPTAIN
CAPTAIN Romans, make way. The good Andronicus,
65 Patron° of virtue, Rome's best champion,   *Representative; pattern*
Successful in the battles that he fights,
With honour and with fortune is returned
From where he circumscribèd° with his sword   *restrained*
And brought to yoke the enemies of Rome.
        Sound drums and trumpets, and then enter [MARTIUS
        and MUTIUS,] *two of Titus' sons, and then men bearing*
        coffin[s] covered with black, then [LUCIUS *and* QUINTUS,]
        two other sons; then TITUS ANDRONICUS [*in his chariot*],
        and then TAMORA *the Queen of Goths and her sons*
        [ALARBUS,] CHIRON, *and* DEMETRIUS, *with* AARON *the*
        Moor[1] *and others as many as can be. Then set down the*
        coffin[s], and TITUS *speaks*
70 TITUS Hail, Rome, victorious in thy mourning weeds!°   *garments*
Lo, as the bark° that hath discharged his° freight   *ship / its*
Returns with precious lading° to the bay   *cargo*
From whence at first she weighed her anchorage,°   *anchor*
Cometh Andronicus, bound with laurel bows,[2]
75 To re-salute his country with his tears,
Tears of true joy for his return to Rome.
Thou great defender[3] of this Capitol,
Stand gracious to the rites that we intend.
Romans, of five-and-twenty valiant sons,
80 Half of the number that King Priam[4] had,
Behold the poor remains, alive and dead.
These that survive let Rome reward with love;
These that I bring unto their latest° home,   *last*
With burial amongst their ancestors.
85 Here Goths have given me leave[5] to sheathe my sword.
Titus unkind,[6] and careless of thine own,

---

1. "Moor" in classical times referred to an inhabitant of Mauretania, in northwest Africa; the term was later applied to Islamic Africans of Arab descent who conquered Spain in the Middle Ages. In Renaissance England, the word often was used of any black-skinned African.
2. Laurel wreath, symbol of victory.

3. Jupiter Capitolinus, king of the Roman gods, to whose shrine on the Capitol victorious generals brought their spoils.
4. King of Troy during the Trojan War.
5. Allowed me (ironic, since the Goths were defeated in battle).
6. Devoid of natural feeling; undutiful.

Why suffer'st thou thy sons unburied yet
To hover on the dreadful shore of Styx?[7]
Make way to lay them by their brethren.
They open the tomb
90 There greet in silence as the dead are wont,
And sleep in peace, slain in your country's wars.
O sacred receptacle of my joys,
Sweet cell of virtue and nobility,
How many sons hast thou of mine in store
95 That thou wilt never render° to me more!°   return / again
LUCIUS   Give us the proudest prisoner of the Goths,
That we may hew his limbs and on a pile
Ad manes fratrum° sacrifice his flesh   To our brothers' shades
Before this earthy prison of their bones,
100 That so the shadows° be not unappeased,   spirits
Nor we disturbed with prodigies° on earth.   evil happenings
TITUS   I give him you, the noblest that survives,
The eldest son of this distressèd Queen.
TAMORA [*kneeling*]   Stay, Roman brethren! Gracious conqueror,
105 Victorious Titus, rue° the tears I shed—   pity
A mother's tears in passion° for her son—   grief
And if thy sons were ever dear to thee,
O, think my son to be as dear to me!
Sufficeth not that we are brought to Rome
110 To beautify thy triumphs,° and return   triumphal processions
Captive to thee and to thy Roman yoke;
But must my sons be slaughtered in the streets
For valiant doings in their country's cause?
O, if to fight for king and commonweal
115 Were piety in thine,° it is in these.°   (your sons) / (my sons)
Andronicus, stain not thy tomb with blood.
Wilt thou draw near the nature of the gods?
Draw near them then in being merciful.
Sweet mercy is nobility's true badge.
120 Thrice-noble Titus, spare my first-born son.
TITUS   Patient° yourself, madam, and pardon me.   Calm
These are their brethren whom your Goths beheld
Alive and dead, and for their brethren slain
Religiously° they ask a sacrifice.   On religious grounds
125 To this your son is marked, and die he must
T'appease their groaning shadows that are gone.
LUCIUS   Away with him, and make a fire straight,°   immediately
And with our swords upon a pile of wood
Let's hew his limbs till they be clean consumed.
Exeunt Titus' sons with ALARBUS
130 TAMORA [*rising*]   O cruel irreligious piety!
CHIRON   Was never Scythia[8] half so barbarous.
DEMETRIUS   Oppose not Scythia to ambitious Rome.
Alarbus goes to rest, and we survive
To tremble under Titus' threat'ning look.
135 Then, madam, stand resolved; but hope withal

---

7. River surrounding the underworld; the dead could   8. Uncivilized region north of the Black Sea.
not cross it until they had been properly buried.

The selfsame gods that armed the Queen of Troy[9]
With opportunity of sharp revenge
Upon the Thracian tyrant in his tent
May favour Tamora, the Queen of Goths—

140 When Goths were Goths and Tamora was queen—
To quit° her bloody wrongs upon her foes.   *revenge*

> *Enter [*QUINTUS, MARCUS, MUTIUS, *and* LUCIUS,] *the sons
> of Andronicus, again, with bloody swords*

LUCIUS   See, lord and father, how we have performed
Our Roman rites. Alarbus' limbs are lopped
And entrails feed the sacrificing fire,

145 Whose smoke like incense doth perfume the sky.
Remaineth naught but to inter our brethren
And with loud 'larums° welcome them to Rome.   *trumpet calls*

TITUS   Let it be so, and let Andronicus
Make this his latest° farewell to their souls.   *last*

> *Flourish. Then sound trumpets and lay the coffins in
> the tomb*

150 In peace and honour rest you here, my sons;
Rome's readiest champions, repose you here in rest,
Secure from worldly chances and mishaps.
Here lurks no treason, here no envy° swells,   *malice*
Here grow no damnèd drugs,° here are no storms,   *poisons*

155 No noise, but silence and eternal sleep.
In peace and honour rest you here, my sons.

> *Enter* LAVINIA

LAVINIA   In peace and honour live Lord Titus long,
My noble lord and father, live in fame.
Lo, at this tomb my tributary° tears   *tribute-bearing*

160 I render for my brethren's obsequies,°   *funeral rites*
[*Kneeling*] And at thy feet I kneel with tears of joy
Shed on this earth for thy return to Rome.
O, bless me here with thy victorious hand,
Whose fortunes Rome's best citizens applaud.

165 TITUS   Kind Rome, that hast thus lovingly reserved
The cordial° of mine age to glad my heart!   *comfort*
Lavinia, live; outlive thy father's days
And fame's eternal date, for virtue's praise.[1]

> [LAVINIA *rises*]

MARCUS [*aloft*]   Long live Lord Titus, my belovèd brother,

170 Gracious triumpher in the eyes of Rome!
TITUS   Thanks, gentle Tribune, noble brother Marcus.
MARCUS   And welcome, nephews, from successful wars,
You that survive and you that sleep in fame.
Fair lords, your fortunes are alike in all,

175 That in your country's service drew your swords,
But safer triumph is this funeral pomp
That hath aspired to Solon's happiness[2]
And triumphs over chance in honour's bed.
Titus Andronicus, the people of Rome,

---

9. In Ovid's *Metamorphoses* 13, Queen Hecuba, enslaved by the Greeks after the defeat of Troy, avenged her son Polydorus by killing the sons of his murderer, Polymnestor, tyrant of Thrace.

1. And may the praise of your virtue outlive eternity.
2. Solon, a Greek statesman, said, "Call no man happy until he is dead."

180   Whose friend in justice thou hast ever been,
        Send thee by me, their tribune and their trust,
        This palliament³ of white and spotless hue,
        And name thee in election for the empire
        With these our late-deceasèd emperor's sons.
185   Be *candidatus*⁴ then, and put it on,
        And help to set a head on headless Rome.
    TITUS   A better head her glorious body fits
        Than his that shakes for age and feebleness.
        What should I don this robe and trouble you?—
190   Be chosen with proclamations today,
        Tomorrow yield up rule, resign my life,
        And set abroad new business for you all.°   *make you busy once again*
        Rome, I have been thy soldier forty years,
        And led my country's strength successfully,
195   And buried one-and-twenty valiant sons
        Knighted in field, slain manfully in arms
        In right° and service of their noble country.   *the just cause*
        Give me a staff of honour for mine age,
        But not a sceptre to control the world.
200   Upright he held it, lords, that held it last.
    MARCUS   Titus, thou shalt obtain and ask° the empery.   *simply by asking*
    SATURNINUS   Proud and ambitious Tribune, canst thou tell?°   *how do you know*
    TITUS   Patience, Prince Saturninus.
    SATURNINUS   Romans, do me right.
        Patricians, draw your swords, and sheathe them not
205   Till Saturninus be Rome's emperor.
        Andronicus, would thou were shipped to hell
        Rather than rob me of the people's hearts!
    LUCIUS   Proud Saturnine, interrupter of the good
        That noble-minded Titus means to thee.
210   TITUS   Content thee, Prince. I will restore to thee
        The people's hearts, and wean them from themselves.
    BASSIANUS   Andronicus, I do not flatter thee
        But honour thee, and will do till I die.
        My faction if thou strengthen with thy friends
215   I will most thankful be; and thanks to men
        Of noble minds is honourable meed.°   *reward*
    TITUS   People of Rome, and people's tribunes here,
        I ask your voices and your suffrages.°   *votes*
        Will ye bestow them friendly on Andronicus?
220   TRIBUNES   To gratify the good Andronicus
        And gratulate° his safe return to Rome   *salute*
        The people will accept whom he admits.°   *allows into office*
    TITUS   Tribunes, I thank you, and this suit I make:
        That you create° our emperor's eldest son   *elect*
225   Lord Saturnine, whose virtues will, I hope,
        Reflect on Rome as Titan's° rays on earth,   *the sun god*
        And ripen justice in this commonweal.°   *community*
        Then if you will elect by my advice,
        Crown him and say, 'Long live our Emperor!'

---

3. Ceremonial garment worn by aspirants to public   4. Candidate (literally, "one wearing the white toga").
office.

230   MARCUS   With voices and applause of every sort,
        Patricians and plebeians, we create
        Lord Saturninus Rome's great emperor,
        And say, 'Long live our Emperor Saturnine!'
            A long flourish [while MARCUS *and the other Tribunes,*
            with SATURNINUS *and* BASSIANUS], *come down*
            [MARCUS *invests*° SATURNINUS *in the white palliament*   dresses
            and hands him a sceptre]
        SATURNINUS   Titus Andronicus, for thy favours done
235   To us in our election this day
        I give thee thanks in part of thy deserts,⁵
        And will with deeds requite thy gentleness.°   pay back your kindness
        And for an onset, Titus, to advance
        Thy name and honourable family,
240   Lavinia will I make my empress,
        Rome's royal mistress, mistress of my heart,
        And in the sacred Pantheon⁶ her espouse.
        Tell me, Andronicus, doth this motion please thee?
        TITUS   It doth, my worthy lord, and in this match
245   I hold me highly honoured of your grace,
        And here in sight of Rome to Saturnine,
        King and commander of our commonweal,
        The wide world's emperor, do I consecrate
        My sword, my chariot, and my prisoners—
250   Presents well worthy Rome's imperious° lord.   imperial
        Receive them, then, the tribute that I owe,
        Mine honour's ensigns° humbled at thy feet.   symbols
        SATURNINUS   Thanks, noble Titus, father of my life.
        How proud I am of thee and of thy gifts
255   Rome shall record; and when I do forget
        The least of these unspeakable° deserts,   inexpressible
        Romans, forget your fealty° to me.   duty
        TITUS [*to* TAMORA]   Now, madam, are you prisoner to an emperor,
        To him that for your honour and your state°   royal dignity
260   Will use you nobly, and your followers.
        SATURNINUS   A goodly lady, trust me, of the hue°   appearance; color
        That I would choose were I to choose anew.⁷
        Clear up, fair queen, that cloudy countenance.
        Though chance of war hath wrought this change of cheer,°   expression
265   Thou com'st not to be made a scorn in Rome.
        Princely shall be thy usage every way.
        Rest° on my word, and let not discontent   Rely
        Daunt all your hopes. Madam, he comforts you
        Can° make you greater than the Queen of Goths.   Who can
270   Lavinia, you are not displeased with this?
        LAVINIA   Not I, my lord, sith° true nobility   since
        Warrants° these words in princely courtesy.   Justifies
        SATURNINUS   Thanks, sweet Lavinia. Romans, let us go.
        Ransomless here we set our prisoners free.
275   Proclaim our honours, lords, with trump° and drum.   trumpet
            [*Flourish. Exeunt* SATURNINUS, TAMORA,
            DEMETRIUS, CHIRON, *and* AARON *the Moor*]

5. *in . . . deserts:* as part of what you deserve.   7. *A goodly . . . anew:* these two lines may be spoken as
6. Roman temple dedicated to all the gods.   an aside.

BASSIANUS   Lord Titus, by your leave, this maid° is mine.   (*Lavinia*)
TITUS   How, sir, are you in earnest then, my lord?
BASSIANUS   Ay, noble Titus, and resolved withal
      To do myself this reason and this right.
280 MARCUS   *Suum cuique*° is our Roman justice.   *To each his own*
      This prince in justice seizeth but his own.
LUCIUS   And that he will and shall, if Lucius live.
TITUS   Traitors, avaunt!° Where is the Emperor's guard?[8]   *be off*
283.1   TITUS   *Treason, my lord! Lavinia is surprised.*
      SATURNINUS   *Surprised, by whom?*
      BASSIANUS   *By him that justly may*
         Bear his betrothed from all the world away.
MUTIUS   Brothers, help to convey her hence away,
285   And with my sword I'll keep this door safe.
            [*Exeunt* BASSIANUS, MARCUS, QUINTUS, *and*
                        MARTIUS, *with* LAVINIA]
      [*To* TITUS] My lord, you pass not here.
TITUS   What, villain boy,
      Barr'st me my way in Rome?
         [*He attacks* MUTIUS]
MUTIUS   Help, Lucius, help!
         [TITUS] *kills him*
LUCIUS [*to* TITUS]   My lord, you are unjust; and more than so,
      In wrongful quarrel you have slain your son.
290 TITUS   Nor thou nor he are any sons of mine.
      My sons would never so dishonour me.
      Traitor, restore Lavinia to the Emperor.
LUCIUS   Dead, if you will, but not to be his wife
      That is another's lawful promised love.
               [*Exit with Mutius' body*]
         Enter aloft [SATURNINUS] *the Emperor with* TAMORA
         and [CHIRON *and* DEMETRIUS,] *her two sons, and*
         AARON *the Moor*
295 TITUS   Follow, my lord, and I'll soon bring her back.
SATURNINUS   No, Titus, no. The Emperor needs her not,
      Nor° her, nor thee, nor any of thy stock.   *Neither*
      I'll trust by leisure° him that mocks me once,   *I'm in no hurry to trust*
      Thee never, nor thy traitorous haughty sons,
300   Confederates all thus to dishonour me.
      Was none in Rome to make a stale°   *laughingstock*
      But Saturnine? Full well, Andronicus,
      Agree these deeds with that proud brag of thine
      That saidst I begged the empire at thy hands.
305 TITUS   O monstrous, what reproachful words are these?
SATURNINUS   But go thy ways, go give that changing piece°   *fickle wench*
      To him that flourished for her with his sword.[9]
      A valiant son-in-law thou shalt enjoy,
      One fit to bandy° with thy lawless sons,   *brawl*
310   To ruffle° in the commonwealth of Rome.   *swagger*

---

8. The following indented passage (lines 283.1–283.3), found in the quartos and F, is difficult to reconcile with the apparent need for Saturninus and his party to leave the stage at line 275 stage direction before entering "aloft" at line 294 stage direction. The Oxford editors believe that Shakespeare intended it to be deleted after adding the episode of Mutius's killing to his original draft, and that the printers of Q1 included it by accident.
9. To him who brandished his sword to win her.

TITUS   These words are razors to my wounded heart.

SATURNINUS   And therefore, lovely Tamora, Queen of Goths,
    That like the stately Phoebe° 'mongst her nymphs   *Diana (the moon)*
    Dost overshine the gallant'st dames of Rome,
315   If thou be pleased with this my sudden choice,
    Behold, I choose thee, Tamora, for my bride,
    And will create thee Empress of Rome.
    Speak, Queen of Goths, dost thou applaud my choice?
    And here I swear by all the Roman gods,
320   Sith priest and holy water are so near,
    And tapers burn so bright, and everything
    In readiness for Hymenaeus° stand,   *god of marriage*
    I will not re-salute the streets of Rome,
    Or climb° my palace, till from forth this place   *ascend to*
325   I lead espoused my bride along with me.

TAMORA   And here, in sight of heaven, to Rome I swear
    If Saturnine advance the Queen of Goths
    She will a handmaid be to his desires,
    A loving nurse, a mother to his youth.°   *youthfulness*
330 SATURNINUS   Ascend, fair Queen, Pantheon. Lords, accompany
    Your noble emperor and his lovely bride,
    Sent by the heavens for Prince Saturnine,
    Whose wisdom[1] hath her fortune conquerèd.
    There shall we consummate our spousal rites.

                    Exeunt [all but TITUS]

335 TITUS   I am not bid° to wait upon this bride.   *invited*
    Titus, when wert thou wont to walk alone,
    Dishonoured thus and challengèd° of wrongs?   *accused*

         Enter MARCUS *and Titus' sons* [LUCIUS, QUINTUS, *and*
         MARTIUS, *carrying Mutius' body*]

MARCUS   O Titus, see, O see what thou hast done—
    In a bad quarrel slain a virtuous son.
340 TITUS   No, foolish Tribune, no; no son of mine,
    Nor thou, nor these, confederates in the deed
    That hath dishonoured all our family;
    Unworthy brother and unworthy sons!

LUCIUS   But let us give him burial as becomes,°   *as is proper*
345   Give Mutius burial with our brethren.

TITUS   Traitors, away, he rests not in this tomb.
    This monument five hundred years hath stood,
    Which I have sumptuously re-edified.°   *rebuilt*
    Here none but soldiers and Rome's servitors°   *defenders*
350   Repose in fame, none basely slain in brawls.
    Bury him where you can; he comes not here.

MARCUS   My lord, this is impiety in you.
    My nephew Mutius' deeds do plead for him.
    He must be buried with his brethren.
355 QUINTUS *and* MARTIUS   And shall, or him we will accompany.

TITUS   'And shall'? What villain was it spake that word?

QUINTUS   He that would vouch it° in any place but here.   *back it up*

TITUS   What, would you bury him in my despite?°   *in defiance of me*

MARCUS   No, noble Titus, but entreat of thee

---

1. Wise consent to my proposal

360   To pardon Mutius and to bury him.

TITUS   Marcus, even thou hast struck upon my crest,
    And with these boys mine honour thou hast wounded.
    My foes I do repute° you every one,   *consider*
    So trouble me no more, but get you gone.

365 MARTIUS   He is not with° himself, let us withdraw.   *is beside*

QUINTUS   Not I, till Mutius' bones be burièd.

        [MARCUS, LUCIUS, QUINTUS, *and* MARTIUS] *kneel*

MARCUS   Brother, for in that name doth nature plead—

QUINTUS   Father, and in that name doth nature speak—

TITUS   Speak thou no more, if all the rest will speed.[2]

370 MARCUS   Renownèd Titus, more than half my soul—

LUCIUS   Dear father, soul and substance of us all—

MARCUS   Suffer thy brother Marcus to inter
    His noble nephew here in virtue's nest,
    That died in honour and Lavinia's cause.

375   Thou art a Roman; be not barbarous.
    The Greeks upon advice° did bury Ajax,[3]   *deliberation*
    That slew himself; and wise Laertes' son
    Did graciously plead for his funerals.
    Let not young Mutius then, that was thy joy,
    Be barred his entrance here.

380 TITUS   Rise, Marcus, rise.
    The dismall'st day is this that e'er I saw,
    To be dishonoured by my sons in Rome.
    Well, bury him, and bury me the next.
        They put [MUTIUS] *in the tomb*

LUCIUS   There lie thy bones, sweet Mutius, with thy friends',

385   Till we with trophies° do adorn thy tomb.   *memorial tributes*

ALL BUT TITUS [*kneeling*]   No man shed tears for noble Mutius;
    He lives in fame, that died in virtue's cause.
        Exeunt [*all but* MARCUS *and* TITUS]

MARCUS   My lord—to step out of these dreary dumps°—   *melancholy*
    How comes it that the subtle° Queen of Goths   *cunning*

390   Is of a sudden thus advanced in Rome?

TITUS   I know not, Marcus, but I know it is—
    Whether by device° or no, the heavens can tell.   *scheming*
    Is she not then beholden to the man
    That brought her for this high good turn[4] so far?

395 MARCUS   Yes, and will nobly him remunerate.

        Flourish. Enter the Emperor [SATURNINUS], TAMORA,
        and her two sons [CHIRON *and* DEMETRIUS], *with*
        [AARON] *the Moor at one door.*
        Enter at the other door BASSIANUS *and* LAVINIA *with*
        [LUCIUS, QUINTUS, *and* MARTIUS]

SATURNINUS   So, Bassianus, you have played your prize.°   *won your bout*
    God give you joy, sir, of your gallant bride.

BASSIANUS   And you of yours, my lord. I say no more,
    Nor wish no less; and so I take my leave.

---

2. If the rest of you wish to meet with good fortune (that is, escape my anger).

3. In the Trojan War, after the Greek hero Ajax committed suicide, Odysseus ("wise Laertes' son") convinced Agamemnon, leader of the Greeks, to grant him honorable burial.

4. Recompense; "turn" was also slang for the sexual act. "Remunerate" (line 395) continues the sexual innuendo.

400 SATURNINUS   Traitor, if Rome have law or we have power,
          Thou and thy faction shall repent this rape.°   *abduction*
     BASSIANUS   'Rape' call you it, my lord, to seize my own—
          My true betrothèd love, and now my wife?
          But let the laws of Rome determine all;
405   Meanwhile am I possessed of that° is mine.   *what*
     SATURNINUS   'Tis good, sir; you are very short with us.
          But if we live we'll be as sharp with you.
     BASSIANUS   My lord, what I have done, as best I may
          Answer I must, and shall do with my life.
410   Only thus much I give your grace to know:
          By all the duties that I owe to Rome,
          This noble gentleman, Lord Titus here,
          Is in opinion° and in honour wronged,   *reputation*
          That, in the rescue of Lavinia,
415   With his own hand did slay his youngest son
          In zeal to you, and highly moved to wrath
          To be controlled° in that he frankly gave.⁵   *opposed*
          Receive him then to favour, Saturnine,
          That hath expressed himself in all his deeds
420   A father and a friend to thee and Rome.
     TITUS   Prince Bassianus, leave to plead° my deeds.   *stop defending*
          'Tis thou and those that have dishonoured me.
               [*He kneels*]
          Rome and the righteous heavens be my judge
          How I have loved and honoured Saturnine!
425 TAMORA [*to* SATURNINUS]   My worthy lord, if ever Tamora
          Were gracious in those princely eyes of thine,
          Then hear me speak indifferently° for all;   *impartially*
          And at my suit, sweet, pardon what is past.
     SATURNINUS   What, madam—be dishonoured openly
430   And basely put it up° without revenge?   *ignobly submit*
     TAMORA   Not so, my lord. The gods of Rome forfend°   *forbid*
          I should be author to dishonour⁶ you.
          But on mine honour dare I undertake°   *vouch*
          For good lord Titus' innocence in all,
435   Whose fury not dissembled speaks his griefs.
          Then at my suit look graciously on him.
          Lose not so noble a friend on vain suppose,°   *idle conjecture*
          Nor with sour looks afflict his gentle heart.
          [*Aside to* SATURNINUS] My lord, be ruled by me, be won at last,
440   Dissemble all your griefs and discontents.
          You are but newly planted in your throne;
          Lest then the people, and patricians too,
          Upon a just survey° take Titus' part,   *examination*
          And so supplant you for ingratitude,
445   Which Rome reputes to be a heinous sin,
          Yield at entreats;° and then let me alone: *to entreaty*
          I'll find a day to massacre them all,
          And raze their faction and their family,
          The cruel father and his traitorous sons
450   To whom I suèd for my dear son's life,

---

5. Freely bestowed (Lavinia upon Saturninus).   6. I should be responsible for dishonoring.

And make them know what 'tis to let a queen
Kneel in the streets and beg for grace in vain.
[*Aloud*] Come, come, sweet Emperor; come, Andronicus,°   *(Marcus)*
Take up° this good old man, and cheer the heart   *Raise to his feet*
455   That dies in tempest of thy angry frown.
SATURNINUS   Rise, Titus, rise; my empress hath prevailed.
TITUS [*rising*]   I thank your majesty and her, my lord,
These words, these looks, infuse new life in me.
TAMORA   Titus, I am incorporate in° Rome,   *made a part of*
460   A Roman now adopted happily,
And must advise the Emperor for his good.
This day all quarrels die, Andronicus;
And let it be mine honour, good my lord,
That I have reconciled your friends and you.
465   For you, Prince Bassianus, I have passed
My word and promise to the Emperor
That you will be more mild and tractable.
And fear not, lords, and you, Lavinia;
By my advice, all humbled on your knees,
470   You shall ask pardon of his majesty.
     [BASSIANUS, LAVINIA, LUCIUS, QUINTUS, *and* MARTIUS
     kneel]
LUCIUS   We do, and vow to heaven and to his highness
That what we did was mildly as we might,°   *possible*
Tend'ring° our sister's honour and our own.   *Having regard for*
MARCUS [*kneeling*]   That on mine honour here do I protest.°   *solemnly declare*
475   SATURNINUS   Away, and talk not, trouble us no more.
TAMORA   Nay, nay, sweet Emperor, we must all be friends.
The Tribune and his nephews kneel for grace.
I will not be denied; sweetheart, look back.
SATURNINUS   Marcus, for thy sake and thy brother's here,
480   And at my lovely Tamora's entreats,
I do remit° these young men's heinous faults.   *forgive*
Stand up!
     [MARCUS, BASSIANUS, LAVINIA, *and Titus' sons stand*]
     Lavinia, though you left me like a churl,°   *boorishly*
I found a friend, and sure as death I swore
I would not part° a bachelor from the priest.   *depart*
485   Come, if the Emperor's court can feast two brides
You are my guest, Lavinia, and your friends.
This day shall be a love-day,[7] Tamora.
TITUS   Tomorrow an° it please your majesty   *if*
To hunt the panther and the hart with me,
490   With horn and hound we'll give your grace *bonjour*.°   *good day*
SATURNINUS   Be it so, Titus, and gramercy,° too.   *thank you*
        Exeunt. Flourish

2.1

[*Enter* AARON *alone*]
AARON   Now climbeth Tamora Olympus' top,[1]
Safe out of fortune's shot,° and sits aloft,   *range*
Secure of° thunder's crack or lightning flash,   *from*

7. Day for love; day appointed to settle disputes amica-   2.1 Scene continues, but the tomb is no longer needed.
bly.   1. Mountain home of the Greek gods.

Advanced above pale envy's° threat'ning reach.   *malice's*
5 As when the golden sun salutes the morn
And, having gilt the ocean with his beams,
Gallops° the zodiac in his glistering coach   *Gallops through*
And overlooks the highest-peering hills,
So Tamora.
10 Upon her wit° doth earthly honour wait,°   *intelligence / attend*
And virtue stoops and trembles at her frown.
Then, Aaron, arm thy heart and fit thy thoughts
To mount aloft with thy imperial mistress,
And mount her pitch² whom thou in triumph long
15 Hast prisoner held fettered in amorous chains,
And faster bound to Aaron's charming eyes
Than is Prometheus tied to Caucasus.³
Away with slavish weeds° and servile thoughts!   *clothes*
I will be bright, and shine in pearl and gold
20 To wait upon this new-made empress.
To wait, said I?—to wanton° with this queen,   *play amorously*
This goddess, this Semiramis,⁴ this nymph,
This siren⁵ that will charm Rome's Saturnine
And see his shipwreck and his commonweal's.
25 Hollo, what storm is this?
    Enter CHIRON *and* DEMETRIUS, *braving*°   *defying each other*
DEMETRIUS Chiron, thy years wants° wit, thy wits wants edge°   *lack / sharpness*
And manners to intrude where I am graced°   *favored*
And may, for aught thou knowest, affected° be.   *loved*
CHIRON Demetrius, thou dost overween° in all,   *behave presumptuously*
30 And so in this, to bear me down with braves.°   *threats*
'Tis not the difference of a year or two
Makes me less gracious, or thee more fortunate.
I am as able and as fit as thou
To serve, and to deserve my mistress' grace,
35 And that my sword upon thee shall approve,°   *prove*
And plead my passions for Lavinia's love.
AARON [*aside*] Clubs, clubs!⁶ These lovers will not keep the peace.
DEMETRIUS Why, boy, although our mother, unadvised,°   *rashly*
Gave you a dancing-rapier° by your side,   *an ornamental sword*
40 Are you so desperate grown to threat° your friends?   *threaten*
Go to, have your lath⁷ glued within your sheath
Till you know better how to handle it.
CHIRON Meanwhile, sir, with the little skill I have
Full well shalt thou perceive how much I dare.
DEMETRIUS Ay, boy, grow ye so brave?
    They draw
45 AARON   Why, how now, lords?
So near the Emperor's palace dare ye draw
And maintain such a quarrel openly?⁸

---

2. Rise to her height, a hawking term (sexually suggestive).
3. In Greek mythology, Zeus punished Prometheus by chaining him to a rock in the Caucasus Mountains; a vulture fed on his liver daily.
4. In Mesopotamian mythology, the Assyrian Queen who founded and ruled Babylon, and who also had attributes of Ishtar, goddess associated with sexual lust.
5. In Greek mythology, sirens were female creatures that lured sailors to destruction.
6. Here's a brawl (a cry among London apprentices to join or quell a fight).
7. Wooden sword used in theatrical productions.
8. In the Renaissance, it was illegal to draw a sword in the presence of the sovereign or at court.

Full well I wot° the ground of all this grudge.° *know / quarrel*
I would not for a million of gold
50   The cause were known to them it most concerns,
Nor would your noble mother for much more
Be so dishonoured in the court of Rome.
For shame, put up.° *sheathe your swords*
DEMETRIUS   Not I, till I have sheathed
My rapier in his bosom, and withal
55   Thrust those reproachful speeches down his throat
That he hath breathed in my dishonour here.
CHIRON   For that I am prepared and full resolved,
Foul-spoken coward, that thund'rest with thy tongue,
And with thy weapon nothing dar'st perform.
60 AARON   Away, I say.
Now, by the gods that warlike Goths adore,
This petty brabble° will undo us all. *quarrel*
Why, lords, and think you not how dangerous
It is to jet° upon a prince's right? *encroach*
65   What, is Lavinia then become so loose,
Or Bassianus so degenerate,
That for her love such quarrels may be broached° *begun*
Without controlment,° justice, or revenge? *restraint*
Young lords, beware; and should the Empress know
70   This discord's ground,[9] the music would not please.
CHIRON   I care not, I, knew she° and all the world, *if she knew*
I love Lavinia more than all the world.
DEMETRIUS   Youngling, learn thou to make some meaner° *lesser*
     choice.
Lavinia is thine elder brother's hope.
75 AARON   Why, are ye mad? Or know ye not in Rome
How furious and impatient they be,
And cannot brook° competitors in love? *endure*
I tell you, lords, you do but plot your deaths
By this device.
CHIRON   Aaron, a thousand deaths
80   Would I propose° to achieve her whom I love. *face*
AARON   To achieve her how?
DEMETRIUS   Why makes thou it so strange?
She is a woman, therefore may be wooed;
She is a woman, therefore may be won;
She is Lavinia, therefore must be loved.
85   What, man, more water glideth by the mill
Than wots the miller of, and easy it is
Of a cut loaf to steal a shive,° we know. *slice*
Though Bassianus be the Emperor's brother,
Better than he have worn Vulcan's badge.[1]
90 AARON [*aside*]   Ay, and as good as Saturninus may.
DEMETRIUS   Then why should he despair that knows to court it° *carry on a courtship*
With words, fair looks, and liberality?° *generosity*
What, hast not thou full often struck° a doe *struck dead*

---

9. Basis; in music, the bass line.
1. *worn Vulcan's badge*: been cuckolded, as the god Vulcan was by Venus, the goddess of love.

And borne her cleanly° by the keeper's nose? · · · · · · · · · · · *deftly and unnoticed*
95 AARON Why then, it seems some certain snatch[2] or so
Would serve your turns.
CHIRON · · · · · · · · · · · · · · · · Ay, so the turn were served.° · · · · · *(with sexual innuendo)*
DEMETRIUS Aaron, thou hast hit it.
AARON · · · · · · · · · · · · · · · · Would you had hit it[3] too,
Then should not we be tired with this ado.
Why, hark ye, hark ye, and are you such fools
100 To square° for this? Would it offend you then · · · · · · · · · *quarrel*
That both should speed?° · *succeed*
CHIRON Faith, not me.
DEMETRIUS Nor me, so° I were one. · · · · · · · · · · · · · · · *provided that*
AARON For shame, be friends, and join for that you jar.[4]
105 'Tis policy° and stratagem must do · · · · · · · · · · · · · · · *cunning*
That° you affect,° and so must you resolve · · · · · · · · *What / desire*
That what you cannot as you would achieve,
You must perforce accomplish as you may.
Take this of me: Lucrece[5] was not more chaste
110 Than this Lavinia, Bassianus' love.
A speedier course than ling'ring languishment° · · · · · · · *lovesickness*
Must we pursue, and I have found the path.
My lords, a solemn° hunting is in hand; · · · · · · · · · · · *ceremonial*
There will the lovely Roman ladies troop.° · · · · · · · · · *walk together*
115 The forest walks are wide and spacious,
And many unfrequented plots° there are, · · · · · · · · · · · *places*
Fitted by kind° for rape and villainy. · · · · · · · · · · · · · · *nature*
Single° you thither then this dainty doe, · · · · · · · · · · · *Isolate*
And strike her home by force, if not by words,
120 This way or not at all stand you in hope.
Come, come; our Empress, with her sacred wit
To villainy and vengeance consecrate,
Will we acquaint with all what we intend,
And she shall file our engines° with advice · · · · · · · · · *sharpen our wits*
125 That will not suffer you to square yourselves,° · · · · · · · *be at odds*
But to your wishes' height advance you both.
The Emperor's court is like the house of Fame,[6]
The palace full of tongues, of eyes and ears,
The woods are ruthless, dreadful, deaf, and dull.° · · · · · *insensible*
130 There speak and strike, brave boys, and take your turns.
There serve your lust, shadowed from heaven's eye,
And revel in Lavinia's treasury.
CHIRON Thy counsel, lad, smells of no cowardice.
DEMETRIUS *Sit fas aut nefas,*° till I find the stream · · · · · *Be it right or wrong*
135 To cool this heat, a charm to calm these fits,
Per Styga, per manes vehor.[7] · *Exeunt*

2. Bite (with sexual innuendo).
3. Hit the nail on the head; "scored" sexually.
4. And join to get what you fight over.
5. Virtuous Roman matron raped by Tarquin, a member of the Roman royal family; after her suicide, her kin avenged her by overthrowing the King and establishing the Roman Republic. Shakespeare retells the story in

The Rape of Lucrece.
6. Rumor; the House of Fame is described by Ovid in *Metamorphoses* 12 and by Chaucer in *The House of Fame.*
7. I am carried through the underworld, through the spirits (that is, I am in hell). Adapted from Seneca's *Hippolytus.*

2.2

Enter TITUS ANDRONICUS *and his three sons* [QUINTUS,
LUCIUS, *and* MARTIUS], *and* MARCUS, *making a noise*
with hounds and horns

TITUS   The hunt is up, the morn is bright and grey,°   *(used of dawn light)*
The fields are fragrant and the woods are green.
Uncouple[1] here, and let us make a bay°   *deep barking*
And wake the Emperor and his lovely bride,
5   And rouse the Prince, and ring° a hunter's peal,   *sound*
That all the court may echo with the noise.
Sons, let it be your charge, as it is ours,
To attend the Emperor's person carefully.
I have been troubled in my sleep this night,
10   But dawning day new comfort hath inspired.

> *Here a cry of hounds, and wind° horns in a peal; then*   *blow*
> *enter* SATURNINUS, TAMORA, BASSIANUS, LAVINIA,
> CHIRON, DEMETRIUS, *and their attendants*

Many good-morrows to your majesty.
Madam, to you as many, and as good.
I promisèd your grace a hunter's peal.
SATURNINUS   And you have rung it lustily,° my lords,   *heartily*
15   Somewhat too early for new-married ladies.
BASSIANUS   Lavinia, how say you?
LAVINIA   I say no.
I have been broad awake two hours and more.
SATURNINUS   Come on then, horse and chariots let us have,
And to our sport. [*To* TAMORA] Madam, now shall ye see
Our Roman hunting.
20   MARCUS   I have dogs, my lord,
Will rouse the proudest panther in the chase,°   *hunting ground*
And climb the highest promontory top.
TITUS   And I have horse will follow where the game
Makes way, and run like swallows o'er the plain.
25   DEMETRIUS [*aside*]   Chiron, we hunt not, we, with horse nor hound,
But hope to pluck a dainty doe to ground.   *Exeunt*

2.3

Enter AARON *alone* [*with gold*]

AARON   He that had wit would think that I had none,
To bury so much gold under a tree
And never after to inherit° it.   *possess*
Let him that thinks of me so abjectly
5   Know that this gold must coin a stratagem
Which, cunningly effected, will beget
A very excellent piece of villainy.
And so repose, sweet gold, for their unrest
That have their alms out of the Empress' chest.[1]
[*He hides the gold*]
Enter TAMORA *alone to the Moor*
10   TAMORA   My lovely Aaron, wherefore look'st thou sad

2.2 Location: A forest near the Emperor's palace.   1. *That . . . chest*: Who get this gold, which comes from
1. Unleash the hounds.   the Empress's treasury.
2.3 Location: The forest.

When everything doth make a gleeful boast?°   *display*
The birds chant melody on every bush,
The snakes lies rollèd in the cheerful sun,
The green leaves quiver with the cooling wind
15   And make a chequered shadow on the ground.
Under their sweet shade, Aaron, let us sit,
And whilst the babbling echo mocks the hounds,
Replying shrilly to the well-tuned horns,
As if a double hunt were heard at once,
20   Let us sit down and mark their yellowing° noise,   *bellowing*
And after conflict such as was supposed
The wand'ring prince and Dido once enjoyed²
When with a happy storm they were surprised,
And curtained with a counsel-keeping° cave,   *secret-keeping*
25   We may, each wreathèd in the other's arms,
Our pastimes done, possess a golden slumber
Whiles hounds and horns and sweet melodious birds
Be unto us as is a nurse's song
Of lullaby to bring her babe asleep.
30   AARON   Madam, though Venus govern your desires,
Saturn is dominator over mine.³
What signifies my deadly-standing° eye,   *murderously glaring*
My silence, and my cloudy° melancholy,   *gloomy*
My fleece of woolly hair that now uncurls
35   Even as an adder when she doth unroll
To do some fatal execution?
No, madam, these are no venereal⁴ signs.
Vengeance is in my heart, death in my hand,
Blood and revenge are hammering in my head.
40   Hark, Tamora, the empress of my soul,
Which never hopes more heaven than rests in thee,
This is the day of doom for Bassianus.
His Philomel⁵ must lose her tongue today,
Thy sons make pillage of her chastity
45   And wash their hands in Bassianus' blood.
Seest thou this letter? [*Giving a letter*] Take it up, I pray thee,
And give the King this fatal-plotted scroll.
Now question me no more. We are espied.
Here comes a parcel° of our hopeful° booty,   *part / hoped-for*
50   Which dreads not yet their lives' destruction.
          Enter BASSIANUS *and* LAVINIA
TAMORA [*aside to* AARON]   Ah, my sweet Moor, sweeter to me than life!
AARON [*aside to* TAMORA]   No more, great Empress; Bassianus comes.
Be cross with him, and I'll go fetch thy sons
To back thy quarrels, whatsoe'er they be.   *Exit*
55   BASSIANUS   Who have we here? Rome's royal empress
Unfurnished of her well-beseeming troop?⁶

---

2. In Virgil's *Aeneid* 4, the Carthaginian Queen Dido
and Aeneas, later founder of Rome, make love in a cave
where they have taken refuge.
3. Those born when the planet Venus was ascendant
were supposed to be amorous; Saturn produced a
colder, gloomier temperament.
4. Sexual; derived from Venus.

5. In Greek mythology, an Athenian princess raped by
her brother-in-law Tereus; he cut out her tongue, but
she wove a tapestry incriminating him (see Introduction and Ovid, *Metamorphoses* 6).
6. *Unfurnished . . . troop*: Not accompanied by an
appropriate escort.

Or is it Dian,[7] habited° like her   *dressed*
Who hath abandonèd her holy groves
To see the general hunting in this forest?

60 TAMORA Saucy controller° of my private steps, *Insolent observer*
Had I the power that some say Dian had,
Thy temples should be planted presently° *immediately*
With horns, as was Actaeon's, and the hounds
Should drive° upon thy new-transformèd limbs, *rush*
65 Unmannerly intruder as thou art![8]

LAVINIA Under your patience, gentle Empress,
'Tis thought you have a goodly gift in horning,[9]
And to be doubted° that your Moor and you *suspected*
Are singled forth° to try experiments. *drawn apart*
70 Jove shield your husband from his hounds today—
'Tis pity they should take him for a stag.

BASSIANUS Believe me, Queen, your swart° Cimmerian[1] *swarthy*
Doth make your honour of his body's hue,
Spotted, detested, and abominable.
75 Why are you sequestered from all your train,
Dismounted from your snow-white goodly steed,
And wandered hither to an obscure plot,
Accompanied but with a barbarous Moor,
If foul desire had not conducted you?

80 LAVINIA And being intercepted in your sport,
Great reason that my noble lord be rated° *scolded*
For sauciness. [*To* BASSIANUS] I pray you, let us hence,
And let her joy° her raven-coloured love. *enjoy*
This valley fits the purpose passing well.

85 BASSIANUS The King my brother shall have note of this.

LAVINIA Ay, for these slips have made him noted° long. *notorious*
Good King, to be so mightily abused!° *deceived*

TAMORA Why have I patience to endure all this?

     Enter CHIRON *and* DEMETRIUS

DEMETRIUS How now, dear sovereign and our gracious mother,
90 Why doth your highness look so pale and wan?

TAMORA Have I not reason, think you, to look pale?
These two have 'ticed° me hither to this place. *enticed*
A barren detested vale you see it is;
The trees, though summer, yet forlorn and lean,
95 Overcome° with moss and baleful[2] mistletoe. *Overgrown*
Here never shines the sun, here nothing breeds
Unless the nightly owl or fatal° raven, *ominous*
And when they showed me this abhorrèd pit
They told me here at dead time of the night
100 A thousand fiends, a thousand hissing snakes,
Ten thousand swelling toads, as many urchins° *goblins*
Would make such fearful and confusèd cries
As any mortal body hearing it

---

7. Diana, chaste goddess of the hunt (sarcastic).
8. In Greek mythology, the hunter Actaeon came upon Diana naked; she turned him into a stag, and his own hounds tore him apart (see Ovid, *Metamorphoses* 3).
9. The husbands of unfaithful women were supposed to grow staglike horns.
1. The Cimmerians were a legendary people upon whom the sun never shone.
2. Harmful (mistletoe is parasitic).

Should straight fall mad or else die suddenly.
105 No sooner had they told this hellish tale
But straight they told me they would bind me here
Unto the body of a dismal yew[3]
And leave me to this miserable death.
And then they called me foul adulteress,
110 Lascivious Goth,[4] and all the bitterest terms
That ever ear did hear to such effect.
And had you not by wondrous fortune come,
This vengeance on me had they executed.
Revenge it as you love your mother's life,
115 Or be ye not henceforward called my children.
DEMETRIUS   This is a witness that I am thy son.
            [*He*] *stab*[*s* BASSIANUS]
CHIRON   And this for me, struck home to show my strength.
            [*He stabs* BASSIANUS, *who dies.*
            TAMORA *turns to* LAVINIA]
LAVINIA   Ay, come, Semiramis[5]—nay, barbarous Tamora,
For no name fits thy nature but thy own.
120 TAMORA [*to* CHIRON]   Give me the poniard. You shall know, my boys,
Your mother's hand shall right your mother's wrong.
DEMETRIUS   Stay, madam, here is more belongs to her.
First thresh the corn, then after burn the straw.
This minion stood° upon her chastity,   *hussy prided herself*
125 Upon her nuptial vow, her loyalty,
And with that quaint° hope braves° your mightiness.   *fine / defies*
And shall she carry this unto her grave?
CHIRON   An if° she do I would I were an eunuch.   *An if = If*
Drag hence her husband to some secret hole,
130 And make his dead trunk pillow to our lust.
TAMORA   But when ye have the honey ye desire
Let not this wasp outlive, us both to sting.
CHIRON   I warrant you, madam, we will make that sure.
Come, mistress, now perforce we will enjoy
135 That nice-preservèd honesty[6] of yours.
LAVINIA   O Tamora, thou bearest a woman's face—
TAMORA   I will not hear her speak. Away with her!
LAVINIA   Sweet lords, entreat her hear me but a word.
DEMETRIUS [*to* TAMORA]   Listen, fair madam, let it be your glory
140 To see her tears, but be your heart to them
As unrelenting flint to drops of rain.
LAVINIA   When did the tiger's young ones teach the dam?°   *mother*
O, do not learn her wrath! She taught it thee.
The milk thou sucked'st from her did turn to marble,
145 Even at thy teat thou hadst° thy tyranny.   *took in*
Yet every mother breeds not sons alike.
            [*To* CHIRON] Do thou entreat her show a woman's pity.
CHIRON   What, wouldst thou have me prove myself a bastard?
LAVINIA   'Tis true, the raven doth not hatch a lark.
150 Yet have I heard—O, could I find it now!—

---

3. The yew tree is associated with sadness.   5. See note to 2.1.22.
4. Punning on "goat," a proverbially lustful animal. 6. Fastidiously guarded chastity.

The lion, moved with pity, did endure
To have his princely paws° pared all away.   *claws*
Some say that ravens foster forlorn children°   *abandoned baby birds*
The whilst their own birds famish in their nests.
155   O, be to me, though thy hard heart say no,
Nothing so kind, but something pitiful.[7]

TAMORA   I know not what it means. Away with her!

LAVINIA   O, let me teach thee for my father's sake,
That gave thee life when well he might have slain thee.
160   Be not obdurate, open thy deaf ears.

TAMORA   Hadst thou in person ne'er offended me
Even for his sake am I pitiless.
Remember, boys, I poured forth tears in vain
To save your brother from the sacrifice,
165   But fierce Andronicus would not relent.
Therefore away with her, and use her as you will—
The worse to her, the better loved of me.

LAVINIA   O Tamora, be called a gentle queen,
And with thine own hands kill me in this place;
170   For 'tis not life that I have begged so long;
Poor I was slain when Bassianus died.

TAMORA   What begg'st thou then, fond° woman? Let me go.   *foolish*

LAVINIA   'Tis present° death I beg, and one thing more   *immediate*
That womanhood denies° my tongue to tell.   *forbids*
175   O, keep me from their worse-than-killing lust,
And tumble me into some loathsome pit
Where never man's eye may behold my body.
Do this, and be a charitable murderer.

TAMORA   So should I rob my sweet sons of their fee.
180   No, let them satisfy their lust on thee.

DEMETRIUS [*to* LAVINIA]   Away, for thou hast stayed us here
    too long.

LAVINIA   No grace, no womanhood—ah, beastly creature,
The blot and enemy to our general name,°   *the reputation of women*
Confusion° fall—   *Destruction*

CHIRON   Nay then, I'll stop your mouth. [*To* DEMETRIUS]
185   Bring thou her husband.
This is the hole where Aaron bid us hide him.

[DEMETRIUS *and* CHIRON *cast Bassianus' body into the pit*
and cover the mouth of it with branches, then exeunt
dragging LAVINIA]

TAMORA   Farewell, my sons. See that you make her sure.[8]
Ne'er let my heart know merry cheer indeed
Till all the Andronici[9] be made away.°   *murdered*
190   Now will I hence to seek my lovely Moor,
And let my spleenful° sons this trull° deflower.   *Exit*   *lustful / whore*

Enter AARON *with* [QUINTUS *and* MARTIUS,] *two of*
Titus' sons

AARON   Come on, my lords, the better foot before.
Straight will I bring you to the loathsome pit
Where I espied the panther fast asleep.

---

7. Not so kind as the raven, but showing some pity.   9. Family of Andronicus.
8. Make sure of her, keep her from doing harm; kill her.

195 QUINTUS My sight is very dull, whate'er it bodes.[1]
 MARTIUS And mine, I promise you. Were it not for shame,
　　Well could I leave our sport to sleep awhile.
　　　　[*He falls into the pit*]
 QUINTUS What, art thou fallen? What subtle° hole is this, ___treacherous
　　Whose mouth is covered with rude-growing briers
200　　Upon whose leaves are drops of new-shed blood
　　As fresh as morning dew distilled on flowers?
　　A very fatal° place it seems to me. ___ill-omened
　　Speak, brother. Hast thou hurt thee with the fall?
 MARTIUS O brother, with the dismall'st object hurt
205　　That ever eye with sight made heart lament.
 AARON [*aside*] Now will I fetch the King to find them here,
　　That he thereby may have a likely guess
　　How these were they that made away his brother. ___*Exit*
 MARTIUS Why dost not comfort me and help me out
210　　From this unhallowed and bloodstainèd hole?
 QUINTUS I am surprisèd with an uncouth° fear. ___uncanny
　　A chilling sweat o'erruns my trembling joints;
　　My heart suspects more than mine eye can see.
 MARTIUS To prove thou hast a true-divining heart,
215　　Aaron and thou look down into this den,
　　And see a fearful sight of blood and death.
 QUINTUS Aaron is gone, and my compassionate heart
　　Will not permit mine eyes once to behold
　　The thing whereat it trembles by surmise.° ___merely by imagining it
220　　O, tell me who it is, for ne'er till now
　　Was I a child to fear I know not what.
 MARTIUS Lord Bassianus lies berayed° in blood ___defiled
　　All on a heap, like to a slaughtered lamb,
　　In this detested, dark, blood-drinking pit.
225 QUINTUS If it be dark how dost thou know 'tis he?
 MARTIUS Upon his bloody finger he doth wear
　　A precious ring[2] that lightens all this hole,
　　Which like a taper° in some monument ___candle
　　Doth shine upon the dead man's earthy° cheeks ___clay-colored
230　　And shows the ragged entrails° of this pit. ___rough interior
　　So pale did shine the moon on Pyramus[3]
　　When he by night lay bathed in maiden° blood. ___innocent
　　O brother, help me with thy fainting hand—
　　If fear hath made thee faint, as me it hath—
235　　Out of this fell° devouring receptacle, ___dreadful
　　As hateful as Cocytus'° misty mouth. ___a river of hell
 QUINTUS Reach me thy hand, that I may help thee out,
　　Or, wanting° strength to do thee so much good, ___lacking
　　I may be plucked into the swallowing womb
240　　Of this deep pit, poor Bassianus' grave.
　　I have no strength to pluck thee to the brink,
 MARTIUS Nor I no strength to climb without thy help.
 QUINTUS Thy hand once more, I will not loose again
　　Till thou art here aloft or I below.

1. Sleepiness was a bad omen.
2. Perhaps a carbuncle, thought to emit light.
3. In Ovid's version of a classical legend (*Metamor-*

phoses 4), Pyramus thinks his beloved Thisbe dead and
kills himself; this is the subject of the mechanicals' play
in *A Midsummer Night's Dream.*

245   Thou canst not come to me; I come to thee.
               [He] fall[s into the pit]
               Enter [SATURNINUS] *the Emperor* [*with attendants*],
               and AARON *the Moor*

SATURNINUS   Along with me! I'll see what hole is here,
    And what he is that now is leapt into it.
               [He speaks into the pit]
    Say, who art thou that lately didst descend
    Into this gaping hollow of the earth?

250 MARTIUS   The unhappy sons of old Andronicus,
    Brought hither in a most unlucky hour
    To find thy brother Bassianus dead.

SATURNINUS   My brother dead! I know thou dost but jest.
    He and his lady both are at the lodge
255   Upon the north side of this pleasant chase.°   *hunting ground*
    'Tis not an hour since I left them there.

MARTIUS   We know not where you left them all alive,
    But, out° alas, here have we found him dead!   *(emphatic)*
               Enter TAMORA, TITUS ANDRONICUS, *and* LUCIUS

TAMORA   Where is my lord the King?

260 SATURNINUS   Here, Tamora, though gripped with killing grief.

TAMORA   Where is thy brother Bassianus?

SATURNINUS   Now to the bottom dost thou search° my wound.   *probe*
    Poor Bassianus here lies murderèd.

TAMORA   Then all too late I bring this fatal writ,°   *document*
265   The complot° of this timeless° tragedy,   *plot / untimely*
    And wonder greatly that man's face can fold
    In pleasing smiles such murderous tyranny.
               She giveth SATURNINE *a letter*

SATURNINUS [*reads*]   'An if we miss to meet him handsomely,°   *conveniently*
    Sweet huntsman—Bassianus 'tis we mean—
270   Do thou so much as dig the grave for him.
    Thou know'st our meaning. Look for thy reward
    Among the nettles at the elder tree
    Which overshades the mouth of that same pit
    Where we decreed to bury Bassianus.
275   Do this, and purchase us thy lasting friends.'
    O Tamora, was ever heard the like!
    This is the pit, and this the elder tree.
    Look, sirs, if you can find the huntsman out
    That should° have murdered Bassianus here.   *was to*

280 AARON   My gracious lord, here is the bag of gold.

SATURNINUS [*to* TITUS]   Two of thy whelps,° fell curs of bloody   *puppies; literally, sons*
    kind,°   *nature; breed*
    Have here bereft my brother of his life.
    Sirs, drag them from the pit unto the prison.
    There let them bide until we have devised
285   Some never-heard-of torturing pain for them.

TAMORA   What, are they in this pit? O wondrous thing!
    How easily murder is discoverèd!°   *revealed*
               [Attendants drag QUINTUS, MARTIUS, *and Bassianus'*
               body from the pit]

TITUS [*kneeling*]   High Emperor, upon my feeble knee
    I beg this boon with tears not lightly shed:
290   That this fell fault of my accursèd sons—

Accursèd if the fault be proved in them—
SATURNINUS   If it be proved? You see it is apparent.°   obvious
Who found this letter? Tamora, was it you?
TAMORA   Andronicus himself did take it up.
295   TITUS   I did, my lord, yet let me be their bail,
For by my father's reverend tomb I vow
They shall be ready at your highness' will
To answer their suspicion⁴ with their lives.
SATURNINUS   Thou shalt not bail them. See thou follow me.
300   Some bring the murdered body, some the murderers.
Let them not speak a word—the guilt is plain;
For by my soul, were there worse end than death
That end upon them should be executed.   [Exit]
TAMORA   Andronicus, I will entreat the King.
305   Fear not° thy sons, they shall do well enough.   Fear not for
TITUS [rising]   Come, Lucius, come, stay not to talk with
them.°   Exeunt   (Quintus and Marcus)

2.4

*Enter the Empress' sons, [CHIRON and DEMETRIUS,] with
LAVINIA, her hands cut off and her tongue cut out, and
ravished*

DEMETRIUS   So, now go tell, an if thy tongue can speak,
Who 'twas that cut thy tongue and ravished thee.
CHIRON   Write down thy mind, bewray° thy meaning so,   reveal
An if thy stumps will let thee play the scribe.
5   DEMETRIUS   See how with signs and tokens she can scrawl.
CHIRON [to LAVINIA]   Go home, call for sweet° water, wash thy   perfumed
hands.
DEMETRIUS   She hath no tongue to call nor hands to wash,
And so let's leave her to her silent walks.
CHIRON   An 'twere my cause¹ I should go hang myself.
10   DEMETRIUS   If thou hadst hands to help thee knit° the cord.   knot
Exeunt [CHIRON and DEMETRIUS]
Wind° horns. Enter MARCUS from hunting to LAVINIA   Blow
MARCUS   Who is this—my niece that flies away so fast?
Cousin,° a word. Where is your husband?   Kinswoman
If I do dream, would all my wealth would wake me.²
If I do wake, some planet strike me down
15   That I may slumber an eternal sleep.
Speak, gentle niece, what stern ungentle hands
Hath lopped and hewed and made thy body bare
Of her two branches, those sweet ornaments
Whose circling shadows kings have sought to sleep in,
20   And might not gain so great a happiness
As half thy love. Why dost not speak to me?
Alas, a crimson river of warm blood,
Like to a bubbling fountain stirred with wind,
Doth rise and fall between thy rosèd lips,
25   Coming and going with thy honey breath.
But sure some Tereus³ hath deflowered thee

---

4. The suspicion they are under.   2. *would all . . . me*: I would give all I had to wake up.
2.4 Location: Scene continues.   3. See note to 2.3.43.
1. If I were in her position.

And, lest thou shouldst detect° him, cut thy tongue.   *expose*
Ah, now thou turn'st away thy face for shame,
And notwithstanding all this loss of blood,
30   As from a conduit with three issuing spouts,
Yet do thy cheeks look red as Titan's face°   *(the sun)*
Blushing to be encountered with a cloud.
Shall I speak for thee? Shall I say 'tis so?
O that I knew thy heart,° and knew the beast,   *what is in thy heart*
35   That I might rail at him to ease my mind!
Sorrow concealèd, like an oven stopped,°   *stopped up*
Doth burn the heart to cinders where it is.
Fair Philomel, why she but lost her tongue
And in a tedious sampler° sewed her mind.   *laborious tapestry*
40   But, lovely niece, that mean° is cut from thee.   *method*
A craftier Tereus, cousin, hast thou met,
And he hath cut those pretty fingers off
That could have better sewed than Philomel.
O, had the monster seen those lily hands
45   Tremble like aspen leaves upon a lute
And make the silken strings delight to kiss them,
He would not then have touched them for his life.
Or had he heard the heavenly harmony
Which that sweet tongue hath made,
50   He would have dropped his knife and fell asleep,
As Cerberus at the Thracian poet's feet.[4]
Come, let us go and make thy father blind,
For such a sight will blind a father's eye.
One hour's storm will drown the fragrant meads:°   *meadows*
55   What will whole months of tears thy father's eyes?
Do not draw back, for we will mourn with thee.
O, could our mourning ease thy misery!   *Exeunt*

3.1

*Enter the Judges, [Tribunes,][1] and Senators with Titus'
two sons, [MARTIUS and QUINTUS,] bound, passing [over]
the stage to the place of execution, and TITUS going
before, pleading*

TITUS   Hear me, grave fathers; noble Tribunes, stay.
For pity of mine age, whose youth was spent
In dangerous wars whilst you securely slept;
For all my blood in Rome's great quarrel shed;
5   For all the frosty nights that I have watched,
And for these bitter tears which now you see
Filling the agèd wrinkles in my cheeks,
Be pitiful to my condemnèd sons,
Whose souls is not corrupted as 'tis thought.
10   For two-and-twenty sons I never wept,
Because they died in honour's lofty bed.

   ANDRONICUS *lieth down, and the Judges pass by him*

For these two, Tribunes, in the dust I write

---

4. The Thracian poet Orpheus, attempting to rescue
his dead wife, Eurydice, used his music to lull to sleep
Cerberus, the watchdog of the underworld.

3.1 Location: A Roman street.
1. Not including Marcus, who enters at line 58.

My heart's deep languor° and my soul's sad tears.   *grief*

Let my tears stanch° the earth's dry appetite;   *satisfy*

15 My sons' sweet blood will make it shame° and blush.   *feel shame*

Exeunt [*all but* TITUS]

O earth, I will befriend thee more with rain

That shall distil from these two ancient ruins°   *(his eyes)*

Than youthful April shall with all his showers.

In summer's drought I'll drop upon thee still.

20 In winter with warm tears I'll melt the snow

And keep eternal springtime on thy face,

So° thou refuse to drink my dear sons' blood.   *Provided that*

Enter LUCIUS *with his weapon drawn*

O reverend Tribunes, O gentle, agèd men,

Unbind my sons, reverse the doom of death,

25 And let me say, that never wept before,

My tears are now prevailing° orators!   *persuasive*

LUCIUS   O noble father, you lament in vain.

The Tribunes hear you not. No man is by,

And you recount your sorrows to a stone.

30 TITUS   Ah Lucius, for thy brothers let me plead.

Grave Tribunes, once more I entreat of you—

LUCIUS   My gracious lord, no tribune hears you speak.

TITUS   Why, 'tis no matter, man. If they did hear,

They would not mark° me; if they did mark,   *attend to*

35 They would not pity me; yet plead I must.

Therefore I tell my sorrows to the stones,

Who, though they cannot answer my distress,

Yet in some sort they are better than the Tribunes

For that they will not intercept° my tale.   *interrupt*

40 When I do weep they humbly at my feet

Receive my tears and seem to weep with me,

And were they but attirèd in grave weeds°   *sober garments*

Rome could afford° no tribunes like to these.   *provide*

A stone is soft as wax, tribunes more hard than stones.

45 A stone is silent and offendeth not,

And tribunes with their tongues doom men to death.

But wherefore stand'st thou with thy weapon drawn?

LUCIUS   To rescue my two brothers from their death,

For which attempt the Judges have pronounced

50 My everlasting doom of banishment.

TITUS [*rising*]   O happy man, they have befriended thee!

Why, foolish Lucius, dost thou not perceive

That Rome is but a wilderness of tigers?

Tigers must prey, and Rome affords no prey

55 But me and mine. How happy art thou then

From these devourers to be banishèd!

But who comes with our brother Marcus here?

Enter MARCUS *with* LAVINIA

MARCUS   Titus, prepare thy agèd eyes to weep,

Or if not so, thy noble heart to break.

60 I bring consuming sorrow to thine age.

TITUS   Will it consume me? Let me see it then.

MARCUS   This was thy daughter.

TITUS   Why, Marcus, so she is.

LUCIUS [*falling on his knees*]   Ay me, this object° kills me.   *spectacle*

65	TITUS	Faint-hearted boy, arise and look upon her.	
		[LUCIUS *rises*]	
		Speak, Lavinia, what accursèd hand	
		Hath made thee handless in thy father's sight?	
		What fool hath added water to the sea,	
		Or brought a faggot° to bright-burning Troy?²	*piece of firewood*
70		My grief was at the height before thou cam'st,	
		And now like Nilus it disdaineth bounds.³	
		Give me a sword, I'll chop off my hands too,	
		For they have fought for Rome, and all in vain;	
		And they have nursed this woe in feeding life;⁴	
75		In bootless° prayer have they been held up,	*useless*
		And they have served me to effectless° use.	*fruitless*
		Now all the service I require of them	
		Is that the one will help to cut the other.	
		'Tis well, Lavinia, that thou hast no hands,	
80		For hands to do Rome service is but vain.	
	LUCIUS	Speak, gentle sister, who hath martyred° thee.	*mutilated*
	MARCUS	O, that delightful engine° of her thoughts,	*instrument*
		That blabbed° them with such pleasing eloquence,	*uttered*
		Is torn from forth that pretty hollow cage	
85		Where, like a sweet melodious bird, it sung	
		Sweet varied notes, enchanting every ear.	
	LUCIUS	O, say thou for her, who hath done this deed?	
	MARCUS	O, thus I found her, straying in the park,	
		Seeking to hide herself, as doth the deer	
90		That hath received some unrecuring° wound.	*incurable*
	TITUS	It was my dear, and he that wounded her	
		Hath hurt me more than had he killed me dead;	
		For now I stand as one upon a rock	
		Environed° with a wilderness of sea,	*Surrounded*
95		Who marks the waxing tide grow wave by wave,	
		Expecting° ever when some envious° surge	*Awaiting / malignant*
		Will in his° brinish bowels swallow him.	*its*
		This way to death my wretched sons are gone.	
		Here stands my other son, a banished man,	
100		And here my brother, weeping at my woes.	
		But that which gives my soul the greatest spurn°	*contemptuous blow*
		Is dear Lavinia, dearer than my soul.	
		Had I but seen thy picture in this plight	
		It would have madded me.° What shall I do	*made me insane*
105		Now I behold thy lively° body so?	*living*
		Thou hast no hands to wipe away thy tears,	
		Nor tongue to tell me who hath martyred thee.	
		Thy husband he is dead, and for his death	
		Thy brothers are condemned and dead by this.°	*this time*
110		Look, Marcus, ah, son Lucius, look on her!	
		When I did name her brothers, then fresh tears	
		Stood on her cheeks, as doth the honey-dew	
		Upon a gathered lily almost witherèd.	

---

2. Troy was torched by the Greeks after their victory.
3. Before it was dammed, the river Nile flooded annually.
4. And by defending Rome, they have induced this misery.

MARCUS   Perchance she weeps because they killed her husband;
115   Perchance because she knows them innocent.
TITUS   If they did kill thy husband, then be joyful,
         Because the law hath ta'en revenge on them.
         No, no, they would not do so foul a deed;
         Witness the sorrow that their sister makes.
120   Gentle Lavinia, let me kiss thy lips;
         Or make some sign how I may do thee ease.
         Shall thy good uncle, and thy brother Lucius,
         And thou, and I, sit round about some fountain,
         Looking all downwards to behold our cheeks
125   How they are stained, like meadows yet not dry
         With miry slime left on them by a flood?
         And in the fountain shall we gaze so long
         Till the fresh taste be taken from that clearness,
         And made a brine pit with our bitter tears?
130   Or shall we cut away our hands like thine?
         Or shall we bite our tongues, and in dumb shows
         Pass the remainder of our hateful days?
         What shall we do? Let us that have our tongues
         Plot some device° of further misery,   contrivance
135   To make us wondered at in time to come.
LUCIUS   Sweet father, cease your tears, for at your grief
         See how my wretched sister sobs and weeps.
MARCUS   Patience, dear niece. Good Titus, dry thine eyes.
TITUS   Ah, Marcus, Marcus, brother, well I wot°   know
140   Thy napkin° cannot drink a tear of mine,   handkerchief
         For thou, poor man, hast drowned it with thine own.
LUCIUS   Ah, my Lavinia, I will wipe thy cheeks.
TITUS   Mark, Marcus, mark. I understand her signs.
         Had she a tongue to speak, now would she say
145   That to her brother which I said to thee.
         His napkin with his true tears all bewet
         Can do no service on her sorrowful cheeks.
         O, what a sympathy° of woe is this—   consensus
         As far from help as limbo⁵ is from bliss.
         Enter AARON *the Moor, alone*
150 AARON   Titus Andronicus, my lord the Emperor
         Sends thee this word: that, if thou love thy sons,
         Let Marcus, Lucius or thyself, old Titus,
         Or any one of you, chop off your hand
         And send it to the King. He for the same
155   Will send thee hither both thy sons alive,
         And that shall be the ransom for their fault.
TITUS   O gracious Emperor! O gentle Aaron,
         Did ever raven sing so like a lark
         That gives sweet tidings of the sun's uprise?
160   With all my heart I'll send the Emperor my hand.
         Good Aaron, wilt thou help to chop it off?
LUCIUS   Stay, father, for that noble hand of thine,
         That hath thrown down so many enemies,

---

5. Region in hell dedicated to those denied entrance to heaven ("bliss") through no fault of their own: for instance, unbaptized infants, or virtuous people who lived before the advent of Christianity.

Shall not be sent. My hand will serve the turn.
165 My youth can better spare my blood than you,
And therefore mine shall save my brothers' lives.
MARCUS   Which of your hands hath not defended Rome
And reared aloft the bloody battleaxe,
Writing destruction on the enemy's castle?
170 O, none of both but are of high desert.
My hand hath been but idle; let it serve
To ransom my two nephews from their death,
Then have I kept it to a worthy end.
AARON   Nay, come, agree whose hand shall go along,
175 For fear they die before their pardon come.
MARCUS   My hand shall go.
LUCIUS   By heaven it shall not go.
TITUS   Sirs, strive no more. Such withered herbs as these
Are meet° for plucking up, and therefore mine.   *proper*
LUCIUS   Sweet father, if I shall be thought thy son,
180 Let me redeem my brothers both from death.
MARCUS   And for our father's sake and mother's care,
Now let me show a brother's love to thee.
TITUS   Agree between you. I will spare my hand.
LUCIUS   Then I'll go fetch an axe.
MARCUS   But I will use the axe.
                    Exeunt [LUCIUS *and* MARCUS]
185 TITUS   Come hither, Aaron. I'll deceive them both.
Lend me thy hand, and I will give thee mine.
AARON [*aside*]   If that be called deceit, I will be honest
And never whilst I live deceive men so.
But I'll deceive you in another sort,°   *way*
190 And that you'll say ere half an hour pass.
                    He cuts off Titus' hand.
                    Enter LUCIUS *and* MARCUS *again*
TITUS   Now stay your strife. What shall be is dispatched.
Good Aaron, give his majesty my hand.
Tell him it was a hand that warded° him   *defended*
From thousand dangers; bid him bury it.
195 More hath it merited; that° let it have.   *(burial)*
As for my sons, say I account of them
As jewels purchased at an easy price,
And yet dear too, because I bought mine own.
AARON   I go, Andronicus; and for thy hand
200 Look by and by to have thy sons with thee.
[*Aside*] Their heads, I mean. O, how this villainy
Doth fat° me with the very thoughts of it!   *feast*
Let fools do good, and fair men call for grace:
Aaron will have his soul black like his face.   *Exit*
205 TITUS   O, here I lift this one hand up to heaven
And bow this feeble ruin to the earth.
        [*He kneels*]
If any power pities wretched tears,
To that I call. [*To* LAVINIA, *who kneels*] What, wouldst thou
        kneel with me?
Do then, dear heart; for heaven shall hear our prayers,
210 Or with our sighs we'll breathe the welkin dim°   *make the heavens misty*
And stain the sun with fog, as sometime° clouds   *sometimes do*

When they do hug him in their melting° bosoms.   (with rain)

MARCUS   O brother, speak with possibility,°   what is possible
   And do not break into these deep extremes.

215 TITUS   Is not my sorrows deep, having no bottom?
   Then be my passions° bottomless with them.   expression of suffering

MARCUS   But yet let reason govern thy lament.

TITUS   If there were reason for these miseries,
   Then into limits could I bind my woes.

220 When heaven doth weep, doth not the earth o'erflow?
   If the winds rage, doth not the sea wax mad,
   Threat'ning the welkin with his big-swoll'n face?
   And wilt thou have a reason for this coil?°   turmoil
   I am the sea. Hark how her sighs doth blow.

225 She is the weeping welkin, I the earth.
   Then must my sea be movèd with° her sighs,   by
   Then must my earth with her continual tears
   Become a deluge overflowed and drowned,
   Forwhy° my bowels⁶ cannot hide her woes,   Because

230 But like a drunkard must I vomit them.
   Then give me leave, for losers will have leave
   To ease their stomachs⁷ with their bitter tongues.

     Enter a MESSENGER *with two heads and a hand*

MESSENGER   Worthy Andronicus, ill art thou repaid
   For that good hand thou sent'st the Emperor.

235 Here are the heads of thy two noble sons,
   And here's thy hand in scorn to thee sent back—
   Thy grief their sports, thy resolution mocked,
   That° woe is me to think upon thy woes   So that
   More than remembrance of my father's death.

     [He sets down the heads and hand]   *Exit*

240 MARCUS   Now let hot Etna° cool in Sicily,   volcano in Sicily
   And be my heart an ever-burning hell.
   These miseries are more than may be borne.
   To weep with them that weep doth ease some deal,°   somewhat
   But sorrow flouted° at is double death.   mocked

245 LUCIUS   Ah, that this sight should make so deep a wound
   And yet detested life not shrink thereat—
   That ever death should let life bear his name°   be called life
   Where life hath no more interest but to breathe!⁸

     [LAVINIA kisses TITUS]

MARCUS   Alas, poor heart, that kiss is comfortless

250 As frozen water to a starvèd° snake.   numb with cold

TITUS   When will this fearful slumber° have an end?   nightmare

MARCUS   Now farewell, flatt'ry;° die, Andronicus.   pleasing delusion
   Thou dost not slumber. See thy two sons' heads,
   Thy warlike hand, thy mangled daughter here,

255 Thy other banished son with this dear sight
   Struck pale and bloodless, and thy brother, I,
   Even like a stony image, cold and numb.
   Ah, now no more will I control° thy griefs.   try to restrain
   Rend off thy silver hair, thy other hand

---

6. The bowels were thought to be the seat of compassion.

7. Resentments (with play on "vomit").

8. Where nothing is left of life but breathing.

260   Gnawing with thy teeth, and be this dismal sight
     The closing up° of our most wretched eyes.   *(in death)*
     Now is a time to storm. Why art thou still?
     TITUS   Ha, ha, ha!
     MARCUS   Why dost thou laugh? It fits not with this hour.
265   TITUS   Why, I have not another tear to shed.
     Besides, this sorrow is an enemy,
     And would usurp upon my wat'ry eyes
     And make them blind with tributary⁹ tears.
     Then which way shall I find Revenge's cave?—
270   For these two heads do seem to speak to me
     And threat me I shall never come to bliss
     Till all these mischiefs° be returned° again   *calamities / turned back*
     Even in their throats that hath committed them.
     Come, let me see what task I have to do.
           [He and LAVINIA *rise]*
275   You heavy° people, circle me about,   *sad*
     That I may turn me to each one of you
     And swear unto my soul to right your wrongs.
        *[*MARCUS, LUCIUS, *and* LAVINIA *circle* TITUS. *He pledges them]*
     The vow is made. Come, brother, take a head,
     And in this hand the other will I bear.
280   And Lavinia, thou shalt be employed.
     Bear thou my hand, sweet wench, between thine arms.
     As for thee, boy, go get thee from my sight.
     Thou art an exile and thou must not stay.
     Hie° to the Goths, and raise an army there,   *Hurry*
285   And if ye love me, as I think you do,
     Let's kiss and part, for we have much to do.
         [They kiss.] Exeunt [all but LUCIUS*]*
     LUCIUS   Farewell, Andronicus, my noble father,
     The woefull'st man that ever lived in Rome.
     Farewell, proud Rome, till Lucius come again;
290   He loves his pledges¹ dearer than his life.
     Farewell, Lavinia, my noble sister:
     O, would thou wert as thou tofore° hast been!   *formerly*
     But now nor° Lucius nor Lavinia lives   *neither*
     But in oblivion and hateful griefs.
295   If Lucius live he will requite your wrongs
     And make proud Saturnine and his empress
     Beg at the gates like Tarquin and his queen.²
     Now will I to the Goths and raise a power,°   *an army*
     To be revenged on Rome and Saturnine.   *Exit*

3.2

     A banquet.° Enter ANDRONICUS, MARCUS, LAVINIA, *and*   *light meal*
     the boy [YOUNG LUCIUS]
     TITUS   So, so, now sit, and look you eat no more
     Than will preserve just so much strength in us
     As will revenge these bitter woes of ours.
           [They sit]

---

9. Paying tribute (to sorrow, the enemy).
1. Vows; hostages (family members left behind in Rome).

2. Tarquin and his family were banished from Rome after the rape of Lucrece; see note to 2.1.109.
3.2 Location: In Titus's house.

Marcus, unknit° that sorrow-wreathen knot.   *unfold (your arms)*
5   Thy niece and I, poor creatures, want° our hands,   *lack*
And cannot passionate° our tenfold grief   *feelingly express*
With folded arms. This poor right hand of mine
Is left to tyrannize° upon my breast,   *(by beating)*
Who,° when my heart, all mad with misery,   *Which*
10   Beats in this hollow prison of my flesh,
Then thus I thump it down.
        [He beats his breast]
    [*To* LAVINIA] Thou map° of woe, that thus dost talk in signs,   *image*
When thy poor heart beats with outrageous beating
Thou canst not strike it thus to make it still!
15   Wound it with sighing,[1] girl; kill it with groans,
Or get some little knife between thy teeth
And just against° thy heart make thou a hole,   *next to*
That all the tears that thy poor eyes let fall
May run into that sink° and, soaking in,   *receptacle*
20   Drown the lamenting fool[2] in sea-salt tears.
    MARCUS   Fie, brother, fie! Teach her not thus to lay
Such violent hands upon her tender life.
    TITUS   How now! Has sorrow made thee dote° already?   *insane*
Why, Marcus, no man should be mad but I.
25   What violent hands can she lay on her life?
Ah, wherefore dost thou urge the name of hands
To bid Aeneas tell the tale twice o'er
How Troy was burnt and he made miserable?[3]
O, handle not the theme, to talk of hands,
30   Lest we remember still that we have none.
Fie, fie, how franticly I square° my talk,   *regulate*
As if we should forget we had no hands
If Marcus did not name the word of hands!
Come, let's fall to; and, gentle girl, eat this.
35   Here is no drink! Hark, Marcus, what she says.
I can interpret all her martyred signs.
She says she drinks no other drink but tears,
Brewed with her sorrow, mashed[4] upon her cheeks.
Speechless complainer, I will learn thy thought.
40   In thy dumb action° will I be as perfect°   *gesture / expert*
As begging hermits in their holy prayers.
Thou shalt not sigh, nor hold thy stumps to heaven,
Nor wink, nor nod, nor kneel, nor make a sign,
But I of these will wrest an alphabet,
45   And by still° practice learn to know thy meaning.   *continual*
    YOUNG LUCIUS   Good grandsire, leave these bitter deep laments.
Make my aunt merry with some pleasing tale.
    MARCUS   Alas, the tender boy in passion° moved   *sorrow*
Doth weep to see his grandsire's heaviness.
50   TITUS   Peace, tender sapling, thou art made of tears,°   *(i.e., still soft)*
And tears will quickly melt thy life away.
        MARCUS *strikes the dish with a knife*

---

1. Sighs were thought to draw blood from the heart.
2. Often a term of endearment.
3. In Virgil's *Aeneid* 2, Aeneas tells Dido the story of

Troy's fall.
4. Mixed with water, like beer for brewing.

What dost thou strike at, Marcus, with thy knife?
MARCUS   At that that I have killed, my lord—a fly.
TITUS   Out on thee, murderer! Thou kill'st my heart.
55   Mine eyes are cloyed with view of tyranny.
A deed of death done on the innocent
Becomes not Titus' brother. Get thee gone.
I see thou art not for my company.
MARCUS   Alas, my lord, I have but killed a fly.
60   TITUS   'But'? How if that fly had a father, brother?
How would he° hang his slender gilded wings   (the father)
And buzz lamenting dirges in the air!
Poor harmless fly,
That with his pretty buzzing melody
65   Came here to make us merry—and thou hast killed him!
MARCUS   Pardon me, sir, it was a black ill-favoured° fly,   ugly
Like to the Empress' Moor. Therefore I killed him.
TITUS   O, O, O!
Then pardon me for reprehending thee,
70   For thou hast done a charitable deed.
Give me thy knife. I will insult on° him,   triumph over
Flattering myself as if⁵ it were the Moor
Come hither purposely to poison me.
        [He takes a knife, and strikes]
There's for thyself, and that's for Tamora. Ah, sirrah!
75   Yet I think we are not brought so low
But that between us we can kill a fly
That comes in likeness of a coal-black Moor.
MARCUS   Alas, poor man! Grief has so wrought on him
He takes false shadows for true substances.
80   TITUS   Come, take away.° Lavinia, go with me.   (the meal)
I'll to thy closet° and go read with thee   private room
Sad stories chancèd° in the times of old.   that happened
Come, boy, and go with me. Thy sight is young,
And thou shalt read when mine begin to dazzle.°   Exeunt   my eyes grow dim

4.1

Enter Lucius' son and LAVINIA *running after him, and
the boy flies from her with his books under his arm.
Enter* TITUS *and* MARCUS
YOUNG LUCIUS   Help, grandsire, help! My aunt Lavinia
Follows me everywhere, I know not why.
Good uncle Marcus, see how swift she comes.
Alas, sweet aunt, I know not what you mean.
        [He drops his books]
5   MARCUS   Stand by me, Lucius. Do not fear thine aunt.
TITUS   She loves thee, boy, too well to do thee harm.
YOUNG LUCIUS   Ay, when my father was in Rome¹ she did.
MARCUS   What means my niece Lavinia by these signs?
TITUS   Fear her not, Lucius; somewhat° doth she mean.   something
10   MARCUS   See, Lucius, see how much she makes of thee.
Somewhither° would she have thee go with her.   Somewhere

---

5. Pleasing myself with the thought that.
4.1 Location: Titus's garden.

1. That is, here to protect me.

Ah, boy, Cornelia² never with more care
Read to her sons than she hath read to thee
Sweet poetry and Tully's³ *Orator*.

15 Canst thou not guess wherefore she plies° thee thus?   *importunes*

YOUNG LUCIUS My lord, I know not, I, nor can I guess,
Unless some fit or frenzy do possess her;
For I have heard my grandsire say full oft
Extremity of griefs would make men mad,
20 And I have read that Hecuba of Troy⁴
Ran mad for sorrow. That made me to fear,
Although, my lord, I know my noble aunt
Loves me as dear as e'er my mother did,
And would not but in fury° fright my youth,   *except in madness*
25 Which made me down to throw my books and fly,
Causeless, perhaps. But pardon me, sweet aunt;
And, madam, if my uncle Marcus go°   *go with us*
I will most willingly attend your ladyship.

MARCUS Lucius, I will
    [LAVINIA *turns the books over with her stumps*]
30 TITUS How now, Lavinia? Marcus, what means this?
Some book there is that she desires to see.
Which is it, girl, of these?—Open them, boy.
[*To* LAVINIA] But thou art deeper read and better skilled.⁵
Come and take choice of all my library,
35 And so beguile thy sorrow till the heavens
Reveal the damned contriver of this deed.—
Why lifts she up her arms in sequence° thus?   *one after the other*

MARCUS I think she means that there were more than one
Confederate in the fact.° Ay, more there was,   *crime*
40 Or else to heaven she heaves them for revenge.

TITUS Lucius, what book is that she tosseth⁶ so?

YOUNG LUCIUS Grandsire, 'tis Ovid's *Metamorphoses*.
My mother gave it me.

MARCUS   For love of her that's gone,
Perhaps, she culled° it from among the rest.   *picked*

45 TITUS Soft, so busily she turns the leaves.
Help her. What would she find? Lavinia, shall I read?
This is the tragic tale of Philomel,
And treats of Tereus' treason and his rape,⁷
And rape, I fear, was root of thy annoy.°   *injury*
50 MARCUS See, brother, see. Note how she quotes° the leaves.   *examines*

TITUS Lavinia, wert *thou* thus surprised, sweet girl,
Ravished and wronged as Philomela was,
Forced in the ruthless, vast, and gloomy woods?
See, see. Ay, such a place there is where we did hunt—
55 O, had we never, never hunted there!—
Patterned by° that the poet here describes,   *On the pattern of*
By nature made for murders and for rapes.

MARCUS O, why should nature build so foul a den,
Unless the gods delight in tragedies?

---

2. Mother of the two Gracchi, famous tribunes; Cornelia was viewed as the ideal Roman mother because of her devotion to their education.
3. Cicero's; his *Orator* and *De Oratore*, treatises on rhetoric written c. 50 B.C.E., were both standard texts in

Renaissance grammar schools.
4. See 1.1.136 and note.
5. Than to read schoolbooks.
6. Clumsily turns the pages.
7. See note to 2.3.43.

60   TITUS   Give signs, sweet girl, for here are none but friends,
       What Roman lord it was durst do the deed.
       Or slunk not Saturnine,[8] as Tarquin erst,°   *once*
       That left the camp to sin in Lucrece' bed?[9]

   MARCUS   Sit down, sweet niece. Brother, sit down by me.
       [They sit]

65   Apollo, Pallas, Jove, or Mercury[1]
       Inspire me, that I may this treason find.°   *discover the truth of*
       My lord, look here. Look here, Lavinia.
       This sandy plot is plain.° Guide if thou canst   *flat*
       This after me.

           He writes his name with his staff, and guides it with feet
           and mouth
             I here have writ my name
70   Without the help of any hand at all.
       Cursed be that heart that forced us to this shift!°   *contrivance*
       Write thou, good niece, and here display at last
       What God will have discovered° for revenge.   *revealed*
       Heaven guide thy pen to print thy sorrows plain,
75   That we may know the traitors and the truth.

           She takes the staff in her mouth, and guides it with her
           stumps, and writes[2]
       O, do ye read, my lord, what she hath writ?

   TITUS   'Stuprum°—Chiron—Demetrius.'   *Defilement*

   MARCUS   What, what!—The lustful sons of Tamora
       Performers of this heinous bloody deed?

80   TITUS   *Magni dominator poli,*
       Tam lentus audis scelera, tam lentus vides?[3]

   MARCUS   O, calm thee, gentle lord, although I know
       There is enough written upon this earth
       To stir a mutiny in the mildest thoughts,
85   And arm the minds of infants to exclaims.°   *exclamations*
       My lord, kneel down with me; Lavinia, kneel;
       And kneel, sweet boy, the Roman Hector's[4] hope,
       [All kneel]
       And swear with me—as, with the woeful fere°   *husband*
       And father of that chaste dishonoured dame
90   Lord Junius Brutus[5] sware for Lucrece' rape—
       That we will prosecute by good advice°   *after careful planning*
       Mortal revenge upon these traitorous Goths,
       And see their blood, or die with this reproach.°   *dishonor*
       [They rise]

   TITUS   'Tis sure enough an° you knew how,   *if*
95   But if you hunt these bear-whelps, then beware.
       The dam° will wake, and if she wind° ye once   *mother / scent*
       She's with the lion deeply still in league,

---

8. Was it Saturninus who slunk.
9. See note to 2.1.109.
1. Roman gods: Apollo was the god of prophecy, Pallas (Minerva) of wisdom, Mercury of hidden knowledge. Jove (Jupiter), the king of the gods, was often imagined as all-knowing.
2. This action recalls Io in Ovid's *Metamorphoses* 1, who after her rape by Jove was turned into a heifer by

Jove's jealous wife, Juno; she revealed her identity to her family by writing her story in the dust with her hoof.
3. Ruler of the great heavens, are you so slow to hear and see crimes? (adapted from Seneca's *Hippolytus*).
4. Lucius the elder, champion of Rome as Hector was of Troy.
5. Leader of those who drove the Tarquins from Rome.

And lulls him whilst she playeth on her back,
And when he sleeps will she do what she list.°   *pleases*
100   You are a young huntsman, Marcus. Let alone,
And come, I will go get a leaf° of brass   *sheet*
And with a gad° of steel will write these words,   *spike*
And lay it by. The angry northern wind
Will blow these sands like Sibyl's leaves abroad,[6]
105   And where's our lesson then? Boy, what say you?
YOUNG LUCIUS   I say, my lord, that if I were a man
    Their mother's bedchamber should not be safe
    For these base bondmen to the yoke of Rome.
MARCUS   Ay, that's my boy! Thy father hath full oft
110   For his ungrateful country done the like.[7]
YOUNG LUCIUS   And, uncle, so will I, an if I live.
TITUS   Come go with me into mine armoury.
    Lucius, I'll fit° thee; and withal,° my boy   *equip / in addition*
    Shall carry from me to the Empress' sons
115   Presents that I intend to send them both.
    Come, come, thou'lt do my message, wilt thou not?
YOUNG LUCIUS   Ay, with my dagger in their bosoms, grandsire.
TITUS   No, boy, not so. I'll teach thee another course.
    Lavinia, come. Marcus, look to my house.
120   Lucius and I'll go brave it° at the court.   *cut a fine figure*
    Ay, marry, will we, sir, and we'll be waited on.
                    Exeunt [all but MARCUS]
MARCUS   O heavens, can you hear a good man groan
    And not relent, or not compassion° him?   *pity*
    Marcus, attend him in his ecstasy,°   *madness*
125   That hath more scars of sorrow in his heart
    Than foemen's marks upon his battered shield,
    But yet so just that he will not revenge.
    Revenge the heavens[8] for old Andronicus!   *Exit*

4.2

*Enter AARON, CHIRON, and DEMETRIUS at one door, and
at the other door young LUCIUS and another with a
bundle of weapons, and verses writ upon them*

CHIRON   Demetrius, here's the son of Lucius.
    He hath some message to deliver us.
AARON   Ay, some mad message from his mad grandfather.
YOUNG LUCIUS   My lords, with all the humbleness I may
5   I greet your honours from Andronicus
    [*Aside*] And pray the Roman gods confound° you both.   *destroy*
DEMETRIUS   Gramercy,° lovely Lucius. What's the news?   *Thank you*
YOUNG LUCIUS [*aside*]   That you are both deciphered,° that's the   *detected*
    news,
    For villains marked with rape. [*Aloud*] May it please you,
10   My grandsire, well advised, hath sent by me
    The goodliest weapons of his armoury
    To gratify° your honourable youth,   *grace*

---

6. The Sybil of Cumae (in Italy) wrote prophecies on
leaves and placed them outside her cave; they sometimes blew away before they could be read.

7. That is, fought against the Goths.
8. May the heavens take revenge.
4.2 Location: The imperial palace.

The hope of Rome, for so he bid me say;
    [*His attendant gives the weapons*]
And so I do, and with his gifts present
15 Your lordships that, whenever you have need,
You may be armèd and appointed° well;   *equipped*
And so I leave you both [*aside*] like bloody villains.
                            Exit [*with attendant*]

DEMETRIUS What's here—a scroll, and written round about?
Let's see.
20 'Integer vitae, scelerisque purus,
Non eget Mauri iaculis, nec arcu.'[1]
CHIRON O, 'tis a verse in Horace, I know it well.
I read it in the grammar long ago.
AARON Ay, just,° a verse in Horace; right, you have it.   *exactly*
25 [*Aside*] Now what a thing it is to be an ass!
Here's no sound° jest. The old man hath found their guilt,   *wholesome*
And sends them weapons wrapped about with lines
That wound beyond their feeling to the quick.[2]
But were our witty° Empress well afoot°   *clever / up and about*
30 She would applaud Andronicus' conceit.°   *device*
But let her rest in her unrest[3] a while.
[*To* CHIRON *and* DEMETRIUS] And now, young lords, was't not a
    happy star
Led us to Rome, strangers and, more than so,
Captives, to be advancèd to this height?
35 It did me good before the palace gate
To brave[4] the Tribune in his brother's hearing.
DEMETRIUS But me more good to see so great a lord
Basely insinuate° and send us gifts.   *curry favor*
AARON Had he not reason, Lord Demetrius?
40 Did you not use his daughter very friendly?
DEMETRIUS I would we had a thousand Roman dames
At such a bay,° by turn to serve our lust.   *Cornered like that*
CHIRON A charitable wish, and full of love.
AARON Here lacks but your mother for to say amen.
45 CHIRON And that would she, for twenty thousand more.
DEMETRIUS Come, let us go and pray to all the gods
For our belovèd mother in her pains.°   *(labor pains)*
AARON Pray to the devils; the gods have given us over.
    Trumpets sound
DEMETRIUS Why do the Emperor's trumpets flourish thus?
50 CHIRON Belike° for joy the Emperor hath a son.   *Probably*
DEMETRIUS Soft, who comes here?
    Enter NURSE *with a blackamoor child*
NURSE   Good morrow, lords.
O tell me, did you see Aaron the Moor?
AARON Well, more° or less, or ne'er a whit at all,   *(punning on "Moor")*
Here Aaron is; and what with Aaron now?
55 NURSE O gentle Aaron, we are all undone.

---

1. "The man upright in life and free from crime needs neither the Moorish javelin nor the bow" (Horace, *Odes* 1.22.1–2); quoted in William Lily's Latin grammar, standard in Elizabethan schools.

2. That pierce them deeply though they are too dull to feel it.
3. Remain in her distress (Tamora is in childbirth).
4. To defy (not shown in the play).

Now help, or woe betide thee evermore!
AARON   Why, what a caterwauling dost thou keep!
What dost thou wrap and fumble° in thy arms?   *bundle up*
NURSE   O, that which I would hide from heaven's eye,
60   Our Empress' shame and stately Rome's disgrace.
She is delivered, lords, she is delivered.
AARON   To whom?
NURSE   I mean she is brought abed.°   *delivered of a child*
AARON   Well, God give her good rest. What hath he sent her?
NURSE   A devil.[5]
AARON   Why then, she is the devil's dam.
65   A joyful issue!°   *outcome; child*
NURSE   A joyless, dismal, black, and sorrowful issue.
Here is the babe, as loathsome as a toad
Amongst the fair-faced breeders of our clime.
The Empress sends it thee, thy stamp, thy seal,[6]
70   And bids thee christen it with thy dagger's point.
AARON   Zounds,° ye whore, is black so base a hue?   *God's wounds*
Sweet blowze,° you are a beauteous blossom, sure.   *red-cheeked wench*
DEMETRIUS   Villain, what hast thou done?
AARON   That which thou canst not undo.
75   CHIRON   Thou hast undone our mother.
AARON   Villain, I have done° thy mother.   *used sexually*
DEMETRIUS   And therein, hellish dog, thou hast undone her.
Woe to her chance, and damned her loathèd choice,
Accursed the offspring of so foul a fiend.
CHIRON   It shall not live.
80   AARON   It shall not die.
NURSE   Aaron, it must; the mother wills it so.
AARON   What, must it, nurse? Then let no man but I
Do execution on my flesh and blood.
DEMETRIUS   I'll broach° the tadpole on my rapier's point.   *impale*
85   Nurse, give it me. My sword shall soon dispatch it.
AARON   Sooner this sword shall plough thy bowels up.
    [*He takes the child and draws his sword*]
Stay, murderous villains, will you kill your brother?
Now, by the burning tapers of the sky
That shone so brightly when this boy was got,°   *conceived*
90   He dies upon my scimitar's sharp point
That touches this, my first-born son and heir.
I tell you, younglings, not Enceladus[7]
With all his threat'ning band of Typhon's° brood,   *father of the Titans*
Nor great Alcides,[8] nor the god of war
95   Shall seize this prey out of his father's hands.
What, what, ye sanguine,[9] shallow-hearted boys,
Ye whitelimed° walls, ye alehouse painted signs,[1]   *whitewashed*
Coal-black is better than another hue
In that it scorns to bear another hue;
100   For all the water in the ocean
Can never turn the swan's black legs to white,

5. The devil was often imagined as black, and Africans as devils.
6. *thy stamp, thy seal*: bearing your imprint.
7. In Greek mythology, a Titan who warred against the gods.
8. Hercules (literally, descendant of Alcaeus).
9. Ruddy (as opposed to black).
1. Cheap, garish images of men.

Although she lave° them hourly in the flood.[2]   *bathe*
Tell the Empress from me I am of age
To keep mine own, excuse it how she can.

105 DEMETRIUS   Wilt thou betray thy noble mistress thus?

AARON   My mistress is my mistress, this myself,
The figure° and the picture of my youth.   *image*
This before all the world do I prefer;
This maugre° all the world will I keep safe,   *in spite of*
110 Or some of you shall smoke° for it in Rome.   *suffer*

DEMETRIUS   By this our mother is for ever shamed.

CHIRON   Rome will despise her for this foul escape.°   *escapade*

NURSE   The Emperor in his rage will doom° her death.   *decree*

CHIRON   I blush to think upon this ignomy.°   *ignominy*

115 AARON   Why, there's the privilege your beauty bears.
Fie, treacherous hue, that will betray with blushing
The close enacts° and counsels of thy heart.   *secret purposes*
Here's a young lad framed of another leer.°   *complexion*
Look how the black slave smiles upon the father,
120 As who should say 'Old lad, I am thine own.'
He is your brother, lords, sensibly° fed   *manifestly*
Of that self° blood that first gave life to you,   *same*
And from that womb where you imprisoned were
He is enfranchisèd° and come to light.   *freed*
125 Nay, he is your brother by the surer side,°   *(the mother's)*
Although my seal be stampèd in his face.

NURSE   Aaron, what shall I say unto the Empress?

DEMETRIUS   Advise thee,° Aaron, what is to be done,   *Consider*
And we will all subscribe to° thy advice.   *follow*
130 Save thou the child, so° we may all be safe.   *provided that*

AARON   Then sit we down, and let us all consult.
My son and I will have the wind of you.[3]
Keep there; now talk at pleasure of your safety.
    [*They sit*]

DEMETRIUS [*to the* NURSE]   How many women saw this child of his?

135 AARON   Why, so, brave lords, when we do join in league
I am a lamb; but if you brave the Moor,
The chafèd° boar, the mountain lioness,   *enraged*
The ocean swells not so as Aaron storms.
    [*To the* NURSE] But say again, how many saw the child?

140 NURSE   Cornelia the midwife, and myself,
And no one else but the delivered Empress.

AARON   The Empress, the midwife, and yourself.
Two may keep counsel when the third's away.
Go to the Empress, tell her this I said.
    He kills her
145 'Wheak, wheak'[4]—so cries a pig preparèd to the spit.

DEMETRIUS   What mean'st thou, Aaron? Wherefore didst thou this?

AARON   O Lord, sir, 'tis a deed of policy.°   *prudence*
Shall she live to betray this guilt of ours—
A long-tongued, babbling gossip? No, lords, no.

---

2. Stream; alluding to the proverb "One cannot wash an Ethiop white."
3. Will keep downwind (as a wary hunter does when stalking game).
4. Aaron imitates her death cry.

150 And now be it known to you my full intent.
Not far, one Muliteus my countryman
His wife⁵ but yesternight was brought to bed.
His child is like to° her, fair as you are.   resembles
Go pack° with him, and give the mother gold,   conspire
155 And tell them both the circumstance of all,°   the full details
And how by this their child shall be advanced
And be receivèd for the Emperor's heir,
And substituted in the place of mine,
To calm this tempest whirling in the court;
160 And let the Emperor dandle him for his own.
Hark ye, lords, you see I have given her physic,°   medicine
And you must needs bestow her funeral.
The fields are near, and you are gallant grooms.°   fellows
This done, see that you take no longer days,°   waste no time
165 But send the midwife presently to me.
The midwife and the nurse well made away,
Then let the ladies tattle what they please.
CHIRON   Aaron, I see thou wilt not trust the air
   With secrets.
DEMETRIUS   For this care of Tamora,
170 Herself and hers are highly bound to thee.
        Exeunt [CHIRON *and* DEMETRIUS *with the Nurse's body*]
AARON   Now to the Goths, as swift as swallow flies,
   There to dispose° this treasure in mine arms   bestow
   And secretly to greet the Empress' friends.
   Come on, you thick-lipped slave, I'll bear you hence,
175 For it is you that puts us to our shifts.°   force us to scheme
   I'll make you feed on berries and on roots,
   And fat on curds and whey, and suck the goat,
   And cabin in a cave, and bring you up
   To be a warrior and command a camp.° *Exit* [*with the child*]   an army

4.3

Enter TITUS, *old* MARCUS, [*his son* PUBLIUS,] YOUNG
LUCIUS, *and other gentlemen* [SEMPRONIUS, CAIUS] *with*
bows; and TITUS *bears the arrows with letters on the*
ends of them

TITUS   Come, Marcus, come; kinsmen, this is the way.
   Sir boy, let me see your archery.
   Look ye draw home° enough, and 'tis there straight.°   fully / immediately
   *Terras Astraea reliquit.*¹
5   Be you remembered,° Marcus: she's gone, she's fled.   Remember
   Sirs, take you to your tools. You, cousins, shall
   Go sound the ocean and cast your nets.
   Happily° you may catch her in the sea;   Perhaps
   Yet there's as little justice as at land.
10 No, Publius and Sempronius, you must do it.
   'Tis you must dig with mattock and with spade
   And pierce the inmost centre of the earth.

5. *one . . . wife*: the wife of a certain Muliteus, my
countryman.
4.3 Location: Outside the Emperor's palace.

1. "Astraea [goddess of justice] has abandoned the
earth" (Ovid, *Metamorphoses* 1.150).

Then, when you come to Pluto's region,[2]
I pray you deliver him this petition.
15 Tell him it is for justice and for aid,
And that it comes from old Andronicus,
Shaken with sorrows in ungrateful Rome.
Ah, Rome! Well, well, I made thee miserable
What time° I threw the people's suffrages°   *When / votes*
20 On him that thus doth tyrannize o'er me.
Go, get you gone, and pray be careful all,
And leave you not a man-of-war unsearched.
This wicked Emperor may have shipped her[3] hence,
And, kinsmen, then we may go pipe[4] for justice.
25 MARCUS O, Publius, is not this a heavy case,°   *sad situation*
To see thy noble uncle thus distraught?
PUBLIUS Therefore, my lords, it highly us concerns
By day and night t'attend him carefully
And feed his humour° kindly as we may,   *humor him*
30 Till time beget some careful° remedy.   *solicitous; laborious*
MARCUS Kinsmen, his sorrows are past remedy,
But [   ][5]
Join with the Goths, and with revengeful war
Take wreak on Rome for this ingratitude,
35 And vengeance on the traitor Saturnine.
TITUS Publius, how now? How now, my masters?
What, have you met with her?
PUBLIUS No, my good lord, but Pluto sends you word
If you will have Revenge from hell, you shall.
40 Marry, for° Justice, she is now employed,   *as for*
He thinks, with Jove, in heaven or somewhere else,
So that perforce you must needs stay a time.[6]
TITUS He doth me wrong to feed me with delays.
I'll dive into the burning lake[7] below
45 And pull her out of Acheron° by the heels.   *river of the underworld*
Marcus, we are but shrubs, no cedars we,
No big-boned men framed of the Cyclops'[8] size,
But metal, Marcus, steel to the very back,
Yet wrung with wrongs more than our backs can bear;
50 And sith° there's no justice in earth nor hell,   *since*
We will solicit heaven and move the gods
To send down Justice for to wreak° our wrongs.   *revenge*
Come, to this gear.° You are a good archer, Marcus.   *business*
        He gives them the arrows
'Ad Iovem', that's for you. Here, 'ad Apollinem'.
55 'Ad Martem',[9] that's for myself.
Here, boy, 'to Pallas'.° Here 'to Mercury'.   *Minerva*
'To Saturn',° Caius—not 'to Saturnine'!   *father of Jove*
You were as good to° shoot against the wind.   *might as well*
To it, boy! Marcus, loose° when I bid.   *(the arrows)*

---

2. The underworld, ruled by Pluto.
3. Astraea, whom the mad Titus imagines being smuggled out of Rome in a war boat.
4. Whistle (that is, seek in vain).
5. A line may be missing here; see Textual Variants.

6. So that by necessity ("preface") you must wait a while.
7. Phlegethon, river of fire of the underworld.
8. One-eyed giants of Greek legend.
9. "To Jove," "to Apollo," "to Mars"; Mars was the god of war.

60 Of° my word, I have written to effect.   *On*
There's not a god left unsolicited.
MARCUS Kinsmen, shoot all your shafts into the court.
We will afflict the Emperor in his pride.
TITUS Now, masters, draw.
[*They shoot*]
O, well said,° Lucius!   *done*
65 Good boy, in Virgo's¹ lap! Give it Pallas.
MARCUS My lord, I aim a mile beyond the moon.²
Your letter is with Jupiter by this.
TITUS Ha, ha! Publius, Publius, what hast thou done?
See, see, thou hast shot off one of Taurus'³ horns.
70 MARCUS This was the sport, my lord. When Publius shot,
The Bull, being galled,° gave Aries⁴ such a knock   *angered*
That down fell both the Ram's horns in the court,
And who should find them but the Empress' villain!°   *servant; scoundrel*
She laughed, and told the Moor he should not choose
75 But give them⁵ to his master for a present.
TITUS Why, there it goes. God give his lordship joy.
Enter the CLOWN° *with a basket and two pigeons in it*   *rustic*
News, news from heaven; Marcus, the post is come.
Sirrah, what tidings? Have you any letters?
Shall I have justice? What says Jupiter?
80 CLOWN Ho, the gibbet-maker?⁶ He says that he hath taken them
down again, for the man must not be hanged till the next week.
TITUS But what says Jupiter, I ask thee?
CLOWN Alas, sir, I know not 'Jupiter'. I never drank with him in
all my life.
TITUS Why, villain, art not thou the carrier?
85 CLOWN Ay, of my pigeons, sir; nothing else.
TITUS Why, didst thou not come from heaven?
CLOWN From heaven? Alas, sir, I never came there. God forbid
I should be so bold to press to heaven in my young days. Why,
I am going with my pigeons to the tribunal plebs⁷ to take up
90 a matter of brawl betwixt my uncle and one of the Emperal's°   *(for "Emperor")*
men.⁸
91.1   MARCUS [*to* TITUS]   *Why, sir, that is as fit as can be to serve*
          for your oration, and let him deliver the pigeons to the
          Emperor from you.
          TITUS [*to the* CLOWN]   *Tell me, can you deliver an oration to*
          the Emperor with a grace?
91.6   CLOWN   *Nay, truly, sir, I could never say grace in all my life.*
TITUS Sirrah, come hither. Make no more ado,
But give your pigeons to the Emperor.
By me thou shalt have justice at his hands.
95 Hold, hold—[*giving money*] meanwhile, here's money for thy
          charges.

---

1. Constellation identified with Astraea after her flight
from earth.
2. Marcus, humoring Titus, expects him to take the
words literally; but they also mean "talk wildly, make
extravagant claims."
3. Constellation of the bull.
4. Constellation of the ram.

5. The horns, as the sign of the cuckold.
6. The Clown hears "gibbetter" for "Jupiter."
7. *Tribunus plebis*, tribune of the common people.
8. The following indented passage (lines 91.1–91.6),
found in the early texts, appear to be a draft of the subsequent six lines.

Give me pen and ink. Sirrah, can you with a grace
Deliver up a supplication?

CLOWN Ay, sir.

100 TITUS [*writing and giving the* CLOWN *a paper*] Then here is a
supplication for you, and when you come to him, at the first
approach you must kneel, then kiss his foot, then deliver up
your pigeons, and then look for your reward. I'll be at hand,
sir; see you do it bravely.°   *handsomely*

105 CLOWN I warrant you, sir. Let me alone.°   *Leave it to me*

TITUS Sirrah, hast thou a knife? Come, let me see it.
Here, Marcus, fold it in the oration,
For thou hast made it like an humble suppliant.
And when thou hast given it to the Emperor,

110 Knock at my door and tell me what he says.

CLOWN God be with you, sir. I will.   *Exit*

TITUS Come, Marcus, let us go. Publius, follow me.   *Exeunt*

4.4

Enter [SATURNINUS,] *the Emperor, and* [TAMORA,] *the*
Empress, and [CHIRON *and* DEMETRIUS,] *her two sons,*
and others. The Emperor brings the arrows in his hand
that TITUS *shot at him*

SATURNINUS Why, lords, what wrongs are these! Was ever seen
An emperor in Rome thus overborne,°   *insolently treated*
Troubled, confronted thus, and for the extent
Of egall justice¹ used in such contempt?

5 My lords, you know, as know the mightful gods,
However these disturbers of our peace
Buzz in the people's ears, there naught hath passed
But even with° law against the wilful sons   *according to*
Of old Andronicus. And what an if

10 His sorrows have so overwhelmed his wits?
Shall we be thus afflicted in his wreaks,°   *vindictive deeds*
His fits, his frenzy, and his bitterness?
And now he writes to heaven for his redress.
See, here's 'to Jove' and this 'to Mercury',

15 This 'to Apollo', this 'to the god of war'—
Sweet scrolls to fly about the streets of Rome!
What's this but libelling against the Senate
And blazoning° our unjustice everywhere?   *proclaiming*
A goodly humour,° is it not, my lords?—   *whim*

20 As who would° say, in Rome no justice were.   *As if one were to*
But, if I live, his feignèd ecstasies°   *pretended insanity*
Shall be no shelter to these outrages,
But he and his shall know that justice lives
In Saturninus' health, whom if he sleep

25 He'll so awake² as he in fury shall
Cut off the proud'st conspirator that lives.

TAMORA My gracious lord, my lovely Saturnine,

4.4 Location: The Emperor's Palace.
1. *for . . . justice*: in return for exercising impartial justice.
2. *whom . . . awake*: A confusing passage. If the first "he" (in line 24) refers to Titus, then the meaning is "If Titus impairs Saturninus's health (tries to 'put him to sleep'), then Saturninus will rouse himself angrily." If the first "he" refers to Saturninus, then "Although Saturninus seems not to respond now, he will awaken." Some editors change the first and third (line 25) "he"s to "she"s, making the phrase refer to justice.

Lord of my life, commander of my thoughts,
Calm thee, and bear the faults of Titus' age,
30　Th'effects of sorrow for his valiant sons
Whose loss hath pierced him deep and scarred his heart;
And rather comfort his distressèd plight
Than prosecute the meanest or the best[3]
For these contempts. (Aside) Why, thus it shall become
35　High-witted° Tamora to gloze° with all.　　　　　　　*Intelligent / delude*
But, Titus, I have touched thee to the quick.
Thy life blood out if Aaron now be wise,
Then is all safe, the anchor in the port.
　　　　　Enter CLOWN
How now, good fellow, wouldst thou speak with us?
40　CLOWN　Yea, forsooth, an° your mistress-ship be Emperial.　　*if*
TAMORA　Empress I am, but yonder sits the Emperor.
CLOWN　'Tis he. God and Saint Stephen give you good-e'en.°　　*good evening*
I have brought you a letter and a couple of pigeons here.
　　　　[SATURNINUS] *reads the letter*
SATURNINUS [*to an attendant*]　Go, take him away, and hang
　　　him presently.°　　　　　　　　　　　　　　　　　　*instantly*
45　CLOWN　How much money must I° have?　　　　　　　　*am I to*
TAMORA　Come, sirrah, you must be hanged.
CLOWN　Hanged, by' Lady?[4] Then I have brought up a neck to a
fair end.　　　　　　　　　　　*Exit* [*with attendant*]
SATURNINUS　Despiteful and intolerable wrongs!
50　Shall I endure this monstrous villainy?
I know from whence this same device proceeds.
May this be borne?—As if his traitorous sons,
That died by law for murder of our brother,
Have by my means been butchered wrongfully!
55　Go, drag the villain hither by the hair.
Nor° age nor honour shall shape privilege.°　　　*Neither / afford immunity*
For this proud mock I'll be thy slaughterman,
Sly frantic wretch, that holp'st° to make me great　　　*helped*
In hope thyself should govern Rome and me.
　　　　　Enter AEMILIUS [*a messenger*]
60　SATURNINUS　What news with thee, Aemilius?
AEMILIUS　Arm, my lords! Rome never had more cause.
The Goths have gathered head,° and with a power　　　*an army*
Of high-resolvèd men bent to the spoil°　　　　　*eager to plunder*
They hither march amain° under conduct°　　　*swiftly / command*
65　Of Lucius, son to old Andronicus,
Who threats in course of this revenge to do
As much as ever Coriolanus[5] did.
SATURNINUS　Is warlike Lucius general of the Goths?
These tidings nip me, and I hang the head,
70　As flowers with frost, or grass beat down with storms.
Ay, now begins our sorrows to approach.
'Tis he the common people love so much.
Myself hath often heard them say,

---

3. Lowest or highest ranking.
4. By our Lady (the Virgin Mary).
5. Early Roman warrior who, after he was banished,

joined his former enemies and led an army against
Rome; the subject of Shakespeare's *Coriolanus*.

When I have walkèd like a private man,[6]

75 That Lucius' banishment was wrongfully,°   *wrongfully imposed*

And they have wished that Lucius were their emperor.

TAMORA   Why should you fear? Is not your city strong?

SATURNINUS   Ay, but the citizens favour Lucius,

And will revolt from me to succour him.

80 TAMORA   King, be thy thoughts imperious like thy name.

Is the sun dimmed, that° gnats do fly in it?   *because*

The eagle suffers little birds to sing,

And is not careful° what they mean thereby,   *troubled*

Knowing that with the shadow of his wings

85 He can at pleasure stint° their melody.   *stop*

Even so mayst thou the giddy° men of Rome.   *fickle*

Then cheer thy spirit; for know thou, Emperor,

I will enchant the old Andronicus

With words more sweet and yet more dangerous

90 Than baits to fish or honey-stalks[7] to sheep

Whenas° the one is wounded with the bait,   *When*

The other rotted[8] with delicious feed.

SATURNINUS   But he will not entreat his son for us.

TAMORA   If Tamora entreat him, then he will,

95 For I can smooth° and fill his agèd ears   *flatter*

With golden promises that, were his heart

Almost impregnable, his old ears deaf,

Yet should both ear and heart obey my tongue.

[*To* AEMILIUS] Go thou before to be our ambassador.

100 Say that the Emperor requests a parley

Of warlike Lucius, and appoint the meeting

Even at his father's house, the old Andronicus.

SATURNINUS   Aemilius, do this message honourably,

And if he stand on hostage[9] for his safety,

105 Bid him demand what pledge will please him best.

AEMILIUS   Your bidding shall I do effectually.   *Exit*

TAMORA   Now will I to that old Andronicus,

And temper° him with all the art I have   *work on*

To pluck proud Lucius from the warlike Goths.

110 And now, sweet Emperor, be blithe again,

And bury all thy fear in my devices.

SATURNINUS   Then go incessantly,° and plead to him.   *immediately*

                  Exeunt [*severally*]°   *separately*

5.1

Flourish. Enter LUCIUS *with an army of Goths with*
drums° and soldiers   *drummers*

LUCIUS   Approvèd° warriors and my faithful friends,   *Proven*

I have receivèd letters from great Rome

Which signifies what hate they bear their emperor

And how desirous of our sight they are.

5 Therefore, great lords, be as your titles witness,

Imperious, and impatient of your wrongs,

And wherein Rome hath done you any scath°   *harm*

---

6. Disguised as an ordinary man.
7. Clover (large quantities make sheep ill).
8. Afflicted by the rot, a liver disease in sheep.

9. If he demand a hostage (to be killed if Titus is threatened).
5.1 Location: Outside Rome.

Let him make treble satisfaction.

A GOTH   Brave slip° sprung from the great Andronicus,   offspring
10   Whose name was once our terror, now our comfort,
     Whose high exploits and honourable deeds
     Ingrateful Rome requites with foul contempt,
     Be bold° in us. We'll follow where thou lead'st,   confident
     Like stinging bees in hottest summer's day
15   Led by their master[1] to the flowered fields,
     And be avenged on cursèd Tamora.

GOTHS   And as he saith, so say we all with him.

LUCIUS   I humbly thank him, and I thank you all.
     But who comes here, led by a lusty Goth?

          Enter a GOTH, *leading of* AARON *with his child in his arms*

20 GOTH   Renownèd Lucius, from our troops I strayed
     To gaze upon a ruinous monastery,
     And as I earnestly did fix mine eye
     Upon the wasted° building, suddenly   ruined
     I heard a child cry underneath a wall.
25   I made unto the noise, when soon I heard
     The crying babe controlled° with this discourse: calmed
     'Peace, tawny slave,[2] half me and half thy dam!
     Did not thy hue bewray° whose brat thou art,   show
     Had nature lent thee but thy mother's look,
30   Villain, thou mightst have been an emperor.
     But where the bull and cow are both milk-white
     They never do beget a coal-black calf.
     Peace, villain, peace!'—even thus he rates° the babe—   scolds
     'For I must bear thee to a trusty Goth
35   Who, when he knows thou art the Empress' babe,
     Will hold thee dearly for thy mother's sake.'
     With this, my weapon drawn, I rushed upon him,
     Surprised him suddenly, and brought him hither
     To use as you think needful of° the man.   appropriate to

40 LUCIUS   O worthy Goth, this is the incarnate devil
     That robbed Andronicus of his good hand.
     This is the pearl that pleased your Empress' eye,
     And here's the base fruit of her burning lust.
     [*To* AARON] Say, wall-eyed slave, whither wouldst thou convey
45   This growing image of thy fiendlike face?
     Why dost not speak? What, deaf? What, not a word?
     A halter, soldiers! Hang him on this tree,
     And by his side his fruit of bastardy.

AARON   Touch not the boy; he is of royal blood.

50 LUCIUS   Too like the sire for ever being° good.   ever to be
     First hang the child, that he may see it sprawl°—   twitch convulsively
     A sight to vex the father's soul withal.
     Get me a ladder.

          [*A* GOTH *brings a ladder, which* AARON *climbs*]

AARON   Lucius, save the child,
     And bear it from me to the Empress.
55   If thou do this, I'll show thee wondrous things
     That highly may advantage thee to hear.

---

1. The queen bee was thought to be male.   2. Used affectionately, like "brat," and "villain," below.

If thou wilt not, befall what may befall,
I'll speak no more but 'Vengeance rot you all!'
LUCIUS   Say on, and if it please me which thou speak'st
60   Thy child shall live, and I will see it nourished.
AARON   And if it please thee? Why, assure thee, Lucius,
'Twill vex thy soul to hear what I shall speak;
For I must talk of murders, rapes, and massacres,
Acts of black night, abominable deeds,
65   Complots° of mischief, treason, villainies   Conspiracies
Ruthful° to hear yet piteously[3] performed,   Lamentable
And this shall all be buried in my death
Unless thou swear to me my child shall live.
LUCIUS   Tell on thy mind. I say thy child shall live.
70   AARON   Swear that he shall, and then I will begin.
LUCIUS   Who should I swear by? Thou believest no god.
That granted, how canst thou believe an oath?
AARON   What if I do not?—as indeed I do not—
Yet for I know thou art religious
75   And hast a thing within thee callèd conscience,
With twenty popish tricks and ceremonies
Which I have seen thee careful to observe,
Therefore I urge° thy oath; for that I know   insist on
An idiot holds his bauble° for a god,   jester's stick
80   And keeps the oath which by that god he swears,
To that I'll urge him, therefore thou shalt vow
By that same god, what god soe'er it be,
That thou adorest and hast in reverence,
To save my boy, to nurse and bring him up,
85   Or else I will discover naught to thee.
LUCIUS   Even by my god I swear to thee I will.
AARON   First know thou I begot him on the Empress.
LUCIUS   O most insatiate and luxurious° woman!   lascivious
AARON   Tut, Lucius, this was but a deed of charity
90   To° that which thou shalt hear of me anon.   Compared to
'Twas her two sons that murdered Bassianus.
They cut thy sister's tongue, and ravished her,
And cut her hands, and trimmed her as thou sawest.
LUCIUS   O detestable villain! Call'st thou that trimming?
95   AARON   Why, she was washed and cut and trimmed, and 'twas
Trim° sport for them which had the doing of it.   Fine
LUCIUS   O barbarous beastly villains, like thyself!
AARON   Indeed, I was their tutor to instruct them.
That codding° spirit had they from their mother,   lustful
100   As sure a card as ever won the set.°   game
That bloody mind I think they learned of me,
As true a dog as ever fought at head.[4]
Well, let my deeds be witness of my worth.
I trained° thy brethren to that guileful hole   lured
105   Where the dead corpse of Bassianus lay.
I wrote the letter that thy father found,
And hid the gold within that letter mentioned,

3. In a way that would excite pity.
4. As ever went for the bull's head (in the sport of bullbaiting).

Confederate with the Queen and her two sons;
And what not done that thou hast cause to rue
110   Wherein I had no stroke of mischief in it?
I played the cheater[5] for thy father's hand,
And when I had it drew myself apart,°   *went off alone*
And almost broke my heart° with extreme laughter.   *died*
I pried me° through the crevice of a wall   *I peered*
115   When for his hand he had his two sons' heads,
Beheld his tears, and laughed so heartily
That both mine eyes were rainy like to his;
And when I told the Empress of this sport
She swoonèd almost at my pleasing tale,
120   And for my tidings gave me twenty kisses.
     A GOTH   What, canst thou say all this and never blush?
     AARON   Ay, like a black dog, as the saying is.
     LUCIUS   Art thou not sorry for these heinous deeds?
     AARON   Ay, that I had not done a thousand more.
125   Even now I curse the day—and yet I think
Few come within the compass of my curse—
Wherein I did not some notorious ill,
As kill a man, or else devise his death;
Ravish a maid, or plot the way to do it;
130   Accuse some innocent and forswear myself;
Set deadly enmity between two friends;
Make poor men's cattle break their necks;
Set fire on barns and haystacks in the night,
And bid the owners quench them with their tears.
135   Oft have I digged up dead men from their graves
And set them upright at their dear friends' door,
Even when their sorrows almost was forgot,
And on their skins, as on the bark of trees,
Have with my knife carvèd in Roman letters
140   'Let not your sorrow die though I am dead.'
But I have done a thousand dreadful things
As willingly as one would kill a fly,
And nothing grieves me heartily indeed
But that I cannot do ten thousand more.
145   LUCIUS   Bring down the devil, for he must not die
So sweet a death as hanging presently.°   *immediately*
         [*Goths bring* AARON *down the ladder*]
     AARON   If there be devils, would I were a devil,
To live and burn in everlasting fire,
So I might have your company in hell
150   But to torment you with my bitter tongue.
     LUCIUS   Sirs, stop his mouth, and let him speak no more.
         [*Goths gag* AARON]
         Enter AEMILIUS
     A GOTH   My lord, there is a messenger from Rome
Desires to be admitted to your presence.
     LUCIUS   Let him come near.
155   Welcome, Aemilius. What's the news from Rome?
     AEMILIUS   Lord Lucius, and you princes of the Goths,

---

5. Swindler; escheator, an officer appointed to look after property forfeited to the crown.

The Roman Emperor greets you all by me,
And for he understands you are in arms,
He craves a parley at your father's house,
160 Willing you to demand your hostages,
And they shall be immediately delivered.
A GOTH   What says our general?
LUCIUS   Aemilius, let the Emperor give his pledges
Unto my father and my uncle Marcus,
165 And we will come. Away!   *Flourish. Exeunt [marching]*

5.2

Enter TAMORA *and* [CHIRON *and* DEMETRIUS,] *her two*
    sons, disguised

TAMORA   Thus, in this strange and sad habiliment,°   somber costume
    I will encounter with Andronicus
    And say I am Revenge, sent from below
    To join with him and right his heinous wrongs.
5   Knock at his study, where they say he keeps°   stays
    To ruminate strange plots of dire revenge.
    Tell him Revenge is come to join with him
    And work confusion on his enemies.
          They knock, and TITUS [*aloft*] *opens his study door*
TITUS   Who doth molest my contemplation?
10   Is it your trick to make me ope the door,
    That so my sad decrees° may fly away   solemn resolutions
    And all my study be to no effect?
    You are deceived; for what I mean to do,
    See here, in bloody lines I have set down,
15   And what is written shall be executed.
TAMORA   Titus, I am come to talk with thee.
TITUS   No, not a word. How can I grace my talk,
    Wanting° a hand to give it action?°   Lacking / gesture
    Thou hast the odds° of me, therefore no more.   advantage
20 TAMORA   If thou didst know me thou wouldst talk with me.
TITUS   I am not mad, I know thee well enough;
    Witness this wretched stump, witness these crimson lines,
    Witness these trenches° made by grief and care,   wrinkles
    Witness the tiring day and heavy night,
25   Witness all sorrow that I know thee well
    For our proud empress, mighty Tamora.
    Is not thy coming for my other hand?
TAMORA   Know, thou sad man, I am not Tamora.
    She is thy enemy, and I thy friend.
30   I am Revenge, sent from th'infernal kingdom
    To ease the gnawing vulture[1] of thy mind
    By working wreakful° vengeance on thy foes.   vindictive
    Come down, and welcome me to this world's light.
    Confer with me of murder and of death.
35   There's not a hollow cave or lurking-place,
    No vast obscurity° or misty vale   dark wasteland
    Where bloody murder or detested rape

5.2 Location: Titus's courtyard.
1. Alluding to the story of Prometheus; see note to 2.1.17.

Can couch° for fear, but I will find them out,   hide
And in their ears tell them my dreadful name,
40 Revenge, which makes the foul offender quake.
TITUS Art thou Revenge, and art thou sent to me
    To be a torment to mine enemies?
TAMORA I am; therefore come down, and welcome me.
TITUS Do me some service ere I come to thee.
45 Lo by thy side where Rape and Murder stands.
    Now give some surance° that thou art Revenge,   proof
    Stab them, or tear them on thy chariot wheels,
    And then I'll come and be thy wagoner,
    And whirl along with thee about the globe,
50 Provide two proper palfreys,° black as jet,   handsome horses
    To hale° thy vengeful wagon swift away   draw
    And find out murderers in their guilty caves.
    And when thy car is loaden with their heads
    I will dismount, and by thy wagon wheel
55 Trot like a servile footman all day long,
    Even from Hyperion's° rising in the east   the sun god
    Until his very downfall in the sea;
    And day by day I'll do this heavy task,
    So° thou destroy Rapine and Murder there.   Provided that
60 TAMORA These are my ministers, and come with me.
TITUS Are they thy ministers? What are they called?
TAMORA Rape and Murder, therefore callèd so
    'Cause they take vengeance of such kind of men.
TITUS Good Lord, how like the Empress' sons they are,
65 And you the Empress! But we worldly° men   mortal
    Have miserable, mad, mistaking eyes.
    O sweet Revenge, now do I come to thee,
    And if one arm's embracement will content thee,
    I will embrace thee in it by and by.   [Exit aloft]
70 TAMORA This closing° with him fits his lunacy.   agreeing
    Whate'er I forge° to feed his brainsick humours   invent
    Do you uphold and maintain in your speeches,
    For now he firmly takes me for Revenge,
    And being credulous in this mad thought
75 I'll make him send for Lucius his son,
    And whilst I at a banquet hold him sure
    I'll find some cunning practice out of hand[2]
    To scatter and disperse the giddy Goths,
    Or at the least make them his enemies.
80 See, here he comes, and I must ply my theme.°   keep up the act
        [Enter TITUS, below]
TITUS Long have I been forlorn, and all for thee.
    Welcome, dread Fury, to my woeful house.
    Rapine and Murder, you are welcome, too.
    How like the Empress and her sons you are!
85 Well are you fitted, had you but a Moor.
    Could not all hell afford you such a devil?—
    For well I wot° the Empress never wags°   know / stirs
    But in her company there is a Moor,
    And would you represent our Queen aright

2. I'll find some scheme on the spur of the moment.

90   It were convenient° you had such a devil.   *fitting*
           But welcome as you are. What shall we do?
    TAMORA   What wouldst thou have us do, Andronicus?
    DEMETRIUS   Show me a murderer, I'll deal with him.
    CHIRON   Show me a villain that hath done a rape,
95   And I am sent to be revenged on him.
    TAMORA   Show me a thousand that hath done thee wrong,
           And I will be revengèd on them all.
    TITUS [*to* DEMETRIUS]   Look round about the wicked streets of Rome,
           And when thou find'st a man that's like thyself,
100   Good Murder, stab him; he's a murderer.
           [*To* CHIRON] Go thou with him, and when it is thy hap°   *chance*
           To find another that is like to thee,
           Good Rapine, stab him; he is a ravisher.
           [*To* TAMORA] Go thou with them, and in the Emperor's court
105   There is a queen attended by a Moor.
           Well shalt thou know her by thine own proportion,
           For up and down° she doth resemble thee.   *top to toe*
           I pray thee, do on them some violent death;
           They have been violent to me and mine.
110   TAMORA   Well hast thou lessoned us. This shall we do;
           But would it please thee, good Andronicus,
           To send for Lucius, thy thrice-valiant son,
           Who leads towards Rome a band of warlike Goths,
           And bid him come and banquet at thy house—
115   When he is here, even at thy solemn° feast,   *ceremonious*
           I will bring in the Empress and her sons,
           The Emperor himself, and all thy foes,
           And at thy mercy shall they stoop and kneel,
           And on them shalt thou ease thy angry heart.
120   What says Andronicus to this device?
    TITUS   Marcus, my brother! 'Tis sad Titus calls.
           Enter MARCUS
           Go, gentle Marcus, to thy nephew Lucius.
           Thou shalt enquire him out among the Goths.
           Bid him repair° to me, and bring with him   *come*
125   Some of the chiefest princes of the Goths.
           Bid him encamp his soldiers where they are.
           Tell him the Emperor and the Empress too
           Feast at my house, and he shall feast with them.
           This do thou for my love, and so let him,
130   As he regards his agèd father's life.
    MARCUS   This will I do, and soon return again.   [*Exit*]
    TAMORA   Now will I hence about thy business,
           And take my ministers along with me.
    TITUS   Nay, nay, let Rape and Murder stay with me,
135   Or else I'll call my brother back again,
           And cleave to no revenge but Lucius.[3]
    TAMORA [*aside to her sons*]   What say you, boys, will you abide
              with him
           Whiles I go tell my lord the Emperor

---

3. That is, depend on Lucius's invading army for revenge.

How I have governed our determined jest?[4]

140 Yield to his humour, smooth and speak him fair,°   *flatter and humor him*
And tarry with him till I turn° again.   *return*

TITUS [*aside*]   I knew them all, though they supposed me mad,
And will o'erreach them in their own devices—
A pair of cursèd hell-hounds and their dam.

145 DEMETRIUS   Madam, depart at pleasure. Leave us here.

TAMORA   Farewell, Andronicus. Revenge now goes
To lay a complot to betray thy foes.

TITUS   I know thou dost, and sweet Revenge, farewell.
[*Exit* TAMORA]

CHIRON   Tell us, old man, how shall we be employed?

150 TITUS   Tut, I have work enough for you to do.
Publius, come hither; Caius and Valentine.
[*Enter* PUBLIUS, CAIUS, *and* VALENTINE]

PUBLIUS   What is your will?

TITUS   Know you these two?

PUBLIUS   The Empress' sons I take them°—Chiron, Demetrius.   *take them to be*

TITUS   Fie, Publius, fie! Thou art too much deceived.

155 The one is Murder, and Rape is the other's name.
And therefore bind them, gentle Publius;
Caius and Valentine, lay hands on them.
Oft have you heard me wish for such an hour,
And now I find it. Therefore bind them sure,

160 And stop their mouths if they begin to cry.   [*Exit*]

CHIRON   Villains, forbear! We are the Empress' sons.

PUBLIUS   And therefore do we what we are commanded.
[PUBLIUS, CAIUS, *and* VALENTINE *bind and gag* CHIRON
and DEMETRIUS]
Stop close their mouths. Let them not speak a word.
Is he sure° bound? Look that you bind them fast.   *securely*
Enter TITUS ANDRONICUS *with a knife, and* LAVINIA
with a basin

165 TITUS   Come, come, Lavinia. Look, thy foes are bound.
Sirs, stop their mouths. Let them not speak to me,
But let them hear what fearful words I utter.
O villains, Chiron and Demetrius!
Here stands the spring whom you have stained with mud,

170 This goodly summer with your winter mixed.
You killed her husband, and for that vile fault
Two of her brothers were condemned to death,
My hand cut off and made a merry jest,
Both her sweet hands, her tongue, and that more dear

175 Than hands or tongue, her spotless chastity,
Inhuman traitors, you constrained and forced.
What would you say if I should let you speak?
Villains, for shame. You could not beg for grace.°   *mercy*
Hark, wretches, how I mean to martyr you.

180 This one hand yet is left to cut your throats,
Whiles that Lavinia 'tween her stumps doth hold
The basin that receives your guilty blood.

---

4. How have I managed the jest we planned?

You know your mother means to feast with me,
And calls herself Revenge, and thinks me mad.
185 Hark, villains, I will grind your bones to dust,
And with your blood and it I'll make a paste,°   *dough*
And of the paste a coffin° I will rear,   *piecrust (with wordplay)*
And make two pasties of your shameful heads,
And bid that strumpet, your unhallowed dam,
190 Like to the earth swallow her own increase.°   *progeny*
This is the feast that I have bid her to,
And this the banquet she shall surfeit on;
For worse than Philomel you used my daughter,
And worse than Progne I will be revenged.⁵
195 And now, prepare your throats. Lavinia, come.
Receive the blood, and when that they are dead
Let me go grind their bones to powder small,
And with this hateful liquor temper° it,   *mix*
And in that paste let their vile heads be baked.
200 Come, come, be everyone officious°   *busy*
To make this banquet, which I wish may prove
More stern and bloody than the Centaurs' feast.⁶
    He cuts their throats
So, now bring them in, for I'll play the cook
And see them ready against° their mother comes.   *by the time*
           Exeunt [carrying the bodies]

5.3

Enter LUCIUS, MARCUS, *and the Goths [with* AARON, *pris-
oner, and an attendant with his child]*
LUCIUS   Uncle Marcus, since 'tis my father's mind
    That I repair to Rome, I am content.
A GOTH   And ours with thine,¹ befall what fortune will.
LUCIUS   Good uncle, take you in this barbarous Moor,
5   This ravenous tiger, this accursèd devil.
    Let him receive no sust'nance, fetter him
    Till he be brought unto the Empress' face
    For testimony of her foul proceedings,
    And see the ambush° of our friends be strong.   *troops lying in wait*
10   I fear the Emperor means no good to us.
AARON   Some devil whisper curses in my ear
    And prompt me, that my tongue may utter forth
    The venomous malice of my swelling heart.
LUCIUS   Away, inhuman dog, unhallowed slave!
15   Sirs, help our uncle to convey him in.
          [Exeunt Goths with AARON *and his child]*
    Flourish
    The trumpets show the Emperor is at hand.
    *Enter [*SATURNINUS*] the Emperor, and [*TAMORA*] the
    Empress, with [*AEMILIUS,*] Tribunes, [Senators,] and
    others*

---

5. Philomela's sister, Progne, revenged herself on her
rapist husband, Tereus, by killing their son Itys and
serving his flesh in a meal (see Introduction).
6. In Greek legend, the wedding feast of Hippodamia
ended in a bloody battle when the Centaurs tried to

carry off the bride and other women (see Ovid, *Metamorphoses* 12).
5.3 Location: Titus's courtyard.
1. Our minds accord with yours.

SATURNINUS What, hath the firmament more suns than one?

LUCIUS What boots° it thee to call thyself a sun? *avails*

MARCUS Rome's emperor and nephew, break the parle.° *stop the dispute*

20 These quarrels must be quietly debated.

The feast is ready which the careful° Titus *assiduous; troubled*

Hath ordained to an honourable end,

For peace, for love, for league, and good to Rome.

Please you therefore draw nigh, and take your places.

25 SATURNINUS Marcus, we will.

> Hautboys.[2] *A table brought in.* [*They sit.*]
> Enter TITUS *like a cook, placing the dishes, and* LAVINIA
> *with a veil over her face;* [YOUNG LUCIUS, *and others*]

TITUS Welcome, my gracious lord; welcome, dread Queen;

Welcome, ye warlike Goths; welcome, Lucius;

And welcome, all. Although the cheer° be poor, *refreshments*

'Twill fill your stomachs. Please you, eat of it.

30 SATURNINUS Why art thou thus attired, Andronicus?

TITUS Because I would be sure to have all well

To entertain your highness and your Empress.

TAMORA We are beholden to you, good Andronicus.

TITUS An if your highness knew my heart, you were.

35 My lord the Emperor, resolve me this:

Was it well done of rash Virginius[3]

To slay his daughter with his own right hand

Because she was enforced, stained, and deflowered?

SATURNINUS It was, Andronicus.

TITUS   Your reason, mighty lord?

40 SATURNINUS Because the girl should not survive her shame,

And by her presence still renew his sorrows.

TITUS A reason mighty, strong, effectual;

A pattern, precedent, and lively warrant

For me, most wretched, to perform the like.

45 Die, die, Lavinia, and thy shame with thee,

And with thy shame thy father's sorrow die.

> *He kills her*

SATURNINUS What hast thou done, unnatural and unkind?

TITUS Killed her for whom my tears have made me blind.

I am as woeful as Virginius was,

50 And have a thousand times more cause than he

To do this outrage, and it now is done.

SATURNINUS What, was she ravished? Tell who did the deed.

TITUS Will't please you eat? Will't please your highness feed?

TAMORA Why hast thou slain thine only daughter thus?

55 TITUS Not I, 'twas Chiron and Demetrius.

They ravished her, and cut away her tongue,

And they, 'twas they, that did her all this wrong.

SATURNINUS Go, fetch them hither to us presently.° *at once*

TITUS [*revealing the heads*] Why, there they are, both bakèd in
        this pie,

60 Whereof their mother daintily hath fed,

---

2. Oboes, used to provide music for ceremonial occasions.
3. A Roman centurion who in some versions of the
story killed his daughter to prevent her rape; in other
versions, he acted as Titus describes.

Eating the flesh that she herself hath bred.
'Tis true, 'tis true, witness my knife's sharp point.°   (*with pun on "period"*)
    He stabs the Empress
SATURNINUS   Die, frantic° wretch, for this accursèd deed.   *deranged*
    [*He kills* TITUS]
LUCIUS   Can the son's eye behold his father bleed?
65   There's meed for meed,° death for a deadly deed.   *measure for measure*
    [*He kills* SATURNINUS. *Confusion follows.*
    Enter Goths. LUCIUS, MARCUS, *and others go aloft*]
MARCUS   You sad-faced men, people and sons of Rome,
     By uproars severed, as a flight of fowl
     Scattered by winds and high tempestuous gusts,
     O, let me teach you how to knit again
70   This scattered corn° into one mutual° sheaf,   *grain / unified*
     These broken limbs again into one body.
A ROMAN LORD   Let Rome herself be bane° unto herself,   *destroyer*
     And she whom mighty kingdoms curtsy to,
     Like a forlorn and desperate castaway,
75   Do shameful execution on herself.
     But if my frosty signs and chaps° of age,   *white hair and wrinkles*
     Grave witnesses of true experience,
     Cannot induce you to attend my words.
     [*To* LUCIUS] Speak, Rome's dear friend, as erst° our ancestor[4]   *once*
80   When with his solemn tongue he did discourse
     To lovesick Dido's sad-attending° ear   *seriously listening*
     The story of that baleful-burning night
     When subtle Greeks surprised King Priam's Troy.
     Tell us what Sinon[5] hath bewitched our ears,
85   Or who hath brought the fatal engine[6] in
     That gives our Troy, our Rome, the civil° wound.   *incurred in civil war*
     My heart is not compact° of flint nor steel,   *composed*
     Nor can I utter all our bitter grief,
     But floods of tears will drown my oratory
90   And break° my utt'rance even in the time   *interrupt*
     When it should move ye to attend me most,
     And force you to commiseration.
     Here's Rome's young captain. Let him tell the tale,
     While I stand by and weep to hear him speak.
95 LUCIUS   Then, gracious auditory,° be it known to you   *audience*
     That Chiron and the damned Demetrius
     Were they that murderèd our Emperor's brother,
     And they it were that ravishèd our sister.
     For their fell° faults our brothers were beheaded,   *cruel*
100   Our father's tears despised, and basely cozened°   *cheated*
     Of that true hand that fought Rome's quarrel out°   *to the finish*
     And sent her enemies unto the grave.
     Lastly myself, unkindly° banishèd,   *unnaturally*
     The gates shut on me, and turned weeping out
105   To beg relief among Rome's enemies,
     Who drowned their enmity in my true tears
     And oped their arms to embrace me as a friend.

4. Aeneas, Trojan ancestor of the Roman people.
5. The Greek who persuaded the Trojans to admit the
wooden horse full of soldiers.
6. Instrument (the wooden horse).

I am the turned-forth, be it known to you,
That have preserved her° welfare in my blood,   *(Rome's)*
110 And from her bosom took the enemy's point,
Sheathing the steel in my advent'rous body.
Alas, you know I am no vaunter,° I.   *boaster*
My scars can witness, dumb although they are,
That my report is just and full of truth.
115 But soft, methinks I do digress too much,
Citing my worthless praise. O, pardon me,
For when no friends are by, men praise themselves.

MARCUS   Now is my turn to speak. Behold the child.
Of this was Tamora deliverèd,
120 The issue of an irreligious Moor,
Chief architect and plotter of these woes.
The villain is alive in Titus' house,
And as he is to witness, this is true.
Now judge what cause had Titus to revenge
125 These wrongs unspeakable, past patience,°   *endurance*
Or more than any living man could bear.
Now have you heard the truth. What say you, Romans?
Have we° done aught amiss, show us wherein,   *If we have*
And from the place where you behold us pleading
130 The poor remainder of Andronici
Will hand in hand all headlong hurl ourselves[7]
And on the ragged stones beat forth our souls
And make a mutual closure° of our house.°   *end / family*
Speak, Romans, speak, and if you say we shall,
135 Lo, hand in hand Lucius and I will fall.

AEMILIUS   Come, come, thou reverend man of Rome,
And bring our emperor gently in thy hand,
Lucius, our emperor—for well I know
The common voice do cry it shall be so.
140 ROMANS   Lucius, all hail, Rome's royal emperor!
MARCUS *[to attendants]*   Go, go into old Titus' sorrowful house
And hither hale that misbelieving Moor
To be adjudged some direful slaught'ring death
As punishment for his most wicked life.   *[Exeunt some]*
         [LUCIUS, MARCUS, and the others come down]
145 ROMANS   Lucius, all hail, Rome's gracious governor!
LUCIUS   Thanks, gentle Romans. May I govern so
To heal Rome's harms and wipe away her woe.
But, gentle people, give me aim° awhile,   *encourage me*
For nature puts me to° a heavy task.   *sets me*
150 Stand all aloof, but, uncle, draw you near
To shed obsequious° tears upon this trunk.   *mournful*
[Kissing TITUS] O, take this warm kiss on thy pale cold lips,
These sorrowful drops upon thy bloodstained face,
The last true duties of thy noble son.
155 MARCUS *[kissing TITUS]*   Tear for tear, and loving kiss for kiss,
Thy brother Marcus tenders on thy lips.
O, were the sum of these that I should pay
Countless and infinite, yet would I pay them.

---

7. Traditionally, traitors were thrown from the Tarpeian Rock on the Capitoline Hill.

LUCIUS [*to* YOUNG LUCIUS]   Come hither, boy, come, come, and
        learn of us
160   To melt in showers. Thy grandsire loved thee well.
    Many a time he danced thee on his knee,
    Sung thee asleep, his loving breast thy pillow.
    Many a story hath he told to thee,
    And bid thee bear his pretty tales in mind,
165   And talk of them when he was dead and gone.
MARCUS   How many thousand times hath these poor lips,
    When they were living, warmed themselves on thine!
    O now, sweet boy, give them their latest° kiss.   *last*
    Bid him farewell. Commit him to the grave.
170   Do them° that kindness, and take leave of them.   *(his lips)*
YOUNG LUCIUS [*kissing* TITUS]   O grandsire, grandsire, ev'n with
        all my heart
    Would I were dead, so° you did live again.   *provided that*
    O Lord, I cannot speak to him for weeping.
    My tears will choke me if I ope my mouth.
        [*Enter some with* AARON]
175 A ROMAN   You sad Andronici, have done with woes.
    Give sentence on this execrable wretch
    That hath been breeder of these dire events.
LUCIUS   Set him breast-deep in earth and famish him.
    There let him stand, and rave, and cry for food.
180   If anyone relieves or pities him,
    For the offence he dies. This is our doom.°   *judgment*
    Some stay to see him fastened in the earth.
AARON   Ah, why should wrath be mute and fury dumb?
    I am no baby, I, that with base prayers
185   I should repent the evils I have done.
    Ten thousand worse than ever yet I did
    Would I perform if I might have my will.
    If one good deed in all my life I did
    I do repent it from my very soul.
190 LUCIUS   Some loving friends convey the Emperor hence,
    And give him burial in his father's grave.°   *ancestral tomb*
    My father and Lavinia shall forthwith
    Be closèd in our household's monument.
    As for that ravenous tiger, Tamora,
195   No funeral rite nor man in mourning weed,°   *garments*
    No mournful bell shall ring her burial;
    But throw her forth to beasts and birds to prey.°   *prey upon*
    Her life was beastly and devoid of pity,
    And being dead, let birds on her take pity.
                   Exeunt [*with the bodies*]

The First Part of Henry the Sixth

Battles dominate *1 Henry VI*. Set in the fifteenth century, the play depicts England's attempts to retain a military and political foothold in France. Orléans, Rouen, Angiers (modern Angers), Bordeaux—the English and French clash at each place, spilling vast amounts of blood to assert control over the territories to which each laid claim. The English claimed parts of France both by treaty and by inheritance. In 1360, the English King, Edward III, was granted sovereignty over Calais and Bordeaux by the Treaty of Bretigny, which concluded part of what came to be known as the Hundred Years' War. This same Edward, from whom Henry VI was descended, also claimed the French Crown itself through his mother, Isabella, the daughter of Philip IV of France. Philip's three sons died without producing male heirs, but Isabella, married to Edward II of England, gave birth to Edward III, who vigorously pursued both the Crown and the territory of France. In the fifteenth century, his great-grandson, Henry V, renewed these efforts and achieved remarkable military successes at Harfleur and Agincourt (see Shakespeare's *Henry V* for an account of his reign). His son, Henry VI, struggled to retain what his father had won.

In this struggle, depicted in the present play, England has one incomparable hero, the valiant Lord Talbot, who fights with such ferocity that the French flee at the very sound of his name. In 1592, probably just a few months after the play was first performed, Thomas Nashe, Shakespeare's contemporary (and himself a playwright who may have had a hand in the composition of the play—see Textual Note), wrote: "How would it have joyed brave Talbot (the terror of the French) to think that after he had lain two hundred yeares in his tomb, he should triumph again on the stage, and have his bones new embalmed with the tears of ten thousand spectators at least (at several times), who, in the Tragedian that represents his person, imagine they behold him fresh bleeding?" This comment—which imagines the long-dead Talbot cheered by the thought of having his mighty victories and lamentable death played again and again—forms part of Nashe's extended defense of stage plays. While many Elizabethan writers attacked the theater as a place of idleness where lies and lewd stories were circulated, Nashe used plays like *1 Henry VI* to argue for the value of the stage, partly because of its role in preserving the memory of England's glorious heroes. As Nashe says, "For the subject of them (for the most part) it is borrowed out of our English Chronicles, wherein our forefathers' valiant acts (that have lain long buried in rusty brass and worm-eaten books) are revived, and they themselves raised from the grave of oblivion, and brought to plead their aged honors in open presence." For Nashe, Talbot is one of those worthy forefathers, pleased to be resurrected in the person of an English actor.

Shakespeare was instrumental in creating the vogue in the 1590s for stage plays based on events from the reigns of England's former monarchs. The division of the 1623 First Folio into histories, comedies, and tragedies indicates that the plays dealing with English history were perceived as a distinct and important group of works. From the beginning of his career until 1599, when *Henry V* was first acted, Shakespeare contributed to the writing of at least eight plays based loosely on the reigns of English Kings from Richard II, who was deposed in 1399, to Henry VII, who assumed the English throne in 1485 after the Battle of Bosworth Field; in addition, there was one play on the reign of King John (1199–1216). Some of these plays chronicle the English wars in France. And some depict the lengthy struggle, known as the Wars of the Roses, between two branches of England's royal family for possession of the English throne:

on one side of this struggle were the Lancastrians, who wore the red rose as their badge; on the other side were the Yorkists, who wore the white. Both groups claimed descent from King Edward III. (For charts showing the genealogies of the Lancastrians and the Yorkists, see the endpapers at back.) The Battle of Bosworth Field ended this civil strife when Henry Tudor, a descendant of John of Gaunt, Duke of Lancaster, defeated Richard III, the last of the Yorkist Kings, and then married Elizabeth of York, the daughter of an earlier Yorkist King, Edward IV. Henry Tudor thus united the red rose and the white, and the Tudors ruled England until 1603, when Elizabeth I, granddaughter of Henry VII, died without issue. It was during the final years of Elizabeth's reign that Shakespeare wrote his history plays.

Many have speculated about why these plays about England's past became so popular. Nashe gives us a clue when he emphasizes their role in celebrating martial heroes and in creating for the common people a collective memory of their national past. In the sixteenth century, many chronicle histories of England were written, such as Edward Hall's *Union of the Two Noble and Illustre Famelies of Lancastre & Yorke* (1548) and Raphael Holinshed's *Chronicles of England, Scotland, and Ireland;* the second edition of Holinshed, published in 1587, was used extensively by Shakespeare in composing his history plays. These prose chronicles, in fact, may have been some of the "worm-eaten" books from which Nashe imagined Talbot being revived for a more pleasurable life on the stage. The theater, unlike obscure and musty texts, made a version of English history accessible even to those who could not read. For a penny, a common person could go to the theater, stand in the pit, and thrill to the exploits of Talbot, the embodiment of English martial valor. Dramatized history thus contributed to an emerging sense of national identity that depended not only on allegiance to a monarch, but also on pride in a shared English culture, language, and identity. The theater played a role in constructing this shared identity, providing ordinary people with riveting representations of a common national past.

In the early 1590s, there were good reasons why arousing patriotic sentiment for an English military hero like Talbot might have been popular. In 1588, England had, with the help of bad weather, repulsed an attack by the Spanish Armada, an invasion fleet sent by Europe's most powerful Catholic power, Spain. This victory had encouraged many English people to feel that their country should play a more active role in supporting the Protestant powers of Europe against their Catholic enemies. In 1591–92, Elizabeth had with some reluctance sent her charismatic nobleman the Earl of Essex into France to aid Henry IV of Navarre and the French Protestant faction. In this campaign, Essex participated in a struggle for control of the city of Rouen. We can date *1 Henry VI* to sometime in 1592 both because Nashe's comments on Talbot were published that year and because the play seems to refer to this French campaign. It depicts fifteenth-century Englishmen invading French soil—and attacking Rouen—at the very moment an English army was once again before the city's walls. Many in England might thus have seen in Talbot an image of their contemporary champion, the dashing Earl of Essex.

Shakespeare was involved in writing two more plays on the reign of Henry VI; in the First Folio, these were entitled, respectively, *The Second Part of Henry the Sixth* and *The Third Part of Henry the Sixth*. These two plays, however, were also published in earlier Octavo or quarto versions, where they bore the titles *The First Part of the Contention of the Two Famous Houses of York and Lancaster* and *The True Tragedy of Richard Duke of York and the Good King Henry the Sixth*. No one is certain whether these plays were written before or after *1 Henry VI*, although the Oxford editors believe they precede *Part 1*. Whatever the exact order of composition, these three plays represent Shakespeare's earliest efforts in the history genre. They were quickly followed by *Richard III*, about the Yorkist monarchs Edward IV and Richard III, who pushed their way to the throne after Henry VI and his son had been killed. This completed Shakespeare's treatment of the reign of Henry VI and of the bloody civil war that erupted during it. Only later in the decade did Shakespeare dramatize the events leading up to Henry VI's kingship. These

The title page of the third volume of Raphael Holinshed's *Chronicles* (1587 ed.).

King Henry VI. Artist and date unknown.

later history plays—*Richard II, 1* and *2 Henry IV,* and *Henry V*—take us from the late fourteenth century to that moment at which the present play begins: Henry V's death in 1422.

Today, when Shakespeare's plays are far more popular than prose histories, many people assume that the history of England in the late fourteenth and fifteenth centuries is accurately and adequately depicted in his dramas. This is a mistake. In composing *1 Henry VI,* the author or authors drew on the 1587 edition of Holinshed's *Chronicles,* Hall's history of the Wars of the Roses, and a number of other historical works; but literally dozens of changes, both large and small, were made in these source materials to give dramatic shape to their sprawling succession of battles, deaths, and diplomatic stratagems. For example, *1 Henry VI* opens with the funeral of Henry V, the great Lancastrian King who won much of France for England. In the midst of this scene comes news that many of the French territories captured by Henry V have already been lost. In actuality, these French towns did not fall until years after Henry's death. But the alteration heightens the sense of crisis attendant upon the great warrior's death. English interests are imperiled; a vigorous military King has been succeeded on the throne by a mere child and his squabbling advisers. Indeed, Henry VI was only nine months old when his father died. Again, the play changes the facts so that Henry, while not old enough to govern without the aid of a Lord Protector, is certainly not an infant when the play opens and is ready to marry when it ends.

Much else was changed. Talbot's capture of Rouen, though unhistorical, may have been added to indicate the desired outcome of Essex's adventures in France. Other events Shakespeare or his collaborators made up from whole cloth: for example, the striking scene in the Temple Garden when the followers of York and Somerset pluck red and white roses to indicate whose side they choose in a quarrel over a point in law. The bloody conflict that was to result in the fall of kings and the death of thousands of nobles and common soldiers is thus given a moment of origin, traced back to an obscure event that—in the unstable conditions of Henry's tenuous reign—flares into a conflagration of blood and death. In some cases, Shakespeare simply repeats the historical confusion of his sources. In this play, for example, the Edmund Mortimer who had a claim to the throne is conflated with his cousin John Mortimer, who was imprisoned in the Tower for many years for supporting his kinsman's royal ambitions. Sir John Fastolf is treated as a cowardly knight, when in actuality he was a distinguished officer of Henry's in the French wars. Both of these inaccuracies were probably repetitions of what Shakespeare or his possible collaborators would have found in texts available to them. (Later, a cowardly character named Falstaff appears in Shakespeare's *1* and *2 Henry IV* and in *The Merry Wives of Windsor.*)

Indisputably, the play depicts events neither exactly as they were presented in the chronicles nor as a modern historian might present them. In turning historical materials into effective drama, Shakespeare or his collaborators gave one of many possible shapes to the welter of events recorded in the various sources. Many have tried to discern what Shakespeare's "philosophy of history" could have been. Did he, for example, subscribe to the view expressed in Edward Hall's history that the turmoil of the fifteenth century was God's punishment for Henry IV's crime in deposing a rightful King, Richard II—a crime for which England paid in blood for over a hundred years? Or did he take a more secular view of history, in which events unfold as they do because of human choices and actions rather than because of God's intervention? One must read the plays to decide about these questions, and the answers may differ from play to play. An early and possibly a collaborative work, *1 Henry VI* does not necessarily adopt a single point of view toward why historical events unfold as they do. Unlike some of Shakespeare's other history plays, such as *Richard III*, this one contains very little language suggesting that an angry God is punishing England for Henry IV's earlier deposition of Richard II. Rather, events seem to unfold as a direct consequence of human decisions and human rivalries. That demons actually appear to Joan of Arc in Act V, however, complicates matters. Their presence suggests the existence of a supernatural realm that has some influence, however ambiguous, on the course of human affairs.

In dramatic terms, *1 Henry VI* is structured by juxtaposing two conflicts. In the foreground is the struggle between the French and English forces in France. The English, led by Talbot, clash repeatedly with the army of Charles, the French Dauphin. He, in turn, is given aid throughout much of the play by a remarkable figure: the martial maid, Joan of Arc. But a counterpoint to the struggle between French and English emerges by way of the feuding the play depicts among the English nobility. These two lines of action impinge on one another, as the internal squabbling among the English leaders keeps them from giving proper support to their soldiers in the field, eventually allowing Joan and Charles to kill Talbot before the walls of Bordeaux.

If the play has a message to deliver to the English, it would seem to be that petty rivalries and divisions among the English nobility can destroy England from within. As the boy King says to his quarreling nobles, Gloucester and Winchester,

> Believe me, lords, my tender years can tell
> Civil dissension is a viperous worm
> That gnaws the bowels of the commonwealth.
> (3.1.72–74)

The play seldom lets the audience forget about this worm. As early as the first scene, Winchester, whose status as bishop and then later as cardinal connects him to the Church of Rome, quarrels with Gloucester, who has been appointed the Protector of the Realm—that is, the one who effectively holds royal power while the King is still a child. Secular and religious authority clash, and the rent that this causes in the fabric of the commonwealth finds visual embodiment in the several arguments and stage fights that break out between Winchester's tawny-clothed followers and Gloucester's blue-coated serving men. This striking visual juxtaposition of the two factions vividly reveals the cankerworm of civil dissension at work. The red and white roses worn by the followers, respectively, of Somerset and York serve the same purpose, splitting England into two parties just when a united front is needed to sustain the French wars. Young Henry, although aware of the danger of civil dissension, can do little to stop it. On the one hand, he empowers Richard of York by returning to him the lands and titles taken from his father, the Earl of Cambridge, who had been accused of treason; and on the other hand, he decides to wear the red rose of the House of Lancaster. Striving, perhaps, for even-handedness, he inadvertently encourages the dissension he would suppress.

Yet to modern readers, perhaps the most interesting part of the play is not its demonstration of the dangers of civil dissension but its handling of the opposition between Talbot, terror of the French, and Joan, scourge of the English. In contrast to the rivalrous and selfish nobles who surround the young Henry, Talbot is the epitome of the unselfish heroism that Nashe found so compelling. Like a good feudal lord, he lives to serve his King in battle, an arena in which he repeatedly confirms his noble lineage and demonstrates his masculinity. Captured by the French when stabbed in the back by "a base Walloon" (an inhabitant of a French-speaking province now in Belgium), he nonetheless so terrifies his captors that they keep a guard of armed bowmen around him even when he sleeps. Talbot embodies the play's nostalgia for an idealized feudal world in which the values of valor and loyalty are shared by a community of men and passed on by them to their sons. In this regard, the play quite possibly spoke to a longing on the part of some of Elizabeth's subjects to be ruled once more by a king, not by an aging female monarch. When *1 Henry VI* was written, Elizabeth, no longer young and with no heir, was entering the fourth decade of her long reign. The play seems to tap into a yearning for a return to masculine rule and martial values.

In France, Talbot is surrounded by other great English warriors: most notably Salisbury, who dies at the siege of Orléans, and Bedford, who, though sick and dying, insists on being carried in a chair to the battlefield at Rouen in order to give courage to his men. Perhaps most touchingly, at Bordeaux, where the warring English nobles refuse to send him aid, Talbot is joined on the battlefield by his son John, a fledgling warrior come to learn from his father the skills and the values of the warrior class he aspires to join. Urged to flee, he refuses, certain that flight would prove him both effeminate and baseborn. Instead, he is initiated into the rites of manhood by shedding blood and sustaining wounds in what can only be described as an erotics of battle. Having rescued him from the Bastard of Orléans, his father says:

> When from the Dauphin's crest thy sword struck fire
> It warmed thy father's heart with proud desire
> Of bold-faced victory. Then leaden age,
> Quickened with youthful spleen and warlike rage,
> Beat down Alençon, Orléans, Burgundy,
> And from the pride of Gallia rescued thee.
> The ireful Bastard Orléans, that drew blood
> From thee, my boy, and had the maidenhood
> Of thy first fight, I soon encounterèd,
> And interchanging blows, I quickly shed
> Some of his bastard blood. . . .

(4.6.10–20)

Young Talbot, shedding blood in his first battle, is compared to a young girl who bleeds during her first experience of intercourse. The cut and thrust of battle is thus imaged as a sexual encounter in which the goal is to penetrate the body and shed the blood of one's enemy. Young Talbot's willingness to participate in such struggles, no matter how inevitable his ultimate defeat, signifies the purity of his lineage and blood. Bound together by a code of chivalric values and by the rites of blood, Talbot, his son, and Bedford, Salisbury, and those who fight with them upon the fields of France embody the heroism Nashe suggested would stir the hearts of English theatergoers. By play's end, however, all these warriors are dead. With young Talbot's premature slaughter on the plains of Bordeaux, the bright flame of English chivalry flickers out. England passes into the hands of mere politicians and rivalrous churchmen who, if they fight, fight not for king and country but for their own particular interests.

The English in this play are defeated in part because of their failure to live up to and support their own best ideals as embodied in the figure of Talbot. Their defeat, however, also owes much to Talbot's chief antagonist, Joan of Arc, in Shakespeare's play a magnetic and complicated figure. Depending on the vantage point from which she is viewed, Joan is a holy maid sent by God to aid her country, a servant of the devil, or a deceitful whore. When the Bastard of Orléans first introduces her to the Dauphin, he calls Joan a holy maid and a prophet, and after she both sees through the Dauphin's trick to substitute René for himself and defeats the Dauphin in single combat, he proclaims her an Amazon (one of the legendary race of women warriors) and a Deborah (an Old Testament prophet and judge who accompanied an Israelite army against their Canaanite oppressors). These comparisons suggest how highly the French at first value their female champion. For a time, Joan seems possessed of uncanny powers. Not only does she recognize the Dauphin without ever having seen him before, but, perhaps more remarkably, she seems to suck away the great Talbot's strength, leaving him confused and ashamed before the walls of Orléans.

The English respond to this powerful but disarmingly down-to-earth peasant girl by calling her a witch and a whore. Much of their language concerning Joan is filled with bawdy double meanings, beginning with their play on the word *pucelle*, meaning "maid" or "virgin" in French, but sounding like "puzzel," English slang for "whore." From the first time he meets her in battle, Talbot assumes that Joan's powers can come only from witchcraft, rather than from a heavenly or merely human source. Joan's circumstances invite this kind of denigration. She is an unmarried woman who has turned

Fifteenth-century Franco-Flemish portrait of Joan of Arc.

soldier and assumed the garments of a man. In the early modern period, to dress like a man was often read as a violation of woman's assigned place in the gender hierarchy and an indication of the cross-dresser's uncontrolled will and appetites. Such women were easily assumed to be sexually transgressive, as well as vulnerable to the temptations of the devil.

Even Elizabeth, the unmarried Queen, was subject to endless rumors concerning her sexuality. Some whispered that she had had bastard children with the Earl of Leicester, some that her hymen was so thick that no man could penetrate her. The virgin and the whore, the heaven-sent exception and the unnatural monster—the one could easily be turned into the other. While it seems implausible that Joan was constructed explicitly to remind spectators of the English Queen, nonetheless the shepherd girl serves as a lightning rod to capture some of the ambivalent emotions attached to the Queen and to the idea of powerful public women more generally. Occasionally Joan is portrayed in language echoing that used of Elizabeth. Charles, for example, calls her Astraea's daughter—that is, daughter of the goddess of justice—a title often applied to Elizabeth. Several critics have argued that Joan's battlefield exploits recall the stories circulated about Elizabeth in 1588, when she was said to have appeared in armor before her troops at Tilbury as they prepared to go into battle against the Spanish. Having the body of a woman but the role and the clothing of a man, each of these women could incite reverence but also demonization. Anomalies, they could be read as criminals or fiends rather than as miraculous exceptions to their cultures' expectations concerning virtuous women.

Shakespeare's Joan is built of contradictions. At first, she seems a miracle worker who speaks confidently of her role as servant of "God's mother" (1.3.57) and savior of France. At times, she demonstrates Amazonian strength and shrewd military leadership. At other times, she speaks with the sharp tongue and pragmatic realism of a shepherd girl. When, for example, the English herald delivers an extended eulogy over the body of Talbot on the plains of Bordeaux, Joan interrupts him: "Him that thou magnifi'st with all these titles / Stinking and flyblown lies here at our feet" (4.7.75–76). Elsewhere, having persuaded Burgundy to leave his alliance with Talbot and rejoin the French side, she remarks with irony: "Done like a Frenchman—[*aside*] turn and turn again" (3.7.85).

The greatest shift in the presentation of Joan, however, occurs in Act 5, when she unexpectedly dwindles into a frightened and ineffectual practitioner of witchcraft. Summoning demons, she offers to let them suck her blood in return for doing her bidding. They refuse, leaving her vainly attempting to save herself from burning by pleading pregnancy. This diminished Joan of the last act—who, when directly depicted as a witch, is presented as an impotent one—seems deployed in part to bring the play to a closure acceptable to English pride. Talbot may have been defeated, but Joan is not allowed to win the war or even to live. This ending also echoes historical fact. The English handed the actual Joan of Arc over to the Inquisition, and, found guilty of heresy and witchcraft, she was burned in May 1431.

Joan's connection with witchcraft also capitalizes on the widespread interest in the phenomenon in the early 1590s. In 1591, accounts had reached England of the Scottish King James's prosecution of witches; and some had dared to hint that Elizabeth herself had used witchcraft to defeat the Spanish Armada. Several English treatises had been published in the 1580s debating whether witches were indeed the servants of the devil or were simply people, usually old women, scapegoated by their communities or deluded into thinking they had powers they actually lacked. The play, of course, doesn't settle the matter, giving us a Joan whose success against the English could have either a supernatural cause or a more mundane origin in her own strength, cleverness, and ability to inspire others. And while she does summon demons in the last act, they fail to aid her.

But Joan is not the only woman in *1 Henry VI*. There are two others: the Countess of Auvergne and Margaret of Anjou, both French and both allied to Joan in the threat they pose to English manhood. While the play certainly highlights the political and military damage done to England by dissension among the English nobility, it also constructs women, especially French women, as a source of danger to England and her male leaders. While no English women appear in *1 Henry VI,* three French women play important roles, and all threaten English interests. Joan almost ousts the English from France. The Countess of Auvergne attempts to imprison Talbot in her castle. Margaret conquers men's hearts by her great beauty, causing Henry VI to accept the dowerless Margaret as his bride, despite his promise to marry another woman. Suffolk, the King's retainer, has already fallen prey to her charms, setting up the possibility that, Joan gone, yet another French woman will cause rivalries and dissension in England.

In the warrior culture idealized in the person of Talbot, women would not seem to figure very importantly, except perhaps as mothers who give birth to sons who will continue the lineage and the values of the fathers. But *1 Henry VI* depicts a more complicated reality. It shows, for example, how a potential wife, like Margaret, can incite uncontrollable desires in men and so become much more than a vehicle for reproduction or a pawn in a dynastic settlement. It also shows that some men, like the French of this play, seem unable to be martial heroes without the extraordinary and exceptional help of a woman. And it acknowledges that sometimes fathers don't beget sons worthy of the paternal name, as seems to be the case with Henry VI. Sometimes women must fill the void left by masculine failings; occasionally, as with Elizabeth I, a woman must even become King. *1 Henry VI* puts all of these complex and contradictory knowledges in play. While it creates heroes for men weary of feminine rule, in the process it also acknowledges the potential weaknesses of men, the occasional failures of the patriarchal gender system to function as it should, and the sometimes surprising and terrifying powers of women. As it turns out, Nashe painted too simple a picture of the history plays. They are not only about the valiant acts of "our forefathers" but also about the failings of less admirable Englishmen and indeed about the actions of women, some of whom, though foreign, seem to have spoken to anxieties generated very close to home.

JEAN E. HOWARD

TEXTUAL NOTE

The only text of *1 Henry VI* is found in the First Folio (F) of 1623. Using several types of stylistic and metrical evidence, the Oxford editors have returned to an existing editorial tradition of assigning authorship to several dramatists. Much of Act 1, they believe, was written by Thomas Nashe; Shakespeare is assigned only 2.4, the scene in the Temple Garden in which the followers of York and Somerset pluck the white roses and the red, and 4.2 through 4.7.32, the battle scenes at Bordeaux in which Talbot and his son meet their deaths after being denied aid by the quarreling English nobles. While the identities of other collaborators are suggested with less certainty, Robert Greene and George Peele are possibilities. Other contemporary textual critics, who attribute the entire play to Shakespeare, feel that the kinds of textual evidence used to adduce multiple authorship are unreliable for work produced so early in Shakespeare's career and discern no marked differences between the quality of this and other plays attributed to him in the early 1590s.

Act and scene divisions are incomplete in the Folio text and may not be theatrical in origin. The Oxford editors have divided the text in Acts 1, 3, and 5 into more scenes than are found in most modern editions. Generally, additional scenes are marked at points during a battle when the stage appears momentarily to be clear of all characters, the traditional indication in the Renaissance theater that one scene has ended and another begun. Thus, during the battle for Orléans, what are traditionally designated as 1.2 and 1.4 are each divided into two shorter scenes (1.2–1.3 and 1.5–1.6); during the struggle for Rouen, the scene traditionally designated as 3.2 is divided into five parts (3.2–3.6); and during the battle for Angiers, 5.3 is divided in this text into three scenes (5.3–5.5).

In addition, the Oxford editors have disposed of what has long been a confusion in F concerning whether Winchester is a cardinal for the whole duration of the play or is elevated to cardinal in Act 5. In Act 1, he is referred to both as a bishop and as a cardinal. The Oxford editors have taken the liberty of deleting or altering all Act 1 references to Winchester as a cardinal. Thus, for example, at 1.4.41, the Oxford text refers to Winchester's "purple robes," while F refers to his "scarlet robes," the color traditionally worn by cardinals.

SELECTED BIBLIOGRAPHY

Hodgdon, Barbara. "Enclosing Contention: *1, 2,* and *3 Henry VI.*" *The End Crowns All: Closure and Contradiction in Shakespeare's History.* Princeton: Princeton University Press, 1991. 44–99. Analyzes techniques for creating or disrupting dramatic closure in Shakespeare's early histories.

Jackson, Gabriele Bernhard. "Topical Ideology: Witches, Amazons, and Shakespeare's Joan of Arc." *English Literary Renaissance* 18 (1988): 40–65. Examines the contradictory aspects of the characterization of Joan of Arc, arguing that she is represented both as a positive force and analogue of Queen Elizabeth and also as a witch and strumpet.

Knowles. Ric. "The First Tetralogy in Performance." *A Companion to Shakespeare's Works.* Vol. II: *The Histories.* Ed. Richard Dutton and Jean E. Howard. Malden, Mass.: Blackwell, 2003. 263–86. Discusses key theatrical performances of Shakespeare's earliest history plays, including *1 Henry VI.*

Lee, Patricia-Ann. "Reflections of Power: Margaret of Anjou and the Dark Side of Queenship." *Renaissance Quarterly* 39 (1986): 183–217. Analyzes how the historical Margaret was represented not only in Shakespeare's plays but in the historical chronicles of the fifteenth and sixteenth centuries.

Rackin, Phyllis. *Stages of History: Shakespeare's English Chronicles.* Ithaca, N.Y.: Cornell University Press, 1990. 146–200. Discusses how women in Shakespeare's English history plays subvert and challenge the masculine writing of history.

Riggs, David. *Shakespeare's Heroical Histories: Henry VI and Its Literary Tradition*. Cambridge, Mass.: Harvard University Press, 1971. 93–139. Explores the deterioration of heroic ideals in Shakespeare's early English histories with special attention paid to the opposition of Talbot, the English hero, and Joan of Arc, his French antithesis.

Saccio, Peter. *Shakespeare's English Kings: History, Chronicle, and Drama*. 2nd ed. New York: Oxford University Press, 2000. 90–113. Discusses the differences between the historical events of Henry VI's reign and Shakespeare's representation of them.

Taylor, Gary. "Shakespeare and Others: The Authorship of *Henry the Sixth, Part I*." *Medieval and Renaissance Drama in England* 7 (1995) : 145–205. Lays out evidence for his view that *1 Henry VI* was collaboratively written.

Tricomi, Albert. "Joan la Pucelle and the Inverted Saints Play in *1 Henry VI*." *Renaissance and Reformation* 25 (2001): 5–31. Reads *1 Henry VI* as a Reformation critique of Joan of Arc as a false prophet who incites men to idolatry and of *1 Henry VI* as an inversion of a Catholic saint's play.

Walsh, Brian. "'Unkind Division': The Double Absence of Performing History in *1 Henry VI*." *Shakespeare Quarterly* 55 (2004): 119–47. Discusses the role of performance in evoking, but never fully capturing, the historical past to which *1 Henry VI* refers.

FILM

Henry VI, Part One. 1983. Dir. Jane Howell. UK/USA. 112 min. A BBC-TV production featuring Trevor Peacock as Talbot, Peter Benson as Henry VI, and Brenda Blethyn as Joan. Lavish costumes and some strong performances in a textually faithful version of the play.

The First Part of Henry the Sixth

THE PERSONS OF THE PLAY

The English

KING HENRY VI
Duke of GLOUCESTER, Lord Protector, uncle of King Henry
Duke of BEDFORD, Regent of France
Duke of EXETER
Bishop of WINCHESTER (later Cardinal), uncle of King Henry
Duke of SOMERSET
RICHARD PLANTAGENET, later DUKE OF YORK, and Regent of France
Earl of WARWICK
Earl of SALISBURY
Earl of SUFFOLK
Lord TALBOT
JOHN Talbot
Edmund MORTIMER
Sir William GLASDALE
Sir Thomas GARGRAVE
Sir John FASTOLF
Sir William LUCY
WOODVILLE, Lieutenant of the Tower of London
MAYOR of London
VERNON
BASSET
A LAWYER
A LEGATE and ambassadors
Messengers, warders and keepers of the Tower of London,
    servingmen, officers, captains, soldiers, heralds, watch

The French

CHARLES, Dauphin of France
RENÉ, Duke of Anjou, King of Naples
MARGARET, his daughter
Duke of ALENÇON
BASTARD of Orléans
Duke of BURGUNDY, uncle of King Henry
GENERAL of the French garrison at Bordeaux
COUNTESS of Auvergne
MASTER GUNNER of Orléans
A BOY, his son
JOAN la Pucelle
A SHEPHERD, father of Joan
Porter, French sergeant, French sentinels, French scout,
    French herald, the Governor of Paris, fiends, and soldiers

1.1

Dead march.° Enter the funeral of King Henry the   *Funeral march*
Fifth, attended on by the Duke of BEDFORD *(Regent of*
France), the Duke of GLOUCESTER *(Protector), the Duke*
of EXETER, *[the Earl of]* WARWICK, *the Bishop of* WIN-
CHESTER, *and the Duke of* SOMERSET

BEDFORD   Hung be the heavens with black!¹ Yield, day, to night!
Comets, importing° change of times and states,   *foretelling*
Brandish your crystal tresses² in the sky,
And with them scourge the bad revolting° stars   *rebellious*
5   That have consented unto Henry's death—
King Henry the Fifth, too famous to live long.³
England ne'er lost a king of so much worth.
GLOUCESTER   England ne'er had a king until his time.
Virtue° he had, deserving to command.   *Merit; power*
10   His brandished sword did blind men with his° beams.   *its*
His arms spread wider than a dragon's wings.
His sparkling eyes, replete with wrathful fire,
More dazzled and drove back his enemies
Than midday sun, fierce bent against their faces.
15   What should I say? His deeds exceed all speech.
He ne'er lift up his hand but conquerèd.⁴
EXETER   We mourn in black; why mourn we not in blood?°   *by shedding blood*
Henry is dead, and never shall revive.
Upon a wooden coffin we attend,
20   And death's dishonourable victory
We with our stately presence glorify,
Like captives bound to a triumphant car.°   *chariot*
What, shall we curse the planets of mishap,
That plotted thus our glory's overthrow?
25   Or shall we think the subtle-witted French
Conjurers and sorcerers, that, afraid of him,
By magic verses have contrived his end?
WINCHESTER   He was a king blest of the King of Kings.⁵
Unto the French, the dreadful judgement day
30   So dreadful will not be as was his sight.
The battles of the Lord of Hosts⁶ he fought.
The Church's prayers made him so prosperous.°   *successful*
GLOUCESTER   The Church? Where is it? Had not churchmen prayed,⁷
His thread of life had not so soon decayed.°   *grown weak*
35   None do you like but an effeminate prince,
Whom like a schoolboy you may overawe.
WINCHESTER   Gloucester, whate'er we like, thou art Protector,⁸
And lookest to command the Prince and realm.

1.1 Location: Westminster Abbey, England.
1. Alluding to the theatrical practice, when a tragedy was to be performed, of hanging black draperies from the "heavens," or roof projecting over the stage.
2. Flash your bright hair (the tails of the comets).
3. Henry V, the English conqueror of France who is the subject of a later play by Shakespeare, lived from 1387 until 1422. The assertion that he was too famous to live long may refer to the popular belief that jealous fate (the stars of line 4) prematurely cut down those whose fame became too great.

4. He never lifted up his hand (in battle) without conquering.
5. The name for God in biblical descriptions of the Last Judgment (see Revelation 19:16).
6. Another biblical name for God (see Psalms 24:10, Isaiah 13:13).
7. Punning on "preyed" and implying that Winchester conspired against the King.
8. Ruler of the kingdom during the King's youth. (Henry VI was an infant when his father died.)

Thy wife[9] is proud: she holdeth thee in awe,°   *overawes or rules you*

40 More than God or religious churchmen may.

GLOUCESTER   Name not religion, for thou lov'st the flesh,

And ne'er throughout the year to church thou go'st,

Except it be to pray against thy foes.

BEDFORD   Cease, cease these jars,° and rest your minds in peace.   *discords*

45 Let's to the altar. Heralds, wait on us.°   *attend us*

     [*Exeunt* WARWICK, SOMERSET, *and heralds with coffin*][1]

Instead of gold, we'll offer up our arms—

Since arms avail not, now that Henry's dead.

Posterity, await for° wretched years,   *expect*

When, at their mothers' moistened eyes, babes shall suck,[2]

50 Our isle be made a marish° of salt tears,   *marsh*

And none but women left to wail the dead.

Henry the Fifth, thy ghost I invocate:

Prosper this realm; keep it from civil broils;°   *wars*

Combat with adverse planets in the heavens.

55 A far more glorious star thy soul will make

Than Julius Caesar[3] or bright—

     Enter a MESSENGER

MESSENGER   My honourable lords, health to you all.

Sad tidings bring I to you out of France,

Of loss, of slaughter, and discomfiture.

60 Guyenne, Compiègne, Rouen, Rheims, Orléans,

Paris, Gisors, Poitiers are all quite lost.

BEDFORD   What sayst thou, man, before dead Henry's corpse?

Speak softly, or the loss of those great towns

Will make him burst his lead° and rise from death.   *lead lining of coffin*

65 GLOUCESTER [*to the* MESSENGER]   Is Paris lost? Is Rouen yielded up?

If Henry were recalled to life again,

These news would cause him once more yield the ghost.°   *to die*

EXETER [*to the* MESSENGER]   How were they lost? What

     treachery was used?

MESSENGER   No treachery, but want° of men and money.   *lack*

70 Amongst the soldiers this is mutterèd:

That here you maintain several factions,

And whilst a field° should be dispatched and fought,   *an army; battle*

You are disputing of° your generals.   *about*

One would have ling'ring wars, with little cost;

75 Another would fly swift, but wanteth wings;

A third thinks, without expense at all,

By guileful fair words peace may be obtained.

Awake, awake, English nobility!

Let not sloth dim your honours new-begot.

80 Cropped° are the flower-de-luces[4] in your arms;   *Plucked*

---

9. Eleana Cobham. Accused of pride and overweening ambition, she is found guilty of witchcraft in *The First Part of the Contention*.
1. F does not indicate when the funeral procession exits. If it exits now rather than at the end of the scene, then Henry's coffin is not onstage when the messengers from France arrive; but the actors carrying the coffin would have more time to prepare for their parts in the battle scene in 1.2.
2. When babies are fed only with their mother's tears.
3. According to Roman tradition, Caesar's soul was turned into a shining star (Ovid's *Metamorphoses*) or comet (Suetonius) after his murder.
4. English name for the French national emblem, the fleur-de-lis (lily flower), which appeared in the English coat of arms and signified the English claim to the French throne. By the Treaty of Troyes (1420), Henry V was named heir to the French King Charles VI, but Henry died shortly before Charles; at Charles's death, the French throne passed to his son, the Dauphin, leading to the renewed struggles between the French and English depicted here.

Of England's coat,° one half is cut away.   [*Exit*]   *coat of arms*
EXETER   Were our tears wanting to this funeral,
These tidings would call forth her° flowing tides.   *(England's)*
BEDFORD   Me they concern; Regent⁵ I am of France.
85   Give me my steelèd coat. I'll fight for France.
Away with these disgraceful wailing robes!
[*He removes his mourning robe*]
Wounds will I lend the French, instead of eyes,
To weep⁶ their intermissive° miseries.   *temporarily interrupted*
Enter to them another MESSENGER [*with letters*]
SECOND MESSENGER   Lords, view these letters, full of bad mischance.
90   France is revolted from the English quite,
Except some petty towns of no import.
The Dauphin⁷ Charles is crownèd king in Rheims;
The Bastard of Orléans⁸ with him is joined;
René, Duke of Anjou, doth take his part;
95   The Duke of Alençon flyeth to his side.   *Exit*
EXETER   The Dauphin crownèd King? All fly to him?
O whither shall *we* fly from this reproach?
GLOUCESTER   We will not fly, but to our enemies' throats.
Bedford, if thou be slack, I'll fight it out.
100   BEDFORD   Gloucester, why doubt'st thou of my forwardness?
An army have I mustered in my thoughts,
Wherewith already France is overrun.
Enter another MESSENGER
THIRD MESSENGER   My gracious lords, to add to your laments,
Wherewith you now bedew King Henry's hearse,
105   I must inform you of a dismal° fight   *disastrous*
Betwixt the stout° Lord Talbot⁹ and the French.   *brave*
WINCHESTER   What, wherein Talbot overcame—is't so?
THIRD MESSENGER   O no, wherein Lord Talbot was o'erthrown.
The circumstance I'll tell you more at large.°   *in greater detail*
110   The tenth of August last, this dreadful° lord,   *fear-inspiring*
Retiring from the siege of Orléans,
Having full scarce° six thousand in his troop,   *barely*
By three-and-twenty thousand of the French
Was round encompassèd and set upon.
115   No leisure had he to enrank° his men.   *to set in battle lines*
He wanted pikes¹ to set before his archers—
Instead whereof, sharp stakes plucked out of hedges
They pitchèd in the ground confusèdly,
To keep the horsemen off from breaking in.
120   More than three hours the fight continuèd,

---

5. Ruler in the King's absence.
6. *Wounds . . . weep:* I will give the French wounds, so that they will weep blood (from the wounds, instead of tears from the eyes).
7. Charles VII (1403–1461) held the title of Dauphin (heir to the French throne) until he became King in 1422. Historically, his coronation at Reims did not occur until 1429.
8. Jean, Count of Dunois (1403–1468), illegitimate

son of the Duke of Orléans and nephew of King Charles VI.
9. John Talbot, first Earl of Shrewsbury (1388–1453) and perhaps the most celebrated English military hero of his day, was captured by the French at the Battle of Patay, the "dismal fight" described here.
1. He lacked ironbound stakes (normally set in the ground in front of archers to protect against attacking cavalry).

Where valiant Talbot above human thought
Enacted wonders with his sword and lance.
Hundreds he sent to hell, and none durst stand° him;   *face*
Here, there, and everywhere, enraged he slew.
125 The French exclaimed the devil was in arms:
All the whole army stood agazed on° him.   *astonished at*
His soldiers, spying his undaunted spirit,
'A° Talbot! A Talbot!' cried out amain,°   *To / strongly*
And rushed into the bowels of the battle.
130 Here had the conquest fully been sealed up,
If Sir John Fastolf² had not played the coward.
He, being in the vanguard placed behind,³
With purpose to relieve and follow them,
Cowardly fled, not having struck one stroke.
135 Hence grew the general wrack° and massacre.   *destruction*
Enclosèd were they with° their enemies.   *by*
A base Walloon,⁴ to win the Dauphin's grace,
Thrust Talbot with a spear into the back—
Whom all France, with their chief assembled strength,
140 Durst not presume to look once in the face.
BEDFORD   Is Talbot slain then? I will slay myself,
For living idly here in pomp and ease
Whilst such a worthy leader, wanting aid,
Unto his dastard foemen° is betrayed.   *enemies*
145 THIRD MESSENGER   O no, he lives, but is took prisoner,
And Lord Scales with him, and Lord Hungerford;
Most of the rest slaughtered, or took likewise.
BEDFORD   His ransom there is none but I shall pay.
I'll hale the Dauphin headlong from his throne;
150 His crown shall be the ransom of my friend.
Four of their lords I'll change° for one of ours.   *exchange (kill)*
Farewell, my masters; to my task will I.
Bonfires in France forthwith I am to make,
To keep our great Saint George's feast⁵ withal.
155 Ten thousand soldiers with me I will take,
Whose bloody deeds shall make all Europe quake.
THIRD MESSENGER   So you had need. Fore Orléans, besieged,
The English army is grown weak and faint.
The Earl of Salisbury craveth supply,°   *reinforcements*
160 And hardly keeps his men from mutiny,
Since they, so few, watch such a multitude.   [*Exit*]
EXETER   Remember, lords, your oaths to Henry sworn:
Either to quell the Dauphin utterly,
Or bring him in obedience to your yoke.
165 BEDFORD   I do remember it, and here take my leave
To go about my preparation.   *Exit*

---

2. Shakespeare follows a doubtful historical tradition here. Even though in some chronicles depicted as a coward, Sir John Fastolf (1378?–1459) was actually a distinguished soldier and officer of Henry V in the French wars. For this character's relationship with the cowardly knight Falstaff in (1 and 2) *Henry IV*, see the Introduction to *1 Henry IV*.

3. He being stationed in the rear of the vanguard.
4. Inhabitant of a French-speaking province in what is now southern Belgium.
5. The feast day of St. George, England's patron saint, April 23, was traditionally celebrated with bonfires. Bedford suggests that he will celebrate it every day with military victories over the French.

GLOUCESTER   I'll to the Tower[6] with all the haste I can,
    To view th'artillery and munition,
    And then I will proclaim young Henry king.   *Exit*
170 EXETER   To Eltham[7] will I, where the young King is,
    Being ordained his special governor,
    And for his safety there I'll best devise.   *Exit*
WINCHESTER   Each hath his place and function to attend;
    I am left out; for me, nothing remains.
175   But long I will not be Jack-out-of-office.[8]
    The King from Eltham I intend to steal,
    And sit at chiefest stern° of public weal.   *Exit* (*as steersman*)

1.2

Sound a flourish.° Enter CHARLES [*the Dauphin, the*   *fanfare of trumpets*
Duke of] ALENÇON, *and* RENÉ [*Duke of Anjou*], *march-*
ing with drum[mer] and soldiers

CHARLES   Mars his true moving—even as in the heavens,
    So in the earth—to this day is not known.[1]
    Late° did he shine upon the English side;   *Recently*
    Now we are victors: upon us he smiles.
5   What towns of any moment° but we have?   *importance*
    At pleasure here we lie near Orléans
    Otherwhiles° the famished English, like pale ghosts,   *Occasionally*
    Faintly besiege us one hour in a month.
ALENÇON   They want their porrage° and their fat bull beeves.   *porridge; stew*
10   Either they must be dieted° like mules,   *fed*
    And have their provender tied to their mouths,
    Or piteous they will look, like drownèd mice.
RENÉ   Let's raise the siege. Why live we idly here?
    Talbot is taken, whom we wont° to fear.   *were accustomed*
15   Remaineth none but mad-brained Salisbury,
    And he may well in fretting spend his gall:°   *exhaust his anger*
    Nor° men nor money hath he to make war.   *Neither*
CHARLES   Sound, sound, alarum!° We will rush on them.   (*the call to arms*)
    Now for the honour of the forlorn[2] French,
20   Him I forgive my death that killeth me
    When he sees me go back one foot or flee.   *Exeunt*

1.3

Here alarum. They [the French] are beaten back by the
English with great loss. Enter CHARLES [*the Dauphin,*
the Duke of] ALENÇON, *and* RENÉ [*Duke of Anjou*]

CHARLES   Who ever saw the like? What men have I?
    Dogs, cowards, dastards! I would ne'er have fled,
    But that they left me 'midst my enemies.
RENÉ   Salisbury is a desperate homicide.
5   He fighteth as one weary of his life.
    The other lords, like lions wanting food,
    Do rush upon us as their hungry prey.°   *prey to their hunger*

---

6. The Tower of London, which served as both a royal
residence and an arsenal.
7. Another royal residence, located south of London.
8. Proverbial for someone who had been dismissed
from a job.
1.2 Location: Near Orléans, France.

1. The precise nature of the planet Mars's orbit was a
subject of debate until Johannes Kepler described it in
1609. Mars, the god of war, was known for his unpre-
dictability.
2. Performing their duty at the risk of death.
1.3 Location: Near Orléans.

ALENÇON Froissart,[1] a countryman of ours, records
     England all Olivers and Rolands[2] bred
10   During the time Edward the Third did reign.
     More truly now may this be verified,
     For none but Samsons and Goliases[3]
     It sendeth forth to skirmish. One to ten?
     Lean raw-boned rascals,° who would e'er suppose   *thin, inferior deer*
15   They had such courage and audacity?
CHARLES Let's leave this town, for they are hare-brained slaves,
     And hunger will enforce them to be more eager.°   *fierce*
     Of old I know them: rather with their teeth
     The walls they'll tear down, than forsake the siege.
20 RENÉ I think by some odd gimmers[4] or device
     Their arms are set, like clocks, still to strike on,
     Else ne'er could they hold out so as they do.
     By my consent we'll even let them alone.
ALENÇON Be it so.
          Enter the BASTARD *of Orléans*
25 BASTARD Where's the Prince Dauphin? I have news for him.
CHARLES Bastard of Orléans, thrice welcome to us.
BASTARD Methinks your looks are sad, your cheer appalled.°   *countenance made pale*
     Hath the late overthrow wrought this offence?
     Be not dismayed, for succour is at hand.
30   A holy maid hither with me I bring,
     Which, by a vision sent to her from heaven,
     Ordainèd is to raise this tedious siege
     And drive the English forth° the bounds of France.   *out of*
     The spirit of deep prophecy she hath,
35   Exceeding the nine sibyls of old Rome.[5]
     What's past and what's to come she can descry.
     Speak: shall I call her in? Believe my words,
     For they are certain and unfallible.
CHARLES Go call her in.   [*Exit* BASTARD][6]
                    But first, to try her skill,
40   René stand thou as Dauphin in my place.
     Question her proudly; let thy looks be stern.
     By this means shall we sound° what skill she hath.   *test*
          Enter [the BASTARD *of Orléans with]* JOAN *[la]*
          Pucelle[7] [armed]
RENÉ [*as Charles*] Fair maid, is't thou wilt do these wondrous feats?
JOAN René, is't thou that thinkest to beguile me?
45   Where is the Dauphin? [*To* CHARLES] Come, come from behind.
     I know thee well, though never seen before.
     Be not amazed. There's nothing hid from me.
     In private will I talk with thee apart.

---

1. Jean Froissart, author of a history of medieval France and England.
2. The most famous of Charlemagne's knights.
3. The biblical warriors Samson and Goliath were noted for their exceptional strength.
4. Gimmals, mechanical parts for transmitting motion (as in clockwork).
5. Sibyls were women in antiquity possessing the power of prophecy, perhaps "nine" here because of confusion with the nine prophetic books offered to Tarquin, the ruler of Rome, by the Cumaean Sibyl.
6. F does not indicate who brings in Joan, but it seems likely that it is the Bastard himself rather than a servant.
7. French for "the maid" or "the virgin." Joan of Arc (1412–1431) was celebrated by the French as the "Maid of Orléans" after she fought in the battle depicted here. A formidable warrior, she eventually became a prisoner of the English and was burned alive for heresy.

Stand back you lords, and give us leave awhile.
  [RENÉ, ALENÇON *and* BASTARD *stand apart*]
RENÉ [*to* ALENÇON *and* BASTARD] She takes upon her bravely, at
50   first dash.[8]
JOAN Dauphin, I am by birth a shepherd's daughter,
  My wit untrained in any kind of art.
  Heaven and our Lady gracious° hath it pleased   *(the Virgin Mary)*
  To shine on my contemptible estate.
55 Lo, whilst I waited on my tender lambs,
  And to sun's parching heat displayed my cheeks,
  God's mother deignèd to appear to me,
  And in a vision, full of majesty,
  Willed me to leave my base vocation
60 And free my country from calamity.
  Her aid she promised, and assured success.
  In complete glory she revealed herself—
  And whereas I was black[9] and swart° before,   *dark; swarthy*
  With those clear rays which she infused° on me   *shed*
65 That beauty am I blest with, which you may see.
  Ask me what question thou canst possible,
  And I will answer unpremeditated.
  My courage try by combat, if thou dar'st,
  And thou shalt find that I exceed my sex.
70 Resolve on° this: thou shalt be fortunate,   *Be sure of*
  If thou receive me for thy warlike mate.°   *co-worker; lover*
CHARLES Thou hast astonished me with thy high terms.°   *lofty phrases*
  Only this proof ° I'll of thy valour make: *test*
  In single combat thou shalt buckle° with me.   *contend; make love*
75 An if° thou vanquishest, thy words are true;   *An if=If*
  Otherwise, I renounce all confidence.
JOAN I am prepared. Here is my keen-edged sword,
  Decked with five flower-de-luces on each side—
  The which at Touraine, in Saint Katherine's[1] churchyard,
80 Out of a great deal of old iron I chose forth.
CHARLES Then come a° God's name. I fear no woman.   *in*
JOAN And while I live, I'll ne'er fly from a man.
   Here they fight and JOAN [*la*] *Pucelle overcomes*
CHARLES Stay, stay thy hands! Thou art an Amazon,[2]
  And fightest with the sword of Deborah.[3]
85 JOAN Christ's mother helps me, else I were too weak.
CHARLES Whoe'er helps thee, 'tis thou that must help me.
  Impatiently I burn with thy desire.°   *with desire for you*
  My heart and hands thou hast at once subdued.
  Excellent Pucelle if thy name be so,
90 Let me thy servant,° and not sovereign be.   *lover*
  'Tis the French Dauphin sueth to thee thus.
JOAN I must not yield to any rites of love,
  For my profession's sacred from above.
  When I have chasèd all thy foes from hence,
95 Then will I think upon a recompense.

---

8. She plays her part well from the start.
9. Dark-skinned (probably from the sun).
1. Patroness of young maidens and female students;
reputed to be the holiest of Christ's virgins.
2. One of the tribe of legendary female warriors

claimed by Herodotus to live in Scythia.
3. An Old Testament prophet and judge who accompanied Barak as he led a victorious Israelite army
against the Canaanites (see Judges 4–5).

CHARLES   Meantime, look gracious on thy prostrate thrall.

RENÉ [*to the other lords apart*]   My lord, methinks, is very long
　　　in talk.

ALENÇON   Doubtless he shrives this woman to her smock,[4]
　　　Else ne'er could he so long protract his speech.

100   RENÉ   Shall we disturb him, since he keeps no mean?°   *moderation*

ALENÇON   He may mean more than we poor men do know.
　　　These women are shrewd tempters with their tongues.

RENÉ [*to* CHARLES]   My lord, where are you? What devise° you on?   *decide*
　　　Shall we give o'er Orléans, or no?

105   JOAN   Why, no, I say. Distrustful recreants,°   *cowards*
　　　Fight till the last gasp; I'll be your guard.

CHARLES   What she says, I'll confirm. We'll fight it out.

JOAN   Assigned am I to be the English scourge.[5]
　　　This night the siege assuredly I'll raise.

110   Expect Saint Martin's summer, halcyon's days,[6]
　　　Since I have entered into these wars.
　　　Glory is like a circle in the water,
　　　Which never ceaseth to enlarge itself
　　　Till, by broad spreading, it disperse to naught.

115   With Henry's death, the English circle ends.
　　　Dispersèd are the glories it included.
　　　Now am I like that proud insulting° ship   *exultant*
　　　Which Caesar and his fortune bore at once.[7]

CHARLES   Was Mohammed inspirèd with a dove?[8]

120   Thou with an eagle[9] art inspirèd then.
　　　Helen,[1] the mother of great Constantine,
　　　Nor yet Saint Philip's daughters[2] were like thee.
　　　Bright star of Venus,° fall'n down on the earth,   *Roman goddess of love*
　　　How may I reverently worship thee enough?

125   ALENÇON   Leave off delays, and let us raise the siege.

RENÉ   Woman, do what thou canst to save our honours.
　　　Drive them from Orléans, and be immortalized.

CHARLES   Presently° we'll try. Come, let's away about it.   *Immediately*
　　　No prophet will I trust, if she prove false.   *Exeunt*

1.4

Enter [the Duke of] GLOUCESTER, *with his* SERVINGMEN
[in blue coats][1]

GLOUCESTER   I am come to survey the Tower this day.
　　　Since Henry's death, I fear there is conveyance.°   *dishonesty*
　　　Where be these warders,° that they wait not here?   *guards*
　　　[A SERVINGMAN *knocketh on the gates*]

---

4. Hears her confession completely; examines her intimately (to her "smock," or undergarments).

5. An individual sent by God to punish sin.

6. A period of unseasonable calm (the sea was thought to grow calm in December so that halcyons, or kingfishers, could build their nests upon it). *Saint Martin's summer*: Indian summer (St. Martin's Day falls on November 11).

7. According to Plutarch, an anxious sea captain was calmed when Caesar told him that his ship contained both Caesar and Caesar's natural good fortune.

8. Mohammed was the prophet and founder of Islam. Some Elizabethans claimed he was a fraud who fooled followers into thinking he was divinely inspired by training a dove to take seeds from his ear. Christians saw the dove as an incarnation of the Holy Spirit.

9. Attribute of the apostle St. John and hence a symbol of divine inspiration; also an aggressive enemy of the dove.

1. St. Helena, the mother of the emperor who made Christianity the official religion of the Roman Empire, was said to have been led by a vision to discover Jesus' cross and sepulcher.

2. Four virgins noted in the New Testament (Acts 21:9) for their powers of prophecy.

1.4 Location: The Tower of London.

1. The typical attire of Elizabethan servants.

Open the gates: 'tis Gloucester that calls.
FIRST WARDER [*within the Tower*]   Who's there that knocketh so
5   imperiously?
GLOUCESTER'S FIRST MAN   It is the noble Duke of Gloucester.
SECOND WARDER [*within the Tower*]   Whoe'er he be, you may
      not be let in.
GLOUCESTER'S FIRST MAN   Villains,° answer you so the Lord   *Scoundrels; peasants*
      Protector?
FIRST WARDER [*within the Tower*]   The Lord protect him, so we
      answer him.
10   We do no otherwise than we are willed.°   *commanded*
GLOUCESTER   Who willèd you? Or whose will stands, but mine?
      There's none Protector of the realm but I.
      [*To* SERVINGMEN] Break up the gates. I'll be your warrantize.°   *surety; authorization*
      Shall I be flouted thus by dunghill grooms?
            Gloucester's men rush at the Tower gates
WOODVILLE[2] [*within the Tower*][3]   What noise is this? What
15   traitors have we here?
GLOUCESTER   Lieutenant, is it you whose voice I hear?
      Open the gates! Here's Gloucester, that would enter.
WOODVILLE [*within the Tower*]   Have patience, noble duke:
      I may not open.
      My lord of Winchester forbids.
20   From him I have express commandèment
      That thou, nor none of thine, shall be let in.
GLOUCESTER   Faint-hearted Woodville! Prizest him fore me?—
      Arrogant Winchester, that haughty prelate,
      Whom Henry, our late sovereign, ne'er could brook?°   *tolerate*
25   Thou art no friend to God or to the King.
      Open the gates, or I'll shut thee out shortly.
SERVINGMEN   Open the gates unto the Lord Protector,
      Or we'll burst them open, if that you come not quickly.
            Enter, to the [Lord] Protector at the Tower gates, [the
            Bishop of] WINCHESTER *and his men in tawny coats*[4]
WINCHESTER   How now, ambitious vizier![5] What means this?
GLOUCESTER   Peeled° priest, dost thou command me to be   *Shaven; tonsured*
30   shut out?
WINCHESTER   I do, thou most usurping proditor,°   *traitor*
      And not 'Protector', of the King or realm.
GLOUCESTER   Stand back, thou manifest conspirator.
      Thou that contrived'st to murder our dead lord,
35   Thou that giv'st whores indulgences to sin,[6]
      If thou proceed in this thy insolence—
WINCHESTER   Nay, stand thou back! I will not budge a foot.

2. Richard Woodville (died c. 1441) was a loyal follower of the Lancastrian King Henry VI. His granddaughter Elizabeth married the Yorkist King Edward IV
in 1464, a marriage Shakespeare depicts in *Richard III.*
3. The original stage direction at 1.4.14 reads:
"Gloucester's men rush at the Tower gates, and
Woodville the Lieutenant speaks within." The First and
Second Warders most likely also speak here from within
the Tower, but it is unclear whether they speak from the
upper stage or from behind some stage device suggesting a grate or window.

4. Typically worn by attendants of important churchmen.
5. A high state official in the Turkish Empire, which
Elizabethans frequently denounced as barbaric.
6. In 1426, Gloucester charged Winchester with
attempting to have King Henry V ("our dead lord")
killed. He here also accuses Winchester of encouraging
prostitution, referring to the revenues that the Bishop
of Winchester collected from the brothels on the south
bank of the Thames (where, in Shakespeare's time,
many theaters were also located).

This be Damascus,[7] be thou cursèd Cain,
To slay thy brother Abel, if thou wilt.

40 GLOUCESTER   I will not slay thee, but I'll drive thee back.
Thy purple robes, as a child's bearing-cloth,°   *christening gown*
I'll use to carry thee out of this place.

WINCHESTER   Do what thou dar'st, I beard° thee to thy face.   *defy*

GLOUCESTER   What, am I dared and bearded to my face?

45 Draw, men, for all this privilegèd place.[8]

     [*All draw their swords*]

Blue coats to tawny coats!—Priest, beware your beard.
I mean to tug it, and to cuff you soundly.
Under my feet I'll stamp thy bishop's mitre.
In spite of Pope, or dignities of church,

50 Here by the cheeks I'll drag thee up and down.

WINCHESTER   Gloucester, thou wilt answer this before the Pope.

GLOUCESTER   Winchester goose! I cry, 'A rope, a rope!'[9]
[*To his* SERVINGMEN] Now beat them hence. Why do you let them stay?
[*To* WINCHESTER] Thee I'll chase hence, thou wolf in sheep's array.

55 Out, tawny coats! Out, cloakèd hypocrite!

     Here Gloucester's men beat out the Bishop's men.[1] *Enter*
     in the hurly-burly the MAYOR *of London and his Officers*

MAYOR   Fie, lords!—that you, being supreme magistrates,
Thus contumeliously° should break the peace.   *contemptuously*

GLOUCESTER   Peace, mayor, thou know'st little of my wrongs.
Here's Beaufort—that regards nor° God nor king—   *neither*

60 Hath here distrained° the Tower to his use.   *seized*

WINCHESTER [*to* MAYOR]   Here's Gloucester—a foe to citizens,
One that still motions° war, and never peace,   *who always advocates*
O'ercharging your free purses[2] with large fines°—   *taxes*
That seeks to overthrow religion,

65 Because he is Protector of the realm,
And would have armour here out of the Tower
To crown himself king and suppress the Prince.

GLOUCESTER   I will not answer thee with words but blows.

     Here they [*the factions*] *skirmish again*

MAYOR   Naught rests° for me, in this tumultuous strife,   *is left*

70 But to make open proclamation.
Come, officer, as loud as e'er thou canst, cry.

OFFICER   All manner of men, assembled here in arms this day
against God's peace and the King's, we charge and command
you in his highness' name to repair to your several dwelling

75 places, and not to wear, handle, or use any sword, weapon, or
dagger henceforward, upon pain of death.

     [*The skirmishes cease*]

GLOUCESTER   Bishop, I'll be no breaker of the law.
But we shall meet and break our minds° at large.   *express our views*

---

7. Damascus, in Syria, was believed to have been built on the spot where Adam and Eve's son Cain murdered his brother Abel (see Genesis 4).
8. It was illegal to draw swords near "privileged" sites, including royal residences. *for all this:* though this is a.
9. A call for a hangman's noose. *Winchester goose:* slang expression for a swelling in the groin caused by venereal disease; a prostitute or a victim of venereal disease.
1. F's stage direction reads: "Cardinal's men." Here, as elsewhere, the Oxford editors have removed the confusion about when Winchester is made a cardinal by assuming him to be a bishop until Act 5.
2. Overburdening your generous purses.

WINCHESTER   Gloucester, we'll meet to thy cost, be sure.
80 Thy heart-blood I will have for this day's work.
MAYOR   I'll call for clubs,[3] if you will not away.
   [*Aside*] This bishop is more haughty than the devil.
GLOUCESTER   Mayor, farewell. Thou dost but what thou mayst.
WINCHESTER   Abominable Gloucester, guard thy head,
85 For I intend to have it ere long.

                      Exeunt [*both factions severally*]°   separately

MAYOR [*to* OFFICERS]   See the coast cleared, and then we will depart.—
   Good God, these nobles should such stomachs° bear!   angry tempers
   I myself fight not once in forty year.   *Exeunt*

1.5

Enter the MASTER GUNNER *of Orléans and his* BOY

MASTER GUNNER   Sirrah,[1] thou know'st how Orléans is besieged,
   And how the English have the suburbs won.
BOY   Father, I know, and oft have shot at them;
   Howe'er, unfortunate, I missed my aim.
5 MASTER GUNNER   But now thou shalt not. Be thou ruled by me.
   Chief Master Gunner am I of this town;
   Something I must do to procure me grace.°   honor
   The Prince's spials° have informèd me   spies
   How the English, in the suburbs close entrenched,
10 Wont,° through a secret grate of iron bars   *Are accustomed*
   In yonder tower, to overpeer the city,
   And thence discover how with most advantage
   They may vex us with shot or with assault.
   To intercept this inconvenience,°   harm
15 A piece of ordnance 'gainst° it I have placed,   directed toward
   And even these three days have I watched, if I could see them.
   Now do thou watch, for I can stay no longer.
   If thou spy'st any, run and bring me word,
   And thou shalt find me at the governor's.
20 BOY   Father, I warrant you, take you no care°—   don't worry

                      Exit [MASTER GUNNER *at one door*]

   I'll never trouble you, if I may spy them.

                      Exit [*at the other door*]

1.6

Enter [*the Earl of*] SALISBURY *and* [*Lord*] TALBOT
[*above*] *on the turrets with others* [*among them*
Sir Thomas GARGRAVE *and Sir William* GLASDALE]

SALISBURY   Talbot, my life, my joy, again returned?
   How wert thou handled, being prisoner?
   Or by what means got'st thou to be released?
   Discourse, I prithee, on this turret's top.
5 TALBOT   The Duke of Bedford had a prisoner,
   Called the brave Lord Ponton de Santrailles;
   For him was I exchanged and ransomèd.

---

3. I'll shout for London apprentices to bring their clubs
and quell this riot. "Prentices and clubs" was a common
rallying cry.
1.5 Location: Orléans.

1. Normally used to address social inferiors, but here
used to address the Master Gunner's young son.
1.6 Location: Tower before the walls of Orléans.

But with a baser man-of-arms° by far   *soldier of lower rank*
Once in contempt they would have bartered me—
10 Which I, disdaining, scorned, and cravèd death
Rather than I would be so pilled esteemed.°   *so cheaply valued*
In fine,° redeemed I was, as I desired.   *In short*
But O, the treacherous Fastolf wounds my heart,
Whom with my bare fists I would execute
15 If I now had him brought into my power.
SALISBURY Yet tell'st thou not how thou wert entertained.°   *treated*
TALBOT With scoffs and scorns and contumelious taunts.
In open market place produced they me,
To be a public spectacle to all.
20 'Here', said they, 'is the terror of the French,
The scarecrow that affrights our children so.'
Then broke I from the officers that led me
And with my nails digged stones out of the ground
To hurl at the beholders of my shame.
25 My grisly countenance made others fly.
None durst come near, for fear of sudden death.
In iron walls they deemed me not secure:
So great fear of my name 'mongst them were spread
That they supposed I could rend bars of steel
30 And spurn° in pieces posts of adamant.[1]   *kick*
Wherefore a guard of chosen shot° I had   *selected marksmen*
That walked about me every minute while;°   *constantly*
And if I did but stir out of my bed,
Ready they were to shoot me to the heart.
The BOY [*passes over the stage*] *with a linstock*[2]
35 SALISBURY I grieve to hear what torments you endured.
But we will be revenged sufficiently.
Now it is supper time in Orléans.
Here, through this grate, I count each one,
And view the Frenchmen how they fortify.
40 Let us look in: the sight will much delight thee.—
Sir Thomas Gargrave and Sir William Glasdale,
Let me have your express° opinions   *precise*
Where is best place to make our batt'ry next.
[*They look through the grate*]
GARGRAVE I think at the north gate, for there stands Lou.°   *fortress of St. Lou*
45 GLASDALE And I here, at the bulwark of the Bridge.
TALBOT For aught I see, this city must be famished°   *starved out*
Or with light skirmishes enfeeblèd.
Here they° *shoot* [*off chambers within*] *and* SALISBURY   *(the French)*
[*and* GARGRAVE] *fall down*
SALISBURY O Lord have mercy on us, wretched sinners!
GARGRAVE O Lord have mercy on me, woeful man!
50 TALBOT What chance is this that suddenly hath crossed us?
Speak, Salisbury—at least, if thou canst, speak.
How far'st thou, mirror° of all martial men?   *best example*
One of thy eyes and thy cheek's side struck off?

---

1. A legendary stony substance said to be impregnable.
2. F's stage direction reads: "Enter the Boy with a linstock." He probably does not stay onstage, however, but
passes from one side to the other on his way to light the

charge that will strike down Salisbury and Gargrave.
linstock: a stick used to hold a lighted match or torch
for firing cannon.

Accursèd tower! Accursèd fatal hand
55 That hath contrived this woeful tragedy!
In thirteen battles Salisbury o'ercame;
Henry the Fifth he first trained to the wars;
Whilst any trump did sound or drum struck up
His sword did ne'er leave striking in the field.
60 Yet liv'st thou, Salisbury? Though thy speech doth fail,
One eye thou hast to look to heaven for grace.
The sun with one eye vieweth all the world.
Heaven, be thou gracious to none alive
If Salisbury wants° mercy at thy hands.—   lacks
65 Sir Thomas Gargrave, hast thou any life?
Speak unto Talbot. Nay, look up to him.—
Bear hence his body; I will help to bury it.

                    [*Exit one with Gargrave's body*]
Salisbury, cheer thy spirit with this comfort:
Thou shalt not die whiles°—   until
70 He beckons with his hand, and smiles on me,
As who should say, 'When I am dead and gone,
Remember to avenge me on the French.'
Plantagenet, I will—and like thee, Nero,[3]
Play on the lute, beholding the towns burn.
75 Wretched shall France be only in° my name.   at the mere sound of

                    Here an alarum, and it thunders and lightens
What stir is this? What tumult's in the heavens?
Whence cometh this alarum and the noise?

                    Enter a MESSENGER

MESSENGER   My lord, my lord, the French have gathered head.°   assembled an army
The Dauphin, with one Joan la Pucelle joined,
80 A holy prophetess new risen up,
Is come with a great power° to raise the siege.   army

                    Here SALISBURY *lifteth himself up and groans*

TALBOT   Hear, hear, how dying Salisbury doth groan!
It irks his heart he cannot be revenged.
Frenchmen, I'll be a Salisbury to you.
85 *Pucelle* or pucelle,[4] Dauphin or dog-fish,[5]
Your hearts I'll stamp out with my horse's heels
And make a quagmire of your mingled brains.—
Convey me° Salisbury into his tent,   for me
And then we'll try what these dastard Frenchmen dare.

                    Alarum. Exeunt [*carrying* SALISBURY]

1.7

                    Here an alarum again, and [*Lord*] TALBOT *pursueth the*
                    Dauphin and driveth him. Then enter JOAN [*la*] *Pucelle*
                    driving Englishmen before her [*and exeunt*]. *Then enter*
                    [*Lord*] TALBOT

TALBOT   Where is my strength, my valour, and my force?
Our English troops retire; I cannot stay them.
A woman clad in armour chaseth men.

---

3. Talbot here compares himself with Nero, the emperor who played music while he watched Rome burn. Salisbury was a descendant of the Plantagenet dynasty, which ruled England from 1154 to 1485.
4. Talbot puns on the French word for "virgin" (*pucelle*),

which sounds like the English slang for "slut" ("puzzel").
5. Punning on the Elizabethan spelling of "dauphin" as "dolphin": hence the taunt that the Dauphin is a "dog-fish."
1.7 Location: In and before Orléans.

Enter [JOAN *la*] *Pucelle*

Here, here she comes. [*To* JOAN] I'll have a bout¹ with thee.

5   Devil or devil's dam,° I'll conjure thee.   *mother*
Blood will I draw on thee—thou art a witch²—
And straightway give thy soul to him thou serv'st.

JOAN   Come, come, 'tis only I that must disgrace thee.
        Here they fight

TALBOT   Heavens, can you suffer hell so to prevail?

10   My breast I'll burst with straining of my courage°   *vital energy*
And from my shoulders crack my arms asunder
But I will° chastise this high-minded° strumpet.   *If I do not / arrogant*
        They fight again

JOAN   Talbot, farewell. Thy hour is not yet come.
I must go victual° Orléans forthwith.   *supply with provisions*
        A short alarum, then [*the French pass over the stage*
        and] *enter the town with soldiers*

15   O'ertake me if thou canst. I scorn thy strength.
Go, go, cheer up thy hungry-starvèd° men.   *starving to death*
Help Salisbury to make his testament.
This day is ours, as many more shall be.   *Exit* [*into the town*]

TALBOT   My thoughts are whirlèd like a potter's wheel.

20   I know not where I am nor what I do.
A witch by fear, not force, like Hannibal³
Drives back our troops and conquers as she lists.
So bees with smoke and doves with noisome° stench   *noxious*
Are from their hives and houses driven away.

25   They called us, for our fierceness, English dogs;
Now, like to whelps, we crying run away.
        A short alarum. [*Enter English soldiers*]
Hark, countrymen: either renew the fight
Or tear the lions out of England's coat.°   *coat of arms*
Renounce your style;° give sheep in lions' stead.⁴   *distinguishing mark*

30   Sheep run not half so treacherous° from the wolf,   *cowardly*
Or horse or oxen from the leopard,
As you fly from your oft-subduèd slaves.
        Alarum. Here another skirmish
It will not be. Retire into your trenches.
You all consented unto Salisbury's death,

35   For none would strike a stroke in his revenge.°   *in revenge of his death*
Pucelle is entered into Orléans
In spite of us or aught that we could do.   [*Exeunt Soldiers*]
O would I were to die with Salisbury!
The shame hereof will make me hide my head.
        *Exit. Alarum. Retreat*⁵

1.8

Flourish. Enter on the walls [JOAN *la*] *Pucelle,* [CHARLES
the] *Dauphin,* RENÉ [*Duke of Anjou, the Duke of*]
ALENÇON *and* [*French*] *Soldiers* [*with colours*]

JOAN   Advance° our waving colours on the walls;   *Raise*
Rescued is Orléans from the English.

---

1. Fight; sexual encounter. Much of the speech to and about Joan has sexual overtones.
2. Whoever drew blood from a witch was supposed to be protected from her magic.
3. The Carthaginian military leader who once put to flight his Roman enemies by tying firebrands to the horns of two thousand oxen.
4. Display (on your coat of arms) sheep instead of lions.
5. A trumpet call to signal a retreat.
1.8 Location: Scene continues.

Thus Joan la Pucelle hath performed her word.
CHARLES Divinest creature, Astraea's[1] daughter,
5   How shall I honour thee for this success?
Thy promises are like Adonis' garden,[2]
That one day bloomed and fruitful were the next.
France, triumph in thy glorious prophetess!
Recovered is the town of Orléans.
10 More blessèd hap° did ne'er befall our state.   event
RENÉ Why ring not out the bells aloud throughout the town?
Dauphin, command the citizens make bonfires
And feast and banquet in the open streets
To celebrate the joy that God hath given us.
15 ALENÇON All France will be replete with mirth and joy
When they shall hear how we have played the men.°   acted like men
CHARLES 'Tis Joan, not we, by whom the day is won—
For which I will divide my crown with her,
And all the priests and friars in my realm
20 Shall in procession sing her endless praise.
A statelier pyramid to her I'll rear
Than Rhodope's[3] of Memphis ever was.
In memory of her, when she is dead
Her ashes, in an urn more precious
25 Than the rich-jewelled coffer of Darius,[4]
Transported shall be at high festivals
Before the kings and queens of France.
No longer on Saint Denis° will we cry,   patron saint of France
But Joan la Pucelle shall be France's saint.
30 Come in, and let us banquet royally
After this golden day of victory.

Flourish. Exeunt

2.1

Enter [on the walls] a [French] SERGEANT *of a band,
with two* SENTINELS

SERGEANT Sirs, take your places and be vigilant.
If any noise or soldier you perceive
Near to the walls, by some apparent° sign   obvious
Let us have knowledge at the court of guard.°   guardroom
A SENTINEL Sergeant, you shall.   [*Exit* SERGEANT]
5   Thus are poor servitors,
When others sleep upon their quiet beds,
Constrained to watch in darkness, rain, and cold.

Enter [Lord] TALBOT, *[the Dukes of]* BEDFORD *and* BUR-
GUNDY *[and soldiers], with scaling ladders, their drums
beating a dead march*[1]

TALBOT Lord regent, and redoubted° Burgundy—   distinguished
By whose approach the regions of Artois,
10 Wallon, and Picardy are friends to us[2]—

---

1. Greek goddess of justice; she lived on earth during the Golden Age but fled to the heavens during the corruption of the Iron Age. Queen Elizabeth I was often compared to Astraea.
2. A mythical garden noted for its fertility and described by Spenser in *The Faerie Queene*.
3. A Greek courtesan who married the King of Memphis (city in Egypt) and reputedly built the third pyramid.
4. A jeweled treasure chest that Alexander allegedly won from the Persian King Darius III and used to store the works of Homer.
2.1 Location: In and before Orléans.
1. Either a funeral march for Salisbury or the muffled march that signifies a secret attack.
2. *By . . . us*: during Henry V's reign, the Duke of Burgundy became an English ally and won support for the English from the French and Netherlandish regions to which Talbot refers.

This happy night the Frenchmen are secure,°   *overconfident*
Having all day caroused and banqueted.
Embrace we then this opportunity,
As fitting best to quittance° their deceit,   *repay*
15   Contrived by art° and baleful sorcery.   *craftiness*

BEDFORD   Coward of France!³ How much he wrongs his fame,°   *reputation*
Despairing of his own arms' fortitude,
To join with witches and the help of hell.

BURGUNDY   Traitors have never other company.
20   But what's that 'Pucelle' whom they term so pure?

TALBOT   A maid, they say.

BEDFORD   A maid? And be so martial?

BURGUNDY   Pray God she prove not masculine ere long.⁴
If underneath the standard of the French⁵
She carry armour⁶ as she hath begun—

25 TALBOT   Well, let them practise and converse⁷ with spirits.
God is our fortress, in whose conquering name
Let us resolve to scale their flinty bulwarks.

BEDFORD   Ascend, brave Talbot. We will follow thee.

TALBOT   Not all together. Better far, I guess,
30   That we do make our entrance several ways—
That, if it chance the one of us do fail,
The other yet may rise against their force.⁸

BEDFORD   Agreed. I'll to yon corner.

BURGUNDY   And I to this.

[Exeunt severally BEDFORD *and* BURGUNDY
*with some soldiers]*⁹

TALBOT   And here will Talbot mount, or make his grave.
35   Now, Salisbury, for thee, and for the right
Of English Henry, shall this night appear
How much in duty I am bound to both.

*[*TALBOT *and his soldiers scale the walls]*

SENTINELS   Arm! Arm! The enemy doth make assault!

ENGLISH SOLDIERS   Saint George! A Talbot!¹   *[Exeunt above.]*

*[Alarum.] The French [soldiers] leap o'er the walls in
their shirts [and exeunt]. Enter several ways [the]*
BASTARD *[of Orléans, the Duke of]* ALENÇON, *[and]* RENÉ
*[Duke of Anjou], half ready and half unready*²

40 ALENÇON   How now, my lords? What, all unready so?

BASTARD   Unready? Ay, and glad we scaped so well.

RENÉ   'Twas time, I trow,° to wake and leave our beds,   *believe*
Hearing alarums at our chamber doors.

ALENÇON   Of all exploits since first I followed arms
45   Ne'er heard I of a warlike enterprise
More venturous or desperate than this.

---

3. The Dauphin.
4. She does not turn out to be a man; she does not turn out to be carrying a male child. The following lines are full of sexual innuendoes.
5. French ensign; French penis.
6. Wear armor; bear the weight of an armed man (in intercourse).
7. Scheme and talk; have sex and be intimate.
8. May scale the walls despite French resistance.
9. The staging of this scene is complex. Bedford and Burgundy may stay onstage and attack different parts of the tiring-house wall, or, as here, they may exit in several directions and fight offstage.

1. To Talbot. This cry is included in the actual stage directions in F, but here it is assigned to nameless "English soldiers" (see also line 79).
2. In this complicated piece of stage business, Talbot's men ascend ladders to the upper stage, which represents the walls of Orléans. They there surprise French soldiers, some of whom leap down from the upper to the lower stage as if fleeing from Orléans. On the lower stage, the fleeing and defeated French nobles debate their plight. *half ready and half unready*: half dressed and half undressed.

BASTARD   I think this Talbot be a fiend of hell.

RENÉ   If not of hell, the heavens sure favour him.

ALENÇON   Here cometh Charles. I marvel how he sped.°   *fared*

    Enter CHARLES [*the Dauphin*] *and* JOAN [*la Pucelle*]

50 BASTARD   Tut, holy Joan³ was his defensive guard.

CHARLES [*to* JOAN]   Is this thy cunning,° thou deceitful dame?   *skill; sorcery*

    Didst thou at first, to flatter us withal,

    Make us partakers of a little gain

    That now our loss might be ten times so much?

55 JOAN   Wherefore is Charles impatient with his friend?

    At all times will you have my power alike?

    Sleeping or waking must I still prevail,

    Or will you blame and lay the fault on me?—

    Improvident° soldiers, had your watch been good,   *Negligent*

60   This sudden mischief never could have fall'n.

CHARLES   Duke of Alençon, this was your default,

    That, being captain of the watch tonight,

    Did look no better to that weighty charge.

ALENÇON   Had all your quarters been as safely kept

65   As that whereof I had the government,

    We had not been thus shamefully surprised.

BASTARD   Mine was secure.

RENÉ   And so was mine, my lord.

CHARLES   And for myself, most part of all this night

    Within her° quarter and mine own precinct   *(Joan's)*

70   I was employed in passing to and fro

    About relieving of the sentinels.

    Then how or which way should they first break in?

JOAN   Question, my lords, no further of the case,

    How or which way. 'Tis sure they found some place

75   But weakly guarded, where the breach was made.

    And now there rests° no other shift° but this—   *remains / device*

    To gather our soldiers, scattered and dispersed,

    And lay new platforms° to endamage them.   *plots; schemes*

    Alarum. Enter [*an* ENGLISH] SOLDIER

ENGLISH SOLDIER   A Talbot! A Talbot!

    They [*the French*] *fly, leaving their clothes behind*

80 ENGLISH SOLDIER   I'll be so bold to take what they have left.

    The cry of 'Talbot' serves me for a sword,

    For I have loaden me with many spoils,

    Using no other weapon but his name.   *Exit* [*with spoils*]

2.2

    Enter [*Lord*] TALBOT, [*the Dukes of*] BEDFORD [*and*]

    BURGUNDY [*a* CAPTAIN, *and soldiers*]

BEDFORD   The day begins to break and night is fled,

    Whose pitchy mantle overveiled the earth.

    Here sound retreat and cease our hot pursuit.

    Retreat [*is sounded*]

TALBOT   Bring forth the body of old Salisbury

5   And here advance it° in the market place,   *raise it up (on a bier)*

---

3. A reference to her sexual availability; "hole" was   **2.2 Location:** Within Orléans.
slang for "vagina."

The middle centre of this cursèd town.   [*Exit one or more*]
Now have I paid my vow unto his soul:
For every drop of blood was° drawn from him   *that was*
There hath at least five Frenchmen died tonight.
10 And that hereafter ages may behold
What ruin happened in revenge of him,
Within their chiefest temple I'll erect
A tomb, wherein his corpse shall be interred—
Upon the which, that everyone may read,
15 Shall be engraved the sack of Orléans,
The treacherous manner of his mournful death,
And what a terror he had been to France.
But, lords, in all our bloody massacre
I muse° we met not with the Dauphin's grace,   *wonder*
20 His new-come champion, virtuous[1] Joan of Arc,
Nor any of his false confederates.
BEDFORD   'Tis thought, Lord Talbot, when the fight began,
Roused on the sudden from their drowsy beds,
They did amongst the troops of armèd men
25 Leap o'er the walls for refuge in the field.
BURGUNDY   Myself, as far as I could well discern
For smoke and dusky vapours of the night,
Am sure I scared the Dauphin and his trull,°   *whore*
When arm-in-arm they both came swiftly running,
30 Like to a pair of loving turtle-doves
That could not live asunder day or night.
After that things are set in order here,
We'll follow them with all the power we have.
        Enter a MESSENGER
MESSENGER   All hail, my lords! Which of this princely train
35 Call ye the warlike Talbot, for his acts
So much applauded through the realm of France?
TALBOT   Here is the Talbot. Who would speak with him?
MESSENGER   The virtuous lady, Countess of Auvergne,
With modesty admiring thy renown,
40 By me entreats, great lord, thou wouldst vouchsafe
To visit her poor castle where she lies,°   *dwells*
That she may boast she hath beheld the man
Whose glory fills the world with loud report.°   *acclaim; din of war*
BURGUNDY   Is it even so? Nay, then I see our wars
45 Will turn unto a peaceful comic sport,
When ladies crave to be encountered with.
You may not, my lord, despise her gentle suit.°   *well-bred request*
TALBOT   Ne'er trust me then, for when a world of men
Could not prevail with all their oratory,
50 Yet hath a woman's kindness overruled.—
And therefore tell her I return great thanks,
And in submission will attend on her.—
Will not your honours bear me company?
BEDFORD   No, truly, 'tis more than manners will.°   *etiquette allows*
55 And I have heard it said, 'Unbidden guests

___

1. Full of virtue or manly courage; chaste (said ironically).

Are often welcomest when they are gone'.

TALBOT Well then, alone—since there's no remedy—
I mean to prove° this lady's courtesy.   *test*
Come hither, captain.

[*He*] *whispers*

You perceive my mind?

60 CAPTAIN I do, my lord, and mean° accordingly.   *intend to act*

Exeunt [*severally*]

2.3

Enter [*the*] COUNTESS [*of Auvergne and her* PORTER]

COUNTESS Porter, remember what I gave in charge,°   *I commanded*
And when you have done so, bring the keys to me.

PORTER Madam, I will.   *Exit*

COUNTESS The plot is laid. If all things fall out right,
5   I shall as famous be by this exploit
As Scythian Tomyris[1] by Cyrus' death.
Great is the rumour° of this dreadful° knight,   *fame / fear-inspiring*
And his achievements of no less account.
Fain° would mine eyes be witness with mine ears,   *Gladly*
10 To give their censure° of these rare° reports.   *opinion / remarkable*

Enter MESSENGER *and* [*Lord*] TALBOT

MESSENGER Madam, according as your ladyship desired,
By message craved, so is Lord Talbot come.

COUNTESS And he is welcome. What, is this the man?

MESSENGER Madam, it is.

COUNTESS   Is this the scourge[2] of France?
15 Is this the Talbot, so much feared abroad
That with his name the mothers still their babes?
I see report is fabulous and false.
I thought I should have seen some Hercules,[3]
A second Hector,[4] for his grim aspect°   *appearance*
20 And large proportion of his strong-knit limbs.
Alas, this is a child, a seely° dwarf.   *feeble*
It cannot be this weak and writhled° shrimp   *wrinkled*
Should strike such terror to his enemies.

TALBOT Madam, I have been bold to trouble you.
25 But since your ladyship is not at leisure,
I'll sort some other time to visit you.

[*He is going*]

COUNTESS [*to* MESSENGER] What means he now? Go ask him
whither he goes.

MESSENGER Stay, my Lord Talbot, for my lady craves
To know the cause of your abrupt departure.

30 TALBOT Marry,[5] for that° she's in a wrong belief,   *because*
I go to certify her Talbot's here.

Enter PORTER *with keys*

COUNTESS If thou be he, then art thou prisoner.

TALBOT Prisoner? To whom?

2.3 Location: The Countess's castle, Auvergne.
1. Asian queen who, in revenge for her son's death,
killed the Persian King Cyrus and kept his head in a
wineskin filled with human blood.
2. Individual sent by God to punish sin. Joan describes

herself as "the English scourge" at 1.3.108.
3. Mythical hero famous for his immense strength.
4. Greatest of the Trojan warriors, celebrated in Homer's
Iliad.
5. By the Virgin Mary, a mild oath.

COUNTESS   To me, bloodthirsty lord;
And for that cause I trained° thee to my house.   *enticed*

35   Long time thy shadow° hath been thrall° to me,   *image / slave*
    For in my gallery thy picture hangs;
    But now the substance shall endure the like,
    And I will chain these legs and arms of thine
    That hast by tyranny these many years

40   Wasted our country, slain our citizens,
    And sent our sons and husbands captive°—   *into captivity*

TALBOT   Ha, ha, ha!

COUNTESS   Laughest thou, wretch? Thy mirth shall turn to moan.

TALBOT   I laugh to see your ladyship so fond°   *foolish*

45   To think that you have aught but Talbot's shadow
    Whereon to practise your severity.

COUNTESS   Why? Art not thou the man?

TALBOT   I am indeed.

COUNTESS   Then have I substance too.

50 TALBOT   No, no, I am but shadow of myself.
    You are deceived; my substance is not here.
    For what you see is but the smallest part
    And least proportion of humanity.[6]
    I tell you, madam, were the whole frame[7] here,

55   It is of such a spacious lofty pitch°   *height*
    Your roof were not sufficient to contain't.

COUNTESS   This is a riddling merchant for the nonce.[8]
    He will be here, and yet he is not here.
    How can these contrarieties agree?

60 TALBOT   That will I show you presently.°   *immediately*
    [*He*] *winds*° *his horn.* [*Within,*] *drums strike up; a peal*   *blows*
    of ordnance. Enter [*English*] *soldiers*
    How say you, madam? Are you now persuaded
    That Talbot is but shadow of himself?
    These are his substance, sinews, arms, and strength,
    With which he yoketh your rebellious necks,

65   Razeth your cities and subverts° your towns,   *overthrows*
    And in a moment makes them desolate.

COUNTESS   Victorious Talbot, pardon my abuse.°   *error; deception*
    I find thou art no less than fame hath bruited,°   *proclaimed*
    And more than may be gathered by thy shape.

70   Let my presumption not provoke thy wrath,
    For I am sorry that with reverence
    I did not entertain° thee as thou art.   *receive*

TALBOT   Be not dismayed, fair lady, nor misconster°   *misconstrue*
    The mind of Talbot, as you did mistake

75   The outward composition of his body.
    What you have done hath not offended me;
    Nor other satisfaction do I crave
    But only, with your patience,° that we may   *permission*
    Taste of your wine and see what cates° you have: *delicacies*

80   For soldiers' stomachs always serve them well.

---

6. Smallest part of the whole man (and, by implication, of the whole army that constitutes Talbot's military presence).
7. The entire structure of my body (and of my army).
8. This is a dealer in riddles as occasion requires.

COUNTESS   With all my heart; and think me honourèd
To feast so great a warrior in my house.   *Exeunt*

2.4

[*A rose brier.*] *Enter* RICHARD PLANTAGENET, [*the Earl*
of] WARWICK, [*the Duke of*] SOMERSET, [*William de la*]
Pole [*the Earl of* SUFFOLK], *and others* [VERNON, *and a*
LAWYER]

RICHARD PLANTAGENET   Great lords and gentlemen, what
    means this silence?
Dare no man answer in a case of truth?
SUFFOLK   Within the Temple hall we were° too loud.   would have been
    The garden here is more convenient.
5 RICHARD PLANTAGENET   Then say at once if I maintained the truth;
    Or else was wrangling Somerset in th'error?
SUFFOLK   Faith, I have been a truant° in the law,   neglectful of study
    And never yet could frame° my will to it,   adapt
    And therefore frame the law unto my will.
10 SOMERSET   Judge you, my lord of Warwick, then between us.
WARWICK   Between two hawks, which flies the higher pitch,°   height
    Between two dogs, which hath the deeper mouth,°   voice
    Between two blades, which bears the better temper,[1]
    Between two horses, which doth bear him best,
15   Between two girls, which hath the merriest eye,
    I have perhaps some shallow spirit of judgement;
    But in these nice° sharp quillets° of the law,   precise / distinctions
    Good faith, I am no wiser than a daw.[2]
RICHARD PLANTAGENET   Tut, tut, here is a mannerly forbearance.
20   The truth appears so naked on my side
    That any purblind° eye may find it out.   half-blind
SOMERSET   And on my side it is so well apparelled,
    So clear, so shining, and so evident,
    That it will glimmer through a blind man's eye.
25 RICHARD PLANTAGENET   Since you are tongue-tied and so loath to speak,
    In dumb significants° proclaim your thoughts.   silent gestures
    Let him that is a true-born gentleman
    And stands upon the honour of his birth,
    If he suppose that I have pleaded truth,[3]
30   From off this briar pluck a white rose[4] with me.
        [*He plucks a white rose*].
SOMERSET   Let him that is no coward nor no flatterer,
    But dare maintain the party° of the truth,   side
    Pluck a red rose[5] from off this thorn with me.
        [*He plucks a red rose*]

2.4 Location: The Temple Garden, near the Middle
and Inner Temple, two buildings that housed the London law schools known as the Inns of Court.
1. *the better temper:* this refers to the degree of hardness attained by a steel sword blade when it is tempered
(that is, heated to a required temperature and then
plunged into cold liquid).
2. Jackdaw (a proverbially stupid bird).
3. Presented the case for truth according to proper
procedures. (This scene contains many legal terms.)

4. Badge of the House of York. In the mid-fifteenth
century, two branches of the Plantagenet dynasty, the
Yorkists and the Lancastrians, fought what was termed
the Wars of the Roses over who would hold the English
throne. Shakespeare invented this scene to provide a
point of origin for the quarrel that grew into the civil
wars he depicted in his plays on the reigns of Henry VI,
Edward IV, and Richard III.
5. Badge of the House of Lancaster.

WARWICK   I love no colours,° and without all colour   *hues; pretenses*
35   Of base insinuating flattery
     I pluck this white rose with Plantagenet.
SUFFOLK   I pluck this red rose with young Somerset,
     And say withal° I think he held the right.   *besides*
VERNON   Stay, lords and gentlemen, and pluck no more
40   Till you conclude that he upon whose side
     The fewest roses from the tree are cropped
     Shall yield° the other in the right opinion.   *concede*
SOMERSET   Good Master Vernon, it is well objected.°   *urged*
     If I have fewest, I subscribe° in silence.   *submit*
45 RICHARD PLANTAGENET   And I.
VERNON   Then for the truth and plainness of the case
     I pluck this pale and maiden blossom here,
     Giving my verdict on the white rose' side.
SOMERSET   Prick not your finger as you pluck it off,
50   Lest, bleeding, you do paint the white rose red,
     And fall on my side so against your will.
VERNON   If I, my lord, for my opinion° bleed,   *conviction*
     Opinion° shall be surgeon to my hurt   *Reputation*
     And keep me on the side where still I am.
55 SOMERSET   Well, well, come on! Who else?
LAWYER   Unless my study and my books be false,
     The argument you held was wrong in law;
     In sign whereof I pluck a white rose too.
RICHARD PLANTAGENET   Now Somerset, where is your argument?
60 SOMERSET   Here in my scabbard, meditating that°   *thinking of what*
     Shall dye your white rose in a bloody red.
RICHARD PLANTAGENET   Meantime your cheeks do counterfeit° our roses,   *imitate*
     For pale they look with fear, as witnessing
     The truth on our side.
SOMERSET   No, Plantagenet,
65   'Tis not for fear, but anger, that thy cheeks
     Blush for pure shame to counterfeit our roses,
     And yet thy tongue will not confess thy error.
RICHARD PLANTAGENET   Hath not thy rose a canker,° Somerset?   *cankerworm; grub*
SOMERSET   Hath not thy rose a thorn, Plantagenet?
70 RICHARD PLANTAGENET   Ay, sharp and piercing, to maintain his° truth,   *its*
     Whiles thy consuming canker eats his falsehood.
SOMERSET   Well, I'll find friends to wear my bleeding roses,
     That shall maintain what I have said is true,
     Where false Plantagenet dare not be seen.
75 RICHARD PLANTAGENET   Now, by this maiden blossom in my hand,
     I scorn thee and thy fashion,° peevish boy.   *sort*
SUFFOLK   Turn not thy scorns this way, Plantagenet.
RICHARD PLANTAGENET   Proud Pole,[6] I will, and scorn both him
       and thee.
SUFFOLK   I'll turn my part thereof into thy throat.[7]
80 SOMERSET   Away, away, good William de la Pole.

---

6. The Duke of Suffolk's family name.   7. I'll throw the slanders back into your throat.

We grace° the yeoman[8] by conversing with him.   *do honor to*
WARWICK   Now, by God's will, thou wrong'st him, Somerset.
    His grandfather was Lionel Duke of Clarence,
    Third son to the third Edward, King of England.[9]
85   Spring crestless° yeomen from so deep a root?   *without a coat of arms*
RICHARD PLANTAGENET   He bears him on the place's privilege,[1]
    Or durst not for his craven° heart say thus.   *cowardly*
SOMERSET   By him that made me, I'll maintain my words
    On any plot of ground in Christendom.
90   Was not thy father, Richard Earl of Cambridge,
    For treason executed in our late king's days?
    And by his treason stand'st not thou attainted,[2]
    Corrupted, and exempt° from ancient gentry?   *excluded*
    His trespass yet lives guilty in thy blood,
95   And till thou be restored[3] thou art a yeoman.
RICHARD PLANTAGENET   My father was attachèd, not attainted;[4]
    Condemned to die for treason, but no traitor—
    And that I'll prove on better men than Somerset,
    Were growing time once ripened to my will.[5]
100   For your partaker° Pole, and you yourself,   *As for your ally*
    I'll note you in my book of memory,
    To scourge you for this apprehension.°   *opinion*
    Look to it well, and say you are well warned.
SOMERSET   Ah, thou shalt find us ready for thee still,
105   And know us by these colours for thy foes,
    For these my friends, in spite of° thee, shall wear.   *in contempt of*
RICHARD PLANTAGENET   And, by my soul, this pale and angry rose,
    As cognizance° of my blood-drinking hate,   *an emblem*
    Will I forever, and my faction, wear
110   Until it wither with me to my grave,
    Or flourish to the height of my degree.°   *noble rank*
SUFFOLK   Go forward, and be choked with thy ambition.
    And so farewell until I meet thee next.   *Exit*
SOMERSET   Have with thee,° Pole.—Farewell, ambitious Richard.   *Let us go*
    Exit
115 RICHARD PLANTAGENET   How I am braved,° and must perforce endure it!   *insulted*
WARWICK   This blot that they object° against your house   *allege*
    Shall be wiped out in the next parliament,
    Called for the truce of° Winchester and Gloucester.   *to make peace between*
    An if° thou be not then created York,   *An if=If*
120   I will not live to be accounted Warwick.
    Meantime, in signal of my love to thee,

8. A man, below the rank of gentleman, holding a small estate. (Richard Plantagenet lost his lands and titles when Henry V executed his father, Richard, Earl of Cambridge, for treason.)
9. Clarence was actually Richard's great-great-grandfather on his mother's side. Edmund, Duke of York, fifth son of Edward III, was his paternal grandfather; thus Richard could trace his descent from Edward III through both his mother and his father.
1. He takes advantage of the safety provided by a privileged place. Quarreling with drawn weapons was prohibited in some precincts, but the Temple, though

originally founded as a religious house, was not one of them.
2. Condemned for treason. One so convicted lost his estate and property. His blood was declared "corrupted" (see line 93), so he could neither inherit nor transmit property and titles.
3. Are given back your lands and titles.
4. Was arrested, not convicted. Plantagenet implies that his father's execution was illegal because there was no parliamentary bill of attainder.
5. If the unfolding of time brings me my desire.

Against proud Somerset and William Pole,
Will I upon thy party wear this rose.
And here I prophesy: this brawl today,
125 Grown to this faction° in the Temple garden,   *conflict*
Shall send, between the red rose and the white,
A thousand souls to death and deadly night.

RICHARD PLANTAGENET   Good Master Vernon, I am bound to you,
That you on my behalf would pluck a flower.
130 VERNON   In your behalf still will I wear the same.
LAWYER   And so will I.
RICHARD PLANTAGENET   Thanks, gentles.
Come, let us four to dinner. I dare say
This quarrel will drink blood another day.

                   Exeunt. [The rose brier is removed]

2.5

Enter [Edmund] MORTIMER, *brought in a chair*
[by his KEEPERS]*[1]*

MORTIMER   Kind keepers of my weak decaying age,
Let dying Mortimer here rest himself.
Even like a man new-halèd° from the rack,[2]   *newly dragged*
So fare my limbs with long imprisonment;
5 And these grey locks, the pursuivants° of death,   *heralds*
Argue the end of Edmund Mortimer,[3]
Nestor-like[4] agèd in an age of care.
These eyes, like lamps whose wasting oil is spent,
Wax dim, as drawing to their exigent;°   *end*
10 Weak shoulders, overborne with burdening grief,
And pithless° arms, like to a withered vine   *strengthless*
That droops his° sapless branches to the ground.   *its*
Yet are these feet—whose strengthless stay° is numb,   *support*
Unable to support this lump of clay—
15 Swift-wingèd with desire to get a grave,
As witting° I no other comfort have.   *knowing*
But tell me, keeper, will my nephew come?
KEEPER   Richard Plantagenet, my lord, will come.
We sent unto the Temple, unto his chamber,
20 And answer was returned that he will come.
MORTIMER   Enough. My soul shall then be satisfied.
Poor gentleman, his wrong° doth equal mine.   *(wrong done to him)*
Since Henry Monmouth° first began to reign—   *(Henry V)*
Before whose glory I was great in arms—
25 This loathsome sequestration° have I had;   *imprisonment*

2.5 Location: A cell in the Tower of London.
1. F's stage direction reads: "Enter Mortimer, brought
in in a Chair and Jailors."
2. Instrument of torture on which the victim's body
was stretched.
3. As in the sources that Shakespeare probably used,
several historical Mortimers are conflated here. In
1385, Richard II declared Roger Mortimer, fourth
Earl of March, his heir. When Roger died in battle in

1398, his claim passed to Edmund Mortimer, fifth
Earl of March and uncle of Richard Plantagenet, who
in turn inherited the Mortimer claim to the throne. It
was Edmund's cousin Sir John Mortimer, however,
who lay imprisoned in the Tower until 1424, when he
was executed for advocating Edmund's claim to the
throne.
4. Like Nestor, the aged Homeric hero and adviser
famous for his wisdom.

And even since then hath Richard been obscured,
Deprived of honour and inheritance.
But now the arbitrator of despairs,
Just Death, kind umpire of men's miseries,
30 With sweet enlargement° doth dismiss me hence.   release
I would his° troubles likewise were expired,   (Richard's)
That so he might recover what was lost.
            Enter RICHARD [PLANTAGENET]
KEEPER   My lord, your loving nephew now is come.
MORTIMER   Richard Plantagenet, my friend, is he come?
35 RICHARD PLANTAGENET   Ay, noble uncle, thus ignobly used:
Your nephew, late° despisèd Richard, comes.   recently
MORTIMER [*to* KEEPERS]   Direct mine arms I may embrace his neck
And in his bosom spend my latter° gasp.   final
O tell me when my lips do touch his cheeks,
40 That I may kindly give one fainting kiss.
            [*He embraces* RICHARD]
And now declare, sweet stem from York's great stock,°   trunk
Why didst thou say of late thou wert despised?
RICHARD PLANTAGENET   First lean thine agèd back against mine arm,
And in that ease I'll tell thee my dis-ease.°   trouble
45 This day in argument upon a case
Some words there grew 'twixt Somerset and me;
Among which terms he used his lavish tongue
And did upbraid me with my father's death;
Which obloquy° set bars before my tongue,   disgrace
50 Else with the like I had requited him.
Therefore, good uncle, for my father's sake,
In honour of a true Plantagenet,
And for alliance'° sake, declare the cause   kinship's
My father, Earl of Cambridge, lost his head.
55 MORTIMER   That cause, fair nephew, that imprisoned me,
And hath detained me all my flow'ring youth
Within a loathsome dungeon, there to pine,
Was cursèd instrument of his decease.
RICHARD PLANTAGENET   Discover° more at large what cause that was,   Explain
60 For I am ignorant and cannot guess.
MORTIMER   I will, if that my fading breath permit
And death approach not ere my tale be done.
Henry the Fourth, grandfather to this King,
Deposed his nephew° Richard, Edward's son,   kinsman (here, cousin)
65 The first begotten and the lawful heir
Of Edward king, the third of that descent;
During whose° reign the Percies of the north,   (Henry IV's)
Finding his usurpation most unjust,
Endeavoured my advancement to the throne.
70 The reason moved° these warlike lords to this   that moved
Was for that°—young King Richard thus removed,   Was because
Leaving no heir begotten of his body—
I was the next° by birth and parentage,   (in line for the throne)
For by my mother I derivèd° am   descended
75 From Lionel Duke of Clarence, the third son
To King Edward the Third—whereas the King
From John of Gaunt doth bring his pedigree,

Being but fourth of that heroic line.
But mark: as in this haughty° great attempt   *lofty*
80 They laboured to plant the rightful heir,
I lost my liberty, and they their lives.
Long after this, when Henry the Fifth,
Succeeding his father Bolingbroke, did reign,
Thy father, Earl of Cambridge then, derived
85 From famous Edmund Langley, Duke of York,
Marrying my sister that thy mother was,
Again, in pity of my hard distress,
Levied an army, weening° to redeem   *intending*
And have installed me in the diadem;°   *crown*
90 But, as the rest, so fell that noble earl,
And was beheaded. Thus the Mortimers,
In whom the title rested, were suppressed.
RICHARD PLANTAGENET Of which, my lord, your honour is the last.
MORTIMER True, and thou seest that I no issue have,
95 And that my fainting words do warrant° death.   *promise*
Thou art my heir. The rest I wish thee gather°—   *infer*
But yet be wary in thy studious° care.   *diligent*
RICHARD PLANTAGENET Thy grave admonishments prevail with me.
But yet methinks my father's execution
100 Was nothing less than bloody tyranny.
MORTIMER With silence, nephew, be thou politic.°   *prudent*
Strong-fixèd is the house of Lancaster,
And like a mountain, not to be removed.
But now thy uncle is removing° hence,   *departing*
105 As princes do their courts, when they are cloyed°   *sickened*
With long continuance in a settled place.
RICHARD PLANTAGENET O uncle, would some part of my young years
Might but redeem the passage of your age.
MORTIMER Thou dost then wrong me, as that slaughterer doth
110 Which giveth many wounds when one will kill.
Mourn not, except° thou sorrow for my good.   *unless*
Only give order for my funeral.
And so farewell, and fair be all thy hopes,
And prosperous be thy life in peace and war. *Dies*
115 RICHARD PLANTAGENET And peace, no war, befall thy parting soul.
In prison hast thou spent a pilgrimage,
And like a hermit overpassed° thy days.   *spent*
Well, I will lock his counsel in my breast,
And what I do imagine, let that rest.
120 Keepers, convey him hence, and I myself
Will see his burial better than his life.[5]
    Exeunt [KEEPERS *with Mortimer's body*]
Here dies the dusky torch of Mortimer,
Choked with° ambition of the meaner sort.[6]   *by*
And for° those wrongs, those bitter injuries,   *And as for*

---

5. *better than his life:* more sumptuous than the life he 6. *meaner sort:* people of lower rank (referring to Bol-
led (in prison). ingbroke and his line).

125 Which Somerset hath offered to my house,
I doubt not but with honour to redress.
And therefore haste I to the Parliament,
Either to be restorèd to my blood,°   inherited rights
Or make mine ill th'advantage of my good.[7]   *Exit*

3.1

Flourish. Enter [young] KING [HENRY],[1] *[the Dukes of]*
EXETER, *[and]* GLOUCESTER, *[the Bishop of]*
WINCHESTER, *[the Duke of]* SOMERSET, *[and the Earl*
of] SUFFOLK, *[with red roses, the Earl of]* WARWICK,
[and] RICHARD PLANTAGENET *[with white roses].[2]*
GLOUCESTER *offers to put up a bill;*° WINCHESTER   written statement
snatches it, tears it

WINCHESTER Com'st thou with deep premeditated lines?
With written pamphlets studiously devised?
Humphrey of Gloucester, if thou canst accuse,
Or aught intend'st to lay unto my charge,
5   Do it without invention,° suddenly,   premeditated design
As I with sudden and extemporal speech
Purpose to answer what thou canst object.°   lay to my charge
GLOUCESTER Presumptuous priest, this place° commands my patience, (Parliament)
Or thou shouldst find thou hast dishonoured me.
10   Think not, although in writing I preferred°   set out
The manner of thy vile outrageous crimes,
That therefore I have forged, or am not able
Verbatim° to rehearse the method of my pen.[3]   Orally
No, prelate, such is thy audacious wickedness,
15   Thy lewd,° pestiferous,° and dissentious pranks, base / deadly
As very° infants prattle of thy pride.   That even
Thou art a most pernicious usurer,[4]
Froward° by nature, enemy to peace,   Perverse
Lascivious, wanton, more than well beseems
20   A man of thy profession and degree.°   rank
And for° thy treachery, what's more manifest?—   And as for
In that thou laid'st a trap to take my life,
As well at London Bridge as at the Tower.
Beside, I fear me, if thy thoughts were sifted,°   closely examined
25   The King thy sovereign is not quite exempt
From envious malice of thy swelling heart.
WINCHESTER Gloucester, I do defy thee.—Lords, vouchsafe
To give me hearing what I shall reply.
If I were covetous, ambitious, or perverse,
30   As he will have me, how am I so poor?
Or how haps it I seek not to advance
Or raise myself, but keep my wonted° calling?   customary

---

7. Or turn the injuries I have suffered to my advantage.
3.1 Location: The Parliament House, London.
1. The historical Henry VI was five years old at the time
of this Parliament in 1327. In this scene, Shakespeare
refers to the King's "tender years" but does not specify
his age.
2. F does not mention that roses are worn in this scene,
but in 2.4 the rival factions promised to wear them forever. This edition indicates their presence throughout

the ensuing action.
3. To recount the order of the argument I wrote.
4. Alluding to the fact that Winchester's wealth was
partly derived from his use of a papal bull and partly
from the Southwark brothels (see 1.4.35 and note). In
Measure for Measure, Shakespeare refers to prostitution
as one of the "two usuries" (3.1.263). Moneylending
bred interest; prostitution bred both illicit offspring and
financial profit.

And for dissension, who preferreth peace
More than I do?—except I be provoked.
35 No, my good lords, it is not that offends;
It is not that that hath incensed the Duke.
It is because no one should sway° but he,   rule
No one but he should be about the King—
And that engenders thunder in his breast
40 And makes him roar these accusations forth.
But he shall know I am as good—
GLOUCESTER   As good?—
Thou bastard of my grandfather.[5]
WINCHESTER   Ay, lordly sir; for what are you, I pray,
45 But one imperious° in another's throne?   ruling
GLOUCESTER   Am I not Protector, saucy priest?
WINCHESTER   And am not I a prelate of the Church?
GLOUCESTER   Yes—as an outlaw in a castle keeps°   dwells
And useth it to patronage° his theft.   protect
WINCHESTER   Unreverent Gloucester.
50 GLOUCESTER   Thou art reverend
Touching° thy spiritual function, not thy life.   With regard to
WINCHESTER   Rome shall remedy this.
GLOUCESTER[6]   Roam thither then.
WARWICK [to WINCHESTER]   My lord, it were your duty to forbear.
SOMERSET   Ay, so° the bishop be not overborne:°   as long as / overruled
55 Methinks my lord° should be religious,°   (Gloucester) / pious
And know the office° that belongs to such.°   duty / (prelates)
WARWICK   Methinks his lordship° should be humbler.   (Winchester)
It fitteth not a prelate so to plead.°   wrangle
SOMERSET   Yes, when his holy state is touched so near.° affected so directly
60 WARWICK   State holy or unhallowed, what of that?
Is not his grace Protector to the King?
RICHARD PLANTAGENET [aside]   Plantagenet, I see, must hold his tongue,
Lest it be said, 'Speak, sirrah,[7] when you should;
Must your bold verdict intertalk° with lords?'   hold opinion; converse
65 Else would I have a fling at Winchester.
KING HENRY   Uncles of Gloucester and of Winchester,
The special watchmen of our English weal,°   well-being; state
I would prevail, if prayers might prevail,
To join your hearts in love and amity.
70 O what a scandal is it to our crown
That two such noble peers as ye should jar!°   quarrel
Believe me, lords, my tender years can tell
Civil dissension is a viperous worm
That gnaws the bowels of the commonwealth.
        A noise within
75 SERVINGMEN [within]   Down with the tawny coats![8]
KING HENRY   What tumult's this?
WARWICK   An uproar, I dare warrant,

---

5. Winchester was born an illegitimate son of Gloucester's grandfather, John of Gaunt, though later he was
made legitimate by an act of Parliament.
6. F assigns this line to Warwick, but giving it to
Gloucester further heightens the antipathy between
Winchester and the Lord Protector.

7. Term used to address social inferiors.
8. Again, this line is included as part of the stage directions in F and is here plausibly assigned to "Servingmen." The same is true at line 78, where F's stage
direction reads: "A noise again, Stones, Stones."

Begun through malice of the Bishop's men.
A noise again
SERVINGMEN [*within*]   Stones, stones!
Enter [the] MAYOR [*of London*]
MAYOR   O my good lords, and virtuous Henry,
80   Pity the city of London, pity us!
The Bishop and the Duke of Gloucester's men,
Forbidden late° to carry any weapon,   *lately*
Have filled their pockets full of pebble stones
And, banding themselves in contrary parts,°   *opposing parties*
85   Do pelt so fast at one another's pate
That many have their giddy brains knocked out.
Our windows are broke down in every street,
And we for fear compelled to shut our shops.
Enter in skirmish, with bloody pates[, Winchester's
SERVINGMEN *in tawny coats and Gloucester's in blue*
coats]
KING HENRY   We charge you, on allegiance to ourself,
90   To hold your slaught'ring hands and keep the peace.
[The skirmish ceases]
Pray, Uncle Gloucester, mitigate this strife.
FIRST SERVINGMAN   Nay, if we be forbidden stones, we'll fall to
it with our teeth.
SECOND SERVINGMAN   Do what ye dare, we are as resolute.
Skirmish again
95   GLOUCESTER   You of my household, leave this peevish broil,°   *this foolish fight*
And set this unaccustomed° fight aside.   *unusual; disorderly*
THIRD SERVINGMAN   My lord, we know your grace to be a man
Just and upright and, for your royal birth,
Inferior to none but to his majesty;
100   And ere that° we will suffer such a prince,   *And before*
So kind a father of the commonweal,
To be disgracèd° by an inkhorn mate,°   *insulted / scribbler*
We and our wives and children all will fight
And have our bodies slaughtered by thy foes.
105   FIRST SERVINGMAN   Ay, and the very parings of our nails
Shall pitch a field⁹ when we are dead.
[They] begin [to skirmish] again
GLOUCESTER   Stay, stay, I say!
An if you love me as you say you do,
Let me persuade you to forbear a while.
KING HENRY   O how this discord doth afflict my soul!
110   Can you, my lord of Winchester, behold
My sighs and tears, and will not once relent?
Who should be pitiful° if you be not?   *merciful*
Or who should study to prefer° a peace,   *propose*
If holy churchmen take delight in broils?
115   WARWICK   Yield, my lord Protector; yield, Winchester—
Except you mean with obstinate repulse°   *refusal*
To slay your sovereign and destroy the realm.
You see what mischief—and what murder, too—
Hath been enacted through your enmity.
120   Then be at peace, except° ye thirst for blood.   *unless*

_____
9. Shall fortify a battlefield (usually with defensive wood or iron stakes).

WINCHESTER He shall submit, or I will never yield.

GLOUCESTER Compassion on the King commands me stoop,
Or I would see his heart out ere the priest
Should ever get that privilege of° me.   *advantage over*

125 WARWICK Behold, my lord of Winchester, the Duke
Hath banished moody° discontented fury,   *sullen*
As by his smoothèd brows it doth appear.
Why look you still so stern and tragical?

GLOUCESTER Here, Winchester, I offer thee my hand.

130 KING HENRY [*to* WINCHESTER] Fie, Uncle Beaufort! I have heard you preach
That malice was a great and grievous sin;
And will not you maintain the thing you teach,
But prove a chief offender in the same?

WARWICK Sweet King! The Bishop hath a kindly gird.°   *a gentle rebuke*

135 For shame, my lord of Winchester, relent.
What, shall a child instruct you what to do?

WINCHESTER Well, Duke of Gloucester, I will yield to thee
Love for thy love, and hand for hand I give.

GLOUCESTER [*aside*] Ay, but I fear me with a hollow° heart.   *an insincere*

140 [*To the others*] See here, my friends and loving countrymen,
This token serveth for a flag of truce
Betwixt ourselves and all our followers.
So help me God, as I dissemble not.

WINCHESTER So help me God [*aside*] as I intend it not.

145 KING HENRY O loving uncle, kind Duke of Gloucester,
How joyful am I made by this contract!
[*To* SERVINGMEN] Away, my masters, trouble us no more,
But join in friendship as your lords have done.

FIRST SERVINGMAN Content. I'll to the surgeon's.

150 SECOND SERVINGMAN And so will I.

THIRD SERVINGMAN And I will see what physic° the tavern   *medicine*
affords.

Exeunt [the MAYOR *and* SERVINGMEN]

WARWICK Accept this scroll, most gracious sovereign,
Which in the right of Richard Plantagenet

155 We do exhibit to your majesty.

GLOUCESTER Well urged, my lord of Warwick—for, sweet prince,
An if your grace mark every circumstance,
You have great reason to do Richard right,
Especially for those occasions°   *reasons*

160 At Eltham Place I told your majesty.

KING HENRY And those occasions, uncle, were of force.—
Therefore, my loving lords, our pleasure is
That Richard be restorèd to his blood.

WARWICK Let Richard be restorèd to his blood.

165 So shall his father's wrongs be recompensed.

WINCHESTER As will the rest, so willeth Winchester.

KING HENRY If Richard will be true,° not that alone   *loyal*
But all the whole inheritance I give
That doth belong unto the house of York,

170 From whence you spring by lineal descent.[1]

---

1. *But . . . descent*: The King restores Richard not only to the earldom of Cambridge (inherited from his father) but also to the dukedom of York (inherited from his uncle).

RICHARD PLANTAGENET   Thy humble servant vows obedience
And humble service till the point of death.
KING HENRY   Stoop then, and set your knee against my foot.
   [RICHARD *kneels*]
And in reguerdon° of that duty done,   *reward*
175   I gird thee with the valiant sword of York.
Rise, Richard, like a true Plantagenet,
And rise created princely Duke of York.
RICHARD DUKE OF YORK [*rising*]   And so thrive Richard, as thy
   foes may fall;
And as my duty springs, so perish they
180   That grudge one thought° against your majesty.   *hold any grudges*
ALL BUT RICHARD AND SOMERSET   Welcome, high prince, the
   mighty Duke of York!
SOMERSET [*aside*]   Perish, base prince, ignoble Duke of York!
GLOUCESTER   Now will it best avail your majesty
To cross the seas and to be crowned in France.
185   The presence of a king engenders love
Amongst his subjects and his loyal friends,
As it disanimates° his enemies.   *discourages*
KING HENRY   When Gloucester says the word, King Henry goes,
For friendly counsel cuts off many foes.
190   GLOUCESTER   Your ships already are in readiness.
   Sennet.[2] *Exeunt. Manet*° EXETER   *Remains*
EXETER   Ay, we may march in England or in France,
Not seeing what is likely to ensue.
This late° dissension grown betwixt the peers   *recent*
Burns under feignèd ashes of forged love,
195   And will at last break out into a flame.
As festered members° rot but by degree   *parts of the body*
Till bones and flesh and sinews fall away,
So will this base and envious discord breed.
And now I fear that fatal prophecy
200   Which, in the time of Henry named the Fifth,
Was in the mouth of every sucking babe:
That 'Henry born at Monmouth° should win all,   *(Henry V)*
And Henry born at Windsor° should lose all'—   *(Henry VI)*
Which is so plain that Exeter doth wish
205   His days may finish, ere that hapless time.   *Exit*

3.2

Enter [JOAN *la*] *Pucelle, disguised, with four* [*French*]
SOLDIERS *with sacks upon their backs*
JOAN   These are the city gates, the gates of Rouen,
Through which our policy° must make a breach.   *trickery*
Take heed. Be wary how you place your words.
Talk like the vulgar° sort of market men   *common*
5   That come to gather money for their corn.°   *grain*
If we have entrance, as I hope we shall,
And that° we find the slothful watch but weak,   *if*

---

2. Trumpet notes that accompany a procession.   3.2. Location: In and around Rouen, France.

I'll by a sign give notice to our friends,
That Charles the Dauphin may encounter them.

10 A SOLDIER   Our sacks shall be a mean° to sack the city,   *means*
And we be lords and rulers over Rouen.
Therefore we'll knock.

        [They] knock

WATCH *[within]*   *Qui là?*°   *Who is there*

JOAN   *Paysans, la pauvre gens de France:*[1]
Poor market folks that come to sell their corn.

15 WATCH *[opening the gates]*   Enter, go in. The market bell is rung.

JOAN *[aside]*   Now, Rouen, I'll shake thy bulwarks to the ground.

                                   Exeunt

3.3

Enter CHARLES *[the Dauphin, the]* BASTARD
[of Orléans, the Duke of] ALENÇON*[*, RENÉ *Duke of*
Anjou, and French soldiers]

CHARLES   Saint Denis bless this happy stratagem,
And once again we'll sleep secure in Rouen.

BASTARD   Here entered Pucelle and her practisants.°   *conspirators*
Now she is there, how will she specify

5 'Here is the best and safest passage in'?

RENÉ   By thrusting out a torch from yonder tower—
Which, once discerned, shows that her meaning is:
No way to that, for weakness, which she entered.[1]

       Enter [JOAN *la*] *Pucelle on the top, thrusting out a torch*
       burning

JOAN   Behold, this is the happy wedding torch

10 That joineth Rouen unto her countrymen,
But burning fatal to the Talbonites.°   *followers of Talbot*

BASTARD   See, noble Charles, the beacon of our friend.
The burning torch in yonder turret stands.

CHARLES   Now shine it° like a comet of revenge,   *may it shine*

15 A prophet to the fall of all our foes!

RENÉ   Defer no time; delays have dangerous ends.
Enter and cry, 'The Dauphin!', presently,°   *at once*
And then do execution on the watch.°   *Alarum. [Exeunt]*   *then kill the guards*

3.4

An alarum. [Enter Lord] TALBOT *in an excursion*°   *a skirmish*

TALBOT   France, thou shalt rue this treason with thy tears,
If Talbot but survive thy treachery.
Pucelle, that witch, that damnèd sorceress,
Hath wrought this hellish mischief unawares,°   *unexpectedly*

5 That hardly we escaped the pride of France.[1]   *Exit*

---

1. Peasants, the poor folk of France.
3.3 Location: Scene continues.
1. No entrance is as weakly guarded as the one she
entered.

3.4 Location: Scene continues.
1. That only with difficulty we escaped the princely
power of France.

3.5

An alarum. Excursions. [The Duke of] BEDFORD
brought in sick, in a chair. Enter [Lord] TALBOT *and*
[the Duke of] BURGUNDY, *without; within,*[1] *[*JOAN la*]*
Pucelle, CHARLES *[the Dauphin, the]* BASTARD
[of Orléans, the Duke of ALENÇON*], and* RENÉ *[Duke*
of Anjou] on the walls

JOAN   Good morrow gallants. Want ye corn for bread?
I think the Duke of Burgundy will fast
Before he'll buy again at such a rate.
'Twas full of darnel.° Do you like the taste?   *weeds*

5 BURGUNDY   Scoff on, vile fiend and shameless courtesan.
I trust ere long to choke thee with thine own,°   *your own bread*
And make thee curse the harvest of that corn.

CHARLES   Your grace may starve, perhaps, before that time.

BEDFORD   O let no words, but deeds, revenge this treason.

10 JOAN   What will you do, good graybeard? Break a lance
And run a-tilt at° death within a chair?   *joust with*

TALBOT   Foul fiend of France, and hag of all despite,°   *most despicable*
Encompassed with thy lustful paramours,
Becomes it thee to taunt his valiant age

15 And twit with cowardice a man half dead?
Damsel, I'll have a bout° with you again,   *fight; sexual struggle*
Or else let Talbot perish with this shame.

JOAN   Are ye so hot,° sir?—Yet, Pucelle, hold thy peace.   *angry; lustful*
If Talbot do but thunder, rain will follow.

They [the English] whisper together in counsel

20 God speed the parliament; who shall be the Speaker?

TALBOT   Dare ye come forth and meet us in the field?

JOAN   Belike your lordship takes us then for fools,
To try if that our own be ours or no.

TALBOT   I speak not to that railing Hecate[2]

25 But unto thee, Alençon, and the rest.
Will ye, like soldiers, come and fight it out?

ALENÇON   Seignieur, no.

TALBOT   Seignieur, hang! Base muleteers° of   *Lowborn mule drivers*
France,
Like peasant footboys do they keep° the walls   *stay near*
And dare not take up arms like gentlemen.

30 JOAN   Away, captains, let's get us from the walls,
For Talbot means no goodness by his looks.
Goodbye, my lord. We came but to tell you
That we are here.   *Exeunt [French] from the walls*

TALBOT   And there will we be, too, ere it be long,

35 Or else reproach be Talbot's greatest fame.
Vow Burgundy, by honour of thy house,
Pricked on° by public wrongs sustained in France,   *Urged on*
Either to get the town again or die.
And I—as sure as English Henry lives,

40 And as his father here was conqueror;[3]

3.5 Location: Scene continues.
1. The stage directions suggest that Talbot's party is on the main stage; Joan's party may appear on the upper stage gallery.
2. In classical mythology, the goddess of night and the underworld and the patron of witchcraft.
3. Henry V had captured Rouen in 1419.

As sure as in this late° betrayèd town   *recently*
Great Cœur-de-lion's heart was buried⁴—
So sure I swear to get the town or die.

BURGUNDY   My vows are equal partners with thy vows.

45   TALBOT   But ere we go, regard this dying prince,
The valiant Duke of Bedford. [*To* BEDFORD] Come, my lord,
We will bestow you in some better place,
Fitter for sickness and for crazy° age.   *feeble*

BEDFORD   Lord Talbot, do not so dishonour me.

50   Here will I sit before the walls of Rouen,
And will be partner of your weal° or woe.   *happiness*

BURGUNDY   Courageous Bedford, let us now persuade you.

BEDFORD   Not to be gone from hence; for once I read
That stout Pendragon,⁵ in his litter sick,

55   Came to the field and vanquishèd his foes.
Methinks I should revive the soldiers' hearts,
Because I ever found them as myself.

TALBOT   Undaunted spirit in a dying breast!
Then be it so; heavens keep old Bedford safe.

60   And now no more ado, brave Burgundy,
But gather we our forces out of hand,°   *at once*
And set upon our boasting enemy.   *Exit* [*with* BURGUNDY]

        An alarum. Excursions. Enter Sir John FASTOLF
        and a CAPTAIN

CAPTAIN   Whither away, Sir John Fastolf, in such haste?

FASTOLF   Whither away? To save myself by flight.

65   We are like to have the overthrow° again.   *to be defeated*

CAPTAIN   What, will you fly, and leave Lord Talbot?

FASTOLF   Ay, all the Talbots in the world, to save my life.   *Exit*

CAPTAIN   Cowardly knight, ill fortune follow thee!   *Exit*

        Retreat. Excursions. [JOAN *la*] *Pucelle,* ALENÇON,
        and CHARLES *fly*

BEDFORD   Now, quiet soul, depart when heaven please,

70   For I have seen our enemies' overthrow.
What is the trust or strength of foolish man?
They that of late were daring with their scoffs
Are glad and fain° by flight to save themselves.   *eager*

        BEDFORD *dies, and is carried in by two in his chair*

3.6

        An alarum. Enter [*Lord*] TALBOT, [*the Duke of*]
        BURGUNDY, *and the rest* [*of the English soldiers*]

TALBOT   Lost and recovered in a day again!
This is a double honour, Burgundy;
Yet heavens have glory for this victory!

BURGUNDY   Warlike and martial Talbot, Burgundy

5   Enshrines thee in his heart, and there erects
Thy noble deeds as valour's monuments.

TALBOT   Thanks, gentle° Duke. But where is Pucelle now?   *noble*
I think her old familiar° is asleep.   *attendant demon*

---

4. According to Holinshed's *Chronicles*, Richard
Cœur-de-Lion (the Lion-Hearted), who ruled England
from 1189 to 1199, willed that his heart be buried in
Rouen as a sign of his love for the city.

5. Uther Pendragon, the father of King Arthur. This
story is told in Geoffrey of Monmouth's history of
Britain (*Historia Regum Britanniae*). stout: brave.
3.6 Location: Scene continues.

Now where's the Bastard's braves,° and Charles his gleeks?°   boasts / Charles's jests
10   What, all amort?° Rouen hangs her head for grief   dispirited
That such a valiant company are fled.
Now will we take some order° in the town,   establish order
Placing therein some expert officers,
And then depart to Paris, to the King,
15   For there young Henry with his nobles lie.°   lives
BURGUNDY   What wills Lord Talbot pleaseth Burgundy.
TALBOT   But yet, before we go, let's not forget
The noble Duke of Bedford late deceased,
But see his exequies° fulfilled in Rouen.   funeral rites
20   A braver soldier never couchèd° lance;   leveled (for attack)
A gentler heart did never sway in court.
But kings and mightiest potentates must die,
For that's the end of human misery.   *Exeunt*

3.7

Enter CHARLES [*the Dauphin, the*] BASTARD [*of Orléans,*
the Duke of] ALENÇON, [JOAN *la*] Pucelle [*and French*
soldiers]

JOAN   Dismay not, princes, at this accident,
Nor grieve that Rouen is so recoverèd.
Care° is no cure, but rather corrosive,°   Sorrow / destructive
For things that are not to be remedied.
5   Let frantic° Talbot triumph for a while,   mad
And like a peacock sweep along his tail;
We'll pull his plumes and take away his train,°   peacock's tail; army
If Dauphin and the rest will be but ruled.
CHARLES   We have been guided by thee hitherto,
10   And of thy cunning had no diffidence.°   doubt
One sudden foil° shall never breed distrust.   defeat
BASTARD [*to* JOAN]   Search out thy wit for secret policies,°   stratagems
And we will make thee famous through the world.
ALENÇON [*to* JOAN]   We'll set thy statue in some holy place
15   And have thee reverenced like a blessèd saint.
Employ thee then, sweet virgin, for our good.
JOAN   Then thus it must be; this doth Joan devise:
By fair persuasions mixed with sugared words
We will entice the Duke of Burgundy
20   To leave the Talbot and to follow us.
CHARLES   Ay, marry, sweeting,° if we could do that   (a lover's nickname)
France were no place for Henry's warriors,
Nor should that nation boast it so with us,
But be extirpèd° from our provinces.   rooted out
25   ALENÇON   For ever should they be expulsed from France
And not have title of an earldom here.
JOAN   Your honours shall perceive how I will work
To bring this matter to the wishèd end.
   Drum sounds afar off
Hark, by the sound of drum you may perceive
30   Their powers are marching unto Paris-ward.°   toward Paris
   Here sound an English march

3.7 Location: Plains near Rouen.

There goes the Talbot, with his colours spread,°   *flags unfurled*
And all the troops of English after him.
     [*Here sound a*] *French march*
Now in the rearward comes the Duke and his;
Fortune in favour° makes him lag behind.   *as a favor to us*
35   Summon a parley.[1] We will talk with him.
     Trumpets sound a parley
CHARLES [*calling*]   A parley with the Duke of Burgundy.
     [*Enter the Duke of* BURGUNDY]
BURGUNDY   Who craves a parley with the Burgundy?
JOAN   The princely Charles of France, thy countryman.
BURGUNDY   What sayst thou, Charles?—for I am marching hence.
40   CHARLES   Speak, Pucelle, and enchant him with thy words.
JOAN   Brave Burgundy, undoubted° hope of France,   *certain*
  Stay. Let thy humble handmaid speak to thee.
BURGUNDY   Speak on, but be not over-tedious.
JOAN   Look on thy country, look on fertile France,
45   And see the cities and the towns defaced
  By wasting ruin of the cruel foe.
  As looks the mother on her lowly babe
  When death doth close his tender-dying° eyes,   *young-dying*
  See, see the pining malady of France;
50   Behold the wounds, the most unnatural wounds,
  Which thou thyself hast given her woeful breast.
  O turn thy edgèd sword another way,
  Strike those that hurt, and hurt not those that help.
  One drop of blood drawn from thy country's bosom
55   Should grieve thee more than streams of foreign gore.
  Return thee, therefore, with a flood of tears,
  And wash away thy country's stainèd spots.[2]
BURGUNDY [*aside*]   Either she hath bewitched me with her words,
  Or nature makes me suddenly relent.
60   JOAN   Besides, all French and France exclaims on° thee,   *denounces*
  Doubting thy birth and lawful progeny.°   *ancestry*
  Who join'st thou with but with a lordly nation
  That will not trust thee but for profit's sake?
  When Talbot hath set footing once in France
65   And fashioned thee that instrument of ill,
  Who then but English Henry will be lord,
  And thou be thrust out like a fugitive?
  Call we to mind, and mark but this for proof:
  Was not the Duke of Orléans thy foe?
70   And was he not in England prisoner?
  But when they heard he was thine enemy
  They set him free, without his ransom paid,
  In spite of Burgundy and all his friends.[3]
  See, then, thou fight'st against thy countrymen,
75   And join'st with them will be thy slaughtermen.
  Come, come, return; return, thou wandering lord,

---

1. Sound a trumpet to request a conference.
2. And wash away the spots of blood that defile your country.
3. The historical Orléans was not released by the English until five years after Burgundy abandoned the English alliance.

Charles and the rest will take thee in their arms.

BURGUNDY [*aside*]   I am vanquishèd.[4] These haughty° words of hers   *lofty*
Have battered me like roaring cannon-shot
80   And made me almost yield upon my knees.
[*To the others*] Forgive me, country, and sweet countrymen;
And lords, accept this hearty kind embrace.
My forces and my power of men are yours.
So farewell, Talbot. I'll no longer trust thee.

85   JOAN   Done like a Frenchman—[*aside*] turn and turn again.

CHARLES   Welcome, brave Duke. Thy friendship makes us fresh.

BASTARD   And doth beget new courage in our breasts.

ALENÇON   Pucelle hath bravely played her part in this,
And doth deserve a coronet of gold.

90   CHARLES   Now let us on, my lords, and join our powers,
And seek how we may prejudice° the foe.   *Exeunt*   *hurt*

3.8

[*Flourish.*] *Enter* KING [HENRY, *the Duke of*] GLOUCES-
TER, [*the Bishop of*] WINCHESTER, [*the Duke of*] EXE-
TER; [RICHARD DUKE OF] YORK, [*the Earl of*] WARWICK,
[*and* VERNON *with white roses; the Earl of*] SUFFOLK,
[*the Duke of*] SOMERSET [*and* BASSET *with red roses*]. *To
them, with his soldiers,* [*enter Lord*] TALBOT

TALBOT   My gracious prince and honourable peers,
Hearing of your arrival in this realm
I have a while given truce unto my wars
To do my duty° to my sovereign;   *give homage*
5   In sign whereof, this arm that hath reclaimed
To your obedience fifty fortresses,
Twelve cities, and seven walled towns of strength,
Beside five hundred prisoners of esteem,°   *noble rank*
Lets fall his sword before your highness' feet,
10   And with submissive loyalty of heart
Ascribes the glory of his conquest got
First to my God, and next unto your grace.
            [*He kneels*][1]

KING HENRY   Is this the Lord Talbot, uncle Gloucester,
That hath so long been resident in France?

15   GLOUCESTER   Yes, if it please your majesty, my liege.

KING HENRY [*to* TALBOT]   Welcome, brave captain and victorious lord.
When I was young—as yet I am not old—
I do remember how my father said
A stouter champion never handled sword.
20   Long since we were resolvèd° of your truth,°   *convinced / loyalty*
Your faithful service and your toil in war,
Yet never have you tasted our reward,
Or been reguerdoned° with so much as thanks,   *rewarded*
Because till now we never saw your face.

---

4. The historical Burgundy did not return to the
French side until four years after Joan's death.
3.8 Location: The palace, Paris.

1. F does not indicate when Talbot kneels, but he must
do so: at line 25, he is urged to "stand up."

Therefore stand up,
    [TALBOT *rises*]

25   and for these good deserts
We here create you Earl of Shrewsbury;
And in our coronation take your place.[2]
       Sennet. Exeunt. Manent° VERNON *and* BASSET   *Remain*

VERNON   Now sir, to you that were so hot° at sea,   *angry*
Disgracing of these colours° that I wear   *this badge (the rose)*

30 In honour of my noble lord of York,
Dar'st thou maintain the former words thou spak'st?

BASSET   Yes, sir, as well as you dare patronage°   *defend*
The envious barking of your saucy tongue
Against my lord the Duke of Somerset.

35 VERNON   Sirrah, thy lord I honour as he is.

BASSET   Why, what is he?—as good a man as York.

VERNON   Hark ye, not so. In witness, take ye that.
        [VERNON] *strikes him*

BASSET   Villain, thou know'st the law of arms[3] is such
That whoso draws a sword 'tis present° death,   *immediate*

40 Or else this blow should broach° thy dearest blood.   *tap (as a wine vat)*
But I'll unto his majesty and crave
I may have liberty° to venge this wrong,   *permission*
When thou shalt see I'll meet thee to thy cost.

VERNON   Well, miscreant,° I'll be there as soon as you,   *villain*

45 And after meet you sooner than you would.°   *Exeunt*   *would wish*

4.1

[*Flourish.*] *Enter* KING [HENRY, *the Duke of*]
GLOUCESTER, [*the Bishop of*] WINCHESTER, [*the Duke*
of] EXETER, [RICHARD DUKE OF] YORK, [*and the Earl of*]
WARWICK, [*with white roses; the Earl of*] SUFFOLK, [*and*
the Duke of] SOMERSET, [*with red roses; Lord*] TALBOT,
and [*the*] Governor [*of Paris*]

GLOUCESTER   Lord Bishop, set the crown upon his head.

WINCHESTER   God save King Henry, of that name the sixth!
      [WINCHESTER *crowns the* KING]

GLOUCESTER   Now, Governor of Paris, take your oath
That you elect° no other king but him;   *acknowledge*

5 Esteem none friends but such as are his friends,
And none your foes but such as shall pretend°   *propose*
Malicious practices against his state.
This shall ye do, so help you righteous God.
      Enter [*Sir John*] FASTOLF [*with a letter*]

FASTOLF   My gracious sovereign, as I rode from Calais

10 To haste unto your coronation
A letter was delivered to my hands,
      [*He presents the letter*]
Writ to your grace from th' Duke of Burgundy.

TALBOT   Shame to the Duke of Burgundy and thee!
I vowed, base knight, when I did meet thee next,

---

2. The historical Talbot was created Earl of Shrewsbury in 1442, more than ten years after Henry's
coronation.

3. The law that forbade fighting near a royal residence
(see also 1.4.45 and 2.4.86).
4.1 Location: The palace, Paris.

15   To tear the Garter¹ from thy craven's° leg,   *coward's*
         [*He tears it off*]
    Which I have done because unworthily
    Thou wast installèd in that high degree.—
    Pardon me, princely Henry and the rest.
    This dastard° at the battle of Patay   *coward*
20   When but in all° I was six thousand strong,   *When all told*
    And that the French were almost ten to one,
    Before we met, or that a stroke was given,
    Like to a trusty° squire did run away;   *faithful (here ironic)*
    In which assault we lost twelve hundred men.
25   Myself and divers gentlemen beside
    Were there surprised and taken prisoners.
    Then judge, great lords, if I have done amiss,
    Or whether that such cowards ought to wear
    This ornament of knighthood: yea or no?
30 GLOUCESTER   To say the truth, this fact° was infamous   *deed*
    And ill beseeming any common man,
    Much more a knight, a captain and a leader.
    TALBOT   When first this order was ordained, my lords,
    Knights of the Garter were of noble birth,
35   Valiant and virtuous, full of haughty° courage,   *lofty*
    Such as were grown to credit° by the wars;   *fame*
    Not fearing death nor shrinking for distress,
    But always resolute in most extremes.°   *in greatest extremities*
    He then that is not furnished in this sort°   *not endowed like this*
40   Doth but usurp the sacred name of knight,
    Profaning this most honourable order,
    And should—if I were worthy to be judge—
    Be quite degraded,° like a hedge-born swain²   *reduced in rank*
    That doth presume to boast of gentle° blood.   *noble*
    KING HENRY [*to* FASTOLF]   Stain to thy countrymen, thou hear'st
45   thy doom.°   *sentence*
    Be packing, therefore, thou that wast a knight.
    Henceforth we banish thee on pain of death.   [*Exit* FASTOLF]
    And now, my Lord Protector, view the letter
    Sent from our uncle, Duke of Burgundy.³
    GLOUCESTER   What means his grace that he hath changed his
50   style?°   *form of address*
    No more but plain and bluntly 'To the King'?
    Hath he forgot he is his sovereign?
    Or doth this churlish superscription°   *rude address*
    Pretend° some alteration in good will?   *Indicate*
55   What's here? 'I have upon especial cause,
    Moved with compassion of my country's wrack°   *destruction*
    Together with the pitiful complaints
    Of such as your oppression feeds upon,
    Forsaken your pernicious faction
60   And joined with Charles, the rightful King of France.'
    O monstrous treachery! Can this be so?

---

1. A ribbon, worn below the left knee, signifying membership in the Order of the Garter, the highest rank of English knighthood.

2. A lowly or illegitimate country person.

3. Henry VI's uncle, the Duke of Bedford, married Burgundy's sister Anne.

That in alliance, amity, and oaths
There should be found such false dissembling guile?
KING HENRY   What? Doth my uncle Burgundy revolt?
65 GLOUCESTER   He doth, my lord, and is become your foe.
KING HENRY   Is that the worst this letter doth contain?
GLOUCESTER   It is the worst, and all, my lord, he writes.
KING HENRY   Why then, Lord Talbot there shall talk with him
And give him chastisement for this abuse.
70 [*To* TALBOT] How say you, my lord? Are you not content?
TALBOT   Content, my liege? Yes. But that I am prevented,°   anticipated
I should have begged I might have been employed.
KING HENRY   Then gather strength and march unto him straight.°   at once
Let him perceive how ill we brook° his treason,   tolerate
75 And what offence it is to flout his friends.
TALBOT   I go, my lord, in heart desiring still°   always
You may behold confusion of your foes.   [*Exit*]
Enter VERNON [*wearing a white rose,*] *and* BASSET [*wear-
ing a red rose*]
VERNON [*to* KING HENRY]   Grant me the combat,° gracious   permission to duel
sovereign.
BASSET [*to* KING HENRY]   And me, my lord; grant me the combat, too.
RICHARD DUKE OF YORK [*to* KING HENRY, *pointing to* VERNON]
80 This is my servant;° hear him, noble Prince.   follower
SOMERSET [*to* KING HENRY, *pointing to* BASSET]   And this is mine,
sweet Henry; favour him.
KING HENRY   Be patient, lords, and give them leave to speak.
Say, gentlemen, what makes you thus exclaim,
And wherefore crave you combat, or with whom?
85 VERNON   With him, my lord; for he hath done me wrong.
BASSET   And I with him; for he hath done me wrong.
KING HENRY   What is that wrong whereof you both complain?
First let me know, and then I'll answer you.
BASSET   Crossing the sea from England into France,
90 This fellow here with envious carping tongue
Upbraided me about the rose I wear,
Saying the sanguine° colour of the leaves°   blood-red / petals
Did represent my master's blushing cheeks
When stubbornly he did repugn° the truth   reject
95 About a certain question[4] in the law
Argued betwixt the Duke of York and him,
With other vile and ignominious terms;
In confutation of which rude reproach,
And in defence of my lord's worthiness,
100 I crave the benefit of law of arms.[5]
VERNON   And that is my petition, noble lord;
For though he seem with forgèd quaint conceit°   false cunning words
To set a gloss° upon his bold intent,   good appearance
Yet know, my lord, I was provoked by him,
105 And he first took exceptions at this badge,
Pronouncing that the paleness of this flower
Bewrayed° the faintness of my master's heart.   Revealed

---

4. The "certain question" apparently concerns the
question of York's succession to the throne and the
attainder of his father. See 2.4 and 2.5.45–129.
5. The right to decide the matter in a duel.

RICHARD DUKE OF YORK   Will not this malice, Somerset, be left?°   *put aside*
SOMERSET   Your private grudge, my lord of York, will out,
110   Though ne'er so cunningly you smother it.
KING HENRY   Good Lord, what madness rules in brainsick men
When for so slight and frivolous a cause
Such factious emulations° shall arise?   *divisive jealousies*
Good cousins both of York and Somerset,
115   Quiet yourselves, I pray, and be at peace.
RICHARD DUKE OF YORK   Let this dissension first be tried by fight,
And then your highness shall command a peace.
SOMERSET   The quarrel toucheth none but us alone;
Betwixt ourselves let us decide it then.
120   RICHARD DUKE OF YORK   There is my pledge.⁶ Accept it, Somerset.
VERNON [*to* KING HENRY]   Nay, let it rest where it began at first.⁷
BASSET [*to* KING HENRY]   Confirm it so, mine honourable lord.
GLOUCESTER   Confirm it so? Confounded be your strife,
And perish ye with your audacious prate!°   *prattling*
125   Presumptuous vassals, are you not ashamed
With this immodest clamorous outrage
To trouble and disturb the King and us?
And you, my lords, methinks you do not well
To bear with their perverse objections,°   *accusations*
130   Much less to take occasion° from their mouths   *the opportunity*
To raise a mutiny betwixt yourselves.
Let me persuade you take a better course.
EXETER   It grieves his highness. Good my lords, be friends.
KING HENRY   Come hither, you that would be combatants.
135   Henceforth I charge you, as you love our favour,
Quite to forget this quarrel and the cause.
And you, my lords, remember where we are—
In France, amongst a fickle wavering nation.
If they perceive dissension in our looks,
140   And that within ourselves we disagree,
How will their grudging stomachs° be provoked   *resentful tempers*
To wilful disobedience, and rebel!
Beside, what infamy will there arise
When foreign princes shall be certified°   *informed*
145   That for a toy,° a thing of no regard,   *trifle*
King Henry's peers and chief nobility
Destroyed themselves and lost the realm of France!
O, think upon the conquest of my father,
My tender years, and let us not forgo
150   That for a trifle that was bought with blood.⁸
Let me be umpire in this doubtful° strife.   *uncertain*
I see no reason, if I wear this rose,
      [*He takes a red rose*]
That anyone should therefore be suspicious
I more incline to Somerset than York.
155   Both are my kinsmen, and I love them both.

---

6. A glove or gauntlet thrown down in a duel.
7. Let the quarrel remain with me and Basset, who began it.

8. *let . . . blood:* let us not lose for a trifle what was bought with blood (that is, let us not lose France).

As well they may upbraid me with my crown
Because, forsooth, the King of Scots is crowned.
But your discretions better can persuade
Than I am able to instruct or teach,
160 And therefore, as we hither came in peace,
So let us still continue peace and love.
Cousin of York, we institute° your grace   *appoint*
To be our regent in these parts of France;
And good my lord of Somerset, unite
165 Your troops of horsemen with his bands of foot,°   *infantry*
And like true subjects, sons of your progenitors,
Go cheerfully together and digest°   *dissipate*
Your angry choler on your enemies.
Ourself, my Lord Protector, and the rest,
170 After some respite, will return to Calais,
From thence to England, where I hope ere long
To be presented by your victories
With Charles, Alençon, and that traitorous rout.°   *rabble*
      [Flourish.] Exeunt. Manent YORK, WARWICK,
                  VERNON, *[and]* EXETER

WARWICK   My lord of York, I promise you, the King
175 Prettily, methought, did play the orator.
RICHARD DUKE OF YORK   And so he did; but yet I like it not
In that he wears the badge of Somerset.
WARWICK   Tush, that was but his fancy; blame him not.
I dare presume, sweet Prince, he thought no harm.
180 RICHARD DUKE OF YORK   An if I wist° he did—but let it rest.   *If I knew for certain*
Other affairs must now be managèd. *Exeunt. Manet* EXETER
EXETER   Well didst thou, Richard, to suppress thy voice;
For had the passions of thy heart burst out
I fear we should have seen deciphered° there   *revealed*
185 More rancorous spite, more furious raging broils,
Than yet can be imagined or supposed.
But howsoe'er, no simple man that sees
This jarring discord of nobility,
This shouldering of each other in the court,
190 This factious bandying° of their favourites,°   *quarreling / followers*
But that° it doth presage some ill event.°   *But sees that / outcome*
'Tis much when sceptres are in children's hands,
But more when envy breeds unkind° division: *unnatural*
There comes the ruin, there begins confusion.   *Exit*

4.2
    Enter [Lord] TALBOT *with [a] trump[eter] and*
    drum[mer and soldiers] before Bordeaux
TALBOT   Go to the gates of Bordeaux, trumpeter.
Summon their general unto the wall.
    [The trumpeter] sounds [a parley]. Enter [French]
    GENERAL, *aloft*
English John Talbot, captain, calls you forth,
Servant in arms to Harry King of England;
5 And thus he would:° open your city gates,   *desires*
Be humble to us, call my sovereign yours

4.2 Location: Before Bordeaux.

And do him homage as obedient subjects,
And I'll withdraw me and my bloody power.
But if you frown upon this proffered peace,
10 You tempt the fury of my three attendants—
Lean famine, quartering° steel, and climbing fire—   *dismembering*
Who in a moment even° with the earth   *level*
Shall lay your stately and air-braving° towers   *air-defying; lofty*
If you forsake the offer of their love.
15 GENERAL   Thou ominous and fearful owl[1] of death,
Our nation's terror and their bloody scourge,
The period° of thy tyranny approacheth.   *end*
On us thou canst not enter but by death,
For I protest we are well fortified
20 And strong enough to issue out and fight.
If thou retire, the Dauphin well appointed°   *equipped*
Stands with the snares of war to tangle thee.
On either hand thee° there are squadrons pitched[2]   *On both sides of you*
To wall thee from the liberty of flight,
25 And no way canst thou turn thee for redress
But death doth front thee with apparent spoil,[3]
And pale destruction meets thee in the face.
Ten thousand French have ta'en the sacrament[4]
To fire their dangerous artillery
30 Upon no Christian soul but English Talbot.
Lo, there thou stand'st, a breathing valiant man
Of an invincible unconquered spirit.
This is the latest° glory of thy praise,   *final*
That I thy enemy due° thee withal,   *endow*
35 For ere the glass° that now begins to run   *hourglass*
Finish the process of his° sandy hour,   *progress of its*
These eyes that see thee now well colourèd°   *in good health*
Shall see thee withered, bloody, pale, and dead.
       Drum afar off
Hark, hark, the Dauphin's drum, a warning bell,
40 Sings heavy music to thy timorous soul,
And mine shall ring thy dire departure out.[5]   *Exit*
TALBOT   He fables not. I hear the enemy.
Out, some light horsemen, and peruse their wings.°   *survey their flanks*
       [*Exit one or more*]
O negligent and heedless° discipline,   *careless*
45 How are we parked° and bounded in a pale!°—   *enclosed / fenced area*
A little herd of England's timorous deer
Mazed with[6] a yelping kennel of French curs.
If we be English deer, be then in blood,°   *vigorous*
Not rascal-like[7] to fall down with a pinch,°   *nip (from hounds)*
50 But rather, moody-mad° and desperate stags,   *enraged*
Turn on the bloody hounds with heads of steel
And make the cowards stand aloof at bay.
Sell every man his life as dear as mine

---

1. The owl's cry was thought to portend evil or death (see Ovid's *Metamorphoses* 10.521–52 and *Macbeth* 2.2.3).
2. Arranged on the field for battle.
3. But death confronts you with obvious destruction.
4. Have received the Christian sacrament of Holy Communion (as a way of confirming their oaths).
5. And my drum—the alarm signal given when the general's army is to "issue out and fight" (line 20) against Talbot—shall signal your death.
6. Bewildered by; trapped in maze with.
7. Not like lean, worthless deer.

And they shall find dear° deer of us, my friends.   costly
55 God and Saint George,° Talbot and England's right,   England's patron saint
Prosper our colours in this dangerous fight!   [*Exeunt*]

4.3

Enter a MESSENGER *that meets* [*the* DUKE OF] YORK.
Enter [RICHARD DUKE OF] YORK *with* [*a*] *trumpet*[*er*] *and
many soldiers*

RICHARD DUKE OF YORK   Are not the speedy scouts returned again
That dogged° the mighty army of the Dauphin?   tracked
MESSENGER   They are returned, my lord, and give it out
That he is marched to Bordeaux with his power
5 To fight with Talbot. As he marched along,
By your espials° were discoverèd   spies
Two mightier troops than that the Dauphin led,
Which joined with him and made their march for Bordeaux.
RICHARD DUKE OF YORK   A plague upon that villain Somerset
10 That thus delays my promisèd supply
Of horsemen that were levied for this siege!
Renownèd Talbot doth expect my aid,
And I am louted° by a traitor villain   made a fool of
And cannot help the noble chevalier.
15 God comfort him in this necessity;
If he miscarry,° farewell wars in France!   come to harm
Enter another messenger [*Sir William* LUCY]
LUCY[1]   Thou princely leader of our English strength,
Never so needful on the earth of France,
Spur to the rescue of the noble Talbot,
20 Who now is girdled with a waste° of iron   vast expanse; belt
And hemmed about with grim destruction.
To Bordeaux, warlike Duke; to Bordeaux, York,
Else farewell Talbot, France, and England's honour.
RICHARD DUKE OF YORK   O God, that Somerset, who in proud heart
25 Doth stop my cornets,° were in Talbot's place!   troops of cavalry
So should we save a valiant gentleman
By forfeiting a traitor and a coward.
Mad ire and wrathful fury makes me weep,
That thus we die while remiss° traitors sleep.   idle; negligent
30 LUCY   O, send some succour to the distressed lord.
RICHARD DUKE OF YORK   He dies, we lose; I break my warlike word;
We mourn, France smiles; we lose, they daily get,
All 'long° of this vile traitor Somerset.   because
LUCY   Then God take mercy on brave Talbot's soul,
35 And on his son young John, who two hours since
I met in travel toward his warlike father.
This seven years did not Talbot see his son,
And now they meet where both their lives are done.
RICHARD DUKE OF YORK   Alas, what joy shall noble Talbot have
40 To bid his young son welcome to his grave?

4.3 Location: An unspecified field in France.
1. In F, this and the subsequent three speeches
assigned to Lucy are spoken by "Second Messenger"
and "Messenger." However, at line 43, York addresses
the speaker as "Lucy."

Away—vexation almost stops my breath
That sundered friends greet in the hour of death.
Lucy, farewell. No more my fortune can°   *can do*
But curse the cause I cannot aid the man.
45 Maine, Blois, Poitiers, and Tours are won away
'Long all° of Somerset and his delay. *Exeunt [all but* LUCY]   *All because*
LUCY Thus while the vulture of sedition
Feeds in the bosom of such great commanders,
Sleeping neglection° doth betray to loss   *Careless disregard*
50 The conquest of our scarce-cold conqueror,[2]
That ever-living man of memory[3]
Henry the Fifth. Whiles they each other cross,
Lives, honours, lands, and all hurry to loss.   [*Exit*][4]

4.4

Enter [the Duke of] SOMERSET *with his army*

SOMERSET [*to a* CAPTAIN] It is too late, I cannot send them now.
This expedition was by York and Talbot
Too rashly plotted. All our general force
Might with a sally of the very town
5 Be buckled with.[1] The over-daring Talbot
Hath sullied all his gloss of former honour
By this unheedful, desperate, wild adventure.
York set him on to fight and die in shame
That, Talbot dead, great York might bear the name.°   *claim preeminence*
[*Enter* LUCY]
10 CAPTAIN Here is Sir William Lucy, who with me
Set from our o'ermatched forces forth for aid.
SOMERSET How now, Sir William, whither were you sent?
LUCY Whither, my lord? From bought and sold[2] Lord Talbot,
Who, ringed about with bold adversity,
15 Cries out for noble York and Somerset
To beat assailing death from his weak legions;
And whiles the honourable captain there
Drops bloody sweat from his war-wearied limbs
And, unadvantaged,° ling'ring looks for rescue,   *disadvantaged*
20 You his false hopes, the trust of England's honour,
Keep off aloof with worthless emulation.°   *rivalry*
Let not your private discord keep away
The levied succours° that should lend him aid,   *reinforcements*
While he, renownèd noble gentleman,
25 Yield up his life unto a world of ° odds.   *immense*
Orléans the Bastard, Charles, and Burgundy,
Alençon, René, compass him about,
And Talbot perisheth by your default.
SOMERSET York set him on; York should have sent him aid.

2. The conquest made by our recently dead conqueror. (The events of this scene actually took place thirty-one years after the death of the historical Henry V.)
3. That man who will live forever in memory.
4. F does not mark Lucy's exit at this point. Conceivably, he stays onstage as Somerset enters to him.
4.4 Location: Scene continues.
1. *All . . . with:* Our entire army might be engaged by

an attack simply from the French garrison in the town (without taking into account the other French forces coming as reinforcements).
2. *bought and sold:* a proverbial expression meaning "betrayed," perhaps alluding to the biblical account of Christ's betrayal by his disciple Judas for forty pieces of silver.

30 LUCY   And York as fast upon your grace exclaims,
        Swearing that you withhold his levied horse
        Collected for this expedition.
    SOMERSET   York lies. He might have sent° and had the horse.   *sent for*
        I owe him little duty and less love,
35   And take foul scorn° to fawn on him by sending.   *find it disgraceful*
    LUCY   The fraud of England, not the force of France,
        Hath now entrapped the noble-minded Talbot.
        Never to England shall he bear his life,
        But dies betrayed to fortune by your strife.
40 SOMERSET   Come, go. I will dispatch the horsemen straight.°   *immediately*
        Within six hours they will be at his aid.
    LUCY   Too late comes rescue. He is ta'en or slain,
        For fly he could not if he would have fled,
        And fly would Talbot never, though he might.
45 SOMERSET   If he be dead, brave Talbot, then adieu.
    LUCY   His fame lives in the world, his shame in you.

Exeunt [*severally*]

4.5

Enter [*Lord*] TALBOT *and his son* [JOHN]

    TALBOT   O young John Talbot, I did send for thee
        To tutor thee in stratagems of war,
        That Talbot's name might be in thee revived
        When sapless° age and weak unable limbs   *withered*
5   Should bring thy father to his drooping chair.[1]
        But O—malignant and ill-boding stars!—
        Now thou art come unto a feast of death,
        A terrible and unavoided° danger.   *unavoidable*
        Therefore, dear boy, mount on my swiftest horse,
10   And I'll direct thee how thou shalt escape
        By sudden flight. Come, dally not, be gone.
    JOHN   Is my name Talbot, and am I your son,
        And shall I fly? O, if you love my mother,
        Dishonour not her honourable name
15   To make a bastard and a slave of me.
        The world will say he is not Talbot's blood
        That basely fled when noble Talbot stood.
    TALBOT   Fly to revenge my death if I be slain.
    JOHN   He that flies so will ne'er return again.
20 TALBOT   If we both stay, we both are sure to die.
    JOHN   Then let me stay and, father, do you fly.
        Your loss is great; so your regard° should be.   *concern for yourself*
        My worth unknown, no loss is known in me.
        Upon my death the French can little boast;
25   In yours they will: in you all hopes are lost.
        Flight cannot stain the honour you have won,
        But mine it will, that no exploit have done.
        You fled for vantage,° everyone will swear,   *military advantage*
        But if I bow, they'll say it was for fear.
30   There is no hope that ever I will stay
        If the first hour I shrink and run away.

4.5 Location: Battlefield near Bordeaux.
1. Chair where he sits wearily, as his strength and life decline.

Here on my knee I beg mortality°   *death*
Rather than life preserved with infamy.
TALBOT   Shall all thy mother's hopes lie in one tomb?
35   JOHN   Ay, rather than I'll shame my mother's womb.
TALBOT   Upon my blessing I command thee go.
JOHN   To fight I will, but not to fly the foe.
TALBOT   Part of thy father may be saved in thee.
JOHN   No part of him but will be shamed in me.
40   TALBOT   Thou never hadst renown, nor canst not lose it.
JOHN   Yes, your renownèd name—shall flight abuse it?
TALBOT   Thy father's charge° shall clear thee from that stain.   *order*
JOHN   You cannot witness for me, being slain.°   *if you are slain*
If death be so apparent,° then both fly.   *appear so likely*
45   TALBOT   And leave my followers here to fight and die?
My age° was never tainted with such shame.   *life*
JOHN   And shall my youth be guilty of such blame?
No more can I be severed from your side
Than can yourself your self in twain divide.
50   Stay, go, do what you will: the like do I,
For live I will not if my father die.
TALBOT   Then here I take my leave of thee, fair son,
Born to eclipse° thy life this afternoon.   *extinguish*
Come, side by side together live and die,
55   And soul with soul from France to heaven fly.   *Exeunt*

4.6

Alarum. Excursions, wherein [Lord] Talbot's son [JOHN]
is hemmed about [by French soldiers] and TALBOT
rescues him. [The English drive off the French]
TALBOT   Saint George° and victory! Fight, soldiers, fight!   *patron saint of England*
The Regent[1] hath with Talbot broke his word,
And left us to the rage of France his° sword.   *(France's)*
Where is John Talbot? [*To* JOHN] Pause and take thy breath.
5   I gave thee life, and rescued thee from death.
JOHN   O twice my father, twice am I thy son:
The life thou gav'st me first was lost and done
Till with thy warlike sword, despite of fate,
To my determined° time thou gav'st new date.°   *exactly defined / limit*
10   TALBOT   When from the Dauphin's crest thy sword struck fire
It warmed thy father's heart with proud desire
Of bold-faced victory. Then leaden age,
Quickened with youthful spleen° and warlike rage,   *courage*
Beat down Alençon, Orléans, Burgundy,
15   And from the pride of Gallia° rescued thee.   *France*
The ireful Bastard Orléans, that drew blood
From thee, my boy, and had the maidenhood
Of thy first fight,[2] I soon encounterèd,
And interchanging blows, I quickly shed
20   Some of his bastard blood, and in disgrace°   *disdain*
Bespoke him thus: 'Contaminated, base,
And misbegotten blood I spill of thine,

4.6 Location: Scene continues.
1. York, who was appointed regent at 4.1.162–63.
2. *that drew . . . fight:* an allusion to the notion that a

woman bleeds during her first experience of heterosexual intercourse. So young Talbot has bled during his first battle.

Mean° and right poor, for that pure blood of mine   *Base*
Which thou didst force from Talbot, my brave boy.'
25 Here, purposing° the Bastard to destroy,   *as I was intending*
Came in strong rescue. Speak thy father's care:
Art thou not weary, John? How dost thou fare?
Wilt thou yet leave the battle, boy, and fly,
Now thou art sealed° the son of chivalry?   *confirmed*
30 Fly to revenge my death when I am dead;
The help of one stands me in little stead.°   *does me little good*
O, too much folly is it, well I wot,°   *knew*
To hazard all our lives in one small boat.
If I today die not with Frenchmen's rage,
35 Tomorrow I shall die with mickle° age.   *great*
By me they nothing gain, and if I stay
'Tis but the short'ning of my life one day.
In thee thy mother dies, our household's name,
My death's revenge, thy youth, and England's fame.
40 All these and more we hazard by thy stay;
All these are saved if thou wilt fly away.
JOHN   The sword of Orléans hath not made me smart;°   *suffer*
These words of yours draw life-blood from my heart.
On that advantage,³ bought with such a shame,
45 To save a paltry life and slay bright fame,
Before young Talbot from old Talbot fly
The coward horse that bears me fall° and die;   *may it fall*
And like me° to the peasant boys of France,   *compare me*
To be shame's scorn and subject of mischance!⁴
50 Surely, by all the glory you have won,
An if I fly I am not Talbot's son.
Then talk no more of flight; it is no boot.°   *use; profit*
If son to Talbot, die at Talbot's foot.
TALBOT   Then follow thou thy desp'rate sire of Crete,
55 Thou Icarus;⁵ thy life to me is sweet.
If thou wilt fight, fight by thy father's side,
And commendable proved, let's die in pride.   *Exeunt*

4.7

Alarum. Excursions. Enter old [Lord] TALBOT *led*
[by a SERVANT*]*
TALBOT   Where is my other life? Mine own is gone.
O where's young Talbot, where is valiant John?
Triumphant death smeared with captivity,°   *the blood of captives*
Young Talbot's valour makes me smile at thee.
5 When he perceived me shrink° and on my knee,   *weaken*
His bloody sword he brandished over me,
And like a hungry lion did commence
Rough deeds of rage and stern impatience.
But when my angry guardant° stood alone,   *protector*
10 Tend'ring° my ruin and assailed of none,   *Concerned for*

---

3. For the sake of that advantage (of safety).
4. To be an ashamed object of scorn and a victim of misfortune.
5. According to classical mythology, Icarus and his father, Daedalus, tried to escape imprisonment in Crete using artificial wings of feathers and wax. Daedalus succeeded, but Icarus flew too close to the sun and died.

4.7 Location: Scene continues.

Dizzy-eyed fury and great rage of heart
Suddenly made him from my side to start
Into the clust'ring battle° of the French,   *crowded ranks*
And in that sea of blood my boy did drench°   *drown*
15   His over-mounting spirit; and there died
My Icarus, my blossom, in his pride.

     Enter [English soldiers] with John Talbot['s body], borne

SERVANT   O my dear lord, lo where your son is borne.
TALBOT   Thou antic° death, which laugh'st us here to scorn,   *grotesquely grinning*
Anon° from thy insulting tyranny,   *Soon*
20   Coupled in bonds of perpetuity,
Two Talbots wingèd through the lither° sky   *yielding*
In thy despite shall scape mortality.
[*To* JOHN] O thou whose wounds become hard-favoured death,[1]
Speak to thy father ere thou yield thy breath.
25   Brave° death by speaking, whether he will or no;   *Defy*
Imagine him a Frenchman and thy foe.—
Poor boy, he smiles, methinks, as who° should say   *as one who*
'Had death been French, then death had died today'.
Come, come, and lay him in his father's arms.

     [*Soldiers lay* JOHN *in Talbot's arms*]

30   My spirit can no longer bear these harms.
Soldiers, adieu. I have what I would have,
Now my old arms are young John Talbot's grave.

     [*He*] *dies.* [*Alarum. Exeunt soldiers leaving the bodies*]
     Enter CHARLES [*the Dauphin, the dukes of*] ALENÇON
     [*and*] BURGUNDY, [*the*] BASTARD [*of Orléans*], *and* [JOAN
     la] *Pucelle*

CHARLES   Had York and Somerset brought rescue in,
We should have found a bloody day of this.
35   BASTARD   How the young whelp of Talbot's,[2] raging wood,°   *mad*
Did flesh his puny sword[3] in Frenchmen's blood!
JOAN   Once I encountered[4] him, and thus I said:
'Thou maiden[5] youth, be vanquished by a maid.'
But with a proud, majestical high scorn
40   He answered thus: 'Young Talbot was not born
To be the pillage of a giglot° wench.'   *plunder of a wanton*
So rushing in the bowels° of the French,   *center*
He left me proudly, as unworthy fight.
BURGUNDY   Doubtless he would have made a noble knight.
45   See where he lies inhearsèd° in the arms   *(as in a coffin)*
Of the most bloody nurser of his harms.[6]
BASTARD   Hew them to pieces, hack their bones asunder,
Whose life was England's glory, Gallia's° wonder.   *France's*
CHARLES   O no, forbear; for that which we have fled
50   During the life, let us not wrong it dead.

     Enter [*Sir William*] LUCY [*with a French herald*]

LUCY   Herald, conduct me to the Dauphin's tent

---

1. Whose wounds make ugly death attractive.
2. The young puppy of Talbot's (John Talbot). The Bastard is punning on "talbot" as the name for a kind of hunting dog.
3. Plunged in his inexperienced sword for the first time, with a sexual wordplay: plunged in his inexperienced or diminutive penis for the first time.
4. Another bawdy pun: "encounter" may mean "to meet sexually."
5. Virginal; inexperienced in battle.
6. Person who taught him to harm his enemies; person who caused his injuries.

To know who hath obtained the glory of the day.

CHARLES   On what submissive message art thou sent?

LUCY   Submission, Dauphin? 'Tis a mere° French word.   *pure*

55   We English warriors wot° not what it means.   *know*
I come to know what prisoners thou hast ta'en,
And to survey the bodies of the dead.

CHARLES   For prisoners ask'st thou? Hell our prison is.[7]
But tell me whom thou seek'st.

60   LUCY   But where's the great Alcides[8] of the field,
Valiant Lord Talbot, Earl of Shrewsbury,
Created for his rare success in arms
Great Earl of Wexford, Waterford, and Valence,
Lord Talbot of Goodrich and Urchinfield,

65   Lord Strange of Blackmere, Lord Verdun of Alton,
Lord Cromwell of Wingfield, Lord Furnival of Sheffield,
The thrice victorious lord of Falconbridge,
Knight of the noble order of Saint George,
Worthy[9] Saint Michael and the Golden Fleece,

70   Great *Maréhal*° to Henry the Sixth   *commander in chief*
Of all his wars within the realm of France?

JOAN   Here's a silly, stately style° indeed.   *list of titles*
The Turk,° that two-and-fifty kingdoms hath,   *Sultan of Turkey*
Writes not so tedious a style as this.

75   Him that thou magnifi'st with all these titles
Stinking and flyblown° lies here at our feet.   *putrified*

LUCY   Is Talbot slain, the Frenchmen's only scourge,
Your kingdom's terror and black Nemesis?[1]
O, were mine eye-balls into bullets turned,

80   That I in rage might shoot them at your faces!
O, that I could but call these dead to life!—
It were enough to fright the realm of France.
Were but his picture left amongst you here
It would amaze° the proudest of you all.   *terrify*

85   Give me their bodies, that I may bear them hence
And give them burial as beseems° their worth.   *as is appropriate to*

JOAN [*to* CHARLES]   I think this upstart is old Talbot's ghost,
He speaks with such a proud commanding spirit.
For God's sake let him have them. To keep them here

90   They would but stink and putrefy the air.

CHARLES   Go, take their bodies hence.

LUCY   I'll bear them hence, but from their ashes shall be reared
A phoenix[2] that shall make all France afeard.

CHARLES   So we be rid of them, do with them what thou wilt.

[*Exeunt* LUCY *and herald with the bodies*]

95   And now to Paris in this conquering vein.
All will be ours, now bloody Talbot's slain.   *Exeunt*

---

7. Charles implies that the French have killed their enemies (sent them to hell) rather than taking prisoners.
8. Hercules (a descendant of Alcaeus), the hero of
classical mythology, famous for performing difficult
feats of strength and bravery.
9. Worthy of; equal in value to. The Order of St.
Michael was a French chivalric order established in

1469, after the events of the play occurred. The Order
of the Golden Fleece was formed in Burgundy in 1430.
1. The Greek goddess of avenging justice.
2. A legendary bird that was said to live five hundred
years, burn itself to ashes, and then be reborn from the
ashes.

5.1

Sennet. Enter KING [HENRY, *the Dukes of*]
GLOUCESTER, *and* EXETER [*and others*]

KING HENRY [*to* GLOUCESTER]   Have you perused the letters from the Pope,
The Emperor, and the Earl of Armagnac?
GLOUCESTER   I have, my lord, and their intent is this:
They humbly sue unto your excellence
5   To have a godly peace concluded of
Between the realms of England and of France.
KING HENRY   How doth your grace affect their motion?°   *like their proposal*
GLOUCESTER   Well, my good lord, and as the only means
To stop effusion° of our Christian blood   *spilling*
10   And 'stablish quietness on every side.
KING HENRY   Ay, marry, uncle; for I always thought
It was both impious and unnatural
That such immanity° and bloody strife   *barbarity*
Should reign among professors of one faith.
15   GLOUCESTER   Beside, my lord, the sooner to effect
And surer bind this knot of amity,
The Earl of Armagnac, near knit° to Charles—   *closely related*
A man of great authority in France—
Proffers his only daughter to your grace
20   In marriage, with a large and sumptuous dowry.
KING HENRY   Marriage, uncle? Alas, my years are young,
And fitter is my study and my books
Than wanton dalliance with a paramour.
Yet call th'ambassadors,   [*Exit one or more*]
and as you please,
25   So let them have their answers every one.
I shall be well content with any choice
Tends° to God's glory and my country's weal.°   *That tends / welfare*

Enter [*the Bishop of*] WINCHESTER, [*now in cardinal's
habit,*] *and three ambassadors* [*one a Papal* LEGATE]

EXETER [*aside*]   What, is my lord of Winchester installed
And called unto a cardinal's degree?
30   Then I perceive that will be verified
Henry the Fifth did sometime° prophesy: *at one time*
'If once he come to be a cardinal,
He'll make his cap° co-equal with the crown.'   *(a cardinal's red hat)*
KING HENRY   My lords ambassadors, your several suits
35   Have been considered and debated on.
Your purpose is both good and reasonable,
And therefore are we certainly resolved
To draw° conditions of a friendly peace,   *draft*
Which by my lord of Winchester we mean
40   Shall be transported presently to France.
GLOUCESTER [*to ambassadors*]   And for the proffer of my lord your master,
I have informed his highness so at large°   *in full*
As,° liking of the lady's virtuous gifts,   *That*
Her beauty, and the value of her dower,
45   He doth intend she shall be England's queen.

5.1 Location: The palace, London.

KING HENRY [*to ambassadors*]   In argument° and proof of which   *As evidence*
    contract
Bear her this jewel, pledge of my affection.
[*To* GLOUCESTER] And so, my lord Protector, see them guarded
And safely brought to Dover, wherein shipped,°   *where once embarked*
50   Commit them to the fortune of the sea.
           Exeunt [*severally all but* WINCHESTER *and* LEGATE]
WINCHESTER   Stay, my lord legate; you shall first receive
The sum of money which I promisèd
Should be delivered to his holiness
For clothing me in these grave ornaments.°   *solemn robes of office*
55 LEGATE   I will attend upon your lordship's leisure.   [*Exit*]¹
WINCHESTER   Now Winchester will not submit, I trow,°   *trust*
Or be inferior to the proudest peer.
Humphrey of Gloucester, thou shalt well perceive
That nor° in birth or for authority   *neither*
60   The Bishop will be overborne° by thee.   *overruled*
I'll either make thee stoop and bend thy knee,
Or sack this country with a mutiny.°   *Exit*   *an open revolt*

5.2

Enter CHARLES [*the Dauphin reading a letter,*
the Dukes of] BURGUNDY [*and*] ALENÇON, [*the*]
BASTARD [*of Orléans*], RENÉ [*Duke of Anjou*], *and* JOAN
[*la Pucelle*]

CHARLES   These news, my lords, may cheer our drooping spirits.
'Tis said the stout° Parisians do revolt   *valiant*
And turn again unto the warlike French.
ALENÇON   Then march to Paris, royal Charles of France,
5   And keep not back your powers in dalliance.°   *idleness*
JOAN   Peace be amongst them if they turn to us;
Else, ruin combat with their palaces!¹
           Enter [*a*] SCOUT
SCOUT   Success unto our valiant general,
And happiness to his accomplices.°   *allies*
10 CHARLES   What tidings send our scouts? I prithee speak.
SCOUT   The English army, that divided was
Into two parties, is now conjoined in one,²
And means to give you battle presently.°   *immediately*
CHARLES   Somewhat too sudden, sirs, the warning is;
15   But we will presently provide for them.
BURGUNDY   I trust the ghost of Talbot is not there.
JOAN   Now he is gone, my lord, you need not fear.³
Of all base passions, fear is most accursed.
Command the conquest, Charles, it shall be thine;
20   Let Henry fret and all the world repine.°   *complain*
CHARLES   Then on, my lords; and France be fortunate!   *Exeunt*

---

1. The legate may leave at this point, but there is no
exit marked in F. He may simply step to the side while
Winchester makes his final speech and then exit with
the prelate.

5.2 Location: Plains in Anjou, France.
1. Otherwise, let ruin destroy their palaces.
2. In other words, York and Suffolk have joined forces.
3. F assigns this line to Burgundy.

5.3

Alarum. Excursions. Enter JOAN *[la] Pucelle*

JOAN The Regent° conquers, and the Frenchmen fly.   *(Richard Duke of York)*
Now help, ye charming° spells and periapts,°   *magic / amulets*
And ye choice spirits that admonish° me   *forewarn*
And give me signs of future accidents.°   *events*
    Thunder
5 You speedy helpers, that are substitutes°   *deputies*
Under the lordly monarch of the north,¹
Appear, and aid me in this enterprise.
    Enter Fiends
This speed and quick appearance argues° proof   *offers*
Of your accustomed° diligence to me.   *customary*
10 Now, ye familiar spirits² that are culled
Out of the powerful regions under earth,
Help me this once, that France may get the field.°   *win the battle*
    They walk and speak not
O, hold me not with silence overlong!
Where I was wont to feed you with my blood,³
15 I'll lop a member° off and give it you   *limb*
In earnest° of a further benefit,   *As an advance payment*
So you do condescend to help me now.
    They hang their heads
No hope to have redress? My body shall
Pay recompense if you will grant my suit.
    They shake their heads
20 Cannot my body nor blood-sacrifice
Entreat you to your wonted furtherance?°   *usual assistance*
Then take my soul—my body, soul, and all—
Before that England give the French the foil.°   *defeat*
    They depart
See, they forsake me. Now the time is come
25 That France must vail her lofty-plumèd crest⁴
And let her head fall into England's lap.
My ancient° incantations are too weak,   *former*
And hell too strong for me to buckle° with.   *fight; do combat*
Now, France, thy glory droopeth to the dust.   *Exit*

5.4

Excursions. [The Dukes of] BURGUNDY *and* YORK *fight*
*hand to hand. [The] French fly. [*JOAN *la Pucelle*
is taken]

RICHARD DUKE OF YORK Damsel of France, I think I have you fast.
Unchain your spirits now with spelling° charms,   *conjuring*
And try if they can gain your liberty.
A goodly prize, fit for the devil's grace!¹
5 [*To his soldiers*] See how the ugly witch doth bend her brows,°   *scowls*
As if with Circe² she would change my shape.

5.3 Location: Before Angiers (i.e., Angers), France.
1. The devil and his demons were frequently associated with the north.
2. Attendant spirits that could be summoned by a witch; often they inhabited the bodies of animals.
3. Witches were thought to have extra nipples with which they fed their familiars, or attendant spirits.

4. Must lower her high-feathered helmet.
5.4 Location: Scene continues.
1. Fit for his grace, the devil (said sarcastically).
2. According to Greek mythology, a witch who seduced Odysseus and turned his men into swine (see Homer, *Odyssey* 10).

JOAN   Changed to a worser shape thou canst not be.

RICHARD DUKE OF YORK   O, Charles the Dauphin is a proper° man.   *handsome*
    No shape but his can please your dainty° eye.   *fastidious*

10 JOAN   A plaguing mischief light on Charles and thee,
    And may ye both be suddenly surprised
    By bloody hands in° sleeping on your beds!   *while*

RICHARD DUKE OF YORK   Fell banning° hag, enchantress, hold   *Fierce cursing*
    thy tongue.

JOAN   I prithee give me leave to curse awhile.

RICHARD DUKE OF YORK   Curse, miscreant,° when thou comest   *heretic*
15   to the stake.   *Exeunt*

5.5

Alarum. Enter [the Earl of] SUFFOLK *with* MARGARET
    in his hand°   *led by the hand*

SUFFOLK   Be what thou wilt, thou art my prisoner.
    [He] gazes on her
    O fairest beauty, do not fear nor fly,
    For I will touch thee but with reverent hands,
    And lay them gently on thy tender side.
5   I kiss these fingers for eternal peace.
    Who art thou? Say, that I may honour thee.

MARGARET   Margaret my name, and daughter to a king,
    The King of Naples,[1] whosoe'er thou art.

SUFFOLK   An earl I am, and Suffolk am I called.
10   Be not offended, nature's miracle,
    Thou art allotted° to be ta'en by me.   *destined*
    So doth the swan his downy cygnets save,°   *young swans protect*
    Keeping them prisoner underneath his wings.
    Yet if this servile usage° once offend,   *treatment as a slave*
15   Go, and be free again, as Suffolk's friend.
    She is going
    O stay! *[Aside]* I have no power to let her pass.
    My hand would free her, but my heart says no.
    As plays the sun upon the glassy stream,
    Twinkling another counterfeited° beam,   *reflected*
20   So seems this gorgeous beauty to mine eyes.
    Fain would I woo her, yet I dare not speak.
    I'll call for pen and ink, and write my mind.
    Fie, de la Pole,[2] disable° not thyself!   *disparage*
    Hast not a tongue? Is she not here to hear?
25   Wilt thou be daunted at a woman's sight?[3]
    Ay, beauty's princely majesty is such
    Confounds° the tongue, and makes the senses rough.°   *That it confuses / dull*

MARGARET   Say, Earl of Suffolk—if thy name be so—
    What ransom must I pay before I pass?
30   For I perceive I am thy prisoner.

SUFFOLK *[aside]*   How canst thou tell she will deny° thy suit   *refuse*

5.5 Location: Scene continues.
1. That is, the René of earlier scenes, Duke of Anjou and also titular King of Naples and Sicily.

2. Suffolk's family name.
3. At the sight of a woman; at a woman's gaze.

Before thou make a trial of her love?

MARGARET   Why speak'st thou not? What ransom must I pay?

SUFFOLK [aside]   She's beautiful, and therefore to be wooed;

35   She is a woman, therefore to be won.

MARGARET   Wilt thou accept of ransom, yea or no?

SUFFOLK [aside]   Fond° man, remember that thou hast a wife;   Foolish
Then how can Margaret be thy paramour?°   mistress

MARGARET [aside]   I were best to leave him, for he will not hear.

40   SUFFOLK [aside]   There° all is marred; there lies a cooling card.⁴   By that fact

MARGARET [aside]   He talks at random; sure the man is mad.

SUFFOLK [aside]   And yet a dispensation⁵ may be had.

MARGARET   And yet I would that you would answer me.

SUFFOLK [aside]   I'll win this Lady Margaret. For whom?

45   Why, for my king—tush, that's a wooden⁶ thing.

MARGARET [aside]   He talks of wood. It is some carpenter.

SUFFOLK [aside]   Yet so my fancy° may be satisfied,   love
And peace establishèd between these realms.
But there remains a scruple° in that too,   an objection

50   For though her father be the King of Naples,
Duke of Anjou and Maine, yet is he poor,
And our nobility will scorn the match.

MARGARET   Hear ye, captain? Are you not at leisure?

SUFFOLK [aside]   It shall be so, disdain they ne'er so much.

55   Henry is youthful, and will quickly yield.
[To MARGARET] Madam, I have a secret to reveal.

MARGARET [aside]   What though I be enthralled,° he seems a knight   taken captive
And will not any way dishonour me.

SUFFOLK   Lady, vouchsafe to listen° what I say.   listen to

60   MARGARET [aside]   Perhaps I shall be rescued by the French,
And then I need not crave his courtesy.

SUFFOLK   Sweet madam, give me hearing in a cause.

MARGARET [aside]   Tush, women have been captivate⁷ ere now.

SUFFOLK   Lady, wherefore talk you so?

65   MARGARET   I cry you mercy, 'tis but quid for quo.°   tit for tat

SUFFOLK   Say, gentle Princess, would you not suppose
Your bondage happy to be° made a queen?   if you were to be

MARGARET   To be a queen in bondage is more vile
Than is a slave in base servility,°   slavery
For princes should be free.

70   SUFFOLK   And so shall you,
If happy England's royal king be free.

MARGARET   Why, what concerns his freedom unto me?

SUFFOLK   I'll undertake to make thee Henry's queen,
To put a golden sceptre in thy hand,

75   And set a precious crown upon thy head,
If thou wilt condescend° to be my—   agree

MARGARET   What?

SUFFOLK   His love.

MARGARET   I am unworthy to be Henry's wife.

---

4. An obstacle; literally, a card that, when played, dashes the hopes of one's opponent.
5. Special permission from the Pope to dissolve a marriage.

6. Stupid (referring either to King Henry or to his own scheme to woo Margaret).
7. Have been taken prisoner; have fallen in love against their will.

SUFFOLK   No, gentle madam, I unworthy am
80 To woo so fair a dame to be his wife
    [*Aside*] And have no portion° in the choice myself.—   *share*
    How say you, madam; are ye so content?
MARGARET   An if my father please, I am content.
SUFFOLK   Then call our captains and our colours forth,
    [*Enter captains, colours, and trumpeters*]
85 And, madam, at your father's castle walls
    We'll crave a parley to confer with him.
        Sound [*a parley*]. *Enter* RENÉ [*Duke of Anjou*]
        on the walls
    See, René, see thy daughter prisoner.
RENÉ   To whom?
SUFFOLK   To me.
RENÉ   Suffolk, what remedy?
    I am a soldier, and unapt° to weep   *unsuited*
90 Or to exclaim on° fortune's fickleness.   *complain of*
SUFFOLK   Yes, there is remedy enough, my lord.
    Assent, and for thy honour give consent
    Thy daughter shall be wedded to my king,
    Whom I with pain have wooed and won thereto;
95 And this her easy-held° imprisonment   *easily endured*
    Hath gained thy daughter princely liberty.
RENÉ   Speaks Suffolk as he thinks?
SUFFOLK   Fair Margaret knows
    That Suffolk doth not flatter, face° or feign.   *deceive*
RENÉ   Upon thy princely warrant° I descend   *guarantee*
100 To give thee answer of thy just demand.
SUFFOLK   And here I will expect° thy coming.   *await*
                    [*Exit* RENÉ *above*]
        Trumpets sound. Enter RENÉ
RENÉ   Welcome, brave Earl, into our territories.
    Command in Anjou what your honour pleases.
SUFFOLK   Thanks, René, happy for° so sweet a child,   *fortunate in having*
105 Fit to be made companion with a king.
    What answer makes your grace unto my suit?
RENÉ   Since thou dost deign to woo her little worth
    To be the princely bride of such a lord,
    Upon condition I may quietly
110 Enjoy mine own, the countries Maine and Anjou,
    Free from oppression or the stroke of war,
    My daughter shall be Henry's, if he please.
SUFFOLK   That is her ransom. I deliver her,
    And those two counties° I will undertake   *domains of a count*
115 Your grace shall well and quietly enjoy.
RENÉ   And I again° in Henry's royal name,   *in return*
    As deputy unto that gracious king,
    Give thee her hand for sign of plighted faith.°   *a marriage pledge*
SUFFOLK   René of France, I give thee kingly thanks,
120 Because this is in traffic° of a king.   *business*
    [*Aside*] And yet methinks I could be well content
    To be mine own attorney in this case.[8]
    [*To* RENÉ] I'll over then to England with this news,

---

8. To act on my own behalf in this instance, with a pun on "case" as slang for "vagina."

And make this marriage to be solemnized.
125 So farewell, René; set this diamond safe
In golden palaces, as it becomes.°   *as befits it*
RENÉ   I do embrace thee as I would embrace
The Christian prince King Henry, were he here.
MARGARET [*to* SUFFOLK]   Farewell, my lord. Good wishes, praise, and prayers
130 Shall Suffolk ever have of Margaret.
            She is going
SUFFOLK   Farewell, sweet madam; but hark you, Margaret—
No princely commendations° to my king?   *greetings*
MARGARET   Such commendations as becomes a maid,
A virgin, and his servant, say to him.
135 SUFFOLK   Words sweetly placed, and modestly directed.
            [*She is going*]
But madam, I must trouble you again—
No loving token to his majesty?
MARGARET   Yes, my good lord: a pure unspotted heart,
Never yet taint° with love, I send the King.   *tinged*
140 SUFFOLK   And this withal.°   *in addition*
            [*He*] kiss[*es*] *her*
MARGARET   That for thyself; I will not so presume
To send such peevish° tokens to a king.   *trifling*
            [*Exeunt* RENÉ *and* MARGARET]
SUFFOLK [*aside*]   O, wert thou for myself!—but Suffolk, stay.
Thou mayst not wander in that labyrinth.⁹
145 There Minotaurs and ugly treasons lurk.
Solicit° Henry with her wondrous praise.   *Entice*
Bethink thee on her virtues that surmount,
Mad° natural graces that extinguish° art.   *Extravagant / eclipse*
Repeat their semblance¹ often on the seas,
150 That when thou com'st to kneel at Henry's feet
Thou mayst bereave° him of his wits with wonder.   *Exeunt*   *dispossess*

5.6

            Enter [RICHARD DUKE OF] YORK, [*the Earl of*]
            WARWICK, [*and a*] SHEPHERD
RICHARD DUKE OF YORK   Bring forth that sorceress condemned
    to burn.
            [*Enter* JOAN *la Pucelle guarded*]¹
SHEPHERD   Ah, Joan, this kills thy father's heart outright.
Have I sought° every country far and near,   *searched*
And now it is my chance to find thee out°   *discover you*
5 Must I behold thy timeless° cruel death?   *untimely*
Ah Joan, sweet daughter Joan, I'll die with thee.
JOAN   Decrepit miser,° base ignoble wretch,   *miserable person*
I am descended of a gentler° blood.   *more aristocratic*
Thou art no father nor no friend° of mine.   *kinsman*
10 SHEPHERD   Out, out!—My lords, an't please you, 'tis not so.

---

9. A maze built by Daedalus for King Minos of Crete,
who kept in it the Minotaur (a monster born from
Queen Pasiphaë's sexual encounter with a bull).
1. Recall the image or description of her virtues.
5.6 Location: Camp of the Duke of York, France.

1. In F, Joan is included in the list of those who enter
at the beginning of this scene, but it makes sense to
have her enter after York commands that she be
brought forth.

I did beget her, all the parish knows.
Her mother liveth yet, can testify
She was the first fruit of my bach'lorship.[2]

WARWICK [*to* JOAN]   Graceless,° wilt thou deny thy parentage?   *Depraved person*

RICHARD DUKE OF YORK   This argues° what her kind of life hath   *testifies to*
15   been—
Wicked and vile; and so her death concludes.°   *confirms; ends*

SHEPHERD   Fie, Joan, that thou wilt be so obstacle.[3]
God knows thou art a collop° of my flesh,   *slice*
And for thy sake have I shed many a tear.
20   Deny me not, I prithee, gentle Joan.

JOAN   Peasant, avaunt! [*To the English*] You have suborned[4] this man
Of purpose to obscure my noble birth.

SHEPHERD [*to the English*]   'Tis true I gave a noble[5] to the priest
The morn that I was wedded to her mother.
25   [*To* JOAN] Kneel down, and take my blessing, good my girl.
Wilt thou not stoop? Now cursèd be the time
Of thy nativity. I would the milk
Thy mother gave thee when thou sucked'st her breast
Had been a little ratsbane° for thy sake.   *rat poison*
30   Or else, when thou didst keep° my lambs afield,   *tend*
I wish some ravenous wolf had eaten thee.
Dost thou deny thy father, cursèd drab?°   *whore*
[*To the English*] O burn her, burn her! Hanging is too good.

Exit

RICHARD DUKE OF YORK [*to guards*]   Take her away, for she hath
                lived too long,
35   To fill the world with vicious qualities.

JOAN   First let me tell you whom you have condemned:
Not one begotten of a shepherd swain,
But issued from the progeny of kings;
Virtuous and holy, chosen from above
40   By inspiration of celestial grace
To work exceeding° miracles on earth.   *exceptional*
I never had to do with wicked spirits;
But you that are polluted with your lusts,
Stained with the guiltless blood of innocents,
45   Corrupt and tainted with a thousand vices—
Because you want° the grace that others have,   *lack*
You judge it straight° a thing impossible   *immediately*
To compass° wonders but by help of devils.   *accomplish*
No, misconceivèd[6] Joan of Arc hath been
50   A virgin from her tender infancy,
Chaste and immaculate in very thought,
Whose maiden-blood thus rigorously effused°   *cruelly shed*
Will cry for vengeance at the gates of heaven.

RICHARD DUKE OF YORK   Ay, ay, [*to guards*] away with her to execution.
55   WARWICK [*to guards*]   And hark ye, sirs: because she is a maid,
Spare for no faggots. Let there be enough.

---

2. The first child I had as an unmarried man.
3. Obstinate. This use of "obstacle" suggests the shepherd's country dialect.
4. Hired to give false evidence.

5. English gold coin worth about one-third of a pound.
6. Misunderstood, with a pun on "misconceived" as "miscreated in the womb."

Place barrels of pitch upon the fatal stake,
That so her torture may be shortenèd.[7]
JOAN Will nothing turn° your unrelenting hearts?   *change*
60   Then Joan, discover° thine infirmity,   *reveal*
That warranteth by law to be thy privilege:[8]
I am with child, ye bloody homicides.
Murder not then the fruit within my womb,
Although ye hale° me to a violent death.   *drag*
RICHARD DUKE OF YORK Now heaven forfend—the holy maid
65   with child?
WARWICK [*to* JOAN] The greatest miracle that e'er ye wrought.
Is all your strict preciseness° come to this?   *propriety*
RICHARD DUKE OF YORK She and the Dauphin have been
      ingling.°   *having sex; dallying*
I did imagine° what would be her refuge.°   *wonder / last defense*
70 WARWICK Well, go to, we will have no bastards live,
Especially since Charles must father it.
JOAN You are deceived. My child is none of his.
It was Alençon[9] that enjoyed my love.
RICHARD DUKE OF YORK Alençon, that notorious Machiavel?[1]
75   It dies an if it had a thousand lives.
JOAN O give me leave, I have deluded you.
'Twas neither Charles nor yet the Duke I named,
But René King of Naples that prevailed.
WARWICK A married man?—That's most intolerable.
80 RICHARD DUKE OF YORK Why, here's a girl; I think she knows not well—
There were so many—whom she may accuse.
WARWICK It's sign she hath been liberal° and free.   *generous; promiscuous*
RICHARD DUKE OF YORK And yet forsooth she is a virgin pure!
[*To* JOAN] Strumpet, thy words condemn thy brat and thee.
85   Use no entreaty, for it is in vain.
JOAN Then lead me hence; with whom I leave my curse.
May never glorious sun reflex° his beams   *throw*
Upon the country where you make abode,
But darkness and the gloomy shade of death
90   Environ you till mischief° and despair   *misfortune*
Drive you to break your necks or hang yourselves.
       Enter [*the Bishop of* WINCHESTER, *now*] *Cardinal*
RICHARD DUKE OF YORK [*to* JOAN] Break thou in pieces, and
      consume° to ashes,   *burn away*
Thou foul accursèd minister of hell.   [*Exit* JOAN, *guarded*]
WINCHESTER Lord Regent, I do greet your excellence
95   With letters of commission from the King.
For know, my lords, the states of Christendom,
Moved with remorse of° these outrageous broils,   *pity for*
Have earnestly implored a general peace
Betwixt our nation and the aspiring French,

---

7. The orders for wood and pitch are meant to ensure either that Joan will die quickly as a result of asphyxiation from the smoke, rather than from the flames themselves, or that she will die swiftly from the intensity of the fire.
8. The legal right of a pregnant woman to postpone her execution until after she has given birth.
9. Jean, second Duke of Alençon, was cousin to Charles, the Dauphin.
1. Scheming politician. Niccolò Machiavelli (1469–1527), author of *The Prince*, became associated with principles of cunning statecraft.

100   And here at hand the Dauphin and his train
         Approacheth to confer about some matter.
         RICHARD DUKE OF YORK   Is all our travail° turned to this effect?   *labor*
         After the slaughter of so many peers,
         So many captains, gentlemen, and soldiers
105   That in this quarrel have been overthrown
         And sold their bodies for their country's benefit,
         Shall we at last conclude effeminate peace?
         Have we not lost most part of all the towns
         By treason, falsehood, and by treachery,
110   Our great progenitors had conquerèd?
         O Warwick, Warwick, I foresee with grief
         The utter loss of all the realm of France!
         WARWICK   Be patient, York. If we conclude a peace
         It shall be with such strict and severe covenants
115   As° little shall the Frenchmen gain thereby.   *That*
           Enter CHARLES [*the Dauphin, the Duke of*] ALENÇON,
           [*the*] BASTARD [*of Orléans, and*] RENÉ [*Duke of Anjou*]
         CHARLES   Since, lords of England, it is thus agreed
         That peaceful truce shall be proclaimed in France,
         We come to be informèd by yourselves
         What the conditions of that league° must be.   *treaty*
120   RICHARD DUKE OF YORK   Speak, Winchester; for boiling choler° chokes   *anger*
         The hollow passage of my poisoned voice
         By sight of these our baleful° enemies.   *deadly*
         WINCHESTER   Charles and the rest, it is enacted thus:
         That, in regard° King Henry gives consent,   *since*
125   Of mere° compassion and of lenity,°   *Out of pure / mildness*
         To ease your country of distressful war
         And suffer° you to breathe in fruitful peace,   *allow*
         You shall become true liegemen[2] to his crown.
         And, Charles, upon condition thou wilt swear
130   To pay him tribute and submit thyself,
         Thou shalt be placed as viceroy under him,
         And still enjoy thy regal dignity.
         ALENÇON   Must he be then as shadow of himself?—
         Adorn his temples with a coronet,[3]
135   And yet in substance and authority
         Retain but privilege of a private man?
         This proffer is absurd and reasonless.
         CHARLES   'Tis known already that I am possessed
         With more than half the Gallian° territories,   *French*
140   And therein reverenced for their lawful king.
         Shall I, for lucre° of the rest° unvanquished,   *gain / rest that are*
         Detract so much from that prerogative
         As to be called but° viceroy of the whole?   *merely*
         No, lord ambassador, I'll rather keep
145   That which I have than, coveting for more,
         Be cast° from possibility of all.   *excluded*
         RICHARD DUKE OF YORK   Insulting Charles, hast thou by secret means
         Used intercession to obtain a league

---

2. Those bound to serve a feudal lord; faithful subjects.   3. Small crown worn by nobles.

And, now the matter grows to compromise,°   *toward resolution*
150 Stand'st thou aloof upon comparison?⁴
Either accept the title thou usurp'st,
Of benefit° proceeding from our king   *As a benefaction*
And not of any challenge of desert,⁵
Or we will plague thee with incessant wars.
155 RENÉ [*aside to* CHARLES]   My lord, you do not well in obstinacy
To cavil⁶ in the course of this contract.
If once it be neglected,° ten to one   *disregarded*
We shall not find like opportunity.
ALENÇON [*aside to* CHARLES]   To say the truth, it is your policy°   *astute course*
160 To save your subjects from such massacre
And ruthless slaughters as are daily seen
By our proceeding in hostility;
And therefore take this compact of a truce,
Although you break it when your pleasure serves.
165 WARWICK   How sayst thou, Charles? Shall our condition stand?
CHARLES   It shall,
Only reserved° you claim no interest   *With the reservation*
In any of our towns of garrison.°   *fortified towns*
RICHARD DUKE OF YORK   Then swear allegiance to his majesty,
170 As thou art knight, never to disobey
Nor be rebellious to the crown of England,
Thou nor thy nobles, to the crown of England.
[*They swear*]
So, now dismiss your army when ye please.
Hang up your ensigns, let your drums be still;
175 For here we entertain a solemn peace.   *Exeunt*

5.7

Enter [the Earl of] SUFFOLK, *in conference with* KING
[HENRY, *and the Dukes of*] GLOUCESTER *and* EXETER
KING HENRY [*to* SUFFOLK]   Your wondrous rare description, noble Earl,
Of beauteous Margaret hath astonished me.
Her virtues gracèd with external gifts
Do breed love's settled° passions in my heart,   *unchanging*
5   And like as rigour° of tempestuous gusts   *violent force*
Provokes° the mightiest hulk° against the tide,   *Drives / ship*
So am I driven by breath of her renown°   *word of her fame*
Either to suffer shipwreck or arrive
Where I may have fruition of her love.
10   SUFFOLK   Tush, my good lord, this superficial tale
Is but a preface of her worthy praise.°   *the praise she deserves*
The chief perfections of that lovely dame,
Had I sufficient skill to utter them,
Would make a volume of enticing lines
15   Able to ravish any dull conceit;°   *imagination*
And, which is more, she is not so divine,
So full° replete with choice of all delights,   *fully*
But with as humble lowliness of mind
She is content to be at your command—

---

4. Do you hold off in order to quibble about the terms?   6. To raise frivolous objections.
5. And not by any claim of inherent right.   5.7 Location: The palace, London.

20   Command, I mean, of virtuous chaste intents,
          To love and honour Henry as her lord.
          KING HENRY   And otherwise will Henry ne'er presume.
          [*To* GLOUCESTER] Therefore, my lord Protector, give consent
          That Marg'ret may be England's royal queen.
25   GLOUCESTER   So should I give consent to flatter sin.
          You know, my lord, your highness is betrothed
          Unto another lady of esteem.[1]
          How shall we then dispense with that contract
          And not deface your honour with reproach?
30   SUFFOLK   As doth a ruler with unlawful oaths,
          Or one that, at a triumph[2] having vowed
          To try his strength, forsaketh yet the lists[3]
          By reason of his adversary's odds.
          A poor earl's daughter is unequal odds,
35   And therefore may be broke[4] without offence.
          GLOUCESTER   Why, what, I pray, is Margaret more than that?
          Her father is no better than an earl,
          Although in glorious titles he excel.
          SUFFOLK   Yes, my lord; her father is a king,
40   The King of Naples and Jerusalem,
          And of such great authority in France
          As his alliance will confirm our peace
          And keep the Frenchmen in allegiance.
          GLOUCESTER   And so the Earl of Armagnac may do,
45   Because he is near kinsman unto Charles.
          EXETER   Beside, his wealth doth warrant° a liberal dower,   *guarantee*
          Where René sooner will receive than give.
          SUFFOLK   A dower, my lords? Disgrace not so your King
          That he should be so abject, base, and poor
50   To choose for wealth and not for perfect love.
          Henry is able to enrich his queen,
          And not to seek a queen to make him rich.
          So worthless peasants bargain for their wives,
          As market men for oxen, sheep, or horse.
55   Marriage is a matter of more worth
          Than to be dealt in by attorneyship.°   *proxy*
          Not whom *we* will but whom his grace affects°   *desires*
          Must be companion of his nuptial bed.
          And therefore, lords, since he affects her most,
60   That most of all these reasons bindeth us:
          In our opinions she should be preferred.
          For what is wedlock forcèd° but a hell,   *enforced marriage*
          An age of discord and continual strife,
          Whereas the contrary bringeth bliss,
65   And is a pattern° of celestial peace.   *an example*
          Whom should we match with Henry, being a king,
          But Margaret, that is daughter to a king?
          Her peerless feature° joinèd with her birth°   *form / high rank*
          Approves her° fit for none but for a king.   *Confirms that she is*
70   Her valiant courage and undaunted spirit,

---

1. The daughter of the Earl of Armagnac (see 5.1.15–20).
2. Tournament or combat between two opponents on horseback and armed with lances.
3. *forsaketh yet the lists*: nevertheless leaves the tournament grounds.
4. That is, the marriage pledge may be broken.

More than in women commonly is seen,
Will answer our hope in issue of a king.[5]
For Henry, son unto a conqueror,
Is likely to beget more conquerors
75 If with a lady of so high resolve°   determination
As is fair Margaret he be linked in love.
Then yield, my lords, and here conclude with me:
That Margaret shall be queen, and none but she.
KING HENRY   Whether it be through force of your report,
80 My noble lord of Suffolk, or for that°   or because
My tender youth was never yet attaint°   infected
With any passion of inflaming love,
I cannot tell; but this I am assured:
I feel such sharp dissension in my breast,
85 Such fierce alarums° both of hope and fear,   alarms
As I am sick with working of my thoughts.
Take therefore shipping; post,° my lord, to France;   hasten
Agree to any covenants, and procure
That Lady Margaret do vouchsafe° to come   promise
90 To cross the seas to England and be crowned
King Henry's faithful and anointed queen.
For your expenses and sufficient charge,°   money to spend
Among the people gather up a tenth.[6]
Be gone, I say; for till you do return
95 I rest perplexèd° with a thousand cares.   I remain troubled
[To GLOUCESTER] And you, good uncle, banish all offence.°   hostility
If you do censure me by what you were,[7]
Not what you are, I know it will excuse
This sudden execution of my will.
100 And so conduct me where from° company   away from
I may revolve and ruminate my grief.[8]   Exit [with EXETER]
GLOUCESTER   Ay, grief, I fear me, both at first and last.   Exit
SUFFOLK   Thus Suffolk hath prevailed, and thus he goes
As did the youthful Paris[9] once to Greece,
105 With hope to find the like event° in love,   the same outcome
But prosper better than the Trojan did.
Margaret shall now be queen and rule the King;
But I will rule both her, the King, and realm.   Exit

5. Will satisfy our hopes by bringing forth a king.
6. A tax of 10 percent on income or property.
7. If you judge me by how you behaved when you were young.
8. I may return again and again in my mind to my grief.

9. According to Greek mythology, Paris went to Greece from Troy and abducted Helen, the wife of Menelaus. This act was said to have brought about the Trojan War, in which Paris was killed.

Richard III

Among the very few anecdotes about Shakespeare that date from his own lifetime is a ribald story recorded in 1602 in the diary of a London law student, John Manningham:

> Upon a time when Burbage played Richard III there was a citizen grew so far in liking with him, that before she went from the play she appointed him to come that night unto her by the name of Richard III. Shakespeare, overhearing their conclusion, went before, was entertained and at his game ere Burbage came. The message being brought that Richard III was at the door, Shakespeare caused return to be made that William the Conqueror was before Richard III.

Like most stories about celebrities, this one probably says more about those who circulated it than about those it describes. But it does at least suggest that Richard Burbage, the famous actor who first played Richard III (as well as such parts as Romeo and Hamlet), had not by virtue of his villainous role lost all of his glamour. Indeed, it is striking that Richard—the "elvish-marked, abortive, rooting hog" (1.3.225), the "poisonous bunch-backed toad" (1.3.244), the heartless cur sent, as he himself puts it, "deformed" and "unfinished" (1.1.20) into the world—has seemed weirdly and compellingly attractive to generations of playgoers. From the start, the play seems to have aroused intense interest: first performed in 1592 or 1593, *Richard III* was published in quarto no fewer than five times during Shakespeare's lifetime.

What can account for this attraction? It is not an obvious feature in the chronicle histories upon which Shakespeare relied, nor does Richard seem to have a comparable allure in another play of unknown authorship that dates from the same period, *The True Tragedy of Richard III*. In these works, Richard figures as the pitiless, treacherous villain of what has been called the "Tudor Myth"—that is, the officially sanctioned account of the origin and legitimacy of the Tudor dynasty. That dynasty was founded by Henry, Earl of Richmond, who defeated Richard III at the Battle of Bosworth Field (1485), reigned until his death in 1509 as Henry VII, and was the grandfather of Queen Elizabeth (1533–1603). It is hardly surprising that the new regime, whose claim to the throne was somewhat shaky, would wish to discredit the old. Modern historians emphasize Richard's solid administrative skills; Tudor apologists depict Richard not merely as venal or unscrupulous but as a monster of evil, a creature whose moral viciousness was vividly stamped on his twisted body.

The principal literary source for this spectacularly partisan depiction was not a piece of simple propaganda but an unusually subtle and complex *History of King Richard the Third* (c. 1513) by the great humanist Thomas More. Later sixteenth-century historians, notably Edward Halle in *The Union of the Two Noble and Illustre Fameilies of Lancastre & Yorke* (1548) and Raphael Holinshed in *The Chronicles of England, Scotland, and Ireland* (1577, revised in 1587), followed closely in More's wake, repeating many of the details that Shakespeare in turn borrowed: Richard's habit of gnawing his lip, for example, or his restlessness, or the rumor that he was born with teeth. More and his followers deftly interwove three distinct explanatory accounts of Richard's behavior: political, psychological, and metaphysical. As a politician (a word with nasty connotations in the Renaissance), More's Richard is a particularly cunning player in a corrupt world, a schemer plotting to seize power and destroy all real or potential rivals. Psychologically, he is a strange blend of courage, wit, skillful dissembling, and fathomless malice. And on the metaphysical plane, he is a horrible instrument of God's wrath, a virtual devil incarnate.

Most sixteenth-century historians and chroniclers were, by our standards, far more interested in conveying moral meanings than in impartially recounting facts. Shakespeare allowed himself an even greater latitude, freely reshaping and condensing his historical materials in order to heighten dramatic effect and to intensify the political, psychological, and metaphysical dimensions of his villainous antihero. The play compresses events that in reality occurred over a long period of time, so that, for example, Richard's murderous plot against his brother George, Duke of Clarence (1478), is cleverly twined around his cynical courtship of Lady Anne (1472), which is in turn depicted as occurring during the funeral procession of King Henry (1471). The historical Lady Anne had only been betrothed to King Henry's son Edward, but Shakespeare writes as if she had actually been married to him; likewise, he folds Richmond's unsuccessful attempt to invade England in 1483 into his successful invasion of 1485, and he has old Queen Margaret, who was not even in England during most of the events that the play depicts, haunting the royal court like a bitter, half-crazed Greek tragic chorus.

Manipulating the insecurities, factional rivalries, and ambitions of everyone around him, Shakespeare's Richard is a consummate portrait of what sixteenth-century Englishmen termed a "machiavel"—that is, a person who acts on the immoral advice allegedly offered by the Florentine humanist Niccolò Machiavelli in *The Prince* (written in 1513, first printed in 1532). According to the period's lurid and grossly distorted account of this advice, Machiavelli had counseled princes to lie, cheat, and murder under the cover of hypocritical professions of virtue and piety. "I count Religion but a childish Toy," declares the character called Machevil, who speaks the prologue to Marlowe's *Jew of Malta* (c. 1590). Shakespeare's Richard, at first terrified by the apparition of the ghosts in Act 5, rallies to express comparable sentiments: "Conscience is but a word that cowards use, / Devised at first to keep the strong in awe" (5.6.39–40). These are sentiments that, for the most part, Richard keeps to himself—or, rather, shares only with the audience in a succession of gleeful asides—for he is highly skilled at assuming the pose of religious faith. Aided by his fellow hypocrite Buckingham, Richard appears in a memorable scene, prayer book in hand, miming "devotion and right Christian zeal" (3.7.103) while cynically stage-managing the supposedly popular call for his coronation.

Richard III. Portrait by unknown artist (c. 1590).

Shakespeare's vision of Richard as a consummate role-player goes back to a brilliant sketch of the same character in one of the three earlier plays he had written on fifteenth-century English history. Taken together, these plays—*The First Part of Henry the Sixth, The First Part of the Contention of the Two Famous Houses of York and Lancaster (2 Henry VI)*, and *The True Tragedy of Richard Duke of York and the Good King Henry the Sixth (3 Henry VI)*—depict the chaotic, violent struggle known as the Wars of the Roses, between two noble houses, the Lancastrians and the Yorkists. At the close of *Richard Duke of York (3 Henry VI)*, the Yorkist faction, led by the Duke of York's three surviving sons (Edward, George, and Richard), has triumphed. The last Lancastrian king, Henry VI, has been killed, and Richard's eldest brother has been crowned King Edward IV. But a shadow is cast across this decisive Yorkist victory by the ruthless and unsatisfied ambition of Richard.

Even though it can stand (and be performed) entirely on its own, *Richard III* may be regarded as the fourth part of a tetralogy, for it picks up directly from the turbulent events depicted in *Richard Duke of York* and, more particularly, from the project Richard announces in a long soliloquy. He declares that since nature has seen fit to deform his body and so exclude him from sensual pleasures, he will instead pursue the crown. "I can add colours to the chameleon," he boasts, "change shapes with Proteus for advantages, / And set the murderous Machiavel to school" (*Richard Duke of York* 3.2.191–93). Here Shakespeare is beginning to psychologize the machiavel, to provide inner motives for his violent ambition and his compulsive shape changing. *Richard III* continues and intensifies this process: as his opening soliloquy suggests, Richard feels that from birth he has been cruelly cheated by dissembling nature. Deprived of the normal satisfactions of nurturing and kindness—it is as if his mother's womb itself had rejected him—he tries to find compensatory satisfaction in cruelty and dissembling of his own. He seeks not only vengeance against an unloving world but also the pleasure of cherishing himself. Yet at the end, in a vigorous if crude moment of self-analysis, he discovers that even self-love eludes him: "I love myself. Wherefore? . . . O no, alas, I rather hate myself" (5.5.141–43).

Richard's self-hatred is psychologically revealing—evidently, he has internalized the loathing that he inspires in virtually everyone around him—but it is not simply generated from within: there is, the play's characters continually imply, a divinely sanctioned, objective moral order independent of both individuals and society, and by the fixed norms of this order Richard *is* hateful. It is possible for villains like Richard or the murderers of Clarence to close their ears to the admonitions of conscience, but all human actions are part of a larger design and will ultimately be judged by a heavenly power. From this higher perspective, Richard's deformity is less the *cause* of his evil nature than its *sign*. Similarly, the ghosts in Act 5 are not merely psychological projections but metaphysical emissaries. The dead do not simply rot and disappear, nor do they survive only in the memories and dreams of the living: they are an ineradicable presence, a part of the structure of reality, an uncanny age group capable of blessing and cursing. Richard tries to shake off their condemnation, as earlier he had jauntily deflected Margaret's elaborate curse, but their words bring beads of sweat to his trembling flesh. For while he may tell himself that his victims' words are merely the impotent weapons of the powerless, he cannot escape the play's pervasive sense that there is something eerie and disturbing about curses, as if through incantatory verbal ritual they magically touch the hidden order of things.

Despite Richard's disruptive mockery and unceremonious violence, an atmosphere of ritual lingers over much of *Richard III*, tingeing the rhetorically elaborate expressions of grief and

Henry VII. Portrait by Michael Sittow (1505).

"For they account his head upon the bridge" (3.2.67). London Bridge adorned with the heads of traitors. From Claes Jansz. Visscher, *Londinum florentissima Britanniae urbs* (1625).

anger, solemnizing formal ceremonies, and shaping the perceptions of the guilt-ridden characters. Although the play gives us historical figures with psychological motivations and political stratagems, often we seem less in the secular world of disenchanted politics than in the world of classical tragedy or medieval rite. Thus, for example, Clarence's terrible nightmare just before his murder recalls the hell of the Roman playwright Seneca and, still more, the hell of fourteenth-century Christian painting, with its howling fiends and damned souls. Clarence is haunted by the sense of an unappeasable God preparing to punish him for his crimes, and his dream discloses what he does not yet consciously know: that the agent of divine retribution is his own brother, Richard.

This ritual process—the inexorable working out, through the agency of Richard, of retributive justice or (as ancient tragedians personified it) Nemesis—is best conveyed perhaps by the chorus of grief-crazed women, above all by old Queen Margaret, who identifies Richard as "hell's black intelligencer" (4.4.71), or secret agent. In a series of stiff antiphonal laments (4.4.35ff.), Margaret (the widow of the slain Henry VI), Queen Elizabeth (the widow of Edward IV), and the Duchess of York (the widowed mother of Edward and his brothers, including Richard) tease out the strict eye-for-an-eye logic of the action. And at one startling moment, Richard himself comes close to acknowledging his role within this scheme: he likens himself to "the formal Vice, Iniquity" (3.1.82).

The character called the Vice is an inheritance of the medieval morality play: the busy enemy of mankind, the Vice was at once the agent of hell and the tool of divine providence, a master plotter and a puppet in a play that is not of his own making. Yet this fixed place in the divine plan did not preclude his acquiring an extraordinary theatrical power and resourcefulness, qualities that Shakespeare would later exploit in characters as different (and as magnificent) as Falstaff and Iago. Shakespeare constructs Richard out of many elements in the Vice tradition: a jaunty use of asides, a delight in sharing his schemes with the audience, a grotesque appearance, a penchant for disguise, a manic energy and humor, and a wickedly engaging ability to defer though not finally to escape well-deserved punishment. Richard's own allusion to the Vice calls attention to yet another element, a skill in playing with the doubleness of words and exploiting the slipperiness of language: "Thus like the formal Vice, Iniquity, / I moralize two meanings in one word" (3.1.82–83). *Richard III* puts the demonic master of this vicious skill on display and, in the end, stages his destruction: in a sense, the ritual that lingers over the play is an exorcism.

But, of course, *Richard III* is not in fact a ritual, and Shakespeare's subtle blending of psychological, metaphysical, and political perspectives carefully suspends any determination of their relative significance in the events he dramatizes. The psychological development of Richard is arrested by the intimation that psychology is itself the tool of a supernatural scheme; the supernatural is subverted (at least until the ghost scene) by the Machiavellian subordination of religion to power politics; but power politics is itself undermined by the suggestion that individuals act in the grip not of rational calculation but of psychological pressures and passions over which they have little or no control. The complex interplay of forces is reflected perhaps in an ambiguity about the play's genre: first appearing in print as *The Tragedy of King Richard the Third,* it was rechristened in the First Folio as one of Shakespeare's history plays, *The Life & Death of Richard the Third.*

That these multiple perspectives do not simply cancel each other out is the result of the extraordinary theatrical force of Richard himself. Only *Hamlet,* of all Shakespeare's plays, is comparably dominated by a single character, and only *Macbeth* is comparably structured around an evil hero. (The villains Richard most anticipates—Philip the Bastard in *King John,* Don John in *Much Ado About Nothing,* Iago in *Othello,* and Edmund in *King Lear*—are all at varying degrees of distance from the main protagonist.) Without for a moment concealing from the audience Richard's appalling, monstrous evil, Shakespeare makes his villain immensely captivating. In large part, his allure derives from what Keats called the "gusto," the overwhelming liveliness, of Shakespeare's characters: "Your eyes drop millstones when fools' eyes fall tears," says Richard to the murderers; "I like you, lads" (1.3.351–52). The startling frankness of this villainy has a comic charge, a charge renewed in the open wickedness of his plans for unsuspecting Hastings—"Chop off his head" (3.1.190)—or for the innocent young princes: "I wish the bastards dead" (4.2.19). There is gusto in Richard's slyness as well as in his frankness, a slyness that also is often comic: "So wise so young, they say, do never live long" (3.1.79).

The allure of such moments seems to be bound up with the allure of the theater itself, with its capacity for emotional intensification, surprise, deception, and heightened energy. The religious enemies of the theater in Shakespeare's age charged that this energy was essentially erotic—the playhouse, they complained, aroused sexual desire—and before dismissing their charges as preposterous, we might recall the comic anecdote from John Manningham's diary with which this introduction began. Shakespeare himself in *Richard III* seems to play with the seductive power of theatrical performance in the bizarre scene in which Richard successfully courts Lady Anne over the body of her father-in-law, the King, whom he has murdered: "Was ever woman in this humour wooed?" Richard exults; "Was ever woman in this humour won?" (1.2.215–16). Richard's wooing has nothing to do with tenderness, affection, sympathy, or even physical attraction; we witness an aggressive male assault upon Lady Anne's rooted, eloquently expressed, and eminently justified fear and loathing. Here, as elsewhere, Richard gets what he wants because he possesses greater power to control the scenario: more than Anne, more than anyone, he knows how to initiate action, conceal motives, threaten, intimidate, and hurt. He has killed Anne's husband as well as her father-in-law; he will, when she has served his purpose, kill Anne too. Anne knows this well enough—"Ill rest betide the chamber where thou liest" (1.2.112)—but she virtually invents uncertainties to mask the calculating murderousness she herself has perceived with cold clarity: "I would I knew thy heart," she muses, seconds after she has thoroughly inventoried Richard's villainous heart (1.2.180).

Anne is shallow, corruptible, naively ambitious, and, above all, frightened—all qualities that help to account for her spectacular surrender—but the scene's theatrical power rests less upon a depiction of her character than upon the spectacle of Richard's restless aggression transformed during the rapid-fire exchange of one-liners (called in rhetoric *stichomythia*) into a perverse form of sexual provocation and of Anne's verbal violence transformed, in spite of itself, into an erotic response. In light of this transformation, the misshapen Richard's celebration of his sexual attractiveness—

> I do mistake my person all this while.
> Upon my life she finds, although I cannot,
> Myself to be a marv'lous proper man—

is not wholly ironic, even if he himself thinks it is (1.2.239–50).

Eros has not been excluded from Richard's career; it has found a new and com-pelling form in his energetic, witty, and murderous chafing against the obstacles in his path. These obstacles are not simply set in opposition to his desire; rather they virtu-ally constitute it, for it is the extent of his distance from power that generates Richard's craving for it. His politics, and hence the sexuality implied by that politics, is trans-gressive; it thrives on the violation of social and natural bonds. His is the psychology of the rapist, and the character in Shakespeare closest to Richard III is the rapist Tarquin (in *The Rape of Lucrece*), whose lust is excited precisely by the barriers he is forced to overcome. This chafing structure is why the violent verbal assaults upon Richard, most intense from the women in the play, seem only to intensify his aggressive energies. It is perhaps also why Richard seems to lose much of his erotic power as soon as he has established himself on the throne. When the obstacles in his path to the crown have been removed, when there is no legitimate authority to transgress, the erotic quality of his ambition immediately begins to wane.

The play has allowed Richard to be a perverse erotic champion—a role probably possible only in this highly theatrical vision of history—but the desire he embodies can-not be integrated into any viable social or natural order; nor does it constitute a coher-ent, stable inner life. By the play's end, he seems a hollow man, a set of theatrical masks that project grotesque shadows upon the world. Fittingly, when "shadows," in the form of those he has murdered, return to terrify him, he can only express his fear in histri-onic terms, staging a miniature dialogue with himself and then imagining his con-science as the audience, with its thousand tongues condemning him for a villain.

Richard's manifest theatricality is only the extreme form of a theatricality diffused throughout the play. Virtually all of the speeches—lamentation, cursing, debate, persuasion—are cast as self-conscious performances: "What means this scene of rude impatience?" asks the Duchess of York; Queen Elizabeth replies, "To mark an act of tragic violence" (2.2.38–39). Moreover, there is a pervasive sense that the characters exist as figures in someone else's play: through most of the performance, they are fig-ures, without knowing it, in Richard's play, but Richard himself is a figure in another play, larger than himself. That larger play is at once the drama of history, scripted (as Tudor ideology claimed) by God, and the historical drama or tragedy, scripted by Shake-speare. If the script obliges all of the characters to display the power of divine provi-dence, it obliges them at the same time to display the power of the theater. For if the stage pays homage to the state, it also makes the state into a histrionic spectacle on the public stage. *Richard III* manages to imply that the whole vast enterprise of Tudor power exists to make this play, and the theater in which it is performed, possible.

STEPHEN GREENBLATT

TEXTUAL NOTE

Richard III first appeared in quarto (Q1) in 1597, without the playwright's name but with a very full title page:

> THE TRAGEDY OF King Richard the third. Containing, His treacherous Plots against his brother Clarence: the pittiefull murther of his iunocent nephewes: his tyrannicall vsurpation: with the whole course of his detested life, and most deserued death. As it hath beene lately Acted by the Right honourable the Lord Chamberlaine his seruants AT LONDON Printed by Valentine Sims, for Andrew Wise, dwelling in Paules Chu[r]chyard, at the Signe of the Angell. 1597.

The play proved to be a popular one: so much so that five more quarto versions came out before the appearance of the First Folio (F) in 1623. These quarto editions (Q2–Q6) can claim no textual authority, because of their means of composition; each was based on the text of the one immediately preceding it. Each not only carried forward, therefore, the accumulated errors of its predecessors but added some of its own. The main editorial questions revolve, then, about the authority of, and the relationship between, Q1 and F.

Certainly the quarto text influenced F. But the hundreds of differences between the two suggest that a further source, an independent manuscript, was also used in the construction of F. The Oxford editor Gary Taylor believes that this manuscript was probably a transcript, presumably done by a scribe, of Shakespeare's "foul papers," that is, a version of the play in Shakespeare's own hand, with whatever additions, corrections, and revisions he may have inserted in the course of its composition.

It appears that neither Q nor F derives directly from Shakespeare's own manuscript. It has, however, been proposed that Q, the shorter text, might represent a first draft of the play. Gary Taylor rejects this hypothesis. In his view, Q is a "bad" Quarto—that is, one reconstructed from memory of the play as performed. If so, it is a surprisingly thorough reconstruction, carried out, probably, not by one or two renegade players of minor roles but by Shakespeare's company itself, or rather by those members to hand when the reconstructed text was being written down. Some part of the company on tour in the provinces, for example, could have found itself without a prompt copy of *Richard III*. A text hurriedly assembled in such circumstances might be substantially complete, except for gaps in the minor roles, which would have been played by hired men. Such gaps, showing up as omissions and textual variants, do in fact occur in the quarto version of the play and therefore lend support to Taylor's theory. Given that the passages Q omits tend to slow down the dramatic action and that its only substantial additional passage is a particularly impressive one (the "clock" dialogue, 4.2.101–20), it seems to follow that Q is a later text—one more theatrically attuned, one trimmed of some superfluous bulk. Hence, Oxford adopts a substantial number of the quarto variants.

Other omissions appear to show the effects of censorship. The exclamation "Zounds" ("by His wounds") appears four times in Q but not in F, as does a reference to "Christ's dear blood shed for our grievous sins." The name "God," however, appears frequently in both texts. Political rather than purely religious concerns seem to have caused a further omission. Hastings's lines at the conclusion of 3.4, in which he prophesies "the fearful'st time" in a coming "miserable England," could well be seen as unsettling to an audience that laid great store by prophecy. These lines do not appear in F. But what of the inclusion only in Q of the "clock" dialogue mentioned above? In fact, this seeming anomaly (it is the only major passage not in F) adds weight to the early F hypothesis. The very singular nature of this passage leads Oxford to see it as "an inspired afterthought." No political considerations—far less theatrical ones—could justify its deletion. We might also note that in what was an already very long play, Shakespeare might have been more inclined to deletion than to addition.

F, we can see, is closer to its sources, Halle and Holinshed, and is manifestly the superior text. Many passages are better crafted in meter and meaning than their quarto counterparts. F, then, is the control text for substantive readings. Recalling, however, that the quarto reconstruction would have taken place at a time when Shakespeare himself was active in the company and may have had a hand in revision for the stage, an unusually large number of departures from the control text have been retained. The reader is thus presented, we hope, with the play in its most fully realized theatrical form.

In this edition, Folio passages that were omitted from Q and relegated in the *Oxford Shakespeare* to an appendix are printed inset and in italics.

SELECTED BIBLIOGRAPHY

Burnett, Mark Thornton. "'Monsters' and 'Molas': Body Politics in *Richard III*." *Constructing "Monsters" in Shakespearean Drama and Early Modern Culture*. New York: Palgrave Macmillan, 2002. 65–94. Fluctuating between images of monsters shaped and unfinished, Richard represents the anxieties of a barren Tudor line seeking new political form.

Carroll, William. " 'The Form of Law': Ritual and Succession in *Richard III*." *True Rites and Maimed Rites: Ritual and Anti-Ritual in Shakespeare and His Age*. Ed. Linda Woodbridge and Edward Berry. Urbana: University of Illinois Press, 1992. 203–19.

Howard, Jean E., and Phyllis Rackin. "Weak Kings, Warrior Women, and the Assault on Dynastic Authority." *Engendering a Nation: A Feminist Account of Shakespeare's English Histories*. London: Routledge, 1997. 100–18. Shifting from history to tragedy, *Richard III* ennobles and disempowers women as passive emblems of pity, while Richard appropriates their seductive theatrical energy.

Hunter, Robert G. *Shakespeare and the Mystery of God's Judgments*. Athens: University of Georgia Press, 1976. Poised between Augustinian and Calvinist conceptions of God's will, Richard's seemingly contradictory status as a tragic figures acting in a providential frame generates the complexity of Shakespeare's art.

Marche, Stephen. "Mocking Dead Bones: Historical Memory and the Theater of the Dead in *Richard III*." *Comparative Drama* 37.1 (2003): 37–57. The play's ambivalent generic status—between tragedy and history—is reflected in Richard's tragic inability to overcome history by silencing the dead who challenge his shaping narrative.

Moulton, Ian Frederick. " 'A Monster Great Deformed': The Unruly Masculinities of *Richard III*." *Shakespeare Quarterly* 47.3 (1996): 251–68. Shakespeare both critiques and celebrates masculine aggression, revealing the incoherence of masculinity as an early modern cultural concept.

Rossiter, A. P. *Angel with Horns, and Other Shakespeare Lectures*. Ed. Graham Storey. New York: Theatre Arts Books, 1961. Richard's demonic appeal as God's avenging angel makes the play less moral history than comic history built on paradoxical irony and inversion.

Targoff, Ramie. " 'Dirty' Amens: Devotion, Applause, and Consent in *Richard III*." *Renaissance Drama* 31 (2002): 61–84. The question of what constitutes true consent on the part of the English toward their King can be tracked through the play's odd use of the liturgical term "Amen," which both Richard and Richmond solicit in different ways from their audiences in order to legitimate their rule.

Torey, Michael. " 'The Plain Devil and Dissembling Looks': Ambivalent Physiognomy and Shakespeare's *Richard III*." *English Literary Renaissance* 30.2 (2000): 123–53. Richard's ability to deceive his victims and manipulate his corporal image complicates the seeming intelligibility of his deformity.

Wheeler, Richard P. "History, Character, and Conscience in *Richard III*." *Comparative Drama* 5 (1971–72): 301–21. The play dramatizes the struggle between divine and profane views of history, between conscience and egoism, that troubled the late Elizabethan era.

Films

Richard III. 1912. Dir. André Calmettes and James Keane. USA. 55 min. The silent film version, with Robert Gemp as Edward IV and Frederick Warde as Richard.

Richard III. 1955. Dir. Laurence Olivier. UK. 161 min. A deformed and morally twisted yet seductively charismatic Richard, played by Olivier, with John Gielgud as Clarence.

Richard III. 1995. Dir. Richard Loncraine. UK/USA. 104 min. Richard as a sly and ruthless fascist dictator in a stylishly corrupt 1930s Britain. Ian McKellan is Richard, Robert Downey, Jr. is Lord Rivers.

Looking for Richard. 1996. Dir. Al Pacino. USA. 111 min. Part adaptation, part behind-the-scenes documentary about bringing the Shakespeare play to modern audiences. With Pacino playing Richard and Kevin Spacey playing Buckingham.

The Tragedy of
King Richard the Third

THE PERSONS OF THE PLAY

KING EDWARD IV
DUCHESS OF YORK, his mother
PRINCE EDWARD
Richard, the young Duke of YORK } his sons
George, Duke of CLARENCE
RICHARD, Duke of GLOUCESTER, later KING RICHARD III } his brothers
Clarence's SON
Clarence's DAUGHTER
QUEEN ELIZABETH, King Edward's wife
Anthony Woodeville, Earl RIVERS, her brother
Marquis of DORSET }
Lord GRAY } her sons
Sir Thomas VAUGHAN
GHOST OF KING HENRY VI
QUEEN MARGARET, his widow
GHOST OF PRINCE EDWARD, his son
LADY ANNE, Prince Edward's widow
William, LORD HASTINGS, Lord Chamberlain
Lord STANLEY, Earl of Derby, his friend
HENRY EARL OF RICHMOND, later KING HENRY VII, Stanley's son-in-law
Earl of OXFORD }
Sir James BLUNT } Richmond's followers
Sir Walter HERBERT }
Duke of BUCKINGHAM }
Duke of NORFOLK }
Sir Richard RATCLIFFE }
Sir William CATESBY } Richard Gloucester's followers
Sir James TYRRELL }
Two MURDERERS }
A PAGE }
CARDINAL
BISHOP OF ELY
John, a PRIEST
SIR CHRISTOPHER, a Priest
Sir Robert BRACKENBURY, Lieutenant of the Tower of London
Lord MAYOR of London
A SCRIVENER
Hastings, a PURSUIVANT
SHERIFF
Aldermen and Citizens
Attendants, two bishops, messengers, soldiers

1.1

Enter RICHARD *Duke of* GLOUCESTER[1]

RICHARD GLOUCESTER   Now is the winter of our discontent
Made glorious summer by this son of York;[2]
And all the clouds that loured° upon our house°   glowered / family
In the deep bosom of the ocean buried.
5   Now are our brows bound with victorious wreaths,
Our bruisèd arms° hung up for monuments,°   armor / memorials
Our stern alarums° changed to merry meetings,   call to arms
Our dreadful marches to delightful measures.°   dances
Grim-visaged war hath smoothed his wrinkled front,°   forehead
10   And now—instead of mounting barbèd° steeds   armored
To fright the souls of fearful adversaries—
He capers[3] nimbly in a lady's chamber
To the lascivious pleasing of a lute.
But I, that am not shaped for sportive° tricks   amorous
15   Nor made to court an amorous looking-glass,
I that am rudely stamped[4] and want° love's majesty   lack
To strut before a wanton ambling nymph,
I that am curtailed of this fair proportion,°   shape
Cheated of feature° by dissembling nature,   good appearance
20   Deformed, unfinished, sent before my time
Into this breathing world scarce half made up—
And that so lamely and unfashionable°   badly formed
That dogs bark at me as I halt° by them—   limp
Why, I in this weak piping[5] time of peace
25   Have no delight to pass away the time,
Unless to spy my shadow in the sun
And descant on° mine own deformity.   remark upon
And therefore since I cannot prove° a lover   prove to be
To entertain these fair well-spoken days,
30   I am determinèd° to prove a villain   resolved; fated
And hate the idle pleasures of these days.
Plots have I laid, inductions[6] dangerous,
By drunken prophecies, libels and dreams
To set my brother Clarence[7] and the King
35   In deadly hate the one against the other.
And if King Edward be as true and just
As I am subtle false and treacherous,
This day should Clarence closely be mewed up°   caged (like a hawk)
About a prophecy which says that 'G'[8]
40   Of Edward's heirs the murderer shall be.
        Enter [*George Duke of*] CLARENCE, *guarded, and* [*Sir
        Robert*] BRACKENBURY
Dive, thoughts, down to my soul: here Clarence comes.
Brother, good day. What means this armèd guard
That waits upon your grace?

1.1 Location: A street in London.
1. Pronounced "Gloster."
2. *son of York*: Edward IV, son of Richard, Duke of York; with wordplay on Edward's emblem, a sun in splendor.
3. In court dances, men often made "capers," or showy leaps; also suggests a sexual escapade.
4 Roughly, imperfectly shaped (alluding to the stamping of a coin with an image).
5. Characterized by the music of a peaceful shepherd's

flute: shrill-voiced, like women or children.
6. Initial moves, prologues.
7. George, Duke of Clarence, Richard, Duke of Gloucester, and King Edward IV were brothers; Clarence, being older than Richard, would become King if Edward and his heirs died.
8. Which Edward interprets as "George," but which could—and does—mean "Gloucester."

CLARENCE His majesty,
Tend'ring° my person's safety, hath appointed   *Caring about*
45 This conduct° to convey me to the Tower.⁹   *escort*
RICHARD GLOUCESTER Upon what cause?
CLARENCE Because my name is George.
RICHARD GLOUCESTER Alack, my lord, that fault is none of yours.
He should for that commit your godfathers.¹
Belike° his majesty hath some intent   *Probably*
50 That you should be new-christened in the Tower.
But what's the matter, Clarence? May I know?
CLARENCE Yea, Richard, when I know—for I protest
As yet I do not. But as I can learn
He hearkens after prophecies and dreams,
55 And from the cross-row° plucks the letter 'G'   *alphabet*
And says a wizard told him that by 'G'
His issue° disinherited should be.   *children*
And for my name of George begins with 'G',
It follows in his thought that I am he.
60 These, as I learn, and suchlike toys° as these,   *trifles*
Hath moved his highness to commit° me now.   *arrest*
RICHARD GLOUCESTER Why, this it is when men are ruled by women.
'Tis not the King that sends you to the Tower;
My Lady Gray,² his wife—Clarence, 'tis she
65 That tempts him to this harsh extremity.
Was it not she, and that good man of worship³
Anthony Woodeville her brother there,
That made him send Lord Hastings to the Tower,
From whence this present day he is delivered?
70 We are not safe, Clarence; we are not safe.
CLARENCE By heaven, I think there is no man secure
But the Queen's kindred, and night-walking heralds°   *secret go-betweens*
That trudge betwixt the King and Mrs Shore.⁴
Heard ye not what an humble suppliant
75 Lord Hastings was for his delivery?
RICHARD GLOUCESTER Humbly complaining to her deity⁵
Got my Lord Chamberlain⁶ his liberty.
I'll tell you what: I think it is our way,°   *strategy*
If we will keep in favour with the King,
80 To be her men and wear her livery.⁷
The jealous, o'erworn widow⁸ and herself,°   *(Jane Shore)*
Since that our brother dubbed them⁹ gentlewomen,
Are mighty gossips° in our monarchy.   *busybodies*
BRACKENBURY I beseech your graces both to pardon me.
85 His majesty hath straitly given in charge°   *has strictly ordered*

9. Tower of London, used to house noble prisoners as well as (in Elizabethan England) traitors and political agitators.
1. The godfather was responsible for the naming of a newborn child.
2. A sarcastic reference to the Queen, widow of Sir John Gray before her marriage to the King. Her maiden name was Elizabeth Woodeville (also Woodville).
3. Honor (here, a sarcastic phrase, more appropriate to a solid, middle-class citizen than to the Queen's brother, Anthony Woodeville, who succeeded his father as Earl Rivers).
4. Jane Shore, wife of a London goldsmith. Her liaison

with Edward was notorious. *Mrs*: Mistress (here in both the polite and the abusive sense).
5. Jane Shore (ironically, by analogy with "her majesty").
6. Hastings's title. According to Shakespeare's sources, Jane Shore became his mistress when her affair with the King ended.
7. Servants ("men") in noble households wore the colors ("livery") of the family.
8. The Queen, a widow before she married Edward IV. *o'erworn*: faded.
9. Invested them with the status of (usually used of knights). Richard grossly exaggerates the lowly status of the Queen's family before her marriage.

That no man shall have private conference,
Of what degree soever,[1] with your brother.
RICHARD GLOUCESTER   Even so. An't° please your worship, Brackenbury,   *If it*
You may partake of anything we say.
90   We speak no treason, man. We say the King
Is wise and virtuous, and his noble Queen
Well struck° in years, fair, and not jealous.   *advanced*
We say that Shore's wife hath a pretty foot,
A cherry lip,
95   A bonny eye, a passing° pleasing tongue,   *an exceedingly*
And that the Queen's kin are made gentlefolks.
How say you, sir? Can you deny all this?
BRACKENBURY   With this, my lord, myself have naught° to do.   *nothing*
RICHARD GLOUCESTER   Naught[2] to do with Mrs Shore? I tell thee, fellow:
100   He that doth naught with her—excepting one—
Were best to do it secretly alone.
BRACKENBURY   What one, my lord?
RICHARD GLOUCESTER   Her husband, knave. Wouldst thou betray me?
BRACKENBURY   I beseech your grace to pardon me, and do withal°   *moreover*
105   Forbear your conference with the noble Duke.
CLARENCE   We know thy charge, Brackenbury, and will obey.
RICHARD GLOUCESTER   We are the Queen's abjects,° and must obey.   *base subjects*
Brother, farewell. I will unto the King,
And whatsoe'er you will employ me in—
110   Were it to call King Edward's widow° 'sister'—   *(Queen Elizabeth)*
I will perform it to enfranchise° you.   *free*
Meantime, this deep disgrace in brotherhood
Touches me dearer[3] than you can imagine.
CLARENCE   I know it pleaseth neither of us well.
115   RICHARD GLOUCESTER   Well, your imprisonment shall not be long.
I will deliver you or lie for you.[4]
Meantime, have patience.
CLARENCE   I must perforce.° Farewell.   *of necessity*
    Exeunt CLARENCE[, BRACKENBURY, *and guard, to the Tower*]
RICHARD GLOUCESTER   Go tread the path that thou shalt ne'er return.
Simple plain Clarence, I do love thee so
120   That I will shortly send thy soul to heaven,
If heaven will take the present at° our hands.   *from*
But who comes here? The new-delivered° Hastings?   *newly released*
    Enter LORD HASTINGS [*from the Tower*]
LORD HASTINGS   Good time of day unto my gracious lord.
RICHARD GLOUCESTER   As much unto my good Lord Chamberlain.
125   Well are you welcome to the open air.
How hath your lordship brooked° imprisonment?   *tolerated*
LORD HASTINGS   With patience, noble lord, as prisoners must.
But I shall live, my lord, to give them thanks
That were the cause of my imprisonment.
130   RICHARD GLOUCESTER   No doubt, no doubt—and so shall Clarence too,
For they that were your enemies are his,
And have prevailed as much on him as you.

---

1. *no . . . soever:* that is, despite Richard's high rank ("degree"), he must not speak with the prisoner.
2. Wickedness; here, specifically sexual intercourse.
3. Wounds me more, but also (as a hidden meaning),

implicates me more.
4. In prison, in place of Clarence (with a pun on "lie" as "tell falsehoods about"). "Deliver" and "lie for" rhyme.

LORD HASTINGS   More pity that the eagles should be mewed
    While kites° and buzzards prey at liberty.   *scavenger birds*

135 RICHARD GLOUCESTER   What news abroad?°   *circulating*

LORD HASTINGS   No news so bad abroad as this at home:
    The King is sickly, weak, and melancholy,
    And his physicians fear° him mightily.   *fear for*

RICHARD GLOUCESTER   Now by Saint Paul, that news is bad indeed.

140   O he hath kept an evil diet° long,   *way of life*
    And overmuch consumed his royal person,[5]
    'Tis very grievous to be thought upon.
    Where is he? In his bed?

LORD HASTINGS   He is.

RICHARD GLOUCESTER   Go you before and I will follow you.

                                 Exit HASTINGS

145   He cannot live, I hope, and must not die
    Till George be packed with post-haste° up to heaven.   *by express*
    I'll in to urge his hatred more to Clarence,
    With lies well steeled° with weighty arguments.   *made strong*
    And if I fail not in my deep intent,
150   Clarence hath not another day to live—
    Which done, God take King Edward to his mercy
    And leave the world for me to bustle in.
    For then I'll marry Warwick's youngest daughter.[6]
    What though I killed her husband and her father?[7]
155   The readiest way to make the wench amends
    Is to become her husband and her father,
    The which will I: not all so much for love,
    As for another secret close intent,°   *private purpose*
    By marrying her, which I must reach unto.
160   But yet I run before my horse to market.
    Clarence still breathes, Edward still lives and reigns;
    When they are gone, then must I count my gains.   *Exit*

1.2

Enter [gentlemen, bearing] the corpse of [King] Henry VI
[in an open coffin], with halberdiers[1] to guard it,
    LADY ANNE *being the mourner*

LADY ANNE   Set down, set down your honourable load,
    If honour may be shrouded in a hearse,°   *an open coffin*
    Whilst I a while obsequiously° lament   *mournfully*
    Th'untimely fall of virtuous Lancaster.[2]
    [They set the coffin down]
5   Poor key-cold[3] figure of a holy king,
    Pale ashes of the house of Lancaster,
    Thou bloodless remnant of that royal blood:
    Be it lawful that I invocate thy ghost[4]
    To hear the lamentations of poor Anne,
10   Wife to thy Edward, to thy slaughtered son,

---

5. And has been weakened by extravagant living.
6. Lady Anne Neville, who had been betrothed (but not married) to Edward, Prince of Wales, the son of King Henry VI. Shakespeare, however, writes of Anne as Edward's widow.
7. *her father:* Henry VI (father-in-law).
1.2 Location: A street in London.
1. Men carrying halberds (a spearlike weapon with a

blade as well as a point).
2. Henry VI, of the house of Lancaster, was deposed and murdered by the Yorkists. The dynastic quarrel dates from the deposition of Richard II and is dramatized in Shakespeare's three *Henry VI* plays.
3. Proverbial for "cold as death."
4. Conjuring of spirits was generally condemned. *invocate:* invoke.

Stabbed by the selfsame hand that made these wounds.
Lo, in these windows⁵ that let forth thy life,
I pour the helpless° balm of my poor eyes.   useless
O cursèd be the hand that made these holes,
15 Cursèd the blood that let this blood from hence,
Cursèd the heart that had the heart to do it.
More direful hap betide° that hated wretch   fate befall
That makes us wretched by the death of thee
Than I can wish to wolves, to spiders, toads,
20 Or any creeping venomed thing that lives.
If ever he have child, abortive° be it,   incompletely formed
Prodigious,° and untimely brought to light,   Monstrous
Whose ugly and unnatural aspect°   appearance
May fright the hopeful mother at the view,
25 And that be heir to his unhappiness.⁶
If ever he have wife, let her be made
More miserable by the death of him
Than I am made by my young lord and thee.⁷—
Come now towards Chertsey° with your holy load,   monastery near London
30 Taken from Paul's⁸ to be interrèd there,
      [*The gentlemen lift the coffin*]
And still as° you are weary of this weight   Whenever
Rest you, whiles I lament King Henry's corpse.
      Enter RICHARD *Duke of* GLOUCESTER
RICHARD GLOUCESTER [*to the gentlemen*] Stay, you that bear
      the corpse, and set it down.
LADY ANNE   What black magician conjures up this fiend
35 To stop devoted charitable deeds?
RICHARD GLOUCESTER [*to the gentlemen*] Villains,° set down   Scoundrels; peasants
      the corpse, or by Saint Paul
I'll make a corpse of him that disobeys.
HALBERDIER   My lord, stand back and let the coffin pass.
RICHARD GLOUCESTER   Unmannered dog, stand thou when I command.
40 Advance⁹ thy halberd higher than my breast,
Or by Saint Paul I'll strike thee to my foot
And spurn° upon thee, beggar, for thy boldness.   kick
      [*They set the coffin down*]
LADY ANNE [*to gentlemen and halberdiers*] What, do you tremble?
      Are you all afraid?
Alas, I blame you not, for you are mortal,
45 And mortal eyes cannot endure the devil.—
Avaunt,° thou dreadful minister of hell.   Be gone
Thou hadst but power over his mortal body;
His soul thou canst not have; therefore be gone.
RICHARD GLOUCESTER   Sweet saint, for charity be not so cursed.°   bad-tempered
50 LADY ANNE   Foul devil, for God's sake hence and trouble us not,
For thou hast made the happy earth thy hell,
Filled it with cursing cries and deep exclaims.
If thou delight to view thy heinous deeds,
Behold this pattern° of thy butcheries.—   example
55 O gentlemen, see, see! Dead Henry's wounds

---

5. Stab wounds (possibly referring to the custom of
opening the windows to let a dying soul pass).
6. Evil nature; ill fortune.

7. By the deaths of Prince Edward and King Henry VI.
8. St. Paul's, cathedral of the City of London.
9. Raise upright (rather than hold it pointing at Richard).

Ope their congealèd mouths and bleed afresh.[1]
Blush, blush, thou lump of foul deformity,
For 'tis thy presence that ex-hales° this blood   *calls forth*
From cold and empty veins where no blood dwells.
60   Thy deed, inhuman and unnatural,
Provokes this deluge supernatural.[2]
O God, which this blood mad'st, revenge his death.
O earth, which this blood drink'st, revenge his death.
Either heav'n with lightning strike the murd'rer dead,
65   Or earth gape open wide and eat him quick°   *alive*
As thou dost swallow up this good king's blood,
Which his hell-governed arm hath butcherèd.
RICHARD GLOUCESTER   Lady, you know no rules of charity,
     Which renders good for bad, blessings for curses.
70   LADY ANNE   Villain, thou know'st no law of God nor man.
     No beast so fierce but knows some touch of pity.
RICHARD GLOUCESTER   But I know none, and therefore am no beast.
LADY ANNE   O wonderful, when devils tell the truth![3]
RICHARD GLOUCESTER   More wonderful, when angels are so angry.
75   Vouchsafe,° divine perfection of a woman,   *Grant*
     Of these supposèd crimes to give me leave
     By circumstance° but to acquit myself.   *detailed argument*
LADY ANNE   Vouchsafe, diffused[4] infection of a man,
     Of these known evils but to give me leave
80   By circumstance t'accuse thy cursèd self.
RICHARD GLOUCESTER   Fairer than tongue can name thee, let me have
     Some patient leisure to excuse myself.
LADY ANNE   Fouler than heart can think thee, thou canst make
     No excuse current° but to hang thyself.   *valid*
85   RICHARD GLOUCESTER   By such despair I should accuse myself.
LADY ANNE   And by despairing shalt thou stand excused,
     For doing worthy vengeance on thyself
     That didst unworthy slaughter upon others.
RICHARD GLOUCESTER   Say that I slew them not.
LADY ANNE   Then say they were not slain.
90   But dead they are—and, devilish slave, by thee.
RICHARD GLOUCESTER   I did not kill your husband.
LADY ANNE   Why, then he is alive.
RICHARD GLOUCESTER   Nay, he is dead, and slain by Edward's hand.
LADY ANNE   In thy foul throat thou liest. Queen Margaret saw
     Thy murd'rous falchion° smoking in his blood,[5]   *curved sword*
95   The which thou once didst bend against° her breast,   *turn toward*
     But that thy brothers beat aside the point.
RICHARD GLOUCESTER   I was provokèd by her sland'rous tongue,
     That laid their guilt upon my guiltless shoulders.
LADY ANNE   Thou wast provokèd by thy bloody mind,
100   That never dream'st on aught° but butcheries.   *anything*
     Didst thou not kill this king?
RICHARD GLOUCESTER   I grant ye.

---

1. A murdered victim's wounds were supposed to bleed again in the presence of the murderer.
2. Q, F: most unnatural. The emendation underscores Anne's call (in the next line) for divine intervention.
3. That is, Richard is a devil, not man or beast.
4. Misshapen, but also an infection whose harmful effects are dispersed widely.
5. In *Richard Duke of York* (3 *Henry VI*) 5.5, King Edward stabbed the Prince first, and Richard followed.

LADY ANNE Dost grant me, hedgehog?[6] Then God grant me, too,
    Thou mayst be damnèd for that wicked deed.
    O he was gentle, mild, and virtuous.
105 RICHARD GLOUCESTER The better for the King of Heaven that hath him.
    LADY ANNE He *is* in heaven, where thou shalt never come.
    RICHARD GLOUCESTER Let him thank me that holp° that to send him thither,   helped
    For he was fitter for that place than earth.
    LADY ANNE And thou unfit for any place but hell.
110 RICHARD GLOUCESTER Yes, one place else, if you will hear me name it.
    LADY ANNE Some dungeon.
    RICHARD GLOUCESTER   Your bedchamber.
    LADY ANNE Ill rest betide° the chamber where thou liest.   befall
    RICHARD GLOUCESTER So will it, madam, till I lie with you.
    LADY ANNE I hope so.
    RICHARD GLOUCESTER I know so. But gentle Lady Anne,
115 To leave this keen encounter of our wits
    And fall something into a slower method,[7]
    Is not the causer of the timeless° deaths   untimely
    Of these Plantagenets,[8] Henry and Edward,
    As blameful as the executioner?
120 LADY ANNE Thou wast the cause of that accursed effect.
    RICHARD GLOUCESTER Your beauty was the cause of that effect—
    Your beauty that did haunt me in my sleep
    To undertake the death of all the world
    So I might live one hour in your sweet bosom.
125 LADY ANNE If I thought that, I tell thee, homicide,°   murderer
    These nails should rend that beauty from my cheeks.
    RICHARD GLOUCESTER These eyes could not endure sweet beauty's wreck.
    You should not blemish it if I stood by.
    As all the world is cheerèd by the sun,
130 So I by that: it is my day, my life.
    LADY ANNE Black night o'ershade thy day, and death thy life.
    RICHARD GLOUCESTER Curse not thyself, fair creature: thou art both.
    LADY ANNE I would I were, to be revenged on thee.[9]
    RICHARD GLOUCESTER It is a quarrel most unnatural,
135 To be revenged on him that loveth you.
    LADY ANNE It is a quarrel just and reasonable,
    To be revenged on him that killed my husband.
    RICHARD GLOUCESTER He that bereft thee, lady, of thy husband,
    Did it to help thee to a better husband.
140 LADY ANNE His better doth not breathe upon the earth.
    RICHARD GLOUCESTER He lives that loves thee better than he° could.   (Edward)
    LADY ANNE Name him.
    RICHARD GLOUCESTER Plantagenet.
    LADY ANNE   Why, that was he.
    RICHARD GLOUCESTER The selfsame name, but one of better nature.
    LADY ANNE Where is he?
    RICHARD GLOUCESTER   Here.

              She spits at him
              Why dost thou spit at me?
145 LADY ANNE Would it were mortal poison for thy sake.

---

6. Term of abuse applied to someone who pays no attention to others' feelings; alluding to Richard's humped back and his heraldic badge, the boar.
7. And argue somewhat less hastily.
8. The royal house from which both Lancastrians,

including Henry and his son Edward, and Yorkists, including Richard himself, descended.
9. That is, if Anne were Richard's day and his life, she could end both and thus be revenged on him.

RICHARD GLOUCESTER Never came poison from so sweet a place.

LADY ANNE Never hung poison on a fouler toad.[1]
　Out of my sight! Thou dost infect mine eyes.

RICHARD GLOUCESTER Thine eyes, sweet lady, have infected mine.

150 **LADY ANNE** Would° they were basilisks[2] to strike thee dead.　　　　*I wish that*

RICHARD GLOUCESTER I would they were, that I might die at once,°　*once and for all*
　For now they kill me with a living death.
　Those eyes of thine from mine have drawn salt tears,
　Shamed their aspects° with store of childish drops.[3]　　　　*appearance*

154.1　　　*These eyes, which never shed remorseful tear—*
　　　　No, when my father York and Edward[4] wept
　　　　To hear the piteous moan that Rutland[5] made
　　　　When black-faced° Clifford shook his sword at him;　　　*threatening*
154.5　　*Nor when thy warlike father° like a child*　　　　*(Warwick)*
　　　　Told the sad story of my father's death
　　　　And twenty times made pause to sob and weep,
　　　　That all the standers-by had wet their cheeks
　　　　Like trees bedashed with rain. In that sad time
154.10　　*My manly eyes did scorn an humble tear,*
　　　　And what these sorrows could not thence exhale°　　　*draw out*
　　　　Thy beauty hath, and made them blind with weeping.

155 I never sued° to friend nor enemy;　　　　*petitioned*
　My tongue could never learn sweet smoothing° word;　　*flattering*
　But now thy beauty is proposed my fee,°　　　　*recompense*
　My proud heart sues and prompts my tongue to speak.

　　　　She looks scornfully at him

　Teach not thy lip such scorn, for it was made
160 For kissing, lady, not for such contempt.
　If thy revengeful heart cannot forgive,

　　　　[*He kneels and offers her his sword*]

　Lo, here I lend thee this sharp-pointed sword,
　Which if thou please to hide in this true breast
　And let the soul forth that adoreth thee,
165 I lay it naked to the deadly stroke
　And humbly beg the death upon my knee.

　　　　He lays his breast open;° she offers° at [*it*] *with his sword*　　*bare / thrusts*

　Nay, do not pause, for I did kill King Henry;
　But 'twas thy beauty that provokèd me.
　Nay, now dispatch: 'twas I that stabbed young Edward;
170 But 'twas thy heavenly face that set me on.

　　　　She lets fall the sword

　Take up the sword again, or take up me.

LADY ANNE Arise, dissembler.

　　　　[*He rises*]

　　　　　　　　Though I wish thy death,
　I will not be thy executioner.

RICHARD GLOUCESTER Then bid me kill myself, and I will do it.

LADY ANNE I have already.

175 **RICHARD GLOUCESTER** 　　　　That was in thy rage.
　Speak it again, and even with the word

---

1. Toads were popularly regarded as "ugly and venomous" (*As You Like It* 2.1.13).
2. Legendary monsters, supposed to kill with a glance.
3. The indented passage that follows, 154.1–154.12, appears only in F.

4. His brother, now the King.
5. Historically, Rutland was Richard's older brother. Shakespeare unhistorically makes him a child. His death is dramatized in *Richard Duke of York* 1.3–2.1.

This hand—which for thy love did kill thy love—
Shall, for thy love, kill a far truer love.
To both their deaths shalt thou be accessary.
180 LADY ANNE   I would I knew thy heart.
RICHARD GLOUCESTER   'Tis figured in my tongue.
LADY ANNE   I fear me both are false.
RICHARD GLOUCESTER   Then never man was true.
LADY ANNE   Well, well, put up your sword.
185 RICHARD GLOUCESTER   Say then my peace is made.
LADY ANNE   That shalt thou know hereafter.
RICHARD GLOUCESTER   But shall I live in hope?
LADY ANNE   All men, I hope, live so.
RICHARD GLOUCESTER   Vouchsafe° to wear this ring.   Consent
190 LADY ANNE   To take is not to give.⁶
RICHARD GLOUCESTER   Look how my ring encompasseth° thy finger;   encircles
Even so thy breast encloseth my poor heart.
Wear both of them, for both of them are thine.
And if thy poor devoted servant° may   lover
195 But beg one favour at thy gracious hand,
Thou dost confirm his happiness for ever.
LADY ANNE   What is it?
RICHARD GLOUCESTER   That it may please you leave these sad designs°   affairs
To him that hath most cause to be a mourner,
200 And presently° repair to Crosby House,⁷   at once
Where—after I have solemnly interred
At Chertsey monast'ry this noble king,
And wet his grave with my repentant tears—
I will with all expedient° duty see you.   prompt
205 For divers unknown° reasons, I beseech you   various secret
Grant me this boon.°   favor
LADY ANNE   With all my heart—and much it joys me, too,
To see you are become so penitent.
Tressell and Berkeley, go along with me.
RICHARD GLOUCESTER   Bid me farewell.
210 LADY ANNE   'Tis more than you deserve.⁸
But since you teach me how to flatter you,
Imagine I have said farewell already.   *Exeunt two with* ANNE
RICHARD GLOUCESTER   Sirs, take up the corpse.
GENTLEMAN   Towards Chertsey, noble lord?
RICHARD GLOUCESTER   No, to Blackfriars; there attend° my coming.   await
                 Exeunt [with] corpse. Manet° GLOUCESTER   Remains
215 Was ever woman in this humour° wooed?   mood; manner
Was ever woman in this humour won?
I'll have her, but I will not keep her long.
What, I that killed her husband and his father,
To take her in her heart's extremest hate,
220 With curses in her mouth, tears in her eyes,
The bleeding witness of my hatred by,
Having God, her conscience, and these bars° against me,   obstacles
And I no friends to back my suit withal
But the plain devil and dissembling looks—
225 And yet to win her, all the world to nothing?° Ha!   against such odds

6. To take your ring is not to give myself.   8. That is, to fare well is more than you deserve.
7. One of Richard's London residences.

Hath she forgot already that brave prince,
Edward her lord, whom I some three months since
Stabbed in my angry mood at Tewkesbury?
A sweeter and a lovelier gentleman,
230 Framed in the prodigality of nature,[9]
Young, valiant, wise, and no doubt right royal,
The spacious world cannot again afford°—   *provide*
And will she yet abase° her eyes on me,   *lower; humble*
That cropped the golden prime[1] of this sweet prince
235 And made her widow to a woeful bed?
On me, whose all not equals Edward's moiety?°   *half*
On me, that halts° and am misshapen thus?   *limp*
My dukedom to a beggarly *denier*,[2]
I do mistake my person all this while.
240 Upon my life she finds, although I cannot,
Myself to be a marv'lous proper° man.   *handsome*
I'll be at charges for° a looking-glass   *I'll buy*
And entertain° a score or two of tailors   *hire*
To study fashions to adorn my body.
245 Since I am crept in° favour with myself,   *into*
I will maintain it with some little cost.
But first I'll turn yon fellow in his grave,
And then return lamenting to my love.
Shine out, fair sun, till I have bought a glass,
250 That I may see my shadow as I pass.   *Exit*

1.3

Enter QUEEN [ELIZABETH], *Lord* RIVERS, [*Marquis* DORSET],
and Lord GRAY

RIVERS [*to* ELIZABETH]   Have patience, madam. There's no doubt his majesty
Will soon recover his accustomed health.
GRAY [*to* ELIZABETH]   In that you brook it ill,° it makes him worse.   *take it badly*
Therefore, for God's sake entertain good comfort,
5   And cheer his grace with quick° and merry eyes.   *lively*
QUEEN ELIZABETH   If he were dead, what would betide on° me?   *befall*
RIVERS[1]   No other harm but loss of such a lord.
QUEEN ELIZABETH   The loss of such a lord includes all harms.
GRAY   The heavens have blessed you with a goodly son
10   To be your comforter when he is gone.
QUEEN ELIZABETH   Ah, he is young, and his minority
Is put unto the trust of Richard Gloucester,
A man that loves not me—nor none of you.
RIVERS   Is it concluded° he shall be Protector?   *officially decreed*
15 QUEEN ELIZABETH   It is determined,° not concluded yet;   *decided*
But so it must be, if the King miscarry.°   *die*

Enter [*the Duke of*] BUCKINGHAM *and* [*Lord* STANLEY
Earl of] *Derby*

GRAY   Here come the Lords of Buckingham and Derby.
BUCKINGHAM   [*to* ELIZABETH]   Good time of day unto your royal grace.
STANLEY   [*to* ELIZABETH]   God make your majesty joyful, as you have been.

---

9. Made when nature in its gift giving was being lavish.   *to*: against (as in betting).
1. Springtime (Richard "cropped," or harvested,   1.3 Location: The royal palace of Westminster.
Edward's life prematurely).   1. F: Gray. Rivers's role in the conversation is far fuller
2. French coin, one-twelfth of a sou (extremely little).   in Q than in F (see lines 30, 54).

20 QUEEN ELIZABETH   The Countess Richmond,[2] good my lord of Derby,
        To your good prayer will scarcely say 'Amen'.
        Yet, Derby—notwithstanding she's your wife,
        And loves not me—be you, good lord, assured
        I hate not you for her proud arrogance.
25 STANLEY   I do beseech you, either not believe
        The envious° slanders of her false accusers   *malicious*
        Or, if she be accused on true report,
        Bear with her weakness, which I think proceeds
        From wayward° sickness, and no grounded malice.   *not easily treated*
30 RIVERS   Saw you the King today, my lord of Derby?
   STANLEY   But° now the Duke of Buckingham and I   *Just*
        Are come from visiting his majesty.
   QUEEN ELIZABETH   With likelihood of his amendment,° lords?   *recovery*
   BUCKINGHAM   Madam, good hope: his grace speaks cheerfully.
35 QUEEN ELIZABETH   God grant him health. Did you confer with him?
   BUCKINGHAM   Ay, madam. He desires to make atonement°   *reconciliation*
        Between the Duke of Gloucester and your brothers,
        And between them and my Lord Chamberlain,°   *(Hastings)*
        And sent to warn° them to his royal presence.   *summon*
40 QUEEN ELIZABETH   Would all were well! But that will never be.
        I fear our happiness is at the height.[3]
            Enter RICHARD [*Duke of*] GLOUCESTER [*and* LORD
            HASTINGS]
   RICHARD GLOUCESTER   They do me wrong, and I will not endure it.
        Who are they that complain unto the King
        That I forsooth am stern and love them not?
45   By holy Paul, they love his grace but lightly
        That fill his ears with such dissentious rumours.
        Because I cannot flatter and look fair,
        Smile in men's faces, smooth,° deceive, and cog,°   *flatter / cheat*
        Duck with French nods[4] and apish° courtesy,   *imitative; clumsy*
50   I must be held a rancorous enemy.
        Cannot a plain man live and think no harm,
        But thus his simple truth must be abused
        With° silken, sly, insinuating jacks?°   *By / nobodies*
   RIVERS   To whom in all this presence° speaks your grace?   *present company*
55 RICHARD GLOUCESTER   To thee, that hast nor honesty nor grace.
        When have I injured thee? When done thee wrong?
        Or thee? Or thee? Or any of your faction?
        A plague upon you all! His royal grace—
        Whom God preserve better than you would wish—
60   Cannot be quiet scarce a breathing while[5]
        But you must trouble him with lewd° complaints.   *ignorant*
   QUEEN ELIZABETH   Brother of Gloucester, you mistake the matter.
        The King—on his own royal disposition,°   *inclination*
        And not provoked by any suitor else—
65   Aiming belike° at your interior hatred,   *Guessing probably*
        That in your outward action shows itself
        Against my children, brothers, and myself,

2. Lady Margaret Beaufort, Lord Stanley's wife, was (by an earlier marriage) the mother of Henry Tudor, Earl of Richmond, who at play's end succeeds Richard and becomes Henry VII. As a descendant of the house of Lancaster, she was unlikely to have friendly feelings toward the Yorkist King Edward IV or his family.
3. At its highest point on Fortune's proverbial wheel, and thus about to decline.
4. *French nods*: elaborate bows.
5. Long enough to catch his breath.

Makes[6] him to send, that he may learn the ground
Of your ill will, and thereby to remove it.

70 RICHARD GLOUCESTER   I cannot tell. The world is grown so bad
That wrens make prey where eagles dare not perch.
Since every jack became a gentleman,
There's many a gentle person made a jack.

QUEEN ELIZABETH   Come, come, we know your meaning, brother Gloucester.
75 You envy my advancement, and my friends'.
God grant we never may have need of you.

RICHARD GLOUCESTER   Meantime, God grants that I have need of you.
Our brother° is imprisoned by your means,   (Clarence)
Myself disgraced, and the nobility
80 Held in contempt, while great promotions
Are daily given to ennoble those
That scarce some two days since were worth a noble.[7]

QUEEN ELIZABETH   By him° that raised me to this care-full height   (God)
From that contented hap° which I enjoyed,   fortune; lot
85 I never did incense his majesty
Against the Duke of Clarence, but have been
An earnest advocate to plead for him.
My lord, you do me shameful injury
Falsely to draw me in these vile suspects.°   suspicions
90 RICHARD GLOUCESTER   You may deny that you were not the mean°   instigation
Of my Lord Hastings' late imprisonment.

RIVERS   She may, my lord, for—

RICHARD GLOUCESTER   She may, Lord Rivers; why, who knows not so?
She may do more, sir, than denying that.
95 She may help you to many fair preferments,°   lucrative positions
And then deny her aiding hand therein,
And lay those honours on[8] your high desert.
What may she not? She may—ay, marry,[9] may she.

RIVERS   What 'marry, may she'?

100 RICHARD GLOUCESTER   What marry, may she? Marry with a king:
A bachelor, and a handsome stripling,° too.   young man
Iwis your grandam had a worser match.[1]

QUEEN ELIZABETH   My lord of Gloucester, I have too long borne
Your blunt upbraidings and your bitter scoffs.
105 By heaven, I will acquaint his majesty
Of those gross taunts that oft I have endured.
I had rather be a country servant-maid
Than a great queen, with this condition:
To be so baited,° scorned, and stormèd at.   provoked
        Enter old QUEEN MARGARET[2] [unseen behind them]
110 Small joy have I in being England's queen.

QUEEN MARGARET [aside]   And lessened be that small, God I beseech him.
Thy honour, state,° and seat° is due to me.   rank / throne

RICHARD GLOUCESTER [to ELIZABETH]   What? Threat you me
        with telling of the King?
Tell him, and spare not. Look what° I have said,   Whatever

---

6. The grammatical subject is still "the King."
7. Gold coin, worth one-third of a pound sterling.
8. And attribute those honors to.
9. Indeed (originally, an oath on the Virgin Mary), with pun in nest line on "wed."
1. Your mother (and the Queen's) was born of a less

distinguished union. *Iwis:* Assuredly (already archaic).
2. Historically, Margaret—widow of the Lancastrian King Henry VI—was held prisoner in England for five years after her husband's defeat at the Battle of Tewkesbury and then exiled to France.

115   I will avouch't in presence of the King.
     I dare adventure to be° sent to th' Tower.   *I risk being*
     'Tis time to speak; my pains³ are quite forgot.
     QUEEN MARGARET [*aside*]   Out, devil! I remember them too well.
     Thou killed'st my husband Henry in the Tower,
120   And Edward, my poor son, at Tewkesbury.
     RICHARD GLOUCESTER [*to* ELIZABETH]   Ere you were queen—
         ay, or your husband king—
     I was a packhorse° in his great affairs,   *beast of burden*
     A weeder-out of his proud adversaries,
     A liberal rewarder of his friends.
125   To royalize his blood, I spent mine own.
     QUEEN MARGARET [*aside*]   Ay, and much better blood than his or thine.
     RICHARD GLOUCESTER [*to* ELIZABETH]   In all which time you
         and your husband Gray
     Were factious° for the house of Lancaster;   *partisan*
     And Rivers, so were you.—Was not your husband
130   In Margaret's battle° at Saint Albans slain?⁴   *army*
     Let me put in your minds, if you forget,
     What you have been ere this, and what you are;
     Withal,° what I have been, and what I am.   *In addition; also*
     QUEEN MARGARET [*aside*]   A murd'rous villain, and so still thou art.
135   RICHARD GLOUCESTER   Poor Clarence did forsake his father⁵ Warwick—
     Ay, and forswore himself, which Jesu pardon—
     QUEEN MARGARET [*aside*]   Which God revenge!
     RICHARD GLOUCESTER   To fight on Edward's party° for the crown,   *side*
     And for his meed,° poor lord, he is mewed up.   *reward*
140   I would to God my heart were flint like Edward's,
     Or Edward's soft and pitiful like mine.
     I am too childish-foolish for this world.
     QUEEN MARGARET [*aside*]   Hie° thee to hell for shame, and leave this world,   *Hurry*
     Thou cacodemon;° there thy kingdom is.   *evil spirit*
145   RIVERS   My lord of Gloucester, in those busy days
     Which here you urge° to prove us enemies,   *recall*
     We followed then our lord, our sovereign king.
     So should we you, if you should be our king.
     RICHARD GLOUCESTER   If I should be? I had rather be a pedlar.
150   Far be it from my heart, the thought thereof.
     QUEEN ELIZABETH   As little joy, my lord, as you suppose
     You should enjoy, were you this country's king,
     As little joy may you suppose in me,
     That I enjoy being the queen thereof.
155   QUEEN MARGARET [*aside*]   Ah, little joy enjoys the queen thereof,
     For I am she, and altogether joyless.
     I can no longer hold me patient.
         [*She comes forward*]
     Hear me, you wrangling pirates, that fall out
     In sharing that which you have pilled° from me.   *pillaged*
160   Which of you trembles not that looks on me?
     If not that I am Queen, you bow like subjects;

3. Efforts, trouble (on the King's behalf).
4. Queen Elizabeth's first husband, Sir John Gray, died fighting for the Lancastrian faction.
5. Father-in-law. Clarence married Warwick's daughter Isabella, sister of this play's Lady Anne, and for a time defied his brothers by supporting the Lancastrian faction. He "forswore himself" (line 136) by returning to fight for the Yorkish faction.

Yet that by you deposed, you quake like rebels.[6]
[*To* RICHARD] Ah, gentle villain,[7] do not turn away.

RICHARD GLOUCESTER   Foul wrinkled witch, what mak'st thou°   *what are you doing*
in my sight?

165   QUEEN MARGARET   But repetition° of what thou hast marred: *recounting*
That will I make before I let thee go.[8]

166.1   RICHARD GLOUCESTER   *Wert thou not banishèd on pain of death?*
        QUEEN MARGARET   *I was, but I do find more pain in banishment*
        Than death can yield me here by my abode.
A husband and a son thou ow'st to me,
[*To* ELIZABETH] And thou a kingdom; [*to the rest*] all of you allegiance.
This sorrow that I have by right is yours,
170   And all the pleasures you usurp are mine.

RICHARD GLOUCESTER   The curse my noble father laid on thee—
When thou didst crown his warlike brows with paper,
And with thy scorns° drew'st rivers from his eyes,   *mocking speeches*
And then, to dry them, gav'st the duke a clout°   *rag; handkerchief*
175   Steeped in the faultless° blood of pretty Rutland[9]—   *innocent*
His curses then, from bitterness of soul
Denounced against thee, are all fall'n upon thee,
And God, not we, hath plagued thy bloody deed.

QUEEN ELIZABETH [*to* MARGARET]   So just is God to right the innocent.

LORD HASTINGS [*to* MARGARET]   O 'twas the foulest deed to slay
180   that babe,°   *(Rutland)*
And the most merciless that e'er was heard of.

RIVERS [*to* MARGARET]   Tyrants themselves wept when it was reported.

DORSET [*to* MARGARET]   No man but prophesied revenge for it.

BUCKINGHAM [*to* MARGARET]   Northumberland, then present, wept to see it.

185   QUEEN MARGARET   What? Were you snarling all before I came,
Ready to catch each other by the throat,
And turn you all your hatred now on me?
Did York's dread curse prevail so much with heaven
That Henry's death, my lovely Edward's death,
190   Their kingdom's loss, my woeful banishment,
Should all but answer for° that peevish brat?   *Should merely equal*
Can curses pierce the clouds and enter heaven?
Why then, give way, dull clouds, to my quick° curses!   *lively*
Though not by war, by surfeit° die your king,   *high living*
195   As ours by murder to make him a king.
[*to* ELIZABETH] Edward thy son, that now is Prince of Wales,
For Edward my son, that was Prince of Wales,
Die in his youth by like° untimely violence.   *similarly*
Thyself, a queen, for me that was a queen,
200   Outlive thy glory like my wretched self.
Long mayst thou live—to wail thy children's death,
And see another, as I see thee now,
Decked° in thy rights, as thou art 'stalled° in mine.   *Dressed / installed*
Long die thy happy days before thy death,
205   And after many lengthened hours of grief
Die, neither mother, wife, nor England's queen.—

6. *If . . . rebels:* Even if you do not bow because I am
Queen, at least you tremble like rebels because you
deposed me.
7. Well-born peasant; kindly scoundrel.
8. The indented passage that follows, 166.1–166.3,

appears only in F.
9. This is dramatized in *Richard Duke of York*
1.4.80–96, in which Margaret crowns the Duke of York
with a paper crown and waves a handkerchief dipped in
his son Rutland's blood in front of his eyes.

Rivers and Dorset, you were standers-by,
And so wast thou, Lord Hastings,[1] when my son
Was stabbed with bloody daggers. God I pray him,
210 That none of you may live his natural age,
But by some unlooked° accident cut off.   *unlooked-for*
RICHARD GLOUCESTER   Have done thy charm,° thou hateful,   *spell; curse*
    withered hag.
QUEEN MARGARET   And leave out thee? Stay, dog, for thou shalt hear me.
If heaven have any grievous plague in store
215 Exceeding those that I can wish upon thee,
O let them keep it till thy sins be ripe,
And then hurl down their indignation
On thee, the troubler of the poor world's peace.
The worm of conscience still begnaw thy soul.
220 Thy friends suspect for° traitors while thou liv'st,   *to be*
And take deep traitors for thy dearest friends.
No sleep close up that deadly eye of thine,
Unless it be while some tormenting dream
Affrights thee with a hell of ugly devils.
225 Thou elvish-marked, abortive, rooting hog,[2]
Thou that wast sealed° in thy nativity   *stamped*
The slave of nature[3] and the son of hell,
Thou slander of thy heavy° mother's womb,   *sorrowful*
Thou loathèd issue of thy father's loins,
230 Thou rag of honour, thou detested—
RICHARD GLOUCESTER   Margaret.
QUEEN MARGARET   Richard.
RICHARD GLOUCESTER   Ha?
QUEEN MARGARET   I call thee not.
RICHARD GLOUCESTER   I cry thee mercy° then, for I did think   *I beg your pardon*
That thou hadst called me all these bitter names.
235 QUEEN MARGARET   Why so I did, but looked for no reply.
O let me make the period° to my curse.   *full stop; finish*
RICHARD GLOUCESTER   'Tis done by me, and ends in 'Margaret'.
QUEEN ELIZABETH [*to* MARGARET]   Thus have you breathed your
    curse against yourself.
QUEEN MARGARET   Poor painted Queen, vain flourish[4] of my fortune,
240 Why strew'st thou sugar on that bottled° spider   *bottle-shaped; swollen*
Whose deadly web ensnareth thee about?
Fool, fool, thou whet'st a knife to kill thyself.
The day will come that thou shalt wish for me
To help thee curse this poisonous bunch-backed° toad.   *hunchbacked*
245 LORD HASTINGS   False-boding° woman, end thy frantic curse,   *Falsely prophesying*
Lest to thy harm thou move our patience.
QUEEN MARGARET   Foul shame upon you, you have all moved mine.
RIVERS   Were you well served, you would be taught your duty.
QUEEN MARGARET   To serve me well you all should do me duty.°   *show me deference*
250 Teach me to be your queen, and you my subjects:
O serve me well, and teach yourselves that duty.
DORSET   Dispute not with her: she is lunatic.

---

1. Rivers, Dorset, and Hastings were not present at Prince Edward's murder at Tewkesbury as dramatized in *Richard Duke of York* 5.5, but they are in the chronicles that served as Shakespeare's sources. The Prince, in fact, was slain by unknown combatants during the battle.

2. Richard's emblem was the white boar. *elvish-marked:* deformed by evil fairies. *abortive:* misshapen.
3. Because he was deformed from birth.
4. *painted:* counterfeit, with play on "use of cosmetics." *vain flourish:* empty, meaningless decoration.

QUEEN MARGARET   Peace, master Marquis, you are malapert.°   *impertinent*
    Your fire-new stamp of honour is scarce current.⁵
255 O that your young nobility could judge
    What 'twere to lose it and be miserable.
    They that stand high have many blasts to shake them,
    And if they fall they dash themselves to pieces.
RICHARD GLOUCESTER   Good counsel, marry!—Learn it, learn it, Marquis.
260 DORSET   It touches you, my lord, as much as me.
RICHARD GLOUCESTER   Ay, and much more; but I was born so high.
    Our eyrie⁶ buildeth in the cedar's top,
    And dallies with the wind, and scorns the sun.
QUEEN MARGARET   And turns the sun to shade. Alas, alas!
265 Witness my son, now in the shade of death,
    Whose bright outshining beams thy cloudy wrath
    Hath in eternal darkness folded up.
    Your eyrie buildeth in our eyrie's nest.—
    O God that seest it, do not suffer it;
270 As it was won with blood, lost be it so.
RICHARD GLOUCESTER   Peace, peace! For shame, if not for charity.
QUEEN MARGARET   Urge neither charity nor shame to me.
    Uncharitably with me have you dealt,
    And shamefully my hopes by you are butchered.
275 My charity is outrage; life, my shame;°   *my life is one of shame*
    And in that shame still live my sorrow's rage.
BUCKINGHAM   Have done, have done.
QUEEN MARGARET   O princely Buckingham, I'll kiss thy hand
    In sign of league and amity with thee.
280 Now fair befall° thee and thy noble house!   *good fortune to*
    Thy garments are not spotted with our blood,
    Nor thou within the compass° of my curse.   *scope*
BUCKINGHAM   Nor no one here, for curses never pass
    The lips of those that breathe them in the air.⁷
285 QUEEN MARGARET   I will not think but they ascend the sky
    And there awake God's gentle sleeping peace.
    O Buckingham, take heed of yonder dog.
        [*She points at* RICHARD]
    Look when he fawns, he bites; and when he bites,
    His venom tooth will rankle⁸ to the death.
290 Have naught to do with him; beware of him;
    Sin, death, and hell have set their marks on him,
    And all their ministers attend on him.
RICHARD GLOUCESTER   What doth she say, my lord of Buckingham?
BUCKINGHAM   Nothing that I respect, my gracious lord.
295 QUEEN MARGARET   What, dost thou scorn me for my gentle counsel,
    And soothe the devil that I warn thee from?
    O but remember this another day,
    When he shall split thy very heart with sorrow,
    And say, 'Poor Margaret was a prophetess'.—
300 Live each of you the subjects to his hate,
    And he to yours, and all of you to God's.   *Exit*
HASTINGS   My hair doth stand on end to hear her curses.

---

5. Your recently acquired title is not yet secure (as newly minted coins that have not yet achieved common currency).
6. Eagle's brood (the sons of York).

7. *curses . . . air*: it is as if curses were never spoken or afflict only the curser.
8. Will cause a wound that will fester.

RIVERS   And so doth mine. I muse why she's at liberty.

RICHARD GLOUCESTER   I cannot blame her, by God's holy mother.
305   She hath had too much wrong, and I repent
My part thereof that I have done to her.

QUEEN ELIZABETH   I never did her any, to my knowledge.

RICHARD GLOUCESTER   Yet you have all the vantage of her wrong.[9]
I was too hot° to do somebody good,   *eager*
310   That° is too cold° in thinking of it now.   *Who / ungrateful*
Marry, as for Clarence, he is well repaid:
He is franked up to fatting[1] for his pains.
God pardon them that are the cause thereof.

RIVERS   A virtuous and a Christian-like conclusion,
315   To pray for them that have done scathe° to us.   *harm*

RICHARD GLOUCESTER   So do I ever—(*speaks to himself*) being well advised:
For had I cursed now, I had cursed myself.
                    Enter [Sir William] CATESBY

CATESBY   Madam, his majesty doth call for you,
And for your grace, and you my gracious lords.

320   QUEEN ELIZABETH   Catesby, I come.—Lords, will you go with me?

RIVERS   We wait upon your grace.   *Exeunt. Manet* RICHARD

RICHARD GLOUCESTER   I do the wrong, and first begin to brawl.°   *complain; protest*
The secret mischiefs that I set abroach°   *set in motion*
I lay unto the grievous charge of[2] others.
325   Clarence, whom I indeed have cast in darkness,
I do beweep to many simple gulls°—   *credulous fools*
Namely to Derby, Hastings, Buckingham—
And tell them, ''Tis the Queen and her allies
That stir the King against the Duke my brother'.
330   Now they believe it, and withal whet me
To be revenged on Rivers, Dorset, Gray;
But then I sigh, and with a piece of scripture
Tell them that God bids us do good for evil;
And thus I clothe my naked villainy
335   With odd old ends,° stol'n forth of Holy Writ,   *old bits and pieces*
And seem a saint when most I play the devil.
                    Enter two MURDERERS
But soft, here come my executioners.—
How now, my hardy, stout, resolvèd° mates!   *resolute*
Are you now going to dispatch this thing?
340   A MURDERER   We are, my lord, and come to have the warrant,
That we may be admitted where he is.

RICHARD GLOUCESTER   Well thought upon; I have it here about me.
                    [*He gives them the warrant*]
When you have done, repair° to Crosby Place.   *return*
But sirs, be sudden° in the execution,   *swift*
345   Withal obdurate; do not hear him plead,
For Clarence is well spoken, and perhaps
May move your hearts to pity, if you mark° him.   *listen to*

A MURDERER   Tut, tut, my lord, we will not stand to prate.
Talkers are no good doers. Be assured,
350   We go to use our hands, and not our tongues.

---

9. All the benefits acquired as a result of the wrong she   2. I make into a serious accusation against.
has suffered.
1. He is penned up to fatten (for slaughter, like a pig).

RICHARD GLOUCESTER   Your eyes drop millstones when fools'
    eyes fall° tears.   *let fall*
  I like you, lads. About your business straight.°   *straightaway*
  Go, go, dispatch.
MURDERERS   We will, my noble lord.
        Exeunt [RICHARD *at one door, the* MURDERERS *at another*]

1.4

Enter [*George Duke of*] CLARENCE [*and Sir Robert*
  BRACKENBURY[1]]

BRACKENBURY   Why looks your grace so heavily° today?   *melancholy*
CLARENCE   O I have passed a miserable night,
  So full of fearful dreams, of ugly sights,
  That as I am a Christian faithful man,
5 I would not spend another such a night
  Though 'twere to buy a world of happy days,
  So full of dismal terror was the time.
BRACKENBURY   What was your dream, my lord? I pray you, tell me.
CLARENCE   Methoughts that I had broken from the Tower,
10 And was embarked to cross to Burgundy,
  And in my company my brother Gloucester,
  Who from my cabin tempted me to walk
  Upon the hatches;[2] there we looked toward England,
  And cited up° a thousand heavy times   *recalled*
15 During the wars of York and Lancaster
  That had befall'n us. As we paced along
  Upon the giddy footing of the hatches,
  Methought that Gloucester stumbled, and in falling
  Struck me—that sought to stay° him—overboard   *steady*
20 Into the tumbling billows of the main.
  O Lord! Methought what pain it was to drown,
  What dreadful noise of waters in my ears,
  What sights of ugly death within my eyes.
  Methoughts I saw a thousand fearful wrecks,
25 Ten thousand men that fishes gnawed upon,
  Wedges of gold, great ouches,[3] heaps of pearl,
  Inestimable° stones, unvalued° jewels,   *Countless / invaluable*
  All scattered in the bottom of the sea.
  Some lay in dead men's skulls; and in those holes
30 Where eyes did once inhabit, there were crept—
  As 'twere in scorn of eyes—reflecting gems,
  Which wooed the slimy bottom of the deep
  And mocked the dead bones that lay scattered by.
BRACKENBURY   Had you such leisure in the time of death,
35 To gaze upon these secrets of the deep?
CLARENCE   Methought I had, and often did I strive
  To yield the ghost,° but still° the envious° flood   *To die / always / malicious*
  Stopped-in° my soul and would not let it forth   *Stopped up*
  To find the empty, vast, and wand'ring air,
40 But smothered it within my panting bulk,°   *body*
  Who° almost burst to belch it in the sea.   *Which*

1.4 Location: In the Tower of London.
1. F gives this part to an anonymous keeper, Brackenbury not entering until line 72.

2. Planks laid across the hold of a ship, forming a temporary deck.
3. Gold or silver brooches set with jewels. Q, F: anchors.

BRACKENBURY   Awaked you not in this sore agony?

CLARENCE   No, no, my dream was lengthened after life.[4]

O then began the tempest to my soul!

45 I passed, methought, the melancholy flood,[5]

With that sour ferryman which poets write of,

Unto the kingdom of perpetual night.

The first that there did greet my stranger soul

Was my great father-in-law, renownèd Warwick,

50 Who cried aloud, 'What scourge° for perjury   punishment

Can this dark monarchy afford false Clarence?'

And so he vanished. Then came wand'ring by

A shadow[6] like an angel, with bright hair,

Dabbled in blood, and he shrieked out aloud,

55 'Clarence is come: false, fleeting,° perjured Clarence,   fickle

That stabbed me in the field by Tewkesbury.

Seize on him, furies![7] Take him unto torment!'

With that, methoughts a legion of foul fiends

Environed° me, and howlèd in mine ears   Surrounded

60 Such hideous cries that with the very noise

I trembling waked, and for a season after

Could not believe but that I was in hell,

Such terrible impression made my dream.

BRACKENBURY   No marvel, lord, though° it affrighted you;   that

65 I am afraid, methinks, to hear you tell it.

CLARENCE   Ah, Brackenbury, I have done these things,

That now give evidence against my soul,

For Edward's sake; and see how he requites me.[8]

68.1 *O God! If my deep prayers cannot appease thee*

But thou wilt be avenged on my misdeeds,

Yet execute thy wrath in me alone.

O spare my guiltless wife and my poor children.

Keeper, I pray thee, sit by me awhile.

70 My soul is heavy, and I fain would° sleep.   *I desire to*

BRACKENBURY   I will, my lord. God give your grace good rest.

[CLARENCE *sleeps*]

Sorrow breaks seasons and reposing hours,[9]

Makes the night morning and the noontide night.

Princes have but their titles for their glories,

75 An outward honour for an inward toil,

And for unfelt imaginations[1]

They often feel a world of restless cares;

So that, between their titles and low name,

There's nothing differs but the outward fame.

Enter two MURDERERS

80 FIRST MURDERER   Ho, who's here?

BRACKENBURY   What wouldst thou, fellow? And how cam'st thou hither?

SECOND MURDERER   I would speak with Clarence, and I came

hither on my legs.

4. My dream also depicted my fate after death.
5. The river Styx, across which Charon (the "sour ferryman" of the next line) ferried souls to Hades, the classical hell.
6. Shade, ghost (Edward, Prince of Wales—son of
Henry VI, and Clarence's brother-in-law—whom
Clarence helped to murder; see *Richard Duke of York*
5.5.40).

7. In Greek mythology, female spirits who enacted
vengeance for blood crimes against relatives.
8. The indented passage that follows, 68.1–68.4,
appears only in F. *requites*: repays.
9. Sorrow disrupts life's normal rhythms and disregards the hours appropriate to sleep.
1. *for unfelt imaginations*: "for the sake of imaginary
and unreal gratifications" (Dr. Johnson).

BRACKENBURY   What, so brief?

85   FIRST MURDERER   'Tis better, sir, than to be tedious. [*To* SECOND
MURDERER] Let him see our commission,° and talk no more.   authorization
[BRACKENBURY] *reads*

BRACKENBURY   I am in this commanded to deliver
The noble Duke of Clarence to your hands.
I will not reason what is meant hereby,

90   Because I will be° guiltless of the meaning.   wish to be
There lies the Duke asleep, and there the keys.
[*He throws down the keys*]
I'll to the King and signify to him
That thus I have resigned to you my charge.°   responsibility

FIRST MURDERER   You may, sir; 'tis a point of wisdom. Fare you

95   well.   *Exit* [BRACKENBURY]

SECOND MURDERER   What, shall I stab him as he sleeps?

FIRST MURDERER   No. He'll say 'twas done cowardly, when he
wakes.

SECOND MURDERER   Why, he shall never wake until the great

100   judgement day.

FIRST MURDERER   Why, then he'll say we stabbed him sleeping.

SECOND MURDERER   The urging of that word 'judgement' hath
bred a kind of remorse in me.

FIRST MURDERER   What, art thou afraid?

105   SECOND MURDERER   Not to kill him, having a warrant, but to
be damned for killing him, from the which no warrant can
defend me.

FIRST MURDERER   I thought thou hadst been resolute.

SECOND MURDERER   So I am—to let him live.

110   FIRST MURDERER   I'll back to the Duke of Gloucester and tell
him so.

SECOND MURDERER   Nay, I pray thee. Stay a little. I hope this
passionate humour° of mine will change. It was wont to hold   compassionate mood
me but while one tells° twenty.   counts
[*He counts to twenty*]

115   FIRST MURDERER   How dost thou feel thyself now?

SECOND MURDERER   Some certain dregs of conscience are yet
within me.

FIRST MURDERER   Remember our reward, when the deed's done.

SECOND MURDERER   'Swounds,° he dies. I had forgot the reward.   By God's wounds

120   FIRST MURDERER   Where's thy conscience now?

SECOND MURDERER   O, in the Duke of Gloucester's purse.

FIRST MURDERER   When he opens his purse to give us our
reward, thy conscience flies out.

SECOND MURDERER   'Tis no matter. Let it go. There's few or

125   none will entertain° it.   host; employ

FIRST MURDERER   What if it come to thee again?

SECOND MURDERER   I'll not meddle with it. It makes a man a coward. A man cannot steal but it accuseth him. A man cannot
swear but it checks him. A man cannot lie with his neighbour's

130   wife but it detects him. 'Tis a blushing, shamefaced spirit, that
mutinies in a man's bosom. It fills a man full of obstacles. It
made me once restore a purse of gold that by chance I found.
It beggars any man that keeps it. It is turned out of towns and
cities for a dangerous thing, and every man that means to live

135   well endeavours to trust to himself and live without it.

FIRST MURDERER 'Swounds, 'tis even now at my elbow, persuading me not to kill the Duke.

SECOND MURDERER Take the devil in thy mind, and believe him°   *(conscience)*
not: he would insinuate with thee but to make thee sigh.²

140 FIRST MURDERER I am strong framed; he cannot prevail with
me.

SECOND MURDERER Spoke like a tall° man that respects thy reputation. Come, shall we fall to work?   *valiant*

FIRST MURDERER Take him on the costard with the hilts of thy
145 sword, and then throw him into the malmsey butt³ in the next
room.

SECOND MURDERER O excellent device!—and make a sop⁴ of
him.

FIRST MURDERER Soft,° he wakes.   *Hush*

150 SECOND MURDERER Strike!

FIRST MURDERER No, we'll reason with him.

CLARENCE Where art thou, keeper? Give me a cup of wine.

SECOND MURDERER You shall have wine enough, my lord, anon.

CLARENCE In God's name, what art thou?

FIRST MURDERER   A man, as you are.

155 CLARENCE But not as I am, royal.

FIRST MURDERER Nor you as we are, loyal.

CLARENCE Thy voice is thunder, but thy looks are humble.

FIRST MURDERER My voice is now the King's;⁵ my looks, mine own.

CLARENCE How darkly and how deadly dost thou speak.
160 Your eyes do menace me. Why look you pale?
Who sent you hither? Wherefore do you come?

SECOND MURDERER To, to, to—

CLARENCE   To murder me.

BOTH MURDERERS   Ay, ay.

CLARENCE You scarcely have the hearts to tell me so,
And therefore cannot have the hearts to do it.
165 Wherein, my friends, have I offended you?

FIRST MURDERER Offended us you have not, but the King.

CLARENCE I shall be reconciled to him again.

SECOND MURDERER Never, my lord; therefore prepare to die.

CLARENCE Are you drawn forth° among a world of men   *selected from*
170 To slay the innocent? What is my offence?
Where is the evidence that doth accuse me?
What lawful quest° have given their verdict up   *jury*
Unto the frowning judge, or who pronounced
The bitter sentence of poor Clarence' death?
175 Before I be convict by course of law,
To threaten me with death is most unlawful.
I charge you, as you hope to have redemption
By Christ's dear blood, shed for our grievous sins,
That you depart and lay no hands on me.
180 The deed you undertake is damnable.

FIRST MURDERER What we will do, we do upon command.

SECOND MURDERER And he that hath commanded is our king.

CLARENCE Erroneous vassals,° the great King of Kings   *Misguided subjects*

---

2. he . . . sight: he (conscience) would ingratiate himself with you simply to cause you grief.
3. Wine barrel (malmsey is a strong, sweet wine).

costard: head (literally, a large apple).
4. Piece of bread or wafer soaked in wine.
5. I am now acting on the King's command.

Hath in the table of his law° commanded   *the Ten Commandments*
185 That thou shalt do no murder. Will you then
Spurn at his edict, and fulfil a man's?
Take heed, for he holds vengeance in his hand
To hurl upon their heads that break his law.
SECOND MURDERER   And that same vengeance doth he hurl on thee,
190 For false forswearing, and for murder too.
Thou didst receive the sacrament[6] to fight
In quarrel of° the house of Lancaster.   *On the side of*
FIRST MURDERER   And, like a traitor to the name of God,
Didst break that vow, and with thy treacherous blade
195 Unripped'st the bowels of thy sov'reign's son.[7]
SECOND MURDERER   Whom thou wast sworn to cherish and defend.
FIRST MURDERER   How canst thou urge God's dreadful law to us,
When thou hast broke it in such dear degree?
CLARENCE   Alas, for whose sake did I that ill deed?
200 For Edward, for my brother, for his sake.
He sends ye not to murder me for this,
For in that sin he is as deep as I.
If God will be avengèd for the deed,
O know you yet, he doth it publicly.
205 Take not the quarrel from his pow'rful arm;
He needs no indirect or lawless course
To cut off those that have offended him.
FIRST MURDERER   Who made thee then a bloody minister°   *agent*
When gallant springing° brave Plantagenet,°   *sprightly / (Edward)*
210 That princely novice,° was struck dead by thee?   *youth*
CLARENCE   My brother's love,° the devil, and my rage.   *My love for my brother*
FIRST MURDERER   Thy brother's love, our duty, and thy faults
Provoke us hither now to slaughter thee.
CLARENCE   If you do love my brother, hate not me.
215 I am his brother, and I love him well.
If you are hired for meed,° go back again,   *reward*
And I will send you to my brother Gloucester,
Who shall reward you better for my life
Than Edward will for tidings of my death.
220 SECOND MURDERER   You are deceived. Your brother Gloucester hates you.
CLARENCE   O no, he loves me, and he holds me dear.
Go you to him from me.
FIRST MURDERER   Ay, so we will.
CLARENCE   Tell him, when that our princely father York
Blessed his three sons with his victorious arm,
225 And charged us from his soul to love each other,
He little thought of this divided friendship.
Bid Gloucester think of this, and he will weep.
FIRST MURDERER   Ay, millstones, as he lessoned° us to weep.   *taught*
CLARENCE   O do not slander him, for he is kind.[8]
230 FIRST MURDERER   As snow in harvest. Come, you deceive yourself.
'Tis he that sends us to destroy you here.
CLARENCE   It cannot be, for he bewept my fortune,

---

6. Take communion and in doing so swear by the body of God.
7. That is, Prince Edward, son of the then sovereign, Henry VI.
8. He is full of natural feelings (and hence a loving brother).

And hugged me in his arms, and swore with sobs
That he would labour° my delivery.   *work for*

235 FIRST MURDERER   Why, so he doth, when he delivers you
From this earth's thraldom to the joys of heaven.
SECOND MURDERER   Make peace with God, for you must die, my lord.
CLARENCE   Have you that holy feeling in your souls
To counsel me to make my peace with God,
240 And are you yet to your own souls so blind
That you will war with God by murd'ring me?
O sirs, consider: they that set you on
To do this deed will hate you for the deed.
SECOND MURDERER [*to* FIRST]   What shall we do?
CLARENCE   Relent? and save your souls.
245 FIRST MURDERER   Relent? No. 'Tis cowardly and womanish.
CLARENCE   Not to relent is beastly, savage, devilish.—
My friend, I spy some pity in thy looks.
O if thine eye be not a flatterer,°   *deceiver (of Clarence)*
Come thou on my side, and entreat for me.
250 A begging prince, what beggar pities not?
Which of you, if you were a prince's son,
Being pent° from liberty as I am now,   *restrained*
If two such murderers as yourselves came to you,
Would not entreat for life? As you would beg
255 Were you in my distress—
SECOND MURDERER   Look behind you, my lord!
FIRST MURDERER (*He stabs* [CLARENCE]) Take that, and that! If
         all this will not serve,
I'll drown you in the malmsey butt within.
                                     Exit [*with Clarence's body*]
SECOND MURDERER   A bloody deed, and desperately dispatched!
260 How fain,° like Pilate, would I wash my hands   *gladly*
Of this most grievous, guilty murder done.
         Enter FIRST MURDERER
FIRST MURDERER   How now? What mean'st thou, that thou help'st me not?
By heaven, the Duke shall know how slack you have been.
SECOND MURDERER   I would he knew that I had saved his brother.
265 Take thou the fee, and tell him what I say,
For I repent me that the Duke is slain.   *Exit*
FIRST MURDERER   So do not I. Go, coward as thou art.—
Well, I'll go hide the body in some hole
Till that the Duke give order for his burial.
270 And, when I have my meed, I will away,
For this will out,⁹ and then I must not stay.   *Exit*

2.1

Flourish.° Enter KING [EDWARD], *sick,* QUEEN [ELIZA-   *Trumpet call*
BETH], *Lord Marquis* DORSET, [*Lord*] RIVERS, [LORD]
HASTINGS, [*Sir William*] CATESBY, [*the Duke of*] BUCK-
INGHAM [*and Lord Gray*]
KING EDWARD   Why, so! Now have I done a good day's work.
You peers, continue this united league.
I every day expect an embassage
From my redeemer to redeem me hence,

9. "Murder will out" was proverbial.   2.1 Location: The palace, London.

5   And more in peace my soul shall part to heaven
       Since I have made my friends at peace on earth.
       Hastings and Rivers, take each other's hand.
       Dissemble not¹ your hatred; swear your love.
       RIVERS   By heaven, my soul is purged from grudging hate,
10   And with my hand I seal my true heart's love.
       [*He takes Hastings' hand*]
       LORD HASTINGS   So thrive I,° as I truly swear the like.   *May I prosper*
       KING EDWARD   Take heed you dally° not before your king,   *trifle*
       Lest he that is the supreme King of Kings
       Confound° your hidden falsehood, and award°   *Defeat / cause*
15   Either of you to be the other's end.²
       LORD HASTINGS   So prosper I, as I swear perfect love.
       RIVERS   And I, as I love Hastings with my heart.
       KING EDWARD [*to* ELIZABETH]   Madam, yourself is not exempt from this,
       Nor your son Dorset;—Buckingham, nor you.
20   You have been factious one against the other.
       Wife, love Lord Hastings, let him kiss your hand—
       And what you do, do it unfeignedly.
       QUEEN ELIZABETH [*giving* HASTINGS *her hand to kiss*] There,
           Hastings. I will never more remember
       Our former hatred: so thrive I, and mine.°   *my family*
25   KING EDWARD   Dorset, embrace him. Hastings, love Lord Marquis.
       DORSET   This interchange of love, I here protest,°   *affirm*
       Upon my part shall be inviolable.
       LORD HASTINGS   And so swear I.
           [*They embrace*]
       KING EDWARD   Now, princely Buckingham, seal thou this league
30   With thy embracements to my wife's allies,
       And make me happy in your unity.
       BUCKINGHAM [*to* ELIZABETH]   Whenever Buckingham doth turn his hate
       Upon your grace, but° with all duteous love   *nor*
       Doth cherish you and yours, God punish me
35   With hate in those where I expect most love.
       When I have most need to employ a friend,
       And most assurèd that he is a friend,
       Deep,° hollow, treacherous, and full of guile   *Crafty*
       Be he unto me. This do I beg of heaven,
40   When I am cold in love to you or yours.
           [*They*] embrace
       KING EDWARD   A pleasing cordial,° princely Buckingham,   *health-giving drink*
       Is this thy vow unto my sickly heart.
       There wanteth now our brother Gloucester here,
       To make the blessèd period° of this peace.   *conclusion*
       Enter [*Sir Richard*] RATCLIFFE *and* [RICHARD *Duke of*]
       GLOUCESTER
45   BUCKINGHAM   And in good time,
       Here comes Sir Richard Ratcliffe and the Duke.
       RICHARD GLOUCESTER   Good morrow to my sovereign King and Queen.—
       And princely peers, a happy time of day.
       KING EDWARD   Happy indeed, as we have spent the day.
50   Brother, we have done deeds of charity,
       Made peace of enmity, fair love of hate,

---

1. Do not merely disguise.   2. Each of you to cause the death of the other.

Between these swelling wrong-incensèd³ peers.

RICHARD GLOUCESTER   A blessèd labour, my most sovereign lord.

Among this princely heap° if any here,   *company*
55 By false intelligence° or wrong surmise,   *information*
Hold me a foe,
If I unwittingly or in my rage
Have aught committed that is hardly borne°   *is deeply resented*
By any in this presence, I desire
60 To reconcile me to his friendly peace.
'Tis death to me to be at enmity.
I hate it, and desire all good men's love.—
First, madam, I entreat true peace of you,
Which I will purchase with my duteous service.—
65 Of you, my noble cousin Buckingham,
If ever any grudge were lodged between us.—
Of you, Lord Rivers, and Lord Gray of you,
That all without desert° have frowned on me.—   *entirely without cause*
Dukes, earls, lords, gentlemen, indeed of all!
70 I do not know that Englishman alive
With whom my soul is any jot at odds
More than the infant that is born tonight.
I thank my God for my humility.

QUEEN ELIZABETH   A holy day shall this be kept hereafter.
75 I would to God all strifes were well compounded.°—   *resolved*
My sovereign lord, I do beseech your highness
To take our brother Clarence to your grace.

RICHARD GLOUCESTER   Why, madam, have I offered love for this,
To be so flouted° in this royal presence?   *mocked*
80 Who knows not that the gentle Duke is dead?
        They all start
You do him injury to scorn his corpse.⁴

RIVERS⁵   Who knows not he is dead? Who knows he is?

QUEEN ELIZABETH   All-seeing heaven, what a world is this?

BUCKINGHAM   Look I so pale, Lord Dorset, as the rest?

85 DORSET   Ay, my good lord, and no one in the presence°   *(of the King)*
But his red colour hath forsook his cheeks.

KING EDWARD   Is Clarence dead? The order was reversed.

RICHARD GLOUCESTER   But he, poor man, by your first order died,
And that a wingèd Mercury⁶ did bear;
90 Some tardy cripple bore the countermand,
That came too lag° to see him buried.   *late*
God grant that some, less noble and less loyal,
Nearer in bloody thoughts, but not in blood,⁷
Deserve not worse than wretched Clarence did,
95 And yet go current from suspicion.⁸
        Enter [Lord STANLEY] *Earl of Derby*

STANLEY [*kneeling*]   A boon,° my sovereign, for my service done.   *favor*

KING EDWARD   I pray thee, peace! My soul is full of sorrow.

STANLEY   I will not rise, unless your highness hear me.

---

3. *swelling:* inflated with anger and pride. *wrong-incensèd:* mistakenly provoked; provoked by wrongs, injuries.
4. *to scorn his corpse:* by (supposedly) speaking ironically of him.
5. F assigns this line to King Edward.

6. The speedy messenger of the gods in classical mythology.
7. That is, nearer to bloody plots than was the innocent Clarence, but not so near the King in blood (another dig at the Queen's upstart relatives).
8. And yet are accepted at face value without suspicion.

KING EDWARD Then say at once, what is it thou requests?

100 STANLEY The forfeit, sovereign, of my servant's life,[9]
Who slew today a riotous gentleman,
Lately attendant on the Duke of Norfolk.

KING EDWARD Have I a tongue to doom° my brother's death,   order
And shall that tongue give pardon to a slave?
105 My brother slew no man; his fault was thought;
And yet his punishment was bitter death.
Who sued to me for him? Who in my wrath
Kneeled at my feet, and bid me be advised?°   consider carefully
Who spoke of brotherhood? Who spoke of love?
110 Who told me how the poor soul did forsake
The mighty Warwick and did fight for me?
Who told me, in the field at Tewkesbury,
When Oxford had me down, he rescued me,
And said, 'Dear brother, live, and be a king'?
115 Who told me, when we both lay in the field,
Frozen almost to death, how he did lap° me   wrap
Even in his garments, and did give himself
All thin° and naked to the numb-cold night?   thinly clad
All this from my remembrance brutish wrath
120 Sinfully plucked, and not a man of you
Had so much grace to put it in my mind.
But when your carters° or your waiting vassals   cart drivers
Have done a drunken slaughter, and defaced
The precious image[1] of our dear redeemer,
125 You straight° are on your knees for 'Pardon, pardon!'—   straightaway
And I, unjustly too, must grant it you.
But, for my brother, not a man would speak,
Nor I, ungracious, speak unto myself
For him, poor soul. The proudest of you all
130 Have been beholden to him in his life,
Yet none of you would once beg for his life.
O God, I fear thy justice will take hold
On me—and you, and mine, and yours, for this.—
Come, Hastings, help me to my closet.°   private (bed)room
135 Ah, poor Clarence!   Exeunt some with KING and QUEEN

RICHARD GLOUCESTER This is the fruits of rashness. Marked you not
How that the guilty kindred of the Queen
Looked pale, when they did hear of Clarence' death?
O, they did urge it still unto the King.
140 God will revenge it. Come, lords, will you go
To comfort Edward with our company?

BUCKINGHAM We wait upon your grace.   Exeunt

2.2

Enter the old DUCHESS OF YORK *with the two children of*
Clarence[1]

BOY Good grannam, tell us, is our father dead?

DUCHESS OF YORK No, boy.

GIRL Why do you weep so oft, and beat your breast,

---

9. That is, the release of his servant from a sentence of
death.
1. A man, thought to be created in God's image.

2.2 Location: The palace, London.
1. Edward and Margaret Plantagenet (not to be confused
with King Edward, Prince Edward, or Queen Margaret).

And cry, 'O Clarence, my unhappy son'?
5   BOY   Why do you look on us and shake your head,
And call us orphans, wretches, castaways,
If that our noble father were alive?
DUCHESS OF YORK   My pretty cousins,° you mistake me both.   kinsmen
I do lament the sickness of the King,
10   As loath to lose him, not your father's death.
It were lost sorrow to wail one that's lost.
BOY   Then you conclude, my grannam, he is dead.
The King mine uncle is to blame for this.
God will revenge it—whom I will importune°   beg
15   With earnest prayers, all to that effect.
GIRL   And so will I.
DUCHESS OF YORK   Peace, children, peace! The King doth love you well.
Incapable° and shallow innocents,   Uncomprehending
You cannot guess who caused your father's death.
20   BOY   Grannam, we can. For my good uncle Gloucester
Told me the King, provoked to it by the Queen,
Devised impeachments° to imprison him,   charges
And when my uncle told me so he wept,
And pitied me, and kindly kissed my cheek,
25   Bade me rely on him as on my father,
And he would love me dearly as his child.
DUCHESS OF YORK   Ah, that deceit should steal such gentle shapes,°   appearances
And with a virtuous visor° hide deep vice!   mask
He is my son, ay, and therein my shame;
30   Yet from my dugs° he drew not this deceit.   breasts
BOY   Think you my uncle did dissemble, grannam?
DUCHESS OF YORK   Ay, boy.
BOY   I cannot think it. Hark, what noise is this?
        Enter QUEEN [ELIZABETH] *with her hair about her ears*[2]
QUEEN ELIZABETH   Ah, who shall hinder me to wail and weep?
35   To chide my fortune, and torment myself?
I'll join with black despair against my soul,
And to myself become an enemy.
DUCHESS OF YORK   What means this scene of rude° impatience?   violent
QUEEN ELIZABETH   To mark an act of tragic violence.
40   Edward, my lord, thy son, our king, is dead.[3]
Why grow the branches when the root is gone?
Why wither not the leaves that want° their sap?   lack
If you will live, lament; if die, be brief,
That our swift-wingèd souls may catch the King's,
45   Or like obedient subjects follow him
To his new kingdom of ne'er-changing night.
DUCHESS OF YORK   Ah, so much interest° have I in thy sorrow   right to share
As I had title[4] in thy noble husband.
I have bewept a worthy husband's[5] death,
50   And lived with looking on his images.°   likenesses (his sons)
But now two mirrors[6] of his princely semblance

2. Disheveled hair was a conventional expression of grief
on the Elizabethan stage. F adds "Rivers and Dorset after
her" and gives them lines to speak later in the scene.
3. Shakespeare is telescoping events. Edward actually
died some five years after Clarence.

4. Legal right (as Edward's mother, the Duchess of York
has a right to mourn).
5. The Duke of York (whose death is dramatized in
Richard Duke of York).
6. Clarence and King Edward.

Are cracked in pieces by malignant death,
And I for comfort have but one false glass,°   *(Richard)*
That grieves me when I see my shame in him.
55 Thou art a widow, yet thou art a mother,
And hast the comfort of thy children left.
But death hath snatched my husband from mine arms
And plucked two crutches from my feeble hands,
Clarence and Edward. O what cause have I,
60 Thine being but a moiety° of my moan,   *half*
To overgo° thy woes, and drown thy cries?   *exceed*
BOY [*to* ELIZABETH]   Ah, aunt, you wept not for our father's death.
How can we aid you with our kindred tears?°   *tears of relatives*
DAUGHTER [*to* ELIZABETH]   Our fatherless distress was left unmoaned;
65 Your widow-dolour° likewise be unwept.   *widow's grief*
QUEEN ELIZABETH   Give me no help in lamentation.
I am not barren to bring forth complaints.[7]
All springs reduce[8] their currents to mine eyes,
That I, being governed by the wat'ry moon,
70 May send forth plenteous tears to drown the world.
Ah, for my husband, for my dear Lord Edward!
CHILDREN   Ah, for our father, for our dear Lord Clarence!
DUCHESS OF YORK   Alas, for both, both mine, Edward and Clarence!
QUEEN ELIZABETH   What stay° had I but Edward, and he's gone?   *support*
75 CHILDREN   What stay had we but Clarence, and he's gone?
DUCHESS OF YORK   What stays had I but they, and they are gone?
QUEEN ELIZABETH   Was never widow had so dear° a loss!   *grievous*
CHILDREN   Were never orphans had so dear a loss!
DUCHESS OF YORK   Was never mother had so dear a loss!
80 Alas, I am the mother of these griefs.
Their woes are parcelled;° mine is general.   *inclusive*
She for an Edward weeps, and so do I;
I for a Clarence weep, so doth not she.
These babes for Clarence weep, and so do I;
85 I for an Edward weep, so do not they.
Alas, you three on me, threefold distressed,
Pour all your tears. I am your sorrow's nurse,
And I will pamper° it with lamentation.[9]   *(over)feed*
88.1   DORSET   *Comfort, dear mother. God is much displeased*
        That you take with unthankfulness his doing.
        In common worldly things 'tis called ungrateful
        With dull unwillingness to pay a debt
88.5   *Which with a bounteous hand was kindly lent;*
        Much more to be thus opposite with° heaven   *in opposition to*
        For it requires° the royal debt it lent you.   *calls back*
    RIVERS   *Madam, bethink you like a careful mother*
        Of the young Prince your son. Send straight for him;
88.10   *Let him be crowned. In him your comfort lives.*
        Drown desperate sorrow in dead Edward's grave
        And plant your joys in living Edward's throne.

---

7. I can deliver my own lamentations.   9. The indented passage that follows, 88.1–88.12,
8. Lead back (as to the sea, which is governed by the   appears only in F.
moon).

Enter RICHARD [*Duke of*] GLOUCESTER, *the* [*Duke of*]
BUCKINGHAM, [*Lord* STANLEY *Earl of*] *Derby,* [LORD]
HASTINGS, *and* [*Sir Richard*] RATCLIFFE

RICHARD GLOUCESTER [*to* ELIZABETH]   Sister, have comfort. All of us have cause
90   To wail the dimming of our shining star,
But none can help our harms by wailing them.—
Madam, my mother, I do cry you mercy.°   *I beg your pardon*
I did not see your grace. Humbly on my knee
I crave your blessing.
95   DUCHESS OF YORK   God bless thee, and put meekness in thy breast,
Love, charity, obedience, and true duty.
RICHARD GLOUCESTER   Amen. [*Aside*] 'And make me die a good old man.'
That is the butt-end° of a mother's blessing;   *conclusion*
I marvel that her grace did leave it out.
100   BUCKINGHAM   You cloudy° princes and heart-sorrowing peers   *sad; raining (tears)*
That bear this heavy mutual load of moan,°   *lamentation*
Now cheer each other in each other's love.
Though we have spent our harvest of this king,
We are to reap the harvest of his son.
105   The broken rancour[1] of your high-swoll'n hearts
But lately° splinted, knit, and joined together,   *Only recently*
Must gently be preserved, cherished, and kept.
Meseemeth° good that, with some little train,°   *I think it / entourage*
Forthwith from Ludlow[2] the young Prince be fet°   *fetched*
110   Hither to London to be crowned our king.[3]
110.1   RIVERS   *Why with some little train, my lord of Buckingham?*
          BUCKINGHAM   *Marry, my lord, lest by a multitude°*   *large entourage*
          The new-healed wound of malice should break out,
          Which would be so much the more dangerous
110.5   *By how much the estate is green and yet ungoverned.*[4]
          Where every horse bears his commanding rein[5]
          And may direct his course as please himself°   *as he pleases*
          As well the fear of harm as harm apparent°   *as actual harm*
          In my opinion ought to be prevented.
110.10   RICHARD GLOUCESTER   *I hope the King made peace with all of us,*
          And the compact is firm and true in me.
          RIVERS   *And so in me, and so I think in all.*
          Yet since it is but green, it should be put
          To no apparent likelihood of breach,
110.15   *Which haply° by much company might be urged.*   *perhaps*
          Therefore I say, with noble Buckingham,
          That it is meet° so few should fetch the Prince.   *fitting*
          HASTINGS   *And so say I.*
RICHARD GLOUCESTER   Then be it so, and go we to determine
Who they shall be that straight shall post° to Ludlow.—   *ride speedily*
Madam, and you my sister, will you go
To give your censures° in this weighty business?   *opinions*
115   QUEEN ELIZABETH *and* DUCHESS OF YORK   With all our hearts.
          Exeunt. Manent RICHARD *and* BUCKINGHAM

1. Bitterness that caused you to be divided (unnaturally, like a broken limb).
2. Royal castle in Shropshire, near the Welsh border,
where Prince Edward, as Prince of Wales, was staying.
3. The indented passage that follows, 110.1–110.18,

appears only in F.
4. *By . . . ungoverned*: Considering that the government is newly established and not yet in full control.
5. *bears . . . rein*: takes charge of the rein that should
restrain him.

BUCKINGHAM My lord, whoever journeys to the Prince,
  For God's sake let not us two stay at home,
  For by the way I'll sort° occasion,   *find*
  As index° to the story we late° talked of,   *prologue / lately*
120 To part the Queen's proud kindred from the Prince.
RICHARD GLOUCESTER My other self, my counsel's consistory,° *council chamber*
  My oracle, my prophet, my dear cousin!
  I, as a child, will go by thy direction.
  Towards Ludlow then, for we'll not stay behind.   *Exeunt*

2.3

Enter one CITIZEN *at one door and another at the other*
FIRST CITIZEN Good morrow, neighbour. Whither away so fast?
SECOND CITIZEN I promise° you, I scarcely know myself.   *assure*
  Hear you the news abroad?
FIRST CITIZEN   Yes, that the King is dead.
SECOND CITIZEN Ill news, by'r Lady;° seldom comes the better.[1] *by the Virgin Mary*
5 I fear, I fear, 'twill prove a giddy° world.   *mad*
Enter another CITIZEN
THIRD CITIZEN Neighbours, God speed.
FIRST CITIZEN   Give you good morrow, sir.
THIRD CITIZEN Doth the news hold of good King Edward's death?
SECOND CITIZEN Ay, sir, it is too true. God help the while.
THIRD CITIZEN Then, masters,° look to see a troublous world. *sirs*
10 FIRST CITIZEN No, no, by God's good grace his son shall reign.
THIRD CITIZEN Woe to that land that's governed by a child.
SECOND CITIZEN In him there is a hope of government,
  Which in his nonage council under him,[2]
  And in his full and ripened years himself,
15 No doubt shall then, and till then, govern well.
FIRST CITIZEN So stood the state when Henry the Sixth
  Was crowned in Paris but at nine months old.
THIRD CITIZEN Stood the state so? No, no, good friends, God wot.° *knows*
  For then this land was famously enriched
20 With politic,° grave counsel;° then the King   *astute / advisers*
  Had virtuous uncles to protect his grace.
FIRST CITIZEN Why, so hath this, both by his father and mother.
THIRD CITIZEN Better it were they all came by his father,
  Or by his father there were none at all.
25 For emulation° who shall now be near'st[3]   *competition*
  Will touch us all too near, if God prevent not.
  O full of danger is the Duke of Gloucester,
  And the Queen's sons and brothers haught° and proud. *haughty*
  And were they° to be ruled, and not to rule,   *(both factions)*
30 This sickly land might solace° as before.   *prosper*
FIRST CITIZEN Come, come, we fear the worst. All will be well.
THIRD CITIZEN When clouds are seen, wise men put on their cloaks;
  When great leaves fall, then winter is at hand;
  When the sun sets, who doth not look for night?
35 Untimely storms make men expect a dearth.

2.3 Location: A street in London.   years of his minority.
1. Things rarely change for the better (proverbial).   3. Most influential with the King.
2. The Privy Council governing in his name during the

All may be well, but if God sort° it so   *ordain*
'Tis more than we deserve, or I expect.

SECOND CITIZEN   Truly the hearts of men are full of fear.
You cannot reason° almost with a man   *converse*
40   That looks not heavily and full of dread.

THIRD CITIZEN   Before the days of change still is it so.
By a divine instinct men's minds mistrust°   *suspect*
Ensuing danger, as by proof° we see   *experience*
The water swell before a boist'rous storm.
45   But leave it all to God. Whither away?

SECOND CITIZEN   Marry, we were sent for to the justices.

THIRD CITIZEN   And so was I. I'll bear you company.   *Exeunt*

2.4

Enter [Lord] CARDINAL, *young [Duke of]* YORK, QUEEN
[ELIZABETH], *and the [old]* DUCHESS OF YORK

CARDINAL   Last night, I hear, they lay them at Northampton.
At Stony Stratford[1] they do rest tonight.
Tomorrow, or next day, they will be here.

DUCHESS OF YORK   I long with all my heart to see the Prince.
5   I hope he is much grown since last I saw him.

QUEEN ELIZABETH   But I hear, no. They say my son of York
Has almost overta'en him in his growth.

YORK   Ay, mother, but I would not have it so.

DUCHESS OF YORK   Why, my young cousin, it is good to grow.

10   YORK   Grandam, one night as we did sit at supper,
My uncle Rivers talked how I did grow
More than my brother. 'Ay', quoth my nuncle° Gloucester,   *uncle (colloquial)*
'Small herbs have grace; gross weeds do grow apace'.°   *rapidly*
And since, methinks I would not grow so fast,
15   Because sweet flow'rs are slow, and weeds make haste.

DUCHESS OF YORK   Good faith, good faith, the saying did not hold°   *hold true*
In him that did object° the same to thee.   *argue*
He was the wretched'st thing when he was young,
So long a-growing, and so leisurely,
20   That if his rule were true he should be gracious.

CARDINAL   Why, so no doubt he is, my gracious madam.

DUCHESS OF YORK   I hope he is, but yet let mothers doubt.

YORK   Now, by my troth, if I had been remembered,
I could have given my uncle's grace a flout[2]
25   To touch his growth, nearer than he touched° mine.   *hit*

DUCHESS OF YORK   How, my young York? I pray thee, let me hear it.

YORK   Marry, they say my uncle grew so fast
That he could gnaw a crust at two hours old.
'Twas full two years ere I could get a tooth.
30   Grannam, this would have been a biting jest.

DUCHESS OF YORK   I pray thee, pretty York, who told thee this?

YORK   Grannam, his nurse.

DUCHESS OF YORK   His nurse? Why, she was dead ere thou wast born.

YORK   If 'twere not she, I cannot tell who told me.

2.4 Location: The palace, London.   2. *if . . . flout:* if I had been told this, I could have
1. Town in Buckinghamshire (south of Northampton).   taunted my noble uncle.
F reverses the order of the towns.

35 QUEEN ELIZABETH A parlous° boy! Go to,[3] you are too shrewd.°   *mischievous / sharp*
CARDINAL Good madam, be not angry with the child.
QUEEN ELIZABETH Pitchers have ears.[4]
            Enter [Marquis] DORSET
CARDINAL   Here comes your son, Lord Dorset.
    What news, Lord Marquis?
DORSET   Such news, my lord,
    As grieves me to report.
QUEEN ELIZABETH   How doth the Prince?
DORSET Well, madam, and in health.
40 DUCHESS OF YORK   What is thy news then?
DORSET Lord Rivers and Lord Gray are sent to Pomfret,[5]
    And with them Thomas Vaughan, prisoners.
DUCHESS OF YORK Who hath committed them?
DORSET   The mighty dukes,
    Gloucester and Buckingham.
CARDINAL   For what offence?
45 DORSET The sum of all I can,° I have disclosed.   *know*
    Why or for what the nobles were committed
    Is all unknown to me, my gracious lord.
QUEEN ELIZABETH Ay me! I see the ruin of our house.
    The tiger now hath seized the gentle hind.°   *doe*
50 Insulting tyranny begins to jet°   *encroach; strut*
    Upon the innocent and aweless[6] throne.
    Welcome destruction, blood, and massacre!
    I see, as in a map, the end of all.
DUCHESS OF YORK Accursèd and unquiet wrangling days,
55 How many of you have mine eyes beheld?
    My husband lost his life to get the crown,
    And often up and down my sons were tossed,
    For me to joy and weep their gain and loss.
    And being seated,° and domestic broils°   *enthroned / disorders*
60 Clean overblown,° themselves the conquerors   *Completely ended*
    Make war upon themselves, brother to brother,
    Blood to blood, self against self. O preposterous
    And frantic outrage, end thy damnèd spleen,°   *malice*
    Or let me die, to look on death no more.
65 QUEEN ELIZABETH [*to* YORK] Come, come, my boy, we will to sanctuary.[7]—
    Madam, farewell.
DUCHESS OF YORK Stay, I will go with you.
QUEEN ELIZABETH You have no cause.
CARDINAL [*to* ELIZABETH]   My gracious lady, go,
    And thither bear your treasure and your goods.
    For my part, I'll resign° unto your grace   *hand over*
70 The seal[8] I keep, and so betide° to me   *and so may it happen*
    As well I tender° you and all of yours.   *care for*
    Go, I'll conduct you to the sanctuary.   *Exeunt*

3. Expression of disapproval.
4. Proverbially said of children who overhear remarks made by adults: "Little pitchers have big ears."
5. Modern Pontefract, in west Yorkshire, site of the castle where Richard II was murdered.
6. Not able to command respect (because the King is so young).

7. Anyone, including criminals, could claim the protection of the church ("sanctuary") and thus immunity from civil law, initially for forty days. The Queen sought sanctuary at Westminster Abbey.
8. An engraved stamp, signifying the authority of the bearer, used to authenticate legal documents; here, the Great Seal of England.

3.1[1]

The Trumpets sound. Enter young PRINCE [EDWARD],
the Dukes of GLOUCESTER *and* BUCKINGHAM, *Lord* CAR-
DINAL, *with others* [*including Lord* STANLEY *Earl of*
Derby and Sir William CATESBY]

BUCKINGHAM   Welcome, sweet Prince, to London, to your chamber.[2]
RICHARD GLOUCESTER [*to* PRINCE EDWARD]   Welcome, dear
    cousin, my thoughts' sovereign.°   *ruler of my thoughts*
The weary way hath made you melancholy.
PRINCE EDWARD   No, uncle, but our crosses[3] on the way
5   Have made it tedious, wearisome, and heavy.
I want° more uncles here to welcome me.   *lack; desire*
RICHARD GLOUCESTER   Sweet Prince, the untainted virtue of your years
    Hath not yet dived into the world's deceit,
Nor more can you distinguish of a man
10   Than of his outward show, which God he knows
Seldom or never jumpeth° with the heart.   *coincides*
Those uncles[4] which you want were dangerous.
Your grace attended to their sugared words,
But looked not on the poison of their hearts.
15   God keep you from them, and from such false friends.
PRINCE EDWARD   God keep me from false friends; but they were none.
    Enter Lord MAYOR [*and his train*]
RICHARD GLOUCESTER   My lord, the Mayor of London comes to greet you.
MAYOR [*kneeling to* PRINCE EDWARD]   God bless your grace with
    health and happy days.
PRINCE EDWARD   I thank you, good my lord, and thank you all.—
20   I thought my mother and my brother York
Would long ere this have met us on the way.
Fie, what a slug° is Hastings, that he hastes not   *sluggard*
To tell us whether they will come or no.
    Enter LORD HASTINGS
BUCKINGHAM   In happy time here comes the sweating lord.
25 PRINCE EDWARD [*to* HASTINGS]   Welcome, my lord. What, will
    our mother come?
LORD HASTINGS   On what occasion° God he knows, not I,   *For what reason*
The Queen your mother, and your brother York,
Have taken sanctuary. The tender° Prince   *young; affectionate*
Would fain have° come with me to meet your grace,   *Would have liked to*
30   But by his mother was perforce° withheld.   *forcibly*
BUCKINGHAM   Fie, what an indirect and peevish° course   *perverse*
Is this of hers!—Lord Cardinal, will your grace
Persuade the Queen to send the Duke of York
Unto his princely brother presently?°—   *immediately*
35   If she deny, Lord Hastings, go with him,
And from her jealous° arms pluck him perforce.   *suspicious; mistrustful*
CARDINAL   My lord of Buckingham, if my weak oratory
    Can from his mother win the Duke of York,

3.1 Location: A street in London.
1. Either because of defects in the original manuscript
or because of blunders in the printing house, the text of
this scene, up to line 148, is exceptionally corrupt and
has been editorially reconstructed.
2. Capital (London was known as *camera regis*, "the
King's chamber").

3. Referring to the arrests of his uncle and half-
brothers on the journey.
4. Of the two arrested, only Rivers, being Elizabeth's
brother, was Prince Edward's real uncle; Gray, a son by
Elizabeth's previous marriage, was therefore actually
half brother to the Prince.

Anon° expect him. But if she be obdurate   *Very soon*
40 To mild entreaties, God in heaven forbid
We should infringe the sacred privilege
Of blessèd sanctuary. Not for all this land
Would I be guilty of so deep a sin.
BUCKINGHAM You are too senseless-obstinate, my lord,
45 Too ceremonious° and traditional.   *rule-bound*
Weigh it not with the grossness° of this age. *coarseness*
You break not sanctuary in seizing him.
The benefit thereof is always granted
To those whose dealings have deserved the place,
50 And those who have the wit to claim the place.
This prince hath neither claimed it nor deserved it,
And therefore, in my mind, he cannot have it.
Then taking him from thence that 'longs not there,[5]
You break thereby no privilege nor charter.
55 Oft have I heard of 'sanctuary men',[6]
But 'sanctuary children' ne'er till now.
CARDINAL My lord, you shall o'errule my mind for once.—
Come on, Lord Hastings, will you go with me?
LORD HASTINGS I come, my lord.
60 PRINCE EDWARD Good lords, make all the speedy haste you may.—
       Exeunt CARDINAL *and* HASTINGS
Say, uncle Gloucester, if our brother come,
Where shall we sojourn° till our coronation?   *stay*
RICHARD GLOUCESTER Where it seems best unto your royal self.
If I may counsel you, some day or two
65 Your highness shall repose you at the Tower,[7]
Then where you please and shall be thought most fit
For your best health and recreation.
PRINCE EDWARD I do not like the Tower of any place.°— *of all places*
Did Julius Caesar build that place, my lord?
70 BUCKINGHAM He did, my gracious lord, begin that place,
Which since succeeding ages have re-edified.° *built further*
PRINCE EDWARD Is it upon record, or else reported[8]
Successively from age to age, he built it?
BUCKINGHAM Upon record, my gracious liege.
75 PRINCE EDWARD But say, my lord, it were not registered,° *documented*
Methinks the truth should live from age to age,
As 'twere retailed° to all posterity   *related orally*
Even to the general all-ending day.°   *Day of Judgment*
RICHARD GLOUCESTER [*aside*] So wise so young, they say, do
   never live long.
80 PRINCE EDWARD What say you, uncle?
RICHARD GLOUCESTER I say, 'Without characters° fame lives long'. *writing*
[*Aside*] Thus like the formal Vice, Iniquity,[9]
I moralize two meanings in one word.[1]
PRINCE EDWARD That Julius Caesar was a famous man:

---

5. Taking the Prince from a place he has not claimed as sanctuary.
6. Criminals seeking to avoid prosecution.
7. It was customary for Kings of England (before James II) to spend the night before their coronation in the Tower, it being a royal palace and one of the strongest fortresses in the country. But Edward fears its other aspect, as a prison.
8. Is it on written record or otherwise told orally.
9. The conventional Vice figure, called Iniquity, who in sixteenth-century morality plays symbolized all of the vices.
1. As the Vice often did, Richard makes the same phrase have a double meaning.

85 With what his valour did t'enrich his wit,
His wit set down to make his valour live.²
Death made no conquest of this conqueror,
For yet he lives in fame though not in life.
I'll tell you what, my cousin Buckingham.
90 BUCKINGHAM   What, my good lord?
PRINCE EDWARD   An if° I live until I be a man,   An if = If
I'll win our ancient right³ in France again,
Or die a soldier, as I lived a king.
RICHARD GLOUCESTER [aside]   Short summers lightly have a
forward spring.⁴
        Enter young [Duke of.] YORK, [LORD] HASTINGS, and
        [Lord] CARDINAL
95 BUCKINGHAM   Now in good time, here comes the Duke of York.
PRINCE EDWARD   Richard of York, how fares our loving brother?
YORK   Well, my dread⁵ lord—so must I call you now.
PRINCE EDWARD   Ay, brother, to our grief, as it is yours.
Too late° he died that might have kept that title,   recently
100 Which by his death hath lost much majesty.
RICHARD GLOUCESTER   How fares our noble cousin, Lord of York?
YORK   I thank you, gentle uncle, well. O, my lord,
You said that idle° weeds are fast in growth;   useless
The Prince, my brother, hath outgrown me far.
105 RICHARD GLOUCESTER   He hath, my lord.
YORK   And therefore is he idle?
RICHARD GLOUCESTER   O my fair cousin, I must not say so.
YORK   He is more beholden to you then than I.
RICHARD GLOUCESTER   He may command me as my sovereign,
But you have power in me as a kinsman.
110 YORK   I pray you, uncle, render me this dagger.
RICHARD GLOUCESTER   My dagger, little cousin? With all my heart.
PRINCE EDWARD   A beggar, brother?
YORK   Of my kind uncle that I know will give,
It being but a toy° which is no grief to give.   trifle
115 RICHARD GLOUCESTER   A greater gift than that I'll give my cousin.
YORK   A greater gift? O, that's the sword to it.⁶
RICHARD GLOUCESTER   Ay, gentle cousin, were it light enough.
YORK   O, then I see you will part but° with light° gifts.   only / trivial
In weightier things you'll say a beggar nay.
120 RICHARD GLOUCESTER   It is too heavy for your grace to wear.
YORK   I'd weigh it lightly, were it heavier.⁷
RICHARD GLOUCESTER   What, would you have my weapon, little lord?
YORK   I would, that I might thank you as you call me.
RICHARD GLOUCESTER   How?
125 YORK   Little.
PRINCE EDWARD   My lord of York will still be cross° in talk.—   perverse; quarrelsome
Uncle, your grace knows how to bear with him.
YORK   You mean to bear me, not to bear with me.—
Uncle, my brother mocks both you and me.

---

2. *With . . . live:* The same valorous deeds that
enlivened Caesar's writing were themselves made
immortal by his retelling of them.
3. Right to the throne (claimed by Henry V and his son
Henry VI).
4. Proverbial: Those who die young ("forward") are

often ("lightly") precocious.
5. Held in awe (a common formula for addressing a
king).
6. *to it:* that is, to the dagger (the sword is to the dagger as the greater gift is to the lesser).
7. I'd consider it of little value, even if it were heavier.

130 Because that I am little like an ape,[8]
He thinks that you should bear me on your shoulders.
BUCKINGHAM   With what a sharp, prodigal wit[9] he reasons.
To mitigate the scorn he gives his uncle,
He prettily and aptly taunts himself.
135 So cunning and so young is wonderful.°   *a cause of wonder*
RICHARD GLOUCESTER [*to* PRINCE EDWARD]   My lord, will't
please you pass along?
Myself and my good cousin Buckingham
Will° to your mother to entreat of her   *Will go*
To meet you at the Tower and welcome you.
140 YORK [*to* PRINCE EDWARD]   What, will you go unto the Tower, my lord?
PRINCE EDWARD   My Lord Protector needs will have it so.
YORK   I shall not sleep in quiet at the Tower.
RICHARD GLOUCESTER   Why, what should you fear there?
YORK   Marry, my uncle Clarence' angry ghost.
145 My grannam told me he was murdered there.
PRINCE EDWARD   I fear no uncles dead.
RICHARD GLOUCESTER   Nor none that live, I hope.
PRINCE EDWARD   An if they[1] live, I hope I need not fear.
[*To* YORK] But come, my lord, and with a heavy heart,
Thinking on them, go we unto the Tower.
A sennet.[2]
          Exeunt. Manent RICHARD, BUCKINGHAM, *and* CATESBY
BUCKINGHAM [*to* RICHARD]   Think you, my lord, this little prating°   *chattering*
150   York
Was not incensèd° by his subtle mother   *incited*
To taunt and scorn you thus opprobriously?
RICHARD GLOUCESTER   No doubt, no doubt. O, 'tis a parlous° boy,   *shrewd*
Bold, quick, ingenious, forward, capable.
155 He is all the mother's, from the top to toe.
BUCKINGHAM   Well, let them rest.—Come hither, Catesby. Thou art sworn
As deeply° to effect what we intend   *cunningly*
As closely° to conceal what we impart.   *secretly*
Thou know'st our reasons, urged upon the way.[3]
160 What think'st thou? Is it not an easy matter
To make Lord William Hastings of our mind,[4]
For the instalment° of this noble duke   *enthroning*
In the seat royal of this famous isle?
CATESBY   He for his father's sake so loves the Prince[5]
165 That he will not be won to aught against him.
BUCKINGHAM   What think'st thou then of Stanley?° Will not he?   *(Earl of Derby)*
CATESBY   He will do all-in-all as Hastings doth.
BUCKINGHAM   Well then, no more but this. Go, gentle Catesby,
And, as it were far off, sound thou Lord Hastings
170 How he doth stand affected to our purpose.[6]
170.1   *And summon him tomorrow to the Tower*
          To sit about° the coronation.   *To discuss in council*
If thou dost find him tractable° to us,   *compliant*

---

8. Alluding to Richard's hunched back, which is compared to the saddle worn by jesters who carried monkeys about at carnivals and fairs.
9. A nimble wit (intelligence); a wit both sharp and prodigal (abundant or excessive).
1. Richard meant himself; Edward refers to Rivers and Gray.

2. Trumpet notes to signal a procession.
3. On the journey from London to Ludlow.
4. To have Hastings share in our opinion.
5. Hastings loves the Prince as the son of the beloved King Edward.
6. The following indented passage, 170.1–170.2, appears only in F. *stand affected to:* regard, like.

Encourage him, and tell him all our reasons.
If he be leaden, icy, cold, unwilling,
Be thou so too, and so break off your talk,
175 And give us notice of his inclination,
For we tomorrow hold divided counsels,[7]
Wherein thyself shalt highly° be employed.   *importantly*
RICHARD GLOUCESTER Commend me to Lord William.° Tell   (Hastings)
        him, Catesby,
His ancient knot[8] of dangerous adversaries
180 Tomorrow are let blood° at Pomfret Castle,   *are executed*
And bid my lord, for joy of this good news,
Give Mrs Shore[9] one gentle kiss the more.
BUCKINGHAM Good Catesby, go effect this business soundly.°   *thoroughly; well*
CATESBY My good lords both, with all the heed I can.
185 RICHARD GLOUCESTER Shall we hear from you, Catesby, ere we sleep?
CATESBY You shall, my lord.
RICHARD GLOUCESTER At Crosby House,° there shall you find   (Richard's residence)
        us both.   *Exit* CATESBY
BUCKINGHAM My lord, what shall we do if we perceive
Lord Hastings will not yield to our complots?°   *plots*
190 RICHARD GLOUCESTER Chop off his head. Something we will determine.
And look when° I am king, claim thou of me   *And as soon as*
The earldom of Hereford, and all the movables[1]
Whereof the King my brother was possessed.
BUCKINGHAM I'll claim that promise at your grace's hand.
195 RICHARD GLOUCESTER And look° to have it yielded with all kindness.   *And expect*
Come, let us sup betimes,° that afterwards   *early*
We may digest our complots in some form.[2]   *Exeunt*

3.2

Enter a MESSENGER *to the door of* LORD HASTINGS
MESSENGER [*knocking*] My lord, my lord!
LORD HASTINGS [*within*]   Who knocks?
MESSENGER   One from Lord Stanley.
        Enter LORD HASTINGS
LORD HASTINGS What is't o'clock?
MESSENGER   Upon the stroke of four.
LORD HASTINGS Cannot my Lord Stanley sleep these tedious nights?
MESSENGER So it appears by that I have to say.
5   First he commends him to your noble self.
LORD HASTINGS What then?
MESSENGER Then certifies° your lordship that this night   *assures*
He dreamt the boar had razèd off his helm.[1]
Besides, he says there are two councils kept,
10   And that may be determined at the one
Which may make you and him to rue at° th'other.   *regret*
Therefore he sends to know your lordship's pleasure,
If you will presently° take horse with him,   *immediately*

---

7. There will be two separate council meetings, one public to plan the Prince's coronation, the other private to plot Richard's seizing of the crown.
8. Conspiracy, with additional meaning of "tumor," picked up in the next line in the image of bloodletting as medical treatment.
9. After Edward's death, Jane Shore (see 1.1.71–77) became Hastings's mistress.

1. Personal as opposed to real property: furnishings, rather than land.
2. We may break plans down into an orderly system (with pun on "digest").
3.2 Location: Outside Lord Hastings's house, in London.
1. He dreamed the boar (Richard's emblem) had sheared off his helmet (figuratively, cut off his head).

And with all speed post with him toward the north
15 To shun the danger that his soul divines.°   *prophesies*
LORD HASTINGS   Go, fellow, go, return unto thy lord.
Bid him not fear the separated councils.
His honour and myself are at the one,
And at the other is my good friend Catesby,
20 Where nothing can proceed that toucheth° us   *concerns; harms*
Whereof I shall not have intelligence.°   *secret information*
Tell him his fears are shallow, without instance.°   *evidence*
And for his dreams, I wonder he's so simple,°   *childish*
To trust the mock'ry of unquiet slumbers.
25 To fly the boar before the boar pursues
Were to incense the boar to follow us,
And make pursuit where he did mean° no chase.   *intend*
Go, bid thy master rise, and come to me,
And we will both together to the Tower,
30 Where he shall see the boar will use us kindly.[2]
MESSENGER   I'll go, my lord, and tell him what you say.   *Exit*
                    Enter CATESBY
CATESBY   Many good morrows to my noble lord.
LORD HASTINGS   Good morrow, Catesby. You are early stirring.
What news, what news, in this our tott'ring state?
35 CATESBY   It is a reeling° world indeed, my lord,   *an unstable*
And I believe will never stand upright
Till Richard wear the garland of the realm.
LORD HASTINGS   How? 'Wear the garland'? Dost thou mean the crown?
CATESBY   Ay, my good lord.
40 LORD HASTINGS   I'll have this crown° of mine cut from my shoulders   *head*
Before I'll see the crown so foul misplaced.
But canst thou guess that he doth aim at it?
CATESBY   Ay, on my life, and hopes to find you forward°   *a strong supporter*
Upon his party° for the gain thereof—   *On his side*
45 And thereupon he sends you this good news:
That this same very day your enemies,
The kindred of the Queen, must die at Pomfret.
LORD HASTINGS   Indeed I am no mourner for that news,
Because they have been still my adversaries.
50 But that I'll give my voice on Richard's side
To bar my master's heirs in true descent,
God knows I will not do it, to the death.[3]
CATESBY   God keep your lordship in that gracious mind!
LORD HASTINGS   But I shall laugh at this a twelvemonth hence:
55 That they which brought me in my master's hate,[4]
I live to look upon their tragedy.
Well, Catesby, ere a fortnight make me older,
I'll send some packing that yet think not on't.
CATESBY   'Tis a vile thing to die, my gracious lord,
60 When men are unprepared, and look not for it.
LORD HASTINGS   O monstrous, monstrous! And so falls it out
With Rivers, Vaughan, Gray—and so 'twill do
With some men else, that think themselves as safe

---

2. Gently (but also, with unintended irony, characteristically).
3. Even at the risk of death.

4. That those (Rivers, Vaughan, and Gray) who turned
King Edward against me.

As thou and I, who as thou know'st are dear
65 To princely Richard and to Buckingham.
CATESBY   The Princes both make high account of° you—   highly esteem
[*Aside*] For they account° his head upon the bridge.[5]   expect
LORD HASTINGS   I know they do, and I have well deserved it.
    Enter Lord STANLEY
Come on, come on, where is your boar-spear,[6] man?
70 Fear you the boar, and go so unprovided?[7]
STANLEY   My lord, good morrow.—Good morrow, Catesby.—
You may jest on, but by the Holy Rood°   Cross
I do not like these several° councils, I.   separate
LORD HASTINGS   My lord, I hold my life as dear as you do yours,
75 And never in my days, I do protest,
Was it so precious to me as 'tis now.
Think you, but° that I know our state secure,   if it were not
I would be so triumphant as I am?
STANLEY   The lords at Pomfret, when they rode from London,
80 Were jocund,° and supposed their states were sure,°   merry / secure
And they indeed had no cause to mistrust;
But yet you see how soon the day o'ercast.°   became overcast
This sudden stab of rancour I misdoubt.[8]
Pray God, I say, I prove a needless coward.
85 What, shall we toward the Tower? The day is spent.[9]
LORD HASTINGS   Come, come, have with you!° Wot° you what,   I'll go with you / Know
    my lord?
Today the lords you talked of are beheaded.
STANLEY   They for their truth° might better wear their heads   honesty
Than some that have accused them wear their hats.°   retain their offices
90 But come, my lord, let us away.
    Enter a PURSUIVANT [*named*] *Hastings*[1]
LORD HASTINGS   Go on before; I'll follow presently.
    Exeunt STANLEY *and* CATESBY
Well met, Hastings. How goes the world with thee?
PURSUIVANT   The better that your lordship please° to ask.   is pleased
LORD HASTINGS   I tell thee, man, 'tis better with me now
95 Than when I met thee last, where now we meet.
Then was I going prisoner to the Tower,
By the suggestion° of the Queen's allies;   incitement
But now, I tell thee—keep it to thyself—
This day those enemies are put to death,
100 And I in better state than e'er I was.
PURSUIVANT   God hold it[2] to your honour's good content.
LORD HASTINGS   Gramercy,° Hastings. There, drink that for me.   Many thanks
    He throws him his purse
PURSUIVANT   God save your lordship.   *Exit*
    Enter a PRIEST

---

5. London Bridge (where the heads of traitors were displayed high on poles).
6. Specialized hunting spear with a crossbar to prevent the impaled boar's tusks from wounding the hunter.
7. Do you fear the boar, and (yet) go unprepared?
8. I mistrust such sudden attacks (as those that befell Rivers, Vaughan, and Gray).
9. It's getting late (in the morning). The scene had opened at 4:00 A.M.
1. F omits his name (taken from Holinshed's *Chroni-*

cles), here and in the dialogue. The name may be important in calling attention to the significance of Lord Hastings's own name: the word means either "someone who hurries" (here, to his destruction) or "a fruit that ripens early or before its time." *pursuivant*: state messenger with authority to execute warrants (particularly of treason). Figuratively, a pursuivant was any summoner or messenger.
2. May God maintain your prosperity.

PRIEST   Well met, my lord. I am glad to see your honour.

105 LORD HASTINGS   I thank thee, good Sir³ John, with all my heart.
I am in your debt for your last exercise.°   *sermon*
Come the next sabbath, and I will content you.⁴

He whispers in his ear.

Enter BUCKINGHAM

BUCKINGHAM   What, talking with a priest, Lord Chamberlain?
Your friends at Pomfret, they do need the priest;
110 Your honour hath no shriving work⁵ in hand.

LORD HASTINGS   Good faith, and when I met this holy man
The men you talk of came into my mind.
What, go you toward the Tower?

BUCKINGHAM   I do, my lord, but long I cannot stay there;
115 I shall return before your lordship thence.

LORD HASTINGS   Nay, like enough, for I stay dinner⁶ there.

BUCKINGHAM [*aside*]   And supper° too, although thou⁷ know'st it not.   *evening meal*
Come, will you go?

LORD HASTINGS   I'll wait upon° your lordship.   *Exeunt*   *attend; go with*

3.3

Enter Sir Richard RATCLIFFE *with halberdiers carrying
Lords* RIVERS, GRAY, *and [Sir Thomas]* VAUGHAN *to
death at Pomfret*¹

RIVERS   Sir Richard Ratcliffe, let me tell thee this:
Today shalt thou behold a subject die
For truth, for duty, and for loyalty.

GRAY [*to* RATCLIFFE]   God bless the Prince from all the pack of you!
5 A knot° you are of damnèd bloodsuckers.   *group*

VAUGHAN [*to* RATCLIFFE]   You live, that shall cry woe for° this   *shall regret*
hereafter.

RATCLIFFE   Dispatch.° The limit of your lives is out.   *Be quick*

RIVERS   O Pomfret, Pomfret! O thou bloody prison,
Fatal and ominous to noble peers!
10 Within the guilty closure° of thy walls,   *enclosure*
Richard the Second here was hacked to death,
And, for more slander to thy dismal seat,²
We give to thee our guiltless blood to drink.

GRAY   Now Margaret's curse is fall'n upon our heads,
15 For standing by when Richard stabbed her son.

RIVERS   Then cursed she Hastings; then cursed she Buckingham;
Then cursed she Richard. O remember, God,
To hear her prayer for them as now for us.
And for° my sister and her princely sons,   *as for*
20 Be satisfied, dear God, with our true blood,
Which, as thou know'st, unjustly must be spilt.

RATCLIFFE   Make haste: the hour of death is expiate.°   *fully come*

RIVERS   Come, Gray; come, Vaughan; let us here embrace.
Farewell, until we meet again in heaven.   *Exeunt*

---

3. Courteous title of respect for clergymen.
4. I will pay your "debt" with a donation.
5. Confession and absolution (here, before execution).
6. I stay for dinner (eaten at about 11:00 A.M.).
7. Here, used contemptuously, as opposed to the formal "you" in line 118.

3.3 Location: Pontefract Castle.
1. Q has an extra opening line for this scene: RATCLIFFE Come, bring forth the prisoners.
2. And, in order to increase the notoriety of this gloomy place.

3.4

Enter [the Duke of] BUCKINGHAM, *[Lord* STANLEY *Earl of] Derby,* [LORD] HASTINGS, BISHOP OF ELY, *[the Duke of]* NORFOLK, *[Sir William* CATESBY,]¹ *with others at a table*

LORD HASTINGS   Now, noble peers, the cause why we are met
Is to determine of° the coronation.   *decide upon*
In God's name, speak: when is the royal day?

BUCKINGHAM   Is all things ready for that solemn time?

5   STANLEY   It is, and wants but nomination.°   *naming the day*

BISHOP OF ELY   Tomorrow, then, I judge a happy° day.   *suitable*

BUCKINGHAM   Who knows the Lord Protector's mind herein?
Who is most inward° with the noble Duke?   *intimate*

BISHOP OF ELY   Your grace, methinks, should soonest know his mind.

10 BUCKINGHAM   We know each other's faces. For° our hearts,   *As for*
He knows no more of mine than I of yours,
Or I of his, my lord, than you of mine.—
Lord Hastings, you and he are near in love.

LORD HASTINGS   I thank his grace; I know he loves me well.

15 But for his purpose in the coronation,
I have not sounded him,° nor he delivered   *sounded him out*
His gracious pleasure any way therein.
But you, my honourable lords, may name the time,
And in the Duke's behalf I'll give my voice,°   *vote*

20 Which I presume he'll take in gentle part.°   *he'll graciously approve*
                *Enter [*RICHARD *Duke of]* GLOUCESTER

BISHOP OF ELY   In happy time, here comes the Duke himself.

RICHARD GLOUCESTER   My noble lords, and cousins all, good morrow.
I have been long a sleeper, but I trust
My absence doth neglect no great design²

25 Which by my presence might have been concluded.

BUCKINGHAM   Had not you come upon your cue, my lord,
William Lord Hastings had pronounced your part—
I mean, your voice, for crowning of the King.

RICHARD GLOUCESTER   Than my Lord Hastings no man might be bolder.³

30 His lordship knows me well, and loves me well.—
My lord of Ely, when I was last in Holborn⁴
I saw good strawberries in your garden there.
I do beseech you send for some of them.

BISHOP OF ELY   Marry, and will, my lord, with all my heart.   *Exit*

35 RICHARD GLOUCESTER   Cousin of Buckingham, a word with you.
[*Aside*] Catesby hath sounded Hastings in° our business,   *in respect to*
And finds the testy gentleman so hot
That he will lose his head ere give consent
His 'master's child'—as worshipful° he terms it—   *reverentially*

40 Shall lose the royalty° of England's throne.   *sovereignty*

BUCKINGHAM   Withdraw yourself a while; I'll go with you.
                *Exeunt [*RICHARD *and* BUCKINGHAM]⁵

STANLEY   We have not yet set down this day of triumph.

3.4 Location: The Tower of London.
1. F has Ratcliffe and Lovell (Sir Thomas Lovell; see 4.4.449) instead of Catesby.
2. My absence delays no important project.
3. No one could more confidently speak for me than

Lord Hastings; but also, no one could be more presumptuous.
4. The Bishop of Ely's official London residence.
5. Q keeps Buckingham on, and changes "I'll go with you" to "I'll follow you."

Tomorrow, in my judgement, is too sudden,

For I myself am not so well provided°   well equipped

45   As else I would be, were the day prolonged.°   further off

        Enter BISHOP OF ELY

BISHOP OF ELY   Where is my lord, the Duke of Gloucester?

I have sent for these strawberries.

LORD HASTINGS   His grace looks cheerfully and smooth° this morning.   untroubled

There's some conceit° or other likes° him well,   thought / pleases

50   When that he bids good morrow with such spirit.

I think there's never a man in Christendom

Can lesser hide his love or hate than he,

For by his face straight° shall you know his heart.   immediately

STANLEY   What of his heart perceive you in his face

55   By any likelihood° he showed today?   appearance

LORD HASTINGS   Marry, that with no man here he is offended—

For were he, he had shown it in his looks.

STANLEY   I pray God he be not.

        Enter RICHARD[6] *and* BUCKINGHAM

RICHARD GLOUCESTER   I pray you all, tell me what they deserve

60   That do conspire my death with devilish plots

Of damnèd witchcraft, and that have prevailed

Upon my body with their hellish charms?

LORD HASTINGS   The tender love I bear your grace, my lord,

Makes me most forward in this princely presence

65   To doom th'offenders, whatsoe'er they be.

I say, my lord, they have deservèd death.

RICHARD GLOUCESTER   Then be your eyes the witness of their evil:

See how I am bewitched. Behold, mine arm

Is like a blasted sapling withered up.

70   And this is° Edward's wife, that monstrous witch,   this is the work of

Consorted° with that harlot, strumpet Shore,   In league with

That by their witchcraft thus have markèd me.

LORD HASTINGS   If they have done this deed, my noble lord—

RICHARD GLOUCESTER   'If'? Thou protector of this damnèd strumpet,

75   Talk'st thou to me of 'ifs'? Thou art a traitor.—

Off with his head. Now, by Saint Paul I swear,

I will not dine until I see the same.

Some see it done.

The rest that love me, rise and follow me.

        Exeunt. Manent CATESBY[7] *with* HASTINGS

80 LORD HASTINGS   Woe, woe for England! Not a whit for me,

For I, too fond,° might have prevented this.   foolish

Stanley did dream the boar did raze our helms,

But I did scorn it and disdain to fly.

Three times today my footcloth horse[8] did stumble,

85   And started when he looked upon the Tower,

As° loath to bear me to the slaughterhouse.   As though

O now I need the priest that spake to me.

I now repent I told the pursuivant,

As too triumphing,° how mine enemies   exulting

6. According to Holinshed, "He returned into the chamber . . . with a wonderful sour, angry countenance, knitting the brows, frowning and fretting, and gnawing on his lips."

7. F calls for Ratcliffe and Lovell.
8. Horse draped with a richly ornamented covering reaching almost to the ground.

90   Today at Pomfret bloodily were butchered,
        And I myself secure in grace and favour.
        O Margaret, Margaret! Now thy heavy curse
        Is lighted on poor Hastings' wretched head.
CATESBY   Come, come, dispatch: the Duke would be at dinner.
95   Make a short shrift;° he longs to see your head.   confession (to a priest)
LORD HASTINGS   O momentary grace of mortal men,
        Which we more hunt for than the grace of God.
        Who builds his hope in th'air of your good looks⁹
        Lives like a drunken sailor on a mast,
100   Ready with every nod¹ to tumble down
        Into the fatal bowels of the deep.²
CATESBY   Come, come, dispatch. 'Tis bootless to exclaim.°   pointless to protest
LORD HASTINGS   O bloody Richard! Miserable England!
        I prophesy the fearful'st time to thee
105   That ever wretched age hath looked upon.—
        Come lead me to the block; bear him my head.
        They smile at me, who shortly shall be dead.   *Exeunt*

3.5

Enter RICHARD *Duke of* GLOUCESTER *and* [*the Duke of*]
        BUCKINGHAM *in rotten*° *armour, marvellous ill-favoured*°   rusty / ugly
RICHARD GLOUCESTER   Come, cousin, canst thou quake and change thy
        colour?
        Murder thy breath in middle of a word?
        And then again begin, and stop again,
        As if thou wert distraught and mad with terror?
5   BUCKINGHAM   Tut, I can counterfeit the deep tragedian,
        Tremble and start at wagging of a straw,¹
        Speak, and look back, and pry° on every side,   peer
        Intending° deep suspicion; ghastly looks   Suggesting
        Are at my service, like enforcèd smiles,
10   And both are ready in their offices²
        At any time to grace my stratagems.
        Enter the [*Lord*] MAYOR
RICHARD GLOUCESTER [*aside to* BUCKINGHAM]   Here comes the Mayor.
BUCKINGHAM [*aside to* RICHARD]   Let me alone to entertain him.—Lord Mayor—
RICHARD GLOUCESTER [*calling as to one within*]   Look to the drawbridge there!
15 BUCKINGHAM   Hark, a drum!
RICHARD GLOUCESTER [*calling as to one within*]   Catesby, o'erlook°   look (out) over
        the walls!
BUCKINGHAM   Lord Mayor, the reason we have sent—
RICHARD GLOUCESTER   Look back, defend thee! Here are enemies.
BUCKINGHAM   God and our innocence defend and guard us.
        Enter [*Sir William*] CATESBY³ *with Hastings' head*
20 RICHARD GLOUCESTER   O, O, be quiet! It is Catesby.
CATESBY   Here is the head of that ignoble traitor,
        The dangerous and unsuspected Hastings.
RICHARD GLOUCESTER   So dear I loved the man that I must weep.

---

9. *Who . . . looks*: Anyone who puts his faith in your
seemingly favorable glances.
1. Complex play on words: Ready as he dozes off; as the
ship rolls; as the monarch, whose "good looks" upheld
him, condemns him with a silent nod.
2. Lines 102–7 appear only in F. Censorship or the fear
of censorship may well be why Hastings's ominous pre-

diction was omitted from Q.
3.5 Location: The Tower of London.
1. Act startled by the least movement or gesture.
2. Both are eager to perform their functions.
3. F calls for Ratcliffe and Lovell, and brings on
Catesby earlier, with the Mayor.

I took him for the plainest° harmless creature   *most manifestly*
25   That breathed upon the earth, a Christian,
Made him my book° wherein my soul recorded   *diary*
The history of all her secret thoughts.
So smooth he daubed his vice with show of virtue
That, his apparent open guilt omitted—
30   I mean, his conversation[4] with Shore's wife—
He lived from all attainture of suspect.[5]
     BUCKINGHAM   The covert'st sheltered° traitor that ever lived.   *The most hidden*
     [*To the* MAYOR] Would you imagine, or almost believe—
Were't not that, by great preservation,[6]
35   We live to tell it—that the subtle traitor
This day had plotted in the Council house
To murder me and my good lord of Gloucester?
     MAYOR   Had he done so?
     RICHARD GLOUCESTER   What, think you we are Turks or infidels,
40   Or that we would against the form of law
Proceed thus rashly in the villain's death
But that the extreme peril of the case,
The peace of England, and our persons' safety,
Enforced us to this execution?
45   MAYOR   Now fair befall you, he deserved his death,
And your good graces both have well proceeded,°   *acted*
To warn false traitors from the like° attempts.   *similar*
I never looked for better at his hands
After he once fell in with Mrs Shore.
50   RICHARD GLOUCESTER[7]   Yet had not we determined he should die,
Until your lordship came to see his end,
Which now the loving haste of these our friends°—   *(Catesby and Buckingham)*
Something against our meanings°—have prevented;   *intentions*
Because, my lord, we would have had you hear
55   The traitor speak, and timorously confess
The manner and the purpose of his treason,
That you might well have signified the same
Unto the citizens, who haply° may   *perhaps*
Misconster us in him,[8] and wail his death.
60   MAYOR   But, my good lord, your graces' word shall serve
As well as° I had seen and heard him speak.   *As well as = As if*
And do not doubt, right noble princes both,
But° I'll acquaint our duteous citizens   *That*
With all your just proceedings in this cause.°   *action*
65   RICHARD GLOUCESTER   And to that end we wished your lordship here,
T'avoid the censures of the carping° world.   *overcritical*
     BUCKINGHAM   Which, since you come too late of our intent,°   *for what we intended*
Yet witness° what you hear we did intend,   *bear witness to*
And so, my good Lord Mayor, we bid farewell.   *Exit* MAYOR
70   RICHARD GLOUCESTER   Go after; after, cousin Buckingham!
The Mayor towards Guildhall[9] hies him in all post;°   *haste*
There, at your meetest vantage of the time,[1]
Infer° the bastardy of Edward's children.   *Allege*
Tell them how Edward put to death a citizen

---

4. Intercourse (in both senses).
5. He lived free from all taint of suspicion.
6. By the most fortunate preservation (of our lives).
7. F assigns this speech and the two preceding lines to

Buckingham.
8. Misunderstand our treatment of him.
9. Center of municipal government in London.
1. At your most appropriate and advantageous moment.

75 Only for saying he would make his son
'Heir to the Crown'—meaning indeed, his house,°   *tavern*
Which by the sign thereof was termèd so.
Moreover, urge his hateful luxury°   *lasciviousness*
And bestial appetite in change of lust,²
80 Which stretched unto their servants, daughters, wives,
Even where° his raging eye, or savage heart,   *Wherever*
Without control, listed° to make a prey.   *desired*
Nay, for a need, thus far come near my person:³
Tell them, when that my mother went with child
85 Of that insatiate Edward,⁴ noble York,
My princely father, then had wars in France,
And by true computation of the time
Found that the issue° was not his begot—   *offspring*
Which well appearèd in his lineaments,°   *features*
90 Being nothing like the noble Duke my father.
Yet touch this sparingly, as 'twere far off,
Because, my lord, you know my mother lives.
BUCKINGHAM   Doubt not, my lord, I'll play the orator
As if the golden fee⁵ for which I plead
95 Were for myself. And so, my lord, adieu.   *[He starts to go]*
RICHARD GLOUCESTER   If you thrive well, bring them to Baynard's Castle,⁶
Where you shall find me well accompanied
With reverend fathers and well-learnèd bishops.
BUCKINGHAM   I go, and towards three or four o'clock
100 Look for the news that the Guildhall affords.⁷   *Exit*
100.1   KING RICHARD *Go, Lovell, with all speed to Doctor Shaw;*
[To RATCLIFFE*] Go thou to Friar Penker.*⁸ *Bid them both*
Meet me within this hour at Baynard's Castle.
[Exeunt LOVELL *and* RATCLIFFE*]*
RICHARD GLOUCESTER   Now will I in, to take some privy order⁹
To draw the brats of Clarence¹ out of sight,
And to give notice that no manner² person
Have any° time recourse unto the Princes.   *Exeunt*   *at any*

3.6

Enter a SCRIVENER° *with a paper in his hand*   *scribe*
SCRIVENER   Here is the indictment of the good Lord Hastings,
Which in a set hand fairly is engrossed,¹
That it may be today read o'er in Paul's²—
And mark how well the sequel° hangs together: *sequence of events*
5 Eleven hours I have spent to write it over,
For yesternight by Catesby was it sent me;
The precedent° was full as long a-doing;   *rough draft*
And yet, within these five hours, Hastings lived,

---

2. In continually shifting the object of his lust.
3. *for . . . person:* if necessary, impugn even to this extent my own honor (by implying that his mother was unfaithful).
4. *went . . . Edward:* was pregnant with dissolute Edward. *insatiate:* impossible to satisfy.
5. The crown (punning on "lawyer's fee").
6. Richard's stronghold, between Blackfriars and London Bridge.
7. The indented passage that follows, 100.1–100.3, appears only in F.
8. Dr. Shaw, brother to the Lord Mayor, and Friar

Perkins, provincial of the Augustinian Order, were prominent clerics who made public speeches supporting Richard's claim to the throne.
9. To make some secret arrangements.
1. The two children seen in 2.2.
2. No kind of (in other words, of whatever status or importance).
3.6 Location: Somewhere in London.
1. Which is written in official script (as opposed to a draft copy) and in the format of a legal document.
2. St. Paul's Cathedral, which served as a secular as well as sacred gathering place.

Untainted,° unexamined, free, at liberty.   *Unaccused*
10   Here's a good world the while! Who is so gross°   *stupid*
That cannot see this palpable device?°   *obvious stratagem*
Yet who so bold but says he sees it not?
Bad is the world, and all will come to naught,°   *wickedness; nothing*
When such ill dealing must be seen in thought.³   *Exit*

3.7

Enter RICHARD [*Duke of*] GLOUCESTER *at one door and*
[*the Duke of*] BUCKINGHAM *at another*

RICHARD GLOUCESTER   How now, how now! What say the citizens?
BUCKINGHAM   Now, by the holy mother of our Lord,
The citizens are mum, say not a word.
RICHARD GLOUCESTER   Touched you° the bastardy of Edward's   *Did you touch on*
children?
5   BUCKINGHAM   I did, with his contract with Lady Lucy,¹
And his contract by deputy² in France,
Th'insatiate greediness of his desire,
And his enforcement° of the city wives,   *violation*
His tyranny for trifles, his own bastardy—
10   As being got° your father then in France,   *conceived*
And his resemblance,° being not like the Duke.   *appearance*
Withal, I did infer your lineaments°—   *lineage*
Being the right idea° of your father   *true image*
Both in your face³ and nobleness of mind;
15   Laid open all your victories in Scotland,⁴
Your discipline in war, wisdom in peace,
Your bounty, virtue, fair humility—
Indeed, left nothing fitting for your purpose
Untouched or slightly handled° in discourse.   *lightly mentioned*
20   And when mine oratory grew toward end,
I bid them that did love their country's good
Cry 'God save Richard, England's royal king!'
RICHARD GLOUCESTER   And did they so?
BUCKINGHAM   No, so God help me. They spake not a word,
25   But, like dumb statues or breathing stones,
Stared each on other and looked deadly pale—
Which, when I saw, I reprehended them,
And asked the Mayor, what meant this wilful silence?
His answer was, the people were not used
30   To be spoke to but by the Recorder.°   *(a city official)*
Then he was urged to tell my tale again:
'Thus saith the Duke . . . thus hath the Duke inferred'°—   *asserted*
But nothing spoke in warrant from himself.°   *on his own authority*
When he had done, some followers of mine own,
35   At lower end of the Hall, hurled up their caps,

---

3. Must be perceived but not spoken of.
3.7 Location: Baynard's Castle.
1. Lady Elizabeth Lucy bore Edward a child. If, as
Buckingham alleges, there had been a formal engagement between them, Edward's subsequent marriage to
Elizabeth Gray would have been ruled invalid. His children by that marriage would have been bastards and
hence ineligible to inherit the throne.
2. The Earl of Warwick, as deputy, had contracted with
Louis XI of France for the marriage of Edward to Bona

of Savoy, the French queen's sister (see *Richard Duke
of York* 3.3).
3. Q, F: forme. The Oxford editors observe that since
Richard is prominently deformed, "form" is inappropriate; in the chronicles, it is Richard's *face* that is compared with his father's.
4. In 1482, as leader of an English expeditionary force
against the Scots, Richard had advanced all the way to
Edinburgh.

And some ten voices cried 'God save King Richard!'
And thus I took the vantage of° those few: *opportunity presented by*
'Thanks, gentle citizens and friends', quoth I;
'This general applause and cheerful shout
40 Argues your wisdoms and your love to Richard'—
And even here brake off and came away.
RICHARD GLOUCESTER What tongueless blocks were they!
  Would they not speak?
BUCKINGHAM[5] No, by my troth, my lord.
RICHARD GLOUCESTER Will not the Mayor then, and his brethren, come?
45 BUCKINGHAM The Mayor is here at hand. Intend° some fear; *Pretend*
Be not you spoke with, but by mighty suit;[6]
And look you get a prayer book in your hand,
And stand between two churchmen, good my lord,
For on that ground I'll build a holy descant.[7]
50 And be not easily won to our request.
Play the maid's part:[8] still answer 'nay'—and take it.
RICHARD GLOUCESTER I go. An if you plead as well for them
As I can say nay to thee for myself,
No doubt we'll bring it to a happy issue.
   [*One knocks within*]
55 BUCKINGHAM Go, go, up to the leads![9] The Lord Mayor knocks.—
           Exit [RICHARD]
  Enter the [*Lord*] MAYOR, [*aldermen,*] *and citizens*
Welcome, my lord. I dance attendance° here. *am kept waiting*
I think the Duke will not be spoke withal.
  Enter CATESBY
Now Catesby, what says your lord to my request?
CATESBY He doth entreat your grace, my noble lord,
60 To visit him tomorrow, or next day.
He is within with two right reverend fathers,
Divinely bent to meditation,
And in no worldly suits would he be moved,
To draw him from his holy exercise.
65 BUCKINGHAM Return, good Catesby, to the gracious Duke.
Tell him myself, the Mayor, and aldermen,
In deep designs, in matter of great moment,
No less importing than[1] our general good,
Are come to have some conference with his grace.
70 CATESBY I'll signify so much unto him straight. *Exit*
BUCKINGHAM Ah ha! My lord, this prince is not an Edward.
He is not lolling on a lewd day-bed,
But on his knees at meditation;
Not dallying with a brace° of courtesans, *pair*
75 But meditating with two deep° divines; *profoundly learned*
Not sleeping to engross° his idle body, *fatten*
But praying to enrich his watchful° soul. *vigilant*
Happy were England would this virtuous prince
Take on his grace the sovereignty thereof.
80 But, sure I fear, we shall not win him to it.

---

5. F omits this line.
6. Do not let them speak with you unless they beg you.
7. Comment; improvised musical variation, usually the highest part. *ground*: basis; musical theme or air, often the bass line.

8. Keep refusing, but at the same time take whatever is offered (proverbial, with sexual innuendo).
9. Flat roof covered with lead.
1. Of no less significance than.

MAYOR   Marry, God defend° his grace should say us nay.   *forbid*
BUCKINGHAM   I fear he will. Here Catesby comes again.

Enter CATESBY

Now Catesby, what says his grace?
CATESBY   He wonders to what end you have assembled
85   Such troops of citizens to come to him,
His grace not being warned thereof before.
He fears, my lord, you mean no good to him.
BUCKINGHAM   Sorry I am my noble cousin should
Suspect me that I mean no good to him.
90   By heaven, we come to him in perfect love,
And so once more return and tell his grace.   *Exit* CATESBY
When holy and devout religious men
Are at their beads,° 'tis much to draw them thence.   *prayers*
So sweet is zealous contemplation.

Enter RICHARD *aloft, between two bishops.* [*Enter*
CATESBY *below*]

95   MAYOR   See where his grace stands 'tween two clergymen.
BUCKINGHAM   Two props of virtue for a Christian prince,
To stay him from the fall of vanity;[2]
And see, a book of prayer in his hand—
True ornaments to know[3] a holy man.—
100   Famous Plantagenet, most gracious prince,
Lend favourable ear to our request,
And pardon us the interruption
Of thy devotion and right Christian zeal.
RICHARD GLOUCESTER   My lord, there needs no such apology.
105   I do beseech your grace to pardon me,
Who, earnest in the service of my God,
Deferred the visitation of my friends.
But leaving this, what is your grace's pleasure?
BUCKINGHAM   Even that, I hope, which pleaseth God above,
110   And all good men of this ungoverned isle.
RICHARD GLOUCESTER   I do suspect I have done some offence
That seems disgracious° in the city's eye,   *displeasing*
And that you come to reprehend my ignorance.
BUCKINGHAM   You have, my lord. Would it might please your grace
115   On our entreaties to amend your fault.
RICHARD GLOUCESTER   Else wherefore breathe I in a Christian land?[4]
BUCKINGHAM   Know then, it is your fault that you resign
The supreme seat, the throne majestical,
The sceptred office of your ancestors,
120   Your state of fortune[5] and your due of birth,
The lineal glory of your royal house,
To the corruption of a blemished stock,[6]
Whiles in the mildness of your sleepy° thoughts—   *contemplative*
Which here we waken to our country's good—
125   The noble isle doth want her proper° limbs: *lack her own*
Her face defaced with scars of infamy,
Her royal stock graft with ignoble plants
And almost shouldered in° the swallowing gulf   *shoved into*

---

2. To prevent him from falling into the sin of vanity.
3. *True . . . know*: Prayer books (and also, perhaps, the clergymen) by which to recognize.
4. Why else do I lead a Christian life?

5. The position that fortune has given you.
6. Edward's "family tree" is degraded by bastardy and immorality.

Of dark forgetfulness and deep oblivion,
130 Which to recure° we heartily solicit   restore
Your gracious self to take on you the charge
And kingly government of this your land—
Not as Protector, steward, substitute,
Or lowly factor° for another's gain,   agent
135 But as successively,° from blood to blood,   in order of succession
Your right of birth, your empery,° your own.   absolute dominion
For this, consorted° with the citizens,   together
Your very worshipful° and loving friends,   respectful
And by their vehement instigation,
140 In this just cause come I to move your grace.
     RICHARD GLOUCESTER   I cannot tell if to depart in silence
Or bitterly to speak in your reproof
Best fitteth my degree° or your condition.[7]   rank
143.1 *If not to answer, you might haply° think*   *perhaps*
       Tongue-tied ambition, not replying, yielded°   *agreed*
       To bear the golden yoke of sovereignty,
       Which fondly° you would here impose on me.   *foolishly*
143.5 *If to reprove you for this suit of yours,*
       So seasoned° with your faithful love to me,   *made palatable*
       Then on the other side I checked° my friends.   *rebuked*
       Therefore to speak, and to avoid the first,
       And then in speaking not to incur the last,
143.10 *Definitively thus I answer you.*
     Your love deserves my thanks; but my desert,
145 Unmeritable,° shuns your high request.   Undeserving
First, if all obstacles were cut away
And that my path were even° to the crown,   smooth
As the ripe revenue and due of birth,
Yet so much is my poverty of spirit,
150 So mighty and so many my defects,
That I would rather hide me from my greatness—
Being a barque to brook° no mighty sea—   a boat to endure
Than in my greatness covet to be hid,[8]
And in the vapour of my glory smothered.
155 But God be thanked, there is no need of me,
And much I need° to help you, were there need.   lack (ability)
The royal tree hath left us royal fruit,
Which, mellowed by the stealing hours of time,
Will well become the seat of majesty
160 And make, no doubt, us happy by his reign.
On him I lay that° you would lay on me,   what
The right and fortune of his happy° stars,   auspicious
Which God defend that I should wring from him.
     BUCKINGHAM   My lord, this argues conscience in your grace,
165 But the respects thereof are nice and trivial,[9]
All circumstances well considerèd.
You say that Edward is your brother's son;
So say we, too—but not by Edward's wife.
For first was he contract° to Lady Lucy—   betrothed

---

7. Social rank. The indented passage that follows, 143.1–143.10, appears only in F.
8. Than desire to be enveloped by my greatness.
9. But the reasons you advance are nit-picking (thus, overscrupulous).

170 Your mother lives a witness to his vow[1]—
And afterward, by substitute,° betrothed   *proxy*
To Bona, sister to the King of France.
These both put off, a poor petitioner,
A care-crazed mother to a many sons,
175 A beauty-waning and distressèd widow
Even in the afternoon of her best days,
Made prize and purchase° of his wanton eye,   *booty*
Seduced the pitch and height of his degree[2]
To base declension° and loathed bigamy.   *degradation*
180 By her in his unlawful bed he got
This Edward, whom our manners° call the Prince.   *we in politeness*
More bitterly could I expostulate,
Save that for reverence to some alive[3]
I give a sparing limit to my tongue.
185 Then, good my lord, take to your royal self
This proffered benefit° of dignity—   *bestowal*
If not to bless us and the land withal,
Yet to draw forth° your noble ancestry   *to rescue*
From the corruption of abusing times,
190 Unto a lineal, true-derivèd course.
MAYOR [*to* RICHARD]   Do, good my lord; your citizens entreat you.
BUCKINGHAM [*to* RICHARD]   Refuse not, mighty lord, this proffered love.
CATESBY [*to* RICHARD]   O make them joyful: grant their lawful suit.
RICHARD GLOUCESTER   Alas, why would you heap this care on me?
195 I am unfit for state and majesty.
I do beseech you, take it not amiss.
I cannot, nor I will not, yield to you.
BUCKINGHAM   If you refuse it—as, in love and zeal,
Loath to depose the child, your brother's son,
200 As well we know your tenderness of heart
And gentle, kind, effeminate remorse,[4]
Which we have noted in you to your kindred,
And equally indeed to all estates°—   *social classes*
Yet know, whe'er° you accept our suit or no,   *whether*
205 Your brother's son shall never reign our king,
But we will plant some other in the throne,
To the disgrace and downfall of your house.
And in this resolution here we leave you.—
Come, citizens. 'Swounds,° I'll entreat no more.   *By God's wounds*
210 RICHARD GLOUCESTER   O do not swear, my lord of Buckingham.
                    Exeunt [BUCKINGHAM *and some others*]
CATESBY   Call him again, sweet prince. Accept their suit.
ANOTHER[5]   If you deny them, all the land will rue° it.   *suffer for*
RICHARD GLOUCESTER   Will you enforce° me to a world of cares?   *condemn*
Call them again.   [*Exit one or more*]
                    I am not made of stone,
215 But penetrable to your kind entreats,°   *entreaties*
Albeit against my conscience and my soul.

---

1. Buckingham draws attention to the Duchess of York's objection to her son Edward's marriage to Elizabeth Gray; Edward's supposed betrothals (see notes to lines 5–6), along with the fact of Elizabeth's widowhood, are put forward as evidence that the marriage should be considered bigamous and hence the offspring illegitimate.
2. Drew him down from the eminence appropriate to his noble rank.
3. Richard's own mother, the Duchess of York.
4. And natural, tender pity (feelings thought of at that time as primarily feminine).
5. One of the remaining citizens, city officials, or bishops. In F, Catesby speaks this line.

Enter BUCKINGHAM *and the rest*
Cousin of Buckingham, and sage, grave men,
Since you will buckle fortune on my back,
To° bear her burden, whe'er I will or no,   *To make me*
220   I must have patience to endure the load.
But if black scandal or foul-faced reproach
Attend the sequel of your imposition,°   *what you impose on me*
Your mere° enforcement shall acquittance° me   *outright / acquit*
From all the impure blots and stains thereof;
225   For God doth know, and you may partly see,
How far I am from the desire of this.
MAYOR   God bless your grace! We see it, and will say it.
RICHARD GLOUCESTER   In saying so, you shall but say the truth.
BUCKINGHAM   Then I salute you with this royal title:
230   Long live kind Richard, England's worthy king!
ALL BUT RICHARD[6]   Amen.
BUCKINGHAM   Tomorrow may it please you to be crowned?
RICHARD GLOUCESTER   Even when you please, for you will have it so.
BUCKINGHAM   Tomorrow then, we will attend your grace.
235   And so, most joyfully, we take our leave.
RICHARD GLOUCESTER [*to the bishops*]   Come, let us to our holy work again.—
Farewell, my cousin. Farewell, gentle friends.
        Exeunt [RICHARD *and bishops above, the rest below*]

4.1

Enter QUEEN [ELIZABETH], *the* [*old*] DUCHESS OF YORK,
and Marquis DORSET *at one door;* [LADY] ANNE *Duchess*
of Gloucester [*with Clarence's daughter*] *at another door*
DUCHESS OF YORK   Who meets us here? My niece° Plantagenet,   *granddaughter*
Led in° the hand of her kind aunt of Gloucester?   *by*
Now for° my life, she's wand'ring to the Tower,   *upon*
On pure heart's love, to greet the tender° Prince.—   *young*
Daughter,° well met.   *Daughter-in-law*
5   LADY ANNE   God give your graces both
A happy and a joyful time of day.
QUEEN ELIZABETH   As much to you, good sister.° Whither away?   *sister-in-law*
LADY ANNE   No farther than the Tower, and—as I guess—
Upon the like devotion° as yourselves: *devout duty*
10   To gratulate° the gentle princes there.   *greet*
QUEEN ELIZABETH   Kind sister, thanks. We'll enter all together—
Enter [*from the Tower* BRACKENBURY] *the Lieutenant*
And in good time, here the Lieutenant comes.
Master Lieutenant, pray you by your leave,
How doth the Prince, and my young son of York?
15   BRACKENBURY   Right well, dear madam. By your patience,
I may not suffer° you to visit them.   *permit*
The King hath strictly charged the contrary.
QUEEN ELIZABETH   The King? Who's that?
BRACKENBURY   I mean, the Lord Protector.
QUEEN ELIZABETH   The Lord protect him from that kingly title.[1]
20   Hath he set bounds° between their love and me?   *barriers*

---

6. Q assigns this word to the Mayor only.
4.1 Location: Before the Tower.

1. May God prevent Richard from acquiring the title of
King.

I am their mother; who shall bar me from them?

DUCHESS OF YORK   I am their father's mother; I will see them.

LADY ANNE   Their aunt I am in law, in love their mother;
  Then bring me to their sights. I'll bear thy blame,
25 And take thy office from thee on my peril.[2]

BRACKENBURY   No, madam, no; I may not leave it° so.   *give up my office*
  I am bound by oath, and therefore pardon me.   *Exit*

Enter Lord STANLEY *[Earl of Derby]*

STANLEY   Let me but meet you ladies one hour hence,
  And I'll salute your grace of York as mother
30 And reverend looker-on° of two fair queens.[3]   *beholder*
  [To ANNE*]* Come, madam, you must straight to Westminster,[4]
  There to be crownèd Richard's royal queen.

QUEEN ELIZABETH   Ah, cut my lace asunder,[5] that my pent heart
  May have some scope to beat, or else I swoon
35 With this dead-killing news.

LADY ANNE   Despiteful tidings! O unpleasing news!

DORSET *[to* ANNE*]*   Be of good cheer.—Mother, how fares your grace?

QUEEN ELIZABETH   O Dorset, speak not to me. Get thee gone.
  Death and destruction dogs thee at thy heels.
40 Thy mother's name is ominous to children.[6]
  If thou wilt outstrip death, go cross the seas,
  And live with Richmond from[7] the reach of hell.
  Go, hie thee! Hie thee from this slaughterhouse,
  Lest thou increase the number of the dead,
45 And make me die the thrall° of Margaret's curses: *slave*
  'Nor mother, wife, nor counted° England's Queen'.   *regarded as*

STANLEY   Full of wise care is this your counsel, madam.
  [To DORSET*]* Take all the swift advantage of the hours.
  You shall have letters from me to my son°   *stepson (Richmond)*
50 In your behalf, to meet you on the way.
  Be not ta'en tardy by unwise delay.

DUCHESS OF YORK   O ill-dispersing° wind of misery!   *misfortune-scattering*
  O my accursèd womb, the bed° of death!   *birthplace*
  A cockatrice[8] hast thou hatched to the world,
55 Whose unavoided eye is murderous.

STANLEY *[to* ANNE*]*   Come, madam, come. I in all haste was sent.

LADY ANNE   And I in all unwillingness will go.
  O would to God that the inclusive verge°   *enclosing rim*
  Of golden metal that must round° my brow   *encircle*
60 Were red-hot steel, to sear me to the brains.
  Anointed let me be with deadly venom,[9]
  And die ere men can say 'God save the Queen'.

QUEEN ELIZABETH   Go, go, poor soul. I envy not thy glory.
  To feed my humour,° wish thyself no harm.   *To humor me*
65 LADY ANNE   No? Why? When he that is my husband now
  Came to me as I followed Henry's corpse,
  When scarce the blood was well washed from his hands,

2. And take on the responsibilities of your position at
my own risk.
3. Elizabeth, widow of Edward IV, and Anne, wife of
Richard III.
4. To Westminster Abbey, where English monarchs are
traditionally crowned.
5. Elizabethan women wore tightly laced bodices.

6. The fact that you are my son places you in danger.
7. Away from. Henry Tudor, Earl of Richmond, had
fled to Brittany in 1472, when Edward IV secured his
grasp on the throne.
8. Basilisk (see note to 1.2.150).
9. Instead of the holy oil used in the ceremony of coronation.

Which issued from my other angel husband
And that dear saint which then I weeping followed—
70 O when, I say, I looked on Richard's face,
This was my wish: 'Be thou', quoth I, 'accursed
For making me, so young, so old a widow,[1]
And when thou wedd'st, let sorrow haunt thy bed;
And be thy wife—if any be so mad—
75 More miserable made by the life of thee
Than thou hast made me by my dear lord's death.'
Lo, ere I can repeat this curse again,
Within so small a time, my woman's heart
Grossly° grew captive to his honey words   Stupidly
80 And proved the subject of mine own soul's curse,
Which hitherto hath held mine eyes from rest—
For never yet one hour in his bed
Did I enjoy the golden dew of sleep,
But with his timorous° dreams was still° awaked.   fearful / continually
85 Besides, he hates me for° my father Warwick,   because of
And will, no doubt, shortly be rid of me.
QUEEN ELIZABETH   Poor heart, adieu. I pity thy complaining.°   lamenting
LADY ANNE   No more than with my soul I mourn for yours.
DORSET   Farewell, thou woeful welcomer of glory.
90 LADY ANNE   Adieu, poor soul, that tak'st thy leave of it.
DUCHESS OF YORK [to DORSET] Go thou to Richmond, and good fortune guide thee.
    [To ANNE, STANLEY, and Clarence's daughter] Go thou to Richard, and good angels
        tend thee.
    [To ELIZABETH] Go thou to sanctuary, and good thoughts possess thee.
    I to my grave, where peace and rest lie with me.
95 Eighty odd years of sorrow have I seen,
And each hour's joy racked with a week of teen.[2]   [Exit]
96.1   QUEEN ELIZABETH   Stay: yet look back with me unto the Tower.—
            Pity, you ancient stones, those tender babes,
            Whom envy° hath immured within your walls.   malice; jealousy
            Rough cradle for such little pretty ones,
96.5   Rude ragged nurse, old sullen playfellow
            For tender princes: use my babies well.
            So foolish sorrow bids your stones farewell.   Exeunt

4.2

Sound a sennet. Enter [KING] RICHARD in pomp, [the
Duke of] BUCKINGHAM, [Sir William] CATESBY, other
nobles[1] [and a PAGE]
KING RICHARD   Stand all apart.°—Cousin of Buckingham.   aside
BUCKINGHAM   My gracious sovereign?
KING RICHARD   Give me thy hand.
            Sound [a sennet]. Here he ascendeth the throne
    Thus high by thy advice
5 And thy assistance is King Richard seated.
But shall we wear these glories for a day?
Or shall they last, and we rejoice in them?
BUCKINGHAM   Still° live they, and for ever let them last.   Perpetually

1. Doomed to a long life of widowhood.
2. Grief. The indented passage that follows,
96.1–96.7, appears only in F; the other characters
remain onstage.
4.2 Location: The palace, London.
1. In F, specifically Ratcliffe and Lovell.

KING RICHARD   Ah, Buckingham, now do I play the touch,[2]

10   To try if thou be current° gold indeed.   *real, genuine*
     Young Edward lives. Think now what I would speak.

BUCKINGHAM   Say on, my loving lord.

KING RICHARD   Why, Buckingham, I say I would be king.

BUCKINGHAM   Why, so you are, my thrice-renownèd liege.

15   KING RICHARD   Ha? Am I king? 'Tis so. But Edward lives.

BUCKINGHAM   True, noble prince.

KING RICHARD   O bitter consequence,°   *conclusion; retort*
     That Edward still should live 'true noble prince'.
     Cousin, thou wast not wont° to be so dull.   *accustomed*
     Shall I be plain? I wish the bastards dead,

20   And I would have it immediately performed.
     What sayst thou now? Speak suddenly,° be brief.   *at once*

BUCKINGHAM   Your grace may do your pleasure.

KING RICHARD   Tut, tut, thou art all ice. Thy kindness freezes.
     Say, have I thy consent that they shall die?

25   BUCKINGHAM   Give me some little breath, some pause, dear lord,
     Before I positively speak in this.
     I will resolve° you herein presently.°   *Exit*   *answer / shortly*

CATESBY [*to another, aside*]   The King is angry. See, he gnaws his lip.

KING RICHARD [*aside*]   I will converse with iron-witted fools

30   And unrespective° boys. None are for me   *unobservant*
     That look into me with considerate° eyes.   *critical*
     High-reaching° Buckingham grows circumspect.—   *Ambitious*
     Boy.

PAGE   My lord?

35   KING RICHARD   Know'st thou not any whom corrupting gold
     Will tempt unto a close° exploit of death?   *secret*

PAGE   I know a discontented gentleman
     Whose humble means match not his haughty spirit.
     Gold were as good as twenty orators,

40   And will no doubt tempt him to anything.

KING RICHARD   What is his name?

PAGE   His name, my lord, is Tyrrell.

KING RICHARD   I partly know the man. Go call him hither, boy.
                                                          Exit [PAGE]
     [*Aside*] The deep-revolving,° witty° Buckingham   *deeply scheming / clever*
     No more shall be the neighbour to my counsels.

45   Hath he so long held out° with me untired,   *kept up*
     And stops he now for breath? Well, be it so.
                    Enter [*Lord*] STANLEY [*Earl of*] *Derby*
     How now, Lord Stanley? What's the news?

STANLEY   Know, my loving lord,
     The Marquis Dorset, as I hear, is fled

50   To Richmond, in those parts beyond the seas
     Where he abides.

KING RICHARD   Come hither, Catesby. [*Aside to* CATESBY] Rumour it abroad
     That Anne, my wife, is very grievous sick.
     I will take order for her keeping close.[3]

55   Enquire me out some mean-born gentleman,
     Whom I will marry straight to Clarence' daughter.

---

2. Touchstone: a means of testing gold.   3. I will arrange to have her kept out of sight.

The boy⁴ is foolish,° and I fear not him.   *simpleminded*
Look how thou dream'st. I say again, give out
That Anne, my queen, is sick, and like to die.
60   About it, for it stands me much upon°   *is very important to me*
To stop all hopes whose growth may damage me.
                                               [*Exit* CATESBY]
      [*Aside*] I must be married to my brother's daughter,⁵
      Or else my kingdom stands on brittle glass.
      Murder her brothers, and then marry her?
65   Uncertain way of gain, but I am in
      So far in blood that sin will pluck on° sin.   *incite*
      Tear-falling pity dwells not in this eye.—
            Enter [*Sir James*] TYRRELL; [*he kneels*]
      Is thy name Tyrrell?
TYRRELL   James Tyrrell, and your most obedient subject.
KING RICHARD   Art thou indeed?
70   TYRRELL   Prove° me, my gracious lord.   *Test*
KING RICHARD   Dar'st thou resolve to kill a friend of mine?
TYRRELL   Please you,° but I had rather kill two enemies.   *If you wish*
KING RICHARD   Why there thou hast it: two deep enemies,
      Foes to my rest, and my sweet sleep's disturbers,
75   Are they that I would have thee deal upon.°   *set to work upon*
      Tyrrell, I mean those bastards in the Tower.
TYRRELL   Let me have open means to come⁶ to them,
      And soon I'll rid you from the fear of them.
KING RICHARD   Thou sing'st sweet music. Hark, come hither, Tyrrell.
80   Go, by this token. Rise, and lend thine ear.
            [RICHARD] *whispers in his ear*
      'Tis no more but so.° Say it is done,   *That's all*
      And I will love thee, and prefer° thee for it.   *promote*
TYRRELL   I will dispatch it straight.
KING RICHARD   Shall we hear from thee, Tyrrell, ere we sleep?⁷
            Enter BUCKINGHAM
85   TYRRELL   Ye shall, my lord.   *Exit*
BUCKINGHAM   My lord, I have considered in my mind
      The late request that you did sound me in.
KING RICHARD   Well, let that rest. Dorset is fled to Richmond.
BUCKINGHAM   I hear the news, my lord.
90   KING RICHARD   Stanley, he° is your wife's son. Well, look to it.   *(Richmond)*
BUCKINGHAM   My lord, I claim the gift, my due by promise,
      For which your honour and your faith is pawned:
      Th'earldom of Hereford, and the movables
      Which you have promisèd I shall possess.
95   KING RICHARD   Stanley, look to your wife. If she convey
      Letters to Richmond, you shall answer it.°   *for it*
BUCKINGHAM   What says your highness to my just request?
KING RICHARD   I do remember me, Henry the Sixth
      Did prophesy that Richmond should be king,
100   When Richmond was a little peevish boy.
      A king . . . perhaps . . . perhaps.⁸
BUCKINGHAM   My lord?

---

4. Clarence's eldest son, Edward, Earl of Warwick.
5. To Edward's daughter, Elizabeth of York, who was later to unite the two houses by becoming queen to the Lancastrian Henry VII, formerly the Earl of Richmond.
6. Let me have free access.
7. F omits this and the following line.
8. The passage that follows, lines 101–119, appears only in Q.

KING RICHARD   How chance the prophet could not at that time
　　　Have told me, I being by, that I should kill him?
BUCKINGHAM   My lord, your promise for the earldom.
105 KING RICHARD   Richmond? When last I was at Exeter,
　　　The Mayor in courtesy showed me the castle,
　　　And called it 'Ruge-mount'⁹—at which name I started,
　　　Because a bard of Ireland¹ told me once
　　　I should not live long after I saw 'Richmond'.
110 BUCKINGHAM   My lord?
KING RICHARD   Ay? What's o'clock?
BUCKINGHAM   I am thus bold to put your grace in mind
　　　Of what you promised me.
KING RICHARD   　　　　　　　But what's o'clock?
BUCKINGHAM   Upon the stroke of ten.
115 KING RICHARD   Well, let it strike!
BUCKINGHAM   Why 'let it strike'?
KING RICHARD   Because that, like a jack,² thou keep'st the stroke
　　　Betwixt thy begging and my meditation.
　　　I am not in the giving vein today.
120 BUCKINGHAM   Why then resolve me,° whe'er you will or no?　　　*answer me resolutely*
KING RICHARD   Thou troublest me. I am not in the vein.°　　　*mood*
　　　　　　　Exit [RICHARD, *followed by all but* BUCKINGHAM]
BUCKINGHAM   And is it thus? Repays he my deep° service　　　*i.e., rendered at great risk*
　　　With such contempt? Made I him king for this?
　　　O let me think on Hastings, and be gone
125 To Brecon,° while my fearful head is on.　　　*manor house in Wales*
　　　　　　　　Exit [*at another door*]

4.3

Enter Sir [*James*] TYRRELL

TYRRELL   The tyrannous and bloody act is done—
　　　The most arch° deed of piteous massacre　　　*preeminent*
　　　That ever yet this land was guilty of.
　　　Dighton and Forrest,¹ whom I did suborn°　　　*induce*
5 To do this piece of ruthless butchery,
　　　Albeit they were fleshed² villains, bloody dogs,
　　　Melted with tenderness and mild compassion,
　　　Wept like two children in their deaths' sad story.³
　　　'O thus', quoth Dighton, 'lay the gentle babes';
10 'Thus, thus', quoth Forrest, 'girdling° one another　　　*embracing*
　　　Within their alabaster° innocent arms.　　　*marble-white*
　　　Their lips were four red roses on a stalk,
　　　And in their summer beauty kissed each other.
　　　A book of prayers on their pillow lay,
15 'Which once', quoth Forrest, 'almost changed my mind.
　　　But O, the devil'—there the villain stopped,
　　　When° Dighton thus told on, 'We smotherèd　　　*At which point*
　　　The most replenishéd° sweet work of nature,　　　*complete*

9. Redhill (but punning on "Richmond").
1. Celtic bards, or poets, were also considered prophets.
2. A Jack was the mechanical figure who appeared to strike the hours in early clocks. By clockwork reiterations of his suit, Richard suggests, Buckingham is behaving like an annoying beggar and interfering with Richard's "meditation."
4.3 Location: The palace, London.

1. For the murder of the princes, Tyrrell recruited his servant, John Dighton, along with Myles Forrest and two others.
2. Experienced in killing; applied to hounds that had been fed part of their first kill in order to give them a taste for blood.
3. Wept in telling the sad story of the Princes' deaths.

That from the prime° creation e'er she framed.'   *first*
20   Hence both are gone,° with conscience and remorse.   *overcome*
They could not speak, and so I left them both,
To bear this tidings to the bloody king.
     Enter KING RICHARD
And here he comes.—All health, my sovereign lord.
KING RICHARD   Kind Tyrrell, am I happy in thy news?
25   TYRRELL   If to have done the thing you gave in charge
Beget your happiness,[4] be happy then,
For it is done.
KING RICHARD   But didst thou see them dead?
TYRRELL   I did, my lord.
KING RICHARD   And buried, gentle Tyrrell?
TYRRELL   The chaplain of the Tower hath buried them;
30   But where, to say the truth, I do not know.
KING RICHARD   Come to me, Tyrrell, soon, at after-supper,°   *dessert*
When thou shalt tell the process° of their death.   *story*
Meantime, but think how I may do thee good,
And be inheritor of thy desire.[5]
Farewell till then.
35   TYRRELL   I humbly take my leave.   *Exit*
KING RICHARD   The son of Clarence have I pent° up close.   *locked*
His daughter meanly have I matched in marriage.[6]
The sons of Edward sleep in Abraham's bosom,[7]
And Anne, my wife, hath bid this world goodnight.
40   Now, for° I know the Breton[8] Richmond aims   *because*
At young Elizabeth, my brother's daughter,
And by that knot° looks proudly o'er the crown,   *marriage; alliance*
To her go I, a jolly thriving wooer[9]—
     Enter [Sir Richard] RATCLIFFE[1] *[running]*
RATCLIFFE   My lord.
45   KING RICHARD   Good news or bad, that thou com'st in so bluntly?
RATCLIFFE   Bad news, my lord. Ely° is fled to Richmond,   *(Bishop of Ely)*
And Buckingham, backed with the hardy Welshmen,
Is in the field, and still his power increaseth.
KING RICHARD   Ely with Richmond troubles me more near°   *deeply*
50   Than Buckingham and his rash-levied strength.°   *hastily raised army*
Come, I have learned that fearful commenting
Is leaden servitor[2] to dull delay.
Delay leads impotent and snail-paced beggary.°   *ruin*
Then fiery expedition° be my wing: *speed*
55   Jove's Mercury,[3] an herald for a king.
Go, muster men. My counsel is my shield.[4]
We must be brief, when traitors brave the field.[5]   *Exeunt*

---

4. *If . . . happiness:* If it pleases you to have accomplished what you ordered done.
5. *but . . . desire:* you have only to think what you want of me, and you will possess it.
6. I have married off to a poor man.
7. In heaven (see Luke 16:22–23).
8. Person from Brittany; Richmond spent fourteen years in exile there before returning to England to face Richard III in 1485.
9. It was widely rumored that Anne was poisoned in order to facilitate a plan by Richard to marry Elizabeth,

sister to the missing princes; modern historians believe that these allegations are probably untrue. Richard's alleged actions regarding Clarence's son and daughter (lines 36–37) are certainly untrue.
1. Q calls for Catesby.
2. *fearful . . . servitor:* frightened talk is the sluggish attendant.
3. The swift messenger of the gods.
4. *My . . . shield:* I do not talk, but arm myself to fight. *counsel:* adviser.
5. When traitors defy (us on) the battlefield.

4.4

Enter old QUEEN MARGARET

QUEEN MARGARET   So now prosperity begins to mellow°   *ripen*
  And drop into the rotten mouth of death.
  Here in these confines slyly have I lurked
  To watch the waning of mine enemies.
5 A dire induction° am I witness to,   *prologue (as to a play)*
  And will to France, hoping the consequence°   *conclusion (as of a play)*
  Will prove as bitter, black, and tragical.

Enter the [old] DUCHESS OF YORK *and* QUEEN [ELIZABETH]

  Withdraw thee, wretched Margaret. Who comes here?

QUEEN ELIZABETH   Ah, my poor princes! Ah, my tender babes!
10 My unblown° flowers, new-appearing sweets!°   *unopened / blooms*
  If yet your gentle souls fly in the air,
  And be not fixed in doom perpetual,[1]
  Hover about me with your airy wings
  And hear your mother's lamentation.

15 QUEEN MARGARET [*aside*]   Hover about her, say that right for right
  Hath dimmed your infant morn to agèd night.[2]

DUCHESS OF YORK[3]   So many miseries have crazed° my voice   *cracked*
  That my woe-wearied tongue is still and mute.
  Edward Plantagenet, why art thou dead?

20 QUEEN MARGARET [*aside*]   Plantagenet doth quit° Plantagenet;   *pay for (the deeds of)*
  Edward for Edward pays a dying debt.[4]

QUEEN ELIZABETH   Wilt thou, O God, fly from such gentle lambs
  And throw them in the entrails of the wolf?
  When° didst thou sleep, when such a deed was done?   *Whenever (up until now)*

25 QUEEN MARGARET [*aside*]   When holy Harry[5] died, and my sweet son.

DUCHESS OF YORK   Dead life, blind sight, poor mortal living ghost,[6]
  Woe's scene, world's shame, grave's due by life usurped,[7]
  Brief abstract° and record of tedious days,   *epitome; summary*
  Rest thy unrest on England's lawful earth,
30 Unlawfully made drunk with innocents' blood.

[*They sit*]

QUEEN ELIZABETH   Ah that thou[8] wouldst as soon afford a grave
  As thou canst yield a melancholy seat.
  Then would I hide my bones, not rest them here.
  Ah, who hath any cause to mourn but we?

35 QUEEN MARGARET [*coming forward*]   If ancient sorrow be most reverend,
  Give mine the benefit of seniory,[9]
  And let my griefs frown on the upper hand.[1]
  If sorrow can admit society,
  Tell o'er° your woes again by viewing mine.   *Count; narrate*
40 I had an Edward, till a Richard killed him;
  I had a husband, till a Richard killed him.

4.4 Location: Before the palace.
1. *fixed in doom perpetual*: assigned by an irrevocable sentence to your final place of punishment or reward.
2. *right for . . . night*: evenhanded justice has destroyed the bright hopes of your young lives.
3. Q places this after line 34 (making it the last speech before Margaret's intervention) and omits lines 20–21.
4. A debt for which payment is death. *Edward for Edward*: Prince Edward (Elizabeth's son) for Prince Edward (Margaret's son, whose murder is dramatized in *Richard Duke of York*).

5. Henry VI (Margaret's husband).
6. *mortal living ghost*: a dead person doomed to exist among the living.
7. *graves . . . usurped*: person who ought to be dead, unlawfully alive.
8. Here, Elizabeth is addressing the earth directly.
9. Seniority; Q1–5 have "signorie," F "signeurie," which suggests that Margaret may mean "sovereignty" or "lordship" ("seigniory").
1. *frown . . . hand*: have precedence in mourning.

[*To* ELIZABETH] Thou hadst an Edward, till a Richard killed him;
Thou hadst a Richard,[2] till a Richard killed him.
DUCHESS OF YORK [*rising*] I had a Richard too, and thou didst kill him;
45   I had a Rutland too,[3] thou holpst to kill him.
QUEEN MARGARET   Thou hadst a Clarence too, and Richard killed him.
From forth the kennel of thy womb hath crept
A hell-hound that doth hunt us all to death:
That dog that had his teeth before his eyes,[4]
50   To worry° lambs and lap their gentle blood;   *tear apart*
That foul defacer of God's handiwork,
That reigns in gallèd° eyes of weeping souls;   *sore (from crying)*
That excellent grand tyrant of the earth
Thy womb let loose to chase us to our graves.
55   O upright, just, and true-disposing God,
How do I thank thee that this charnel[5] cur
Preys on the issue° of his mother's body,   *offspring*
And makes her pewfellow° with others' moan.   *companion at church*
DUCHESS OF YORK   O Harry's wife, triumph not in my woes.
60   God witness with me, I have wept for thine.
QUEEN MARGARET   Bear with me. I am hungry for revenge,
And now I cloy me° with beholding it.   *gorge myself*
Thy Edward, he is dead, that killed my Edward;
Thy other Edward dead, to quite° my Edward;   *requite*
65   Young York, he is but boot,[6] because both they
Matched not the high perfection of my loss;
Thy Clarence, he is dead, that stabbed my Edward,
And the beholders of this frantic° play—   *insane*
Th'adulterate° Hastings, Rivers, Vaughan, Gray—   *adulterous*
70   Untimely smothered° in their dusky graves.   *buried*
Richard yet lives, hell's black intelligencer,°   *spy*
Only reserved their factor[7] to buy souls
And send them thither; but at hand, at hand
Ensues his piteous and unpitied end.
75   Earth gapes, hell burns, fiends roar, saints pray,
To have him suddenly conveyed from hence.
Cancel his bond of life, dear God, I plead,
That I may live and say, 'The dog is dead'.
QUEEN ELIZABETH   O thou didst prophesy the time would come
80   That I should wish for thee to help me curse
That bottled spider, that foul bunch-backed toad.
QUEEN MARGARET   I called thee then 'vain flourish of my fortune';
I called thee then, poor shadow,° 'painted queen'[8]—   *semblance*
The presentation° of but what I was,   *copy*
85   The flattering index° of a direful pageant,°   *prologue / play*
One heaved a-high to be hurled down below,
A mother only mocked with two fair babes,
A dream of what thou wast, a garish flag

---

2. Edward and Richard were Queen Elizabeth's two sons (smothered in the Tower).
3. Her husband (Richard, Duke of York) and youngest son; both deaths are dramatized in Act 1 of *Richard Duke of York*.
4. His enemies rumored that the savage Richard was born with teeth.

5. Of the charnel house or tomb. Q, F print "carnal."
6. He is thrown in simply to make the bargain even.
7. *Only . . . factor*: Retained (or preserved from death) only in order to serve as hell's agent. *their*: the demonic inhabitants of hell.
8. See 1.3.239.

To be the aim of every dangerous shot,[9]

90 A sign° of dignity, a breath, a bubble,   *mere symbol*

A queen in jest, only to fill the scene.

Where is thy husband now? Where be thy brothers?

Where are thy two sons? Wherein dost thou joy?

Who sues, and kneels, and says 'God save the Queen'?

95 Where be the bending° peers that flattered thee?   *bowing; yielding*

Where be the thronging troops that followed thee?

Decline[1] all this, and see what now thou art:

For happy wife, a most distressèd widow;

For joyful mother, one that wails the name;

100 For queen, a very caitiff,° crowned with care;   *wretch*

For one being sued to, one that humbly sues;

For she that scorned at me, now scorned of° me;   *by*

For she being feared of all, now fearing one;

For she commanding all, obeyed of none.

105 Thus hath the course of justice whirled about,

And left thee but a very prey to time,

Having no more but thought of what thou wert

To torture thee the more, being what thou art.

Thou didst usurp my place, and dost thou not

110 Usurp the just proportion of my sorrow?

Now thy proud neck bears half my burdened° yoke—   *burdensome*

From which, even here, I slip my weary head,

And leave the burden of it all on thee.

Farewell, York's wife, and queen of sad mischance.

115 These English woes shall make me smile in France.

QUEEN ELIZABETH [*rising*] O thou, well skilled in curses, stay a while,

And teach me how to curse mine enemies.

QUEEN MARGARET Forbear to sleep the nights, and fast the days;

Compare dead happiness with living woe;

120 Think that thy babes were sweeter than they were,

And he that slew them fouler than he is.

Bett'ring° thy loss makes the bad causer worse.   *Magnifying*

Revolving° this will teach thee how to curse.   *Musing on*

QUEEN ELIZABETH My words are dull. O quicken° them with   *enliven; sharpen*
     thine!

QUEEN MARGARET Thy woes will make them sharp and pierce

125   like mine.   *Exit*

DUCHESS OF YORK Why should calamity be full of words?

QUEEN ELIZABETH Windy attorneys to their client woes,[2]

Airy recorders of intestate joys,[3]

Poor breathing° orators of miseries.   *speaking*

130 Let them have scope. Though what they will impart

Help nothing else, yet do they ease the heart.

DUCHESS OF YORK If so, then be not tongue-tied; go with me,

And in the breath of bitter words let's smother

My damnèd son, that thy two sweet sons smothered.

     [*A march within*]

135 The trumpet sounds. Be copious in exclaims.°   *exclamation*

---

9. *garish . . . shot:* bearer of a brightly colored standard who draws the enemy fire.
1. Recite in order with the proper endings (as a noun in Latin grammar).

2. Words are long-winded pleaders for the sufferings that have hired them.
3. Words record joys that have died without bequeathing anything.

Enter KING RICHARD *and his train marching with drummers and trumpeters*

KING RICHARD   Who intercepts me in my expedition?°   haste; march

DUCHESS OF YORK   O, she that might have intercepted thee,
By strangling thee in her accursèd womb,
From all the slaughters, wretch, that thou hast done.

140 QUEEN ELIZABETH   Hid'st thou that forehead with a golden crown,
Where should be branded—if that right were right—
The slaughter of the prince that owed° that crown,   *rightfully owned*
And the dire death of my poor sons and brothers?
Tell me, thou villain-slave, where are my children?

145 DUCHESS OF YORK   Thou toad, thou toad, where is thy brother Clarence?
And little Ned Plantagenet his son?

QUEEN ELIZABETH   Where is the gentle Rivers, Vaughan, Gray?

DUCHESS OF YORK   Where is kind Hastings?

KING RICHARD *[to his train]*   A flourish, trumpets! Strike
   alarum,° drums!   *Call to arms*

150 Let not the heavens hear these tell-tale women
Rail on the Lord's anointed. Strike, I say!
   Flourish. Alarums
[To the women] Either be patient and entreat me fair,°   *treat me courteously*
Or with the clamorous report° of war   *noise*
Thus will I drown your exclamations.

155 DUCHESS OF YORK   Art thou my son?

KING RICHARD   Ay, I thank God, my father, and yourself.

DUCHESS OF YORK   Then patiently hear my impatience.

KING RICHARD   Madam, I have a touch of your condition,°   *temperament*
That cannot brook the accent° of reproof.   *abide the language*

DUCHESS OF YORK   O let me speak!

160 KING RICHARD   Do, then; but I'll not hear.

DUCHESS OF YORK   I will be mild and gentle in my words.

KING RICHARD   And brief, good mother, for I am in haste.

DUCHESS OF YORK   Art thou so hasty? I have stayed° for thee,   *waited*
God knows, in torment and in agony—

165 KING RICHARD   And came I not at last to comfort you?

DUCHESS OF YORK   No, by the Holy Rood,° thou know'st it well.   *Cross*
Thou cam'st on earth to make the earth my hell.
A grievous burden was thy birth to me;
Tetchy° and wayward was thy infancy;   *Irritable*

170 Thy schooldays frightful,° desp'rate, wild, and furious;   *frightening*
Thy prime° of manhood daring, bold, and venturous;   *beginning*
Thy age confirmed,° proud, subtle, sly, and bloody;   *settled maturity*
More mild, but yet more harmful; kind in hatred.⁴
What comfortable hour canst thou name

175 That ever graced me⁵ in thy company?

KING RICHARD   Faith, none but Humphrey Hewer,⁶ that called your grace
To breakfast once, forth° of my company.   *out*
If I be so disgracious° in your eye,   *unpleasing*
Let me march on, and not offend you, madam.—
Strike up the drum.

180 DUCHESS OF YORK   I pray thee, hear me speak.

---

4. Concealing hatred under cover of kindness.
5. Gave me pleasure; but Richard interprets as "called me by the title 'your grace.'"
6. A proper name, based on "ewer" (a servant who waits at table), but also suggesting "huer" (someone who makes a hue or cry) and playing on "hour" (line 174). Proverbially, "to dine with Duke Humphrey" was not to dine at all.

KING RICHARD   You speak too bitterly.

DUCHESS OF YORK   Hear me a word,
For I shall never speak to thee again.

KING RICHARD   So.

DUCHESS OF YORK   Either thou wilt die by God's just ordinance
185   Ere from this war thou turn° a conqueror,   *return*
Or I with grief and extreme age shall perish,
And never more behold thy face again.
Therefore take with thee my most heavy curse,
Which in the day of battle tire thee more
190   Than all the complete armour that thou wear'st.
My prayers on the adverse party° fight,   *opposite side*
And there the little souls of Edward's children
Whisper° the spirits of thine enemies,   *Whisper to*
And promise them success and victory.
195   Bloody thou art, bloody will be thy end;
Shame serves° thy life, and doth thy death attend.   *Exit*   *accompanies*

QUEEN ELIZABETH   Though far more cause, yet much less spirit to curse
Abides in me; I say 'Amen' to all.

KING RICHARD   Stay, madam. I must talk a word with you.

200   QUEEN ELIZABETH   I have no more sons of the royal blood
For thee to slaughter. For my daughters, Richard,
They shall be praying nuns, not weeping queens,
And therefore level not to hit their lives.[7]

KING RICHARD   You have a daughter called Elizabeth,
205   Virtuous and fair, royal and gracious.

QUEEN ELIZABETH   And must she die for this? O let her live,
And I'll corrupt her manners,° stain her beauty,   *morals*
Slander myself as false to Edward's bed,
Throw over her the veil of infamy.
210   So° she may live unscarred of bleeding slaughter,   *Provided that*
I will confess she was not Edward's daughter.

KING RICHARD   Wrong not her birth. She is a royal princess.

QUEEN ELIZABETH   To save her life I'll say she is not so.

KING RICHARD   Her life is safest only in her birth.[8]

215   QUEEN ELIZABETH   And only in that safety died her brothers.

KING RICHARD   Lo, at their births good stars were opposite.°   *adverse*

QUEEN ELIZABETH   No, to their lives ill friends were contrary.°   *opposed*

KING RICHARD   All unavoided° is the doom° of destiny—   *unavoidable / sentence*

QUEEN ELIZABETH   True, when avoided grace[9] makes destiny.
220   My babes were destined to a fairer death,
If grace had blessed thee with a fairer life.[1]

221.1   KING RICHARD   *You speak as if that I had slain my cousins.*

         QUEEN ELIZABETH   *Cousins indeed, and by their uncle cozened°*   *cheated*
         Of comfort, kingdom, kindred, freedom, life.
         Whose hand soever lanced their tender hearts,
221.5   *Thy head all indirectly gave direction.[2]*
         No doubt the murd'rous knife was dull and blunt
         Till it was whetted on thy stone-hard heart
         To revel in the entrails of my lambs.
         But that still° use of grief makes wild grief tame,   *Except that continual*

---

7. And therefore do not take aim to kill them.
8. Her life is safe only because of her high birth.
9. When a man who has rejected God's grace (that is, Richard).

1. The indented passage that follows, 221.1–221.14, appears only in F.
2. *Whose . . . direction:* No matter who killed them, it was you, though indirectly, who caused it.

221.10
                My tongue should to thy ears not name my boys
                Till that my nails were anchored in thine eyes—
                And I in such a desp'rate bay³ of death,   boat / deprived
                Like a poor barque° of sails and tackling reft,°
                Rush all to pieces on thy rocky bosom.

KING RICHARD   Madam, so thrive I in my enterprise
                And dangerous success of bloody wars,
                As I intend more good to you and yours
225   Than ever you or yours by me were harmed.⁴

QUEEN ELIZABETH   What good is covered with the face of heaven,⁵
                To be discovered, that can do me good?

KING RICHARD   Th'advancement of your children, gentle lady.

QUEEN ELIZABETH   Up to some scaffold, there to lose their heads.

230 KING RICHARD   Unto the dignity and height of fortune,
                The high imperial type° of this earth's glory.   symbol

QUEEN ELIZABETH   Flatter my sorrow with report of it.
                Tell me what state, what dignity, what honour,
                Canst thou demise° to any child of mine?   transmit

235 KING RICHARD   Even all I have—ay, and myself and all,
                Will I withal endow a child of thine,
                So° in the Lethe⁶ of thy angry soul   If
                Thou drown the sad remembrance of those wrongs,
                Which thou supposest I have done to thee.

240 QUEEN ELIZABETH   Be brief, lest that the process° of thy kindness   story
                Last longer telling° than thy kindness' date.°   in the telling / duration

KING RICHARD   Then know that, from my soul,⁷ I love thy daughter.

QUEEN ELIZABETH   My daughter's mother thinks that with her soul.

KING RICHARD   What do you think?

245 QUEEN ELIZABETH   That thou dost love my daughter *from* thy soul;
                So *from* thy soul's love didst thou love her brothers,
                And *from* my heart's love I do thank thee for it.

KING RICHARD   Be not so hasty to confound° my meaning.   deliberately misconstrue
                I mean, that *with* my soul I love thy daughter,
250   And do intend to make her queen of England.

QUEEN ELIZABETH   Well then, who dost thou mean shall be her king?

KING RICHARD   Even he that makes her queen. Who else should be?

QUEEN ELIZABETH   What, thou?

KING RICHARD   Even so. How think you of it?

QUEEN ELIZABETH   How canst thou woo her?

KING RICHARD   That would I learn of you,
255   As one being best acquainted with her humour.°   temperament

QUEEN ELIZABETH   And wilt thou learn of me?

KING RICHARD   Madam, with all my heart.

QUEEN ELIZABETH   Send to her, by the man that slew her brothers,
                A pair of bleeding hearts; thereon engrave
                'Edward' and 'York'; then haply° will she weep.   perhaps
260   Therefore present to her—as sometimes° Margaret   once
                Did to thy father, steeped in Rutland's blood⁸—
                A handkerchief which, say to her, did drain

---

3. Inlet; the situation of a cornered animal when it turns to face its hunters.
4. *Madam . . . harmed:* (I pray) that the success of my upcoming battles be as certain as is my intention to do to you more good in the future than I have done you harm in the past. *success:* consequence.
5. What good is there on earth.
6. A river in the underworld whose waters induced forgetfulness.
7. With all my soul (but Queen Elizabeth takes it as "separated from," "at variance with").
8. Dramatized in *Richard Duke of York* 1.4.

The purple sap° from her sweet brother's body,   blood
And bid her wipe her weeping eyes withal.°   with it
265   If this inducement move her not to love,
Send her a letter of thy noble deeds.
Tell her thou mad'st away her uncle Clarence,
Her uncle Rivers—ay, and for her sake
Mad'st quick conveyance with° her good aunt Anne.   Got rid of
270   KING RICHARD   You mock me, madam. This is not the way
To win your daughter.
QUEEN ELIZABETH   There is no other way,
Unless thou couldst put on some other shape,
And not be Richard, that hath done all this.⁹
273.1   KING RICHARD   *Say that I did all this for love of her.*
QUEEN ELIZABETH   *Nay, then indeed she cannot choose but hate thee,*
Having bought love with such a bloody spoil.°   slaughter
KING RICHARD   *Look what° is done cannot be now amended.*   Whatever
273.5   *Men shall deal° unadvisedly sometimes,*   act
Which after-hours gives leisure to repent.
If I did take the kingdom from your sons,
To make amends I'll give it to your daughter.
If I have killed the issue of your womb,
273.10   *To quicken your increase¹ I will beget*
Mine issue of your blood upon your daughter.
A grandam's name is little less in love
Than is the doting title of a mother.
They are as children but one step below,
273.15   *Even of your mettall,° of your very blood:*   spirit
Of all one pain, save for a night of groans
Endured of her for whom you bid like sorrow.²
Your children were vexation to your youth,
But mine shall be a comfort to your age.
273.20   *The loss you have is but a son being king,*
And by that loss your daughter is made queen.
I cannot make you what amends I would,
Therefore accept such kindness as I can.°   can give
Dorset your son, that with a fearful soul
273.25   *Leads discontented steps in foreign soil,*
This fair alliance quickly shall call home
To high promotions and great dignity.
The king that calls your beauteous daughter wife,
Familiarly shall call thy Dorset brother.
273.30   *Again shall you be mother to a king,*
And all the ruins of distressful times
Repaired with double riches of content.
What? We have many goodly days to see.
The liquid drops of tears that you have shed
273.35   *Shall come again, transformed to orient° pearl,*   shining
Advantaging° their loan with interest   Augmenting
Of ten times double gain of happiness.
Go then, my mother, to thy daughter go.
Make bold her bashful years with your experience.

9. The indented passage that follows, 273.1–273.55,   2. *Of all . . . sorrow:* Originating from a single bout of
appears only in F.   labor (Elizabeth's), with the addition of just one more
1. To give (new) life to your offspring.   night of pain by the daughter you bore.

273.40   *Prepare her ears to hear a wooer's tale.*
        Put in her tender heart th'aspiring flame
        Of golden sovereignty. Acquaint the Princess
        With the sweet silent hours of marriage joys.
        And when this arm of mine hath chastisèd
273.45   *The petty rebel, dull-brained Buckingham,*
        Bound with triumphant garlands will I come
        And lead thy daughter to a conqueror's bed—
        To whom I will retail°　my conquest won,   *relate*
        And she shall be sole victoress: Caesar's Caesar.
273.50   QUEEN ELIZABETH   *What were I best to say? Her father's brother*
        Would°　be her lord?°　Or shall I say her uncle?   *Wishes to / husband*
        Or he that slew her brothers and her uncles?
        Under what title shall I woo for thee,
        That God, the law, my honour, and her love
273.55   *Can make seem pleasing to her tender years?*
  KING RICHARD   Infer°　fair England's peace by this alliance.   *Give as a reason*
275   QUEEN ELIZABETH   Which she shall purchase with still-lasting°　war.   *perpetual*
  KING RICHARD   Tell her the King, that may command, entreats.
  QUEEN ELIZABETH   That at her hands which the King's King°　forbids.   *(God)*
  KING RICHARD   Say she shall be a high and mighty queen.
  QUEEN ELIZABETH   To vail°　the title,°　as her mother doth.   *yield / (of Queen)*
280   KING RICHARD   Say I will love her everlastingly.
  QUEEN ELIZABETH   But how long shall that title 'ever' last?
  KING RICHARD   Sweetly in force unto her fair life's end.
  QUEEN ELIZABETH   But how long fairly°　shall her sweet life last?   *without foul play*
  KING RICHARD   As long as heaven and nature lengthens it.
285   QUEEN ELIZABETH   As long as hell and Richard likes of it.
  KING RICHARD   Say I, her sovereign, am her subject love.
  QUEEN ELIZABETH   But she, your subject, loathes such sovereignty.
  KING RICHARD   Be eloquent in my behalf to her.
  QUEEN ELIZABETH   An honest tale speeds°　best being plainly told.   *succeeds*
290   KING RICHARD   Then plainly to her tell my loving tale.
  QUEEN ELIZABETH   Plain and not honest is too harsh a style.[3]
  KING RICHARD   Your reasons are too shallow and too quick.[4]
  QUEEN ELIZABETH   O no, my reasons are too deep and dead—
        Too deep and dead, poor infants, in their graves.
295   KING RICHARD   Harp not on that string, madam. That is past.
  QUEEN ELIZABETH   Harp on it still shall I, till heart-strings break.
  KING RICHARD   Now by my George, my garter,[5] and my crown—
  QUEEN ELIZABETH   Profaned, dishonoured, and the third usurped.
  KING RICHARD   I swear—
  QUEEN ELIZABETH   By nothing, for this is no oath.
300   Thy George, profaned, hath lost his°　holy honour;   *its*
        Thy garter, blemished, pawned his lordly virtue;
        Thy crown, usurped, disgraced his kingly glory.
        If something thou wouldst swear to be believed,
        Swear then by something that thou hast not wronged.
  KING RICHARD   Then by myself—
305   QUEEN ELIZABETH   Thy self is self-misused.
  KING RICHARD   Now by the world—

---

3. The plain style (as in the proverb "Truth is plain"), unless it is truth telling, will be too harsh; lies need elaborate decoration.

4. Rash, ill considered; but Elizabeth's response plays on "quick" as "alive."

5. A garter and a jeweled pendant with the figure of St. George were parts of the insignia of the Order of the Garter, the highest order of knighthood.

QUEEN ELIZABETH	'Tis full of thy foul wrongs.	
KING RICHARD	My father's death—	
QUEEN ELIZABETH	Thy life hath that dishonoured.	
KING RICHARD	Why then, by God—	
QUEEN ELIZABETH	God's wrong is most of all.	

If thou didst fear to break an oath with him,
310 The unity the King my husband made[6]
Thou hadst not broken, nor my brothers died.
If thou hadst feared to break an oath by him,
Th'imperial metal circling now thy head
Had graced the tender temples of my child,
315 And both the princes had been breathing here,
Which now—two tender bedfellows for dust—
Thy broken faith hath made the prey for worms.
What canst thou swear by now?

KING RICHARD The time to come.

QUEEN ELIZABETH That thou hast wrongèd in the time o'erpast,
320 For I myself have many tears to wash
Hereafter time,° for time past wronged by thee.   *The future*
The children live, whose fathers thou hast slaughtered—
Ungoverned youth,[7] to wail it in their age.°   *when they grow older*
The parents live, whose children thou hast butchered—
325 Old barren plants, to wail it with° their age.   *along with*
Swear not by time to come, for that thou hast
Misused ere used, by times ill-used o'erpast.[8]

KING RICHARD As I intend[9] to prosper and repent,
So thrive I in my dangerous affairs
330 Of hostile arms—myself myself confound,°   *may I ruin myself*
Heaven and fortune bar me happy hours,
Day yield me not thy light nor night thy rest;
Be opposite, all planets of good luck,
To my proceeding—if, with dear heart's love,
335 Immaculate devotion, holy thoughts,
I tender° not thy beauteous, princely daughter.   *love*
In her consists my happiness and thine.
Without her follows—to myself and thee,
Herself, the land, and many a Christian soul—
340 Death, desolation, ruin, and decay.
It cannot be avoided but by this;
It will not be avoided but by this.
Therefore, good-mother°—I must call you so—   *mother-in-law*
Be the attorney of my love to her.
345 Plead what I will be, not what I have been;
Not my deserts, but what I will deserve.
Urge the necessity and state of times,°   *state of affairs*
And be not peevish-fond° in great designs.   *foolishly obstinate*

QUEEN ELIZABETH Shall I be tempted of the devil thus?
350 KING RICHARD Ay, if the devil tempt you to do good.

QUEEN ELIZABETH Shall I forget myself to be myself?[1]

KING RICHARD Ay, if yourself 's remembrance wrong yourself.

---

6. The "reconciliation" staged in 2.1 between Queen
Elizabeth and her enemies.
7. Youth without a father's guidance.
8. *thou . . . o'erpast:* you have, by the continuing effects
of your past crimes, misused the future even before it

comes to pass.
9. *As I intend:* the formulation has the force of "I swear
that as I intend."
1. Am I to overlook all wrongs done me in order to
become Queen Mother (as I already have been)?

QUEEN ELIZABETH Yet thou didst kill my children.

KING RICHARD But in your daughter's womb I bury them,

355   Where, in that nest of spicery,² they will breed

Selves of themselves, to your recomfiture.°   *consolation*

QUEEN ELIZABETH Shall I go win my daughter to thy will?

KING RICHARD And be a happy mother by the deed.

QUEEN ELIZABETH I go. Write to me very shortly,

360   And you shall understand from me her mind.

KING RICHARD Bear her my true love's kiss,

       [*He kisses her*]   and so farewell—

                          Exit [ELIZABETH]

Relenting fool, and shallow, changing woman.

       Enter [*Sir Richard*] RATCLIFFE

How now, what news?

RATCLIFFE Most mighty sovereign, on the western coast

365   Rideth a puissant° navy. To our shores   *mighty*

Throng many doubtful, hollow-hearted friends,

Unarmed and unresolved, to beat them back.

'Tis thought that Richmond is their° admiral,   *(the navy's)*

And there they hull,° expecting but the aid   *drift; wait*

370   Of Buckingham to welcome them ashore.

KING RICHARD Some light-foot° friend post° to the Duke of   *swift-footed / hasten*

       Norfolk.

Ratcliffe thyself, or Catesby—where is he?³

CATESBY Here, my good lord.

KING RICHARD   Catesby, fly to the Duke.

CATESBY I will, my lord, with all convenient° haste.   *due*

375 KING RICHARD Ratcliffe, come hither. Post to Salisbury;

When thou com'st thither—[*to* CATESBY] dull, unmindful villain,

Why stay'st thou here, and goest not to the Duke?

CATESBY First, mighty liege, tell me your highness' pleasure:

What from your grace I shall deliver to him?

380 KING RICHARD O true, good Catesby. Bid him levy straight

The greatest strength and power that he can make,°   *raise*

And meet me suddenly° at Salisbury.   *without delay*

CATESBY I go.   *Exit*

RATCLIFFE What, may it please you, shall I do at Salisbury?

385 KING RICHARD Why, what wouldst thou do there before I go?

RATCLIFFE Your highness told me I should post before.

KING RICHARD My mind is changed.

       Enter Lord STANLEY

                          Stanley, what news with you?

STANLEY None, good my liege, to please you with the hearing,

Nor none so bad but well may be reported.

390 KING RICHARD Hoyday,° a riddle! Neither good nor bad.   *(an exclamation)*

Why need'st thou run so many mile about

When thou mayst tell thy tale the nearest° way?   *most direct*

Once more, what news?

STANLEY   Richmond is on the seas.

KING RICHARD There let him sink, and be the seas on him.

395   White-livered° renegade, what doth he there?   *Cowardly*

---

2. Fragrant spices—in contrast to the stench of other burial places; the spices on the phoenix's pyre. *nest:* place where eggs are hatched, but also specifically the nest or pyre on which the legendary phoenix burned itself and then rose from its own ashes.

3. Parts of lines 373–74 appear only in F.

STANLEY   I know not, mighty sovereign, but by guess.

KING RICHARD   Well, as you guess?

STANLEY   Stirred up by Dorset, Buckingham, and Ely,
He makes for England, here to claim the crown.

400 KING RICHARD   Is the chair° empty? Is the sword unswayed?   *throne*
Is the King dead? The empire° unpossessed?   *state*
What heir of York is there alive but we?
And who is England's king but great York's heir?
Then tell me, what makes he° upon the seas?   *what is he doing*

405 STANLEY   Unless for that, my liege, I cannot guess.

KING RICHARD   Unless for that° he comes to be your liege,   *because*
You cannot guess wherefore the Welshman[4] comes.
Thou wilt revolt and fly to him, I fear.

STANLEY   No, my good lord, therefore mistrust me not.

410 KING RICHARD   Where is thy power then? To beat him back,
Where be thy tenants and thy followers?
Are they not now upon the western shore,
Safe-conducting the rebels from their ships?

STANLEY   No, my good lord, my friends are in the north.

415 KING RICHARD   Cold friends to me. What do they in the north,
When they should serve their sovereign in the west?

STANLEY   They have not been commanded, mighty King.
Pleaseth° your majesty to give me leave,   *If it please*
I'll muster up my friends and meet your grace

420 Where and what time your majesty shall please.

KING RICHARD   Ay, ay, thou wouldst be gone to join with Richmond.
But I'll not trust thee.

STANLEY   Most mighty sovereign,
You have no cause to hold my friendship doubtful.
I never was, nor never will be, false.

425 KING RICHARD   Go then and muster men—but leave behind
Your son George Stanley. Look your heart be firm,
Or else his head's assurance is but frail.

STANLEY   So deal with him as I prove true to you.   *Exit*
Enter a MESSENGER

MESSENGER   My gracious sovereign, now in Devonshire,

430 As I by friends am well advertisèd,°   *well informed*
Sir Edward Courtenay and the haughty prelate,
Bishop of Exeter, his elder brother,
With many more confederates are in arms.
Enter another MESSENGER

SECOND MESSENGER   In Kent, my liege, the Guildfords are in arms,

435 And every hour more competitors°   *associates*
Flock to the rebels, and their power grows strong.
Enter another MESSENGER

THIRD MESSENGER   My lord, the army of great Buckingham—

KING RICHARD   Out on ye, owls![5] Nothing but songs of death?
He striketh him
There, take thou that, till thou bring better news.

440 THIRD MESSENGER   The news I have to tell your majesty
Is that, by sudden flood and fall of water,°   *rain*
Buckingham's army is dispersed and scattered,
And he himself wandered away alone,

___

4. Richmond's grandfather, Owen Tudor, was Welsh.   5. The cry of the owl was thought to portend evil.

No man knows whither.

KING RICHARD   I cry thee mercy.°—   *I beg your pardon*
445 Ratcliffe, reward him for the blow I gave him.—
Hath any well-advisèd° friend proclaimed   *foresighted*
Reward to him that brings the traitor in?

THIRD MESSENGER   Such proclamation hath been made, my lord.

    Enter another MESSENGER

FOURTH MESSENGER   Sir Thomas Lovell and Lord Marquis Dorset—
450 'Tis said, my liege—in Yorkshire are in arms.
But this good comfort bring I to your highness:
The Breton navy is dispersed by tempest.
Richmond in Dorsetshire sent out a boat
Unto the shore, to ask those on the banks
455 If they were his assistants,° yea or no?   *allies*
Who answered him they came from Buckingham
Upon his party.° He, mistrusting them,   *faction*
Hoist sail and made his course again for Bretagne.°   *Brittany*

KING RICHARD   March on, march on, since we are up in arms,
460 If not to fight with foreign enemies,
Yet to beat down these rebels here at home.

    Enter CATESBY

CATESBY   My liege, the Duke of Buckingham is taken.
That is the best news. That the Earl of Richmond
Is with a mighty power landed at Milford[6]
465 Is colder tidings, yet they must be told.

KING RICHARD   Away, towards Salisbury! While we reason° here,   *talk*
A royal battle might be won and lost.
Someone take order Buckingham be brought
To Salisbury. The rest march on with me.   *Flourish. Exeunt*

4.5

    Enter [Lord STANLEY *Earl of] Derby and* SIR CHRISTO-
    PHER *[a priest]*

STANLEY   Sir Christopher, tell Richmond this from me:
That in the sty of this most deadly boar
My son George Stanley is franked up in hold.[1]
If I revolt, off goes young George's head.
5 The fear of that holds off my present aid.
But tell me, where is princely Richmond now?

SIR CHRISTOPHER   At Pembroke, or at Ha'rfordwest[2] in Wales.

STANLEY   What men of name° resort to him?   *rank*

SIR CHRISTOPHER   Sir Walter Herbert, a renownèd soldier,
10 Sir Gilbert Talbot, Sir William Stanley,[3]
Oxford, redoubted° Pembroke,[4] Sir James Blunt,   *dreaded*
And Rhys-ap-Thomas with a valiant crew,
And many other of great name and worth—
And towards London do they bend their power,°   *lead their troops*

---

6. Milford Haven, a large, deep natural harbor on the Welsh coast, far enough from centers of population to be ideal for an invading army. The events of Richmond's successful invasion at Milford in 1485 are telescoped, in the mouths of the four messengers, with those of his unsuccessful rebellion against Richard two years earlier.

4.5 Location: A private place, perhaps Derby's house.
1. Is shut up (in a sty) in custody.
2. Haverford West, town at the northern end of Milford Haven. Pembroke was the county town of Pembrokeshire, situated on Milford Haven.
3. Lord Stanley, the Earl of Derby's brother.
4. Jasper Tudor, Richmond's uncle.

15　　If by the way they be not fought withal.

STANLEY　Well, hie° thee to thy lord. Commend me to him. 　　　*hasten*
　　　Tell him the Queen hath heartily consented
　　　He should espouse Elizabeth her daughter.
　　　My letter will resolve him of my mind.[5]

20　　Farewell.　　　　　　　　　　　　　　*Exeunt [severally]*

5.1

Enter [the Duke of] BUCKINGHAM *with halberdiers, led*
[by a SHERIFF*] to execution*

BUCKINGHAM　Will not King Richard let me speak with him?

SHERIFF　No, my good lord, therefore be patient.

BUCKINGHAM　Hastings, and Edward's children, Gray and Rivers,
　　　Holy King Henry and thy fair son Edward,
5　　Vaughan, and all that have miscarrièd° 　　　　　　*died*
　　　By underhand, corrupted, foul injustice:
　　　If that your moody, discontented souls[1]
　　　Do through the clouds behold this present hour,
　　　Even for revenge mock my destruction.
10　　This is All-Souls' day,[2] fellow, is it not?

SHERIFF　It is.

BUCKINGHAM　Why then All-Souls' day is my body's doomsday.
　　　This is the day which, in King Edward's time,
　　　I wished might fall on me,[3] when I was found
15　　False to his children and his wife's allies.° 　　　　　*kinsmen*
　　　This is the day wherein I wished to fall
　　　By the false faith of him whom most I trusted.
　　　This, this All-Souls' day to my fearful soul
　　　Is the determined respite of my wrongs.[4]
20　　That high all-seer which I dallied with
　　　Hath turned my feignèd prayer on my head,
　　　And given in earnest what I begged in jest.
　　　Thus doth he force the swords of wicked men
　　　To turn their own points in their masters' bosoms.
25　　Thus Margaret's curse falls heavy on my neck.
　　　'When he', quoth she, 'shall split thy heart with sorrow,
　　　Remember Margaret was a prophetess.'[5]
　　　Come lead me, officers, to the block of shame.
　　　Wrong hath but wrong, and blame the due of blame.　　　*Exeunt*

5.2

*Enter [*HENRY EARL OF*]* RICHMOND *[with a letter, the*
Earl of] OXFORD, *[Sir James]* BLUNT, *[Sir Walter]* HER-
BERT, *and others, with drum and colours*

HENRY EARL OF RICHMOND　Fellows in arms, and my most loving friends,
　　　Bruised underneath the yoke of tyranny,
　　　Thus far into the bowels° of the land 　　　　　　　*center*

---

5. Will make my intentions clear to him.
5.1 Location: Salisbury.
1. Because they are unable to rest in peace until their
violent deaths have been avenged. *moody*: angry.
2. November 2, the day on which the Roman Catholic
Church intercedes for all Christian souls and on which
spirits were supposed to walk (as in the following
scenes at Shrewsbury).

3. See Buckingham's prophetic speech in 2.1.32–40.
4. Is the preordained ending of my wrongdoing (but
alluding to the more usual significance of All Souls'
Day, "preordained final rest from suffering"). *respite*:
day to which something is postponed.
5. See 1.3.298–99.
5.2 Location: Near Tamworth in Staffordshire.

Have we marched on without impediment,
5 And here receive we from our father¹ Stanley
Lines of fair comfort and encouragement.
The wretched, bloody, and usurping boar,
That spoils your summer fields and fruitful vines,
Swills your warm blood like wash,° and makes his trough   *pig fodder*
10 In your inbowelled° bosoms, this foul swine   *disemboweled*
Lies now even in the centry° of this isle,   *center; sentry post*
Near to the town of Leicester, as we learn.
From Tamworth thither is but one day's march.
In God's name, cheerly° on, courageous friends,   *cheerfully*
15 To reap the harvest of perpetual peace
By this one bloody trial of sharp war.
OXFORD   Every man's conscience is a thousand swords
To fight against this guilty homicide.°   *murderer*
HERBERT   I doubt not but his friends will turn to us.
20 BLUNT   He hath no friends but what are friends for fear,
Which in his dearest° need will fly from him.   *most extreme*
HENRY EARL OF RICHMOND   All for our vantage.° Then, in God's   *advantage*
name, march.
True hope is swift, and flies with swallows' wings;
Kings it makes gods, and meaner° creatures kings.   *baser*
                         Exeunt [marching]

5.3

Enter KING RICHARD *in arms, with* [*the Duke of*] NOR-
FOLK, [*Sir Richard*] RATCLIFFE, *Sir William* [CATESBY,
and others]¹

KING RICHARD   Here pitch our tent, even here in Bosworth field.
   [*Soldiers begin to pitch a tent*]
Why, how now, Catesby? Why look you so sad?
CATESBY   My heart is ten times lighter than my looks.
KING RICHARD   My lord of Norfolk.
NORFOLK   Here, most gracious liege.
5 KING RICHARD   Norfolk, we must have knocks.° Ha, must we not?   *blows*
NORFOLK   We must both give and take, my loving lord.
KING RICHARD   Up with my tent! Here will I lie tonight.
But where tomorrow? Well, all's one for that.°   *it makes no difference*
Who hath descried° the number of the traitors?   *discerned*
10 NORFOLK   Six or seven thousand is their utmost power.
KING RICHARD   Why, our battalia° trebles that account.°   *army / number*
Besides, the King's name is a tower of strength,
Which they upon the adverse faction want.°   *lack*
Up with the tent! Come, noble gentlemen,
15 Let us survey the vantage of the ground.²
Call for some men of sound direction.°   *military judgment*
Let's lack no discipline, make no delay—
For, lords, tomorrow is a busy day.   *Exeunt [at one door]*

---

1. Stepfather (Richmond was the son of Edmund Tudor
and Margaret Beaufort; Lord Stanley, Earl of Derby, was
his mother's third husband). *our:* royal plural.
5.3 Location: The rest of the play takes place on
Bosworth Field.

1. Instead of Catesby, the stage direction in F has the
Earl of Surrey, who speaks with Richard at line 3.
2. *vantage of the ground:* military advantages offered by
the spot chosen for battle.

5.4

Enter [at another door HENRY EARL OF] RICHMOND,
[Sir James BLUNT,] *Sir William Brandon, [the Earl of]*
OXFORD, [*Marquis*] DORSET [*and others*]¹

HENRY EARL OF RICHMOND   The weary sun hath made a golden set,
And by the bright track of his fiery car²
Gives token of a goodly day tomorrow.
Sir William Brandon, you shall bear my standard.
5   The Earl of Pembroke keeps° his regiment;   *stays with*
Good Captain Blunt, bear my good night to him,
And by the second hour in the morning
Desire the Earl to see me in my tent.
Yet one thing more, good Captain, do for me:
10   Where is Lord Stanley quartered, do you know?
BLUNT   Unless I have mista'en his colours much,
Which well I am assured I have not done,
His regiment lies half a mile, at least,
South from the mighty power of the King.
15   HENRY EARL OF RICHMOND   If without peril it be possible,
Sweet Blunt, make some good means to speak with him,
And give him from me this most needful note.
BLUNT   Upon my life, my lord, I'll undertake it.
And so God give you quiet rest tonight.
HENRY EARL OF RICHMOND   Good night, good Captain Blunt.
                                                                                   [*Exit* BLUNT]
20   Come, gentlemen.
Give me some ink and paper in my tent.
I'll draw the form and model° of our battle,   *plan*
Limit° each leader to his several charge,°   *Appoint / separate duty*
And part° in just proportion our small power.   *divide*
25   Let us consult upon tomorrow's business.
Into my tent: the dew is raw and cold.
                                        They withdraw into the tent

5.5

[*A table brought in.*] *Enter* KING RICHARD, [*Sir
Richard*] RATCLIFFE, [*the Duke of*] NORFOLK, [*Sir
William*] CATESBY [*and others*]

KING RICHARD   What is't o'clock?
CATESBY   It's supper-time, my lord. It's nine o'clock.
KING RICHARD   I will not sup tonight. Give me some ink and paper.
What, is my beaver easier° than it was?   *my helmet visor looser*
5   And all my armour laid into my tent?
CATESBY   It is, my liege, and all things are in readiness.
KING RICHARD   Good Norfolk, hie thee° to thy charge.   *hasten*
Use careful watch; choose trusty sentinels.
NORFOLK   I go, my lord.
10   KING RICHARD   Stir with the lark tomorrow, gentle Norfolk.
NORFOLK   I warrant° you, my lord.   *Exit*   *assure; guarantee*
KING RICHARD   Catesby.
CATESBY   My lord?

5.4
1. Although Q and F are silent on the question of how
many tents are onstage at the end of this scene, most
editors direct these attendants to pitch another for Richmond during the following dialogue. Oxford and Dorset
are specified in F but not in Q, which calls only for "the
lords."
2. Chariot (of the sun god Phoebus).
5.5

KING RICHARD   Send out a pursuivant-at-arms°   *one who attends a herald*
    To Stanley's regiment. Bid him bring his power°   *forces*
    Before sun-rising, lest his son George fall
15   Into the blind cave of eternal night.   [*Exit* CATESBY]
    Fill me a bowl of wine. Give me a watch.[1]
    Saddle white Surrey[2] for the field tomorrow.
    Look that my staves° be sound, and not too heavy.   *lance shafts*
    Ratcliffe.
20 RATCLIFFE   My lord?
    KING RICHARD   Saw'st thou the melancholy Lord Northumberland?
    RATCLIFFE   Thomas the Earl of Surrey and himself,
    Much about cockshut° time, from troop to troop   *twilight*
    Went through the army, cheering up the soldiers.
25 KING RICHARD   So, I am satisfied. Give me some wine.
    I have not that alacrity of spirit,
    Nor cheer of mind, that I was wont to have.
    [*The wine is brought*]
    Set it down. Is ink and paper ready?
    RATCLIFFE   It is, my lord.
    KING RICHARD   Leave me. Bid my guard watch.
30   About the mid of night come to my tent,
    Ratcliffe, and help to arm me. Leave me, I say.
    Exit RATCLIFFE [*with others.* RICHARD *writes, and later sleeps*]
    Enter [*Lord* STANLEY *Earl of*] *Derby to* HENRY EARL
    OF] RICHMOND [*and the lords*] *in his tent*
    STANLEY   Fortune and victory sit on thy helm!°   *helmet*
    HENRY EARL OF RICHMOND   All comfort that the dark night can afford
    Be to thy person, noble father-in-law.°   *stepfather*
35   Tell me, how fares our loving mother?
    STANLEY   I, by attorney,° bless thee from thy mother,   *by proxy*
    Who prays continually for Richmond's good.
    So much for that. The silent hours steal on,
    And flaky° darkness breaks within the east.   *streaked with light*
40   In brief—for so the season° bids us be—   *time of day*
    Prepare thy battle early in the morning,
    And put thy fortune to th'arbitrement°   *determination; verdict*
    Of bloody strokes and mortal-sharing[3] war.
    I, as I may—that which I would, I cannot—
45   With best advantage will deceive the time,[4]
    And aid thee in this doubtful shock° of arms.   *this uncertain clash*
    But on thy side I may not be too forward—
    Lest, being seen, thy brother,° tender° George,   *stepbrother / young*
    Be executed in his father's sight.
50   Farewell. The leisure° and the fearful time   *time available*
    Cuts off the ceremonious vows of love
    And ample interchange of sweet discourse,
    Which so long sundered friends should dwell upon.
    God give us leisure for these rights of love.
55   Once more, adieu. Be valiant, and speed well.

---

1. Probably a watch light (a slow-burning candle, to write by); possibly a special guard (see line 29).
2. The chroniclers report that Richard was mounted on a "great white course," but the name is Shakespeare's.
3. Apportioning to mortals their lot; shearing or cutting down mortals. Q has "mortal staring," giving the commonplace image of war as both evil-looking and able to cause damage with its glance (like a basilisk).
4. *as . . . time:* as best I can—for I cannot fight openly on your side—I will mislead Richard.

HENRY EARL OF RICHMOND   Good lords, conduct him to his regiment.
   I'll strive with° troubled thoughts to take a nap,   *despite*
   Lest leaden slumber peise° me down tomorrow,   *weigh*
   When I should mount with wings of victory.
60   Once more, good night, kind lords and gentlemen.
        Exeunt [STANLEY *and the lords*]. *Manet* RICHMOND
        [RICHMOND *kneels*]
   O thou, whose captain I account myself,
   Look on my forces with a gracious eye.
   Put in their hands thy bruising irons° of wrath,   *swords*
   That they may crush down with a heavy fall
65   Th'usurping helmets of our adversaries.
   Make us thy ministers of chastisement,
   That we may praise thee in the victory.
   To thee I do commend my watchful° soul,   *alert*
   Ere I let fall the windows° of mine eyes.   *eyelids*
70   Sleeping and waking, O defend me still!   [*He*] *sleeps*
     Enter the GHOST OF *young* PRINCE EDWARD [*above*][5]
GHOST OF PRINCE EDWARD (*to* RICHARD)   Let me sit heavy on
    thy soul tomorrow,
   Prince Edward, son to Henry the Sixth.[6]
   Think how thou stabbedst me in my prime of youth
   At Tewkesbury. Despair, therefore, and die.
75   (*To* RICHMOND) Be cheerful, Richmond, for the wrongèd souls
   Of butchered princes fight in thy behalf.
   King Henry's issue,° Richmond, comforts thee.   [*Exit*][7] *offspring*
     Enter [*above*] *the* GHOST OF [KING] HENRY VI
GHOST OF KING HENRY (*to* RICHARD)   When I was mortal, my
    anointed° body   (*with sacred oil*)
   By thee was punchèd full of deadly holes.
80   Think on the Tower[8] and me. Despair and die.
   Harry the Sixth bids thee despair and die.
   (*To* RICHMOND) Virtuous and holy, be thou conqueror.
   Harry that prophesied[9] thou shouldst be king
   Comforts thee in thy sleep. Live and flourish!   [*Exit*]
     Enter [*above*] *the* GHOST OF [*George Duke of*] CLARENCE
85 GHOST OF CLARENCE [*to* RICHARD]   Let me sit heavy on thy soul tomorrow,
   I that was washed to death with fulsome° wine,   *sickening*
   Poor Clarence, by thy guile betrayed to death.
   Tomorrow in the battle think on me,
   And fall° thy edgeless sword. Despair and die.   *drop*
90   (*To* RICHMOND) Thou offspring of the house of Lancaster,
   The wrongèd heirs of York do pray for thee.
   Good angels guard thy battle.° Live and flourish!   [*Exit*] *army*
     Enter [*above*] *the* GHOSTS OF [*Lords*] RIVERS, GRAY, *and*
     [*Sir Thomas*] VAUGHAN
GHOST OF RIVERS [*to* RICHARD]   Let me sit heavy on thy soul tomorrow,
   Rivers that died at Pomfret. Despair and die.
95 GHOST OF GRAY [*to* RICHARD]   Think upon Gray, and let thy soul despair.

5. Q, F do not specify how or where the ghosts enter.
6. Line not present in Q, F; it is added here because Edward is the one character not seen previously, and it is possible that information originally intended as dialogue ended up as the stage direction when the text was printed.
7. Exits not given in Q, F. The ghosts could exeunt together at the end.
8. Where Henry VI was supposedly murdered.
9. See *Richard Duke of York* 4.7, in which King Henry (sometimes "Harry"), declaring the young Richmond "England's hope," foresees Richmond's accession to the throne and the beginning of what was to become the Tudor dynasty.

GHOST OF VAUGHAN [*to* RICHARD]   Think upon Vaughan, and with guilty fear
Let fall thy pointless lance. Despair and die.
ALL THREE (*to* RICHMOND)   Awake, and think our wrongs in Richard's bosom
Will conquer him. Awake, and win the day!   [*Exeunt* GHOSTS]
Enter [*above*] *the* GHOSTS OF THE *two young* PRINCES
GHOSTS OF THE PRINCES (*to* RICHARD)   Dream on thy cousins,[1]
100   smothered in the Tower.
Let us be lead within thy bosom, Richard,
And weigh thee down to ruin, shame, and death.
Thy nephews' souls bid thee despair and die.
(*To* RICHMOND) Sleep, Richmond, sleep in peace and wake in joy.
105 Good angels guard thee from the boar's annoy.
Live, and beget a happy race of kings!
Edward's unhappy sons do bid thee flourish. [*Exeunt* GHOSTS]
Enter [*above*] *the* GHOST OF *Lord* HASTINGS[2]
GHOST OF HASTINGS [*to* RICHARD]   Bloody and guilty, guiltily awake,
And in a bloody battle end thy days.
110 Think on Lord Hastings, then despair and die.
(*To* RICHMOND) Quiet, untroubled soul, awake, awake!
Arm, fight, and conquer for fair England's sake.   [*Exit*]
Enter [*above*] *the* GHOST OF LADY ANNE
GHOST OF LADY ANNE (*to* RICHARD)   Richard, thy wife, that wretched Anne thy wife,
That never slept a quiet hour with thee,
115 Now fills thy sleep with perturbations.
Tomorrow in the battle think on me,
And fall thy edgeless sword. Despair and die.
(*To* RICHMOND) Thou quiet soul, sleep thou a quiet sleep.
Dream of success and happy victory.
120 Thy adversary's wife doth pray for thee.   [*Exit*]
Enter [*above*] *the* GHOST [OF *the Duke*] *of* BUCKINGHAM
GHOST OF BUCKINGHAM (*to* RICHARD)   The first was I that helped thee to the crown;
The last was I that felt thy tyranny.
O in the battle think on Buckingham,
And die in terror of thy guiltiness!
125 Dream on, dream on, of bloody deeds and death;
Fainting,° despair; despairing, yield thy breath.   *Losing heart*
(*To* RICHMOND) I died for hope[3] ere I could lend thee aid.
But cheer thy heart, and be thou not dismayed.
God and good angels fight on Richmond's side,
130 And Richard falls in height of all his pride.   [*Exit*]
RICHARD *starteth up out of a dream*
KING RICHARD   Give me another horse! Bind up my wounds!
Have mercy, Jesu!—Soft, I did but dream.
O coward conscience, how dost thou afflict me?
The lights burn blue.[4] It is now dead midnight.
135 Cold fearful drops stand on my trembling flesh.
What do I fear? Myself? There's none else by.
Richard loves Richard; that is, I am I.
Is there a murderer here? No. Yes, I am.
Then fly! What, from myself? Great reason. Why?

---

1. Nephews ("cousins" was a term used for any kinsmen).
2. Q has him enter before the princes, as he had died before them.
3. I died hoping I could aid you.
4. Thought to indicate the presence of ghosts.

140 Lest I revenge. Myself upon myself?
Alack, I love myself. Wherefore?° For any good   *Why*
That I myself have done unto myself?
O no, alas, I rather hate myself
For hateful deeds committed by myself.
145 I am a villain. Yet I lie: I am not.
Fool, of thyself speak well.—Fool, do not flatter.
My conscience hath a thousand several° tongues,   *separate*
And every tongue brings in a several tale,
And every tale condemns me for a villain.
150 Perjury, perjury, in the high'st degree!⁵
Murder, stern murder, in the dir'st degree!
All several sins, all used in each degree,
Throng to the bar,° crying all, 'Guilty, guilty!'   *(of the court)*
I shall despair.⁶ There is no creature loves me,
155 And if I die no soul will pity me.
Nay, wherefore should they?—Since that I myself
Find in myself no pity to myself.
Methought the souls of all that I had murdered
Came to my tent, and every one did threat
160 Tomorrow's vengeance on the head of Richard.
      Enter RATCLIFFE
RATCLIFFE   My lord?
KING RICHARD   'Swounds, who is there?
RATCLIFFE   My lord, 'tis I. The early village cock
    Hath twice done salutation to the morn.
165   Your friends are up, and buckle on their armour.
KING RICHARD   O Ratcliffe, I have dreamed a fearful dream.
    What thinkest thou, will all our friends prove true?
RATCLIFFE   No doubt, my lord.
KING RICHARD   Ratcliffe, I fear, I fear.
RATCLIFFE   Nay, good my lord, be not afraid of shadows.°   *illusions; ghosts*
170 KING RICHARD   By the Apostle Paul, shadows tonight
    Have struck more terror to the soul of Richard
    Than can the substance of ten thousand soldiers
    Armèd in proof° and led by shallow Richmond.   *impenetrable armor*
    'Tis not yet near day. Come, go with me.
175   Under our tents I'll play the eavesdropper,
    To see if any mean to shrink from me.
        Exeunt RICHARD *and* RATCLIFFE
      Enter the lords to [HENRY EARL OF] RICHMOND, *sitting*
      in his tent
LORDS   Good morrow, Richmond.
HENRY EARL OF RICHMOND   Cry mercy,° lords and watchful   *Beg your pardon*
    gentlemen,
    That you have ta'en a tardy sluggard here.
180 A LORD   How have you slept, my lord?
HENRY EARL OF RICHMOND   The sweetest sleep and fairest
    boding° dreams   *most propitious*
    That ever entered in a drowsy head
    Have I since your departure had, my lords.

5. Every kind of sin, from least to most wicked.
6. Despair was considered the only unforgivable sin; see 1.2.85–88.

Methought their souls whose bodies Richard murdered
185   Came to my tent and cried on[7] victory.
    I promise you, my soul is very jocund°   *joyful*
    In the remembrance of so fair a dream.
    How far into the morning is it, lords?
A LORD   Upon the stroke of four.
190 HENRY EARL OF RICHMOND   Why then, 'tis time to arm, and give direction.
          His oration to his soldiers
    Much that I could say, loving countrymen,
    The leisure° and enforcement of the time   *time available*
    Forbids to dwell on. Yet remember this:
    God and our good cause fight upon our side.
195   The prayers of holy saints and wrongèd souls,
    Like high-reared bulwarks, stand before our forces.
    Richard except,° those whom we fight against   *excepted*
    Had rather have us win than him they follow.
    For what is he they follow? Truly, friends,
200   A bloody tyrant and a homicide;
    One raised in blood, and one in blood established;[8]
    One that made means° to come by what he hath,   *that contrived*
    And slaughtered those that were the means to help him;
    A base, foul stone, made precious by the foil[9]
205   Of England's chair, where he is falsely set;[1]
    One that hath ever been God's enemy.
    Then if you fight against God's enemy,
    God will, in justice, ward° you as his soldiers.   *guard*
    If you do sweat to put a tyrant down,
210   You sleep in peace, the tyrant being slain.
    If you do fight against your country's foes,
    Your country's foison° pays your pains the hire.   *abundance*
    If you do fight in safeguard of your wives,
    Your wives shall welcome home the conquerors.
215   If you do free your children from the sword,
    Your children's children quites° it in your age.   *requites*
    Then, in the name of God and all these rights,
    Advance° your standards! Draw your willing swords!   *Raise*
    For me, the ransom of this bold attempt
220   Shall be my cold corpse on the earth's cold face;[2]
    But if I thrive,° to gain of my attempt,   *succeed*
    The least of you shall share his part thereof.
    Sound, drums and trumpets, bold and cheerfully!
    God and Saint George!° Richmond and victory!   *patron saint of England*
         [*Exeunt to the sound of drums and trumpets*]

5.6

    Enter KING RICHARD, [*Sir Richard*] RATCLIFFE, [*Sir
    William*] CATESBY [*and others*]
KING RICHARD   What said Northumberland, as touching° Richmond?   *regarding*
RATCLIFFE   That he was never trainèd up in arms.

---

7. And called out (a hunting term); here, urged me on to.

8. *One raised . . . established:* One who has come to the throne by bloodshed and has held it through further bloodshed.

9. Metal leaf was often placed under a jewel as a part of its setting, in order to increase its radiance.

1. Of the throne of England, on which he is wrongly placed; with a pun on "being set like a jewel."

2. *the ransom . . . face:* the only ransom I will give them is my dead body.

5.6

KING RICHARD   He said the truth. And what said Surrey then?

RATCLIFFE   He smiled and said, 'The better for our purpose.'

5   KING RICHARD   He was in the right, and so indeed it is.

    Clock strikes

Tell the clock there.[1] Give me a calendar.°   *an almanac*

Who saw the sun today?

    [A book is brought]

RATCLIFFE   Not I, my lord.

KING RICHARD   Then he disdains to shine, for by the book°   *(the almanac)*

He should have braved° the east an hour ago.   *made resplendent*

10   A black day will it be to somebody.

Ratcliffe.

RATCLIFFE   My lord?

KING RICHARD   The sun will not be seen today.

The sky doth frown and lour° upon our army.   *glower*

I would these dewy tears were from° the ground.   *gone from*

15   Not shine today—why, what is that to me

More than to Richmond? For the selfsame heaven

That frowns on me looks sadly upon him.

    Enter [the Duke of] NORFOLK

NORFOLK   Arm, arm, my lord! The foe vaunts° in the field.   *flaunts his strength*

KING RICHARD   Come, bustle, bustle! Caparison° my horse.   *Put the trappings on*

    [RICHARD arms]

20   Call up Lord Stanley, bid him bring his power.°   *[Exit one]*   *forces*

I will lead forth my soldiers to the plain,

And thus my battle° shall be orderèd.   *army*

My forward° shall be drawn out all in length,   *front rank*

Consisting equally of horse and foot,

25   Our archers placèd strongly in the midst.

John Duke of Norfolk, Thomas Earl of Surrey,

Shall have the leading of this multitude.

They thus directed,° we ourself will follow   *positioned*

In the main battle, whose puissance° on both sides   *power*

30   Shall be well wingèd° with our chiefest horse.°   *flanked / best cavalry*

This, and Saint George to boot![2] What think'st thou, Norfolk?

NORFOLK   A good direction, warlike sovereign.

    He showeth him a paper

This paper found I on my tent this morning.

    [He reads]

    'Jackie of Norfolk be not too bold,

35   For Dickon thy master is bought and sold.'[3]

KING RICHARD   A thing devisèd by the enemy.—

Go, gentlemen, each man unto his charge.

Let not our babbling dreams affright our souls.

Conscience is but a word that cowards use,

40   Devised at first to keep the strong in awe.

Our strong arms be our conscience; swords, our law.

March on, join° bravely! Let us to't, pell mell—   *join battle*

If not to heaven, then hand in hand to hell.

    His oration to his army

What shall I say, more than I have inferred?°   *put forward*

45   Remember whom you are to cope withal:°   *with*

---

1. Count the clock's strokes.
2. *and . . . boot:* with the aid of our patron saint as a bonus.

3. Is betrayed. *Jackie of Norfolk:* John, Duke of Norfolk. *Dickon:* Dick (that is, Richard).

A sort° of vagabonds, rascals and runaways,   *gang*
A scum of Bretons and base lackey° peasants,   *lowly*
Whom their o'ercloyèd° country vomits forth   *nauseously overfull*
To desperate ventures and assured destruction.
50   You sleeping safe, they bring to you unrest;
You having lands and blessed with beauteous wives,
They would distrain° the one, distain° the other.   *confiscate / dishonor*
And who doth lead them, but a paltry fellow?
Long kept in Bretagne at our mother's[4] cost;
55   A milksop; one that never in his life
Felt so much cold as over shoes in snow.[5]
Let's whip[6] these stragglers o'er the seas again,
Lash hence these overweening rags of France,
These famished beggars, weary of their lives,
60   Who—but for° dreaming on this fond° exploit—   *were it not for / foolish*
For want of means,° poor rats, had hanged themselves.   *livelihood*
If we be conquered, let *men* conquer us,
And not these bastard Bretons, whom our fathers
Have in their own land beaten, bobbed,° and thumped,   *pounded*
65   And in record left them the heirs of shame.[7]
Shall these enjoy our lands? Lie with our wives?
Ravish our daughters?
         Drum afar off
                              Hark, I hear their drum.
Fight, gentlemen of England! Fight, bold yeomen!
Draw, archers, draw your arrows to the head!
70   Spur your proud horses hard, and ride in blood!
Amaze the welkin° with your broken staves!   *sky*
         Enter a MESSENGER
What says Lord Stanley? Will he bring his power?
MESSENGER   My lord, he doth deny° to come.   *refuse*
KING RICHARD   Off with young George's head!
75   NORFOLK   My lord, the enemy is past the marsh.
After the battle let George Stanley die.
KING RICHARD   A thousand hearts are great within my bosom.
Advance our standards! Set upon our foes!
Our ancient word° of courage, fair Saint George,   *battle cry*
80   Inspire us with the spleen° of fiery dragons.   *anger*
Upon them! Victory sits on our helms!°   *Exeunt*   *helmets*

5.7

Alarum. Excursions.° Enter [Sir William] CATESBY   *Military sallies*
CATESBY *[calling]*[1]   Rescue, my lord of Norfolk! Rescue, rescue!
[To a soldier] The King enacts more wonders than a man,[2]
Daring an opposite° to every danger.   *to oppose himself*
His horse is slain, and all on foot he fights,
5   Seeking for Richmond in the throat of death.
[Calling] Rescue, fair lord, or else the day is lost!

---

4. Apparently from a misprint in Holinshed, which should have read "brother's" (that is, Richard's brother-in-law, Charles, Duke of Burgundy, who supported Richmond in exile). Possibly: to the detriment of England, the mother country.
5. *as . . . snow:* as one does who walks in snow that covers the tops of his shoes.

6. English vagabonds were whipped out of the parish by a local official.
7. And gave them a shameful record in history.
5.7
1. Some editors bring Norfolk onstage, although the stage directions do not call for him in either Q or F.
2. More wonders than seems possible for a man.

*Alarums. Enter [*KING*]* RICHARD

KING RICHARD   A horse! A horse! My kingdom for a horse!

CATESBY   Withdraw, my lord. I'll help you to a horse.

KING RICHARD   Slave, I have set my life upon a cast,³

10   And I will stand the hazard of the die.

I think there be six Richmonds⁴ in the field.

Five have I slain today, instead of him.

A horse! A horse! My kingdom for a horse!   [*Exeunt*]

5.8

*Alarum. Enter [*KING*]* RICHARD *[at one door] and*
*[*HENRY EARL OF*]* RICHMOND *[at another]. They fight.*
RICHARD *is slain. [Exit* RICHMOND.*] Retreat¹ and flour-*
*ish. Enter [*HENRY EARL OF*]* RICHMOND *and [Lord* STAN-
LEY *Earl of] Derby, with divers other lords [and soldiers]*

HENRY EARL OF RICHMOND   God and your arms be praised, victorious friends!

The day is ours. The bloody dog is dead.

STANLEY *[bearing the crown]*   Courageous Richmond, well hast

thou acquit° thee.   acquitted; conducted

Lo, here this long usurpèd royalty²

5   From the dead temples of this bloody wretch

Have I plucked off, to grace thy brows withal.°   with

Wear it, enjoy it, and make much of it.

[He sets the crown on Henry's head]

KING HENRY VII   Great God of heaven, say 'Amen' to all.

But tell me—young George Stanley, is he living?

10   STANLEY   He is, my lord, and safe in Leicester town,

Whither, if it please you, we may now withdraw us.

KING HENRY VII   What men of name are slain on either side?

STANLEY *[reads]*   John Duke of Norfolk, Robert Brackenbury,

Walter Lord Ferrers, and Sir William Brandon.

15   KING HENRY VII   Inter their bodies as becomes their births.°   befits their rank

Proclaim a pardon to the soldiers fled

That in submission will return to us,

And then—as we have ta'en the sacrament³—

We will unite the white rose and the red.⁴

20   Smile, heaven, upon this fair conjunction,°   union

That long have frowned upon their enmity.

What traitor hears me and says not 'Amen'?

England hath long been mad, and scarred herself;

The brother blindly shed the brother's blood;

25   The father rashly slaughtered his own son;

The son, compelled, been butcher to the sire;

All that divided York and Lancaster,

United in their dire division.⁵

O now let Richmond and Elizabeth,

30   The true succeeders of each royal house,

By God's fair ordinance° conjoin together,   decree

3. A throw of the die (one of a pair of dice) in line 10.
4. In addition to Richmond, five other men dressed and
armed to resemble him (a common safety measure).
5.8
1. A trumpet signal for (Richard's) men to retire.
2. Emblem of sovereignty; here, the crown.
3. Referring to the oath, taken by Richmond in the
cathedral at Rheims, that he would marry Princess

Elizabeth as soon as he was crowned.
4. The badges of the Yorkist (white) and Lancastrian
(red) factions. The marriage of Richmond (Lancastrian) and Princess Elizabeth (Yorkist) brought to an
end the so-called Wars of the Roses, dramatized in the
three *Henry VI* plays.
5. Joined by hatred, having nothing in common but
mutual antagonism.

And let their heirs—God, if his will be so—
Enrich the time to come with smooth-faced peace,
With smiling plenty, and fair prosperous days.
35 Abate° the edge of traitors, gracious Lord,   Blunt
That would reduce° these bloody days again   bring back
And make poor England weep forth streams of blood.
Let them not live to taste this land's increase,°   prosperity
That would with treason wound this fair land's peace.
40 Now civil wounds are stopped; peace lives again.
That she may long live here, God say 'Amen'.

[*Flourish.*] *Exeunt*

Venus and Adonis

When Shakespeare wrote the narrative poem *Venus and Adonis,* he was already an up-and-coming playwright; but he called his poem "the first heir of my invention" because, in 1593, it was his earliest work to see print. While plays were considered the property of the theater company and found their way to the printing house erratically if at all, an author could publish nondramatic works like *Venus and Adonis* and *The Rape of Lucrece* without impediment. It was customary to dedicate such published poems to aristocrats who might provide financial support or other form of patronage. Shakespeare dedicated *Venus and Adonis* to Henry Wriothesley, Earl of Southampton, a handsome nineteen-year-old aristocrat with sophisticated literary tastes, who was soon to come into a substantial fortune. But despite the conventionally flattering language of the dedication, Shakespeare intended to appeal to a larger audience than merely the patron to whom the poem was nominally addressed. Indeed, *Venus and Adonis* was exceedingly popular in Shakespeare's lifetime: it went through nine editions, and his contemporaries quote passages from it more often than they quote from any other Shakespearean play or poem.

Part of the attraction of the poem for Shakespeare's contemporaries was its extended and apparently effortless deployment of an elaborate poetic form. The poem's *ababcc* stanza, a quatrain followed by a couplet, was popular among many Elizabethan poets—George Gascoigne, Thomas Lodge, Edmund Spenser, and Philip Sidney, among others—but Shakespeare's virtuosity was so widely recognized that it has henceforth been known in English not by its Italian name, *sesta rima,* but as the "Venus and Adonis stanza." A sort of abbreviated sonnet, this stanza, in Shakespeare's hands, tends often to proffer a snatch of narrative in the quatrain, followed by a summarizing or reflective couplet, thus alternating between advancing the plot and commenting, pithily and wittily, upon the action.

Shakespeare found the story of Venus and Adonis in Ovid's *Metamorphoses,* a poem in fifteen books that retells, in beautiful Latin, more than two hundred pagan myths of transformation. Since Elizabethan schoolboys were required to memorize long passages from the *Metamorphoses,* many of Shakespeare's readers knew Ovid in the original; others read him in a popular 1567 English translation by Arthur Golding. Shakespeare would have been aware that the cult of Adonis was widespread in antiquity, a cult that involved rites of fertility and seasonal renewal and was associated with the adoration of a mother goddess variously identified as Venus, Aphrodite, Astoreth, Isis, or Cybele. In the Old Testament, the Israelites are periodically chastised for abandoning their male divinity for the worship of this heathen goddess; her cult thus seems, at least for the Jews of antiquity, to have constituted an alluring alternative to patriarchal monotheism. For Christian interpreters, the myth of the mutilated, transformed Adonis resembles the story of Christ closely enough to be read, on the one hand, as a pagan analogue to Christ's death and resurrection and, on the other hand, as a demonstration of the superior power of the Judeo-Christian God, who, unlike Venus, can confer true immortality.

Shakespeare was not the only Elizabethan writer to adapt Ovid's stories to an English idiom. *Venus and Adonis* is an erotic narrative poem of a type that had become popular in the 1580s and grew even more so in the 1590s, partly because of the success of Shakespeare's poem and of Christopher Marlowe's roughly contemporaneous *Hero and Leander.* The writers of such poems acquired their plots from classical sources, but they got their idea of how to treat those plots from a medieval and Renaissance tradition of erotic

Two horses mating. From Antonio Tempesta, *Horses of Different Lands.*

poetry, deriving from the Italian poet Petrarch and developed in English by such poets as Thomas Wyatt, Philip Sidney, and Edmund Spenser. In *Venus and Adonis*, Shakespeare reconceives his mythological protagonists so that his poem might in some respects more closely approximate a Petrarchan norm. When Ovid's Venus is dazzled by Adonis, she resolves to appeal to him by feigning an interest in his favorite sport. By donning hunting gear and resolutely chasing rabbits, she successfully captures the gorgeous huntsman, her true quarry. Shakespeare's Venus declares herself in a much more forthright fashion, but his Adonis, unlike Ovid's, remains unresponsive to her charms. Thus *Venus and Adonis* reproduces a dynamic that Petrarch and his followers had made familiar by the late sixteenth century, in which a yearning lover pleads endlessly with a chilly love object.

The enduring fascination of this scenario for Renaissance poets lay in their recognition that the absence of sexual gratification can enhance erotic desire: "An oven that is stopped, or river stayed, / Burneth more hotly, swelleth with more rage" (lines 331–32). In Petrarchan poetry, little of consequence seems to happen, but the apparent lack of momentum is actually a prime stimulus to creativity. Frustration hones techniques of erotic persuasion; it energizes lament; it interestingly complicates the poet-lover's state of mind. The sophisticated pleasure of intense self-awareness replaces the straightforward, even mindless pleasure of the sex act itself. In *Venus and Adonis*, Shakespeare's concentration on psychological detail produces an extraordinary slowing-down and drawing-out of the action. Ovid spends about eighty-five lines on Adonis, beginning with a brisk description of his birth and ending with an equally succinct account of his metamorphosis into an anemone flower. Shakespeare manages to devote almost twelve hundred lines to the last twenty-four hours of Adonis's life.

In some important respects, however, Shakespeare departs from his Petrarchan precedents. The Ovidian retelling of the story of Venus and Adonis appears in *Metamor-*

phoses 10, a book that, as Ovid's translator Arthur Golding writes, "chiefly doth contain one kind of argument / Reproving most prodigious lusts." Taken together, the stories of Book 10 treat necrophilia, homosexuality, bestiality, fetishism, and incest; in this context, the story of Venus and Adonis seems relatively tame. But the "prodigiousness" of the Venus and Adonis story becomes clear when it is compared with similar Ovidian tales, which usually involve gods—Jove, Neptune, Apollo, or Pluto—who rape or attempt to rape beautiful young women. The story of Venus and Adonis reverses the "normal" gender of eager divinity and reluctant mortal.

Shakespeare's revisions of the story exaggerate the effects of this transposition. He attributes some conventionally "masculine" traits to his heroine and some conventionally "feminine" ones to his hero. His Venus is experienced, immensely strong, and apparently quite a bit larger than the Adonis whom she effortlessly tucks under one arm. Shakespeare's Adonis is dimpled, tender, coy, and virginal. At the same time, a female, even one as formidable as Venus, is imagined to be incapable of rape, so Venus cannot simply overpower her beloved as Apollo or Jove might do. Anatomical constraints force her to play a quite different but also conventionally masculine part: the pleading, unsatisfied role conventionally assigned to the male lover in Petrarchan poetry.

Since in Renaissance erotic poetry the positions of actively desiring, rhetorically fluent male and passive, unwilling female are ordinarily strictly demarcated, the sexual transpositions in the Venus and Adonis story have immediate consequences for Shakespeare's use of poetic conventions. Obviously they give those conventions a fresh twist. In Shakespeare's hands, such novelty is often comic: the aggressive, rhetorically hyperbolic Venus and the fastidious Adonis are funny, because now as then they violate conventional notions of appropriate gender-specific behavior. Some of these reversals are obvious to a modern reader, since our courtship rituals retain vestiges of the assumption that males are naturally dominant and inclined to take the sexual initiative. Other reversals are more specific to the poetic tradition in which Shakespeare wrote. In traditional love poetry, for instance, the enamored man "blazons," or elaborately describes, the features of the woman he desires, dwelling on the incomparable beauty of her eyes, hair, lips, hands, voice, gestures, and so forth. But in *Venus and Adonis,* Venus is compelled to blazon her own charms, because Adonis will not do it for her.

> Mine eyes are grey, and bright, and quick in turning.
> My beauty as the spring doth yearly grow.
> My flesh is soft and plump, my marrow burning.
> . . . .
> Bid me discourse, I will enchant thine ear;
> Or like a fairy, trip upon the green;
> Or like a nymph, with long, dishevelled hair,
> Dance on the sands, and yet no footing seen.
> (lines 140–48)

While in the conventional love situation the blazon is a man's cry of yearning for an exquisite object, here it becomes a woman's calculated, but unsuccessful, advertising campaign.

Shakespeare also dwells on the comic quality of Venus's divine attributes, such as the miraculous weightlessness of her robust body. At one point, Venus describes herself as a kind of giant balloon: "Witness this primrose bank whereon I lie: / These forceless flowers like sturdy trees support me" (lines 151–52). Her physical strength contrasts vividly with her quintessentially feminine body: when Venus "locks her lily fingers one in one" (line 228), she turns out to have a grip of steel. Shakespeare's interest in such apparent incongruities foreshadowed his much more elaborate exploration of the effects of transvestism and sexual reversal in such plays as *As You Like It, Twelfth Night, All's Well That Ends Well, Macbeth,* and *Antony and Cleopatra.* The humor of *Venus and Adonis* is two-edged, however, for it implicitly mocks not merely the aberrant protagonists but the standards from which they deviate. In what sense are particular

Cupid taking aim. From George Wither, *A Collection of Emblemes* (1635). The motto reads: "Be wary, whosoe're thou be, / For from Love's arrows, none are free."

traits or behaviors "naturally" masculine or feminine if actual males and females do not possess them?

The upending of gender stereotypes in *Venus and Adonis* is only one of the strategies of reversal that structure the imagery of the poem. Again and again, its metaphors and similes insist on the similarity of what seems different, the difference in what seems the same. Hunting is and is not like sexual pursuit; killing is and is not like loving; female sexual desire is and is not like maternal nurture; the boar, savagely rooting in Adonis's groin, is and is not like Venus; Adonis is and is not like the sun god or the flower into which he eventually transforms. Many of these comparisons or implied comparisons are traditional ones; Shakespeare's virtuosity is evident not as much in the originality of his individual conceits as in their extraordinary profusion and in the surprising way in which apparently incompatible images are tellingly juxtaposed.

The handling of imagery corresponds with the poem's abrupt reversals of mood and with the unpredictable, accidental quality of the story. The frank comedy of the beginning swerves into tragedy, or at least pathos, at the close, as the immortal goddess confronts the death of her reluctant beloved. Over the course of the poem, our estimation of both characters undergoes dizzying shifts. Venus—goddess, whore, cradle robber, and queen—is funny, scary, eloquent, and pitiable by turns. Adonis's sexual diffidence at first seems as ridiculous to the readers as it does to Venus; but he suddenly seems less absurd when he replies, gravely even if rather too sanctimoniously, to Venus's importunities.

Venus's frank joy in the pleasures of sex suggests an uninhibited pagan universe, in which gods, animals, and human beings all are ruled by the same laws of generation and sensual enjoyment. Shakespeare's lavish attention to the forest setting in which the poem takes place suggests his keen appreciation of the sensuous possibilities of a purely natural world. The bodies of animals—Adonis's splendid courser, inflamed by lust; the ferocious boar, bursting through the thorniest thickets; the zigzagging hunted hare— all are accorded blazons of their own, as if they, not merely the human lovers, were full participants in the story of love and death. At such moments, the poem seems enthusiastically to endorse the original religious significance of the Venus and Adonis story, which linked human lives with the rhythms of a natural environment.

But Shakespeare's poem hardly evokes a sexual utopia. Even though the pagan setting of the poem presumably frees the characters from the sexually abstemious culture of Christianity, the heroine and hero still disagree vehemently about the value of sexual indulgence. Chastity has its attractions even apart from whatever supernatural reinforcement Christian faith might lend to it—especially, as Adonis notes, for those who are not yet fully adult. The

The boar attacking Adonis. From Henry Peacham, *Minerva Britanna* (1612).

immortal Venus thinks of experience as an endless series of pleasurable present-tense moments; the mortal Adonis wants to conceive of his life in terms of narrative development, building slowly and coherently to a future maturity. His untimely death suggests the risks of thinking of one's life in this fashion; he seems unwisely to have forgone present satisfaction in the hope of a reward that will never materialize.

On the other hand, why should Adonis, the victim of a sexual attack, enjoy caresses he has neither invited nor encouraged? Just as Shakespeare's reversal of gender stereotypes calls into question the adequacy of those stereotypes, so Adonis's recoil from Venus calls into question the naturalness of reproductive sexuality. Venus, the goddess of love, is supposed to be the apex of heterosexual desirability, both source and goal of every man's desire. Adonis, however, does not desire her even when she presses herself upon him. The congress of male and female thus seems simultaneously natural—what Adonis's palfrey and a passing mare know without tutelage—and optional, a possibility that some males, at any rate, may be willing to do without.

Shakespeare writes almost entirely from Venus's perspective: the boy, not the woman, is the sex object of *Venus and Adonis*. In an age lacking our comparatively rigid conception of sexual orientation, lovely androgynous boys were assumed to be attractive to adult men and women alike. Shakespeare returned to the subject of the adolescent boy's ambiguous, half-conscious sexiness in his transvestite comedies, and to the adult man's reluctance to commit himself to exclusively heterosexual alliances in those plays as well as in *The Merchant of Venice. Venus and Adonis* can thus be read both as a narrative of frustrated heterosexual desire and, perhaps, as a parable of desire for a beautiful, aloof boy by a male poet—a scenario also sketched in many of Shakespeare's sonnets.

What is the meaning of sexuality? *Venus and Adonis* suggests a wide variety of possibilities: it is both a joke and a cosmic principle, a function of stern reproductive necessity and of sheer animal exuberance, a link with the animal world and an escape from it, a necessity and an option, a reminder of mortality and an intimation of immortality, a celebration of personal uniqueness and a threat to the formation of an individual identity. The shifting perspectives of the poem exploit the ambivalence with which Shakespeare's culture, as well as our own, treats sexual matters as simultaneously comical and deeply serious. The language of *Venus and Adonis* is especially good at capturing the confusing, contradictory array of sensations produced by another person's unfamiliar body close to one's own, a sensation at once grand, comic, oppressive, arousing, and repellant. The sweating, reeking, melting, and liquefying that at first seem specific to Venus's courtship of Adonis appear, by the end of the poem, to represent a principle of mortal existence and moral evaluation, as one thing merges unsteadily, unexpectedly, into another.

Biographical critics have found in *Venus and Adonis* ample grounds for speculation. Does the sexual dynamic of this poem reflect Shakespeare's experience with the older

Anne Hathaway, hauling him into some bosky nook outside Stratford, or alternatively an infatuation with Henry Wriothesley, the gorgeous youth to whom, some speculate, the early sonnets are devoted in both senses of the word? Given the scanty biographical data that have come down to us, it is impossible to know. What is clear is that *Venus and Adonis* inaugurates many of the distinctive features of Shakespeare's later work: a fascination, and capacity to sympathize, with sexually assertive women and self-contained, immature young men; an erotic energy that is both exuberant and hard to pin down; a complex moral sensibility capable of apprehending contradictory ethical imperatives at the same time; and an uncanny ability to combine comic, tragic, pathetic, and sensuous effects in a single work, even in a single poetic moment.

KATHARINE EISAMAN MAUS

TEXTUAL NOTE

The textual history of *Venus and Adonis* is much less tangled than that of most of the plays. Critics have theorized that Shakespeare wrote the narrative poems in 1592 and 1593, when an epidemic of bubonic plague forced the London theaters to close. At the time, it was unclear whether the playhouses would be allowed to reopen, so Shakespeare may have had not merely plenty of time on his hands but an urgent practical motive for establishing his credentials as a nondramatic writer. *Venus and Adonis* was first published in quarto in 1593 by the printer Richard Field, who was, like Shakespeare, a native of Stratford-upon-Avon. Only one copy of this edition survives. It contains very few obvious misprints and was presumably prepared from Shakespeare's manuscript, perhaps under his direct supervision. *Venus and Adonis* was frequently reprinted during Shakespeare's lifetime, but there is little substantive variation from one printing to another.

SELECTED BIBLIOGRAPHY

Bate, Jonathan. "Sexual Poetry." *Shakespeare and Ovid.* Oxford: Clarendon, 1993. 48–65. Shakespeare's adaptation of Ovid's story of transgressive desire.

Hughes, Ted. "Conception and Gestation of the Equation's Tragic Myth." *Shakespeare and the Goddess of Complete Being.* London: Faber and Faber, 1992. 49–92. *Venus and Adonis* as Shakespeare's version of an ancient myth, filtered through Roman Catholicism, of goddess and sacrificed consort.

Hulse, Clark. *Metamorphic Verse: The Elizabethan Minor Epic.* Princeton: Princeton University Press, 1981. 141–75. *Venus and Adonis* in relation to its sources and immediate predecessors.

Kahn, Coppélia. "Self as Eros in *Venus and Adonis.*" *Man's Estate: Masculine Identity in Shakespeare.* Berkeley: University of California Press, 1981. 21–46. Adonis as narcissist.

Keach, William. "Venus and Adonis." *Elizabethan Erotic Narratives: Irony and Pathos in the Ovidian Poetry of Shakespeare, Marlowe, and Their Contemporaries.* New Brunswick, N.J.: Rutgers University Press, 1977. 52–84. The poem considered among others of its genre.

Kolin, Philip C. *Venus and Adonis: Critical Essays.* New York: Garland, 1997. A collection of articles.

Rambuss, Richard. "What It Feels Like for a Boy: Shakespeare's *Venus and Adonis.*" *A Companion to Shakespeare's Works,* vol. IV: *Poems, Problem Comedies, Late Plays.* Ed. Richard Dutton and Jean Howard. Malden, Mass.: Blackwell, 2003. *Venus and Adonis* as a "proto-gay" poem.

Venus and Adonis

Vilia miretur vulgus; mihi flavus Apollo
Pocula Castalia plena ministret aqua.[1]

TO THE RIGHT HONOURABLE
HENRY WRIOTHESLEY,
EARL OF SOUTHAMPTON, AND
BARON OF TITCHFIELD[2]

Right Honourable, I know not how I shall offend in dedicating
my unpolished lines to your lordship, nor how the world will
censure° me for choosing so strong a prop to support so weak a   *judge*
burden. Only, if your honour seem but pleased, I account myself
highly praised, and vow to take advantage of all idle hours till I
have honoured you with some graver labour. But if the first heir[3]
of my invention prove deformed, I shall be sorry it had so noble
a godfather, and never after ear° so barren a land for fear it yield   *cultivate*
me still° so bad a harvest. I leave it to your honourable survey,   *always*
and your honour to your heart's content, which I wish may always
answer your own wish and the world's hopeful expectation.

    YOUR HONOUR'S IN ALL DUTY,
    WILLIAM SHAKESPEARE

Even as the sun with purple-coloured face
Had ta'en his last leave of the weeping morn,[1]
Rose-cheeked Adonis hied him° to the chase.   *hurried*
Hunting he loved, but love he laughed to scorn.
5   Sick-thoughted° Venus makes amain° unto him,   *Lovesick / speedily*
    And like a bold-faced suitor 'gins to woo him.

'Thrice fairer than myself,' thus she began,
'The fields' chief flower, sweet above compare,
Stain to all nymphs,° more lovely than a man,   *Eclipsing all women*
10 More white and red than doves or roses are—
    Nature that made thee with herself at strife
    Saith that the world hath ending with thy life.[2]

'Vouchsafe, thou wonder, to alight thy steed
And rein his proud head to the saddle-bow;

Dedication
1. "Let vile people admire vile things; may fair-haired
Apollo serve me goblets filled with Castalian water"
(Ovid, *Amores* 1.15.35–36). Apollo is the god of poetry;
the Castalian spring is sacred to the Muses.
2. Prominent courtier, nineteen years old at the time of
Venus and Adonis's publication. Shakespeare also dedicated *The Rape of Lucrece* to him.

3. *Venus and Adonis* was Shakespeare's first published
work.
Poem
1. Aurora, goddess of the dawn, weeps tears of dew
when forsaken each morning by her lover, the sun.
2. *Nature . . . life*: Nature, who strove to surpass herself in making you, says that if you die, the world will
end.

15 If thou wilt deign this favour, for thy meed°   *reward*
    A thousand honey secrets shalt thou know.
      Here come and sit where never serpent hisses;
      And, being sat, I'll smother thee with kisses,

    'And yet not cloy thy lips with loathed satiety,
20 But rather famish them amid their plenty,
    Making them red, and pale, with fresh variety;
    Ten kisses short as one, one long as twenty.
      A summer's day will seem an hour but short,
      Being wasted° in such time-beguiling sport.'   *spent*

25 With this, she seizeth on his sweating palm,
    The precedent of pith and livelihood,[3]
    And, trembling in her passion, calls it balm—
    Earth's sovereign° salve to do a goddess good.   *potent*
      Being so enraged, desire doth lend her force
30   Courageously to pluck him from his horse.

    Over one arm, the lusty courser's rein;
    Under her other was the tender boy,
    Who blushed and pouted in a dull disdain
    With leaden appetite, unapt to toy.[4]
35   She red and hot as coals of glowing fire;
      He red for shame, but frosty in desire.

    The studded bridle on a ragged bough
    Nimbly she fastens—O, how quick is love!
    The steed is stallèd° up, and even now   *fastened*
40 To tie the rider she begins to prove.°   *try*
      Backward she pushed him, as she would be thrust,
      And governed him in strength, though not in lust.

    So soon was she along° as he was down,   *alongside him*
    Each leaning on their elbows and their hips.
45 Now doth she stroke his cheek, now doth he frown
    And 'gins to chide, but soon she stops his lips,
      And, kissing, speaks, with lustful language broken:°   *interrupted*
      'If thou wilt chide, thy lips shall never open.'

    He burns with bashful shame; she with her tears
50 Doth quench the maiden burning of his cheeks.
    Then, with her windy sighs and golden hairs,
    To fan and blow them dry again she seeks.
      He saith she is immodest, blames her miss;°   *misbehavior*
      What follows more she murders with a kiss.

55 Even as an empty eagle, sharp by fast,°   *hungry from fasting*
    Tires° with her beak on feathers, flesh, and bone,   *Tears*
    Shaking her wings, devouring all in haste
    Till either gorge° be stuffed or prey be gone,   *stomach*
      Even so she kissed his brow, his cheek, his chin,
60   And where she ends she doth anew begin.

---

3. The evidence of strength and liveliness.   4. Uninterested in sex play.

Forced to content,° but never to obey,°   *acquiesce / respond*
Panting he lies and breatheth in her face.
She feedeth on the steam as on a prey
And calls it heavenly moisture, air of grace,
65   Wishing her cheeks were gardens full of flowers,
    So they were dewed with such distilling° showers.   *gently dropping*

Look how a bird lies tangled in a net,
So fastened in her arms Adonis lies.
Pure shame and awed° resistance made him fret,   *overpowered*
70 Which bred more beauty in his angry eyes.
    Rain added to a river that is rank°   *full*
    Perforce will force it overflow the bank.

Still she entreats, and prettily entreats,
For to a pretty ear she tunes her tale.
75 Still is he sullen, still he lours° and frets   *frowns*
'Twixt crimson shame and anger ashy-pale.
    Being red, she loves him best; and being white,
    Her best is bettered with a more delight.

Look how he can, she cannot choose but love;
80 And by her fair immortal hand she swears
From his soft bosom never to remove
Till he take truce° with her contending tears,   *come to terms*
    Which long have rained, making her cheeks all wet;
    And one sweet kiss shall pay this countless debt.

85 Upon this promise did he raise his chin,
Like a divedapper[5] peering through a wave
Who, being looked on, ducks as quickly in—
So offers he to give what she did crave.
    But when her lips were ready for his pay,
90   He winks,° and turns his lips another way.   *shuts his eyes*

Never did passenger° in summer's heat   *traveler*
More thirst for drink than she for this good turn.
Her help she sees, but help she cannot get.
She bathes in water, yet her fire must burn.
95   'O pity,' gan she cry, 'flint-hearted boy!
    'Tis but a kiss I beg—why art thou coy?

'I have been wooed as I entreat thee now
Even by the stern and direful god of war,°   *Mars*
Whose sinewy neck in battle ne'er did bow,
100 Who conquers where he comes in every jar.°   *conflict*
    Yet hath he been my captive and my slave,
    And begged for that which thou unasked shalt have.

'Over my altars hath he hung his lance,
His battered shield, his uncontrollèd° crest,   *unvanquished*
105 And for my sake hath learned to sport and dance,

5. Grebe (small English waterbird).

To toy, to wanton, dally, smile, and jest,
　　Scorning his churlish drum and ensign red,
　　Making my arms° his field, his tent my bed.　　　　　　*(a pun)*

'Thus he that over-ruled I overswayed,
110　Leading him prisoner in a red-rose chain.
　　Strong-tempered steel his stronger strength obeyed,
　　Yet was he servile to my coy disdain.
　　　　O, be not proud, nor brag not of thy might,
　　　　For mast'ring her that foiled° the god of fight.　　　*conquered*

115　'Touch but my lips with those fair lips of thine—
　　Though mine be not so fair, yet are they red—
　　The kiss shall be thine own as well as mine.
　　What seest thou in the ground? Hold up thy head.
　　　　Look in mine eyeballs: there thy beauty lies.°　　*lies reflected*
120　　Then why not lips on lips, since eyes in eyes?

'Art thou ashamed to kiss? Then wink again,
　　And I will wink. So shall the day seem night.
　　Love keeps his revels where there are but twain.
　　Be bold to play—our sport is not in sight.°　　　　*unobserved*
125　　These blue-veined violets whereon we lean
　　　　Never can blab, nor know not⁶ what we mean.

'The tender spring° upon thy tempting lip　　　*growth of new beard*
　　Shows thee unripe; yet mayst thou well be tasted.
　　Make use of time; let not advantage slip.
130　Beauty within itself should not be wasted.
　　　　Fair flowers that are not gathered in their prime
　　　　Rot, and consume themselves in little time.

'Were I hard-favoured,° foul, or wrinkled-old,　　　*ugly*
　　Ill-nurtured, crooked, churlish, harsh in voice,
135　O'er-worn,° despisèd, rheumatic, and cold,　　　*Worn out*
　　Thick-sighted,° barren, lean, and lacking juice,　　*Partly blind*
　　　　Then mightst thou pause, for then I were not for thee.
　　　　But having no defects, why dost abhor me?

'Thou canst not see one wrinkle in my brow.
140　Mine eyes are grey,⁷ and bright, and quick in turning.
　　My beauty as the spring doth yearly grow.°　　　*rejuvenate*
　　My flesh is soft and plump, my marrow° burning.　　*vital spirits*
　　　　My smooth moist hand, were it with thy hand felt,
　　　　Would in thy palm dissolve, or seem to melt.

145　'Bid me discourse, I will enchant thine ear;
　　Or like a fairy, trip upon the green;
　　Or like a nymph, with long, dishevelled hair,
　　Dance on the sands, and yet no footing° seen.　　　*footprint*
　　　　Love is a spirit all compact° of fire,　　　*made up*
150　　Not gross° to sink, but light, and will aspire.°　　*heavy / rise*

6. The double negative ("nor . . . not") was acceptable　　7. Considered the best eye color by medieval and Renais-
in Elizabethan English.　　　　　　　　　　　　　　　sance love poets.

'Witness this primrose bank whereon I lie:
These forceless flowers like sturdy trees support me.
Two strengthless doves⁸ will draw me through the sky
From morn till night, even where I list° to sport me.   *wherever I wish*
155   Is love so light, sweet boy, and may it be
    That thou should think it heavy unto thee?

'Is thine own heart to thine own face affected?°   *attracted*
Can thy right hand seize love upon thy left?°   *by clasping the left*
Then woo thyself, be of thyself rejected;
160 Steal thine own freedom,° and complain on theft.   *Capture your affections*
    Narcissus⁹ so himself himself forsook,
    And died to kiss his shadow in the brook.

'Torches are made to light, jewels to wear,
Dainties to taste, fresh beauty for the use,
165 Herbs for their smell, and sappy plants to bear.
Things growing to themselves° are growth's abuse.   *only for themselves*
    Seeds spring from seeds, and beauty breedeth beauty:
    Thou wast begot; to get° it is thy duty.   *beget*

'Upon the earth's increase why shouldst thou feed
170 Unless the earth with thy increase be fed?
By law of nature thou art bound to breed,
That thine° may live when thou thyself art dead;   *(your children)*
    And so in spite of death thou dost survive,
    In that thy likeness still is left alive.'

175 By this,° the lovesick queen began to sweat,   *By this time*
For where they lay the shadow had forsook them,
And Titan,° tired in the midday heat,   *the sun god*
With burning eye did hotly overlook them,
    Wishing Adonis had his team° to guide   *(of sun horses)*
180   So he° were like him,° and by Venus' side.   *(Titan) / (Adonis)*

And now Adonis, with a lazy sprite°   *dull spirit*
And with a heavy, dark, disliking eye,
His louring brows o'erwhelming° his fair sight,   *overhanging*
Like misty vapours when they blot the sky,
185   Souring his cheeks,° cries, 'Fie, no more of love!   *Frowning*
    The sun doth burn my face; I must remove.'°   *leave*

'Ay me,' quoth Venus, 'young, and so unkind?°   *unnatural*
What bare° excuses mak'st thou to be gone?   *poor*
I'll sigh celestial breath, whose gentle wind
190 Shall cool the heat of this descending sun.
    I'll make a shadow for thee of my hairs;
    If they burn too, I'll quench them with my tears.

'The sun that shines from heaven shines but warm,°   *merely warms me*
And lo, I lie between that sun and thee.

---

8. Traditionally, Venus's chariot was drawn by swans or doves; see lines 1190–92.
9. In classical mythology, a young man who fell in love with his own image reflected in the water; after he pined to death, he was turned into a flower.

195 The heat I have from thence doth little harm;
Thine eye darts forth the fire that burneth me,
    And were I not immortal, life were done°   destroyed
    Between this heavenly and earthly sun.

'Art thou obdurate, flinty, hard as steel?
200 Nay, more than flint, for stone at rain relenteth.°   wears away
Art thou a woman's son, and canst not feel
What 'tis to love, how want of love° tormenteth?   being denied love
    O, had thy mother borne so hard a mind,
    She had not brought forth thee, but died unkind.

205 'What am I, that thou shouldst contemn° me this?   deny; scorn
Or what great danger dwells upon my suit?
What were thy lips the worse for one poor kiss?
Speak, fair; but speak fair words, or else be mute.
    Give me one kiss, I'll give it thee again,
210 And one for int'rest, if thou wilt have twain.

'Fie, lifeless picture, cold and senseless° stone,   insensible
Well painted idol, image dull and dead,
Statue contenting but the eye alone,
Thing like a man, but of no woman bred:
215 Thou art no man, though of a man's complexion,°   appearance
    For men will kiss even by their own direction.'°   inclination

This said, impatience chokes her pleading tongue,
And swelling passion doth provoke a pause.
Red cheeks and fiery eyes blaze forth° her wrong.   display; flame out
220 Being judge in love, she cannot right her cause;[1]
    And now she weeps, and now she fain° would speak,   gladly
    And now her sobs do her intendments° break.   intended words

Sometime she shakes her head, and then his hand;
Now gazeth she on him, now on the ground.
225 Sometime her arms enfold him like a band;°   fetter
She would, he will not in her arms be bound.
    And when from thence he struggles to be gone,
    She locks her lily fingers one in one.

'Fondling,'° she saith, 'since I have hemmed thee here   Foolish one; beloved
230 Within the circuit of this ivory pale,°   fence
I'll be a park, and thou shalt be my deer.
Feed where thou wilt, on mountain or in dale;
    Graze on my lips, and if those hills be dry,
    Stray lower, where the pleasant fountains lie.

235 'Within this limit is relief[2] enough,
Sweet bottom-grass,[3] and high delightful plain,
Round rising hillocks, brakes obscure and rough,°   dark, shaggy thickets
To shelter thee from tempest and from rain.

---

1. Although (or because) she is love's arbiter, she can-   3. Valley grass (pubic hair); Venus's body-landscape is
not win her own case.   intentionally suggestive throughout.
2. Pasture; variety of landscape; sexual gratification.

Then be my deer, since I am such a park;
240 No dog shall rouse thee,° though a thousand bark.'   *drive you from cover*

At this Adonis smiles as in disdain,
That in each cheek appears a pretty dimple.
Love made those hollows, if° himself were slain,   *so that if*
He might be buried in a tomb so simple,
245   Foreknowing well, if there he came to lie,
  Why, there love lived, and there he could not die.

These lovely caves, these round enchanting pits,
Opened their mouths to swallow Venus' liking.°   *to engulf her desire*
Being mad before, how doth she now for wits?[4]
250 Struck dead at first, what needs a second striking?
  Poor queen of love, in thine own law forlorn,°   *condemned to suffer*
  To love a cheek that smiles at thee in scorn!

Now which way shall she turn? What shall she say?
Her words are done, her woes the more increasing.
255 The time is spent; her object will away,
And from her twining arms doth urge releasing.
  'Pity,' she cries; 'some favour, some remorse!'°   *compassion*
  Away he springs, and hasteth to his horse.

But lo, from forth a copse° that neighbours by   *thicket*
260 A breeding jennet,° lusty, young, and proud,   *mare in heat*
Adonis' trampling courser doth espy,
And forth she rushes, snorts, and neighs aloud.
  The strong-necked steed, being tied unto a tree,
  Breaketh his rein, and to her straight goes he.

265 Imperiously he leaps, he neighs, he bounds,
And now his woven girths he breaks asunder.
The bearing[5] earth with his hard hoof he wounds,
Whose hollow womb resounds like heaven's thunder.
  The iron bit he crusheth 'tween his teeth,
270   Controlling what he was controllèd with.

His ears up-pricked, his braided hanging mane
Upon his compassed crest° now stand on end;   *arched neck*
His nostrils drink the air, and forth again,
As from a furnace, vapours doth he send.
275   His eye, which scornfully glisters like fire,
  Shows his hot courage° and his high desire.   *lust*

Sometime he trots, as if he told° the steps,   *counted*
With gentle majesty and modest pride.
Anon he rears upright, curvets,[6] and leaps,
280 As who° should say, 'Lo, thus my strength is tried,°   *one who / tested*
  And this I do to captivate the eye
  Of the fair breeder that is standing by.'

4. How does she keep her sanity now?   6. Bounds on his hind legs with raised forelegs.
5. Supporting; suffering; generative.

What recketh he° his rider's angry stir,°   *cares he about / noise*
His flattering° 'Holla', or his 'Stand, I say!'?   *cajoling*
285   What cares he now for curb° or pricking spur,   *bit*
For rich caparisons or trappings gay?
  He sees his love, and nothing else he sees,
  For nothing else with his proud sight agrees.

Look when° a painter would surpass the life   *Just as*
290   In limning out° a well proportioned steed,   *depicting*
His art with nature's workmanship at strife,
As if the dead the living should exceed:
  So did this horse excel a common one
  In shape, in courage, colour, pace, and bone.°   *frame*

295   Round-hoofed, short-jointed, fetlocks shag and long,⁷
Broad breast, full eye, small head, and nostril wide,
High crest, short ears, straight legs, and passing° strong;   *extremely*
Thin mane, thick tail, broad buttock, tender hide—
  Look what° a horse should have he did not lack,   *Whatever*
300   Save a proud rider on so proud a back.

Sometime he scuds far off, and there he stares;
Anon he starts at stirring of a feather.
To bid the wind a base⁸ he now prepares,
And whe'er° he run or fly they know not whether;°   *whether / which*
305   For through his mane and tail the high wind sings,
  Fanning the hairs, who wave like feathered wings.

He looks upon his love, and neighs unto her;
She answers him as if she knew his mind.
Being proud, as females are, to see him woo her,
310   She puts on outward strangeness,° seems unkind,   *reserve*
  Spurns at° his love, and scorns the heat he feels,   *Repels; kicks*
  Beating his kind° embracements with her heels.   *amorous; natural*

Then, like a melancholy malcontent,
He vails° his tail that, like a falling plume,   *lowers*
315   Cool shadow to his melting buttock lent.
He stamps, and bites the poor flies in his fume.°   *anger*
  His love, perceiving how he was enraged,
  Grew kinder, and his fury was assuaged.

His testy° master goeth about° to take him,   *angry / tries*
320   When lo, the unbacked breeder,⁹ full of fear,
Jealous of catching,° swiftly doth forsake him,   *Fearful of being caught*
With her the horse, and left Adonis there.
  As they were mad unto the wood they hie them,
  Outstripping crows that strive to overfly them.

325   All swoll'n with chafing,° down Adonis sits,   *anger*
Banning° his boist'rous and unruly beast;   *Cursing*

---

7. *short-jointed . . . long:* with short pasterns (the bone   8. To dare the wind to run (from a children's game,
just above the horse's hoof) and shaggy joints above the   prisoner's base).
hooves.   9. Mare without mount (rider or stallion).

And now the happy season once more fits°   *is suited*
That lovesick love by pleading may be blessed;
    For lovers say the heart hath treble wrong
330   When it is barred the aidance of the tongue.

An oven that is stopped, or river stayed,°   *dammed*
Burneth more hotly, swelleth with more rage.
So of concealèd sorrow may be said
Free vent of words love's fire doth assuage.
335   But when the heart's attorney° once is mute,   *pleader (the tongue)*
    The client breaks,[1] as desperate in his suit.

He sees her coming, and begins to glow,
Even as a dying coal revives with wind,
And with his bonnet° hides his angry brow,   *hat*
340 Looks on the dull earth with disturbèd mind,
    Taking no notice that she is so nigh,
    For all askance he holds her in his eye.

O, what a sight it was wistly° to view   *intently*
How she came stealing to the wayward boy,
345 To note the fighting conflict of her hue,
How white and red each other did destroy!
    But now her cheek was pale; and by and by
    It flashed forth fire, as lightning from the sky.

Now was she just before him as he sat,
350 And like a lowly lover down she kneels;
With one fair hand she heaveth up his hat;
Her other tender hand his fair cheek feels.
    His tend'rer cheek receives her soft hand's print
    As apt as new-fall'n snow takes any dint.°   *dent*

355 O, what a war of looks was then between them,
Her eyes petitioners to his eyes suing!
His eyes saw her eyes as they had not seen them;
Her eyes wooed still; his eyes disdained the wooing;
    And all this dumb play had his° acts made plain   *its*
360   With tears which, chorus-like, her eyes did rain.[2]

Full gently now she takes him by the hand,
A lily prisoned in a jail of snow,
Or ivory in an alabaster band;
So white a friend engirds so white a foe.
365   This beauteous combat, wilful and unwilling,
    Showed° like two silver doves that sit a-billing.   *Looked*

Once more the engine of her thoughts began:
'O fairest mover on this mortal round,°   *earth*
Would thou wert as I am, and I a man,
370 My heart all whole as thine, thy heart my wound;°   *suffering my wound*

1. Breaks apart; goes bankrupt.
2. Venus's tears interpret her mute gestures as the chorus in a play explains a dumb show.

For one sweet look thy help I would assure thee,
Though nothing but my body's bane° would cure thee.'   *destruction*

'Give me my hand,' saith he. 'Why dost thou feel it?'
'Give me my heart,' saith she, 'and thou shalt have it.
375   O, give it me, lest thy hard heart do steel it,³
And, being steeled, soft sighs can never grave° it;   *engrave*
Then love's deep groans I never shall regard,
Because Adonis' heart hath made mine hard.'

'For shame,' he cries, 'let go, and let me go!
380   My day's delight is past; my horse is gone,
And 'tis your fault I am bereft him so.
I pray you hence, and leave me here alone;
For all my mind, my thought, my busy care
Is how to get my palfrey° from the mare.'   *riding horse*

385   Thus she replies: 'Thy palfrey, as he should,
Welcomes the warm approach of sweet desire.
Affection° is a coal that must be cooled,   *Passion*
Else, suffered,° it will set the heart on fire.   *allowed to persist*
The sea hath bounds, but deep desire hath none;
390   Therefore no marvel though thy horse be gone.

'How like a jade° he stood tied to the tree,   *nag*
Servilely mastered with a leathern rein!
But when he saw his love, his youth's fair fee,°   *reward*
He held such petty bondage in disdain,
395   Throwing the base thong from his bending crest,
Enfranchising his mouth, his back, his breast.

'Who sees his true-love in her naked bed,
Teaching the sheets a whiter hue than white,
But when his glutton eye so full hath fed
400   His other agents° aim at like delight?   *faculties*
Who is so faint that dares not be so bold
To touch the fire, the weather being cold?

'Let me excuse thy courser, gentle boy;
And learn of him, I heartily beseech thee,
405   To take advantage on° presented joy.   *of*
Though I were dumb, yet his proceedings teach thee.
O, learn to love! The lesson is but plain,
And, once made perfect,° never lost again.'   *learned by heart*

'I know not love,' quoth he, 'nor will not know it,
410   Unless it be a boar, and then I chase it.
'Tis much to borrow, and I will not owe it.
My love to love is love but to disgrace it;⁴
For I have heard it is a life in death,
That laughs and weeps, and all but with a breath.

3. Turn my heart to steel; steal my heart.   4. My only interest in love is in discrediting it.

415 'Who wears a garment shapeless and unfinished?
Who plucks the bud before one leaf put forth?
If springing° things be any jot diminished,   °immature
They wither in their prime, prove nothing worth.
 The colt that's backed° and burdened being young,   °ridden
420 Loseth his pride, and never waxeth strong.

'You hurt my hand with wringing. Let us part,
And leave this idle° theme, this bootless° chat.   °useless / pointless
Remove your siege from my unyielding heart;
To love's alarms° it will not ope the gate.   °assaults
425 Dismiss your vows, your feignèd tears, your flatt'ry;
 For where a heart is hard they make no batt'ry.'°   °breach

'What, canst thou talk?' quoth she. 'Hast thou a tongue?
O, would thou hadst not, or I had no hearing!
Thy mermaid's voice[5] hath done me double wrong.
430 I had my load before, now pressed° with bearing: °oppressed
 Melodious discord, heavenly tune harsh sounding,
 Ears' deep-sweet music, and heart's deep-sore wounding.

'Had I no eyes but ears, my ears would love
That inward beauty and invisible;
435 Or were I deaf, thy outward parts would move
Each part in me that were but sensible.°   °perceiving
 Though neither eyes nor ears to hear nor see,
 Yet should I be in love by touching thee.

'Say that the sense of feeling were bereft me,
440 And that I could not see, nor hear, nor touch,
And nothing but the very smell were left me,
Yet would my love to thee be still as much;
 For from the stillitory[6] of thy face excelling°   °incomparable
 Comes breath perfumed, that breedeth love by smelling.

445 'But O, what banquet wert thou to the taste,
Being nurse and feeder of the other four!
Would they not wish the feast might ever last
And bid suspicion° double-lock the door   °wariness
 Lest jealousy, that sour unwelcome guest,
450 Should by his stealing-in disturb the feast?'

Once more the ruby-coloured portal° opened   °threshold (mouth)
Which to his speech did honey passage yield,
Like a red morn that ever yet betokened
Wrack° to the seaman, tempest to the field,   °Shipwreck
455 Sorrow to shepherds, woe unto the birds,
 Gusts and foul flaws° to herdmen and to herds.   °winds

This ill presage advisedly she marketh.[7]
Even as the wind is hushed before it raineth,
Or as the wolf doth grin° before he barketh,   °show his teeth

5. Which, irresistible in song, was supposed to lure sailors onto rocks.
6. Apparatus used to distill perfume.
7. She notices this bad omen carefully.

460 Or as the berry breaks before it staineth,
　　Or like the deadly bullet of a gun,
　　His meaning struck her ere his words begun,

And at his look she flatly falleth down,
For looks kill love, and love by looks reviveth;
465 A smile recures° the wounding of a frown,　　　　　　　　　　　*cures*
But blessèd bankrupt that by loss so thriveth!
　　The silly° boy, believing she is dead,　　　　　　　　　　　*naive*
　　Claps her pale cheek till clapping makes it red,

And, all amazed,° brake° off his late intent,　　　　　*perplexed / broke*
470 For sharply he did think to reprehend her,
Which cunning love did wittily prevent.
Fair fall[8] the wit that can so well defend her!
　　For on the grass she lies as she were slain,
　　Till his breath breatheth life in her again.

475 He wrings her nose, he strikes her on the cheeks,
He bends her fingers, holds her pulses hard;°　　　　　*takes her pulse*
He chafes her lips; a thousand ways he seeks
To mend the hurt that his unkindness marred.°　　　*caused to injure her*
　　He kisses her; and she, by her good will,°　　　　　　　　*consent*
480　　Will never rise, so he will kiss her still.°　　　　　　*keep kissing her*

The night of sorrow now is turned to day.
Her two blue windows° faintly she upheaveth,　　　　　　*(her eyes)*
Like the fair sun when, in his fresh array,
He cheers the morn, and all the earth relieveth;
485　　And as the bright sun glorifies the sky,
　　So is her face illumined with her eye,

Whose beams upon his hairless face are fixed,
As if from thence they borrowed all their shine.
Were never four such lamps together mixed,
490 Had not his clouded with his brow's repine.°　　　　　　*discontent*
　　But hers, which through the crystal tears gave light,
　　Shone like the moon in water seen by night.

'O, where am I?' quoth she; 'in earth or heaven,
Or in the ocean drenched,° or in the fire?　　　　　　　　*submerged*
495 What hour is this: or° morn or weary even?°　　　　*either / evening*
Do I delight to die, or life desire?
　　But now I lived, and life was death's annoy;°　　　　*deathly pain*
　　But now I died, and death was lively° joy.　　　　　　　*living*

'O, thou didst kill me; kill me once again!
500 Thy eyes' shrewd° tutor, that hard heart of thine,　　　　　*stern*
Hath taught them scornful tricks, and such disdain
That they have murdered this poor heart of mine,
　　And these mine eyes, true leaders° to their queen,　　　　*guides*
　　But for thy piteous° lips no more had seen.　　　　　　*pitying*

8. Good luck befall (with wordplay on "fall down").

505 'Long may they kiss each other, for this cure!
O, never let their crimson liveries wear,°   *wear out*
And as they last, their verdure° still endure
To drive infection from the dangerous year,
  That the star-gazers, having writ on death,°   *predicted plague*
510   May say the plague is banished by thy breath!

'Pure lips, sweet seals in my soft lips imprinted,
What bargains may I make still to be sealing?°   *kissing; making deals*
To sell myself I can be well contented,
So° thou wilt buy, and pay, and use good dealing;   *If*
515   Which purchase if thou make, for fear of slips°   *fraud*
  Set thy seal manual° on my wax-red lips.   *identifying stamp*

'A thousand kisses buys my heart from me;
And pay them at thy leisure, one by one.
What is ten hundred touches° unto thee?   *(of the lips)*
520 Are they not quickly told,° and quickly gone?   *counted*
  Say for non-payment that the debt should double,
  Is twenty hundred kisses such a trouble?'

'Fair queen,' quoth he, 'if any love you owe me,
Measure my strangeness° with my unripe years.   *Explain my coldness*
525 Before I know myself, seek not to know me.
No fisher but the ungrown fry forbears.[1]
  The mellow plum doth fall, the green sticks fast,
  Or, being early plucked, is sour to taste.

'Look, the world's comforter° with weary gait   *(the sun)*
530 His day's hot task hath ended in the west.
The owl, night's herald, shrieks 'tis very late;
The sheep are gone to fold, birds to their nest,
  And coal-black clouds, that shadow heaven's light,
  Do summon us to part and bid good night.

535 'Now let me say good night, and so say you.
If you will say so, you shall have a kiss.'
'Good night,' quoth she; and ere he says adieu
The honey° fee of parting tendered° is.   *sweet / given*
  Her arms do lend his neck a sweet embrace.
540   Incorporate° then they seem; face grows to face,   *United in one body*

Till breathless he disjoined, and backward drew
The heavenly moisture, that sweet coral mouth,
Whose precious taste her thirsty lips well knew,
Whereon they surfeit, yet complain on drought.
545   He with her plenty pressed, she faint with dearth,
  Their lips together glued, fall to the earth.

Now quick desire hath caught the yielding prey,
And glutton-like she feeds, yet never filleth.
Her lips are conquerors, his lips obey,

---

9. Literally, greenness; here, freshness. The lips ward   1. Every fisherman spares the young fish.
off disease as fresh parsley was believed to do.

550   Paying what ransom the insulter° willeth,   *conqueror*
      Whose vulture° thought doth pitch the price so high   *ravenous*
      That she will draw his lips' rich treasure dry,

      And, having felt the sweetness of the spoil,
      With blindfold fury she begins to forage.
555   Her face doth reek° and smoke, her blood doth boil,   *steam*
      And careless° lust stirs up a desperate courage,   *reckless*
        Planting° oblivion, beating reason back,   *Implanting*
        Forgetting shame's pure blush and honour's wrack.°   *ruin*

      Hot, faint, and weary with her hard embracing,
560   Like a wild bird being tamed with too much handling,
      Or as the fleet-foot roe that's tired with chasing,
      Or like the froward° infant stilled with dandling,   *fretful*
        He now obeys, and now no more resisteth,
        While she takes all she can, not all she listeth.°   *desires*

565   What wax so frozen but dissolves with temp'ring°   *fingering*
      And yields at last to every light impression?
      Things out of° hope are compassed° oft with vent'ring,   *beyond / accomplished*
      Chiefly in love, whose leave° exceeds commission.°   *liberty / warrant*
        Affection faints° not, like a pale-faced coward,   *Passion relents*
570   But then woos best when most his choice is froward.

      When he did frown, O, had she then gave over,
      Such nectar from his lips she had not sucked.
      Foul° words and frowns must not repel a lover.   *Harsh*
      What though the rose have prickles, yet 'tis plucked!
575   Were beauty under twenty locks kept fast,
        Yet love breaks through, and picks them all at last.

      For pity now she can no more detain him.
      The poor fool° prays her that he may depart.   *(term of affection)*
      She is resolved no longer to restrain him,
580   Bids him farewell, and look well to° her heart,   *take good care of*
        The which, by Cupid's bow she doth protest,
        He carries thence encagèd in his breast.

      'Sweet boy,' she says, 'this night I'll waste in sorrow,
      For my sick heart commands mine eyes to watch.
585   Tell me, love's master, shall we meet tomorrow?
      Say, shall we, shall we? Wilt thou make the match?'
        He tells her no, tomorrow he intends
        To hunt the boar with certain of his friends.

      'The boar!' quoth she; whereat a sudden pale,
590   Like lawn° being spread upon the blushing rose,   *fine linen*
      Usurps her cheek. She trembles at his tale,
      And on his neck her yoking arms she throws.
        She sinketh down, still hanging by his neck.
        He on her belly falls, she on her back.

595 Now is she in the very lists² of love,
Her champion mounted for the hot encounter.
All is imaginary she doth prove.³
He will not manage her,° although he mount her,   *ride her (like a horse)*
That worse than Tantalus' is her annoy,⁴
600 To clip Elysium,⁵ and to lack her joy.

Even so poor birds, deceived with painted grapes,
Do surfeit by the eye, and pine the maw;⁶
Even so she languisheth in her mishaps
As° those poor birds that helpless° berries saw.   *Like / unusable*
605 The warm effects° which she in him finds missing   *outward signs*
She seeks to kindle with continual kissing.

But all in vain, good queen! It will not be.
She hath assayed° as much as may be proved;°   *attempted / tried*
Her pleading hath deserved a greater fee:⁷
610 She's Love; she loves; and yet she is not loved.
'Fie, fie,' he says, 'you crush me. Let me go.
You have no reason to withhold me so.'

'Thou hadst been gone,' quoth she, 'sweet boy, ere this,
But that thou told'st me thou wouldst hunt the boar.
615 O, be advised; thou know'st not what it is
With javelin's point a churlish swine to gore,
Whose tushes,° never sheathed, he whetteth still,°   *tusks / continually*
Like to a mortal° butcher, bent° to kill.   *deadly / intending*

'On his bow-back° he hath a battle⁸ set   *arched back*
620 Of bristly pikes that ever threat his foes.
His eyes like glow-worms shine; when he doth fret
His snout digs sepulchres where'er he goes.
Being moved,° he strikes, whate'er is in his way,   *angered*
And whom he strikes his crooked tushes slay.

625 'His brawny sides with hairy bristles armed
Are better proof° than thy spear's point can enter.   *armor*
His short thick neck cannot be easily harmed.
Being ireful,° on the lion he will venture.   *angry*
The thorny brambles and embracing bushes,
630 As° fearful of him, part; through whom° he rushes.   *As if / which*

'Alas, he naught esteems that face of thine,
To which love's eyes pays tributary gazes,
Nor thy soft hands, sweet lips, and crystal eyne,°   *eyes (archaic)*
Whose full perfection all the world amazes;
635 But having thee at vantage°—wondrous dread!—   *his mercy*
Would root° these beauties as he roots the mead.°   *root up / meadow*

---

2. Enclosed tournament arena.
3. The hot encounter is only imaginary, she finds.
4. Torment. In classical mythology, Tantalus was punished by eternal hunger and thirst; food and water were always visible but receded at his approach.
5. In classical mythology, the abode of the blessed dead. *clip*: embrace.
6. Starve the stomach. The ancient Greek artist Zeuxis painted grapes so realistic that birds pecked at them.
7. A legal metaphor: Venus, acting as an attorney, deserves a better payment.
8. Row of armed soldiers.

'O, let him keep° his loathsome cabin° still.   *stay in / lair*
Beauty hath naught to do with such foul fiends.
Come not within his danger by thy will.
640   They that thrive well take counsel of their friends.
      When thou didst name the boar, not to dissemble,⁹
      I feared thy fortune, and my joints did tremble.

'Didst thou not mark my face? Was it not white?
Saw'st thou not signs of fear lurk in mine eye?
645   Grew I not faint, and fell I not downright?
Within my bosom, whereon thou dost lie,
      My boding heart pants, beats, and takes no rest,
      But like an earthquake shakes thee on my breast.

'For where love reigns, disturbing jealousy°   *apprehension*
650   Doth call himself affection's sentinel,
Gives false alarms, suggesteth mutiny,°   *incites rebellion*
And in a peaceful hour doth cry, "Kill, kill!",°   *(a battle cry)*
      Distemp'ring° gentle love in his desire,   *Quenching*
      As air and water do abate the fire.

655   'This sour informer, this bate-breeding° spy,   *conflict-breeding*
This canker° that eats up love's tender spring,°   *cankerworm / sprout*
This carry-tale, dissentious jealousy,
That sometime true news, sometime false doth bring,
      Knocks at my heart, and whispers in mine ear
660   That if I love thee, I thy death should fear;

'And, more than so, presenteth to mine eye
The picture of an angry chafing boar,
Under whose sharp fangs on his back doth lie
An image like thyself, all stained with gore,
665   Whose blood upon the fresh flowers being shed
      Doth make them droop with grief, and hang the head.

'What should I do, seeing thee so indeed,
That tremble at th'imagination?
The thought of it doth make my faint heart bleed,
670   And fear doth teach it divination.
      I prophesy thy death, my living sorrow,
      If thou encounter with the boar tomorrow.

'But if thou needs wilt hunt, be ruled by me:
Uncouple° at the timorous flying° hare,   *Unleash the dogs / fleeing*
675   Or at the fox which lives by subtlety,
Or at the roe which no encounter dare.
      Pursue these fearful° creatures o'er the downs,   *timid*
      And on thy well-breathed horse keep with thy hounds.

'And when thou hast on foot the purblind° hare,   *dim-sighted*
680   Mark the poor wretch, to overshoot° his troubles,   *run past*
How he outruns the wind, and with what care
He cranks and crosses° with a thousand doubles.   *twists and turns*

9. *not to dissemble*: to tell the truth.

The many musits° through the which he goes   *hedge gaps*
Are like a labyrinth to amaze° his foes.   *confuse*

685 'Sometime he runs among a flock of sheep
To make the cunning hounds mistake their smell,
And sometime where earth-delving conies° keep,   *rabbits*
To stop the loud pursuers in their yell;
    And sometime sorteth° with a herd of deer,   *consorts*
690   Danger deviseth shifts;° wit waits on fear.   *tricks*

'For there his smell with others being mingled,
The hot scent-snuffing hounds are driven to doubt,
Ceasing their clamorous cry till they have singled,
With much ado, the cold fault° cleanly out.   *lost scent*
695   Then do they spend their mouths.° Echo replies,   *give tongue*
    As if another chase were in the skies.

'By this, poor Wat,° far off upon a hill,   *(name for a hare)*
Stands on his hinder legs with list'ning ear,
To hearken if his foes pursue him still.
700 Anon their loud alarums he doth hear,
    And now his grief may be comparèd well
    To one sore sick that hears the passing-bell.[1]

'Then shalt thou see the dew-bedabbled wretch
Turn, and return, indenting° with the way.   *zigzagging*
705 Each envious° brier his weary legs do scratch;   *malicious*
Each shadow makes him stop, each murmur stay;
    For misery is trodden on by many,
    And, being low, never relieved by any.

'Lie quietly, and hear a little more;
710 Nay, do not struggle, for thou shalt not rise.
To make thee hate the hunting of the boar
Unlike myself thou hear'st me moralize,[2]
    Applying° this to that, and so to so,   *Showing the pertinence of*
    For love can comment upon every woe.

715 'Where did I leave?'° 'No matter where,' quoth he;   *leave off*
'Leave me, and then the story aptly ends.
The night is spent.' 'Why what of that?' quoth she.
'I am,' quoth he, 'expected of° my friends,   *by*
    And now 'tis dark, and going I shall fall.'
720   'In night,' quoth she, 'desire sees best of all.

'But if thou fall, O, then imagine this:
The earth, in love with thee, thy footing trips,
And all is but to rob thee of a kiss.
Rich preys° make true° men thieves; so do thy lips   *spoils / honest*
725   Make modest Dian[3] cloudy and forlorn
    Lest she should steal a kiss, and die forsworn.[4]

---

1. Bell tolled for one who has just died.
2. Although I (the goddess of love) do not usually make moral points, I do so now.
3. Goddess of the moon, hunting, and virginity, also called "Cynthia" (line 728); "cloudy" because covered with clouds and because made sorrowful by her love of Adonis.
4. Die having violated her oath of chastity.

'Now of this dark night I perceive the reason.
Cynthia, for shame, obscures her silver shine
Till forging° nature be condemned of treason   *counterfeiting*
730   For stealing moulds from heaven, that were divine,
    Wherein she framed thee, in high heaven's despite,°   *defiance*
    To shame the sun by day and her by night.

'And therefore hath she bribed the destinies
To cross the curious° workmanship of nature,   *elaborate*
735   To mingle beauty with infirmities,
    And pure perfection with impure defeature,°   *disfigurement*
      Making it subject to the tyranny
      Of mad mischances and much misery;

'As burning fevers, agues pale and faint,
740   Life-poisoning pestilence, and frenzies wood,°   *insane fits*
The marrow-eating sickness⁵ whose attaint°   *infection*
Disorder breeds by heating of the blood;
    Surfeits, impostumes,° grief, and damned despair   *abscesses*
    Swear nature's death for framing° thee so fair.   *making*

745   'And not the least of all these maladies
But in one minute's fight brings beauty under.
Both favour, savour,° hue, and qualities,   *beauty; smell*
Whereat th'impartial gazer late did wonder,
    Are on the sudden wasted,° thawed, and done,   *wasted away*
750   As mountain snow melts with the midday sun.

'Therefore, despite of fruitless° chastity,   *defying barren*
Love-lacking vestals and self-loving nuns,
That on the earth would breed a scarcity
And barren dearth of daughters and of sons,
755   Be prodigal. The lamp that burns by night
      Dries up his oil to lend the world his light.

'What is thy body but a swallowing grave,
Seeming to bury that posterity
Which, by the rights of time, thou needs must have
760   If thou destroy them not in dark obscurity?
    If so, the world will hold thee in disdain,
    Sith° in thy pride so fair a hope is slain.   *Since*

'So in thyself thyself art made away,°   *destroyed*
A mischief° worse than civil, home-bred strife,   *An evil*
765   Or theirs whose desperate hands themselves do slay,
Or butcher sire that reaves° his son of life.   *robs*
    Foul cank'ring rust the hidden treasure frets,°   *eats away*
    But gold that's put to use more gold begets.'

'Nay, then,' quoth Adon, 'You will fall again
770   Into your idle,° over-handled theme.   *unprofitable*
The kiss I gave you is bestowed in vain,
And all in vain you strive against the stream;

5. Syphilis, which attacks the bones.

For, by this black-faced night, desire's foul nurse,
Your treatise° makes me like you worse and worse.   *discussion; plea*

775 'If love have lent you twenty thousand tongues,
And every tongue more moving than your own,
Bewitching like the wanton mermaid's songs,
Yet from mine ear the tempting tune is blown;
For know, my heart stands armèd in mine ear,
780   And will not let a false sound enter there,

'Lest the deceiving harmony should run
Into the quiet closure° of my breast,   *enclosure*
And then my little heart were quite undone,
In his bedchamber to be barred of rest.
785   No, lady, no. My heart longs not to groan,
        But soundly sleeps, while now it sleeps alone.

'What have you urged that I cannot reprove?
The path is smooth that leadeth on to danger.
I hate not love, but your device° in love,   *tactics*
790 That lends embracements unto every stranger.
        You do it for increase—O strange excuse,
        When reason is the bawd to lust's abuse!

'Call it not love, for love to heaven is fled
Since sweating lust on earth usurped his name,
795 Under whose simple° semblance he hath fed   *innocent*
Upon fresh beauty, blotting it with blame;
        Which the hot tyrant stains, and soon bereaves,
        As caterpillars do the tender leaves.

'Love comforteth, like sunshine after rain,
800 But lust's effect is tempest after sun.
Love's gentle spring doth always fresh remain;
Lust's winter comes ere summer half be done.
        Love surfeits not; lust like a glutton dies.
        Love is all truth, lust full of forgèd lies.

805 'More I could tell, but more I dare not say;
The text is old, the orator too green.
Therefore in sadness° now I will away;   *truly*
My face is full of shame, my heart of teen.°   *grief*
        Mine ears that to your wanton talk attended
810   Do burn themselves for having so offended.'

With this he breaketh from the sweet embrace
Of those fair arms which bound him to her breast,
And homeward through the dark laund° runs apace,   *glade*
Leaves love upon her back, deeply distressed.
815   Look how a bright star shooteth from the sky,
        So glides he in the night from Venus' eye,

Which after him she darts, as one on shore
Gazing upon a late-embarkèd friend
Till the wild waves will have him seen no more,

820 Whose ridges with the meeting clouds contend.
   So did the merciless and pitchy night
   Fold in the object that did feed her sight.

   Whereat amazed,° as one that unaware   *shocked*
   Hath dropped a precious jewel in the flood,
825 Or stonished,° as night wand'rers often are,   *confused*
   Their light blown out in some mistrustful° wood: *anxiety-producing*
      Even so, confounded in the dark she lay,
      Having lost the fair discovery of her way.[6]

   And now she beats her heart, whereat it groans,
830 That all the neighbour caves, as seeming troubled,
   Make verbal repetition of her moans;
   Passion° on passion deeply is redoubled.   *Lamentation*
      'Ay me,' she cries, and twenty times 'Woe, woe!'
      And twenty echoes twenty times cry so.

835 She, marking them, begins a wailing note,
   And sings extemporally a woeful ditty,
   How love makes young men thrall,° and old men dote,   *enslaved*
   How love is wise in folly, foolish-witty.
      Her heavy° anthem still concludes in woe,   *sorrowful*
840   And still the choir of echoes answer so.

   Her song was tedious, and outwore the night;
   For lovers' hours are long, though seeming short.
   If pleased themselves, others, they think, delight
   In such-like circumstance, with such-like sport.
845   Their copious stories oftentimes begun
      End without audience, and are never done.

   For who hath she to spend the night withal°   *with*
   But idle sounds resembling parasites,°   *flattering hangers-on*
   Like shrill-tongued tapsters° answering every call,   *tavern keepers*
850 Soothing the humour of fantastic wits?[7]
      She says ''Tis so'; they answer all ''Tis so',
      And would say after her, if she said 'No'.

   Lo, here the gentle lark, weary of rest,
   From his moist cabinet° mounts up on high   *nest*
855 And wakes the morning,° from whose silver breast   *(Aurora)*
   The sun ariseth in his majesty,
      Who doth the world so gloriously behold
      That cedar tops and hills seem burnished gold.

   Venus salutes him with this fair good-morrow:
860 'O thou clear° god, and patron of all light,   *bright*
   From whom each lamp and shining star doth borrow
   The beauteous influence[8] that makes him bright:

---

6. *the fair . . . way*: a clear view of her path; a beautiful
guide.
7. Catering to the moods of erratic people.

8. The ethereal stream that in Renaissance astrology
was supposed to flow from stars and planets.

There lives a son° that sucked an earthly mother   (Adonis)
May° lend thee light, as thou dost lend to other.'   Who may

865   This said, she hasteth to a myrtle grove,
Musing° the morning is so much o'erworn°   Wondering / spent
And yet she hears no tidings of her love.
She hearkens for his hounds, and for his horn.
    Anon she hears them chant it lustily,°   sing out heartily
870   And all in haste she coasteth° to the cry.   rushes

And as she runs, the bushes in the way
Some catch her by the neck, some kiss her face,
Some twine about her thigh to make her stay.
She wildly breaketh from their strict° embrace,   restricting
875   Like a milch° doe whose swelling dugs° do ache,   milk / udders
    Hasting to feed her fawn hid in some brake.°   thicket

By this° she hears the hounds are at a bay,[9]   By now
Whereat she starts, like one that spies an adder
Wreathed up in fatal folds just in his way,
880 The fear whereof doth make him shake and shudder;
    Even so the timorous yelping of the hounds
    Appals her senses, and her spirit confounds.

For now she knows it is no gentle chase,
But the blunt° boar, rough bear, or lion proud,   rude
885 Because the cry remaineth in one place,
Where fearfully the dogs exclaim aloud.
    Finding their enemy to be so curst,°   vicious
    They all strain court'sy[1] who shall cope° him first.   contend with

This dismal cry rings sadly in her ear,
890 Through which it enters to surprise° her heart,   assault
Who, overcome by doubt and bloodless fear,
With cold-pale weakness numbs each feeling part;°   sense organ
    Like soldiers when their captain once doth yield,
    They basely fly, and dare not stay° the field.   remain in

895 Thus stands she in a trembling ecstasy,°   stupor
Till, cheering up her senses all dismayed,
She tells them 'tis a causeless fantasy
And childish error that they are afraid;
    Bids them leave quaking, bids them fear no more;
900   And with that word she spied the hunted boar,

Whose frothy mouth, bepainted all with red,
Like milk and blood being mingled both together,
A second fear through all her sinews spread,
Which madly hurries her, she knows not whither.
905   This way she runs, and now she will no further,
    But back retires to rate° the boar for murder.   berate

---

9. Stopped by the quarry, which is making a stand.   1. Politely defer to one another.

A thousand spleens° bear her a thousand ways.   impulses
She treads the path that she untreads again.
Her more than haste is mated° with delays,   counteracted
910 Like the proceedings of a drunken brain,
    Full of respects,° yet naught at all respecting;   considerations
    In hand with all things, naught at all effecting.[2]

Here kennelled in a brake she finds a hound,
And asks the weary caitiff° for his master;   wretch
915 And there another licking of his wound,
    'Gainst venomed sores the only sovereign plaster.°   effective remedy
    And here she meets another, sadly scowling,
    To whom she speaks; and he replies with howling.

When he hath ceased his ill-resounding noise,
920 Another flap-mouthed mourner, black and grim,
Against the welkin° volleys out his voice.   sky
Another, and another, answer him,
    Clapping their proud tails to the ground below,
    Shaking their scratched ears, bleeding as they go.

925 Look how the world's poor people are amazed
At apparitions, signs, and prodigies,°   strange occurrences
Whereon with fearful eyes they long have gazed,
Infusing them with° dreadful prophecies: Reading into them
    So she at these sad signs draws up her breath,
930 And, sighing it again, exclaims on° death.   berates

'Hard-favoured tyrant, ugly, meagre, lean,
Hateful divorce of love'—thus chides she death;
'Grim-grinning° ghost, earth's worm: what dost thou mean   (like a skull)
To stifle beauty, and to steal his breath
935 Who, when he lived, his breath and beauty set
    Gloss on the rose, smell to the violet?

'If he be dead—O no, it cannot be,
Seeing his beauty, thou shouldst strike at it.
O yes, it may; thou hast no eyes to see,[3]
940 But hatefully, at random dost thou hit.
    Thy mark° is feeble age; but thy false dart   target
    Mistakes that aim, and cleaves an infant's heart.

'Hadst thou but bid beware, then he° had spoke,   (Adonis)
And, hearing him, thy power had lost his° power.   its
945 The destinies will curse thee for this stroke.
They bid thee crop a weed; thou pluck'st a flower.
    Love's golden arrow at him should have fled,°   flown
    And not death's ebon dart to strike him dead.

'Dost thou drink tears, that thou provok'st such weeping?
950 What may a heavy groan advantage° thee?   benefit
Why hast thou cast into eternal sleeping
Those eyes that taught all other eyes to see?

2. Full of notions, yet actually attending to nothing.   3. Death's eye sockets are empty, like a skull's.

Now nature cares not for thy mortal vigour,[4]
Since her best work is ruined with thy rigour.'

955   Here overcome, as one full of despair,
    She vailed° her eyelids, who like sluices stopped   *lowered*
    The crystal tide that from her two cheeks fair
    In the sweet channel of her bosom dropped.
        But through the flood-gates breaks the silver rain,
960   And with his strong course opens them again.

    O, how her eyes and tears did lend and borrow!°   *(by reflection)*
    Her eye seen in the tears, tears in her eye,
    Both crystals, where they viewed each other's sorrow:
    Sorrow, that friendly° sighs sought still to dry,   *consoling; like-minded*
965   But, like a stormy day, now wind, now rain,
        Sighs dry her cheeks, tears make them wet again.

    Variable passions throng her constant woe,
    As striving who should best become° her grief.   *fit*
    All entertained,° each passion labours so   *permitted to enter*
970   That every present sorrow seemeth chief,
        But none is best. Then join they all together,
        Like many clouds consulting° for foul weather.   *gathering*

    By this, far off she hears some huntsman hollo;°   *(hunting call)*
    A nurse's song ne'er pleased her babe so well.
975   The dire imagination° she did follow   *train of thought*
    This sound of hope doth labour to expel;
        For now reviving joy bids her rejoice
        And flatters her it is Adonis' voice.

    Whereat her tears began to turn their tide,°   *to ebb*
980   Being prisoned in her eye like pearls in glass;
    Yet sometimes falls an orient° drop beside,   *a glistening*
    Which her cheek melts, as° scorning it should pass   *as if*
        To wash the foul° face of the sluttish ground,   *dirty*
        Who is but drunken when she seemeth drowned.

985   O hard-believing love—how strange it seems
    Not to believe, and yet too credulous!
    Thy weal° and woe are both of them extremes.   *prosperity*
    Despair, and hope, makes thee ridiculous.
        The one doth flatter thee in thoughts unlikely;
990   In likely thoughts the other kills thee quickly.

    Now she unweaves the web that she hath wrought.
    Adonis lives, and death is not to blame.
    It was not she that called him all to naught.[5]
    Now she adds honours to his hateful name.
995   She clepes° him king of graves, and grave for kings,   *calls (archaic)*
        Imperious supreme° of all mortal things.   *Imperial ruler*

---

4. Nature does not heed your lethal power.   5. She who called Death everything bad.

'No, no,' quoth she, 'sweet death, I did but jest.
Yet pardon me, I felt a kind of fear
Whenas I met the boar, that bloody beast,
1000   Which knows no pity, but is still severe.
      Then, gentle shadow—truth I must confess—
      I railed on thee, fearing my love's decease.

''Tis not my fault; the boar provoked my tongue.
Be wreaked° on him, invisible commander.   *revenged*
1005   'Tis he, foul creature, that hath done thee wrong.
I did but act;° he's author of thy slander.   *(as an agent)*
      Grief hath two tongues,° and never woman yet   *is doubly loud*
      Could rule them both, without ten women's wit.'

Thus, hoping that Adonis is alive,
1010   Her rash suspect° she doth extenuate,   *suspicion*
And, that his beauty may the better thrive,
With death she humbly doth insinuate;°   *curry favor*
      Tells him of trophies, statues, tombs; and stories
      His victories, his triumphs, and his glories.

1015   'O Jove,' quoth she, 'how much a fool was I
To be of such a weak and silly mind
To wail his death who lives, and must not die
Till mutual° overthrow of mortal kind!   *universal*
      For he being dead, with him is beauty slain,
1020   And beauty dead, black chaos comes again.

'Fie, fie, fond° love, thou art as full of fear   *foolish; affectionate*
As one with treasure laden, hemmed with thieves.
Trifles unwitnessèd with eye or ear
Thy coward heart with false bethinking° grieves.'   *imagination*
1025   Even at this word she hears a merry horn,
      Whereat she leaps,° that was but late° forlorn.   *(for joy) / lately*

As falcons to the lure, away she flies.
The grass stoops not, she treads on it so light;
And in her haste unfortunately spies
1030   The foul boar's conquest on her fair delight;
      Which seen, her eyes, as murdered with the view,
      Like stars ashamed of° day, themselves withdrew.°   *put to shame by / shut*

Or as the snail, whose tender horns being hit
Shrinks backward in his shelly cave with pain,
1035   And there, all smothered up, in shade doth sit,
Long after fearing to creep forth again;
      So at his bloody view her eyes are fled
      Into the deep dark cabins of her head,

Where they resign their office and their light
1040   To the disposing of her troubled brain,
Who bids them still consort with° ugly night,   *always accompany*
And never wound the heart with looks again,
      Who,° like a king perplexèd° in his throne,   *(the heart) / troubled*
      By their suggestion° gives a deadly groan,   *(the eyes') incitement*

1045　Whereat each tributary subject⁶ quakes,
　　　As when the wind, imprisoned in the ground,
　　　Struggling for passage, earth's foundation shakes,⁷
　　　Which with cold terror doth men's minds confound.
　　　　This mutiny each part doth so surprise°　　　　　　*assail*
1050　That from their dark beds once more leap her eyes,

　　　And, being opened, threw unwilling light
　　　Upon the wide wound that the boar had trenched
　　　In his soft flank, whose wonted° lily-white　　　　　　*usual*
　　　With purple tears that his wound wept was drenched.
1055　　No flower was nigh, no grass, herb, leaf, or weed,
　　　　But stole his blood, and seemed with him to bleed.

　　　This solemn sympathy poor Venus noteth.
　　　Over one shoulder doth she hang her head.
　　　Dumbly° she passions,° franticly she doteth.　　　*Mutely / suffers*
1060　She thinks he could not die, he is not dead.
　　　　Her voice is stopped, her joints forget to bow,°　　*cannot bend*
　　　　Her eyes are mad that they have wept till° now.　　*before*

　　　Upon his hurt she looks so steadfastly
　　　That her sight, dazzling,° makes the wound seem three;　*blurring*
1065　And then she reprehends her mangling eye,
　　　That makes more gashes where no breach should be.
　　　　His face seems twain; each several limb is doubled;
　　　　For oft the eye mistakes, the brain being troubled.

　　　'My tongue cannot express my grief for one,
1070　And yet,' quoth she, 'behold two Adons dead!
　　　My sighs are blown away, my salt tears gone,
　　　Mine eyes are turned to fire, my heart to lead.
　　　　Heavy heart's lead, melt at mine eyes' red fire!
　　　　So shall I die by drops of hot desire.

1075　'Alas, poor world, what treasure hast thou lost,
　　　What face remains alive that's worth the viewing?
　　　Whose tongue is music now? What canst thou boast
　　　Of things long since, or anything ensuing?
　　　　The flowers are sweet, their colours fresh and trim;
1080　　But true sweet beauty lived and died with him.

　　　'Bonnet nor veil henceforth no creature wear:°　*(to preserve complexion)*
　　　Nor sun nor wind will ever strive to kiss you.
　　　Having no fair° to lose, you need not fear.　　　　　*beauty*
　　　The sun doth scorn you, and the wind doth hiss you.
1085　　But when Adonis lived, sun and sharp air
　　　　Lurked like two thieves to rob him of his fair;

　　　'And therefore would he put his bonnet on,
　　　Under whose brim the gaudy sun would peep.
　　　The wind would blow it off, and, being gone,

---

6. Each inferior organ of Venus's body.　　　　7. Sixteenth-century explanation of earthquakes.

1090   Play with his locks; then would Adonis weep,
        And straight,° in pity of his tender years,   *immediately*
        They both would strive who first should dry his tears.

    'To see his face the lion walked along
    Behind some hedge, because he would not fear° him.   *frighten*
1095   To recreate° himself° when he hath sung,   *entertain / (Adonis)*
    The tiger would be tame, and gently hear him.
        If he had spoke, the wolf would leave his prey,
        And never fright the silly° lamb that day.   *innocent*

    'When he beheld his shadow in the brook,
1100   The fishes spread on it their golden gills.
    When he was by, the birds such pleasure took
    That some would sing, some other in their bills
        Would bring him mulberries and ripe-red cherries.
        He fed them with his sight, they him with berries.

1105   'But this foul, grim, and urchin-snouted° boar,   *hedgehog-snouted*
    Whose downward eye still looketh for a grave,
    Ne'er saw the beauteous livery[8] that he wore:
    Witness the entertainment° that he gave.   *reception*
        If he did see his face, why then, I know
1110   He thought to kiss him, and hath killed him so.

    ''Tis true, 'tis true; thus was Adonis slain;
    He ran upon the boar with his sharp spear,
    Who did not whet his teeth at him again,°   *in return*
    But by a kiss thought to persuade him° there,   *win him over*
1115   And, nuzzling in his flank, the loving swine
        Sheathed unaware the tusk in his soft groin.

    'Had I been toothed like him, I must confess
    With kissing him I should have killed him first;
    But he is dead, and never did he bless
1120   My youth with his, the more am I accursed.'
        With this she falleth in the place she stood,
        And stains her face with his congealèd blood.

    She looks upon his lips, and they are pale.
    She takes him by the hand, and that is cold.
1125   She whispers in his ears a heavy tale,
    As if they heard the woeful words she told.
        She lifts the coffer-lids° that close his eyes,   *treasure-chest lids*
        Where lo, two lamps burnt out in darkness lies;

    Two glasses, where herself herself beheld
1130   A thousand times, and now no more reflect,
    Their virtue° lost, wherein they late excelled,   *power*
    And every beauty robbed of his° effect.   *its*
        'Wonder of time,' quoth she, 'this is my spite,°   *torment*
        That, thou being dead, the day should yet be light.

---

8. His appearance (literally, garment).

1135 'Since thou art dead, lo, here I prophesy
Sorrow on love hereafter shall attend.
It° shall be waited on with jealousy,   *(Love)*
Find sweet beginning, but unsavoury end;
    Ne'er settled equally, but high or low,⁹
1140   That all love's pleasure shall not match his woe.

'It shall be fickle, false, and full of fraud,
Bud, and be blasted,° in a breathing-while:°   *blighted / moment*
The bottom poison, and the top o'erstrawed°   *strewn over*
With sweets that shall the truest sight beguile.
1145   The strongest body shall it make most weak,
    Strike the wise dumb,° and teach the fool to speak.   *mute*

'It shall be sparing,° and too full of riot,°   *miserly / excess*
Teaching decrepit age to tread the measures.¹
The staring° ruffian shall it keep in quiet,   *glaring*
1150 Pluck down the rich, enrich the poor with treasures;
    It shall be raging-mad, and silly-mild;
    Make the young old, the old become a child.

'It shall suspect where is no cause of fear;
It shall not fear where it should most mistrust.
1155 It shall be merciful, and too severe,
And most deceiving when it seems most just.°   *honest*
    Perverse it shall be where it shows most toward,²
    Put fear to valour, courage to the coward.

'It shall be cause of war and dire events,
1160 And set dissension 'twixt the son and sire;
Subject and servile to all discontents,³
As dry combustious matter is to fire.
    Sith° in his prime death doth my love destroy,   *Since*
    They that love best their loves shall not enjoy.'

1165 By this, the boy that by her side lay killed
Was melted like a vapour from her sight,
And in his blood that on the ground lay spilled
A purple flower sprung up, chequered with white,°   *(the anemone)*
    Resembling well his pale cheeks, and the blood
1170   Which in round drops upon their whiteness stood.

She bows her head the new-sprung flower to smell,
Comparing it to her Adonis' breath,
And says within her bosom it shall dwell,
Since he himself is reft° from her by death.   *torn*
1175   She crops the stalk, and in the breach appears
    Green-dropping sap, which she compares to tears.

'Poor flower,' quoth she, 'this was thy father's guise°—   *habit*
Sweet issue° of a more sweet-smelling sire—   *offspring; emission*

---

9. *Ne'er . . . low:* Love shall involve extremes of happiness and grief rather than equanimity; lovers shall
come from different social stations.

1. To dance (inappropriately).
2. It shall be stubborn where it seems most compliant.
3. Cause and slave of all discontentedness.

For every little grief to wet his eyes.
1180 To grow unto himself° was his desire,   *mature independently*
    And so 'tis thine; but know it is as good
    To wither in my breast as in his blood.

'Here was thy father's bed, here in my breast.
Thou art the next of blood,° and 'tis thy right.   *heir (with wordplay)*
1185 Lo, in this hollow cradle take thy rest;
My throbbing heart shall rock thee day and night.
    There shall not be one minute in an hour
    Wherein I will not kiss my sweet love's flower.'

Thus, weary of the world, away she hies,
1190 And yokes her silver doves, by whose swift aid
Their mistress, mounted, through the empty skies
In her light chariot quickly is conveyed,
    Holding their course to Paphos,[4] where their queen
    Means to immure° herself, and not be seen.   *confine*

---

4. Venus's abode in Cyprus.

The Rape of Lucrece

In the dedication to *Venus and Adonis* in 1593, Shakespeare promised his patron the Earl of Southampton a "graver labor"; a year later, *The Rape of Lucrece* delivered on his pledge. Like most nondramatic poems of the period, in other words, this one was dedicated to a wealthy individual whom Shakespeare hoped would reward his efforts, and presumably reflected Shakespeare's awareness of that individual's literary preferences. Perhaps not surprisingly, then, the two poems have much in common: their classical inspiration; their lush, highly rhetorical narrative verse; their interest in the dynamic of a one-sided sexual passion. Yet both poems were intended for a wider audience, and both were popular successes: *The Rape of Lucrece* was reprinted at least six times during Shakespeare's lifetime. Moreover, as Shakespeare suggests in his dedication, whereas *Venus and Adonis,* despite its sad end, remains playful even in its pathos, *The Rape of Lucrece* treats a tragic subject of political as well as sexual consequence. It is written in rime royal, a seven-line iambic-pentameter stanza with the rhyme scheme *ababbcc,* a verse form reserved since the time of Chaucer for elevated, tragic subjects. Shakespeare's contemporary Gabriel Harvey captures the difference in the two poems when he comments that *Venus and Adonis* pleases "the younger sort," while *The Rape of Lucrece,* like *Hamlet,* pleases "the wiser sort."

Today *The Rape of Lucrece* is commonly regarded far less highly than the play with which Harvey classifies it. The change in estimation suggests that Shakespeare's original readers came to the poem with generic expectations, literary tastes, and interpretive equipment different from our own. One important difference is the greater familiarity many Renaissance readers would have had with Shakespeare's sources, a familiarity that left them free to concentrate on the ways in which the poet was varying or amplifying on well-known prototypes. Slightly different versions of the tale of Tarquin and Lucretia were available in Livy's history of Rome and in Ovid's *Fasti,* both commonly read in Elizabethan grammar schools. In 509 B.C.E., Rome's King was Tarquin the Proud, a good military leader but an oppressive ruler over his own subjects. Sextus Tarquinius, the King's son, raped Lucretia, the wife of Collatinus, one of his aristocratic retainers. Lucretia committed suicide after revealing the crime to her male relatives and exhorting them to revenge her. After her corpse was exhibited in the Roman Forum, a wholesale revolt against the Tarquins erupted, led by the King's nephew Lucius Junius Brutus. The royal family was exiled, and Rome became a republic, ruled by a senate and administered by one or more elected "consuls," of which Lucius Junius Brutus was the first.

For the Renaissance as well as for its original Roman audience, the story of Tarquin and Lucrece displayed vividly the inextricability of domestic and civic order, of public and private realms, of sexual and political violence. As a political fable, it suggested circumstances in which subjects were permitted, even obliged, to challenge the authority of their sovereign. When Tarquin rapes Lucrece, he does not merely perpetrate an act of brutal violence against her, but he defies Collatinus's exclusive claim on his wife's body, imagined as the husband's property. The story thus exemplifies a ruler's reckless disregard for the rights of his *male* subjects. In the late sixteenth century, when monarchies in western Europe were strengthening their power at the expense of parliaments and the higher aristocracy, the story could be cited as a precedent for resisting tyranny.

Purely as a sexual melodrama too, the story had wide appeal. Again and again, Renaissance painters portrayed Tarquin stealing into Lucretia's bed, Lucretia stabbing herself, and Lucius Junius Brutus exhorting over her body in the marketplace, often incorporating all three scenes into the same picture. Lucretia became a focus of especially fierce

Lucretia. Raphael.

debate. On the one hand, she seemed a model of wifely duty, a woman to whom marital fidelity was not merely a matter of social respectability but a fundamental life principle. On the other hand, suicide by the sword—the traditional last, defiant gesture of heroic Roman men—could seem improperly self-assertive in a woman. Moreover, some Christian writers considered Lucretia's suicide not merely indecorous but sinful. In *The City of God,* Augustine argued that since virtues are properties of the will and not the body, Lucretia was innocent of unchastity. But ironically, her sexual blamelessness rendered her suicide completely inexcusable; Augustine considered her a murderess who had taken her own life out of unchristian pride. By Shakespeare's time, therefore, Lucretia could be held up, variously, as a model of female propriety and as an example of pagan willfulness, as a woman who both upholds and breaks from the usual constraints upon her sex.

Adapting the story to his own purposes, Shakespeare makes interesting changes of detail and emphasis. As Ovid and Livy recount it, the story of violation, suicide, and revolution is full of turbulent physical action and unexpected revelations: and in Livy especially, the political consequences of the rape receive much more attention than the sexual assault itself. Shakespeare's version downplays—though it does not eliminate—the political aspects of the story, and it contains most of the feverish momentum of the original story in the prefatory "Argument": "The same night he treacherously stealeth into her chamber, violently ravished her, and early in the morning speedeth away. Lucrece, in this lamentable plight, hastily dispatcheth messengers." The poem itself, by contrast, concentrates not upon moments of violence or haste but upon what precedes and follows those moments: what Tarquin thinks on his way to Lucrece's bedchamber, how Lucrece occupies herself between the time she sends off her messenger and Collatine's return.

Like *Venus and Adonis, The Rape of Lucrece* eschews eventfulness for elaborate psychological analysis, attempting to capture in verse the uneven surge and flow of troubled, self-divided consciousnesses. In Shakespeare's hands, the story of Tarquin and Lucrece becomes a story about how people make choices that lead to violence. Everything in the poem is the consequence of a decision, not an accident of fate, and nothing seems inevitable. The poem teases the reader with alternative possibilities. What if Collatine had kept his marital happiness to himself? What if Tarquin's conscience had overcome his lust? What if Lucrece's beauty had blinded Tarquin permanently instead of temporarily? What if Collatine had arrived to save Lucrece at the last moment? What if Lucrece had resolved to kill Tarquin rather than herself?

In large part, these alternatives receive so much attention because both Tarquin and Lucrece make decisions that fail to reflect their best interests. The poem is constantly suggesting that they would be better off doing something else; and, interestingly, the characters themselves at times seem lucidly aware of that fact. Tarquin tells himself that his assault will desecrate the very virtue he admires in Lucrece, destroy his own self-respect, and bring dishonor upon his family. Then he rapes Lucrece. Lucrece argues to herself what her husband and father will tell her later: that she cannot incur guilt by a sexual act to which she has not consented, and that therefore she need not take her own life. Then she commits suicide.

In both cases, the characters' stubborn refusal to acknowledge the obvious seems to follow from their tendency to conceive of themselves in terms of a few crucial metaphors. In Tarquin's case, the metaphors are military: "Affection is my captain, and he leadeth, / . . . My heart shall never countermand mine eye" (lines 271, 276). Such images attract Tarquin because they portray a rash, grossly disorderly act in terms of strict discipline. Even as he overturns the proper subordination of passion to reason, he elaborates a clear, if perverse, hierarchy of priorities. Moreover, by casting himself as a warrior and Lucrece as an enemy territory, Tarquin minimizes the blame that attaches to rape, an act conventionally associated with (and often excused in) soldiers pillaging an enemy town.

Of course, as Lucrece reminds him, she is not his foe, and Tarquin's actions violate not only her bodily integrity but her husband's trust in a friend and superior. Her pleas show how tendentious are Tarquin's interpretations of the metaphors he attaches to himself. When Tarquin describes himself as an "uncontrollèd tide," and therefore intractable to entreaties, Lucrece attempts to modify the sense of the metaphor:

> 'Thou art,' quoth she, 'a sea, a sovereign king,
> And lo, there falls into thy boundless flood
> Black lust, dishonour, shame, misgoverning,
> Who seek to stain the ocean of thy blood.'
> (lines 652–55)

Likewise, her account of his psychological state replaces the military metaphor of battle against an enemy with one of civil order temporarily disrupted:

> I sue for exiled majesty's repeal;
> Let him return, and flatt'ring thoughts retire.
> His true respect will prison false desire.
> (lines 640–42)

Eventually, the rape that Tarquin tries to think of as an orderly military maneuver leads not only to his psychological fragmentation and self-torment but to literal exile, an exile Lucrece describes as already having occurred metaphorically.

After the rape and Tarquin's departure, the narrative focus shifts to Lucrece. Although she knows that she is not intentionally guilty of breaking her marital vows, she nonetheless construes herself as culpable. Like her violator, Lucrece thinks of herself and her body in symbolic terms, although in her case the governing metaphors are fortress, house, mansion, temple, tree. By emphasizing the protective function of the body, these metaphors make it easy for Lucrece to think of herself as irreparably damaged once her body has been assaulted by Tarquin's lust:

> Ay me, the bark peeled from the lofty pine
> His leaves will wither and his sap decay;
> So must my soul, her bark being peeled away.
> (lines 1167–69)

Once Tarquin sacks and batters Lucrece's fortress, she suffers regardless of her innocence, like the inhabitant of a plundered town. Of course, like Tarquin, Lucrece interprets such metaphors tendentiously: she could just as well think of the "bark" or the "house" that shelters her soul as a morally insignificant excrescence. Instead, when the condition of her body seems to conflict with the condition of her soul, she desperately attempts to resolve the inconsistency by declaring herself irredeemably contaminated. In doing so, she endorses—indeed, almost celebrates—a literally fatal ambivalence in the definition of female chastity. For despite Augustine's objections, female chastity ordinarily refers to a physical condition as well as to a mental attitude in cultures that value female bodily intactness; this ambivalence still haunts rape survivors today, who often blame themselves for their own victimization.

Comprehensible though Lucrece's suicide may be in these terms, however, it is ironically fraught with the very contradictions she seeks to avoid. She "revenges" herself

Tarquino e Lucrezia. Titian (c. 1570).

upon Tarquin by completing the assault he began, plunging the phallic blade into what Shakespeare calls the "sheath" of her breast (the Latin word for "sheath" is *vagina*). She insists that she is acting in Collatine's interests even while she ignores his wishes; she proves her innocence by demanding of herself that she pay the penalty for guilt; she validates her version of the rape story by silencing herself more effectively than Tarquin had with the bedclothes.

Although the metaphors Tarquin and Lucrece use to think about their respective situations are, therefore, highly problematic, they are definitely not arbitrary. Both protagonists derive their figures of speech from the same medieval and Renaissance poetic tradition Shakespeare had already drawn upon in *Venus and Adonis.* The configuration of characters—the warrior-lover desperately pursuing his passion, the beautiful woman whose chastity makes her irresistibly desirable—is likewise conventional. Shakespeare suggests the importance of this poetic mentality for *The Rape of Lucrece* by anachronistically importing the language of chivalry into a poem about ancient Rome: Tarquin agonizes about the consequences of his transgression for his family's coat of arms, and Lucrece accuses him of breaking "knighthood, gentry, and sweet friendship's oath" (line 569). This is closer to the world of Thomas Malory's Arthurian romances, Thomas Wyatt's sonnets, Philip Sidney's *Arcadia,* or Edmund Spenser's *Faerie Queene* than it is to the world of Livy or Ovid.

In fact, it is possible to see *The Rape of Lucrece,* like *Venus and Adonis,* as attempting to renovate a rhetoric of sexual passion that had begun to seem trite by Shakespeare's time. But the two poems employ almost exactly opposite strategies of renewal. *Venus and Adonis* surprises the reader by turning conventional expectations of gendered behavior upside down, assigning the aggressive, desiring role to the woman and casting the male as an uncorrupted fortress of virtue. *The Rape of Lucrece,* on the other hand, pushes the conventional language of love poetry in a relentlessly literal direction, making it interesting by unleashing the latent ferocity and misogyny of a courtly love aesthetic. Lovers in the poetry of Spenser and Sidney, Petrarch and Wyatt, think of themselves as soldiers of desire, but they are so awed by their mistresses that aggressive thoughts are quenched by a mere glance from their imperious beloveds. Shakespeare's Tarquin, in contrast, more consistent and less exquisitely sensitive, uses the implicitly coercive rhetoric of love poetry as a pretext for rape.

Given the poem's intense concern with the use and misuse of language, it is not surprising that *The Rape of Lucrece* is also attentive to the relationship of rhetoric to other forms of representation. Again and again, the poem pauses to consider the relative power and conviction of linguistic and visual experience, of the ear and the eye. At some points in the poem, vision seems the privileged sense, giving immediate access to the unquestionably real. "Beauty itself doth of itself persuade / The eyes of men without an orator," the narrator declares; "To see sad sights moves more than hear them told" (lines 29–30, 1324). Yet Shakespeare alters his sources to have Tarquin provoked to lust not by the sight of Lucrece but by Collatine's report of her; and he dwells too on Lucrece's inability to divine Tarquin's motives from his appearance.

The rape and death of Lucretia. From Jost Amman, *Icones Livianae* (1572).

This persistent concern with the relative adequacy of different representational modes culminates in a long passage in which Lucrece contemplates a tapestry of Troy. In multiple ways, the tapestry is relevant to her own case, for the Trojan War was the consequence of a rape, and after the city's destruction, Trojan exiles were supposed to have founded Rome. After Lucrece's suicide, the account of her rape will provide the pretext for another founding, that of the Roman Republic. Eventually, her story will be displayed by artists in the same way that the legend of Troy is illustrated here—a series of chronologically distinct episodes represented simultaneously on the same panel. As Lucrece gazes at the painter's vast panorama of violation, the poet emphasizes both the vivid realism of the depiction and the artificial means by which that realism is produced: "Here one man's hand leaned on another's head, / His nose being shadowed by his neighbour's ear" (lines 1415–16). Portraying people according to the laws of perspective makes them look "natural," but it also reduces them to a collection of grotesquely amputated shapes. Like *Venus and Adonis*, *The Rape of Lucrece* invokes nature as a category of value and then subverts it; but whereas the earlier poem undermines "nature" by suggesting that its supposed precepts are inadequate, the later poem undermines "nature" by suggesting that its effect is only achieved by extraordinary artifice. Shakespeare will consider the issue again in such plays as *A Midsummer Night's Dream*, *The Winter's Tale*, *The Tempest*, and, of course, *Hamlet*.

KATHARINE EISAMAN MAUS

TEXTUAL NOTE

Richard Field was the printer for *The Rape of Lucrece*, published in 1594, as he had been for *Venus and Adonis* the previous year. Like *Venus and Adonis*, *Lucrece* in its printed state probably derives directly from Shakespeare's manuscript, and it presents relatively few textual difficulties. Some editors question whether Shakespeare wrote the prefatory "Argument." A few variations among surviving copies of the First Quarto represent proof corrections; in Elizabethan times, proofreading was done while the work was in the process of being printed, so corrections could appear in some copies but not in others.

SELECTED BIBLIOGRAPHY

Belsey, Catherine. "Tarquin Dispossessed: Expropriation and Consent in *The Rape of Lucrece*." *Shakespeare Quarterly* 52 (2001): 45–70. Lucrece as property and as person.

Donaldson, Ian. *The Rapes of Lucretia: A Myth and Its Transformations*. Oxford: Clarendon, 1982. Discusses Shakespeare's poem alongside other literary and artistic treatments of the story.

Fineman, Joel. "Shakespeare's Will: The Temporality of Rape." *Representations* 20 (Fall 1987): 25–76. Features an ingenious discussion of the "let" as both hindering Tarquin and spurring him to action.

Hadfield, Andrew. "Tarquin's Everlasting Banishment: Republicanism and Constitutionalism in *The Rape of Lucrece* and *Titus Andronicus*." *Parergon: Journal of the Australian and New Zealand Association for Medieval and Renaissance Studies* 19 (2002): 77–104. A discussion of the political issues in the poem.

Kahn, Coppélia. "The Rape in Shakespeare's *Lucrece*." *Shakespeare Studies* 9 (1976): 45–72. Feminist account of rape and patriarchy in the poem.

Maus, Katharine Eisaman. "Taking Tropes Seriously: Language and Violence in Shakespeare's *Rape of Lucrece*." *Shakespeare Quarterly* 37 (1986): 66–82. *The Rape of Lucrece* as a literalization of Petrarchan metaphors.

Vickers, Nancy. "The Blazon of Sweet Beauty's Best: Shakespeare's *Lucrece*." *Shakespeare and the Question of Theory*. Ed. Patricia Parker and Geoffrey Hartman. New York: Methuen, 1985. 95–115. The sexual politics of the blazon or detailed description of Lucrece's body.

The Rape of Lucrece

TO THE RIGHT HONOURABLE
HENRY WRIOTHESLEY,
EARL OF SOUTHAMPTON AND
BARON OF TITCHFIELD[1]

The love I dedicate to your lordship is without end, whereof this pamphlet° without beginning[2] is but a superfluous moiety.° The warrant° I have of your honourable disposition, not the worth of my untutored lines, makes it assured of acceptance. What I have done is yours; what I have to do is yours, being part in all I have, devoted yours. Were my worth greater my duty would show greater, meantime, as it is, it is bound to your lordship, to whom I wish long life still° lengthened with all happiness.

short work / part
assurance

continually

YOUR LORDSHIP'S IN ALL DUTY,
WILLIAM SHAKESPEARE

THE ARGUMENT°

plot

Lucius Tarquinius (surnamed Superbus for his excessive pride),° after he had caused his own father-in-law Servius Tullius to be cruelly murdered, and, contrary to the Roman laws and customs, not requiring[3] or staying for the people's suffrages° had possessed himself of the kingdom, went accompanied with his sons and other noblemen of Rome to besiege Ardea,[4] during which siege the principal men of the army meeting one evening at the tent of Sextus Tarquinius, the King's son, in their discourses after supper everyone commended the virtues of his own wife, among whom Collatinus extolled the incomparable chastity of his wife, Lucretia. In that pleasant humour° they all posted° to Rome, and, intending by their secret and sudden arrival to make trial of that which everyone had before avouched, only Collatinus finds his wife (though it were late in the night) spinning amongst her maids. The other ladies were all found dancing, and revelling, or in several disports.° Whereupon the noblemen yielded Collatinus the victory and his wife the fame. At that time Sextus Tarquinius, being enflamed with Lucrece' beauty, yet smothering his passions for the present, departed with the rest back to the camp, from whence he shortly after privily° withdrew himself and was, according to his estate,° royally entertained and lodged by Lucrece at Collatium.[5] The same night he treacherously stealeth into her chamber, violently

"the Proud"

approval

merry mood
hurried

diversions

secretly / rank

Dedication and **Argument**
1. See *Venus and Adonis*, note 2 to Dedication.
2. *The Rape of Lucrece* begins *in medias res* (in the middle of the story), as the Latin poet Horace recommends in *The Art of Poetry.*

3. Not asking for.
4. City 25 miles south of Rome.
5. Town 10 miles east of Rome; the ancestral home of Collatinus's family.

ravished her, and early in the morning speedeth away. Lucrece, in this lamentable plight, hastily dispatcheth messengers—one to Rome for her father, another to the camp for Collatine. They came, the one accompanied with Junius Brutus, the other with Publius Valerius, and, finding Lucrece attired in mourning habit, demanded the cause of her sorrow. She, first taking an oath of them for her revenge, revealed the actor° and whole manner of his dealing, and withal° suddenly stabbed herself. Which done, with one consent they all vowed to root out the whole hated family of the Tarquins, and, bearing the dead body to Rome, Brutus acquainted the people with the doer and manner of the vile deed, with a bitter invective against the tyranny of the King; wherewith the people were so moved that with one consent and a general acclamation the Tarquins were all exiled and the state government changed from kings to consuls.⁶

doer
moreover

From the besieged Ardea all in post,°   *haste*
Borne by the trustless wings of false desire,
Lust-breathèd° Tarquin leaves the Roman host   *Lust-inspired*
And to Collatium bears the lightless° fire   *smoldering*
5   Which, in pale embers hid, lurks to aspire°   *rise up*
     And girdle with embracing flames the waist
     Of Collatine's fair love, Lucrece the chaste.

Haply° that name of chaste unhapp'ly° set   *Perhaps / unfortunately*
This bateless° edge on his keen appetite,   *unbluntable*
10   When Collatine unwisely did not let°   *forbear*
To praise the clear unmatchèd red and white
Which triumphed in that sky of his delight,°   *(Lucrece's face)*
     Where mortal stars° as bright as heaven's beauties   *(her eyes)*
     With pure aspects¹ did him peculiar° duties.   *exclusive*

15   For he the night before in Tarquin's tent
Unlocked the treasure of his happy state,
What priceless wealth the heavens had him lent
In the possession of his beauteous mate,
Reck'ning his fortune at such high-proud rate
20   That kings might be espousèd to more fame,
     But° king nor peer to such a peerless dame.   *But neither*

O happiness enjoyed but of° a few,   *only by*
And, if possessed, as soon decayed and done
As is the morning's silver melting dew
25   Against the golden splendour of the sun,
An expired date° cancelled ere well begun!   *time limit*
     Honour and beauty in the owner's arms
     Are weakly fortressed from a world of harms.

Beauty itself doth of° itself persuade   *by*
30   The eyes of men without an orator.
What needeth then apology be made

---

6. Chief magistrates, elected for one-year terms.   **Poem**
                                                  1. Looks; astral influences.

To set forth that which is so singular?°   *unique*
Or why is Collatine the publisher°   *publicizer*
  Of that rich jewel he should keep unknown
35   From thievish ears, because it is his own?

Perchance his boast of Lucrece' sov'reignty°   *superiority*
Suggested° this proud issue° of a king,   *Tempted / offspring*
For by our ears our hearts oft tainted be.
Perchance that envy of so rich a thing,
40   Braving compare,° disdainfully did sting   *Defying comparison*
  His high-pitched thoughts, that meaner° men should vaunt°   *inferior / boast*
  That golden hap° which their superiors want.°   *luck / lack*

But some untimely thought did instigate
His all-too-timeless° speed, if none of those.   *untimely; rapid*
45   His honour, his affairs, his friends, his state°   *rank*
Neglected all, with swift intent he goes
To quench the coal which in his liver° glows.   *(seat of lust)*
  O rash false heat, wrapped in repentant cold,
  Thy hasty spring still blasts° and ne'er grows old!   *is always frostbitten*

50   When at Collatium this false lord arrived,
Well was he welcomed by the Roman dame,
Within whose face beauty and virtue strived
Which of them both should underprop her fame.
When virtue bragged, beauty would blush for shame;
55   When beauty boasted blushes, in despite°   *defiance*
  Virtue would stain° that or° with silver white.   *dye / gold*

But beauty, in that white entitulèd°   *claiming title*
From Venus' doves, doth challenge that fair field.[2]
Then virtue claims from beauty beauty's red,
60   Which virtue gave the golden age to gild[3]
  Their silver cheeks, and called it then their shield,
    Teaching them thus to use it in the fight:
    When shame assailed, the red should fence° the white.   *defend*

This heraldry in Lucrece' face was seen,
65   Argued° by beauty's red and virtue's white.   *Demonstrated; disputed*
Of either's colour was the other queen,
Proving from world's minority° their right.   *earliest age*
Yet their ambition makes them still to fight,
  The sovereignty of either being so great
70   That oft they interchange each other's seat.

This silent war of lilies and of roses
Which Tarquin viewed in her fair face's field
In their pure ranks his traitor eye encloses,
Where, lest between them both it should be killed,
75   The coward captive vanquishèd doth yield
    To those two armies that would let him go
    Rather than triumph in° so false a foe.   *over*

2. Territory; battlefield; surface on which a coat of arms is displayed. *Venus' doves*: white turtledoves draw the chariot of Venus, the love goddess.

3. Coat with gold; cover with red (as in a blush). *the golden age*: a mythical, ideal era of innocence and plenty.

Now thinks he that her husband's shallow tongue,
The niggard prodigal that praised her so,
80 In that high task hath done her beauty wrong,
Which far exceeds his barren skill to show.°   *describe*
Therefore that praise which Collatine doth owe°   *fail to render*
    Enchanted Tarquin answers° with surmise   *compensates for*
    In silent wonder of still-gazing eyes.

85 This earthly saint adorèd by this devil
Little suspecteth the false worshipper,
For unstained thoughts do seldom dream on evil.
Birds never limed° no secret bushes fear,   *trapped*
So guiltless she securely° gives good cheer⁴   *unsuspectingly*
90   And reverent welcome to her princely guest,
    Whose inward ill no outward harm expressed,

For that he coloured° with his high estate,   *disguised*
Hiding base sin in pleats° of majesty,   *folds*
That° nothing in him seemed inordinate   *So that*
95 Save sometime too much wonder of his eye,
Which, having all, all could not satisfy,
    But poorly rich so wanteth in his store°   *plenty*
    That, cloyed with much, he pineth still for more.

But she that never coped with stranger° eyes   *strangers'*
100 Could pick no meaning from their parling° looks,   *persuasive*
Nor read the subtle shining secrecies
Writ in the glassy margins⁵ of such books.
She touched no unknown baits nor feared no hooks,
    Nor could she moralize° his wanton sight°   *interpret / looking*
105   More than his eyes were opened to the light.⁶

He stories to her ears her husband's fame
Won in the fields of fruitful Italy,
And decks with praises Collatine's high name
Made glorious by his manly chivalry
110 With bruisèd arms° and wreaths of victory.   *dented weapons*
    Her joy with heaved-up hand she doth express,
    And wordless so greets heaven for his success.

Far from the purpose of his coming thither
He makes excuses for his being there.
115 No cloudy show of stormy blust'ring weather
Doth yet in his fair welkin° once appear   *sky (face)*
Till sable° night, mother of dread and fear,   *black*
    Upon the world dim darkness doth display
    And in her vaulty prison stows the day.

120 For then is Tarquin brought unto his bed,
Intending° weariness with heavy sprite;°   *Pretending / spirit*
For after supper long he questionèd°   *conversed*
With modest Lucrece, and wore out the night.

---

4. Hospitable entertainment.   often placed.
5. Where summaries and interpretive remarks were   6. Were made obvious.

Now leaden slumber with life's strength doth fight,
125   And everyone to rest himself betakes
   Save thieves, and cares, and troubled minds that wakes.

As one of which doth Tarquin lie revolving°   *considering*
The sundry dangers of his will's obtaining,°   *gratifying his desire*
Yet ever to obtain his will resolving,
130 Though weak-built hopes[7] persuade him to abstaining.
Despair to gain doth traffic oft for gaining,[8]
   And when great treasure is the meed° proposed,   *prize*
   Though death be adjunct,[9] there's no death supposed.°   *thought of*

Those that much covet are with gain so fond°   *infatuated*
135 That what° they have not, that which they possess,   *That for what*
They scatter and unloose it from their bond,°   *ownership*
And so by hoping more they have but less,
Or, gaining more, the profit° of excess   *advantage*
   Is but to surfeit and such griefs[1] sustain
140   That they° prove bankrupt in this poor-rich gain.   *(the covetous)*

The aim of all is but to nurse the life
With honour, wealth, and ease in waning age,
And in this aim there is such thwarting strife
That one for all, or all for one, we gage,°   *risk*
145 As° life for honour in fell° battle's rage,   *For instance / cruel*
   Honour for wealth; and oft that wealth doth cost
   The death of all, and all together lost.

So that, in vent'ring ill,[2] we leave to be
The things we are for that which we expect,
150 And this ambitious foul infirmity
In having° much, torments us with defect   *While we have*
Of that we have; so then we do neglect
   The thing we have, and all for want of wit°   *lack of sense*
   Make something nothing by augmenting it.

155 Such hazard now must doting Tarquin make,
Pawning his honour to obtain his lust,
And for himself himself he must forsake.
Then where is truth if there be no self-trust?°   *truth to oneself*
When shall he think to find a stranger just
160   When he himself himself confounds, betrays
   To sland'rous tongues and wretched hateful days?

Now stole upon the time the dead of night
When heavy sleep had closed up mortal eyes.
No comfortable star did lend his° light,   *its*
165 No noise but owls' and wolves' death-boding cries
Now serves the season, that they may surprise
   The silly° lambs. Pure thoughts are dead and still,   *innocent*
   While lust and murder wakes to stain° and kill.   *defile*

---

7. The fact that his hopes are flimsy.   9. Be joined with it.
8. Despair of gaining her (rightfully) often encourages   1. That is, the ills that accompany excess.
him to gain her (by any means possible).   2. In taking serious risks; in undertaking evil deeds.

And now this lustful lord leapt from his bed,
170 Throwing his mantle rudely o'er his arm,
Is madly tossed between desire and dread.
Th'one sweetly flatters, th'other feareth harm,
But honest fear, bewitched with lust's foul charm,
 Doth too-too oft betake him to retire,°   *retreat*
175 Beaten away by brainsick rude desire.

His falchion° on a flint he softly smiteth,   *curved sword*
That from the cold stone sparks of fire do fly,
Whereat a waxen torch forthwith he lighteth,
Which must be lodestar° to his lustful eye,   *guiding light*
180 And to the flame thus speaks advisedly:°   *deliberately*
 'As from this cold flint I enforced this fire,
 So Lucrece must I force to my desire.'

Here pale with fear he doth premeditate
The dangers of his loathsome enterprise,
185 And in his inward mind he doth debate
What following sorrow may on this arise.
Then, looking scornfully, he doth despise
 His naked armour of still-slaughtered lust,[3]
 And justly thus controls° his thoughts unjust: *rebukes; restrains*

190 'Fair torch, burn out thy light, and lend it not
To darken her whose light excelleth thine;
And die, unhallowed thoughts, before you blot
With your uncleanness that which is divine.
Offer pure incense to so pure a shrine.
195 Let fair humanity abhor the deed
 That spots and stains love's modest snow-white weed.° *attire (chastity)*

'O shame to knighthood and to shining arms!
O foul dishonour to my household's grave!°   *ancestral tomb*
O impious act including° all foul harms!   *encompassing*
200 A martial man to be soft fancy's° slave!   *love's*
True valour still a true respect[4] should have;
 Then my digression° is so vile, so base,   *error*
 That it will live engraven in my face.

'Yea, though I die the scandal will survive
205 And be an eyesore in my golden coat.°   *(of arms)*
Some loathsome dash[5] the herald will contrive
To cipher me how fondly° I did dote,   *To show how foolishly*
That my posterity, shamed with the note,°   *stigma*
 Shall curse my bones and hold it for no sin
210 To wish that I their father had not been.

'What win I if I gain the thing I seek?
A dream, a breath, a froth of fleeting joy.
Who buys a minute's mirth to wail a week,

---

3. His ineffective defense against his lust, always quenched in the moment of fulfillment; his not-yet-erect penis.
4. A suitable awareness of virtue.
5. Bar in a coat of arms, indicating a dishonorable action by an ancestor.

Or sells eternity to get a toy?°   *trifle*
215 For one sweet grape who will the vine destroy?
　　　Or what fond beggar, but to touch the crown,
　　　Would with the sceptre straight be strucken down?

'If Collatinus dream of my intent
Will he not wake, and in a desp'rate rage
220 Post hither this vile purpose to prevent?—
This siege that hath engirt° his marriage,   *surrounded*
This blur° to youth, this sorrow to the sage,   *blot*
　　　This dying virtue, this surviving shame,
　　　Whose crime will bear an ever-during° blame.   *everlasting*

225 'O what excuse can my invention° make   *ingenuity*
When thou shalt charge me with so black a deed?
Will not my tongue be mute, my frail joints shake,
Mine eyes forgo their light,° my false heart bleed?   *power of vision*
The guilt being great, the fear doth still exceed,
230 　　And extreme fear can neither fight nor fly,
　　　But coward-like with trembling terror die.

'Had Collatinus killed my son or sire,
Or lain in ambush to betray my life,
Or were he not my dear friend, this desire
235 Might have excuse to work upon his wife
As in revenge or quittal° of such strife.   *requital*
　　　But as he is my kinsman, my dear friend,
　　　The shame and fault finds no excuse nor end.

'Shameful it is—ay, if the fact° be known.   *deed*
240 Hateful it is—there is no hate in loving.
I'll beg her love—but she is not her own.
The worst is but denial and reproving;
My will is strong past reason's weak removing.
　　　Who fears a sentence° or an old man's saw°   *maxim / proverb*
245 　　Shall by a painted cloth be kept in awe.'⁶

Thus graceless holds he disputation
'Tween frozen conscience and hot-burning will,
And with good thoughts makes dispensation,°   *dispenses*
Urging the worser sense for vantage still;
250 Which in a moment doth confound and kill
　　　All pure effects,° and doth so far proceed   *tendencies*
　　　That what is vile shows like a virtuous deed.

Quoth he, 'She took me kindly by the hand,
And gazed for tidings in my eager eyes,
255 Fearing some hard news from the warlike band
Where her belovèd Collatinus lies.
O how her fear did make her colour rise!
　　　First red as roses that on lawn° we lay,   *fine linen*
　　　Then white as lawn, the roses took away.

6. Will be awed by a tapestry (often depicting morally significant narratives, as in lines 1366ff.).

260 'And how her hand, in my hand being locked,
     Forced it to tremble with her loyal fear,
     Which struck her sad, and then it faster rocked
     Until her husband's welfare she did hear,
     Whereat she smilèd with so sweet a cheer°   *an expression*
265   That had Narcissus⁷ seen her as she stood
         Self-love had never drowned him in the flood.

     'Why hunt I then for colour° or excuses?   *pretext*
     All orators are dumb when beauty pleadeth.
     Poor wretches have remorse in poor abuses;°   *regret minor lapses*
270 Love thrives not in the heart that shadows° dreadeth;   *illusory scruples*
     Affection° is my captain, and he leadeth,   *Passion*
         And when his gaudy banner is displayed,
         The coward fights, and will not be dismayed.

     'Then childish fear avaunt,° debating die,   *begone*
275 Respect° and reason wait on° wrinkled age!   *Circumspection / attend*
     My heart shall never countermand mine eye,
     Sad° pause and deep regard beseems the sage.   *Serious*
     My part is youth, and beats these from the stage.⁸
         Desire my pilot is, beauty my prize.°   *pirate's booty*
280   Then who fears sinking where such treasure lies?'

     As corn° o'ergrown by weeds, so heedful fear   *grain*
     Is almost choked by unresisted lust.
     Away he steals, with open list'ning ear,
     Full of foul hope and full of fond° mistrust,   *foolish; passionate*
285 Both which as servitors to the unjust
         So cross him with their opposite persuasion
         That now he vows a league, and now invasion.

     Within his thought her heavenly image sits,
     And in the selfsame seat sits Collatine.
290 That eye which looks on her confounds his wits,
     That eye which him beholds, as° more divine,   *because it is*
     Unto a view so false will not incline,
         But with a pure appeal seeks° to the heart,   *applies*
         Which once corrupted, takes the worser part,

295 And therein heartens up his servile powers⁹
     Who, flattered by their leader's jocund show,
     Stuff up his lust as minutes fill up hours,
     And as their captain, so their pride doth grow,
     Paying more slavish tribute than they owe.¹
300   By reprobate desire thus madly led
         The Roman lord marcheth to Lucrece' bed.

     The locks between her chamber and his will,
     Each one by him enforced, retires his ward;°   *withdraws its bolt*
     But as they open they all rate° his ill,   *berate (by squeaking)*

---

7. In classical mythology, a youth who fell in love with
his reflection in a pool; in some versions of the tale, he
drowned attempting to kiss the image.
8. Like the Vice character in the medieval morality play.

9. Appetites or passions, imagined as servants of the
heart, the seat of conscience.
1. That is, debasing themselves by collaborating and
encouraging the corrupted heart.

305 Which drives the creeping thief to some regard.°   *caution*
    The threshold grates the door to have him heard,
      Night-wand'ring weasels² shriek to see him there.
      They fright him, yet he still pursues his fear.°   *what makes him fear*

    As each unwilling portal yields him way,
310 Through little vents and crannies of the place
    The wind wars with his torch to make him stay,
    And blows the smoke of it into his face,
    Extinguishing his conduct° in this case.   *guide; behavior*
      But his hot heart, which fond desire doth scorch,
315   Puffs forth another wind that fires the torch,

    And being lighted, by the light he spies
    Lucretia's glove wherein her needle sticks.
    He takes it from the rushes where it lies,
    And gripping it, the needle his finger pricks,
320 As who should say 'This glove to wanton tricks
      Is not inured. Return again in haste.
      Thou seest our mistress' ornaments are chaste.'

    But all these poor forbiddings could not stay him;
    He in the worst sense consters° their denial.   *construes*
325 The doors, the wind, the glove that did delay him
    He takes for accidental things of trial,°   *tests of resolve*
    Or as those bars which stop the hourly dial,³
      Who with a ling'ring stay his course doth let°   *hinder; permit*
      Till every minute pays the hour his debt.

330 'So, so,' quoth he, 'these lets attend the time,
    Like little frosts that sometime threat the spring
    To add a more rejoicing to the prime,°   *spring*
    And give the sneapèd° birds more cause to sing.   *pinched with cold*
    Pain pays the income° of each precious thing.   *is the price of*
335   Huge rocks, high winds, strong pirates, shelves,° and sands   *reefs*
      The merchant fears, ere rich at home he lands.'

    Now is he come unto the chamber door
    That shuts him from the heaven of his thought,
    Which with a yielding latch, and with no more,
340 Hath barred him from the blessèd thing he sought.
    So from° himself impiety hath wrought°   *unlike / made him*
      That for his prey to pray he doth begin,
      As if the heavens should countenance his sin.

    But in the midst of his unfruitful prayer
345 Having solicited th'eternal power
    That his foul thoughts might compass° his fair fair,⁴   *obtain; embrace*
    And they would stand auspicious to the hour,
    Even there he starts.° Quoth he, 'I must deflower.   *is startled*
      The powers to whom I pray abhor this fact;°   *deed*
350   How can they then assist me in the act?

---

2. Weasels were kept to catch vermin.   before jerking forward.
3. The marks on a clock face, where the hands pause   4. His virtuous and beautiful one.

'Then love and fortune be my gods, my guide!
My will is backed with resolution.
Thoughts are but dreams till their effects be tried;
The blackest sin is cleared with absolution.
355   Against love's fire fear's frost hath dissolution.
       The eye of heaven is out,° and misty night   extinguished
       Covers the shame that follows sweet delight.'

This said, his guilty hand plucked up the latch,
And with his knee the door he opens wide.
360   The dove sleeps fast that this night-owl will catch.
Thus treason works ere traitors be espied.
Who sees the lurking serpent steps aside,
       But she, sound sleeping, fearing no such thing,
       Lies at the mercy of his mortal° sting.   lethal

365   Into the chamber wickedly he stalks,°   steals
And gazeth on her yet-unstainèd bed.
The curtains being close,° about he walks,   shut
Rolling his greedy eye-balls in his head.
By their high treason is his heart misled,
370   Which gives the watchword to his hand full soon
       To draw the cloud° that hides the silver moon.   (the bed curtain)

Look as° the fair and fiery-pointed sun   See how
Rushing from forth a cloud bereaves our sight,
Even so, the curtain drawn, his eyes begun
375   To wink,° being blinded with a greater light.   close
Whether it is that she reflects so bright
       That dazzleth them, or else some shame supposed,
       But blind they are, and keep themselves enclosed.

O had they in that darksome prison died,
380   Then had they seen the period° of their ill.   end
Then Collatine again by Lucrece' side
In his clear° bed might have reposèd still.   undefiled
But they must ope, this blessèd league° to kill,   marriage
       And holy-thoughted Lucrece to their sight
385   Must sell her joy, her life, her world's delight.

Her lily hand her rosy cheek lies under,
Coz'ning° the pillow of a lawful kiss,   Cheating
Who therefore angry seems to part in sunder,°   in two
Swelling on either side to want his bliss;[5]
390   Between whose hills her head entombèd is,
       Where like a virtuous monument she lies
       To be admired of lewd unhallowed eyes.

Without the bed her other fair hand was,
On the green coverlet, whose perfect white
395   Showed like an April daisy on the grass,
With pearly sweat resembling dew of night.

---

5. Because it is denied its pleasure (of her lips touching its surface).

Her eyes like marigolds[6] had sheathed their light,
   And canopied in darkness sweetly lay
   Till they might open to adorn the day.

400 Her hair like golden threads played with her breath—
O modest wantons, wanton modesty!—
Showing life's triumph in the map° of death,   *image*
And death's dim look in life's mortality.
Each° in her sleep themselves so beautify   *(life and death)*
405   As if between them twain there were no strife,
   But that life lived in death, and death in life.

Her breasts like ivory globes circled with blue,
A pair of maiden[7] worlds unconquerèd,
Save of their lord no bearing yoke they knew,
410 And him by oath they truly honourèd.
These worlds in Tarquin new ambition bred,
   Who like a foul usurper went about
   From this fair throne to heave the owner out.

What could he see but mightily he noted?
415 What did he note but strongly he desired?
What he beheld, on that he firmly doted,
And in his will° his wilful eye he tired.[8]   *lust*
   With more than admiration he admired
   Her azure veins, her alabaster skin,
420   Her coral lips, her snow-white dimpled chin.

As the grim lion fawneth° o'er his prey,   *shows delight*
Sharp hunger by the conquest satisfied,
So o'er this sleeping soul doth Tarquin stay,
His rage of lust by gazing qualified,°   *mollified*
425 Slaked not suppressed for standing by her side.
   His eye which late this mutiny restrains
   Unto a greater uproar tempts his veins,

And they like straggling slaves° for pillage fighting,   *lowborn soldiers*
Obdurate vassals fell° exploits effecting,   *fierce*
430 In bloody death and ravishment delighting,
Nor children's tears nor mothers' groans respecting,
Swell in their pride, the onset still° expecting.   *at any moment*
   Anon his beating heart, alarum° striking,   *signal to attack*
   Gives the hot charge, and bids them do their liking.

435 His drumming heart cheers up his burning eye,
His eye commends° the leading to his hand.   *entrusts*
His hand, as proud of such a dignity,
Smoking with pride marched on to make his stand
On her bare breast, the heart of all her land,
440   Whose ranks of blue veins as his hand did scale°   *climb*
   Left their round turrets destitute and pale.

---

6. The pot marigold folds up its flowers at day's end.
7. Used of an unconquered citadel.
8. Wearied; fed greedily (as a hawk tears flesh with its beak).

They, must'ring° to the quiet cabinet°   *gathering / room (heart)*
Where their dear governess° and lady lies,   *ruler*
Do tell her she is dreadfully beset,
445 And fright her with confusion of their cries.
      She much amazed breaks ope her locked-up eyes,
          Who, peeping forth this tumult to behold,
          Are by his flaming torch dimmed and controlled.°   *overwhelmed*

      Imagine her as one in dead of night
450 From forth dull sleep by dreadful fancy waking,
      That thinks she hath beheld some ghastly sprite
      Whose grim aspect sets every joint a-shaking.
      What terror 'tis! But she in worser taking,°   *plight*
          From sleep disturbèd, heedfully doth view
455   The sight which makes supposèd terror true.

      Wrapped and confounded in a thousand fears,
      Like to a new-killed bird she trembling lies.
      She dares not look, yet, winking,° there appears   *shutting her eyes*
      Quick-shifting antics,° ugly in her eyes.   *grotesque shapes*
460 Such shadows are the weak brain's forgeries,
          Who, angry that the eyes fly from their lights,
          In darkness daunts them with more dreadful sights.

      His hand that yet remains upon her breast—
      Rude ram,° to batter such an ivory wall—   *battering ram*
465 May feel her heart, poor citizen, distressed,
      Wounding itself to death, rise up and fall,
      Beating her bulk,° that his hand shakes withal.°   *chest / as well*
          This moves in him more rage and lesser pity
          To make the breach and enter this sweet city.

470 First like a trumpet doth his tongue begin
      To sound a parley⁹ to his heartless° foe,   *terrified*
      Who o'er the white sheet peers her whiter chin,
      The reason of this rash alarm to know,
      Which he by dumb demeanour° seeks to show.   *mute gesture*
475   But she with vehement prayers urgeth still
          Under what colour° he commits this ill.   *pretext*

      Thus he replies: 'The colour in thy face,
      That even for anger makes the lily pale
      And the red rose blush at her own disgrace,
480 Shall plead for me and tell my loving tale.
      Under that colour° am I come to scale   *pretext; hue; flag*
          Thy never-conquered fort. The fault is thine,
          For those thine eyes betray thee unto mine.

      'Thus I forestall thee, if thou mean to chide:
485 Thy beauty hath ensnared thee to this night,
      Where thou with patience must my will abide,
      My will that marks thee for my earth's° delight,   *earthly; bodily*
      Which I to conquer sought with all my might.

9. A call to a negotiation.

But as reproof and reason beat it° dead,   *(my lust)*
490   By thy bright beauty was it newly bred.

'I see what crosses° my attempt will bring,   *misfortunes*
I know what thorns the growing rose defends;
I think° the honey guarded with a sting;   *know*
All this beforehand counsel° comprehends.   *wisdom*
495   But will is deaf, and hears no heedful friends.
    Only he hath an eye to gaze on beauty,
    And dotes on what he looks, 'gainst law or duty.

'I have debated even in my soul
What wrong, what shame, what sorrow I shall breed;
500   But nothing can affection's° course control,   *passion's*
Or stop the headlong fury of his speed.
I know repentant tears ensue° the deed,   *follow*
    Reproach, disdain, and deadly enmity,
    Yet strive I to embrace mine infamy.'

505   This said, he shakes aloft his Roman blade,
Which like a falcon tow'ring in the skies
Coucheth the fowl° below with his wings' shade   *Makes the prey crouch*
Whose crooked beak threats, if he° mount he dies.   *(the fowl)*
So under his insulting° falchion lies   *triumphantly exulting*
510   Harmless Lucretia, marking what he tells
    With trembling fear, as fowl hear falcons' bells.[1]

'Lucrece,' quoth he, 'this night I must enjoy thee.
If thou deny, then force must work my way,
For in thy bed I purpose to destroy thee.
515   That done, some worthless slave of thine I'll slay
To kill thine honour with thy life's decay;[2]
    And in thy dead arms do I mean to place him,
    Swearing I slew him seeing thee embrace him.

'So thy surviving husband shall remain
520   The scornful mark of every open eye,°   *observer*
Thy kinsmen hang their heads at this disdain,
Thy issue blurred with nameless bastardy,[3]
And thou, the author of their obloquy,
    Shalt have thy trespass cited up in rhymes°   *described in ballads*
525   And sung by children in succeeding times.

'But if thou yield, I rest thy secret friend.
The fault unknown is as a thought unacted.
A little harm done to a great good end
For lawful policy remains enacted.[4]
530   The poisonous simple° sometime is compacted°   *ingredient / mixed*
    In a pure° compound; being so applied,   *benign*
    His venom in effect is purified.

---

1. Hunting falcons had bells attached to their legs.   father's name is unknown.
2. To destroy your reputation along with your life.   4. For . . . enacted: Is allowed as proper statesmanship.
3. Your children suspected of being bastards whose

'Then for thy husband and thy children's sake
Tender my suit;° bequeath not to their lot   *Regard my plea*
535   The shame that from them no device[5] can take,
The blemish that will never be forgot,
Worse than a slavish wipe or birth-hour's blot;[6]
   For marks descried in men's nativity
   Are nature's faults, not their own infamy.'

540   Here with a cockatrice'[7] dead-killing eye
He rouseth up himself, and makes a pause,
While she, the picture of pure piety,
Like a white hind° under the gripe's° sharp claws,   *doe / griffin*
Pleads in a wilderness where are no laws
545   To the rough beast that knows no gentle right,°   *law of gentility*
   Nor aught obeys but his foul appetite.

But when a black-faced cloud the world doth threat,
In his dim mist th'aspiring mountains hiding,
From earth's dark womb some gentle gust doth get
550   Which blows these pitchy vapours from their biding,°   *place*
Hind'ring their present° fall by this dividing;   *immediate*
   So his unhallowed haste her words delays,
   And moody Pluto winks while Orpheus plays.[8]

Yet, foul night-waking cat, he doth but dally
555   While in his holdfast foot the weak mouse panteth.
Her sad behaviour feeds his vulture folly,°   *ravenous insanity*
A swallowing gulf° that even in plenty wanteth.   *whirlpool; belly*
His ear her prayers admits, but his heart granteth
   No penetrable entrance to her plaining.°   *lament*
560   Tears harden lust, though marble wear with raining.

Her pity-pleading eyes are sadly fixed
In the remorseless wrinkles of his face.
Her modest eloquence with sighs is mixed,
Which to her oratory adds more grace.
565   She puts the period often from his° place,   *its*
   And midst the sentence so her accent breaks
   That twice she doth begin ere once she speaks.

She conjures him by high almighty Jove,
By knighthood, gentry,° and sweet friendship's oath,   *noble birth*
570   By her untimely tears, her husband's love,
By holy human law and common troth,[9]
By heaven and earth and all the power of both,
   That to his borrowed° bed he make retire,   *(guest)*
   And stoop[1] to honour, not to foul desire.

---

5. Ingenuity; heraldic emblem.
6. A slave's brand or birthmark.
7. Legendary monster whose glance was deadly.
8. When Orpheus, a legendary musician and poet, attempted to regain his dead wife from the underworld, he charmed Pluto, god of the underworld, by playing on the lyre.
9. *common troth:* the good faith that binds communities together.
1. Swoop down to a lure (in falconry); lie down; subject himself.

575 Quoth she, 'Reward not hospitality
    With such black payment as thou hast pretended.°   *offered*
    Mud not the fountain that gave drink to thee;
    Mar not the thing that cannot be amended;
    End thy ill aim before thy shoot be ended.
580 He is no woodman° that doth bend his bow   *sportsman*
    To strike a poor unseasonable° doe.   *out-of-season*

    'My husband is thy friend; for his sake spare me.
    Thyself art mighty; for thine own sake leave me;
    Myself a weakling; do not then ensnare me.
585 Thou look'st not like deceit; do not deceive me.
    My sighs like whirlwinds labour hence to heave thee.
        If ever man were moved with woman's moans,
        Be movèd with my tears, my sighs, my groans.

    'All which together, like a troubled ocean,
590 Beat at thy rocky and wreck-threat'ning heart
    To soften it with their continual motion,
    For stones dissolved to water do convert.
        O, if no harder than a stone thou art,
        Melt at my tears, and be compassionate.
595   Soft pity enters at an iron gate.

    'In Tarquin's likeness I did entertain thee.
    Hast thou put on his shape to do him shame?
    To all the host of heaven I complain me.
    Thou wrong'st his honour, wound'st his princely name.
600 Thou art not what thou seem'st, and if the same,
        Thou seem'st not what thou art, a god, a king,
        For kings like gods should govern everything.

    'How will thy shame be seeded° in thine age   *ripened*
    When thus thy vices bud before thy spring?
605 If in thy hope° thou dar'st do such outrage,   *If not yet in power*
    What dar'st thou not when once thou art a king?
    O be remembered, no outrageous thing
        From vassal actors° can be wiped away;   *lowborn criminals*
        Then kings' misdeeds cannot be hid in clay.°   *(even after death)*

610 'This deed will make thee only loved for° fear,   *obeyed out of*
    But happy monarchs still° are feared for love.   *always*
    With foul offenders thou perforce must bear
    When they in thee the like offences prove.
    If but for fear of this, thy will remove;
615   For princes are the glass,° the school, the book   *mirror*
        Where subjects' eyes do learn, do read, do look.

    'And wilt thou be the school where lust shall learn?
    Must he in thee read lectures of such shame?
    Wilt thou be glass wherein it shall discern
620 Authority for sin, warrant for blame,
    To privilege° dishonour in thy name?   *justify*
        Thou back'st° reproach against long-living laud,°   *support / praise*
        And mak'st fair reputation but a bawd.

'Hast thou command?° By him° that gave it thee,   *authority / (God)*
625 From a pure heart command thy rebel will.
Draw not thy sword to guard iniquity,
For it was lent thee all that brood° to kill.   *kind of thing*
Thy princely office how canst thou fulfil
    When, patterned° by thy fault, foul sin may say   *given a precedent*
630   He learned to sin, and thou didst teach the way?

'Think but how vile a spectacle it were
To view thy present trespass in another.
Men's faults do seldom to themselves appear;
Their own transgressions partially they smother.°   *hide (from themselves)*
635 This guilt would seem death-worthy in thy brother.
    O, how are they wrapped in with infamies
    That from their own misdeeds askance° their eyes!   *turn away*

'To thee, to thee my heaved-up hands appeal,
Not to seducing lust, thy rash relier.[2]
640 I sue for exiled majesty's repeal;°   *recall from exile*
Let him return, and flatt'ring thoughts retire.
His true respect° will prison false desire,   *judgment*
    And wipe the dim mist from thy doting eyne,°   *eyes (archaic)*
    That thou shalt see thy state, and pity mine.'

645 'Have done,' quoth he; 'my uncontrollèd tide
Turns not, but swells the higher by this let.°   *restraint*
Small lights are soon blown out; huge fires abide,
And with the wind in greater fury fret.
The petty streams, that pay a daily debt
650   To their salt sovereign,° with their fresh falls' haste   *(the sea)*
    Add to his flow, but alter not his taste.'

'Thou art,' quoth she, 'a sea, a sovereign king,
And lo, there falls into thy boundless flood
Black lust, dishonour, shame, misgoverning,
655 Who seek to stain the ocean of thy blood.°   *disposition; birthright*
If all these petty ills shall change thy good,
    Thy sea within a puddle's womb is hearsed,°   *enclosed*
    And not the puddle in thy sea dispersed.

'So shall these slaves° be king, and thou their slave;   *(lust, dishonor, etc.)*
660 Thou nobly base, they basely dignified;
Thou their fair life, and they thy fouler grave;
Thou loathèd in their shame, they in thy pride.
The lesser thing should not the greater hide.
    The cedar stoops not to the base shrub's foot,
665   But low shrubs wither at the cedar's root.

'So let thy thoughts, low vassals to thy state'—
'No more,' quoth he, 'by heaven, I will not hear thee.
Yield to my love. If not, enforcèd hate
Instead of love's coy° touch shall rudely tear thee.   *gentle*
670 That done, despitefully° I mean to bear thee   *maliciously*

---

2. *thy rash relier*: on which you rashly rely.

Unto the base bed of some rascal groom°   *servant*
To be thy partner in this shameful doom.'

This said, he sets his foot upon the light;
For light and lust are deadly enemies.
675 Shame folded up in blind concealing night
When most unseen, then most doth tyrannize.
The wolf hath seized his prey, the poor lamb cries,
 Till with her own white fleece° her voice controlled° *(bedclothes) / overpowered*
 Entombs her outcry in her lips' sweet fold.°   *crevice; sheep pen*

680 For with the nightly linen that she wears
He pens her piteous clamours in her head,
Cooling his hot face in the chastest tears
That ever modest eyes with sorrow shed.
O that prone° lust should stain so pure a bed,   *headlong; eager*
685 The spots whereof could weeping purify,
 Her tears should drop on them perpetually!

But she hath lost a dearer thing than life,
And he hath won what he would lose again.
This forcèd league doth force a further strife,
690 This momentary joy breeds months of pain;
This hot desire converts to cold disdain.
 Pure chastity is rifled of her store,
 And lust, the thief, far poorer than before.

Look° as the full-fed hound or gorgèd hawk,   *Just*
695 Unapt for tender° smell or speedy flight,   *delicate*
Make slow pursuit, or altogether balk°   *turn from*
The prey wherein by nature they delight,
So surfeit-taking Tarquin fares° this night.   *behaves; feeds*
 His taste delicious, in digestion souring,
700 Devours his will that lived by foul devouring.

O deeper sin than bottomless conceit°   *unlimited fantasy*
Can comprehend in still imagination!
Drunken desire must vomit his receipt°   *what he swallowed*
Ere he can see his own abomination.
705 While lust is in his pride, no exclamation
 Can curb his heat or rein his rash desire,
 Till like a jade° self-will himself doth tire. *recalcitrant horse*

And then with lank and lean discoloured cheek,
With heavy eye, knit brow, and strengthless pace,
710 Feeble desire, all recreant,[3] poor, and meek,
Like to a bankrupt beggar wails his case.
The flesh being proud, desire doth fight with grace,
 For there it revels, and when that decays,°   *subsides*
 The guilty rebel for remission° prays.   *pardon*

715 So fares it with this faultful lord of Rome
Who this accomplishment so hotly chased;

3. Cowardly; faithless; exhausted.

For now against himself he sounds° this doom,°   *pronounces / sentence*
That through the length of times he stands disgraced.
Besides, his soul's fair temple is defaced,
720   To whose weak ruins muster troops of cares
     To ask the spotted princess° how she fares.   *(the defiled soul)*

She says her subjects with foul insurrection
Have battered down her consecrated wall,
And by their mortal° fault brought in subjection   *deadly*
725   Her immortality, and made her thrall
To living death and pain perpetual,
     Which° in her prescience she controllèd still,   *(the soul's subjects)*
     But her foresight could not forestall their will.

Ev'n in this thought through the dark night he stealeth,
730   A captive victor that hath lost in gain,
Bearing away the wound that nothing healeth,
The scar that will, despite of cure, remain;
Leaving his spoil° perplexed in greater pain.   *prey*
     She bears the load of lust he left behind,
735   And he the burden of a guilty mind.

He like a thievish dog creeps sadly thence;
She like a wearied lamb lies panting there.
He scowls, and hates himself for his offence;
She, desperate, with her nails her flesh doth tear.
740   He faintly flies, sweating with guilty fear;
     She stays, exclaiming on° the direful night.   *denouncing*
     He runs, and chides his vanished loathed delight.

He thence departs, a heavy convertite;°   *sad penitent*
She there remains, a hopeless castaway.
745   He in his speed looks for the morning light;
She prays she never may behold the day.
'For day,' quoth she, 'night's scapes° doth open lay,   *sins*
     And my true eyes have never practised how
     To cloak offences with a cunning brow.

750   'They think not but that every eye can see
The same disgrace which they themselves behold,
And therefore would they still in darkness be,
To have their unseen sin remain untold.
For they their guilt with weeping will unfold,
755   And grave,° like water that doth eat in steel,[4]   *engrave*
     Upon my cheeks what helpless shame I feel.'

Here she exclaims against repose and rest,
And bids her eyes hereafter still be blind.
She wakes her heart by beating on her breast,
760   And bids it leap from thence where it may find
Some purer chest to close° so pure a mind.   *enclose*
     Frantic with grief, thus breathes she forth her spite°   *reproach*
     Against the unseen secrecy of night:

---

4. Aqua fortis (literally, "strong water"), nitric acid.

'O comfort-killing night, image of hell,
765 Dim register° and notary of shame,   *recorder*
Black stage for tragedies and murders fell,
Vast sin-concealing chaos, nurse of blame!
Blind muffled bawd, dark harbour for defame,°   *infamy*
   Grim cave of death, whisp'ring conspirator
770   With close-tongued treason and the ravisher!

'O hateful, vaporous, and foggy night,
Since thou art guilty of my cureless crime,
Muster thy mists to meet the eastern light,
Make war against proportioned° course of time.   *orderly*
775 Or if thou wilt permit the sun to climb
   His wonted height, yet ere he go to bed
   Knit poisonous clouds about his golden head.

'With rotten damps° ravish the morning air,   *vapors*
Let their exhaled unwholesome breaths make sick
780 The life of purity, the supreme fair,°   *(the sun)*
Ere he arrive his weary noon-tide prick;°   *mark on a clock*
And let thy musty vapours march so thick
   That in their smoky ranks his smothered light
   May set at noon, and make perpetual night.

785 'Were Tarquin night, as he is but night's child,
The silver-shining queen[5] he would distain;°   *stain*
Her twinkling handmaids° too, by him defiled,   *(the stars)*
Through night's black bosom should not peep again.
So should I have co-partners in my pain,
790   And fellowship in woe doth woe assuage,
   As palmers'° chat makes short their pilgrimage.   *pilgrims'*

'Where now I have no one to blush with me,
To cross their arms[6] and hang their heads with mine,
To mask their brows and hide their infamy,
795 But I alone, alone must sit and pine,
Seasoning the earth with showers of silver brine,
   Mingling my talk with tears, my grief with groans,
   Poor wasting monuments° of lasting moans.   *short-lived tokens*

'O night, thou furnace of foul reeking smoke,
800 Let not the jealous° day behold that face   *suspicious*
Which underneath thy black all-hiding cloak
Immodestly lies martyred with disgrace!
Keep still possession of thy gloomy place,
   That all the faults which in thy reign are made
805   May likewise be sepulchred in thy shade.

'Make me not object° to the tell-tale day: *manifest*
The light will show charactered° in my brow   *written*
The story of sweet chastity's decay,
The impious breach of holy wedlock vow.
810 Yea, the illiterate that know not how

---

5. The moon, symbol of chastity.   6. This is a conventional gesture of melancholy.

To cipher° what is writ in learnèd books   *decipher*
Will quote° my loathsome trespass in my looks.   *note*

'The nurse to still her child will tell my story,
And fright her crying babe with Tarquin's name.
815 The orator to deck his oratory
Will couple my reproach to Tarquin's shame.
Feast-finding minstrels[7] tuning my defame
    Will tie the hearers to attend° each line,   *listen to*
    How Tarquin wrongèd me, I Collatine.

820 'Let my good name, that senseless° reputation,   *intangible*
For Collatine's dear love be kept unspotted;
If that be made a theme for disputation,
The branches of another root are rotted,[8]
And undeserved reproach to him allotted
825   That is as clear from this attaint° of mine   *stain*
    As I ere this was pure to Collatine.

'O unseen shame, invisible disgrace!
O unfelt sore, crest-wounding[9] private scar!
Reproach° is stamped in Collatinus' face,   *Reproof; dishonor*
830 And Tarquin's eye may read the mot° afar,   *motto*
How he in peace is wounded, not in war.
    Alas, how many bear such shameful blows,
    Which not themselves but he that gives them knows!

'If, Collatine, thine honour lay in me,
835 From me by strong assault it is bereft;
My honey lost, and I, a drone-like bee,
Have no perfection of my summer left,[1]
But robbed and ransacked by injurious theft.
    In thy weak hive a wandering wasp hath crept,
840   And sucked the honey which thy chaste bee kept.

'Yet am I guilty of thy honour's wrack;°   *ruin*
Yet for thy honour did I entertain him.
Coming from thee, I could not put him back,
For it had been dishonour to disdain him.
845 Besides, of weariness he did complain him,
    And talked of virtue—O unlooked-for evil,
    When virtue is profaned in such a devil!

'Why should the worm intrude the maiden bud,
Or hateful cuckoos hatch in sparrows' nests,
850 Or toads infect fair founts with venom° mud,   *venomous*
Or tyrant folly° lurk in gentle breasts,   *cruel lewdness*
Or kings be breakers of their own behests?°   *commands*
    But no perfection is so absolute
    That some impurity doth not pollute.

---

7. Minstrels were paid to perform at banquets.
8. That is, Collatine's reputation is also destroyed.
9. Damaging the coat of arms, hence family honor (cf.

lines 204–10).
1. Have nothing left of what I made in the summer; have none of the purity of my prime remaining.

855 'The agèd man that coffers up his gold
Is plagued with cramps, and gouts, and painful fits,
And scarce hath eyes his treasure to behold,
But like still-pining Tantalus² he sits,
And useless barns° the harvest of his wits,   *hoards*
860   Having no other pleasure of his gain
    But torment that it cannot cure his pain.

'So then he hath it when he cannot use it,
And leaves it to be mastered° by his young,°   *possessed / children*
Who in their pride do presently° abuse it.   *immediately*
865 Their father was too weak and they too strong
To hold their cursèd-blessèd fortune long.
    The sweets we wish for turn to loathèd sours
    Even in the moment that we call them ours.

'Unruly blasts wait on the tender spring,
870 Unwholesome weeds take root with precious flowers,
The adder hisses where the sweet birds sing,
What virtue breeds, iniquity devours.
We have no good that we can say is ours
    But ill-annexèd opportunity³
875   Or° kills his life or else his quality.   *Either*

'O opportunity, thy guilt is great!
'Tis thou that execut'st the traitor's treason;
Thou sets the wolf where he the lamb may get;
Whoever plots the sin, thou point'st° the season.   *appoint*
880 'Tis thou that spurn'st at right, at law, at reason;
    And in thy shady cell where none may spy him
    Sits sin, to seize the souls that wander by him.

'Thou mak'st the vestal⁴ violate her oath,
Thou blow'st the fire when temperance is thawed,
885 Thou smother'st honesty, thou murd'rest troth,
Thou foul abettor, thou notorious bawd;°   *procurer*
Thou plantest scandal and displacest laud.
    Thou ravisher, thou traitor, thou false thief,
    Thy honey turns to gall, thy joy to grief.

890 'Thy secret pleasure turns to open shame,
Thy private feasting to a public fast,
Thy smoothing° titles to a ragged name,   *flattering*
Thy sugared tongue to bitter wormwood taste.
Thy violent vanities can never last.
895   How comes it then, vile opportunity,
    Being so bad, such numbers seek for thee?

'When wilt thou be the humble suppliant's friend,
And bring him where his suit may be obtained?
When wilt thou sort° an hour great strifes to end,   *select*

2. A mythological figure who was punished in Hades by eternal hunger and thirst; food and water were always visible but receded at his approach.
3. Bad circumstances joined to or following from the good.
4. The priestess of Vesta, Roman goddess of the hearth and household; vestals were sworn to lifelong virginity.

900   Or free that soul which wretchedness hath chained,
    Give physic° to the sick, ease to the pained?   *medicine*
       The poor, lame, blind, halt,° creep, cry out for thee,   *limp*
       But they ne'er meet with opportunity.

    'The patient dies while the physician sleeps,
905   The orphan pines while the oppressor feeds,
    Justice is feasting while the widow weeps,
    Advice° is sporting while infection breeds.   *(medical advice)*
    Thou grant'st no time for charitable deeds.
       Wrath, envy, treason, rape, and murder's rages,
910   Thy heinous hours wait on them as their pages.

    'When truth and virtue have to do with thee
    A thousand crosses° keep them from thy aid.   *impediments*
    They buy° thy help, but sin ne'er gives a fee;   *(must pay for)*
    He gratis comes, and thou art well appaid°   *satisfied*
915   As well to hear as grant what he hath said.
       My Collatine would else have come to me
       When Tarquin did, but he was stayed by thee.

    'Guilty thou art of murder and of theft,
    Guilty of perjury and subornation,[5]
920   Guilty of treason, forgery, and shift,°   *fraud*
    Guilty of incest, that abomination:
    An accessory by thine inclination°   *nature*
       To all sins past and all that are to come
       From the creation to the general doom.

925   'Misshapen time, copesmate° of ugly night,   *comrade*
    Swift subtle post,° carrier of grisly care,   *messenger*
    Eater of youth, false slave to false delight,
    Base watch° of woes, sin's pack-horse, virtue's snare,   *town crier; announcer*
    Thou nursest all, and murd'rest all that are.
930   O hear me then, injurious shifting° time;   *changing; traitorous*
       Be guilty of my death, since° of my crime.   *as thou art*

    'Why hath thy servant opportunity
    Betrayed the hours thou gav'st me to repose,
    Cancelled my fortunes, and enchainèd me
935   To endless date° of never-ending woes?   *duration*
    Time's office is to fine° the hate of foes,   *end; punish*
       To eat up errors by opinion° bred,   *rumor*
       Not spend the dowry of a lawful bed.

    'Time's glory is to calm contending kings,
940   To unmask falsehood and bring truth to light,
    To stamp the seal of time in agèd things,
    To wake the morn and sentinel° the night,   *guard*
    To wrong the wronger till he render right,
       To ruinate proud buildings with thy hours
945   And smear with dust their glitt'ring golden towers;

---

5. Bribing others to give false testimony.

'To fill with worm-holes stately monuments,
To feed oblivion with decay of things,
To blot old books and alter their contents,
To pluck the quills from ancient ravens' wings,
950   To dry the old oak's sap and blemish° springs,   *contaminate*
    To spoil antiquities of hammered steel,
    And turn the giddy round of fortune's wheel;

'To show the beldame° daughters of her daughter,   *old woman*
To make the child a man, the man a child,
955   To slay the tiger that doth live by slaughter,
To tame the unicorn and lion wild,
To mock the subtle in themselves beguiled,[6]
    To cheer the ploughman with increaseful crops,
    And waste huge stones with little water drops.

960   'Why work'st thou mischief in thy pilgrimage,
Unless thou couldst return to make amends?
One poor retiring[7] minute in an age
Would purchase thee a thousand thousand friends,
Lending him wit that to bad debtors lends.
965   O this dread night, wouldst thou one hour come back,
    I could prevent this storm and shun thy wrack!

'Thou ceaseless lackey° to eternity,   *eternal servant*
With some mischance cross Tarquin in his flight.
Devise extremes beyond extremity
970   To make him curse this cursèd crimeful night.
Let ghastly shadows his lewd eyes affright,
    And the dire thought of his committed evil
    Shape every bush a hideous shapeless devil.

'Disturb his hours of rest with restless trances;°   *dreams; seizures*
975   Afflict him in his bed with bedrid groans;
Let there bechance him pitiful mischances
To make him moan, but pity not his moans.
Stone him with hardened hearts harder than stones,
    And let mild women to him lose their mildness,
980   Wilder to him than tigers in their wildness.

'Let him have time to tear his curlèd hair,
Let him have time against himself to rave,
Let him have time of time's help to despair,
Let him have time to live a loathèd slave,
985   Let him have time a beggar's orts° to crave,   *scraps*
    And time to see one that by alms doth live
    Disdain to him disdainèd scraps to give.

'Let him have time to see his friends his foes,
And merry fools to mock at him resort.°   *gather*
990   Let him have time to mark how slow time goes
In time of sorrow, and how swift and short

---

6. The cunning, taken in by their own schemes.
7. Returning (thus permitting people to do things differently).

His time of folly and his time of sport;
    And ever let his unrecalling crime[8]
    Have time to wail th'abusing of his time.

995 'O time, thou tutor both to good and bad,
Teach me to curse him that thou taught'st this ill;
At his own shadow let the thief run mad,
Himself himself seek every hour to kill;
Such wretched hands such wretched blood should spill,
1000   For who so base would such an office have
    As sland'rous deathsman° to so base a slave?   *detested executioner*

'The baser is he, coming from a king,
To shame his hope with deeds degenerate.
The mightier man, the mightier is the thing
1005 That makes him honoured or begets him hate,
For greatest scandal waits on greatest state.[9]
    The moon being clouded presently° is missed,   *immediately*
    But little stars may hide them when they list.°   *wish*

'The crow may bathe his coal-black wings in mire
1010 And unperceived fly with the filth away,
But if the like the snow-white swan desire,
The stain upon his silver down will stay.
Poor grooms° are sightless° night, kings glorious day.   *servants / dark*
    Gnats are unnoted wheresoe'er they fly,
1015   But eagles gazed upon with every eye.

'Out, idle words, servants to shallow fools,
Unprofitable sounds, weak arbitrators!
Busy yourselves in skill-contending schools,°   *(of rhetoric)*
Debate where leisure serves with dull debaters,
1020 To trembling clients be you mediators;
    For me, I force° not argument a straw,   *value*
    Since that my case is past the help of law.

'In vain I rail at opportunity,
At time, at Tarquin, and uncheerful night.
1025 In vain I cavil with° mine infamy,   *object to*
In vain I spurn at my confirmed despite.°   *irreparable injury*
This helpless° smoke of words doth me no right;   *unhelpful; weak*
    The remedy indeed to do me good
    Is to let forth my foul defilèd blood.

1030 'Poor hand, why quiver'st thou at this decree?
Honour thyself to rid me of this shame,
For if I die, my honour lives in thee,
But if I live, thou liv'st in my defame.°   *infamy*
Since thou couldst not defend thy loyal dame,
1035   And wast afeard to scratch her wicked foe,
    Kill both thyself and her for yielding so.'

8. Crime that cannot be undone.   9. Attends those of highest rank.

This said, from her betumbled couch she starteth,
To find some desp'rate instrument of death.
But this, no slaughterhouse, no tool imparteth°　　　　　*furnishes*
1040 To make more vent° for passage of her breath,　　　　　*a bigger hole*
Which thronging through her lips so vanisheth
　　As smoke from Etna that in air consumes,
　　Or that which from dischargèd cannon fumes.

'In vain,' quoth she, 'I live, and seek in vain
1045 Some happy mean to end a hapless life.
I feared by Tarquin's falchion to be slain,
Yet for the selfsame purpose seek a knife.
But when I feared I was a loyal wife;
　　So am I now—O no, that cannot be,
1050 　　Of that true type° hath Tarquin rifled me.　　　　　*pattern of virtue*

'O, that is gone for which I sought to live,
And therefore now I need not fear to die.
To clear this spot by death, at least I give
A badge of fame to slander's livery,°　　　　　*servant's uniform*
1055 A dying life to living infamy.
　　Poor helpless help, the treasure stol'n away,
　　To burn the guiltless casket where it lay!

'Well, well, dear Collatine, thou shalt not know
The stainèd taste of violated troth.
1060 I will not wrong thy true affection so
To flatter thee with an infringèd oath.
This bastard graft[1] shall never come to growth.
　　He shall not boast, who did thy stock pollute,
　　That thou art doting father of his fruit,

1065 'Nor shall he smile at thee in secret thought,
Nor laugh with his companions at thy state.
But thou shalt know thy int'rest° was not bought　　　　　*property*
Basely with gold, but stol'n from forth thy gate.
For me, I am the mistress of my fate,
1070 　　And with my trespass never will dispense°　　　　　*dispense with = excuse*
　　Till life to death acquit° my forced offence.　　　　　*atone for*

'I will not poison thee with my attaint,°　　　　　*contamination*
Nor fold° my fault in cleanly coined excuses.　　　　　*envelop*
My sable ground[2] of sin I will not paint
1075 To hide the truth of this false night's abuses.
My tongue shall utter all; mine eyes, like sluices,
　　As from a mountain spring that feeds a dale
　　Shall gush pure streams to purge my impure tale.'

1080 By this, lamenting Philomel[3] had ended
The well-tuned warble of her nightly sorrow,

---

1. Lucrece assumes that Tarquin has made her pregnant. Her image is from the grafting of plants, in which
two different kinds of plants are artificially forced to
grow as one; a "bastard slip" is an unwanted shoot.
2. Black background (a heraldic term).

3. The nightingale. In classical mythology, Philomela
was raped by King Tereus, her sister's husband, and
with her sister took vengeance on him. All three were
changed into birds (see Ovid, *Metamorphoses* 6).

And solemn night with slow sad gait descended
To ugly hell, when lo, the blushing morrow
Lends light to all fair eyes that light will borrow.
    But cloudy° Lucrece shames° herself to see,   *melancholy / is ashamed*
1085   And therefore still in night would cloistered be.

Revealing day through every cranny spies,
And seems to point her out where she sits weeping;
To whom she sobbing speaks, 'O eye of eyes,
Why pry'st thou through my window? Leave thy peeping,
1090   Mock with thy tickling beams eyes that are sleeping,
        Brand not my forehead with thy piercing light,
        For day hath naught to do what's done by night.'

Thus cavils she with everything she sees:
True grief is fond° and testy as a child   *foolish*
1095   Who, wayward once,° his mood with naught agrees;   *once out of sorts*
Old woes, not infant sorrows, bear them mild.°   *bear themselves mildly*
Continuance tames the one; the other wild,
        Like an unpractised swimmer plunging still,°   *constantly*
        With too much labour drowns for want of skill.

1100   So she, deep drenchèd in a sea of care,
Holds disputation with each thing she views,
And to herself all sorrow doth compare;
No object but her passion's strength renews,
And as one shifts,° another straight° ensues.   *moves / immediately*
1105   Sometime her grief is dumb° and hath no words,   *mute*
        Sometime 'tis mad and too much talk affords.

The little birds that tune their morning's joy
Make her moans mad with their sweet melody,
For mirth doth search° the bottom of annoy;°   *probe / vexation*
1110   Sad souls are slain° in merry company;   *overcome with distress*
Grief best is pleased with grief's society.
        True sorrow then is feelingly sufficed°   *properly contented*
        When with like semblance it is sympathized.°   *matched*

'Tis double death to drown in ken° of shore;   *sight*
1115   He ten times pines° that pines beholding food;   *starves*
To see the salve doth make the wound ache more;
Great grief grieves most at that would do it good;
Deep woes roll forward like a gentle flood
        Who, being stopped, the bounding° banks o'erflows.   *confining*
1120   Grief dallied° with nor° law nor limit knows.   *trifled / neither*

'You mocking birds,' quoth she, 'your tunes entomb
Within your hollow-swelling feathered breasts,
And in my hearing be you mute and dumb;
My restless discord loves no stops nor rests;
1125   A woeful hostess brooks° not merry guests.   *tolerates*
        Relish° your nimble notes to pleasing ears;   *Warble; make pleasing*
        Distress likes dumps° when time is kept with tears.   *sad songs*

'Come, Philomel, that sing'st of ravishment,
Make thy sad grove in my dishevelled hair.
1130　As the dank earth weeps at thy languishment,°　　　　　　　　*lamentation*
So I at each sad strain will strain a tear,
And with deep groans the diapason° bear;　　　　　　　　*bass accompaniment*
　　For burden-wise[4] I'll hum on Tarquin still,
　　While thou on Tereus descants better skill.[5]

1135　'And whiles against a thorn[6] thou bear'st thy part
To keep thy sharp woes waking, wretched I,
To imitate thee well, against my heart
Will fix a sharp knife to affright mine eye,
Who° if it wink° shall thereon fall and die.　　　　　　　　*(I) / (my eye) close*
1140　　These means, as frets° upon an instrument,　　　　　*(punning on "vexation")*
　　Shall tune our heart-strings to true languishment.

'And for, poor bird, thou sing'st not in the day,
As shaming any eye should thee behold,
Some dark deep desert seated from the way,[7]
1145　That knows not parching heat nor freezing cold,
Will we find out, and there we will unfold
　　To creatures stern sad tunes to change their kinds.°　　　*natures*
　　Since men prove beasts, let beasts bear gentle minds.'

As the poor frighted deer that stands at gaze,
1150　Wildly determining which way to fly,
Or one encompassed with a winding maze,
That cannot tread the way out readily,
So with herself is she in mutiny,
　　To live or die which of the twain were better
1155　　When life is shamed and death reproach's debtor.°　　　*will incur reproach*

'To kill myself,' quoth she, 'alack, what were it
But with my body my poor soul's pollution?[8]
They that lose half with greater patience bear it
Than they whose whole is swallowed in confusion.°　　　　　*ruin*
1160　That mother tries a merciless conclusion°　　　　　　　　*experiment*
　　Who, having two sweet babes, when death takes one
　　Will slay the other and be nurse to none.

'My body or my soul, which was the dearer,
When the one pure the other made divine?
1165　Whose love of either to myself was nearer,
When both were kept for heaven and Collatine?
Ay me, the bark peeled from the lofty pine
　　His leaves will wither and his sap decay;
　　So must my soul, her bark being peeled away.

1170　'Her house is sacked, her quiet interrupted,
Her mansion battered by the enemy,
Her sacred temple spotted, spoiled, corrupted,

4. Like a bass line; playing on "burden" as sorrow, weight.
5. Sings the treble part more skillfully.
6. The nightingale was imagined to press against a thorn to keep itself awake during the night.
7. Some uninhabited place located far from the road.
8. To pollute my poor soul, as my body has already been polluted.

Grossly engirt with daring° infamy.   *unrestrained*
Then let it not be called impiety
1175 If in this blemished fort° I make some hole   *(my body)*
Through which I may convey° this troubled soul. *steal away*

'Yet die I will not till my Collatine
Have heard the cause of my untimely death,
That he may vow in that sad hour of mine
1180 Revenge on him that made me stop my breath.
My stainèd blood to Tarquin I'll bequeath,
 Which by him tainted shall for him be spent,
 And as his due writ° in my testament.° *written / last will*

'My honour I'll bequeath unto the knife
1185 That wounds my body so dishonourèd.
'Tis honour to deprive° dishonoured life;   *take away*
The one° will live, the other° being dead. *(honor) / (life)*
So of shame's ashes shall my fame be bred,⁹
 For in my death I murder shameful scorn;
1190 My shame so dead, mine honour is new born.

'Dear lord of that dear jewel° I have lost,   *(chastity)*
What legacy shall I bequeath to thee?
My resolution, love, shall be thy boast,
By whose example thou revenged mayst be.
1195 How Tarquin must be used, read it in me.
 Myself, thy friend, will kill myself, thy foe;
 And for my sake serve° thou false Tarquin so. *treat*

'This brief abridgement of my will I make:
My soul and body to the skies and ground;
1200 My resolution, husband, do thou take;
Mine honour be the knife's that makes my wound;
My shame be his that did my fame confound;
 And all my fame that lives disbursèd be° *that remains be paid out*
 To those that live and think no shame of me.

1205 'Thou, Collatine, shalt oversee° this will.   *execute*
How was I overseen° that thou shalt see it! *deluded*
My blood shall wash the slander of mine ill;
My life's foul deed my life's fair end shall free it.
Faint not, faint heart, but stoutly say "So be it".
1210 Yield to my hand, my hand shall conquer thee;
 Thou dead, both die, and both shall victors be.'

This plot of death when sadly she had laid,
And wiped the brinish° pearl from her bright eyes, *salty*
With untuned° tongue she hoarsely calls her maid, *inharmonious*
1215 Whose swift obedience to her mistress hies;° *hastens*
For fleet-winged duty with thought's feathers flies.
 Poor Lucrece' cheeks unto her maid seem so
 As winter meads when sun doth melt their snow.

---

9. My honor will be like the mythological phoenix, consumed in fire only to be reborn from the ashes.

Her mistress she doth give demure good-morrow
1220 With soft slow tongue, true mark of modesty,
And sorts° a sad look to her lady's sorrow,   *suits*
For why° her face wore sorrow's livery;°   *Because / attire*
But durst not ask of her audaciously
    Why her two suns were cloud-eclipsèd so,
1225   Nor why her fair cheeks over-washed with woe.

But as the earth doth weep, the sun being set,
Each flower moistened like a melting eye,
Even so the maid with swelling drops gan wet
Her circled° eyne, enforced° by sympathy   *rounded / compelled*
1230 Of those fair suns set in her mistress' sky,
    Who in a salt-waved ocean quench their light;
    Which makes the maid weep like the dewy night.

A pretty while° these pretty creatures stand,   *fair amount of time*
Like ivory conduits coral cisterns filling.
1235 One justly weeps, the other takes in hand°   *acknowledges*
No cause but company of her drops' spilling.
Their gentle sex to weep are often willing,
    Grieving themselves to guess at° others' smarts,°   *conjecture / pains*
    And then they drown their eyes or break their hearts.

1240 For men have marble, women waxen minds,
And therefore are they formed as marble will.
The weak oppressed, th'impression of strange kinds°   *alien natures*
Is formed in them by force, by fraud, or skill.
Then call them not the authors of their ill,
1245   No more than wax shall be accounted evil
    Wherein is stamped the semblance of a devil.

Their smoothness like a goodly champaign plain°   *open field*
Lays open° all the little worms that creep;   *Reveals*
In men as in a rough-grown grove remain
1250 Cave-keeping° evils that obscurely° sleep.   *Concealed / unseen*
Through crystal walls each little mote° will peep;   *speck*
    Though men can cover crimes with bold stern looks,
    Poor women's faces are their own faults' books.

No man° inveigh against the withered flower,   *Let no man*
1255 But chide rough winter that the flower hath killed.
Not that devoured, but that which doth devour
Is worthy blame. O, let it not be held
Poor women's faults that they are so full-filled
    With men's abuses. Those proud lords, to blame,
1260   Make weak-made women tenants to their shame.

The precedent° whereof in Lucrece view,   *proof*
Assailed by night with circumstances strong
Of present° death, and shame that might ensue   *immediate*
By that her death, to do her husband wrong.
1265 Such danger to resistance did belong
    That dying fear through all her body spread;
    And who cannot abuse a body dead?

By this,° mild patience bid fair Lucrece speak   *this time*
To the poor counterfeit of her complaining.°   *(the weeping maid)*
1270 'My girl,' quoth she, 'on what occasion break
Those tears from thee that down thy cheeks are raining?
If thou dost weep for grief of my sustaining,°   *borne by me*
    Know, gentle wench, it small avails° my mood.   *little helps*
    If tears could help, mine own would do me good.

1275 'But tell me, girl, when went'—and there she stayed,
Till after a deep groan—'Tarquin from hence?'
'Madam, ere I was up,' replied the maid,
'The more to blame my sluggard negligence.
Yet with the fault I thus far can dispense:°   *excuse*
1280   Myself was stirring ere the break of day,
    And ere I rose was Tarquin gone away.

'But lady, if your maid may be so bold,
She would request to know your heaviness.'°   *sorrow*
'O, peace,' quoth Lucrece, 'if it should be told,
1285 The repetition cannot make it less;
For more it is than I can well express,
    And that deep torture may be called a hell
    When more is felt than one hath power to tell.

'Go, get me hither paper, ink, and pen;
1290 Yet save that labour, for I have them here.
What should I say? One of my husband's men
Bid thou be ready by and by to bear
A letter to my lord, my love, my dear.
    Bid him with speed prepare to carry it;
1295   The cause craves° haste, and it will soon be writ.'   *requires*

Her maid is gone, and she prepares to write,
First hovering o'er the paper with her quill.
Conceit° and grief an eager combat fight;   *Imagination*
What wit° sets down is blotted straight with will;°   *thought / passion*
1300 This is too curious-good,° this blunt and ill.   *elaborate*
    Much like a press° of people at a door   *crowd*
    Throng her inventions, which shall go before.°   *first*

At last she thus begins: 'Thou worthy lord
Of that unworthy wife that greeteth thee,
1305 Health to thy person! Next, vouchsafe t'afford—
If ever, love, thy Lucrece thou wilt see—
Some present° speed to come and visit me.   *immediate*
    So I commend me,° from our house in grief;   *ask to be remembered*
    My woes are tedious, though my words are brief.'

1310 Here folds she up the tenor° of her woe,   *gist*
Her certain sorrow writ uncertainly.
By this short schedule° Collatine may know   *summary*
Her grief, but not her grief's true quality.
She dares not thereof make discovery,°   *revelation*
1315   Lest he should hold it her own gross abuse,°   *trespass*
    Ere she with blood had stained her stain's excuse.

Besides, the life and feeling of her passion
She hoards, to spend when he is by to hear her,
When sighs and groans and tears may grace the fashion°   *appearance; fashioning*
1320   Of her disgrace, the better so to clear her
From that suspicion which the world might bear her.
    To shun this blot she would not blot the letter
    With words, till action might become° them better.   *suit*

To see sad sights moves more than hear them told,
1325   For then the eye interprets to the ear
The heavy motion° that it doth behold,   *sad action*
When every part a part of woe doth bear.
'Tis but a part of sorrow that we hear;
    Deep sounds make lesser noise than shallow fords,
1330   And sorrow ebbs, being blown with wind of words.

Her letter now is sealed, and on it writ
'At Ardea to my lord with more than haste'.
The post attends,° and she delivers it,   *messenger waits*
Charging the sour-faced groom to hie as fast
1335   As lagging fowls before the northern blast.
    Speed more than speed° but dull and slow she deems;   *Even unusual speed*
    Extremity still urgeth such extremes.

The homely villain° curtsies to her low,   *unpolished menial*
And blushing on her with a steadfast eye
1340   Receives the scroll without or° yea or no,   *either*
And forth with bashful innocence doth hie.
But they whose guilt within their bosoms lie
    Imagine every eye beholds their blame,
    For Lucrece thought he blushed to see her shame,

1345   When, silly groom,° God wot,° it was defect   *simple servant / knows*
Of spirit, life, and bold audacity.
Such harmless creatures have a true respect
To talk in deeds,[1] while others saucily
Promise more speed, but do it leisurely.
1350   Even so this pattern of the worn-out age°   *old-fashioned model*
    Pawned° honest looks, but laid no words to gage.°   *Offered / as a pledge*

His kindled duty[2] kindled her mistrust,
That two red fires in both their faces blazed.
She thought he blushed as knowing Tarquin's lust,
1355   And blushing with him, wistly° on him gazed.   *attentively*
Her earnest eye did make him more amazed.°   *bewildered*
    The more she saw the blood his cheeks replenish,
    The more she thought he spied in her some blemish.

But long she thinks° till he return again,   *she thinks it long*
1360   And yet the duteous vassal scarce is gone.
The weary time she cannot entertain,°   *while away*
For now 'tis stale to sigh, to weep, and groan.

1. *have . . . deeds*: rightly express their deference by   2. His blushing bow; his ardent loyalty.
their actions (rather than merely by their words).

So woe hath wearied woe, moan tired moan,
   That she her plaints a little while doth stay,
1365   Pausing for means to mourn some newer way.

At last she calls to mind where hangs a piece
   Of skilful painting made for° Priam's Troy,   *representing*
   Before the which is drawn the power° of Greece,   *army*
   For Helen's rape the city to destroy,
1370   Threat'ning cloud-kissing Ilion° with annoy;°   *high-built Troy / injury*
      Which the conceited° painter drew so proud   *ingenious*
      As heaven, it seemed, to kiss the turrets bowed.

A thousand lamentable objects there,
   In scorn of° nature, art gave lifeless life.   *Defying*
1375   Many a dry drop seemed a weeping tear
   Shed for the slaughtered husband by the wife.
   The red blood reeked° to show the painter's strife,[3]   *smoked*
      And dying eyes gleamed forth their ashy lights
      Like dying coals burnt out in tedious nights.

1380   There might you see the labouring pioneer°   *trench digger*
   Begrimed with sweat and smearèd all with dust,
   And from the towers of Troy there would appear
   The very eyes of men through loop-holes thrust,
   Gazing upon the Greeks with little lust.°   *pleasure*
1385   Such sweet observance° in this work was had   *verisimilitude*
      That one might see those far-off eyes look sad.

In great commanders grace and majesty
   You might behold, triumphing in their faces;
   In youth, quick° bearing and dexterity;   *lively*
1390   And here and there the painter interlaces
   Pale cowards marching on with trembling paces,
      Which heartless° peasants did so well resemble   *dejected*
      That one would swear he saw them quake and tremble.

In Ajax and Ulysses, O what art
1395   Of physiognomy might one behold!
   The face of either ciphered° either's heart;   *represented*
   Their face their manners most expressly told.
   In Ajax' eyes blunt° rage and rigour rolled,   *rude*
      But the mild glance that sly Ulysses lent
1400   Showed deep regard° and smiling government.°   *judgment / self-control*

There pleading° might you see grave Nestor stand,   *persuading*
   As 'twere encouraging the Greeks to fight,
   Making such sober action with his hand
   That it beguiled attention, charmed the sight.
1405   In speech it seemed his beard all silver-white
      Wagged up and down, and from his lips did fly
      Thin winding breath which purled° up to the sky.   *curled*

---

3. Conflict between Trojans and Greeks; conflict between nature and art.

About him were a press of gaping faces
Which seemed to swallow up his sound advice,
1410 All jointly list'ning, but with several graces,° *various attitudes*
As if some mermaid did their ears entice;
Some high, some low, the painter was so nice.° *skillful; subtle*
    The scalps of many, almost hid behind,
    To jump up higher seemed, to mock the mind.° *(by artistic illusion)*

1415 Here one man's hand leaned on another's head,
His nose being shadowed by his neighbour's ear;
Here one being thronged bears° back, all boll'n° and red; *crowded pushes / swollen*
Another, smothered, seems to pelt° and swear, *scold*
And in their rage such signs of rage they bear
1420   As but for loss of° Nestor's golden words *That except they might miss*
    It seemed they would debate with angry swords.

For much imaginary° work was there; *creative*
Conceit deceitful, so compact,° so kind,° *efficient / natural*
That for Achilles' image stood his spear
1425 Gripped in an armèd hand; himself behind
Was left unseen save to the eye of mind;
    A hand, a foot, a face, a leg, a head,
    Stood for the whole to be imaginèd.

And from the walls of strong-besiegèd Troy
1430 When their brave hope, bold Hector, marched to field,
Stood many Trojan mothers sharing joy
To see their youthful sons bright weapons wield;
And to their hope they such odd action° yield *contrary gestures*
    That through their light joy seemèd to appear,
1435   Like bright things stained, a kind of heavy fear.

And from the strand° of Dardan where they fought *shore*
To Simois'° reedy banks the red blood ran, *Trojan river*
Whose waves to imitate the battle sought
With swelling ridges, and their ranks began
1440   To break upon the gallèd° shore, and then *eroded; injured*
    Retire again, till meeting greater ranks
    They join, and shoot their foam at Simois' banks.

To this well painted piece is Lucrece come,
To find a face where all distress is stelled.° *engraved*
1445 Many she sees where cares have carvèd some,
But none where all distress and dolour dwelled
Till she despairing Hecuba° beheld *Queen of Troy*
    Staring on Priam's° wounds with her old eyes, *King of Troy*
    Which bleeding under Pyrrhus' proud foot lies.

1450 In her the painter had anatomized° *laid open*
Time's ruin, beauty's wreck, and grim care's reign.
Her cheeks with chaps° and wrinkles were disguised;° *cracks / disfigured*
Of what she was no semblance did remain.
Her blue blood changed to black in every vein,
1455   Wanting° the spring that those shrunk pipes had fed, *Lacking*
    Showed life imprisoned in a body dead.

On this sad shadow Lucrece spends her eyes,
And shapes her sorrow to the beldame's° woes,   *old woman's*
Who nothing wants to answer her⁴ but cries
1460 And bitter words to ban° her cruel foes.   *curse*
    The painter was no god to lend her those,
      And therefore Lucrece swears he did her wrong
      To give her so much grief, and not a tongue.

'Poor instrument,' quoth she, 'without a sound,
1465 I'll tune° thy woes with my lamenting tongue,   *sing*
    And drop sweet balm in Priam's painted wound,
    And rail on Pyrrhus that hath done him wrong,
    And with my tears quench Troy that burns so long,
      And with my knife scratch out the angry eyes
1470   Of all the Greeks that are thine enemies.

'Show me the strumpet° that began this stir,°   *(Helen) / dispute*
That with my nails her beauty I may tear.
Thy heat of lust, fond Paris, did incur
This load of wrath that burning Troy doth bear;
1475 Thine eye kindled the fire that burneth here,
      And here in Troy, for trespass of thine eye,
      The sire, the son, the dame and daughter die.

'Why should the private pleasure of someone
Become the public plague of many moe?°   *more*
1480 Let sin alone° committed light alone   *by one person*
Upon his head that hath transgressèd so;
Let guiltless souls be freed from guilty woe.
    For one's offence why should so many fall,
    To plague a private sin in general?°   *collectively*

1485 'Lo, here weeps Hecuba, here Priam dies,
Here manly Hector faints, here Troilus swoons,
Here friend by friend in bloody channel° lies,   *gutter*
And friend to friend gives unadvisèd° wounds,   *unintended*
And one man's lust these many lives confounds.
1490   Had doting Priam checked his son's desire,
      Troy had been bright with fame, and not with fire.'

Here feelingly she weeps Troy's painted woes;
For sorrow, like a heavy hanging bell
Once set on ringing, with his° own weight goes;   *its*
1495 Then little strength rings out the doleful knell.
So Lucrece, set a-work, sad tales doth tell
    To pencilled pensiveness and coloured sorrow.
    She lends them words, and she their looks doth borrow.

She throws her eyes about the painting round,
1500 And who she finds forlorn she doth lament.
At last she sees a wretched image bound,
That piteous looks to Phrygian shepherds lent.⁵

---

4. Who lacks nothing to resemble her.
5. That made Phrygian shepherds look on in pity (Phrygia was the area around Troy).

His face, though full of cares, yet showed content.
　Onward to Troy with the blunt swains° he goes, *rough rustics*
1505　So mild that patience° seemed to scorn his woes. *his patience*

In him the painter laboured with his skill
To hide deceit and give the harmless show° *appearance*
An humble gait, calm looks, eyes wailing still,° *weeping continually*
A brow unbent that seemed to welcome woe;
1510 Cheeks neither red nor pale, but mingled so
　That blushing red no guilty instance° gave, *sign*
　Nor ashy pale the fear that false hearts have.

But like a constant and confirmèd devil
He entertained° a show so seeming just, *maintained*
1515 And therein so ensconced° his secret evil *concealed*
That jealousy° itself could not mistrust° *suspicion / suspect*
False creeping craft and perjury should thrust
　Into so bright a day such blackfaced storms,
　Or blot with hell-born sin such saint-like forms.

1520 The well skilled workman this mild image drew
For perjured Sinon,[6] whose enchanting° story *deluding*
The credulous old Priam after slew;
Whose words like wildfire[7] burnt the shining glory
Of rich-built Ilion, that the skies were sorry,
1525　And little stars shot from their fixèd places
　When their glass° fell wherein they viewed their faces. *mirror (Troy)*

This picture she advisedly° perused, *carefully*
And chid° the painter for his wondrous skill, *scolded*
Saying some shape° in Sinon's was abused, *(other person's shape)*
1530 So fair a form lodged not a mind so ill;
And still on him she gazed, and gazing still,
　Such signs of truth in his plain° face she spied *open*
　That she concludes the picture was belied.° *shown to be false*

'It cannot be,' quoth she, 'that so much guile'—
1535 She would have said 'can lurk in such a look',
But Tarquin's shape came in her mind the while,
And from her tongue 'can lurk' from 'cannot' took.
'It cannot be' she in that sense forsook,
　And turned it thus: 'It cannot be, I find,
1540　But such a face should bear a wicked mind.

'For even as subtle Sinon here is painted,
So sober-sad, so weary, and so mild,
As if with grief or travail he had fainted,
To me came Tarquin armèd, too beguiled° *disguised*
1545 With outward honesty, but yet defiled
　With inward vice. As Priam him did cherish,
　So did I Tarquin, so my Troy did perish.

---

6. Sinon was a Greek who pretended to have fled from his own people; once "rescued" and brought to Troy, he persuaded the Trojans to receive the wooden horse into their city.
7. A mixture of sulfur, tar, and other combustible substances, used to set fires during battle.

'Look, look, how list'ning Priam wets his eyes
To see those borrowed° tears that Sinon sheds.   *inauthentic*
1550 Priam, why art thou old and yet not wise?
For every tear he falls° a Trojan bleeds.   *(Sinon) lets fall*
His eye drops fire, no water thence proceeds.
    Those round clear pearls of his that move thy pity
    Are balls of quenchless fire to burn thy city.

1555 'Such devils steal effects° from lightless hell,   *illusions*
For Sinon in his fire doth quake with cold,
And in that cold hot-burning fire doth dwell.
These contraries such unity do hold
Only to flatter° fools and make them bold;   *encourage*
1560 So Priam's trust false Sinon's tears doth flatter
    That he finds means to burn his Troy with water.'

Here, all enraged, such passion her assails
That patience is quite beaten from her breast.
She tears the senseless° Sinon with her nails,   *unfeeling*
1565 Comparing him to that unhappy° guest   *misfortune-bringing*
Whose deed hath made herself herself detest.
    At last she smilingly with this gives o'er:
    'Fool, fool,' quoth she, 'his wounds will not be sore.'

Thus ebbs and flows the current of her sorrow,
1570 And time doth weary time with her complaining.
She looks for night, and then she longs for morrow,
And both she thinks too long with her remaining.
Short time seems long in sorrow's sharp sustaining.°   *painful enduring*
    Though woe be heavy, yet it seldom sleeps,
1575 And they that watch° see time how slow it creeps.   *remain awake*

Which all this time hath overslipped her thought
That she with painted images hath spent,
Being from the feeling of her own grief brought
By deep surmise° of others' detriment,°   *contemplation / suffering*
1580 Losing her woes in shows of discontent.°   *pictures of sorrow*
    It easeth some, though none it ever cured,
    To think their dolour others have endured.

But now the mindful° messenger come back   *dutiful*
Brings home his lord and other company,
1585 Who finds his Lucrece clad in mourning black,
And round about her tear-distainèd° eye   *tear-stained*
Blue circles streamed, like rainbows in the sky.
    These water-galls° in her dim element°   *rainbow fragments / sky*
    Foretell new storms to° those already spent.   *in addition to*

1590 Which when her sad beholding husband saw,
Amazedly in her sad face he stares.
Her eyes, though sod° in tears, looked red and raw,   *sodden*
Her lively colour killed with deadly cares.
He hath no power to ask her how she fares.
1595   Both stood like old acquaintance in a trance,
    Met far from home, wond'ring each other's chance.°   *fortune*

At last he takes her by the bloodless hand,
And thus begins: 'What uncouth° ill event   *strange*
Hath thee befall'n, that thou dost trembling stand?
1600 Sweet love, what spite° hath thy fair colour spent?   *harm*
Why art thou thus attired in discontent?[8]
   Unmask,° dear dear, this moody heaviness,   *Disclose*
   And tell thy grief, that we may give redress.'

Three times with sighs she gives her sorrow fire[9]
1605 Ere once she can discharge one word of woe.
At length addressed° to answer his desire,   *ready*
She modestly prepares to let them know
Her honour is ta'en prisoner by the foe,
   While Collatine and his consorted° lords   *accompanying*
1610   With sad attention long to hear her words.

And now this pale swan in her wat'ry nest
Begins the sad dirge of her certain ending.[1]
'Few words,' quoth she, 'shall fit the trespass best,
Where no excuse can give the fault amending.
1615 In me more woes than words are now depending,°   *weighing; belonging*
   And my laments would be drawn out too long
   To tell them all with one poor tired tongue.

'Then be this all the task it hath to say:
Dear husband, in the interest° of thy bed   *claiming possession*
1620 A stranger came, and on that pillow lay
Where thou wast wont to rest thy weary head;
And what wrong else may be imaginèd
   By foul enforcement might be done to me,
   From that, alas, thy Lucrece is not free.

1625 'For in the dreadful dead of dark midnight
With shining falchion in my chamber came
A creeping creature with a flaming light,
And softly cried, "Awake, thou Roman dame,
And entertain° my love; else lasting shame   *receive*
1630   On thee and thine this night I will inflict,
   If thou my love's desire do contradict.

"'For some hard-favoured° groom of thine," quoth he,   *ugly*
"Unless thou yoke thy liking to my will,
I'll murder straight,° and then I'll slaughter thee,   *immediately*
1635 And swear I found you where you did fulfil
The loathsome act of lust, and so did kill
   The lechers in their deed. This act will be
   My fame, and thy perpetual infamy."

'With this I did begin to start and cry,
1640 And then against my heart he set his sword,
Swearing unless I took all patiently

---

8. Black; see line 1585.
9. As sixteenth-century gunners lighted firearms with matches.
1. Swans were supposed to sing only when they were on the point of death.

I should not live to speak another word.
So should my shame still rest upon record,
   And never be forgot in mighty Rome
1645   Th'adulterate° death of Lucrece and her groom.   *adulterous*

'Mine enemy was strong, my poor self weak,
And far the weaker with so strong a fear.
My bloody judge forbade my tongue to speak;
No rightful plea might plead for justice there.
1650   His scarlet lust came° evidence to swear   *gave*
   That my poor beauty had purloined his eyes;
   And when the judge is robbed, the prisoner dies.

'O teach me how to make mine own excuse,
Or at the least this refuge let me find:
1655   Though my gross blood be stained with this abuse,
Immaculate and spotless is my mind.
   That was not forced, that never was inclined
      To accessory yieldings,[2] but still pure
      Doth in her poisoned closet yet endure.'

1660   Lo, here the hopeless merchant° of this loss,   *owner (Collatine)*
With head declined° and voice dammed up with woe,   *bent*
With sad set eyes and wreathèd arms across,[3]
From lips new waxen° pale begins to blow   *newly grown*
The grief away that stops his answer so;
1665   But wretched as he is, he strives in vain.
   What he breathes out, his breath drinks up again.

As through an arch° the violent roaring tide   *(under a bridge)*
Outruns the eye that doth behold his haste,
Yet in the eddy boundeth in his pride
1670   Back to the strait that forced him on so fast,
In rage sent out, recalled in rage being past;
   Even so his sighs, his sorrows, make a saw,[4]
   To push grief on, and back the same grief draw.

Which speechless woe of his poor she attendeth,°   *poor Lucrece notes*
1675   And his untimely frenzy° thus awaketh: *delirium*
'Dear lord, thy sorrow to my sorrow lendeth
Another power;° no flood by raining slaketh.   *Greater strength*
My woe too sensible° thy passion maketh,   *acutely felt*
   More feeling-painful. Let it then suffice
1680   To drown on woe one pair of weeping eyes.

'And for my sake, when I might charm thee so,[5]
For she that was thy Lucrece, now attend me.
Be suddenly revengèd on my foe—
Thine, mine, his own. Suppose thou dost defend me
1685   From what is past. The help that thou shalt lend me

---

2. To yielding that would make me an accessory to the crime.
3. See line 793 and note.
4. Go back and forth (inhaling and exhaling), like a saw cutting wood.
5. As I used to be when I charmed you (before the rape).

Comes all too late, yet let the traitor die,
For sparing° justice feeds° iniquity.   *lenient / encourages*

'But ere I name him, you fair lords,' quoth she,
Speaking to those that came with Collatine,
1690 'Shall plight° your honourable faiths to me   *pledge*
With swift pursuit to venge this wrong of mine;
For 'tis a meritorious fair design°   *intention*
    To chase injustice with revengeful arms.
    Knights, by their oaths, should right poor ladies' harms.'

1695 At this request with noble disposition°   *purpose*
Each present lord began to promise aid,
As bound in knighthood to her imposition,°   *imposed task*
Longing to hear the hateful foe bewrayed.°   *revealed*
But she that yet her sad task hath not said°   *completed*
1700   The protestation stops. 'O speak,' quoth she;
    'How may this forcèd stain be wiped from me?'

'What is the quality of my offence,
Being constrained with dreadful circumstance?
May my pure mind with the foul act dispense,
1705 My low-declinèd honour to advance?°   *raise*
May any terms acquit me from this chance?°   *mishap*
    The poisoned fountain clears itself again,
    And why not I from this compellèd stain?'

With this they all at once began to say
1710 Her body's stain her mind untainted clears,
While with a joyless smile she turns away
The face, that map which deep impression bears
Of hard misfortune, carved in it with tears.
    'No, no,' quoth she, 'no dame hereafter living
1715   By my excuse shall claim excuse's giving.'

Here with a sigh as if her heart would break
She throws forth Tarquin's name. 'He, he,' she says—
But more than he her poor tongue could not speak,
Till after many accents° and delays,   *sighs*
1720 Untimely breathings, sick and short essays,°   *attempts*
    She utters this: 'He, he, fair lords, 'tis he
    That guides this hand to give this wound to me.'

Even here she sheathèd in her harmless° breast   *innocent*
A harmful knife, that thence her soul unsheathed.
1725 That blow did bail° it from the deep unrest   *liberate*
Of that polluted prison where it breathed.
Her contrite sighs unto the clouds bequeathed
    Her wingèd sprite,° and through her wounds doth fly   *spirit*
    Life's lasting date[6] from cancelled destiny.

---

6. Eternal duration. The line is difficult, and could
mean that Lucrece's immortal soul separates from her
earthly life and body (canceled destiny), or that
Lucrece, by taking her fate into her own hands (can-
celing her destiny), makes her fame eternal.

1730 Stone-still, astonished° with this deadly deed   *stunned*
       Stood Collatine and all his lordly crew,
       Till Lucrece' father that beholds her bleed
       Himself on her self-slaughtered body threw;
       And from the purple fountain Brutus[7] drew
1735   The murd'rous knife; and as it left the place
         Her blood in poor revenge held it in chase,

       And bubbling from her breast it doth divide
       In two slow rivers, that the crimson blood
       Circles her body in on every side,
1740   Who like a late-sacked° island vastly° stood,   *just-looted / devastated*
       Bare and unpeopled in this fearful° flood.   *fearsome*
         Some of her blood still pure and red remained,
         And some looked black, and that false Tarquin-stained.

       About the mourning and congealèd face
1745   Of that black blood a wat'ry rigol° goes,   *circle*
       Which seems to weep upon the tainted place;
       And ever since, as pitying Lucrece' woes,
       Corrupted blood some watery token shows;
         And blood untainted still doth red abide,
1750   Blushing at that which is so putrefied.

       'Daughter, dear daughter,' old Lucretius cries,
       'That life was mine which thou hast here deprived.
       If in the child the father's image lies,
       Where shall I live now Lucrece is unlived?°   *slain*
1755   Thou wast not to this end from me derived.
         If children predecease progenitors,
         We are their offspring, and they none of ours.

       'Poor broken glass,° I often did behold   *mirror*
       In thy sweet semblance my old age new born;
1760   But now that fair fresh mirror, dim and old,
       Shows me a bare-boned death° by time outworn.   *skull*
       O, from thy cheeks my image thou hast torn,
         And shivered all the beauty of my glass,
         That I no more can see what once I was.

1765   'O time, cease thou thy course and last no longer,
       If they surcease° to be that should survive!   *cease*
       Shall rotten death make conquest of the stronger,
       And leave the falt'ring feeble souls alive?
       The old bees die, the young possess their hive.
1770   Then live, sweet Lucrece, live again and see
         Thy father die, and not thy father thee.'

       By this starts Collatine as from a dream,
       And bids Lucretius give his sorrow place;
       And then in key-cold° Lucrece' bleeding stream   *cold as metal*
1775   He falls, and bathes the pale fear in his face,

7. Lucius Junius Brutus. Tarquin the Proud, the   pretending to be mentally retarded. After Lucrece's
rapist's father, had killed Brutus's brother, but Brutus,   rape, he led the coup that overthrew the Tarquins and
whose name means "stupid," escaped royal suspicion by   established republican government in Rome.

And counterfeits to die with her a space,
   Till manly shame bids him possess his breath,
   And live to be revengèd on her death.

The deep vexation of his inward soul
1780   Hath served a dumb arrest° upon his tongue,   *silent injunction*
Who, mad that sorrow should his use control,°   *prevent*
Or keep him from heart-easing words so long,
Begins to talk; but through his lips do throng
   Weak words, so thick come in his poor heart's aid
1785   That no man could distinguish what he said.

Yet sometime 'Tarquin' was pronouncèd plain,
But through his teeth, as if the name he tore.
This windy tempest, till it blow up rain,
Held back his sorrow's tide to make it more.
1790   At last it rains, and busy winds give o'er.
   Then son and father weep with equal strife
   Who should weep most, for daughter or for wife.

The one doth call her his, the other his,
Yet neither may possess the claim they lay.
1795   The father says 'She's mine'; 'O, mine she is,'
Replies her husband, 'do not take away
My sorrow's interest;° let no mourner say   *title of possession*
   He weeps for her, for she was only mine,
   And only must be wailed by Collatine.'

1800   'O,' quoth Lucretius, 'I did give that life
Which she too early and too late hath spilled.'
'Woe, woe,' quoth Collatine, 'she was my wife.
I owed° her, and 'tis mine that she hath killed.'   *owned*
'My daughter' and 'my wife' with clamours filled
1805   The dispersed air, who, holding Lucrece' life,[8]
   Answered° their cries, 'my daughter' and 'my wife'.   *Echoed*

Brutus, who plucked the knife from Lucrece' side,
Seeing such emulation° in their woe   *competition*
Began to clothe his wit in state° and pride,   *dignity*
1810   Burying in Lucrece' wound his folly's show.°   *pretended stupidity*
He with the Romans was esteemèd so
   As silly jeering idiots° are with kings,   *court jesters*
   For sportive words and utt'ring foolish things.

But now he throws that shallow habit° by   *foolish appearance*
1815   Wherein deep policy° did him disguise,   *shrewdness*
And armed his long-hid wits advisedly°   *prudently*
To check the tears in Collatinus' eyes.
'Thou wrongèd lord of Rome,' quoth he, 'arise.
   Let my unsounded° self, supposed a fool,   *of unknown depth*
1820   Now set thy long-experienced wit to school.

'Why, Collatine, is woe the cure for woe?
Do wounds help wounds, or grief help grievous deeds?

8. See lines 1727ff.

Is it revenge to give thyself a blow
For his foul act by whom thy fair wife bleeds?
1825　　Such childish humour° from weak minds proceeds;　　　　　*silly behavior*
　　　　　Thy wretched wife mistook the matter so
　　　　　To slay herself, that should have slain her foe.

　　　　'Courageous Roman, do not steep thy heart
　　　　In such relenting dew of lamentations,
1830　　But kneel with me, and help to bear thy part
　　　　To rouse our Roman gods with invocations
　　　　That they will suffer° these abominations—　　　　　*allow*
　　　　　Since Rome herself in them doth stand disgraced—
　　　　　By our strong arms from forth her fair streets chased.°　　　*to be chased*

1835　　'Now by the Capitol that we adore,
　　　　And by this chaste blood so unjustly stained,
　　　　By heaven's fair sun that breeds the fat° earth's store,°　　*fertile / plenty*
　　　　By all our country° rights in Rome maintained,　　　　　*civic*
　　　　And by chaste Lucrece' soul that late complained
1840　　　Her wrongs to us, and by this bloody knife,
　　　　　We will revenge the death of this true wife.'

　　　　This said, he struck his hand upon his breast,
　　　　And kissed the fatal knife to end his vow,
　　　　And to his protestation urged the rest,
1845　　Who, wond'ring at him, did his words allow.°　　　　　*approve*
　　　　　Then jointly to the ground their knees they bow,
　　　　　And that deep vow which Brutus made before
　　　　　He doth again repeat, and that they swore.

　　　　When they had sworn to this advisèd doom°　　　*considered judgment*
1850　　They did conclude to bear dead Lucrece thence,
　　　　To show her bleeding body thorough° Rome,　　　　　*throughout*
　　　　And so to publish° Tarquin's foul offence;　　　　　*publicize*
　　　　　Which being done with speedy diligence,
　　　　　The Romans plausibly° did give consent　　　　　*with applause*
1855　　To Tarquin's everlasting banishment.

The Reign of
King Edward the Third

Did Shakespeare write *The Reign of King Edward the Third*? The jury is out, but the Oxford editors have come to believe that he wrote at least part of it. In that view, they are joined by an increasing number of scholars who find in this chronicle history traces of the issues that preoccupied Shakespeare in his early years as a dramatist, as well as a number of lines and scenes that recall other plays and poems he authored both in the early 1590s and later in his career, including *The Rape of Lucrece*, the sonnets, *The Life of Henry V*, and *Measure for Measure*. *Edward III*, written entirely in verse, was first printed in 1596, with a second edition appearing in 1599, but the title page gave no indication of authorship, only that *"it hath bin sundrie times plaied about the Citie of London."* Many scholars believe that it was first performed by Lord Pembroke's Men, a company that staged several of Shakespeare's early plays before he became a member of the Lord Chamberlain's Men in 1594. In 1656, two printers attributed *Edward III* to Shakespeare in a list of printed plays, but the list has many errors. In 1760, Shakespearean editor and scholar Edward Capell seconded the idea but admitted that there was little external evidence to support it. He, however, provided the first modern version of the text, leaving it to readers to decide the authorship question on their own. Seldom acted, until recent years the play has not been included in collected editions of Shakespeare's works.

The tide, however, has begun to turn. *King Edward III* has been given several recent stage productions, mostly notably by the Royal Shakespeare Company in 2002; and it is now printed in several collected editions of Shakespeare's works, including the second edition of the *Oxford Shakespeare* upon which the *Norton Shakespeare* is based. (For the complete text of the play, go to wwnorton.com/shakespeare.) What caused this new willingness to entertain the possibility that the play is in part or in its entirety by Shakespeare? First, scholars have increasingly realized that a number of early modern plays were collaboratively written, including some traditionally assigned to Shakespeare such as *Pericles*, *The Two Noble Kinsmen*, and a number of his early history plays. Why, then, exclude *King Edward III*, which, on stylistic and thematic grounds, seems to many scholars to contain several scenes indicating Shakespeare's authorship? While only a few scholars believe the play to be entirely his, a number find it likely that he had a hand in those parts involving the Countess of Salisbury and possibly some involving Prince Edward. The Oxford editors assign the bulk of Scene 2, all of Scenes 3 and 12, and possibly Scene 13 to Shakespeare. Second, the play, which most scholars believe was written between 1590 and 1594, mirrors many of Shakespeare's preoccupations during that time. Its central characters are the great Plantagenet king, Edward III, and his oldest son, Edward the Black Prince; its central action their heroic conquest of France. Throughout the 1590s, Shakespeare wrote about the aftermath of this king's reign as, after the Black Prince's early death, the Yorkist and Lancastrian branches of the Plantagenet family began a bitter fight over the crown, in the process losing effective control of England's French territories. In most of Shakespeare's other history plays, Edward III and his eldest son are revered as exemplars of English chivalry and military prowess. It is plausible, then, to think that Shakespeare would have been drawn to the direct dramatization of the king so often alluded to in his other histories.

Whether or not the play is in part by Shakespeare, *King Edward III* is an interesting and highly patriotic example of dramatized English history, a genre popular throughout

THE RAIGNE OF KING EDVVARD the third:

As it hath bin sundrie times plaied about the Citie of London.

LONDON,
Printed for Cuthbert Burby.
1596.

The title page for *The Raigne of King Edward the Third* (1596) gives no indication of who wrote the play.

the 1590s. Written in the wake of the destruction of the Spanish Armada in 1588, an event to which the play several times alludes, it presents England as a nearly invincible military force. As the action opens, Scottish forces have invaded England's northern borders, and Edward III has been insultingly summoned to France to pay tribute to its king. By play's end, Edward has captured both David, King of Scotland, and Jean of Valois, King of France, and he has triumphed in the great naval battle of Sluys as well as in land battles at Crécy, Poitiers, and Calais, a series of events that historically took place over a number of years but are here conveniently collapsed into one continuous arc of action.

Particular attention is paid to the exploits of Prince Edward, who, a little like Prince Hal of the *Henry IV* plays, is shown growing into his role as military hero and prospective monarch. Before the all-important Battle of Crécy, to mark the significance of the Prince's participation in it, his father ritualistically invests his son with the accoutrements of knighthood:

> And, Ned, because this battle is the first
> That ever yet thou fought'st in pitched field,
> As ancient custom is of martialists
> To dub thee with the type of chivalry,
> In solemn manner we will give thee arms.
> Come, therefore, heralds; orderly bring forth
> A strong attirement for the Prince my son.
>   (Scene 6, lines 171–77)

The Prince is then ceremoniously given a coat of armor, and then a helmet, a lance, a shield, and finally the honor of leading the vanguard in the coming battle. In the midst of that battle, when the Prince is surrounded by an overwhelming number of foes, the English nobles plead with King Edward to rescue him. Edward refuses. Demonstrating a species of "tough love," he says that the Prince's courage and skill are being tested and that he must fight this battle by himself, whatever the outcome. Miraculously, the Prince returns to his father in triumph *"bearing in his hand his shivered lance. The body of the King of Bohemia is borne before, wrapped in the colours of Bohemia"* (after Scene 8, line 60). This induction into the ways of chivalry recalls *1 Henry VI* and the exploits of the English hero, Talbot, and his son John, although in that play these mighty English warriors are slain by the French, but only after making a remarkable account of themselves against great odds; and it looks ahead to *Henry V* and King Henry's miraculous victory over the French at Agincourt. Not mentioned in this play, but probably known to many in the audience, was the fact that Edward III established the Order of the Garter, a chivalric institution that honored England's most distinguished warrior nobles. In the play, King Edward, his son, and his chief officers all come to embody Garter values of honor, courage, and military prowess.

The stage deeds of Edward and his son must have been memorable. They were explicitly recalled by Thomas Heywood in *An Apology for Actors* (1612), when he exclaims:

> What English Prince should hee behold the true portrature of that famous King *Edward* the third, foraging France, taking so great a King captive in his owne country, quartering the English Lyons with the French Flower-delyce, ... would not bee suddenly Inflam'd with so royall a spectacle, being made apt and fit for the like achievement. So of *Henry* the fift.

The play clearly could make an impression on spectators, and its consistent emphasis on the overconfidence and pride of the French allowed for easy identification with the courageous and ultimately victorious English forces.

King Edward III's opening scenes, however, offer more complex pleasures, and those scenes are the ones most often attributed to Shakespeare. Edward III does not start the play as a paragon of virtue, even though he is a mighty warrior. Moving north to repel the Scots, who have besieged the castle where the Countess of Salisbury is

ensconced, Edward falls swiftly and irrevocably in love with her, despite the fact that
both he and she have spouses and children. In several remarkable encounters in which
he pursues and she resists, the author dramatizes a moral struggle between two equally
matched antagonists. In the end, she prevails, after threatening to kill herself should
Edward insist on making her violate her marriage vows. As if waking from a dream,
he says:

> Even by that power I swear, that gives me now
> The power to be ashamèd of myself,
> I never mean to part my lips again
> In any words that tends to such a suit.
> Arise, true English lady, whom our isle
> May better boast of than ever Roman might
> Of her, whose ransacked treasury hath tasked
> The vain endeavour of so many pens.
> Arise, and be my fault thy honour's fame
> Which after-ages shall enrich thee with.
>
> (Scene 3, lines 186–95)

A homegrown Lucrece, the Countess is Edward's ideal of an English lady, her
chastity the guarantor of the purity of English bloodlines and, finally, the spur to
Edward's own sense of honor. Prior to this moment, however, the play has vividly
depicted the psychological torment of a man caught in the throes of a passion he can't
control, a passion that draws him from affairs of state and very nearly makes him willing to murder his own wife and the Countess's husband. It is only after Edward overcomes this passion, with the Countess's help, that he is able to lead his army to France.
Self-conquest seems the prerequisite for military conquest.

Interestingly, this part of the play contains its only memorably comic character, the
hapless Lodowick, secretary to King Edward, who is commanded by the King to pen a
letter to the Countess expressing Edward's passion. Lodowick is not much of a love poet
and seems completely flummoxed by the task. After he ekes out a few lines, the King
critiques them roundly, especially for commending the Countess's chastity, for, as he
says, "I had rather have her chased than chaste!" (Scene 2, line 320), and for likening
her to the moon when Edward would have her likened to the sun. The scene is both a
sly comment on the frustrations of writing poetry at somebody else's command and also
a lovely example of the ironic tonal juxtapositions so often found in early modern
drama, especially drama by Shakespeare. The King is wrapped up in his own passion,
forgetful of all the world, and both the grandeur and the dangerous self-absorption of
his passion are highlighted through the contrast provided by the commonsensical, non-
lyrical voice of his secretary just trying to do a job. Edward is in raptures over his
beloved; Lodowick needs the facts: "To whom, my lord, shall I direct my style?" (Scene
2, line 246); "Write I to a woman?" (Scene 2, line 261). "Of what condition or estate
she is / 'Twere requisite that I should know, my lord" (Scene 2, lines 265–66). Eventually, in frustration, the King grabs Lodowick's pen and paper, and vows to write the letter himself.

As the Countess of Salisbury scenes predict, throughout *Edward III* English women
are given unusually powerful roles. Salisbury may be the English Lucrece, but the play's
most striking embodiment of female power is Queen Philippa, Edward's wife, who,
though pregnant, actively takes part in the suppression of the Scots while her husband
is in France. As one lord describes her, she, "big with child, was every day in arms"
(Scene 10, line 45). At the end of the play, she appears in France, still pregnant, for the
moment when the Scottish and French kings both surrender to Edward. In *King
Edward III*, women can be warriors without causing scandal. While the central battles
in France make war seem an affair between men, the edges of the text suggest that this
is not so, that women, too, can be warriors, and important ones.

Their key role in dynastic continuity is equally acknowledged. Edward's claim to

France rests on his mother's status as the only direct heir of the French King, King Philippe. As the Comte d'Artois says, she

> Was all the daughters that this Philippe had,
> Whom afterward your father took to wife.
> And from the fragrant garden of her womb
> Your gracious self, the flower of Europe's hope,
> Derivèd is inheritor to France.
>
> (Scene 1, lines 12–16)

The womb as a fragrant garden is a striking image, suggesting the beauty of his mother's fecundity, which in this instance has brought forth "the flower of Europe's hope" and secured that son a kingdom. Edward's wife, in turn, has brought forth heirs, in this play exemplified by the Black Prince, upon whose face his mother's image is vividly stamped. Looking at his young son while adulterously pursuing the Countess of Salisbury, Edward exclaims: "O, how his mother's face, / Modelled in his, corrects my strayed desire, / And rates my heart, and chides my thievish eye, / Who, being rich enough in seeing her, / Yet seek elsewhere" (Scene 3, lines 74–78). Rather than passive matter molded by the active father's impress, the mother in this instance has shaped the features of her son. Bearing his father's name, he bears his mother's face. It is women like the Countess whose chastity guarantees the purity of bloodlines and women like Edward's mother and wife who make dynastic lineage possible. The pregnant Philippa's appearance onstage at the end of the play brings together in one body the powerful martial and procreative roles that women in this play exemplify.

If *King Edward III* is primarily concerned with establishing English claims to French territory, its treatment of the Scots may be one factor in its seeming disappearance from print and stage at the end of the sixteenth century. The Scots are depicted as craven opportunists who besiege Roxburgh Castle, the Countess of Salisbury's home, and invade the northern shires of England once Edward's attention turns toward France. The Countess fears their "rough insulting barbarism" and the "vile, uncivil, skipping jigs" in which they will "bray forth" their imagined conquest of her castle (Scene 2, lines 9, 12, 13). Despite their boasting, however, the Scots run away when Edward unexpectedly appears to lift the siege of the castle. Later, these same Scots are defeated by English forces led by Queen Philippa, and the dramatist invents an unhistorical scene in which David, their King, is brought to France to be part of Edward's spectacle of conquest. It might not be surprising if, under a Scottish king like James I, who ascended the English throne in 1603, canny theater companies who wished to avoid his displeasure might have ceased to make *King Edward III* an active part of their repertory. Whatever the cause, the play fell from sight for most of the four hundred years following its first appearance in the 1590s. Now, however, it is available for all to judge what hand Shakespeare may have had—if any—in its composition, but also simply as another interesting example of how the early modern playwrights told the story of their nation's past.

JEAN E. HOWARD

SELECTED BIBLIOGRAPHY

Cahill, Patricia. "Biopower in the English Pale: Generation and Genocide in *King Edward III*." *Unto the Breach: Martial Formations, Historical Trauma, and the Early Modern Stage*. London: Oxford University Press, 2008. Argues that the play by indirection is concerned with the conquest of Ireland and with the military and procreative strategies by which that conquest could be achieved.

Conlan, J. P. "Shakespeare's *Edward III*: A Consolation for English Recusants." *Comparative Drama* 35.2 (2001): 177–207. Proposes that the play critiques the persecution of recusants after the English defeat of the Spanish Armada in 1588.

Melchiori, Giorgio, ed. *King Edward III*. Cambridge: Cambridge University Press, 1998. The introduction to this edition discusses the play's date of composition, the authorship question, and matters of style, theme, and dramatic structure.

———. *Shakespeare's Garter Plays: "Edward III" to "Merry Wives of Windsor."* Newark: University of Delaware Press, 1994. Argues that because the historical Edward III founded the Order of the Garter and because *King Edward III* deals with the theme of honor and the education of princes, it should be grouped with five other Shakespeare plays preoccupied with the Order and its values.

Metz, G. Harold, ed. *Sources of Four Plays Ascribed to Shakespeare: "The Reign of King Edward III," "Sir Thomas More," "The History of Cardenio," "The Two Noble Kinsmen."* Columbia: University of Missouri Press, 1989. Summarizes scholarship on the play and provides primary source material from Jean Froissart, Raphael Holinshed, and William Painter.

Proudfoot, Richard. "*The Reign of Edward III* (1596) and Shakespeare." *Proceedings of the British Academy* 71 (1985): 159–85. Discusses many aspects of the play, including arguing that it has a three-part structure and was first performed by Lord Pembroke's Men.

Rackin, Phyllis. "Women's Roles in the Elizabethan History Plays." *The Cambridge Companion to Shakespeare's History Plays*. Ed. Michael Hattaway. Cambridge: Cambridge University Press, 2002. 71–85. Questioning Shakespeare's authorship of *King Edward III*, Rackin argues that, unlike most of Shakespeare's history plays, it shows women who are both virtuous and powerful in the persons of the Countess of Salisbury and Queen Philippa.

Sams, Eric, ed. *Shakespeare's "Edward III."* New Haven: Yale University Press, 1996. Argues strenuously that Shakespeare was the author of *Edward III* because of parallels to other Shakespeare plays and poems, and on the basis of diction, versification, imagery, and so forth.

The Comedy of Errors

In his essay "On Cripples," Shakespeare's great contemporary Montaigne alludes to a strange case of impersonation in a small rural community in southwestern France. There, a cunning imposter succeeded in assuming the identity of Martin Guerre, a man who had disappeared some years before. The imposter lived in the community for three years, sleeping with Guerre's wife and farming his land, until the real Martin Guerre unexpectedly returned. Convicted of fraud, the imposter confessed and was hanged.

Montaigne was dismayed by the execution, for he felt that the evidence was too murky, the imposture too convincing, and human identity too elusive a possession to justify capital punishment. The court, he writes, should have emulated the ancient Greek tribunal that, confronted by a similarly baffling case, ordered the parties to come back in a hundred years. Montaigne was not only advising judicial caution; he was urging his readers to take everyday life less automatically, to acknowledge the inevitability of ignorance and error, and to respond to their own existence with wonder. "I have seen no more evident monstrosity and miracle in the world than myself," he writes in the same essay in which he talks about Martin Guerre. "We become habituated to anything strange by use and time; but the more I frequent myself and know myself, the more my deformity astonishes me, and the less I understand myself."

Montaigne's reflections on Martin Guerre have no direct bearing on *The Comedy of Errors*, but they alert us to the play's wholesale unsettling of the familiar. The comfortable assumptions that condition a normal life—I know who I am; these things belong to me and not to someone else; these are the people I love, work for, do business with, or avoid—are undermined by the tangled interactions of two sets of identical (and identically named) twins. Antipholus of Syracuse and Antipholus of Ephesus, along with their servants, Dromio of Syracuse and Dromio of Ephesus, have been raised apart from one another in separate cities and are unaware that their paths are now unexpectedly crossing. Through a breathless succession of zany doublings and confusions, Shakespeare's comedy discloses the hidden strangeness of ordinary existence. An invitation to dinner, a simple transaction with a goldsmith, the operation of commercial and civil laws, the relation between master and servant, the bond between husband and wife (or mistress or sister-in-law)—all become unhinged, as if by sorcery. "There's not a man I meet but doth salute me," says Antipholus of Syracuse, "as if I were their well-acquainted friend, / And everyone doth call me by my name" (4.3.1–3). These are the practices of everyday life, but to this stranger who is, unbeknownst to him, being mistaken for his identical (and identically named) twin, they confirm the unsavory reputation of Ephesus as a place of "nimble jugglers," "Dark-working sorcerers," "Soul-killing witches," and "Disguisèd cheaters" (1.2.98–101).

The audience knows, of course, that Antipholus's uncanny experiences have been caused neither by witchcraft nor by the larcenous wiles that so astonished Montaigne. The wonder that seems to suffuse everything is the result of nothing more magical or malicious than twinship and a shared name, and hence, we could say, such wonder is spurious or misplaced, the result of misunderstandings. "This is the fairy land" (2.2.189), exclaims one of the Dromios, mystified by the succession of inexplicable events, and his similarly disoriented master invokes the notorious wiles of far-off Lapland. But in *The Comedy of Errors*, there is in reality only daylight and the familiar city

An Italian merchant pictured on a Florentine playing card.

street of Roman comedy, a street reassuringly adapted to the commercial world of Shakespeare's London. Disorientation and danger lurk, to be sure, in this conventional urban landscape—Antipholus of Syracuse thinks he is the victim of sorcery, Antipholus of Ephesus is treated as a madman, Adriana fears the loss of her husband's love, Luciana is convinced that her brother-in-law is trying to seduce her, the servants are constantly beaten, and poor Egeon is condemned to die at day's end. The pressure of time weighs heavily on virtually all of the characters, enmeshed as they are in humiliating, menacing, and apparently insoluble difficulties, but these confusions are neatly resolved by the appointed hour of 5:00 P.M.

Yet this comic resolution does not quite make wonder altogether evaporate from the play. Montaigne urged his readers to abandon their confident belief in the ordered rationality of life and to find the marvelous in the everyday. Identical twins are fairly commonplace and the fact that two people can bear the same name even more so, but Shakespeare's play calls attention to all that is potentially disorienting in the routine circumstances of life. The end of *The Comedy of Errors* seems to restore order and reason—to make the ordinary world ordinary again—but the closing gestures lightly unsettle this restoration. The abbess, who turns out to be Egeon's long-lost wife and the mother of the twin Antipholuses, finds a strange image, at once touching and grotesque, to describe her experiences: she declares that she has been pregnant for thirty-three years and has only now given birth. And the twin Dromios, unable to determine which of them is the elder and should therefore go first through the door, decide that they will draw lots for seniority; meanwhile, they will dispense with hierarchy and go through the door hand in hand.

More telling, perhaps, the questions raised by the strange case of Martin Guerre linger unresolved at the end of Shakespeare's comedy: What is the self? What are the guarantees of identity? Who possesses a name and by what right? How is individuality secured? How can one person represent another? The drama is the perfect medium for an exploration of these questions, for the form of the drama itself invites reflection on the extent to which it is possible for one person to assume the identity of another. From this perspective, *The Comedy of Errors* is not, as it is sometimes said to be, a simple and even simpleminded farce, the crude work of a novice playwright, but a remarkably subtle and acute deployment of the very conditions of the theater to engage with problems that haunted Shakespeare throughout his career.

While it is a mistake to view it as mere apprentice work, *The Comedy of Errors* is nonetheless one of the earliest of Shakespeare's plays (and it is also, perhaps not coincidentally, the shortest). Its exact date of composition and first performance are unknown; there was a performance at Gray's Inn, one of London's law schools, on December 28, 1594, but its thematic and stylistic resemblances to Shakespeare's other early comedies, *The Two Gentlemen of Verona, Love's Labour's Lost*, and *The Taming of the Shrew*, have led many scholars to conclude that he wrote it some years earlier. It was not printed until 1623, as part of the First Folio.

The anonymous recorder of the Gray's Inn performance—apparently something of a debacle because of the pushing and shoving of unexpectedly large crowds—noted the play's resemblance to an ancient comedy, the *Menaechmi*, written by the Roman playwright Plautus. Shakespeare probably read this much-admired play in Latin, since an English translation, by William Warner, was not printed until 1595. The *Menaechmi* is a brilliant, energetic farce, fast-paced, funny, and, as farces often are, cold at heart. A prologue carefully explains the premise: a Syracusan merchant took one of his twin sons, seven years old, on a business trip abroad. During a festival, he accidentally became separated from the son. The boy was found by a childless trader, who took him off to Epidamnum; the father, crazed with grief, died a few days later. When news of the catastrophe reached Syracuse, the remaining son was given the name of his missing brother.

The action of Plautus's play is set some years later, when Menaechmus of Syracuse, searching for his twin, finds himself in Epidamnum. Greeted warmly by perfect strangers, Menaechmus realizes that some mistake is being made, but he is not filled with dread. "I can lose nothing," he cheerfully tells his slave, as he accepts food, gifts, and sexual favors from a woman who has inexplicably confused him with someone else and imagines that she is his mistress. What most strikes him is that it is all free of charge. His twin, a prosperous citizen normally comfortable in an entourage that includes wife, household slaves, mistress, and an obnoxious hanger-on nicknamed the Sponge, is frustrated by the fact that everyone seems to have gone mad and becomes enraged when he himself is treated as a madman. The dizzying confusions steadily mount until the brothers find themselves face-to-face and, with delicious slowness, figure out that they are the long-separated identical twins. The brothers plan to return together to Syracuse, and the play ends with the announcement of the forthcoming auction of Menaechmus's property: "slaves, household effects, house, land, etcetera—and a wife, should there be any purchaser."

A scene in the street/the street as scene. Woodcut from a German edition of Terence's *Eunuchus* (1486).

Though he took over much of Plautus's farce, Shakespeare made highly revealing changes and additions. For a start, he shifted the setting from Epidamnum to Ephesus, a city associated with sorcery, exorcism, mystery cults, and early Christianity. As if to multiply the comic confusion generated by one set of identical twins, he added a second set—the servants, who, for reasons that are not really explained, bear like their masters a single name. (The device of the identical slaves is borrowed from another play by Plautus, the *Amphitruo*.) Shakespeare also chose in effect to double the plot by framing the main action with the anguished figure of the Syracusan merchant Egeon, caught up in his city's murderous commercial struggle with rival Ephesus. The melancholy personal history that Egeon relates is adapted not from the ancient comedy but from a medieval romance, the tale of Apollonius of Tyre as told by the fourteenth-century poet John Gower in his *Confessio Amantis* (a tale to which Shakespeare again turned many years later for the plot of *Pericles*). Egeon's fate quickly recedes from the audience's attention, but the threat to his life provides a somber context for the play's hilarity, and his return to the stage at the close, on the way to the place of execution, suddenly raises the stakes of the resolution. The closing scene highlights the romance elements that Shakespeare introduced into his frenetic scheme of mistaken identity: the reuniting of parents and children who had been tragically separated, the miraculous recovery of a beloved spouse long presumed dead, and a sense of wonder that does not entirely evaporate with the solving of the puzzle. Plautus's Epidamnum is a city full of rogues, parasites, and courtesans, a place where you can lose your cloak, your chain, and your money; Shakespeare's Ephesus is a place where you can lose—or regain—your life.

Egeon's story in *The Comedy of Errors* has a shape that merits attention: he is condemned to death through the operation of an inflexible law that even the sympathetic duke cannot mitigate, and then, through a wondrous turn of events, his life is spared, and he recovers the loved ones he thought he had lost forever. Even though the play is set in pagan antiquity, in this shape we may sense the psychic and moral rhythm of Christianity: the mortal penalty of the harsh law is wiped out, altogether unexpectedly and gratuitously, by a miraculous, loving dispensation. The farcical core of the play is at a considerable remove from this portentous rhythm, but Christianity's influence is not restricted to the frame. Since Shakespeare and his age were relatively indifferent to anachronism, Antipholus of Syracuse can say to his servant, "Now, as I am a Christian, answer me" (1.2.77), and the servant can call for his rosary beads and cross himself (2.2.188). The fear of demonic possession takes a specifically Christian form when Satan himself is exorcised by Doctor Pinch. And although pagan antiquity had shrines such as the Temple of Diana at Ephesus (where the tale of Apollonius of Tyre reaches it climax), the priory and its Abbess seem to belong in a Christian community, a community invoked by the very name of Ephesus, where St. Paul preached and to which he wrote an influential epistle.

A central concern of Paul's Epistle to the Ephesians is Christian marriage: men are urged to love their wives as their own bodies, while women are urged to submit themselves unto their husbands as unto the Lord. These strikingly asymmetrical admonitions make themselves felt throughout *The Comedy of Errors*. Where Plautus's Menaechmus cheerfully cheats on his wife, Shakespeare's married twin seems to have an inward principle of moral restraint. Antipholus is driven to the courtesan only when his wife, Adriana, seems to turn him away from his own house—and even then, protesting to his friends that his wife's suspicions are unfounded, he seems mainly interested in dinner and pleasant conversation. Where the nameless wife in Plautus is above all outraged that her husband has stolen from her a gown and a bracelet to bestow as presents on his mistress, Shakespeare's Adriana is obsessed with the possibility that her husband no longer loves her. It is this tormenting fear of marital estrangement that has driven her to a querulousness that only confirms her overwhelming craving for perfect union:

"I'll to the mart" (3.2.182). London's Royal Exchange, founded by Sir Thomas Gresham, 1565. Etching by Wenceslaus Hollar (1644).

> Ah, do not tear away thyself from me;
> For know, my love, as easy mayst thou fall
> A drop of water in the breaking gulf,
> And take unmingled thence that drop again
> Without addition or diminishing,
> As take from me thyself, and not me too.
>
> (2.2.124–29)

The oneness that is envisioned here, the poignant longing for wholeness, and the fear of pollution and self-loss have no place in the emotional register of the *Menaechmi*. Where Plautus's farce ends with a joke about offering the wife for sale, *The Comedy of Errors* ends with the characters, reconciled and reunited, entering the abbey for a feast.

Near the close of Shakespeare's play, the Abbess seems to reflect the spirit of St. Paul's admonition to wives when she observes that by robbing her husband of the "sweet recreation" that he should find at home, Adriana's "jealous fits" have driven him mad (5.1.69–87). This criticism echoes both Antipholus's own complaint that his wife is "shrewish" and the distinctly Pauline opinions voiced by Adriana's sister, Luciana. Luciana—a character for whom there is no precedent in Plautus—argues that males of every species are "masters to their females, and their lords" (2.1.24) and therefore that Adriana should patiently submit to her husband. Such views, similar to those expressed by the "reformed" Katherine in *The Taming of the Shrew*, are given considerable prominence in *The Comedy of Errors*, and yet they are neither unchallenged nor unequivocally endorsed. Adriana observes that her sister is single and hence that her views on marriage are untested by experience. And the Abbess's moralizing diagnosis—that Antipholus would not have mistreated Adriana or gone mad if she had reined in her tongue—turns out to be merely another of the mistaken conjectures that all of the characters incessantly advance in their attempts to account for the day's weird events.

There is a kind of laughter that functions as social regulation: comedy, writes Sir Philip Sidney in his *Defense of Poesie* (c. 1583), "is an imitation of the common errors of our life," which the dramatist represents "in the most ridiculous and scornful sort that may be, so as it is impossible that any beholder can be content to be such a one." The errors in *The Comedy of Errors* are ridiculous, but they are hardly common, and the audience's laughter seems something other than scornful or regulative. None of the explanatory accounts, not even the moral values and providential rhythm of Christianity with which Shakespeare has infused his pagan plot, seems entirely adequate as a response to the chain of mad mistakings. The characters are subject not to a divine plan or to the social order but to fortune. And if this fortune turns out to have the happy air of providence—epitomized by the reuniting of the divided and dispersed family—there seems to be no particularly uplifting lesson to be learned.

Shakespeare's play, to be sure, is cannily alert to social inequities—an innocent merchant is condemned to death for being in the wrong place at the wrong time; a husband is "master of his liberty," while a wife must "practise to obey" (2.1.7, 29); one set of twins is destined through poverty to be the servants, casually beaten and abused, of the other set—but it does not mount a strenuous protest or imagine a radical transformation. In the midst of the farcical confusions, characters repeatedly long for greater justice, equality, and emotional fulfillment, but *The Comedy of Errors* does not encourage us to believe that such an existence can be realized. There may be a happy resolution, but there is no escape from the pervasive, fundamentally inequitable social order and from the mercantile world based on credit, trade, exchange, bonds, and debt.

Several of Shakespeare's best-loved comedies are structured around alternative worlds: the familiar, daylit realm of the court or city is set against the magical realm of the woods and the enchanted night. But in *The Comedy of Errors*, there is only the single urban setting, a setting that would have reminded contemporary audiences of the bustling city that stretched out beyond the walls of the playhouse. In the sixteenth century, London had become the center of a commercial culture that Shakespeare deftly sketches with quick strokes. We learn that Antipholus keeps a purse of ducats locked "in the desk / That's covered o'er with Turkish tapestry" (4.1.103–4), that the courtesan considers a ring worth 40 ducats "too much to lose" (4.3.91), and that the goldsmith plans to discharge his overdue debt to a merchant with the money that Antipholus has promised to pay him for the gold chain. That gold chain functions as a convenient symbol of the interlinked network of obligations and exchanges in which the twins—who seem as like one another as two coins of equal value—are caught and which their uncontrolled interchangeability temporarily disrupts.

A closer look reveals that Antipholus of Ephesus and Antipholus of Syracuse are not perfectly interchangeable: the former is confident, well connected, and somewhat irascible; the latter is anxious, insecure, driven by restless longing:

> I to the world am like a drop of water
> That in the ocean seeks another drop,
> Who, falling there to find his fellow forth,
> Unseen, inquisitive, confounds himself.
>   (1.2.35–38)

This poignant sense of self-loss, which anticipates the alienation and existential anxiety of the tragedies, is intensified by the mad confusions that follow: the events of *The Comedy of Errors* may be deliciously amusing to the audience, but to the characters they are mystifying and even nightmarish. Antonin Artaud, a modern writer who championed what he called the "Theater of Cruelty," praises the Marx Brothers' movies in terms that seem at least as relevant to Shakespeare's comedy: "In order to understand the powerful, total, definitive, absolute originality . . . of films like *Animal Crackers*," Artaud writes, "you would have to add to humor the notion of something disquieting and tragic, a fatality (neither happy nor unhappy, difficult to formulate) which would hover over it like the cast of an appalling malady upon an exquisitely beautiful profile." And yet it is not the nightmare that triumphs but laughter, laughter at what another sixteenth-century writer, George Gascoigne, called "supposes." Gascoigne defined a suppose as "a mistaking or imagination of one thing for another," and it is with a frantic succession of these supposes, all equally wide of the mark, that the baffled characters of *The Comedy of Errors* occupy themselves.

The "imagination of one thing for another" could serve as a definition of the theater. The spectators of Shakespeare's comedy have paid for the pleasure of watching identity slip away from the characters' grasp, as if in the home or the marketplace who you are is no more secure than it is onstage. They have paid too for the pleasure of watching identity serendipitously return, as if Shakespeare's theater had the magic power to restore the human family, however broken and scattered, and restore stability to the battered self. If neither the loss nor the recovery is altogether plausible, the delicious intertwining of the two seems designed to provoke what Montaigne urged upon his readers: a skeptical wonder.

STEPHEN GREENBLATT

TEXTUAL NOTE

The Comedy of Errors was first printed in the 1623 First Folio, which is therefore the only authoritative text of the play. Scholars generally believe that the text was based on Shakespeare's own autograph manuscript. Evidence for this belief centers on features of the stage directions and speech prefixes that are likely to derive from the playwright himself rather than a compositor or playhouse bookkeeper. For example, the stage direction before 4.4.36 calls for "a Schoole-master, call'd Pinch," although there is no mention in the dialogue that Pinch is a schoolmaster. Similarly, while the prompter's copy would normally call only for a particular character by name, the stage direction at 2.1.0 specifies that Adriana is "wife to Antipholis Sereptus." ("Sereptus" is from the Latin *surreptus*, "stolen away," an epithet applied several times by Plautus to the twin who corresponds to Antipholus of Ephesus. At his first appearance, Antipholus of Syracuse is referred to as "Antipholus Erotes"; some critics have conjectured that "Erotes" is a corruption of *erraticus*, "wandering," by analogy with *surreptus*.)

The Folio text indicates act divisions (and specifies "Scena Prima" at the beginning of Acts 1, 3, 4, and 5).

SELECTED BIBLIOGRAPHY

Baldwin, T. W. *Shakespere's Five-Act Structure: Shakespere's Early Plays on the Background of Renaissance Theories of Five-Act Structure from 1470*. Urbana: University of Illinois Press, 1947.

Christensen, Ann C. "'Because their business still lies out a' door': Resisting the Separation of the Spheres in Shakespeare's *The Comedy of Errors*." *Literature and History* 5 (1996): 19–37.

Frye, Northrop. "The Argument of Comedy." *English Institute Essays*. New York: AMS Press, 1948. 58–73.

Hunt, Maurice. "Slavery, English Servitude and *The Comedy of Errors*." *English Literary Renaissance* 27 (1997): 31–56.

Miola, Robert S., ed. *"The Comedy of Errors": Critical Essays*. New York: Routledge, 2001.

Parker, Patricia. "The Bible and the Marketplace: *The Comedy of Errors*." *Shakespeare from the Margins: Language, Culture, Context*. Chicago: University of Chicago Press, 1996. 56–82.

Perry, Curtis. "Commerce, Community, and Nostalgia in *The Comedy of Errors*." *Money and the Age of Shakespeare: Essays in New Economic Criticism*. Ed. Linda Woodbridge. New York: Palgrave Macmillan, 2003. 39–51.

Salgādo, Gāmini. " 'Time's Deformed Hand': Sequence, Consequence, and Inconsequence in *The Comedy of Errors*." *Shakespeare Survey* 25 (1972): 81–92.

Taylor, Gary. "Textual and Sexual Criticism: A Crux in *The Comedy of Errors*." *Renaissance Drama* 19 (1988): 195–225.

Witmore, Michael. "The Avoidance of Ends in *The Comedy of Errors*." *Culture of Accidents: Unexpected Knowledges in Early Modern England*. Stanford: Stanford University Press, 2001. 62–81.

FILM

The Comedy of Errors. 1983. Dir. James Cellan Jones. UK. 109 min. A BBC-TV production, with Roger Daltrey (lead singer of The Who) as the Dromios.

The Comedy of Errors

THE PERSONS OF THE PLAY

Solinus, DUKE of Ephesus
EGEON, a merchant of Syracuse, father of the Antipholus twins
ANTIPHOLUS OF EPHESUS ⎫ twin brothers, sons of Egeon
ANTIPHOLUS OF SYRACUSE ⎭
DROMIO OF EPHESUS ⎫ twin brothers, and bondmen of the
DROMIO OF SYRACUSE ⎭ Antipholus twins
ADRIANA, wife of Antipholus of Ephesus
LUCIANA, her sister
NELL, Adriana's kitchen-maid
ANGELO, a goldsmith
BALTHASAR, a merchant
A COURTESAN
Doctor PINCH, a schoolmaster and exorcist
MERCHANT OF EPHESUS, a friend of Antipholus of Syracuse
SECOND MERCHANT, Angelo's creditor
Emilia, an ABBESS at Ephesus
Jailer, messenger, headsman, officers, and other attendants

1.1

Enter [Solinus], the DUKE *of Ephesus, with* [EGEON] *the
Merchant of Syracuse,* JAILER, *and other attendants*

EGEON   Proceed, Solinus, to procure my fall,
  And by the doom° of death end woes and all.   *sentence*
DUKE   Merchant of Syracusa, plead no more.
  I am not partial° to infringe our laws.   *inclined*
5 The enmity and discord which of late
  Sprung from the rancorous outrage of your Duke
  To merchants, our well-dealing[1] countrymen,
  Who, wanting° guilders[2] to redeem° their lives,   *lacking / ransom*
  Have sealed° his rigorous statutes with their bloods,   *ratified*
10 Excludes all pity from our threat'ning looks.
  For since the mortal° and intestine jars°   *deadly / bitter strife*
  'Twixt thy seditious countrymen and us,
  It hath in solemn synods° been decreed,   *assemblies*
  Both by the Syracusians and ourselves,
15 To admit no traffic to[3] our adverse° towns.   *hostile*
  Nay more: if any born at Ephesus
  Be seen at Syracusian marts° and fairs;   *markets*
  Again, if any Syracusian born
  Come to the bay of Ephesus—he dies,

1.1 Location: A street in Ephesus. The setting of the
entire play was probably modeled after that of ancient
Roman comedy: a conjunction of city streets, with
three doors to represent houses, each marked with a
sign. The house of Antipholus of Ephesus, identified as
the Phoenix, is flanked by the courtesan's house
(marked with the sign of a porcupine) and the priory
(perhaps marked anachronistically with a cross). When
the action is not focused on these houses, the stage
serves as a generalized urban space, most often called
the "mart"—that is, the marketplace.
1. Honest-trading; more generally, civil or well-behaved.
2. Money, not specifically referring to Dutch or German coins.
3. To allow no trade between.

20   His goods confiscate to the Duke's dispose,°   *disposal*
        Unless a thousand marks⁴ be levièd°   *raised*
        To quit° the penalty and ransom him.   *pay*
        Thy substance,° valued at the highest rate,   *goods*
        Cannot amount unto a hundred marks.
25   Therefore by law thou art condemned to die.
        EGEON   Yet this my comfort: when your words are done,
        My woes end likewise with the evening sun.
        DUKE   Well, Syracusian, say in brief the cause
        Why thou departed'st from thy native home,
30   And for what cause thou cam'st to Ephesus.
        EGEON   A heavier task could not have been imposed
        Than I° to speak my griefs unspeakable.   *Than for me*
        Yet, that the world may witness that my end
        Was wrought by nature,⁵ not by vile offence,
35   I'll utter what my sorrow gives me leave.
        In Syracusa was I born, and wed
        Unto a woman happy but for me,⁶
        And by me° happy, had not our hap° been bad.   *by me made / luck*
        With her I lived in joy, our wealth increased
40   By prosperous voyages I often made
        To Epidamnum,⁷ till my factor's° death,   *agent's*
        And the great care of goods at random° left,   *untended*
        Drew me from kind embracements of my spouse,
        From whom my absence was not six months old
45   Before herself—almost at fainting under
        The pleasing punishment that women bear°—   *(pregnancy)*
        Had made provision for her following me,
        And soon and safe arrivèd where I was.
        There had she not been long but she became
50   A joyful mother of two goodly sons;
        And, which was strange, the one so like the other
        As° could not be distinguished but by names.   *That they*
        That very hour, and in the selfsame inn,
        A mean-born woman° was deliverèd   *woman of low birth*
55   Of such a burden male, twins both alike.
        Those, for° their parents were exceeding poor,   *because*
        I bought, and brought up to attend my sons.
        My wife, not meanly° proud of two such boys,   *in no small degree*
        Made daily motions° for our home return.   *requests*
60   Unwilling, I agreed. Alas! Too soon
        We came aboard.
        A league from Epidamnum had we sailed
        Before the always-wind-obeying deep
        Gave any tragic instance° of our harm.   *sign*
65   But longer did we not retain much hope,
        For what obscurèd light the heavens did grant
        Did but convey unto our fearful minds
        A doubtful warrant° of immediate death,   *A fearsome confirmation*
        Which though myself would gladly have embraced,
70   Yet the incessant weepings of my wife—

---

4. A mark was two-thirds of a pound in English money,   6. Fortunate except in her association with me.
although there was no coin of this amount.   7. Plautus's setting for the *Meneachmi*, now Durrës in
5. Was brought about by natural feeling: a father's   Albania; Shakespeare's play, however, seems to treat it
love.   as if it were in Greece.

Weeping before° for what she saw must come—   *in advance*
And piteous plainings° of the pretty babes,   *cries*
That mourned for fashion, ignorant what to fear,[8]
Forced me to seek delays° for them and me.   *reprieves*
75   And this it was—for other means was none:
The sailors sought for safety by our boat,°   *lifeboat*
And left the ship, then sinking-ripe,[9] to us.
My wife, more careful° for the latter-born,°   *anxious / younger*
Had fastened him unto a small spare mast
80   Such as seafaring men provide for storms.
To him one of the other twins was bound,
Whilst I had been like heedful of° the other.   *equally attentive to*
The children thus disposed,° my wife and I,   *placed*
Fixing our eyes on whom our care was fixed,
85   Fastened ourselves at either end the mast,
And floating straight,° obedient to the stream,   *immediately*
Was carried towards Corinth, as we thought.
At length the sun, gazing upon the earth,
Dispersed those vapours° that offended° us,   *clouds / harmed*
90   And by the benefit of his wishèd light
The seas waxed calm, and we discoverèd
Two ships from far, making amain° to us: *speeding*
Of Corinth that, of Epidaurus[1] this.
But ere they came—O let me say no more!
95   Gather the sequel by that went before.[2]
DUKE   Nay, forward, old man; do not break off so,
For we may pity though not pardon thee.
EGEON   O, had the gods done so, I had not now
Worthily° termed them merciless to us.   *Justly*
100   For, ere the ships could meet by° twice five leagues,   *come within*
We were encountered by a mighty rock,
Which being violently borne upon,
Our helpful ship° was splitted in the midst,   *(the mast)*
So that in this unjust divorce of us
105   Fortune had left to both of us alike°   *equally*
What° to delight in, what to sorrow for.   *Something*
Her° part, poor soul, seeming as burdenèd   *(My wife's)*
With lesser weight[3] but not with lesser woe,
Was carried with more speed before the wind,
110   And in our sight they three were taken up
By fishermen of Corinth, as we thought.
At length another ship had seized on us,°   *hauled us up*
And, knowing whom it was their hap° to save,   *luck*
Gave healthful welcome to their shipwrecked guests,
115   And would have reft° the fishers of their prey[4]   *deprived*
Had not their barque° been very slow of sail;   *vessel*
And therefore homeward did they bend their course.
Thus have you heard me severed from my bliss,
That by misfortunes was my life prolonged
120   To tell sad stories of my own mishaps.

8. That imitated the adults' lamentation without understanding it.
9. At the point of sinking; softened and ready to drop.
1. Either modern Dubrovnik, on the Adriatic and north of Durrës (Epidamnum), or the Greek city actually called Epidaurus, near Corinth.
2. Deduce what followed from that which I have already recounted.
3. Lighter than her husband and the other child.
4. Those whom they have fished out of the sea.

DUKE   And for the sake of them thou sorrow'st for,
　　Do me the favour to dilate at° full   *relate in*
　　What have befall'n of them and thee till now.

EGEON   My youngest boy,[5] and yet my eldest care,
125　At eighteen years became inquisitive
　　After his brother, and importuned me
　　That his attendant—so his case was like,[6]
　　Reft of his brother, but retained his name[7]—
　　Might bear him company in the quest of him;
130　Whom whilst I laboured of a love to see,[8]
　　I hazarded the loss of whom I loved.
　　Five summers have I spent in farthest Greece,
　　Roaming clean through the bounds of Asia,
　　And coasting° homeward came to Ephesus,   *sailing*
135　Hopeless to find,° yet loath to leave unsought   *find them*
　　Or° that or any place that harbours men.   *Either*
　　But here must end the story of my life,
　　And happy were I in my timely death
　　Could all my travels[9] warrant° me they live.   *assure*
140　DUKE   Hapless° Egeon, whom the fates have marked   *Unlucky*
　　To bear the extremity of dire mishap,
　　Now trust me, were it not against our laws—
　　Which princes, would they, may not disannul[1]—
　　Against my crown, my oath, my dignity,
145　My soul should sue as advocate for thee.
　　But though thou art adjudgèd° to the death,   *sentenced*
　　And passèd sentence may not be recalled
　　But° to our honour's great disparagement,°   *Except / disgrace*
　　Yet will I favour thee in what I can.[2]
150　Therefore, merchant, I'll limit° thee this day   *allot*
　　To seek thy health° by beneficial help.   *deliverance*
　　Try all the friends thou hast in Ephesus:
　　Beg thou or borrow to make up the sum,
　　And live. If no, then thou art doomed to die.
155　Jailer, take him to thy custody.

JAILER   I will, my lord.

EGEON   Hopeless and helpless doth Egeon wend,°   *go*
　　But to procrastinate° his lifeless end.   *Exeunt*   *postpone*

1.2

Enter [from the bay] ANTIPHOLUS [OF SYRACUSE], MER-
CHANT [OF EPHESUS], *and* DROMIO [OF SYRACUSE]

MERCHANT OF EPHESUS   Therefore give out° you are of Epidamnum,   *say*
　　Lest that your goods too soon be confiscate.
　　This very day a Syracusian merchant
　　Is apprehended for arrival here,
5　And, not being able to buy out° his life,   *ransom*
　　According to the statute of the town
　　Dies ere the weary sun set in the west.
　　There is your money that I had to keep.°   *in my keeping*

---

5. An inconsistency of detail (see line 78).
6. *so . . . like:* in this way his situation was similar.
7. Bore the name of the brother from whom he was separated.
8. *Whom . . . see:* Since I longed to see my lost son.

9. Journeys; "travails," efforts.
1. *would . . . disannul:* even if they wished to, cannot cancel or make void.
2. Yet I will bend the law's strictness as much as I can.
1.2 Location: A street in Ephesus.

ANTIPHOLUS OF SYRACUSE [*to* DROMIO] Go bear it to the
      Centaur,[1] where we host,°   *lodge*
10   And stay there, Dromio, till I come to thee.
    Within this hour it will be dinner-time.[2]
    Till that° I'll view the manners of the town,   *then*
    Peruse° the traders, gaze upon the buildings,   *Observe*
    And then return and sleep within mine inn;
15   For with long travel I am stiff and weary.
    Get thee away.
DROMIO OF SYRACUSE Many a man would take you at your word,
    And go indeed, having so good a mean.[3]   *Exit*
ANTIPHOLUS OF SYRACUSE A trusty villain,[4] sir, that very oft,
20   When I am dull° with care and melancholy,   *gloomy*
    Lightens my humour[5] with his merry jests.
    What,° will you walk with me about the town,   *Now then*
    And then go to my inn and dine with me?
MERCHANT OF EPHESUS I am invited, sir, to certain merchants
25   Of whom I hope to make much benefit.
    I crave your pardon. Soon° at five o'clock,   *Promptly*
    Please° you, I'll meet with you upon the mart,   *If it please*
    And afterward consort° you till bedtime.   *accompany*
    My present business calls me from you now.
30 ANTIPHOLUS OF SYRACUSE Farewell till then. I will go lose myself,
    And wander up and down to view the city.
MERCHANT OF EPHESUS Sir, I commend you to your own
      content.°   *Exit*   *pleasures; peace*
ANTIPHOLUS OF SYRACUSE He that commends me to mine own
      content
    Commends me to the thing I cannot get.
35   I to the world am like a drop of water
    That in the ocean seeks another drop,
    Who, falling there to find his fellow forth,[6]
    Unseen, inquisitive, confounds° himself.   *mingles; destroys*
    So I, to find a mother and a brother,
40   In quest of them, unhappy, lose myself.
        Enter DROMIO OF EPHESUS
    Here comes the almanac of my true date.[7]
    What now? How chance° thou art returned so soon?   *What happened that*
DROMIO OF EPHESUS Returned so soon? Rather approached too late.
    The capon burns, the pig falls from the spit.
45   The clock hath strucken twelve upon the bell;
    My mistress made it one[8] upon my cheek.
    She is so hot° because the meat is cold.   *angry*
    The meat is cold because you come not home.
    You come not home because you have no stomach.° *appetite*
50   You have no stomach, having broke your fast;°   *having eaten*
    But we that know what 'tis to fast and pray
    Are penitent[9] for your default° today.   *fault*

---

1. The name of an inn; taverns, inns, and shops were frequently identified by a pictorial sign.
2. Noon, time for the midday meal.
3. Opportunity, but punning on "means" (wealth).
4. Servant or slave (villein); also rogue or scoundrel (often used affectionately).
5. Mood, determined by the humors, bodily fluids that formed the basis of Elizabethan medical psychology.
6. To locate a matching drop.
7. The measure of my exact age (because born on the same date).
8. *made it one:* struck one o'clock.
9. Are doing penance in the ordinary way by prayer and fasting (since the meal is delayed), and also through being beaten.

ANTIPHOLUS OF SYRACUSE   Stop in your wind,° sir. Tell me this,   *Shut your mouth*
    I pray:
    Where have you left the money that I gave you?
55 DROMIO OF EPHESUS   O—sixpence that I had o' Wednesday last
    To pay the saddler for my mistress' crupper?[1]
    The saddler had it, sir; I kept it not.
ANTIPHOLUS OF SYRACUSE   I am not in a sportive humour now.
    Tell me, and dally not: where is the money?
60 We being strangers here, how dar'st thou trust
    So great a charge from° thine own custody?   *responsibility out of*
DROMIO OF EPHESUS   I pray you, jest, sir, as° you sit at dinner.   *when*
    I from my mistress come to you in post.°   *haste*
    If I return I shall be post[2] indeed,
65 For she will scour° your fault upon my pate.°   *score; flog / head*
    Methinks your maw,° like mine, should be your clock,   *stomach*
    And strike[3] you home without a messenger.
ANTIPHOLUS OF SYRACUSE   Come, Dromio, come, these jests are
        out of season.
    Reserve them till a merrier hour than this.
70 Where is the gold I gave in charge to thee?
DROMIO OF EPHESUS   To me, sir? Why, you gave no gold to me.
ANTIPHOLUS OF SYRACUSE   Come on, sir knave,[4] have done your
        foolishness,
    And tell me how thou hast disposed° thy charge.   *dealt with*
DROMIO OF EPHESUS   My charge was but to fetch you from the mart
75 Home to your house, the Phoenix,[5] sir, to dinner.
    My mistress and her sister stays° for you.   *wait*
ANTIPHOLUS OF SYRACUSE   Now, as I am a Christian,[6] answer me
    In what safe place you have bestowed my money,
    Or I shall break that merry sconce° of yours   *head*
80 That stands° on tricks when I am undisposed.°   *insists / not in the mood*
    Where is the thousand marks thou hadst of me?
DROMIO OF EPHESUS   I have some marks of yours upon my pate,
    Some of my mistress' marks upon my shoulders,
    But not a thousand marks between you both.
85 If I should pay your worship those again,°   *back*
    Perchance you will not bear them patiently.
ANTIPHOLUS OF SYRACUSE   Thy mistress' marks? What mistress,
        slave, hast thou?
DROMIO OF EPHESUS   Your worship's wife, my mistress, at the Phoenix:
    She that doth fast till you come home to dinner,
90 And prays that you will hie° you home to dinner.   *hasten*
ANTIPHOLUS OF SYRACUSE   What, wilt thou flout° me thus unto   *mock; disobey*
        my face,
    Being forbid? There, take you that, sir knave!
        [*He beats* DROMIO]
DROMIO OF EPHESUS   What mean you, sir? For God's sake,
        hold° your hands!   *stop*

---

1. A strap passed under a horse's tail to prevent the saddle from slipping forward.
2. Beaten, like a wooden doorpost on which tavern charges were tallied (scored).
3. Beat; ring time like a clock.
4. Ironic: "knave," like "villain," means both "servant" and "rogue."

5. Antipholus of Ephesus's house is, like the inn (line 9), identified by a sign, this one depicting the mythological bird that symbolized resurrection. Many Londoners lived above their places of business.
6. A common oath, though anachronistic in classical Greece.

Nay, an° you will not, sir, I'll take my heels.°   *Exit*   if / run away
95 ANTIPHOLUS OF SYRACUSE   Upon my life, by some device° or other   trick
The villain is o'er-raught° of all my money.   cheated
They say this town is full of cozenage,°   deception
As° nimble jugglers[7] that deceive the eye,   Such as
Dark-working[8] sorcerers that change the mind,
100 Soul-killing witches that deform[9] the body,
Disguisèd cheaters, prating mountebanks,°   fast-talking quacks
And many suchlike libertines of sin.[1]
If it prove so, I will be gone the sooner.
I'll to the Centaur to go seek this slave.
105 I greatly fear my money is not safe.   *Exit*

2.1

Enter [from the Phoenix] ADRIANA, *wife to* ANTIPHOLUS
*[*OF EPHESUS*], with* LUCIANA, *her sister*

ADRIANA   Neither my husband nor the slave returned
That in such haste I sent to seek his master?
Sure,° Luciana, it is two o'clock.   Surely
LUCIANA   Perhaps some merchant hath invited him,
5 And from the mart he's somewhere gone to dinner.
Good sister, let us dine, and never fret.
A man is master of his liberty.
Time is their mistress, and when they see time
They'll go or come. If so, be patient, sister.
10 ADRIANA   Why should their liberty than ours be more?
LUCIANA   Because their business still° lies out o' door.   always
ADRIANA   Look when I serve him so, he takes it ill.[1]
LUCIANA   O, know he is the bridle of your will.[2]
ADRIANA   There's none but° asses will be bridled so.   Only
15 LUCIANA   Why, headstrong liberty is lashed° with woe.   beaten; tied down
There's nothing situate under heaven's eye
But hath his bound° in earth, in sea, in sky.   its limits
The beasts, the fishes, and the wingèd fowls
Are their males' subjects and at their controls.°   under their control
20 Man, more divine,[3] the master of all these,
Lord of the wide world and wild wat'ry seas,
Indued with intellectual sense and souls,
Of more pre-eminence than fish and fowls,
Are masters to their females, and their lords.[4]
25 Then let your will attend on their accords.[5]
ADRIANA   This servitude makes you to keep unwed.
LUCIANA   Not this, but troubles of the marriage bed.[6]
ADRIANA   But were you wedded, you would bear some sway.°   wield some power
LUCIANA   Ere I learn love, I'll practise to obey.

---

7. Performers skilled in manipulating appearances; the term could mean either an actual sorcerer or a mere illusionist.
8. Operating secretly or producing darkness.
9. Injure, disfigure; change the shape of (like the enchantress Circe of Homer's *Odyssey*, who transformed Odysseus's men into swine).
1. Unrestrained sinners. F prints "Liberties," possibly referring to the district where many theaters of London (including Shakespeare's company) operated, just outside the city's legal jurisdiction.
2.1 Location: Before the house of Antipholus of Ephesus.

1. Whenever I treat him so, he takes it badly.
2. He is meant to restrain your desires.
3. Nearer to God (in the great hierarchy of all beings).
4. *Man . . . lords:* Man's dominion over the creatures of earth and water derives from Genesis 1:28–29; his rule over woman is expressed in Paul's epistles, especially 1 Corinthians 11:3ff. and Ephesians 5:22ff. ("Wives, submit yourselves unto your husbands, as unto the Lord").
5. *attend . . . accords:* serve their wishes.
6. Compare 1 Corinthians 7:28: "And if a virgin marry, she sinneth not: nevertheless such shall have trouble in the flesh."

30	ADRIANA How if your husband start° some otherwhere?°	*strays; wanders / elsewhere*
	LUCIANA Till he come home again, I would forbear.°	*be patient*
	ADRIANA Patience unmoved! No marvel though she pause:[7]	
	They can be meek that have no other cause.°	*reason not to be*
	A wretched soul, bruised with adversity,	
35	We bid be quiet when we hear it cry.	
	But were we burdened with like° weight of pain,	*equal*
	As much or more we should ourselves complain.	
	So thou, that hast no unkind mate to grieve thee,	
	With urging helpless° patience would relieve° me.	*futile / comfort*
40	But if thou live to see like right bereft,[8]	
	This fool-begged[9] patience in thee will be left.°	*abandoned*
	LUCIANA Well, I will marry one day, but to try.°	*test*

Enter DROMIO OF EPHESUS

	Here comes your man.° Now is your husband nigh.°	*servant / near*
	ADRIANA Say, is your tardy master now at hand?	
45	DROMIO OF EPHESUS Nay, he's at two hands with me, and that	
	my two ears can witness.[1]	
	ADRIANA Say, didst thou speak with him? Know'st thou his mind?	
	DROMIO OF EPHESUS I? Ay, he told[2] his mind upon mine ear.	
	Beshrew° his hand, I scarce could understand it.	*Curse*
50	LUCIANA Spake he so doubtfully° thou couldst not feel his meaning?	*ambiguously*
	DROMIO OF EPHESUS Nay, he struck so plainly I could too well	
	feel his blows, and withal so doubtfully° that I could scarce	*dreadfully; stoutly*
	under-stand° them.	*stand under*
	ADRIANA But say, I prithee,° is he coming home?	*pray thee*
55	It seems he hath great care to please his wife.[3]	
	DROMIO OF EPHESUS Why, mistress, sure my master is horn-mad.	
	ADRIANA Horn-mad,[4] thou villain?	
	DROMIO OF EPHESUS I mean not cuckold-mad, but sure he is stark mad.	
	When I desired him to come home to dinner,	
60	He asked me for a thousand marks in gold.	
	''Tis dinner-time,' quoth I. 'My gold,' quoth he.	
	'Your meat doth burn,' quoth I. 'My gold,' quoth he.	
	'Will you come home?' quoth I. 'My gold,' quoth he;	
	'Where is the thousand marks I gave thee, villain?'	
65	'The pig', quoth I, 'is burned.' 'My gold!' quoth he.	
	'My mistress, sir—' quoth I. 'Hang up° thy mistress!	*Enough of*
	I know thy mistress not. Out° on thy mistress!'	*A curse*
	LUCIANA Quoth who?	
	DROMIO OF EPHESUS Quoth my master.	
70	'I know', quoth he, 'no house, no wife, no mistress.'	
	So that my errand,° due unto my tongue,[5]	*delivery; message*
	I thank him, I bare° home upon my shoulders;	*bore*
	For, in conclusion, he did beat me there.	
	ADRIANA Go back again, thou slave, and fetch him home.	
75	DROMIO OF EPHESUS Go back again and be new° beaten home?	*again*

7. That she hesitates (to marry).
8. *like . . . bereft:* yourself similarly deprived of rights.
9. Declaredly foolish; to "beg a person for a fool" was to petition the Court of Wards for custody of a lunatic (and thus custody of all his possessions).
1. *he's . . . witness:* he boxed my ears with both of his hands.
2. Communicated, but playing on "struck" ("tolled").
3. Ironic: compare 1 Corinthians 7:32–33: "The unmar-

ried careth for the things of the Lord, how he may please the Lord: But he that is married careth for the things that are of the world, how he may please his wife."
4. Uncontrolled and wild as a horned beast (a common expression, as intended by Dromio); enraged at being made a cuckold, who by popular repute grew horns (as Adriana takes it).
5. *due . . . tongue:* which I should have carried back in words.

For God's sake, send some other messenger.

ADRIANA   Back, slave, or I will break thy pate across.

DROMIO OF EPHESUS   An he will bless that cross with other beating,⁶
Between you I shall have a holy⁷ head.

80 ADRIANA   Hence, prating peasant.° Fetch thy master home.   *babbling fellow*
      [*She beats* DROMIO]

DROMIO OF EPHESUS   Am I so round⁸ with you as you with me,
That like a football you do spurn° me thus?   *maltreat; kick*
You spurn me hence, and he will spurn me hither.
If I last in this service, you must case me in leather.⁹   [*Exit*]

85 LUCIANA [*to* ADRIANA]   Fie, how impatience loureth° in your face!   *frowns*

ADRIANA   His company must do his minions grace,¹
Whilst I at home starve for a merry look.
Hath homely age th'alluring beauty took
From my poor cheek? Then he hath wasted it.²

90 Are my discourses dull? Barren my wit?
If voluble and sharp° discourse be marred,   *witty*
Unkindness blunts it more than marble hard.³
Do their° gay vestments° his affections bait?⁴   *(the minions')*/*clothing*
That's not my fault: he's master of my state.⁵

95 What ruins are in me that can be found
By him not ruined?⁶ Then is he the ground°   *cause*
Of my defeatures.° My decayèd fair°   *disfigurement*/*beauty*
A sunny look of his would soon repair.
But, too unruly deer, he breaks the pale,⁷

100 And feeds from° home. Poor I am but his stale.⁸   *away from*

LUCIANA   Self-harming jealousy! Fie, beat it hence.

ADRIANA   Unfeeling fools can with such wrongs dispense.
I know his eye doth homage otherwhere,
Or else what lets° it but he would be here?   *prevents*

105 Sister, you know he promised me a chain.
Would that alone o' love he would detain,⁹
So° he would keep fair quarter° with his bed.   *If then*/*faith*
I see the jewel best enamellèd
Will lose her beauty. Yet the gold bides° still   *remains*

110 That others touch;¹ and often touching will
Wear gold, and yet no man that hath a name°   *reputation*
By falsehood and corruption doth it shame.²
Since that my beauty cannot please his eye,
I'll weep what's left away, and weeping die.

115 LUCIANA   How many fond° fools serve mad jealousy!   *infatuated*

Exeunt [into the Phoenix]

---

6. If he will give me another beating (playing on "across," a cross made by blows on my head, and "bless," the French *blesser*, "to injure").
7. Blessed (because marked with the sign of the cross); also, full of holes.
8. Blunt, disrespectful (with a play on "spherical," like a football).
9. If I survive as your servant, you must cover me with leather, like a football; with a play on "last," a wooden model of a foot used in making leather shoes.
1. Must grace his paramours.
2. Caused it to waste away; squandered it.
3. More than hard marble would blunt a sharp tool.
4. Lure away (bait); lessen (abate) toward Adriana.
5. Estate or general condition, including clothes; also,

metaphorically, kingdom.
6. *What . . . ruined*: What deterioration can be found in me that he is not responsible for?
7. He goes beyond the park boundary ("pale").
8. Lover held up to the ridicule of her rivals; prostitute.
9. *Would . . . detain*: I wish he would withhold that one manifestation of love.
1. *touch*: test (the fineness of gold was tested by rubbing it on a touchstone); caress, referring to her husband's infidelities.
2. *I see . . . shame*: a difficult passage, possibly owing to omitted lines. The general idea is that reputation, like gold, withstands corruption and yet may be worn away. Her husband's infidelities have not tarnished his name, but they may diminish her substance.

2.2

Enter ANTIPHOLUS [OF SYRACUSE]

ANTIPHOLUS OF SYRACUSE   The gold I gave to Dromio is laid up
  Safe at the Centaur, and the heedful° slave   careful
  Is wandered forth in care to seek me out.
  By computation and mine host's report,[1]
5 I could not speak° with Dromio since at first   could not have spoken
  I sent him from the mart! See, here he comes.

Enter DROMIO [OF] SYRACUSE

  How now, sir, is your merry humour altered?
  As you love strokes,° so jest with me again.   blows
  You know no Centaur? You received no gold?
10 Your mistress sent to have me home to dinner?
  My house was at the Phoenix?—Wast thou mad,
  That thus so madly thou didst answer me?
DROMIO OF SYRACUSE   What answer, sir? When spake I such a word?
ANTIPHOLUS OF SYRACUSE   Even now, even here, not half an hour since.
15 DROMIO OF SYRACUSE   I did not see you since you sent me hence
  Home to the Centaur with the gold you gave me.
ANTIPHOLUS OF SYRACUSE   Villain, thou didst deny the gold's
      receipt,°   receiving the gold
  And told'st me of a mistress and a dinner,
  For which I hope thou felt'st[2] I was displeased.
20 DROMIO OF SYRACUSE   I am glad to see you in this merry vein.°   disposition
  What means this jest? I pray you, master, tell me.
ANTIPHOLUS OF SYRACUSE   Yea, dost thou jeer and flout me in
      the teeth?°   to my face
  Think'st thou I jest? Hold,° take thou that, and that.   Stop
      [*He*] *beats* DROMIO
DROMIO OF SYRACUSE   Hold, sir, for God's sake—now your jest is earnest![3]
25 Upon what bargain[4] do you give it me?
ANTIPHOLUS OF SYRACUSE   Because that I familiarly sometimes
  Do use you for my fool,° and chat with you,   jester
  Your sauciness will jest upon my love,[5]
  And make a common[6] of my serious hours.
30 When the sun shines, let foolish gnats make sport,°   play
  But creep in crannies when he hides his beams.
  If you will jest with me, know my aspect,[7]
  And fashion your demeanour to° my looks,   to match
  Or I will beat this method° in your sconce.°   rule / head
35 DROMIO OF SYRACUSE   'Sconce'° call you it? So° you would leave   Small fort / If
  battering,[8] I had rather have it a head. An° you use these   If
  blows long, I must get a sconce° for my head, and ensconce°   protective screen / shelter
  it too, or else I shall seek my wit° in my shoulders. But I pray,   brains
  sir, why am I beaten?
40 ANTIPHOLUS OF SYRACUSE   Dost thou not know?
DROMIO OF SYRACUSE   Nothing, sir, but that I am beaten.

2.2 Location: A street in Ephesus.
1. Based on a calculation of the time elapsed and the
innkeeper's account of Dromio's doings.
2. Perceived, with an allusion to the beating.
3. Serious, with a play on "earnest" as a deposit to
secure a business transaction.
4. Transaction (playing on the financial sense of
"earnest"); in this context, contention or quarrel.

5. *Your . . . love:* You impertinently assume the right to
joke because of my benevolence.
6. Land belonging to the whole community (Dromio
maintains an egalitarian spirit at inappropriate times).
7. Countenance, expression; (in astrology) the position
of a heavenly body, as the sun (lines 30–31).
8. Beating; here, with a play on "sconce," attacking
with a battering ram.

ANTIPHOLUS OF SYRACUSE Shall I tell you why?

DROMIO OF SYRACUSE Ay, sir, and wherefore;° for they say every *for what reason*
why hath a wherefore.

45 ANTIPHOLUS OF SYRACUSE 'Why' first: for flouting me; and then 'wherefore':
For urging° it the second time to me. *repeating*

DROMIO OF SYRACUSE Was there ever any man thus beaten out
of season,° *unjustly*
When in the why and the wherefore is neither rhyme nor reason?—
Well, sir, I thank you.

ANTIPHOLUS OF SYRACUSE Thank me, sir, for what?

50 DROMIO OF SYRACUSE Marry,[9] sir, for this something that you
gave me for nothing.

ANTIPHOLUS OF SYRACUSE I'll make you amends next, to give° *by giving*
you nothing for something. But say, sir, is it dinner-time?

DROMIO OF SYRACUSE No, sir, I think the meat wants that° I *lacks what*
55 have.

ANTIPHOLUS OF SYRACUSE In good time,[1] sir. What's that?

DROMIO OF SYRACUSE Basting.[2]

ANTIPHOLUS OF SYRACUSE Well, sir, then 'twill be dry.

DROMIO OF SYRACUSE If it be, sir, I pray you eat none of it.

60 ANTIPHOLUS OF SYRACUSE Your reason?

DROMIO OF SYRACUSE Lest it make you choleric[3] and purchase
me another dry basting.° *severe beating*

ANTIPHOLUS OF SYRACUSE Well, sir, learn to jest in good time.[4]
There's a time for all things.

65 DROMIO OF SYRACUSE I durst° have denied that before you were *dared*
so choleric.

ANTIPHOLUS OF SYRACUSE By what rule,° sir? *principle*

DROMIO OF SYRACUSE Marry, sir, by a rule as plain as the plain
bald pate of Father Time himself.[5]

70 ANTIPHOLUS OF SYRACUSE Let's hear it.

DROMIO OF SYRACUSE There's no time for a man to recover his
hair that grows bald by nature.

ANTIPHOLUS OF SYRACUSE May he not do it by fine and
recovery?[6]

75 DROMIO OF SYRACUSE Yes, to pay a fine° for a periwig, and *fee*
recover the lost hair of another man.[7]

ANTIPHOLUS OF SYRACUSE Why is Time such a niggard of hair,
being, as it is, so plentiful an excrement?° *outward growth*

DROMIO OF SYRACUSE Because it is a blessing that he bestows on
80 beasts, and what he hath scanted° men in hair he hath given *given less to*
them in wit.° *intellect*

ANTIPHOLUS OF SYRACUSE Why, but there's many a man hath
more hair than wit.

DROMIO OF SYRACUSE Not a man of those but he hath the wit to
85 lose his hair.[8]

---

9. By the Virgin Mary, a mild oath.
1. Indeed! (an expression of ironical acquiescence).
2. Punning on a second meaning, "beating."
3. Angry. Choler was the hot, dry humor (see note to 1.2.21); diet and climate were thought to affect the humors sympathetically, so that overly dry meat might lead to a choleric disposition.
4. Opportunely; in a merry or good-humored time.

5. Time was commonly depicted as a bald old man.
6. *fine and recovery*: the legal method of transferring the ownership of property that could not normally be sold, especially to break an entail.
7. *to pay . . . man*: to buy a wig made from someone else's hair (as wigs usually were).
8. *wit . . . hair*: ironic—clever enough to catch syphilis (which may cause hair loss).

ANTIPHOLUS OF SYRACUSE   Why, thou didst conclude hairy men
plain dealers, without wit.[9]
DROMIO OF SYRACUSE   The plainer dealer,[1] the sooner lost. Yet
he loseth it in a kind of jollity.°   *(sexual pleasure)*
90   ANTIPHOLUS OF SYRACUSE   For what reason?
DROMIO OF SYRACUSE   For two, and sound° ones too.   *strong*
ANTIPHOLUS OF SYRACUSE   Nay, not sound,° I pray you.   *healthy*
DROMIO OF SYRACUSE   Sure° ones, then.   *Certain*
ANTIPHOLUS OF SYRACUSE   Nay, not sure,° in a thing falsing.[2]   *trustworthy*
95   DROMIO OF SYRACUSE   Certain ones, then.
ANTIPHOLUS OF SYRACUSE   Name them.
DROMIO OF SYRACUSE   The one, to save the money that he
spends in tiring;° the other, that at dinner they should not drop   *hairstyling*
in his porridge.
100   ANTIPHOLUS OF SYRACUSE   You would all this time have proved
there is no time for all things.
DROMIO OF SYRACUSE   Marry, and did, sir: namely, e'en° no time   *even; precisely*
to recover hair lost by nature.
ANTIPHOLUS OF SYRACUSE   But your reason was not substantial,°   *firmly based*
105   why there is no time to recover.
DROMIO OF SYRACUSE   Thus I mend° it: Time himself is bald,   *improve*
and therefore to the world's end will have bald followers.
ANTIPHOLUS OF SYRACUSE   I knew 'twould be a bald° conclusion.   *an inane*
            Enter [from the Phoenix] ADRIANA *and* LUCIANA
But soft—who wafts° us yonder?   *beckons*
110   ADRIANA   Ay, ay, Antipholus, look strange[3] and frown:
Some other mistress hath thy sweet aspects.°   *loving looks*
I am not Adriana, nor thy wife.
The time was once when thou unurged wouldst vow
That never words were music to thine ear,
115   That never object pleasing in thine eye,
That never touch well welcome to thy hand,
That never meat sweet-savoured in thy taste,
Unless I spake, or looked, or touched, or carved to° thee.   *for*
How comes it now, my husband, O how comes it
120   That thou art then estrangèd from thyself?—
Thy 'self' I call it, being strange to me
That, undividable, incorporate,°   *united in one body*
Am better than thy dear self's better part.[4]
Ah, do not tear away thyself from me;
125   For know, my love, as easy mayst thou fall°   *let fall*
A drop of water in the breaking gulf,
And take unmingled thence that drop again
Without addition or diminishing,
As take from me thyself, and not me too.[5]
130   How dearly° would it touch thee to the quick   *deeply*
Shouldst thou but° hear I were licentious,   *only*
And that this body, consecrate to thee,
By ruffian lust should be contaminate?

9. *conclude . . . wit:* argue that hairy men were simple,
lacking in cunning and therefore honest (plain dealers).
1. With pun on "deal," have sex.
2. In a deceptive matter; perhaps punning on "thing"
as "sexual organ."
3. Look distant, but suggesting "without recognition,"
as if a foreigner—which he is.

4. Either his better qualities or his soul (which is better than his body). Adriana's plea depends on the doctrine of marriage as "one flesh" articulated in Genesis
2:23–24 and echoed in Paul's mystical view of the
church as wedded to God. Compare Ephesians
5:28–33.
5. *not me too:* not take me away from myself as well.

Wouldst thou not spit at me, and spurn° at me,   *strike*
135 And hurl the name of husband in my face,[6]
And tear the stained skin[7] off my harlot brow,
And from my false hand cut the wedding ring,
And break it with a deep-divorcing vow?
I know thou canst, and therefore see° thou do it!   *make sure*
140 I am possessed with° an adulterate blot;[8]   *in possession of*
My blood is mingled with the crime of lust.
For if we two be one, and thou play false,
I do digest the poison of thy flesh,
Being strumpeted° by thy contagion.   *made a whore*
145 Keep then fair league[9] and truce with thy true bed,
I live unstained, thou undishonourèd.
ANTIPHOLUS OF SYRACUSE   Plead you to *me*, fair dame? I know you not.
In Ephesus I am but two hours old,
As strange unto your town as to your talk,
150 Who, every word by all my wit being scanned,°   *analyzed*
Wants° wit in all one word to understand.   *Lacks*
LUCIANA   Fie, brother,° how the world is changed with you!   *brother-in-law*
When were you wont to use° my sister thus?   *treat*
She sent for you by Dromio home to dinner.
155 ANTIPHOLUS OF SYRACUSE   By Dromio?
DROMIO OF SYRACUSE   By me?
ADRIANA   By thee; and this thou didst return° from him—   *bring back*
That he did buffet thee, and in his blows
Denied my house for° his, me for his wife.   *to be*
160 ANTIPHOLUS OF SYRACUSE   Did you converse, sir, with this gentlewoman?
What is the course and drift of your compact?[1]
DROMIO OF SYRACUSE   I, sir? I never saw her till this time.
ANTIPHOLUS OF SYRACUSE   Villain, thou liest; for even her very° words   *exact*
Didst thou deliver to me on the mart.
165 DROMIO OF SYRACUSE   I never spake with her in all my life.
ANTIPHOLUS OF SYRACUSE   How can she thus then call us by our
    names?—
Unless it be by inspiration.°   *divine revelation*
ADRIANA   How ill agrees it° with your gravity°   *does it suit / dignity*
To counterfeit° thus grossly° with your slave,   *dissemble / blatantly*
170 Abetting him to thwart me in my mood!
Be it my wrong you are from me exempt,[2]
But wrong not that wrong with a more contempt.[3]
Come, I will fasten on this sleeve of thine.
Thou art an elm, my husband; I a vine,[4]
175 Whose weakness, married to thy stronger state,°   *condition*
Makes me with thy strength to communicate.°   *share*
If aught possess thee from me,[5] it is dross,°   *worthless*
Usurping ivy, brier, or idle moss,
Who, all° for want of pruning, with intrusion°   *entirely / invasively*
180 Infect thy sap, and live on thy confusion.[6]

---

6. And bitterly confront me with my degraded marriage vow.

7. Mark of impure character, as if she had been legally branded as a harlot.

8. The stain, or disgrace, of adultery.

9. *Keep . . . league*: If you keep faithful alliance.

1. What is the purpose and meaning of your conspiracy?

2. *Be . . . exempt*: Grant that it is my fault that you are alienated from me.

3. But do not add to that injury with mockery.

4. This image occurs both in Ovid's *Metamorphoses* 14.665–66 and in Psalm 128:3, included in the Elizabethan homily on marriage.

5. If anything takes possession of you away from (or apart from) me.

6. *live . . . confusion*: take life from your destruction.

ANTIPHOLUS OF SYRACUSE [*aside*]   To me she speaks, she moves°   *uses*
    me for her theme.°   *topic*
What, was I married to her in my dream?
Or sleep I now, and think I hear all this?
What error drives our eyes and ears amiss?
185 Until I know this sure uncertainty,
I'll entertain° the offered fallacy.°   *accept / delusion*
LUCIANA   Dromio, go bid the servants spread° for dinner.   *lay the table*
DROMIO OF SYRACUSE [*aside*]   O, for my beads!° I cross me[7] for°   *rosary beads / as*
    a sinner.
This is the fairy land. O spite of spites,
190 We talk with goblins, oafs,[8] and sprites.°   *spirits*
If we obey them not, this will ensue:
They'll suck our breath or pinch us black and blue.[9]
LUCIANA   Why prat'st° thou to thyself, and answer'st not?   *babble*
Dromio, thou drone,° thou snail, thou slug, thou sot.°   *idler / blockhead*
DROMIO OF SYRACUSE [*to* ANTIPHOLUS]   I am transformèd,
195   master, am not I?
ANTIPHOLUS OF SYRACUSE   I think thou art in mind, and so am I.
DROMIO OF SYRACUSE   Nay, master, both in mind and in my shape.
ANTIPHOLUS OF SYRACUSE   Thou hast thine own form.
DROMIO OF SYRACUSE   No, I am an ape.[1]
LUCIANA   If thou art changed to aught,° 'tis to an ass.   *anything*
DROMIO OF SYRACUSE [*to* ANTIPHOLUS]   'Tis true she rides° me,   *tyrannizes*
200   and I long for grass.[2]
'Tis so, I am an ass; else it could never be
But I should know her as well as she knows me.
ADRIANA   Come, come, no longer will I be a fool,
To put the finger in the eye and weep
205 Whilst man and master laughs my woes to scorn.[3]
[*To* ANTIPHOLUS] Come, sir, to dinner.—Dromio, keep the gate.—
Husband, I'll dine above with you today,
And shrive you of[4] a thousand idle pranks.—
Sirrah,[5] if any ask you for your master,
210 Say he dines forth,° and let no creature enter.—   *out*
Come, sister.—Dromio, play the porter well.
ANTIPHOLUS OF SYRACUSE [*aside*]   Am I in earth, in heaven, or in hell?
Sleeping or waking? Mad or well advised?°   *sane*
Known unto these, and to myself disguised!
215 I'll say as they say, and persever so,
And in this mist at all adventures° go.   *whatever occurs*
DROMIO OF SYRACUSE   Master, shall I be porter at the gate?
ADRIANA   Ay, and let none enter, lest I break your pate.°   *head*
LUCIANA   Come, come, Antipholus, we dine too late.
              Exeunt [*into the Phoenix*]

---

7. Make the sign of the cross (to ward off evil).
8. Changelings, goblin children left in the place of abducted human infants. F reads "owles," a possible reference to witchcraft.
9. Traditional recreations for fairies.

1. An imitation (of myself); a fool.
2. Freedom, as when a horse is put out to pasture.
3. *laughs . . . scorn:* make a mockery of my pain.
4. And act as your confessor to hear and pardon.
5. Standard term for addressing inferiors.

3.1

Enter ANTIPHOLUS OF EPHESUS, *his man* DROMIO,
ANGELO *the goldsmith, and* BALTHASAR *the merchant*

ANTIPHOLUS OF EPHESUS   Good Signor Angelo, you must excuse us all.
My wife is shrewish° when I keep not hours.°   *ill tempered / am late*
Say that I lingered with you at your shop
To see the making of her carcanet,°   *jeweled necklace*
5   And that tomorrow you will bring it home.—
But here's a villain that would face me down[1]
He met me on the mart, and that I beat him,
And charged him with[2] a thousand marks in gold,
And that I did deny my wife and house.
10   Thou drunkard, thou, what didst thou mean by this?
DROMIO OF EPHESUS   Say what you will, sir, but I know what I know—
That you beat me at the mart I have your hand[3] to show.
If the skin were parchment, and the blows you gave were ink,
Your own handwriting would tell you what I think.
ANTIPHOLUS OF EPHESUS   I think thou art an ass.
15   DROMIO OF EPHESUS   Marry, so it doth appear
By the wrongs I suffer and the blows I bear.
I should kick being kicked, and, being at that pass,°   *in that predicament*
You would keep from my heels, and beware of an ass.
ANTIPHOLUS OF EPHESUS   You're sad,° Signor Balthasar. Pray   *serious*
    God our cheer°   *fare*
20   May answer° my good will, and your good welcome here.   *equal*
BALTHASAR   I hold your dainties cheap, sir, and your welcome dear.[4]
ANTIPHOLUS OF EPHESUS   O, Signor Balthasar, either at flesh or fish
A table full of welcome makes scarce° one dainty dish.   *scarcely makes*
BALTHASAR   Good meat, sir, is common; that every churl° affords.   *peasant*
ANTIPHOLUS OF EPHESUS   And welcome more common, for
25   that's nothing but words.
BALTHASAR   Small cheer° and great welcome makes a merry feast.   *Little food*
ANTIPHOLUS OF EPHESUS   Ay, to a niggardly host and more spar-
    ing° guest.   *temperate*
But though my cates° be mean,° take them in good part.   *provisions / poor*
Better cheer may you have, but not with better heart.
30   But soft,[5] my door is locked. [*To* DROMIO] Go bid them let us in.
DROMIO OF EPHESUS [*calling*]   Maud, Bridget, Marian, Cicely, Gillian, Ginn!
    [*Enter* DROMIO OF SYRACUSE *within the Phoenix*]
DROMIO OF SYRACUSE [*within the Phoenix*]   Mome, malt-horse,
    capon, coxcomb, idiot, patch![6]
Either get thee from the door or sit down at the hatch.[7]
Dost thou conjure for° wenches, that thou call'st for such   *summon by spells*
    store°   *plenty*
35   When one is one too many? Go, get thee from the door.
DROMIO OF EPHESUS   What patch is made our porter? My mas-
    ter stays° in the street.   *waits*
DROMIO OF SYRACUSE [*within*]   Let him walk from whence he
    came, lest he catch cold on's° feet.   *on his*

3.1 Location: Before the house of Antipholus of Ephesus.
1. That would insist despite my denial that.
2. And accused him of possessing.
3. The mark of Antipholus's hand.
4. I value your welcome more highly than the delicacies of your table.
5. An exclamation of surprise.
6. Dolt, plodding oaf, eunuch, fool, idiot, clown.
7. Literally, sit down at the gate or half door, but playing on the proverbial phrase "set a hatch (gate) before
the door" of the tongue: keep silent.

ANTIPHOLUS OF EPHESUS   Who talks within there? Ho, open the door!

DROMIO OF SYRACUSE [*within the Phoenix*]   Right, sir, I'll tell
    you when, an° you'll tell me wherefore.   *if*

40 ANTIPHOLUS OF EPHESUS   Wherefore? For my dinner—I have not dined today.

DROMIO OF SYRACUSE [*within the Phoenix*]   Nor today here you
    must not. Come again when you may.

ANTIPHOLUS OF EPHESUS   What art thou that keep'st me out
    from the house I owe?°   *own*

DROMIO OF SYRACUSE [*within the Phoenix*]   The porter for this
    time,° sir, and my name is Dromio.   *for now*

DROMIO OF EPHESUS   O villain, thou hast stol'n both mine
    office° and my name.   *function*

45 The one ne'er got me credit, the other mickle blame.[8]

If thou hadst been Dromio today in my place,

Thou wouldst have changed thy pate° for an aim,[9] or thy name   *exchanged your head*
    for an ass.

        Enter NELL [*within the Phoenix*]

NELL [*within the Phoenix*]   What a coil° is there, Dromio? Who   *disturbance*
    are those at the gate?

DROMIO OF EPHESUS   Let my master in, Nell.[1]

NELL [*within the Phoenix*]   Faith no, he comes too late;
    And so tell your master.

50 DROMIO OF EPHESUS   O Lord, I must laugh.

Have at you[2] with a proverb: 'Shall I set in my staff?'[3]

NELL [*within the Phoenix*]   Have at you with another—that's
    'When? Can you tell?'[4]

DROMIO OF SYRACUSE [*within the Phoenix*]   If thy name be
    called Nell, Nell, thou hast answered him well.

ANTIPHOLUS OF EPHESUS [*to* NELL]   Do you hear, you minion?°   *subordinate*
    You'll let us in, I hope?

55 [   ]⁵

NELL [*within the Phoenix*]   I thought to have asked you.

DROMIO OF SYRACUSE [*within*]   And you said no.°   *(already)*

DROMIO OF EPHESUS   So, come help.

      [*He and* ANTIPHOLUS *beat the door*]

           Well struck! There was blow for blow.[6]

ANTIPHOLUS OF EPHESUS [*to* NELL]   Thou baggage,° let me in.   *good-for-nothing*

NELL [*within the Phoenix*]   Can you tell for whose sake?

DROMIO OF EPHESUS   Master, knock the door hard.

NELL [*within the Phoenix*]   Let him knock till it ache.

60 ANTIPHOLUS OF EPHESUS   You'll cry for this, minion, if I beat the door down.

NELL [*within the Phoenix*]   What needs all that, and a pair of stocks in the town?[7]

      Enter ADRIANA [*within the Phoenix*]

ADRIANA [*within the Phoenix*]   Who is that at the door that
    keeps° all this noise?   *keeps up*

DROMIO OF SYRACUSE [*within the Phoenix*]   By my troth, your
    town is troubled with unruly boys.

---

8. My reputation ("name") has never brought me credit, but in the course of my duties I have received much reproof ("mickle").

9. A target or butt, punning on "a name."

1. In F, Nell is designated "Luce" throughout this scene.

2. A challenge or warning in a fight (as with a quarter staff): Now I attack you.

3. Shall I take up residence? (proverbial).

4. Proverbial response of defiance.

5. Since line 54 has no rhyme in this consistently rhymed passage, it seems likely that either "hope" should be emended to "trow" (believe), or there is a line missing.

6. Blows to the door in response to verbal blows from within.

7. Why should I worry when there is a legal punishment for such behavior? *stocks:* instrument of punishment in which a person was seated with his or her legs locked in a wooden frame.

ANTIPHOLUS OF EPHESUS [*to* ADRIANA]   Are you there, wife? You
    might have come before.

ADRIANA [*within the Phoenix*]   Your wife, sir knave? Go, get you
65   from the door.   [*Exit with* NELL]

DROMIO OF EPHESUS [*to* ANTIPHOLUS]   If you went in pain, mas-
    ter, this knave would go sore.[8]

ANGELO [*to* ANTIPHOLUS]   Here is neither cheer, sir, nor wel-
    come; we would fain° have either.   *gladly*

BALTHASAR   In° debating which was best, we shall part° with   *After / depart*
    neither.

DROMIO OF EPHESUS [*to* ANTIPHOLUS]   They stand at the door,
    master. Bid them welcome hither.

ANTIPHOLUS OF EPHESUS   There is something in the wind,° that   *afoot*
70   we cannot get in.

DROMIO OF EPHESUS   You would say so, master, if your gar-
    ments were thin.°   *(taking "wind" literally)*
    Your cake[9] here is warm within: you stand here in the cold.
    It would make a man mad as a buck[1] to be so bought and sold.°   *betrayed*

ANTIPHOLUS OF EPHESUS   Go fetch me something. I'll break
    ope° the gate.   *open*

DROMIO OF SYRACUSE [*within the Phoenix*]   Break° any breaking   *Do*
75   here, and I'll break your knave's pate.

DROMIO OF EPHESUS   A man may break° a word with you, sir,   *speak*
    and words are but wind;
    Ay, and break it in your face, so he break it° not behind.   *break wind*

DROMIO OF SYRACUSE [*within the Phoenix*]   It seems thou
    want'st breaking.[2] Out upon thee, hind!°   *slave; fellow*

DROMIO OF EPHESUS   Here's too much 'Out upon thee!' I pray
    thee, let me in.

DROMIO OF SYRACUSE [*within the Phoenix*]   Ay, when fowls have
80   no feathers, and fish have no fin.

ANTIPHOLUS OF EPHESUS   Well, I'll break in.—Go borrow me a crow.°   *crowbar*

DROMIO OF EPHESUS   A crow without feather? Master, mean you so?
    For a fish without a fin, there's a fowl without a feather.
    [*To* DROMIO OF SYRACUSE]
    If a crow help us in, sirrah, we'll pluck a crow° together.   *settle accounts*

85 ANTIPHOLUS OF EPHESUS   Go, get thee gone. Fetch me an iron crow.

BALTHASAR   Have patience, sir. O, let it not be so!
    Herein you war against your reputation,
    And draw within the compass of suspect°   *scope of suspicion*
    Th'unviolated honour of your wife.
90   Once this:° your long experience of her wisdom,   *In brief*
    Her sober virtue, years,° and modesty,   *maturity*
    Plead on her part some cause° to you unknown;   *explanation; excuse*
    And doubt not, sir, but she will well excuse°   *explain*
    Why at this time the doors are made° against you.   *barred*
95   Be ruled by me. Depart in patience,
    And let us to the Tiger[3] all to dinner,
    And about evening come yourself alone
    To know the reason of this strange restraint.°   *exclusion*
    If by strong hand you offer° to break in   *attempt*
100   Now in the stirring passage° of the day,   *traffic*

---

8. If you, the master, get punished as a knave, so will I,
the actual servant ("knave").
9. Referring either to Adriana or to the meal.
1. Angry, with an allusion to cuckoldry (see 2.1.57 and

note).
2. Need a beating; need to be "broken in," or tamed
like a horse.
3. The name of an inn; see 1.2.9.

A vulgar° comment will be made of it,   *public; lewd*
And that supposèd° by the common rout°   *accepted / mob*
Against your yet ungallèd estimation,[4]
That may with foul intrusion enter in
105 And dwell upon your grave when you are dead.
For slander lives upon succession,°   *perpetuates itself*
For ever housed where once it gets possession.
ANTIPHOLUS OF EPHESUS   You have prevailed. I will depart in quiet,
And in despite of mirth° mean to be merry.   *ridicule*
110 I know a wench of excellent discourse,
Pretty and witty; wild,° and yet, too, gentle.°   *lively / refined*
There will we dine. This woman that I mean,
My wife—but, I protest, without desert°—   *my deserving*
Hath oftentimes upbraided me withal.°   *scolded me about*
115 To her will we to dinner. [*To* ANGELO] Get you home
And fetch the chain. By this,° I know, 'tis made.   *this time*
Bring it, I pray you, to the Porcupine,
For there's the house.° That chain will I bestow—   *That is where she lives*
Be it for nothing but to spite my wife—
120 Upon mine hostess there. Good sir, make haste:
Since mine own doors refuse to entertain° me,   *welcome*
I'll knock elsewhere, to see if they'll disdain me.
ANGELO   I'll meet you at that place some hour hence.
ANTIPHOLUS OF EPHESUS   Do so.   [*Exit* ANGELO]
               This jest shall cost me some expense.
        Exeunt [DROMIO OF SYRACUSE *within the*
        Phoenix, and the others into the Porcupine]

3.2

Enter [*from the Phoenix*] LUCIANA *with* ANTIPHOLUS OF
    SYRACUSE
LUCIANA   And may it be that you have quite forgot
A husband's office?° Shall, Antipholus,   *duty*
Even in the spring of love thy love-springs° rot?   *young shoots of love*
Shall love, in building, grow so ruinous?[1]
5 If you did wed my sister for her wealth,
Then for her wealth's sake use° her with more kindness;   *treat*
Or if you like elsewhere, do it by stealth:
Muffle° your false love with some show of blindness.[2]   *Hide*
Let not my sister read it in your eye.
10 Be not thy tongue thy own shame's orator.
Look sweet, speak fair, become disloyalty;[3]
Apparel vice like virtue's harbinger.°   *herald*
Bear a fair presence,° though your heart be tainted: *Present a pleasant front*
Teach sin the carriage° of a holy saint.   *bearing*
15 Be secret-false. What° need she be acquainted?   *Why*
What simple thief brags of his own attaint?°   *crime*
'Tis double wrong to truant with° your bed,   *be unfaithful to*
And let her read it in thy looks at board.°   *table*
Shame hath a bastard fame, well managèd;°   *if properly handled*
20 Ill deeds is° doubled with an evil word.   *are*

---

4. *yet . . . estimation:* as yet uninjured reputation.
3.2 Location: Scene continues.
1. Shall love become a ruin at the time of its building?
2. Seem to blindfold yourself so that your glances do

not reveal your faithlessness.
3. *become disloyalty:* put an attractive face on your
unfaithfulness.

Alas, poor women, make us but believe—
    Being compact of credit[4]—that you love us.
Though others have the arm, show us the sleeve.[5]
    We in your motion turn,[6] and you may move° us.   *control; touch*
25 Then, gentle brother, get you in again.
    Comfort my sister, cheer her, call her wife:
'Tis holy sport to be a little vain°   *false*
    When the sweet breath of flattery conquers strife.
ANTIPHOLUS OF SYRACUSE   Sweet mistress—what your name is else I know not,
30   Nor by what wonder you do hit of° mine.   *on*
Less in your knowledge and your grace you show not
    Than our earth's wonder,[7] more than earth° divine.   *mortal flesh*
Teach me, dear creature, how to think and speak.
    Lay open to my earthy gross conceit,[8]
35 Smothered in errors, feeble, shallow, weak,
    The folded° meaning of your words' deceit.   *hidden*
Against my soul's pure truth why labour you
    To make it wander in an unknown field?
Are you a god? Would you create me new?°   *anew*
40   Transform me, then, and to your power I'll yield.
But if that I am I, then well I know
    Your weeping sister is no wife of mine,
Nor to her bed no homage° do I owe.   *duty*
    Far more, far more, to you do I decline.°   *incline; submit*
45 O, train° me not, sweet mermaid,[9] with thy note   *entice*
    To drown me in thy sister's flood of tears.
Sing, siren, for thyself, and I will dote.°   *grow infatuated*
    Spread o'er the silver waves thy golden hairs,
And as a bed I'll take them, and there lie,
50   And in that glorious supposition° think   *(that the hair is a bed)*
He gains by death that° hath such means to die.[1]   *who*
    Let love, being light,[2] be drownèd if she sink.
LUCIANA   What, are you mad, that you do reason so?
ANTIPHOLUS OF SYRACUSE   Not mad, but mated[3]—how, I do not know.
55 LUCIANA   It is a fault that springeth from your eye.°   *(from looking lustfully)*
ANTIPHOLUS OF SYRACUSE   For gazing on your beams,° fair sun,   *eyes*
    being by.
LUCIANA   Gaze where you should, and that will clear your sight.
ANTIPHOLUS OF SYRACUSE   As good to wink,° sweet love, as look   *shut one's eyes*
    on° night.   *at*
LUCIANA   Why call you me 'love'? Call my sister so.
ANTIPHOLUS OF SYRACUSE   Thy sister's sister.
LUCIANA   That's my sister.
60 ANTIPHOLUS OF SYRACUSE   No,
    It is thyself, mine own self's better part,
Mine eye's clear eye, my dear heart's dearer heart,

---

4. Being made of credulity, gullible.
5. Although others have the reality of your love, present us the appearance.
6. We are subject to your influence (as heavenly bodies were believed to follow the rotations of concentric celestial spheres).
7. *Less . . . wonder:* You seem as wise and as gracious as the wonder of the world (probably an allusion to Queen Elizabeth, before whom the play may have been performed).
8. *earthy gross conceit:* clumsy mortal understanding.
9. Siren; in Greek legend, mermaids' singing lured sailors to their death (see line 47).
1. Perhaps with a pun on "to die" as the Elizabethan expression for "orgasm."
2. The line has two implications: only false love could sink, because true love is too light and buoyant; and love deserves drowning because it is giddy and wanton.
3. Amazed, confounded; in love; married.

My food, my fortune, and my sweet hope's aim,
My sole earth's heaven, and my heaven's claim.[4]

65 LUCIANA All this my sister is, or else should be.

ANTIPHOLUS OF SYRACUSE Call thyself sister, sweet, for I am thee.°   thine
Thee will I love, and with thee lead my life.
Thou hast no husband yet, nor I no wife.
Give me thy hand.

LUCIANA   O soft, sir, hold you still;
70 I'll fetch my sister to get her good will. *Exit [into the Phoenix]*
                Enter [from the Phoenix] DROMIO [OF] SYRACUSE

ANTIPHOLUS OF SYRACUSE Why, how now, Dromio! Where
runn'st thou so fast?

DROMIO OF SYRACUSE Do you know me, sir? Am I Dromio? Am
I your man? Am I myself?

75 ANTIPHOLUS OF SYRACUSE Thou art Dromio, thou art my man,
thou art thyself.

DROMIO OF SYRACUSE I am an ass, I am a woman's man, and
besides° myself.   in addition

ANTIPHOLUS OF SYRACUSE What woman's man? And how
80 besides thyself?

DROMIO OF SYRACUSE Marry, sir, besides myself I am due to a
woman: one that claims me, one that haunts me, one that will
have me.

ANTIPHOLUS OF SYRACUSE What claim lays she to thee?

85 DROMIO OF SYRACUSE Marry, sir, such claim as you would lay to
your horse; and she would have me as a beast—not that, I being
a beast, she would have me, but that she, being a very beastly
creature, lays claim to me.

ANTIPHOLUS OF SYRACUSE What is she?

90 DROMIO OF SYRACUSE A very reverend° body; ay, such a one as a   worthy
man may not speak of without he say 'sir-reverence'.[5] I have but
lean luck in the match, and yet is she a wondrous fat marriage.

ANTIPHOLUS OF SYRACUSE How dost thou mean, a fat marriage?

DROMIO OF SYRACUSE Marry, sir, she's the kitchen wench,° and   servant
95 all grease; and I know not what use to put her to but to make
a lamp of her, and run from her by her own light. I warrant°   guarantee
her rags and the tallow in them will burn a Poland winter.[6] If
she lives till doomsday, she'll burn a week longer than the
whole world.[7]

100 ANTIPHOLUS OF SYRACUSE What complexion is she of?

DROMIO OF SYRACUSE Swart° like my shoe, but her face nothing   Dark
like so clean kept. For why?°—She sweats a man may go over-   How so?
shoes[8] in the grime of it.

ANTIPHOLUS OF SYRACUSE That's a fault that water will mend.

105 DROMIO OF SYRACUSE No, sir, 'tis in grain.° Noah's flood could   ingrained
not do it.

ANTIPHOLUS OF SYRACUSE What's her name?

DROMIO OF SYRACUSE Nell, sir. But her name and three-
quarters—that's an ell° and three-quarters—will not measure   more than a yard
110 her from hip to hip.

4. My only heaven on earth and only claim on heaven.
5. "Saving your reverence," an apology for a potentially
offensive remark.
6. The length of a winter in Poland—a long time.

7. Than the rest of the world (the popular Christian
belief being that the earth would end in fire).
8. She sweats so much a man may be up to his ankles.

ANTIPHOLUS OF SYRACUSE   Then she bears some breadth?

DROMIO OF SYRACUSE   No longer from head to foot than from
hip to hip. She is spherical, like a globe. I could find out°   *discover*
countries in her.

115 ANTIPHOLUS OF SYRACUSE   In what part of her body stands Ireland?

DROMIO OF SYRACUSE   Marry, sir, in her buttocks. I found it out
by the bogs.°   *peat marsh; sponginess*

ANTIPHOLUS OF SYRACUSE   Where Scotland?

DROMIO OF SYRACUSE   I found it by the barrenness, hard in the
120 palm of her hand.[9]

ANTIPHOLUS OF SYRACUSE   Where France?

DROMIO OF SYRACUSE   In her forehead, armed and reverted,[1]
making war against her heir.[2]

ANTIPHOLUS OF SYRACUSE   Where England?

125 DROMIO OF SYRACUSE   I looked for the chalky cliffs,[3] but I could
find no whiteness in them. But I guess it stood in her chin, by°   *judging by*
the salt rheum° that ran between France and it.   *mucus*

ANTIPHOLUS OF SYRACUSE   Where Spain?

DROMIO OF SYRACUSE   Faith, I saw it not, but I felt it hot in her
130 breath.[4]

ANTIPHOLUS OF SYRACUSE   Where America, the Indies?

DROMIO OF SYRACUSE   O, sir, upon her nose, all o'er embellished
with rubies, carbuncles, sapphires,[5] declining their rich aspect[6]
to the hot breath of Spain, who sent whole armadas of car-
135 racks to be ballast[7] at her nose.

ANTIPHOLUS OF SYRACUSE   Where stood Belgia, the Netherlands?

DROMIO OF SYRACUSE   O, sir, I did not look so low.[8] To conclude,
this drudge or diviner° laid claim to me, called me Dromio,   *witch*
swore I was assured° to her, told me what privy° marks I had   *betrothed / private; secret*
140 about me—as the mark of my shoulder, the mole in my neck,
the great wart on my left arm—that I, amazed, ran from her
as a witch. And I think if my breast had not been made of faith,
and my heart of steel,[9] she had transformed me to a curtal°   *tailless*
dog, and made me turn i'th' wheel.°   *turn a roasting spit*

ANTIPHOLUS OF SYRACUSE   Go, hie thee presently.° Post° to the   *now / Hasten*
145 road.°   *harbor*
An if° the wind blow any way from shore,°   *An if = If / out to sea*
I will not harbour in this town tonight.
If any barque put forth, come to the mart,
Where I will walk till thou return to me.
150 If everyone knows us, and we know none,
'Tis time, I think, to trudge,° pack, and be gone.   *depart*

DROMIO OF SYRACUSE   As from a bear a man would run for life,
So fly I from her that would be my wife.   *Exit [to the bay]*

ANTIPHOLUS OF SYRACUSE   There's none but witches do inhabit here,
155 And therefore 'tis high time that I were hence.
She that doth call me husband, even my° soul   *my very*

---

9. Hard with calluses and dry (a moist hand proverbially indicated fertility; hence a dry hand could con-
note barrenness).
1. In rebellion (perhaps referring to syphilitic sores).
2. A possible allusion to contemporary French politics;
a pun on "hair," which she is losing, probably on
account of venereal disease.
3. Teeth; an allusion to the white chalk cliffs of Dover.
4. As if she had been eating pungent food.

5. Glistening skin blemishes (as if precious stones).
6. Casting their gaze down; paying tribute to.
7. *armadas . . . ballast:* fleets of galleons to be loaded.
8. The Netherlands and Belgium were also known as
the Low Countries.
9. Compare Ephesians 6:11ff.: "Put on the whole
armour of God, that ye may be able to stand against the
assaults of the devil. . . . having on the breast plate of
righteousness. . . . Above all, take the shield of faith."

Doth for a wife abhor. But her fair sister,
Possessed with such a gentle sovereign° grace,   *excellent*
Of such enchanting presence and discourse,
160   Hath almost made me traitor to myself.
But lest myself be guilty to° self-wrong,   *of*
I'll stop mine ears against the mermaid's song.

Enter ANGELO *with the chain*

ANGELO   Master Antipholus.
ANTIPHOLUS OF SYRACUSE   Ay, that's my name.
ANGELO   I know it well, sir. Lo, here's the chain.
165   I thought to have ta'en° you at the Porcupine.   *overtaken*
The chain unfinished made me stay° thus long.   *delay*
ANTIPHOLUS OF SYRACUSE [*taking the chain*]   What is your will
     that I shall do with this?
ANGELO   What please° yourself, sir. I have made it for you.   *pleases*
ANTIPHOLUS OF SYRACUSE   Made it for me, sir? I bespoke° it not.   *ordered*
170   ANGELO   Not once, nor twice, but twenty times you have.
Go home with it, and please your wife withal,°   *with it*
And soon at supper-time I'll visit you,
And then receive my money for the chain.
ANTIPHOLUS OF SYRACUSE   I pray you, sir, receive the money now,
175   For fear you ne'er see chain nor money more.
ANGELO   You are a merry man, sir. Fare you well.   *Exit*
ANTIPHOLUS OF SYRACUSE   What I should think of this I cannot tell.
But this I think: there's no man is so vain°   *foolish*
That would refuse so fair an offered chain.
180   I see a man here needs not live by shifts,°   *his own efforts*
When in the streets he meets such golden gifts.
I'll to the mart, and there for Dromio stay.
If any ship put out, then straight° away!   *Exit*   *immediately*

4.1

Enter [SECOND] MERCHANT, [ANGELO *the*] *goldsmith,*
     and an OFFICER

SECOND MERCHANT [*to* ANGELO]   You know since Pentecost[1] the sum is due,
And since I have not much importuned you;
Nor now I had not,° but° that I am bound   *I would not have / except*
To Persia, and want° guilders for my voyage.   *lack*
5   Therefore make present satisfaction,°   *immediate payment*
Or I'll attach° you by this officer.   *arrest*
ANGELO   Even just the sum that I do owe to you
Is growing° to me by Antipholus,   *owing*
And in the instant that I met with you
10   He had of me a chain. At five o'clock
I shall receive the money for the same.
Pleaseth you° walk with me down to his house,   *If it please you to*
I will discharge my bond, and thank you too.

Enter ANTIPHOLUS [OF] EPHESUS, DROMIO [OF EPHESUS]
     from the Courtesan's [*house, the Porcupine*]

OFFICER   That labour may you save. See where he comes.

4.1 Location: A street in Ephesus.
1. Christian festival observed on the seventh Sunday after Easter, in commemoration of the descent of the

Holy Ghost on the disciples on the day of the Jewish harvest holiday of Shavuoth.

ANTIPHOLUS OF EPHESUS [*to* DROMIO]   While I go to the gold-
15   smith's house, go thou
       And buy a rope's end.° That will I bestow°   *piece of rope / employ (as a whip)*
       Among my wife and her confederates
       For locking me out of my doors by day.
       But soft,° I see the goldsmith. Get thee gone.   *wait*
20   Buy thou a rope, and bring it home to me.
DROMIO OF EPHESUS   I buy a thousand pound a year, I buy a
       rope.[2]   *Exit*
ANTIPHOLUS OF EPHESUS [*to* ANGELO]   A man is well holp up°   *helped*
       that trusts to you!
       I promisèd your presence and the chain,
       But neither chain nor goldsmith came to me.
25   Belike° you thought our love° would last too long   *Perhaps / friendship*
       If it were chained together, and therefore came not.
ANGELO   Saving° your merry humour, here's the note   *Without offense to*
       How much your chain weighs to the utmost carat,
       The fineness of the gold, and chargeful fashion,°   *costly craftsmanship*
30   Which doth amount to three odd ducats° more   *gold coins*
       Than I stand debted° to this gentleman.   *indebted*
       I pray you see him presently discharged,°   *paid off now*
       For he is bound to sea, and stays but° for it.   *waits only*
ANTIPHOLUS OF EPHESUS   I am not furnished with the present° money.   *ready*
35   Besides, I have some business in the town.
       Good signor, take the stranger to my house,
       And with you take the chain, and bid my wife
       Disburse the sum on the receipt thereof.
       Perchance° I will be there as soon as you.   *Perhaps*
40 ANGELO   Then you will bring the chain to her yourself?
ANTIPHOLUS OF EPHESUS   No, bear it with you, lest I come not
       time° enough.   *soon*
ANGELO   Well, sir, I will. Have you the chain about you?
ANTIPHOLUS OF EPHESUS   An if I have not, sir, I hope you have;
       Or else you may return without your money.
45 ANGELO   Nay, come, I pray you, sir, give me the chain.
       Both wind and tide stays° for this gentleman,   *wait*
       And I, to blame, have held him here too long.
ANTIPHOLUS OF EPHESUS   Good Lord! You use this dalliance° to   *trifling delay*
       excuse
       Your breach of promise to° the Porcupine.   *to go to*
50   I should have chid you for not bringing it,
       But like a shrew° you first begin to brawl.   *sour person*
SECOND MERCHANT [*to* ANGELO]   The hour steals on. I pray you,
       sir, dispatch.°   *hurry*
ANGELO [*to* ANTIPHOLUS]   You hear how he importunes me. The chain!
ANTIPHOLUS OF EPHESUS   Why, give it to my wife, and fetch
       your money.
55 ANGELO   Come, come, you know I gave it you even° now.   *just*
       Either send the chain, or send me by some token.[3]
ANTIPHOLUS OF EPHESUS   Fie, now you run this humour out of
       breath.°   *exhaust this joke*
       Come, where's the chain? I pray you let me see it.

---

2. Perhaps in exasperated contrast with Antipholus of   3. With some sign of yours (so that Adriana will know
Syracuse's earlier demand for a thousand marks (2.1.60).   to pay me).

SECOND MERCHANT   My business cannot brook° this dalliance.   tolerate
60   Good sir, say whe'er° you'll answer° me or no;   whether / repay
   If not, I'll leave him to the officer.
   ANTIPHOLUS OF EPHESUS   I answer you? What should I answer you?
   ANGELO   The money that you owe me for the chain.
   ANTIPHOLUS OF EPHESUS   I owe you none till I receive the chain.
65   ANGELO   You know I gave it you half an hour since.
   ANTIPHOLUS OF EPHESUS   You gave me none. You wrong me much to say so.
   ANGELO   You wrong me more, sir, in denying it.
   Consider how it stands upon° my credit.[4]   affects
   SECOND MERCHANT   Well, officer, arrest him at my suit.
70   OFFICER [to ANGELO]   I do, and charge you in the Duke's name to obey me.
   ANGELO [to ANTIPHOLUS]   This touches° me in reputation.   injures
   Either consent to pay this sum for me,
   Or I attach° you by this officer.   arrest
   ANTIPHOLUS OF EPHESUS   Consent to pay thee that° I never had?   for what
75   Arrest me, foolish fellow, if thou dar'st.
   ANGELO   Here is thy fee:[5] arrest him, officer.
   I would not spare my brother in this case
   If he should scorn me so apparently.°   openly
   OFFICER [to ANTIPHOLUS]   I do arrest you, sir. You hear the suit.
80   ANTIPHOLUS OF EPHESUS   I do obey thee till I give thee bail.
   [To ANGELO] But, sirrah, you shall buy this sport as dear[6]
   As all the metal in your shop will answer.°   amount to
   ANGELO   Sir, sir, I shall have law° in Ephesus,   my legal rights
   To your notorious shame, I doubt it not.
                  Enter DROMIO [OF] SYRACUSE, *from the bay*
85   DROMIO OF SYRACUSE   Master, there's a barque of Epidamnum
   That stays but till her owner comes aboard,
   And then she bears away. Our freightage,° sir,   luggage; goods
   I have conveyed aboard, and I have bought
   The oil, the balsamum,[7] and aqua-vitae.
90   The ship is in her trim;° the merry wind   ready to sail
   Blows fair from land. They stay for naught° at all   nothing
   But for their owner, master, and yourself.
   ANTIPHOLUS OF EPHESUS   How now? A madman? Why, thou
      peevish° sheep,[8]   bleating
   What ship of Epidamnum stays for me?
95   DROMIO OF SYRACUSE   A ship you sent me to, to hire waftage.°   buy our passage
   ANTIPHOLUS OF EPHESUS   Thou drunken slave, I sent thee for a rope,
   And told thee to what purpose and what end.
   DROMIO OF SYRACUSE   You sent me for a ropes end° as soon.   a beating
   You sent me to the bay, sir, for a barque.
100   ANTIPHOLUS OF EPHESUS   I will debate this matter at more leisure,
   And teach your ears to list° me with more heed.   listen to
   To Adriana, villain, hie thee straight.°   go immediately
   Give her this key, and tell her in the desk
   That's covered o'er with Turkish tapestry
105   There is a purse of ducats. Let her send it.
   Tell her I am arrested in the street,
   And that shall bail me.° Hie thee, slave. Be gone!—   pay my bail

---

4. Financial standing; more generally, reputation.
5. Public officers were entitled to private payment.
6. You shall pay as dearly for this amusement.
7. A healing resin; alcoholic spirit.
8. Idiot, punning on "ship" in the next line (the words were similarly pronounced).

On, officer, to prison, till it come.

Exeunt [all but DROMIO OF SYRACUSE]

DROMIO OF SYRACUSE   To Adriana. That is where we dined,
110   Where Dowsabel⁹ did claim me for her husband.
She is too big, I hope, for me to compass.¹
Thither I must, although against my will;
For servants must their masters' minds° fulfil.   *Exit*   wishes

4.2

Enter [from the Phoenix] ADRIANA *and* LUCIANA

ADRIANA   Ah, Luciana, did he tempt thee so?
Mightst thou perceive austerely in his eye¹
That he did plead in earnest, yea or no?
Looked he or° red or pale, or sad or merrily?   either
5   What observation mad'st thou in this case
Of his heart's meteors tilting² in his face?
LUCIANA   First he denied you had in him no° right.   any
ADRIANA   He meant he did me none, the more my spite.°   grief
LUCIANA   Then swore he that he was a stranger here.
10   ADRIANA   And true he swore, though yet forsworn³ he were.
LUCIANA   Then pleaded I for you.
ADRIANA   And what said he?
LUCIANA   That love I begged for you, he begged of me.
ADRIANA   With what persuasion did he tempt thy love?
LUCIANA   With words that in an honest suit° might move.   courtship
15   First he did praise my beauty, then my speech.
ADRIANA   Didst speak him fair?°   encourage him
LUCIANA   Have patience, I beseech.
ADRIANA   I cannot, nor I will not, hold me still.°   silent
My tongue, though not my heart, shall have his° will.   its
He is deformèd, crookèd, old, and sere,°   withered
20   Ill-faced, worse-bodied, shapeless° everywhere,   ill shaped
Vicious, ungentle, foolish, blunt, unkind,
Stigmatical in making,⁴ worse in mind.
LUCIANA   Who would be jealous, then, of such a one?
No evil lost is wailed when it is gone.
25   ADRIANA   Ah, but I think him better than I say,
And yet would herein others' eyes were worse.⁵
Far from her nest the lapwing⁶ cries away.
My heart prays for him, though my tongue do curse.

Enter DROMIO [OF] SYRACUSE *running*

DROMIO OF SYRACUSE   Here, go—the desk, the purse! Sweet now, make haste!⁷
LUCIANA   How?⁸ Hast thou lost thy breath?
30   DROMIO OF SYRACUSE   By running fast.

---

9. English form of "Dulcibella," a generic name for a sweetheart.
1. Embrace or gain; probably also alluding to her geographical extent (see 3.2.113–37).
4.2 Location: Before the house of Antipholus of Ephesus.
1. By the seriousness of his expression.
2. Conflicting emotions, as if heavenly bodies were engaged in combat ("tilting").
3. *true . . . forsworn:* he is behaving like a stranger to me, but he is lying and false to his marriage vows if he claims to be one.

4. Deformed in his physical makeup.
5. And nevertheless wish others' eyes to be deceived (and so think him ugly).
6. A bird (the peewit) that diverts attention away from her nest to protect her young; Adriana wishes to turn other women's attention from Antipholus's attractions.
7. Dromio is possibly speaking to himself as he rushes in.
8. What's this? Although F treats Luciana's word as one sentence, Dromio's answer is obviously a comic misunderstanding.

ADRIANA   Where is thy master, Dromio? Is he well?

DROMIO OF SYRACUSE   No, he's in Tartar limbo,[9] worse than hell.
     A devil in an everlasting[1] garment hath him,
     One whose hard heart is buttoned up with steel;
35   A fiend, a fairy,[2] pitiless and rough;
     A wolf, nay worse, a fellow all in buff;[3]
     A back-friend,[4] a shoulder-clapper,° one that countermands°   arresting officer / prohibits
     The passages of alleys, creeks, and narrow launds;[5]
     A hound that runs counter,[6] and yet draws dryfoot well;[7]
40   One that before the Judgement[8] carries poor souls to hell.

ADRIANA   Why, man, what is the matter?

DROMIO OF SYRACUSE   I do not know the matter,° he is 'rested°   dispute / arrested
     on the case.[9]

ADRIANA   What, is he arrested? Tell me at whose suit.

DROMIO OF SYRACUSE   I know not at whose suit he is arrested well,
45   But is in a suit of buff which 'rested him, that can I tell.
     Will you send him, mistress, redemption—the money in his desk?

ADRIANA   Go fetch it, sister.   Exit LUCIANA [into the Phoenix]
                              This I wonder at,
     That he unknown to me should be in debt.
     Tell me, was he arrested on° a bond?   for breaking
50   DROMIO OF SYRACUSE   Not on a bond but on a stronger thing:
     A chain, a chain—do you not hear it ring?

ADRIANA   What, the chain?

DROMIO OF SYRACUSE   No, no, the bell. 'Tis time that I were gone:
     It was two ere I left him, and now the clock strikes one.[1]

ADRIANA   The hours come back! That did I never hear.

DROMIO OF SYRACUSE   O yes, if any hour[2] meet a sergeant, a°   he
55   turns back for very fear.

ADRIANA   As if time were in debt. How fondly° dost thou reason!   foolishly

DROMIO OF SYRACUSE   Time is a very bankrupt, and owes more
     than he's worth to season.[3]
     Nay, he's a thief too. Have you not heard men say
     That time comes stealing on by night and day?
60   If a be in debt and theft, and a sergeant in° the way,   stands in
     Hath he not reason to turn back an hour in a day?
          Enter LUCIANA [from the Phoenix, with the money]

ADRIANA   Go, Dromio, there's the money. Bear it straight,°   quickly
     And bring thy master home immediately.   [Exit DROMIO]
     Come, sister, I am pressed° down with conceit:°   depressed / imaginings
65   Conceit, my comfort and my injury.
               Exeunt [into the Phoenix]

---

9. Hellish prison. "Tartar" is short for "Tartarus," the
classical hell, but it also suggests the Tartars, central
Asian people reputed by Elizabethans to be particularly
savage. "Limbo" was common slang for "prison."
1. Term for the durable material used in the period for
the uniform of prison officers; eternal, like hell's punishments.
2. Malevolent fairy, like the goblins in 2.2.190–92.
3. Stout leather used in uniforms.
4. False friend; also referring to the officer's hand on
the culprit's back during an arrest.
5. The traffic through alleys, small passageways, and
narrow pathways. launds: glades or clearings, pathways
through woods.

6. Runs in the opposite direction to the prey; also perhaps alluding to the Counter, as several debtors' prisons
in London were known.
7. draws . . . well: tracks game by the scent of its foot.
8. before the Judgement: in a court of law, with an allusion to the Day of Judgment.
9. on the case: in a legal action where the injury was not
specifically addressed by precedent; by means of the
officer's hand on his outer clothing ("case").
1. "On" and "one" were pronounced similarly.
2. Perhaps a pun on "ower" (debtor), or "whore."
3. "Seisin," a legal term for "possession"; opportunity;
thus, there is too little time to make good the promises
of the occasion.

4.3

Enter ANTIPHOLUS [OF] SYRACUSE [*wearing the chain*]

ANTIPHOLUS OF SYRACUSE   There's not a man I meet but doth salute° me   greet
As if I were their well-acquainted friend,
And everyone doth call me by my name.
Some tender° money to me, some invite me,   offer
5   Some other give me thanks for kindnesses.
Some offer me commodities to buy.
Even now a tailor called me in his shop,
And showed me silks that he had bought for me,
And therewithal° took measure of my body.   with that
10   Sure, these are but imaginary wiles,°   delusions
And Lapland sorcerers[1] inhabit here.

Enter DROMIO [OF] SYRACUSE [*with the money*]

DROMIO OF SYRACUSE   Master, here's the gold you sent me for.
What, have you got redemption from the picture of old Adam
new apparelled?[2]

ANTIPHOLUS OF SYRACUSE   What gold is this? What Adam dost
15   thou mean?

DROMIO OF SYRACUSE   Not that Adam that kept the Paradise,
but that Adam that keeps the prison—he that goes in the calf 's
skin,[3] that was killed for the Prodigal;[4] he that came behind
you, sir, like an evil angel, and bid you forsake your liberty.[5]

20   ANTIPHOLUS OF SYRACUSE   I understand thee not.

DROMIO OF SYRACUSE   No? Why, 'tis a plain case: he that went
like a bass viol[6] in a case of leather; the man, sir, that when
gentlemen are tired gives them a sob[7] and 'rests them; he, sir,
that takes pity on decayed° men and gives them suits of   ruined
25   durance;[8] he that sets up his rest[9] to do more exploits with his
mace° than a Moorish pike.   staff of office

ANTIPHOLUS OF SYRACUSE   What, thou mean'st an officer?

DROMIO OF SYRACUSE   Ay, sir, the sergeant of the band: he that
brings any man to answer it° that breaks his bond; one that   for it
30   thinks a man always going to bed, and says 'God give you good
rest.'°   arrest

ANTIPHOLUS OF SYRACUSE   Well, sir, there rest in° your foolery.   cease
Is there any ships puts forth tonight? May we be gone?

DROMIO OF SYRACUSE   Why, sir, I brought you word an hour
35   since that the barque *Expedition* put forth tonight, and then
were you hindered by the sergeant to tarry for the hoy[1] *Delay*.
Here are the angels[2] that you sent for to deliver you.

ANTIPHOLUS OF SYRACUSE The fellow is distraught,° and so am I,   distracted; mad
And here we wander in illusions.
40   Some blessèd power deliver us from hence.

Enter a COURTESAN [*from the Porcupine*]

4.3 Location: A street in Ephesus.
1. Lapland was known for witches.
2. *from . . . apparelled:* from the sergeant in his leather
uniform. Old Adam is the figure of man's sinful nature,
dressed, after the Fall, in skins (Genesis 3:21). There is
also a possible reference to Ephesians 4:22–24 ("put
off . . . the old man, which is corrupt . . . put on the
new man, which after God is created in righteousness"). The text is emended from F: What have
you got the picture of old Adam new apparelled?
3. The buff of the officer's garments.
4. The prodigal son of Luke 15:11–32; his father killed

a calf for a feast on his return home.
5. *bid . . . liberty:* arrested you.
6. Large stringed instrument, like a cello (continuing
the jokes about the officer's leather uniform).
7. A rest (for tired horses) as well as a lament, picked
up in the following puns of " 'rests" and "pity."
8. *suits of durance:* lawsuits or prosecutions ending in
imprisonment; clothes of hard-wearing material.
9. *sets up his rest:* gambles all (punning on "arrest").
1. A small, slow vessel used in coastal waters. The
names of the ships are Dromio's improvisations.
2. Gold coins bearing a figure of the archangel Michael.

COURTESAN Well met, well met, Master Antipholus.
I see, sir, you have found the goldsmith now.
Is that the chain you promised me today?
ANTIPHOLUS OF SYRACUSE Satan, avoid!³ I charge thee, tempt
me not!

45 DROMIO OF SYRACUSE Master, is this Mistress Satan?
ANTIPHOLUS OF SYRACUSE It is the devil.
DROMIO OF SYRACUSE Nay, she is worse, she is the devil's dam;° mother
and here she comes in the habit° of a light° wench. And thereof clothing / wanton
comes that the wenches say 'God damn me'—that's as much to
50 say, 'God make me a light wench.' It is written they appear to
men like angels of light.⁴ Light is an effect of fire, and fire will
burn. Ergo,° light wenches will burn.⁵ Come not near her. Therefore
COURTESAN Your man and you are marvellous merry, sir.
Will you go with me? We'll mend° our dinner here. complete
55 DROMIO OF SYRACUSE Master, if you do, expect spoon-meat,⁶
and bespeak° a long spoon. request
ANTIPHOLUS OF SYRACUSE Why, Dromio?
DROMIO OF SYRACUSE Marry, he must have a long spoon that
must eat with the devil.
ANTIPHOLUS OF SYRACUSE [to COURTESAN Avoid, thou fiend!
60 What tell'st thou me of supping?
Thou art, as you are all, a sorceress.
I conjure° thee to leave me and be gone. order; charge
COURTESAN Give me the ring of mine you had at dinner,
Or for my diamond the chain you promised,
65 And I'll be gone, sir, and not trouble you.
DROMIO OF SYRACUSE Some devils ask but° the parings of one's nail, only
A rush,° a hair, a drop of blood, a pin, straw
A nut, a cherry-stone;
But she, more covetous, would have a chain.
70 Master, be wise; an if° you give it her, an if=if
The devil will shake her chain,⁷ and fright us with it.
COURTESAN [to ANTIPHOLUS] I pray you, sir, my ring, or else the chain.
I hope you do not mean to cheat me so?
ANTIPHOLUS OF SYRACUSE Avaunt, thou witch!—Come, Dromio, let us go.
75 DROMIO OF SYRACUSE 'Fly pride' says the peacock.⁸ Mistress, that you know.
Exeunt [ANTIPHOLUS OF SYRACUSE
and DROMIO OF SYRACUSE]
COURTESAN Now, out of doubt, Antipholus is mad;
Else would he never so demean° himself. conduct; debase
A ring he hath of mine worth forty ducats,
And for the same he promised me a chain.
80 Both one and other he denies me now.
The reason that I gather he is mad,
Besides this present instance of his rage,
Is a mad tale he told today at dinner
Of his own doors being shut against his entrance.
85 Belike° his wife, acquainted with his fits, Probably

3. Away. An echo of Jesus' words to Satan in Matthew
4:10: "Avoid Satan."
4. From 2 Corinthians 11:14: "Satan himself is transformed into an angel of light."
5. Will transmit venereal disease; will suffer in hell.
6. Soft food for babies or invalids, mentioned for the

sake of the proverb in lines 58–59.
7. Alluding to the binding of the devil in a chain in Revelation 20:1.
8. For the conniving courtesan to complain about
cheating is, in Dromio's view, analogous to a proud peacock decrying pride.

On purpose shut the doors against his way.°   *entrance*
My way is now to hie° home to his house,   *hasten*
And tell his wife that, being lunatic,
He rushed into my house, and took perforce°   *forcibly*
90   My ring away. This course I fittest choose,
For forty ducats is too much to lose.   [*Exit*]

4.4

Enter ANTIPHOLUS [OF] EPHESUS *with a Jailor* [*an*
OFFICER]

ANTIPHOLUS OF EPHESUS   Fear me not, man, I will not break away.
I'll give thee ere I leave thee so much money
To warrant thee° as I am 'rested for.   *As surety*
My wife is in a wayward mood today,
5   And will not lightly° trust the messenger   *readily*
That I should be attached° in Ephesus.   *arrested*
I tell you 'twill sound harshly in her ears.

Enter DROMIO [OF] EPHESUS *with a rope's end*

Here comes my man. I think he brings the money.—
How now, sir? Have you that I sent you for?
10 DROMIO OF EPHESUS   Here's that, I warrant you, will pay[1] them all.
ANTIPHOLUS OF EPHESUS   But where's the money?
DROMIO OF EPHESUS   Why, sir, I gave the money for the rope.
ANTIPHOLUS OF EPHESUS   Five hundred ducats, villain, for a rope?
DROMIO OF EPHESUS   I'll serve° you, sir, five hundred at the rate.°   *provide / for that price*
ANTIPHOLUS OF EPHESUS   To what end did I bid thee hie thee
15   home?
DROMIO OF EPHESUS   To° a rope's end, sir, and to that end am I   *For*
    returned.
ANTIPHOLUS OF EPHESUS   And to that end, sir, I will welcome you.[2]
    [*He beats* DROMIO]
OFFICER   Good sir, be patient.
DROMIO OF EPHESUS   Nay, 'tis for me to be patient: I am in adversity.[3]
20 OFFICER   Good now,° hold thy tongue.   *Please*
DROMIO OF EPHESUS   Nay, rather persuade *him* to hold° his   *hold off*
    hands.
ANTIPHOLUS OF EPHESUS   Thou whoreson,[4] senseless villain!
DROMIO OF EPHESUS   I would I were senseless, sir, that I might
    not feel your blows.
25 ANTIPHOLUS OF EPHESUS   Thou art sensible in° nothing but   *responsive to*
    blows, and so is an ass.
DROMIO OF EPHESUS   I am an ass indeed. You may prove it by
    my long ears.[5]—I have served him from the hour of my nativity
    to this instant, and have nothing at his hands for my service
30   but blows. When I am cold, he heats me with beating. When
    I am warm, he cools me with beating. I am waked with it when
    I sleep, raised with it when I sit, driven out of doors with it when
    I go from home, welcomed home with it when I return. Nay, I
    bear it on my shoulders, as a beggar wont her brat,[6] and I think

---

4.4 Location: Scene continues.
1. With a beating. (See 4.1.15–21.)
2. I will treat you to a rope's end (a beating).
3. In painful circumstances; alluding to Psalms 94:13.
4. Literally, son of a whore; more generally, a term of

contemptuous familiarity.
5. Playing on "ears/years," which were pronounced in the same way.
6. *wont her brat:* is accustomed to carrying her child.

35   when he hath lamed me I shall beg with it[7] from door to door.

    Enter ADRIANA, LUCIANA, COURTESAN, *and a schoolmas-*
    ter called PINCH

ANTIPHOLUS OF EPHESUS   Come, go along: my wife is coming
    yonder.

DROMIO OF EPHESUS [*to* ADRIANA]   Mistress, *respice finem*[8]—
    respect your end—or rather, to prophesy like the parrot,[9]
    'Beware the rope's end'.

ANTIPHOLUS OF EPHESUS   Wilt thou still talk?

    [*He*] *beats* DROMIO

40 COURTESAN [*to* ADRIANA]   How say you now? Is not your husband mad?

ADRIANA   His incivility confirms no less.—
    Good Doctor Pinch, you are a conjurer.[1]
    Establish him in his true sense[2] again,
    And I will please you° what you will demand.   *repay you with*

45 LUCIANA   Alas, how fiery and how sharp° he looks!   *fierce*

COURTESAN   Mark how he trembles in his ecstasy.°   *frenzy*

PINCH [*to* ANTIPHOLUS]   Give me your hand, and let me feel your pulse.

ANTIPHOLUS OF EPHESUS   There is my hand, and let it feel your ear.

    [*He strikes* PINCH]

PINCH   I charge thee, Satan, housed within this man,

50   To yield possession to my holy prayers,
    And to thy state of darkness hie thee straight:
    I conjure thee by all the saints in heaven.

ANTIPHOLUS OF EPHESUS   Peace, doting wizard, peace! I am not mad.

ADRIANA   O that thou wert not, poor distressèd soul.

55 ANTIPHOLUS OF EPHESUS   You minion,° you, are these your customers?   *hussy*
    Did this companion° with the saffron° face   *rascal / yellow*
    Revel and feast it at my house today,
    Whilst upon me the guilty doors were shut,
    And I denied to enter in my house?

60 ADRIANA   O husband, God doth know you dined at home,
    Where would you had remained until this time,
    Free from these slanders° and this open shame.   *scandals*

ANTIPHOLUS OF EPHESUS   Dined at home?

    [*To* DROMIO]   Thou villain, what sayst thou?

DROMIO OF EPHESUS   Sir, sooth to say,° you did not dine at home.   *to speak truly*

65 ANTIPHOLUS OF EPHESUS   Were not my doors locked up, and I shut out?

DROMIO OF EPHESUS   Pardie,° your doors were locked, and you   *By God (pardieu)*
    shut out.

ANTIPHOLUS OF EPHESUS   And did not she herself revile me there?

DROMIO OF EPHESUS   Sans° fable, she herself reviled you there.   *Without*

ANTIPHOLUS OF EPHESUS   Did not her kitchen-maid rail, taunt, and scorn me?

70 DROMIO OF EPHESUS   Certes° she did. The kitchen vestal[3] scorned you.   *Certainly*

ANTIPHOLUS OF EPHESUS   And did not I in rage depart from thence?

DROMIO OF EPHESUS   In verity you did. My bones bears witness,
    That since have felt the vigour of his rage.

---

7. I shall receive a beating (a frequent punishment for begging).

8. A religious injunction to "think on your end," but punning on *respice funem*, "think on the rope" (on hanging).

9. Parrots were often taught to cry "rope," an exclamation or curse; the "prophecy" is that the hearer deserves to be hanged.

1. Capable of exorcising devils; exorcism required a "doctor"—a learned man—since it was thought that devils needed to be addressed in Latin.

2. His right mind. Possession and lunacy were not necessarily medically distinct, since both involved the displacement of reason (by passion, sickness, or demons).

3. Ironic: a virgin priestess of the household goddess Vesta's temple, responsible for keeping the fire burning.

ADRIANA [*aside to* PINCH] Is't good to soothe° him in these contraries? *humor*

75 PINCH [*aside to* ADRIANA] It is no shame.° The fellow finds his vein, *harm*
And, yielding to him, humours well his frenzy.

ANTIPHOLUS OF EPHESUS [*to* ADRIANA] Thou hast suborned° the *induced*
goldsmith to arrest me.

ADRIANA Alas, I sent you money to redeem you,
By Dromio here, who came in haste for it.

80 DROMIO OF EPHESUS Money by me? Heart and good will you might,
But surely, master, not a rag° of money. *farthing*

ANTIPHOLUS OF EPHESUS Went'st not thou to her for a purse of ducats?

ADRIANA He came to me, and I delivered it.

LUCIANA And I am witness with her that she did.

85 DROMIO OF EPHESUS God and the ropemaker bear me witness
That I was sent for nothing but a rope.

PINCH [*aside to* ADRIANA] Mistress, both man and master is possessed.
I know it by their pale and deadly° looks. *deathlike*
They must be bound and laid in some dark room.[4]

ANTIPHOLUS OF EPHESUS [*to* ADRIANA] Say wherefore didst thou
90 lock me forth° today, *out*
[*To* DROMIO] And why dost thou deny the bag of gold?

ADRIANA I did not, gentle husband, lock thee forth.

DROMIO OF EPHESUS And, gentle master, I received no gold.
But I confess, sir, that we were locked out.

95 ADRIANA Dissembling villain, thou speak'st false in both.

ANTIPHOLUS OF EPHESUS Dissembling harlot, thou art false in all,
And art confederate with a damnèd pack° *conspiracy*
To make a loathsome abject scorn of me.
But with these nails I'll pluck out those false eyes,
100 That would behold in me this shameful sport.
[*He reaches for* ADRIANA; *she shrieks.*] *Enter three or
four, and offer to bind him. He strives*

ADRIANA O, bind him, bind him. Let him not come near me.

PINCH More company!° The fiend is strong within him. *Get help*

LUCIANA Ay me, poor man, how pale and wan he looks.

ANTIPHOLUS OF EPHESUS What, will you murder me?—Thou, jailer, thou,
105 I am thy prisoner. Wilt thou suffer them
To make a rescue?[5]

OFFICER   Masters, let him go.
He is my prisoner, and you shall not have him.

PINCH Go, bind his man, for he is frantic too.
[*They bind* DROMIO]

ADRIANA What wilt thou do, thou peevish° officer? *stupid*
110 Hast thou delight to see a wretched man
Do outrage and displeasure° to himself? *harm*

OFFICER He is my prisoner. If I let him go,
The debt he owes will be required of me.

ADRIANA I will discharge° thee ere I go from thee. *repay*
115 Bear me forthwith unto his creditor,
And, knowing how the debt grows,[6] I will pay it.—
Good Master Doctor, see him safe conveyed
Home to my house. O most unhappy day!

ANTIPHOLUS OF EPHESUS O most unhappy strumpet!

---

4. An ordinary sixteenth-century treatment for insanity.   6. *knowing . . . grows:* when I know how the debt came
5. To release by force from legal custody.   about.

120 DROMIO OF EPHESUS   Master, I am here entered in bond for you.

ANTIPHOLUS OF EPHESUS   Out on thee, villain! Wherefore dost
thou mad° me?   goad

DROMIO OF EPHESUS   Will you be bound for nothing? Be mad, good master—
Cry, 'The devil!'⁷

LUCIANA   God help, poor souls, how idly do they talk!

125 ADRIANA   Go bear him hence. Sister, go you with me.
Exeunt [into the Phoenix, PINCH *and others*
carrying off ANTIPHOLUS OF EPHESUS *and* DROMIO OF
EPHESUS]. *Manent*° OFFICER, ADRIANA, LUCIANA, COURTESAN   Remain
[To the OFFICER] Say now, whose suit is he arrested at?

OFFICER   One Angelo, a goldsmith. Do you know him?

ADRIANA   I know the man. What is the sum he owes?

OFFICER   Two hundred ducats.

ADRIANA   Say, how grows it due?

130 OFFICER   Due for a chain your husband had of him.

ADRIANA   He did bespeak° a chain for me, but had it not.   order

COURTESAN   Whenas your husband all in rage today
Came to my house, and took away my ring—
The ring I saw upon his finger now—

135 Straight after did I meet him with a chain.

ADRIANA   It may be so, but I did never see it.
Come, jailer, bring me where the goldsmith is.
I long to know the truth hereof at large.°   in full
Enter ANTIPHOLUS [OF] SYRACUSE [*wearing the chain*]
with his rapier drawn, and DROMIO [OF] SYRACUSE [*also*
with rapier]

LUCIANA   God, for thy mercy, they are loose again!

140 ADRIANA   And come with naked° swords. Let's call more help   drawn
To have them bound again.

OFFICER   Away, they'll kill us!
Run all out. Exeunt omnes,° *as fast as may be, frighted.*   all
[ANTIPHOLUS *and* DROMIO *remain*]

ANTIPHOLUS OF SYRACUSE   I see these witches are afraid of swords.

DROMIO OF SYRACUSE   She that would be your wife now ran from you.

ANTIPHOLUS OF SYRACUSE   Come to the Centaur. Fetch our stuff from thence.

145 I long that we were safe and sound aboard.

DROMIO OF SYRACUSE   Faith, stay here this night. They will
surely do us no harm. You saw they speak us fair, give us gold.
Methinks they are such a gentle nation that, but for the
mountain of mad flesh that claims marriage of me, I could

150 find in my heart to stay here still,° and turn witch.   always

ANTIPHOLUS OF SYRACUSE   I will not stay tonight for all the town.
Therefore away, to get our stuff aboard.   *Exeunt*

5.1

Enter [SECOND] MERCHANT *and* [ANGELO] *the goldsmith*

ANGELO   I am sorry, sir, that I have hindered you,
But I protest he had the chain of me,
Though most dishonestly he doth deny it.

SECOND MERCHANT   How is the man esteemed here in the city?

---

7. A cry of exasperation; a direct address to the devil,   possessed.
which would lend support to the view that he is   5.1 Location: Before a priory.

5 ANGELO Of very reverend reputation, sir,
      Of credit infinite, highly beloved,
      Second to none that lives here in the city.
      His word might bear my wealth at any time.[1]
   SECOND MERCHANT Speak softly. Yonder, as I think, he walks.

   Enter ANTIPHOLUS [OF SYRACUSE, *wearing the chain,*]
   and DROMIO [OF SYRACUSE] *again*

10 ANGELO 'Tis so, and that self° chain about his neck   *same*
      Which he forswore° most monstrously to have.   *denied on oath*
      Good sir, draw near to me. I'll speak to him.—
      Signor Antipholus, I wonder much
      That you would put me to this shame and trouble,
15   And not without some scandal to yourself,
      With circumstance° and oaths so to deny   *detailed argument*
      This chain, which now you wear so openly.
      Beside the charge,° the shame, imprisonment,   *cost*
      You have done wrong to this my honest friend,
20   Who, but for staying on° our controversy,   *as a result of*
      Had hoisted sail and put to sea today.
      This chain you had of me. Can you deny it?
   ANTIPHOLUS OF SYRACUSE I think I had. I never did deny it.
   SECOND MERCHANT Yes, that you did, sir, and forswore it too.
25 ANTIPHOLUS OF SYRACUSE Who heard me to deny it or forswear it?
   SECOND MERCHANT These ears of mine, thou know'st, did hear thee.
      Fie on thee, wretch! 'Tis pity that thou liv'st
      To walk where any honest men resort.
   ANTIPHOLUS OF SYRACUSE Thou art a villain to impeach me thus.
30   I'll prove mine honour and mine honesty
      Against thee presently,° if thou dar'st stand.°   *now / defend yourself*
   SECOND MERCHANT I dare, and do defy thee for a villain.

   They draw. Enter ADRIANA, LUCIANA, COURTESAN, *and*
   others [*from the Phoenix*]

   ADRIANA Hold, hurt him not, for God's sake; he is mad.
      Some get within him,° take his sword away.   *his guard*
35   Bind Dromio too, and bear them to my house.
   DROMIO OF SYRACUSE Run, master, run! For God's sake take° a   *take cover in*
      house.
      This is some priory—in, or we are spoiled.°   *ruined*

   Exeunt ANTIPHOLUS [OF SYRACUSE *and*
   DROMIO OF SYRACUSE] *to the priory*
   Enter [*from the priory*] *the Lady* ABBESS

   ABBESS Be quiet, people. Wherefore throng you hither?
   ADRIANA To fetch my poor distracted husband hence.
40   Let us come in, that we may bind him fast,
      And bear him home for his recovery.
   ANGELO I knew he was not in his perfect wits.
   SECOND MERCHANT I am sorry now that I did draw on him.
   ABBESS How long hath this possession held the man?
45 ADRIANA This week he hath been heavy, sour, sad,
      And much, much different from the man he was;
      But till this afternoon his passion°   *insanity*
      Ne'er brake° into extremity of rage.   *broke*
   ABBESS Hath he not lost much wealth by wreck at sea?

---

1. His word alone would be enough security to borrow all I have.

50	Buried some dear friend? Hath not else his eye
	Strayed° his affection in unlawful love—	*Led astray*
	A sin prevailing much in youthful men,
	Who give their eyes the liberty of gazing?
	Which of these sorrows is he subject to?
55	ADRIANA To none of these, except it be the last,
	Namely some love that drew him oft from home.
	ABBESS You should for that have reprehended him.
	ADRIANA Why, so I did.
	ABBESS Ay, but not rough enough.
	ADRIANA As roughly as my modesty would let me.
60	ABBESS Haply° in private.	*Perhaps*
	ADRIANA And in assemblies too.
	ABBESS Ay, but not enough.
	ADRIANA It was the copy° of our conference.°	*theme / conversation*
	In bed he slept not for my urging it.
65	At board° he fed not for my urging it.	*table*
	Alone, it was the subject of my theme.
	In company I often glancèd° it.	*alluded to*
	Still° did I tell him it was vile and bad.	*Continually*
	ABBESS And thereof came it that the man was mad.
70	The venom° clamours of a jealous woman	*venomous*
	Poisons more deadly than a mad dog's tooth.
	It seems his sleeps were hindered by thy railing,
	And thereof comes it that his head is light.
	Thou sayst his meat was sauced with thy upbraidings.
75	Unquiet meals make ill digestions.
	Thereof the raging fire of fever bred,
	And what's a fever but a fit of madness?[2]
	Thou sayst his sports were hindered by thy brawls.
	Sweet recreation barred, what doth ensue
80	But moody and dull melancholy,
	Kinsman to grim and comfortless despair,
	And at her heels a huge infectious troop
	Of pale distemperatures° and foes to life?	*illnesses; imbalances*
	In food, in sport, and life-preserving rest
85	To be disturbed would mad or° man or beast.	*would make mad either*
	The consequence is, then, thy jealous fits
	Hath scared thy husband from the use of wits.
	LUCIANA She never reprehended him but mildly
	When he demeaned himself rough, rude, and wildly.
90	[To ADRIANA] Why bear you these rebukes, and answer not?
	ADRIANA She did betray me to my own reproof.—
	Good people, enter, and lay hold on him.
	ABBESS No, not a creature enters in my house.
	ADRIANA Then let your servants bring my husband forth.
95	ABBESS Neither. He took this place for sanctuary,[3]
	And it shall privilege him from your hands
	Till I have brought him to his wits again,
	Or lose my labour in essaying it.
	ADRIANA I will attend my husband, be his nurse,
100	Diet° his sickness, for it is my office,°	*Treat / duty*

---

2. Both are imbalances in the body's humors; see note to 4.4.43.   3. Churches and other sacred buildings provided refuge from legal prosecution until the seventeenth century.

And will have no attorney° but myself.   *proxy*
And therefore let me have him home with me.

ABBESS   Be patient, for I will not let him stir
Till I have used the approvèd° means I have,   *tested*
105   With wholesome syrups, drugs, and holy prayers
To make of him a formal° man again.   *complete; sane*
It is a branch and parcel° of mine oath,   *part*
A charitable duty of my order.
Therefore depart, and leave him here with me.

110 ADRIANA   I will not hence, and leave my husband here;
And ill it doth beseem your holiness
To separate the husband and the wife.

ABBESS   Be quiet and depart. Thou shalt not have him.
                        [Exit into the priory]

LUCIANA *[to* ADRIANA*]*   Complain unto the Duke of this indignity.

115 ADRIANA   Come, go, I will fall prostrate at his feet,
And never rise until my tears and prayers
Have won his grace to come in person hither
And take perforce my husband from the Abbess.

SECOND MERCHANT   By this, I think, the dial point's at five.
120   Anon,° I'm sure, the Duke himself in person   *Soon*
Comes this way to the melancholy vale,
The place of death and sorry execution,
Behind the ditches of the abbey here.

ANGELO   Upon what cause?

125 SECOND MERCHANT   To see a reverend Syracusian merchant,
Who put unluckily into this bay
Against the laws and statutes of this town,
Beheaded publicly for his offence.

ANGELO   See where they come. We will behold his death.

130 LUCIANA   Kneel to the Duke before he pass the abbey.
        *Enter [*Solinus*]* DUKE *of Ephesus, and [*EGEON*] the mer-*
        chant of Syracuse, bareheaded, with the headsman° and   *executioner*
        other officers

DUKE   Yet once again proclaim it publicly:
If any friend will pay the sum for him,
He shall not die, so much we tender⁴ him.

ADRIANA *[kneeling]*   Justice, most sacred Duke, against the Abbess!

135 DUKE   She is a virtuous and a reverend lady.
It cannot be that she hath done thee wrong.

ADRIANA   May it please your grace, Antipholus my husband,
Who I made lord of me and all I had
At your important° letters⁵—this ill day   *urgent*
140   A most outrageous fit of madness took him,
That desp'rately he hurried through the street,
With him his bondman, all as mad as he,
Doing displeasure to the citizens
By rushing in their houses, bearing thence
145   Rings, jewels, anything his rage° did like.   *he in his madness*
Once did I get him bound, and sent him home,
Whilst to take order for° the wrongs I went   *settle up*
That here and there his fury had committed.

4. Offer; feel tender regard for.
5. Formal instructions. Adriana may have been the Duke's ward.

Anon, I wot° not by what strong° escape,   *know / forcible*
150 He broke from those that had the guard of him,
And with his mad attendant and himself,
Each one with ireful passion, with drawn swords,
Met us again, and, madly bent on us,
Chased us away; till, raising of more aid,
155 We came again to bind them. Then they fled
Into this abbey, whither we pursued them,
And here the Abbess shuts the gates on us,
And will not suffer us to fetch him out,
Nor send him forth that we may bear him hence.
160 Therefore, most gracious Duke, with thy command
Let him be brought forth, and borne hence for help.
DUKE [*raising* ADRIANA]   Long since, thy husband served me in my wars,
And I to thee engaged a prince's word,
When thou didst make him master of thy bed,
165 To do him all the grace° and good I could.—   *favor; patronage*
Go, some of you, knock at the abbey gate,
And bid the Lady Abbess come to me.
I will determine this before I stir.
       Enter a MESSENGER [*from the Phoenix*]
MESSENGER [*to* ADRIANA]   O mistress, mistress, shift° and save   *do what you can*
       yourself!
170 My master and his man are both broke loose,
Beaten the maids a-row,° and bound the Doctor,   *one after another*
Whose beard they have singed off with brands° of fire,   *torches*
And ever as it blazed they threw on him
Great pails of puddled° mire to quench the hair.   *foul*
175 My master preaches patience to him, and the while
His man with scissors nicks him like a fool;[6]
And sure—unless you send some present help—
Between them they will kill the conjurer.
ADRIANA   Peace, fool. Thy master and his man are here,
180 And that is false thou dost report to us.
MESSENGER   Mistress, upon my life I tell you true.
I have not breathed almost since I did see it.
He cries for you, and vows, if he can take you,
To scorch your face and to disfigure you.
       Cry within
185 Hark, hark, I hear him, mistress. Fly, be gone!
DUKE [*to* ADRIANA]   Come stand by me. Fear nothing. Guard
       with halberds!°   *spears with blades*
       Enter ANTIPHOLUS OF EPHESUS *and* DROMIO [OF]
       EPHESUS [*from the Phoenix*]
ADRIANA   Ay me, it is my husband! Witness you
That he is borne about invisible.
Even now we housed him in° the abbey here,   *chased him into*
190 And now he's there, past thought of human reason.
ANTIPHOLUS OF EPHESUS   Justice, most gracious Duke, O grant me justice,
Even for the service that long since I did thee,
When I bestrid thee[7] in the wars, and took
Deep scars to save thy life; even for the blood
195 That then I lost for thee, now grant me justice!

---

6. Cuts his hair in a foolish or fantastical fashion.   7. Stood over you (to defend you when you were down).

EGEON [*aside*]   Unless the fear of death doth make me dote,°   *grow senile*
    I see my son Antipholus, and Dromio.

ANTIPHOLUS OF EPHESUS   Justice, sweet prince, against that woman there,
    She whom thou gav'st to me to be my wife,
200   That hath abusèd and dishonoured me
    Even in the strength and height of injury.
    Beyond imagination is the wrong
    That she this day hath shameless thrown on me.

DUKE   Discover° how, and thou shalt find me just.   *Reveal*

205 ANTIPHOLUS OF EPHESUS   This day, great Duke, she shut the doors upon me
    While she with harlots° feasted in my house.   *scoundrels*

DUKE   A grievous fault!—Say, woman, didst thou so?

ADRIANA   No, my good lord. Myself, he, and my sister
    Today did dine together. So befall my soul
210   As this is false he burdens me withal.[8]

LUCIANA   Ne'er may I look on day nor sleep on night
    But° she tells to your highness simple truth.   *Unless*

ANGELO [*aside*]   O perjured woman! They are both forsworn.
    In this the madman justly chargeth them.

215 ANTIPHOLUS OF EPHESUS   My liege, I am advisèd° what I say,   *fully aware*
    Neither disturbed with the effect of wine,
    Nor heady-rash provoked with raging ire,
    Albeit my wrongs might make one wiser mad.
    This woman locked me out this day from dinner.
220   That goldsmith there, were he not packed° with her,   *conspiring*
    Could witness it, for he was with me then,
    Who parted with me to go fetch a chain,
    Promising to bring it to the Porcupine,
    Where Balthasar and I did dine together.
225   Our dinner done, and he not coming thither,
    I went to seek him. In the street I met him,
    And in his company that gentleman.
    [*He points to the* SECOND MERCHANT]
    There did this perjured goldsmith swear me down°   *contradict me in swearing*
    That I this day of him received the chain,
230   Which, God he knows, I saw not. For the which
    He did arrest me with an officer.
    I did obey, and sent my peasant° home   *servant*
    For certain ducats. He with none returned.
    Then fairly° I bespoke° the officer   *courteously / asked*
235   To go in person with me to my house.
    By th' way, we met my wife, her sister, and a rabble more
    Of vile confederates. Along with them
    They brought one Pinch, a hungry lean-faced villain,
    A mere anatomy,° a mountebank,°   *skeleton / quack*
240   A threadbare juggler,° and a fortune-teller,   *illusionist*
    A needy, hollow-eyed, sharp-looking° wretch,   *emaciated*
    A living dead man. This pernicious slave,
    Forsooth, took on him as° a conjurer,   *posed as*
    And gazing in mine eyes, feeling my pulse,
245   And with no face, as 'twere, outfacing me,[9]
    Cries out I was possessed. Then all together

---

8. *So . . . withal:* Let the fate of my soul depend on   9. And with his thin face staring me down.
whether what he charges me with is false.

They fell upon me, bound me, bore me thence,
And in a dark and dankish vault at home
There left me and my man, both bound together,

250   Till, gnawing with my teeth my bonds in sunder,°   *apart*
I gained my freedom, and immediately
Ran hither to your grace, whom I beseech
To give me ample satisfaction
For these deep shames and great indignities.

255 ANGELO   My lord, in truth, thus far I witness with him:
That he dined not at home, but was locked out.

DUKE   But had he such a chain of thee, or no?

ANGELO   He had, my lord, and when he ran in here
These people saw the chain about his neck.

260 SECOND MERCHANT [*to* ANTIPHOLUS]   Besides, I will be sworn these ears of mine
Heard you confess you had the chain of him,
After you first forswore it on the mart,
And thereupon I drew my sword on you;
And then you fled into this abbey here,

265   From whence I think you are come by miracle.

ANTIPHOLUS OF EPHESUS   I never came within these abbey walls,
Nor ever didst thou draw thy sword on me.
I never saw the chain, so help me heaven,
And this is false you burden me withal.°   *with*

270 DUKE   Why, what an intricate impeach° is this!   *complex charge*
I think you all have drunk of Circe's cup.[1]
If here you housed° him, here he would have been.   *cornered*
If he were mad, he would not plead so coldly.°   *rationally*
[*To* ADRIANA] You say he dined at home, the goldsmith here

275   Denies that saying. [*To* DROMIO] Sirrah, what say you?

DROMIO OF EPHESUS [*pointing out the* COURTESAN]   Sir, he
        dined with her there, at the Porcupine.

COURTESAN   He did, and from my finger snatched that ring.

ANTIPHOLUS OF EPHESUS   'Tis true, my liege, this ring I had of her.

DUKE [*to* COURTESAN]   Saw'st thou him enter at the abbey here?

280 COURTESAN   As sure, my liege, as I do see your grace.

DUKE   Why, this is strange. Go call the Abbess hither.
I think you are all mated,° or stark mad.   *bewildered*

Exit one to the ABBESS

EGEON [*coming forward*]   Most mighty Duke, vouchsafe me speak a word.
Haply° I see a friend will save my life,   *Maybe*

285   And pay the sum that may deliver me.

DUKE   Speak freely, Syracusian, what thou wilt.

EGEON [*to* ANTIPHOLUS]   Is not your name, sir, called Antipholus?
And is not that your bondman Dromio?

DROMIO OF EPHESUS   Within this hour I was his bondman,[2] sir,

290   But he, I thank him, gnawed in two my cords.
Now am I Dromio, and his man, unbound.

EGEON   I am sure you both of you remember me.

DROMIO OF EPHESUS   Ourselves we do remember, sir, by you;[3]
For lately we were bound as you are now.

295   You are not Pinch's patient, are you, sir?

---

1. The drink by means of which the enchantress Circe
turned men into swine.
2. His indentured servant; tied up with him. (The pun
continues in line 291.)
3. By looking at you, we remember how we were
(bound).

EGEON   Why look you strange° on me? You know me well.   *unknowingly*

ANTIPHOLUS OF EPHESUS   I never saw you in my life till now.

EGEON   O, grief hath changed me since you saw me last,
And careful° hours with time's deformèd° hand   *sorrowful / deforming*

300   Have written strange defeatures° in my face.   *disfigurements*
But tell me yet, dost thou not know my voice?

ANTIPHOLUS OF EPHESUS   Neither.

EGEON   Dromio, nor thou?

DROMIO OF EPHESUS   No, trust° me sir, nor I.   *believe*

305   EGEON   I am sure thou dost.

DROMIO OF EPHESUS   Ay, sir, but I am sure I do not, and whatsoever a man denies, you are now bound to believe him.

EGEON   Not know my voice? O time's extremity,
Hast thou so cracked and splitted my poor tongue

310   In seven short years that here my only son
Knows not my feeble key of untuned cares?⁴
Though now this grainèd° face of mine be hid   *lined*
In sap-consuming winter's drizzled snow,
And all the conduits of my blood froze up,

315   Yet hath my night of life some memory,
My wasting lamps° some fading glimmer left,   *failing eyes*
My dull deaf ears a little use to hear.
All these old witnesses, I cannot err,
Tell me thou art my son Antipholus.

320   ANTIPHOLUS OF EPHESUS   I never saw my father in my life.

EGEON   But° seven years since,° in Syracusa bay,   *Only / ago*
Thou know'st we parted. But perhaps, my son,
Thou sham'st to acknowledge me in misery.

ANTIPHOLUS OF EPHESUS   The Duke, and all that know me in the city,

325   Can witness with me that it is not so.
I ne'er saw Syracusa in my life.

DUKE [*to* EGEON]   I tell thee, Syracusian, twenty years
Have I been patron to Antipholus,
During which time he ne'er saw Syracusa.

330   I see thy age and dangers make thee dote.

Enter [*from the priory*] *the* ABBESS, *with* ANTIPHOLUS
[OF] SYRACUSE, [*wearing the chain,*] *and* DROMIO [OF]
SYRACUSE

ABBESS   Most mighty Duke, behold a man much wronged.

All gather to see them

ADRIANA   I see two husbands, or mine eyes deceive me.

DUKE   One of these men is *genius*⁵ to the other:
And so of these, which is the natural° man,   *human; mortal*

335   And which the spirit? Who deciphers them?

DROMIO OF SYRACUSE   I, sir, am Dromio. Command him away.

DROMIO OF EPHESUS   I, sir, am Dromio. Pray let me stay.

ANTIPHOLUS OF SYRACUSE   Egeon, art thou not? Or else his ghost.

DROMIO OF SYRACUSE   O, my old master, who hath bound him here?

340   ABBESS   Whoever bound him, I will loose his bonds,
And gain a husband by his liberty.
Speak, old Egeon, if thou beest the man
That hadst a wife once called Emilia,

4. My weak voice born of harsh sorrows.
5. Attendant spirit. It was a classical belief that each person had such a spirit, identical in appearance, allotted to him at birth.

That bore thee at a burden° two fair sons.   *in one birth*
345   O, if thou beest the same Egeon, speak,
    And speak unto the same Emilia.
  DUKE   Why, here begins his morning story right:
    These two Antipholus', these two so like,
    And these two Dromios, one in semblance—
350   Besides his urging° of her wreck at sea.   *claim*
    These are the parents to these children,
    Which accidentally are met together.
  EGEON   If I dream not, thou art Emilia.
    If thou art she, tell me, where is that son
355   That floated with thee on the fatal° raft?   *ill-fated*
  ABBESS   By men of Epidamnum he and I
    And the twin Dromio all were taken up.
    But, by and by, rude° fishermen of Corinth   *harsh; boorish*
    By force took Dromio and my son from them,
360   And me they left with those of Epidamnum.
    What then became of them I cannot tell;
    I, to this fortune that you see me in.
  DUKE *[to* ANTIPHOLUS OF SYRACUSE*]* Antipholus, thou cam'st
      from Corinth first.°   *originally*
  ANTIPHOLUS OF SYRACUSE   No, sir, not I. I came from Syracuse.
365   DUKE   Stay, stand apart. I know not which is which.
  ANTIPHOLUS OF EPHESUS   I came from Corinth, my most gracious lord.
  DROMIO OF EPHESUS   And I with him.
  ANTIPHOLUS OF EPHESUS   Brought to this town by that most famous warrior,
    Duke Menaphon, your most renownèd uncle.
370   ADRIANA   Which of you two did dine with me today?
  ANTIPHOLUS OF SYRACUSE   I, gentle mistress.
  ADRIANA   And are not you my husband?
  ANTIPHOLUS OF EPHESUS   No, I say nay to that.
  ANTIPHOLUS OF SYRACUSE   And so do I. Yet did she call me so;
375   And this fair gentlewoman, her sister here,
    Did call me brother. *[To* LUCIANA*]* What I told you then
    I hope I shall have leisure° to make good,   *opportunity*
    If this be not a dream I see and hear.
  ANGELO   That is the chain, sir, which you had of me.
380   ANTIPHOLUS OF SYRACUSE   I think it be, sir. I deny it not.
  ANTIPHOLUS OF EPHESUS *[to* ANGELO*]* And you, sir, for this chain arrested me.
  ANGELO   I think I did, sir. I deny it not.
  ADRIANA *[to* ANTIPHOLUS OF EPHESUS*]* I sent you money, sir, to be your bail,
    By Dromio, but I think he brought it not.
385   DROMIO OF EPHESUS   No, none by me.
  ANTIPHOLUS OF SYRACUSE *[to* ADRIANA*]* This purse of ducats I received from you,
    And Dromio my man did bring them me.
    I see we still° did meet each other's man,   *constantly*
    And I was ta'en for him, and he for me,
390   And thereupon these errors are arose.
  ANTIPHOLUS OF EPHESUS   These ducats pawn I for my father here.
  DUKE   It shall not need. Thy father hath his life.
  COURTESAN   Sir, I must have that diamond from you.
  ANTIPHOLUS OF EPHESUS   There, take it, and much thanks for my good cheer.
395   ABBESS   Renownèd Duke, vouchsafe to take the pains
    To go with us into the abbey here,
    And hear at large discoursèd° all our fortunes,   *recounted in full*

And all that are assembled in this place,
That by this sympathizèd° one day's error   *shared*
400   Have suffered wrong. Go, keep us company,
And we shall make full satisfaction.
Thirty-three years have I but gone in travail°   *labor*
Of you, my sons, and till this present hour
My heavy burden ne'er deliverèd.
405   The Duke, my husband, and my children both,
And you the calendars of their nativity,[6]
Go to a gossips' feast,[7] and joy with me.
After so long grief, such festivity!
DUKE   With all my heart I'll gossip at° this feast.   *join in*

Exeunt omnes [into the priory]. Manent the two DROMIOS *and two*
*brothers [*ANTIPHOLUS*]*

DROMIO OF SYRACUSE *[to* ANTIPHOLUS OF EPHESUS*]*   Master,
410   shall I fetch your stuff from shipboard?
ANTIPHOLUS OF EPHESUS   Dromio, what stuff of mine hast thou
embarked?°   *placed on board*
DROMIO OF SYRACUSE   Your goods that lay at host, sir, in the
Centaur.
ANTIPHOLUS OF SYRACUSE   He speaks to me.—I am your master, Dromio.
Come, go with us. We'll look to that anon.
415   Embrace thy brother there; rejoice with him.
Exeunt [the brothers ANTIPHOLUS*]*
DROMIO OF SYRACUSE   There is a fat friend at your master's house,
That kitchened me for you[8] today at dinner.
She now shall be my sister, not my wife.
DROMIO OF EPHESUS   Methinks you are my glass° and not my brother. *mirror*
420   I see by you° I am a sweet-faced youth.   *by means of you*
Will you walk in to see their gossiping?°   *merrymaking*
DROMIO OF SYRACUSE   Not I, sir, you are my elder.[9]
DROMIO OF EPHESUS   That's a question. How shall we try° it?   *test*
DROMIO OF SYRACUSE   We'll draw cuts° for the senior. Till then, *straws*
lead thou first.
425 DROMIO OF EPHESUS   Nay, then thus:
We came into the world like brother and brother,
And now let's go hand in hand, not one before another.
Exeunt [to the priory]

---

6. (Addressed to the Dromios): the two servants are a record of their masters' age, having been born at the same time.
7. A feast attended by the godparents ("gossips") to celebrate the christening of a child.

8. Who entertained me in the kitchen in mistake for you.
9. The elder customarily takes precedence and enters first.

Love's Labour's Lost

Love's Labour's Lost (1594–95) is an experimental play disguised as a conventional one. Its most striking feature—sexualized verbal wit—goes well with its aristocratic love plot. Yet the work is complicated by an unexpected concluding twist; challenges to hierarchies of gender, class, nation, and race; a scatological and homoerotic view of bodily function; and partly buried political and religious references. Without jettisoning the spirit of romantic comedy, then, Love's Labour's Lost offers a complex view of wooing and wedding with broader social implications.

Initially, Shakespeare telegraphs what is coming next. King Ferdinand of Navarre and his three courtiers—Biron, Dumaine, and Longueville—swear to shun women for three years to pursue the studious life of an ancient Greek or Renaissance Italian philosophical academy. Yet the arrival of a diplomatic embassy led by the Princess of France that includes three ladies-in-waiting—Rosaline, Catherine, and Maria—induces the men to fall in love. They are ridiculed for their about-face. In a multiple eavesdropping scene, they overhear each other confessing this change of heart and hypocritically denounce such oath breaking. In a court masque (a dramatic form where costumed aristocrats are the performers), they disguise themselves as Russians to advance their claims, but the ladies' own disguises lead each man to woo the wrong woman. Then, two hundred lines from the end, a messenger reports that the Princess's father, the King of France, has died. The world of romantic comedy—Navarre's rural retreat from the ordinary affairs of life—is invaded by death. When the men obliviously continue their wooing, the women, who all along have mistrusted their forsworn suitors, insist on a year's separation, which returns the plot to the opening rejection of heterosexual life.

From Two Gentlemen of Verona (1590–91) to Twelfth Night (1601), Shakespeare's young lovers marry off. Love's Labour's Lost's open-ended conclusion thus sets its apart from the other romantic comedies, pointing instead to the problem plays, Troilus and Cressida (1601–02), Measure for Measure (1604), and All's Well That Ends Well (1604–05). Here, as Biron remarks with the work's typical dramaturgical self-consciousness, "Our wooing doth not end like an old play. / Jack hath not Jill" (5.2.851–52). Both the romantic plot and the deflating outcome are suggested by the concluding poetic dialogue between Spring, associated with fertility and love, and Winter, linked to coldness and suffering. Yet Spring also brings "unpleasing" cuckoldry and Winter "a merry note" (5.2.877, 893).

Before then, the aristocrats' verbal ingenuity dominates Love's Labour's Lost. No other Shakespearean play so emphasizes its own brilliance, so centrally concerns language itself, so heavily draws on bookishness, so revels in courtly style. Love's Labour's Lost possesses the highest ratio of rhyme to blank verse among the dramatic works—rivaled only by A Midsummer Night's Dream (1594–96). Shakespeare's most heavily rhymed tragedy, Romeo and Juliet (1595), and history, Richard II (1595), also date from these years, sometimes thought of as Shakespeare's lyrical period. Rhyming calls attention to the medium of language itself. By contrast, when Shakespeare seeks to render speech naturalistically, to make his language a neutral expression of thought, he characteristically resorts to blank verse or prose.

In Love's Labour's Lost, Shakespeare generally employs blank verse for serious moments in long speeches, while reserving rhyme for the witty repartee of love—itself a microcosm of the play's larger debate structure. In the opening scene, each male courtier discusses, in blank verse, the vow of abstinence from women before capping his speech with a concluding couplet (lines 1–48, couplets at 22–23, 26–27, 31–32,

47–48). But when the King and Biron then debate the plan, they switch to rhyme—usually rhymed pentameter couplets, sometimes known as heroic couplets. At times, Shakespeare shifts to quatrains rhymed *abab*. If such a passage is followed by a couplet (see, for example, 1.1.61–66), the result is the six-line stanza of Shakespeare's amatory narrative poem *Venus and Adonis* (1592–93), a work that meditates comically on gender reversal. If three quatrains are followed by a couplet, a sonnet is born (for instance, 1.1.80–93). Loosely speaking, there are at least seven sonnets in the play (also 1.1.160–74; 4.3.22–37 and 55–68; 5.2.274–89, 343–56, and 402–15). Six of the seven are romantic. In love with the peasant Jaquenetta, Armado from the subplot remarks, "I am sure I shall turn sonnet" (that is, sonneteer; 1.2.162–63). The boom of the English love sonnet begins in 1591 with the publication of Sidney's *Astrophil and Stella*, and Shakespeare is thought to have started his own sequence around 1592–93. Three of the lords' poems to the ladies were lifted from the 1598 quarto of the play for an unauthorized 1599 collection attributed to Shakespeare. Within the play, the sonnets function complexly. The ladies coolly receive their suitors' poetic protestations, the King deploys a sonnet to describe Armado, and the two sonnets in dialogue further extend the form while belittling the men. This turning of the sonnet upon itself achieves self-contradiction when Biron, having embraced plain speaking, avows his love to Rosaline—"O never will I . . . woo in rhyme" (5.2.402–05)—in what proves to be the opening of a sonnet.

This wooing rhetoric is also associated with male bonding. The lords begin by misogynistically excluding any woman from their company "'on pain of losing her tongue'" (1.1.122). Once in love, they switch to the Renaissance courtier's amatory style, derived from two influential Italian writers—the fourteenth-century lyric poet Petrarch, founder of the European sonnet craze, and the fifteenth-century Neoplatonic philosopher Ficino. But in the eavesdropping scene, their feelings are expressed not through direct address to the ladies but through intended soliloquies inadvertently delivered to each other. The scene enacts the rhetorical figure of chiasmus—common to many passages in the play—in which the second of two parallel structures inverts the order of the first. Here Biron, the King, Longueville, and Dumaine successively confess their love, whereupon Dumaine's oath breaking is denounced by Longueville, Longueville's by the King, and the King's by Biron. And just as Biron, who shares with Armado's page Mote the privilege of speaking directly to the audience, is the only courtier whose initial confession is not overheard, he alone denounces himself, albeit under compulsion. Thereafter, the courtiers imagine their wooing as collective sexual attack: "Advance your standards, and upon them, lords. / Pell-mell, down with them" (4.3.341–42). In short, the play casts a jaundiced eye on the sexual style of men in groups. Fittingly, then, the courtiers' year of isolation separates them not only from women but also from each other. As in *The Merchant of Venice* (1596–97), another play that punishes male lovers who break their vows, the dissolution of male bonds precedes durable heterosexual attachment.

But, of course, the language of *Love's Labour's Lost* is marked not just by the poetry of love but also by an often sexualized punning. Even though the men excel at this language of romantic combat, they are no match for the women. The following exchange occurs during the Russian masque:

CATHERINE   What, was your visor made without a tongue?
LONGUEVILLE   [*taking* CATHERINE *for Maria*] I know the reason, lady, why you ask.
CATHERINE   O, for your reason! Quickly, sir, I long.
LONGUEVILLE   You have a double tongue within your mask,
    And would afford my speechless visor half.
CATHERINE   'Veal', quoth the Dutchman. Is not veal a calf?
LONGUEVILLE   A calf, fair lady?
CATHERINE   No, a fair lord calf.
LONGUEVILLE   Let's part the word.

CATHERINE	No, I'll not be your half.
	Take all and wean it, it may prove an ox.
LONGUEVILLE	Look how you butt yourself in these sharp mocks!
	Will you give horns, chaste lady? Do not so.
CATHERINE	Then die a calf before your horns do grow.
LONGUEVILLE	One word in private with you ere I die.
CATHERINE	Bleat softly, then. The butcher hears you cry.

(5.2.242–55)

Referring to the mouthpiece keeping the mask in place, Catherine evokes Longueville's silence ("without a tongue"). Longueville's second reply ("double tongue") accuses Catherine of punning, concealing her identity, being deceptive, and speaking enough for two, and then urges her to relinquish one tongue so he can speak and she will reveal her identity. Catherine's "Veal" combines Dutch for "well," German for "much," and a pun on "veil" with the end of her second comment ("long"). The result is "long-veal," veiled assertion of her interlocutor's identity. "Veal" also anticipates "calf" at line's end—source of the passage's remaining jokes. Catherine reverses Longueville's question, branding him "a fair lord calf," a dolt. Longueville's offer of compromise ("part the word") inspires Catherine's construal of "part" as "divide"; hence her refusal to "be your half" (better half, wife) and covert acknowledgment that the first half of the word ("ca") suggests her name. Longueville should raise the calf into an "ox," a castrated dolt with "horns," symbol of cuckoldry. This argument sullies her reputation, he warns, but Catherine tells him that to avoid cuckoldry he should drop dead. Longueville asks for a tête-à-tête "ere I die" (have an orgasm), to which Catherine agrees, while warning him of his impending doom.

The ladies also best the lords by critique of male verbal excess (*sans* is French for "without"):

| BIRON | My love to thee is sound, sans crack or flaw. |
| ROSALINE | Sans 'sans', I pray you. |

(5.2.415–16)

The men, Biron realizes, must drop their bookish language to approximate the women's norm: "Honest plain words best pierce the ear of grief" (5.2.735). Rosaline sentences him to a year of jesting among "the speechless sick and . . . groaning wretches" (5.2.828–29), where he will learn the value—or valuelessness—of wit. And the Princess usually exercises a dignified stylistic restraint that eludes the men. Yet the women's actual practice often repudiates their theory. Early on, Rosaline sympathetically evokes Biron's wit. The ladies then embrace the game of verbal one-upmanship and obscene punning, as the Catherine-Longueville exchange demonstrates. Thus they violate the principle Rosaline claims Biron has ignored:

A jest's prosperity lies in the ear
Of him that hears it, never in the tongue
Of him that makes it.

(5.2.838–40)

The women's self-contradictory avowal of wit and sobriety alike renders them romantically desirable in a fashion alien to the stereotypes of love poetry. Their possibly cynical economic mission may depend, as Boyet, their attending lord, suggests, on the Princess's ability to win the King's love. There are repeated jibes at their appearance as well as accusations of unchastity leveled at Rosaline by Biron, Boyet, and Catherine. The sexual innuendos in Catherine and Rosaline's exchange turn on "light" (bright, frivolous, or wanton), contrasted with both "heavy" (serious, overweight) and "dark" (black, obscure, wanton; 5.2.14–46, 4.3.228–78). While not erasing the ladies' moral superiority, these countertendencies justify modern productions that have treated them without idealism or sentimentality.

The subplot offers a different kind of critique. More a series of set pieces than a continuous story, it offers both structural parallel and social contrast to the main plot. The first eight scenes (in modern editions) alternate between main plot and subplot; the concluding, ninth scene unites the two sets of characters. In each plot, the characters are divided into two groups, one of which intrudes from the outside—the ladies in the main plot, Armado and Mote in the subplot. Such symmetries, which reinforce the work's formalized, dancelike structure and give it an aristocratic feel, recall the comedies that John Lyly wrote in the 1580s for boy actors. But this formalism acquires special force from the subplot's rootedness in popular culture, a culture reinvoked in the concluding speeches of Spring and Winter. Costard and Jaquenetta are from the rural lower classes; Dull, the constable, who anticipates Dogberry in *Much Ado About Nothing* (1598), barely stands above them. Mote is a page; Nathaniel, Holofernes, and Armado, although of higher rank, derive from the stock characters (minister, schoolmaster, braggart) of Italian commedia dell'arte, an originally popular, improvisational theater.

The juxtaposition of the two plots exalts and deflates the aristocrats. The subplot's fractured prose and doggerel verse sets off Biron's polished poetry to advantage. Holofernes is the leading practitioner of the popular characters' penchant for synonyms. An apple hangs in the "*caelo,* the sky, the welkin, the heaven, and . . . falleth . . . on . . . *terra,* the soil, the land, the earth" (4.2.5–6). Armado's forte is schematic syntax: "The time when? . . . Now for the ground which. . . . Then for the place where" (1.1.227–31). But if Armado's language is excessive, Biron's is only slightly less so. Similarly, Costard's violation of the edict against being "taken with a wench" (1.1.270–71) anticipates the failure of the aristocrats. This leveling continues when Armado's love letter to Jaquenetta is echoed by those of the lords. Armado and Biron both have their epistles delivered by Costard, whose confusion of the two exposes each writer to ridicule. The courtiers' Muscovite masque is paralleled by the popular pageant of the Nine Worthies, a scene resembling the humble theatricals of *A Midsummer Night's Dream.* Moreover, both masque and pageant anticipate the larger plot of *Love's Labour's Lost* in their failure to end as their performers wish.

Garden scene. From Thomas Hill, *The Gardener's Labyrinth* (1577).

Queen Elizabeth hunting. From George Gascoigne, *The Noble Art of Venerie or Hunting* (1575).

Costard's verbal sparring with the King and Princess, in which he holds his own, also reduces the sense of social superiority. His pointed response to dismissal by the forsworn courtiers—"Walk aside the true folk, and let the traitors stay" (4.3.209)—recalls his, but not their, honesty from the start. The lords' ridicule of the Nine Worthies prompts Holofernes' telling reply: "This is not generous, not gentle, not humble" (5.2.617). Although the aristocrats learn nothing from Mercadé's announcement of the death of the Princess's father, Armado, whom Costard has just accused of getting Jaquenetta pregnant, sees the need to reform. The lords accept their one-year sentences reluctantly, whereas his voluntary longer commitment echoes and reverses their opening oaths: "I am a votary, I have vowed to Jaquenetta / To hold the plough for her sweet love three year" (5.2.860–61). The oddity here is Biron. More than any other aristocratic character, he internalizes popular culture, moving from refined verse to colloquial and proverbial expression in what is one of Shakespeare's most proverb-rich plays. For instance, he is the only figure from the main plot with an extended prose speech (4.3.1–17). In Shakespeare, this sort of linguistic range is often integral to a character's unique ability to negotiate life's complexities for good or for ill. Yet Biron, despite his wit, intelligence, and insight, proves almost as hapless as his fellow suitors.

The subplot also reflects on the main plot through often scatological or homo-erotic bodily imagery, which includes a series of terms for constipation and its release—"immured," "restrained," "bound," "purgation," "loose" (3.1.113–16)—as well as Armado's boast of intimacy with the King, who has a tendency "with his royal finger thus [to] dally with my excrement" (5.1.87–88). In the play of the Nine Worthies, Holofernes as Judas Maccabeus is reduced to Judas (Iscariot), betrayer of Jesus.

> BOYET   Therefore, as he is an ass, let him go.
> And so adieu, sweet Jude. Nay, why dost thou stay?
> DUMAINE   For the latter end of his name.
> BIRON   For the ass to the Jude. Give it him. Jud-as, away.
> (5.2.613–16)

Here, emphasis on "ass" activates the synonymous connotation of "end," which thus proves the end of his body as well as "of his name." This primarily popular material suggests that the main courtship plot is not the whole story. The romantic and sexual language of the aristocrats is balanced by a less exalted, more excremental view of the body. Such passages also exploit some of the possibilities of a transvestite theater, in which boys played the women's parts. Specifically, the normative heterosexuality of the main plot is answered by hints of homosexuality emanating from the subplot. In short, this verbal patterning expands the play's notions of the body and sexuality beyond what events themselves overtly offer.

This imagery also feeds into a consideration of religious, national, and racial xenophobia. Costard calls Mote "my incony [fine-quality] Jew" (3.1.124), where "incony" inspires "inkle" [tape] (3.1.127), which suggests "ingle" (catamite, a boy kept by a pederast; see also 1.2.7). When Judas Maccabeus is "clipped" of his surname, Jewish circumcision is apparently glanced at. As we have seen, Holofernes is expelled by the lords as "Jud-as"—sign of the age's association of Jews with both excrement and sodomy. Coming from "tawny Spain," "Dun"-colored Armado, "in all the world's new fashion planted" and hence perhaps associated with New World plantations, is also an alien figure (1.1.171, 4.3.195, 1.1.162). Yet he is less foreign than the Russians, much less their accompanying blackamoors, whose presence glances at racial subjugation. They could be based on a report of an earlier Tudor masque or on a contemporary amateur entertainment at one of London's law schools. Alternatively, the play and these two performances all may draw on the period's link of Russia with dark skin. Although Love's Labour's Lost dramatizes a practice of scapegoating foreigners, however, it does not ratify this practice. Holofernes as Judas issues a pointed rebuke to the aristocrats; Armado reveals a depth of commitment foreign to them; the Russian masque backfires. Just as the play undermines convention in the central love plot, here, too, it calls into question—without openly attacking—cultural norms.

But the aristocrats themselves, unlike most of the popular characters, are also foreign. Behind the play lie contemporary political events that assume importance, given the plot's lack of literary sources. The comedy's King of Navarre draws on King Henry of Navarre, who established a philosophical academy and was accused of withdrawing from life. His three courtiers are named for the historical king's aristocratic contemporaries, two of whom (the play's Biron and Dumaine) served him. The Princess may derive from Princess Marguerite de Valois, daughter of King Henry II of France. Marguerite was already Henry of Navarre's estranged wife when she led an embassy of reconciliation to him in 1578, accompanied by her famous ladies-in-waiting. As in Love's Labour's Lost, one topic of discussion was "Aquitaine, a dowry for a queen" (2.1.8). Negotiations proceeded amid rampant adultery that undermined the vows of reconciliation and, contemporaries believed, caused renewal of France's Wars of Religion (1562–98), the bloody conflict between Protestant and Catholic aristocrats arguably noticed in the play's "civil war of wits" (2.1.225). Boyet, Mercadé, and perhaps Mote also have prominent namesakes from these wars. To end the conflict and secure his claim on the French throne, Henry converted to Catholicism in 1593, a further oath breaking that provoked criticism in Protestant England. The sympathy and judgment directed toward the play's lords, the serious treatment of their repudiated vows, the current of threatening sexuality, the emphasis on conflict, the invasion of death into the festive aristocratic world—all are compatible with this background.

Foreignness and sexuality converge in the debate about the aristocrats' own colors. A 1984 production of the play cast a black actress as Rosaline. Although only Rosaline's hair and eyes are black, metaphorically the play cannot leave darkness alone. Unwillingly in love with Rosaline, Biron initially complains of her color (3.1.181–84, 4.3.2–3). But echoing Shakespeare's sonnets to the "dark lady," he later takes blackness as the standard of beauty:

> KING   By heaven, thy love is black as ebony
>
> . . . .
>
> BIRON   No face is fair that is not full so black.
> KING   O paradox! Black is the badge of hell.
> (4.3.243, 249–50)

For the King, if black is beautiful, even "Ethiops," who presumably share his distaste for their appearance, "of their sweet complexion crack [boast]" (4.3.264). But it is not only the women whose faces evoke darkness. "Biron they call him," Rosaline remarks, "but a merrier man . . . I never spent an hour's talk withal" (2.1.66–68). The implied contrast is between "Merrier" and "Biron," punning on the brown in brown study, or seriousness. Before "the heavenly Rosaline," Biron imagines himself "a rude and savage man of Ind" (4.3.217–18), a claim that he repeats in her presence: "Vouchsafe to show the sunshine of your face / That we, like savages, may worship it" (5.2.200–01). The inclusion of the blackamoors thus accords with the play's unconventional association of its central and most attractive couple with blackness.

Love's Labour's Lost went unperformed from 1642 to 1839, remaining unpopular until the mid-twentieth century. But modern enthusiasm for wordplay and demonstrations of the comedy's theatrical potential have led to an upward revaluation. Perhaps today its significance lies in linguistic artifice that is and is not rejected, an upper class that learns its manners from the lower, a capacious sense of bodily and sexual experience, a sympathetic evocation of blackness, a plot that takes a clear-eyed but not dismissive view of romantic love, and a company of women who ride off into the sunset without their men.

WALTER COHEN

TEXTUAL NOTE

Although the date of *Love's Labour's Lost* is hard to pin down with much certainty, most scholars today locate the original and only composition of the play in 1594–95. Perhaps Shakespeare designed it for the Lord Chamberlain's Men, a recently formed professional company that worked in London's suburban, open-air, commercial theaters and of which he was an actor and a shareholder. The first printing of the play, in quarto, is lost. Another quarto, dated 1598 (Q), is the earliest extant printed version of a Shakespearean play that names its author. Q supposedly reproduces the play "as it was presented before her Highnes / this last Christmas." It is the basis for all modern editions. The title page calls the work *Loues labors lost,* a spelling that, in accord with the punning ethos of the play, leaves open various meanings, depending on where the apostrophe goes in the first word and whether there is an apostrophe—as a contraction for "is"—in the second. To complicate the semantic possibilities, *Loue labors lost* and *Loues Labour lost* are also among the early designations for the work.

Q derives from an authorial manuscript—either directly or, more probably, indi-

Berowne. Did not I dance with you in *Brabant* once?
Kather. Did not I dance with you in *Brabant* once?
Ber. I know you did.
Kath. How needles was it then to afke the queftion?
Ber. You muft not be fo quicke.
Kath. Tis long of you that fpur me with fuch queftions,
Ber. Your wit's too hot,it fpeedes too faft, twill tire.
Kath. Not till it leaue the rider in the mire,
Ber. What time a day?
Kath. The houre that fooles fhould afke.
Ber. Now faire befall your mafke,
Kath. Faire fall the face it couers,
Ber. And fend you manie louers,
Kath. Amen,fo you be none.
Ber. Nay then will I be gon.

Berow. Did not I dance with you in *Brabant* once?
Rofa. Did not I dance with you in *Brabant* once?
Ber. I know you did.
Rofa. How needleffe was it then to ask the queftic
Ber. You muft not be fo quicke.
Ber. 'Tis long of you ẙ fpur me with fuch queftior
Ber. Your wit's too hot,it fpeeds too faft, 'twill tii
Rofa. Not till it leaue the Rider in the mire.
Ber. What time a day?
Rofa. The howre that fooles fhould aske.
Ber. Now faire befall your maske.
Rofa. Faire fall the face it couers.
Ber. And fend you many louers.
Rofa. Amen,fo you be none.
Ber. Nay then will I be gone.

Biron's first flirtatious exchange with Catherine in Q (2.1.113–26) (left); revised to Rosaline in F (2.1.113–26) (right).

rectly via the lost quarto, which seems to have been printed from that manuscript. For an edition with an authorial manuscript behind it, it is extremely problematic, despite evidence that part of it was proofread. It is full of errors, uncorrected false starts, and the juxtaposition of original and revised versions of the same passages, although many of these are obvious and easily remedied. In this edition, the earlier renditions of subsequently rewritten text, beginning at 4.3.291, 5.2.130, and 5.2.798, are indented in the text. It is difficult to judge whether Q's foreign-language errors are Shakespeare's, the character's, or the compositor's. Here, they are usually corrected but occasionally attributed to the character. Q's speech prefixes often employ generic tags ("King," "Braggart," "Boy," "Page," "Princess," "Queen," "Lady 1–3," "Clown," "Maid," "Curate," "Pedant"). These tags function in various ways, but as a group they suggest that Shakespeare developed his characters out of stock dramatic, mainly comic, figures, especially from Italian commedia dell'arte (this legacy is discussed in the Introduction). *The Norton Shakespeare,* however, substitutes characters' names in the speech prefixes wherever possible, with the exception of Ferdinand of Navarre, who is identified as "King." At 4.2.60–97 and occasionally thereafter in the same scene, Q's speech prefixes attribute Nathaniel's lines to Holofernes and vice versa. These have been corrected. The biggest problem in Q involves the naming of the French ladies in 2.1, who are often referred to as "Lady," "Lady 1," "Lady 2," and "Lady 3." Most important, Catherine seems to be paired with Biron, Rosaline with Dumaine: Biron engages in witty exchanges first with Catherine (2.1.113–26) and then with Rosaline (2.1.178–92) before asking after Catherine (2.1.208–09), while Dumaine inquires about Rosaline (2.1.193–94). The remainder of the play reverses the pairings.

The version of *Love's Labour's Lost* printed in the First Folio of 1623 (F) is derived from either the lost or the extant quarto. F adds poorly conceived and mislabeled act divisions, which, along with scene divisions introduced by eighteenth-century editors, are reproduced here for ease of reference. F also introduces several new readings and speech attributions, at least some of them probably derived from manuscript annotations added to Q. Notably, it appends a new last line to the play, "You that way, we this way." Still more crucial is the replacement of Catherine by Rosaline in Biron's first flirtatious exchange (2.1.113–26). These shifts go much of the way toward aligning the scene's action with what happens thereafter, thus rejecting the apparent meaning of Q—that Biron and Dumaine each first express interest in one woman and then abruptly fall in love with another.

All subsequent editions of *Love's Labour's Lost,* even when based on Q, have followed F in this respect. Most current textual scholars believe that Q reveals Shakespeare's initial indecision about how to pair the men and women off, and that the annotations in the copy of Q on which F is based record a version of the text closer to performance than Q is. In short, F's linkage of Biron with Rosaline from the start is correct. But proponents of this position disagree among themselves on important points, disagreements that suggest the speculative character of the hypothesis. The fundamental problem is uncertainty about the source, nature, and authority of the annotations to Q that lie behind F: the available evidence is too frail and contradictory to inspire confidence.

Although the version printed here is based on the near consensus among recent textual scholars, an alternative position has existed since the eighteenth century. In a relatively recent essay, Manfred Draudt ("The 'Rosaline-Katherine Tangle' of *Love's Labour's Lost*," *The Library* 6 [1982]: 381–96) suggestively argues that Q 2.1 may provide the most accurate rendition available of the romantic relations in *Love's Labour's Lost*. Retaining Q's speech attributions would have various advantages. Biron's and Dumaine's feelings are not obvious in 2.1, and the abrupt switching of male love interest and the casual transfer of women between men have analogues in other Shakespearean plays of the period—*The Two Gentlemen of Verona, Romeo and Juliet,* and *A Midsummer Night's Dream*. The quarto readings are also closer to the events of the court of the historical Henry of Navarre than is the revised text. Further, if Biron and Dumaine are inconstant, it is easier to understand why in 5.2 Catherine and Rosaline attack each other in sexualized language so harsh the Princess has to intervene (lines 14–46); why Catherine accuses Dumaine of "hypocrisy" and Rosaline plans to "torture" Biron (51, 60), whereas the Princess and Maria criticize their suitors more mildly; why Catherine's and Rosaline's concluding promises to their lovers (lines 807, 840–46) are more equivocal than those of the Princess and Maria (lines 783–89, 810–11); and why Rosaline seems only recently to have met Biron (lines 818–19). Finally, the Quarto lends greater force to the ladies' disguises in 5.2, which trick the men into wooing the wrong women; to the women's skeptical, almost cruel treatment of the men throughout; and to the oft-noted near interchangeability of the aristocratic characters. The notes, therefore, list the rejected quarto readings in 2.1 to facilitate a running comparison of the two approaches to the text.

SELECTED BIBLIOGRAPHY

Archer, John Michael. "*Love's Labour's Lost*." *A Companion to Shakespeare's Works*. Vol. 3: *The Comedies*. Ed. Richard Dutton and Jean E. Howard. Malden, Mass.: Blackwell, 2003. 320–37. Treats issues of race and nation in relation to language, gender, and sexuality.

Booth, Stephen. *King Lear, Macbeth, Indefinition, and Tragedy*. New Haven: Yale University Press, 1983. 69–82. The problem of the unexpected end, both of the plot and of the body.

Carroll, William C. *The Great Feast of Language in "Love's Labour's Lost."* Princeton: Princeton University Press, 1976. Wordplay, self-conscious theatricality, and poetic set pieces in relation to the larger debate structure of the play.

Elam, Keir. *Shakespeare's Universe of Discourse: Language-Games in the Comedies*. New York: Cambridge University Press, 1984. 289–308. Emphasis on the play's highly rhetorical critique of rhetoric.

Evans, Malcolm. *Signifying Nothing: Truth's True Contents in Shakespeare's Text*. Athens: University of Georgia Press, 1986. 50–65. The impact of writing on the speech of both aristocratic lovers and comic pedants.

Gilbert, Miriam. "*Love's Labour's Lost*": *Shakespeare in Performance*. Manchester: Manchester University Press, 1993. Survey of its topic, with detailed analysis of important recent performances.

Londré, Felicia Hardison, ed. "*Love's Labour's Lost*": *Critical Essays*. New York: Garland, 1997. Critical accounts of *Love's Labour's Lost,* both text and performance, 1598–1995, but primarily since World War II.

Maus, Katharine Eisaman. "Transfer of Title in *Love's Labour's Lost*: Language, Individualism, Gender." *Shakespeare Left and Right*. Ed. Ivo Kamps. New York: Routledge,

1991. 206–23. The relationship between the play's reversal of standard gender hierarchy and its questioning of the naturalness of meaningful language.

Mazzio, Carla. "The Melancholy of Print: *Love's Labour's Lost.*" *Historicism, Psycho-analysis, and Early Modern Culture.* Ed. Carla Mazzio and Douglas Trevor. New York: Routledge, 2000. 186–227. The intersection in the play of the speech(less-ness) of love and early modern print culture, especially pedagogical manuals.

Parker, Patricia. "Preposterous Reversals: *Love's Labour's Lost.*" *Modern Language Quarterly* 54 (1993): 435–82. The centrality of wordplay, especially obscene bodily punning, to the work's dramatic structure and particularly to its challenge to class, gender, and sexual hierarchy.

FILM

Love's Labour's Lost. 2000. Dir. Kenneth Branagh. UK. 93 min. Musical comedy with 1930s songs and settings, half of Shakespeare's lines retained, and the play's events shadowed by the coming of World War II. Cast includes Branagh, Alicia Silverstone, and Nathan Lane.

Love's Labour's Lost

The Persons of the Play

Ferdinand, KING of Navarre

BIRON
LONGUEVILLE } lords attending on the King
DUMAINE

Don Adriano de ARMADO, an affected Spanish braggart
MOTE, his page
PRINCESS of France

ROSALINE
CATHERINE } ladies attending on the
MARIA } Princess

BOYET
Two other LORDS } attending on the Princess
COSTARD, a clown
JAQUENETTA, a country wench
Sir NATHANIEL, a curate
HOLOFERNES, a schoolmaster
Anthony DULL, a constable
MERCADÉ, a messenger
A FORESTER

1.1

Enter Ferdinand, KING *of Navarre,* BIRON, LONGUEVILLE,
and DUMAINE[1]

KING   Let fame, that all hunt after in their lives,
    Live registered upon our brazen° tombs,   *brass; long-lasting*
    And then grace° us in the disgrace° of death   *honor / disfigurement*
    When, spite of cormorant° devouring time,[2]   *despite ravenous*
5   Th'endeavour of this present breath° may buy   *speech; life*
    That honour which shall bate° his scythe's keen edge   *blunt*
    And make us heirs of all eternity.
    Therefore, brave conquerors—for so you are,
    That war against your own affections°   *passions*
10   And the huge army of the world's desires—
    Our late° edict shall strongly stand in force.   *recent*
    Navarre shall be the wonder of the world.
    Our court shall be a little academe,
    Still° and contemplative in living art.[3]   *Peaceful*
15   You three—Biron, Dumaine, and Longueville—
    Have sworn for three years' term to live with me
    My fellow scholars, and to keep those statutes

1.1 Location: The action of the whole play takes place in the King of Navarre's park.
1. For the historical background to these figures, see the Introduction. Until Henry of Navarre's accession to the French throne in 1589, Navarre was an independent kingdom in southwestern France. "Biron" is pronounced "Be-roon." The pronunciation of "Longueville" fluctuates, rhyming with "ill" (4.3.120), "compile" (4.3.130),

and, by implication, "veal" (5.2.247).
2. Proverbial; one of many indications of the recourse to proverbs in this play by aristocrats and commoners alike.
3. The art of living (the term in this sense goes back to ancient Stoic thought); learning invigorated by life. *academe* (line 13): a philosophical academy of the sort initiated by Plato and revived in the Renaissance.

That are recorded in this schedule° here.   *document*
Your oaths are passed;° and now subscribe° your names,   *pledged / sign*
20   That his own hand may strike his honour down
That violates the smallest branch° herein.   *clause*
If you are armed° to do as sworn to do,   *equipped*
Subscribe to your deep oaths, and keep it, too.[4]
LONGUEVILLE   I am resolved. 'Tis but a three years' fast.
25   The mind shall banquet, though the body pine.
Fat paunches have lean pates,° and dainty bits°   *heads / bites*
Make rich the ribs but bankrupt quite the wits.
          [*He signs*]
DUMAINE   My loving lord, Dumaine is mortified.°   *dead to worldliness*
The grosser manner of these world's delights
30   He throws upon the gross world's baser slaves.
To love, to wealth, to pomp I pine and die,
With all these[5] living in philosophy.
          [*He signs*]
BIRON   I can but say their protestation over.°   *again*
So much, dear liege,° I have already sworn: *lord*
35   That is, to live and study here three years.
But there are other strict observances,
As not to see a woman in that term,
Which I hope well is not enrollèd° there;   *listed*
And one day in a week to touch no food,
40   And but one meal on every day beside,
The which I hope is not enrollèd there;
And then to sleep but three hours in the night,
And not be seen to wink of° all the day,   *close my eyes during*
When I was wont to think no harm° all night,[6]   *it harmless (to sleep)*
45   And make a dark night too of half the day,
Which I hope well is not enrollèd there.
O, these are barren tasks, too hard to keep—
Not to see ladies, study, fast, not sleep.
KING   Your oath is passed to pass away from these.
50   BIRON   Let me say no, my liege, an if° you please.   *an if = if*
I only swore to study with your grace,
And stay here in your court, for three years' space.
LONGUEVILLE   You swore to that, Biron, and to the rest.
BIRON   By yea and nay,[7] sir, then I swore in jest.
55   What is the end of study, let me know?
KING   Why, that to know which else we should not know.
BIRON   Things hid and barred, you mean, from common sense.°   *ordinary perception*
KING   Ay, that is study's god-like recompense.
BIRON   Come on,[8] then, I will swear to study so
60   To know the thing I am forbid[9] to know,
As thus: to study where I well may dine
When I to feast expressly am forbid;
Or study where to meet some mistress fine
When mistresses from common sense are hid;

---

4. The first use of a couplet to cap a blank-verse speech. See also 1.1.26–27, 31–32, 47–48, the last of which begins the pattern of rhyming couplets. For an *abab* quatrain followed by a couplet to form the six-line *Venus and Adonis* stanza, see 1.1.61–66.
5. His three companions; the conditions prescribed in the document; or the suggestion that philosophy is a source or substitute for the worldly attractions of line 31.

6. Proverbial.
7. Earnestly (a solemn oath based on Matthew 5:37); ambiguously.
8. Q has "Com'on," possibly indicating a pun on "common" (line 57).
9. Deliberately misinterpreting "should" (line 56) as "ought" rather than "would."

65	Or having sworn too hard a keeping° oath,	*a too-demanding*
	Study to break it and not break my troth.	
	If study's gain be thus, and° this be so,	*if*
	Study knows that which yet it doth not know.¹	
	Swear me to this, and I will ne'er say no.°	*(first rhyming triplet)*
70	KING These be the stops° that hinder study quite,	*obstacles*
	And train° our intellects to vain delight.	*allure*
	BIRON Why, all delights are vain, but that most vain	
	Which, with pain° purchased, doth inherit pain;°	*labor / suffering*
	As° painfully to pore upon a book	*such as*
75	To seek the light of truth while truth the while	
	Doth falsely° blind the eyesight of his look.°	*deceitfully / its vision*
	Light, seeking light, doth light of light beguile;²	
	So ere you find where light in darkness lies	
	Your light grows dark by losing of your eyes.	
80	Study me³ how to please the eye indeed	
	By fixing it upon a fairer° eye,	*woman's*
	Who dazzling so,⁴ that eye shall be his heed,°	*guard; what he heeds*
	And give him light that it° was blinded by.	*(his eye)*
	Study is like the heavens' glorious sun,	
85	That will not be deep searched with saucy° looks.	*presumptuous; insolent*
	Small° have continual plodders ever won	*Little*
	Save base° authority from others' books.	*Except commonplace*
	These earthly godfathers of heaven's lights,°	*astronomers*
	That give a name to every fixèd star,	
90	Have no more profit of their shining nights	
	Than those that walk and wot° not what they are.	*know*
	Too much to know is to know naught but fame,°	*hearsay; reputation*
	And every godfather can give a name.°	*(as astronomers do)*
	KING How well he's read, to reason against reading!	
95	DUMAINE Proceeded° well, to stop all good proceeding.⁵	*Argued*
	LONGUEVILLE He weeds° the corn° and still lets grow the	*pulls up / wheat*
	weeding.°	*weeds*
	BIRON The spring is near when green geese are a-breeding.⁶	
	DUMAINE How follows that?	
	BIRON Fit in his° place and time.	*its*
	DUMAINE In reason nothing.	
	BIRON Something then in rhyme.⁷	
100	KING Biron is like an envious sneaping° frost,	*a malicious biting*
	That bites the first-born infants° of the spring.	*buds*
	BIRON Well, say I am! Why should proud° summer boast	*splendid*
	Before the birds have any cause to sing?	
	Why should I joy in any abortive° birth?	*premature*
105	At Christmas I no more desire a rose	
	Than wish a snow in May's new-fangled shows,°	*displays of flowers*
	But like of° each thing that in season grows.	*But enjoy*
	So you to study, now it is too late,°	*(for us to be students)*

1. *If . . . know:* If study means experiencing the forbidden (line 60), study does indeed enable one to know what isn't yet known (line 56).
2. The eye, from too much study (reading), is blinded (as if from looking at a bright light).
3. Study, I say: the beginning of the first sonnet (lines 80–93; see also 1.1.160–74, 4.3.22–37, 4.3.55–68, 5.2.274–89, 5.2.343–56, 5.2.402–15). This is the earliest of Biron's claims that a man's spiritual enlightenment depends not on reading books but on gazing into a beautiful woman's eyes. This idea reached England

especially through the fourteenth-century Italian lyric poet Petrarch and the fifteenth-century Italian Neoplatonic philosopher Ficino.
4. The man (who does this) being thus bedazzled.
5. Toward a university degree.
6. When young geese are mating (as will the young lords, Biron implies). A goose is also a prostitute.
7. "In reason," it follows "nothing" (not at all); but in rhyme, "something" (somewhat)—an allusion to the proverbial phrase "neither rhyme nor reason" and perhaps to their own rhyming repartee.

Climb o'er the house to unlock the little gate.[8]

110 KING   Well, sit you out.° Go home, Biron. Adieu.   *don't take part*
BIRON   No, my good lord, I have sworn to stay with you.
And though I have for barbarism° spoke more   *on behalf of ignorance*
Than for that angel knowledge you can say,
Yet confident I'll keep what I have sworn,
115   And bide the penance of each three years' day.°   *day of the three years*
Give me the paper. Let me read the same,
And to the strict'st decrees I'll write my name.

KING [*giving a paper*]   How well this yielding rescues thee from
shame!

BIRON [*reads*]   'Item: that no woman shall come within a mile of
120   my court.' Hath this been proclaimed?
LONGUEVILLE   Four days ago.
BIRON   Let's see the penalty. 'On pain of losing her tongue.'
Who devised this penalty?
LONGUEVILLE   Marry,[9] that did I.
125 BIRON   Sweet lord, and why?
LONGUEVILLE   To fright them hence with that dread penalty.
BIRON   A dangerous law against gentility.°   *courtesy*
'Item: if any man be seen to talk with a woman within the term
of three years, he shall endure such public shame as the rest of
130   the court can possible° devise.'   *possibly*
This article, my liege, yourself must break;
For well you know here comes in embassy
The French King's daughter with yourself to speak—
A maid of grace and complete majesty—
135   About surrender-up of Aquitaine[1]
To her decrepit, sick, and bedrid father.
Therefore this article is made in vain,
Or vainly comes th'admirèd Princess hither.

KING   What say you, lords? Why, this was quite forgot.
140 BIRON   So study evermore is overshot.°   *wide of the mark*
While it doth study to have what it would,
It doth forget to do the thing it should;
And when it hath the thing it hunteth most,
'Tis won as towns with fire[2]—so won, so lost.
145 KING   We must of force° dispense with this decree.   *necessity*
She must lie° here, on mere° necessity.   *lodge / absolute*
BIRON   Necessity will make us all forsworn
Three thousand times within this three years' space;
For every man with his affects° is born,   *passions*
150   Not by° might mastered, but by special grace.°   *by his own / (of God)*
If I break faith, this word° shall speak for me: *motto*
I am forsworn on mere necessity.
So to the laws at large° I write my name,   *in general*
And he that breaks them in the least degree
155   Stands in attainder of° eternal shame.   *condemned to*
[*He signs*]
Suggestions° are to other as to me,   *Temptations*
But I believe, although I seem so loath,
I am the last that will last° keep his oath.   *longest; least likely*

---

8. Set about things in a senseless, backward way—   1. A large area in southern France.
rather than climbing over the gate to unlock the house.   2. That is, destroyed in being captured.
9. Indeed (invocation of the Virgin Mary).

But is there no quick° recreation granted?   *lively*

160 KING   Ay, that there is.° Our court, you know, is haunted[3]   *frequented*
With° a refinèd traveller of° Spain,   *By/from*
A man in all the world's new fashion planted,[4]
That hath a mint of phrases in his brain.
One who° the music of his own vain tongue   *whom*
165 Doth ravish like enchanting harmony;
A man of complements,° whom right and wrong   *fashion; attainments?*
Have chose as umpire of their mutiny.°   *discord*
This child of fancy,° that Armado hight,°   *absurd being/is called*
For interim° to our studies shall relate   *interlude*
170 In high-borne words the worth of many a knight
From tawny° Spain lost in the world's debate.°   *sunburned/warfare*
How you delight, my lords, I know not, I;
But I protest I love to hear him lie,
And I will use him for my minstrelsy.°   *entertainment*
175 BIRON   Armado is a most illustrious wight,°   *person*
A man of fire-new° words, fashion's own knight.   *newly coined*
LONGUEVILLE   Costard the swain[5] and he shall be our sport,
And so to study three years is but short.

Enter a constable [Anthony DULL] with a letter, with
COSTARD

DULL   Which is the Duke's° own person?   *King's*
180 BIRON   This, fellow. What wouldst?
DULL   I myself reprehend° his own person, for I am his grace's   *(blunder for "represent")*
farborough.[6] But I would see his own person in flesh and blood.
BIRON   This is he.
DULL   Señor Arm—Arm—commends° you. There's villainy   *greets*
185 abroad. This letter will tell you more.
COSTARD   Sir, the contempts[7] thereof are as touching me.
KING   A letter from the magnificent Armado.[8]
BIRON   How low soever the matter, I hope in God for high
words.
190 LONGUEVILLE   A high hope for a low heaven.° God grant us   *a small blessing*
patience.
BIRON   To hear, or forbear laughing?
LONGUEVILLE   To hear meekly, sir, and to laugh moderately, or
to forbear both.
195 BIRON   Well, sir, be it as the style shall give us cause to climb
in the merriness.[9]
COSTARD   The matter° is to me, sir, as concerning Jaquenetta.   *(perhaps sexual)*
The manner of it is, I was taken with the manner.°   *caught red-handed*
BIRON   In what manner?
200 COSTARD   In manner and form[1] following, sir—all those three. I
was seen with her in the manor house, sitting with her upon
the form,° and taken following her into the park; which put   *bench*
together is 'in manner and form following'. Now, sir, for the
manner: it is the manner of a man to speak to a woman. For
205 the form: in some form.

---

3. The beginning of a sonnet that actually extends to fifteen lines (lines 160–74).
4. Established. *World's new fashion planted:* may also refer to Spanish New World plantations.
5. The costard is a large apple; the word is also used comically to refer to the head. *swain:* country lad.
6. Blunder for "thirdborough," a petty constable.
7. Blunder for "contents"; but also, inadvertently, "con-

tempt."
8. Phrase used of the Spanish Armada (1588).
9. *style . . . merriness:* stile=fence; the humble subject of "merriness" does not ordinarily lead one "to climb" to a high prose "style." A "style" is also a pen and, hence, perhaps a penis that will "climb" (swell) in "merriness" (pleasure).
1. Legal, then proverbial phrase.

BIRON   For the 'following', sir?

COSTARD   As it shall follow in my correction;° and God defend   *punishment*
the right.°   *(prayer before combat)*

KING   Will you hear this letter with attention?

210 BIRON   As we would hear an oracle.

COSTARD   Such is the simplicity² of man to hearken after the
flesh.

KING [*reads*]   'Great deputy, the welkin's vicegerent° and sole   *heaven's deputy*
dominator of Navarre, my soul's earth's° god, and body's foster-   *earthly*
215 ing patron'—

COSTARD   Not a word of Costard yet.

KING   'So it is'—

COSTARD   It may be so; but if he say it is so, he is, in telling true,
but so.°   *truly only so-so*

220 KING   Peace!

COSTARD   Be to me and every man that dares not fight.

KING   No words!

COSTARD   Of other men's secrets, I beseech you.

KING   'So it is, besieged with sable-coloured° melancholy, I did   *black*
225 commend the black-oppressing humour° to the most whole-   *melancholy*
some physic° of thy health-giving air, and, as I am a gentleman,   *medicine*
betook myself to walk. The time when? About the sixth hour,
when beasts most graze, birds best peck, and men sit down to
that nourishment which is called supper. So much for the time
230 when. Now for the ground which—which, I mean, I walked
upon. It is yclept° thy park. Then for the place where—where,   *called (archaic)*
I mean, I did encounter that obscene° and most preposterous³   *disgusting; wanton*
event that draweth from my snow-white pen° the ebon-   *goose quill*
coloured° ink which here thou viewest, beholdest, surveyest, or   *black*
235 seest. But to the place where. It standeth north-north-east and
by east from the west corner of thy curious-knotted° garden.   *intricately patterned*
There did I see that low-spirited° swain, that base minnow° of   *base / shrimp*
thy mirth'—

COSTARD   Me?

240 KING   'That unlettered,° small-knowing soul'—   *illiterate*

COSTARD   Me?

KING   'That shallow vassal'°—   *base wretch; vessel*

COSTARD   Still me?

KING   'Which, as I remember, hight Costard'—

245 COSTARD   O, me!

KING   'Sorted° and consorted, contrary to thy established pro-   *Associated*
claimed edict and continent canon,° with, with, O with—but   *restraining law*
with this I passion° to say wherewith'—   *grieve*

COSTARD   With a wench.

250 KING   'With a child of our grandmother Eve, a female, or for thy
more sweet understanding a woman. Him I, as my ever-
esteemed duty pricks⁴ me on, have sent to thee, to receive the
meed° of punishment, by thy sweet grace's officer Anthony   *reward*
Dull, a man of good repute, carriage, bearing, and estimation.'

255 DULL   Me, an't° shall please you. I am Anthony Dull.   *if it*

KING   'For Jaquenetta—so is the weaker vessel° called—which I   *woman (I Peter 3:7)*
apprehended with the aforesaid swain, I keep her as a vessel of

---

2. Folly; Q has "sinplicitie"—perhaps a pun.
3. Unnatural; in reversed position—with "obscene"
(line 232) anatomically suggesting placement of the

rear, or posterior, in front. See 5.1.75, 77, 101.
4. Spurs (sexual). For other uses of the word, see
2.1.188; 4.1.128, 134; 4.2.11, 18, 45, 48, 53, 56.

thy law's fury, and shall at the least of thy sweet notice° bring   *as soon as you order*
her to trial.° Thine in all compliments of devoted and heart-   *(legally; sexually)*
260   burning heat of duty,

> Don Adriano de Armado.'

BIRON   This is not so well as I looked for, but the best that ever I
heard.

KING   Ay, the best for° the worst. [*To* COSTARD]But, sirrah,[5] what   *best example of*
265   say you to this?

COSTARD   Sir, I confess the wench.

KING   Did you hear the proclamation?

COSTARD   I do confess much of the hearing it, but little of the
marking of° it.   *paying attention to*

270   KING   It was proclaimed a year's imprisonment to be taken with
a wench.

COSTARD   I was taken with none, sir. I was taken with a damsel.

KING   Well, it was proclaimed 'damsel'.

COSTARD   This was no damsel, neither, sir. She was a virgin.

275   KING   It is so varied,° too, for it was proclaimed 'virgin'.   *covers that variation*

COSTARD   If it were, I deny her virginity. I was taken with a maid.

KING   This 'maid' will not serve your turn, sir.

COSTARD   This maid will serve my turn,° sir.   *(sexually)*

KING   Sir, I will pronounce your sentence. You shall fast a week
280   with bran and water.

COSTARD   I had rather pray a month with mutton and porridge.[6]

KING   And Don Armado shall be your keeper.
My lord Biron, see him delivered o'er,
And go we, lords, to put in practice that
285   Which each to other hath so strongly sworn.

> [*Exeunt the* KING, LONGUEVILLE, *and* DUMAINE]

BIRON   I'll lay° my head to any good man's hat   *bet*
These oaths and laws will prove an idle scorn.
Sirrah, come on.

COSTARD   I suffer for the truth, sir; for true it is I was taken with
290   Jaquenetta, and Jaquenetta is a true° girl, and therefore, wel-   *an honest*
come the sour cup of prosperity, affliction[7] may one day smile
again; and till then, sit thee down,° sorrow.   *Exeunt*   *stay with me*

1.2

Enter ARMADO *and* MOTE,[1] *his page*

ARMADO   Boy, what sign is it° when a man of great spirit grows   *what does it mean*
melancholy?

MOTE   A great sign, sir, that he will look sad.

ARMADO   Why, sadness is one and the selfsame thing,° dear imp.°   *(as melancholy) / child*

5   MOTE   No, no, O Lord, sir, no.

ARMADO   How canst thou part° sadness and melancholy, my   *distinguish between*
tender juvenal?[2]

MOTE   By a familiar° demonstration of the working,° my tough   *plain / their operation*
señor.°   *sir; senior*

10   ARMADO   Why 'tough señor'? Why 'tough señor'?

MOTE   Why 'tender juvenal'? Why 'tender juvenal'?

ARMADO   I spoke it, tender juvenal, as a congruent epitheton

---

5. Standard term for addressing social inferiors.
6. Mutton soup; "mutton" is also slang for "prostitute."
7. Blunder for reverse order: "affliction, prosperity."
1.2 Location: The King's park.

1. Q has "Moth," meaning "moth" or "mote" (speck). It
is pronounced like the latter word, and that sense may
be primary.
2. Youth; Juvenal, ancient Roman satirist.

appertaining to° thy young days, which we may nominate°   *suitable term for / call*
'tender'.

15 MOTE   And I, tough señor, as an appertinent° title to your old   *appropriate*
time, which we may name 'tough'.

ARMADO   Pretty and apt.

MOTE   How mean you, sir? I 'pretty' and my saying 'apt'? Or I
'apt' and my saying 'pretty'?

20 ARMADO   Thou 'pretty', because little.°   *(proverbial)*

MOTE   Little pretty, because little. Wherefore 'apt'?

ARMADO   And therefore 'apt' because quick.°   *quick-witted*

MOTE   Speak you this in my praise, master?

ARMADO   In thy condign° praise.   *well-deserved*

25 MOTE   I will praise an eel with the same praise.

ARMADO   What—that an eel is ingenious?

MOTE   That an eel is quick.°   *alive*

ARMADO   I do say thou art quick in answers. Thou heatest my
blood.°   *You make me angry*

30 MOTE   I am answered, sir.

ARMADO   I love not to be crossed.

MOTE [aside]   He speaks the mere° contrary—crosses³ love not
him.   *absolute*

ARMADO   I have promised to study three years with the Duke.

35 MOTE   You may do it in an hour, sir.

ARMADO   Impossible.

MOTE   How many is one, thrice told?°   *counted*

ARMADO   I am ill at reckoning; it fitteth the spirit of a tapster.°   *bartender*

MOTE   You are a gentleman and a gamester,° sir.   *gambler*

40 ARMADO   I confess both. They are both the varnish of a complete
man.

MOTE   Then I am sure you know how much the gross sum of
deuce-ace° amounts to.   *a two and a one (dice)*

ARMADO   It doth amount to one more than two.

45 MOTE   Which the base vulgar° do call three.   *common people*

ARMADO   True.

MOTE   Why, sir, is this such a piece° of study? Now here is 'three'   *masterpiece*
studied ere ye'll thrice wink, and how easy it is to put 'years' to
the word 'three' and study 'three years' in two words, the danc-
50 ing horse⁴ will tell you.

ARMADO   A most fine figure.°   *verbal turn; number*

MOTE [aside]   To prove you a cipher.°   *zero*

ARMADO   I will hereupon confess I am in love; and as it is base°   *ignoble*
for a soldier to love, so am I in love with a base° wench. If   *lowborn*
55 drawing my sword against the humour of affection° would   *inclination to love*
deliver me from the reprobate thought of it, I would take desire
prisoner and ransom him to any French courtier for a new-
devised curtsy.° I think scorn° to sigh. Methinks I should out-   *bowing fashion / disdain*
swear° Cupid. Comfort me, boy. What great men have been in   *renounce*
60 love?

MOTE   Hercules, master.

ARMADO   Most sweet Hercules! More authority, dear boy. Name
more—and, sweet my child, let them be men of good repute
and carriage.°   *behavior*

---

3. Coins (often imprinted with crosses).
4. Morocco, a performing horse trained to "count" with   its hooves, was a London sensation in 1591. Mote jok-
ingly takes "three years" as the object of "study" (line 34).

65	MOTE Samson, master; he was a man of good carriage, great carriage, for he carried the town-gates on his back[5] like a porter, and he was in love.
	ARMADO O well-knit Samson, strong-jointed Samson! I do excel thee in my rapier as much as thou didst me in carrying gates. I
70	am in love, too. Who was Samson's love, my dear Mote?
	MOTE A woman, master.
	ARMADO Of what complexion?[6]
	MOTE Of all the four, or the three, or the two, or one of the four.
	ARMADO Tell me precisely of what complexion?
75	MOTE Of the sea-water green,[7] sir.
	ARMADO Is that one of the four complexions?
	MOTE As I have read, sir; and the best of them, too.
	ARMADO Green indeed is the colour of lovers, but to have a love of that colour, methinks Samson had small reason for it. He
80	surely affected° her for her wit.°

loved / intelligence

MOTE It was so, sir, for she had a green wit.[8]

ARMADO My love is most immaculate white and red.

MOTE Most maculate° thoughts, master, are masked under such colours.° — impure; hues; pretexts

85 ARMADO Define,° define, well-educated infant. — Explain your meaning

MOTE My father's wit and my mother's tongue assist me!

ARMADO Sweet invocation of a child!—most pretty and pathetical.° — touching

MOTE If she be made° of white and red, — also "maid"

90 Her faults will ne'er be known,
For blushing cheeks by faults are bred
And fears by pale white shown.
Then if she fear or be to blame,
By this you shall not know;
95 For still her cheeks possess the same
Which native° she doth owe.° — naturally / own

A dangerous rhyme, master, against the reason of white and red.

ARMADO Is there not a ballad, boy, of the King and the Beggar?[9]

100 MOTE The world was very guilty of such a ballad some three ages since, but I think now 'tis not to be found; or if it were, it would neither serve° for the writing nor the tune. — be acceptable

ARMADO I will have that subject newly writ o'er, that I may example my digression° by some mighty precedent. Boy, I do — justify my lapse

105 love that country girl that I took in the park with the rational hind[1] Costard. She deserves well.

MOTE [aside] To be whipped°—and yet a better love than my — (as a prostitute) master.

ARMADO Sing, boy. My spirit grows heavy in love.

110 MOTE And that's great marvel, loving a light° wench. — wanton

ARMADO I say, sing.

MOTE Forbear till this company be past.

5. For the gates, see Judges 16:3. Love proved disastrous for both Hercules and Samson.
6. Temperament (Armado's meaning), as determined by the balance of bodily humors; blood, phlegm, melancholy (from black bile), choler; skin coloring (Mote's meaning).
7. Ill colored; evidence of chlorosis, an anemic condition affecting young women.
8. Immature understanding (proverbial).
9. The ballad concerns the love of King Cophetua for the beggar maid Zenelophon. See also 4.1.65.
1. Peasant (or deer?) capable of reason.

Enter[COSTARD *the*] *clown, Constable* [DULL], *and*
[JAQUENETTA, *a*] *wench*

DULL [*to* ARMADO]   Sir, the Duke's pleasure is that you keep
Costard safe, and you must suffer° him to take no delight, nor   allow
no penance,° but a° must fast three days a week. For this   (for "pleasance"?) / he
damsel, I must keep her at the park. She is allowed for the
dey-woman.° Fare you well.   approved as dairymaid

ARMADO [*aside*]   I do betray myself with blushing.—Maid.

JAQUENETTA   Man.

ARMADO   I will visit thee at the lodge.

JAQUENETTA   That's hereby.²

ARMADO   I know where it is situate.

JAQUENETTA   Lord, how wise you are!

ARMADO   I will tell thee wonders.

JAQUENETTA   With that face?°   Really?

ARMADO   I love thee.

JAQUENETTA   So I heard you say.°   You don't say so

ARMADO   And so farewell.

JAQUENETTA   Fair weather after you.°   (proverbial)

DULL   Come, Jaquenetta, away. *Exeunt* [DULL *and* JAQUENETTA]

ARMADO   Villain,° thou shalt fast for thy offences ere thou be   Peasant; rascal
pardoned.

COSTARD   Well, sir, I hope when I do it I shall do it on a full
stomach.°   well fed; bravely

ARMADO   Thou shalt be heavily punished.

COSTARD   I am more bound to you than your fellows,° for they   servants
are but lightly rewarded.

ARMADO   Take away this villain. Shut him up.

MOTE   Come, you transgressing slave. Away!

COSTARD   Let me not be pent up,° sir. I will fast, being loose.³   jailed; constipated

MOTE   No, sir. That were fast and loose.° Thou shalt to prison.   a cheating trick

COSTARD   Well, if ever I do see the merry days of desolation°   (for "elation"?)
that I have seen, some shall see.

MOTE   What shall some see?

COSTARD   Nay, nothing, Master Mote, but what they look upon.
It is not for prisoners to be too silent in their words, and therefore I will say nothing. I thank God I have as little patience as
another man, and therefore I can be quiet.

Exeunt [MOTE *and* COSTARD]

ARMADO   I do affect° the very ground—which is base—where her   love
shoe—which is baser—guided by her foot—which is basest—
doth tread. I shall be forsworn—which is a great argument° of   proof
falsehood—if I love. And how can that be true love which is
falsely attempted? Love is a familiar;° love is a devil. There is   an attendant evil spirit
no evil angel but love. Yet was Samson so tempted, and he had
an excellent strength. Yet was Solomon so seduced, and he had
a very good wit. Cupid's butt-shaft° is too hard for Hercules'   unbarbed arrow
club, and therefore too much odds for a Spaniard's rapier. The
first and second cause° will not serve my turn: the passado⁴ he   (in the dueling code)
respects not, the duello° he regards not. His disgrace is to be   dueling code
called boy, but his glory is to subdue men. Adieu, valour; rust,
rapier; be still, drum: for your manager° is in love; yea, he   wielder

2. Nearby; neither here nor there(?)
3. Being free; being loose in the bowels.

4. Fencing thrust.

loveth. Assist me, some extemporal° god of rhyme, for I am sure   *impromptu*
I shall turn sonnet.° Devise wit, write pen, for I am for whole   *sonneteer*
volumes, in folio.°   *Exit*   *largest size of book*

2.1

Enter the PRINCESS *of France with three attending ladies*
[MARIA, CATHERINE, *and* ROSALINE] *and three lords* [*one
named* BOYET][1]

BOYET   Now, madam, summon up your dearest spirits.°   *utmost energies*
Consider who the King your father sends,
To whom he sends, and what's his embassy:
Yourself, held precious in the world's esteem,
5   To parley with the sole inheritor°   *owner*
Of all perfections that a man may owe,
Matchless Navarre; the plea° of no less weight   *that which is claimed*
Than Aquitaine, a dowry for a queen.
Be now as prodigal of all dear grace
10   As nature was in making graces dear[2]
When she did starve the general world beside°   *except (you)*
And prodigally gave them all to you.
PRINCESS   Good Lord Boyet, my beauty, though but mean,°   *average*
Needs not the painted flourish° of your praise.   *embellishment*
15   Beauty is bought by judgement of the eye,
Not uttered[3] by base sale of chapmen's° tongues.   *salesmen's*
I am less proud to hear you tell° my worth   *speak of; reckon up*
Than you much willing to be counted wise
In spending your wit in the praise of mine.
20   But now to task the tasker:[4] good Boyet,
You are not ignorant all-telling fame°   *rumor*
Doth noise abroad° Navarre hath made a vow   *spread the rumor that*
Till painful° study shall outwear three years   *taxing*
No woman may approach his silent court.
25   Therefore to's° seemeth it a needful course,   *to us*
Before we enter his forbidden gates,
To know his pleasure; and in that behalf,
Bold° of your worthiness, we single you   *Confident*
As our best-moving fair° solicitor.   *most eloquent and just*
30   Tell him the daughter of the King of France
On serious business, craving quick dispatch,
Importunes personal conference with his grace.
Haste, signify so much while we attend,
Like humble-visaged suitors, his high will.
35 BOYET   Proud of° employment, willingly I go.   *Honored with*
PRINCESS   All pride is willing pride,° and yours is so. *Exit* BOYET   *vanity*
Who are the votaries,° my loving lords,   *vow takers*
That are vow-fellows with this virtuous duke?
A LORD   Lord Longueville is one.
PRINCESS   Know you the man?
40 MARIA   I know him, madam. At a marriage feast
Between Lord Périgord[5] and the beauteous heir

2.1 Location: Outside the gates of the King's court.
1. Pronounced "Boy-ett."
2. *dear grace . . . graces dear:* chiasmus, an *abba* rhetorical structure common to the aristocrats' speech and the larger movement of the play. See 4.3 and Introduc-

tion. The second "dear" means costly (because rare).
3. Not spoken; not offered for sale.
4. Impose a task on you who have given me one; chastise the task setter.
5. Not otherwise mentioned; Périgord was in Aquitaine.

Of Jaques Fauconbridge solemnizèd
In Normandy saw I this Longueville.
A man of sovereign parts° he is esteemed,   outstanding qualities
45 Well fitted in arts, glorious in arms.
Nothing becomes him ill that he would° well.   wishes to do
The only soil of° his fair virtue's gloss—   stain on
If virtue's gloss will stain with any soil—
Is a sharp wit matched with too blunt° a will,   rough; unfeeling
50 Whose edge hath power to cut, whose will still° wills   always
It should none spare that come within his° power.   its
PRINCESS   Some merry mocking lord, belike°—is't so?   probably
MARIA   They say so most that most his humours know.
PRINCESS   Such short-lived wits do wither as they grow.
55 Who are the rest?
CATHERINE[6]   The young Dumaine, a well-accomplished youth,
Of° all that virtue love for virtue loved.   By
Most power to do most harm, least knowing ill,[7]
For he hath wit to make an ill shape good,
60 And shape to win grace, though he had no wit.[8]
I saw him at the Duke Alençon's once,
And much too little° of that good I saw   short
Is my report to° his great worthiness.   my report compared with
ROSALINE[9]   Another of these students at that time
65 Was there with him, if I have heard a truth.
Biron[1] they call him, but a merrier man,
Within the limit of becoming° mirth,   decorous
I never spent an hour's talk withal.°   with
His eye begets occasion° for his wit,   finds opportunities
70 For every object that the one doth catch
The other turns to a mirth-moving jest,
Which his fair tongue, conceit's expositor,°   thought's expounder
Delivers in such apt and gracious words
That agèd ears play truant at° his tales,   neglect work to hear
75 And younger hearings are quite ravishèd,
So sweet and voluble° is his discourse.   fluent
PRINCESS   God bless my ladies, are they all in love,
That every one her own hath garnishèd
With such bedecking ornaments of praise?
A LORD   Here comes Boyet.

            Enter BOYET

80 PRINCESS   Now, what admittance,° lord?   reception
BOYET   Navarre had notice of your fair approach,
And he and his competitors° in oath   partners
Were all addressed° to meet you, gentle lady,   ready
Before I came. Marry, thus much I have learnt:
85 He rather means to lodge you in the field,

6. Q, F: 2 Lady. The remainder of the scene strongly
suggests that Lady 2 is Rosaline, not Catherine. The
last three acts imply that Lady 2 is Catherine, however.
For the issues involved in this emendation and others in
2.1 (lines 64, 113–26, 178–92, 194, and 209), see the
Textual Note.
7. Potentially dangerous by virtue of his very innocence; although he theoretically could do harm, he is
free of all misdeeds.
8. *For . . . wit:* He is intelligent enough to make up for
a displeasing appearance, if he had one (or perhaps to
make something evil seem virtuous), and good-looking

enough to win favor (from people or perhaps God),
even if he lacked intelligence.
9. Q: 3 Lady; F: Rosaline. The remainder of the scene
in Q strongly suggests that Lady 3 is Catherine, not
Rosaline. The last three acts of Q imply that Lady 3 is
Rosaline, however.
1. Probable pun on "Biron/brown." "Brown" was pronounced much like "Biron" ("Be-roon"); Q's spelling of
"Biron" is "Berowne." "Brown" was associated with
somberness or melancholy (as in a "brown study"), and is
contrasted in this line with "merrier" by means of "but."

Like one that comes here to besiege his court,
Than seek a dispensation for his oath
To let you enter his unpeopled° house.   *servantless*

Enter NAVARRE, LONGUEVILLE, DUMAINE, *and* BIRON
Here comes Navarre.

90   KING   Fair Princess, welcome to the court of Navarre.

     PRINCESS   'Fair' I give you back again, and welcome I have not
    yet. The roof of this court° is too high to be yours, and welcome   *sky*
    to the wide fields too base to be mine.

     KING   You shall be welcome, madam, to my court.

95   PRINCESS   I will be welcome, then. Conduct me thither.

     KING   Hear me, dear lady. I have sworn an oath—

     PRINCESS   Our Lady help my lord! He'll be forsworn.

     KING   Not for the world, fair madam, by my will.°   *willingly (mild oath)*

     PRINCESS   Why, will° shall break it—will and nothing else.   *(sexual) desire*

100   KING   Your ladyship is ignorant what it is.

     PRINCESS   Were my lord so his ignorance were wise,
    Where now his knowledge must prove ignorance.
    I hear your grace hath sworn out housekeeping.°   *repudiated hospitality*
    'Tis deadly sin to keep that oath, my lord,

105   And sin to break it.
    But pardon me, I am too sudden°-bold.   *rashly*
    To teach a teacher ill beseemeth me.
    Vouchsafe to read the purpose of my coming,
    And suddenly resolve° me in my suit.   *immediately answer*
    [*She gives him a paper*]

110   KING   Madam, I will, if suddenly I may.

     PRINCESS   You will the sooner that I were away,°   *so that I'll go*
    For you'll prove perjured if you make me stay.
    [*Navarre reads the paper*]

     BIRON [*to* ROSALINE]   Did not I dance with you in Brabant once?

     ROSALINE[2]   Did not I dance with you in Brabant once?

     BIRON   I know you did.

115   ROSALINE   How needless was it then
    To ask the question!

     BIRON   You must not be so quick.°   *sharp; hasty; witty*

     ROSALINE   'Tis 'long of° you, that spur° me with such questions.   *due to / prod*

     BIRON   Your wit's too hot, it speeds too fast, 'twill tire.

     ROSALINE   Not till it leave the rider in the mire.

120   BIRON   What time o' day?

     ROSALINE   The hour that fools should ask.

     BIRON   Now fair befall° your mask.   *good luck to*

     ROSALINE   Fair fall° the face it covers.   *befall*

     BIRON   And send you many lovers.

125   ROSALINE   Amen, so you be none.

     BIRON   Nay, then will I be gone.

     KING [*to the* PRINCESS]   Madam, your father here doth intimate
    The payment of[3] a hundred thousand crowns,
    Being but the one-half of an entire sum

130   Disbursèd by my father in his° wars.   *(the King of France's)*
    But say that he° or we—as neither have—   *(Navarre's father)*
    Received that sum, yet there remains unpaid
    A hundred thousand more, in surety of the which

2. Lines 114–25—Q: Catherine; F: Rosaline.   3. *intimate . . . of:* suggest he paid.

One part of Aquitaine is bound to us,
135 Although not valued° to the money's worth.   *equal in value*
If then the King your father will restore
But that one half which is unsatisfied,
We will give up our right in Aquitaine
And hold fair friendship with his majesty.
140 But that, it seems, he little purposeth,
For here he doth demand to have repaid°   *insists he has repaid*
A hundred thousand crowns, and not demands,°   *rather than offering*
On payment of a hundred thousand crowns,
To have his title live in Aquitaine,
145 Which we much rather had depart withal,°   *surrender*
And have the money by our father lent,
Than Aquitaine, so gelded° as it is.[4]   *reduced; castrated*
Dear Princess, were not his requests so far
From reason's yielding, your fair self should make
150 A yielding 'gainst some reason in my breast,
And go well satisfied to France again.
      PRINCESS   You do the King my father too much wrong,
And wrong the reputation of your name,
In so unseeming° to confess receipt   *seeming unwilling*
155 Of that° which hath so faithfully been paid.   *200,000 crowns*
      KING   I do protest I never heard of it,
And if you prove it I'll repay it back
Or yield up Aquitaine.
      PRINCESS   We arrest° your word.   *seize as security*
Boyet, you can produce acquittances°   *receipts*
160 For such a sum from special officers
Of Charles, his° father.   *(Navarre's)*
      KING   Satisfy me so.
      BOYET   So please your grace, the packet is not come
Where that and other specialties° are bound.   *legal contracts*
Tomorrow you shall have a sight of them.
165 KING   It shall suffice me, at which interview
All liberal° reason I will yield unto.   *civilized*
Meantime receive such welcome at my hand
As honour, without breach of honour, may
Make tender of to thy true worthiness.
170 You may not come, fair princess, within my gates,
But here without° you shall be so received   *outside*
As you shall deem yourself lodged in my heart,
Though so denied fair harbour in my house.
Your own good thoughts excuse me, and farewell.
175 Tomorrow shall we visit you again.
      PRINCESS   Sweet health and fair desires consort° your grace.   *accompany*
      KING   Thy own wish wish I thee in every place.
                    Exit [with LONGUEVILLE *and* DUMAINE]
      BIRON[5] [*to* ROSALINE]   Lady, I will commend you to mine own
            heart.
180 ROSALINE   Pray you, do my commendations. I would be glad to
            see it.[6]

---

4. Navarre says that of the 200,000 crowns he's owed, the King of France falsely claims to have paid back half and has given him Aquitaine as collateral for the other half, even though it isn't worth that much. Navarre is willing to return Aquitaine and forget the entire debt in return for 100,000 crowns, but France wants Navarre to pay that sum and keep Aquitaine.
5. Lines 178–92—Q: Biron; F: Boyet.
6. Know your real feelings; literally, behold your heart and, hence, see you dead.

BIRON   I would you heard it groan.

ROSALINE   Is the fool° sick?   *poor thing*

BIRON   Sick at the heart.

185   ROSALINE   Alack, let it blood.°   *bleed it (medically)*

BIRON   Would that do it good?

ROSALINE   My physic° says 'Ay'.   *medical knowledge*

BIRON   Will you prick't with your eye?[7]

ROSALINE   *Non point,*° with my knife.   *Not at all; it's blunt*

190   BIRON   Now God save thy life.

ROSALINE   And yours, from long living.

BIRON   I cannot stay thanksgiving.[8]   *Exit*

          Enter DUMAINE

DUMAINE [*to* BOYET]   Sir, I pray you a word. What lady is that same?

BOYET   The heir of Alençon, Catherine[9] her name.

195   DUMAINE   A gallant lady. Monsieur, fare you well.   *Exit*

          [*Enter* LONGUEVILLE]

LONGUEVILLE [*to* BOYET]   I beseech you a word, what is she in
          the white?

BOYET   A woman sometimes, an° you saw her in the light.   *if*

LONGUEVILLE   Perchance light in the light.° I desire her name.   *wanton if seen clearly*

BOYET   She hath but one for herself; to desire that were a shame.

200   LONGUEVILLE   Pray you, sir, whose daughter?

BOYET   Her mother's, I have heard.

LONGUEVILLE   God's blessing on your beard!°   *(insult)*

BOYET   Good sir, be not offended.
          She is an heir of Fauconbridge.

205   LONGUEVILLE   Nay, my choler° is ended.   *anger*
          She is a most sweet lady.

BOYET   Not unlike,° sir. That may be.   *Exit* LONGUEVILLE   *unlikely*

          Enter BIRON

BIRON   What's her name in the cap?

BOYET   Rosaline,[1] by good hap.

210   BIRON   Is she wedded or no?

BOYET   To her will, sir, or so.°   *or something like that*

BIRON   O, you are welcome, sir. Adieu.

BOYET   Farewell to me, sir, and welcome to you.°   *Exit* BIRON   *you're welcome to go*

MARIA   That last is Biron, the merry madcap lord.
          Not a word with him but a jest.

215   BOYET   And every jest but a word.

PRINCESS   It was well done of you to take him at his word.°   *(literally; punningly)*

BOYET   I was as willing to grapple as he was to board.[2]

CATHERINE[3]   Two hot sheeps,[4] marry.

BOYET   And wherefore not ships?
          No sheep, sweet lamb, unless we feed on your lips.

220   CATHERINE[5]   You sheep and I pasture[6]—shall that finish the jest?

BOYET   So° you grant pasture for me.   *So long as*

CATHERINE   Not so, gentle beast.
          My lips are no common, though several they be.[7]

BOYET   Belonging to whom?

---

7. "Eye" puns on "Ay" (line 187), suggesting a needle
but also a vagina, impossibly serving as a penis.
8. Stay long enough to thank you (for that rude remark).
9. Q, F: Rosaline.
1. Q, F: Catherine.
2. Join ships ("grapple") for hand-to-hand combat
("board"): metaphor for competitive wordplay, with sexual overtones.

3. F: Maria.
4. "Sheeps" was pronounced like "ships."
5. Lines 220, 221, 223—Q, F: Lady.
6. Pun on "pastor" (shepherd).
7. My lips are not commonly owned grazing land,
though they are pasture—they are privately owned,
enclosed land (*several*: more than one; separate).

CATHERINE   To my fortunes and me.

PRINCESS   Good wits will be jangling;° but, gentles,° agree.   *quarreling / gentlefolk*

225   This civil war of wits were much better used
      On Navarre and his bookmen,° for here 'tis abused.°   *scholars / misapplied*

BOYET   If my observation, which very seldom lies,
      By the heart's still rhetoric° disclosèd with eyes,   *silent eloquence*
      Deceive me not now, Navarre is infected.

230   PRINCESS   With what?

BOYET   With that which we lovers entitle 'affected'.°   *being in love*

PRINCESS   Your reason?

BOYET   Why, all his behaviours did make their retire°   *withdrawal*
      To the court of his eye, peeping thorough° desire.   *through*

235   His heart like an agate with your print impressed,[8]
      Proud with his form,° in his eye pride expressed.   *the Princess's image*
      His tongue, all impatient to speak[9] and not see,
      Did stumble with haste in his eyesight to be.
      All senses to that sense did make their repair,°   *resort*

240   To feel° only looking° on fairest of fair.   *experience / by looking*
      Methought all his senses were locked in his eye,
      As jewels in crystal, for some prince to buy,
      Who, tendering° their own worth from where they were   *displaying*
         glassed,°   *encased in crystal*
      Did point° you to buy them along as you passed.   *direct*

245   His face's own margin[1] did quote° such amazes   *indicate*
      That all eyes saw his eyes enchanted with gazes.
      I'll give you° Aquitaine and all that is his   *bet you get*
      An you give him for my sake but one loving kiss.

PRINCESS   Come, to our pavilion. Boyet is disposed.°   *(to be merry)*

250   BOYET   But to speak that in words which his eye hath disclosed.
      I only have made a mouth of his eye
      By adding a tongue, which I know will not lie.

ROSALINE[2]   Thou art an old love-monger, and speak'st skilfully.

MARIA   He is Cupid's grandfather, and learns news of him.

255   CATHERINE   Then was Venus° like her mother, for her father is   *Cupid's mother*
         but grim.°   *not handsome*

BOYET   Do you hear, my mad° wenches?   *high-spirited*

MARIA   No.

BOYET   What then, do you see?

CATHERINE   Ay—our way to be gone.

BOYET   You are too hard for me.

                                        Exeunt

3.1

Enter [ARMADO *the*] *braggart,*[1] *and* [MOTE] *his boy*

ARMADO   Warble, child; make passionate° my sense of hearing.   *responsive*

MOTE [*sings*]   Concolinel.°   *song title or opening*

ARMADO   Sweet air!° Go, tenderness of years, take this key. Give   *tune*
      enlargement° to the swain. Bring him festinately° hither. I must   *freedom / in a hurry*
5   employ him in a letter to my love.

8. Engraved with your image. Agates were engraved
and set in rings.
9. Impatient at being able only to speak.
1. The part of a book in which comments were printed.
2. Lines 253, 254, 255, 256, 257: Q—Lady, Lady 2,
Lady 3, Lady, Lady; F—Rosaline, Maria, Lady 2, Lady
1, Lady 2. It is uncertain which of the ladies should

speak these lines.
3.1 Location: The King's park.
1. The braggart soldier was a stock figure in the contemporary Italian commedia dell'arte, a theatrical form
with popular roots. His theatrical ancestry can be
traced back to ancient Roman comedy.

MOTE Master, will you win your love with a French brawl?° *dance*

ARMADO How meanest thou—brawling in French?[2]

MOTE No, my complete master; but to jig off a tune° at the *sing a jiglike tune*

tongue's end, canary° to it with your feet, humour° it with turn- *dance / adapt to*

10   ing up your eyelids, sigh a note and sing a note, sometime

through the throat as if you swallowed love with singing love,

sometime through the nose as if you snuffed up love by smell-

ing love, with your hat penthouse-like° o'er the shop of your *like an awning*

eyes, with your arms crossed° on your thin-belly[3] doublet like a *(from love melancholy)*

15   rabbit on a spit, or your hands in your pocket like a man after° *in the style of*

the old painting, and keep not too long in one tune, but a snip° *snatch*

and away. These are complements, these are humours; these

betray nice° wenches that would be betrayed without these, *seduce wanton*

and make them men of note—do you note? *men*—that most

20   are affected° to these. *given*

ARMADO How hast thou purchased this experience?

MOTE By my penny of observation.

ARMADO But O, but O—

MOTE 'The hobby-horse is forgot.'[4]

25   ARMADO Call'st thou my love hobby-horse?

MOTE No, master, the hobby-horse is but a colt,° and your love *young horse; wanton*

perhaps a hackney.° But have you forgot your love? *riding horse; whore*

ARMADO Almost I had.

MOTE Negligent student, learn her by heart.

30   ARMADO By heart and in heart, boy.

MOTE And out of heart,° master. All those three I will prove. *disheartened*

ARMADO What wilt thou prove?

MOTE A man, if I live; and this, 'by', 'in', and 'without', upon

the instant: 'by' heart you love her because your heart cannot

35   come *by* her; 'in' heart you love her because your heart is *in*

love with her; and 'out' of heart you love her, being *out* of heart

that you cannot enjoy her.

ARMADO I am all these three.

MOTE [*aside*] And three times as much more, and yet nothing

40   at all.

ARMADO Fetch hither the swain. He must carry me° a letter. *for me*

MOTE [*aside*] A message well sympathized°—a horse to be *matched*

ambassador for an ass.

ARMADO Ha, ha! What sayst thou?

45   MOTE Marry, sir, you must send the ass upon the horse, for he

is very slow-gaited. But I go.

ARMADO The way is but short. Away!

MOTE As swift as lead, sir.

ARMADO The meaning, pretty ingenious?

50   Is not lead a metal heavy, dull, and slow?

MOTE *Minime*,° honest master—or rather, master, no. *By no means*

ARMADO I say lead is slow.

MOTE   You are too swift, sir, to say so.

Is that lead slow which is fired from a gun?

ARMADO Sweet smoke of rhetoric!

---

2. "Brawling" means "quarreling," but the phrase may
also refer to popular rioting against immigrant French
merchants and artisans.
3. Unpadded belly or lower part; also suggesting that
Armado is wasting away for love.

4. A lament for the passing of the good old days; perhaps the refrain of a song. A hobbyhorse—a person costumed as a horse—was used in popular dancing; the
word also meant "whore," perhaps suggested by the
association between "O" (line 23) and "vagina."

55   He reputes me a cannon, and the bullet, that's he.
         I shoot thee at the swain.
    MOTE   Thump,° then, and I flee.   [*Exit*]   *Bang*
    ARMADO   A most acute juvenal—voluble° and free of grace.   *quick-witted*
         By thy favour, sweet welkin,° I must sigh in thy face.   *sky*
         Most rude melancholy, valour gives thee place.°   *gives way to you*
60   My herald is returned.
             Enter [MOTE *the*] *page, and* [COSTARD *the*] *clown*
    MOTE   A wonder, master—here's a costard broken in a shin.[5]
    ARMADO   Some enigma, some riddle; come, thy *l'envoi*.° Begin.   *explanation*
    COSTARD   No egma, no riddle, no *l'envoi*, no salve in the mail,[6]
         sir. O sir, plantain,° a plain plantain—no *l'envoi*, no *l'envoi*, no   *healing herb*
65   salve, sir, but a plantain.
    ARMADO   By virtue, thou enforcest laughter—thy silly thought
         my spleen.[7] The heaving of my lungs provokes me to ridicu-
         lous° smiling. O pardon me, my stars! Doth the inconsiderate[8]   *mocking; absurd*
         take salve for *l'envoi*, and the word *l'envoi* for a salve?
70   MOTE   Do the wise think them other? Is not *l'envoi* a salve?
    ARMADO   No, page, it is an epilogue or discourse to make plain
         Some obscure precedence that hath tofore been sain.[9]
         I will example° it.   *give an example of*
             The fox, the ape, and the humble-bee°   *bumblebee*
75   Were still at odds,[1] being but three.
         There's the moral.° Now the *l'envoi*.   *lesson*
    MOTE   I will add the *l'envoi*. Say the moral again.
    ARMADO   The fox, the ape, and the humble-bee
             Were still at odds, being but three.
80   MOTE   Until the goose came out of door
             And stayed° the odds by adding four.°   *stopped / a fourth*
         Now will I begin your moral, and do you follow with my
         l'envoi.
             The fox, the ape, and the humble-bee
85   Were still at odds, being but three.
    ARMADO   Until the goose came out of door,
             Staying the odds by adding four.
    MOTE   A good *l'envoi*, ending in the goose.[2] Would you desire
         more?
90   COSTARD   The boy hath sold him a bargain—a goose,° that's flat.°   *made him a fool / certain*
         Sir, your pennyworth° is good an° your goose be fat.   *bargain / if*
         To sell a bargain well is as cunning as fast and loose.°   *cheating; (of bowels)*
         Let me see, a fat *l'envoi*—ay, that's a fat goose.°   *buttocks?*
    ARMADO   Come hither, come hither. How did this argument°   *topic*
95   begin?
    MOTE   By saying that a costard was broken in a shin.
         Then called you for the *l'envoi*.
    COSTARD   True, and I for a plantain. Thus came your argument°   *enema?*

---

5. A head with a cut shin (an anatomical impossibility that provokes Mote's amusement); disappointed in love or sex (alluding to Armado's triumph over Costard); taking a loan.
6. Costard takes Armado to be proposing remedies for his shin. "Egma" for "enigma" may be an error for an "egg" solution or "enema." *L'envoi* refers to a salve or ointment, perhaps by confusion with "lenify" (to soothe or purge). There is also a pun on the Latin *salve* (greetings), the opposite of *l'envoi*'s sense of "farewell." *mail:* traveling bag. In addition, a salve inserted in or an anal salvo discharged from the male.

7. Amusement: the spleen was regarded as the organ controlling laughter.
8. The thoughtless person.
9. *Some . . . sain:* What was obscurely said before. The couplet is in poulter's measure—fourteen syllables, then twelve.
1. Were always quarreling; were always an odd number.
2. Punning on the French *oie* (goose), the final sound in *envoi*, "ending in the goose" also because it is inserted in the end of the goose (prostitute, victim of venereal disease).

in. Then the boy's fat *l'envoi,* the goose that you bought, and
100   he ended the market.°   *bargaining*
ARMADO   But tell me, how was there a costard broken in a shin?
MOTE   I will tell you sensibly.°   *clearly; feelingly*
COSTARD   Thou hast no feeling of it. Mote, I will speak that
l'envoi.
105   I, Costard, running out, that was safely within,[3]
Fell over the threshold and broke my shin.
ARMADO   We will talk no more of this matter.
COSTARD   Till there be more matter° in the shin.   *pus; semen*
ARMADO   Sirrah Costard, I will enfranchise° thee.   *free*
110 COSTARD   O, marry me to one Frances![4] I smell some *l'envoi,*
some goose, in this.
ARMADO   By my sweet soul, I mean setting thee at liberty, enfree-
doming thy person. Thou wert immured,° restrained, capti-   *shut in*
vated, bound.°   *(of bowels)*
115 COSTARD   True, true, and now you will be my purgation° and let   *liberator; enema*
me loose.°   *(my bowels)*
ARMADO   I give thee thy liberty, set° thee from durance,° and in   *free/imprisonment*
lieu thereof impose on thee nothing but this: bear this signif-
icant° to the country maid, Jaquenetta.   *token*
120   [*Giving him a letter*] There is remuneration [*giving him*
money], for the best ward° of mine honour is rewarding my   *guard*
dependants. Mote, follow.   [*Exit*]
MOTE   Like the sequel, I. Signor Costard, adieu.   *Exit*
COSTARD   My sweet ounce of man's flesh, my incony Jew![5]
125   Now will I look to his remuneration. Remuneration—O, that's
the Latin word for three-farthings.° Three-farthings—remuner-   *¾-pence coin*
ation. 'What's the price of this inkle?'[6] 'One penny.' 'No, I'll give
you a remuneration.' Why, it carries it!° Remuneration! Why,   *carries the day*
it is a fairer name than French crown.[7] I will never buy and
130   sell out of° this word.   *without using*
        Enter BIRON
BIRON   My good knave Costard, exceedingly well met.
COSTARD   Pray you, sir, how much carnation° ribbon may a man   *flesh-colored*
buy for a remuneration?
BIRON   What is a remuneration?
135 COSTARD   Marry, sir, halfpenny-farthing.°   *three farthings*
BIRON   Why, then, three-farthing-worth of silk.
COSTARD   I thank your worship. God be wi' you.
BIRON   Stay, slave, I must employ thee.
  As thou wilt win my favour, good my knave,
140   Do one thing for me that I shall entreat.
COSTARD   When would you have it done, sir?
BIRON   This afternoon.
COSTARD   Well, I will do it, sir. Fare you well.
BIRON   Thou knowest not what it is.
145 COSTARD   I shall know, sir, when I have done it.
BIRON   Why, villain, thou must know first.

---

3. *running out . . . within:* possible reference to bodily
emissions.
4. Punning on "enfranchise" (line 109); "Frances" was
probably a common name for a prostitute.
5. Religious reference from the mishearing of "adieu"
(line 123); playful diminutive of "jewel" or "juvenal."
incony: fine, quality.

6. Linen tape, suggested by "incony" (line 124); near
homonym of "ingle," a catamite (boy kept by a pederast), and perhaps thereby evoking the period's association of the "Jew" (line 124) with sodomy.
7. A coin; syphilis (the "French disease") results in a
bald head ("crown").

COSTARD I will come to your worship tomorrow morning.

BIRON It must be done this afternoon. Hark, slave,
 It is but this:

150 The Princess comes to hunt here in the park,
 And in her train there is a gentle lady.
 When tongues speak sweetly, then they name her name,
 And Rosaline they call her. Ask for her,
 And to her white hand see thou do commend
 This sealed-up counsel.° There's thy guerdon° [*giving him a*   *message / reward*
155 *letter and money*], go.

COSTARD Guerdon! O sweet guerdon!—better than remuneration, elevenpence-farthing better[8]—most sweet guerdon! I will
do it, sir, in print.° Guerdon—remuneration.   *Exit*   *to the letter*

BIRON And I, forsooth, in love—I that have been love's whip,
160 A very beadle[9] to a humorous° sigh,   *moody*
 A critic, nay, a night-watch constable,
 A domineering pedant° o'er the boy,°   *schoolmaster / Cupid*
 Than whom no mortal so magnificent.
 This wimpled,° whining, purblind,° wayward boy, *blindfolded / all-blind*
165 This Signor° Junior, giant dwarf, Dan° Cupid, *Sir; senior / Master*
 Regent of love-rhymes, lord of folded arms,
 Th'anointed sovereign of sighs and groans,
 Liege of all loiterers and malcontents,
 Dread prince of plackets, king of codpieces,[1]
170 Sole imperator° and great general   *Absolute ruler*
 Of trotting paritors[2]—O my little heart!
 And I to be a corporal of his field,°   *field officer*
 And wear his colours like a tumbler's hoop!° *(adorned with ribbons)*
 What? I love, I sue, I seek a wife?—
175 A woman, that is like a German clock,
 Still° a-repairing, ever out of frame,°   *Always / order*
 And never going aright, being° a watch,   *though*
 But being° watched that it may still go right. *Except when*
 Nay, to be perjured, which is worst of all,
180 And among three to love the worst of all—
 A whitely° wanton with a velvet° brow,   *pale / smooth*
 With two pitch°-balls stuck in her face for eyes— *tar black*
 Ay, and, by heaven, one that will do the deed° *sexual act*
 Though Argus[3] were her eunuch° and her guard. *harem guard*
185 And I to sigh for her, to watch° for her, *stay awake at night*
 To pray for her—go to,° it is a plague   *come now*
 That Cupid will impose for my neglect
 Of his almighty dreadful little might.
 Well, I will love, write, sigh, pray, sue, groan:
190 Some men must love my lady, and some Joan.°   [*Exit*] *lower-class woman*

---

8. Biron has given Costard a "guerdon" of one shilling, or twelve pence, which is "elevenpence-farthing" (eleven pence and one farthing) "better than remuneration," defined earlier by Costard as "three-farthings" (where four farthings equal one pence; line 126).

9. Minor parish official who punished lesser offenses (for instance, by whipping).

1. The parts of clothes covering the male sexual organ (hence, penises, or men). *plackets*: slits in petticoats (hence, female genitalia, or women).

2. Officers who summoned sexual offenders to ecclesiastical courts.

3. Mythical watchman with a hundred eyes.

4.1

Enter the PRINCESS, *a* FORESTER, *her ladies* [ROSALINE,
MARIA, *and* CATHERINE] *and her lords* [*among them*
BOYET]

PRINCESS Was that the King that spurred his horse so hard
　　Against the steep uprising of the hill?

BOYET I know not, but I think it was not he.

PRINCESS Whoe'er a° was, a showed a mounting mind.　　　　　*he*
　　Well, lords, today we shall have our dispatch.

5　　Ere Saturday we will return to France.
　　Then, forester my friend, where is the bush
　　That we must stand and play the murderer in?

FORESTER Hereby, upon the edge of yonder coppice°—　　　　　*thicket*
　　A stand° where you may make the fairest° shoot.　　*hunter's station / best*

10 PRINCESS I thank my beauty, I am fair that shoot,
　　And thereupon thou speak'st 'the fairest shoot'.

FORESTER Pardon me, madam, for I meant not so.

PRINCESS What, what? First praise me, and again say no?
　　O short-lived pride! Not fair? Alack, for woe!

15 FORESTER Yes, madam, fair.

PRINCESS　　　　　　　　Nay, never paint° me now.　　　　　*flatter*
　　Where fair° is not, praise cannot mend the brow.　　　　*beauty*
　　Here, good my glass,° take this for telling true.　　*my good mirror*
　　[*She gives him money*]
　　Fair payment for foul words is more than due.

FORESTER Nothing but fair is that which you inherit.°　　　　　*own*

20 PRINCESS See, see, my beauty will be saved by merit![1]
　　O heresy in fair,° fit for these days[2]—　　　　*in regard to beauty*
　　A giving hand, though foul, shall have fair praise.
　　But come, the bow. Now mercy° goes to kill,　　*the merciful Princess*
　　And shooting well is then accounted ill.°　　　　*unmerciful*

25　　Thus will I save my credit in the shoot,
　　Not wounding—pity would not let me do't.[3]
　　If wounding, then it was to show my skill,
　　That more for praise than purpose meant to kill.
　　And, out of question,° so it is sometimes—　　　　*beyond doubt*

30　　Glory° grows guilty of detested crimes　　*The desire for glory*
　　When for fame's sake, for praise, an outward part,
　　We bend to that the working of the heart,
　　As I for praise alone now seek to spill
　　The poor deer's blood that my heart means no ill.

35 BOYET Do not curst° wives hold that self-sovereignty　　　*shrewish*
　　Only for praise' sake when they strive to be
　　Lords o'er their lords?

PRINCESS Only for praise, and praise we may afford
　　To any lady that subdues a lord.

40　　　　　*Enter* [COSTARD *the*] *clown*

BOYET Here comes a member of the commonwealth.°　　*common people*

COSTARD God dig-you-de'en,° all. Pray you, which is the head　　*give you good evening*
　　lady?

4.1 Location: A hunter's station in the King's park.
1. Desert; good works (her "payment").
2. Believing in salvation by faith, Protestants considered it a common "heresy" "these days" to think, as

Catholics did, that one could be "saved by merit."
3. *Thus . . . do't:* I will save my reputation as a hunter by saying, if I miss, that pity for the deer caused me to miss deliberately.

PRINCESS   Thou shalt know her, fellow, by the rest that have no
45   heads.[4]
COSTARD   Which is the greatest lady, the highest?
PRINCESS   The thickest and the tallest.
COSTARD   The thickest and the tallest—it is so, truth is truth.
        An your waist, mistress, were as slender as my wit
50   One o' these maids' girdles for your waist should be fit.
        Are not you the chief woman? You are the thickest here.
PRINCESS   What's your will, sir? What's your will?
COSTARD   I have a letter from Monsieur Biron to one Lady Rosaline.
PRINCESS   O, thy letter, thy letter! [*She takes it*] He's a good
        friend of mine.
55   [*To* COSTARD] Stand aside, good bearer. Boyet, you can carve.°   cut meat; act affected
        Break up° this capon.[5]   Cut up; open
            [*She gives the letter to* BOYET]
BOYET   I am bound to serve.
        This letter is mistook. It importeth° none here.   matters to
        It is writ to Jaquenetta.
PRINCESS   We will read it, I swear.
        Break the neck of the wax,° and everyone give ear.   seal; (capon)
60   BOYET [*reads*] 'By heaven, that thou art fair is most infallible,°   certain
        true that thou art beauteous, truth itself that thou art lovely.
        More fairer than fair, beautiful than beauteous, truer than truth
        itself, have commiseration on thy heroical vassal. The magnan-
        imous and most illustrate° King Cophetua set's° eye upon the   illustrious / set his
65   penurious and indubitate° beggar Zenelophon,[6] and he it was   undoubted
        that might rightly say "*Veni, vidi, vici*",[7] which to annothanize°   anatomize; annotate
        in the vulgar—O base and obscure vulgar!°—*videlicet*° "He   vernacular / namely
        came, see, and overcame." He came, one; see, two; overcame,
        three. Who came? The King. Why did he come? To see. Why
70   did he see? To overcome. To whom came he? To the beggar.
        What saw he? The beggar. Who overcame he? The beggar.
        The conclusion is victory. On whose side? The King's. The
        captive is enriched. On whose side? The beggar's. The catastro-
        phe° is a nuptial. On whose side? The King's—no, on both in   outcome
75   one, or one in both. I am the King—for so stands the compari-
        son—thou the beggar, for so witnesseth thy lowliness. Shall I
        command thy love? I may. Shall I enforce thy love? I could.
        Shall I entreat thy love? I will. What shalt thou exchange for
        rags? Robes. For tittles?° Titles. For thyself? Me. Thus,   jots; specks
80   expecting thy reply, I profane my lips on thy foot, my eyes on
        thy picture, and my heart on thy every part.
                Thine in the dearest design of industry,°   gallantry?; diligence
                        Don Adriano de Armado.
        Thus dost thou hear the Nemean lion[8] roar
85   'Gainst thee, thou lamb, that standest as his prey.
        Submissive fall his princely feet before,
            And he from forage° will incline to play.   raging
        But if thou strive, poor soul, what art thou then?
        Food for his rage, repasture° for his den.'   food
90   PRINCESS   What plume of feathers° is he that indited° this   silly bird / wrote
        letter?

---

4. Part of the body, literalizing metaphorical use of
"head" as "leader" (line 42); maidenhead.
5. Love letter; castrated male chicken.

6. See 1.2.99.
7. Originally said by Julius Caesar.
8. Killed by Hercules as the first of his labors.

What vane?[9] What weathercock?° Did you ever hear better? *(example of showiness)*

BOYET I am much deceived but I remember the style.

PRINCESS Else your memory is bad, going o'er[1] it erewhile.

BOYET This Armado is a Spaniard that keeps° here in court, *dwells*

95 A phantasim,° a Monarcho,[2] and one that makes sport *fantastic being*

To° the Prince and his bookmates. *For*

PRINCESS [*to* COSTARD] Thou, fellow, a word.

Who gave thee this letter?

COSTARD I told you—my lord.

PRINCESS To whom shouldst thou give it?

COSTARD From my lord to my lady.

PRINCESS From which lord to which lady?

100 COSTARD From my lord Biron, a good master of mine,

To a lady of France that he called Rosaline.

PRINCESS Thou hast mistaken his letter. Come, lords, away.

[*To* ROSALINE, *giving her the letter*]

Here, sweet, put up this, 'twill be thine another day.° *your turn will come*

Exit [*attended*]

BOYET Who is the suitor? Who is the suitor?° *(with pun on "shooter")*

ROSALINE Shall I teach you to know?

BOYET Ay, my continent° of beauty. *container of all*

105 ROSALINE Why, she that bears the bow.

Finely put off.° *evaded*

BOYET My lady goes to kill horns, but if thou marry,

Hang me by the neck if horns that year miscarry.[3]

Finely put on.° *applied*

ROSALINE Well then, I am the shooter.

110 BOYET And who is your deer?° *prey; dear*

ROSALINE If we choose by the horns, yourself come not near.[4]

Finely put on indeed!

MARIA You still wrangle with her, Boyet, and she strikes at the brow.[5]

BOYET But she herself is hit lower[6]—have I hit her° now? *found her out*

115 ROSALINE Shall I come upon thee with an old saying that was a man when King Pépin of France was a little boy,[7] as touching the hit it?[8]

BOYET So I may answer thee with one as old that was a woman when Queen Guinevere of Britain[9] was a little wench, as

120 touching the hit it.

ROSALINE [*sings*]

Thou canst not hit it, hit it, hit it,

Thou canst not hit it, my good man.

BOYET [*sings*]

An I cannot, cannot, cannot,

An I cannot, another can. *Exit* [ROSALINE]

125 COSTARD By my troth, most pleasant! How both did fit it!° *sing well; (bawdy)*

MARIA A mark° marvellous well shot, for they both did hit it. *target*

---

9. Weathervane, often in the form of a heraldic banner; vanity.

1. Having read; having climbed (taking "style" in line 92 as "stile," "fence").

2. Pretentious person—from the nickname of an eccentric Italian of Shakespeare's time who claimed to be a monarch of the world.

3. If you do not soon cuckold your husband; possibly, if penises fail or lead to a miscarriage. From here through line 135, there are almost continuous sexual references.

4. Probably: If you want to be safe, don't come close, because you have cuckold's horns.

5. Aims well; taunts you about your cuckold's horns.

6. In the heart; in the genitals.

7. Was already old when Charlemagne's father (d. 768) was a little boy.

8. *the hit it:* bawdy popular round and the dance done to it.

9. Notoriously unfaithful wife of the legendary King Arthur.

BOYET   A mark—O mark but that mark! A mark, says my lady.
       Let the mark have a prick° in't to mete° at, if it may be.   bull's-eye; penis / aim
MARIA   Wide o' the bow hand[1]—i'faith, your hand is out.°   out of practice
COSTARD   Indeed, a must shoot nearer, or he'll ne'er hit the
130   clout.°   bull's-eye; (bawdy)
BOYET   An if my hand be out, then belike your hand is in.[2]
COSTARD   Then will she get the upshoot[3] by cleaving the pin.°   center
MARIA   Come, come, you talk greasily,° your lips grow foul.   indecently
COSTARD   She's too hard for you at pricks,° sir. Challenge her to   archery; sex
         bowl.
135 BOYET   I fear too much rubbing.[4] Goodnight, my good owl.[5]

                    [*Exeunt* BOYET, MARIA, *and* CATHERINE]

COSTARD   By my soul, a swain, a most simple clown.
       Lord, Lord, how the ladies and I have put him down!
       O' my troth, most sweet jests, most incony° vulgar wit,   fine-quality
       When it comes so smoothly off, so obscenely,[6] as it were, so fit!
140   Armado o'th' t'other side°—O, a most dainty° man!—   by contrast / elegant
       To see him walk before a lady and to bear her fan!
       To see him kiss his hand, and how most sweetly° a will swear,   stylishly
       And his page o' t'other side, that handful of wit—
       Ah heavens, it is a most pathetical nit!°   affecting little fellow
           Shout° *within*   Loud voice; shooting
145   Sola, sola!°   *Exit*   hunting cry

                              4.2

       Enter DULL, HOLOFERNES *the pedant,*[1] *and* NATHANIEL
       [*the curate*]

NATHANIEL   Very reverend° sport, truly, and done in the testi-   respectable
       mony° of a good conscience.   with the warrant
HOLOFERNES   The deer was, as you know—*sanguis*[2]—in blood,°   robust
       ripe as the pomewater° who now hangeth like a jewel in the   kind of apple
5   ear of *caelo*, the sky, the welkin, the heaven, and anon° falleth   soon after
       like a crab° on the face of *terra*, the soil, the land, the earth.   crab apple
NATHANIEL   Truly, Master Holofernes, the epithets are sweetly
       varied, like a scholar at the least. But, sir, I assure ye it was a
       buck of the first head.[3]
10 HOLOFERNES   Sir[4] Nathaniel, *haud credo*.°   I hardly think so
DULL   'Twas not a 'auld grey doe', 'twas a pricket.[5]
HOLOFERNES   Most barbarous intimation!° Yet a kind of insinu-   intrusion
       ation, as it were *in via*, in way, of explication, *facere*,° as it were,   to make
       replication,° or rather *ostentare*, to show, as it were, his inclina-   explanation
15   tion after his undressed, unpolished, uneducated, unpruned,
       untrained, or rather unlettered, or ratherest unconfirmed,°   inexperienced
       fashion, to insert again° my '*haud credo*' for a deer.   interpret

---

1. Too far to the left side (a cry in archery).
2. If I'm out of practice (at archery, at sex), you're not.
3. Winning shot; ejaculation.
4. In the game of bowls, touching obstacles; sexual
friction.
5. "Owl," a bird of night, is suggested by "Goodnight";
to "take owl" is to take offense; rhyming with "bowl,"
"owl" suggests "ole" (hole) in the sexual sense.
6. Inadvertently accurate; perhaps a blunder for
"seemly."
4.2 Location: The King's park.
1. Holofernes—a character based on a warrior whose
decapitation by the heroine of the apocryphal Book
of Judith saves Jerusalem—was a familiar tyrant in
medieval religious plays; also a doctor of theology and

tutor to Gargantua in Rabelais's *Gargantua and Panta-
gruel*. Like the braggart soldier, the pedant or schoolmaster was a stock character in commedia dell'arte (see
Introduction); his prominence is due to the humanist-
inspired, early Tudor educational reforms that presumably shaped Shakespeare's own formal education.
2. The Latin in this scene, some of it inaccurate, is
translated only when the characters themselves fail to
do so. It is often unclear whether an error is the character's or the printer's.
3. With his first head of antlers; in his fifth year.
4. Used generally of graduates, including priests (like
"Reverend").
5. Buck in its second year, with a sexual hint.

DULL   I said the deer was not a 'auld grey doe', 'twas a pricket.

HOLOFERNES   Twice-sod simplicity, *bis coctus*!°

20   O thou monster ignorance, how deformed dost thou look!

NATHANIEL   Sir, he hath never fed of the dainties that are bred
in a book.

He hath not eat paper, as it were, he hath not drunk ink. His
intellect is not replenished, he is only an animal, only sensible°   *capable of feeling*
in the duller parts,

And such barren plants are set before us that we thankful

25   should be,

Which we of taste and feeling are, for those parts that do fruc-
tify° in us more than he.   *bear fruit*

For as it would ill become me to be vain, indiscreet, or a fool,

So were there a patch set on learning[7] to see *him* in a school.

But *omne bene*° say I, being of an old father's° mind: *all is well / sage's*

30   'Many can brook the weather that love not the wind.'[8]

DULL   You two are bookmen. Can you tell me by your wit
What was a month old at Cain's birth that's not five weeks old
as yet?

HOLOFERNES   *Dictynna*, Goodman° Dull, *Dictynna*, Goodman   *Yeoman*
Dull.

35   DULL   What is *'Dictima'*?

NATHANIEL   A title to° Phoebe, to *luna*, to the moon.   *name for*

HOLOFERNES   The moon was a month old when Adam was no
more,

And raught° not to five weeks when he came to five score.   *reached*
Th'allusion holds in the exchange.[9]

40   DULL   'Tis true, indeed, the collusion° holds in the exchange.   *(for "allusion")*

HOLOFERNES   God comfort° thy capacity, I say th'allusion holds   *pity*
in the exchange.

DULL   And I say the pollution[1] holds in the exchange, for the
moon is never but a month old—and I say beside that 'twas a

45   pricket that the Princess killed.

HOLOFERNES   Sir Nathaniel, will you hear an extemporal epitaph on the death of the deer? And to humour the ignorant call
I the deer the Princess killed a pricket.

NATHANIEL   *Perge*,° good Master Holofernes, *perge*, so it shall   *Proceed*

50   please you to abrogate scurrility.[2]

HOLOFERNES   I will something affect the letter,[3] for it argues°   *shows*
facility.

The preyful° Princess pierced and pricked a pretty pleasing   *desirous of prey*
pricket.

Some say a sore,[4] but not a sore till now made sore with
shooting.

The dogs did yell; put 'l' to 'sore', then 'sorel'° jumps from   *buck in its third year*

55   thicket—

Or° pricket sore, or else sorel. The people fall a-hooting.   *Either*

---

6. *Twice . . . coctus*: Twice-boiled folly, twice-cooked; *"coctus"* also continues the sexual innuendo of "pricket" (line 18) with the suggestion of "cock."

7. It would mean that a fool ("patch") had been put to his studies; there would be a black mark on learning.

8. Many can endure the weather while disliking some of its features (?); one must live with what one cannot change (proverbial).

9. The riddle works as well with Adam as with Cain.

1. Dull's blunder for "allusion" again, but in each case a commentary on his interlocutors. "Collusion" can refer to a verbal trick designed to promote collusion in the sense of conspiracy; linguistic pollution occurs when one favors difficult foreign words over straightforward English.

2. *Perge . . . scurrility*: proceed . . . avoid indecency. Nathaniel is probably worrying about "pricket"—justifiably, given line 53, below. *"Perge"* may suggest "purging."

3. I will to some extent aspire to alliteration.

4. Deer in its fourth year.

If sore be sore, then 'l'° to 'sore' makes fifty sores—O sore 'l'!   *Roman numeral for 50*
Of one sore I an hundred make by adding but one more 'l'.°   *50 more; moral*

NATHANIEL   A rare talent!°   *talon; ability*

60   DULL   If a talent be a claw, look how he claws° him with a talent.   *scratches; flatters*

HOLOFERNES   This is a gift that I have, simple, simple—a foolish
extravagant° spirit, full of forms, figures, shapes, objects, ideas,   *wandering*
apprehensions, motions,° revolutions.° These are begot in the   *impulses / reflections*
ventricle° of memory, nourished in the womb of *pia mater*,[5] and   *part of the brain*
65   delivered upon the mellowing of occasion.° But the gift is good   *when the time is ripe*
in those in whom it is acute, and I am thankful for it.

NATHANIEL   Sir, I praise the Lord for you, and so may my parishioners; for their sons are well tutored by you, and their daughters profit very greatly under you.[6] You are a good member of
70   the commonwealth.

HOLOFERNES   *Mehercle*,° if their sons be ingenious they shall   *By Hercules*
want° no instruction; if their daughters be capable, I will put it   *lack*
to them. But *Vir sapit qui pauca loquitur*;[7] a soul feminine
saluteth us.

Enter JAQUENETTA, *and* [COSTARD] *the clown*

75   JAQUENETTA   God give you good-morrow, Master Parson.

HOLOFERNES   Master Parson, *quasi*° 'pierce one'?[8] And if one   *as if*
should be pierced, which is the one?

COSTARD   Marry, Master Schoolmaster, he that is likeliest to° a   *most like*
hogshead.[9]

80   HOLOFERNES   'Of piercing a hogshead'°—a good lustre of con-   *getting drunk?*
ceit° in a turf of earth, fire enough for a flint, pearl enough for   *spark of imagination*
a swine[1]—'tis pretty, it is well.

JAQUENETTA   Good Master Parson, be so good as read me this
letter. It was given me by Costard, and sent me from Don Arm-
85   ado. I beseech you read it.

[*She gives the letter to* NATHANIEL, *who reads it*]

HOLOFERNES [*to himself*]   '*Facile precor gelida quando pecas
omnia sub umbra ruminat*',[2] and so forth. Ah, good old Mantuan! I may speak of thee as the traveller doth of Venice:

          Venezia, Venezia,
90   *Chi non ti vede, chi non ti prezia*.[3]

Old Mantuan, old Mantuan— who understandeth thee not,
loves thee not. [*He sings*] Ut, re, sol, la, mi, fa.[4] [*To* NATHANIEL]
Under pardon, sir, what are the contents? Or rather, as
Horace° says in his—what, my soul—verses?   *ancient Roman poet*

95   NATHANIEL   Ay, sir, and very learned.

HOLOFERNES   Let me hear a staff,° a stanza, a verse. *Lege*,   *stanza*
domine.°   *Read, sir*

---

5. Membrane surrounding the brain.
6. In conjunction with "member" (line 69), "capable" (line 72), and "put it to them" (lines 72–73), probably bawdy.
7. "That man is wise that speaketh few things or words" (Lily's Latin grammar, translating a common proverb).
8. Pronounced like "parson" or "person"; bawdy.
9. Large cask used for beer or wine; fool.
1. To "cast pearls before swine," a biblical phrase, was already proverbial.
2. "Easily, I pray, since you are getting everything wrong under the cool shade, it ruminates." A nonsensical mis-

quotation of the first line of a Latin poem by the Italian poet (1448–1516) Mantuan, a poem well known even to schoolboys in Shakespeare's time. The correct Latin means: "Faustus, I pray, since the whole herd are chewing their cud in the cool shade." The errors may be the printer's rather than Holofernes' or Shakespeare's.
3. Italian proverb, translated by John Florio as "Venice, who seeth thee not, praiseth thee not" (*First Fruits*, 1578).
4. Notes of the scale ("ut" is the modern "do"). If Holofernes sings them as a scale, he gets them in the wrong order; but they may represent a tune.

NATHANIEL [*reads*] 'If love make me forsworn, how shall I swear
    to love?[5]
  Ah, never faith could hold, if not to beauty vowed.
100 Though to myself forsworn, to thee I'll faithful prove.
    Those thoughts to me were oaks,[6] to thee like osiers° bowed.   *willows*
  Study his bias leaves,° and makes his book thine eyes,   *goes off course*
    Where all those pleasures live that art would comprehend.
  If knowledge be the mark,° to know thee shall suffice.   *aim*
105 Well learnèd is that tongue that well can thee commend;
    All ignorant that soul that sees thee without wonder;
  Which is to me some praise that I thy parts° admire.   *qualities*
    Thy eye Jove's lightning bears, thy voice his dreadful thunder,
  Which, not to anger bent, is music and sweet fire.
110 Celestial as thou art, O pardon, love, this wrong,
    That singeth heaven's praise with such an earthly tongue.'
HOLOFERNES   You find not the apostrophus,° and so miss the   *elision mark*
  accent. Let me supervise° the canzonet.° Here are only num-   *look over / little poem*
  bers ratified,° but for the elegancy, facility, and golden cadence   *correct meters*
115 of poesy—*caret*.° Ovidius Naso[7] was the man. And why indeed   *it is lacking*
  'Naso' but for smelling out the odoriferous flowers of fancy, the
  jerks of invention?[8] *Imitari*° is nothing. So doth the hound his   *To imitate*
  master, the ape his keeper, the tired° horse his rider. But *domi-*   *attired*
  cella—virgin—was this directed to you?
120 JAQUENETTA   Ay, sir.[9]
HOLOFERNES   I will overglance the superscript.° 'To the snow-   *address*
  white hand of the most beauteous Lady Rosaline.' I will look
  again on the intellect° of the letter for the nomination of the   *meaning; contents*
  party writing to the person written unto. 'Your ladyship's in all
125 desired employment, Biron.' Sir Nathaniel, this Biron is one of
  the votaries with the King, and here he hath framed a letter to
  a sequent° of the stranger° Queen's, which, accidentally or by   *follower / foreign*
  the way of progression,° hath miscarried. [*To* JAQUENETTA] Trip   *in transit*
  and go,[1] my sweet, deliver this paper into the royal hand of the
130 King. It may concern much. Stay not thy compliment, I forgive
  thy duty.[2] Adieu.
JAQUENETTA   Good Costard, go with me.—Sir, God save your
  life.
COSTARD   Have with thee,° my girl.   *Exit* [*with* JAQUENETTA]   *I'll come with you*
135 NATHANIEL   Sir, you have done this in the fear of God very religiously, and, as a certain father° saith—   *church father*
HOLOFERNES   Sir, tell not me of the father; I do fear colourable
  colours.[3] But to return to the verses—did they please you, Sir
  Nathaniel?
140 NATHANIEL   Marvellous well for the pen.°   *penmanship*

---

5. The beginning of a sonnet (lines 98–111), with six
stresses per line. Like the poems of Longueville
(4.3.55–68) and Dumaine (4.3.97–116), it was
reprinted in *The Passionate Pilgrime* (1599), a collection attributed to Shakespeare on the title page but
actually containing poetry by various writers.
6. Those resolutions that seemed to me to be as strong
as oaks.
7. The full name of the ancient Roman poet Ovid was
Publius Ovidius Naso; *nasus* is Latin for "nose."
8. The strokes of imagination.
9. Q reads: "sir from one mounsier *Berowne*, one of the

strange Queenes Lordes." Jaquenetta has just said
(lines 84–85) that Armado wrote and Costard gave her
the letter, and she can't know that Biron, who is not a
"strange" (foreign) courtier, actually composed it.
Probably the errors are Shakespeare's.
1. A common expression, the title of a popular song
and dance.
2. Do not delay in order to take leave politely. I excuse
you from making a curtsy.
3. I do mistrust plausible—but specious—arguments
(a rejection of popishness?).

HOLOFERNES I do dine today at the father's of a certain pupil of
mine where, if before repast it shall please you to gratify° the   *grace; please*
table with a grace, I will on my privilege I have with the parents
of the foresaid child or pupil undertake your *ben venuto*,[4]
145 where I will prove those verses to be very unlearned, neither
savouring of poetry, wit, nor invention. I beseech your society.

NATHANIEL And thank you too, for society, saith the text,[5] is the
happiness of life.

HOLOFERNES And certes° the text most infallibly concludes it.   *certainly*
150 [*To* DULL] Sir, I do invite you too. You shall not say me nay.
Pauca verba.° Away, the gentles are at their game,[6] and we will   *Few words*
to our recreation.   *Exeunt*

4.3

Enter BIRON *with a paper in his hand, alone*

BIRON The King, he is hunting the deer. I am coursing° myself.   *pursuing*
They have pitched a toil,° I am toiling in a pitch[1]—pitch that   *set a snare*
defiles. Defile—a foul word. Well, set thee down,° sorrow; for   *stay with me*
so they say the fool said, and so say I, and I the fool. Well
5 proved, wit! By the Lord, this love is as mad as Ajax, it kills
sheep,[2] it kills me, I a sheep—well proved again o' my side. I
will not love. If I do, hang me; i'faith, I will not. O, but her
eye! By this light, but for her eye I would not love her. Yes, for
her two eyes. Well, I do nothing in the world but lie, and lie in
10 my throat.° By heaven, I do love, and it hath taught me to   *scandalously*
rhyme and to be melancholy, and here [*showing a paper*] is
part of my rhyme, and here [*touching his breast*] my melancholy. Well, she hath one o' my sonnets already. The clown
bore it, the fool sent it, and the lady hath it. Sweet clown,
15 sweeter fool, sweetest lady. By the world, I would not care a pin
if the other three were in.° Here comes one with a paper. God   *similarly involved*
give him grace to groan.°   *(out of love)*

He stands aside.[3] *The* KING *entereth* [*with a paper*]

KING Ay me!

BIRON [*aside*] Shot, by heaven! Proceed, sweet Cupid, thou hast
20 thumped him with thy birdbolt under the left pap.° In faith,   *your arrow in the heart*
secrets.

KING [*reads*] 'So sweet a kiss the golden sun gives not[4]
To those fresh morning drops upon the rose
As thy eyebeams when their fresh rays have smote
25   The night of dew° that on my cheeks down flows.   *nightly tears*
Nor shines the silver moon one-half so bright
Through the transparent bosom of the deep
As doth thy face through tears of mine give light.
Thou shin'st in every tear that I do weep.
30 No drop but as a coach doth carry thee,
So ridest thou triumphing in my woe.
Do but behold the tears that swell in me
And they thy glory through my grief will show.

---

4. Undertake your welcome (Italian).
5. No convincing source has been identified.
6. The gentlefolk are at their sport (hunting).
4.3. Location: Scene continues.
1. In tar; in Rosaline's eyes(?)
2. At the Greek siege of Troy, when Agamemnon
awards Achilles' armor to Odysseus, Ajax goes mad with

rage and kills a flock of sheep, believing them to be the
Greek army.
3. At line 74, Biron says, "here sit I in the sky." At some
point before then—perhaps here—he mounts to a
higher level.
4. The beginning of a sonnet that actually extends to
sixteen lines (lines 22–37).

But do not love thyself; then thou wilt keep
35   My tears for glasses,° and still make me weep.   *mirrors*
O Queen of queens, how far dost thou excel,
No thought can think nor tongue of mortal tell.'
How shall she know my griefs? I'll drop the paper.
Sweet leaves, shade° folly. Who is he comes here?   *hide*

Enter LONGUEVILLE [*with papers*]. *The* KING *steps aside*

40   What, Longueville, and reading—listen, ear!
BIRON [*aside*]   Now in thy° likeness one more fool appear!   *(the King's)*
LONGUEVILLE   Ay me! I am forsworn.
BIRON [*aside*]   Why, he comes in like a perjure,° wearing papers.[5]   *perjurer*
KING [*aside*]   In love, I hope! Sweet fellowship in shame.
45   BIRON [*aside*]   One drunkard loves another of the name.
LONGUEVILLE   Am I the first that have been perjured so?
BIRON [*aside*]   I could put thee in comfort, not by two that I know.
Thou makest the triumviry,[6] the corner-cap° of society,   *three-cornered cap*
The shape of love's Tyburn,[7] that hangs up simplicity.°   *folly*
50   LONGUEVILLE   I fear these stubborn° lines lack power to move.   *rough*
O sweet Maria, empress of my love,
These numbers° will I tear, and write in prose.   *verses*
BIRON [*aside*]   O, rhymes are guards° on wanton Cupid's hose,   *decorative bands*
Disfigure not his slop.°   *breeches*
LONGUEVILLE   This same shall go.[8]

He reads the sonnet

55   'Did not the heavenly rhetoric of thine eye,
     'Gainst whom the world cannot hold argument,
Persuade my heart to this false perjury?
Vows for thee broke deserve not punishment.
A woman I forswore, but I will prove,
60   Thou being a goddess, I forswore not thee.
My vow was earthly, thou a heavenly love.
Thy grace° being gained cures all disgrace in me.   *favor*
Vows are but breath, and breath a vapour is.
Then thou, fair sun, which on my earth dost shine,
65   Exhal'st° this vapour-vow; in thee it is.   *Draw up*
If broken then, it is no fault of mine.
If by me broke, what fool is not so wise
To lose an oath to win a paradise?'
BIRON [*aside*]   This is the liver vein,[9] which makes flesh a deity,
70   A green goose° a goddess, pure, pure idolatry.   *silly girl; whore*
God amend us, God amend: we are much out o'th' way.°   *badly astray*

Enter DUMAINE [*with a paper*]

LONGUEVILLE [*aside*]   By whom shall I send this? Company? Stay.
     [*He steps aside*]
BIRON [*aside*]   All hid, all hid—an old infant play.[1]
Like a demigod here sit I in the sky,
75   And wretched fools' secrets heedfully o'er-eye.
More sacks to the mill!° O heavens, I have my wish.   *More to come!*
Dumaine transformed—four woodcocks° in a dish!   *fools*
DUMAINE   O most divine Kate!

5. Wearing a poem (lines 55–68). Convicted perjurers were exposed by having to wear papers that explained their guilt.
6. You complete the triumvirate (group of three rulers).
7. The common place of execution in London, here metaphorically for gallows, which were triangular.
8. Either he has hesitated before tearing the paper, or he pieces it together, as if in response to Biron's aside.
9. Style of the lover (the liver was thought of as the seat of love).
1. Hide-and-seek ("play" means "game"); perhaps also a medieval religious play in which God views the actions from above, like Biron (line 74).

BIRON [*aside*]   O most profane coxcomb!°   fool
80 DUMAINE   By heaven, the wonder in a mortal eye!
BIRON [*aside*]   By earth, she is not, corporal;² there you lie.
DUMAINE   Her amber hairs for foul hath amber quoted.³
BIRON [*aside*]   An amber-coloured raven was well noted.⁴
DUMAINE   As upright as the cedar.
BIRON [*aside*]   Stoop,⁵ I say.
Her shoulder is with child.°   bulging; bowed down
85 DUMAINE   As fair as day.
BIRON [*aside*]   Ay, as some days; but then no sun must shine.
DUMAINE   O that I had my wish!
LONGUEVILLE [*aside*]   And I had mine!
KING [*aside*]   And I mine too, good Lord!
90 BIRON [*aside*]   Amen, so I had mine. Is not that a good word?⁶
DUMAINE   I would forget her, but a fever she
Reigns in my blood and will remembered be.
BIRON [*aside*]   A fever in your blood—why then, incision°   bloodletting
Would let her out in saucers⁷—sweet misprision.°   misinterpretation
95 DUMAINE   Once more I'll read the ode that I have writ.
BIRON [*aside*]   Once more I'll mark how love can vary° wit.   inspire; impair

DUMAINE *reads his sonnet*

DUMAINE   'On a day—alack the day—
Love, whose month is ever May,
Spied a blossom passing° fair   surpassingly
100 Playing in the wanton° air.   playful
Through the velvet leaves the wind
All unseen can° passage find,   did
That° the lover, sick to death,   So that
Wished himself the heavens' breath.
105 "Air", quoth he, "thy cheeks may blow;
Air, would I might triumph so.
But, alack, my hand is sworn
Ne'er to pluck thee from thy thorn—
Vow, alack, for youth unmeet,°   inappropriate
110 Youth so apt to pluck a sweet.
Do not call it sin in me
That I am forsworn for thee,
Thou for whom great Jove would swear
Juno but an Ethiop⁸ were,
115 And deny himself for° Jove,   to be
Turning mortal for thy love.'"
This will I send, and something else more plain,
That shall express my true love's fasting pain.
O, would the King, Biron, and Longueville
120 Were lovers too! Ill to example° ill   be a precedent for
Would from my forehead wipe a perjured note,⁹
For none offend where all alike do dote.

---

2. Officer in Cupid's army; perhaps, (she is merely) corporeal, or human. The possible application to both Dumaine and Catherine, but in different ways, is characteristic of Biron's asides here.
3. Her amber-colored hairs have caused amber itself to be regarded as foul by comparison.
4. Dumaine is an acute observer, Biron remarks ironically, in describing Catherine's black hair as amber. (Catherine is the raven, a black fowl, punningly sug-

gested by "foul," line 82.)
5. She's stooped; come down to earth.
6. Isn't that a kind wish; isn't "Amen" a "good word"?
7. Into basins used to catch the blood; by the basinful.
8. Black African (used here in racist fashion to signify ugliness).
9. Inscription (and see Biron's description of Longueville, line 43).

LONGUEVILLE [*coming forward*]   Dumaine, thy love is far from
    charity,°   *Christian love*
    That in love's grief desir'st society.°   *company*
125   You may look pale, but I should blush, I know,
    To be o'erheard and taken napping so.
    KING [*coming forward*]   Come, sir, you blush. As his, your case
        is such.
    You chide at him, offending twice as much.
    You do not love Maria? Longueville
130   Did never sonnet for her sake compile,
    Nor never lay his wreathèd arms athwart[1]
    His loving bosom to keep down his heart?
    I have been closely° shrouded in this bush,   *secretly*
    And marked you both, and for you both did blush.
135   I heard your guilty rhymes, observed your fashion,
    Saw sighs reek° from you, noted well your passion.   *rise*
    'Ay me!' says one, 'O Jove!' the other cries.
    One, her hairs were gold; crystal the other's eyes.
    [*To* LONGUEVILLE] You would for paradise break faith and troth,
140   [*To* DUMAINE] And Jove for your love would infringe an oath.
    What will Biron say when that he shall hear
    Faith so infringèd, which such zeal did swear?
    How will he scorn, how will he spend his wit!
    How will he triumph, leap, and laugh at it!
145   For all the wealth that ever I did see
    I would not have him know so much by° me.   *about*
    BIRON [*coming forward*]   Now step I forth to whip hypocrisy.
    Ah, good my liege, I pray thee pardon me.
    Good heart, what grace hast thou thus to reprove
150   These worms for loving, that art most in love?
    Your eyes do make no coaches.° In your tears   (*see lines 31–32*)
    There is no certain princess that appears.
    You'll not be perjured, 'tis a hateful thing;
    Tush, none but minstrels like of sonneting!
155   But are you not ashamed, nay, are you not,
    All three of you, to be thus much o'ershot?°   *wide of the mark*
    [*To* LONGUEVILLE] You found his° mote, the King your mote   (*Dumaine's*)
        did see,
    But I a beam[2] do find in each of three.
    O, what a scene of fool'ry have I seen,
160   Of sighs, of groans, of sorrow, and of teen!°   *grief*
    O me, with what strict patience have I sat,
    To see a king transformèd to a gnat!
    To see great Hercules whipping a gig,°   *spinning a top*
    And profound Solomon to tune° a jig,   *play*
165   And Nestor[3] play at pushpin° with the boys,   *child's game*
    And critic Timon[4] laugh at idle toys!°   *foolish fancies*
    Where lies thy grief, O tell me, good Dumaine?
    And, gentle Longueville, where lies thy pain?
    And where my liege's? All about the breast.

---

1. Folded arms across. (Folded arms were a sign of love melancholy.)
2. Larger defect: "And why beholdest thou the mote that is in thy brother's eye, but considerest [or "perceivest"] not the beam that is in thine own eye?"
(Matthew 7:3–5; Luke 6:41–42).
3. Homeric hero, a type figure of wise old age; later portrayed in Shakespeare's *Troilus and Cressida*.
4. Cynical Greek misanthrope; later, the central character of Shakespeare's *Timon of Athens*.

A caudle,° ho!   *warm, healing drink*

170 KING   Too bitter is thy jest.
Are we betrayed thus to thy over-view?
BIRON   Not you to me, but I betrayed by you.
I that am honest, I that hold it sin
To break the vow I am engagèd in.
175 I am betrayed by keeping company
With men like you, men of inconstancy.
When shall you see me write a thing in rhyme,
Or groan for Joan, or spend a minute's time
In pruning me?° When shall you hear that I   *preening myself*
180 Will praise a hand, a foot, a face, an eye,
A gait, a state,° a brow, a breast, a waist,   *an attitude; bearing*
A leg, a limb?
KING   Soft, whither away so fast?
A true° man or a thief, that gallops so?   *an honest*
BIRON   I post° from love; good lover, let me go.   *hasten*
        Enter JAQUENETTA *[with a letter,] and* [COSTARD *the*]
        clown
JAQUENETTA   God bless the King!
185 KING   What present° hast thou there?   *writing; gift*
COSTARD   Some certain treason.
KING   What makes treason° here?   *is treason doing*
COSTARD   Nay, it makes nothing, sir.
KING   If it mar nothing neither,
The treason and you go in peace away together!
JAQUENETTA   I beseech your grace, let this letter be read.
190 Our parson misdoubts° it; 'twas treason, he said.   *suspects*
KING   Biron, read it over.
        [BIRON *takes and*] *reads the letter*
        [*To* JAQUENETTA] Where hadst thou it?
JAQUENETTA   Of Costard.
KING [*to* COSTARD]   Where hadst thou it?
195 COSTARD   Of Dun Adramadio,⁵ Dun Adramadio.
        [BIRON *tears the letter*]
KING [*to* BIRON]   How now, what is in you? Why dost thou tear it?
BIRON   A toy, my liege, a toy. Your grace needs not fear it.
LONGUEVILLE   It did move him to passion, and therefore let's hear it.
DUMAINE [*taking up a piece of the letter*]   It is Biron's writing,
        and here is his name.
BIRON [*to* COSTARD]   Ah, you whoreson loggerhead,° you were   *foolish blockhead*
200 born to do me shame!
Guilty, my lord, guilty! I confess, I confess.
KING   What?
BIRON   That you three fools lacked me fool to make up the
        mess.°   *group of four at table*
He, he, and you—e'en you, my liege—and I
205 Are pickpurses° in love, and we deserve to die.   *cheaters*
O, dismiss this audience, and I shall tell you more.
DUMAINE   Now the number is even.
BIRON   True, true; we are four.
Will these turtles° be gone?   *turtledoves; lovers*
KING   Hence, sirs; away.

---

5. *Dun*: error for Don meaning "gray-brown," referring to skin color and recalling "tawny Spain" (1.1.171). *Adramadio*: error for Adriano that encompasses "drama," "mad," "amado" (loved).

COSTARD   Walk aside the true folk, and let the traitors stay.

                [*Exeunt* COSTARD *and* JAQUENETTA]

210 BIRON   Sweet lords, sweet lovers!—O, let us embrace.
      As true we are as flesh and blood can be.
      The sea will ebb and flow, heaven show his face.
      Young blood doth not obey an old decree.
      We cannot cross° the cause why we were born,   *oppose*
215   Therefore of all hands° must we be forsworn.   *in any case*
  KING   What, did these rent° lines show some love of thine?   *torn*
  BIRON   'Did they', quoth you? Who sees the heavenly Rosaline
      That, like a rude° and savage man of Ind°   *an ignorant / India*
      At the first op'ning of the gorgeous east,
220   Bows not his vassal head and, strucken blind,
      Kisses the base ground with obedient breast?
      What peremptory° eagle-sighted eye[6]   *determined*
      Dares look upon the heaven of her brow
      That is not blinded by her majesty?
225 KING   What zeal, what fury hath inspired thee now?
      My love, her mistress, is a gracious moon,
      She an attending star, scarce seen a light.°   *hardly visible*
  BIRON   My eyes are then no eyes, nor I Biron.
      O, but for my love, day would turn to night.
230   Of all complexions the culled sovereignty°   *those chosen as best*
      Do meet as at a fair in her fair cheek,
      Where several worthies make one dignity,[7]
      Where nothing wants° that want° itself doth seek.   *lacks / desire*
      Lend me the flourish of all gentle tongues—
235   Fie, painted rhetoric! O, she needs it not.
      To things of sale a seller's praise belongs.
      She passes praise—then praise too short doth blot.[8]
      A withered hermit fivescore winters worn
      Might shake off fifty, looking in her eye.
240   Beauty doth varnish age as if new-born,
      And gives the crutch the cradle's infancy.
      O, 'tis the sun that maketh all things shine.
  KING   By heaven, thy love is black as ebony.
  BIRON   Is ebony like her? O word divine!
245   A wife of such wood were felicity.
      O, who can give an oath? Where is a book,°   *a Bible*
      That I may swear beauty doth beauty lack
      If that she learn not of her eye to look?[9]
      No face is fair that is not full so° black.   *just as*
250 KING   O paradox! Black is the badge of hell,
      The hue of dungeons and the style[1] of night,
      And beauty's crest becomes the heavens well.[2]
  BIRON   Devils soonest tempt, resembling spirits of light.[3]
      O, if in black my lady's brows be decked,
255   It mourns that painting and usurping hair°   *makeup and false hair*

---

6. The eagle, king of birds, was thought to be the only one able to look directly at the sun.
7. Various kinds of excellence together produce a single preeminent beauty.
8. Hence praise inevitably falls short and mars her reputation.
9. If beauty doesn't learn from Rosaline's eye how she (beauty) could look.
1. Title. Q, F: Schoole. The phrase "school of night"

has been supposed to refer to a secret society of Shakespeare's time; alternatively, it may mean that night learns to be black in black's school.
2. (And yet, you say,) the badge of your dark beauty is heavenly (said incredulously); it is the sun, not your dark beauty, that is heavenly.
3. Fair beauties are not to be trusted, "for Satan himself is transformed into an angel of light" (2 Corinthians 11:14).

Should ravish doters with a false aspect,
    And therefore is she born to make black fair.
Her favour° turns the fashion of the days,   °appearance
    For native blood° is counted painting now,   °natural red coloring
260 And therefore red that would avoid dispraise
    Paints itself black to imitate her brow.
DUMAINE   To look like her are chimney-sweepers black.
LONGUEVILLE   And since her time are colliers counted bright.
KING   And Ethiops of their sweet complexion crack.°   °boast
265 DUMAINE   Dark needs no candles now, for dark is light.
BIRON   Your mistresses dare never come in rain,
    For fear their colours should be washed away.
KING   'Twere good yours did; for, sir, to tell you plain,
    I'll find a fairer face not washed today.
270 BIRON   I'll prove her fair, or talk till doomsday here.
KING   No devil will fright thee then° so much as she.   °(at doomsday)
DUMAINE   I never knew man hold vile stuff so dear.
LONGUEVILLE [showing his foot]   Look, here's thy love—my foot
    and her face see.⁴
BIRON   O, if the streets were pavèd with thine eyes
275 Her feet were much too dainty for such tread.
DUMAINE   O vile! Then as she goes, what upward lies°   °(bawdy)
    The street should see as she walked overhead.
KING   But what of this? Are we not all in love?
BIRON   Nothing so sure, and thereby all forsworn.
280 KING   Then leave this chat and, good Biron, now prove
    Our loving lawful and our faith not torn.
DUMAINE   Ay, marry there, some flattery° for this evil.   °excuse
LONGUEVILLE   O, some authority how to proceed,
    Some tricks, some quillets° how to cheat the devil.   °verbal tricks
DUMAINE   Some salve for perjury.°   °oath breaking; purging
285 BIRON   O, 'tis more than need.
    Have at you,° then, affection's° men-at-arms.   °Here goes / love's
    Consider what you first did swear unto:
    To fast, to study, and to see no woman—
    Flat treason 'gainst the kingly state of youth.
290 Say, can you fast? Your stomachs are too young,
    And abstinence engenders maladies.⁵
291.1 *And where that° you have vowed to study, lords,*   *°And whereas*
    In that⁶ each of you have forsworn his book,
    Can you still dream, and pore, and thereon look?
    For when would you, my lord, or you, or you,
291.5 *Have found the ground of study's excellence*
    Without the beauty of a woman's face?
    From women's eyes this doctrine I derive.
    They are the ground, the books, the academes,
    From whence doth spring the true Promethean fire.
291.10 *Why, universal plodding poisons up*
    The nimble° spirits in the arteries,   *°life-giving*
    As motion and long-during° action tires   *°long-lasting*

---

4. You may see her face in my (black) shoes.
5. The following twenty-three indented lines (291.1–291.23) represent an unrevised version of parts of Biron's long speech, 4.3.285–91, 292–339. The first six lines form the basis of 292–97; the next three are revised at 4.3.324–28; the next four at 4.3.298–300; the last nine are less directly related to the revised version.
6. Inasmuch as; in that vow.

The sinewy vigour of the traveller.
Now, for not looking on a woman's face
291.15 You have in that forsworn the use of eyes,
And study, too, the cause of your vow.
For where is any author in the world
Teaches such beauty as a woman's eye?
Learning is but an adjunct to ourself,
291.20 And where we are, our learning likewise is.
Then when ourselves we see in ladies' eyes
With ourselves.
Do we not likewise see our learning there?
O, we have made a vow to study, lords,
And in that vow we have forsworn our books;[7]
For when would you, my liege, or you, or you
295 In leaden contemplation have found out
Such fiery numbers° as the prompting eyes   *passionate verses*
Of beauty's tutors have enriched you with?
Other slow arts° entirely keep° the brain,   *disciplines / inhabit*
And therefore, finding barren practisers,
300 Scarce show a harvest of their heavy toil.
But love, first learnèd in a lady's eyes,
Lives not alone immurèd° in the brain,   *only shut up*
But with the motion of all elements[8]
Courses as swift as thought in every power,°   *faculty*
305 And gives to every power a double power
Above° their functions and their offices.°   *Beyond / normal duties*
It adds a precious seeing to the eye—
A lover's eyes will gaze an eagle blind.[9]
A lover's ear will hear the lowest sound
310 When the suspicious head of theft is stopped.[1]
Love's feeling is more soft and sensible°   *sensitive*
Than are the tender horns of cockled snails.°   *snails with shells*
Love's tongue proves dainty Bacchus° gross in taste. *Greek god of wine*
For valour, is not love a Hercules,
315 Still° climbing trees in the Hesperides?[2]   *Constantly*
Subtle as Sphinx,[3] as sweet and musical
As bright Apollo's° lute strung with his hair;   *Greek god of music*
And when love speaks, the voice of all the gods
Make heaven drowsy with the harmony.
320 Never durst poet touch a pen to write
Until his ink were tempered with love's sighs.
O, then his lines would ravish savage ears,
And plant in tyrants mild humility.
From women's eyes this doctrine I derive.
325 They sparkle still the right Promethean fire.[4]
They are the books, the arts, the academes
That show, contain, and nourish all the world,
Else none° at all in aught proves excellent.   *Without them no one*
Then fools you were these women to forswear,

7. Our true books, women's eyes.
8. Earth, air, fire, and water.
9. Can stare at the sun (here, the beloved woman) without injury longer than even an eagle can.
1. When even an alert thief (or someone listening for a thief) hears nothing.

2. Garden of golden apples that Hercules had to pick as his eleventh labor.
3. Monster in Greek mythology that killed travelers who failed to solve her riddle.
4. Divine fire. In Greek mythology Prometheus stole fire from heaven and gave it to humanity.

330 Or keeping what is sworn, you will prove fools.
For wisdom's sake—a word that all men love—
Or for love's sake—a word that loves[5] all men—
Or for men's sake—the authors of these women—
Or women's sake—by whom we men are men—
335 Let us once lose our oaths to find ourselves,[6]
Or else we lose ourselves to keep our oaths.
It is religion to be thus forsworn,
For charity itself fulfils the law,[7]
And who can sever love from charity?

340 KING   Saint Cupid, then, and, soldiers, to the field!

BIRON   Advance your standards,° and upon them, lords.   *(with a sexual sense)*
Pell-mell, down with them; but be first advised
In conflict that you get the sun of them.[8]

LONGUEVILLE   Now to plain dealing. Lay these glozes° by.   *verbal sophistries*
345 Shall we resolve to woo these girls of France?

KING   And win them, too! Therefore let us devise
Some entertainment for them in their tents.

BIRON   First, from the park let us conduct them thither;
Then homeward every man attach° the hand   *seize*
350 Of his fair mistress. In the afternoon
We will with some strange° pastime solace them,   *novel*
Such as the shortness of the time can shape,
For revels, dances, masques, and merry hours
Forerun° fair love, strewing her way with flowers.   *Run before*

355 KING   Away, away, no time shall be omitted
That will be time,° and may by us be fitted.°   *long enough / used well*

BIRON   *Allons, allons!*° Sowed cockle reaped no corn,[9]   *Come on*
And justice always whirls in equal measure.°   *acts impartially*
Light° wenches may prove plagues to men forsworn.   *Frivolous*
360 If so, our copper buys° no better treasure.   [*Exeunt*]   *base coin deserves*

5.1

Enter [HOLOFERNES] *the pedant,* [NATHANIEL] *the
curate, and* [Anthony] DULL

HOLOFERNES   *Satis quid sufficit.*[1]

NATHANIEL   I praise God for you, sir. Your reasons° at dinner   *discourses*
have been sharp and sententious, pleasant without scurrility,
witty without affection,° audacious without impudency,   *affectation*
5 learned without opinion,° and strange° without heresy. I did   *arrogance / original*
converse this quondam day° with a companion of the King's   *the other day*
who is intituled, nominated, or called Don Adriano de
Armado.

HOLOFERNES   *Novi hominum tanquam te.*[2] His humour° is lofty,   *temperament*
10 his discourse peremptory,° his tongue filed,° his eye ambitious,   *overbearing / polished*
his gait majestical, and his general behaviour vain, ridiculous,

---

5. Meaning uncertain: is a friend to; values; pleases; inspires with love; is lovable to.
6. "For whosoever will save his life shall lose it: and whosoever will lose his life for my sake shall find it" (Matthew 16:25).
7. "He that loveth another hath fulfilled the law" (Romans 13:8). "Love worketh no ill to his neighbour: therefore is love the fulfilling of the law" (Romans 13:10).
8. Get the sun in their eyes (get the advantage); also, probably bawdy, playing on "beget the son."
9. Wheat ("corn") was never reaped where weeds

("cockle") were sown (proverbial): in other words, we won't get something for nothing; we must make an effort.
5.1 Location: The King's park.
1. Should be *Satis est quod sufficit:* Enough is enough, but recalling the English proverb "Enough is as good as a feast." The Latin in this scene, some of it inaccurate, again is translated only when the characters themselves fail to do so. Here, too, it is often unclear whether the error is the character's, the printer's, or Shakespeare's.
2. I know the man as well as I know you.

and thrasonical.³ He is too picked,° too spruce, too affected, *fastidious*
    too odd, as it were, too peregrinate,° as I may call it. *exotic*
NATHANIEL A most singular and choice epithet.
       Draw[s] out his table-book° *notebook*
15 HOLOFERNES He draweth out the thread of his verbosity finer
    than the staple of his argument.⁴ I abhor such fanatical phan-
    tasims,⁵ such insociable and point-device° companions, such *extremely precise*
    rackers of orthography⁶ as to speak 'dout', *sine*° 'b', when he *without*
    should say 'doubt'; 'det' when he should pronounce 'debt'—'d,
20   e, b, t', not 'd, e, t'. He clepeth° a calf 'cauf', half 'hauf', *calls*
    neighbour *vocatur*° 'nebour'—'neigh' abbreviated 'ne'. This is *is called*
    abhominable—which he would call 'abominable'. It insinu-
    ateth me of *insanire*⁷—*ne intelligis, domine?*⁸—to make frantic,
    lunatic.
25 NATHANIEL *Laus deo, bone intelligo.*⁹
  HOLOFERNES *Bone? Bon, fort bon*—Priscian a little scratched¹—
    'twill serve.
       Enter [ARMADO *the*] *braggart,* [MOTE *his*] *boy* [*and* COS-
       TARD *the clown*]
  NATHANIEL *Videsne quis venit?*° *Do you see who's coming?*
  HOLOFERNES *Video, et gaudio.*° *I see, and rejoice*
30 ARMADO [*to* MOTE] Chirrah.²
  HOLOFERNES [*to* NATHANIEL] *Quare*° 'chirrah', not 'sirrah'? *Why*
  ARMADO Men of peace, well encountered.
  HOLOFERNES Most military sir, salutation!
  MOTE [*aside to* COSTARD] They have been at a great feast of lan-
35   guages and stolen the scraps.
  COSTARD [*aside to* MOTE] O, they have lived long on the alms-
    basket³ of words. I marvel thy master hath not eaten thee for a
    word, for thou art not so long by the head as *honorificabilitu-*
    dinitatibus.⁴ Thou art easier swallowed than a flapdragon.⁵
40 MOTE [*aside to* COSTARD] Peace, the peal° begins. *jangling; babble*
  ARMADO [*to* HOLOFERNES] Monsieur, are you not lettered?° *learned; literate*
  MOTE Yes, yes, he teaches boys the horn-book.° What is 'a, b' *alphabet book*
    spelled backward, with the horn on his head?° *a cuckold*
  HOLOFERNES *Ba, pueritia,*° with a horn added. *child(ishness)*
45 MOTE *Ba*, most silly sheep, with a horn! You hear his learning.
  HOLOFERNES *Quis, quis,*° thou consonant?⁶ *Who*
  MOTE The last of the five vowels if you repeat them, or the
    fifth° if I. *"u"; you; ewe*
  HOLOFERNES I will repeat them: a, e, i—
50 MOTE The sheep.⁷ The other two concludes it: o, u.⁸

3. Boastful, bragging. From "Thraso," the braggart soldier in *Eunuchus*, by the Roman dramatist Terence.
4. He's wordy. (Unintentionally ironic, coming from
Holofernes; "staple" means "fiber," "argument" means
"subject matter.")
5. Extravagant, fantastic beings.
6. Tormentors of spelling. Holofernes speaks for those
educational theorists who urged, unsuccessfully, that
English words be spelled and pronounced like their
Latin roots.
7. Puts me in mind of madness; perhaps, drives me mad.
8. Don't you understand, master?
9. Praise God, I understand well.
1. Bone? Bon, fort bon: Well? Good, that's good
(French; ironical). *Priscian a little scratched:* imperfect
Latin (Priscian was a sixth-century Latin grammarian).
Holofernes is ridiculing Nathaniel's mistake of using

bone for *bene*.
2. Pseudo-Spanish or dialectal pronunciation of "Sirrah"; or garbled Greek for "Hail."
3. Basket in which the leftovers of a feast were collected for the poor.
4. Dative and ablative plural of a Latin word meaning
"honorableness," renowned for its length. *word:* "mote"
equals the French *mot*, which means "word."
5. A raisin floated on flaming brandy, which had to be
snapped up with the mouth and eaten in the game of
snapdragon.
6. Nonentity (because a consonant alone is soundless).
7. The Spanish for "sheep"—*oveja*, often spelled
oueia—seems to have been used as a device for memo-
rizing the vowels.
8. Proves what I say (or completes the list): oh, you.

ARMADO   Now by the salt° wave of the *Mediterraneum* a sweet   *salty; witty*
touch,° a quick venue° of wit; snip, snap, quick, and home.⁹ It   *hit / thrust*
rejoiceth my intellect—true wit.

MOTE   Offered by a child to an old man, which is 'wit-old'.¹

55   HOLOFERNES   What is the figure?° What is the figure?   *figure of speech*

MOTE   Horns.

HOLOFERNES   Thou disputes like an infant. Go whip thy gig.°   *spin your top*

MOTE   Lend me your horn to make one, and I will whip about
your infamy *circum circa*²—a gig of° a cuckold's horn.   *made of*

60   COSTARD   An° I had but one penny in the world, thou shouldst   *If*
have it to buy gingerbread. [*Giving money*] Hold, there is the
very remuneration I had of thy master, thou halfpenny° purse   *tiny*
of wit, thou pigeon-egg of discretion. O, an the heavens were
so pleased that thou wert but my bastard, what a joyful father

65   wouldst thou make me! Go to, thou hast it *ad dunghill,* at the
fingers' ends,° as they say.   *exactly; scatological*

HOLOFERNES   O, I smell false Latin—'*dunghill*' for *unguem.*°   *fingernail*

ARMADO   Arts-man, *preambulate.*³ We will be singled° from the   *separated*
barbarous. Do you not educate youth at the charge-house° on   *endowed school*

70   the top of the mountain?

HOLOFERNES   Or *mons*, the hill.

ARMADO   At your sweet pleasure, for the mountain.

HOLOFERNES   I do, sans° question.   *without*

ARMADO   Sir, it is the King's most sweet pleasure and affection°   *wish*

75   to congratulate° the Princess at her pavilion in the posteriors⁴   *greet*
of this day, which the rude multitude call the afternoon.

HOLOFERNES   The posterior of the day, most generous° sir, is lia-   *noble*
ble, congruent, and measurable° for the afternoon. The word   *suitable (synonyms)*
is well culled,⁵ choice, sweet, and apt, I do assure you, sir, I do

80   assure.

ARMADO   Sir, the King is a noble gentleman, and my familiar,° I   *close friend*
do assure ye, very good friend. For what is inward° between us,   *confidential*
let it pass. I do beseech thee, remember thy courtesy. I beseech
thee, apparel thy head.⁶ And, among other important and most

85   serious designs, and of great import indeed, too—but let that
pass,⁷ for I must tell thee it will please his grace, by the world,
sometime to lean upon my poor shoulder and with his royal
finger thus dally with my excrement,° with my mustachio. But,   *growth of hair; feces*
sweetheart, let that pass. By the world, I recount no fable. Some

90   certain special honours it pleaseth his greatness to impart to
Armado, a soldier, a man of travel, that hath seen the world.
But let that pass. The very all of all° is—but, sweetheart, I do   *sum of everything*
implore secrecy—that the King would have me present the
Princess—sweet chuck°—with some delightful ostentation,° or   *chick / spectacular show*

95   show, or pageant, or antic,° or firework. Now, understanding   *grotesque pageant*
that the curate and your sweet self are good at such eruptions°   *(scatological)*
and sudden breaking-out° of mirth, as it were, I have acquainted   *(scatological)*
you withal° to the end to crave your assistance.   *with it*

---

9. And to the target.
1. Mentally feeble; "wittol," a content cuckold.
2. Around and around.
3. Scholar, walk ahead, with a play on "arse."
4. End (temporal and anatomical).
5. With a play on "cul," French for backside.

6. *remember . . . head:* remember that you removed
your hat in courtesy (perhaps at line 33). I beseech you,
put it back on.
7. Suggestion of sodomy, developed in the repeated
phrase "but [butt] let that pass" (lines 85–86, 88–89,
92).

HOLOFERNES   Sir, you shall present before her the Nine Wor-
100 thies.⁸ Sir Nathaniel, as concerning some entertainment of°   *way of spending*
time, some show in the posterior of this day to be rendered by
our assistance, the King's command, and this most gallant,
illustrate,° and learned gentlemen before the Princess, I say   *illustrious*
none so fit as to present the Nine Worthies.

105 NATHANIEL   Where will you find men worthy enough to present
them?

HOLOFERNES   Joshua, yourself;⁹ myself, Judas Maccabeus; and
this gallant gentleman, Hector. This swain, because of his great
limb or joint, shall pass Pompey the Great;¹ the page, Hercules.

110 ARMADO   Pardon, sir, error! He is not quantity enough for that
Worthy's thumb. He is not so big as the end of his club.

HOLOFERNES   Shall I have audience?° He shall present Hercules   *attention*
in minority.° His enter° and exit shall be strangling a snake,²   *childhood / entrance*
and I will have an apology° for that purpose.   *explanatory speech*

115 MOTE   An excellent device! So, if any of the audience hiss, you
may cry 'Well done, Hercules, now thou crushest the snake!'—
that is the way to make an offence gracious, though few have
the grace to do it.

ARMADO   For the rest of the Worthies?

120 HOLOFERNES   I will play three myself.

MOTE   Thrice-worthy gentleman!

ARMADO   Shall I tell you a thing?

HOLOFERNES   We attend.°   *listen*

ARMADO   We will have, if this fadge° not, an antic. I beseech you,   *succeed*
125 follow.

HOLOFERNES   *Via,*° goodman Dull! Thou hast spoken no word   *Come on*
all this while.

DULL   Nor understood none neither, sir.

HOLOFERNES   *Allons!*° We will employ thee.   *Come on*

130 DULL   I'll make one° in a dance or so, or I will play on the tabor°   *join / small drum*
to the Worthies, and let them dance the hay.°   *reel*

HOLOFERNES   Most dull, honest Dull! To our sport, away.

Exeunt

5.2

Enter the [PRINCESS *and her*] *ladies* [ROSALINE, MARIA,
and CATHERINE]

PRINCESS   Sweethearts, we shall be rich ere we depart,
If fairings° come thus plentifully in.   *gifts*
A lady walled about with diamonds¹—
Look you what I have from the loving King.

5 ROSALINE   Madam, came nothing else along with that?

PRINCESS   Nothing but this?—yes, as much love in rhyme
As would be crammed up in a sheet of paper
Writ o' both sides the leaf, margin and all,
That he was fain to seal on Cupid's name.²

---

8. Famous conquerors often represented in folk plays
and pageants. Usually three pagans—Hector, Alexander,
Julius Caesar; three Jews—Joshua, David, Judas Maccabeus; and three Christians—Arthur, Charlemagne,
and Godfrey of Bouillon or Guy of Warwick. Of these,
only Alexander, Judas Maccabeus, and Hector appear in
the next scene; Shakespeare adds Pompey and Hercules.
9. In the event, Nathaniel plays Alexander.
1. *great . . . Great:* Costard's considerable size allows

him to "pass" for Pompey the Great, suggesting "penis"
through "limb" or "joint," and, through the jingle with
"pump" in "Pompey," both "penis" and "pudendum."
2. Hercules strangled two snakes sent by Juno to kill
him in his cradle.
5.2 Location: The ladies' lodgings in the King's park.
1. This describes the gift (a pendant or brooch).
2. So that he was obliged to obliterate Cupid's name
with his seal.

10	ROSALINE That was the way to make his godhead wax,°	grow; sealing wax
	For he hath been five thousand year° a boy.	(age of the world)
	CATHERINE Ay, and a shrewd unhappy gallows,[3] too.	
	ROSALINE You'll ne'er be friends with him, a° killed your sister.	he
	CATHERINE He made her melancholy, sad, and heavy,	
15	And so she died. Had she been light like you,	
	Of such a merry, nimble, stirring spirit,	
	She might ha' been a grandam ere she died;	
	And so may you, for a light heart lives long.	
	ROSALINE What's your dark° meaning, mouse, of this light°	covert / careless
	word?	
20	CATHERINE A light° condition in a beauty dark.	frivolous; wanton
	ROSALINE We need more light to find your meaning out.	
	CATHERINE You'll mar the light by taking it in snuff,[4]	
	Therefore I'll darkly end the argument.	
	ROSALINE Look what° you do, you do it still i'th' dark.°	whatever / (bawdy)
25	CATHERINE So do not you, for you are a light wench.	
	ROSALINE Indeed I weigh not° you, and therefore light.	weigh less than
	CATHERINE You weigh me not? O, that's you care not for me.	
	ROSALINE Great reason, for past care is still past cure.	
	PRINCESS Well bandied, both; a set of wit well played.	
30	But Rosaline, you have a favour,° too.	love token
	Who sent it? And what is it?	
	ROSALINE I would you knew.	
	An if my face were but as fair as yours	
	My favour° were as great, be witness this.	appearance
	Nay, I have verses, too, I thank Biron,	
35	The numbers° true, and were the numb'ring,° too,	meter / evaluation
	I were the fairest goddess on the ground.	
	I am compared to twenty thousand fairs.°	beauties
	O, he hath drawn my picture in his letter.	
	PRINCESS Anything like?	
40	ROSALINE Much in the letters,° nothing in the praise.	penmanship
	PRINCESS Beauteous as ink°—a good conclusion.	(that is, black)
	CATHERINE Fair as a text° B in a copy-book.	formally written black
	ROSALINE Ware pencils,[5] ho! Let me not die your debtor,°	I'll pay you back
	My red dominical,[6] my golden letter.[7]	
45	O, that your face were not so full of O's!°	pockmarks; pudendum
	PRINCESS A pox of that jest; I beshrew° all shrews.	wish mischief upon
	But Catherine, what was sent to you from fair Dumaine?	
	CATHERINE Madam, this glove.	
	PRINCESS Did he not send you twain?	
	CATHERINE Yes, madam; and moreover,	
50	Some thousand verses of a faithful lover.	
	A huge translation° of hypocrisy	expression
	Vilely compiled, profound simplicity.°	folly
	MARIA This° and these pearls to me sent Longueville.	(A chain)
	The letter is too long by half a mile.	
55	PRINCESS I think no less. Dost thou not wish in heart	
	The chain were longer and the letter short?	

3. Ill-natured, pernicious gallows bird, deserving to be hanged.
4. Taking it amiss; snuffing a candle.
5. Beware of introducing the subject of brushes (used for cosmetic purposes as well as for drawing portraits).

6. Red letter marking Sundays and feast days in an almanac; reference to Catherine's ruddy complexion.
7. Also used to mark Sunday; reference to Catherine's fair hair.

MARIA   Ay, or I would these hands might never part.[8]

PRINCESS   We are wise girls to mock our lovers so.

ROSALINE   They are worse fools to purchase mocking so.

60   That same Biron I'll torture ere I go.

O that I knew he were but in by th' week!°—   *permanently caught*

How I would make him fawn, and beg, and seek,

And wait the season, and observe the times,°   *dance attendance*

And spend his prodigal wits in bootless° rhymes,   *fruitless*

65   And shape his service wholly to my hests,°   *commands*

And make him proud to make me proud that jests![9]

So pursuivant°-like would I o'ersway his state   *arresting officer*

That he should be my fool, and I his fate.

PRINCESS   None are so surely caught when they are catched

70   As wit turned fool. Folly in wisdom hatched

Hath wisdom's warrant, and the help of school,

And wit's own grace, to grace a learnèd fool.

ROSALINE   The blood of youth burns not with such excess

As gravity's° revolt to wantonness.   *a wise person's*

75 MARIA   Folly in fools bears not so strong a note°   *stigma*

As fool'ry in the wise when wit doth dote,°   *act foolishly*

Since all the power thereof it doth apply

To prove, by wit, worth in simplicity.°   *folly*

      Enter BOYET

PRINCESS   Here comes Boyet, and mirth is in his face.

80 BOYET   O, I am stabbed with laughter! Where's her grace?

PRINCESS   Thy news, Boyet?

BOYET   Prepare, madam, prepare.

Arm, wenches, arm. Encounters mounted are°   *An attack is prepared*

Against your peace. Love doth approach disguised,

Armèd in arguments. You'll be surprised.[1]

85   Muster your wits, stand in your own defence,

Or hide your heads like cowards and fly hence.

PRINCESS   Saint Denis to Saint Cupid![2] What are they

That charge° their breath against us? Say, scout, say.   *level (a weapon)*

BOYET   Under the cool shade of a sycamore

90   I thought to close mine eyes some half an hour

When lo, to interrupt my purposed rest

Toward that shade I might behold addressed°   *I could see approaching*

The King and his companions. Warily

I stole into a neighbour thicket by

95   And overheard what you shall overhear:°   *hear over again*

That by and by disguised they will be here.

Their herald is a pretty knavish page

That well by heart hath conned his embassage.°   *learned his message*

Action and accent° did they teach him there.   *Gesture and intonation*

100   'Thus must thou speak', and 'thus thy body bear'.

And ever and anon they made a doubt°   *expressed fear*

Presence majestical would put him out,[3]

'For', quoth the King, 'an angel shalt thou see,

Yet fear not thou, but speak audaciously.'

8. Perhaps she has twisted the chain around them; or, she'd never separate her hands to give one hand in marriage to so ungenerous a man.

9. And be pleased to praise the one who mocks him; and be glad to be ridiculed.

1. Overcome by a surprise attack.

2. St. Denis (the patron saint of France) against St. Cupid.

3. Would make him forget his lines.

105   The boy replied, 'An angel is not evil.
       I should have feared her had she been a devil.'
       With that all laughed and clapped him on the shoulder,
       Making the bold wag by their praises bolder.
       One rubbed his elbow⁴ thus, and fleered,° and swore   *grinned*
110   A better speech was never spoke before.
       Another with his finger and his thumb°   (*snapping his fingers*)
       Cried '*Via*,° we will do't, come what will come!'   *Come on*
       The third he capered and cried 'All goes well!'
       The fourth turned on the toe° and down he fell.   *did a pirouette*
115   With that they all did tumble on the ground
       With such a zealous laughter, so profound,
       That in this spleen° ridiculous appears,   *fit (of laughter)*
       To check their folly, passion's solemn tears.
       PRINCESS   But what, but what—come they to visit us?
120   BOYET   They do, they do, and are apparelled thus
       [   ]⁵
       Like Muscovites or Russians, as I guess.
       Their purpose is to parley, to court and dance,
       And every one his love-suit will advance
125   Unto his several° mistress, which they'll know   *particular*
       By favours several which they did bestow.
       PRINCESS   And will they so? The gallants shall be tasked,°   *put to the test*
       For, ladies, we will every one be masked,
       And not a man of them shall have the grace,°   *luck*
130   Despite of suit,° to see a lady's face.⁶   *pleading; costume*
130.1   *Hold, Rosaline. This favour thou shalt wear,*
             And then the King willcourt thee for his dear.
       [*To* ROSALINE] Hold, take thou this, my sweet, and give me
             thine.
       So shall Biron take me for Rosaline.
             [*She changes favours with* ROSALINE]
             [*To* CATHERINE *and* MARIA]
       And change you favours, too. So shall your loves
       Woo contrary, deceived by these removes.°   *exchanges*
             [CATHERINE *and* MARIA *change favours*]
135   ROSALINE   Come on, then, wear the favours most in sight.°   *conspicuously*
       CATHERINE   But in this changing what is your intent?
       PRINCESS   The effect of my intent is to cross theirs.
       They do it but in mockery-merriment,°   *satirical mirth*
       And mock for mock is only my intent.
140   Their several counsels° they unbosom shall   *confidences*
       To loves mistook, and so be mocked withal
       Upon the next occasion that we meet
       With visages displayed to talk and greet.
       ROSALINE   But shall we dance if they desire us to't?
145   PRINCESS   No, to the death we will not move a foot,
       Nor to their penned speech render we no grace,
       But while 'tis spoke each turn away her face.
       BOYET   Why, that contempt will kill the speaker's heart,
       And quite divorce his memory from his part.

---

4. Sign of satisfaction.
5. Absence of a rhyme for "guess" and a referent for "thus" suggests that a line describing the lords' costumes has been lost.
6. The following two indented lines (130.1–130.2), spoken by the Princess, seem to represent a first draft of 5.2.131–32.

150 PRINCESS   Therefore I do it; and I make no doubt
       The rest will ne'er come in if he be out.[7]
       There's no such sport as sport by sport o'erthrown,
       To make theirs ours, and ours none but our own.
       So shall we stay, mocking intended game,
155   And they well mocked depart away with shame.
              Sound trumpet
       BOYET   The trumpet sounds, be masked, the masquers come.
              [*The ladies mask.*]
              Enter blackamoors with music;[8] the boy [MOTE] *with a*
              speech; the [KING *and his*] *lords, disguised* [*as Russians*]
       MOTE   All hail, the richest beauties on the earth!
       BIRON [*aside*]   Beauties no richer than rich taffeta.°   (*masks of taffeta*)
       MOTE   A holy parcel° of the fairest dames—   *party*
              The ladies turn their backs to him
160   That ever turned their—backs to mortal views.
       BIRON   'Their eyes', villain, 'their eyes'!
       MOTE   That ever turned their eyes to mortal views.
              Out . . .
       BOYET   True, out° indeed!   (*of his part*)
165   MOTE   Out of your favours, heavenly spirits, vouchsafe°   *be willing*
              Not to behold—
       BIRON   'Once to behold', rogue!
       MOTE   Once to behold with your sun-beamèd eyes—
              With your sun-beamèd eyes—
170   BOYET   They will not answer to that epithet.
              You were best call it 'daughter-beamèd' eyes.
       MOTE   They do not mark° me, and that brings me out.   *listen to*
       BIRON   Is this your perfectness?° Be gone, you rogue!   (*in saying your lines*)
              [*Exit* MOTE]
       ROSALINE [*as the Princess*][9]   What would these strangers?° Know   *foreigners*
              their minds, Boyet.
175   If they do speak our language, 'tis our will
       That some plain° man recount their purposes.   *plainspoken*
       Know what they would.
       BOYET   What would you with the Princess?
       BIRON   Nothing but peace and gentle visitation.°   *visiting*
       ROSALINE   What would they, say they?
180   BOYET   Nothing but peace and gentle visitation.
       ROSALINE   Why, that they have, and bid them so be gone.
       BOYET   She says you have it, and you may be gone.
       KING   Say to her we have measured° many miles   *paced*
              To tread a measure° with her on this grass.   *dance*
185   BOYET   They say that they have measured many a mile
              To tread a measure with you on this grass.
       ROSALINE   It is not so. Ask them how many inches
              Is in one mile. If they have measured many,
              The measure then of one is easily told.°   *counted*
190   BOYET   If to come hither you have measured miles,
              And many miles, the Princess bids you tell
              How many inches doth fill up one mile.

---

7. The rest of his prepared speech will be forgotten if
he's confused ("out" of his part).
8. Presumably nonspeaking musicians dressed as black
Africans to provide an exotic accompaniment (see

Introduction).
9. From here to line 229, Rosaline speaks as the
Princess.

BIRON   Tell her we measure them by weary steps.
BOYET   She hears herself.
ROSALINE   How many weary steps
195   Of many weary miles you have o'ergone
        Are numbered in the travel of one mile?
BIRON   We number nothing that we spend for you.
        Our duty is so rich, so infinite,
        That we may do it still° without account.°   *always / reckoning*
200   Vouchsafe to show the sunshine of your face
        That we, like savages, may worship it.
ROSALINE   My face is but a moon,¹ and clouded,° too.   *masked; dark*
KING   Blessed are clouds to do as such clouds do.
        Vouchsafe, bright moon, and these thy stars,° to shine,   *companions*
205   Those clouds removed, upon our watery eyne.°   *eyes*
ROSALINE   O vain petitioner, beg a greater matter.
        Thou now requests but moonshine in the water.°   *nothing*
KING   Then in our measure do but vouchsafe one change.²
        Thou bidd'st me beg; this begging is not strange.°   *odd; foreign*
ROSALINE   Play, music, then.
            [*Music plays*]³
210   Nay, you must do it soon.
        Not yet?—no dance! Thus change I like the moon.
KING   Will you not dance? How come you thus estranged?
ROSALINE   You took the moon at full, but now she's changed.
KING   Yet still she is the moon, and I the man.°   *(in the moon)*
215   [   ]⁴
        The music plays, vouchsafe some motion° to it.   *movement; response*
ROSALINE   Our ears vouchsafe it.
KING   But your legs should do it.
ROSALINE   Since you are strangers and come here by chance
        We'll not be nice.° Take hands. We will not dance.   *coy*
KING   Why take we hands, then?
220   ROSALINE   Only to part friends.
        Curtsy, sweethearts, and so the measure ends.
KING   More measure° of this measure, be not nice.   *A larger amount*
ROSALINE   We can afford no more at such a price.
KING   Price you yourselves. What buys your company?
ROSALINE   Your absence only.
225   KING   That can never be.
ROSALINE   Then cannot we be bought, and so adieu—
        Twice to your visor, and half once to you.⁵
KING   If you deny to dance, let's hold more chat.
ROSALINE   In private, then.
KING   I am best pleased with that.
            [*The* KING *and* ROSALINE *talk apart*]
        BIRON [*to the* PRINCESS, *taking her for Rosaline*]
230   White-handed mistress, one sweet word with thee.
PRINCESS   Honey and milk and sugar—there is three.
BIRON   Nay then, two treys,° an if you grow so nice°—   *threes (dice) / subtle*

---

1. Because it shines with a borrowed light.
2. Of the moon; of the figure in the dance, *measure*:
dance.
3. It is not certain whether the music should start here
or later.

4. A line rhyming with "man" seems to have dropped
out.
5. Perhaps: your masked ("visor") (double) face
deserves two farewells, but yourself less than one (for
behaving so foolishly).

Metheglin, wort, and malmsey°—well run, dice!   *three sweet drinks*
There's half-a-dozen sweets.

PRINCESS   Seventh sweet, adieu.

235   Since you can cog,° I'll play no more with you.   *cheat*

BIRON   One word in secret.

PRINCESS   Let it not be sweet.

BIRON   Thou griev'st my gall.°   *chafe my sore place*

PRINCESS   Gall°—bitter!   *Liver bile*

BIRON   Therefore meet.°   *fitting; let's meet?*

          [BIRON *and the* PRINCESS *talk apart*]

DUMAINE [*to* MARIA, *taking her for Catherine*]
     Will you vouchsafe with me to change a word?°   *exchange words*

MARIA   Name it.

DUMAINE   Fair lady—

MARIA   Say you so? Fair lord—
     Take that for° your 'fair lady'.   *in exchange for*

240   DUMAINE   Please it you,
     As much in private, and I'll bid adieu.

          [DUMAINE *and* MARIA *talk apart*]

CATHERINE   What, was your visor made without a tongue?[6]

LONGUEVILLE [*taking* CATHERINE *for Maria*]   I know the reason,
     lady, why you ask.

CATHERINE   O, for your reason! Quickly, sir, I long.

245   LONGUEVILLE   You have a double tongue within your mask,
     And would afford my speechless visor half.[7]

CATHERINE   'Veal', quoth the Dutchman. Is not veal a calf?[8]

LONGUEVILLE   A calf, fair lady?

CATHERINE   No, a fair lord calf.°   *dolt*

LONGUEVILLE   Let's part the word.°   *compromise*

CATHERINE   No, I'll not be your half.[9]

250   Take all and wean° it, it may prove an ox.[1]   *raise*

LONGUEVILLE   Look how you butt° yourself in these sharp mocks!   *attack*
     Will you give horns,[2] chaste lady? Do not so.

CATHERINE   Then die a calf before your horns do grow.

LONGUEVILLE   One word in private with you ere I die.°   *have an orgasm*

255   CATHERINE   Bleat softly, then. The butcher hears you cry.

          [LONGUEVILLE *and* CATHERINE *talk apart*]

BOYET   The tongues of mocking wenches are as keen
     As is the razor's edge invisible,
     Cutting a smaller hair than may be seen,
     Above the sense of sense; so sensible[3]

260   Seemeth their conference.° Their conceits° have wings   *conversation / fancies*
     Fleeter than arrows, bullets, wind, thought, swifter things.

ROSALINE   Not one word more, my maids. Break off, break off.

---

6. A projection within a mask permitting it to be held in place with the mouth. Catherine is also alluding to Longueville's silence.
7. *You . . . half:* You are double-tongued (masked; punning; deceptive; speaking enough for two) and ask about my silence because you'd be wise to give up half your speech by giving me one of the tongues (the one that keeps her mask on; this would reveal her identity).
8. *'Veal':* Well (ironic: Dutch pronunciation of "well" or German *viel,* meaning "much"; "Dutch" could mean "German"); veil (mask). Combined with Catherine's previous word, "long" (line 244), the result is "Longueville"—thus demonstrating that she knows the identity of her disguised suitor and had anticipated his "half" (line 246) by uttering half his name. *Veau,* French for "veal," does also mean "calf" (a dunce in Renaissance English).
9. Taking "part" as "divide": half of what you are the other half of; your better half (your wife); half of "calf" ("ca," for "Catherine").
1. Dolt; castrated male.
2. Butt with horns; equip with horns; cuckold.
3. *Above . . . sense:* Above the power of the senses to apprehend (perhaps with the ironic meaning of "nonsense"). *so sensible:* so acutely felt by the hearer.

BIRON   By heaven, all dry-beaten with pure scoff![4]
KING   Farewell, mad wenches, you have simple wits.
                        Exeunt [the KING, *lords, and blackamoors]*
                [*The ladies unmask*]
265   PRINCESS   Twenty adieus, my frozen Muscovites.
        Are these the breed of wits so wondered at?
        BOYET   Tapers they are, with your sweet breaths puffed out.
        ROSALINE   Well-liking° wits they have; gross, gross; fat, fat.   *Plump*
        PRINCESS   O poverty in wit, kingly-poor flout![5]
270   Will they not, think you, hang themselves tonight,
            Or ever but in visors show their faces?
        This pert Biron was out of count'nance° quite.   *disconcerted; masked*
        ROSALINE   Ah, they were all in lamentable cases.°   *states; outfits*
        The King was weeping-ripe for° a good word.[6]   *near tears for lack of*
275   PRINCESS   Biron did swear himself out of all suit.[7]
        MARIA   Dumaine was at my service, and his sword.
            'Non point,'° quoth I. My servant straight was mute.   *Not at all; it's blunt*
        CATHERINE   Lord Longueville said I came o'er his heart,
            And trow you° what he called me?   *can you believe*
        PRINCESS   'Qualm',[8] perhaps.
        CATHERINE   Yes, in good faith.
280   PRINCESS   Go, sickness as thou art.
        ROSALINE   Well, better wits have worn plain statute-caps.[9]
        But will you hear? The King is my love sworn.
        PRINCESS   And quick Biron hath plighted faith to me.
        CATHERINE   And Longueville was for my service born.
285   MARIA   Dumaine is mine, as sure as bark on tree.
        BOYET   Madam, and pretty mistresses, give ear.
            Immediately they will again be here
            In their own shapes,° for it can never be   *Undisguised*
            They will digest° this harsh indignity.   *accept*
        PRINCESS   Will they return?
290   BOYET   They will, they will, God knows,
            And leap for joy, though they are lame with blows.
            Therefore change favours, and when they repair,°   *return*
            Blow° like sweet roses in this summer air.   *Bloom*
        PRINCESS   How 'blow'? How 'blow'? Speak to be understood.
295   BOYET   Fair ladies masked are roses in their bud;
            Dismasked, their damask sweet commixture[1] shown,
            Are angels vailing° clouds, or roses blown.°   *letting fall / blooming*
        PRINCESS   Avaunt, perplexity!° What shall we do   *Be off, riddler*
            If they return in their own shapes to woo?
300   ROSALINE   Good madam, if by me you'll be advised,
            Let's mock them still, as well known[2] as disguised.
            Let us complain to them what fools were here,
            Disguised like Muscovites in shapeless gear,°   *ill-cut clothes*
            And wonder what they were, and to what end

---

4. Soundly beaten without bloodshed; battered by mocking words.
5. Reversed wordplay ("kingly-poor") on "well-li-king" (or like-king," line 268), criticizing Rosaline's "flout" (gibe) and perhaps the King's as well (line 264).
6. The beginning of a sixteen-line dialogue sonnet.
7. Avowed his passion—beyond all reason; out of character for his Russian "suit" (costume); in a mistaken "suit" at love (to the wrong woman).

8. Heartburn: perhaps punning on "came" (line 278) and picked up in "go" (line 280).
9. Cleverer people have been ordinary apprentices (whose headwear was regulated by statute); perhaps an allusion to fancy caps forming part of the lords' disguise.
1. Sweet red and white complexion.
2. Let's mock them just as much now that they are known for themselves.

305 Their shallow shows, and prologue vilely penned,
And their rough carriage° so ridiculous,   *awkward manner*
Should be presented at our tent to us.
BOYET   Ladies, withdraw. The gallants are at hand.
PRINCESS   Whip, to our tents, as roes° run over land!   *deer*

Exeunt [the ladies]

Enter the KING[, BIRON, DUMAINE, *and* LONGUEVILLE, *as themselves*]

310 KING   Fair sir, God save you. Where's the Princess?
BOYET   Gone to her tent. Please it your majesty
Command me any service to her thither?
KING   That she vouchsafe me audience for one word.
BOYET   I will, and so will she, I know, my lord.   *Exit*
315 BIRON   This fellow pecks up wit as pigeons peas,
And utters° it again when God doth please.   *speaks; sells*
He is wit's pedlar, and retails his wares
At wakes and wassails,° meetings, markets, fairs.   *festivals and revels*
And we that sell by gross,° the Lord doth know,   *wholesale*
320 Have not the grace to grace it with such show.
This gallant pins the wenches on his sleeve.°   *attracts all the girls*
Had he been Adam, he had° tempted Eve.   *would have*
A can carve³ too, and lisp,° why, this is he   *speak affectedly*
That kissed his hand away in courtesy.
325 This is the ape of form,° Monsieur the Nice,°   *good form / fastidious*
That when he plays at tables° chides the dice   *backgammon*
In honourable° terms. Nay, he can sing   *polite*
A mean most meanly,⁴ and in ushering°   *as a gentleman usher*
Mend° him who can. The ladies call him sweet.   *Improve on*
330 The stairs as he treads on them kiss his feet.
This is the flower that smiles on everyone
To show his teeth as white as whales' bone,°   *walrus ivory*
And consciences that will not die in debt
Pay him the due of 'honey-tongued' Boyet.
335 KING   A blister on his sweet tongue with my heart,
That put Armado's page out of his part!

Enter the ladies [and BOYET]

BIRON   See where it° comes. Behaviour,° what wert thou   *(Boyet) / Fine manners*
Till this madman° showed thee, and what art thou now?   *madcap*
KING   All hail, sweet madam, and fair time of day!
340 PRINCESS   'Fair' in 'all hail'° is foul, as I conceive.   *(as in "hailstorm")*
KING   Construe my speeches better, if you may.
PRINCESS   Then wish me better. I will give you leave.
KING   We came to visit you,⁵ and purpose now
To lead you to our court. Vouchsafe it, then.
345 PRINCESS   This field shall hold me, and so hold your vow.
Nor° God nor I delights in perjured men.   *Neither*
KING   Rebuke me not for that which you provoke.
The virtue° of your eye must break my oath.   *power*
PRINCESS   You nickname virtue.° 'Vice' you should have spoke,   *misname goodness*
350 For virtue's office° never breaks men's troth.   *action*
Now by my maiden honour, yet as pure
As the unsullied lily, I protest,

---

3. He can act with social grace, flirt.
4. *he . . . meanly:* he can sing an in-between vocal part (tenor or alto) in the appropriate way (make himself generally useful).
5. The beginning of another dialogue sonnet.

A world of torments though I should endure,
I would not yield to be your house's guest,
355 So much I hate a breaking cause° to be   *cause of breaking*
Of heavenly oaths, vowed with integrity.
KING   O, you have lived in desolation here,
    Unseen, unvisited, much to our shame.
PRINCESS   Not so, my lord. It is not so, I swear.
360   We have had pastimes here, and pleasant game.
    A mess of° Russians left us but of late.   *group of four*
KING   How, madam? Russians?
PRINCESS   Ay, in truth, my lord.
    Trim gallants, full of courtship and of state.
ROSALINE   Madam, speak true.—It is not so, my lord.
365   My lady, to the manner of the days,°   *in the present fashion*
    In courtesy gives undeserving praise.
    We four indeed confronted were with four
    In Russian habit. Here they stayed an hour,
    And talked apace, and in that hour, my lord,
370   They did not bless us with one happy° word.   *well-chosen*
    I dare not call them fools, but this I think:
    When they are thirsty, fools would fain have drink.
BIRON   This jest is dry° to me. Gentle sweet,   *barren (punningly)*
    Your wits makes wise things foolish. When we greet,
375   With eyes' best seeing, heaven's fiery eye,
    By light we lose light.[6] Your capacity
    Is of that nature that to° your huge store   *compared to*
    Wise things seem foolish, and rich things but poor.
ROSALINE   This proves you wise and rich, for in my eye—
380 BIRON   I am a fool, and full of poverty.
ROSALINE   But that you take what doth to you belong
    It were a fault to snatch words from my tongue.
BIRON   O, I am yours, and all that I possess.
ROSALINE   All the fool mine!
BIRON   I cannot give you less.
385 ROSALINE   Which of the visors was it that you wore?
BIRON   Where? When? What visor? Why demand° you this?   *ask*
ROSALINE   There, then, that visor, that superfluous case,°   *mask*
    That hid the worse and showed the better face.
KING [*aside to the lords*]   We were descried.° They'll mock us *uncovered*
    now, downright.
390 DUMAINE [*aside to the* KING]   Let us confess, and turn it to a jest.
PRINCESS   Amazed, my lord? Why looks your highness sad?
ROSALINE   Help, hold his° brows, he'll swoon. Why look you pale? *(Biron's)*
    Seasick, I think, coming from Muscovy.
BIRON   Thus pour the stars down plagues for perjury.
395   Can any face of brass° hold longer out?   *brazen shamelessness*
    Here stand I, lady. Dart thy skill at me—
    Bruise me with scorn, confound me with a flout,
    Thrust thy sharp wit quite through my ignorance,
    Cut me to pieces with thy keen conceit,°   *intelligence*
400   And I will wish° thee nevermore to dance,   *invite*
    Nor nevermore in Russian habit wait.°   *attend on you*
    O, never will I trust to speeches penned,[7]

---

6. When we gaze intently at the sun, we go blind.
7. The beginning of a sonnet (lines 402–15)—ironic,
    considering Biron's renunciation of literary effects.

Nor to the motion of a schoolboy's tongue,
Nor never come in visor to my friend,°   *sweetheart*
405   Nor woo in rhyme, like a blind harper's song.
Taffeta phrases, silken terms precise,
Three-piled° hyperboles, spruce affectation,   *Rich velvet; Elaborate*
Figures° pedantical—these summer flies   *(of speech)*
Have blown me full of maggot ostentation.°   *laid maggot eggs in me*
410   I do forswear them, and I here protest,
By this white glove—how white the hand, God knows!—
Henceforth my wooing mind shall be expressed
In russet° yeas, and honest kersey° noes.   *homely / plain*
And to begin, wench, so God help me, law!°   *indeed (humble oath)*
415   My love to thee is sound, sans° crack or flaw.   *without*
ROSALINE   Sans 'sans', I pray you.
BIRON   Yet° I have a trick°   *Still / touch*
Of the old rage.° Bear with me, I am sick.   *fever*
I'll leave it by degrees. Soft, let us see.
Write 'Lord have mercy on us'[8] on those three.°   *(his companions)*
420   They are infected, in their hearts it lies.
They have the plague, and caught it of your eyes.
These lords are visited,° you are not free;   *afflicted by plague*
For the Lord's tokens° on you do I see.   *favors; plague spots*
PRINCESS   No, they are free[9] that gave these tokens to us.
425   BIRON   Our states are forfeit.[1] Seek not to undo us.[2]
ROSALINE   It is not so, for how can this be true,
That you stand forfeit, being those that sue?°   *sue at law; beg; woo*
BIRON   Peace, for I will not have to do° with you.   *deal; copulate*
ROSALINE   Nor shall not, if I do as I intend.
430   BIRON [*to the lords*]   Speak for yourselves. My wit is at an end.
KING   Teach us, sweet madam, for our rude transgression
Some fair excuse.
PRINCESS   The fairest is confession.
Were not you here but even now disguised?
KING   Madam, I was.
PRINCESS   And were you well advised?°   *in your right mind*
KING   I was, fair madam.
435   PRINCESS   When you then were here,
What did you whisper in your lady's ear?
KING   That more than all the world I did respect° her.   *value*
PRINCESS   When she shall challenge° this, you will reject her.   *assert her claim to*
KING   Upon mine honour, no.
PRINCESS   Peace, peace, forbear.
440   Your oath once broke, you force not° to forswear.   *find it easy*
KING   Despise me when I break this oath of mine.
PRINCESS   I will, and therefore keep it. Rosaline,
What did the Russian whisper in your ear?
ROSALINE   Madam, he swore that he did hold me dear
445   As precious eyesight, and did value me
Above this world, adding thereto moreover
That he would wed me, or else die my lover.

8. A common inscription on the doors of plague-visited houses.
9. Generous; at liberty; free of love; free of obligation.
1. (Denying the Princess's claim in line 424 that the men are "free"): Our estates are subject to confiscation; our condition as bachelors is ended; because we're in love, we've lost power over ourselves; as would-be husbands, we owe you our estates; we've acted dishonorably.
2. Don't undo our forfeiture (don't ruin us) by calling us "free" (by rejecting our love).

PRINCESS   God give thee joy of him! The noble lord
Most honourably doth uphold his word.

450   KING   What mean you, madam? By my life, my troth,
I never swore this lady such an oath.

ROSALINE   By heaven, you did, and to confirm it plain,
You gave me this. But take it, sir, again.

KING   My faith and this the Princess I did give.

455   I knew her by this jewel on her sleeve.

PRINCESS   Pardon me, sir, *this* jewel did she wear,
And Lord Biron, I thank him, is my dear.
[*To* BIRON] What, will you have me, or your pearl again?

BIRON   Neither of either.° I remit° both twain.   *the two / surrender*
460   I see the trick on't.° Here was a consent,°   *of it / plot*
Knowing aforehand of our merriment,
To dash it like a Christmas comedy.
Some carry-tale, some please-man, some slight zany,
Some mumble-news, some trencher-knight, some Dick[3]
465   That smiles his cheek in years,° and knows the trick   *into wrinkles*
To make my lady laugh when she's disposed,
Told our intents before, which once disclosed,
The ladies did change favours, and then we,
Following the signs, wooed but the sign of she.°   *each mistress*
470   Now, to our perjury to add more terror,
We are again forsworn, in will° and error.°   *willfully / mistakenly*
Much upon this 'tis,[4] [*to* BOYET] and might not you
Forestall° our sport, to make us thus untrue?   *Have undermined*
Do not you know my lady's foot by th' square,[5]
475   And laugh upon the apple[6] of her eye,
And stand between her back, sir, and the fire,°   *keep the heat from her*
Holding a trencher,° jesting merrily?   *serving plate*
You put our page out. Go, you are allowed.°   *privileged (as a fool)*
Die when you will, a smock[7] shall be your shroud.
480   You leer° upon me, do you? There's an eye   *look malevolently at*
Wounds like a leaden sword.°   *harmless stage sword*

BOYET   Full merrily
Hath this brave manège, this career been run.

BIRON   Lo, he is tilting straight.[8] Peace, I have done.
       Enter [COSTARD *the*] *clown*
Welcome, pure wit. Thou partest a fair fray.

485   COSTARD   O Lord, sir, they would know
Whether the three Worthies shall come in or no.

BIRON   What, are there but three?

COSTARD   No, sir, but it is vara° fine,   *very*
For everyone pursents° three.   *(re)presents*

BIRON   And three times thrice is nine.

COSTARD   Not so, sir, under° correction, sir, I hope it is not so.   *subject to*
You cannot beg us,° sir. I can assure you, sir, we know what   *show we're fools*
490   we know.

---

3. *carry-tale:* talebearer. *please-man:* toady. *zany:* clownish, rustic servant in commedia dell'arte. *mumble-news:* gossip. *trencher-knight:* parasite, who dines from his lord's dish ("trencher") or who has a lordly appetite. *Dick:* low fellow.
4. It happened very much like this.
5. Know how to please your mistress. *square:* a carpenter's rule (Boyet "has her measure"); possible pun on "squire" (an "apple-squire" was a pimp; see "apple," line 475 and note).
6. Pupil. Boyet can wittily catch the Princess's eye; he is on intimate terms with her.
7. Woman's garment (either a charge of effeminacy or equivalent to "women will be the death of you").
8. Jousting (linguistically) at once. *manège* (line 482): feat of horsemanship. *career:* short gallop at full speed.

I hope, sir, three times thrice, sir—

BIRON   Is not nine?

COSTARD   Under correction, sir, we know whereuntil° it doth   *to what*
amount.

BIRON   By Jove, I always took three threes for nine.

495 COSTARD   O Lord, sir, it were pity you should get your living by
reck'ning,[9] sir.

BIRON   How much is it?

COSTARD   O Lord, sir, the parties themselves, the actors, sir, will
show whereuntil it doth amount. For mine own part, I am, as
500 they say, but to parfect° one man in one poor man, Pompion[1]   *present; perfect*
the Great, sir.

BIRON   Art thou one of the Worthies?

COSTARD   It pleased them to think me worthy of Pompey the
Great. For mine own part, I know not the degree° of the Wor-   *rank*
505 thy, but I am to stand for him.

BIRON   Go, bid them prepare.

COSTARD   We will turn it finely off, sir. We will take some care.
Exit

KING   Biron, they will shame us. Let them not approach.

BIRON   We are shame-proof, my lord, and 'tis some policy°   *clever strategy*
510 To have one show worse than the King's and his company.

KING   I say they shall not come.

PRINCESS   Nay, my good lord, let me o'errule you now.
That sport best pleases that doth least know how.
Where zeal strives to content, and the contents
515 Dies in the zeal of that which it presents,[2]
There form confounded makes most form in mirth,[3]
When great things labouring° perish in their birth.   *(to be born)*

BIRON   A right description of our sport,° my lord.   *(the Russian masque)*
Enter [ARMADO the] braggart

ARMADO [to the KING]   Anointed, I implore so much expense of
520 thy royal sweet breath as will utter a brace° of words.   *pair*
[ARMADO *and the* KING *speak apart*]

PRINCESS   Doth this man serve God?

BIRON   Why ask you?

PRINCESS   A° speaks not like a man of God his° making.   *He / (God's)*

ARMADO   That is all one, my fair sweet honey monarch,° for, I   *King or Princess?*
525 protest, the schoolmaster is exceeding fantastical, too-too vain,
too-too vain. But we will put it, as they say, to *fortuna de la*
guerra.° I wish you the peace of mind, most royal couplement.   *the fortune of war*
Exit

KING   Here is like to be a good presence of Worthies. He pres-
ents Hector of Troy, the swain Pompey the Great, the parish-
530 curate Alexander, Armado's page Hercules, the pedant Judas
Maccabeus,
And if these four Worthies in their first show thrive,
These four will change habits° and present the other five.   *costumes*

BIRON   There is five in the first show.

535 KING   You are deceived, 'tis not so.

BIRON   The pedant, the braggart, the hedge-priest,° the fool,   *illiterate priest*
and the boy,

9. It would be a shame if you had to earn your living by
arithmetic.
1. Pumpkin (blunder for "Pompey").

2. *and . . . presents*: and the enthusiasm of those who
present the play is fatal to the substance.
3. Artistry defeated produces the greatest comic effect.

Abate throw at novum[4] and the whole world again
Cannot pick out five such, take each one in his vein.°   *characteristic manner*
KING   The ship is under sail, and here she comes amain.°   *at full speed*
     Enter [COSTARD *the clown as*] *Pompey*

540   COSTARD [*as Pompey*]   I Pompey am—
BIRON   You lie, you are not he.
COSTARD [*as Pompey*]   I Pompey am—
BOYET   With leopard's head on knee.[5]
BIRON   Well said, old mocker. I must needs be friends with thee.
COSTARD [*as Pompey*]   I Pompey am, Pompey surnamed the Big.°   *(sexual)*
DUMAINE   'The Great'.
545   COSTARD   It is 'Great', sir—
     [*As Pompey*] Pompey surnamed the Great,
     That oft in field with targe° and shield did make my foe to sweat,[6]   *shield*
     And travelling along this coast I here am come by chance,
     And lay my arms before the legs° of this sweet lass of France.—   *(bawdy)*
550   If your ladyship would say 'Thanks, Pompey', I had done.
PRINCESS[7]   Great thanks, great Pompey.
COSTARD   'Tis not so much worth, but I hope I was perfect.° I   *I recited correctly*
     made a little fault in 'great'.
BIRON   My hat to a halfpenny° Pompey proves the best Worthy.   *I'll bet anything*
     [COSTARD *stands aside*.]
     Enter [NATHANIEL *the*] *curate* [*as*] *Alexander*
NATHANIEL [*as Alexander*]   When in the world I lived I was the
555   world's commander.
     By east, west, north, and south, I spread my conquering
         might.
     My scutcheon° plain° declares that I am Alisander.   *coat of arms / clearly*
BOYET   Your nose says no, you are not, for it stands too right.[8]
BIRON [*to* BOYET]   Your nose smells 'no'[9] in this, most tender-
     smelling° knight.   *sensitive-to-smell*
560   PRINCESS   The conqueror is dismayed. Proceed, good Alexander.
NATHANIEL [*as Alexander*]   When in the world I lived I was the
     world's commander.
BOYET   Most true, 'tis right, you were so, Alisander.
BIRON [*to* COSTARD]   Pompey the Great.
COSTARD   Your servant, and Costard.
565   BIRON   Take away the conqueror, take away Alisander.
COSTARD [*to* NATHANIEL]   O, sir, you have overthrown Alisander
     the Conqueror. You will be scraped out of the painted cloth[1]
     for this. Your lion that holds his pole-axe sitting on a close-stool
     will be given to Ajax.[2] He will be the ninth Worthy. A con-
570   queror and afeard to speak? Run away for shame, Alisander.
     Exit [NATHANIEL *the*] *curate*
There, an't° shall please you, a foolish mild man, an honest   *if it*
man, look you, and soon dashed. He is a marvellous good

---

4. Barring a lucky chance in the dice game of novum (in which the main throws were five and nine—like the five actors playing the Nine Worthies).
5. Embossed either on the knee piece of his armor or on his shield, which he might then be holding upside down.
6. The first of three lines in fourteeners (14-syllable lines)—an archaic meter by the 1590s, like most of those used by the nonaristocratic characters.
7. Q gives the line to "Lady": perhaps Costard kneels to the wrong woman.
8. Straight (alluding to Alexander's reputed crooked neck).

9. Implying that Nathaniel smells bad; according to the Greek biographer Plutarch, Alexander was reputed to have "a marvellous good savour" (Thomas North's translation).
1. Referring to the practice of representing the Worthies on wall hangings.
2. Alexander's arms, which showed a lion holding a battle-ax (or penis) and seated (a "close-stool" is a toilet), will be given to another warrior, Ajax (punning on "a jakes," a toilet), a Greek hero from the Trojan War who coveted the armor of Achilles. See 4.3.6 and note.

neighbour, faith, and a very good bowler, but for Alisander—
alas, you see how 'tis—a little o'erparted.° But there are Wor-   *given too hard a role*
575 thies a-coming will speak their mind in some other sort.
PRINCESS   Stand aside, good Pompey.

*Enter [HOLOFERNES the] pedant [as] Judas, and the boy
[MOTE as] Hercules*

HOLOFERNES   Great Hercules is presented by this imp,°   *child*
Whose club killed Cerberus, that three-headed *canus*,[3]
And when he was a babe, a child, a shrimp,
580 Thus did he strangle serpents in his *manus*.°   *hands; (play on "anus")*
Quoniam° he seemeth in minority,°   *Since / a child*
Ergo° I come with this apology.   *Therefore*
[*To* MOTE] Keep some state° in thy exit, and vanish.   *dignity*

Exit [MOTE]

HOLOFERNES [*as Judas*]   Judas I am—
585 DUMAINE   A Judas?
HOLOFERNES   Not Iscariot, sir.
[*As Judas*] Judas I am, yclept° Maccabeus.   *named*
DUMAINE   Judas Maccabeus clipped° is plain Judas.   *shortened; circumcised*
BIRON   A kissing traitor.[4] How art thou proved Judas?
590 HOLOFERNES [*as Judas*]   Judas I am—
DUMAINE   The more shame for you, Judas.
HOLOFERNES   What mean you, sir?
BOYET   To make Judas hang himself.
HOLOFERNES   Begin,° sir. You are my elder.   *You go first*
595 BIRON   Well followed—Judas was hanged on an elder.°   *(tree)*
HOLOFERNES   I will not be put out of countenance.°   *be upset*
BIRON   Because thou hast no face.°   *countenance*
HOLOFERNES   What is this?[5]
BOYET   A cittern-head.°   *guitar*
600 DUMAINE   The head of a bodkin.°   *hairpin; small dagger*
BIRON   A death's face° in a ring.   *death's head*
LONGUEVILLE   The face of an old Roman coin, scarce seen.°   *worn down*
BOYET   The pommel° of Caesar's falchion.°   *handle / sword*
DUMAINE   The carved-bone face on a flask.°   *gunpowder horn*
605 BIRON   Saint George's half-cheek° in a brooch.   *profile*
DUMAINE   Ay, and in a brooch of lead.°   *(indicating low rank)*
BIRON   Ay, and worn in the cap of a tooth-drawer.[6] And now for-
ward, for we have put thee in countenance.°   *depicted you*
HOLOFERNES   You have put me out of countenance.
610 BIRON   False, we have given thee faces.
HOLOFERNES   But you have outfaced° them all.   *mocked*
BIRON   An thou wert a lion, we would do so.
BOYET   Therefore, as he is an ass,[7] let him go.
And so adieu, sweet Jude. Nay, why dost thou stay?
615 DUMAINE   For the latter end of his name.
BIRON   For the ass to the Jude. Give it him. Jud-as, away.[8]
HOLOFERNES   This is not generous,° not gentle,° not humble.°   *noble / courteous / kind*
BOYET   A light for Monsieur Judas. It grows dark, he may stumble.

[*Exit* HOLOFERNES]

---

3. In classical mythology, the three-headed watchdog ("canis") of Hades.
4. Alluding to the kiss with which Judas Iscariot betrayed Jesus, with a pun on "clipped" (embraced, kissed), itself punning on "yclept."
5. Indicating his face. The replies refer to ornamental faces on objects.

6. Worn by a lowly dentist as a sign of his trade.
7. An ass disguises himself as a lion in one of Aesop's tables—only to have his own nature undo him. "Ass" in the sense of "backside" is punningly evoked by "end" (line 615).
8. As, in "Jud-as," is "the latter end of his name" (line 615), but "end" also means "ass."

PRINCESS Alas, poor Maccabeus, how hath he been baited!

Enter [ARMADO *the*] *braggart* [*as Hector*]

620 BIRON Hide thy head, Achilles,⁹ here comes Hector in arms.

DUMAINE Though my mocks come home by° me, I will now be   *later rebound on*
merry.

KING Hector was but a Trojan¹ in respect of° this.   *in comparison with*

BOYET But is this Hector?

625 KING I think Hector was not so clean-timbered.°   *well built*

LONGUEVILLE His leg is too big for Hector's.

DUMAINE More calf,° certain.   *part of the leg; fool*

BOYET No, he is best endowed in the small.°   *leg below the calf*

BIRON This cannot be Hector.

630 DUMAINE He's a god, or a painter, for he makes faces.°   *grimaces; creates life*

ARMADO [*as Hector*] The armipotent° Mars, of lances the   *powerful in arms*
almighty,
Gave Hector a gift—

DUMAINE A gilt nutmeg.²

BIRON A lemon.

635 LONGUEVILLE Stuck with cloves.

DUMAINE No, cloven.

ARMADO Peace!
[*As Hector*] The armipotent Mars, of lances the almighty,
Gave Hector a gift, the heir of Ilion,°   *Troy*

640 A man so breathèd° that certain he would fight, yea,   *fit*
From morn till night, out of his pavilion.°   *jousting tent*
I am that flower—

DUMAINE   That mint.

LONGUEVILLE   That colombine.

ARMADO Sweet Lord Longueville, rein thy tongue.

LONGUEVILLE I must rather give it the rein, for it runs° against   *jousts; races; speaks*

645 Hector.

DUMAINE Ay, and Hector's a greyhound.³

ARMADO The sweet war-man is dead and rotten. Sweet chucks,
beat not the bones of the buried. When he breathed he was a
man. But I will forward with my device.° [*To the* PRINCESS]   *performance*

650 Sweet royalty, bestow on me the sense of hearing.

BIRON *steps forth*

PRINCESS Speak, brave Hector, we are much delighted.

ARMADO I do adore thy sweet grace's slipper.

BOYET Loves her by the foot.

DUMAINE He may not by the yard.°   *penis (slang)*

655 ARMADO [*as Hector*] This Hector far surmounted Hannibal.⁴
[   ]⁵

ARMADO The party is gone.°   *Hector is dead*

COSTARD Fellow Hector, she is gone, she is two months on her
way.⁶

---

9. Leading Greek hero in the Trojan War; Hector's
chief opponent and slayer in Homer, but his inferior
and a coward in *Troilus and Cressida.*
1. An ordinary guy (slang).
2. A nutmeg glazed with egg yolk, used, like "lemon"
and "cloves" (lines 634, 635), to flavor drinks. A common lover's gift, the "gilt nutmeg" may also allude to
Armado's makeup. "Lemon" perhaps puns on "leman"
(lover, sweetheart), in which case "cloven" (line 636)
would have a sexual innuendo.
3. Famous as a runner; "Hector" was a common name
for a greyhound.

4. Surpassed Hannibal, leader of Carthage against
Rome (with the unintentional homosexual innuendo of
"surmounted").
5. An interjection may be missing here.
6. Jaquenetta is two months pregnant. Since at most only
a few days seem to have passed in the aristocratic plot, it
is possible to infer that Costard is the actual father; but
this may be an example of Shakespearean double time.
The stage direction "Biron steps forth" following line 650
may indicate that he urges Costard to make this declaration. Alternatively, he may merely be trying to prevent
Armado from speaking, an effort the Princess thwarts.

660 ARMADO What meanest thou?

COSTARD Faith, unless you play the honest Trojan the poor
wench is cast away. She's quick.° The child brags in her belly   *pregnant*
already. 'Tis yours.°   *(because it brags)*

ARMADO Dost thou infamonize° me among potentates? Thou   *defame (a coinage)*
665 shalt die.

COSTARD Then° shall Hector be whipped for Jaquenetta that is   *In that case*
quick by him, and hanged for Pompey that is dead by him.⁷

DUMAINE Most rare Pompey!

BOYET Renowned Pompey!

670 BIRON Greater than great—great, great, great Pompey, Pompey
the Huge.°   *(bawdy)*

DUMAINE Hector trembles.

BIRON Pompey is moved. More Ates,° more Ates—stir them on,   *goddess of discord*
stir them on!

675 DUMAINE Hector will challenge him.

BIRON Ay, if a° have no more man's blood in his belly than will   *he*
sup° a flea.   *feed*

ARMADO By the North Pole, I do challenge thee.

COSTARD I will not fight with a pole, like a northern° man. I'll   *an uncivilized (Scot)*
680 slash, I'll do it by the sword. I bepray you, let me borrow my
arms° again.   *(from the Princess)*

DUMAINE Room for the incensed Worthies.

COSTARD I'll do it in my shirt.

DUMAINE Most resolute Pompey.

685 MOTE [*aside to* ARMADO] Master, let me take you a button-hole
lower.⁸ Do you not see Pompey is uncasing° for the combat?   *undressing*
What mean you? You will lose your reputation.

ARMADO Gentlemen and soldiers, pardon me. I will not combat
in my shirt.

690 DUMAINE You may not deny it, Pompey hath made the challenge.

ARMADO Sweet bloods,° I both may and will.   *men of fiery spirit*

BIRON What reason have you for't?

ARMADO The naked truth of it is, I have no shirt. I go woolward
695 for penance.⁹

MOTE True, and it was enjoined him in Rome° for want of   *center of Catholicism*
linen, since when I'll be sworn he wore none but a dish-clout°   *dishcloth*
of Jaquenetta's, and that a wears next his heart, for a favour.

Enter a messenger, Monsieur MERCADÉ¹

MERCADÉ God save you, madam.

PRINCESS   Welcome, Mercadé,
700 But that thou interrupt'st our merriment.

MERCADÉ I am sorry, madam, for the news I bring
Is heavy in my tongue. The King your father—

PRINCESS Dead, for° my life.   *upon*

MERCADÉ   Even so. My tale is told.

BIRON Worthies, away. The scene begins to cloud.

705 ARMADO For mine own part, I breathe free breath. I have seen

---

7. Whom Armado has killed; whose hopes of Jaquenetta Armado has killed.
8. Help you to take off your doublet; take you down a
peg or two; (both proverbial).
9. He has no linen between his wool outer garments

and his skin—a form of Catholic self-punishment.
1. Possibly Mercury, the classical messenger of the
gods and guide of souls to the underworld; perhaps also
Mar-Arcadia, a reminder that death enters even the
pastoral, Arcadian world of Navarre's park.

the day of wrong through the little hole of discretion, and I will
right myself like a soldier.[2]   *Exeunt Worthies*

KING   How fares your majesty?°   *(her new title)*

QUEEN   Boyet, prepare. I will away tonight.

710 KING Madam, not so, I do beseech you stay.

QUEEN   Prepare, I say. I thank you, gracious lords,
For all your fair endeavours, and entreat,
Out of a new-sad soul, that you vouchsafe
In your rich wisdom to excuse or hide°   *overlook*
715 The liberal° opposition of our spirits.   *unrestrained*
If overboldly we have borne ourselves
In the converse of breath,° your gentleness°   *conversation / courtesy*
Was guilty of it. Farewell, worthy lord.
A heavy heart bears not a nimble tongue.
720 Excuse me so coming too short of thanks,
For my great suit so easily obtained.[3]

KING   The extreme parts of time extremely forms
All causes to the purpose of his speed,[4]
And often at his very loose° decides   *the last moment*
725 That which long process could not arbitrate.
And though the mourning brow of progeny
Forbid the smiling courtesy of love
The holy suit which fain it would convince,°   *give proof of*
Yet since love's argument was first° on foot,   *already*
730 Let not the cloud of sorrow jostle it
From what it purposed, since to wail friends lost
Is not by much so wholesome-profitable
As to rejoice at friends but newly found.

QUEEN   I understand you not. My griefs are double.[5]

735 BIRON Honest plain words best pierce the ear of grief,
And by these badges° understand the King.   *signs; words*
For your fair sakes have we neglected time,
Played foul play with our oaths. Your beauty, ladies,
Hath much deformed us, fashioning our humours
740 Even to the opposèd end of our intents,[6]
And what in us hath seemed ridiculous—
As love is full of unbefitting strains,°   *impulses*
All wanton° as a child, skipping and vain,   *careless*
Formed by the eye and therefore like the eye,
745 Full of strange shapes, of habits and of forms,
Varying in subjects as the eye doth roll
To every varied object in his glance;
Which parti-coated° presence of loose° love   *foolish / unrestrained*
Put on by us, if in your heavenly eyes
750 Have misbecomed° our oaths and gravities,   *been unbecoming to*
Those heavenly eyes that look into these faults
Suggested° us to make them. Therefore, ladies,   *Tempted*
Our love being yours, the error that love makes
Is likewise yours. We to ourselves prove false
755 By being once false for ever to be true

---

2. I have enough sense to acknowledge my wrongdoing
and will honorably put myself in the right.

3. Even though there is no mention of the suit after
2.1, we must assume that it was settled.

4. *The extreme . . . speed:* Final moments enforce rapid

decisions.

5. Doubled because I cannot understand you.

6. *fashioning . . . intents:* distorting our behavior into
the opposite of what we intended.

To those that make us both—fair ladies, you.
And even that falsehood, in itself a sin,
Thus purifies itself and turns to grace.
QUEEN   We have received your letters full of love,
760   Your favours the ambassadors of love,
And in our maiden council rated them
At° courtship, pleasant jest, and courtesy,   *As*
As bombast[7] and as lining to the time.
But more devout° than this in our respects°   *serious / consideration*
765   Have we not been, and therefore met your loves
In their own fashion, like a merriment.
DUMAINE   Our letters, madam, showed much more than jest.
LONGUEVILLE   So did our looks.
ROSALINE   We did not quote° them so.   *interpret*
KING   Now, at the latest minute of the hour,
Grant us your loves.
770   QUEEN   A time, methinks, too short
To make a world-without-end° bargain in.   *an everlasting (biblical)*
No, no, my lord, your grace is perjured much,
Full of dear° guiltiness, and therefore this: *grievous; precious*
If for my love—as there is no such cause[8]—
775   You will do aught,° this shall you do for me: *anything*
Your oath I will not trust, but go with speed
To some forlorn and naked hermitage
Remote from all the pleasures of the world.
There stay until the twelve celestial signs°   *(of the zodiac)*
780   Have brought about the annual reckoning.
If this austere, insociable life
Change not your offer made in heat of blood;
If frosts and fasts, hard lodging and thin weeds°   *clothes*
Nip not the gaudy blossoms of your love,
785   But that it bear this trial and last° love,   *remain*
Then at the expiration of the year
Come challenge° me, challenge me by these deserts,   *claim*
And, by this virgin palm now kissing thine,
I will be thine, and till that instance° shut   *instant*
790   My woeful self up in a mourning house,
Raining the tears of lamentation
For the remembrance of my father's death.
If this thou do deny, let our hands part,
Neither entitled in the other's heart.
795   KING   If this, or more than this, I would deny,
To flatter up° these powers of mine with rest   *pamper*
The sudden hand of death close up mine eye.
Hence, hermit,° then. My heart is in thy breast.[9]   *I'm off to be a hermit*
[*They talk apart*]
798.1   BIRON   *And what to me, my love? And what to me?*
ROSALINE   *You must be purgèd, too. Your sins are rank.*
You are attaint° with faults and perjury.   *dishonored; infected*
Therefore if you my favour mean to get
798.5   *A twelvemonth shall you spend, and never rest*
But seek the weary beds of people sick.

7. Wool stuffing for clothes; inflated rhetoric.   9. The following six indented lines (798.1–798.6) rep-
8. No reason why you should feel obliged to do so.   resent a draft version of 5.2.814–31.

DUMAINE [*to* CATHERINE]   But what to me, my love? But what
     to me?
800   A wife?
CATHERINE   A beard,[1] fair health, and honesty.
     With three-fold love I wish you all these three.
DUMAINE   O, shall I say 'I thank you, gentle wife'?
CATHERINE   Not so, my lord. A twelvemonth and a day
805   I'll mark no words that smooth-faced wooers say.
     Come when the King doth to my lady come;
     Then if I have much love, I'll give you some.
DUMAINE   I'll serve thee true and faithfully till then.
CATHERINE   Yet swear not, lest ye be forsworn again.
     [*They talk apart*]
LONGUEVILLE   What says Maria?
810   MARIA   At the twelvemonth's end
     I'll change my black gown for a faithful friend.°   *lover*
LONGUEVILLE   I'll stay° with patience; but the time is long.   *wait*
MARIA   The liker you—few taller are so young.[2]
     [*They talk apart*]
BIRON [*to* ROSALINE]   Studies my lady?° Mistress, look on me.   *Are you preoccupied*
815   Behold the window of my heart, mine eye,
     What humble suit attends° thy answer there.   *waits for*
     Impose some service on me for thy love.
ROSALINE   Oft have I heard of you, my lord Biron,
     Before I saw you; and the world's large tongue
820   Proclaims you for a man replete with mocks,
     Full of comparisons° and wounding flouts,   *satirical similes*
     Which you on all estates° will execute   *classes of people*
     That lie within the mercy of your wit.
     To weed this wormwood° from your fruitful brain,   *bitterness*
825   And therewithal to win me if you please,
     Without the which I am not to be won,
     You shall this twelvemonth term from day to day
     Visit the speechless sick and still converse°   *always associate*
     With groaning wretches, and your task shall be
830   With all the fierce° endeavour of your wit   *forceful*
     To enforce the painèd impotent° to smile.   *sick*
BIRON   To move wild laughter in the throat of death?—
     It cannot be, it is impossible.
     Mirth cannot move a soul in agony.
835   ROSALINE   Why, that's the way to choke a gibing spirit,
     Whose influence is begot of that loose grace°   *uncritical acceptance*
     Which shallow laughing hearers give to fools.
     A jest's prosperity lies in the ear
     Of him that hears it, never in the tongue
840   Of him that makes it. Then if sickly ears,
     Deafed with the clamours of their own dear groans,
     Will hear your idle scorns, continue then,
     And I will have you and that fault withal.°   *as well*
     But if they will not, throw away that spirit,
845   And I shall find you empty of that fault,
     Right joyful of your reformation.

---

1. Implying that he looks immature; perhaps also that
as a hermit he'll grow a beard.

2. The more like you—although tall ("long"), you are
still young.

BIRON   A twelvemonth? Well, befall what will befall,
    I'll jest a twelvemonth in an hospital.

QUEEN [*to the* KING]   Ay, sweet my lord, and so I take my leave.

850   KING   No, madam, we will bring° you on your way.   *escort*

BIRON   Our wooing doth not end like an old play.
    Jack hath not Jill. These ladies' courtesy
    Might well have made our sport a comedy.

KING   Come, sir, it wants° a twelvemonth an' a day,   *lacks*
    And then 'twill end.

855   BIRON   That's too long for a play.

        Enter [ARMADO *the*] *braggart*

ARMADO [*to the* KING]   Sweet majesty, vouchsafe me.

QUEEN   Was not that Hector?

DUMAINE   The worthy knight of Troy.

ARMADO   I will kiss thy royal finger and take leave.
860   I am a votary, I have vowed to Jaquenetta
    To hold the plough° for her sweet love three year. But, most   *To farm (bawdy)*
    esteemed greatness, will you hear the dialogue° that the two   *debate*
    learned men[3] have compiled in praise of the owl and the
    cuckoo? It should have followed in the end of our show.

865   KING   Call them forth quickly, we will do so.

ARMADO   Holla, approach!

        Enter [HOLOFERNES, NATHANIEL, COSTARD, MOTE, DULL,
        JAQUENETTA, *and others*]
                        This side is Hiems, winter,
    This Ver, the spring, the one maintained° by the owl,   *supported*
    The other by the cuckoo. Ver, begin.

SPRING [*sings*]
        When daisies pied° and violets blue,[4]   *multicolored*
870   And lady-smocks° all silver-white,   *cuckoo flowers*
        And cuckoo-buds° of yellow hue   *buttercups?*
            Do paint the meadows with delight,
        The cuckoo then on every tree
        Mocks married men, for thus sings he:
875   Cuckoo!
        Cuckoo, cuckoo—O word of fear,[5]
        Unpleasing to a married ear.
        When shepherds pipe on oaten straws,
            And merry larks are ploughmen's clocks;
880   When turtles tread,° and rooks and daws,   *turtledoves mate*
            And maidens bleach their summer smocks,
        The cuckoo then on every tree
        Mocks married men, for thus sings he:
            Cuckoo!
885   Cuckoo, cuckoo—O word of fear,
        Unpleasing to a married ear.

WINTER [*sings*]
        When icicles hang by the wall,
            And Dick the shepherd blows his nail,[6]
        And Tom bears logs into the hall,
890   And milk comes frozen home in pail;
        When blood is nipped,° and ways° be foul,   *chilled / pathways*

---

3. Holofernes and Nathaniel(?)
4. The dialogue is in iambic tetrameter, a song meter.
5. Because it sounds like "cuckold."
6. Blows on his hands to keep warm; is idle.

Then nightly sings the staring owl:
Tu-whit, tu-whoo!⁷—a merry note,
While greasy Joan doth keel° the pot.   *stir to cool*
895   When all aloud the wind doth blow,
And coughing drowns the parson's saw,°   *moralizing*
And birds sit brooding in the snow,
And Marian's nose looks red and raw;
When roasted crabs° hiss in the bowl,°   *crab apples / (of ale)*
900   Then nightly sings the staring owl:
Tu-whit, tu-whoo!—a merry note,
While greasy Joan doth keel the pot.

ARMADO   The words of Mercury are harsh after the songs of
Apollo.⁸ You that way, we this way.⁹   *Exeunt* [*severally*]°   *separately*

---

7. Perhaps: to it (a hunting cry, with possible sexual overtones), to woo.

8. Presumably the love poetry of the King and courtiers. *words of Mercury:* probably referring to Mercadé's somber message. (See note to the stage direction following line 698.)

9. This line may distinguish the audience ("you") from the actors ("we"), the aristocratic from the humbler characters, the French ladies from the inhabitants of Navarre, or even the actor playing Spring from the one playing Winter.

Love's Labour's Won

In 1598, Francis Meres called as witnesses to Shakespeare's excellence in comedy 'his *Gētlemē of Verona*, his *Errors*, his *Loue labors lost*, his *Loue labours wonne*, his *Midsummers night dreame*, & his *Merchant of Venice*'. This was the only evidence that Shakespeare wrote a play called *Love's Labour's Won* until the discovery in 1953 of a fragment of a bookseller's list that had been used in the binding of a volume published in 1637/8. The fragment itself appears to record items sold from 9 to 17 August 1603 by a book dealer in the south of England. Among items headed '[inte]rludes & tragedyes' are

> marchant of vennis
> taming of a shrew
> knak to know a knave
> knak to know an honest man
> loves labor lost
> loves labor won

No author is named for any of the items. All the plays named in the list except *Love's Labour's Won* are known to have been printed by 1600; all were written by 1596–97. Taken together, Meres's reference in 1598 and the 1603 fragment appear to demonstrate that a play by Shakespeare called *Love's Labour's Won* had been performed by the time Meres wrote and was in print by August 1603. Conceivably the phrase served as an alternative title for one of Shakespeare's other comedies, though the only one believed to have been written by 1598 but not listed by Meres is *The Taming of the Shrew*, which is named (as *The Taming of a Shrew*) in the bookseller's fragment. Otherwise we must suppose that *Love's Labour's Won* is the title of a lost play by Shakespeare, that no copy of the edition mentioned in the bookseller's list is extant, and that Heminges and Condell failed to include it in the 1623 Folio.

None of these suppositions is implausible. We know of at least one other lost play attributed to Shakespeare (see *Cardenio*, below), and of many lost works by contemporary playwrights. No copy of the first edition of *Titus Andronicus* was known until 1904; for *I Henry IV* and *The Passionate Pilgrim* only a fragment of the first edition survives. And we now know that *Troilus and Cressida* was almost omitted from the 1623 Folio (probably for copyright reasons) despite its evident authenticity. It is also possible that, like most of the early editions of Shakespeare's plays, the lost edition of *Love's Labour's Won* did not name him on the title-page, and this omission might go some way to explaining the failure of the edition to survive, or (if it does still survive) to be noticed. *Love's Labour's Won* stands a much better chance of having survived, somewhere, than *Cardenio*: because it was printed, between 500 and 1,500 copies were once in circulation, whereas for *Cardenio* we know of only a single manuscript.

The evidence for the existence of the lost play (unlike that for *Cardenio*) gives us little indication of its content. Meres explicitly states, and the title implies, that it was a comedy. Its titular pairing with *Love's Labour's Lost* suggests that they may have been written at about the same time. Both Meres and the bookseller's catalogue place it after *Love's Labour's Lost*; although neither list is necessarily chronological, Meres's does otherwise agree with our own view of the order of composition of Shakespeare's comedies.

THE OXFORD EDITORS

A Midsummer Night's Dream

Imagine an aristocratic wedding in a grand English country house. Imagine that after the solemnities and the wedding supper, the newlyweds and their distinguished guests—including the most distinguished guest of all, Queen Elizabeth I—are treated to a private entertainment, a play written especially for them. Imagine that the play is Shakespeare's *A Midsummer Night's Dream,* a comedy that culminates not only in three marriages but in a play, *Pyramus and Thisbe,* performed for the newlyweds with delicious incompetence by well-meaning, hopelessly bumbling artisans. Their inept performance amuses the happy couples and helps to "wear away this long age of three hours," as the amorously impatient Duke Theseus puts it, "between our after-supper and bed-time" (5.1.33–34). At the end of the play within the play, the stage brides and grooms exit to consummate their marriages—"Sweet friends, to bed"—and so, too, amid the blessings and sly jokes of their guests, the real newlyweds retire to bed.

Scholars have told and retold this story of the aristocratic wedding for which Shakespeare wrote his most enchanting comedy until it has come to seem like an established truth, one of the few things we actually know about the composition of the plays. But while the story is both charming and plausible, there is not a shred of actual evidence that *A Midsummer Night's Dream* was ever performed at, let alone written expressly for, such a wedding. What we do know is that this play was performed on the London stage: the title page of the First Quarto says that it "hath been sundry times publikely acted" by the Lord Chamberlain's Men and that it was written by William Shakespeare.

The precise date that *A Midsummer Night's Dream* was written and first performed is unknown; the Elizabethan writer Francis Meres mentions it admiringly in 1598, and certain of its stylistic features have led many scholars to place it around 1594–96, the probable period of the comparably lyrical *Romeo and Juliet* and *Richard II.* Attempts to find more precise coordinates by locating an allusion to a particular Royal Progress in Oberon's lines about the "fair vestal thronèd by the west" (2.1.158) or to a particular wet season in Titania's lines about the miserable weather (2.1.88ff.) have been defeated by the frequency of both Queen Elizabeth's travels and English rainstorms.

What accounts, then, for all the speculation about the wedding ceremony, complete with royal attendance? In part, the answer lies in the comedy's thematic focus on love consummated in marriage. The final ritual blessing of the bride beds—the fairies' version of a traditional Catholic practice deemed superstitious by zealous Protestants—can be seen as the culmination of the elaborate festivities, including song, music, dancing, and plays, that often accompanied upper-class Elizabethan marriages. In part, imagining a specific historical occasion helps to highlight an uncertainty, at once pleasurable and disturbing, about the borderline between reality and illusion: as in a hall of mirrors, the real-life newlyweds whiling away the hours before bedtime by watching a play would see onstage other newlyweds whiling away the hours before bedtime by watching a play.

But, as four centuries of readers and playgoers have found, you do not need to see *A Midsummer Night's Dream* on your wedding day, nor do you need to be an aristocrat, to savor its delights. There have, to be sure, been a few dissenters: the diarist Samuel Pepys wrote after seeing a production in 1662 that "it is the most insipid ridiculous play that ever I saw in my life," although he took note of "some good dancing and some handsome women." Most audiences have been vastly more enthusiastic. The play has inspired a succession of musical adaptations and settings, along with famously lavish productions. By the nineteenth century, Shakespeare's bare stage had given way to

Cupid and his victims. From Gilles Corrozet, *Hecatomgraphie* (1540).

gorgeous sets, with twinkling lights, fairies rising on midnight mushrooms, the moon shining over the Acropolis, and live rabbits hopping across carpets of flowers. Film is, of course, well suited to such fantasies, as a series of famous motion pictures have shown, but *A Midsummer Night's Dream* has proved equally at home in the simplest of settings. Generations of schoolchildren have romped through cardboard forests, while in Peter Brook's influential 1970 production for the Royal Shakespeare Company the actors performed (often on trapeze) in a three-sided, brightly lit, bare white box.

Working its magic on the imagination, Shakespeare's visionary poetic drama appeals to an unusually broad spectrum of spectators. The play may induce fantasies of aristocratic or private pleasure, but it does so with the resources of the public stage. If it mocks working-class artisans (skilled craftsmen who are simply called "the rabble" in one quarto stage direction), it also laughs at well-born young lovers. Its language reflects an unusually high incidence of the tropes familiar to those who had received rhetorical and literary training, but you do not have to learn the Greek names for these tropes—*anaphora, isocolon, epizeuxis,* and the like—to enjoy their effects. Take, for example, the exchange between Lysander and Hermia in the wake of Egeus's attempt to block their betrothal:

> LYSANDER   The course of true love never did run smooth,
>   But either it was different in blood—
> HERMIA   O cross!—too high to be enthralled to low.
> LYSANDER   Or else misgrafted in respect of years—
> HERMIA   O spite!—too old to be engaged to young.
> LYSANDER   Or merit stood upon the choice of friends—
> HERMIA   O hell!—to choose love by another's eyes.
>   (1.1.134–40)

The alternation of single lines, called *stichomythia,* is a scheme that Shakespeare borrowed from the Roman playwright Seneca and used in different ways in many of his plays. The effect here is to convey the lovers' mutual anguish, tinging it slightly perhaps with a gently ironic distance that evaporates in the poignant lament that follows (lines 141–49). The rhetorical devices, along with the subtle modulations from blank verse to rhymed couplets to boisterous comic prose, are so deftly handled that their pleasures are accessible to the learned and unlearned alike. This breadth also reflects the very wide range of cultural materials that the playwright has cunningly woven together, from the classical heritage of the educated elite to popular ballads and folk customs, from refined and sophisticated entertainments to the coarser delights of farce.

The exquisite lyricism of much of the play, the celebration of aristocratic pastimes such as the hunt, and a vision of courtly glamour conjure up an upper-class milieu. There is no single literary source for Shakespeare's depiction of this world, or indeed for the play as a whole, but he is indebted for the legendary Theseus and Hippolyta to Thomas North's translation (1579) of Plutarch's *Lives of the Noble Grecians and Romanes,* and still more to Chaucer's *Knight's Tale.* The *Dream* repeatedly echoes Chaucer's references to observing "the rite of May," a folk custom still current in Elizabethan England and quite possibly known to Shakespeare personally. To the dismay of Puritans, who regarded the celebration as a lascivious remnant of paganism, young men and women of all classes would go out into the woods and fields to welcome the

Pyramus and Thisbe. From George Wither, *A Collection of Emblemes* (1635).

May with singing and dancing. Shakespeare's title associates this custom with another occasion for festive release: Midsummer Eve (June 23), when the solstice was marked not only by holiday license but by tales of fairy spells and temporary madness.

Some Elizabethan aristocrats kept theatrical troupes as liveried servants, along with young pages who could sing and perform, and powerful magnates, both secular and religious, often had plays, masquerades, and elaborate shows staged in their houses. From this milieu, Shakespeare derives a vision of what we can call the revels of power, performances designed to entertain, gratify, and reflect the values of those at the top. From this milieu too Shakespeare absorbs a sense of social hierarchy: a distinction between Duke Theseus, at once imperious and genteel, and Egeus, wealthy but distinctly lower in rank and harping on what is his by law, along with a more marked distinction between these characters and the artisans, loyal members of the lower orders, regarded by their social superiors with condescending indulgence.

The artisans—or "rude mechanicals," as they are called—enable Shakespeare to introduce wonderful swoops into earthy prose, snatches of jigs, a comical taste for the grotesque, a glimpse of a world that usually resides beyond the horizon of courtly vision. The lovers at the pinnacle of the play's society do not know the names and trades of the "hard-handed men that work in Athens here" (5.1.72) who have come to offer them entertainment, but we the audience do, and we even know something of their hopes and dreams. As with the Pageant of the Nine Worthies in *Love's Labour's Lost*, we are invited at once to join in the mockery of the inept performers and to distance ourselves from the mockers. That is, the audience of *A Midsummer Night's Dream* is not simply mirrored in the play's upper classes: the real audience is given a broader perspective, a more capacious understanding than anyone onstage.

This understanding is signaled not only in our ability to take in both the courtly and popular dimensions of the play, but also in our ability to see what escapes both aristocrats and artisans: the world of the fairies. But what are the fairies? From what social milieu do they spring? It is tempting to reply that they are denizens of the country—that is, characters drawn from the semipagan folklore of rural England. This is at least partially true: Reginald Scot, who wrote a brilliant attack on witchcraft persecutions (*The Discoverie of Witchcraft*, 1584), suggests that Robin Goodfellow, the mischievous spirit also called a Puck, was once feared by villagers, but was now widely recognized to be a figure of mere "illusion and knaverie." Yet intensive scholarly research over several generations has suggested that Shakespeare's fairies are quite unlike those his audience might have credited, half-credited, or—as Scot hoped—discredited.

The fairies of Elizabethan popular belief were often threatening and dangerous, while those of *A Midsummer Night's Dream* are generally benevolent. The former steal human infants, perhaps to sacrifice them to the devil, while the latter, even when they quarrel over the possession of a young boy, do so to bestow love and favor upon him; the former leave deformed, emaciated children in place of those they have stolen, while the latter trip nimbly through the palace blessing the bride beds and warding off deformities. Shakespeare's fairies have some of the menacing associations of "real" fairies—Puck speaks of shrouds and gaping graves, while the quarrel between Oberon and Titania has disrupted the seasons and damaged the crops, as wicked spirits were said to do. But the fairies we see are, as Oberon says, "spirits of another sort." Oberon and Titania (whose names Shakespeare took from the French romance *Huon of Bordeaux* and from Ovid, respectively) repeatedly demonstrate their good will toward mortals, though they have very little good will toward each other. The fairy king and queen are distressed at the unintended consequences of their quarrel, and each is involved, with romantic generosity, in the happiness of Theseus and Hippolyta. This generosity extends beyond the immediate range of their interests: in the midst of plotting to humiliate Titania, Oberon attempts to intervene on behalf of the spurned Helena, and though this intervention proves, through Puck's mistake, to lead to hopeless confusion, the fairies make amends.

Indeed, if Puck takes mischievous delight in the discord he has helped to sow among the four young lovers—"Lord, what fools these mortals be!" (3.2.115)—he is not the originator of that discord, and he is the indispensable agent for setting things right. In his role as both mischief-maker and matchmaker, Puck resembles the crafty slave in comedies by the Latin playwrights Plautus and Terence, a stock character who sometimes seems to enjoy and contribute to the plot's tangles but who manages in the end to remove the obstacles that stand in the way of the young lovers.

This resemblance brings us to yet another of the cultural elements that Shakespeare cunningly interweaves in the plot of *A Midsummer Night's Dream*. From the classical literary tradition, which he must have first encountered in grammar school, Shakespeare derives the ancient Greek setting, the story of Pyramus and Thisbe as told in Ovid's *Metamorphoses*, the comic transformation of a man into an ass as told in Apuleius's *Golden Ass*, and, above all, the basic plot device of young lovers contriving to escape the rigid will of a stern father. This device was one of the staples of the New Comedy of ancient Greece and was a mainstay as well in Roman comedy. The literary convention corresponds to certain aspects of actual life in Shakespeare's England, where lawsuits provide records of parents trying to compel children to marry against their will. But the historical problem of marital consent has a complex relation to its artistic representation. Not only does the play exaggerate the actual punitive power of the father—Egeus threatens his disobedient daughter with death (to which Theseus offers, as a grim alternative, the nunnery)—but it also exaggerates the release from this power by staging the giddy possibility of a marriage based entirely on love and desire rather than parental will.

In *A Midsummer Night's Dream*, this release, a highly implausible dream for any Elizabethan member of the middle or upper classes, is brought about by a further plot device: the escape from the court or city to the "green world" of the forest. This theatrical structure is not characteristic of the New Comedy, but it somewhat resembles the Saturnalian rhythms of the Old Comedy of Aristophanes, with its festive release from the discipline and sobriety of everyday life, and, still more perhaps, it reflects certain English folk customs, such as Maying. When Theseus comes upon the four exhausted lovers asleep in the woods, he thinks that "they rose up early to observe / The rite of May" (4.1.129–30).

But, of course, Theseus is wrong. The lovers were not out a-Maying, but had spent the night stumbling through the woods in a confused state of fear, anger, and desire. When it enters the charmed, moonlit space of *A Midsummer Night's Dream,* "the rite of May," along with the other rituals and representations Shakespeare stitched together in creating his play, is transformed; to use Peter Quince's term for the metamorphosed Bottom, the rites and rituals are "translated." Folk customs, the revels of power, the classical tradition as taught in schools, all are displaced from their points of origin, their enabling institutions and assumptions, and brought into a new space, the space of the Shakespearean stage.

This "translation" has, in every case, the odd effect of simultaneous elevation and enervation, celebration and parody. Thus the minor Ovidian tale of Pyramus and Thisbe is greatly elaborated but also travestied; the popular realm is at once lovingly represented and mercilessly ridiculed; the revels of power are reproduced but also ironically distanced.

Some of the play's most wonderful moments spring from the zany conjunction of distinct and even opposed theatrical modes (a conjunction characteristically parodied in the oxymoronic title of the artisans' play, "A tedious brief scene of young Pyramus / And his love Thisbe: very tragical mirth" [5.1.56–57]). Thus, for example, exquisite love poetry and low comedy meet in the wonderful moment in which the queen of fairies awakens to become enraptured at the sight of the most flatulently absurd of the mechanicals, Bottom. Bottom has been transformed with perfect appropriateness into an ass, yet it is he who is granted the play's most exquisite vision of delight and who articulates, in a comically confused burlesque of St. Paul (1 Corinthians 2:9), the deepest sense of wonder: "The eye of man hath not heard, the ear of man hath not seen, man's hand is not able to taste, his tongue to conceive, nor his heart to report what my dream was" (4.1.204–07).

It would be asinine, the play suggests, to try to expound this dream, but we can at least suggest that, whatever its meaning, its existence is closely linked to the nature of

A fairy hill. From Olaus Magnus, *Historia de Gentibus Septentrionalibus* (1555).

the theater itself. Puck suggests as much when he proposes in the Epilogue that the audience imagine that it has all along been slumbering: the play it has seen has been a collective hallucination. The play, then, is a dream about watching a play about dreams. Fittingly, the comedy devotes much of its last act to a parody of a theatrical performance, as if its most enduring concern were not the fate of the lovers but the possibility of performing plays. The entire last act of *A Midsummer Night's Dream* is unnecessary in terms of the plot: by Oberon's intervention and Theseus's fiat, the plot complications have all been resolved at the end of Act 4. Knots that had seemed almost impossible to untangle—Theseus had declared in Act 1 that he was powerless to over-turn the ancient privilege of Athens invoked by Egeus—suddenly dissolve. The absurdly easy resolution of an apparently hopeless dilemma characterizes not only the lovers' legal but also their emotional condition, a blend of mad confusion and geometric logic that is settled, apparently permanently, with the aid of the fairies' magical love juice.

But this diagrammatic settling of affairs sits uncomfortably with all that the lovers have experienced in the woods. Both critics and directors have given different weight to this experience. Some treat the lovers as mindless comic puppets, jerked by the play-wright's invisible strings, while others take more seriously the darkness that shadows their words and actions. This darkness includes emotional violence and masochism, the betrayal of friendship, the radical fickleness of desire. It extends to the play's sexual politics. Under the strain of the night's adventures, the friendship between Hermia and Helena begins to crack apart, while Lysander and Demetrius become bitter rivals. Although they are eventually reconciled, it is as if the heterosexual couplings can only be formed by painfully sundering the intimate same-sex bonds that preceded them. Shakespeare had begun to reflect on this problem as early as *The Two Gentlemen of Verona,* possibly his first play, and throughout his career he returned to it repeatedly, including in what is possibly his last play, *The Two Noble Kinsmen.* For the most part, the broken friendships are repaired, but, as with Antonio and Sebastian in *Twelfth Night* and Leontes and Polixenes in *The Winter's Tale,* there is usually a lingering sense of loss, from which even the sunnier *Midsummer Night's Dream* is not completely exempt.

In another very early play, *The Taming of the Shrew,* Shakespeare had also begun his lifelong reflection on the struggle between men and women, a struggle frequently focused on the male desire to dominate and subdue the female. In *A Midsummer Night's Dream,* tension flares in the case of the fairies into open conflict over the Indian boy, the locus of Oberon's assertion of patriarchal power and Titania's claim to independence. In the human world of the play, this tension is less immediately apparent, but in the first scene Theseus alludes to his military conquest of the Amazon queen Hippolyta, and there are other brief glimpses of cruelty, indifference, and rage. Those who see *A Midsummer Night's Dream* as lighthearted entertainment must somehow laugh off this darkness; those who wish to emphasize the play's more troubling and discordant notes must somehow neutralize the comic register in which such notes are sounded. For example, the brutal insults hurled at Hermia by the young man who had loved her and with whom she has eloped might well seem extremely painful, but the fantastic language in which these insults are expressed—

> Get you gone, you dwarf,
> You *minimus* of hind'ring knot-grass made,
> You bead, you acorn
>
> (3.2.329–31)

—distances audiences from the pain and generates laughter.

Audiences for most productions tend to oscillate between engagement and detachment. In the young lovers' choices and sufferings, we encounter a situation where the final outcome doesn't matter greatly to us but matters greatly to them. And while we see the characters from a distance—although Hermia and Helena are distinct enough, even attentive readers occasionally find it difficult to remember which is Lysander and which Demetrius—we also experience at least glancingly *their* sense of how important the difference is, how unbearable to be matched against one's consent, how painfully difficult to make a match that corresponds to one's desires.

Desires in *A Midsummer Night's Dream* are intense, irrational, and alarmingly mobile. This mobility, the speed with which desire can be detached from one object and attached to a different object, does not diminish the exigency of the passion, for the lovers are convinced at every moment that their choices are irrefutably rational and irresistibly compelling. But there is no security in these choices, and the play is repeatedly haunted by a fear of abandonment. The emblem, as well as agent, of a dangerously mobile desire is the fairies' love juice. No human being in the play experiences a purely abstract, objectless desire; when you desire, you desire *someone*. But the love juice is the distilled essence of erotic mobility itself, and it is appropriately in the power of the fairies. For the fairies seem to embody the principle of what we might call polytropic desire—that is, desire that can instantaneously alight on any object, including an ass-headed man, and that can with equal instantaneousness swerve away from that object and on to another. Oberon and Titania have, we learn, long histories of amorous adventures; they are aware of each other's wayward passions; and, endowed with an extraordinary, eroticizing rhetoric, they move endlessly through the spiced, moonlit night.

If there is a link between the fairies and the erotic, there is a still more powerful link between the fairies and the imagination. Theseus makes the connection explicit when he rejects the stories that the lovers have told him: "I never may believe / These antique fables, nor these fairy toys." In a famous speech (5.1.2–22), he accounts for such fables and toys as products of the imagination. The speech reflects Theseus's misplaced confidence in his own sense of waking reality, a reality that does not include fairies. Yet paradoxically, in dismissively categorizing the lunatic, the lover, and the poet as "of imagination all compact," he manages to articulate insights that the play seems to uphold. Those in the grip of a powerful imagination may be loosed from the moorings of reason and nature, and they may inhabit a world of wish fulfillment and its converse, nightmare. But the poet whose imagination "bodies forth / The forms of things unknown" (5.1.14–15) has created *A Midsummer Night's Dream,* giving his fantasies—including the fantasy called "Theseus"—"a local habitation and a name." Finally, it is the imagination that enables giddy, restless, changeable mortals to attach their desires to a particular person.

For Theseus, the imagination is the agent of delusion—and there is much in the play that would seem to support this conclusion. But his account is not complete without Hippolyta's insistence that the story the four young lovers tell seems to have something that goes beyond delusion. Their minds, she observes, have been "transfigured" together, and this shared transfiguration bears witness to "something of great constancy; / But howsoever, strange and admirable" (5.1.26–27). It is as if we were all to wake up one morning and discover we had had the same dream.

And, of course, *we* in the audience have, as Puck's epilogue suggests, had just this experience: the experience of the theater. In the theater, we confront a living representation of the complex relation between transfiguration and delusion, a relation explored with fantastic, anxious literalness in the artisans' performance of *Pyramus and Thisbe.* In reassuring the ladies that the lion is only Snug the Joiner, that nothing is what it claims to be, the players simultaneously burlesque the stage and call attention to the basic elements from which any performance is made: rudimentary scenery, artisans, language, imagination, desire.

There is precious little evidence, to be sure, of either imagination or desire in the artisans' performance of *Pyramus and Thisbe.* Their absence is part of the comical awfulness of the play within the play, the reason in effect that it does not become the Shakespearean tragedy it so strikingly resembles, *Romeo and Juliet.* And yet, as Theseus says, "The best in this kind are but shadows, and the worst are no worse if imagination amend them." "It must be your imagination, then," Hippolyta points out, "and not theirs" (5.1.208–10). But that is true of performances far greater than that of which the artisans are capable. If we are to see fairies onstage in *A Midsummer Night's Dream,* and not simply flesh-and-blood actors (probably boy actors in Shakespeare's theater), it must be our imagination that makes amends. So too if we are to believe in the lovers' desire and sympathize with their predicament, it must be *our* desire that animates their words.

Such, at least, is the vision of the theater suggested by the play that Bottom and company offer to the newlyweds. There is nothing really out there, their performance implies, except what the audience graciously consents to dream. Yet in the closing moments of the play, when the fairies emerge from the woods and venture into Theseus's mansion to bless the bride beds, a quite different vision of theater is suggested, one in which the dreams and desires that we have are determined by forces over which we have no control, forces that only a playwright's love juice can make visible under an imaginary moon.

STEPHEN GREENBLATT

TEXTUAL NOTE

A Midsummer Night's Dream was entered in the Stationers' Register on October 8, 1600, and printed that same year in quarto:

> A Midsommer nights dreame. As it hath beene sundry times pub*lickely acted, by the Right honourable,* the Lord Chamberlaine his *seruants. Written by William Shakespeare.* Imprinted at London, for *Thomas Fisher,* and are to be soulde at his shoppe, at the Signe of the White Hart, in *Fleetestreete.* 1600.

This quarto (Q1) was evidently prepared from a manuscript in Shakespeare's hand. A second quarto (Q2), printed in 1619 (though falsely dated 1600), corrects some errors in Q1, but it also introduces new errors. This second quarto was used as the basis for the 1623 First Folio text of the play (F), though the Folio editors also had recourse to a theatrical manuscript, probably a promptbook in the possession of Shakespeare's company, the King's Men. Evidence for this manuscript includes a Folio stage direction before 5.1.126: "Tawyer with a Trumpet before them." "Tawyer" presumably refers to William Tawyer, a musician employed by the King's Men.

From this theatrical manuscript evidently derived several alterations in stage directions and in speech prefixes, the most notable of which is the substitution in Act 5 of Egeus for Philostrate as the master of ceremonies. The substitution may simply be a mistake: in an early performance, the same actor may have played the parts of both Egeus and Philostrate, and this doubling may have led to an error in the speech prefix. But it is also possible that the play was revised in order to integrate the disgruntled Egeus more fully into the festive conclusion.

Act and scene divisions all derive from F; there are none in the quarto text. Traditionally, Act 3, Scene 2 continues to the end of the act, but since the stage is apparently cleared at 3.2.413, this edition marks a break (perhaps indicating a gap in time and place) by dividing the scene in two and designating a third scene. In F, at the end of Act 3 there is a stage direction, "They sleepe all the Act," which indicates that the four lovers remain asleep onstage during the interval customary between acts and that the action that resumes in the next act is understood to be continuous.

On the basis of mislined verses in 5.1.1–84, scholars have conjectured that Shakespeare may have revised Theseus's speech as originally conceived and added lines in the margin of his copy. Since these revisions may give us a glimpse of Shakespeare's process of composition, this book appends a reconstruction of what would have been the original speech.

The control text for this edition of *A Midsummer Night's Dream* is Q1 (1600). But in keeping with the Oxford editors' principle of basing their text on the most theatrical early version of each play—that is, the version closest to the play as performed by Shakespeare's company during the playwright's own lifetime—changes in speech prefixes and other substantive variants have been adopted from F.

SELECTED BIBLIOGRAPHY

Barber, C. L. "May Games and Metamorphoses on a Midsummer's Night." *Shakespeare's Festive Comedy: A Study of Dramatic Form and Its Relation to Social Custom*. Princeton: Princeton University Press, 1959. 119–62. *A Midsummer Night's Dream* combines folk customs, Ovidian fancy, and Elizabethan pageantry to produce a clarifying release of imagination.

Bate, Jonathan. *Shakespeare and Ovid*. New York: Oxford University Press, 1993. *A Midsummer Night's Dream* indirectly dramatizes Ovid, gathering themes of myth, metamorphosis, and love into a mixed mode typical of sixteenth-century mythography.

Briggs, K. M. *The Anatomy of Puck: An Examination of Fairy Beliefs Among Shakespeare's Contemporaries and Successors*. London: Routledge and Kegan Paul, 1959. A survey of early modern notions about fairies, especially in English literary tradition, describing also the influence of Shakespeare's innovations.

Dash, Irene G. *Women's Worlds in Shakespeare's Plays*. London: Associated University Presses, 1997. Looks at *A Midsummer Night's Dream* in performance, arguing that traditional staging practices have tended reductively to simplify Shakespeare's women.

Girard, René. "Myth and Ritual in Shakespeare: *A Midsummer Night's Dream*." *Textual Strategies: Perspectives in Post-Structuralist Criticism*. Ed. Josué V. Harari. Ithaca, N.Y.: Cornell University Press, 1979. 189–212. This play presents a genetic theory of myth, charting a collective mental transformation.

Loomba, Ania. "The Great Indian Vanishing Trick—Colonialism, Property, and the Family in *A Midsummer Night's Dream*." *A Feminist Companion to Shakespeare*. Ed. Dympna Callaghan. Malden, Mass.: Blackwell, 2000. 163–87. Argues that the Indian boy represents the shaping dialectic between non-European practices and Western domestic ideology.

Montrose, Louis. *The Purpose of Playing: Shakespeare and the Cultural Politics of the Elizabethan Theatre*. Chicago: University of Chicago Press, 1996. Examines the play's relationship to Elizabethan ideology through discourses of gender, physiology, social rank, and royal iconography.

Traub, Valerie. *The Renaissance of Lesbianism in Early Modern England*. Cambridge: Cambridge University Press, 2002. Observes how renovated classical idioms and new scientific knowledge made female-female desire intelligible in the Renaissance.

Williams, Gary Jay. *Our Moonlight Revels: "A Midsummer Night's Dream" in the Theatre*. Iowa City: University of Iowa Press, 1997. The major stage, film, and opera adaptations, understood in relation to the cultures that produced them.

Young, David P. *Something of Great Constancy: The Art of "A Midsummer Night's Dream."* New Haven: Yale University Press, 1966. Extensive, variegated study covering sources, structure, performance, and contexts.

FILMS

A Midsummer Night's Dream. 1935. Dir. William Dieterle and Max Reinhardt. USA. 133 min. Sumptuous production, with balletic fairies, a serpentine Hippolyta, an elaborate Mendelssohn score, and Mickey Rooney as Puck.

A Midsummer Night's Dream. 1968. Dir. Peter Hall. UK. 124 min. Noted for its mini-skirted sensuality, body paint, and extremely gnarled and muddy forest. With Diana Rigg and Helen Mirren.

A Midsummer Night's Dream. 1996. Dir. Adrian Noble. UK. 105 min. Theseus and Hippolyta double as Oberon and Titania, with a frame device of a boy dreaming the play. Starring Lindsay Duncan and Alex Jennings.

A Midsummer Night's Dream. 1999. Dir. Michael Hoffman. USA. 116 min. In Victorian costume against the Tuscan backdrop, this dreamy and erotic version amplifies Bottom's role. With Kevin Kline and Michelle Pfeiffer.

A Midsummer Night's Dream

The Persons of the Play

THESEUS, Duke of Athens
HIPPOLYTA, Queen of the Amazons, betrothed to Theseus
PHILOSTRATE, Master of the Revels to Theseus
EGEUS, father of Hermia
HERMIA, daughter of Egeus, in love with Lysander
LYSANDER, loved by Hermia
DEMETRIUS, suitor to Hermia
HELENA, in love with Demetrius
OBERON, King of Fairies
TITANIA, Queen of Fairies
ROBIN GOODFELLOW, a puck
PEASEBLOSSOM ⎫
COBWEB ⎪
MOTE ⎬ fairies
MUSTARDSEED ⎭
Peter QUINCE, a carpenter
Nick BOTTOM, a weaver
Francis FLUTE, a bellows-mender
Tom SNOUT, a tinker
SNUG, a joiner
Robin STARVELING, a tailor
Attendant lords and fairies

1.1

Enter THESEUS, HIPPOLYTA, [*and* PHILOSTRATE,] *with others*

THESEUS Now, fair Hippolyta, our nuptial hour
　　Draws on apace. Four happy days bring in
　　Another moon—but O, methinks how slow
　　This old moon wanes! She lingers° my desires　　*delays fulfillment of*
5　　Like to a stepdame° or a dowager　　　　　　　*stepmother*
　　Long withering out a young man's revenue.[1]
HIPPOLYTA Four days will quickly steep° themselves in night,　　*plunge*
　　Four nights will quickly dream away the time;
　　And then the moon, like to a silver bow
10　　New bent in heaven, shall behold the night
　　Of our solemnities.
THESEUS　　　　　　　　Go, Philostrate,
　　Stir up the Athenian youth to merriments.
　　Awake the pert and nimble spirit of mirth.
　　Turn melancholy forth to funerals—
15　　The pale companion is not for our pomp. [*Exit* PHILOSTRATE]
　　Hippolyta, I wooed thee with my sword,
　　And won thy love doing thee injuries.[2]

1.1 Location: Theseus's palace in Athens.
1. *a dowager . . . revenue*: a widow using up the inheritance that will go to her husband's (young) heir on her
death.
2. Theseus captured Hippolyta in his military conquest
of the Amazons.

But I will wed thee in another key—
With pomp, with triumph,° and with revelling.   *public festivity*

    Enter EGEUS[3] *and his daughter* HERMIA, *and* LYSANDER
    and DEMETRIUS

20 EGEUS   Happy be Theseus, our renownèd Duke.

    THESEUS   Thanks, good Egeus. What's the news with thee?

    EGEUS   Full of vexation come I, with complaint
Against my child, my daughter Hermia.—
Stand forth Demetrius.—My noble lord,
25 This man hath my consent to marry her.—
Stand forth Lysander.—And, my gracious Duke,
This hath bewitched the bosom of my child.
Thou, thou, Lysander, thou hast given her rhymes,
And interchanged love tokens with my child.
30 Thou hast by moonlight at her window sung
With feigning[4] voice verses of feigning love,
And stol'n the impression of her fantasy[5]
With bracelets of thy hair, rings, gauds,° conceits,°   *trinkets / clever gifts*
Knacks,° trifles, nosegays,° sweetmeats—messengers   *Knickknacks / bouquets*
35 Of strong prevailment° in unhardened youth.   *persuasiveness*
With cunning hast thou filched my daughter's heart,
Turned her obedience which is due to me
To stubborn harshness. And, my gracious Duke,
Be it so° she will not here before your grace   *If*
40 Consent to marry with Demetrius,
I beg the ancient privilege of Athens:
As she is mine, I may dispose of her,
Which shall be either to this gentleman
Or to her death, according to our law
45 Immediately° provided in that case.   *Expressly*

    THESEUS   What say you, Hermia? Be advised, fair maid.
To you your father should be as a god,
One that composed° your beauties, yea, and one   *fashioned*
To whom you are but as a form in wax,
50 By him imprinted,[6] and within his power
To leave° the figure or disfigure° it.   *maintain / destroy*
Demetrius is a worthy gentleman.

    HERMIA   So is Lysander.

    THESEUS   In himself he is,
But in this kind,° wanting your father's voice,[7]   *respect*
55 The other must be held the worthier.

    HERMIA   I would my father looked but with my eyes.

    THESEUS   Rather your eyes must with his judgement look.

    HERMIA   I do entreat your grace to pardon me.
I know not by what power I am made bold,
60 Nor how it may concern° my modesty   *befit*
In such a presence here to plead my thoughts,
But I beseech your grace that I may know
The worst that may befall me in this case
If I refuse to wed Demetrius.

---

3. Pronounced "Ege-us," accented on the second syllable.
4. A triple pun: desiring; feigning; soft (in music).
5. *stol'n . . . fantasy:* by craftily impressing your image
on her imagination, like a seal in wax, you have stolen
her love.
6. *you are . . . imprinted:* you are a wax impression of
his seal.
7. Lacking your father's consent or vote.

65	THESEUS Either to die the death,° or to abjure	*be executed*
	For ever the society of men.	
	Therefore, fair Hermia, question your desires.	
	Know° of your youth, examine well your blood,°	*Inquire / passions*
	Whether, if you yield not to your father's choice,	
70	You can endure the livery° of a nun,⁸	*habit*
	For aye° to be in shady cloister mewed,°	*ever / caged in*
	To live a barren sister all your life,	
	Chanting faint hymns to the cold fruitless moon.⁹	
	Thrice blessèd they that master so their blood	
75	To undergo such maiden pilgrimage;°	*life as a virgin*
	But earthlier happy is the rose distilled¹	
	Than that which, withering on the virgin thorn,	
	Grows, lives, and dies in single blessedness.°	*celibate*
	HERMIA So will I grow, so live, so die, my lord,	
80	Ere I will yield my virgin patent² up	
	Unto his lordship whose unwishèd yoke	
	My soul consents not to give sovereignty.	
	THESEUS Take time to pause, and by the next new moon—	
	The sealing day betwixt my love and me	
85	For everlasting bond of fellowship—	
	Upon that day either prepare to die	
	For disobedience to your father's will,	
	Or else to wed Demetrius, as he would,	
	Or on Diana's altar to protest°	*vow*
90	For aye austerity and single life.	
	DEMETRIUS Relent, sweet Hermia; and, Lysander, yield	
	Thy crazèd title° to my certain right.	*unsound claim*
	LYSANDER You have her father's love, Demetrius;	
	Let me have Hermia's. Do you marry him.	
95	EGEUS Scornful Lysander! True, he hath my love;	
	And what is mine my love shall render him,	
	And she is mine, and all my right of her	
	I do estate° unto Demetrius.	*settle; bestow*
	LYSANDER [*to* THESEUS] I am, my lord, as well derived° as he,	*descended*
100	As well possessed.° My love is more than his,	*endowed with wealth*
	My fortunes every way as fairly ranked,	
	If not with vantage,° as Demetrius;	*superiority*
	And—which is more than all these boasts can be—	
	I am beloved of beauteous Hermia.	
105	Why should not I then prosecute° my right?	*pursue*
	Demetrius—I'll avouch it to his head°—	*face*
	Made love to Nedar's daughter, Helena,	
	And won her soul, and she, sweet lady, dotes,	
	Devoutly dotes, dotes in idolatry	
110	Upon this spotted and inconstant³ man.	
	THESEUS I must confess that I have heard so much,	
	And with Demetrius thought to have spoke thereof;	
	But, being over-full of self affairs,°	*my own concerns*
	My mind did lose it. But, Demetrius, come;	
115	And come, Egeus. You shall go with me.	

8. Orders of nuns were established in the Christian Middle Ages, but Elizabethans used the term as well for women devoted to a religious life in classical antiquity.
9. The emblem of Diana, goddess of chastity.

1. Made use of (roses were distilled to make perfumes). *earthlier happy:* happier on earth.
2. My right to remain a virgin.
3. *spotted and inconstant:* stained with fickleness.

I have some private schooling° for you both. *advice*
For you, fair Hermia, look you arm° yourself *prepare*
To fit your fancies° to your father's will, *desires*
Or else the law of Athens yields you up—
120 Which by no means we may extenuate°— *mitigate*
To death or to a vow of single life.
Come, my Hippolyta; what cheer, my love?—
Demetrius and Egeus, go along.
I must employ you in some business
125 Against° our nuptial, and confer with you *In preparation for*
Of something nearly that⁴ concerns yourselves.
EGEUS With duty and desire we follow you.

Exeunt. Manent° LYSANDER *and* HERMIA *Remain*

LYSANDER How now, my love? Why is your cheek so pale?
How chance the roses there do fade so fast?
130 HERMIA Belike° for want of rain, which I could well *Probably*
Beteem° them from the tempest of my eyes. *Afford; grant*
LYSANDER Ay me, for aught that I could ever read,
Could ever hear by tale or history,
The course of true love never did run smooth,
135 But either it was different in blood°— *hereditary rank*
HERMIA O cross!°—too high to be enthralled to low. *vexation*
LYSANDER Or else misgrafted° in respect of years— *badly matched*
HERMIA O spite!—too old to be engaged to young.
LYSANDER Or merit stood° upon the choice of friends°— *rested / kin*
140 HERMIA O hell!—to choose love by another's eyes.
LYSANDER Or if there were a sympathy° in choice, *an agreement*
War, death, or sickness did lay siege to it,
Making it momentany° as a sound, *momentary*
Swift as a shadow, short as any dream,
145 Brief as the lightning in the collied° night, *coal-black*
That, in a spleen,° unfolds° both heaven and earth, *swift impulse / reveals*
And, ere a man hath power to say 'Behold!',
The jaws of darkness do devour it up.
So quick⁵ bright things come to confusion.
150 HERMIA If then true lovers have been ever° crossed, *always*
It stands as an edict in destiny.
Then let us teach our trial patience,⁶
Because it is a customary cross,
As due to love as thoughts, and dreams, and sighs,
155 Wishes, and tears, poor fancy's° followers. *love's*
LYSANDER A good persuasion.° Therefore hear me, Hermia. *principle; doctrine*
I have a widow aunt, a dowager
Of great revenue, and she hath no child,
And she respects° me as her only son. *regards*
160 From Athens is her house remote seven leagues.
There, gentle Hermia, may I marry thee,
And to that place the sharp Athenian law
Cannot pursue us. If thou lov'st me then,
Steal forth thy father's house tomorrow night,
165 And in the wood, a league without° the town, *outside*
Where I did meet thee once with Helena

4. *nearly that*: that closely. 6. Let us teach ourselves to be patient in this trial.
5. Quickly (adverb); vital, lively (adjective).

To do observance to a morn of May,°   *celebrate May Day*
There will I stay for thee.

HERMIA   My good Lysander,
I swear to thee by Cupid's strongest bow,
170   By his best arrow with the golden head,[7]
By the simplicity° of Venus' doves,[8]   *innocence*
By that which knitteth souls and prospers loves,
And by that fire which burned the Carthage queen
When the false Trojan under sail was seen;[9]
175   By all the vows that ever men have broke—
In number more than ever women spoke—
In that same place thou hast appointed me
Tomorrow truly will I meet with thee.

LYSANDER   Keep promise, love. Look, here comes Helena.

       Enter HELENA

180   HERMIA   God speed, fair[1] Helena. Whither away?

HELENA   Call you me fair? That 'fair' again unsay.
Demetrius loves your fair—O happy fair!°   *fortunate beauty*
Your eyes are lodestars,° and your tongue's sweet air°   *guiding stars / melody*
More tuneable° than lark to shepherd's ear   *tuneful*
185   When wheat is green, when hawthorn buds appear.
Sickness is catching. O, were favour° so!   *looks; charms*
Your words I catch, fair Hermia; ere I go,
My ear should catch your voice, my eye your eye,
My tongue should catch your tongue's sweet melody.
190   Were the world mine, Demetrius being bated,°   *excepted*
The rest I'd give to be to you translated.°   *transformed*
O, teach me how you look, and with what art
You sway the motion° of Demetrius' heart.   *desire*

HERMIA   I frown upon him, yet he loves me still.
195   HELENA   O that your frowns would teach my smiles such skill!

HERMIA   I give him curses, yet he gives me love.

HELENA   O that my prayers could such affection move!

HERMIA   The more I hate, the more he follows me.

HELENA   The more I love, the more he hateth me.
200   HERMIA   His folly, Helen, is no fault of mine.

HELENA   None but your beauty; would that fault were mine!

HERMIA   Take comfort. He no more shall see my face.
Lysander and myself will fly this place.
Before the time I did Lysander see
205   Seemed Athens as a paradise to me.
O then, what graces in my love do dwell,
That he hath turned a heaven unto a hell?

LYSANDER   Helen, to you our minds we will unfold.
Tomorrow night, when Phoebe° doth behold   *Diana (the moon)*
210   Her silver visage in the wat'ry glass,
Decking with liquid pearl the bladed grass—
A time that lovers' sleights doth still° conceal—   *always*
Through Athens' gates have we devised to steal.

HERMIA   And in the wood where often you and I
215   Upon faint° primrose beds were wont° to lie,   *pale / accustomed*

---

7. Cupid's sharp golden arrow was said to create love; his blunt lead arrow caused dislike.
8. Said to draw Venus's chariot.
9. *fire . . . seen:* Dido, Queen of Carthage, burned herself

on a funeral pyre when her lover, Aeneas, sailed away.
1. The dialogue plays on the meanings "blonde," "beautiful," "beauty." Helena is presumably fair-haired and Hermia (called a "raven" at 2.2.120) a brunette.

Emptying our bosoms of their counsel sweet,
There my Lysander and myself shall meet,
And thence from Athens turn away our eyes
To seek new friends and stranger companies.°   *the company of strangers*
220 Farewell, sweet playfellow. Pray thou for us,
And good luck grant thee thy Demetrius.—
Keep word, Lysander. We must starve our sight
From lovers' food till morrow deep midnight.
LYSANDER   I will, my Hermia.   *Exit* HERMIA
Helena, adieu.
225 As you on him, Demetrius dote on you.   *Exit*
HELENA   How happy some o'er other some² can be!
Through Athens I am thought as fair as she.
But what of that? Demetrius thinks not so.
He will not know what all but he do know.
230 And as he errs, doting on Hermia's eyes,
So I, admiring of his qualities.
Things base and vile, holding no quantity,°   *shape; proportion*
Love can transpose to form and dignity.
Love looks not with the eyes, but with the mind,³
235 And therefore is winged Cupid painted blind.
Nor hath love's mind of any judgement taste;°   *any trace of judgment*
Wings and no eyes figure° unheedy haste.   *symbolize*
And therefore is love said to be a child
Because in choice he is so oft beguiled.
240 As waggish° boys in game° themselves forswear,   *playful / sport; play*
So the boy Love is perjured everywhere.
For ere Demetrius looked on Hermia's eyne°   *eyes*
He hailed down oaths that he was only mine,
And when this hail some heat from Hermia felt,
245 So he dissolved,° and showers of oaths did melt.   *broke faith; melted*
I will go tell him of fair Hermia's flight.
Then to the wood will he tomorrow night
Pursue her, and for this intelligence°   *information*
If I have thanks it is a dear expense.⁴
250 But herein mean I to enrich my pain,
To have his sight thither and back again.   *Exit*

1.2

Enter QUINCE *the carpenter, and* SNUG *the joiner, and*
BOTTOM *the weaver, and* FLUTE *the bellows-mender, and*
SNOUT *the tinker, and* STARVELING *the tailor*¹
QUINCE   Is all our company here?
BOTTOM   You were best to call them generally,² man by man,
according to the scrip.°   *script; list*
QUINCE   Here is the scroll of every man's name which is thought

---

2. *o'er other some:* in comparison with others.
3. Love is promoted not by the evidence of the senses, but by the fancies of the mind.
4. Costly (because of the betrayal of secrecy and because it leads Demetrius to Hermia); or welcome (because the potential return is Demetrius's love regained).
1.2 Location: Somewhere in the city of Athens.
1. The artisans' names recall their occupations. Quince's name is probably derived from "quoins," wooden wedges used by carpenters who made buildings

such as houses and theaters. The name "Snug" evokes well-finished wooden furniture made by joiners. A bottom was the piece of wood on which thread was wound; Bottom's name also connotes "ass" and "lowest point." As Flute's name suggests, domestic bellows whistle through holes when needing repair. Snout's name may refer to the spouts of the kettles he repairs, or to his nose. Tailors, as Starveling's name recalls, were proverbially thin.
2. Bottom's error for "individually" (he frequently mistakes words in this manner).

5   fit through all Athens to play in our interlude° before the Duke   *brief play*
    and the Duchess on his wedding day at night.

BOTTOM   First, good Peter Quince, say what the play treats on;
    then read the names of the actors; and so grow to a point.[3]

QUINCE   Marry,° our play is *The Most Lamentable Comedy and*   *By the Virgin Mary*
10   *Most Cruel Death of Pyramus and Thisbe.*[4]

BOTTOM   A very good piece of work, I assure you, and a merry.
    Now, good Peter Quince, call forth your actors by the scroll.
    Masters, spread yourselves.

QUINCE   Answer as I call you. Nick Bottom, the weaver?

15 BOTTOM   Ready. Name what part I am for, and proceed.

QUINCE   You, Nick Bottom, are set down for Pyramus.

BOTTOM   What is Pyramus? A lover or a tyrant?

QUINCE   A lover, that kills himself most gallant for love.

BOTTOM   That will ask some tears in the true performing of it. If
20   I do it, let the audience look to their eyes. I will move stones.
    I will condole,° in some measure. To the rest.—Yet my chief   *lament; arouse pity*
    humour° is for a tyrant. I could play 'erc'les[5] rarely,° or a part   *inclination / excellently*
    to tear a cat° in, to make all split.°   *rant / go to pieces*

                 The raging rocks
25   And shivering shocks
                 Shall break the locks
                 Of prison gates,
                 And Phibus' car[6]
                 Shall shine from far
30   And make and mar
                 The foolish Fates.

    This was lofty. Now name the rest of the players.—This is
    'erc'les' vein, a tyrant's vein. A lover is more condoling.

QUINCE   Francis Flute, the bellows-mender?

35 FLUTE   Here, Peter Quince.

QUINCE   Flute, you must take Thisbe on you.

FLUTE   What is Thisbe? A wand'ring knight?°   *knight-errant*

QUINCE   It is the lady that Pyramus must love.

FLUTE   Nay, faith, let not me play a woman.[7] I have a beard
40   coming.

QUINCE   That's all one.° You shall play it in a mask,[8] and you   *irrelevant*
    may speak as small° as you will.   *high-pitched; shrill*

BOTTOM   An° I may hide my face, let me play Thisbe too. I'll   *If*
    speak in a monstrous° little voice: 'Thisne, Thisne!'[9]—'Ah   *exceptionally*
45   Pyramus, my lover dear, thy Thisbe dear and lady dear.'

QUINCE   No, no, you must play Pyramus; and Flute, you Thisbe.

BOTTOM   Well, proceed.

QUINCE   Robin Starveling, the tailor?

STARVELING   Here, Peter Quince.

50 QUINCE   Robin Starveling, you must play Thisbe's mother. Tom
    Snout, the tinker?

SNOUT   Here, Peter Quince.

QUINCE   You, Pyramus' father; myself, Thisbe's father. Snug the

---

3. *grow to a point:* draw to a conclusion.
4. Parodying titles such as that of Thomas Preston's *Cambyses: A Lamentable Tragedy Mixed Full of Pleasant Mirth . . .* (c. 1570).
5. Hercules (a stock ranting role in early plays).
6. The chariot of Phoebus Apollo, the sun god (the odd spelling may represent Bottom's pronunciation).

7. On the Elizabethan stage, women's parts were played by boys and young men.
8. Elizabethan ladies regularly wore masks for anonymity and to protect their complexions.
9. Probably intended as a pet name for Thisbe; or it may mean "in this manner."

joiner, you the lion's part; and I hope here is a play fitted.°   *(well) cast*
55   SNUG   Have you the lion's part written? Pray you, if it be, give it
    me; for I am slow of study.
    QUINCE   You may do it extempore, for it is nothing but roaring.
    BOTTOM   Let me play the lion too. I will roar that I will do any
    man's heart good to hear me. I will roar that I will make the
60   Duke say 'Let him roar again; let him roar again'.
    QUINCE   An you should do it too terribly you would fright the
    Duchess and the ladies that they would shriek, and that were
    enough to hang us all.
    ALL THE REST   That would hang us, every mother's son.
65   BOTTOM   I grant you, friends, if you should fright the ladies out
    of their wits they would have no more discretion but to hang us,
    but I will aggravate° my voice so that I will roar you as gently   *(for "moderate")*
    as any sucking dove.[1] I will roar you an 'twere° any nightingale.   *as though it were*
    QUINCE   You can play no part but Pyramus; for Pyramus is a
70   sweet-faced man; a proper° man as one shall see in a summer's   *handsome*
    day; a most lovely, gentlemanlike man. Therefore you must
    needs play Pyramus.
    BOTTOM   Well, I will undertake it. What beard were I best to
    play it in?
75   QUINCE   Why, what you will.
    BOTTOM   I will discharge° it in either your straw-colour beard,   *perform*
    your orange-tawny[2] beard, your purple-in-grain° beard, or your   *very deep red*
    French-crown-colour° beard, your perfect yellow.   *gold-coin-colored*
    QUINCE   Some of your French crowns have no hair at all,[3] and
80   then you will play bare faced.° But masters, here are your   *beardless; undisguised*
    parts,[4] and I am to entreat you, request you, and desire you to
    con° them by tomorrow night, and meet me in the palace wood   *memorize*
    a mile without the town by moonlight. There will we rehearse;
    for if we meet in the city we shall be dogged with company,
85   and our devices° known. In the meantime I will draw a bill°   *plans / list*
    of properties such as our play wants. I pray you fail me not.
    BOTTOM   We will meet, and there we may rehearse most
    obscenely[5] and courageously. Take pains; be perfect.[6] Adieu.
    QUINCE   At the Duke's oak we meet.
90   BOTTOM   Enough. Hold, or cut bowstrings.[7]   *Exeunt*

2.1

Enter a FAIRY *at one door and* ROBIN GOODFELLOW [*a
puck*][1] *at another*

    ROBIN   How now, spirit, whither wander you?
    FAIRY   Over hill, over dale,
       Thorough° bush, thorough brier,   *Through*
       Over park, over pale,°   *enclosure; fence*
5   Thorough flood, thorough fire:
       I do wander everywhere

---

1. Bottom confuses "sitting dove" and "sucking lamb."
2. Dark yellow, a recognized name for the dye. (Bottom the weaver shows his professional knowledge.)
3. Referring to the baldness caused by venereal disease ("the French disease").
4. Literally; an Elizabethan actor was generally given only his own lines and cues.
5. A comic blunder, possibly for "out of sight" (from the

scene or from being seen).
6. Letter perfect in learning your parts.
7. *Hold, or cut bowstrings* (from archery): Keep your word, or be disgraced (?).
2.1 Location: A wood near Athens.
1. A puck is a devil or an imp; in Elizabethan folklore, Robin Goodfellow (also known as Puck) was a mischievous spirit who would do housework if well treated.

Swifter than the moonës sphere,[2]
And I serve the Fairy Queen
To dew her orbs[3] upon the green.
10 The cowslips tall her pensioners° be.   *royal bodyguards*
In their gold coats spots you see;
Those be rubies, fairy favours;°   *gifts*
In those freckles live their savours.°   *scent*
I must go seek some dewdrops here,
15 And hang a pearl in every cowslip's ear.
Farewell, thou lob° of spirits; I'll be gone.   *country bumpkin*
Our Queen and all her elves come here anon.
ROBIN   The King doth keep his revels here tonight.
Take heed the Queen come not within his sight,
20 For Oberon is passing fell and wroth[4]
Because that she, as her attendant, hath
A lovely boy stol'n from an Indian king.
She never had so sweet a changeling;[5]
And jealous Oberon would have the child
25 Knight of his train, to trace° the forests wild.   *range*
But she perforce° withholds the lovèd boy,   *forcibly*
Crowns him with flowers, and makes him all her joy.
And now they never meet in grove, or green,
By fountain° clear, or spangled starlight sheen,°   *spring / shining starlight*
30 But they do square,° that all their elves for fear   *quarrel*
Creep into acorn cups, and hide them there.
FAIRY   Either I mistake your shape and making° quite   *form*
Or else you are that shrewd° and knavish sprite   *mischievous*
Called Robin Goodfellow. Are not you he
35 That frights the maidens of the villag'ry,°   *villages*
Skim milk, and sometimes labour in the quern,°   *hand mill*
And bootless° make the breathless housewife churn,   *in vain*
And sometime° make the drink to bear no barm°—   *at times / froth on ale*
Mislead night wanderers, laughing at their harm?
40 Those that 'hobgoblin' call you, and 'sweet puck',
You do their work, and they shall have good luck.
Are not you he?
ROBIN   Thou speak'st aright;
I am that merry wanderer of the night.
I jest to Oberon, and make him smile
45 When I a fat and bean-fed horse beguile,°   *trick*
Neighing in likeness of a filly foal;
And sometime lurk I in a gossip's° bowl   *an old woman's*
In very likeness of a roasted crab,[6]
And when she drinks, against her lips I bob.
50 And on her withered dewlap° pour the ale.   *loose skin on neck*
The wisest aunt° telling the saddest° tale   *old woman / most serious*
Sometime for three-foot stool mistaketh me;
Then slip I from her bum. Down topples she,
And 'tailor' cries,[7] and falls into a cough,
55 And then the whole choir° hold their hips, and laugh,   *company*

---

2. Each planet, including the moon, was thought to be fixed in a transparent hollow globe revolving round the earth. *moonës*: the obsolete genitive of "moon."
3. Sprinkle her fairy rings (circles of dark grass).
4. *passing fell and wroth*: exceedingly fierce and angry.
5. Usually a child left by fairies in exchange for one

stolen, but here the stolen child.
6. Crab apple ("lamb's wool," a winter drink, was made with roasted apples and warm ale).
7. Possibly the old woman cries this because she ends up cross-legged on the floor as tailors sat to work or because she falls on her "tail."

And waxen° in their mirth, and sneeze, and swear   *increase*
A merrier hour was never wasted there.—
    Enter [OBERON] *King of Fairies at one door, with his*
    train, and [TITANIA] *Queen at another, with hers*
But make room, fairy: here comes Oberon.

FAIRY   And here my mistress. Would that he were gone.

60 OBERON   Ill met by moonlight, proud Titania.

TITANIA   What, jealous Oberon?—Fairies, skip hence.
  I have forsworn his bed and company.

OBERON   Tarry, rash wanton.° Am not I thy lord?   *impetuous creature*

TITANIA   Then I must be thy lady; but I know
65   When thou hast stol'n away from fairyland
    And in the shape of Corin[8] sat all day,
    Playing on pipes of corn, and versing love[9]
    To amorous Phillida. Why art thou here
    Come from the farthest step° of India,   *limit*
70   But that, forsooth, the bouncing° Amazon,   *vigorous*
    Your buskined° mistress and your warrior love,   *wearing hunting boots*
    To Theseus must be wedded, and you come
    To give their bed joy and prosperity?

OBERON   How canst thou thus for shame, Titania,
75   Glance at my credit° with Hippolyta,   *Question my good name*
    Knowing I know thy love to Theseus?
    Didst not thou lead him through the glimmering night
    From Perigouna whom he ravishèd,
    And make him with fair Aegles[1] break his faith,
80   With Ariadne and Antiopa?[2]

TITANIA   These are the forgeries of jealousy,
    And never since the middle summer's spring°   *beginning of midsummer*
    Met we on hill, in dale, forest, or mead,
    By pavèd fountain or by rushy[3] brook,
85   Or in° the beachèd margin° of the sea   *on / shore*
    To dance our ringlets° to the whistling wind,   *circular dances*
    But with thy brawls thou hast disturbed our sport.
    Therefore the winds, piping to us in vain,
    As in revenge have sucked up from the sea
90   Contagious fogs which, falling in the land,
    Hath every pelting° river made so proud   *paltry*
    That they have overborne their continents.°   *banks*
    The ox hath therefore stretched his yoke in vain,
    The ploughman lost his sweat, and the green corn°   *grain*
95   Hath rotted ere his youth attained a beard.
    The fold stands empty in the drownèd field,
    And crows are fatted with the murrain° flock.   *dead of disease*
    The nine men's morris[4] is filled up with mud,
    And the quaint mazes in the wanton green[5]
100   For lack of tread are undistinguishable.

---

8. Corin and Phillida are typical names for a shepherd and shepherdess in pastoral poetry.
9. Making or reciting love poetry. *pipes of corn:* musical instruments made of oat stalks.
1. Perigouna and Aegles were previous mistresses of Theseus (taken from Plutarch's *Life of Theseus*).
2. Taken from Plutarch; some writers used "Antiopa" as an alternative name for the Amazonian queen Theseus married, although here it seems to refer to a different

woman. Ariadne helped Theseus kill the Minotaur and escape from his labyrinth on Crete; she fled with Theseus, but he deserted her on Naxos.
3. Fringed with reeds. *pavèd:* pebbled.
4. The playing area for this outdoor game (traditionally, a board game played with nine pebbles or pegs) was cut in turf.
5. Luxuriant grass. *quaint mazes:* intricate arrangements of paths (kept visible by use).

The human mortals want° their winter cheer.[6]   *lack*
No night is now with hymn or carol blessed.
Therefore[7] the moon, the governess of floods,
Pale in her anger washes° all the air,   *moistens; wets*
105   That rheumatic[8] diseases do abound;
And thorough this distemperature° we see   *bad weather; disturbance*
The seasons alter: hoary-headed frosts
Fall in the fresh lap of the crimson rose,
And on old Hiems'° thin and icy crown   *winter's*
110   An odorous chaplet° of sweet summer buds   *wreath*
Is, as in mock'ry, set. The spring, the summer,
The childing° autumn, angry winter change   *fruitful*
Their wonted liveries,[9] and the mazèd° world   *bewildered*
By their increase° now knows not which is which;   *crop yield*
115   And this same progeny of evils comes
From our debate,° from our dissension.   *quarrel*
We are their parents and original.°   *origin*
OBERON   Do you amend it, then. It lies in you.
Why should Titania cross her Oberon?
120   I do but beg a little changeling boy
To be my henchman.°   *page of honor*
TITANIA   Set your heart at rest.[1]
The fairyland buys not the child of me.
His mother was a vot'ress[2] of my order,
And in the spicèd Indian air by night
125   Full often hath she gossiped by my side,
And sat with me on Neptune's yellow sands,
Marking th'embarkèd traders° on the flood,°   *merchant ships / tide*
When we have laughed to see the sails conceive
And grow big-bellied with the wanton° wind,   *playful; amorous*
130   Which she with pretty and with swimming[3] gait
Following,° her womb then rich with my young squire,   *Copying*
Would imitate, and sail upon the land
To fetch me trifles, and return again
As from a voyage, rich with merchandise.
135   But she, being mortal, of that boy did die;
And for her sake do I rear up her boy;
And for her sake I will not part with him.
OBERON   How long within this wood intend you stay?
TITANIA   Perchance till after Theseus' wedding day.
140   If you will patiently dance in our round,
And see our moonlight revels, go with us.
If not, shun me, and I will spare° your haunts.   *avoid*
OBERON   Give me that boy and I will go with thee.
TITANIA   Not for thy fairy kingdom.—Fairies, away.
145   We shall chide° downright if I longer stay.   *quarrel*
           Exeunt [TITANIA *and her train*]
OBERON   Well, go thy way. Thou shalt not from° this grove   *go from*
Till I torment thee for this injury.°—   *insult*
My gentle puck, come hither. Thou rememb'rest

---

6. Winter cheer would include the hymns and carols of the Yuletide. But Q, F reading: here.
7. As in lines 88 and 93 above, referring to the consequences of their quarrel.
8. Characterized by rheum: colds, coughs, etc.

9. Customary clothing.
1. Proverbial expression for "Abandon that idea."
2. Woman who has taken a vow to serve (often religious).
3. As though gliding through the waves.

150	Since° once I sat upon a promontory	*When*
	And heard a mermaid on a dolphin's back	
	Uttering such dulcet° and harmonious breath°	*sweet / voice; song*
	That the rude° sea grew civil at her song	*rough*
	And certain stars shot madly from their spheres°	*orbits*
	To hear the sea-maid's music?	
	ROBIN I remember.	
155	OBERON That very time I saw, but thou couldst not,	
	Flying between the cold moon and the earth	
	Cupid, all armed. A certain aim he took	
	At a fair vestal thronèd by the west,[4]	
	And loosed his love-shaft° smartly from his bow	*golden arrow*
160	As° it should pierce a hundred thousand hearts.	*As though*
	But I might° see young Cupid's fiery shaft	*could*
	Quenched in the chaste beams of the wat'ry moon,	
	And the imperial vot'ress passèd on,	
	In maiden meditation, fancy-free.°	*free of love thoughts*
165	Yet marked I where the bolt° of Cupid fell.	*arrow*
	It fell upon a little western flower—	
	Before, milk-white; now, purple with love's wound—	
	And maidens call it love-in-idleness.[5]	
	Fetch me that flower; the herb I showed thee once.	
170	The juice of it on sleeping eyelids laid	
	Will make or° man or woman madly dote	*either*
	Upon the next live creature that it sees.	
	Fetch me this herb, and be thou here again	
	Ere the leviathan[6] can swim a league.	
175	ROBIN I'll put a girdle° round about the earth	*circle*
	In forty minutes. *Exit*	
	OBERON Having once this juice	
	I'll watch Titania when she is asleep,	
	And drop the liquor° of it in her eyes.	*juice*
	The next thing then she waking looks upon—	
180	Be it on lion, bear, or wolf, or bull,	
	On meddling monkey, or on busy ape—	
	She shall pursue it with the soul of love.	
	And ere I take this charm from off her sight—	
	As I can take it with another herb—	
185	I'll make her render up her page to me.	
	But who comes here? I am invisible,	
	And I will overhear their conference.	
	Enter DEMETRIUS, HELENA *following him*	
	DEMETRIUS I love thee not, therefore pursue me not.	
	Where is Lysander, and fair Hermia?	
190	The one I'll slay, the other slayeth me.	
	Thou told'st me they were stol'n unto this wood,	
	And here am I, and wood° within this wood	*insane*
	Because I cannot meet my Hermia.	
	Hence, get thee gone, and follow me no more.	
195	HELENA You draw me, you hard-hearted adamant,[7]	

---

4. To the west of India; in England. *vestal:* virgin (a compliment to Queen Elizabeth, the Virgin Queen, and possibly an allusion to a specific entertainment in her honor, such as the water pageant at Elvetham in 1591).
5. Pansy. (Classical legend describes how the mulberry turned purple with Pyramus's blood and the hyacinth with Hyacinthus's, but does not mention the pansy.)
6. Biblical sea monster, identified with the whale.
7. Very hard stone supposed to have magnetic properties. *draw me:* the magnetic power of attraction.

But yet you draw not iron; for my heart
Is true as steel.[8] Leave you° your power to draw,   *Relinquish*
And I shall have no power to follow you.

DEMETRIUS   Do I entice you? Do I speak you fair?[9]

200   Or rather do I not in plainest truth
Tell you I do not nor I cannot love you?

HELENA   And even for that do I love you the more.
I am your spaniel, and, Demetrius,
The more you beat me I will fawn on you.

205   Use me but as your spaniel: spurn me, strike me,
Neglect me, lose me; only give me leave,
Unworthy as I am, to follow you.
What worser place can I beg in your love—
And yet a place of high respect with me—

210   Than to be usèd as you use your dog?

DEMETRIUS   Tempt not too much the hatred of my spirit;
For I am sick when I do look on thee.

HELENA   And I am sick when I look not on you.

DEMETRIUS   You do impeach° your modesty too much,   *call into question*

215   To leave the city and commit yourself
Into the hands of one that loves you not;
To trust the opportunity of night,
And the ill counsel of a desert° place,   *deserted*
With the rich worth of your virginity.

220   HELENA   Your virtue is my privilege,° for that°   *protection / because*
It is not night when I do see your face;
Therefore I think I am not in the night,
Nor doth this wood lack worlds of company;
For you in my respect° are all the world.   *As far as I am concerned*

225   Then how can it be said I am alone,
When all the world is here to look on me?

DEMETRIUS   I'll run from thee, and hide me in the brakes,°   *thickets*
And leave thee to the mercy of wild beasts.

HELENA   The wildest hath not such a heart as you.

230   Run when you will. The story shall be changed:
Apollo flies, and Daphne holds the chase.[1]
The dove pursues the griffin,[2] the mild hind°   *doe*
Makes speed to catch the tiger: bootless° speed,   *useless*
When cowardice pursues, and valour flies.

235   DEMETRIUS   I will not stay thy questions.[3] Let me go;
Or if thou follow me, do not believe
But I shall do thee mischief in the wood.

HELENA   Ay, in the temple, in the town, the field,
You do me mischief. Fie, Demetrius,

240   Your wrongs do set a scandal on my sex.[4]
We cannot fight for love as men may do;
We should be wooed, and were not made to woo.
I'll follow thee, and make a heaven of hell,
To die upon the hand I love so well.

---

8. Hermia contrasts the base metal iron with steel, which holds its temper.
9. Do I speak kindly to you?
1. A reversal of the traditional myth in which the nymph Daphne, flying from Apollo, was transformed into a laurel tree to escape him.

2. Fabulous monster with a lion's body and an eagle's head and wings.
3. I will not wait here any longer to hear you talk.
4. Your injustice to me causes me to behave in a way that disgraces my sex (by wooing him rather than being wooed).

Exit [DEMETRIUS, HELENA *following him*]

245 OBERON   Fare thee well, nymph. Ere he do leave this grove
    Thou shalt fly him, and he shall seek thy love.

    Enter [ROBIN GOODFELLOW *the*] *puck*

    Hast thou the flower there? Welcome, wanderer.

ROBIN   Ay, there it is.

OBERON   I pray thee give it me.
    I know a bank where the wild thyme blows,
250   Where oxlips⁵ and the nodding violet grows,
    Quite overcanopied with luscious woodbine,°   *honeysuckle*
    With sweet musk-roses,⁶ and with eglantine.°   *sweetbrier, a type of rose*
    There sleeps Titania sometime of the night,
    Lulled in these flowers with dances and delight;
255   And there the snake throws° her enamelled skin,   *throws off; casts*
    Weed° wide enough to wrap a fairy in;   *Garment*
    And with the juice of this I'll streak° her eyes,   *anoint*
    And make her full of hateful fantasies.
    Take thou some of it, and seek through this grove.
260   A sweet Athenian lady is in love
    With a disdainful youth. Anoint his eyes;
    But do it when the next thing he espies
    May be the lady. Thou shalt know the man
    By the Athenian garments he hath on.
265   Effect it with some care, that he may prove
    More fond° on her than she upon her love;   *doting*
    And look thou meet me ere the first cock crow.⁷

ROBIN   Fear not, my lord. Your servant shall do so.

                    Exeunt [*severally*]°   *separately*

2.2

Enter TITANIA, *Queen of Fairies, with her train*

TITANIA   Come, now a roundel° and a fairy song,   *circular dance*
    Then for the third part of a minute¹ hence:
    Some to kill cankers° in the musk-rose buds,   *caterpillars*
    Some war with reremice° for their leathern wings   *bats*
5   To make my small elves coats, and some keep back
    The clamorous owl, that nightly hoots and wonders
    At our quaint° spirits. Sing me now asleep;   *dainty*
    Then to your offices, and let me rest.

    [*She lies down.*] FAIRIES *sing*

FIRST FAIRY   You spotted snakes with double° tongue,   *forked*
10   Thorny hedgehogs, be not seen;
             Newts and blindworms,² do no wrong;
             Come not near our Fairy Queen.
CHORUS [*dancing*]   Philomel³ with melody,
             Sing in our sweet lullaby;
15   Lulla, lulla, lullaby; lulla, lulla, lullaby.
             Never harm
             Nor spell nor charm

---

5. Hybrid between primrose and cowslip.
6. Large rambling white roses.
7. Some spirits were thought unable to bear daylight (compare *Hamlet* 1.1.28–36).
2.2 Location: The wood.
1. The fairies are quick enough to do their tasks in

twenty seconds.
2. Newts (water lizards) and blindworms were thought to be poisonous, as were spiders (line 20).
3. Philomel, the nightingale (in classical mythology, a woman who, raped by her sister's husband, was transformed into a bird).

Come our lovely lady nigh.
So good night, with lullaby.

20   FIRST FAIRY   Weaving spiders, come not here;
Hence, you long-legged spinners, hence;
Beetles black, approach not near;
Worm nor snail do no offence.

CHORUS [*dancing*]   Philomel with melody,
25   Sing in our sweet lullaby;
Lulla, lulla, lullaby; lulla, lulla, lullaby.
Never harm
Nor spell nor charm
Come our lovely lady nigh.
30   So good night, with lullaby.

[TITANIA] *sleeps*

SECOND FAIRY   Hence, away. Now all is well.
One aloof° stand sentinel.   *at a distance*

[*Exeunt all but* TITANIA *and the sentinel*]
Enter OBERON. [*He drops the juice on Titania's eyelids*]

OBERON   What thou seest when thou dost wake,
Do it for thy true love take;
35   Love and languish for his sake.
Be it ounce,° or cat, or bear,   *lynx*
Pard,° or boar with bristled hair,   *Leopard*
In thy eye that shall appear
When thou wak'st, it is thy dear.
40   Wake when some vile thing is near.   [*Exit*]

Enter LYSANDER *and* HERMIA

LYSANDER   Fair love, you faint with wand'ring in the wood,
And, to speak truth, I have forgot our way.
We'll rest us, Hermia, if you think it good,
And tarry for the comfort of the day.

45   HERMIA   Be it so, Lysander. Find you out a bed;
For I upon this bank will rest my head.

[*She lies down*]

LYSANDER   One turf shall serve as pillow for us both;
One heart, one bed; two bosoms, and one troth.°   *pledged faith*

HERMIA   Nay, good Lysander; for my sake, my dear,
50   Lie further off yet; do not lie so near.

LYSANDER   O, take the sense,° sweet, of my innocence!   *true meaning*
Love takes the meaning in love's conference[4]—
I mean that my heart unto yours is knit,
So that but one heart we can make of it.
55   Two bosoms interchainèd with an oath;
So, then, two bosoms and a single troth.
Then by your side no bed-room me deny;
For lying so, Hermia, I do not lie.[5]

HERMIA   Lysander riddles very prettily.
60   Now much beshrew[6] my manners and my pride
If Hermia meant to say Lysander lied.
But, gentle friend, for love and courtesy,
Lie further off, in humane° modesty.   *courteous*

---

4. Love enables lovers truly to understand one another.   6. Curse (used in a mild sense).
5. Deceive; punning on "lie down."

Such separation as may well be said
65 Becomes a virtuous bachelor and a maid,
So far be distant; and good night, sweet friend.
Thy love ne'er alter till thy sweet life end.

LYSANDER   Amen, amen, to that fair prayer say I;
And then end life when I end loyalty.
70 Here is my bed; sleep give thee all his rest.
        [*He lies down*]
HERMIA   With half that wish the wisher's eyes be pressed.[7]
        They sleep [*apart.*]
        Enter [ROBIN GOODFELLOW *the*] *puck*
ROBIN   Through the forest have I gone,
But Athenian found I none
On whose eyes I might approve°   *test*
75 This flower's force in stirring love.
Night and silence. Who is here?
Weeds of Athens he doth wear.
This is he my master said
Despisèd the Athenian maid—
80 And here the maiden, sleeping sound
On the dank and dirty ground.
Pretty soul, she durst not lie
Near this lack-love, this kill-courtesy.
Churl,° upon thy eyes I throw   *Rude fellow*
85 All the power this charm doth owe.°   *own*
        [*He drops the juice on Lysander's eyelids*]
When thou wak'st, let love forbid
Sleep his seat on thy eyelid.[8]
So, awake when I am gone.
For I must now to Oberon.   *Exit*
        Enter DEMETRIUS *and* HELENA, *running*
90 HELENA   Stay, though thou kill me, sweet Demetrius.
DEMETRIUS   I charge thee hence, and do not haunt me thus.
HELENA   O, wilt thou darkling° leave me? Do not so.   *in darkness*
DEMETRIUS   Stay, on thy peril;[9] I alone will go.   *Exit*
HELENA   O, I am out of breath in this fond° chase.   *foolish*
95 The more my prayer, the lesser is my grace.°   *reward*
Happy is Hermia, wheresoe'er she lies;
For she hath blessèd and attractive° eyes.   *magnetic*
How came her eyes so bright? Not with salt tears—
If so, my eyes are oft'ner washed than hers.
100 No, no; I am as ugly as a bear,
For beasts that meet me run away for fear.
Therefore no marvel though Demetrius
Do, as° a monster, fly my presence thus.   *as if I were*
What wicked and dissembling glass of mine
105 Made me compare° with Hermia's sphery eyne!°   *compete / starry eyes*
But who is here? Lysander, on the ground?
Dead, or asleep? I see no blood, no wound.
Lysander, if you live, good sir, awake.
LYSANDER [*awaking*]   And run through fire I will for thy sweet sake.
110 Transparent[1] Helena, nature shows art°   *skill; magic power*

---

7. May sleep's rest be shared between us. *pressed:* closed in sleep.
8. *forbid . . . eyelid:* prevent you from sleeping.
9. Stay here or risk peril (if you follow me).
1. Radiant; capable of being seen through.

That through thy bosom makes me see thy heart.
Where is Demetrius? O, how fit a word
Is that vile name to perish on my sword!

HELENA   Do not say so, Lysander; say not so.
115 What though he love your Hermia? Lord, what though?
Yet Hermia still loves you; then be content.

LYSANDER   Content with Hermia? No, I do repent
The tedious minutes I with her have spent.
Not Hermia but Helena I love.
120 Who will not change a raven for a dove?
The will of man is by his reason swayed,[2]
And reason says you are the worthier maid.
Things growing are not ripe until their season,
So I, being young, till now ripe not to reason.
125 And, touching now the point of human skill,[3]
Reason becomes the marshal[4] to my will,
And leads me to your eyes, where I o'erlook°   look over; read
Love's stories written in love's richest book.

HELENA   Wherefore was I to this keen° mockery born?   sharp
130 When at your hands did I deserve this scorn?
Is't not enough, is't not enough, young man,
That I did never—no, nor never can—
Deserve a sweet look from Demetrius' eye,
But you must flout my insufficiency?[5]
135 Good troth,° you do me wrong; good sooth,° you do,   Truly / indeed
In such disdainful manner me to woo.
But fare you well. Perforce I must confess
I thought you lord of more true gentleness.°   courtesy; breeding
O, that a lady of one man refused
140 Should of ° another therefore be abused!   Exit   by

LYSANDER   She sees not Hermia. Hermia, sleep thou there,
And never mayst thou come Lysander near;
For as a surfeit of the sweetest things
The deepest loathing to the stomach brings,
145 Or as the heresies that men do leave
Are hated most of those they did deceive,[6]
So thou, my surfeit and my heresy,
Of all be hated, but the most of me;
And all my powers, address° your love and might   direct; apply
150 To honour Helen, and to be her knight.   Exit

HERMIA [awaking]   Help me, Lysander, help me! Do thy best
To pluck this crawling serpent from my breast!
Ay me, for pity. What a dream was here?
Lysander, look how I do quake with fear.
155 Methought a serpent ate my heart away,
And you sat smiling at his cruel prey.°   act of preying
Lysander—what, removed? Lysander, lord—
What, out of hearing, gone? No sound, no word?
Alack, where are you? Speak an if ° you hear,   an if = if
160 Speak, of ° all loves. I swoon almost with fear.   for the sake of

---

2. Renaissance psychology considered the will (that is, the passions) to be in constant conflict with, and ideally subject to, the faculty of reason.
3. Reaching (only) now the highest point of human judgment.

4. Officer who led guests to their appointed places.
5. *flout my insufficiency:* mock my shortcomings by pretending they are wonderful qualities.
6. *as the heresies . . . deceive:* as men most hate the false opinions they once held.

No? Then I well perceive you are not nigh.
Either death or you I'll find immediately.   *Exit*

3.1

Enter the clowns:° [QUINCE, SNUG, BOTTOM, FLUTE,   *rustics*
SNOUT, *and* STARVELING]

BOTTOM   Are we all met?

QUINCE   Pat,° pat; and here's a marvellous convenient place for   *On the dot*
our rehearsal. This green plot shall be our stage, this hawthorn
brake° our tiring-house,° and we will do it in action as we will   *thicket / dressing room*
5   do it before the Duke.

BOTTOM   Peter Quince?

QUINCE   What sayst thou, bully° Bottom?   *good fellow; jolly*

BOTTOM   There are things in this comedy of Pyramus and
Thisbe that will never please. First, Pyramus must draw a sword
10   to kill himself, which the ladies cannot abide. How answer you
that?

SNOUT   By'r la'kin,[1] a parlous° fear.   *perilous*

STARVELING   I believe we must leave the killing out, when all is
done.[2]

15   BOTTOM   Not a whit. I have a device to make all well. Write me
a prologue, and let the prologue seem to say we will do no
harm with our swords, and that Pyramus is not killed indeed;
and for the more better assurance, tell them that I, Pyramus,
am not Pyramus, but Bottom the weaver. This will put them
20   out of fear.

QUINCE   Well, we will have such a prologue; and it shall be written in eight and six.[3]

BOTTOM   No, make it two more: let it be written in eight and
eight.

25   SNOUT   Will not the ladies be afeard of the lion?

STARVELING   I fear it, I promise you.

BOTTOM   Masters, you ought to consider with yourself, to bring
in—God shield us—a lion among ladies is a most dreadful
thing;[4] for there is not a more fearful° wild fowl than your lion   *frightening*
30   living, and we ought to look to't.

SNOUT   Therefore another prologue must tell he is not a lion.

BOTTOM   Nay, you must name his name, and half his face must
be seen through the lion's neck, and he himself must speak
through, saying thus or to the same defect:° 'ladies', or 'fair   *(for "effect")*
35   ladies, I would wish you' or 'I would request you' or 'I would
entreat you not to fear, not to tremble. My life for yours.[5] If you   *a threat to*
think I come hither as a lion, it were pity of ° my life. No, I am
no such thing. I am a man, as other men are'—and there,
indeed, let him name his name, and tell them plainly he is
40   Snug the joiner.

QUINCE   Well, it shall be so; but there is two hard things: that is,
to bring the moonlight into a chamber—for you know Pyramus
and Thisbe meet by moonlight.

3.1 Location: Remains the same, although F introduces an act break.
1. By our ladykin (Virgin Mary): a mild oath.
2. When all is said and done.
3. Alternate lines of eight and six syllables (a common
ballad measure).

4. In 1594, at a feast in honor of the christening of
King James's son, a tame lion that was supposed to draw
a chariot was replaced by a black African in order to
avoid frightening the audience.
5. I pledge my life to defend yours.

45 SNOUT[6] Doth the moon shine that night we play our play?

BOTTOM A calendar, a calendar—look in the almanac, find out moonshine, find out moonshine.

Enter [ROBIN GOODFELLOW[7] *the*] *puck* [*invisible*]

QUINCE [*with a book*][8] Yes, it doth shine that night.

BOTTOM Why, then may you leave a casement of the great chamber window where we play open, and the moon may
50 shine in at the casement.

QUINCE Ay, or else one must come in with a bush of thorns and a lantern and say he comes to disfigure,[9] or to present,° the   *represent* person of Moonshine. Then there is another thing: we must have a wall in the great chamber; for Pyramus and Thisbe, says
55 the story, did talk through the chink of a wall.

SNOUT You can never bring in a wall. What say you, Bottom?

BOTTOM Some man or other must present Wall; and let him have some plaster, or some loam, or some rough-cast[1] about him, to signify 'wall'; and let him hold his fingers thus, and
60 through that cranny shall Pyramus and Thisbe whisper.

QUINCE If that may be, then all is well. Come, sit down every mother's son, and rehearse your parts. Pyramus, you begin. When you have spoken your speech, enter into that brake; and so everyone according to his cue.

65 ROBIN [*aside*] What hempen homespuns[2] have we swagg'ring here
So near the cradle of the Fairy Queen?
What, a play toward?° I'll be an auditor—   *in preparation*
An actor, too, perhaps, if I see cause.

QUINCE Speak, Pyramus. Thisbe, stand forth.

70 BOTTOM [*as Pyramus*] Thisbe, the flowers of odious° savours   (*for "odorous"*)
sweet.

QUINCE Odours, odours.

BOTTOM [*as Pyramus*] Odours savours sweet.
So hath thy breath, my dearest Thisbe dear.
But hark, a voice. Stay thou but here a while,
75 And by and by I will to thee appear.   *Exit*

ROBIN[3] [*aside*] A stranger Pyramus than e'er played here. [*Exit*]

FLUTE Must I speak now?

QUINCE Ay, marry must you. For you must understand he goes but to see a noise that he heard, and is to come again.

80 FLUTE [*as Thisbe*] Most radiant Pyramus, most lily-white of hue,
Of colour like the red rose on triumphant brier;
Most bristly juvenile,° and eke° most lovely Jew,[4]   *lively youth / also*
As true as truest horse that yet would never tire:
I'll meet thee, Pyramus, at Ninny's° tomb.   *fool's*

85 QUINCE Ninus'[5] tomb, man!—Why, you must not speak that yet. That you answer to Pyramus. You speak all your part at

---

6. Or Snug: Q2, F abbreviate as "Sn."
7. Robin's entrance here (in F only) is also noted (in both F and Q) at line 65.
8. The book, perhaps comically supplied by Robin, is an editorial conjecture.
9. Blunder for "figure," represent. *bush of thorns:* bundle of thornbush kindling (like the lantern, a traditional accessory of the man in the moon).
1. Mixture of lime and gravel used to plaster outside walls.

2. Peasants, country bumpkins, dressed in coarse homespun fabric made from hemp.
3. Q gives this line to Quince.
4. Not often considered "lovely" by Elizabethan Christians; usually a term of abuse (here echoing the first syllable of "juvenile").
5. Mythical founder of Nineveh, whose wife, Semiramis, was believed to have founded Babylon, the setting for the story of Pyramus and Thisbe.

once, cues and all.—Pyramus, enter: your cue is past; it is
'never tire'.

FLUTE   O.

90   [*As Thisbe*] As true as truest horse that yet would never tire.
         [*Enter* ROBIN *leading* BOTTOM *with the ass-head*]

BOTTOM [*as Pyramus*]   If I were fair,° Thisbe, I were° only thine.   *handsome / would be*

QUINCE   O monstrous! O strange! We are haunted. Pray, masters; fly, masters: help!   *The clowns all exeunt*

ROBIN   I'll follow you, I'll lead you about a round,°   *in circles*
95   Through bog, through bush, through brake, through brier.
Sometime a horse I'll be, sometime a hound,
    A hog, a headless bear, sometime a fire,°   *will-o'-the-wisp*
And neigh, and bark, and grunt, and roar, and burn,
Like horse, hound, hog, bear, fire, at every turn.   *Exit*
         Enter [BOTTOM[6] *again,*] *with the ass-head*

100 BOTTOM   Why do they run away? This is a knavery of them to
make me afeard.
         Enter SNOUT

SNOUT   O Bottom, thou art changed. What do I see on thee?

BOTTOM   What do you see? You see an ass-head of your own,[7]
do you?   [*Exit* SNOUT]
         Enter QUINCE

105 QUINCE   Bless thee, Bottom, bless thee. Thou art translated.°   *transformed*
                                                Exit

BOTTOM   I see their knavery. This is to make an ass of me, to
fright me, if they could; but I will not stir from this place, do
what they can. I will walk up and down here, and I will sing,
that they shall hear I am not afraid.

110   [*Sings*]   The ousel cock° so black of hue,   *male blackbird*
                    With orange-tawny bill;
                    The throstle° with his note so true,   *song thrush*
                    The wren with little quill.°   *reed pipe*

TITANIA [*awaking*]   What angel wakes me from my flow'ry bed?

115 BOTTOM [*sings*]   The finch, the sparrow, and the lark,
                    The plainsong[8] cuckoo grey,
                    Whose note full many a man doth mark,
                        And dares not answer 'Nay'[9]—
for indeed, who would set his wit to° so foolish a bird? Who   *pay heed to*
120   would give a bird the lie,[1] though he cry 'Cuckoo' never so?°   *ever so much*

TITANIA   I pray thee, gentle mortal, sing again.
Mine ear is much enamoured of thy note;
So is mine eye enthrallèd to thy shape;
And thy fair virtue's force[2] perforce doth move me
125   On the first view to say, to swear, I love thee.

BOTTOM   Methinks, mistress, you should have little reason for
that. And yet, to say the truth, reason and love keep little company together nowadays—the more the pity that some honest
neighbours will not make them friends. Nay, I can gleek° upon   *make jokes*
130   occasion.

TITANIA   Thou art as wise as thou art beautiful.

6. He might have remained onstage when the others
left. Entrance noted in F only.
7. You see a figment of your own asinine imagination.
8. A melody sung without adornment; the repeated

"cuckoo" (associated with cuckoldry).
9. Deny (that he is a cuckold).
1. Who would call a bird a liar.
2. Your patience; power of your good qualities.

BOTTOM   Not so, neither; but if I had wit enough to get out of
this wood, I have enough to serve mine own turn.°   *purpose*
TITANIA   Out of this wood do not desire to go.
135   Thou shalt remain here, whether thou wilt or no.
I am a spirit of no common rate:°   *rank*
The summer still° doth tend upon my state;[3]   *always; continually*
And I do love thee. Therefore go with me.
I'll give thee fairies to attend on thee,
140   And they shall fetch thee jewels from the deep,
And sing while thou on pressèd flowers dost sleep;
And I will purge thy mortal grossness° so   *fleshly being*
That thou shalt like an airy spirit go.
Peaseblossom, Cobweb, Mote, and Mustardseed!

> *Enter four fairies:* PEASEBLOSSOM, COBWEB, MOTE,[4] *and*
> MUSTARDSEED

A FAIRY   Ready.
ANOTHER   And I.
ANOTHER   And I.
ANOTHER   And I.
145   ALL FOUR   Where shall we go?
TITANIA   Be kind and courteous to this gentleman.
Hop in his walks, and gambol in his eyes.
Feed him with apricots and dewberries,
With purple grapes, green figs, and mulberries;
150   The honeybags steal from the humble-bees,°   *bumblebees*
And for night tapers crop their waxen thighs
And light them at the fiery glow-worms' eyes
To have° my love to bed, and to arise;   *lead*
And pluck the wings from painted butterflies
155   To fan the moonbeams from his sleeping eyes.
Nod to him, elves, and do him courtesies.
A FAIRY   Hail, mortal.
ANOTHER   Hail.
ANOTHER   Hail.
160   ANOTHER   Hail.
BOTTOM   I cry your worships mercy,[5] heartily.—I beseech your
worship's name.
COBWEB   Cobweb.
BOTTOM   I shall desire you of more acquaintance, good Master
165   Cobweb. If I cut my finger,[6] I shall make bold with you.—Your
name, honest gentleman?
PEASEBLOSSOM   Peaseblossom.
BOTTOM   I pray you commend me to Mistress Squash, your
mother, and to Master Peascod,[7] your father. Good Master
170   Peaseblossom, I shall desire you of more acquaintance, too.—
Your name, I beseech you, sir?
MUSTARDSEED   Mustardseed.
BOTTOM   Good Master Mustardseed, I know your patience[8] well.
That same cowardly giantlike ox-beef[9] hath devoured many a
175   gentleman of your house. I promise you your kindred hath

---

3. Serves me, as part of my royal retinue.
4. Speck. "Mote" and "moth" were pronounced alike.
5. I beg pardon of your honors.
6. Cobwebs were used to stop bleeding.

7. Ripe pea pod (called "your father" because it suggests "codpiece"). *Squash:* unripe pea pod.
8. What you have suffered with fortitude.
9. Because beef is often eaten with mustard.

made my eyes water ere now. I desire you of more acquaintance, good Master Mustardseed.

TITANIA [*to the fairies*]   Come, wait upon him, lead him to my bower.
The moon, methinks, looks with a wat'ry eye,

180   And when she weeps, weeps every little flower,[1]
Lamenting some enforcèd° chastity.   *violated; involuntary*
Tie up my love's tongue;[2] bring him silently.   *Exeunt*

3.2

*Enter [*OBERON,] *King of Fairies*

OBERON   I wonder if Titania be awaked,
Then what it was that next came in her eye,
Which she must dote on in extremity.

*Enter [*ROBIN GOODFELLOW *the*] *puck*

Here comes my messenger. How now, mad spirit?

5   What nightrule° now about this haunted grove?   *night revels; sports*

ROBIN   My mistress with a monster is in love.
Near to her close° and consecrated bower   *private*
While she was in her dull° and sleeping hour   *drowsy*
A crew of patches,° rude mechanicals°   *fools / rough workmen*

10   That work for bread upon Athenian stalls,°   *market stands*
Were met together to rehearse a play
Intended for great Theseus' nuptial day.
The shallowest thickskin of that barren sort,°   *witless lot*
Who Pyramus presented,° in their sport   *acted*

15   Forsook his scene° and entered in a brake,   *stage*
When I did him at this advantage take.
An ass's nole° I fixèd on his head.   *noddle; head*
Anon his Thisbe must be answerèd,
And forth my mimic° comes. When they him spy—   *burlesque actor*

20   As wild geese that the creeping fowler° eye,   *hunter of birds*
Or russet-pated choughs, many in sort,[1]
Rising and cawing at the gun's report,
Sever° themselves and madly sweep the sky—   *Scatter*
So, at his sight, away his fellows fly,

25   And at our stamp[2] here o'er and o'er one falls.
He° 'Murder' cries, and help from Athens calls.   *One (workman)*
Their sense thus weak, lost with their fears thus strong,
Made senseless things begin to do them wrong.
For briers and thorns at their apparel snatch;

30   Some sleeves, some hats—from yielders all things catch.[3]
I led them on in this distracted fear,
And left sweet Pyramus translated there;
When in that moment, so it came to pass,
Titania waked and straightway loved an ass.

35   OBERON   This falls out better than I could devise.
But hast thou yet latched° the Athenian's eyes   *anointed*
With the love juice, as I did bid thee do?

ROBIN   I took him sleeping; that is finished, too;
And the Athenian woman by his side,

---

1. Dew was thought to originate on the moon.
2. Bottom is perhaps making involuntary asinine noises.
3.2 Location: The wood.
1. Together, in a flock. *russet-pated choughs:* gray-

headed jackdaws.
2. Editors have wondered how a fairy's presumably
tiny foot could cause the human to fall.
3. Everything robs the timid.

40 That° when he waked of force° she must be eyed.   *So that / necessity*

        Enter DEMETRIUS *and* HERMIA

OBERON   Stand close. This is the same Athenian.

ROBIN   This is the woman, but not this the man.

        [They stand apart]

DEMETRIUS   O, why rebuke you him that loves you so?

    Lay breath so bitter on your bitter foe.

45 HERMIA   Now I but chide, but I should use thee worse;

    For thou, I fear, hast given me cause to curse.

    If thou hast slain Lysander in his sleep,

    Being o'er shoes° in blood, plunge in the deep,   *Having waded so far*

    And kill me too.

50   The sun was not so true unto the day

    As he to me. Would he have stolen away

    From sleeping Hermia? I'll believe as soon

    This whole° earth may be bored, and that the moon   *solid*

    May through the centre creep, and so displease

55   Her brother's noontide with th'Antipodes.[4]

    It cannot be but thou hast murdered him.

    So should a murderer look—so dead,° so grim.   *deathly pale*

DEMETRIUS   So should the murdered look, and so should I,

    Pierced through the heart with your stern cruelty.

60   Yet you, the murderer, look as bright, as clear

    As yonder Venus in her glimmering sphere.°   *orbit*

HERMIA   What's this to my Lysander? Where is he?

    Ah, good Demetrius, wilt thou give him me?

DEMETRIUS   I had rather give his carcass to my hounds.

65 HERMIA   Out, dog; out, cur. Thou driv'st me past the bounds

    Of maiden's patience. Hast thou slain him then?

    Henceforth be never numbered among men.

    O, once tell true; tell true, even for my sake.

    Durst thou have looked upon him being awake,

70   And hast thou killed him sleeping? O brave touch!°   *noble stroke*

    Could not a worm,° an adder do so much?—   *serpent*

    An adder did it, for with doubler[5] tongue

    Than thine, thou serpent, never adder stung.

DEMETRIUS   You spend your passion on a misprised mood.°   *in misconceived anger*

75   I am not guilty of Lysander's blood,

    Nor is he dead, for aught that I can tell.

HERMIA   I pray thee, tell me then that he is well.

DEMETRIUS   And if I could, what should I get therefor?°   *for that*

HERMIA   A privilege never to see me more;

80   And from thy hated presence part I so.

    See me no more, whether he be dead or no.   *Exit*

DEMETRIUS   There is no following her in this fierce vein.

    Here therefore for a while I will remain.

    So sorrow's heaviness[6] doth heavier grow

85   For debt that bankrupt sleep doth sorrow owe,[7]

    Which now in some slight measure it will pay,

---

4. *that . . . Antipodes:* that the moon could creep through a hole bored through the earth's center and emerge on the other side, the Antipodes, displeasing the inhabitants by displacing the noontime sun with the darkness of night. (Apollo, the sun god, was the brother of Diana, the moon goddess.)

5. More forked (of the adder); more duplicitous (of Demetrius).

6. Sadness (punning on "heavy": drowsy).

7. *For . . . owe:* Because of the sleeplessness sorrow causes.

If for his tender here I make some stay.[8]
    [*He lies*] *down* [*and sleeps*]
OBERON [*to* ROBIN]   What hast thou done? Thou hast mistaken quite,
  And laid the love juice on some true love's sight.
90   Of thy misprision° must perforce ensue   *mistake*
  Some true love turned, and not a false turned true.
ROBIN   Then fate o'errules, that, one man holding troth,°   *faith*
  A million fail, confounding oath on oath.[9]
OBERON   About the wood go swifter than the wind,
95   And Helena of Athens look° thou find.   *be sure*
  All fancy-sick° she is, and pale of cheer°   *lovesick / face*
  With sighs of love that costs the fresh blood dear.[1]
  By some illusion see thou bring her here.
  I'll charm his eyes against° she do appear.   *in readiness for when*
100 ROBIN   I go, I go—look how I go,
  Swifter than arrow from the Tartar's bow.[2]   *Exit*
OBERON   Flower of this purple dye,
              Hit with Cupid's archery,
              Sink in apple° of his eye.   *pupil*
    [*He drops the juice on Demetrius' eyelids*]
105   When his love he doth espy,
              Let her shine as gloriously
              As the Venus of the sky.
              When thou wak'st, if she be by,
              Beg of her for remedy.
    Enter [ROBIN GOODFELLOW *the*] *puck*
110 ROBIN   Captain of our fairy band,
              Helena is here at hand,
              And the youth mistook by me,
              Pleading for a lover's fee.°   *reward*
              Shall we their fond° pageant see?   *foolish*
115   Lord, what fools these mortals be!
OBERON   Stand aside. The noise they make
              Will cause Demetrius to awake.
ROBIN   Then will two at once woo one.
              That must needs be sport alone;°   *unique*
120   And those things do best please me
              That befall prepost'rously.°   *ass backward*
    [*They stand apart.*]
    Enter HELENA, LYSANDER [*following her*]
LYSANDER   Why should you think that I should woo in scorn?
    Scorn and derision never come in tears.
  Look when I vow, I weep; and vows so born,
125   In their nativity all truth appears.[3]
  How can these things in me seem scorn to you,
  Bearing the badge of faith[4] to prove them true?
HELENA   You do advance° your cunning more and more,   *increase; display*
    When truth kills truth[5]—O devilish holy fray!
130 These vows are Hermia's. Will you give her o'er?

---

8. *Which . . . stay:* I will rest here awhile to give sleep
the opportunity to pay off some of its debt to sorrow.
9. Among the millions of faithless men, the one true
man's oath has been subverted by fate.
1. Sighs were thought to cause loss of blood.
2. Tartars, a dark-skinned, supposedly savage people in

Asia Minor, were famed for their archery.
3. *Look . . . appears:* The fact that I am weeping
authenticates my vow's sincerity.
4. Insignia, such as worn on a servant's livery (here, his
tears).
5. When one vow nullifies another.

Weigh oath with oath, and you will nothing weigh.[6]
Your vows to her and me put in two scales
Will even weigh, and both as light as tales.°   *lies; fiction*
LYSANDER   I had no judgement when to her I swore.
135   HELENA   Nor none, in my mind, now you give her o'er.
LYSANDER   Demetrius loves her, and he loves not you.
HELENA[7]   [   ].
DEMETRIUS [*awaking*]   O Helen, goddess, nymph, perfect, divine!
To what, my love, shall I compare thine eyne?
140   Crystal is muddy. O, how ripe in show°   *appearance*
Thy lips, those kissing cherries, tempting grow!
That pure congealèd white—high Taurus'[8] snow,
Fanned with the eastern wind—turns to a crow[9]
When thou hold'st up thy hand. O, let me kiss
145   This princess of pure white, this seal° of bliss!   *pledge*
HELENA   O spite! O hell! I see you all are bent
To set against me for your merriment.
If you were civil, and knew courtesy,
You would not do me thus much injury.
150   Can you not hate me—as I know you do—
But you must join in souls to mock me too?
If you were men, as men you are in show,
You would not use a gentle° lady so,   *well-born; mild*
To vow and swear and superpraise my parts°   *overpraise my qualities*
155   When I am sure you hate me with your hearts.
You both are rivals and love Hermia,
And now both rivals to mock Helena.
A trim° exploit, a manly enterprise—   *fine*
To conjure tears up in a poor maid's eyes
160   With your derision. None of noble sort°   *rank; nature*
Would so offend a virgin, and extort°   *torture*
A poor soul's patience, all to make you sport.
LYSANDER   You are unkind, Demetrius. Be not so.
For you love Hermia; this you know I know.
165   And here with all good will, with all my heart,
In Hermia's love I yield you up my part;
And yours of Helena to me bequeath,
Whom I do love, and will do till my death.
HELENA   Never did mockers waste more idle breath.
170   DEMETRIUS   Lysander, keep thy Hermia. I will none.[1]
If e'er I loved her, all that love is gone.
My heart to her but as guestwise° sojourned   *as a guest*
And now to Helen is it home returned,
There to remain.
LYSANDER   Helen, it is not so.
175   DEMETRIUS   Disparage not the faith thou dost not know,
Lest to thy peril thou aby it dear.°   *pay for it dearly*
         Enter HERMIA
Look where thy love comes; yonder is thy dear.
HERMIA   Dark night, that from the eye his° function takes,   *its*
The ear more quick of apprehension makes.

---

6. *you . . . weigh:* you will find that neither oath has any substance; you, Lysander, will be found to have no substance.
7. Helena's retort, awakening Demetrius, may have been inadvertently omitted by the Q and F texts.
8. Range of high mountains in Asia Minor.
9. *turns to a crow:* appears black by contrast.
1. I will have nothing to do with her.

180 Wherein it doth impair the seeing sense,
It pays the hearing double recompense.
Thou art not by mine eye, Lysander, found;
Mine ear, I thank it, brought me to thy sound.
But why unkindly didst thou leave me so?

185 LYSANDER Why should he stay whom love doth press to go?
HERMIA What love could press Lysander from my side?
LYSANDER Lysander's love, that would not let him bide:
Fair Helena, who more engilds the night
Than all yon fiery O's and eyes of light.[2]

190 Why seek'st thou me? Could not this make thee know
The hate I bare thee made me leave thee so?
HERMIA You speak not as you think. It cannot be.
HELENA [aside] Lo, she is one of this confederacy.
Now I perceive they have conjoined all three

195 To fashion this false sport in spite of° me.—   *to spite*
Injurious Hermia, most ungrateful maid,
Have you conspired, have you with these contrived
To bait[3] me with this foul derision?
Is all the counsel° that we two have shared—   *confidences*

200 The sisters' vows, the hours that we have spent
When we have chid the hasty-footed time
For parting us—O, is all quite forgot?
All schooldays' friendship, childhood innocence?
We, Hermia, like two artificial gods

205 Have with our needles created both one flower,
Both on one sampler, sitting on one cushion,
Both warbling of one song, both in one key,
As if our hands, our sides, voices, and minds
Had been incorporate.° So we grew together,   *of one body*

210 Like to a double cherry: seeming parted,
But yet an union in partition,
Two lovely berries moulded on one stem.
So, with two seeming bodies but one heart,
Two of the first[4]—like coats in heraldry,

215 Due but to one and crownèd with one crest.
And will you rend our ancient love asunder,
To join with men in scorning your poor friend?
It is not friendly, 'tis not maidenly.
Our sex as well as I may chide you for it,

220 Though I alone do feel the injury.
HERMIA I am amazèd at your passionate words.
I scorn you not. It seems that you scorn me.
HELENA Have you not set Lysander, as in scorn,
To follow me, and praise my eyes and face?

225 And made your other love, Demetrius—
Who even but now° did spurn me with his foot—   *just now*
To call me goddess, nymph, divine, and rare,
Precious, celestial? Wherefore speaks he this
To her he hates? And wherefore doth Lysander

230 Deny your love so rich within his soul,

2. Stars (punning on the vowels and on lovers' exclamatory "oh"s and "ay"s). An "o" was a spangle.
3. To torment (as Elizabethans set dogs to bait a bear).
4. A technical phrase in heraldry, referring to the first

quartering in a coat of arms, which may be repeated. The friends then have two bodies but a single, overarching identity.

And tender° me, forsooth, affection,   *offer*
But by your setting on, by your consent?
What though I be not so in grace° as you,   *favor*
So hung upon with love, so fortunate,
235   But miserable most, to love unloved—
This you should pity rather than despise.

HERMIA   I understand not what you mean by this.

HELENA   Ay, do. Persever, counterfeit sad° looks,   *serious*
Make mouths upon° me when I turn my back,   *Make faces at*
240   Wink each at other, hold the sweet jest up.°   *keep up the joke*
This sport well carried shall be chronicled.
If you have any pity, grace, or manners,
You would not make me such an argument.°   *a subject of merriment*
But fare ye well. 'Tis partly my own fault,
245   Which death or absence soon shall remedy.

LYSANDER   Stay, gentle Helena, hear my excuse,
My love, my life, my soul, fair Helena.

HELENA   O excellent!

HERMIA [*to* LYSANDER]   Sweet, do not scorn her so.

DEMETRIUS [*to* LYSANDER]   If she cannot entreat I can compel.[5]

250   LYSANDER   Thou canst compel no more than she entreat.
Thy threats have no more strength than her weak prayers.—
Helen, I love thee; by my life I do.
I swear by that which I will lose for thee
To prove him false that says I love thee not.

255   DEMETRIUS [*to* HELENA]   I say I love thee more than he can do.

LYSANDER   If thou say so, withdraw,[6] and prove it too.

DEMETRIUS   Quick, come.

HERMIA   Lysander, whereto tends all this?

[*She takes him by the arm*]

LYSANDER   Away, you Ethiope.[7]

DEMETRIUS   No, no, sir, yield.°   (*to Hermia*)
Seem to break loose, take on as° you would follow,   *pretend*
260   But yet come not. You are a tame man; go.

LYSANDER [*to* HERMIA]   Hang off,° thou cat, thou burr; vile thing, let loose,   *Let go*
Or I will shake thee from me like a serpent.

HERMIA   Why are you grown so rude? What change is this,
Sweet love?

LYSANDER   Thy love? Out, tawny Tartar, out;
265   Out, loathèd med'cine;[8] O hated potion, hence.

HERMIA   Do you not jest?

HELENA   Yes, sooth,° and so do you.   *truly*

LYSANDER   Demetrius, I will keep my word with thee.

DEMETRIUS   I would I had your bond, for I perceive
A weak bond[9] holds you. I'll not trust your word.

270   LYSANDER   What, should I hurt her, strike her, kill her dead?
Although I hate her, I'll not harm her so.

HERMIA   What, can you do me greater harm than hate?
Hate me—wherefore? O me, what news,° my love?   *what has happened*
Am not I Hermia? Are not you Lysander?

---

5. If Hermia cannot entreat you to stop, I can make you do it.
6. Come with me ("step outside").
7. Allusion to Hermia's dark hair and complexion. Elizabethans generally regarded light complexions as more beautiful than dark and often stigmatized dark-skinned peoples (such as Ethiopians or Tartars) as ugly.
8. Any drug (including poison).
9. Hermia's weak grasp (with a pun on "bond": oath, in the previous line).

275   I am as fair now as I was erewhile.°   *a while ago*
       Since night you loved me, yet since night you left me.
       Why then, you left me—O, the gods forbid—
       In earnest, shall I say?

LYSANDER   Ay, by my life,
       And never did desire to see thee more.

280   Therefore be out of hope, of question, doubt.
       Be certain, nothing truer; 'tis no jest
       That I do hate thee and love Helena.

HERMIA [*to* HELENA]   O me, you juggler,° you canker blossom,[1]   *trickster*
       You thief of love—what, have you come by night
       And stol'n my love's heart from him?

285   HELENA   Fine, i'faith.
       Have you no modesty, no maiden shame,
       No touch of bashfulness? What, will you tear
       Impatient answers from my gentle tongue?
       Fie, fie, you counterfeit, you puppet,[2] you!

290   HERMIA   Puppet? Why, so! Ay, that way goes the game.
       Now I perceive that she hath made compare
       Between our statures; she hath urged her height,
       And with her personage, her tall personage,
       Her height, forsooth, she hath prevailed with him—

295   And are you grown so high in his esteem
       Because I am so dwarfish and so low?
       How low am I, thou painted maypole?[3] Speak,
       How low am I? I am not yet so low
       But that my nails can reach unto thine eyes.

HELENA [*to* DEMETRIUS *and* LYSANDER]   I pray you, though you
300   mock me, gentlemen,
       Let her not hurt me. I was never curst.°   *quarrelsome*
       I have no gift at all in shrewishness.
       I am a right° maid for my cowardice.   *proper*
       Let her not strike me. You perhaps may think

305   Because she is something° lower than myself   *somewhat*
       That I can match her—

HERMIA   Lower? Hark again.

HELENA   Good Hermia, do not be so bitter with me.
       I evermore did love you, Hermia,
       Did ever keep your counsels, never wronged you—

310   Save that in love unto Demetrius
       I told him of your stealth° unto this wood.   *stealing away*
       He followed you; for love I followed him.
       But he hath chid me hence, and threatened me
       To strike me, spurn me, nay, to kill me too.

315   And now, so° you will let me quiet go,   *if only*
       To Athens will I bear my folly back,
       And follow you no further. Let me go.
       You see how simple and how fond° I am.   *foolish*

HERMIA   Why, get you gone. Who is't that hinders you?

320   HELENA   A foolish heart that I leave here behind.

HERMIA   What, with Lysander?

---

1. Worm that devours blossoms (of love).   3. Proverbial for someone tall and skinny. *painted:*
2. Fraudulent imitation; but Hermia interprets "pup-   insulting allusion to the use of cosmetics.
pet" as a reference to her height.

HELENA   With Demetrius.

LYSANDER   Be not afraid; she shall not harm thee, Helena.

DEMETRIUS   No, sir, she shall not, though you take her part.

HELENA   O, when she is angry she is keen° and shrewd.°   *sharp / shrewish*

325   She was a vixen when she went to school,
And though she be but little, she is fierce.

HERMIA   Little again? Nothing but 'low' and 'little'?—
Why will you suffer her to flout me thus?
Let me come to her.

LYSANDER   Get you gone, you dwarf,

330   You *minimus* of hind'ring knot-grass⁴ made,
You bead, you acorn.

DEMETRIUS   You are too officious
In her behalf that scorns your services.
Let her alone. Speak not of Helena.
Take not her part. For if thou dost intend

335   Never so little° show of love to her,   *Even the smallest*
Thou shalt aby° it.   *pay for*

LYSANDER   Now she holds me not.
Now follow, if thou dar'st, to try whose right,
Of thine or mine, is most in Helena.

DEMETRIUS   Follow? Nay, I'll go with thee, cheek by jowl.⁵

Exeunt LYSANDER *and* DEMETRIUS

340 HERMIA   You, mistress, all this coil° is long° of you.   *turmoil / because*
Nay, go not back.

HELENA   I will not trust you, I,
Nor longer stay in your curst company.
Your hands than mine are quicker for a fray;°   *fight*
My legs are longer, though, to run away.   [*Exit*]

345 HERMIA   I am amazed, and know not what to say.   *Exit*

OBERON *and* ROBIN [*come forward*]

OBERON   This is thy negligence. Still° thou mistak'st,   *Always*
Or else commit'st thy knaveries wilfully.

ROBIN   Believe me, king of shadows,° I mistook.   *fairy spirits*
Did not you tell me I should know the man

350   By the Athenian garments he had on?—
And so far° blameless proves my enterprise   *to this extent*
That I have 'nointed an Athenian's eyes;
And so far am I glad it so did sort°   *turn out*
As° this their jangling° I esteem a sport.   *Since / bickering*

355 OBERON   Thou seest these lovers seek a place to fight.
Hie° therefore, Robin, overcast the night;   *Hurry*
The starry welkin° cover thou anon   *sky*
With drooping fog as black as Acheron,°   *river of hell*
And lead these testy rivals so astray

360   As° one come not within another's way.   *So that*
Like to Lysander sometime frame thy tongue,
Then stir Demetrius up with bitter wrong;°   *insults*
And sometime rail thou like Demetrius,
And from each other look thou lead them thus

365   Till o'er their brows death-counterfeiting sleep

---

4. Creeping binding weed (its sap was thought to stunt   5. Proverbial for "side by side."
human growth). *minimus*: diminutive thing (Latin).

With leaden legs and batty° wings doth creep.   *batlike*
Then crush this herb into Lysander's eye—
Whose liquor hath this virtuous° property,   *potent*
To take from thence all error with his might,
370   And make his eyeballs roll with wonted° sight.   *normal*
When they next wake, all this derision
Shall seem a dream and fruitless° vision,   *inconsequential*
And back to Athens shall the lovers wend°   *go*
With league° whose date° till death shall never end.   *covenant / duration*
375   Whiles I in this affair do the employ,
I'll to my queen and beg her Indian boy;
And then I will her charmèd° eye release   *enchanted*
From monster's view, and all things shall be peace.
ROBIN   My fairy lord, this must be done with haste,
380   For night's swift dragons[6] cut the clouds full fast,
And yonder shines Aurora's harbinger,[7]
At whose approach ghosts, wand'ring here and there,
Troop home to churchyards; damnèd spirits all
That in cross-ways and floods[8] have burial
385   Already to their wormy beds are gone,
For fear lest day should look their shames upon.
They wilfully themselves exiled from light,
And must for aye° consort with black-browed night.   *forever*
OBERON   But we are spirits of another sort.
390   I with the morning's love[9] have oftmade sport,
And like a forester[1] the groves may tread
Even till the eastern gate, all fiery red,
Opening on Neptune° with fair blessèd beams   *the sea*
Turns into yellow gold his salt° green streams.   *salty*
395   But notwithstanding, haste, make no delay;
We may effect this business yet ere day.   [*Exit*]
ROBIN   Up and down, up and down,
I will lead them up and down.
I am feared in field and town.
400   Goblin,° lead them up and down.   (*Puck himself*)
Here comes one.
    Enter LYSANDER
LYSANDER   Where art thou, proud Demetrius? Speak thou now.
ROBIN [*shifting place*][2]   Here, villain, drawn° and ready. Where   *with sword drawn*
    art thou?
LYSANDER   I will be with thee straight.°   *immediately*
ROBIN [*shifting place*]   Follow me then
To plainer° ground.   [*Exit* LYSANDER][3]   *clearer*
    Enter DEMETRIUS
405   DEMETRIUS [*shifting place*]   Lysander, speak again.
Thou runaway, thou coward, art thou fled?
Speak! In some bush? Where dost thou hide thy head?

6. Imagined as drawing the chariots of the goddess of night.
7. Herald of the goddess of dawn; the morning star.
8. In which the drowned were "buried," without Christian sacrament. *cross-ways:* crossroads (where suicides were buried, also without Christian sacrament). Robin is differentiating here between two types of spirits: those who wandered from their churchyard graves and those who have no proper resting place. These two types, both

ghosts of former humans, are differentiated in turn from the fairy spirits by Oberon in the ensuing lines.
9. The love of Aurora, goddess of dawn (or Cephalus, a brave hunter, Aurora's lover).
1. Keeper of a royal forest or private park.
2. In F, this direction is placed in the margin in the middle of this episode. (In what follows, Robin presumably mimics the voices of Demetrius and Lysander.)
3. He might instead wander about the stage.

ROBIN [*shifting place*]   Thou coward, art thou bragging to the stars,
Telling the bushes that thou look'st for wars,
410 And wilt not come? Come, recreant;° come, thou child,   *coward; wretch*
I'll whip thee with a rod. He is defiled
That draws a sword on thee.⁴
DEMETRIUS [*shifting place*]   Yea, art thou there?
ROBIN [*shifting place*]   Follow my voice; we'll try° no manhood here.   *test*
                                 Exeunt

3.3

[*Enter* LYSANDER]

LYSANDER   He goes before me, and still dares me on;
When I come where he calls, then he is gone.
The villain is much lighter heeled than I;
I followed fast, but faster he did fly,
5 That° fallen am I in dark uneven way,   *With the result that*
And here will rest me.
       [*He lies*] *down*
                   Come, thou gentle day;
For if but once thou show me thy grey light,
I'll find Demetrius, and revenge this spite.   [*He sleeps*]
      Enter ROBIN [GOODFELLOW] *and* DEMETRIUS
ROBIN [*shifting place*]   Ho, ho, ho, coward, why com'st thou not?
10 DEMETRIUS   Abide° me if thou dar'st, for well I wot°   *Wait for / know*
Thou runn'st before me, shifting every place,
And dar'st not stand nor look me in the face.
Where art thou now?
ROBIN [*shifting place*]   Come hither, I am here.
DEMETRIUS   Nay, then thou mock'st me. Thou shalt buy° this   *pay for*
    dear°   *dearly*
15 If ever I thy face by daylight see.
Now go thy way. Faintness constraineth me
To measure out my length on this cold bed.
     [*He lies down*]
By day's approach look to be visited.   [*He sleeps*]
     Enter HELENA
HELENA   O weary night, O long and tedious night,
20 Abate° thy hours; shine comforts from the east   *Shorten*
That I may back to Athens by daylight
From these that my poor company detest;
And sleep, that sometimes shuts up sorrow's eye,
Steal me a while from mine own company.
    [*She lies down and sleeps*]
25 ROBIN   Yet but three? Come one more,
Two of both kinds makes up four.
     Enter HERMIA
Here she comes, curst° and sad.   *angry*
Cupid is a knavish lad
Thus to make poor females mad.
30 HERMIA   Never so weary, never so in woe,
Bedabbled° with the dew, and torn with briers,   *Sprinkled*
I can no further crawl, no further go.
My legs can keep no pace with my desires.

---

4. I.e., it would be a disgrace to treat you as an honorable opponent.   3.3 Location: Scene continues.

Here will I rest me till the break of day.
[*She lies down*]
35 Heavens shield Lysander, if they mean a fray.
[*She sleeps*]

ROBIN   On the ground sleep sound.
I'll apply to your eye,
Gentle lover, remedy.
[*He drops the juice on Lysander's eyelids*]
When thou wak'st thou tak'st
40 True delight in the sight
Of thy former lady's eye,
And the country proverb known,
That 'every man should take his own',
In your waking shall be shown.
45 Jack shall have Jill,
Naught shall go ill,
the man shall have his mare again, and all shall be well.   [*Exit*]

4.1

Enter [TITANIA,] *Queen of Fairies, and* [BOTTOM *the*]
clown [*with the ass-head*], *and fairies:* [PEASEBLOSSOM,
COBWEB, MOTE, *and* MUSTARDSEED]

TITANIA [*to* BOTTOM]   Come, sit thee down upon this flow'ry bed,
While I thy amiable° cheeks do coy,°   *lovable / caress*
And stick musk-roses in thy sleek smooth head,
And kiss thy fair large ears, my gentle joy.
5 BOTTOM   Where's Peaseblossom?
PEASEBLOSSOM   Ready.
BOTTOM   Scratch my head, Peaseblossom. Where's Monsieur
Cobweb?
COBWEB   Ready.
10 BOTTOM   Monsieur Cobweb, good monsieur, get you your
weapons in your hand and kill me a red-hipped humble-bee
on the top of a thistle; and, good monsieur, bring me the hon-
eybag. Do not fret yourself too much in the action, monsieur;
and, good monsieur, have a care the honeybag break not. I
15 would be loath to have you overflowen with° a honeybag, signor.   *submerged by*
[*Exit* COBWEB]
Where's Monsieur Mustardseed?
MUSTARDSEED   Ready.
BOTTOM   Give me your neaf,° Monsieur Mustardseed. Pray you,   *fist*
leave your courtesy,[1] good monsieur.
20 MUSTARDSEED   What's your will?
BOTTOM   Nothing, good monsieur, but to help Cavaliery[2] Peaseblossom[3] to scratch. I must to the barber's, monsieur, for
methinks I am marvellous hairy about the face; and I am such
a tender ass, if my hair do but tickle me I must scratch.
25 TITANIA   What, wilt thou hear some music, my sweet love?
BOTTOM   I have a reasonable good ear in music. Let's have the
tongs and the bones.[4]

4.1 Location: The wood. The original text has no act
break here. F has the four lovers sleep through the
action onstage.
1. *leave your courtesy:* stop bowing, or do not stand
bareheaded.

2. Blunder for "Cavalier," perhaps influenced by the
Italian term *cavaliere*.
3. The early texts have "Cobweb" (Shakespeare's or the
printer's error).
4. Triangle and clappers (rustic musical instruments).

Rural music[5]

TITANIA   Or say, sweet love, what thou desir'st to eat.

BOTTOM   Truly, a peck of provender.° I could munch your good
30   dry oats. Methinks I have a great desire to a bottle° of hay. Good
    hay, sweet hay, hath no fellow.°

    fodder
    bundle
    equal

TITANIA   I have a venturous fairy that shall seek
    The squirrel's hoard, and fetch thee off new nuts.

BOTTOM   I had rather have a handful or two of dried peas. But I
35   pray you, let none of your people stir me. I have an exposition
    of° sleep come upon me.   *disposition to*

TITANIA   Sleep thou, and I will wind thee in my arms.
    Fairies, be gone, and be all ways° away.   [*Exeunt* fairies]   *in every direction*
    So° doth the woodbine[6] the sweet honeysuckle   *Thus*
40   Gently entwist; the female ivy so
    Enrings the barky fingers of the elm.
    O how I love thee, how I dote on thee!
    [*They sleep.*]
    Enter ROBIN GOODFELLOW [*the puck*] *and* OBERON[7]
    [*King of Fairies, meeting*]

OBERON   Welcome, good Robin. Seest thou this sweet sight?
    Her dotage now I do begin to pity,
45   For meeting her of late behind the wood,
    Seeking sweet favours° for this hateful fool,   *love tokens*
    I did upbraid her and fall out with her,
    For she his hairy temples then had rounded
    With coronet of fresh and fragrant flowers,
50   And that same dew which sometime° on the buds   *formerly*
    Was wont° to swell like round and orient[8] pearls   *accustomed*
    Stood now within the pretty flow'rets' eyes,
    Like tears that did their own disgrace bewail.
    When I had at my pleasure taunted her,
55   And she in mild terms begged my patience,
    I then did ask of her her changeling child,
    Which straight she gave me, and her fairy sent
    To bear him to my bower in fairyland.
    And now I have the boy, I will undo
60   This hateful imperfection of her eyes.
    And, gentle puck, take this transformèd scalp
    From off the head of this Athenian swain,
    That he, awaking when the other° do,   *others*
    May all to Athens back again repair,
65   And think no more of this night's accidents
    But as the fierce vexation of a dream.
    But first I will release the Fairy Queen.
    [*He drops the juice on Titania's eyelids*]
    Be as thou wast wont to be,
    See as thou wast wont to see.
70   Dian's bud o'er Cupid's flower[9]
    Hath such force and blessèd power.

---

5. Probably background music, which continues during the following dialogue, rather than a separate musical interlude. The direction only occurs in F.
6. Here, "woodbine" cannot mean "honeysuckle," as it did at 2.1.251, and thus must refer to a different plant.
7. In Q, he enters earlier, unseen, with Titania and her train.
8. Lustrous (the best pearls were from the Far East).
9. "Dian's bud," the herb of 2.1.184 and 3.2.367, is perhaps *Agnus castus*, or chaste tree: said to preserve chastity and hence the antidote to "Cupid's flower," or the love-in-idleness of 2.1.166 etc.

Now, my Titania, wake you, my sweet queen.
TITANIA [*awaking*]   My Oberon, what visions have I seen!
Methought I was enamoured of an ass.
OBERON   There lies your love.
75 TITANIA   How came these things to pass?
O, how mine eyes do loathe his visage now!
OBERON   Silence a while.—Robin, take off this head.—
Titania, music call, and strike more dead
Than common sleep of all these five¹ the sense.
80 TITANIA   Music, ho—music such as charmeth sleep.
Still° music   Soft
ROBIN [*taking the ass-head off* BOTTOM]   Now when thou wak'st
with thine own fool's eyes peep.
OBERON   Sound music.
[*The music changes*]
Come, my queen, take hands with me,
And rock the ground whereon these sleepers be.
[OBERON *and* TITANIA *dance*]
Now thou and I are new in amity,
85 And will tomorrow midnight solemnly
Dance in Duke Theseus' house, triumphantly,
And bless it to all fair prosperity.
There shall the pairs of faithful lovers be
Wedded with Theseus, all in jollity.
90 ROBIN   Fairy King, attend and mark.
I do hear the morning lark.
OBERON   Then, my queen, in silence sad
Trip we after nightës² shade.
We the globe can compass° soon,   orbit
95 Swifter than the wand'ring moon.
TITANIA   Come, my lord, and in our flight
Tell me how it came this night
That I sleeping here was found
With these mortals on the ground.
Exeunt [OBERON, TITANIA, *and*
ROBIN. *The*] *sleepers lie still*
Wind horns [*within*]. *Enter* THESEUS [*with*] EGEUS, HIP-
POLYTA, *and all his train*
100 THESEUS   Go, one of you, find out the forester,
For now our observation³ is performed;
And since we have the vanguard° of the day,   earliest part
My love shall hear the music of my hounds.
Uncouple⁴ in the western valley; let them go.
105 Dispatch, I say, and find the forester.   [*Exit one*]
We will, fair Queen, up to the mountain's top,
And mark the musical confusion
Of hounds and echo in conjunction.
HIPPOLYTA   I was with Hercules and Cadmus⁵ once
110 When in a wood of Crete they bayed° the bear   brought to bay
With hounds of Sparta.⁶ Never did I hear

---

1. The lovers and Bottom.
2. The obsolete genitive inflection.
3. "Observance to a morn of May," as at 1.1.167.
4. Release (the dogs, leashed in pairs).

5. Mythical founder of Thebes. (No source for the anecdote is known.)
6. Famous in antiquity as hunting dogs.

Such gallant chiding;° for besides the groves,   *barking*
The skies, the fountains, every region near
Seemed all one mutual cry. I never heard
115 So musical a discord, such sweet thunder.
    THESEUS   My hounds are bred out of the Spartan kind,
So flewed,[7] so sanded;° and their heads are hung   *sandy-colored*
With ears that sweep away the morning dew,
Crook-kneed, and dewlapped[8] like Thessalian bulls,
120 Slow in pursuit, but matched in mouth like bells,
Each under each.[9] A cry more tuneable[1]
Was never holla'd to nor cheered with horn
In Crete, in Sparta, nor in Thessaly.
Judge when you hear. But soft:° what nymphs are these?   *stop; look*
125 EGEUS   My lord, this is my daughter here asleep,
    And this Lysander; this Demetrius is;
    This Helena, old Nedar's Helena.
    I wonder of their being here together.
    THESEUS   No doubt they rose up early to observe
130 The rite of May, and, hearing our intent,
Came here in grace of our solemnity.°   *ceremony*
But speak, Egeus: is not this the day
That Hermia should give answer of her choice?
    EGEUS   It is, my lord.
135 THESEUS   Go bid the huntsmen wake them with their horns.
                             [*Exit one*]
        Shout within: wind horns. [*The lovers*] *all start up*
Good morrow, friends. Saint Valentine[2] is past.
Begin these wood-birds but to couple now?
    LYSANDER   Pardon, my lord.
             [*The lovers kneel*]
    THESEUS   I pray you all stand up.
             [*The lovers stand*]
    [*To* DEMETRIUS *and* LYSANDER] I know you two are rival enemies.
140 How comes this gentle concord in the world,
That hatred is so far from jealousy°   *suspicion*
To sleep by hate, and fear no enmity?
    LYSANDER   My lord, I shall reply amazèdly,°   *confusedly*
Half sleep, half waking. But as yet, I swear,
145 I cannot truly say how I came here,
But as I think—for truly would I speak,
And, now I do bethink me, so it is—
I came with Hermia hither. Our intent
Was to be gone from Athens where° we might,   *wherever*
150 Without° the peril of the Athenian law—   *Outside*
    EGEUS [*to* THESEUS]   Enough, enough, my lord, you have enough.
    I beg the law, the law upon his head.—
    They would have stol'n away, they would, Demetrius,
    Thereby to have defeated° you and me—   *defrauded*
155 You of your wife, and me of my consent,
    Of my consent that she should be your wife.
    DEMETRIUS [*to* THESEUS]   My lord, fair Helen told me of their stealth,

---

7. Flews were large hanging, fleshy chaps.
8. With hanging folds of skin under the neck (compare 2.1.50).
9. *matched . . . each:* harmoniously matched in the pitch of their barking, like a set of bells.
1. A pack of hounds more well tuned.
2. Birds were said to choose their mates on Valentine's Day.

Of this their purpose hither to this wood,
And I in fury hither followed them,
160 Fair Helena in fancy° following me.   *love*
But, my good lord, I wot not by what power—
But by some power it is—my love to Hermia,
Melted as the snow, seems to me now
As the remembrance of an idle gaud°   *a worthless trinket*
165 Which in my childhood I did dote upon,
And all the faith, the virtue of my heart,
The object and the pleasure of mine eye
Is only Helena. To her, my lord,
Was I betrothed ere I saw Hermia.
170 But like in sickness³ did I loathe this food;
But, as in health come to my natural taste,
Now I do wish it, love it, long for it,
And will for evermore be true to it.
THESEUS Fair lovers, you are fortunately met.
175 Of this discourse we more will hear anon.—
Egeus, I will overbear your will,
For in the temple by and by with us
These couples shall eternally be knit.—
And, for° the morning now is something° worn,   *since / somewhat*
180 Our purposed hunting shall be set aside.
Away with us to Athens. Three and three,
We'll hold a feast in great solemnity.
Come, Hippolyta.
                    Exit Duke [THESEUS *with* HIPPOLYTA, EGEUS,
                                            and all his train]
DEMETRIUS These things seem small and undistinguishable,
185 Like far-off mountains turnèd into clouds.
HERMIA Methinks I see these things with parted° eye,   *improperly focused*
When everything seems double.
HELENA   So methinks,
And I have found Demetrius like a jewel,
Mine own and not mine own.⁴
DEMETRIUS   It seems to me
190 That yet we sleep, we dream. Do not you think
The Duke was here and bid us follow him?
HERMIA Yea, and my father.
HELENA   And Hippolyta.
LYSANDER And he did bid us follow to the temple.
DEMETRIUS Why then, we are awake. Let's follow him,
195 And by the way let us recount our dreams.   *Exeunt lovers*
            BOTTOM *wakes*
BOTTOM When my cue comes, call me, and I will answer. My
next is 'most fair Pyramus'. Heigh-ho.° Peter Quince? Flute the   *(Perhaps a yawn)*
bellows-mender? Snout the tinker? Starveling? God's my life!°   *Good Lord*
Stolen hence, and left me asleep?—I have had a most rare
200 vision. I have had a dream past the wit of man to say what
dream it was. Man is but an ass if he go about° t'expound this   *try*
dream. Methought I was—there is no man can tell what.
Methought I was, and methought I had—but man is but a

---

3. Only as a person does when ill or nauseated.
4. Mine on the principle of "finders keepers," but once someone else's.

patched fool[5] if he will offer° to say what methought I had. The   *venture*

205 eye of man hath not heard, the ear of man hath not seen, man's
hand is not able to taste, his tongue to conceive, nor his heart
to report[6] what my dream was. I will get Peter Quince to write
a ballad of this dream. It shall be called 'Bottom's Dream',
because it hath no bottom,[7] and I will sing it in the latter end

210 of a play, before the Duke. Peradventure,° to take it the more   *Perhaps*
gracious, I shall sing it at her° death.   *Exit*   *(Thisbe's?)*

4.2

Enter QUINCE, FLUTE, SNOUT, *and* STARVELING

QUINCE   Have you sent to Bottom's house? Is he come home
yet?

STARVELING   He cannot be heard of. Out of doubt° he is trans-   *Doubtless*
ported.[1]

5 FLUTE   If he come not, then the play is marred. It goes not forward. Doth it?

QUINCE   It is not possible. You have not a man in all Athens able
to discharge° Pyramus but he.   *perform*

FLUTE   No, he hath simply the best wit° of any handicraft-man   *intellect*

10 in Athens.

QUINCE   Yea, and the best person,° too; and he is a very para-   *looks*
mour for a sweet voice.

FLUTE   You must say 'paragon'. A paramour is, God bless us, a
thing of naught.°   *something wicked*

Enter SNUG *the joiner*

15 SNUG   Masters, the Duke is coming from the temple, and there
is two or three lords and ladies more married. If our sport° had   *entertainment*
gone forward we had all been made men.[2]

FLUTE   O sweet bully Bottom! Thus hath he lost sixpence a day[3]
during his life. He could not have scaped sixpence a day. An°   *If*

20 the Duke had not given him sixpence a day for playing Pyramus, I'll be hanged. He would have deserved it. Sixpence a
day in Pyramus, or nothing.

Enter BOTTOM

BOTTOM   Where are these lads? Where are these hearts?°   *mates*

QUINCE   Bottom! O most courageous[4] day! O most happy hour!

25 BOTTOM   Masters, I am to discourse wonders; but ask me not
what. For if I tell you, I am no true Athenian. I will tell you
everything right as it fell out.

QUINCE   Let us hear, sweet Bottom.

BOTTOM   Not a word of° me. All that I will tell you is that the   *out of*

30 Duke hath dined. Get your apparel together, good strings° to   *(to attach the beards)*
your beards, new ribbons to your pumps. Meet presently° at the   *immediately*
palace; every man look o'er his part. For the short and the long
is, our play is preferred.° In any case let Thisbe have clean   *recommended*
linen, and let not him that plays the lion pare his nails, for they

35 shall hang out for the lion's claws. And, most dear actors, eat
no onions nor garlic, for we are to utter sweet breath, and I do

---

5. Jester in a patchwork or motley costume.
6. *The eye . . . report:* burlesque of Scripture: "The eye
hath not seen, and the ear hath not heard, neither have
entered into the heart of man" those things that God
has prepared (1 Corinthians 2:9–10 [Bishops' Bible]).
7. Because it is unfathomable, has no substance (foundation).

4.2 Location: Athens.
1. Carried away (by the fairies); transformed.
2. *we . . . men:* our fortunes would have been made.
3. As a royal pension, considerably more than the average daily wage of an Elizabathan workman.
4. Blunder for "brave," meaning "splendid."

not doubt but to hear them say it is a sweet comedy. No more
words. Away, go, away!   *Exeunt*

5.1

Enter THESEUS, HIPPOLYTA, EGEUS,[1] *and* [*attendant*]
  lords

HIPPOLYTA   'Tis strange, my Theseus, that° these lovers speak of.   *that which*
THESEUS   More strange than true. I never may believe
    These antique[2] fables, nor these fairy toys.°   *trifles*
    Lovers and madmen have such seething brains,
5   Such shaping fantasies,° that apprehend°   *imaginations / conceive*
    More than cool reason ever comprehends.
    The lunatic, the lover, and the poet
    Are of imagination all compact.°   *composed*
    One sees more devils than vast hell can hold:
10   That is the madman. The lover, all as frantic,
    Sees Helen's beauty in a brow of Egypt.[3]
    The poet's eye, in a fine frenzy rolling,
    Doth glance from heaven to earth, from earth to heaven,
    And as imagination bodies forth
15   The forms of things unknown, the poet's pen
    Turns them to shapes, and gives to airy nothing
    A local habitation and a name.
    Such tricks hath strong imagination
    That if it would but apprehend some joy
20   It comprehends some bringer° of that joy;   *source*
    Or in the night, imagining some fear,°   *object to be feared*
    How easy is a bush supposed a bear!
HIPPOLYTA   But all the story of the night told over,
    And all their minds transfigured so together,
25   More witnesseth than fancy's images,[4]
    And grows to something of great constancy;°   *consistency*
    But howsoever,° strange and admirable.°   *in any case / wondrous*

Enter lovers: LYSANDER, DEMETRIUS, HERMIA, *and*
  HELENA

THESEUS   Here come the lovers, full of joy and mirth.
    Joy, gentle friends—joy and fresh days of love
    Accompany your hearts.
30 LYSANDER   More than to us
    Wait in your royal walks, your board, your bed.[5]
THESEUS   Come now, what masques, what dances shall we have
    To wear away this long age of three hours
    Between our after-supper and bed-time?
35   Where is our usual manager of mirth?
    What revels are in hand? Is there no play
    To ease the anguish of a torturing hour?
    Call Egeus.
EGEUS   Here, mighty Theseus.
THESEUS   Say, what abridgement[6] have you for this evening?

5.1 Location: Athens. Theseus's palace.
1. Q does not call for Egeus, but gives all his speeches
to Philostrate (the character briefly addressed in 1.1).
F's substitution of Egeus here may be a mistake (the
possible result of the same actor playing both parts in
an early performance) or an attempt to incorporate the
angry father into the festive close.

2. Ancient; strange, grotesque (as in "antic").
3. In a gypsy's face. *Helen:* Helen of Troy.
4. *More . . . images:* Testifies to something more than
mere figments of the imagination.
5. *More . . . bed:* May even more joy and love attend
your daily lives.
6. Pastime, something to make the evening seem shorter.

40 What masque, what music? How shall we beguile
The lazy time if not with some delight?
EGEUS   There is a brief° how many sports are ripe.   *short list*
Make choice of which your highness will see first.
LYSANDER[7] [*reads*]   'The battle with the centaurs,[8] to be sung
45 By an Athenian eunuch to the harp.'
THESEUS   We'll none of that. That have I told my love
In glory of my kinsman Hercules.[9]
LYSANDER [*reads*]   'The riot of the tipsy bacchanals
Tearing the Thracian singer in their rage.'[1]
50 THESEUS   That is an old device,° and it was played   *show*
When I from Thebes came last a conqueror.
LYSANDER [*reads*]   'The thrice-three muses mourning for the death
Of learning, late deceased in beggary.'[2]
THESEUS   That is some satire, keen and critical,
55 Not sorting with° a nuptial ceremony.   *befitting*
LYSANDER [*reads*]   'A tedious brief scene of young Pyramus
And his love Thisbe: very tragical mirth.'
THESEUS   'Merry' *and* 'tragical'? 'Tedious' *and* 'brief'?—
That is, hot ice and wondrous strange black[3] snow.
60 How shall we find the concord of this discord?
EGEUS   A play there is, my lord, some ten words long,
Which is as 'brief' as I have known a play;
But by ten words, my lord, it is too long,
Which makes it 'tedious'; for in all the play
65 There is not one word apt, one player fitted.°   *appropriately cast*
And 'tragical', my noble lord, it is,
For Pyramus therein doth kill himself;
Which when I saw rehearsed, I must confess,
Made mine eyes water; but more merry tears
70 The passion of loud laughter never shed.
THESEUS   What are they that do play it?
EGEUS   Hard-handed men that work in Athens here,
Which never laboured in their minds till now,
And now have toiled° their unbreathed° memories   *taxed / unexercised*
75 With this same play against° your nuptial.   *in preparation for*
THESEUS   And we will hear it.
EGEUS   No, my noble lord,
It is not for you. I have heard it over,
And it is nothing, nothing in the world,
Unless you can find sport in their intents
80 Extremely stretched,° and conned° with cruel pain   *strained / memorized*
To do you service.
THESEUS   I will hear that play;
For never anything can be amiss
When simpleness and duty tender it.
Go, bring them in; and take your places, ladies. [*Exit* EGEUS]

---

7. In Q, Theseus both reads the list and comments on it himself.
8. Probably the battle that occurred when the Centaurs tried to carry off the bride of Theseus's friend Pirithous.
9. According to Plutarch, Hercules and Theseus were cousins.
1. The murder of the poet Orpheus by drunken women, devotees of Dionysus.

2. Possibly a topical reference: Robert Greene, Christopher Marlowe, and Thomas Kyd, university wits who began writing for the stage in the 1580s, all died in desperate circumstances in 1592–94. But satiric laments on the poverty of scholars and poets were commonplace.
3. "Black" is an editorial conjecture. Q and F omit a word that would make "snow" an oxymoron comparable to "hot ice."

85 HIPPOLYTA I love not to see wretchedness o'ercharged,[4]
And duty in his service° perishing.   *its attempt to serve*
THESEUS Why, gentle sweet, you shall see no such thing.
HIPPOLYTA He says they can do nothing in this kind.°   *kind of thing*
THESEUS The kinder we, to give them thanks for nothing.
90 Our sport shall be to take what they mistake,
And what poor duty cannot do,
Noble respect° takes it in might, not merit.[5]   *consideration*
Where I have come, great clerks° have purposèd   *scholars*
To greet me with premeditated welcomes,
95 Where I have seen them shiver and look pale,
Make periods in the midst of sentences,
Throttle their practised accent[6] in their fears,
And in conclusion dumbly have broke off,
Not paying me a welcome. Trust me, sweet,
100 Out of this silence yet I picked a welcome,
And in the modesty of fearful° duty   *frightened*
I read as much as from the rattling tongue
Of saucy and audacious eloquence.
Love, therefore, and tongue-tied simplicity
105 In least speak most, to my capacity.°   *in my judgment*
          [*Enter* EGEUS]
EGEUS So please your grace, the Prologue is addressed.[7]
THESEUS Let him approach.
          Flourish trumpets. Enter [QUINCE *as*] *the Prologue*
QUINCE [*as Prologue*] If we offend, it is with our good will.
That you should think: we come not to offend
110 But with good will. To show our simple skill,
That is the true beginning of our end.
Consider then we come but in despite.
We do not come as minding° to content you,   *intending*
Our true intent is. All for your delight
115 We are not here. That you should here repent you
The actors are at hand, and by their show
You shall know all that you are like to know.[8]
THESEUS This fellow doth not stand upon points.[9]
LYSANDER He hath rid his prologue like a rough° colt: he knows   *an unbroken*
120 not the stop.[1] A good moral, my lord: it is not enough to speak,
but to speak true.
HIPPOLYTA Indeed, he hath played on this prologue like a child
on a recorder[2]—a sound, but not in government.°   *control*
THESEUS His speech was like a tangled chain—nothing°   *not at all*
125 impaired, but all disordered. Who is next?
          Enter with a trumpeter before them [BOTTOM *as*] *Pyra-*
          mus, [FLUTE *as*] *Thisbe,* [SNOUT *as*] *Wall,* [STARVELING
          as] *Moonshine, and* [SNUG *as*] *Lion* [*for the dumb*
          show][3]

---

4. Overburdened. *wretchedness:* incompetence or
weakness; poor people.
5. *in . . . merit:* with respect to the giver's capacity, not
the merit of the performance.
6. Rehearsed eloquence; usual manner of speaking.
7. The speaker of the Prologue is ready.
8. The humor of Quince's speech rests in its mis-
punctuation; repunctuated, it becomes a typical courteous address.

9. Bother about niceties; heed punctuation marks.
1. How to rein the colt to a stop; punctuation mark.
2. A woodwind instrument resembling a flute.
3. Elizabethan plays were often prefaced by a "dumb
show" in which the actors silently mimed the main
action, occasionally to the accompaniment (as here) of
a narrator. The artisans may enact the story as Quince
tells it, merely adopt symbolic attitudes, or introduce
themselves.

QUINCE [*as Prologue*] Gentles, perchance you wonder at this show,
    But wonder on, till truth make all things plain.
  This man is Pyramus, if you would know;
    This beauteous lady Thisbe is, certain.
130 This man with lime and roughcast doth present
    Wall, that vile wall which did these lovers sunder;
  And through Wall's chink, poor souls, they are content
    To whisper; at the which let no man wonder.
  This man, with lantern, dog, and bush of thorn,
135   Presenteth Moonshine. For if you will know,
  By moonshine did these lovers think no scorn°   *(it) no disgrace*
    To meet at Ninus' tomb, there, there to woo.
  This grizzly beast, which 'Lion' hight° by name,   *is called*
    The trusty Thisbe coming first by night
140   Did scare away, or rather did affright;
    And as she fled, her mantle she did fall,°   *drop*
  Which Lion vile with bloody mouth did stain.
  Anon comes Pyramus, sweet youth and tall,°   *brave*
    And finds his trusty Thisbe's mantle slain;
145 Whereat with blade—with bloody, blameful blade—
    He bravely broached° his boiling bloody breast;   *stabbed*
  And Thisbe, tarrying in mulberry shade,
    His dagger drew and died. For all the rest,
  Let Lion, Moonshine, Wall, and lovers twain
150 At large° discourse, while here they do remain.   *length*
              *Exeunt all [the clowns] but [*SNOUT *as*] Wall*

THESEUS   I wonder if the lion be to speak.
DEMETRIUS   No wonder, my lord—one lion may when many
  asses do.
SNOUT [*as Wall*]   In this same interlude° it doth befall   *play*
155 That I, one Snout by name, present a wall;
  And such a wall as I would have you think
  That had in it a crannied hole or chink,
  Through which the lovers Pyramus and Thisbe
  Did whisper often, very secretly.
160 This loam, this roughcast, and this stone doth show
  That I am that same wall; the truth is so.
  And this the cranny is, right and sinister,[4]
  Through which the fearful lovers are to whisper.
THESEUS   Would you desire lime and hair to speak better?
165 DEMETRIUS   It is the wittiest partition[5] that ever I heard dis-
  course, my lord.
              *Enter [*BOTTOM *as*] Pyramus*
THESEUS   Pyramus draws near the wall. Silence.
BOTTOM [*as Pyramus*]   O grim-looked° night, O night with hue   *grim-looking*
  so black,
    O night which ever art when day is not;
170 O night, O night, alack, alack, alack,
    I fear my Thisbe's promise is forgot.
  And thou, O wall, O sweet O lovely wall,
    That stand'st between her father's ground and mine,
  Thou wall, O wall, O sweet and lovely wall,

---

4. Left; running horizontally. Or on the one side   5. Wall; formal term for part of an oration.
(Pyramus's) and the other (Thisbe's).

175   Show me thy chink, to blink through with mine eyne.
            [*Wall shows his chink*]
         Thanks, courteous wall. Jove shield thee well for this.
         But what see I? No Thisbe do I see.
         O wicked wall, through whom I see no bliss,
         Cursed be thy stones[6] for thus deceiving me.

180   THESEUS   The wall methinks, being sensible,° should curse   *capable of feeling*
         again.°   *back*
       BOTTOM [*to* THESEUS]   No, in truth, sir, he should not. 'Deceiv-
         ing me' is Thisbe's cue. She is to enter now, and I am to spy
         her through the wall. You shall see, it will fall pat° as I told you.   *precisely*
            Enter [FLUTE *as*] *Thisbe*
185   Yonder she comes.
       FLUTE [*as Thisbe*]   O wall, full often hast thou heard my moans
         For parting my fair Pyramus and me.
         My cherry lips have often kissed thy stones,
         Thy stones with lime and hair knit up in thee.
190   BOTTOM [*as Pyramus*]   I see a voice. Now will I to the chink
         To spy an° I can hear my Thisbe's face.   *if*
         Thisbe?
       FLUTE [*as Thisbe*]   My love—thou art my love, I think.
       BOTTOM [*as Pyramus*]   Think what thou wilt, I am thy lover's
           grace°   *gracious lover*
         And like Lemander[7] am I trusty still.
195   FLUTE [*as Thisbe*]   And I like Helen,[8] till the fates me kill.
       BOTTOM [*as Pyramus*]   Not Shaphalus to Procrus[9] was so true.
       FLUTE [*as Thisbe*]   As Shaphalus to Procrus, I to you.
       BOTTOM [*as Pyramus*]   O kiss me through the hole of this vile wall.
       FLUTE [*as Thisbe*]   I kiss the wall's hole, not your lips at all.
       BOTTOM [*as Pyramus*]   Wilt thou at Ninny's tomb meet me
200   straightway?
       FLUTE [*as Thisbe*]   Tide° life, tide death, I come without delay.   *Betide; come*
               [*Exeunt* BOTTOM *and* FLUTE *severally*]
       SNOUT [*as Wall*]   Thus have I, Wall, my part dischargèd so;
         And being done, thus Wall away doth go.   *Exit*
       THESEUS   Now is the wall down between the two neighbours.
205   DEMETRIUS   No remedy, my lord, when walls are so wilful to°   *as to*
         hear without warning.[1]
       HIPPOLYTA   This is the silliest stuff that ever I heard.
       THESEUS   The best in this kind are but shadows,[2] and the worst
         are no worse if imagination amend them.
210   HIPPOLYTA   It must be your imagination, then, and not theirs.
       THESEUS   If we imagine no worse of them than they of them-
         selves, they may pass for excellent men. Here come two noble
         beasts in: a man and a lion.
            Enter [SNUG *as*] *Lion,* [*and* STARVELING *as*] *Moonshine*
            [*with a lantern, thorn bush, and dog*]
       SNUG [*as Lion*]   You, ladies, you whose gentle hearts do fear

---

6. Punning on "testicles."
7. Blunder for "Leander," who drowned while swimming across the Hellespont to meet his lover, Hero.
8. Helen of Troy was notoriously untrustworthy; a
blunder for "Hero."
9. Blunder for "Cephalus" and "Procris." Procris was in

fact seduced by her husband in disguise as another
man; he later accidentally killed her.
1. Informing the parents. *hear:* proverbially, "walls
have ears."
2. Mere likenesses without substance. *kind:* profession
(that is, actors)

215   The smallest monstrous mouse that creeps on floor,
    May now perchance both quake and tremble here
      When lion rough in wildest rage doth roar.
    Then know that I as Snug the joiner am
    A lion fell,[3] nor else no lion's dam.
220   For if I should as Lion come in strife
    Into this place, 'twere pity on my life.

THESEUS   A very gentle beast, and of a good conscience.

DEMETRIUS   The very best at a beast, my lord, that e'er I saw.

LYSANDER   This lion is a very fox[4] for his valour.

225 THESEUS   True, and a goose[5] for his discretion.

DEMETRIUS   Not so, my lord, for his valour cannot carry his discretion, and the fox carries the goose.

THESEUS   His discretion, I am sure, cannot carry his valour, for
the goose carries not the fox. It is well. Leave it to his discretion,
230 and let us listen to the moon.

STARVELING [*as Moonshine*]   This lantern doth the hornèd°   *crescent*
moon present.

DEMETRIUS   He should have worn the horns on his head.[6]

THESEUS   He is no crescent,° and his horns are invisible within   *waxing moon*
the circumference.

235 STARVELING [*as Moonshine*]   This lantern doth the hornèd moon present.
    Myself the man i'th' moon do seem to be.

THESEUS   This is the greatest error of all the rest—the man
should be put into the lantern. How is it else the man i'th'
moon?

240 DEMETRIUS   He dares not come there for° the candle; for you see   *for fear of*
it is already in snuff.[7]

HIPPOLYTA   I am aweary of this moon. Would he would change.

THESEUS   It appears by his small light of discretion that he is in
the wane; but yet in courtesy, in all reason, we must stay the
245 time.

LYSANDER   Proceed, Moon.

STARVELING   All that I have to say is to tell you that the lantern
is the moon, I the man i'th' moon, this thorn bush my thorn
bush, and this dog my dog.

250 DEMETRIUS   Why, all these should be in the lantern, for all these
are in the moon. But silence; here comes Thisbe.

      Enter [FLUTE *as*] *Thisbe*

FLUTE [*as Thisbe*]   This is old Ninny's tomb. Where is my love?

SNUG [*as Lion*]   O.

      Lion roars. Thisbe [*drops her mantle and*] *runs off*

DEMETRIUS   Well roared, Lion.

255 THESEUS   Well run, Thisbe.

HIPPOLYTA   Well shone, Moon.—Truly, the moon shines with a
good grace.

      [*Lion worries Thisbe's mantle*]

THESEUS   Well moused,[8] Lion.

DEMETRIUS   And then came Pyramus.

      Enter [BOTTOM *as*] *Pyramus*

260 LYSANDER   And so the lion vanished.   [*Exit Lion*]

---

3. Fierce; or skin (punning on the costume to which
Snug reassuringly calls attention).
4. Symbolic of low cunning, rather than courage.
5. Symbolic of foolishness.

6. The symbol of a cuckold.
7. In need of snuffing; angry.
8. The mantle is like a mouse in the mouth of a cat.

BOTTOM [*as Pyramus*]   Sweet moon, I thank thee for thy sunny beams.
    I thank thee, moon, for shining now so bright;
  For by thy gracious, golden, glittering gleams
    I trust to take of truest Thisbe sight.

265   But stay, O spite!
        But mark, poor knight,
    What dreadful dole° is here?   *grief*
        Eyes, do you see?
        How can it be?

270   O dainty duck, O dear!
        Thy mantle good,
    What, stained with blood?
    Approach, ye furies fell.
        O fates,⁹ come, come,

275   Cut thread and thrum,¹
    Quail,° crush, conclude, and quell.°   *Overpower / kill*

THESEUS   This passion—and² the death of a dear friend—would
  go near to make a man look sad.

HIPPOLYTA   Beshrew my heart, but I pity the man.

280 BOTTOM [*as Pyramus*]   O wherefore, nature, didst thou lions frame,
    Since lion vile hath here deflowered³ my dear?—
  Which is—no, no, which *was*—the fairest dame
    That lived, that loved, that liked, that looked, with cheer.
        Come tears, confound;

285   Out sword, and wound
    The pap° of Pyramus.   *breast*
        Ay, that left pap,
        Where heart doth hop.
    Thus die I: thus, thus, thus.
        [*He stabs himself*]

290   Now am I dead,
        Now am I fled,
    My soul is in the sky.
        Tongue, lose thy light;
        Moon, take thy flight.   [*Exit Moonshine*]

295   Now die, die, die, die, die.   [*He dies*]

DEMETRIUS   No die but an ace for him; for he is but one.⁴

LYSANDER   Less than an ace, man; for he is dead; he is nothing.

THESEUS   With the help of a surgeon he might yet recover and
  prove an ass.

300 HIPPOLYTA   How chance Moonshine is gone before Thisbe
  comes back and finds her lover.

THESEUS   She will find him by starlight.
      Enter [FLUTE *as*] *Thisbe*
  Here she comes, and her passion° ends the play.   *passionate speech*

HIPPOLYTA   Methinks she should not use a long one for such a

305 Pyramus. I hope she will be brief.

DEMETRIUS   A mote° will turn the balance which Pyramus,   *speck*

---

9. The three Fates in Greek mythology spun and cut
the thread of a person's life.
1. A technical term from Bottom's occupation: the
tufted end of a weaver's warp, or set of yarns placed
lengthwise in a loom when the woven fabric is cut.
2. Only if combined with. *passion:* suffering; extravagant

speech.
3. Ruined (but commonly suggesting "deprived of her
virginity"); his error for "devoured."
4. Pun on "die" as one of a pair of dice. *one:* the ace, or
lowest throw.

which[5] Thisbe, is the better—he for a man, God warrant us;
she for a woman, God bless us.

LYSANDER She hath spied him already with those sweet eyes.

310 DEMETRIUS And thus she means, videlicet:[6]

FLUTE [as Thisbe] Asleep, my love?
　　What, dead, my dove?
　　O Pyramus, arise.
　　Speak, speak. Quite dumb?
315 　　Dead, dead? A tomb
　　Must cover thy sweet eyes.
　　These lily lips,
　　This cherry nose,
　　These yellow cowslip cheeks
320 　　Are gone, are gone.
　　Lovers, make moan.
　　His eyes were green as leeks.
　　O sisters three,°　　　　　　　　　　　　　　　　　*the Fates*
　　Come, come to me
325 　　With hands as pale as milk.
　　Lay them in gore,
　　Since you have shore°　　　　　　　　　　　　　　　*shorn*
　　With shears his thread of silk.
　　Tongue, not a word.
330 　　Come, trusty sword,
　　Come, blade, my breast imbrue.°　　　　　　*stain with blood*
　　　　[She stabs herself]
　　And farewell friends,
　　Thus Thisbe ends.
　　Adieu, adieu, adieu.　　　　　　　　　　　　　　　[She dies]

335 THESEUS Moonshine and Lion are left to bury the dead.

DEMETRIUS Ay, and Wall too.

BOTTOM[7] No, I assure you, the wall is down that parted their
fathers. Will it please you to see the epilogue or to hear a bergamask dance[8] between two of our company?

340 THESEUS No epilogue, I pray you; for your play needs no excuse.
Never excuse; for when the players are all dead there need
none to be blamed. Marry, if he that writ it had played Pyramus
and hanged himself in Thisbe's garter it would have been a
fine tragedy; and so it is, truly, and very notably discharged. But
345 come, your bergamask. Let your epilogue alone.

　　[BOTTOM and FLUTE[9] dance a bergamask, then exeunt]
　　The iron tongue of midnight hath told° twelve.　　*counted; tolled*
　　Lovers, to bed; 'tis almost fairy time.
　　I fear we shall outsleep the coming morn
　　As much as we this night have overwatched.°　　*stayed awake too late*
350 　　This palpable-gross° play hath well beguiled　　*palpably crude*
　　The heavy° gait of night. Sweet friends, to bed.　　*drowsy; slow*
　　A fortnight hold we this solemnity
　　In nightly revels and new jollity.　　　　　　　　　　*Exeunt*

---

5. *which . . . which:* whether . . . or.
6. As follows. *means:* moans; lodges a formal legal complaint.
7. Spoken by Snug, the Lion, in Q.

8. A dance named after Bergamo, in Italy (commonly ridiculed for its rusticity).
9. The only "two of our company" onstage at the end of the play.

5.2

Enter Puck [ROBIN GOODFELLOW, with a broom]

ROBIN   Now the hungry lion roars,
    And the wolf behowls the moon,
whilst the heavy° ploughman snores,   *weary*
    All with weary task fordone.°   *"done in"; exhausted*
5   Now the wasted brands° do glow   *burned-out logs*
    Whilst the screech-owl, screeching loud,
    Puts the wretch that lies in woe
        In remembrance of a shroud.
    Now it is the time of night
10   That the graves, all gaping wide,
    Every one lets forth his sprite[1]
        In the churchway paths to glide;
    And we fairies that do run
        By the triple Hecate's[2] team
15   From the presence of the sun,
        Following darkness like a dream,
    Now are frolic.° Not a mouse   *merry*
    Shall disturb this hallowed house.
    I am sent with broom[3] before
20   To sweep the dust behind° the door.   *from behind*

Enter [OBERON and TITANIA,] King and Queen of
Fairies, with all their train

OBERON   Through the house give glimmering light.
    By the dead and drowsy fire
    Every elf and fairy sprite
        Hop as light as bird from brier,
25   And this ditty after me
    Sing, and dance it trippingly.

TITANIA   First rehearse your song by rote,
    To each word a warbling note.
    Hand in hand with fairy grace
30   Will we sing and bless this place.

The song.[4] *[The fairies dance]*

OBERON   Now until the break of day
    Through this house each fairy stray.
    To the best bride bed will we,[5]
    Which by us shall blessèd be,
35   And the issue there create°   *created; conceived*
    Ever shall be fortunate.
    So shall all the couples three
    Ever true in loving be,
    And the blots of nature's hand
40   Shall not in their issue stand.
    Never mole, harelip, nor scar,
    Nor mark prodigious° such as are *ominous birthmark*
    Despisèd in nativity
    Shall upon their children be.

5.2 Location: Theseus's palace.
1. Each grave lets forth its ghost.
2. Hecate was goddess of the moon and night, and had three realms: heaven (as Cynthia), earth (as Diana), and hell (as Proserpine).
3. One of his traditional emblems; he helped good

housekeepers and punished lazy ones.
4. F does not assign lines 31–52 to Oberon. They are indented and printed in italics as "The Song."
5. Oberon and Titania will bless the bed of Theseus and Hippolyta.

45   With this field-dew consecrate[6]

                Every fairy take his gait°   *way*

                And each several° chamber bless   *separate*

                Through this palace with sweet peace;

                And the owner of it blessed

50   Ever shall in safety rest.

                Trip away, make no stay,

                Meet me all by break of day.

                          Exeunt [all but ROBIN]

Epilogue

ROBIN   If we shadows have offended,

                Think but this, and all is mended:

                That you have but slumbered here,

                While these visions did appear;

5   And this weak and idle theme,

                No more yielding but° a dream,   *than*

                Gentles, do not reprehend.

                If you pardon, we will mend.

                And as I am an honest puck,

10   If we have unearnèd luck

                Now to 'scape the serpent's tongue,[1]

                We will make amends ere long,

                Else the puck a liar call.

                So, good night unto you all.

15   Give me your hands,° if we be friends,   *applause*

                And Robin shall restore amends.

Additional Passage

An unusual quantity and kind of mislineation in Q1 has persuaded most scholars that the text at the beginning of 5.1 was revised, with new material written in the margins. The Oxford editors here offer a reconstruction of the passage as originally drafted, which can be compared with 5.1.1–86 of the edited text.

5.1

Enter THESEUS, HIPPOLYTA, *and* PHILOSTRATE

HIPPOLYTA   'Tis strange, my Theseus, that these lovers speak of.

THESEUS   More strange than true. I never may believe

    These antique fables, nor these fairy toys.

    Lovers and mad men have such seething brains.

5   One sees more devils than vast hell can hold:

    That is the madman. The lover, all as frantic,

    Sees Helen's beauty in a brow of Egypt.

    Such tricks hath strong imagination

    That if it would but apprehend some joy

10   It comprehends some bringer of that joy;

    Or in the night, imagining some fear,

    How easy is a bush supposed a bear!

HIPPOLYTA   But all the story of the night told over,

    And all their minds transfigured so together,

---

6. Consecrated, blessed. Playfully alludes to traditional Catholic custom of blessing the bride bed with holy water.

Epilogue
1. Hissing from the audience.

15 More witnesseth than fancy's images,
And grows to something of great constancy;
But howsoever, strange and admirable.

Enter the lovers: LYSANDER, DEMETRIUS, HERMIA, *and*
HELENA

THESEUS Here come the lovers, full of joy and mirth.
Come now, what masques, what dances shall we have
20 To ease the anguish of a torturing hour?
Call Philostrate.

PHILOSTRATE   Here mighty Theseus.

THESEUS Say, what abridgement have you for this evening?
What masque, what music? How shall we beguile
The lazy time if not with some delight?

25 PHILOSTRATE There is a brief how many sports are ripe.
Make choice of which your highness will see first.

THESEUS 'The battle with the centaurs to be sung
By an Athenian eunuch to the harp.'
We'll none of that. That have I told my love
30 In glory of my kinsman Hercules.
'The riot of the tipsy Bacchanals
Tearing the Thracian singer in their rage.'
That is an old device, and it was played
When I from Thebes came last a conquerer.
35 'The thrice-three Muses mourning for the death
Of learning, late deceased in beggary.'
That is some satire, keen and critical,
Not sorting with a nuptial ceremony.
'A tedious brief scene of young Pyramus
40 And his love Thisby.' 'Tedious' *and* 'brief'?

PHILOSTRATE A play there is, my lord, some ten words long,
Which is as 'brief' as I have known a play;
But by ten words, my lord, it is too long,
Which makes it 'tedious'; for in all the play
45 There is not one word apt, one player fitted.

THESEUS What are they that do play it?

PHILOSTRATE Hard-handed men that work in Athens here,
Which never laboured in their minds till now,
And now have toiled their unbreathed memories
50 With this same play against your nuptial.

THESEUS Go, bring them in; and take your places, ladies.

Exit PHILOSTRATE

HIPPOLYTA I love not to see wretchedness o'ercharged
And duty in his service perishing.

Romeo and Juliet

Plato's dialogue *The Symposium* recounts a dinner party where the guests spent a long night in impassioned, brilliant philosophical conversation about love. By daybreak, most of the guests had fallen asleep, but Socrates, who had spoken with particularly luminous intelligence, was still awake, trying to prove that a single playwright was capable of writing both comedy and tragedy. As he clinched his case, his weary interlocutors nodded off to sleep. Thus we never learn the argument that Socrates was making for the convergence of the tragic and comic visions in one dramatist, and neither the ancient Greek nor the Roman world has left us an instance of that convergence. But we have its supreme embodiment in Shakespeare. The achievement is particularly striking in two plays probably written around 1595. Scholars have been unable to determine with certainty whether *Romeo and Juliet* was written before or after *A Midsummer Night's Dream*; one of Shakespeare's most delightful comedies and one of his most beloved tragedies appear to have been written at virtually the same time and out of some very similar materials.

In the entertainment performed for the newlyweds at the close of *A Midsummer Night's Dream*, the young lovers, Pyramus and Thisbe, are separated by a "vile wall." They attempt to elope together, but Pyramus, mistakenly thinking that Thisbe has been killed, rashly commits suicide, whereupon Thisbe in despair stabs herself. A strange way, it would seem, to celebrate festive nuptials, but Shakespeare's comedy continually triumphs over fears of rashness, mutability, and death by staging and laughing at them. The inept amateur actors call attention so crudely to the tragedy's artificiality and contrivance that it provokes derisive laughter: "This is the silliest stuff that ever I heard" (5.1.207).

In *Romeo and Juliet,* whose climax closely resembles that of Pyramus and Thisbe, Shakespeare does not shy away from artifice and contrivance. His tragedy is unusually dependent on coincidence, mischance, and accident to produce what the Chorus, in the sonnet that serves as the prologue, calls the lovers' "misadventured piteous overthrows." Nor does he forswear the note of witty, wicked parody that transformed the woes of Pyramus and Thisbe into an occasion for mirth. Romeo's friend Mercutio gives voice to an irrepressible spirit of mockery, a spirit that seems to challenge the very possibility of romantic love or tragic destiny. (There is a seventeenth-century report—it doesn't date from the playwright's own lifetime—that Shakespeare remarked that he was forced to kill Mercutio in the third act to prevent being killed by him.) But Shakespeare manages to make the story of his reckless, star-crossed lovers immensely moving, resistant at once to corrosive irony and to moralizing disapproval. He does so principally through his mastery of what the bumbling performers in *A Midsummer Night's Dream* conspicuously lack: the power of language to make and unmake the world.

It is this poetic power—"poetic" derives from the Greek word for "making"—that provides Shakespeare with the key to resolving the paradox addressed by Socrates in *The Symposium* and that enables him to transform his rather shopworn source materials into something rich and strange. The story of the ill-fated lovers from bitterly feuding families had been told many times in the sixteenth century by Italian and French writers and had already appeared more than once in English. Shakespeare's direct source is Arthur Brooke's *Tragicall Historye of Romeus and Juliet* (1562), a long, leaden English poem based on a French prose version by Pierre Boaistuau (1559), who was in turn adapting an Italian version by Bandello (1554), who in turn based his narrative on Luigi da Porto's version (1525) of a tale by Masuccio Salernitano (1476). Shakespeare follows the main outline of Brooke's narrative, although he makes many changes in the interests of theatrical compression and intensification. Hence the events that in Brooke take nine months are telescoped into a few days. The figure of Mercutio is brilliantly developed, as is the vulgar, meddling, earthy Nurse. Juliet, eighteen years old in Bandello's version and sixteen in Brooke's, is depicted as only thirteen, a young girl suddenly awakening to passionate desires that set her against the will of her family.

But it is principally by means of the incandescent brilliance of its language that *Romeo and Juliet* has earned its place as one of the greatest love stories in world literature. Shakespeare makes linguistic power figure thematically in the play by insisting on the crucial importance of naming and, more generally, by repeatedly calling attention to the force of verbal actions. This was by no means the playwright's private obsession. His play is the product of a rhetorical culture, a culture steeped in an awareness—in the philosopher J. L. Austin's phrase—of "how to do things with words." What are some of the things that characters do with words? For a start, they insult each other, a dangerous pastime of both servants and masters. They also invite one another (Capulet's favorite pastime); they confess (formally, to a priest; informally, to friends); they conjure; they curse; they make contracts; they vow; and, if they have the power of the prince, they banish. And through all of these verbal actions, no matter how serious or even deadly they may be, they constantly play with language.

Romeo and Juliet is saturated with language games: paradoxes, oxymorons, double entendres, rhyming tricks, verbal echoings, multiple puns. The obvious question is, why? One possible answer, proposed as early as the eighteenth century, is that Shakespeare could not resist: verbal wit was an addiction, an obsession, the object of an irrational passion. He could indulge this passion because a display of wit would appeal to those segments of the audience most attuned to rhetorical acrobatics. Another answer

Two gallants fight a duel in the street. From George Wither, *A Collection of Emblemes* (1635).

is that puns are a clarifying challenge, an assault on sentiments to test whether they are genuine or merely forced and empty. Hence Mercutio attempts to mock Romeo's passion with a set of ribald jests, jests that are reiterated unconsciously by the Nurse in such exclamations as "Stand up, stand up, stand an you be a man" (3.3.88). To survive the corrosive effect of such mockery is a measure of true love and a sign of authenticity: "He jests at scars that never felt a wound" (2.1.43).

But this explanation for the tragedy's pervasive wordplay is not wholly adequate, since at the height of both their love and their despair, Romeo and Juliet also pun. Romeo on the verge of suicide plays with the word "engrossing" (death as wholesaler; monopolist; lawyer); Juliet plays with the word "restorative" (the kiss as medicine; poison; death; resurrection); and both play with the Elizabethan "die" as a term for "orgasm." Here wordplay functions not to deflate but to cram into brief utterances more meanings than language would ordinarily hold and to force us to confront both unresolvable contradictions and hidden connections. That is, puns work to juxtapose or hold open possibilities that normally are viewed as mutually exclusive. Thus they may be said to reach both a psychological and a thematic level at which oppositions—pain and joy, loss and restoration, love and death, comedy and tragedy—are canceled.

Wordplay would be impossible in a language in which words were strictly bound to things in a perfect correspondence between naming and nature. Punning is possible only if there is some slippage in sound and meaning, so that one sign can refer to two or more objects or, as Mercutio wittily demonstrates in his Queen Mab speech, to nothing at all. Yet wordplay can also suggest surprising linkages and secret realities. Hence, for example, the punning in Romeo and Juliet's initial exchange at the Capulet ball derives its power from the lovers' conviction that there really is an essential relation between the touching of their hands and lips and a religious experience. This relation, invisible to the ordinary social world around them, is disclosed in the language game they spontaneously play, a game that takes the form of a shared sonnet.

Even to speak of this first exchange as a game is to risk diminishing its intense seriousness. For Mercutio, words are fantastic trifles in a world fit only for satire, sexual teasing, and make-believe. He is a young man in love with masks; indeed, as he readies himself for the masked ball, he seems to regard his own face as a mask: "Give me a case to put my visage in, / A visor for a visor" (1.4.29–30). The moment Romeo and Juliet meet, all masks seem to fall away, all prior emotions fade into nothingness, and all games become earnest. "Did my heart love till now?" asks Romeo, and Juliet, sending the Nurse to find out Romeo's name, declares, "If he be marrièd, / My grave is like to be my wedding bed" (1.5.131–32).

At some moments in *Romeo and Juliet,* then, wordplay reveals the arbitrariness of language; at other moments, it seems to reveal a hidden reality, even a sacred truth. These contradictory revelations are explored in the famous balcony scene in Act 2. Mercutio's mockery gives way, after Romeo's abrupt, one-line dismissal, to incantatory language so intense as to create a new heaven and a new earth. A bare, daylit stage (as it would have been in the Elizabethan playhouse) becomes a dark garden above which Juliet appears like the sun. Visibility is canceled and then restored, by means of metaphor, to the "white upturnèd wond'ring eyes / Of mortals" (2.1.71–72). Romeo's ecstatic words are the poetic record of a revelation, a vision of a creature unique, perfect, and infinitely beautiful.

The visionary moment turns into a moment of auditory revelation as well, as Romeo, in an intense, eroticized version of what audiences routinely do, overhears Juliet's soliloquy. He has entered into her most intimate thoughts and longings and has an overpowering proof of their authenticity, since she speaks with no awareness of his presence. The inner world his lyrical utterance has conjured up is miraculously united with her own. But her words at once offer a complete fulfillment of this union and a shattering of fulfillment: "O Romeo, Romeo, wherefore art thou Romeo?" (2.1.75). Only if Romeo's name is an arbitrary sign, to be stripped away, discarded, and replaced, can her love be realized. But in a world in which words are divorced from reality, what

"Then I defy you, stars" (5.1.24). *Imagines Constellationum*. From Ptolemy, *Almagest* (1541 ed.), after Dürer.

would be the status of a love made by language? In a world in which names are mere empty signs, how could language create a new reality?

If words are arbitrary, then Romeo and Juliet's love, woven of words, is wedded to nothingness. If they are not arbitrary, if they cannot float free of the body and society, then their love will be destroyed by the rage of feuding parents—the parents who have bestowed proper names on their offspring—and by the whole daylight world of social exchange that gives ordinary language its normal meanings. Against the magical, passionate, transformative language of Romeo and Juliet is set not only Mercutio's mockery but the Nurse's garrulous evocation of the inescapable life cycle: birth, weaning, sexual maturity, and death.

In the Nurse's view, all lives have a certain interchangeability. Juliet's value can be measured in gold coins—"I tell you, he that can lay hold of her / Shall have the chinks" (1.5.113–14)—and an exiled husband can be replaced: Paris is "a lovely gentleman," she tells the grieving Juliet, "Romeo's a dishclout to him" (3.5.218–19). Romeo and Juliet insist by contrast on the absolute singularity of their love, on the stilling of cyclical time, and on the cancellation of the social network of form and compliment. For a moment on her balcony, Juliet regrets that Romeo has heard her declare her "true-love passion," but then she bids farewell to conventional restraint and boldly steps forward into the magical realm of reciprocal desire. This realm is not without its own solemn order: their love must be formally confirmed in honorable vows of holy matrimony spoken before the friar. But first in the garden, away from church and family and friends, the fullness of the lovers' matched longings finds expression in words that seem to possess mythic power, power to transform darkness into intense light and at the same time to block out the harsh, unforgiving light of the everyday.

The everyday has its own powerful resources, however, and forces its way back into the world that love has transformed. It does so through the ability of names like "Capulet" and "Montague" to conjure up bitter social rivalries. For, as *Romeo and Juliet* repeatedly discloses, words as we ordinarily use them are rarely wholly arbitrary or wholly mythic. They are social constructions, communal creations that are neither complete unto themselves nor empty and hence malleable by individuals. Both language as arbitrary and language as mythic are radical attempts to challenge this notion of words as shared creations carrying with them the tensions and resolutions present in communities, but the community in effect kills off the challenge—whether it comes from Mercutio, who tries to turn social hatred and love alike into a game about "nothing," or from Romeo and Juliet, who try to escape through darkness, subterfuge, and the language of love into a realm apart.

How does the communitarian spirit of language, and with it a sense of the inescapability of the social, manifest itself in *Romeo and Juliet*? It does so, first of all, through a series of characters such as those we glimpse in the opening moments of the play, when the Capulet servants, Samson and Gregory, provoke the absurd quarrel with the Montague servants, Abraham and Balthasar. The point is not only the foolishness of the social codes—"Do you bite your thumb at us, sir?" "I do bite my thumb, sir" (1.1.39–40)—but also their pervasiveness. In a tragedy memorable for its dreams of the most intense privacy—Juliet longs for Romeo to leap to her arms "untalked of and unseen" (3.2.7)—the bustling world makes its presence felt as insistently as the Nurse's voice calling again and again to Juliet as she stands at her window. Shakespeare is wonderfully resourceful in conveying this presence. There is, for example, the nameless servant whose inability to read the list of those invited to the Capulets' ball leads him to turn for assistance to Romeo and Benvolio, who chance at that moment to be walking by. The list itself deftly conjures up the social elite of Verona, with its network of kinship bonds:

> Signor Placentio and his lovely nieces,
> Mercutio and his brother Valentine,
> Mine uncle Capulet, his wife and daughters,

and so on through the whole "fair assembly" (1.2.63ff). At the ball itself, Shakespeare is careful to include a glimpse of the servants, hurrying to clear the dishes but finding time to put aside a piece of marzipan for themselves or arranging for a private party with Susan Grindstone and Nell. And, in the midst of the horror and lamenting when Juliet's cold and stiff body is discovered on the morning she was to be married to Paris, Shakespeare turns our attention to the musicians who had been hired to entertain the wedding guests and who now stand around cracking lame jokes and hoping for a bit of dinner (as if—to invert a celebrated line from *Hamlet*—the marriage-baked meats will coldly furnish forth the funeral table).

There are, besides the servants, other social units that carry the glacial weight of the collective norms and ordinary interests against which Romeo and Juliet struggle. The exclusiveness and intensity of their love is clearly in tension with the bond that links Romeo to his male friends. "Now art thou sociable," says Mercutio with evident relief, when Romeo briefly resumes the old mocking repartee; "now art thou Romeo" (2.3.77). But neither Romeo nor Juliet is any longer the same person, and the passionate love that divides Romeo from his friends sets both lovers still more decisively against the values of their powerful families. Those values involve a complex intertwining of honor, dignity, love, will, and property, a blend that can manifest itself as gracious hospitality or as murderous feuding, as gentle nostalgia or as cold calculation, as a father's indulgent affection for his daughter or as blind rage when she attempts to thwart his will. Romeo and Juliet's love and clandestine marriage can find no place

The city of Verona. From John Speed, *Prospect of the Most Famous Parts of the World* (1676).

in this familial order of things, just as its absoluteness is incompatible with the familial sense of cyclical time.

Beyond the structure of the family in the society of Verona, though linked to that structure by ties of kinship, lies the state, embodied in the figure of Prince Escalus. Formally, *Romeo and Juliet* is built around the well-meaning ruler's attempt to stop the "civil brawls" (1.1.82) at the play's beginning, his banishment of Romeo at its midpoint, and his final inquiry, to "clear these ambiguities" (5.3.216), at its close. But this necessary principle of civic order, even though it has important consequences, seems almost beside the point, as inadequate and uncomprehending as the statues in pure gold that the grieving fathers propose to erect.

A much deeper social principle is figured in Friar Laurence, who embodies the collective wisdom and sanctity of the community. Although set apart, the friar is not a hermit or a recluse; he is an active agent in the community's affairs. His attempt to use Romeo and Juliet's love as a means to resolve the feud between the Montagues and the Capulets disastrously backfires, and with his sleeping potions, his elaborate plots, and, at the close, his fatal cowardice, he has some of the qualities of the stereotypical meddling friar of anticlerical satire. But Friar Laurence is a more complex figure, with a subtle grasp of the doubleness—both poison and medicine—of the natural world and a thoughtful advocacy of moderation. This advocacy draws on an ancient and powerful critique of extremes in passion, which the play's tragic outcome would seem to endorse.

Yet few readers or spectators come away from *Romeo and Juliet* with the conviction that it would be better to love moderately. The intensity of the lovers' passion seems to have its own compelling, self-justifying force, which quietly brushes away all social obstacles and moralizing warnings: "Think true love acted simple modesty" (3.2.16). And the play's incantatory language of love—braiding together the wildly fanciful and the exquisitely simple—has after four hundred years an unforgettable freshness:

> Come, gentle night; come, loving, black-browed night,
> Give me my Romeo, and when I shall die
> Take him and cut him out in little stars,
> And he will make the face of heaven so fine
> That all the world will be in love with night
> And pay no worship to the garish sun.   (3.2.20–25)

If the society of the play will not tolerate such ecstatic desire, if the contingencies of the ordinary world manage to destroy it, *Romeo and Juliet* offers us the consoling realization that the lovers themselves have all along been in love with night.

STEPHEN GREENBLATT

TEXTUAL NOTE

Romeo and Juliet was first published in quarto in 1597 (Q1). A second edition (Q2), advertised on the title page as "newly corrected, augmented, and amended," was published two years later. Q2 provided copy for a third quarto published in 1609 (Q3), from which in turn was printed another quarto (Q4) and the First Folio (F) text (both in 1623). Since Q3 and Q4, along with the Folio version of the play, all depend on Q2, the complex textual problems posed by *Romeo and Juliet* are focused on the precise nature of Q2 and its relation to the substantially different versions of the play, Q1.

Scholars generally agree that Q1 is a so-called bad Quarto, a defective text that derives not from the author's manuscript but from the recollection of actors. Since Elizabethan playing companies usually tried to keep the plays out of print, Q1 would in all likelihood have been an unauthorized and illicit transcript; modern analysis has directed suspicion on the actors who played Romeo and Paris. The title page identifies neither author nor publisher, and the text was evidently not licensed in the Stationers' Register.

Q2 is a fuller, more authoritative text. Certain of its features—inconsistent speech prefixes, "permissive" stage directions (e.g., "Enter three or four Citizens," 1.1.66 stage direction), and the preservation of lines that Shakespeare evidently meant to cross out after revision—indicate that Q2 was set from the author's own rough draft, or "foul papers." The draft appears to have posed difficulties for the printing house, for the compositors seem on a number of occasions to have had difficulty making sense of the manuscript. Moreover, perhaps because a page of the manuscript was missing, one passage in Q2—from 1.2.51 to 1.3.36—is taken directly from Q1. With the exception of this passage, for which Q1 serves as the control text, the text of *Romeo and Juliet* is based on Q2.

SELECTED BIBLIOGRAPHY

Belsey, Catherine. "The Name of the Rose in *Romeo and Juliet*." *Yearbook of English Studies* 23 (1993): 126–42. *Romeo and Juliet* dramatizes both the desire to transcend the realm of signifiers into a metaphysical ideal and the impossibility of attaining it.

Goldberg, Jonathan. "*Romeo and Juliet*'s Open Rs." *Queering the Renaissance*. Ed. Jonathan Goldberg. Durham, N.C.: Duke University Press, 1994. 218–35. Homosocial rivalry challenges the play's heterosexual order, implying the interchangeability of male and female love objects.

Kahn, Coppélia. "Coming of Age in Verona." *The Woman's Part: Feminist Criticism of Shakespeare*. Ed. Carolyn Ruth Swift Lenz, Gayle Greene, and Carol Thomas Neely. Urbana: University of Illinois Press, 1983. 171–93. The oppressive mores of a patriarchal society are chiefly responsible for the tragic determinism that suffocates the lovers.

Kristeva, Julia. "*Romeo and Juliet*: Love-Hatred in the Couple." *Shakespearean Tragedy*. Ed. John Drakakis. New York: Longman, 1992. 296–315. We benefit from a closer look, informed by Freud and Lacan, at the symptomatic (unconscious) response to transgressive and fantastic love as manifested in the characters, the playwright, and ourselves.

Liebler, Naomi Conn. "'There is no world without Verona walls': The City in *Romeo and Juliet.*" *A Companion to Shakespeare's Works*, vol. 1: *The Tragedies.* Ed. Richard Dutton and Jean E. Howard. Malden, Mass.: Blackwell, 2003. 303–18. Shakespeare's Verona is a matrix of violence and disorder, becoming the play's tragic protagonist as it collapses the ideal of the walled city.

Moisan, Thomas. "'O Any Thing of Nothing, First Create!': Gender and Patriarchy and the Tragedy of *Romeo and Juliet.*" *In Another Country: Feminist Perspectives on Renaissance Drama.* Ed. Dorothea Kehler and Susan Baker. Metuchen, N.J.: Scarecrow Press, 1991. 113–36. *Romeo and Juliet's* tragic love story subverts patriarchy, but its gender prescriptions recuperate male authority.

Nevo, Ruth. "Tragic Form in *Romeo and Juliet.*" *Studies in English Literature* 9 (1969): 241–58. Shakespeare develops a distinctive style of tragedy, predicated on the heroic embodiment of opposing forces, the subversion of appearances, the presence of the uncanny, and the complex ideal of sexual love.

Porter, Joseph A. *Shakespeare's Mercutio: His History and Drama.* Chapel Hill, N.C.: University of North Carolina Press, 1988. From a patchwork of sources, classical and contemporary, Shakespeare breathed life into the complex, subversive, homosexual Mercutio.

Snow, Edward. "Language and Sexual Difference in *Romeo and Juliet.*" *Shakespeare's "Rough Magic": Renaissance Essays in Honor of C. L. Barber.* Ed. Peter Erickson and Coppélia Kahn. Newark: University of Delaware Press, 1985. 168–92. If the language of Juliet and Romeo articulates their profound interconnectedness, it also discloses ominous differences between them and suggests that gender difference is the tragedy's deepest dichotomy.

Snyder, Susan. "*Romeo and Juliet:* Comedy into Tragedy." *Essays in Criticism* 20 (1970): 391–402. At first possessing all the makings of a comedy, *Romeo and Juliet* morphs from one genre to another: the descent into tragedy becomes ineluctable upon the death of Mercutio.

FILMS

Romeo and Juliet. 1936. Dir. George Cukor. USA. 125 min. A lavish, big-studio release, Cukor's black-and-white film stars Leslie Howard, who was then forty-two, and Norma Shearer in the lead roles. John Barrymore plays Mercutio.

West Side Story. 1961. Dir. Jerome Robbins and Robert Wise. USA. 152 min. A musical, modernized adaptation of the play set in New York with rival ethnic gangs. Leonard Bernstein wrote the celebrated score.

Romeo and Juliet. 1968. Dir. Franco Zeffirelli. UK/Italy. 138 min. A flower-power, 1960s youth-culture interpretation of the play, featuring teenaged actors Leonard Whiting and Olivia Hussey in the title roles.

William Shakespeare's Romeo + Juliet. 1996. Dir. Baz Luhrmann. USA. 120 min. Starring Leonardo DiCaprio and Claire Danes, Luhrmann's frenetic update, set in modern-day "Verona Beach," explains the family feud in terms of a gang conflict.

Qing ren jie (A Time to Love). 2005. Dir. Jianqi Huo. China. 113 min. Set during the Cultural Revolution, two Chinese lovers read and watch versions of Shakespeare's play together, and enact the balcony scene. In Mandarin.

The Most Excellent and Lamentable Tragedy of Romeo and Juliet

THE PERSONS OF THE PLAY

CHORUS
ROMEO
MONTAGUE, his father
MONTAGUE'S WIFE
BENVOLIO, Montague's nephew
ABRAHAM, Montague's servingman
BALTHASAR, Romeo's man
JULIET
CAPULET, her father
CAPULET'S WIFE
TYBALT, her nephew
His page
PETRUCCIO
CAPULET'S COUSIN
Juliet's NURSE
PETER
SAMSON } servingmen of the Capulets
GREGORY
Other SERVINGMEN
MUSICIANS
Escalus, PRINCE of Verona
MERCUTIO
County PARIS } his kinsmen
PAGE to Paris
FRIAR LAURENCE
FRIAR JOHN
An APOTHECARY
CHIEF WATCHMAN
Other CITIZENS OF THE WATCH
Masquers, guests, gentlewomen, followers of the Montague and Capulet factions

Prologue

[*Enter*] CHORUS

CHORUS Two households, both alike in dignity°   *status*
    In fair Verona, where we lay our scene,
    From ancient grudge break to new mutiny,°   *wrangling*
    Where civil blood makes civil hands unclean.[1]
5   From forth the fatal° loins of these two foes   *ill-fated*
    A pair of star-crossed[2] lovers take their life,
    Whose misadventured° piteous overthrows   *unfortunate*
    Doth with their death bury their parents' strife.

Prologue
1. Where citizens' hands are stained with the blood of their fellow citizens.

2. Thwarted by the adverse influence of the stars appearing at the time of their birth, which controlled their destinies.

The fearful passage of their death-marked love
10   And the continuance of their parents' rage—
Which but their children's end, naught could remove—
Is now the two-hours' traffic° of our stage;   *business; movement*
The which if you with patient ears attend,
What here shall miss, our toil shall strive to mend.³   [*Exit*]

1.1

Enter SAMSON *and* GREGORY, *of the house of Capulet,*
with swords and bucklers°   *small round shields*

SAMSON   Gregory, on my word, we'll not carry coals.¹
GREGORY   No, for then we should be colliers.²
SAMSON   I mean an° we be in choler,° we'll draw.°   *if / anger / draw swords*
GREGORY   Ay, while you live, draw your neck out of collar.°   *a noose*
5 SAMSON   I strike quickly,° being moved.³   *vigorously*
GREGORY   But thou art not quickly° moved to strike.   *speedily*
SAMSON   A dog of the house of Montague moves me.
GREGORY   To move is to stir, and to be valiant is to stand,⁴ there-
    fore if thou art moved, thou runn'st away.
10 SAMSON   A dog of that house shall move me to stand. I will take
    the wall of⁵ any man or maid of Montague's.
GREGORY   That shows thee a weak slave, for the weakest goes to
    the wall.⁶
SAMSON   'Tis true, and therefore women, being the weaker ves-
15   sels,⁷ are ever thrust to the wall;° therefore I will push Mon-   *ravished*
    tague's men from the wall, and thrust his maids to the wall.
GREGORY   The quarrel is between our masters and us their men.
SAMSON   'Tis all one.° I will show myself a tyrant: when I have   *the same*
    fought with the men I will be civil with the maids—I will cut
20   off their heads.
GREGORY   The heads of the maids?
SAMSON   Ay, the heads of the maids, or their maidenheads, take
    it in what sense thou wilt.
GREGORY   They must take it in sense° that feel it.   *through sensation*
25 SAMSON   Me they shall feel while I am able to stand, and 'tis
    known I am a pretty piece of flesh.⁸
GREGORY   'Tis well thou art not fish. If thou hadst, thou hadst
    been poor-john.⁹
    Enter [ABRAHAM *and another servingman*] *of the Mon-*
    tagues
    Draw thy tool.¹ Here comes of the house of Montagues.
30 SAMSON   My naked weapon is out. Quarrel, I will back thee.
GREGORY   How—turn thy back and run?
SAMSON   Fear me not.²
GREGORY   No, marry³—I fear thee!
SAMSON   Let us take the law of our side. Let them begin.

---

3. *What . . . mind:* The actors will try to rectify whatever is missing or ill told in the Prologue.
1.1 Location: A street or public place in Verona.
1. We'll not suffer humiliation.
2. Professional coal porters, proverbially sneaky.
3. Being roused to anger.
4. Stand firm against assault. Playing, as with "strike"
and "stir," on sexual arousal.
5. I will assert superiority over. The sidewalk nearest
the wall was cleaner than that nearer the street.
6. Proverbial: The weakest are always pushed aside.

7. Paul's description of women in 1 Peter 3:7.
8. An attractive fellow possessed of an impressive
member.
9. Dried salted hake, appropriate as a taunt because
shriveled and cheap. "Neither fish nor flesh" was
proverbial for an uncategorizable oddity.
1. Weapon (and continuing the bawdy wordplay).
2. Do not doubt my fortitude; in the next line, Gregory
takes it in the modern sense of "Do not be afraid of me."
3. By the Virgin Mary, a mild oath with a meaning similar to "indeed."

35   GREGORY   I will frown as I pass by, and let them take it as they
      list.°   *like*

     SAMSON   Nay, as they dare. I will bite my thumb at them,[4] which
      is disgrace to them if they bear it.
         [*He bites his thumb*]

     ABRAHAM   Do you bite your thumb at us, sir?

40   SAMSON   I do bite my thumb, sir.

     ABRAHAM   Do you bite your thumb at us, sir?

     SAMSON [*to* GREGORY]   Is the law of our side if I say 'Ay'?

     GREGORY   No.

     SAMSON [*to* ABRAHAM]   No, sir, I do not bite my thumb at you,
45   sir, but I bite my thumb, sir.

     GREGORY [*to* ABRAHAM]   Do you quarrel, sir?

     ABRAHAM   Quarrel, sir? No, sir.

     SAMSON   But if you do, sir, I am for you.[5] I serve as good a man
      as you.

50   ABRAHAM   No better.

     SAMSON   Well, sir.
         Enter BENVOLIO

     GREGORY   Say 'better'. Here comes one of my master's kinsmen.

     SAMSON [*to* ABRAHAM]   Yes, better, sir.

     ABRAHAM   You lie.

55   SAMSON   Draw, if you be men. Gregory, remember thy washing°   *slashing; violent*
      blow.   *blow*
         They [*draw and*] *fight*

     BENVOLIO [*drawing*]   Part, fools. Put up your swords. You know
      not what you do.
         Enter TYBALT

     TYBALT [*drawing*]   What, art thou drawn among these heartless
      hinds?[6]

60   Turn thee, Benvolio. Look upon thy death.

     BENVOLIO   I do but keep the peace. Put up thy sword,
      Or manage° it to part these men with me.   *wield*

     TYBALT   What, drawn and talk of peace? I hate the word
      As I hate hell, all Montagues, and thee.
65   Have at thee, coward.
         They fight. Enter three or four CITIZENS [OF THE
         WATCH], *with clubs or partisans*°   *broad-tipped spears*

     CITIZENS OF THE WATCH   Clubs, bills° and partisans! Strike! Beat   *ax-bladed spears*
      them down!
      Down with the Capulets. Down with the Montagues.
         Enter old CAPULET *in his gown, and his* WIFE

     CAPULET   What noise is this? Give me my long sword, ho!

     CAPULET'S WIFE   A crutch, a crutch—why call you for a sword?
         Enter old MONTAGUE [*with his sword drawn*], *and his*
         WIFE

70   CAPULET   My sword, I say. Old Montague is come,
      And flourishes his blade in spite° of me.   *defiance*

     MONTAGUE   Thou villain Capulet!
         [*His* WIFE *holds him back*]
                     Hold me not, let me go.

---

4. Flick the thumbnail from behind the upper teeth, an
insulting gesture.
5. I accept your invitation to fight.

6. These cowardly servants, punning on female deer
("hinds") unprotected by a stag ("hart/heart").

MONTAGUE'S WIFE   Thou shalt not stir one foot to seek a foe.
  [*The* CITIZENS OF THE WATCH *attempt to*] *part them.*
  Enter PRINCE *Escalus with his train*
PRINCE   Rebellious subjects, enemies to peace,
75   Profaners of this neighbour-stainèd steel[7]—
  Will they not hear? What ho, you men, you beasts,
  That quench the fire of your pernicious rage
  With purple° fountains issuing from your veins: crimson
  On pain of torture, from those bloody hands
80   Throw your mistempered[8] weapons to the ground,
  And hear the sentence of your movèd° Prince.   furious
  [MONTAGUE, CAPULET, *and their followers throw*
    down their weapons]
  Three civil brawls bred of an airy° word   unsubstantial
  By thee, old Capulet, and Montague,
  Have thrice disturbed the quiet of our streets
85   And made Verona's ancient° citizens   elderly
  Cast by° their grave-beseeming ornaments[9]   Cast away
  To wield old partisans in hands as old,
  Cankered° with peace, to part your cankered° hate.   Rusty / malignant
  If ever you disturb our streets again
90   Your lives shall pay the forfeit° of the peace.   ransom
  For this time all the rest depart away.
  You, Capulet, shall go along with me;
  And Montague, come you this afternoon
  To know our farther pleasure in this case
95   To old Freetown,[1] our common judgement-place.
  Once more, on pain of death, all men depart.
              Exeunt [*all but* MONTAGUE,
                his WIFE, *and* BENVOLIO]
MONTAGUE   Who set this ancient quarrel new abroach?°   open
  Speak, nephew: were you by when it began?
BENVOLIO   Here were the servants of your adversary
100   And yours, close fighting ere I did approach.
  I drew to part them. In the instant came
  The fiery Tybalt with his sword prepared,
  Which, as he breathed° defiance to my ears,   uttered
  He swung about his head and cut the winds
105   Who, nothing hurt withal,° hissed him in scorn.   by that
  While we were interchanging thrusts and blows,
  Came more and more, and fought on part and part[2]
  Till the Prince came, who parted either part.
MONTAGUE'S WIFE   O where is Romeo—saw you him today?
110   Right glad I am he was not at this fray.
BENVOLIO   Madam, an hour before the worshipped sun
  Peered forth° the golden window of the east,   out from
  A troubled mind drive° me to walk abroad,   drove
  Where, underneath the grove of sycamore[3]
115   That westward rooteth° from this city side,   grows out

7. You who defile weapons with the stains of your
neighbors' blood.
8. Badly shaped and hardened, as well as unnecessarily wrathful by disposition.
9. Attire and symbolic staffs appropriate to grave old
age. Possibly playing on the old men's proximity to the
grave.
1. In Brooke's translation from the Italian source, the
Capulet house is called Villa Franca.
2. Fought for one side and the other.
3. Associated with melancholy lovers, who are "sick-
amour."

So early walking did I see your son.
Towards him I made, but he was ware° of me,   *wary*
And stole into the covert° of the wood.   *covering*
I, measuring his affections° by my own—   *inclination*
120   Which then most sought where most might not be found,[4]
Being one too many by my weary self—
Pursued my humour° not pursuing his,   *mood*
And gladly shunned who gladly fled from me.
MONTAGUE   Many a morning hath he there been seen,
125   With tears augmenting the fresh morning's dew,
Adding to clouds more clouds with his deep sighs.
But all so soon as the all-cheering sun
Should in the farthest east begin to draw
The shady curtains from Aurora's[5] bed,
130   Away from light steals home my heavy° son,   *melancholy*
And private in his chamber pens himself,
Shuts up his windows, locks fair daylight out,
And makes himself an artificial night.
Black and portentous° must this humour[6] prove,   *ominous (of illness)*
135   Unless good counsel may the cause remove.
BENVOLIO   My noble uncle, do you know the cause?
MONTAGUE   I neither know it nor can learn of him.
BENVOLIO   Have you importuned him by any° means?   *all*
MONTAGUE   Both by myself and many other friends,
140   But he, his own affection's counsellor,°   *confidant*
Is to himself—I will not say how true,[7]
But to himself so secret and so close,°   *discreet*
So far from sounding and discovery,°   *fathoming and revelation*
As is the bud bit with an envious worm°   *a spiteful grub (larva)*
145   Ere he can spread his sweet leaves° to the air   *petals*
Or dedicate his beauty to the sun.
Could we but learn from whence his sorrows grow
We would as willingly give cure as know.
              Enter ROMEO
BENVOLIO   See where he comes. So please you° step aside,   *please you = please*
150   I'll know his grievance or be much denied.
MONTAGUE   I would° thou wert so happy° by thy stay   *wish / fortunate*
To hear true shrift.° Come, madam, let's away.   *confession*
              Exeunt [MONTAGUE *and his* WIFE]
BENVOLIO   Good morrow, cousin.
ROMEO   Is the day so young?
BENVOLIO   But new° struck nine.   *only just*
ROMEO   Ay me, sad hours seem long.
155   Was that my father that went hence so fast?
BENVOLIO   It was. What sadness lengthens Romeo's hours?
ROMEO   Not having that which, having, makes them short.
BENVOLIO   In love.
ROMEO   Out.
160   BENVOLIO   Of love?
ROMEO   Out of her favour where I am in love.

---

4. *where . . . found:* in a place where I was unlikely to
have company.
5. Goddess of the dawn in classical legend.
6. "Humors," essential bodily fluids, were considered
the basis of human beings' physical and psychological

constitution. Too much black bile caused melancholy
and a host of illnesses and derangements.
7. Loyal, but also invoking the proverbial wisdom that
only one who is "true to him- or herself" can be
upstanding in dealing with others.

BENVOLIO   Alas that love, so gentle in his view,°   *appearance*
          Should be so tyrannous and rough in proof.°   *experience*
ROMEO   Alas that love, whose view is muffled still,[8]
165   Should without eyes see pathways to his will.°   *intention; lust*
          Where shall we dine? [*Seeing blood*] O me! What fray was here?
          Yet tell me not, for I have heard it all.
          Here's much to do with hate, but more with love.
          Why then, O brawling love, O loving hate,
170   O anything of nothing first create;[9]
          O heavy lightness, serious vanity,
          Misshapen chaos of well-seeming forms,
          Feather of lead, bright smoke, cold fire, sick health,
          Still-waking° sleep, that is not what it is!   *Always awake*
175   This love feel I, that feel no love in this.
          Dost thou not laugh?
BENVOLIO   No, coz,° I rather weep.   *cousin*
ROMEO   Good heart, at what?
BENVOLIO   At thy good heart's oppression.°   *affliction*
ROMEO   Why, such is love's transgression.
          Griefs of mine own lie heavy in my breast,
180   Which thou wilt propagate° to have it pressed[1]   *multiply*
          With more of thine. This love that thou hast shown
          Doth add more grief to too much of mine own.
          Love is a smoke made with the fume of sighs,
          Being purged,° a fire sparkling in lovers' eyes,   *clarified*
185   Being vexed,° a sea nourished with lovers' tears.   *stirred up*
          What is it else? A madness most discreet,°   *wise*
          A choking gall and a preserving sweet.
          Farewell, my coz.
BENVOLIO   Soft,° I will go along;   *Wait*
          An if° you leave me so, you do me wrong.   *An If = if*
190 ROMEO   Tut, I have lost myself. I am not here.
          This is not Romeo; he's some other where.
BENVOLIO   Tell me in sadness,[2] who is that you love?
ROMEO   What, shall I groan and tell thee?
BENVOLIO   Groan? Why no; but sadly tell me who.
195 ROMEO   Bid a sick man in sadness make his will,
          A word ill urged to one that is so ill.
          In sadness, cousin, I do love a woman.
BENVOLIO   I aimed so near when I supposed you loved.
ROMEO   A right good markman; and she's fair I love.
200 BENVOLIO   A right fair mark,° fair coz, is soonest hit.   *target; vulva*
ROMEO   Well, in that hit you miss. She'll not be hit
          With Cupid's arrow; she hath Dian's wit,[3]
          And, in strong proof° of chastity well armed,°   *tested armor / covered*
          From love's weak childish bow she lives unharmed.
205   She will not stay° the siege of loving terms,   *undergo*
          Nor bide th'encounter of assailing eyes,[4]

8. Who cannot see. Cupid was often depicted as blind
or blindfolded.
9. *create:* created. Inverting the proverb "Nothing can
come of nothing" and also recalling the doctrine that
God made the world out of nothing. Romeo catalogues
the "miraculous" paradoxes of love.
1. Burdened; embraced.

2. Seriousness, although Romeo plays on the sense
"melancholy."
3. The scruples and cleverness of Diana, the classical
goddess of hunting and chastity.
4. *th'encounter of assailing eyes:* military metaphors for
courtship conventionally used in Petrarchan love
poetry.

Nor ope her lap to saint-seducing gold.[5]
O, she is rich in beauty, only poor
That when she dies, with beauty dies her store.°   *wealth*

210   BENVOLIO   Then she hath sworn that she will still° live chaste?   *always*

ROMEO   She hath, and in that sparing° makes huge waste;   *refraining; thrift*
For beauty starved with her severity
Cuts beauty off from all posterity.[6]
She is too fair, too wise, wisely too fair,°   *just*

215   To merit bliss° by making me despair.[7]   *heaven's blessing*
She hath forsworn to love, and in that vow
Do I live dead, that live to tell it now.

BENVOLIO   Be ruled by me; forget to think of her.

ROMEO   O, teach me how I should forget to think!

220   BENVOLIO   By giving liberty unto thine eyes.
Examine other beauties.

ROMEO   'Tis the way
To call hers, exquisite, in question more.[8]
These happy masks that kiss fair ladies' brows,
Being black, puts us in mind they hide the fair.

225   He that is strucken blind cannot forget
The precious treasure of his eyesight lost.
Show me a mistress that is passing° fair,   *surpassingly*
What doth her beauty serve but as a note
Where I may read who passed that passing fair?

230   Farewell, thou canst not teach me to forget.

BENVOLIO   I'll pay° that doctrine, or else die in debt.[9]   *Exeunt*   *impart*

1.2

Enter old CAPULET, *County*° PARIS, *and the Clown*   *Count*
[PETER, *a servingman*]

CAPULET   But Montague is bound° as well as I,   *under oath*
In penalty alike, and 'tis not hard, I think,
For men so old as we to keep the peace.

PARIS   Of honourable reckoning[1] are you both,

5   And pity 'tis you lived at odds so long.
But now, my lord: what say you to my suit?

CAPULET   But saying o'er what I have said before.
My child is yet a stranger in the world;
She hath not seen the change of fourteen years.

10   Let two more summers wither in their pride
Ere we may think her ripe to be a bride.

PARIS   Younger than she are happy mothers made.

CAPULET   And too soon marred are those so early made.[2]
But woo her, gentle Paris, get her heart;

15   My will to her consent is but a part,
And, she agreed, within her scope of choice
Lies my consent and fair-according voice.
This night I hold an old-accustomed feast

---

5. To golden gifts that are irresistibly persuasive. Also, in classical legend, Jupiter descended upon Danaë as a shower of gold.
6. *For . . . posterity:* Since she will not have children, her beauty will die with her. *starved:* killed.
7. Despair of salvation, a grave sin.
8. *in question more:* more intensely to mind.
9. Die whatever the cost to me; die still owing you the

doctrine of forgetfulness.
1.2 Location: A street or plaza in Verona.
1. Repute, with a play on "accounting."
2. Q2 includes two more lines following line 13, probably rejected by Shakespeare in the writing process: "Earth hath swallowed all my hopes but she, / She's the hopeful Lady of my earth" (*earth:* body).

Whereto I have invited many a guest
20 Such as I love, and you among the store,
One more most welcome, makes my number more.
At my poor house look to behold this night
Earth-treading stars that make dark heaven light.
Such comfort as do lusty young men feel
25 When well-apparelled April on the heel
Of limping winter treads—even such delight
Among fresh female buds shall you this night
Inherit° at my house; hear all, all see,   *Enjoy*
And like her most whose merit most shall be,
30 Which on more view of many, mine, being one,
May stand in number, though in reck'ning none.³
Come, go with me. [*Giving* PETER *a paper*] Go, sirrah,° trudge   (*address to an inferior*)
    about;
Through fair Verona find those persons out
Whose names are written there, and to them say
35 My house and welcome on their pleasure stay.°   *wait*
                        Exeunt [CAPULET *and* PARIS]
PETER   Find them out whose names are written here? It is written that the shoemaker should meddle with his yard° and the   *yardstick*
tailor with his last,° the fisher with his pencil° and the painter   *shoe form / paintbrush*
with his nets; but I am sent to find those persons whose names
40 are here writ, and can never find° what names the writing per-   *figure out*
son hath here writ. I must to the learned.
                Enter BENVOLIO *and* ROMEO
In good time.
BENVOLIO [*to* ROMEO]   Tut, man, one fire burns out another's burning,
    One pain is lessened by another's anguish.
45 Turn giddy,° and be holp° by backward turning.   *Turn until dizzy / helped*
    One desperate grief cures with another's languish.⁴
Take thou some new infection⁵ to thy eye,
And the rank poison of the old will die.
ROMEO   Your plantain leaf⁶ is excellent for that.
50 BENVOLIO   For what, I pray thee?
ROMEO   For your broken° shin.   *gashed*
BENVOLIO   Why, Romeo, art thou mad?
ROMEO   Not mad, but bound more than a madman is;
    Shut up in prison, kept without my food,
    Whipped and tormented and— [*to* PETER] Good e'en,° good   *evening (afternoon)*
55   fellow.
PETER   God gi'° good e'en. I pray, sir, can you read?   *give you*
ROMEO   Ay, mine own fortune in my misery.⁷
PETER   Perhaps you have learned it without book.⁸ But I pray,
    can you read anything you see?
60 ROMEO   Ay, if I know the letters and the language.
PETER   Ye say honestly. Rest you merry.⁹
ROMEO   Stay, fellow, I can read.
            He reads the letter

---

3. *Which . . . none:* Upon closer inspection of the many young women, my daughter may make a part of the gorgeous display, but be of no account by herself. "One" was proverbially "no number."
4. Is displaced by the languishing pain of a new grief.
5. New object of passion, which causes a distortion of sight in the lover.
6. The ordinary plaintain leaf, used to dress wounds or bruises and thought to have curative powers.
7 Romeo takes "read" to mean "understand" or "perceive," as in "to read one's fortune."
8. *without book:* from memory or by ear, as well as through experience rather than education.
9. A farewell. Peter takes Romeo to mean "if only I knew the letters and the language."

'Signor Martino and his wife and daughters,
County° Anselme and his beauteous sisters,
65 The lady widow of Vitruvio,
Signor Placentio and his lovely nieces,
Mercutio and his brother Valentine,
Mine uncle Capulet, his wife and daughters,
My fair niece Rosaline and Livia,
70 Signor Valentio and his cousin Tybalt,
Lucio and the lively Helena.'
A fair assembly. Whither should they come?

PETER   Up.[1]

ROMEO   Whither?

75 PETER   To supper to our house.

ROMEO   Whose house?

PETER   My master's.

ROMEO   Indeed, I should have asked thee that before.

PETER   Now I'll tell you without asking. My master is the great
80 rich Capulet, and if you be not of the house of Montagues, I
pray come and crush° a cup of wine. Rest you merry.   *Exit*   *drink*

BENVOLIO   At this same ancient° feast of Capulet's   *traditional*
Sups the fair Rosaline, whom thou so loves,
With all the admirèd beauties of Verona.
85 Go thither, and with unattainted° eye   *unbiased*
Compare her face with some that I shall show,
And I will make thee think thy swan a crow.

ROMEO   When the devout religion° of mine eye   *pious belief*
Maintains such falsehood, then turn tears to fires;
90 And these° who, often drowned, could never die,   *these eyes*
Transparent° heretics, be burnt for liars.   *Obvious; self-evident*
One fairer than my love!—the all-seeing sun
Ne'er saw her match since first the world begun.

BENVOLIO   Tut, you saw her fair, none else being by,
95 Herself poised with° herself in either eye;   *balanced against*
But in that crystal scales let there be weighed
Your lady's love against some other maid
That I will show you shining at this feast,
And she shall scant show well that now seems best.

100 ROMEO   I'll go along, no such sight to be shown,
But to rejoice in splendour of mine own.   [*Exeunt*]

1.3

Enter CAPULET'S WIFE *and* NURSE

CAPULET'S WIFE   Nurse, where's my daughter? Call her forth to me.

NURSE   Now, by my maidenhead at twelve year old,[1]
I bade her come. What,[2] lamb, what, ladybird—
God forbid[3]—where is this girl? What, Juliet!

Enter JULIET

5 JULIET   How now, who calls?

NURSE   Your mother.

JULIET   Madam, I am here. What is your will?

---

1. "Come up" is a phrase expression scorn.
1.3 Location: Capulet's house.
1. Presumably the latest date that the Nurse could swear by her virginity.

2. An expression of impatience.
3. Either an apology for the promiscuous connotation of "ladybird" of fearing something amiss in Juliet's absence.

CAPULET'S WIFE This is the matter.—Nurse, give leave° a while.   *excuse us*
   We must talk in secret.—Nurse, come back again.
10 I have remembered me, thou's° hear our counsel.°   *you shall / secrets*
   Thou knowest my daughter's of a pretty age.
NURSE Faith, I can tell her age unto an hour.
CAPULET'S WIFE She's not fourteen.
NURSE I'll lay fourteen of my teeth—and yet, to my teen° be it   *sorrow*
15 spoken, I have but four—she's not fourteen. How long is it now
   to Lammastide?[4]
CAPULET'S WIFE A fortnight and odd days.
NURSE Even or odd, of all days in the year
   Come Lammas Eve at night shall she be fourteen.
20 Susan[5] and she—God rest all Christian souls!—
   Were of an age. Well, Susan is with God;
   She was too good for me. But, as I said,
   On Lammas Eve at night shall she be fourteen,
   That shall she, marry, I remember it well.
25 'Tis since the earthquake now eleven years,
   And she was weaned—I never shall forget it—
   Of all the days of the year upon that day,
   For I had then laid wormwood[6] to my dug,°   *on my nipple*
   Sitting in the sun under the dovehouse wall.
30 My lord and you were then at Mantua.
   Nay, I do bear a brain!° But, as I said,   *memory*
   When it did taste the wormwood on the nipple
   Of my dug and felt it bitter, pretty fool,°   *(an endearment)*
   To see it tetchy° and fall out wi'th' dug!   *peevish*
35 'Shake', quoth the dove-house![7] 'Twas no need, I trow,
   To bid me trudge;°   *remove myself*
   And since that time it is eleven years,
   For then she could stand high-lone.° Nay, by th' rood,° *upright alone / cross*
   She could have run and waddled all about,
40 For even the day before, she broke her brow,°   *cut her forehead*
   And then my husband—God be with his soul,
   A° was a merry man!—took up the child.   *He*
   'Yea,' quoth he, 'dost thou fall upon thy face?
   Thou wilt fall backward when thou hast more wit,° *knowledge*
45 Wilt thou not, Jule?' And, by my halidom,°   *holiness; holy relic*
   The pretty wretch left° crying and said 'Ay'.   *stopped*
   To see now how a jest shall come about!°   *come true*
   I warrant an° I should live a thousand years   *if*
   I never should forget it. 'Wilt thou not, Jule?' quoth he,
50 And, pretty fool, it stinted° and said 'Ay'.   *she ceased*
CAPULET'S WIFE Enough of this. I pray thee hold thy peace.
NURSE Yes, madam. Yet I cannot choose but laugh
   To think it should leave crying and say 'Ay'.
   And yet, I warrant,° it had upon it° brow   *assure you / its*
55 A bump as big as a young cock'rel's stone.°   *rooster's testicle*
   A perilous knock, and it cried bitterly.
   'Yea,' quoth my husband, 'fall'st upon thy face?
   Thou wilt fall backward when thou com'st to age,

---

4. August 1, originally celebrated by the church as a harvest festival.
5. The Nurse evidently suckled Juliet after her own daughter died.
6. A proverbially bitter plant extract.
7. The dove house shook with the earthquake.

Wilt thou not, Jule?' It stinted and said 'Ay'.

60   JULIET   And stint thou too, I pray thee, Nurse, say I.

NURSE   Peace, I have done. God mark° thee to his grace,   *elect*
Thou wast the prettiest babe that e'er I nursed.
An° I might live to see thee married once,°   *If / one day*
I have my wish.

65   CAPULET'S WIFE   Marry,° that 'marry' is the very theme   *Truly*
I came to talk of. Tell me, daughter Juliet,
How stands your dispositions to be married?

JULIET   It is an honour that I dream not of.

NURSE   'An honour'! Were not I thine only nurse,
70   I would say thou hadst sucked wisdom from thy teat.[8]

CAPULET'S WIFE   Well, think of marriage now. Younger than you
Here in Verona, ladies of esteem,
Are made already mothers. By my count
I was your mother much upon these years
75   That you are now a maid. Thus then, in brief :
The valiant Paris seeks you for his love.

NURSE   A man, young lady, lady, such a man
As all the world—why, he's a man of wax.[9]

CAPULET'S WIFE   Verona's summer hath not such a flower.

80   NURSE   Nay, he's a flower, in faith, a very flower.

CAPULET'S WIFE [*to* JULIET]   What say you? Can you love the gentleman?
This night you shall behold him at our feast.
Read o'er the volume of young Paris' face,
And find delight writ there with beauty's pen.
85   Examine every married lineament,[1]
And see how one° another lends content;[2]   *one to*
And what obscured in this fair volume lies
Find written in the margin[3] of his eyes.
This precious book of love, this unbound° lover,   *single; unrestrained*
90   To beautify him only lacks a cover.
The fish lives in the sea, and 'tis much pride
For fair without the fair within to hide.[4]
That book in many's eyes doth share the glory
That in gold clasps locks in the golden story.[5]
95   So shall you share all that he doth possess
By having him, making yourself no less.

NURSE   No less, nay, bigger. Women grow° by men.   *swell with child*

CAPULET'S WIFE [*to* JULIET]   Speak briefly: can you like of Paris' love?

JULIET   I'll look° to like, if looking liking move;[6]   *expect; examine*
100   But no more deep will I endart[7] mine eye
Than your consent gives strength to make it fly.

Enter a servingman [PETER]

PETER   Madam, the guests are come, supper served up, you
called, my young lady asked for, the Nurse cursed in the pantry,
and everything in extremity.° I must hence to wait.° I beseech   *a terrible state / serve*
105   you follow straight.°   *immediately*

8. From the teat that nourished you.
9. Model of perfection, as if sculpted rather than born.
1. Harmoniously composed feature; a joined line of
flowing handwriting.
2. Meaning; happiness.
3. Glosses to difficult passage of text were set in the
margin.
4. For a lovely setting (Juliet) to frame and enrich the
fair Paris.
5. *That book . . . story:* Many esteem a book's golden
binding as highly as the story it contains. The speech
thoroughly confuses who is covering whom.
6. If looking can motivate liking.
7. Sink itself like an arrow into its target; shoot glances
that, like Cupid's arrows, inflame his passions.

CAPULET'S WIFE   We follow thee.   *Exit a servingman* [PETER]
                          Juliet, the County stays.°   *the Count awaits*
NURSE   Go, girl; seek happy nights to° happy days.   *Exeunt*   *at the end of*

1.4

Enter ROMEO, MERCUTIO, *and* BENVOLIO, [*as masquers,*]
with five or six other masquers[1] [*bearing a drum and*
torches]

ROMEO   What, shall this speech° be spoke for our excuse,   *prologue*
   Or shall we on without apology?
BENVOLIO   The date is out of° such prolixity.   *past for*
   We'll have no Cupid hoodwinked[2] with a scarf,
5   Bearing a Tartar's painted bow of lath,[3]
   Scaring the ladies like a crowkeeper,°   *scarecrow*
   Nor no without-book° Prologue faintly spoke   *memorized*
   After° the prompter for our entrance.   *Repeating after*
   But let them measure° us by what they will,   *judge*
10   We'll measure° them a measure,° and be gone.   *apportion / dance*
ROMEO   Give me a torch. I am not for this ambling;°   *dancing*
   Being but heavy,° I will bear the light.   *melancholy*
MERCUTIO   Nay, gentle° Romeo, we must have you dance.   *noble; softhearted*
ROMEO   Not I, believe me. You have dancing shoes
15   With nimble soles; I have a soul of lead
   So stakes me to the ground I cannot move.
MERCUTIO   You are a lover; borrow Cupid's wings,
   And soar with them above a common bound.[4]
ROMEO   I am too sore° empiercèd with his shaft   *deeply*
20   To soar with his light° feathers, and so bound   *cheery; agile; wanton*
   I cannot bound a pitch[5] above dull woe;
   Under love's heavy burden do I sink.
MERCUTIO   And to sink in it should you burden love—
   Too great oppression for a tender thing.[6]
25   ROMEO   Is love a tender thing? It is too rough,
   Too rude, too boist'rous, and it pricks like thorn.
MERCUTIO   If love be rough with you, be rough with love.
   Prick° love for pricking, and you beat love down.[7]   *Stab; sexually penetrate*
   Give me a case[8] to put my visage in,
30   A visor for a visor.[9] What care I
   What curious eye doth quote° deformity?   *notice*
   Here are the beetle brows° shall blush for me.   *protruding eyebrows*
   [*They put on visors*]
BENVOLIO   Come, knock and enter, and no sooner in
   But every man betake him to his legs.°   *to dancing; to flight*
35   ROMEO   A torch for me. Let wantons light of heart
   Tickle the sense-less rushes° with their heels,   *floor matting*
   For I am proverbed with a grandsire° phrase.   *an ancient*

1.4 Location: Before Capulet's house.
1. Performers or participants in an aristocratic masked
entertainment, consisting of dances and sometimes
dumb shows and set speeches.
2. Blindfolded and foolish Cupid, a typical costume for
the presenter of the masque's theme.
3. Short bow shaped like the upper lip, made of the
thin wood used for theatrical properties.

4. A normal limit; an average dancer's leap.
5. Height from which a hawk stoops to kill.
6. Suggesting a pudendum.
7. *Prick . . . down:* Playing on the sense "satiate desire
by fulfilling it."
8. Literally, "mask," but also slang for the vagina.
9. Mask for an ugly face. Proverbial: "A well-favored
visor to hide an ill-favored face."

I'll be a candle-holder and look on.[1]
The game was ne'er so fair, and I am done.[2]
    [*He takes a torch*]

40 MERCUTIO   Tut, dun's the mouse,[3] the constable's own word.°   *phrase*
If thou art dun we'll draw thee from the mire[4]
Of—save your reverence[5]—love, wherein thou stickest
Up to the ears. Come, we burn daylight,° ho!   *waste time*
ROMEO   Nay, that's not so.
MERCUTIO   I mean, sir, in delay
45 We waste our lights in vain, like lights by day.
Take our good meaning, for our judgement sits
Five times in that ere once in our five wits.[6]
ROMEO   And we mean° well in going to this masque,   *intend*
But 'tis no wit° to go.   *intelligence*
MERCUTIO   Why, may one ask?
ROMEO   I dreamt a dream tonight.°   *last night*
50 MERCUTIO   And so did I.
ROMEO   Well, what was yours?
MERCUTIO   That dreamers often lie.
ROMEO   In bed asleep while they do dream things true.
MERCUTIO   O, then I see Queen Mab[7] hath been with you.
BENVOLIO   Queen Mab, what's she?
55 MERCUTIO   She is the fairies' midwife, and she comes
In shape no bigger than an agate stone[8]
On the forefinger of an alderman,
Drawn with a team of little atomi°   *atoms*
Athwart men's noses as they lie asleep.
60 Her wagon spokes made of long spinners'° legs;   *spiders'*
The cover, of the wings of grasshoppers;
Her traces, of the moonshine's wat'ry beams;
Her collars, of the smallest spider web;
Her whip, of cricket's bone, the lash of film;°   *spider's-web thread*
65 Her wagoner,° a small grey-coated gnat   *driver*
Not half so big as a round little worm
Pricked from the lazy finger of a maid.[9]
Her chariot is an empty hazelnut
Made by the joiner° squirrel or old grub,[1]   *carpenter*
70 Time out o' mind the fairies' coachmakers.
And in this state° she gallops night by night   *regal finery*
Through lovers' brains, and then they dream of love;
O'er courtiers' knees, that dream on curtsies straight;[2]
O'er ladies' lips, who straight on kisses dream,
75 Which oft the angry Mab with blisters plagues
Because their breaths with sweetmeats° tainted are.   *candies*
Sometime she gallops o'er a lawyer's lip,

---

1. Proverbial: "A good candleholder proves a good gamester. A spectator loses nothing."
2. Proverbial: "When play is best, it is time to leave."
3. Proverbial: Keep silent and unseen, like a mouse.
4. In the Christmas game "Dun is in the mire," players pantomimed drawing a log representing a horse out of a boggy road. Mercutio is suggesting that Romeo is a stick-in-the-mud.
5. An apology for crude language, here used mockingly.
6. *Take . . . wits:* Understand my intended good meaning using common sense ("judgement"), which is five times as trustworthy as the five senses.

7. Possibly Celtic, but probably Shakespeare's invention. "Queen" meant "whore," and "Mab" was a stereotypical name for prostitutes.
8. A small human figure was often carved on agate stones set in seal rings.
9. According to popular belief, worms generated in idle girls' fingers.
1. Grubs bore holes. Lines 68–70, from Q1, do not appear in Q2 at all; numerous other changes in the order and wording of his speech suggest that Q1 incorporated revisions that Q2 and later revisions did not.
2. Dream of respectful bows immediately.

And then dreams he of smelling out a suit;[3]
And sometime comes she with a tithe-pig's[4] tail
80 Tickling a parson's nose as a° lies asleep;   *he*
Then dreams he of another benefice.[5]
Sometime she driveth o'er a soldier's neck,
And then dreams he of cutting foreign throats,
Of breaches, ambuscados, Spanish blades,[6]
85 Of healths five fathom deep;[7] and then anon°   *soon*
Drums in his ear, at which he starts and wakes,
And being thus frighted, swears a prayer or two,
And sleeps again. This is that very Mab
That plaits° the manes of horses in the night,   *entangles*
90 And bakes the elf-locks[8] in foul sluttish° hairs,   *dirty*
Which once untangled much misfortune bodes.
This is the hag, when maids lie on their backs,
That presses them[9] and learns° them first to bear,   *teaches*
Making them women of good carriage.[1]
This is she—

95 ROMEO   Peace, peace, Mercutio, peace!
Thou talk'st of nothing.°   *imaginings; a vagina*
MERCUTIO   True. I talk of dreams,
Which are the children of an idle brain,
Begot of nothing but vain fantasy,°   *empty imagination*
Which is as thin of substance as the air,
100 And more inconstant than the wind, who woos
Even now the frozen bosom of the north,
And, being angered, puffs away from thence,
Turning his face to the dew-dropping south.
BENVOLIO   This wind you talk of blows us from ourselves.
105 Supper is done, and we shall come too late.
ROMEO   I fear too early, for my mind misgives°   *fears*
Some consequence yet hanging in the stars
Shall bitterly begin his fearful date°   *period*
With this night's revels, and expire° the term   *finish*
110 Of a despisèd life, closed in my breast,
By some vile forfeit of untimely death.[2]
But he° that hath the steerage of my course   *(God)*
Direct my sail! On, lusty gentlemen.
BENVOLIO   Strike, drum.
They march about the stage and [exeunt]

1.5

*[*PETER *and other* SERVINGMEN*] come forth with napkins*
PETER   Where's Potpan, that he helps not to take away? He shift
a trencher,° he scrape a trencher!   *wooden plate*
FIRST SERVINGMAN   When good manners shall lie all in one or
two men's hands, and they unwashed too, 'tis a foul° thing.   *bad; dirty*

---

3. A petition at court, which the lawyer could facilitate
for a fee.
4. Pig paid as a tithe to the parish for the support of the
priest.
5. Pluralism—holding multiple benefices simultaneously—was a common source of corruption in the
early modern Church.
6. *breaches:* burst fortifications. *ambuscados:*
ambushes. *Spanish blades:* swords made in Toledo were
famous for their quality.

7. Fantastically deep cups of liquor.
8. And hardens the tangles. According to folk legend,
unknotting them would anger the malicious elves.
9. Evil spirits were supposed to be responsible for
erotic dreams, taking the form of an illusory sexual
partner.
1. Excellent deportment; the capacity for carrying the
weight of a lover; childbearing.
2. As fate prematurely foreclosing on a mortgaged life.
1.5. Location: Capulet's house.

5   PETER   Away with the joint-stools,[1] remove the court-cupboard,°   *sideboard*
    look to the plate.° Good thou, save me a piece of marzipan,   *silverware*
    and, as thou loves me, let the porter let in Susan Grindstone
    and Nell. Anthony and Potpan!
    SECOND SERVINGMAN   Ay, boy, ready.
10   PETER   You are looked for and called for, asked for and sought
    for, in the great chamber.
    FIRST SERVINGMAN   We cannot be here and there too. Cheerly,
    boys! Be brisk a while, and the longest liver take all.[2]
           [They come and go, setting forth tables and chairs]
           Enter old CAPULET *[and family and] all the guests and*
           gentlewomen to the masquers
    CAPULET *[to the masquers]*   Welcome, gentlemen. Ladies that
    have their toes
15   Unplagued with corns will walk a bout° with you.   *dance a turn*
    Aha, my mistresses, which of you all
    Will now deny to dance? She that makes dainty,°   *coyly demurs*
    She, I'll swear, hath corns. Am I come near ye now?[3]
    Welcome, gentlemen. I have seen the day
20   That I have worn a visor, and could tell
    A whispering tale in a fair lady's ear
    Such as would please. 'Tis gone, 'tis gone, 'tis gone.
    You are welcome, gentlemen. Come, musicians, play.
           Music plays, and they dance. [ROMEO *stands apart*]
    A hall,[4] a hall! Give room, and foot it, girls.
25   *[To* SERVINGMEN*]*   More light, you knaves, and turn the tables up,[5]
    And quench the fire, the room is grown too hot.
    [To his COUSIN*]* Ah sirrah, this unlooked-for° sport comes well.   *unexpected*
    Nay, sit, nay, sit, good cousin° Capulet,   *kinsman*
    For you and I are past our dancing days.
           *[*CAPULET *and his* COUSIN *sit]*
30   How long is't now since last yourself and I
    Were in a masque?
    CAPULET'S COUSIN   By'r Lady, thirty years.
    CAPULET   What, man, 'tis not so much, 'tis not so much.
    'Tis since the nuptial of Lucentio,
    Come Pentecost[6] as quickly as it will,
35   Some five-and-twenty years; and then we masqued.
    CAPULET'S COUSIN   'Tis more, 'tis more. His son is elder, sir.
    His son is thirty.
    CAPULET   Will you tell me that?
    His son was but a ward[7] two years ago.
    ROMEO *[to a* SERVINGMAN*]*   What lady's that which doth enrich the hand
    Of yonder knight?
40   SERVINGMAN   I know not, sir.
    ROMEO   O, she doth teach the torches to burn bright!
    It seems she hangs upon the cheek of night
    As a rich jewel in an Ethiope's ear—
    Beauty too rich for use, for earth too dear.[8]

1. Stools made by a furniture maker, commonly used for seating at large banquets.
2. Proverbial, meaning "Life is short."
3. Does that strike home?
4. Make space in the hall.
5. Dismantle and stack the trestle tables.
6. The seventh Sunday after Easter, a standard reference point in the medieval and Renaissance calendar.
7. Subject to a guardian; a minor.
8. Too precious for this world; too valuable to die and be buried in earth.

45   So shows a snowy dove trooping° with crows   *flocking*
     As yonder lady o'er her fellows shows.
     The measure° done, I'll watch her place of stand,°   *dance / standing*
     And, touching hers, make blessèd my rude hand.
     Did my heart love till now? Forswear it, sight,
50   For I ne'er saw true beauty till this night.
TYBALT   This, by his voice, should be a Montague.
     Fetch me my rapier, boy.   [*Exit* page]
                         What, dares the slave
     Come hither, covered with an antic face,⁹
     To fleer° and scorn at our solemnity?°   *sneer / festivity*
55   Now, by the stock and honour of my kin,
     To strike him dead I hold it not a sin.
CAPULET [*standing*]   Why, how now, kinsman? Wherefore storm you so?
TYBALT   Uncle, this is a Montague, our foe,
     A villain° that is hither come in spite   *An ill-doer; a slave*
60   To scorn at our solemnity this night.
CAPULET   Young Romeo, is it?
TYBALT   'Tis he, that villain Romeo.
CAPULET   Content° thee, gentle coz, let him alone.   *Calm*
     A bears him like a portly° gentleman,   *dignified*
     And, to say truth, Verona brags of him
65   To be a virtuous and well-governed° youth.   *sensible*
     I would not for the wealth of all this town
     Here in my house do him disparagement.
     Therefore be patient, take no note of him.
     It is my will, the which if thou respect,
70   Show a fair presence° and put off these frowns,   *demeanor*
     An ill-beseeming semblance° for a feast.   *expression*
TYBALT   It fits when such a villain is a guest.
     I'll not endure him.
CAPULET   He shall be endured.
     What, goodman¹ boy, I say he shall. Go to,²
75   Am I the master here or you? Go to—
     You'll not endure him! God shall mend my soul.
     You'll make a mutiny° among my guests,   *brawl*
     You will set cock-a-hoop!³ You'll be the man!
TYBALT   Why, uncle, 'tis a shame.
CAPULET   Go to, go to,
80   You are a saucy boy. Is't so, indeed?
     This trick° may chance to scathe° you. I know what,⁴   *stupidity / harm*
     You must contrary me. Marry, 'tis time⁵—
         [A *dance ends.* JULIET *retires to her place of stand, where*
         ROMEO *awaits her*]
     [*To the guests*] Well said,° my hearts! [*To* TYBALT] You are a   *done*
         princox,° go.   *cheeky boy*
     Be quiet, or— [*to* SERVINGMEN] more light, more light!— [*to*
         TYBALT] for shame,
85   I'll make you quiet. [*To the guests*] What, cheerly, my hearts!
         [*The music plays again, and the guests dance*]

9. A grotesque mask; a playful mask.
1. Courtesy title applied to a commoner (and thus an insult to the noble Tybalt).
2. An expression of impatience.
3. You will abandon restraint, like a drinker who

removes the tap ("cock") from the barrel or like a boastfully crowing rooster.
4. Know what I'll do; mean what I say.
5. Time to teach you a lesson; time that you became obedient.

TYBALT   Patience perforce° with wilful choler° meeting   *enforced / rash anger*
　　　　Makes my flesh tremble in their different° greeting.   *hostile*
　　　　I will withdraw, but this intrusion shall,
　　　　Now seeming sweet, convert to bitt'rest gall.   *Exit*
90   ROMEO [*to* JULIET, *touching her hand*]   If I profane with my unworthiest hand[6]
　　　　This holy shrine, the gentler sin is this:
　　　　My lips, two blushing pilgrims,[7] ready stand
　　　　To smooth that rough touch with a tender kiss.
　　　　JULIET   Good pilgrim, you do wrong your hand too much,
95   　　　　Which mannerly° devotion shows in this.   *seemly*
　　　　For saints[8] have hands that pilgrims' hands do touch,
　　　　And palm to palm is holy palmers'° kiss.   *pilgrims'*
　　ROMEO   Have not saints lips, and holy palmers, too?
　　JULIET   Ay, pilgrim, lips that they must use in prayer.
100 ROMEO   O then, dear saint, let lips do what hands do:
　　　　They pray; grant thou, lest faith turn to despair.
　　JULIET   Saints do not move, though grant for prayers' sake.[9]
　　ROMEO   Then move not while my prayer's effect I take.
　　　　　　[*He kisses her*]
　　　　Thus from my lips, by thine my sin is purged.
105 JULIET   Then have my lips the sin that they have took.
　　ROMEO   Sin from my lips? O trespass sweetly urged![1]
　　　　Give me my sin again.°   *back*
　　　　　　[*He kisses her*]
　　JULIET   You kiss by th' book.[2]
　　NURSE   Madam, your mother craves a word with you.
　　　　　　[JULIET *departs to her mother*]
　　ROMEO   What is her mother?
　　NURSE   Marry, bachelor,°   *young man*
110 Her mother is the lady of the house,
　　　　And a good lady, and a wise and virtuous.
　　　　I nursed her daughter that you talked withal.°   *with*
　　　　I tell you, he that can lay hold of her
　　　　Shall have the chinks.°   *plenty of coins*
　　ROMEO [*aside*]   Is she a Capulet?
115 O dear account!° My life is my foe's debt.[3]   *costly reckoning*
　　BENVOLIO   Away, be gone, the sport is at the best.
　　ROMEO   Ay, so I fear, the more is my unrest.
　　CAPULET   Nay, gentlemen, prepare not to be gone.
　　　　We have a trifling foolish banquet towards.[4]
　　　　　　[*They whisper in his ear*]
120 Is it e'en so? Why then, I thank you all.
　　　　I thank you, honest gentlemen. Good night.
　　　　More torches here! Come on then, let's to bed.
　　　　[*To his* COUSIN] Ah, sirrah, by my fay,° it waxes late.   *faith*
　　　　I'll to my rest.

---

6. Romeo and Juliet here address each other in the form of a sonnet.
7. Florio's *World of Wordes* (1598) translates the Italian word *romeo* as "wanderer" or "palmer" (pilgrim to the Holy Land).
8. Statues or pictures of saints, which attracted Catholic pilgrims. The Elizabethan Anglican Church held that the worship of such images was blasphemy; to an English audience, therefore, Romeo's description of his love could sound like idolatry.

9. Again identifying the saint with her image. As a statue she does not move, but as a saint in heaven she can intercede with God on behalf of the worshipper.
1. Sweetly argued that the first kiss was a transgression, and sweetly advocated that the transgression of a second kiss is needed to take the sin of the first away.
2. According to the rules; implies "proficiently," "politely," or "with poetic flatteries."
3. A debt owing to my foe; in the power of my foe.
4. A trifling, paltry dessert coming.

Exeunt [CAPULET, *his* WIFE, *and his* COUSIN. *The*
guests, gentlewomen, masquers, musicians, and
servingmen begin to leave]

125 JULIET   Come hither, Nurse. What is yon gentleman?
NURSE   The son and heir of old Tiberio.
JULIET   What's he that now is going out of door?
NURSE   Marry, that, I think, be young Petruccio.
JULIET   What's he that follows here, that would not dance?
130 NURSE   I know not.
JULIET   Go ask his name.
[NURSE *goes*]
                        If he be marrièd,
    My grave is like° to be my wedding bed.   likely
NURSE [*returning*]   His name is Romeo, and a Montague,
    The only son of your great enemy.
135 JULIET [*aside*]   My only love sprung from my only hate!
    Too early seen unknown, and known too late!
    Prodigious° birth of love it is to me   Monstrous; ominous
    That I must love a loathèd enemy.
NURSE   What's tis?° what's tis?   this
JULIET   A rhyme I learnt even now
    Of one I danced withal.
        One calls within 'Juliet!'
140 NURSE   Anon,° anon.   Right away
    Come, let's away. The strangers all are gone.   *Exeunt*

                        2.0

[*Enter*] CHORUS
CHORUS   Now old° desire doth in his deathbed lie,   Romeo's former
    And young affection gapes° to be his heir.   longs
    That fair for which love groaned for and would die,
    With tender Juliet matched,° is now not fair.   compared
    Now Romeo is beloved and loves again,°   in return; once more
5   Alike bewitchèd by the charm of looks;[1]
    But to his foe supposed° he must complain,[2]   presumed
    And she steal love's sweet bait from fearful° hooks.   fearsome
    Being held a foe, he may not have access
    To breathe such vows as lovers use° to swear,   are accustomed
10 And she as much in love, her means much less
    To meet her new belovèd anywhere.
    But passion lends them power, time means, to meet,
    Temp'ring extremities° with extreme sweet.   [*Exit*] Modifying dangers

                        2.1

Enter ROMEO *alone*[1]
ROMEO   Can I go forward when my heart is here?
    Turn back, dull earth,[2] and find thy centre[3] out.
        [*He turns back and withdraws.*]
    Enter BENVOLIO *with* MERCUTIO

2.0
1. Appearances; desirous glances.
2. Conventionally, make lovesick speeches.
2.1 Location: Outside Capulet's house.
1. The main stage represents the area outside the wall of
Capulet's orchard and then the inside of the orchard
below the window of Juliet's room. Romeo is imagined to

leap over the garden wall when he withdraws at line 2.
2. Romeo's flesh, drawing on two traditional views of the
human body: animated dust or clay, and a "microcosm,"
or little world, which mirrors the order of the universe.
Earth was the most sluggish and immobile element.
3. The point in the earth toward which everything falls;
or Romeo's heart (metaphorically, Juliet).

BENVOLIO [*calling*]   Romeo, my cousin Romeo, Romeo!

MERCUTIO   He is wise, and, on my life, hath stol'n him° home to bed.   *himself*

5 BENVOLIO   He ran this way, and leapt this orchard wall.
Call, good Mercutio.

MERCUTIO   Nay, I'll conjure° too.   *summon as a spirit*
Romeo! Humours!⁴ Madman! Passion! Lover!
Appear thou in the likeness of a sigh.
Speak but one rhyme and I am satisfied.

10 Cry but 'Ay me!' Pronounce but 'love' and 'dove'.
Speak to my gossip° Venus one fair word,   *crony*
One nickname for her purblind° son and heir,   *dim-sighted; blind*
Young Adam⁵ Cupid, he that shot so trim°   *accurately*
When King Cophetua loved the beggar maid.⁶—

15 He heareth not, he stirreth not, he moveth not.
The ape⁷ is dead, and I must conjure him.—
I conjure thee by Rosaline's bright eyes,
By her high forehead and her scarlet lip,
By her fine foot, straight leg, and quivering thigh,

20 And the demesnes° that there adjacent lie,   *estates*
That in thy likeness thou appear to us.

BENVOLIO   An if he hear thee, thou wilt anger him.

MERCUTIO   This cannot anger him. 'Twould anger him
To raise a spirit⁸ in his mistress' circle

25 Of some strange° nature, letting it there stand   *other person's*
Till she had laid it and conjured it down.
That were some spite. My invocation
Is fair and honest. In his mistress' name,
I conjure only but to raise up him.

30 BENVOLIO   Come, he hath hid himself among these trees
To be consorted° with the humorous⁹ night.   *in company*
Blind is his love, and best befits the dark.

MERCUTIO   If love be blind, love cannot hit the mark.°   *target; vulva*
Now will he sit under a medlar¹ tree

35 And wish his mistress were that kind of fruit
As maids call medlars when they laugh alone.
O Romeo, that she were, O that she were
An open-arse,° and thou a popp'rin' pear.²   *medlar*
Romeo, good night. I'll to my truckle-bed.³

40 This field-bed⁴ is too cold for me to sleep.
Come, shall we go?

BENVOLIO   Go then, for 'tis in vain
To seek him here that means not to be found.

Exeunt [BENVOLIO *and* MERCUTIO]

ROMEO [*coming forward*]   He jests at scars that never felt a wound.⁵
But soft,° what light through yonder window breaks?   *wait; hush*

---

4. Pure moods, not mixed together to form an even "temper."
5. Probably alluding to Adam Bell, a famously accurate sixteenth-century archer.
6. The story of a king who falls in love with a beggar and makes her his queen was the subject of a popular ballad.
7. Foolish creature (a disrespectful endearment), or alluding to a magician's trick of "reviving" an ape that had been trained to play dead.
8. A word for "semen"; the entire speech is filled with obscene wordplay.
9. Damp; melancholy.

1. A fruit thought to resemble the female sex organs, with a play on "meddle" in the sense "have sexual intercourse with."
2. A pear from Poperinghe in Flanders, punning on "popper-in" or "pop her in."
3. Small bed, often for a child, which was stored under a larger one.
4. A lying place in the open, and a soldier's portable bed.
5. Rhymes with "found." This line precedes a scene change in most editions, although the location remains the same if both the inside and the outside of the orchard are supposed to be visible onstage.

45 It is the east, and Juliet is the sun.
    Arise, fair sun, and kill the envious moon,[6]
    Who is already sick and pale with grief
    That thou, her maid, art far more fair than she.
    Be not her maid, since she is envious.
50 Her vestal° livery is but sick and green,[7]   virginal
    And none but fools do wear it; cast it off.
         [*Enter* JULIET *aloft*]
    It is my lady, O, it is my love.
    O that she knew she were!
    She speaks, yet she says nothing. What of that?
55 Her eye discourses; I will answer it.
    I am too bold. 'Tis not to me she speaks.
    Two of the fairest stars in all the heaven,
    Having some business, do entreat her eyes
    To twinkle in their spheres[8] till they return.
60 What if her eyes were there, they in her head?—
    The brightness of her cheek would shame those stars
    As daylight doth a lamp; her eye in heaven
    Would through the airy region° stream so bright   ethereal sky
    That birds would sing and think it were not night.
65 See how she leans her cheek upon her hand.
    O, that I were a glove upon that hand,
    That I might touch that cheek!
JULIET   Ay me.
ROMEO [*aside*]   She speaks.
    O, speak again, bright angel; for thou art
    As glorious to this night, being o'er my head,
70 As is a wingèd messenger° of heaven   angel
    Unto the white upturnèd[9] wond'ring eyes
    Of mortals that fall back to gaze[1] on him
    When he bestrides the lazy-passing clouds
    And sails upon the bosom of the air.
JULIET [*not knowing* ROMEO *hears her*]   O Romeo, Romeo,
75   wherefore° art thou Romeo?   why
    Deny thy father and refuse thy name,
    Or if thou wilt not, be but sworn my love,
    And I'll no longer be a Capulet.
ROMEO [*aside*]   Shall I hear more, or shall I speak at this?
80 JULIET   'Tis but thy name that is my enemy.
    Thou art thyself, though° not a Montague.   even if
    What's Montague? It is nor hand, nor foot,
    Nor arm, nor face, nor any other part
    Belonging to a man. O, be some other name!
85 What's in a name? That which we call a rose
    By any other word would smell as sweet.
    So Romeo would, were he not Romeo called,
    Retain that dear perfection which he owes°   owns
    Without that title. Romeo, doff° thy name,   shed
90 And for thy name—which is no part of thee—
    Take all myself.

---

6. Emblem of Diana, goddess of chastity.
7. Unfulfilled sexual desire was thought to cause green
sickness (anemia) in adolescent girls; also alluding to
the moon's pallor.

8. In Ptolemaic astrology, crystalline spheres around the
earth that carried the heavenly bodies in their rotations.
9. Turned up, revealing the whites at the bottoms.
1. Fall backward in gazing.

ROMEO [*to* JULIET] I take thee at thy word.[2]
Call me but love and I'll be new baptized.[3]
Henceforth I never will be Romeo.

JULIET   What man art thou that, thus bescreened in night,
So stumblest on my counsel?°   *private thoughts*

95 ROMEO   By a name
I know not how to tell thee who I am.
My name, dear saint, is hateful to myself
Because it is an enemy to thee.
Had I it written, I would tear the word.

100 JULIET   My ears have yet not drunk a hundred words
Of thy tongue's uttering, yet I know the sound.
Art thou not Romeo, and a Montague?

ROMEO   Neither, fair maid, if either thee dislike.°   *displeases you*

JULIET   How cam'st thou hither, tell me, and wherefore?

105 The orchard walls are high and hard to climb,
And the place death, considering who thou art,
If any of my kinsmen find thee here.

ROMEO   With love's light wings did I o'erperch° these walls,   *fly over*
For stony limits cannot hold love out,

110 And what love can do, that dares love attempt.
Therefore thy kinsmen are no stop° to me.   *obstacle*

JULIET   If they do see thee, they will murder thee.

ROMEO   Alack, there lies more peril in thine eye
Than twenty of their swords. Look thou but sweet,

115 And I am proof° against their enmity.   *armed*

JULIET   I would not for the world they saw thee here.

ROMEO   I have night's cloak to hide me from their eyes,
And but° thou love me, let them find me here.   *unless*
My life were better ended by their hate

120 Than death proroguèd,° wanting of° thy love.   *deferred / lacking*

JULIET   By whose direction found'st thou out this place?

ROMEO   By love, that first did prompt me to enquire.
He lent me counsel, and I lent him eyes.
I am no pilot, yet wert thou as far

125 As that vast shore washed with the farthest sea,
I should adventure° for such merchandise.   *voyage*

JULIET   Thou knowest the mask of night is on my face,
Else would a maiden blush bepaint my cheek
For that which thou hast heard me speak tonight.

130 Fain° would I dwell on form,° fain, fain deny   *Gladly / propriety*
What I have spoke; but farewell, compliment.°   *polite convention*
Dost thou love me? I know thou wilt say 'Ay',
And I will take thy word. Yet if thou swear'st
Thou mayst prove false. At lovers' perjuries,

135 They say, Jove laughs. O gentle Romeo,
If thou dost love, pronounce° it faithfully;   *utter*
Or if thou think'st I am too quickly won,
I'll frown, and be perverse,° and say thee nay,   *contrary*
So thou wilt woo; but else,° not for the world.   *otherwise*

140 In truth, fair Montague, I am too fond,°   *infatuated*
And therefore thou mayst think my 'haviour light.°   *licentious; capricious*

---

2. At face value; as you have asked me to.   3. Given a new name; born into a new persona.

But trust me, gentleman, I'll prove more true
Than those that have more cunning to be strange.°   *distant*
I should have been more strange, I must confess,
145 But that thou overheard'st, ere I was ware,°   *aware*
My true-love passion. Therefore pardon me,
And not° impute this yielding to light love,   *do not*
Which the dark night hath so discoverèd.°   *revealed*
ROMEO   Lady, by yonder blessèd moon I vow,
150 That tips with silver all these fruit-tree tops—
JULIET   O swear not by the moon, th'inconstant moon
That monthly changes in her circled orb,°   *orbital sphere*
Lest that thy love prove likewise variable.
ROMEO   What shall I swear by?
JULIET   Do not swear at all,
155 Or if thou wilt, swear by thy gracious self,
Which is the god of my idolatry,[4]
And I'll believe thee.
ROMEO   If my heart's dear love—
JULIET   Well, do not swear. Although I joy in thee,
I have no joy of this contract° tonight.   *exchange of vows*
160 It is too rash, too unadvised,° too sudden,   *undeliberated*
Too like the lightning which doth cease to be
Ere one can say it lightens. Sweet, good night.
This bud of love by summer's ripening breath
May prove a beauteous flower when next we meet.
165 Good night, good night. As sweet repose and rest
Come to thy heart as that within my breast.
ROMEO   O, wilt thou leave me so unsatisfied?
JULIET   What satisfaction canst thou have tonight?
ROMEO   Th'exchange of thy love's faithful vow for mine.
170 JULIET   I gave thee mine before thou didst request it,
And yet I would it were° to give again.   *were available*
ROMEO   Wouldst thou withdraw it? For what purpose, love?
JULIET   But to be frank° and give it thee again.   *generous; honest*
And yet I wish but for the thing I have.
175 My bounty is as boundless as the sea,
My love as deep. The more I give to thee
The more I have, for both are infinite.
                    [NURSE] *calls within*
I hear some noise within. Dear love, adieu.—
Anon,° good Nurse!—Sweet Montague, be true.   *One moment*
180 Stay but a little; I will come again.   [*Exit*]
ROMEO   O blessèd, blessèd night! I am afeard,
Being in night, all this is but a dream,
Too flattering-sweet to be substantial.
                    [*Enter* JULIET *aloft*]
JULIET   Three words, dear Romeo, and good night indeed.
185 If that thy bent of love be honourable,
Thy purpose marriage, send me word tomorrow,
By one that I'll procure to come to thee,
Where and what time thou wilt perform the rite,
And all my fortunes at thy foot I'll lay,
190 And follow thee, my lord, throughout the world.

---

4. Not only was loving a man more than God idolatrous, but so was swearing oaths by anything other than God.

NURSE (*within*) Madam!

JULIET I come, anon. [*To* ROMEO] But if thou mean'st not well,
        I do beseech thee—

NURSE (*within*) Madam!

195 JULIET By and by I come.—
             To cease thy strife° and leave me to my grief.   striving
             Tomorrow will I send.

ROMEO So thrive my soul⁵—

JULIET A thousand times good night.   *Exit*

200 ROMEO A thousand times the worse to want° thy light.   lack
             Love goes toward love as schoolboys from their books,
             But love from love, toward school with heavy looks.

                       [*He is going*]

             Enter JULIET [*aloft*] *again*

JULIET Hist,° Romeo! Hist! O for a falconer's voice   (*falconer's call*)
        To lure this tassel-gentle⁶ back again.

205   Bondage⁷ is hoarse, and may not speak aloud,
        Else would I tear° the cave where Echo⁸ lies,   split with cries
        And make her airy tongue more hoarse than mine
        With repetition of my Romeo's name. Romeo!

ROMEO It is my soul that calls upon my name.

210   How silver-sweet sound lovers' tongues by night,
        Like softest music to attending ears!

JULIET Romeo!

ROMEO   My nyas?°   young hawk

JULIET   What o'clock tomorrow
        Shall I send to thee?

ROMEO   By the hour of nine.

JULIET I will not fail; 'tis twenty year till then.

215   I have forgot why I did call thee back.

ROMEO Let me stand here till thou remember it.

JULIET I shall forget, to have thee still° stand there,   always
        Rememb'ring how I love thy company.

ROMEO And I'll still stay, to have thee still forget,

220   Forgetting any other home but this.

JULIET 'Tis almost morning. I would have thee gone—
        And yet no farther than a wanton's° bird,   spoiled child's
        That lets it hop a little from his hand,
        Like a poor prisoner in his twisted gyves,°   fetters

225   And with a silk thread plucks it back again,
        So loving-jealous of his liberty.

ROMEO I would° I were thy bird.   wish

JULIET   Sweet, so would I.
        Yet I should kill thee with much cherishing.
        Good night, good night. Parting is such sweet sorrow

230   That I shall say good night till it be morrow.

ROMEO Sleep dwell upon thine eyes, peace in thy breast.

                            [*Exit* JULIET]

        Would I were sleep and peace, so sweet to rest.
        Hence will I to my ghostly° sire's close° cell,   spiritual / small; private
        His help to crave, and my dear hap° to tell.   *Exit*   fortune

---

5. On peril of damnation.

6. Tercel-gentle, a male peregrine falcon. Literally, a noble ("gentle") hawk.

7. Confinement within her family's home; duty owed her family.

8. In classical legend, a woman who, scorned by Narcissus, wasted away with grief until only a voice remained to haunt empty caves.

2.2

Enter FRIAR [LAURENCE] *alone, with a basket*

FRIAR LAURENCE The grey°-eyed morn smiles on the frowning night,   *pale blue*
Chequ'ring the eastern clouds with streaks of light,
And fleckled° darkness like a drunkard reels   *dappled*
From forth° day's path and Titan's¹ fiery wheels.   *out of*
5 Now, ere the sun advance° his burning eye   *brings up*
The day to cheer and night's dank dew to dry,
I must up-fill this osier cage° of ours   *willow basket*
With baleful weeds and precious-juicèd flowers.
The earth, that's nature's mother, is her tomb.
10 What is her burying grave, that is her womb,
And from her womb children of divers° kind   *several; varied*
We sucking on her natural bosom find,
Many for many virtues° excellent,   *healthful properties*
None but for some,² and yet all different.
15 O mickle° is the powerful grace° that lies   *great / divine beneficence*
In plants, herbs, stones, and their true qualities,
For naught° so vile that on the earth doth live   *nothing is*
But to the earth some special good doth give;
Nor aught so good but, strained° from that fair use,   *twisted*
20 Revolts from true birth, stumbling on abuse.³
Virtue itself turns vice being misapplied,
And vice sometime's by action dignified.

Enter ROMEO

Within the infant rind of this weak flower
Poison hath residence, and medicine power,
25 For this, being smelt, with that part° cheers each part;°   *act / bodily member*
Being tasted, slays all senses with the heart.
Two such opposèd kings encamp them still°   *always*
In man as well as herbs—grace and rude will;
And where the worser is predominant,
30 Full soon the canker° death eats up that plant.   *grub; cancer*
ROMEO Good morrow, father.
FRIAR LAURENCE   *Benedicite.°*   *God bless you*
What early tongue so sweet saluteth me?
Young son, it argues a distempered head
So soon to bid good morrow to thy bed.
35 Care keeps his watch in every old man's eye,
And where care lodges, sleep will never lie,
But where unbruisèd° youth with unstuffed° brain   *fresh / unanxious*
Doth couch his limbs, there golden sleep doth reign.
Therefore thy earliness doth me assure
40 Thou art uproused with some distemp'rature;
Or if not so, then here I hit it right:
Our Romeo hath not been in bed tonight.
ROMEO That last is true; the sweeter rest was mine.
FRIAR LAURENCE God pardon sin!—Wast thou with Rosaline?
45 ROMEO With Rosaline, my ghostly father? No,
I have forgot that name and that name's woe.
FRIAR LAURENCE That's my good son; but where hast thou been then?

2.2 Location: A street in Verona.
1. Helios, a classical sun god, was descended from the Titans. He traveled across the sky in a chariot.

2. None that is not excellent for some use.
3. Turns from its intended benefits if it happens to be misused.

ROMEO   I'll tell thee ere thou ask it me again.
I have been feasting with mine enemy,
50   Where on a sudden one hath wounded me
That's by me wounded. Both our remedies
Within thy help and holy physic° lies.   *medicine*
I bear no hatred, blessèd man, for lo,
My intercession° likewise steads° my foe.   *request / benefits*
55 FRIAR LAURENCE   Be plain, good son, and homely° in thy drift.   *direct*
Riddling confession finds but riddling shrift.°   *absolution*
ROMEO   Then plainly know my heart's dear love is set
On the fair daughter of rich Capulet.
As mine on hers, so hers is set on mine,
60   And all combined save what thou must combine
By holy marriage. When and where and how
We met, we wooed, and made exchange of vow
I'll tell thee as we pass; but this I pray,
That thou consent to marry us today.
65 FRIAR LAURENCE   Holy Saint Francis, what a change is here!
Is Rosaline, that thou didst love so dear,
So soon forsaken? Young men's love then lies
Not truly in their hearts, but in their eyes.
Jesu Maria, what a deal of brine
70   Hath washed thy sallow° cheeks for Rosaline!   *yellowed*
How much salt water thrown away in waste
To season° love, that of it doth not taste!   *preserve; flavor*
The sun not yet thy sighs⁴ from heaven clears.
Thy old° groans yet ring in mine ancient ears.   *former*
75   Lo, here upon thy cheek the stain doth sit
Of an old tear that is not washed off yet.
If e'er thou wast thyself, and these woes thine,
Thou and these woes were all for Rosaline.
And art thou changed? Pronounce this sentence° then: *maxim; verdict*
80   Women may fall when there's no strength in men.
ROMEO   Thou chidd'st me oft for loving Rosaline.
FRIAR LAURENCE   For doting, not for loving, pupil mine.
ROMEO   And bad'st me bury love.
FRIAR LAURENCE   Not in a grave
To lay one in, another out to have.
85 ROMEO   I pray thee, chide me not. Her I love now
Doth grace for grace and love for love allow.
The other did not so.
FRIAR LAURENCE   O, she knew well
Thy love did read by rote, that could not spell.⁵
But come, young waverer, come, go with me.
90   In one respect I'll thy assistant be;
For this alliance may so happy prove
To turn your households' rancour to pure love.
ROMEO   O, let us hence! I stand° on sudden haste.   *depend; insist*
FRIAR LAURENCE   Wisely and slow. They stumble that run fast.
                                        Exeunt

---

4. The mist Romeo's exhalations produced.
5. Did recite the memorized phrases of love poetry, without understanding or meaning them.

2.3

Enter BENVOLIO *and* MERCUTIO

MERCUTIO   Where the devil should this Romeo be? Came he
not home tonight?°   *last night*

BENVOLIO   Not to his father's. I spoke with his man.

MERCUTIO   Why, that same pale° hard-hearted wench, that   *fair-skinned; frigid*
Rosaline,

5   Torments him so that he will sure run mad.

BENVOLIO   Tybalt, the kinsman to old Capulet,
Hath sent a letter to his father's house.

MERCUTIO   A challenge, on my life.

BENVOLIO   Romeo will answer° it.   *accept*

MERCUTIO   Any man that can write may answer a letter.

10 BENVOLIO   Nay, he will answer the letter's master, how he dares,
being dared.

MERCUTIO   Alas, poor Romeo, he is already dead—stabbed with
a white wench's black eye, run through the ear with a love
song, the very pin[1] of his heart cleft with the blind bow-boy's
15 butt-shaft;[2] and is he a man to encounter Tybalt?

BENVOLIO   Why, what is Tybalt?

MERCUTIO   More than Prince of Cats.[3] O, he's the courageous
captain of compliments.° He fights as you sing pricksong:[4]   *formalities of dueling*
keeps time, distance,[5] and proportion.° He rests his minim   *harmony; form*
20 rests:[6] one, two, and the third in your bosom; the very butcher
of a silk button.[7] A duellist, a duellist; a gentleman of the very
first house of the first and second cause.[8] Ah, the immortal
passado, the *punto reverso,* the *hai.*[9]

BENVOLIO   The what?

25 MERCUTIO   The pox of° such antic,° lisping, affecting° phan-   *on / grotesque / affected*
tasims,° these new tuners of accent![1] 'By Jesu, a very good blade,   *bizarrely mannered men*
a very tall° man, a very good whore.' Why° is not this a lamen-   *valiant / Why, now*
table thing, grandsire, that we should be thus afflicted with
these strange[2] flies,° these fashionmongers, these 'pardon-   *gaudy buzzers*
30 me's',[3] who stand so much on the new form that they cannot
sit at ease on the old bench?[4] O, their bones, their bones![5]

Enter ROMEO

BENVOLIO   Here comes Romeo, here comes Romeo!

MERCUTIO   Without his roe, like a dried herring.[6] O flesh, flesh,

---

2.3 Location: Scene continues.

1. Peg in the center of an archery target.

2. Blunt practice arrow, fit for children and hence for
Cupid.

3. Called Tybalt or Tibert in medieval stories of Rey-
nard the fox. "Catso," from the Italian word for "penis,"
was also a slang term for a rogue.

4. Sung from sheet music and thus more precise and
invariable than extempore or remembered music.

5. Musical intervals between notes; also, a set space to
be kept between combatants.

6. Short musical rests, referring to the brief strategic
pauses in a duel.

7. Alluding to the boast of an Italian fencing master in
London that he could "hit any Englishman with a
thrust upon any button."

8. *gentleman . . . cause:* superior practitioner of taking
up quarrels as duels. *first house:* the best fencing school.
cause: a reason that according to the etiquette of fencing
would require an honorable gentleman to seek a duel.

9. Italian fencing terms for a lunging sword thrust,
backhanded thrust, and thrust that reaches through.

1. These faddishly novel speakers, such as those
importing foreign phrases. A typical Renaissance English satire, here seemingly unaffected by the fact that
Italian is the native tongue of Verona.

2. Newfangled; foreign.

3. *pardon-me's:* the fastidiously mannered, affecting
the French *pardonnez-moi.*

4. *who . . . bench:* as if both Mercutio and Benvolio
were elderly ("grandsire"), viewing the decline of the
young. *stand:* insist. *form:* etiquette; fashion; bench.

5. *O . . . bones:* Aching on the austere furniture of their
predecessors; infected with the "bone disease," syphilis.
Mercutio may also be satirizing the courtly habit of crying "Bon! Bon!" (French for "good") as a kind of inane
flattery.

6. Emaciated, since the roe is removed in curing. This
leaves Romeo's name a mournful wail, "Me, O." He is
also missing his roe deer (female, named Rosaline).

how art thou fishified![7] Now is he for the numbers° that *verses*
35 Petrarch[8] flowed in. Laura to° his lady was a kitchen wench— *compared to*
marry, she had a better love to berhyme her—Dido[9] a dowdy,
Cleopatra a gypsy,[1] Helen and Hero[2] hildings° and harlots, *hussies*
Thisbe[3] a grey° eye or so, but not to the purpose.° Signor *blue / of consequence*
Romeo, *bonjour*. There's a French salutation to your French
40 slop.° You gave us the counterfeit fairly last night. *loose breeches*

ROMEO Good morrow to you both. What counterfeit did I give
you?

MERCUTIO The slip,[4] sir, the slip. Can you not conceive?° *understand*

ROMEO Pardon, good Mercutio. My business was great, and in
45 such a case as mine a man may strain° courtesy. *nearly abandon*

MERCUTIO That's as much as to say such a case as yours constrains a man to bow in the hams.[5]

ROMEO Meaning to curtsy.[6]

MERCUTIO Thou hast most kindly hit[7] it.

50 ROMEO A most courteous exposition.

MERCUTIO Nay, I am the very pink° of courtesy. *nonpareil; carnation*

ROMEO Pink for flower.° *dianthus; vulva*

MERCUTIO Right.

ROMEO Why, then is my pump° well flowered.[8] *shoe; penis*

55 MERCUTIO Sure wit, follow me° this jest now till thou hast worn *chase; respond to*
out thy pump, that when the single° sole of it is worn, the jest *thin*
may remain, after the wearing, solely singular.° *utterly unique*

ROMEO O single-soled° jest, solely° singular for the singleness!° *shoddy / only / foolishness*

MERCUTIO Come between us, good Benvolio. My wits faints.[9]

60 ROMEO Switch and spurs,[1] switch and spurs, or I'll cry a match.° *claim a victory*

MERCUTIO Nay, if our wits run the wild-goose chase,[2] I am done,
for thou hast more of the wild goose° in one of thy wits than I *folly*
am sure I have in my whole five. Was I with° you there for the *even with*
goose?

65 ROMEO Thou wast never with me for anything when thou wast
not there for the goose.[3]

MERCUTIO I will bite thee by the ear[4] for that jest.

ROMEO Nay, good goose, bite not.[5]

MERCUTIO Thy wit is very bitter sweeting,° it is a most sharp *apple*
70 sauce.° *mockery*

ROMEO And is it not then well served in to a sweet goose?

MERCUTIO O, here's a wit of cheveril,° that stretches from an *kid leather*
inch narrow to an ell broad.[6]

---

7. Gone pale and limp, turned into a herring. Fish, thought weak and relatively unnourishing, was the substitute for "flesh" (meat) during fasts.
8. Petrarch's sonnets addressed to Laura were the model for an English love-sonnet craze.
9. The beautiful queen of Carthage who fell in love with Aeneas but was deserted by him in Virgil's *Aeneid*.
1. A term of abuse. Gypsies were supposed to have come from Egypt, where Cleopatra was queen and lover of Julius Caesar and Mark Antony.
2. Helen's abduction by Paris initiated the Trojan War. Hero was Leander's lover in a tragic legend.
3. Beloved of Pyramus in a classical legend that parallels *Romeo and Juliet*. The young lovers, coming from hostile families, die as a result of a missed meeting and misinterpreted evidence.
4. Counterfeit coin.

5. Playing on "business" as "sexual intercourse" and "case" as "vagina." Mercutio suggests that Romeo needs to flex his buttocks or he may wind up with a leg-weakening venereal disease.
6. Pronounced the same as "courtesy."
7. Most truly guessed it; most truly sexually penetrated it.
8. Pinked, or decoratively perforated.
9. Treating the exchange of wit as a duel.
1. Flog your wits to a full gallop; continue.
2. A cross-country horse race in which the leader chose the course and the rest had to follow.
3. Silliness; whore's company.
4. Usually suggesting affectionate nibbling.
5. A proverbial cry for mercy, here used ironically.
6. That spreads itself very thin (an ell was forty-five inches).

ROMEO   I stretch it out for that word 'broad', which, added to the
75   goose, proves thee far and wide a broad goose.[7]

MERCUTIO   Why, is not this better now than groaning for love?
Now art thou sociable, now art thou Romeo, now art thou what
thou art by art° as well as by nature, for this drivelling love is   learning
like a great natural° that runs lolling up and down to hide his   idiot
80   bauble[8] in a hole.

BENVOLIO   Stop there, stop there.

MERCUTIO   Thou desirest me to stop in[9] my tale° against the   story; penis
hair.[1]

BENVOLIO   Thou wouldst else have made thy tale large.

85   MERCUTIO   O, thou art deceived, I would have made it short, for
I was come to the whole depth of my tale, and meant indeed
to occupy the argument° no longer.   topic

Enter NURSE, *and her man* [PETER]

ROMEO   Here's goodly gear.[2]

BENVOLIO   A sail, a sail![3]

90   MERCUTIO   Two, two—a shirt° and a smock.°   man / woman

NURSE   Peter.

PETER   Anon.°   At your service

NURSE   My fan, Peter.

MERCUTIO   Good Peter, to hide her face, for her fan's the fairer
95   face.

NURSE   God ye° good morrow,° gentlemen.   give you / morning

MERCUTIO   God ye good e'en,° fair gentlewoman.   afternoon

NURSE   Is it good e'en?

MERCUTIO   'Tis no less, I tell ye: for the bawdy hand of the dial
100   is now upon the prick° of noon.   mark; penis

NURSE   Out upon you,[4] what° a man are you!   what sort of

ROMEO   One, gentlewoman, that God hath made for himself to
mar.[5]

NURSE   By my troth, it is well said. 'For himself to mar', quoth
105   a?° Gentlemen, can any of you tell me where I may find the   he
young Romeo?

ROMEO   I can tell you, but young Romeo will be older when you
have found him than he was when you sought him. I am the
youngest of that name, for fault° of a worse.   lack

110   NURSE   You say well.

MERCUTIO   Yea, is the worst well? Very well took, i'faith, wisely,
wisely.

NURSE   [*to* ROMEO]   If you be he, sir, I desire some confidence
with you.

115   BENVOLIO   She will endite[6] him to some supper.

MERCUTIO   A bawd, a bawd, a bawd. So ho![7]

ROMEO   What hast thou found?°   spotted; figured out

---

7. A gross idiot; a licentious fellow; a goose fattened for
the table.
8. *that . . . bauble:* who runs with his tongue hanging
out to cover up a Jester's wand, at one end either
grotesquely carved or adorned with an inflated pig's
bladder; penis.
9. Cease; stuff in.
1. Against the grain; against the pubic hair.
2. Spoken ironically of Mercutio's witticisms or the
Nurse's voluminous appearance.
3. A sailor's cry upon sighting another ship.

4. An expression of indignation.
5. *One . . . . mar:* combines two proverbial expressions.
"It is his to make or mar" suggests that Mercutio has
the free will to determine his own character. "He is a
man of God's making" places the blame for Mercutio's
character on God.
6. Deliberately substituted for "invite," to mock the
Nurse's erroneous use of "confidence" for "conference"
in the line above.
7. The cry of a hunter who has spotted his quarry.

MERCUTIO   No hare,° sir, unless a hare, sir, in a lenten pie,[8] that   *prostitute*
is something stale and hoar ere it be spent.[9]

He walks by them and sings

120   An old hare hoar
               And an old hare hoar
               Is very good meat in Lent.
               But a hare that is hoar
               Is too much for a score[1]
125   When it hoars° ere it be spent.   *turns moldy; whores*
Romeo, will you come to your father's? We'll to dinner thither.

ROMEO   I will follow you.

MERCUTIO   Farewell, ancient lady. Farewell, [*sings*] 'lady, lady,
lady'.[2]   *Exeunt* MERCUTIO [*and*] BENVOLIO

130 NURSE   I pray you, sir, what saucy merchant° was this that was so   *commoner*
full of his ropery?°   *knavery*

ROMEO   A gentleman, Nurse, that loves to hear himself talk, and
will speak more in a minute than he will stand to° in a month.   *perform*

NURSE   An a° speak anything against me, I'll take him down° an   *If he / humble him*
135 a were lustier[3] than he is, and twenty such jacks;° an if I cannot,   *scoundrels*
I'll find those that shall. Scurvy knave! I am none of his flirt-
jills,° I am none of his skeans-mates.[4] [*To* PETER] And thou   *loose women*
must stand by, too, and suffer every knave to use me at his
pleasure.

140 PETER   I saw no man use you at his pleasure. If I had, my weapon
should quickly have been out; I warrant you, I dare draw as
soon as another man if I see occasion in a good quarrel, and
the law on my side.

NURSE   Now, afore God, I am so vexed that every part about me
145 quivers. Scurvy knave! [*To* ROMEO] Pray you, sir, a word; and,
as I told you, my young lady bid me enquire you out. What she
bid me say I will keep to myself, but first let me tell ye if ye
should lead her in a fool's paradise, as they say, it were a very
gross° kind of behaviour, as they say, for the gentlewoman is   *outrageous*
150 young; and therefore if you should deal double° with her, truly   *falsely; forcefully*
it were an ill thing to be offered to any gentlewoman, and very
weak° dealing.   *poor*

ROMEO   Nurse, commend me to thy lady and mistress. I protest°   *swear*
unto thee—

155 NURSE   Good heart, and i'faith I will tell her as much. Lord,
Lord, she will be a joyful woman.

ROMEO   What wilt thou tell her, Nurse? Thou dost not mark°   *pay attention to*
me.

NURSE   I will tell her, sir, that you do protest;[5] which as I take it
160 is a gentlemanlike offer.

ROMEO   Bid her devise
Some means to come to shrift this afternoon,
And there she shall at Friar Laurence' cell
Be shrived° and married. [*Offering money*] Here is for thy pains.   *absolved after confession*
165 NURSE   No, truly, sir, not a penny.

---

8. Meat illicitly eaten during Lent by disguising it in a
pie, just as the Nurse's unattractiveness hides whatever
promiscuity she may practice.
9. Somewhat stale and moldy by the time the last of the
rationed luxury is consumed.
1. Is too much to pay for.

2. Refrain to a ballad about a perfectly chaste woman,
intended derisively.
3. Stronger; hornier.
4. Knife-wielding rogues.
5. The Nurse takes this as a marriage offer, probably
confusing "protest" with "propose."

ROMEO   Go to, I say, you shall.

NURSE [*taking the money*]   This afternoon, sir. Well, she shall be there.

ROMEO   And stay, good Nurse, behind the abbey wall.
    Within this hour my man shall be with thee
170   And bring thee cords made like a tackled stair,°   *a knotted ladder*
    Which to the high topgallant[6] of my joy
    Must be my convoy° in the secret night.   *means of conveyance*
    Farewell. Be trusty, and I'll quit° thy pains.   *repay*
    Farewell. Commend me to thy mistress.

175   NURSE   Now God in heaven bless thee! Hark you, sir.

ROMEO   What sayst thou, my dear Nurse?

NURSE   Is your man secret?° Did you ne'er hear say   *discreet*
    'Two may keep counsel, putting one away'?

ROMEO   I warrant thee my man's as true as steel.

180   NURSE   Well, sir, my mistress is the sweetest lady.
    Lord, Lord, when 'twas a little prating thing—
    O, there is a nobleman in town, one Paris,
    That would fain lay knife aboard;[7] but she, good soul,
    Had as lief° see a toad, a very toad,   *gladly*
185   As see him. I anger her sometimes,
    And tell her that Paris is the properer° man;   *more handsome*
    But I'll warrant you, when I say so she looks
    As pale as any clout° in the versal° world.   *sheet / entire*
    Doth not rosemary[8] and Romeo begin
190   Both with a° letter?   *the same*

ROMEO   Ay, Nurse, what of that? Both with an 'R'.

NURSE   Ah, mocker—that's the dog's name.[9] 'R' is for the—no, I
    know it begins with some other letter, and she hath the pret-
    tiest sententious[1] of it, of you and rosemary, that it would do
195   you good to hear it.

ROMEO   Commend me to thy lady.

NURSE   Ay, a thousand times. Peter!

PETER   Anon.

NURSE [*giving* PETER *her fan*]   Before,° and apace.°   *Lead / quickly*

                    Exeunt [PETER *and* NURSE *at one door,*
                    ROMEO *at another door*]

2.4

Enter JULIET

JULIET   The clock struck nine when I did send the Nurse.
    In half an hour she promised to return.
    Perchance she cannot meet him. That's not so.
    O, she is lame! Love's heralds should be thoughts,
5   Which ten times faster glides than the sun's beams
    Driving back shadows over louring° hills.   *dark; threatening*
    Therefore do nimble-pinioned° doves draw Love,°   *winged / Venus*
    And therefore hath the wind-swift Cupid wings.
    Now is the sun upon the highmost hill°   *zenith*
10   Of this day's journey, and from nine till twelve
    Is three long hours, yet she is not come.
    Had she affections° and warm youthful blood   *passions*

---

6. The highest platform on a mast, from which the top-
gallant sail was handled.
7. One claimed a place at dinner by laying one's personal knife on the table ("board").
8. A token of remembrance, between lovers and also of

the dead.
9. "R"—the sound "arr"—was thought to resemble a
dog's snarl.
1. Blunder for "sentences"; sayings.
2.4 Location: Capulet's orchard.

She would be as swift in motion as a ball.
My words would bandy° her to my sweet love,   *volley (as in tennis)*
15   And his to me.
But old folks, many feign° as they were dead—   *act*
Unwieldy, slow, heavy, and pale as lead.

Enter NURSE [*and* PETER]

O God, she comes! O honey Nurse, what news?
Hast thou met with him? Send thy man away.

20   NURSE   Peter, stay° at the gate.   [*Exit* PETER]   *wait*

JULIET   Now, good sweet Nurse—O Lord, why look'st thou sad?
Though news be sad, yet tell them merrily;
If good, thou sham'st the music of sweet news
By playing it to me with so sour a face.

25   NURSE   I am a-weary. Give me leave° a while.   *Let me alone*
Fie, how my bones ache. What a jaunce° have I!   *trotting about*

JULIET   I would thou hadst my bones and I thy news.
Nay, come, I pray thee speak, good, good Nurse, speak.

NURSE   Jesu, what haste! Can you not stay a while?
30   Do you not see that I am out of breath?

JULIET   How art thou out of breath when thou hast breath
To say to me that thou art out of breath?
The excuse that thou dost make in this delay
Is longer than the tale thou dost excuse.
35   Is thy news good or bad? Answer to that.
Say either, and I'll stay° the circumstance.°   *wait for / full details*
Let me be satisfied: is't good or bad?

NURSE   Well, you have made a simple° choice. You know not   *foolish*
how to choose a man. Romeo? No, not he; though his face be
40   better than any man's, yet his leg excels all men's, and for a
hand and a foot and a body, though they be not to be talked
on,° yet they are past compare. He is not the flower of cour-   *worth mentioning*
tesy, but, I'll warrant him, as gentle as a lamb. Go thy ways,[1]
wench. Serve God. What, have you dined at home?

45   JULIET   No, no. But all this did I know before.
What says he of our marriage—what of that?

NURSE   Lord, how my head aches! What a head have I!
It beats as it would fall in twenty pieces.
My back—

[JULIET *rubs her back*]

       a' t'other side—ah, my back, my back!
50   Beshrew° your heart for sending me about   *Curse (mild oath)*
To catch my death with jauncing up and down.

JULIET   I'faith, I am sorry that thou art not well.
Sweet, sweet, sweet Nurse, tell me, what says my love?

NURSE   Your love says, like an honest° gentleman, and a courte-   *honorable*
55   ous, and a kind,° and a handsome, and, I warrant, a virtuous—   *true*
where is your mother?

JULIET   Where is my mother? Why, she is within.
Where should she be? How oddly thou repliest!
'Your love says like an honest gentleman
"Where is your mother?"'

60   NURSE   O, God's Lady° dear!   *Mary, Mother of God*
Are you so hot?° Marry come up, I trow.[2]   *impatient; aroused*

---

1. Off you go; do as you will do.
2. *Marry . . . trow*: an expression of indignant or amused surprise and reproof.

Is this the poultice for my aching bones?
Henceforward do your messages yourself.
JULIET   Here's such a coil!° Come, what says Romeo?   to-do
65   NURSE   Have you got leave to go to shrift today?
JULIET   I have.
NURSE   Then hie° you hence to Friar Laurence' cell.   hurry
There stays a husband to make you a wife.
Now comes the wanton° blood up in your cheeks.   fickle; lustful
70   They'll be in scarlet straight° at any news.   immediately
Hie you to church. I must another way,
To fetch a ladder by the which your love
Must climb a bird's nest soon, when it is dark.
I am the drudge, and toil in your delight,
75   But you shall bear the burden[3] soon at night.
Go, I'll to dinner. Hie you to the cell.
JULIET   Hie to high fortune! Honest Nurse, farewell.
                                        Exeunt [*severally*]°   separately

2.5

Enter FRIAR [LAURENCE] *and* ROMEO
FRIAR LAURENCE   So smile the heavens upon this holy act
That after-hours with sorrow chide us not!
ROMEO   Amen, amen. But come what sorrow can,
It cannot countervail the exchange of joy
5   That one short minute gives me in her sight.
Do thou but close° our hands with holy words,   join
Then love-devouring death do what he dare—
It is enough I may but call her mine.
FRIAR LAURENCE   These violent° delights have violent ends,   sudden; intense
10   And in their triumph die like fire and powder,[1]
Which as they kiss consume. The sweetest honey
Is loathsome in his own deliciousness,
And in the taste confounds the appetite.[2]
Therefore love moderately. Long love doth so.
15   Too swift arrives as tardy as too slow.
                Enter JULIET *somewhat fast, and embraceth* ROMEO
Here comes the lady. O, so light[3] a foot
Will ne'er wear out the everlasting flint.[4]
A lover may bestride the gossamers°   spiders' threads
That idles in the wanton° summer air,   playful
20   And yet not fall, so light is vanity.[5]
JULIET   Good even° to my ghostly° confessor.   evening / spiritual
FRIAR LAURENCE   Romeo shall thank thee, daughter, for us both.
JULIET   As much to him,[6] else is his thanks too much.
ROMEO   Ah, Juliet, if the measure° of thy joy   measuring vessel
25   Be heaped like mine, and that thy skill be more
To blazon° it, then sweeten with thy breath°   describe; trumpet / speech
This neighbour air, and let rich music's tongue
Unfold the imagined° happiness that both   unexpressed ideas of

3. Do the work; carry a lover; sing the theme of a duet, overwhelms.
alluding to the sounds of lovemaking.   3. Swift; dainty; free of care; sexually open.
2.5 Location: Friar Laurence's cell.   4. Will never endure or subdue the hard road of life.
1. Gunpowder. *triumph:* victory; celebration.   5. Temporary worldly pleasure
2. *The sweetest . . . appetite:* from the proverb "Too   6. An equal amount. Both greetings consist of a kiss.
much honey cloys the stomach." *his:* its. *confounds:*

Receive in either by this dear encounter.

30   JULIET   Conceit,° more rich in matter than in words,   *Imagination*
Brags of his substance,[7] not of ornament.°   *rhetoric; form*
They are but beggars that can count their worth,
But my true love is grown to such excess
I cannot sum up some of half my wealth.[8]

35   FRIAR LAURENCE   Come, come with me, and we will make short work,
For, by your leaves, you shall not stay alone
Till Holy Church incorporate two in one.[9]   *Exeunt*

3.1

Enter MERCUTIO [*with his page*], BENVOLIO, *and men*

BENVOLIO   I pray thee, good Mercutio, let's retire.
The day is hot, the Capels are abroad,°   *about*
And if we meet we shall not scape a brawl,
For now, these hot days, is the mad blood stirring.

5   MERCUTIO   Thou art like one of these fellows that, when he
enters the confines of a tavern, claps me° his sword upon the   *claps me = claps*
table and says 'God send me no need of thee', and by the oper-
ation° of the second cup, draws him on the drawer[1] when   *effect*
indeed there is no need.

10   BENVOLIO   Am I like such a fellow?

MERCUTIO   Come, come, thou art as hot a jack° in thy mood as   *rogue*
any in Italy, and as soon moved° to be moody,° and as soon   *provoked / angry*
moody to be° moved.   *at being*

BENVOLIO   And what to?

15   MERCUTIO   Nay, an there were two such, we should have none
shortly, for one would kill the other. Thou—why, thou wilt
quarrel with a man that hath a hair more or a hair less in his
beard than thou hast. Thou wilt quarrel with a man for cracking nuts, having no other reason but because thou hast hazel
20   eyes. What eye but such an eye would spy out such a quarrel?
Thy head is as full of quarrels as an egg is full of meat,° and yet   *foodstuff*
thy head hath been beaten as addle° as an egg for quarrelling.   *rotten; confused*
Thou hast quarrelled with a man for coughing in the street
because he hath wakened thy dog that hath lain asleep in the
25   sun. Didst thou not fall out with a tailor for wearing his new
doublet before Easter;[2] with another for tying his new shoes
with old ribbon? And yet thou wilt tutor me from quarrelling!

BENVOLIO   An I were so apt to quarrel as thou art, any man
should buy the fee-simple[3] of my life for an hour and a quarter.

30   MERCUTIO   The fee simple? O, simple!°   *foolish*

Enter TYBALT, PETRUCCIO, *and others*

BENVOLIO   By my head, here comes the Capulets.

MERCUTIO   By my heel, I care not.

TYBALT [*to* PETRUCCIO *and the others*]   Follow me close, for I
will speak to them.
[*To the Montagues*] Gentlemen, good e'en. A word with one
of you.

---

7. Wealth; content.
8. *I . . . wealth:* The amount is too large to be understood precisely.
9. Literally, put two into one body. Marriage mystically
united man and woman in "one flesh" (Genesis 2:2).
3.1 Location: A street in Verona.

1. Draws his sword on the server.
2. New fashions came out at Easter, after the austere
penitence of Lent.
3. Outright possession of land, usually an inherited
right; here, the whole value of Benvolio's life.

35 MERCUTIO And but one word with one of us? Couple it with
        something: make it a word and a blow.
    TYBALT You shall find me apt enough to that, sir, an you will
        give me occasion.
    MERCUTIO Could you not take some occasion without giving?
40 TYBALT Mercutio, thou consort'st° with Romeo.   associate
    MERCUTIO 'Consort'?° What, dost thou make us minstrels? An   Play in a band
        thou make minstrels of us, look to hear nothing but discords.
        [Touching his rapier] Here's my fiddlestick; here's that shall
        make you dance. Zounds°—'Consort'!   By God's wounds
45 BENVOLIO We talk here in the public haunt° of men.   gathering place
        Either withdraw unto some private place,
        Or reason coldly° of your grievances,   dispassionately
        Or else depart.° Here all eyes gaze on us.   separate
    MERCUTIO Men's eyes were made to look, and let them gaze.
50   I will not budge for no man's pleasure, I.

                        Enter ROMEO

    TYBALT Well, peace be with you, sir. Here comes my man.
    MERCUTIO But I'll be hanged, sir, if he wear your livery.[4]
        Marry, go before to field, he'll be your follower.°   servant; pursuer
        Your worship in that sense may call him 'man'.
55 TYBALT Romeo, the love I bear thee can afford
        No better term than this: thou art a villain.°   base commoner; rogue
    ROMEO Tybalt, the reason that I have to love thee
        Doth much excuse the appertaining rage
        To[5] such a greeting. Villain am I none.
60   Therefore, farewell. I see thou knowest me not.
    TYBALT Boy, this shall not excuse the injuries
        That thou hast done me. Therefore turn and draw.
    ROMEO I do protest I never injured thee,
        But love thee better than thou canst devise
65   Till thou shalt know the reason of my love.
        And so, good Capulet—which name I tender°   regard; love
        As dearly as mine own—be satisfied.
    MERCUTIO [drawing] O calm, dishonourable, vile submission!
        Alla stoccado carries it away.[6]
70   Tybalt, you ratcatcher, come, will you walk?°   withdraw to fight
    TYBALT What wouldst thou have with me?
    MERCUTIO Good King of Cats, nothing but one of your nine
        lives. That I mean to make bold withal,° and, as you shall use   be so bold as to take
        me hereafter,[7] dry-beat° the rest of the eight. Will you pluck   soundly thrash
75   your sword out of his pilcher° by the ears? Make haste, lest mine   leather scabbard
        be about your ears ere it be out.
    TYBALT [drawing] I am for you.
    ROMEO Gentle Mercutio, put thy rapier up.
    MERCUTIO [to TYBALT] Come, sir, your passado.°   forward thrust
        [They fight]
80 ROMEO [drawing] Draw, Benvolio. Beat down their weapons.
        Gentlemen, for shame forbear this outrage.°   violence
        Tybalt, Mercutio, the Prince expressly hath
        Forbid this bandying° in Verona streets.   strife

---

4. Mercutio obnoxiously mistakes Tybalt's "my man"   appropriate anger at.
for "personal servant."   6. The rapier thrust wins the day.
5. Doth . . . / To: Permits me to put aside my otherwise   7. And, according to how you subsequently treat me.

Hold, Tybalt, good Mercutio.
[ROMEO *beats down their points and rushes between*
them.] TYBALT *under Romeo's arm thrusts* MERCUTIO *in*

85 PETRUCCIO   Away, Tybalt!

Exeunt TYBALT [PETRUCCIO, *and their followers*]

MERCUTIO   I am hurt.
A plague o' both your houses. I am sped.°   finished
Is he gone, and hath nothing?

BENVOLIO   What, art thou hurt?

MERCUTIO   Ay, ay, a scratch, a scratch; marry, 'tis enough.

90 Where is my page? Go, villain. Fetch a surgeon.

[*Exit page*]

ROMEO   Courage, man. The hurt cannot be much.

MERCUTIO   No, 'tis not so deep as a well, nor so wide as a church
door, but 'tis enough. 'Twill serve. Ask for me tomorrow, and
you shall find me a grave man. I am peppered,° I warrant, for   done for
95 this world. A plague o' both your houses! Zounds, a dog, a rat,
a mouse, a cat, to scratch a man to death! A braggart, a rogue,
a villain, that fights by the book of arithmetic!⁸ Why the devil
came you between us? I was hurt under your arm.

ROMEO   I thought all for the best.

100 MERCUTIO   Help me into some house, Benvolio,
Or I shall faint. A plague o' both your houses.
They have made worms' meat of me.
I have it, and soundly, too. Your houses!

Exeunt [*all but* ROMEO]

ROMEO   This gentleman, the Prince's near ally,°   relative
105 My very° friend, hath got this mortal hurt   true
In my behalf, my reputation stained
With Tybalt's slander—Tybalt, that an hour
Hath been my cousin! O sweet Juliet,
Thy beauty hath made me effeminate,
110 And in my temper⁹ softened valour's steel.

Enter BENVOLIO

BENVOLIO   O Romeo, Romeo, brave Mercutio is dead!
That gallant spirit hath aspired° the clouds,   ascended to
Which too untimely here did scorn the earth.

ROMEO   This day's black fate on more days doth depend.°   hang over
115 This but begins the woe others must end.

Enter TYBALT

BENVOLIO   Here comes the furious Tybalt back again.

ROMEO   He gad° in triumph, and Mercutio slain?   gallivanting
Away to heaven, respective lenity,°   respectful lenience
And fire-eyed fury be my conduct° now.   guide
120 Now, Tybalt, take the 'villain' back again
That late thou gav'st me, for Mercutio's soul
Is but a little way above our heads,
Staying for thine to keep him company.
Either thou, or I, or both must go with him.

125 TYBALT   Thou, wretched boy, that didst consort° him here,   accompany
Shalt with him hence.

8. By the numbers; according to a fencing manual.   was believed that too much time with or passion for
9. Emotional makeup, here suggesting the hardened   women would cause a man to become effeminate.
character of a fighting man (*temper*: to harden steel). It

ROMEO   This shall determine that.

They fight. TYBALT *falls [and dies]*

BENVOLIO   Romeo, away, be gone.
The citizens are up,° and Tybalt slain.   up in arms
Stand not amazed.° The Prince will doom° thee death   stupefied / sentence
130 If thou art taken. Hence, be gone, away.
ROMEO   O, I am fortune's fool!°   dupe
BENVOLIO   Why dost thou stay?

Exit ROMEO

Enter CITIZENS [OF THE WATCH]

CITIZEN OF THE WATCH   Which way ran he that killed Mercutio?
Tybalt, that murderer, which way ran he?
BENVOLIO   There lies that Tybalt.
CITIZEN OF THE WATCH   Up, sir, go with me.
135 I charge thee in the Prince's name, obey.

Enter PRINCE, *old* MONTAGUE, CAPULET, *their* WIVES,
and all

PRINCE   Where are the vile beginners of this fray?
BENVOLIO   O noble Prince, I can discover° all   reveal
The unlucky manage° of this fatal brawl.   handling
There lies the man, slain by young Romeo,
140 That slew thy kinsman, brave Mercutio.
CAPULET'S WIFE   Tybalt, my cousin, O, my brother's child!
O Prince, O cousin, husband! O, the blood is spilled
Of my dear kinsman! Prince, as thou art true,
For blood of ours shed blood of Montague!
O cousin, cousin!
145 PRINCE   Benvolio, who began this fray?
BENVOLIO   Tybalt, here slain, whom Romeo's hand did slay.
Romeo, that spoke him° fair,° bid him bethink   to him / courteously
How nice° the quarrel was, and urged withal°   trivial / also
Your high displeasure. All this—utterèd
150 With gentle breath, calm look, knees humbly bowed—
Could not take° truce with the unruly spleen°   arrange / bitter mood
Of Tybalt deaf to peace, but that he tilts
With piercing steel at bold Mercutio's breast,
Who, all as hot, turns deadly point to point,
155 And, with a martial scorn, with one hand beats
Cold death aside,[1] and with the other sends
It back to Tybalt, whose dexterity
Retorts° it. Romeo, he cries aloud,   Returns
'Hold, friends, friends, part!' and swifter than his tongue
160 His agent° arm beats down their fatal points,   effective
And 'twixt them rushes, underneath whose arm
An envious° thrust from Tybalt hit the life   A malicious
Of stout° Mercutio, and then Tybalt fled,   courageous
But by and by comes back to Romeo,
165 Who had but newly entertained° revenge,   considered
And to't they go like lightning; for ere I
Could draw to part them was stout Tybalt slain,
And as he fell did Romeo turn and fly.
This is the truth, or let Benvolio die.

---

1. *with . . . aside:* the two would have been fighting either with daggers in or cloaks rolled about their second hand to ward off the other's weapon.

170 CAPULET'S WIFE He is a kinsman to the Montague.
　　　Affection makes him false; he speaks not true.
　　　Some twenty of them fought in this black strife,
　　　And all those twenty could but kill one life.
　　　I beg for justice, which thou, Prince, must give.
175 Romeo slew Tybalt; Romeo must not live.
　　PRINCE Romeo slew him, he slew Mercutio.
　　　Who now the price of his° dear blood doth owe?　　　　　　(Mercutio's)
　　MONTAGUE Not Romeo, Prince. He was Mercutio's friend.
　　　His fault° concludes but what the law should end,　　　　　offense
　　　The life of Tybalt.
180 PRINCE　　　　　　And for that offence
　　　Immediately we do exile him hence.
　　　I have an interest in your hate's proceeding;
　　　My blood° for your rude brawls doth lie a-bleeding.　　　kinsman
　　　But I'll amerce° you with so strong a fine　　　　　　　　penalize
185 That you shall all repent the loss of mine.
　　　I will be deaf to pleading and excuses.
　　　Nor tears nor prayers shall purchase out° abuses.　　　　compensate for
　　　Therefore use none. Let Romeo hence in haste,
　　　Else, when he is found, that hour is his last.
190 Bear hence this body, and attend our will.
　　　Mercy but murders, pardoning those that kill.

Exeunt [with the body]

3.2

Enter JULIET *alone*

　　JULIET Gallop apace,° you fiery-footed steeds,　　　　　　　quickly
　　　Towards Phoebus' lodging.¹ Such a waggoner°　　　　　　charioteer
　　　As Phaëton² would whip you to the west
　　　And bring in cloudy night immediately.
5 Spread thy close° curtain, love-performing night,　　　　　covering
　　　That runaways'³ eyes may wink,° and Romeo　　　　　　close
　　　Leap to these arms untalked of and unseen.
　　　Lovers can see to do their amorous rites
　　　By their own beauties; or, if love be blind,
10 It best agrees with night. Come, civil° night,　　　　　　　solemn
　　　Thou sober-suited matron all in black,
　　　And learn me how to lose a winning match⁴
　　　Played for a pair of stainless maidenhoods.
　　　Hood my unmanned° blood, bating⁵ in my cheeks,　　　untamed; virgin
15 With thy black mantle till strange° love grown bold　　　shy
　　　Think true love acted simple° modesty.　　　　　　　　　mere; innocent
　　　Come night, come Romeo; come, thou day in night,
　　　For thou wilt lie upon the wings of night
　　　Whiter than new snow on a raven's back.
20 Come, gentle night; come, loving, black-browed night,
　　　Give me my Romeo, and when I shall die

3.2 Location: Capulet's house.
1. Under the world to the west, where the sun god
Phoebus Apollo was imagined to rest with his fiery chariot at night.
2. The son of Apollo, who rashly attempted to steer his
father's chariot across the sky. To save the earth from
scorching, Jupiter struck him down with a lightning bolt.

3. Either the runaway horses of the sun or roving and
curious vagabonds.
4. *match*: competition. A husband and a marriage
("match") are won by surrendering.
5. Fluttering like a restless falcon before its eyes are
covered with a "hood" to calm it.

Take him and cut him out in little stars,[6]
And he will make the face of heaven so fine
That all the world will be in love with night

25 And pay no worship to the garish sun.
O, I have bought the mansion of a love
But not possessed it, and though I am sold,[7]
Not yet enjoyed. So tedious is this day
As is the night before some festival

30 To an impatient child that hath new robes
And may not wear them.

> *Enter* NURSE, *[wringing her hands,] with the ladder of*
> *cords in her lap*°   bodice fold

O, here comes my Nurse,
And she brings news, and every tongue that speaks
But Romeo's name speaks heavenly eloquence.
Now, Nurse, what news? What, hast thou there
The cords that Romeo bid thee fetch?

35 NURSE [*putting down the cords*]   Ay, ay, the cords.

JULIET   Ay me, what news? Why dost thou wring thy hands?

NURSE   Ah, welladay!° He's dead, he's dead, he's dead!   alas
We are undone, lady, we are undone.
Alack the day, he's gone, he's killed, he's dead!

JULIET   Can heaven be so envious?°   spiteful; jealous

40 NURSE   Romeo can,
Though heaven cannot. O Romeo, Romeo,
Who ever would have thought it Romeo?

JULIET   What devil art thou that dost torment me thus?
This torture should be roared in dismal hell.

45 Hath Romeo slain himself? Say thou but 'Ay',
And that bare vowel 'I' shall poison more
Than the death-darting eye of cockatrice.[8]
I am not I if there be such an 'Ay',
Or those eyes shut that makes thee answer 'Ay'.

50 If he be slain, say 'Ay'; or if not, 'No'.
Brief sounds determine of my weal° or woe.   welfare

NURSE   I saw the wound, I saw it with mine eyes,
God save the mark,[9] here on his manly breast—
A piteous corpse, a bloody, piteous corpse—

55 Pale, pale as ashes, all bedaubed in blood,
All in gore° blood; I swoonèd at the sight.   clotted

JULIET   O, break, my heart, poor bankrupt, break at once!
To prison,[1] eyes; ne'er look on liberty.
Vile earth,[2] to earth resign; end motion° here,   movement; emotion

60 And thou and Romeo press[3] one heavy° bier!   weighty; sad

NURSE   O Tybalt, Tybalt, the best friend I had!
O courteous Tybalt, honest° gentleman,   honorable
That ever I should live to see thee dead!

JULIET   What storm is this that blows so contrary?

65 Is Romeo slaughtered, and is Tybalt dead?

---

6. *Take . . . stars*: an imagined tranformation, based on those in Ovid's *Metamorphoses*, whereby Romeo also dies and is immortalized. Q4's reading of "he" for "I" (line 21) makes more immediate sense and is often accepted. Also, "die" could mean "have an orgasm."
7. *O . . . sold*: the image is inverted: first Juliet buys the mansion, and then she becomes the "sold" house.
8. A mythical serpent that kills by merely looking.

9. An apology for mentioning something unpleasant, but also emphasizing the fatal "mark" of the rapier.
1. Bankruptcy—to "break" financially—was punishable by imprisonment.
2. The despised body, echoing Ecclesiastes 12:7: "Then shall the dust return to the earth as it was."
3. Burden; embrace.

My dearest cousin and my dearer lord?
Then, dreadful trumpet, sound the general doom,[4]
For who is living if those two are gone?
NURSE   Tybalt is gone and Romeo banishèd.
70   Romeo that killed him—he is banishèd.
JULIET   O God, did Romeo's hand shed Tybalt's blood?
NURSE   It did, it did, alas the day, it did.
JULIET   O serpent heart hid with° a flow'ring° face!   by / lovely; benign
Did ever dragon keep° so fair a cave?   guard
75   Beautiful tyrant, fiend angelical!
Dove-feathered raven, wolvish-ravening lamb!
Despisèd substance of divinest show!°   appearance
Just opposite to what thou justly° seem'st—   precisely; rightfully
A damnèd saint, an honourable villain.
80   O nature, what hadst thou to do[5] in hell
When thou didst bower[6] the spirit of a fiend
In mortal paradise of such sweet flesh?
Was ever book containing such vile matter
So fairly bound? O, that deceit should dwell
85   In such a gorgeous palace!
NURSE   There's no trust, no faith, no honesty in men;
All perjured, all forsworn, all naught,° dissemblers all.   wicked
Ah, where's my man? Give me some aqua vitae.°   brandy
These griefs, these woes, these sorrows make me old.
Shame come to Romeo!
90   JULIET   Blistered be thy tongue
For such a wish! He was not born to shame.
Upon his brow shame is ashamed to sit,
For 'tis a throne where honour may be crowned
Sole monarch of the universal earth.
95   O, what a beast was I to chide at him!
NURSE   Will you speak well of him that killed your cousin?
JULIET   Shall I speak ill of him that is my husband?
Ah, poor my° lord, what tongue shall smooth° thy name   my poor / praise
When I, thy three-hours wife, have mangled it?
100   But wherefore, villain, didst thou kill my cousin?
That villain cousin would have killed my husband.
Back, foolish tears, back to your native spring!
Your tributary[7] drops belong to woe,
Which you, mistaking, offer up to joy.[8]
105   My husband lives, that Tybalt would have slain;
And Tybalt's dead, that would have slain my husband.
All this is comfort. Wherefore° weep I then?   Why
Some word there was, worser than Tybalt's death,
That murdered me. I would forget it fain,°   gladly
110   But O, it presses to my memory
Like damnèd guilty deeds to sinners' minds!
'Tybalt is dead, and Romeo banishèd.'
That 'banishèd', that one word 'banishèd'
Hath slain ten thousand Tybalts. Tybalt's death
115   Was woe enough, if it had ended there;

---

4. The Last Judgment announced with angel's trumpets.
5. What were you doing.
6. Lodge or enclose, suggesting a surrounding garden.

7. Tribute-paying; in-flowing.
8. Offer up to a joyful (and thus inappropriate) occasion.

Or, if sour woe delights in fellowship
And needly° will be ranked with⁹ other griefs,   *necessarily*
Why followed not, when she said 'Tybalt's dead',
'Thy father', or 'thy mother', nay, or both,
120   Which modern° lamentation might have moved?°   *ordinary / produced*
But with a rearward¹ following Tybalt's death,
'Romeo is banishèd'—to speak that word
Is father, mother, Tybalt, Romeo, Juliet,
All slain, all dead. 'Romeo is banishèd'—
125   There is no end, no limit, measure, bound,
In that word's death. No words can that woe sound.°   *utter; fathom*
Where is my father and my mother, Nurse?
NURSE   Weeping and wailing over Tybalt's corpse.
Will you go to them? I will bring you thither.
130 JULIET   Wash they his wounds with tears; mine shall be spent
When theirs are dry, for Romeo's banishment.
Take up those cords. Poor ropes, you are beguiled,°   *cheated*
Both you and I, for Romeo is exiled.
He made you for a highway to my bed,
135   But I, a maid, die maiden-widowèd.
Come, cords; come, Nurse; I'll to my wedding bed,
And death, not Romeo, take my maidenhead!
NURSE [*taking up the cords*]   Hie to your chamber. I'll find Romeo
To comfort you. I wot° well where he is.   *know*
140   Hark ye, your Romeo will be here at night.
I'll to him. He is hid at Laurence' cell.
JULIET [*giving her a ring*]   O, find him! Give this ring to my true knight,
And bid him come to take his last farewell. *Exeunt* [*severally*]

3.3

Enter FRIAR [LAURENCE]
FRIAR LAURENCE   Romeo, come forth, come forth, thou fear-full man.
Affliction is enamoured of thy parts,°   *qualities*
And thou art wedded to calamity.
Enter ROMEO
ROMEO   Father, what news? What is the Prince's doom?°   *sentence*
5   What sorrow craves acquaintance at my hand
That I yet know not?
FRIAR LAURENCE   Too familiar
Is my dear son with such sour company.
I bring thee tidings of the Prince's doom.
ROMEO   What less than doomsday is the Prince's doom?
10 FRIAR LAURENCE   A gentler judgement vanished° from his lips: *escaped*
Not body's death, but body's banishment.
ROMEO   Ha, banishment? Be merciful, say 'death',
For exile hath more terror in his look,
Much more than death. Do not say 'banishment'.
15 FRIAR LAURENCE   Hence from Verona art thou banishèd.
Be patient,° for the world is broad and wide.   *able to endure*
ROMEO   There is no world without° Verona walls   *outside*
But purgatory, torture, hell itself.
Hence banishèd is banished from the world,
20   And world's exile is death. Then 'banishèd'

---

9. Will be accompanied by.   3.3 Location: Friar Laurence's cell.
1. *rearward*: rearguard action, with a pun on "afterword."

Is death mistermed. Calling death 'banishèd'
Thou cutt'st my head off with a golden axe,
And smil'st upon the stroke that murders me.

FRIAR LAURENCE   O deadly° sin, O rude unthankfulness!   *damnable*
25   Thy fault our law calls death,° but the kind Prince,   *a capital offense*
Taking thy part, hath rushed° aside the law   *forced*
And turned that black word 'death' to banishment.
This is dear mercy, and thou seest it not.

ROMEO   'Tis torture, and not mercy. Heaven is here
30   Where Juliet lives, and every cat and dog
And little mouse, every unworthy thing,
Live here in heaven and may look on her,
But Romeo may not. More validity,°   *health*
More honourable state, more courtship° lives   *courtly state; wooing*
35   In carrion flies than Romeo. They may seize
On the white wonder of dear Juliet's hand,
And steal immortal blessing from her lips,
Who, even in pure and vestal° modesty,   *virginal*
Still° blush, as thinking their own kisses[1] sin.   *Always*
40   But Romeo may not, he is banishèd.
Flies may do this, but I from this must fly.
They are free men, but I am banishèd.
And sayst thou yet that exile is not death?
Hadst thou no poison mixed, no sharp-ground knife,
45   No sudden mean° of death, though ne'er so mean,°   *method / ignoble*
But 'banishèd' to kill me—'banishèd'?
O friar, the damnèd use that word in hell.[2]
Howling attends it. How hast thou the heart,
Being a divine, a ghostly confessor,
50   A sin-absolver and my friend professed,
To mangle me with that word 'banishèd'?

FRIAR LAURENCE   Thou fond° mad man, hear me a little speak.   *foolish; infatuated*
ROMEO   O, thou wilt speak again of banishment.
FRIAR LAURENCE   I'll give thee armour to keep off that word—
55   Adversity's sweet milk, philosophy,
To comfort thee though thou art banishèd.

ROMEO   Yet 'banishèd'? Hang up° philosophy!   *Hang up = Hang*
Unless philosophy can make a Juliet,
Displant° a town, reverse a prince's doom,   *Uproot*
60   It helps not, it prevails not. Talk no more.

FRIAR LAURENCE   O, then I see that madmen have no ears.
ROMEO   How should they, when that wise men have no eyes?
FRIAR LAURENCE   Let me dispute° with thee of thy estate.°   *discuss / position*
ROMEO   Thou canst not speak of that thou dost not feel.
65   Wert thou as young as I, Juliet thy love,
An hour but° married, Tybalt murderèd,   *only*
Doting like me, and like me banishèd,
Then mightst thou speak, then mightst thou tear thy hair,
And fall upon the ground, as I do now,
[*He falls upon the ground*]
70   Taking the measure of an unmade grave.
Knock [*within*]
FRIAR LAURENCE   Arise, one knocks. Good Romeo, hide thyself.

---

1. Their touching each other in closing.   2. Because they are banished from heaven.

ROMEO   Not I, unless the breath of heartsick groans
    Mist-like enfold me from the search of eyes.
        Knock [*within*]
FRIAR LAURENCE   Hark, how they knock!—Who's there?—
    Romeo, arise.
75   Thou wilt be taken.—Stay a while.—Stand up.
        [*Still*] *knock* [*within*]
    Run to my study.—By and by!—God's will,°   *By providence*
    What simpleness° is this?   *stupidity*
        Knock [*within*]
                        I come, I come.
    Who knocks so hard? Whence come you? What's your will?
NURSE [*within*][3]   Let me come in, and you shall know my errand.
    I come from Lady Juliet.
80 FRIAR LAURENCE [*opening the door*] Welcome then.
        Enter NURSE
NURSE   O holy friar, O tell me, holy friar,
    Where is my lady's lord? Where's Romeo?
FRIAR LAURENCE   There on the ground, with his own tears
    made drunk.
NURSE   O, he is even° in my mistress' case,°   *exactly / condition; vagina*
85   Just in her case! O woeful sympathy,
    Piteous predicament! Even so lies she,
    Blubb'ring and weeping, weeping and blubb'ring.
    [*To* ROMEO]   Stand up, stand up, stand an° you be a man,   *if*
    For Juliet's sake, for her sake, rise and stand.
90   Why should you fall into so deep an O?°   *a groaning*
ROMEO [*rises*]   Nurse.
NURSE   Ah sir, ah sir, death's the end of all.[4]
ROMEO   Spak'st thou of Juliet? How is it with her?
    Doth not she think me an old° murderer,   *a practiced*
    Now I have stained the childhood of our joy
95   With blood removed but little from her own?
    Where is she, and how doth she, and what says
    My concealed lady° to our cancelled° love?   *secret wife / invalidated*
NURSE   O, she says nothing, sir, but weeps and weeps,
    And now falls on her bed, and then starts up,
100   And 'Tybalt' calls, and then on Romeo cries,
    And then down falls again.
ROMEO   As if that name
    Shot from the deadly level° of a gun   *aim*
    Did murder her as that name's cursèd hand
    Murdered her kinsman. O tell me, friar, tell me,
105   In what vile part of this anatomy
    Doth my name lodge? Tell me, that I may sack
    The hateful mansion.
        He offers to stab himself, and NURSE *snatches the dagger*
        away
FRIAR LAURENCE   Hold° thy desperate hand.   *Restrain*
    Art thou a man? Thy form cries out thou art.
    Thy tears are womanish, thy wild acts denote
110   The unreasonable° fury of a beast.   *incapable of reason*

---

3. Behind one of the doors at the back of the stage, rep-   4. A proverbial consolation.
resenting the door of the cell.

Unseemly° woman in a seeming man,   *Inappropriate; immodest*
And ill-beseeming beast in seeming both!⁵
Thou hast amazed me. By my holy order,
I thought thy disposition better tempered.
115   Hast thou slain Tybalt? Wilt thou slay thyself,
And slay thy lady that in thy life lives
By doing damnèd° hate upon thyself?   *sinful*
Why rail'st thou on thy birth, the heaven, and earth,
Since birth° and heaven° and earth,° all three, do meet   *nobility / soul / body*
120   In thee at once, which thou at once wouldst lose?
Fie, fie, thou sham'st thy shape, thy love, thy wit,
Which like a usurer abound'st in all,
And usest none in that true use indeed
Which should bedeck thy shape, thy love, thy wit.⁶
125   Thy noble shape is but a form° of wax,   *figure*
Digressing° from the valour of a man;   *If it deviates*
Thy dear love sworn but hollow perjury,
Killing that love which thou hast vowed to cherish;
Thy wit, that ornament° to shape and love,   *necessary accessory*
130   Misshapen° in the conduct° of them both,   *Inept / management*
Like powder in a skilless soldier's flask
Is set afire by thine own ignorance,
And thou dismembered with thine own defence.°   *weapon*
What, rouse thee, man! Thy Juliet is alive,
135   For whose dear sake thou wast but lately dead:
There art thou happy. Tybalt would kill thee,
But thou slewest Tybalt: there art thou happy.
The law that threatened death becomes thy friend,
And turns it to exile: there art thou happy.
140   A pack of blessings light upon thy back,
Happiness courts thee in her best array,
But, like a mishavèd° and sullen wench,   *misbehaved*
Thou pout'st upon thy fortune and thy love.
Take heed, take heed, for such die miserable.
145   Go, get thee to thy love, as was decreed.
Ascend her chamber; hence and comfort her.
But look thou stay not till the watch be set,⁷
For then thou canst not pass to Mantua,
Where thou shalt live till we can find a time
150   To blaze° your marriage, reconcile your friends,°   *make public / kin*
Beg pardon of the Prince, and call thee back
With twenty hundred thousand times more joy
Than thou went'st forth in lamentation.
Go before, Nurse. Commend me to thy lady,
155   And bid her hasten all the house to bed,
Which heavy sorrow makes them apt unto.
Romeo is coming.
NURSE   O Lord, I could have stayed here all the night
To hear good counsel! O, what learning is!
160   My lord, I'll tell my lady you will come.
ROMEO   Do so, and bid my sweet prepare to chide.

---

5. An unnatural beast in seeming both man and unreasoning animal, or both man and woman.
6. *thou sham'st . . . wit:* you abound in looks, love, and intelligence ("wit"), but you do not use them judiciously

and are therefore like a usurer who acquires money for its own sake, without putting it to good use.
7. Until the guards take up their positions (at the city gates).

NURSE *offers to go in, and turns again*
NURSE [*giving the ring*]   Here, sir, a ring she bid me give you, sir.
Hie you,° make haste, for it grows very late.   *Hurry*
ROMEO   How well my comfort° is revived by this.   *Exit* NURSE   *happiness*
FRIAR LAURENCE   Go hence, good night, and here stands° all   *and on this depends*
165   your state.
Either be gone before the watch be set,
Or by the break of day disguised from hence.
Sojourn in Mantua. I'll find out your man,
And he shall signify from time to time
170   Every good hap° to you that chances here.   *event*
Give me thy hand. 'Tis late. Farewell. Good night.
ROMEO   But that a joy past joy calls out on me,
It were a grief so brief° to part with thee.   *hastily*
Farewell.   *Exeunt* [*severally*]

3.4

Enter old CAPULET, *his* WIFE, *and* PARIS
CAPULET   Things have fall'n out, sir, so unluckily
That we have had no time to move° our daughter.   *persuade*
Look you, she loved her kinsman Tybalt dearly,
And so did I. Well, we were born to die.
5   'Tis very late. She'll not come down tonight.
I promise you, but for your company
I would have been abed an hour ago.
PARIS   These times of woe afford no times to woo.
Madam, good night. Commend me to your daughter.
10   CAPULET'S WIFE   I will, and know her mind early tomorrow.
Tonight she's mewed up to¹ her heaviness.°   *sadness*
PARIS *offers to go in, and* CAPULET *calls him again*
CAPULET   Sir Paris, I will make a desperate tender°   *a reckless offer*
Of my child's love. I think she will be ruled
In all respects by me. Nay, more, I doubt it not.
15   Wife, go you to her ere you go to bed.
Acquaint her here of my son Paris' love,
And bid her—mark you me?—on Wednesday next—
But soft—what day is this?
PARIS   Monday, my lord.
CAPULET   Monday. Ha, ha! Well, Wednesday is too soon.
20   O' Thursday let it be. O' Thursday, tell her,
She shall be married to this noble earl.
Will you be ready? Do you like this haste?
We'll keep° no great ado—a friend or two.   *celebrate with*
For hark you, Tybalt being slain so late,°   *recently*
25   It may be thought we held° him carelessly,°   *regarded / indifferently*
Being our kinsman, if we revel much.
Therefore we'll have some half a dozen friends,
And there an end. But what say you to Thursday?
PARIS   My lord, I would° that Thursday were tomorrow.   *wish*
30   CAPULET   Well, get you gone. O' Thursday be it, then.
[*To his* WIFE]   Go you to Juliet ere you go to bed.
Prepare her, wife, against° this wedding day.—   *for*

3.4 Location: Capulet's house.   1. Shut in with. The "mews" are hawks' housing.

Farewell, my lord.—Light to my chamber, ho!—
Afore me,² it is so very late that we
35 May call it early by and by. Good night.

Exeunt [CAPULET *and his* WIFE *at*
one door, PARIS *at another door*]

3.5

Enter ROMEO *and* JULIET *aloft* [*with the ladder of cords*]

JULIET Wilt thou be gone? It is not yet near day.
It was the nightingale, and not the lark,
That pierced the fear-full hollow of thine ear.
Nightly she sings on yon pom'granate tree.
5 Believe me, love, it was the nightingale.
ROMEO It was the lark, the herald of the morn,
No nightingale. Look, love, what envious° streaks   spiteful
Do lace the severing° clouds in yonder east.   parting
Night's candles are burnt out, and jocund day
10 Stands tiptoe on the misty mountain tops.
I must be gone and live, or stay and die.
JULIET Yon light is not daylight; I know it, I.
It is some meteor that the sun exhaled¹
To be to thee this night a torchbearer
15 And light thee on thy way to Mantua.
Therefore stay yet. Thou need'st not to be gone.
ROMEO Let me be ta'en, let me be put to death.
I am content, so° thou wilt have it so.   as long as
I'll say yon grey is not the morning's eye,
20 'Tis but the pale reflex° of Cynthia's° brow;   reflection / the moon's
Nor that is not the lark whose notes do beat
The vaulty heaven so high above our heads.
I have more care° to stay than will to go.   desire
Come, death, and welcome; Juliet wills it so.
25 How is't, my soul? Let's talk. It is not day.
JULIET It is, it is. Hie hence, be gone, away.
It is the lark that sings so out of tune,
Straining° harsh discords and unpleasing sharps.²   Distorting; tuning up
Some say the lark makes sweet division;°   variations on a melody
30 This doth not so, for she divideth us.
Some say the lark and loathèd toad changed eyes.³
O, now I would they had changed voices, too,
Since arm from arm that voice doth us affray,°   frighten
Hunting thee hence with hunt's-up⁴ to the day.
35 O, now be gone! More light and light it grows.
ROMEO More light and light, more dark and dark our woes.

Enter NURSE *hastily*

NURSE Madam.
JULIET Nurse.
NURSE Your lady mother is coming to your chamber.
40 The day is broke; be wary, look about.   [*Exit*]

---

2. **Afore me**: A mild oath, or possibly an address to the torchbearing servant to walk in front of him.
3.5 Location: The upper acting area represents Juliet's window or balcony. The main stage represents Capulet's orchard until line 59, then the interior of Capulet's house from line 64.
1. Breathed. Meteors were thought to be impure vapors that the sun had drawn up from the earth and

ignited and were usually considered bad omens.
2. Harsh sounds, too-high tones.
3. A folk explanation for the supposed ugliness of the lark's eyes and the beauty of the toad's. *changed*: exchanged.
4. Morning song used to wake the bride after the wedding night.

JULIET   Then, window, let day in, and let life out.

ROMEO   Farewell, farewell! One kiss, and I'll descend.

He [lets down the ladder of cords and] goes down

JULIET   Art thou gone so, love, lord, my husband, friend?°   lover

I must hear from thee every day in the hour,

45   For in a minute there are many days.

O, by this count I shall be much in years

Ere I again behold my Romeo.

ROMEO   Farewell.

I will omit no opportunity

50   That may convey my greetings, love, to thee.

JULIET   O, think'st thou we shall ever meet again?

ROMEO   I doubt it not, and all these woes shall serve

For sweet discourses° in our times to come.   conversations

JULIET   O God, I have an ill-divining° soul!   a misfortune-predicting

55   Methinks I see thee, now thou art so low,

As one dead in the bottom of a tomb.

Either my eyesight fails, or thou look'st pale.

ROMEO   And trust me, love, in my eye so do you.

Dry sorrow drinks our blood.⁵ Adieu, adieu.   *Exit*

JULIET [*pulling up the ladder and weeping*]   O fortune, fortune,

60   all men call thee fickle.

If thou art fickle, what dost thou with him

That is renowned for faith?° Be fickle, fortune,   fidelity

For then I hope thou wilt not keep him long,

But send him back.

*Enter [*CAPULET'S WIFE *below*]

CAPULET'S WIFE   Ho, daughter, are you up?

65   JULIET   Who is't that calls? It is my lady mother.

Is she not down° so late, or up so early?   in bed

What unaccustomed cause procures° her hither?   brings

*She goes down [*and enters below*]

CAPULET'S WIFE   Why, how now, Juliet?

JULIET   Madam, I am not well.

CAPULET'S WIFE   Evermore weeping for your cousin's death?

70   What, wilt thou wash him from his grave with tears?

An if thou couldst, thou couldst not make him live,

Therefore have done. Some grief shows much of love,

But much of grief shows still° some want° of wit.   always / lack

JULIET   Yet let me weep for such a feeling° loss.   profound

75   CAPULET'S WIFE   So shall you feel° the loss, but not the friend°   experience; touch / kin

Which you so weep for.

JULIET   Feeling so the loss,

I cannot choose but ever weep the friend.°   lover

CAPULET'S WIFE   Well, girl, thou weep'st not so much for his death

As that the villain lives which slaughtered him.

JULIET   What villain, madam?

80   CAPULET'S WIFE   That same villain Romeo.

JULIET [*aside*]   Villain and he be many miles asunder.

[*To her mother*] God pardon him—I do, with all my heart,

And yet no man like° he doth grieve my heart.   so much as; resembling

CAPULET'S WIFE   That is because the traitor murderer lives.

---

5. *Dry . . . blood*: Each sigh supposedly cost the heart a drop of blood. Thus, the lovers are pale. *Dry*: Thirsty.

85   JULIET   Ay, madam, from the reach of these my hands.
       Would none but I might venge my cousin's death.
      CAPULET'S WIFE   We will have vengeance for it, fear thou not.
       Then weep no more. I'll send to one in Mantua,
       Where that same banished runagate° doth live,   *runaway; fugitive*
90   Shall give him such an unaccustomed dram
       That he shall soon keep Tybalt company;
       And then I hope thou wilt be satisfied.°   *sufficiently avenged*
      JULIET   Indeed, I never shall be satisfied
       With Romeo till I behold him, dead,
95   Is my poor heart[6] so for a kinsman vexed.
       Madam, if you could find out but a man
       To bear a poison, I would temper° it   *mix; dilute*
       That Romeo should, upon receipt thereof,
       Soon sleep in quiet. O, how my heart abhors
100   To hear him named and cannot come to him
       To wreak the love I bore my cousin
       Upon his body that hath slaughtered him!
      CAPULET'S WIFE   Find thou the means, and I'll find such a man.
       But now I'll tell thee joyful tidings, girl.
105   JULIET   And joy comes well in such a needy time.
       What are they, I beseech your ladyship?
      CAPULET'S WIFE   Well, well, thou hast a careful° father, child;   *solicitous*
       One who, to put thee from thy heaviness,
       Hath sorted out a sudden° day of joy   *chosen an immediate*
110   That thou expect'st not, nor I looked not for.
      JULIET   Madam, in happy° time. What day is that?   *at a fortunate*
      CAPULET'S WIFE   Marry, my child, early next Thursday morn
       The gallant, young, and noble gentleman
       The County Paris at Saint Peter's Church
115   Shall happily make thee there a joyful bride.
      JULIET   Now, by Saint Peter's Church, and Peter too,
       He shall not make me there a joyful bride.
       I wonder° at this haste, that I must wed   *am astonished*
       Ere he that should be husband comes to woo.
120   I pray you, tell my lord and father, madam,
       I will not marry yet; and when I do, I swear
       It shall be Romeo—whom you know I hate—
       Rather than Paris. These are news indeed.
       Enter old CAPULET *and* NURSE
      CAPULET'S WIFE   Here comes your father. Tell him so yourself,
125   And see how he will take it at your hands.
      CAPULET   When the sun sets, the earth doth drizzle° dew,   *weep out*
       But for the sunset of my brother's son
       It rains downright.
       How now, a conduit,° girl? What, still in tears?   *fountain*
130   Evermore show'ring? In one little body
       Thou counterfeit'st a barque,° a sea, a wind,   *represent a ship*
       For still thy eyes—which I may call the sea—
       Do ebb and flow with tears. The barque thy body is,
       Sailing in this salt flood; the winds thy sighs,
135   Who,° raging with thy tears and they with them,   *Which*

---

6. *till . . . heart:* Juliet allows her mother to understand that she will not be satisfied "till I behold him dead," while privately meaning that until she beholds him, "dead is my poor heart."

Without a sudden calm will overset

Thy tempest-tossèd body.—How now, wife?

Have you delivered to her our decree?

CAPULET'S WIFE Ay, sir, but she will none,° she gives you thanks.   *not agree*

140 I would the fool° were married to her grave.   *peevish child*

CAPULET Soft, take me with you,[7] take me with you, wife.

How, will she none? Doth she not give us thanks?

Is she not proud?° Doth she not count her blest,   *gratified*

Unworthy as she is, that we have wrought°   *contrived for*

145 So worthy a gentleman to be her bride?°   *bridegroom*

JULIET Not proud you have, but thankful that you have.

Proud can I never be of what I hate,

But thankful even for hate° that is meant love.°   *a hateful thing / as love*

CAPULET How, how, how, how—chopped logic?° What is this?   *mere sophistry*

150 'Proud', and 'I thank you', and 'I thank you not',

And yet 'not proud'? Mistress minion,° you,   *spoiled child*

Thank me no thankings, nor proud me no prouds,

But fettle° your fine joints 'gainst° Thursday next   *prepare / for*

To go with Paris to Saint Peter's Church,

155 Or I will drag thee on a hurdle[8] thither.

Out,[9] you green-sickness carrion! Out, you baggage,

You tallow-face!

CAPULET'S WIFE Fie, fie, what, are you mad?

JULIET (*kneels down*) Good father, I beseech you on my knees,

Hear me with patience but to speak a word.

160 CAPULET Hang thee, young baggage, disobedient wretch!

I tell thee what: get thee to church o' Thursday,

Or never after look me in the face.

Speak not, reply not, do not answer me.

                    [JULIET *rises*]

My fingers itch. Wife, we scarce thought us blest

165 That God had lent us but this only child,

But now I see this one is one too much,

And that we have a curse in having her.

Out on her, hilding!°   *hussy*

NURSE   God in heaven bless her!

You are to blame, my lord, to rate° her so.   *berate*

170 CAPULET And why, my lady Wisdom? Hold your tongue,

Good Prudence. Smatter° with your gossips,° go!   *Chatter / cronies*

NURSE I speak no treason.

CAPULET   O, God-i'-good-e'en!°   *for God's sake*

NURSE May not one speak?

CAPULET   Peace, you mumbling fool,

Utter your gravity° o'er a gossip's bowl,°   *wisdom / drinking bowl*

For here we need it not.

175 CAPULET'S WIFE   You are too hot.°   *irascible, rash*

CAPULET God's bread,° it makes me mad. Day, night;   *By the communion bread*

    work, play;

Alone, in company, still my care° hath been   *business*

To have her matched; and having now provided

A gentleman of noble parentage,

---

7. Not so fast, let me understand you.   execution.

8. A sledge used to draw traitors through the streets to   9. An expression of disgust and impatience.

180 Of fair demesnes,° youthful, and nobly lined,°   estates / descended
Stuffed, as they say, with honourable parts,°   qualities
Proportioned as one's thought would wish a man[1]—
And then to have a wretched puling fool,
A whining maumet,° in her fortune's tender,[2]   puppet
185 To answer 'I'll not wed, I cannot love;
I am too young, I pray you pardon me'!
But an you will not wed, I'll pardon you!°   excuse you (to leave)
Graze where you will, you shall not house with me.
Look to't, think on't. I do not use° to jest.   make it customary
190 Thursday is near. Lay hand on heart.[3] Advise.°   Consider
An you be mine, I'll give you to my friend.
An you be not, hang, beg, starve, die in the streets,
For, by my soul, I'll ne'er acknowledge thee,
Nor what is mine shall never do thee good.
195 Trust to't. Bethink you. I'll not be forsworn.   *Exit*
JULIET   Is there no pity sitting in the clouds
That sees into the bottom of my grief?
O sweet my° mother, cast me not away!   my sweet
Delay this marriage for a month, a week;
200 Or if you do not, make the bridal bed
In that dim monument° where Tybalt lies.   sepulchre
CAPULET'S WIFE   Talk not to me, for I'll not speak a word.
Do as thou wilt, for I have done with thee.   *Exit*
JULIET   O, God—O Nurse, how shall this be prevented?
205 My husband is on earth, my faith° in heaven.   marriage vows
How shall that faith return again to earth
Unless that husband send it me from heaven
By leaving earth?[4] Comfort me, counsel me.
Alack, alack, that heaven should practise stratagems
210 Upon so soft a subject as myself!
What sayst thou? Hast thou not a word of joy?
Some comfort, Nurse.
NURSE   Faith, here it is: Romeo
Is banishèd, and all the world to nothing[5]
That he dares ne'er come back to challenge you,
215 Or if he do, it needs must be by stealth.
Then, since the case so stands as now it doth,
I think it best you married with the County.
O, he's a lovely gentleman!
Romeo's a dishclout° to him. An eagle, madam,   dishcloth
220 Hath not so green, so quick, so fair an eye
As Paris hath. Beshrew° my very heart,   Curse
I think you are happy° in this second match,   lucky
For it excels your first; or if it did not,
Your first is dead, or 'twere as good he were
225 As living hence and you no use of him.
JULIET   Speak'st thou from thy heart?
NURSE   And from my soul, too, else beshrew them both.
JULIET   Amen.
NURSE   What?

---

1. Shaped as handsomely as you can imagine.
2. When good fortune is offered her.
3. Ascertain your feelings.
4. *How . . . earth:* How can I swear marriage vows

again unless Romeo dies first, thus releasing me from
my vows to him?
5. And it's a sure bet.

230 JULIET   Well, thou hast comforted me marvellous much.
　　　Go in; and tell my lady I am gone,
　　　Having displeased my father, to Laurence' cell
　　　To make confession and to be absolved.
　　NURSE   Marry, I will; and this is wisely done.　　　　[Exit]
235 JULIET (looks after NURSE)   Ancient damnation!⁶ O most wicked fiend!
　　　Is it more sin to wish me thus forsworn,
　　　Or to dispraise my lord with that same tongue
　　　Which she hath praised him with above compare
　　　So many thousand times? Go, counsellor!
240 　　Thou and my bosom° henceforth shall be twain.°　　　heart's contents / divided
　　　I'll to the friar, to know his remedy.
　　　If all else fail, myself have power to die.　　　　　Exit

4.1

Enter FRIAR [LAURENCE] *and County* PARIS

FRIAR LAURENCE   On Thursday, sir? The time is very short.
PARIS   My father Capulet will have it so,
　　And I am nothing slow¹ to slack his haste.
FRIAR LAURENCE   You say you do not know the lady's mind?
5 　　Uneven is the course.² I like it not.
PARIS   Immoderately she weeps for Tybalt's death,
　　And therefore have I little talked of love,
　　For Venus smiles not in a house of tears.
　　Now, sir, her father counts it dangerous
10 　That she do give her sorrow so much sway,
　　And in his wisdom hastes our marriage
　　To stop the inundation of her tears,
　　Which, too much minded° by herself alone,　　　　brooded over
　　May be put from her by society.°　　　　　　　　company
15 　Now do you know the reason of this haste.
FRIAR LAURENCE [aside]   I would I knew not why it should be slowed.—
　　　　　Enter JULIET
　　Look, sir, here comes the lady toward my cell.
PARIS   Happily met, my lady and my wife.
JULIET   That may be, sir, when I may be a wife.
20 PARIS   That 'may be' must be, love, on Thursday next.
JULIET   What must be shall be.
FRIAR LAURENCE　　　　　　　That's a certain text.
PARIS   Come you to make confession to this father?
JULIET   To answer that, I should confess to you.
PARIS   Do not deny to him that you love me.
25 JULIET   I will confess to you that I love him.
PARIS   So will ye, I am sure, that you love me.
JULIET   If I do so, it will be of more price,°　　　　value
　　Being spoke behind your back, than to your face.
PARIS   Poor soul, thy face is much abused with tears.
30 JULIET   The tears have got small victory by that,
　　For it was bad enough before their spite.°　　　　injury
PARIS   Thou wrong'st it more than tears with that report.
JULIET   That is no slander, sir, which is a truth,
　　And what I spake, I spake it to my face.

6. Damnable old woman (with a hint of "original sin").
4.1. Location: Friar Laurence's cell.
1. Not reluctant; not trying to drag behind him.
2. The plan is irregular; this is a tricky road to follow.

35 PARIS   Thy face is mine, and thou hast slandered it.

JULIET   It may be so, for it is not mine own.[3]—
    Are you at leisure, holy father, now,
    Or shall I come to you at evening mass?

FRIAR LAURENCE   My leisure serves me, pensive° daughter, now.   *sorrowful*
40   My lord, we must entreat the time alone.

PARIS   God shield° I should disturb devotion!—   *forbid*
    Juliet, on Thursday early will I rouse ye.
    [*Kissing her*] Till then, adieu, and keep this holy kiss.   *Exit*

JULIET   O, shut the door, and when thou hast done so,
45   Come weep with me, past hope, past cure, past help!

FRIAR LAURENCE   O Juliet, I already know thy grief.°   *grievous situation*
    It strains me past the compass° of my wits.   *limit*
    I hear thou must, and nothing may prorogue° it,   *postpone*
    On Thursday next be married to this County.

50 JULIET   Tell me not, friar, that thou hear'st of this,
    Unless thou tell me how I may prevent it.
    If in thy wisdom thou canst give no help,
    Do thou but call my resolution wise,
        [*She draws a knife*]
    And with this knife I'll help it presently.°   *immediately*
55   God joined my heart and Romeo's, thou our hands;
    And ere this hand, by thee to Romeo's sealed,
    Shall be the label[4] to another deed,
    Or my true heart with treacherous revolt
    Turn to another, this shall slay them both.
60   Therefore, out of thy long-experienced time,
    Give me some present counsel; or, behold,
    'Twixt my extremes° and me this bloody knife   *extreme difficulties*
    Shall play the umpire, arbitrating that
    Which the commission° of thy years and art°   *authority / learning*
65   Could to no issue of true honour bring.
    Be not so long to speak. I long to die
    If what thou speak'st speak not of remedy.

FRIAR LAURENCE   Hold, daughter, I do spy a kind of hope
    Which craves as desperate° an execution[5]   *reckless*
70   As that is desperate° which we would prevent.   *hopeless*
    If, rather than to marry County Paris,
    Thou hast the strength of will to slay thyself,
    Then is it likely thou wilt undertake
    A thing like death to chide away this shame,
75   That cop'st° with death himself to scape from it;°   *Who wrestles / (shame)*
    And, if thou dar'st, I'll give thee remedy.

JULIET   O, bid me leap, rather than marry Paris,
    From off the battlements of any tower,
    Or walk in thievish° ways, or bid me lurk   *thief-infested*
80   Where serpents are. Chain me with roaring bears,
    Or hide me nightly in a charnel house,°   *burial vault*
    O'ercovered quite with dead men's rattling bones,
    With reeky° shanks and yellow chapless[6] skulls;   *foully damp*

---

3. Because it belongs to Romeo; also because Juliet, in her ambiguous replies, is not showing Paris her true face.
4. Ribbon attaching a seal to a legal document (deed),

and so a pledge confirming another marriage.
5. A performance; a killing.
6. Without a lower jaw.

Or bid me go into a new-made grave
85 And hide me with a dead man in his tomb—
Things that, to hear them told, have made me tremble—
And I will do it without fear or doubt,°   *dread; hesitation*
To live an unstained wife to my sweet love.
FRIAR LAURENCE   Hold, then; go home, be merry, give consent
90 To marry Paris. Wednesday is tomorrow.
Tomorrow night look° that thou lie alone.   *be sure*
Let not the Nurse lie with thee in thy chamber.
Take thou this vial, being then in bed,
And this distilling° liquor drink thou off,   *permeating*
95 When presently through all thy veins shall run
A cold and drowsy humour;° for no pulse   *bodily fluid*
Shall keep his° native progress, but surcease.°   *its / cease*
No warmth, no breath shall testify thou livest.
The roses in thy lips and cheeks shall fade
100 To wanny° ashes, thy eyes' windows° fall   *pale / lids*
Like death when he shuts up the day of life.
Each part, deprived of supple government,°   *control of movement*
Shall, stiff and stark and cold, appear like death;
And in this borrowed likeness of shrunk death
105 Thou shalt continue two-and-forty hours,
And then awake as from a pleasant sleep.
Now, when the bridegroom in the morning comes
To rouse thee from thy bed, there art thou dead.
Then, as the manner of our country is,
110 In thy best robes, uncovered on the bier
Thou shalt be borne to that same ancient vault
Where all the kindred of the Capulets lie.
In the meantime, against° thou shalt awake,   *in preparation for when*
Shall Romeo by my letters know our drift,°   *scheme*
115 And hither shall he come, and he and I
Will watch° thy waking, and that very night   *keep vigil for*
Shall Romeo bear thee hence to Mantua.
And this shall free thee from this present shame,
If no inconstant toy° nor womanish fear   *fickle whim*
120 Abate thy valour in the acting it.
JULIET   Give me, give me! O, tell not me of fear!
FRIAR LAURENCE [*giving her the vial*]   Hold, get you gone. Be
    strong and prosperous
In this resolve. I'll send a friar with speed
To Mantua with my letters° to thy lord.   *letter*
125 JULIET   Love give me strength, and strength shall help afford.
Farewell, dear father.   *Exeunt* [*severally*]

4.2

Enter old CAPULET, *his* WIFE, NURSE, *and two or three*
    SERVINGMEN
CAPULET [*giving a* SERVINGMAN *a paper*]   So many guests invite
    as here are writ.   [*Exit* SERVINGMAN]
[*To the other* SERVINGMAN] Sirrah, go hire me twenty
    cunning° cooks.   *skillful*

4.2 Location: Capulet's house.

SERVINGMAN   You shall have none ill, sir, for I'll try° if they can   test
    lick their fingers.
5   CAPULET   How canst thou try them so?
SERVINGMAN   Marry, sir, 'tis an ill cook that cannot lick his own
    fingers, therefore he that cannot lick his fingers goes not with
    me.
CAPULET   Go, be gone.   [*Exit* SERVINGMAN]
10   We shall be much unfurnished° for this time.   unprepared
    [*To* NURSE] What, is my daughter gone to Friar Laurence?
NURSE   Ay, forsooth.
CAPULET   Well, he may chance to do some good on her.
    A peevish,° self-willed harlotry° it° is.   *An obstinate / brat / she*
        Enter JULIET
15   NURSE   See where she comes from shrift° with merry look.   absolution
CAPULET [*to* JULIET]   How now, my headstrong, where have you
        been gadding?
JULIET   Where I have learned me to repent the sin
    Of disobedient opposition
    To you and your behests, and am enjoined
20   By holy Laurence to fall prostrate here
    To beg your pardon. (*She kneels down*) Pardon, I beseech you.
    Henceforward I am ever ruled by you.
CAPULET [*to* NURSE]   Send for the County; go tell him of this.
    I'll have this knot knit up tomorrow morning.
25   JULIET   I met the youthful lord at Laurence' cell,
    And gave him what becoming° love I might,   suitable
    Not stepping o'er the bounds of modesty.
CAPULET   Why, I am glad on't.° This is well. Stand up.   of it
    [JULIET *rises*]
    This is as't should be. Let me see the County.
30   [*To* NURSE] Ay, marry, go, I say, and fetch him hither.
    Now, afore God, this reverend holy friar,
    All our whole city is much bound to him.
JULIET   Nurse, will you go with me into my closet°   chamber
    To help me sort such needful ornaments
35   As you think fit to furnish me tomorrow?
CAPULET'S WIFE   No, not till Thursday. There is time enough.
CAPULET   Go, Nurse, go with her. We'll to church tomorrow.
        Exeunt JULIET *and* NURSE
CAPULET'S WIFE   We shall be short in our provision.
    'Tis now near night.
CAPULET   Tush, I will stir about,
40   And all things shall be well, I warrant thee, wife.
    Go thou to Juliet, help to deck up her.
    I'll not to bed tonight. Let me alone.
    I'll play the housewife for this once. What, ho!
    They are all forth. Well, I will walk myself
45   To County Paris to prepare up him
    Against tomorrow. My heart is wondrous light,
    Since this same wayward girl is so reclaimed.[1]
        Exeunt [*severally*]

1. Reformed; claimed in marriage.

4.3

Enter JULIET *and* NURSE [*with garments*]¹

JULIET Ay, those attires are best. But, gentle Nurse,
I pray thee leave me to myself tonight,
For I have need of many orisons°   prayers
To move the heavens to smile upon my state,
5   Which—well thou knowest—is cross° and full of sin.   adverse

Enter [CAPULET'S WIFE]

CAPULET'S WIFE What, are you busy, ho? Need you my help?
JULIET No, madam, we have culled such necessaries
As are behoveful° for our state° tomorrow.   needful / ceremony
So please° you, let me now be left alone,   If it pleases
10 And let the Nurse this night sit up with you,
For I am sure you have your hands full all
In this so sudden business.
CAPULET'S WIFE   Good night.
Get thee to bed, and rest, for thou hast need.

Exeunt [CAPULET'S WIFE *and* NURSE]

JULIET Farewell. God knows when we shall meet again.
15 I have a faint cold fear thrills° through my veins   pierces
That almost freezes up the heat of life.
I'll call them back again to comfort me.
Nurse!—What should she do here?

[*She opens curtains, behind which is seen her bed*]

My dismal° scene I needs must act alone.   calamitous
20 Come, vial. What if this mixture do not work at all?
Shall I be married then tomorrow morning?
No, no, this shall forbid it. Lie thou there.

[*She lays down a knife*]

What if it be a poison which the friar
Subtly hath ministered to have me dead,
25 Lest in this marriage he should be dishonoured
Because he married me before to Romeo?
I fear it is—and yet methinks it should not,°   not be
For he hath still° been tried° a holy man.   always / proved
How if, when I am laid into the tomb,
30 I wake before the time that Romeo
Come to redeem me? There's a fearful point.
Shall I not then be stifled in the vault,
To whose foul mouth no healthsome air breathes in,
And there die strangled° ere my Romeo comes?   suffocated
35 Or, if I live, is it not very like°   likely
The horrible conceit of death and night,
Together with the terror of the place—
As° in a vault, an ancient receptacle   As it is
Where for this many hundred years the bones
40 Of all my buried ancestors are packed;
Where bloody Tybalt, yet but green° in earth,   newly
Lies fest'ring in his shroud; where, as they say,
At some hours in the night spirits resort—
Alack, alack, is it not like that I,
45 So early waking—what with loathsome smells,

4.3 Location: Capulet's house.
1. Juliet's chamber may be represented by a bed onstage for this scene and the next.

And shrieks like mandrakes² torn out of the earth,
That living mortals, hearing them, run mad—
O, if I wake, shall I not be distraught,
Environèd with all these hideous fears,
50 And madly play with my forefathers' joints,
And pluck the mangled Tybalt from his shroud,
And, in this rage,° with some great kinsman's bone   insanity
As with a club dash out my desp'rate brains?
O, look! Methinks I see my cousin's ghost
55 Seeking out Romeo that did spit his body
Upon a rapier's point. Stay, Tybalt, stay!
Romeo, Romeo, Romeo! Here's drink. I drink to thee.
[*She drinks from the vial and*] *falls upon her bed within
the curtains*

4.4

Enter [CAPULET'S WIFE,] *and* NURSE *with herbs*
CAPULET'S WIFE   Hold, take these keys, and fetch more spices, Nurse.
NURSE   They call for dates and quinces in the pastry.°   *pastry kitchen*
Enter old CAPULET
CAPULET   Come, stir, stir, stir! The second cock hath crowed.
The curfew bell¹ hath rung. 'Tis three o'clock.
5 Look to the baked meats, good Angelica.²
Spare not for cost.
NURSE   Go, you cot-quean,° go.   *old housewife*
Get you to bed. Faith, you'll be sick tomorrow
For this night's watching.°   *wakefulness*
CAPULET   No, not a whit. What, I have watched ere now
10 All night for lesser cause, and ne'er been sick.
CAPULET'S WIFE   Ay, you have been a mouse-hunt° in your time,   *skirt chaser*
But I will watch° you from such watching now.   *guard*
Exeunt [CAPULET'S WIFE] *and* NURSE
CAPULET   A jealous-hood,³ a jealous-hood!
Enter three or four SERVINGMEN, *with spits and logs and
baskets*
                    Now, fellow, what is there?
FIRST SERVINGMAN   Things for the cook, sir, but I know not what.
CAPULET   Make haste, make haste.
[*Exit* FIRST SERVINGMAN *and one or two others*]
15   Sirrah, fetch drier logs.
Call Peter. He will show thee where they are.
SECOND SERVINGMAN   I have a head, sir, that will find out logs⁴
And never trouble Peter for the matter.
CAPULET   Mass,° and well said! A merry whoreson,° ha!   *By the mass / rogue*
Thou shalt be loggerhead.°   *Exit* [SECOND SERVINGMAN]   *wooden-headed*
20   Good faith, 'tis day.
The County will be here with music straight,
For so he said he would.
Play music [*within*]
                    I hear him near.

2. Plants with forked roots thought to resemble a man.
Popular belief held that they uttered a death- or
madness-producing shriek upon being pulled up.
4.4 Location: Scene continues.
1. Also rung at daybreak.
2. Unclear whether Capulet refers to his wife or the

nurse.
3. Jealousy; jealous woman.
4. I have a good head for finding things, so I can certainly find the logs; my head knows all about logs (I am
a blockhead).

Nurse! Wife! What ho, what, Nurse, I say!

Enter NURSE

Go waken Juliet. Go and trim her up.
25 I'll go and chat with Paris. Hie, make haste,
Make haste, the bridegroom he is come already.
Make haste, I say.   *[Exit]*
NURSE   Mistress, what, mistress! Juliet! Fast,° I warrant her, she.   *Asleep*
Why, lamb, why, lady! Fie, you slug-abed!
30 Why, love, I say, madam, sweetheart, why, bride!
What, not a word? You take your pennyworths° now.   *bits (of sleep)*
Sleep for a week, for the next night, I warrant,
The County Paris hath set up his rest[5]
That you shall rest but little. God forgive me!
35 Marry, and amen. How sound is she asleep!
I needs must wake her. Madam, madam, madam!
Ay, let the County take° you in your bed.   *catch; sexually possess*
He'll fright you up, i'faith. Will it not be?
       [She draws back the curtains]
What, dressed and in your clothes, and down again?
40 I must needs wake you. Lady, lady, lady!
Alas, alas! Help, help! My lady's dead.
O welladay,° that ever I was born!   *alas*
Some aqua-vitae, ho! My lord, my lady!
       Enter [CAPULET'S WIFE]
CAPULET'S WIFE   What noise is here?
NURSE   O lamentable day!
CAPULET'S WIFE   What is the matter?
45 NURSE   Look, look. O heavy day!
CAPULET'S WIFE   O me, O me, my child, my only life!
Revive, look up, or I will die with thee.
Help, help, call help!
       Enter [CAPULET]
CAPULET   For shame, bring Juliet forth. Her lord is come.
50 NURSE   She's dead, deceased. She's dead, alack the day!
CAPULET'S WIFE   Alack the day, she's dead, she's dead, she's dead!
CAPULET   Ha, let me see her! Out,° alas, she's cold.   *Woe*
Her blood is settled,° and her joints are stiff.   *motionless*
Life and these lips have long been separated.
55 Death lies on her like an untimely frost
Upon the sweetest flower of all the field.
NURSE   O lamentable day!
CAPULET'S WIFE   O woeful time!
CAPULET   Death, that hath ta'en her hence to make me wail,
Ties up my tongue, and will not let me speak.
       Enter FRIAR [LAURENCE] *and* PARIS [*with Musicians*]
60 FRIAR LAURENCE   Come, is the bride ready to go to church?
CAPULET   Ready to go, but never to return.
[*To* PARIS] O son, the night before thy wedding day
Hath death lain with thy wife. See, there she lies,
Flower as she was, deflowerèd by him.
65 Death is my son-in-law, death is my heir.
My daughter he hath wedded. I will die,
And leave him all. Life, living,° all is death's.   *property*

---

5. Has resolved (from staking everything in the card game primero), with bawdy pun.

All at once wring their hands and cry out

PARIS Have I thought° long to see this morning's face,   *expected*
And doth it give me such a sight as this?
70 Beguiled,° divorcèd, wrongèd, spited,° slain!   *Cheated / injured*
Most detestable death, by thee beguiled,
By cruel, cruel thee quite overthrown.
O love, O life: not life, but love in death.

CAPULET'S WIFE Accursed, unhappy, wretched, hateful day!
75 Most miserable hour that e'er time saw
In lasting° labour of his pilgrimage!   *eternal*
But one, poor one, one poor and loving child,
But one thing to rejoice and solace in,
And cruel death hath catched° it from my sight!   *seized*

80 NURSE O woe! O woeful, woeful, woeful day!
Most lamentable day! Most woeful day
That ever, ever, I did yet behold!
O day, O day, O day, O hateful day,
Never was seen so black a day as this!
85 O woeful day, O woeful day!

CAPULET Despised, distressèd, hated, martyred, killed!
Uncomfortable° time, why cam'st thou now   *Comfortless*
To murder, murder our solemnity?°   *festivity*
O child, O child, my soul and not my child!⁶
90 Dead art thou, alack, my child is dead,
And with my child my joys are burièd.

FRIAR LAURENCE Peace, ho, for shame! Confusion's° cure lives   *Destruction's*
not
In these confusions.° Heaven and yourself   *commotions*
Had part in this fair maid. Now heaven hath all,
95 And all the better is it for the maid.
Your part in her you could not keep from death,
But heaven keeps his part in eternal life.
The most you sought was her promotion,°   *social advancement*
For 'twas your heaven° she should be advanced,   *highest ambition*
100 And weep ye now, seeing she is advanced
Above the clouds as high as heaven itself?
O, in this love you love your child so ill
That you run mad, seeing that she is well.
She's not well married that lives married long,
105 But she's best married that dies married young.
Dry up your tears, and stick your rosemary
On this fair corpse, and, as the custom is,
All in her best array bear her to church;
For though fond° nature° bids us all lament,   *foolish; doting / affection*
110 Yet nature's tears are reason's merriment.°   *laughable idiocy*

CAPULET All things that we ordainèd festival
Turn from their office° to black funeral.   *due function*
Our instruments to melancholy bells,
Our wedding cheer° to a sad burial feast,   *fare*
115 Our solemn° hymns to sullen° dirges change;   *ceremonial / mournful*
Our bridal flowers serve for a buried corpse,
And all things change them to the contrary.

FRIAR LAURENCE Sir, go you in; and madam, go with him,
And go, Sir Paris. Everyone prepare

---

6. *not my child:* because dead and only a corpse.

120 To follow this fair corpse unto her grave.
The heavens do lour° upon you for some ill.°   *hang threatening / offense*
Move° them no more by crossing their high will.   *Anger*

All but NURSE *go forth, casting rosemary on* JULIET *and*
shutting the curtains. Manent° NURSE *and* MUSICIANS   *Remain*

FIRST MUSICIAN   Faith, we may put° up our pipes and be gone.   *pack*
NURSE   Honest good fellows, ah, put up, put up,
125 For well you know this is a pitiful case.
FIRST MUSICIAN   Ay, by my troth, the case may be amended.[7]

                                   Exit [NURSE]

         Enter PETER
PETER   Musicians, O, musicians! 'Heart's ease',° 'Heart's ease';   *(popular song)*
O, an you will have me live, play 'Heart's ease'.
FIRST MUSICIAN   Why 'Heart's ease'?
130 PETER   O, musicians, because my heart itself plays 'My heart is
full of woe'. O, play me some merry dump° to comfort me.   *sad tune*
FIRST MUSICIAN   Not a dump, we. 'Tis no time to play now.
PETER   You will not then?
FIRST MUSICIAN   No.
135 PETER   I will then give it you soundly.°   *thoroughly; in sound*
FIRST MUSICIAN   What will you give us?
PETER   No money, on my faith, but the gleek.[8] I will give you
the minstrel.[9]
FIRST MUSICIAN   Then will I give you the serving-creature.
140 PETER [*drawing his dagger*]   Then will I lay the serving-creature's
dagger on your pate. I will carry° no crotchets.[1] I'll re you, I'll   *bear; sing*
fa you. Do you note° me?   *heed*
FIRST MUSICIAN   An you re us and fa us, you note° us.   *give notes to*
SECOND MUSICIAN   Pray you, put up your dagger and put out°   *show; quench*
145 your wit.
PETER   Then have at you with my wit. I will dry-beat° you with   *thrash*
an iron° wit, and put up my iron dagger. Answer[2] me like men.   *a merciless*
[*Sings*]   When griping grief the heart doth wound,
         And doleful dumps° the mind oppress,   *melancholy*
150   Then music with her silver sound[3]—
Why 'silver sound', why 'music with her silver sound'? What
say you, Matthew Minikin?°   *small lute string*
FIRST MUSICIAN   Marry, sir, because silver hath a sweet sound.
PETER   Prates!° What say you, Hugh Rebec?[4]   *Chatter*
155 SECOND MUSICIAN   I say 'silver sound' because musicians sound
for silver.
PETER   Prates too! What say you, Simon Soundpost?[5]
THIRD MUSICIAN   Faith, I know not what to say.
PETER   O, I cry you mercy,° you are the singer. I will say for you.   *beg your pardon*
160 It is 'music with her silver sound' because musicians have no
gold for sounding.[6]
[*Sings*]   Then music with her silver sound
           With speedy help doth lend redress.   *Exit*
FIRST MUSICIAN   What a pestilent knave is this same!

---

7. Things could be better; the instrument case can be
repaired.
8. To "give the gleek" was to make a fool of or play a
trick on.
9. I will insultingly call you a minstrel.
1. Whimsy; quarter notes.
2. Defy; respond to.

3. Lines from the song "In Commendation of Music."
4. Three-stringed instrument.
5. Supporting peg fixed between the sounding board
and back of a stringed instrument.
6. Musicians are given no gold for playing; they are
poor and have no gold to jingle.

165 SECOND MUSICIAN   Hang him, jack! Come, we'll in here, tarry
for the mourners, and stay° dinner.   *Exeunt*   *await*

5.1

Enter ROMEO

ROMEO   If I may trust the flattering° truth of sleep,   *encouraging*
My dreams presage some joyful news at hand.
My bosom's lord sits lightly in his throne,[1]
And all this day an unaccustomed spirit
5   Lifts me above the ground with cheerful thoughts.
I dreamt my lady came and found me dead—
Strange dream, that gives a dead man leave to think!—
And breathed such life with kisses in° my lips   *into*
That I revived and was an emperor.
10   Ah me, how sweet is love itself possessed°   *enjoyed in reality*
When but love's shadows° are so rich in joy!   *dreams; images*

Enter BALTHASAR, *his man, booted*[2]

News from Verona! How now, Balthasar?
Dost thou not bring me letters from the friar?
How doth my lady? Is my father well?
15   How fares my Juliet? That I ask again,
For nothing can be ill if she be well.

BALTHASAR   Then she is well, and nothing can be ill.
Her body sleeps in Capel's monument,
And her immortal part with angels lives.
20   I saw her laid low in her kindred's vault,
And presently° took post[3] to tell it you.   *immediately*
O, pardon me for bringing these ill news,
Since you did leave it for my office,° sir.   *duty*

ROMEO   Is it e'en so? Then I defy you, stars.
25   Thou knowest my lodging. Get me ink and paper,
And hire posthorses. I will hence tonight.

BALTHASAR   I do beseech you, sir, have patience.
Your looks are pale and wild, and do import°   *signify*
Some misadventure.

ROMEO   Tush, thou art deceived.
30   Leave me, and do the thing I bid thee do.
Hast thou no letters to me from the friar?

BALTHASAR   No, my good lord.

ROMEO   No matter. Get thee gone,
And hire those horses. I'll be with thee straight.

Exit BALTHASAR

Well, Juliet, I will lie with thee tonight.
35   Let's see for means. O mischief, thou art swift
To enter in the thoughts of desperate men!
I do remember an apothecary,
And hereabouts a dwells, which late I noted,
In tattered weeds,° with overwhelming° brows,   *clothes / overhanging*
40   Culling of simples.° Meagre were his looks.   *herbs*
Sharp misery had worn him to the bones,
And in his needy° shop a tortoise hung,   *poor*
An alligator stuffed, and other skins

5.1 Location: A street in Mantua.
1. Love rules in the heart; the heart is at ease in the
chest.
2. *booted:* as if he has just dismounted.
3. Set out on post horses.

Of ill-shaped fishes; and about his shelves
45   A beggarly account° of empty boxes,   *A sparse collection*
Green earthen pots, bladders, and musty seeds,
Remnants of packthread,° and old cakes of roses⁴   *twine*
Were thinly scattered to make up a show.
Noting this penury, to myself I said
50   'An if a man did need a poison now,
Whose sale is present death⁵ in Mantua,
Here lives a caitiff ° wretch would sell it him.'   *pitiful*
O, this same thought did but forerun my need,
And this same needy man must sell it me.
55   As I remember, this should be the house.
Being holiday, the beggar's shop is shut.
What ho, apothecary!
            Enter APOTHECARY
APOTHECARY   Who calls so loud?
ROMEO   Come hither, man. I see that thou art poor.
            [*He offers money*]
Hold, there is forty ducats.⁶ Let me have
60   A dram of poison—such soon-speeding gear⁷
As will disperse itself through all the veins,
That the life-weary taker may fall dead,
And that the trunk° may be discharged of breath   *body*
As violently as hasty powder fired
65   Doth hurry from the fatal cannon's womb.
APOTHECARY   Such mortal drugs I have, but Mantua's law
Is death to any he° that utters° them.   *man / offers to sell*
ROMEO   Art thou so bare° and full of wretchedness,   *destitute*
And fear'st to die? Famine is in thy cheeks,
70   Need and oppression starveth in thy eyes,
Contempt and beggary hangs upon thy back.
The world is not thy friend, nor the world's law.
The world affords° no law to make thee rich.   *provides*
Then be not poor, but break it, and take this.
75   APOTHECARY   My poverty but not my will consents.
ROMEO   I pay thy poverty and not thy will.
APOTHECARY [*handing* ROMEO *poison*]   Put this in any liquid
            thing you will
And drink it off, and if you had the strength
Of twenty men it would dispatch you straight.°   *immediately*
ROMEO [*giving money*]   There is thy gold—worse poison to
80   men's souls,
Doing more murder in this loathsome world,
Than these poor compounds that thou mayst not sell.
I sell thee poison; thou hast sold me none.
Farewell, buy food, and get thyself in flesh.°   *grow fatter*
                                        [*Exit* APOTHECARY]
85   Come, cordial° and not poison, go with me   *restorative; heart's ease*
To Juliet's grave, for there must I use thee.   *Exit*

---

4. Rose petals pressed into cake form and used as a   and Shakespeare's usual currency for plays not set in
sachet.   England.
5. Punishable by immediate death.   7. Quick-working stuff; quick-killing stuff.
6. Various gold coins used at times in much of Europe,

5.2

Enter FRIAR JOHN [*at one door*]

FRIAR JOHN   Holy Franciscan friar, brother, ho!

Enter FRIAR LAURENCE [*at another door*]

FRIAR LAURENCE   This same should be the voice of Friar John.
Welcome from Mantua! What says Romeo?
Or if his mind° be writ, give me his letter.   thoughts

5   FRIAR JOHN   Going to find a barefoot brother out—
One of our order—to associate me[1]
Here in this city visiting the sick,
And finding him, the searchers[2] of the town,
Suspecting that we both were in a house

10   Where the infectious pestilence did reign,
Sealed up the doors, and would not let us forth,
So that my speed to Mantua there was stayed.°   stopped

FRIAR LAURENCE   Who bare my letter then to Romeo?

FRIAR JOHN   I could not send it—here it is again—

15   Nor get a messenger to bring it thee,
So fearful were they of infection.°   contagion

FRIAR LAURENCE   Unhappy fortune! By my brotherhood,
The letter was not nice,° but full of charge,°   trivial / importance
Of dear import,° and the neglecting it   serious consequence

20   May do much danger. Friar John, go hence.
Get me an iron crow,° and bring it straight   crowbar
Unto my cell.

FRIAR JOHN   Brother, I'll go and bring it thee.   *Exit*

FRIAR LAURENCE   Now must I to the monument alone.
Within this three hours will fair Juliet wake.

25   She will beshrew° me much that Romeo   curse
Hath had no notice of these accidents.°   events
But I will write again to Mantua,
And keep her at my cell till Romeo come.
Poor living corpse, closed in a dead man's tomb!   *Exit*

5.3

Enter County PARIS *and his* PAGE, *with flowers, sweet°*   perfumed
water [*and a torch*]

PARIS   Give me thy torch, boy. Hence, and stand aloof.°   stay apart
Yet put it out, for I would not be seen.
[*His* PAGE *puts out the torch*]
Under yon yew trees lay thee all along,°   stretched out
Holding thy ear close to the hollow ground.

5   So shall no foot upon the churchyard tread,
Being° loose, unfirm, with digging up of graves,   The ground being
But thou shalt hear it. Whistle then to me
As signal that thou hear'st something approach.
Give me those flowers. Do as I bid thee. Go.

10   PAGE [*aside*]   I am almost afraid to stand alone
Here in the churchyard, yet I will adventure.°   risk it
[*He hides himself at a distance from* PARIS]

5.2 Location: Friar Laurence's cell.
1. Franciscan friars (barefoot because the order is
sworn to poverty) traveled only in pairs. *associate:*
accompany.

2. Health officers appointed to examine corpses and
identify houses infected with the plague.
5.3 Location: The Capulet mausoleum.

PARIS (*strews the tomb with flowers*)　Sweet flower, with flowers
　　　　thy bridal bed I strew.
　　　　　[*He sprinkles water*]
　　　O woe! Thy canopy° is dust and stones,　　　　　　　covering; bed hangings
　　　Which with sweet water nightly I will dew,
15　　Or, wanting that, with tears distilled by moans.
　　　The obsequies that I for thee will keep°　　　　　　　perform
　　　Nightly shall be to strew thy grave and weep.
　　　　　[PAGE *whistles*]
　　　The boy gives warning. Something doth approach.
　　　What cursèd foot wanders this way tonight
20　　To cross° my obsequies and true love's rite?　　　　　thwart
　　　　　Enter ROMEO *and* BALTHASAR, *with a torch, a mattock,*°　　pickax
　　　　　and a crow of iron
　　　What, with a torch? Muffle me, night, a while.
　　　　　[*He stands aside*]
ROMEO　Give me that mattock and the wrenching iron.
　　　Hold, take this letter. Early in the morning
　　　See thou deliver it to my lord and father.
25　　Give me the light. Upon thy life I charge thee,
　　　Whate'er thou hear'st or seest, stand all aloof,
　　　And do not interrupt me in my course.
　　　Why I descend into this bed of death
　　　Is partly to behold my lady's face,
30　　But chiefly to take thence from her dead finger
　　　A precious ring, a ring that I must use
　　　In dear° employment. Therefore hence, be gone.　　　important; tender
　　　But if thou, jealous,° dost return to pry　　　　　　　suspicious
　　　In what I farther shall intend to do,
35　　By heaven, I will tear thee joint by joint,
　　　And strew this hungry churchyard with thy limbs.
　　　The time and my intents are savage-wild,
　　　More fierce and more inexorable far
　　　Than empty tigers or the roaring sea.
40　BALTHASAR　I will be gone, sir, and not trouble ye.
　　ROMEO　So shalt thou show me friendship. Take thou that.
　　　　　[*He gives money*]
　　　Live and be prosperous, and farewell, good fellow.
　　BALTHASAR [*aside*]　For all this same, I'll hide me hereabout.
　　　His looks I fear, and his intents I doubt.°　　　　　　suspect
　　　　　[*He hides himself at a distance from* ROMEO.]
　　　　　ROMEO *begins to open the tomb*
45　ROMEO　Thou detestable maw, thou womb[1] of death,
　　　Gorged with the dearest morsel of the earth,
　　　Thus I enforce thy rotten jaws to open,
　　　And in despite° I'll cram thee with more food.　　　　defiant ill will
　　PARIS [*aside*]　This is that banished haughty Montague
50　　That murdered my love's cousin, with which grief
　　　It is supposèd the fair creature died;
　　　And here is come to do some villainous shame
　　　To the dead bodies. I will apprehend him.
　　　　　[*Drawing*] Stop thy unhallowed° toil, vile Montague!　unholy

---

1. Belly; also playing on the birthplace of Romeo's death.

55   Can vengeance be pursued further than death?
Condemnèd villain, I do apprehend thee.
Obey and go with me, for thou must die.

ROMEO   I must indeed, and therefore came I hither.
Good gentle youth, tempt not a desp'rate° man.   *despairing; violent*
60   Fly hence, and leave me. Think upon these gone.
Let them affright thee. I beseech thee, youth,
Put not another sin upon my head
By urging me to fury. O, be gone.
By heaven, I love thee better than myself,
65   For I come hither armed against myself.
Stay not, be gone. Live, and hereafter say
A madman's mercy bid thee run away.

PARIS   I do defy thy conjuration,°   *entreaty*
And apprehend thee for a felon here.

70   ROMEO [*drawing*]   Wilt thou provoke me? Then have at thee, boy.
     They fight

PAGE   O Lord, they fight! I will go call the watch.   [*Exit*]

PARIS   O, I am slain! If thou be merciful,
Open the tomb, lay me with Juliet.

ROMEO   In faith, I will.   [PARIS *dies*]
     Let me peruse this face.
75   Mercutio's kinsman, noble County Paris!
What said my man when my betossèd° soul   *storm-tossed*
Did not attend° him as we rode? I think   *listen to*
He told me Paris should have married Juliet.
Said he not so? Or did I dream it so?
80   Or am I mad, hearing him talk of Juliet,
To think it was so? O, give me thy hand,
One writ with me in sour misfortune's book.
I'll bury thee in a triumphant° grave.   *magnificent*
     [*He opens the tomb, revealing* JULIET]
A grave—O no, a lantern,° slaughtered youth,   *lighthouse*
85   For here lies Juliet, and her beauty makes
This vault a feasting presence² full of light.
     [*He bears the body of Paris to the tomb*]
Death, lie thou there, by a dead man interred.
How oft, when men are at the point of death,
Have they been merry, which their keepers° call   *sick nurses; jailors*
90   A lightning before death! O, how may I
Call this a lightning? O my love, my wife!
Death, that hath sucked the honey of thy breath,
Hath had no power yet upon thy beauty.
Thou art not conquered.° Beauty's ensign° yet   *overpowered; seduced / flag*
95   Is crimson in thy lips and in thy cheeks,
And death's pale flag is not advancèd there.
Tybalt, liest thou there in thy bloody sheet?
O, what more favour can I do to thee
Than with that hand that cut thy youth in twain
100   To sunder his° that was thine enemy?   *the youth of him*
Forgive me, cousin. Ah, dear Juliet,
Why art thou yet so fair? Shall I believe
That unsubstantial° death is amorous,   *immaterial*

---

2. Festive royal chamber for receiving guests.

And that the lean abhorrèd monster keeps
105   Thee here in dark to be his paramour?
For fear of that I still will stay with thee,
And never from this pallet of dim night
Depart again. Here, here will I remain
With worms that are thy chambermaids. O, here
110   Will I set up my everlasting rest,³
And shake the yoke of inauspicious stars
From this world-wearied flesh. Eyes, look your last.
Arms, take your last embrace, and lips, O you
The doors of breath, seal with a righteous kiss
115   A dateless° bargain to engrossing⁴ death.   *An eternal*
      [*He kisses* JULIET, *then pours poison into the cup*]
Come, bitter conduct°, come, unsavoury guide,   *conductor; leader*
Thou desperate pilot, now at once run on
The dashing rocks thy seasick weary° barque!   *travel-weary*
Here's to my love.
      [*He drinks the poison*]
              O true apothecary,
120   Thy drugs are quick!° Thus with a kiss I die.   *fast; vigorous*
      [*He kisses* JULIET,] *falls* [*and dies.*]
      Enter FRIAR [LAURENCE] *with lantern, crow,*
      and spade
FRIAR LAURENCE   Saint Francis be my speed!° How oft tonight   *help*
  Have my old feet stumbled at graves? Who's there?
BALTHASAR   Here's one, a friend, and one that knows you well.
FRIAR LAURENCE   Bliss be upon you. Tell me, good my friend,
125   What torch is yon that vainly lends his light
To grubs and eyeless skulls? As I discern,
It burneth in the Capels' monument.
BALTHASAR   It doth so, holy sir, and there's my master,
  One that you love.
FRIAR LAURENCE   Who is it?
BALTHASAR   Romeo.
FRIAR LAURENCE   How long hath he been there?
130   BALTHASAR   Full half an hour.
FRIAR LAURENCE   Go with me to the vault.
BALTHASAR   I dare not, sir.
My master knows not but I am gone hence,
And fearfully° did menace me with death   *fearsomely*
If I did stay to look on his intents.
135   FRIAR LAURENCE   Stay then, I'll go alone. Fear comes upon me.
O, much I fear some ill unthrifty° thing.   *unfortunate*
BALTHASAR   As I did sleep under this yew tree here
I dreamt my master and another fought,
And that my master slew him.
FRIAR LAURENCE   Romeo!
      [*He*] *stoops and looks on the blood and weapons*
140   Alack, alack, what blood is this which stains
The stony entrance of this sepulchre?
What mean these masterless and gory swords
To lie discoloured by this place of peace?

---

3. Make my final determination.
4. Buying up in large quantities to monopolize; writing a legal document.

Romeo! O, pale! Who else? What, Paris, too,
145 And steeped in blood? Ah, what an unkind° hour   *unnatural; a cruel*
Is guilty of this lamentable chance!°   *event*
    JULIET [*awakes and*] *rises*
The lady stirs.
JULIET   O comfortable° friar, where is my lord?   *solace-giving*
I do remember well where I should be,
150 And there I am. Where is my Romeo?
FRIAR LAURENCE   I hear some noise. Lady, come from that nest
Of death, contagion, and unnatural sleep.
A greater power than we can contradict
Hath thwarted our intents. Come, come away.
155 Thy husband in thy bosom there lies dead,
And Paris, too. Come, I'll dispose of thee
Among a sisterhood of holy nuns.
Stay not to question, for the watch is coming.
Come, go, good Juliet. I dare no longer stay.   *Exit*
160 JULIET   Go, get thee hence, for I will not away.
What's here? A cup closed in my true love's hand?
Poison, I see, hath been his timeless° end.   *untimely; lasting*
O churl!—drunk all, and left no friendly drop
To help me after? I will kiss thy lips.
165 Haply° some poison yet doth hang on them,   *Perhaps*
To make me die with a restorative.[5]
    [*She kisses Romeo's lips*]
Thy lips are warm.
CHIEF WATCHMAN [*within*]   Lead, boy. Which way?
JULIET   Yea, noise? Then I'll be brief.
    [*She takes Romeo's dagger*]
                    O happy° dagger,   *fortunate*
This is thy sheath! There rust, and let me die.
    She stabs herself, falls [*and dies*]
    Enter [PAGE] *and* WATCH
170 PAGE   This is the place, there where the torch doth burn.
CHIEF WATCHMAN   The ground is bloody. Search about the churchyard.
Go, some of you. Whoe'er you find, attach.°   *arrest*
    [*Exeunt some* WATCHMEN]
Pitiful sight! Here lies the County slain,
And Juliet bleeding, warm, and newly dead,
175 Who here hath lain this two days burièd.
Go tell the Prince. Run to the Capulets,
Raise up the Montagues. Some others search.
    [*Exeunt other* WATCHMEN *severally*]
We see the ground° whereon these woes do lie,   *earth*
But the true ground° of all these piteous woes   *cause*
180 We cannot without circumstance° descry.   *a fuller account*
    Enter [WATCHMEN] *with Romeo's man* [BALTHASAR]
SECOND WATCHMAN   Here's Romeo's man. We found him in
  the churchyard.
CHIEF WATCHMAN   Hold him in safety° till the Prince come   *securely*
hither.
    Enter another WATCHMAN WITH FRIAR [LAURENCE]
THIRD WATCHMAN   Here is a friar that trembles, sighs, and weeps.

---

5. Both the kiss, which is healing, and the poison, which restores them to each other.

We took this mattock and this spade from him
185   As he was coming from this churchyard's side.[6]
     CHIEF WATCHMAN   A great suspicion. Stay° the friar, too.   *Hold*
         Enter PRINCE *with others*
     PRINCE   What misadventure is so early up,
     That calls our person from our morning rest?
         Enter old CAPULET *and his* WIFE
     CAPULET   What should it be that is so shrieked abroad?
190   CAPULET'S WIFE   O, the people in the street cry 'Romeo',
     Some 'Juliet', and some 'Paris', and all run
     With open° outcry toward our monument.   *public; open-mouthed*
     PRINCE   What fear is this which startles° in our ears?   *bursts out*
     CHIEF WATCHMAN   Sovereign, here lies the County Paris slain,
195   And Romeo dead, and Juliet, dead before,
     Warm, and new killed.
     PRINCE   Search, seek, and know how this foul murder comes.
     CHIEF WATCHMAN   Here is a friar, and slaughtered Romeo's man,
     With instruments upon them fit to open
200   These dead men's tombs.
     CAPULET   O heavens! O wife, look how our daughter bleeds!
     This dagger hath mista'en, for lo, his house°   *scabbard*
     Is empty on the back of Montague,
     And it mis-sheathèd in my daughter's bosom.
205   CAPULET'S WIFE   O me, this sight of death is as a bell
     That warns° my old age to a sepulchre.   *summons*
         Enter old MONTAGUE
     PRINCE   Come, Montague, for thou art early up
     To see thy son and heir more early down.
     MONTAGUE   Alas, my liege, my wife is dead tonight.
210   Grief of my son's exile hath stopped her breath.
     What further woe conspires against mine age?
     PRINCE   Look, and thou shalt see.
     MONTAGUE [*seeing Romeo's body*]   O thou untaught! What
          manners is in this,
     To press before° thy father to a grave?   *To shove ahead of*
215   PRINCE   Seal up the mouth of outrage[7] for a while,
     Till we can clear these ambiguities
     And know their spring, their head, their true descent;
     And then will I be general of your woes,
     And lead you even to death. Meantime, forbear,
220   And let mischance be slave to° patience.   *overruled by*
     Bring forth the parties of suspicion.
     FRIAR LAURENCE   I am the greatest,° able to do least,   *most suspect*
     Yet most suspected, as the time and place
     Doth make against me, of this direful murder;
225   And here I stand, both to impeach and purge
     Myself condemnèd and myself excused.[8]
     PRINCE   Then say at once what thou dost know in this.
     FRIAR LAURENCE   I will be brief, for my short date° of breath   *duration*
     Is not so long as is a tedious tale.
230   Romeo, there dead, was husband to that Juliet,
     And she, there dead, that Romeo's faithful wife.

---

6. This side of the churchyard.
7. Of impassioned exclamation.

8. *to . . . excused:* to accuse myself of what I am guilty
of and clear myself of what I am not.

I married them, and their stol'n marriage day
Was Tybalt's doomsday, whose untimely death
Banished the new-made bridegroom from this city,
235   For whom, and not for Tybalt, Juliet pined.
You, to remove that siege of grief from her,
Betrothed and would have married her perforce°   *forcibly*
To County Paris. Then comes she to me,
And with wild looks bid me devise some mean°   *method*
240   To rid her from this second marriage,
Or in my cell there would she kill herself.
Then gave I her—so tutored by my art[9]—
A sleeping potion, which so took effect
As I intended, for it wrought on her
245   The form° of death. Meantime I writ to Romeo   *appearance*
That he should hither come as this° dire night   *as this = this*
To help to take her from her borrowed grave,
Being the time the potion's force should cease.
But he which bore my letter, Friar John,
250   Was stayed by accident, and yesternight
Returned my letter back. Then all alone,
At the prefixéd° hour of her waking,   *prearranged*
Came I to take her from her kindred's vault,
Meaning to keep her closely° at my cell   *secretly*
255   Till I conveniently° could send to Romeo.   *befittingly*
But when I came, some minute ere the time
Of her awakening, here untimely lay
The noble Paris and true Romeo dead.
She wakes, and I entreated her come forth
260   And bear this work of heaven with patience.
But then a noise did scare me from the tomb,
And she, too desperate, would not go with me,
But, as it seems, did violence on herself.
All this I know, and to the marriage
265   Her nurse is privy; and if aught in this
Miscarried by my fault, let my old life
Be sacrificed, some hour before his° time,   *its*
Unto the rigour of severest law.
PRINCE   We still° have known thee for a holy man.   *always*
270   Where's Romeo's man? What can he say to this?
BALTHASAR   I brought my master news of Juliet's death,
And then in post° he came from Mantua   *haste*
To this same place, to this same monument.
This letter he early bid me give his father,
275   And threatened me with death, going in the vault,
If I departed not and left him there.
PRINCE   Give me the letter. I will look on it.
         [He *takes the letter*]
Where is the County's page that raised the watch?
Sirrah, what made° your master in this place?   *did*
280   PAGE   He came with flowers to strew his lady's grave,
And bid me stand aloof, and so I did.
Anon° comes one with light to ope the tomb,   *Soon*

---

9. As I knew through my medical study to do.

And by and by my master drew on him,
And then I ran away to call the watch.
285 PRINCE   This letter doth make good the friar's words,
Their course of love, the tidings of her death;
And here he writes that he did buy a poison
Of a poor 'pothecary, and therewithal
Came to this vault to die, and lie with Juliet.
290 Where be these enemies? Capulet, Montague,
See what a scourge is laid upon your hate,
That heaven finds means to kill your joys° with love.   *happiness; children*
And I, for winking at° your discords, too   *closing my eyes to*
Have lost a brace of kinsmen. All are punishèd.
295 CAPULET   O brother Montague, give me thy hand.
This is my daughter's jointure,° for no more   *marriage portion*
Can I demand.
MONTAGUE   But I can give thee more,
For I will raise her statue in pure gold,
That whiles Verona by that name is known
300 There shall no figure at such rate be set[1]
As that of true and faithful Juliet.
CAPULET   As rich shall Romeo's by his lady's lie,
Poor sacrifices of our enmity.
PRINCE   A glooming° peace this morning with it brings.   *frowning; dark*
305 The sun for sorrow will not show his head.
Go hence, to have more talk of these sad things.
Some shall be pardoned, and some punishèd;
For never was a story of more woe
Than this of Juliet and her Romeo.
                                        [*The tomb is closed.*] Exeunt

---

1. No figure shall be so valued; no figure shall be erected at such a price.

Richard II

In the first scene of *Richard II*, two armed noblemen face each other before the royal throne. They hurl insults at one another, their deadly antagonism barely held in check by the formality of the occasion. This is an "appeal for treason," a kind of trial already archaic in Shakespeare's time, in which plaintiff and defendant present their cases in their own persons before the king, who instantly dispenses justice. The structure of the situation suggests what the men themselves insist upon: that one lies and one tells the truth, that one is a traitor and one a true subject. But even while we are implicitly asked to judge between rival claims, we have no way of knowing what has happened or whom to trust.

In the ensuing scenes, we learn that Bolingbroke and Mowbray are fighting about the murder of Thomas of Woodstock, the uncle of King Richard II. Apparently Bolingbroke knows that Richard secretly ordered Woodstock's death. Since he cannot say so, he picks Richard's agent Mowbray as his target, for Woodstock had been in Mowbray's safekeeping. Meanwhile, Mowbray, likewise unable to blame the true culprit openly, is outraged at being called a traitor when it was his allegiance to Richard that led him to acquiesce in the killing.

This is a far more tangled situation than the simple yes-or-no structure of the appeal for treason or, several scenes later, the "trial by combat" could allow anyone to acknowledge. Moreover, the King's participation in the crime upon which he is supposed to be passing judgment obviously compromises his impartiality. The institution of the appeal for treason is premised on the assumptions that, as Richard himself states emphatically, the king has no part in his subjects' quarrels and that it is in his best interests to have the truth revealed. Here, neither assumption is correct. The ceremonies of royal authority so colorfully staged in the first few scenes turn out to be inconclusive, postponing rather than confronting real sources of discord.

As the play continues, we come to realize that the confusion of the first few scenes, a confusion Shakespeare forces his audience momentarily to share, results from an intractable problem in a system of monarchical government. Since the king's subjects are obliged to obey him, it is not clear how, short of direct divine intervention, his follies or vices may be checked. To admit that subjects have a right to judge or even to remove their king threatens the stability of the realm, since any subject, discontented for any reason, might incite a revolt. But to allow the king to have his own way no matter what opens the way to tyranny.

The proper extent of a monarch's power was a crucial, and unresolved, political issue in sixteenth- and early seventeenth-century England, when first the Tudors and then the Stuarts struggled to extend their traditional prerogatives. A few decades after Shakespeare's death, disagreement about the nature of royal authority would provoke the English Civil War. In the 1590s, when Shakespeare was writing his history plays, the lines of stress upon which the country would eventually fracture were already apparent, even though the disasters to come would not have seemed inevitable.

When Shakespeare wrote about the medieval reign of Richard II, in other words, he saw the conflicts of that reign through the lens of the late sixteenth century. His meticulous re-creation of antiquated judicial processes did not conceal from audiences in his own time the contemporary relevance of the play. In all sixteenth-century texts and perhaps in performance, the lines in which Richard gives up his crown were omitted: many scholars theorize that this episode was considered too inflammatory to print or stage. When the Earl of Essex rebelled against Elizabeth I in 1601, some of his supporters cited Richard's reign as providing a historical precedent for the deposition of a monarch. They paid Shakespeare's company to perform a play about Richard's reign—almost certainly Shakespeare's play—in an attempt to rally supporters to their cause. "I am Richard II," snapped the furious Queen. "Know you not that?"

To acknowledge the contemporary relevance of Richard's reign is not to claim that Shakespeare wrote his play purely as a means of commenting obliquely on the policies of Elizabeth I. Rather, the urgent contemporary task of defining a nation-state led Shakespeare to an extended historical inquiry into the institution of the English monarchy, an inquiry of which *Richard II* is a part. By looking at points at which the normal order of royal succession is challenged, Shakespeare illuminates interesting inconsistencies in Renaissance theories of kingship and political authority. Several years earlier, he had written the three *Henry VI* plays and *Richard III,* which while not originally conceived as a series eventually constituted what critics call the "first tetralogy": a group of plays that together present a continuous chronicle of the long Wars of the Roses in the fifteenth century. Soon after finishing *Richard III,* Shakespeare began writing another group of history plays, the "second tetralogy," which backtrack in time to treat the origins of the conflicts he had already brought to the stage.

As he had for his earlier history plays, Shakespeare turned to Raphael Holinshed's *Chronicles of England, Scotland, and Ireland* (1587). There he found in the reign of Richard II a remote cause of the war to be waged many years hence. Richard II was grandson of Edward III, whose formidable precedent haunts all the plays of the second tetralogy. King Edward had five sons who survived to adulthood, but his eldest, Edward the Black Prince, predeceased him. The Black Prince left a son of his own, however, the future Richard II, to whom the throne descended after Edward III's death. At the time of his accession, Richard was ten years old, and during his adolescence his powerful uncles, the younger brothers of the Black Prince, administered his kingdom on his behalf. After Richard reached young adulthood and began to rule in his own name, he found it difficult to gain the respect of his uncles, experienced middle-aged men who had become accustomed to command. His own rashness and ineffectuality only compounded his troubles. Shakespeare's play opens upon the young Richard, already complicit in the murder of one of his uncles; the remaining uncles, who scorn Richard's maladroit rule but realize they owe allegiance to him; and Richard's cousins Bolingbroke and Northumberland, who are more willing than their elders to act on the recognition of the ruler's weakness.

Early in the play, Richard reacts to Bolingbroke's veiled challenge by exiling him; shortly thereafter, he confiscates Bolingbroke's estate. When, exasperated, Bolingbroke invades England and successfully seizes the crown from his cousin, his action neatly ruptures two traditional sources of royal authority. Unquestionably, Bolingbroke is the more astute tactician, the more effective leader. Richard, however, is equally undoubtedly the rightful heir of Edward III, and as such has been anointed king in a sacred coronation ceremony. Thus

Richardus ii. From John Rastell, *The Pastyme of People* (1529).

"Like perspectives, which, rightly gazed upon, / Show nothing but confusion; / eyed awry, / Distinguish form" (*Richard II* 2.2.18–20). The most famous Renaissance example of such a "perspective" or anamorphic picture is Hans Holbein's *The Ambassadors* (1533); when the painting is viewed from the side ("awry"), the elongated object in the foreground reveals itself to be a skull.

one character has all the advantages when considered from a material and practical point of view, while the other derives his claim to authority from the more abstract principle of divinely sanctioned hereditary right.

Shakespeare imagines the division between the two men not merely as a political issue but as a question of character. A vivid sense of Bolingbroke's personality emerges in his confrontation with Mowbray. Mowbray harps on Bolingbroke's lies, laments the damage Bolingbroke's accusation has done to his reputation, and experiences Bolingbroke's verbal accusation as a physical attack: he is "pierced to the soul with slander's venomed spear" (1.1.171). Bolingbroke, by contrast, trusts not words but physical strength: "What my tongue speaks my right-drawn sword may prove," he stoutly declares (1.1.46). Tellingly, his word "right" conflates his proficiency as a warrior with the uprightness of his cause, suggesting that he does not care to recognize the potential difference. Likewise, Bolingbroke repeatedly speaks of making his words *good*, by which he means backing them up by force. As a corollary, he is suspicious or dismissive of anything that seems merely imaginary, verbal, or abstract. When his father, Gaunt, encourages him to reconcile himself to his exile by renaming it an educational tour or a pleasure junket, Bolingbroke replies:

> O, who can hold a fire in his hand
> By thinking on the frosty Caucasus,
> Or cloy the hungry edge of appetite
> By bare imagination of a feast . . . ?
> (1.3.257–60)

As the play proceeds, this insistence on material facts rather than words or imagination comes to seem entirely characteristic of a man who has no legal claim on the throne, but who takes it because he is able to do so.

Unlike Bolingbroke, Richard is an inept manager of practical affairs. In the first act, most of his powerful kinfolk let him literally get away with murder; but in the second act, it becomes clear that they will not tolerate his infringement of property rights. Medieval kings were expected to cover most of the expenses of government from their own large estates, but to raise additional funds Richard "farms out" the realm—that is, grants the power to tax to private individuals who can confiscate subjects' property virtually as they please, provided the king gets a share of the spoils. Not surprisingly, such legalized theft produces widespread resentment. For the upper aristocracy, the last straw is Richard's seizure of the duchy of Lancaster upon John of Gaunt's death: the encroachment seems to them worse than homicide, because it directly threatens the social structure upon which their status depends. Inherited property distinguishes noblemen from "men of no name": in fact, noble names are derived from property, the lands of Lancaster, Gloucester, York, Northumberland, and so forth. In *Richard II,* both social disruptions and identity crises are marked by a struggle over such titles and the power they signify. Bolingbroke, returning to England, insists on being called "Lancaster," not "Hereford"; Northumberland presumptuously forgets to call Richard "King"; Richard himself laments, upon his deposition, that "I must nothing be . . . I have no name, no title" (4.1.191, 245).

Although technically aristocrats did not own their land outright but held it in trust from the sovereign, by Richard's time Magna Carta protected the right of property holders to pass their lands to their heirs. Only a conviction for treason could forfeit the family claim. Ironically, at the moment Richard commandeers the Lancastrian estates, Bolingbroke is apparently on the verge of invading England with an armed force, so he is actually a traitor and Richard could eventually have appropriated his property in a perfectly legal manner. But Richard's characteristic neglect of proper procedure makes Bolingbroke's return seem a response to dispossession and thus turns the nobility toward the rebel cause.

Richard does not imagine that he must earn the respect of the people he governs, or balance his budget, or follow laws. He does not believe that his authority depends on the consent of the governed or on the effective manipulation of material resources. Whereas Bolingbroke thinks of power as emanating from "below"—from the King's subjects, from the deployment of material resources—Richard thinks of it as descending from "above," from the God whose representative on earth he was born to be. His assertion in 3.2.50–53 is entirely characteristic:

> Not all the water in the rough rude sea
> Can wash the balm from an anointed king.
> The breath of worldly men cannot depose
> The deputy elected by the Lord.

Later in the same scene, deserted by all but a few supporters, he exclaims: "Is not the King's name forty thousand names? / Arm, arm, my name!" (3.2.81–82). What Richard needs now, of course, is not names but soldiers, but he deliberately refuses to acknowledge the difference.

Richard's drastic impracticalities derive from his conviction that the God who put him on the throne is immanent in the created universe and vigilant in defense of His deputy. Richard is not unique in this conviction: the assumption that God intervenes continuously in human affairs in order to guarantee just outcomes underlies the ritual of the trial by combat as it is staged in 1.3. The way spirit informs and controls the material world can render "dead matter" sympathetic to human beings. "This earth shall have a feeling," Richard claims (3.2.24). Thus he is confident that the earth will put toads in the way of traitors, and that angels will rush to save a king in trouble.

Medieval histories are full of such narratives: the ground opens up and swallows an atheist; lightning strikes a perjurer dead.

By Shakespeare's time, the trial by combat had been discredited and the conception of the world to which Richard adheres was beginning to seem obsolete. Some thinkers were increasingly discarding anthropocentric ways of thinking and conceiving of the material world as something alien to human consciousness, ruled by purely physical laws of cause and effect. This change in mentality affected historians, who were subjecting long-accepted myths to critical scrutiny; scientists, who began to place a new value on empirical experimentation; and theologians, who were becoming more skeptical of the continuation of miracles in postbiblical times. Political theorists such as Machiavelli pragmatically insisted on describing political power as it really was exercised, and not as God or moral scruples might dictate that it ought to be exercised. The pragmatic Bolingbroke, then, is associated with a new, effective, but not necessarily moral or satisfying way of thinking about the manipulation of men and matter.

Richard's assumptions about the world and his place in it turn out to be wrong. His naïveté about the relationship of language and power, spirit and matter, leaves him vulnerable to Bolingbroke's assault. Bolingbroke's supplanting of Richard, then, might be seen not merely as a personal or even a political victory, but as the uprooting of one worldview by another. Whether this displacement represents an advance or a deterioration is, however, another question. The second part of the play, in which Bolingbroke emerges victorious, reexamines the nature of the conflict between the two men and the principles they represent.

In a pivotal scene in Act 3, Bolingbroke, Northumberland, and York approach the castle in which Richard has sequestered himself. When Richard finally emerges on the battlements, Bolingbroke exclaims:

> See, see, King Richard doth himself appear,
> As doth the blushing discontented sun
> From out the fiery portal of the east
> When he perceives the envious clouds are bent
> To dim his glory and to stain the track
> Of his bright passage to the occident.
>
> (3.3.61–66)

Bolingbroke is untypically eloquent here, but interestingly, his extended simile works against his own interests. The comparison between king and sun, a traditional figure of speech, implies that the king is both unique and indispensable. Rebels are not rival suns; they are transient clouds that the mighty king will eventually burn away. Even while he mutinies against Richard's misgovernment, Bolingbroke seems unable to escape a conservative conception of monarchy in which rebellion is a form of envy doomed to failure.

Bolingbroke's linguistic slip suggests that it may be easier to amass an army and seize the throne than to put aside one's inherited convictions about the nature of royal authority. Bolingbroke does not have an alternative vocabulary in which to justify his own behavior. Thus, throughout the play, it is hard to be sure whether he is cunningly concealing his true motives or simply incapable of articulating them even to himself. In the opening scenes, although Richard recognizes Bolingbroke's challenge to his authority, Bolingbroke himself seems a bit obtuse about his own purposes, as if his accusation of Mowbray were merely an effect of his sturdy loyalty to Richard. Likewise, it is unclear whether he initially realizes that his return from exile commits him not merely to regaining the Lancastrian estates but to a more thorough attack on Richard's sovereignty. Bolingbroke never appears before us, alone or in company, to ponder his own conduct and motives. In this regard, he differs not only from the obsessively self-reflective Richard but from other Shakespearean usurpers: Richard III, Macbeth, *Hamlet*'s Claudius.

In Act 4, however unable he may be to justify the grounds of his own authority, Bolingbroke—now King Henry IV—astutely recognizes that he must convince his subjects that he is legitimately entitled to the crown. Henry needs, somehow, to transfer to himself that mysterious sense of royal sanctity in which Richard initially places so much confidence and to which Henry has no plausible claim. Henry and his followers thus attempt to paper over his gross procedural breach with procedural punctiliousness. Richard cannot be summarily imprisoned or executed; rather, he must seem voluntarily and publicly to resign his sovereignty to Henry.

Unfortunately for Henry, he is not good at managing such rituals, while Richard is in his element. In 4.1, Richard masterfully seizes the symbolic initiative from the apparent victors. "Now mark me how I will undo myself," he announces (line 193).

> I give this heavy weight from off my head,
> And this unwieldy sceptre from my hand,
> The pride of kingly sway from out my heart.
> With mine own tears I wash away my balm,
> With mine own hands I give away my crown,
> With mine own tongue deny my sacred state,
> With mine own breath release all duteous oaths.
> All pomp and majesty I do forswear.
> My manors, rents, revenues I forgo.
> My acts, decrees, and statutes I deny.
>
> (lines 194–203)

Richard's actions and words here are meant to recall a coronation ceremony, in which the king is invested with the crown and scepter as his insignia of office, anointed with balm as a sign that he is God's chosen, promised the allegiance of his subjects, given formal title to the royal domains. One of the main points of this ceremony is its permanence: it cannot be undone. By referring to this ritual at the moment of his deposition, Richard implies that giving up the crown is an impossible act, a kind of absurdity. Moreover, reversing the ceremonies—taking off the crown rather than putting it on, relinquishing rather than accepting the scepter—suggests a special scandal. In medieval and early modern Europe, as among some fundamentalist religious groups today, reversing beneficent ceremonies supposedly evoked their diabolical opposites. One called up devils by reciting Scripture passages backward, or bound oneself to Satan by performing an inversion of baptismal rites. Richard's enthusiastic self-dramatization of his plight does not quell doubts about the legitimacy of the usurpation, but encourages those doubts. Immediately after Richard departs, his friends begin to conspire on his behalf; and although their plot is eventually crushed, Henry's reign will never be quiet thereafter.

As the play proceeds, the view of politics associated with Bolingbroke, a view that initially seems hardheaded and realistic, begins to seem not very practical after all. An acceptable social order requires more than the brute force Henry deploys so expertly. It requires a common set of ideas and practices, a common language and attitude, a set of rituals—all the immaterial abstractions Henry had originally been inclined to disregard.

Just as Shakespeare, over the course of the play, alters our view of the political dilemma represented by the rebellion, so he manipulates our outlook on its main characters. As soon as Richard has lost his throne, we need no longer evaluate him in terms of his effectiveness as a ruler. Immediately his talents seem more obvious, his faults less reprehensible. Richard's extraordinary poetic and introspective gifts allow him to analyze his own situation with a delicacy and insight of which Bolingbroke is entirely incapable. He is acutely aware of the figure he cuts to the only audience that matters to him, himself; in fact, his self-destructive behavior might be seen as an unconscious quest for the expressive opportunities provided only by misery. Always preoccupied with analogies between kingship and godhead, Richard identifies more and more, as the play

Death of Phaeton. From Antonio Tempesta, *Ovid's "Metamorphoses"* (1606).

continues, with the suffering Christ, consoling himself with the comparison and deriving from it a certain sad grandeur. Obviously Richard's particular strengths are intrinsically connected to his weaknesses, but that does not mean that those strengths are negligible. They are especially hard to ignore in a *play,* in which poetic language, symbolic thought, and the effective deployment of spectacle are central concerns.

Our shifting view of Richard has produced, in both Shakespeare's time and our own, a certain ambiguity as to the play's genre. When Shakespeare's friends and fellow actors compiled his works in the First Folio, they grouped *Richard II* with the history plays—understandably, since it concerns itself with problems of rule and the legitimacy of rulers, is based on historical materials, and inaugurates a series of plays that deals with the reigns of three successive kings. Yet in its earliest printed version the play was called "The Tragedie of Richard II," a title that suggests a focus not on the fate of a nation but on the disastrous career of a fascinating, flawed individual.

Richard's case encourages us to reflect on the way the politics and the values of political life—the dominant concerns of history plays—constrain our evaluation of him. In *Richard II,* Shakespeare uses female characters to suggest the possibility of an alternative perspective on the events he depicts. In the second scene, the Duchess of Gloucester urges Gaunt to revenge Thomas of Woodstock, her husband and his brother. Gaunt refuses: in his view, the subject's duty to his monarch must outweigh his obligation to his kin. Their conversation reminds us that England's political crisis is also a familial disaster, and that construing it as one rather than the other has important consequences.

Throughout the play, the men, like Gaunt, tend to subordinate domestic concerns to civic ones, family bonds to the all-important relationship between king and subject. The women, like the Duchess of Gloucester, do the opposite. Although the historical Richard was married to a ten-year-old queen, Shakespeare makes Isabella a mature young woman and invents touching, wholly nonfactual scenes in which she intuitively senses her husband's trouble, then discovers the usurpation in a garden and suffers through an imposed parting from her husband. The pathos of these scenes derives from the Queen's utter helplessness. She is imagined as Richard's wife, a domestic function, not England's Queen, a public one. All her responses are thus founded on her singleminded loyalty to the marital tie, as sharply distinguished from the bonds of politics. "Banish us both, and send the King with me," she begs Northumberland, when he informs them that she will be exiled and her husband kept under house arrest in England. "That were some love, but little policy," Northumberland replies (5.1.83, 84). The last thing Bolingbroke needs is a legitimate child of Richard's to confuse his claims on the throne even more. But the Queen fails to grasp Northumberland's meaning, because she does not understand "policy"—that is, politics. It is not her sphere.

The difference between civic and domestic domains also appears in the scenes immediately following, which stage a dispute between the Duke and Duchess of York over their son, Aumerle. Here again Shakespeare altered his sources, unhistorically making Aumerle an only child and the Duchess his natural mother. Having discovered that Aumerle is involved in a plot to kill the new Henry IV and reinstate Richard, York feels bound to inform Henry of the treason. He puts what he sees as his civic duty above the ties of blood. The Duchess is outraged. "Wilt thou not hide the trespass of thine own?" she asks. "Have we more sons? Or are we like to have?" (5.2.89–90). For her, the familial relationship takes precedence over the public one.

This dividing of the "public" male role from the "private" female role is hardly a Shakespearean invention. But Shakespeare puts that division of perspective to thematic use in *Richard II*. In 2.2, when Isabella has a presentiment of ruin, Bushy tries to console her in an elaborate speech about perspective glasses and "anamorphic" paintings. These two Renaissance inventions encourage speculation about the difference between the "right" or "centered" way of seeing and an oblique outlook from which shapes look very different. Of course, Isabella's inexplicable presentiment of disaster turns out to be more apt than her male companions' optimism. Perhaps the women's different perspective implies that the history play's focus on traditionally masculine political concerns may exclude whole realms of human experience.

In the fifth act, Richard—weeping, enclosed, suffering, and excluded from authority—finds himself in the position the play has defined as a feminine one. Politically marginalized, he nonetheless dominates the closing moments of the play, first by his powerful soliloquizing and later by his courageous defiance of his murderers. In some respects, the final scenes of *Richard II* recall its opening. What seems to be a simple opposition turns out to be far more complex, as categories of expedience and impracticality, power and weakness, right and wrong mutate and change places. Once again, the apparent conclusion of a conflict merely postpones its resolution. The *Henry IV* plays will stage the aftermath.

KATHARINE EISAMAN MAUS

TEXTUAL NOTE

The first printed version of *Richard II* was a Quarto published in 1597 (Q1). The quality of the text is good, and most scholars have assumed that it was printed either directly from Shakespeare's manuscript or (because the stage directions are very brief) from a transcript of Shakespeare's manuscript not designed to provide the basis for theatrical performance. Two more Quartos, printed in 1598 (Q2 and Q3), mention Shakespeare as the author of the play on their title pages. In 1608, a fourth Quarto appeared (Q4), and in 1615, a fifth (Q5); each Quarto seems based on the one that had appeared before it. However, Q4 was the first to print the "new additions of the parliament scene, and the deposing of King Richard," scenes not present in the earlier Quartos.

The First Folio of 1623 (F) text was probably printed with reference to a promptbook, because it has much more detailed stage directions than the quarto texts. Editors disagree, however, over whether this promptbook text was based on Shakespeare's manuscript or on a corrected copy of Q1 or Q3. F includes a version of the abdication scene that is different, and better, than the one in Q4 and Q5. F omits some lines that are present in Q1, and there are also a number of single-word divergences between the two texts. In cases where only a single line is missing, the deletion may represent a compositor's error, so the Oxford editors have followed Q1. In cases where more substantial passages have been excluded, the editors assume that Shakespeare himself was responsible; these passages are indented in the text.

The most important difference between Q1 and F is F's inclusion of the deposition scene. Some scholars have argued that Elizabeth's censors considered the passage too provocative to stage and insisted that it be deleted; after Elizabeth's death, it was possible to reinstate the offending material. Others argue that Shakespeare revised the play during the first decade of the seventeenth century and wrote the deposition scene at that time.

The Oxford editors have generally based their text on Q1, except for the deposition scene, where they have followed F. They have, however, assimilated many of F's more complete stage directions and many of its single-word variants from Q1, when in the editors' opinion those variants represent Shakespeare's revisions to his own text rather than compositorial corruptions.

SELECTED BIBLIOGRAPHY

Calderwood, James L. "*Richard II* and the Fall of Speech." *Shakespearean Metadrama: The Argument of the Play in "Titus Andronicus," "Love's Labour's Lost," "Romeo and Juliet," and "Richard II."* Minneapolis: University of Minnesota Press, 1971. 149–86. The transfer of power from Richard to Bolingbroke as a version of Shakespeare's move from lyric stylization to a sparer dramatic language.

Doran, Madeline. "Imagery in *Richard II* and *Henry IV.*" *Modern Language Review* 37 (1942): 113–22. Changes in handling metaphor and simile as key to the differences between *Richard II* and *Henry IV, Part 1*.

Gaudet, Paul. "The 'Parasitical Counselors' in Shakespeare's *Richard II*: A Problem in Dramatic Interpretation." *Shakespeare Quarterly* 33 (1982): 142–54. Bushy, Bagot, and Greene: innocent or guilty?

Hamilton, Donna. "The State of Law in *Richard II.*" *Shakespeare Quarterly* 34 (1983): 5–17. The relation between monarchy and law in *Richard II* and in early modern political theory.

Kantorowicz, Ernst H. Chapter 2. *The King's Two Bodies: A Study in Mediaeval Political Theology.* Princeton: Princeton University Press, 1957. 24–41. Theory of kingship in *Richard II*.

Kastan, David. "Proud Majesty Made a Subject: Shakespeare and the Spectacle of Rule." *Shakespeare Quarterly* 37 (1986): 459–75. Theatrical representation destabilizes kingship in *Richard II*.

McMillin, Scott. "*Richard II*: Eyes of Sorrow, Eyes of Desire." *Shakespeare Quarterly* 35 (1984): 40–52. An impulse to self-expressiveness is at odds with the exercise of political power in *Richard II*.

Moore, Jeanie Grant. "Queen of Sorrow, King of Grief: Reflections and Perspectives in *Richard II.*" *In Another Country: Feminist Perspectives on Renaissance Drama.* Ed. Dorothea Kehler and Susan Baker. Metuchen, N.J.: Scarecrow Press, 1991. 19–35. Special attention to imagery of mirrors and anamorphic pictures.

Saccio, Peter. *Shakespeare's English Kings: History, Chronicle, and Drama.* 2nd ed. New York: Oxford University Press, 2000. 17–35. Succinct account of the historical background to Shakespeare's play.

Tillyard, E. M. W. *Shakespeare's History Plays.* London: Chatto & Windus, 1944. 244–63. *Richard II* shows the transition from the medieval to the modern world.

Zitner, Sheldon. "Aumerle's Conspiracy." *Studies in English Literature* 14 (1974): 238–57. The importance of the Aumerle scenes for the end of *Richard II.*

Film

King Richard the Second. 1978. Dir. David Giles, UK. 158 mins. In this BBC-TV production, Derek Jacobi as an effeminate Richard II confronts Jon Finch as the calculating Bolingbroke. John Gielgud is a notable John of Gaunt.

The Tragedy of King Richard the Second

THE PERSONS OF THE PLAY

KING RICHARD II
The QUEEN, his wife
JOHN OF GAUNT, Duke of Lancaster, Richard's uncle
Harry BOLINGBROKE, Duke of Hereford, John of Gaunt's son,
    later KING HENRY IV
DUCHESS OF GLOUCESTER, widow of Gaunt's and York's brother
Duke of YORK, King Richard's uncle
DUCHESS OF YORK
Duke of AUMERLE, their son
Thomas MOWBRAY, Duke of Norfolk
GREEN
BAGOT } followers of King Richard
BUSHY
Percy, Earl of NORTHUMBERLAND
HARRY PERCY, his son
Lord ROSS } of Bolingbroke's party
Lord WILLOUGHBY
Earl of SALISBURY
BISHOP OF CARLISLE } of King Richard's party
Sir Stephen SCROPE
Lord BERKELEY
Lord FITZWALTER
Duke of SURREY
ABBOT OF WESTMINSTER
Sir Piers EXTON
LORD MARSHAL
HERALDS
CAPTAIN of the Welsh army
LADIES attending the Queen
GARDENER
Gardener's MEN
Exton's MEN
KEEPER of the prison at Pomfret
GROOM of King Richard's stable
Lords, soldiers, attendants

1.1

Enter KING RICHARD, JOHN OF GAUNT, *with* [*the* LORD
MARSHAL], *other nobles, and attendants*

KING RICHARD   Old John of Gaunt,[1] time-honoured Lancaster,
    Hast thou according to thy oath and bond
    Brought hither Henry Hereford, thy bold son,
    Here to make good the boist'rous late appeal,°   *violent recent accusation*

1.1. Location: Windsor Castle.
1. Named after his birthplace, Ghent (in Flanders); his

title was Duke of Lancaster. He was fifty-eight years
old.

5 Which then our leisure² would not let us hear,
Against the Duke of Norfolk, Thomas Mowbray?
JOHN OF GAUNT I have, my liege.
KING RICHARD Tell me moreover, hast thou sounded° him   *inquired of*
If he appeal the Duke on ancient malice³
10 Or worthily, as a good subject should,
On some known ground of treachery in him?
JOHN OF GAUNT As near as I could sift° him on that argument,° *discover from / topic*
On some apparent° danger seen in him   *manifest*
Aimed at your highness, no inveterate malice.
KING RICHARD Then call them to our presence.

         [*Exit one or more*]
15   Face to face
And frowning brow to brow, ourselves will hear
The accuser and the accusèd freely speak.
High-stomached° are they both and full of ire;   *Haughty*
In rage, deaf as the sea, hasty as fire.

   Enter BOLINGBROKE [*Duke of Hereford*], *and* MOWBRAY
   [*Duke of Norfolk*]
20 BOLINGBROKE Many years of happy days befall
My gracious sovereign, my most loving liege!
MOWBRAY Each day still better others' happiness,⁴
Until the heavens, envying earth's good hap,°   *fortune*
Add an immortal title to your crown!
25 KING RICHARD We thank you both. Yet one but flatters us,
As well appeareth by the cause you come,
Namely, to appeal each other of high treason.
Cousin of Hereford, what dost thou object°   *charge*
Against the Duke of Norfolk, Thomas Mowbray?
30 BOLINGBROKE First—heaven be the record to my speech—
In the devotion of a subject's love,
Tend'ring° the precious safety of my Prince,   *Having care for*
And free from other misbegotten hate,
Come I appellant° to this princely presence.   *as accuser*
35 Now, Thomas Mowbray, do I turn to thee;
And mark my greeting° well, for what I speak   *address*
My body shall make good upon this earth,
Or my divine° soul answer it in heaven.   *Immortal*
Thou art a traitor and a miscreant,
40 Too good° to be so, and too bad to live,   *wellborn*
Since the more fair and crystal is the sky,
The uglier seem the clouds that in it fly.
Once more, the more to aggravate the note,°   *emphasize the reproach*
With a foul traitor's name stuff I thy throat,
45 And wish, so please my sovereign, ere I move
What my tongue speaks my right-drawn sword may prove.
MOWBRAY Let not my cold words here accuse my zeal.°   *cast doubt on my loyalty*
'Tis not the trial of a woman's war,
The bitter clamour of two eager° tongues,   *sharp*
50 Can arbitrate⁵ this cause betwixt us twain.
The blood is hot that must be cooled for this.

2. That is, lack of leisure. Richard uses the royal "we." 4. May each day be better than the last.
3. Out of long-standing enmity. 5. Judge (without implying compromise).

Yet can I not of such tame patience boast
As to be hushed and naught at all to say.
First, the fair reverence of your highness curbs me
55 From giving reins and spurs to my free speech,
Which else would post° until it had returned   *ride fast*
These terms of treason doubled down his throat.
Setting aside his high blood's royalty,[6]
And let him be° no kinsman to my liege,   *And as if he were*
60 I do defy him, and I spit at him,
Call him a slanderous coward and a villain;
Which to maintain I would allow him odds,
And meet him, were I tied° to run afoot   *obliged*
Even to the frozen ridges of the Alps,
65 Or any other ground inhabitable,
Wherever Englishman durst set his foot.
Meantime let this defend my loyalty:
By all my hopes, most falsely doth he lie.

BOLINGBROKE [*throwing down his gage*][7] Pale trembling coward,
      there I throw my gage,
70 Disclaiming here the kindred of[8] the King,
And lay aside my high blood's royalty,
Which fear, not reverence, makes thee to except.°   *set aside*
If guilty dread have left thee so much strength
As to take up mine honour's pawn,° then stoop.   *(the gage)*
75 By that, and all the rites of knighthood else,
Will I make good against thee, arm to arm,
What I have spoke or thou canst worse devise.

MOWBRAY [*taking up the gage*]   I take it up,[9] and by that sword I swear
Which gently laid my knighthood on my shoulder,
80 I'll answer thee in any fair degree°   *honorable manner*
Or chivalrous design of knightly trial;
And when I mount, alive may I not light°   *dismount*
If I be traitor or unjustly fight!

KING RICHARD [*to* BOLINGBROKE]   What doth our cousin lay to
      Mowbray's charge?
85 It must be great that can inherit us°   *make us have*
So much as of a thought of ill in him.

BOLINGBROKE   Look what I speak, my life shall prove it true:
That Mowbray hath received eight thousand nobles°   *gold coins*
In name of lendings° for your highness' soldiers,   *As advances on pay*
90 The which he hath detained for lewd employments,°   *improper uses*
Like a false traitor and injurious villain.
Besides I say, and will in battle prove,
Or° here or elsewhere, to the furthest verge°   *Either / horizon*
That ever was surveyed by English eye,
95 That all the treasons for these eighteen years[1]
Complotted° and contrivèd in this land   *Plotted*
Fetch° from false Mowbray their first head° and spring.   *Derive / source*
Further I say, and further will maintain
Upon his bad life, to make all this good,

---

6. Bolingbroke as well as Richard was a grandson of
Edward III.
7. Pledge to combat—probably a glove.
8. The privilege of kinship with.
9. Thereby accepting the challenge.
1. Since the Peasants' Revolt of 1381.

100	That he did plot the Duke of Gloucester's death,[2]
	Suggest° his soon-believing° adversaries,
	And consequently,° like a traitor-coward,
	Sluiced° out his innocent soul through streams of blood;
	Which blood, like sacrificing Abel's,[3] cries
105	Even from the tongueless caverns of the earth

Incite / credulous
subsequently
Let flow

To me for justice and rough chastisement.
And, by the glorious worth of my descent,
This arm shall do it or this life be spent.
KING RICHARD　How high a pitch[4] his resolution soars!
110　Thomas of Norfolk, what sayst thou to this?
MOWBRAY　O, let my sovereign turn away his face,
And bid his ears a little while be deaf,
Till I have told this slander of his blood°　　　*disgrace to his ancestry*
How God and good men hate so foul a liar!
115　KING RICHARD　Mowbray, impartial are our eyes and ears.
Were he my brother, nay, my kingdom's heir,
As he is but my father's brother's son,
Now by my sceptre's awe I make a vow
Such neighbour-nearness to our sacred blood
120　Should nothing privilege him, nor partialize°　　　*bias*
The unstooping firmness of my upright soul.
He is our subject, Mowbray; so art thou.
Free speech and fearless I to thee allow.
MOWBRAY　Then, Bolingbroke, as low as to thy heart
125　Through the false passage of thy throat thou liest!
Three parts of that receipt° I had for Calais　　　*money received*
Disbursed I duly to his highness' soldiers.
The other part reserved I by consent,
For that my sovereign liege was in my debt
130　Upon remainder of a dear account[5]
Since last I went to France to fetch his queen.
Now swallow down that lie. For Gloucester's death,
I slew him not, but to my own disgrace
Neglected my sworn duty in that case.[6]
135　For you, my noble lord of Lancaster,
The honourable father to my foe,
Once did I lay an ambush for your life,
A trespass that doth vex my grievèd soul;
But ere I last received the Sacrament
140　I did confess it, and exactly° begged　　　*expressly*
Your grace's pardon, and I hope I had it.
This is my fault. As for the rest appealed,°　　　*accused*
It issues from the rancour of a villain,
A recreant° and most degenerate° traitor,　　　*faithless / cowardly*
145　Which in myself° I boldly will defend,　　　*my own person*
　　　[*He throws down his gage*]
And interchangeably° hurl down my gage　　　*reciprocally*

Upon this overweening traitor's foot,
To prove myself a loyal gentleman
Even in the best blood chambered° in his bosom;   *enclosed*
150   In haste whereof° most heartily I pray   *To hasten which*
Your highness to assign our trial day.
[BOLINGBROKE *takes up the gage*]
KING RICHARD   Wrath-kindled gentlemen, be ruled by me.
Let's purge this choler without letting blood.[7]
This we prescribe, though no physician:
155   Deep malice[8] makes too deep incision;
Forget, forgive, conclude,° and be agreed;   *come to terms*
Our doctors say this is no time to bleed.
Good uncle, let this end where it begun.
We'll calm the Duke of Norfolk, you your son.
160   JOHN OF GAUNT   To be a make-peace shall become my age.
Throw down, my son, the Duke of Norfolk's gage.[9]
KING RICHARD   And, Norfolk, throw down his.
JOHN OF GAUNT   When, Harry, when?
Obedience bids I should not bid again.
KING RICHARD   Norfolk, throw down! We bid; there is no boot.°   *help for it*
165   MOWBRAY [*kneeling*]   Myself I throw, dread sovereign, at thy foot.
My life thou shalt command, but not my shame,
The one my duty owes, but my fair name,
Despite of death that lives upon my grave,
To dark dishonour's use thou shalt not have.
170   I am disgraced, impeached, and baffled[1] here,
Pierced to the soul with slander's venomed spear,
The which no balm can cure but his heart blood
Which breathed° this poison.   *uttered*
KING RICHARD   Rage must be withstood.
Give me his gage. Lions make leopards tame.[2]
175   MOWBRAY [*standing*]   Yea, but not change his spots.[3] Take but my shame,
And I resign my gage. My dear dear lord,
The purest treasure mortal times° afford   *earthly lives*
Is spotless reputation; that away,
Men are but gilded loam, or painted clay.
180   A jewel in a ten-times barred-up chest
Is a bold spirit in a loyal breast.
Mine honour is my life. Both grow in one.°   *united*
Take honour from me, and my life is done.
Then, dear my liege, mine honour let me try.°   *put to the test*
185   In that I live, and for that will I die.
KING RICHARD   Cousin, throw down your gage. Do you begin.
BOLINGBROKE   O God defend my soul from such deep sin!
Shall I seem crest-fallen in my father's sight?
Or with pale beggar-fear impeach my height°   *disgrace my rank*
190   Before this out-dared dastard?° Ere my tongue   *coward*
Shall wound my honour with such feeble wrong,
Or sound so base a parle,° my teeth shall tear   *trumpet call for a truce*
The slavish motive° of recanting fear,   *instrument (the tongue)*

---

7. Let's expel the bile (thought to be the physiological cause of anger) without bloodletting (in combat; as a medical remedy).
8. Enmity; virulence (of a disease).
9. As a gesture of reconciliation.

1. Publicly stripped of knighthood (a chivalric term).
2. Lions were the King's emblem; leopards were Mowbray's. Heraldic banners are likely to be displayed onstage in this scene.
3. Leopard spots; stains of reproach.

And spit it bleeding in his° high disgrace   *its*
195   Where shame doth harbour, even in Mowbray's face.

Exit [JOHN OF] GAUNT

KING RICHARD   We were not born to sue, but to command;
Which since we cannot do to make you friends,
Be ready, as your lives shall answer it,
At Coventry upon Saint Lambert's day.°   *September 17*
200   There shall your swords and lances arbitrate
The swelling difference of your settled hate.
Since we cannot atone° you, we shall see   *reconcile*
Justice design the victor's chivalry.⁴
Lord Marshal, command our officers-at-arms
205   Be ready to direct these home alarms.°   *Exeunt*   *domestic disturbances*

1.2

Enter JOHN OF GAUNT [*Duke of Lancaster*], *with*
DUCHESS OF GLOUCESTER

JOHN OF GAUNT   Alas, the part I had in Gloucester's blood¹
Doth more solicit me than your exclaims°   *exclamations*
To stir against the butchers of his life.
But since correction lieth in² those hands
5   Which made the fault that we cannot correct,
Put we our quarrel to the will of heaven,
Who, when they see the hours ripe on earth,
Will rain hot vengeance on offenders' heads.
DUCHESS OF GLOUCESTER   Finds brotherhood in thee no sharper spur?
10   Hath love in thy old blood no living fire?
Edward's° seven sons, whereof thyself art one,   *Edward III's*
Were as seven vials of his sacred blood,
Or seven fair branches springing from one root.
Some of those seven are dried by nature's course,
15   Some of those branches by the destinies cut;
But Thomas, my dear lord, my life, my Gloucester,
One vial full of Edward's sacred blood,
One flourishing branch of his most royal root,
Is cracked, and all the precious liquor spilt;
20   Is hacked down, and his summer leaves all faded
By envy's° hand and murder's bloody axe.   *hatred's*
Ah, Gaunt, his blood was thine! That bed, that womb,
That mettle,° that self° mould that fashioned thee,   *substance / same*
Made him a man; and though thou liv'st and breathest,
25   Yet art thou slain in him. Thou dost consent
In some large measure to thy father's death
In that thou seest thy wretched brother die,
Who was the model of thy father's life.
Call it not patience, Gaunt, it is despair.
30   In suff'ring thus thy brother to be slaughtered
Thou show'st the naked° pathway to thy life,   *defenseless; obvious*
Teaching stern murder how to butcher thee.
That which in mean° men we entitle patience   *common*
Is pale cold cowardice in noble breasts.

---

4. Indicate the victor in knightly combat.
1.2 Location: John of Gaunt's house.
1. Thomas of Woodstock, Duke of Gloucester, was

Gaunt's younger brother.
2. Since punishment depends on (Gaunt blames
Richard for Woodstock's death).

35 What shall I say? To safeguard thine own life
The best way is to venge° my Gloucester's death.　　　　*avenge*
JOHN OF GAUNT　God's is the quarrel; for God's substitute,
His deputy anointed in his sight,
Hath caused his death; the which if wrongfully,
40 Let heaven revenge, for I may never lift
An angry arm against his minister.°　　　　*agent*
DUCHESS OF GLOUCESTER　Where then, alas, may I complain myself?
JOHN OF GAUNT　To God, the widow's champion and defence.
DUCHESS OF GLOUCESTER　Why then, I will. Farewell, old Gaunt.
45 Thou goest to Coventry, there to behold
Our cousin° Hereford and fell° Mowbray fight.　　　*Kinsman / ruthless*
O, set my husband's wrongs on Hereford's spear,
That it may enter butcher Mowbray's breast!
Or if misfortune miss the first career,³
50 Be Mowbray's sins so heavy in his bosom
That they may break his foaming courser's back
And throw the rider headlong in the lists,
A caitiff,° recreant° to my cousin Hereford!　　　*A wretch / yielding*
Farewell, old Gaunt. Thy sometimes° brother's wife　*former*
55 With her companion, grief, must end her life.
JOHN OF GAUNT　Sister, farewell. I must to Coventry.
As much good stay with thee as go with me.
DUCHESS OF GLOUCESTER　Yet one word more. Grief boundeth⁴
　　　where it falls,
Not with the empty hollowness, but weight.⁵
60 I take my leave before I have begun,
For sorrow ends not when it seemeth done.
Commend me to thy brother, Edmund York.
Lo, this is all.—Nay, yet depart not so!
Though this be all, do not so quickly go.
65 I shall remember more. Bid him—ah, what?—
With all good speed at Pleshey⁶ visit me.
Alack, and what shall good old York there see
But empty lodgings° and unfurnished walls,　　　*rooms*
Unpeopled offices,° untrodden stones,　　　*servants' quarters*
70 And what hear there for welcome but my groans?
Therefore commend me; let him not come there
To seek out sorrow that dwells everywhere.
Desolate, desolate will I hence and die.
The last leave of thee takes my weeping eye. *Exeunt [severally]°*　*separately*

1.3

*Enter LORD MARSHAL [with officers setting out chairs],
and Duke [of] AUMERLE*

LORD MARSHAL　My lord Aumerle, is Harry Hereford armed?
AUMERLE　Yea, at all points,° and longs to enter in.　　*completely*
LORD MARSHAL　The Duke of Norfolk, sprightfully° and bold,　*spiritedly*
Stays° but the summons of the appellant's° trumpet.　*Awaits / accuser's*
5 AUMERLE　Why then, the champions are prepared, and stay
For nothing but his majesty's approach.

3. If (Mowbray's) downfall fail to occur at the first encounter.
4. Rebounds (causing further sound; the Duchess apologizes for continuing to speak).
5. Not because it is hollow, like a bouncing ball, but because it is heavy.
6. Gloucester's house in Essex.
1.3 Location: The lists (tournament arena) at Coventry.

The trumpets sound, and KING [RICHARD] *enters with*
[JOHN OF] GAUNT, BUSHY, BAGOT, GREEN, *and other*
nobles. When they are set, enter MOWBRAY *Duke of Nor-*
folk, defendant, in arms, and a HERALD [*to Mowbray*]

KING RICHARD   Marshal, demand of yonder champion
The cause of his arrival here in arms.
Ask him his name, and orderly° proceed   *according to the rules*
10   To swear him in the justice of his cause.
LORD MARSHAL [*to* MOWBRAY]   In God's name and the King's,
say who thou art,
And why thou com'st thus knightly clad in arms,
Against what man thou com'st, and what thy quarrel.
Speak truly on thy knighthood and thy oath,
15   As so defend thee heaven and thy valour!
MOWBRAY   My name is Thomas Mowbray, Duke of Norfolk,
Who hither come engagèd by my oath—
Which God defend° a knight should violate—   *forbid*
Both to defend my loyalty and truth
20   To God, my king, and my succeeding issue,
Against the Duke of Hereford that appeals me;
And by the grace of God and this mine arm
To prove him, in defending of myself,
A traitor to my God, my king, and me.
25   And as I truly fight, defend me heaven!
[*He sits.*]
The trumpets sound. Enter [BOLINGBROKE] *Duke of*
Hereford, appellant, in armour, and HERALD
KING RICHARD   Marshal, ask yonder knight in arms
Both who he is and why he cometh hither
Thus plated in habiliments of war;[1]
And formally, according to our law,
30   Depose° him in the justice of his cause.   *Take testimony from*
LORD MARSHAL [*to* BOLINGBROKE]   What is thy name? And
wherefore com'st thou hither
Before King Richard in his royal lists?
Against whom comest thou? And what's thy quarrel?
Speak like a true knight, so defend thee heaven!
35   BOLINGBROKE   Harry of Hereford, Lancaster, and Derby
Am I, who ready here do stand in arms
To prove by God's grace and my body's valour
In lists on Thomas Mowbray, Duke of Norfolk,
That he is a traitor foul and dangerous
40   To God of heaven, King Richard, and to me.
And as I truly fight, defend me heaven!
[*He sits*]
LORD MARSHAL   On pain of death, no person be so bold
Or daring-hardy as to touch the lists
Except the Marshal and such officers
45   Appointed to direct these fair designs.°   *procedures*
BOLINGBROKE [*standing*]   Lord Marshal, let me kiss my sovereign's hand
And bow my knee before his majesty,
For Mowbray and myself are like two men
That vow a long and weary pilgrimage;

1. Wearing plated battle armor.

50   Then let us take a ceremonious leave
         And loving farewell of our several° friends.   *respective*
     LORD MARSHAL [*to* KING RICHARD]   The appellant in all duty
         greets your highness,
         And craves to kiss your hand and take his leave.
     KING RICHARD   We will descend and fold him in our arms.
         [*He descends from his seat and embraces* BOLINGBROKE]
55   Cousin of Hereford, as° thy cause is just,   *insofar as*
     So be thy fortune in this royal fight.
     Farewell, my blood, which if today thou shed,
     Lament we may, but not revenge thee dead.
     BOLINGBROKE   O, let no noble eye profane° a tear   *misuse*
60   For me if I be gored with Mowbray's spear.
     As confident as is the falcon's flight
     Against a bird do I with Mowbray fight.
     [*To the* LORD MARSHAL] My loving lord, I take my leave of you;
     [*To* AUMERLE] Of you, my noble cousin, Lord Aumerle;
65   Not sick, although I have to do with death,
     But lusty,° young, and cheerly drawing breath.   *vigorous*
     Lo, as at English feasts, so I regreet°   *greet*
     The daintiest² last, to make the end most sweet.
     [*To* GAUNT, *kneeling*] O thou, the earthly author of my blood,
70   Whose youthful spirit in me regenerate°   *reborn*
     Doth with a two-fold vigour lift me up
     To reach at victory above my head,
     Add proof° unto mine armour with thy prayers,   *invulnerability*
     And with thy blessings steel° my lance's point,   *harden*
75   That it may enter Mowbray's waxen° coat   *(that is, soft)*
     And furbish new the name of John a Gaunt
     Even in the lusty haviour° of his son.   *conduct*
     JOHN OF GAUNT   God in thy good cause make thee prosperous!
     Be swift like lightning in the execution,
80   And let thy blows, doubly redoublèd,
     Fall like amazing° thunder on the casque°   *stupefying / helmet*
     Of thy adverse pernicious enemy.
     Rouse up thy youthful blood, be valiant, and live.
     BOLINGBROKE [*standing*]   Mine innocence and Saint George
         to thrive!
85   MOWBRAY [*standing*]   However God or fortune cast my lot,
     There lives or dies, true to King Richard's throne,
     A loyal, just, and upright gentleman.
     Never did captive with a freer heart
     Cast off his chains of bondage and embrace
90   His golden uncontrolled enfranchisement°   *unrestrained liberation*
     More than my dancing soul doth celebrate
     This feast of battle with mine adversary.
     Most mighty liege, and my companion peers,
     Take from my mouth the wish of happy years.
95   As gentle and as jocund as to jest°   *take part in revels*
     Go I to fight. Truth hath a quiet breast.
     KING RICHARD   Farewell, my lord. Securely° I espy   *Confidently*
     Virtue with valour couchèd³ in thine eye.—
     Order the trial, Marshal, and begin.

---

2. Finest thing, like a dessert.   3. Lodged; aimed in readiness (like a lance).

100 LORD MARSHAL   Harry of Hereford, Lancaster, and Derby,
Receive thy lance; and God defend the right!
[*An officer bears a lance to* BOLINGBROKE]
BOLINGBROKE   Strong as a tower in hope, I cry 'Amen!'°   *from Psalm 61:3*
LORD MARSHAL [*to an officer*]   Go bear this lance to Thomas,
Duke of Norfolk.
[*An officer bears a lance to* MOWBRAY]
FIRST HERALD   Harry of Hereford, Lancaster, and Derby
105 Stands here for God, his sovereign, and himself,
On pain to be found false and recreant,
To prove the Duke of Norfolk, Thomas Mowbray,
A traitor to his God, his king, and him,
And dares him to set forward to the fight.
110 SECOND HERALD   Here standeth Thomas Mowbray, Duke of Norfolk,
On pain to be found false and recreant,
Both to defend himself and to approve°   *prove*
Henry of Hereford, Lancaster, and Derby
To God his sovereign and to him disloyal,
115 Courageously and with a free desire
Attending but the signal to begin.
LORD MARSHAL   Sound trumpets, and set forward combatants!
[*A charge is sounded.*]
[KING RICHARD *throws down his warder*]°   *staff*
Stay, the King hath thrown his warder down.
KING RICHARD   Let them lay by their helmets and their spears,
120 And both return back to their chairs again.
[BOLINGBROKE *and* MOWBRAY *disarm and sit*]
[*To the nobles*] Withdraw with us, and let the trumpets sound
While we return° these dukes what we decree.   *Until we deliver to*
A long flourish° [*during which* KING RICHARD *and his*   *extended trumpet call*
nobles withdraw and hold council, then come forward.
KING RICHARD *addresses* BOLINGBROKE *and* MOWBRAY]
Draw near, and list what with our council we have done.
For that° our kingdom's earth should not be soiled   *Because*
125 With that dear blood which it hath fosterèd,
And for° our eyes do hate the dire aspect°   *because / spectacle*
Of civil wounds ploughed up with neighbours' swords,⁴
127.1   *And for we think the eagle-wingèd pride*
Of sky-aspiring and ambitious thoughts
With rival-hating envy set on you°   *malice set you on*
To wake our peace, which in our country's cradle
127.5   *Draws the sweet infant breath of gentle sleep,*
Which, so roused up with boist'rous untuned drums,
With harsh-resounding trumpets' dreadful bray,
130 And grating shock of wrathful iron arms,
Might from our quiet confines fright fair peace
And make us wade even in our kindred's blood,
Therefore we banish you our territories.
You, cousin Hereford, upon pain° of life,   *loss*
135 Till twice five summers have enriched our fields
Shall not regreet° our fair dominions,   *greet again*
But tread the stranger° paths of banishment.   *foreign*

---

4. The following indented passage (lines 127.1–127.5) appears in Q1 but not in F. Shakespeare probably deleted it as part of his limited revisions to the text.

BOLINGBROKE   Your will be done. This must my comfort be:
That sun that warms you here shall shine on me,
140   And those his golden beams to you here lent
Shall point on me and gild my banishment.
KING RICHARD   Norfolk, for thee remains a heavier doom,°   *sentence*
Which I with some unwillingness pronounce.
The sly° slow hours shall not determinate°   *stealthy / bring to an end*
145   The dateless limit° of thy dear° exile.   *limitless period / grievous*
The hopeless word of 'never to return'
Breathe I against thee, upon pain of life.
MOWBRAY   A heavy sentence, my most sovereign liege,
And all unlooked-for from your highness' mouth.
150   A dearer merit,° not so deep a maim°   *better reward / an injury*
As to be cast forth in the common air,
Have I deservèd at your highness' hands.
The language I have learnt these forty years,
My native English, now I must forgo,
155   And now my tongue's use is to me no more
Than an unstringèd viol° or a harp,   *six-stringed instrument*
Or like a cunning° instrument cased up,   *skillfully made*
Or, being open, put into his hands
That knows no touch to tune the harmony.
160   Within my mouth you have enjailed my tongue,
Doubly portcullised° with my teeth and lips,   *Shut in by an iron gate*
And dull unfeeling barren ignorance
Is made my jailer to attend on me.
I am too old to fawn upon a nurse,
165   Too far in years to be a pupil now.
What is thy sentence then but speechless death,
Which robs my tongue from breathing native breath?
KING RICHARD   It boots° thee not to be compassionate.°   *helps / sorrowful*
After our sentence, plaining° comes too late.   *lamenting*
170   MOWBRAY   Then thus I turn me from my country's light,
To dwell in solemn shades of endless night.
KING RICHARD   Return again, and take an oath with thee.
[*To both*] Lay on our royal sword your banished hands.
Swear by the duty that you owe to God—
175   Our part therein⁵ we banish with yourselves—
To keep the oath that we administer.
You never shall, so help you truth and God,
Embrace each other's love in banishment,
Nor never look upon each other's face,
180   Nor never write, regreet, nor reconcile
This low'ring tempest of your home-bred hate,
Nor never by advisèd° purpose meet   *deliberated*
To plot, contrive, or complot any ill
'Gainst us, our state, our subjects, or our land.
BOLINGBROKE   I swear.
185   MOWBRAY   And I, to keep all this.
BOLINGBROKE   Norfolk, so far as to mine enemy
By this time, had the King permitted us,
One of our souls had wandered in the air,

5. Your allegiance to me as God's deputy.

Banished this frail sepulchre of our flesh,
190 As now our flesh is banished from this land.
Confess thy treasons ere thou fly the realm.
Since thou hast far to go, bear not along
The clogging° burden of a guilty soul.   *encumbering*
MOWBRAY   No, Bolingbroke, if ever I were traitor,
195 My name be blotted from the book of life,°   *eternal life*
And I from heaven banished as from hence.
But what thou art, God, thou, and I do know,
And all too soon I fear the King shall rue.
Farewell, my liege. Now no way can I stray:°   *lose my way*
200 Save back to England, all the world's my way.   *Exit*
KING RICHARD   Uncle, even in the glasses° of thine eyes   *windows*
I see thy grievèd heart. Thy sad aspect°   *appearance*
Hath from the number of his banished years
Plucked four away. [*To* BOLINGBROKE] Six frozen winters spent,
205 Return with welcome home from banishment.
BOLINGBROKE   How long a time lies in one little word!
Four lagging winters and four wanton° springs   *luxuriant*
End in a word: such is the breath of kings.
JOHN OF GAUNT   I thank my liege that in regard of me
210 He shortens four years of my son's exile.
But little vantage° shall I reap thereby,   *profit*
For ere the six years that he hath to spend
Can change their moons and bring their times about,
My oil-dried lamp and time-bewasted° light   *extinguished by time*
215 Shall be extinct with age and endless night.
My inch of taper will be burnt and done,
And blindfold[6] death not let me see my son.
KING RICHARD   Why, uncle, thou hast many years to live.
JOHN OF GAUNT   But not a minute, King, that thou canst give.
220 Shorten my days thou canst with sudden sorrow,
And pluck nights from me, but not lend a morrow.
Thou canst help time to furrow me with age,
But stop no wrinkle in his pilgrimage.
Thy word is current° with him for my death,   *valid*
225 But dead, thy kingdom cannot buy my breath.
KING RICHARD   Thy son is banished upon good advice,
Whereto thy tongue a party verdict[7] gave.
Why at our justice seem'st thou then to lour?°   *frown*
JOHN OF GAUNT   Things sweet to taste prove in digestion sour.
230 You urged me as a judge, but I had rather
You would have bid me argue like a father.
Alas, I looked when° some of you should say   *I expected that*
I was too strict to make mine own away,
But you gave leave to my unwilling tongue
235 Against my will to do myself this wrong.[8]
235.1   *O, had't been a stranger, not my child,*
            To smooth° his fault I should have been more mild.   *To gloss over*
            A partial slander° sought I to avoid,   *A suspicion of partiality*
            And in the sentence my own life destroyed.

---

6. Because death's emblem is a hooded figure or an
eyeless skull, and because the dead cannot see.
7. A share in the joint verdict.

8. The following indented passage (lines 235.1–235.4)
appears only in Q1.

KING RICHARD   Cousin, farewell; and uncle, bid him so.
Six years we banish him, and he shall go.
      Flourish. Exeunt [all but AUMERLE, *the* LORD MARSHAL,
      JOHN OF GAUNT, *and* BOLINGBROKE]
AUMERLE [*to* BOLINGBROKE]   Cousin, farewell. What presence
      must not know,[9]
From where you do remain° let paper show.   [*Exit*]   *stay*
LORD MARSHAL [*to* BOLINGBROKE]   My lord, no leave take I, for
240   I will ride
As far as land will let me by your side.
JOHN OF GAUNT [*to* BOLINGBROKE]   O, to what purpose dost
      thou hoard thy words,
That thou return'st no greeting to thy friends?
BOLINGBROKE   I have too few to take my leave of you,
245 When the tongue's office° should be prodigal   *function*
To breathe the abundant dolour of the heart.
JOHN OF GAUNT   Thy grief is but thy absence for a time.
BOLINGBROKE   Joy absent, grief is present for that time.
JOHN OF GAUNT   What is six winters? They are quickly gone.
250 BOLINGBROKE   To men in joy, but grief makes one hour ten.
JOHN OF GAUNT   Call it a travel that thou tak'st for pleasure.
BOLINGBROKE   My heart will sigh when I miscall it so,
Which finds it an enforcèd pilgrimage.
JOHN OF GAUNT   The sullen passage of thy weary steps
255 Esteem as foil[1] wherein thou art to set
The precious jewel of thy home return.[2]
256.1   BOLINGBROKE   *Nay, rather every tedious stride I make*
      Will but remember° what a deal° of world   *remind me / an extent*
      I wander from the jewels that I love.
      Must I not serve a long apprenticehood
256.5   *To foreign passages, and in the end,*
      Having my freedom, boast of nothing else
      But that I was a journeyman[3] to grief?
    JOHN OF GAUNT   *All places that the eye of heaven° visits* *sun; God's presence*
      Are to a wise man ports and happy havens.
256.10   *Teach thy necessity to reason thus;*
      There is no virtue like necessity.
      Think not the King did banish thee,
      But thou the King. Woe doth the heavier sit
      Where it perceives it is but faintly° borne.   *faintheartedly*
256.15   *Go, say I sent thee forth to purchase° honour,*   *acquire*
      And not the King exiled thee; or suppose
      Devouring pestilence hangs in our air
      And thou art flying to a fresher clime.
      Look what° thy soul holds dear, imagine it   *Whatever*
256.20   *To lie that way thou goest, not whence thou com'st.*
      Suppose the singing birds musicians,
      The grass whereon thou tread'st the presence strewed,[4]
      The flowers fair ladies, and thy steps no more
      Than a delightful measure° or a dance;   *a stately dance*

---

9. What you cannot tell me personally because of your absence.
1. Thin metal against which jewels were set to enhance their luster.

2. The following indented passage (lines 256.1–256.26) appears only in Q1.
3. Person who has finished an apprenticeship.
4. The royal presence chamber strewn with rushes.

256.25 　　　For gnarling° sorrow hath less power to bite　　　　　snarling
　　　　　The man that mocks at it and sets it light.°　　　　values it lightly
BOLINGBROKE　O, who can hold a fire in his hand
　　　By thinking on the frosty Caucasus,[5]
　　　Or cloy the hungry edge of appetite
260　　By bare imagination of a feast,
　　　Or wallow naked in December snow
　　　By thinking on fantastic° summer's heat?　　　　　　　imagined
　　　O no, the apprehension of the good
　　　Gives but the greater feeling to the worse.
265　　Fell sorrow's tooth doth never rankle° more　　　　　　irritate
　　　Than when he bites, but lanceth[6] not the sore.
JOHN OF GAUNT　Come, come, my son, I'll bring thee on thy way.
　　　Had I thy youth and cause, I would not stay.°　　　　　linger
BOLINGBROKE　Then England's ground, farewell. Sweet soil, adieu,
270　My mother and my nurse that bears me yet!
　　　Where'er I wander, boast of this I can:
　　　Though banished, yet a trueborn Englishman.　　　Exeunt

1.4

Enter KING [RICHARD] *with* GREEN *and* BAGOT *at one
door, and the Lord* AUMERLE *at another*

KING RICHARD　We did observe.[1]—Cousin Aumerle,
　　　How far brought you high Hereford on his way?
AUMERLE　I brought high Hereford, if you call him so,
　　　But to the next highway, and there I left him.
5　KING RICHARD　And say, what store of parting tears were shed?
AUMERLE　Faith, none for me,° except the north-east wind,　my part
　　　Which then grew bitterly against our faces,
　　　Awaked the sleeping rheum,° and so by chance　　　　tears
　　　Did grace our hollow parting with a tear.
10　KING RICHARD　What said our cousin when you parted with him?
AUMERLE　'Farewell.' And for° my heart disdainèd that my tongue　because
　　　Should so profane the word, that[2] taught me craft
　　　To counterfeit oppression of such grief
　　　That words seemed buried in my sorrow's grave.
15　Marry,° would the word 'farewell' have lengthened hours　Indeed
　　　And added years to his short banishment,
　　　He should have had a volume of farewells;
　　　But since it would not, he had none of me.
KING RICHARD　He is our cousin, cousin;[3] but 'tis doubt,
20　When time shall call him home from banishment,
　　　Whether our kinsman come to see his friends.°　　　relatives
　　　Ourself and Bushy, Bagot here, and Green
　　　Observed his courtship to the common people,
　　　How he did seem to dive into their hearts
25　With humble and familiar courtesy,
　　　What reverence he did throw away on slaves,
　　　Wooing poor craftsmen with the craft of smiles
　　　And patient underbearing° of his fortune,　　　　　enduring

5. Mountain range between the Black and Caspian seas.
6. Probes (to release the pus from an abscess).
1.4 Location: The court.
1. The scene begins in mid-conversation; the King is replying to a remark by Bagot or Green.

2. His heart. Unwilling to give Hereford good wishes insincerely, Aumerle pretends to be overwhelmed with grief.
3 Richard, Bolingbroke, and Aumerle were sons of three brothers.

As 'twere to banish their affects with him.[4]
30 Off goes his bonnet° to an oysterwench.   *cap*
A brace of draymen° bid God speed him well,   *A couple of cart drivers*
And had the tribute of his supple knee
With 'Thanks, my countrymen, my loving friends',
As were our England in reversion[5] his,
35 And he our subjects' next degree in hope.
GREEN   Well, he is gone, and with him go these thoughts.
Now for the rebels which stand out in Ireland.
Expedient manage° must be made, my liege,   *Hasty arrangements*
Ere further leisure yield them further means
40 For their advantage and your highness' loss.
KING RICHARD   We will ourself in person to this war,
And for° our coffers with too great a court   *because*
And liberal largess are grown somewhat light,
We are enforced to farm our royal realm,[6]
45 The revenue whereof shall furnish us
For our affairs in hand. If that come short,
Our substitutes° at home shall have blank charters,[7]   *deputies*
Whereto, when they shall know what men are rich,
They shall subscribe them° for large sums of gold,   *write down their names*
50 And send them after to supply our wants;
For we will make for Ireland presently.°   *at once*
        Enter BUSHY
Bushy, what news?
BUSHY   Old John of Gaunt is grievous sick, my lord,
Suddenly taken, and hath sent post-haste
55 To entreat your majesty to visit him.
KING RICHARD   Where lies he?
BUSHY   At Ely House.
KING RICHARD   Now put it, God, in his physician's mind
To help him to his grave immediately.
60 The lining[8] of his coffers shall make coats
To deck our soldiers for these Irish wars.
Come, gentlemen, let's all go visit him.
Pray God we may make haste and come too late!   *Exeunt*

2.1

Enter JOHN OF GAUNT [*Duke of Lancaster*], *sick*, [*carried
in a chair*], *with Duke of* YORK

JOHN OF GAUNT   Will the King come, that I may breathe my last
In wholesome counsel to his unstaid° youth?   *unruly*
YORK   Vex not yourself, nor strive not with your breath,
For all in vain comes counsel to his ear.
5 JOHN OF GAUNT   O, but they say the tongues of dying men
Enforce attention, like deep harmony.
Where words are scarce they are seldom spent in vain,
For they breathe truth that breathe their words in pain.
He that no more must say is listened more
10   Than they whom youth and ease have taught to glose.°   *talk speciously*

4. As if taking their affections with him into exile.
5. A legal term for property that reverts to the original
owner on the expiring of a contract.
6. To lease the King's right to tax.
7. Documents enabling the King to raise money by
forced loans; the deputies can fill in the blanks with any
amount they see fit.
8. Contents (playing on "lining cloth").
2.1 Location: Ely House.

More are men's ends marked than their lives before.
　The setting sun, and music at the close,
As the last taste of sweets, is sweetest last,
Writ in remembrance more than things long past.
15　Though Richard my life's counsel would not hear,
My death's sad tale may yet undeaf his ear.
　YORK　No, it is stopped with other, flattering sounds,
As praises of whose taste the wise are feared,°　　　　　　　*wary*
Lascivious metres to whose venom sound
20　The open ear of youth doth always listen,
Report of fashions in proud Italy,
Whose manners still° our tardy-apish¹ nation　　　　　　　*always*
Limps after in base imitation.
Where doth the world thrust forth a vanity—
25　So° it be new there's no respect° how vile—　　　*Provided / regard for*
That is not quickly buzzed into his ears?
Then all too late comes counsel, to be heard
Where will doth mutiny with wit's regard.²
Direct not him whose way himself will choose:
30　'Tis breath thou lack'st, and that breath wilt thou lose.
　JOHN OF GAUNT　Methinks I am a prophet new-inspired,
And thus, expiring, do foretell of him.
His rash, fierce blaze of riot° cannot last,　　　　　　　*wastefulness*
For violent fires soon burn out themselves.
35　Small showers last long, but sudden storms are short.
He tires betimes° that spurs too fast betimes.　　　　　*soon*
With eager feeding food doth choke the feeder.
Light vanity, insatiate cormorant,³
Consuming means, soon preys upon itself.
40　This royal throne of kings, this sceptred isle,
This earth of majesty, this seat of Mars,°　　　　　*war god's dwelling*
This other Eden, demi-paradise,
This fortress built by nature for herself
Against infection° and the hand of war,　　　　　*disease; depravity*
45　This happy breed of men, this little world,
This precious stone set in the silver sea,
Which serves it in the office° of a wall,　　　　　　　*function*
Or as a moat defensive to a house
Against the envy° of less happier lands;　　　　　　　*malice*
50　This blessèd plot, this earth, this realm, this England,
This nurse, this teeming womb of royal kings,
Feared by their breed⁴ and famous by their birth,
Renownèd for their deeds as far from home
For Christian service and true chivalry⁵
55　As is the sepulchre, in stubborn Jewry,⁶
Of the world's ransom, blessèd Mary's son;
This land of such dear souls, this dear dear land,
Dear for her reputation through the world,
Is now leased out—I die pronouncing it—
60　Like to a tenement° or pelting° farm.　　　　*rental property / worthless*
England, bound in with the triumphant sea,

1. Imitative but outmoded.
2. Where willfulness overthrows sound judgment.
3. Glutton (literally, a bird that swallows fish whole).
4. For their inherited valor.

5. Alluding to the English kings' accomplishments in the Crusades.
6. Judaea, stubborn in its resistance to Christianity.

Whose rocky shore beats back the envious siege
Of wat'ry Neptune, is now bound in with shame,
With inky blots and rotten parchment bonds.[7]
65 That England that was wont to conquer others
Hath made a shameful conquest of itself.
Ah, would the scandal vanish with my life,
How happy then were my ensuing death!

Enter KING [RICHARD], QUEEN, [*Duke of*] AUMERLE,
BUSHY, GREEN, BAGOT, [*Lord*] ROSS, *and* [*Lord*]
WILLOUGHBY

YORK   The King is come. Deal mildly with his youth,
70 For young hot colts, being reined, do rage the more.
QUEEN   How fares our noble uncle Lancaster?
KING RICHARD   What comfort, man? How is't with agèd Gaunt?
JOHN OF GAUNT   O, how that name befits my composition!°   constitution
Old Gaunt indeed, and gaunt in being old.
75 Within me grief hath kept a tedious fast,
And who abstains from meat° that is not gaunt?   food
For sleeping England long time have I watched.°   stayed awake
Watching breeds leanness, leanness is all gaunt.
The pleasure that some fathers feed upon
80 Is my strict fast: I mean my children's looks.[8]
And therein fasting, hast thou made me gaunt.
Gaunt am I for the grave, gaunt as a grave,
Whose hollow womb inherits naught but bones.
KING RICHARD   Can sick men play so nicely° with their names?   subtly
85 JOHN OF GAUNT   No, misery makes sport to mock itself.
Since thou dost seek to kill my name in me,[9]
I mock my name, great King, to flatter thee.
KING RICHARD   Should dying men flatter with those that live?
JOHN OF GAUNT   No, no, men living flatter those that die.
90 KING RICHARD   Thou now a-dying sayst thou flatt'rest me.
JOHN OF GAUNT   O no: thou diest, though I the sicker be.
KING RICHARD   I am in health; I breathe, and see thee ill.
JOHN OF GAUNT   Now He that made me knows I see thee ill:
Ill in myself to see, and in thee seeing ill.[1]
95 Thy deathbed is no lesser than thy land,
Wherein thou liest in reputation sick;
And thou, too careless patient as thou art,
Committ'st thy anointed body to the cure
Of those physicians[2] that first wounded thee.
100 A thousand flatterers sit within thy crown,
Whose compass° is no bigger than thy head,   circumference
And yet, encagèd in so small a verge,[3]
The waste[4] is no whit lesser than thy land.
O, had thy grandsire with a prophet's eye
105 Seen how his son's son should destroy his sons,
From forth° thy reach he would have laid thy shame,   out of
Deposing thee before thou wert possessed,[5]
Which art possessed° now to depose thyself.   in a diabolical frenzy

7. Richard's "blank charters."
8. Since Bolingbroke is exiled.
9. Destroy my family (by exiling Bolingbroke).
1. Too ill to see well, and seeing evil in you.
2. Richard's favorites, or his own bad impulses.

3. Area; distance of 12 miles around the court, to which special rules applied.
4. Destruction (specifically, injury done to a property by a tenant); waist, narrowest part.
5. In possession of the crown.

Why, cousin,° wert thou regent° of the world   *kinsman / ruler*
110 It were a shame to let this land by lease.
But, for thy world, enjoying but this land,[6]
Is it not more than shame to shame it so?
Landlord of England art thou now, not king.
Thy state of law[7] is bondslave to the law,
115 And—

KING RICHARD   And thou, a lunatic lean-witted fool,
Presuming on an ague's privilege,°   *the privilege of the sick*
Dar'st with thy frozen° admonition   *rigid; caused by a chill*
Make pale our cheek, chasing the royal blood
120 With fury from his native residence.°   *its natural place*
Now by my seat's° right royal majesty,   *throne's*
Wert thou not brother to great Edward's son,[8]
This tongue that runs so roundly° in thy head   *freely*
Should run thy head from thy unreverent shoulders.
125 JOHN OF GAUNT   O, spare me not, my brother Edward's son,
For that I was his father Edward's son.
That blood already, like the pelican,[9]
Hast thou tapped out[1] and drunkenly caroused.
My brother Gloucester, plain well-meaning soul—
130 Whom fair befall in heaven 'mongst happy souls—
May be a precedent and witness good
That thou respect'st not spilling° Edward's blood.   *don't hesitate to spill*
Join with the present sickness that I have,
And thy unkindness be like crookèd age,
135 To crop° at once a too-long withered flower.   *cut*
Live in thy shame, but die not shame with thee.[2]
These words hereafter thy tormentors be.
[*To attendants*] Convey me to my bed, then to my grave.
Love they to live that love and honour have.
                    Exit [carried in a chair]
140 KING RICHARD   And let them die that age and sullens° have,   *sulks*
For both hast thou, and both become the grave.
YORK   I do beseech your majesty impute his words
To wayward sickliness and age in him.
He loves you, on my life, and holds you dear
145 As Harry Duke of Hereford, were he here.
KING RICHARD   Right, you say true: as Hereford's love, so his.[3]
As theirs, so mine; and all be as it is.
                    Enter [Earl of] NORTHUMBERLAND
NORTHUMBERLAND   My liege, old Gaunt commends him to your majesty.
KING RICHARD   What says he?
NORTHUMBERLAND   Nay, nothing: all is said.
150 His tongue is now a stringless instrument.
Words, life, and all, old Lancaster hath spent.
YORK   Be York the next that must be bankrupt so!
Though death be poor, it ends a mortal woe.
KING RICHARD   The ripest fruit first falls, and so doth he.

6. Since this realm alone constitutes your world.
7. Legal status (as landlord, not King).
8. Edward the Black Prince, Edward III's son and Richard's father.
9. A mother pelican was thought to wound her breast so her ungrateful young could feed on her blood.

1. Let run as from a barrel tap.
2. May your shame outlive you.
3. York claims that Gaunt loves Richard as much as he loves his own son; Richard deliberately misconstrues York to mean Gaunt loves Richard as much as Hereford does.

155 His time is spent; our pilgrimage must be.°   *continue*
So much for that. Now for our Irish wars.
We must supplant those rough rug-headed kerns,[4]
Which live like venom where no venom else
But only they have privilege to live.[5]

160 And for° these great affairs do ask some charge,[6]   *because*
Towards our assistance we do seize to us
The plate, coin, revenues, and movables°   *personal property*
Whereof our uncle Gaunt did stand possessed.

YORK   How long shall I be patient? Ah, how long

165 Shall tender° duty make me suffer wrong?   *scrupulous*
Not Gloucester's death, nor Hereford's banishment,
Nor Gaunt's rebukes, nor England's private wrongs,[7]
Nor the prevention of poor Bolingbroke
About his marriage,[8] nor my own disgrace,

170 Have ever made me sour my patient cheek,
Or bend one wrinkle° on my sovereign's face.   *one frown*
I am the last of noble Edward's sons,
Of whom thy father, Prince of Wales, was first.
In war was never lion raged more fierce,

175 In peace was never gentle lamb more mild,
Than was that young and princely gentleman.
His face thou hast, for even so looked he,
Accomplished with the number of thy hours.°   *When he was your age*
But when he frowned it was against the French,

180 And not against his friends. His noble hand
Did win what he did spend, and spent not that
Which his triumphant father's hand had won.
His hands were guilty of no kindred blood,
But bloody with the enemies of his kin.

185 O, Richard, York is too far gone with grief,
Or else he never would compare between.

KING RICHARD   Why uncle, what's the matter?

YORK   O my liege,
Pardon me if you please; if not, I, pleased
Not to be pardoned, am content withal.°   *nevertheless*

190 Seek you to seize and grip into your hands
The royalties[9] and rights of banished Hereford?
Is not Gaunt dead? And doth not Hereford live?
Was not Gaunt just? And is not Harry true?
Did not the one deserve to have an heir?

195 Is not his heir a well-deserving son?
Take Hereford's rights away, and take from Time
His° charters and his customary rights   *Its*
Let not tomorrow then ensue° today;   *follow*
Be not thyself, for how art thou a king

200 But by fair sequence and succession?
Now afore God—God forbid I say true!—
If you do wrongfully seize Hereford's rights,
Call in° the letters patents that he hath   *Revoke*

---

4. Shaggy Irish foot soldiers.
5. Alluding to the legend that St. Patrick drove snakes out of Ireland.
6. Do demand some expenditure.
7. Wrongs committed against private individuals.

8. Richard intervened against Bolingbroke's proposed marriage to the King of France's cousin.
9. Privileges granted by a king through "letters patents" (line 203).

By his attorneys general to sue
205 His livery, and deny his offered homage,[1]
You pluck° a thousand dangers on your head,   *pull*
You lose a thousand well-disposèd hearts,
And prick my tender patience to those thoughts
Which honour and allegiance cannot think.
210 KING RICHARD   Think what you will, we seize into our hands
His plate, his goods, his money, and his lands.
YORK   I'll not be by the while.[2] My liege, farewell.
What will ensue hereof there's none can tell.
But by bad courses may be understood
215 That their events° can never fall out good.   *Exit*   *outcomes*
KING RICHARD   Go, Bushy, to the Earl of Wiltshire straight.
Bid him repair° to us to Ely House   *go*
To see° this business. Tomorrow next   *attend to*
We will for Ireland, and 'tis time, I trow.°   *think*
220 And we create, in absence of ourself,
Our uncle York Lord Governor of England;
For he is just and always loved us well.—
Come on, our Queen; tomorrow must we part.
Be merry, for our time of stay is short.
        Flourish. Exeunt KING [RICHARD], QUEEN[, AUMERLE,
        GREEN, *and* BAGOT *at one door,* BUSHY *at another door*].
        Manent° NORTHUMBERLAND, WILLOUGHBY, *and* ROSS   *Remain*
225 NORTHUMBERLAND   Well, lords, the Duke of Lancaster is dead.
ROSS   And living too, for now his son is Duke.
WILLOUGHBY   Barely in title, not in revenues.
NORTHUMBERLAND   Richly in both, if justice had her right.
ROSS   My heart is great,° but it must break with silence   *full of emotion*
230 Ere't be disburdened with a liberal° tongue.   *unrestrained*
NORTHUMBERLAND   Nay, speak thy mind, and let him ne'er
        speak more
That speaks thy words again to do thee harm.
WILLOUGHBY   Tends that that thou wouldst speak to[3] the Duke
        of Hereford?
If it be so, out with it boldly, man.
235 Quick is mine ear to hear of good towards him.
ROSS   No good at all that I can do for him,
Unless you call it good to pity him,
Bereft and gelded of his patrimony.
NORTHUMBERLAND   Now afore God, 'tis shame such wrongs are borne
240 In him, a royal prince, and many more
Of noble blood in this declining land.
The King is not himself, but basely led
By flatterers; and what they will inform
Merely in° hate 'gainst any of us all,   *Purely out of*
245 That will the King severely prosecute
'Gainst us, our lives, our children, and our heirs.
ROSS   The commons° hath he pilled° with grievous taxes,   *common people / stripped*
And quite lost their hearts. The nobles hath he fined
For ancient quarrels, and quite lost their hearts.

---

1. The letters patents allow Hereford, through his
legal representatives ("attorneys general"), to make a
legal claim for the inheritance of his land ("sue" for
delivery), provided he swears allegiance to the King
("offers homage").
2. Present during the seizure.
3. Does what you would say concern.

250 WILLOUGHBY   And daily new exactions are devised,
      As blanks, benevolences,° and I wot° not what.   *forced loans / know*
      But what, a' God's name, doth become of this?°   *this money*
   NORTHUMBERLAND   Wars hath not wasted it; for warred he hath not,
      But basely yielded upon compromise
255   That which his ancestors achieved with blows.⁴
      More hath he spent in peace than they in wars.
   ROSS   The Earl of Wiltshire hath the realm in farm.⁵
   WILLOUGHBY   The King's grown bankrupt like a broken man.
   NORTHUMBERLAND   Reproach and dissolution hangeth over him.
260 ROSS   He hath not money for these Irish wars,
      His burdenous taxations notwithstanding,
      But by the robbing of the banished Duke.
   NORTHUMBERLAND   His noble kinsman. Most degenerate King!
      But, lords, we hear this fearful tempest sing,
265   Yet seek no shelter to avoid the storm.
      We see the wind sit sore° upon our sails,   *blow hard*
      And yet we strike⁶ not, but securely° perish.   *heedlessly*
   ROSS   We see the very wreck that we must suffer,
      And unavoided° is the danger now   *unavoidable*
270   For suffering° so the causes of our wreck.   *enduring*
   NORTHUMBERLAND   Not so: even through the hollow eyes° of death   *eye sockets*
      I spy life peering; but I dare not say
      How near the tidings of our comfort is.
   WILLOUGHBY   Nay, let us share thy thoughts, as thou dost ours.
275 ROSS   Be confident to speak, Northumberland.
      We three are but thyself, and, speaking so,
      Thy words are but as thoughts. Therefore be bold.
   NORTHUMBERLAND   Then thus. I have from Port le Blanc,
      A bay in Brittaine,⁷ received intelligence
280   That Harry Duke of Hereford, Reinold Lord Cobham,
      Thomas son and heir to the Earl of Arundel⁸
      That late broke from the Duke of Exeter,
      His⁹ brother, Archbishop late° of Canterbury,   *until recently*
      Sir Thomas Erpingham, Sir Thomas Ramston,
285   Sir John Norbery,
      Sir Robert Waterton, and Francis Coint,
      All these well furnished by the Duke of Brittaine
      With eight tall ships, three thousand men of war,°   *soldiers*
      Are making hither with all due expedience,
290   And shortly mean to touch our northern shore.
      Perhaps they had ere this, but that they stay
      The first departing of the King¹ for Ireland.
      If then we shall shake off our slavish yoke,
      Imp out² our drooping country's broken wing,
295   Redeem from broking pawn° the blemished crown,   *pawnbrokers*
      Wipe off the dust that hides our sceptre's gilt,
      And make high majesty look like itself,
      Away with me in post° to Ravenspurgh.³   *speedily*

---

4. Referring to the ceding of Brest, a city in western France, to the Duke of Brittany.
5. *in farm*: on lease (as in 1.4.44–46).
6. Lower sails; deliver blows.
7. Brittany, in northwest France.
8. An editorial approximation of a line missing from early texts. Shakespeare's source states that Arundel's son escaped from Exeter's custody.
9. The Earl of Arundel's.
1. *they stay . . . King*: they wait for the King to depart first.
2. Engraft new feathers on (from falconry).
3. Then a port on the river Humber, in Yorkshire.

But if you faint,° as fearing to do so,   *are fainthearted*
300   Stay, and be secret, and myself will go.
ROSS   To horse, to horse! Urge doubts to them that fear.
WILLOUGHBY   Hold out my horse,° and I will first be there.   *If my horse holds up*

                                                                        Exeunt

2.2

Enter the QUEEN, BUSHY, [*and*] BAGOT
BUSHY   Madam, your majesty is too much sad.[1]
        You promised when you parted with the King
        To lay aside life-harming heaviness°   *melancholy*
        And entertain° a cheerful disposition.   *assume*
5   QUEEN   To please the King I did; to please myself
        I cannot do it. Yet I know no cause
        Why I should welcome such a guest as grief,
        Save bidding farewell to so sweet a guest
        As my sweet Richard. Yet again, methinks
10   Some unborn sorrow, ripe in fortune's womb,
        Is coming towards me; and my inward soul
        At nothing trembles. With something it grieves
        More than with parting from my lord the King.
     BUSHY   Each substance of a grief hath twenty shadows
15   Which shows like grief itself but is not so.
        For sorrow's eye, glazèd with blinding tears,
        Divides one thing entire to many objects—
        Like perspectives, which, rightly gazed upon,
        Show nothing but confusion; eyed awry,
20   Distinguish form.[2] So your sweet majesty,
        Looking awry upon your lord's departure,
        Find shapes° of grief more than himself to wail,°   *images / bewail*
        Which, looked on as it is, is naught but shadows
        Of what it is not. Then, thrice-gracious Queen,
25   More than your lord's departure weep not: more is not seen,
        Or if it be, 'tis with false sorrow's eye,
        Which for things true weeps things imaginary.
     QUEEN   It may be so, but yet my inward soul
        Persuades me it is otherwise. Howe'er it be,
30   I cannot but be sad: so heavy-sad
        As thought—on thinking on no thought I think[3]–
        Makes me with heavy nothing faint and shrink.
     BUSHY   'Tis nothing but conceit,° my gracious lady.   *imagination*
     QUEEN   'Tis nothing less:[4] conceit is still° derived   *always*
35   From some forefather grief; mine is not so;
        For nothing hath begot my something° grief—   *substantial*
        Or something hath the nothing that I grieve[5]—
        'Tis in reversion that I do possess[6]—

2.2. Location: Windsor Castle.
1. Shakespeare makes Richard's queen a mature young woman; the historical Isabella was married to Richard at seven years and was ten at the time of Bolingbroke's invasion.
2. *For . . . from*: Bushy compares the Queen's eye first to a perspective glass that multiplies one image into many, then to a perspective picture that looks distorted unless viewed at an angle ("awry").
3. *As thought . . . think*: a difficult line. The Oxford

editors adopt the Q1 version, "thought"; other editors adopt the F version, "though," which is hardly less obscure. The Queen is playing with the paradox that her premonition, a thought of nothing, or "no thought," is nonetheless almost physically oppressive.
4. Anything but conceit.
5. Or the grief that I feel apparently over nothing actually has some cause.
6. It will come at a later date (that is, her grief anticipates its occasion).

But what it is that is not yet known what,
40 I cannot name; 'tis nameless woe, I wot.
        Enter GREEN
GREEN   God save your majesty, and well met, gentlemen.
    I hope the King is not yet shipped for Ireland.
QUEEN   Why hop'st thou so? 'Tis better hope he is,
    For his designs crave° haste, his haste good hope.   *need*
45 Then wherefore dost thou hope he is not shipped?
GREEN   That he, our hope, might have retired his power,°   *brought back his forces*
    And driven into despair an enemy's hope,
    Who strongly hath set footing in this land.
    The banished Bolingbroke repeals° himself,   *recalls from exile*
50 And with uplifted arms° is safe arrived   *weapons*
    At Ravenspurgh.
QUEEN   Now God in heaven forbid!
GREEN   Ah madam, 'tis too true! And, that is worse,
    The Lord Northumberland, his son young Harry Percy,
    The Lords of Ross, Beaumont, and Willoughby,
55 With all their powerful friends, are fled to him.
BUSHY   Why have you not proclaimed Northumberland,
    And all the rest, revolted faction-traitors?°   *treasonous conspirators*
GREEN   We have; whereupon the Earl of Worcester
    Hath broke his staff,[7] resigned his stewardship,
60 And all the household servants fled with him
    To Bolingbroke.
QUEEN   So, Green, thou art the midwife to my woe,
    And Bolingbroke my sorrow's dismal heir.
    Now hath my soul brought forth her prodigy,°   *monstrous birth; portent*
65 And I, a gasping new-delivered mother,
    Have woe to woe, sorrow to sorrow joined.
BUSHY   Despair not, madam.
QUEEN   Who shall hinder me?
    I will despair, and be at enmity
    With cozening° hope. He° is a flatterer,   *cheating / (Hope)*
70 A parasite, a keeper-back of death,
    Who° gently would dissolve° the bonds of life,   *(Death) / loosen*
    Which false hope lingers in extremity.
          Enter [Duke of] YORK *[wearing a gorget]*[8]
GREEN   Here comes the Duke of York.
QUEEN   With signs of war about his agèd neck.
75 O, full of careful business° are his looks!   *anxious preoccupation*
    Uncle, for God's sake speak comfortable° words.   *comforting*
YORK   Should I do so, I should belie my thoughts.
    Comfort's in heaven, and we are on the earth,
    Where nothing lives but crosses,° cares, and grief.   *misfortunes*
80 Your husband, he is gone to save far off,
    Whilst others come to make him lose at home.
    Here am I, left to underprop his land,
    Who, weak with age, cannot support myself.
    Now comes the sick hour that his surfeit made.
85 Now shall he try° his friends that flattered him.   *test*
          *Enter a [*SERVINGMAN*]*

---

7. Symbolically resigning his office as lord steward of   brother.
the King's household. Worcester is Northumberland's   8. Piece of armor protecting the throat.

SERVINGMAN My lord, your son was gone before I came.

YORK He was? Why so, go all which way it will.
The nobles they are fled. The commons° they are cold,   *common people*
And will, I fear, revolt on Hereford's side.
90 Sirrah, get thee to Pleshey, to my sister° Gloucester.   *sister-in-law*
Bid her send me presently° a thousand pound—   *immediately*
Hold; take my ring.⁹

SERVINGMAN My lord, I had forgot to tell your lordship,
Today as I came by I callèd there—
95 But I shall grieve you to report the rest.

YORK What is't, knave?°   *fellow*

SERVINGMAN An hour before I came, the Duchess died.

YORK God for his mercy, what a tide of woes
Comes rushing on this woeful land at once!
100 I know not what to do. I would to God,
So my untruth° had not provoked him to it,   *disloyalty*
The King had cut off my head with my brother's.
What, are there no posts° dispatched for Ireland?   *fast messengers*
How shall we do for money for these wars?
105 [*To the* QUEEN] Come, sister—cousin, I would say; pray pardon me.¹
[*To the* SERVINGMAN] Go, fellow, get thee home. Provide some carts,
And bring away the armour that is there. [*Exit* SERVINGMAN]
Gentlemen, will you go muster men?
If I know how or which way to order these affairs
110 Thus disorderly thrust into my hands,
Never believe me. Both are my kinsmen.
T'one is my sovereign, whom both my oath
And duty bids defend; t'other again
Is my kinsman, whom the King hath wronged,
115 Whom conscience and my kindred bids to right.
Well, somewhat we must do. [*To the* QUEEN] Come, cousin,
I'll dispose of° you.—   *make arrangements for*
Gentlemen, go muster up your men,
And meet me presently at Berkeley Castle.²
120 I should to Pleshey too, but time will not permit.
All is uneven,
And everything is left at six and seven.°   *in confusion*

                    Exeunt Duke [*of* YORK *and*] QUEEN.
                    Manent BUSHY, GREEN [*and* BAGOT]

BUSHY The wind sits fair³ for news to go for Ireland,
But none returns. For us to levy power
125 Proportionable to the enemy
Is all unpossible.

GREEN Besides, our nearness to the King in love
Is near° the hate of those love not the King.   *Implies*

BAGOT And that is the wavering commons; for their love
130 Lies in their purses, and whoso empties them
By so much fills their hearts with deadly hate.

BUSHY Wherein the King stands generally condemned.

BAGOT If judgement lie in them,° then so do we,   *is in the people's hands*
Because we ever have been near the King.

---

9. As proof that he comes with York's authorization.   2. In Gloucestershire, in western England.
1. The Duchess's death is uppermost in York's mind.   3. The wind blows from a favorable direction.

135 GREEN Well, I will for refuge straight to Bristol Castle.
　　　　　The Earl of Wiltshire is already there.
　　BUSHY Thither will I with you; for little office°　　　　　　　　°service
　　　　　Will the hateful commoners perform for us,
　　　　　Except like curs to tear us all to pieces.
140 　　　　[*To* BAGOT] Will you go along with us?
　　BAGOT No, I will to Ireland, to his majesty.
　　　　　Farewell: if heart's presages be not vain
　　　　　We three here part that ne'er shall meet again.
　　BUSHY That's as York thrives[4] to beat back Bolingbroke.
145 GREEN Alas, poor Duke, the task he undertakes
　　　　　Is numb'ring sands and drinking oceans dry.
　　　　　Where one on his side fights, thousands will fly.
　　BAGOT Farewell at once, for once, for all and ever.
　　BUSHY Well, we may meet again.
　　BAGOT 　　　　　　　　　　　　　I fear me never.
　　　　　　　　　　Exeunt [BUSHY *and* GREEN *at one door,*
　　　　　　　　　　　　and BAGOT *at another door*]

2.3

Enter [BOLINGBROKE *Duke of Lancaster and*] *Hereford,*
and [*the Earl of*] NORTHUMBERLAND

　　BOLINGBROKE How far is it, my lord, to Berkeley now?
　　NORTHUMBERLAND Believe me, noble lord,
　　　　　I am a stranger here in Gloucestershire.
　　　　　These high wild hills and rough uneven ways
5　　　　Draws out our miles and makes them wearisome;
　　　　　And yet your fair discourse hath been as sugar,
　　　　　Making the hard way sweet and delectable.
　　　　　But I bethink me what a weary way
　　　　　From Ravenspurgh to Cotswold[1] will be found
10　　　　In° Ross and Willoughby, wanting° your company,　　　°By / lacking
　　　　　Which I protest hath very much beguiled
　　　　　The tediousness and process° of my travel.　　　　　°tedious course
　　　　　But theirs is sweetened with the hope to have
　　　　　The present benefit which I possess;
15　　　　And hope to joy is little less in joy
　　　　　Than hope enjoyed. By this° the weary lords　　　　°this expectation
　　　　　Shall make their way seem short as mine hath done
　　　　　By sight of what I have: your noble company.
　　BOLINGBROKE Of much less value is my company
　　　　　Than your good words.
　　　　　　　Enter HARRY PERCY
20　　　　　　　　　　　　　　　　But who comes here?
　　NORTHUMBERLAND It is my son, young Harry Percy,[2]
　　　　　Sent from my brother Worcester, whencesoever.°　　　°wherever he may be
　　　　　Harry, how fares your uncle?°　　　　　　　　　　°Worcester
　　HARRY PERCY I had thought, my lord, to have learned his
　　　　　health of you.
25　　NORTHUMBERLAND Why, is he not with the Queen?
　　HARRY PERCY No, my good lord; he hath forsook the court,

---

4. That depends on York's success.
2.3 Location: Gloucestershire.
1. Hilly part of Gloucestershire.

2. Shakespeare makes Harry Percy, the Hotspur of
1 Henry IV, a boy here; the historical Percy was two
years older than Bolingbroke.

Broken his staff of office, and dispersed
The household of the King.

NORTHUMBERLAND   What was his reason?
He was not so resolved when last we spake together.

30 HARRY PERCY   Because your lordship was proclaimèd traitor.
But he, my lord, is gone to Ravenspurgh
To offer service to the Duke of Hereford,
And sent me over by Berkeley to discover
What power the Duke of York had levied there,

35   Then with directions to repair to Ravenspurgh.

NORTHUMBERLAND   Have you forgot the Duke of Hereford, boy?³

HARRY PERCY   No, my good lord, for that is not forgot
Which ne'er I did remember. To my knowledge,
I never in my life did look on him.

40 NORTHUMBERLAND   Then learn to know him now. This is the Duke.

HARRY PERCY   My gracious lord, I tender you my service,
Such as it is, being tender, raw, and young,
Which elder days shall ripen and confirm
To more approvèd° service and desert.   *more fully demonstrated*

45 BOLINGBROKE   I thank thee, gentle Percy, and be sure
I count myself in nothing else so happy
As in a° soul rememb'ring my good friends;   *my*
And as my fortune ripens with thy love,
It shall be still thy true love's recompense.

50 My heart this covenant makes; my hand thus seals it.
    [*He gives* PERCY *his hand*]

NORTHUMBERLAND   How far is it to Berkeley, and what stir°   *activity*
Keeps good old York there with his men of war?

HARRY PERCY   There stands the castle, by yon tuft of trees,
Manned with three hundred men, as I have heard,

55 And in it are the Lords of York, Berkeley, and Seymour,
None else of name° and noble estimate.°   *title / reputation*
    Enter [*Lord*] ROSS *and* [*Lord*] WILLOUGHBY

NORTHUMBERLAND   Here come the Lords of Ross and Willoughby,
Bloody with spurring, fiery red with haste.

BOLINGBROKE   Welcome, my lords. I wot° your love pursues   *know*

60 A banished traitor. All my treasury
Is yet but unfelt° thanks, which, more enriched,   *immaterial*
Shall be your love and labour's recompense.

ROSS   Your presence makes us rich, most noble lord.

WILLOUGHBY   And far surmounts our labour to attain it.

65 BOLINGBROKE   Evermore thank's the exchequer⁴ of the poor,
Which till my infant fortune comes to years°   *of age*
Stands for° my bounty.   *in place of*
    Enter BERKELEY
                But who comes here?

NORTHUMBERLAND   It is my lord of Berkeley, as I guess.

BERKELEY   My lord of Hereford, my message is to you.

70 BOLINGBROKE   My lord, my answer is to 'Lancaster',⁵
And I am come to seek that name in England,

---

3. Northumberland scolds his son for not greeting Bolingbroke respectfully.
4. Gratitude is always the treasury.

5. I only reply to the title of Lancaster (which Richard
took away).

And I must find that title in your tongue
Before I make reply to aught you say.

BERKELEY   Mistake me not, my lord, 'tis not my meaning

75 To raze one title of your honour out.
To you, my lord, I come—what lord you will—
From the most gracious regent of this land,
The Duke of York, to know what pricks you on°   *incites you*
To take advantage of the absent time°   *time of absence*

80 And fright our native peace with self-borne⁶ arms.

Enter [Duke of] YORK

BOLINGBROKE   I shall not need transport my words by you.
Here comes his grace in person.—My noble uncle!

[He kneels]

YORK   Show me thy humble heart, and not thy knee,
Whose duty is deceivable° and false.   *deceptive*

85 BOLINGBROKE   My gracious uncle—

YORK   Tut, tut, grace me no grace, nor uncle me no uncle.
I am no traitor's uncle, and that word 'grace'
In an ungracious mouth is but profane.
Why have those banished and forbidden legs

90 Dared once to touch a dust° of England's ground?   *speck*
But then more 'why': why have they dared to march
So many miles upon her peaceful bosom,
Frighting her pale-faced villages with war
And ostentation° of despisèd arms?   *display*

95 Com'st thou because the anointed King is hence?
Why, foolish boy, the King is left behind,
And in my loyal bosom lies his power.
Were I but now the lord of such hot youth
As when brave Gaunt, thy father, and myself

100 Rescued the Black Prince, that young Mars of men,
From forth the ranks of many thousand French,
O then how quickly should this arm of mine,
Now prisoner to the palsy, chastise thee
And minister correction° to thy fault!   *administer punishment*

105 BOLINGBROKE   My gracious uncle, let me know my fault.
On what condition stands it and wherein?⁷

YORK   Even in condition of the worst degree:
In gross rebellion and detested treason.
Thou art a banished man, and here art come

110 Before the expiration of thy time
In braving° arms against thy sovereign.   *defiant*

BOLINGBROKE   *[standing]*   As I was banished, I was banished Hereford;
But as I come, I come for Lancaster.
And, noble uncle, I beseech your grace,

115 Look on my wrongs with an indifferent° eye.   *impartial*
You are my father, for methinks in you
I see old Gaunt alive. O then, my father,
Will you permit that I shall stand condemned
A wandering vagabond, my rights and royalties

120 Plucked from my arms perforce and given away
To upstart unthrifts?° Wherefore was I born?   *spendthrifts*

6. Borne for oneself, not for the King; borne against   7. What is its nature, and in what does it consist?
fellow countrymen.

If that my cousin King be King in England,
It must be granted I am Duke of Lancaster.
You have a son, Aumerle my noble kinsman.
125 Had you first died and he been thus trod down,
He should have found his uncle Gaunt a father
To rouse his wrongs and chase them to the bay.[8]
I am denied to sue my livery[9] here,
And yet my letters patents give me leave.
130 My father's goods are all distrained° and sold,   *confiscated*
And these and all are all amiss employed.
What would you have me do? I am a subject,
And I challenge law;° attorneys are denied me;   *demand my rights*
And therefore personally I lay my claim
135 To my inheritance of free descent.°   *legal succession*
NORTHUMBERLAND   The noble Duke hath been too much abused.
ROSS   It stands your grace upon[1] to do him right.
WILLOUGHBY   Base men by his endowments° are made great.   *property*
YORK   My lords of England, let me tell you this.
140 I have had feeling of my cousin's wrongs,
And laboured all I could to do him right.
But in this kind° to come, in braving arms,   *manner*
Be his own carver,[2] and cut out his way
To find out right with wrong[3]—it may not be.
145 And you that do abet him in this kind
Cherish rebellion, and are rebels all.
NORTHUMBERLAND   The noble Duke hath sworn his coming is
But for his own, and for the right of that
We all have strongly sworn to give him aid;
150 And let him never see joy that breaks that oath.
YORK   Well, well, I see the issue° of these arms.   *consequence*
I cannot mend it, I must needs confess,
Because my power° is weak and all ill-left.   *army*
But if I could, by Him that gave me life,
155 I would attach° you all, and make you stoop   *arrest*
Unto the sovereign mercy of the King.
But since I cannot, be it known to you
I do remain as neuter.° So fare you well—   *neutral*
Unless you please to enter in the castle
160 And there repose you for this night.
BOLINGBROKE   An offer, uncle, that we will accept.
But we must win° your grace to go with us   *persuade*
To Bristol Castle, which they say is held
By Bushy, Bagot, and their complices,°   *accomplices*
165 The caterpillars° of the commonwealth,   *devourers*
Which I have sworn to weed and pluck away.
YORK   It may be I will go with you—but yet I'll pause,
For I am loath to break our country's laws.
Nor° friends nor foes, to me welcome you are.   *Neither*
170 Things past redress are now with me past care.   *Exeunt*

---

8. *rouse*: startle an animal from its cover. *bay*: point
where the animal turns on its pursuers.
9. See note to 2.1.205.

1. It is incumbent on your grace.
2. Help himself to meat (instead of waiting to be served).
3. To illegally obtain what he deserves.

2.4

Enter Earl of SALISBURY *and a* WELSH CAPTAIN

WELSH CAPTAIN   My lord of Salisbury, we have stayed° ten days,   *waited*
And hardly° kept our countrymen together,   *with difficulty*
And yet we hear no tidings from the King.
Therefore we will disperse ourselves. Farewell.

5   SALISBURY   Stay yet another day, thou trusty Welshman.
The King reposeth all his confidence in thee.

WELSH CAPTAIN   'Tis thought the King is dead. We will not stay.
The bay trees in our country are all withered,
And meteors fright the fixèd stars of heaven.

10   The pale-faced moon looks bloody on the earth,[1]
And lean-looked prophets whisper fearful change.
Rich men look sad, and ruffians dance and leap;
The one in fear to lose what they enjoy,
The other to enjoy° by rage and war.   *hoping to profit*

15   These signs forerun the death or fall of kings.
Farewell. Our countrymen are gone and fled,
As well assured Richard their king is dead.   *Exit*

SALISBURY   Ah, Richard! With the eyes of heavy mind
I see thy glory, like a shooting star,

20   Fall to the base earth from the firmament.
Thy sun sets weeping in the lowly west,
Witnessing° storms to come, woe, and unrest.   *Testifying to*
Thy friends are fled to wait upon thy foes,
And crossly° to thy good all fortune goes.   *Exit*   *adversely*

3.1

Enter BOLINGBROKE [*Duke of Lancaster and Hereford,*
Duke of] YORK, [*Earl of*] NORTHUMBERLAND, [*Lord*]
ROSS, [HARRY] PERCY, [*and Lord*] WILLOUGHBY

BOLINGBROKE   Bring forth these men.

[*Enter*] BUSHY *and* GREEN, [*guarded as*] *prisoners*

Bushy and Green, I will not vex° your souls,   *afflict*
Since presently° your souls must part your bodies,   *immediately*
With too much urging° your pernicious lives,   *emphasizing*

5   For 'twere no charity. Yet to wash your blood
From off my hands, here in the view of men
I will unfold some causes of your deaths.
You have misled a prince, a royal king,
A happy° gentleman in blood and lineaments,[1]   *fortunate*

10   By you unhappied and disfigured clean.°   *utterly*
You have, in manner,° with your sinful hours   *so to speak*
Made a divorce betwixt his queen and him,
Broke the possession of a royal bed,
And stained the beauty of a fair queen's cheeks

15   With tears drawn from her eyes by your foul wrongs.[2]
Myself—a prince by fortune of my birth,
Near to the King in blood, and near in love
Till you did make him misinterpret me—
Have stooped my neck under your injuries,

2.4 Location: A camp in Wales.
1. Holinshed records the first of these omens (line 8); the others are poetic commonplaces.
3.1 Location: Before Bristol Castle.

1. In descent and qualities.
2. Bolingbroke implies that Bushy and Green had homosexual relations with Richard; Holinshed claims that they procured female paramours for him.

20 And sighed my English breath in foreign clouds,°   *air*
Eating the bitter bread of banishment,
Whilst you have fed upon my signories,°   *estates*
Disparked my parks³ and felled my forest woods,
From my own windows torn my household coat,⁴
25 Razed° out my imprese,° leaving me no sign,   *Scraped / heraldic emblem*
Save men's opinions and my living blood,
To show the world I am a gentleman.
This and much more, much more than twice all this,
Condemns you to the death.—See them delivered over
30 To execution and the hand of death.
BUSHY   More welcome is the stroke of death to me
Than Bolingbroke to England.
GREEN   My comfort is that heaven will take our souls,
And plague injustice with the pains of hell.
35 BOLINGBROKE   My lord Northumberland, see them dispatched.
        [*Exit* NORTHUMBERLAND, *with* BUSHY *and* GREEN, *guarded*]
Uncle, you say the Queen is at your house.
For God's sake, fairly° let her be intreated.°   *courteously / treated*
Tell her I send to her my kind commends.°   *greetings*
Take special care my greetings be delivered.
40 YORK   A gentleman of mine I have dispatched
With letters of your love to her at large.°   *fully described*
BOLINGBROKE   Thanks, gentle uncle.—Come, lords, away,
To fight with Glyndŵr⁵ and his complices.
A while to work, and after, holiday.   *Exeunt*

3.2

Drums. Flourish. Enter [KING] RICHARD, [*Duke of*]
AUMERLE, [BISHOP OF] CARLISLE, *and soldiers* [*with*]
colours°   *flags*
KING RICHARD   Harlechly Castle call they this at hand?
AUMERLE   Yea, my lord. How brooks° your grace the air   *enjoys*
After your late° tossing on the breaking seas?   *recent*
KING RICHARD   Needs must° I like it well. I weep for joy   *Necessarily*
5 To stand upon my kingdom once again.
        [*He touches the ground*]
Dear earth, I do salute thee with my hand,
Though rebels wound thee with their horses' hoofs.
As a long-parted mother with her child
Plays fondly with her tears, and smiles in meeting,
10 So, weeping, smiling, greet I thee my earth,
And do thee favours with my royal hands.
Feed not thy sovereign's foe, my gentle earth,
Nor with thy sweets° comfort his ravenous sense;¹   *bounty*
But let thy spiders that suck up thy venom²
15 And heavy-gaited toads³ lie in their way,
Doing annoyance to the treacherous feet
Which with usurping steps do trample thee.
Yield stinging nettles to mine enemies,

3. Put my hunting lands to other use.
4. Removed the stained glass bearing my coat of arms.
5. This character appears in *1 Henry IV* and is perhaps
to be identified with the Welsh captain of 2.4.
3.2 Location: Near Harlech Castle, on the coast of

Gwynedd, Wales.
1. Appetite; intention.
2. It was thought that spiders drew their venom from
the earth.
3. Also thought to be poisonous.

And when they from thy bosom pluck a flower
20 Guard it, I pray thee, with a lurking adder,
Whose double° tongue may with a mortal touch   *forked*
Throw death upon thy sovereign's enemies.—
Mock not my senseless conjuration,[4] lords.
This earth shall have a feeling, and these stones
25 Prove armèd soldiers, ere her native king°   *King entitled by birth*
Shall falter under foul rebellion's arms.
BISHOP OF CARLISLE   Fear not, my lord. That power that made you king
Hath power to keep you king in spite of all.[5]
28.1   *The means that heavens yield must be embraced*
          And not neglected; else° heaven would,   *otherwise*
          And we will not: heaven's offer we refuse,
          The proffered means of succour and redress.
AUMERLE   He means, my lord, that we are too remiss,
30 Whilst Bolingbroke, through our security,°   *overconfidence*
Grows strong and great in substance and in friends.
KING RICHARD   Discomfortable° cousin, know'st thou not   *Disheartening*
That when the searching eye of heaven is hid
Behind the globe, that lights the lower world,
35 Then thieves and robbers range abroad unseen
In murders and in outrage bloody here;
But when from under this terrestrial ball
He fires° the proud tops of the eastern pines,   *lights up*
And darts his light through every guilty hole,
40 Then murders, treasons, and detested sins,
The cloak of night being plucked from off their backs,
Stand bare and naked, trembling at themselves?
So when this thief, this traitor, Bolingbroke,
Who all this while hath revelled in the night
45 Whilst we were wand'ring with the Antipodes,
Shall see us rising in our throne, the east,[6]
His treasons will sit blushing in his face,
Not able to endure the sight of day,
But, self-affrighted, tremble at his sin.
50 Not all the water in the rough rude sea
Can wash the balm° from an anointed king.   *oil of consecration*
The breath of worldly men cannot depose
The deputy elected by the Lord.
For every man that Bolingbroke hath pressed°   *drafted*
55 To lift shrewd° steel against our golden crown,   *wicked; sharp*
God for his Richard hath in heavenly pay
A glorious angel. Then if angels fight,
Weak men must fall; for heaven still° guards the right.   *always*
          Enter [Earl of] SALISBURY
Welcome, my lord. How far off lies your power?
60 SALISBURY   Nor nea'er° nor farther off, my gracious lord,   *Neither nearer*
Than this weak arm. Discomfort guides my tongue,
And bids me speak of nothing but despair.
One day too late, I fear me, noble lord,
Hath clouded all thy happy days on earth.

---

4. Injunction addressed to an insentient being (the earth).
5. The following indented passage (lines 28.1–28.4) appears only in Q1.
6. *That when . . . east:* Richard compares the sun ("the searching eye of heaven," line 33), the antipodes, or "lower world" on the other side of the globe, to himself leaving England to visit Ireland. Unlike the sun, however, Richard arrives from the west.

65   O, call back yesterday, bid time return,
     And thou shalt have twelve thousand fighting men.
     Today, today, unhappy day too late,
     Overthrows thy joys, friends, fortune, and thy state;°   *prosperity; nation*
     For all the Welshmen, hearing thou wert dead,
70   Are gone to Bolingbroke, dispersed, and fled.
AUMERLE   Comfort, my liege. Why looks your grace so pale?
KING RICHARD   But now° the blood of twenty thousand men   *A moment ago*
     Did triumph° in my face, and they are fled;   *shine*
     And till so much blood thither come again
75   Have I not reason to look pale and dead?
     All souls that will be safe fly from my side,
     For time hath set a blot upon my pride.
AUMERLE   Comfort, my liege. Remember who you are.
KING RICHARD   I had forgot myself. Am I not King?
80   Awake, thou sluggard majesty, thou sleep'st!
     Is not the King's name forty thousand names?
     Arm, arm, my name! A puny subject strikes
     At thy great glory. Look not to the ground,
     Ye favourites of a king: are we not high?
85   High be our thoughts. I know my uncle York
     Hath power enough to serve our turn.
               Enter SCROPE
                                                       But who comes here?
SCROPE   More health and happiness betide my liege
     Than can my care-tuned[7] tongue deliver° him.   *offer*
KING RICHARD   Mine ear is open and my heart prepared.
90   The worst is worldly loss thou canst unfold.
     Say, is my kingdom lost? Why 'twas my care,°   *trouble*
     And what loss is it to be rid of care?
     Strives Bolingbroke to be as great as we?
     Greater he shall not be. If he serve God
95   We'll serve Him too, and be his fellow so.[8]
     Revolt our subjects? That we cannot mend.
     They break their faith to God as well as us.
     Cry° woe, destruction, ruin, loss, decay: *Though you may cry*
     The worst is death, and death will have his° day.   *its*
100 SCROPE   Glad am I that your highness is so armed
     To bear the tidings of calamity.
     Like an unseasonable stormy day,
     Which makes the silver rivers drown their shores
     As if the world were all dissolved to tears,
105 So high above his limits° swells the rage   *bounds; banks*
     Of Bolingbroke, covering your fearful° land   *alarmed*
     With hard bright steel, and hearts harder than steel.
     Whitebeards have armed their thin and hairless scalps
     Against thy majesty. Boys with women's voices
110 Strive to speak big, and clap their female° joints   *weak*
     In stiff unwieldy arms° against thy crown.   *armor*
     Thy very beadsmen[9] learn to bend their bows
     Of double-fatal[1] yew against thy state.

7. Tuned to the key sorrow.
8. Be Bolingbroke's equal in that regard.
9. Poor elderly men who received charity in return for   praying for their benefactors' souls.
                                                          1. Because yew is poisonous, and its wood was used to make bows.

Yea, distaff-women° manage rusty bills²   *spinners*

115   Against thy seat.° Both young and old rebel,   *throne*

And all goes worse than I have power to tell.

KING RICHARD   Too well, too well thou tell'st a tale so ill.

Where is the Earl of Wiltshire? Where is Bagot?³

What is become of Bushy, where is Green,

120   That they have let the dangerous enemy

Measure our confines⁴ with such peaceful° steps?   *unopposed*

If we prevail, their heads shall pay for it.

I warrant they have made peace with Bolingbroke.

SCROPE   Peace have they made with him indeed, my lord.

125   KING RICHARD   O villains, vipers damned without redemption!

Dogs easily won to fawn on any man!

Snakes in my heart-blood warmed, that sting my heart!

Three Judases, each one thrice-worse than Judas!⁵

Would they make peace? Terrible hell make war

130   Upon their spotted° souls for this offence!   *blemished*

SCROPE   Sweet love, I see, changing his property,°   *its quality*

Turns to the sourest and most deadly hate.

Again uncurse their souls. Their peace is made

With heads, and not with hands. Those whom you curse

135   Have felt the worst of death's destroying wound,

And lie full low, graved in the hollow ground.

AUMERLE   Is Bushy, Green, and the Earl of Wiltshire dead?

SCROPE   Ay, all of them at Bristol lost their heads.

AUMERLE   Where is the Duke my father, with his power?

140   KING RICHARD   No matter where. Of comfort no man speak.

Let's talk of graves, of worms and epitaphs,

Make dust our paper, and with rainy eyes

Write sorrow on the bosom of the earth.

Let's choose executors and talk of wills—

145   And yet not so, for what can we bequeath

Save our deposèd° bodies to the ground?   *dethroned; prostrate*

Our lands, our lives, and all are Bolingbroke's;

And nothing can we call our own but death,

And that small model⁶ of the barren earth

150   Which serves as paste⁷ and cover to our bones.

[*Sitting*] For God's sake, let us sit upon the ground,

And tell sad stories of the death of kings—

How some have been deposed, some slain in war,

Some haunted by the ghosts they have deposed,

155   Some poisoned by their wives, some sleeping killed,

All murdered. For within the hollow crown

That rounds° the mortal temples of a king   *encircles*

Keeps Death his court; and there the antic° sits,   *jester*

Scoffing his state⁸ and grinning at his pomp,

160   Allowing him a breath, a little scene,

To monarchize,° be feared, and kill with looks,⁹   *play the monarch*

Infusing him with self and vain conceit,¹

As if this flesh which walls about our life

---

2. Spiked axes on long shafts.

3. Bagot is not one of the "three Judases" (line 128) actually executed by Bolingbroke; he reappears in 4.1.

4. Travel over our territories.

5. Disciple who betrayed Jesus.

6. Microcosm (the body); enveloping shape (the grave).

7. Pastry shell (also known as "coffin").

8. Mocking the King's regality.

9. Order executions with a glance.

1. Instilling in him vain ideas about himself.

Were brass impregnable; and humoured thus,[2]
165 Comes at the last, and with a little pin
Bores through his castle wall; and farewell, king.
Cover your heads,[3] and mock not flesh and blood
With solemn reverence. Throw away respect,
Tradition, form, and ceremonious duty,
170 For you have but mistook me all this while.
I live with bread, like you; feel want,
Taste grief, need friends. Subjected thus,[4]
How can you say to me I am a king?
BISHOP OF CARLISLE My lord, wise men ne'er wail their present woes,
175 But presently prevent the ways to wail.[5]
To fear the foe, since fear oppresseth° strength,   *suppresses*
Gives in your weakness strength unto your foe;
And so your follies fight against yourself.
Fear, and be slain. No worse can come to fight;°   *in fighting*
180 And fight and die is death destroying death,[6]
Where fearing dying pays death servile breath.
AUMERLE My father hath a power.° Enquire of him,   *an army*
And learn to make a body of a limb.
KING RICHARD [*standing*] Thou chid'st me well. Proud Boling-
   broke, I come
185 To change blows with thee for our day of doom.[7]
This ague-fit° of fear is overblown.°   *chill / blown over*
An easy task it is to win our own.
Say, Scrope, where lies our uncle with his power?
Speak sweetly, man, although thy looks be sour.
190 SCROPE Men judge by the complexion° of the sky   *appearance*
   The state and inclination of the day.
So may you by my dull and heavy eye
   My tongue hath but a heavier tale to say.
I play the torturer by small and small°   *little by little*
195 To lengthen out the worst that must be spoken.
Your uncle York is joined with Bolingbroke,
And all your northern castles yielded up,
And all your southern gentlemen° in arms   *men of rank*
Upon his faction.
KING RICHARD   Thou hast said enough.
200 [*To* AUMERLE] Beshrew° thee, cousin, which didst lead me forth   *Woe to*
Of that sweet way I was in to despair.
What say you now? What comfort have we now?
By heaven, I'll hate him everlastingly
That bids me be of comfort any more.
205 Go to Flint Castle;° there I'll pine away.   *Welsh castle near Chester*
A king, woe's slave, shall kingly woe obey.
That power I have, discharge, and let them go
To ear° the land that hath some hope to grow;   *till*
For I have none. Let no man speak again
210 To alter this, for counsel is but vain.
AUMERLE My liege, one word.
KING RICHARD   He does me double wrong

2. And Death having thus amused himself.
3. Replace your hats (do not respectfully remain bare-
headed).
4. Made a subject to such needs (with pun).

5. But immediately vanquish the causes of grief.
6. To die fighting is to destroy death's power by dying.
7. To exchange blows with you in order to determine
our fates.

That wounds me with the flatteries of his tongue.
Discharge my followers. Let them hence away
From Richard's night to Bolingbroke's fair day.   *Exeunt*

3.3

Enter BOLINGBROKE [*Duke of Lancaster and Hereford,*
Duke of] YORK, [*Earl of*] NORTHUMBERLAND, [*and sol-*
diers] *with drum and colours*

BOLINGBROKE   So that by this intelligence° we learn   *information*
  The Welshmen are dispersed, and Salisbury
  Is gone to meet the King, who lately landed
  With some few private friends upon this coast.
5 NORTHUMBERLAND   The news is very fair and good, my lord.
  Richard not far from hence hath hid his head.
  YORK   It would beseem the Lord Northumberland
  To say 'King Richard'. Alack the heavy day
  When such a sacred king should hide his head!
10 NORTHUMBERLAND   Your grace mistakes. Only to be brief
  Left I his title out.
  YORK   The time hath been,
  Would you have been so brief with him, he would
  Have been so brief with you to shorten you,
  For taking so the head,[1] your whole head's length.
15 BOLINGBROKE   Mistake not, uncle, further than you should.
  YORK   Take not, good cousin, further than you should,
  Lest you mistake° the heavens are over our heads.   *forget*
  BOLINGBROKE   I know it, uncle, and oppose not myself
  Against their will.

Enter [HARRY] PERCY [*and a trumpeter*]

          But who comes here?
20 Welcome, Harry. What, will not this castle yield?
  HARRY PERCY   The castle royally is manned, my lord,
  Against thy entrance.
  BOLINGBROKE   Royally?
  Why, it contains no king.
  HARRY PERCY   Yes, my good lord,
  It doth contain a king. King Richard lies
25 Within the limits of yon lime and stone,
  And with him are the Lord Aumerle, Lord Salisbury,
  Sir Stephen Scrope, besides a clergyman
  Of holy reverence; who, I cannot learn.
  NORTHUMBERLAND   O, belike° it is the Bishop of Carlisle.   *probably*
30 BOLINGBROKE [*to* NORTHUMBERLAND]   Noble lord,
  Go to the rude ribs° of that ancient castle;   *rough walls*
  Through brazen trumpet send the breath of parley
  Into his ruined ears,° and thus deliver.   *its battered loopholes*
  Henry Bolingbroke
35 Upon his knees doth kiss King Richard's hand,
  And sends allegiance and true faith of heart
  To his most royal person, hither come
  Even at his feet to lay my arms and power,
  Provided that my banishment repealed°   *revoked*
40 And lands restored again be freely granted.

3.3 Location: Before Flint Castle.   1. For omitting the title thus; for acting without restraint.

If not, I'll use the advantage of my power,
And lay° the summer's dust with showers of blood   make settle
Rained from the wounds of slaughtered Englishmen;
The which how far off from the mind of Bolingbroke
45 It is such crimson tempest should bedrench
The fresh green lap of fair King Richard's land,
My stooping duty° tenderly shall show.   submissive kneeling
Go, signify as much, while here we march
Upon the grassy carpet of this plain.
50 Let's march without the noise of threat'ning drum,
That from this castle's tottered° battlements   dilapidated
Our fair appointments° may be well perused.   equipment
Methinks King Richard and myself should meet
With no less terror than the elements
55 Of fire and water° when their thund'ring shock   lightning and rain
At meeting tears the cloudy cheeks of heaven.
Be he the fire, I'll be the yielding water.
The rage be his, whilst on the earth I rain°   (punning on "reign"?)
My waters: on the earth, and not on him.—
60 March on, and mark King Richard, how he looks.
       [*They march about the stage; then* BOLINGBROKE, YORK,
       PERCY, *and soldiers stand at a distance from the walls;*
       NORTHUMBERLAND *and a trumpeter advance to the
       walls.*] *The trumpets sound [a] parley without, and [an]
       answer within; then a flourish [within.* KING] RICHARD
       appeareth on the walls,[2] [*with* BISHOP OF] CARLISLE,
       [*Duke of*] AUMERLE, SCROPE, [*and Earl of*] SALISBURY
See, see, King Richard doth himself appear,
As doth the blushing[3] discontented sun
From out the fiery portal of the east
When he perceives the envious° clouds are bent   malicious
65 To dim his glory and to stain the track
Of his bright passage to the occident.
YORK Yet looks he like a king. Behold, his eye,
As bright as is the eagle's, lightens forth[4]
Controlling majesty. Alack, alack for woe
70 That any harm should stain so fair a show!
KING RICHARD [*to* NORTHUMBERLAND] We are amazed; and
       thus long have we stood
To watch° the fearful bending of thy knee,   wait for
Because we thought ourself thy lawful king.
An if° we be, how dare thy joints forget   An if = If
75 To pay their aweful° duty to our presence?   reverential
If we be not, show us the hand of God
That hath dismissed us from our stewardship.
For well we know no hand of blood and bone
Can grip° the sacred handle of our sceptre,   seize
80 Unless he do profane, steal, or usurp.
And though you think that all—as you have done—
Have torn° their souls by turning them from us,   ruined (by disloyalty)
And we are barren and bereft of friends,

---

2. That is, on the balcony of the tiring-house at the   weather).
back of the stage.   4. Flashes out (the eagle is a traditional royal symbol).
3. Red (proverbially, a red morning sky anticipates bad

threaten

85 Yet know my master, God omnipotent,
    Is mustering in his clouds on our behalf
    Armies of pestilence; and they shall strike
    Your children yet unborn and unbegot,
    That lift your vassal hands against my head
    And threat° the glory of my precious crown.
90 Tell Bolingbroke, for yon methinks he is,
    That every stride he makes upon my land
    Is dangerous treason. He is come to open
    The purple testament° of bleeding war;
    But ere the crown he looks for live in peace
95 Ten thousand bloody crowns° of mothers' sons
    Shall ill become the flower of England's face,⁵
    Change the complexion of her maid-pale° peace
    To scarlet indignation, and bedew
    Her pastures' grass with faithful English blood.
    NORTHUMBERLAND [*kneeling*] The King of heaven forbid our
100   lord the King
    Should so with civil and uncivil⁶ arms
    Be rushed upon. Thy thrice-noble cousin
    Harry Bolingbroke doth humbly kiss thy hand,
    And by the honourable tomb he swears,
105 That stands upon your royal grandsire's° bones,
    And by the royalties of both your bloods,
    Currents that spring from one most gracious head,°
    And by the buried hand of warlike Gaunt,
    And by the worth and honour of himself,
110 Comprising all that may be sworn or said,
    His coming hither hath no further scope°
    Than for his lineal royalties,° and to beg
    Enfranchisement° immediate on his knees;
    Which on thy royal party° granted once,
115 His glittering arms he will commend° to rust,
    His barbèd° steeds to stables, and his heart
    To faithful service of your majesty.
    This swears he as he is a prince and just,
    And as I am a gentleman I credit° him.
120 KING RICHARD Northumberland, say thus the King returns:°
    His noble cousin is right welcome hither,
    And all the number of his fair demands
    Shall be accomplished without contradiction.
    With all the gracious utterance thou hast,
125 Speak to his gentle hearing kind commends.°
         [NORTHUMBERLAND *and the trumpeter return to*
         BOLINGBROKE]
    [*To* AUMERLE] We do debase ourself, cousin, do we not,
    To look so poorly° and to speak so fair?
    Shall we call back Northumberland, and send
    Defiance to the traitor, and so die?
130 AUMERLE No, good my lord, let's fight with gentle words
    Till time lend friends, and friends their helpful swords.
    KING RICHARD O God, O God, that e'er this tongue of mine,
    That laid the sentence of dread banishment

Marginal glosses:
- (line 89) *threaten*
- (line 93) *blood-red document*
- (line 95) *heads*
- (line 97) *innocent white*
- (line 105) *(Edward III's)*
- (line 107) *source*
- (line 111) *aim*
- (line 112) *hereditary rights*
- (line 113) *Recall from exile*
- (line 114) *part*
- (line 115) *commit*
- (line 116) *armed*
- (line 119) *believe*
- (line 120) *replies*
- (line 125) *regards*
- (line 127) *abjectly*

---

5. Blooming surface of England; faces of England's choicest youth.   6. Of the same country and violent; playing on "civil" as "peaceful" and "uncivil" as "alien."

On yon proud man, should take it off again
135 With words of sooth!° O, that I were as great   *soothing words*
As is my grief, or lesser than my name,
Or that I could forget what I have been,
Or not remember what I must be now!
Swell'st thou, proud heart? I'll give thee scope to beat,
140 Since foes have scope to beat both thee and me.
　　　　　[NORTHUMBERLAND *advances to the walls*]
AUMERLE　Northumberland comes back from Bolingbroke.
KING RICHARD　What must the King do now? Must he submit?
The King shall do it. Must he be deposed?
The King shall be contented. Must he lose
145 The name of King? A° God's name, let it go.   *In*
I'll give my jewels for a set of beads,°   *rosary*
My gorgeous palace for a hermitage,
My gay apparel for an almsman's° gown,   *a beggar's*
My figured° goblets for a dish of wood,   *engraved*
150 My sceptre for a palmer's° walking staff,   *pilgrim's*
My subjects for a pair of carvèd saints,
And my large kingdom for a little grave,
A little, little grave, an obscure grave;
Or I'll be buried in the King's highway,°   *(as suicides were)*
155 Some way of common trade° where subjects' feet   *passage*
May hourly trample on their sovereign's head,
For on my heart they tread now, whilst I live,
And buried once, why not upon my head?
Aumerle, thou weep'st, my tender-hearted cousin.
160 We'll make foul weather with despisèd tears.
Our sighs and they shall lodge° the summer corn,   *beat down*
And make a dearth° in this revolting° land.   *famine / rebellious*
Or shall we play the wantons° with our woes,   *we frolic*
And make some pretty match° with shedding tears;   *clever game*
165 As thus to drop them still° upon one place   *continually*
Till they have fretted° us a pair of graves   *eroded for*
Within the earth, and therein laid? 'There lies
Two kinsmen digged their graves with weeping eyes.'
Would not this ill do well? Well, well, I see
170 I talk but idly° and you mock at me.   *foolishly*
Most mighty prince, my lord Northumberland,
What says King Bolingbroke? Will his majesty
Give Richard leave to live till Richard die?
You make a leg,° and Bolingbroke says 'Ay'.   *an obeisance*
175 NORTHUMBERLAND　My lord, in the base court° he doth attend   *outer courtyard*
To speak with you. May it please you to come down?
KING RICHARD　Down, down I come like glist'ring Phaethon,[7]
Wanting the manage° of unruly jades.[8]   *Lacking control*
In the base court: base court where kings grow base
180 To come at traitors' calls, and do them grace.°   *favor them*
In the base court, come down: down court, down King,
For night-owls shriek where mounting larks should sing.
　　　　　[*Exeunt* KING RICHARD *and his party*]

---

7. In Greek mythology, the son of the sun god. He attempted to drive his father's sun chariot but was too weak to control the horses; Zeus, king of the gods, struck him down with a thunderbolt to prevent him from destroying the earth.
8. Horses (contemptuous).

[NORTHUMBERLAND *returns to* BOLINGBROKE]

BOLINGBROKE   What says his majesty?

NORTHUMBERLAND   Sorrow and grief of heart

Makes him speak fondly,° like a frantic° man.   *foolishly / an insane*

[*Enter* KING RICHARD *and his party below*]

Yet he is come.

185   BOLINGBROKE   Stand all apart,

And show fair duty to his majesty.

He kneels down

My gracious lord.

KING RICHARD   Fair cousin, you debase your princely knee

To make the base earth proud with kissing it.

190   Me rather had° my heart might feel your love   *I had rather*

Than my unpleased eye see your courtesy.

Up, cousin, up. Your heart is up, I know,

Thus high at least,⁹ although your knee be low.

BOLINGBROKE   My gracious lord, I come but for mine own.

195   KING RICHARD   Your own is yours, and I am yours, and all.

BOLINGBROKE   So far be mine, my most redoubted° lord,   *dreaded*

As my true service shall deserve your love.

KING RICHARD   Well you deserve. They well deserve to have

That know the strong'st and surest way to get.

[BOLINGBROKE *rises*]

200   [*To* YORK] Uncle, give me your hands. Nay, dry your eyes.

Tears show their love, but want their remedies.°   *do no good*

[*To* BOLINGBROKE] Cousin, I am too young to be your father,

Though you are old enough to be my heir.

What you will have I'll give, and willing too;

205   For do we must what force will have us do.

Set on towards London, cousin: is it so?

BOLINGBROKE   Yea, my good lord.

KING RICHARD   Then I must not say no.

Flourish. Exeunt.

3.4

Enter the QUEEN *with her two* LADIES

QUEEN   What sport shall we devise here in this garden,

To drive away the heavy thought of care?

FIRST LADY   Madam, we'll play at bowls.°   *lawn bowling*

QUEEN   'Twill make me think the world is full of rubs,¹

5   And that my fortune runs against the bias.²

SECOND LADY   Madam, we'll dance.

QUEEN   My legs can keep no measure° in delight   *dance step*

When my poor heart no measure° keeps in grief;   *moderation*

Therefore no dancing, girl. Some other sport.

10   FIRST LADY   Madam, we'll tell tales.

QUEEN   Of sorrow or of joy?

FIRST LADY   Of either, madam.

QUEEN   Of neither, girl.

For if of joy, being altogether wanting,

15   It doth remember° me the more of sorrow.   *remind*

---

9. Richard touches his crown.   2. Runs askew. *bias*: literally, a lead weight in the bowl
3.4 Location: The Duke of York's garden.   that makes it run smoothly.
1. Impediments (a term from the game of bowls).

Or if of grief, being altogether had,°   *possessed*
It adds more sorrow to my want of joy.
For what I have I need not to repeat,
And what I want it boots° not to complain.   *helps*
SECOND LADY   Madam, I'll sing.
20 QUEEN   'Tis well that thou hast cause;
But thou shouldst please me better wouldst thou weep.
SECOND LADY   I could weep, madam, would it do you good.
QUEEN   And I could sing, would weeping do me good,
And never borrow any tear of thee.
        Enter a GARDENER *and two* [MEN]
25 But stay; here come the gardeners.
Let's step into the shadow of these trees.
My wretchedness unto a row of pins³
They will talk of state, for everyone doth so
Against° a change. Woe is forerun with woe.   *In anticipation of*
    [*The* QUEEN *and her* LADIES *stand apart*]
30 GARDENER [*to* FIRST MAN]   Go, bind thou up young dangling apricots
Which, like unruly children, make their sire
Stoop with oppression of their prodigal° weight.   *excessive*
Give some supportance to the bending twigs.
[*To* SECOND MAN] Go thou, and, like an executioner,
35 Cut off the heads of too fast-growing sprays
That look too lofty in our commonwealth.
All must be even° in our government.   *equal*
You thus employed, I will go root away
The noisome° weeds which without profit suck   *harmful*
40 The soil's fertility from wholesome flowers.
FIRST MAN   Why should we, in the compass of a pale,⁴
Keep law and form and due proportion,
Showing as in a model our firm estate,°   *stable government*
When our sea-wallèd garden, the whole land,
45 Is full of weeds, her fairest flowers choked up,
Her fruit trees all unpruned, her hedges ruined,
Her knots⁵ disordered, and her wholesome herbs
Swarming with caterpillars?
GARDENER   Hold thy peace.
He that hath suffered° this disordered spring   *permitted*
50 Hath now himself met with the fall of leaf.
The weeds which his broad spreading leaves did shelter,
That seemed in eating him to hold him up,
Are plucked up, root and all, by Bolingbroke—
I mean the Earl of Wiltshire, Bushy, Green.
SECOND MAN   What, are they dead?
55 GARDENER   They are; and Bolingbroke
Hath seized the wasteful King. O, what pity is it
That he had not so trimmed and dressed° his land   *cultivated*
As we this garden! We at time of year°   *in season*
Do wound the bark, the skin of our fruit trees,⁶
60 Lest, being over-proud in° sap and blood,   *excessively swollen with*
With too much riches it confound° itself.   *ruin*

---

3. I'll bet my great wretchedness against a trivial row of pins.
4. In the limits of a fenced enclosure.

5. Intricate flower beds; social bonds.
6. *Do . . . trees:* this restricts the tree's food supply, encouraging fruit buds to form.

Had he done so to great and growing men,
They might have lived to bear, and he to taste,
Their fruits of duty. Superfluous branches
65 We lop away, that bearing boughs may live.
Had he done so, himself had borne° the crown,[7]   *retained*
Which waste of idle hours hath quite thrown down.
FIRST MAN   What, think you then the King shall be deposed?
GARDENER   Depressed° he is already, and deposed   *Brought low*
70 'Tis doubt° he will be. Letters came last night   *feared*
To a dear friend of the good Duke of York's
That tell black tidings.
QUEEN   O, I am pressed to death through want of speaking![8]
          [*She comes forward*]
Thou, old Adam's[9] likeness, set to dress° this garden,   *cultivate*
75 How dares thy harsh rude° tongue sound this unpleasing news?   *ignorant*
What Eve, what serpent hath suggested° thee   *tempted*
To make a second fall of cursèd man?
Why dost thou say King Richard is deposed?
Dar'st thou, thou little better thing than earth,
80 Divine° his downfall? Say where, when, and how   *Prophesy*
Cam'st thou by this ill tidings? Speak, thou wretch!
GARDENER   Pardon me, madam. Little joy have I
To breathe this news, yet what I say is true.
King Richard he is in the mighty hold
85 Of Bolingbroke. Their fortunes both are weighed.
In your lord's scale is nothing but himself
And some few vanities that make him light.
But in the balance of great Bolingbroke,
Besides himself, are all the English peers,
90 And with that odds he weighs King Richard down.
Post° you to London and you will find it so.   *Hasten*
I speak no more than everyone doth know.
QUEEN   Nimble mischance that art so light of foot,
Doth not thy embassage° belong to me,   *message*
95 And am I last that knows it? O, thou think'st
To serve me last, that I may longest keep
Thy sorrow in my breast. Come, ladies, go
To meet at London London's king in woe.
What, was I born to this, that my sad look
100 Should grace the triumph° of great Bolingbroke?   *triumphal procession*
Gard'ner, for telling me these news of woe,
Pray God the plants thou graft'st may never grow.
          Exit [*with her* LADIES]
GARDENER   Poor Queen, so that° thy state might be no worse   *if as a result*
I would my skill were subject to thy curse.
105 Here did she fall° a tear. Here in this place   *drop*
I'll set a bank of rue,[1] sour herb-of-grace.
Rue even for ruth° here shortly shall be seen   *pity*
In the remembrance of a weeping queen.
                              Exeunt

7. Playing on the "crown" of a tree.
8. In medieval and Renaissance England, indicted persons who refused to plead guilty or not guilty were
killed with weights laid on the stomach.
9. Adam was the first gardener.
1. Herb associated with compassion and repentance.

4.1

Enter, as to Parliament, BOLINGBROKE [*Duke of Lancaster and Hereford, Duke of*] AUMERLE, [*Earl of*]
NORTHUMBERLAND, [HARRY] PERCY, [*Lord*] FITZWALTER,
[*Duke of*] SURREY, [BISHOP OF] CARLISLE, [*and the*]
ABBOT OF WESTMINSTER

BOLINGBROKE   Call forth Bagot.

Enter BAGOT, [*with*] *officers*

                    Now, Bagot, freely speak thy mind:
  What thou dost know of noble Gloucester's death,
  Who wrought it with[1] the King, and who performed
  The bloody office° of his timeless° end.   *deed / untimely*

5 BAGOT   Then set before my face the Lord Aumerle.

BOLINGBROKE [*to* AUMERLE]   Cousin, stand forth, and look
    upon that man.

      [AUMERLE *stands forth*]

BAGOT   My lord Aumerle, I know your daring tongue
  Scorns to unsay° what once it hath delivered.   *deny*
  In that dead° time when Gloucester's death was plotted   *fatal; dark*

10 I heard you say 'Is not my arm of length,°   *long enough*
  That reacheth from the restful English court
  As far as Calais, to mine uncle's head?'
  Amongst much other talk that very time[2]
  I heard you say that you had rather refuse

15 The offer of an hundred thousand crowns
  Than° Bolingbroke's return to England,   *Than accept*
  Adding withal° how blest this land would be   *besides*
  In this your cousin's death.

AUMERLE   Princes and noble lords,
  What answer shall I make to this base man?

20 Shall I so much dishonour my fair stars°   *honorable birth*
  On equal terms to give him chastisement?[3]
  Either I must, or have mine honour soiled
  With the attainder° of his slanderous lips.   *accusation*

      [*He throws down his gage*]

  There is my gage, the manual seal of death

25 That marks thee out for hell. I say thou liest,
  And will maintain° what thou hast said is false   *will uphold in combat*
  In thy heart blood, though being all too base
  To stain the temper[4] of my knightly sword.

BOLINGBROKE   Bagot, forbear. Thou shalt not take it up.

30 AUMERLE   Excepting one,° I would he° were the best *(Bolingbroke) / (Bagot)*
  In all this presence that hath moved° me so.   *angered*

FITZWALTER   If that thy valour stand on sympathy,[5]
  There is my gage, Aumerle, in gage to thine.

      [*He throws down his gage*]

  By that fair sun which shows me where thou stand'st,

35 I heard thee say, and vauntingly° thou spak'st it,   *boastfully*
  That thou wert cause of noble Gloucester's death.
  If° thou deny'st it twenty times, thou liest,   *Even if*

4.1 Location: Westminster Hall.
1. Who persuaded; who collaborated with.
2. *that very time:* inconsistent, since Gloucester was
killed long before Bolingbroke's exile.

3. Punishment (a lord could refuse to fight a lowborn
man in the trial by combat).
4. Quality (literally, "hardness").
5. Insists on equality of rank.

And I will turn thy falsehood to thy heart,
Where it was forgèd, with my rapier's point.

40 AUMERLE   Thou dar'st not, coward, live to see that day.

FITZWALTER   Now by my soul, I would it were this hour.

AUMERLE   Fitzwalter, thou art damned to hell for this.

HARRY PERCY   Aumerle, thou liest. His honour is as true
In this appeal° as thou art all unjust;   accusation

45 And that thou art so, there I throw my gage
    [*He throws down his gage*]
To prove it on thee to the extremest point
Of mortal breathing. Seize it if thou dar'st.

AUMERLE   An if I do not, may my hands rot off,
And never brandish more° revengeful steel   again

50 Over the glittering helmet of my foe.[6]

50.1 ANOTHER LORD   *I task the earth to the like, forsworn Aumerle,*
    And spur thee on with full as many lies°   accusations of lying
    As may be hollowed° in thy treacherous ear   shouted
    From sun to sun.° There is my honour's pawn.   sunrise to sunset

50.5 *Engage it to[7] the trial if thou darest.*
    [*He throws down his gage*]

AUMERLE   *Who sets° me else? By heaven, I'll throw[8] at all.*   challenges (in gambling)
I have a thousand spirits in one breast
To answer twenty thousand such as you.

SURREY   My lord Fitzwalter, I do remember well
The very time Aumerle and you did talk.

FITZWALTER   'Tis very true. You were in presence° then,   were present
And you can witness with me this is true.

55 SURREY   As false, by heaven, as heaven itself is true.

FITZWALTER   Surrey, thou liest.

SURREY   Dishonourable boy,
That lie shall lie so heavy on my sword
That it shall render vengeance and revenge,
Till thou, the lie-giver, and that lie do lie

60 In earth as quiet as thy father's skull;
In proof whereof, there is my honour's pawn.
    [*He throws down his gage*]
Engage it to the trial if thou dar'st.

FITZWALTER   How fondly dost thou spur a forward horse!
If I dare eat, or drink, or breathe, or live,

65 I dare meet Surrey in a wilderness
And spit upon him whilst I say he lies,
And lies, and lies.[9] There is my bond of faith
To tie thee to my strong correction.
As I intend to thrive in this new world,

70 Aumerle is guilty of my true appeal.°   accusation
Besides, I heard the banished Norfolk° say   (Mowbray)
That thou, Aumerle, didst send two of thy men
To execute the noble Duke at Calais.

AUMERLE   Some honest Christian trust me with° a gage.   lend me
    [*He takes another's gage and throws it down*]

---

6. The following indented passage (lines 50.1–50.8)   8. Defeat (as by throwing dice).
appears only in Q1.   9. Fitzwalter may throw down another gage here.
7. Accept it as a pledge ("gage") for.

75 That Norfolk lies, here do I throw down this,
If he may be repealed,° to try his honour.   *recalled from exile*
BOLINGBROKE   These differences shall all rest under gage[1]
Till Norfolk be repealed. Repealed he shall be,
And, though mine enemy, restored again
80 To all his lands and signories.° When he is returned,   *estates*
Against Aumerle we will enforce his trial.
BISHOP OF CARLISLE   That honourable day shall never be seen.
Many a time hath banished Norfolk fought
For Jesu Christ in glorious Christian field,[2]
85 Streaming the ensign of the Christian cross
Against black pagans, Turks, and Saracens;
And, toiled° with works of war, retired himself   *exhausted*
To Italy, and there at Venice gave
His body to that pleasant country's earth,
90 And his pure soul unto his captain, Christ,
Under whose colours he had fought so long.
BOLINGBROKE   Why, Bishop of Carlisle, is Norfolk dead?
BISHOP OF CARLISLE   As surely as I live, my lord.
BOLINGBROKE   Sweet peace conduct his sweet soul to the bosom
95 Of good old Abraham![3] Lords appellants,
Your differences° shall all rest under gage   *disputes*
Till we assign you to your days of trial.
      Enter [Duke of] YORK
YORK   Great Duke of Lancaster, I come to thee
From plume-plucked° Richard, who with willing soul   *humbled*
100 Adopts thee heir, and his high sceptre yields
To the possession of thy royal hand.
Ascend his throne, descending now from him,
And long live Henry, of that name the fourth!
BOLINGBROKE   In God's name I'll ascend the regal throne.
105 BISHOP OF CARLISLE   Marry, God forbid!
Worst° in this royal presence may I speak,   *Least worthy*
Yet best beseeming° me to speak the truth.   *fitting (as a clergyman)*
Would God that any in this noble presence
Were enough noble to be upright judge
110 Of noble Richard. Then true noblesse° would   *nobility*
Learn° him forbearance from so foul a wrong.   *Teach*
What subject can give sentence on his king?
And who sits here that is not Richard's subject?
Thieves are not judged but° they are by° to hear,   *except when / present*
115 Although apparent° guilt be seen in them;   *obvious*
And shall the figure° of God's majesty,   *image*
His captain, steward, deputy elect,°   *chosen*
Anointed, crownèd, planted many years,
Be judged by subject and inferior breath,
120 And he himself not present? O, forfend° it, God,   *prohibit*
That in a Christian climate souls refined[4]
Should show so heinous, black, obscene° a deed!   *odious*
I speak to subjects, and a subject speaks
Stirred up by God thus boldly for his king.

---

1. Shall remain as standing challenges.
2. In battle for the Christian cause.
3. *the bosom . . . Abraham:* that is, heavenly rest; see

Luke 16:22.
4. Spiritually improved; aristocratic.

125 My lord of Hereford here, whom you call king,
Is a foul traitor to proud Hereford's king;
And, if you crown him, let me prophesy
The blood of English shall manure the ground,
And future ages groan for this foul act.

130 Peace shall go sleep with Turks and infidels,
And in this seat° of peace tumultuous wars   *region; throne*
Shall kin with kin and kind with kind confound.⁵
Disorder, horror, fear, and mutiny
Shall here inhabit, and this land be called

135 The field of Golgotha⁶ and dead men's skulls.
O, if you rear this house against this house°   *(Lancaster against York)*
It will the woefullest division prove
That ever fell upon this cursèd earth!
Prevent, resist it; let it not be so,

140 Lest child, child's children, cry against you woe.

NORTHUMBERLAND   Well have you argued, sir, and for your pains
Of capital treason we arrest you here.
My lord of Westminster, be it your charge
To keep him safely till his day of trial.⁷

145 May it please you, lords, to grant the Commons' suit?⁸

BOLINGBROKE   Fetch hither Richard, that in common° view   *public*
He may surrender.⁹ So we shall proceed
Without suspicion.

YORK   I will be his conduct.°   *Exit*   *escort*

BOLINGBROKE   Lords, you that here are under our arrest,

150 Procure your sureties for your days of answer.¹
Little are we beholden to your love,
And little looked for° at your helping hands.   *expected*

Enter RICHARD *and* [*Duke of*] YORK [*with attendants*
bearing the crown and sceptre]

RICHARD   Alack, why am I sent for to a king
Before I have shook off the regal thoughts

155 Wherewith I reigned? I hardly yet have learned
To insinuate, flatter, bow, and bend my knee.
Give sorrow leave awhile to tutor me
To this submission. Yet I well remember
The favours° of these men. Were they not mine?   *faces; benefits*

160 Did they not sometime cry 'All hail!' to me?
So Judas did to Christ. But He in twelve
Found truth in all but one; I, in twelve thousand, none.
God save the King! Will no man say 'Amen'?
Am I both priest and clerk?² Well then, Amen.

165 God save the King, although I be not he.
And yet Amen, if heaven do think him me.
To do what service am I sent for hither?

YORK   To do that office° of thine own good will   *task; ceremony*
Which tired majesty did make thee offer:

---

5. Shall destroy kinsman by fellow kinsman and countryman by fellow countryman.
6. Place of Christ's crucifixion, the name of which
means "place of dead men's skulls."
7. The passage that follows, to line 308, is not included
in the earliest texts. See Textual Note.
8. The House of Commons' request that Richard

should have judgment passed on him.
9. Abdicate (the legitimacy of the Commons' suit
depended on Richard's having given up the crown and
thus his royal immunity from prosecution).
1. Procure persons guaranteeing your appearance on
the day of trial.
2. Priest's assistant who utters the responses to prayers.

170　The resignation of thy state and crown
　　To Henry Bolingbroke.
　　RICHARD [*to an attendant*]　Give me the crown. [*To* BOLINGBROKE]
　　Here, cousin, seize the crown.
　　Here, cousin. On this side my hand, on that side thine.
　　Now is this golden crown like a deep well
175　That owes° two buckets filling one another,³ *has*
　　The emptier ever dancing in the air,
　　The other down, unseen, and full of water.
　　That bucket down and full of tears am I,
　　Drinking my griefs, whilst you mount up on high.
180　BOLINGBROKE　I thought you had been willing to resign.
　　RICHARD　My crown I am, but still my griefs are mine.
　　You may my glories and my state° depose, *royal status*
　　But not my griefs; still° am I king of those. *permanently*
　　BOLINGBROKE　Part of your cares you give me with your crown.
185　RICHARD　Your cares set up do not pluck my cares down.
　　My care is loss of care by old care done;
　　Your care is gain of care by new care won.⁴
　　The cares I give I have, though given away;
　　They 'tend° the crown, yet still with me they stay. *attend; accompany*
190　BOLINGBROKE　Are you contented to resign the crown?
　　RICHARD　Ay, no; no, ay; for I must nothing be;⁵
　　Therefore no, no, for I resign to thee.
　　Now mark me how I will undo° myself. *ruin; strip*
　　I give this heavy weight from off my head,
　　　　[BOLINGBROKE *accepts the crown*]
195　And this unwieldy sceptre from my hand,
　　　　[BOLINGBROKE *accepts the sceptre*]
　　The pride of kingly sway from out my heart.
　　With mine own tears I wash away my balm,
　　With mine own hands I give away my crown,
　　With mine own tongue deny my sacred state,° *divine right to be King*
200　With mine own breath release all duteous oaths.° *oaths of allegiance*
　　All pomp and majesty I do forswear.
　　My manors, rents, revenues I forgo.
　　My acts, decrees, and statutes I deny.° *repudiate*
　　God pardon all oaths that are broke to me.
205　God keep all vows unbroke are made to thee.
　　Make me, that nothing have, with nothing grieved,⁶
　　And thou with all pleased, that hast all achieved.
　　Long mayst thou live in Richard's seat to sit,
　　And soon lie Richard in an earthy pit.
210　'God save King Henry,' unkinged Richard says,
　　'And send him many years of sunshine° days.' *sunny*
　　What more remains?
　　NORTHUMBERLAND [*giving* RICHARD *papers*]
　　　　　　　　No more but that you read° *read aloud*
　　These accusations and these grievous crimes
　　Committed by your person and your followers

---

3. That is, the raising of one causing the other to descend and fill.
4. *Your cares . . . won:* an extended wordplay on "care": Your assuming cares of state does not relieve me of grief. I mourn the loss of responsibility, by lack of diligence in the past; you concern yourself with gaining responsibility, won by effort.
5. Playing on "ay" (yes) and "I": since I am no thing, then "I," that is, "ay," is "no."
6. Grieved at nothing; grieved at having nothing.

215   Against the state and profit° of this land,   *established prosperity*
       That by confessing them, the souls of men
       May deem that you are worthily deposed.
       RICHARD   Must I do so? And must I ravel out
       My weaved-up follies? Gentle Northumberland,
220   If thy offences were upon record,
       Would it not shame thee in so fair a troop°   *company*
       To read a lecture° of them? If thou wouldst,   *give a public reading*
       There shouldst thou find one heinous article
       Containing the deposing of a king
225   And cracking the strong warrant of an oath,
       Marked with a blot, damned in the book of heaven.
       Nay, all of you that stand and look upon
       Whilst that my wretchedness doth bait[7] myself,
       Though some of you, with Pilate, wash your hands,[8]
230   Showing an outward pity, yet you Pilates
       Have here delivered me to my sour° cross,   *bitter*
       And water cannot wash away your sin.
       NORTHUMBERLAND   My lord, dispatch.° Read o'er these articles.   *hurry up*
       RICHARD   Mine eyes are full of tears; I cannot see.
235   And yet salt water blinds them not so much
       But they can see a sort° of traitors here.   *pack*
       Nay, if I turn mine eyes upon myself
       I find myself a traitor with the rest,
       For I have given here my soul's consent
240   T'undeck the pompous° body of a king,   *splendidly dressed*
       Made glory base and sovereignty a slave,
       Proud majesty a subject, state° a peasant.   *royalty*
       NORTHUMBERLAND   My lord—
       RICHARD   No lord of thine, thou haught°-insulting man,   *haughty*
245   Nor no man's lord. I have no name, no title,
       No, not that name was given me at the font,
       But 'tis usurped. Alack the heavy day,
       That I have worn so many winters out
       And know not now what name to call myself!
250   O, that I were a mockery king of snow,
       Standing before the sun of Bolingbroke
       To melt myself away in water-drops!
       Good king, great king—and yet not greatly good—
       An if my word be sterling° yet in England,   *valid (like currency)*
255   Let it command a mirror hither straight,°   *immediately*
       That it may show me what a face I have,
       Since it is bankrupt of his° majesty.   *its*
       BOLINGBROKE   Go some of you and fetch a looking-glass.
                                                                [*Exit one or more*]
       NORTHUMBERLAND   Read o'er this paper while the glass° doth   *until the mirror*
           come.
260   RICHARD   Fiend, thou torment'st me ere I come to hell.
       BOLINGBROKE   Urge it no more, my lord Northumberland.
       NORTHUMBERLAND   The Commons will not then be satisfied.
       RICHARD   They shall be satisfied. I'll read enough
           When I do see the very book indeed

---

7. Torment (as in bearbaiting).
8. Pilate, Jesus' judge, washed his hands to signify his   disclaiming of responsibility for the death sentence he
                                                             imposed at the request of the Jews.

265 Where all my sins are writ, and that's myself.
     Enter one with a glass
  Give me that glass, and therein will I read.
    [RICHARD *takes the glass and looks in it*]
  No deeper wrinkles yet? Hath sorrow struck
  So many blows upon this face of mine
  And made no deeper wounds? O flatt'ring glass,
270 Like to my followers in prosperity,
  Thou dost beguile me! Was this face the face
  That every day under his household roof
  Did keep ten thousand men? Was this the face
  That like the sun did make beholders wink?°   *shut their eyes*
275 Is this the face which faced⁹ so many follies,
  That was at last outfaced° by Bolingbroke?   *stared down*
  A brittle glory shineth in this face.
  As brittle as the glory is the face,
    [*He shatters the glass*]
  For there it is, cracked in an hundred shivers.
280 Mark, silent King, the moral of this sport:
  How soon my sorrow hath destroyed my face.
  BOLINGBROKE The shadow¹ of your sorrow hath destroyed
  The shadow° of your face.   *image*
  RICHARD   Say that again:
  'The shadow of my sorrow'—ha, let's see.
285 'Tis very true: my grief lies all within,
  And these external manner of laments
  Are merely shadows to the unseen grief
  That swells with silence in the tortured soul.
  There lies the substance, and I thank thee, King,
290 For thy great bounty that not only giv'st
  Me cause to wail, but teachest me the way
  How to lament the cause. I'll beg one boon,°   *favor*
  And then be gone and trouble you no more.
  Shall I obtain it?
  BOLINGBROKE   Name it, fair cousin.
295 RICHARD Fair cousin? I am greater than a king;
  For when I was a king my flatterers
  Were then but subjects; being now a subject,
  I have a king here to my flatterer.
  Being so great, I have no need to beg.
300 BOLINGBROKE Yet ask.
  RICHARD And shall I have?
  BOLINGBROKE You shall.
  RICHARD Then give me leave to go.
  BOLINGBROKE Whither?
305 RICHARD Whither you will, so° I were from your sights.   *provided that*
  BOLINGBROKE Go some of you, convey° him to the Tower.   *conduct*
  RICHARD O good, 'convey'!° Conveyors are you all,   *steal*
  That rise thus nimbly by a true king's fall.
            [*Exit, guarded*]
  BOLINGBROKE On Wednesday next we solemnly set down

9. Countenanced; adorned (as a garment trimmed with
"facings").
1. Darkness; outward display; image, reflection; un-

happiness (Richard plays on the word's various meanings in the following passage).

310   Our coronation. Lords, prepare yourselves.

                  Exeunt. Manent [ABBOT OF] WESTMINSTER,

                      [BISHOP OF] CARLISLE, [*and*] AUMERLE

ABBOT OF WESTMINSTER   A woeful pageant have we here beheld.

BISHOP OF CARLISLE   The woe's to come, the children yet unborn

    Shall feel this day as sharp to them as thorn.

AUMERLE   You holy clergymen, is there no plot

315   To rid the realm of this pernicious blot?

ABBOT OF WESTMINSTER   My lord, before I freely speak my

       mind herein,

    You shall not only take the sacrament[2]

    To bury mine intents,[3] but also to effect

    Whatever I shall happen to devise.

320   I see your brows are full of discontent,

    Your hearts of sorrow, and your eyes of tears.

    Come home with me to supper. I will lay

    A plot shall show us all a merry day.   *Exeunt*

5.1

      Enter the QUEEN *with her* LADIES

QUEEN   This way the King will come. This is the way

    To Julius Caesar's ill-erected Tower,[1]

    To whose flint bosom my condemnèd lord

    Is doomed a prisoner by proud Bolingbroke.

5   Here let us rest, if this rebellious earth

    Have any resting for her true king's queen.

      Enter RICHARD, *and guard*

    But soft,° but see—or rather do not see—   *wait*

    My fair rose wither. Yet look up, behold,

    That you in pity may dissolve to dew,

10   And wash him fresh again with true-love tears.—

    Ah, thou the model where old Troy did stand![2]

    Thou map° of honour, thou King Richard's tomb,   *epitome*

    And not King Richard! Thou most beauteous inn:

    Why should hard-favoured° grief be lodged in thee,   *ugly; unfortunate*

15   When triumph is become an alehouse[3] guest?

RICHARD   Join not with grief, fair woman, do not so,

    To make my end too sudden. Learn, good soul,

    To think our former state a happy dream,

    From which awaked, the truth of what we are

20   Shows us but this. I am sworn brother, sweet,

    To grim necessity, and he and I

    Will keep a league till death. Hie° thee to France,   *Hasten*

    And cloister thee in some religious house.°   *convent*

    Our holy lives must win a new world's° crown,   *(heaven's)*

25   Which our profane hours here have stricken down.

QUEEN   What, is my Richard both in shape and mind

    Transformed and weakenèd? Hath Bolingbroke

    Deposed thine intellect? Hath he been in thy heart?

    The lion dying thrusteth forth his paw

---

2. A solemn oath, accompanied by the rite of Communion.
3. To keep my intentions secret.
5.1 Location: A street near the Tower of London.
1. The Tower of London (popularly thought to have

been built by Caesar). *ill-erected:* poorly built; erected for evil ends.
2. The pattern of fallen greatness, like Troy.
3. Poorer class of lodging (referring to Bolingbroke) than an "inn."

30 And wounds the earth, if nothing else, with rage
To be° o'erpowered; and wilt thou, pupil-like,   *At being*
Take the correction, mildly kiss the rod,
And fawn on rage with base humility,
Which art a lion and the king of beasts?

35 RICHARD A king of beasts[4] indeed! If aught but beasts,
I had been still a happy king of men.
Good sometimes° Queen, prepare thee hence for France.   *former*
Think I am dead, and that even here thou tak'st,
As from my death-bed, thy last living leave.

40 In winter's tedious nights, sit by the fire
With good old folks, and let them tell thee tales
Of woeful ages long ago betid;[5]
And ere thou bid goodnight, to quit their griefs°   *repay their sad tales*
Tell thou the lamentable fall of me,

45 And send the hearers weeping to their beds;
Forwhy the senseless brands will sympathize[6]
The heavy accent of thy moving[7] tongue,
And in compassion weep the fire out;
And some° will mourn in ashes, some coal black,   *(firebrands)*

50 For the deposing of a rightful king.
        Enter [Earl of] NORTHUMBERLAND

NORTHUMBERLAND My lord, the mind of Bolingbroke is changed.
You must to Pomfret,° not unto the Tower.   *castle in Yorkshire*
And, madam, there is order ta'en[8] for you.
With all swift speed you must away to France.

55 RICHARD Northumberland, thou ladder wherewithal
The mounting Bolingbroke ascends my throne,
The time shall not be many hours of age
More than it is ere foul sin, gathering head,
Shall break into corruption.[9] Thou shalt think,

60 Though he divide the realm and give thee half,
It is too little helping[1] him to all.
He shall think that thou, which know'st the way
To plant unrightful kings, wilt know again,
Being ne'er so little urged another way,

65 To pluck him headlong from the usurpèd throne.
The love of wicked friends converts to fear,
That fear to hate, and hate turns one or both
To worthy° danger and deservèd death.   *severe*

NORTHUMBERLAND My guilt be on my head, and there an end.[2]

70 Take leave and part,° for you must part° forthwith.   *separate / depart*

RICHARD Doubly divorced! Bad men, you violate
A twofold marriage: 'twixt my crown and me,
And then betwixt me and my married wife.
[*To the* QUEEN] Let me unkiss the oath 'twixt thee and me—

75 And yet not so, for with a kiss 'twas made.
Part us, Northumberland: I towards the north,
Where shivering cold and sickness pines the clime;°   *afflicts the region*

---

4. Lion (Richard's emblem); ruler of beastly men.
5. Woe that happened long ago.
6. Because even the insentient firewood will respond empathetically.
7. Physically and emotionally.
8. Arrangements have been made.
9. Pus (the image is of a swelling abscess). *Henry IV,*

Parts 1 and 2, the sequels to *Richard II,* dramatize Northumberland's rebellion against "the mounting Bolingbroke."
1. *helping:* since you helped.
2. Recalling the cry of the Jews at Jesus' trial: "His death be upon our heads, and the heads of our children."

My queen to France, from whence set forth in pomp
She came adornèd hither like sweet May,
80 Sent back like Hallowmas° or short'st of day.³   *November 1*
QUEEN   And must we be divided? Must we part?
RICHARD   Ay, hand from hand, my love, and heart from heart.
QUEEN   Banish us both, and send the King with me.
NORTHUMBERLAND   That were some love, but little policy.°   *but politically naive*
85 QUEEN   Then whither he goes, thither let me go.
RICHARD   So two together weeping make one woe.
Weep thou for me in France, I for thee here.
Better far off than, near, be ne'er the nea'er.⁴
Go count thy way with sighs, I mine with groans.
90 QUEEN   So longest way shall have the longest moans.
RICHARD   Twice for one step I'll groan, the way being short,
And piece the way out° with a heavy heart.   *lengthen the way*
Come, come, in wooing sorrow let's be brief,
Since, wedding it, there is such length in grief.
95 One kiss shall stop our mouths, and dumbly° part.   *silently*
Thus give I mine, and thus take I thy heart.
     [*They kiss*]
QUEEN   Give me mine own again. 'Twere no good part⁵
To take on me to keep and kill thy heart.
     [*They kiss*]
So now I have mine own again, be gone,
100 That I may strive to kill it with a groan.
RICHARD   We make woe wanton⁶ with this fond delay.
Once more, adieu. The rest let sorrow say.
     Exeunt [RICHARD, *guarded, and* NORTHUMBERLAND *at
one door, the* QUEEN *and her* LADIES *at another door*]

5.2

Enter DUKE *and* DUCHESS OF YORK
DUCHESS OF YORK   My lord, you told me you would tell the rest,
When weeping made you break the story off,
Of our two cousins'° coming into London.   *kinsmen's*
YORK   Where did I leave?
DUCHESS OF YORK   At that sad stop, my lord,
5 Where rude misgoverned° hands from windows' tops°   *unruly / upper windows*
Threw dust and rubbish on King Richard's head.
YORK   Then, as I said, the Duke, great Bolingbroke,
Mounted upon a hot and fiery steed,
Which his aspiring rider¹ seemed to know,
10 With slow but stately pace kept on his course,
Whilst all tongues cried 'God save thee, Bolingbroke!'
You would have thought the very windows spake,
So many greedy looks of young and old
Through casements darted their desiring eyes
15 Upon his visage, and that all the walls
With painted imagery² had said at once,
'Jesu preserve thee! Welcome, Bolingbroke!'

---

3. Winter solstice.
4. Better to be far away than to be near but never
nearer to our happiness.
5. It would not be good of me.
6. We make our woe unrestrained; we make a sport of
our grief.
5.2 Location: The Duke of York's house.
1. Object of "seemed to know."
2. Painted cloths that were hung on walls in pageants;
figures in these sometimes had "speech bubbles."

Whilst he, from the one side to the other turning,
Bare-headed, lower than his proud steed's neck,
20 Bespake° them thus: 'I thank you, countrymen',   *Addressed*
And thus still doing, thus he passed along.
DUCHESS OF YORK   Alack, poor Richard! Where rode he the whilst?
YORK   As in a theatre the eyes of men,
After a well-graced actor leaves the stage,
25 Are idly bent on him that enters next,
Thinking his prattle to be tedious,
Even so, or with much more contempt, men's eyes
Did scowl on gentle Richard. No man cried 'God save him!'
No joyful tongue gave him his welcome home;
30 But dust was thrown upon his sacred head,
Which with such gentle sorrow he shook off,
His face still combating° with tears and smiles,   *continually struggling*
The badges° of his grief and patience,   *emblems*
That had not God for some strong purpose steeled
35 The hearts of men, they must perforce have melted,
And barbarism itself have pitied him.
But heaven hath a hand in these events,
To whose high will we bound our calm contents.[3]
To Bolingbroke are we sworn subjects now,
40 Whose state and honour I for aye allow.°   *forever acknowledge*
    Enter [Duke of] AUMERLE
DUCHESS OF YORK   Here comes my son Aumerle.
YORK   Aumerle that was;[4]
But that is lost for being Richard's friend,
And, madam, you must call him 'Rutland' now.
I am in Parliament pledge for his truth°   *guarantor of his loyalty*
45 And lasting fealty° to the new-made King.   *fidelity*
DUCHESS OF YORK   Welcome, my son. Who are the violets now
That strew the green lap of the new-come spring?
AUMERLE   Madam, I know not, nor I greatly care not.
God knows I had as lief° be none as one.   *had rather*
50 YORK   Well, bear you well in this new spring of time,
Lest you be cropped° before you come to prime.   *cut*
What news from Oxford? Hold these jousts and triumphs?°   *processions*
AUMERLE   For aught I know, my lord, they do.
YORK   You will be there, I know.
55 AUMERLE   If God prevent it not, I purpose so.
YORK   What seal is that that hangs without thy bosom?[5]
Yea, look'st thou pale? Let me see the writing.
AUMERLE   My lord, 'tis nothing.
YORK   No matter, then, who see it.
I will be satisfied. Let me see the writing.
60 AUMERLE   I do beseech your grace to pardon me.
It is a matter of small consequence,
Which for some reasons I would not have seen.
YORK   Which for some reasons, sir, I mean to see.
I fear, I fear!
DUCHESS OF YORK   What should you fear?

---

3. Bound ourselves to be calmly contented.
4. Aumerle has been deprived of his dukedom; he remains Earl of Rutland.

5. The document is in Aumerle's doublet, with the seal on a visibly dangling slip of attached paper.

65   'Tis nothing but some bond that he is entered into
    For gay apparel 'gainst° the triumph day.   *in time for*
YORK   Bound to himself?[6] What doth he with a bond
    That he is bound to? Wife, thou art a fool.
    Boy, let me see the writing.
70   AUMERLE   I do beseech you, pardon me. I may not show it.
YORK   I will be satisfied. Let me see it, I say.
          He plucks it out of [Aumerle's] bosom, and reads it
    Treason, foul treason! Villain, traitor, slave!
DUCHESS OF YORK   What is the matter, my lord?
YORK   Ho, who is within there? Saddle my horse.—
75   God for his mercy, what treachery is here!
DUCHESS OF YORK   Why, what is it, my lord?
YORK   Give me my boots, I say. Saddle my horse.—
    Now by mine honour, by my life, my troth,
    I will appeach° the villain.   *accuse*
80   DUCHESS OF YORK   What is the matter?
YORK   Peace, foolish woman.
DUCHESS OF YORK   I will not peace. What is the matter, son?
AUMERLE   Good mother, be content. It is no more
    Than my poor life must answer.
DUCHESS OF YORK   Thy life answer?
85   YORK   Bring me my boots. I will unto the King.
          His man enters with his boots
DUCHESS OF YORK   Strike him,° Aumerle! Poor boy, thou art   *(the servant)*
    amazed.°   *distraught*
    [*To York's man*]   Hence, villain! Never more come in my sight.
YORK   Give me my boots, I say.
DUCHESS OF YORK   Why, York, what wilt thou do?
    Wilt thou not hide the trespass of thine own?
90   Have we more sons?[7] Or are we like to have?
    Is not my teeming date° drunk up with time?   *my period of childbearing*
    And wilt thou pluck my fair son from mine age,
    And rob me of a happy mother's name?
    Is he not like thee? Is he not thine own?
95   YORK   Thou fond,° mad woman,   *foolish*
    Wilt thou conceal this dark conspiracy?
    A dozen of them here have ta'en the sacrament,
    And interchangeably set down their hands[8]
    To kill the King at Oxford.
DUCHESS OF YORK   He shall be none.°   *not be one of them*
100   We'll keep him here, then what is that to him?
YORK   Away, fond woman! Were he twenty times my son
    I would appeach him.
DUCHESS OF YORK   Hadst thou groaned° for him   *suffered labor pains*
    As I have done thou wouldst be more pitiful.
    But now I know thy mind: thou dost suspect
105   That I have been disloyal to thy bed,
    And that he is a bastard, not thy son.
    Sweet York, sweet husband, be not of that mind.
    He is as like thee as a man may be,

---

6. If Aumerle had signed a bond to borrow money, the
creditor would have the bond.
7. Actually, Aumerle had a brother and a sister, and the

Duchess of York, the Duke's second wife, was Aumerle's
stepmother.
8. And mutually committed themselves in writing.

Not like to me or any of my kin,
And yet I love him.
110 YORK   Make way, unruly woman.

Exit [with his man]

DUCHESS OF YORK   After, Aumerle! Mount thee upon his horse.
Spur, post,° and get before him to the King,   Ride fast
And beg thy pardon ere he do accuse thee.
I'll not be long behind—though I be old,
115 I doubt not but to ride as fast as York—
And never will I rise up from the ground
Till Bolingbroke have pardoned thee. Away, be gone!

Exeunt [severally]

5.3

*Enter BOLINGBROKE, [crowned KING HENRY,] with
[HARRY] PERCY, and other nobles*

KING HENRY   Can no man tell of my unthrifty son?¹
'Tis full three months since I did see him last.
If any plague hang over us, 'tis he.
I would to God, my lords, he might be found.
5 Enquire at London 'mongst the taverns there,
For there, they say, he daily doth frequent
With unrestrainèd loose companions—
Even such, they say, as stand in narrow lanes
And beat our watch° and rob our passengers°—   watchmen / wayfarers
10 Which he, young wanton and effeminate° boy,   pleasure-seeking
Takes on° the point of honour to support   Makes it
So dissolute a crew.
HARRY PERCY   My lord, some two days since,° I saw the Prince,   ago
And told him of these triumphs held at Oxford.
15 KING HENRY   And what said the gallant?
HARRY PERCY   His answer was he would unto the stews,°   brothels
And from the common'st creature pluck a glove,
And wear it as a favour,² and with that
He would unhorse the lustiest° challenger.   most vigorous
20 KING HENRY   As dissolute as desperate.° Yet through both   reckless
I see some sparks of better hope, which elder days
May happily³ bring forth.
Enter [Duke of] AUMERLE, amazed
                    But who comes here?
AUMERLE   Where is the King?
KING HENRY   What means our cousin that he stares and looks so wildly?
25 AUMERLE [*kneeling*]   God save your grace! I do beseech your majesty
To have some conference with your grace alone.
KING HENRY [*to lords*]   Withdraw yourselves, and leave us here alone.
                    [*Exeunt all but KING HENRY and AUMERLE*]
What is the matter with our cousin now?
AUMERLE   For ever may my knees grow° to the earth,   be fixed
30 My tongue cleave to the roof within my mouth,
Unless a pardon ere I rise or speak.
KING HENRY   Intended or committed was this fault?

5.3 Location: Windsor Castle.
1. Henry's oldest son is Prince Hal of *1* and *2 Henry IV,*
later King Henry V. *unthrifty:* dissolute.

2. Lady's gift to a knight that is worn in combat.
3. Perhaps; with good fortune.

If on the first,° how heinous e'er it be,   *If only intended*
To win thy after-love I pardon thee.
35 AUMERLE [*rising*]   Then give me leave that I may turn the key,
That no man enter till my tale be done.
KING HENRY   Have thy desire.
[AUMERLE *locks the door.*]
The Duke of YORK *knocks at the door and crieth*
YORK [*within*]   My liege, beware! Look to thyself!
Thou hast a traitor in thy presence there.
[KING HENRY *draws his sword*]
KING HENRY [*to* AUMERLE]   Villain, I'll make thee safe.°   *harmless*
40 AUMERLE   Stay° thy revengeful hand! Thou hast no cause to fear.   *Restrain*
YORK [*knocking within*]   Open the door, secure° foolhardy King!   *overconfident*
Shall I for° love speak treason⁴ to thy face?   *out of*
Open the door, or I will break it open.
[KING HENRY *opens the door.*] *Enter* [*Duke of*] YORK
KING HENRY   What is the matter, uncle? Speak,
45 Recover breath, tell us how near is danger,
That we may arm us to encounter it.
YORK   Peruse this writing here, and thou shalt know
The treason that my haste⁵ forbids me show.°   *explain*
[*He gives* KING HENRY *the paper*]
AUMERLE   Remember, as thou read'st, thy promise past.
50 I do repent me. Read not my name there.
My heart is not confederate with my hand.°   *signature*
YORK   It was, villain, ere thy hand did set it down.
I tore it° from the traitor's bosom, King.   *(the bond)*
Fear, and not love, begets his penitence.
55 Forget to pity him, lest pity prove
A serpent that will sting thee to the heart.
KING HENRY   O, heinous, strong, and bold conspiracy!
O loyal father of a treacherous son!
Thou sheer,° immaculate, and silver fountain,   *clear*
60 From whence this stream through muddy passages
Hath held his current and defiled himself,
Thy overflow of good converts to bad,
And thy abundant goodness shall excuse
This deadly° blot in thy digressing⁶ son.   *damnable; death-dealing*
65 YORK   So shall my virtue be his vice's bawd,
And he shall spend mine honour with his shame,
As thriftless sons their scraping fathers' gold.
Mine honour lives when his dishonour dies,
Or my shamed life in his dishonour lies.
70 Thou kill'st me in his life: giving him breath
The traitor lives, the true man's put to death.
DUCHESS OF YORK [*within*]   What ho, my liege, for God's sake let me in!
KING HENRY   What shrill-voiced suppliant makes this eager cry?
DUCHESS OF YORK [*within*]   A woman, and thy aunt, great King; 'tis I.
75 Speak with me, pity me! Open the door!
A beggar begs that never begged before.
KING HENRY   Our scene is altered from a serious thing,
And now changed to 'The Beggar and the King'.°   *(the name of a ballad)*

4. Disrespectfully criticize (as "secure" and "foolhardy").   6. Diverging from course (as of a stream); transgressing.
5. York is out of breath.

My dangerous cousin, let your mother in.
80 I know she is come to pray for your foul sin.

[AUMERLE *opens the door.*] *Enter* DUCHESS [OF YORK]

YORK If thou do pardon, whosoever pray,
More sins for this forgiveness prosper may.
This festered joint° cut off, the rest rest sound.   *infected limb*
This let alone will all the rest confound.°   *destroy*
DUCHESS OF YORK [*kneeling*]   O King, believe not this
85   hard-hearted man.
Love loving not itself, none other can.[7]
YORK Thou frantic woman, what dost thou make° here?   *do*
Shall thy old dugs° once more a traitor rear?   *breasts*
DUCHESS OF YORK Sweet York, be patient.—Hear me, gentle liege.
KING HENRY Rise up, good aunt.
90 DUCHESS OF YORK   Not yet, I thee beseech.
Forever will I kneel upon my knees,
And never see day that the happy sees,
Till thou give joy, until thou bid me joy
By pardoning Rutland, my transgressing boy.
95 AUMERLE [*kneeling*] Unto° my mother's prayers I bend my knee.   *In support of*
YORK [*kneeling*] Against them both my true joints bended be.
Ill mayst thou thrive if thou grant any grace.
DUCHESS OF YORK Pleads he in earnest? Look upon his face.
His eyes do drop no tears, his prayers are in jest.
100 His words come from his mouth; ours from our breast.
He prays but faintly, and would be denied;
We pray with heart and soul, and all beside.
His weary joints would gladly rise, I know;
Our knees shall kneel till to the ground they grow.
105 His prayers are full of false hypocrisy;
Ours of true zeal and deep integrity.
Our prayers do outpray his; then let them have
That mercy which true prayer ought to have.
KING HENRY Good aunt, stand up.
DUCHESS OF YORK   Nay, do not say 'Stand up'.
110 Say 'Pardon' first, and afterwards 'Stand up'.
An if° I were thy nurse, thy tongue to teach,   *An if = If*
'Pardon' should be the first word of thy speech.
I never longed to hear a word till now.
Say 'Pardon', King. Let pity teach thee how.
115 The word is short, but not so short as sweet;
No word like 'Pardon' for kings' mouths so meet.°   *fit*
YORK Speak it in French, King: say 'Pardonnez-moi'.[8]
DUCHESS OF YORK Dost thou teach pardon pardon to destroy?[9]
Ah, my sour° husband, my hard-hearted lord   *harsh*
120 That sets the word itself against the word!
Speak 'Pardon' as 'tis current in our land;
The chopping[1] French we do not understand.
Thine eye begins to speak; set thy tongue there;
Or in thy piteous heart plant thou thine ear,
125 That hearing how our plaints and prayers do pierce,

7. If one does not love one's own flesh and blood, one   9. Rhymes with "moi" in anglicized pronunciation.
can love no one else (not even the King).   1. Logic-chopping, changing the meaning.
8. "Excuse me," a polite refusal.

Pity may move thee 'Pardon' to rehearse.°　　　　　　　*recite*

KING HENRY　Good aunt, stand up.

DUCHESS OF YORK　　　　　　　　I do not sue to stand.

Pardon is all the suit I have in hand.

KING HENRY　I pardon him as God shall pardon me.

[YORK and AUMERLE *rise]*

130　DUCHESS OF YORK　O, happy vantage° of a kneeling knee!　　*gain; position*

Yet am I sick for fear. Speak it again.

Twice saying pardon doth not pardon twain,°　　　　　　*divide*

But makes one pardon strong.

KING HENRY　　　　　　　　I pardon him

With all my heart.

DUCHESS OF YORK *[rising]*　A god on earth thou art.

135　KING HENRY　But for our trusty brother-in-law[2] and the Abbot,

With all the rest of that consorted° crew,　　　　　*confederated*

Destruction straight shall dog them at the heels.

Good uncle, help to order several powers°　　　　　　*forces*

To Oxford, or where'er these traitors are.

140　They shall not live within this world, I swear,

But I will have them if I once know where.

Uncle, farewell; and cousin, so adieu.

Your mother well hath prayed; and prove you true.°　　　*loyal*

DUCHESS OF YORK　Come, my old[3] son. I pray God make thee new.

*Exeunt [*KING HENRY *at one door;* YORK,

DUCHESS OF YORK, *and* AUMERLE

at another door]

5.4

Enter Sir Piers EXTON, *and* [MEN]

EXTON　Didst thou not mark the King, what words he spake?

'Have I no friend will rid me of this living fear?'

Was it not so?

FIRST MAN　　　　Those were his very words.

EXTON　'Have I no friend?' quoth he. He spake it twice,

5　And urged it twice together, did he not?

SECOND MAN　He did.

EXTON　And speaking it, he wishtly° looked on me,　　　　*intently*

As who° should say 'I would thou wert the man　　　　*As if he*

That would divorce this terror from my heart',

10　Meaning the King at Pomfret. Come, let's go.

I am the King's friend, and will rid° his foe.　　*Exeunt*　　*will get rid of*

5.5

Enter RICHARD, *alone*

RICHARD　I have been studying how I may compare

This prison where I live unto the world;

And for because the world is populous,

And here is not a creature but myself,

5　I cannot do it. Yet I'll hammer° it out.　　　　　　　*work*

My brain I'll prove the female° to my soul,　　　*(that is, receptive)*

My soul the father, and these two beget

---

2. The Duke of Exeter and Earl of Huntingdon, husband of Bolingbroke's sister; like Aumerle, he had been deprived of his dukedom.
3. Unregenerate (recalling the baptism service: "O

merciful God, grant that the old Adam in this child may be so buried that the new man may be raised up in him").
5.4 Location: Windsor Castle.
5.5 Location: Pomfret Castle.

A generation of still-breeding° thoughts;   *ever-breeding*
And these same thoughts people this little world
10   In humours[1] like the people of this world.°   *(the real world)*
For no thought is contented. The better sort,
As thoughts of things divine, are intermixed
With scruples,° and do set the faith itself   *doubts*
Against the faith,[2] as thus: 'Come, little ones',[3]
15   And then again,
'It is as hard to come as for a camel
To thread the postern of a small needle's eye.'[4]
Thoughts° tending to ambition, they do plot   *Other thoughts*
Unlikely wonders:° how these vain weak nails   *miracles*
20   May tear a passage through the flinty ribs
Of this hard world, my ragged° prison walls;   *rugged*
And for they cannot, die in their own pride.°   *prime of life; arrogance*
Thoughts tending to content° flatter themselves   *contentment*
That they are not the first of fortune's slaves,
25   Nor shall not be the last—like seely° beggars,   *simpleminded*
Who, sitting in the stocks, refuge[5] their shame
That many have, and others must, set there;
And in this thought they find a kind of ease,
Bearing their own misfortunes on the back
30   Of such as have before endured the like.
Thus play I in one person many people,
And none contented. Sometimes am I king;
Then treason makes me wish myself a beggar,
And so I am. Then crushing penury
35   Persuades me I was better when a king.
Then am I kinged again, and by and by
Think that I am unkinged by Bolingbroke,
And straight° am nothing. But whate'er I be,   *at once*
Nor I, nor any man that but° man is,   *merely*
40   With nothing shall be pleased till he be eased
With being nothing.
       The music plays
                    Music do I hear.
Ha; ha; keep time! How sour sweet music is
When time is broke and no proportion kept.
So is it in the music of men's lives.
45   And here have I the daintiness of ear
To check° time broke in a disordered string;°   *rebuke / string instrument*
But for the concord° of my state and time   *harmony*
Had not an ear to hear my true time broke.
I wasted time, and now doth time waste me,
50   For now hath time made me his numb'ring clock.[6]
My thoughts are minutes, and with sighs they jar
Their watches° on unto mine eyes, the outward watch[7]   *periods of vigil*
Whereto my finger, like a dial's point,°   *clock's hand*

---

1. Temperaments; caprices.
2. *the faith . . . faith*: scriptural passage against scriptural passage.
3. From Matthew 19:14, Mark 10:14, and Luke 18:25, implying the ease of obtaining salvation.
4. Adapting Matthew 19:24, Mark 10:25, or Luke

18:25, which describe the unlikeliness of the rich reaching heaven.
5. Find refuge for; rationalize.
6. Clock that counts hours and minutes, not an hourglass.
7. Clockface; mind's external watcher.

Is pointing still° in cleansing them from tears.[8]   *always*
55   Now, sir, the sounds that tell what hour it is
  Are clamorous groans that strike upon my heart,
  Which is the bell. So sighs, and tears, and groans
  Show minutes, hours, and times. But my time
  Runs posting° on in Bolingbroke's proud joy,   *speeding*
60   While I stand fooling here, his jack of the clock.[9]
  This music mads° me. Let it sound no more,   *maddens*
  For though it have holp° madmen to their wits,   *helped*
  In me it seems it will make wise men mad.
        [*The music ceases*]
  Yet blessing on his heart that gives it me,
65   For 'tis a sign of love, and love to Richard
  Is a strange brooch° in this all-hating world.   *rare ornament*
      Enter a GROOM *of the stable*
GROOM   Hail, royal Prince!
RICHARD   Thanks, noble peer.
  The cheapest of us is ten groats too dear.[1]
  What art thou, and how com'st thou hither,
70   Where no man never comes but that sad dog
  That brings me food to make misfortune live?
GROOM   I was a poor groom of thy stable, King,
  When thou wert king; who, travelling towards York,
  With much ado at length have gotten leave
75   To look upon my sometimes° royal master's face.   *former*
  O, how it erned° my heart when I beheld   *grieved*
  In London streets, that coronation day,
  When Bolingbroke rode on roan Barbary,
  That horse that thou so often hast bestrid,
80   That horse that I so carefully have dressed!°   *groomed*
RICHARD   Rode he on Barbary? Tell me, gentle friend,
  How went he under him?
GROOM   So proudly as if he disdained the ground.
RICHARD   So proud that Bolingbroke was on his back.
85   That jade° hath eat bread from my royal hand;   *nag*
  This hand hath made him proud with clapping° him.   *patting*
  Would he not stumble, would he not fall down—
  Since pride must have a fall—and break the neck
  Of that proud man that did usurp his back?
90   Forgiveness, horse! Why do I rail on thee,
  Since thou, created to be awed by man,
  Wast born to bear? I was not made a horse,
  And yet I bear a burden like an ass,
  Spur-galled[2] and tired by jauncing° Bolingbroke.   *rough-riding*
      Enter KEEPER *to* RICHARD, *with meat*
95 KEEPER [*to* GROOM]   Fellow, give place.° Here is no longer stay.   *leave*
RICHARD [*to* GROOM]   If thou love me, 'tis time thou wert away.
GROOM   What my tongue dares not, that my heart shall say.
                    Exit
KEEPER   My lord, will't please you to fall to?

---

8. Wiping tears from my eyes.
9. Manikin that strikes the clock's bell.
1. You have overpriced the cheaper of us (me, a prisoner) in calling me "royal." The difference between the coins "royal" (10 shillings) and "noble" (6 shillings 8 pence) is "ten groats" (40 pence). In other words, we are equal in worth.
2. Made sore by spurring.

RICHARD Taste of it first,[3] as thou art wont to do.
100 KEEPER My lord, I dare not. Sir Piers of Exton,
Who lately came from the King, commands the contrary.
RICHARD [*striking the* KEEPER] The devil take Henry of Lancaster and thee!
Patience is stale, and I am weary of it.
KEEPER Help, help, help!
EXTON and his [men] rush in
105 RICHARD How now! What means death in this rude assault?
[*He seizes a weapon from a man, and kills him*]
Villain, thy own hand yields thy death's instrument.
[*He kills another*]
Go thou, and fill another room in hell.
Here EXTON *strikes him down*
RICHARD That hand shall burn in never-quenching fire
That staggers thus my person.° Exton, thy fierce hand   *thus makes me stagger*
110 Hath with the King's blood stained the King's own land.
Mount, mount, my soul; thy seat° is up on high,   *residence*
Whilst my gross flesh sinks downward, here to die. [*He dies*]
EXTON As full of valour as of royal blood.
Both have I spilt. O, would the deed were good!
115 For now the devil that told me I did well
Says that this deed is chronicled in hell.
This dead King to the living King I'll bear.
Take hence the rest, and give them burial here.
Exeunt [EXTON *with Richard's body at one door, and
his men with the other bodies at another door*]

5.6

Flourish. Enter [KING HENRY] *with* [*Duke of*] YORK, *with
other lords and attendants*
KING HENRY Kind uncle York, the latest news we hear
Is that the rebels have consumed with fire
Our town of Ci'cester° in Gloucestershire;   *Cirencester*
But whether they be ta'en or slain we hear not.
Enter [*Earl of*] NORTHUMBERLAND
5 Welcome, my lord. What is the news?
NORTHUMBERLAND First, to thy sacred state wish I all happiness.
The next news is, I have to London sent
The heads of Salisbury, Spencer, Blunt, and Kent.
The manner of their taking may appear
10 At large discoursèd° in this paper here.   *Narrated in full*
[*He gives the paper to* KING HENRY]
KING HENRY We thank thee, gentle Percy, for thy pains,
And to thy worth will add right worthy° gains.   *valuable; well-deserved*
Enter Lord FITZWALTER
FITZWALTER My lord, I have from Oxford sent to London
The heads of Brocas and Sir Bennet Seely,
15 Two of the dangerous consorted° traitors   *confederated*
That sought at Oxford thy dire overthrow.
KING HENRY Thy pains, Fitzwalter, shall not be forgot.
Right noble is thy merit, well I wot.°   *know*
Enter HARRY PERCY [*with the* BISHOP OF] CARLISLE
[*guarded*]

3. To make sure it is not poisoned.   5.6 Location: Windsor Castle.

HARRY PERCY   The grand conspirator Abbot of Westminster,

20   With clog° of conscience and sour melancholy,   *burden*
      Hath yielded up his body to the grave.
      But here is Carlisle living, to abide
      Thy kingly doom° and sentence of his pride.   *judgment*
KING HENRY   Carlisle, this is your doom.

25   Choose out some secret place, some reverent room
      More than thou hast,[1] and with it joy° thy life.   *enjoy*
      So as thou liv'st in peace, die free from strife.
      For though mine enemy thou hast ever been,
      High sparks of honour in thee have I seen.
          Enter EXTON *with [his men bearing] a coffin*

30 EXTON   Great King, within this coffin I present
      Thy buried fear. Herein all breathless lies
      The mightiest of thy greatest enemies,
      Richard of Bordeaux, by me hither brought.
KING HENRY   Exton, I thank thee not, for thou hast wrought

35   A deed of slander° with thy fatal hand   *disgrace*
      Upon my head and all this famous land.
EXTON   From your own mouth, my lord, did I this deed.
KING HENRY   They love not poison that do poison need;
      Nor do I thee. Though I did wish him dead,

40   I hate the murderer, love him murderèd.
      The guilt of conscience take thou for thy labour,
      But neither my good word nor princely favour.
      With Cain[2] go wander through the shades of night,
      And never show thy head by day nor light.
          [*Exeunt* EXTON *and his men*]

45   Lords, I protest my soul is full of woe
      That blood should sprinkle me to make me grow.
      Come mourn with me for what I do lament,
      And put on sullen black incontinent.°   *immediately*
      I'll make a voyage to the Holy Land

50   To wash this blood off from my guilty hand.
      March sadly after. Grace my mournings here
      In weeping after this untimely bier.   *Exeunt [with the coffin]*

---

1. More reverent than the prison cell you inhabit now.
2. After Cain murdered his brother Abel, he was condemned to be a vagabond (Genesis 4:14).

The Life and Death of King John

Historical narrative often attributes meaning to history. *The Life and Death of King John* (1596) does not. Although it focuses on historical process, on how events fit together over time, it suggests the larger significance of John's reign (1199–1216) only in disorienting fashion. The plot promises more coherence than it delivers; the apparent trajectory of events repeatedly proves illusory; seemingly decisive moments turn out to be mere episodes in the open-ended, ironic, unpredictable movement of history. The play thus breaks with the providential conclusion to Shakespeare's first tetralogy (four related plays on English history) provided by *Richard III* (1592–93) and, more generally, with the moralizing strategy of Renaissance humanist historians. A transitional work, it moves Shakespeare closer to the pragmatic, secular political thinking of Niccolò Machiavelli and to the concerns with the problematic relationship between hereditary legitimacy and fitness to rule characteristic of his second tetralogy, from *Richard II* to *Henry V* (1595–99).

The logic of the plot is to undermine logic, to frustrate expectation, to reveal the uncertain relationship between intention and outcome in a world that offers only fragments of an overarching consolation—religious or otherwise—for the frequent futility of human endeavor. The basic antagonisms arise from John's efforts to retain the crown and its overseas French territories. John faces challenges from the French, ostensibly acting on behalf of his young nephew Arthur, whose hereditary claim to the throne is stronger, and from the Catholic Church, with which John is also at odds. These conflicts repeatedly take surprising turns. The first-act struggle over inheritance between the Bastard and his younger half brother Robert Falconbridge leads to the unexpected conclusion that illegitimate birth is no barrier to legitimate inheritance. Even more surprisingly, the Bastard quickly renounces that inheritance. Similarly, when the English and French battle to a stalemate in seeking the loyalty of Angers, they join forces to level the town to punish its autonomy and then instead resolve to end their quarrel—sparing the town—through a cynical political marriage. But this resolution proves as transitory as the previous ones when Pandolf, the papal legate, excommunicates John, and France, as a result, repudiates the deal.

Although John now seems in trouble, his ensuing military triumph shifts his fortunes. Yet by ordering the murder of Arthur, he undermines his own position. It looks as if John will be rescued from the consequences of his crime when Hubert, the executioner, spares Arthur. But Arthur dies attempting to escape, an accident the English lords interpret as murder. Their defection to the invading French army apparently seals John's fate. Even though John submits to the Pope to eliminate the invasion's rationale, this tactic has no effect. But when the lords learn that the Dauphin, son of the French king, plans to kill them after securing the English throne, they return to John.

The war itself is marked less by climactic battles than by both sides' careless habit of losing their armies at sea: nature, too, subverts expectations. But even this does not save John. Hated by the English clergy for his earlier extortions from the monasteries, he is poisoned by a vengeful monk. This outcome lacks dramatic logic: the pillaging of the monasteries is undramatized and given very little weight; royal resistance to Catholic domination is viewed positively if peripherally; John has been reconciled with Rome; and he is apparently dying of a fever even before his poisoning. Finally, Prince Henry, the King's young son, is conveniently produced just as peace breaks out between England and France. Accordingly, the orthodox ending, in which the legitimate heir succeeds his father, feels highly contingent. And this feeling is reinforced by the characters'

The coronation of King John. From Matthew of Westminster, *Flores Historiarum* (late thirteenth or early fourteenth century).

routine repudiation of their oaths, by shifts in dramatic register—from long public, ceremonial set pieces to rapidly shifting, increasingly private introspective scenes—and by the numerous unexplained acts whose significance remains obscure.

This view of history, in which the meaning of events proves unstable and problematic, is of a piece with Shakespeare's treatment of his sources, his major characters, his central themes, and his possible allusions to contemporary Elizabethan politics, as well as with the play's later theatrical fortunes. *King John*'s closest analogue is the anonymous play *The Troublesome Reign of John, King of England* (published 1591). Most critics believe it to be Shakespeare's primary source rather than the other way around; but regardless of the chronology (on which see the Textual Note), comparison of the two works is instructive. If *The Troublesome Reign* is the earlier work, as is assumed here, it relies in part on Raphael Holinshed's *Chronicles of England, Scotland, and Ireland* (second edition, 1587), the nonfictional narrative of English history on which Shakespeare himself drew extensively during the 1590s for his other national history plays. *The Troublesome Reign*'s author reshapes chronology and invents episodes, alterations that *King John* generally adopts, and promotes conventional Protestant and national chauvinism, which *King John* mutes. From early in the English Reformation, John was seen as a proto-Protestant royal martyr who temporarily challenged Roman Catholicism by rejecting the papal choice for archbishop of Canterbury and heavily taxing the church. Hence he was thought to have anticipated Queen Elizabeth's father, Henry VIII, whose break with Rome and expropriation of the monasteries initiated the Reformation. But Shakespeare weakens the connection to Henry, toning down the rhetoric of *The Troublesome Reign* by more closely following Holinshed, who combines the Protestant view with a centuries-old Catholic hostility to John. While the anonymous play portrays monks engaged in outrageous sexual conduct, Shakespeare omits the scene and calls John's ecclesiastical tax policy pillaging. Similarly, although John's submission to Rome is lamented in *King John,* Shakespeare hardly makes the decision catastrophic. But he does retain some of *The Troublesome Reign*'s anti-Catholicism—for instance, in John's defense of an English church. Overall, however, the play's Protestantism is unmilitant: *King John* offers scant comfort to Catholics but little more to Protestants. This outlook may reflect Shakespeare's antipathy to Christian theological controversy and perhaps his partly Catholic family background and education.

Shakespeare also softens *The Troublesome Reign*'s English national chauvinism, despite concluding with the Bastard's patriotic credo:

> This England never did, nor never shall,
> Lie at the proud foot of a conqueror
> But when it first did help to wound itself.
> Now these her princes are come home again,
> Come the three corners of the world in arms
> And we shall shock them. Naught shall make us rue
> If England to itself do rest but true.
>
> (5.7.112–18)

These lines are more ambiguous than they first appear. Although they oppose foreign conquest of England, the play has considered the possibility that such domination is preferable to continued rule by a murderous English monarch. Moreover, the "But when" in the first sentence and the "if" in the third temper optimism, especially given the prior conduct of the aristocracy.

This skeptical view of traditional authority—ecclesiastical and secular alike—shapes the characterization of *King John.* Most striking is the relative inattention to John himself, the figure whose "life and death" the play claims to dramatize. The resulting vacuum is filled by women and a bastard, personages generally peripheral to dynastic history. Nowhere in Shakespeare's two historical tetralogies do women play so active a role. In the first act, John's mother, Queen Eleanor, challenges the French ambassador even before her son has a chance to do so. She then recognizes the Bastard as the illegitimate offspring of her dead son King Richard I, the Lionheart, John's oldest brother and predecessor on the throne, and (1.1.150) recruits her newly found grandson into royal service.

In Acts 2 and 3, the verbal dispute between John and Arthur (represented by the King of France) is partly carried out by proxy. Eleanor and especially Arthur's mother, Constance, whose role Shakespeare expanded from his sources, are more active than their children and (with the Bastard) rhetorically dominate the stage—especially in their confrontation in Act 2, Scene 1 and in Constance's subsequent lamentations for her son. Going beyond the common female role—victim of history—these women attempt to direct the action. Moreover, Constance and Eleanor question each other's sexual honor—an issue broached earlier when the Bastard's mother acknowledges her adulterous affair with King Richard. This recurrent concern underscores the uncertainly of biologically legitimate patriarchal succession. Hereditary descent from father to son accords a central role to women, whose sexual fidelity is considered necessary to that descent but unreliable. *King John* emphasizes the dubious fidelity of women but denies any consequence for hereditary succession. Although the mothers' attacks on each other weaken traditional notions of male legitimacy and Constance powerfully points up the unprincipled maneuvering of the two kings, she changes no one's mind, and midway through the play both she and Eleanor disappear from the plot. Their offstage deaths are reported shortly thereafter.

With them go the challenges they pose but not necessarily all they represent. Rather than executing Arthur, Hubert protects the boy, assuming a nurturing, arguably maternal, role. The Bastard's relationship to John late in the play is similar, and Prince Henry sheds tears over his dying father. Pandolf calls the Church "our Holy mother" (3.1.67,

King John's tomb in Worcester Cathedral. From Francis Sandford, *A Genealogical History of the Kings and Queens of England* (1707).

182), and the Bastard taxes the treasonous lords for "ripping up the womb / Of your dear mother England" (5.2.152–53). But it is unclear how effective these surrogates prove. Following the mothers' deaths, the sons become increasingly inept. They are memorable less in themselves than for the way that physical imagery running through *King John,* often as personification, is reliteralized in the accounts of their suffering. Arthur leaps to his accidental death when the "Good ground" of England, which he hopes does "not break my limbs," proves to be inhospitable "stones" (4.3.2, 6, 9). Earlier, the motif of fire and heat is picked up in the threat to burn out Arthur's eyes, a threat echoed in, to use John's words, the "tyrant fever [that] burns me up" and the poison that produces "so hot a summer in my bosom" (5.3.14, 5.7.30). More generally, John's stunned response to his mother's death helps explain the transformation in his behavior from confident leadership to helpless passivity. By the last part of the play, he is neither tragic nor even entirely villainous but simply beside the point, his fall coinciding with the Bastard's rise.

That rise enables a defense of illegitimacy. An almost entirely unhistorical personage in the least historical of Shakespeare's history plays, the Bastard is the work's most prominent character. Although critics have traced the development of his character, he is arguably less a coherent fictional figure than a series of discontinuous theatrical functions. His changes seem dictated more by twists of the plot than shifts in personality. The Bastard initially embodies a mischievous popular culture. Theatrically, he descends from the devilish Vice figure, a character in the earlier English morality plays. The Vice combined a commitment to evil, an intimacy with the audience, and a penchant for fun. Similarly, the Bastard speaks to and for the audience in verbally playful asides and soliloquies, denouncing the moral failings of the powerful while cheerfully conceding that he, too, is out for himself. He takes pleasure in promoting discord, and he appears immune to bodily harm, an immunity that wins him repeated description as the devil.

Unlike Shakespeare's earlier transmutations of the Vice such as Richard III, however, the Bastard is obviously a positive character. Thus, there is another side to this figure, which becomes dominant only later in the play. After John deems him legitimate and the Bastard rejects his patrimony in order to be knighted and recognized as King Richard's illegitimate son, his simultaneous financial fall and social rise allow the identification of royalty with illegitimacy. His unswerving loyalty contrasts with the self-serving deal between John and the King of France, a deal that the Bastard memorably denounces as "commodity," or self-interest (2.1.562–99). Later, that loyalty casts a harsh light on the English aristocrats' treasonous alliance with the French. The Bastard thus becomes more responsible, if less entertaining—a transformation managed by keeping the character offstage for five hundred lines. Horrified by the death of Arthur, whom he now views as the legitimate monarch, but persuaded that it was accidental, he undertakes the defense of crown and realm alike, even as John declines. In this endeavor, he proves the ethical center of a world otherwise almost devoid of positive value.

The Bastard owes this authority to his social and theatrical range. As the reembodiment of his biological father, he reflects both badly and well on the King. It is the Bastard rather than John who exacts family vengeance by killing the Duke of Austria, in this play—but not historically—slayer of King Richard. And it is the Bastard who offers the appropriate response to the death and possible murder of Arthur, for which the King bears partial—arguably full—responsibility. By comparison, John looks at best mediocre and at worst evil. Yet the Bastard's presence also suggests that the spirit of Richard guards the throne and, hence, that John is the right person for the job. As the Bastard insists in referring to John, "his royalty doth speak in me" (5.2.129).

Thus a man whose birth is illegitimate validates the fitness to rule of a man whose claim to the crown is already disputed in *The Troublesome Reign*. Shakespeare further weakens John's legal position, which is based on King Richard's will naming him successor. When Constance asserts Arthur's right to the throne, Eleanor retorts, "I can produce / A will that bars the title of thy son" (2.1.191–92). But a will is trumped by the rule of succession, which stipulates that the crown go to the firstborn male or his oldest male descendant. Here that is Arthur, son of the deceased Geoffrey, younger brother of Richard but, crucially, older brother of John. Hence, when John explains why he will prevail against the French and Arthur—"Our strong possession and our right for us" (1.1.39)—Eleanor cautions, "Your strong possession much more than your right" (line 40). Her denial of legality has authority because she supports John. John unwittingly concedes the decisiveness of order of birth when he awards the Falconbridge inheritance to the illegitimate Bastard rather than to the Bastard's younger, legitimate brother, whose claim is based only on his father's will. Even though Arthur is, therefore, legitimate and John is not, legitimacy and fitness are not synonymous. After undermining John's hereditary right, Shakespeare complicates the question. He departs from his sources by making Arthur a helpless child heavily dependent on his mother, the King of France, and the Duke of Austria. Arthur also has no interest in being King: his unfitness to rule—recognized by most commentators on *King John*—means that John's "strong possession" carries real weight.

But by ordering Arthur's murder, John squanders his authority, thereby also weakening the play's conflict between hereditary legitimacy and rightful rule. *King John's* skepticism about the meaningfulness of historical process thus undermines this central theme. A similar fate is reserved even for the Bastard, despite his crucial role in recognizing John's heir and articulating a vision of national unity. In Holinshed, John "lost a great part of his army" to drowning; in *The Troublesome Reign*, the Bastard informs John that the sea has "swallowed up the most of all our men." *King John* has the Bastard narrate this event twice, both times making him more responsible for the debacle—"half my power," "the best part of my power" (5.6.40, 5.7.61). Ineptitude is soon replaced by irrelevance: the Bastard opts for war after others have already negotiated peace. Although he is not simply shunted aside by the unpredictable concatenation of historical events, the resolution has less to do with human intention and achievement than with the collapse of both contending parties.

Where does this leave England? Temporally, *King John* differs from Shakespeare's other history plays of the 1590s: it treats the early thirteenth rather than the late fourteenth and fifteenth centuries. Standing alone rather than in a tetralogy, it does not develop a dynastic sense of "England" by depicting the sequence of reigns. Sociologically, the play is also atypical. John's reign is remembered for the Magna Carta and—without historical warrant—Robin Hood. Both concern resistance to royal tyranny—by the aristocracy and the lower class, respectively. Although these stories were available in the 1590s, neither appears in the play. The lords rebel late in the action, but the balance of power between king and nobility remains secondary. And despite a brief reference to popular unrest, *King John* accords the English people an even more marginal role in constituting the nation. This treatment of aristocracy and populace contrasts with Shakespeare's approach in his history plays of the next three years from the second tetralogy, *1* and *2 Henry IV* and *Henry V*.

King John points elsewhere. Richard the Lionheart's legacy is dispersed among three of his blood relatives—John, Arthur, and the Bastard—none of whom is a fully adequate successor. Like the Bastard, Constance and Eleanor are part of the royal family. But these three characters, who, as noted earlier, belong to peripheral groups, suggest an expansion of outlook, a shift from dynasty to nation and, hence, a repudiation of absolutist rule. That expansion is implied by the importance accorded in Act 2 to the political will of the citizens of Angers, who are asked to decide which claimant is their legitimate king, and arguably by the valorization of humane feeling and personal loyalty late in the play. Yet the Bastard's social rise from obscurity to protector of England suggests a partial analogue to the sixteenth-century emergence of a nonhereditary political elite to fill crucial positions in the new state bureaucracy. On this reading, the play ends not with an expanded, less authoritarian view of the polity, but with a redeployed ruling apparatus. If so, this reorganization of the state remains barely realized in *King John*. So, too, does a properly national sense of England. It may be that no national perspective was fully available without the traditional legitimacy of dynastic succession. The second tetralogy may be seen as an effort to fuse the people and the crown. *King John,* however, devoid of climactic battle or concluding marriage, is more effective at undermining than at reconstituting authority: it is here that its distinctiveness lies.

The play may thus have provided its initial audiences with a compelling projection back into the thirteenth century of the charged issue of the legitimacy of Queen Elizabeth and competing claims of Mary, Queen of Scots. First, just as John's monarchical claim depends on Richard's will, the will of Henry VIII named Elizabeth heir. But the legitimacy of appointing one's successors by will had been challenged even in Henry's lifetime. Second, Shakespeare's John is accused of being a bastard and excommunicated by the pope; Elizabeth was declared a bastard by her father and excommunicated by the pope. And just as Arthur is the son of John's older brother, Mary, Queen of Scots, was the daughter of Henry's older sister. Elizabeth's legal claim to the crown was thus arguably weaker than Mary's.

Fourth, Arthur's cause is championed by King Philip of France; Mary, too, enjoyed the support of foreign Catholic monarchs, including King Philip II of Spain. Fifth, after ordering Arthur's death, John tries to absolve himself of the crime that he commissioned but did not commit; in 1587, Elizabeth ordered Mary's execution and then distanced herself from the judicial murder. Sixth, Arthur's death provokes an invasion from France to impose foreign Catholic rule. The invaders are led by the Dauphin, whose claim to the English crown rests on his marriage to John's niece, Blanche. Analogous motives led Philip II, widowed husband of Mary—the older sister of Elizabeth and her predecessor as queen—to launch the Spanish Armada the year after Mary's death. Finally, in *King John*, England is saved by a providential storm that destroys much of the French navy. So, too, a storm wrecked the Armada, a catastrophe interpreted by the victors as God's deliverance of Protestant England from enemies intent on conquest and Catholic rule.

Although these summaries oversimplify theater and history alike, they suggest the explosive issues that Shakespeare dramatized—the struggle with the papacy, the threat of invasion, and especially the problem of legitimate rule. There were risks in questioning Elizabeth's royal legitimacy or accusing her of murdering the rightful queen— even by covert historical analogy. Yet *King John* raises these matters not to resolve them but to meditate on their complexity. John both is and is not Arthur's murderer; he both is and is not the legitimate king.

Finally, the enigmatic logic of *King John's* plot has affected its theatrical fortunes. Since the eighteenth century, the play has been cut to render its uncertain nationalism unambiguous. In the nineteenth century, its discontinuities and powerful confrontations between characters encouraged productions in which narrative sweep was sacrificed to pageantry and individual scenes, especially involving Constance. *King John* has also proven useful for political allegory in times of crisis. It was prominent in the battle against the censorship legislation of the 1737 Licensing Act, and it was marshaled to support loyalist opposition to the Catholic Jacobite invasion of England in 1745. It served similar ends in the French and Indian War fifteen years later, during the Napoleonic Wars at the beginning of the nineteenth century, as a justification for British imperialism during the Boer War in South Africa in 1899, and as a rallying cry before and during World War II. A 1961 production took the contested city of Angers as an image of Berlin, recently divided between East and West, and subsequent decades saw performances in several Eastern European Communist countries. Although *King John* was the first of Shakespeare's plays to be filmed (in 1899, an extremely brief version consisting of three scenes—John's temptation of Hubert, Constance's lamentation, and John's death scene), the work's theatrical standing declined in the twentieth century. There may be promise, however, in the recent rebellion against politically orthodox interpretations in criticism and performance alike. The 1988–89 production directed by Deborah Warner is noteworthy for its often satiric view of male authority in an unstable world. Perhaps a revival of interest depends less on the play's pageantry or jingoism than on its disabused view of power and its refusal to find reassurance in the interconnected, yet uncertain, sequence of historical events.

WALTER COHEN

TEXTUAL NOTE

The initial printing of *The Life and Death of King John* was in the First Folio of 1623 (F). That text probably goes back to an authorial manuscript, or "foul papers," from 1596 that was subsequently copied between 1609 and 1623 by two scribes. Their transcript, though not a promptbook, seems to have been designed with future theatrical performance in mind. The second scribe moved further from Shakespeare's manuscript toward stage-ready copy than did the first. In response to a 1606 law prohibiting oaths, the scribes presumably sanitized Shakespeare's language, replacing, for instance, "God" with "heaven."

The *Norton Shakespeare* reverses that process, restoring what Shakespeare wrote but retaining other scribal innovations, such as the introduction of act and scene divisions. In F, these are messy and illogical, perhaps in part because two compositors set the type for the play. This edition follows earlier editors in treating F's "Scaena Secunda" as 2.1 and its "Actus Secundus" as 2.2, even though this is not the only reasonable solution. Beginning at the present edition's 2.1.325, F starts calling the Citizen of Angers "Hubert." The shift may indicate a desire to double the parts (have the same actor play both roles) or conflate the two characters. If the latter, the extant text does not complete the job: the two men do not seem like the same person. Accordingly, this edition emends F to keep the two characters separate.

Partly on the basis of *King John's* recourse to rhetoric reminiscent of the Spanish Armada era (1588), a few scholars place its composition in 1590 or earlier and see it as a source for the anonymous play *The Troublesome Reign of John, King of England* (published in 1591). Yet a direct link between the wording of two stage directions in *The Troublesome Reign* and their analogues in *King John* is easily explained only if the anonymous play came first and Shakespeare was familiar with it. Shakespeare could have read the relevant stage directions in the 1591 edition of *The Troublesome Reign,* but it is not clear how the author of *The Troublesome Reign* could have seen Shakespeare's unpublished stage directions. Stylistic and metrical tests, which date *King John* to roughly 1596, support this hypothesis.

SELECTED BIBLIOGRAPHY

Anderson, Thomas. "'Legitimation, name, and all is gone': Bastardy and Bureaucracy in Shakespeare's *King John.*" *Journal for Early Modern Cultural Studies* 4.2 (Fall/Winter 2004): 35–61. The Bastard's rise as indicative less of monarchical power than of the emergence of a new model of impersonal bureaucratic efficiency.

Braunmuller, A. R. "*King John* and Historiography." *English Literary History* 55 (1988): 309–32. Conflict between theater and historical writing, exemplified in the Bastard's ahistorical character and Arthur's death.

Burckhardt, Sigurd. *Shakespearean Meanings.* Princeton: Princeton University Press, 1968. 116–43. *King John* as a modern, rather than traditional, play, rejecting divine sanction for both religious and secular authority.

Candido, Joseph, ed. *"King John."* Shakespeare: The Critical Tradition series. Atlantic Highlands, N.J.: Athlone, 1996. Selection from criticisms of the play, 1790–1919; focus on individual characters and emotionally powerful scenes.

Cousin, Geraldine. *King John.* Manchester: Manchester University Press, 1994. Performance history, including 1984 BBC film (see below).

Curren-Aquino, Deborah T., ed. *"King John": New Perspectives.* Newark: University of Delaware Press, 1989. Twelve essays, various perspectives, but generally seeing the play as an experiment with the form of the national history play.

Dusinberre, Juliet. "*King John* and Embarrassing Women." *Shakespeare Survey* 42 (1989): 37–52. Women as a structurally unifying force in the first three acts. The play disintegrates with their disappearance.

Howard, Jean E., and Phyllis Rackin. *Engendering a Nation: A Feminist Account of Shakespeare's English Histories.* London: Routledge, 1997. 119–33. *King John* as a challenge to patriarchal, dynastic orthodoxy through skeptical women's voices.

Shirley, Frances A., ed. *"King John" and "Henry VIII": Critical Essays.* New York: Garland, 1988. The twelve essays on *King John*, mostly from the 1930s to 1960s, are diverse in outlook but generally more concerned with structural and national unity than is recent criticism.

Vaughan, Virginia Mason. *"King John." A Companion to Shakespeare's Works.* Vol. 2: *The Histories.* Ed. Richard Dutton and Jean E. Howard. Malden, Mass.: Blackwell, 2003. 379–94. Overview of the play, seen as advocating limits on absolute secular or religious power.

FILMS

King John. 1899. Dir. Walter Pfeffer Dando and William K. L. Dickson. UK. 2 min. The first Shakespeare film, a black-and-white silent. See Introduction.

The Life and Death of King John. 1984. Dir. David Giles. UK. 155 min. A relatively conservative BBC production notable for Claire Bloom's innovative, coolly rational Constance.

The Life and Death of King John

The Persons of the Play

KING JOHN of England
QUEEN ELEANOR, his mother
LADY FALCONBRIDGE
Philip the BASTARD, later knighted as Sir Richard Plantagenet,
    her illegitmate son by King Richard I (Cœur-de-lion)
Robert FALCONBRIDGE, her legitimate son
James GURNEY, her attendant
Lady BLANCHE of Spain, niece of King John
PRINCE HENRY, son of King John
HUBERT, a follower of King John
Earl of SALISBURY
Earl of PEMBROKE
Earl of ESSEX
Lord BIGOT
KING PHILIP of France
LOUIS THE DAUPHIN, his son
ARTHUR, Duke of Brittaine, nephew of King John
Lady CONSTANCE, his mother
Duke of AUSTRIA (Limoges)
CHÂTILLON, ambassador from France to England
Count MELUN
A CITIZEN of Angers
Cardinal PANDOLF, a legate from the Pope
PETER OF POMFRET, a prophet
HERALDS
EXECUTIONERS
MESSENGERS
SHERIFF
Lords, soldiers, attendants

1.1

[*Flourish.*] *Enter* KING JOHN, QUEEN ELEANOR,[1] [*and the
Earls of*] PEMBROKE, ESSEX, *and* SALISBURY; *with the*[m]
    CHÂTILLON *of France*

KING JOHN   Now say, Châtillon, what would France with us?[2]
CHÂTILLON   Thus, after greeting, speaks the King of France,
    In my behaviour,° to the majesty—   *person*
    The borrowed° majesty—of England here.   *usurped*
5 QUEEN ELEANOR   A strange beginning: 'borrowed majesty'?
KING JOHN   Silence, good mother, hear the embassy.°   *message*
CHÂTILLON   Philip of France, in right and true behalf

1.1 Location: John's court in London.
1. This scene, which occupies the first act, is unhistorical. The youngest son of Henry II and "Queen
Eleanor" (Eleanor of Aquitaine), John (1167–1216)
succeeded his brother, the famed crusader Richard I

(the Lionheart), in 1199 and ruled until his death.
Eleanor of Aquitaine (c. 1122–1204) was Queen first of
France and then of England. See "A Shakespearean
Genealogy," on the front endpapers.
2. What does (the King of) France want with us?

Of thy deceasèd brother Geoffrey's³ son,
Arthur Plantagenet,⁴ lays most lawful claim
10   To this fair island and the territories,
To Ireland, Poitou, Anjou, Touraine, Maine;⁵
Desiring thee to lay aside the sword
Which sways° usurpingly these several titles,°   rules / separate lands
And put the same into young Arthur's hand,
15   Thy nephew and right royal sovereign.
KING JOHN   What follows if we disallow of this?
CHÂTILLON   The proud control° of fierce and bloody war,   compulsion
To enforce these rights so forcibly withheld—
KING JOHN   Here have we war for war, and blood for blood,
20   Controlment for controlment: so answer France.
CHÂTILLON   Then take my king's defiance from my mouth,
The farthest limit of my embassy.
KING JOHN   Bear mine° to him, and so depart in peace.   my defiance
Be thou as lightning in the eyes of France,
25   For ere thou canst report,⁶ I will be there;
The thunder of my cannon° shall be heard.   (anachronism)
So hence. Be thou the trumpet of our wrath,
And sullen presage° of your own decay.°—   gloomy omen / downfall
An honourable conduct° let him have;   escort
30   Pembroke, look to't.—Farewell, Châtillon.

                    Exeunt CHÂTILLON *and* PEMBROKE

QUEEN ELEANOR   What now, my son? Have I not ever° said   always
How that ambitious Constance⁷ would not cease
Till she had kindled France and all the world
Upon° the right and party of her son?   On behalf of
35   This might have been prevented and made whole°   settled
With very easy arguments of love,°   friendly discussions
Which now the manage° of two kingdoms must   government
With fearful-bloody issue° arbitrate.   outcome
KING JOHN   Our strong possession and our right for us.°   on our side
QUEEN ELEANOR [*aside to* KING JOHN]   Your strong possession
40   much more than your right,
Or else it must go wrong with you and me:
So much my conscience whispers in your ear,
Which none but heaven and you and I shall hear.

                    Enter a SHERIFF [*who whispers to* ESSEX]

ESSEX   My liege,° here is the strangest controversy,   lord
45   Come from the country to be judged by you,
That e'er I heard. Shall I produce the men?
KING JOHN   Let them approach.—   [*Exit* SHERIFF]

---

3. Geoffrey was older than John and younger than Richard I; he died before Henry II. Because of changes in the laws of inheritance, John's claims to the throne would have been weaker in Shakespeare's lifetime—and are so represented—than they were in his own day, the early thirteenth century.
4. "Plantagenet" was the family name of most English monarchs from the accession of Henry II in 1154 to the deposition of Richard III in 1485. The historical Arthur was in his late teens; Shakespeare makes him much younger.

5. Except for Ireland, English territories in western and central France. Historically, it was these French territories, rather than the English crown itself, that Arthur claimed.
6. Before you can deliver your message (pun on noise of thunder or cannon).
7. Arthur's mother, Geoffrey's widow in Shakespeare and in his main source, *The Troublesome Reign of King John*. Historically, Constance remarried twice after Geoffrey's death.

Our abbeys and our priories shall pay[8]
This expeditious charge.°   *sudden cost (of war)*
    Enter Robert FALCONBRIDGE *and Philip [the* BASTARD,[9]
    with the Sheriff]
                       What men are you?

50 BASTARD   Your faithful subject I, a gentleman
Born in Northamptonshire, and eldest son,
As I suppose, to Robert Falconbridge,
A soldier, by the honour-giving hand
Of Cœur-de-lion° knighted in the field.   *Richard the Lionheart*

55 KING JOHN   What art thou?
FALCONBRIDGE   The son and heir to that same Falconbridge.
KING JOHN   Is that the elder, and art thou the heir?
You came not of one mother then, it seems.
BASTARD   Most certain of one mother, mighty King—
60 That is well known—and, as I think, one father.
But for the certain knowledge of that truth
I put you o'er to° heaven, and to my mother.   *refer you to*
Of that° I doubt as all men's children may.   *(truth)*
QUEEN ELEANOR   Out on thee,° rude man! Thou dost shame thy   *Away with you*
   mother
65 And wound her honour with this diffidence.°   *distrust*
BASTARD   I, Madam? No, I have no reason for it.
That is my brother's plea and none of mine,
The which if he can prove, a pops me out°   *he deprives me of*
At least from fair five hundred pound a year.
70 Heaven guard my mother's honour, and my land!
KING JOHN   A good blunt fellow.—Why, being younger born,
Doth he lay claim to thine inheritance?
BASTARD   I know not why, except to get the land;
But once he slandered me with bastardy.
75 But whe'er° I be as true° begot or no,   *whether / legitimately*
That still I lay upon my mother's head;°   *I let my mother answer*
But that I am as well begot, my liege—
Fair fall the bones that took the pains for me[1]—
Compare our faces and be judge yourself.
80 If old Sir Robert did beget us both
And were our father, and this son like him,
O old Sir Robert, father, on my knee
I give heaven thanks I was not like to thee.
KING JOHN   Why, what a madcap hath heaven lent us here!
85 QUEEN ELEANOR[2]   He hath a trick° of Cœur-de-lion's face;   *distinguishing trait*
The accent of his tongue affecteth° him.   *resembles*
Do you not read some tokens of my son
In the large composition° of this man?   *openness; build*
KING JOHN   Mine eye hath well examinèd his parts,°   *attributes*
And finds them perfect Richard.
90   [*To Robert* FALCONBRIDGE]   Sirrah,° speak: *(used to inferiors)*
What doth move you to claim your brother's land?

---

8. Alluding to John's much-resented taxation of the monastic orders.
9. Drawing upon a passing reference in Holinshed's *Chronicles, The Troublesome Reign* invents a major role for this character, a role that Shakespeare further

expands.
1. May good fortune befall the bones (of the dead man) who went to the trouble of begetting me.
2. The Queen may speak the following lines privately to John.

BASTARD   Because he hath a half-face° like my father!   profile; thin face
   With half that face[3] would he have all my land,
   A half-faced groat[4] five hundred pound a year.

95   FALCONBRIDGE   My gracious liege, when that my father lived,
   Your brother° did employ my father much—   (Richard)
   BASTARD   Well, sir, by this you cannot get my land.
   Your tale must be how he employed my mother.
   FALCONBRIDGE   And once dispatched him in an embassy
100   To Germany, there with the Emperor
   To treat of high affairs touching that time.
   Th'advantage of his absence took the King,
   And in the meantime sojourned at my father's,
   Where how he did prevail I shame to speak.
105   But truth is truth: large lengths of seas and shores
   Between my father and my mother lay,
   As I have heard my father speak himself,
   When this same lusty° gentleman was got.°   vigorous / conceived
   Upon his deathbed he by will bequeathed
110   His lands to me, and took it on his death°   solemnly swore
   That this my mother's son was none of his;
   And if he were, he came into the world
   Full fourteen weeks before the course of time.
   Then, good my liege, let me have what is mine,
115   My father's land, as was my father's will.
   KING JOHN   Sirrah, your brother is legitimate.°   (legally correct)
   Your father's wife did after wedlock bear him,
   And if she did play false, the fault was hers,
   Which fault lies on the hazards of° all husbands   is a risk for
120   That marry wives. Tell me, how if my brother,
   Who, as you say, took pains to get this son,
   Had of your father claimed this son for his?
   In sooth, good friend, your father might have kept
   This calf, bred from his cow, from all the world;
125   In sooth he might. Then if he were my brother's,
   My brother might not claim him, nor your father,
   Being none of his, refuse him.[5] This concludes:
   My mother's son did get your father's heir;
   Your father's heir must have your father's land.
130   FALCONBRIDGE   Shall then my father's will be of no force
   To dispossess that child which is not his?
   BASTARD   Of no more force to dispossess me, sir,
   Than was his will° to get me, as I think.   legal instrument; lust
   QUEEN ELEANOR   Whether hadst° thou rather be: a Falconbridge,   Which would
135   And like thy brother to enjoy thy land,
   Or the reputed son of Cœur-de-lion,
   Lord of thy presence,° and no land beside?   yourself
   BASTARD   Madam, an if° my brother had my shape,   an If=if
   And I had his, Sir Robert's his° like him,   Sir Robert's
140   And if my legs were two such riding-rods,°   their riding switches
   My arms such eel-skins stuffed, my face so thin
   That in mine ear I durst not stick a rose

---

3. Half of his father's face, since Falconbridge inherits
maternal features as well; "face" is also "impudence."
4. A coin showing the monarch's head in profile; also
Falconbridge, who as a person is worth only as much as

a groat (4 pence), despite his inheritance.
5. *nor . . . him:* nor could your father, though not the
biological father to the Bastard, disown him.

Lest men should say 'Look where three-farthings goes!',[6]
And, to° his shape, were heir to all this land,   *in addition to*
145   Would I might never stir from off this place.[7]
I would give it every foot° to have this face;   *every foot of it*
It would not be Sir Nob in any case.[8]
QUEEN ELEANOR   I like thee well. Wilt thou forsake thy fortune,
Bequeath thy land to him, and follow me?
150   I am a soldier and now bound to France.
BASTARD   Brother, take you my land; I'll take my chance.
Your face hath got five hundred pound a year,
Yet sell your face for fivepence and 'tis dear.°—   *expensive*
Madam, I'll follow you unto the death.
155 QUEEN ELEANOR   Nay, I would have you go before me thither.
BASTARD   Our country manners give our betters way.[9]
KING JOHN   What is thy name?
BASTARD   Philip, my liege, so is my name begun:
Philip, good old Sir Robert's wife's eldest son.
160 KING JOHN   From henceforth bear his name whose form thou bear'st.
Kneel thou down Philip, but arise more great:
    [*He knights the* BASTARD]
Arise Sir Richard and Plantagenet.[1]
BASTARD   Brother by th' mother's side, give me your hand.
My father gave me honour, yours gave land.
165   Now blessèd be the hour, by night or day,
When I was got, Sir Robert was away.
QUEEN ELEANOR   The very spirit of Plantagenet!
I am thy grandam, Richard; call me so.
BASTARD   Madam, by chance, but not by truth;° what though?°   *chastely / but so what?*
170   Something about,° a little from the right,°   *a bit off / unlawful*
In at the window, or else o'er the hatch;[2]
Who dares not stir by day must walk° by night,   *go; rob (sexually)*
And have is have, however men do catch.[3]
Near or far off, well won is still well shot,[4]
175   And I am I, howe'er I was begot.
KING JOHN   Go, Falconbridge, now hast thou thy desire:
A landless knight° makes thee a landed squire.—   *(the Bastard)*
Come, madam, and come, Richard; we must speed
For France; for France, for it is more than need.
180 BASTARD   Brother, adieu. Good fortune come to thee,
For thou wast got i'th' way of honesty.
    Exeunt all but [*the*] BASTARD
A foot of honour[5] better than I was,
But many a many foot of land the worse.
Well, now can I make any Joan° a lady.   *lower-class woman*

---

6. A rose appeared behind the Queen's head on a three-farthing coin, which was thin and of small value (less than a penny).
7. May I be struck dead here and now.
8. My appearance would not be that of Sir Robert under any circumstances. The speech is full of sexual innuendo. "Riding-rods" (line 140) and "eel-skins" (line 141) hint at sexual inadequacy associated with a thin penis. "Nob" (line 147) is also slang for "penis." "Rose" (line 142), "shape" (line 144), and "case" (line 147) may refer to the vagina; "riding" (line 140), "stuffed" (line 141), "stick a rose" (line 142), and "foot" (line 146) suggest copulation; and "stir" (line 145) can mean "sexually arouse."

9. The Bastard jokes that it's proper to let social superiors go first.
1. Perhaps the shift from blank verse to rhyme (lines 145–81), though not fully systematic, reinforces the Bastard's social elevation here.
2. Both phrases are proverbial for birth out of wedlock. *hatch:* the lower half of a divided door.
3. That is, possession is nine-tenths of the law.
4. Archery metaphor, with sexual innuendo, as with "stir" (line 172). The entire passage is also marked by mock-proverbial expressions.
5. A degree of status. The Bastard contrasts his aristocratic "honour" with Falconbridge's middle-class "honesty" (line 181).

185 'Good e'en, Sir Richard'—'God-a-mercy[6] fellow';
And if his name be George I'll call him Peter,
For new-made honour doth forget men's names;
'Tis too respective and too sociable
For your conversion.[7] Now your traveller,
190 He and his toothpick at my worship's mess;
And when my knightly stomach is sufficed,
Why then I suck my teeth[8] and catechize
My pickèd° man of countries. 'My dear sir,'   *affected; tooth-picked*
Thus leaning on mine elbow I begin,
195 'I shall beseech you—'. That is Question now;
And then comes Answer like an Absey book.°   *a school (ABC) primer*
'O sir,' says Answer, 'at your best command,
At your employment, at your service, sir.'
'No sir,' says Question, 'I, sweet sir, at yours.'
200 And so, ere Answer knows what Question would,°   *wishes*
Saving in dialogue of compliment,°   *Except empty flattery*
And talking of the Alps and Apennines,
The Pyrenean and the River Po,
It draws toward supper° in conclusion so.   *(another meal)*
205 But this is worshipful society,
And fits the mounting spirit° like myself;   *ambitious character*
For he is but a bastard to° the time   *no true child of*
That doth not smack of observation;°   *courtly obsequiousness*
And so am I°—whether I smack or no,   *so I intend*
210 And not alone in habit° and device,°   *clothes / heraldic emblem*
Exterior form, outward accoutrement,
But from the inward motion°—to deliver   *impulse*
Sweet, sweet, sweet poison° for the age's tooth;°   *flattery / appetite*
Which,° though I will not practise° to deceive,   *(flattery) / make a habit*
215 Yet to avoid deceit° I mean to learn;   *being deceived*
For it shall strew the footsteps of my rising.[9]
                Enter LADY FALCONBRIDGE *and James* GURNEY
But who comes in such haste in riding-robes?
What woman-post° is this? Hath she no husband   *female dispatch rider*
That will take pains to blow a horn[1] before her?
220 O me, 'tis my mother! How now, good lady?
What brings you here to court so hastily?
LADY FALCONBRIDGE   Where is that slave thy brother? Where is he
That holds in chase° mine honour up and down?   *Who hunts*
BASTARD   My brother Robert, old Sir Robert's son?
225 Colbrand the Giant,[2] that same mighty man?
Is it Sir Robert's son that you seek so?
LADY FALCONBRIDGE   Sir Robert's son, ay, thou unreverent boy,

6. God reward you: the patronizing reply of a social superior. The Bastard imagines himself, newly promoted, encountering a social inferior who says "Good evening." His soliloquy continues in this vein, parodying the affectation of courtiers and foreign travelers, in part through the ironic use of religious rhetoric—"conversion" (line 189, referring to his new rank), "my worship's mess" (line 190; "my worship" means both "a lord" and "the Lord"; "mess" means both "a dinner table" and "the Mass," the commemoration of Christ's Last Supper), and "catechize" (line 192; orally question, usually about religious principles).

7. 'Tis . . . conversion: Remembering names is beneath the dignity of a newly created knight.
8. The Bastard defiantly cleans his teeth in the vulgar English fashion, rather than resorting to the traveler's and courtier's affectation of a toothpick.
9. For flattery will ease my ascent; awareness of deceptive flattery will do so.
1. Post horn announcing the rider's approach; also, the symbol of a cuckold.
2. Danish giant killed by Guy in the popular romance *Guy of Warwick*.

Sir Robert's son. Why scorn'st thou at Sir Robert?
He is Sir Robert's son, and so art thou.

230 BASTARD   James Gurney, wilt thou give us leave° awhile?   *leave us*
GURNEY   Good leave, good Philip.
BASTARD   Philip Sparrow,[3] James!
There's toys abroad;[4] anon I'll tell thee more.

Exit James [GURNEY]

Madam, I was not old Sir Robert's son.
Sir Robert might have eat his part in me
235 Upon Good Friday, and ne'er broke his fast.
Sir Robert could do° well, marry° to confess,   *(sexual) / indeed*
Could a get° me! Sir Robert could not do it: *Could he have begotten*
We know his handiwork.° Therefore, good mother,   *(Falconbridge)*
To whom am I beholden for these limbs?
240 Sir Robert never holp° to make this leg.   *helped*
LADY FALCONBRIDGE   Hast thou conspirèd with thy brother too,
That for thine own gain shouldst defend mine honour?
What means this scorn, thou most untoward° knave?   *unmannerly*
BASTARD   Knight, knight, good mother, Basilisco-like![5]
245 What! I am dubbed; I have it° on my shoulder.   *(a sword tap)*
But, mother, I am not Sir Robert's son.
I have disclaimed Sir Robert; and my land,
Legitimation, name, and all is gone.
Then, good my mother, let me know my father;
250 Some proper man, I hope; who was it, mother?
LADY FALCONBRIDGE   Hast thou denied thyself a Falconbridge?
BASTARD   As faithfully as I deny the devil.
LADY FALCONBRIDGE   King Richard Cœur-de-lion was thy father.
By long and vehement suit I was seduced
255 To make room for him in my husband's bed.
Heaven lay not my transgression to my charge!
Thou art the issue° of my dear° offence,   *result / costly; loving*
Which was so strongly urged past my defence.
BASTARD   Now by this light, were I to get° again,   *be conceived*
260 Madam, I would not wish a better father.
Some sins do bear their privilege° on earth,   *are pardonable*
And so doth yours; your fault was not your folly.°   *your sin wasn't foolish*
Needs must you lay your heart at his dispose,°   *disposal*
Subjected tribute to commanding love,
265 Against whose fury and unmatchèd force
The aweless° lion could not wage the fight,   *fearless*
Nor keep his princely heart from Richard's hand.
He that perforce° robs lions of their hearts[6]   *by his strength*
May easily win a woman's. Ay, my mother,
270 With all my heart I thank thee for my father.
Who lives and dares but say thou didst not well
When I was got, I'll send his soul to hell.
Come, lady, I will show thee to my kin,
   And they shall say, when Richard me begot,

3. Recalling the popularity of Philip as a name for a
mere bird, the Bastard considers the name beneath him.
4. There's trivial news (ironic).
5. The cowardly braggart Basilisco in an anonymous
play *Solyman and Perseda,* probably from the early
1590s, calls himself a knight while his servant calls him
a knave.
6. Alluding to Richard I's legendary feat of killing a lion
by putting his hand down its throat and pulling out its
heart (hence the epithet Cœur-de-lion, Lionheart).

275 If thou hadst said him nay, it had been sin.⁷
    Who says it was, he lies: I say 'twas not.⁷

                            Exeunt

2.1

[Flourish.] Enter before Angers [at one door] PHILIP
King of France, LOUIS [THE] DAUPHIN, *[Lady]* CON-
STANCE, *and* ARTHUR *[Duke of Brittaine, with soldiers;
at another door the Duke of]* AUSTRIA *[wearing a lion's
hide, with soldiers]*¹

KING PHILIP   Before Angers well met, brave Austria.—
  Arthur, that great forerunner of thy blood,
  Richard° that robbed the lion of his heart   *(Arthur's uncle)*
  And fought the holy wars in Palestine,°   *Third Crusade (1189–92)*
5 By this brave duke came early to his grave;²
  And, for amends to his posterity,
  At our importance° hither is he come   *urgent request*
  To spread his colours,° boy, in thy behalf,   *battle flags*
  And to rebuke the usurpation
10 Of thy unnatural uncle, English John.
  Embrace him, love him, give him welcome hither.
ARTHUR *[to* AUSTRIA]   God shall forgive you Cœur-de-lion's death,
  The rather that° you give his offspring life,   *All the more because*
  Shadowing° their right under your wings of war.   *Protecting*
15   I give you welcome with a powerless hand,
  But with a heart full of unstainèd love.
  Welcome before the gates of Angers, Duke.
KING PHILIP   A noble boy. Who would not do thee right?
AUSTRIA *[kissing* ARTHUR]   Upon thy cheek lay I this zealous kiss
20 As seal to this indenture° of my love: *contract*
  That to my home I will no more return
  Till Angers and the right thou hast in France,
  Together with that pale, that white-faced shore,°   *chalk cliffs of Dover*
  Whose foot° spurns back the ocean's roaring tides   *(of the cliffs)*
25 And coops° from other lands her islanders,   *protects*
  Even till that England, hedged in with the main,°   *ocean*
  That water-wallèd bulwark, still° secure   *always*
  And confident from foreign purposes,
  Even till that utmost corner of the west
30 Salute thee for her king. Till then, fair boy,
  Will I not think of home, but follow arms.
CONSTANCE   O, take his mother's thanks, a widow's thanks,
  Till your strong hand shall help to give him strength
  To make a more° requital to your love.   *greater*
35 AUSTRIA   The peace of heaven is theirs that lift their swords
  In such a just and charitable war.
KING PHILIP   Well then, to work! Our cannon shall be bent°   *aimed*

---

7. Not a sin; nought (nothing); naughty, and hence
something, a sin.
2.1 Location: Before the town wall of Angers.
1. This is "Scaena Secunda" in F (see the Textual
Note). The back of the stage represents the town wall,
with the town notionally behind it. The Citizen's entry
"upon the walls" (s.d. after line 200) is onto the upper
stage. Below the upper stage, central tiring-house doors

would probably represent the gates of Angers, the capital of John's French holdings. These remain closed; the
French and English armies appear from side entrances.
2. Austria, the "brave duke," imprisoned Richard, but
Richard was actually killed while besieging the castle of
the Viscount of Limoges in France. Shakespeare follows his main source in combining the two historical
figures in the character of Austria.

Against the brows° of this resisting town.   *walls*
Call for our chiefest men of discipline°   *military skill*
40   To cull the plots of best advantages.³
We'll lay before this town our royal bones,
Wade to the market-place in Frenchmen's blood,
But we will° make it subject to this boy.   *In order to; unless we*
     CONSTANCE   Stay for an answer to your embassy,
45   Lest unadvised° you stain your swords with blood.   *rashly*
My lord Châtillon may from England bring
That right in peace which here we urge° in war,   *seek*
And then we shall repent each drop of blood
That hot rash haste so indirectly° shed.   *wrongfully*
     Enter CHÂTILLON
50   KING PHILIP   A wonder, lady: lo upon thy wish
Our messenger Châtillon is arrived.—
What England° says, say briefly, gentle lord;   *the King of England*
We coldly° pause for thee. Châtillon, speak.   *calmly*
     CHÂTILLON   Then turn your forces from this paltry siege,
55   And stir them up against a mightier task.
England, impatient of your just demands,
Hath put himself in arms. The adverse winds,
Whose leisure I have stayed,° have given him time   *Which I had to wait out*
To land his legions all as soon as I.
60   His marches are expedient° to this town,   *coming quickly*
His forces strong, his soldiers confident.
With him along is come the Mother-Queen,
An Ate° stirring him to blood and strife;   *goddess of discord*
With her her niece,⁴ the Lady Blanche of Spain;
65   With them a bastard of the King's deceased;°   *of Richard's*
And all th'unsettled humours⁵ of the land—
Rash, inconsiderate,° fiery voluntaries,°   *imprudent / volunteers*
With ladies'° faces and fierce dragons' spleens°—   *beardless / tempers*
Have sold their fortunes at their native homes,
70   Bearing their birthrights proudly on their backs,⁶
To make a hazard of° new fortunes here.   *To take a chance on*
In brief, a braver choice of dauntless spirits
Than now the English bottoms° have waft o'er   *ships*
Did never float upon the swelling tide
75   To do offence and scathe° in Christendom.   *damage*
     Drum beats
The interruption of their churlish drums
Cuts off more circumstance.° They are at hand;   *detail*
To parley or to fight therefore prepare.
     KING PHILIP   How much unlooked-for is this expedition!°   *military force; speed*
80   AUSTRIA   By how much unexpected, by so much
We must awake endeavour for defence,
For courage mounteth with occasion.°   *necessity*
Let them be welcome then: we are prepared.

---

3. To pick the positions of greatest advantage (for the cannons).
4. Actually, Eleanor's granddaughter: "niece" is used in a broad sense.
5. Men of discontented spirits; masterless men of no fixed abode. The soldiers are seen as "humors" (physical elements of the body, which affect temperament) discharged from the body of England.
6. In the form of armor bought by selling their land ("birthrights" and "fortunes," line 69). "All his clothes are on his back" is proverbial.

Enter [*marching*] KING [JOHN] *of England,* [*the*] BAS-
TARD, QUEEN [ELEANOR], [*Lady*] BLANCHE, [*the Earl of*]
PEMBROKE, *and* [*soldiers*]

KING JOHN   Peace be to France, if France in peace permit
85   Our just and lineal° entrance to our own.°   *hereditary / Angers*
Ⅰf not, bleed France,° and peace ascend to heaven,   *let France bleed*
Whiles we, God's wrathful agent, do correct°   *punish*
Their proud contempt that beats his peace to heaven.

KING PHILIP   Peace be to England, if that war° return   *if the English forces*
90   From France to England, there to live in peace.
England we love, and for that England's° sake   *that land's; Arthur's*
With burden of our armour here we sweat.
This toil of ours should be a work of thine;
But thou from loving England art so far
95   That thou hast underwrought° his lawful king,   *undermined*
Cut off the sequence of posterity,°   *the succession*
Outfacèd infant state,° and done a rape   *Defied Arthur's right*
Upon the maiden virtue of the crown.
[*Pointing to* ARTHUR]
Look here upon thy brother Geoffrey's face.
100   These eyes, these brows, were moulded out of his;
This little abstract° doth contain that large°   *précis / full version*
Which died in Geoffrey; and the hand of time
Shall draw this brief° into as huge a volume.   *summary*
That Geoffrey was thy elder brother born,
105   And this his son; England was Geoffrey's right,
And this is Geoffrey's.° In the name of God,   *(son and heir)*
How comes it then that thou art called a king,
When living blood doth in these temples beat,
Which owe° the crown that thou o'ermasterest?   *own*
110   KING JOHN   From whom hast thou this great commission, France,
To draw my answer from thy articles?°   *charges*
KING PHILIP   From that supernal° judge that stirs good thoughts   *heavenly*
In any breast of strong authority°   *In any powerful ruler*
To look into the blots and stains of right.
115   That judge hath made me guardian to this boy,
Under whose warrant I impeach° thy wrong,   *challenge*
And by whose help I mean to chastise it.
KING JOHN   Alack, thou dost usurp authority.
KING PHILIP   Excuse it is to beat usurping down.[7]
120   QUEEN ELEANOR   Who is it thou dost call usurper, France?
CONSTANCE   Let me make answer: thy usurping son.
QUEEN ELEANOR   Out,° insolent! Thy bastard shall be king   *Begone*
That thou mayst be a queen and check° the world.   *master*
CONSTANCE   My bed was ever° to thy son as true   *always*
125   As thine was to thy husband; and this boy
Liker in feature to his father Geoffrey
Than thou and John in manners, being as like
As rain to water, or devil to his dam.°   *mother*
My boy a bastard? By my soul I think
130   His father never was so true begot.
It cannot be, an if° thou wert his mother.   *an if = if*

---

7. My (so-called) usurpation is excusable because I am using it to put down (real) usurpation.

QUEEN ELEANOR [*to* ARTHUR]   There's a good mother, boy, that
          blots° thy father.   *slanders*
  CONSTANCE [*to* ARTHUR]   There's a good grandam, boy, that
          would blot thee.
  AUSTRIA   Peace!
  BASTARD   Hear the crier!⁸
  AUSTRIA   What the devil art thou?
135 BASTARD   One that will play the devil, sir, with you,
          An a° may catch your hide⁹ and you alone.   *If he (I)*
          You are the hare° of whom the proverb goes,   *coward*
          Whose valour plucks dead lions by the beard.°   *(an insult)*
          I'll smoke your skin-coat° an I catch you right—   *thrash your hide*
140   Sirrah,° look to't—i'faith I will, i'faith!   *Boy (an insult)*
  BLANCHE   O, well did he° become that lion's robe   *(Richard)*
          That did disrobe the lion of that robe!
  BASTARD   It lies as sightly° on the back of him   *fitly*
          As great Alcides' shows¹ upon an ass.
145   But, ass, I'll take that burden from your back,
          Or lay on that° shall make your shoulders crack.   *that burden which*
  AUSTRIA   What cracker° is this same that deafs our ears   *boaster*
          With this abundance of superfluous breath?—
          King Philip, determine what we shall do straight.°   *immediately*
150 KING PHILIP   Women and fools,° break off your conference.—   *children*
          King John, this is the very sum of all:
          England and Ireland, Anjou,² Touraine, Maine,
          In right of Arthur do I claim of thee.
          Wilt thou resign them and lay down thy arms?
155 KING JOHN   My life as soon. I do defy thee, France.—
          Arthur of Brittaine, yield thee to my hand,
          And out of my dear love I'll give thee more
          Than e'er the coward hand of France can win.
          Submit thee, boy.
  QUEEN ELEANOR [*to* ARTHUR]   Come to thy grandam, child.
160 CONSTANCE [*to* ARTHUR]   Do, child, go to it° grandam, child.   *its*
          Give grandam kingdom, and it grandam will
          Give it a plum, a cherry, and a fig.°   *(obscene)*
          There's a good grandam.°   *(sarcastic baby talk)*
  ARTHUR   Good my mother, peace.
          I would that I were low laid in my grave.
165   I am not worth this coil° that's made for me.   *commotion*
          [*He weeps*]
  QUEEN ELEANOR   His mother shames him so, poor boy, he weeps.
  CONSTANCE   Now shame upon you, whe'er° she does or no!   *whether*
          His grandam's wrongs, and not his mother's shames,
          Draw those heaven-moving pearls from his poor eyes,
170   Which heaven shall take in nature° of a fee;   *as a kind*
          Ay, with these crystal beads° heaven shall be bribed   *tears*
          To do him justice and revenge on you.
  QUEEN ELEANOR   Thou monstrous slanderer of heaven and earth!

---

8. The Bastard mockingly compares Austria to an officer in a law court who calls for order.
9. The lion skin Austria wears, which, as a memento of
his father's death, antagonizes the Bastard.
1. As the lion skin of Hercules would appear (alluding
to his legendary size and strength, and to the proverbial

"ass in a lion's skin").
2. Here and at line 488, Shakespeare appears to confuse the province (Anjou) with the besieged town
(Angers; French: Angiers). Elsewhere, he maintains a
distinction, as do his sources.

CONSTANCE   Thou monstrous injurer of heaven and earth!

175   Call not me slanderer. Thou and thine usurp
The dominations, royalties° and rights   *royal powers*
Of this oppressèd boy. This is thy eld'st son's son,³
Infortunate in nothing but in thee.
Thy sins are visited° in this poor child;   *punished*

180   The canon of the law° is laid on him,   *biblical decree*
Being but the second generation
Removèd from thy sin-conceiving womb.⁴

KING JOHN   Bedlam,° have done.   *Lunatic*

CONSTANCE   I have but this to say:
That he° is not only plaguèd for her sin,°   *(Arthur) / (adultery)*

185   But God hath made her sin° and her the plague   *(John)*
On this removèd issue,° plaguèd for her   *(Arthur)*
And with her plague;⁵ her sin his injury,
Her injury the beadle to her sin;
All punished in the person of this child,

190   And all for her.⁶ A plague upon her!

QUEEN ELEANOR   Thou unadvisèd° scold, I can produce   *rash*
A will that bars the title of thy son.

CONSTANCE   Ay, who doubts that? A will, a wicked will,
A woman's will,⁷ a cankered grandam's will!

195   KING PHILIP   Peace, lady; pause or be more temperate.
It ill beseems this presence° to cry aim   *royal assembly*
To⁸ these ill-tunèd repetitions.—
Some trumpet summon hither to the walls
These men of Angers. Let us hear them speak

200   Whose title they admit, Arthur's or John's.

Trumpet sounds. Enter a CITIZEN⁹ *upon the walls*

CITIZEN   Who is it that hath warned° us to the walls?   *summoned*

KING PHILIP   'Tis France for England.

KING JOHN   England for itself.
You men of Angers and my loving subjects—

KING PHILIP   You loving men of Angers, Arthur's subjects,

205   Our trumpet called you to this gentle parle°—   *parley*

KING JOHN   For our° advantage; therefore hear us first.   *(England's; John's)*
These flags of France that are advancèd here
Before the eye and prospect of your town,
Have hither marched to your endamagement.

210   The cannons have their bowels full of wrath,
And ready mounted are they to spit forth
Their iron indignation 'gainst your walls.
All preparation for a bloody siege
And merciless proceeding by these French

215   Confront your city's eyes, your winking° gates;   *closed (in sleep)*
And but for our approach, those sleeping stones

---

3. Oldest grandson; but perhaps deliberately meant to produce the false inference that Arthur is really the "eld'st son's [Richard's] son."

4. Implying sexual infidelity in the conception of John. These lines (especially 179) echo the Second Commandment (Exodus 20:5, "the law" of line 180): "visiting the iniquity of the fathers upon the children unto the third and fourth generation."

5. *plagued . . . plague:* punished because of and by her.

6. *her sin his injury . . . her:* her wrongful action is like a parish constable (a "beadle," who whipped petty criminals) urging on her son to afflict Arthur; all (Eleanor's

sin, John as its embodiment) are punished in Arthur, and all because of Eleanor.

7. Testament influenced by a woman (Eleanor; ironically, it was illegal for women to make wills themselves, for fear their husbands would influence them); a woman's desire (as in the proverbial "A woman will have her will").

8. *to cry aim / To:* to encourage.

9. Shakespeare may have taken some steps toward conflating this character with Hubert, who figures prominently later in the play (see note to line 325 and Textual Note), but no early text survives in which such an identification of characters has been fully effected.

	That as a waist° doth girdle you about,	*girdle*
	By the compulsion of their ordinance,°	*artillery*
	By this time from their fixèd beds of lime°	*their foundations*
220	Had been dishabited,¹ and wide havoc made	
	For bloody power to rush upon your peace.	
	But on the sight of us your lawful king,	
	Who painfully,° with much expedient° march,	*laboriously / hurried*
	Have brought a countercheck before your gates	
225	To save unscratched your city's threatened cheeks,	
	Behold the French, amazed,° vouchsafe° a parle;	*terrified / grant*
	And now instead of bullets wrapped in fire	
	To make a shaking fever in your walls,	
	They shoot but calm words folded up in smoke°	*deceit*
230	To make a faithless error° in your ears;	*lie*
	Which trust accordingly, kind citizens,	
	And let us in, your king, whose laboured° spirits,	*worn out*
	Forwearied in this action of swift speed,	
	Craves harbourage within your city walls.	
235	KING PHILIP When I have said, make answer to us both.	
	[He takes Arthur's hand]	
	Lo, in this° right hand, whose protection	*(Philip's)*
	Is most divinely vowed upon the right	
	Of him° it holds, stands young Plantagenet,	*(Arthur)*
	Son to the elder brother of this man°	*(John)*
240	And king o'er him and all that he enjoys.	
	For this downtrodden equity° we tread	*right*
	In warlike march these greens before your town,	
	Being no further enemy to you	
	Than the constraint° of hospitable zeal	*necessity*
245	In the relief of this oppressèd child	
	Religiously° provokes. Be pleasèd then	*Solemnly*
	To pay that duty which you truly owe	
	To him that owes° it, namely this young prince;	*has a right to*
	And then our arms, like to a muzzled bear,	
250	Save in aspect,° hath all offence° sealed up:	*appearance / aggression*
	Our cannons' malice vainly shall be spent	
	Against th'invulnerable clouds of heaven,	
	And with a blessèd and unvexed retire,°	*unmolested retreat*
	With unhacked swords and helmets all unbruised,	
255	We will bear home that lusty blood again	
	Which here we came to spout against your town,	
	And leave your children, wives, and you in peace.	
	But if you fondly° pass our proffered offer,	*foolishly*
	'Tis not the roundure° of your old-faced walls	*roundness; circumference*
260	Can hide you from our messengers of war,°	*cannonballs*
	Though all these English and their discipline°	*military skill*
	Were harboured in their rude° circumference.	*rugged*
	Then tell us, shall your city call us lord	
	In that behalf which° we have challenged it,	*in which; for whom*
265	Or shall we give the signal to our rage,	
	And stalk in blood to our possession?	
	CITIZEN In brief, we are the King of England's subjects.	
	For him and in his right we hold this town.	

1. Dislodged, unclothed ("habit" picking up "waist," "girdle," line 217). Angers continues to be personified here ("cheeks," line 225; "fever," line 228) and later in the scene.

KING JOHN Acknowledge then the King, and let me in.
270 CITIZEN That can we not; but he that proves° the king,   proves to be
        To him will we prove loyal; till that time
        Have we rammed up our gates against the world.
KING JOHN Doth not the crown of England prove the king?
        And if not that, I bring you witnesses:
275   Twice fifteen thousand hearts of England's breed—
BASTARD [aside] Bastards and else.°   others
KING JOHN To verify our title with their lives.
KING PHILIP As many and as well-born bloods as those—
BASTARD [aside] Some bastards too.
280 KING PHILIP Stand in his face° to contradict his claim.   against him
CITIZEN Till you compound° whose right is worthiest,   settle
        We for the worthiest hold° the right from both.   withhold
KING JOHN Then God forgive the sin of all those souls
        That to their everlasting residence,
285   Before the dew of evening fall, shall fleet°   leave their bodies
        In dreadful trial of° our kingdom's king.   contest to determine
KING PHILIP Amen, Amen! Mount, chevaliers!° To arms!   horsemen
BASTARD Saint George that swinged° the dragon, and e'er since   thrashed
        Sits on's horseback at mine hostess' door,[2]
290   Teach us some fence!° [To AUSTRIA] Sirrah, were I at home swordsmanship
        At your den, sirrah, with your lioness,°   whore; wife
        I would set an ox-head° to your lion's hide   add cuckold's horns
        And make a monster of you.
AUSTRIA   Peace, no more.
BASTARD O tremble, for you hear the lion roar!
295 KING JOHN Up higher to the plain, where we'll set forth
        In best appointment° all our regiments.   readiness
BASTARD Speed then, to take advantage of the field.°   best battle positions
KING PHILIP It shall be so, and at the other hill
        Command the rest to stand.[3] God and our right!°   (English royal motto)
            Exeunt [severally° KING JOHN and KING PHILIP with their   separately
            powers. The CITIZEN remains on the walls]
            [Alarum.] Here, after excursions,° enter [at one door] the   onstage skirmishes
            HERALD of France, with [a] trumpet[er], to the gates
300 FRENCH HERALD You men of Angers, open wide your gates
        And let young Arthur Duke of Brittaine in,
        Who by the hand of France this day hath made
        Much work for tears in many an English mother,
        Whose sons lie scattered on the bleeding ground;
305   Many a widow's husband grovelling lies,
        Coldly embracing the discoloured earth;
        And victory with little loss doth play
        Upon the dancing banners of the French,
        Who are at hand, triumphantly displayed,°   drawn up
310   To enter conquerors, and to proclaim
        Arthur of Brittaine England's king and yours.
            Enter [at another door the] English HERALD, with [a]
            trumpet[er]
ENGLISH HERALD Rejoice, you men of Angers, ring your bells!
        King John, your king and England's, doth approach,

---

2. The idea that St. George, England's patron saint, is ever on horseback yet never rides was proverbial. *at mine hostess' door*: on an inn sign.

3. Command the reserves to be in readiness. (This concludes an unheard conversation in parallel with John's.)

Commander of this hot malicious day.
315 Their armours that marched hence so silver-bright
Hither return all gilt° with Frenchmen's blood.   *smeared; golden*
There stuck no plume in any English crest°   *(on a helmet)*
That is removèd by a staff° of France;   *spear*
Our colours° do return in those same hands   *banners*
320 That did display them when we first marched forth;
And like a jolly troop of huntsmen come
Our lusty English, all with purpled hands
Dyed in the dying slaughter of their foes.
Open your gates and give the victors way.
325 CITIZEN[4]   Heralds, from off our towers we might° behold   *could*
From first to last the onset and retire
Of both your armies, whose equality
By our best eyes cannot be censurèd.°   *differentiated*
Blood hath bought blood and blows have answered blows,
330 Strength matched with strength and power confronted power.
Both are alike, and both alike we like.
One must prove greatest. While they weigh so even,
We hold our town for neither, yet for both.
         Enter the two kings with their powers,° at several doors   *armies*
         [*at one door* KING JOHN, *the* BASTARD, QUEEN ELEANOR
         and Lady BLANCHE, *with soldiers; at another door* KING
         PHILIP, LOUIS THE DAUPHIN, *and the Duke of* AUSTRIA
         with soldiers][5]
KING JOHN   France, hast thou yet more blood to cast away?
335 Say, shall the current of our right run on,
Whose passage, vexed with thy impediment,
Shall leave his native channel° and o'erswell°   *normal course / flood*
With course disturbed even thy confining shores,
Unless thou let his silver water keep
340 A peaceful progress to the ocean?
KING PHILIP   England, thou hast not saved one drop of blood
In this hot trial more than we of France;
Rather, lost more. And by this hand I swear,
That sways the earth this climate° overlooks,   *part of the sky*
345 Before we will lay down our just-borne arms,
We'll put thee down 'gainst whom these arms we bear,
Or add a royal number° to the dead,   *(Philip)*
Gracing the scroll that tells of this war's loss
With slaughter coupled to the name of kings.
350 BASTARD   Ha, majesty! How high thy glory towers
When the rich blood of kings is set on fire!
O, now doth Death line his dead chaps° with steel;   *deadly jaws*
The swords of soldiers are his teeth, his fangs;
And now he feasts, mousing° the flesh of men   *tearing; biting*
355 In undetermined differences° of kings.   *unresolved disputes*
Why stand these royal fronts° amazèd thus?   *faces*
Cry havoc,[6] Kings! Back to the stainèd field,
You equal potents,° fiery-kindled spirits!   *equally strong rulers*

---

4. This and subsequent speeches of the Citizen are attributed to Hubert in the earliest Folio text. See note to line 200.
5. F calls for "the two Kings with their powers"; this
seems to exclude Constance and Arthur.
6. Order given to troops for pillaging and merciless slaughter.

Then let confusion° of one part° confirm   *let overthrow / side*
360   The other's peace; till then, blows, blood, and death!

KING JOHN   Whose party do the townsmen yet admit?

KING PHILIP   Speak, citizens, for England: who's your king?

CITIZEN   The King of England, when we know the King.

KING PHILIP   Know him in us,° that here hold up his right.   *me*

365   KING JOHN   In us, that are our own great deputy°   *representative*
And bear possession of our person° here,   *represent my own claim*
Lord of our presence,° Angers, and of you.   *myself*

CITIZEN   A greater power than we denies all this,
And, till it be undoubted, we do lock
370   Our former scruple in our strong-barred gates,
Kinged of° our fear, until our fears resolved   *Commanded by*
Be by some certain king, purged and deposed.

BASTARD   By heaven, these scroyles° of Angers flout you, Kings,   *scoundrels*
And stand securely on their battlements
375   As in a theatre, whence they gape and point
At your industrious scenes and acts of death.
Your royal presences° be ruled by me.   *persons*
Do like the mutines of Jerusalem:[7]
Be friends awhile, and both conjointly° bend   *together*
380   Your sharpest deeds of malice on this town.
By east and west let France and England mount
Their battering cannon, chargèd to° the mouths,   *loaded to*
Till their soul-fearing° clamours have brawled° down   *terrifying / broken*
The flinty ribs° of this contemptuous city.   *walls*
385   I'd play incessantly upon these jades,[8]
Even till unfencèd° desolation   *unwalled*
Leave them as naked as the vulgar° air.   *common*
That done, dissever your united strengths,
And part your mingled colours once again;
390   Turn face to face, and bloody point to point.
Then in a moment Fortune shall cull° forth   *choose*
Out of one side her happy minion,°   *darling*
To whom in favour she shall give the day,°   *victory*
And kiss him with a glorious victory.
395   How like you this wild counsel, mighty states?°   *rulers*
Smacks it not something of the policy?°   *political cunning*

KING JOHN   Now, by the sky that hangs above our heads,
I like it well.—France, shall we knit° our powers,   *join*
And lay this Angers even with the ground,
400   Then after fight who shall be king of it?

BASTARD [*to* KING PHILIP]   An if thou hast the mettle of a king,
Being wronged as we are by this peevish° town,   *obstinate*
Turn thou the mouth of thy artillery,
As we will ours, against these saucy° walls;   *presumptuous*
405   And when that we have dashed them to the ground,
Why, then defy each other, and pell-mell°   *quickly*
Make work upon ourselves, for[9] heaven or hell.

KING PHILIP   Let it be so.—Say, where will you assault?

---

7. Warring factions of Jerusalem who temporarily united against besieging Roman forces in 70 C.E.
8. I'd unceasingly fire at (or torment) these wretches. (A "jade" was a decrepit horse or an insulting term for a woman—and hence a double insult when applied to a man.)
9. On behalf of; for the destination of.

KING JOHN   We from the west will send destruction
410   Into this city's bosom.
AUSTRIA   I from the north.
KING PHILIP   Our thunder° from the south   *cannon*
    Shall rain their drift of bullets° on this town.   *shower of cannonballs*
BASTARD [*to* KING JOHN]   O prudent discipline!° From north to south   *tactics*
415   Austria and France shoot in each other's mouth.
    I'll stir them to it. Come, away, away!
CITIZEN   Hear us, great Kings, vouchsafe a while to stay,
    And I shall show you peace and fair-faced league.
    Win you this city without stroke or wound;
420   Rescue those breathing lives to die in beds,
    That here come sacrifices for the field.
    Persever not, but hear me, mighty Kings.
KING JOHN   Speak on with favour;° we are bent° to hear.   *permission / willing*
CITIZEN   That daughter there of Spain, the Lady Blanche,
425   Is niece to England. Look upon the years°   *ages*
    Of Louis the Dauphin and that lovely maid.
    If lusty love should go in quest of beauty,
    Where should he find it fairer than in Blanche?
    If zealous° love should go in search of virtue,   *pious*
430   Where should he find it purer than in Blanche?
    If love ambitious sought a match of birth,
    Whose veins bound° richer blood than Lady Blanche?   *contain*
    Such as she is in beauty, virtue, birth,
    Is the young Dauphin every way complete;°   *perfect*
435   If not complete, O, say he is not she;
    And she again wants nothing—to name want—
    If want it be not that she is not he.[1]
    He is the half part of a blessèd man,
    Left to be finishèd by such as she;
440   And she a fair divided excellence,
    Whose fullness of perfection lies in him.
    O, two such silver currents when they join
    Do glorify the banks that bound them in,
    And two such shores to two such streams made one,
445   Two such controlling bounds, shall you be, Kings,
    To these two princes if you marry them.
    This union shall do more than battery can
    To our fast-closèd gates, for at this match,[2]
    With swifter spleen° than powder can enforce,   *passion*
450   The mouth of passage shall we fling wide ope,
    And give you entrance. But without this match
    The sea enragèd is not half so deaf,
    Lions more confident, mountains and rocks
    More free from motion, no, not Death himself
455   In mortal fury half so peremptory,°   *resolved*
    As we to keep this city.
BASTARD [*aside*]   Here's a stay°   *an obstacle; cease-fire*
    That shakes the rotten carcass of old Death
    Out of his rags.[3] Here's a large mouth,° indeed,   *(of a cannon or human)*

---

1. *If not . . . he:* The Dauphin is perfect insofar as he lacks Blanche, and vice versa. *wants:* lacks. *to:* if I must.

2. Marriage; device for lighting gun "powder" (line 449).

3. *That . . . rags:* That steals what belongs to death.

That spits forth Death and mountains, rocks and seas,
460 Talks as familiarly of roaring lions
As maids of thirteen do of puppy-dogs.
What cannoneer begot this lusty blood?
He speaks plain cannon: fire, and smoke, and bounce;°   *bang*
He gives the bastinado° with his tongue;   *a cudgeling*
465 Our ears are cudgelled; not a word of his
But buffets better than a fist of France.
Zounds!° I was never so bethumped with words   *God's wounds*
Since I first called my brother's father Dad.
     QUEEN ELEANOR [*aside to* KING JOHN] Son, list° to this conjunc-   *listen*
     tion,° make this match,   *proposition*
470 Give with our niece a dowry large enough;
For, by this knot, thou shalt so surely tie
Thy now unsured assurance to the crown
That yon green° boy shall have no sun to ripe   *unripe; young*
The bloom that promiseth a mighty fruit.
475 I see a yielding in the looks of France;
Mark how they whisper. Urge them while their souls
Are capable of° this ambition,   *susceptible to*
Lest zeal,° now melted by the windy breath   *(on Arthur's behalf)*
Of soft petitions, pity, and remorse,
480 Cool and congeal° again to what it was.   *freeze*
     CITIZEN Why answer not the double majesties
This friendly treaty° of our threatened town?   *entreaty; proposal*
     KING PHILIP Speak England first, that hath been forward first
To speak unto this city: what say you?
485   KING JOHN If that the Dauphin there, thy princely son,
Can in this book of beauty° read 'I love',   *(Blanche)*
Her dowry shall weigh equal with a queen;
For Anjou and fair Touraine, Maine, Poitou,[4]
And all that we upon this side the sea—
490 Except this city now by us besieged—
Find liable° to our crown and dignity,   *subject*
Shall gild her bridal bed, and make her rich
In titles, honours, and promotions,°   *elevations in rank*
As she in beauty, education, blood,
495 Holds hand with° any princess of the world.   *Is equal to*
     KING PHILIP What sayst thou, boy? Look in the lady's face.
     LOUIS THE DAUPHIN I do, my lord, and in her eye I find
A wonder, or a wondrous miracle,
The shadow of myself formed in her eye;
500 Which, being but the shadow of your son,
Becomes a sun and makes your son a shadow.[5]
I do protest I never loved myself
Till now enfixèd° I beheld myself   *imprinted*
Drawn in the flattering table° of her eye.   *surface*
     [*He*] *whispers with* BLANCHE
505   BASTARD [*aside*] Drawn in the flattering table of her eye,
Hanged in the frowning wrinkle of her brow,

---

4. The French territories claimed by both John and Arthur will go to the Dauphin.
5. *The shadow of myself . . . a shadow:* The Dauphin speaks in elaborate clichés of courtly love poetry: the conceit is common, as is the "sun/son" wordplay. He claims that his "shadow," from being a mere reflection or pale imitation of the King's son (or a shadow of the sun) in Blanche's eyes, becomes a "sun" because her eyes are so bright, with the result that the actual "son" becomes a mere "shadow" of his own reflection.

And quartered in her heart:[6] he doth espy
Himself love's traitor. This is pity now,
That hanged and drawn and quartered there should be
510 In such a love so vile a lout as he.
BLANCHE [*to* LOUIS THE DAUPHIN]   My uncle's will in this respect is mine.
If he see aught° in you that makes him like,   *anything*
That anything he sees which moves his liking
I can with ease translate it to my will;
515 Or if you will, to speak more properly,°   *precisely*
I will enforce it easily to my love.
Further I will not flatter you, my lord,
That all I see in you is worthy° love,   *deserving of*
Than this:[7] that nothing do I see in you,
520 Though churlish° thoughts themselves should be your judge,   *grudging*
That I can find should merit any hate.
KING JOHN   What say these young ones? What say you, my niece?
BLANCHE   That she is bound in honour still° to do   *always*
What you in wisdom shall vouchsafe° to say.   *deign*
525 KING JOHN   Speak then, Prince Dauphin, can you love this lady?
LOUIS THE DAUPHIN   Nay, ask me if I can refrain from love,
For I do love her most unfeignedly.
KING JOHN   Then do I give Volquessen,[8] Maine,
Poitou, and Anjou, these five provinces,
530 With her to thee, and this addition more:
Full thirty thousand marks° of English coin.   *£20,000*
Philip of France, if thou be pleased withal,°   *with this*
Command thy son and daughter to join hands.
KING PHILIP   It likes° us well.—Young princes, close your hands.   *pleases*
535 AUSTRIA   And your lips too, for I am well assured
That I did so when I was first assured.°   *betrothed*
[LOUIS THE DAUPHIN *and Lady* BLANCHE *join hands and kiss*]
KING PHILIP   Now citizens of Angers, ope your gates.
Let in that amity which you have made,
For at Saint Mary's chapel presently°   *immediately*
540 The rites of marriage shall be solemnized.—
Is not the Lady Constance in this troop?
[*Aside*] I know she is not, for this match made up
Her presence would have interrupted much.
[*Aloud*] Where is she and her son? Tell me who knows.
545 LOUIS THE DAUPHIN   She is sad and passionate° at your highness' tent.   *sorrowful*
KING PHILIP   And by my faith this league that we have made
Will give her sadness very little cure.—
Brother of England, how may we content
This widow lady? In her right we came,
550 Which we, God knows, have turned another way
To our own vantage.°   *advantage*
KING JOHN   We will heal up all,
For we'll create young Arthur Duke of Brittaine[9]
And Earl of Richmond, and this rich fair town
We make him lord of. Call the Lady Constance.

---

6. *Drawn . . . heart:* the Bastard alludes to the punishment of being hanged, drawn (disemboweled; but also,
painted, line 504), and quartered (cut in pieces; but also,
lodged) for treason. The rhyme scheme of lines 505–10
mimics the last six lines of a Shakespearean sonnet.

7. Taking up "Further," line 517.
8. Modern Vexin, northwest of Paris.
9. An inconsistency: Arthur already holds this title, as
John himself acknowledges (line 156).

555	Some speedy messenger bid her repair°	come
	To our solemnity.° I trust we shall,	(marriage) ceremony
	If not fill up the measure of her will,	
	Yet in some measure satisfy her so	
	That we shall stop her exclamation.°	loud reproaches
560	Go we as well as haste will suffer° us	allow
	To this unlooked-for, unprepared pomp.°	ceremony

[*Flourish.*] *Exeunt* [*all but the* BASTARD]

	BASTARD Mad world, mad kings, mad composition!°	treaty
	John, to stop Arthur's title in the whole,	
	Hath willingly departed° with a part;	parted
565	And France, whose armour conscience buckled on,	
	Whom zeal and charity brought to the field	
	As God's own soldier, rounded° in the ear	whispered to
	With° that same purpose-changer,[1] that sly devil,	By
	That broker that still breaks the pate[2] of faith,	
570	That daily break-vow, he that wins of° all,	gets the best of
	Of kings, of beggars, old men, young men, maids,—	
	Who° having no external° thing to lose	(maids) / material
	But the word 'maid',° cheats° the poor maid of that—	virginity / he cheats
	That smooth-faced° gentleman, tickling° commodity;	plausible / cajoling
575	Commodity, the bias[3] of the world,	
	The world who of itself is peised° well,	balanced
	Made to run even upon even ground,	
	Till this advantage, this vile-drawing° bias,	drawing to evil
	This sway° of motion, this commodity,	swayer; swerver
580	Makes it take head° from all indifferency,°	flee / impartiality
	From all direction, purpose, course, intent;	
	And this same bias, this commodity,	
	This bawd,° this broker, this all-changing word,	procurer
	Clapped on the outward eye[4] of fickle France,	
585	Hath drawn him from his own determined aid,	
	From a resolved and honourable war,	
	To a most base and vile-concluded peace.	
	And why rail I on this commodity?	
	But for° because he hath not wooed me yet—	Only
590	Not that I have the power to clutch° my hand	clench (in refusal)
	When his fair angels would salute[5] my palm,	
	But for° my hand, as unattempted° yet,	Because / untempted
	Like a poor beggar raileth on the rich.	
	Well, whiles I am a beggar I will rail,	
595	And say there is no sin but to be rich,	
	And being rich, my virtue then shall be	
	To say there is no vice but beggary.	
	Since kings break faith upon° commodity,	on account of
	Gain, be my lord, for I will worship thee. *Exit*	

1. "Purpose-changer," as well as the subsequent noun phrases in lines 568–70, is in apposition to those in line 574, in particular "commodity" (self-interest, profit seeking; that which translates everything into its market value to the exclusion of noneconomic considerations).
2. Cracks the skull (giving colloquial vigor to "breaks faith"). *broker:* go-between, procurer (leading to word-play in "breaks" and "break-vow," lines 569–70).
3. Literally, in the game of bowls, the off-center weight of a bowl that causes it to veer from a straight course.
4. Fixed its hold on the outer edge of a bowl so as to make it swerve from a true course; suddenly caught the "outward eye" of self-interest as opposed to the inward eye of conscience. Both meanings are applicable to King Philip.
5. *angels would salute:* 10-shilling coins (with the archangel Michael on them) would kiss (greet); alluding to the Annunciation and Michael's "salute" to the Virgin Mary.

2.2

Enter [Lady] CONSTANCE, ARTHUR *[Duke of Brittaine],
and [the Earl of]* SALISBURY[1]

CONSTANCE [*to* SALISBURY]   Gone to be married? Gone to swear a peace?
False blood to false blood joined! Gone to be friends?
Shall Louis have Blanche, and Blanche those provinces?
It is not so, thou hast misspoke, misheard.

5   Be well advised,° tell o'er thy tale again.   *Consider carefully*
It cannot be, thou dost but say 'tis so.
I trust I may not trust thee, for thy word
Is but the vain breath of a common° man.   *(as opposed to royal)*
Believe me, I do not believe thee, man;

10   I have a king's oath to the contrary.
Thou shalt be punished for thus frighting me;
For I am sick and capable of° fears;   *susceptible to*
Oppressed with wrongs, and therefore full of fears;
A widow husbandless, subject to fears;

15   A woman naturally born to fears;
And though° thou now confess thou didst but jest,   *even if*
With my vexed spirits I cannot take a truce,°   *make peace*
But they will quake and tremble all this day.
What dost thou mean by shaking of thy head?

20   Why dost thou look so sadly on my son?
What means that hand upon that breast of thine?
Why holds thine eye that lamentable rheum,°   *tears*
Like a proud° river peering o'er his bounds?°   *swollen / banks*
Be these sad signs confirmers of thy words?

25   Then speak again—not all thy former tale,
But this one word: whether thy tale be true.
SALISBURY   As true as I believe you think them° false   *(the French and English)*
That give you cause to prove my saying true.
CONSTANCE   O, if thou teach me to believe this sorrow,

30   Teach thou this sorrow how to make me die;
And let belief and life encounter so
As doth the fury of two desperate men
Which in the very meeting fall and die.[2]
Louis marry Blanche! [*To* ARTHUR] O boy, then where art thou?

35   France friend with England!—What becomes of me?
[*To* SALISBURY] Fellow,° be gone, I cannot brook° thy sight;   *(an insult) / endure*
This news hath made thee a most ugly man.
SALISBURY   What other harm have I, good lady, done,
But spoke the harm that is by others done?

40   CONSTANCE   Which harm within itself so heinous is
As it makes harmful all that speak of it.
ARTHUR   I do beseech you, madam, be content.°   *calm*
CONSTANCE   If thou that bidd'st me be content wert grim,
Ugly and sland'rous to thy mother's womb,[3]

45   Full of unpleasing blots and sightless° stains,   *unsightly*
Lame, foolish, crooked, swart,° prodigious,[4]   *dark*
Patched° with foul moles and eye-offending marks,   *Blotched*
I would not care, I then would be content,

2.2 Location: The French camp by Angers.
1. This is "Actus Secundus" in F (see Textual Note).
2. O . . . *die:* in this image, drawn from emblem-book
representations of Fury, sorrow (or belief) dies as

Constance does.
3. Malformed babies were seen as a divine punishment
for wickedness.
4. Monstrous (and thereby foretelling evil).

For then I should not love thee, no, nor thou
50   Become thy great birth, nor deserve a crown.
But thou art fair, and at thy birth, dear boy,
Nature and Fortune joined to make thee great.
Of Nature's gifts thou mayst with lilies boast,
And with the half-blown° rose. But Fortune, O,   *half-blossomed; young*
55   She is corrupted, changed, and won from thee;
Sh'adulterates° hourly with thine uncle John,   *prostitutes herself*
And with her golden hand hath plucked on° France   *enticed*
To tread down fair respect of sovereignty,°   *(Arthur's rights)*
And made his majesty the bawd to theirs.[5]
60   France is a bawd to Fortune and King John,
That strumpet Fortune, that usurping John.
[*To* SALISBURY] Tell me, thou fellow, is not France forsworn?°   *an oath breaker*
Envenom° him with words, or get thee gone   *Poison*
And leave those woes alone, which I alone
Am bound to underbear.°   *suffer under*
65 SALISBURY   Pardon me, madam,
I may not go without you to the Kings.
CONSTANCE   Thou mayst, thou shalt; I will not go with thee.
I will instruct my sorrows to be proud,
For grief is proud and makes his owner stoop.
[*She sits upon the ground*]
70   To me and to the state° of my great grief   *throne (ironic)*
Let kings assemble, for my grief's so great
That no supporter but the huge firm earth
Can hold it up. Here I and sorrows sit;
Here is my throne; bid kings come bow to it.
[*Exeunt* SALISBURY *and* ARTHUR]

3.1

[*Flourish.*] Enter KING JOHN [*and* KING PHILIP *of*]
France [*hand in hand;* LOUIS THE] DAUPHIN [*and Lady*]
BLANCHE, [*married;* QUEEN] ELEANOR, *Philip* [*the* BAS-
TARD, *and the Duke of*] AUSTRIA[1]
KING PHILIP [*to* BLANCHE] 'Tis true,[2] fair daughter, and this blessèd day
Ever in France shall be kept festival.
To solemnize this day, the glorious sun
Stays in his course° and plays the alchemist,[3]   *Stands still*
5   Turning with splendour of his precious eye
The meagre cloddy earth to glittering gold.
The yearly course that brings this day about
Shall never see it but a holy day.
CONSTANCE [*rising*] A wicked day, and not a holy day!
10   What hath this day deserved? What hath it done,
That it in golden letters should be set

---

5. And made Philip the go-between for John and Fortune.
3.1 Location: The French camp by Angers.
1. Shakespeare originally intended no act break,
though that division, which appears in F, probably indicates a pause in the performance when the play was
revived with act divisions. Salisbury and Arthur might
stay onstage, but they have no further part in the
scene's action. Their exit, if it occurs, may be followed
by a brief pause with Constance alone onstage. She

remains unobserved until line 9. F's stage directions
have her enter with the others at the start of the act,
perhaps because they merely list all the characters who
need to be onstage after a break in the action. But her
words of 2.2.67–74 are incompatible with her entry
here, which is therefore omitted.
2. King Philip enters in mid-conversation.
3. Alchemists sought to turn base metals such as lead
into gold.

Among the high tides° in the calendar? · *great festivals*
Nay, rather turn this day out of the week,
This day of shame, oppression, perjury.
15 Or if it must stand still,° let wives with child · · · · · · · · · · · · · · · · · · *remain*
Pray that their burdens may not fall° this day, · · · · · · · · · · · · · · *they not give birth*
Lest that their hopes prodigiously[4] be crossed;
But° on this day let seamen fear no wreck; · *Except*
No bargains break that are not this day made;
20 This day all things begun come to ill end,
Yea, faith itself to hollow falsehood change.
KING PHILIP   By heaven, lady, you shall have no cause
To curse the fair proceedings of this day.
Have I not pawned° to you my majesty?° · · · · · · · · · · · · · · · *pledged / royal word*
25 CONSTANCE   You have beguiled me with a counterfeit° · · · · · · *false coin or portrait*
Resembling majesty, which being touched and tried° · · · · · · · · · · *tested for gold*
Proves valueless. You are forsworn, forsworn.
You came in arms to spill mine enemies' blood,
But now in arms° you strengthen it with yours. · · · · · · · · · *arm in arm; militarily*
30 The grappling vigour and rough frown of war
Is cold in amity and painted° peace, · *counterfeit*
And our oppression° hath made up° this league. · · · · · · · · · *affliction / possible*
Arm, arm, you heavens, against these perjured Kings!
A widow cries, be husband to me, God!
35 Let not the hours of this ungodly day
Wear out° the day in peace, but ere sun set · *Finish*
Set armèd discord 'twixt these perjured Kings.
Hear me, O hear me!
AUSTRIA   Lady Constance, peace.
CONSTANCE   War, war, no peace! Peace is to me a war.
40 O Limoges, O Austria,[5] thou dost shame
That bloody spoil.° Thou slave, thou wretch, thou coward! · · · · · · · · *(the lion skin)*
Thou little valiant, great in villainy;
Thou ever strong upon the stronger side;
Thou Fortune's champion, that dost never fight
45 But when her humorous ladyship° is by · · · · · · · · · · · · · · · *changeable Fortune*
To teach thee safety. Thou art perjured too,
And sooth'st up greatness.° What a fool art thou, · · · · · · · · · *flatter the powerful*
A ramping° fool, to brag and stamp, and swear · · · · · · · · · · *showily threatening*
Upon my party!° Thou cold-blooded slave, · *cause*
50 Hast thou not spoke like thunder on my side,° · *behalf*
Been sworn my soldier, bidding me depend
Upon thy stars, thy fortune, and thy strength?
And dost thou now fall over° to my foes? · *defect*
Thou wear a lion's hide! Doff it, for shame,
55 And hang a calf's-skin[6] on those recreant° limbs. · · · · · · · · · *cowardly; traitorous*
AUSTRIA   O, that a man should speak those words to me!
BASTARD   And hang a calf's-skin on those recreant limbs.
AUSTRIA   Thou dar'st not say so, villain, for thy life.
BASTARD   And hang a calf's-skin on those recreant limbs.
KING JOHN [*to the* BASTARD]   We like not this. Thou dost forget
60   thyself.° · *your rank; protocol*

4. By an ominously monstrous child.
5. See note to 2.1.5.
6. Symbolizing cowardice or folly.

Enter [Cardinal] PANDOLF

KING PHILIP   Here comes the holy legate of the Pope.[7]

PANDOLF   Hail, you anointed deputies of God.°—   *kings*
To thee, King John, my holy errand is.
I Pandolf, of fair Milan Cardinal,
65   And from Pope Innocent the legate here,
Do in his name religiously demand
Why thou against the Church, our Holy Mother,
So wilfully dost spurn,° and force perforce°   *kick / and forcibly*
Keep Stephen Langton, chosen° Archbishop   *(by the Pope)*
70   Of Canterbury, from that holy see.
This, in our foresaid Holy Father's name,
Pope Innocent, I do demand of thee.

KING JOHN   What earthy name to interrogatories
Can task the free breath of a sacred king?[8]
75   Thou canst not, Cardinal, devise a name
So slight, unworthy, and ridiculous
To charge me to an° answer, as the Pope.   *to make an*
Tell him this tale, and from the mouth of England
Add thus much more: that no Italian priest°   *the Pope*
80   Shall tithe or toll° in our dominions;   *collect church revenue*
But as we, under God, are supreme head,[9]
So, under him, that great supremacy°   *sovereignty*
Where we do reign we will alone uphold
Without th'assistance of a mortal hand.
85   So tell the Pope, all reverence set apart°   *rejected*
To him and his usurped authority.

KING PHILIP   Brother of England, you blaspheme in this.

KING JOHN   Though you and all the kings of Christendom
Are led so grossly by this meddling priest,
90   Dreading the curse that money may buy out,[1]
And by the merit of vile gold, dross, dust,
Purchase corrupted pardon of a man,[2]
Who in that sale sells pardon from himself;[3]
Though you and all the rest so grossly led
95   This juggling° witchcraft with revenue cherish;   *deceiving*
Yet I alone, alone do me oppose
Against the Pope, and count his friends my foes.

PANDOLF   Then by the lawful power that I have
Thou shalt stand cursed and excommunicate;°   *excommunicated*
100   And blessèd shall he be that doth revolt
From his allegiance to an heretic;
And meritorious shall that hand be called,
Canonizèd and worshipped as a saint,
That takes away by any secret course
Thy hateful life.

---

7. Shakespeare follows his main source in combining two papal legates in one, as he does in the use of Austria to represent two of Richard I's adversaries.
8. *What . . . king?*: What person holding an earthly title (the Pope or his deputy) can demand answers from a King who governs by divine right? John attributes to himself the divine authority he has just denied the Pope.
9. "Supreme head" of the English Church is the title adopted in 1534 by Henry VIII, Elizabeth's father, in defiance of the papacy. This passage is perhaps the

most openly and anachronistically Protestant, anti-Catholic moment in the play.
1. Excommunication is the "curse" that a bribe can buy off, or reverse.
2. An allusion to the sale of indulgences, or papal dispensations for sin, by a member of the Catholic clergy ("a man").
3. The clergyman "sells" (gives up) hope of God's forgiveness for himself and is hence damned by his selling. The pardon he sells lacks efficacy because it comes "from himself," rather than from God.

105 CONSTANCE   O lawful let it be
That I have room° with Rome to curse awhile.   *opportunity*
Good Father Cardinal, cry thou 'Amen'
To my keen curses, for without my wrong°   *the wrongs done to me*
There is no tongue hath power to curse him right.°   *properly*
110 PANDOLF   There's law and warrant, lady, for my curse.
CONSTANCE   And for mine too. When law can do no right,
Let it be lawful that law bar no wrong.°   *cursing*
Law cannot give my child his kingdom here,
For he that holds his kingdom holds the law.
115 Therefore, since law° itself is perfect wrong,   *(secular)*
How can the law° forbid my tongue to curse?   *(ecclesiastical)*
PANDOLF   Philip of France, on peril of a curse,°   *excommunication*
Let go the hand of that arch-heretic,
And raise the power of France upon his head,
120 Unless he do submit himself to Rome.
QUEEN ELEANOR   Look'st thou pale, France? Do not let go thy hand.
CONSTANCE [*to* KING JOHN]   Look to it, devil, lest that France repent,
And by disjoining hands hell lose a soul.
AUSTRIA   King Philip, listen to the Cardinal.
125 BASTARD   And hang a calf's-skin on his recreant limbs.
AUSTRIA   Well, ruffian, I must pocket up° these wrongs,   *put up with*
Because—
BASTARD   Your breeches best may carry them.[4]
KING JOHN   Philip, what sayst thou to the Cardinal?
CONSTANCE   What should he say, but as° the Cardinal?   *the same as*
130 LOUIS THE DAUPHIN   Bethink you, Father, for the difference
Is purchase of a heavy curse from Rome,
Or the light loss of England for a friend.
Forgo the easier.
BLANCHE   That's the curse of Rome.
CONSTANCE   O Louis, stand fast; the devil tempts thee here
135 In likeness of a new untrimmèd° bride.   *virginal*
BLANCHE   The Lady Constance speaks not from her faith,
But from her need.
CONSTANCE [*to* KING PHILIP]   O if thou grant my need,
Which only lives but by the death of faith,[5]
That need must needs infer this principle:[6]
140 That faith would live again by death of need.°   *by the end of my woes*
O, then tread down my need, and faith mounts up;
Keep my need up, and faith is trodden down.
KING JOHN   The King is moved, and answers not to this.
CONSTANCE [*to* KING PHILIP]   O, be removed from him, and answer well.
145 AUSTRIA   Do so, King Philip, hang no more in doubt.
BASTARD   Hang nothing but a calf's-skin, most sweet lout.
KING PHILIP   I am perplexed, and know not what to say.
PANDOLF   What canst thou say but will perplex° thee more,   *trouble*
If thou stand excommunicate and cursed?
150 KING PHILIP   Good Reverend Father, make my person yours,°   *put yourself in my place*
And tell me how you would bestow yourself.°   *what you would do*
This royal hand and mine are newly knit,°   *joined*

4. Probably, you may best carry them (the "wrongs" of line 126, or kicks) in the pocket of your breeches; possibly implying that Austria will be kicked in the breeches.
5. Which (my need) exists only because of your broken faith (the pledge to support Arthur) or my loss of faith in you; perhaps, which will live only if you break your faith (to the Church).
6. That need necessarily implies this truth.

And the conjunction of our inward souls
Married in league, coupled and linked together
155 With all religious strength of sacred vows;
The latest breath that gave the sound of words
Was deep-sworn faith, peace, amity, true love,
Between our kingdoms and our royal selves;
And even° before this truce, but new° before,   *just / only just*
160 No longer than we well could wash our hands°   *(of blood)*
To clap this royal bargain up of peace,[7]
God knows, they were besmeared and over-stained
With slaughter's pencil,° where Revenge did paint   *paintbrush*
The fearful difference° of incensèd kings;   *dispute*
165 And shall these hands, so lately purged of blood,
So newly joined in love, so strong in both,°   *(blood and love)*
Unyoke this seizure[8] and this kind regreet,°   *return of salutation*
Play fast and loose with faith, so jest with heaven,
Make such unconstant children of ourselves,
170 As now again to snatch our palm from palm,
Unswear faith sworn, and on the marriage-bed
Of smiling peace to march a bloody host,
And make a riot on the gentle brow
Of true sincerity? O holy sir,
175 My Reverend Father, let it not be so.
Out of your grace, devise, ordain, impose
Some gentle order, and then we shall be blessed
To do your pleasure and continue friends.
PANDOLF All form is formless, order orderless,
180 Save what is opposite to England's love.
Therefore to arms, be champion of our Church,
Or let the Church, our mother, breathe her curse,
A mother's curse, on her revolting son.
France, thou mayst hold° a serpent by the tongue,   *may more easily hold*
185 A crazèd lion by the mortal° paw,   *deadly*
A fasting tiger safer by the tooth,
Than keep in peace that hand which thou dost hold.
KING PHILIP I may disjoin my hand, but not my faith.
PANDOLF So mak'st thou faith an enemy to faith,[9]
190 And like a civil war, sett'st oath to oath,
Thy tongue against thy tongue. O, let thy vow,
First made to heaven, first be to heaven performed;
That is, to be the champion of our Church.
What since thou swor'st[1] is sworn against thyself,
195 And may not be performèd by thyself;
For that which thou hast sworn to do amiss
Is not amiss when it is truly done;[2]
And being not done where doing tends to ill,
The truth is then most done not doing it.
200 The better act of purposes mistook[3]
Is to mistake again; though indirect,°   *circuitous; wrong*
Yet indirection thereby grows direct,

---

7. To seal this royal peace treaty by shaking hands.
8. Of hands joined together.
9. You set your faith to John against your faith to the Church. The confusing rhetoric of this speech exemplifies the elaborate and sometimes equivocal reasoning known as casuistry that was practiced by sixteenth-

century Catholics and hated by English Protestants.
1. What you've subsequently sworn (amity with John).
2. For . . . done: For it's not immoral to break an immoral vow. truly done: not done at all because it is immoral.
3. The better act when you've done wrong.

And falsehood falsehood cures, as fire cools fire
Within the scorchèd veins of one new burned.[4]
205 It is religion that doth make vows kept;°   *make us honor our vows*
But thou hast sworn against religion;
By what thou swear'st, against the thing thou swear'st;[5]
And mak'st an oath the surety for thy troth:[6]
Against an oath, the truth. Thou art unsure
210 To swear: swear'st only not to be forsworn—[7]
Else what a mockery should it be to swear!—
But thou dost swear only to be forsworn,
And most forsworn to keep what thou dost swear;[8]
Therefore thy later vows against thy first
215 Is in thyself rebellion to° thyself,   *against*
And better conquest never canst thou make
Than arm thy constant and thy nobler parts
Against these giddy loose suggestions;°   *dissolute temptations*
Upon° which better part° our prayers come in   *On behalf of / side*
220 If thou vouchsafe° them. But if not, then know   *accept*
The peril of our curses light on thee
So heavy as thou shalt not shake them off,
But in despair° die under their black weight.   *(because damned)*
AUSTRIA   Rebellion, flat rebellion!
BASTARD   Wilt not be?[9]
225 Will not a calf's-skin stop that mouth of thine?
LOUIS THE DAUPHIN   Father, to arms!
BLANCHE   Upon thy wedding day?
Against the blood that thou hast marrièd?
What, shall our feast be kept with° slaughtered men?   *attended by*
Shall braying trumpets and loud churlish drums,
230 Clamours of hell, be measures° to our pomp?°   *music / celebration*
[*She kneels*]
O husband, hear me! Ay, alack, how new
Is 'husband' in my mouth! Even for that name
Which till this time my tongue did ne'er pronounce,
Upon my knee I beg, go not to arms
Against mine uncle.
235 CONSTANCE [*kneeling*]   O, upon my knee
Made hard with kneeling, I do pray to thee,
Thou virtuous Dauphin, alter not the doom°   *fate*
Forethought by heaven.[1]
BLANCHE [*to* LOUIS THE DAUPHIN]   Now shall I see thy love:
what motive may
240 Be stronger with thee than the name of wife?
CONSTANCE   That which upholdeth him that thee upholds:°   *who supports you*
His honour.—O thine honour, Louis, thine honour!
LOUIS THE DAUPHIN [*to* KING PHILIP]   I muse your majesty doth
seem so cold

4. *as fire . . . burned:* the theory that one fire cools another was proverbial but false.
5. By your oath to John, you break your oath to your religion, the basis for all other vows.
6. You make an oath the guarantee of your "troth" (agreement with John); but with a pun on its opposite— the "truth" (or religious faith) of the next line.
7. *Thou art . . . forsworn:* You waver over swearing, and do so only not to break faith (with John).
8. *But thou . . . dost swear:* But your (secular) oath-taking leads only to (religious) oath-breaking, especially in maintaining your oath to John.
9. Is it all in vain; won't you be quiet?
1. Constance self-interestedly treats as a single issue John's two separate matters—Arthur's right to the throne and Pandolf's insistence on papal right. The belief that people are preordained for either salvation or damnation ("doom / Forethought by heaven") is more Protestant than Catholic.

When such profound respects° do pull you on.   *weighty considerations*
245   PANDOLF   I will denounce a curse upon his head.
    KING PHILIP   Thou shalt not need.—England, I will fall from° thee.   *desert*
        [*He takes his hand from King John's hand.* BLANCHE
          and CONSTANCE *rise*]
    CONSTANCE   O, fair return of banished majesty!
    QUEEN ELEANOR   O, foul revolt of French inconstancy!
    KING JOHN   France, thou shalt rue this hour within this hour.
250   BASTARD   Old Time the clock-setter, that bald sexton Time,
      Is it as he will?—Well then, France shall rue.[2]
    BLANCHE   The sun's o'ercast with blood; fair day, adieu!
      Which is the side that I must go withal?°   *with*
      I am with both, each army hath a hand,
255   And in their rage, I having hold of both,
      They whirl asunder° and dismember me.   *dash apart*
      Husband, I cannot pray that thou mayst win.—
      Uncle, I needs must pray that thou mayst lose.—
      Father,° I may not wish the fortune thine.—   *Father-in-law (Philip)*
260   Grandam, I will not wish thy wishes thrive.
      Whoever wins, on that side shall I lose,
      Assurèd loss before the match be played.
    LOUIS THE DAUPHIN   Lady, with me, with me thy fortune° lies.   *prosperity*
    BLANCHE   There where my fortune° lives, there° my life dies.   *fate / (with Louis)*
    KING JOHN [*to the* BASTARD]   Cousin, go draw our puissance°   *army*
265   together.—   *Exit the* BASTARD]
      France, I am burned up with inflaming wrath,
      A rage whose heat hath this condition:
      That nothing can allay,° nothing but blood,   *cure*
      The blood, and dearest-valued blood, of France.
270   KING PHILIP   Thy rage shall burn thee up, and thou shalt turn
      To ashes ere our blood shall quench that fire.
      Look to thyself, thou art in jeopardy.
    KING JOHN   No more than he that threats.—To arms let's hie!°   *hasten*
                 Exeunt [*severally*]

3.2

      Alarum;° excursions.° Enter [*the*] BASTARD, *with* [*the*]   *Call to arms / battles*
       Duke of] *Austria's head*
    BASTARD   Now, by my life, this day grows wondrous hot;
      Some airy devil[1] hovers in the sky
      And pours down mischief. Austria's head lie there,
      While Philip breathes.
          Enter [KING] JOHN, ARTHUR [*Duke of Brittaine, and*]
         HUBERT
5   KING JOHN   Hubert, keep this boy.—Philip,° make up!°   *(the Bastard) / press on*
      My mother is assailèd in our tent,
      And ta'en° I fear.   *captured*
    BASTARD   My lord, I rescued her;

---

2. *Old . . . rue*: The sexton set the church clock and dug graves. Hence, the "hour" (line 249), or time, which was usually portrayed as bald, will indeed be fatal. "Time" and "rue" recall the punning proverb about herbs, "Thyme and rue grow both in one garden," in which the pleasant taste of thyme is contrasted with the bitterness of rue: the passage of time is accompa-

nied by regret. Together the two lines mean something like "If things proceed according to the fatal effects of time, France will indeed be sorry, because time (thyme) and rue go together."
3.2 Location: Plains near Angers.
1. Aerial devils or spirits held to cause thunderstorms and subsequent death.

Her highness is in safety; fear you not.
But on, my liege, for very little pains
10   Will bring this labour to an happy end.

        Exeunt [KING JOHN *and the* BASTARD *at one door,*
           HUBERT *and* ARTHUR *at another door*]

3.3

Alarum; excursions; retreat.° *Enter* [KING] JOHN,   *signal for retreat*
  [QUEEN] ELEANOR, ARTHUR [*Duke of Brittaine, the*] BAS-
  TARD, HUBERT, *lords* [*with soldiers*][1]

KING JOHN [*to* QUEEN ELEANOR]   So shall it be; your grace shall
    stay behind[2]
  So° strongly guarded. [*To* ARTHUR] Cousin,° look not sad;   *Thus / Kinsman*
  Thy grandam loves thee, and thy uncle will
  As dear be to thee as thy father was.
5 ARTHUR   O, this will make my mother die with grief.
  KING JOHN [*to the* BASTARD]   Cousin, away for England! Haste before,°   *Go ahead*
  And ere our coming, see thou shake the bags
  Of hoarding abbots.[3] The fat ribs of peace
  Must by the hungry now be fed upon.
10 Imprisoned angels° set at liberty.[4]   *gold coins; spirits*
  Use our commission° in his° utmost force.   *(to tax) / its*
  BASTARD   Bell, book, and candle[5] shall not drive me back
  When gold and silver becks° me to come on.   *beckons*
  I leave your highness.—Grandam, I will pray,
15 If ever I remember to be holy,
  For your fair safety. So I kiss your hand.
  QUEEN ELEANOR   Farewell, gentle cousin.
  KING JOHN   Coz, farewell.
                           [*Exit the* BASTARD]
  QUEEN ELEANOR   Come hither, little kinsman. Hark, a word.
    [*She takes* ARTHUR *aside*]
  KING JOHN   Come hither, Hubert.
    [*He takes* HUBERT *aside*]
                      O my gentle Hubert,
20 We owe thee much. Within this wall of flesh°   *(John's body)*
  There is a soul counts thee her creditor,
  And with advantage° means to pay thy love;   *interest*
  And, my good friend, thy voluntary oath°   *oath of allegiance*
  Lives in this bosom, dearly cherishèd.
  Give me thy hand.
    [*He takes Hubert's hand*]
25   I had a thing to say,
  But I will fit it with some better tune.°   *words; reward*
  By heaven, Hubert, I am almost ashamed
  To say what good respect° I have of thee.   *opinion*
  HUBERT   I am much bounden° to your majesty.   *indebted*

3.3 Location: Scene continues.
1. F does not begin a new scene here, but it does empty
the stage—hence the scene division adopted here and
in most modern editions.
2. In France, to control the French possessions while
John returns to England.
3. *shake . . . abbots*: pillage the monasteries, which

have hoarded wealth. When Henry VIII made himself
head of the English Church, he confiscated monastic
treasure.
4. F places this line right after "abbots" (line 8), perhaps because a marginal addition in the foul papers was
misplaced in the scribal transcript.
5. Articles used in the rite of excommunication.

30 KING JOHN   Good friend, thou hast no cause to say so yet,
But thou shalt have; and creep time ne'er so slow,
Yet it shall come for me to do thee good.
I had a thing to say—but let it go.
The sun is in the heaven, and the proud day,
35 Attended with the pleasures of the world,
Is all too wanton° and too full of gauds°   *merry / playthings*
To give me audience.° If the midnight bell   *For you to listen*
Did with his iron tongue and brazen mouth
Sound on into the drowsy race° of night;   *course*
40 If this same were a churchyard° where we stand,   *graveyard*
And thou possessèd° with a thousand wrongs;   *obsessed*
Or if that surly spirit, melancholy,
Had baked° thy blood and made it heavy, thick,   *congealed*
Which else° runs tickling up and down the veins,   *otherwise*
45 Making that idiot,° laughter, keep° men's eyes   *jester / stay in*
And strain their cheeks to idle merriment—
A passion° hateful to my purposes—   *mood*
Or if that thou couldst see me without eyes,
Hear me without thine ears, and make reply
50 Without a tongue, using conceit° alone,   *understanding*
Without eyes, ears, and harmful sound of words;
Then in despite° of broad-eyed watchful day   *defiance*
I would into thy bosom pour my thoughts.
But, ah, I will not. Yet I love thee well,
55 And by my troth,° I think thou lov'st me well.   *faith*
HUBERT   So well that what you bid me undertake,
Though that° my death were adjunct to my act,   *Even if*
By heaven, I would do it.
KING JOHN   Do not I know thou wouldst?
Good Hubert, Hubert, Hubert, throw thine eye
60 On yon young boy. I'll tell thee what, my friend,
He is a very serpent in my way,
And wheresoe'er this foot of mine doth tread,
He lies before me. Dost thou understand me?
Thou art his keeper.
HUBERT   And I'll keep him so
65 That he shall not offend your majesty.
KING JOHN   Death.
HUBERT   My lord.
KING JOHN   A grave.
HUBERT   He shall not live.
KING JOHN   Enough.
I could be merry now. Hubert, I love thee.
Well, I'll not say what I intend for thee.
Remember. [*To* QUEEN ELEANOR] Madam, fare you well.
70 I'll send those powers° o'er to your majesty.   *troops*
QUEEN ELEANOR   My blessing go with thee.
KING JOHN [*to* ARTHUR]   For England, cousin, go.
Hubert shall be your man, attend on you
With all true duty.—On toward Calais, ho!
              Exeunt [QUEEN ELEANOR, *attended, at one door,*
                      the rest at another door]

3.4

Enter [KING PHILIP *of*] *France*, [LOUIS THE] DAUPHIN,
[*Cardinal*] PANDOLF, [*and*] *attendants*

KING PHILIP   So, by a roaring tempest on the flood,
A whole armada of convicted sail
Is scattered and disjoined from fellowship.[1]

PANDOLF   Courage and comfort; all shall yet go well.

5 KING PHILIP   What can go well when we have run° so ill?   *performed; run away*
Are we not beaten? Is not Angers lost,
Arthur ta'en prisoner, divers° dear friends slain,   *various*
And bloody England° into England gone,   *John*
O'erbearing interruption, spite[2] of France?

10 LOUIS THE DAUPHIN   What he hath won, that hath he fortified.
So hot a speed, with such advice disposed,°   *judgment regulated*
Such temperate° order in so fierce a cause,   *calm*
Doth want example.° Who hath read or heard   *lack precedent*
Of any kindred action like to this?

15 KING PHILIP   Well could I bear that England had this praise,
So° we could find some pattern° of our shame.   *If / precedent*

Enter CONSTANCE [*distracted,° with her hair about her*   *wild; mad*
ears]

Look who comes here! A grave° unto a soul,   *(Constance's body)*
Holding th'eternal spirit against her will[3]
In the vile prison of afflicted breath.°—   *life*
20 I prithee, lady, go away with me.

CONSTANCE   Lo, now, now see the issue° of your peace!   *outcome*

KING PHILIP   Patience, good lady; comfort, gentle Constance.

CONSTANCE   No, I defy all counsel, all redress,°   *comfort*
But that which ends all counsel, true redress:
25 Death, Death, O amiable, lovely Death!
Thou odoriferous° stench, sound rottenness!   *fragrant*
Arise forth from the couch of lasting° night,   *bed of everlasting*
Thou hate and terror to prosperity,
And I will kiss thy detestable bones,
30 And put my eyeballs in thy vaulty brows,[4]
And ring these fingers with thy household worms,[5]
And stop this gap of breath with fulsome dust,[6]
And be a carrion° monster like thyself.   *corpse-eating*
Come grin on me, and I will think thou smil'st,
35 And buss° thee as thy wife. Misery's love,   *kiss*
O, come to me!

KING PHILIP   O fair affliction,° peace!   *afflicted one*

CONSTANCE   No, no, I will not, having breath to cry.
O, that my tongue were in the thunder's mouth!
Then with a passion° would I shake the world,   *an emotional outcry*
40 And rouse from sleep that fell anatomy,°   *fierce skeleton*
Which cannot hear a lady's feeble voice,
Which scorns a modern invocation.°   *an ordinary plea*

PANDOLF   Lady, you utter madness, and not sorrow.

3.4 Location: The French camp by Angers.
1. *So . . . fellowship:* This French naval defeat is not in
Shakespeare's sources. It is probably a reference to the
Spanish Armada of 1588 (see the Introduction). *convicted sail:* doomed ships.
2. Overcoming hindrances, in spite.

3. *Holding . . . will:* that is, she wants to die.
4. Hollow forehead; the eye sockets of the imagined
skull of death's corpse.
5. And wear the worms that serve you and live inside
you as rings around my fingers.
6. And kiss this mouth with nauseous dust.

CONSTANCE   Thou art not holy to belie me so.
45   I am not mad: this hair I tear is mine;
       My name is Constance; I was Geoffrey's wife;
       Young Arthur is my son; and he is lost.
       I am not mad; I would to God I were,
       For then 'tis like° I should forget myself.   *likely*
50   O, if I could, what grief should I forget!
       Preach some philosophy to make me mad,
       And thou shalt be canonized, Cardinal.
       For, being not mad, but sensible° of grief,   *subject to feelings*
       My reasonable part produces reason
55   How I may be delivered of° these woes,   *freed from*
       And teaches me to kill or hang myself.
       If I were mad I should forget my son,
       Or madly think a babe of clouts° were he.   *cloth doll*
       I am not mad; too well, too well I feel
60   The different plague° of each calamity.   *distinct affliction*
KING PHILIP   Bind up those tresses. O, what love I note
       In the fair multitude of those her hairs!
       Where but by chance a silver drop° hath fallen,   *tear*
       Even to that drop ten thousand wiry friends°   *hairs*
65   Do glue themselves° in sociable grief,   *mat together*
       Like true, inseparable, faithful loves,
       Sticking together in calamity.
CONSTANCE   To England, if you will.[7]
KING PHILIP   Bind up your hairs.
CONSTANCE   Yes, that I will. And wherefore will I do it?
70   I tore them from their bonds, and cried aloud,
       'O that these hands could so redeem my son,
       As they have given these hairs their liberty!'
       But now I envy at their liberty,
       And will again commit them to their bonds,
75   Because my poor child is a prisoner.
           [*She binds up her hair*]
       And Father Cardinal, I have heard you say
       That we shall see and know our friends in heaven.
       If that be true, I shall see my boy again;
       For since the birth of Cain, the first male child,
80   To him that did but yesterday suspire,°   *take his first breath*
       There was not such a gracious creature born.
       But now will canker-sorrow eat my bud,[8]
       And chase the native beauty from his cheek;
       And he will look as hollow as a ghost,
85   As dim and meagre° as an ague's° fit,   *pale and thin / fever's*
       And so he'll die; and rising so again,
       When I shall meet him in the court of heaven,
       I shall not know him; therefore never, never
       Must I behold my pretty Arthur more.
90 PANDOLF   You hold too heinous a respect° of grief.   *view*
CONSTANCE   He talks to me that never had a son.
KING PHILIP   You are as fond of grief as of your child.

---

7. Apparently a reply to line 20, delayed because of Constance's distraction. Possibly the intervening passage is a revision interpolated after the original composition.

8. But now sorrow, like a cankerworm, will eat my flower (Arthur); this is proverbial.

CONSTANCE   Grief fills the room up of my absent child,
Lies in his bed, walks up and down with me,
95   Puts on his pretty looks, repeats his words,
Remembers° me of all his gracious parts,   *Reminds*
Stuffs out his vacant garments with his form;
Then have I reason to be fond of grief.
Fare you well. Had you such a loss as I,
100   I could give better comfort than you do.
     [*She unbinds her hair*]
I will not keep this form upon my head
When there is such disorder in my wit.
O Lord, my boy, my Arthur, my fair son,
My life, my joy, my food, my all the world,
105   My widow-comfort, and my sorrow's cure!   *Exit*
KING PHILIP   I fear some outrage,° and I'll follow her.   *(perhaps suicide)*
                                                    Exit [*attended*]
LOUIS THE DAUPHIN   There's nothing in this world can make me joy.
Life is as tedious as a twice-told tale,
Vexing the dull ear of a drowsy man;
110   And bitter shame hath spoiled the sweet world's taste,
That° it yields naught but shame and bitterness.   *So that*
PANDOLF   Before the curing of a strong disease,
Even in the instant of repair and health,
The fit° is strongest. Evils that take leave,   *symptom*
115   On their departure most of all show evil.
What have you lost by losing of this day?
LOUIS THE DAUPHIN   All days of glory, joy, and happiness.
PANDOLF   If you had won it, certainly you had.
No, no; when Fortune means° to men most good,   *intends*
120   She looks upon them with a threat'ning eye.
'Tis strange to think how much King John hath lost
In this which he accounts so clearly won.
Are not you grieved that Arthur is his prisoner?
LOUIS THE DAUPHIN   As heartily as he is glad he hath him.
125   PANDOLF   Your mind is all as youthful as your blood.
Now hear me speak with a prophetic spirit,
For even the breath of what I mean to speak
Shall blow each dust,° each straw, each little rub,°   *speck / obstacle*
Out of the path which shall directly lead
130   Thy foot to England's throne. And therefore mark.
John hath seized Arthur, and it cannot be
That whiles warm life plays in that infant's veins
The misplaced° John should entertain an hour,   *usurping*
One minute, nay, one quiet breath of rest.
135   A sceptre snatched with an unruly hand
Must be as boisterously° maintained as gained;   *violently*
And he that stands upon a slipp'ry place
Makes nice of no vile hold to stay⁹ him up.
That John may stand, then Arthur needs must fall;
140   So be it, for it cannot be but so.
LOUIS THE DAUPHIN   But what shall I gain by young Arthur's fall?
PANDOLF   You, in the right of Lady Blanche your wife,
May then make all the claim that Arthur did.¹

9. Is not fussy about the vileness of any hold to keep.   1. In Shakespeare's sources but not historical.

LOUIS THE DAUPHIN   And lose it, life and all, as Arthur did.

145 PANDOLF   How green you are, and fresh in this old world!
John lays you plots;° the times conspire with you; — plots to your benefit
For he that steeps his safety in true° blood — legitimate
Shall find but bloody safety and untrue.[2]
This act, so vilely born, shall cool the hearts

150 Of all his people, and freeze up their zeal,° — enthusiastic loyalty
That none so small advantage shall step forth
To check his reign but they will cherish it;[3]
No natural exhalation° in the sky, — meteor
No scope° of nature, no distempered° day, — effect / stormy

155 No common wind, no customèd° event, — everyday
But they will pluck away his° natural cause, — its
And call them meteors,° prodigies, and signs, — portents
Abortives,[4] presages, and tongues of° heaven — signs from
Plainly denouncing vengeance upon John.

160 LOUIS THE DAUPHIN   Maybe he will not touch young Arthur's life,
But hold° himself safe in his prisonment. — consider
PANDOLF   O sir, when he shall hear of your approach,
If that young Arthur be not gone already,
Even at that news he dies; and then the hearts

165 Of all his people shall revolt from him,
And kiss the lips of unacquainted° change, — unfamiliar
And pick strong matter of° revolt and wrath — reasons for
Out of the bloody fingers' ends of John.
Methinks I see this hurly all on foot,° — commotion all under way

170 And O, what better matter breeds for you
Than I have named! The Bastard Falconbridge
Is now in England, ransacking the Church,
Offending charity. If but a dozen French
Were there in arms, they would be as a call° — decoy; call to arms

175 To train° ten thousand English to their side, — draw
Or as a little snow tumbled about
Anon becomes a mountain. O noble Dauphin,
Go with me to the King. 'Tis wonderful
What may be wrought out of their discontent

180 Now that their souls are top-full of offence.° — grievances
For England, go! I will whet on° the King. — provoke
LOUIS THE DAUPHIN   Strong reasons make strange actions. Let us go.
If you say ay, the King will not say no.   *Exeunt*

4.1

Enter HUBERT, *and* EXECUTIONERS [*with a rope and irons*]
HUBERT   Heat me these irons hot, and look thou stand
Within the arras.[1] When I strike my foot
Upon the bosom of the ground, rush forth
And bind the boy which you shall find with me

5 Fast to the chair. Be heedful. Hence, and watch!
EXECUTIONER   I hope your warrant will bear out° the deed. — authorize
HUBERT   Uncleanly° scruples: fear not you. Look to't!° — Improper / Do it
[*The* EXECUTIONERS *withdraw behind the arras*]

---

2. Compare Genesis 9:6: "Whoso sheddeth man's blood, by man shall his blood be shed." *untrue*: untrustworthy.
3. *none . . . it*: they will seize the smallest opportunity

to dethrone him.
4. Untimely or monstrous births (seen as portents).
4.1 Location: A castle prison in England.
1. Behind the tapestry hangings.

Young lad, come forth, I have to say° with you.   *something to discuss*

    Enter ARTHUR [*Duke of Brittaine*]

ARTHUR   Good morrow, Hubert.

HUBERT   Good morrow, little Prince.

10 ARTHUR   As little prince, having so great a title

    To be more prince, as may be.[2] You are sad.

HUBERT   Indeed I have been merrier.

ARTHUR   Mercy on me!

    Methinks nobody should be sad but I.

    Yet I remember, when I was in France,

15   Young gentlemen would be as sad as night

    Only for wantonness.° By my christendom,°   *affectation / faith*

    So° I were out of prison and kept sheep,   *If*

    I should be as merry as the day is long;

    And so I would be here, but that I doubt°   *fear*

20   My uncle practises° more harm to me.   *plots*

    He is afraid of me, and I of him.

    Is it my fault that I was Geoffrey's son?

    No, indeed is't not, and I would to God

    I were your son, so you would love me, Hubert.

25 HUBERT [*aside*]   If I talk to him, with his innocent prate°   *prattle*

    He will awake my mercy, which lies dead;

    Therefore I will be sudden, and dispatch.

ARTHUR   Are you sick, Hubert? You look pale today.

    In sooth, I would° you were a little sick,   *Truly, I wish*

30   That I might sit all night and watch with you.

    I warrant I love you more than you do me.

HUBERT [*aside*]   His words do take possession of my bosom.

    [*He shows* ARTHUR *a paper*]

    Read here, young Arthur. [*aside*] How now: foolish rheum,°   *tears*

    Turning dispiteous° torture out of door?   *pitiless*

35   I must be brief, lest resolution drop

    Out at mine eyes in tender womanish tears.

    [*To* ARTHUR] Can you not read it? Is it not fair writ?°   *legible; legal*

ARTHUR   Too fairly, Hubert, for so foul effect.

    Must you with hot irons burn out both mine eyes?[3]

HUBERT   Young boy, I must.

ARTHUR   And will you?

40 HUBERT   And I will.

ARTHUR   Have you the heart? When your head did but ache

    I knit my handkerchief about your brows,

    The best I had—a princess wrought it° me,   *made it for*

    And I did never ask it you° again—   *back from you*

45   And with my hand at midnight held your head,

    And like the watchful minutes to the hour

    Still and anon° cheered up the heavy time,[4]   *Continually*

    Saying 'What lack you?' and 'Where lies your grief?'°   *pain*

    Or 'What good love° may I perform for you?'   *loving deed*

50   Many a poor man's son would have lain still

    And ne'er have spoke a loving word to you,

---

2. *As . . . be:* Although I have title to be a great prince (king), I am as little a prince as is possible.
3. The order to blind Arthur here is at odds with the death sentence of 3.3.66, as well as with Hubert's deci-sion later in this scene (line 127) falsely to report Arthur's death, a decision he makes good on in 4.2.
4. The minutes are seen as breaking up the time to make it pass easily.

But you at your sick service had a prince.
Nay, you may think my love was crafty love,
And call it cunning. Do, an if you will.
55 If heaven be pleased that you must use me ill,
Why then you must. Will you put out mine eyes,
These eyes that never did, nor never shall,
So much as frown on you?

HUBERT   I have sworn to do it,
And with hot irons must I burn them out.

60 ARTHUR   Ah, none but in this iron age[5] would do it.
The iron of itself, though heat° red hot,   heated
Approaching near these eyes would drink my tears,
And quench his° fiery indignation   its
Even in the matter° of mine innocence;   substance; tears
65 Nay, after that, consume° away in rust,   dissolve
But° for containing fire to harm mine eye.   Merely
Are you more stubborn-hard than hammered iron?
An if an angel should have come to me
And told me Hubert should put out mine eyes,
70 I would not have believed him; no tongue but Hubert's.

        [HUBERT stamps his foot]

HUBERT   Come forth!

        [The EXECUTIONERS come forth]

                        Do as I bid you do.

ARTHUR   O, save me, Hubert, save me! My eyes are out
Even with the fierce looks of these bloody men.

HUBERT [to the EXECUTIONERS]   Give me the iron, I say, and bind him here.

        [He takes the iron]

75 ARTHUR   Alas, what need you be so boisterous-rough?
I will not struggle; I will stand stone-still.
For God's sake, Hubert, let me not be bound.
Nay, hear me, Hubert! Drive these men away,
And I will sit as quiet as a lamb;
80 I will not stir, nor wince, nor speak a word,
Nor look upon the iron angerly.°   angrily
Thrust but these men away, and I'll forgive you,
Whatever torment you do put me to.

HUBERT [to the EXECUTIONERS]   Go stand within. Let me alone with him.

85 EXECUTIONER   I am best pleased to be from° such a deed.   away from

        [Exeunt EXECUTIONERS]

ARTHUR   Alas, I then have chid° away my friend!   scolded
He hath a stern look, but a gentle heart.
Let him come back, that his compassion may
Give life to yours.

HUBERT   Come, boy, prepare yourself.

ARTHUR   Is there no remedy?

90 HUBERT   None but to lose your eyes.

ARTHUR   O God, that there were but a mote° in yours,   speck of dust
A grain, a dust, a gnat, a wandering hair,
Any annoyance in that precious sense,°   sight
Then, feeling what small things are boisterous° there,   painful
95 Your vile intent must needs seem horrible.

HUBERT   Is this your promise? Go to,° hold your tongue!   Stop it (rebuke)

5. Cruel, degenerate world, in contrast to the legendary "golden" and "silver" ages; with a play on the hot irons.

ARTHUR   Hubert, the utterance of a brace of tongues
   Must needs want pleading for a pair of eyes.[6]
   Let° me not hold my tongue, let me not, Hubert;   *Make*
100 Or, Hubert, if you will, cut out my tongue,
   So° I may keep mine eyes. O, spare mine eyes,   *If*
   Though to no use but still to look on you.
   Lo, by my troth,° the instrument is cold   *faith*
   And would not harm me.
HUBERT   I can heat it, boy.
105 ARTHUR   No, in good sooth:° the fire is dead with grief,   *truly*
   Being create° for comfort, to be° used   *created / at being*
   In undeserved extremes.° See else° yourself.   *extreme suffering / for*
   There is no malice in this burning coal;
   The breath of heaven hath blown his spirit° out,   *(dead person's) soul*
110 And strewed repentant ashes° on his head.   *(of a penitent sinner)*
HUBERT   But with my breath I can revive it, boy.
ARTHUR   An if you do, you will but make it blush
   And glow with shame of your proceedings, Hubert.
   Nay, it perchance will sparkle° in your eyes,   *cast sparks*
115 And like a dog that is compelled to fight,
   Snatch at his master that doth tarre° him on.   *set*
   All things that you should° use to do me wrong   *would*
   Deny their office;° only you do lack   *Disobey*
   That mercy which fierce fire and iron extends,
120 Creatures of note° for mercy-lacking uses.   *Things noteworthy*
HUBERT   Well, see to live.[7] I will not touch thine eye
   For all the treasure that thine uncle owes.°   *owns*
   Yet am I sworn, and I did purpose, boy,
   With this same very iron to burn them out.
125 ARTHUR   O, now you look like Hubert. All this while
   You were disguisèd.
HUBERT   Peace, no more. Adieu.
   Your uncle must not know but° you are dead.   *otherwise than that*
   I'll fill these doggèd° spies with false reports;   *unfeeling*
   And, pretty child, sleep doubtless° and secure   *without fear*
130 That Hubert, for the wealth of all the world,
   Will not offend° thee.   *harm*
ARTHUR   O God! I thank you, Hubert.
HUBERT   Silence, no more. Go closely° in with me.   *secretly*
   Much danger do I undergo for thee.   *Exeunt*

4.2

[*Flourish.*] *Enter* [KING] JOHN, [*the Earls of*] PEMBROKE
and SALISBURY, *and other lords.* [KING JOHN *ascends the
throne*]

KING JOHN   Here once again we sit, once again crowned,[1]
   And looked upon, I hope, with cheerful eyes.
PEMBROKE   This 'once again', but that your highness pleased,
   Was once superfluous.[2] You were crowned before,

---

6. *the utterance . . . eyes*: not even a pair of tongues
would be enough to plead for a pair of eyes.
7. Live, and retain your sight.
4.2 Location: John's court in England.
1. John has had a second coronation. Its purpose,
according to Shakespeare's main source, was to get the
English lords again to swear allegiance to him.
2. *but . . . superfluous*: but for the fact that you wanted
this second coronation, it would have been one too
many.

5 And that high royalty was ne'er plucked off,
The faiths of men ne'er stainèd with revolt;
Fresh expectation° troubled not the land   Hope of a new king
With any longed-for change or better state.[3]
SALISBURY   Therefore to be possessed with double pomp,
10 To guard° a title that was rich before,   adorn
To gild refinèd gold, to paint the lily,
To throw a perfume on the violet,
To smooth the ice, or add another hue
Unto the rainbow, or with taper-light°   candlelight
15 To seek the beauteous eye of heaven to garnish,°   the sun to adorn
Is wasteful and ridiculous excess.
PEMBROKE   But that your royal pleasure must be done,
This act is as an ancient tale new-told,
And in the last repeating troublesome,
20 Being urgèd at a time unseasonable.°   inappropriate
SALISBURY   In this the antique and well-noted° face   familiar
Of plain old form° is much disfigurèd,   custom
And like a shifted wind unto a sail,
It makes the course of thoughts to fetch about,°   change directions
25 Startles and frights consideration,[4]
Makes sound opinion sick, and truth suspected
For putting on so new a fashioned robe.[5]
PEMBROKE   When workmen strive to do better than well,
They do confound° their skill in covetousness;[6]   destroy
30 And oftentimes excusing of a fault
Doth make the fault the worser by th'excuse;
As patches set upon a little breach°   tear
Discredit more in hiding of the fault
Than did the fault before it was so patched.
35 SALISBURY   To this effect: before you were new-crowned
We breathed our counsel,° but it pleased your highness   spoke our advice
To overbear° it; and we are all well pleased,   overrule
Since all and every part of what we would°   wish
Doth make a stand° at what your highness will.°   stop; resist / desires
40 KING JOHN   Some reasons of this double coronation
I have possessed you with,° and think them strong.   instructed you in
And more, more strong, when lesser is my fear
I shall endue° you with. Meantime but ask   supply
What you would have reformed that is not well,
45 And well shall you perceive how willingly
I will both hear and grant you your requests.[7]
PEMBROKE   Then I, as one that am the tongue° of these   spokesman
To sound° the purposes of all their hearts,   express
Both for myself and them, but chief of all
50 Your safety, for the which myself and them
Bend° their best studies,° heartily request   Direct / efforts
Th'enfranchisement° of Arthur, whose restraint   release

3. Better government; better living conditions.
4. Encourages questions about John's claim to the throne.
5. For behaving so uncustomarily; for donning a coronation robe.
6. By greedily trying to do even better.
7. Lines 43–46 may allude to the historical King John's submission to the baronial demands spelled out in the Magna Carta. See also line 168 and 5.2.20–23.

Doth move the murmuring lips of discontent
To break into this dangerous argument:
55 If what in rest° you have, in right you hold,   *in peace*
Why then your fears—which, as they say, attend
The steps of wrong—should move you to mew up°   *confine*
Your tender kinsman, and to choke his days
With barbarous ignorance, and deny his youth
60 The rich advantage of good exercise?°   *education*
That the time's enemies may not have this
To grace occasions,° let it be our suit   *To justify opposition*
That you have bid us ask, his liberty;
Which for our goods we do no further ask
65 Than whereupon our weal, on you depending,
Counts it your weal he have his liberty.[8]

     Enter HUBERT

KING JOHN   Let it be so. I do commit his youth
To your direction.—Hubert, what news with you?
     [*He takes* HUBERT *aside*]

PEMBROKE   This is the man should do the bloody deed:
70 He showed his warrant to a friend of mine.
The image of a wicked heinous fault°   *crime*
Lives in his eye; that close aspect° of his   *furtive appearance*
Does show the mood of a much troubled breast;
And I do fearfully believe 'tis done
75 What we so feared he had a charge to do.

SALISBURY   The colour of the King doth come and go
Between his purpose and his conscience,
Like heralds 'twixt two dreadful battles set.°   *armies set for battle*
His passion is so ripe it needs must break.°   *burst (like a boil)*
80 PEMBROKE   And when it breaks, I fear will issue thence
The foul corruption° of a sweet child's death.   *pus*

KING JOHN [*coming forward*]   We cannot hold° mortality's strong hand.   *hold back*
Good lords, although my will to give is living,
The suit which you demand is gone and dead.
85 He tells us Arthur is deceased tonight.°   *last night*

SALISBURY   Indeed we feared his sickness was past cure.

PEMBROKE   Indeed we heard how near his death he was,
Before the child himself felt he was sick.
This must be answered,° either here or hence.°   *answered for / in heaven*
90 KING JOHN   Why do you bend such solemn brows on me?
Think you I bear the shears of destiny?[9]
Have I commandment on the pulse of life?

SALISBURY   It is apparent° foul play, and 'tis shame   *blatant*
That greatness should so grossly offer° it.   *brazenly flaunt*
95 So thrive it in your game;[1] and so, farewell.

PEMBROKE   Stay yet, Lord Salisbury; I'll go with thee,
And find th'inheritance of this poor child,
His little kingdom of a forcèd° grave.   *violently imposed*
That blood which owed° the breadth of all this isle   *owned (by right)*
100 Three foot of it doth hold. Bad world the while.°   *while such deeds occur*

---

8. *Which . . . liberty*: Which we ask for ourselves only
insofar as concern for our benefit, which depends on
you, leads to the conclusion that it is to your benefit to
free him.

9. The shears with which, in Greek mythology, the
Fates cut the thread of life.
1. May you suffer a similar fate.

This must not be thus borne. This will break out°   *break out in conflict*
To all our sorrows; and ere long, I doubt.°   *fear*
          Exeunt [PEMBROKE, SALISBURY, *and other lords*]
KING JOHN   They burn in indignation. I repent.
There is no sure foundation set on blood,
105   No certain life achieved by others' death.
          Enter [*a*] MESSENGER
A fearful eye thou hast. Where is that blood
That I have seen inhabit in those cheeks?
So foul a sky° clears not without a storm;   *(his face)*
Pour down thy weather: how goes all° in France?   *everything; everyone*
110 MESSENGER   From France to England. Never such a power
For any foreign preparation°   *military expedition*
Was levied in the body of a land.
The copy° of your speed is learned by them,   *example*
For when you should be told they do prepare,
115   The tidings comes that they are all arrived.
KING JOHN   O, where hath our intelligence° been drunk?   *spy network*
Where hath it slept? Where is my mother's ear,
That such an army could be drawn in France,
And she not hear of it?
MESSENGER   My liege, her ear
120   Is stopped with dust. The first of April died
Your noble mother. And as I hear, my lord,
The Lady Constance in a frenzy died
Three days before; but this from rumour's tongue
I idly heard; if true or false I know not.
125 KING JOHN   Withhold thy speed,° dreadful Occasion;°   *Slow down / events*
O, make a league with me till I have pleased
My discontented peers. What, Mother dead?
How wildly then walks my estate° in France!—   *fare my possessions*
Under whose conduct came those powers of France
130   That thou for truth giv'st out° are landed here?   *claim*
MESSENGER   Under the Dauphin.
          Enter [*the*] BASTARD *and* PETER OF POMFRET[2]
KING JOHN   Thou hast made me giddy
With these ill tidings. [*To the* BASTARD] Now, what says the world
To your proceedings?° Do not seek to stuff   *(monastic pillaging)*
My head with more ill news, for it is full.
135 BASTARD   But if you be afeard to hear the worst,
Then let the worst, unheard, fall on your head.
KING JOHN   Bear with me, cousin, for I was amazed°   *confused; stunned*
Under the tide;° but now I breathe again   *sea (of bad tidings)*
Aloft the flood, and can give audience
140   To any tongue, speak it of what it will.
BASTARD   How I have sped° among the clergymen   *fared*
The sums I have collected shall express.
But as I travelled hither through the land,
I find the people strangely fantasied,°   *full of peculiar ideas*
145   Possessed with rumours, full of idle° dreams,   *foolish*
Not knowing what they fear, but full of fear.
And here's a prophet that I brought with me
From forth the streets of Pomfret, whom I found

2. Modern Pontefract, west Yorkshire.

With many hundreds treading on his heels;
150 To whom he sung, in rude,° harsh-sounding rhymes,   *unpolished*
That ere the next Ascension Day³ at noon
Your highness should deliver up° your crown.   *give up*
KING JOHN   Thou idle dreamer, wherefore didst thou so?
PETER OF POMFRET   Foreknowing that the truth will fall out so.
155 KING JOHN   Hubert, away with him! Imprison him,
And on that day, at noon, whereon he says
I shall yield up my crown, let him be hanged.
Deliver him to safety,° and return,   *custody*
For I must use thee. [*Exeunt* HUBERT *and* PETER OF POMFRET]
O my gentle cousin,
160 Hear'st thou the news abroad, who are arrived?
BASTARD   The French, my lord: men's mouths are full of it.
Besides, I met Lord Bigot and Lord Salisbury
With eyes as red° as new-enkindled fire,   *(in rage)*
And others more, going to seek the grave
165 Of Arthur, whom they say is killed tonight°   *last night*
On your suggestion.
KING JOHN   Gentle kinsman, go
And thrust thyself into their companies.
I have a way to win their loves again.
Bring them before me.
BASTARD   I will seek them out.
170 KING JOHN   Nay, but make haste, the better foot before.°   *go quickly*
O, let me have no subject° enemies   *subjects who are my*
When adverse foreigners affright my towns
With dreadful pomp of stout invasion!
Be Mercury, set feathers to thy heels,⁴
175 And fly like thought° from them to me again.   *(proverbially swift)*
BASTARD   The spirit of the time° shall teach me speed.   *Exit*   *present occasion*
KING JOHN   Spoke like a sprightful° noble gentleman!—   *spirited*
Go after him, for he perhaps shall need
Some messenger betwixt me and the peers,
180 And be thou he.
MESSENGER   With all my heart, my liege.   [*Exit*]
KING JOHN   My mother dead!
            Enter HUBERT
HUBERT   My lord, they say five moons° were seen tonight,   *(an ominous portent)*
Four fixèd, and the fifth did whirl about
185 The other four in wondrous motion.
KING JOHN   Five moons?
HUBERT   Old men and beldams° in the streets   *crones*
Do prophesy upon it dangerously.
Young Arthur's death is common in their mouths,
And when they talk of him they shake their heads,
190 And whisper one another in the ear;
And he that speaks doth grip the hearer's wrist,
Whilst he that hears makes fearful action,°   *shows fear*
With wrinkled brows, with nods, with rolling eyes.
I saw a smith stand with his hammer, thus,
195 The whilst his iron did on the anvil cool,

---

3. The Thursday, forty days after Easter, on which   4. Mercury, swift messenger of the Roman gods, wore
Christ is supposed to have ascended to heaven.   winged sandals.

With open mouth swallowing a tailor's news,
Who, with his shears and measure in his hand,
Standing on slippers which his nimble haste
Had falsely thrust upon contrary° feet,   *the wrong*
200   Told of a many thousand warlike French
That were embattailèd° and ranked in Kent.   *in battle order*
Another lean unwashed artificer°   *artisan*
Cuts off his° tale, and talks of Arthur's death.   *(the tailor's)*
KING JOHN   Why seek'st thou to possess me with these fears?
205   Why urgest thou so oft young Arthur's death?
Thy hand hath murdered him. I had a mighty cause
To wish him dead, but thou hadst none to kill him.
HUBERT   No had,° my lord? Why, did you not provoke me? *Hadn't I*
KING JOHN   It is the curse of kings to be attended
210   By slaves that take their humours° for a warrant   *whims*
To break within the bloody house of life,[5]
And on the winking° of authority   *hint; lapse*
To understand a law,° to know the meaning   *To infer a command*
Of dangerous majesty, when perchance it frowns
215   More upon humour than advised respect.°   *considered opinion*
HUBERT   Here is your hand° and seal for what I did.   *signature*
    [*He shows a paper*]
KING JOHN   O, when the last account 'twixt heaven and earth
Is to be made,[6] then shall this hand and seal
Witness against us to damnation!
220   How oft the sight of means to do ill deeds
Make deeds ill done! Hadst not thou been by,°   *on hand*
A fellow by the hand of nature marked,°   *(by ugliness)*
Quoted,° and signed° to do a deed of shame, *Noted / marked*
This murder had not come into my mind.
225   But taking note of thy abhorred aspect,°   *appearance*
Finding thee fit for bloody villainy,
Apt, liable° to be employed in danger,° *suitable / doing harm*
I faintly broke° with thee of Arthur's death;   *vaguely spoke*
And thou, to be endearèd to a king,
230   Made it no conscience° to destroy a prince. *no matter of conscience*
HUBERT   My lord—
KING JOHN   Hadst thou but shook thy head or made a pause
When I spake darkly° what I purposed,   *insinuated*
Or turned an eye of doubt upon my face,
235   As° bid me tell my tale in express° words, *As if to / plain*
Deep shame had struck me dumb, made me break off,
And those thy fears might have wrought fears in me.
But thou didst understand me by my signs,
And didst in signs again parley° with sin;   *negotiate*
240   Yea, without stop, didst let thy heart consent,
And consequently thy rude° hand to act   *rough*
The deed which both our tongues held vile° to name. *refused*
Out of my sight, and never see me more!
My nobles leave me, and my state is braved,°   *challenged*
245   Even at my gates, with ranks of foreign powers;
Nay, in the body of this fleshly land,°   *(John's body)*

---

5. The human body, which contains blood and which
murder makes bloody.

6. *when . . . made*: when Judgment Day arrives.

This kingdom, this confine° of blood and breath,   *territory*
Hostility and civil tumult reigns
Between my conscience and my cousin's death.

250   HUBERT   Arm you against your other enemies;
I'll make a peace between your soul and you.
Young Arthur is alive. This hand of mine
Is yet a maiden° and an innocent hand,   *virgin*
Not painted with the crimson spots of blood.

255   Within this bosom never entered yet
The dreadful motion° of a murderous thought;   *impulse*
And you have slandered nature° in my form,°   *my nature / appearance*
Which, howsoever rude exteriorly,
Is yet the cover of a fairer mind

260   Than to be butcher of an innocent child.

   KING JOHN   Doth Arthur live? O, haste thee to the peers;
Throw this report° on their incensèd° rage,   *(like water) / burning*
And make them tame to their obedience.°   *(to John)*
Forgive the comment that my passion made

265   Upon thy feature,° for my rage was blind,   *features*
And foul imaginary eyes of blood[7]
Presented thee more hideous than thou art.
O, answer not, but to my closet° bring   *private room*
The angry lords with all expedient° haste.   *quick*

270   I conjure° thee but slowly; run more fast. *Exeunt [severally]*   *urge*

4.3

Enter ARTHUR *[Duke of Brittaine] on the walls [disguised as a ship-boy]*

   ARTHUR   The wall is high, and yet will I leap down.
Good ground, be pitiful, and hurt me not.
There's few or none do know me; if they did,
This ship-boy's semblance° hath disguised me quite.°   *disguise / completely*

5   I am afraid, and yet I'll venture it.
If I get down and do not break my limbs,
I'll find a thousand shifts° to get away.   *stratagems*
As good to die and go, as die and stay.
     [He leaps down]
O me! My uncle's spirit is in these stones.

10   Heaven take my soul, and England keep my bones!
     [He] dies

Enter [the Earls of] PEMBROKE *[and]* SALISBURY, *and
[Lord]* BIGOT

   SALISBURY   Lords, I will meet him° at Saint Edmundsbury.[1]   *(the Dauphin)*
It is our safety,° and we must embrace   *means of safety*
This gentle offer of the perilous time.

   PEMBROKE   Who brought that letter from the Cardinal?°   *Pandolf*

15   SALISBURY   The Count Melun, a noble lord of France,
Who's private with° me of the Dauphin's love;   *Who has confided in*
'Tis much more general° than these lines import.   *much greater*

   BIGOT   Tomorrow morning let us meet him then.

   SALISBURY   Or rather, then set forward, for 'twill be

20   Two long days' journey, lords, or ere° we meet.   *before*

---

7. John's, bloody from rage; Hubert's, bloody from   4.3 Location: Outside the castle.
guilt; Arthur's, bloody from murder.   1. Bury St. Edmunds, Suffolk (a place of pilgrimage).

Enter [the] BASTARD

BASTARD   Once more today well met, distempered° lords.   *ill-humored*
  The King by me requests your presence straight.°   *immediately*
SALISBURY   The King hath dispossessed himself of us.
  We will not line his thin bestainèd cloak
25   With our pure honours, nor attend the foot
  That leaves the print of blood where'er it walks.
  Return and tell him so; we know the worst.
BASTARD   Whate'er you think, good words I think were best.
SALISBURY   Our griefs and not our manners reason now.
30 BASTARD   But there is little reason in your grief.
  Therefore 'twere reason° you had manners now.   *reasonable*
PEMBROKE   Sir, sir, impatience hath his privilege.°   *its particular right*
BASTARD   'Tis true—to hurt his master, no man else.[2]
SALISBURY   This is the prison.
      [He sees Arthur's body]
                  What is he lies here?
35 PEMBROKE   O death, made proud with pure and princely beauty!
  The earth had not a hole° to hide this deed.   *grave*
SALISBURY   Murder, as° hating what himself hath done,   *as though*
  Doth lay it open° to urge on revenge.   *on public display*
BIGOT   Or when he° doomed this beauty to a grave,   *(murder)*
40   Found it too precious-princely for a grave.
SALISBURY *[to the* BASTARD*]*   Sir Richard, what think you? You have beheld.
  Or have you° read or heard; or could you think,   *Have you either*
  Or do you almost think, although you see,
  That you do see? Could thought, without this object,
45   Form such another?[3] This is the very top,
  The height, the crest,° or crest unto the crest,   *(atop a coat of arms)*
  Of murder's arms; this is the bloodiest shame,
  The wildest savagery, the vilest stroke
  That ever wall-eyed° wrath or staring rage   *glaring*
50   Presented to the tears of soft remorse.°   *pity*
PEMBROKE   All murders past do stand excused in° this,   *in comparison with*
  And this, so sole° and so unmatchable,   *unique*
  Shall give a holiness, a purity,
  To the yet-unbegotten sin of times,°   *the future*
55   And prove a deadly bloodshed but a jest,
  Exampled by° this heinous spectacle.   *Given the precedent of*
BASTARD   It is a damnèd and a bloody work,
  The graceless° action of a heavy° hand—   *impious / an oppressive*
  If that it be the work of any hand.
60 SALISBURY   If that it be the work of any hand?
  We had a kind of light° what would ensue: *premonition*
  It is the shameful work of Hubert's hand,
  The practice° and the purpose of the King;   *plot*
  From whose obedience I forbid my soul,
65   Kneeling before this ruin of sweet life,
  And breathing to his breathless excellence
  The incense of a vow, a holy vow,
  Never to taste the pleasures of the world,

---

2. Angry words hurt no one but the speaker (proverbial).
3. *Or do . . . another:* Could you even approach the thought of what you actually see here? Without seeing Arthur's body, would it be possible to imagine such a sight?

Never to be infected with delight,
70　Nor conversant with ease and idleness,
　　Till I have set a glory to this hand°　　　　　　　　　　*(his own; Arthur's)*
　　By giving it the worship° of revenge.　　　　　　　　　　　　　*honor*
PEMBROKE *and* BIGOT　Our souls religiously confirm thy words.

　　　　　　Enter HUBERT

HUBERT　Lords, I am hot with haste in seeking you.
75　Arthur doth live; the King hath sent for you.
SALISBURY　O, he is bold, and blushes not at death!—
　　Avaunt,° thou hateful villain, get thee gone!　　　　　　　　　　*Begone*
HUBERT　I am no villain.
SALISBURY　　　　　　　　　　Must I rob the law?[4]
　　　　[*He draws his sword*]
BASTARD　Your sword is bright,° sir; put it up° again.　　*unused / sheathe it*
80　SALISBURY　Not till I sheathe it in a murderer's skin.
HUBERT [*drawing his sword*]　Stand back, Lord Salisbury, stand back, I say!
　　By heaven, I think my sword's as sharp as yours.
　　I would not have you, lord, forget yourself,[5]
　　Nor tempt° the danger of my true° defence,　　　　　　*test / honest; able*
85　Lest I, by marking of° your rage, forget　　　　　　　　*responding to*
　　Your worth, your greatness and nobility.
BIGOT　Out, dunghill! Dar'st thou brave° a nobleman?　　　　　　　*defy*
HUBERT　Not for my life; but yet I dare defend
　　My innocent life against an emperor.
SALISBURY　Thou art a murderer.
90　HUBERT　　　　　　　　　　Do not prove me so;°　　*(by making me kill)*
　　Yet° I am none. Whose tongue soe'er speaks false,　　　　　*Up to now*
　　Not truly speaks; who speaks not truly, lies.
PEMBROKE　Cut him to pieces!
BASTARD [*drawing his sword*]　　Keep the peace, I say!
SALISBURY　Stand by,° or I shall gall° you, Falconbridge.　　*aside / wound*
95　BASTARD　Thou wert better gall the devil, Salisbury.
　　If thou but frown on me, or stir thy foot,
　　Or teach thy hasty spleen° to do me shame,　　　　　　　　*temper*
　　I'll strike thee dead. Put up thy sword betime,°　　　　　*immediately*
　　Or I'll so maul you and your toasting-iron°　　　　*sword (belittling)*
100　That you shall think the devil is come from hell.
BIGOT　What wilt thou do, renownèd Falconbridge,
　　Second° a villain and a murderer?　　　　　　　　　　　　*Back up*
HUBERT　Lord Bigot, I am none.
BIGOT　　　　　　　　　　Who killed this prince?
HUBERT　'Tis not an hour since I left him well.
105　I honoured him, I loved him, and will weep
　　My date° of life out for his sweet life's loss.　　　　　　　　*term*
SALISBURY　Trust not those cunning waters of his eyes,
　　For villainy is not without such rheum,
　　And he, long traded° in it, makes it seem　　　　　　　*experienced*
110　Like rivers of remorse and innocency.
　　Away with me, all you whose souls abhor
　　Th'uncleanly savours° of a slaughter-house,　　　　　　　　*odors*
　　For I am stifled with this smell of sin.
BIGOT　Away toward Bury,° to the Dauphin there.　　　*Bury St. Edmunds*

───────────────────

4. Deprive the law of its due by killing Hubert.　　orable for a lord to challenge a commoner, or vice
5. Lose self-control; forget your rank (it not being hon-　　versa, as lines 85–86 suggest).

115 PEMBROKE   There, tell the King, he may enquire° us out.   seek

                  Exeunt Lords [PEMBROKE, SALISBURY, *and* BIGOT]

  BASTARD   Here's a good world! Knew you of this fair work?
    Beyond the infinite and boundless reach
    Of mercy, if thou didst this deed of death
    Art thou damned, Hubert.

120 HUBERT   Do but hear me, sir.

  BASTARD   Ha! I'll tell thee what:
    Thou'rt damned as black—nay nothing is so black—
    Thou art more deep damned than Prince Lucifer;
    There is not yet so ugly a fiend of hell

125   As thou shalt be if thou didst kill this child.

  HUBERT   Upon my soul—

  BASTARD   If thou didst but consent
    To this most cruel act, do but despair;⁶
    And if thou want'st° a cord, the smallest thread   lack
    That ever spider twisted from her womb

130   Will serve to strangle thee; a rush° will be a beam   reed
    To hang thee on; or wouldst thou° drown thyself,   *if you wish to*
    Put but a little water in a spoon
    And it shall be, as all the ocean,
    Enough to stifle such a villain up.

135   I do suspect thee very grievously.

  HUBERT   If I in act, consent, or sin of thought
    Be guilty of the stealing that sweet breath
    Which was embounded° in this beauteous clay,°   *enclosed / (Arthur's body)*
    Let hell want pains enough to torture me.
    I left him well.

140 BASTARD   Go bear him in thine arms.
    I am amazed,° methinks, and lose my way   *bewildered*
    Among the thorns and dangers of this world.

           [HUBERT *takes up* ARTHUR *in his arms*]

    How easy dost thou take all England up!
    From forth° this morsel of dead royalty,   *Out of*

145   The life, the right, and truth of all this realm
    Is fled to heaven, and England now is left
    To tug and scramble, and to part by th' teeth
    The unowed interest⁷ of proud swelling state.
    Now for the bare-picked bone of majesty

150   Doth doggèd° war bristle his angry crest,⁸   *cruel*
    And snarleth in the gentle eyes of peace;
    Now powers from home° and discontents at home   *foreign armies*
    Meet in one line,° and vast confusion waits,°   *rank / chaos awaits*
    As doth a raven on a sick-fall'n beast,

155   The imminent decay of wrested pomp.°   *usurped power*
    Now happy he whose cloak and cincture° can   *belt*
    Hold out this tempest. Bear away that child,
    And follow me with speed. I'll to the King.
    A thousand businesses are brief in hand,°   *need urgent action*

160   And heaven itself doth frown upon the land. *Exeunt* [*severally*]

---

6. Lose all hope of salvation and hence commit suicide.
7. Contested or unowned possession; obedience ("interest") that is not due ("unowed"), because John

lacks legitimacy.
8. Dog's hackles (hairs on neck and back); crest on a coat of arms.

5.1

[*Flourish.*] *Enter* KING JOHN *and* [*Cardinal*] PANDOLF,
[*with*] *attendants*

KING JOHN [*giving* PANDOLF *the crown*]   Thus have I yielded up
    into your hand
    The circle of my glory.

PANDOLF [*giving back the crown*]   Take again
    From this my hand, as holding of° the Pope,   *as land rented from*
    Your sovereign greatness and authority.

5 KING JOHN   Now keep your holy word: go meet the French,
    And from his Holiness° use all your power   *the Pope*
    To stop their marches 'fore we are enflamed.
    Our discontented counties° do revolt,   *shires; nobles*
    Our people quarrel with obedience,
10   Swearing allegiance and the love of soul
    To stranger° blood, to foreign royalty.   *foreign*
    This inundation of mistempered humour
    Rests by you only to be qualified.[1]
    Then pause not, for the present time's so sick
15   That present° med'cine must be ministered,   *immediate*
    Or overthrow incurable ensues.

PANDOLF   It was my breath° that blew this tempest up,   *words*
    Upon your stubborn usage of the Pope,
    But since you are a gentle convertite,°   *convert*
20   My tongue shall hush again this storm of war
    And make fair weather in your blust'ring land.
    On this Ascension Day, remember well,
    Upon your oath of service to the Pope,
    Go I to make the French lay down their arms.

                Exeunt [*all but* KING JOHN][2]

25 KING JOHN   Is this Ascension Day? Did not the prophet
    Say that before Ascension Day at noon
    My crown I should give off?[3] Even so I have.
    I did suppose it should be on constraint,
    But, heaven be thanked, it is but voluntary.

    Enter BASTARD

30 BASTARD   All Kent hath yielded; nothing there holds out
    But Dover Castle. London hath received,
    Like a kind host, the Dauphin and his powers.°   *army*
    Your nobles will not hear you, but are gone
    To offer service to your enemy;
35   And wild amazement hurries° up and down   *confusion drives*
    The little number of your doubtful° friends.   *untrustworthy; fearful*

KING JOHN   Would not my lords return to me again
    After they heard young Arthur was alive?

BASTARD   They found him dead and cast into the streets,
40   An empty casket, where the jewel of life
    By some damned hand was robbed and ta'en away.

KING JOHN   That villain Hubert told me he did live.

BASTARD   So on my soul he did, for aught he knew.
    But wherefore do you droop? Why look you sad?

5.1 Location: John's court.
1. *This . . . qualified:* Only you can cure this surge of
diseased behavior.

2. F leaves the attendants onstage with John. But even
in that case, this speech could easily be a soliloquy.
3. See 4.2.147–52.

45   Be great in act as you have been in thought.
Let not the world see fear and sad distrust
Govern the motion of a kingly eye.
Be stirring as the time,[4] be fire with° fire;   *against*
Threaten the threat'ner, and outface the brow
50   Of bragging horror. So shall inferior eyes,
That borrow their behaviours from the great,
Grow great by your example, and put on
The dauntless spirit of resolution.
Away, and glisten like the god of war
55   When he intendeth to become the field.°   *adorn the battlefield*
Show boldness and aspiring confidence.
What, shall they seek the lion in his den
And fright him there, and make him tremble there?
O, let it not be said! Forage,° and run   *Range (for prey)*
60   To meet displeasure farther from the doors,
And grapple with him ere he come so nigh.
    KING JOHN   The legate of the Pope hath been with me,
And I have made a happy peace with him,
And he hath promised to dismiss the powers
Led by the Dauphin.
65   BASTARD   O inglorious league!
Shall we, upon the footing of our land,°   *standing on our own soil*
Send fair-play orders,° and make compromise,   *equitable conditions*
Insinuation,° parley, and base truce   *Ingratiating proposals*
To arms invasive?° Shall a beardless boy,   *invading*
70   A cockered silken wanton,° brave our fields   *spoiled dandyish child*
And flesh his spirit[5] in a warlike soil,
Mocking the air with colours idly° spread,   *carelessly*
And find no check? Let us, my liege, to arms!
Perchance the Cardinal cannot make your peace,
75   Or if he do, let it at least be said
They saw we had a purpose of defence.
    KING JOHN   Have thou the ordering of this present time.
    BASTARD   Away, then, with good courage! [*Aside*] Yet I know
Our party may well meet a prouder foe.[6]   *Exeunt*

5.2

Enter [marching] (in arms) [LOUIS THE] DAUPHIN, [*the
Earl of*] SALISBURY, [*Count*] MELUN, [*the Earl of*] PEM-
BROKE, [*and Lord*] BIGOT, [*with*] *soldiers*
    LOUIS THE DAUPHIN   My Lord Melun, let this[1] be copied out,
And keep it safe for our remembrance.
Return the precedent° to these lords again,   *original copy*
That having our fair order° written down,   *arrangements*
5   Both they and we, perusing o'er these notes,
May know wherefore we took the sacrament[2]
And keep our faiths firm and inviolable.
    SALISBURY   Upon our sides it never shall be broken.
And, noble Dauphin, albeit we swear

---

4. Be as vigorous as the times demand.
5. Initiate himself in bloodshed (in the "soil," as a
sword is "fleshed" in a body).
6. Is well able to handle an even stronger enemy than
the French; may be up against an enemy more powerful than we are.
5.2 Location: St. Edmundsbury (Bury St. Edmunds) in
Suffolk.
1. This agreement with the English lords.
2. The Mass, taken as a solemn dedication to the task.

10	A voluntary zeal° and an unurgèd° faith	*commitment / unforced*
	To your proceedings, yet believe me, Prince,	
	I am not glad that such a sore of time	
	Should seek a plaster° by contemnèd° revolt,	*bandage / despised*
	And heal the inveterate canker° of one wound	*infection*
15	By making many. O, it grieves my soul	
	That I must draw this metal° from my side	*(his sword)*
	To be a widow-maker! O, and there	
	Where honourable rescue and defence	
	Cries out upon[3] the name of Salisbury!	
20	But such is the infection of the time,	
	That for the health and physic° of our right,	*cure*
	We cannot deal but with the very hand	
	Of stern injustice and confusèd wrong.[4]	
	And is't not pity, O my grievèd friends,	
25	That we the sons and children of this isle	
	Was born to see so sad an hour as this,	
	Wherein we step after a stranger,° march	*foreigner*
	Upon her gentle bosom, and fill up	
	Her enemies' ranks? I must withdraw and weep	
30	Upon the spot° of this enforcèd cause—	*place; stain*
	To grace the gentry of a land remote,	
	And follow unacquainted colours° here.	*unfamiliar banners*
	What, here? O nation, that thou couldst remove;°	*move elsewhere*
	That Neptune's arms° who clippeth thee about°	*the sea / embraces you*
35	Would bear thee from the knowledge of thyself	
	And gripple° thee unto a pagan shore,	*join*
	Where these two Christian armies might combine	
	The blood of malice in a vein of league,°	*(against a pagan foe)*
	And not to spend° it so unneighbourly.	*shed*
40	**LOUIS THE DAUPHIN** A noble temper° dost thou show in this,	*disposition*
	And great affections,° wrestling in thy bosom,	*emotions; loyalties*
	Doth make an earthquake of nobility.°	*out of a noble nature*
	O, what a noble combat hast thou fought	
	Between compulsion° and a brave respect!°	*necessity / patriotism*
45	Let me wipe off this honourable dew	
	That silverly doth progress on thy cheeks.	
	My heart hath melted at a lady's tears,	
	Being an ordinary inundation;	
	But this effusion of such manly drops,	
50	This shower blown up by tempest of the soul,	
	Startles mine eyes, and makes me more amazed	
	Than had I seen the vaulty° top of heaven	*arched*
	Figured quite o'er° with burning meteors.[5]	*Adorned thoroughly*
	Lift up thy brow, renownèd Salisbury,	
55	And with a great heart heave away this storm;	
	Commend° these waters to those baby eyes	*Leave*
	That never saw the giant° world enraged,	*grown-up*
	Nor met with Fortune other than at feasts,	
	Full warm of° blood, of mirth, of gossiping.	*with*
60	Come, come, for thou shalt thrust thy hand as deep	

3. Exclaim against; appeal to.

4. *We . . . wrong:* We cannot act except with unjust means; or, possibly, we cannot act except against the unjust hand of John.

5. Meteors were seen as portents of disaster.

Into the purse of rich prosperity
As Louis himself. So, nobles, shall you all
That knit your sinews° to the strength of mine.   *join your powers*
    [*A trumpet sounds*]
And even there methinks an angel⁶ spake!
    Enter [*Cardinal*] PANDOLF

65   Look where the holy legate comes apace,
To give us warrant from the hand of heaven,°   *the Pope; God*
And on our actions set the name of right
With holy breath.

PANDOLF   Hail, noble prince of France!
The next° is this. King John hath reconciled   *next thing I have to say*
70   Himself to Rome; his spirit is come in°   *has submitted*
That so stood out against the Holy Church,
The great metropolis and See of Rome;
Therefore thy threat'ning colours° now wind up,°   *banners / put away*
And tame the savage spirit of wild war,
75   That like a lion fostered up at hand°   *by human hand*
It may lie gently at the foot of peace,
And be no further harmful than in show.

LOUIS THE DAUPHIN   Your grace shall pardon me: I will not back.° *go back*
I am too high-born to be propertied,°   *manipulated*
80   To be a secondary° at control,   *subordinate*
Or useful serving-man and instrument
To any sovereign state° throughout the world.   *(the papacy)*
Your breath first kindled the dead coal of wars
Between this chastised kingdom and myself,
85   And brought in matter° that should feed this fire;   *fuel*
And now 'tis far too huge to be blown out
With that same weak wind which enkindled it.
You taught me how to know the face of right,°   *my rightful claim*
Acquainted me with interest° to this land,   *my claim*
90   Yea, thrust this enterprise into my heart;
And come ye now to tell me John hath made
His peace with Rome? What is that peace to me?
I, by the honour of my marriage bed,
After young Arthur, claim this land for mine;
95   And now it is half conquered, must I back
Because that John hath made his peace with Rome?
Am I Rome's slave? What penny hath Rome borne,°   *contributed*
What men provided, what munition sent
To underprop° this action? Is't not I   *support*
100 That undergo this charge? Who else but I,
And such as to my claim are liable,°   *are liable to me*
Sweat in this business and maintain° this war?   *pay for*
Have I not heard these islanders shout out
'Vive le Roi!' as I have banked their towns?
105 Have I not here the best cards for the game,
To win this easy match played for a crown?

---

6. The trumpet, an editorial addition, is seen as an angel's affirmation of the Dauphin's speech. The stage direction may not be necessary, however. "Angel" might also mean "gold coin," developing the money imagery of lines 61–63—"purse of rich prosperity," "nobles" (also a coin), and perhaps "sinews" (where "sinews of war" connotes money). The Dauphin's point, perhaps made in an aside, would be that money talks in persuading the English peers to join his cause.

And shall I now give o'er the yielded set?[7]
No, no, on my soul, it never shall be said.

PANDOLF   You look but on the outside of this work.

110   LOUIS THE DAUPHIN   Outside or inside, I will not return
Till my attempt° so much be glorified   *warlike enterprise*
As to my ample hope was promisèd
Before I drew° this gallant head of war,°   *gathered / army*
And culled° these fiery spirits from the world   *picked out*
115   To outlook conquest° and to win renown   *To defy defeat*
Even in the jaws of danger and of death.
        [*A trumpet sounds*]
What lusty° trumpet thus doth summon us?   *vigorous*
        Enter [*the*] BASTARD

BASTARD   According to the fair play° of the world,   *code of chivalry*
Let me have audience; I am sent to speak.
120   My holy lord of Milan, from the King
I come to learn how you have dealt for him,
And as° you answer I do know the scope   *according to how*
And warrant limited unto my tongue.

PANDOLF   The Dauphin is too wilful-opposite,°   *stubbornly hostile*
125   And will not temporize with° my entreaties.   *will not heed*
He flatly says he'll not lay down his arms.

BASTARD   By all the blood that ever fury breathed,
The youth says well. Now hear our English king,
For thus his royalty doth speak in me.
130   He is prepared, and reason too he should.°   *as he should be*
This apish and unmannerly approach,
This harnessed masque and unadvisèd revel,[8]
This unhaired° sauciness and boyish troops,   *youthful*
The King doth smile at, and is well prepared
135   To whip this dwarfish war, these pigmy arms,
From out the circle° of his territories.   *confines*
That hand which had the strength even at your door
To cudgel you and make you take the hatch,°   *beat a hasty retreat*
To dive like buckets in concealèd wells,
140   To crouch in litter° of your stable planks,   *animal's bedding*
To lie like pawns° locked up in chests and trunks,   *pawned goods*
To hug° with swine, to seek sweet safety out   *bed down*
In vaults and prisons, and to thrill° and shake   *shiver*
Even at the crying of your nation's crow,°   *the cock*
145   Thinking his voice an armèd Englishman;
Shall that victorious hand be feebled here
That in your chambers° gave you chastisement?   *your own home*
No! Know the gallant monarch is in arms,
And like an eagle o'er his eyrie towers°   *soars over his nest*
150   To souse° annoyance that comes near his nest.   *swoop down on*
        [*To the English lords*]
And you degenerate, you ingrate revolts,°   *ungrateful rebels*
You bloody Neros, ripping up the womb
Of your dear mother England,[9] blush for shame;

---

7. 'Vive . . . set: The Dauphin uses an extended card-playing metaphor, including "Vive le Roi" ("Long live the King"), "banked" (put in the bank, won; but also, sailed by the banks of or perhaps besieged), "cards," "game," "match played," "crown" (the coin as a stake in a card game; John's crown), and "yielded set" (the hand already won).
8. This courtly entertainment in armor and rashly undertaken revelry.
9. The Roman Emperor Nero was supposed to have murdered his mother by ripping open her womb.

For your own ladies and pale-visaged maids
155 Like Amazons¹ come tripping after drums;
Their thimbles into armèd gauntlets° change,   *steel-plated gloves*
Their needles to lances, and their gentle hearts
To fierce and bloody inclination.°   *disposition*
LOUIS THE DAUPHIN   There end thy brave,° and turn thy face°   *defiance / return*
    in peace.
160 We grant thou canst outscold us. Fare thee well:
We hold our time too precious to be spent
With such a brabbler.°   *quarreler*
PANDOLF   Give me leave to speak.
BASTARD   No, I will speak.
LOUIS THE DAUPHIN   We will attend° to neither.—   *listen*
Strike up the drums, and let the tongue of war
165 Plead for our interest and our being here.
BASTARD   Indeed your drums, being beaten, will cry out;
And so shall you, being beaten. Do but start
An echo with the clamour of thy drum,
And even at hand a drum is ready braced°   *ready to be struck*
170 That shall reverberate all as loud as thine.
Sound but another, and another shall
As loud as thine rattle the welkin's° ear,   *sky's*
And mock° the deep-mouthed thunder; for at hand,   *outrival*
Not trusting to this halting° legate here,   *wavering*
175 Whom he hath used rather for sport than need,
Is warlike John; and in his forehead sits
A bare-ribbed Death, whose office° is this day   *task*
To feast upon whole thousands of the French.
LOUIS THE DAUPHIN   Strike up our drums to find this danger out.
180 BASTARD   And thou shalt find it, Dauphin, do not doubt.
            [Drums beat.] Exeunt [the BASTARD *at one door,*
            all the rest, marching, at another door]

5.3

Alarum. Enter [KING] JOHN [*at one door*] *and* HUBERT
[*at another door*]
KING JOHN   How goes the day with us? O, tell me, Hubert.
HUBERT   Badly, I fear. How fares your majesty?
KING JOHN   This fever that hath troubled me so long
Lies heavy on me. O, my heart is sick!
    Enter a MESSENGER
5 MESSENGER   My lord, your valiant kinsman Falconbridge
Desires your majesty to leave the field,
And send him word by me which way you go.
KING JOHN   Tell him toward Swineshead,° to the abbey there.   *(in Lincolnshire)*
MESSENGER   Be of good comfort, for the great supply°   *reinforcements*
10 That was expected by the Dauphin here
Are wrecked three nights ago on Goodwin Sands.°   *shoals off Kent*
This news was brought to Richard,° but even now   *(the Bastard)*
The French fight coldly and retire themselves.°   *retreat*
KING JOHN   Ay me, this tyrant fever burns me up,

---

1. Female warriors of classical legend.   **5.3** Location: The battlefield.

15 And will not let me welcome this good news.
Set on toward Swineshead. To my litter straight;°   *portable bed at once*
Weakness possesseth me, and I am faint.   *Exeunt*

5.4

[*Alarum.*] *Enter* [*the Earls of*] SALISBURY [*and*] PEM-
BROKE, *and* [*Lord*] BIGOT

SALISBURY   I did not think the King so stored° with friends.   *well provided*
PEMBROKE   Up once again; put spirit in the French.
If they miscarry,° we miscarry too.   *fail*
SALISBURY   That misbegotten devil Falconbridge,
5 In spite of spite,° alone upholds the day.°   *everything / battle*
PEMBROKE   They say King John, sore° sick, hath left the field.   *grievously*

Enter [*Count*] MELUN, *wounded* [*led by a soldier*]

MELUN   Lead me to the revolts° of England here.   *rebels*
SALISBURY   When we were happy, we had other names.
PEMBROKE   It is the Count Melun.
SALISBURY   Wounded to death.
10 MELUN   Fly, noble English, you are bought and sold.°   *betrayed*
Unthread the rude eye of rebellion,[1]
And welcome home again discarded faith;
Seek out King John and fall before his feet,
For if the French be lords of° this loud° day   *win / hectic*
15 He° means to recompense the pains you take   *(Louis)*
By cutting off your heads. Thus hath he sworn,
And I with him, and many more with me,
Upon the altar at Saint Edmundsbury,
Even on that altar where we swore to you
20 Dear amity and everlasting love.
SALISBURY   May this be possible? May this be true?
MELUN   Have I not hideous death within my view,
Retaining but a quantity of life,
Which bleeds away, even as a form of wax
25 Resolveth from his figure° 'gainst the fire?   *Melts out of shape*
What in the world should make me now deceive,
Since I must lose the use of all deceit?
Why should I then be false, since it is true
That I must die here, and live hence° by truth?   *in the next world*
30 I say again, if Louis do win the day,
He is forsworn° if e'er those eyes of yours   *perjured*
Behold another daybreak in the east;
But even this night, whose black contagious breath
Already smokes about the burning cresset°   *suspended torch*
35 Of the old, feeble, and day-wearied sun,
Even this ill night your breathing shall expire,
Paying the fine of rated° treachery   *assessed (as penalty)*
Even with a treacherous fine° of all your lives,   *payment; end*
If Louis by your assistance win the day.
40 Commend me to one Hubert with your king.
The love of him, and this respect° besides,   *consideration*
For that° my grandsire was an Englishman,   *Because*

5.4 Location: Scene continues.
1. Turn back from the barbarous path of rebellion   down which you've been led (like a thread that has been
inserted into the needle's eye and must be pulled out).

Awakes my conscience to confess all this;
In lieu° whereof, I pray you bear me hence   *recompense*
45 From forth the noise and rumour° of the field,   *tumult*
Where I may think the remnant of my thoughts
In peace, and part this body and my soul
With contemplation and devout desires.
SALISBURY   We do believe thee; and beshrew° my soul   *woe to*
50 But° I do love the favour° and the form   *Unless / look*
Of this most fair occasion; by the which
We will untread° the steps of damnèd flight,°   *retrace / desertion*
And like a bated° and retirèd flood,   *an abated*
Leaving our rankness° and irregular course,   *flooding*
55 Stoop low within those bounds we have o'erlooked,°   *overflowed; ignored*
And calmly run on in obedience
Even to our ocean, to our great King John.
My arm shall give thee help to bear thee hence,
For I do see the cruel pangs of death
60 Right in thine eye.—Away, my friends! New flight,°   *change of allegiance*
And happy newness that intends old right.[2]   *Exeunt*

5.5

[*Alarum; retreat.*] Enter [LOUIS THE] DAUPHIN, *and his*
    train

LOUIS THE DAUPHIN   The sun of heaven, methought, was loath to set,
But stayed and made the western welkin blush,
When English measured° backward their own ground   *crossed*
In faint retire.° O, bravely came we off,[1]   *weak retreat*
5 When with a volley of our needless° shot,   *unnecessary*
After such bloody toil, we bid good night,
And wound our tatt'ring colours clearly up,[2]
Last in the field and almost lords of it.
     Enter a MESSENGER
MESSENGER   Where is my prince the Dauphin?
LOUIS THE DAUPHIN   Here. What news?
10 MESSENGER   The Count Melun is slain; the English lords
By his persuasion are again fall'n off;°   *changed in allegiance*
And your supply° which you have wished so long   *supplies*
Are cast away and sunk on Goodwin Sands.
LOUIS THE DAUPHIN   Ah, foul shrewd° news! Beshrew° thy very   *harmful / Curse*
    heart!
15 I did not think to be so sad tonight
As this hath made me. Who was he that said
King John did fly an hour or two before
The stumbling night[3] did part our weary powers?
MESSENGER   Whoever spoke it, it is true, my lord.
20 LOUIS THE DAUPHIN   Well, keep good quarter° and good care tonight.   *guard*
The day shall not be up so soon as I,
To try the fair adventure° of tomorrow.   *Exeunt*   *chance*

---

2. That intends to restore the ancient right—John's
claim to rule and our just conduct.
5.5 Location: Scene continues.
1. We acquitted ourselves valiantly.

2. We rolled our tattered (waving) banners up without
obstruction from the English.
3. That is, night that causes stumbling.

5.6

Enter [the] BASTARD *[with a light] and* HUBERT *[with a pistol], severally*

HUBERT   Who's there? Speak, ho! Speak quickly, or I shoot.

BASTARD   A friend. What art thou?

HUBERT   Of the part° of England.   *side*

BASTARD   Whither dost thou go?

HUBERT   What's that to thee?

Why may not I demand of thine affairs

5   As well as thou of mine?

BASTARD   Hubert, I think.

HUBERT   Thou hast a perfect° thought.   *correct*

I will upon all hazards° well believe   *against all odds*

Thou art my friend that know'st my tongue so well.

Who art thou?

10   BASTARD   Who thou wilt. An if thou please,

Thou mayst befriend me so much as to think

I come one way° of the Plantagenets.   *by one parent*

HUBERT   Unkind remembrance!¹ Thou and eyeless° night   *blind*

Have done me shame. Brave soldier, pardon me

15   That any accent° breaking from thy tongue   *sound*

Should 'scape the true acquaintance of mine ear.

BASTARD   Come, come, sans compliment.° What news abroad?   *no formalities*

HUBERT   Why, here walk I in the black brow of night

To find you out.

BASTARD   Brief, then, and what's the news?

20   HUBERT   O my sweet sir, news fitting to the night:

Black, fearful, comfortless, and horrible.

BASTARD   Show me the very wound of this ill news;

I am no woman, I'll not swoon at it.

HUBERT   The King, I fear, is poisoned by a monk.

25   I left him almost speechless, and broke out°   *hurried away*

To acquaint you with this evil, that you might

The better arm you to the sudden time°   *for this emergency*

Than if you had at leisure° known of this.   *later*

BASTARD   How did he take it?° Who did taste to° him?   *(poison) / (the food) for*

30   HUBERT   A monk, I tell you, a resolvèd villain,²

Whose bowels suddenly burst out. The King

Yet° speaks, and peradventure may recover.   *Still*

BASTARD   Who didst thou leave to tend his majesty?

HUBERT   Why, know you not? The lords are all come back,

35   And brought Prince Henry³ in their company,

At whose request the King hath pardoned them,

And they are all about his majesty.

BASTARD   Withhold thine indignation, mighty heaven,

And tempt us not to bear above our power.⁴

40   I'll tell thee, Hubert, half my power this night,

Passing these flats, are taken° by the tide.   *drowned*

These Lincoln Washes⁵ have devourèd them;

5.6 Location: Near Swineshead Abbey.

1. Bad memory (criticizing himself for not recognizing the Bastard).

2. A "resolvèd villain" since, as the person whose job it was to protect the King by tasting his food, he knowingly took poison himself just so that he could succeed in poisoning the King.

3. John's son; later, King Henry III.

4. And don't push us (or me) past our power to endure. "Bear above our power" may hint at the Bastard's previous thoughts, here put aside, of assuming the throne himself.

5. The tides of the Wash (tidal flatlands south of Lincolnshire).

Myself, well mounted, hardly° have escaped.   *barely; with trouble*
Away before!° Conduct me to the King.   *Go on ahead*
45   I doubt° he will be dead or ere° I come.   *Exeunt*   *fear / before*

5.7

Enter PRINCE HENRY, [*the Earl of*] SALISBURY, *and*
[*Lord*] BIGOT
PRINCE HENRY   It is too late. The life of all his blood
Is touched° corruptibly, and his pure° brain,   *infected / (once) lucid*
Which some suppose the soul's frail dwelling-house,
Doth by the idle° comments that it makes   *foolish*
5   Foretell the ending of mortality.°   *mortal life*
Enter [*the Earl of*] PEMBROKE
PEMBROKE   His highness yet doth speak, and holds belief
That being brought into the open air,
It would allay the burning quality
Of that fell° poison which assaileth him.   *savage*
10   PRINCE HENRY   Let him be brought into the orchard here.—
[*Exit Lord* BIGOT][1]
Doth he still rage?
PEMBROKE   He is more patient
Than when you left him. Even° now, he sung.   *Just*
PRINCE HENRY   O, vanity° of sickness! Fierce extremes°   *delusion / (of pain)*
In their continuance will not feel themselves.[2]
15   Death, having preyed upon the outward parts,°   *the body*
Leaves them invincible,° and his siege is now   *(because overcome)*
Against the mind; the which he pricks and wounds
With many legions of strange fantasies,
Which in their throng and press to that last hold°   *stronghold (the mind)*
20   Confound° themselves. 'Tis strange that death should sing. *Destroy*
I am the cygnet° to this pale faint swan,   *young swan*
Who chants a doleful hymn to his own death,[3]
And from the organ-pipe° of frailty sings   *voice box*
His soul and body to their lasting rest.
25   SALISBURY   Be of good comfort, Prince, for you are born
To set a form upon that indigest°   *chaos*
Which he hath left so shapeless and so rude.°   *formless*
[KING] JOHN [*is*] **brought in** [*with Lord* BIGOT *attending*]
KING JOHN   Ay marry, now° my soul hath elbow-room;   *now being outdoors*
It would not out at° windows nor at doors.   *go out through*
30   There is so hot a summer in my bosom
That all my bowels crumble up to dust;
I am a scribbled form, drawn with a pen
Upon a parchment, and against° this fire°   *before / (of poison)*
Do I shrink up.
PRINCE HENRY   How fares your majesty?
35   KING JOHN   Poisoned, ill fare!° Dead, forsook, cast off; *food; state of things*
And none of you will bid the winter come
To thrust his icy fingers in my maw,°   *stomach; mouth; throat*
Nor let my kingdom's rivers take their course
Through my burned bosom, nor entreat the north

5.7 Location: The orchard of Swinestead Abbey.
1. F has no stage direction. Someone must fetch John:
either Bigot here or Pembroke after line 12.

2. By continuing for a long time will cease to be felt.
3. John's swan song; swans were thought to sing only
as they died.

40   To make his bleak winds kiss my parchèd lips
    And comfort me with cold. I do not ask you much;
    I beg cold° comfort, and you are so strait°   *slight; cooling / mean*
    And so ingrateful you deny me that.
  PRINCE HENRY   O, that there were some virtue° in my tears   *remedial power*
    That might relieve you!
45 KING JOHN   The salt in them is hot.
    Within me is a hell, and there the poison
    Is, as a fiend, confined to tyrannize
    On unreprievable condemnèd blood.
         Enter [the] BASTARD
  BASTARD   O, I am scalded with my violent motion°   *haste*
50   And spleen° of speed to see your majesty!   *impetuosity*
  KING JOHN   O cousin, thou art come to set° mine eye.   *close*
    The tackle° of my heart is cracked and burnt,   *rigging (heartstrings)*
    And all the shrouds° wherewith my life should sail   *sail ropes*
    Are turnèd to one thread, one little hair;
55   My heart hath one poor string to stay° it by,   *support*
    Which holds but till thy news be utterèd,
    And then all this thou seest is but a clod
    And module° of confounded° royalty.   *counterfeit / destroyed*
  BASTARD   The Dauphin is preparing° hitherward,   *coming*
60   Where God He knows how we shall answer him;
    For in a° night the best part of my power,   *a single*
    As I upon° advantage did remove,   *to gain*
    Were in the Washes all unwarily
    Devourèd by the unexpected flood.
        [KING JOHN *dies*]
65 SALISBURY   You breathe these dead° news in as dead an ear.   *fatal*
    [*To* KING JOHN] My liege, my lord!—But° now a king, now thus.   *Just*
  PRINCE HENRY   Even so must I run on, and even so stop.
    What surety of the world, what hope, what stay,°   *support; continuation*
    When this was now a king and now is clay?
70 BASTARD [*to* KING JOHN]   Art thou gone so? I do but stay behind
    To do the office° for thee of revenge,   *duty*
    And then my soul shall wait on° thee to heaven,   *follow*
    As it on earth hath been thy servant still.°   *always*
    [*To the lords*] Now, now, you stars° that move in your right spheres,[4]   *(the nobles)*
75   Where be your powers?° Show now your mended faiths,°   *armies / loyalties*
    And instantly return with me again,
    To push destruction and perpetual shame
    Out of the weak door of our fainting° land.   *dispirited*
    Straight° let us seek, or straight we shall be sought.   *Immediately*
80   The Dauphin rages at our very heels.
  SALISBURY   It seems you know not, then, so much as we.
    The Cardinal Pandolf is within at rest,
    Who half an hour since came from the Dauphin,
    And brings from him such offers of our peace
85   As we with honour and respect may take,
    With purpose presently° to leave this war.   *immediately*
  BASTARD   He will the rather do it when he sees
    Ourselves well-sinewed° to our own defence.   *strongly armed*
  SALISBURY   Nay, 'tis in a manner done already,

4. Proper orbits, around the King, as the stars were thought to orbit the earth.

90 For many carriages° he hath dispatched   *vehicles*
To the sea-side, and put his cause and quarrel
To the disposing of the Cardinal,
With° whom yourself, myself, and other lords,   *To*
If you think meet,° this afternoon will post°   *fit / hurry*
95 To consummate° this business happily.   *conclude*
BASTARD Let it be so.—And you, my noble prince,
With other princes° that may best be spared,   *nobles*
Shall wait upon° your father's funeral.   *attend*
PRINCE HENRY At Worcester must his body be interred,
For so he willed it.
100 BASTARD   Thither shall it then,
And happily° may your sweet self put on   *with good fortune*
The lineal state° and glory of the land,   *inherited kingship*
To whom with all submission, on my knee,
I do bequeath° my faithful services   *give*
105 And true subjection everlastingly.
      [*He kneels*]
SALISBURY And the like tender° of our love we make,   *offer*
To rest° without a spot° for evermore.   *remain / blemish*
      [SALISBURY, PEMBROKE *and* BIGOT *kneel*]
PRINCE HENRY I have a kind of soul that would give thanks,
And knows not how to do it but with tears.
      [*He weeps*]
110 BASTARD [*rising*] O, let us pay the time but needful° woe,   *only the necessary*
Since it hath been beforehand with our griefs.⁵
This England never did, nor never shall,
Lie at the proud foot of a conqueror
But° when it first did help to wound itself.   *Except*
115 Now these her princes are come home again,
Come the three corners of the world⁶ in arms
And we shall shock° them. Naught shall make us rue   *resist; repel*
If England to itself do rest but true.
      [*Flourish.*] *Exeunt* [*with the body*]

---

5. Since we have already suffered and grieved—
perhaps with the additional implication that the suffering is now over.
6. England itself is seen as the fourth corner.

The Merchant of Venice

Jew. Jew. Jew. The word echoes through *The Merchant of Venice.* The play has generated controversy for centuries. Is it anti-Semitic? Does it criticize anti-Semitism? Does it merely represent anti-Semitism without either endorsement or condemnation? Are the Christians right to call Shylock, the Jewish moneylender, a "devil," an "inexorable dog"; or is he merely the understandably resentful victim of their bigotry? Does Portia, Shylock's antagonist in the courtroom, exemplify the best in womanly virtue, or is she a manipulative virago? These questions about character suggest others that might be phrased more generally. What are the obligations of majority cultures to minorities in their midst? Do universally shared human characteristics outweigh racial and religious differences, or are such differences decisive?

Perhaps these issues seem more pressing nowadays than they did for Shakespeare. He could hardly could have predicted Nazi genocide or other modern forms of "ethnic cleansing." Nor could he have foreseen the opportunities and problems faced by multiracial societies centuries after his death. Nevertheless, by Shakespeare's time, the legacy of Jew hating in western Europe was already long and bitter. Depictions of fiendish Jews were routine in medieval and Renaissance drama; the villainous protagonist of Christopher Marlowe's *Jew of Malta,* a popular success in the early 1590s, was only the latest precedent. In 1594, shortly before Shakespeare wrote *The Merchant of Venice,* an outpouring of anti-Semitic outrage was triggered by the case of Roderigo Lopez, a Portuguese Jewish convert to Christianity accused of attempting to murder Queen Elizabeth.

Of course, the existence of anti-Semitism in sixteenth-century England says little about Shakespeare's own attitudes. He could have written *The Merchant of Venice* either to capitalize on or to criticize the prejudices of his society. Interestingly, Shakespeare had probably never encountered practicing Jews, since they had been forcibly expelled from England in the Middle Ages. And England was not alone in its intolerance. In 1492, Spain banished all non-Christians. Christians fought among themselves as well: during the sixteenth century, northern Europe saw decades of bloody conflict between Catholics and Protestants, while much of southern Europe was in the grip of the Inquisition. The impulse behind these persecutions was the conviction that a stable society required a shared belief system. A community based on consensus can indeed be impressively cohesive. Its homogeneity, however, makes it impatient of those who do not share its assumptions. Moreover, by the 1590s, when Shakespeare wrote *The Merchant of Venice,* bloody religious conflict all over Europe was making such consensus seem increasingly elusive—something obtainable, if at all, only at appalling human cost.

Possibly Venice seemed to Shakespeare to offer an alternative social prototype. Although it had no natural resources to speak of, it was the richest city in Renaissance Europe, located where the products of Asia could most conveniently be exchanged with those of western Europe. As a town of traders, Venice was full of foreigners: Turks, Jews, Arabs, Africans, Christians of various nationalities and denominations. By sixteenth-century standards, the city was unusually tolerant of diversity. This relative toleration was intimately linked with the city's wealth: its legal guarantees of fair treatment for all were designed to keep its markets running smoothly. Antonio tells Solanio:

> The Duke cannot deny the course of law,
> For the commodity that strangers have

Prospect of Venice. From George Braun and Franz Hogenberg, *Civitates Orbis Terrarum* (1593).

> With us in Venice, if it be denied,
> Will much impeach the justice of the state,
> Since that the trade and profit of the city
> Consisteth of all nations.
>
> (3.3.26–31)

Shakespeare stresses, even exaggerates, this evenhanded cosmopolitanism. Historically, for instance, Venetian Jews were confined to a ghetto, gated and locked at night, but Shakespeare either did not know this fact or chose to ignore it. Venice thus provided Shakespeare with an example—perhaps the only example in sixteenth-century Europe—of a place where people with little in common culturally might coexist peacefully solely because it was materially expedient to do so. The laws of the marketplace seemed to have little to do with religion or nationality.

In *The Merchant of Venice,* Shakespeare juxtaposes social relations based on similarity with social relations based on economic self-interest. The Christian gentlemen who populate the opening scenes comprise a community with a common value system. Acutely aware of what they have in common, these individuals are openhanded to others in their group. When Bassanio asks Antonio for a loan, Antonio rushes to supply him even though he does not have the money at hand. When Graziano asks a favor of Bassanio, Bassanio grants it before he even hears what it is. Later in the play, when Portia finds out that Antonio's life is forfeit because of 3,000 ducats, she instantly offers to pay twelve times that sum to redeem him. Not entirely surprisingly, Bassanio is an amiable spendthrift whose plan to recoup his monetary losses involves considerable risk:

> In my schooldays, when I had lost one shaft,
> I shot his fellow of the selfsame flight
> The selfsame way, with more advisèd watch,
> To find the other forth; and by adventuring both,
> I oft found both.
>
> (1.1.140–44)

"Oft" is not "always." Sometimes, presumably, Bassanio lost both arrows. His temperamental similarity to his friend Antonio, the merchant-adventurer, is an optimism about gambling at long odds.

Such prodigal panache is undeniably attractive, especially in comedy, where generic conventions typically ensure that characters beat long odds. It generates, moreover, some of the most gorgeous poetry of the play, a language of risky munificence, in which phenomenal wealth is accumulated only to be splendidly dispersed. Salerio, for instance, describes a shipwreck as a beautiful squandering of luxury goods:

> dangerous rocks,
> Which, touching but my gentle vessel's side,
> Would scatter all her spices on the stream,
> Enrobe the roaring waters with my silks.
>
> (1.1.31–34)

Likewise, Portia tells Bassanio:

> for myself alone
> I would not be ambitious in my wish
> To wish myself much better, yet for you
> I would be trebled twenty times myself,
> A thousand times more fair, ten thousand times more rich,
> That only to stand high in your account
> I might in virtues, beauties, livings, friends,
> Exceed account.
>
> (3.2.150–57)

Unfortunately, it soon becomes obvious that the Christians' generosity, grace, and self-assurance have a disconcerting racist tinge. The magnanimous, depressive Antonio proudly acknowledges kicking and spitting on Shylock. The charming Portia rejoices in the failure of her black suitor to choose the correct casket: "Let all of his complexion choose me so" (2.7.79). These people find it hard to deal with those different from themselves: their society is based as much on the exclusion of the alien as on the inclusion of the similar. The moral ambiguity of the Christians' outlook is captured in their fondness for the loaded word "kind," which in Renaissance English meant not only "compassionate" but "similar," or "akin." People act benevolently toward those who are of the same *kind* as themselves.

Shylock's relation to the Venetian Christians exemplifies a different social mechanism. Unable to trust to love and generosity, Shylock relies instead on contractually enforceable promises and networks of mutual material need. Shylock's emphasis on purely economic factors means that he does not think about money the way Antonio and Bassanio do. He tends not to spend but to conserve, not to expand but to defend, not to seek risk but to minimize it. When he imagines disaster, he envisions not a spectacular swirl of silk and spices, but a sordid scenario of thievery and nibbling rats.

Although Shylock identifies strongly with his "sacred nation," his "tribe," and although he apparently relies on fellow Jews like Tubal, the play gives little sense of Jewish community. The play represents Shylock as an isolated figure, shunned by his daughter, abandoned by his servant. His calculating, loveless existence seems to result from the way he manages his property. Or perhaps isolation has made him cautious and selfish. Shylock has little motive to be generous with the Christians who despise him, and every reason to believe that he cannot depend on others to rescue him from misfortune.

The psychological and social contrasts between the Christians and Shylock reflect both class and religious differences. The Christians' magnificent improvidence is, in Shakespeare's time, a distinctively aristocratic trait. A true gentleman refuses to be too obviously concerned with monetary expenditure, especially where friends are concerned. He also feels socially obliged to display himself properly. Bassanio spends huge sums of borrowed money equipping himself for his trip to Belmont, even though all he technically need do is arrive alone and select the correct casket. Coming to Portia unattended or in shabby clothes is unthinkable even though (or perhaps because) "all the wealth I had," as Bassanio freely admits, "ran in my veins" (3.2.253–54). By contrast Shylock, despite his evident wealth, is obviously no gentleman. He locks up his possessions, regrets how much his servant eats, fumes over the money he spends searching for his missing daughter.

At the same time, the opposition between the Christians and Shylock seems rooted in religious disparities. Judaism in the play is presented not in its actual complexity but as a sixteenth-century Christian like Shakespeare would have construed it, as a set of dramatically vivid contrasts with Christian norms. The law of Moses, as set down in Deuteronomy and Leviticus, specifies

"Jews." From Jost Amman, *The Panoplia* (1568).

numerous aspects of the observant Jew's life—what to eat and wear, how to worship, how to conduct business, how to punish crimes. The Mosaic code places a high value upon justice and emphasizes the importance of adhering to the letter of the law. Shylock's Judaism reveals itself not merely in his distinctive dress and his avoidance of pork, but in his trust of literal meanings, his respect for observable facts, his expectation that contracts will be rigorously enforced.

The typical Christian outlook is different. Christians obtain divine approval not by wearing certain garments, avoiding particular foods, or circumcising their boys, but by believing in Christ's power to save them. The central virtues in this religious system are not justice and scrupulous compliance with the law but charity, mercy, and a willingness to believe what seems incredible. In the terms Shakespeare provides in *The Merchant of Venice*, the Christian demeanor is entrepreneurial, even reckless, the spiritual equivalent of what Antonio does with his ships or Bassanio does with the money he borrows from his friend. "Give up everything you have and follow me," Jesus tells his would-

Young man in Venice. From Cesare Vecellio, *De gli habiti antichi et moderni* (1590).

be follower, advice echoed in the inscription on the lead casket: "Who chooseth me must give and hazard all he hath." Like the word "kind," the similarly complex word "gentle" is used repeatedly in the play to describe this distinctive set of traits: the word simultaneously refers to considerate behavior, to aristocratic family background, and to "gentile," or Christian, religious convictions.

The differences between Christian and Jew become starkly apparent over the issue of usury. Antonio thinks he ought to lend money to friends as an act of charity, properly performed as freely as God Himself dispenses grace. "For when did friendship take / A breed for barren metal of his friend?" (1.3.128–29). The charging of interest seems improperly to generate money from money alone: wealth loses its purely instrumental quality and acquires an uncanny capacity to "breed," or reproduce, like a live organism. Usury, blurring the distinction between the domain of the spirit and the merely material realm, threatens to collapse friendship, a spiritual relationship, into a mere economic transaction.

Shylock, by contrast, refuses to distinguish between human relations and money relations. His "pound of flesh" proposal, baldly insisting that flesh is convertible to ducats, demands that the Christians violate their own taboo against confusing categories of spirit and matter, flesh and money, live and dead. Thus Bassanio initially finds the bargain absolutely unacceptable. At the same time, the very existence of the taboo encourages the Christians to accept Shylock's characterization of the contract as a "merry sport": they simply cannot believe he is serious. Antonio mistakenly binds himself under the gross but entirely typical misapprehension that Shylock has mysteriously become "kind."

As the play proceeds, it modifies somewhat these initially vivid contrasts between Christian and Jew. Shylock pretends that he thinks of people in purely material, economic terms; but he becomes a moving character precisely at those moments when he admits another kind of value. After Jessica's flight, Solanio claims that Shylock has been seen running through the streets crying, "O, my ducats! O, my daughter! . . . My ducats and my daughter!" (2.8.15ff.). It is impossible to know how accurate this rumor might be: the equation of ducats and daughter is exactly what Christians expect of Shylock. But when Shylock finally appears onstage, he says nothing of the kind. When Tubal tells him that Jessica has exchanged a turquoise ring for a monkey, Shylock replies: "Out upon her! Thou torturest me, Tubal. It was my turquoise. I had it of Leah when I was a bachelor. I would not have given it for a wilderness of monkeys" (3.1.100–02). Insisting upon the sentimental value of the turquoise ring, Shylock seems directly to deny the convertibility of human into monetary relations. His grief over his daughter's defection, and her insensitivity to his relation with her dead mother, exceeds his financial loss. Likewise in the courtroom, Shylock is remarkable not for his calculating prudence but for his refusal to be swayed by monetary appeals. There is something in the quality of his oppression that he refuses to convert into a payoff.

The Christians are also more complicated than they profess to be. Although human values, in their view, transcend marketplace values, and they are commanded to love not only neighbors but even enemies, only some persons elicit a humane response. Others are disregarded or treated as nonhuman. When Salerio and Solanio ridicule Shylock, he protests: "Hath not a Jew eyes? Hath not a Jew hands, organs, dimensions, senses, affections, passions; fed with the same food, hurt with the same weapons, subject to the same diseases, healed by the same means, warmed and cooled by the same winter and summer as a Christian is?" (3.1.49–54). Shylock asserts that a common human experience of embodiment ought to override considerations of religious or racial difference. These lines are among the most memorable in the play, but the argument does not follow from the position Shylock has taken earlier. Rather, it is effective because it exposes Christian hypocrisy. Similarly, in the trial scene, Shylock points out that the Christian practice of slavery plainly sets a monetary value upon human beings. The Christians' creed mandates universal love, but they fail to behave in accord with their precepts.

These inconsistencies haunt the play's friendships and marriages. Marriage is a hybrid social relation: obviously associated with love and with the reproduction of living organisms, it is simultaneously a property relation, involving the economic alliance of individuals and families. Bassanio's courtship of Portia is doubly motivated: he loves her, and he needs her money. The language of his attraction, even at its most generous and disinterested, is full of the metaphors of commerce and exchange. And although Antonio protests against thinking of friendship as an economic transaction, it is not difficult to construe his generosity as an attempt to buy Bassanio's love. So although the Christians attempt to differentiate spiritual values from economic ones, those values continually turn out to be intimately intertwined.

The casket test directly confronts this problem. The failures of Morocco and Aragon demonstrate that it is possible to find a plausible reason for choosing any one of the three caskets. But when Bassanio makes his choice, we see how the test works: it can be solved only by one who views its puzzles from the correct point of view. Bassanio must abstract from his particular relation with Portia to a general distinction between "ornament" and "truth":

> Look on beauty
> And you shall see 'tis purchased by the weight,
> Which therein works a miracle in nature,
> Making them lightest that wear most of it.
> (3.2.88–91)

Surely Bassanio does not believe that because Portia is lovely, she must be unchaste. Instead, his upbringing as a Christian gentleman has acquainted him with a particular frame of mind that prefers invisible over visible things, spirit over body, metaphor over literal meaning. The same cultural background makes him willing to take chances: to "hazard all he hath" on the unprepossessing lead casket. Because every suitor gets the same chance, the casket test seems to be fair; in fact, it is rather like those "objective" intelligence tests that, in subtle or not-so-subtle ways, reward the belief systems of dominant groups while stigmatizing outsiders. In this case, the person best fitted to be Portia's husband is one who, by Christian standards, knows the limitations and right use of wealth. This knowledge enables him to value characteristics in his wife—virtue, intelligence, and beauty—that make her precious in more than monetary ways.

One of the surprises of the casket test is that it takes place at all. Portia's obedience to her dead father's apparently irrational plans for her is remarkable in comedy, for comic heroines more often, like Jessica, defy their fathers than conscientiously follow their orders. Perhaps Portia could be seen as synthesizing the best of Jewish and Christian characteristics; obeying the letter of a wise Father's law, even while cultivating the spiritual virtues of love and generosity. Perhaps, then, Jewish and Christian outlooks are not *necessarily* in conflict (any more than there is a necessary conflict in being, as Portia is, both rich and beautiful). Certainly Portia's respect for the letter of the law, combined with her willingness to go beyond that letter, makes her the only character who can effectively confront Shylock in the trial scene.

When she disguises herself as a young lawyer, Portia becomes one of many Shakespearean comic heroines to assume male attire. The power that she achieves by her transvestism signals an interesting development in Shakespeare's treatment of the relations between men and women. Earlier plays often differentiate sharply between the sexes: between the male political domain and the female domestic domain in *Richard II,* between the male street and the female bedchamber in *Romeo and Juliet.* In *The Merchant of Venice* and the comedies Shakespeare wrote immediately thereafter, women seem to possess a new liberty of action. Their freedom coincides with another new development in Shakespearean comedy, the presence of a scapegoat character—someone like Shylock, who cannot be assimilated into the comic society at the end of the play. Perhaps when the most serious social threats seem to be posed by outsiders, there is more freedom for women within the "in" group: the crucial bifurcation is no longer between male and female but between "us" and "them."

Portia's legal strategy is complex, and thus the trial has several stages. At first, she both offers and recommends generosity:

> Therefore, Jew,
> Though justice be thy plea, consider this:
> That in the course of justice none of us
> Should see salvation. We do pray for mercy,
> And that same prayer doth teach us all to render
> The deeds of mercy.
>
> (4.1.192–97)

Not surprisingly, Shylock is deaf to this eloquence. Portia's argument is based on the distinctively Christian premise that salvation is an undeserved gift. She derives her authority from the Lord's Prayer: "forgive us our trespasses as we forgive those who trespass against us." But Shylock doesn't accept, or even perhaps know the existence of, a prayer that supposedly "teaches us all." Portia's plea for tolerance and compassion might seem to rest on universal premises, but in fact Portia's "we" who "pray for mercy" neatly excludes the Jew.

The judgment upon Shylock at the end of the trial has disturbed many critics and audiences. After the Christians win the case—not only saving Antonio's life but also keeping the 3,000 ducats Shylock had lent Bassanio—Portia seems to take exactly the revenge she has up to now deplored. Her legal ground is provided by a previously unmentioned law against any alien who plots the death of a Venetian citizen. The law in which Shylock trusted, because it seemed to provide a refuge from prejudice, turns out to have prejudice inscribed within it from the start. In this respect, it resembles the casket test—everybody seems to get the same chance, but in fact the test blatantly favors the insider.

Portia and the Duke apparently regard the dismissal of Shylock as merciful; his *life* is preserved, although half or all of his mere money is taken away. Portia's sentence forces Shylock to behave as a Christian citizen and father should: to worship in a Christian church, to grant money to his daughter, to recognize the difference between spiritual and economic well-being. Eschewing lethal force, the Duke demands that Shylock acquiesce in his punishment: "I am content," he says at last. But what else can he say? The coercive inclusion of Shylock in the Christian community seems all the more violent because it professes to renounce coercion, dropping "as the gentle rain from heaven." If designating people outcasts is bad, compelling them to participate in a society they find intolerable may be even worse.

The Merchant of Venice thus hovers on the edge of tragedy. Shylock's ferocious negativity is poised against, and arguably elicited by, the Christians' hypocritical refusal to admit the way their spiritual lives depend on material prosperity. The presence of the scapegoated Jew lays bare the mechanisms by which Venetian society works. Shylock can be reviled and dismissed, but the possibilities that he represents do not simply vanish when he flees the courtroom. Thus the moral disquiet the play raises among directors, readers, and audiences: Christian and Jewish perspectives seem mutually invalidating, and both finally inadequate.

Shakespeare suggests the stubbornness of the problems broached by the play in the way he structures the last act. Most Shakespeare comedies return to the city or the court at the end, or at least look forward to that return; but in *The Merchant of Venice*, the play ends at Belmont, the nostalgically depicted, magically copious "green world." It is as if the formal demand for comic closure conflicts with Shakespeare's awareness that no neat resolution of Venice's problems is forthcoming.

Indeed, some muted version of those problems pursues the Christians even to Portia's estate. The act begins with the banter between the newlyweds Jessica and Lorenzo, who have stayed behind at Belmont in Portia's absence. It is a bit ominous that all the love stories they recall are unhappy ones. Still, the couple's affectionate banter makes the scene a welcome change from what has immediately preceded it. Showing Jessica and Lorenzo in married bliss minutes after the brutal expulsion of Shylock seems an attempt to confine the punitive energies of the play to the usurer alone. The scene offers an alternative vision of interaction between racial groups, one that involves love rather than hatred. Jessica's marriage to a Christian has exempted her from Shylock's fate. Of course, this is a vision not of mutual tolerance but of assimilation: majority cultures do not need to exterminate people unlike themselves if they can merely exterminate their differences. Lorenzo describes to his wife the "music of the spheres"—a perfect heavenly harmony made inaudible by the corruption of this life. Perhaps, analogously, the Christians' failure lies not in the nature of their ideals, but in the imperfect realization of those ideals in the everyday world. The inevitable dissonance between the mundane and the ideal world does not necessarily, however, simply drain the ideal of its meaning.

The moral dilemmas posed by high but perhaps unrealizable ideals come under scrutiny yet again in the ring tricks with which the play ends. After Antonio's trial, Portia-as-Balthazar asks Bassanio for his wedding ring as payment for legal services. This request poses Bassanio a harder problem than Shylock had. Bassanio can imagine breaking a written contract, but not denying the request of an ally to whom he's indebted. By giving the ring to Balthazar, Bassanio demonstrates both that his loyalty to Antonio still outweighs his allegiance to Portia and that he has trouble governing his generous impulses. Portia's trick teaches Bassanio and Antonio that the marital relationship involves unique responsibilities and that those responsibilities impose a limit on munificence.

Again and again in *The Merchant of Venice* oppositions between potentially tragic alternatives miraculously dissolve—between being rich and being virtuous, marrying for money and marrying for love, following paternal orders and making one's own choice, enforcing the letter of the law and enforcing its spirit, remaining faithful to one's wife and loving one's male friend. Balthazar turns out to have been Portia, Bassanio has given his ring to its original owner, and all seems to be well. But by setting the play's last act in a magical world of trust and abundance, Shakespeare stresses the artifice involved in his resolution. Even as this beautiful, troubling play comes to a close, it pointedly emphasizes the distance between the final act's charmed fictional world and the intransigent real one.

KATHARINE EISAMAN MAUS

TEXTUAL NOTE

The textual history of *The Merchant of Venice* is not as complicated as that of some other Shakespeare plays. Two quarto editions exist, both dated 1600 on the title page. One, printed "by I. R. for Thomas Heys," is now called Q1; nineteen copies of this text have survived. Another Quarto (Q2), printed "by I. Roberts," is a falsely dated text actually produced in 1619 by William Jaggard (the same man who printed the First Folio four years later). Yet another version of *The Merchant of Venice* appears in the 1623 First Folio (F).

Q1 seems to have been prepared either directly from Shakespeare's own manuscript or from an accurate transcript of that manuscript. Internal evidence indicates that both Q2 and F were based on copies of Q1. F has some additions, chiefly stage directions, which suggests that a text marked up for stage production was likely to have been consulted at some point in preparing this text. Q1 is not divided into acts or scenes; F adds act divisions. Scene divisions were not added until the eighteenth century.

Q1, therefore, with the exception of some stage directions, is the most reliable authority for a modern text of *The Merchant of Venice*. The Oxford text follows Q1 closely, adopting from F and later editors the traditional divisions into acts and scenes, and accepting many of the Folio stage directions as representing the performance practice of Shakespeare's company.

The title *The Jew of Venice* does not appear in any printed text of the play. It was used, however, when the play was entered on the Stationers' Register in 1598. Since the theatrical company, not a bookseller, was responsible for the entry, the Oxford editors believe that members of Shakespeare's company considered *The Jew of Venice* an acceptable alternative title.

SELECTED BIBLIOGRAPHY

Barber, C. L. "The Merchants and the Jew of Venice: Wealth's Communion and an Intruder." *Shakespeare's Festive Comedy: A Study of Dramatic Form and Its Relation to Social Custom*. Princeton: Princeton University Press, 1959. The Christian's opulent festivity challenged by Shylock's fiercely reductive attitude toward money.

Burckhardt, Sigurd. "*The Merchant of Venice*: The Gentle Bond." *Shakespearean Meanings*. Princeton: Princeton University Press, 1968. 206–89. The importance of various kinds of bonds in *The Merchant of Venice*.

Cohen, Walter. "*The Merchant of Venice* and the Possibilities of Historical Criticism." *English Literary History* 49 (1982): 765–89. The play's theatrical artifice as reflecting economic conflicts in early modern Europe.

Danson, Lawrence. *The Harmonies of "The Merchant of Venice."* New Haven: Yale University Press, 1978. Describes the play's conflicts in detail, and argues for their satisfactory resolution.

Engle, Lars. "Money and Moral Luck in *The Merchant of Venice*." *Shakespearean Pragmatism: Market of His Time*. Chicago: University of Chicago Press, 1993. 77–106. Emotional and financial balance sheets, and their ethical consequences: *The Merchant of Venice* read through the lens of late twentieth-century ethical philosophy.

Gross, Kenneth. *Shylock Is Shakespeare.* Chicago: University of Chicago Press, 2006. Shakespeare's personal connection to Shylock.

Lewalski, Barbara. "Biblical Allusion and Allegory in *The Merchant of Venice.*" *Shakespeare Quarterly* 13 (1962): 327–43. Shakespeare's use of biblical typology.

Lupton, Julia Reinhard. "Merchants of Venice, Circles of Citizenship." *Citizen-Saints: Shakespeare and Political Theology.* Chicago: University of Chicago Press, 2005. 75–101. Judaism and citizenship in early modern Venice.

Newman, Karen. "Portia's Ring: Unruly Women and the Structure of Exchange in *The Merchant of Venice.*" *Shakespeare Quarterly* 38 (1987): 19–33. Portia, as gift-giver, occupies a position of power usually coded as masculine.

Shapiro, James. *Shakespeare and the Jews.* New York: Columbia University Press, 1996. Anti-Semitism in Shakespeare's time.

Shell, Marc. "'The Wether and the Ewe': Verbal Usury in *The Merchant of Venice.*" *Kenyon Review* 1.4 (1979): 65–92. A close analysis of exchange and redemption in *Merchant of Venice*, focusing particularly on Shylock's story of Laban and Jacob.

Wilson, Luke. "Drama and Marine Insurance in Shakespeare's London." *The Law in Shakespeare.* Ed. Constance Jordan and Karen Cunningham. London: Palgrave Macmillan, 2007. 127–42.

FILMS

The Merchant of Venice. 1973. Dir. John Sichel. UK. 131 min. Laurence Olivier as Shylock.

The Merchant of Venice. 1980. Dir. Jack Gold. UK. 157 min. Textually faithful but stilted. Gemma Jones is a chilly, calculating Portia.

The Merchant of Venice. 2001. Dir. Trevor Nunn. UK. 141 min. A film version of an acclaimed Royal National Theatre production, set in Europe between the world wars. Vividly acted, with many interesting directorial choices. Henry Goodman's Shylock is especially memorable.

The Merchant of Venice. 2004. Dir. Michael Radford. UK. 131 min. Al Pacino as Shylock, Lynn Collins as Portia. Sumptuous period costumes and sets. This production emphasizes the disquieting aspects of the play, not only the Venetians' anti-Semitism but the struggle between Portia and Antonio over Bassanio's allegiance.

The Comical History of the Merchant
of Venice, or Otherwise Called
the Jew of Venice

The Persons of the Play

ANTONIO, a merchant of Venice
BASSANIO, his friend and Portia's suitor
LEONARDO, Bassanio's servant
LORENZO ⎫
GRAZIANO ⎪
SALERIO ⎬ friends of Antonio and Bassanio
SOLANIO ⎭
SHYLOCK, a Jew
JESSICA, his daughter
TUBAL, a Jew
LANCELOT, a clown, first Shylock's servant and then Bassanio's
GOBBO, his father
PORTIA, an heiress
NERISSA, her waiting-gentlewoman
BALTHASAR ⎫
STEFANO ⎬ Portia's servants
Prince of MOROCCO ⎫
Prince of ARAGON ⎬ Portia's suitors
DUKE of Venice
Magnificoes of Venice
A jailer, attendants, and servants

1.1

Enter ANTONIO, SALERIO, *and* SOLANIO

ANTONIO   In sooth,° I know not why I am so sad.   *truth*
   It wearies me, you say it wearies you,
   But how I caught it, found it, or came by it,
   What stuff 'tis made of, whereof it is born,
5 I am to learn;°   *have yet to discover*
   And such a want-wit° sadness makes of me   *dullard*
   That I have much ado to know myself.
SALERIO   Your mind is tossing on the ocean,
   There where your argosies° with portly° sail,   *merchant ships / stately*
10 Like signors° and rich burghers on the flood—   *lords*
   Or as it were the pageants[1] of the sea—
   Do overpeer° the petty traffickers   *tower over*
   That curtsy[2] to them, do them reverence,
   As they fly by them with their woven wings.

1.1 Location: Venice.
1. Movable stages used by itinerant actors or in parades.

2. By bobbing on the waves or by lowering their flags in salute.

1121

SOLANIO [*to* ANTONIO]   Believe me, sir, had I such venture°   *a risky undertaking*
15   forth
          The better part of my affections would
          Be with my hopes abroad. I should be still°   *always*
          Plucking the grass to know where sits the wind,
          Peering in maps for ports and piers and roads,°   *open harbors*
20   And every object that might make me fear
          Misfortune to my ventures out of doubt
          Would make me sad.
SALERIO   My wind cooling my broth
          Would blow me to an ague° when I thought   *make me shiver*
          What harm a wind too great might do at sea.
25   I should not see the sandy hour-glass run
          But I should think of shallows and of flats,°   *shoals*
          And see my wealthy Andrew,[3] decks in sand,
          Vailing her hightop° lower than her ribs   *Lowering her topmast*
          To kiss her burial.° Should I go to church   *burial place*
30   And see the holy edifice of stone
          And not bethink me straight° of dangerous rocks   *immediately think*
          Which, touching but my gentle vessel's side,
          Would scatter all her spices on the stream,
          Enrobe the roaring waters with my silks,
35   And, in a word, but even now° worth this,°   *moments ago / so much*
          And now worth nothing? Shall I have the thought
          To think on this, and shall I lack the thought
          That such a thing bechanced° would make me sad?   *having occurred*
          But tell not me. I know Antonio
40   Is sad to think upon his merchandise.
ANTONIO   Believe me, no. I thank my fortune for it,
          My ventures are not in one bottom° trusted,   *ship*
          Nor to one place;° nor is my whole estate   *destination*
          Upon the fortune of this present year.
45   Therefore my merchandise makes me not sad.
SOLANIO   Why then, you are in love.
ANTONIO   Fie, fie.
SOLANIO   Not in love neither? Then let us say you are sad
          Because you are not merry, and 'twere as easy
          For you to laugh, and leap, and say you are merry
50   Because you are not sad. Now, by two-headed Janus,[4]
          Nature hath framed strange fellows in her time:
          Some that will evermore peep through their eyes[5]
          And laugh like parrots° at a bagpiper,[6]   *(screeching loudly)*
          And other of such vinegar aspect°   *sour looks*
55   That they'll not show their teeth in way of smile
          Though Nestor[7] swear the jest be laughable.
                    Enter BASSANIO, LORENZO, *and* GRAZIANO
          Here comes Bassanio, your most noble kinsman,
          Graziano, and Lorenzo. Fare ye well.
          We leave you now with better company.
60 SALERIO   I would have stayed till I had made you merry
          If worthier friends had not prevented me.

---

3. Name of a Spanish galleon captured by the English
at Cádiz in 1596.
4. Roman god with faces looking both forward and
backward.
5. Eyes almost shut by violent laughter.
6. Whose music was considered woeful.
7. Sober, elderly Greek hero in *The Iliad*.

ANTONIO   Your worth is very dear in my regard.
          I take it your own business calls on you,
          And you embrace th'occasion to depart.
65 SALERIO   Good morrow, my good lords.
    BASSANIO   Good signors both, when shall we laugh?° Say, when?   *make merry together*
               You grow exceeding strange.° Must it be so?   *reserved*
    SALERIO   We'll make our leisures to attend on° yours.   *suit*

                           Exeunt SALERIO *and* SOLANIO

    LORENZO   My lord Bassanio, since you have found Antonio,
70   We two will leave you; but at dinner-time
           I pray you have in mind where we must meet.
    BASSANIO   I will not fail you.
    GRAZIANO   You look not well, Signor Antonio.
           You have too much respect upon the world.°   *anxiety about business*
75   They lose it that do buy it with much care.
           Believe me, you are marvellously changed.
    ANTONIO   I hold the world but as the world, Graziano—
           A stage where every man must play a part,
           And mine a sad one.
    GRAZIANO   Let me play the fool.
80   With mirth and laughter let old⁸ wrinkles come,
           And let my liver⁹ rather heat with wine
           Than my heart cool with mortifying¹ groans.
           Why should a man whose blood is warm within
           Sit like his grandsire cut in alabaster,²
85   Sleep when he wakes, and creep into the jaundice³
           By being peevish? I tell thee what, Antonio—
           I love thee, and 'tis my love that speaks—
           There are a sort of men whose visages
           Do cream and mantle⁴ like a standing° pond,   *stagnant*
90   And do a wilful stillness entertain
           With purpose to be dressed in an opinion°   *a reputation*
           Of wisdom, gravity, profound conceit,°   *judgment*
           As who should say 'I am Sir Oracle,
           And when I ope my lips, let no dog bark.'
95   O my Antonio, I do know of these
           That therefore only are reputed wise
           For saying nothing, when I am very sure,
           If they should speak, would almost damn those ears
           Which, hearing them, would call their brothers fools.⁵
100   I'll tell thee more of this another time.
           But fish not with this melancholy bait
           For this fool gudgeon,° this opinion.—   *tiny, easily caught fish*
           Come, good Lorenzo.—Fare ye well a while.
           I'll end my exhortation after dinner.
    LORENZO   [*to* ANTONIO *and* BASSANIO]   Well, we will leave you
105   then till dinner-time.
           I must be one of these same dumb° wise men,   *mute*
           For Graziano never lets me speak.

<hr>

8. Accompanying old age; abundant.
9. The liver was considered the seat of passion.
1. Deadly (groans were believed to drain blood from the heart).
2. Stone from which tomb effigies were carved.
3. Thought to result from too much yellow bile, a bodily

substance associated with irritability.
4. *cream and mantle:* grow a scum; that is, assume a fixed countenance.
5. *would . . . fools:* alluding to Matthew 5:22: "And whosoever shall say to his brother . . . , fool, shall be in danger of hell fire."

GRAZIANO Well, keep me company but two years more
    Thou shalt not know the sound of thine own tongue.
110 ANTONIO Fare you well. I'll grow a talker for this gear.⁶
GRAZIANO Thanks, i'faith, for silence is only commendable
    In a neat's° tongue dried and a maid not vendible.⁷   *an ox's*
               Exeunt [GRAZIANO *and* LORENZO]
ANTONIO Yet is that anything now?
BASSANIO Graziano speaks an infinite deal of nothing, more
115   than any man in all Venice. His reasons° are as two grains of   *sensible remarks*
    wheat hid in two bushels of chaff: you shall seek all day ere
    you find them, and when you have them they are not worth
    the search.
ANTONIO Well, tell me now what lady is the same
120   To whom you swore a secret pilgrimage,
    That you today promised to tell me of.
BASSANIO 'Tis not unknown to you, Antonio,
    How much I have disabled mine estate
    By something showing a more swelling port°   *extravagant lifestyle*
125   Than my faint means would grant continuance,°   *allow to continue*
    Nor do I now make moan to be abridged°   *reduced*
    From such a noble rate;° but my chief care   *style*
    Is to come fairly off from the great debts
    Wherein my time, something too prodigal,
130   Hath left me gaged.° To you, Antonio,   *pledged*
    I owe the most in money and in love,
    And from your love I have a warranty°   *sanction*
    To unburden all my plots and purposes
    How to get clear of all the debts I owe.
135 ANTONIO I pray you, good Bassanio, let me know it,
    And if it stand as you yourself still do,
    Within the eye of honour, be assured
    My purse, my person, my extremest means
    Lie all unlocked to your occasions.°   *requirements*
140 BASSANIO In my schooldays, when I had lost one shaft,
    I shot his° fellow of the selfsame flight°   *its / size and weight*
    The selfsame way, with more advisèd° watch,   *careful*
    To find the other forth; and by adventuring° both,   *hazarding*
    I oft found both. I urge this childhood proof
145   Because what follows is pure innocence.
    I owe you much, and, like a wilful youth,
    That which I owe is lost; but if you please
    To shoot another arrow that self° way   *same*
    Which you did shoot the first, I do not doubt,
150   As I will watch the aim, or° to find both   *either*
    Or bring your latter hazard° back again,   *risk*
    And thankfully rest debtor for the first.
ANTONIO You know me well, and herein spend but° time   *only lose*
    To wind about my love with circumstance;°   *circumlocution*
155   And out of doubt you do me now more wrong
    In making question of my uttermost⁸
    Than if you had made waste of all I have.
    Then do but say to me what I should do

6. *for this gear:* as a result of your talk.
7. Sellable—that is, marriageable.
8. In doubting that I would do my utmost to help you.

That in your knowledge may by me be done,
160 And I am pressed unto° it. Therefore speak.   *obliged to do*
BASSANIO   In Belmont is a lady richly left,°   *left a fortune*
And she is fair, and, fairer than that word,
Of wondrous virtues. Sometimes° from her eyes   *At times*
I did receive fair speechless messages.
165 Her name is Portia, nothing undervalued
To⁹ Cato's daughter, Brutus' Portia;¹
Nor is the wide world ignorant of her worth,
For the four winds blow in from every coast
Renownèd suitors, and her sunny locks
170 Hang on her temples like a golden fleece,
Which makes her seat of Belmont Colchis' strand,²
And many Jasons come in quest of her.
O my Antonio, had I but the means
To hold a rival place with one of them,
175 I have a mind presages me such thrift°   *prosperity*
That I should questionless be fortunate.
ANTONIO   Thou know'st that all my fortunes are at sea,
Neither have I money nor commodity°   *goods*
To raise a present sum. Therefore go forth—
180 Try what my credit can in Venice do;
That shall be racked° even to the uttermost   *stretched*
To furnish thee to Belmont, to fair Portia.
Go presently enquire, and so will I,
Where money is; and I no question make
185 To have it of my trust or for my sake.³   Exeunt [severally]°   *separately*

1.2

Enter PORTIA *with her waiting-woman*, NERISSA

PORTIA   By my troth,° Nerissa, my little body is aweary of this   *faith*
great world.
NERISSA   You would be,¹ sweet madam, if your miseries were in
the same abundance as your good fortunes are; and yet, for
5 aught I see, they are as sick that surfeit with too much as they
that starve with nothing. It is no mean° happiness, therefore,   *slight*
to be seated in the mean.° Superfluity comes sooner by° white   *middle / sooner gets*
hairs, but competency° lives longer.   *moderate estate*
PORTIA   Good sentences,° and well pronounced.   *aphorisms*
10 NERISSA   They would be better if well followed.
PORTIA   If to do were as easy as to know what were good to do,
chapels had been churches, and poor men's cottages princes'
palaces. It is a good divine° that follows his own instructions.   *clergyman*
I can easier teach twenty what were good to be done than to
15 be one of the twenty to follow mine own teaching. The brain
may devise laws for the blood,° but a hot temper² leaps o'er a   *passion*
cold decree. Such a hare is madness, the youth, to skip o'er
the meshes° of good counsel, the cripple.³ But this reasoning   *snares*
is not in the fashion° to choose me a husband. O me, the word   *of a kind*

9. *nothing . . . / To:* no less worthy than.
1. Roman matron famous for heroic fidelity to her husband; a character in *Julius Caesar.*
2. Coast of Colchis, where in classical mythology Jason
won the Golden Fleece.
3. *of . . . sake:* because of my creditworthiness or as a

personal favor.
1.2 Location: Belmont.
1. You would have reason to be weary.
2. An impetuous disposition.
3. Because wisdom is imagined as elderly.

20 'choose'! I may neither choose who I would nor refuse who I
dislike; so is the will° of a living daughter curbed by the will°   *wish / testament*
of a dead father. Is it not hard, Nerissa, that I cannot choose
one nor refuse none?

NERISSA   Your father was ever virtuous, and holy men at their
25 death have good inspirations; therefore the lottery that he
hath devised in these three chests of gold, silver, and lead,
whereof who chooses his meaning chooses you, will no doubt
never be chosen by any rightly but one who you shall rightly
love. But what warmth is there in your affection towards any
30 of these princely suitors that are already come?

PORTIA   I pray thee overname them, and as thou namest them
I will describe them; and according to my description, level°   *guess*
at my affection.

NERISSA   First there is the Neapolitan prince.

35 PORTIA   Ay, that's a colt[4] indeed, for he doth nothing but talk of
his horse, and he makes it a great appropriation° to his own   *augmentation*
good parts° that he can shoe him himself. I am much afeard   *own abilities*
my lady his mother played false with a smith.

NERISSA   Then is there the County Palatine.[5]

40 PORTIA   He doth nothing but frown, as who should say 'An° you   *If*
will not have me, choose'.° He hears merry tales and smiles   *do as you wish*
not. I fear he will prove the weeping philosopher[6] when he
grows old, being so full of unmannerly° sadness in his youth.   *immoderate*
I had rather be married to a death's-head with a bone in his
45 mouth than to either of these. God defend me from these two!

NERISSA   How say you by the French lord, Monsieur le Bon?

PORTIA   God made him, and therefore let him pass for a man. In
truth, I know it is a sin to be a mocker, but he—why, he hath
a horse better than the Neapolitan's, a better bad habit of
50 frowning than the Count Palatine. He is every man in no man.
If a throstle° sing, he falls straight° a-cap'ring. He will fence   *thrush / immediately*
with his own shadow. If I should marry him, I should marry
twenty husbands. If he would despise me, I would forgive him,
for if he love me to madness, I shall never requite him.

55 NERISSA   What say you then to Falconbridge, the young baron
of England?

PORTIA   You know I say nothing to him, for he understands not
me, nor I him. He hath neither Latin, French, nor Italian, and
you will come into the court and swear that I have a poor pen-
60 nyworth in the English. He is a proper° man's picture, but   *handsome*
alas, who can converse with a dumb show?° How oddly he is   *pantomime*
suited! I think he bought his doublet° in Italy, his round hose[7]   *upper garment*
in France, his bonnet° in Germany, and his behaviour every-   *hat*
where.

65 NERISSA   What think you of the Scottish lord, his neighbour?

PORTIA   That he hath a neighbourly charity in him, for he borrowed a box of the ear of the Englishman and swore he would
pay him again when he was able. I think the Frenchman
became his surety, and sealed under for another.[8]

---

4. Foolish young man. Neapolitans were excellent
horsemen.
5. Count possessing royal powers.
6. Heracleitus, a melancholy Greek philosopher.
7. Puffed breeches.

8. The Frenchman vouched for the Scot's payment (of
a box on the ear) and promised to add another himself
(referring to France's frequent promises to help the
Scots against the English).

70 NERISSA   How like you the young German, the Duke of Saxony's nephew?

PORTIA   Very vilely in the morning when he is sober, and most vilely in the afternoon when he is drunk. When he is best he is a little worse than a man, and when he is worst he is little 75 better than a beast. An the worst fall that ever fell, I hope I shall make shift° to go without him.   *manage*

NERISSA   If he should offer° to choose, and choose the right   *endeavor* casket, you should refuse to perform your father's will if you should refuse to accept him.

80 PORTIA   Therefore, for fear of the worst, I pray thee set a deep glass of Rhenish wine° on the contrary casket; for if the devil   *white German wine* be within and that temptation without, I know he will choose it. I will do anything, Nerissa, ere I will be married to a sponge.

NERISSA   You need not fear, lady, the having any of these lords. 85 They have acquainted me with their determinations, which is indeed to return to their home and to trouble you with no more suit unless you may be won by some other sort° than   *way* your father's imposition° depending on the caskets.   *conditions*

PORTIA   If I live to be as old as Sibylla[9] I will die as chaste as 90 Diana unless I be obtained by the manner of my father's will. I am glad this parcel of wooers are so reasonable, for there is not one among them but I dote on his very absence; and I pray God grant them a fair departure.

NERISSA   Do you not remember, lady, in your father's time, a 95 Venetian, a scholar and a soldier, that came hither in company of the Marquis of Montferrat?

PORTIA   Yes, yes, it was Bassanio—as I think, so was he called.

NERISSA   True, madam. He of all the men that ever my foolish eyes looked upon was the best deserving a fair lady.

100 PORTIA   I remember him well, and I remember him worthy of thy praise.

Enter a SERVINGMAN

How now, what news?

SERVINGMAN   The four strangers seek for you, madam, to take their leave, and there is a forerunner come from a fifth, the 105 Prince of Morocco, who brings word the Prince his master will be here tonight.

PORTIA   If I could bid the fifth welcome with so good heart as I can bid the other four farewell, I should be glad of his approach. If he have the condition° of a saint and the complex-   *character* 110 ion of a devil,[1] I had rather he should shrive me° than wive me.   *absolve me of my sins* Come, Nerissa. [*To the* SERVINGMAN] Sirrah, go before. Whiles we shut the gate upon one wooer, Another knocks at the door.   *Exeunt*

1.3

Enter BASSANIO *with* SHYLOCK *the Jew*

SHYLOCK   Three thousand ducats.[1] Well.

BASSANIO   Ay, sir, for three months.

SHYLOCK   For three months. Well.

---

9. In classical mythology, the Cumaean Sibyl asked Apollo for as many years of life as the grains of sand she held in her hand; she forgot to ask for eternal youth.

1. Devils were imagined as black.
1.3 Location: Street in Venice.
1. Gold coins. The sum is very large.

	BASSANIO For the which, as I told you, Antonio shall be bound.°	contractually responsible
5	SHYLOCK Antonio shall become bound. Well.	
	BASSANIO May you stead° me? Will you pleasure me? Shall I	accommodate
	know your answer?	
	SHYLOCK Three thousand ducats for three months, and Antonio	
	bound.	
10	BASSANIO Your answer to that.	
	SHYLOCK Antonio is a good man.	
	BASSANIO Have you heard any imputation to the contrary?	
	SHYLOCK Ho, no, no, no, no! My meaning in saying he is a good	
	man is to have you understand me that he is sufficient.° Yet	of adequate wealth
15	his means are in supposition.° He hath an argosy bound to	doubt

Tripolis, another to the Indies. I understand moreover upon
the Rialto[2] he hath a third at Mexico, a fourth for England,
and other ventures he hath squandered abroad. But ships are
but boards, sailors but men. There be land rats and water rats,
20   water thieves and land thieves—I mean pirates—and then
there is the peril of waters, winds, and rocks. The man is,
notwithstanding, sufficient. Three thousand ducats. I think I
may take his bond.

BASSANIO Be assured you may.
25 SHYLOCK I will be assured[3] I may, and that I may be assured,
I will bethink me. May I speak with Antonio?

BASSANIO If it please you to dine with us.

SHYLOCK Yes, to smell pork, to eat of the habitation which your
prophet the Nazarite[4] conjured the devil into! I will buy with
30   you, sell with you, talk with you, walk with you, and so following, but I will not eat with you, drink with you, nor pray
with you.

    Enter ANTONIO
[*To* ANTONIO] What news on the Rialto? [*To* BASSANIO] Who is
he comes here?
35 BASSANIO This is Signor Antonio.

    [BASSANIO *and* ANTONIO *speak silently to one another*]

	SHYLOCK [*aside*] How like a fawning publican[5] he looks.	
	I hate him for he is a Christian;	
	But more, for that in low simplicity[6]	
	He lends out money gratis,° and brings down	free
40	The rate of usance° here with us in Venice.	interest
	If I can catch him once upon the hip[7]	
	I will feed fat the ancient grudge I bear him.	
	He hates our sacred nation,° and he rails,	(the Jews)
	Even there where merchants most do congregate,	
45	On me, my bargains, and my well-won thrift°—	profit
	Which he calls interest. Cursèd be my tribe	
	If I forgive him.	
	BASSANIO Shylock, do you hear?	
	SHYLOCK I am debating of my present store,°	supply of money
	And by the near guess of my memory	

2. Merchants' exchange in Venice.
3. Sure (but Shylock uses the word to mean "given financial guarantees").
4. Jesus, who cast devils into a herd of swine.
5. Tax collector; he robs me, but now, like the publican

in Luke 18:10–14 who prays to Jesus for mercy, tries to ingratiate himself because he wants a favor.
6. In meek honesty; in base folly.
7. *upon the hip*: at a disadvantage (wrestling terminology).

50 I cannot instantly raise up the gross°   *total*
    Of full three thousand ducats. What of that?
    Tubal, a wealthy Hebrew of my tribe,
    Will furnish me. But soft°—how many months   *wait*
    Do you desire? [*To* ANTONIO] Rest you fair, good signor.
55 Your worship was the last man in our mouths.[8]
    ANTONIO Shylock, albeit I neither lend nor borrow
    By taking nor by giving of excess,
    Yet to supply the ripe° wants of my friend   *urgent*
    I'll break a custom. [*To* BASSANIO] Is he yet possessed°   *informed*
60 How much ye would?
    SHYLOCK Ay, ay, three thousand ducats.
    ANTONIO And for three months.
    SHYLOCK I had forgot—three months. [*To* BASSANIO] You told me so.—
    Well then, your bond; and let me see—but hear you,
65 Methoughts you said you neither lend nor borrow
    Upon advantage.°   *interest*
    ANTONIO   I do never use it.
    SHYLOCK When Jacob grazed his uncle Laban's sheep—
    This Jacob from our holy Abram was,
    As his wise mother wrought in his behalf,
70 The third possessor; ay, he was the third[9]—
    ANTONIO And what of him? Did he take interest?
    SHYLOCK No, not take interest, not, as you would say,
    Directly int'rest. Mark what Jacob did:
    When Laban and himself were compromised°   *agreed*
75 That all the eanlings° which were streaked and pied°   *lambs / spotted*
    Should fall as Jacob's hire, the ewes, being rank,°   *in heat*
    In end of autumn turnèd to the rams,
    And when the work of generation° was   *mating*
    Between these woolly breeders in the act,
80 The skilful shepherd peeled me certain wands,[1]
    And in the doing of the deed of kind°   *nature*
    He stuck them up before the fulsome ewes
    Who, then conceiving, did in eaning° time   *lambing*
    Fall° parti-coloured lambs; and those were Jacob's.   *Deliver*
85 This was a way to thrive; and he was blest;
    And thrift is blessing, if men steal it not.
    ANTONIO This was a venture, sir, that Jacob served for[2]—
    A thing not in his power to bring to pass,
    But swayed and fashioned by the hand of heaven.
90 Was this inserted to make interest good,[3]
    Or is your gold and silver ewes and rams?
    SHYLOCK I cannot tell. I make it breed as fast.
    But note me, signor—
    ANTONIO   Mark you this, Bassanio?
    The devil can cite Scripture for his purpose.
95 An evil soul producing holy witness
    Is like a villain with a smiling cheek,

8. We were just mentioning you.
9. After Abraham and Isaac; his mother, Rebecca, helped him cheat his brother Esau of his birthright. The story of Laban's sheep is told in Genesis 30:25–43.

1. Stripped part of the bark off some sticks ("me" is colloquial).
2. This was a speculative enterprise on which Jacob staked his wages as a servant.
3. Was this brought up to defend taking interest.

A goodly apple rotten at the heart.

O, what a goodly outside falsehood hath!

SHYLOCK   Three thousand ducats. 'Tis a good round sum.

100 Three months from twelve—then let me see the rate.

ANTONIO   Well, Shylock, shall we be beholden to you?

SHYLOCK   Signor Antonio, many a time and oft

In the Rialto you have rated° me   berated

About my moneys and my usances.

105 Still° have I borne it with a patient shrug,   Always

For suff 'rance is the badge⁴ of all our tribe.

You call me misbeliever, cut-throat, dog,

And spit upon my Jewish gaberdine,°   long coat

And all for use of that which is mine own.

110 Well then, it now appears you need my help.

Go to, then. You come to me, and you say

'Shylock, we would have moneys'—you say so,

You, that did void your rheum° upon my beard,   spit

And foot me as you spurn° a stranger cur   contemptuously kick

115 Over your threshold. Moneys is your suit.

What should I say to you? Should I not say

'Hath a dog money? Is it possible

A cur can lend three thousand ducats?' Or

Shall I bend low, and in a bondman's° key,   slave's

120 With bated breath and whisp'ring humbleness

Say this: 'Fair sir, you spat on me on Wednesday last;

You spurned me such a day; another time

You called me dog; and for these courtesies

I'll lend you thus much moneys'?

125 ANTONIO   I am as like to call thee so again,

To spit on thee again, to spurn thee too.

If thou wilt lend this money, lend it not

As to thy friends; for when did friendship take

A breed⁵ for barren metal of his friend?

130 But lend it rather to thine enemy,

Who if he break,° thou mayst with better face   fail to repay

Exact the penalty.

SHYLOCK   Why, look you, how you storm!

I would be friends with you, and have your love,

Forget the shames that you have stained me with,

135 Supply your present wants, and take no doit°   small coin

Of usance for my moneys; and you'll not hear me.

This is kind⁶ I offer.

BASSANIO   This were° kindness.   would be

SHYLOCK   This kindness will I show.

140 Go with me to a notary, seal me there

Your single bond,⁷ and, in a merry sport,

If you repay me not on such a day,

In such a place, such sum or sums as are

Expressed in the condition, let the forfeit°   penalty

145 Be nominated for an equal° pound   Be stipulated as an exact

---

4. For enduring insult is the characteristic.
5. Offspring (interest); alluding to an ancient argument that it was unnatural to use money to "breed," or make, more money.

6. Benevolent; natural (but perhaps with the covert suggestion "in kind").
7. Bond signed by the debtor alone (Antonio) without additional guarantors.

Of your fair flesh to be cut off and taken
In what part of your body pleaseth me.
ANTONIO   Content, in faith. I'll seal to such a bond,
And say there is much kindness in the Jew.
150   BASSANIO   You shall not seal to such a bond for me.
I'll rather dwell in my necessity.°   *remain in need*
ANTONIO   Why, fear not, man; I will not forfeit it.
Within these two months—that's a month before
This bond expires—I do expect return
155   Of thrice three times the value of this bond.
SHYLOCK   O father Abram, what these Christians are,
Whose own hard dealings teaches them suspect
The thoughts of others! [*To* BASSANIO] Pray you tell me this:
If he should break his day, what should I gain
160   By the exaction of the forfeiture?
A pound of man's flesh taken from a man
Is not so estimable,° profitable neither,   *valuable*
As flesh of muttons, beeves, or goats. I say,
To buy his favour I extend this friendship.
165   If he will take it, so. If not, adieu,
And, for my love, I pray you wrong me not.
ANTONIO   Yes, Shylock, I will seal unto this bond.
SHYLOCK   Then meet me forthwith at the notary's.
Give him direction for this merry bond,
170   And I will go and purse the ducats straight,
See to my house—left in the fearful° guard   *doubtful*
Of an unthrifty knave—and presently
I'll be with you.
ANTONIO   Hie thee,° gentle Jew.   *Exit* [SHYLOCK]   *Hurry*
The Hebrew will turn Christian; he grows kind.
175   BASSANIO   I like not fair terms and a villain's mind.
ANTONIO   Come on. In this there can be no dismay.
My ships come home a month before the day.   *Exeunt*

2.1

[*Flourish of cornets.*] *Enter* [*the Prince of*] MOROCCO,
*a tawny Moor all in white, and three or four followers
accordingly,*[1] *with* PORTIA, NERISSA, *and their train*
MOROCCO [*to* PORTIA]   Mislike me not for my complexion,
The shadowed livery° of the burnished sun,   *servant's uniform*
To whom I am a neighbour and near bred.°   *close kin*
Bring me the fairest creature northward born,
5   Where Phoebus'° fire scarce thaws the icicles,   *the sun god*
And let us make incision for your love
To prove whose blood is reddest,[2] his or mine.
I tell thee, lady, this aspect° of mine   *countenance*
Hath feared° the valiant. By my love I swear,   *frightened*
10   The best regarded virgins of our clime
Have loved it too. I would not change this hue
Except to steal your thoughts, my gentle queen.
PORTIA   In terms of choice I am not solely led
By nice direction° of a maiden's eyes.   *fastidious guidance*

2.1 Location: Belmont.   2. Red blood was considered a sign of valor.
1. Of similar complexion and dress.

15   Besides, the lott'ry of my destiny
      Bars me the right of voluntary choosing.
      But if my father had not scanted° me,   *limited*
      And hedgèd° me by his wit° to yield myself   *restricted / wisdom*
      His wife who wins me by that means I told you,
20   Yourself, renownèd Prince, then stood as fair[3]
      As any comer I have looked on yet
      For my affection.
MOROCCO   Even for that I thank you.
      Therefore I pray you lead me to the caskets
      To try my fortune. By this scimitar,
25   That slew the Sophy° and a Persian prince   *Shah of Persia*
      That won three fields of Sultan Suleiman,°   *Turkish ruler*
      I would o'erstare the sternest eyes that look,
      Outbrave the heart most daring on the earth,
      Pluck the young sucking cubs from the she-bear,
30   Yea, mock the lion when a° roars for prey,   *he*
      To win the lady. But alas the while,
      If Hercules and Lichas° play at dice   *Hercules' servant*
      Which is the better man, the greater throw
      May turn by fortune from the weaker hand.
35   So is Alcides° beaten by his rage,[4]   *Hercules*
      And so may I, blind Fortune leading me,
      Miss that which one unworthier may attain,
      And die with grieving.
PORTIA   You must take your chance,
      And either not attempt to choose at all,
40   Or swear before you choose, if you choose wrong
      Never to speak to lady afterward
      In way of marriage. Therefore be advised.°   *careful*
MOROCCO   Nor will not. Come, bring me unto my chance.
PORTIA   First, forward to the temple. After dinner
      Your hazard shall be made.
45 MOROCCO   Good fortune then,
      To make me blest or cursèd'st among men.
                    [*Flourish of*] *cornets. Exeunt*

2.2

                    Enter [LANCELOT] *the clown*
LANCELOT   Certainly my conscience will serve° me to run from   *allow*
      this Jew my master. The fiend is at mine elbow and tempts me,
      saying to me 'Gobbo, Lancelot Gobbo, good Lancelot,' or
      'good Gobbo,' or 'good Lancelot Gobbo—use your legs, take the
5   start,° run away.' My conscience says 'No, take heed, honest   *begone*
      Lancelot, take heed, honest Gobbo,' or, as aforesaid, 'honest
      Lancelot Gobbo—do not run, scorn running with thy heels.'°   *indignantly (with pun)*
      Well, the most courageous fiend bids me pack. '*Via!*'° says the   *Away*
      fiend; 'Away!' says the fiend. 'For the heavens, rouse up a brave
10   mind,' says the fiend, 'and run.' Well, my conscience hanging
      about the neck of my heart says very wisely to me, 'My honest
      friend Lancelot'—being an honest man's son, or rather an hon-
      est woman's son, for indeed my father did something smack,

---

3. Seemed as attractive; stood as good a chance.   2.2 Location: Venice.
4. Often amended to "page."

something grow to; he had a kind of taste¹—well, my conscience says, 'Lancelot, budge not'; 'Budge!' says the fiend;
'Budge not', says my conscience. 'Conscience,' say I, 'you
counsel well'; 'Fiend,' say I, 'you counsel well.' To be ruled by
my conscience I should stay with the Jew my master who, God
bless the mark,² is a kind of devil; and to run away from the
Jew I should be ruled by the fiend who, saving your reverence,
is the devil himself. Certainly the Jew is the very devil incar-
nation;° and in my conscience, my conscience is but a kind of   *(for "incarnate")*
hard conscience to offer to counsel me to stay with the Jew.
The fiend gives the more friendly counsel. I will run, fiend.
My heels are at your commandment. I will run.

    Enter old GOBBO, *[blind,] with a basket*

GOBBO Master young man, you, I pray you, which is the way to
  Master Jew's?
LANCELOT *[aside]* O heavens, this is my true-begotten father
  who, being more than sand-blind—high-gravel-blind³—
  knows me not. I will try confusions⁴ with him.
GOBBO Master young gentleman, I pray you which is the way
  to Master Jew's?
LANCELOT Turn up on your right hand at the next turning, but
  at the next turning of all on your left, marry at the very next
  turning, turn of no hand but turn down indirectly to the Jew's
  house.
GOBBO By God's sonties,° 'twill be a hard way to hit. Can you   *saints*
  tell me whether one Lancelot that dwells with him dwell with
  him or no?
LANCELOT Talk you of young Master⁵ Lancelot? *[Aside]* Mark
  me now, now will I raise the waters.⁶ *[To* GOBBO*]* Talk you of
  young Master Lancelot?
GOBBO No master, sir, but a poor man's son. His father, though
  I say't, is an honest exceeding poor man, and, God be thanked,
  well to live.⁷
LANCELOT Well, let his father be what a° will, we talk of young   *he*
  Master Lancelot.
GOBBO Your worship's friend, and Lancelot, sir.
LANCELOT But I pray you, *ergo*° old man, *ergo* I beseech you,   *therefore*
  talk you of young Master Lancelot?
GOBBO Of Lancelot, an't° please your mastership.   *if it*
LANCELOT *Ergo* Master Lancelot. Talk not of Master Lancelot,
  father,⁸ for the young gentleman, according to fates and destinies and such odd sayings—the sisters three° and such branches   *the Fates*
  of learning—is indeed deceased; or, as you would say in plain
  terms, gone to heaven.
GOBBO Marry, God forbid! The boy was the very staff of my age,
  my very prop.
LANCELOT *[aside]* Do I look like a cudgel or a hovel-post,° a   *shed post*
  staff or a prop? *[To* GOBBO*]* Do you know me, father?

---

1. *my father . . . taste:* that is, my father was licentious.
2. Conventional apology before a rude remark, like "saving your reverence."
3. Lancelot's coinage for a degree of blindness between sand-blind (partly blind) and stone-blind.
4. Lancelot's version of "try conclusions" (experiment).
5. "Master" was only applied to gentlemen's sons.
6. Start something; bring on tears.
7. Well-to-do (contradicts the previous line).
8. Customary address to an old man.

GOBBO   Alack the day, I know you not, young gentleman. But I
pray you tell me, is my boy—God rest his soul—alive or dead?

LANCELOT   Do you not know me, father?

GOBBO   Alack, sir, I am sand-blind. I know you not.

65 LANCELOT   Nay, indeed, if you had your eyes you might fail of
the knowing me. It is a wise father that knows his own child.⁹
Well, old man, I will tell you news of your son. [*Kneeling*]
Give me your blessing. Truth will come to light; murder cannot be hid long—a man's son may, but in the end truth will

70 out.

GOBBO   Pray you, sir, stand up. I am sure you are not Lancelot,
my boy.

LANCELOT   Pray you, let's have no more fooling about it, but give
me your blessing. I am Lancelot, your boy that was, your son

75 that is, your child that shall be.

GOBBO   I cannot think you are my son.

LANCELOT   I know not what I shall think of that, but I am
Lancelot the Jew's man, and I am sure Margery your wife is
my mother.

80 GOBBO   Her name is Margery indeed. I'll be sworn, if thou be
Lancelot thou art mine own flesh and blood.
[*He feels Lancelot's head*]
Lord worshipped might he be, what a beard hast thou got!¹
Thou hast got more hair on thy chin than Dobbin my fill-
horse° has on his tail.   cart horse

85 LANCELOT   It should seem then that Dobbin's tail grows back-
ward.² I am sure he had more hair of his tail than I have of my
face when I last saw him.

GOBBO   Lord, how art thou changed! How dost thou and thy
master agree?° I have brought him a present. How 'gree you   get along

90 now?

LANCELOT   Well, well; but for mine own part, as I have set up
my rest³ to run away, so I will not rest till I have run some
ground. My master's a very Jew.⁴ Give him a present?—give
him a halter!° I am famished in his service. You may tell° every   noose / count

95 finger I have with my ribs. Father, I am glad you are come.
Give me° your present to one Master Bassanio, who indeed   Give
gives rare new liveries.° If I serve not him, I will run as far as   servants' uniforms
God has any ground.
Enter BASSANIO *with* [LEONARDO *and*] *follower*[s]
O rare fortune! Here comes the man. To him, father, for I am

100 a Jew if I serve the Jew any longer.

BASSANIO   [*to one of his men*]   You may do so, but let it be so
hasted° that supper be ready at the farthest° by five of the   hurried / latest
clock. See these letters delivered, put the liveries to making,
and desire° Graziano to come anon° to my lodging. [*Exit one*]   tell / at once

105 LANCELOT   [*to* GOBBO]   To him, father.

GOBBO   [*to* BASSANIO]   God bless your worship.

BASSANIO   Gramercy.° Wouldst thou aught° with me?   Many thanks / anything

GOBBO   Here's my son, sir, a poor boy—

---

9. Transposing the proverb "A wise child knows his
own father."
1. Gobbo mistakes Lancelot's hair for a beard.
2. Gets shorter; grows from the wrong end.

3. As I have definitely determined (phrase in the card
game primero meaning "risk everything").
4. Cruel, grasping person; Hebrew. *a very:* an absolute.

LANCELOT [*to* BASSANIO]   Not a poor boy, sir, but the rich Jew's
110 man that would, sir, as my father shall specify.
GOBBO [*to* BASSANIO]   He hath a great infection,° sir, as one   (for "affection"; wish)
would say, to serve—
LANCELOT   Indeed, the short and the long is, I serve the Jew,
and have a desire as my father shall specify.
115 GOBBO [*to* BASSANIO]   His master and he, saving your worship's
reverence, are scarce cater-cousins.°   close friends
LANCELOT [*to* BASSANIO]   To be brief, the very truth is that the
Jew, having done me wrong, doth cause me, as my father—
being, I hope, an old man—shall frutify° unto you.   (for "certify")
120 GOBBO [*to* BASSANIO]   I have here a dish of doves that I would
bestow upon your worship, and my suit is—
LANCELOT [*to* BASSANIO]   In very brief, the suit is impertinent°   (for "pertinent")
to myself, as your worship shall know by this honest old man;
and though I say it, though old man, yet, poor man, my father.
125 BASSANIO   One speak for both. What would you?
LANCELOT   Serve you, sir.
GOBBO [*to* BASSANIO]   That is the very defect° of the matter, sir.   (for "effect")
BASSANIO [*to* LANCELOT]   I know thee well. Thou hast obtained
thy suit.
130 Shylock thy master spoke with me this day,
And hath preferred thee, if it be preferment[5]
To leave a rich Jew's service to become
The follower of so poor a gentleman.
LANCELOT   The old proverb[6] is very well parted between my
135 master Shylock and you, sir: you have the grace of God, sir,
and he hath enough.
BASSANIO   Thou speak'st it well. [*To* GOBBO]   Go, father, with thy son.
[*To* LANCELOT]   Take leave of thy old master and enquire
My lodging out. [*To one of his men*]   Give him a livery
140 More guarded° than his fellows'. See it done.   decorated
LANCELOT [*to* GOBBO]   Father, in. I cannot get a service, no, I
have ne'er a tongue in my head—well!
[*He looks at his palm.*]
If any man in Italy have a fairer table[7] which doth offer to swear
upon a book,[8] I shall have good fortune. Go to, here's a simple°   unremarkable (ironic)
145 line of life, here's a small trifle of wives—alas, fifteen wives is
nothing. Eleven widows and nine maids is a simple coming-in[9]
for one man, and then to scape drowning thrice, and to be in
peril of my life with the edge of a featherbed[1]—here are simple
scapes. Well, if Fortune be a woman, she's a good wench for
150 this gear.° Father, come. I'll take my leave of the Jew in the   matter
twinkling. *Exit [with old* GOBBO]
BASSANIO   I pray thee, good Leonardo, think on this.
These things being bought and orderly bestowed,°   stowed on ship
Return in haste, for I do feast tonight
155 My best-esteemed acquaintance. Hie thee. Go.
LEONARDO   My best endeavours shall be done herein.
[*He begins to leave.*] *Enter* GRAZIANO

5. And has recommended you, if it be advancement.
6. "The grace of God is gear enough."
7. Palm (Lancelot reads the lines of his palm to predict
the future).
8. To tell the truth (referring to the practice of taking
an oath with the palm on the Bible).
9. A scanty income; an easy sexual entrance.
1. Alluding to a sexual adventure.

GRAZIANO [*to* LEONARDO]   Where's your master?
LEONARDO   Yonder, sir, he walks.

                                                                                          Exit

GRAZIANO   Signor Bassanio.
BASSANIO   Graziano.
GRAZIANO   I have a suit to you.
BASSANIO   You have obtained it.
160   GRAZIANO   You must not deny me. I must go with you to Belmont.
BASSANIO   Why then, you must. But hear thee, Graziano,
          Thou art too wild, too rude and bold of voice—
          Parts° that become thee happily enough,   *Attributes*
          And in such eyes as ours appear not faults;
165   But where thou art not known, why, there they show
          Something too liberal.° Pray thee, take pain   *unrestrained*
          To allay with some cold drops of modesty
          Thy skipping spirit, lest through thy wild behaviour
          I be misconstered° in the place I go to,   *misconstrued*
          And lose my hopes.
170   GRAZIANO   Signor Bassanio, hear me.
          If I do not put on a sober habit,°   *behavior; clothing*
          Talk with respect, and swear but now and then,
          Wear prayer books in my pocket, look demurely—
          Nay more, while grace is saying hood mine eyes
175   Thus with my hat,² and sigh, and say 'Amen',
          Use all the observance of civility,
          Like one well studied in a sad ostent°   *solemn appearance*
          To please his grandam,° never trust me more.°   *grandmother / again*
BASSANIO   Well, we shall see your bearing.
180   GRAZIANO   Nay, but I bar tonight. You shall not gauge me
          By what we do tonight.
BASSANIO   No, that were pity.
          I would entreat you rather to put on
          Your boldest suit of mirth, for we have friends
          That purpose merriment. But fare you well.
185   I have some business.
GRAZIANO   And I must to Lorenzo and the rest.
          But we will visit you at supper-time.   *Exeunt* [*severally*]

2.3
Enter JESSICA *and* [LANCELOT] *the clown*

JESSICA   I am sorry thou wilt leave my father so.
          Our house is hell, and thou, a merry devil,
          Didst rob it of some taste of tediousness.
          But fare thee well. There is a ducat for thee.
5   And, Lancelot, soon at supper shalt thou see
          Lorenzo, who is thy new master's guest.
          Give him this letter, do it secretly;
          And so farewell. I would not have my father
          See me in talk with thee.
10   LANCELOT   Adieu. Tears exhibit° my tongue, most beautiful   *(for "inhibit")*
          pagan; most sweet Jew; if a Christian do not play the knave and
          get thee, I am much deceived. But adieu. These foolish drops
          do something drown my manly spirit. Adieu.

---

2. Hats were worn at meals but taken off for grace.   2.3 Location: Shylock's house in Venice.

JESSICA Farewell, good Lancelot.   *Exit* [LANCELOT]

15   Alack, what heinous sin is it in me
         To be ashamed to be my father's child!
         But though I am a daughter to his blood,
         I am not to his manners.° O Lorenzo,   behavior
         If thou keep promise I shall end this strife,
20   Become a Christian and thy loving wife.   *Exit*

2.4

Enter GRAZIANO, LORENZO, SALERIO, *and* SOLANIO

LORENZO Nay, we will slink away in° supper-time,   during
         Disguise us at my lodging, and return
         All in an hour.

GRAZIANO We have not made good preparation.

5 SALERIO We have not spoke as yet of ° torchbearers.   not yet arranged for

SOLANIO 'Tis vile, unless it may be quaintly ordered,°   cleverly managed
         And better in my mind not undertook.

LORENZO 'Tis now but four o'clock. We have two hours
         To furnish us.

Enter LANCELOT *with a letter*

         Friend Lancelot, what's the news?

10 LANCELOT [*presenting the letter*] An° it shall please you to break   If
         up° this, it shall seem to signify.   open

LORENZO [*taking the letter*] I know the hand. In faith, 'tis a fair
         hand,
         And whiter than the paper it writ on
         Is the fair hand that writ.

GRAZIANO   Love-news, in faith.

15 LANCELOT [*to* LORENZO] By your leave, sir.

LORENZO Whither goest thou?

LANCELOT Marry, sir, to bid my old master the Jew to sup tonight
         with my new master the Christian.

LORENZO Hold,° here, take this. [*Giving money*] Tell gentle Jessica   Wait
20   I will not fail her. Speak it privately.
         Go.   *Exit* [LANCELOT *the*] *clown*
             Gentlemen,
         Will you prepare you for this masque tonight?
         I am provided of a torchbearer.

SALERIO Ay, marry, I'll be gone about it straight.°   immediately

SOLANIO And so will I.

25 LORENZO   Meet me and Graziano
         At Graziano's lodging some hour hence.

SALERIO 'Tis good we do so.   *Exit* [*with* SOLANIO]

GRAZIANO Was not that letter from fair Jessica?

LORENZO I must needs tell thee all. She hath directed
30   How I shall take her from her father's house,
         What gold and jewels she is furnished with,
         What page's suit she hath in readiness.
         If e'er the Jew her father come to heaven
         It will be for his gentle daughter's sake;
35   And never dare misfortune cross her foot
         Unless she° do it under this excuse: (*misfortune*)

2.4 Location: Street in Venice.

That she° is issue° to a faithless Jew.   *(Jessica) / offspring*
Come, go with me. Peruse this as thou goest.
    [*He gives* GRAZIANO *the letter*]
Fair Jessica shall be my torchbearer.   *Exeunt*

2.5

Enter [SHYLOCK *the*] *Jew and his man that was,*°   *former servant*
[LANCELOT] *the clown*

SHYLOCK   Well, thou shalt see, thy eyes shall be thy judge,
The difference of old Shylock and Bassanio.
[*Calling*] What, Jessica! [*To* LANCELOT] Thou shalt not gormandize°   *overeat*
As thou hast done with me. [*Calling*] What, Jessica!
5 [*To* LANCELOT] And sleep and snore and rend apparel out.°   *wear out clothes*
[*Calling*] Why, Jessica, I say!
LANCELOT [*calling*]   Why, Jessica!
SHYLOCK   Who bids thee call? I do not bid thee call.
LANCELOT   Your worship was wont to tell me I could do nothing
  without bidding.
    Enter JESSICA
10 JESSICA [*to* SHYLOCK]   Call you? What is your will?
SHYLOCK   I am bid forth to supper, Jessica.
There are my keys. But wherefore° should I go?   *why*
I am not bid for love. They flatter me,
But yet I'll go in hate, to feed upon
15 The prodigal Christian. Jessica, my girl,
Look to my house. I am right loath° to go.   *very unwilling*
There is some ill a-brewing towards my rest,
For I did dream of money-bags tonight.°   *last night*
LANCELOT   I beseech you, sir, go. My young master doth expect
20   your reproach.°   *(for "approach")*
SHYLOCK   So do I his.
LANCELOT   And they have conspired together. I will not say you
  shall see a masque, but if you do, then it was not for nothing
  that my nose fell a-bleeding on Black Monday° last at six   *Easter Monday*
25   o'clock i'th' morning, falling out that year on Ash Wednesday
  was four year in th'afternoon.[1]
SHYLOCK   What, are there masques? Hear you me, Jessica,
Lock up my doors; and when you hear the drum
And the vile squealing of the wry-necked[2] fife,
30 Clamber not you up to the casements then,
Nor thrust your head into the public street
To gaze on Christian fools with varnished° faces,   *painted; masked*
But stop my house's ears—I mean my casements.
Let not the sound of shallow fopp'ry° enter   *frivolity*
35 My sober house. By Jacob's staff[3] I swear
I have no mind of feasting forth° tonight.   *away from home*
But I will go. [*To* LANCELOT] Go you before me, sirrah.
Say I will come.
LANCELOT   I will go before, sir.
    [*Aside to* JESSICA]
Mistress, look out at window for all this.[4]

2.5 Location: Outside Shylock's house.
1. Lancelot mocks Shylock's superstition.
2. Fifes were played with the head turned sideways.

3. See Genesis 32:10 and Hebrews 11:21.
4. *for all this*: despite Shylock's instructions.

40 There will come a Christian by
Will be worth a Jeẅes eye. *[Exit]*

SHYLOCK *[to JESSICA]* What says that fool of Hagar's offspring,[5] ha?

JESSICA His words were 'Farewell, mistress'; nothing else.

SHYLOCK The patch° is kind enough, but a huge feeder,   *fool*
45 Snail-slow in profit,° and he sleeps by day   *proficiency*
More than the wildcat. Drones hive not with me;
Therefore I part with him, and part with him
To one that I would have him help to waste
His borrowed purse. Well, Jessica, go in.
50 Perhaps I will return immediately.
Do as I bid you. Shut doors after you.
Fast bind, fast find[6]—
A proverb never stale in thrifty mind.   *Exit [at one door]*

JESSICA Farewell; and if my fortune be not crossed,
55 I have a father, you a daughter lost.   *Exit [at another door]*

2.6

Enter the masquers, GRAZIANO and SALERIO [with torchbearers]

GRAZIANO This is the penthouse[1] under which Lorenzo
Desired us to make stand.

SALERIO   His hour is almost past.

GRAZIANO And it is marvel he outdwells his hour,
For lovers ever run before the clock.

5 SALERIO O, ten times faster Venus' pigeons[2] fly
To seal love's bonds new made than they are wont
To keep obligèd° faith unforfeited.°   *pledged / unbroken*

GRAZIANO That ever holds.° Who riseth from a feast   *remains true*
With that keen appetite that he sits down?
10 Where is the horse that doth untread° again   *retrace*
His tedious measures with the unbated fire
That he did pace them first? All things that are
Are with more spirit chasèd than enjoyed.
How like a younker or a prodigal[3]
15 The scarfèd barque° puts from her native bay,   *streamer-bedecked ship*
Hugged and embracèd by the strumpet wind!
How like the prodigal doth she return,
With over-weathered ribs° and raggèd sails,   *weatherbeaten timbers*
Lean, rent,° and beggared by the strumpet wind!   *torn*

Enter LORENZO [with a torch]

20 SALERIO Here comes Lorenzo. More of this hereafter.

LORENZO Sweet friends, your patience for my long abode.°   *delay*
Not I but my affairs have made you wait.
When you shall please to play the thieves for wives
I'll watch° as long for you therein. Approach.   *wait*
25 Here dwells my father° Jew. *[Calling]* Ho, who's within?   *father-in-law*

[Enter] JESSICA above [in boy's apparel]

JESSICA Who are you? Tell me for more certainty,

---

5. That despicable gentile. Hagar, Abraham's gentile
servant, bore him a son, Ishmael; she and her child
were cast out after the birth of Abraham's legitimate
son, Isaac.
6. Something firmly secured will remain fastened.

2.6 Location: Scene continues.
1. Projecting roof of an upper story.
2. Doves that drew the love goddess's chariot.
3. See Luke 15:11–31. *younker:* fashionable youth;
junior seaman.

Albeit I'll swear that I do know your tongue.

LORENZO Lorenzo, and thy love.

JESSICA Lorenzo, certain, and my love indeed,
30   For who love I so much? And now who knows
But you, Lorenzo, whether I am yours?

LORENZO Heaven and thy thoughts are witness that thou art.

JESSICA Here, catch this casket. It is worth the pains.
I am glad 'tis night, you do not look on me,
35   For I am much ashamed of my exchange;°   *change of clothes*
But love is blind, and lovers cannot see
The pretty° follies that themselves commit;   *ingenious*
For if they could, Cupid himself would blush
To see me thus transformèd to a boy.

40   LORENZO Descend, for you must be my torchbearer.

JESSICA What, must I hold a candle to my shames?
They in themselves, good sooth,° are too too light.°   *in truth / clear; wanton*
Why, 'tis an office of discovery,⁴ love,
And I should be obscured.

LORENZO   So are you, sweet,
45   Even in the lovely garnish° of a boy.   *dress*
But come at once,
For the close° night doth play the runaway,°   *secret / steals away*
And we are stayed° for at Bassanio's feast.   *waited*

JESSICA I will make fast the doors, and gild myself
50   With some more ducats, and be with you straight.
                                                                     [*Exit above*]

GRAZIANO Now, by my hood, a gentile, and no Jew.

LORENZO Beshrew° me but I love her heartily,   *Evil befall*
For she is wise, if I can judge of her;
And fair she is, if that mine eyes be true;
55   And true she is, as she hath proved herself;
And therefore like herself, wise, fair, and true,
Shall she be placèd in my constant soul.
                         Enter JESSICA [*below*]
What, art thou come? On, gentlemen, away.
Our masquing mates by this time for us stay.
                         Exit [*with* JESSICA *and* SALERIO]
                         Enter ANTONIO

ANTONIO Who's there?

60   GRAZIANO   Signor Antonio?

ANTONIO Fie, fie, Graziano, where are all the rest?
'Tis nine o'clock. Our friends all stay for you.
No masque tonight. The wind is come about.
Bassanio presently° will go aboard.   *immediately*
65   I have sent twenty out to seek for you.

GRAZIANO I am glad on't. I desire no more delight
Than to be under sail and gone tonight.   *Exeunt*

2.7

[*Flourish of cornets.*] *Enter* PORTIA *with* MOROCCO *and
both their trains*

PORTIA Go, draw aside the curtains, and discover°   *reveal*
The several caskets to this noble prince.

---

4. (Torchbearing) is a task of disclosure.   2.7 Location: Belmont.

[*The curtains are drawn aside, revealing three caskets*]

[*To* MOROCCO]   Now make your choice.

MOROCCO   This first of gold, who° this inscription bears: *which*

5 'Who chooseth me shall gain what many men desire.'

The second silver, which this promise carries:

'Who chooseth me shall get as much as he deserves.'

This third dull lead, with warning all as blunt:[1]

'Who chooseth me must give and hazard all he hath.'

10 How shall I know if I do choose the right?

PORTIA   The one of them contains my picture, Prince.

If you choose that, then I am yours withal.°   *with it*

MOROCCO   Some god direct my judgement! Let me see.

I will survey th'inscriptions back again.

15 What says this leaden casket?

'Who chooseth me must give and hazard all he hath.'

Must give, for what? For lead? Hazard for lead?

This casket threatens. Men that hazard all

Do it in hope of fair advantages.

20 A golden mind stoops not to shows of dross.°   *rubbish*

I'll then nor° give nor hazard aught for lead.   *neither*

What says the silver with her virgin hue?

'Who chooseth me shall get as much as he deserves.'

'As much as he deserves': pause there, Morocco,

25 And weigh thy value with an even° hand.   *impartial*

If thou beest rated by thy estimation

Thou dost deserve enough, and yet 'enough'

May not extend so far as to the lady.

And yet to be afeard of my deserving

30 Were but a weak disabling° of myself.   *disparagement*

As much as I deserve—why, that's the lady!

I do in birth deserve her, and in fortunes,

In graces, and in qualities of breeding;

But more than these, in love I do deserve.

35 What if I strayed no farther, but chose here?

Let's see once more this saying graved in gold:

'Who chooseth me shall gain what many men desire.'

Why, that's the lady! All the world desires her.

From the four corners of the earth they come

40 To kiss this shrine, this mortal breathing saint.

The Hyrcanian deserts[2] and the vasty° wilds   *vast*

Of wide Arabia are as throughfares° now   *main roads*

For princes to come view fair Portia.

The watery kingdom, whose ambitious head°   *(of a storm)*

45 Spits in the face of heaven, is no bar

To stop the foreign spirits, but they come

As o'er a brook to see fair Portia.

One of these three contains her heavenly picture.

Is't like° that lead contains her? 'Twere damnation   *probable*

50 To think so base a thought. It° were too gross   *(lead)*

To rib her cerecloth[3] in the obscure grave.

Or shall I think in silver she's immured,°   *enclosed*

Being ten times undervalued to tried° gold?   *purified*

O sinful thought! Never so rich a gem
55   Was set in worse than gold. They have in England
A coin that bears the figure of an angel[4]
Stamped in gold, but that's insculped° upon;   *engraved*
But here an angel in a golden bed
Lies all within. Deliver me the key.
60   Here do I choose, and thrive I as I may.
         [*He is given a key*]
PORTIA   There, take it, Prince; and if my form° lie there,   *image*
Then I am yours.
         [MOROCCO *opens the golden casket*]
MOROCCO   O hell! What have we here?
A carrion death,° within whose empty eye   *A skull*
There is a written scroll. I'll read the writing.
65   'All that glisters is not gold;
Often have you heard that told.
Many a man his life hath sold
But my outside[5] to behold.
Gilded tombs do worms infold.°   *enclose*
70   Had you been as wise as bold,
Young in limbs, in judgement old,
Your answer had not been enscrolled.
Fare you well; your suit is cold.'
Cold indeed, and labour lost.
75   Then farewell heat, and welcome frost.
Portia, adieu. I have too grieved a heart
To take a tedious leave. Thus losers part.
                 Exit [*with his train*]. *Flourish* [*of*] *cornets*
PORTIA   A gentle riddance. Draw the curtains, go.
Let all of his complexion choose me so.
         [*The curtains are drawn.*] *Exeunt*

2.8

Enter SALERIO *and* SOLANIO
SALERIO   Why, man, I saw Bassanio under sail.
With him is Graziano gone along,
And in their ship I am sure Lorenzo is not.
SOLANIO   The villain Jew with outcries raised° the Duke,   *roused*
5   Who went with him to search Bassanio's ship.
SALERIO   He came too late. The ship was under sail.
But there the Duke was given to understand
That in a gondola were seen together
Lorenzo and his amorous Jessica.
10   Besides, Antonio certified the Duke
They were not with Bassanio in his ship.
SOLANIO   I never heard a passion° so confused,   *an outburst*
So strange, outrageous, and so variable
As the dog Jew did utter in the streets.
15   'My daughter! O, my ducats! O, my daughter!
Fled with a Christian! O, my Christian ducats!
Justice! The law! My ducats and my daughter!
A sealèd bag, two sealèd bags of ducats,

---

4. The gold coin called angel had the figure of St.   5. Gold; face that once covered the skull.
Michael on its face.   2.8 Location: Venice.

Of double ducats, stol'n from me by my daughter!

20 And jewels, two stones, two rich and precious stones,[1]
Stol'n by my daughter! Justice! Find the girl!
She hath the stones upon her, and the ducats!'

SALERIO Why, all the boys in Venice follow him,
Crying, 'His stones, his daughter, and his ducats!'

25 SOLANIO Let good Antonio look he keep his day,°   repay his debt on time
Or he shall pay for this.

SALERIO   Marry, well remembered.
I reasoned° with a Frenchman yesterday,   conversed
Who told me in the narrow seas° that part   (English Channel)
The French and English there miscarried°   wrecked

30 A vessel of our country, richly fraught.°   laden
I thought upon Antonio when he told me,
And wished in silence that it were not his.

SOLANIO You were best to tell Antonio what you hear—
Yet do not suddenly, for it may grieve him.

35 SALERIO A kinder gentleman treads not the earth.
I saw Bassanio and Antonio part.
Bassanio told him he would make some speed
Of his return. He answered, 'Do not so.
Slubber° not business for my sake, Bassanio,   Hastily perform

40 But stay the very riping of the time;
And for the Jew's bond which he hath of me,
Let it not enter in your mind° of love.   interrupt your thoughts
Be merry, and employ your chiefest thoughts
To courtship and such fair ostents° of love   displays

45 As shall conveniently° become you there.'   properly
And even there, his eye being big with tears,
Turning his face, he put his hand behind him
And, with affection wondrous sensible,°   obvious; heartfelt
He wrung Bassanio's hand; and so they parted.

50 SOLANIO I think he only loves the world for him.
I pray thee let us go and find him out,
And quicken his embracèd heaviness[2]
With some delight or other.

SALERIO   Do we so.   *Exeunt*

2.9

Enter NERISSA *and a servitor*

NERISSA Quick, quick, I pray thee, draw the curtain straight.°   immediately
The Prince of Aragon hath ta'en his oath,
And comes to his election presently.°   his choice at once
[*The servitor draws aside the curtain, revealing the three
caskets. Flourish of cornets.*] *Enter* ARAGON, *his train,
and* PORTIA

PORTIA Behold, there stand the caskets, noble Prince.

5 If you choose that wherein I am contained,
Straight shall our nuptial rites be solemnized.
But if you fail, without more speech, my lord,
You must be gone from hence immediately.

1. With the suggestion "testicles," taken up by the mocking boys in line 24.
2. And lighten the grief he embraces.
2.9 Location: Belmont.

ARAGON   I am enjoined by oath to observe three things:
10 First, never to unfold to anyone
Which casket 'twas I chose. Next, if I fail
Of the right casket, never in my life
To woo a maid in way of marriage.
Lastly, if I do fail in fortune of my choice,
15 Immediately to leave you and be gone.
PORTIA   To these injunctions everyone doth swear
That comes to hazard° for my worthless self.   gamble
ARAGON   And so have I addressed° me. Fortune now   prepared
To my heart's hope! Gold, silver, and base lead.
    [He reads the leaden casket]
20 'Who chooseth me must give and hazard all he hath.'
You shall look fairer ere I give or hazard.
What says the golden chest? Ha, let me see.
'Who chooseth me shall gain what many men desire.'
'What many men desire'—that 'many' may be meant
25 By° the fool multitude, that choose by show,   For
Not learning more than the fond° eye doth teach,   foolish
Which pries not to th'interior but, like the martlet,°   swallow
Builds in the weather° on the outward wall   open air
Even in the force and road of casualty.°   mishap
30 I will not choose what many men desire,
Because I will not jump° with common spirits   agree
And rank me with the barbarous multitudes.
Why then, to thee, thou silver treasure-house.
Tell me once more what title thou dost bear.
35 'Who chooseth me shall get as much as he deserves'—
And well said too, for who shall go about
To cozen° fortune, and be honourable   cheat
Without the stamp° of merit? Let none presume   official seal
To wear an undeservèd dignity.
40 O, that estates, degrees,° and offices   social ranks
Were not derived° corruptly, and that clear honour   gained
Were purchased° by the merit of the wearer!   acquired
How many then should cover that stand bare,[1]
How many be commanded that command?
45 How much low peasantry would then be gleaned°   separated
From the true seed of honour, and how much honour
Picked from the chaff and ruin of the times
To be new varnished?° Well; but to my choice.   regain its luster
'Who chooseth me shall get as much as he deserves.'
50 I will assume° desert. Give me a key for this,   claim
And instantly unlock my fortunes here.
    [He is given a key, and opens the silver casket]
PORTIA   Too long a pause for that which you find there.
ARAGON   What's here? The portrait of a blinking idiot
Presenting me a schedule.° I will read it.   document
55 How much unlike art thou to Portia!
How much unlike my hopes and my deservings!
'Who chooseth me shall have as much as he deserves.'

1. Should wear hats who now stand bareheaded (before their social superiors).

Did I deserve no more than a fool's head?
Is that my prize? Are my deserts no better?

60 PORTIA   To offend and judge are distinct offices,[2]
And of opposèd natures.

ARAGON   What is here?
[*He reads the schedule*]
'The fire seven times tried° this;   *purified*
Seven times tried that judgement is
That did never choose amiss.
65 Some there be that shadows kiss;[3]
Such have but a shadow's bliss.
There be fools alive, iwis,°   *in truth*
Silvered[4] o'er; and so was this.
Take what wife you will to bed,
70 I° will ever be your head.   (*the blinking idiot*)
So be gone; you are sped.'°   *finished*
Still more fool I shall appear
By the time I linger here.
With one fool's head I came to woo,
75 But I go away with two.
Sweet, adieu. I'll keep my oath
Patiently to bear my wroth.°   *grief*
[*Flourish of cornets. Exit with his train*]
PORTIA   Thus hath the candle singed the moth.
O, these deliberate° fools! When they do choose   *careful*
80 They have the wisdom by their wit to lose.
NERISSA   The ancient saying is no heresy:
Hanging and wiving goes by destiny.
PORTIA   Come, draw the curtain, Nerissa.
[NERISSA *draws the curtain*]
Enter MESSENGER
MESSENGER   Where is my lady?
PORTIA   Here. What would my lord?
85 MESSENGER   Madam, there is alighted at your gate
A young Venetian, one that comes before
To signify th'approaching of his lord,
From whom he bringeth sensible regrets,°   *tangible greetings*
To wit, besides commends and courteous breath,
90 Gifts of rich value. Yet° I have not seen   *Until now*
So likely° an ambassador of love.   *suitable*
A day in April never came so sweet
To show how costly° summer was at hand   *lavish*
As this fore-spurrer comes before his lord.
95 PORTIA   No more, I pray thee, I am half afeard
Thou wilt say anon° he is some kin to thee,   *soon*
Thou spend'st such high-day[5] wit in praising him.
Come, come, Nerissa, for I long to see
Quick Cupid's post° that comes so mannerly.   *messenger*
100 NERISSA   Bassanio, Lord Love,° if thy will it be!   *Exeunt*   *Cupid*

---

2. To err and to judge are different functions.
3. Like Narcissus in classical mythology, a youth who
fell in love with his own reflection.
4. Silver-haired (thus apparently wise).
5. Holiday (fit for special occasions).

3.1

Enter SOLANIO *and* SALERIO

SOLANIO Now, what news on the Rialto?

SALERIO Why, yet it lives there unchecked[1] that Antonio hath
a ship of rich lading wrecked on the narrow seas—the Good-
wins[2] I think they call the place—a very dangerous flat, and
5 fatal, where the carcasses of many a tall ship lie buried, as they
say, if my gossip Report° be an honest woman of her word.   *Dame Rumor*

SOLANIO I would she were as lying a gossip in that as ever
knapped° ginger or made her neighbours believe she wept for   *nibbled*
the death of a third husband. But it is true, without any slips
10 of prolixity° or crossing the plain highway of talk, that the   *any wordy lies*
good Antonio, the honest Antonio—O that I had a title good
enough to keep his name company—

SALERIO Come, the full stop.°   *period*

SOLANIO Ha, what sayst thou? Why, the end is he hath lost a
15 ship.

SALERIO I would it might prove the end of his losses.

SOLANIO Let me say amen betimes, lest the devil cross° my   *thwart*
prayer—

Enter SHYLOCK

for here he comes in the likeness of a Jew. How now, Shylock,
20 what news among the merchants?

SHYLOCK You knew, none so well, none so well as you, of my
daughter's flight.

SALERIO That's certain. I for my part knew the tailor that made
the wings[3] she flew withal.

25 SOLANIO And Shylock for his own part knew the bird was
fledge,° and then it is the complexion° of them all to leave the   *feathered / disposition*
dam.°   *mother (here, parent)*

SHYLOCK She is damned for it.

SALERIO That's certain, if the devil may be her judge.

30 SHYLOCK My own flesh and blood to rebel![4]

SOLANIO Out upon it, old carrion, rebels it at these years?

SHYLOCK I say my daughter is my flesh and my blood.

SALERIO There is more difference between thy flesh and hers
than between jet° and ivory; more between your bloods than   *black mineral*
35 there is between red wine and Rhenish.° But tell us, do you   *white wine*
hear whether Antonio have had any loss at sea or no?

SHYLOCK There I have another bad match.° A bankrupt, a   *bad deal*
prodigal, who dare scarce show his head on the Rialto; a beggar, that was used to come so smug upon the mart. Let him look
40 to his bond. He was wont to call me usurer: let him look to his
bond. He was wont to lend money for a° Christian courtesy: let   *out of*
him look to his bond.

SALERIO Why, I am sure if he forfeit thou wilt not take his
flesh. What's that good for?

45 SHYLOCK To bait fish withal.° If it will feed nothing else it will   *with*
feed my revenge. He hath disgraced me, and hindered me half
a million; laughed at my losses, mocked at my gains, scorned

3.1 Location: Venice.
1. It circulates there without denial.
2. Goodwin Sands, where the Thames joins the sea.
"Goodwin" means "friend."

3. Playing on "wing," a decorative flap on the upper
sleeve.
4. Shylock means "my own offspring"; Solanio pretends
he means "carnal appetite."

my nation, thwarted my bargains, cooled my friends, heated
mine enemies, and what's his reason?—I am a Jew. Hath not a
50 Jew eyes? Hath not a Jew hands, organs, dimensions,° senses, *bodily form*
affections, passions; fed with the same food, hurt with the
same weapons, subject to the same diseases, healed by the
same means, warmed and cooled by the same winter and
summer as a Christian is? If you prick us do we not bleed? If
55 you tickle us do we not laugh? If you poison us do we not die?
And if you wrong us shall we not revenge? If we are like you
in the rest, we will resemble you in that. If a Jew wrong a
Christian, what is his° humility? Revenge. If a Christian *(the Christian's)*
wrong a Jew, what should his sufferance° be by Christian *patience*
60 example? Why, revenge. The villainy you teach me I will execute, and it shall go hard but I will better the instruction.

   Enter a MAN *from Antonio*

MAN [*to* SOLANIO *and* SALERIO] Gentlemen, my master Antonio
 is at his house and desires to speak with you both.
SALERIO We have been up and down to seek him.

   Enter TUBAL

65 SOLANIO Here comes another of the tribe. A third cannot be
 matched° unless the devil himself turn Jew. *found to match*

   Exeunt [SOLANIO *and* SALERIO, *with Antonio's* MAN]

SHYLOCK How now, Tubal? What news from Genoa? Hast thou
 found my daughter?
TUBAL I often came where I did hear of her, but cannot find
70 her.
SHYLOCK Why, there, there, there, there. A diamond gone cost
 me two thousand ducats in Frankfurt.⁵ The curse never fell
 upon our nation till now—I never felt it till now. Two thousand
 ducats in that and other precious, precious jewels. I would my
75 daughter were dead at my foot and the jewels in her ear! Would
 she were hearsed° at my foot and the ducats in her coffin! No *coffined*
 news of them? Why, so. And I know not what's spent in the
 search. Why thou, loss upon loss: the thief gone with so
 much, and so much to find the thief, and no satisfaction, no
80 revenge, nor no ill luck stirring but what lights o' my shoulders,
 no sighs but o' my breathing, no tears but o' my shedding.
TUBAL Yes, other men have ill luck too. Antonio, as I heard in
 Genoa—
SHYLOCK What, what, what? Ill luck, ill luck?
85 TUBAL Hath an argosy cast away coming from Tripolis.
SHYLOCK I thank God, I thank God! Is it true, is it true?
TUBAL I spoke with some of the sailors that escaped the wreck.
SHYLOCK I thank thee, good Tubal. Good news, good news! Ha,
 ha—heard in Genoa?
90 TUBAL Your daughter spent in Genoa, as I heard, one night
 fourscore ducats.
SHYLOCK Thou stick'st a dagger in me. I shall never see my gold
 again. Fourscore ducats at a sitting? Fourscore ducats?
TUBAL There came divers of Antonio's creditors in my company
95 to Venice that swear he cannot choose but break.° *go bankrupt*
SHYLOCK I am very glad of it. I'll plague him, I'll torture him.
 I am glad of it.

---

5. Site of a jewel market.

TUBAL   One of them showed me a ring that he had of your
        daughter for a monkey.
100 SHYLOCK   Out upon her! Thou torturest me, Tubal. It was my
        turquoise. I had it of Leah when I was a bachelor. I would not
        have given it for a wilderness of monkeys.
TUBAL   But Antonio is certainly undone.
SHYLOCK   Nay, that's true, that's very true. Go, Tubal, fee° me   hire
105   an officer. Bespeak him a fortnight before. I will have the heart
        of him if he forfeit, for were he out of Venice I can make what
        merchandise° I will. Go, Tubal, and meet me at our synagogue.   drive what bargains
        Go, good Tubal; at our synagogue, Tubal.

                                                        Exeunt [*severally*]

                              3.2
        Enter BASSANIO, PORTIA, NERISSA, GRAZIANO, *and all
        their trains.* [*The curtains are drawn aside, revealing the
        three caskets*]
PORTIA [*to* BASSANIO]   I pray you tarry. Pause a day or two
        Before you hazard, for in choosing° wrong   *if you choose*
        I lose your company. Therefore forbear a while.
        There's something tells me—but it is not love—
5   I would not lose you; and you know yourself
        Hate counsels not in such a quality.°   *way*
        But lest you should not understand me well—
        And yet a maiden hath no tongue but thought—
        I would detain you here some month or two
10   Before you venture for me. I could teach you
        How to choose right, but then I am forsworn.
        So° will I never be; so may you miss me.[1]   *(forsworn)*
        But if you do, you'll make me wish a sin,
        That I had been forsworn. Beshrew your eyes,
15   They have o'erlooked° me and divided me.   *bewitched*
        One half of me is yours, the other half yours—
        Mine own, I would say, but if mine, then yours,
        And so all yours. O, these naughty° times   *evil*
        Puts bars between the owners and their rights;
20   And so, though yours, not yours. Prove it so,
        Let fortune go to hell for it, not I.[2]
        I speak too long, but tis to piece° the time,   *extend*
        To eke° it, and to draw it out in length   *augment*
        To stay° you from election.°   *delay/choosing*
BASSANIO   Let me choose,
25   For as I am, I live upon the rack.[3]
PORTIA   Upon the rack, Bassanio? Then confess
        What treason there is mingled with your love.
BASSANIO   None but that ugly treason of mistrust°   *uncertainty*
        Which makes me fear° th'enjoying of my love.   *doubt*
30   There may as well be amity and life
        'Tween snow and fire as treason and my love.
PORTIA   Ay, but I fear you speak upon the rack,
        Where men enforcèd do speak anything.

3.2 Location: Belmont.   fault, not mine (for breaking my oath).
1. Fail to attain me.   3. Instrument of torture used on traitors.
2. *Prove . . . I*: If it turns out thus, let it be fortune's

BASSANIO Promise me life and I'll confess the truth.

PORTIA Well then, confess and live.

35 **BASSANIO**   'Confess and love'
    Had been the very sum of my confession.
    O happy torment, when my torturer
    Doth teach me answers for deliverance!°   *release*
    But let me to my fortune and the caskets.

40 **PORTIA** Away then. I am locked in one of them.
    If you do love me, you will find me out.
    Nerissa and the rest, stand all aloof.
    Let music sound while he doth make his choice.
    Then if he lose he makes a swanlike end,[4]
45   Fading in music. That the comparison
    May stand more proper, my eye shall be the stream
    And wat'ry deathbed for him. He may win,
    And what is music then? Then music is
    Even as the flourish° when true subjects bow   *fanfare*
50   To a new-crownèd monarch. Such it is
    As are those dulcet sounds in break of day
    That creep into the dreaming bridegroom's ear
    And summon him to marriage.[5] Now he goes,
    With no less presence° but with much more love   *dignity*
55   Than young Alcides when he did redeem
    The virgin tribute paid by howling Troy
    To the sea-monster.[6] I stand for sacrifice.
    The rest aloof are the Dardanian° wives,   *Trojan*
    With blearèd° visages come forth to view   *weepy*
60   The issue° of th'exploit. Go, Hercules.   *outcome*
    Live thou,° I live. With much much more dismay   *If you live*
    I view the fight than thou that mak'st the fray.

    Here music. A song the whilst BASSANIO *comments on*
    the caskets to himself

[ONE FROM PORTIA'S TRAIN]
        Tell me where is fancy° bred,   *love; infatuation*
        Or° in the heart, or in the head?   *Whether*
65   How begot, how nourishèd?
[ALL]   Reply, reply.
[ONE FROM PORTIA'S TRAIN]
        It is engendered in the eyes,[7]
        With gazing fed; and fancy dies
        In the cradle[8] where it lies.
70   Let us all ring fancy's knell.
        I'll begin it: ding, dong, bell.
ALL   Ding, dong, bell.

BASSANIO [*aside*] So may the outward shows be least themselves.[9]
    The world is still° deceived with ornament.   *continually*
75   In law, what plea so tainted and corrupt
    But, being seasoned with a gracious voice,
    Obscures the show of evil? In religion,

---

4. The swan was thought to sing only once, just before its death.
5. It was customary to play music under a bridegroom's window on the morning of his wedding.
6. Alcides (Hercules) saved the Trojan princess Hesione when she was to be sacrificed to a sea monster,

not because he loved her but to win two horses her father offered as a reward.
7. Love was imagined to enter through the eyes.
8. In infancy, in the eyes (?)
9. Least express the truth.

What damnèd error but some sober brow
Will bless it and approve° it with a text,   *prove*
80 Hiding the grossness with fair ornament?
There is no vice so simple° but assumes   *unalloyed; stupid*
Some mark of virtue on his° outward parts.   *its*
How many cowards whose hearts are all as false
As stairs of sand, wear yet upon their chins
85 The beards of Hercules and frowning Mars,
Who, inward searched,° have livers white as milk?[1]   *examined*
And these assume but valour's excrement[2]
To render them redoubted.° Look on beauty   *feared*
And you shall see 'tis purchased by the weight,°   *(like cosmetics)*
90 Which therein works a miracle in nature,
Making them lightest° that wear most of it.   *most licentious*
So are those crispèd,° snaky, golden locks   *curled*
Which makes such wanton gambols with the wind
Upon supposèd fairness,° often known   *beauty*
95 To be the dowry° of a second head,   *endowment (in a wig)*
The skull that bred them in the sepulchre.
Thus ornament is but the guilèd° shore   *beguiling*
To a most dangerous sea, the beauteous scarf
Veiling an Indian° beauty; in a word,   *a swarthy (pejorative)*
100 The seeming truth which cunning times put on
To entrap the wisest. [*Aloud*] Therefore, thou gaudy gold,
Hard food for Midas,[3] I will none of thee.
[*To the silver casket*] Nor none of thee, thou pale and com-
            mon drudge°   *laborer (in coins)*
'Tween man and man. But thou, thou meagre lead,
105 Which rather threaten'st than dost promise aught,
Thy paleness moves me more than eloquence,
And here choose I. Joy be the consequence!
PORTIA [*aside*] How all the other passions fleet to air,
As° doubtful thoughts, and rash-embraced despair,   *Such as*
110 And shudd'ring fear, and green-eyed jealousy.
O love, be moderate! Allay thy ecstasy.
In measure rain thy joy; scant° this excess.[4]   *lessen*
I feel too much thy blessing: make it less,
For fear I surfeit.
            [BASSANIO *opens the leaden casket*]
BASSANIO   What find I here?
115 Fair Portia's counterfeit.° What demi-god[5]   *likeness*
Hath come so near creation? Move these eyes?
Or whether, riding on the balls of mine,°   *my eyes*
Seem they in motion? Here are severed lips
Parted with sugar breath. So sweet a bar
120 Should sunder such sweet friends. Here in her hairs
The painter plays the spider, and hath woven
A golden mesh t'untrap° the hearts of men   *entrap (phonetic?)*
Faster than gnats in cobwebs. But her eyes—
How could he see to do them? Having made one,

1. Lily-livered (the liver was considered the seat of   turned to gold.
courage).   4. Synonym for "interest" or "usury."
2. External attribute; hair (the beard).   5. Supernaturally gifted painter.
3. Everything King Midas touched, including his food,

125 Methinks it should have power to steal both his
And leave itself unfurnished.° Yet look how far   *unaccompanied*
The substance of my praise doth wrong this shadow°   *portrait*
In underprizing° it, so far this shadow   *understating*
Doth limp behind the substance.° Here's the scroll,   *real thing (Portia)*
130 The continent° and summary of my fortune.   *container*
   'You that choose not by the view
   Chance as fair° and choose as true.   *Gamble as luckily*
   Since this fortune falls to you,
   Be content, and seek no new.
135   If you be well pleased with this,
   And hold your fortune for your bliss,
   Turn you where your lady is,
   And claim her with a loving kiss.'
A gentle scroll. Fair lady, by your leave,
140 I come by note to give[6] and to receive,
Like one of two contending in a prize,°   *contest*
That thinks he hath done well in people's eyes,
Hearing applause and universal shout,
Giddy in spirit, still gazing in a doubt
145 Whether those peals of praise be his° or no.   *for him*
So, thrice-fair lady, stand I even so,
As doubtful whether what I see be true
Until confirmed, signed, ratified by you.
PORTIA   You see me, Lord Bassanio, where I stand,
150 Such as I am. Though for myself alone
I would not be ambitious in my wish
To wish myself much better, yet for you
I would be trebled twenty times myself,
A thousand times more fair, ten thousand times more rich,
155 That only to stand high in your account°   *estimation*
I might in virtues, beauties, livings,° friends,   *possessions*
Exceed account. But the full sum of me
Is sum of something which, to term in gross,°   *to describe fully*
Is an unlessoned girl, unschooled, unpractisèd,
160 Happy° in this, she is not yet so old   *Fortunate*
But she may learn; happier than this,
She is not bred so dull but she can learn;
Happiest of all is that her gentle spirit
Commits itself to yours to be directed
165 As from her lord, her governor, her king.
Myself and what is mine to you and yours
Is now converted.° But° now I was the lord   *transferred / Just*
Of this fair mansion, master of my servants,
Queen o'er myself; and even now, but now,
170 This house, these servants, and this same myself
Are yours, my lord's. I give them with this ring,
Which when you part from, lose, or give away,
Let it presage the ruin of your love,
And be my vantage to exclaim on you.[7]
175 BASSANIO   Madam, you have bereft me of all words.
Only my blood speaks to you in my veins,

---

6. I come by written authorization to give a kiss; to give myself.   7. And be my opportunity to reproach you.

And there is such confusion in my powers°   *faculties*
As after some oration fairly spoke
By a belovèd prince there doth appear
180 Among the buzzing pleasèd multitude,
Where every something being blent° together   *blended*
Turns to a wild° of nothing save of joy,   *chaos*
Expressed and not expressed. But when this ring
Parts from this finger, then parts life from hence.
185 O, then be bold to say° Bassanio's dead.   *say confidently*

NERISSA   My lord and lady, it is now our time
That have stood by and seen our wishes prosper
To cry 'Good joy, good joy, my lord and lady!'

GRAZIANO   My lord Bassanio, and my gentle lady,
190 I wish you all the joy that you can wish,
For I am sure you can wish none from me.[8]
And when your honours mean to solemnize
The bargain of your faith, I do beseech you
Even at that time I may be married too.

195 BASSANIO   With all my heart, so° thou canst get a wife.   *if*

GRAZIANO   I thank your lordship, you have got me one.
My eyes, my lord, can look as swift as yours.
You saw the mistress, I beheld the maid.
You loved, I loved; for intermission°   *delay*
200 No more pertains to me, my lord, than you.
Your fortune stood upon the caskets there,
And so did mine too, as the matter falls;
For wooing here until I sweat again,°   *repeatedly*
And swearing till my very roof° was dry   *(of his mouth)*
205 With oaths of love, at last—if promise[9] last—
I got a promise of this fair one here
To have her love, provided that your fortune
Achieved her mistress.

PORTIA   Is this true, Nerissa?

NERISSA   Madam, it is, so you stand pleased withal.

210 BASSANIO   And do you, Graziano, mean good faith?

GRAZIANO   Yes, faith, my lord.

BASSANIO   Our feast shall be much honoured in your marriage.

GRAZIANO [*to* NERISSA]   We'll play° with them the first boy for a   *wager*
thousand ducats.

215 NERISSA   What, and stake down?[1]

GRAZIANO   No, we shall ne'er win at that sport and stake down.

Enter LORENZO, JESSICA, *and* SALERIO, *a messenger from*
Venice

But who comes here? Lorenzo and his infidel!
What, and my old Venetian friend Salerio!

BASSANIO   Lorenzo and Salerio, welcome hither,
220 If that the youth of my new int'rest° here   *position*
Have power° to bid you welcome. [*To* PORTIA] By your leave,   *Gives me the right*
I bid my very° friends and countrymen,   *true*
Sweet Portia, welcome.

PORTIA   So do I, my lord. They are entirely welcome.

225 LORENZO   I thank your honour. For my part, my lord,

8. You do not need my good wishes.
9. Nerissa's, to wed Graziano.

1. Put the money down now (Graziano follows with a bawdy joke on "flaccid penis").

My purpose was not to have seen you here,
But meeting with Salerio by the way
He did entreat me past all saying nay
To come with him along.

SALERIO   I did, my lord,
230   And I have reason for it. Signor Antonio
Commends him° to you.   *Sends greeting*
        [*He gives* BASSANIO *a letter*]
BASSANIO   Ere I ope his letter
I pray you tell me how my good friend doth.
SALERIO   Not sick, my lord, unless it be in mind;
Nor well, unless in mind. His letter there
235   Will show you his estate.°   *situation*
        [BASSANIO] *opens the letter* [*and reads*]
GRAZIANO   Nerissa, [*indicating* JESSICA] cheer yon stranger. Bid
her welcome.
Your hand, Salerio. What's the news from Venice?
How doth that royal° merchant good Antonio?   *princely*
I know he will be glad of our success.
240   We are the Jasons; we have won the fleece.
SALERIO   I would you had won the fleece° that he hath lost.   *(punning on "fleets")*
PORTIA   There are some shrewd° contents in yon same paper   *evil*
That steals the colour from Bassanio's cheek.
Some dear friend dead, else nothing in the world
245   Could turn° so much the constitution   *change*
Of any constant° man. What, worse and worse?   *resolute*
With leave, Bassanio, I am half yourself,
And I must freely have the half of anything
That this same paper brings you.
BASSANIO   O sweet Portia,
250   Here are a few of the unpleasant'st words
That ever blotted paper. Gentle lady,
When I did first impart my love to you
I freely told you all the wealth I had
Ran in my veins: I was a gentleman;
255   And then I told you true; and yet, dear lady,
Rating myself at nothing, you shall see
How much I was a braggart. When I told you
My state° was nothing, I should then have told you   *wealth*
That I was worse than nothing, for indeed
260   I have engaged° myself to a dear friend,   *pledged*
Engaged my friend to his mere° enemy,   *utter*
To feed my means. Here is a letter, lady,
The paper° as the body of my friend,   *(ripped open)*
And every word in it a gaping wound
265   Issuing life-blood. But is it true, Salerio?
Hath all his ventures failed? What, not one hit?°   *success*
From Tripolis, from Mexico, and England,
From Lisbon, Barbary, and India,
And not one vessel scape the dreadful touch
270   Of merchant-marring rocks?
SALERIO   Not one, my lord.
Besides, it should appear that if he had
The present° money to discharge° the Jew   *ready / pay*
He° would not take it. Never did I know   *(Shylock)*

A creature that did bear the shape of man
275 So keen° and greedy to confound° a man.   *eager/destroy*
He plies the Duke at morning and at night,
And doth impeach the freedom of the state²
If they deny him justice. Twenty merchants,
The Duke himself, and the magnificoes°   *Venetian magnates*
280 Of greatest port,° have all persuaded° with him,   *dignity/argued*
But none can drive him from the envious° plea   *malicious*
Of forfeiture, of justice, and his bond.
JESSICA   When I was with him I have heard him swear
To Tubal and to Cush, his countrymen,
285 That he would rather have Antonio's flesh
Than twenty times the value of the sum
That he did owe him; and I know, my lord,
If law, authority, and power deny not,
It will go hard with poor Antonio.
290 PORTIA [*to* BASSANIO]   Is it your dear friend that is thus in trouble?
BASSANIO   The dearest friend to me, the kindest man,
The best-conditioned° and unwearied spirit   *best-natured*
In doing courtesies, and one in whom
The ancient Roman honour more appears
295 Than any that draws breath in Italy.
PORTIA   What sum owes he the Jew?
BASSANIO   For me, three thousand ducats.
PORTIA   What, no more?
Pay him six thousand and deface° the bond.   *destroy*
Double six thousand, and then treble that,
300 Before a friend of this description
Shall lose a hair thorough Bassanio's fault.
First go with me to church and call me wife,
And then away to Venice to your friend;
For never shall you lie by Portia's side
305 With an unquiet soul. You shall have gold
To pay the petty debt twenty times over.
When it is paid, bring your true friend along.
My maid Nerissa and myself meantime
Will live as maids and widows. Come, away,
310 For you shall hence upon your wedding day.
Bid your friends welcome, show a merry cheer.°   *countenance*
Since you are dear° bought, I will love you dear.°   *expensively/dearly*
But let me hear the letter of your friend.
BASSANIO [*reads*]   'Sweet Bassanio, my ships have all miscarried,
315 my creditors grow cruel, my estate is very low, my bond to the
Jew is forfeit, and since in paying it, it is impossible I should
live, all debts are cleared between you and I if I might but see
you at my death. Notwithstanding, use your pleasure.° If your   *follow your wishes*
love do not persuade you to come, let not my letter.'
320 PORTIA   O, love! Dispatch all business, and be gone.
BASSANIO   Since I have your good leave to go away
I will make haste, but till I come again
No bed shall e'er be guilty of my stay
Nor rest be interposer 'twixt us twain.   *Exeunt*

---

2. Accuse the state of not preserving commercial liberty.

3.3

Enter [SHYLOCK] *the Jew,* SOLANIO, ANTONIO, *and the*
jailer

SHYLOCK   Jailer, look to him. Tell not me of mercy.
This is the fool that lent out money gratis.
Jailer, look to him.

ANTONIO   Hear me yet, good Shylock.

SHYLOCK   I'll have my bond. Speak not against my bond.
5   I have sworn an oath that I will have my bond.
Thou called'st me dog before thou hadst a cause,
But since I am a dog, beware my fangs.
The Duke shall grant me justice. I do wonder,
Thou naughty° jailer, that thou art so fond°   wicked/foolish
10   To come abroad° with him at his request.   outside

ANTONIO   I pray thee hear me speak.

SHYLOCK   I'll have my bond. I will not hear thee speak.
I'll have my bond, and therefore speak no more.
I'll not be made a soft and dull-eyed° fool   gullible
15   To shake the head, relent, and sigh, and yield
To Christian intercessors. Follow not.
I'll have no speaking. I will have my bond.   *Exit*

SOLANIO   It is the most impenetrable cur
That ever kept° with men.   lived

ANTONIO   Let him alone.
20   I'll follow him no more with bootless° prayers.   fruitless
He seeks my life. His reason well I know:
I oft delivered° from his forfeitures   saved
Many that have at times made moan to me.
Therefore he hates me.

SOLANIO   I am sure the Duke
25   Will never grant this forfeiture to hold.

ANTONIO   The Duke cannot deny° the course of law,   prevent
For the commodity that strangers[1] have
With us in Venice, if it be denied,
Will much impeach the justice of the state,
30   Since that the trade and profit of the city
Consisteth of all nations. Therefore go.
These griefs and losses have so bated° me   diminished
That I shall hardly spare a pound of flesh
Tomorrow to my bloody creditor.
35   Well, jailer, on. Pray God Bassanio come
To see me pay his debt, and then I care not.   *Exeunt*

3.4

Enter PORTIA, NERISSA, LORENZO, JESSICA, *and*
[BALTHASAR,] *a man of Portia's*

LORENZO [*to* PORTIA]   Madam, although I speak it in your presence,
You have a noble and a true conceit°   conception
Of godlike amity, which appears most strongly
In bearing thus the absence of your lord.
5   But if you knew to whom you show this honour,

3.3 Location: Street in Venice.   3.4 Location: Belmont.
1. For the trading privileges that foreigners (including
Jews).

How true a gentleman you send relief,
How dear a lover° of my lord your husband,   *friend*
I know you would be prouder of the work
Than customary bounty can enforce you.[1]

10 PORTIA I never did repent for doing good,
Nor shall not now; for in companions
That do converse and waste° the time together,   *spend (not pejorative)*
Whose souls do bear an equal yoke of love,
There must be needs a like proportion
15 Of lineaments, of manners, and of spirit,
Which makes me think that this Antonio,
Being the bosom lover of my lord,
Must needs be like my lord. If it be so,
How little is the cost I have bestowed
20 In purchasing the semblance of my soul[2]
From out the state of hellish cruelty.
This comes too near the praising of myself,
Therefore no more of it. Hear other things:
Lorenzo, I commit into your hands
25 The husbandry° and manage of my house   *care*
Until my lord's return. For mine own part,
I have toward heaven breathed a secret vow
To live in prayer and contemplation,
Only attended by Nerissa here,
30 Until her husband and my lord's return.
There is a monastery two miles off,
And there we will abide. I do desire you
Not to deny this imposition,°   *decline this charge*
The which my love and some necessity
Now lays upon you.

35 LORENZO   Madam, with all my heart,
I shall obey you in all fair commands.

PORTIA My people do already know my mind,
And will acknowledge you and Jessica
In place of Lord Bassanio and myself.
40 So fare you well till we shall meet again.

LORENZO Fair thoughts and happy hours attend on you!

JESSICA I wish your ladyship all heart's content.

PORTIA I thank you for your wish, and am well pleased
To wish it back on you. Fare you well, Jessica.

         Exeunt [LORENZO *and* JESSICA]
45 Now, Balthasar,
As I have ever found thee honest-true,
So let me find thee still. Take this same letter,
And use thou all th'endeavour of a man
In speed to Padua. See thou render this
50 Into my cousin's hands, Doctor Bellario,
And look what notes and garments he doth give thee,
Bring them, I pray thee, with imagined° speed   *all imaginable*
Unto the traject,° to the common° ferry   *ferry / public*
Which trades° to Venice. Waste no time in words,   *goes back and forth*
55 But get thee gone. I shall be there before thee.

BALTHASAR Madam, I go with all convenient° speed.   [*Exit*]   *due*

---

1. Than ordinary generosity permits you.   2. In redeeming the likeness of my Bassanio (Antonio).

PORTIA   Come on, Nerissa. I have work in hand
         That you yet know not of. We'll see our husbands
         Before they think of us.
NERISSA   Shall they see us?
60 PORTIA   They shall, Nerissa, but in such a habit°   *garb*
         That they shall think we are accomplishèd°   *equipped*
         With that we lack.° I'll hold thee any wager,   *(i.e., penises)*
         When we are both accoutered like young men
         I'll prove the prettier fellow of the two,
65   And wear my dagger with the braver grace,
         And speak between the change of man and boy
         With a reed° voice, and turn two mincing steps   *piping*
         Into a manly stride, and speak of frays
         Like a fine bragging youth, and tell quaint° lies   *elaborate*
70   How honourable ladies sought my love,
         Which I denying, they fell sick and died.
         I could not do withal.° Then I'll repent,   *help it*
         And wish for all that that I had not killed them;
         And twenty of these puny lies I'll tell,
75   That men shall swear I have discontinued° school   *been out of*
         Above° a twelvemonth. I have within my mind   *At least*
         A thousand raw tricks of these bragging Jacks°   *fellows*
         Which I will practise.
NERISSA   Why, shall we turn to³ men?
80 PORTIA   Fie, what a question's that
         If thou wert near a lewd interpreter!
         But come, I'll tell thee all my whole device°   *plan*
         When I am in my coach, which stays for us
         At the park gate; and therefore haste away,
85   For we must measure twenty miles today.   *Exeunt*

3.5

Enter [LANCELOT] the clown, and JESSICA

LANCELOT   Yes, truly; for look you, the sins of the father are to
         be laid upon the children, therefore I promise you I fear° you.   *fear for*
         I was always plain with you, and so now I speak my agitation°   *(for "cogitation")*
         of the matter, therefore be o' good cheer, for truly I think you
5   are damned. There is but one hope in it that can do you any
         good, and that is but a kind of bastard hope, neither.
JESSICA   And what hope is that, I pray thee?
LANCELOT   Marry, you may partly hope that your father got you
         not, that you are not the Jew's daughter.
10 JESSICA   That were a kind of bastard hope indeed. So the sins
         of my mother should be visited upon me.
LANCELOT   Truly then, I fear you are damned both by father and
         mother. Thus, when I shun Scylla your father, I fall into
         Charybdis your mother.¹ Well, you are gone° both ways.   *doomed*
15 JESSICA   I shall be saved by my husband.² He hath made me a
         Christian.
LANCELOT   Truly, the more to blame he! We were Christians

---

3. Turn into (with bawdy suggestion).
3.5 Location: Portia's garden in Belmont.
1. Scylla was a mythological sea monster, Charybdis a
whirlpool in the Strait of Messina. Mariners had to avoid
both, a proverbially difficult task.
2. "The unbelieving wife is sanctified by the husband"
(1 Corinthians 7:14).

enough before, e'en as many as could well live one by another.[3]
This making of Christians will raise the price of hogs. If we
20   grow all to be pork-eaters we shall not shortly have a rasher° on   *bacon strip*
the coals for money.°   *any price*

     Enter LORENZO

JESSICA   I'll tell my husband, Lancelot, what you say. Here he
comes.
LORENZO   I shall grow jealous of you shortly, Lancelot, if you
25   thus get my wife into corners.
JESSICA   Nay, you need not fear us, Lorenzo. Lancelot and I are
out.° He tells me flatly there's no mercy for me in heaven   *quarreling*
because I am a Jew's daughter, and he says you are no good
member of the commonwealth, for in converting Jews to Chris-
30   tians you raise the price of pork.
LORENZO [*to* LANCELOT]   I shall answer° that better to the com-   *explain*
monwealth than you can the getting up of the Negro's belly.
The Moor[4] is with child by you, Lancelot.
LANCELOT   It is much that the Moor should be more than rea-
35   son,[5] but if she be less than an honest° woman, she is indeed   *a chaste*
more than I took her for.
LORENZO   How every fool can play upon the word! I think the
best grace of wit will shortly turn into silence, and discourse
grow commendable in none only but parrots. Go in, sirrah, bid
40   them prepare for dinner.
LANCELOT   That is done, sir. They have all stomachs.°   *appetites*
LORENZO   Goodly Lord, what a wit-snapper are you! Then bid
them prepare dinner.
LANCELOT   That is done too, sir; only 'cover'[6] is the word.
45   LORENZO   Will you cover then, sir?
LANCELOT   Not so, sir, neither. I know my duty.
LORENZO   Yet more quarrelling with occasion![7] Wilt thou show
the whole wealth of thy wit in an instant? I pray thee understand a plain man in his plain meaning. Go to thy fellows; bid
50   them cover the table, serve in the meat, and we will come in
to dinner.
LANCELOT   For the table,° sir, it shall be served in. For the meat,   *meal*
sir, it shall be covered.[8] For your coming in to dinner, sir, why,
let it be as humours and conceits° shall govern.   *Exit*   *whims and notions*
55   LORENZO   O dear discretion, how his words are suited![9]
The fool hath planted in his memory
An army of good words, and I do know
A many fools that stand in better place,
Garnished° like him, that for a tricksy word   *Provided (with words)*
60   Defy the matter.° How cheer'st thou,[1] Jessica?   *Refuse to talk sense*
And now, good sweet, say thy opinion:
How dost thou like the Lord Bassanio's wife?
JESSICA   Past all expressing. It is very meet°   *proper*
The Lord Bassanio live an upright life,
65   For, having such a blessing in his lady,

---

3. *well . . . another*: reside next door to one another;
earn a living off one another.
4. Apparently an African woman of Portia's household.
5. Should be bigger than is reasonable (punning on
"more/ Moor").
6. Set the table; but Lancelot puns on "cover" as meaning "put on the hat."

7. Playing on words whenever possible.
8. Served in covered dishes (playfully or unconsciously
reversing Lorenzo's instructions).
9. Adapted to the occasion. *dear discretion*: precious
discrimination (ironic).
1. How are you.

He finds the joys of heaven here on earth,
And if on earth he do not merit it,
In reason he should never come to heaven.
Why, if two gods should play some heavenly match
70 And on the wager lay two earthly women,
And Portia one, there must be something else
Pawned° with the other; for the poor rude world   *Wagered*
Hath not her fellow.

LORENZO   Even such a husband
Hast thou of me as she is for a wife.

75 JESSICA   Nay, but ask my opinion too of that!

LORENZO   I will anon.° First let us go to dinner.   *soon*

JESSICA   Nay, let me praise you while I have a stomach.°   *an appetite; desire*

LORENZO   No, pray thee, let it serve for table-talk.
Then, howsome'er° thou speak'st, 'mong other things   *however*
I shall digest° it.   *ingest; analyze*

80 JESSICA   Well, I'll set you forth.²   *Exeunt*

4.1

Enter the DUKE, *the magnificoes,* ANTONIO, BASSANIO,
      GRAZIANO, *and* [SALERIO]

DUKE   What, is Antonio here?

ANTONIO   Ready, so please your grace.

DUKE   I am sorry for thee. Thou art come to answer
A stony adversary, an inhuman wretch
Uncapable of pity, void and empty
From any dram° of mercy.   *trace*

5 ANTONIO   I have heard
Your grace hath ta'en great pains to qualify°   *alleviate*
His rigorous course, but since he stands obdurate,
And that no lawful means can carry me
Out of his envy's° reach, I do oppose   *malice's*
10 My patience to his fury, and am armed°   *prepared*
To suffer with a quietness of spirit
The very tyranny° and rage of his.   *cruelty*

DUKE   Go one, and call the Jew into the court.

SALERIO   He is ready at the door. He comes, my lord.

Enter SHYLOCK

15 DUKE   Make room, and let him stand before our° face.   *(the royal "we")*
Shylock, the world thinks—and I think so too—
That thou but lead'st this fashion° of thy malice   *sustain the pretense*
To the last hour of act,° and then 'tis thought   *brink of performance*
Thou'lt show thy mercy and remorse° more strange°   *compassion / extraordinary*
20 Than is thy strange apparent cruelty,
And where thou now exacts the penalty—
Which is a pound of this poor merchant's flesh—
Thou wilt not only loose° the forfeiture,   *waive*
But, touched with human gentleness and love,
25 Forgive a moiety° of the principal,   *part*
Glancing an eye of pity on his losses,
That have of late so huddled° on his back   *piled*
Enough to press a royal merchant down

2. I'll serve you up (like a dinner); I'll extol you.   4.1 Location: The Venetian court.

And pluck commiseration of his state
30 From brassy° bosoms and rough hearts of flint,   *unfeeling*
From stubborn Turks and Tartars never trained
To offices° of tender courtesy.   *acts*
We all expect a gentle answer, Jew.

SHYLOCK   I have possessed° your grace of what I purpose,   *informed*
35 And by our holy Sabbath have I sworn
To have the due and forfeit of my bond.
If you deny it, let the danger° light   *damage*
Upon your charter and your city's freedom.
You'll ask me why I rather choose to have
40 A weight of carrion flesh than to receive
Three thousand ducats. I'll not answer that,
But say it is my humour.° Is it answered?   *caprice*
What if my house be troubled with a rat,
And I be pleased to give ten thousand ducats
45 To have it baned?° What, are you answered yet?   *poisoned*
Some men there are love not a gaping pig,[1]
Some that are mad if they behold a cat,
And others when the bagpipe sings i'th' nose
Cannot contain their urine; for affection,°   *impulse*
50 Mistress of passion, sways it to the mood
Of what it likes or loathes. Now for your answer:
As there is no firm reason to be rendered
Why he° cannot abide a gaping pig,   *one man*
Why he° a harmless necessary cat,   *another*
55 Why he° a woollen bagpipe, but of force°   *yet another / necessarily*
Must yield to such inevitable shame
As to offend himself being offended,
So can I give no reason, nor I will not,
More than a lodged° hate and a certain loathing   *settled*
60 I bear Antonio, that I follow thus
A losing° suit against him. Are you answered?   *An unprofitable*

BASSANIO   This is no answer, thou unfeeling man,
To excuse the current of thy cruelty.

SHYLOCK   I am not bound to please thee with my answers.
65 BASSANIO   Do all men kill the things they do not love?

SHYLOCK   Hates any man the thing he would not kill?

BASSANIO   Every offence is not a hate at first.

SHYLOCK   What, wouldst thou have a serpent sting thee twice?

ANTONIO   I pray you think you question° with the Jew.   *dispute*
70 You may as well go stand upon the beach
And bid the main flood bate his° usual height;   *high tide reduce its*
You may as well use question with the wolf
Why he hath made the ewe bleat for the lamb;
You may as well forbid the mountain pines
75 To wag their high tops and to make no noise
When they are fretten° with the gusts of heaven,   *fretted; agitated*
You may as well do anything most hard
As seek to soften that—than which what's harder?—
His Jewish heart. Therefore, I do beseech you,
80 Make no more offers, use no farther means,

---

1. Roasted pig with its mouth propped open.

But with all brief and plain conveniency°   *suitability*
Let me have judgement and the Jew his will.
BASSANIO [*to* SHYLOCK]   For thy three thousand ducats here is six.
SHYLOCK   If every ducat in six thousand ducats
85   Were in six parts, and every part a ducat,
I would not draw° them. I would have my bond.   *take*
DUKE   How shalt thou hope for mercy, rend'ring none?
SHYLOCK   What judgement shall I dread, doing no wrong?
You have among you many a purchased slave
90   Which, like your asses and your dogs and mules,
You use in abject and in slavish parts°   *roles*
Because you bought them. Shall I say to you
'Let them be free, marry them to your heirs.
Why sweat they under burdens? Let their beds
95   Be made as soft as yours, and let their palates
Be seasoned with such viands.'° You will answer   *food*
'The slaves are ours.' So do I answer you.
The pound of flesh which I demand of him
Is dearly bought. 'Tis mine, and I will have it.
100   If you deny me, fie upon your law:
There is no force in the decrees of Venice.
I stand for judgement. Answer: shall I have it?
DUKE   Upon° my power I may dismiss this court   *In accordance with*
Unless Bellario, a learnèd doctor
105   Whom I have sent for to determine° this,   *resolve*
Come here today.
SALERIO   My lord, here stays without°   *waits outside*
A messenger with letters from the doctor,
New come from Padua.
DUKE   Bring us the letters. Call the messenger. [*Exit* SALERIO]
110 BASSANIO   Good cheer, Antonio. What, man, courage yet!
The Jew shall have my flesh, blood, bones, and all
Ere thou shalt lose for me one drop of blood.
ANTONIO   I am a tainted wether° of the flock,   *castrated ram*
Meetest for death.° The weakest kind of fruit   *Most fit for slaughter*
115   Drops earliest to the ground; and so let me.
You cannot better be employed, Bassanio,
Than to live still and write mine epitaph.

       Enter [SALERIO, *with*] NERISSA [*apparelled as a judge's*
       clerk]

DUKE   Came you from Padua, from Bellario?
NERISSA   From both, my lord. Bellario greets your grace.
       [*She gives a letter to the* DUKE.
       SHYLOCK *whets his knife on his shoe*]
120 BASSANIO [*to* SHYLOCK]   Why dost thou whet thy knife so earnestly?
SHYLOCK   To cut the forfeit from that bankrupt there.
GRAZIANO   Not on thy sole but on thy soul, harsh Jew,
Thou mak'st thy knife keen. But no metal can,
No, not the hangman's° axe, bear° half the keenness   *executioner's / have*
125   Of thy sharp envy.° Can no prayers pierce thee?   *malice*
SHYLOCK   No, none that thou hast wit enough to make.
GRAZIANO   O, be thou damned, inexorable dog,
And for thy life° let justice be accused!   *for allowing you to live*
Thou almost mak'st me waver in my faith

130 To hold opinion with Pythagoras[2]
That souls of animals infuse themselves
Into the trunks of men. Thy currish spirit
Governed a wolf who, hanged for human slaughter,[3]
Even from the gallows did his fell soul fleet,°   *his cruel soul flit*
135 And, whilst thou lay'st in thy unhallowed dam,
Infused itself in thee; for thy desires
Are wolvish, bloody, starved, and ravenous.
SHYLOCK   Till thou canst rail the seal from off my bond
Thou but offend'st° thy lungs to speak so loud.   *hurt*
140 Repair thy wit, good youth, or it will fall
To cureless° ruin. I stand here for law.   *incurable*
DUKE   This letter from Bellario doth commend
A young and learnèd doctor to our court.
Where is he?
NERISSA   He attendeth here hard by
145 To know your answer, whether you'll admit him.
DUKE   With all my heart. Some three or four of you
Go give him courteous conduct° to this place.   *escort*
                                    [Exeunt three or four]
Meantime the court shall hear Bellario's letter.
[Reads] 'Your grace shall understand that at the receipt of your
150 letter I am very sick, but in the instant that your messenger
came, in loving visitation was with me a young doctor of Rome;
his name is Balthasar. I acquainted him with the cause in controversy between the Jew and Antonio, the merchant. We
turned o'er many books together. He is furnished with my opin-
155 ion which, bettered with his own learning—the greatness
whereof I cannot enough commend—comes with him at my
importunity to fill up° your grace's request in my stead. I   *answer*
beseech you let his lack of years be no impediment to let him
lack° a reverend estimation, for I never knew so young a body   *keep him from having*
160 with so old a head. I leave him to your gracious acceptance,
whose trial shall better publish his commendation.'[4]
        Enter [three or four with] PORTIA *[as Balthasar]*
You hear the learn'd Bellario, what he writes;
And here, I take it, is the doctor come.
[To PORTIA   Give me your hand. Come you from old Bellario?
PORTIA   I did, my lord.
165 DUKE   You are welcome. Take your place.
Are you acquainted with the difference°   *dispute*
That holds this present question[5] in the court?
PORTIA   I am informèd throughly° of the cause.°   *thoroughly / case*
Which is the merchant here, and which the Jew?
170 DUKE   Antonio and old Shylock, both stand forth.
        *[*ANTONIO *and* SHYLOCK *stand forth]*
PORTIA   Is your name Shylock?
SHYLOCK   Shylock is my name.
PORTIA   Of a strange nature is the suit you follow,
Yet in such rule° that the Venetian law   *order*

---

2. Greek philosopher who believed in the transmigration of souls.
3. In Elizabethan times, animals were tried and hanged
for wrongdoing; possibly an allusion to the 1594 execution of the Jewish physician Lopez (Latin *lupus*, "wolf").
4. Whose performance ("trial") shall better make
known his worth.
5. That is now being tried.

Cannot impugn you as you do proceed.

175 [*To* ANTONIO] You stand within his danger,° do you not?   *power to harm*

ANTONIO   Ay, so he says.

PORTIA   Do you confess the bond?

ANTONIO   I do.

PORTIA   Then must the Jew be merciful.

SHYLOCK   On what compulsion must I? Tell me that.

PORTIA   The quality of mercy is not strained.°   *compelled*

180 It droppeth as the gentle rain from heaven
Upon the place beneath. It is twice blest:
It blesseth him that gives, and him that takes.
'Tis mightiest in the mightiest. It becomes
The thronèd monarch better than his crown.

185 His sceptre shows the force of temporal power,
The attribute to° awe and majesty,   *of*
Wherein doth sit the dread and fear of kings;
But mercy is above this sceptred sway.
It is enthronèd in the hearts of kings;

190 It is an attribute to God himself,
And earthly power doth then show likest° God's   *most like*
When mercy seasons° justice. Therefore, Jew,   *moderates*
Though justice be thy plea, consider this:
That in the course of justice none of us

195 Should see salvation. We do pray for mercy,
And that same prayer° doth teach us all to render   *(the Lord's Prayer)*
The deeds of mercy. I have spoke thus much
To mitigate the justice of thy plea,°   *your demand for justice*
Which if thou follow, this strict court of Venice

200 Must needs give sentence 'gainst the merchant there.

SHYLOCK   My deeds upon my head![6] I crave the law,
The penalty and forfeit of my bond.

PORTIA   Is he not able to discharge the money?

BASSANIO   Yes, here I tender it for him in the court,

205 Yea, twice the sum. If that will not suffice
I will be bound to pay it ten times o'er
On forfeit of my hands, my head, my heart.
If this will not suffice, it must appear
That malice bears down° truth. And, I beseech you,   *overwhelms*

210 Wrest once° the law to your authority.   *For once twist*
To do a great right, do a little wrong,
And curb this cruel devil of his will.

PORTIA   It must not be. There is no power in Venice
Can alter a decree establishèd.

215 'Twill be recorded for a precedent,
And many an error by the same example
Will rush into the state. It cannot be.

SHYLOCK   A Daniel come to judgement, yea, a Daniel![7]
O wise young judge, how I do honour thee!

220 PORTIA   I pray you let me look upon the bond.

SHYLOCK   Here 'tis, most reverend doctor, here it is.

PORTIA   Shylock, there's thrice thy money offered thee.

---

6. The Jewish crowd at Jesus' trial cried, "His blood be   of Susanna, accused of inchastity by the Elders; he res-
on us, and on our children" (Matthew 27:25).   cues her and convicts them.
7. In the Apocrypha, the youth Daniel judges the case

SHYLOCK An oath, an oath! I have an oath in heaven.
Shall I lay perjury upon my soul?
No, not for Venice.

225 PORTIA   Why, this bond is forfeit,
And lawfully by this the Jew may claim
A pound of flesh, to be by him cut off
Nearest the merchant's heart. [*To* SHYLOCK] Be merciful.
Take thrice thy money. Bid me tear the bond.

230 SHYLOCK When it is paid according to the tenor.°   *condition*
It doth appear you are a worthy judge.
You know the law. Your exposition
Hath been most sound. I charge you, by the law
Whereof you are a well-deserving pillar,

235 Proceed to judgement. By my soul I swear
There is no power in the tongue of man
To alter me. I stay° here on my bond.   *insist*
ANTONIO Most heartily I do beseech the court
To give the judgement.
PORTIA   Why, then thus it is:

240 You must prepare your bosom for his knife—
SHYLOCK O noble judge, O excellent young man!
PORTIA For the intent and purpose of the law
Hath full relation to[8] the penalty
Which here appeareth due upon the bond.

245 SHYLOCK 'Tis very true. O wise and upright judge!
How much more elder art thou than thy looks!
PORTIA [*to* ANTONIO] Therefore lay bare your bosom.
SHYLOCK   Ay, his breast.
So says the bond, doth it not, noble judge?
'Nearest his heart'—those are the very words.

250 PORTIA It is so. Are there balance° here to weigh the flesh?   *scales*
SHYLOCK I have them ready.
PORTIA Have by some surgeon, Shylock, on your charge°   *expense*
To stop his wounds, lest he do bleed to death.
SHYLOCK Is it so nominated in the bond?

255 PORTIA It is not so expressed, but what of that?
'Twere good you do so much for charity.
SHYLOCK I cannot find it. 'Tis not in the bond.
PORTIA [*to* ANTONIO] You, merchant, have you anything to say?
ANTONIO But little. I am armed and well prepared.

260 Give me your hand, Bassanio; fare you well.
Grieve not that I am fall'n to this for you,
For herein Fortune shows herself more kind
Than is her custom; it is still her use°   *commonly her habit*
To let the wretched man outlive his wealth

265 To view with hollow eye and wrinkled brow
An age of poverty, from which ling'ring penance
Of such misery doth she cut me off.
Commend me to your honourable wife.
Tell her the process° of Antonio's end.   *tale*

270 Say how I loved you. Speak me fair° in death,   *well of me*
And when the tale is told, bid her be judge
Whether Bassanio had not once a love.

8. Is entirely in agreement with.

Repent but you° that you shall lose your friend, *Sorrow only*
And he repents not that he pays your debt;
275   For if the Jew do cut but deep enough,
I'll pay it instantly, with all my heart.
BASSANIO   Antonio, I am married to a wife
Which is as dear to me as life itself,
But life itself, my wife, and all the world
280   Are not with me esteemed above thy life.
I would lose all, ay, sacrifice them all
Here to this devil, to deliver you.
PORTIA [*aside*]   Your wife would give you little thanks for that
If she were by to hear you make the offer.
285   GRAZIANO   I have a wife who, I protest, I love.
I would she were in heaven so she could
Entreat some power to change this currish Jew.
NERISSA [*aside*]   'Tis well you offer it behind her back;
The wish would make else an unquiet house.
290   SHYLOCK [*aside*]   These be the Christian husbands. I have a daughter.
Would any of the stock of Barabbas⁹
Had been her husband rather than a Christian.
[*Aloud*] We trifle° time. I pray thee pursue° sentence. *waste / proceed with*
PORTIA   A pound of that same merchant's flesh is thine.
295   The court awards it, and the law doth give it.
SHYLOCK   Most rightful judge!
PORTIA   And you must cut this flesh from off his breast.
The law allows it, and the court awards it.
SHYLOCK   Most learnèd judge! A sentence: [*to* ANTONIO] come, prepare.
300   PORTIA   Tarry a little. There is something else.
This bond doth give thee here no jot of blood.
The words expressly are 'a pound of flesh'.
Take then thy bond. Take thou thy pound of flesh.
But in the cutting it, if thou dost shed
305   One drop of Christian blood, thy lands and goods
Are by the laws of Venice confiscate
Unto the state of Venice.
GRAZIANO   O upright judge!
Mark, Jew! O learnèd judge!
SHYLOCK   Is that the law?
310   PORTIA   Thyself shalt see the act;
For as thou urgest justice, be assured
Thou shalt have justice more than thou desir'st.
GRAZIANO   O learnèd judge! Mark, Jew! O learnèd judge!
SHYLOCK   I take this offer, then. Pay the bond thrice,
And let the Christian go.
315   BASSANIO   Here is the money.
PORTIA   Soft,° the Jew shall have all justice. Soft, no haste. *Not so fast*
He shall have nothing but the penalty.
GRAZIANO   O Jew, an upright judge, a learnèd judge!
PORTIA [*to* SHYLOCK]   Therefore prepare thee to cut off the flesh.
320   Shed thou no blood, nor cut thou less nor more
But just° a pound of flesh. If thou tak'st more *exactly*
Or less than a just pound, be it but so much

---

9. Thief whom the Jews asked Pilate to set free instead of Jesus (Mark 15:6–15).

As makes it light or heavy in the substance°   *weight*
Or the division° of the twentieth part   *fraction*
325 Of one poor scruple°—nay, if the scale do turn   *tiny weight*
But in the estimation° of a hair,   *amount*
Thou diest, and all thy goods are confiscate.
GRAZIANO   A second Daniel, a Daniel, Jew!
Now, infidel, I have you on the hip.[1]
330 PORTIA   Why doth the Jew pause? Take thy forfeiture.
SHYLOCK   Give me my principal, and let me go.
BASSANIO   I have it ready for thee. Here it is.
PORTIA   He hath refused it in the open court.
He shall have merely justice and his bond.
335 GRAZIANO   A Daniel, still say I, a second Daniel!
I thank thee, Jew, for teaching me that word.
SHYLOCK   Shall I not have barely° my principal?   *even*
PORTIA   Thou shalt have nothing but the forfeiture
To be so taken at thy peril, Jew.
340 SHYLOCK   Why then, the devil give him good of it.
I'll stay no longer question.[2]
PORTIA   Tarry, Jew.
The law hath yet another hold on you.
It is enacted in the laws of Venice,
If it be proved against an alien
345 That by direct or indirect attempts
He seek the life of any citizen,
The party 'gainst the which he doth contrive°   *plot*
Shall seize one half his goods; the other half
Comes to the privy coffer° of the state,   *private treasury*
350 And the offender's life lies in° the mercy   *at*
Of the Duke only, 'gainst all other voice—
In which predicament I say thou stand'st,
For it appears by manifest proceeding
That indirectly, and directly too,
355 Thou hast contrived against the very life
Of the defendant, and thou hast incurred
The danger° formerly by me rehearsed.°   *penalty / described*
Down, therefore, and beg mercy of the Duke.
GRAZIANO [*to* SHYLOCK]   Beg that thou mayst have leave to hang thyself—
360 And yet, thy wealth being forfeit to the state,
Thou hast not left the value of a cord.
Therefore thou must be hanged at the state's charge.°   *expense*
DUKE [*to* SHYLOCK]   That thou shalt see the difference of our spirit,
I pardon thee thy life before thou ask it.
365 For half thy wealth, it is Antonio's.
The other half comes to the general state,
Which humbleness may drive° unto a fine.   *reduce*
PORTIA   Ay, for the state, not for Antonio.[3]
SHYLOCK   Nay, take my life and all, pardon not that.
370 You take my house when you do take the prop
That doth sustain my house; you take my life
When you do take the means whereby I live.[4]

---

1. At a disadvantage (see 1.3.41).
2. I'll press my case no further.
3. With respect to the state's half, not Antonio's.

4. "He that taketh away his neighbor's living, slayeth
him" (Ecclesiasties 34:22).

PORTIA   What mercy can you render him, Antonio?
GRAZIANO   A halter,° gratis. Nothing else, for God's sake. *hangman's noose*
375 ANTONIO   So please my lord the Duke and all the court
To quit the fine for one half of his goods,
I am content, so he will let me have
The other half in use,⁵ to render it
Upon his death unto the gentleman
380 That lately stole his daughter.
Two things provided more: that for this favour
He presently° become a Christian; *immediately*
The other, that he do record a gift
Here in the court of all he dies possessed
385 Unto his son, Lorenzo, and his daughter.
DUKE   He shall do this, or else I do recant° *withdraw*
The pardon that I late pronouncèd here.
PORTIA   Art thou contented, Jew? What dost thou say?
SHYLOCK   I am content.
390 PORTIA [*to* NERISSA]   Clerk, draw a deed of gift.
SHYLOCK   I pray you give me leave to go from hence.
I am not well. Send the deed after me,
And I will sign it.
DUKE   Get thee gone, but do it.
GRAZIANO [*to* SHYLOCK]   In christ'ning shalt thou have two godfathers.
395 Had I been judge thou shouldst have had ten more,° *(to constitute a jury)*
To bring thee to the gallows, not the font.   *Exit* [SHYLOCK]
DUKE [*to* PORTIA]   Sir, I entreat you home with me to dinner.
PORTIA   I humbly do desire your grace of pardon.
I must away this night toward Padua,
400 And it is meet° I presently set forth. *proper*
DUKE   I am sorry that your leisure serves you not.° *you haven't the time*
Antonio, gratify° this gentleman, *reward*
For in my mind you are much bound to him.
                              Exit DUKE *and his train*
BASSANIO [*to* PORTIA]   Most worthy gentleman, I and my friend
405 Have by your wisdom been this day acquitted
Of grievous penalties, in lieu whereof
Three thousand ducats due unto the Jew
We freely cope° your courteous pains withal. *repay*
ANTONIO   And stand indebted over and above
410 In love and service to you evermore.
PORTIA   He is well paid that is well satisfied,
And I, delivering you, am satisfied,
And therein do account myself well paid.
My mind was never yet more mercenary.
415 I pray you know me when we meet again.
I wish you well; and so I take my leave.
BASSANIO   Dear sir, of force° I must attempt you further. *necessity*
Take some remembrance of us as a tribute,
Not as fee. Grant me two things, I pray you:
420 Not to deny me, and to pardon me.° *excuse my urging*

5. Antonio's conditions are unclear, because "quit" in line 376 (requite) could mean "pardon" or "make him pay," and "in use" (line 378) could mean either "in trust" or "for my own purposes." But the arrangements for Shylock's property later in the scene suggest that Antonio succeeds in getting Shylock's penalty reduced: Shylock retains half of his wealth, and Antonio holds the other half in trust for Jessica and Lorenzo until Shylock dies, at which point they inherit the whole estate.

PORTIA You press me far, and therefore I will yield.
[*To* ANTONIO] Give me your gloves. I'll wear them for your sake.
[*To* BASSANIO] And for your love I'll take this ring from you.
Do not draw back your hand. I'll take no more,
425 And you in love shall not deny me this.
BASSANIO This ring, good sir? Alas, it is a trifle.
I will not shame myself to give you this.
PORTIA I will have nothing else, but only this;
And now, methinks, I have a mind to it.
430 BASSANIO There's more depends on this° than on the value.   *involved here*
The dearest ring in Venice will I give you,
And find it out by proclamation.
Only for this, I pray you pardon me.
PORTIA I see, sir, you are liberal in offers.
435 You taught me first to beg, and now methinks
You teach me how a beggar should be answered.
BASSANIO Good sir, this ring was given me by my wife,
And when she put it on she made me vow
That I should neither sell, nor give, nor lose it.
440 PORTIA That 'scuse serves many men to save their gifts.
An if° your wife be not a madwoman,   *An if = If*
And know how well I have deserved this ring,
She would not hold out enemy for ever
For giving it to me. Well, peace be with you.
                        Exeunt [PORTIA *and* NERISSA]
445 ANTONIO My lord Bassanio, let him have the ring.
Let his deservings and my love withal
Be valued 'gainst your wife's commandëment.
BASSANIO Go, Graziano, run and overtake him.
Give him the ring, and bring him, if thou canst,
450 Unto Antonio's house. Away, make haste.   *Exit* GRAZIANO
Come, you and I will thither presently,
And in the morning early will we both
Fly toward Belmont. Come, Antonio.   *Exeunt*

4.2

Enter PORTIA *and* NERISSA [*still disguised*]
PORTIA Enquire the Jew's house out, give him this deed,[1]
And let him sign it. We'll away tonight,
And be a day before our husbands home.
This deed will be well welcome to Lorenzo.
                        Enter GRAZIANO
5 GRAZIANO Fair sir, you are well o'erta'en.
My lord Bassanio upon more advice°   *further thought*
Hath sent you here this ring, and doth entreat
Your company at dinner.
PORTIA   That cannot be.
His ring I do accept most thankfully,
10 And so I pray you tell him. Furthermore,
I pray you show my youth old Shylock's house.
GRAZIANO That will I do.
NERISSA   Sir, I would speak with you.
[*Aside to* PORTIA] I'll see if I can get my husband's ring

4.2 Location: Street in Venice.   1. Mentioned in 4.1.390.

Which I did make him swear to keep for ever.

15 PORTIA [*aside to* NERISSA] Thou mayst; I warrant we shall have
  old° swearing   *lots of*
  That they did give the rings away to men.
  But we'll outface them, and outswear them too.
  Away, make haste. Thou know'st where I will tarry.

  [*Exit at one door*]

NERISSA [*to* GRAZIANO] Come, good sir, will you show me to this house?

  Exeunt [*at another door*]

5.1

Enter LORENZO *and* JESSICA

LORENZO The moon shines bright. In such a night as this,
  When the sweet wind did gently kiss the trees
  And they did make no noise—in such a night
  Troilus, methinks, mounted the Trojan walls,
5 And sighed his soul toward the Grecian tents
  Where Cressid lay that night.[1]

JESSICA   In such a night
  Did Thisbe fearfully o'ertrip the dew
  And saw the lion's shadow ere himself,
  And ran dismayed away.[2]

LORENZO   In such a night
10 Stood Dido with a willow in her hand
  Upon the wild sea banks, and waft her love
  To come again to Carthage.[3]

JESSICA   In such a night
  Medea gatherèd the enchanted herbs
  That did renew old Aeson.[4]

LORENZO   In such a night
15 Did Jessica steal° from the wealthy Jew,   *escape; rob*
  And with an unthrift° love did run from Venice   *a spendthrift*
  As far as Belmont.

JESSICA   In such a night
  Did young Lorenzo swear he loved her well,
  Stealing her soul with many vows of faith,
  And ne'er a true one.

20 LORENZO   In such a night
  Did pretty Jessica, like a little shrew,
  Slander her love, and he forgave it her.

JESSICA I would outnight you, did nobody come.
  But hark, I hear the footing° of a man.   *footsteps*

  Enter [STEFANO,] *a messenger*

25 LORENZO Who comes so fast in silence of the night?

STEFANO A friend.

LORENZO A friend—what friend? Your name, I pray you, friend?

STEFANO Stefano is my name, and I bring word

5.1 Location: Belmont.
1. Troilus was a Trojan Prince whose lover, Cressida, forsook him for the Greek Diomedes after she was sent from Troy to the Greek camp. See *Troilus and Cressida*.
2. Thisbe, going at night to meet her lover, Pyramus, was frightened by a lion and fled. Pyramus, assuming she was dead, killed himself; when she found his body, Thisbe committed suicide too. The story is dramatized

by "the rude mechanicals" in *A Midsummer Night's Dream*.
3. Dido, Queen of Carthage, was abandoned by her lover, the Trojan hero Aeneas. *willow*: emblem of forsaken love. *waft*: waved to.
4. Medea was a sorceress who loved Jason and helped him win the Golden Fleece; she magically restored Aeson, Jason's father, to youth.

My mistress will before the break of day
30 Be here at Belmont. She doth stray about
By holy crosses,° where she kneels and prays   *roadside shrines*
For happy wedlock hours.
LORENZO   Who comes with her?
STEFANO   None but a holy hermit and her maid.
I pray you, is my master yet returned?
35 LORENZO   He is not, nor we have not heard from him.
But go we in, I pray thee, Jessica,
And ceremoniously let us prepare
Some welcome for the mistress of the house.
        Enter [LANCELOT] *the clown*
LANCELOT [*calling*]   Sola, sola! Wo, ha, ho! Sola, sola!⁵
40 LORENZO   Who calls?
LANCELOT [*calling*]   Sola!—Did you see Master Lorenzo? [*Call-
ing*] Master Lorenzo! Sola, sola!
LORENZO   Leave hollering, man: here.
LANCELOT [*calling*]   Sola!—Where, where?
45 LORENZO   Here.
LANCELOT   Tell him there's a post° come from my master with his   *messenger*
horn full of good news. My master will be here ere morning.
                                        [*Exit*]
LORENZO [*to* JESSICA]   Sweet soul, let's in, and there expect°   *await*
        their coming.
And yet no matter. Why should we go in?
50 My friend Stefano, signify,° I pray you,   *announce*
Within the house your mistress is at hand,
And bring your music forth into the air.   *Exit* STEFANO
How sweet the moonlight sleeps upon this bank!
Here will we sit, and let the sounds of music
55 Creep in our ears. Soft stillness and the night
Become the touches⁶ of sweet harmony.
Sit, Jessica.
        [*They sit*]
                Look how the floor of heaven
Is thick inlaid with patens° of bright gold.   *disks*
There's not the smallest orb which thou behold'st
60 But in his motion like an angel sings,
Still° choiring to the young-eyed⁷ cherubins.   *Continually*
Such harmony⁸ is in immortal souls,
But whilst this muddy vesture of decay°   *this mortal body*
Doth grossly close it° in, we cannot hear it.°   *(the soul) / (the music)*
        [*Enter Musicians*]
65 [*To the Musicians*] Come, ho, and wake Diana⁹ with a hymn.
With sweetest touches pierce your mistress'° ear,   *(Portia's)*
And draw her home with music.
        [*The Musicians*] *play*
JESSICA   I am never merry when I hear sweet music.
LORENZO   The reason is your spirits are attentive,
70 For do but note a wild and wanton herd
Or race° of youthful and unhandled colts,   *group*

5. Imitating a messenger's horn.
6. Suit the notes (literally, the fingering of a stringed instrument).
7. Keen-sighted.
8. The music of the spheres.
9. Goddess of the moon and of chastity.

Fetching mad bounds, bellowing and neighing loud,
Which is the hot condition of their blood,
If they but hear perchance a trumpet sound,
75   Or any air of music touch their ears,
You shall perceive them make a mutual° stand,   *simultaneous*
Their savage eyes turned to a modest gaze
By the sweet power of music. Therefore the poet[1]
Did feign that Orpheus drew° trees, stones, and floods,   *allured*
80   Since naught so stockish,° hard, and full of rage   *stolid*
But music for the time doth change his nature.
The man that hath no music in himself,
Nor is not moved with concord of sweet sounds,
Is fit for treasons, stratagems,° and spoils.°   *plots / plunder*
85   The motions of his spirit are dull as night,
And his affections° dark as Erebus.°   *inclinations / hell*
Let no such man be trusted. Mark the music.

Enter PORTIA *and* NERISSA [*as themselves*]

PORTIA   That light we see is burning in my hall.
How far that little candle throws his beams—
90   So shines a good deed in a naughty° world.   *an evil*
NERISSA   When the moon shone we did not see the candle.
PORTIA   So doth the greater glory dim the less.
A substitute° shines brightly as a king   *deputy*
Until a king be by, and then his state
95   Empties itself as doth an inland brook
Into the main of waters.° Music, hark.   *the ocean*
NERISSA   It is your music, madam, of the house.
PORTIA   Nothing is good, I see, without respect.°   *reference to context*
Methinks it sounds much sweeter than by day.
100   NERISSA   Silence bestows that virtue on it, madam.
PORTIA   The crow doth sing as sweetly as the lark
When neither is attended,[2] and I think
The nightingale, if she should sing by day,
When every goose is cackling, would be thought
105   No better a musician than the wren.
How many things by season seasoned are[3]
To their right praise and true perfection!

[*She sees* LORENZO *and* JESSICA]

Peace, ho!

[*Music ceases*]

           The moon sleeps with Endymion,[4]
And would not be awaked.
LORENZO [*rising*]   That is the voice,
110   Or I am much deceived, of Portia.
PORTIA   He knows me as the blind man knows the cuckoo—
By the bad voice.
LORENZO   Dear lady, welcome home.
PORTIA   We have been praying for our husbands' welfare,
Which speed° we hope the better for our words.   *Who prosper*
Are they returned?
115   LORENZO   Madam, they are not yet,

---

1. Ovid, in *Metamorphoses* 10, tells the story of Orpheus,
a legendary musician.
2. Is listened to; is accompanied.

3. *by season . . . are:* by proper time are adapted.
4. In classical mythology, a shepherd beloved of the
moon goddess, who caused him to sleep forever.

But there is come a messenger before
To signify their coming.

PORTIA   Go in, Nerissa.
Give order to my servants that they take
No note at all of our being absent hence;
120 Nor you, Lorenzo; Jessica, nor you.
        A tucket° sounds   trumpet flourish
LORENZO   Your husband is at hand. I hear his trumpet.
We are no tell-tales, madam. Fear you not.
PORTIA   This night, methinks, is but the daylight sick.
It looks a little paler. 'Tis a day
125 Such as the day is when the sun is hid.
        Enter BASSANIO, ANTONIO, GRAZIANO, *and their follow-*
        ers. [GRAZIANO *and* NERISSA *speak silently to one*
        another]
BASSANIO   We should hold day with the Antipodes
If you would walk in absence of the sun.⁵
PORTIA   Let me give light, but let me not be light;°   unfaithful
For a light wife doth make a heavy° husband,   sad
130 And never be Bassanio so for me.
But God sort° all. You are welcome home, my lord.   decide
BASSANIO   I thank you, madam. Give welcome to my friend.
This is the man, this is Antonio,
To whom I am so infinitely bound.
135 PORTIA   You should in all° sense be much bound to him,   every
For as I hear he was much bound for you.
ANTONIO   No more than I am well acquitted° of.   freed
PORTIA   Sir, you are very welcome to our house.
It must appear in other ways than words,
140 Therefore I scant this breathing courtesy.⁶
GRAZIANO [*to* NERISSA]   By yonder moon I swear you do me wrong.
In faith, I gave it to the judge's clerk.
Would he were gelt° that had it for my part,   gelded; castrated
Since you do take it, love, so much at heart.
145 PORTIA   A quarrel, ho, already! What's the matter?
GRAZIANO   About a hoop of gold, a paltry ring
That she did give me, whose posy° was   motto
For all the world like cutlers' poetry
Upon a knife—'Love me and leave me not'.
150 NERISSA   What talk you of the posy or the value?
You swore to me when I did give it you
That you would wear it till your hour of death,
And that it should lie with you in your grave.
Though not for me, yet for your vehement oaths
155 You should have been respective° and have kept it.   careful
Gave it a judge's clerk?—no, God's my judge,
The clerk will ne'er wear hair on's face that had it.
GRAZIANO   He will an if he live to be a man.
NERISSA   Ay, if a woman live to be a man.
160 GRAZIANO   Now by this hand, I gave it to a youth,
A kind of boy, a little scrubbèd° boy   stunted

---

5. *We . . . sun:* We would share daylight with the
other side of the world (Antipodes) if you habitually
walked when the sun was gone (implying "such is your

radiance").
6. I make brief this verbal welcome.

No higher than thyself, the judge's clerk,
A prating° boy that begged it as a fee.   *chattering*
I could not for my heart deny it him.

165 PORTIA   You were to blame, I must be plain with you,
To part so slightly with your wife's first gift,
A thing stuck on with oaths upon your finger,
And so riveted with faith unto your flesh.
I gave my love a ring, and made him swear
170 Never to part with it; and here he stands.
I dare be sworn for him he would not leave° it,   *part with*
Nor pluck it from his finger for the wealth
That the world masters.° Now, in faith, Graziano,   *possesses*
You give your wife too unkind a cause of grief.
175 An 'twere to me, I should be mad at it.

BASSANIO [*aside*]   Why, I were best to cut my left hand off
And swear I lost the ring defending it.

GRAZIANO [*to* PORTIA]   My lord Bassanio gave his ring away
Unto the judge that begged it, and indeed
180 Deserved it, too, and then the boy his clerk,
That took some pains in writing, he begged mine,
And neither man nor master would take aught
But the two rings.

PORTIA [*to* BASSANIO]   What ring gave you, my lord?
Not that, I hope, which you received of me.

185 BASSANIO   If I could add a lie unto a fault
I would deny it; but you see my finger
Hath not the ring upon it. It is gone.

PORTIA   Even so void is your false heart of truth.
By heaven, I will ne'er come in your bed
Until I see the ring.

190 NERISSA [*to* GRAZIANO]   Nor I in yours
Till I again see mine.

BASSANIO   Sweet Portia,
If you did know to whom I gave the ring,
If you did know for whom I gave the ring,
And would conceive for what I gave the ring,
195 And how unwillingly I left the ring
When naught would be accepted but the ring,
You would abate the strength of your displeasure.

PORTIA   If you had known the virtue° of the ring,   *power*
Or half her worthiness that gave the ring,
200 Or your own honour to contain° the ring,   *retain*
You would not then have parted with the ring.
What man is there so much unreasonable,
If you had pleased to have defended it
With any terms of zeal, wanted° the modesty°   *would lack / moderation*
205 To urge° the thing held as a ceremony?°   *insist on / sacred symbol*
Nerissa teaches me what to believe.
I'll die for't but some woman had the ring.

BASSANIO   No, by my honour, madam, by my soul,
No woman had it, but a civil doctor°   *doctor of civil law*
210 Which did refuse three thousand ducats of me,
And begged the ring, the which I did deny him,
And suffered° him to go displeased away,   *permitted*
Even he that had held up the very life

Of my dear friend. What should I say, sweet lady?
215 I was enforced to send it after him.
I was beset with shame and courtesy.
My honour would not let ingratitude
So much besmear it. Pardon me, good lady,
For by these blessèd candles of the night,
220 Had you been there I think you would have begged
The ring of me to give the worthy doctor.
PORTIA   Let not that doctor e'er come near my house.
Since he hath got the jewel that I loved,
And that which you did swear to keep for me,
225 I will become as liberal° as you.   *generous; licentious*
I'll not deny him anything I have,
No, not my body nor my husband's bed.
Know° him I shall, I am well sure of it.   *(with sexual suggestion)*
Lie not a night from home. Watch me like Argus.[7]
230 If you do not, if I be left alone,
Now by mine honour, which is yet mine own,
I'll have that doctor for my bedfellow.
NERISSA [*to* GRAZIANO]   And I his clerk, therefore be well advised
How you do leave me to mine own protection.
235 GRAZIANO   Well, do you so. Let not me take him then,
For if I do, I'll mar the young clerk's pen.°   *(with sexual suggestion)*
ANTONIO   I am th'unhappy subject of these quarrels.
PORTIA   Sir, grieve not you. You are welcome notwithstanding.
BASSANIO   Portia, forgive me this enforcèd wrong,
240 And in the hearing of these many friends
I swear to thee, even by thine own fair eyes,
Wherein I see myself—
PORTIA   Mark you but that?
In both my eyes he doubly sees himself,
In each eye one. Swear by your double° self,   *twofold; deceitful*
And there's an oath of credit.[8]
245 BASSANIO   Nay, but hear me.
Pardon this fault, and by my soul I swear
I never more will break an oath with thee.
ANTONIO [*to* PORTIA]   I once did lend my body for his wealth
Which, but for him that had your husband's ring,
250 Had quite miscarried. I dare be bound again,
My soul upon the forfeit, that your lord
Will never more break faith advisedly.°   *intentionally*
PORTIA   Then you shall be his surety.° Give him this,   *guarantor of a loan*
And bid him keep it better than the other.
255 ANTONIO   Here, Lord Bassanio, swear to keep this ring.
BASSANIO   By heaven, it is the same I gave the doctor!
PORTIA   I had it of him. Pardon me, Bassanio,
For by this ring, the doctor lay with me.
NERISSA   And pardon me, my gentle Graziano,
260 For that same scrubbèd boy, the doctor's clerk,
In lieu of° this last night did lie with me.   *In exchange for*
GRAZIANO   Why, this is like the mending of highways
In summer where the ways are fair enough![9]

---

7. Mythical many-eyed monster.
8. An oath to be believed (ironic).

9. *where . . . enough:* when repair is not required.

What, are we cuckolds ere we have deserved it?

265 PORTIA   Speak not so grossly. You are all amazed.°   *confused*
Here is a letter. Read it at your leisure.
It comes from Padua, from Bellario.
There you shall find that Portia was the doctor,
Nerissa there her clerk. Lorenzo here
270 Shall witness I set forth as soon as you,
And even but now returned. I have not yet
Entered my house. Antonio, you are welcome,
And I have better news in store for you
Than you expect. Unseal this letter soon.
275 There you shall find three of your argosies
Are richly come to harbour suddenly.
You shall not know by what strange accident
I chancèd on this letter.

ANTONIO   I am dumb!°   *dumbstruck*

BASSANIO [*to* PORTIA]   Were you the doctor and I knew you not?

280 GRAZIANO [*to* NERISSA]   Were you the clerk that is to make me cuckold?

NERISSA   Ay, but the clerk that never means to do it
Unless he live until he be a man.

BASSANIO [*to* PORTIA]   Sweet doctor, you shall be my bedfellow.
When I am absent, then lie with my wife.

285 ANTONIO [*to* PORTIA]   Sweet lady, you have given me life and
          living,°   *possessions*
For here I read for certain that my ships
Are safely come to road.°   *harbor*

PORTIA   How now, Lorenzo?
My clerk hath some good comforts, too, for you.

NERISSA   Ay, and I'll give them him without a fee.
290 There do I give to you and Jessica
From the rich Jew a special deed of gift,
After his death, of all he dies possessed of.

LORENZO   Fair ladies, you drop manna in the way
Of starvèd people.

PORTIA   It is almost morning,
295 And yet I am sure you are not satisfied
Of these events at full. Let us go in,
And charge us there upon inter'gatories,¹
And we will answer all things faithfully.

GRAZIANO   Let it be so. The first inter'gatory
300 That my Nerissa shall be sworn on is
Whether till the next night she had rather stay,
Or go to bed now, being two hours to day.
But were the day come, I should wish it dark
Till I were couching° with the doctor's clerk.   *lying*
305 Well, while I live I'll fear no other thing
So sore as keeping safe Nerissa's ring.°   *Exeunt   (with sexual suggestion)*

---

1. And question us under oath.

I Henry IV

A roadside inn that fails to provide chamber pots for its customers, a castle in Wales where a magician summons spirits to be his musicians, the royal palace in London from which the King of England launches a campaign against rebel forces—these are but a few of the disparate venues where the action of *1 Henry IV* occurs. With this drama, the Shakespearean history play broadens out to encompass a rich diversity of languages, characters, and locales. Nothing in Shakespeare's earlier English histories quite antici-pates this one. The great prose chronicles of the sixteenth century, such as Raphael Holinshed's *Chronicles of England, Scotland, and Ireland* (second edition, 1587), which Shakespeare consulted and whose materials he freely adapted and supplemented, stand behind all his history plays. The earlier plays, however, like the chronicles, focus pri-marily on the world of court and battlefield in which the monarch and his nobles appear as history's significant players, their rivalries and their achievements the focal point of the action. Common people such as Jack Cade have roles in these works, but their sto-ries are typically subordinated to the monarchical plot. In *1 Henry IV*, something differ-ent happens. Several lines of action unfold at once, each connected to particular geographical locales, and each commenting upon, without simply displacing, the oth-ers. Henry IV, who had seized the throne from Richard II, is the play's title character, but from the start he is a beleaguered figure kept from his dream of making a Crusade to the Holy Land by discontent and rebellion among his nobles, especially the Percy family, and burdened with an oldest son, Prince Hal, who acts more like a prodigal child than the heir to the throne. The King appears in some key scenes, but for long stretches the action focuses on other characters and on places, like a common London tavern, that the King would never deign to visit.

Some events take place in the north of England, in the Northumberland stronghold of the Percy family. The play is set in the early fifteenth century, but even in the late sixteenth century the north of England was popularly regarded as lawless, wild, and linked to marginalized Catholic practices and beliefs, its nobility not fully incorporated into the increasingly centralized state being constructed by the Tudor monarchs. In 1569, members of the Percy family had been prominent in the Northern Rebellion, an attempt to overthrow Queen Elizabeth and put Mary Queen of Scots, a Catholic, on the throne. In drawing his portrait of the Percys, Shakespeare makes their champion, Hotspur, an impassioned embodiment of medieval chivalry, eager above all for honor and for the glory to be won in battle. While the historical Hotspur was actually much older than the King's son, Prince Hal, Shakespeare follows Samuel Daniel's poem *The Civile Wars Between the Two Houses of Lancaster and York* (1595) in making him Hal's coequal in years and his rival for preeminence in the kingdom. He is joined in rebel-lion by other figures from the threatening territories on the perimeter of England: by the Earl of Douglas, a formidable Scottish warrior, and by the Welshman Owain Glyndŵr, a self-proclaimed magician with a fiery temper, a lyrical temperament, and a daughter who marries Edmund Mortimer, the man presented in this play as Richard II's designated heir to the throne. Wales thus harbors both rebellion and the man who was arguably the legitimate King of England.

Another of the play's crucial locales is a tavern in Eastcheap, a commercial district in the east of London. This tavern is Prince Hal's second home where he comes to drink and amuse himself, and particularly to carouse with Falstaff, the dissipated knight who is the young Prince's tutor in folly, his intimate friend, and surrogate father. In Eastcheap, Hal rubs elbows with commoners such as Mistress Quickly, the Hostess,

The historical Owain Glyndŵr claimed the title of Prince of Wales. His great seal, both sides of which are shown here, bears the inscription "Owain, by the grace of God, prince of Wales" and depicts four upreared (rampant) lions, the coat of arms of the Gwynedd dynasty, to which Glyndŵr belonged.

and with Francis, the inarticulate apprentice tapster. Shakespeare took his cue about Hal's presence amid this crew from the many popular accounts of the Prince's dissolute youth, especially from a play printed in 1598 called *The Famous Victories of Henry the Fifth,* some version of which seems to have been staged in the late 1580s. It depicts not only episodes from Hal's madcap youth but also his eventual reformation and assumption of the throne. Shakespeare elaborated extensively on this story of youthful prodigality. Mistress Quickly, for example, is entirely his invention, and the character of Falstaff, while loosely modeled on a figure in *The Famous Victories,* is utterly transformed by Shakespeare into what has remained one of the great comic creations of the English theater. Witty, opportunistic, and utterly indifferent to the decorum expected of a knight of advanced years, Falstaff makes the tavern a place of perpetual play and the antithesis of the duty-driven world of the court. That the Prince seems irresistibly drawn to Eastcheap makes others, especially his father, question his fitness to rule, but the high-spirited playfulness of Falstaff's world suggests why the Prince might take refuge there from the demands of his public role and the exacting expectations of the King, his father.

One of the objections to English popular theater voiced by a contemporary poet, Sir Philip Sidney, was that it mingled clowns with kings in a way that violated codes of aesthetic and social decorum; these codes insisted on the strict separation of high and low subject matter, language, and people. In contrast to Sidney's dicta, *1 Henry IV* is thoroughly hybrid in its mingling of the high matter of rebellion and affairs of state with the low matter of drinking, jokes, and highway robbery. The play is also a temporal hybrid in that the tavern scenes seem to take place not in the early fifteenth century, when Henry IV was struggling to secure his rule, but more nearly in the late sixteenth century, when Shakespeare was actually writing his play. In the tavern scenes, for example, characters make fun of plays and modes of writing popular in the 1570s and 1580s, such as Thomas Preston's ranting tyrant play *Cambyses* (1569) and the baroquely ornate rhetoric popularized by John Lyly in his *Euphues* (1578). The tavern world is also filled with references to the commodities that passed through London's markets in the late sixteenth century. The characters there drink sack, Madeira, and bastard—popular alcoholic beverages, some (such as Madeira) imported from as far away as an island off the coast of west Africa; and they refer to articles of clothing, such as the Spanish-leather wallets and leather jerkins with crystal buttons, worn by London's aspiring mercantile classes. Eastcheap itself, where the tavern is located, was a major market street in Shakespeare's London, and the tavern scenes are steeped in references to the commercial culture, including the theatrical culture, of early modern England.

There is every indication, however, that if a Sidney would have found the hybridity of the play a problem, ordinary consumers did not. Judging by its publication history, in its own time 1 Henry IV was one of Shakespeare's most popular plays. It appeared in two quarto versions in 1598 and then in five more before the First Folio was printed in 1623. Even after that, individual quarto editions of the play continued to appear. Part of its popularity undoubtedly derived from the fact that with 1 Henry IV, the Shakespearean history play began to supplement chronicle history, which focuses on monarchs, nobles, and affairs of state, with chorography: that is, with a mode of writing popular in the late sixteenth century that described and surveyed the land of England focusing on the products, the terrain, and the customs of England's various regions. 1 Henry IV is a chorography in the sense that while the play's distinct lines of action comment on one another, each is defined in relation to specific places, customs, and social groups. The commercial, bawdy world of the tavern, with its cast of lowlife characters and its rituals of drinking and play, is very different from the more formal milieu of Westminster, where the King and his nobles are immersed in the tasks of statecraft, and different again from the world of passion and magic centered in Glyndŵr's Welsh castle. Through the multiple plots, the spectator watching the play experiences the illusion of complex temporal simultaneity and social and geographic heterogeneity. Thus in successive scenes, the rebels, in Wales, plot the dismemberment of England and listen to a song sung in Welsh (3.1); King Henry, in Westminster, berates his wayward son (3.2); Falstaff, in Eastcheap, tries to cheat Mistress Quickly by claiming that his ring was stolen in her tavern (3.3). All these actions go on cotemporally but in widely disparate locales, creating a theatrical illusion of the diversity encompassed by the ongoing life of the nation and its bordering regions.

But the play's complex elaboration of difference also makes evident its monarch's central problem: how to maintain control over and enforce unity upon the territories over which he claims dominion but which threaten to break away or assert a worrisome autonomy. As in Henry V, Shakespeare here dramatizes the tension between efforts at nation building and the cultural, religious, and political differences that promote fragmentation. The problem of furthering national unity is especially pressing for Henry IV because he did not lineally inherit the throne; he seized it from Richard II. He is on shaky ground, then, should he attempt to unify England under the banner of his own legitimacy. In fact, for much of the play, Henry is a king in search of a strategy of rule. He had hoped to unify his people and quiet his conscience for his part in Richard's deposition and death by undertaking a Crusade to recover Jerusalem for European Christianity. But trouble at home keeps him from enacting his plan as rebellion bubbles up on the Scottish border, on the Welsh border, in the northern counties, and even in the Church, in the person of the Archbishop of York. The land seethes with the murmurings of rebels.

In the England of the 1590s, the monarch's most pressing problem of control was posed by Ireland; there, after 1595, the Earl of Tyrone led the challenge to English rule. Like Glyndŵr, Tyrone was educated in England and in some accounts was even Glyndŵr's descendant. While Ireland is not directly depicted in 1 Henry IV, Hotspur verbally links Wales and Ireland. Urged to listen to a song sung in Welsh, he says that he would rather hear his hunting dog "howl in Irish" (3.1.232), thereby confirming the common English view that Welsh and Irish were equally barbarous languages. More important, Wales stands in the play as a displaced image of the contemporary Irish situation. In the popular imagination, Wales often seemed a foreign place of mystery and danger, even though it had been officially incorporated in England in the 1530s and the Welsh language banned as unnatural and barbarous. In 1 Henry IV, Wales represents the threat not only of rebellion but also of effeminization and seduction. Mortimer, the supposed heir to the English throne, falls in love with Glyndŵr's daughter, promises to learn her language, and never appears on the battlefield against Henry's forces. In essence, he "goes native," a persistent fear voiced by the English concerning their soldiers and settlers in Ireland. The English had long worried that through prolonged contact with the Irish, English men and women might adopt their barbarous ways and forfeit their English identity. They even feared that their children, in drinking the milk of Irish wet nurses, could be transformed into people more Irish than English.

In *1 Henry IV,* the threat posed by the dangerous Welsh borderlands and by the northern Percy faction directly challenges the King's authority. Hampered by the questionable means by which he came to the throne, Henry ultimately finds force and guile the most effective instruments for maintaining his power. He can win battles, and he is willing to use deception to improve his position. At Shrewsbury, his major battle against the rebels, a number of Henry's nobles dress like the King, frustrating the enemy's ability to identify the true King and encouraging Henry's own forces by the seeming ubiquity of their monarch. Perpetual battle, however, is a costly way to rule, and having many nobles dress like him runs counter to Henry's stated belief that the King should be seldom seen in order to be the more wondered at when he does appear. To have many men marching in the King's clothing and answering to the King's name might, in fact, subversively suggest that "King" is a part any man could play, given the right accoutrements.

Prince Hal faces the pressing task of finding better strategies for ruling the changed world his father brought into being by his deposition of King Richard. He cannot assume that his kingship will be uncontested simply because he is Henry's son. A usurper's offspring has more legitimacy than a usurper, but not much. Rather, Hal must *make* himself King by a convincing performance of the part, and he must beat out those who would be his rivals, such as Harry Hotspur. Viewed one way, *1 Henry IV* is a study in the political and theatrical skills necessary for rule in a world where the inevitability and assumed legitimacy of inherited kingship has been called into question. In 1532, Niccolò Machiavelli's *The Prince,* a manual of practical statecraft, was published and quickly became notorious throughout Europe. Machiavelli taught rulers how to maintain their power through a mixture of guile, alliance, warfare, and personal force of character. Popularly viewed as irreligious and amoral, Machiavelli nonetheless was a byword for political pragmatism.

In his sophisticated manipulation of power, Hal shows himself a good student of Machiavelli, and the Machiavellian strand of his characterization has caused a split in critical assessments of him. To many, Hal personifies the ideal English king, the perfect mean between the self-indulgence of a Falstaff and the impassioned inflexibility of a Hotspur. He is thus an object of desire and emulation. Other critics focus on what they perceive as a lack of humanity at the heart of this consummate politician and recoil from his calculated use of other people to serve his own ends. For example, at the end of the first scene in which he appears, Hal in soliloquy speaks about his tavern mates:

> I know you all, and will a while uphold
> The unyoked humour of your idleness.
> Yet herein will I imitate the sun,
> Who doth permit the base contagious clouds
> To smother up his beauty from the world,
> That when he please again to be himself,
> Being wanted he may be more wondered at
> By breaking through the foul and ugly mists
> Of vapours that did seem to strangle him.
>   (1.2.173–81)

These lines reveal the calculation that is one part of this character's representation. Comparing himself to the royal symbol, the sun, Hal casts his companions as the contaminating clouds and ugly mists that temporarily obscure his own radiance. Hal is chillingly disdainful of those he elsewhere treats as boon companions, but he also finds their baseness *useful*, since it will set in high relief his own glory, once he has cast them off.

Hal is an interesting dramatic character and not merely a personification of political expediency, however, precisely because his calculated use of his companions does not necessarily preclude his being attracted to them and to the world of play and good fellowship that they represent. In *1 Henry IV*, Hal is not yet King, and the moment of repudiation is not yet upon him. In this play, he can both enjoy his time in Eastcheap and also acquire skills there that he will need when he ascends his father's troubled throne. In the tavern, for example, he and Falstaff take turns playing King and Prince in a theatrical staging of the prodigal Hal's encounter with his reproving father. Hal rehearses the cadences and the sentiments of royal speech, trying out a part, learning to inhabit it convincingly. But it is not just his own part he masters. Unlike his father, Hal does not hold himself aloof from his would-be subjects. His ventures into Eastcheap are in part a mapping of one corner of England, a survey of the customs and strange languages of this locale. To Ned Poins he boasts that having been instructed by three tapsters in the terminology of drinking, "I can drink with any tinker in his own language during my life" (2.5.16–17).

In the tavern, Hal also meditates on the strange tongue of his great rival, Hotspur, whose impatient but impassioned speech Hal parodies:

> I am not yet of Percy's mind, the Hotspur of the North—he that kills me some six or seven dozen of Scots at a breakfast, washes his hands, and says to his wife, 'Fie upon this quiet life! I want work.' 'O my sweet Harry,' says she, 'how many hast thou killed today?' 'Give my roan horse a drench,' says he, and answers, 'Some fourteen,' an hour after; 'a trifle, a trifle.' I prithee call in Falstaff. I'll play Percy, and that damned brawn shall play Dame Mortimer his wife. (2.5.94–101)

Learning the language of others and rehearsing their tongues is, for Hal, one of the arts of power. He can—and later he will—repudiate some of those whose language and customs he has imbibed, making the repudiation a justification for his own rule. Knowing disorderliness, the King will use his office to punish it. He can also appropriate the language of others, as at Shrewsbury he appropriates the chivalric accents of Hotspur; or he can co-opt others to serve his own purposes by speaking to them in a tongue they can comprehend. By his own account, Hal is beloved of the tapsters who have taught him their language, and they have promised that when he is king, he "shall command all the good lads in Eastcheap" (2.5.12–13). Many of them he will eventually command in his wars in France. It can be argued, therefore, that there is a profound instrumentality to Hal's sojourn outside the court milieu that should be his "natural" home. He is acquiring theatrical skills, linguistic skills, and above all a knowledge of the diverse corners of an England he must rule by a mixture of charm, guile, and strategic severity—demonizing some subjects to win the loyalty of others, outstripping rivals by outdoing them at their own particular strengths.

Yet Hal is only part of this play, and *1 Henry IV*'s uniqueness consists in good part in the way it plays off one dramatic perspective, one line of action, against another. The young Prince is certainly the focus of the play's narrative of reform, and he is the only character who can move with seeming ease among the worlds of tavern, court, and battlefield. Yet even as he surveys and judges those around him, the play's structure of geographical juxtapositions and its vivid depiction of other characters and other modes of being invite the audience to submit the Prince himself to critical scrutiny. Consider, for example, 3.1 and 3.2, the scenes at the center of the play that take the audience first to Glyndŵr's castle in Wales, where he, Hotspur, Mortimer, and Worcester are plotting their rebellion, and then to the King's palace at Westminster to which Henry has summoned his son. The first scene graphically establishes the kingdom-cleaving threat posed by the rebels. They have a map and are planning how they will divide the territory of England into three parts. But the scene also establishes the danger, mystery, and beauty of this borderland. Glyndŵr is a man trained in occult arts who boasts that the earth shook at his birth and that he can summon spirits to do his bidding. Hotspur scoffs, but when Glyndŵr's daughter promises to sing in Welsh, Glyndŵr says:

> Do so, and those musicians that shall play to you
> Hang in the air a thousand leagues from hence,
> And straight they shall be here. Sit and attend.
>
> (3.1.220–22)

Three lines later, music plays, its origins a mystery. When Glyndŵr speaks, Wales seems a land of enchantment, haunted by spirits.

Wales is also a place where women are integral to the action as they seldom are elsewhere in the play. Except for Mistress Quickly, Kate Percy and Glyndŵr's daughter are the play's only two female characters; and 3.1, the play's only scene in which two women are onstage at the same time, is set in Wales and is largely Shakespeare's invention. In the chronicles, Glyndŵr, Mortimer, and Hotspur's proposed division of conquered territory is negotiated by representatives in the Archbishop of Bangor's house. By contrast, in *1 Henry IV* it occurs at Glyndŵr's home with the women present. In short, Shakespeare went to some trouble to link the rebels with women—more specifically, with wives and daughters. The question is why. In part, the choice portrays the rebels, unlike the Lancastrians, as having private as well as public lives. Glyndŵr is fond of his daughter and worries about her happiness. Mortimer dotes on this same daughter and seems to have married her for love as much as for political alliance. Hotspur's affection for his wife is displayed through the teasing banter with which he persistently addresses her. Scornful of mooning lovers, he nonetheless is careful to take his wife with him when he journeys to Wales.

The passions so nakedly on display in 3.1 clearly signal the rebels' vulnerabilities. In the patriarchal thought of the period, men were presented as superior to women because they were supposedly more rational and less subject to their passions. If men loved women too much, they risked becoming effeminate—that is, *like* a woman in placing desire above reason, especially if that desire kept a man from performing his public duties, such as going to war. Hotspur prizes his masculinity and the public honor to be won in battle. He is contemptuous of the affected courtier who appeared at Holmedon after the fighting, demanding Hotspur's prisoners (1.3.28–68). In his dealings with his wife, Hotspur seems to use banter and jokes to maintain control of his affection for her. He would not, for a woman, forgo the man-to-man erotics of battle when, "hot horse to horse" (4.1.123), he clashes against the bosom of Prince Hal. Mortimer, by contrast, simply succumbs to the charms of the Welsh woman. He never appears in battle: Wales and a wife swallow him up.

This Welsh world of danger, mystery, and passion sits strangely against the world of calculation that unfolds immediately thereafter, when in 3.2 King Henry castigates Prince Hal for his dissolute life and together they discuss strategies of monarchical self-presentation. The throne room is a place not of enchantment but of business. No women are shown at court, and passion manifests itself most strongly as the desire to rule. Father and son are both preoccupied with the tactics and strategies by which they can most effectively command the loyalty of subjects. While Henry fears his son misunderstands the task before him, Hal shows that he is every bit as astute as his father. But after the high emotions and alluring lyricism of the Welsh scene, the throne room at Westminster can seem a pragmatic and claustrophobic space. In concentrating their energies on rule, Henry and Hal here are divorced from many things that give the rebel world its charm.

Falstaff and the tavern pose a different challenge to the values of Westminster. As critics have shown, the fat man's tutoring of Hal in riotous living mimics the pedagogical relationship of master to student that was sometimes eroticized in the early modern period. Much of the poignancy of the play's depiction of the friendship between the two comes from the tension between their apparent intimacy and the Prince's stated intention to repudiate his companion. Falstaff's threat to monarchical values is obvious. Against the future-oriented calculations of Hal and his father, he insists on living in the present. As his huge body testifies, he demands the immediate gratification of physical desires. To eat, drink, and jest—these are pleasures that for Falstaff brook no delay. Hal can discipline himself. He is thin, as Falstaff points out, and he can plot a personal reformation sometime far in the future and work toward that end. Falstaff cannot or will not; and yet, while a figure of disorder, he has for many readers been the play's most interesting and memorable character. Aside from Hamlet, no other Shakespearean figure has attracted as much critical attention as the fat knight.

Falstaff and Prince Hal. Pen and watercolor drawing on paper by William Blake (c. 1780).

When Shakespeare first wrote the play, he called this character Sir John Oldcastle. The choice was unfortunate, for the Cobham family, descendants of the historical Oldcastle, protested. William Brooke, the tenth Baron Cobham, had been Lord Chamberlain from August 1596 to March 1597, the very months when most scholars believe Shakespeare completed *1 Henry IV*. Since the Lord Chamberlain oversaw the licensing of plays through the office of the Master of the Revels, Cobham was in an especially favorable position to object to this comic rendition of his ancestor. Shakespeare apparently changed the character's name in response to this act of censorship, though traces of his original intentions can be discerned, including the fact that in 1.2.37–38 Falstaff is still referred to as "my old lad of the castle." In addition, in the first complete Quarto of *1 Henry IV*, there are a few traces of the fact that Peto once bore the name "Harvey," and Bardolph the name "Russell." Again, the objections of powerful figures may have forced changes. "Russell" was the family name of the prominent earls of Bedford, and "Harvey" the name of the stepfather of the Earl of Southampton.

Recently, some critics (including the editors of the Oxford text) have argued that the names "Peto," "Bardolph," and "Falstaff" should be replaced by the names Shakespeare originally intended—namely, "Harvey," "Russell," and "Oldcastle." They suggest that such a replacement would undo an act of censorship that thwarted Shakespeare's original intentions. This edition retains the substituted names primarily because these are the names Shakespeare consistently used after the initial act of censorship, and they have become part of the textual and dramatic history of this and other plays. While it is important to point out that an act of censorship occurred, to "undo" it creates new erasures in the textual and cultural history of the play. For Shakespeare, "Falstaff," not "Oldcastle," became the word linking the various textual manifestations of his fat knight as he appeared both in *1* and *2 Henry IV* and then in *The Merry Wives of Windsor*.

It is of interest, however, to ask why Shakespeare first used the name "Oldcastle" in his play. The historical Oldcastle was a knight who served Henry IV in battle in both France and Wales, but who was also a Lollard; that is, he was connected with the religious group often seen as a forerunner of English Protestantism for its critiques of the Catholic Church and its advocacy of a vernacular Bible to be made available to lay people. At first, Henry IV treated Oldcastle's religious views leniently, but eventually Oldcastle was sent to the Tower of London and condemned as a heretic by the Archbishop of Canterbury. He escaped, and Henry was warned that Oldcastle was leading an armed force against him. Oldcastle was captured in 1417 and eventually hung in chains and then burned on the gallows.

This knight suggests Shakespeare's portrait of the chivalric heroes Prince Hal and Hotspur at the battle of Shrewsbury. From Henry Peacham's *Minerva Britanna* (1612).

In the sixteenth century, how one viewed Oldcastle depended largely on one's religious perspective. To many zealous Protestants, such as John Foxe, Oldcastle was a Protestant hero, a victim of Catholic oppression rather than a traitor; Foxe included Oldcastle in his *Book of Martyrs*. But by the 1590s, Lollards were also sometimes linked with "extremist" Protestant groups pushing for radical reforms in the Church of England. Making a well-known Lollard martyr a fat figure of disorder therefore did not necessarily signal Catholic sympathies. It might simply be a way of suggesting the hypocrisy of zealous reformers. In other plays, especially in his portrait of Malvolio in *Twelfth Night*, Shakespeare makes fun of "Puritans" who claimed a greater righteousness and strictness of life than their more moderate contemporaries. In *1 Henry IV*, Falstaff's language is liberally studded with biblical quotations, most of which he misapplies or contradicts by his behavior. Thus he tells Hal that one must labor in one's vocation (1.2.92–93), an injunction found in 1 Corinthians 7:20 and in Ephesians 4:1. But the vocation in which *he* would labor is that of thief—not exactly what Protestant divines meant when discussing the virtues of a vocation. Moreover, by making Falstaff so obviously a glutton and lover of sack, Shakespeare could be making fun of the hypocrisy of Puritans, as Ben Jonson was to do in *Bartholomew Fair* and Thomas Middleton in *A Chaste Maid in Cheapside*.

The name Shakespeare fastened upon to replace Oldcastle had its own history. The historical Fastolf (1378?–1459) was a courageous officer in Henry VI's war in France, though in some chronicles he appears erroneously to have been called a coward, a detail that Shakespeare repeats in *1 Henry VI*. Having once used the name without repercussion in the former play, Shakespeare may have felt it was safe to employ it as a replacement for "Oldcastle" and to play upon the figure's reputation for cowardice.

Yet it may be a mistake to connect Shakespeare's character too strictly to any historical counterpart. As scholarship has shown, Falstaff is a rich amalgam of popular and literary traditions. In part, he resembles the irreverent Vice figure from the medieval morality plays. Traditionally, the Vice, a comic and clever character, tempted the hero to sin while voices of virtue or duty tried to steer him along a more reputable path. In *1 Henry IV*, Hal is torn between his allegiances to Falstaff and his father, to vice and virtue, to the tavern and the court. Falstaff also conjures up the topsy-turvy world of Carnival in which rulers were temporarily displaced and the body's pleasures (eating, drinking, breaking wind, having sex) were celebrated before the arrival of abstemious Lent. The unending jokes about Falstaff's fat paunch highlight his symbolic connection to bodily excess, and his contempt for the law and for military duty make him the antithesis of the King and a perpetual emblem of disorder. In creating Falstaff, Shakespeare also drew on the figure from classical tradition of the braggart warrior who is really a coward. At Shrewsbury, Falstaff plays the coward, and yet he falsely claims credit for having killed Hotspur. The gap between his words and his deeds is enormous, though in this instance, as in many others, the Prince graciously does not reveal this lie for what it is. Above all, however, Falstaff embodies traditions of popular critique associated with the stage clown. In early productions, Will Kemp, the famous clown in Shakespeare's company, probably played the part. Sometimes speaking from a downstage position near the audience, the clown traditionally poked fun at upstage authority figures. Falstaff does so in spades, whether mocking the elevated speech of King Henry or twitting Hal for being so skinny. But Falstaff is more than a gadfly or a parasite swollen fat on others' folly. He also embodies a mode of being in the world that serves as a powerful alternative both to the calculations of Hal and to Hotspur's headlong, death-courting pursuit of honor. For example, before the Battle of Shrewsbury Falstaff meditates witheringly on just what honor means and on its value:

> Can honour set-to a leg? No. Or an arm? No. Or take away the grief of a wound?
> No. Honour hath no skill in surgery, then? No. What is honour? A word. What is in
> that word 'honour'? What is that 'honour'? Air. A trim reckoning! Who hath it?
> He that died o'Wednesday. Doth he feel it? No. Doth he hear it? No. 'Tis insensible
> then? Yea, to the dead. But will it not live with the living? No. Why? Detraction will
> not suffer it. Therefore I'll none of it. Honour is a mere scutcheon. And so ends my
> catechism. (5.1.130–39)

Others, like Hotspur, find honor worth dying for, and generations of men have gone into battle believing the same thing. But for Falstaff, honor is worth the loss of neither a leg nor a life. During the ensuing battle, Falstaff carries a bottle of sack in his pistol case and ingloriously feigns death when attacked by Douglas. But though Hotspur and others are slain, Falstaff rises up. He embraces neither honor nor death, but life, and many readers and theatergoers have cheered his choice while others have been repulsed by his opportunism and cowardice.

Shrewsbury, then, is not only the place where the play's disparate strands of action come together as the King, Prince Hal, Hotspur, and even Falstaff assemble in one spot; it is also where the audience is invited to judge the relative worth of the values embraced by these different characters. Among those who fare well is Prince Hal. Shrewsbury is perhaps his happiest hour. During the battle, he finds a way to redeem his reputation and distinguish himself from Falstaff without being forced to repudiate his friend, just as he kills Hotspur while paying homage to his courage. But the equipoise of this battle's conclusion is precarious. Hal is not yet king and must still delay his assumption of the throne. Falstaff has not reformed and probably never will. And the rebels have not been destroyed. Hotspur is dead, but the Archbishop of York, Glyndŵr, and Mortimer are still in arms. In other words, it is an illusion that Hal has carried all before him. In the corners and crevices of the realm, dissension and difference remain. In such conditions, the work of rule is a performance with no end.

JEAN E. HOWARD

TEXTUAL NOTE

The first quarto edition of *1 Henry IV* was printed in 1598. Only a fragment, comprising 1.3.199 through 2.3.19 of a single copy, now remains. This Quarto, usually designated as Q0 but in the Oxford edition called Q1, was the basis for a second quarto edition printed later in 1598. This text, Q2, serves as the control text for most modern editions. The manuscript behind Q1 does not seem to have been marked up for the theater, so it was probably not the promptbook. The manuscript was either a corrected copy of Shakespeare's "foul papers" or, more probably, a transcription of them made by a professional scribe. This manuscript was prepared with unusual care, perhaps to show that changes required by the Master of the Revels had been made in the text. Originally, the characters Falstaff, Peto, and Bardolph had been assigned the names "Oldcastle," "Harvey," and "Russell." Objections from the Cobham family, descendants of Oldcastle, and perhaps from other powerful people seem to have forced Shakespeare to change these names (see the Introduction for a fuller discussion of this act of censorship).

Five other quarto editions were published, in 1599, 1604, 1608, 1613, and 1622, before the publication of the First Folio (F) in 1623. These all derive from Q2 and have no independent authority. The Folio text derives from the 1613 Quarto, but act and scene divisions were added, speech prefixes and stage directions altered, and oaths were softened or removed and biblical allusions altered in compliance with the 1606 edict forbidding profanity on the stage. The party responsible for these changes is uncertain. Some changes may have been made by the compositors who set the text or by someone acting as editor (perhaps John Heminges or Henry Condell, Shakespeare's fellow share-holders in the King's Men who oversaw the production of the First Folio). The Oxford editors plausibly argue that these changes may in part derive from a manuscript pre-pared by the same scribe who prepared a similarly "literary" manuscript for 2 *Henry IV*—that is, a manuscript less attuned to playhouse requirements than to the ration-alization of the text as a written document. This scribal manuscript may itself have derived from a promptbook whose theatrical features were largely obscured by the tran-scription. The Oxford editors also believe that a few of the changes made in F may reflect Shakespeare's own revisions of Q.

The act and scene divisions of F are followed except for the marking of new scenes at 2.3 and 5.3. The latter scene break, regularly inserted in most modern editions, indi-cates a clearing of the stage in the middle of the Battle of Shrewsbury; 2.3 is added to mark the moment at Gad's Hill when, Falstaff and his friends having led off the travel-ers they have captured, Hal and Poins come onstage disguised in their buckram suits.

As explained in the Introduction, for this play Norton is using the names "Falstaff," "Peto," and "Bardolph" (rather than Oxford's "Oldcastle," "Harvey," and "Russell"). Consequently, Oxford speech prefixes and stage directions, and in a few places the Oxford text, have been silently altered where these three characters are concerned in order to return to the names and language appearing in the printed quarto texts of 1598. Textual deviations from Q are marked in the variants, and Norton's standardiza-tion of quarto speech prefixes is delineated immediately before those variants. In par-ticular, "Falstaff," rather than Oxford's "Sir John," has been used in speech prefixes in this play as well as in 2 *Henry IV*.

SELECTED BIBLIOGRAPHY

Barber, C. L. "Rule and Misrule in *Henry IV.*" *Shakespeare's Festive Comedy: A Study of Dramatic Form and Its Relation to Social Custom*. Princeton: Princeton University Press, 1959. 192–221. Explores the ritual subtext of *Henry IV, Parts I and II*, argu-ing that Falstaff becomes a scapegoat whose banishment rids the community of bad luck.

Barker, Roberta. "Tragical-Comical-Historical Hotspur." *Shakespeare Quarterly* 54 (2003): 288–307. Examines how Hotspur has been interpreted through the cen-turies and argues that the role is central to the play's examination of masculine hero-ism.

Greenblatt, Stephen. "Invisible Bullets." *Shakespearean Negotiations: The Circulation of Social Energy in Renaissance England*. Berkeley: University of California Press, 1988. 21–65. Discusses how Renaissance texts such as Thomas Hariot's *A Brief and True Report of the New Found Land of Virginia* and Shakespeare's 1 *Henry IV* sub-vert their culture's dominant values regarding religious belief and political author-ity and yet contain or mitigate the doubts they raise.

Greenfield, Matthew. "*1 Henry IV*: Metatheatrical Britain." *British Identities and En-glish Renaissance Literature*. Ed. David J. Baker and Willy Maley. New York: Cam-bridge University Press, 2002. 71–80. Discusses the interplay of different characters, locales, and genres in the play, arguing that it fails to create a single onstage community but instead reveals the distance between groups.

Highley, Christopher. "Wales, Ireland, and 1 *Henry IV.*" *Renaissance Drama*, n.s., 21 (1990): 91–114. Discusses England's Elizabethan wars in Ireland as a subtext for

1 Henry IV and Glyndŵr as a displaced image of the Irish leader Hugh O'Neill, Earl of Tyrone.

Howard, Jean E., and Phyllis Rackin. "Gender and Nation: Anticipations of Modernity in the Second Tetralogy." *Engendering a Nation: A Feminist Account of Shakespeare's English Histories*. London: Routledge, 1997. 137–215. Focuses on the disruptive role of women in the play, both the Welsh women, including Glyndŵr's daughter, and the women of the Eastcheap tavern.

Kastan, David Scott. "'The King Hath Many Marching in His Coats'; or, What Did You Do During the War, Daddy?" *Shakespeare Left and Right*. Ed. Ivo Kamps. New York: Routledge, 1991. 241–58. Argues that the theater does not just reproduce the political ideologies of the powerful but instead makes space for unauthorized and heterogeneous views, including, in *Henry IV*, the view that kingship itself is just a role.

Laroque, François. "Shakespeare's 'Battle of Carnival and Lent': The Falstaff Scenes Reconsidered (*1* and *2 Henry IV*)." *Shakespeare and Carnival: After Bakhtin*. Ed. Ronald Knowles. New York: St. Martin's, 1998. 83–96. Discusses the connections between Shakespeare's *Henry IV* plays and the opposition in Carnival between the fat and the lean, Falstaff and the Prince.

McMillin, Scott. *Henry IV, Part One*. Shakespeare in Performance series. Manchester: Manchester University Press, 1991. Analyzes theatrical, film, and television performances of *1 Henry IV* in the second half of the twentieth century, arguing that this is the period when Hal, rather than Falstaff or Hotspur, became the focus of critical and theatrical attention.

Mullaney, Steven. "The Rehearsal of Cultures." *The Place of the Stage: License, Play, and Power in Renaissance England*. Chicago: University of Chicago Press, 1988. 60–87. Discusses the sixteenth-century fascination with collecting artifacts from distant cultures and argues that the stage also represented and rehearsed otherness.

FILMS

Chimes at Midnight. 1965. Dir. Orson Welles. UK. 115 min. In black and white, the film combines scenes from several plays to focus on Falstaff and his relationship with Prince Hal. An imaginative and moving adaptation, it boasts memorable performances by Welles as Falstaff, John Gielgud as Henry IV, and Keith Baxter as the Prince.

Henry IV, Part I. 1979. Dir. David Giles. UK. 155 min. A BBC-TV production with strong performances by Anthony Quayle as Falstaff and Tim Pigott-Smith as Hotspur in an otherwise dutifully faithful version of the play.

My Own Private Idaho. 1991. Dir. Gus Van Sant. USA. 102 min. Set in modern-day Portland, Oregon, and loosely based on the *Henry IV* plays, the film stars River Phoenix and Keanu Reeves as two young men who for a time join William Richert, the Falstaff figure, in a life of dissipation.

The History of Henry the Fourth

THE PERSONS OF THE PLAY

KING HENRY IV

PRINCE HARRY, Prince of Wales,
 familiarly known as Hal ⎫
Lord JOHN OF LANCASTER   ⎬ King Henry's sons
Earl of WESTMORLAND
Sir Walter BLUNT

Earl of WORCESTER
Percy, Earl of NORTHUMBERLAND, his brother
Henry Percy, known as HOTSPUR,
 Northumberland's son
Kate, LADY PERCY, Hotspur's wife
Lord Edmund MORTIMER, called Earl of March,
 Lady Percy's brother ⎫
LADY MORTIMER, his wife   ⎬ rebels against King Henry
Owain GLYNDŴR, Lady Mortimer's father
Earl of DOUGLAS
Sir Richard VERNON
Scrope, ARCHBISHOP of York
SIR MICHAEL, a member of the Archbishop's
 household

Sir John FALSTAFF ⎫
Edward (Ned) POINS
BARDOLPH
PETO   ⎬ associates of Prince Harry
Mistress Quickly, HOSTESS of
 a tavern in Eastcheap
FRANCIS, a drawer
VINTNER ⎭

GADSHILL
CARRIERS
CHAMBERLAIN
OSTLER
TRAVELLERS
SHERIFF
MESSENGERS
SERVANT
Lords, soldiers

1.1

Enter KING [HENRY], *Lord* JOHN OF LANCASTER, [*and
the*] *Earl of* WESTMORLAND, *with other* [*lords*]

KING HENRY So shaken as we are, so wan with care,
 Find we° a time for frighted peace to pant   *Let us find*
 And breathe short-winded accents° of new broils   *words*

1.1 Location: The palace, London.

To be commenced in strands afar remote.[1]
5 No more the thirsty entrance° of this soil   *parched mouth*
Shall daub her lips with her own children's blood.
No more shall trenching° war channel° her fields,   *cutting / furrow*
Nor bruise her flow'rets with the armèd hoofs
Of hostile paces.° Those opposèd eyes,   *horses' footsteps*
10 Which, like the meteors of a troubled heaven,[2]
All of one nature, of one substance bred,
Did lately meet in the intestine° shock   *internal*
And furious close° of civil butchery,   *hand-to-hand combat*
Shall now in mutual well-beseeming° ranks   *orderly*
15 March all one way, and be no more opposed
Against acquaintance, kindred, and allies.
The edge of war, like an ill-sheathèd knife,
No more shall cut his master. Therefore, friends,
As far as to the sepulchre of Christ—
20 Whose soldier now, under whose blessèd cross
We are impressèd° and engaged to fight—   *conscripted*
Forthwith a power of English shall we levy,
Whose arms were moulded in their mothers' womb
To chase these pagans in those holy fields
25 Over whose acres walked those blessèd feet
Which fourteen hundred years ago were nailed,
For our advantage, on the bitter cross.
But this our purpose now is twelve month old,
And bootless° 'tis to tell you we will go.   *useless*
30 Therefor° we meet not now. Then let me hear   *On that account*
Of you, my gentle cousin° Westmorland,   *my noble kinsman*
What yesternight our Council did decree
In forwarding this dear expedience.°   *urgent undertaking*
WESTMORLAND   My liege, this haste was hot in question,°   *under urgent debate*
35 And many limits of the charge[3] set down
But yesternight, when all athwart° there came   *at cross-purposes*
A post° from Wales, loaden with heavy news,   *messenger*
Whose worst was that the noble Mortimer,
Leading the men of Herefordshire to fight
40 Against the irregular and wild Glyndŵr,[4]
Was by the rude hands of that Welshman taken,
A thousand of his people butcherèd,
Upon whose dead corpse'° there was such misuse,   *corpses*
Such beastly shameless transformation,[5]
45 By those Welshwomen done as may not be
Without much shame retold or spoken of.
KING HENRY   It seems then that the tidings of this broil
Brake° off our business for the Holy Land.   *Broke*

---

1. On distant shores. King Henry is alluding to the Holy Land, to which he vowed to lead a crusade at the close of *Richard II*.
2. Unusual events in the sky, such as comets or shooting stars, were thought to portend strife and disaster.
3. Many particulars concerning responsibilities and expenses.
4. In most editions, Glyndŵr's name is given as "Glendower," an anglicized version of the Welsh word used in this text. Glyndŵr is probably "irregular" in the sense of

using guerrilla tactics in his warfare; possibly, the word alludes to his alleged sorcery.
5. Mutilation. Holinshed's 1587 *Chronicles*, one of Shakespeare's sources, says the Welsh women's acts on this occasion were too shameful to relate, but contemporary editor Abraham Fleming, in the same edition of the *Chronicles*, includes an account of another battle in which Welsh women cut off the sexual organs and the noses of conquered enemies and put them, respectively, in the mouths and anuses of those enemies.

WESTMORLAND   This matched with other did, my gracious lord,
50   For more uneven° and unwelcome news   °disturbing
        Came from the north, and thus it did import:
        On Holy-rood day[6] the gallant Hotspur there—
        Young Harry Percy—and brave Archibald,
        That ever valiant and approvèd° Scot,   °worthy
55   At Holmedon[7] met,
        Where they did spend a sad and bloody hour,
        As by° discharge of their artillery   °As judging by
        And shape of likelihood° the news was told;   °And probable outcome
        For he that brought them° in the very heat   °(the news)
60   And pride° of their contention did take horse,   °height
        Uncertain of the issue° any way.   °outcome
KING HENRY   Here is a dear, a true industrious friend,
        Sir Walter Blunt,[8] new lighted from his horse,
        Stained with the variation of each soil
65   Betwixt that Holmedon and this seat° of ours;   °dwelling
        And he hath brought us smooth° and welcome news.   °agreeable
        The Earl of Douglas is discomfited.
        Ten thousand bold Scots, two-and-twenty knights,
        Balked° in their own blood did Sir Walter see   °Heaped up; thwarted
70   On Holmedon's plains. Of prisoners Hotspur took
        Mordake the Earl of Fife and eldest son
        To beaten Douglas,[9] and the Earl of Athol,
        Of Moray, Angus, and Menteith;
        And is not this an honourable spoil,
75   A gallant prize? Ha, cousin, is it not?
WESTMORLAND   In faith, it is a conquest for a prince to boast of.
KING HENRY   Yea, there thou mak'st me sad, and mak'st me sin
        In envy that my lord Northumberland
        Should be the father to so blest a son—
80   A son who is the theme of honour's tongue,
        Amongst a grove the very straightest plant,
        Who is sweet Fortune's minion° and her pride—   °favorite
        Whilst I by looking on the praise of him
        See riot and dishonour stain the brow
85   Of my young Harry. O, that it could be proved
        That some night-tripping fairy[1] had exchanged
        In cradle clothes our children where they lay,
        And called mine Percy, his Plantagenet![2]
        Then would I have his Harry, and he mine.
90   But let him° from my thoughts. What think you, coz,°   °let him go / kinsman
        Of this young Percy's pride? The prisoners
        Which he in this adventure hath surprised°   °captured
        To his own use[3] he keeps, and sends me word

---

6. Holy Cross Day, September 14.
7. Holmedon (also spelled "Humbleton") in Northumberland was the site in 1402 of a Scottish invasion of England.
8. It is not clear whether Blunt comes onstage now. He could have entered at the beginning of the scene; alternatively, as in this edition, he may not come onstage at all. Blunt has no lines in the scene, and Henry could at this point receive a letter containing Blunt's news or could be reporting news he has already learned. "Here" would thus refer in a general way to Blunt's being at

court.
9. Mordake was not actually Douglas's son, but an understandable misreading of Holinshed led Shakespeare to believe he was.
1. It was popularly believed that fairies stole beautiful children and left bad or malformed ones in their place.
2. Henry was descended from the Plantagenet dynasty; and the Percys were a distinguished family from the north of England to which Hotspur belonged.
3. Prisoners were routinely used as a source of revenue.

I shall have none but Mordake Earl of Fife.

95 WESTMORLAND This is his uncle's teaching. This is Worcester,
Malevolent to you in all aspects,[4]
Which makes him prune[5] himself, and bristle up
The crest of youth against your dignity.

KING HENRY But I have sent for him to answer this;
100 And for this cause awhile we must neglect
Our holy purpose to Jerusalem.
Cousin, on Wednesday next our Council we
Will hold at Windsor. So inform the lords.
But come yourself with speed to us again,
105 For more is to be said and to be done
Than out of anger can be utterèd.

WESTMORLAND I will, my liege.

Exeunt [KING HENRY, LANCASTER, *and other lords*
at one door; WESTMORLAND *at another door*]

1.2

Enter [HARRY][1] *Prince of Wales and Sir John* FALSTAFF[2]

FALSTAFF Now, Hal, what time of day is it, lad?

PRINCE HARRY Thou art so fat-witted° with drinking of old   *thick-witted*
sack,[3] and unbuttoning thee after supper, and sleeping upon
benches after noon, that thou hast forgotten to demand that
5 truly which thou wouldst truly know. What a devil hast thou to
do with the time of the day? Unless hours were cups of sack, and
minutes capons,[4] and clocks the tongues of bawds, and dials°   *clock faces; sundials*
the signs of leaping-houses,° and the blessed sun himself a   *brothels*
fair hot wench in flame-coloured taffeta,[5] I see no reason why
10 thou shouldst be so superfluous° to demand the time of the day.   *needlessly curious*

FALSTAFF Indeed you come near me° now, Hal, for we that take   *are near the mark*
purses go by the moon and the seven stars,[6] and not 'By Phoe-
bus, he, that wand'ring knight so fair'.[7] And I prithee, sweet
wag,° when thou art a king, as God save thy grace—'majesty'   *mischievous boy*
15 I should say, for grace[8] thou wilt have none—

PRINCE HARRY What, none?

FALSTAFF No, by my troth, not so much as will serve to be prologue to an egg and butter.[9]

PRINCE HARRY Well, how then? Come, roundly,° roundly.   *to the point*

20 FALSTAFF Marry° then, sweet wag, when thou art king let not   *By Mary (a mild oath)*
us that are squires of the night's body[1] be called thieves of the

---

4. Habitually hostile to you. The line suggests that
Worcester is a planet whose influence is always harmful, whatever his position, or "aspect," in the sky.
5. A term from falconry suggesting the hawk's trimming of its feathers as preparation for action.
1.2 Location: A room in the Prince's apartments, London.
1. F's stage direction reads, "Henry Prince of Wales"; Q
reads, "prince of Wales." Norton speech prefixes refer
to this character as "Prince Harry," and the same designation is used, as here, in stage directions.
2. See Introduction and Textual Note for a discussion
of Falstaff's name.
3. Spanish white wine.
4. Castrated male chickens (an Elizabethan delicacy).
5. Silk cloth, which in some contexts was associated

with prostitutes.
6. The constellation known as the Pleiades. *go by the
moon*: go about at moonlight; tell time by the light of
the moon.
7. Evidently a line from a contemporary ballad or
romance about Phoebus, the sun god of classical
mythology.
8. Virtue; with a pun also on "grace" as meaning "God's
favor" and "a prayer before meals." Falstaff asserts that
Hal has none of these and so must be called "your
majesty," rather than "your grace," which was also a
title of honor.
9. *egg and butter*: a mere snack needing only the shortest grace.
1. Let not we who steal by night. Falstaff alludes to the
attendants of knights known as "squires of the body."

day's beauty. Let us be 'Diana's foresters',² 'gentlemen of the
shade', 'minions of the moon', and let men say we be men of
good government,° being governed, as the sea is, by our noble *conduct*
25 and chaste mistress the moon, under whose countenance° we *face; protection*
steal.

PRINCE HARRY   Thou sayst well, and it holds well° too, for the *the comparison is apt*
fortune of us that are the moon's men doth ebb and flow like
the sea, being governed as the sea is by the moon. As for proof
30 now: a purse of gold most resolutely snatched on Monday
night, and most dissolutely spent on Tuesday morning; got
with swearing 'lay by!',³ and spent with crying 'bring in!';⁴ now
in as low an ebb as the foot of the ladder, and by and by in as
high a flow as the ridge° of the gallows.⁵ *crossbar*

35 FALSTAFF   By the Lord, thou sayst true, lad; and is not my Hostess of the tavern a most sweet wench?

PRINCE HARRY   As the honey of Hybla,⁶ my old lad of the cas-
tle;⁷ and is not a buff jerkin⁸ a most sweet robe of durance?° *durability; imprisonment*

FALSTAFF   How now, how now, mad wag? What, in thy quips
40 and thy quiddities?° What a plague have I to do with a buff *quibbles (wordplay)*
jerkin?

PRINCE HARRY   Why, what a pox⁹ have I to do with my Hostess
of the tavern?

FALSTAFF   Well, thou hast called her to a reckoning¹ many a
45 time and oft.

PRINCE HARRY   Did I ever call for thee to pay thy part?²

FALSTAFF   No, I'll give thee thy due, thou hast paid all there.

PRINCE HARRY   Yea, and elsewhere so far as my coin would
stretch;³ and where it would not, I have used my credit.

50 FALSTAFF   Yea, and so used it that were it not here apparent that
thou art heir apparent—but I prithee, sweet wag, shall there
be gallows standing in England when thou art king, and resolution thus fubbed⁴ as it is with the rusty curb of old father
Antic° the law? Do not thou when thou art king hang a thief. *buffoon*

55 PRINCE HARRY   No, thou shalt.

FALSTAFF   Shall I? O, rare! By the Lord, I'll be a brave° judge! *fine; well-dressed*

PRINCE HARRY   Thou judgest false already. I mean thou shalt
have the hanging of the thieves, and so become a rare hangman.

60 FALSTAFF   Well, Hal, well; and in some sort it jumps° with my *agrees*
humour° as well as waiting in the court,⁵ I can tell you. *temperament*

PRINCE HARRY   For obtaining of suits?⁶

2. Hunters by moonlight; thieves. In classical mythology, Diana was goddess of the moon.
3. A thief's cry similar to "Hands up!"
4. A tavern customer's call for more food or wine.
5. The Prince's speech is riddled with sexual slang,
including "purse" (line 30) as meaning "vagina" or
"scrotum"; "snatched" (line 30) as "forcibly had sexual
relations with"; "spent" (line 31) as "exhausted by sexual activity"; "lay by" (line 32) as "lie back"; "spent with"
(line 32) as "reached orgasm with"; and "low" (line 33)
and "high" (line 34) as referring to a penis, first limp
and then erect.
6. Region of Sicily renowned for its honey.
7. Slang for "roisterer"; also a play on the name "Old-

castle" (see Introduction).
8. Leather jacket often worn by jailers.
9. The equivalent of "what the devil." The pox literally
was plague or syphilis.
1. You have asked that she present the bill; asked that
she show her value sexually.
2. To pay your bill; to use your penis.
3. So far as my money would go; so far as my ability to
engender, or "coin," a child would take me.
4. And valor (of thieves) thus thwarted.
5. Being in attendance at the royal court or at the court
of justices.
6. Petitions; clothing. The hangman was entitled to
claim the victims' clothing.

FALSTAFF Yea, for obtaining of suits, whereof the hangman
hath no lean wardrobe. 'Sblood,[7] I am as melancholy as a gib
65 cat,° or a lugged bear.[8]   *tomcat*

PRINCE HARRY Or an old lion, or a lover's lute.

FALSTAFF Yea, or the drone of a Lincolnshire bagpipe.

PRINCE HARRY What sayst thou to a hare,[9] or the melancholy of
Moor-ditch?[1]

70 **FALSTAFF** Thou hast the most unsavoury similes, and art
indeed the most comparative,° rascalliest sweet young Prince.   *quick at comparisons*
But Hal, I prithee trouble me no more with vanity.° I would   *worthless things*
to God thou and I knew where a commodity° of good names°   *supply / reputations*
were to be bought. An old lord of the Council rated me the
75 other day in the street about you, sir, but I marked him not;
and yet he talked very wisely, but I regarded him not; and yet
he talked wisely, and in the street too.

PRINCE HARRY Thou didst well, for wisdom cries out in the
streets, and no man regards it.[2]

80 **FALSTAFF** O, thou hast damnable iteration,[3] and art indeed
able to corrupt a saint. Thou hast done much harm upon me,
Hal, God forgive thee for it. Before I knew thee, Hal, I knew
nothing; and now am I, if a man should speak truly, little better than one of the wicked. I must give over this life, and I will
85 give it over. By the Lord, an° I do not, I am a villain. I'll be   *if*
damned for never a° king's son in Christendom.   *for no*

PRINCE HARRY Where shall we take a purse tomorrow, Jack?

FALSTAFF Zounds,[4] where thou wilt, lad! I'll make one;° an I do   *I'll take part*
not, call me villain and baffle me.[5]

90 **PRINCE HARRY** I see a good amendment of life in thee, from
praying to purse-taking.

FALSTAFF Why, Hal, 'tis my vocation,° Hal. 'Tis no sin for a   *calling*
man to labour in his vocation.[6]

Enter POINS

Poins! Now shall we know if Gadshill[7] have set a match.° O,   *planned a theft*
95 if men were to be saved by merit,[8] what hole in hell were hot
enough for him? This is the most omnipotent villain that ever
cried 'Stand!' to a true° man.   *an honest*

PRINCE HARRY Good morrow, Ned.

POINS Good morrow, sweet Hal. [*To* FALSTAFF] What says
100 Monsieur Remorse? What says Sir John, sack-and-sugar
Jack?[9] How agrees the devil and thee about thy soul, that thou
soldest him on Good Friday[1] last, for a cup of Madeira[2] and a
cold capon's leg?

---

7. By His blood (an oath alluding to Christ's crucifixion).
8. A baited bear. In a popular form of entertainment,
bears were led in chains and set upon by dogs.
9. The hare's sadness was proverbial. Its flesh, when
eaten, was supposed to generate melancholy.
1. An open sewer outside the walls of London.
2. A biblical allusion to Proverbs 1:20–24.
3. You have a soul-endangering way of reading Scripture. This is one of several speeches in which Falstaff
uses a language associated with Puritans.
4. By Christ's wounds (a strong oath).
5. And subject me to public disgrace. Falstaff alludes
to the practice of "baffling," in which perjured knights
or effigies of them were hung upside down in public
places.

6. Allusion to 1 Corinthians 7:20 and Ephesians 4:1.
Falstaff is misusing the biblical injunction to work at
one's vocation to justify robbery.
7. A thief named after Gad's Hill, the place where he
practices his robberies. This hill, near Rochester on the
road from Canterbury to London, was notorious for
highway robberies.
8. By good works (as opposed to salvation by God's
grace).
9. "Jack" is a nickname for "John," but the word also
means "a drinking vessel" or "a knave." Falstaff likes
sugar in his sack, or sweet white wine.
1. The strictest of fast days in the Christian calendar.
2. A white wine exported from Madeira, an island off
the coast of west Africa.

PRINCE HARRY Sir John stands to° his word, the devil shall have   *keeps*
105   his bargain, for he was never yet a breaker of proverbs: he will
       give the devil his due.
POINS [*to* FALSTAFF] Then art thou damned for keeping thy
       word with the devil.
PRINCE HARRY Else he had been damned for cozening° the   *cheating*
110   devil.
POINS But my lads, my lads, tomorrow morning by four o'clock
       early, at Gads Hill, there are pilgrims going to Canterbury
       with rich offerings, and traders riding to London with fat
       purses. I have visors° for you all; you have horses for your-   *masks*
115   selves. Gadshill lies° tonight in Rochester. I have bespoke°   *lodges / ordered*
       supper tomorrow night in Eastcheap.³ We may do it as secure°   *safely*
       as sleep. If you will go, I will stuff your purses full of crowns;
       if you will not, tarry at home and be hanged.
FALSTAFF Hear ye, Edward, if I tarry at home and go not, I'll
120   hang you for going.
POINS You will, chops?°   *fat cheeks*
FALSTAFF Hal, wilt thou make one?
PRINCE HARRY Who, I rob? I a thief? Not I, by my faith.
FALSTAFF There's neither honesty,° manhood, nor good fel-   *honor*
125   lowship in thee, nor thou camest not of the blood royal, if
       thou darest not stand for° ten shillings.⁴   *fight for; be worth*
PRINCE HARRY Well then, once in my days I'll be a madcap.
FALSTAFF Why, that's well said.
PRINCE HARRY Well, come what will, I'll tarry at home.
130   FALSTAFF By the Lord, I'll be a traitor then, when thou art king.
PRINCE HARRY I care not.
POINS Sir John, I prithee leave the Prince and me alone. I will
       lay him down such reasons for this adventure that he shall go.
FALSTAFF Well, God give thee the spirit of persuasion and him
135   the ears of profiting, that what thou speakest may move and
       what he hears may be believed, that the true prince may, for
       recreation' sake, prove a false thief; for the poor abuses of the
       time want countenance.⁵ Farewell. You shall find me in
       Eastcheap.
140   PRINCE HARRY Farewell, the latter spring; farewell, All-hallown
       summer.⁶   [*Exit* FALSTAFF]
POINS Now, my good sweet honey lord, ride with us tomorrow.
       I have a jest to execute that I cannot manage alone. Falstaff,
       Peto, Bardolph, and Gadshill shall rob those men that we
145   have already waylaid—yourself and I will not be there—and
       when they have the booty, if you and I do not rob them, cut
       this head off from my shoulders.
PRINCE HARRY But how shall we part with them in setting forth?
POINS Why, we will set forth before or after them and appoint
150   them a place of meeting, wherein it is at our pleasure to fail.
       And then will they adventure upon the exploit themselves,
       which they shall have no sooner achieved but we'll set upon
       them.

3. A street and market district in London, evidently the   6. Addressing Falstaff as youth in age (a second spring)
location of the play's tavern.   and likening him to a period of unusually mild weather
4. A 10-shilling coin was called a "royal," thus punning   (a second summer) occurring around All Hallows' Day,
on the Prince's "blood royal."   November 1.
5. Lack encouragement (from those of high rank).

PRINCE HARRY Ay, but 'tis like that they will know us by our
155   horses, by our habits,° and by every other appointment,° to be   *clothing / item*
  ourselves.
POINS Tut, our horses they shall not see—I'll tie them in the
  wood; our visors we will change after we leave them; and, sirrah,[7] I have cases of buckram for the nonce,[8] to immask° our   *hide*
160   noted° outward garments.   *known*
PRINCE HARRY But I doubt they will be too hard for us.[9]
POINS Well, for two of them, I know them to be as true-bred
  cowards as ever turned back; and for the third, if he fight
  longer than he sees reason, I'll forswear arms. The virtue of
165   this jest will be the incomprehensible° lies that this same fat   *boundless*
  rogue will tell us when we meet at supper: how thirty at least
  he fought with, what wards,° what blows, what extremities he   *parries*
  endured; and in the reproof° of this lives the jest.   *disproof*
PRINCE HARRY Well, I'll go with thee. Provide us all things nec-
170   essary, and meet me tomorrow night in Eastcheap; there I'll
  sup. Farewell.
POINS Farewell, my lord.   *Exit*
PRINCE HARRY I know you all, and will a while uphold
  The unyoked humour° of your idleness.   *unbridled whims*
175   Yet herein will I imitate the sun,
  Who doth permit the base contagious° clouds   *disease-carrying*
  To smother up his beauty from the world,
  That° when he please again to be himself,   *So that*
  Being wanted° he may be more wondered at   *Having been missed*
180   By breaking through the foul and ugly mists
  Of vapours that did seem to strangle him.
  If all the year were playing holidays,
  To sport would be as tedious as to work;
  But when they seldom come, they wished-for come,
185   And nothing pleaseth but rare accidents.°   *exceptional events*
  So when this loose behaviour I throw off
  And pay the debt I never promisèd,
  By how much better than my word I am,
  By so much shall I falsify men's hopes;°   *expectations*
190   And like bright metal on a sullen ground,°   *dull background*
  My reformation, glitt'ring o'er my fault,
  Shall show more goodly and attract more eyes
  Than that which hath no foil to set it off.
  I'll so offend to° make offence a skill,°   *as to / an art*
195   Redeeming time[1] when men think least I will.   *Exit*

1.3

Enter the KING, [*the Earls of*] NORTHUMBERLAND [*and*]
WORCESTER, HOTSPUR, *Sir Walter* BLUNT, *with other*
[*lords*]

KING HENRY [*to* HOTSPUR, NORTHUMBERLAND, *and* WORCESTER]
  My blood hath been too cold and temperate,
  Unapt° to stir at these indignities,   *Slow*

---

7. A familiar form of address, conventionally used with
social inferiors.
8. I have suits of coarse cloth for the purpose.
9. But I fear they will be more than we can manage.
1. Making amends for misspent time. Injunctions to

redeem time were both proverbial and biblical: see
Ephesians 5:16 or Colossians 4:5.
1.3. Location: A royal residence, probably Windsor
Castle.

And you have found me,° for accordingly   *discovered this fact*
You tread upon my patience; but be sure
5   I will from henceforth rather be myself,°   *(i.e., my royal self)*
Mighty and to be feared, than my condition,[1]
Which hath been smooth as oil, soft as young down,
And therefore lost that title of° respect   *claim to*
Which the proud soul ne'er pays but to the proud.
10   WORCESTER   Our house,[2] my sovereign liege, little deserves
The scourge of greatness to be used on it,
And that same greatness too, which our own hands
Have holp° to make so portly.°   *helped / majestic*
NORTHUMBERLAND [*to the* KING]   My lord—
KING HENRY   Worcester, get thee gone, for I do see
15   Danger and disobedience in thine eye.
O sir, your presence is too bold and peremptory,°   *proud*
And majesty might never yet endure
The moody frontier[3] of a servant brow.
You have good leave° to leave us. When we need   *full permission*
20   Your use and counsel we shall send for you. *Exit* WORCESTER
You were about to speak.
NORTHUMBERLAND   Yea, my good lord.
Those prisoners in your highness' name demanded,
Which Harry Percy here at Holmedon took,
Were, as he says, not with such strength denied
25   As was delivered° to your majesty,   *reported*
Who either through envy° or misprision°   *malice / error*
Was guilty of this fault, and not my son.
HOTSPUR [*to the* KING]   My liege, I did deny no prisoners;
But I remember, when the fight was done,
30   When I was dry° with rage and extreme toil,   *thirsty*
Breathless and faint, leaning upon my sword,
Came there a certain lord, neat and trimly dressed,
Fresh as a bridegroom, and his chin, new-reaped,[4]
Showed° like a stubble-land at harvest-home.[5]   *Looked*
35   He was perfumèd like a milliner,[6]
And 'twixt his finger and his thumb he held
A pouncet-box,[7] which ever and anon
He gave his nose and took't away again—
Who° therewith angry, when it next came there   *(the nose)*
40   Took it in snuff[8]—and still he smiled and talked;
And as the soldiers bore dead bodies by,
He called them untaught knaves, unmannerly
To bring a slovenly° unhandsome corpse   *base; nasty*
Betwixt the wind and his nobility.
45   With many holiday and lady° terms   *dainty and effeminate*
He questioned me; amongst the rest demanded
My prisoners in your majesty's behalf.
I then, all smarting with my wounds being cold—
To be so pestered with a popinjay!°—   *parrot; vain dandy*

---

1. My natural (mild) temperament.
2. The Percy family, which had supported Henry against Richard II.
3. The angry expression (punning on "frontier" as meaning both "forehead" and "military fortifications").
4. Newly trimmed. London in the 1590s witnessed a fashion for close-shaved beards.

5. At the end of harvest (when the fields are cut back to stubble).
6. Seller of finely scented apparel such as bonnets, ribbons, and gloves. The name derives from the fact that these goods were often imports from Milan.
7. Perfume box with a perforated lid.
8. Took offense at it; inhaled it.

50 Out of my grief° and my impatience   *pain*
    Answered neglectingly,° I know not what—   *negligently*
    He should, or should not—for he made me mad
    To see him shine so brisk, and smell so sweet,
    And talk so like a waiting gentlewoman
55 Of guns, and drums, and wounds, God save the mark!⁹
    And telling me the sovereign'st° thing on earth   *best*
    Was parmacity¹ for an inward bruise,
    And that it was great pity, so it was,
    This villainous saltpetre² should be digged
60 Out of the bowels of the harmless earth,
    Which many a good tall° fellow had destroyed   *brave*
    So cowardly, and but for these vile guns
    He would himself have been a soldier.
    This bald unjointed° chat of his, my lord,   *This trivial incoherent*
65 Made me to answer indirectly, as I said,
    And I beseech you, let not his report
    Come current° for an accusation   *Be taken as valid*
    Betwixt my love and your high majesty.
    BLUNT [*to the* KING]   The circumstance considered, good my lord,
70 Whate'er Lord Harry Percy then had said
    To such a person, and in such a place,
    At such a time, with all the rest retold,
    May reasonably die, and never rise
    To do him wrong or any way impeach
75 What then he said, so° he unsay it now.   *if*
    KING HENRY   Why, yet he doth deny° his prisoners,   *refuse to hand over*
    But with proviso and exception
    That we at our own charge shall ransom straight°   *immediately*
    His brother-in-law the foolish Mortimer,³
80 Who, on my soul, hath wilfully betrayed
    The lives of those that he did lead to fight
    Against that great magician, damned Glyndŵr—
    Whose daughter, as we hear, the Earl of March
    Hath lately married. Shall our coffers, then,
85 Be emptied to redeem a traitor home?
    Shall we buy treason, and indent with fears⁴
    When they have lost and forfeited themselves?
    No, on the barren mountains let him starve;
    For I shall never hold that man my friend
90 Whose tongue shall ask me for one penny cost
    To ransom home revolted° Mortimer—   *rebellious*
    HOTSPUR   Revolted Mortimer?
    He never did fall off,° my sovereign liege,   *change allegiance*
    But by the chance of war. To prove that true
95 Needs no more but one tongue for all those wounds,
    Those mouthèd° wounds, which valiantly he took   *gaping; eloquent*

---

9. God keep evil away (an expression of indignation).
1. Spermaceti, an oily substance from the sperm whale that was used in various medicines and potions. The spelling "parmacity" probably derives from the ointment's association with the Italian city of Parma.
2. The main ingredient of gunpowder.
3. Shakespeare follows Holinshed's *Chronicles* in confusing or conflating two Edmund Mortimers. One was

captured by Glyndŵr and later became Glyndŵr's son-in-law and Hotspur's brother-in-law. The other, the fifth Earl of March, was his nephew and claimed the English throne as a descendant of Lionel, Duke of Clarence, third son of Edward III. This Mortimer was the one named by Richard II as his presumptive heir.
4. And bargain with those whom we have reason to fear.

	When on the gentle Severn's[5] sedgy° bank,	*marshy*
	In single opposition, hand to hand,	
	He did confound° the best part of an hour	*consume*
100	In changing hardiment° with great Glyndŵr.	*matching valor*
	Three times they breathed,° and three times did they drink,	*rested*
	Upon agreement, of swift Severn's flood,	
	Who, then affrighted with their bloody looks,	
	Ran fearfully among the trembling reeds,	
105	And hid his crisp° head in the hollow bank,	*rippled*
	Bloodstainèd with these valiant combatants.	
	Never did bare and rotten policy°	*cunning*
	Colour° her working with such deadly wounds,	*Disguise*
	Nor never could the noble Mortimer	
110	Receive so many, and all willingly.	
	Then let not him be slandered with revolt.[6]	

KING HENRY   Thou dost belie° him, Percy, thou dost belie him.   *misrepresent*
He never did encounter with Glyndŵr. I tell thee,
He durst as well have met the devil alone
As Owain Glyndŵr for an enemy.
Art thou not ashamed? But, sirrah, henceforth
Let me not hear you speak of Mortimer.
Send me your prisoners with the speediest means,
Or you shall hear in such a kind from me
As will displease you.—My lord Northumberland,
We license your departure with your son.
[*To* HOTSPUR] Send us your prisoners, or you'll hear of it.
Exeunt [all but HOTSPUR *and* NORTHUMBERLAND]

HOTSPUR   An if° the devil come and roar for them   *An if=If*
I will not send them. I will after straight°   *go after him at once*
And tell him so, for I will ease my heart,
Although it be with hazard of my head.

NORTHUMBERLAND   What, drunk with choler?° Stay and pause awhile.   *anger*
Enter [the Earl of] WORCESTER
Here comes your uncle.

HOTSPUR   Speak of Mortimer?
Zounds, I will speak of him, and let my soul
Want mercy° if I do not join with him.   *Be damned*
In his behalf I'll empty all these veins,
And shed my dear blood drop by drop in the dust,
But I will lift the downfall° Mortimer   *downfallen*
As high in the air as this unthankful King,
As this ingrate and cankered° Bolingbroke.[7]   *corrupted*

NORTHUMBERLAND [*to* WORCESTER]   Brother, the King hath
made your nephew mad.

WORCESTER   Who struck this heat up after I was gone?

HOTSPUR   He will forsooth have all my prisoners;
And when I urged the ransom once again
Of my wife's brother, then his cheek looked pale,
And on my face he turned an eye of death,°   *a menacing look*
Trembling even at the name of Mortimer.

---

5. The Severn River flows from Wales into Bristol
Channel in England.
6. With the accusation of having revolted.

7. Henry's family name. Hotspur's use of it suggests his
unwillingness to acknowledge Henry as King.

WORCESTER   I cannot blame him: was not he proclaimed
By Richard, that dead is, the next of blood?°   *heir to the throne*
145 NORTHUMBERLAND   He was; I heard the proclamation.
And then it was when the unhappy° King,   *unfortunate*
Whose wrongs in us° God pardon, did set forth   *done by us*
Upon his Irish expedition,[8]
From whence he, intercepted,° did return   *interrupted*
150 To be deposed, and shortly murderèd.
WORCESTER   And for whose death we in the world's wide mouth
Live scandalized° and foully spoken of.   *disgraced*
HOTSPUR   But soft,° I pray you; did King Richard then   *wait*
Proclaim my brother° Edmund Mortimer   *brother-in-law*
Heir to the crown?
155 NORTHUMBERLAND   He did; myself did hear it.
HOTSPUR   Nay, then I cannot blame his cousin[9] King
That wished him on the barren mountains starve.
But shall it be that you that set the crown
Upon the head of this forgetful man,
160 And for his sake wear the detested blot
Of murderous subornation,[1] shall it be
That you a world of curses undergo,
Being the agents or base second means,
The cords, the ladder, or the hangman, rather?
165 O, pardon me that I descend so low
To show the line and the predicament
Wherein you range[2] under this subtle° King!   *cunning*
Shall it for shame be spoken in these days,
Or fill up chronicles in time to come,
170 That men of your nobility and power
Did gage° them both in an unjust behalf,°   *pledge / cause*
As both of you, God pardon it, have done:
To put down Richard, that sweet lovely rose,
And plant this thorn, this canker,[3] Bolingbroke?
175 And shall it in more shame be further spoken
That you are fooled, discarded, and shook off
By him for whom these shames ye underwent?
No; yet time serves° wherein you may redeem   *is available*
Your banished honours, and restore yourselves
180 Into the good thoughts of the world again,
Revenge the jeering and disdained° contempt   *disdainful*
Of this proud King, who studies day and night
To answer° all the debt he owes to you   *satisfy*
Even with the bloody payment of your deaths.
Therefore, I say—
185 WORCESTER   Peace, cousin, say no more.
And now I will unclasp a secret book,
And to your quick-conceiving discontents
I'll read you matter deep and dangerous,
As full of peril and adventurous spirit

---

8. As Shakespeare dramatizes in *Richard II,* Bolingbroke returned to England from exile in France while
Richard was at war in Ireland.
9. Punning on "cozen" (cheat).
1. Of assisting with a murder.
2. *To . . . range:* To show the degree and category into

which you might be classified (with a pun on "line" as
meaning "hangman's rope" and on "predicament" as
meaning "an unpleasant situation").
3. Wild and inferior kind of rose; also, cankerworm
(which destroys plants), or ulcerated sore.

190   As to o'erwalk° a current roaring loud   *walk across*
     On the unsteadfast footing of a spear.
     HOTSPUR   If he fall in, good night, or sink or swim.[4]
     Send danger from the east unto the west,
     So° honour cross it from the north to south;   *Provided*
195   And let them grapple. O, the blood more stirs
     To rouse a lion than to start a hare!
     NORTHUMBERLAND [*to* WORCESTER]   Imagination of some great exploit
     Drives him beyond the bounds of patience.
     HOTSPUR   By heaven, methinks it were an easy leap
200   To pluck bright honour from the pale-faced moon,
     Or dive into the bottom of the deep,
     Where fathom-line[5] could never touch the ground,
     And pluck up drownèd honour by the locks,
     So he that doth redeem her thence might wear,
205   Without corrival,° all her dignities.   *competitor*
     But out upon this half-faced fellowship!°   *paltry sharing of honors*
     WORCESTER [*to* NORTHUMBERLAND]   He apprehends a world of
         figures[6] here,
     But not the form of what he should attend.°   *pay attention to*
     [*To* HOTSPUR] Good cousin, give me audience for a while,
210   And list° to me.   *listen*
     HOTSPUR   I cry you mercy.°   *I beg your pardon*
     WORCESTER   Those same noble Scots[7]
     That are your prisoners—
     HOTSPUR   I'll keep them all.
     By God, he shall not have a Scot of them;
     No, if a scot would save his soul he shall not.
     I'll keep them, by this hand.
215   WORCESTER   You start away,
     And lend no ear unto my purposes.
     Those prisoners you shall keep.
     HOTSPUR   Nay, I will; that's flat.
     He said he would not ransom Mortimer,
     Forbade my tongue to speak of Mortimer;
220   But I will find him when he lies asleep,
     And in his ear I'll hollo 'Mortimer!'
     Nay, I'll have a starling shall be taught to speak
     Nothing but 'Mortimer', and give it him
     To keep his anger still° in motion.   *constantly*
225   WORCESTER   Hear you, cousin, a word.
     HOTSPUR   All studies here I solemnly defy,°   *renounce*
     Save how to gall and pinch° this Bolingbroke.   *torture*
     And that same sword-and-buckler[8] Prince of Wales—
     But that I think his father loves him not
230   And would be glad he met with some mischance—
     I would have him poisoned with a pot of ale.[9]
     WORCESTER   Farewell, kinsman. I'll talk to you
     When you are better tempered to attend.

---

4. Farewell to him, whether he sinks or manages to swim for a short time.
5. A weighted line used in testing the depth of the sea.
6. Figures of speech; fantasies.
7. Inhabitants of Scotland (with a pun in the following lines on "scot" as meaning "a small sum").
8. In Elizabethan England, the sword and buckler, or small shield, were associated with ordinary fighting men. A prince should use rapier and dagger.
9. A drink associated with the common people.

NORTHUMBERLAND [*to* HOTSPUR]   Why, what a wasp-stung and
      impatient fool
235   Art thou to break into this woman's mood,¹
      Tying thine ear to no tongue but thine own!
   HOTSPUR   Why, look you, I am whipped and scourged with rods,
      Nettled and stung with pismires,° when I hear   *ants*
      Of this vile politician° Bolingbroke.   *schemer*
240   In Richard's time—what d'ye call the place?
      A plague upon't, it is in Gloucestershire.
      'Twas where the madcap Duke his uncle kept—
      His uncle York—where I first bowed my knee
      Unto this king of smiles, this Bolingbroke.²
245   'Sblood, when you and he came back from Ravenspurgh.³
   NORTHUMBERLAND   At Berkeley castle.
   HOTSPUR   You say true.
      Why, what a candy deal of° courtesy   *quantity of sweet*
      This fawning greyhound then did proffer me!
      'Look when° his infant fortune came to age',   *Whenever; as soon as*
250   And 'gentle Harry Percy', and 'kind cousin'.
      O, the devil take such cozeners!°—God forgive me.   *cheaters*
      Good uncle, tell your tale; I have done.
   WORCESTER   Nay, if you have not, to't again.
      We'll stay° your leisure.   *await*
   HOTSPUR   I have done, i'faith.
255   WORCESTER   Then once more to your Scottish prisoners.
      Deliver them up° without their ransom straight;   *Release them*
      And make the Douglas'⁴ son your only mean°   *agent; means*
      For powers° in Scotland, which, for divers reasons   *raising an army*
      Which I shall send you written, be assured
260   Will easily be granted. [*To* NORTHUMBERLAND] You, my lord,
      Your son in Scotland being thus employed,
      Shall secretly into the bosom creep
      Of that same noble prelate well-beloved,
      The Archbishop.
   HOTSPUR   Of York, is't not?
   WORCESTER   True, who bears hard°   *resents*
265   His brother's death at Bristol, the Lord Scrope.⁵
      I speak not this in estimation,°   *as a guess*
      As what I think might be, but what I know
      Is ruminated, plotted, and set down,
      And only stays° but to behold the face   *waits*
270   Of that occasion that shall bring it on.
   HOTSPUR   I smell it; upon my life, it will do well!
   NORTHUMBERLAND   Before the game is afoot thou still lett'st slip.⁶
   HOTSPUR   Why, it cannot choose but be a noble plot—
      And then the power° of Scotland and of York   *army*
      To join with Mortimer, ha?
275   WORCESTER   And so they shall.

---

1. Alluding to the commonplace that women were, by nature, unable to hold their tongues.
2. This event is depicted in *Richard II* 2.3.20–56.
3. Bolingbroke's landing place at the mouth of the Humber River in Yorkshire upon his return from exile.
4. The "the" before Douglas's name indicates that he is head of a Scottish clan or noble family.
5. Richard Scroop (or le Scrope), the Archbishop of York and an ally of the rebels in this play, was actually a distant cousin of William Scroop, Earl of Wiltshire, who was a favorite of Richard II and was executed by Henry IV in 1399. His death is mentioned in *Richard II* 3.2.
6. Before the quarry is even in the field, you always let loose the dogs. This image from hunting implies that Hotspur habitually jumps the gun.

HOTSPUR   In faith, it is exceedingly well aimed.

WORCESTER   And 'tis no little reason bids us speed
    To save our heads by raising of a head;°   *an army*
    For, bear ourselves as even° as we can,   *carefully*
280   The King will always think him in our debt,
    And think we think ourselves unsatisfied
    Till he hath found a time to pay us home.°   *repay us fully*
    And see already how he doth begin
    To make us strangers to his looks of love.

285 HOTSPUR   He does, he does. We'll be revenged on him.

WORCESTER   Cousin, farewell. No further go in this
    Than I by letters shall direct your course.
    When time is ripe, which will be suddenly,°   *soon*
    I'll steal to Glyndŵr and Lord Mortimer,
290   Where you and Douglas and our powers at once,
    As I will fashion it, shall happily meet,
    To bear our fortunes in our own strong arms,
    Which now we hold at° much uncertainty.   *with*

NORTHUMBERLAND   Farewell, good brother. We shall thrive, I
    trust.

295 HOTSPUR [*to* WORCESTER]   Uncle, adieu. O, let the hours be short
    Till fields° and blows and groans applaud our sport!   *battlefields*

          Exeunt [WORCESTER *at one door,*
        NORTHUMBERLAND *and* HOTSPUR *at another door*]

2.1

Enter a CARRIER,[1] *with a lantern in his hand*

FIRST CARRIER   Heigh-ho! An't° be not four by the day,° I'll be   *If it / in the morning*
hanged. Charles's Wain[2] is over the new chimney, and yet our
horse° not packed. What, ostler![3]   *horses*

OSTLER [*within*]   Anon,° anon!   *Right away*

5 FIRST CARRIER   I prithee, Tom, beat cut's saddle,[4] put a few
flocks in the point.[5] Poor jade is wrung in the withers,[6] out of
all cess.°   *measure*

Enter another CARRIER

SECOND CARRIER   Peas and beans° are as dank here as a dog,   *(horse feed)*
and that is the next way to give poor jades the bots.° This   *intestinal worms*
10 house is turned upside down since Robin Ostler died.

FIRST CARRIER   Poor fellow never joyed since the price of oats
rose; it was the death of him.

SECOND CARRIER   I think this be the most villainous house in all
London road for fleas. I am stung like a tench.[7]

15 FIRST CARRIER   Like a tench? By the mass, there is ne'er a king
christen° could be better bit than I have been since the first   *Christian king*
cock.°   *midnight*

2.1 Location: An innyard in Rochester, Kent.
1. One who transports goods for hire.
2. The constellation now known as the Plow or the
Great Bear.
3. One who attends to horses at an inn.
4. Soften the horse's saddle. "Cut" was a term for a
horse with a docked tail or a gelding; here, it may be the

horse's name.
5. Put a few tufts of wood in the saddle's pommel (to
soften it).
6. The poor old horse is extremely sore in the ridge
between its shoulder blades.
7. A spotted fish whose markings may have looked like
flea bites.

SECOND CARRIER   Why, they will allow us ne'er a jordan,° and   *chamber pot*
          then we leak° in your chimney, and your chamber-lye° breeds   *urinate / urine*
20   fleas like a loach.[8]

FIRST CARRIER   What, ostler! Come away, and be hanged, come
          away!

SECOND CARRIER   I have a gammon of bacon° and two races°   *a ham / roots*
          of ginger to be delivered as far as Charing Cross.[9]

25   FIRST CARRIER   God's body, the turkeys in my pannier° are   *basket*
          quite starved! What, ostler! A plague on thee, hast thou never
          an eye in thy head? Canst not hear? An° 'twere not as good deed   *If*
          as drink to break the pate° on thee, I am a very villain. Come,   *skull*
          and be hanged! Hast no faith° in thee?   *responsibility*

          Enter GADSHILL

30   GADSHILL   Good morrow, carriers. What's o'clock?

FIRST CARRIER   I think it be two o'clock.

GADSHILL   I prithee lend me thy lantern to see my gelding in the
          stable.

FIRST CARRIER   Nay, by God, soft.° I know a trick worth two of   *wait*
35   that, i'faith.

GADSHILL [*to* SECOND CARRIER]   I pray thee, lend me thine.

SECOND CARRIER   Ay, when? Canst tell?[1] 'Lend me thy lantern,'
          quoth a.° Marry, I'll see thee hanged first.   *says he*

GADSHILL   Sirrah carrier, what time do you mean to come to
40   London?

SECOND CARRIER   Time enough to go to bed with a candle, I
          warrant° thee.—Come, neighbour Mugs, we'll call up the   *assure*
          gentlemen. They will along° with company, for they have great   *travel*
          charge.°   *Exeunt* [CARRIERS]   *have valuable cargo*

45   GADSHILL   What ho, chamberlain![2]

          Enter CHAMBERLAIN

CHAMBERLAIN   'At hand' quoth Pickpurse.[3]

GADSHILL   That's even as fair° as "'At hand" quoth the cham-   *good*
          berlain', for thou variest no more from picking of purses than
          giving direction doth from labouring:[4] thou layest the plot°   *plan*
50   how.

CHAMBERLAIN   Good morrow, Master Gadshill. It holds current
          that° I told you yesternight. There's a franklin in the   *holds true what*
          Weald[5] of Kent hath brought three hundred marks[6] with him
          in gold. I heard him tell it to one of his company last night at
55   supper—a kind of auditor, one that hath abundance of charge
          too, God knows what. They are up already, and call for eggs
          and butter; they will away presently.

GADSHILL   Sirrah, if they meet not with Saint Nicholas's
          clerks,[7] I'll give thee this neck.

60   CHAMBERLAIN   No, I'll none of it; I pray thee keep that for the
          hangman, for I know thou worshippest Saint Nicholas as truly
          as a man of falsehood may.

---

8. A fish. The comparison means that urine breeds
fleas either as a loach breeds loaches or as a loach
breeds fleas. There was a popular belief that some fish
spawned flies or fleas.
9. A marketplace between London and Westminster.
1. A retort similar to "Never."
2. Bedroom attendant. In popular discourse, chamberlains were notorious for their complicity with thieves.
3. "I am at your disposal," as the thief said (evidently a

popular tag).
4. For you are not more different from a pickpocket
than an overseer is from a laborer.
5. There's a small landowner in the wooded region.
6. Coins worth two-thirds of a pound each.
7. Slang for "highway robbers." St. Nicholas was variously regarded as the patron saint of travelers and of
thieves.

GADSHILL   What talkest thou to me of the hangman? If I hang,
I'll make a fat pair of gallows, for if I hang, old Sir John hangs
65   with me, and thou knowest he's no starveling. Tut, there are
other Trojans[8] that thou dreamest not of, the which° for sport'   who
sake are content to do the profession° some grace, that would,   (of robbery)
if matters should be looked into, for their own credit' sake
make all whole.° I am joined with no foot-landrakers,[9] no   set things right
70   long-staff sixpenny strikers,[1] none of these mad mustachio
purple-hued maltworms,[2] but with nobility and tranquillity,
burgomasters and great 'oyez'-ers;[3] such as can hold in,° such   can keep a secret
as will strike sooner than speak, and speak sooner than drink,
and drink sooner than pray. And yet, zounds, I lie, for they
75   pray continually to their saint the commonwealth; or rather,
not pray to her, but prey on her; for they ride up and down[4]
on her and make her their boots.°   booty; footwear
CHAMBERLAIN   What, the commonwealth their boots? Will she
hold out water in foul way?[5]
80   GADSHILL   She will, she will, justice hath liquored her.[6] We steal
as in a castle,° cocksure; we have the recipe of fern-seed,[7] we   in complete safety
walk invisible.
CHAMBERLAIN   Nay, by my faith, I think you are more beholden
to the night than to fern-seed for your walking invisible.
85   GADSHILL   Give me thy hand; thou shalt have a share in our
purchase,° as I am a true man.   plunder
CHAMBERLAIN   Nay, rather let me have it as you are a false thief.
GADSHILL   Go to, 'homo'° is a common name to all men. Bid the   man
ostler bring my gelding out of the stable. Farewell, you muddy°   stupid
90   knave.   Exeunt [severally]°   separately

2.2

Enter PRINCE [HARRY], POINS, PETO [and BARDOLPH][1]
POINS   Come, shelter, shelter!
          [Exeunt PETO and BARDOLPH at another door]
I have removed Falstaff's horse, and he frets° like a gummed   worries; frays
velvet.[2]
PRINCE HARRY   Stand close!°   [Exit POINS]   concealed
          Enter FALSTAFF
5   FALSTAFF   Poins! Poins, and be hanged! Poins!
PRINCE HARRY   Peace, ye fat-kidneyed rascal! What a brawling
dost thou keep!
FALSTAFF   Where's Poins, Hal?
PRINCE HARRY   He is walked up to the top of the hill. I'll go seek
10   him.   [Exit]

8. Slang for "roisterers."
9. Highwaymen who travel on foot (rather than on
horse).
1. Thieves who carried crude weapons and robbed for
small sums.
2. These drunkards with wild mustaches and purple
faces.
3. Court officials who cried "Oyez," or "Hear ye."
4. They travel (with a pun on "ride" as meaning "to
mount sexually").
5. Will she keep water out (off your feet) on a muddy

road; will she protect you in difficulty?
6. Greased her (as one waterproofs leather); bribed
her.
7. Popularly supposed to make those who wore it invisible.
2.2 Location: The highway, Gad's Hill.
1. For a discussion of the names of "Bardolph" and
"Peto," see the Textual Note and Introduction.
2. Like cheap velvet treated with gum. Gummed velvet
was shiny but wore out quickly.

FALSTAFF   I am accursed to rob in that thief's company. The
rascal hath removed my horse and tied him I know not where.
If I travel but four foot by the square° further afoot, I shall   *(a measuring tool)*
break my wind.° Well, I doubt not but to die a fair death, for[3]   *be breathless; fart*
15   all this—if I scape hanging for killing that rogue. I have forsworn his company hourly any time this two-and-twenty
years, and yet I am bewitched with the rogue's company. If the
rascal have not given me medicines° to make me love him, I'll   *love potions*
be hanged. It could not be else: I have drunk medicines.
20   Poins! Hal! A plague upon you both! Bardolph! Peto! I'll starve
ere I'll rob a foot further. An 'twere not as good a deed as drink
to turn true man° and to leave these rogues, I am the veriest   *repent; turn informer*
varlet that ever chewed with a tooth. Eight yards of uneven
ground is threescore and ten miles afoot with me, and the
25   stony-hearted villains know it well enough. A plague upon't
when thieves cannot be true one to another!

They whistle. [Enter PRINCE HARRY, POINS, PETO, *and*
BARDOLPH]*[4]

Whew! A plague upon you all! Give me my horse, you rogues,
give me my horse, and be hanged!

PRINCE HARRY   Peace, ye fat-guts. Lie down, lay thine ear close
30   to the ground, and list if thou canst hear the tread of travellers.

FALSTAFF   Have you any levers to lift me up again, being down?
'Sblood, I'll not bear my own flesh so far afoot again for all the
coin in thy father's exchequer. What a plague mean ye to colt°   *trick*
35   me thus?

PRINCE HARRY   Thou liest: thou art not colted, thou art
uncolted.°   *unhorsed*

FALSTAFF   I prithee, good Prince Hal, help me to my horse,
good king's son.

PRINCE HARRY   Out, ye rogue, shall I be your ostler?

40   FALSTAFF   Hang thyself in thine own heir-apparent garters![5] If
I be ta'en, I'll peach° for this. An I have not ballads made on   *inform against you*
you all and sung to filthy tunes,[6] let a cup of sack be my poi-
son. When a jest is so forward, and afoot too![7] I hate it.

Enter GADSHILL *[visored]°*   *wearing a mask*

GADSHILL   Stand!

45   FALSTAFF   So I do, against my will.

POINS   O, 'tis our setter,° I know his voice. Gadshill, what   *one who sets up a crime*
news?

GADSHILL[8]   Case ye,° case ye, on with your visors! There's   *Disguise yourselves*
money of the King's coming down the hill; 'tis going to the
50   King's exchequer.

FALSTAFF   You lie, ye rogue, 'tis going to the King's tavern.

---

3. Die a natural death, despite.
4. It is not clear exactly when the Prince and his companions show themselves to the frustrated Falstaff.
They can all enter here, or the Prince and Poins could
enter at line 28 and Bardolph and Peto at the same time
as Gadshill at line 43.
5. Falstaff's version of the proverb "He may hang himself in his own garters." As the heir to the throne, the
Prince was a member of the Order of the Garter, the
highest order of English knighthood.
6. Ballads on topical themes were sung by ballad
singers and sold cheaply as broadsides in streets, the-

aters, and other public places.
7. When a plot (to rob) is so advanced and goes so well;
when a joke (on me) goes so far and makes me go on
foot.
8. In Q, this speech is assigned to Bardolph; but Poins
has just asked Gadshill a question, so one expects an
answer to come from him. It has been conjectured that
the confusion here may reflect confusion in Shakespeare's foul papers about whether Bardolph and Gadshill were to be two characters or one. See note to
2.5.159.

GADSHILL There's enough to make° us all.   *make fortunes for*

FALSTAFF To be hanged.

[They put on visors]

PRINCE HARRY Sirs, you four shall front° them in the narrow   *confront*
55 lane. Ned Poins and I will walk lower. If they scape from your
encounter, then they light on us.

PETO How many be there of them?

GADSHILL Some eight or ten.

FALSTAFF Zounds, will they not rob us?

60 PRINCE HARRY What, a coward, Sir John Paunch?

FALSTAFF Indeed I am not John of Gaunt[9] your grandfather,
but yet no coward, Hal.

PRINCE HARRY Well, we leave that to the proof.°   *test*

POINS Sirrah Jack, thy horse stands behind the hedge. When
65 thou needest him, there thou shalt find him. Farewell, and
stand fast.

FALSTAFF Now cannot I strike him if I should be hanged.

PRINCE HARRY *[aside to POINS]* Ned, where are our disguises?

POINS *[aside to the PRINCE]* Here, hard by. Stand close.

[Exeunt the PRINCE and POINS]

70 FALSTAFF Now, my masters, happy man be his dole,[1] say I;
every man to his business.

[They stand aside.]

Enter the TRAVELLERS [amongst them the CARRIERS]

FIRST TRAVELLER Come, neighbour, the boy shall lead our
horses down the hill. We'll walk afoot a while, and ease their
legs.

75 THIEVES *[coming forward]* Stand!

SECOND TRAVELLER Jesus bless us!

FALSTAFF Strike, down with them, cut the villains' throats! Ah,
whoreson caterpillars,[2] bacon-fed knaves! They hate us youth.
Down with them, fleece them!

80 FIRST TRAVELLER O, we are undone, both we and ours for ever!

FALSTAFF Hang ye, gorbellied° knaves, are ye undone? No, ye   *potbellied*
fat chuffs;[3] I would your store° were here. On, bacons,° on!   *all you own / fat men*
What, ye knaves! Young men must live. You are grand-jurors,[4]
are ye? We'll jure ye, faith.

*Here they rob them and bind them. Exeunt [the THIEVES
with the TRAVELLERS]*

2.3

*Enter PRINCE [HARRY] and POINS [disguised in buckram
suits]*

PRINCE HARRY The thieves have bound the true° men; now   *honest*
could thou and I rob the thieves, and go merrily to London. It
would be argument° for a week, laughter for a month, and a   *topic for discussion*
good jest for ever.

5 POINS Stand close; I hear them coming.

[They stand aside]

*Enter [FALSTAFF, BARDOLPH, PETO, and GADSHILL, with
the travellers' money]*

---

9. Henry IV's father. Falstaff puns on "Gaunt" as meaning "lean"; in fact, his name is derived from "Ghent,"
his birthplace.
1. Proverbial expression meaning "Good luck to everyone."
2. Parasites. *whoreson*: an insult derived from "whore's

son."
3. Rude, churlish fellows; misers.
4. Referring to the fact that only prosperous citizens
served on grand juries.
2.3 Location: Scene continues.

FALSTAFF   Come, my masters, let us share, and then to horse
before day. An° the Prince and Poins be not two arrant cow-   *If*
ards, there's no equity stirring.° There's no more valour in that   *justice to be found*
Poins than in a wild duck.

     As they are sharing, the PRINCE *and* POINS *set upon*
     them

10 PRINCE HARRY   Your money!

POINS   Villains!

     They all [GADSHILL, BARDOLPH, *and* PETO] *run away*
     [*severally*] *and* FALSTAFF, *after a blow or two,* [*roars and*]
     runs away too, leaving the booty behind them

PRINCE HARRY   Got with much ease. Now merrily to horse.
The thieves are all scattered, and possessed with fear
So strongly that they dare not meet each other.
15 Each takes his fellow for an officer.
Away, good Ned. Falstaff sweats to death,
And lards° the lean earth as he walks along.   *drips fat on*
Were't not for laughing, I should pity him.

POINS   How the fat rogue roared!   *Exeunt* [*with the booty*]

2.4

     Enter HOTSPUR, *reading a letter*

HOTSPUR   'But for mine own part, my lord, I could be well con-
tented to be there, in respect of° the love I bear your house.'°—   *because of / family*
He could be contented; why is he not then? In respect of the
love he bears our house! He shows in this he loves his own barn
5 better than he loves our house. Let me see some more.—'The
purpose you undertake is dangerous'— Why, that's certain: 'tis
dangerous to take a cold, to sleep, to drink; but I tell you, my
lord fool, out of this nettle danger we pluck this flower safety.—
'The purpose you undertake is dangerous, the friends you have
10 named uncertain, the time itself unsorted,° and your   *unsuitable*
whole plot too light for the counterpoise of° so great an   *to counterbalance*
opposition.'— Say you so, say you so? I say unto you again, you
are a shallow, cowardly hind,° and you lie. What a lack-brain   *peasant*
is this! By the Lord, our plot is a good plot as ever was laid,
15 our friends true and constant; a good plot, good friends, and
full of expectation; an excellent plot, very good friends. What
a frosty-spirited rogue is this! Why, my lord of York° commends   *(Archbishop Scrope)*
the plot and the general course of the action. Zounds, an I
were now by this rascal, I could brain him with his lady's fan!
20 Is there not my father, my uncle, and myself? Lord Edmund
Mortimer, my lord of York, and Owain Glyndŵr? Is there not
besides the Douglas? Have I not all their letters, to meet me
in arms by the ninth of the next month? And are they not
some of them set forward already? What a pagan rascal is this,
25 an infidel! Ha, you shall see now, in very sincerity of fear and
cold heart will he to the King, and lay open all our proceedings! O, I could divide myself and go to buffets[1] for moving°   *urging*
such a dish of skim-milk with so honourable an action! Hang
him! Let him tell the King we are prepared; I will set forward
30 tonight.

     Enter his Lady [LADY PERCY]

2.4 Location: The Percys' home, Warkworth Castle, in
Northumberland.

1. I could split myself into two and fall to blows with
myself.

How now, Kate? I must leave you within these two hours.

LADY PERCY   O my good lord, why are you thus alone?
For what offence have I this fortnight been
A banished woman from my Harry's bed?

35 Tell me, sweet lord, what is't that takes from thee
Thy stomach,° pleasure, and thy golden sleep?   °appetite
Why dost thou bend thine eyes upon the earth,
And start so often when thou sitt'st alone?
Why hast thou lost the fresh blood in thy cheeks,

40 And given my treasures and my rights² of thee
To thick-eyed° musing and curst melancholy?   °vacantly staring
In thy faint° slumbers I by thee have watched,   °restless
And heard thee murmur tales of iron wars,
Speak terms of manège° to thy bounding steed,   °horsemanship

45 Cry 'Courage! To the field!' And thou hast talked
Of sallies and retires,° of trenches, tents,   °advances and retreats
Of palisadoes,³ frontiers,° parapets,   °ramparts
Of basilisks, of cannon, culverin,⁴
Of prisoners ransomed, and of soldiers slain,

50 And all the currents of a heady° fight.   °headlong
Thy spirit within thee hath been so at war,
And thus hath so bestirred thee in thy sleep,
That beads of sweat have stood upon thy brow
Like bubbles in a late-disturbèd° stream;   °recently disturbed

55 And in thy face strange motions have appeared,
Such as we see when men restrain their breath
On some great sudden hest.° O, what portents are these?   °command
Some heavy° business hath my lord in hand,   °serious; sad
And I must know it, else he loves me not.

HOTSPUR   What ho!
            [*Enter* SERVANT]

60   Is Gilliams with the packet gone?

SERVANT   He is, my lord, an hour ago.

HOTSPUR   Hath Butler brought those horses from the sheriff?

SERVANT   One horse, my lord, he brought even now.

HOTSPUR   What horse? A roan, a crop-ear, is it not?

SERVANT   It is, my lord.

65 HOTSPUR   That roan shall be my throne.
Well, I will back him straight.—O, *Esperance!*⁵—
Bid Butler lead him forth into the park.

LADY PERCY   But hear you, my lord.

HOTSPUR   What sayst thou, my lady?

LADY PERCY   What is it carries you away?

HOTSPUR   Why, my horse,
My love, my horse.

70 LADY PERCY   Out, you mad-headed ape!
A weasel⁶ hath not such a deal of spleen°   °impulsiveness; anger
As you are tossed with.
In faith, I'll know your business, Harry, that I will.

2. Marriage rights. Alluding to the belief that husbands
and wives owe a mutual marriage debt that obliges
them regularly to engage in sexual relations with one
another.
3. Pointed stakes driven into the ground as defensive
barriers.
4. *basilisks*: large cannons, named after a deadly

mythological reptile. *culverin:* a name for both a kind of
long cannon and a firearm noted for its ability to fire
over a long range.
5. Referring to the Percy motto *Esperance ma comforte,*
or "Hope is my reliance."
6. Weasels were proverbially quarrelsome.

I fear my brother Mortimer doth stir
75   About his title, and hath sent for you
     To line° his enterprise; but if you go—   strengthen
HOTSPUR   So far afoot? I shall be weary, love.
LADY PERCY   Come, come, you paraquito,° answer me   little parrot
     Directly to this question that I ask.
80   In faith, I'll break thy little finger,° Harry,   (euphemism for "penis")
     An if thou wilt not tell me all things true.
HOTSPUR   Away, away, you trifler! Love? I love thee not,
     I care not for thee, Kate. This is no world
     To play with maumets⁷ and to tilt° with lips.   duel
85   We must have bloody noses and cracked crowns,⁸
     And pass them current,⁹ too. God's me,° my horse!—   God save me
     What sayst thou, Kate? What wouldst thou have with me?
LADY PERCY   Do you not love me? Do you not indeed?
     Well, do not, then, for since you love me not
90   I will not love myself. Do you not love me?
     Nay, tell me if you speak in jest or no.
HOTSPUR   Come, wilt thou see me ride?
     And when I am a-horseback,¹ I will swear
     I love thee infinitely. But hark you, Kate.
95   I must not have you henceforth question me
     Whither I go, nor reason whereabout.°   discuss about what
     Whither I must, I must; and, to conclude,
     This evening must I leave you, gentle Kate.
     I know you wise, but yet no farther wise
100 Than Harry Percy's wife; constant you are,
     But yet a woman;² and for secrecy
     No lady closer,° for I well believe   more secretive
     Thou wilt not utter what thou dost not know.
     And so far will I trust thee, gentle Kate.
105 LADY PERCY   How, so far?
HOTSPUR   Not an inch further. But hark you, Kate,
     Whither I go, thither shall you go too.
     Today will I set forth, tomorrow you.
     Will this content you, Kate?
LADY PERCY   It must, of force.°   Exeunt   of necessity

2.5

          Enter PRINCE [HARRY]
PRINCE HARRY   Ned, prithee come out of that fat° room, and   stuffy
     lend me thy hand to laugh a little.
          Enter POINS [*at another door*]
POINS   Where hast been, Hal?
PRINCE HARRY   With three or four loggerheads,° amongst three   blockheads
5   or fourscore hogsheads.° I have sounded the very bass-string of casks for liquor
     humility. Sirrah, I am sworn brother to a leash of drawers,° and group of three tapsters
     can call them all by their christen names, as 'Tom', 'Dick', and
     'Francis'. They take it already, upon their salvation, that

---

7. Breasts; dolls; false gods. The term derived from "mahomet," whom English Protestants viewed as a false god worshipped by heathen peoples.
8. Punning on "cracked crowns" as meaning "broken heads" and "counterfeit currency." Hotspur may be alluding to the acts of rape associated with warfare: "nose" is slang for "penis," and a "cracked crown" can

mean a "whore" or "deflowered woman."
9. Establish them as the norm; let them circulate.
1. On my horse; having sexual intercourse.
2. Women were assumed to be great talkers who could keep no secrets.
2.5 Location: An inn in Eastcheap, London.

though I be but Prince of Wales yet I am the king of courtesy,
10 and tell me flatly I am no proud jack° like Falstaff, but a   *fellow*
Corinthian,¹ a lad of mettle, a good boy—by the Lord, so they
call me; and when I am King of England I shall command all
the good lads in Eastcheap. They call drinking deep 'dyeing
scarlet',² and when you breathe in your watering³ they cry
15 'Hem!' and bid you 'Play it off!'° To conclude, I am so good a   *Drink up*
proficient in one quarter of an hour that I can drink with any
tinker° in his own language during my life. I tell thee, Ned,   *itinerant pot mender*
thou hast lost much honour that thou wert not with me in this
action. But, sweet Ned—to sweeten which name of Ned I give
20 thee this penny-worth of sugar,⁴ clapped even now into my
hand by an underskinker,° one that never spake other English   *assistant tapster*
in his life than 'Eight shillings and sixpence', and 'You are wel-
come', with this shrill addition, 'Anon,° anon, sir! Score° a   *At once / Chalk up*
pint of bastard⁵ in the Half-moon!'⁶ or so. But, Ned, to drive
25 away the time till Falstaff come, I prithee do thou stand in
some by-room, while I question my puny° drawer to what end   *inexperienced*
he gave me the sugar, and do thou never leave calling 'Fran-
cis!', that his tale to me may be nothing but 'Anon!' Step aside,
and I'll show thee a precedent.°   [*Exit* POINS]   *give you a foretaste*
30 POINS [*within*]   Francis!
PRINCE HARRY   Thou art perfect.
POINS [*within*]   Francis!
          Enter [FRANCIS, *a*] *drawer*
FRANCIS   Anon, anon, sir!—Look down into the Pomegranate,⁷
Ralph!
35 PRINCE HARRY   Come hither, Francis.
FRANCIS   My lord.
PRINCE HARRY   How long hast thou to serve,⁸ Francis?
FRANCIS   Forsooth, five years, and as much as to—
POINS [*within*]   Francis!
40 FRANCIS   Anon, anon, sir!
PRINCE HARRY   Five year! By'r Lady,⁹ a long lease for the clink-
ing of pewter. But Francis, darest thou be so valiant as to play
the coward with thy indenture,° and show it a fair pair of   *contract*
heels, and run from it?
45 FRANCIS   O Lord, sir, I'll be sworn upon all the books° in En-   *(Bibles)*
gland, I could find in my heart—
POINS [*within*]   Francis!
FRANCIS   Anon, sir!
PRINCE HARRY   How old art thou, Francis?
50 FRANCIS   Let me see, about Michaelmas¹ next I shall be—
POINS [*within*]   Francis!
FRANCIS   Anon, sir! [*To the* PRINCE] Pray, stay a little, my lord.

1. A rich, licentious man. In contemporary texts, ancient Corinth was famous for wealth and sensuality.
2. Referring to the ruddy complexion associated with drunkards or to the fact that urine, a product of drink, was used to dye wool.
3. When you pause to breathe in your drink.
4. Tapsters sold sugar to sweeten wine.
5. A Spanish wine, so named because it was mixed or adulterated with honey.

6. Name of the inn room to which the wine is to be charged.
7. Name of another room in the inn.
8. Serve as apprentice. Apprenticeship typically began at age twelve or fourteen and lasted seven years.
9. By our Lady (an oath invoking the Virgin Mary).
1. September 29, a holy day honoring the archangel Michael and signifying to tradespeople the close of an accounting period.

PRINCE HARRY   Nay, but hark you, Francis. For the sugar thou
    gavest me, 'twas a pennyworth, was't not?

55 FRANCIS   O Lord, I would it had been two!

PRINCE HARRY   I will give thee for it a thousand pound. Ask me
    when thou wilt, and thou shalt have it—

POINS [*within*]   Francis!

FRANCIS   Anon, anon!

60 PRINCE HARRY   Anon, Francis? No, Francis, but tomorrow,
    Francis; or, Francis, o' Thursday; or, indeed, Francis, when
    thou wilt. But Francis.

FRANCIS   My lord.

PRINCE HARRY   Wilt thou rob this leathern-jerkin, crystal-
65 button, knot-pated, agate-ring, puke-stocking, caddis-garter,
    smooth-tongue, Spanish-pouch?[2]

FRANCIS   O Lord, sir, who do you mean?

PRINCE HARRY   Why, then, your brown bastard is your only
    drink![3] For look you, Francis, your white canvas doublet will
70 sully.° In Barbary,[4] sir, it cannot come to° so much.   *get dirty / be worth*

FRANCIS   What, sir?

POINS [*within*]   Francis!

PRINCE HARRY   Away, you rogue! Dost thou not hear them call?
    [*As he departs* POINS *and the* PRINCE] *both call him. The
    Drawer stands amazed, not knowing which way to go.*
    Enter VINTNER°   *Innkeeper*

VINTNER   What, standest thou still, and hearest such a calling?
75 Look to the guests within.   [*Exit* FRANCIS]
    My lord, old Sir John with half a dozen more are at the door.
    Shall I let them in?

PRINCE HARRY   Let them alone a while, and then open the door.
    [*Exit* VINTNER]
    Poins!

80 POINS [*within*]   Anon, anon, sir!
    Enter POINS

PRINCE HARRY   Sirrah, Falstaff and the rest of the thieves are at
    the door. Shall we be merry?

POINS   As merry as crickets, my lad. But hark ye, what cunning
    match° have you made with this jest of the drawer? Come,   *game*
85 what's the issue?°   *outcome*

PRINCE HARRY   I am now of all humours that have showed
    themselves humours[5] since the old days of goodman° Adam to   (*title for a farmer*)
    the pupil° age of this present twelve o'clock at midnight.   *youthful*
    [*Enter* FRANCIS]
    What's o'clock, Francis?

90 FRANCIS   Anon, anon, sir!   [*Exit at another door*]

---

2. Referring (satirically) to Francis's employer, who
would be robbed of Francis's labor if the apprentice
were to run away. This employer is imagined as dressing in the manner of an upwardly mobile Londoner,
wearing a leather jacket ("jerkin") with crystal buttons
and keeping his hair close-cropped ("knot-pated"). He
also wears a signet ring with a carved agate, dark
("puke") stockings, and garters made from caddis ribbon (a cheaper alternative to silk). He has a simpering
style of speech and carries a vintner's pouch made of
Spanish leather.

3. The best of all drinks; the only drink you'll get (if you
stay in the tavern). This entire speech seems meant to
mystify Francis while obliquely warning him that he
will get dirty and be poor if he fulfills his apprenticeship.
4. North African region from which England acquired
sugar.
5. That is, I am in the mood for anything. Renaissance
medical theory held that four body fluids, or humors,
determined by their relative proportions the health,
temperament, and moods of an individual.

PRINCE HARRY   That ever this fellow should have fewer words than a parrot, and yet the son of a woman! His industry is upstairs and downstairs, his eloquence the parcel of a reckoning.° I am not yet of Percy's mind, the Hotspur of the North—he that kills me° some six or seven dozen of Scots at a breakfast, washes his hands, and says to his wife, 'Fie upon this quiet life! I want work.' 'O my sweet Harry,' says she, 'how many hast thou killed today?' 'Give my roan horse a drench,'° says he, and answers, 'Some fourteen,' an hour after; 'a trifle, a trifle.' I prithee call in Falstaff. I'll play Percy, and that damned brawn° shall play Dame Mortimer his wife. 'Rivo!'[6] says the drunkard. Call in Ribs, call in Tallow.°

items of a bill
he that slays

dose of medicine

fat boar
fat drippings

Enter FALSTAFF [*with sword and buckler,* BARDOLPH, PETO, *and* GADSHILL, *followed by* FRANCIS, *with wine*]

POINS   Welcome, Jack. Where hast thou been?

FALSTAFF   A plague of all cowards, I say, and a vengeance too, marry and amen!—Give me a cup of sack, boy.—Ere I lead this life long, I'll sew netherstocks,° and mend them and foot° them too. A plague of all cowards!—Give me a cup of sack, rogue. Is there no virtue extant?

stockings / making a new foot for

He drinketh

PRINCE HARRY   Didst thou never see Titan° kiss a dish of butter— pitiful hearted Titan—that melted at the sweet tale of the sun's? If thou didst, then behold that compound.[7]

the sun

FALSTAFF [*to* FRANCIS]   You rogue, here's lime[8] in this sack too. There is nothing but roguery to be found in villainous man, yet a coward is worse than a cup of sack with lime in it.

[*Exit* FRANCIS][9]

A villainous coward! Go thy ways, old Jack, die when thou wilt. If manhood, good manhood, be not forgot upon the face of the earth, then am I a shotten herring.[1] There lives not three good men unhanged in England, and one of them is fat and grows old, God help the while.° A bad world, I say. I would I were a weaver[2]—I could sing psalms, or anything. A plague of all cowards, I say still.

these times

PRINCE HARRY   How now, woolsack, what mutter you?

FALSTAFF   A king's son! If I do not beat thee out of thy kingdom with a dagger of lath,[3] and drive all thy subjects afore thee like a flock of wild geese, I'll never wear hair on my face more. You, Prince of Wales!

PRINCE HARRY   Why, you whoreson round man, what's the matter?

FALSTAFF   Are not you a coward? Answer me to that. And Poins there?

POINS   Zounds, ye fat paunch, an ye call me coward, by the Lord I'll stab thee.

---

6. An exclamation associated with boisterous drinking.
7. Combination; that is, the melted butter (referring to Falstaff).
8. Often added to bad wine to make it dry and sparkling.
9. Neither Q nor F indicates when Francis leaves the stage. He plays no further part in the action after this, so an exit here avoids the problem of having a character onstage with no obvious function.

1. A herring that has spawned its roe and is thus very thin.
2. Weavers were reputed to sing the Psalms of the Bible at work. Many were Puritans, and some had emigrated from the zealously Protestant Low Countries.
3. A wooden dagger, which was the weapon associated with the Vice figure in medieval morality plays (see note to line 413).

FALSTAFF   I call thee coward? I'll see thee damned ere I call
thee coward, but I would give a thousand pound I could run
135   as fast as thou canst. You are straight enough in the shoulders;
you care not who sees your back. Call you that backing of your
friends? A plague upon such backing! Give me them that will
face me. Give me a cup of sack. I am a rogue if I drunk today.

PRINCE HARRY   O villain, thy lips are scarce wiped since thou
140   drunkest last.

FALSTAFF   All is one for that.°   *It doesn't matter*

He drinketh

A plague of all cowards, still say I.

PRINCE HARRY   What's the matter?

FALSTAFF   What's the matter? There be four of us here have
145   ta'en a thousand pound this day morning.°   *this morning*

PRINCE HARRY   Where is it, Jack, where is it?

FALSTAFF   Where is it? Taken from us it is. A hundred upon
poor four of us.

PRINCE HARRY   What, a hundred, man?

150   FALSTAFF   I am a rogue if I were not at half-sword° with a dozen   *dueling closely*
of them, two hours together. I have scaped by miracle. I am
eight times thrust through the doublet,° four through the hose,°   *short jacket / breeches*
my buckler° cut through and through, my sword hacked like   *shield*
a handsaw. *Ecce signum.*[4]

[*He shows his sword*]

155   I never dealt better since I was a man. All would not do.[5] A
plague of all cowards! [*Pointing to* GADSHILL, PETO, *and* BAR-
DOLPH] Let them speak. If they speak more or less than truth,
they are villains and the sons of darkness.

PRINCE HARRY[6]   Speak, sirs, how was it?

160   GADSHILL   We four set upon some dozen—

FALSTAFF [*to the* PRINCE]   Sixteen at least, my lord.

GADSHILL   And bound them.

PETO   No, no, they were not bound.

FALSTAFF   You rogue, they were bound every man of them, or
165   am a Jew else, an Hebrew Jew.

GADSHILL   As we were sharing, some six or seven fresh men set
upon us.

FALSTAFF   And unbound the rest; and then come in the other.

PRINCE HARRY   What, fought you with them all?

170   FALSTAFF   All? I know not what you call all, but if I fought not
with fifty of them, I am a bunch of radish. If there were not
two- or three-and-fifty upon poor old Jack, then am I no two-
legged creature.

PRINCE HARRY   Pray God you have not murdered some of them.

175   FALSTAFF   Nay, that's past praying for. I have peppered° two of   *made it hot for*
them. Two I am sure I have paid°—two rogues in buckram   *killed*
suits. I tell thee what, Hal, if I tell thee a lie, spit in my face,
call me horse. Thou knowest my old ward°—   *posture of defense*

[*He stands as to fight*]

---

4. Behold the evidence (Latin).
5. All I did was not enough; the whole group was insufficient opposition.
6. This is a second place (see 2.2.48) where textual
confusion surrounds the character of Gadshill. In Q,
this line is assigned to Gadshill and the following line
to Russell (whose name was changed to "Bardolph" as

a result of censorship; see Introduction). In F, this line
is assigned to the Prince and the following line to Gadshill. The next two speeches here assigned to Gadshill
were also given to Russell in Q. The F assignment of
these lines to Gadshill may indicate that at some point
Shakespeare divided between two characters a role
originally designed for one.

here I lay,° and thus I bore my point.° Four rogues in buckram   *stood / sword point*
180   let drive at me.

PRINCE HARRY   What, four? Thou saidst but two even now.

FALSTAFF   Four, Hal, I told thee four.

POINS   Ay, ay, he said four.

FALSTAFF   These four came all afront,° and mainly° thrust at me.   *abreast / mightily*
185   I made me no more ado, but took all their seven points in my
     target,° thus.   *shield*

         [*He wards himself with his buckler*]

PRINCE HARRY   Seven? Why, there were but four even now.

FALSTAFF   In buckram?

POINS   Ay, four in buckram suits.

190 FALSTAFF   Seven, by these hilts,° or I am a villain else.   *sword handle*

PRINCE HARRY [*aside to* POINS]   Prithee, let him alone. We shall
     have more anon.

FALSTAFF   Dost thou hear me, Hal?

PRINCE HARRY   Ay, and mark° thee too, Jack.   *pay attention to; count*

195 FALSTAFF   Do so, for it is worth the listening to. These nine in
     buckram that I told thee of—

PRINCE HARRY [*aside to* POINS]   So, two more already.

FALSTAFF   Their points[7] being broken—

POINS [*aside to the* PRINCE]   Down fell their hose.

200 FALSTAFF   Began to give me ground. But I followed me° close,   *I followed*
     came in foot and hand, and, with a thought,° seven of the eleven   *swift as thought*
     I paid.

PRINCE HARRY [*aside to* POINS]   O monstrous! Eleven buckram
     men grown out of two!

205 FALSTAFF   But, as the devil would have it, three misbegotten
     knaves in Kendal green[8] came at my back and let drive at me;
     for it was so dark, Hal, that thou couldst not see thy hand.

PRINCE HARRY   These lies are like their father that begets
     them—gross as a mountain, open, palpable. Why, thou clay-
210   brained guts, thou knotty-pated° fool, thou whoreson obscene   *blockheaded*
     greasy tallow-catch[9]—

FALSTAFF   What, art thou mad? Art thou mad? Is not the truth
     the truth?

PRINCE HARRY   Why, how couldst thou know these men in
215   Kendal green when it was so dark thou couldst not see thy
     hand? Come, tell us your reason. What sayst thou to this?

POINS   Come, your reason, Jack, your reason.

FALSTAFF   What, upon compulsion? Zounds, an I were at the
     strappado,[1] or all the racks[2] in the world, I would not tell you
220   on compulsion. Give you a reason on compulsion? If reasons
     were as plentiful as blackberries, I would give no man a rea-
     son upon compulsion, I.

PRINCE HARRY   I'll be no longer guilty of this sin. This sanguine°   *red-faced*
     coward, this bed-presser,° this horse-back-breaker, this huge hill   *licentious man*
225   of flesh—

---

7. Sword points, but Poins takes it as meaning "fasten-
ings for hose."
8. A coarse green cloth made in Kendal, Cumbria. It
was associated with poor country people, especially
forest dwellers, as well as outlaws.
9. Greasy lump of fat (gathered by butchers for candle

making).
1. A torture device in which victims were lifted off the
ground by ropes attached to their hands, which were
tied behind their backs, and then let fall.
2. A torture device in which victims' limbs were pulled
apart.

FALSTAFF 'Sblood, you starveling, you elf-skin, you dried neat's°   ox's
tongue, you bull's pizzle, you stock-fish[3]—O, for breath to utter
what is like thee!— you tailor's yard,[4] you sheath, you bow-
case, you vile standing tuck[5]—

230 PRINCE HARRY Well, breathe awhile, and then to't again, and
when thou hast tired thyself in base comparisons, hear me
speak but this.

POINS Mark, Jack.

PRINCE HARRY We two saw you four set on four, and bound
235 them, and were masters of their wealth.—Mark now how a
plain tale shall put you down.—Then did we two set on you
four, and, with a word, outfaced you from your prize, and have
it; yea, and can show it you here in the house. And Falstaff,
you carried your guts away as nimbly, with as quick dexterity,
240 and roared for mercy, and still run and roared, as ever I heard
bull-calf. What a slave art thou, to hack thy sword as thou
hast done, and then say it was in fight! What trick, what
device, what starting-hole° canst thou now find out to hide   refuge
thee from this open and apparent shame?

245 POINS Come, let's hear, Jack; what trick hast thou now?

FALSTAFF By the Lord, I knew ye as well as he that made ye.
Why, hear you, my masters. Was it for me to kill the heir-
apparent? Should I turn upon the true prince? Why, thou
knowest I am as valiant as Hercules;[6] but beware instinct. The
250 lion will not touch the true prince[7]—instinct is a great matter. I was now a coward on instinct. I shall think the better of
myself and thee during my life—I for a valiant lion, and thou
for a true prince. But by the Lord, lads, I am glad you have the
money.—[Calling] Hostess, clap to the doors.—Watch to-
255 night, pray tomorrow.[8] Gallants, lads, boys, hearts of gold, all
the titles of good fellowship come to you! What, shall we be
merry, shall we have a play extempore?

PRINCE HARRY Content, and the argument° shall be thy running   subject
away.

260 FALSTAFF Ah, no more of that, Hal, an thou lovest me.

Enter HOSTESS

HOSTESS O Jesu, my lord the Prince!

PRINCE HARRY How now, my lady the Hostess, what sayst thou
to me?

HOSTESS Marry, my lord, there is a nobleman of the court at door
265 would speak with you. He says he comes from your father.

PRINCE HARRY Give him as much as will make him a royal
man,[9] and send him back again to my mother.

FALSTAFF What manner of man is he?

HOSTESS An old man.

---

3. *bull's pizzle:* a bull's penis that when dried and
stretched was used as a whip. *stock-fish:* dried cod.
4. Tailors were popularly imagined to lack virility. Falstaff puns on "yard" as referring both to a tailor's measuring stick and to his penis.
5. *sheath:* empty case (punning on "sheath" as meaning
"foreskin"). *bow-case:* a long, thin case for unstrung
bows. *standing tuck:* a stiff rapier (with a pun on "standing" as meaning "sexually erect").

6. In classical mythology, a hero who performed prodigious acts of strength and courage.
7. A popular belief derived from classical texts.
8. Falstaff alludes here to Matthew 26:41: "Watch and
pray, that ye enter not into temptation." He puns on
"watch" as meaning "keep vigil" and "carouse" and on
"pray" as meaning "prey."
9. Punning on "nobles" and "royals" as names of coins,
the latter being more valuable.

270 FALSTAFF What doth gravity out of his bed at midnight? Shall
I give him his answer?

PRINCE HARRY Prithee do, Jack.

FALSTAFF Faith, and I'll send him packing.   *Exit*

PRINCE HARRY Now, sirs; [*to* GADSHILL] by'r Lady, you fought
275 fair—so did you, Peto, so did you, Bardolph. You are lions
too—you ran away upon instinct, you will not touch the true
prince; no, fie!

BARDOLPH Faith, I ran when I saw others run.

PRINCE HARRY Faith, tell me now in earnest, how came Fal-
280 staff's sword so hacked?

PETO Why, he hacked it with his dagger, and said he would
swear truth out of England[1] but he would make you believe it
was done in fight, and persuaded us to do the like.

BARDOLPH Yea, and to tickle our noses with speargrass,[2] to make
285 them bleed; and then to beslubber our garments with it, and
swear it was the blood of true men. I did that° I did not this   *what*
seven year before—I blushed to hear his monstrous devices.

PRINCE HARRY O villain, thou stolest a cup of sack eighteen years
ago, and wert taken with the manner,° and ever since thou hast   *caught in the act*
290 blushed extempore.° Thou hadst fire[3] and sword on thy side,   *spontaneously*
and yet thou rannest away. What instinct hadst thou for it?

BARDOLPH [*indicating his face*] My lord, do you see these meteors? Do you behold these exhalations?[4]

PRINCE HARRY I do.

295 BARDOLPH What think you they portend?°   *signify*

PRINCE HARRY Hot livers,[5] and cold° purses.   *empty*

BARDOLPH Choler,[6] my lord, if rightly taken.°   [*Exit*][7]   *understood*

PRINCE HARRY No, if rightly taken, halter.[8]

        Enter FALSTAFF

Here comes lean Jack; here comes bare-bone. How now, my
300 sweet creature of bombast?[9] How long is't ago, Jack, since
thou sawest thine own knee?

FALSTAFF My own knee? When I was about thy years, Hal, I was
not an eagle's talon in the waist; I could have crept into any
alderman's thumb-ring. A plague of sighing and grief—it blows
305 a man up like a bladder. There's villainous news abroad. Here
was Sir John Bracy from your father; you must to the court in
the morning. That same mad fellow of the North, Percy, and
he of Wales that gave Amamon° the bastinado,° and made Luc-   *(a devil) / a beating*
ifer cuckold,[1] and swore the devil his true liegeman° upon the   *subject*
310 cross of a Welsh hook[2]—what a plague call you him?

1. Swear so excessively that Truth, imagined as an allegorical figure, would run out of England to escape him.
2. A plant with sharply pointed leaves.
3. A reference to Bardolph's red face, the focus of the
jests that follow.
4. "Meteors" and "exhalations" refer to the red
blotches on Bardolph's face, here compared to disturbances in the heavens.
5. Short tempers; livers inflamed by drink.
6. The humor associated with an angry disposition.
7. Neither Q nor F marks an exit for Bardolph here,
but both indicate that he reenters at line 439. The nec-

essary exit might well follow this discussion of his
inflamed face.
8. No, if rightly arrested, a noose. The Prince forces a
legal reading on the previous line, playing on "choler"
as "collar," or "noose," and taking "taken" to mean
"arrested."
9. Cotton padding; pompous speech.
1. Slept with the devil's own wife; gave the devil his
horns (the proverbial sign of a cuckold).
2. A heavy weapon with a crooked end, lacking the
cross shape on which oaths were usually made.

POINS   Owain Glyndŵr.

FALSTAFF   Owain, Owain, the same; and his son-in-law Mortimer, and old Northumberland, and that sprightly Scot of Scots
Douglas, that runs a-horseback up a hill perpendicular—

315 PRINCE HARRY   He that rides at high speed and with his pistol
kills a sparrow flying.

FALSTAFF   You have hit it.

PRINCE HARRY   So did he never the sparrow.

FALSTAFF   Well, that rascal hath good mettle in him; he will not

320 run.

PRINCE HARRY   Why, what a rascal art thou, then, to praise him
so for running!

FALSTAFF   A-horseback, ye cuckoo, but afoot he will not budge
a foot.

325 PRINCE HARRY   Yes, Jack, upon instinct.

FALSTAFF   I grant ye, upon instinct. Well, he is there too, and
one Mordake, and a thousand blue-caps° more. Worcester is   Scottish soldiers
stolen away tonight. Thy father's beard is turned white with the
news. You may buy land now as cheap as stinking mackerel.

330 PRINCE HARRY   Why then, it is like, if there come a hot June and
this civil buffeting hold,° we shall buy maidenheads as they buy   continue
hobnails: by the hundreds.³

FALSTAFF   By the mass, lad, thou sayst true; it is like we shall
have good trading that way. But tell me, Hal, art not thou hor-

335 rible afeard? Thou being heir-apparent, could the world pick
thee out three such enemies again as that fiend Douglas, that
spirit Percy, and that devil Glyndŵr? Art thou not horribly
afraid? Doth not thy blood thrill° at it?   shudder

PRINCE HARRY   Not a whit, i'faith. I lack some of thy instinct.

340 FALSTAFF   Well, thou wilt be horribly chid tomorrow when thou
comest to thy father. If thou love me, practise an answer.

PRINCE HARRY   Do thou stand for° my father, and examine me   impersonate
upon the particulars of my life.

FALSTAFF   Shall I? Content. This chair shall be my state,° this   throne

345 dagger my sceptre, and this cushion my crown.
[He sits]

PRINCE HARRY   Thy state is taken for a joint-stool,⁴ thy golden
sceptre for a leaden dagger, and thy precious rich crown for a
pitiful bald crown.

FALSTAFF   Well, an° the fire of grace be not quite out of thee,   if

350 now shalt thou be moved. Give me a cup of sack to make my
eyes look red, that it may be thought I have wept; for I must
speak in passion, and I will do it in King Cambyses' vein.⁵

PRINCE HARRY   [bowing]   Well, here is my leg.°   bow

FALSTAFF   And here is my speech. [To PETO, POINS, and GADS-

355 HILL] Stand aside, nobility.

HOSTESS   O Jesu, this is excellent sport, i'faith.

FALSTAFF   Weep not, sweet Queen,⁶ for trickling tears are vain.

---

3. Alluding to rape as a practice of war or to the notion
that women would be likely to relinquish their virginity
cheaply during wartime.
4. A stool made of wooden pieces fitted or joined
together.
5. In the exaggerated rhetorical style associated with

such early Elizabethan plays as *Cambyses*, a tragedy
about a despotic Persian king.
6. Possibly addressed to the Hostess, with a pun on
"quean" as slang for "whore."

	HOSTESS O the Father, how he holds his countenance!°	*keeps a straight face*
	FALSTAFF For God's sake, lords, convey° my tristful° Queen,	*lead away / sad*
360	For tears do stop° the floodgates of her eyes.	*fill*
	HOSTESS O Jesu, he doth it as like one of these harlotry° players	*vagabond; scurvy*
	as ever I see!	
	FALSTAFF Peace, good pint-pot; peace, good tickle-brain.⁷—	
	Harry, I do not only marvel where thou spendest thy time, but	
365	also how thou art accompanied. For though the camomile,°	*an herb*
	the more it is trodden on, the faster it grows, yet youth, the	
	more it is wasted, the sooner it wears.⁸ That thou art my son	
	I have partly thy mother's word, partly my own opinion, but	
	chiefly a villainous trick° of thine eye, and a foolish hanging	*trait*
370	of thy nether° lip, that doth warrant° me. If then thou be son	*lower / assure*
	to me, here lies the point. Why, being son to me, art thou so	
	pointed at?° Shall the blessed sun of heaven prove a micher,°	*criticized / truant*
	and eat blackberries?—A question not to be asked. Shall the	
	son of England prove a thief, and take purses?—A question to	
375	be asked. There is a thing, Harry, which thou hast often heard	
	of, and it is known to many in our land by the name of pitch.°	*sticky, black tar*
	This pitch, as ancient writers do report, doth defile.⁹ So doth	
	the company thou keepest. For Harry, now I do not speak to	
	thee in drink, but in tears; not in pleasure, but in passion; not	
380	in words only, but in woes also. And yet there is a virtuous	
	man whom I have often noted in thy company, but I know not	
	his name.	
	PRINCE HARRY What manner of man, an it like your majesty?	
	FALSTAFF A goodly, portly man, i'faith, and a corpulent; of a	
385	cheerful look, a pleasing eye, and a most noble carriage;° and,	*bearing*
	as I think, his age some fifty, or, by'r Lady, inclining to three-	
	score. And now I remember me, his name is Falstaff. If that	
	man should be lewdly given,° he deceiveth me; for, Harry, I	*be lustful*
	see virtue in his looks. If, then, the tree may be known by the	
390	fruit, as the fruit by the tree,¹ then peremptorily I speak it—	
	there is virtue in that Falstaff. Him keep with; the rest ban-	
	ish. And tell me now, thou naughty varlet, tell me, where hast	
	thou been this month?	
	PRINCE HARRY Dost thou speak like a king? Do thou stand for	
395	me, and I'll play my father.	
	FALSTAFF [*standing*] Depose me. If thou dost it half so gravely,	
	so majestically both in word and matter, hang me up by the	
	heels for a rabbit sucker,° or a poulter's hare.²	*an unweaned rabbit*
	PRINCE HARRY [*sitting*] Well, here I am set.°	*seated*
400	FALSTAFF And here I stand. [*To the others*] Judge, my masters.	
	PRINCE HARRY Now, Harry, whence come you?	
	FALSTAFF My noble lord, from Eastcheap.	
	PRINCE HARRY The complaints I hear of thee are grievous.	

---

7. Slang term for a strong alcoholic drink, and hence
for the drinker.
8. Falstaff's entire speech is a parody of the previously
fashionable ornate rhetoric exemplified by John Lyly's
Euphues (1578).

9. See Ecclesiasticus 13:1 (also cited in Lyly's
Euphues).
1. An allusion to Matthew 12:33 (which also appears
in Lyly's *Euphues*).
2. A hare sold in a poultry shop.

FALSTAFF 'Sblood, my lord, they are false. [*To the others*] Nay,
405 I'll tickle ye for° a young prince, i'faith. *amuse you as*
PRINCE HARRY Swearest thou, ungracious boy? Henceforth ne'er
look on me. Thou art violently carried away from grace. There
is a devil haunts thee in the likeness of an old fat man; a tun° *large barrel*
of man is thy companion. Why dost thou converse° with that *associate*
410 trunk of humours,[3] that bolting-hutch° of beastliness, that *bin for coarse meal*
swollen parcel of dropsies,[4] that huge bombard° of sack, that *leather wine vessel*
stuffed cloak-bag° of guts, that roasted Manningtree[5] ox with *suitcase*
the pudding° in his belly, that reverend Vice,[6] that grey Iniquity, *stuffing*
that father Ruffian, that Vanity in Years? Wherein is he good,° *virtuous; proficient*
415 but to taste sack and drink it? Wherein neat and cleanly,° but *deft*
to carve a capon and eat it? Wherein cunning, but in craft?
Wherein crafty, but in villainy? Wherein villainous, but in all
things? Wherein worthy, but in nothing?
FALSTAFF I would your grace would take me with you.° Whom *explain what you mean*
420 means your grace?
PRINCE HARRY That villainous, abominable misleader of youth,
Falstaff; that old white-bearded Satan.
FALSTAFF My lord, the man I know.
PRINCE HARRY I know thou dost.
425 FALSTAFF But to say I know more harm in him than in myself
were to say more than I know. That he is old, the more the
pity, his white hairs do witness it. But that he is, saving your
reverence,[7] a whoremaster, that I utterly deny. If sack and
sugar be a fault, God help the wicked. If to be old and merry
430 be a sin, then many an old host° that I know is damned. If to *innkeeper*
be fat be to be hated, then Pharaoh's lean kine[8] are to be
loved. No, my good lord, banish Peto, banish Bardolph, banish Poins, but for sweet Jack Falstaff, kind Jack Falstaff, true
Jack Falstaff, valiant Jack Falstaff, and therefore more valiant
435 being, as he is, old Jack Falstaff,
Banish not him thy Harry's company,
Banish not him thy Harry's company.
Banish plump Jack, and banish all the world.
PRINCE HARRY I do; I will.
[*Knocking within. Exit* HOSTESS.][9]
Enter BARDOLPH, *running*
440 BARDOLPH O my lord, my lord, the sheriff with a most mon-
strous watch° is at the door. *group of constables*
FALSTAFF Out, ye rogue! Play out the play! I have much to say
in the behalf of that Falstaff.
Enter the HOSTESS

---

3. A chest full of body fluids, whose excess, according to Renaissance medical theory, was extremely unhealthy.
4. Diseases characterized by retention of water.
5. Market town in Essex, noted for the Manningtree Fair, where a roasted ox may have been part of the festivities.
6. An irreverent, comic, and (usually) youthful character representing evil and sin in the medieval morality plays. Sometimes named "Iniquity."
7. If you will excuse the expression.
8. In a biblical story in Genesis 41:18–21, Pharaoh dreams of seven lean cows ("kine") that portend seven years of famine.
9. Neither F nor Q marks an exit for the Hostess, but both indicate her reentry at line 443. It makes sense for her to exit here to see about the commotion at her door.

HOSTESS   O Jesu! My lord, my lord!
445   PRINCE HARRY   Heigh, heigh, the devil rides upon a fiddlestick!¹
What's the matter?
HOSTESS   The sheriff and all the watch are at the door. They are
come to search the house. Shall I let them in?
FALSTAFF   Dost thou hear, Hal? Never call a true piece of gold
450   a counterfeit—thou art essentially made, without seeming so.²
PRINCE HARRY   And thou a natural coward without instinct.
FALSTAFF   I deny your major.° If you will deny³ the sheriff, so.   main premise
If not, let him enter. If I become° not a cart° as well as another   adorn / hangman's cart
man, a plague on my bringing up. I hope I shall as soon be
455   strangled with a halter as another.
PRINCE HARRY   Go, hide thee behind the arras.° The rest walk up   tapestry wall hanging
above. Now, my masters, for a true face and good conscience.
   [Exeunt POINS, BARDOLPH, and GADSHILL]
FALSTAFF   Both which I have had, but their date is out;° and   has expired
therefore I'll hide me.
   [He withdraws behind the arras]
460   PRINCE HARRY [to HOSTESS]   Call in the sheriff. [Exit HOSTESS]
   Enter SHERIFF and [a] CARRIER
Now, master sheriff, what is your will with me?
SHERIFF   First, pardon me, my lord. A hue and cry⁴
Hath followed certain men unto this house.
PRINCE HARRY   What men?
465   SHERIFF   One of them is well known, my gracious lord,
A gross, fat man.
CARRIER   As fat as butter.
PRINCE HARRY   The man, I do assure you, is not here,
For I myself at this time have employed him.
And, sheriff, I will engage° my word to thee   pledge
470   That I will by tomorrow dinner-time
Send him to answer thee, or any man,
For anything he shall be charged withal.
And so let me entreat you leave the house.
SHERIFF   I will, my lord. There are two gentlemen
475   Have in this robbery lost three hundred marks.
PRINCE HARRY   It may be so. If he have robbed these men,
He shall be answerable. And so, farewell.
SHERIFF   Good night, my noble lord.
PRINCE HARRY   I think it is good morrow, is it not?
480   SHERIFF   Indeed, my lord, I think it be two o'clock.
                    Exeunt [SHERIFF and CARRIER]
PRINCE HARRY   This oily rascal is known as well as Paul's.°   St. Paul's Cathedral
Go call him forth.
PETO   Falstaff!
   [He draws back the arras, revealing FALSTAFF asleep]
             Fast asleep

1. That is, what a row about nothing.
2. A famously difficult passage. Falstaff may be insisting he is true gold, not a counterfeit (and so should not
be turned over to the watch) just as Hal is a true Prince

("essentially made") despite appearances.
3. If you will refuse to let in.
4. A group of citizens who pursue a criminal.

Behind the arras, and snorting like a horse.
PRINCE HARRY   Hark how hard he fetches breath. Search his
485   pockets.

[PETO] *searcheth his pocket and findeth certain papers.*
[*He closeth the arras and cometh forward*]
What hast thou found?
PETO   Nothing but papers, my lord.
PRINCE HARRY   Let's see what they be. Read them.
PETO [*reads*]   Item: a capon.   2s. 2d.
     Item: sauce.   4d.
490   Item: sack, two gallons.   5s. 8d.
     Item: anchovies and sack after supper.   2s. 6d.
     Item: bread.   ob.°   obolus (*halfpenny*)
PRINCE HARRY   O monstrous! But one halfpennyworth of bread
     to this intolerable deal° of sack! What there is else, keep close;   quantity
495   we'll read it at more advantage.° There let him sleep till day.   *a better opportunity*
     I'll to the court in the morning. We must all to the wars, and
     thy place shall be honourable. I'll procure this fat rogue a
     charge of foot,[5] and I know his death will be a march of twelve
     score.[6] The money shall be paid back again, with advantage.°   interest
500   Be with me betimes° in the morning; and so good morrow,   early
     Peto.
PETO   Good morrow, good my lord.   *Exeunt* [*severally*]

3.1

Enter HOTSPUR, [*the Earl of*] WORCESTER, *Lord* MORTI-
MER, [*and*] *Owain* GLYNDŴR [*with a map*]
MORTIMER   These promises are fair, the parties sure,
     And our induction° full of prosperous hope.[1]   beginning
HOTSPUR   Lord Mortimer and cousin Glyndŵr,
     Will you sit down? And uncle Worcester?
     [MORTIMER, GLYNDŴR, *and* WORCESTER *sit*]
5   A plague upon it, I have forgot the map!
GLYNDŴR   No, here it is. Sit, cousin Percy, sit,
     Good cousin Hotspur;
          [HOTSPUR *sits*]
               For by that name
     As oft as Lancaster[2] doth speak of you,
     His cheek looks pale, and with a rising sigh
     He wisheth you in heaven.
10   HOTSPUR   And you in hell,
     As oft as he hears Owain Glyndŵr spoke of.
GLYNDŴR   I cannot blame him. At my nativity
     The front° of heaven was full of fiery shapes,   forehead
     Of burning cressets;[3] and at my birth

---

5. Command of an infantry company.
6. I know it will kill him to march twelve times twenty
yards or paces.
3.1 Location: Glyndŵr's castle, Wales. According to
Holinshed's *Chronicles*, the events of this scene take
place in the house of the Archdeacon of Bangor; but he
is not present in Shakespeare's scene, and Glyndŵr acts

as host throughout.
1. Full of the hope of prospering.
2. Referring to Henry's title as Duke and hence implying a denial of the legitimacy of his kingship.
3. Metal baskets of fire suspended from long poles;
meteors.

15 　　The frame and huge foundation of the earth
　　　　Shaked like a coward.
　　HOTSPUR　　　　　　　　Why, so it would have done
　　　　At the same season if your mother's cat
　　　　Had but kittened, though yourself had never been born.
　　GLYNDŴR　　I say the earth did shake when I was born.
20 　HOTSPUR　　And I say the earth was not of my mind
　　　　If you suppose as fearing you it shook.
　　GLYNDŴR　　The heavens were all on fire, the earth did tremble—
　　HOTSPUR　　O, then the earth shook to see the heavens on fire,
　　　　And not in fear of your nativity.
25 　　Diseasèd nature oftentimes breaks forth
　　　　In strange eruptions; oft the teeming° earth　　　　　　　　　*fertile*
　　　　Is with a kind of colic pinched and vexed
　　　　By the imprisoning of unruly wind
　　　　Within her womb, which for enlargement° striving　　　　*release*
30 　　Shakes the old beldam° earth, and topples down　　　*grandmother*
　　　　Steeples and moss-grown towers. At your birth
　　　　Our grandam earth, having this distemp'rature,°　　　　*disorder*
　　　　In passion shook.
　　GLYNDŴR　　　　　　　Cousin, of many men
　　　　I do not bear these crossings.° Give me leave　　　*contradictions*
35 　　To tell you once again that at my birth
　　　　The front of heaven was full of fiery shapes,
　　　　The goats ran from the mountains, and the herds
　　　　Were strangely clamorous to the frighted fields.
　　　　These signs have marked me extraordinary,
40 　　And all the courses of my life do show
　　　　I am not in the roll of common men.
　　　　Where is he living, clipped in with° the sea　　　*encircled by*
　　　　That chides the banks° of England, Scotland, Wales,　　　*shores*
　　　　Which° calls me pupil or hath read to° me?　　　*Who / tutored*
45 　　And bring him out° that is but woman's son　　　*show me any man*
　　　　Can trace° me in the tedious ways of art,⁴　　　*follow*
　　　　And hold me pace° in deep experiments.　　　*keep up with me*
　　HOTSPUR [*standing*]　　I think there's no man speaketh better Welsh.⁵
　　　　I'll to dinner.
50 　MORTIMER　　Peace, cousin Percy, you will make him mad.
　　GLYNDŴR　　I can call spirits from the vasty deep.°　　　*lower world*
　　HOTSPUR　　Why, so can I, or so can any man;
　　　　But will they come when you do call for them?
　　GLYNDŴR　　Why, I can teach you, cousin, to command the devil.
55 　HOTSPUR　　And I can teach thee, coz, to shame the devil,
　　　　By telling truth: 'Tell truth, and shame the devil'.
　　　　If thou have power to raise him, bring him hither,
　　　　And I'll be sworn I have power to shame him hence.
　　　　O, while you live, tell truth and shame the devil.
60 　MORTIMER　　Come, come, no more of this unprofitable chat.
　　GLYNDŴR　　Three times hath Henry Bolingbroke made head°　　　*raised an army*
　　　　Against my power;° thrice from the banks of Wye　　　*army*

4. The long, laborious ways of magic.
5. The Welsh language was often described by English
writers as a barbaric one, and "to speak Welsh" commonly meant to use a strange, unintelligible language.
Hotspur implies that Glyndŵr speaks nonsense.

And sandy-bottomed Severn have I sent him
Bootless° home, and weather-beaten back.[6]   *Unsuccessful*

65 HOTSPUR Home without boots, and in foul weather too!
How scapes he agues,° in the devil's name?   *fevers*
GLYNDŴR Come, here's the map. Shall we divide our right,°   *what we are entitled to*
According to our threefold order ta'en?[7]
MORTIMER The Archdeacon hath divided it
70 Into three limits° very equally.   *regions*
England from Trent and Severn hitherto°   *to here*
By south and east is to my part assigned;
All westward—Wales beyond the Severn shore
And all the fertile land within that bound—
75 To Owain Glyndŵr; [*to* HOTSPUR] and, dear coz, to you
The remnant northward lying off from Trent.
And our indentures tripartite° are drawn,   *in triplicate*
Which, being sealèd interchangeably[8]—
A business that this night may execute°—   *may be done tonight*
80 Tomorrow, cousin Percy, you and I
And my good lord of Worcester will set forth
To meet your father and the Scottish power,
As is appointed us, at Shrewsbury.
My father,° Glyndŵr, is not ready yet,   *father-in-law*
85 Nor shall we need his help these fourteen days.
Within that space you may have drawn together
Your tenants, friends, and neighbouring gentlemen.
GLYNDŴR A shorter time shall send me to you, lords;
And in my conduct° shall your ladies come,   *escort*
90 From whom you now must steal and take no leave;
For there will be a world of water shed
Upon the parting of your wives and you.
HOTSPUR Methinks my moiety° north from Burton here   *portion*
In quantity equals not one° of yours.   *either*
95 See how this river comes me cranking in,[9]
And cuts me from the best of all my land
A huge half-moon, a monstrous cantle,° out.   *piece*
I'll have the current in this place dammed up,
And here the smug° and silver Trent shall run   *smooth*
100 In a new channel fair and evenly.
It shall not wind with such a deep indent,
To rob me of so rich a bottom° here.   *lowland plain*
GLYNDŴR Not wind? It shall, it must; you see it doth.
MORTIMER Yea, but mark how he bears his course, and runs me up°   *turns upward*
105 With like advantage on the other side,
Gelding the opposèd continent[1] as much
As on the other side it takes from you.
WORCESTER Yea, but a little charge° will trench° him here,   *expense / rechannel*
And on this north side win this cape of land,
110 And then he runs straight and even.
HOTSPUR I'll have it so; a little charge will do it.

---

6. According to Holinshed, Glyndŵr used magic to raise storms that frustrated Henry's attacks.
7. *threefold:* either an agreement made in triplicate (see line 77) or an agreement having three parts (see the rebels' plan to divide the island into three pieces at lines 68–76). *order ta'en:* agreement made.
8. Bearing the seals of all three nobles.
9. Comes bending in on my shores.
1. Cutting a vital piece from ("gelding") the opposite bank.

GLYNDŴR	I'll not have it altered.	
HOTSPUR	Will not you?	
GLYNDŴR	No, nor you shall not.	

115 HOTSPUR   Who shall say me nay?
GLYNDŴR   Why, that will I.
HOTSPUR   Let me not understand you, then: speak it in Welsh.
GLYNDŴR   I can speak English, lord, as well as you;
For I was trained up in the English court,
120   Where, being but young, I framèd to the harp
Many an English ditty lovely well,
And gave the tongue a helpful ornament[2]—
A virtue that was never seen in you.
HOTSPUR   Marry, and I am glad of it, with all my heart.
125   I had rather be a kitten and cry 'mew'
Than one of these same metre ballad-mongers.[3]
I had rather hear a brazen canstick turned,[4]
Or a dry wheel grate on the axle-tree,°   axle
And that would set my teeth nothing on edge,
130   Nothing so much as mincing° poetry.   affected
'Tis like the forced gait of a shuffling° nag.   hobbled
GLYNDŴR   Come, you shall have Trent turned.
HOTSPUR   I do not care. I'll give thrice so much land
To any well-deserving friend;
135   But in the way of bargain—mark ye me—
I'll cavil on° the ninth part of a hair.   quibble about
Are the indentures drawn? Shall we be gone?
GLYNDŴR   The moon shines fair. You may away by night.
I'll haste the writer, and withal°   simultaneously
140   Break with° your wives of your departure hence.   Inform
I am afraid my daughter will run mad,
So much she doteth on her Mortimer.   *Exit*
MORTIMER   Fie, cousin Percy, how you cross my father!
HOTSPUR   I cannot choose. Sometime he angers me
145   With telling me of the moldwarp[5] and the ant,
Of the dreamer Merlin[6] and his prophecies,
And of a dragon and a finless fish,
A clip-winged griffin[7] and a moulten° raven,   moulted
A couching lion and a ramping cat,[8]
150   And such a deal of skimble-skamble° stuff   stupid
As puts me from my faith.[9] I tell you what,
He held me last night at the least nine hours
In reckoning up the several devils' names
That were his lackeys. I cried, 'Hum!' and, 'Well, go to!',
155   But marked him not a word. O, he is as tedious
As a tired horse, a railing wife,
Worse than a smoky house. I had rather live

2. And gave the English language the ornament of a musical setting; and supplemented the English lyrics with pleasing music.
3. Sellers or writers of ballads.
4. A brazen candlestick scraped and polished on a lathe after casting. John Stow's *Survey of London* (1598) records contemporary complaints about the noise of candlestick making.
5. Mole. Holinshed records a prophecy whereby Henry, figured as a mole, would be overthrown by a

dragon, a lion, and a wolf, representing Glyndŵr, Percy, and Mortimer, respectively.
6. Legendary Welsh prophet, wizard, and bard at King Arthur's court.
7. A fabulous beast, part lion and part eagle.
8. Alluding to the heraldic terms "couchant" and "rampant," which mean "crouching" and "rearing fiercely." Hotspur is making fun of Glyndŵr's heraldic preoccupations.
9. As makes me a skeptic, even of religion.

With cheese and garlic, in a windmill, far,
Than feed on cates° and have him talk to me   delicacies
160   In any summer house° in Christendom.   luxurious residence
       MORTIMER   In faith, he is a worthy gentleman,
       Exceedingly well read, and profited°   proficient
       In strange concealments,° valiant as a lion,   In occult arts
       And wondrous affable, and as bountiful
165   As mines of India. Shall I tell you, cousin?
       He holds your temper in a high respect,
       And curbs himself even of his natural scope°   freedom of speech
       When you come 'cross° his humour; faith, he does.   contradict
       I warrant you, that man is not alive
170   Might so have tempted° him as you have done   provoked
       Without the taste of danger and reproof.
       But do not use it oft, let me entreat you.
       WORCESTER [to HOTSPUR]   In faith, my lord, you are too wilful-blame,°   stubborn
       And since your coming hither have done enough
175   To put him quite besides° his patience.   out of
       You must needs learn, lord, to amend this fault.
       Though sometimes it show greatness, courage, blood°—   spirit; noble birth
       And that's the dearest grace° it renders you—   best distinction
       Yet oftentimes it doth present° harsh rage,   show
180   Defect of manners, want of government,
       Pride, haughtiness, opinion,° and disdain,   self-conceit
       The least of which haunting a nobleman
       Loseth men's hearts, and leaves behind a stain
       Upon the beauty of all parts besides,°   all other qualities
185   Beguiling° them of commendation.   Depriving
       HOTSPUR   Well, I am schooled. Good manners be your speed!° give you success
              Enter GLYNDŴR *with the Ladies* [LADY PERCY *and Morti-*
              mer's wife]
       Here come our wives, and let us take our leave.
       [*Mortimer's wife weeps, and speaks to him in Welsh*]
       MORTIMER   This is the deadly spite° that angers me: vexation
       My wife can speak no English, I no Welsh.
190   GLYNDŴR   My daughter weeps she'll not part with you.
       She'll be a soldier, too; she'll to the wars.
       MORTIMER   Good father, tell her that she and my aunt Percy[1]
       Shall follow in your conduct speedily.
              GLYNDŴR *speaks to her in Welsh, and she answers*
              him in the same
       GLYNDŴR   She is desperate here,° a peevish self-willed harlotry,°   on this point / hussy
195   One that no persuasion can do good upon.
              The lady speaks in Welsh
       MORTIMER   I understand thy looks. That pretty Welsh°   (i.e., her tears)
       Which thou down pourest from these swelling heavens°   overflowing eyes
       I am too perfect° in, and but for shame   proficient
       In such a parley° should I answer thee.   In a similar language
              The lady [*kisses him, and speaks*] *again in Welsh*
200   MORTIMER   I understand thy kisses, and thou mine,
       And that's a feeling disputation;[2]
       But I will never be a truant, love,

---

1. Kate, Lady Percy. Her historical counterpart was the sister, not the aunt, of Glyndŵr's son-in-law.   2. A conversation rooted in emotions or in touch.

Till I have learnt thy language, for thy tongue
Makes Welsh as sweet as ditties highly° penned,   *eloquently*
205 Sung by a fair queen in a summer's bower
With ravishing division,° to her lute.   *embellishments*
GLYNDŴR   Nay, if you melt,° then will she run mad.   *weep*
    The lady [sits on the rushes³ and] speaks again in Welsh
MORTIMER   O, I am ignorance itself in this!
GLYNDŴR   She bids you on the wanton° rushes lay you down   *luxurious*
210 And rest your gentle head upon her lap,⁴
And she will sing the song that pleaseth you,
And on your eyelids crown the god of sleep,
Charming your blood with pleasing heaviness,°   *sleepiness*
Making such difference 'twixt wake and sleep
215 As is the difference betwixt day and night
The hour before the heavenly-harnessed team⁵
Begins his golden progress in the east.
MORTIMER   With all my heart, I'll sit and hear her sing.
By that time will our book,° I think, be drawn.   *document*
    [He sits, resting his head on the Welsh lady's lap]
220 GLYNDŴR   Do so, and those musicians that shall play to you
Hang in the air a thousand leagues from hence,
And straight they shall be here. Sit and attend.
HOTSPUR   Come, Kate, thou art perfect in lying down.°   *expert at lovemaking*
Come, quick, quick, that I may lay my head in thy lap.⁶
225 LADY PERCY *[sitting]*   Go, ye giddy goose!
    [HOTSPUR sits, resting his head on Lady Percy's lap.]
    The music plays⁷
HOTSPUR   Now I perceive the devil understands Welsh;
And 'tis no marvel, he is so humorous.°   *eccentric; whimsical*
By'r Lady, he's a good musician.
LADY PERCY   Then should you be nothing but musical,
230 For you are altogether governed by humours.°   *whims*
Lie still, ye thief, and hear the lady sing in Welsh.
HOTSPUR   I had rather hear Lady my brach° howl in Irish.   *female hunting dog*
LADY PERCY   Wouldst thou have thy head broken?
HOTSPUR   No.
235 LADY PERCY   Then be still.
HOTSPUR   Neither—'tis a woman's fault.⁸
LADY PERCY   Now God help thee!
HOTSPUR   To the Welsh lady's bed.
LADY PERCY   What's that?
240 HOTSPUR   Peace; she sings.
    Here the lady sings a Welsh song
HOTSPUR   Come, Kate, I'll have your song too.
LADY PERCY   Not mine, in good sooth.°   *truth*
HOTSPUR   Not yours, in good sooth! Heart,° you swear like a   *By God's heart*
comfit-maker's° wife: 'Not you, in good sooth!' and 'As true as   *confectioner's*
245 I live!' and
'As God shall mend me!' and 'As sure as day!';

---

3. Used as a floor covering, both in houses and on the theater stage.
4. Often a euphemism for the genitals.
5. The sun was supposedly carried in a chariot drawn by horses.
6. "Head" was slang for "penis" and "lap" for "vagina."

7. Instrumental music would probably be played in a so-called music house behind the upper stage in the Elizabethan theater and so might well seem to "hang in the air" (see lines 220–21).
8. No, I won't be still—it is a woman's trait (and I am a man).

And giv'st such sarcenet⁹ surety for thy oaths
As if thou never walk'st further than Finsbury.¹
Swear me, Kate, like a lady as thou art,
250 A good mouth-filling oath, and leave 'in sooth'
And such protest of pepper gingerbread²
To velvet-guards and Sunday citizens.³
Come, sing.

LADY PERCY   I will not sing.

255 HOTSPUR   'Tis the next° way to turn tailor,⁴ or be redbreast   °quickest
teacher.° [Rising] An the indentures be drawn, I'll away within   °or teach birds to sing
these two hours; and so come in when ye will.   Exit

GLYNDŴR   Come, come, Lord Mortimer. You are as slow
As hot Lord Percy is on fire to go.
260 By this° our book is drawn. We'll but seal,   °now
And then to horse immediately.

MORTIMER [rising]   With all my heart.
[The ladies rise, and all] exeunt

3.2

Enter KING [HENRY], PRINCE [HARRY], *and* [lords]

KING HENRY   Lords, give us leave—the Prince of Wales and I
Must have some private conference—but be near at hand,
For we shall presently have need of you.   *Exeunt lords*
I know not whether God will have it so
5 For some displeasing service I have done,
That in his secret doom° out of my blood°   °judgment / lineage
He'll breed revengement and a scourge for me,
But thou dost in thy passages° of life   °course
Make me believe that thou art only marked
10 For° the hot vengeance and the rod of heaven   °To be
To punish my mistreadings. Tell me else,
Could such inordinate° and low desires,   °unsuitable
Such poor, such bare, such lewd, such mean attempts,°   °base undertakings
Such barren pleasures,¹ rude society,
15 As thou art matched withal° and grafted to,   °with
Accompany the greatness of thy blood,
And hold their level° with thy princely heart?   °And claim equality

PRINCE HARRY   So please your majesty, I would I could
Quit° all offences with as clear excuse   °Clear myself of
20 As well as I am doubtless° I can purge   °certain
Myself of many I am charged withal;
Yet such extenuation let me beg
As, in reproof° of many tales devised—   °upon disproof
Which oft the ear of greatness needs must hear
25 By smiling pickthanks° and base newsmongers°—   °flatterers / gossips
I may, for some things true wherein my youth
Hath faulty wandered and irregular,
Find pardon on my true submission.°   °admission of guilt

KING HENRY   God pardon thee! Yet let me wonder, Harry,

9. Flimsy (from the name of a fine silk).
1. Finsbury Fields, north of London, was a popular resort for London's middling classes. Hotspur implies that Kate's mild oaths make her sound like a burgher's wife.
2. Watered-down oaths. Gingerbread was cheaply available at fairs and markets, and sometimes pepper was used as an inexpensive substitute for ginger.

3. Citizens who doff their work clothes and dress up only on Sundays. *To velvet-guards:* To those, like citizens' wives, whose clothes are trimmed ("guarded") with velvet.
4. Tailors were noted for singing.
3.2 Location: The palace, London.
1. Unprofitable habits; nonreproductive erotic pursuits.

30   At thy affections,° which do hold a wing   *inclinations*
      Quite from² the flight of all thy ancestors.
      Thy place in Council thou hast rudely³ lost—
      Which by thy younger brother is supplied—
      And art almost an alien to the hearts
35   Of all the court and princes of my blood.
      The hope and expectation of thy time°   *time of life; youth*
      Is ruined, and the soul of every man
      Prophetically do forethink thy fall.
      Had I so lavish of my presence been,
40   So common-hackneyed⁴ in the eyes of men,
      So stale and cheap to vulgar company,
      Opinion,° that did help me to the crown,   *Public opinion*
      Had still kept loyal to possession,⁵
      And left me in reputeless° banishment,   *inglorious*
45   A fellow of no mark nor likelihood.°   *promise of success*
      By being seldom seen, I could not stir
      But, like a comet, I was wondered at,
      That men would tell their children 'This is he.'
      Others would say 'Where, which is Bolingbroke?'
50   And then I stole all courtesy from heaven,⁶
      And dressed myself in such humility
      That I did pluck allegiance from men's hearts,
      Loud shouts and salutations from their mouths,
      Even in the presence of the crownèd King.
55   Thus did I keep my person fresh and new,
      My presence like a robe pontifical°—   *churchman's rich dress*
      Ne'er seen but wondered at—and so my state,°   *magnificence; royalty*
      Seldom but sumptuous, showed like a feast,
      And won by rareness such solemnity.
60   The skipping King, he ambled up and down
      With shallow jesters and rash bavin° wits,   *brushwood*
      Soon kindled and soon burnt, carded his state,⁷
      Mingled his royalty with cap'ring fools,
      Had his great name profanèd with their scorns,°   *by their scornful manners*
65   And gave his countenance,° against his name,⁸   *approval*
      To laugh at gibing boys, and stand the push°   *tolerate the impudence*
      Of every beardless vain comparative;°   *wit*
      Grew a companion to the common streets,
      Enfeoffed° himself to popularity,   *Surrendered*
70   That, being daily swallowed by men's eyes,
      They surfeited with honey, and began
      To loathe the taste of sweetness, whereof a little
      More than a little is by much too much.
      So when he had occasion to be seen,
75   He was but as the cuckoo is in June,⁹
      Heard, not regarded, seen but with such eyes
      As, sick and blunted with community,°   *familiarity*

2. *which . . . from:* which do fly a course contrary to.
3. By violence. Perhaps alluding to the story, dramatized in *The Famous Victories of Henry V,* that Prince
Hal boxed the Lord Chief Justice on the ear and was
subsequently punished.
4. Cheapened. A hackney was a horse available for
common hire.
5. The possessor of the throne (Richard II).

6. That is, surpassed heaven itself for graciousness.
7. Adulterated his royal dignity. The term refers to a
process ("carding") whereby wool or liquids were mixed
with inferior substances.
8. To the detriment of his reputation.
9. Referring to a proverbial saying, "No one regards the
June cuckoo's song."

Afford no extraordinary gaze
Such as is bent on sun-like majesty
80 When it shines seldom in admiring eyes,
But rather drowsed and hung their eyelids down,
Slept in his face,° and rendered such aspect°   *before his eyes / looks*
As cloudy° men use to their adversaries,   *sullen*
Being with his presence glutted, gorged, and full.
85 And in that very line,° Harry, standest thou;   *category*
For thou hast lost thy princely privilege
With vile participation.° Not an eye   *base companionship*
But is a-weary of thy common sight,
Save mine, which hath desired to see thee more,
90 Which now doth that° I would not have it do—   *what*
Make blind itself with foolish tenderness.
     [*He weeps*]
PRINCE HARRY   I shall hereafter, my thrice-gracious lord,
Be more myself.
KING HENRY   For all the world,
As thou art to this hour was Richard then,
95 When I from France set foot at Ravenspurgh,
And even as I was then is Percy now.
Now by my sceptre, and my soul to boot,
He hath more worthy interest° to the state   *more claim by worth*
Than thou, the shadow° of succession;   *mere image*
100 For, of° no right, nor colour° like to right,   *having / pretext*
He doth fill fields with harness° in the realm,   *armor*
Turns head° against the lion's° armèd jaws,   *Leads a revolt / king's*
And, being no more in debt to years than thou,
Leads ancient lords and reverend bishops on
105 To bloody battles, and to bruising arms.
What never-dying honour hath he got
Against renownèd Douglas!—whose high deeds,
Whose hot incursions and great name in arms,
Holds from all soldiers chief majority°   *preeminence*
110 And military title capital[1]
Through all the kingdoms that acknowledge Christ.
Thrice hath this Hotspur, Mars° in swaddling-clothes, *god of war*
This infant warrior, in his enterprises
Discomfited° great Douglas; ta'en him once;   *Defeated*
115 Enlargèd° him; and made a friend of him   *Released*
To fill the mouth of deep defiance up,[2]
And shake the peace and safety of our throne.
And what say you to this? Percy, Northumberland,
The Archbishop's grace of York, Douglas, Mortimer,
120 Capitulate° against us, and are up.°   *Combine / up in arms*
But wherefore do I tell these news to thee?
Why, Harry, do I tell thee of my foes,
Which° art my near'st and dearest enemy?—   *Who*
Thou that art like enough, through vassal° fear,   *servile*
125 Base inclination, and the start of spleen,°   *fit of temper*
To fight against me under Percy's pay,
To dog his heels, and curtsy at his frowns,

1. And claim to the title of principal (capital) warrior.
2. To add volume to the voice of deep defiance; to fill up the appetite of deep defiance.

To show how much thou art degenerate.

PRINCE HARRY Do not think so; you shall not find it so.
130 And God forgive them that so much have swayed
Your majesty's good thoughts away from me.
I will redeem all this on Percy's head,
And in the closing of some glorious day
Be bold to tell you that I am your son;
135 When I will wear a garment all of blood,
And stain my favours° in a bloody mask,   *features*
Which, washed away, shall scour my shame with it.
And that shall be the day, whene'er it lights,°   *comes*
That this same child of honour and renown,
140 This gallant Hotspur, this all-praisèd knight,
And your unthought-of Harry chance to meet.
For every honour sitting on his helm,
Would they were multitudes, and on my head
My shames redoubled; for the time will come
145 That I shall make this northern youth exchange
His glorious deeds for my indignities.
Percy is but my factor,° good my lord,   *agent*
To engross up° glorious deeds on my behalf;   *amass*
And I will call him to so strict account
150 That he shall render every glory up,
Yea, even the slightest worship of his time,°   *honor of his life*
Or I will tear the reckoning from his heart.
This, in the name of God, I promise here,
The which if he be pleased I shall perform,
155 I do beseech your majesty may salve°   *heal*
The long-grown wounds of my intemperature;°   *disorder; intemperance*
If not, the end of life cancels all bonds,
And I will die a hundred thousand deaths
Ere break the smallest parcel of this vow.
160 **KING HENRY** A hundred thousand rebels die in this.
Thou shalt have charge° and sovereign trust herein.   *military command*
        Enter [Sir Walter] BLUNT
How now, good Blunt? Thy looks are full of speed.
BLUNT So hath the business that I come to speak of.
Lord Mortimer of Scotland[3] hath sent word
165 That Douglas and the English rebels met
The eleventh of this month at Shrewsbury.
A mighty and a fearful head° they are,   *army*
If promises be kept on every hand,
As ever offered foul play in a state.
170 **KING HENRY** The Earl of Westmorland set forth today,
With him my son Lord John of Lancaster,
For this advertisement° is five days old.   *news*
On Wednesday next, Harry, you shall set forward.
On Thursday we ourselves will march.
175 Our meeting is Bridgnorth,[4] and, Harry, you
Shall march through Gloucestershire, by which account,°   *calculation*
Our business valuèd,° some twelve days hence   *taken into account*
Our general forces at Bridgnorth shall meet.

---

3. A Scottish lord who is unrelated to Glyndŵr's son-in-law.   4. A town about 20 miles southeast of Shrewsbury.

Our hands are full of business; let's away.
180   Advantage feeds him fat[5] while men delay.   *Exeunt*

3.3

Enter FALSTAFF [*with a truncheon° at his waist*], *and*   *officer's club*
    BARDOLPH

FALSTAFF   Bardolph, am I not fallen away° vilely since this last   *shrunk*
  action?[1] Do I not bate?° Do I not dwindle? Why, my skin hangs   *grow thin*
  about me like an old lady's loose gown. I am withered like an
  old apple-john.[2] Well, I'll repent, and that suddenly, while I
5   am in some liking.° I shall be out of heart[3] shortly, and then I   *in the mood*
  shall have no strength to repent. An I have not forgotten what
  the inside of a church is made of, I am a peppercorn, a brewer's
  horse°—the inside of a church! Company, villainous company,   *an old workhorse*
  hath been the spoil of me.

10 BARDOLPH   Sir John, you are so fretful you cannot live long.

FALSTAFF   Why, there is it. Come, sing me a bawdy song, make
  me merry. I was as virtuously given° as a gentleman need to   *inclined*
  be: virtuous enough; swore little; diced not—above seven
  times a week; went to a bawdy-house not—above once in a
15   quarter—of an hour; paid money that I borrowed—three or
  four times; lived well, and in good compass.° And now I live   *limits*
  out of all order, out of all compass.

BARDOLPH   Why, you are so fat, Sir John, that you must needs be
  out of all compass,° out of all reasonable compass, Sir John.   *circumference; girth*

20 FALSTAFF   Do thou amend thy face, and I'll amend my life.
  Thou art our admiral,° thou bearest the lantern in the poop[4]—   *flagship*
  but 'tis in the nose of thee. Thou art the Knight of the Burning Lamp.[5]

BARDOLPH   Why, Sir John, my face does you no harm.

25 FALSTAFF   No, I'll be sworn; I make as good use of it as many a
  man doth of a death's head,[6] or a *memento mori*.[7] I never see
  thy face but I think upon hell-fire and Dives that lived in
  purple—for there he is in his robes, burning, burning.[8] If thou
  wert any way given to virtue, I would swear by thy face; my
30   oath should be 'By this fire that's God's angel!' But thou art
  altogether given over,° and wert indeed, but for the light in thy   *dedicated to vice*
  face, the son of utter darkness. When thou rannest up Gads
  Hill in the night to catch my horse, if I did not think thou hadst
  been an *ignis fatuus* or a ball of wildfire,[9] there's no purchase
35   in money. O, thou art a perpetual triumph,° an everlasting   *torchlight procession*
  bonfire-light! Thou hast saved me a thousand marks[1] in links°   *small torches*
  and torches, walking with thee in the night betwixt tavern and

---

5. Opportunities (for rebellion) flourish; the superior
position (of the rebels) improves.
3.3 Location: The inn in Eastcheap, London.
1. This last military engagement (referring to the Gad's
Hill episode).
2. A kind of apple often eaten long after picking, when
its skin was shriveled.
3. Disinclined; weary.
4. The ship's main deck.
5. Parodying figures from popular romance such as
Amadis, the Knight of the Burning Sword.
6. A skull, or representation of a skull, such as was
engraved as an emblem of mortality on seal rings.
7. An object serving as a reminder of mortality (Latin
for "remember you must die").

8. Referring to a biblical parable about a rich man
"clothed in purple and fine linen" who regularly refused
to feed the beggar Lazarus and was ultimately forced to
suffer in hell for his sin (Luke 16:19–23); also referring
to Bardolph's body as bearing the signs of venereal disease. "Burning" implies "on fire with lust" as well as
"infected with syphilitic sores."
9. A flaming explosive used in warfare or in fireworks;
skin marked by erysipelas, an inflammatory disease.
ignis fatuus (Latin for "foolish fire"): a phenomenon in
which phosphorescent light appears on marshy ground;
a false hope.
1. Considerable money (each mark was worth two-
thirds of a pound).

tavern—but the sack that thou hast drunk me° would have   *drunk (at my cost)*
bought me lights as good cheap° at the dearest chandler's² in   *as cheaply*
40   Europe. I have maintained that salamander³ of yours with fire
any time this two-and-thirty years, God reward me for it.

BARDOLPH   'Sblood, I would my face were in your belly!⁴

FALSTAFF   God-a-mercy! So should I be sure to be heartburnt.

Enter HOSTESS

How now, Dame Partlet⁵ the hen, have you enquired yet who
45   picked my pocket?

HOSTESS   Why, Sir John, what do you think, Sir John? Do you
think I keep thieves in my house? I have searched, I have
enquired; so has my husband, man by man, boy by boy, ser-
vant by servant. The tithe° of a hair was never lost in my house   *tenth part*
50   before.

FALSTAFF   Ye lie, Hostess: Bardolph was shaved and lost many
a hair,⁶ and I'll be sworn my pocket was picked. Go to, you are
a woman, go.

HOSTESS   Who, I? No, I defy thee! God's light, I was never
55   called so in mine own house before.

FALSTAFF   Go to, I know you well enough.

HOSTESS   No, Sir John, you do not know me,⁷ Sir John; I know
you, Sir John. You owe me money, Sir John, and now you pick
a quarrel to beguile me of it. I bought you a dozen of shirts to
60   your back.

FALSTAFF   Dowlas,° filthy dowlas. I have given them away to   *Coarse linen*
bakers' wives; they have made bolters° of them.   *sieves*

HOSTESS   Now as I am a true woman, holland° of eight shillings   *fine linen*
an ell.° You owe money here besides, Sir John: for your diet,   *a measure of 45 inches*
65   and by-drinkings,° and money lent you, four-and-twenty pound.   *drinks between meals*

FALSTAFF [*pointing at* BARDOLPH]   He had his part of it. Let him
pay.

HOSTESS   He? Alas, he is poor; he hath nothing.

FALSTAFF   How, poor? Look upon his face. What call you rich?
70   Let them coin his nose, let them coin his cheeks, I'll not pay
a denier.⁸ What, will you make a younker° of me? Shall I not   *novice; gull*
take mine ease in mine inn, but I shall have my pocket picked?
I have lost a seal-ring of my grandfather's worth forty mark.

HOSTESS   O Jesu, [*to* BARDOLPH] I have heard the Prince tell
75   him, I know not how oft, that that ring was copper.

FALSTAFF   How? The Prince is a jack,° a sneak-up.° [*Raising*   *rascal / sly villain*
his truncheon] 'Sblood, an he were here I would cudgel him
like a dog if he would say so.

Enter PRINCE [HARRY *and* PETO], *marching; and* FAL-
STAFF *meets* [*them*], *playing upon his truncheon like a*
fife

How now, lad, is the wind in that door,° i'faith? Must we all   *quarter*
80   march?

BARDOLPH   Yea, two and two, Newgate fashion.⁹

---

2. The most expensive candle maker's.
3. A fabled lizard capable of living in fire. The implication is that Falstaff has maintained the salamander Bardolph with the "fires" of sack or lust.
4. Equivalent to "Stick it down your throat" (a proverbial retort to an insult).
5. A traditional name for hens and for women supposed to talk too much.

6. Had his beard cut; was cheated or robbed of his
money; lost his hair because of syphilis.
7. That is, you don't know how honest I am; you don't
have sexual knowledge of me.
8. French copper coin of little value.
9. Bound like convicts taken to and from London's
Newgate prison.

HOSTESS   My lord, I pray you hear me.

PRINCE HARRY   What sayst thou, Mistress Quickly? How doth
   thy husband?

I love him well; he is an honest man.

85   HOSTESS   Good my lord, hear me!

FALSTAFF   Prithee, let her alone, and list to me.

PRINCE HARRY   What sayst thou, Jack?

FALSTAFF   The other night I fell asleep here behind the arras,
   and had my pocket picked. This house is turned bawdy-
90   house: they pick pockets.

PRINCE HARRY   What didst thou lose, Jack?

FALSTAFF   Wilt thou believe me, Hal, three or four bonds of
   forty pound apiece, and a seal-ring of my grandfather's.

PRINCE HARRY   A trifle, some eightpenny matter.

95   HOSTESS   So I told him, my lord; and I said I heard your grace
   say so; and, my lord, he speaks most vilely of you, like a foul-
   mouthed man as he is, and said he would cudgel you.

PRINCE HARRY   What? He did not!

HOSTESS   There's neither faith, truth, nor womanhood in me
100   else.

FALSTAFF   There's no more faith in thee than in a stewed
   prune,[1] nor no more truth in thee than in a drawn fox;[2] and,
   for womanhood, Maid Marian[3] may be the deputy's wife of
   the ward to° thee. Go, you thing,[4] go!

compared to

105   HOSTESS   Say, what thing, what thing?

FALSTAFF   What thing? Why, a thing to thank God on.

HOSTESS   I am no thing to thank God on. I would thou shouldst
   know it, I am an honest man's wife; and setting thy knighthood aside, thou art a knave to call me so.

110   FALSTAFF   Setting thy womanhood aside, thou art a beast to say
   otherwise.

HOSTESS   Say, what beast, thou knave, thou?

FALSTAFF   What beast? Why, an otter.

PRINCE HARRY   An otter, Sir John? Why an otter?

115   FALSTAFF   Why? She's neither fish nor flesh;[5] a man knows not
   where to have her.[6]

HOSTESS   Thou art an unjust man in saying so. Thou or any
   man knows where to have me, thou knave, thou.

PRINCE HARRY   Thou sayst true, Hostess, and he slanders thee
120   most grossly.

HOSTESS   So he doth you, my lord, and said this other day you
   owed him a thousand pound.

PRINCE HARRY [*to* FALSTAFF]   Sirrah, do I owe you a thousand
   pound?

125   FALSTAFF   A thousand pound, Hal? A million! Thy love is worth
   a million; thou owest me thy love.

HOSTESS   Nay, my lord, he called you 'jack' and said he would
   cudgel you.

FALSTAFF   Did I, Bardolph?

---

1. Symbol of a bawd. Brothels often displayed a dish of
stewed prunes in the window.
2. A hunted fox drawn out from its hiding spot; a dead
fox dragged to lay a false trail.
3. A disreputable character, usually played by a cross-
dressed man, in the boisterous May games and morris
dances denounced by Puritan preachers. The figure is
here juxtaposed to the respectable wife of the deputy of
the ward.
4. A euphemism for "female genitalia."
5. The otter's unusual appearance led to debates about
whether it was a fish or an animal.
6. How to understand her; how to have sexual relations
with her.

130 BARDOLPH   Indeed, Sir John, you said so.

FALSTAFF   Yea, if he said my ring was copper.

PRINCE HARRY   I say 'tis copper; darest thou be as good as thy
word now?

FALSTAFF   Why, Hal, thou knowest as thou art but man I dare,
135 but as thou art prince, I fear thee as I fear the roaring of the
lion's whelp.°   cub

PRINCE HARRY   And why not as the lion?

FALSTAFF   The King himself is to be feared as the lion. Dost
thou think I'll fear thee as I fear thy father? Nay, an I do, I pray
140 God my girdle break.

PRINCE HARRY   O, if it should, how would thy guts fall about thy
knees! But sirrah, there's no room for faith, truth, nor honesty
in this bosom of thine; it is all filled up with guts and midriff.
Charge an honest woman with picking thy pocket? Why, thou
145 whoreson impudent embossed rascal,⁷ if there were anything
in thy pocket but tavern reckonings, memorandums of bawdy-
houses, and one poor pennyworth of sugar-candy to make thee
long-winded°—if thy pocket were enriched with any other   to give you energy
injuries⁸ but these, I am a villain. And yet you will stand to it,°   persist
150 you will not pocket up° wrong. Art thou not ashamed?   keep quiet about

FALSTAFF   Dost thou hear, Hal? Thou knowest in the state of
innocency Adam fell, and what should poor Jack Falstaff do
in the days of villainy? Thou seest I have more flesh than
another man, and therefore more frailty. You confess, then,
155 you picked my pocket.

PRINCE HARRY   It appears so by the story.

FALSTAFF   Hostess, I forgive thee. Go make ready breakfast.
Love thy husband, look to thy servants, cherish thy guests.
Thou shalt find me tractable to any honest reason; thou seest
160 I am pacified still.° Nay, prithee, be gone.   Exit HOSTESS   always
Now, Hal, to the news at court. For the robbery, lad, how is
that answered?°   settled

PRINCE HARRY   O, my sweet beef, I must still be good angel to
thee. The money is paid back again.

165 FALSTAFF   O, I do not like that paying back; 'tis a double labour.

PRINCE HARRY   I am good friends with my father, and may do
anything.

FALSTAFF   Rob me the exchequer the first thing thou dost, and
do it with unwashed hands° too.   do it at once

170 BARDOLPH   Do, my lord.

PRINCE HARRY   I have procured thee, Jack, a charge of foot.°   an infantry command

FALSTAFF   I would it had been of horse! Where shall I find one°   someone
that can steal well? O, for a fine thief of the age of two-and-
twenty or thereabouts! I am heinously unprovided.° Well, God   ill equipped
175 be thanked for these rebels—they offend none but the virtuous.
I laud them, I praise them.

PRINCE HARRY   Bardolph.

BARDOLPH   My lord?

PRINCE HARRY   [giving letters]   Go bear this letter to Lord John
of Lancaster,
180 To my brother John; this to my lord of Westmorland.

---

7. *embossed rascal*: bloated rogue; hunted deer,   8. Any other things whose loss causes you injury.
exhausted and foaming at the mouth.

[*Exit* BARDOLPH]

Go, Peto, to horse, to horse, for thou and I
Have thirty miles to ride yet ere dinner time. [*Exit* PETO]
Jack, meet me tomorrow in the Temple Hall°
At two o'clock in the afternoon.

185 There shalt thou know thy charge, and there receive
Money and order for their furniture.°   *equipment*
The land is burning, Percy stands on high,
And either we or they must lower lie.   [*Exit*]

FALSTAFF   Rare words! Brave world! [*Calling*] Hostess, my
breakfast, come!—

190 O, I could wish this tavern were my drum!¹   *Exit*

4.1

Enter HOTSPUR *and* [*the Earls of*] WORCESTER *and*
DOUGLAS

HOTSPUR   Well said, my noble Scot! If speaking truth
In this fine age were not thought flattery,
Such attribution° should the Douglas have   *praise*
As not a soldier of this season's stamp°   *coinage*

5 Should go so general current° through the world.   *be so widely accepted*
By God, I cannot flatter, I do defy
The tongues of soothers,° but a braver place   *flatterers*
In my heart's love hath no man than yourself.
Nay, task° me to my word, approve° me, lord.   *hold / test*

10 DOUGLAS   Thou art the king of honour.
No man so potent breathes upon the ground
But I will beard° him.   *defy*

HOTSPUR   Do so, and 'tis well.

Enter a MESSENGER *with letters*

What letters hast thou there? I can but thank you.

MESSENGER   These letters come from your father.

15 HOTSPUR   Letters from him? Why comes he not himself?

MESSENGER   He cannot come, my lord, he is grievous sick.

HOTSPUR   Zounds, how has he the leisure to be sick
In such a jostling° time? Who leads his power?   *turbulent*
Under whose government° come they along?   *command*

20 MESSENGER   His letters bears his mind, not I, my lord.

[HOTSPUR *reads the letter*]

WORCESTER   I prithee tell me, doth he keep his bed?

MESSENGER   He did, my lord, four days ere I set forth;
And at the time of my departure thence
He was much feared° by his physicians.   *feared for*

25 WORCESTER   I would the state of time° had first been whole°   *of the times / healthy*
Ere he by sickness had been visited.
His health was never better worth° than now.   *of more value*

HOTSPUR   Sick now? Droop now? This sickness doth infect
The very life-blood of our enterprise.

30 'Tis catching° hither, even to our camp.   *infectious*
He writes me here that inward sickness stays him,
And that his friends by deputation°   *through deputies*

---

9. One of the Inns of Court, London's law schools.
1. A disputed passage. Perhaps Falstaff means he
wishes that he could stay at the tavern rather than go to
war or that he could make the tavern ring with the noise

of his departure. He puns on "taborn" (tabor), a kind of
drum used to call soldiers to battle.
4.1 Location: The rebel camp near Shrewsbury.

Could not so soon be drawn;° nor did he think it meet°   *assembled / suitable*
To lay so dangerous and dear a trust
35   On any soul removed° but on his own.   *not directly involved*
Yet doth he give us bold advertisement°   *counsel*
That with our small conjunction° we should on,   *joint force*
To see how fortune is disposed to us;
For, as he writes, there is no quailing now,
40   Because the King is certainly possessed°   *informed*
Of all our purposes. What say you to it?
WORCESTER   Your father's sickness is a maim to us.
HOTSPUR   A perilous gash, a very limb lopped off.
And yet, in faith, it is not. His present want°   *absence*
45   Seems more than we shall find it. Were it good
To set° the exact wealth of all our states°   *stake / resources*
All at one cast,° to set so rich a main[1]   *throw of the dice*
On the nice hazard° of one doubtful hour?   *precarious chance*
It were not good, for therein should we read
50   The very bottom and the sole[2] of hope,
The very list,° the very utmost bound,   *limit*
Of all our fortunes.
DOUGLAS   Faith, and so we should, where now remains
A sweet reversion°—we may boldly spend   *future inheritance*
55   Upon the hope of what is to come in.
A comfort of retirement[3] lives in this.
HOTSPUR   A rendezvous, a home to fly unto,
If that the devil and mischance look big°   *threateningly*
Upon the maidenhead° of our affairs.   *virgin state; start*
60   WORCESTER   But yet I would your father had been here.
The quality and hair° of our attempt   *character*
Brooks° no division. It will be thought   *Tolerates*
By some that know not why he is away
That wisdom, loyalty, and mere° dislike   *absolute*
65   Of our proceedings kept the Earl from hence;
And think how such an apprehension
May turn the tide of fearful faction,°   *timid support*
And breed a kind of question in our cause.
For, well you know, we of the off'ring° side   *challenging*
70   Must keep aloof from strict arbitrament,°   *rigorous judgment*
And stop all sight-holes, every loop° from whence   *loophole*
The eye of reason may pry in upon us.
This absence of your father's draws° a curtain   *opens*
That shows the ignorant a kind of fear
75   Before not dreamt of.
HOTSPUR   You strain too far.
I rather of his absence make this use:
It lends a lustre, and more great opinion,°   *prestige*
A larger dare° to our great enterprise,   *daring*
Than if the Earl were here; for men must think
80   If we without his help can make a head°   *raise an army*
To push against a kingdom, with his help
We shall o'erturn it topsy-turvy down.
Yet° all goes well, yet all our joints° are whole.   *So far / limbs*

---

1. A stake in gambling; an army.   3. Refuge to which one can retreat.
2. Undersurface (as of a shoe), with a pun on "soul."

DOUGLAS   As heart can think, there is not such a word
85 Spoke of in Scotland as this term of fear.
         Enter Sir Richard VERNON
HOTSPUR   My cousin Vernon! Welcome, by my soul!
VERNON   Pray God my news be worth a welcome, lord.
    The Earl of Westmorland, seven thousand strong,
    Is marching hitherwards; with him Prince John.
HOTSPUR   No harm. What more?
90 VERNON   And further I have learned
    The King himself in person is set forth,
    Or hitherwards intended speedily,
    With strong and mighty preparation.
HOTSPUR   He shall be welcome too. Where is his son,
95 The nimble-footed madcap Prince of Wales,
    And his comrades that daffed° the world aside   tossed
    And bid it pass?
VERNON   All furnished,° all in arms,   equipped
    All plumed like ostriches,⁴ that with the wind
    [   ]
100 Baiting° like eagles having lately bathed,   *Beating their wings*
    Glittering in golden coats like images,°   *gilded statues*
    As full of spirit as the month of May,
    And gorgeous as the sun at midsummer;
    Wanton° as youthful goats, wild as young bulls.   *Frisky*
105 I saw young Harry with his beaver° on,   *visor; helmet*
    His cuishes° on his thighs, gallantly armed,   *armor for the thighs*
    Rise from the ground like feathered Mercury,⁵
    And vaulted with such ease into his seat
    As if an angel dropped down from the clouds
110 To turn and wind° a fiery Pegasus,⁶   *wheel about*
    And witch° the world with noble horsemanship.   *bewitch*
HOTSPUR   No more, no more! Worse than the sun in March,⁷
    This praise doth nourish agues.⁷ Let them come!
    They come like sacrifices in their trim,°   *fine trappings*
115 And to the fire-eyed maid of smoky war°   *Bellona, goddess of war*
    All hot and bleeding will we offer them.
    The mailèd° Mars shall on his altar sit   *dressed in armor*
    Up to the ears in blood. I am on fire
    To hear this rich reprisal° is so nigh,   *prize*
120 And yet not ours! Come, let me taste° my horse,   *test; try*
    Who is to bear me like a thunderbolt
    Against the bosom of the Prince of Wales.
    Harry to Harry shall, hot horse to horse,
    Meet and ne'er part till one drop down a corpse.
    O, that Glyndŵr were come!
125 VERNON   There is more news.
    I learned in Worcester, as I rode along,
    He cannot draw° his power this fourteen days.   *assemble*
DOUGLAS   That's the worst tidings that I hear of yet.

4. Some editors follow Q in printing "estriches" (goshawks, a kind of hawk) here. Various emendations have been proposed for this and the following lines. The Oxford editors assume a line has been lost, as the brackets indicate.
5. The Roman messenger of the gods, often represented as a young man with winged sandals or a winged hat.
6. A winged horse of classical myth.
7. The March sun was popularly imagined as warm enough to kindle feverish diseases ("agues") without being strong enough to dispel them.

WORCESTER   Ay, by my faith, that bears a frosty sound.

130 HOTSPUR   What may the King's whole battle° reach unto?   *army*
VERNON   To thirty thousand.

HOTSPUR   Forty let it be.
My father and Glyndŵr being both away,
The powers° of us may serve so great a day.   *armies*
Come, let us take a muster speedily.

135 Doomsday is near: die all, die merrily.

DOUGLAS   Talk not of dying; I am out of° fear   *free from*
Of death or death's hand for this one half year.   *Exeunt*

4.2

Enter FALSTAFF *and* BARDOLPH

FALSTAFF   Bardolph, get thee before to Coventry; fill me a bottle of sack. Our soldiers shall march through. We'll to Sutton
Coldfield[1] tonight.

BARDOLPH   Will you give me money, captain?

5 FALSTAFF   Lay out,° lay out.   *Use your own*

BARDOLPH   This bottle makes an angel.[2]

FALSTAFF   [*giving* BARDOLPH *money*]   An if° it do, take it for thy   *An if = If*
labour; an if it make twenty, take them all; I'll answer the
coinage.[3] Bid my lieutenant Peto meet me at town's end.

10 BARDOLPH   I will, captain. Farewell.   *Exit*

FALSTAFF   If I be not ashamed of my soldiers, I am a soused
gurnet.° I have misused the King's press[4] damnably. I have got   *a pickled fish*
in exchange of one hundred and fifty soldiers three hundred
and odd pounds. I press me° none but good householders, yeo-   *I draft*
15 men's sons, enquire me out contracted° bachelors, such as had   *engaged to be wed*
been asked twice on the banns,[5] such a commodity° of warm   *quantity*
slaves[6] as had as lief° hear the devil as a drum, such as fear the   *willingly*
report of a caliver° worse than a struck° fowl or a hurt wild   *musket / wounded*
duck. I pressed me none but such toasts and butter,° with hearts   *such weaklings*
20 in their bellies no bigger than pins' heads, and they have
bought out their services;[7] and now my whole charge consists
of ensigns, corporals, lieutenants, gentlemen of companies[8]—
slaves as ragged as Lazarus[9] in the painted cloth,° where the   *cheap wall hangings*
glutton's dogs licked his sores—and such as indeed were never
25 soldiers, but discarded unjust° servingmen, younger sons to   *dishonest*
younger brothers, revolted° tapsters, and ostlers trade-fallen,°   *runaway / out of work*
the cankers° of a calm world and a long peace, ten times more   *cankerworms; parasites*
dishonourable-ragged than an old feazed ensign;° and such   *tattered flag*
have I to fill up the rooms of them as° have bought out their   *places of those who*
30 services, that you would think that I had a hundred and fifty
tattered prodigals lately come from swine-keeping, from eating
draff and husks.[1] A mad fellow met me on the way and told me
I had unloaded all the gibbets° and pressed the dead bodies.   *gallows*

4.2 Location: The road approaching Coventry.
1. Town about 20 miles northwest of Coventry in Warwickshire.
2. Brings my outlay to several shillings (an "angel").
Falstaff retorts by punning on "makes" as meaning
"earns a profit of."
3. I'll be responsible for the money coined.
4. Commission for conscripting soldiers.
5. Proclamations made on three consecutive Sundays
affirming one's intent to marry.

6. Well-off or comfort-loving cowards.
7. They have paid me to excuse them from military service.
8. Gentlemen volunteers who were not officers.
9. For the story of Lazarus and the rich man, see note
to 3.3.28.
1. Alluding to the biblical parable of the prodigal son,
who longs to eat swill ("draff") and corn husks meant
for pigs after he has squandered his inheritance in
debauchery (see Luke 15:11–16).

No eye hath seen such scarecrows. I'll not march through Cov-
35 entry with them, that's flat. Nay, and the villains march wide
    betwixt the legs, as if they had gyves° on, for indeed I had the   *fetters*
    most of them out of prison. There's not a shirt and a half in all
    my company; and the half-shirt is two napkins tacked together
    and thrown over the shoulders like a herald's coat without
40 sleeves; and the shirt, to say the truth, stolen from my host° at   *innkeeper*
    Saint Albans, or the red-nose innkeeper of Daventry.² But that's
    all one; they'll find linen enough on every hedge.³

      Enter PRINCE [HARRY] *and the Lord[Earl] of* WESTMOR-
      LAND

PRINCE HARRY   How now, blown Jack?⁴ How now, quilt?

FALSTAFF   What, Hal! How now, mad wag? What a devil dost
45 thou in Warwickshire? My good lord of Westmorland, I cry
    you mercy!° I thought your honour had already been at   *I beg your pardon*
    Shrewsbury.

WESTMORLAND   Faith, Sir John, 'tis more than time that I were
    there, and you too; but my powers are there already. The King,
50 I can tell you, looks for us all. We must away° all night.   *must march*

FALSTAFF   Tut, never fear° me. I am as vigilant as a cat to steal   *worry about*
    cream.

PRINCE HARRY   I think to steal cream indeed, for thy theft hath
    already made thee butter.⁵ But tell me, Jack, whose fellows are
55 these that come after?

FALSTAFF   Mine, Hal, mine.

PRINCE HARRY   I did never see such pitiful rascals.

FALSTAFF   Tut, tut, good enough to toss,⁶ food for powder,° food   *cannon fodder*
    for powder. They'll fill a pit as well as better. Tush, man, mor-
60 tal men, mortal men.

WESTMORLAND   Ay, but Sir John, methinks they are exceeding
    poor and bare,° too beggarly.   *threadbare*

FALSTAFF   Faith, for their poverty, I know not where they had
    that, and for their bareness, I am sure they never learned that
65 of me.

PRINCE HARRY   No, I'll be sworn, unless you call three fingers in
    the ribs⁷ bare. But sirrah, make haste. Percy is already in the
    field.   *Exit*

FALSTAFF   What, is the King encamped?

70 WESTMORLAND   He is, Sir John. I fear we shall stay too long.
                                 [Exit]

FALSTAFF   Well, to the latter end of a fray
    And the beginning of a feast
    Fits a dull fighter and a keen guest.   *Exit*

4.3

      Enter HOTSPUR, [*the Earls of*] WORCESTER [*and*] DOUG-
      LAS, *and* [*Sir Richard*] VERNON

HOTSPUR   We'll fight with him tonight.

WORCESTER   It may not be.

---

2. Saint Albans is a town north of London, Daventry a
town southeast of Coventry.
3. Where laundresses set it out to dry.
4. Punning on "jack" as referring to what many Elizabethan soldiers wore: a quilted jacket covered with
leather or cloth and worn over iron plates. *blown:*
swollen; short-winded.

5. The riches ("cream") you have stolen have made you
rich, or turned you into fat.
6. Good enough to be tossed on pikes.
7. Three fingers of fat over the ribs. A finger was a measure of three-quarters of an inch.
4.3 Location: The rebels' camp, Shrewsbury.

DOUGLAS	You give him then advantage.	
VERNON	Not a whit.	
HOTSPUR	Why say you so? Looks he not for supply?°	*reinforcements*
VERNON	So do we.	
HOTSPUR	His is certain; ours is doubtful.	

5 WORCESTER Good cousin, be advised. Stir not tonight.

VERNON [*to* HOTSPUR] Do not, my lord.

DOUGLAS You do not counsel well.
  You speak it out of fear and cold heart.

VERNON Do me no slander, Douglas. By my life—
  And I dare well maintain it with my life—
10 If well-respected° honour bid me on,   *well-considered*
  I hold as little counsel with weak fear
  As you, my lord, or any Scot that this day lives.
  Let it be seen tomorrow in the battle
  Which of us fears.

15 DOUGLAS Yea, or tonight.

VERNON Content.

HOTSPUR Tonight, say I.

VERNON Come, come, it may not be. I wonder much,
  Being men of such great leading° as you are,   *leadership*
20 That you foresee not what impediments
  Drag back our expedition.° Certain horse°   *rapid progress / cavalry*
  Of my cousin Vernon's are not yet come up.
  Your uncle Worcester's horse came but today,
  And now their pride° and mettle is asleep,   *spirit*
25 Their courage with hard labour tame and dull,
  That not a horse is half the half himself.

HOTSPUR So are the horses of the enemy
  In general journey-bated° and brought low.   *weary from travel*
  The better part of ours are full of rest.

30 WORCESTER The number of the King exceedeth our.
  For God's sake, cousin, stay° till all come in.   *wait*
      The trumpet sounds a parley[1] [*within*]. *Enter*
      Sir Walter BLUNT

BLUNT I come with gracious offers from the King,
  If you vouchsafe me hearing and respect.

HOTSPUR Welcome, Sir Walter Blunt; and would to God
35 You were of our determination.°   *on our side*
  Some of us love you well, and even those some° *those same persons*
  Envy your great deservings and good name,
  Because you are not of our quality,°   *party*
  But stand against us like an enemy.

40 BLUNT And God defend° but still I should stand so,   *forbid*
  So long as out of limit° and true rule   *bounds of allegiance*
  You stand against anointed majesty.
  But to my charge. The King hath sent to know
  The nature of your griefs,° and whereupon   *grievances*
45 You conjure from the breast of civil peace
  Such bold hostility, teaching his duteous land
  Audacious cruelty. If that the King
  Have any way your good deserts forgot,
  Which he confesseth to be manifold,

---

1. Summons to a conference with the enemy.

50 He bids you name your griefs, and with all speed
    You shall have your desires, with interest,
    And pardon absolute for yourself and these
    Herein misled by your suggestion.°   *instigation*
    HOTSPUR   The King is kind, and well we know the King
55 Knows at what time to promise, when to pay.
    My father and my uncle and myself
    Did give him that same royalty he wears;
    And when he was not six-and-twenty strong,
    Sick in the world's regard, wretched and low,
60 A poor unminded° outlaw sneaking home,   *insignificant*
    My father gave him welcome to the shore;
    And when he heard him swear and vow to God
    He came but to be Duke of Lancaster,
    To sue his livery,² and beg his peace
65 With tears of innocency and terms of zeal,
    My father, in kind heart and pity moved,
    Swore him assistance, and performed it too.
    Now when the lords and barons of the realm
    Perceived Northumberland did lean to him,
70 The more and less came in with cap and knee,³
    Met him in boroughs, cities, villages,
    Attended him on bridges, stood in lanes,⁴
    Laid gifts before him, proffered him their oaths,
    Gave him their heirs as pages, followed him,
75 Even at the heels, in golden° multitudes.   *resplendent*
    He presently, as greatness knows itself,°   *recognizes its power*
    Steps me° a little higher than his vow   *Steps*
    Made to my father while his blood° was poor   *spirit*
    Upon the naked shore at Ravenspurgh,
80 And now forsooth takes on him to reform
    Some certain edicts and some strait° decrees   *strict*
    That lie too heavy on the commonwealth,
    Cries out upon abuses, seems to weep
    Over his country's wrongs; and by this face,°   *outward show*
85 This seeming brow of justice, did he win
    The hearts of all that he did angle for;
    Proceeded further, cut me off° the heads   *cut off*
    Of all the favourites that the absent King
    In deputation° left behind him here   *As deputies*
90 When he was personal° in the Irish war.   *engaged in person*
    BLUNT   Tut, I came not to hear this.
    HOTSPUR   Then to the point.
    In short time after, he deposed the King,
    Soon after that deprived him of his life,
    And in the neck of that tasked° the whole state;   *And immediately taxed*
95 To make that worse, suffered his kinsman March⁵—
    Who is, if every owner were well placed,⁶
    Indeed his king—to be engaged° in Wales,   *held hostage*
    There without ransom to lie forfeited;°   *unredeemed*

2. To plead for the restitution of his lands (which Richard II had seized when John of Gaunt, Bolingbroke's father, died).
3. Those of both high and low social status deferentially presented themselves (with cap in hand and bended knee).
4. Stood in rows along the roadways.
5. The Earl of March. For his claim to the throne, see note to 1.3.79.
6. If everyone had possessions according to his entitlement.

	Disgraced me in my happy victories,	
100	Sought to entrap me by intelligence,°	*spying*
	Rated° mine uncle from the Council-board,	*Drove away*
	In rage dismissed my father from the court,	
	Broke oath on oath, committed wrong on wrong,	
	And in conclusion drove us to seek out	
105	This head of safety,[7] and withal° to pry	*also*
	Into his title, the which we find	
	Too indirect° for long continuance.	*irregular*

BLUNT   Shall I return this answer to the King?

HOTSPUR   Not so, Sir Walter. We'll withdraw awhile.

110	Go to the King, and let there be impawned°	*pledged*
	Some surety for a safe return again;	
	And in the morning early shall mine uncle	
	Bring him our purposes. And so, farewell.	

BLUNT   I would you would accept of grace and love.

HOTSPUR   And maybe so we shall.

115 BLUNT   Pray God you do.

Exeunt [HOTSPUR, WORCESTER, DOUGLAS, *and*
VERNON *at one door,* BLUNT *at another door*]

4.4

Enter the ARCHBISHOP *of York, and* SIR MICHAEL

	ARCHBISHOP [*giving letters*] Hie, good Sir Michael, bear this sealèd brief°	*dispatch*
	With wingèd haste to the Lord Marshal,	
	This to my cousin Scrope, and all the rest	
	To whom they are directed. If you knew	
5	How much they do import, you would make haste.	

SIR MICHAEL   My good lord,
I guess their tenor.

ARCHBISHOP   Like enough you do.

	Tomorrow, good Sir Michael, is a day	
	Wherein the fortune of ten thousand men	
10	Must bide the touch;° for, sir, at Shrewsbury,	*stand the test*
	As I am truly given to understand,	
	The King with mighty and quick-raisèd power	
	Meets with Lord Harry. And I fear, Sir Michael,	
	What with the sickness of Northumberland,	
15	Whose power was in the first proportion,°	*magnitude*
	And what with Owain Glyndŵr's absence thence,	
	Who with them was a rated sinew[1] too,	
	And comes not in, overruled by prophecies,	
	I fear the power of Percy is too weak	
20	To wage an instant° trial with the King.	*immediate*

SIR MICHAEL   Why, my good lord, you need not fear; there is Douglas
And Lord Mortimer.

ARCHBISHOP   No, Mortimer is not there.

SIR MICHAEL   But there is Mordake, Vernon, Lord Harry Percy;

	And there is my lord of Worcester, and a head°	*troop*
25	Of gallant warriors, noble gentlemen.	

ARCHBISHOP   And so there is; but yet the King hath drawn
The special head of all the land together—

7. That is, safety in these gathered forces.
4.4 Location: The Archbishop's palace, York.

1. A much-valued source of strength.

The Prince of Wales, Lord John of Lancaster,
The noble Westmorland, and warlike Blunt,
30 And many more corrivals,° and dear° men   *associates / noble*
Of estimation° and command in arms.   *reputation*
SIR MICHAEL   Doubt not, my lord, they shall be well opposed.
ARCHBISHOP   I hope no less, yet needful 'tis to fear;
And to prevent the worst, Sir Michael, speed.
35 For if Lord Percy thrive not, ere the King
Dismiss his power he means to visit us,
For he hath heard of our confederacy,
And 'tis but wisdom to make strong against him;
Therefore make haste. I must go write again
40 To other friends; and so farewell, Sir Michael.   *Exeunt [severally]*

5.1

Enter KING [HENRY], PRINCE [HARRY], *Lord* JOHN OF LAN-
CASTER, [*the*] *Earl of* WESTMORLAND, *Sir Walter* BLUNT,
and FALSTAFF

KING HENRY   How bloodily the sun begins to peer
Above yon bulky hill! The day looks pale
At his distemp'rature.°   *sick appearance*
PRINCE HARRY   The southern wind
Doth play the trumpet to his° purposes,   *(the sun's)*
5 And by his hollow whistling in the leaves
Foretells a tempest and a blust'ring day.
KING HENRY   Then with the losers let it sympathize,°   *accord*
For nothing can seem foul to those that win.
*The trumpet sounds [a parley within]. Enter [the Earl
of]* WORCESTER [*and Sir Richard* VERNON][1]
How now, my lord of Worcester? 'Tis not well
10 That you and I should meet upon such terms
As now we meet. You have deceived our trust,
And made us doff our easy robes of peace
To crush our old limbs in ungentle steel.
This is not well, my lord, this is not well.
15 What say you to it? Will you again unknit
This churlish knot of all-abhorrèd war,
And move in that obedient orb[2] again
Where you did give a fair and natural light,
And be no more an exhaled meteor,[3]
20 A prodigy of fear,° and a portent   *A fearful omen*
Of broachèd mischief° to the unborn times?   *Of evil set flowing*
WORCESTER   Hear me, my liege.
For mine own part, I could be well content
To entertain the lag-end° of my life   *latter end*
25 With quiet hours; for I protest,
I have not sought the day of this dislike.°   *discord*
KING HENRY   You have not sought it? How comes it, then?
FALSTAFF   Rebellion lay in his way, and he found it.

5.1 Location: King Henry's camp at Shrewsbury.
1. Neither Q nor F indicates that Vernon accompanies
Worcester in this scene, but it seems lacking in ceremony
for Worcester to go to King Henry's camp alone. Also, in
the next scene, Worcester discusses with Vernon what the
King has said and whether to inform Hotspur, making it
appear that Vernon was present at this meeting.

2. Orbit. Henry, drawing on a conventional analogy
between social and cosmological order, compares
Worcester to a star or a planet that, in Ptolemaic cos-
mology, should move properly in its sphere (orbit)
around the earth.
3. Meteors were thought to be made of gas exhaled by
the sun and were considered bad omens.

PRINCE HARRY   Peace, chewet,° peace!   *jackdaw; chatterer*

30   WORCESTER [*to the* KING]   It pleased your majesty to turn your looks
       Of favour from myself and all our house;
       And yet I must remember° you, my lord,   *remind*
       We were the first and dearest of your friends.
       For you my staff of office did I break
35   In Richard's time, and posted° day and night   *rode swiftly*
       To meet you on the way and kiss your hand
       When yet you were in place° and in account°   *social status / esteem*
       Nothing so strong and fortunate as I.
       It was myself, my brother, and his son
40   That brought you home, and boldly did outdare
       The dangers of the time. You swore to us,
       And you did swear that oath at Doncaster,
       That you did nothing purpose° 'gainst the state,   *intend*
       Nor claim no further than your new-fall'n right,[4]
45   The seat° of Gaunt, dukedom of Lancaster.   *estate*
       To this we swore our aid, but in short space
       It rained down fortune show'ring on your head,
       And such a flood of greatness fell on you,
       What with our help, what with the absent King,
50   What with the injuries° of a wanton° time,   *evils / lawless*
       The seeming sufferances° that you had borne,   *wrongs*
       And the contrarious° winds that held the King   *adverse*
       So long in his unlucky Irish wars
       That all in England did repute him dead;
55   And from this swarm of fair advantages
       You took occasion to be quickly wooed
       To gripe° the general sway into your hand,   *seize*
       Forgot your oath to us at Doncaster,
       And being fed by us, you used us so
60   As that ungentle gull,° the cuckoo's bird,   *rude young bird*
       Useth the sparrow[5]—did oppress our nest,
       Grew by our feeding to so great a bulk
       That even our love° durst not come near your sight   *we who loved you*
       For fear of swallowing.° But with nimble wing   *being swallowed*
65   We were enforced for safety' sake to fly
       Out of your sight, and raise this present head,
       Whereby we stand opposèd° by such means   *in opposition to you*
       As you yourself have forged against yourself,
       By unkind usage, dangerous° countenance,   *threatening*
70   And violation of all faith and troth
       Sworn to us in your younger enterprise.
       KING HENRY   These things indeed you have articulate,°   *expressed*
       Proclaimed at market crosses,[6] read in churches,
       To face° the garment of rebellion   *adorn*
75   With some fine colour° that may please the eye   *hue; pretext*
       Of fickle changelings° and poor discontents,   *turncoats*
       Which gape and rub the elbow[7] at the news
       Of hurly-burly innovation;°   *rebellion*

---

4. The right newly descended to you (upon the death
of your father).
5. The female cuckoo lays its eggs in the nests of
smaller birds such as the sparrow, who raises the
cuckoo's young until they grow so large they threaten
the sparrow and her nest.

6. Crosses set up in marketplaces, often atop polygonal
structures with open archways on each of the sides and
vaulted within.
7. And hug themselves with crossed arms (conventional expression of delight).

And never yet did insurrection want°   *lack*
80   Such water-colours to impaint his cause,
Nor moody beggars starving for a time
Of pell-mell° havoc and confusion.   *chaotic*
PRINCE HARRY   In both our armies there is many a soul
Shall pay full dearly for this encounter
85   If once they join in trial.° Tell your nephew   *combat*
The Prince of Wales doth join with all the world
In praise of Henry Percy. By my hopes,
This present enterprise set off his head,°   *not counted against him*
I do not think a braver gentleman,
90   More active-valiant or more valiant-young,
More daring, or more bold, is now alive
To grace this latter age with noble deeds.
For my part, I may speak it to my shame,
I have a truant been to chivalry;
95   And so I hear he doth account me too.
Yet this, before my father's majesty:
I am content that he shall take the odds°   *have the advantage*
Of his great name and estimation,°   *reputation*
And will, to save the blood on either side,
100 Try fortune with him in a single fight.
KING HENRY   And, Prince of Wales, so dare we venture thee,
Albeit° considerations infinite   *Were it not that*
Do make against it. No, good Worcester, no.
We love our people well; even those we love
105 That are misled upon your cousin's° part;   *kinsman's*
And will they take the offer of our grace,°   *mercy*
Both he and they and you, yea, every man
Shall be my friend again, and I'll be his.
So tell your cousin, and bring me word
110 What he will do. But if he will not yield,
Rebuke and dread correction wait on° us,   *serve*
And they shall do their office. So be gone.
We will not now be troubled with reply.
We offer fair; take it advisedly.
                                    Exeunt WORCESTER [*and* VERNON]
115 PRINCE HARRY   It will not be accepted, on my life.
The Douglas and the Hotspur both together
Are confident against the world in arms.
KING HENRY   Hence, therefore, every leader to his charge,
For on their answer will we set on them,
120 And God befriend us as our cause is just!
                      Exeunt. Manent° Prince [HARRY] *and* FALSTAFF   *Remain*
FALSTAFF   Hal, if thou see me down in the battle, and bestride
me,° so.° 'Tis a point of friendship.   *stand over me / good*
PRINCE HARRY   Nothing but a colossus[8] can do thee that friend-
ship. Say thy prayers, and farewell.
125 FALSTAFF   I would 'twere bed-time, Hal, and all well.
PRINCE HARRY   Why, thou owest God a death.   [*Exit*]
FALSTAFF   'Tis not due yet. I would be loath to pay him before
his day. What need I be so forward with him that calls not on
me? Well, 'tis no matter; honour pricks° me on. Yea, but how   *spurs*

---

8. Referring to a massive statue of Apollo that purportedly stood over the entrance to the harbor in ancient Rhodes
and was referred to as the Colossus of Rhodes.

130 if honour prick me off⁹ when I come on? How then? Can honour set-to° a leg? No. Or an arm? No. Or take away the grief   *mend*
of a wound? No. Honour hath no skill in surgery, then? No.
What is honour? A word. What is in that word 'honour'? What
is that 'honour'? Air. A trim reckoning!° Who hath it? He that   *A nice summing up*
135 died o'Wednesday. Doth he feel it? No. Doth he hear it? No.
'Tis insensible¹ then? Yea, to the dead. But will it not live with
the living? No. Why? Detraction° will not suffer° it. Therefore   *Slander / allow*
I'll none of it. Honour is a mere scutcheon.² And so ends my
catechism.   *Exit*

5.2

Enter [the Earl of] WORCESTER *and Sir Richard*
VERNON

WORCESTER   O no, my nephew must not know, Sir Richard,
The liberal and kind offer of the king.
VERNON   'Twere best he did.
WORCESTER   Then are we all undone.
It is not possible, it cannot be,
5 The King should keep his word in loving us.
He will suspect us still,° and find a time   *always*
To punish this offence in other faults.
Supposition all our lives shall be stuck full of eyes,¹
For treason is but trusted like the fox,
10 Who, ne'er so° tame, so cherished, and locked up,   *no matter how*
Will have a wild trick of his ancestors.
Look how we can, or° sad or merrily,   *whether*
Interpretation will misquote our looks,
And we shall feed like oxen at a stall,
15 The better cherished still the nearer death.
My nephew's trespass may be well forgot;
It hath the excuse of youth and heat of blood,
And an adopted name of privilege²—
A hare-brained Hotspur, governed by a spleen.°   *hot temper*
20 All his offences live upon my head,
And on his father's. We did train° him on,   *lead*
And, his corruption being ta'en from us,
We as the spring° of all shall pay for all.   *source*
Therefore, good cousin, let not Harry know
25 In any case the offer of the King.
VERNON   Deliver what you will; I'll say 'tis so.

Enter HOTSPUR [*and the Earl of* DOUGLAS]
Here comes your cousin.
HOTSPUR   My uncle is returned.
Deliver up³ my Lord of Westmorland.
Uncle, what news?
30 WORCESTER   The King will bid you battle presently.
DOUGLAS   Defy him by the Lord of Westmorland.
HOTSPUR   Lord Douglas, go you and tell him so.

9. Selects me to die; marks me off the list.
1. Imperceptible to the senses.
2. Heraldic shield exhibited at funerals displaying the
deceased person's coat of arms.
5.2 Location: The rebels' camp.
1. The King's suspicion will cause him constantly to
spy on us. Worcester is referring to an allegorical rep-

resentation of Suspicion dressed in a coat of eyes or to
secret agents similar to those whom Elizabeth's government maintained.
2. A nickname, "Hotspur," which may excuse his rashness.
3. Release (as the hostage for the safe return of
Worcester and Vernon).

DOUGLAS   Marry, and shall, and very willingly.   *Exit*

WORCESTER   There is no seeming° mercy in the King.   *semblance of*

35 HOTSPUR   Did you beg any? God forbid!

WORCESTER   I told him gently of our grievances,

Of his oath-breaking, which he mended thus:

By now forswearing that he is forsworn.

He calls us 'rebels', 'traitors', and will scourge

40   With haughty arms this hateful name in us.

Enter [the Earl of] DOUGLAS

DOUGLAS   Arm, gentlemen, to arms, for I have thrown

A brave° defiance in King Henry's teeth—   *proud*

And Westmorland that was engaged° did bear it—   *held as hostage*

Which cannot choose but bring him quickly on.

WORCESTER [*to* HOTSPUR]   The Prince of Wales stepped forth

45   before the King

And, nephew, challenged you to single fight.

HOTSPUR   O, would the quarrel lay upon our heads,

And that no man might draw short breath today

But I and Harry Monmouth![4] Tell me, tell me,

50   How showed his tasking?° Seemed it in contempt?   *challenge*

VERNON   No, by my soul, I never in my life

Did hear a challenge urged more modestly,

Unless a brother should a brother dare

To gentle° exercise and proof of arms.[5]   *noble*

55   He gave you all the duties of° a man,   *respect due to*

Trimmed up your praises[6] with a princely tongue,

Spoke your deservings like a chronicle,

Making you ever better than his praise

By still° disprasing praise valued with you;[7]   *constantly*

60   And, which became him like a prince indeed,

He made a blushing cital° of himself,   *mention*

And chid his truant youth with such a grace

As if he mastered there a double spirit

Of teaching and of learning instantly.°   *simultaneously*

65   There did he pause; but let me tell the world,

If he outlive the envy° of this day,   *malice*

England did never owe° so sweet a hope,   *own*

So much misconstrued in his wantonness.°   *self-indulgence*

HOTSPUR   Cousin, I think thou art enamourèd

70   On° his follies. Never did I hear   *Of*

Of any prince so wild a liberty.°   *such unrestrained license*

But be he as he will, yet once ere night

I will embrace him with a soldier's arm,

That he shall shrink under my courtesy.

75   Arm, arm, with speed! And fellows, soldiers, friends,

Better consider what you have to do

Than I, that have not well the gift of tongue,

Can lift your blood[8] up with persuasion.

Enter a MESSENGER

MESSENGER   My lord, here are letters for you.

80 HOTSPUR   I cannot read them now.   [*Exit* MESSENGER]

---

4. Harry of Monmouth, the town in Wales where the
Prince was born.
5. Trial of skill at weapons.
6. Embellished his praises of you.

7. As measured against you (because your merit
exceeds all praise).
8. Rebelliousness; self-indulgence.

O gentlemen, the time of life is short.
To spend that shortness basely were too long
If life did ride upon a dial's point,
Still ending at the arrival of an hour.⁹
85 An if we live, we live to tread on kings;
If die, brave death when princes die with us!
Now for our consciences: the arms are fair
When the intent of bearing them is just.

      Enter another MESSENGER

MESSENGER   My lord, prepare; the King comes on apace.   [*Exit*]
90 HOTSPUR   I thank him that he cuts me from my tale,
For I profess not° talking, only this: *am not skilled at*
Let each man do his best. And here draw I
A sword whose temper° I intend to stain   *tempered steel*
With the best blood that I can meet withal
95 In the adventure of this perilous day.
Now *Esperance!*¹ Percy! And set on!
Sound all the lofty instruments of war,
And by that music let us all embrace,
For, heaven to earth,² some of us never shall
100 A second time do such a courtesy.

    The trumpets sound. Here they embrace. [*Exeunt*]

5.3

KING [HENRY] *enters with his power. Alarum*¹ [*and exe-*
unt] *to the battle. Then enter* [*the Earl of*] DOUGLAS,
and Sir Walter BLUNT [*disguised as the* KING]

BLUNT   What is thy name, that in the battle thus
Thou crossest me? What honour dost thou seek
Upon my head?
DOUGLAS   Know then my name is Douglas,
And I do haunt thee in the battle thus
5 Because some tell me that thou art a king.
BLUNT   They tell thee true.
DOUGLAS   The Lord of Stafford dear today hath bought
Thy likeness,² for instead of thee, King Harry,
This sword hath ended him. So shall it thee,
10 Unless thou yield thee as my prisoner.
BLUNT   I was not born a yielder, thou proud Scot,
And thou shalt find a king that will revenge
Lord Stafford's death.

    They fight. DOUGLAS *kills* BLUNT. *Then enter* HOTSPUR

HOTSPUR   O Douglas, hadst thou fought at Holmedon thus,
15 I never had triumphed upon a Scot.
DOUGLAS   All's done, all's won: here breathless lies the King.
HOTSPUR   Where?
DOUGLAS   Here.
HOTSPUR   This, Douglas? No, I know this face full well.
20 A gallant knight he was; his name was Blunt—

---

9. *To spend . . . hour:* that is, If life only lasted an hour
(*dial's point:* hand of a clock), it would still be too long
if it were basely spent.
1. Hope (the Percy motto; see note to 2.4.66).
2. The odds are as great as the distance from heaven to
earth.

5.3 Location: The remaining scenes take place on the
battlefield at Shrewsbury.
1. A call to arms, usually sounded on drum or trumpets.
2. *hath . . . likeness:* has paid for impersonating you;
has paid for his resemblance to you.

Semblably furnished° like the King himself.   *Similarly equipped*

DOUGLAS [*to Blunt's body*]   A fool go with thy soul,³ whither it goes!
A borrowed title hast thou bought too dear.
Why didst thou tell me that thou wert a king?

25 HOTSPUR   The king hath many marching in his coats.⁴

DOUGLAS   Now by my sword, I will kill all his coats.
I'll murder all his wardrobe, piece by piece,
Until I meet the King.

HOTSPUR   Up and away!
Our soldiers stand full fairly for the day.⁵

              Exeunt [leaving Blunt's body]

    Alarum. Enter FALSTAFF

30 FALSTAFF   Though I could scape shot-free⁶ at London, I fear
the shot here. Here's no scoring⁷ but upon the pate.—Soft,
who are you?— Sir Walter Blunt. There's honour for you.
Here's no vanity. I am as hot as molten lead, and as heavy too.
God keep lead out of me; I need no more weight than mine

35 own bowels. I have led my ragamuffins where they are peppered; there's not three of my hundred and fifty left alive, and
they are for the town's end,⁸ to beg during life.

    Enter PRINCE [HARRY]
But who comes here?

PRINCE HARRY   What, stand'st thou idle here? Lend me thy sword.

40 Many a noble man lies stark and stiff
Under the hoofs of vaunting enemies,
Whose deaths as yet are unrevenged. I prithee
Lend me thy sword.

FALSTAFF   O Hal, I prithee give me leave to breathe awhile.

45 Turk Gregory⁹ never did such deeds in arms
As I have done this day. I have paid° Percy,   *settled with (killed)*
I have made him sure.¹

PRINCE HARRY   He is indeed,
And living to kill thee. I prithee
Lend me thy sword.

FALSTAFF   Nay, before God, Hal,

50 If Percy be alive thou gett'st not my sword;
But take my pistol if thou wilt.

PRINCE HARRY   Give it me. What, is it in the case?

FALSTAFF   Ay, Hal;
'Tis hot, 'tis hot. There's that will sack a city.

    The PRINCE *draws it out, and finds it to be a bottle of
sack*

PRINCE HARRY   What, is it a time to jest and dally now?

    He throws the bottle at him. Exit

55 FALSTAFF   Well, if Percy be alive, I'll pierce him. If he do come
in my way, so; if he do not, if I come in his willingly, let him
make a carbonado² of me. I like not such grinning° honour as *menacing*

---

3. May the title of "fool" go with your soul (for impersonating the King).
4. In his surcoat, or loose robes of rich material,
embroidered with the royal coat of arms and worn over
armor.
5. Our soldiers look as though they will win the day.
6. Escape without paying the tavern bill ("shot"), with
a pun in the following line on "shot" as ammunition
(projectiles, cannon shot, etc.).
7. Recording of debts by means of "scores," or notches

on a board (customary in taverns); wounding or cutting.
8. By the town gates, where people often begged.
9. A conflation of the idea of the Turk, taken to be a
cruel and fierce fighter and an enemy of Protestant England, and either Pope Gregory VII or Pope Gregory
XIII, both regarded as violent and cruel by Protestant
writers.
1. I have killed him; but the Prince takes "sure" to
mean "secure."
2. Meat slashed to grill.

Sir Walter hath. Give me life, which if I can save, so; if not, honour comes unlooked for, and there's an end.

Exit [with Blunt's body]

5.4

Alarum. Excursions. Enter KING [HENRY], PRINCE
[HARRY, *wounded*], *Lord* JOHN OF LANCASTER, *and* [*the*]
Earl of WESTMORLAND

KING HENRY I prithee, Harry, withdraw thyself, thou bleed'st too much.
Lord John of Lancaster, go you with him.

JOHN OF LANCASTER Not I, my lord, unless I did bleed too.

PRINCE HARRY [*to the* KING] I beseech your majesty, make up,°   go forward
5   Lest your retirement do amaze° your friends.   alarm

KING HENRY I will do so. My lord of Westmorland,
Lead him to his tent.

WESTMORLAND [*to the* PRINCE] Come, my lord, I'll lead you to your tent.

PRINCE HARRY Lead me, my lord? I do not need your help,
10   And God forbid a shallow scratch should drive
The Prince of Wales from such a field as this,
Where stained¹ nobility lies trodden on,
And rebels' arms triumph in massacres.

JOHN OF LANCASTER We breathe° too long. Come, cousin Westmorland,   rest
15   Our duty this way lies. For God's sake, come.

[*Exeunt* LANCASTER *and* WESTMORLAND]

PRINCE HARRY By God, thou hast deceived me, Lancaster;
I did not think thee lord of such a spirit.
Before I loved thee as a brother, John,
But now I do respect thee as my soul.

20   KING HENRY I saw him hold Lord Percy at the point°   sword point
With lustier maintenance° than I did look for   more valiant bearing
Of such an ungrown warrior.

PRINCE HARRY O, this boy lends mettle to us all!   *Exit*

Enter [the Earl of] DOUGLAS

DOUGLAS Another king! They grow like Hydra's heads.²
25   I am the Douglas, fatal to all those
That wear those colours on them. What art thou
That counterfeit'st the person of a king?

KING HENRY The King himself, who, Douglas, grieves at heart
So many of his shadows° thou hast met   likenesses
30   And not the very King. I have two boys
Seek° Percy and thyself about the field;   Who seek
But seeing thou fall'st on me so luckily,
I will assay° thee; and defend thyself.   challenge

DOUGLAS I fear thou art another counterfeit;
35   And yet, in faith, thou bear'st thee like a king.
But mine° I am sure thou art, whoe'er thou be,   (my prize of war)
And thus I win thee.

They fight. The KING *being in danger, enter* PRINCE
[HARRY]

PRINCE HARRY Hold up thy head, vile Scot, or thou art like
Never to hold it up again. The spirits

5.4
1. Bloodstained; disgraced by defeat.
2. A monster in classical mythology that grew two

heads whenever one was cut off. The hydra was a common image of political disorder.

40　　Of valiant Shirley, Stafford, Blunt, are in my arms.
　　　It is the Prince of Wales that threatens thee,
　　　Who never promiseth but he means to pay.
　　　　　　They fight. DOUGLAS *flieth*
　　　Cheerly, my lord! How fares your grace?
　　　Sir Nicholas Gawsey hath for succour sent,
45　　And so hath Clifton. I'll to Clifton straight.
　　KING HENRY　Stay and breathe awhile.
　　　Thou hast redeemed thy lost opinion,°　　　　　*reputation*
　　　And showed thou mak'st some tender of° my life,　*have some regard for*
　　　In this fair rescue thou hast brought to me.
50　PRINCE HARRY　O God, they did me too much injury
　　　That ever said I hearkened for° your death.　　*desired*
　　　If it were so, I might have let alone
　　　The insulting° hand of Douglas over you,　　　*scornful*
　　　Which would have been as speedy in your end
55　　As all the poisonous potions in the world,
　　　And saved the treacherous labour of your son.
　　KING HENRY　Make up° to Clifton; I'll to Sir Nicholas Gawsey.　*Go forward*
　　　　　　　　　　　　　　　　　　　Exit

　　　　Enter HOTSPUR
　　HOTSPUR　If I mistake not, thou art Harry Monmouth.
　　PRINCE HARRY　Thou speak'st as if I would deny my name.
　　HOTSPUR　My name is Harry Percy.
60　PRINCE HARRY　　　　　　　　Why then, I see
　　　A very valiant rebel of the name.
　　　I am the Prince of Wales; and think not, Percy,
　　　To share with me in glory any more.
　　　Two stars keep not their motion in one sphere,[3]
65　　Nor can one England brook° a double reign　　*endure*
　　　Of Harry Percy and the Prince of Wales.
　　HOTSPUR　Nor shall it, Harry, for the hour is come
　　　To end the one of us, and would to God
　　　Thy name in arms were now as great as mine.
70　PRINCE HARRY　I'll make it greater ere I part from thee,
　　　And all the budding honours on thy crest°　　*helmet; coat of arms*
　　　I'll crop° to make a garland for my head.　　*cut*
　　HOTSPUR　I can no longer brook thy vanities.°　　*empty boasts*
　　　　　　They fight.
　　　　　　Enter FALSTAFF
　　FALSTAFF　Well said, Hal! To it, Hal! Nay, you shall find no boy's
75　　play here, I can tell you.
　　　　　　Enter DOUGLAS. *He fighteth with* FALSTAFF, *who falls
　　　　　　down as if he were dead.* [*Exit* DOUGLAS.] *The* PRINCE
　　　　　　killeth [HOTSPUR]
　　HOTSPUR　O Harry, thou hast robbed me of my youth.
　　　I better brook the loss of brittle life
　　　Than those proud titles thou hast won of me.
　　　They wound my thoughts worse than thy sword my flesh.
80　　But thoughts, the slaves of life, and life, time's fool,
　　　And time, that takes survey of all the world,
　　　Must have a stop.° O, I could prophesy,　　*an end*

---

3. Alluding to the theory that stars moved in concentric spheres around a center. Only one star could occupy a single sphere.

But that the earthy and cold hand of death
Lies on my tongue. No, Percy, thou art dust,
85 And food for—   *[He dies]*
PRINCE HARRY   For worms, brave Percy. Fare thee well, great heart.
Ill-weaved ambition, how much art thou shrunk!
When that this body did contain a spirit,
A kingdom for it was too small a bound,
90 But now two paces of the vilest earth
Is room enough. This earth that bears thee dead
Bears not alive so stout° a gentleman.   *valiant*
If thou wert sensible° of courtesy,   *conscious*
I should not make so dear° a show of zeal;°   *heartfelt / emotion*
95 But let my favours[4] hide thy mangled face,
       [He covers Hotspur's face]
And even in thy behalf I'll thank myself
For doing these fair rites of tenderness.
Adieu, and take thy praise with thee to heaven.
Thy ignominy sleep with thee in the grave,
100 But not remembered in thy epitaph.
       He spieth FALSTAFF *on the ground*
What, old acquaintance! Could not all this flesh
Keep in a little life? Poor Jack, farewell.
I could have better spared a better man.
O, I should have a heavy° miss of thee,   *sad; weighty*
105 If I were much in love with vanity.
Death hath not struck so fat a deer today,
Though many dearer in this bloody fray.
Embowelled[5] will I see thee by and by.
Till then, in blood by noble Percy lie.   *Exit*
       FALSTAFF *riseth up*
110 FALSTAFF   Embowelled? If thou embowel me today, I'll give you
leave to powder° me, and eat me too, tomorrow. 'Sblood, 'twas   *pickle in salt*
time to counterfeit, or that hot termagant[6] Scot had paid me,
scot and lot° too. Counterfeit? I lie, I am no counterfeit. To   *in full*
die is to be a counterfeit, for he is but the counterfeit of a man
115 who hath not the life of a man. But to counterfeit dying when
a man thereby liveth is to be no counterfeit, but the true and
perfect image of life indeed. The better part of valour is discretion, in the which better part° I have saved my life. Zounds,   *role*
I am afraid of this gunpowder Percy, though he be dead. How
120 if he should counterfeit too, and rise? By my faith, I am afraid
he would prove the better counterfeit. Therefore I'll make him
sure; yea, and I'll swear I killed him. Why may not he rise as
well as I? Nothing confutes me but eyes,[7] and nobody sees
me. Therefore, sirrah, *[stabbing* HOTSPUR*]* with a new wound
125 in your thigh, come you along with me.
       He takes up HOTSPUR *on his back.*
       Enter PRINCE *[*HARRY*] and [Lord]* JOHN OF LANCASTER
PRINCE HARRY   Come, brother John. Full bravely hast thou fleshed

---

4. Ornaments such as plumes or gloves worn into battle.
5. Prepared for embalming and burial as noblemen were; disemboweled in the manner of a hunted deer.
6. A quarrelsome or shrewish person; the name of an imaginary deity who, according to medieval morality plays, was worshipped by followers of Mohammed.
7. No one could confute my story but an eyewitness.

Thy maiden sword.[8]

JOHN OF LANCASTER   But soft; whom have we here?

Did you not tell me this fat man was dead?

PRINCE HARRY   I did; I saw him dead,

Breathless and bleeding on the ground.

130   [*To* FALSTAFF]   Art thou alive?

Or is it fantasy° that plays upon our eyesight?   *hallucination*

I prithee speak; we will not trust our eyes

Without our ears. Thou art not what thou seem'st.

FALSTAFF   No, that's certain: I am not a double man.° But if I   *ghost; two men*

135   be not Jack Falstaff, then am I a jack.° There is Percy. If your   *knave*

father will do me any honour; so; if not, let him kill the next

Percy himself. I look to be either earl or duke, I can assure you.

PRINCE HARRY   Why, Percy I killed myself, and saw thee dead.

FALSTAFF   Didst thou? Lord, Lord, how this world is given to

140   lying! I grant you I was down and out of breath, and so was he;

but we rose both at an instant,° and fought a long hour by   *simultaneously*

Shrewsbury clock. If I may be believed, so; if not, let them that

should reward valour bear the sin upon their own heads. I'll

take't on my death° I gave him this wound in the thigh. If the   *swear on my deathbed*

145   man were alive and would deny it, zounds, I would make him

eat a piece of my sword.

JOHN OF LANCASTER   This is the strangest tale that e'er I heard.

PRINCE HARRY   This is the strangest fellow, brother John.

[*To* FALSTAFF] Come, bring your luggage nobly on your back.

150   For my part, if a lie may do thee grace,°   *get you favor*

I'll gild it with the happiest° terms I have.   *most favorable*

A retreat is sounded

The trumpet sounds retreat; the day is our.

Come, brother, let us to the highest° of the field   *highest ground*

To see what friends are living, who are dead.

Exeunt [*the* PRINCE *and* LANCASTER]

155   FALSTAFF   I'll follow, as they say, for reward. He that rewards me,

God reward him. If I do grow great, I'll grow less; for I'll purge,[9]

and leave sack, and live cleanly, as a nobleman should do.

Exit [*bearing Hotspur's body*]

5.5

The trumpets sound. Enter KING [HENRY], PRINCE
[HARRY], *Lord* JOHN OF LANCASTER, [*the*] *Earl of* WEST-
MORLAND, *with* [*the Earl of*] WORCESTER *and* [*Sir Rich-
ard*] VERNON, *prisoners* [*and soldiers*]

KING HENRY   Thus ever did rebellion find rebuke.

Ill-spirited Worcester, did not we send grace,

Pardon, and terms of love to all of you?

And wouldst thou turn our offers contrary,

5   Misuse the tenor° of thy kinsman's trust?   *Abuse the substance*

Three knights upon our party slain today,

A noble earl, and many a creature else,

---

8. *Full . . . sword:* How courageously or splendidly
have you initiated in bloodshed your untried weapon
(fought your first battle). The phrase alludes to hunting
practices in which hawks or hounds were "fleshed," or
made eager for prey by the taste of blood. Also alluding,
by way of the slang meaning of "sword" as "penis," to a
man's first sexual encounters with the flesh of others.
9. I'll take laxatives (to reduce my weight); I'll repent.

Had been alive this hour
If like a Christian thou hadst truly borne
10 Betwixt our armies true intelligence.°   *information*
WORCESTER   What I have done my safety urged me to,
And I embrace this fortune patiently,
Since not to be avoided it falls on me.
KING HENRY   Bear Worcester to the death, and Vernon too.
15 Other offenders we will pause upon.°   *reflect upon*
        Exeunt WORCESTER *and* VERNON [*guarded*]
How goes the field?
PRINCE HARRY   The noble Scot Lord Douglas, when he saw
The fortune of the day quite turned from him,
The noble Percy slain, and all his men
20 Upon the foot of fear,° fled with the rest;   *Fleeing in fear*
And falling from a hill he was so bruised
That the pursuers took him. At my tent
The Douglas is, and I beseech your grace
I may dispose of him.
25 KING HENRY   With all my heart.
PRINCE HARRY   Then, brother John of Lancaster,
To you this honourable bounty° shall belong.   *act of generosity*
Go to the Douglas, and deliver him
Up to his pleasure ransomless and free.
30 His valours shown upon our crests° today   *helmets*
Have taught us how to cherish such high deeds
Even in the bosom of our adversaries.
JOHN OF LANCASTER   I thank your grace for this high courtesy,
Which I shall give away immediately.
35 KING HENRY   Then this remains, that we divide our power.
You, son John, and my cousin Westmorland,
Towards York shall bend you° with your dearest speed   *direct your course*
To meet Northumberland and the prelate Scrope,
Who, as we hear, are busily in arms.
40 Myself and you, son Harry, will towards Wales,
To fight with Glyndŵr and the Earl of March.
Rebellion in this land shall lose his sway,
Meeting the check of such another day;
And since this business so fair is done,
45 Let us not leave° till all our own be won.   *leave off*
        Exeunt [*the* KING, *the* PRINCE, *and their power*
      at one door, LANCASTER, WESTMORLAND, *and their*
                  power at another door]

The Merry Wives of Windsor

"The first act of the *Merry Wives* alone contains more life and reality than all German literature." So wrote Friedrich Engels to Karl Marx, his fellow German revolutionary and coauthor with Engels of the *Manifesto of the Communist Party*. Perhaps what he admired in *The Merry Wives of Windsor* (1597–98) is the dramatization of the middle class as it is being formed out of social tensions and verbal distinctions, out of disparate and often contradictory elements. Probably Engels also shared the enthusiasm of four centuries of theater audiences for the play's elaborate intrigues and comic stage business. Certainly this is Shakespeare's most middle-class play in its subject matter, setting, and outlook. It is also his most farcical, more so than even such early works as *The Comedy of Errors* and *The Taming of the Shrew*. Farce and intrigue establish the comic tone that informs the play's ultimate spirit of good-humored reconciliation. They also provide the plot mechanisms through which the characters' parochial self-interest is forged into a capacious social unity where hierarchy, though not permanently eliminated, is temporarily suspended. The particular fusion of these two elements—the theatrical and the social—produces the play's distinctiveness.

The Merry Wives celebrates the playful but chaste behavior of the titular characters, Mistress Page and Mistress Ford, each married to a prosperous burgher. The overt message is delivered by Mistress Page: "Wives may be merry, and yet honest, too" (4.2.89), where "honest" means being sexually faithful to their mates. Page's easy and—from a sexual point of view—justified trust of his wife's fidelity provides a norm from which Ford's irrational jealousy of his wife deviates. The two women's plot against the sexually and economically predatory Sir John Falstaff, their would-be seducer, is also designed to dupe and ultimately cure Ford. In the subplot, the concluding love marriage between Fenton, the impoverished gentleman, and the Pages' daughter Anne, who is beneath him socially but above him financially, affirms romantic love in a way that arguably is also assimilable to citizen values.

The play's time and place reinforce this sense of middle-class community. Together they create the impression of life in an English provincial town as it is being lived at the moment of the play's first performance—a rare phenomenon in Renaissance drama. Although such works as *The Comedy of Errors* and *The Merchant of Venice* depict prosperous citizens of a rank below the aristocracy, those characters live either abroad, or in the past, or both. By contrast, *The Merry Wives* retains a contemporary, domestic, and nonaristocratic feel unique in Shakespearean drama. To be sure, this feel is not uniform; the play refers back to the early fifteenth century. Moreover, not all of the materials from which it is constructed are indigenous: the closest analogue and most likely source for the main plot is found in *Il Pecorone* (1558), by the Italian writer Ser Giovanni Fiorentino. This plot and the primary subplot also draw on ancient Roman comedy, medieval farce, and Renaissance Italian drama. Finally, the play liberally includes characters from both above and below the middle class. Yet the historical allusions do not conjure up a bygone era, the foreign literary and theatrical traditions are reworked into English dramatic and cultural stereotypes, and the upper- and lower-class figures ultimately function to underscore the assimilating power of the middle class.

The play takes a jaundiced view of nearly every character with a claim to social standing. Slender's pretensions to gentility are mocked from beginning to end. His uncle, Justice Shallow, does not fare much better. In the opening scene, Shallow, whose authority is based not in the town but in the county and ultimately in the

Cuckold, his unfaithful wife, and the seducer. From *Roxburghe Ballads* (seventeenth century).

monarchy, acts not to preserve the peace but to undermine it. Similarly ineffectual are the peacemaking efforts of the parson, Sir Hugh Evans, whose honorary title and position as parson indicate that he, too, derives authority from the outside (in this case, from the national church). Evans is also foreign (Welsh), and he seeks to fight a duel with another foreigner (the French Doctor Caius), who is well-to-do and has connections at court.

A different kind of conflict pits the wealthy citizens against their social, but not economic, superiors. Page rejects the love suit of Fenton, and Falstaff is subjected to repeated abuse, in Act 5 functioning as a scapegoat against whom the townspeople can unite. This antagonism between citizen and gentleman is given a financial twist appropriate to the dominant ethos of the play. Page believes that Fenton is motivated by money rather than love, a charge that Fenton admits to Anne was originally true, although he insists that the balance has now shifted:

> I found thee of more value
> Than stamps in gold or sums in sealèd bags;
> And 'tis the very riches of thyself
> That now I aim at.
>
> (3.4.15–18)

Falstaff has no romantic concerns at all, attempting his seductions in the interest perhaps of lust and certainly of profit, metaphorically figured as the fruits of mercantile imperialism. Of Mistress Page he exclaims: "She bears the purse too. She is a region in Guiana, all gold and bounty. I will be cheaters to them both, and they shall be exchequers to me. They shall be my East and West Indies, and I will trade to them both. . . . Sail like my pinnace to these golden shores" (1.3.58–62, 70).

Yet the conclusion tells a different story. Page and his wife, although at cross purposes with each other, have each been trying to marry Anne off to an absurdly unsuitable partner. But when they realize there is no alternative, both husband and wife accept their daughter's marriage with good humor. This stance incorporates Fenton, of course, but is immediately extended by Mistress Page to include Falstaff as well. This act reveals not the servility but the capaciousness, generosity, and adaptability of the citizens' world. The marriage of Fenton to Anne—the main accomplishment of the play, with the exception of the simultaneous duping of Falstaff and curing of

Ford—implicitly marks the reconciliation of the middle class with their social betters. Both plots raise the fear of mercenary, sexually threatening aristocratic interlopers only to emphasize the emptiness of that concern—in one instance because of the comic incompetence of the predator and in the other because of the falseness of the suspicion. Even though the language of the play highlights Fenton's lofty rank—he is the sole character to speak primarily in blank verse—in the end he becomes part of the community. Similarly, the tricking of Falstaff in the final scene draws on the royal and aristocratic heritage of the court masque. But this theatrical form, in which the courtiers become the actors, is here recast in a popular, festive mode.

The concluding scene also includes a compliment to the Order of the Garter uttered in blank verse—to reflect the elevated subject matter—by Mistress Quickly disguised as the Queen of the Fairies (5.5.53–70). The Order of the Garter was an aristocratic fraternity under the patronage of the Queen that inducted new members at Windsor Castle. This passage has the effect of placing the town of Windsor under the protection of the castle of Windsor, just as the town's Garter Inn evokes the castle's more elevated Order of the Garter. These references also seem to be a clue to the play's first performance—probably in April 1597 before Elizabeth in London at the Garter Feast, where candidates were elected to the order for induction the following month. One of those to be elected was the new patron of Shakespeare's acting company, and he may well have commissioned the play for the occasion. There also seems to be a comic reference to a German aristocrat elected at the same time (4.5.61–64). But writing in 1702, and hence with uncertain authority, John Dennis records a different tradition. He claims it was the Queen who, after seeing *1 Henry IV*, ordered Shakespeare to write another play about Falstaff, showing him in love, and to complete it within fourteen days.

It is possible that Shakespeare temporarily put aside the composition of *2 Henry IV*, with which *The Merry Wives* has close verbal affinities, to comply either with his patron or with his Queen—indeed, perhaps rather hurriedly. *The Merry Wives* shares at least the names of a number of characters with the two parts of *Henry IV* and with *Henry V*—Falstaff, of course, but also Mistress Quickly, Shallow, Pistol, Bardolph, and Nim. Fenton supposedly "kept company with the wild Prince and Poins" (3.2.61), an allusion to the future Henry V and one of his companions in the *Henry IV* plays. But even though the names are the same, the characters are not. To take only the most prominent example: the easily duped Falstaff of Windsor lacks the indomitable comic resourcefulness that he repeatedly demonstrates in the history plays. Still, the web of political associations lends a national and monarchical aspect to the more circumscribed events of *The Merry Wives*. The effect is ambiguous, even contradictory: on the one hand, royal power is asserted in its absence; on the other, the middling sort who inhabit the town come to stand for all of England.

The play's generalizing force is further enhanced by a degree of indebtedness to popular culture unusual even for Shakespeare. In keeping with its social milieu, *The Merry Wives* has a far higher percentage of prose than does any other Shakespearean work. Much of it satirically reproduces the language of proverb and cliché; Master Slender and Mistress Quickly in particular depend on clichés that verge on the meaningless. Slender's words to Page convey little more than vague good will along with silly ineptitude: "Master Page, I am glad to see you. Much good do it your good heart! . . . And I thank you always with my heart, la, with my heart. . . . Sir, I thank you. By yea and no, I do" (1.1.65–70). Similarly, Quickly can unleash a barrage of only weakly communicative language that somehow enables her to connect with almost all the other characters: "nobody but has his fault," "the very yea and the no," "that's neither here nor there," "what the goodyear," "thereby hangs a tale," "an honest maid as ever broke bread," "Out upon't" (1.4.12, 82, 93, 106, 130, 131–32, 145).

This unintentionally humorous rhetoric is hardly the only evidence of popular culture in the play. *The Merry Wives* also brings on stage a considerable number of lower-class characters. These are not the clowns and fools of the more aristocratic romantic comedies, but servants: John and Robert, who work for the Fords; Peter Simple, who

Elizabeth I and the Knights of the Garter. Engraved by Michael Gheeraerts the Elder (1576).

waits on Slender; John Rugby and Mistress Quickly, who belong to Caius's household; and, set apart from all of these, Falstaff's hangers-on—Bardolph, Pistol, and Nim. Moreover, in the final scene, when the children of Windsor dress up as fairies to punish Falstaff, they mobilize a popular rural belief, evidently shared by their victim, in mischievous immortal spirits who prey upon the local inhabitants. The insults and injuries Falstaff sustains—suffocation, a dunking in the river, a beating, and pinching—belong to the popular tradition of knockabout physical stage action characteristic of both farce and shaming rituals of the time.

Windsor's sense of community also depends on a cheerfully casual ethnocentrism. Hostility to foreigners is part of the throwaway language of the play (especially the Host's): "base Hungarian wight," "Base Phrygian Turk," "Flemish drunkard," "Cathayan," "Ethiopian," "Francisco," "Castalian King Urinal," "Anthropophaginian" (cannibal), "Bohemian Tartar" (1.3.18, 78; 2.1.20–21, 127; 2.3.24, 29; 4.5.8, 16). One of Ford's jealous fits trades in similar stereotypes: "I will rather trust a Fleming with my butter, Parson Hugh the Welshman with my cheese, an Irishman with my aqua-vitae bottle, or a thief to walk my ambling gelding, than my wife with herself" (2.2.265–68). The same effect is produced by the fragmentary, obscure satirical treatment of Germans generally and of a particular German Duke, who is accused of horse stealing in what there is of the third plot of the play, Caius and Evans's revenge on the Host (4.3, 4.5.51–75).

But clearly it is in the fractured English of the French Caius and Welsh Evans themselves, and the good-humored ridicule it evokes, that the English chauvinism of *The Merry Wives* appears most prominently. Evans "makes fritters of English" (5.5.136); he and Caius "hack our English" (3.1.67). Their marked accents, as well as Caius's frequent reversion to French, call attention to their foreignness. Their silly decision to fight a duel is thwarted by the Host out of affection for the two men and perhaps out of hostility to this aristocratic means of settling disputes. Both the intention and the inability to carry it out intensify the other characters' sense of the superiority of the English middle class. This sense, communicated to the audience as well, is clear enough in the First Folio (1623)—which the present edition follows—despite the likelihood that Shakespeare composed the text that lies behind it for an aristocratic event. But it is even more consistently emphasized in the First Quarto (1602), which seems to be based on a revision of the original version for popular performance. (See the Textual Note.)

As the title of the play reveals, however, its conflicts are fought primarily in terms of gender. But the meaning of these conflicts, despite their unambiguous outcomes, is unclear. Is the wives' triumph over Falstaff's sexual adventuring and Ford's fantasy of his wife's infidelity a victory for *middle-class* women (as suggested earlier), for middle-class *women,* or for both? The play celebrates the wives' freedom and autonomy, in short their merriness, but that merriness serves primarily to protect their husbands' wealth. Primarily, but not entirely. Though Page proudly contrasts his liberal attitude toward his wife with Ford's misogynist anxiety, Mistress Page's scheming against her husband's plans for their daughter's marriage reveals that female self-assertion does not necessarily dovetail with male desire. In this different sense, Ford's fears are justified, Page's confidence undermined. As it turns out, neither parent prevails, although a woman does: Anne replicates the companionate marriage of her mother and father, but she does so against their will, by insisting on her right to choose her own husband.

A view of gender relations and sexuality less obviously tied to emerging middle-class norms is produced by Mistress Quickly's language. Although the obsessive sexual innuendo of that language often escapes the speaker herself, she is not alone in her heedless punning. Evans in particular evinces a comparable obliviousness to the sexual implications of his own speech, an obliviousness that Quickly's comic misunderstandings during the seemingly extraneous Latin lesson (4.1) are instrumental in revealing. Evans, who doubles as Windsor's schoolmaster, quizzes young William Page on the fundamentals of Latin grammar as they were taught in the first years of school, specifically asking his pupil to recite the possessive plural form (or "genitive case") of the word for "this" ("of these"). Mistress Quickly looks on and comments uncomprehendingly:

what she overlooks in her own speech she detects in a language she cannot understand.

> WILLIAM   Genitive case?
> EVANS   Ay.
> WILLIAM   *Genitivo: 'horum, harum, horum'.*
> MISTRESS QUICKLY   Vengeance of Jenny's case! Fie on her!
> Never name her, child, if she be a whore.
>
> (4.1.50–54)

Here, "genitive" may suggest "generative" or even "genital" as well as the female name "Jenny"; "case" is slang for "vagina"; and *"horum,"* a genitive plural, evokes the more obvious "whore." The scene turns on conflicts between Latin and English, literacy and illiteracy, middle class and lower, man and woman. This is not an isolated moment. Earlier in the play, the language of grammar, allied to translation as in this scene, acquires a sexual charge as Falstaff boasts of his intention to seduce Mistress Ford:

> FALSTAFF . . . I can construe the action of her familiar style; and
> the hardest voice of her behaviour, to be Englished rightly, is 'I
> am Sir John Falstaff's'.
> PISTOL   He hath studied her well, and translated her will: out of
> honesty, into English.
>
> (1.3.39–43)

A different pattern of sexual allusion emerges when Falstaff finds himself trapped in Ford's house on his second assignation with Mistress Ford, and the wives prevail upon him to escape disguised as the "Aunt of Brentford." Although Ford does not see through the costume, he does spew out a torrent of hostile rhetoric—"A witch, a quean, an old cozening quean!" he begins (4.2.149)—before beating up someone whom he believes, however erroneously, to be an old woman (albeit a disreputable one). But of course the woman he attacks is really Falstaff, whose transvestite outfit anticipates the final moments of *The Merry Wives*. Although neither the Folio nor the Quarto is sufficiently consistent about the colors the various characters wear at the end of the play to make possible an exact reconstruction of how Fenton manages to fool the other suitors and elope with Anne, the central trick is unambiguous. "I came yonder at Eton to marry Mistress Anne Page, and she's a great lubberly boy," Slender laments. "If I had been married to him, for all he was in woman's apparel, I would not have had him" (5.5.169–70, 176–77). Caius finds himself even more deeply entangled in the deception. "Ver is Mistress Page? By Gar, I am cozened! I ha' married *un garçon,* a boy, *un paysan,* by Gar. A boy!" (5.5.186–87). This is not the first such sexual tease. Earlier, Ford comments disapprovingly on the intimacy between the merry wives: "I think if your husbands were dead you two would marry." The charge of what we would now call homosexuality is quickly rejected. "Be sure of that—two other husbands," Mistress Page immediately replies (3.2.11–13). Similarly, the ending entertains the option of man-boy sexual relations only to punish Anne's foolish suitors. Like adultery and financially motivated arranged marriages, these are deviations from the elaborately constructed romantic and sexual norm, whose literal issue is emphasized by the unusual prominence of children in the play.

Yet this is not the whole story. The cross-dressing conclusion points self-referentially beyond the fictional action to the actors who have produced the fiction. Shakespeare wrote for a transvestite theater in which female parts were performed by boys. Members of the audience might well note the distance between the fairy queen—a flattering allusion to Queen Elizabeth—Mistress Quickly, and the fictional character who plays the doubly fictional part. They might also register the real boy actor impersonating these two fictional figures. And at the very end, Slender and Caius are not alone in their predicament: Fenton, too, goes off with a boy dressed as a girl. This conclusion simultaneously celebrates and subverts the theatrical illusion. Renaissance accounts

A "skimmington," a public rite of humiliation for domestic disorder.

praise the lifelike persuasiveness of the best boy actors who impersonated women. Here, the boy gets the girl just as the audience would wish, at the very moment Shakespeare reminds them that they have willingly believed in precisely the falsehood accepted by some of the play's more foolish characters.

This resolution, like *The Merry Wives* as a whole, is at once socially suggestive and visually funny. Much of the pleasure of the play arises from the physical comedy of plot and counterplot—Caius discovering Simple in his closet, Ford in disguise urging Falstaff to seduce his wife, Caius and Evans unknowingly preparing for solo duels, Falstaff repeatedly escaping Ford only to suffer still greater humiliation, the deluded would-be bridegrooms stealing off with the wrong fairies. This effective stage business helps explain the work's success both in the theater and in operatic adaptation (especially Verdi's *Falstaff*, 1893).

Particularly at the end, however, stage business also serves to work out the subplot in a way that unravels the logic of the main plot. By the final scene, the revenge on Falstaff has brought together a socially and verbally heterogeneous and often antagonistic group—not just the merry wives and their servants but also their husbands, Evans, Mistress Quickly, and the children of Windsor. Yet the result is not the expected expulsion of the predatory courtier by a unified town but the undoing of nearly all positions of superiority. The central mechanism for this antiscapegoating outcome is the decision by the Fords and Pages to subject Falstaff to one more round of abuse. Even though they are confident that he no longer poses a threat, perhaps they believe he needs to make amends to the whole town. Thus the main plot, in which Falstaff and Ford are fooled by the wives, is balanced by the subplot, in which the fun at the expense of Caius and Slender is perhaps less important than the thwarting of the Pages, who have plotted against each other and must endure the humiliating reversal of having Ford and Falstaff lecture them. As Falstaff says: "I am glad, though you have ta'en a special stand to strike at me, that your arrow hath glanced" (5.5.211–12). Even Anne acknowledges fault: "Pardon, good father. Good my mother, pardon" (line 194). In the fragmentary third plot, the Host fools Evans and Caius, only to have these two rivals team up to exact revenge from him.

The pattern is that of the duper duped. In the end, the renunciation of plotting and hostility by a compromised group of characters produces a moral leveling. The hierarchies and conflicts that separate man from woman, parent from child, sexual normality from sexual deviancy, town from crown, Englishman from foreigner, upper class from middle class, and middle class from lower are resolved—or, more accurately, evaded—through the good-natured, universal inclusiveness of the conclusion. The middle class at the end of the play is a different, more encompassing category than at the beginning. Its strength lies in its cheerful capacity to absorb all comers despite the conscious efforts of most of the leading characters, its ability to fashion a unity that is felt to be more profound than the multiple conflicts dividing the town. And when Mistress Page invites the other characters to "laugh this sport o'er by a country fire" (5.5.219), she is incorporating within the play an experience that the play itself has sought to provide its audience.

Walter Cohen

TEXTUAL NOTE

The Merry Wives of Windsor, probably composed and first performed in 1597, survives in two important early printed versions—the First Quarto (Q, 1602) and the First Folio (F, 1623). (The Second Quarto, from 1619, simply reprints the First.) This early publication history partly obscures the likely chronology of composition, however. The version in F is printed from a manuscript prepared by a professional scribe named Ralph Crane, who did a fair amount of editing as he copied. His manuscript is in turn based on either a playhouse promptbook or an authorial manuscript. In either case, the Folio text has a close connection with the first performance of the play. Although a date as late as 1601 remains a possibility, most scholars believe that that performance took place in 1597 in a royal and aristocratic setting—for reasons given in the Introduction.

The First Quarto is almost certainly a reported or recollected text (also known as a "memorial reconstruction"): an account of the play in performance prepared largely from memory by the actors who had the parts of the Host (probably) and Falstaff (possibly). Borrowings from *Henry V* mean that it must have been composed between 1598, the earliest year in which *Henry V* could plausibly have been written, and 1602, when the Quarto of *The Merry Wives* was published. Little over half the length of the Folio *Merry Wives,* it seems to be an attempt to recall a version of the play that had already been adapted and cut. Because the First Quarto derives from the memory of a performance rather than from a manuscript that is directly or indirectly Shakespearean, it lacks textual authority.

Accordingly, all modern editions, including the present one, are based on F, in this respect continuing an unbroken tradition tacitly begun with the Third Quarto (1630), which is based not on the first two Quartos but on F. But from 1602 to 1623, the First Quarto was the only written version of the play publicly available. In addition, various problems with the Folio *Merry Wives* make the First Quarto—as truncated, unreliable, and even garbled as it sometimes is—a crucial resource. Thus, where F gives Ford the pseudonym "Broome," Q offers "Brooke." This is surely the original choice, as the wordplay in Falstaff's expression of gratitude for a gift of wine from the character makes clear: "Such Brookes are welcome to me, that o'erflows such liquor" (2.2.135–36). The name was censored at some point from 1597 on, perhaps because "Brooke" was the family name of the patron of Shakespeare's acting company. F's relatively weak and infrequent oaths again suggest censorship, in this instance probably in response to a law of 1606 prohibiting references to God in the theater. Especially in what look like poorly remembered passages, Q's oaths also seem to lack strict textual fidelity to an authorial or theatrical original. But they are fuller and in that sense more accurate. In addition, Q preserves one or more passages that either are omitted from F or are clearly superior to the comparable phrases included there. And because Ralph Crane's editing of the manuscript for F included placing all stage entrances at the very beginning of each scene regardless of where they actually belonged, the stage directions of Q can be quite helpful.

Still other verbal discrepancies between the two versions point to more general thematic differences. Q omits F's Latin lesson (4.1) as well as its allusion in 5.5 to the Order of the Garter ceremony. At least the second of these cuts, both of which seem to indicate a text designed for a more popular audience than the courtly spectators aimed at by F, may well have been made by Shakespeare's company when it put on *The Merry Wives* in the public, commercial theater. References to rural life in Windsor and to the presence of the court are more frequent in F than in Q, which sometimes has urban allusions instead and which simply omits some elite or courtly material. Only in Q are courtiers mocked by name (Brooke, Mömpelgard), and in general F has the more appreciative view of the court.

Many questions remain about both Q and F. At least one intriguing possibility is worth pondering. F may be based on an authorial manuscript that was used for the initial court performance. Q may be based on the memory of stage performances of a promptbook that incorporates revisions of the authorial manuscript for the public theater. If both hypotheses are correct, F accurately preserves a unique, anomalous first performance; Q inaccurately preserves the different version used for the overwhelming majority of the performances in Shakespeare's lifetime. On this interpretation, the textual situation is paradoxical: Q has more value than is usually assumed, despite its inaccuracy. Because it derives from the memory of performance, its language is less authentically Shakespearean than F's. But because those performances reflect revisions that include Shakespeare's own changes as well as other changes made by his company that he accepted, Q may be more authentically Shakespearean than F in presenting the playwright's final treatment of his material, a treatment that accords greater relative weight to popular material both by excluding high-cultural scenes and by including satirical references and additional allusions to everyday life.

SELECTED BIBLIOGRAPHY

Brown, Pamela Allen. *Better a Shrew Than a Sheep: Women, Drama, and the Culture of Jest in Early Modern England.* Ithaca, N.Y.: Cornell University Press, 2003. 33–55. *The Merry Wives* as a play appealing to women. This study focuses on—and differentiates between—the two wives in the context of communal women's culture, female chastity, and neighborhood gender relations.
Buccola, Regina M. "Shakespeare's Fairy Dance with Religio-Political Controversy in *The Merry Wives of Windsor.*" *Shakespeare and the Culture of Christianity in Early Modern England.* Ed. Dennis Taylor and David Beauregard. New York: Fordham University Press, 2003. 159–79. Connections among fairies, Catholicism, the Welsh, and women in the play and society alike seen in *The Merry Wives* as potentially subversive but ultimately incorporated into an orthodox order.
Erickson, Peter. "The Order of the Garter, the Cult of Elizabeth, and Class-Gender Tension in *The Merry Wives of Windsor.*" *Shakespeare Reproduced: The Text in History and Ideology.* Ed. Jean E. Howard and Marion F. O'Connor. New York: Methuen, 1987. 116–42. Tension between a conservative class hierarchy, emblematized by the Order of the Garter, and a less traditional affirmation of female authority, productive of male anxiety and represented by the wives and their linkage to Elizabeth.
Hall, Jonathan. "The Evacuations of Falstaff (*The Merry Wives of Windsor*)." *Shakespeare and Carnival: After Bakhtin.* Ed. Ronald Knowles. New York: St. Martin's, 1998. 123–51. The domestication of the grotesque, carnivalesque body of Falstaff by a stable bourgeois world.
Helgerson, Richard. "Language Lessons: Linguistic Colonialism, Linguistic Postcolonialism, and the Early Modern English Nation." *Yale Journal of Criticism* 11 (1998): 289–99. Latin versus English versus marginal dialects as colonizing and colonized languages.
Kegl, Rosemary. "'The Adoption of Abominable Terms': Middle Classes, Merry Wives, and the Insults That Shape Windsor." *The Rhetoric of Concealment: Figuring Gender and Class in Renaissance Literature.* Ithaca, N.Y.: Cornell University Press, 1994. 77–125. The language of class and gender hierarchy, with attention to issues of ethnocentrism.

Marcus, Leah. "Levelling Shakespeare: Local Customs and Local Texts." *Shakespeare Quarterly* 42 (1991): 168–78. Contrast of the rural, aristocratic Folio version of the play with the urban, middle-class quarto text.

Melchiori, Giorgio, ed. *The Merry Wives of Windsor*. Walton-on-Thames, Surrey: Thomas Nelson, 2000. Outstanding scholarly edition with a lengthy critical introduction.

Parker, Patricia. "*The Merry Wives of Windsor* and Shakespearean Translation." *Modern Language Quarterly* 52 (1991): 225–61. The scene of Latin instruction (4.1) as integral to the play, revealing links between language and sexuality.

Pittenger, Elizabeth. "Dispatch Quickly: The Mechanical Reproduction of Pages." *Shakespeare Quarterly* 42 (1991): 389–408. Connections among printing, pedagogy, language, and gender hierarchy, also with special attention to 4.1.

Salingar, Leo. "The Englishness of the *The Merry Wives of Windsor*." *Cahiers élisabéthains* 59 (2001): 9–25. General reading of the play covering geographical setting, social structure, farce, and especially nationalist linguistic patterns.

FILM

The Merry Wives of Windsor. 1982. Dir. David Hugh Jones. UK. 168 min. BBC production with Ben Kingsley as Ford and Judy Davis as Mistress Ford.

The Merry Wives of Windsor

THE PERSONS OF THE PLAY

MISTRESS Margaret PAGE
Master George PAGE, her husband
ANNE Page, their daughter
WILLIAM Page, their son } citizens of Windsor
MISTRESS Alice FORD
Master Frank FORD, her husband
JOHN }
ROBERT } their servants
Sir John FALSTAFF
BARDOLPH }
PISTOL } Sir John Falstaff's
NIM } followers
ROBIN, Sir John Falstaff's page
The HOST of the Garter Inn
Sir Hugh EVANS, a Welsh parson
Doctor CAIUS, a French physician
MISTRESS QUICKLY, his housekeeper
John RUGBY, his servant
Master FENTON, a young gentleman, in love with Anne Page
Master Abraham SLENDER
Robert SHALLOW, his uncle, a Justice
Peter SIMPLE, Slender's servant
Children of Windsor, appearing as fairies

1.1

Enter Justice SHALLOW, [*Master*] SLENDER, *and Sir*[1]
Hugh EVANS

SHALLOW   Sir Hugh, persuade me not. I will make a Star Cham-
ber° matter of it. If he were twenty Sir John Falstaffs, he shall   *high court*
not abuse Robert Shallow, Esquire.°   *(just below a knight)*
SLENDER   In the county of Gloucester, Justice of Peace and
5 Coram.[2]
SHALLOW   Ay, cousin° Slender, and Custalorum.   *kinsman (here, nephew)*
SLENDER   Ay, and Ratolorum[3] too; and a gentleman born, Mas-
ter Parson, who writes himself 'Armigero'° in any bill, war   *esquire; arms bearer*
rant,quittance,° or obligation: 'Armigero'.   *discharge from debt*
10 SHALLOW   Ay, that I do, and have done any time these three hundred years.
SLENDER   All his successors gone before him hath done't, and all

---

1.1 Location: A street, later moving to the entrance to
Page's house.
1. *Justice:* justice of the peace (line 4), a local judge.
Master: regularly used of Slender (beginning at line 47),
a respectful prefix to a name that is similar in meaning to
the modern "Mr.," which derives from it. *Sir:* clergyman's
honorary title, not indicating knighthood, as it does with
Falstaff (line 2).
2. Blunder for "quorum," designating justices who could

try a felon if a sufficient number of them (two or more)
were present. Literally, *coram* is Latin for "in the presence
of"; to "bring under coram" was to subject someone to
discipline: hence, Slender comically provides an unwittingly accurate account of Shallow's office.
3. "Custalorum" (line 6) and "Ratolorum" are blunders
for *custos rotulorum* (keeper of the rolls), the principal
justice in a county; perhaps a play on "rat."

his ancestors that come after him may. They may give the
dozen white luces° in their coat.°   pike/coat of arms

15 SHALLOW   It is an old coat.

EVANS   The dozen white louses do become an old coad⁴ well. It
agrees well passant:⁵ it is a familiar° beast to man, and signifies   familial; too intimate
love.

SHALLOW   The luce is the fresh fish; the salt fish is an old cod.⁶

20 SLENDER   I may quarter,⁷ coz.°   kinsman

SHALLOW   You may, by marrying.

EVANS   It is marring indeed if he quarter it.

SHALLOW   Not a whit.

EVANS   Yes, py'r Lady.° If he has a quarter of your coat, there is   by our Lady (Mary)
25 but three skirts° for yourself, in my simple conjectures. But that   coattails
is all one. If Sir John Falstaff have committed disparagements
unto you, I am of the Church, and will be glad to do my benevolence to make atonements and compromises between you.

SHALLOW   The Council⁸ shall hear it; it is a riot.

30 EVANS   It is not meet° the Council hear a riot. There is no fear   fitting
of Got in a riot. The Council, look you, shall desire to hear the
fear of Got, and not to hear a riot. Take your 'visaments in
that.⁹

SHALLOW   Ha! O' my life, if I were young again, the sword
35 should end it.

EVANS   It is petter that friends is the sword and end it.¹ And there
is also another device in my prain, which peradventure prings
goot discretions with it. There is Anne Page which is daughter
to Master George Page, which is pretty virginity.

40 SLENDER   Mistress Anne Page? She has brown hair, and speaks
small° like a woman?   in a soprano voice

EVANS   It is that fery person for all the 'orld, as just as you will
desire. And seven hundred pounds of moneys, and gold and
silver, is° her grandsire upon his death's-bed—Got deliver to a   did
45 joyful resurrections—give, when she is able to overtake seventeen years old. It were a goot motion° if we leave our pribbles   plan
and prabbles,° and desire a marriage between Master Abraham   squabbles
and Mistress Anne Page.

SLENDER   Did her grandsire leave her seven hundred pound?

50 EVANS   Ay, and her father is make her a petter penny.°   will give much more

SHALLOW   I know the young gentlewoman. She has good gifts.°   qualities

EVANS   Seven hundred pounds and possibilities° is goot gifts.   financial prospects

SHALLOW   Well, let us see honest Master Page. Is Falstaff there?

EVANS   Shall I tell you a lie? I do despise a liar as I do despise
55 one that is false, or as I despise one that is not true. The knight
Sir John is there, and I beseech you be ruled by your well-

4. Coat; cod; scrotum. Evans, in what is meant to be a
stereotypical Welsh accent, often pronounces "t" for "d,"
"p" for "b," and "f" for "v" and omits initial "w." "Louses"
is Evans's comic error for "luces" (line 14), a term from
heraldry, the branch of knowledge concerned with the
right to bear arms, with family pedigrees, and with coats
of arms. (See also "Armigero" and "coat," lines 8, 14.)
The error is set up by the two meanings of "old coat"
(noble lineage, worn-out clothing, line 15), and Evans's
pronunciation then provokes further uncomprehending
wordplay by Shallow (line 19).
5. Walking, looking to the right with the right paw raised
(heraldic); surpassingly. The heraldic image is absurd for
a fish, only slightly less so for a louse.

6. Meaning unclear—perhaps a joke involving Evans's
pronunciation ("louses/luces"; "coad/coat/cod"). fresh:
freshwater, unpreserved. salt: saltwater, salt-cured,
obscene.
7. I may add another (family's) coat to one of the four
parts of my heraldic arms (for instance, through marriage); but in Evans's reply, cut up in quarters. The
humor of this passage (lines 7–25) results from the deflation of social pretentiousness by unintentionally punning
incomprehension.
8. Star Chamber (lines 1–2); but Evans understands it as
"church council."
9. Take . . . that: Be advised.
1. The intervention of friends should end the dispute.

willers.° I will peat the door for Master Page.   *well-wishers*
    [*He knocks on the door*]
  What ho! Got pless your house here!
  PAGE [*within*]   Who's there?

60 EVANS   Here is Got's plessing and your friend, and Justice Shallow, and here young Master Slender, that peradventures shall
  tell you another tale° if matters grow to your likings.   *(a marriage proposal)*
    Enter Master PAGE
  PAGE   I am glad to see your worships well. I thank you for my
  venison, Master Shallow.

65 SHALLOW   Master Page, I am glad to see you. Much good do it
  your good heart! I wished your venison better; it was ill°   *unlawfully (by Falstaff?)*
  killed.—How doth good Mistress Page?—And I thank you
  always with my heart, la,° with my heart.   *indeed*
  PAGE   Sir, I thank you.

70 SHALLOW   Sir, I thank you. By yea and no,° I do.   *(almost meaningless)*
  PAGE   I am glad to see you, good Master Slender.
  SLENDER   How does your fallow° greyhound, sir? I heard say he   *light-brown*
  was outrun on Cotswold.°   *the Cotswold hills*
  PAGE   It could not be judged, sir.

75 SLENDER   You'll not confess, you'll not confess.°   *(that the dog lost)*
  SHALLOW   That he will not. 'Tis your fault,° 'tis your fault.   *You're in the wrong*
  [*To* PAGE] 'Tis a good dog.
  PAGE   A cur, sir.
  SHALLOW   Sir, he's a good dog and a fair dog. Can there be more

80   said? He is good and fair. Is Sir John Falstaff here?
  PAGE   Sir, he is within; and I would I could do a good office
  between you.
  EVANS   It is spoke as a Christians ought to speak.
  SHALLOW   He hath wronged me, Master Page.

85 PAGE   Sir, he doth in some sort confess it.
  SHALLOW   If it be confessed, it is not redressed. Is not that so,
  Master Page? He hath wronged me; indeed he hath; at a word,°   *in short*
  he hath. Believe me, Robert Shallow, Esquire, saith he is
  wronged.
    Enter Sir John FALSTAFF, BARDOLPH, NIM, *and* PISTOL

90 PAGE   Here comes Sir John.
  FALSTAFF   Now, Master Shallow, you'll complain of me to the
  King?
  SHALLOW   Knight, you have beaten my men, killed my deer, and
  broke open my lodge.°   *keeper's house*

95 FALSTAFF   But not kissed your keeper's daughter?
  SHALLOW   Tut, a pin.° This shall be answered.   *trifling comment*
  FALSTAFF   I will answer it straight: I have done all this. That is
  now answered.
  SHALLOW   The Council shall know this.

100 FALSTAFF   'Twere better for you if it were known in counsel.°   *kept secret*
  You'll be laughed at.
  EVANS   *Pauca verba,*° Sir John, good worts.   *Few words*
  FALSTAFF   Good worts?° Good cabbage!—Slender, I broke your   *words; cabbage*
  head. What matter° have you against me?   *complaint*

105 SLENDER   Marry, sir, I have matter in my head against you, and
  against your cony-catching° rascals, Bardolph, Nim, and Pistol.   *swindling*
  BARDOLPH   You Banbury cheese!°   *thin (like Slender)*
  SLENDER   Ay, it is no matter.

PISTOL   How now, Mephistopheles?[2]
110 SLENDER   Ay, it is no matter.
NIM   Slice, I say *pauca, pauca*. Slice, that's my humour.[3]
SLENDER [*to* SHALLOW]   Where's Simple, my man? Can you tell,
      cousin?
EVANS   Peace, I pray you. Now let us understand. There is three
115 umpires in this matter, as I understand: that is, Master Page,
      fidelicet° Master Page; and there is myself, fidelicet myself; and   *namely*
      the three party is, lastly and finally, mine Host of the Garter.°   *(a Windsor inn)*
PAGE   We three to hear it, and end it between them.
EVANS   Fery goot. I will make a prief of it in my notebook, and
120 we will afterwards 'ork upon the cause with as great discreetly
      as we can.
FALSTAFF   Pistol.
PISTOL   He hears with ears.
EVANS   The tevil and his tam!° What phrase is this? 'He hears   *dam (mother)*
125 with ear'! Why, it is affectations.
FALSTAFF   Pistol, did you pick Master Slender's purse?
SLENDER   Ay, by these gloves did he—or I would I might never
      come in mine own great chamber° again else—of seven groats   *hall; bedroom*
      in mill-sixpences, and two Edward shovel-boards[4] that cost me
130 two shilling and twopence apiece of Ed Miller. By these gloves.
FALSTAFF   Is this true, Pistol?
EVANS   No, it is false, if it° is a pickpurse.   *he*
PISTOL   Ha, thou mountain-foreigner!° Sir John and master mine,   *Welshman*
      I combat challenge of this latten bilbo.[5]—
135 Word of denial in thy *labras*° here,   *lips*
      Word of denial: froth and scum, thou liest.
SLENDER [*pointing to* NIM]   By these gloves, then, 'twas he.
NIM   Be advised, sir, and pass good humours.° I will say 'marry,   *behave properly*
      trap with you'[6] if you run the nuthook's humour on me.[7] That
140 is the very note° of it.   *fact*
SLENDER   By this hat, then, he in the red face° had it. For though   *(Bardolph)*
      I cannot remember what I did when you made me drunk, yet
      I am not altogether an ass.
FALSTAFF [*to* BARDOLPH]   What say you, Scarlet and John?[8]
145 BARDOLPH   Why, sir, for my part I say the gentleman had drunk
      himself out of his five sentences.
EVANS   It is 'his five senses'. Fie, what the ignorance is!
BARDOLPH   And being fap,° sir, was, as they say, cashiered.° And   *drunk / kicked out*
      so conclusions passed the careers.[9]
150 SLENDER   Ay, you spake in Latin[1] then, too. But 'tis no matter.
      I'll ne'er be drunk, whilst I live, again, but in honest, civil,
      godly company, for° this trick. If I be drunk, I'll be drunk with   *on account of*
      those that have the fear of God, and not with drunken knaves.
EVANS   So Got 'udge me,° that is a virtuous mind.   *judge*

2. The devil in Christopher Marlowe's *Dr. Faustus*, perhaps played as a thin, gaunt character.
3. "Slice" takes up the Banbury cheese insult (line 107) and may command Slender to cut off his remarks, to stick to few words ("*pauca*"). Nim's temperament ("humour") is to slice Slender with his sword.
4. *groat*: four-penny coin. *mill-sixpences*: new coins that may have been worth more than their face value. *Edward shovel-boards*: old shillings. Shallow has paid over twice their face value because of their use in the game of shovel board.

5. A sword (from Bilbao, Spain, where fine swords known for their elasticity were made) made of brass or a brasslike, yellow mixed metal; probably alluding to Slender's cowardice and thinness.
6. Get lost; go play a children's game; you'll be caught (?).
7. If you act like a constable in accusing me.
8. Robin Hood's accomplices, Will Scarlet and Little John; alluding to Bardolph's complexion.
9. Things got out of hand; he misinterpreted things.
1. Slender can't understand Bardolph's slang and so assumes it must be Latin.

155 FALSTAFF You hear all these matters denied, gentlemen, you
hear it.

      Enter ANNE *Page [with wine]*

PAGE Nay, daughter, carry the wine in; we'll drink within.

                                            [Exit ANNE]

SLENDER O heaven, this is Mistress Anne Page!

      Enter [at another door] MISTRESS FORD *and* MISTRESS
      PAGE

PAGE How now, Mistress Ford?

160 FALSTAFF Mistress Ford, by my troth, you are very well met. By
your leave, good mistress.

      Sir John FALSTAFF *kisses her*

PAGE Wife, bid these gentlemen welcome.—Come, we have a
hot venison pasty to° dinner. Come, gentlemen, I hope we shall   *pie for*
drink down all unkindness.   *Exeunt all but* SLENDER

165 SLENDER I had rather than forty shillings I had my book of songs
and sonnets here.[2]

      Enter SIMPLE

How now, Simple, where have you been? I must wait on
myself, must I? You have not the book of riddles about you,
have you?

170 SIMPLE Book of riddles? Why, did you not lend it to Alice Short-
cake upon Allhallowmas last, a fortnight afore Michaelmas?[3]

      [Enter SHALLOW *and* EVANS]

SHALLOW *[to* SLENDER] Come, coz; come, coz; we stay° for you.   *wait*
[Aside to him] A word with you, coz.
      [He draws SLENDER *aside]*

Marry, this, coz: there is, as 'twere, a tender,° a kind of tender,   *(marriage) proposal*
175 made afar off ° by Sir Hugh here. Do you understand me?   *indirectly*

SLENDER Ay, sir, you shall find me reasonable.° If it be so, I shall   *(with Falstaff)*
do that that is reason.

SHALLOW Nay, but understand me.

SLENDER So I do, sir.

180 EVANS Give ear to his motions.° Master Slender, I will descrip-   *proposals*
tion the matter to you, if you be capacity of it.

SLENDER Nay, I will do as my cousin Shallow says. I pray you
pardon me. He's a Justice of Peace in his country,° simple°   *district / humble; foolish*
though I stand here.

185 EVANS But that is not the question. The question is concerning
your marriage.

SHALLOW Ay, there's the point, sir.

EVANS Marry, is it, the very point of it—to Mistress Anne Page.

SLENDER Why, if it be so, I will marry her upon any reasonable
190 demands.°   *requests*

EVANS But can you affection the 'oman? Let us command to
know that of your mouth, or of your lips—for divers philoso-
phers hold that the lips is parcel° of the mouth. Therefore,   *part and parcel*
precisely, can you carry your good will to the maid?

195 SHALLOW Cousin Abraham Slender, can you love her?

SLENDER I hope, sir, I will do as it shall become one that would
do reason.

---

2. Probably Richard Tottel's *Miscellany* (1557), an out-
of-date collection of love poetry on whose quotable
quotes Slender wishes to draw in wooing Anne Page.

3. Allhallowmas, or All Saints' Day (November 1), is
actually over a month after Michaelmas, September 29.

EVANS Nay, Got's lords and his ladies, you must speak positable° *positively*
if you can carry her your desires towards her.

200 SHALLOW That you must. Will you, upon good dowry, marry
her?

SLENDER I will do a greater thing than that upon your request,
cousin, in° any reason. *within*

SHALLOW Nay, conceive° me, conceive me, sweet coz. What I *understand*
205 do is to pleasure you, coz. Can you love the maid?

SLENDER I will marry her, sir, at your request. But if there be no
great love in the beginning, yet heaven may decrease° it upon *(for "increase")*
better acquaintance, when we are married and have more occa-
sion to know one another. I hope upon familiarity will grow
210 more contempt.° But if you say 'marry her', I will marry her. *(for "content")*
That I am freely dissolved,° and dissolutely. *(for "resolved")*

EVANS It is a fery discretion answer, save the faul'° is in the 'ord *fault*
'dissolutely'. The 'ort is, according to our meaning, 'resolutely'.
His meaning is good.

215 SHALLOW Ay, I think my cousin meant well.

SLENDER Ay, or else I would I might be hanged, la.

[*Enter* ANNE *Page*]

SHALLOW Here comes fair Mistress Anne.—Would I were young
for your sake, Mistress Anne.

ANNE The dinner is on the table. My father desires your wor-
220 ships' company.

SHALLOW I will wait on him, fair Mistress Anne.

EVANS 'Od's° plessed will, I will not be absence at the grace. *God's*

[*Exeunt* SHALLOW *and* EVANS]

ANNE [*to* SLENDER] Will't please your worship to come in, sir?

SLENDER No, I thank you, forsooth, heartily; I am very well.

225 ANNE The dinner attends° you, sir. *awaits*

SLENDER I am not a-hungry, I thank you, forsooth. [*To* SIMPLE]
Go, sirrah; for all you are my man, go wait upon my cousin
Shallow. [*Exit* SIMPLE]
A Justice of Peace sometime may be beholden to his friend for
230 a man. I keep but three men and a boy yet, till my mother be
dead. But what though?° Yet I live like a poor gentleman born. *what of it*

ANNE I may not go in without your worship. They will not sit
till you come.

SLENDER I'faith, I'll eat nothing. I thank you as much as though
235 I did.

ANNE I pray you, sir, walk in.

[*Dogs bark within*]

SLENDER I had rather walk here, I thank you. I bruised my shin
th'other day, with playing at sword and dagger with a master of
fence°—three veneys° for a dish of stewed prunes[4]—and, by *fencing / bouts*
240 my troth, I cannot abide the smell of hot meat° since. Why do *food; prostitutes*
your dogs bark so? Be there bears i'th' town?

ANNE I think there are, sir. I heard them talked of.

SLENDER I love the sport° well—but I shall as soon quarrel at[5] it *bearbaiting*
as any man in England. You are afraid if you see the bear loose,
245 are you not?

ANNE Ay, indeed, sir.

SLENDER That's meat and drink° to me, now. I have seen Sack- *everyday fare*

4. Prostitutes.   5. Object to (?); brawl at (?).

erson[6] loose twenty times, and have taken him by the chain.
But I warrant you, the women have so cried and shrieked at it
250 that it passed.° But women, indeed, cannot abide 'em. They   *surpassed description*
are very ill-favoured,° rough things.   *ugly*

Enter PAGE

PAGE   Come, gentle Master Slender, come. We stay for you.
SLENDER   I'll eat nothing, I thank you, sir.
PAGE   By cock and pie,° you shall not choose,° sir. Come, come.   *(mild oath) / you must*
255 SLENDER   Nay, pray you lead the way.
PAGE   Come on, sir.
SLENDER   Mistress Anne, yourself shall go first.
ANNE   Not I, sir. Pray you keep on.°   *go on*
SLENDER   Truly, I will not go first, truly, la. I will not do you that
260 wrong.
ANNE   I pray you, sir.
SLENDER   I'll rather be unmannerly than troublesome. You do
yourself wrong, indeed, la.

*Exeunt [*SLENDER *first, the others following]*

1.2

Enter Sir Hugh EVANS *and* SIMPLE, *from dinner*

EVANS   Go your ways, and ask of ° Doctor Caius' house which   *concerning*
is the way. And there dwells one Mistress Quickly, which is in
the manner of his 'oman, or his dry-nurse,° or his cook, or his   *housekeeper*
laundry, his washer, and his wringer.
5 SIMPLE   Well, sir.
EVANS   Nay, it is petter yet. Give her this letter, for it is a 'oman
that altogethers acquaintance° with Mistress Anne Page. And   *is well acquainted*
the letter is to desire and require her to solicit your master's
desires to Mistress Anne Page. I pray you be gone.

[Exit SIMPLE]

10 I will make an end of my dinner; there's pippins° and cheese   *apples*
to come.   *Exit*

1.3

Enter Sir John FALSTAFF, BARDOLPH, NIM, PISTOL, *and*
[ROBIN] *the boy*

FALSTAFF   Mine Host of the Garter!

Enter [the] HOST *of the Garter*

HOST   What says my bully rook?° Speak scholarly and wisely.   *fine fellow*
FALSTAFF   Truly, mine Host, I must turn away some of my followers.
5 HOST   Discard, bully Hercules, cashier.° Let them wag.° Trot,   *dismiss / go their ways*
trot.
FALSTAFF   I sit° at ten pounds a week.   *lodge*
HOST   Thou'rt an emperor: Caesar, kaiser, and pheezer.[1] I will
entertain° Bardolph. He shall draw, he shall tap.° Said I well,   *employ / tend bar*
10 bully Hector?[2]
FALSTAFF   Do so, good mine Host.

6. Famous bear used in bearbaiting.
1.2 Location: Scene continues.
1.3 Location: The Garter Inn.
1. Literally, "one who drives others away"; but the Host
evidently means "vizier" (Turkish viceroy). *Caesar:* the

name of Julius Caesar became a title, "emperor."
2. Greatest of the Trojans who fought in the Trojan War.
Similarly, Hercules (line 5) was the most famous hero of
classical mythology.

HOST   I have spoke; let him follow. [*To* BARDOLPH] Let me see
thee froth and lime.[3] I am at a word:° follow.   *Exit*   °*I mean what I say*

FALSTAFF   Bardolph, follow him. A tapster is a good trade. An
15   old cloak makes a new jerkin;° a withered servingman a fresh   °*jacket*
tapster. Go; adieu.

BARDOLPH   It is a life that I have desired. I will thrive.   *Exit*

PISTOL   O base Hungarian wight,° wilt thou the spigot wield?   °*hungry, hidebound man*

NIM   He was gotten in drink;[4] his mind is not heroic. Is not the
20   humour conceited?°   °*idea witty*

FALSTAFF   I am glad I am so acquit of this tinderbox.[5] His thefts
were too open. His filching was like an unskilful singer: he kept
not time.

NIM   The good humour° is to steal at a minute's rest.°   °*trick / within a minute*

25   PISTOL   'Convey' the wise it call. 'Steal'? Foh, a fico[6] for the
phrase!

FALSTAFF   Well, sirs, I am almost out at heels.°   °*destitute*

PISTOL   Why then, let kibes° ensue.   °*sore heels*

FALSTAFF   There is no remedy: I must cony-catch,° I must shift.°   °*swindle / live by my wits*

30   PISTOL   Young ravens must have food.

FALSTAFF   Which of you know Ford of this town?

PISTOL   I ken the wight.° He is of substance good.°   °*know the man / well-off*

FALSTAFF   My honest lads, I will tell you what I am about.°   °*up to; in girth*

PISTOL   Two yards and more.

35   FALSTAFF   No quips now, Pistol. Indeed, I am in the waist two
yards about. But I am now about no waste; I am about thrift.
Briefly, I do mean to make love to Ford's wife. I spy entertainment[7] in her. She discourses, she carves,[8] she gives the leer of
invitation. I can construe[9] the action of her familiar style; and
40   the hardest voice of her behaviour, to be Englished rightly, is 'I
am Sir John Falstaff's'.

PISTOL   He hath studied her well, and translated her will:[1] out of
honesty,° into English.   °*chastity*

NIM   The anchor is deep.[2] Will that humour pass?°   °*phrase pass muster*

45   FALSTAFF   Now, the report° goes, she has all the rule of her hus-   °*rumor*
band's purse; he hath a legion of angels.°   °*gold coins*

PISTOL   As many devils entertain, and 'To her, boy!'° say I.   °*(hunting cry)*

NIM   The humour rises; it is good. Humour me the angels![3]

FALSTAFF [*showing letters*]   I have writ me here a letter to her—
50   and here another to Page's wife, who even now gave me good
eyes too, examined my parts[4] with most judicious oeillades;°   °*amorous glances*
sometimes the beam of her view gilded my foot, sometimes my
portly belly.

PISTOL   Then did the sun on dunghill shine.

55   NIM   I thank thee for that humour.

---

3. *froth and lime:* both are ways of cheating the customer—by putting a good head on the beer (to give short measure) and by adulterating wine with lime (to remove acidity and make it sparkle).

4. Begotten when his parents were drunk (thought to make one cowardly).

5. Alluding to Bardolph's red complexion and irascible temper. *acquit:* rid.

6. An abusive insult usually accompanied by the gesture of showing the thumb pushed between index and middle fingers: historically, "fig" (Spanish); allusively, "female genitals."

7. Provision of food, drink, and lodging; ability to give sexual pleasure.

8. Perhaps: acts courteously; gestures broadly with her hands; shows pleasing skill in carving meat—hence, somewhere between ordinary friendliness and sexual enticement.

9. Interpret (beginning a grammatical pun that includes "style," "voice," "Englished," and "translated," lines 39, 40, 42).

1. Intention; sexual desires; legal document (thought of as written in Latin).

2. That's a deep plot; you're out of your depth (?).

3. Perhaps: the plot develops; it's good. Get the money. (Here, as elsewhere in Nim's speech, "humour" means whatever the context demands.)

4. My (sexual) capacities.

FALSTAFF   O, she did so course o'er my exteriors, with such a
greedy intention, that the appetite of her eye did seem to scorch
me up like a burning-glass!⁵ Here's another letter to her. She
bears the purse too. She is a region in Guiana,⁶ all gold and
60 bounty. I will be cheaters⁷ to them both, and they shall be
exchequers to me. They shall be my East and West Indies, and
I will trade to them both. [*Giving a letter to* PISTOL] Go bear
thou this letter to Mistress Page, [*giving a letter to* NIM] and
thou this to Mistress Ford. We will thrive, lads, we will thrive.
65 PISTOL [*returning the letter*]   Shall I Sir Pandarus of Troy⁸ become,
And by my side wear steel?° Then Lucifer take all.   *And remain a soldier*
NIM [*returning the letter*]   I will run no base humour. Here, take
the humour-letter. I will keep the haviour of reputation.⁹
FALSTAFF [*to* ROBIN]   Hold,° sirrah. Bear you these letters tightly.°   *Take these / safely*
70 Sail like my pinnace° to these golden shores.   *small, fast boat*
[*He gives* ROBIN *the letters*]
Rogues, hence, avaunt!° Vanish like hailstones! Go!   *be gone*
Trudge, plod, away o'th' hoof, seek shelter, pack!°   *be off*
Falstaff will learn the humour of the age:
French thrift, you rogues—myself and skirted page.¹
Exeunt FALSTAFF *and* [ROBIN] *the boy*
75 PISTOL   Let vultures gripe° thy guts!—for gourd and fullam²   *seize*
holds,°   *are profitable*
And high and low beguiles the rich and poor.
Tester° I'll have in pouch° when thou shalt lack,   *Sixpence/purse*
Base Phrygian Turk!³
NIM   I have operations° which be humours of revenge.   *plans*
PISTOL   Wilt thou revenge?
80 NIM   By welkin° and her stars!   *the sky (poetic)*
PISTOL   With wit or steel?
NIM   With both the humours, I.
I will discuss° the humour of this love to Ford.   *disclose*
PISTOL   And I to Page shall eke° unfold   *also (archaic)*
How Falstaff, varlet vile,
85 His dove will prove,° his gold will hold,   *test; sample*
And his soft couch defile.
NIM   My humour shall not cool. I will incense Ford to deal with
poison; I will possess him with yellowness;⁴ for this revolt of
mine° is dangerous. That is my true humour.   *(against Falstaff)*
90 PISTOL   Thou art the Mars of malcontents.⁵
I second thee. Troop on.   *Exeunt*

5. Glass lens used to concentrate the sun's rays and so
start a fire.
6. South American country famed for its unexploited
wealth and fertility, as were the East and West Indies (line
61).
7. Escheaters, officers of the Exchequer (or Treasury,
line 61) responsible for estates that fell forfeit and so came
to the crown; deceivers, robbers.
8. Pandarus is the aristocrat who, as Troy is besieged by
the Greeks, serves as go-between (or pander) in the affair
between Troilus and Cressida, Pandarus's niece. Shakespeare's play on the subject is several years later than
The Merry Wives.
9. I will behave respectfully.
1. Suggesting that French gentlemen were thought to

retain few, though well-dressed, followers. *skirted:* wearing
a coat with full tails.
2. *gourd and fullam:* false dice and loaded dice—loaded
"high" to produce a four, five, or six, or "low" to produce
one, two, or three. See line 76.
3. Terms of abuse. The Turks, Europe's main military
foe, were Muslims and hence considered infidels. The
Phrygians, early inhabitants of what is now Turkey, were
conquered by Europeans; to the classical Greeks, "Phrygian" was equivalent to "slave."
4. Fill him with jealousy. (An inconsistency: in 2.1,
Nim goes to Page and Pistol to Ford, who is possessed with
yellowness.)
5. Most warlike rebel (Mars was the Roman god of war).

1.4

Enter MISTRESS QUICKLY *and* SIMPLE

MISTRESS QUICKLY What,° John Rugby!   (*a summoning call*)

Enter John RUGBY

I pray thee, go to the casement and see if you can see my master, Master Doctor Caius, coming. If he do, i'faith, and find
anybody in the house, here will be an old° abusing of God's   *will be lots of*
5   patience and the King's English.

RUGBY I'll go watch.

MISTRESS QUICKLY Go; and we'll have a posset[1] for't soon at
night,° in faith, at the latter end of a seacoal[2] fire.   *toward nightfall*

[*Exit* RUGBY]

An honest, willing, kind fellow as ever servant shall come in
10   house withal;° and, I warrant you, no telltale, nor no   *with*
breedbate.° His worst fault is that he is given to prayer; he is   *troublemaker*
something peevish° that way—but nobody but has his fault. But   *foolish*
let that pass. Peter Simple you say your name is?

SIMPLE Ay, for fault° of a better.   *lack*

15   MISTRESS QUICKLY And Master Slender's your master?

SIMPLE Ay, forsooth.

MISTRESS QUICKLY Does he not wear a great round beard, like
a glover's paring-knife?

SIMPLE No, forsooth; he hath but a little whey face, with a little
20   yellow beard, a Cain-coloured° beard.   *yellow or reddish*

MISTRESS QUICKLY A softly spirited° man, is he not?   *meek-spirited*

SIMPLE Ay, forsooth; but he is as tall a man of his hands as any
is between this and his head.[3] He hath fought with a warrener.° *gamekeeper*

MISTRESS QUICKLY How say you?—O, I should remember him:
25   does he not hold up his head, as it were, and strut in his gait?

SIMPLE Yes, indeed does he.

MISTRESS QUICKLY Well, heaven send Anne Page no worse fortune! Tell Master Parson Evans I will do what I can for your
master. Anne is a good girl, and I wish—

[*Enter* RUGBY]

30   RUGBY Out, alas, here comes my master!   [*Exit*]

MISTRESS QUICKLY We shall all be shent.° Run in here, good   *scolded*
young man; for God's sake, go into this closet. He will not stay
long.

[SIMPLE] *steps into the* [*closet*]

What, John Rugby! John! What, John, I say!

[*Enter* RUGBY]

35   [*Speaking loudly*] Go, John, go enquire for my master. I doubt° *suspect*
he be not well, that he comes not home.   [*Exit* RUGBY]

[*Singing*] 'And down, down, adown-a' (*etc.*)

Enter Doctor CAIUS

CAIUS Vat is you sing? I do not like dese toys.° Pray you go and   *frivolous tunes*
vetch me in my closet *un boîtier vert*—a box, a green-a box. Do
40   intend° vat I speak? A green-a box.   *Do you hear*

MISTRESS QUICKLY Ay, forsooth, I'll fetch it you. [*Aside*] I am
glad he went not in himself. If he had found the young man,
he would have been horn-mad.°   *mad as a bull*

[*She goes to fetch the box*]

1.4 Location: Dr. Caius's house.   2. Superior coal brought by sea.
1. Restorative drink of hot milk curdled with wine or ale.   3. But he is as brave a man as any is around here.

CAIUS   *Fe, fe, fe, fe! Ma foi, il fait fort chaud! Je m'en vais à la*
45   *cour. La grande affaire.*[4]

MISTRESS QUICKLY   Is it this, sir?

CAIUS   *Oui. Mets-le à ma pochette.*[5] *Dépêche,* quickly! Vere is
dat knave Rugby?

MISTRESS QUICKLY   What, John Rugby! John!
          Enter John [RUGBY]

50   RUGBY   Here, sir.

CAIUS   You are John Rugby, and you are Jack° Rugby. Come,   *(connotes knavery)*
take-a your rapier, and come after my heel to the court.

RUGBY   'Tis ready, sir, here in the porch.
          [*He fetches the rapier*]

CAIUS   By my trot,° I tarry too long. 'Od's me,° *qu'ai-j' oublié?*[6]   *troth / God save me*
55   Dere is some simples[7] in my closet dat I vill not for the varld I
shall leave behind.

MISTRESS QUICKLY [*aside*]   Ay me, he'll find the young man there,
and be mad.

CAIUS [*discovering* SIMPLE]   O *diable,*° *diable!* Vat is in my   *devil*
60   closet? Villainy, *larron!*° Rugby, my rapier!   *thief*
          [*He takes the rapier*]

MISTRESS QUICKLY   Good master, be content.

CAIUS   Wherefore shall I be content-a?

MISTRESS QUICKLY   The young man is an honest man.

CAIUS   What shall de honest man do in my closet? Dere is no
65   honest man dat shall come in my closet.

MISTRESS QUICKLY   I beseech you, be not so phlegmatic.[8] Hear
the truth of it. He came of an errand to me from Parson Hugh.

CAIUS   Vell.

SIMPLE   Ay, forsooth, to desire her to—

70   MISTRESS QUICKLY   Peace, I pray you.

CAIUS   Peace-a your tongue. [*To* SIMPLE] Speak-a your tale.

SIMPLE   To desire this honest gentlewoman, your maid, to speak
a good word to Mistress Anne Page for my master in the way of
marriage.

75   MISTRESS QUICKLY   This is all, indeed, la; but I'll ne'er put my
finger in the fire an need not.[9]

CAIUS   Sir Hugh send-a you?—Rugby, *baile*° me some paper.   *bring*
          [RUGBY *brings paper*]
     [*To* SIMPLE] Tarry you a little-a while.
          Doctor [CAIUS] *writes*

MISTRESS QUICKLY [*aside to* SIMPLE]   I am glad he is so quiet. If
80   he had been throughly moved,° you should have heard him so   *really angered*
loud and so melancholy.° But notwithstanding, man, I'll do   *(for "choleric"?)*
your master what good I can. And the very yea and the no is,
the French doctor, my master—I may call him my master, look
you, for I keep his house, and I wash, wring, brew, bake, scour,
85   dress meat° and drink, make the beds, and do all myself—   *prepare food*

SIMPLE [*aside to* MISTRESS QUICKLY]   'Tis a great charge° to come   *burden; (sexual)*
under one body's hand.

MISTRESS QUICKLY [*aside to* SIMPLE]   Are you advised o' that?°   *You're telling me*
You shall find it a great charge—and to be up early, and down

4. French: By my faith, it is very hot. I am going to
court—important business. (The French in this scene
is translated only when Caius fails to do so himself.)
5. Yes, put it in my pocket.
6. What have I forgotten?
7. Medicines composed of one herb or constituent;

unknown to Caius, also the character's name.
8. Cold and dull (Quickly's mistake for the opposite
temperament—choleric, or angry).
9. I'll never put myself in danger by getting involved if
I don't have to.

90 late. But notwithstanding, to tell you in your ear—I would have
no words of it—my master himself is in love with Mistress
Anne Page. But notwithstanding that, I know Anne's mind:
that's neither here nor there.

CAIUS [*giving the letter to* SIMPLE] You, jack'nape,° give-a this   idiot
95 letter to Sir Hugh. By Gar,° it is a shallenge. I will cut his troat   God
in de Park, and I will teach a scurvy jackanape priest to meddle
or make.° You may be gone. It is not good you tarry here. By   interfere
Gar, I will cut all his two stones.° By Gar, he shall not have a   testicles
stone to throw at his dog.   [*Exit* SIMPLE]

100 MISTRESS QUICKLY Alas, he speaks but for his friend.

CAIUS It is no matter-a ver° dat. Do not you tell-a me dat I shall   for
have Anne Page for myself? By Gar, I vill kill de jack-priest.°   knave-priest
And I have appointed mine Host of de Jarteer° to measure our   garter
weapon.° By Gar, I will myself have Anne Page.   to referee

105 MISTRESS QUICKLY Sir, the maid loves you, and all shall be well.
We must give folks leave to prate, what the goodyear!°   what the devil

CAIUS Rugby, come to the court with me. [*To* MISTRESS
QUICKLY] By Gar, if I have not Anne Page, I shall turn your
head out of my door. Follow my heels, Rugby.

110 MISTRESS QUICKLY You shall have Anne°—   Anne; an
                    Exeunt Doctor [CAIUS *and* RUGBY]
—ass-head of your own. No, I know Anne's mind for that.
Never a woman in Windsor knows more of Anne's mind than
I do, nor can do more than I do with her, I thank heaven.

FENTON [*within*] Who's within there, ho!

115 MISTRESS QUICKLY Who's there, I trow?°—Come near° the   wonder / Enter
house, I pray you.
                    Enter [*Master*] FENTON

FENTON How now, good woman, how dost thou?

MISTRESS QUICKLY The better that it pleases your good worship
to ask.

120 FENTON What news? How does pretty Mistress Anne?

MISTRESS QUICKLY In truth, sir, and she is pretty, and honest,°   chaste
and gentle,° and one that is your friend. I can tell you that by   well-bred
the way, I praise heaven for it.

FENTON Shall I do any good,° thinkest thou? Shall I not lose my   make any progress
125 suit?

MISTRESS QUICKLY Troth, sir, all is in His hands above. But notwithstanding, Master Fenton, I'll be sworn on a book° she loves   a Bible
you. Have not your worship a wart above your eye?

FENTON Yes, marry, have I. What of that?

130 MISTRESS QUICKLY Well, thereby hangs a tale. Good faith, it is
such another Nan![1]—But I detest,° an honest maid as ever   (for "protest")
broke bread.°—We had an hour's talk of that wart. I shall never   ate (proverbial)
laugh but in that maid's company.—But indeed she is given
too much to allicholy° and musing.—But for you—well—go   (for "melancholy")
135 to!°   come, come

FENTON Well, I shall see her today. Hold, there's money for
thee. Let me have thy voice in my behalf. If thou seest her
before me, commend me.

MISTRESS QUICKLY Will I? I'faith, that I will. And I will tell your
140 worship more of the wart the next time we have confidence,°   confide
and of other wooers.

---

1. Nan (Anne) is such an extraordinary (or lively) one.

FENTON   Well, farewell. I am in great haste now.

MISTRESS QUICKLY   Farewell to your worship.   [*Exit* FENTON]
Truly, an honest gentleman; but Anne loves him not, for I
145   know Anne's mind as well as another° does.—Out upon't,[2]   anyone else
what have I forgot?   *Exit*

2.1

Enter MISTRESS PAGE, [*with*] *a letter*

MISTRESS PAGE   What, have I scaped love-letters in the holiday
time° of my beauty, and am I now a subject for them? Let me   heyday
see.

[*She reads*]
'Ask me no reason why I love you, for though Love use Reason
5   for his precision, he admits him not for his counsellor.[1] You
are not young; no more am I. Go to, then, there's sympathy.°   agreement
You are merry; so am I. Ha, ha, then, there's more sympathy.
You love sack,° and so do I. Would you desire better sympathy?   Spanish wine
Let it suffice thee, Mistress Page, at the least if the love of sol-
10   dier can suffice, that I love thee. I will not say "pity me"—'tis
not a soldier-like phrase—but I say "love me".

    By me, thine own true knight,
    By day or night
    Or any kind of light,
15   With all his might
    For thee to fight,
        John Falstaff.'

What a Herod of Jewry° is this! O, wicked, wicked world! One   bragging stage villain
that is well-nigh worn to pieces with age, to show himself a
20   young gallant! What an unweighed° behaviour hath this Flem-   unbalanced
ish° drunkard picked, i'th' devil's name, out of my conversa-   (proverbially drunk)
tion,° that he dares in this manner assay° me? Why, he hath   conduct / proposition
not been thrice in my company. What should I say° to him? I   can I have said
was then frugal of my mirth, heaven forgive me. Why, I'll
25   exhibit° a bill in the Parliament for the putting down[2] of men.   introduce
O God, that I knew how to be revenged on him! For revenged
I will be, as sure as his guts are made of puddings.°   gut-encased sausages

Enter MISTRESS FORD

MISTRESS FORD   Mistress Page! By my faith, I was going to your
house.
30   MISTRESS PAGE   And by my faith, I was coming to you. You look
very ill.
MISTRESS FORD   Nay, I'll ne'er believe that: I have° to show to   have something
the contrary.
MISTRESS PAGE   Faith, but you do, in my mind.
35   MISTRESS FORD   Well, I do, then. Yet I say I could show you to
the contrary. O Mistress Page, give me some counsel.
MISTRESS PAGE   What's the matter, woman?
MISTRESS FORD   O woman, if it were not for one trifling respect,°   consideration
I could come to such honour!°   rank
40   MISTRESS PAGE   Hang the trifle, woman; take the honour. What
is it? Dispense with trifles. What is it?

---

2. Expression of dismay.
2.1 Location: Outside Page's house.
1. That is, Love employs Reason to make strong arguments, or preach, on Love's behalf (a "precision" was a

Puritan), but Love will not accept Reason's advice.
2. *putting down*: suppression; perhaps also an unconscious sexual suggestion that men are to be put down
for the purpose of intercourse.

MISTRESS FORD   If I would but go to hell for an eternal moment
or so, I could be knighted.[3]

MISTRESS PAGE   What? Thou liest! Sir Alice Ford? These knights
45   will hack,° and so thou shouldst not alter the article of thy   *(military); (sexual?)*
gentry.°   *terms of your station*

MISTRESS FORD   We burn daylight.° Here: read, read.   *waste time*
[*She gives* MISTRESS PAGE *a letter*]
Perceive how I might be knighted.
[MISTRESS PAGE *reads*]
I shall think the worse of fat men as long as I have an eye to
50   make difference of° men's liking.° And yet he would not swear,   *judge among / looks*
praised women's modesty, and gave such orderly and well-
behaved reproof to all uncomeliness° that I would have sworn   *improper behavior*
his disposition would have gone to° the truth of his words. But   *accorded with*
they do no more adhere and keep place together than the hun-
55   dred and fifty psalms to the tune of 'Greensleeves'.° What tem-   *(popular love song)*
pest, I trow, threw this whale, with so many tuns° of oil in his   *casks*
belly, ashore at Windsor? How shall I be revenged on him? I
think the best way were to entertain him with hope, till the
wicked fire of lust have melted him in his own grease. Did you
60   ever hear the like?

MISTRESS PAGE   Letter for letter, but that the name of Page and
Ford differs.
[*She gives* MISTRESS FORD *her letter*]
To thy great comfort in this mystery of ill opinions,[4] here's the
twin brother of thy letter. But let thine inherit first, for I protest
65   mine never shall. I warrant he hath a thousand of these letters,
writ with blank space for different names—sure, more, and
these are of the second edition. He will print them, out of
doubt°—for he cares not what he puts into the press[5] when he   *undoubtedly*
would put us two. I had rather be a giantess, and lie under
70   Mount Pelion.[6] Well, I will find you twenty lascivious turtles[7]
ere one chaste man.

MISTRESS FORD   Why, this is the very same: the very hand, the
very words. What doth he think of us?

MISTRESS PAGE   Nay, I know not. It makes me almost ready to
75   wrangle° with mine own honesty.° I'll entertain° myself like   *argue / chastity / treat*
one that I am not acquainted withal;° for, sure, unless he know   *with*
some strain in me that I know not myself, he would never have
boarded[8] me in this fury.

MISTRESS FORD   'Boarding' call you it? I'll be sure to keep him
80   above deck.

MISTRESS PAGE   So will I. If he come under my hatches, I'll
never to sea again. Let's be revenged on him. Let's appoint him
a meeting, give him a show of comfort° in his suit, and lead   *encouragement*
him on with a fine baited° delay till he hath pawned his horses   *temptingly alluring*
85   to mine Host of the Garter.[9]

MISTRESS FORD   Nay, I will consent to act any villainy against
him that may not sully the chariness° of our honesty. O that   *scrupulous integrity*

---

3. Sexually provided with a knight; dubbed a knight.
4. Falstaff's unfounded and hence mysterious belief that
the wives are promiscuous.
5. Printing press; what he presses sexually.
6. The giants were the Titans, who in Greek mythology
rebelled against the Olympian gods and were punished
by being buried under Mt. Pelion.

7. Turtledoves (proverbially true to their mates).
8. Nautical metaphor: accosted; sexually entered.
9. See note to 4.3.11. The plot does not develop in
exactly the way anticipated: "Brooke" supplies Sir John
with funds, so at first he doesn't have to pawn his
horses to raise money for his courting.

my husband saw this letter! It would give eternal food to his
jealousy.

Enter Master FORD [*with*] PISTOL, *and Master* PAGE
[*with*] NIM

90   MISTRESS PAGE   Why, look where he comes, and my goodman°   husband
too. He's as far from jealousy as I am from giving him cause;
and that, I hope, is an unmeasurable distance.

MISTRESS FORD   You are the happier woman.

MISTRESS PAGE   Let's consult together against this greasy knight.
95   Come hither.

[*They withdraw*]

FORD   Well, I hope it be not so.

PISTOL   Hope is a curtal° dog in some affairs.   an unreliable
Sir John affects° thy wife.   loves; aims at

FORD   Why, sir, my wife is not young.

100 PISTOL   He woos both high and low, both rich and poor,
Both young and old, one with another,° Ford.   indiscriminately
He loves the gallimaufry,° Ford. Perpend.°   mixture / Consider

FORD   Love my wife?

PISTOL   With liver° burning hot. Prevent,   (seat of the passions)
105 Or go thou like Sir Actaeon,[1] he,
With Ringwood[2] at thy heels.
O, odious is the name!

FORD   What name, sir?

PISTOL   The horn,° I say. Farewell.   (of a cuckold)
110 Take heed; have open eye; for thieves do foot° by night.   walk; (sexual)
Take heed ere summer comes, or cuckoo-birds[3] do sing.—
Away, Sir Corporal Nim!—Believe it, Page; he speaks sense.

Exit

FORD [*aside*]   I will be patient. I will find out° this.   investigate

NIM [*to* PAGE]   And this is true. I like not the humour of lying.
115 He hath wronged me in some humours. I should° have borne   was supposed to
the humoured letter to her; but I have a sword, and it shall bite
upon my necessity.° He loves your wife. There's the short and   when I need it to
the long.
My name is Corporal Nim. I speak and I avouch 'tis true.
120 My name is Nim, and Falstaff loves your wife. Adieu.
I love not the humour of bread and cheese.[4] Adieu.   *Exit*

PAGE [*aside*]   The humour of it, quoth a?° Here's a fellow frights   he
English out of his° wits.   its

FORD [*aside*]   I will seek out Falstaff.

125 PAGE [*aside*]   I never heard such a drawling, affecting° rogue.   affectedly speaking

FORD [*aside*]   If I do find° it—well.   ascertain

PAGE [*aside*]   I will not believe such a Cathayan° though the   Chinese; scoundrel
priest o'th' town commended him for° a true man.   as

FORD [*aside*]   'Twas a good, sensible fellow. Well.

[MISTRESS PAGE *and* MISTRESS FORD *come forward*]

130 PAGE   How now, Meg?

MISTRESS PAGE   Whither go you, George? Hark you.

---

1. In Greek mythology, Actaeon was turned into a stag
and consequently hunted and killed by his own dogs. The
stag, in particular its horns, was considered an emblem of
the cuckold, the man whose wife was unfaithful to him.
2. Supposed name of one of Actaeon's dogs.
3. The cuckoo's habit of leaving its eggs to be hatched by
others made it the emblem of cuckolders and made the
sound of its call a taunt to cuckolds. Its song is prevalent
in late spring, after the mating season.
4. Nim's meager fare as Falstaff's retainer, or as now
unemployed; a popular name for wood sorrel, an edible
plant also known as cuckoo-bread or cuckoo-cheese—
hence an allusion to cuckolding.

[They talk apart]

MISTRESS FORD   How now, sweet Frank? Why art thou melancholy?

FORD   I melancholy? I am not melancholy. Get you home, go.

135 MISTRESS FORD   Faith, thou hast some crotchets° in thy head   *strange notions*
now. Will you go, Mistress Page?

MISTRESS PAGE   Have with you.°—You'll come to dinner, George?   *I'm coming*

Enter MISTRESS QUICKLY

[Aside to MISTRESS FORD*]* Look who comes yonder. She shall
be our messenger to this paltry knight.

140 MISTRESS FORD *[aside to* MISTRESS PAGE*]*   Trust me, I thought on
her. She'll fit it.°   *fit the part*

MISTRESS PAGE *[to* MISTRESS QUICKLY*]*   You are come to see my
daughter Anne?

MISTRESS QUICKLY   Ay, forsooth; and I pray how does good Mis-
145 tress Anne?

MISTRESS PAGE   Go in with us and see. We have an hour's talk
with you.

Exeunt MISTRESS PAGE, MISTRESS FORD, *and*
*[*MISTRESS*]* QUICKLY

PAGE   How now, Master Ford?

FORD   You heard what this knave told me, did you not?

150 PAGE   Yes, and you heard what the other told me?

FORD   Do you think there is truth in them?

PAGE   Hang 'em, slaves! I do not think the knight would offer°   *attempt*
it. But these that accuse him in his intent towards our wives are
a yoke° of his discarded men—very rogues, now they be out of   *pair*
155 service.

FORD   Were they his men?

PAGE   Marry, were they.

FORD   I like it never the better for that. Does he lie° at the   *lodge*
Garter?

160 PAGE   Ay, marry, does he. If he should intend this voyage toward
my wife, I would turn her loose to him; and what he gets more
of her than sharp words, let it lie on my head.[5]

FORD   I do not misdoubt° my wife, but I would be loath to turn   *mistrust*
them together. A man may be too confident. I would have
165 nothing lie on my head. I cannot be thus satisfied.

Enter [the] HOST *[of the Garter]*

PAGE   Look where my ranting Host of the Garter comes. There
is either liquor in his pate or money in his purse when he looks
so merrily.—How now, mine Host?

HOST   God bless you, bully rook,° God bless you! Thou'rt a gen-   *fine fellow*
170 tleman.

Enter SHALLOW

Cavaliero Justice,° I say!   *Gallant knight (comic)*

SHALLOW   I follow, mine Host, I follow.—Good even° and   *afternoon*
twenty,° good Master Page. Master Page, will you go with us?   *twenty times over*
We have sport in hand.

175 HOST   Tell him, Cavaliero Justice, tell him, bully rook.

SHALLOW   Sir, there is a fray to be fought between Sir Hugh,
the Welsh priest, and Caius, the French doctor.

FORD   Good mine Host o'th' Garter, a word with you.

5. Let it be my responsibility (but Ford hears an allusion to the cuckold's horns).

HOST   What sayst thou, my bully rook?

FORD *and the* HOST *talk [apart]*

180 SHALLOW [*to* PAGE]   Will you go with us to behold it? My merry
Host hath had the measuring of their weapons,[6] and, I think,
hath appointed them contrary° places. For, believe me, I hear   *different*
the parson is no jester. Hark, I will tell you what our sport shall
be.

[*They talk apart*]

185 HOST [*to* FORD]   Hast thou° no suit against my knight, my guest   *Are you sure you have*
cavaliero?

FORD   None, I protest. But I'll give you a pottle of burnt° sack to   *two quarts of heated*
give me recourse° to him and tell him my name is Brooke[7]—   *access*
only for a jest.

190 HOST   My hand, bully. Thou shalt have egress and regress—said
I well?—and thy name shall be Brooke. It is a merry knight.
[*To* SHALLOW *and* PAGE] Will you go, mijn'heers?°   *gentlemen (Dutch)*

SHALLOW   Have with you, mine Host.

PAGE   I have heard the Frenchman hath good skill in his rapier.

195 SHALLOW   Tut, sir, I could have told you more. In these times
you stand on distance—your passes, stoccados,[8] and I know not
what. 'Tis the heart, Master Page; [*showing his rapier-passes*]
'tis here,° 'tis here. I have seen the time with my long sword[9] I   *like this?*
would have made you four tall° fellows skip like rats.   *valiant*

200 HOST   Here, boys; here, here! Shall we wag?°   *go*

PAGE   Have with you. I had rather hear them scold than fight.

Exeunt HOST, SHALLOW [*and* PAGE]

FORD   Though Page be a secure° fool and stands so firmly on his   *an overconfident*
wife's frailty, yet I cannot put off my opinion so easily. She was
in his company at Page's house, and what they made° there I   *got up to*
205 know not. Well, I will look further into't; and I have a disguise
to sound[1] Falstaff. If I find her honest, I lose° not my labour. If   *waste*
she be otherwise, 'tis labour well bestowed.   *Exit*

2.2

Enter Sir John FALSTAFF *and* PISTOL

FALSTAFF   I will not lend thee a penny.

PISTOL   I will retort° the sum in equipage.°   *repay / equipment?*

FALSTAFF   Not a penny.

PISTOL [*drawing his sword*]   Why then, the world's mine oyster,
5 which I with sword will open.

FALSTAFF   Not a penny. I have been content, sir, you should lay
my countenance to pawn.[1] I have grated upon° my good friends   *harassed*
for three reprieves for you and your coach-fellow° Nim, or else   *companion*
you had looked through the grate° like a gemini° of baboons. I   *prison bars / pair*
10 am damned in hell for swearing to gentlemen my friends you
were good soldiers and tall fellows. And when Mistress Bridget
lost the handle of her fan,[2] I took't° upon mine honour thou   *swore*
hadst it not.

---

6. Has been appointed referee.
7. Q: Brooke; F: Broome. "Brooke" was the family name
of Lord Cobham, who had objected to the characterization of his ancestor Oldcastle in *1 Henry IV*. The name
was changed to "Falstaff." Presumably, another such
objection led to the shift from "Brooke" to "Broome."
8. *In . . . stoccados*: Today, people rely on the distance
between duelists—lunges, thrusts.

9. Obsolete, heavy weapon.
1. To plumb the depths of.
2.2 Location: The Garter Inn.
1. Exploit my reputation (as surety for borrowing money,
etc.).
2. Fans were often made with handles of precious metal
or ivory.

PISTOL   Didst not thou share? Hadst thou not fifteen pence?

15 FALSTAFF   Reason,° you rogue, reason. Thinkest thou I'll endan-   *With good reason*
ger my soul gratis?° At a word, hang no more about me. I am   *for free*
no gibbet° for you. Go, a short knife and a throng, to your   *gallows*
manor of Pickt-hatch, go.³ You'll not bear a letter for me, you
rogue? You stand upon your honour? Why, thou unconfinable
20 baseness, it is as much as I can do to keep the terms of my
honour precise.° Ay, ay, I myself sometimes, leaving the fear of   *pure*
God on the left hand,⁴ and hiding mine honour in my necessity, am fain to shuffle, to hedge, and to lurch;⁵ and yet you,
you rogue, will ensconce° your rags, your cat-a-mountain°   *hide / wildcat*
25 looks, your red-lattice° phrases, and your bold beating° oaths,   *alehouse / battering?*
under the shelter of your honour! You will not do it, you?

PISTOL [*sheathing his sword*]   I do relent. What wouldst thou
more of man?

Enter ROBIN

ROBIN   Sir, here's a woman would speak with you.

30 FALSTAFF   Let her approach.

Enter MISTRESS QUICKLY

MISTRESS QUICKLY   Give your worship good morrow.

FALSTAFF   Good morrow, goodwife.

MISTRESS QUICKLY   Not so, an't please your worship.

FALSTAFF   Good maid, then.

35 MISTRESS QUICKLY   I'll be sworn: as my mother was the first hour
I was born.

FALSTAFF   I do believe the swearer.⁶ What° with me?   *What do you want*

MISTRESS QUICKLY   Shall I vouchsafe⁷ your worship a word or
two?

40 FALSTAFF   Two thousand, fair woman, and I'll vouchsafe thee
the hearing.

MISTRESS QUICKLY   There is one Mistress Ford, sir—I pray come
a little nearer this ways.

[*She draws* FALSTAFF *aside*]

I myself dwell with Master Doctor Caius—

45 FALSTAFF   Well, on. Mistress Ford, you say.

MISTRESS QUICKLY   Your worship says very true. I pray your worship come a little nearer this ways.

FALSTAFF   I warrant thee nobody hears. Mine own people,° mine   *(Pistol and Robin)*
own people.

50 MISTRESS QUICKLY   Are they so? God bless them and make them
His servants!

FALSTAFF   Well, Mistress Ford: what of her?

MISTRESS QUICKLY   Why, sir, she's a good creature. Lord, Lord,
your worship's a wanton! Well, heaven forgive you, and all of
55 us, I pray—

FALSTAFF   Mistress Ford; come, Mistress Ford.

MISTRESS QUICKLY   Marry, this is the short and the long of it. You
have brought her into such a canaries° as 'tis wonderful. The   *(for "quandaries")*
best courtier of them all, when the court lay° at Windsor, could   *resided*

---

3. Pickpockets used a short knife to cut purse strings in a crowd. Pickt-hatch was an area of London infamous for its thieves and prostitutes—hence an unlikely locale for a "manor" (with a possible pun on "manner," or habits).
4. Disregarding the fear of God.
5. Am obliged to cheat, to be devious, and to steal.

6. Quickly thinks she is asserting her virginity, but by confusing the proverbs "as good a maid as her mother" and "as innocent as a newborn babe," she actually claims the opposite. Falstaff expresses his belief in what she has literally, but unintentionally, said.
7. Grant (error for "be vouchsafed, or granted, by").

60　never have brought her to such a canary. Yet there has been
　　knights, and lords, and gentlemen, with their coaches; I war-
　　rant you, coach after coach, letter after letter, gift after gift,
　　smelling so sweetly, all musk; and so rustling, I warrant you, in
　　silk and gold, and in such aligant° terms, and in such wine and　　　　*(for "elegant")*
65　sugar° of the best and the fairest, that would have won any　　　　*flattery*
　　woman's heart; and, I warrant you, they could never get an eye-
　　wink of her. I had myself twenty angels° given me this morn-　　　　*coins (as a bribe)*
　　ing—but I defy° all angels, in any such sort, as they say, but in　　　　*despise*
　　the way of honesty. And, I warrant you, they could never get
70　her so much as sip on a cup with the proudest of them all. And
　　yet there has been earls, nay, which is more, pensioners.[8] But,
　　I warrant you, all is one with her.
FALSTAFF　But what says she to me? Be brief, my good she-
　　Mercury.°　　　　*female messenger*
75　MISTRESS QUICKLY　Marry, she hath received your letter, for the
　　which she thanks you a thousand times, and she gives you to
　　notify° that her husband will be absence from his house　　　　*note*
　　between ten and eleven.
FALSTAFF　Ten and eleven.
80　MISTRESS QUICKLY　Ay, forsooth, and then you may come and
　　see the picture, she says, that you wot° of. Master Ford, her　　　　*know*
　　husband, will be from home. Alas, the sweet woman leads an
　　ill life with him. He's a very jealousy man. She leads a very
　　frampold° life with him, good heart.　　　　*disagreeable*
85　FALSTAFF　Ten and eleven. Woman, commend me to her. I will
　　not fail her.
MISTRESS QUICKLY　Why, you say well. But I have another mes-
　　senger° to your worship. Mistress Page hath her hearty com-　　　　*(for "message")*
　　mendations to you too; and, let me tell you in your ear, she's
90　as fartuous° a civil modest wife, and one, I tell you, that will　　　　*(for "virtuous")*
　　not miss you° morning nor evening prayer, as any is in Wind-　　　　*miss*
　　sor, whoe'er be the other; and she bade me tell your worship
　　that her husband is seldom from home, but she hopes there
　　will come a time. I never knew a woman so dote upon a man.
95　Surely I think you have charms,° la; yes, in truth.　　　　*magic powers*
FALSTAFF　Not I, I assure thee. Setting the attraction of my good
　　parts° aside, I have no other charms.　　　　*(sexual capacities)*
MISTRESS QUICKLY　Blessing on your heart for't!
FALSTAFF　But I pray thee tell me this: has Ford's wife and Page's
100　wife acquainted each other how they love me?
MISTRESS QUICKLY　O God no, sir; that were a jest indeed! They
　　have not so little grace, I hope. That were a trick indeed! But
　　Mistress Page would desire you to send her your little page of
　　all loves.° Her husband has a marvellous infection to[9] the little　　　　*for love's sake*
105　page; and, truly, Master Page is an honest man. Never a wife
　　in Windsor leads a better life than she does. Do what she will;
　　say what she will; take all, pay all; go to bed when she list; rise
　　when she list;° all is as she will. And, truly, she deserves it, for　　　　*wants*
　　if there be a kind woman in Windsor, she is one. You must
110　send her your page, no remedy.
FALSTAFF　Why, I will.
MISTRESS QUICKLY　Nay, but do so, then; and, look you, he may

---

8. Gentlemen of the royal bodyguard.　　　　9. For "affection for."

come and go between you both. And in any case have a nay-
word,° that you may know one another's mind, and the boy   password
115 never need to understand anything—for 'tis not good that
children should know any wickedness. Old folks, you know,
have discretion, as they say, and know the world.

FALSTAFF Fare thee well. Commend me to them both. There's
my purse; I am yet thy debtor.—Boy, go along with this
120 woman.   *Exeunt* MISTRESS QUICKLY [*and* ROBIN]
        [*Aside*] This news distracts° me.   bewilders (with joy)
PISTOL [*aside*]   This punk° is one of Cupid's carriers.°   whore / messengers
        Clap on° more sails! Pursue! Up with your fights!°   Set / fighting screens
        Give fire! She is my prize,° or ocean whelm° them all! [*Exit*] booty/overwhelm
125 FALSTAFF Sayst thou so, old Jack?° Go thy ways! I'll make more   (addressing himself)
        of thy old body than I have done. Will they yet look after° thee?   desire
        Wilt thou, after the expense of so much money, be now a
        gainer? Good body, I thank thee. Let them say 'tis grossly°   crudely
        done; so it be fairly° done, no matter.   successfully
                Enter BARDOLPH [*with sack*]
130 BARDOLPH Sir John, there's one Master Brooke below would
        fain° speak with you and be acquainted with you, and hath sent   be pleased to
        your worship a morning's draught of sack.

FALSTAFF Brooke is his name?
BARDOLPH Ay, sir.
135 FALSTAFF Call him in. [*Drinking sack*] Such Brookes are wel-
        come to me, that o'erflows such liquor.[1] [*Exit* BARDOLPH]
        Aha, Mistress Ford and Mistress Page, have I encompassed°   outwitted
        you? [*Drinking*] Go to. Via!°   On with it
                Enter [BARDOLPH, *and Master*] FORD *disguised like*
                        Brooke
FORD God bless you, sir.
140 FALSTAFF And you, sir. Would you speak with me?
FORD I make bold to press with so little preparation° upon you.   prior notice
FALSTAFF You're welcome. What's your will? [*To* BARDOLPH]
        Give us leave, drawer.°   [*Exit* BARDOLPH]   Leave us, bartender
FORD Sir, I am a gentleman that have spent much. My name is
145 Brooke.
FALSTAFF Good Master Brooke, I desire more acquaintance of
        you.
FORD Good Sir John, I sue for yours—not to charge you,° for I   (with an expense)
        must let you understand I think myself in better plight for a
150 lender than you are;[2] the which hath something° emboldened   somewhat
        me to this unseasoned° intrusion; for they say if money go   ill-timed
        before, all ways do lie open.
FALSTAFF Money is a good soldier, sir, and will on.
FORD Troth, and I have a bag of money here troubles me. If you
155 will help to bear it, Sir John, take half, or all, for easing me of
        the carriage.°   burden of carrying it
FALSTAFF Sir, I know not how I may deserve to be your porter.
FORD I will tell you, sir, if you will give me the hearing.
FALSTAFF Speak, good Master Brooke. I shall be glad to be your
160 servant.
FORD Sir, I hear you are a scholar—I will be brief with you—
        and you have been a man long known to me, though I had

---

1. See the Textual Note for the significance of this
wordplay.

2. I am more able to undertake a risk, an obligation, or
a pledge ("plight") as a lender than you are.

never so good means as desire to make myself acquainted with
you. I shall discover° a thing to you wherein I must very much   *reveal*
165 lay open mine own imperfection; but, good Sir John, as you
have one eye upon my follies, as you hear them unfolded, turn
another into the register° of your own, that I may pass with a   *catalog*
reproof the easier, sith° you yourself know how easy it is to be   *since*
such an offender.

170 FALSTAFF Very well, sir, proceed.

FORD There is a gentlewoman in this town; her husband's name
is Ford.

FALSTAFF Well, sir.

FORD I have long loved her, and, I protest° to you, bestowed   *declare*
175 much on her, followed her with a doting observance,°   *attentiveness*
engrossed° opportunities to meet her, fee'd° every slight occa-   *collected / purchased*
sion that could but niggardly give me sight of her; not only
bought many presents to give her, but have given largely° to   *bountifully*
many to know what she would have given.° Briefly, I have pur-   *would like to be given*
180 sued her as love hath pursued me, which hath been on the
wing of all occasions. But, whatsoever I have merited, either in
my mind or in my means, meed° I am sure I have received   *recompense*
none, unless experience be a jewel. That I have purchased at
an infinite rate,° and that hath taught me to say this: *cost*
185 'Love like a shadow flies when substance love pursues,
Pursuing that that flies, and flying what pursues.'³

FALSTAFF Have you received no promise of satisfaction at her
hands?

FORD Never.

190 FALSTAFF Have you importuned her to such a purpose?

FORD Never.

FALSTAFF Of what quality was your love then?

FORD Like a fair house built on another man's ground, so that I
have lost my edifice by mistaking the place where I erected it.

195 FALSTAFF To what purpose have you unfolded this to me?

FORD When I have told you that, I have told you all. Some say
that though she appear honest° to me, yet in other places she   *chaste*
enlargeth° her mirth so far that there is shrewd° construction   *gives rein to / malicious*
made of her. Now, Sir John, here is the heart of my purpose.
200 You are a gentleman of excellent breeding, admirable dis-
course, of great admittance,⁴ authentic in your place° and per-   *of respectable rank*
son, generally allowed° for your many warlike, court-like, and   *universally approved*
learned preparations.°   *accomplishments*

FALSTAFF O sir!

205 FORD Believe it, for you know it. There is money.
    [*He offers money*]
Spend it, spend it; spend more; spend all I have; only give me
so much of your time in exchange of it as to lay an amiable°   *amorous*
siege to the honesty of this Ford's wife. Use your art of wooing,
win her to consent to you. If any man may, you may as soon as
210 any.

FALSTAFF Would it apply well to the vehemency of your
affection that I should win what you would enjoy? Methinks
you prescribe to yourself very preposterously.

FORD O, understand my drift. She dwells so securely° on the   *relies so confidently*

3. *Love . . . what pursues*: Like a shadow, love pursues a   4. Having qualities ensuring ready admittance into
physical object ("substance")/person/money that flees,   high society.
and flees a physical object/person/money that pursues.

215   excellency of her honour that the folly of my soul dares not
      present itself. She is too bright to be looked against.° Now, *at*
      could I come to her with any detection° in my hand, my desires *accusation*
      had instance° and argument to commend themselves. I could *precedent*
      drive her then from the ward° of her purity, her reputation, her *defense*
220   marriage vow, and a thousand other her° defences which now *of her*
      are too too strongly embattled against me. What say you to't,
      Sir John?

      FALSTAFF   Master Brooke, I will first make bold with your money.
                 [*He takes the money*]
                 Next, give me your hand.
                 [*He takes his hand*]
225   And last, as I am a gentleman, you shall, if you will, enjoy
      Ford's wife.

      FORD   O, good sir!

      FALSTAFF   I say you shall.

      FORD   Want° no money, Sir John, you shall want none. *Lack*

230   FALSTAFF   Want no Mistress Ford, Master Brooke, you shall
      want none. I shall be with her, I may tell you, by her own
      appointment. Even as you came in to me, her spokesmate, or
      go-between, parted from me. I say I shall be with her between
      ten and eleven, for at that time the jealous rascally knave her
235   husband will be forth.° Come you to me at night; you shall *away*
      know how I speed.° *do*

      FORD   I am blessed in your acquaintance. Do you know Ford,
      sir?

      FALSTAFF   Hang him, poor cuckoldly knave, I know him not. Yet
240   I wrong him to call him poor. They say the jealous wittolly[5]
      knave hath masses of money, for the° which his wife seems to *on account of*
      me well favoured.° I will use her as the key of the cuckoldly *good-looking*
      rogue's coffer, and there's my harvest-home.° *profitable harvest*

      FORD   I would you knew Ford, sir, that you might avoid him if
245   you saw him.

      FALSTAFF   Hang him, mechanical salt-butter[6] rogue! I will stare
      him out of his wits. I will awe him with my cudgel; it shall
      hang like a meteor° o'er the cuckold's horns. Master Brooke, *an (ill-omened) comet*
      thou shalt know I will predominate over the peasant, and thou
250   shalt lie with his wife. Come to me soon at night. Ford's a
      knave, and I will aggravate his style:[7] thou, Master Brooke, shalt
      know him for knave and cuckold. Come to me soon at night.

                                                        Exit

      FORD   What a damned epicurean° rascal is this! My heart is *sensual*
      ready to crack with impatience. Who says this is improvident° *baseless*
255   jealousy? My wife hath sent to him, the hour is fixed, the match
      is made. Would any man have thought this? See the hell of
      having a false woman! My bed shall be abused, my coffers ran-
      sacked, my reputation gnawn at, and I shall not only receive
      this villainous wrong, but stand under the adoption of abomi-
260   nable terms, and by him that does me this wrong. Terms!
      Names! 'Amaimon' sounds well, 'Lucifer' well, 'Barbason' well;
      yet they are devils' additions,° the names of fiends. But 'cuck- *names*
      old', 'wittol'! 'Cuckold'—the devil himself hath not such a

5. Willingly cuckolded.
6. *mechanical salt-butter*: lower-class cheap-living;   butter.
Flemish salt butter was less expensive than domestic   7. Increase (irritate) his titles (by adding the title of
                                                           "cuckold" to Ford's name).

name. Page is an ass, a secure ass. He will trust his wife, he will
265 not be jealous. I will rather trust a Fleming with my butter,
Parson Hugh the Welshman with my cheese, an Irishman with
my aqua-vitae° bottle, or a thief to walk my ambling gelding,   *whiskey*
than my wife with herself. Then she plots, then she ruminates,
then she devises; and what they think in their hearts they may
270 effect, they will break their hearts but they will effect. God be
praised for my jealousy! Eleven o'clock the hour. I will prevent
this, detect my wife, be revenged on Falstaff, and laugh at Page.
I will about it. Better three hours too soon than a minute too
late. God's my life: cuckold, cuckold, cuckold!   *Exit*

2.3

Enter Doctor CAIUS *and his man [John]* RUGBY *[with
rapiers]*

CAIUS Jack Rugby!
RUGBY Sir.
CAIUS Vat is the clock, Jack?
RUGBY 'Tis past the hour, sir, that Sir Hugh promised to meet.
5 CAIUS By Gar, he has save his soul dat he is no come; he has
pray his Pible well dat he is no come. By Gar, Jack Rugby, he
is dead already if he be come.
RUGBY He is wise, sir, he knew your worship would kill him if
he came.
10 CAIUS *[drawing his rapier]* By Gar, de herring is no dead so¹ as
I vill kill him. Take your rapier, Jack. I vill tell you how I vill kill
him.
RUGBY Alas, sir, I cannot fence.
CAIUS Villainy,° take your rapier.   *(for "Villain")*
15 RUGBY Forbear: here's company.
[CAIUS *sheathes his rapier.*]
Enter [the] HOST *[of the Garter, Justice]* SHALLOW, *[Mas-
ter]* PAGE, *and [Master]* SLENDER
HOST God bless thee, bully Doctor.
SHALLOW God save you, Master Doctor Caius.
PAGE Now, good Master Doctor.
SLENDER Give you good morrow, sir.
20 CAIUS Vat be all you, one, two, tree, four, come for?
HOST To see thee fight, to see thee foin,° to see thee traverse,²   *thrust*
to see thee here, to see thee there; to see thee pass thy punto,
thy stock, thy reverse, thy distance, thy montant.³ Is he dead,
my Ethiopian?⁴ Is he dead, my Francisco?° Ha, bully? What   *Frenchman*
25 says my Aesculapius, my Galen, my heart of elder,⁵ ha? Is he
dead, bully stale?⁶ Is he dead?
CAIUS By Gar, he is de coward jack-priest° of de vorld. He is not   *knave-priest*
show his face.
HOST Thou art a Castalian King Urinal,⁷ Hector of Greece, my
30 boy.

2.3 Location: Windsor Park (east of Windsor).
1. Not so dead (from the proverbial simile "dead as a herring").
2. Move backward and forward.
3. *pass . . . montant:* use your thrust with the sword
point, your thrust, your backhand sword blow, your skill
in keeping at the right distance, your upward thrust.
4. Dark-skinned person.
5. Replacing "heart of oak"; as the elder is a soft, low-
growing tree, this is an insult disguised as a compliment.
Aesculapius was the classical god of medicine. Galen was
a physician of ancient Greece.
6. Decoy or dupe; wine or urine (often used for medical
diagnosis).
7. Urine bottle. *Castalian:* of the spring Castalia, which
was sacred to the Muses; "cast-stale-ian" (one who diagnoses by inspecting urine; Castilian (Spanish).

CAIUS I pray you bear witness that me have stay six or seven,
two, tree hours for him, and he is no come.

SHALLOW He is the wiser man, Master Doctor. He is a curer of
souls, and you a curer of bodies. If you should fight you go
35 against the hair° of your professions. Is it not true, Master Page? *grain*

PAGE Master Shallow, you have yourself been a great fighter,
though now a man of peace.

SHALLOW Bodykins,° Master Page, though I now be old and of *By God's dear body*
the peace, if I see a sword out my finger itches to make one.° *join in*
40 Though we are justices and doctors and churchmen, Master
Page, we have some salt° of our youth in us. We are the sons of *vigor*
women, Master Page.

PAGE 'Tis true, Master Shallow.

SHALLOW It will be found so, Master Page.—Master Doctor
45 Caius, I am come to fetch you home. I am sworn of the peace.
You have showed yourself a wise physician, and Sir Hugh hath
shown himself a wise and patient churchman. You must go
with me, Master Doctor.

HOST Pardon, guest° Justice. [To CAIUS] A word, Monsieur *(at the Host's inn)*
50 Mockwater.[8]

CAIUS Mockvater? Vat is dat?

HOST Mockwater, in our English tongue, is valour, bully.

CAIUS By Gar, then I have as much mockvater as de
Englishman. Scurvy jack-dog° priest! By Gar, me vill cut his *mongrel*
55 ears.

HOST He will clapper-claw thee tightly,° bully. *maul thee soundly*

CAIUS Clapper-de-claw? Vat is dat?

HOST That is, he will make thee amends.

CAIUS By Gar, me do look° he shall clapper-de-claw me, for, by *anticipate*
60 Gar, me vill have it.

HOST And I will provoke him to't, or let him wag.° *run away*

CAIUS Me tank you for dat.

HOST And moreover, bully—[Aside to the others] But first, master guest and Master Page, and eke° Cavaliero Slender, go *also*
65 you through the town to Frogmore.° *village near Windsor*

PAGE Sir Hugh is there, is he?

HOST He is there. See what humour he is in, and I will bring
the Doctor about by the fields. Will it do well?

SHALLOW We will do it.

70 PAGE, SHALLOW, *and* SLENDER Adieu, good Master Doctor.

Exeunt [PAGE, SHALLOW, *and* SLENDER]

CAIUS[drawing his rapier] By Gar, me vill kill de priest, for he
speak for a jackanape° to Anne Page. *on behalf of an idiot*

HOST Let him die. Sheathe thy impatience; throw cold water on
thy choler. Go about the fields with me through Frogmore. I
75 will bring thee where Mistress Anne Page is, at a farmhouse
a-feasting; and thou shalt woo her. Cried game?[9] Said I well?

CAIUS [sheathing his rapier] By Gar, me dank you vor dat. By
Gar, I love you, and I shall procure-a you de good guest: de
earl, de knight, de lords, de gentlemen, my patiences.° *(for "patients")*

80 HOST For the which I will be thy adversary[1] toward Anne Page.
Said I well?

8. Implying that Caius's diagnoses from urine are quack-
ery, or that Caius is sterile (water being semen) and so
lacking in valor.

9. (Did I say) the chase is on?

1. The Host again makes a joke at the expense of Caius,
who understands "adversary" as "advocate."

CAIUS   By Gar, 'tis good. Vell said.

HOST   Let us wag, then.

CAIUS   Come at my heels, Jack Rugby.   *Exeunt*

3.1

Enter Sir Hugh EVANS [*with a rapier, and bearing a*
book] *and* SIMPLE [*bearing Evans's gown*]

EVANS   I pray you now, good Master Slender's servingman, and
friend Simple by your name, which way have you looked for
Master Caius, that calls himself Doctor of Physic?°   *medicine*

SIMPLE   Marry, sir, the Petty Ward, the Park Ward,[1] every way;
5   old Windsor way,[2] and every way but the town way.

EVANS   I most fehemently desire you you will also look that way.

SIMPLE   I will, sir.   [*Exit*]

EVANS [*opening the book*]°   Jeshu pless me, how full of cholers°   (a Bible?) / anger
I am, and trempling of mind! I shall be glad if he have deceived
10   me. How melancholies I am! I will knog° his urinals about his   knock
knave's costard° when I have good opportunities for the 'ork.°   head / work
Pless my soul!—

[*Singing*]

    To shallow rivers, to whose falls
    Melodious birds sings madrigals.
15   There will we make our peds of roses,
    And a thousand fragrant posies.[3]
    To shallow—

Mercy on me! I have a great dispositions to cry.—

[*Singing*]

    Melodious birds sing madrigals.—
20   When as I sat in Pabylon[4]—
    And a thousand vagram° posies.   *vagrant*
    To shallow (*etc.*)

    [*Enter* SIMPLE]

SIMPLE   Yonder he° is coming. This way, Sir Hugh.   (Caius)

EVANS   He's welcome.

25   [*Singing*] 'To shallow rivers to whose falls—' God prosper the
right! What weapons is° he?   *has*

SIMPLE   No weapons, sir. There comes my master, Master Shallow, and another gentleman, from Frogmore, over the stile this
way.

30   EVANS   Pray you give me my gown—or else keep it in your arms.

[*He reads.*]

Enter [*Justice*] SHALLOW, [*Master*] SLENDER, *and* [*Mas-*
ter] PAGE

SHALLOW   How now, Master Parson? Good morrow, good Sir
Hugh. Keep a gamester from the dice and a good student from
his book, and it is wonderful.

SLENDER [*aside*]   Ah, sweet Anne Page!

35   PAGE   God save you, good Sir Hugh.

EVANS   God pless you from° his mercy sake, all of you.   *for*

3.1 Location: In fields near Frogmore.
1. Toward the Little Park and the Great Park.
2. Toward Old Windsor (a village near Shakespeare's
Windsor).
3. Somewhat misrecalled lines from "Come live with me

and be my love," a song by Christopher Marlowe.
4. Evans inserts the first line of a metrical version of
Psalm 137 (with "I" for "we"), which describes the weeping of the exiled Israelites.

SHALLOW   What, the sword and the Word?° Do you study them   *the Bible*
    both, Master Parson?

PAGE   And youthful still: in your doublet and hose⁵ this raw,
40   rheumatic day!

EVANS   There is reasons and causes for it.

PAGE   We are come to you to do a good office, Master Parson.

EVANS   Fery well. What is it?

PAGE   Yonder is a most reverend gentleman, who, belike° having   *probably*
45   received wrong by some person, is at most odds with his own
    gravity and patience that ever you saw.

SHALLOW   I have lived fourscore years and upward; I never heard
    a man of his place, gravity, and learning so wide of his own
    respect.⁶

50   EVANS   What is he?

PAGE   I think you know him: Master Doctor Caius, the
    renowned French physician.

EVANS   Got's will and his passion of my heart! I had as lief° you   *I had rather*
    would tell me of a mess of pottage.°   *thick soup*

55   PAGE   Why?

EVANS   He has no more knowledge in Hibbocrates⁷ and Galen,
    and he is a knave besides—a cowardly knave as you would
    desires to be acquainted withal.

PAGE [*to* SHALLOW]   I warrant you, he's the man should fight
60   with him.

SLENDER [*aside*]   O sweet Anne Page!

SHALLOW   It appears so by his weapons.

        Enter the HOST [*of the Garter*], *Doctor* CAIUS, *and John*
        RUGBY

    Keep them asunder—here comes Doctor Caius.

        [EVANS *and* CAIUS *draw and*] *offer to fight*

PAGE   Nay, good Master Parson, keep in your weapon.

65   SHALLOW   So do you, good Master Doctor.

HOST   Disarm them and let them question.° Let them keep their   *debate*
    limbs whole, and hack our English.

        [SHALLOW *and* PAGE *take Caius's and Evans's rapiers*]

CAIUS [*to* EVANS]   I pray you let-a me speak a word with your ear.
    Wherefore vill you not meet-a me?

70   EVANS [*aside to* CAIUS]   Pray you use your patience. [*Aloud*] In
    good time!

CAIUS   By Gar, you are de coward, de jack-dog, john-ape.

EVANS [*aside to* CAIUS]   Pray you let us not be laughing-stocks to
    other men's humours. I desire you in friendship, and I will one
75   way or other make you amends. [*Aloud*] By Jeshu, I will knog
    your urinal about your knave's cogscomb.°   *coxcomb; head*

CAIUS   Diable!° Jack Rugby, mine Host de Jarteer, have I not stay   *Devil*
    for him to kill him? Have I not, at de place I did appoint?

EVANS   As I am a Christians soul, now look you, this is the place
80   appointed. I'll be judgement° by mine Host of the Garter.   *judged*

HOST   Peace, I say, Gallia and Gaul,° French and Welsh, soul-   *Wales and France*
    curer and body-curer.

CAIUS   Ay, dat is very good, *excellent.*

HOST   Peace, I say. Hear mine Host of the Garter. Am I politic?°   *devious*

---

5. Close-fitting jacket and tights—that is, without a
cloak.

6. Indifferent to his own good reputation.

7. Hippocrates (ancient Greek physician).

85   Am I subtle?° Am I a Machiavel?[8] Shall I lose my doctor? No,   *crafty*
he gives me the potions and the motions. Shall I lose my par-
son, my priest, my Sir Hugh? No, he gives me the Proverbs and
the No-verbs.[9] [*To* CAIUS] Give me thy hand terrestrial°—so.   *(as bodily curer)*
[*To* EVANS] Give me thy hand celestial—so. Boys of art,° I have   *learning*
90   deceived you both, I have directed you to wrong places. Your
hearts are mighty, your skins are whole, and let burnt sack be
the issue.° [*To* SHALLOW *and* PAGE] Come, lay their swords to   *outcome*
pawn.[1] [*To* CAIUS *and* EVANS] Follow me, lads of peace, follow,
follow, follow.   *Exit*
95 SHALLOW   Afore God, a mad host! Follow, gentlemen, follow.
                             [*Exeunt* SHALLOW *and* PAGE]
SLENDER [*aside*]   O sweet Anne Page!   [*Exit*]
CAIUS   Ha, do I perceive dat? Have you make-a de sot° of us, ha,   *fool*
ha?
EVANS   This is well: he has made us his vlouting-stog.[2] I desire
100   you that we may be friends, and let us knog our prains together
to be revenge on this same scall,° scurvy, cogging companion,°   *scabby / cheating rogue*
the Host of the Garter.
CAIUS   By Gar, with all my heart. He promise to bring me where
is Anne Page. By Gar, he deceive me too.
105 EVANS   Well, I will smite his noddles.° Pray you follow.   *Exeunt*   *head*

3.2
[*Enter*] ROBIN, [*followed by*] MISTRESS PAGE

MISTRESS PAGE   Nay, keep your way,° little gallant. You were   *go on*
wont° to be a follower,° but now you are a leader. Whether had   *accustomed / servant*
you rather,° lead mine eyes, or eye your master's heels?   *Which would you prefer*
ROBIN   I had rather, forsooth, go before you like a man than fol-
5   low him° like a dwarf.   *(Falstaff)*
MISTRESS PAGE   O, you are a flattering boy! Now I see you'll be
a courtier.
                Enter Master FORD
FORD   Well met, Mistress Page. Whither go you?
MISTRESS PAGE   Truly, sir, to see your wife. Is she at home?
10 FORD   Ay, and as idle as she may hang together, for want[1] of
company. I think if your husbands were dead you two would
marry.
MISTRESS PAGE   Be sure of that—two other husbands.
FORD   Where had you this pretty weathercock?°   *(Robin)*
15 MISTRESS PAGE   I cannot tell what the dickens his name is my
husband had him of.°—What do you call your knight's name,   *got him from*
sirrah?
ROBIN   Sir John Falstaff.
FORD   Sir John Falstaff?
20 MISTRESS PAGE   He, he; I can never hit on's name. There is such
a league° between my goodman° and he! Is your wife at home   *friendship / husband*
indeed?
FORD   Indeed she is.

---

8. Follower of Niccolò Machiavelli, Italian political theo-
rist reviled by the Elizabethans, who was held to epito-
mize the "politic" and "subtle."
9. Prohibitions; verbal errors (the Welshman's misuse of
standard English).

1. As a pledge; because they are not needed.
2. Flouting-stock (laughingstock).
3.2 Location: A street in Windsor.
1. And as bored as she can stand to be without falling
apart, for lack.

MISTRESS PAGE   By your leave, sir, I am sick till I see her.

                        [*Exeunt* ROBIN *and* MISTRESS PAGE]

25 FORD   Has Page any brains? Hath he any eyes? Hath he any
thinking? Sure they sleep; he hath no use of them. Why, this
boy will carry a letter twenty mile, as easy as a cannon will
shoot point-blank twelve score.² He pieces out° his wife's incli-   *increases*
nation; he gives her folly motion and advantage.³ And now
30 she's going to my wife, and Falstaff's boy with her. A man may
hear this shower sing in the wind.° And Falstaff's boy with her.   *hear trouble brewing*
Good plots—they are laid; and our revolted° wives share dam-   *disloyal*
nation together. Well, I will take him;° then torture my wife,   *catch him by surprise*
pluck the borrowed veil of modesty from the so-seeming Mis-
35 tress Page, divulge° Page himself for a secure° and wilful   *reveal / an overconfident*
Actaeon,° and to these violent proceedings all my neighbours   *cuckold*
shall cry aim.°   *shall applaud*

            [*Clock strikes*]

The clock gives me my cue, and my assurance bids me search.
There I shall find Falstaff. I shall be rather praised for this than
40 mocked, for it is as positive as the earth is firm that Falstaff is
there. I will go.

            Enter Master PAGE, [*Justice*] SHALLOW, [*Master*] SLEN-
            DER, [*the*] HOST [*of the Garter*], *Sir Hugh* EVANS, *Doctor*
            CAIUS, *and* [*John* RUGBY]

SHALLOW, PAGE, etc.   Well met, Master Ford.

FORD [*aside*]   By my faith, a good knot!° [*To them*] I have good   *group (ironic?)*
cheer° at home, and I pray you all go with me.   *food and drink*

45 SHALLOW   I must excuse myself, Master Ford.

SLENDER   And so must I, sir. We have appointed to dine with
Mistress Anne, and I would not break with° her for more   *break my word to*
money than I'll speak of.

SHALLOW   We have lingered about° a match between Anne Page   *delayed in concluding*
50 and my cousin Slender, and this day we shall have our answer.

SLENDER   I hope I have your good will, father Page.

PAGE   You have, Master Slender: I stand wholly for you. [*To*
CAIUS] But my wife, Master Doctor, is for you altogether.

CAIUS   Ay, be Gar, and de maid is love-a me. My nursh-a°   *housekeeper*
55 Quickly tell me so mush.

HOST [*to* PAGE]   What say you to young Master Fenton? He
capers,° he dances, he has eyes of youth; he writes verses, he   *leaps in dancing*
speaks holiday,° he smells April and May. He will carry't,° he   *gaily / succeed*
will carry't; 'tis in his buttons° he will carry't.   *youth*

60 PAGE   Not by my consent, I promise you. The gentleman is of
no having.° He kept company with the wild Prince⁴ and Poins.   *property*
He is of too high a region;° he knows too much. No, he shall   *rank*
not knit a knot in° his fortunes with the finger of my substance.°   *strengthen / wealth*
If he take her, let him take her simply:° the wealth I have waits   *without dowry*
65 on my consent, and my consent goes not that way.

FORD   I beseech you heartily, some of you go home with me to
dinner. Besides your cheer, you shall have sport: I will show
you a monster.° Master Doctor, you shall go. So shall you, Mas-   *(Falstaff)*
ter Page, and you, Sir Hugh.

---

2. Will shoot straight 240 yards.   in *1* and *2 Henry IV*—actually Falstaff's, rather than Fen-
3. He gives her lust ("folly") prompting and opportunity. ton's, companions.
4. Prince Hal (the future Henry V) and Poins (line 61)

70 SHALLOW Well, God be with you! [*Aside to* SLENDER] We shall
  have the freer wooing at Master Page's.

  Exeunt SHALLOW *and* SLENDER

CAIUS Go home, John Rugby; I come anon. [*Exit* RUGBY]

HOST Farewell, my hearts. I will to my honest knight Falstaff,
  and drink canary° with him. *Exit* °wine

75 FORD [*aside*] I think I shall drink in pipe-wine first with him: I'll
  make him dance.[5] [*To* PAGE, CAIUS, *and* EVANS] Will you go,
  gentles?° °gentlemen

PAGE, CAIUS, *and* EVANS Have with you° to see this monster. °We are coming

  Exeunt

3.3

Enter MISTRESS FORD *and* MISTRESS PAGE

MISTRESS FORD What, John! What, Robert!

MISTRESS PAGE Quickly, quickly! Is the buck-basket°— °laundry basket

MISTRESS FORD I warrant.°—What, Robert, I say! °I'm sure it is

MISTRESS PAGE Come, come, come!

Enter [JOHN *and* ROBERT,] *with a buck-basket*

5 MISTRESS FORD Here, set it down.

MISTRESS PAGE Give your men the charge.° We must be brief. °instructions

MISTRESS FORD Marry, as I told you before, John and Robert, be
  ready here hard by in the brew-house; and when I suddenly
  call you, come forth, and without any pause or staggering take
10 this basket on your shoulders. That done, trudge with it in all
  haste, and carry it among the whitsters° in Datchet Mead,[1] and °linen bleachers
  there empty it in the muddy ditch close by the Thames' side.

MISTRESS PAGE [*to* JOHN *and* ROBERT] You will do it?

MISTRESS FORD I ha' told them over and over; they lack no direc-
15 tion.°—Be gone, and come when you are called. °instructions

  Exeunt [JOHN *and* ROBERT]

Enter ROBIN

MISTRESS PAGE Here comes little Robin.

MISTRESS FORD How now, my eyas-musket,° what news with °young sparrow hawk
  you?

ROBIN My master Sir John is come in at your back door, Mis-
20 tress Ford, and requests your company.

MISTRESS PAGE You little Jack-a-Lent,° have you been true to us? °Lenten puppet

ROBIN Ay, I'll be sworn. My master knows not of your being
  here, and hath threatened to put me into everlasting liberty if I
  tell you of it;° for he swears he'll turn me away.[2] °(Falstaff's visit)

25 MISTRESS PAGE Thou'rt a good boy. This secrecy of thine shall
  be a tailor to thee, and shall make thee a new doublet and
  hose.—I'll go hide me.

MISTRESS FORD Do so. [*To* ROBIN] Go tell thy master I am
  alone. [*Exit* ROBIN]

30 Mistress Page, remember you your cue.

MISTRESS PAGE I warrant thee. If I do not act it, hiss me.

MISTRESS FORD Go to, then. [*Exit* MISTRESS PAGE]

---

5. *drink . . . dance:* make it uncomfortable for Falstaff.
Pipe wine is wine from the cask, with a pun on "the
whine of musical pipes," which are played for a dance.
Ford also puns on "canary" (line 74), which is also a
dance. Drinking becomes a metaphor for Ford's intention

to make Falstaff dance to his tune.
3.3 Location: Ford's house.
1. Meadow situated between Windsor Little Park and the
Thames.
2. He'll dismiss me.

We'll use this unwholesome humidity,° this gross watery pump- ° *body fluids*
kin. We'll teach him to know turtles from jays.³
　　　　Enter Sir John FALSTAFF

35　FALSTAFF　Have I caught thee, my heavenly jewel? Why, now let
　　　me die, for I have lived long enough. This is the period° of my ° *goal*
　　　ambition. O, this blessed hour!
　　MISTRESS FORD　O sweet Sir John!
　　FALSTAFF　Mistress Ford, I cannot cog;° I cannot prate, Mistress ° *lie*
40　　Ford. Now shall I sin in my wish: I would thy husband were
　　　dead. I'll speak it before the best lord. I would make thee my
　　　lady.
　　MISTRESS FORD　I your lady, Sir John? Alas, I should be a pitiful
　　　lady.
45　FALSTAFF　Let the court of France show me such another. I see
　　　how thine eye would emulate the diamond. Thou hast the
　　　right arched beauty of the brow that becomes the ship-tire, the
　　　tire-valiant, or any tire of Venetian admittance.⁴
　　MISTRESS FORD　A plain kerchief, Sir John—my brows become
50　　nothing else, nor that well neither.
　　FALSTAFF　By the Lord, thou art a tyrant° to say so. Thou wouldst ° *(punning on "tire")*
　　　make an absolute° courtier, and the firm fixture of thy foot ° *a perfect*
　　　would give an excellent motion to thy gait in a semicircled
　　　farthingale.⁵ I see what thou wert° if fortune, thy foe, were, with ° *would be*
55　　nature, thy friend. Come, thou canst not hide it.
　　MISTRESS FORD　Believe me, there's no such thing in me.
　　FALSTAFF　What made me love thee? Let that persuade thee
　　　there's something extraordinary in thee. Come, I cannot cog
　　　and say thou art this and that, like a-many of these lisping
60　　hawthorn-buds° that come like women in men's apparel and ° *young perfumed wooers*
　　　smell like Bucklersbury⁶ in simple time;⁷ I cannot. But I love
　　　thee, none but thee; and thou deservest it.
　　MISTRESS FORD　Do not betray° me, sir. I fear you love Mistress ° *deceive*
　　　Page.
65　FALSTAFF　Thou mightst as well say I love to walk by the Counter
　　　gate,° which is as hateful to me as the reek of a lime-kiln. ° *debtors' prison*
　　MISTRESS FORD　Well, heaven knows how I love you; and you
　　　shall one day find it.
　　FALSTAFF　Keep in that mind. I'll deserve it.
70　MISTRESS FORD　Nay, I must tell you, so you do; or else I could
　　　not be in that mind.
　　　　　　[*Enter* ROBIN]
　　ROBIN　Mistress Ford, Mistress Ford! Here's Mistress Page at the
　　　door, sweating and blowing,° and looking wildly, and would ° *puffing*
　　　needs speak with you presently.° ° *immediately*
75　FALSTAFF　She shall not see me. I will ensconce me behind the
　　　arras.° ° *wall curtain*
　　MISTRESS FORD　Pray you do so; she's a very tattling woman.
　　　　　　FALSTAFF *stands behind the arras.*
　　　　　　Enter MISTRESS PAGE
　　What's the matter? How now?

---

3. Gaudy birds, hence flirtatious women. *turtles:* turtledoves, proverbially faithful.
4. Fancifully extravagant headdresses ("tires"), the "ship-
tire" in the form of a ship, that were acceptable in Venice.
"Tire" is from "attire."

5. Skirt shaped with covered hoops at the back.
6. London street where herbs were sold.
7. Summer (when medicinal herbs, or "simples," were
available).

MISTRESS PAGE   O Mistress Ford, what have you done? You're
80 shamed, you're overthrown, you're undone for ever.

MISTRESS FORD   What's the matter, good Mistress Page?

MISTRESS PAGE   O well-a-day,° Mistress Ford! Having an honest   *alas*
man to° your husband, to give him such cause of suspicion!   *as*

MISTRESS FORD   What cause of suspicion?

85 MISTRESS PAGE   What cause of suspicion? Out upon you!° How   *(a reproach)*
am I mistook in you!

MISTRESS FORD   Why, alas, what's the matter?

MISTRESS PAGE   Your husband's coming hither, woman, with all
the officers in Windsor, to search for a gentleman that he says
90 is here now in the house, by your consent, to take an ill advantage of his absence. You are undone.

MISTRESS FORD   'Tis not so, I hope.

MISTRESS PAGE   Pray heaven it be not so that you have such a
man here! But 'tis most certain your husband's coming, with
half Windsor at his heels, to search for such a one. I come
95 before to tell you. If you know yourself clear,° why, I am glad   *innocent*
of it; but if you have a friend° here, convey, convey him out.   *lover*
Be not amazed.° Call all your senses to you. Defend your repu-   *bewildered*
tation, or bid farewell to your good° life for ever.   *respectable*

100 MISTRESS FORD   What shall I do? There is a gentleman, my dear
friend; and I fear not mine own shame so much as his peril. I
had rather than a thousand pound he were out of the house.

MISTRESS PAGE   For shame, never stand° 'you had rather' and   *waste time over*
'you had rather'. Your husband's here at hand. Bethink you of
105 some conveyance:° in the house you cannot hide him. O, how   *trick; transport*
have you deceived me! Look, here is a basket. If he be of any
reasonable stature, he may creep in here; and throw foul linen
upon him as if it were going to bucking.° Or—it is whiting°   *washing / bleaching*
time—send him by your two men to Datchet Mead.

110 MISTRESS FORD   He's too big to go in there. What shall I do?

FALSTAFF [*coming forward*]   Let me see't, let me see't, O let me
see't! I'll in, I'll in. Follow your friend's counsel; I'll in.

MISTRESS PAGE   What, Sir John Falstaff! [*Aside to him*] Are these
your letters, knight?

115 FALSTAFF [*aside to* MISTRESS PAGE]   I love thee. Help me away.
Let me creep in here.
        FALSTAFF *goes into the basket*
I'll never—
        [MISTRESS PAGE *and* MISTRESS FORD] *put [foul] clothes*
        over him

MISTRESS PAGE [*to* ROBIN]   Help to cover your master, boy.—
Call your men, Mistress Ford. [*Aside to* FALSTAFF] You dis-
120 sembling knight!

MISTRESS FORD   What, John! Robert, John!
        [*Enter* JOHN *and* ROBERT]
Go take up these clothes here quickly. Where's the cowl-staff?°   *pole to carry basket*
        [JOHN *and* ROBERT *fit the cowl-staff*]
Look how you drumble!° Carry them to the laundress in Dat-   *dawdle*
chet Mead. Quickly, come!
        [*They lift the basket and start to leave.*]
        [*Enter Master*] FORD, [*Master*] PAGE, *Doctor* CAIUS, *and*
        [*Sir Hugh*] EVANS

125 FORD [*to* PAGE, CAIUS, *and* EVANS]   Pray you come near. If I sus-

pect without cause, why then, make sport at me; then let me
be your jest—I deserve it. [*To* JOHN *and* ROBERT] How now?
Whither bear you this?

JOHN   To the laundress, forsooth.

130   MISTRESS FORD   Why, what have you to do° whither they bear it?   to do with
You were best° meddle with buck-washing!⁸   (sarcastic)

FORD   Buck? I would I could wash myself of the buck! Buck,
buck, buck? Ay, buck, I warrant you, buck. And of the season
too, it shall appear.

                    [*Exeunt* JOHN *and* ROBERT, *with the basket*]

135   Gentlemen, I have dreamt tonight.° I'll tell you my dream.   last night
Here, here, here be my keys. Ascend° my chambers, search,   Go up to
seek, find out. I'll warrant we'll unkennel° the fox. Let me stop   dislodge
this way° first.   passage

                [*He locks the door*]

So, now, uncoop.

140   PAGE   Good Master Ford, be contented. You wrong yourself too
much.

FORD   True, Master Page.—Up, gentlemen! You shall see sport
anon. Follow me, gentlemen.   [*Exit*]

EVANS   This is fery fantastical humours and jealousies.

145   CAIUS   By Gar, 'tis no the fashion of France; it is not jealous in
France.

PAGE   Nay, follow him, gentlemen. See the issue of his search.

                    Exeunt [CAIUS, EVANS, *and* PAGE]

MISTRESS PAGE   Is there not a double excellency in this?

MISTRESS FORD   I know not which pleases me better: that my
150   husband is deceived, or Sir John.

MISTRESS PAGE   What a taking° was he in when your husband   panic
asked what was in the basket!

MISTRESS FORD   I am half afraid he will have need of washing,⁹
so throwing him into the water will do him a benefit.

155   MISTRESS PAGE   Hang him, dishonest rascal! I would all of the
same strain were in the same distress.

MISTRESS FORD   I think my husband hath some special suspicion
of Falstaff's being here, for I never saw him so gross in his
jealousy till now.

160   MISTRESS PAGE   I will lay a plot to try° that, and we will yet have   test
more tricks with Falstaff. His dissolute disease will scarce obey°   be cured by
this medicine.

MISTRESS FORD   Shall we send that foolish carrion° Mistress   rotten flesh
Quickly to him, and excuse his throwing into the water, and
165   give him another hope, to betray him to another punishment?

MISTRESS PAGE   We will do it. Let him be sent for tomorrow
eight o'clock, to have amends.

              Enter [FORD, PAGE, CAIUS, *and* EVANS]

FORD   I cannot find him. Maybe the knave bragged of that he
could not compass.°   accomplish

170   MISTRESS PAGE [*aside to* MISTRESS FORD]   Heard you that?

MISTRESS FORD   You use me well, Master Ford, do you?

FORD   Ay, I do so.

MISTRESS FORD   Heaven make me better than your thoughts!

---

8. Washing that needs bleaching (but Ford thinks of   9. Fear will have made him urinate.
"buck" as "stag," the horned cuckold, and "to copulate").

FORD   Amen.

175 MISTRESS PAGE   You do yourself mighty wrong, Master Ford.

FORD   Ay, ay, I must bear it.

EVANS   If there be anypody in the house, and in the chambers,
and in the coffers, and in the presses,° heaven forgive my sins   *cupboards*
at the day of judgement!

180 CAIUS   Be Gar, nor I too. There is nobodies.

PAGE   Fie, fie, Master Ford, are you not ashamed? What spirit,
what devil suggests this imagination? I would not ha' your distemper in this kind for the wealth of Windsor Castle.

FORD   'Tis my fault, Master Page. I suffer for it.

185 EVANS   You suffer for a pad conscience. Your wife is as honest a
'omans as I will desires among five thousand, and five hundred
too.

CAIUS   By Gar, I see 'tis an honest woman.

FORD   Well, I promised you a dinner. Come, come, walk in the
190 park. I pray you pardon me. I will hereafter make known to you
why I have done this.—Come, wife; come, Mistress Page. I
pray you pardon me. Pray heartily pardon me.

PAGE [*to* CAIUS *and* EVANS]   Let's go in, gentlemen. [*Aside to
them*] But trust me, we'll mock him. [*To* FORD, CAIUS, *and*
195 EVANS] I do invite you tomorrow morning to my house to break-
fast. After, we'll a-birding° together. I have a fine hawk for¹ the   *bird hunting*
bush. Shall it be so?

FORD   Anything.

EVANS   If there is one, I shall make two in the company.

200 CAIUS   If there be one or two, I shall make-a the turd.

FORD   Pray you go, Master Page.

Exeunt [all but EVANS *and* CAIUS]

EVANS   I pray you now, remembrance tomorrow on the lousy
knave mine Host.²

CAIUS   Dat is good, by Gar; with all my heart.

205 EVANS   A lousy knave, to have his gibes and his mockeries.

Exeunt

3.4

Enter Master FENTON *and* ANNE *Page*

FENTON   I see I cannot get thy father's love;
Therefore no more turn me to him, sweet Nan.

ANNE   Alas, how then?

FENTON   Why, thou must be thyself.°   *in charge of yourself*
He doth object I am too great of birth,
5 And that, my state being galled with° my expense,   *estate being hurt by*
I seek to heal it only by his wealth.
Besides these, other bars he lays before me—
My riots past, my wild societies;°   *companionships*
And tells me 'tis a thing impossible
10 I should love thee but as a property.

ANNE   Maybe he tells you true.

FENTON   No, heaven so speed° me in my time to come!   *as heaven may prosper*
Albeit I will confess thy father's wealth
Was the first motive that I wooed thee, Anne,

1. For driving birds into.   3.1.101.
2. A cryptic reference to the "revenge" proposal at   3.4 Location: Outside Page's house.

15   Yet, wooing thee, I found thee of more value
        Than stamps in gold° or sums in sealèd bags;   *stamped gold coins*
        And 'tis the very riches of thyself
        That now I aim at.
ANNE   Gentle Master Fenton,
        Yet seek my father's love, still seek it, sir.
20   If opportunity and humblest suit
        Cannot attain it, why then—

        Enter [Justice] SHALLOW, *[Master]* SLENDER *[richly
        dressed], and* MISTRESS QUICKLY
                                        Hark you hither.
                [They talk apart]
SHALLOW   Break their talk, Mistress Quickly. My kinsman shall
        speak for himself.
SLENDER   I'll make a shaft or a bolt on't.¹ 'Slid,° 'tis but ven-   *By God's eyelid*
25   turing.
SHALLOW   Be not dismayed.
SLENDER   No, she shall not dismay me.
        I care not for that, but that I am afeard.
MISTRESS QUICKLY *[to* ANNE*]*   Hark ye, Master Slender would
        speak a word with you.
30 ANNE   I come to him. *[To* FENTON*]* This is my father's choice.
        O, what a world of vile ill-favoured° faults   *ugly*
        Looks handsome in three hundred pounds a year!°   *(moderate wealth)*
MISTRESS QUICKLY   And how does good Master Fenton? Pray
        you, a word with you.
                [She draws FENTON *aside]*
35 SHALLOW   She's coming. To her, coz! O boy, thou hadst a
        father!°   *be manly; you're manly*
SLENDER   I had a father, Mistress Anne; my uncle can tell you
        good jests of him.—Pray you, uncle, tell Mistress Anne the jest
        how my father stole two geese out of a pen, good uncle.
40 SHALLOW   Mistress Anne, my cousin loves you.
SLENDER   Ay, that I do, as well as I love any woman in Glouces-
        tershire.
SHALLOW   He will maintain you like a gentlewoman.
SLENDER   Ay, by God, that I will, come cut and long-tail,° under   *no matter what*
45   the degree° of a squire.   *in the rank*
SHALLOW   He will make you a hundred and fifty pounds join-
        ture.°   *widowhood settlement*
ANNE   Good Master Shallow, let him woo for himself.
SHALLOW   Marry, I thank you for it, I thank you for that good
50   comfort.—She calls you, coz. I'll leave you.
                [He stands aside]
ANNE   Now, Master Slender.
SLENDER   Now, good Mistress Anne.
ANNE   What is your will?
SLENDER   My will? 'Od's heartlings,° that's a pretty jest indeed! I   *By God's little hearts*
55   ne'er made my will yet, I thank God; I am not such a sickly
        creature, I give God praise.
ANNE   I mean, Master Slender, what would you with me?
SLENDER   Truly, for mine own part, I would little or nothing

---

1. I'll do it one way or another (with possible sexual connotation).

with you. Your father and my uncle hath made motions.° If it   proposals
60 be my luck, so. If not, happy man be his dole.² They can tell
you how things go better than I can.
            Enter Master PAGE [*and*] MISTRESS PAGE
You may ask your father: here he comes.
PAGE   Now, Master Slender.—Love him, daughter Anne.—
Why, how now? What does Master Fenton here?
65 You wrong me, sir, thus still to haunt my house.
I told you, sir, my daughter is disposed of.
FENTON   Nay, Master Page, be not impatient.
MISTRESS PAGE   Good Master Fenton, come not to my child.
PAGE   She is no match for you.
70 FENTON   Sir, will you hear me?
PAGE   No, good Master Fenton.—
Come, Master Shallow; come, son Slender, in.—
Knowing my mind, you wrong me, Master Fenton.
            Exeunt PAGE[, SHALLOW, *and* SLENDER]
MISTRESS QUICKLY [*to* FENTON]   Speak to Mistress Page.
75 FENTON   Good Mistress Page, for that° I love your daughter   because
In such a righteous fashion as I do,
Perforce against all checks,° rebukes, and manners   reproofs
I must advance the colours° of my love,   military banners
And not retire. Let me have your good will.
80 ANNE   Good mother, do not marry me to yon fool.
MISTRESS PAGE   I mean it not; I seek you a better husband.
MISTRESS QUICKLY [*aside to* ANNE]   That's my master, Master
Doctor.
ANNE   Alas, I had rather be set quick i'th' earth°   half-buried alive
85 And bowled to death with turnips.
MISTRESS PAGE   Come, trouble not yourself, good Master Fenton.
I will not be your friend nor enemy.
My daughter will I question how she loves you,
And as I find her, so am I affected.°   inclined
90 Till then, farewell, sir. She must needs go in.
Her father will be angry.
FENTON   Farewell, gentle mistress.—Farewell, Nan.
            Exeunt [MISTRESS PAGE *and* ANNE]
MISTRESS QUICKLY   This is my doing now. 'Nay', said I, 'will you
cast away your child on a fool and a physician? Look on Master
95 Fenton.' This is my doing.
FENTON   I thank thee, [*giving her a ring*] and I pray thee, once°   at some time
tonight
Give my sweet Nan this ring. [*Giving money*] There's for thy
pains.
MISTRESS QUICKLY   Now heaven send thee good fortune!
            Exit FENTON
A kind heart he hath. A woman would run through fire and
100 water for such a kind heart. But yet I would my master had
Mistress Anne; or I would Master Slender had her; or, in sooth,
I would Master Fenton had her. I will do what I can for them
all three, for so I have promised, and I'll be as good as my
word—but speciously° for Master Fenton. Well, I must of°   (*for* "specially") / *run*

2. Good luck to the successful suitor.

105   another errand to Sir John Falstaff from my two mistresses.
       What a beast am I to slack° it!   *Exit*   to be remiss in

                                  3.5

                          Enter Sir John FALSTAFF
FALSTAFF   Bardolph, I say!
                          Enter BARDOLPH
BARDOLPH   Here, sir.
FALSTAFF   Go fetch me a quart of sack; put a toast° in't.   piece of hot toast
                                                   [*Exit* BARDOLPH]
       Have I lived to be carried in a basket like a barrow° of butcher's   wheelbarrow
  5   offal, and to be thrown in the Thames? Well, if I be served
       such another trick, I'll have my brains ta'en out and buttered,[1]
       and give them to a dog for a New Year's gift. 'Sblood, the rogues
       slighted° me into the river with as little remorse as they would   slid; scorned
       have drowned a blind bitch's° puppies, fifteen i'th' litter! And   bitch's blind
 10   you may know by my size that I have a kind of alacrity in sink-
       ing. If the bottom were as deep as hell, I should down.° I had   reach the bottom
       been drowned, but that the shore was shelvy° and shallow—a   made of sandbanks
       death that I abhor, for the water swells a man, and what a thing
       should I have been when I had been swelled? By the Lord, a
 15   mountain of mummy!°   dead flesh
             [*Enter* BARDOLPH, *with two large cups of sack*]
BARDOLPH   Here's Mistress Quickly, sir, to speak with you.
FALSTAFF   Come, let me pour in some sack to the Thames'
       water, for my belly's as cold as if I had swallowed snowballs for
       pills to cool the reins.°   kidneys
             [*He drinks*]
 20   Call her in.
BARDOLPH   Come in, woman!
                          Enter MISTRESS QUICKLY
MISTRESS QUICKLY   [*to* FALSTAFF]   By your leave; I cry you
       mercy.[2] Give your worship good morrow!
FALSTAFF   [*drinking, then speaking to* BARDOLPH]   Take away
 25   these chalices. Go brew° me a pottle° of sack, finely.   prepare / two quarts
BARDOLPH   With eggs, sir?
FALSTAFF   Simple of itself.° I'll no pullet-sperms in my brewage.   Pure
                                              [*Exit* BARDOLPH, *with cups*]
       How now?
MISTRESS QUICKLY   Marry, sir, I come to your worship from Mis-
 30   tress Ford.
FALSTAFF   Mistress Ford? I have had ford enough: I was thrown
       into the ford, I have my belly full of ford.
MISTRESS QUICKLY   Alas the day, good heart, that was not her
       fault. She does so take on with her men; they mistook their
 35   erection.[3]
FALSTAFF   So did I mine, to build upon a foolish woman's
       promise.
MISTRESS QUICKLY   Well, she laments, sir, for it, that it would
       yearn° your heart to see it. Her husband goes this morning a-   grieve
 40   birding. She desires you once more to come to her, between

---

3.5 Location: The Garter Inn.
1. "Buttered" brains may have meant "foolish."
2. *I cry you mercy:* excuse me.

3. Quickly means that Mistress Ford "does take on"
(scold) her servants, who misunderstood her direction,
but there's an obvious, unintentional sexual pun.

eight and nine. I must carry her word° quickly. She'll make
you amends, I warrant you.

FALSTAFF   Well, I will visit her. Tell her so, and bid her think
what a man is; let her consider his frailty, and then judge of my
45   merit.

MISTRESS QUICKLY   I will tell her.

FALSTAFF   Do so. Between nine and ten, sayst thou?

MISTRESS QUICKLY   Eight and nine, sir.

FALSTAFF   Well, be gone. I will not miss° her.

50   MISTRESS QUICKLY   Peace be with you, sir.   *Exit*

FALSTAFF   I marvel I hear not of Master Brooke; he sent me
word to stay° within. I like his money well.

      Enter [Master] FORD, *[disguised as]* Brooke

By the mass, here he comes.

FORD   God bless you, sir.

55   FALSTAFF   Now, Master Brooke, you come to know what hath
passed between me and Ford's wife.

FORD   That indeed, Sir John, is my business.

FALSTAFF   Master Brooke, I will not lie to you. I was at her house
the hour she appointed me.

60   FORD   And sped you,° sir?

FALSTAFF   Very ill-favouredly,° Master Brooke.

FORD   How so, sir? Did she change her determination?

FALSTAFF   No, Master Brooke, but the peaking cornuto° her husband, Master Brooke, dwelling in a continual 'larum° of jeal-
65   ousy, comes me° in the instant of our encounter—after we had
embraced, kissed, protested, and, as it were, spoke the prologue
of our comedy—and at his heels a rabble of his companions,
thither provoked and instigated by his distemper, and, forsooth,
to search his house for his wife's love.

70   FORD   What, while you were there?

FALSTAFF   While I was there.

FORD   And did he search for you, and could not find you?

FALSTAFF   You shall hear. As God would have it, comes in one
Mistress Page, gives intelligence of Ford's approach, and, by
75   her invention and Ford's wife's distraction, they conveyed me
into a buck-basket—

FORD   A buck-basket?

FALSTAFF   By the Lord, a buck-basket!—rammed me in with foul
shirts and smocks, socks, foul stockings, greasy napkins, that,°
80   Master Brooke, there was the rankest compound of villainous
smell that ever offended nostril.

FORD   And how long lay you there?

FALSTAFF   Nay, you shall hear, Master Brooke, what I have suffered to bring this woman to evil, for your good. Being thus
85   crammed in the basket, a couple of Ford's knaves, his hinds,°
were called forth by their mistress, to carry me, in the name of
foul clothes, to Datchet Lane. They took me on their shoulders, met the jealous knave their master in the door, who asked
them once or twice what they had in their basket. I quaked for
90   fear lest the lunatic knave would have searched it, but fate,
ordaining he should be a cuckold, held° his hand. Well, on
went he for a search, and away went I for foul clothes. But mark
the sequel, Master Brooke. I suffered the pangs of three several°
deaths. First, an intolerable fright, to be detected with° a jeal-

your reply

fail

wait for him

did you succeed
badly

sneaking cuckold
alarm
comes

so that

servants (pejorative)

held back

different
by

95 ous rotten bell-wether.⁴ Next, to be compassed like a good
bilbo in the circumference of a peck,⁵ hilt to point, heel to
head. And then, to be stopped° in, like a strong distillation,° *stoppered / liquid*
with stinking clothes that fretted° in their own grease. Think of *fermented*
that—a man of my kidney°—think of that—that am as subject *constitution*
100 to heat as butter, a man of continual dissolution° and thaw. It *melting*
was a miracle to scape suffocation. And in the height of this
bath, when I was more than half stewed in grease like a Dutch
dish, to be thrown into the Thames and cooled, glowing-hot,
in that surge, like a horseshoe. Think of that—hissing hot—
105 think of that, Master Brooke!

FORD In good sadness,° sir, I am sorry that for my sake you have *seriousness*
suffered all this. My suit then is desperate. You'll undertake
her no more?

FALSTAFF Master Brooke, I will be thrown into Etna° as I have *Sicilian volcano*
110 been into Thames ere I will leave her thus. Her husband is
this morning gone a-birding. I have received from her another
embassy° of meeting. 'Twixt eight and nine is the hour, Master *message*
Brooke.

FORD 'Tis past eight already, sir.

115 FALSTAFF Is it? I will then address me to my appointment.
Come to me at your convenient leisure, and you shall know
how I speed; and the conclusion shall be crowned with your
enjoying her. Adieu. You shall have her, Master Brooke; Master
Brooke, you shall cuckold Ford. *Exit*

120 FORD Hum! Ha! Is this a vision? Is this a dream? Do I sleep?
Master Ford, awake! Awake, Master Ford! There's a hole made
in your best coat,⁶ Master Ford. This 'tis to be married! This
'tis to have linen and buck-baskets! Well, I will proclaim myself
what I am. I will now take° the lecher. He is at my house. He *catch*
125 cannot scape me; 'tis impossible he should. He cannot creep
into a halfpenny purse, nor into a pepperbox. But lest the devil
that guides him should aid him, I will search impossible places.
Though what I am I cannot avoid, yet to be what I would not
shall not make me tame. If I have horns to make one mad, let
130 the proverb go with me: I'll be horn-mad.⁷ *Exit*

4.1

Enter MISTRESS PAGE, [MISTRESS] QUICKLY, [*and*] WIL-
LIAM *Page*

MISTRESS PAGE Is he at Mistress Ford's already, thinkest thou?

MISTRESS QUICKLY Sure he is by this,° or will be presently.° But *now / immediately*
truly he is very courageous°-mad about his throwing into the *(for "ragingly")*
water. Mistress Ford desires you to come suddenly.° *at once*

5 MISTRESS PAGE I'll be with her by and by.° I'll but bring my *right away*
young man here to school.

Enter [Sir Hugh] EVANS

Look where his master comes. 'Tis a playing day, I see.—How
now, Sir Hugh, no school today?

---

4. Castrated ram, leader of the flock, with a bell round its
neck and a horn like a cuckold's on its head.
5. To be bent double (encompassed) like a flexible sword
(from Bilbao, Spain, where fine swords known for their
elasticity were made) in the cramped space of a laundry
basket (in a receptacle holding a peck, or a quarter of a

bushel).
6. Proverbial for "Your reputation is spoiled."
7. I'll be as furious as a horned animal in breeding season; furious to be a cuckold.
4.1 Location: Outdoors.

EVANS   No, Master Slender is let° the boys leave° to play.   *asked that / be allowed*

10   MISTRESS QUICKLY   Blessing of his heart!

MISTRESS PAGE   Sir Hugh, my husband says my son profits nothing in the world[1] at his book. I pray you ask him some questions
in his accidence.°   *Latin grammar*

EVANS   Come hither, William. Hold up your head. Come.

15   MISTRESS PAGE   Come on, sirrah. Hold up your head. Answer
your master; be not afraid.

EVANS   William, how many numbers is in nouns?

WILLIAM   Two.°   *(singular and plural)*

MISTRESS QUICKLY   Truly, I thought there had been one number
20   more, because they say ''Od's nouns'.[2]

EVANS   Peace your tattlings!—What is 'fair', William?

WILLIAM   *'Pulcher'.*

MISTRESS QUICKLY   Polecats?° There are fairer things than pole-   *Smelly animals; whores*
cats, sure.

25   EVANS   You are a very simplicity 'oman. I pray you peace.—
What is '*lapis*', William?

WILLIAM   A stone.

EVANS   And what is 'a stone', William?

WILLIAM   A pebble.

30   EVANS   No, it is '*lapis*'. I pray you remember in your prain.

WILLIAM   *'Lapis'.*

EVANS   That is a good William. What is he, William, that does
lend articles?

WILLIAM   Articles are borrowed of the pronoun, and be thus
35   declined. *Singulariter nominativo: 'hic, haec, hoc'.*[3]

EVANS   *Nominativo: 'hig, hag, hog'.*[4] Pray you mark: *genitivo:*°   *genitive*
'huius'. Well, what is your accusative case?

WILLIAM   *Accusativo: 'hinc'*°—   *(for "hunc")*

EVANS   I pray you have your remembrance, child. *Accusativo:*
40   *'hing, hang, hog'.*

MISTRESS QUICKLY   'Hang-hog'[5] is Latin for bacon, I warrant you.

EVANS   Leave your prabbles, 'oman!—What is the focative° case,   *vocative; (obscene)*
William?

WILLIAM   *O—vocativo, O—*

45   EVANS   Remember, William, focative is *caret.*[6]

MISTRESS QUICKLY   And that's a good root.

EVANS   'Oman, forbear.

MISTRESS PAGE [*to* MISTRESS QUICKLY]   Peace.

EVANS   What is your genitive case plural, William?

50   WILLIAM   Genitive case?

EVANS   Ay.

WILLIAM   *Genitivo: 'horum, harum, horum'.*

MISTRESS QUICKLY   Vengeance of° Jenny's case! Fie on her!   *A plague on*
Never name her, child, if she be a whore.[7]

55   EVANS   For shame, 'oman!

MISTRESS QUICKLY   You do ill to teach the child such words. He

---

1. My son fails to improve.
2. God's wounds; three is an odd ("Od's") number.
3. William recites by memory from his textbook. "*Singulariter nominativo*" is "in the nominative singular" (in
which William gives the masculine, feminine, and neuter
of the pronoun "this").
4. The pronunciation in Evans's accent.
5. Alluding to the saying "Hog is not bacon until it be

hanged."
6. Missing. Quickly understands "carrot," whose slang
sense "penis" is supported by a suggestion of "fuck" in
"focative."
7. *Genitive case . . . whore:* "Genitive" is perhaps misun-
derstandable as Latin for "generative" or even "genital"—
as well as "Jenny"; "case" is understood by Quickly to
mean "situation" and also the slang term for "vagina."

teaches him to hick and to hack,° which they'll do fast enough   *drink and copulate?*
of themselves, and to call 'whorum'. Fie upon you!

EVANS   'Oman, art thou lunatics? Hast thou no understandings
60   for thy cases, and the numbers of the genders? Thou art as
foolish Christian creatures as I would desires.

MISTRESS PAGE [*to* MISTRESS QUICKLY]   Prithee, hold thy peace.

EVANS   Show me now, William, some declensions of your pronouns.

65 WILLIAM   Forsooth, I have forgot.

EVANS   It is '*qui, que, quod*'. If you forget your '*qui's*, your '*que's*,
and your '*quod's*,[8] you must be preeches.° Go your ways and   *flogged*
play; go.

MISTRESS PAGE   He is a better scholar than I thought he was.

70 EVANS   He is a good sprag° memory. Farewell, Mistress Page.   *sprack (lively)*

MISTRESS PAGE   Adieu, good Sir Hugh.   [*Exit* EVANS]
Get you home, boy.   [*Exit* WILLIAM]
[*To* MISTRESS QUICKLY] Come, we stay too long.   *Exeunt*

4.2

Enter Sir John FALSTAFF *and* MISTRESS FORD

FALSTAFF   Mistress Ford, your sorrow hath eaten up my sufferance.[1] I see you are obsequious° in your love, and I profess   *devoted*
requital to a hair's breadth:° not only, Mistress Ford, in the   *in full*
simple office of love, but in all the accoutrement, complement,
5   and ceremony of it. But are you sure of your husband now?

MISTRESS FORD   He's a-birding, sweet Sir John.

MISTRESS PAGE [*within*]   What ho, gossip° Ford, what ho!   *friend*

MISTRESS FORD   Step into th' chamber, Sir John.

He steps [*into the chamber*]

Enter MISTRESS PAGE

MISTRESS PAGE   How now, sweetheart, who's at home besides
10   yourself?

MISTRESS FORD   Why, none but mine own people.°   *servants*

MISTRESS PAGE   Indeed?

MISTRESS FORD   No, certainly. [*Aside to her*] Speak louder.

MISTRESS PAGE   Truly, I am so glad you have nobody here.

15 MISTRESS FORD   Why?

MISTRESS PAGE   Why, woman, your husband is in his old lines°   *role*
again. He so takes on° yonder with my husband, so rails against   *raves*
all married mankind, so curses all Eve's daughters° of what   *women*
complexion° soever, and so buffets himself on the forehead,   *temperament*
20   crying 'Peer out,[2] peer out!', that any madness I ever yet beheld
seemed but tameness, civility, and patience to this his distemper he is in now. I am glad the fat knight is not here.

MISTRESS FORD   Why, does he talk of him?

MISTRESS PAGE   Of none but him; and swears he was carried out,
25   the last time he searched for him, in a basket, protests to my
husband he is now here, and hath drawn him and the rest of
their company from their sport to make another experiment° of   *trial*
his suspicion. But I am glad the knight is not here. Now he
shall see his own foolery.

---

8. Possibly pronounced as "keys, case, cods," with "keys"
a euphemism for "penis," "case" a term for "vagina," and
"cods" slang for "testicles."
4.2 Location: Ford's house.

1. Your sorrow has made the memory of my suffering disappear.
2. Emerge (addressed to imagined cuckold's horns).

30   MISTRESS FORD   How near is he, Mistress Page?

MISTRESS PAGE   Hard by at street end. He will be here anon.

MISTRESS FORD   I am undone: the knight is here.

MISTRESS PAGE   Why then, you are utterly shamed, and he's but
a dead man. What a woman are you! Away with him, away
35   with him! Better shame than murder.

MISTRESS FORD   Which way should he go? How should I bestow°   dispose of
him? Shall I put him into the basket again?
     [FALSTAFF comes forth from the chamber]

FALSTAFF   No, I'll come no more i'th' basket. May I not go out
ere he come?

40   MISTRESS PAGE   Alas, three of Master Ford's brothers watch the
door with pistols, that none shall issue out. Otherwise you
might slip away ere he came. But what make you° here?   are you doing

FALSTAFF   What shall I do? I'll creep up into the chimney.

MISTRESS FORD   There they always use to discharge their birding-
45   pieces.°   bird guns

MISTRESS PAGE   Creep into the kiln-hole.°   oven

FALSTAFF   Where is it?

MISTRESS FORD   He will seek there, on my word. Neither press,°   cupboard
coffer, chest, trunk, well, vault, but he hath an abstract° for the   a list
50   remembrance of such places, and goes to them by his note.
There is no hiding you in the house.

FALSTAFF   I'll go out, then.

MISTRESS PAGE   If you go out in your own semblance, you die,
Sir John—unless you go out disguised.

55   MISTRESS FORD   How might we disguise him?

MISTRESS PAGE   Alas the day, I know not. There is no woman's
gown big enough for him; otherwise he might put on a hat, a
muffler,° and a kerchief, and so escape.   face scarf

FALSTAFF   Good hearts, devise something. Any extremity° rather   extravagance
60   than a mischief.°   calamity

MISTRESS FORD   My maid's aunt, the fat woman of Brentford,³
has a gown above.

MISTRESS PAGE   On my word, it will serve him; she's as big as he
is; and there's her thrummed° hat, and her muffler too.—Run   fringed
65   up, Sir John.

MISTRESS FORD   Go, go, sweet Sir John. Mistress Page and I will
look° some linen for your head.   look for

MISTRESS PAGE   Quick, quick! We'll come dress you straight.
Put on the gown the while.   Exit Sir John [FALSTAFF]

70   MISTRESS FORD   I would my husband would meet him in this
shape. He cannot abide the old woman of Brentford. He swears
she's a witch, forbade her my house, and hath threatened to
beat her.

MISTRESS PAGE   Heaven guide him to thy husband's cudgel, and
75   the devil guide his cudgel afterwards!

MISTRESS FORD   But is my husband coming?

MISTRESS PAGE   Ay, in good sadness° is he, and talks of the basket   in all seriousness
too, howsoever⁴ he hath had intelligence.°   information

MISTRESS FORD   We'll try° that, for I'll appoint my men to carry   test

---

3. Gillian of Brentford, a scurrilous comic figure, perhaps historically based, best known for her will, in which
she supposedly "bequeathed a score of farts amongst her
friends." Brentford was a village halfway between Windsor and London.
4. By whatever means.

80   the basket again, to meet him at the door with it as they did
       last time.

    MISTRESS PAGE   Nay, but he'll be here presently. Let's go dress
       him like the witch of Brentford.

    MISTRESS FORD   I'll first direct my men what they shall do with
85   the basket. Go up; I'll bring linen for him straight.°   *immediately*

    MISTRESS PAGE   Hang him, dishonest° varlet! We cannot misuse   *lewd*
       him enough.   [*Exit* MISTRESS FORD]
       We'll leave a proof by that which we will do,
       Wives may be merry, and yet honest,° too.   *chaste*
90   We do not act that° often jest and laugh.   *misbehave who*
       'Tis old but true: 'Still swine eats all the draff'.⁵   *Exit*
           Enter MISTRESS FORD [*with* JOHN *and* ROBERT]

    MISTRESS FORD   Go, sirs, take the basket again on your shoulders.
       Your master is hard at° door. If he bid you set it down, obey   *close to the*
       him. Quickly, dispatch!   [*Exit*]
95   JOHN   Come, come, take it up.

    ROBERT   Pray heaven it be not full of knight again.

    JOHN   I hope not; I had as lief ° bear so much lead.   *I would rather*
        [*They lift*] *the basket.*
        Enter [*Master*] FORD, [*Master*] PAGE, [*Doctor*] CAIUS,
        [*Sir Hugh*] EVANS, *and* [*Justice*] SHALLOW

    FORD   Ay, but if it prove true, Master Page, have you any way
       then to unfool me again?⁶ [*To* JOHN *and* ROBERT] Set down
100   the basket, villains.
        [JOHN *and* ROBERT *set down the basket*]
       Somebody call my wife. Youth in a basket!° O, you panderly   *Fortunate lover?*
       rascals! There's a knot,° a gang, a pack, a conspiracy against   *group*
       me. Now shall the devil be shamed.°—What, wife, I say!   *truth be known*
       Come, come forth! Behold what honest clothes you send forth
105   to bleaching.

    PAGE   Why, this passes,° Master Ford. You are not to go loose   *goes beyond all bounds*
       any longer; you must be pinioned.

    EVANS   Why, this is lunatics; this is mad as a mad dog.

    SHALLOW   Indeed, Master Ford, this is not well, indeed.
110   FORD   So say I too, sir.
        [*Enter* MISTRESS FORD]
       Come hither, Mistress Ford! Mistress Ford, the honest woman,
       the modest wife, the virtuous creature, that hath the jealous
       fool to° her husband! I suspect without cause, mistress, do I?   *for*

    MISTRESS FORD   God be my witness you do, if you suspect me in
115   any dishonesty.

    FORD   Well said, brazen-face; hold it out.°   *keep it up*
        [*He opens the basket and starts to take out clothes*]
       Come forth, sirrah!

    PAGE   This passes.

    MISTRESS FORD [*to* FORD]   Are you not ashamed? Let the clothes
120   alone.

    FORD   I shall find you anon.

    EVANS   'Tis unreasonable: will you take up your wife's clothes?
       Come, away.

---

5. Proverbial: "The quiet swine eats all the hog's wash."   6. Page has evidently accused Ford of making a fool of
In other words, quietness conceals sexual immorality   himself.
(whereas playfulness is innocent; see line 90).

FORD [*to* JOHN *and* ROBERT]   Empty the basket, I say.

125 PAGE   Why, man, why?

FORD   Master Page, as I am a man, there was one conveyed out
of my house yesterday in this basket. Why may not he be there
again? In my house I am sure he is. My intelligence° is true,   *information*
my jealousy is reasonable. [*To* JOHN *and* ROBERT] Pluck me
130 out all the linen.

                [*He takes out clothes*]

MISTRESS FORD   If you find a man there, he shall die a flea's
death.[7]

PAGE   Here's no man.

SHALLOW   By my fidelity, this is not well, Master Ford. This
135 wrongs you.°   *You shame yourself*

EVANS   Master Ford, you must pray, and not follow the imaginations of your own heart. This is jealousies.

FORD   Well, he's not here I seek for.

PAGE   No, nor nowhere else but in your brain.

140 FORD   Help to search my house this one time. If I find not what
I seek, show no colour° for my extremity;° let me for ever be   *excuse / excesses*
your table-sport;° let them say of me, 'As jealous as Ford, that   *laughingstock*
searched a hollow walnut for his wife's leman'.° Satisfy me   *lover*
once more; once more search with me.

                [*Exeunt* JOHN *and* ROBERT *with the basket*]

145 MISTRESS FORD   What ho, Mistress Page! Come you and the old
woman down. My husband will come into the chamber.

FORD   Old woman? What old woman's that?

MISTRESS FORD   Why, it is my maid's Aunt of Brentford.

FORD   A witch, a quean, an old, cozening quean!° Have I not   *cheating hussy*
150 forbid her my house? She comes of errands, does she? We are
simple men; we do not know what's brought to pass under the
profession° of fortune-telling. She works by charms, by spells,   *claim*
by th' figure,[8] and such daubery° as this is, beyond our ele-   *trickery*
ment.° We know nothing.—Come down, you witch, you hag,   *knowledge*
155 you! Come down, I say!

                Enter MISTRESS PAGE, *and* FALSTAFF, *disguised like an*
                old woman.

                [FORD *makes towards them*]

MISTRESS FORD   Nay, good sweet husband!—Good gentlemen,
let him not strike the old woman.

MISTRESS PAGE [*to* FALSTAFF]   Come, Mother Prat.° Come, give   *Buttocks*
me your hand.

160 FORD   I'll prat° her!   *beat; trick*

            FORD *beats* [FALSTAFF]

Out of my door, you witch, you rag, you baggage, you polecat,
you runnion!° Out, out! I'll conjure you, I'll fortune-tell you!   *contemptible woman*

                        [*Exit* FALSTAFF]

MISTRESS PAGE   Are you not ashamed? I think you have killed
the poor woman.

165 MISTRESS FORD   Nay, he will do it.—'Tis a goodly credit for you!

FORD   Hang her, witch!

EVANS   By Jeshu, I think the 'oman is a witch indeed. I like not

---

7. Anyone hiding there must be insignificantly small
and used to living in clothes.

8. Astrological or magical diagrams, or wax effigies used
by witches.

when a 'oman has a great peard. I spy a great peard under his
muffler.

170 FORD   Will you follow, gentlemen? I beseech you, follow. See
but the issue° of my jealousy. If I cry out° thus upon no trail,   *outcome / bark*
never trust me when I open° again.   *start barking*

PAGE   Let's obey his humour° a little further. Come, gentlemen.   *indulge him*
                                         Exeunt [the men]

MISTRESS PAGE   By my troth, he beat him most pitifully.

175 MISTRESS FORD   Nay, by th' mass, that he did not—he beat him
most unpitifully, methought.

MISTRESS PAGE   I'll have the cudgel hallowed and hung o'er the
altar. It hath done meritorious service.

MISTRESS FORD   What think you—may we, with the warrant of
180 womanhood and the witness of a good conscience, pursue
him with any further revenge?

MISTRESS PAGE   The spirit of wantonness is sure scared out of
him. If the devil have him not in fee-simple, with fine and
recovery, he will never, I think, in the way of waste attempt us
185 again.[9]

MISTRESS FORD   Shall we tell our husbands how we have served
him?

MISTRESS PAGE   Yes, by all means, if it be but to scrape the fig-
ures° out of your husband's brains. If they can find in their   *fantasies*
190 hearts the poor, unvirtuous, fat knight shall be any further
afflicted, we two will still be the ministers.

MISTRESS FORD   I'll warrant they'll have him publicly shamed,
and methinks there would be no period° to the jest should he   *conclusion*
not be publicly shamed.

195 MISTRESS PAGE   Come, to the forge with it, then shape it. I would
not have things cool.   *Exeunt*

4.3

Enter [the] HOST *[of the Garter] and* BARDOLPH

BARDOLPH   Sir, the Germans desire to have three of your horses.
The Duke himself will be tomorrow at court, and they° are   *(the Germans)*
going to meet him.

HOST   What duke should that be comes° so secretly? I hear not   *who comes*
5 of him in the court. Let me speak with the gentlemen. They
speak English?

BARDOLPH   Ay, sir. I'll call them to you.

HOST   They shall have my horses, but I'll make them pay; I'll
sauce them.° They have had my house a week at command;[1]   *make them pay dearly*
10 I have turned away my other guests. They must come off.° I'll   *pay up*
sauce them. Come.[2]   *Exeunt*

---

9. Legal terms: If the devil doesn't absolutely own him,
he won't try to despoil us again.
4.3 Location: The Garter Inn.
1. They have had my inn at their disposal for a week.
2. The German Duke is fiction, part of a plot whereby
Caius and Evans revenge themselves on the Host. The

exact details are obscure. A scene or more may have been
censored in which Caius and Evans, or some other characters, disguised themselves as Germans and duped the
Host. Evidently Sir John also parts with his horses: see
5.5.110–11 and 2.1.84–85.

4.4

Enter [Master] PAGE, *[Master]* FORD, MISTRESS PAGE,
MISTRESS FORD, *and Sir Hugh* EVANS

EVANS   'Tis one of the best discretions of a 'oman¹ as ever I did
    look upon.

PAGE   And did he send you both these letters at an instant?°   *at the same time*

MISTRESS PAGE   Within a quarter of an hour.

5 FORD   Pardon me, wife. Henceforth do what thou wilt.

    I rather will suspect the sun with° cold   *of*

    Than thee with wantonness. Now doth thy honour stand,

    In him that was of late an heretic,

    As firm as faith.

PAGE   'Tis well, 'tis well; no more.

10   Be not as extreme in submission

    As in offence.

    But let our plot go forward. Let our wives

    Yet once again, to make us public sport,

    Appoint a meeting with this old fat fellow,

15   Where we may take him and disgrace him for it.

FORD   There is no better way than that they spoke of.

PAGE   How, to send him word they'll meet him in the Park

    At midnight? Fie, fie, he'll never come.

EVANS   You say he has been thrown in the rivers, and has been

20   grievously peaten as an old 'oman. Methinks there should be

    terrors in him, that he should not come. Methinks his flesh is

    punished; he shall have no desires.

PAGE   So think I too.

MISTRESS FORD   Devise but how you'll use° him when he comes,   *treat*

25   And let us two devise to bring him thither.

MISTRESS PAGE   There is an old tale goes that Herne the hunter,

    Sometime° a keeper here in Windsor Forest,   *Once*

    Doth all the winter time at still midnight

    Walk round about an oak with great ragg'd° horns;   *jagged*

30   And there he blasts° the trees, and takes° the cattle,   *blights / bewitches*

    And makes milch-kine° yield blood, and shakes a chain   *dairy cattle*

    In a most hideous and dreadful manner.

    You have heard of such a spirit, and well you know

    The superstitious idle-headed eld°   *people of olden times*

35   Received, and did deliver to our age,

    This tale of Herne the hunter for a truth.

PAGE   Why, yet there want not° many that do fear   *are*

    In deep of night to walk by this Herne's Oak.

    But what of this?

MISTRESS FORD   Marry, this is our device:

40   That Falstaff at that oak shall meet with us,

    Disguised like Herne, with huge horns on his head.

PAGE   Well, let it not be doubted but he'll come,

    And in this shape. When you have brought him thither

    What shall be done with him? What is your plot?

45 MISTRESS PAGE   That likewise have we thought upon, and thus.

    Nan Page my daughter, and my little son,

    And three or four more of their growth,° we'll dress   *size*

    Like urchins,° oafs,° and fairies, green and white,   *goblins / elf children*

4.4 Location: Ford's house.   1. Mistress Page is one of the most discreet women.

|50| With rounds of waxen tapers° on their heads, | *crowns of candles* |

50   With rounds of waxen tapers° on their heads, *crowns of candles*
  And rattles in their hands. Upon a sudden,
  As Falstaff, she, and I are newly met,
  Let them from forth a saw-pit² rush at once,
  With some diffusèd° song. Upon their sight *disordered*
  We two in great amazèdness will fly.
55 Then let them all encircle him about,
  And, fairy-like, to pinch the unclean knight,
  And ask him why, that hour of fairy revel,
  In their so sacred paths he dares to tread
  In shape profane.
MISTRESS FORD   And till he tell the truth,
60 Let the supposèd fairies pinch him sound,° *soundly*
  And burn him with their tapers.
MISTRESS PAGE   The truth being known,
  We'll all present ourselves, dis-horn the spirit,
  And mock him home to Windsor.
FORD   The children must
  Be practised well to this, or they'll ne'er do't.
65 EVANS I will teach the children their behaviours, and I will be
  like a jackanapes° also, to burn the knight with my taber. *monkey; evil spirit*
  FORD That will be excellent. I'll go buy them vizors.° *masks*
  MISTRESS PAGE My Nan shall be the Queen of all the Fairies,
  Finely attirèd in a robe of white.
70 PAGE That silk³ will I go buy—[*aside*] and in that tire° *attire*
  Shall Master Slender steal my Nan away,
  And marry her at Eton.⁴ [*To* MISTRESS PAGE] Go send to Fal-
  staff straight.
FORD Nay, I'll to him again in name of Brooke.
  He'll tell me all his purpose. Sure he'll come.
75 MISTRESS PAGE Fear not you that. [*To* PAGE, FORD, *and* EVANS]
  Go get us properties° *props*
  And tricking° for our fairies. *costumes*
EVANS Let us about it. It is admirable pleasures, and fery honest
  knaveries.   [*Exeunt* FORD, PAGE, *and* EVANS]
MISTRESS PAGE Go, Mistress Ford,
80 Send quickly to Sir John, to know his mind.
           [*Exit* MISTRESS FORD]
  I'll to the Doctor. He hath my good will,
  And none but he, to marry with Nan Page.
  That Slender, though well landed,° is an idiot; *owning much land*
  And he° my husband best of all affects.° *him / likes most*
85 The Doctor is well moneyed, and his friends
  Potent at court. He, none but he, shall have her,
  Though twenty thousand worthier come to crave her. *Exit*

4.5
Enter [the] HOST [*of the Garter*] *and* SIMPLE
HOST What wouldst thou have, boor? What, thick-skin?° Speak, *dullard*
  breathe, discuss. Brief, short, quick, snap.
SIMPLE Marry, sir, I come to speak with Sir John Falstaff, from
  Master Slender.

2. A pit over which wood was sawed.   4. Across the Thames from Windsor.
3. A sign of Page's financial means.   4.5 Location: The Garter Inn.

5   HOST   There's his chamber, his house, his castle, his standing-
        bed and truckle-bed.[1] 'Tis[2] painted about with the story of the
        Prodigal,° fresh and new. Go knock and call. He'll speak like   *prodigal son (Luke 15)*
        an Anthropophaginian° unto thee. Knock, I say.   *cannibal*

   SIMPLE   There's an old woman, a fat woman, gone up into his
10   chamber. I'll be so bold as stay, sir, till she come down. I come
        to speak with her, indeed.

   HOST   Ha, a fat woman? The knight may be robbed. I'll call.—
        Bully knight, bully Sir John! Speak from thy lungs military! Art
        thou there? It is thine Host, thine Ephesian,° calls.   *mate*

15 FALSTAFF [*within*]   How now, mine Host?

   HOST   Here's a Bohemian Tartar tarries° the coming down of thy   *Here a savage awaits*
        fat woman. Let her descend, bully, let her descend. My cham-
        bers are honourable. Fie, privacy!° Fie!   *secret goings-on*

        Enter Sir John FALSTAFF

   FALSTAFF   There was, mine Host, an old fat woman even now
20   with me; but she's gone.

   SIMPLE   Pray you, sir, was't not the wise woman° of Brentford?   *woman skilled in magic*

   FALSTAFF   Ay, marry was it, mussel-shell.° What would you with   *empty head? gaper?*
        her?

   SIMPLE   My master, sir, my master Slender, sent to her, seeing
25   her go through the streets, to know, sir, whether one Nim, sir,
        that beguiled° him of a chain, had the chain or no.   *cheated*

   FALSTAFF   I spake with the old woman about it.

   SIMPLE   And what says she, I pray, sir?

   FALSTAFF   Marry, she says that the very same man that beguiled
30   Master Slender of his chain cozened° him of it.   *tricked*

   SIMPLE   I would I could have spoken with the woman herself. I
        had other things to have spoken with her, too, from him.

   FALSTAFF   What are they? Let us know.

   HOST   Ay, come, quick.

35 SIMPLE   I may not conceal° them, sir.   *(for "reveal")*

   HOST   Conceal them, or thou diest.

   SIMPLE   Why, sir, they were nothing but about Mistress Anne
        Page, to know if it were my master's fortune to have her or no.

   FALSTAFF   'Tis, 'tis his fortune.

40 SIMPLE   What, sir?

   FALSTAFF   To have her or no. Go say the woman told me so.

   SIMPLE   May I be bold to say so, sir?

   FALSTAFF   Ay, Sir Tike;° who more bold?   *cur*

   SIMPLE   I thank your worship. I shall make my master glad with
45   these tidings.   *[Exit]*

   HOST   Thou art clerkly,° thou art clerkly, Sir John. Was there a   *learned*
        wise woman with thee?

   FALSTAFF   Ay, that there was, mine Host, one that hath taught
        me more wit than ever I learned before in my life. And I paid
50   nothing for it, neither, but was paid° for my learning.   *thrashed*

        Enter BARDOLPH [*muddy*]

   BARDOLPH   O Lord, sir, cozenage, mere° cozenage!   *utter*

   HOST   Where be my horses? Speak well of them, varletto.°   *varlet*

   BARDOLPH   Run away with the cozeners. For so soon as I came
        beyond Eton, they threw me off from behind one of them, in a

---

1. Trundle bed, which could be stored under the larger   2. The "it" in "'Tis" refers to either the wall hanging or
standing bed.   the bed hanging.

55   slough of mire, and set spurs and away, like three German
       devils, three Doctor Faustuses.³
    HOST   They are gone but to meet the Duke, villain. Do not say
       they be fled. Germans are honest men.

           Enter Sir Hugh EVANS

    EVANS   Where is mine Host?
60   HOST   What is the matter, sir?
    EVANS   Have a care of your entertainments.° There is a friend   *guests*
       of mine come to town tells me there is three cozen° Garmom-   *related; cheating*
       bles⁴ that has cozened all the hosts of Reading, of Maidenhead,
       of Colnbrook,° of horses and money. I tell you for good will,   *nearby villages*
65   look you. You are wise, and full of gibes and vlouting-stocks,°   *laughingstocks*
       and 'tis not convenient° you should be cozened. Fare you well.   *appropriate*

                                 Exit

       Enter Doctor CAIUS

    CAIUS   Vere is mine Host de Jarteer?
    HOST   Here, Master Doctor, in perplexity and doubtful dilemma.
    CAIUS   I cannot tell vat is dat, but it is tell-a me dat you make
70   grand preparation for a duke de Jamany.° By my trot,° der is no   *Germany/troth*
       duke that the court is know to come. I tell you for good will.
       Adieu.   *Exit*

    HOST [*to* BARDOLPH]   Hue and cry,° villain, go! [*To* FALSTAFF]   *Raise the alarm*
       Assist me, knight. I am undone. [*To* BARDOLPH] Fly, run, hue
75   and cry, villain. I am undone.

         Exeunt HOST *and* BARDOLPH [*severally*]°   *separately*

    FALSTAFF   I would all the world might be cozened, for I have
       been cozened, and beaten too. If it should come to the ear of
       the court how I have been transformed, and how my transfor-
       mation hath been washed and cudgelled, they would melt me
80   out of my fat, drop by drop, and liquor° fishermen's boots with   *grease*
       me. I warrant they would whip me with their fine wits till I
       were as crestfallen° as a dried pear. I never prospered since I   *shriveled*
       forswore myself at primero.° Well, if my wind were but long   *cards*
       enough,° I would repent.   *(to list all my sins)*

          Enter MISTRESS QUICKLY

85   Now; whence come you?
    MISTRESS QUICKLY   From the two parties, forsooth.
    FALSTAFF   The devil take one party, and his dam° the other, and   *mother*
       so they shall be both bestowed. I have suffered more for their
       sakes, more than the villainous inconstancy of man's disposi-
90   tion is able to bear.
    MISTRESS QUICKLY   O Lord, sir, and have not they suffered? Yes,
       I warrant, speciously° one of them. Mistress Ford, good heart,   *(for "specially")*
       is beaten black and blue, that you cannot see a white spot about
       her.
95   FALSTAFF   What tellest thou me of black and blue? I was beaten
       myself into all the colours of the rainbow, and I was like to be
       apprehended for the witch of Brentford. But that my admirable
       dexterity of wit, my counterfeiting the action of an old woman,

---

3. Bardolph alludes to Marlowe's *Doctor Faustus*, whose
titular hero makes a pact with the devil. In one scene,
three devils are conjured to "horse" Benvolio, Frederick,
and Martino on their backs and throw them in "some lake
of mud and dirt" (13.79–85). In the following scene, the

three appear muddy and, anticipating Falstaff's punishment, with horns on their heads.
4. Probably an anagram of "Mömpelgard," the name of a
German count who aspired to—and was elected to—the
Order of the Garter and whom Shakespeare here satirizes.

delivered me, the knave constable had set me i'th' stocks, i'th'
100   common stocks, for a witch.

MISTRESS QUICKLY   Sir, let me speak with you in your chamber.
You shall hear how things go, and, I warrant, to your content.
Here is a letter will say somewhat. Good hearts, what ado here
is to bring you together! Sure one of you does not serve heaven
105   well, that you are so crossed.°   *thwarted*

FALSTAFF   Come up into my chamber.   *Exeunt*

4.6

Enter [Master] FENTON *and [the]* HOST *[of the Garter]*

HOST   Master Fenton, talk not to me. My mind is heavy. I will
give over° all.   *give up*

FENTON   Yet hear me speak. Assist me in my purpose,
And, as I am a gentleman, I'll give thee
5   A hundred pound in gold more than your loss.

HOST   I will hear you, Master Fenton, and I will at the least keep
your counsel.°   *secret*

FENTON   From time to time I have acquainted you
With the dear love I bear to fair Anne Page,
10   Who mutually hath answered my affection,
So far forth as herself might be her chooser,[1]
Even to my wish. I have a letter from her
Of such contents as you will wonder at,
The mirth whereof so larded with my matter°   *mixed with my concern*
15   That neither singly can be manifested
Without the show of both. Fat Falstaff
Hath a great scene. The image° of the jest   *idea*
I'll show you here at large. Hark, good mine Host.
Tonight at Herne's Oak, just 'twixt twelve and one,
20   Must my sweet Nan present° the Fairy Queen—   *play the part of*
    [*Showing the letter*]
The purpose why is here—in which disguise,
While other jests are something rank on foot,°   *somewhat thick afoot*
Her father hath commanded her to slip
Away with Slender, and with him at Eton
25   Immediately to marry. She hath consented.
Now, sir, her mother, ever strong against that match
And firm for Doctor Caius, hath appointed
That he shall likewise shuffle her away,
While other sports are tasking of° their minds,   *engaging*
30   And at the dean'ry,[2] where a priest attends,
Straight marry her. To this her mother's plot
She, seemingly obedient, likewise hath
Made promise to the Doctor. Now, thus it rests.°   *things stand thus*
Her father means she shall be all in white;
35   And in that habit,° when Slender sees his time   *dress*
To take her by the hand and bid her go,
She shall go with him. Her mother hath intended,
The better to denote her to the Doctor—
For they must all be masked and visorèd—
40   That quaint° in green she shall be loose enrobed,   *elegantly*

4.6 Location: Scene continues.
1. Insofar as she might choose her own husband.
2. Residence of the dean (the head of the clergy on the staff of certain churches); (loosely) a parsonage. Here Fenton refers to the deanery attached to St. George's Chapel on the property of Windsor Castle.

With ribbons pendant flaring° 'bout her head;   *waving down*
And when the Doctor spies his vantage ripe,
To pinch her by the hand, and on that token
The maid hath given consent to go with him.

45 HOST   Which means she to deceive, father or mother?

FENTON   Both, my good Host, to go along with me.
And here it rests: that you'll procure the vicar
To stay for me at church 'twixt twelve and one,
And, in the lawful name of ° marrying,   *name of lawful*

50 To give our hearts united ceremony.

HOST   Well, husband° your device. I'll to the vicar.   *manage well; (pun)*
Bring you the maid, you shall not lack a priest.

FENTON   So shall I evermore be bound to thee.
Besides, I'll make a present° recompense.   *Exeunt* [*severally*]   *immediate*

5.1

Enter FALSTAFF *and* [MISTRESS] QUICKLY

FALSTAFF   Prithee, no more prattling; go; I'll hold.° This is the   *keep the appointment*
third time; I hope good luck lies in odd numbers. Away, go!
They say there is divinity° in odd numbers, either in nativity,   *divine power*
chance, or death. Away!

5 MISTRESS QUICKLY   I'll provide you a chain, and I'll do what I
can to get you a pair of horns.

FALSTAFF   Away, I say! Time wears.° Hold up your head, and   *passes*
mince.°   [*Exit* MISTRESS QUICKLY]   *walk affectedly*

Enter [*Master*] FORD [*disguised as Brooke*]

How now, Master Brooke? Master Brooke, the matter will be
10 known tonight or never. Be you in the Park about midnight at
Herne's Oak, and you shall see wonders.

FORD   Went you not to her yesterday, sir, as you told me you had
appointed?

FALSTAFF   I went to her, Master Brooke, as you see,° like a poor   *as I am now*
15 old man; but I came from her, Master Brooke, like a poor old
woman. That same knave Ford, her husband, hath the finest
mad devil of jealousy in him, Master Brooke, that ever governed frenzy. I will tell you, he beat me grievously in the shape
of a woman—for in the shape of man, Master Brooke, I fear
20 not Goliath with a weaver's beam,¹ because I know also life is
a shuttle.² I am in haste. Go along with me; I'll tell you all,
Master Brooke. Since I plucked geese,° played truant, and   *(child's prank)*
whipped top,° I knew not what 'twas to be beaten till lately.   *spun a top*
Follow me. I'll tell you strange things of this knave Ford, on
25 whom tonight I will be revenged, and I will deliver his wife
into your hand. Follow. Strange things in hand, Master Brooke.
Follow.   *Exeunt*

5.2

Enter [*Master*] PAGE, [*Justice*] SHALLOW, [*and Master*]
SLENDER

PAGE   Come, come, we'll couch° i'th' Castle ditch till we see the   *lie*
light of our fairies. Remember, son Slender, my daughter.

SLENDER   Ay, forsooth. I have spoke with her, and we have a nay-

---

5.1 Location: The Garter Inn.
1. The biblical simile for Goliath's spear handle (1 Samuel 17:7).

2. From Job 7:6: "My days are swifter than a weaver's
shuttle."
5.2 Location: An approach to Windsor Park.

word° how to know one another. I come to her in white and   *password*
5   cry 'mum'; she cries 'budget';° and by that we know one   *mumbudget (silence)*
another.

SHALLOW   That's good, too. But what needs either your 'mum'
or her 'budget'? The white will decipher her well enough. [*To*
PAGE] It hath struck ten o'clock.
10 PAGE   The night is dark; lights and spirits will become it well.
God prosper our sport! No man means evil but the devil, and
we shall know him by his horns. Let's away. Follow me.

Exeunt

5.3

Enter MISTRESS PAGE, MISTRESS FORD, [*and Doctor*]
    CAIUS

MISTRESS PAGE   Master Doctor, my daughter is in green. When
you see your time, take her by the hand, away with her to the
deanery, and dispatch it quickly. Go before into the Park. We
two must go together.
5 CAIUS   I know vat I have to do. Adieu.
MISTRESS PAGE   Fare you well, sir.   [*Exit* CAIUS]
My husband will not rejoice so much at the abuse of Falstaff
as he will chafe at the doctor's marrying my daughter. But 'tis
no matter. Better a little chiding than a great deal of heartbreak.
10 MISTRESS FORD   Where is Nan now, and her troop of fairies, and
the Welsh devil Hugh?
MISTRESS PAGE   They are all couched in a pit hard by Herne's
Oak, with obscured lights, which, at the very instant of Falstaff's and our meeting, they will at once display to the night.
15 MISTRESS FORD   That cannot choose but amaze° him.   *That is bound to frighten*
MISTRESS PAGE   If he be not amazed, he will be mocked. If he
be amazed, he will every way be mocked.
MISTRESS FORD   We'll betray him finely.
MISTRESS PAGE   Against such lewdsters and their lechery
20 Those that betray them do no treachery.
MISTRESS FORD   The hour draws on. To the Oak, to the Oak!

Exeunt

5.4

Enter Sir Hugh EVANS [*disguised as a satyr*] *and* [WIL-
LIAM *Page and other children, disguised as*] *fairies*

EVANS   Trib,° trib, fairies! Come! And remember your parts. Be   *Trip*
pold, I pray you. Follow me into the pit, and when I give the
watch'ords, do as I pid you. Come, come; trib, trib!   *Exeunt*

5.5

Enter Sir John FALSTAFF [*disguised as Herne, with horns
on his head, and bearing a chain*]

FALSTAFF   The Windsor bell hath struck twelve; the minute
draws on. Now the hot-blooded gods assist me! Remember,
Jove, thou wast a bull for thy Europa;[1] love set on thy horns. O
powerful love, that in some respects makes a beast a man; in
5 some other, a man a beast! You were also, Jupiter, a swan, for

---

5.3 Location: Scene continues.
5.4 Location: Scene continues.
5.5 Location: Windsor Park.

1. In classical mythology, Jupiter turned himself into a
bull and abducted Europa by swimming across the sea
with her on his back.

the love of Leda.[2] O omnipotent love! How near the god drew
to the complexion of a goose! A fault done first in the form of
a beast—O Jove, a beastly fault!—and then another fault in the
semblance of a fowl—think on't, Jove, a foul fault! When gods
10 have hot° backs, what shall poor men do? For me, I am here a   *lustful*
Windsor stag, and the fattest, I think, i'th' forest. Send me a
cool rut-time,° Jove, or who can blame me to piss my tallow?[3]   *mating season*

Enter MISTRESS FORD [*followed by*] MISTRESS PAGE

Who comes here? My doe!

MISTRESS FORD Sir John! Art thou there, my deer,° my male   *(pun on "dear")*
15 deer?

FALSTAFF My doe with the black scut!° Let the sky rain potatoes,   *tail; pubic hair*
let it thunder to the tune of 'Greensleeves',° hail kissing-   *popular love song*
comfits, and snow eringoes;[4] let there come a tempest of provo-
cation,° I will shelter me here.   *sexual incitement*

[*He embraces her*]

20 MISTRESS FORD Mistress Page is come with me, sweetheart.

FALSTAFF Divide me like a bribed° buck, each a haunch. I will   *stolen*
keep my sides to myself, my shoulders for the fellow° of this   *keeper*
walk,° and my horns° I bequeath your husbands. Am I a wood-   *forest / (of a cuckold)*
man,° ha? Speak I like Herne the hunter? Why, now is Cupid   *hunter; womanizer*
25 a child of conscience; he makes restitution.° As I am a true   *repays my suffering*
spirit, welcome!

A noise [*within*]

MISTRESS PAGE Alas, what noise?

MISTRESS FORD God forgive our sins!

FALSTAFF What should this be?

30 MISTRESS FORD *and* MISTRESS PAGE Away, away!

[*Exeunt* MISTRESS FORD *and* MISTRESS PAGE, *running*]

FALSTAFF I think the devil will not have me damned, lest the oil
that's in me should set hell on fire. He would never else cross
me thus.

Enter Sir Hugh EVANS, [WILLIAM *Page, and children, dis-*
guised as fairies with tapers;] MISTRESS QUICKLY, [*dis-*
guised] *as the Fairy Queen;* ANNE *Page* [*disguised as a*
fairy; and one disguised as Hobgoblin][5]

MISTRESS QUICKLY Fairies black, grey, green, and white,
35 You moonshine revellers, and shades° of night,   *spirits*
You orphan heirs of fixèd destiny,[6]
Attend° your office° and your quality.°—   *Perform/duty/calling*
Crier° hobgoblin, make the fairy oyes.°   *Town crier/hear ye*

HOBGOBLIN Elves, list° your names. Silence, you airy toys.°   *listen for/trifles*
40 Cricket,° to Windsor chimneys shalt thou leap.   *(elf's name)*
Where fires thou find'st unraked° and hearths unswept,   *(hence, likely to die)*
There pinch the maids as blue as bilberry.°   *blueberry*
Our radiant Queen hates sluts and sluttery.°   *dirtiness*

FALSTAFF [*aside*] They are fairies. He that speaks to them shall die.
45 I'll wink° and couch;° no man their works must eye.   *shut my eyes/lie down*

---

2. Jupiter turned himself into a swan in order to rape
Leda.
3. If I urinate or sweat away my fat (as stags were
thought to do at rutting time).
4. Candied roots of sea holly that, like sweet "potatoes"
(line 16), were considered an aphrodisiac. *kissing-*
comfits: breath sweeteners ("comfits" are candies).
5. Anne, who was assigned the part of the Fairy Queen

at 4.4.68, is here replaced by Quickly, either as part of
the marital scheming or simply as an indication that the
boy actor who played Quickly also is to play this role.
Similarly, Hobgoblin may have been played by Pistol or
simply by the actor who played Pistol.
6. You parentless inheritors of fixed duties (?). (Fairies
were supposed to be parentless.)

[*He lies down, and hides his face*]

EVANS Where's Bead? Go you, and, where you find a maid
That ere she sleep has thrice her prayers said,
Raise up° the organs of her fantasy,°   *Stimulate / imagination*
Sleep she[7] as sound as careless° infancy.   *carefree*
50   But those as° sleep and think not on their sins,   *who*
Pinch them, arms, legs, backs, shoulders, sides, and shins.
MISTRESS QUICKLY About,° about!   *To work*
Search Windsor Castle, elves, within and out.
Strew good luck, oafs,° on every sacred room,   *elves*
55   That it may stand till the perpetual doom°   *Judgment Day*
In state° as wholesome as in state° 'tis fit,   *condition / dignity*
Worthy° the owner, and the owner it.   *Worthy of*
The several chairs of order[8] look you scour
With juice of balm and every precious flower.
60   Each fair instalment,° coat,° and sev'ral crest[9]   *seat / coat of arms*
With loyal blazon[1] evermore be blessed;
And nightly, meadow-fairies, look you sing,
Like to the Garter's compass,° in a ring.   *circle*
Th'expressure° that it bears, green let it be,   *image*
65   More fertile-fresh than all the field to see;
And '*Honi soit qui mal y pense*'[2] write
In em'rald tufts, flowers purple, blue, and white,
Like sapphire, pearl, and rich embroidery,
Buckled below fair knighthood's bending knee—
70   Fairies use flowers for their charactery.°   *lettering*
Away, disperse!—But till 'tis one o'clock
Our dance of custom,° round about the oak   *customary dance*
Of Herne the hunter, let us not forget.
EVANS Pray you, lock hand in hand; yourselves in order set;
75   And twenty glow-worms shall our lanterns be
To guide our measure° round about the tree.—   *dance*
But stay; I smell a man of middle earth.°   *a mortal*
FALSTAFF [*aside*] God defend me from that Welsh fairy,
Lest he transform me to a piece of cheese!
80   HOBGOBLIN [*to* FALSTAFF] Vile worm, thou wast o'erlooked° even   *destined to evil*
in thy birth.
MISTRESS QUICKLY [*to fairies*] With trial-fire, touch me° his finger-end. *touch*
If he be chaste, the flame will back descend,
And turn him to no pain; but if he start,
It is the flesh of a corrupted heart.
HOBGOBLIN A trial, come!
85   EVANS   Come, will this wood° take fire?   *(Falstaff's fingers)*
          They [*burn* FALSTAFF *with*] *tapers*
FALSTAFF O, O, O!
MISTRESS QUICKLY Corrupt, corrupt, and tainted in desire.
About him, fairies; sing a scornful rhyme;
And, as you trip, still° pinch him to your time.   *continually*
          They [*dance around* FALSTAFF,] *pinch*[*ing*] *him and*
          sing[*ing*]:

7. Though she is sleeping; may she sleep.
8. The various stalls assigned, in St. George's Chapel, Windsor, to members of the Order of the Garter (a high dignity that the monarch conferred, marked by a garter worn below the knee).

9. Heraldic device on top of the helmet.
1. Together with the coat of arms on a banner.
2. Shame to him who thinks evil of it (the motto of the Order of the Garter).

FAIRIES

90 Fie on sinful fantasy!
Fie on lust and luxury!°   *lechery*
Lust is but a bloody fire,°   *fire of the blood*
Kindled with unchaste desire,
Fed in heart, whose flames aspire,°   *rise up*
95 As thoughts do blow them, higher and higher.
Pinch him, fairies, mutually.°   *all together*
Pinch him for his villainy.
Pinch him, and burn him, and turn him about,
Till candles and starlight and moonshine be out.

[During the song] Doctor CAIUS *comes one way and
steals away a boy in [green]; [enter]* SLENDER *another
way; he takes a boy in [white]; and* FENTON *steals* ANNE.
*[After the song] a noise of hunting within. [*MISTRESS
QUICKLY, EVANS, HOBGOBLIN, *and*] *fairies run away*. FAL-
STAFF *rises [and starts to run away]. Enter Master* PAGE,
Master FORD, *and their wives*

100 PAGE   Nay, do not fly. I think we have watched you° now.   *caught you in the act*
Will none but Herne the hunter serve your turn?
MISTRESS PAGE   I pray you, come, hold up° the jest no higher.°   *prolong / further*
Now, good Sir John, how like you Windsor wives?
[Pointing to Falstaff's horns]
See you these, husband? Do not these fair yokes°   *horns*
105 Become the forest better than the town?
FORD *[to* FALSTAFF*]*   Now, sir, who's a cuckold now? Master
Brooke, Falstaff's a knave, a cuckoldly knave. Here are his
horns, Master Brooke. And, Master Brooke, he hath enjoyed
nothing of Ford's but his buck-basket, his cudgel, and twenty
110 pounds of money which must be paid to Master Brooke; his
horses are arrested° for it,³ Master Brooke.   *seized as security*
MISTRESS FORD   Sir John, we have had ill luck. We could never
mate. I will never take you for my love again, but I will always
count you my deer.
115 FALSTAFF   I do begin to perceive that I am made an ass.
[He takes off the horns]
FORD   Ay, and an ox, too. Both the proofs are extant.⁴
FALSTAFF   And these are not fairies? By the Lord, I was three or
four times in the thought they were not fairies, and yet the
guiltiness of my mind, the sudden surprise of my powers,°   *mind*
120 drove the grossness of the foppery° into a received belief—in   *deceit*
despite of the teeth of° all rhyme and reason—that they were   *against*
fairies. See now how wit may be made a Jack-a-Lent° when 'tis   *butt*
upon ill employment!
EVANS   Sir John Falstaff, serve Got and leave your desires, and
125 fairies will not pinse you.
FORD   Well said, Fairy Hugh.
EVANS   And leave you your jealousies too, I pray you.
FORD   I will never mistrust my wife again till thou art able to
woo her in good English.
130 FALSTAFF   Have I laid my brain in the sun and dried it, that it
wants° matter to prevent so gross o'er-reaching as this? Am I   *lacks*

---

3. See note to 4.3.11.
4. "Ox" (fool, cuckold) is inspired by "yokes" (line 104).

The "proofs" are either the horns, which are "extant"
(existing), or the "ass" and the "ox."

ridden with° a Welsh goat too? Shall I have a coxcomb° of   *harassed by / jester's cap*
frieze? 'Tis time I were choked with a piece of toasted cheese.[5]

EVANS   Seese is not good to give putter; your belly is all putter.

135 FALSTAFF 'Seese' and 'putter'? Have I lived to stand at the taunt
of one that makes fritters of English? This is enough to be the
decay of lust and late walking° through the realm.   *(for sexual purposes)*

MISTRESS PAGE   Why, Sir John, do you think, though° we would   *even if*
have thrust virtue out of our hearts by the head and shoulders,

140 and have given ourselves without scruple to hell, that ever the
devil could have made you our delight?

FORD   What, a hodge-pudding,° a bag of flax?   *sausage*

MISTRESS PAGE   A puffed° man?   *inflated*

PAGE   Old, cold, withered, and of intolerable entrails?

145 FORD   And one that is as slanderous as Satan?

PAGE   And as poor as Job?

FORD   And as wicked as his wife?[6]

EVANS   And given to fornications, and to taverns, and sack, and
wine, and metheglins;° and to drinkings, and swearings, and   *Welsh spiced drink*
150 starings, pribbles and prabbles?°   *raving and squabbles*

FALSTAFF   Well, I am your theme; you have the start° of me. I   *advantage*
am dejected.° I am not able to answer the Welsh flannel. Igno-   *humbled*
rance itself is a plummet o'er me.[7] Use me as you will.

FORD   Marry, sir, we'll bring you to Windsor, to one Master
155 Brooke, that you have cozened of money, to whom you should
have been° a pander. Over and above that° you have suffered,   *intended to be / what*
I think to repay that money will be a biting affliction.

PAGE   Yet be cheerful, knight. Thou shalt eat a posset[8] tonight
at my house, where I will desire thee to laugh at my wife that
160 now laughs at thee. Tell her Master Slender hath married her
daughter.

MISTRESS PAGE [*aside*]   Doctors doubt that!° If Anne Page be my   *(expresses disbelief)*
daughter, she is, by this,° Doctor Caius's wife.   *now*

Enter [Master] SLENDER

SLENDER   Whoa, ho, ho, father Page!

165 PAGE   Son, how now? How now, son? Have you dispatched?°   *settled the business*

SLENDER   Dispatched? I'll make the best in Gloucestershire
know on't;° would I were hanged, la, else.°   *of it / otherwise*

PAGE   Of what, son?

SLENDER   I came yonder at Eton to marry Mistress Anne Page,
170 and she's a great lubberly° boy. If it had not been i'th' church,   *loutish*
I would have swinged° him, or he should have swinged me. If   *beaten; screwed*
I did not think it had been Anne Page, would I might never
stir; and 'tis a postmaster's boy.°   *stableboy*

PAGE   Upon my life, then, you took the wrong.

175 SLENDER   What need you tell me that? I think so, when I took a
boy for a girl. If I had been married to him, for all° he was in   *even though*
woman's apparel, I would not have had him.

---

5. "Welsh goat" (line 132) refers to the large number of
goats in Wales, "frieze" (line 133) to a coarse wool made
there, and "toasted cheese" to what was supposedly a
favorite Welsh food.
6. Satan slanders Job (Job 1:9–11, 2:4–5); Job's wife
tempts him to curse God (2:9).
7. A "plummet" is a "plumb line," used for measuring
depths, with a pun on "plumbet," a woolen fabric and,

hence, connected with "Welsh flannel," one of Falstaff's names here for Evans (along with "Ignorance").
The ignorant Evans, the "Welsh flannel," is a woolen
fabric over Falstaff, by which Falstaff means that even
the ignorant Evans can plumb Flastaff's depths, can see
his true motives.
8. Take a restorative drink of hot milk curdled with
wine or ale.

PAGE   Why, this is your own folly. Did not I tell you how you
should know my daughter by her garments?

180 SLENDER   I went to her in white and cried 'mum', and she cried
'budget', as Anne and I had appointed; and yet it was not Anne,
but a postmaster's boy.

MISTRESS PAGE   Good George, be not angry. I knew of your purpose, turned my daughter into green, and indeed she is now

185 with the Doctor at the deanery, and there married.

       Enter Doctor [CAIUS]

CAIUS   Ver is Mistress Page? By Gar, I am cozened! I ha' married
un garçon, a boy, *un paysan,*° by Gar. A boy! It is not Anne   *a peasant*
Page, by Gar. I am cozened.

PAGE   Why, did you take her in green?

190 CAIUS   Ay, be Gar, and 'tis a boy. Be Gar, I'll raise all Windsor.

FORD   This is strange. Who hath got the right Anne?

       Enter [*Master*] FENTON *and* ANNE

PAGE   My heart misgives me: here comes Master Fenton.—
How now, Master Fenton?

ANNE   Pardon, good father. Good my mother, pardon.

195 PAGE   Now, mistress, how chance you went not with Master Slender?

MISTRESS PAGE   Why went you not with Master Doctor, maid?

FENTON   You do amaze° her. Hear the truth of it.   *confuse*
You would have married her, most shamefully,
Where there was no proportion° held in love.   *balance*

200 The truth is, she and I, long since contracted,°   *betrothed*
Are now so sure° that nothing can dissolve° us.   *united / separate*
Th'offence is holy that she hath committed,
And this deceit loses the name of craft,
Of disobedience, or unduteous title,°   *undutifulness*

205 Since therein she doth evitate° and shun   *avoid*
A thousand irreligious cursèd hours
Which forcèd marriage would have brought upon her.

FORD [*to* PAGE *and* MISTRESS PAGE]   Stand not amazed. Here is no remedy.
In love the heavens themselves do guide the state;

210 Money buys lands, and wives are sold by fate.

FALSTAFF   I am glad, though you have ta'en a special stand° to   *hunter's station*
strike at me, that your arrow hath glanced.°   *missed*

PAGE   Well, what remedy? Fenton, heaven give thee joy!
What cannot be eschewed must be embraced.

215 FALSTAFF   When night-dogs run, all sorts of deer are chased.⁹

MISTRESS PAGE   Well, I will muse° no further. Master Fenton,   *complain*
Heaven give you many, many merry days!
Good husband, let us every one go home,
And laugh this sport o'er by a country fire,
Sir John and all.

220 FORD   Let it be so, Sir John.
To Master Brooke you yet shall hold your word,
For he tonight shall lie with Mistress Ford.   *Exeunt*

---

9. When "dogs" (the failed suitors) run out of control
at night, they may catch "all sorts of deer" (the disguised boys, rather than Anne). In other words, you
can't control nocturnal intrigue.

The Second Part of Henry IV

The title page of the 1600 Quarto of 2 *Henry IV* describes the play as *The Second Part of Henry the Fourth, Continuing to His Death, and Coronation of Henry the Fifth. With the Humours of Sir John Falstaff, and Swaggering Pistol.* Its first focus is the "high" historical matter of the reign of Kings. For this part of the play, Shakespeare drew primarily on the second edition of Raphael Holinshed's *Chronicles of England, Scotland, and Ireland* (1587), although he probably consulted other sources, including Samuel Daniel's *First Four Books of the Civil Wars Between the Two Houses of Lancaster and York* (1595). In regard to this historical material, the title page particularly highlights the delicate moment of succession when one King dies and another is crowned. Shakespeare's audience was facing such a moment at the end of the 1590s. Elizabeth I was old, having been on the English throne since 1558; she had never married, and she had no heirs. The uncertainties of the coming succession may have, by contrast, heightened the pleasure of watching Henry IV followed upon the throne by his male heir, Henry V—the King who, whatever his father's sins in seizing the crown from Richard II, had become in the popular imagination a symbol of kingly perfection and English masculinity. With his customary subtlety, Shakespeare complicates and somewhat darkens the popular image of the wayward prince who undergoes a miraculous transformation, but Hal's coronation nonetheless is the end point toward which the play inexorably moves.

Besides its royal plot, the play also deals in some decidedly "low" and mostly unhistorical matter, suggested on the title page by mention of the "humours" of Falstaff and the presence of swaggering Pistol. These characters hold pride of place alongside Henry IV and Henry V, indicating the popularity of the antic parts of the play—Falstaff's jokes and his flouting of authority or Pistol's madly bombastic language. Some of the matter for the play's comic scenes probably derives from *The Famous Victories of Henry the Fifth,* a popular play about the life of Henry V first published in 1598 but believed to have been performed well before that date. In 2 *Henry IV,* Prince Hal does not mingle with the comic figures as freely as he did in *1 Henry IV*; in fact, he appears only once, in 2.4, in the Eastcheap tavern where Falstaff holds court. Nonetheless, the total number of low, unhistorical characters expands considerably in this play. Pistol is a new character, and Mistress Quickly is joined in her Eastcheap tavern by Doll Tearsheet, a prostitute whose name graphically suggests one consequence of unrestrained fornication. Further, a number of country characters are introduced: the Gloustershire justices of the peace, Shallow and Silence; Shallow's servant, Davy; and the five rural recruits (Mouldy, Bullcalf, Wart, Feeble, and Shadow) whom Falstaff considers for conscription into the army. 2 *Henry IV* is the only history play of which more than half is written in prose, and much of that richly varied prose occurs in the numerous scenes involving these humble figures Shakespeare added to the historical narrative of one king's death and another's coronation.

2 Henry IV was probably written soon after the very popular *1 Henry IV,* which was published in 1598 but probably written and staged in 1596–97. The Quarto was published in 1600, but there is a reference to the character of Justice Silence in Ben Jonson's *Every Man out of His Humour,* published in 1599. 2 *Henry IV* was therefore probably performed sometime between February 1598, when *1 Henry IV* was entered in the Stationers' Register with no indication that it was the first part of a two-part play, and early in 1599. It is likely that censorship of Shakespeare's original naming of Falstaff as "Oldcastle," Bardolph as "Russell," and Peto as "Harvey" (see Introduction to *1 Henry IV*) had occurred before Shakespeare completed 2 *Henry IV,* although a few

THE
Second part of Henrie
the fourth, continuing to his death,
and coronation of Henrie
the fift.

With the humours of sir Iohn Fal-
staffe, and swaggering
Pistoll.

As it hath been sundrie times publikely
acted by the right honourable, the Lord
Chamberlaine his seruants.

Written by William Shakespeare.

LONDON
Printed by V.S. for Andrew Wise, and
William Aspley.
1600.

Title page of the 1600 Quarto of *The Second part of Henrie the fourth . . .* , promising to combine royal history and the comic events involving Falstaff and his tavern companions.

traces of the original names appear in the speech prefixes and stage directions in the first two acts of the quarto text. Shakespeare may have interrupted his composition of 2 *Henry IV* to write *The Merry Wives of Windsor,* a play that could have been performed as early as 1597. If so, he would have written the last acts of 2 *Henry IV* well after the censorship of the offending names in 1 *Henry IV* had occurred, and he would consequently have altered the names in the final acts of the play.

Narrowing down the play's date of composition, however, does not answer the question of why Shakespeare wrote two plays dealing with the reign of Henry IV. Some critics believe that the playwright once intended to encompass all the material of both plays in one, but in writing 1 *Henry IV* he found he had room to depict only the events up to the Battle of Shrewsbury and Hal's emergence as a chivalric hero through his defeat of Hotspur. Therefore, what was "left over" was, in effect, put into 2 *Henry IV* with the patchwork addition of enough comic material to scrape together a play. It is also possible that Shakespeare intended to dramatize only the events now in 1 *Henry IV,* but that having done so, he was encouraged by his success to add another chapter to the story of Hal's reformation and gradual progression toward the throne. Alternatively, Shakespeare may have planned two plays from the beginning, intending to undertake two quite different explorations of the prodigal narrative by which the wild Prince becomes first a chivalric hero and eventually the King of England.

Whatever the original impetus for writing it, the finished play now called 2 *Henry IV* has an integrity of its own and a set of preoccupations that clearly distinguishes it from 1 *Henry IV.* The rebels, for example, are a less flamboyant crew than in the earlier play, and they are not vanquished in combat as at Shrewsbury; rather, at Gaultres, Prince John tricks them into laying down their weapons. Policy, not chivalry, wins the day. Hal's challenge, moreover, is no longer to prove himself the prince of chivalry, with the rebel Henry Percy (Hotspur) as his main antagonist. Rather, he must show himself fit for civil rule. Hence the importance in 2 *Henry IV* of the Lord Chief Justice, a figure who in popular accounts of Hal's life had had the Prince imprisoned for impudently giving him a box on the ear. This event is not dramatized in either of Shakespeare's *Henry IV* plays, as it had been in *The Famous Victories,* but it is several times alluded to. In 2 *Henry IV,* the Chief Justice emerges as the main foil to the disorderly Falstaff. Upon hearing that Henry IV is dead and Hal is King, the fat knight exclaims, "The laws of England are at my commandment" (5.3.125–26). It seems quite possible that under Henry V, law will give way before the appetites and desires of individual subjects. Hal and the Chief Justice do not share the stage until 5.2, but their encounter is a pivotal moment in the text, revealing whether Hal will recognize and honor the authority of the Chief Justice or follow Falstaff in flouting the law.

Also unique to this play is its pervasive concern with the passing of time. As Hastings says at the end of Act 1, "We are time's subjects" (1.3.110); arguably, he sounds the play's central theme. Even the King, to whom so many are subject, is himself subject to time. Shakespeare portrays him as old and sick, though the historical Henry successfully ruled England for ten years after the Battle of Shrewsbury. His sickness and the urgency of the rebel threat pressure the Prince, forcing him to realize that his idle days in the tavern are numbered and that if he lingers longer, he will "profane the precious time" (2.4.330), time he should spend coming to terms with his father and defending a kingdom still threatened by rebels. Even the irrepressible Falstaff now feels time's hand. He enters the play in 1.2 asking what the doctor has said about the urine he has sent for examination, and to Quickly and Tearsheet he confesses, "I am old, I am old" (2.4.243). If 1 *Henry IV* is an expansive work, infused with a feeling of infinite play and infinite possibility, 2 *Henry IV* has a melancholy, autumnal aura. It is a play of limits and constrictions. Shallow intones: "Death, as the Psalmist saith, is certain to all; all shall die" (3.2.33–34). Through its many images of sickness, disease, and old age, the play is permeated with intimations of mortality.

The play's portrayal of Prince Hal shares in the somber mood that suffuses all of 2 *Henry IV.* When the audience first sees him, he is with Poins (2.2), brooding on the impasse to which his own actions have brought him. Rather than keeping a controlling distance from his tavern companion, Hal ruefully acknowledges what he shares with common men. Tired, he desires nothing more exalted than small beer, the common drink of every London apprentice. He admits that he should not, because of his rank, be intimate with Poins; and yet he confesses that he is, revealing how thoroughly he knows his companion's wardrobe and using Poins as a sounding board for his misgivings about his own behavior and its consequences. While the scene's mood changes when Bardolph enters with an absurdly pompous letter from Falstaff, its fretful beginning indicates a new strain in Shakespeare's depiction of Hal's progress toward the throne. In *1 Henry IV*, everything seemed easy for the Prince. He announced a course of reform and enacted it with little apparent cost to himself. In *2 Henry IV*, Shakespeare constructs a more sober Prince who articulates anxiety about the gap between his plebeian taste for small beer and the grandeur of the office he will assume, a Prince who knows that to have acted the wastrel in order to make a dazzling reform may have cost him his father's affection and made it impossible to express his love for the King without appearing a hypocrite. In the opening acts of *2 Henry IV*, Hal's capacity for self-critique and for uncertainty makes him more vulnerable, and perhaps more likable, than the shiny and assured paragon of *1 Henry IV*.

Shakespeare also shows changes in Hal's father, King Henry IV, who in Part 2 reveals a new capacity for introspection. In 3.1, speaking about the burdens of office, he acknowledges the costs of his success and admits that at the start of his reign he could little foresee the changes time would effect in him and in his plans and alliances. Yet like his son, in the end Henry finds his office worth the cost. Power may bring burdens, but for both characters it is irresistible. Each sentimentally envies common men (whose poverty and powerlessness they do not share), but neither renounces the office of King. And neither ever gives up the attempt to control his destiny. Having contemplated the many unforeseen changes of his reign, Henry IV finally breaks off his reverie to plan a campaign against the rebels:

> Are these things then necessities?
> Then let us meet them like necessities;
> And that same word even now cries out on us.
> They say the Bishop and Northumberland
> Are fifty thousand strong.
>
> (3.1.87–91)

This is the pragmatic voice of rule, the blunt determination that Shakespeare attributes both to Prince Hal and to his father.

Yet despite (and perhaps because of) their similarities, Shakespeare makes the relationship of Henry and Hal a troubled one. Part of the complexity of *2 Henry IV* is that while it tellingly anatomizes how these Kings, father and then son, acquire and maintain power, it simultaneously creates the impression of a psychodrama between the two of them that, though inseparable from their political roles, is never fully understood by either. Hal, despite telling Poins he loves his father, does not appear in the King's presence until the end of Act 4, when Henry is on his deathbed. Then, with what has seemed to many to be unseemly haste, Hal, believing his father dead, takes the crown from the sleeping King's pillow and sets it on his own head. Is this, as the King fears, Hal's acting out of a fantasy of parricide? Or, as Hal protests, is it his attempt to come to terms with the burdens of office that have hastened his father's death and that will now fall to him?

In part, the relationship between Hal and Henry is complicated by the guilt each feels about the politically useful and carefully managed "wildness" that each has employed. Hal, of course, has cultivated wildness as a prelude to reform. It is the foil by which he aims to set off his achievement of perfect chivalry and justice. But it is important to remember that to come by his throne, Henry himself had to enact the wildness of usurpation, seizing the crown from a lawfully anointed king, an act Shakespeare depicted in *Richard II*. To be sure, once in the seat of rule, Henry repudiated such wildness and embraced the law, justifying his own reign in part by presenting himself as the bulwark against disorder—that of the rebels and even that of his son. There is no doubt that Hal displays prodigal behavior, spending time in the tavern rather than at court, but his father dwells on and exaggerates his son's lawlessness, picturing England's distress when ruled by a man who "from curbed licence plucks / The muzzle of restraint" (4.3.258–59). This preoccupation with Hal's lawlessness may signal Henry's guilt about his own act of usurpation, for which he has long planned a penitential crusade to the Holy Land (a crusade that we eventually learn would *also* have the effect of distracting his nobles from thoughts of rebellion at home). But Henry does not seem able to see the ways in which his son's tactics resemble his own. Truly his father's child, Hal angles for power with an unerring sense of when to embrace wildness and when to repudiate it. Just as Henry's act of seizing the crown raises the specter of parricide, Henry's obsession with curbing Hal's wildness hints at castration. Without seeming fully to realize the consequences of his own actions, the King would cut off one source of Hal's power, even though he himself once embraced disorder and still needs it to justify his rule.

In Henry's last conversation with Hal and at his death, father and son switch positions in the discourse of "wildness" that runs through the play. The King has been the principle of order, the Prince the ungovernable prodigal. On his deathbed, however, the King acknowledges to Hal:

> God knows, my son,
> By what bypaths and indirect crook'd ways
> I met this crown; and I myself know well
> How troublesome it sat upon my head.
> To thee it shall descend with better quiet,
> Better opinion, better confirmation;
> For all the soil of the achievement goes
> With me into the earth.
>
> (4.3.311–18)

He represents himself as a man stained by his own errancy, but one whose sins can be buried with his death. Hal picks up the theme when he announces after his father's death, "My father is gone wild into his grave" (5.2.122), as if Henry himself embodied the principle of disorder, now buried. Yet Hal continues, suddenly making problematic whose wildness the grave holds:

> For in his tomb lie my affections;
> And with his spirits sadly I survive
> To mock the expectation of the world.
>
> (5.2.123–25)

Now it is *Hal's* wildness that the grave holds, his father's sober spirits that live on in the son. Shedding his prodigality is now not an act of disempowerment but its opposite. The wild Prince has become the order-loving King. It will now be his turn to repudiate those who live outside the compass of the law, beginning with Falstaff.

Critics have argued that *2 Henry IV* looks forward to the tragedies in its somber tone and its focus upon the tortured self-divisions of the King and his son. There is truth in this claim, but one must also recognize that while the play allows the audience to read doubt and self-division in Henry and the Prince, at the end it moves to install Hal unambiguously in the position of the reformed Prince and law-abiding King. Hal's apparent self-division holds the attention of the audience just as his carefully managed reform wins the admiration of his subjects. But when the time is right, whatever the "personal" cost, he embraces the law in the person of the Chief Justice while burying wildness in the person of his father and publicly repudiating it in the person of Falstaff. In so doing, he shows an unerring instinct for the improvisations that allow him to acquire and retain power.

But though Hal publicly repudiates wildness, the play does not. Wildness surges up unpredictably, not only in the actions of the rebels but also in the actions and particularly in the unruly language of those many "minor" characters who are Shakespeare's additions to his historical sources and whose existence is signaled on the title page by reference to the humors of Falstaff and swaggering Pistol. In the late sixteenth century, the English language was undergoing expansion and entering a period of vibrant linguistic experimentation. Many writers were interested in making English a fit language in which to write verse that would rival the achievements of classical literature. They experimented with imitating the verse forms used by Latin writers in particular; they also coined new words, and they attempted to purge English of uncouth or infelicitous elements. But it was not just poets who affected the language. Trade brought new products to England, and those products had to have names. Foreign visitors, merchants, and workers were a common sight in the London landscape, and they, of course, brought their languages with them. Foreign terms were regularly absorbed into the English vernacular. Meanwhile, the theater offered auditors the high-sounding rhetoric of kings and tyrants, while London preachers made their reputations with dazzling displays of oratorical power.

This atmosphere generated an infectious excitement about language, and not all of this excitement was easy to control. Rhetorical handbooks proliferated, each sketching out the styles and figures of speech appropriate to different occasions, and each also listing rhetorical "vices," examples of indecorous or ungrammatical or infelicitous speech. *2 Henry IV* could be considered a casebook of linguistic vices. The minor characters speak a wild farrago of tongues that defy the desire for linguistic order. Swaggering Pistol is a case in point. Much of his speech is composed of scraps of rhetoric he has picked up from going to the London theater, especially, perhaps, to the Rose, where Edward Alleyn, chief actor for the Admiral's Men, specialized in a highly rhetorical and hyperbolic acting style that Pistol seems both to channel and to parody. Pistol, for example, imagines himself as Tamburlaine, the overreaching hero of Marlowe's two-part play about a Scythian shepherd who became one of the great military conquerors of all time. Alleyn was famous for this role, and Pistol's swaggering style aspires to Alleyn's (and Tamburlaine's) rhetorical pyrotechnics. Pistol, however, mangles his references to Marlowe's hero, intermingling what he can remember of Tamburlaine's speeches with a mishmash of fine-sounding names and lines from drinking songs, as when he proclaims:

> Shall pack-horses
> And hollow pampered jades of Asia,
> Which cannot go but thirty mile a day,
> Compare with Caesars and with cannibals,
> And Trojan Greeks?
> Nay, rather damn them with King Cerberus,
> And let the welkin roar. Shall we fall foul for toys?
> (2.4.140–46)

Pistol's "mistakes" are pervasive. First he imitates what he can remember of the moment when Tamburlaine taunts the conquered kings whom he has put in harness to draw his chariot. But then he veers into nonsense, mistaking "cannibal" for "Hannibal," the heroic leader of Carthage; describing Greeks as Trojans, while in *The Iliad* the Greeks and Trojans were two peoples at war with one another; then attributing a crown to Cerberus, the three-headed dog who guarded the gates of hell; and ending with a tag from a drinking song: "And let the welkin roar." The sheer exuberance of the speech is partly what makes it pleasurable—Pistol's delight in the sound of big words, whatever those words may mean—along with the lawless incongruity with which one bit of remembered rhetoric is stitched onto the next. Self-mockingly, but also self-importantly, the passage points to the power of the theater to intoxicate spectators with fine rhetoric. Choleric, explosive, overflowing with the excesses of stage rhetoric, Pistol is a wild card in the play's quest for order and the rule of law.

He is not alone. The play opens with a prologue spoken by Rumour, whose business is telling lies, substituting the untrue for the true. That Shakespeare prefaced the play with this figure indicates his concern with the vagaries and waywardness of language. Sometimes language is maliciously used to deceive, as with Rumour or Prince John's double-edged speech at Gaultres. Sometimes, as with Pistol's bombast, it is used to evoke delight in how words sound, regardless of what they mean. At other times, as with Falstaff's puns, language reveals the double and triple meanings that can be activated from a simple utterance. To take a single example, consider Falstaff's anger in 1.2 at the prosperous merchant who refuses to give him twenty-two yards of satin without his providing adequate security—that is, adequate goods or money to cover the debt. To his Page

The Rumour of Shakespeare's Induction is derived from the classical figure of Fame, here depicted as covered with ears (to gather reports from all quarters) and blowing a horn (to broadcast news abroad). From Vicenzo Cartari, *Imagines deorum* (1581).

Falstaff sputters, "Well, he may sleep in security, for he hath the horn of abundance, and the lightness of his wife shines through it; and yet cannot he see, though he have his own lanthorn to light him" (1.2.39–42). The subversive wittiness of this passage depends on Falstaff's punning on the fact that "horn" can mean the horn lanterns sold by merchants, the cornucopia that is a symbol of abundance, or the horns of a man who has been sexually betrayed by his wife, while "lightness" can mean both illumination and sexual promiscuity. On the surface, Falstaff is grudgingly admitting that the merchant is rich and graced with a wife. But the puns tell another story: that of a blind cuckold whose wife's sexual infidelity is visible to everyone but himself. In Falstaff's mouth, language is a slippery thing and often a devastating tool for confounding an enemy.

One of the play's most remarkable rhetoricians, Mistress Quickly, did not make it to the title page of the Quarto, but her verbal blunders are another example of language's unpredictable qualities. Quickly is not the same person she was in *1 Henry IV*. For one thing, she seems to have lost the husband who was mentioned often, though never glimpsed, in the previous play; and she has acquired a new companion in the person of the prostitute Doll Tearsheet. Unmarried, economically independent, and associated with the criminality of prostitution and perhaps of murder (in 5.4, the women are accused with Pistol of having beaten a man to death), Quickly emerges as a figure of disorder who must be purged from a reformed commonwealth. In part, she represents linguistic anarchy. Her signature utterance is the malapropism, the verbal blunder by which one word is mistaken for another. For example, telling the Chief Justice of Falstaff's whereabouts, she says he was "indited," meaning "invited," to dinner (2.1.24). The malapropism is interesting because it is a kind of lawless speech in which the speaker is guided by the sound of words, or by a private logic, rather than by the usual rules of sense. Quickly, for example, in mistaking "indicted" for "invited" has blundered into her own kind of sense, since she would indeed like to see Falstaff indicted, or brought to legal judgment, for the debts he owes her. Malapropisms, to those who know better, make the speaker appear foolish. Yet they also can disrupt the institutions that depend on clear and predictable communication. Not even the Chief Justice knows quite what to make of Quickly, so persistently does her speech elude the net of common sense, enveloping her in a tangle of meanings—some obscene, some suggestively significant—that she may or may not intend. Sir Francis Bacon called revenge "wild justice"; the malapropism might be called "wild speech," so thoroughly does it defy semantic predictability.

The distinctiveness of the prose assigned to the comic figures in *2 Henry IV* is one of the play's most striking features. It highlights Shakespeare's ability to delineate character by means of linguistic differences. Shallow's mindless repetition of simple words, Falstaff's puns, Quickly's malapropisms, and Pistol's bombast are all ways of individuating these figures. They also suggest the fecundity of speech in Henry's England and register, at the linguistic level, a wild disorder no principle of decorum or law can entirely contain. By means of the double entendre, much of what characters speak in the tavern world alludes to the body and its pleasures, even while they intend or appear to talk of something else. For example, Quickly, complaining of Falstaff to the Chief Justice, says, "He stabbed me in mine own house, most beastly, in good faith. A cares not what mischief he does; if his weapon be out, he will foin like any devil, he will spare neither man, woman, nor child" (2.1.12–15). "Foin" means "thrust" or "strike." Overtly, Quickly describes a Falstaff who takes out his sword or dagger and indiscriminately stabs whoever happens to be handy. Indirectly, and perhaps inadvertently, she describes a Falstaff who, when his sexual "weapon," or penis, is out, will indiscriminately engage in sex with whoever happens to be near. The tavern scenes teem with similar instances of sexualized speech or, more accurately, speech that tells two stories at the same time, one of them a story of sex: its pleasures and diseases and persistence. The bawdy doubleness of tavern

A seventeenth-century tavern scene recalling Mistress Quickly's Eastcheap tavern. From Peter Rollos, *Le Centre de l'amour* (1630?).

prose contrasts sharply with the elevated poetry in which the King most often speaks. Worrying, planning, commanding, the King constructs himself as a bulwark against disorder. But the disorderly, bombastic, vibrant, and lewd speech of the tavern suggests at the level of language the difficulties of controlling the manifold energies of his subjects.

Thinking about the play's control of or its failure to control unsanctioned energies provides a context for considering what traditionally has been the most discussed aspect of *2 Henry IV*: the Prince's final public repudiation of Falstaff. In this play, Falstaff is kept separate from the Prince except for the one scene (2.4) in which the Prince disguises himself as a tavern barman and overhears Falstaff talking with Doll and Quickly. Moreover, the exploitative side of Falstaff is more fully displayed here than in the earlier play. He leeches off Quickly; he takes bribes to release able-bodied men from service in the army; he worms a thousand pounds from Shallow. Yet he is still able, as in the stunning speech in which he indicts Prince John for cold-bloodedness (4.2.78–111), to offer a telling critique of his betters and to embody a frank physicality they eschew. Given Falstaff's wit and his centrality to the pleasure afforded by both *1* and *2 Henry IV*, the new King's repudiation of him—"I know thee not, old man. Fall to thy prayers" (5.5.45)—continues to trouble critics and audiences. Certainly, how the moment is staged can mitigate or harshen its implications. In Terry Hands's 1975 Royal Shakespeare Company production, for example, the newly crowned King came onstage in glittering gold and masked, the epitome of detached and heartless power. In other productions, he rejects his former friend with a sob, emphasizing his own sense of loss and his continuing affection for Falstaff. But however it is staged, there is little doubt that the new King, whatever his "personal" feelings, has turned Falstaff away to consolidate his power.

The final scene, however, is not the play's last word: it is followed by an Epilogue. It is likely that this Epilogue was spoken by the company's clown, in this case Will Kemp, a famed comic actor who in this play is believed to have played Falstaff. It is especially likely that Kemp spoke the Epilogue because of the several references in it to the actor's willingness to use his legs, or to dance, should his words not prove agreeable. Kemp was a skilled dancer, and when he left Shakespeare's company in 1599, he undertook a famous morris dance from London to Norwich. The Epilogue gives the common actor who had played Falstaff the play's last word and its final display of physical skill. At Shrewsbury, Hal had thought Falstaff dead, but, faking death, the fat man had arisen. In *2 Henry IV*, the old knight is banished from the King's presence in the play's final scene, but in the Epilogue, the actor who had played him reappears—soliciting the audience's applause, denying that Falstaff is a representation of the Lollard martyr Sir John Oldcastle (see the Introduction to *1 Henry IV*) and kicking up his heels in a virtuoso display of dancing skill. If in the play proper the forces of order have attempted to demonize the energies associated with popular culture and the low life of the tavern, in the Epilogue those energies have free rein. The body of the common actor holds center stage as Kemp, throwing aside the character Falstaff's mantle of age, delights the audience with a jig.

The Epilogue has another effect. It pluralizes the "authorities" to which the theater is beholden. With its references to the Oldcastle controversy and its final allusion to praying for Queen Elizabeth, the Epilogue acknowledges the power embodied in the person of the monarch and in the state's censorship apparatus. But it also refers to pleasing both the gentlewomen and the gentlemen of the audience—in other words, the paying customers who came to the theater for all sorts of pleasures. If the title page of the Quarto is to be believed, readers, and probably audiences, were as much delighted by the irrepressible and irresponsible antics of Falstaff and swaggering Pistol as by the sober reformation of Hal and the suffering of his father, just as they were undoubtedly as delighted by the mangling of the King's English as by its decorous deployment. In short, while in this play the rule of law officially triumphs over the forces of disorder, the comic actor has the last dance, and theater finds a way to offer pleasures in excess of what the sober historical narrative allows.

JEAN E. HOWARD

TEXTUAL NOTE

2 Henry IV was entered in the Stationers' Register on August 23, 1600, and first printed in a quarto version dated that same year. This Quarto had two issues, the first of which, QA, lacks the present 3.1, in which the sleepless King Henry meditates on the passage of time and the ironies of history. In QB, this scene is included. The text was not printed again until it appeared in a significantly different version in the First Folio of 1623 (F). The Folio text contains eight fairly substantial passages, totaling about 160 lines, not found in Q (A or B). It also differs from the quarto text in a number of other ways: oaths have been excised; punctuation, syntax, and certain aspects of style have been regularized; stage directions have been altered, and in several scenes the names of characters have been "massed" together in an initial stage direction, even if some of these characters only enter at a later point in the scene; some quarto lines are missing, and new part lines appear, as does a table of "The Actors Names" listing all the speaking parts.

The important debate about the play's textual history concerns the relation of Q to F. Q shows signs—such as the use of a number of different speech prefixes for the same character—of having been printed directly from the author's "foul papers," which do not appear to have been marked up for use in a theatrical performance. One explanation for the absence of 3.1 in QA is that the scene was marked for excision in the foul papers, either because it was politically sensitive or to reduce the length of the play. Others have argued that the scene was written on a separate manuscript leaf that became detached from its proper place in the foul papers and so was overlooked by the compositor. The Oxford editors believe that this scene was added by Shakespeare *after* the rest of the manuscript had been written as the first step in his ongoing reworking of the play. They postulate that the compositor who set this part of QA missed the marks indicating where the scene was to be added to the foul papers.

F, by contrast, shows signs of having been prepared by a professional scribe in its regularization of a number of aspects of the text, though these changes also introduce errors and obscure the exact nature of the manuscript underlying the transcription. The excision of oaths is undoubtedly a result of the 1606 statute against profanity on the stage. Some further changes found in F may be due to the special problems facing the compositors setting the text. It appears that too little space had been allocated in F for setting this play in type. Consequently, a group of four additional sheets was added, but the compositor still had to omit words, compressing one part of the text, and to add words and phrases, expanding other parts of the text, in order to fit the play into its allotted space. It is possible that the list of "The Actors Names" was added to fill up a blank page.

Some editors argue that the eight substantial passages found in F but missing from Q were originally present in the manuscript used for setting Q but were marked for excision, either because they were politically sensitive or for theatrical reasons such as the need to reduce the length of the speeches assigned to actors doubling in two roles. These editors grant priority to the quarto text (which appears to be printed from Shakespeare's foul papers and which does not contain the errors and changes made by the scribe who prepared the Folio manuscript), but they usually add the eight additional passages on the grounds that they were originally part of the manuscript behind the Quarto.

The Oxford editors work from different assumptions; specifically, they argue that beginning with 3.1, Shakespeare himself made a series of revisions to the play, perhaps recording these in the fair copy that was to serve as the promptbook. They argue that he did so as part of a consistent strategy to augment the historical portions of the play and to connect it more fully to *Richard II* and *1 Henry IV*. They agree that two of the eight additional Folio passages represent cuts in the quarto text because they deal with the politically sensitive matter of rebellion, but they also hold that the remaining six are Shakespeare's later *additions* to the play. They further argue that some of the other changes in F, such as the deletion of specific lines, show authorial intervention in the interest of making the play more stageworthy. The Oxford editors therefore postulate that the scribe who produced the copy used for setting F, while having a copy of Q to consult, was working primarily from a theatrical promptbook that registered some authorial revisions to the quarto version of the play, though the theatrical nature of that promptbook has been obscured by the "literary" habits of the scribe. As a consequence, this edition of the play, while using Q as its control text, accepts a higher number of Folio readings than is true for many other editions in an attempt to reproduce the stage version of the play the Oxford editors believe underlies F.

The eight substantial new passages found in F deserve further discussion. Interestingly, all of them involve figures who are of the rebels' party. The Oxford editors agree that two of them were censored because they too compellingly justified rebellion. These are 1.1.188–208, Morton's speech announcing that the Archbishop of York has joined the rebellion, using the murder of Richard II as partial justification, and 4.1.55–79, the Archbishop's speech justifying the rebels' position and exclaiming against the King's indifference to their grievances. Other passages are in greater dispute. For example, 2.3.23–45, part of Lady Percy's magnificent speech in praise of Hotspur, does not appear in Q. Is this because Shakespeare had not yet written it? Or had it been cut from the original manuscript because the praise of Hotspur could be read as indirect praise of the Earl of Essex, the dashing, headstrong noble whose triumphal return from a 1599 campaign against the Irish Shakespeare was to anticipate with excitement in *Henry V*—but who in actuality returned home in disgrace and shortly thereafter led an abortive rebellion against Elizabeth? Or was it cut because the boy actor playing Lady Percy also was to play Doll Tearsheet in the next scene and had to have the number of lines he spoke reduced? Each of the eight additional Folio passages, which include 1.1.165–78, 1.3.21–24, 1.3.36–55, 1.3.85–108, and 4.1.101–37 (as well as the three passages already mentioned), is flagged in the notes so that readers can consider each case for themselves. The principal passages deleted from this text but present in Q and in most modern editions of the text are indented and printed as inset passages at the points where they appeared in Q.

Apart from Act 4, this text follows Folio act and scene divisions, although in F the Induction is marked as a separate scene. As for Act 4, F divides it into two scenes, and in many modern editions it is divided into five scenes; this edition divides it into three, ignoring the interpolated scene breaks often added by modern editors after 4.1.226, when Prince John marches onstage to speak with the rebels at Gaultres and after 4.3.132, when the King is carried to the Jerusalem Chamber. It retains, however, the interpolated break after 4.1.349 in which Falstaff enters with Coleville after Prince John has departed the stage, on the grounds that unlike the other two instances, this is a place where the stage is cleared and the action is therefore not continuous. It also retains the Folio scene break (now 4.3) when King Henry first comes onstage sick and in his bed.

SELECTED BIBLIOGRAPHY

Calderwood, James L. *Metadrama in Shakespeare's Henriad: "Richard II" to "Henry V."* Berkeley: University of California Press, 1979. Esp. 88–104. Examines Hal's rejection of Falstaff and the fat knight's inability to escape from history into comic invulnerability.

Crewe, Jonathan. "Reforming Prince Hal: The Sovereign Inheritor in *2 Henry IV*." *Renaissance Drama*, n.s., 21 (1990): 225–42. Discusses the play's obsession with Hal's reform and the role of the father's death in effecting that reform.

Goldberg, Jonathan. "Hal's Desire, Shakespeare's Idaho." *Shakespeare's Hand*. Minneapolis: University of Minnesota Press, 2003. 222–52. Uses Gus Van Sant's film *My Own Private Idaho* to explore sex and gender relations in *1* and *2 Henry IV*, including Hal's potentially sodomitical relations with Falstaff.

Hodgdon, Barbara. "'Let the End Try the Man': *1* and *2 Henry IV*." *The End Crowns All: Closure and Contradiction in Shakespeare's History.* Princeton: Princeton University Press, 1991. 151–84. Discusses the play's problematic ending and different ways it has been staged.

Knights, L. C. "Time's Subjects: The Sonnets and *King Henry IV, Part II*." *Some Shakespearean Themes*. London: Chatto & Windus, 1959. 45–64. Explores the play's themes of time and change as prefigured in the sonnets.

Levine, Nina. "Extending Credit in the *Henry IV* Plays." *Shakespeare Quarterly* 51 (2000): 403–31. Discusses the pervasiveness and ideological complexity of the language of credit in both *Henry IV* plays.

MacDonald, Ronald R. "Uses of Diversity: Bakhtin's Theory of Utterance and Shakespeare's Second Tetralogy." *"Henry IV, Parts One and Two."* Ed. Nigel Wood. Theory in Practice series. Buckingham, Eng.: Open University Press, 1995. 65–91. Uses Bakhtin's theories of language to discuss the heteroglossia, or profusion of disparate voices, in this play.

Rackin, Phyllis. "Historical Kings/Theatrical Clowns." *Stages of History: Shakespeare's English Chronicles*. Ithaca, N.Y.: Cornell University Press, 1990. 201–47. Explores in all the histories the threat to authority embodied in the disorderly conduct and subversive speech of common men and of Falstaff.

Ruiter, David. "'The Unquiet Time' of *2 Henry IV*: Festivity and Order in Flux." *Shakespeare's Festive History: Feasting, Festivity, Fasting, and Lent in the Second Henriad*. Aldershot, Eng.: Ashgate, 2003. 103–41. Probes the difficulties Hal encounters in staging the reform he has so long planned.

Wiles, David. *Shakespeare's Clown: Actor and Text in the Elizabethan Playhouse*. New York: Cambridge University Press, 1987. Esp. "Kemp's Jigs" (43–60) and "Falstaff" (116–35). Argues that Falstaff's role is the clown's part and that it was originally played by Will Kemp, a notable clown in Shakespeare's company who was also famous for his dancing of jigs.

Young, David P., ed. *Twentieth Century Interpretations of "Henry IV, Part II": A Collection of Critical Essays*. Englewood Cliffs, N.J.: Prentice-Hall, 1968. Wide-ranging collection of classic essays from the mid-twentieth century.

FILM

Henry IV, Part II. 1979. Dir. David Giles. UK. 155 min. Judicious cuts and a strong performance by Anthony Quayle as Falstaff strengthen this sober BBC-TV version of the play.

The Second Part of Henry the Fourth

THE PERSONS OF THE PLAY

RUMOUR, the Presenter
EPILOGUE
KING HENRY IV
PRINCE HARRY, later crowned King Henry V ⎱
PRINCE JOHN of Lancaster ⎰ sons of
Humphrey, Duke of GLOUCESTER ⎱ King Henry IV
Thomas, Duke of CLARENCE ⎰
Percy, Earl of NORTHUMBERLAND, of the rebels' party
LADY NORTHUMBERLAND
LADY PERCY, their son Hotspur's widow
TRAVERS, Northumberland's servant
MORTON, a bearer of news from Shrewsbury
Scrope, ARCHBISHOP of York
LORD BARDOLPH ⎫
Thomas, Lord MOWBRAY, the Earl Marshal ⎬ rebels against
Lord HASTINGS ⎭ King Henry IV
Sir John COLEVILLE
LORD CHIEF JUSTICE
His SERVANT
GOWER, a Messenger
Sir John FALSTAFF ⎫
His PAGE ⎪
BARDOLPH ⎬ 'irregular humorists'
POINS ⎪
Ensign PISTOL ⎪
PETO ⎭
MISTRESS QUICKLY, hostess of a tavern
DOLL TEARSHEET, a whore
SNARE ⎱
FANG ⎰ sergeants
Neville, Earl of WARWICK ⎫
Earl of SURREY ⎪
Earl of WESTMORLAND ⎬ supporters of King Henry
HARCOURT ⎪
Sir John Blunt ⎭
Robert SHALLOW ⎱
SILENCE ⎰ country justices
DAVY, Shallow's servant
Ralph MOULDY ⎫
Simon SHADOW ⎪
Thomas WART ⎬ men levied to fight for King Henry
Francis FEEBLE ⎪
Peter BULLCALF ⎭
PORTER of Northumberland's household
DRAWERS

BEADLES
GROOMS
MESSENGER
Sneak and other musicians
Lord Chief Justice's men, soldiers and attendants

Induction

Enter RUMOUR[1] [*in a robe*] *painted full of tongues*

RUMOUR Open your ears; for which of you will stop°   *plug up*
    The vent of hearing° when loud Rumour speaks?   *The ear*
    I from the orient° to the drooping west,   *east*
    Making the wind my post-horse,° still° unfold   *hired horse / continually*
5   The acts commencèd on this ball of earth.
    Upon my tongues continual slanders ride,
    The which in every language I pronounce,
    Stuffing the ears of men with false reports.
    I speak of peace, while covert enmity
10   Under the smile of safety wounds the world;
    And who but Rumour, who but only I,
    Make fearful musters and prepared defence[2]
    Whiles the big° year, swoll'n with some other griefs,   *pregnant*
    Is thought with child by the stern tyrant war,
15   And no such matter? Rumour is a pipe
    Blown by surmises, Jealousy's conjectures,
    And of so easy and so plain a stop[3]
    That the blunt° monster with uncounted° heads,   *stupid / innumerable*
    The still-discordant wav'ring multitude,
20   Can play upon it. But what° need I thus   *why*
    My well-known body to anatomize°   *dissect; lay open*
    Among my household?° Why is Rumour here?   *(the theater audience)*
    I run before King Harry's victory,
    Who in a bloody field by Shrewsbury[4]
25   Hath beaten down young Hotspur and his troops,
    Quenching the flame of bold rebellion
    Even with the rebels' blood. But what mean I
    To speak so true at first? My office is
    To noise abroad that Harry Monmouth[5] fell
30   Under the wrath of noble Hotspur's sword,
    And that the King before the Douglas' rage
    Stooped his anointed head as low as death.
    This have I rumoured through the peasant° towns   *rural*
    Between that royal field of Shrewsbury
35   And this worm-eaten hold° of raggèd stone,   *stronghold*

Induction Location: Outside Northumberland's castle at Warkworth.

1. A personification, possibly based on Virgil's "Fama," depicted as a female monster with many eyes, ears, and tongues who circulated both true and false accounts of events. See *Aeneid* 4.179–90.

2. Cause soldiers, prompted by fear, to assemble and defenses to be made ready. These lines may be topical: fear of imminent Spanish invasion led the Privy Council to mobilize militia forces frequently throughout the latter years of Elizabeth's reign.

3. And whose "stops," or openings, are so easy to play upon. The ease with which Rumour's pipe can be played means that even the common people can do it.

In the next lines, Rumour refers to these commoners as a many-headed monster, a common derogatory image of the people, especially when they aspire to participation in governance. By contrast, the proper head of the realm was held to be the single sovereign.

4. In Shakespeare's rendition of the Battle of Shrewsbury, staged in *1 Henry IV*, Prince Hal kills Henry Percy (Hotspur), and his forces capture the Scottish Earl of Douglas, two of the principal leaders of rebellion. In 1.1 of this play, the announcement of Henry Percy's death invokes considerable wordplay on his nickname, his "hot" spur being transformed into a "cold" spur by death.

5. Prince Hal was called Harry Monmouth in honor of his birthplace, Monmouth, in Wales.

Where Hotspur's father, old Northumberland,
Lies crafty-sick.° The posts come tiring on,[6]   *pretending to be ill*
And not a man of them brings other news
Than they have learnt of me. From Rumour's tongues
40   They bring smooth comforts false, worse than true wrongs.

                                                     Exit

1.1

Enter LORD BARDOLPH[1] *at one door. [He crosses the*
stage to another door]

LORD BARDOLPH
Who keeps the gate here, ho?
                              Enter PORTER *[above]*[2]
                                        Where is the Earl?
PORTER   What shall I say you are?
LORD BARDOLPH   Tell thou the Earl
That the Lord Bardolph doth attend° him here.   *await*
PORTER   His lordship is walked forth into the orchard.
5   Please it your honour knock but at the gate,
And he himself will answer.
              Enter the Earl NORTHUMBERLAND *[at the other door, as*
              sick, with a crutch and coif]°   *nightcap*
LORD BARDOLPH   Here comes the Earl.
                                        [Exit PORTER*]*
NORTHUMBERLAND   What news, Lord Bardolph? Every minute now
Should be the father of some stratagem.
The times are wild; contention, like a horse
10   Full of high feeding,° madly hath broke loose,   *overly rich food*
And bears down all before him.
LORD BARDOLPH   Noble Earl,
I bring you certain news from Shrewsbury.
NORTHUMBERLAND   Good, an° God will.   *if*
LORD BARDOLPH   As good as heart can wish.
The King is almost wounded to the death;
15   And, in the fortune° of my lord your son,   *good luck*
Prince Harry slain outright; and both the Blunts[3]
Killed by the hand of Douglas; young Prince John
And Westmorland and Stafford fled the field;
And Harry Monmouth's brawn,° the hulk Sir John,   *fattened pig*
20   Is prisoner to your son. O, such a day,
So fought, so followed,° and so fairly won,   *carried through*
Came not till now to dignify the times
Since Caesar's fortunes!°   *successes*
NORTHUMBERLAND   How is this derived?
Saw you the field? Came you from Shrewsbury?
25   LORD BARDOLPH   I spake with one, my lord, that came from thence,
A gentleman well bred and of good name,
That freely rendered me these news for true.

---

6. The messengers, exhausting themselves, gallop on.
1.1. Location: Scene continues.
1. A nobleman associated with the rebel Percy faction;
Falstaff's companion with the same name is unrelated.
2. Having the Porter enter on the upper playing
space is conjectural, but it effectively suggests that

Northumberland is in a stronghold where his retainers
are wary of intruders. The upper stage, however, does
not appear to have been used elsewhere in the play.
3. In *1 Henry IV*, only one Blunt, Sir Walter, dies at
Shrewsbury.

Enter TRAVERS

NORTHUMBERLAND   Here comes my servant Travers, who I sent
On Tuesday last to listen after news.

30   LORD BARDOLPH   My lord, I overrode° him on the way,   overtook
And he is furnished with no certainties
More than he haply° may retail from me.   perhaps

NORTHUMBERLAND   Now, Travers, what good tidings comes with you?

TRAVERS   My lord, Lord Bardolph turned me back[4]

35   With joyful tidings, and being better horsed
Outrode me. After him came spurring hard
A gentleman almost forspent° with speed,   worn out
That stopped by me to breathe° his bloodied horse.   rest
He asked the way to Chester,[5] and of him

40   I did demand what news from Shrewsbury.
He told me that rebellion had ill luck,
And that young Harry Percy's spur was cold.
With that he gave his able horse the head,
And, bending forward, struck his armèd heels

45   Against the panting sides of his poor jade°   worn-out horse
Up to the rowel-head;[6] and starting so,
He seemed in running to devour the way,
Staying° no longer question.   Awaiting

NORTHUMBERLAND   Ha? Again:
Said he young Harry Percy's spur was cold?

50   Of Hotspur, 'Coldspur'? that rebellion
Had met ill luck?

LORD BARDOLPH   My lord, I'll tell you what:
If my young lord your son have not the day,
Upon mine honour, for a silken point°   lace for tying a garment
I'll give my barony. Never talk of it.

55   NORTHUMBERLAND   Why should the gentleman that rode by Travers
Give then such instances of loss?

LORD BARDOLPH   Who, he?
He was some hilding° fellow that had stol'n   worthless
The horse he rode on, and, upon my life,
Spoke at a venture.°   at random

Enter MORTON

Look, here comes more news.

60   NORTHUMBERLAND   Yea, this man's brow, like to a title leaf,
Foretells the nature of a tragic volume.[7]
So looks the strand° whereon the imperious flood   shore
Hath left a witnessed usurpation.[8]
Say, Morton, didst thou come from Shrewsbury?

65   MORTON   I ran from Shrewsbury, my noble lord,
Where hateful death put on his ugliest mask
To fright our party.

4. In Q, Travers says that Sir John Umfreuile, not Lord
Bardolph, turned him back. Since Lord Bardolph reports
having met Travers on the road, most critics agree that
Umfreuile and Lord Bardolph are the same character
whose name got changed at some point. At 1.1.161, Q
assigns one line to "Umfr.," another indication that a
character with this name was once to figure in the play.
This line does not appear in F or in the present text.
5. A town north of Shrewsbury.
6. The spiked wheel at the end of the spur.

7. Alluding to the descriptive title pages of early modern printed books, which often indicated the principal
actions of the work and sometimes characterized them
as tragic or comic. For an example, see the descriptive
title page of the quarto version of this play, reprinted in
the Introduction.
8. *whereon . . . usurpation*: where the sea has left evidence of its conquest (of the land). The comparison is
between Morton's brow, wrinkled by sorrow, and sand
furrowed by the sea's encroachment.

NORTHUMBERLAND   How doth my son and brother?[9]
        Thou tremblest, and the whiteness in thy cheek
        Is apter than thy tongue to tell thy errand.
70   Even such a man, so faint, so spiritless,
        So dull, so dead in look, so woebegone,
        Drew Priam's curtain[1] in the dead of night,
        And would have told him half his Troy was burnt;
        But Priam found the fire ere he his tongue,
75   And I my Percy's death ere thou report'st it.
        This thou wouldst say: 'Your son did thus and thus,
        Your brother thus; so fought the noble Douglas',
        Stopping° my greedy ear with their bold deeds;   *Filling*
        But in the end, to stop° my ear indeed,   *plug up; obstruct*
80   Thou hast a sigh to blow away this praise,
        Ending with 'Brother, son, and all are dead.'
MORTON   Douglas is living, and your brother yet;
        But for my lord your son—
NORTHUMBERLAND   Why, he is dead.
        See what a ready tongue suspicion hath!
85   He that but fears the thing he would not know
        Hath by instinct knowledge from others' eyes
        That what he feared is chanced.° Yet speak, Morton.   *has happened*
        Tell thou an earl his divination lies,[2]
        And I will take it as a sweet disgrace,
90   And make thee rich for doing me such wrong.
MORTON   You are too great to be by me gainsaid,
        Your spirit is too true, your fears too certain.
NORTHUMBERLAND   Yet for all this, say not that Percy's dead.
        I see a strange confession in thine eye—
95   Thou shak'st thy head, and hold'st it fear or sin
        To speak a truth. If he be slain, say so.
        The tongue offends not that reports his death;
        And he doth sin that doth belie the dead,
        Not he which says the dead is not alive.
100   Yet the first bringer of unwelcome news
        Hath but a losing office,° and his tongue   *thankless duty*
        Sounds ever after as a sullen° bell   *mournful*
        Remembered knolling a departing friend.
LORD BARDOLPH   I cannot think, my lord, your son is dead.
105 MORTON [*to* NORTHUMBERLAND]   I am sorry I should force you to believe
        That which I would to God I had not seen;
        But these mine eyes saw him in bloody state,
        Rend'ring faint quittance,[3] wearied and out-breathed,°   *out of breath*
        To Harry Monmouth, whose swift wrath beat down
110   The never-daunted Percy to the earth,
        From whence with life he never more sprung up.
        In few,° his death, whose spirit lent a fire   *In short*
        Even to the dullest peasant in his camp,

---

9. The Earl of Worcester, who helped lead the rebellion staged in *1 Henry IV.*
1. Opened Priam's bed curtain. Priam was King of Troy during the Trojan War. This may allude to a scene from Virgil's *Aeneid* in which Hector appears to Aeneas, not Priam, in a dream, warning him of danger. Aeneas

wakes to find Troy in flames.
2. Tell me, who am an earl, that in my prophecy I lie. To say a social superior lies would normally be a grave offense, but Northumberland would be happy to be proven wrong.
3. Repayment (return of blows).

<table>
<tr><td></td><td>Being bruited° once, took fire and heat away</td><td>reported</td></tr>
<tr><td>115</td><td>From the best-tempered courage⁴ in his troops;</td><td></td></tr>
<tr><td></td><td>For from his metal° was his party steeled,</td><td>steel; courage</td></tr>
<tr><td></td><td>Which once in him abated,° all the rest</td><td>blunted</td></tr>
<tr><td></td><td>Turned on themselves,⁵ like dull and heavy lead;</td><td></td></tr>
<tr><td></td><td>And, as the thing that's heavy in itself</td><td></td></tr>
<tr><td>120</td><td>Upon enforcement° flies with greatest speed,</td><td>When forced into motion</td></tr>
</table>

So did our men, heavy in Hotspur's loss,
Lend to this weight such lightness with their fear
That arrows fled not swifter toward their aim
Than did our soldiers, aiming at their safety,
125   Fly from the field. Then was that noble Worcester
Too soon ta'en prisoner; and that furious Scot
The bloody Douglas, whose well-labouring sword
Had three times slain th'appearance of the King,⁶
Gan vail his stomach,⁷ and did grace° the shame   *sanction*
130   Of those that turned their backs, and in his flight,
Stumbling in fear, was took. The sum of all
Is that the King hath won, and hath sent out
A speedy power° to encounter you, my lord,   *quick-moving army*
Under the conduct° of young Lancaster   *command*
135   And Westmorland. This is the news at full.
NORTHUMBERLAND   For this I shall have time enough to mourn.
In poison there is physic;° and these news,   *medicine*
Having been° well, that would have made me sick,   *If I had been*
Being sick, have in some measure made me well;
140   And, as the wretch whose fever-weakened joints,
Like strengthless hinges, buckle under life,⁸
Impatient of his fit, breaks like a fire
Out of his keeper's° arms, even so my limbs,   *nurse's*
Weakened with grief, being now enraged with grief,
Are thrice themselves.
          [*He casts away his crutch*]
145   Hence therefore, thou nice° crutch!   *unmanly*
A scaly° gauntlet now with joints of steel   *mailed*
Must glove this hand.
          [*He snatches off his coif*]
                              And hence, thou sickly coif!
Thou art a guard too wanton° for the head   *effeminate; luxurious*
Which princes fleshed with conquest⁹ aim to hit.
150   Now bind my brows with iron, and approach
The ragged'st° hour that time and spite dare bring   *roughest*
To frown upon th'enraged Northumberland!
Let heaven kiss earth! Now let not nature's hand
Keep the wild flood confined! Let order die!
155   And let this world no longer be a stage
To feed contention in a ling'ring act;¹

---

4. Courage of the finest quality. The implicit comparison is to steel that had been tempered, or made strong, by extreme heat.
5. Bent backward (like soft metal); fled.
6. In *1 Henry IV*, at the Battle of Shrewsbury, members of the rebel faction slew several noblemen dressed in the King's coats whom they mistook for Henry himself. See *1 Henry IV* 5.3.1–13 and 5.4.24–37.

7. Began to lose courage (stomach).
8. Collapse from the burden of living.
9. Which princes made eager for bloody victories by having tasted raw flesh (been victorious). Hounds were "fleshed," given a taste of raw meat, to prepare them for the hunt.
1. *And let . . . act:* And let the world stop being a stage where strife is encouraged in a prolonged action.

But let one spirit of the first-born Cain[2]
Reign in all bosoms, that each heart being set
On bloody courses, the rude scene may end,
160 And darkness be the burier of the dead!
LORD BARDOLPH   Sweet Earl, divorce not wisdom from your honour.
MORTON   The lives of all your loving complices°   *associates*
Lean on your health, the which, if you give o'er
To stormy passion, must perforce decay.[3]
165 You cast th'event° of war, my noble lord,   *calculated the outcome*
And summed° the account of chance, before you said   *added up*
'Let us make head'.° It was your presurmise   *raise an army*
That in the dole° of blows your son might drop.   *dealing out*
You knew he walked o'er perils on an edge,°   *a narrow blade*
170 More likely to fall in than to get o'er.
You were advised° his flesh was capable   *aware*
Of wounds and scars, and that his forward spirit
Would lift him where most trade of° danger ranged.°   *dealing in / was displayed*
Yet did you say, 'Go forth'; and none of this,
175 Though strongly apprehended, could restrain
The stiff-borne° action. What hath then befall'n?   *stubbornly pursued*
Or what doth this bold enterprise bring forth,
More than that being° which was like to be?   *event*
LORD BARDOLPH   We all that are engagèd to° this loss   *involved in*
180 Knew that we ventured on such dangerous seas
That if we wrought out life was ten to one;[4]
And yet we ventured for the gain proposed,
Choked the respect of° likely peril feared;   *Refused to consider*
And since we are o'erset,° venture again.   *overthrown*
185 Come, we will all put forth body and goods.
MORTON   'Tis more than time; and, my most noble lord,
I hear for certain, and dare speak the truth,[5]
The gentle Archbishop of York is up°   *up in arms*
With well-appointed powers.° He is a man   *well-equipped forces*
190 Who with a double surety binds his followers.[6]
My lord, your son had only but the corpse,°   *mere bodies*
But shadows and the shows of men, to fight;
For that same word 'rebellion' did divide
The action of their bodies from their souls,
195 And they did fight with queasiness, constrained,
As men drink potions, that their weapons only
Seemed on our side; but, for their spirits and souls,
This word 'rebellion', it had froze them up,
As fish are in a pond. But now the Bishop
200 Turns insurrection to religion.
Supposed sincere and holy in his thoughts,
He's followed both with body and with mind,
And doth enlarge his rising[7] with the blood
Of fair King Richard, scraped from Pomfret stones;[8]

2. In the Bible, the first human being to be born and the murderer of his brother.
3. Lines 165–78 are not included in Q. (See Textual Note.)
4. The odds were ten to one against our preserving life.
5. Lines 188–208 are missing from Q. It is generally agreed that these lines were cut for political reasons.
6. Referring to the fact that the Archbishop, unlike Hotspur, might use his religious as well as his temporal authority to secure his soldiers' fidelity.
7. And increases the size or enhances the reputation of his rebellion.
8. Alluding to Henry IV's responsibility for the murder of Richard at Pontefract Castle (Pomfret), as staged in Act 5 of *Richard II*. Richard's blood is treated as a holy saint's relic.

205 Derives from heaven his quarrel and his cause;
Tells them he doth bestride° a bleeding land   protect by standing over
Gasping for life under great Bolingbroke;°   (Henry IV)
And more and less° do flock to follow him.   people of all ranks
NORTHUMBERLAND   I knew of this before, but, to speak truth,
210 This present grief had wiped it from my mind.
Go in with me, and counsel every man
The aptest way for safety and revenge.
Get posts° and letters, and make° friends with speed.   messengers / gather
Never so few, and never yet more need.   *Exeunt*

1.2

Enter Sir John FALSTAFF, *[followed by] his* PAGE *bearing
his sword and buckler°*   shield

FALSTAFF   Sirrah,[1] you giant, what says the doctor to my water?°   urine
PAGE   He said, sir, the water itself was a good healthy water,
but, for the party that owed° it, he might have more diseases   owned
than he knew for.°   was aware of
5 FALSTAFF   Men of all sorts take a pride to gird° at me. The brain   mock
of this foolish-compounded clay,[2] man, is not able to invent
anything that tends to laughter more than I invent, or is
invented on me. I am not only witty in myself, but the cause
that wit is in other men. I do here walk before thee like a sow
10 that hath o'erwhelmed° all her litter but one. If the Prince put   crushed
thee into my service for any other reason than to set me off,[3]
why then, I have no judgement. Thou whoreson mandrake,[4]
thou art fitter to be worn in my cap than to wait at my heels. I
was never manned with° an agate[5] till now; but I will set you   attended by
15 neither in gold nor silver, but in vile apparel, and send you
back again to your master for a jewel—the juvenal° the Prince   youth
your master, whose chin is not yet fledge.° I will sooner have a   covered with down
beard grow in the palm of my hand than he shall get one off
his cheek; and yet he will not stick° to say his face is a face-   hesitate
20 royal.[6] God may finish it when he will; 'tis not a hair amiss yet.
He may keep it still at° a face-royal, for a barber shall never   at the value of
earn sixpence out of it. And yet he'll be crowing as if he had
writ man° ever since his father was a bachelor. He may keep   called himself a man
his own grace,° but he's almost out of mine, I can assure him.   title (Prince); favor
25 What said Master Dumbleton about the satin for my short
cloak and slops?[7]
PAGE   He said, sir, you should procure him better assurance
than Bardolph. He would not take his bond and yours; he
liked not the security.
30 FALSTAFF   Let him be damned like the glutton![8] Pray God his

---

1.2 Location: A street in London.
1. Form of address to a social inferior.
2. Clay compounded with foolishness (an image derived from the biblical account of the first human being as formed out of clay).
3. To make me stand out by contrast. The page is tiny, and Falstaff is huge.
4. An herb with a forked root that was popularly supposed to resemble a miniature man. It was believed to shriek when pulled from the ground and to have aphrodisiacal powers. *whoreson*: an insult, derived from the phrase "whore's son."

5. A small jewel often carved with images of people and worn in caps.
6. The face of royalty (with a pun on "royal," a coin worth 10 shillings and stamped with the monarch's face).
7. Baggy knee breeches, fashionable in Elizabethan London.
8. Referring to the biblical parable of Dives, a rich glutton who ignored the pleas of the beggar Lazarus and at death was condemned to hell, where he implored Lazarus to dip his finger in water and lay it on his tongue to cool the flames (see Luke 16:19–31).

tongue be hotter! A whoreson Achitophel,[9] a rascally yea-
forsooth knave,[1] to bear a gentleman in hand° and then stand   *lead a gentleman on*
upon security! The whoreson smooth-pates[2] do now wear noth-
ing but high shoes and bunches of keys at their girdles;[3] and if
35   a man is through with them in honest taking-up,[4] then they
must stand upon security. I had as lief° they would put rats-   *gladly*
bane° in my mouth as offer to stop it with security. I looked a°   *rat poison / that he*
should have sent me two and twenty yards of satin, as I am a
true knight,[5] and he sends me 'security'! Well, he may sleep in
40   security, for he hath the horn of abundance, and the lightness
of his wife shines through it;[6] and yet cannot he see, though he
have his own lanthorn to light him. Where's Bardolph?

PAGE   He's gone in Smithfield[7] to buy your worship a horse.

FALSTAFF   I bought him in Paul's,[8] and he'll buy me a horse in
45   Smithfield. An° I could get me but a wife in the stews,° I were   *If / brothels*
manned, horsed, and wived.

Enter [the] LORD CHIEF JUSTICE *and [his]* SERVANT

PAGE   Sir, here comes the nobleman that committed° the Prince   *imprisoned*
for striking him about Bardolph.[9]

FALSTAFF *[moving away]*   Wait close;° I will not see him.[1]   *concealed*

50   LORD CHIEF JUSTICE *[to his* SERVANT*]*   What's he that goes there?

SERVANT   Falstaff, an't please your lordship.

LORD CHIEF JUSTICE   He that was in question° for the robbery?[2]   *under investigation*

SERVANT   He, my lord; but he hath since done good service at
Shrewsbury, and, as I hear, is now going with some charge° to   *command of soldiers*
55   the Lord John of Lancaster.

LORD CHIEF JUSTICE   What, to York? Call him back again.

SERVANT   Sir John Falstaff!

FALSTAFF   Boy, tell him I am deaf.

PAGE *[to the* SERVANT*]*   You must speak louder; my master is
60   deaf.

LORD CHIEF JUSTICE   I am sure he is to the hearing of anything
good. *[To the* SERVANT*]* Go pluck him by the elbow; I must
speak with him.

SERVANT   Sir John!

65   FALSTAFF   What, a young knave and begging! Is there not wars?[3]
Is there not employment? Doth not the King lack subjects? Do
not the rebels want soldiers? Though it be a shame to be on
any side but one, it is worse shame to beg than to be on the

9. A biblical figure, King David's trusted counselor,
who betrayed him by supporting the treason of the
king's son (2 Samuel 15).
1. A villainous knave who appears to be agreeable. A
"yea-forsooth" knave makes promises with mild oaths
(but then breaks them).
2. Alluding disparagingly to the fashion among tradesmen, especially Puritans, for short hair.
3. Wear the most fashionable shoes and display a mass
of keys (habits suggesting pride and conspicuous consumption).
4. If a man makes a deal with them for a purchase on
credit.
5. Referring to Tudor sumptuary codes, which prescribed the fabrics that could be worn by people of different social ranks. As a knight, Falstaff can wear satin.
6. For he is rich and his wife's promiscuity is visible to
all, with puns on "horn" as referring to the horn
lanterns sold by merchants; to a symbol of overflowing

plenty (a cornucopia); and to cuckoldry (deceived husbands were said to wear horns). "Lightness" can mean
both illumination and sexual promiscuity.
7. A district northwest of London's city walls, used as
a market for animals.
8. St. Paul's Cathedral in London, where masterless
men presented themselves for employment.
9. Alluding to the apocryphal account of the youthful
Prince's assault on the Lord Chief Justice, staged in
The Famous Victories of Henry V, the anonymous play
from which Shakespeare's is partly derived.
1. Falstaff's determination not to acknowledge the
Lord Chief Justice presumably causes him to turn his
back on the magistrate or walk off in another direction.
2. The Gadshill robbery, in which Falstaff took part.
See *1 Henry IV* 2.2.
3. Alluding to the Elizabethan practice of mass conscription of impoverished men.

worst side, were it worse than the name of rebellion can tell
70   how to make° it.   *regard*

SERVANT   You mistake me, sir.

FALSTAFF   Why, sir, did I say you were an honest man? Setting
my knighthood and my soldiership aside, I had lied in my
throat° if I had said so.   *deliberately lied*

75   SERVANT   I pray you, sir, then set your knighthood and your soldiership aside, and give me leave to tell you you lie in your
throat if you say I am any other than an honest man.

FALSTAFF   I give thee leave to tell me so? I lay aside that which
grows to me?° If thou gettest any leave of me, hang me. If thou   *is part of me*
80   takest leave, thou wert better be hanged. You hunt counter.[4]
Hence, avaunt!°   *be gone*

SERVANT   Sir, my lord would speak with you.

LORD CHIEF JUSTICE   Sir John Falstaff, a word with you.

FALSTAFF   My good lord! God give your lordship good time of
85   day. I am glad to see your lordship abroad. I heard say your
lordship was sick. I hope your lordship goes abroad by advice.°   *by medical advice*
Your lordship, though not clean past your youth, have yet some
smack of age in you, some relish of the saltness of time in you;
and I most humbly beseech your lordship to have a reverent
90   care of your health.

LORD CHIEF JUSTICE   Sir John, I sent for you before your expedition to Shrewsbury.

FALSTAFF   An't please your lordship, I hear his majesty is
returned with some discomfort from Wales.[5]

95   LORD CHIEF JUSTICE   I talk not of his majesty. You would not
come when I sent for you.

FALSTAFF   And I hear, moreover, his highness is fallen into this
same whoreson apoplexy.°   *paralysis*

LORD CHIEF JUSTICE   Well, God mend him! I pray you, let me
100   speak with you.

FALSTAFF   This apoplexy is, as I take it, a kind of lethargy, an't
please your lordship, a kind of sleeping in the blood, a
whoreson tingling.

LORD CHIEF JUSTICE   What° tell you me of it? Be it as it is.   *Why*

105   FALSTAFF   It hath it original° from much grief, from study, and   *its origin*
perturbation of the brain. I have read the cause of his effects in
Galen.[6] It is a kind of deafness.

LORD CHIEF JUSTICE   I think you are fallen into the disease, for
you hear not what I say to you.

110   FALSTAFF   Very well, my lord, very well. Rather, an't please you,
it is the disease of not listening, the malady of not marking, that
I am troubled withal.°   *with*

LORD CHIEF JUSTICE   To punish you by the heels[7] would amend
the attention of your ears, and I care not if I do become your
115   physician.

FALSTAFF   I am as poor as Job,[8] my lord, but not so patient. Your
lordship may minister the potion of imprisonment to me in

---

4. You pursue the scent of the game in the wrong
direction.
5. Some discouragement from Wales (where the King
promised to fight Glyndŵr and Mortimer at the end of
1 Henry IV).
6. Ancient Greek physician whose anatomical texts were
widely translated and printed in early modern Europe.

Galen was commonly regarded as the chief authority in
human physiology.
7. By putting your feet in the stocks or in shackles.
8. A biblical figure who, in the Book of Job, patiently
endured the many adversities with which God afflicted
him, including poverty.

respect of° poverty; but how I should be your patient to follow   *on account of*
your prescriptions, the wise may make some dram of a scruple,
120   or indeed a scruple itself.⁹

LORD CHIEF JUSTICE   I sent for you, when there were matters
against you for your life,¹ to come speak with me.

FALSTAFF   As I was then advised by my learned counsel in the
laws of this land-service,° I did not come.   *military duty*

125 LORD CHIEF JUSTICE   Well, the truth is, Sir John, you live in
great infamy.

FALSTAFF   He that buckles himself in my belt cannot live in less.

LORD CHIEF JUSTICE   Your means are very slender, and your waste
is great.

130 FALSTAFF   I would it were otherwise; I would my means were
greater and my waist slenderer.

LORD CHIEF JUSTICE   You have misled the youthful Prince.

FALSTAFF   The young Prince hath misled me. I am the fellow
with the great belly, and he my dog.²

135 LORD CHIEF JUSTICE   Well, I am loath to gall° a new-healed   *to injure by rubbing*
wound. Your day's service at Shrewsbury hath a little gilded
over your night's exploit on Gads Hill. You may thank th'unquiet time for your quiet o'erposting° that action.   *passing swiftly over*

FALSTAFF   My lord—

140 LORD CHIEF JUSTICE   But since all is well, keep it so. Wake not a
sleeping wolf.

FALSTAFF   To wake a wolf is as bad as smell a fox.°   *as being suspicious*

LORD CHIEF JUSTICE   What! You are as a candle, the better part
burnt out.

145 FALSTAFF   A wassail candle,³ my lord, all tallow°—if I did say of   *animal fat*
wax,⁴ my growth would approve° the truth.   *attest to*

LORD CHIEF JUSTICE   There is not a white hair in your face but
should have his effect° of gravity.   *manifestation*

FALSTAFF   His effect of gravy, gravy, gravy.⁵

150 LORD CHIEF JUSTICE   You follow the young Prince up and down
like his ill angel.°   *evil spirit*

FALSTAFF   Not so, my lord; your ill angel is light,⁶ but I hope he
that looks upon me will take me without weighing. And yet in
some respects, I grant, I cannot go.° I cannot tell, virtue is of so   *walk; be circulated*
155   little regard in these costermongers' times⁷ that true valour is
turned bearherd;⁸ pregnancy° is made a tapster, and his quick   *mental agility*
wit wasted in giving reckonings;° all the other gifts appertinent°   *tavern bills / belonging*
to man, as the malice of this age shapes them, are not worth a
gooseberry. You that are old consider not the capacities of us
160   that are young. You do measure the heat of our livers with the
bitterness of your galls.⁹ And we that are in the vanguard° of   *most advanced stage*
our youth, I must confess, are wags too.

---

9. The wise may feel a particle of doubt. Drams and
scruples were small weights used to measure medicines
in apothecary shops.
1. For which your life was at stake.
2. An obscure allusion. It may refer to the man in the
moon, a mythical figure who supposedly carried a bush
and was accompanied by a dog.
3. A large fat candle used at holiday festivities.
4. Beeswax, with pun on "wax" as meaning "grow."
5. Grease; sweat. Falstaff implies that sweat should
drop from his face as fat (gravy) drops from hot meat.

6. Your bad coin weighs less. Falstaff puns on "angel"
as the name of a gold coin that could illegally be clipped
so that it weighed less than it should.
7. In these commercial times. A costermonger sold trifling commodities such as fruits and vegetables.
8. Keeper of bears, such as those used for the popular
entertainment of bearbaiting.
9. You measure the strength of our passions by the bitterness of your melancholy. The liver was believed to be
the seat of youthful passions, and bile or gall produced
the melancholy and anger characteristic of old age.

LORD CHIEF JUSTICE Do you set down your name in the scroll
of youth, that are written down old with all the characters° of   *letters; signs*
165 age? Have you not a moist eye, a dry hand, a yellow cheek, a
white beard, a decreasing leg, an increasing belly? Is not your
voice broken, your wind short, your chin double, your wit single, and every part about you blasted with antiquity? And will
you yet call yourself young? Fie, fie, fie, Sir John!

170 FALSTAFF My lord, I was born about three of the clock in the
afternoon with a white head, and something a° round belly.   *a somewhat*
For my voice, I have lost it with hallowing° and singing of   *shouting to hounds*
anthems. To approve° my youth further, I will not. The truth   *prove*
is, I am only old in judgement and understanding; and he that
175 will caper° with me for a thousand marks,[1] let him lend me the   *dance (in competition)*
money, and have at him! For the box of th'ear that the Prince
gave you, he gave it like a rude° prince, and you took it like a   *violent; an uncivilized*
sensible lord.[2] I have checked him for it, and the young lion
repents—[*aside*] marry,° not in ashes and sackcloth, but in new   *by the Virgin Mary (oath)*
180 silk and old sack.[3]

LORD CHIEF JUSTICE Well, God send the Prince a better companion!

FALSTAFF God send the companion a better prince! I cannot rid
my hands of him.

185 LORD CHIEF JUSTICE Well, the King hath severed you and
Prince Harry. I hear you are going with Lord John of Lancaster against the Archbishop and the Earl of Northumberland.

FALSTAFF Yea, I thank your pretty sweet wit for it. But look° you   *see that*
190 pray, all you that kiss my lady Peace at home, that our armies
join not in a hot day; for, by the Lord, I take but two shirts out
with me, and I mean not to sweat extraordinarily. If it be a hot
day and I brandish anything but my bottle, would I might never
spit white again.[4] There is not a dangerous action° can peep   *military action*
195 out his head but I am thrust upon it. Well, I cannot last ever.
But it was alway yet the trick° of our English nation, if they   *habit*
have a good thing, to make it too common. If ye will needs say
I am an old man, you should give me rest. I would to God my
name were not so terrible to the enemy as it is. I were better to
200 be eaten to death with a rust than to be scoured to nothing with
perpetual motion.

LORD CHIEF JUSTICE Well, be honest, be honest, and God bless
your expedition.

FALSTAFF Will your lordship lend me a thousand pound to fur-
205 nish me forth?

LORD CHIEF JUSTICE Not a penny, not a penny. You are too
impatient to bear crosses.[5] Fare you well. Commend me to my
cousin Westmorland.

[*Exeunt* LORD CHIEF JUSTICE *and his* SERVANT]

---

1. A unit of money; one mark was equal to two-thirds
of a pound.
2. Like a reasonable lord; like a lord capable of feeling
pain. For the story of Hal's striking the Chief Justice,
see note to 1.2.48.
3. A Spanish white wine that improved with age.

4. A disputed passage. Perhaps, may I never drink
again (white spit was thought to be the result of heavy
drinking).
5. To endure afflictions like a good Christian; to carry
silver coins, which bear the sign of a cross.

FALSTAFF   If I do, fillip° me with a three-man beetle.[6] A man can   *strike*
210   no more separate age and covetousness than a° can part young   *he*
       limbs and lechery; but the gout[7] galls the one and the pox
       pinches° the other, and so both the degrees prevent my   *syphilis torments*
       curses.[8] Boy!

PAGE   Sir.

215   FALSTAFF   What money is in my purse?

PAGE   Seven groats° and two pence.   *coins worth fourpence*

FALSTAFF   I can get no remedy against this consumption of the
       purse. Borrowing only lingers and lingers it out, but the disease
       is incurable. [*Giving letters*] Go bear this letter to my lord of
220   Lancaster; this to the Prince; this to the Earl of Westmorland;
       and this to old Mistress Ursula,[9] whom I have weekly sworn to
       marry since I perceived the first white hair of my chin. About
       it. You know where to find me.   [*Exit* PAGE][1]
       A pox of this gout!—or a gout of this pox!—for the one or the
225   other plays the rogue with my great toe. 'Tis no matter if I do
       halt;° I have the wars for my colour,° and my pension shall   *limp / pretext*
       seem the more reasonable. A good wit will make use of any-
       thing. I will turn diseases to commodity.°   *Exit*   *profit*

1.3

Enter the ARCHBISHOP [*of York*], *Thomas* MOWBRAY [*the*]
Earl Marshal,[1] *Lord* HASTINGS, *and* LORD BARDOLPH

ARCHBISHOP OF YORK   Thus have you heard our cause and
          known our means,
       And, my most noble friends, I pray you all
       Speak plainly your opinions of our hopes.
       And first, Lord Marshal, what say you to it?

5   MOWBRAY   I well allow the occasion of our arms,[2]
       But gladly would be better satisfied
       How in our means° we should advance ourselves   *with our resources*
       To look with forehead bold and big enough
       Upon the power and puissance° of the King.   *strength*

10   HASTINGS   Our present musters grow upon the file°   *according to our list*
       To five-and-twenty thousand men of choice,°   *choice men*
       And our supplies° live largely in the hope   *reinforcements*
       Of great Northumberland, whose bosom burns
       With an incensèd fire of injuries.

15   LORD BARDOLPH   The question then, Lord Hastings, standeth thus:
       Whether our present five-and-twenty thousand
       May hold up head° without Northumberland.   *May succeed*

HASTINGS   With him we may.

---

6. A huge sledgehammer designed to be lifted by three laborers at once.

7. A disease characterized by painful inflammation of the joints, often of the toe joints in particular, and associated with the excessive consumption of rich food and alcohol. Falstaff is bothered by gout, and it may have been the reason he sent his urine to be examined by the doctor at the beginning of this scene.

8. So both conditions (age and youth) anticipate my curses. Venereal disease torments young lecherous men; gout afflicts old men.

9. A name nowhere else mentioned in this play. It

could be the first name of Mistress Quickly. It may also be an inadvertent reference to the Ursula of *Much Ado About Nothing*, a play also printed in 1600.

1. Neither Q nor F marks a separate exit for the Page. F indicates a plural "Exeunt" at the end of the scene, suggesting that Falstaff and the Page exit together. But clearly the fat knight's concluding lines are a private meditation on his diseases best spoken after he has sent the Page off to deliver his letters.

1.3 Location: The Archbishop's palace in York.

1. The officer in charge of arranging royal ceremonies.

2. I grant the justice of our taking arms.

LORD BARDOLPH   Yea, marry, there's the point;
    But if without him we be thought too feeble,
20 My judgement is, we should not step too far³
    Till we had his assistance by the hand;
    For in a theme° so bloody-faced as this,   *matter*
    Conjecture, expectation, and surmise
    Of aids uncertain should not be admitted.
25 ARCHBISHOP OF YORK   'Tis very true, Lord Bardolph, for indeed
    It was young Hotspur's case at Shrewsbury.
    LORD BARDOLPH   It was, my lord; who lined° himself with hope,   *strengthened*
    Eating the air on promise of supply,⁴
    Flatt'ring himself with project of a power°   *expectation of an army*
30 Much smaller° than the smallest of his thoughts;   *smaller in actuality*
    And so, with great imagination
    Proper to madmen, led his powers to death,
    And winking° leapt into destruction.   *shutting his eyes*
    HASTINGS   But by your leave, it never yet did hurt
35 To lay down likelihoods and forms of hope.⁵
    LORD BARDOLPH   Yes, if this present quality° of war—   *condition*
    Indeed the instant° action, a cause on foot°—   *present / in motion*
    Lives so in hope; as in an early spring
    We see th'appearing buds, which to prove° fruit   *mature into*
40 Hope gives not so much warrant as despair
    That frosts will bite them.⁶ When we mean to build
    We first survey the plot,⁷ then draw the model;°   *design*
    And when we see the figure° of the house,   *design*
    Then must we rate the cost of the erection,
45 Which if we find outweighs ability,
    What do we then but draw anew the model
    In fewer offices,° or, at least,° desist   *rooms / worst*
    To build at all? Much more in this great work—
    Which is almost to pluck a kingdom down
50 And set another up—should we survey
    The plot of situation and the model,
    Consent° upon a sure foundation,   *Agree*
    Question surveyors,° know our own estate,°   *architects / resources*
    How able such a work to undergo,
55 To weigh against his opposite;⁸ or else
    We fortify in paper and in figures,
    Using the names of men instead of men,
    Like one that draws the model of an house
    Beyond his power to build it, who, half-through,
60 Gives o'er, and leaves his part-created cost⁹
    A naked subject° to the weeping clouds,   *An exposed object*
    And waste for churlish winter's tyranny.
    HASTINGS   Grant that our hopes, yet° likely of fair birth,   *still*
    Should be stillborn, and that we now possessed
65 The utmost man of expectation,¹

---

3. Lines 21–24 are not present in Q.
4. Sustaining himself on nothing but the promise of aid; believing the empty words he had heard concerning promised aid.
5. And hopeful plans. Lines 36–55 are not present in Q.
6. *as in . . . them:* an obscure passage. Bardolph may mean that optimism in this instance is ill advised, just as it is ill advised to hope that early spring buds will

mature into fruit rather than be killed by frost.
7. Plan. What follows is an elaboration on a biblical parable in Luke 14:28–30 about a wise builder.
8. *To weigh . . . opposite:* To put in the balance against contrary arguments. Bardolph is urging the rebels to evaluate their strengths against their weaknesses.
9. And leaves his costly building half completed.
1. The last man whom we can expect.

I think we are a body strong enough,
Even as we are, to equal with the King.
LORD BARDOLPH   What, is the King but five-and-twenty thousand?
HASTINGS   To us no more, nay, not so much, Lord Bardolph;
70   For his divisions, as the times do brawl,°   *are full of conflict*
Are in three heads: one power against the French,
And one against Glyndŵr, perforce a third
Must take up us.° So is the unfirm King   *oppose us*
In three divided, and his coffers sound
75   With hollow poverty and emptiness.
ARCHBISHOP OF YORK   That he should draw his several° strengths together   *separate*
And come against us in full puissance
Need not be dreaded.
HASTINGS   If he should do so,
He leaves his back unarmed, the French and Welsh
80   Baying him at the heels.² Never fear that.
LORD BARDOLPH   Who is it like° should lead his forces hither?   *likely*
HASTINGS   The Duke of Lancaster and Westmorland;
Against the Welsh, himself and Harry Monmouth;
But who is substituted° 'gainst the French   *delegated*
I have no certain notice.³
85   ARCHBISHOP OF YORK   Let us on,
And publish° the occasion of our arms.   *make public*
The commonwealth is sick of their own choice;
Their over-greedy love hath surfeited.⁴
An habitation giddy and unsure
90   Hath he that buildeth on the vulgar° heart.   *common*
O thou fond° many, with what loud applause   *foolish*
Didst thou beat° heaven with blessing Bolingbroke,   *assail*
Before he was what thou wouldst have him be!
And being now trimmed° in thine own desires,   *decked out*
95   Thou, beastly feeder, art so full of him
That thou provok'st thyself to cast him up.
So, so, thou common dog, didst thou disgorge
Thy glutton bosom of the royal Richard;
And now thou wouldst eat thy dead vomit up,
100 And howl'st to find it. What trust is in these times?
They that when Richard lived would have him die
Are now become enamoured on his grave.
Thou that threw'st dust upon his goodly head,
When through proud London he came sighing on
105 After th'admirèd heels of Bolingbroke,
Cri'st now, 'O earth, yield us that king again,
And take thou this!' O thoughts of men accursed!
Past and to come seems best; things present, worst.
MOWBRAY   Shall we go draw our numbers° and set on?   *gather our forces*
110 HASTINGS   We are time's subjects, and time bids be gone.   *Exeunt*

---

2. That is, following him like hunting dogs.
3. Lines 85–108 are not present in Q.

4. Became sick through overindulgence.

2.1

Enter [MISTRESS QUICKLY *the*] *hostess of* [*a*] *tavern, and an officer,* FANG [*followed at a distance by another officer*], SNARE[1]

MISTRESS QUICKLY Master Fang, have you entered the action?°   *begun the lawsuit*
FANG It is entered.
MISTRESS QUICKLY Where's your yeoman?° Is't a lusty[2] yeoman?   *assistant*
Will a stand to't?[3]
5 FANG Sirrah!—Where's Snare?
MISTRESS QUICKLY O Lord, ay, good Master Snare.
SNARE [*coming forward*] Here, here.
FANG Snare, we must arrest Sir John Falstaff.
MISTRESS QUICKLY Yea, good Master Snare, I have entered him[4]
10 and all.
SNARE It may chance° cost some of us our lives, for he will stab.   *perhaps*
MISTRESS QUICKLY Alas the day, take heed of him; he stabbed[5]
me in mine own house, most beastly, in good faith. A cares not
what mischief he does; if his weapon° be out, he will foin° like   *dagger; penis / thrust*
15 any devil, he will spare neither man, woman, nor child.
FANG If I can close[6] with him, I care not for his thrust.
MISTRESS QUICKLY No, nor I neither. I'll be at your elbow.
FANG An I but fist° him once, an a come but within my   *seize; masturbate*
vice°—   *grasp*
20 MISTRESS QUICKLY I am undone by his going, I warrant you; he's
an infinitive thing upon my score.[7] Good Master Fang, hold
him sure. Good Master Snare, let him not scape. A comes continuantly to Pie Corner[8]—saving your manhoods—to buy a
saddle,[9] and he is indited° to dinner to the Lubber's Head[1] in   *(for "invited")*
25 Lombard Street, to Master Smooth's the silkman. I pray you,
since my exion is entered,[2] and my case° so openly known to   *lawsuit; vagina*
the world, let him be brought in to his answer. A hundred mark
is a long one° for a poor lone woman to bear; and I have borne,[3]   *huge account*
and borne, and borne, and have been fobbed off, and fobbed
30 off, and fobbed off, from this day to that day, that it is a shame
to be thought on. There is no honesty in such dealing, unless
a woman should be made an ass and a beast, to bear every
knave's wrong.
Enter Sir John FALSTAFF, BARDOLPH, *and the* [PAGE][4]

2.1 Location: Eastcheap, a street and market in London.
1. That Snare should linger behind Fang is suggested
by the subsequent lines in which Fang cannot locate his
fellow officer. Perhaps Snare is slow and lazy; or perhaps he deliberately lags behind to sniff out trouble and
"ensnare" villains.
2. Sturdy; lustful. The following lines are full of sexual
puns.
3. Will he fight vigorously? Will he maintain an erect
penis?
4. I have brought suit against him, with a pun on
"entered him" as meaning "had sexual relations with
him." The phrase usually denotes a man's sexual entry
into a woman.
5. With a pun on "stabbed" as meaning "sexually penetrated."
6. Fight hand to hand; clinch.
7. "Infinitive" is Quickly's malapropism, or verbal blunder, for "infinite." She implies that the board ("score")

on which her accounts are tallied has innumerable
markings corresponding to Falstaff's debts to her.
8. Piecorner was an area of Smithfield named for its
cooks' shops and known for its commerce in horses and
sex. *continuantly*: blunder for "continually" or "inconti-
nently."
9. With a pun on "saddle" as also meaning "female genitalia."
1. Blunder for "Libbard's," an Elizabethan form of
"Leopard's." The silk merchant's shop sign evidently
contained the image of a leopard's head.
2. Since my legal action has begun, with a pun on
"entered" suggesting sexual penetration.
3. Endured, with a pun on "have borne" as meaning
"have supported the weight of a partner in sexual relations."
4. As here, Q's stage directions sometimes refer to "the
boy" rather than "the page." These have been standardized to "Page" throughout.

Yonder he comes, and that arrant° malmsey-nose[5] knave Bar-   notorious
dolph with him. Do your offices,° do your offices, Master Fang   duties
and Master Snare; do me,[6] do me, do me your offices.

FALSTAFF   How now, whose mare's dead? What's the matter?

FANG   Sir John, I arrest you at the suit of Mistress Quickly.

FALSTAFF [*drawing*]   Away, varlets! Draw, Bardolph! Cut me off
the villain's head! Throw the quean° in the channel!°   whore / street gutter

[BARDOLPH *draws*]

MISTRESS QUICKLY   Throw me in the channel? I'll throw thee in
the channel!

[*A brawl*]

Wilt thou, wilt thou, thou bastardly rogue? Murder, murder!
Ah, thou honeysuckle[7] villain, wilt thou kill God's officers, and
the King's? Ah, thou honeyseed° rogue! Thou art a honeyseed,   (for "homicidal")
a man-queller, and a woman-queller.

FALSTAFF   Keep them off, Bardolph!

FANG   A rescue,[8] a rescue!

MISTRESS QUICKLY   Good people, bring a rescue or two. Thou
wot,° wot thou? Thou wot, wot'a? Do, do, thou rogue, do, thou   You will
hempseed![9]

PAGE   Away, you scullion,° you rampallian,° you fustilarian![1] I'll   kitchen wench / ruffian
tickle your catastrophe![2]

Enter [*the*] LORD CHIEF JUSTICE *and his men*

LORD CHIEF JUSTICE   What is the matter? Keep the peace here,
ho!

[*Brawl ends.* FANG *seizes* FALSTAFF][3]

MISTRESS QUICKLY   Good my lord, be good to me; I beseech you,
stand to me.[4]

LORD CHIEF JUSTICE   How now, Sir John? What, are you brawl-
ing here?
Doth this become your place,° your time° and business?   social place / age
You should have been well on your way to York.
[*To* FANG] Stand from him, fellow. Wherefore hang'st thou
upon him?

MISTRESS QUICKLY   O my most worshipful lord, an't° please your   if it
grace, I am a poor widow of Eastcheap, and he is arrested at
my suit.

LORD CHIEF JUSTICE   For what sum?

MISTRESS QUICKLY   It is more than for some, my lord, it is for all,
all I have. He hath eaten me out of house and home. He hath
put all my substance into that fat belly of his; [*to* FALSTAFF] but
I will have some of it out again, or I will ride thee a-nights like
the mare.[5]

5. Red-nosed from drinking alcohol. Malmsey was a strong red wine named after its place of origin in Greece and available from Spain, Portugal, and their colonies as well as Greece.
6. Do your jobs for me, with a pun on "do me" as slang for "have sexual relations with me."
7. For "homicidal," with a pun on "honey" as slang for "sexual pleasure."
8. A cry for help in resisting arrest. Fang fears Falstaff is being rescued, but Quickly in the next line takes "rescue" to mean "reinforcements" and seems to call for the rescue Fang is trying to stop.
9. Another version of "homicide," with an allusion to the hangman's hempen rope.

1. Fat, unkempt woman.
2. Expression meaning "I'll whip your rear end."
3. There are considerable opportunities for comic stage business here. Someone has to be hanging on Falstaff at this point, because at line 61, the Lord Chief Justice tells a "fellow" to let go. Perhaps Fang has twined himself around Falstaff's legs or has even (living up to his name) lodged his teeth in Falstaff's clothing or anatomy.
4. Support me; be sexually erect for me.
5. Referring to a kind of goblin supposed to produce nightmares by sitting on the chest of a sleeper, with puns on "ride" as meaning "mount sexually" and on "mare" as a disparaging term for "woman."

FALSTAFF   I think I am as like to ride the mare, if I have any
vantage of ground to get up.°   mount

LORD CHIEF JUSTICE   How comes this, Sir John? Fie, what man
of good temper would endure this tempest of exclamation? Are
75   you not ashamed, to enforce a poor widow to so rough a course
to come by her own?

FALSTAFF [to the Hostess]   What is the gross sum that I owe thee?

MISTRESS QUICKLY   Marry, if thou wert an honest man, thyself,
and the money too. Thou didst swear to me upon a parcel-gilt°   partly gilded
80   goblet, sitting in my Dolphin chamber,° at the round table, by   (an inn room)
a sea-coal fire,⁶ upon Wednesday in Wheeson° week, when the   Whitsun (Pentecost)
Prince broke thy head for liking° his father to a singing-man of   likening
Windsor⁷—thou didst swear to me then, as I was washing thy
wound, to marry me, and make me my lady thy wife. Canst
85   thou deny it? Did not goodwife Keech⁸ the butcher's wife
come in then, and call me 'Gossip⁹ Quickly'—coming in to
borrow a mess of° vinegar, telling us she had a good dish of   some
prawns, whereby thou didst desire to eat some, whereby I told
thee they were ill for a green° wound? And didst thou not,   fresh
90   when she was gone downstairs, desire me to be no more so
familiarity° with such poor people, saying that ere long they   (for "familiar")
should call me 'madam'?¹ And didst thou not kiss me, and bid
me fetch thee thirty shillings? I put thee now to thy book-oath;°   oath on the Bible
deny it if thou canst.
    [She weeps]

95   FALSTAFF   My lord, this is a poor mad soul, and she says up and
down the town that her eldest son is like you. She hath been
in good case,° and the truth is, poverty hath distracted her.²   prosperous
But for these foolish officers, I beseech you I may have
redress against them.

100   LORD CHIEF JUSTICE   Sir John, Sir John, I am well acquainted
with your manner of wrenching the true cause the false way. It
is not a confident brow,° nor the throng of words that come   countenance
with such more than impudent sauciness from you, can thrust
me from a level° consideration. You have, as it appears to me,   just
105   practised upon the easy-yielding spirit of this woman, and made
her serve your uses both in purse and in person.

MISTRESS QUICKLY   Yea, in truth, my lord.

LORD CHIEF JUSTICE   Pray thee, peace.   [To FALSTAFF] Pay her
the debt you owe her, and unpay the villainy you have done
110   with her. The one you may do with sterling money, and the
other with current° repentance.   genuine

FALSTAFF   My lord, I will not undergo this sneap° without reply.   reproof
You call honourable boldness 'impudent sauciness'; if a man
will make curtsy and say nothing, he is virtuous. No, my lord,
115   my humble duty° remembered, I will not be your suitor. I say   due respect to you
to you I do desire deliverance from these officers, being upon
hasty employment in the King's affairs.

LORD CHIEF JUSTICE   You speak as having power to do wrong;

---

6. Fire generated from charcoal shipped by sea rather
than by the inferior, locally produced charcoal.
7. One of the professional singers in the chapel at
Windsor, a royal residence west of London.
8. "Goodwife" was the title of a married woman.
"Keech" meant "a lump of animal fat."

9. Familiar form of address for a female friend, derived
from "godmother," the name for the female guardian of
a newly christened child.
1. A form of address for a knight's wife; a whore.
2. Driven her mad.

but answer in th'effect of your reputation,° and satisfy the poor   *as befits your status*
120   woman.
FALSTAFF [*drawing apart*]   Come hither, hostess.
     [*She goes to him*]
     Enter M[aster] GOWER, *a messenger*
LORD CHIEF JUSTICE   Now, Master Gower, what news?
GOWER   The King, my lord, and Harry Prince of Wales
     Are near at hand; the rest the paper tells.
     [LORD CHIEF JUSTICE *reads the paper, and converses*
     apart with GOWER]
125   FALSTAFF   As I am a gentleman!
MISTRESS QUICKLY   Faith, you said so before.
FALSTAFF   As I am a gentleman! Come, no more words of it.
MISTRESS QUICKLY   By this heavenly ground I tread on, I must be
     fain° to pawn both my plate and the tapestry of my dining-   *content*
130   chambers.
FALSTAFF   Glasses, glasses, is the only drinking;[3] and for thy
     walls, a pretty slight drollery,° or the story of the Prodigal,[4] or   *comic painting*
     the German hunting in waterwork,[5] is worth a thousand of
     these bed-hangers° and these fly-bitten tapestries. Let it be ten   *bed curtains*
135   pound if thou canst. Come, an 'twere not for thy humours,°   *moods*
     there's not a better wench in England. Go, wash thy face, and
     draw° the action. Come, thou must not be in this humour with   *withdraw*
     me. Dost not know me? Come, I know thou wast set on to this.
MISTRESS QUICKLY   Pray thee, Sir John, let it be but twenty
140   nobles.[6] I'faith, I am loath to pawn my plate, so God save me,
     la!
FALSTAFF   Let it alone; I'll make other shift.° You'll be a fool   *I'll manage otherwise*
     still.°   *always*
MISTRESS QUICKLY   Well, you shall have it, though I pawn my
145   gown. I hope you'll come to supper. You'll pay me altogether?
FALSTAFF   Will I live? [*To* BARDOLPH *and the* PAGE] Go with her,
     with her. Hook on,° hook on!   *Stick to her*
MISTRESS QUICKLY   Will you have Doll[7] Tearsheet meet you at
     supper?
150   FALSTAFF   No more words; let's have her.
     Exeunt [MISTRESS QUICKLY, BARDOLPH,
     the PAGE, FANG *and* SNARE]
LORD CHIEF JUSTICE [*to* GOWER]   I have heard better news.
FALSTAFF   What's the news, my good lord?
LORD CHIEF JUSTICE [*to* GOWER]   Where lay the King tonight?°   *last night*
GOWER   At Basingstoke,[8] my lord.
155   FALSTAFF [*to* LORD CHIEF JUSTICE]   I hope, my lord, all's well.
     What is the news, my lord?
LORD CHIEF JUSTICE [*to* GOWER]   Come all his forces back?
GOWER   No; fifteen hundred foot, five hundred horse,
     Are marched up to my lord of Lancaster
160   Against Northumberland and the Archbishop.
FALSTAFF [*to* LORD CHIEF JUSTICE]   Comes the King back from
     Wales, my noble lord?

---

3. Glass drinking vessels began to replace metal tankards in the late sixteenth century.
4. Alluding to a biblical parable about a profligate son who repents, which was a frequent subject for cheap painted cloths. See Luke 15:11–32.

5. A hunting scene of German or Dutch origin painted on a wall in imitation of tapestry.
6. Gold coins. Twenty were worth about 6 pounds.
7. A common name for a prostitute.
8. A town 46 miles west of London.

LORD CHIEF JUSTICE [*to* GOWER]   You shall have letters of me
     presently.°   *at once*
Come, go along with me, good Master Gower.
     [*They are going*]
FALSTAFF   My lord!
165 LORD CHIEF JUSTICE   What's the matter?
FALSTAFF   Master Gower, shall I entreat you with me to dinner?
GOWER   I must wait upon my good lord here, I thank you, good
     Sir John.
LORD CHIEF JUSTICE   Sir John, you loiter here too long, being
170   you are to take soldiers up° in counties as you go.   *levy soldiers*
FALSTAFF   Will you sup with me, Master Gower?
LORD CHIEF JUSTICE   What foolish master taught you these man-
     ners, Sir John?
FALSTAFF   Master Gower, if they become me not, he was a fool
175   that taught them me.⁹   [*To* LORD CHIEF JUSTICE] This is the
     right fencing grace,° my lord—tap for tap, and so part fair.°   *style / on good terms*
LORD CHIEF JUSTICE   Now the Lord lighten° thee; thou art a   *enlighten; make thin*
     great fool.   *Exeunt* [LORD CHIEF JUSTICE *and* GOWER *at one*
                                       door, FALSTAFF *at another*]

2.2

Enter PRINCE HARRY *and* POINS¹

PRINCE HARRY   Before God, I am exceeding weary.
POINS   Is't come to that? I had thought weariness durst not have
     attached° one of so high blood.   *laid hold of*
PRINCE HARRY   Faith, it does me, though it discolours the com-
5   plexion of my greatness² to acknowledge it. Doth it not show
     vilely in me to desire small° beer?   *weak*
POINS   Why, a prince should not be so loosely studied° as to   *disposed*
     remember so weak a composition.
PRINCE HARRY   Belike then my appetite was not princely got; for,
10   by my troth, I do now remember the poor creature small beer.
     But indeed, these humble considerations make me out of love
     with my greatness. What a disgrace is it to me to remember thy
     name!³ Or to know thy face tomorrow! Or to take note how
     many pair of silk stockings thou hast—videlicet° these, and   *namely*
15   those that were thy peach-coloured ones! Or to bear° the inven-   *remember*
     tory of thy shirts—as one for superfluity,° and another for use.   *as a spare*
     But that the tennis-court keeper knows better than I, for it is a
     low ebb of linen with thee when thou keepest not racket° there;   *do not play*
     as thou hast not done a great while, because the rest of thy low
20   countries have made a shift to eat up thy holland.⁴

---

9. Falstaff suggests that the habit of ignoring others is
something he learned from a fool, namely the Chief
Justice, who a few lines earlier would not answer Falstaff's questions.
2.2 Location: Prince Hal's dwelling.
1. Q's stage direction reads: "Enter the Prince, Poynes,
Sir John Russel, with other." This is the only place in Q
where the name "Russel" is employed instead of "Bardolph," but it indicates that Shakespeare had been working on some portion of this play before he was forced to
change "Oldcastle" to "Falstaff," "Russell" to "Bardolph,"
and "Harvey" to "Peto" (see Introduction to *1 Henry IV*).
2. It mars my noble countenance (by turning it pale
from weakness or red from shame).
3. Men of high rank should not be on familiar terms
with, or remember the names of, those below them in

status.
4. Because the brothels ("low countries") have contrived
to eat up all the money you would have spent on linen
("holland"). With puns on "low countries" as also meaning "sexual organs" and "the Netherlands" as well as
"brothels"; and with a pun on "holland" as referring to
the country of Holland as well as to the fine linen made
there. Poins has spent his money either on whores or on
providing linen for the babies he has prodigally fathered.
His lack of shirts makes it impossible for him to play at
the tennis courts, where players sweat so much that
shirts were frequently changed. Lines 20.1–20.4, which
follow, do not appear in F but are in Q. The Oxford editors assume they were cut by Shakespeare during revision of the play.

20.1   *And God knows whether those that bawl out the ruins of*
       thy linen[5] shall inherit his kingdom[6]—but the midwives
       say the children are not in the fault, whereupon the world
       increases, and kindreds are mightily strengthened.

POINS   How ill it follows, after you have laboured so hard, you
     should talk so idly! Tell me, how many good young princes
     would do so, their fathers lying so sick as yours is?

PRINCE HARRY   Shall I tell thee one thing, Poins?

25 POINS   Yes, faith, and let it be an excellent good thing.

PRINCE HARRY   It shall serve among wits of no higher breeding
     than thine.

POINS   Go to, I stand the push of° your one thing that you'll tell.   *I can tolerate*

PRINCE HARRY   Marry, I tell thee, it is not meet° that I should be   *appropriate*

30   sad now my father is sick; albeit I could tell to thee, as to one
     it pleases me, for fault° of a better, to call my friend, I could be   *lack*
     sad; and sad indeed too.

POINS   Very hardly,° upon such a subject.   *With great difficulty*

PRINCE HARRY   By this hand, thou thinkest me as far in the devil's

35   book as thou and Falstaff, for obduracy° and persistency. Let   *stubbornness*
     the end try the man. But I tell thee, my heart bleeds inwardly
     that my father is so sick; and keeping such vile company as
     thou art hath, in reason, taken from me all ostentation° of   *signs*
     sorrow.

40 POINS   The reason?

PRINCE HARRY   What wouldst thou think of me if I should weep?

POINS   I would think thee a most princely hypocrite.

PRINCE HARRY   It would be every man's thought, and thou art a
     blessed fellow to think as every man thinks. Never a man's

45   thought in the world keeps the roadway[7] better than thine.
     Every man would think me an hypocrite indeed. And what
     accites° your most worshipful thought to think so?   *induces*

POINS   Why, because you have been so lewd,° and so much   *base*
     engrafted° to Falstaff.   *attached*

50 PRINCE HARRY   And to thee.

POINS   By this light, I am well spoke on;° I can hear it with mine   *of*
     own ears. The worst that they can say of me is that I am a
     second brother,[8] and that I am a proper fellow of my hands;°   *a good fighter*
     and those two things I confess I cannot help.

         Enter BARDOLPH [*followed by the* PAGE]

55   By the mass, here comes Bardolph.

PRINCE HARRY   And the boy that I gave Falstaff. A° had him from   *He*
     me Christian, and look if the fat villain have not transformed
     him ape.[9]

BARDOLPH   God save your grace!

60 PRINCE HARRY   And yours, most noble Bardolph!

POINS   [*to* BARDOLPH]   Come, you virtuous ass, you bashful fool,
     must you be blushing?[1] Wherefore blush you now? What a

---

5. The bastard children who are wrapped in your old
shirts.
6. Go to heaven. With allusions to Matthew 25:34
("Come, ye blessed of my Father, inherit the kingdom
prepared for you from the foundation of the world") and
19:14 ("Suffer little children, and forbid them not, to
come unto me: for of such is the kingdom of heaven").
7. Adheres to the popular viewpoint.

8. That is, a younger brother (and therefore without
prospect of inheritance).
9. Made him look ridiculous, like an ape or a monkey
rather than a human being. Falstaff has perhaps
dressed the Page in an outlandish livery or uniform.
1. The jokes in this portion of the scene often refer to
Bardolph's notoriously red face. The color may be due to
drink, venereal disease, or some form of acne or rosacea.

maidenly man at arms are you become! Is't such a matter° to   *so difficult*
get a pottle-pot's maidenhead?²

65 PAGE   A calls me e'en now, my lord, through a red lattice,³ and
I could discern no part of his face from the window. At last I
spied his eyes, and methought he had made two holes in the
ale-wife's red petticoat, and so peeped through.

PRINCE HARRY [*to* POINS]   Has not the boy profited?°   *(from Falstaff)*

70 BARDOLPH [*to the* PAGE]   Away, you whoreson upright rabbit,
away!

PAGE   Away, you rascally Althea's⁴ dream, away!

PRINCE HARRY   Instruct us, boy; what dream, boy?

PAGE   Marry, my lord, Althea dreamt she was delivered of a
75 firebrand, and therefore I call him her dream.

PRINCE HARRY [*giving him money*]   A crown's-worth of good
interpretation! There 'tis, boy.

POINS   O, that this good blossom could be kept from cankers!°   *cankerworms*
[*Giving the* PAGE *money*] Well, there is sixpence to preserve
80 thee.

BARDOLPH   An° you do not make him hanged among you, the   *If*
gallows shall be wronged.

PRINCE HARRY   And how doth thy master, Bardolph?

BARDOLPH   Well, my good lord. He heard of your grace's coming
85 to town. There's a letter for you.

POINS   Delivered with good respect.° And how doth the Mar-   *(said ironically)*
tlemas⁵ your master?

BARDOLPH   In bodily health, sir.
[PRINCE HARRY *reads the letter*]

POINS   Marry, the immortal part° needs a physician, but that   *the soul*
90 moves not him. Though that be sick, it dies not.

PRINCE HARRY   I do allow this wen° to be as familiar with me as   *wart*
my dog; and he holds his place,° for look you how he writes.   *maintains his position*
[*He gives* POINS *the letter*]⁶

POINS   'John Falstaff, knight'.—Every man must know that,° as   *(Falstaff's rank)*
oft as he has occasion to name himself; even like those that are
95 kin to the King, for they never prick their finger but they say
'There's some of the King's blood spilt.' 'How comes that?' says
he that takes upon him not to conceive.° The answer is as ready   *understand*
as a borrower's cap:⁷ 'I am the King's poor cousin,° sir.'   *relative*

PRINCE HARRY   Nay, they will be kin to us, or they will fetch it°   *derive kinship*
100 from Japhet.⁸ [*Taking the letter*] But the letter. 'Sir John Falstaff, knight, to the son of the King nearest his father, Harry
Prince of Wales, greeting.'

POINS   Why, this is a certificate!°   *legal document*

PRINCE HARRY   Peace!— 'I will imitate the honourable Romans
105 in brevity.'

POINS [*taking the letter*]   Sure he means brevity in breath, short

---

2. To open and drain a two-quart tankard of ale (with implicit comparison to penetrating a virgin).
3. Sign of an alehouse window.
4. A conflation of two dreams from classical mythology. It was Hecuba, the Queen of Troy, who, when pregnant with Paris, dreamed she gave birth to a firebrand that set fire to her city. Althaea was told that her newborn son, Meleager, would live only as long as a brand in the fire was not consumed, so she snatched it from the hearth.
5. Fatted cattle or pigs that were slaughtered on

November 11, the feast day of St. Martin (Martlemas).
6. The reading of the letter is another occasion for comic horseplay. The Prince and Poins may pass it back and forth, or Poins may read it over Prince Harry's shoulder, or snatch it away.
7. As readily produced as the cap of one looking for money.
8. One of Noah's sons (Genesis 10:2–5), imagined to be the common ancestor of all Europeans.

winded. [*Reads*] 'I commend me to thee, I commend thee, and
I leave thee. Be not too familiar with Poins, for he misuses thy
favours so much that he swears thou art to marry his sister Nell.
110   Repent at idle times as thou mayst. And so, farewell.
         Thine by yea and no[9]—which is as much as to say, as
         thou usest him—Jack Falstaff with my familiars,° John   *friends*
         with my brothers and sisters, and Sir John with all
         Europe.'
115   My lord, I'll steep this letter in sack and make him eat it.

PRINCE HARRY   That's to make him eat twenty of his words. But
do you use me thus, Ned? Must I marry your sister?

POINS   God send the wench no worse fortune, but I never said
so.

120 PRINCE HARRY   Well, thus we play the fools with the time, and
the spirits of the wise sit in the clouds and mock us. [*To* BAR-
DOLPH] Is your master here in London?

BARDOLPH   Yea, my lord.

PRINCE HARRY   Where sups he? Doth the old boar feed in the
125   old frank?[1]

BARDOLPH   At the old place, my lord, in Eastcheap.

PRINCE HARRY   What company?

PAGE   Ephesians, my lord, of the old church.[2]

PRINCE HARRY   Sup any women with him?

130 PAGE   None, lord, but old Mistress Quickly and Mistress Doll
Tearsheet.

PRINCE HARRY   What pagan° may that be?   *heathen; prostitute*

PAGE   A proper gentlewoman, sir, and a kinswoman of my master's.

135 PRINCE HARRY   Even such kin as the parish heifers are to the
town bull. Shall we steal upon them, Ned, at supper?

POINS   I am your shadow, my lord; I'll follow you.

PRINCE HARRY   Sirrah, you, boy, and Bardolph, no word to your
master that I am yet come to town. [*Giving money*] There's for
140   your silence.

BARDOLPH   I have no tongue, sir.

PAGE   And for mine, sir, I will govern it.

PRINCE HARRY   Fare you well; go.

             [*Exeunt* BARDOLPH *and the* PAGE]
   This Doll Tearsheet should be some road.[3]

145 POINS   I warrant you, as common as the way between Saint
Albans[4] and London.

PRINCE HARRY   How might we see Falstaff bestow° himself   *behave*
tonight in his true colours, and not ourselves be seen?

POINS   Put on two leathern jerkins° and aprons, and wait upon   *jackets*
150   him at his table like drawers.°   *tavern servants*

PRINCE HARRY   From a god to a bull—a heavy declension°—it   *a sad degradation*
was Jove's case.[5] From a prince to a prentice—a low transfor-

---

9. Parodying the mild oaths associated with Puritans.
1. Pigsty. Possibly a reference to Eastcheap's famous tavern the Boar's Head.
2. Carousers of the usual kind. The Page alludes to the biblical account of the Ephesians, whom St. Paul admonished against lust and drunkenness before their conversion, with a possible reference to Catholics (members of "the old church"), whom English Protestants accused of moral laxity.
3. Some common prostitute. "Road" is slang for "vagina."
4. Town on the heavily traveled road north from London.
5. Referring to Jove's transformation into a bull before his rape of Europa.

mation—that shall be mine; for in everything the purpose
must weigh with° the folly. Follow me, Ned.   *Exeunt*   *match*

2.3
Enter [the Earl of] NORTHUMBERLAND, LADY [NORTHUM-
BERLAND] *and* LADY PERCY[1]

NORTHUMBERLAND   I pray thee, loving wife and gentle
    daughter,°   *daughter-in-law*
    Give even way° unto my rough affairs.   *Allow free scope*
    Put not you on the visage of the times
    And be like them to Percy troublesome.
5 LADY NORTHUMBERLAND   I have given over; I will speak no more.
    Do what you will; your wisdom be your guide.
NORTHUMBERLAND   Alas, sweet wife, my honour is at pawn,
    And, but° my going, nothing can redeem it.   *except by*
LADY PERCY   O yet, for God's sake, go not to these wars!
10   The time was, father, that you broke your word[2]
    When you were more endeared° to it than now—   *bound*
    When your own Percy, when my heart's dear Harry,
    Threw many a northward look to see his father
    Bring up his powers; but he did long in vain.
15   Who then persuaded you to stay at home?
    There were two honours lost, yours and your son's.
    For yours, the God of heaven brighten it!
    For his, it stuck upon him as the sun
    In the grey° vault of heaven, and by his light   *pale blue*
20   Did all the chivalry° of England move   *chivalrous warriors*
    To do brave acts. He was indeed the glass°   *mirror*
    Wherein the noble youth did dress themselves.[3]
    He had no legs that practised not his gait;[4]
    And speaking thick,[5] which nature made his blemish,
25   Became the accents of the valiant;
    For those that could speak low and tardily°   *slowly*
    Would turn their own perfection to abuse
    To seem like him. So that in speech, in gait,
    In diet, in affections° of delight,   *choice*
30   In military rules, humours of blood,°   *disposition*
    He was the mark° and glass, copy° and book,   *target / example*
    That fashioned others. And him—O wondrous him!
    O miracle of men!—him did you leave,
    Second to none, unseconded° by you,   *unsupported*
35   To look upon the hideous god of war
    In disadvantage, to abide a field°   *confront a battle*
    Where nothing but the sound of Hotspur's name
    Did seem defensible;° so you left him.   *to provide a defense*
    Never, O never do his ghost the wrong
40   To hold your honour more precise and nice°   *exacting*
    With others than with him. Let them alone.

2.3 Location: Outside Northumberland's castle at
Warkworth.
1. Q's stage direction designates the women only as
wives: "Enter Northumberland, his wife, and the wife
to Harry Percie."
2. Alluding to Northumberland's absence from the
Battle of Shrewsbury. See *1 Henry IV.*

3. Lines 23–45 do not appear in Q.
4. There was no man able to walk who did not try to
move as Hotspur did.
5. Speaking rapidly. The phrase has often been taken to
mean that Hotspur had a speech defect. A long stage
tradition made him a stutterer.

The Marshal and the Archbishop are strong.
Had my sweet Harry had but half their numbers,
Today might I, hanging on Hotspur's neck,
Have talked of Monmouth's° grave.   *Prince Hal's*

45 NORTHUMBERLAND   Beshrew your heart,
Fair daughter, you do draw my spirits from me
With new lamenting ancient oversights.
But I must go and meet with danger there,
Or it will seek me in another place,
And find me worse provided.

50 LADY NORTHUMBERLAND   O fly to Scotland,
Till that the nobles and the armèd commons
Have of their puissance° made a little taste.   *strength*
LADY PERCY   If they get ground and vantage of the King,
Then join you with them like a rib of steel,

55 To make strength stronger; but, for all our loves,
First let them try themselves. So did your son.
He was so suffered.° So came I a widow,   *allowed to proceed*
And never shall have length of life enough
To rain upon remembrance with mine eyes,[6]

60 That it may grow and sprout as high as heaven
For recordation° to my noble husband.   *As a memorial*
NORTHUMBERLAND   Come, come, go in with me. 'Tis with my mind
As with the tide swelled up unto his height,
That makes a still stand,° running neither way.   *standstill*

65 Fain would I go to meet the Archbishop,
But many thousand reasons hold me back.
I will resolve for Scotland. There am I
Till time and vantage° crave my company.   *Exeunt*   *opportunity*

2.4

[*A table and chairs set forth.*][1] *Enter a* DRAWER° [*with*   *servant in a tavern*
wine and another DRAWER *with a dish of apple-johns*][2]
FIRST DRAWER   What the devil hast thou brought there—apple-
johns? Thou knowest Sir John cannot endure an apple-john.
SECOND DRAWER   Mass,[3] thou sayst true. The Prince once set a
dish of apple-johns before him; and told him, there were five

5   more Sir Johns; and, putting off his hat, said 'I will now take
my leave of these six dry, round, old, withered knights.' It
angered him to the heart. But he hath forgot that.
FIRST DRAWER   Why then, cover,° and set them down; and see if   *spread the cloth*
thou canst find out Sneak's noise.° Mistress Tearsheet would   *band of musicians*

10 fain hear some music.   [*Exit the* SECOND DRAWER]
[*The* FIRST DRAWER *covers the table.*]
[*Enter the* SECOND DRAWER]

6. To rain tears upon his memory, here imagined as a
plant—perhaps rosemary, the conventional symbol of
remembrance.
2.4 Location: A tavern, perhaps the Boar's Head, in
Eastcheap.
1. Changes were made to this scene at some point. In
Q, dialogue occurs between Francis and "a Drawer or
two." At 2.4.13, Q's stage direction reads: "Enter Will."
This character has no lines, and probably his part was
later deleted. In F, the dialogue is somewhat rearranged

and occurs between two drawers, as here. However
many servants are onstage, though, the point of their
scurrying about is to create excitement about Falstaff's
arrival and the trick to be played on him.
2. A kind of apple that could be kept for two years and
was meant to be eaten when the skin was wrinkled and
shriveled up.
3. An oath derived from the name of the Catholic
church service.

SECOND DRAWER   Sirrah, here will be the Prince and Master
    Poins anon,° and they will put on two of our jerkins and aprons,   *soon*
    and Sir John must not know of it. Bardolph hath brought word.
FIRST DRAWER   By the mass, here will be old utis!° It will be an   *merrymaking; a din*
15 excellent stratagem.
SECOND DRAWER   I'll see if I can find out Sneak.   *Exeunt*
        Enter MISTRESS QUICKLY *and* DOLL TEARSHEET [*drunk*]
MISTRESS QUICKLY   I'faith, sweetheart, methinks now you are in
    an excellent good temperality.° Your pulsidge⁴ beats as extraor-   *(for "temper")*
    dinarily as heart would desire, and your colour, I warrant you,
20 is as red as any rose, in good truth, la; but i'faith, you have
    drunk too much canaries,⁵ and that's a marvellous searching°   *strong*
    wine, and it perfumes the blood ere we can say 'What's this?'
    How do you now?
DOLL TEARSHEET   Better than I was.—Hem!
25 MISTRESS QUICKLY   Why, that's well said! A good heart's worth
    gold.
        Enter Sir John FALSTAFF
    Lo, here comes Sir John.
FALSTAFF [*sings*]   'When Arthur first in court'⁶—[*Calls*] Empty
    the jordan!°—[*Sings*] 'And was a worthy king'—How now, Mis-   *chamber pot*
30 tress Doll?
MISTRESS QUICKLY   Sick of a qualm,° yea, good faith.   *fainting fit*
FALSTAFF   So is all her sect;° an they be once in a calm,⁷ they   *kind; sex*
    are sick.
DOLL TEARSHEET   A pox damn you, you muddy rascal!⁸ Is that
35 all the comfort you give me?
FALSTAFF   You make fat rascals, Mistress Doll.
DOLL TEARSHEET   I make them? Gluttony and diseases make
    them; I make them not.
FALSTAFF   If the cook help to make the gluttony, you help to
40 make the diseases, Doll. We catch of you,° Doll, we catch of   *are infected by you*
    you; grant that, my poor virtue, grant that.
DOLL TEARSHEET   Yea, Jesu, our chains and our jewels.⁹
FALSTAFF   'Your brooches, pearls, and ouches'¹—for to serve
    bravely is to come halting off,² you know; to come off the
45 breach with his pike bent bravely,³ and to surgery bravely; to
    venture upon the charged chambers⁴ bravely.
MISTRESS QUICKLY   By my troth, this is the old fashion. You two
    never meet but you fall to some discord. You are both, i' good
    truth, as rheumatic° as two dry toasts; you cannot one bear with   *(for "choleric")*
50 another's confirmities.° What the goodyear, one must bear,⁵ [*to*   *(for "infirmities")*
    DOLL] and that must be you. You are the weaker vessel, as they
    say, the emptier vessel.

---

4. For "pulse."
5. Sweet wine from the Canary Islands.
6. Lines from the ballad "Sir Lancelot du Lake."
7. Quiet; not sexually active (punning on "qualm" in
the prior line).
8. You dull knave. A "rascal" was a young, lean deer.
They were called "muddy" when sluggish and out of
season. In his next speech, Falstaff will accuse Doll of
making even lean deer fat, probably by tempting them
to gluttony and vice.
9. Yes, you steal ("catch") our valuables.
1. Perhaps a line from a ballad, with puns on the three
items of jewelry as slang for the carbuncles and sores

that result from venereal disease.
2. To fight bravely is to return limping; to engage in vigorous sex is to be wounded in the process.
3. To come away from the gap in the fortifications (the
breech) with one's weapon finely bent (with puns on
"breech" as slang for "female genitalia" and "pike" as
slang for "penis").
4. Interior of a mine loaded with munitions; the sexually aroused interior of a woman.
5. Endure; carry goods; support the weight of a sexual
partner; give birth. *What the goodyear*: a phrase probably meaning "What the devil."

DOLL TEARSHEET   Can a weak empty vessel bear such a huge full
hogshead?° There's a whole merchant's venture° of Bordeaux   cask / cargo
55   stuff° in him; you have not seen a hulk better stuffed in the   wine
hold.— Come, I'll be friends with thee, Jack. Thou art going
to the wars, and whether I shall ever see thee again or no there
is nobody cares.
        Enter [a] DRAWER
DRAWER   Sir, Ensign⁶ Pistol's below, and would speak with you.
60   DOLL TEARSHEET   Hang him, swaggering° rascal, let him not   blustering; quarreling
come hither. It is the foul-mouthedest rogue in England.
MISTRESS QUICKLY   If he swagger, let him not come here. No, by
my faith! I must live among my neighbours; I'll no swaggerers.
I am in good name and fame with the very best. Shut the door;
65   there comes no swaggerers here. I have not lived all this while
to have swaggering now. Shut the door, I pray you.
FALSTAFF   Dost thou hear, hostess?
MISTRESS QUICKLY   Pray ye pacify yourself, Sir John. There
comes no swaggerers here.
70   FALSTAFF   Dost thou hear? It is mine ensign.
MISTRESS QUICKLY   Tilly-fally,° Sir John, ne'er tell me. Your   Nonsense
ensign-swaggerer comes not in my doors. I was before Master
Tisick⁷ the debuty° t'other day, and, as he said to me—'twas no   (for "deputy")
longer ago than Wed'sday last, i' good faith—'Neighbour
75   Quickly,' says he—Master Dumb our minister was by then—
'Neighbour Quickly,' says he, 'receive those that are civil, for,'
said he, 'you are in an ill name.' Now a said so, I can tell
whereupon.⁸ 'For,' says he, 'you are an honest woman, and well
thought on; therefore take heed what guests you receive.
80   Receive,' says he, 'no swaggering companions.' There comes
none here. You would bless you° to hear what he said. No, I'll   feel fortunate
no swaggerers.
FALSTAFF   He's no swaggerer, hostess—a tame cheater,⁹ i'faith.
You may stroke him as gently as a puppy greyhound. He'll not
85   swagger with a Barbary hen,° if her feathers turn back in any   guinea hen; prostitute
show of resistance.—Call him up, drawer.   [*Exit* DRAWER]
MISTRESS QUICKLY   Cheater¹ call you him? I will bar no honest
man my house, nor no cheater, but I do not love swaggering,
by my troth, I am the worse when one says 'swagger'. Feel,
90   masters, how I shake, look you, I warrant you.
DOLL TEARSHEET   So you do, hostess.
MISTRESS QUICKLY   Do I? Yea, in very truth do I, an 'twere° an   as if I were
aspen leaf. I cannot abide swaggerers.
        Enter PISTOL, BARDOLPH, *and* [*the* PAGE]
PISTOL   God save you, Sir John.
95   FALSTAFF   Welcome, Ensign Pistol. Here, Pistol, I charge you²
with a cup of sack. Do you discharge³ upon mine hostess.
PISTOL   I will discharge upon her, Sir John, with two bullets.°   (slang for "testicles")
FALSTAFF   She is pistol-proof, sir, you shall not hardly offend°   injure
her.

---

6. A military title for the army's standard-bearer.
7. The name signifies a hacking cough.
8. Now I can tell why he ("a") said so.
9. A decoy in a scheme to defraud people.
1. Quickly apparently understands the word as

"escheator," an officer responsible for returning to the
crown property whose title had lapsed.
2. Toast to you; load you with ammunition (punning on
Pistol's name); arouse you sexually.
3. Return the toast; empty the cup; shoot; ejaculate.

100 MISTRESS QUICKLY   Come, I'll drink no proofs, nor no bullets. I'll
     drink no more than will do me good, for no man's pleasure, I.
     PISTOL   Then to you, Mistress Dorothy! I will charge° you.   *toast; arouse; order*
     DOLL TEARSHEET   Charge me? I scorn you, scurvy companion.
     What, you poor, base, rascally, cheating, lack-linen mate!°   *fellow who has no linen*
105 Away, you mouldy rogue, away! I am meat for your master.[4]
     PISTOL   I know you, Mistress Dorothy.
     DOLL TEARSHEET   Away, you cutpurse° rascal, you filthy bung,[5]   *thieving; castrated*
     away! By this wine, I'll thrust my knife in your mouldy chaps°   *cheeks; buttocks*
     an you play the saucy cuttle with me![6]
     [*She brandishes a knife*]
110 Away, you bottle-ale rascal, you basket-hilt stale juggler,[7] you!
     [PISTOL *draws his sword*]
     Since when, I pray you, sir? God's light, with two points[8] on
     your shoulder! Much!
     PISTOL   God let me not live, but I will murder your ruff° for this.   *starched collar*
     MISTRESS QUICKLY   No, good Captain Pistol; not here, sweet cap-
115 tain.
     DOLL TEARSHEET   Captain? Thou abominable damned cheater,
     art thou not ashamed to be called 'captain'? An captains were
     of my mind, they would truncheon° you out, for taking their   *cudgel*
     names upon you before you have earned them. You a captain?
120 You slave! For what? For tearing a poor whore's ruff in a bawdy-
     house! He a captain? Hang him, rogue, he lives upon mouldy
     stewed prunes[9] and dried cakes. A captain? God's light, these
     villains will make the word 'captain' odious; therefore captains
     had need look to't.
125 BARDOLPH   Pray thee, go down, good ensign.
     FALSTAFF   Hark thee hither, Mistress Doll.
     [*He takes her aside*]
     PISTOL   Not I! I tell thee what, Corporal Bardolph, I could tear
     her! I'll be revenged of her.
     PAGE   Pray thee, go down.
130 PISTOL   I'll see her damned first
     To Pluto's damned lake,° by this hand,[1]   *(the lake of hell)*
     To th'infernal deep,
     Where Erebus,° and tortures vile also.   *the underworld*
     'Hold hook and line!' say I.
135 Down, down, dogs; down, Fates.
     Have we not Hiren here?[2]
     MISTRESS QUICKLY   Good Captain Pizzle,° be quiet. 'Tis very   *Penis*
     late, i'faith. I beseek you now, aggravate° your choler.   *(for "moderate")*
     PISTOL   These be good humours indeed!
140 Shall pack-horses

---

4. That is, I am superior to you; with a pun on "meat"
as meaning "a body available for sexual pleasure."
5. Thief; anus.
6. If you continue to abuse me (with a pun on "cuttle"
as signifying both "knife" and "cuttlefish," which was
supposed to vomit a black liquid to conceal itself from
enemies).
7. You imposter with a cheap, outdated sword. Basket-
work hilts were used on inexpensive weapons or those
used only for practice.
8. Tags for fastening armor.
9. Available in brothels as a supposed preventative of

venereal disease, with a pun on "stew" as meaning
"brothel."
1. In this and subsequent speeches, Pistol rants in an
affected style that recalls and parodies the language of
sensational plays from the 1590s and earlier, which
were often set in non-European locales and involved
military and erotic adventures.
2. Apparently a line from *The Turkish Mohamet and
Hiren [Irene] the Fair Greek*, a lost play by George
Peele. Pistol may be referring to his sword as "Hiren"
with a pun on "iron."

And hollow pampered jades of Asia,[3]
Which cannot go but thirty mile a day,
Compare with Caesars and with cannibals,[4]
And Trojan Greeks?

145 Nay, rather damn them with King Cerberus,[5]
And let the welkin° roar. Shall we fall foul for toys?[6]   *heavens*

MISTRESS QUICKLY   By my troth, captain, these are very bitter
words.

BARDOLPH   Be gone, good ensign; this will grow to a brawl anon.

150 PISTOL   Die men like dogs! Give crowns like pins![7]
Have we not Hiren here?

MISTRESS QUICKLY   O' my word, captain, there's none such here.
What the goodyear, do you think I would deny her? For God's
sake, be quiet.

155 PISTOL   Then feed and be fat, my fair Calipolis.[8]
Come, give's some sack.
Si fortune me tormente, sperato me contento.[9]
Fear we broadsides?[1] No; let the fiend give fire!°   *shoot*
Give me some sack; and, sweetheart, lie thou there.
   [*He lays down his sword*]

160 Come we to full points here? And are etceteras nothings?[2]
   [*He drinks*]

FALSTAFF   Pistol, I would be quiet.

PISTOL   Sweet knight, I kiss thy neaf.° What, we have seen the   *fist*
seven stars![3]

DOLL TEARSHEET   For God's sake, thrust him downstairs. I can
165 not endure such a fustian° rascal.   *worthless*

PISTOL   Thrust him downstairs? Know we not Galloway nags?[4]

FALSTAFF   Quoit° him down, Bardolph, like a shove-groat shil-   *Throw*
ling.[5] Nay, an a do° nothing but speak nothing, a shall be   *if he does*
nothing here.

170 BARDOLPH [*to* PISTOL]   Come, get you downstairs.

PISTOL [*taking up his sword*]   What, shall we have incision?
Shall we imbrue?°   *steep in blood*
Then death rock me asleep, abridge my doleful days.
Why then, let grievous, ghastly, gaping wounds
Untwine the Sisters Three.[6] Come, Atropos, I say!

175 MISTRESS QUICKLY   Here's goodly stuff toward!°   *about to happen*

FALSTAFF   Give me my rapier, boy.

DOLL TEARSHEET   I pray thee, Jack, I pray thee, do not draw.

FALSTAFF [*taking his rapier and speaking to* PISTOL]   Get you downstairs.
   [FALSTAFF, BARDOLPH, *and* PISTOL *brawl*]

---

3. A garbled allusion to Marlowe's *2 Tamburlaine* 4.3.1–2, in which Tamburlaine taunts the Kings whom he has captured and whom he uses in lieu of horses to draw his chariot.
4. Pistol may mean "Hannibals." Hannibal was a famous general of Carthage.
5. In classical mythology, the three-headed dog guarding the underworld.
6. Quarrel over trifles.
7. Alluding to Tamburlaine's extravagance in distributing the crowns of conquered Kings among his followers.
8. Echoing Peele's *Battle of Alcazar,* in which the Moorish King Muly Mahomet offers his starving wife the raw flesh of a lion he has just killed.

9. If fortune torments me, hope contents me (a motto that Pistol renders in a mixture of Italian, French, and Spanish).
1. Shots fired from the side of a ship.
2. That is, have we come to a stop? Is there no further satisfaction to be had in the rest (the "etceteras")? Pistol puns on "etceteras" and "nothings" as slang for "female genitalia."
3. We have caroused all night (with an allusion to the Ursa Major constellation).
4. Small Scottish horses; prostitutes.
5. Shilling coin used in a game like shuffleboard.
6. The three Fates of Greek mythology: Clotho, Lachesis, and Atropos. Atropos cut the thread of life.

MISTRESS QUICKLY   Here's a goodly tumult! I'll forswear keeping
180 house afore I'll be in these tirrits° and frights!   *(for "terrors" or "fits")*
        [FALSTAFF *thrusts at* PISTOL]
     So!
        [PISTOL *thrusts at* FALSTAFF]
     Murder, I warrant now! Alas, alas, put up your naked weapons,
     put up your naked weapons!
        [*Exit* PISTOL, *pursued by* BARDOLPH]

DOLL TEARSHEET   I pray thee, Jack, be quiet; the rascal's gone.
185 Ah, you whoreson little valiant villain, you!

MISTRESS QUICKLY   [*to* FALSTAFF] Are you not hurt i'th' groin?
     Methought a made a shrewd° thrust at your belly.   *vicious*
        [*Enter* BARDOLPH]

FALSTAFF   Have you turned him out o'doors?

BARDOLPH   Yea, sir. The rascal's drunk. You have hurt him, sir,
190 i'th' shoulder.

FALSTAFF   A rascal, to brave° me!   *defy*

DOLL TEARSHEET   Ah, you sweet little rogue, you! Alas, poor ape,
     how thou sweatest! Come, let me wipe thy face; come on, you
     whoreson chops.° Ah rogue, i'faith, I love thee. Thou art as   *fat cheeks*
195 valorous as Hector of Troy,[7] worth five of Agamemnon,[8] and
     ten times better than the Nine Worthies.[9] Ah, villain!

FALSTAFF   A rascally slave! I will toss the rogue in a blanket.[1]

DOLL TEARSHEET   Do, an thou darest for thy heart. An thou dost,
     I'll canvas° thee between a pair of sheets.   *toss*
200   *Enter music[ians]*

PAGE   The music is come, sir.

FALSTAFF   Let them play.—Play, sirs!
        [*Music plays*]
     Sit on my knee, Doll. A rascal bragging slave! The rogue fled
     from me like quicksilver.°   *mercury*

DOLL TEARSHEET   I'faith, and thou followed'st him like a church.°   *(i.e., sedately)*
205 Thou whoreson little tidy° Bartholomew boar-pig,[2] when wilt   *plump*
     thou leave fighting o'days, and foining° o'nights, and begin to   *thrusting*
     patch up thine old body for heaven?
        Enter PRINCE [HARRY] *and* POINS, *disguised* [*as drawers*]

FALSTAFF   Peace, good Doll, do not speak like a death's-head,[3]
     do not bid me remember mine end.

210 DOLL TEARSHEET   Sirrah, what humour's° the Prince of?   *disposition is*

FALSTAFF   A good shallow young fellow. A would have made a
     good pantler;° a would ha' chipped° bread well.   *pantry worker / cut*

DOLL TEARSHEET   They say Poins has a good wit.

FALSTAFF   He a good wit? Hang him, baboon! His wit's as thick
215 as Tewkesbury[4] mustard; there's no more conceit° in him than   *intellect*
     is in a mallet.

DOLL TEARSHEET   Why does the Prince love him so, then?

FALSTAFF   Because their legs are both of a bigness, and a° plays   *he*
     at quoits[5] well, and eats conger and fennel,[6] and drinks off can-

---

7. The greatest Trojan warrior in Homer's *Iliad*.
8. Leader of the Greeks in the battle for Troy.
9. Nine legendary brave men: three Christians—
Arthur, Charlemagne, Godfrey of Boulogne; three
pagans—Hector, Alexander, Julius Caesar; and three
Jews—Joshua, David, Judas Maccabaeus.
1. A punishment for cowardice.
2. A roasted pig associated with an annual London carnival held on August 24, St. Bartholomew's Day.

3. Skull or representation of a skull used as a reminder
of mortality.
4. Market town in Gloucestershire famed for its mustard.
5. A game involving the throwing of a heavy iron ring
toward a target on the ground.
6. Conger eel, a heavy, hard-to-digest food, was served
with fennel.

220   dles' ends for flap-dragons,[7] and rides the wild mare[8] with the
boys, and jumps upon joint-stools, and swears with a good
grace, and wears his boot very smooth like unto the sign of the
leg,[9] and breeds no bate° with telling of discreet stories, and   *discord*
such other gambol° faculties a has that show a weak mind and   *sportive*
225   an able body; for the which the Prince admits him; for the
Prince himself is such another—the weight of a hair will turn
the scales between their avoirdupois.°   *weight*

PRINCE HARRY [*aside to* POINS] Would not this nave° of a wheel   *hub*
have his ears cut off?

230 POINS Let's beat him before his whore.

PRINCE HARRY Look whe'er the withered elder[1] hath not his poll°   *head*
clawed like a parrot.[2]

POINS Is it not strange that desire should so many years outlive
performance?

235 FALSTAFF Kiss me, Doll.
        [*They kiss*]

PRINCE HARRY [*aside to* POINS] Saturn and Venus[3] this year in
conjunction! What says th'almanac to that?

POINS And look whether the fiery Trigon[4] his man be not lisping
to his master's old tables,° his note-book, his counsel-keeper![5]   *writing tablets*

240 FALSTAFF [*to* DOLL] Thou dost give me flattering busses.°   *kisses*

DOLL TEARSHEET By my troth, I kiss thee with a most constant
heart.

FALSTAFF I am old, I am old.

DOLL TEARSHEET I love thee better than I love e'er a scurvy
245   young boy of them all.

FALSTAFF What stuff° wilt have a kirtle° of? I shall receive money   *material / skirt*
o'Thursday; shalt° have a cap tomorrow.—A merry song!   *you shall*
        [*The music plays again*]
Come, it grows late; we'll to bed. Thou'lt forget me when I am
gone.

250 DOLL TEARSHEET By my troth, thou'lt set me a-weeping an thou
sayst so. Prove° that ever I dress myself handsome till thy re-   *If you ever prove*
turn—well, hearken° a'th' end.   *judge*

FALSTAFF Some sack, Francis.

PRINCE *and* POINS [*coming forward*] Anon, anon, sir.

255 FALSTAFF Ha, a bastard son of the King's!—And art not thou
Poins his brother?°   *the brother of Poins*

PRINCE HARRY Why, thou globe of sinful continents,[6] what a life
dost thou lead!

FALSTAFF A better than thou: I am a gentleman, thou art a
260   drawer.

PRINCE HARRY Very true, sir, and I come to draw you out by the
ears.

MISTRESS QUICKLY O, the Lord preserve thy grace! By my troth,

---

7. Referring to a tavern game in which one drank
liquor on which burning objects (flapdragons) had been
set afloat.

8. Plays at a form of leapfrog; has sexual relations with
a woman.

9. As in the sign over the bootmaker's shop (depicting
a well-booted leg).

1. Sapless elder tree; impotent old man.

2. Doll may here be running her hands through Falstaff's hair.

3. The planets governing old age and love.

4. The signs of the zodiac were divided into four sets of
three (trigons). Aries, Leo, and Sagittarius are the "fiery
trigon," being hot and dry. Poins alludes to Bardolph's
red face.

5. Apparently Bardolph is wooing Quickly, here
referred to as Falstaff's confidante and the keeper of his
secrets.

6. World composed of sinful lands; a vast receptacle of
sin.

welcome to London! Now the Lord bless that sweet face of
thine! O Jesu, are you come from Wales?

FALSTAFF [*to* PRINCE HARRY]   Thou whoreson mad compound of
majesty! By this light°—flesh and corrupt blood, thou art wel-   *(a conventional oath)*
come.

DOLL TEARSHEET   How, you fat fool? I scorn you.

POINS [*to* PRINCE HARRY]   My lord, he will drive you out of your
revenge and turn all to a merriment, if you take not the heat.°   *don't act at once*

PRINCE HARRY [*to* FALSTAFF   You whoreson candlemine° you,   *storehouse of tallow*
how vilely did you speak of me now, before this honest,° virtu-   *chaste*
ous, civil gentlewoman!

MISTRESS QUICKLY   God's blessing of your good heart, and so she
is, by my troth!

FALSTAFF [*to* PRINCE HARRY]   Didst thou hear me?

PRINCE HARRY   Yea, and you knew me as you did when you ran
away by Gads Hill;[7] you knew I was at your back, and spoke it
on purpose to try my patience.

FALSTAFF   No, no, no, not so, I did not think thou wast within
hearing.

PRINCE HARRY   I shall drive you, then, to confess the wilful
abuse, and then I know how to handle you.

FALSTAFF   No abuse, Hal; o'mine honour, no abuse.

PRINCE HARRY   Not? To dispraise me, and call me 'pantler' and
'bread-chipper' and I know not what?

FALSTAFF   No abuse, Hal.

POINS   No abuse?

FALSTAFF   No abuse, Ned, i'th' world, honest Ned, none. I dispraised him before the wicked, that the wicked might not fall
in love with him; [*to* PRINCE HARRY] in which doing I have
done the part of a careful° friend and a true subject, and thy   *caring*
father is to give me thanks for it. No abuse, Hal; none, Ned,
none; no, faith, boys, none.

PRINCE HARRY   See now whether pure fear and entire cowardice
doth not make thee wrong this virtuous gentlewoman to close
with° us. Is she of the wicked? Is thine hostess here of the   *in order to pacify*
wicked? Or is thy boy of the wicked? Or honest Bardolph,
whose zeal burns in his nose, of the wicked?

POINS [*to* FALSTAFF]   Answer, thou dead elm, answer.

FALSTAFF   The fiend hath pricked down Bardolph irrecover-
able,[8] and his face is Lucifer's privy° kitchen, where he doth   *private*
nothing but roast malt-worms.° For the boy, there is a good   *weevils; drunkards*
angel about him, but the devil outbids him,° too.   *(the good angel)*

PRINCE HARRY   For the women?

FALSTAFF   For one of them, she's in hell already, and burns°   *infects with syphilis*
poor souls. For th'other, I owe her money, and whether she be
damned for that I know not.[9]

MISTRESS QUICKLY   No, I warrant you.

FALSTAFF   No, I think thou art not; I think thou art quit for° that.   *acquitted of*
Marry, there is another indictment upon thee, for suffering
flesh to be eaten in thy house, contrary to the law,[1] for the
which I think thou wilt howl.

7. Referring to events staged in Act 2 of *1 Henry IV*.
8. Marked Bardolph as beyond redemption.
9. Referring to the view that usury (lending money at
interest) was a sin.

1. Alluding to laws enacted against eating meat during
the Christian penitential days known as Lent as well as
to laws against the sex trade, with a pun on "house" as
"brothel."

315 **MISTRESS QUICKLY** All victuallers° do so. What's a joint of mut-   *innkeepers; bawds*
ton° or two in a whole Lent?   *piece of lamb; whore*
PRINCE HARRY You, gentlewoman—
DOLL TEARSHEET What says your grace?
FALSTAFF His grace says that which his flesh rebels against.[2]
      PETO knocks at door [within]
320 **MISTRESS QUICKLY** Who knocks so loud at door? [*Calls*] Look to
th' door there, Francis.
     Enter PETO
PRINCE HARRY Peto, how now, what news?
PETO The King your father is at Westminster;
And there are twenty weak and wearied posts°   *messengers*
325 Come from the north; and as I came along
I met and overtook a dozen captains,
Bareheaded, sweating, knocking at the taverns,
And asking every one for Sir John Falstaff.
PRINCE HARRY By heaven, Poins, I feel me much to blame
330 So idly to profane the precious time,
When tempest of commotion, like the south°   *the south wind*
Borne° with black vapour, doth begin to melt   *Laden*
And drop upon our bare unarmèd heads.—
Give me my sword and cloak.—Falstaff, good night.
    Exeunt PRINCE [HARRY] and POINS
335 **FALSTAFF** Now comes in the sweetest morsel of the night, and
we must hence and leave it unpicked.
    [Knocking within. Exit BARDOLPH]
More knocking at the door!
    [Enter BARDOLPH]
How now, what's the matter?
BARDOLPH You must away to court, sir, presently.°   *at once*
340 A dozen captains stay° at door for you.   *wait*
FALSTAFF [*to the PAGE*] Pay the musicians, sirrah. Farewell, hostess; farewell, Doll. You see, my good wenches, how men of
merit are sought after. The undeserver° may sleep, when the   *unimportant officer*
man of action is called on. Farewell, good wenches. If I be not
345 sent away post,° I will see you again ere I go.   *hastily*
    [Exeunt musicians]
DOLL TEARSHEET [*weeping*] I cannot speak. If my heart be not
ready to burst—well, sweet Jack, have a care of thyself.
FALSTAFF Farewell, farewell!
    Exit [with BARDOLPH, PETO, and the PAGE]
MISTRESS QUICKLY Well, fare thee well. I have known thee these
350 twenty-nine years come peascod-time,[3] but an honester and
truer-hearted man—well, fare thee well.
    [Enter BARDOLPH]
BARDOLPH Mistress Tearsheet!
MISTRESS QUICKLY What's the matter?
BARDOLPH Bid Mistress Tearsheet come to my master. [*Exit*]
355 **MISTRESS QUICKLY** O run, Doll; run, run, good Doll!
    Exeunt [DOLL at one door, MISTRESS QUICKLY at another door]

2. Implying that the Prince's virtuous speech can't hide a body filled with lust for Tearsheet.

3. The time of year when peas form in the pod (early spring).

3.1

Enter KING [HENRY] *in his nightgown,° with a page*   dressing gown

KING HENRY [*giving letters*]   Go call the Earls of Surrey and of Warwick.
But ere they come, bid them o'er-read these letters
And well consider of them. Make good speed.   *Exit* [*page*]
How many thousand of my poorest subjects

5   Are at this hour asleep? O sleep, O gentle sleep,
Nature's soft nurse, how have I frighted° thee,   frightened
That thou no more wilt weigh my eyelids down
And steep my senses in forgetfulness?
Why rather, sleep, liest thou in smoky cribs,°   hovels

10   Upon uneasy pallets° stretching thee,   hard straw beds
And hushed with buzzing night-flies to thy slumber,
Than in the perfumed chambers of the great,
Under the canopies of costly state,°   splendor
And lulled with sound of sweetest melody?

15   O thou dull° god, why li'st thou with the vile°   drowsy / lowly
In loathsome beds, and leav'st the kingly couch
A watch-case,° or a common 'larum-bell?   sentry box
Wilt thou upon the high and giddy mast
Seal up the ship-boy's eyes, and rock his brains

20   In cradle of the rude° imperious surge,   rough
And in the visitation of the winds,
Who take the ruffian billows by the top,
Curling their monstrous heads, and hanging them
With deafing° clamour in the slippery clouds,   deafening

25   That, with the hurly,° death itself awakes?   tumult
Canst thou, O partial sleep, give thy repose
To the wet sea-boy in an hour so rude,°   wild
And in the calmest and most stillest night,
With all appliances° and means to boot,°   devices / as well

30   Deny it to a king? Then happy low,° lie down.   happy humble people
Uneasy lies the head that wears a crown.
            Enter [*the Earls of*] WARWICK *and* SURREY
WARWICK   Many good morrows to your majesty!
KING HENRY   Is it good morrow, lords?
WARWICK   'Tis one o'clock, and past.
KING HENRY   Why then, good morrow to you all, my lords.

35   Have you read o'er the letter that I sent you?
WARWICK   We have, my liege.°   sovereign
KING HENRY   Then you perceive the body of our kingdom,
How foul it is, what rank° diseases grow,   loathsome
And with what danger near the heart of it.

40   WARWICK   It is but as a body yet distempered,°   sick
Which to his former strength may be restored
With good advice and little medicine.
My lord Northumberland will soon be cooled.
KING HENRY   O God, that one might read the book of fate,

45   And see the revolution of the times¹
Make mountains level, and the continent,°   dry land
Weary of solid firmness, melt itself
Into the sea; and other times to see

3.1 Location: The palace at Westminster.   1. The changes that time will bring.

	The beachy girdle of° the ocean	*girdle of beaches around*
50	Too wide for Neptune's[2] hips; how chance's mocks	
	And changes fill the cup of alteration	
	With divers° liquors![3]	*various*

52.1   *O, if this were seen,*

The happiest youth, viewing his progress through,°   *through life*
What perils past, what crosses° to ensue,   *afflictions*
Would shut the book and sit him down and die.

           'Tis not ten years gone

Since Richard and Northumberland, great friends,
Did feast together; and in two year after

55	Were they at wars. It is but eight years since	
	This Percy° was the man nearest my soul,	*(Northumberland)*
	Who like a brother toiled in my affairs,	
	And laid his love and life under my foot,°	*at my disposal*
	Yea, for my sake, even to° the eyes of Richard	*before*
60	Gave him defiance. But which of you was by—	
	[*To* WARWICK] You, cousin Neville,[4] as I may remember—	
	When Richard, with his eye brimful of tears,	
	Then checked and rated° by Northumberland,	*chided*
	Did speak these words,[5] now proved a prophecy?—	
65	'Northumberland, thou ladder by the which	
	My cousin Bolingbroke ascends my throne'—	
	Though then, God knows, I had no such intent,	
	But that necessity so bowed the state	
	That I and greatness were compelled to kiss—	
70	'The time shall come'—thus did he follow it—	
	'The time will come that foul sin, gathering head,[6]	
	Shall break into corruption'; so went on,	
	Foretelling this same time's condition,	
	And the division of our amity.	
75	WARWICK There is a history in all men's lives	
	Figuring° the natures of the times deceased;°	*Showing / past*
	The which observed, a man may prophesy,	
	With a near aim, of the main chance° of things	*general probability*
	As yet not come to life, who° in their seeds	*which*
80	And weak beginnings lie intreasurèd.°	*stored*
	Such things become the hatch and brood° of time;	*progeny and offspring*
	And by the necessary form of this[7]	
	King Richard might create a perfect guess	
	That great Northumberland, then false to him,	
85	Would of that seed grow to a greater falseness,	
	Which should not find a ground to root upon	
	Unless on you.	
	KING HENRY Are these things then necessities?	
	Then let us meet them like necessities;	

---

2. In classical mythology, the god of the sea. Here the seashore is depicted as a girdle worn by Neptune. That the girdle is too wide or too large indicates that the sea is retreating from the land, in contrast to the prior image of land being absorbed into the ocean.
3. The following three and a half lines (52.1–52.4) do not appear in F, though they are in the 1600 quarto version of the play.
4. An apparent error. The King is addressing the Earl of Warwick, whose surname was Beauchamp, not Neville. Shakespeare may be confusing him with Richard Neville, an important character in his plays on the life of Henry VI.
5. See *Richard II* 5.1, in which similar lines are spoken, though neither Bolingbroke nor Warwick was present.
6. Coming to maturity; coming to a head, like pus on a sore.
7. And by this requisite pattern (of cause and effect).

And that same word even now cries out on° us.   *denounces*
90   They say the Bishop and Northumberland
      Are fifty thousand strong.

WARWICK   It cannot be, my lord.
      Rumour doth double, like the voice and echo,
      The numbers of the feared. Please it your grace
      To go to bed? Upon my soul, my lord,
95   The powers that you already have sent forth
      Shall bring this prize in very easily.
      To comfort you the more, I have received
      A certain instance° that Glyndŵr is dead.   *proof*
      Your majesty hath been this fortnight ill,
100   And these unseasoned° hours perforce must add   *irregular*
      Unto your sickness.

KING HENRY   I will take your counsel.
      And were these inward° wars once out of hand,   *civil*
      We would, dear lords, unto the Holy Land. *Exeunt*

                    3.2
      Enter Justice SHALLOW *and Justice* SILENCE

SHALLOW   Come on, come on, come on! Give me your hand,
      sir, give me your hand, sir. An early stirrer, by the rood!° And   *cross*
      how doth my good cousin° Silence?   *kinsman*

SILENCE   Good morrow, good cousin Shallow.

5   SHALLOW   And how doth my cousin your bedfellow? And your
      fairest daughter and mine, my god-daughter Ellen?

SILENCE   Alas, a black ouzel,[1] cousin Shallow.

SHALLOW   By yea and no, sir, I dare say my cousin William is
      become a good scholar. He is at Oxford still, is he not?

10 SILENCE   Indeed, sir, to my cost.

SHALLOW   A° must then to the Inns o' Court[2] shortly. I was once   *He*
      of Clement's Inn,[3] where I think they will talk of mad Shallow
      yet.

SILENCE   You were called 'lusty Shallow' then, cousin.

15 SHALLOW   By the mass, I was called anything; and I would have
      done anything indeed, too, and roundly,° too. There was I, and   *thoroughly*
      little John Doit of Staffordshire, and black George Barnes, and
      Francis Pickbone, and Will Squeal, a Cotswold man; you had
      not four such swinge-bucklers° in all the Inns o' Court again.   *swashbucklers*
20   And I may say to you, we knew where the bona-robas° were,   *well-dressed prostitutes*
      and had the best of them all at commandment. Then was Jack
      Falstaff, now Sir John, a boy, and page to Thomas Mowbray,
      Duke of Norfolk.

SILENCE   This Sir John, cousin, that comes hither anon° about   *soon*
25   soldiers?

SHALLOW   The same Sir John, the very same. I see him break
      Scoggin's[4] head at the court gate when a was a crack,° not thus   *young fellow*
      high. And the very same day did I fight with one Samson Stock-

---

3.2 Location: Outside Justice Shallow's house in
Gloucestershire.
1. Blackbird. Women with black hair and/or complexions were often viewed as "foul" rather than "fair."
2. Prestigious legal schools in London that admitted
men to the bar.

3. One of the Inns of Chancery, less prestigious legal
colleges.
4. A buffoon (possibly referring to Edward IV's court
jester of that name and famous as the main character
of *Scogin's Jests*, a popular Elizabethan jestbook).

fish, a fruiterer, behind Gray's Inn.[5] Jesu, Jesu, the mad days
30 that I have spent! And to see how many of my old acquaintance
are dead.

SILENCE We shall all follow, cousin.

SHALLOW Certain, 'tis certain; very sure, very sure. Death, as the
Psalmist saith, is certain to all; all shall die. How° a good yoke   *What's the price of*
35 of bullocks at Stamford fair?

SILENCE By my troth, I was not there.

SHALLOW Death is certain. Is old Double of your town living
yet?

SILENCE Dead, sir.

40 SHALLOW Jesu, Jesu, dead! A° drew a good bow; and dead! A   *He*
shot a fine shoot. John o' Gaunt° loved him well, and betted   *(Henry IV's father)*
much money on his head. Dead! A would have clapped i'th'
clout at twelve score,[6] and carried you a forehand shaft a fourteen and fourteen and a half,[7] that it would have done a man's
45 heart good to see. How a score of ewes now?

SILENCE Thereafter as they be.[8] A score of good ewes may be
worth ten pounds.

SHALLOW And is old Double dead?

Enter BARDOLPH *and* [*the* PAGE][9]

SILENCE Here come two of Sir John Falstaff's men, as I think.

50 SHALLOW Good morrow, honest gentlemen.

BARDOLPH I beseech you, which is Justice Shallow?

SHALLOW I am Robert Shallow, sir, a poor esquire of this county,
and one of the King's Justices of the Peace. What is your good
pleasure with me?

55 BARDOLPH My captain, sir, commends him° to you—my captain   *sends his respects*
Sir John Falstaff, a tall° gentleman, by heaven, and a most gal-   *valiant*
lant leader.

SHALLOW He greets me well, sir. I knew him a good backsword
man.° How doth the good knight? May I ask how my lady his   *fencer*
60 wife doth?

BARDOLPH Sir, pardon, a soldier is better accommodated than
with a wife.

SHALLOW It is well said, in faith, sir, and it is well said indeed,
too. 'Better accommodated'—it is good; yea, indeed is it. Good
65 phrases are surely, and ever were, very commendable. 'Accommodated'—it comes of 'accommodo'. Very good, a good phrase.

BARDOLPH Pardon, sir, I have heard the word—'phrase' call you
it?—By this day, I know not the phrase; but I will maintain the
word with my sword to be a soldier-like word, and a word of
70 exceeding good command,° by heaven. 'Accommodated'; that   *fit for many uses*
is, when a man is, as they say, accommodated; or when a man
is being whereby a may be thought to be accommodated;
which is an excellent thing.

Enter Sir John FALSTAFF

SHALLOW It is very just.° Look, here comes good Sir John. [*To*   *true*
75 FALSTAFF] Give me your hand, give me your worship's good

---

5. One of the Inns of Court.
6. Hit the target from 240 yards.
7. He could shoot an arrow straight, to 280 or 290
yards. A "forehand shaft" is an arrow shot in a straight
line rather than with the curved trajectory common for
long shots.
8. The price depends on their quality.

9. In F, Bardolph enters with "his Boy." In Q, he enters
"and one with him." It is reasonable to assume, but not
certain, that Falstaff's page is Bardolph's companion.
The use of a boy actor for this part would allow the
number of adult actors required for the rest of the
scene to be reduced by one.

hand. By my troth, you like well,° and bear your years very well. *you are thriving*
Welcome, good Sir John.

FALSTAFF   I am glad to see you well, good Master Robert Shallow. [*To* SILENCE] Master Surecard, as I think.

80 SHALLOW   No, Sir John, it is my cousin Silence, in commission[1]
with me.

FALSTAFF   Good Master Silence, it well befits you should be of
the peace.

SILENCE   Your good worship is welcome.

85 FALSTAFF   Fie, this is hot weather, gentlemen. Have you provided me here half a dozen sufficient° men? *able*

SHALLOW   Marry, have we, sir. Will you sit?

FALSTAFF   Let me see them, I beseech you.
[*He sits*]

SHALLOW   Where's the roll,° where's the roll, where's the roll? *list*
90 Let me see, let me see, let me see; so, so, so, so, so. Yea, marry,
sir: 'Ralph Mouldy'. [*To* SILENCE] Let them appear as I call,
let them do so, let them do so. Let me see, [*calls*] where is
Mouldy?
[*Enter* MOULDY][2]

MOULDY   Here, an't please you.

95 SHALLOW   What think you, Sir John? A good-limbed fellow,
young, strong, and of good friends.° *well connected*

FALSTAFF   Is thy name Mouldy?

MOULDY   Yea, an't please you.

FALSTAFF   'Tis the more time° thou wert used. *well past time*

100 SHALLOW   Ha, ha, ha, most excellent, i'faith! Things that are
mouldy lack use. Very singular good, in faith, well said, Sir
John, very well said.

FALSTAFF   Prick him.° *Mark his name*

MOULDY   I was pricked[3] well enough before, an you could have
105 let me alone. My old dame° will be undone now for one to do *wife*
her husbandry[4] and her drudgery. You need not to have
pricked me; there are other men fitter to go out than I.

FALSTAFF   Go to, peace, Mouldy. You shall go, Mouldy; it is
time you were spent.° *used up*

110 MOULDY   Spent?

SHALLOW   Peace, fellow, peace. Stand aside; know you where
you are?
[MOULDY *stands aside*]
For th'other, Sir John, let me see: 'Simon Shadow'—

FALSTAFF   Yea, marry, let me have him to sit under. He's like to
115 be a cold° soldier. *dead; cowardly*

SHALLOW [*calls*]   Where's Shadow?
[*Enter* SHADOW]

SHADOW   Here, sir.

FALSTAFF   Shadow, whose son art thou?

SHADOW   My mother's son, sir.

120 FALSTAFF   Thy mother's son! Like enough, and thy father's
shadow.° So the son of the female is the shadow° of the male— *likeness / faint copy*

---

1. Having a position (as justice of the peace).
2. In F, the recruits enter at the beginning of the scene
with Silence and Shallow. But they have nothing to do
until this point in the scene. It is better to have them all
enter with Mouldy and be called forward one by one, or,

as here, to enter separately as each name is called.
3. Vexed; provided with a penis.
4. Will be lacking someone to perform the sexual
duties of a husband; will be lacking someone to do the
work of the farm.

it is often so indeed—but not of the father's substance.[5]

SHALLOW   Do you like him, Sir John?

FALSTAFF   Shadow will serve for summer. Prick him, for we have
125   a number of shadows[6] fill up the muster book.

[SHADOW *stands aside*]

SHALLOW [*calls*]   'Thomas Wart.'

FALSTAFF   Where's he?

[*Enter* WART]

WART   Here, sir.

FALSTAFF   Is thy name Wart?

130   WART   Yea, sir.

FALSTAFF   Thou art a very ragged wart.

SHALLOW   Shall I prick him, Sir John?

FALSTAFF   It were superfluous, for his apparel is built° upon his   *pieced together*
back, and the whole frame stands upon pins.[7] Prick him no
135   more.

SHALLOW   Ha, ha, ha, you can do it, sir, you can do it! I commend you well.

[WART *stands aside*]

[*Calls*] 'Francis Feeble.'

[*Enter* FEEBLE]

FEEBLE   Here, sir.

140   SHALLOW   What trade art thou, Feeble?

FEEBLE   A woman's tailor,[8] sir.

SHALLOW   Shall I prick him, sir?

FALSTAFF   You may, but if he had been a man's tailor, he'd ha'
pricked[9] you. [*To* FEEBLE] Wilt thou make as many holes in an
145   enemy's battle° as thou hast done in a woman's petticoat?   *army*

FEEBLE   I will do my good will,° sir; you can have no more.   *do my best*

FALSTAFF   Well said, good woman's tailor; well said, courageous
Feeble! Thou wilt be as valiant as the wrathful dove or most
magnanimous° mouse. Prick the woman's tailor. Well, Master   *brave*
150   Shallow; deep, Master Shallow.

FEEBLE   I would Wart might have gone, sir.

FALSTAFF   I would thou wert a man's tailor, that thou mightst
mend him and make him fit to go.° I cannot put him to a   *to serve; to have sex*
private soldier[1] that is the leader of so many thousands.° Let   *(of lice)*
155   that suffice, most forcible Feeble.

FEEBLE   It shall suffice, sir.

FALSTAFF   I am bound to thee, reverend Feeble.

[FEEBLE *stands aside*]

Who is next?

SHALLOW [*calls*]   'Peter Bullcalf o'th' green.'

160   FALSTAFF   Yea, marry, let's see Bullcalf.

[*Enter* BULLCALF]

BULLCALF   Here, sir.

FALSTAFF   Fore God, a likely° fellow! Come, prick Bullcalf till   *promising*
he roar again.

---

5. Not born from the father's body (because born from
the mother's); not the father's true son.
6. Fictitious names that officers recorded in order to
collect additional pay from the crown.
7. The whole structure depends upon pegs ("pins");
stands upon legs ("pins").

8. Women's tailors were bywords for effeminacy and
cowardice.
9. Dressed; stabbed; penetrated.
1. Make him a private soldier; offer him sexually to a
private soldier.

BULLCALF   O Lord, good my lord captain!

165   FALSTAFF   What, dost thou roar before thou'rt pricked?

BULLCALF   O Lord, sir, I am a diseased man.

FALSTAFF   What disease hast thou?

BULLCALF   A whoreson cold, sir; a cough, sir, which I caught
with ringing in the King's affairs[2] upon his coronation day, sir.

170   FALSTAFF   Come, thou shalt go to the wars in a gown.° We will   dressing gown
have away° thy cold, and I will take such order° that thy friends   get rid / measures
shall ring for thee.[3]

          [BULLCALF stands aside]

Is here all?

SHALLOW   There is two more called than your number. You

175   must have but four here,[4] sir, and so I pray you go in with me
to dinner.

FALSTAFF   Come, I will go drink with you, but I cannot tarry°   stay for
dinner. I am glad to see you, by my troth, Master Shallow.

SHALLOW   O, Sir John, do you remember since we lay all night

180   in the Windmill in Saint George's Field?[5]

FALSTAFF   No more of that, good Master Shallow, no more of
that.

SHALLOW   Ha, 'twas a merry night! And is Jane Nightwork alive?

FALSTAFF   She lives, Master Shallow.

185   SHALLOW   She never could away with° me.   tolerate

FALSTAFF   Never, never. She would always say she could not
abide Master Shallow.

SHALLOW   By the mass, I could anger her to th' heart. She was
then a bona-roba. Doth she hold her own well?

190   FALSTAFF   Old, old, Master Shallow.

SHALLOW   Nay, she must be old; she cannot choose but be old;
certain she's old; and had Robin Nightwork by old Nightwork
before I came to Clement's Inn.

SILENCE   That's fifty-five year ago.

195   SHALLOW   Ha, cousin Silence, that thou hadst seen that that this
knight and I have seen! Ha, Sir John, said I well?

FALSTAFF   We have heard the chimes at midnight, Master
Shallow.

SHALLOW   That we have, that we have; in faith, Sir John, we

200   have. Our watchword was 'Hem° boys!' Come, let's to dinner;   Drink up
come, let's to dinner. Jesus, the days that we have seen! Come,
come.   Exeunt [SHALLOW, SILENCE, and FALSTAFF]

BULLCALF [coming forward]   Good Master Corporate° Bardolph,   (for "Corporal")
stand° my friend, and here's four Harry ten shillings in French   act as

205   crowns for you.[6] In very truth, sir, I had as lief° be hanged, sir,   willingly
as go. And yet for mine own part, sir, I do not care; but rather
because I am unwilling, and, for mine own part, have a desire
to stay with my friends. Else, sir, I did not care, for mine own
part, so much.

210   BARDOLPH [taking the money]   Go to; stand aside.

          [BULLCALF stands aside]

2. Ringing the church bells in the King's honor.
3. In your place; at your death.
4. An inconsistency: there have been five, not six,
recruits called.
5. A region of London south of the Thames near
Southwark, known as a market for sex. "The Windmill"
was the name of a brothel or an inn.

6. An elaborate way of offering a bribe. The reference
to "Harry ten shillings" is anachronistic; shillings originated during Henry VII's reign and by the 1590s had
been devalued to half their original worth. Therefore,
Bullcalf is offering about 1 pound to be paid in French
crowns (coins worth 4 shillings each).

MOULDY [*coming forward*] And, good Master Corporal Captain, for my old dame's sake stand my friend. She has nobody to do anything about her when I am gone, and she is old and cannot help herself. You shall have forty,° sir.   *(shillings)*

215 BARDOLPH Go to; stand aside.

> [MOULDY *stands aside*]

FEEBLE By my troth, I care not. A man can die but once. We owe God a death. I'll ne'er bear a base mind. An't be my destiny, so; an't be not, so. No man's too good to serve's° prince.   *serve his*
And let it go which way it will, he that dies this year is quit for°   *released from (dying)*
220 the next.

BARDOLPH Well said; thou'rt a good fellow.

FEEBLE Faith, I'll bear no base mind.

> Enter [*Sir John*] FALSTAFF[, SHALLOW, *and* SILENCE]

FALSTAFF Come, sir, which men shall I have?

SHALLOW Four of which you please.

225 BARDOLPH [*to* FALSTAFF] Sir, a word with you. [*Aside to him*] I have three pound to free Mouldy and Bullcalf.

FALSTAFF Go to, well.

SHALLOW Come, Sir John, which four will you have?

FALSTAFF Do you choose for me.

230 SHALLOW Marry, then: Mouldy, Bullcalf, Feeble, and Shadow.

FALSTAFF Mouldy and Bullcalf. For you, Mouldy, stay at home till you are past service;[7] and for your part, Bullcalf, grow till you come unto it.[8] I will none of you.

> [*Exeunt* BULLCALF *and* MOULDY]

SHALLOW Sir John, Sir John, do not yourself wrong. They are
235 your likeliest men, and I would have you served with the best.

FALSTAFF Will you tell me, Master Shallow, how to choose a man? Care I for the limb, the thews,° the stature, bulk, and big   *strength*
assemblance° of a man? Give me the spirit, Master Shallow.   *composition*
Here's Wart; you see what a ragged appearance it is? A shall
240 charge you and discharge you° with the motion of a pewterer's   *load and fire*
hammer,° come off and on swifter than he that gibbets on the   *with a steady motion*
brewer's bucket.[9] And this same half-faced° fellow Shadow;   *thin-faced*
give me this man. He presents no mark° to the enemy; the   *target*
foeman may with as great aim level at° the edge of a penknife.   *fire against*
245 And for a retreat, how swiftly will this Feeble the woman's tailor run off! O, give me the spare men, and spare me the great ones.—Put me a caliver° into Wart's hand, Bardolph.   *musket*

BARDOLPH [*giving* WART *a caliver*] Hold, Wart. Traverse°—thas,   *March*
thas, thas!

> [WART *marches*]

250 FALSTAFF [*to* WART] Come, manage me your caliver. So; very well. Go to, very good, exceeding good. O, give me always a little, lean, old, chapped, bald shot!° Well said, i'faith, Wart;   *marksman*
thou'rt a good scab. Hold; [*giving a coin*] there's a tester° for   *sixpence*
thee.

255 SHALLOW He is not his craft's master; he doth not do it right. I remember at Mile-End Green,[1] when I lay° at Clement's   *lodged*

---

7. Past the time of military duty; past the time of sexual potency.
8. That is, grow until you come into the time of military service; the time of sexual potency. Falstaff plays on the fact that Bullcalf is a *calf*, not a *bull*.

9. Retreat and advance, or raise and lower your gun, faster than he who hangs pails on each end of the wooden bar (gibbet) that a brewer carries on his shoulders.
1. Open land east of London used as a training ground for citizen militias and for fairs and shows.

Inn—I was then Sir Dagonet in Arthur's show²—there was a
little quiver° fellow, and a would manage you his piece thus,   *nimble*
and a would about and about, and come you in° and come you   *thrust at you*
260 in. 'Ra-ta-ta!' would a say; 'Bounce!'° would a say; and away   *Bang*
again would a go; and again would a come. I shall ne'er see
such a fellow.
FALSTAFF   These fellows will do well, Master Shallow. God keep
you, Master Silence; I will not use many words with you. Fare
265 you well, gentlemen both; I thank you. I must° a dozen mile   *must go*
tonight.—Bardolph, give the soldiers coats.
SHALLOW   Sir John, the Lord bless you; God prosper your affairs!
God send us peace! As you return, visit my house; let our old
acquaintance be renewed. Peradventure I will with ye to the
270 court.
FALSTAFF   Fore God, would you would!
SHALLOW   Go to, I have spoke at a word.° God keep you!   *spoken sincerely*
FALSTAFF   Fare you well, gentle gentlemen.
                    Exeunt [SHALLOW *and* SILENCE]
On, Bardolph, lead the men away.
                    [*Exeunt* BARDOLPH, WART, SHADOW, *and* FEEBLE]
275 As I return, I will fetch off° these justices. I do see the bottom   *defraud*
of Justice Shallow. Lord, Lord, how subject we old men are to
this vice of lying! This same starved justice hath done nothing
but prate to me of the wildness of his youth and the feats he
hath done about Turnbull Street;³ and every third word a lie,
280 duer paid° to the hearer than the Turk's tribute.⁴ I do remem-   *sooner paid*
ber him at Clement's Inn, like a man made after supper of a
cheese paring. When a was naked, he was for all the world like
a forked radish,⁵ with a head fantastically carved upon it with a
knife. A was so forlorn° that his dimensions, to any thick° sight,   *thin / imperfect*
285 were invisible. A was the very genius° of famine.⁶   *spirit*
285.1   *yet lecherous as a monkey; and the whores called him*
           'mandrake'. A came ever in the rearward of the fashion,
           and sung those tunes to the overscutched hussies° *that*   *worn-out whores*
           he heard the carmen° *whistle, and sware they were his*   *wagoners*
285.5   *fancies or his good-nights.*°   *his own love songs*
And now is this Vice's dagger⁷ become a squire, and talks as familiarly of John o' Gaunt as if he had been sworn brother to him,
and I'll be sworn a ne'er saw him but once, in the Tilt-yard,°   *tournament arena*
and then he° burst his° head for crowding among the marshal's   *(Gaunt) / (Shallow's)*
290 men. I saw it, and told John o' Gaunt he beat his own
name;⁸ for you might have trussed° him and all his apparel into   *packed*
an eel-skin. The case of a treble hautboy° was a mansion for   *oboe*
him, a court. And now has he land and beeves.° Well, I'll be   *oxen*
acquainted with him if I return; and't shall go hard but I'll
295 make him a philosopher's two stones to me.⁹ If the young dace°   *small fish*

2. Referring to his role as King Arthur's fool in an
archery pageant in which each participant took the
name of one of the knights of the Round Table.
3. An area of Smithfield associated with criminal activities.
4. Money extracted from those the Turkish Sultan conquered or who engaged in trade with him. The penalty
for failure to pay was death, so presumably money was
paid punctually. Shallow is even quicker to tell lies.
5. A mandrake root, said to resemble a man's body. See

note to 1.2.12.
6. The following inset lines (285.1–285.5) appear in Q
but not in F.
7. The wooden dagger used by the Vice, a comic character in medieval morality plays.
8. Attacked someone very gaunt or thin.
9. I'll make him twice as valuable to me as the philosopher's stone that was supposed to transmute base
metals into gold, with a pun on "stones" as meaning
"testicles."

be a bait for the old pike, I see no reason in the law of nature
but I may snap at him. Let time shape, and there an end.

Exit

4.1

Enter [in arms] the ARCHBISHOP *[of York], [Thomas]*
MOWBRAY, *[Lord]* HASTINGS, *[and]* COLEVILLE[1] *within
the Forest of Gaultres*[2]

ARCHBISHOP OF YORK   What is this forest called?

HASTINGS   'Tis Gaultres Forest, an't° shall please your grace.   *if it*

ARCHBISHOP OF YORK   Here stand, my lords, and send discoverers° forth   *scouts*
To know the numbers of our enemies.

HASTINGS   We have sent forth already.

5   ARCHBISHOP OF YORK   'Tis well done.
My friends and brethren in these great affairs,
I must acquaint you that I have received
New-dated° letters from Northumberland,   *Recent*
Their cold intent, tenor, and substance, thus:

10   Here doth he wish his person, with such powers
As might hold sortance° with his quality,°   *accord / rank*
The which he could not levy; whereupon
He is retired to ripe° his growing fortunes   *ripen*
To Scotland, and concludes in hearty prayers

15   That your attempts may overlive the hazard
And fearful meeting of their opposite.°   *enemy*

MOWBRAY   Thus do the hopes we have in him touch ground
And dash themselves to pieces.

Enter a MESSENGER

HASTINGS   Now, what news?

MESSENGER   West of this forest, scarcely off a mile,

20   In goodly form° comes on the enemy;   *battle array*
And, by the ground they hide,° I judge their number   *cover*
Upon or near the rate of thirty thousand.

MOWBRAY   The just proportion° that we gave them out.°   *exact size / estimated*
Let us sway on, and face them in the field.

Enter [the Earl] of WESTMORLAND

25   ARCHBISHOP OF YORK   What well-appointed leader fronts° us here?   *confronts*

MOWBRAY   I think it is my lord of Westmorland.

WESTMORLAND   Health and fair greeting from our general,
The Prince, Lord John and Duke of Lancaster.

ARCHBISHOP OF YORK   Say on, my lord of Westmorland, in peace,
What doth concern your coming.

30   WESTMORLAND   Then, my lord,
Unto your grace do I in chief address
The substance of my speech. If that rebellion
Came like itself, in base and abject routs,°   *lowborn disorderly bands*
Led on by bloody youth, guarded° with rags,   *adorned*

35   And countenanced° by boys and beggary;   *approved*
I say, if damned commotion so appeared

4.1 Location: Gaultres Forest in Yorkshire.
1. In F, this initial stage direction includes Westmorland, who actually enters later in the scene, and Coleville, a rebel captured by Falstaff in 4.2. Most editors delete both figures from the initial stage direction. The Oxford editors speculate that Coleville is the captain who at 4.1.295–97 is sent to tell the rebel army to disperse after peace is made, so they include him in the scene from the beginning.
2. Gaultres was a royal forest north and west of York. In Holinshed's *Chronicles* and in Q and F, it is spelled "Gaultree," a spelling adopted in most editions.

In his true native and most proper shape,
You, reverend father, and these noble lords
Had not been here to dress the ugly form
40 Of base and bloody insurrection
With your fair honours. You, Lord Archbishop,
Whose see° is by a civil peace maintained,   *diocese*
Whose beard the silver hand of peace hath touched,
Whose learning and good letters° peace hath tutored,   *scholarship*
45 Whose white investments figure° innocence,   *robes represent*
The dove and very blessèd spirit of peace,
Wherefore do you so ill translate° yourself   *transform*
Out of the speech of peace that bears such grace
Into the harsh and boist'rous tongue of war,
50 Turning your books to graves, your ink to blood,
Your pens to lances, and your tongue divine
To a loud trumpet and a point° of war?   *signal*
ARCHBISHOP OF YORK Wherefore do I this? So the question stands.
Briefly, to this end: we are all diseased,[3]
55 And with our surfeiting° and wanton hours   *overeating*
Have brought ourselves into a burning fever,
And we must bleed° for it—of which disease   *be bled as a cure*
Our late King Richard, being infected, died.
But, my most noble lord of Westmorland,
60 I take not on me here as a physician,
Nor do I as an enemy to peace
Troop in the throngs of military men;
But rather show° a while like fearful war   *appear*
To diet rank° minds, sick of happiness,   *swollen; overindulged*
65 And purge th'obstructions which begin to stop
Our very veins of life. Hear me more plainly.
I have in equal balance justly weighed
What wrongs our arms may do, what wrongs we suffer,
And find our griefs heavier than our offences.
70 We see which way the stream of time doth run,
And are enforced from our most quiet shore
By the rough torrent of occasion;°   *events*
And have the summary of all our griefs,
When time shall serve, to show in articles,°   *an itemized list*
75 Which long ere this we offered to the King,
And might by no suit gain our audience.
When we are wronged, and would unfold our griefs,
We are denied access unto his person
Even by those men that most have done us wrong.
80 The dangers of the days but newly gone,
Whose memory is written on the earth
With yet° appearing blood, and the examples   *still*
Of every minute's instance,° present now,   *Occurring every minute*
Hath put us in these ill-beseeming° arms,   *unsuitable*
85 Not to break peace, or any branch of it,
But to establish here a peace indeed,
Concurring both in name and quality.
WESTMORLAND Whenever yet was your appeal denied?

---

3. Lines 55–79 are missing from Q, perhaps because they state the case for rebellion too forcefully.

Wherein have you been gallèd° by the King? *vexed; grieved*
90 What peer hath been suborned to grate on° you, *induced to annoy*
That you should seal° this lawless bloody book *license*
Of forged rebellion with a seal divine?[4]
ARCHBISHOP OF YORK   My brother general, the commonwealth
I make my quarrel in particular.[5]
95 WESTMORLAND   There is no need of any such redress;
Or if there were, it not belongs to you.
MOWBRAY   Why not to him in part, and to us all
That feel the bruises of the days before,
And suffer the condition of these times
100 To lay a heavy and unequal° hand *unjust*
Upon our honours?[6]
WESTMORLAND   O my good Lord Mowbray,
Construe the times to° their necessities, *according to*
And you shall say indeed it is the time,
And not the King, that doth you injuries.
105 Yet for your part, it not appears° to me, *it does not appear*
Either from the King or in the present time,
That you should have an inch of any ground
To build a grief on. Were you not restored
To all the Duke of Norfolk's signories,° *properties*
110 Your noble and right well-remembered father's?
MOWBRAY   What thing in honour had my father lost
That need to be revived and breathed° in me? *brought to life*
The King that loved him, as the state stood then,
Was force perforce° compelled to banish him; *against his will*
115 And then that Henry Bolingbroke and he,
Being mounted and both rousèd° in their seats, *raised*
Their neighing coursers daring of the spur,[7]
Their armèd staves in charge,[8] their beavers° down, *helmet visors*
Their eyes of fire sparkling through sights° of steel, *visor slits*
120 And the loud trumpet blowing them together,
Then, then, when there was nothing could have stayed° *kept*
My father from the breast of Bolingbroke—
O, when the King did throw his warder° down, *staff of command*
His own life hung upon the staff he threw;
125 Then threw he down himself and all their lives
That by indictment° and by dint of sword *legal accusations*
Have since miscarried under Bolingbroke.
WESTMORLAND   You speak, Lord Mowbray, now you know not what.
The Earl of Hereford° was reputed then *(Bolingbroke)*
130 In England the most valiant gentleman.
Who knows on whom fortune would then have smiled?
But if your father had been victor there,
He ne'er had borne it out of Coventry;[9]
For all the country in a general voice
135 Cried hate upon him, and all their prayers and love

---

4. Alluding to bishops as official licensers of books with the ability to exercise censorship. Westmorland accuses the Archbishop of *not* censoring the book of rebellion.
5. *My . . . particular*: these two lines are obscure. York seems to be saying he is making the cause of the commonwealth his own because all men are his brothers.
6. The second half of line 101 and lines 102–37 do not

appear in Q. They recount a version of events depicted in Shakespeare's *Richard II* in which Richard stopped a formal combat between Thomas Mowbray, father of the Mowbray of this play, and Bolingbroke, now Henry IV.
7. Daring the spur to prick them forward.
8. Their steel-tipped lances ready for the charge.
9. He never would have carried away the prize from Coventry (where the duel was to take place).

Were set on Hereford, whom they doted on
And blessed and graced, indeed, more than the King.
But this is mere digression from my purpose.
Here come I from our princely general
140 To know your griefs, to tell you from his grace
That he will give you audience; and wherein
It shall appear that your demands are just,
You shall enjoy them, everything set off°   *forgotten*
That might so much as think you enemies.
145 MOWBRAY But he hath forced us to compel this offer,
And it proceeds from policy,° not love.   *political cunning*
WESTMORLAND Mowbray, you overween° to take it so.   *presume too much*
This offer comes from mercy, not from fear;
For lo, within a ken° our army lies,   *the field of vision*
150 Upon mine honour, all too confident
To give admittance to a thought of fear.
Our battle° is more full of names° than yours,   *army / titled men*
Our men more perfect in the use of arms,
Our armour all as strong, our cause the best.
155 Then reason will° our hearts should be as good.   *it follows that*
Say you not then our offer is compelled.
MOWBRAY Well, by my will we shall admit no parley.°   *discussion of terms*
WESTMORLAND That argues but the shame of your offence.
A rotten case° abides no handling.   *cause*
160 HASTINGS Hath the Prince John a full commission,
In very ample virtue° of his father,   *With full authority*
To hear and absolutely to determine
Of what° conditions we shall stand upon?   *whatever*
WESTMORLAND That is intended° in the general's name.   *indicated*
165 I muse° you make so slight a question.   *wonder*
ARCHBISHOP OF YORK Then take, my lord of Westmorland, this schedule;°   *document*
For this contains our general grievances.
Each several° article herein redressed,   *individual*
All members of our cause, both here and hence,
170 That are ensinewed° to this action   *tightly bound (by sinews)*
Acquitted° by a true substantial form,°   *Pardoned / binding act*
And present execution of our wills
To us and to our purposes consigned,[1]
We come within our awe-full banks again,[2]
175 And knit our powers to the arm of peace.
WESTMORLAND [*taking the schedule*] This will I show the general.
Please you, lords,
In sight of both our battles we may meet,
And either end in peace—which God so frame°—   *bring to pass*
Or to the place of diff'rence° call the swords   *conflict*
Which must decide it.
180 ARCHBISHOP OF YORK   My lord, we will do so.   *Exit* WESTMORLAND
MOWBRAY There is a thing within my bosom tells me
That no conditions of our peace can stand.
HASTINGS Fear you not that. If we can make our peace

---

1. *And . . . consigned:* And immediate ("present") fulfillment of our demands allowed us. The emendation to
"consigned" of Q's and F's "confinde" allows three parallel clauses to follow one another, each dealing with one

of the rebels' conditions for putting down their arms.
2. We come again within the bounds of respect (with
the suggestion of a flooded river returning to its banks).

Upon such large° terms and so absolute   *liberal*
185 As our conditions shall consist° upon,   *insist*
Our peace shall stand as firm as rocky mountains.

MOWBRAY   Yea, but our valuation° shall be such   *the value we are held in*
That every slight and false-derivèd° cause,   *wrongly attributed*
Yea, every idle, nice,° and wanton° reason,   *petty / frivolous*
190 Shall to the King taste of this action,°   *(of rebellion)*
That, were our royal faiths martyrs in love,[3]
We shall be winnowed with so rough a wind
That even our corn shall seem as light as chaff,
And good from bad find no partition.°   *distinction*

195 ARCHBISHOP OF YORK   No, no, my lord; note this. The King is weary
Of dainty and such picking° grievances,   *trivial*
For he hath found to end one doubt° by death   *fear*
Revives two greater in the heirs of life;
And therefore will he wipe his tables° clean,   *tablets*
200 And keep no tell-tale to his memory
That may repeat and history° his loss   *retell*
To new remembrance; for full well he knows
He cannot so precisely weed this land
As his misdoubts° present occasion.   *suspicions*
205 His foes are so enrooted with his friends
That, plucking to unfix an enemy,
He doth unfasten so and shake a friend;
So that this land, like an offensive wife
That hath enraged him on to offer strokes,°   *attempt beatings*
210 As he is striking, holds his infant up,
And hangs resolved correction in the arm
That was upreared to execution.[4]

HASTINGS   Besides, the King hath wasted all his rods°   *means of punishment*
On late° offenders, that he now doth lack   *recent*
215 The very instruments of chastisement;
So that his power, like to a fangless lion,
May offer,° but not hold.   *threaten*

ARCHBISHOP OF YORK   'Tis very true.
And therefore be assured, my good Lord Marshal,
If we do now make our atonement° well,   *reconciliation*
220 Our peace will, like a broken limb united,
Grow stronger for the breaking.

MOWBRAY   Be it so.

Enter WESTMORLAND

Here is returned my lord of Westmorland.

WESTMORLAND   The Prince is here at hand. Pleaseth your lordship
To meet his grace just° distance 'tween our armies?   *equal*

225 MOWBRAY   Your grace of York, in God's name then set forward.

ARCHBISHOP OF YORK   Before, and greet his grace!—My lord, we come.

[*They march over the stage.*]

Enter PRINCE JOHN [*with one or more soldiers carrying wine*]

PRINCE JOHN   You are well encountered here, my cousin Mowbray.
Good day to you, gentle lord Archbishop;

---

3. So that even if our loyalty to the King made us lov-   4. *And . . . execution:* And so punishment that was
ing martyrs.   about to be executed is held in suspended action.

And so to you, Lord Hastings, and to all.
230 My lord of York, it better showed with you
When that your flock, assembled by the bell,
Encircled you to hear with reverence
Your exposition on the holy text,
Than now to see you here an iron° man,   *armored; a fierce*
235 Cheering a rout° of rebels with your drum,   *disorderly band*
Turning the word° to sword, and life to death.   *(Scripture)*
That man that sits within a monarch's heart
And ripens in the sunshine of his favour,
Would he° abuse the countenance° of the King,   *Should he / favor*
240 Alack, what mischiefs might he set abroach°   *afoot*
In shadow° of such greatness! With you, Lord Bishop,   *Under cover*
It is even so. Who hath not heard it spoken
How deep you were within the books of God—
To us, the speaker in his° parliament,   *(God's)*
245 To us, th'imagined voice of God himself,
The very opener° and intelligencer°   *interpreter / informer*
Between the grace, the sanctities of heaven
And our dull workings?° O, who shall believe   *ignorant thoughts*
But you misuse the reverence of your place,
250 Employ the countenance and grace of heav'n
As a false favourite doth his prince's name
In deeds dishonourable? You have ta'en up,°   *enlisted*
Under the counterfeited zeal of⁵ God,
The subjects of his substitute, my father;
255 And, both against the peace of heaven and him,
Have here upswarmèd them.⁶
    ARCHBISHOP OF YORK   Good my lord of Lancaster,
I am not here against your father's peace;
But, as I told my lord of Westmorland,
The time misordered doth, in common sense,
260 Crowd us and crush us to this monstrous form,
To hold our safety up. I sent your grace
The parcels° and particulars of our grief,   *items; details*
The which hath been with scorn shoved from the court,
Whereon this Hydra son⁷ of war is born;
265 Whose dangerous eyes may well be charmed asleep⁸
With grant° of our most just and right desires,   *the granting*
And true obedience, of this madness cured,
Stoop tamely to the foot of majesty.
    MOWBRAY   If not, we ready are to try our fortunes
To the last man.
270 HASTINGS   And though we here fall down,
We have supplies° to second our attempt.   *reinforcements*
If they miscarry, theirs shall second them;
And so success of° mischief shall be born,   *from*
And heir from heir shall hold this quarrel up,
275 Whiles° England shall have generation.°   *As long as / offspring*

---

5. Under the pretense of zeal toward God; under the pretense of God's approval.
6. Have raised them up in angry swarms (like bees).
7. Hydra-like offspring. The Archbishop alludes to the many-headed monster of classical mythology, which was almost impossible to kill because its heads grew again as fast as they were cut off.
8. Alluding to another monster of classical mythology, the hundred-eyed Argus, which Hermes overcame by charming it to sleep.

PRINCE JOHN You are too shallow, Hastings, much too shallow,
  To sound the bottom of the after-times.°   *future*
WESTMORLAND Pleaseth your grace to answer them directly
  How far forth you do like their articles?
280 PRINCE JOHN I like them all, and do allow° them well,   *grant*
  And swear here, by the honour of my blood,
  My father's purposes have been mistook,
  And some about him have too lavishly°   *freely*
  Wrested his meaning and authority.
285   [*To the* ARCHBISHOP] My lord, these griefs shall be with speed redressed;
  Upon my soul they shall. If this may please you,
  Discharge your powers unto their several counties,
  As we will ours; and here between the armies
  Let's drink together friendly and embrace,
290   That all their eyes may bear those tokens home
  Of our restorèd love and amity.
ARCHBISHOP OF YORK I take your princely word for these redresses.
PRINCE JOHN I give it you, and will maintain my word;
  And thereupon I drink unto your grace.
    [*He drinks*]
295 HASTINGS [*to* COLEVILLE] Go, captain, and deliver to the army
  This news of peace. Let them have pay, and part.
  I know it will well please them. Hie thee,° captain.   *Get thee gone*
                      Exit [COLEVILLE]
ARCHBISHOP OF YORK To you, my noble lord of Westmorland!
    [*He drinks*]
WESTMORLAND [*drinking*] I pledge your grace. An if you knew what pains
300   I have bestowed to breed this present peace,
  You would drink freely; but my love to ye
  Shall show itself more openly hereafter.
ARCHBISHOP OF YORK I do not doubt you.
WESTMORLAND   I am glad of it.
  [*Drinking*] Health to my lord and gentle cousin Mowbray!
305 MOWBRAY You wish me health in very happy season,°   *at an apt moment*
  For I am on the sudden something ill.
ARCHBISHOP OF YORK Against° ill chances men are ever merry;   *Before*
  But heaviness° foreruns the good event.   *sorrow*
WESTMORLAND Therefore be merry, coz,° since sudden sorrow   *kinsman*
310   Serves to say thus: some good thing comes tomorrow.
ARCHBISHOP OF YORK Believe me, I am passing° light in spirit.   *exceptionally*
MOWBRAY So much the worse, if your own rule be true.
                     Shout [*within*]
PRINCE JOHN The word of peace is rendered. Hark how they
  shout.
MOWBRAY This had° been cheerful after victory.   *would have*
315 ARCHBISHOP OF YORK A peace is of the nature of a conquest,
  For then both parties nobly are subdued,
  And neither party loser.
PRINCE JOHN [*to* WESTMORLAND] Go, my lord,
  And let our army be dischargèd too.   *Exit* [WESTMORLAND]
  [*To the* ARCHBISHOP] And, good my lord, so please you, let our trains°   *troops*
320   March by us, that we may peruse the men
  We should have coped withal.°   *fought against*
ARCHBISHOP OF YORK   Go, good Lord Hastings,
  And ere they be dismissed, let them march by.   *Exit* [HASTINGS]

PRINCE JOHN I trust, lords, we shall lie° tonight together. *lodge*
    Enter [the Earl of] WESTMORLAND *[with captains]*
  Now, cousin, wherefore stands our army still?
325 WESTMORLAND The leaders, having charge from you to stand,
  Will not go off until they hear you speak.
PRINCE JOHN They know their duties.
    Enter [Lord] HASTINGS
HASTINGS *[to the* ARCHBISHOP*]*   Our army is dispersed.
  Like youthful steers unyoked, they take their courses,
  East, west, north, south; or, like a school broke up,
330 Each hurries toward his home and sporting place.
WESTMORLAND Good tidings, my lord Hastings, for the which
  I do arrest thee, traitor, of high treason;
  And you, Lord Archbishop, and you, Lord Mowbray,
  Of capital treason I attach° you both. *arrest*
    [The captains guard HASTINGS, *the* ARCHBISHOP, *and*
    MOWBRAY*]*
335 MOWBRAY Is this proceeding just and honourable?
WESTMORLAND Is your assembly so?
ARCHBISHOP OF YORK Will you thus break your faith?
PRINCE JOHN I pawned° thee none. *pledged*
  I promised you redress of these same grievances
340 Whereof you did complain; which, by mine honour,
  I will perform with a most Christian care.
  But for you rebels, look to taste the due
  Meet° for rebellion and such acts as yours. *Appropriate*
  Most shallowly did you these arms° commence, *military exploits*
345 Fondly° brought here, and foolishly sent hence.— *Foolishly*
  Strike up our drums, pursue the scattered stray.° *stragglers*
  God, and not we, hath safely fought today.
  Some guard these traitors to the block of death,
  Treason's true bed and yielder up of breath. *Exeunt*

4.2

Alarum. Excursions. Enter [Sir John] FALSTAFF *and*
  COLEVILLE
FALSTAFF What's your name, sir, of what condition° are you, *social status*
  and of what place, I pray?
COLEVILLE I am a knight, sir, and my name is Coleville of the
  Dale.
5 FALSTAFF Well then, Coleville is your name, a knight is your
  degree,° and your place the Dale. Coleville shall be still your *rank*
  name, a traitor your degree, and the dungeon your place—a
  place deep enough, so shall you be still Coleville of the Dale.
COLEVILLE Are not you Sir John Falstaff?
10 FALSTAFF As good a man as he, sir, whoe'er I am. Do ye yield,
  sir, or shall I sweat for you? If I do sweat, they are the drops° of *tears*
  thy lovers,° and they weep for thy death; therefore rouse up fear *friends*
  and trembling, and do observance° to my mercy. *pay homage (kneel)*
COLEVILLE *[kneeling]* I think you are Sir John Falstaff, and in
15 that thought yield me.
FALSTAFF *[aside]* I have a whole school of tongues in this belly
  of mine, and not a tongue of them all speaks any other word

but my name. An I had but a belly of any indifferency,° I were   *of moderate size*
simply the most active fellow in Europe. My womb,° my   *belly*
20   womb, my womb undoes me.
                Enter PRINCE JOHN, [*the Earl of*] WESTMORLAND, [*Sir*
                John Blunt,] *and* [*other lords and soldiers*]
        Here comes our general.
        PRINCE JOHN   The heat° is past; follow no further now.   *chase*
                [*A*] *retreat* [*is sounded*]
        Call in the powers, good cousin Westmorland.
                                                    [*Exit* WESTMORLAND]
        Now, Falstaff, where have you been all this while?
25   When everything is ended, then you come.
        These tardy tricks of yours will, on my life,
        One time or other break some gallows' back.¹
        FALSTAFF   I would be sorry, my lord, but it should be thus. I
        never knew yet but rebuke and check° was the reward of valour.   *censure*
30   Do you think me a swallow, an arrow, or a bullet? Have I in
        my poor and old motion the expedition° of thought? I have   *speed*
        speeded hither with the very extremest° inch of possibility; I   *utmost*
        have foundered° nine-score and odd posts;° and here, travel-   *made lame / horses*
        tainted as I am, have in my pure and immaculate valour taken
35   Sir John Coleville of the Dale, a most furious knight and valor-
        ous enemy. But what of that? He saw me, and yielded, that I
        may justly say, with the hook-nosed fellow of Rome, 'I came,
        saw, and overcame.'²
        PRINCE JOHN   It was more of his courtesy than your deserving.
40   FALSTAFF   I know not. Here he is, and here I yield him; and I
        beseech your grace, let it be booked with the rest of this day's
        deeds; or, by the Lord, I will have it in a particular ballad³ else,
        with mine own picture on the top on't, Coleville kissing my
        foot; to the which course if I be enforced, if you do not all show
45   like gilt twopences to me,⁴ and I in the clear sky of fame o'er-
        shine you as much as the full moon doth the cinders of the
        element,° which show like pins' heads to her, believe not the   *the stars*
        word of the noble. Therefore let me have right, and let desert
        mount.°   *merit be rewarded*
50   PRINCE JOHN   Thine's too heavy to mount.
        FALSTAFF   Let it shine then.
        PRINCE JOHN   Thine's too thick° to shine.   *opaque; dim*
        FALSTAFF   Let it do something, my good lord, that may do me
        good, and call it what you will.
        PRINCE JOHN   Is thy name Coleville?
55   COLEVILLE   It is, my lord.
        PRINCE JOHN   A famous rebel art thou, Coleville.
        FALSTAFF   And a famous true subject took him.
        COLEVILLE   I am, my lord, but as my betters are
        That led me hither. Had they been ruled by me,
60   You should have won them dearer° than you have.   *at greater cost*
        FALSTAFF   I know not how—they sold themselves, but thou
        Like a kind fellow gav'st thyself away,
        And I thank thee for thee.

---

1. Cause you to be hanged, which will break the gallows.   3. Ballad specifically about me. Ballads often reported
2. Referring to Julius Caesar, whose portrait and impe-   contemporary scandals and events.
rial exploits would be familiar to Elizabethans through   4. If you do not all look like counterfeits when com-
Thomas North's translation of Plutarch.   pared with me.

Enter [the Earl of] WESTMORLAND

PRINCE JOHN   Have you left pursuit?

WESTMORLAND   Retreat is made, and execution stayed.°   *stopped*

65 PRINCE JOHN   Send Coleville with his confederates
To York, to present° execution.   *immediate*
Blunt, lead him hence, and see you guard him sure.

                                    Exit [Blunt,] with COLEVILLE

And now dispatch we toward the court, my lords.
I hear the King my father is sore° sick.   *severely*

70 [*To* WESTMORLAND] Our news shall go before us to his majesty,
Which, cousin, you shall bear to comfort him;
And we with sober speed will follow you.

FALSTAFF   My lord, I beseech you give me leave to go
Through Gloucestershire, and when you come to court

75 Stand,° my good lord, pray, in your good report.   *Let me stand*

PRINCE JOHN   Fare you well, Falstaff. I in my condition°   *position*
Shall better speak of you than you deserve.

                                    Exeunt [all but FALSTAFF]

FALSTAFF   I would you had but the wit; 'twere better than your
dukedom. Good faith, this same young sober-blooded boy doth

80 not love me, nor a man cannot make him laugh. But that's no
marvel; he drinks no wine. There's never none of these demure
boys come to any proof;° for thin drink° doth so overcool their   *turn out well / beer*
blood, and making many fish meals, that they fall into a kind
of male green-sickness;[5] and then when they marry, they get

85 wenches.° They are generally fools and cowards—which some   *beget females*
of us should be too, but for inflammation.[6] A good sherry-sack°   *Spanish sherry*
hath a two-fold operation in it. It ascends me into the brain,
dries me there[7] all the foolish and dull and crudy° vapours   *coagulated*
which environ° it, makes it apprehensive,° quick, forgetive,[8]   *surround / witty*

90 full of nimble, fiery, and delectable shapes, which, delivered
o'er to the voice, the tongue, which is the birth, becomes excellent wit. The second property of your excellent sherry is the
warming of the blood, which, before cold and settled,° left the   *stagnant*
liver[9] white and pale, which is the badge of pusillanimity and

95 cowardice. But the sherry warms it, and makes it course from
the inwards to the parts' extremes;° it illuminateth the face,   *extremities*
which, as a beacon, gives warning to all the rest of this little
kingdom, man, to arm; and then the vital commoners and
inland° petty spirits[1] muster me° all to their captain, the heart;   *internal / assemble*

100 who, great and puffed up with his retinue, doth any deed of
courage. And this valour comes of sherry. So that skill in the
weapon is nothing without sack, for that sets it a-work; and
learning a mere hoard of gold kept by a devil,[2] till sack com-
mences it and sets it in act and use.[3] Hereof comes it that

---

5. An anemic condition that affected young women in
puberty and that was supposed to be cured through sexual activity. Throughout this speech, Falstaff indicts
John for lacking the heat necessary for masculine valor
and the begetting of male children. Diet was believed to
affect the balance of the four humors, or fluids, that
determined temperament and the relative "heat" of the
body.
6. The passions that alcohol inflames.
7. It ascends into the brain and to my benefit dries up.

8. Inventive.
9. The supposed seat of the passions.
1. Alluding to the medical doctrine of "vital spirits," or
highly refined fluids, that were supposed to suffuse the
blood.
2. Referring to the popular belief that hidden treasures
were guarded by evil spirits.
3. Until sack sets learning free; confers a degree upon
learning (punning on "commencement" and "act," two
terms used for the granting of a university degree).

105   Prince Harry is valiant; for the cold blood he did naturally
      inherit of his father he hath, like lean,° sterile, and bare land,   *barren*
      manured, husbanded,° and tilled, with excellent endeavour of   *cultivated*
      drinking good, and good store of fertile sherry, that he is
      become very hot and valiant. If I had a thousand sons, the first
110   human principle I would teach them should be to forswear
      thin potations, and to addict themselves to sack.
              Enter BARDOLPH
      How now, Bardolph?
BARDOLPH   The army is dischargèd all and gone.
FALSTAFF   Let them go. I'll through Gloucestershire, and there
115   will I visit Master Robert Shallow, Esquire. I have him already
      tempering⁴ between my finger and my thumb, and shortly will
      I seal with him.⁵ Come, away!   *Exeunt*

4.3

              Enter KING [HENRY *in his bed,*¹ *attended by the Earl of*]
              WARWICK, *Thomas Duke of* CLARENCE, *Humphrey*
              [*Duke*] *of* GLOUCESTER [*and others*]
KING HENRY   Now, lords, if God doth give successful end
      To this debate° that bleedeth at our doors,   *conflict*
      We will our youth lead on to higher fields,²
      And draw no swords but what are sanctified.
5   Our navy is addressed,° our power collected,   *prepared*
      Our substitutes in absence well invested,°   *installed in office*
      And everything lies level to° our wish;   *in accordance with*
      Only we want a little personal strength,
      And pause us till these rebels now afoot
10   Come underneath the yoke of government.
WARWICK   Both which we doubt not but your majesty
      Shall soon enjoy.
KING HENRY   Humphrey, my son of Gloucester,
      Where is the Prince your brother?
GLOUCESTER   I think he's gone to hunt, my lord, at Windsor.
KING HENRY   And how accompanied?
15 GLOUCESTER   I do not know, my lord.
KING HENRY   Is not his brother Thomas of Clarence with him?
GLOUCESTER   No, my good lord, he is in presence here.
CLARENCE   What would my lord and father?
KING HENRY   Nothing but well to thee, Thomas of Clarence.
20   How chance thou art not with the Prince thy brother?
      He loves thee, and thou dost neglect him, Thomas.
      Thou hast a better place in his affection
      Than all thy brothers. Cherish it, my boy,
      And noble offices° thou mayst effect   *duties*
25   Of mediation, after I am dead,
      Between his greatness and thy other brethren.
      Therefore omit° him not, blunt not his love,   *neglect*
      Nor lose the good advantage of his grace

---

4. Softening like warm sealing wax.
5. Mold him to my use; conclude with him.
4.3 Location: The Jerusalem Chamber, the palace at
Westminster. (This room is actually in Westminster
Abbey.)

1. Henry may enter walking or carried in a chair or, as
here, in a bed thrust out from behind the stage. The use
of a bed emphasizes the severity of his illness.
2. That is, those of Palestine, where the King proposes
to lead a crusade.

By seeming cold or careless of his will;
30   For he is gracious, if he be observed;°   *shown respect*
  He hath a tear for pity, and a hand
  Open as day for melting° charity.   *compassionate*
  Yet notwithstanding, being incensed, he is flint,
  As humorous° as winter, and as sudden   *changeable*
35   As flaws congealèd° in the spring° of day.   *As snowflakes / dawn*
  His temper therefore must be well observed.
  Chide him for faults, and do it reverently,
  When you perceive his blood inclined to mirth;
  But being moody, give him line and scope°   *free range*
40   Till that his passions, like a whale on ground,
  Confound° themselves with working. Learn this, Thomas,   *Exhaust*
  And thou shalt prove a shelter to thy friends,
  A hoop of gold[3] to bind thy brothers in,
  That the united vessel of their blood,[4]
45   Mingled with venom of suggestion°—   *malicious gossip*
  As force perforce the age will pour it in—
  Shall never leak, though it do work as strong
  As aconitum[5] or rash gunpowder.
  CLARENCE   I shall observe him with all care and love.
50 KING HENRY   Why art thou not at Windsor with him, Thomas?
  CLARENCE   He is not there today; he dines in London.
  KING HENRY   And how accompanied? Canst thou tell that?
  CLARENCE   With Poins and other his continual° followers.   *constant*
  KING HENRY   Most subject is the fattest° soil to weeds,   *richest*
55   And he, the noble image of my youth,
  Is overspread with them; therefore my grief
  Stretches itself beyond the hour of death.
  The blood weeps from my heart when I do shape
  In forms imaginary th'unguided days°   *days lacking a ruler*
60   And rotten times that you shall look upon
  When I am sleeping with my ancestors;
  For when his headstrong riot hath no curb,
  When rage° and hot blood are his counsellors,   *passion*
  When means° and lavish manners meet together,   *opportunity*
65   O, with what wings shall his affections° fly   *desires; inclinations*
  Towards fronting peril and opposed decay?[6]
  WARWICK   My gracious lord, you look beyond° him quite.   *misjudge*
  The Prince but studies his companions,
  Like a strange tongue,° wherein, to gain the language,   *foreign language*
70   'Tis needful that the most immodest word
  Be looked upon and learnt, which once attained,
  Your highness knows, comes to no further use
  But to be known and hated; so, like gross° terms,   *vulgar; common*
  The Prince will in the perfectness of time
75   Cast off his followers, and their memory
  Shall as a pattern or a measure live
  By which his grace must mete° the lives of other,°   *appraise / others*
  Turning past evils to advantages.

---

3. A barrel with a golden hoop; a golden ring.   5. Monkshood, an especially virulent poison.
4. The vessel—a vial or chalice—that holds their blood.   6. Toward the peril and destruction that confront him.

KING HENRY   'Tis seldom when the bee doth leave her comb
In the dead carrion.[7]
     Enter [the Earl of] WESTMORLAND

80   Who's here? Westmorland?

WESTMORLAND   Health to my sovereign, and new happiness
Added to that that I am to deliver!
Prince John your son doth kiss your grace's hand.
Mowbray, the Bishop Scrope, Hastings, and all

85 Are brought to the correction of your law.
There is not now a rebel's sword unsheathed,
But peace puts forth her olive everywhere.
The manner how this action hath been borne
Here at more leisure may your highness read,

90 With every course° in his° particular.   *stage in the action / its*
     [*He gives the* KING *papers*]

KING HENRY   O Westmorland, thou art a summer bird
Which ever in the haunch° of winter sings   *hind part*
The lifting up of day.°   *dawn*
     Enter HARCOURT

               Look, here's more news.

HARCOURT   From enemies heaven keep your majesty;
95 And when they stand against you, may they fall
As those that I am come to tell you of!
The Earl Northumberland and the Lord Bardolph,
With a great power of English and of Scots,
Are by the sheriff of Yorkshire overthrown.

100 The manner and true order of the fight
This packet, please it you, contains at large.
     [*He gives the* KING *papers*]

KING HENRY   And wherefore should these good news make me sick?
Will fortune never come with both hands full,
But write her fair words still in foulest letters?

105 She either gives a stomach° and no food—   *an appetite*
Such are the poor in health—or else a feast,
And takes away the stomach—such are the rich,
That have abundance and enjoy it not.
I should rejoice now at this happy news,

110 And now my sight fails, and my brain is giddy.
O me! Come near me now; I am much ill.
     [*He swoons*]

GLOUCESTER   Comfort, your majesty!

CLARENCE   O my royal father!

WESTMORLAND   My sovereign lord, cheer up yourself, look up.°   *take courage*

WARWICK   Be patient, princes; you do know these fits
115 Are with his highness very ordinary.
Stand from him, give him air; he'll straight be well.

CLARENCE   No, no, he cannot long hold out° these pangs.   *endure*
Th'incessant care and labour of his mind
Hath wrought the mure° that should confine it in   *made the wall*
120 So thin that life looks through and will break out.

GLOUCESTER   The people fear° me, for they do observe   *frighten*

---

7. *'Tis . . . carrion:* It is rare that the bee who has placed her honeycomb in a carcass abandons it. (So the new King will be unlikely to abandon his old pleasures.)

Unfathered heirs and loathly births of nature.[8]
The seasons change their manners, as° the year   *as if*
Had found some months asleep and leaped them over.
125   CLARENCE   The river° hath thrice flowed, no ebb between,   *(the Thames)*
And the old folk, time's doting chronicles,
Say it did so a little time before
That our great grandsire Edward° sicked and died.   *(Edward III)*
WARWICK   Speak lower, princes, for the King recovers.
130   GLOUCESTER   This apoplexy will certain be his end.
KING HENRY   I pray you take me up and bear me hence
Into some other chamber; softly, pray.
       [*The* KING *is carried over the stage in his bed*]
Let there be no noise made, my gentle friends,
Unless some dull° and favourable hand   *restful*
135   Will whisper music to my weary spirit.
WARWICK   Call for the music in the other room.
                        [*Exit one or more. Still° music within*]   *Soft*
KING HENRY   Set me the crown upon my pillow here.
       [CLARENCE *takes the crown from the King's head, and
       sets it on his pillow*][9]
CLARENCE   His eye is hollow, and he changes° much.   *(in complexion)*
       [*A noise within*]
WARWICK   Less noise, less noise!
              Enter PRINCE HARRY
PRINCE HARRY   Who saw the Duke of Clarence?
140   CLARENCE   I am here, brother, full of heaviness.°   *sadness*
PRINCE HARRY   How now, rain within doors, and none abroad?
       How doth the King?
GLOUCESTER   Exceeding ill.
PRINCE HARRY   Heard he the good news yet? Tell it him.
GLOUCESTER   He altered much upon the hearing it.
145   PRINCE HARRY   If he be sick with joy, he'll recover without physic.
WARWICK   Not so much noise, my lords! Sweet prince, speak low.
       The King your father is disposed to sleep.
CLARENCE   Let us withdraw into the other room.
WARWICK   Will't please your grace to go along with us?
150   PRINCE HARRY   No, I will sit and watch here by the King.
              [*Exeunt all but the* KING *and* PRINCE HARRY]
Why doth the crown lie there upon his pillow,
Being so troublesome a bedfellow?
O polished perturbation,° golden care,   *source of unease*
That keep'st the ports° of slumber open wide   *gates (the eyes)*
155   To many a watchful° night!—Sleep with it° now;   *wakeful / (the crown)*
Yet not so sound, and half so deeply sweet,
As he whose brow with homely biggen° bound   *nightcap*
Snores out the watch of night.[1] O majesty,
When thou dost pinch thy bearer, thou dost sit
160   Like a rich armour worn in heat of day,
That scald'st with safety.—By his gates of breath°   *his lips*
There lies a downy feather which stirs not.
Did he suspire,° that light and weightless down   *If he breathed*

8. Children supernaturally begotten and malformed   1. Nighttime. "Watch" alludes to the periods of sentry
offspring resulting from normal conception.   duty into which the night was divided.
9. It is unclear who removes the crown: the weakened
King or his son Clarence, who is the next to speak.

Perforce must move.—My gracious lord, my father!—
165 This sleep is sound indeed. This is a sleep
That from this golden rigol° hath divorced   *ring*
So many English kings.—Thy due from me
Is tears and heavy sorrows of the blood,
Which nature, love, and filial tenderness
170 Shall, O dear father, pay thee plenteously.
My due from thee is this imperial crown,
Which, as immediate from° thy place and blood,   *as next in line to*
Derives itself° to me.   *Descends*
            [*He puts the crown on his head*]
                              Lo where it sits,
Which God shall guard; and put the world's whole strength
175 Into one giant arm, it shall not force
This lineal° honour from me. This from thee   *hereditary*
Will I to mine leave, as 'tis left to me.   *Exit*
            [*Music ceases. The* KING *awakes*]
KING HENRY   Warwick, Gloucester, Clarence!
            Enter [*the Earl of*] WARWICK, [*and the Dukes of*]
            GLOUCESTER [*and*] CLARENCE
CLARENCE   Doth the King call?
WARWICK   What would your majesty? How fares your grace?
180 KING HENRY   Why did you leave me here alone, my lords?
CLARENCE   We left the Prince my brother here, my liege,
    Who undertook to sit and watch by you.
KING HENRY   The Prince of Wales? Where is he? Let me see him.
WARWICK   This door is open; he is gone this way.
185 GLOUCESTER   He came not through the chamber where we stayed.
KING HENRY   Where is the crown? Who took it from my pillow?
WARWICK   When we withdrew, my liege, we left it here.
KING HENRY   The Prince hath ta'en it hence. Go seek him out.
    Is he so hasty that he doth suppose
190 My sleep my death?
    Find him, my lord of Warwick; chide him hither.   [*Exit* WARWICK]
    This part° of his conjoins° with my disease,   *act / unites*
    And helps to end me. See, sons, what things you are,
    How quickly nature falls into revolt
195 When gold becomes her object!
    For this the foolish over-careful fathers
    Have broke their sleep with thoughts, their brains with care,
    Their bones with industry; for this they have
    Engrossèd° and piled up the cankered° heaps   *Gathered / diseased*
200 Of strange-achievèd gold;² for this they have
    Been thoughtful° to invest their sons with arts   *careful*
    And martial exercises; when, like the bee
    Culling from every flower the virtuous sweets,
    Our thighs packed with wax, our mouths with honey,
205 We bring it to the hive; and, like the bees,
    Are murdered for our pains. This bitter taste
    Yields his engrossments to the ending father.³
            Enter [*the Earl of*] WARWICK

---

2. Gold gained in foreign lands or by unnatural or
unusual means.

3. *This . . . father:* This bitter taste is all the dying
father's amassing of wealth amounts to.

Now where is he that will not stay so long
Till his friend sickness have determined° me?   put an end to

210 WARWICK   My lord, I found the Prince in the next room,
Washing with kindly° tears his gentle° cheeks   filial / noble
With such a deep demeanour,° in great sorrow,   sad countenance
That tyranny, which never quaffed° but blood,   drank
Would, by beholding him, have washed his knife
215 With gentle eye-drops.° He is coming hither.   tears
KING HENRY   But wherefore did he take away the crown?

Enter PRINCE HARRY [*with the crown*]

Lo where he comes.—Come hither to me, Harry.
[*To the others*] Depart the chamber; leave us here alone.

Exeunt [*all but the* KING *and* PRINCE HARRY]

PRINCE HARRY   I never thought to hear you speak again.
220 KING HENRY   Thy wish was father, Harry, to that thought.
I stay too long by thee, I weary thee.
Dost thou so hunger for mine empty chair
That thou wilt needs invest thee with my honours
Before thy hour be ripe? O foolish youth,
225 Thou seek'st the greatness that will overwhelm thee!
Stay but a little, for my cloud of dignity°   fragile greatness
Is held from falling with so weak a wind°   (his breath)
That it will quickly drop. My day is dim.
Thou hast stol'n that which after some few hours
230 Were thine without offence, and at my death
Thou hast sealed up° my expectation.   confirmed
Thy life did manifest thou loved'st me not,
And thou wilt have me die assured of it.
Thou hid'st a thousand daggers in thy thoughts,
235 Whom° thou hast whetted on thy stony heart   Which
To stab at half an hour of my life.
What, canst thou not forbear me° half an hour?   grant me but
Then get thee gone and dig my grave thyself,
And bid the merry bells ring to thine ear
240 That thou art crownèd, not that I am dead.
Let all the tears that should bedew my hearse°   coffin
Be drops of balm⁴ to sanctify thy head.
Only compound° me with forgotten dust.   mix
Give that which gave thee life unto the worms.
245 Pluck down my officers, break my decrees;
For now a time is come to mock at form°—   decorum
Harry the Fifth is crowned. Up, vanity!
Down, royal state!° All you sage counsellors, hence!   ceremony
And to the English court assemble now
250 From every region, apes° of idleness!   fools
Now, neighbour confines,° purge you of your scum!   bordering regions
Have you a ruffian that will swear, drink, dance,
Revel the night, rob, murder, and commit
The oldest sins the newest kind of ways?
255 Be happy; he will trouble you no more.
England shall double gild° his treble guilt,   paint over
England shall give him office, honour, might;

---

4. The consecrated oils with which new monarchs were anointed during their coronation.

For the fifth Harry from curbed licence⁵ plucks
The muzzle of restraint, and the wild dog
260 Shall flesh his tooth on° every innocent.   *taste the flesh of*
O my poor kingdom, sick with civil blows!°   *domestic conflicts*
When that my care could not withhold° thy riots,°   *control / strife*
What wilt thou do when riot is thy care?⁶
O, thou wilt be a wilderness again,
265 Peopled with wolves, thy old inhabitants.
PRINCE HARRY   O pardon me, my liege! But for my tears,
The moist impediments unto my speech,
I had forestalled this dear° and deep rebuke   *grievous*
Ere you with grief had spoke and I had heard
270 The course of it so far. There is your crown;
           [*He returns the crown and kneels*]
And He° that wears the crown immortally   *(God)*
Long guard it yours! If I affect° it more   *desire*
Than as your honour and as your renown,
Let me no more from this obedience rise,
275 Which my most true and inward duteous spirit
Teacheth this prostrate and exterior° bending.   *outward*
God witness with me, when I here came in
And found no course of breath within your majesty,
How cold it struck my heart. If I do feign,
280 O, let me in my present wildness° die,   *sinfulness*
And never live to show th'incredulous world
The noble change that I have purposèd.°   *intended*
Coming to look on you, thinking you dead,
And dead almost, my liege, to think you were,
285 I spake unto this crown as having sense,°   *as if it had senses*
And thus upbraided it: 'The care on thee depending⁷
Hath fed upon the body of my father;
Therefore thou best of gold art worst of gold.
Other, less fine in carat, is more precious,
290 Preserving life in medicine potable;⁸
But thou, most fine, most honoured, most renowned,
Hast eat thy bearer up.' Thus, my royal liege,
Accusing it, I put it on my head,
To try° with it, as with an enemy   *struggle*
295 That had before my face murdered my father,
The quarrel of a true inheritor.°   *legitimate heir*
But if it did infect my blood with joy
Or swell my thoughts to any strain of pride,
If any rebel or vain spirit of mine
300 Did with the least affection of° a welcome   *inclination toward*
Give entertainment to the might of it,
Let God for ever keep it from my head,
And make me as the poorest vassal is,
That doth with awe and terror kneel to it.
305 KING HENRY   O my son,
God put it in thy mind to take it hence,

---

5. *Licence*: excessive freedom. The image is of a wild dog that has been curbed, kept under restraint, until his muzzle is removed and chaos ensues.
6. When debauchery (in the person of Hal) is your caretaker; when strife becomes your concern (rather than mine after my death).
7. The trouble that comes along with the crown.
8. Gold in a drinkable solution ("potable") was widely considered healthful.

That thou mightst win the more thy father's love,
Pleading so wisely in excuse of it!
Come hither, Harry; sit thou by my bed,
310 And hear, I think, the very latest° counsel   *last*
That ever I shall breathe.
        [PRINCE HARRY *rises from kneeling and sits by the bed*]
                                    God knows, my son,
By what bypaths and indirect crook'd ways
I met this crown; and I myself know well
How troublesome it sat upon my head.
315 To thee it shall descend with better quiet,
Better opinion,° better confirmation;   *public support*
For all the soil° of the achievement goes   *stain*
With me into the earth. It seemed in me
But as an honour snatched with boist'rous hand;
320 And I had many living to upbraid
My gain of it by their assistances,⁹
Which daily grew to quarrel and to bloodshed,
Wounding supposèd peace. All these bold fears°   *fearful acts*
Thou seest with peril I have answerèd;
325 For all my reign hath been but as a scene
Acting that argument.° And now my death   *theme*
Changes the mood, for what in me was purchased¹
Falls upon thee in a more fairer sort,
So thou the garland wear'st successively.²
330 Yet though thou stand'st more sure than I could do,
Thou art not firm enough, since griefs are green,°   *grievances are fresh*
And all thy friends—which thou must make thy friends—
Have but their stings and teeth newly ta'en out,
By whose fell° working I was first advanced,   *cruel*
335 And by whose power I well might lodge a fear
To be again displaced; which to avoid
I cut them off, and had a purpose now
To lead out many to the Holy Land,
Lest rest and lying still might make them look°   *examine*
340 Too near° unto my state. Therefore, my Harry,   *Too closely*
Be it thy course to busy giddy° minds   *restless*
With foreign quarrels, that action° hence borne out   *military exploits*
May waste° the memory of the former days.   *obliterate*
More would I, but my lungs are wasted so
345 That strength of speech is utterly denied me.
How I came by the crown, O God forgive,
And grant it may with thee in true peace live!
PRINCE HARRY   My gracious liege,
You won it, wore it, kept it, gave it me;
350 Then plain and right must my possession be,
Which I with more than with a common pain°   *effort*
'Gainst all the world will rightfully maintain.
        Enter [PRINCE] JOHN *of Lancaster* [*followed by the Earl
        of*] WARWICK [*and others*]
KING HENRY   Look, look, here comes my John of Lancaster.

---

9. *And . . . assistances:* And many were living who made
demands on me and reproved me on the strength of the
fact that they had helped me to seize the throne.

1. Was acquired by acts, not by inheritance.
2. So that you wear the sign of victory (the crown) by
right of succession.

PRINCE JOHN   Health, peace, and happiness to my royal father!

355 KING HENRY   Thou bring'st me happiness and peace, son John;
But health, alack, with youthful wings is flown
From this bare withered trunk. Upon thy sight
My worldly business makes a period.°   *an end*
Where is my lord of Warwick?

PRINCE HARRY   My lord of Warwick!
[WARWICK *comes forward to the* KING]

360 KING HENRY   Doth any name particular belong
Unto the lodging° where I first did swoon?   *room*

WARWICK   'Tis called Jerusalem, my noble lord.

KING HENRY   Laud be to God! Even there my life must end.
It hath been prophesied to me many years

365 I should not die but in Jerusalem,
Which vainly I supposed the Holy Land;
But bear me to that chamber; there I'll lie;
In that Jerusalem shall Harry die.

Exeunt [*bearing the* KING *in his bed*]

5.1

Enter SHALLOW, SILENCE,[1] [*Sir John*] FALSTAFF, BAR-
DOLPH, *and* [*the*] PAGE

SHALLOW [*to* FALSTAFF]   By cock and pie,[2] you shall not away
tonight.—What, Davy, I say!

FALSTAFF   You must excuse me, Master Robert Shallow.

SHALLOW   I will not excuse you; you shall not be excused;
5 excuses shall not be admitted; there is no excuse shall serve;
you shall not be excused.—Why, Davy!
[*Enter* DAVY]

DAVY   Here, sir.

SHALLOW   Davy, Davy, Davy; let me see, Davy; let me see.
William Cook—bid him come hither.—Sir John, you shall not
10 be excused.

DAVY   Marry, sir, thus: those precepts° cannot be served. And   *warrants*
again,° sir: shall we sow the headland[3] with wheat?   *Moreover*

SHALLOW   With red wheat, Davy. But for William Cook; are there
no young pigeons?

15 DAVY   Yes, sir. Here is now the smith's note° for shoeing and   *bill*
plough-irons.

SHALLOW   Let it be cast° and paid. Sir John, you shall not be   *calculated*
excused.

DAVY   Sir, a new link° to the bucket must needs be had; and, sir,   *chain*
20 do you mean to stop any of William's wages, about the sack he
lost at Hinkley[4] Fair?

SHALLOW   A° shall answer° it. Some pigeons, Davy, a couple of   *He / pay for*
short-legged hens, a joint of mutton, and any pretty little tiny
kickshaws,° tell William Cook.   *fancy dishes*

25 DAVY   Doth the man of war stay all night, sir?

SHALLOW   Yea, Davy. I will use him well; a friend i'th' court is

---

5.1 Location: Shallow's house in Gloucestershire.
1. F includes Silence in this scene; Q does not. If present, he lives up to his name, getting no lines.
2. A mild oath. "Cock" was a euphemism for "God,"
and "pie" was a colloquial word for the collection of

rules by which the pre-Reformation Church ordered
the Church calendar.
3. Unplowed strip of land between two plowed fields.
4. A market town near Coventry.

better than a penny in purse. Use his men well, Davy, for they
are arrant knaves, and will backbite.°   *slander*

DAVY   No worse than they are back-bitten,° sir, for they have mar-   *(by fleas)*
30   vellous° foul linen.   *amazingly*

SHALLOW   Well conceited,° Davy. About thy business, Davy.   *quipped*

DAVY   I beseech you, sir, to countenance° William Visor of   *favor*
Wo'ncot against Clement Perks o'th' Hill.[5]

SHALLOW   There is many complaints, Davy, against that Visor.
35   That Visor is an arrant knave, on my knowledge.

DAVY   I grant your worship that he is a knave, sir; but yet God
forbid, sir, but a knave should have some countenance at his
friend's request. An honest man, sir, is able to speak for himself,
when a knave is not. I have served your worship truly, sir, this
40   eight years. An I cannot once or twice in a quarter bear out° a   *support*
knave against an honest man, I have little credit with your worship. The knave is mine honest friend, sir; therefore I beseech
you let him be countenanced.

SHALLOW   Go to; I say he shall have no wrong. Look about,
45   Davy.   [*Exit* DAVY]
Where are you, Sir John? Come, off with your boots.— Give
me your hand, Master Bardolph.

BARDOLPH   I am glad to see your worship.

SHALLOW   I thank thee with all my heart, kind Master Bardolph.
50   [*To the* PAGE] And welcome, my tall° fellow.—Come, Sir John.   *valiant*

FALSTAFF   I'll follow you, good Master Robert Shallow.
                                   [*Exit* SHALLOW *with* SILENCE]
Bardolph, look to our horses.   [*Exit* BARDOLPH *with the* PAGE]
If I were sawed into quantities,° I should make four dozen of   *pieces*
such bearded hermits' staves as Master Shallow. It is a wonder-
55   ful thing to see the semblable coherence° of his men's spirits   *close correspondence*
and his. They, by observing him, do bear themselves like
foolish justices; he, by conversing° with them, is turned into a   *associating*
justice-like servingman. Their spirits are so married in con-
junction, with the participation of society,° that they flock   *by close association*
60   together in consent like so many wild geese. If I had a suit to
Master Shallow, I would humour his men with the imputation
of being near their master; if to his men, I would curry° with   *employ flattery*
Master Shallow that no man could better command his ser-
vants. It is certain that either wise bearing or ignorant carriage° *demeanor*
65   is caught as men take° diseases, one of another; therefore let   *catch*
men take heed of their company. I will devise matter enough
out of this Shallow to keep Prince Harry in continual laughter
the wearing out of six fashions—which is four terms,[6] or two
actions°—and a shall laugh without intervallums.[7] O, it is   *lawsuits*
70   much that a lie with a slight oath, and a jest with a sad° brow,   *serious*
will do with a fellow that never had the ache in his shoulders![8]
O, you shall see him laugh till his face be like a wet cloak ill
laid up![9]

SHALLOW [*within*]   Sir John!
75   FALSTAFF   I come, Master Shallow; I come, Master Shallow.
                                                              Exit

5. Possibly Stinchcombe Hill, not far from "Wo'ncot"
(the local pronunciation of Woodmancot in Gloucestershire).
6. Alluding to the four divisions of the judicial year.
7. Time between terms.
8. With someone who has not experienced old age or
troubles.
9. *ill laid up*: carelessly put away (so that it is wrinkled).

5.2

Enter the Earl of WARWICK [*at one door*], *and the* LORD
CHIEF JUSTICE [*at another door*]

WARWICK How now, my Lord Chief Justice, whither away?
LORD CHIEF JUSTICE How doth the King?
WARWICK Exceeding well: his cares are now all ended.
LORD CHIEF JUSTICE I hope not dead.
WARWICK   He's walked the way of nature,
5 And to our purposes he lives no more.
LORD CHIEF JUSTICE I would his majesty had called me with him.
    The service that I truly did his life
    Hath left me open to all injuries.
WARWICK Indeed I think the young King loves you not.
10 LORD CHIEF JUSTICE I know he doth not, and do arm myself
    To welcome the condition° of the time,   *(new) circumstances*
    Which cannot look more hideously upon me
    Than I have drawn it in my fantasy.

Enter [PRINCE] JOHN *of Lancaster,* [*and the Dukes of*]
CLARENCE *and* GLOUCESTER

WARWICK Here come the heavy issue° of dead Harry.   *sad offspring*
15 O, that the living Harry had the temper
    Of he the worst of these three gentlemen!
    How many nobles then should hold their places,
    That must strike sail° to spirits of vile sort!°   *submit / low rank*
LORD CHIEF JUSTICE O God, I fear all will be overturned.
20 PRINCE JOHN Good morrow, cousin Warwick, good morrow.
GLOUCESTER *and* CLARENCE Good morrow, cousin.
PRINCE JOHN We meet like men that had forgot to speak.
WARWICK We do remember, but our argument°   *subject matter*
    Is all too heavy to admit much talk.
25 PRINCE JOHN Well, peace be with him that hath made us heavy!
LORD CHIEF JUSTICE Peace be with us, lest we be heavier!
GLOUCESTER O good my lord, you have lost a friend indeed;
    And I dare swear you borrow not that face
    Of seeming sorrow—it is sure your own.
PRINCE JOHN [*to* LORD CHIEF JUSTICE] Though no man be
30   assured what grace to find,°   *favor he will find*
    You stand in coldest expectation.
    I am the sorrier; would 'twere otherwise.
CLARENCE [*to* LORD CHIEF JUSTICE] Well, you must now speak
    Sir John Falstaff fair,
    Which swims against your stream of quality.°   *character; rank*
35 LORD CHIEF JUSTICE Sweet princes, what I did I did in honour,
    Led by th'impartial conduct of my soul;
    And never shall you see that I will beg
    A raggèd° and forestalled remission.[1]   *base*
    If truth and upright innocency fail me,
40 I'll to the King my master, that is dead,
    And tell him who hath sent me after him.

Enter PRINCE HARRY [*as King*]

WARWICK Here comes the Prince.
LORD CHIEF JUSTICE Good morrow, and God save your majesty!

5.2 Location: The palace at Westminster.
1. Either a pardon sure to be denied or a pardon secured in advance (by an act of submission).

PRINCE HARRY This new and gorgeous garment, majesty,
45   Sits not so easy on me as you think.
      Brothers, you mix your sadness with some fear.
      This is the English not the Turkish court;
      Not Amurath an Amurath succeeds,[2]
      But Harry Harry. Yet be sad, good brothers,
50   For, by my faith, it very well becomes you.
      Sorrow so royally in you appears
      That I will deeply° put the fashion on,   *solemnly*
      And wear it in my heart. Why then, be sad;
      But entertain no more of it, good brothers,
55   Than a joint burden laid upon us all.
      For me, by heaven, I bid you be assured
      I'll be your father and your brother too.
      Let me but bear° your love, I'll bear your cares.   *have; carry*
      Yet weep that Harry's dead, and so will I;
60   But Harry lives that shall convert those tears
      By number° into hours of happiness.   *One by one*
PRINCE JOHN, GLOUCESTER, *and* CLARENCE We hope no other
         from your majesty.
PRINCE HARRY You all look strangely on me, [*to* LORD CHIEF
         JUSTICE] and you most.
      You are, I think, assured I love you not.
65 LORD CHIEF JUSTICE I am assured, if I be measured rightly,
      Your majesty hath no just cause to hate me.
PRINCE HARRY No? How might a prince of my great hopes forget
      So great indignities you laid upon me?
      What—rate,° rebuke, and roughly send to prison   *chide*
70   Th'immediate heir of England? Was this easy?
      May this be washed in Lethe[3] and forgotten?
LORD CHIEF JUSTICE I then did use the person° of your father.   *act as a deputy*
      The image of his power lay then in me;
      And in th'administration of his law,
75   Whiles I was busy for the commonwealth,
      Your highness pleasèd to forget my place,°   *rank; position*
      The majesty and power of law and justice,
      The image of the King whom I presented,
      And struck me in my very seat of judgement;
80   Whereon, as° an offender to your father,   *as you were*
      I gave bold way to my authority
      And did commit° you. If the deed were ill,   *imprison*
      Be you contented, wearing now the garland,°   *crown*
      To have a son set your decrees at naught—
85   To pluck down justice from your awe-full° bench,   *awe-inspiring*
      To trip the course of law, and blunt the sword
      That guards the peace and safety of your person,
      Nay, more, to spurn at your most royal image,
      And mock your workings in a second body?°   *representative*
90   Question your royal thoughts, make the case yours,
      Be now the father, and propose° a son;   *imagine*
      Hear your own dignity so much profaned,

---

2. An English name for the Turkish Sultan Murad III,
who had his brothers executed upon his succession in
1574. Turks were bywords for cruelty and tyranny in
early modern England.
3. The river in Hades that induced forgetfulness.

See your most dreadful laws so loosely slighted,
Behold yourself so by a son disdained;
95 And then imagine me taking your part,
And in your power soft° silencing your son.   *gently*
After this cold considerance, sentence me;
And, as you are a king, speak in your state°   *role as monarch*
What I have done that misbecame my place,
100 My person, or my liege's sovereignty.
PRINCE HARRY   You are right Justice,° and you weigh this well.   *perfect justice*
Therefore still bear the balance and the sword;[4]
And I do wish your honours may increase
Till you do live to see a son of mine
105 Offend you and obey you as I did.
So shall I live to speak my father's words:
'Happy am I that have a man so bold
That dares do justice on my proper° son,   *own*
And not less happy having such a son
110 That would deliver up his greatness so
Into the hands of justice.' You did commit° me,   *imprison*
For which I do commit° into your hand   *place*
Th'unstainèd sword that you have used° to bear,   *were accustomed*
With this remembrance:° that you use the same   *reminder*
115 With the like bold, just, and impartial spirit
As you have done 'gainst me. There is my hand.
You shall be as a father to my youth;
My voice shall sound° as you do prompt mine ear,   *speak*
And I will stoop and humble my intents
120 To your well-practised wise directions.—
And princes all, believe me, I beseech you,
My father is gone wild into his grave,
For in his tomb lie my affections;°   *wild passions*
And with his spirits sadly I survive
125 To mock° the expectation of the world,   *defy*
To frustrate prophecies, and to raze out
Rotten opinion, who hath writ me down
After my seeming.[5] The tide of blood° in me   *of passion*
Hath proudly flowed in vanity till now.
130 Now doth it turn, and ebb back to the sea,
Where it shall mingle with the state of floods,°   *the majesty of the sea*
And flow henceforth in formal majesty.
Now call we our high court of Parliament,
And let us choose such limbs° of noble counsel   *members*
135 That the great body of our state may go
In equal rank with the best-governed nation;
That war, or peace, or both at once, may be
As things acquainted and familiar to us;
[*to* LORD CHIEF JUSTICE] In which you, father, shall have foremost hand.
140 [*To all*] Our coronation done, we will accite,°   *summon*
As I before remembered, all our state;°   *nobility*
And, God consigning to° my good intents,   *endorsing*
No prince nor peer shall have just cause to say,
'God shorten Harry's happy life one day.'   *Exeunt*

4. The traditional emblems of justice.   5. According to my (false) appearance.

5.3

[*A table and chairs set forth.*] *Enter Sir John* FALSTAFF,
SHALLOW, SILENCE, DAVY [*with vessels for the table*],
BARDOLPH, *and* [*the*] PAGE

SHALLOW [*to* FALSTAFF]   Nay, you shall see my orchard, where,
in an arbour, we will eat a last year's pippin[1] of mine own
grafting, with a dish of caraways,[2] and so forth—come, cousin
Silence—and then to bed.

5 FALSTAFF   Fore God, you have here a goodly dwelling and a rich.

SHALLOW   Barren, barren, barren; beggars all, beggars all, Sir
John. Marry, good air.—Spread, Davy; spread, Davy.
      [DAVY *begins to spread the table*]
Well said,° Davy.   done

FALSTAFF   This Davy serves you for good uses; he is your serving-
10 man and your husband.°   steward

SHALLOW   A good varlet,° a good varlet, a very good varlet, Sir   servant
John.—By the mass, I have drunk too much sack at supper.—A
good varlet. Now sit down, now sit down. [*To* SILENCE] Come,
cousin.

15 SILENCE   Ah, sirrah, quoth-a,° we shall   said he
      [*sings*]   Do nothing but eat and make good cheer,
            And praise God for the merry year,
            When flesh is cheap and females dear,
            And lusty lads roam here and there
20   So merrily,
            And ever among so merrily.

FALSTAFF   There's a merry heart, good Master Silence! I'll give
you a health° for that anon.   drink a toast to you

SHALLOW   Good Master Bardolph!—Some wine, Davy.

25 DAVY [*to* FALSTAFF]   Sweet sir, sit. [*To* BARDOLPH] I'll be with you
anon. [*To* FALSTAFF] Most sweet sir, sit. Master page, good master page, sit.
      [*All but* DAVY *sit.* DAVY *pours wine*]
Proface![3] What you want° in meat, we'll have in drink; but you   lack
must bear;° the heart's all.   be forbearing

30 SHALLOW   Be merry, Master Bardolph and my little soldier there,
be merry.

SILENCE [*sings*]   Be merry, be merry, my wife has all,
            For women are shrews, both short and tall,
            'Tis merry in hall when beards wags all,
35   And welcome merry shrovetide.[4]
Be merry, be merry.

FALSTAFF   I did not think Master Silence had been a man of this
mettle.°   boldness

SILENCE   Who, I? I have been merry twice and once ere now.
      Enter DAVY [*with a dish of apples*]
40 DAVY   There's a dish of leather-coats° for you.   russet apples

SHALLOW   Davy!

DAVY   Your worship! I'll be with you straight. [*To* FALSTAFF] A
cup of wine, sir?

5.3 Location: Shallow's garden in Gloucestershire.
1. A kind of apple traditionally kept for a year before
eating.
2. Caraway seeds or sweet biscuits containing these
seeds, often eaten with apples.

3. A greeting used as a welcome to a meal, from an Italian phrase meaning "May it do you good."
4. The season of festivities preceding the Christian
penitential season, Lent.

SILENCE [*sings*] A cup of wine

45   That's brisk and fine,

                        And drink unto thee, leman° mine,   *sweetheart*

                        And a merry heart lives long-a.

FALSTAFF Well said, Master Silence.

SILENCE And we shall be merry; now comes in the sweet o'th'

50 night.

FALSTAFF Health and long life to you, Master Silence!

          [*He drinks*]

SILENCE Fill the cup and let it come. I'll pledge you a mile to

      th' bottom.⁵

SHALLOW Honest Bardolph, welcome! If thou want'st anything

55 and wilt not call, beshrew thy heart! [*To the* PAGE] Welcome,

      my little tiny thief, and welcome indeed, too!—I'll drink to

      Master Bardolph, and to all the cavalieros° about London.   *fine fellows*

          [*He drinks*]

DAVY I hope to see London once ere I die.

BARDOLPH An I might see you there, Davy!

60 SHALLOW By the mass, you'll crack° a quart together, ha, will   *drink*

      you not, Master Bardolph?

BARDOLPH Yea, sir, in a pottle-pot.°   *two-quart glass*

SHALLOW By God's liggens,⁶ I thank thee. The knave will stick

      by thee, I can assure thee that; a will not out;° 'tis true-bred.   *drop out*

65 BARDOLPH And I'll stick by him, sir.

SHALLOW Why, there spoke a king! Lack nothing, be merry!

          One knocks at [*the*] *door* [*within*]

      Look who's at door there, ho! Who knocks?   [*Exit* DAVY]

          [SILENCE *drinks*]

FALSTAFF [*to* SILENCE] Why, now you have done me right!⁷

SILENCE [*sings*]   Do me right,

70   And dub me knight—

                        Samingo.⁸

      Is't not so?

FALSTAFF 'Tis so.

SILENCE Is't so?—Why then, say an old man can do somewhat.

          [*Enter* DAVY]

75 DAVY An't please your worship, there's one Pistol come from the

      court with news.

FALSTAFF From the court? Let him come in.

          Enter PISTOL

      How now, Pistol?

PISTOL Sir John, God save you.

80 FALSTAFF What wind blew you hither, Pistol?

PISTOL Not the ill wind which blows no man to good.

      Sweet knight, thou art now one of the greatest men in this

      realm.

SILENCE By'r Lady, I think a be—but goodman° Puff of Bar'son.⁹   *except for yeoman*

85 PISTOL Puff?

      Puff in thy teeth, most recreant coward base!—

---

5. I'll drink to the bottom of the cup, even if it were a mile.

6. An obscure oath, possibly derived from "by God's (eye)lid."

7. Done me justice (by drinking well).

8. Translated lines from a French drinking song,

"Monsieur Mingo." "Sa" may be a mispronunciation of "Sir." "Mingo" means "I urinate."

9. Referring either to Barcheston, a town 10 miles south of Stratford, or Barston, a town between Coventry and Solihull.

Sir John, I am thy Pistol and thy friend,
And helter-skelter have I rode to thee,
And tidings do I bring, and lucky joys,
90 And golden times, and happy news of price.
FALSTAFF I pray thee now, deliver them like a man of this world.
PISTOL A foutre° for the world and worldlings base!   *fig*
I speak of Africa and golden joys.
FALSTAFF O base Assyrian knight,[1] what is thy news?
95 Let King Cophetua[2] know the truth thereof.
SILENCE [*singing*] 'And Robin Hood, Scarlet, and John.'[3]
PISTOL Shall dunghill curs confront the Helicons?[4]
And shall good news be baffled?°   *disgraced*
Then Pistol lay thy head in Furies'[5] lap.
100 SHALLOW Honest gentleman, I know not your breeding.
PISTOL Why then, lament therefor.
SHALLOW Give me pardon, sir. If, sir, you come with news from
the court, I take it there's but two ways: either to utter them, or
conceal them. I am, sir, under the King in some authority.
105 PISTOL Under which king, besonian?° Speak, or die.   *beggarly fellow*
SHALLOW Under King Harry.
PISTOL   Harry the Fourth, or Fifth?
SHALLOW Harry the Fourth.
PISTOL   A foutre for thine office!
Sir John, thy tender lambkin now is king.
Harry the Fifth's the man. I speak the truth.
110 When Pistol lies, do this, [*making the fig*][6] and fig me,
Like the bragging Spaniard.
FALSTAFF   What, is the old King dead?
PISTOL As nail in door. The things I speak are just.°   *true*
FALSTAFF Away, Bardolph, saddle my horse! Master Robert
Shallow, choose what office thou wilt in the land; 'tis thine.
115 Pistol, I will double-charge thee[7] with dignities.
BARDOLPH O joyful day!
I would not take a knighthood for my fortune.
PISTOL What, I do bring good news?
FALSTAFF [*to DAVY*] Carry Master Silence to bed.
                      [*Exit DAVY with SILENCE*]
120 Master Shallow—my lord Shallow—be what thou wilt, I am
fortune's steward—get on thy boots; we'll ride all night.—O
sweet Pistol!—Away, Bardolph!   [*Exit BARDOLPH*]
Come, Pistol, utter more to me, and withal° devise something   *at the same time*
to do thyself good. Boot, boot, Master Shallow! I know the
125 young King is sick for me. Let us take any man's horses—the
laws of England are at my commandment. Blessed are they
that have been my friends, and woe to my Lord Chief Justice.
PISTOL Let vultures vile seize on his lungs also!

1. Adopting Pistol's elevated rhetorical style, Falstaff calls him a knight of Assyria, an Asian empire that the Elizabethans associated with pillage and robbery.
2. Alluding to the African King who marries a beggar in the popular ballad "A Beggar and a King."
3. A line from the ballad "Robin Hood and the Jolly Pinder of Wakefield."
4. That is, "the true Muses." Pistol conflates the Muses of classical mythology with Mt. Helicon, part of the

Parnassus mountain range on which they dwelt.
5. Then let Pistol appeal to the goddesses of revenge.
6. An obscene gesture, known as "the Spanish fig," in which the thumb is put between the fore and middle fingers in a way meant to be suggestive of genitalia and sex acts. In the next line, Pistol refers to a "bragging" (lying) Spaniard who was "figged."
7. Load you (with honors) twice over; load you like a gun twice over, with a pun on Pistol's name.

'Where is the life that late I led?'[8] say they.
130   Why, here it is. Welcome these pleasant days.   *Exeunt*

5.4

Enter Beadles, [dragging in MISTRESS] QUICKLY *and*
     DOLL TEARSHEET[1]

MISTRESS QUICKLY   No, thou arrant knave! I would to God that I
    might die, that I might have thee hanged. Thou hast drawn my
    shoulder out of joint.

FIRST BEADLE   The constables have delivered her over to me;
5   and she shall have whipping-cheer,[2] I warrant her. There hath
    been a man or two killed about her.[3]

DOLL TEARSHEET   Nut-hook,[4] nut-hook, you lie! Come on, I'll
    tell thee what, thou damned tripe-visaged° rascal, an° the child   *flabby-faced / if*
    I go with do miscarry,[5] thou wert better thou hadst struck thy
10   mother, thou paper-faced° villain.   *white-faced*

MISTRESS QUICKLY   O the Lord, that Sir John were come! He
    would make this a bloody day to somebody. But I pray God the
    fruit of her womb miscarry!

FIRST BEADLE   If it do, you shall have a dozen of cushions again;
15   you have but eleven now.[6] Come, I charge you both go with
    me, for the man is dead that you and Pistol beat amongst you.

DOLL TEARSHEET   I'll tell you what, you thin man in a censer,[7] I
    will have you as soundly swinged° for this, you bluebottle[8]   *beaten*
    rogue, you filthy famished correctioner! If you be not swinged,
20   I'll forswear half-kirtles.°   *give up wearing skirts*

FIRST BEADLE   Come, come, you she knight-errant, come!

MISTRESS QUICKLY   O God, that right should thus o'ercome might!
    Well, of sufferance° comes ease.   *from suffering*

DOLL TEARSHEET   Come, you rogue, come; bring me to a justice.

25 MISTRESS QUICKLY   Ay, come, you starved bloodhound.

DOLL TEARSHEET   Goodman death, goodman bones!

MISTRESS QUICKLY   Thou atomy,° thou!   *(for "anatomy"; skeleton)*

DOLL TEARSHEET   Come, you thin thing; come, you rascal.°   *lean deer*

FIRST BEADLE   Very well.   *Exeunt*

5.5

Enter two GROOMS[, *strewing rushes*[1]]

FIRST GROOM   More rushes, more rushes!

SECOND GROOM   The trumpets have sounded twice.

FIRST GROOM   'Twill be two o'clock ere they come from the cor-
    onation.   *Exeunt*

---

8. A line from a lost poem or ballad.
5.4 Location: A street in London.
1. Q says, "Enter Sinklo and three or foure officers."
Sinklo was probably an actor's name. He was evidently
very thin, for this scene contains a number of unflat-
tering references to one of the officer's skinniness.
2. That is, a whipping for her entertainment or supper
("cheer"). Beadles (the parish officers responsible for
enforcing laws) commonly meted out this punishment
for prostitution.
3. Because of her; in her company.
4. A hook for pulling nuts from trees; the arresting

constable.
5. Women who were pregnant might escape the full
force of the law until after they gave birth.
6. Implying that Tearsheet feigns pregnancy by carrying one of Quickly's pillows under her gown.
7. You figure of a man embossed on the lid of a pot for
burning incense.
8. Alluding to the blue tunics worn by beadles.
5.5 Location: A public place near Westminster Abbey.
1. Floor coverings, here strewn on the ground before
the King's entrance.

Enter [Sir John] FALSTAFF, SHALLOW, PISTOL, BAR-
DOLPH, *and [the]* PAGE²

5   FALSTAFF   Stand here by me, Master Robert Shallow. I will make
the King do you grace.° I will leer upon him as a comes by,   *honor*
and do but mark the countenance that he will give me.

PISTOL   God bless thy lungs, good knight.

FALSTAFF   Come here, Pistol; stand behind me. [*To* SHALLOW]
10   O, if I had had time to have made new liveries,³ I would have
bestowed° the thousand pound I borrowed of you! But 'tis no   *spent*
matter; this poor show doth better; this doth infer° the zeal I   *imply*
had to see him.

SHALLOW   It doth so.

15   FALSTAFF   It shows my earnestness of affection—

PISTOL   It doth so.

FALSTAFF   My devotion—

PISTOL   It doth, it doth, it doth.

FALSTAFF   As it were, to ride day and night, and not to deliberate,
20   not to remember, not to have patience to shift me°—   *change my clothes*

SHALLOW   It is most certain.

FALSTAFF   But to stand stained with travel and sweating with
desire to see him, thinking of nothing else, putting all affairs
in oblivion, as if there were nothing else to be done but to see
25   him.

PISTOL   'Tis *semper idem*, for *absque hoc nihil est*:⁴ 'tis all in every
part.

SHALLOW   'Tis so indeed.

PISTOL   My knight, I will inflame thy noble liver,
30   And make thee rage.
Thy Doll, and Helen⁵ of thy noble thoughts,
Is in base durance° and contagious° prison,   *imprisonment / noxious*
Haled° thither   *Dragged*
By most mechanical° and dirty hand.   *menial*
35   Rouse up Revenge from ebon den° with fell Alecto's snake,⁶   *dark cave (hell)*
For Doll is in. Pistol speaks naught but truth.

FALSTAFF   I will deliver her.
    [*Shouts within.*] *Trumpets sound*

PISTOL   There roared the sea, and trumpet-clangour sounds!
    Enter KING HARRY *the Fifth,* [PRINCE JOHN *of Lancaster,*
    the Dukes of CLARENCE *and* GLOUCESTER, *the*] LORD
    CHIEF JUSTICE [*and others*]

FALSTAFF   God save thy grace, King Hal, my royal Hal!

40   PISTOL   The heavens thee guard and keep, most royal imp° of fame!   *offspring*

FALSTAFF   God save thee, my sweet boy!

KING HARRY   My Lord Chief Justice, speak to that vain° man.   *foolish*

LORD CHIEF JUSTICE [*to* FALSTAFF]   Have you your wits? Know
you what 'tis you speak?

FALSTAFF   My king, my Jove,⁷ I speak to thee, my heart!

---

2. In Q, Falstaff and his friends enter after "Trumpets
sound, and the King, and his train passe over the stage."
There are thus two royal processions, one before Falstaff enters and one later in the scene. F contains only
the latter procession, which immediately precedes the
climactic moment when Hal rejects Falstaff.
3. Uniforms such as those worn by the retainers in a
noble household.

4. The first Latin motto, "ever the same," was associated with Queen Elizabeth; the second means "apart
from this, there is nothing."
5. The famously beautiful woman whose abduction by
Paris is said to have started the Trojan War.
6. Alecto was one of the Furies of classical mythology;
her head was covered with snakes.
7. In classical mythology, the ruler of the gods.

45   KING HARRY   I know thee not, old man. Fall to thy prayers.
        How ill white hairs becomes a fool and jester!
        I have long dreamt of such a kind of man,
        So surfeit-swelled,° so old, and so profane;   *bloated from excess*
        But being awake, I do despise my dream.
50   Make less thy body hence,° and more thy grace.   *henceforth*
        Leave gormandizing;° know the grave doth gape   *gluttony*
        For thee thrice wider than for other men.
        Reply not to me with a fool-born jest.
        Presume not that I am the thing I was,
55   For God doth know, so shall the world perceive,
        That I have turned away my former self;
        So will I those that kept me company.
        When thou dost hear I am as I have been,
        Approach me, and thou shalt be as thou wast,
60   The tutor and the feeder of my riots.
        Till then I banish thee, on pain of death,
        As I have done the rest of my misleaders,
        Not to come near our person by ten mile.
        For competence of life[8] I will allow you,
65   That lack of means enforce you not to evils;
        And as we hear you do reform yourselves,
        We will, according to your strengths and qualities,°   *attainments*
        Give you advancement. [*To* LORD CHIEF JUSTICE] Be it your
           charge, my lord,
        To see performed the tenor of our word. [*To his train*] Set on!
                              Exeunt KING [HARRY *and his train*]
70   FALSTAFF   Master Shallow, I owe you a thousand pound.
      SHALLOW   Yea, marry, Sir John; which I beseech you to let me
      have home with me.
      FALSTAFF   That can hardly be, Master Shallow. Do not you
      grieve at this. I shall be sent for in private to him. Look you, he
75   must seem thus to the world. Fear not your advancements. I
      will be the man yet that shall make you great.
      SHALLOW   I cannot perceive how, unless you give me your dou-
      blet and stuff me out with straw. I beseech you, good Sir John,
      let me have five hundred of my thousand.
80   FALSTAFF   Sir, I will be as good as my word. This that you heard
      was but a colour.°   *pretense*
      SHALLOW   A colour[9] I fear that you will die in, Sir John.
      FALSTAFF   Fear no colours. Go with me to dinner. Come, Lieu-
      tenant Pistol; come, Bardolph. I shall be sent for soon at
85   night.
                  Enter [*the* LORD CHIEF] JUSTICE *and* PRINCE JOHN [*with
                  officers*]
      LORD CHIEF JUSTICE [*to officers*]   Go carry Sir John Falstaff to
      the Fleet.°   *(a London prison)*
      Take all his company along with him.
      FALSTAFF   My lord, my lord!
      LORD CHIEF JUSTICE   I cannot now speak. I will hear you soon.—
90   Take them away.

---

8. An allowance sufficient to supply life's necessities.   9. Punning on "collar" as meaning "hangman's noose."

PISTOL *Si fortuna me tormenta, spero me contenta.*[1]

        Exeunt. Manent° Lancaster [PRINCE JOHN]   *Remain*

             and [LORD] CHIEF JUSTICE

PRINCE JOHN I like this fair proceeding of the King's.

  He hath intent his wonted° followers   *customary*

  Shall all be very well provided for,

95 But all are banished till their conversations°   *conduct*

  Appear more wise and modest to the world.

LORD CHIEF JUSTICE And so they are.

PRINCE JOHN The King hath called his parliament, my lord.

LORD CHIEF JUSTICE He hath.

100 PRINCE JOHN I will lay odds that, ere this year expire,

  We bear our civil swords and native fire[2]

  As far as France. I heard a bird so sing,

  Whose music, to my thinking, pleased the King.

  Come, will you hence?   *Exeunt*

Epilogue

[*Enter* EPILOGUE]

EPILOGUE First my fear, then my curtsy,° last my speech.   *bow*

    My fear is your displeasure; my curtsy, my duty; and my
speech to beg your pardons. If you look for a good speech now,
5 you undo° me; for what I have to say is of mine own making,   *ruin*
and what indeed I should say will, I doubt,° prove mine own   *fear*
marring. But to the purpose, and so to the venture.° Be it   *hazard*
known to you, as it is very well, I was lately here in the end of
a displeasing play, to pray your patience for it, and to promise
10 you a better. I did mean indeed to pay you with this; which, if
like an ill venture[1] it come unluckily home, I break,° and you,   *go bankrupt*
my gentle creditors, lose. Here I promised you I would be, and
here I commit my body to your mercies. Bate° me some, and   *Excuse*
I will pay you some, and, as most debtors do, promise you infi-
15 nitely.[2]

    If my tongue cannot entreat you to acquit me, will you com-
mand me to use my legs? And yet that were but light payment,
to dance out of your debt. But a good conscience will make
any possible satisfaction, and so would I. All the gentlewomen
20 here have forgiven me; if the gentlemen will not, then the gentlemen do not agree with the gentlewomen, which was never
seen before in such an assembly.

    One word more, I beseech you. If you be not too much
cloyed with fat meat, our humble author will continue the story
25 with Sir John in it,[3] and make you merry with fair Catherine of
France; where, for anything I know, Falstaff shall die of a
sweat[4]—unless already a° be killed with your hard opinions.   *he*

---

1. See note to 2.4.157.
2. Our swords used up to now in civil war and our native zeal.
Epilogue
1. An unlucky commercial speculation, especially in a cargo at sea.
2. Q here inserts the lines "and so I kneele downe before you; but indeed, to pray for the Queene," which

conclude the Epilogue in F. This is one of several indications that the Epilogue was rewritten and expanded at some point, but that in Q these lines, with their reference to the Queen, were not moved to their proper place at the end of the speech.
3. In fact, Sir John Falstaff does not appear in *Henry V*, the play here anticipated.
4. A sweating sickness; the plague; a venereal disease.

For Oldcastle[5] died a martyr, and this is not the man. My tongue is weary; when my legs are too, I will bid you good night, and so kneel down before you—but, indeed, to pray for
30   the Queen.

[*He dances, then kneels for applause. Exit*]

---

5. Alluding to the fact that Sir John was originally called "Oldcastle" in *1 Henry IV.* See the Introduction to that play.

Much Ado About Nothing

Much Ado About Nothing, first published in 1600 and probably written in 1598, weaves together two stories: the benevolent luring of Beatrice and Benedick into mutual declarations of love and the villainous luring of Claudio into the mistaken belief that Hero is unchaste. For the former plot, there seems to be no specific source, though Shakespeare would have encountered stories of scorners of love who fall in love (including Chaucer's *Troilus and Criseyde*). For the story of the virtuous lady falsely accused, sources abound, including Ludovico Ariosto's wonderful version in Canto V of *Orlando Furioso* (1516, translated into English by Sir John Harington in 1591) and Matteo Bandello's twenty-second *Novella* (1554, translated into French by François de Belleforest in 1574). Shakespeare probably knew these and other versions, both dramatic and nondramatic, among them a tragic retelling by Edmund Spenser in Book II of *The Faerie Queene* (1590). By deftly intertwining the two plots, *Much Ado About Nothing* mingles lightheartedness with a certain haunting sadness.

This sadness is a recurrent note in Shakespeare's earlier comedies: *The Comedy of Errors* opens with a condemned man's lament, *The Merchant of Venice* is darkened by Antonio's melancholy and Shylock's bitter rage, and *Love's Labour's Lost* (which features in Biron and Rosaline a pair of sparring lovers who strikingly anticipate Benedick and Beatrice) ends with a death. In several later comedies, most notably *Measure for Measure,* the darkness is so intensified as to make the term "comedy" seem a problem. But in *Much Ado About Nothing,* Shakespeare creates a balance of laughter, longing, and pain that he equals only in two other great romantic comedies from the same period, *As You Like It* and *Twelfth Night, or What You Will.* The titles of all three plays convey an impression of easy, festive wit, a magical effortlessness that is in fact the product of an extraordinary discipline and skill.

This cunning use of effort to produce the effect of effortlessness can be understood in the light of Baldassare Castiglione's famous courtesy manual *The Book of the Courtier* (1528). Castiglione's remarkable book, published in an English translation in 1561, depicts a witty and sophisticated group of men and women who, in several extended conversations, discuss the qualities that must be possessed by the ideal courtier. The courtier, as they envisage him, must be equally adept at making war and at making love. He must be able to assist the Prince and to dance elegantly, to grasp the subtleties of diplomacy and to sing in a pleasant, unaffected voice, to engage in philosophical speculation and to tell amusing after-dinner stories. In similar fashion, court ladies must be at once modest and spirited, chaste and slyly knowing, unspoiled and elegant. These are, in less idealized and rarefied form, the social roles that Benedick and Beatrice are called upon to play. They are roles that demand exceptionally versatile actors.

Such courtly performances, Castiglione's conversationalists acknowledge, risk seeming stilted and artificial; will be successful only if they appear entirely spontaneous and natural. However carefully they prepare their parts, courtiers should hide all signs of study and rehearsal. To achieve grace, they must practice what Castiglione calls *sprezzatura,* a cultivated nonchalance. *Sprezzatura* is a technique for the manipulation of appearance, for masking the hard work that underlies successful performances. This masking is an open secret: others know that you are masking, but they must keep this knowledge suspended in the belief that it is a breach of decorum to acknowledge their own knowledge.

The society of *The Book of the Courtier* lives with other open secrets. Dark forces lie just outside the charmed circle of delightful lords and ladies: war, arbitrary power, the high risk of betrayal and double-dealing, the commodification of women, the grinding labor to which the great mass of human beings are condemned. The courtier's artful refusal to acknowledge any of these forces could be a mode of escapism, but Castiglione is alert to reality's harsh demands. For him, fashioning the self is a means not of withdrawing from a treacherous world, but of operating successfully within it.

Like Castiglione's *Courtier, Much Ado About Nothing* (whose title suggests the playwright's own mastery of *sprezzatura*) is pervasively concerned with social performance that seems at once spontaneous and calculated. Beatrice and Benedick, at the play's center, are both exquisitely self-conscious, but their self-consciousness takes the paradoxical form of a jaunty indifference to conventional niceties, an almost reckless exuberance that masks a heightened sensitivity to the social currents in which they swim.

By contrast, Don John, the bastard brother, characterizes himself from the start as a radically antisocial creature: "I had rather be a canker in a hedge than a rose in his grace, and it better fits my blood to be disdained of all than to fashion a carriage to rob love from any" (1.3.21–23). These are the sentiments of the outsider, one who, like the bastard Edmund in *King Lear*, is not properly part of the family and kinship network, and they are sufficient, in this play, to account for Don John's relentless, curiously disinterested villainy. He is a man who refuses to "fashion a carriage"—to observe the appropriate code of manners—and this refusal is itself a sign of rebellion. For manners are the lived texture of social life in *Much Ado*, not in the sense of a compulsory set of rules but rather in the sense of an evolving awareness of mutual obligation and interconnectedness.

There is, to be sure, something like compulsion in the obligations and pressures within which the men and women of *Much Ado* live, but the play frustrates any attempt to strip away the fabric of graciousness, apparent choice, and pretended spontaneity with which the compulsions are dressed. An exchange in the comedy's opening moments exemplifies the perfect balance between obligation and will that governs the play's vision of social life. Leonato, the Governor of Messina, is informed by letter of the imminent arrival of Don Pedro of Aragon. Entertainment must be provided at once, and Don Pedro's first words call attention to the pressure of compulsory courtesy: "Good Signor Leonato, are you come to meet your trouble? The fashion of the world is to avoid cost, and you encounter it." It is obviously the fashion of the world to apologize in just this way for imposition, and such an apology calls for an equally conventional denial that any trouble is involved. Leonato duly produces such a denial, a particularly gracious and well-turned one: "Never came trouble to my house in the likeness of your grace; for trouble being gone, comfort should remain, but when you depart from me, sorrow abides and happiness takes his leave." Don Pedro responds to this exquisite compliment with an elegantly modified renewal of his first words and then a polite turn toward Leonato's daughter, Hero: "You embrace your charge too willingly. I think this is your daughter" (1.1.77–85).

In a strict calculation of power politics, these words are meaningless: they posture emptily above the "real" social exchange, which involves the obligation of the civilian authority toward the military authority (as it happens, a foreign military) at the close of a successful campaign. But such a view neglects the importance of graceful social performance, performance whose ease signals the elite status of the speakers and tacitly acknowledges the possibility of failure or refusal. With a ceremonial greeting such as this, the possibility may seem merely theoretical, but in fact it comes to hover over the entire play (whose main plot is in effect formally initiated by Don Pedro's polite notice of Leonato's daughter). By the fifth act, after Don Pedro's officer Claudio has publicly humiliated and repudiated his intended bride, all courtesy has withered away, and only bitterness and recrimination exist between the gracious host and his princely guest.

Dogberry's zany sleuthing resolves the crisis, but the crucial point is that there is nothing absolute and automatic about the code of manners. Social rituals are vulnerable to disruption and misunderstanding, and this vulnerability underscores the importance of consciously keeping up appearances, patrolling social perimeters, and fabricating civility.

In Castiglione's world, there is a high premium placed on the concealment of the labor expended in this fabrication, but Shakespeare's comedy gives us glimpses in the frequent references to the support staff and attentiveness involved in entertainment: "Where is my cousin, your son? Hath he provided this music?" (1.2.1–2); "Being entertained for a perfumer, as I was smoking a musty room . . ." (1.3.46–47); "The revellers are entering, brother. Make good room" (2.1.70). Social labor is still more visible in the diverse kinds of discourse in which the characters participate or to which they refer: greeting, entertainment, embassy, formal letter, conjuration, courtship, epigraph, sonneteering, gossip, legal deposition, aggressive wit, formal denunciation, ritualized apology.

Each of these forms of speech requires a display of skill and hence confers a measure of the honor or shame to which the characters of *Much Ado About Nothing* are intensely attuned. Honor and shame are particularly social emotions, the emotions of those who exist in a world of watching and being watched. "Nothing" in Shakespeare's time was pronounced "noting": this is a play obsessed with characters noting other characters. Hence the special force of *masking*, where the serious business of watching is playfully disrupted by disguise, and hence too the crucial significance of those scenes in which Beatrice and Benedick think they are noting others and are in reality being noted (and tricked). Sensitivity to the possibility of being shamed—which includes being laughed at, rejected, insulted, dishonored, humiliated, and so forth—is never very far from the characters of *Much Ado*. It extends from Leonato, who thinks that death is the fairest cover for his daughter's public humiliation, to Benedick, whose intellectual and sexual endurance is ridiculed by Beatrice when he ducks out of their first exchange with "a jade's trick" (1.1.118), to Dogberry, who longs to be writ down an ass. At its core is intense male anxiety about female infidelity, manifested in the constant nervous jokes about cuckoldry and played on viciously by Don John. "If I see anything tonight why I should not marry her, tomorrow," Claudio tells Don John, "in the congregation where I should wed, there will I shame her." Don Pedro promises to join with his friend "to disgrace her" (3.2.103–07).

Honor and shame, as the play develops them, are closely bound up with linguistic performance. Language is society's way of being intimately present in the individual; the characters may adjust to that social presence, may like Beatrice and Benedick playfully resist it, may like Dogberry distort it unintentionally, but the shared codes of language are more powerful than any individual.

Close attention to the language of *Much Ado About Nothing* begins with the observation that the comedy is written largely, though not entirely, in prose, a medium far more familiar to modern audiences than the blank verse that dominates many of Shakespeare's plays. This prose, however, is of a kind to which we are no longer accustomed. Modern prose tends by design to be rather plain and colorless; Elizabethan prose is often playful, rhetorically inventive, and richly metaphorical. *Much Ado About Nothing* at once plays elaborate prose games and pokes fun at them, as when Benedick complains that lovesick Claudio "was wont to speak plain and to the purpose, like an honest man and a soldier, and now is he turned orthography. His words are a very fantastical banquet, just so many strange dishes" (2.3.16–19). Shakespeare was certainly capable of writing what we would regard as clear, uncluttered prose: "I learn in this letter that Don Pedro of Aragon comes this night to Messina" (1.1.1–2). But he could also produce astonishing rhetorical effects:

> She told me—not thinking I had been myself—that I was the Prince's jester, that I was duller than a great thaw, huddling jest upon jest with such impossible conveyance upon me that I stood like a man at a mark, with a whole army shooting at me. She speaks poniards, and every word stabs. If her breath were as terrible as her terminations, there were no living near her, she would infect to the North Star. I would not marry her though she were endowed with all that Adam had left him before he transgressed. She would have made Hercules have turned spit, yea, and have cleft his club to make the fire, too. (2.1.212–21)

A night watchman. From Thomas Dekker, *The Belman of London* (1608).

The wonderful improvisational piling up of images, each at once subtly linked to the preceding one and yet swerving in a new direction, captures the movement of Benedick's mind: the rush of genuine anger and hurt feelings mingled with the impulse to turn his pain into a comically misogynistic performance to entertain Don Pedro (a performance that, ironically, confirms the charge—that he is the Prince's jester—that originally stung him).

Linguistic performance is the social equivalent of the performance in warfare that is both alluded to and conspicuously excluded from the play's action. Language is violence, and language is the alternative to violence: the play entertains both hypotheses and plays them off against each other. "There is a kind of merry war betwixt Signor Benedick and her," says Leonato of his niece. "They never meet but there's a skirmish of wit between them" (1.1.49–51). If words are the agents of civility, they are also dangerous weapons: "Thy slander hath gone through and through her heart, / And she lies buried with her ancestors"; "God knows, I loved my niece, / And she is dead, slandered to death by villains" (5.1.68–69, 87–88). What we glimpse in the symbolic murder of Hero is not only the maligning power of slander, but also the aggressive potential of even polite or playful speech. The "merry war" between Beatrice and Benedick leaves scars.

The more one attends to the language of *Much Ado About Nothing,* the more it seems saturated with violence. In the lighthearted opening scene alone, there are almost constant comic references to war, plague, betrayal, heresy, burning at the stake, blinding, hanging, spying, poisoning. To be sure, the horrors are not themselves realized dramatically in the play; they are present as mere jokes. Nonetheless, they are present, recalled again and again by the constant threat of disaster, by symbolic death, by public shaming. Even in the tidal rush of the comic resolution, amid the marriages, the music, and the dance, Benedick's final words, indeed the final words of the play, deliberately call attention to the violence that the language has continually, if obliquely, registered. Informed of Don John's capture, Benedick declares, "Think not on him till tomorrow, I'll devise thee brave punishments for him. Strike up, pipers." *Dance* (5.4.121–22).

Viewed in the light of the close, with its conspicuous deferral of torture, but only until tomorrow, the play does not simply transform human misery and violence into wit, but rather addresses itself to the ways in which society manages to endure, to reproduce, to avoid immersion in its own destructive element, to dance. It does so by conscious and unconscious deferral, by the manipulation of appearances, by the deployment of illusions that are known by at least some of its members (the worst and the best) to be illusions.

Illusions are tricks and deceptions, but they are also the social fictions men and women live by. Claudio and Hero exist in the play almost entirely in and as such fictions: their emotions seem less something they possess inwardly than something constructed for them out of the appropriate conventions and rituals. A more complex manifestation in the play of the primacy of illusion is the relation between Beatrice and Benedick. The plot to trick the celebrated skirmishers into marriage originates with Don Pedro, who promises, if Leonato, Hero, and Claudio cooperate with him, to "fash-

Lovers sparring with torches. From George Wither, *A Collection of Emblemes* (1635).

tricked to marry

ion" the match. The key to his success is his ability to mobilize the social code of shame and honor to which Beatrice and Benedick are bound and to use this code as a means to discipline—to shape into a plot that will culminate in marriage—the powerful chafing between them. For both Beatrice and Benedick, the force that pushes them toward declarations of love and hence toward marriage vows is as much hearing themselves criticized by their friends as hearing that the other is desperately in love. "Can this be true?" asks Beatrice, her ears burning. "Stand I condemned for pride and scorn so much?" (3.1.108–09). "I hear how I am censured," Benedick declares, resolving that he "must not seem proud" (2.3.199–200, 202–03).

The conspiratorial fabrication of appearances so as to manipulate the code of shame and honor has the odd effect of establishing a link between the socially approved practices of Don Pedro and the wicked practices of Don John, his bastard brother. Shakespeare seems to go out of his way to call attention to this link: moments after Don Pedro undertakes to "fashion" the affection between Beatrice and Benedick, the villainous Borachio declares that he "will so fashion the matter that Hero shall be absent" and hence can be impersonated by Margaret. In effect, the play's term for the social system in which all the characters—evil as well as virtuous—are involved is "fashion." Shakespeare deftly uses the term both as noun and verb—that is, both to designate the images (including the fashionable costumes) that elicit emotions and to describe the process that shapes these images.

Fashion is closely related not only to image but also to verbal style, which in the aesthetics of the period was regarded as a kind of dress. "The body of your discourse," laughs Benedick, "is sometimes guarded with fragments, and the guards are but slightly basted on neither" (1.1.232–34). The pervasiveness of fashion allows the possibility of drastic deception, but it is also society's redemptive principle. The movement

clothing as of love

of the play is not so much the unmasking of fraud to reveal the true, virtuous essence within as rather the refashioning, after a dangerous illusion, of the proper image and the appropriate words: "Sweet Hero," cries Claudio after his eyes have been opened to the deception, "now thy image doth appear / In the rare semblance that I loved it first" (5.1.235–36).

The fashioning with which the play is concerned complicates any simple opposition between authentic inner feelings and social norms. This is, after all, a plot that features a wooing by masked proxy instead of direct wooing, a theatrical ritual of remorse instead of remorse, a declaration of love based upon a set of illusions and motivated by the fear of shame. Near the play's close, we see Benedick struggling to compose the required sonnet to Beatrice—an entirely conventional exercise performed to fulfill the theatrical role in which he has been cast ("myself in love"). And in the final moments, when the deception is revealed, it is this exercise, rather than any feelings of the heart, that confirms the match. "I'll be sworn upon't that he loves her," declares Claudio:

> For here's a paper written in his hand,
> A halting sonnet of his own pure brain,
> Fashioned to Beatrice.

When a similar sonnet by Beatrice is produced, Benedick cries, "A miracle! Here's our own hands against our hearts" (5.4.85–88, 91).

Many readers of the play, and most performers, have tried to reverse this formulation: Beatrice and Benedick's conversations may be hostile, the interpretation goes, but in their hearts they are, and have long been, deeply in love. Beatrice seems to refer to an earlier time when she had given her heart to Benedick and had evidently been disappointed: "once before he won it of me, with false dice" (2.1.243–44). If they do not declare their love, it is because they are too defensive or, alternatively, too wise to play society's conventional game. In a world of pervasive conventionality and social control, one clever way to insist upon some spontaneity and hence to achieve some authenticity is to quarrel. Perhaps. But what if we do not dismiss their own words? What if we take the conspiracy against them seriously? Beatrice and Benedick would in that case not "love" each other from the start; it would not at all be clear that they love each other, entirely independent of social manipulation, at the close. They are, at least to some extent, tricked into marriage; without the pressure that moves them to professions of love, they would have remained unmarried. Beatrice and Benedick constantly tantalize us with the possibility of an identity quite different from that of Claudio and Hero, an identity deliberately fashioned to resist the constant pressure of society. But that pressure finally prevails. Marriage is a social conspiracy.

If such a view seems ultimately too unsentimental to be tenable in a romantic comedy, it nonetheless makes possible the brilliant scene in which Benedick asks what he can do to prove his love for Beatrice, and Beatrice replies, "Kill Claudio" (4.1.287). Similarly, it helps to account for the laughter provoked by the disillusioned exchange very near the play's close: "Do not you love me?" "Why no, no more than reason" (5.4.74). In both cases, where we might expect tender words, we get the opposite. If we feel nonetheless that romantic love triumphs in the end, we do so in effect because we—audience and readers—participate in the conspiracy to gull the pair into marriage by insisting that they love each other more than reason. In doing so, we confer upon the general restoration of civility at the play's close something more deeply pleasurable.

Benedick and Beatrice have rational arguments, grounded in the gender politics of their world, for remaining single. Benedick knows that a married man must put his honor at risk by entrusting it to a woman, while Beatrice knows that a married woman must put her integrity at risk by submitting herself to a man: "Would it not grieve a woman to be overmastered with a piece of valiant dust?" (2.1.51–52). Even when they are manipulated into declaring their love, they cannot settle into the language of conventional courtship: "Thou and I are too wise," Benedick tells Beatrice, "to woo peaceably" (5.2.61). Their union at the close is a triumph of folly over the "wisdom" of the

A man trapped in the yoke of matrimony. From Henry Peacham. *Minerva Britanna* (1612).

single life, a triumph that recalls Erasmus's *Praise of Folly,* where love is said to be possible only because men and women are induced to put aside their reason and plunge into saving foolishness. Why should they do so? The answer is that it is better to live in illusion than in social isolation and that, as Benedick says, "the world must be peopled" (2.3.213–14).

In most productions of the play, audiences are made to feel that submission to the discipline of love and marriage—"taming my wild heart" (3.1.113), as Beatrice so wonderfully puts it—is a magnificent release of love and energy. Shakespeare had already experimented with comparable themes in *The Taming of the Shrew,* but Petruchio's conquest of Kate seems, at least for many modern viewers, too brutal to accept without a lingering sense of constriction and loss. What keeps the conclusion of *Much Ado About Nothing* from appearing brittle or bitter is a sense that the triumph of illusion is life-affirming, a sense that the friction between Beatrice and Benedick can be turned into mutual pleasure.

If the Claudio/Hero plot and the Beatrice/Benedick plot are two ways in which Shakespeare's comedy shows the saving necessity of illusion, there is a third manifestation: the illusion that evil manifests itself as Don John—that is, in a supremely incompetent and finally impotent form—and that, although it fools clear-eyed and sophisticated observers like Don Pedro, it may be exposed by a bumbling idiot like Dogberry. Some years later, Shakespeare returned to a ruthlessly disillusioned version of the same story, the lover tricked into believing that his beloved has been unfaithful, and called it not *Much Ado About Nothing* but *Othello.*

STEPHEN GREENBLATT

TEXTUAL NOTE

"Much adoe about Nothing . . . *Written by William Shakespeare*" was first published in 1600, in a quarto (Q) printed by Valentine Simmes (or Sims) for Andrew Wise and William Aspley. This is the only version of the play that appeared during Shakespeare's lifetime. The title page states that the play "hath been sundrie times publikely acted by the right honourable, the Lord Chamberlaine his seruants."

Much Ado About Nothing is listed in a Stationers' Register entry of August 4, 1600, along with *As You Like It, Henry V,* and Ben Jonson's *Every Man in His Humour.* All are marked "to be staied"—that is, not published without further permission. It is generally thought that the Lord Chamberlain's Men were attempting to ensure that they would be paid for any printing of these popular plays and that the release of *Much Ado About Nothing* later that same year indicates that the company had resolved whatever dispute had led them to stay publication.

Most scholars, including the Oxford editors, believe that the 1600 Quarto of *Much Ado About Nothing* was set from Shakespeare's "foul papers"—that is, his own manuscript of the play. Evidence includes the omission of several entrances and exits, certain loose ends in the dialogue, and the presence of "ghost" characters. For example, Q's stage directions at the beginning of Acts 1 and 2 list Leonato's wife, Innogen, but Innogen neither speaks nor is spoken to in the course of the play. Evidently she is the ghostly trace of an idea that the playwright abandoned.

Q's speech prefixes are inconsistent, another characteristic feature of foul papers, and in 4.2 they preserve the names of the actors Shakespeare had in mind for two of the comic parts: Will Kemp for Dogberry and Richard Cowley for Verges. Since Kemp left the Lord Chamberlain's Men in 1599, scholars think the play must have been first performed before the date of his departure. And since Francis Meres does not include *Much Ado About Nothing* in a list of Shakespeare's plays he compiled in September 1598 (unless that is what he meant by the play he calls *Loue Labours wonne*), scholars think it probable that the play was first performed after that date. Therefore the likeliest date of the first performance is the winter of 1598–99.

The First Folio (1623) text of the play (F) was based on Q. There are no act or scene divisions in Q; F indicates only act divisions (with the exception of 1.1).

SELECTED BIBLIOGRAPHY

Barish, Jonas A. "Pattern and Purpose in the Prose of *Much Ado About Nothing.*" *Rice University Studies* 60.2 (Spring 1974): 19–30. Variations in the play's mannered rhetorical scheme offer insights into its characters and situations.

Berger, Harry, Jr. "Against the Sink-a-Pace: Sexual and Family Politics in *Much Ado About Nothing.*" *Shakespeare Quarterly* 33 (1982): 302–13. Characterizes Messina's gender conventions in terms of virtue, constancy, reputation, deception, and fashion.

Berry, Ralph. *Shakespeare's Comedies: Explorations in Form.* Princeton: Princeton University Press, 1972. 154–74. Focusing on the difficult reconciliation of sensory experience and judgment, *Much Ado About Nothing* explores the limits of knowledge.

Cook, Carol. "'The Sign and Semblance of Her Honor': Reading Gender Difference in *Much Ado About Nothing.*" *PMLA* 101.2 (1986): 186–202. The play presents the polysemous threat of woman in a world where men are the manipulators and interpreters of signs.

Everett, Barbara. "*Much Ado About Nothing*: The Unsociable Comedy." *English Comedy.* Ed. Michael Cordner, Peter Holland, and John Kerrigan. New York: Cambridge University Press, 1994. 68–84. Shakespeare's realistic portrait of love in society typically mixes its comic nothings with serious concerns.

Gay, Penny. "*Much Ado About Nothing*: A Kind of Merry War." *As She Likes It: Shakespeare's Unruly Women.* London: Routledge, 1994. 143–77. Performance history since the 1950s, spotlighting representations of Beatrice and Benedick.

Howard, Jean. "Renaissance Antitheatricality and the Politics of Gender and Rank in *Much Ado About Nothing.*" *Shakespeare Reproduced: The Text in History and Ideology.* Ed. Jean E. Howard and Marion F. O'Connor. New York: Methuen, 1987. 163–87. *Much Ado About Nothing* supports Elizabethan ideology, condemning marginal social groups through accusations of illegitimate theatrical practice.

Moisan, Thomas. "Deforming Sources: Literary Antecedents and Their Traces in *Much Ado About Nothing.*" *Shakespeare Studies* 31 (2003): 165–83. The play's furtive and ambivalent relationship to its sources reflects its depiction of character, politics, power, and representation.

Myhill, Nova. "Spectatorship in/of *Much Ado About Nothing.*" *Studies in English Literature* 39.2 (1999): 291–311. Considers how *Much Ado About Nothing*'s unreliable "notings" challenge the theater audience's assumptions of omniscience and invulnerability.

Salingar, Leo. "Borachio's Indiscretion: Some Noting about Much Ado." *The Italian World of English Renaissance Drama: Cultural Exchange and Intertextuality.* Ed. Michele Marrapodi. London: Associated University Presses, 1998. 225–38. *Much Ado About Nothing* as a bittersweet masquerade of social ambiguity and false communications.

Traugott, John. "Creating a Rational Rinaldo: A Study in the Mixture of the Genres of Comedy and Romance in *Much Ado About Nothing.*" *Genre* 15 (1982): 157–81. Shows how comedy and romance contaminate and purify each other, one becoming ennobled and the other cured of cruelty.

FILM

Much Ado About Nothing. 1993. Dir. Kenneth Branagh. UK/USA. 111 min. Festive romp set in sunny, country-house Italy. With Kenneth Branagh and Emma Thompson.

Much Ado About Nothing

THE PERSONS OF THE PLAY

DON PEDRO, Prince of Aragon
BENEDICK, of Padua
CLAUDIO, of Florence } lords, companions of Don Pedro
BALTHASAR, attendant on Don Pedro, a singer
DON JOHN, the bastard brother of Don Pedro
BORACHIO
CONRAD } followers of Don John
LEONATO, governor of Messina
HERO, his daughter
BEATRICE, an orphan, his niece
ANTONIO, an old man, brother of Leonato
MARGARET
URSULA } waiting-gentlewomen attendant on Hero
FRIAR FRANCIS
DOGBERRY, the Constable in charge of the Watch
VERGES, the Headborough, Dogberry's partner
A SEXTON
WATCHMEN
A BOY, serving Benedick
Attendants and messengers

1.1

Enter LEONATO, *governor of Messina,* HERO *his
daughter, and* BEATRICE *his niece, with a*
MESSENGER

LEONATO   I learn in this letter that Don Pedro of Aragon comes
this night to Messina.

MESSENGER   He is very near by this. He was not three leagues off
when I left him.

5   LEONATO   How many gentlemen have you lost in this action?°   *campaign*

MESSENGER   But few of any sort,° and none of name.°   *rank / distinction*

LEONATO   A victory is twice itself when the achiever brings home
full numbers. I find here that Don Pedro hath bestowed much
honour on a young Florentine called Claudio.

10   MESSENGER   Much deserved on his part, and equally remem-
bered° by Don Pedro. He hath borne himself beyond the prom-   *rewarded*
ise of his age, doing in the figure of a lamb the feats of a lion.
He hath indeed better bettered° expectation than you must   *exceeded*
expect of me to tell you how.

15   LEONATO   He hath an uncle here in Messina will be very much
glad of it.

MESSENGER   I have already delivered him letters, and there
appears much joy in him—even so much that joy could not
show itself modest° enough without a badge° of bitterness.°   *moderate / show / grief*

1.1 Location: Messina (a city in Sicily). Before the house of Leonato.

20 LEONATO   Did he break out into tears?

MESSENGER   In great measure.

LEONATO   A kind° overflow of kindness,° there are no faces truer   *natural / tenderness*
than those that are so washed. How much better is it to weep
at joy than to joy at weeping!

25 BEATRICE   I pray you, is Signor Montanto[1] returned from the
wars, or no?

MESSENGER   I know none of that name, lady. There was none
such in the army, of any sort.

LEONATO   What is he that you ask for, niece?

30 HERO   My cousin means Signor Benedick of Padua.[2]

MESSENGER   O, he's returned, and as pleasant° as ever he was.   *entertaining*

BEATRICE   He set up his bills° here in Messina, and challenged   *public notices*
Cupid at the flight;[3] and my uncle's fool,° reading the chal-   *jester*
lenge, subscribed for Cupid and challenged him at the bird-

35 bolt.[4] I pray you, how many hath he killed and eaten in these
wars? But how many hath he killed? For indeed I promised to
eat all of his killing.

LEONATO   Faith, niece, you tax° Signor Benedick too much. But   *abuse*
he'll be meet° with you, I doubt it not.   *even*

40 MESSENGER   He hath done good service, lady, in these wars.

BEATRICE   You had musty victual, and he hath holp° to eat it. He   *helped*
is a very valiant trencherman,° he hath an excellent stomach.   *eater*

MESSENGER   And a good soldier too, lady.

BEATRICE   And a good soldier° to a lady, but what is he to a lord?   *servant; lady-killer*

45 MESSENGER   A lord to a lord, a man to a man, stuffed° with all   *well furnished*
honourable virtues.

BEATRICE   It is so, indeed. He is no less than a stuffed man.° But   *mannequin*
for the stuffing—well, we are all mortal.[5]

LEONATO   You must not, sir, mistake my niece. There is a kind

50 of merry war betwixt Signor Benedick and her. They never
meet but there's a skirmish of wit between them.

BEATRICE   Alas, he gets nothing by that. In our last conflict four
of his five wits[6] went halting° off, and now is the whole man   *limping*
governed with one, so that if he have wit enough to keep him-

55 self warm,[7] let him bear it for a difference[8] between himself
and his horse, for it is all the wealth that he hath left to be
known a reasonable creature. Who is his companion now? He
hath every month a new sworn brother.

MESSENGER   Is't possible?

60 BEATRICE   Very easily possible. He wears his faith° but as the   *loyalty*
fashion of his hat, it ever changes with the next block.[9]

MESSENGER   I see, lady, the gentleman is not in your books.°   *favor*

BEATRICE   No. An° he were, I would burn my study. But I pray   *If*
you, who is his companion? Is there no young squarer° now   *boisterous quarreler*

65 that will make a voyage with him to the devil?

MESSENGER   He is most in the company of the right noble
Claudio.

---

1. In fencing, a montanto is an upright blow or thrust.
2. A city in northern Italy.
3. To an archery match. (He claimed to surpass Cupid
at arousing love.)
4. To a contest using bird bolts, or blunt, short-range
arrows allowed to fools and children (and thus appropriate to young Cupid). *subscribed for*: took up the
challenge on behalf of.

5. But as for what he is made of (his "stuffing"), he is
probably as faulty as the rest of us.
6. *five wits*: mental faculties (memory, imagination,
judgment, fantasy, and common sense).
7. If he have minimal common sense.
8. Let him display the fact in his coat of arms in order
to distinguish himself.
9. Newest mold for a hat; fashion.

BEATRICE O Lord, he will hang upon him like a disease. He is
sooner caught than the pestilence,° and the taker° runs pres-   *plague / victim*
70 ently° mad. God help the noble Claudio. If he have caught the   *immediately*
Benedick, it will cost him a thousand pound ere a° be cured.   *he*
MESSENGER I will hold friends[1] with you, lady.
BEATRICE Do, good friend.
LEONATO You will never run mad,[2] niece.
75 BEATRICE No, not till a hot January.
MESSENGER Don Pedro is approached.

Enter DON PEDRO, CLAUDIO, BENEDICK, BALTHASAR, *and*
[DON] JOHN *the bastard*

DON PEDRO Good Signor Leonato, are you come to meet your
trouble? The fashion° of the world is to avoid cost, and you   *custom*
encounter° it.   *go to meet*
80 LEONATO Never came trouble to my house in the likeness of
your grace; for trouble being gone, comfort should remain, but
when you depart from me, sorrow abides and happiness takes
his leave.
DON PEDRO You embrace your charge° too willingly. I think this   *duty*
85 is your daughter.
LEONATO Her mother hath many times told me so.
BENEDICK Were you in doubt, sir, that you asked her?
LEONATO Signor Benedick, no, for then were you a child.
DON PEDRO You have it full,[3] Benedick. We may guess by this
90 what you are, being a man. Truly, the lady fathers herself.[4] Be
happy, lady, for you are like an honourable father.
BENEDICK If Signor Leonato be her father, she would not have
his head;[5] on her shoulders for all Messina, as like him as she
is.
95 BEATRICE[6] I wonder that you will still° be talking, Signor Bene-   *always*
dick. Nobody marks you.
BENEDICK What, my dear Lady Disdain! Are you yet living?
BEATRICE Is it possible disdain should die while she hath such
meet° food to feed it as Signor Benedick? Courtesy itself must   *suitable*
100 convert° to disdain if you come in her presence.   *turn*
BENEDICK Then is courtesy a turncoat. But it is certain I am
loved of° all ladies, only you excepted. And I would I could   *by*
find in my heart that I had not a hard heart, for truly I love
none.
105 BEATRICE A dear happiness to women. They would else have
been troubled with a pernicious suitor. I thank God and my
cold blood I am of your humour° for that. I had rather hear my   *disposition*
dog bark at a crow than a man swear he loves me.
BENEDICK God keep your ladyship still in that mind. So some
110 gentleman or other shall scape a predestinate° scratched face.   *escape an inevitable*
BEATRICE Scratching could not make it worse an 'twere such a
face as yours were.
BENEDICK Well, you are a rare parrot-teacher.[7]
BEATRICE A bird of my tongue is better than a beast of yours.[8]

---

1. I will stay on good terms (so as not to provoke your
sarcasm).
2. "Catch the Benedick."
3. Your sarcasm is fully repaid.
4. She shows by her looks who her father is.
5. The head of an old man.

6. During Beatrice and Benedick's conversation, Don
Pedro talks with Leonato (see line 119).
7. Chatterer (repetitive, like one who teaches a parrot
to speak).
8. A bird with my powers of speech is better than a
dumb beast who, like you, has none.

115 BENEDICK I would my horse had the speed of your tongue, *carry on*
and so good a continuer.⁹ But keep your way,° i' God's name. I
have done.

BEATRICE You always end with a jade's trick.¹ I know you of old.

DON PEDRO That is the sum of all, Leonato. Signor Claudio and
120 Signor Benedick, my dear friend Leonato hath invited you all.
I tell him we shall stay here at the least a month, and he heartily prays some occasion may detain us longer. I dare swear he
is no hypocrite, but prays from his heart.

LEONATO If you swear, my lord, you shall not be forsworn. [*To* *Since you are*
125 DON JOHN] Let me bid you welcome, my lord. Being° reconciled to the Prince your brother, I owe you all duty.

DON JOHN I thank you. I am not of many words, but I thank you.

LEONATO [*to* DON PEDRO] Please it your grace lead on?

DON PEDRO Your hand, Leonato. We will go together.²

Exeunt. Manent° BENEDICK *and* CLAUDIO *Remain*

130 CLAUDIO Benedick, didst thou note the daughter of Signor Leonato?

BENEDICK I noted her not,³ but I looked on her.

CLAUDIO Is she not a modest young lady?

BENEDICK Do you question me as an honest man should do, for
135 my simple true judgement, or would you have me speak after
my custom, as being a professed tyrant° to their sex? *pitiless critic*

CLAUDIO No, I pray thee speak in sober judgement.

BENEDICK Why, i'faith, methinks she's too low° for a high *short*
praise, too brown for a fair praise, and too little for a great
140 praise. Only this commendation I can afford her, that were she
other than she is she were unhandsome, and being no other
but as she is, I do not like her.

CLAUDIO Thou thinkest I am in sport.° I pray thee tell me truly *jest*
how thou likest her.

145 BENEDICK Would you buy her, that you enquire after her?

CLAUDIO Can the world buy such a jewel?

BENEDICK Yea, and a case to put it into. But speak you this with
a sad° brow, or do you play the flouting jack, to tell us Cupid *serious*
is a good hare-finder and Vulcan a rare carpenter?⁴ Come, in
150 what key shall a man take° you to go° in the song? *understand / join*

CLAUDIO In mine eye she is the sweetest lady that ever I looked
on.

BENEDICK I can see yet without spectacles, and I see no such
matter. There's her cousin, an she were not possessed with a
155 fury, exceeds her as much in beauty as the first of May doth the
last of December. But I hope you have no intent to turn husband, have you?

CLAUDIO I would scarce trust myself though I had sworn the
contrary, if Hero would be my wife.

160 BENEDICK Is't come to this? In faith, hath not the world one
man but he will wear his cap with suspicion?⁵ Shall I never see

---

9. And had your staying power ("continuer," in horsemanship, means "stayer").
1. A trick worthy of a badly trained horse (here, dropping out of a race).
2. We will walk out hand in hand (and thus avoid taking precedence).
3. I paid her no special attention.
4. *play . . . carpenter*: spout praises contrary to fact and

intended satirically. Blind Cupid is poorly suited to the
sharp-sighted sport of hunting hares, while Vulcan, the
god of fire, was an excellent ("rare") blacksmith, not a
carpenter. *flouting jack*: mocking rogue.
5. *but . . . suspicion*: who will not be suspected of wearing his cap in order to hide a cuckold's horns (conventional sign of a wife's infidelity).

a bachelor of three-score again? Go to,° i'faith, an thou wilt   *Go on*
needs thrust thy neck into a yoke, wear the print of it, and sigh
away Sundays.[6] Look, Don Pedro is returned to seek you.

    Enter DON PEDRO

165 DON PEDRO   What secret hath held you here that you followed
not to Leonato's?

BENEDICK   I would your grace would constrain me to tell.

DON PEDRO   I charge thee on thy allegiance.

BENEDICK   You hear, Count Claudio? I can be secret as a dumb
170 man, I would have you think so. But on my allegiance, mark
you this, on my allegiance! He is in love. With who? Now that
is your grace's part. Mark how short his answer is: with Hero,
Leonato's short daughter.

CLAUDIO   If this were so, so were it uttered.[7]

175 BENEDICK   Like the old tale, my lord—it is not so, nor 'twas not
so, but indeed, God forbid it should be so.[8]

CLAUDIO   If my passion change not shortly, God forbid it should
be otherwise.

DON PEDRO   Amen, if you love her, for the lady is very well
180 worthy.

CLAUDIO   You speak this to fetch me in,° my lord.   *to trick me*

DON PEDRO   By my troth, I speak my thought.

CLAUDIO   And in faith, my lord, I spoke mine.

BENEDICK   And by my two faiths and troths,[9] my lord, I spoke
185 mine.

CLAUDIO   That I love her, I feel.

DON PEDRO   That she is worthy, I know.

BENEDICK   That I neither feel how she should be loved nor know
how she should be worthy is the opinion that fire cannot melt
190 out of me. I will die in it at the stake.

DON PEDRO   Thou wast ever an obstinate heretic in the despite°   *contempt*
of beauty.

CLAUDIO   And never could maintain his part° but in the force of   *argument*
his will.[1]

195 BENEDICK   That a woman conceived me, I thank her. That she
brought me up, I likewise give her most humble thanks. But
that I will have a recheat winded in my forehead, or hang my
bugle in an invisible baldric,[2] all women shall pardon me.
Because I will not do them the wrong to mistrust any,[3] I will
200 do myself the right to trust none. And the fine° is—for the   *conclusion*
which I may go the finer[4]—I will live a bachelor.

DON PEDRO   I shall see thee ere I die look pale with love.

BENEDICK   With anger, with sickness, or with hunger, my lord;
not with love. Prove° that ever I lose more blood with love than   *If you prove*
205 I will get again with drinking,[5] pick out mine eyes with a bal-

6. *thrust . . . Sundays:* take on the burdens and tedium
of marriage, when you might be enjoying yourself as a
bachelor.
7. *so . . . uttered:* this is how Benedick would tell it.
8. In an English fairy tale (a variant on the Bluebeard
story), a man suspected by his bride-to-be of having
killed his former wives denies his guilt with the refrain
Benedick quotes.
9. His loyalty to both Don Pedro and Claudio, and jok-
ingly, his duplicity.
1. But through prideful obstinacy rather than reason.
2. *But . . . baldric:* But that I should wear a cuckold's

horns. A recheat was a call sounded ("winded") on a
horn to recall the hounds. A baldric was a belt to hold
a horn ("bugle"); it was invisible, a sign of the cuckold's
ignorance.
3. Because I do not wish to wrong women by suspecting any of infidelity.
4. I may dress better (because he will have more money
to spare).
5. *lose . . . drinking:* alluding to the belief that sighing
like a lover caused the blood to evaporate, and drinking
wine renewed it.

lad-maker's[6] pen and hang me up at the door of a brothel house
for the sign of blind Cupid.[7]

DON PEDRO   Well, if ever thou dost fall from this faith thou wilt
prove a notable argument.°   *subject of talk*

210   BENEDICK   If I do, hang me in a bottle like a cat, and shoot at
me,[8] and he that hits me, let him be clapped on the shoulder
and called Adam.[9]

DON PEDRO   Well, as time shall try.° 'In time the savage bull doth   *prove*
bear the yoke.'[1]

215   BENEDICK   The savage bull may, but if ever the sensible° Bene-   *rational*
dick bear it, pluck off the bull's horns and set them in my fore-
head, and let me be vilely painted, and in such great letters as
they write 'Here is good horse to hire' let them signify under
my sign 'Here you may see Benedick, the married man'.

220   CLAUDIO   If this should ever happen thou wouldst be horn-mad.[2]

DON PEDRO   Nay, if Cupid have not spent all his quiver in Venice[3] thou wilt quake for this shortly.

BENEDICK   I look for an earthquake[4] too, then.

DON PEDRO   Well, you will temporize with the hours.[5] In the
225   mean time, good Signor Benedick, repair° to Leonato's, com-   *go*
mend me to him, and tell him I will not fail him at supper, for
indeed he hath made great preparation.

BENEDICK   I have almost matter° enough in me for such an   *intelligence*
embassage.° And so I commit you—   *errand*

230   CLAUDIO   To the tuition[6] of God, from my house if I had it—

DON PEDRO   The sixth of July,

Your loving friend,

Benedick.

BENEDICK   Nay, mock not, mock not. The body of your discourse is sometime guarded with fragments,[7] and the guards
are but slightly basted on[8] neither. Ere you flout° old ends° any   *mock / clichés*
235   further, examine your conscience. And so I leave you.   *Exit*

CLAUDIO   My liege, your highness now may do me good.

DON PEDRO   My love is thine to teach. Teach it but how
And thou shalt see how apt it is to learn
Any hard lesson that may do thee good.

240   CLAUDIO   Hath Leonato any son, my lord?

DON PEDRO   No child but Hero. She's his only heir.
Dost thou affect° her, Claudio?   *love*

CLAUDIO   O my lord,
When you went onward on this ended action°   *campaign*
I looked upon her with a soldier's eye,
245   That liked, but had a rougher task in hand
Than to drive liking to the name of love.
But now I am returned, and that° war-thoughts   *now that*

---

6. Popular love poet or satirist.
7. A painted sign, such as might hang before a brothel.
8. *hang . . . me:* cats in baskets ("bottles") were common Elizabethan targets for recreational archery.
9. Perhaps Adam Bell, a celebrated archer.
1. Proverbial; here, apparently a variation on a line
from Thomas Kyd's *Spanish Tragedy* (c. 1587): "In time
the savage bull sustains the yoke" (2.1.3).
2. Furious, raving like a wild beast (referring to the
rage of a cuckolded husband).
3. Venice was famous in Shakespeare's time for its beautiful courtesans. *spent all his quiver:* used all his arrows.

4. An earthquake would be as unlikely as my quaking
with love.
5. You will soften as time passes; with perhaps a bawdy
pun on "hours," "whores" (pronounced similarly).
6. Protection (Claudio and Don Pedro parody a conventional formula for ending a letter).
7. *The body . . . fragments:* The substance (also punning on the dressmaker's "bodice") of what you say is
sometimes ornamented ("guarded") with odds and ends
("fragments") such as you are mocking me for using.
8. And the decorative phrases are barely relevant.

Have left their places vacant, in their rooms
Come thronging soft and delicate desires,
250 All prompting me how fair young Hero is,
Saying I liked her ere I went to wars.

DON PEDRO   Thou wilt be like a lover presently,
And tire the hearer with a book of words.°   *lover's set speeches*
If thou dost love fair Hero, cherish it,
255 And I will break° with her, and with her father,   *speak*
And thou shalt have her. Was't not to this end
That thou began'st to twist° so fine a story?   *spin*

CLAUDIO   How sweetly you do minister to love,
That know love's grief by his complexion!°   *by its appearance*
260 But lest my liking might too sudden seem
I would have salved° it with a longer treatise.   *smoothed*

DON PEDRO   What need the bridge much broader than the flood?°   *river*
The fairest grant is the necessity.⁹
Look what° will serve is fit. 'Tis once:° thou lovest,   *Whatever / In brief*
265 And I will fit thee with the remedy.
I know we shall have revelling° tonight.   *festivity; masked ball*
I will assume thy part° in some disguise,   *role*
And tell fair Hero I am Claudio.
And in her bosom I'll unclasp my heart¹
270 And take her hearing prisoner with the force
And strong encounter° of my amorous tale.   *assault*
Then after to her father will I break,
And the conclusion is, she shall be thine.
In practice let us put it presently.°   *Exeunt*   *at once*

1.2

Enter LEONATO *and* [ANTONIO,] *an old man brother to*
Leonato, [*severally*]°   *separately*

LEONATO   How now, brother, where is my cousin,° your son?   *kinsman (nephew)*
Hath he provided this music?

ANTONIO   He is very busy about it. But brother, I can tell you
strange news that you yet dreamt not of.

5 LEONATO   Are they good?

ANTONIO   As the event stamps them.¹ But they have a good
cover, they show well outward. The Prince and Count Clau-
dio, walking in a thick-pleached² alley in mine orchard,° were   *garden*
thus much overheard by a man of mine: the Prince discovered°   *revealed*
10 to Claudio that he loved my niece, your daughter, and meant
to acknowledge it this night in a dance, and if he found her
accordant° he meant to take the present time by the top³ and   *consenting*
instantly break° with you of it.   *speak*

LEONATO   Hath the fellow any wit° that told you this?   *intelligence*

15 ANTONIO   A good sharp fellow. I will send for him, and question
him yourself.

LEONATO   No, no. We will hold it as a dream till it appear° itself.   *manifest*
But I will acquaint my daughter withal,° that she may be the   *with it*

---

9. The best gift is something that is truly needed.
1. And I will privately reveal to her my feelings (as if
I were you).
1.2 Location: Leonato's house.
1. As good as the outcome ("event") proves ("stamps")

them. The image is of news bound in a book with a
handsome cover.
2. Enclosed by trees with intertwining boughs.
3. He meant to seize the opportunity. (Time is proverbially bald except for the "top," or forelock.)

better prepared for an answer if peradventure° this be true. Go   *by chance*
20   you and tell her of it.
        [*Enter Attendants*]⁴
        Cousins, you know what you have to do. O, I cry you mercy,⁵
        friend. Go you with me and I will use your skill.—Good
        cousin, have a care this busy time.   *Exeunt*

1.3

Enter [DON] JOHN *the bastard and* CONRAD, *his com-*
        panion

CONRAD   What the goodyear, my lord, why are you thus out of
        measure¹ sad?

DON JOHN   There is no measure in the occasion that breeds it,
        therefore the sadness is without limit.

5   CONRAD   You should hear reason.

DON JOHN   And when I have heard it, what blessing brings it?

CONRAD   If not a present° remedy, at least a patient sufferance.   *an immediate*

DON JOHN   I wonder that thou—being, as thou sayst thou art,
        born under Saturn²—goest about to apply a moral medicine to
10   a mortifying mischief.° I cannot hide what I am. I must be sad   *a deadly sickness*
        when I have cause, and smile at no man's jests; eat when I have
        stomach,° and wait for no man's leisure; sleep when I am   *appetite*
        drowsy, and tend on° no man's business; laugh when I am   *attend to*
        merry, and claw° no man in his humour.°   *flatter / mood*

15   CONRAD   Yea, but you must not make the full show of this till
        you may do it without controlment.° You have of late stood   *restraint*
        out° against your brother, and he hath ta'en you newly into his   *rebelled*
        grace,° where it is impossible you should take true root but by   *favor*
        the fair weather that you make yourself. It is needful that you
20   frame the season for your own harvest.

DON JOHN   I had rather be a canker° in a hedge than a rose³ in   *wild rose; weed*
        his grace, and it better fits my blood° to be disdained of all than   *disposition*
        to fashion° a carriage° to rob love from any. In this, though I   *affect; feign / behavior*
        cannot be said to be a flattering honest man, it must not be
25   denied but I am a plain-dealing villain. I am trusted with a
        muzzle, and enfranchised with a clog.⁴ Therefore I have
        decreed° not to sing in my cage. If I had my mouth I would   *determined*
        bite. If I had my liberty I would do my liking. In the mean
        time, let me be that I am, and seek not to alter me.

30   CONRAD   Can you make no use of your discontent?

DON JOHN   I make all use of it, for I use it only. Who comes
        here?
        Enter BORACHIO⁵
        What news, Borachio?

BORACHIO   I came yonder from a great supper. The Prince your

---

4. The attendants are evidently engaged in preparations for the reveling (2.1). "Cousins" (line 21) may be
dependents in Leonato's household.
5. I beg your pardon (perhaps because he has not initially recognized one of the attendants, or because he
has bumped into him). Leonato's reference to "skill"
suggests that he might be talking to a musician.
1.3 Location: Leonato's house.
1. *What the goodyear*: unexplained exclamation. *out of
measure*: disproportionately.

2. Born when Saturn was in the ascendant (therefore
"saturnine," melancholy).
3. Cultivated rose.
4. I am trusted by being muzzled (in other words, not
trusted at all), and given my freedom with a clog (a
heavy block of wood attached to an animal or man as a
restraint).
5. The name, from the Spanish for "wine bottle," was
used for drunkards.

20   sending that way, for it is said God sends a curst cow short
      horns,[4] but to a cow too curst he sends none.

LEONATO   So, by being too curst, God will send you no horns.

BEATRICE   Just,° if he send me no husband,[5] for the which bless-   *Just so*
      ing I am at him upon my knees every morning and evening.

25   Lord, I could not endure a husband with a beard on his face. I
      had rather lie in the woollen.[6]

LEONATO   You may light on a husband that hath no beard.

BEATRICE   What should I do with him—dress him in my apparel
      and make him my waiting gentlewoman? He that hath a beard

30   is more than a youth, and he that hath no beard is less than a
      man; and he that is more than a youth is not for me, and he
      that is less than a man, I am not for him. Therefore I will even
      take sixpence in earnest of the bearherd and lead his apes into
      hell.[7]

35   LEONATO   Well then, go you into hell?

BEATRICE   No, but° to the gate, and there will the devil meet me   *only*
      like an old cuckold with horns on his head, and say, 'Get you
      to heaven, Beatrice, get you to heaven. Here's no place for you
      maids.' So deliver I up my apes and away to Saint Peter fore

40   the heavens.[8] He shows me where the bachelors[9] sit, and there
      live we as merry as the day is long.

ANTONIO [*to* HERO]   Well, niece, I trust you will be ruled by your
      father.

BEATRICE   Yes, faith, it is my cousin's duty to make curtsy and

45   say, 'Father, as it please you.' But yet for all that, cousin, let
      him be a handsome fellow, or else make another curtsy and
      say, 'Father, as it please me.'

LEONATO   Well, niece, I hope to see you one day fitted with a
      husband.

50   BEATRICE   Not till God make men of some other mettle° than   *substance*
      earth. Would it not grieve a woman to be overmastered with° a   *by*
      piece of valiant dust?—to make an account of her life to a clod
      of wayward marl?° No, uncle, I'll none. Adam's sons are my   *clay*
      brethren, and truly I hold it a sin to match in my kindred.[1]

55   LEONATO [*to* HERO]   Daughter, remember what I told you. If the
      Prince do solicit you in that kind,[2] you know your answer.

BEATRICE   The fault will be in the music, cousin, if you be not
      wooed in good time. If the Prince be too important,° tell him   *importunate*
      there is measure[3] in everything, and so dance out the answer.

60   For hear me, Hero, wooing, wedding, and repenting is as a
      Scotch jig, a measure, and a cinquepace.[4] The first suit° is hot   *courtship*
      and hasty, like a Scotch jig—and full as fantastical; the wed-
      ding mannerly° modest, as a measure, full of state and   *graciously*
      ancientry.° And then comes repentance, and with his bad legs   *old-fashioned decorum*

---

4. Proverbial: God makes sure that the vicious ("curst")
have little power to do harm.
5. That is, if God sent her a husband, she would cuckold him.
6. Sleep between rough blankets (without sheets).
7. *take . . . hell:* take advance payment from the bear
keeper (who trained bears for the popular sport of bearbaiting and who usually had charge of other animals);
leading apes into hell was the proverbial fate of old
maids.

8. Peter is gatekeeper of heaven. Q prints "Peter: for
the heavens"; it is possible that Beatrice means "as far
as heaven is concerned."
9. Unwed men or women.
1. *to . . . kindred:* to marry incestuously.
2. *in that kind:* that is, to marry him.
3. Moderation (punning on the name of a slow, stately
dance [line 63] and continuing the link between dancing and wooing "in good time" [line 58]).
4. A lively five-step dance.

65 falls into the cinquepace faster and faster till he sink into his
grave.
LEONATO   Cousin, you apprehend passing° shrewdly.   *understand more than*
BEATRICE   I have a good eye, uncle. I can see a church by daylight.[5]
70 LEONATO   The revellers are entering, brother. Make good room.
*Enter [DON] PEDRO [the] Prince, CLAUDIO, BENEDICK,
and BALTHASAR, DON JOHN, [and BORACHIO, as] Mask-
ers, with a drum*
DON PEDRO [to HERO]   Lady, will you walk a bout with your
friend?[6]
HERO   So you walk softly, and look sweetly, and say nothing, I
am yours for the walk; and especially when I walk away.
75 DON PEDRO   With me in your company?
HERO   I may say so when I please.
DON PEDRO   And when please you to say so?
HERO   When I like your favour;° for God defend the lute should   *face*
be like the case.[7]
80 DON PEDRO   My visor° is Philemon's roof. Within the house is   *mask*
Jove.[8]
HERO   Why, then, your visor should be thatched.[9]
DON PEDRO   Speak low if
you speak love.
[*They move aside*]
BALTHASAR [to MARGARET]   Well, I would you did like me.
MARGARET   So would not I, for your own sake, for I have many
85 ill° qualities.   *bad*
BALTHASAR   Which is one?
MARGARET   I say my prayers aloud.
BALTHASAR   I love you the better—the hearers may cry amen.
MARGARET   God match me with a good dancer.
90 BALTHASAR   Amen.
MARGARET   And God keep him out of my sight when the dance
is done. Answer, clerk.[1]
BALTHASAR   No more words. The clerk is answered.
[*They move aside*]
URSULA [to ANTONIO]   I know you well enough, you are Signor
95 Antonio.
ANTONIO   At a word,° I am not.   *In short*
URSULA   I know you by the waggling of your head.
ANTONIO   To tell you true, I counterfeit him.
URSULA   You could never do him so ill-well[2] unless you were the
100 very man. Here's his dry hand up and down.[3] You are he, you
are he.
ANTONIO   At a word, I am not.
URSULA   Come, come, do you think I do not know you by your

---

5. That is, see what's in front of me.
6. Often used to mean "lover." *walk a bout:* take a turn
(apparently a term in dancing).
7. God forbid your face should be as unappealing as
your mask.
8. The peasant Philemon and his wife, Baucis, entertained Jove, disguised, in their humble cottage (Ovid,
Metamorphoses 8). This and the following line are in
"fourteeners," a verse form old-fashioned in Shake-

speare's time but used by Arthur Golding in his 1567
translation of the *Metamorphoses.*
9. According to Golding, Philemon's roof was
"thatched all with straw"; Hero means that the mask
should be fitted with false hair or beard.
1. That is, say "Amen" again. The parish clerk led the
responses in church services.
2. *do him so ill-well:* mime his imperfections so ably.
3. His wrinkled hand exactly.

excellent wit? Can virtue° hide itself ? Go to, mum,° you are   *excellence / be quiet*
105   he. Graces will appear, and there's an end.[4]
       [*They move aside*]

BEATRICE [*to* BENEDICK]   Will you not tell me who told you so?

BENEDICK   No, you shall pardon me.

BEATRICE   Nor will you not tell me who you are?

BENEDICK   Not now.

110 BEATRICE   That I was disdainful, and that I had my good wit out
      of the Hundred Merry Tales[5]—well, this was Signor Benedick
      that said so.

BENEDICK   What's he?

BEATRICE   I am sure you know him well enough.

115 BENEDICK   Not I, believe me.

BEATRICE   Did he never make you laugh?

BENEDICK   I pray you, what is he?

BEATRICE   Why, he is the Prince's jester, a very dull fool. Only
      his° gift is in devising impossible° slanders. None but libertines   *His only / unbelievable*
120   delight in him, and the commendation is not in his wit but in
      his villainy,° for he both pleases men and angers them, and   *rudeness*
      then they laugh at him, and beat him. I am sure he is in the
      fleet.° I would he had boarded me.[6]   *company (of dancers)*

BENEDICK   When I know the gentleman, I'll tell him what you
125 say.

BEATRICE   Do, do. He'll but break a comparison[7] or two on me,
      which peradventure° not marked, or not laughed at, strikes him   *perhaps*
      into melancholy, and then there's a partridge wing saved, for
      the fool will eat no supper that night.
       Music

130 We must follow the leaders.°   *leaders in the dance*

BENEDICK   In every good thing.

BEATRICE   Nay, if they lead to any ill I will leave them at the
      next turning.
       Dance. Exeunt [*all but* DON JOHN, BORACHIO, *and*
       CLAUDIO]

DON JOHN [*aside to* BORACHIO]   Sure my brother is amorous on
135   Hero, and hath withdrawn her father to break with him about
      it. The ladies follow her, and but one visor° remains.   *(man wearing a) mask*

BORACHIO [*aside to* DON JOHN]   And that is Claudio. I know him
      by his bearing.

DON JOHN   Are not you Signor Benedick?

140 CLAUDIO   You know me well. I am he.

DON JOHN   Signor, you are very near my brother in his love.° He   *favor*
      is enamoured on Hero. I pray you dissuade him from her. She
      is no equal for his birth. You may do the part of an honest man
      in it.

145 CLAUDIO   How know you he loves her?

DON JOHN   I heard him swear his affection.

BORACHIO   So did I, too, and he swore he would marry her
      tonight.

DON JOHN   Come, let us to the banquet.°   *after-dinner sweets*
       Exeunt. Manet° CLAUDIO   *Remains*

---

4. And that is all there is to be said.   7. He'll only try out, or "crack," a satirical comparison
5. A famously bad joke-book, first published in 1526.   (as one "breaks" a lance).
6. Assaulted me like a ship.

150 CLAUDIO Thus answer I in name of Benedick,
But hear these ill news with the ears of Claudio.
'Tis certain° so, the Prince woos for himself.   certainly
Friendship is constant in all other things
Save in the office° and affairs of love.   business
155 Therefore all° hearts in love use their own tongues.   let all
Let every eye negotiate for itself,
And trust no agent; for beauty is a witch
Against whose charms faith° melteth into blood.°   loyalty / passion
This is an accident of hourly proof,[8]
160 Which I mistrusted° not. Farewell, therefore, Hero.   suspected

        Enter BENEDICK

BENEDICK Count Claudio?
CLAUDIO Yea, the same.
BENEDICK Come, will you go with me?
CLAUDIO Whither?
165 BENEDICK Even to the next willow,[9] about your own business,
County.° What fashion will you wear the garland° of? About   Count / (of willow)
your neck, like an usurer's chain?[1] Or under your arm, like a
lieutenant's scarf?[2] You must wear it one° way, for the Prince   some
hath got your Hero.
170 CLAUDIO I wish him joy of her.
BENEDICK Why, that's spoken like an honest drover;° so they sell cattle dealer
bullocks. But did you think the Prince would have served you
thus?
CLAUDIO I pray you leave me.
175 BENEDICK Ho, now you strike like the blind man—'twas the boy
that stole your meat, and you'll beat the post.[3]
CLAUDIO If it° will not be, I'll leave you.   *Exit*   (your departure)
BENEDICK Alas, poor hurt fowl, now will he creep into sedges.[4]
But that my Lady Beatrice should know me, and not know me!
180 The Prince's fool! Ha, it may be I go under that title because I
am merry. Yea, but so I am apt to do myself wrong. I am not so
reputed. It is the base, though bitter, disposition of Beatrice
that puts the world into her person, and so gives me out.[5] Well,
I'll be revenged as I may.

        Enter [DON PEDRO *the*] *Prince*

185 DON PEDRO Now, signor, where's the Count? Did you see him?
BENEDICK Troth, my lord, I have played the part of Lady Fame.°   Lady Rumor
I found him here as melancholy as a lodge in a warren.[6] I told
him—and I think I told him true—that your grace had got the
good will of this young lady, and I offered him my company to
190 a willow tree, either to make him a garland, as being forsaken,
or to bind him up a rod,° as being worthy to be whipped.   bundle of sticks
DON PEDRO To be whipped—what's his fault?
BENEDICK The flat° transgression of a schoolboy who, being   stupid
overjoyed with finding a bird's nest, shows it his companion,
195 and he steals it.

---

8. This is an occurrence demonstrated every hour, common event.
9. Symbol of unrequited love.
1. A gold chain worn by a moneylender.
2. A sash across the chest.
3. Probably alluding to a folktale, which existed in various forms, of a boy who robbed and played a trick on his blind master. *post:* pillar (with play on Benedick as

the "post," or messenger, who bears bad news).
4. *creep into sedges:* hide to nurse his wounds, as an injured bird crawls into the tall grass along a riverbank.
5. It is Beatrice's low but sarcastic disposition that makes her believe the whole world is of her opinion and represents me accordingly.
6. As a burrow in a rabbit warren. (The rabbit was a traditional symbol of melancholy.)

DON PEDRO   Wilt thou make a trust a transgression? The transgression is in the stealer.

BENEDICK   Yet it had not been amiss the rod had been made,
and the garland too, for the garland he might have worn him-
200 self, and the rod he might have bestowed on you, who, as I take
it, have stolen his bird's nest.

DON PEDRO   I will but teach them° to sing, and restore them to   (the chicks)
the owner.

BENEDICK   If their singing answer your saying, by my faith you
205 say honestly.[7]

DON PEDRO   The Lady Beatrice hath a quarrel to° you. The gen-   with
tleman that danced with her told her she is much wronged by
you.

BENEDICK   O, she misused° me past the endurance of a block.   abused
210 An oak but with one green leaf on it[8] would have answered
her. My very visor began to assume life and scold with her.
She told me—not thinking I had been myself—that I was the
Prince's jester, that I was duller than a great thaw,[9] huddling
jest upon jest with such impossible conveyance° upon me that   speed
215 I stood like a man at a mark,° with a whole army shooting at   target
me. She speaks poniards,° and every word stabs. If her breath   daggers
were as terrible as her terminations,° there were no living near   expressions
her, she would infect to the North Star.[1] I would not marry her
though she were endowed with all that Adam had left him
220 before he transgressed. She would have made Hercules have
turned spit, yea, and have cleft his club to make the fire, too.[2]
Come, talk not of her. You shall find her the infernal Ate° in   goddess of discord
good apparel. I would to God some scholar would conjure[3]
her, for certainly, while she is here a man may live as quiet in
225 hell as in a sanctuary, and people sin upon purpose because
they would go thither, so indeed all disquiet, horror, and perturbation follows° her.   attends upon

Enter CLAUDIO *and* BEATRICE, [*and*] LEONATO [*with*]
HERO

DON PEDRO   Look, here she comes.

BENEDICK   Will your grace command me any service to the
230 world's end? I will go on the slightest errand now to the Antipodes that you can devise to send me on. I will fetch you a tooth-
picker° now from the furthest inch of Asia, bring you the length   toothpick
of Prester John's foot, fetch you a hair off the Great Cham's
beard, do you any embassage to the pigmies,[4] rather than hold
235 three words' conference with this harpy.[5] You have no employment for me?

DON PEDRO   None but to desire your good company.

BENEDICK   O God, sir, here's a dish I love not. I cannot endure
my Lady Tongue.   *Exit*

7. If they sing as you say they will—if you have wooed
Hero for Claudio—then you are talking honorably.
8. An oak with barely any life remaining in it.
9. When the muddy roads kept everyone at home.
1. Thought to be the remotest star.
2. The Amazon Omphale made Hercules wear her
clothes and spin; Benedick imagines an even greater
humiliation and more menial duty—turning the spit.
3. Conjure the evil spirits out of, or supernaturally

consign to hell. *scholar:* learned person (who could
speak Latin, the language of exorcism).
4. *Prester John's . . . pigmies:* all distant, fantastic figures. In legend, Prester John ruled in Ethiopia, while
the Great Cham (Kublai Khan) reigned in Mongolia,
and a race of dwarfs was said to inhabit the mountains
of India.
5. Mythical creature with the face and body of a
woman and the wings and claws of a bird of prey.

240 DON PEDRO   Come, lady, come, you have lost the heart of Signor
       Benedick.
    BEATRICE   Indeed, my lord, he lent it me a while, and I gave
       him use° for it, a double heart for his single one. Marry, once   *interest*
       before he won it of ° me, with false dice. Therefore your grace   *from*
245   may well say I have lost it.
    DON PEDRO   You have put him down, lady, you have put him
       down.[6]
    BEATRICE   So I would not he should do me, my lord, lest I
       should prove the mother of fools. I have brought Count Clau-
250   dio, whom you sent me to seek.
    DON PEDRO   Why, how now, Count, wherefore are you sad?
    CLAUDIO   Not sad, my lord.
    DON PEDRO   How then? Sick?
    CLAUDIO   Neither, my lord.
255 BEATRICE   The Count is neither sad, nor sick, nor merry, nor
       well, but civil° count, civil[7] as an orange, and something° of   *serious / somewhat*
       that jealous complexion.[8]
    DON PEDRO   I'faith, lady, I think your blazon° to be true, though   *formal description*
       I'll be sworn, if he be so, his conceit° is false. Here, Claudio, I   *imagined idea*
260   have wooed in thy name, and fair Hero is won. I have broke°   *spoken*
       with her father and his good will obtained. Name the day of
       marriage, and God give thee joy.
    LEONATO   Count, take of me my daughter, and with her my for-
       tunes. His grace hath made the match, and all grace say amen
265   to it.[9]
    BEATRICE   Speak, Count, 'tis your cue.
    CLAUDIO   Silence is the perfectest herald of joy. I were but little
       happy if I could say how much. [*To* HERO] Lady, as you are
       mine, I am yours. I give away myself for you, and dote upon
270   the exchange.
    BEATRICE [*to* HERO]   Speak, cousin. Or, if you cannot, stop his
       mouth with a kiss, and let not him speak, neither.
    DON PEDRO   In faith, lady, you have a merry heart.
    BEATRICE   Yea, my lord, I thank it. Poor fool, it keeps on the
275   windy° side of care.—My cousin tells him in his ear that he is   *windward; safe*
       in her heart.
    CLAUDIO   And so she doth, cousin.
    BEATRICE   Good Lord, for alliance![1] Thus goes everyone to the
       world but I, and I am sunburnt.[2] I may sit in a corner and cry
280   'Heigh-ho for a husband'.[3]
    DON PEDRO   Lady Beatrice, I will get you one.
    BEATRICE   I would rather have one of your father's getting.° Hath   *begetting*
       your grace ne'er a° brother like you? Your father got excellent   *no*
       husbands if a maid could come by them.
285 DON PEDRO   Will you have me, lady?
    BEATRICE   No, my lord, unless I might have another for working

---

6. Humiliated him. (Beatrice, in reply, puns on the
physical sense.)
7. Punning on "Seville," famous for its bitter oranges.
8. Yellow (the traditional color of jealousy).
9. And may God, the source of all grace, confirm it.
1. Kinship through marriage. (Claudio has just

addressed Beatrice as one of the family.)
2. Unattractive, and therefore unlikely to marry.
(Suntans, like dark complexions, were unfashionable.)
goes . . . to the world: gets married.
3. Title of a ballad; probably a catchphrase in Shakespeare's time.

days. Your grace is too costly to wear every day. But I beseech
your grace, pardon me. I was born to speak all mirth and no
matter.°   *substance*

290   DON PEDRO   Your silence most offends me, and to be merry best
becomes you; for out o' question, you were born in a merry
hour.

BEATRICE   No, sure, my lord, my mother cried. But then there
was a star danced, and under that was I born. [*To* HERO *and*

295   CLAUDIO] Cousins, God give you joy.

LEONATO   Niece, will you look to those things I told you of?

BEATRICE   I cry you mercy,° uncle. [*To* DON PEDRO] By your   *I beg your pardon*
grace's pardon.   *Exit* BEATRICE

DON PEDRO   By my troth, a pleasant-spirited lady.

300   LEONATO   There's little of the melancholy element in her, my
lord. She is never sad° but when she sleeps, and not ever° sad   *serious / not always*
then; for I have heard my daughter say she hath often dreamt
of unhappiness and waked herself with laughing.

DON PEDRO   She cannot endure to hear tell of a husband.

305   LEONATO   O, by no means. She mocks all her wooers out of suit.°   *wooing (her)*

DON PEDRO   She were an excellent wife for Benedick.

LEONATO   O Lord, my lord, if they were but a week married they
would talk themselves mad.

DON PEDRO   County Claudio, when mean you to go to church?

310   CLAUDIO   Tomorrow, my lord. Time goes on crutches till love
have all his rites.

LEONATO   Not till Monday, my dear son, which is hence a just
sevennight, and a time too brief, too, to have all things answer°   *match*
my mind.°   *wishes*

315   DON PEDRO   Come, you shake the head at so long a breathing,°   *an interval*
but I warrant° thee, Claudio, the time shall not go dully by us.   *assure*
I will in the interim undertake one of Hercules' labours, which
is to bring Signor Benedick and the Lady Beatrice into a mountain of affection th'one with th'other. I would fain° have it a   *gladly*

320   match, and I doubt not but to fashion it, if you three will but
minister such assistance as I shall give you direction.

LEONATO   My lord, I am for you, though it cost me ten nights'
watchings.°   *staying awake*

CLAUDIO   And I, my lord.

325   DON PEDRO   And you too, gentle Hero?

HERO   I will do any modest office,° my lord, to help my cousin   *task*
to a good husband.

DON PEDRO   And Benedick is not the unhopefullest° husband   *least promising*
that I know. Thus far can I praise him: he is of a noble strain,°   *descent*

330   of approved° valour and confirmed honesty.° I will teach you   *proven / honor*
how to humour your cousin that she shall fall in love with
Benedick, and I, with your two helps, will so practise on°   *so trick*
Benedick that, in despite of his quick wit and his queasy stom-
ach,° he shall fall in love with Beatrice. If we can do this,   *qualms (about love)*

335   Cupid is no longer an archer; his glory shall be ours, for we are
the only love-gods. Go in with me, and I will tell you my drift.°   *scheme*

                                                      Exeunt

2.2

Enter [DON] JOHN *and* BORACHIO

DON JOHN   It is so. The Count Claudio shall marry the daughter
of Leonato.

BORACHIO   Yea, my lord, but I can cross° it.   *thwart*

DON JOHN   Any bar, any cross, any impediment will be medi-
5   cinable° to me. I am sick in displeasure to him, and whatsoever   *medicinal*
comes athwart his affection ranges evenly with mine.[1] How
canst thou cross this marriage?

BORACHIO   Not honestly, my lord, but so covertly that no dishonesty shall appear in me.

10   DON JOHN   Show me briefly how.

BORACHIO   I think I told your lordship a year since how much
I am in the favour of Margaret, the waiting gentlewoman to
Hero.

DON JOHN   I remember.

15   BORACHIO   I can at any unseasonable instant of the night
appoint° her to look out at her lady's chamber window.   *arrange with*

DON JOHN   What life is in that to be the death of this marriage?

BORACHIO   The poison of that lies in you to temper.° Go you to   *concoct*
the Prince your brother. Spare not to tell him that he hath
20   wronged his honour in marrying the renowned Claudio—
whose estimation° do you mightily hold up°—to a contami-   *reputation / esteem*
nated stale,° such a one as Hero.   *prostitute*

DON JOHN   What proof shall I make of that?

BORACHIO   Proof enough to misuse° the Prince, to vex° Claudio,   *deceive / torment*
25   to undo Hero, and kill Leonato. Look you for any other issue?°   *result*

DON JOHN   Only to despite° them I will endeavour anything.   *Merely to spite*

BORACHIO   Go then. Find me a meet hour to draw Don Pedro
and the Count Claudio alone. Tell them that you know that
Hero loves me. Intend° a kind of zeal both to the Prince and   *Pretend*
30   Claudio as in° love of your brother's honour who hath made   *as if for*
this match, and his friend's reputation who is thus like to be
cozened with the semblance of a maid,[2] that you have discovered thus. They will scarcely believe this without trial. Offer
them instances, which shall bear no less likelihood than to see
35   me at her chamber window, hear me call Margaret Hero, hear
Margaret term me Claudio.[3] And bring them to see this the
very night before the intended wedding, for in the mean time
I will so fashion the matter that Hero shall be absent, and there
shall appear such seeming truth of Hero's disloyalty that jeal-
40   ousy shall be called assurance,[4] and all the preparation° over-   *wedding preparation*
thrown.

DON JOHN   Grow this° to what adverse issue it can, I will put it   *Let this lead*
in practice. Be cunning in the working this,° and thy fee is a   *of this*
thousand ducats.°   *gold coins*

45   BORACHIO   Be you constant in the accusation, and my cunning
shall not shame me.

DON JOHN   I will presently go learn their day of marriage.

Exeunt

2.2 Location: Leonato's house.
1. And whatever frustrates his wishes conforms with
mine.
2. To be cheated with the mere appearance of a virgin.

3. Most editors assume an error here and emend to
"Borachio."
4. That suspicion shall be called certainty.

2.3

Enter BENEDICK

BENEDICK Boy!

[*Enter* BOY]

BOY Signor?

BENEDICK In my chamber window lies a book. Bring it hither to
me in the orchard.

5 BOY I am here already,[1] sir.

BENEDICK I know that, but I would have thee hence and here
again.   *Exit* [BOY]

I do much wonder that one man, seeing how much another
man is a fool when he dedicates his behaviours to love, will,

10 after he hath laughed at such shallow follies in others, become
the argument° of his own scorn by falling in love. And such a   subject
man is Claudio. I have known when there was no music with
him but the drum and the fife, and now had he rather hear the
tabor and the pipe.[2] I have known when he would have walked

15 ten mile afoot to see a good armour, and now will he lie ten
nights awake carving° the fashion of a new doublet.° He was   designing / jacket
wont° to speak plain and to the purpose, like an honest man   accustomed
and a soldier, and now is he turned orthography.[3] His words
are a very fantastical° banquet, just so many strange dishes. May   poetic

20 I be so converted, and see° with these eyes? I cannot tell. I   still see
think not. I will not be sworn but love may transform me to an
oyster, but I'll take my oath on it, till he have made an oyster
of me he shall never make me such a fool. One woman is fair,
yet I am well. Another is wise, yet I am well. Another virtuous,

25 yet I am well. But till all graces be in one woman, one woman
shall not come in my grace.° Rich she shall be, that's certain.   favor
Wise, or I'll none.[4] Virtuous, or I'll never cheapen° her. Fair,   bargain for
or I'll never look on her. Mild, or come not near me. Noble, or
not I for an angel.[5] Of good discourse, an excellent musician,

30 and her hair shall be of what colour it please God. Ha! The
Prince and Monsieur Love. I will hide me in the arbour.

[*He hides.*]

Enter [DON PEDRO *the*] *Prince,* LEONATO, *and* CLAUDIO[6]

DON PEDRO Come, shall we hear this music?

CLAUDIO Yea, my good lord. How still the evening is,
As° hushed on purpose to grace harmony.   As if

35 DON PEDRO [*aside*] See you where Benedick hath hid himself?

CLAUDIO [*aside*] O, very well, my lord. The music ended,
We'll fit the hid-fox with a pennyworth.[7]

Enter BALTHASAR *with music*

DON PEDRO Come, Balthasar, we'll hear that song again.

BALTHASAR O good my lord, tax° not so bad a voice   task

40 To slander music any more than once.

DON PEDRO It is the witness still° of excellency   the mark always

---

2.3 Location: Leonato's garden.
1. That is, it's as good as done. (Benedick takes him literally.)
2. The drum and fife were used by the military; the
tabor (a small drum) and pipe were used in social festivities.
3. Become overelaborate in his speech.
4. Or I'll have none (of her).
5. Not I, though she be an angel (punning on coins: an

angel was worth 10 shillings, and a noble 6 shillings 8
pence).
6. Q's stage direction includes "Music," which seems
premature as the singer, Balthasar, enters at line 38.
7. We'll give our sly eavesdropper more than he bargained for. *hid-fox:* apparently refers to the game of
hide-and-seek (compare *Hamlet* 4.2.28: "Hide, fox, and
all after").

To put a strange face on[8] his own perfection.
I pray thee sing, and let me woo° no more.   cajole
BALTHASAR   Because you talk of wooing[9] I will sing,
45   Since many a wooer doth commence his suit
To her he thinks not worthy, yet he woos,
Yet will he swear he loves.
DON PEDRO   Nay pray thee, come;
Or if thou wilt hold longer argument,
Do it in notes.°   music
BALTHASAR   Note this before my notes:
50   There's not a note of mine that's worth the noting.
DON PEDRO   Why, these are very crotchets[1] that he speaks—
Note notes, forsooth, and nothing![2]
[*The accompaniment begins*]
BENEDICK   Now, divine air! Now is his soul ravished. Is it not
strange that sheep's guts[3] should hale° souls out of men's bod-   drag
55   ies? Well, a horn[4] for my money, when all's done.
BALTHASAR [*sings*]
Sigh no more, ladies, sigh no more.
Men were deceivers ever,
One foot in sea, and one on shore,
To one thing constant never.
60   Then sigh not so, but let them go,
And be you blithe and bonny,°   beautiful
Converting all your sounds of woe
Into hey nonny, nonny.

Sing no more ditties, sing no more
65   Of dumps[5] so dull and heavy.
The fraud of men was ever so
Since summer first was leafy.
Then sigh not so, but let them go,
And be you blithe and bonny,
70   Converting all your sounds of woe
Into hey nonny, nonny.

DON PEDRO   By my troth, a good song.
BALTHASAR   And an ill singer, my lord.
DON PEDRO   Ha, no, no, faith. Thou singest well enough for a
75   shift.°   to make do
BENEDICK [*aside*]   An° he had been a dog that should have   If
howled thus, they would have hanged him; and I pray God his
bad voice bode no mischief. I had as lief° have heard the night-   as gladly
raven,° come what plague could have come after it.   bird of ill omen
80   DON PEDRO   Yea, marry,[6] dost thou hear, Balthasar? I pray thee
get us some excellent music, for tomorrow night we would
have it at the Lady Hero's chamber window.

---

8. *To put . . . on:* Not to admit.
9. Because you put it in terms of wooing (and so are
likely to continue to flatter me insincerely).
1. Whimsies; quarter notes (in music).
2. *Note . . . nothing:* Get on with your singing, and
nothing else. ("Nothing" and "noting" sounded the
same in Elizabethan pronunciation. Compare the same

play on words in the title.)
3. Used to string musical instruments.
4. Military or hunting horn.
5. Melancholy tunes or moods.
6. A mild oath. (Don Pedro is continuing the speech
interrupted by Benedick's aside.)

BALTHASAR   The best I can, my lord.   *Exit*

DON PEDRO   Do so. Farewell. Come hither, Leonato. What was
85   it you told me of today, that your niece Beatrice was in love
      with Signor Benedick?

CLAUDIO [*aside*]   O, ay, stalk on, stalk on. The fowl sits.[7]—I did
      never think that lady would have loved any man.

LEONATO   No, nor I neither. But most wonderful° that she   astounding
90   should so dote on Signor Benedick, whom she hath in all out-
      ward behaviours seemed ever to abhor.

BENEDICK [*aside*]   Is't possible? Sits the wind in that corner?

LEONATO   By my troth, my lord, I cannot tell what to think of it.
      But that she loves him with an enraged° affection, it is past the   a frenzied
95   infinite° of thought.   furthest bounds

DON PEDRO   Maybe she doth but counterfeit.

CLAUDIO   Faith, like° enough.   likely

LEONATO   O God! Counterfeit? There was never counterfeit of
      passion came so near the life of passion as she discovers° it.   exhibits

100   DON PEDRO   Why, what effects of passion shows she?

CLAUDIO [*aside*]   Bait the hook well. This fish will bite.

LEONATO   What effects, my lord? She will sit you[8]—you heard
      my daughter tell you how.

CLAUDIO   She did indeed.

105   DON PEDRO   How, how, I pray you? You amaze me. I would have
      thought her spirit had been invincible against all assaults of
      affection.

LEONATO   I would have sworn it had, my lord, especially against
      Benedick.

110   BENEDICK [*aside*]   I should think this a gull,° but that the white-   trick
      bearded fellow speaks it. Knavery cannot, sure, hide himself in
      such reverence.

CLAUDIO [*aside*]   He hath ta'en th'infection. Hold° it up.   Keep

DON PEDRO   Hath she made her affection known to Benedick?

115   LEONATO   No, and swears she never will. That's her torment.

CLAUDIO   'Tis true, indeed, so your daughter says. 'Shall I,' says
      she, 'that have so oft encountered him with scorn, write to him
      that I love him?'

LEONATO   This says she now when she is beginning to write to
120   him, for she'll be up twenty times a night, and there will she sit
      in her smock° till she have writ a sheet of paper. My daughter   slip
      tells us all.

CLAUDIO   Now you talk of a sheet of paper, I remember a pretty
      jest your daughter told us of.

125   LEONATO   O, when she had writ it and was reading it over, she
      found Benedick and Beatrice between the sheet.

CLAUDIO   That.

LEONATO   O, she tore the letter into a thousand halfpence,°   small pieces
      railed at herself that she should be so immodest to write to one
130   that she knew would flout° her. 'I measure him,' says she, 'by   jeer at
      my own spirit, for I should flout him if he writ to me, yea,
      though I love him I should.'

CLAUDIO   Then down upon her knees she falls, weeps, sobs,
      beats her heart, tears her hair, prays, curses, 'O sweet Benedick,
135   God give me patience.'

---

7. *stalk . . . sits:* go on quietly. Our prey has alighted.   8. She will sit down (i.e., weak with lovesickness).

LEONATO She doth indeed, my daughter says so, and the ecstasy° *passion*
hath so much overborne her that my daughter is sometime
afeard she will do a desperate outrage° to herself. It is very true. *injury*

DON PEDRO It were good that Benedick knew of it by some
140 other, if she will not discover° it. *reveal*

CLAUDIO To what end? He would make but a sport of it and
torment the poor lady worse.

DON PEDRO An he should, it were an alms° to hang him. She's *a charitable deed*
an excellent sweet lady, and, out of all suspicion,° she is vir- *doubt*
145 tuous.

CLAUDIO And she is exceeding wise.

DON PEDRO In everything but in loving Benedick.

LEONATO O my lord, wisdom and blood° combating in so tender *passion*
a body, we have ten proofs to one that blood hath the victory. I
150 am sorry for her, as I have just cause, being her uncle and her
guardian.

DON PEDRO I would she had bestowed this dotage° on me. I *infatuation*
would have doffed⁹ all other respects° and made her half *considerations*
myself. I pray you tell Benedick of it, and hear what a° will say. *he*
155 LEONATO Were it good, think you?

CLAUDIO Hero thinks surely she will die, for she says she will die
if he love her not, and she will die ere she make her love
known, and she will die if he woo her, rather than she will
bate° one breath of her accustomed crossness.° *abate / contrariness*
160 DON PEDRO She doth well. If she should make tender° of her *make an offer*
love 'tis very possible he'll scorn it, for the man, as you know
all, hath a contemptible° spirit. *contemptuous*

CLAUDIO He is a very proper° man. *handsome*

DON PEDRO He hath indeed a good outward happiness.¹
165 CLAUDIO Before God; and in my mind, very wise.

DON PEDRO He doth indeed show some sparks that are like wit.

CLAUDIO And I take him to be valiant.

DON PEDRO As Hector,² I assure you; and in the managing of
quarrels you may say he is wise, for either he avoids them with
170 great discretion or undertakes them with a most Christianlike
fear.

LEONATO If he do fear God, a must necessarily keep peace. If
he break the peace, he ought to enter into a quarrel with fear
and trembling.
175 DON PEDRO And so will he do, for the man doth fear God, howsoever it seems not in him by some large° jests he will make. *broad*
Well, I am sorry for your niece. Shall we go seek Benedick and
tell him of her love?

CLAUDIO Never tell him, my lord. Let her wear it out with good
180 counsel.° *advice*

LEONATO Nay, that's impossible. She may wear her heart out
first.

DON PEDRO Well, we will hear further of it by° your daughter. *from*
Let it cool the while. I love Benedick well, and I could wish he
185 would modestly examine himself to see how much he is unworthy so good a lady.

9. Set aside or cast off.   2. The noblest and bravest Trojan warrior.
1. He is well endowed with looks and bearing.

LEONATO My lord, will you walk? Dinner is ready.

CLAUDIO [*aside*] If he do not dote on her upon this, I will never trust my expectation.°   predictions

190 DON PEDRO [*aside*] Let there be the same net spread for her, and that must your daughter and her gentlewomen carry.° The   manage sport will be when they hold one an opinion of another's dotage, and no such matter.³ That's the scene that I would see, which will be merely a dumb show.⁴ Let us send her to call

195 him in to dinner.

                    Exeunt [DON PEDRO, CLAUDIO, *and* LEONATO]

BENEDICK [*coming forward*] This can be no trick. The conference was sadly borne.° They have the truth of this from Hero.   seriously conducted They seem to pity the lady. It seems her affections have their full bent.⁵ Love me! Why, it must be requited. I hear how I am

200 censured. They say I will bear myself proudly if I perceive the love come from her. They say too that she will rather die than give any sign of affection. I did never think to marry. I must not seem proud. Happy are they that hear their detractions and can put them to mending.° They say the lady is fair. 'Tis a truth, I   amending

205 can bear them witness. And virtuous—'tis so, I cannot reprove°   contradict it. And wise, but for loving me. By my troth, it is no addition to her wit⁶—nor no great argument of her folly, for I will be horribly in love with her. I may chance have some odd quirks° and   quips remnants of wit broken on° me because I have railed so long   cracked against

210 against marriage; but doth not the appetite alter? A man loves the meat in his youth that he cannot endure in his age. Shall quips and sentences° and these paper bullets of the brain awe   epigrams a man from the career° of his humour?° No. The world must   swift course / liking be peopled. When I said I would die a bachelor, I did not think

215 I should live till I were married. Here comes Beatrice.

                    Enter BEATRICE

By this day, she's a fair lady. I do spy some marks of love in her.

BEATRICE Against my will I am sent to bid you come in to dinner.

BENEDICK Fair Beatrice, I thank you for your pains.

220 BEATRICE I took no more pains for those thanks than you take pains to thank me. If it had been painful I would not have come.

BENEDICK You take pleasure, then, in the message?

BEATRICE Yea, just so much as you may take upon a knife's

225 point and choke a daw withal.° You have no stomach,° signor?   jackdaw with / appetite Fare you well.   *Exit*

BENEDICK Ha! 'Against my will I am sent to bid you come in to dinner.' There's a double meaning in that. 'I took no more pains for those thanks than you took pains to thank me.' That's

230 as much as to say 'Any pains that I take for you is as easy as thanks.'—If I do not take pity of her I am a villain. If I do not love her I am a Jew.⁷ I will go get her picture.⁸   *Exit*

---

3. *when . . . matter:* when each believes that the other is madly in love, without any basis in fact.
4. A pantomime (because words for once will fail them).
5. Are stretched to the limit (like a bent bow).

6. No additional proof of her intelligence.
7. That is, lacking in Christian charity (an anti-Semitic stereotype).
8. *get her picture:* have her portrait painted (for a love locket) or sketch it himself.

3.1

Enter HERO *and two gentlewomen,* MARGARET *and*
URSULA

HERO   Good Margaret, run thee to the parlour.
There shalt thou find my cousin Beatrice
Proposing° with the Prince and Claudio.   Talking
Whisper her ear, and tell her I and Ursula
5   Walk in the orchard, and our whole discourse
Is all of her. Say that thou overheard'st us,
And bid her steal into the pleachèd¹ bower
Where honeysuckles, ripened by the sun,
Forbid the sun to enter—like favourites
10   Made proud by princes, that advance their pride
Against that power that bred it.² There will she hide her
To listen° our propose.° This is thy office.   hear / conversation
Bear thee well in it, and leave us alone.
MARGARET   I'll make her come, I warrant you, presently. [*Exit*]
15   HERO   Now, Ursula, when Beatrice doth come,
As we do trace° this alley up and down   pace
Our talk must only be of Benedick.
When I do name him, let it be thy part
To praise him more than ever man did merit.
20   My talk to thee must be how Benedick
Is sick in love with Beatrice. Of this matter
Is little Cupid's crafty arrow made,
That only wounds by hearsay.³
         Enter BEATRICE
                                 Now begin,
For look where Beatrice like a lapwing⁴ runs
25   Close by the ground to hear our conference.
URSULA   The pleasant'st angling is to see the fish
Cut with her golden oars the silver stream
And greedily devour the treacherous bait.
So angle we for Beatrice, who even now
30   Is couchèd° in the woodbine coverture.⁵   hidden
Fear you not my part of the dialogue.
HERO   Then go we near her, that her ear lose nothing
Of the false-sweet bait that we lay for it.—
         [*They approach Beatrice's hiding-place*]
No, truly, Ursula, she is too disdainful.
35   I know her spirits are as coy° and wild   disdainful; shy
As haggards° of the rock.   wild female hawks
URSULA   But are you sure
That Benedick loves Beatrice so entirely?
HERO   So says the Prince and my new trothèd lord.
URSULA   And did they bid you tell her of it, madam?
40   HERO   They did entreat me to acquaint her of it,
But I persuaded them, if they loved Benedick,
To wish him wrestle with affection
And never to let Beatrice know of it.
URSULA   Why did you so? Doth not the gentleman

3.1 Location: Leonato's garden.
1. Screened by intertwining branches.
2. *that advance . . . it*: who presumptuously oppose the
power that created them.

3. Wounds by rumor or gossip.
4. A peewit, a bird that scuttles along the ground.
5. In the honeysuckle arbor.

45   Deserve as full° as fortunate a bed   *fully*
           As ever Beatrice shall couch upon?

HERO   O god of love! I know he doth deserve
           As much as may be yielded to a man.
           But nature never framed a woman's heart

50   Of prouder stuff than that of Beatrice.
           Disdain and scorn ride sparkling in her eyes,
           Misprising° what they look on, and her wit   *Despising*
           Values itself so highly that to her
           All matter else seems° weak. She cannot love,   *other matters seem*

55   Nor take no shape nor project of affection,[6]
           She is so self-endearèd.

URSULA   Sure, I think so.
           And therefore certainly it were not good
           She knew his love, lest she'll make sport at it.

HERO   Why, you speak truth. I never yet saw man,

60   How° wise, how noble, young, how rarely° featured,   *However / finely*
           But she would spell him backward.[7] If fair-faced,
           She would swear the gentleman should be her sister.
           If black,° why nature, drawing of an antic,°   *dark / a buffoon*
           Made a foul blot.° If tall, a lance ill headed;   *error*

65   If low, an agate[8] very vilely cut;
           If speaking, why, a vane blown with all winds;
           If silent, why, a block movèd with° none.   *by*
           So turns she every man the wrong side out,
           And never gives to truth and virtue that

70   Which simpleness° and merit purchaseth.°   *integrity / deserve*

URSULA   Sure, sure, such carping is not commendable.

HERO   No, not to be so odd and from all fashions[9]
           As Beatrice is cannot be commendable.
           But who dare tell her so? If I should speak

75   She would mock me into air, O, she would laugh me
           Out of myself, press me to death[1] with wit.
           Therefore let Benedick, like covered fire,
           Consume away in sighs,[2] waste inwardly.
           It were a better death than die with mocks,

80   Which is as bad as die with tickling.

URSULA   Yet tell her of it, hear what she will say.

HERO   No. Rather I will go to Benedick
           And counsel him to fight against his passion.
           And truly, I'll devise some honest° slanders   *harmless*

85   To stain my cousin with. One doth not know
           How much an ill word may empoison liking.

URSULA   O, do not do your cousin such a wrong.
           She cannot be so much without true judgement,
           Having so swift and excellent a wit

90   As she is prized° to have, as to refuse   *esteemed*
           So rare a gentleman as Signor Benedick.

---

6. *Nor take . . . affection:* Nor form the image or even the concept of love.
7. She would speak of his virtues as faults.
8. Tiny figures were carved in agates and used as seals or in rings.
9. *from all fashions:* contrary to normal behavior.

1. Crushing weights were loaded upon accused criminals who refused to enter a plea; Hero suggests that she will be silenced with mockery and then mocked for her silence.
2. Each sigh was said to draw a drop of blood from the heart.

HERO   He is the only man of Italy,
    Always excepted my dear Claudio.

URSULA   I pray you be not angry with me, madam,
95   Speaking my fancy. Signor Benedick,
    For shape, for bearing, argument,[3] and valour
    Goes foremost in report through Italy.

HERO   Indeed, he hath an excellent good name.

URSULA   His excellence did earn it ere he had it.
100   When are you married, madam?

HERO   Why, every day, tomorrow.[4] Come, go in.
    I'll show thee some attires and have thy counsel
    Which is the best to furnish me tomorrow.

URSULA [*aside*]   She's limed,[5] I warrant you. We have caught
105   her, madam.

HERO [*aside*]   If it prove so, then loving goes by haps.°   *chance*
    Some Cupid kills with arrows, some with traps.

                    Exeunt [HERO *and* URSULA]

BEATRICE [*coming forward*]   What fire is in mine ears?[6] Can this be true?
    Stand I condemned for pride and scorn so much?
110   Contempt, farewell; and maiden pride, adieu.
    No glory lives behind the back of such.[7]
    And, Benedick, love on. I will requite thee,
    Taming my wild heart to thy loving hand.[8]
    If thou dost love, my kindness shall incite thee
115   To bind our loves up in a holy band.
    For others say thou dost deserve, and I
    Believe it better than reportingly.°   *Exit*   *than as mere rumor*

3.2

Enter [DON PEDRO *the*] *Prince,* CLAUDIO, BENEDICK,
    and LEONATO

DON PEDRO   I do but stay till your marriage be consummate, and
    then go I toward Aragon.

CLAUDIO   I'll bring° you thither, my lord, if you'll vouchsafe° me.   *accompany / allow*

DON PEDRO   Nay, that would be as great a soil in the new gloss
5   of your marriage as to show a child his new coat and forbid
    him to wear it. I will only be bold with° Benedick for his com-   *only ask*
    pany, for from the crown of his head to the sole of his foot he
    is all mirth. He hath twice or thrice cut Cupid's bow-string,
    and the little hangman° dare not shoot at him. He hath a heart   *rogue; executioner*
10   as sound as a bell, and his tongue is the clapper, for what his
    heart thinks his tongue speaks.

BENEDICK   Gallants, I am not as I have been.

LEONATO   So say I. Methinks you are sadder.°   *more serious*

CLAUDIO   I hope he be in love.
15
DON PEDRO   Hang him, truant! There's no true drop of blood
    in him to be truly touched with love. If he be sad, he wants°   *lacks*
    money.

---

3. Intellect and rhetorical skill.
4. From tomorrow on, I shall be a married woman
every day.
5. Snared with birdlime, a glue spread on branches to
catch birds.
6. Proverbially, if others were talking about you else-

where, your ears would burn.
7. No one praises such people behind their backs.
8. In falconry, the bird is tamed by the hand of the falconer.
3.2 Location: Leonato's house.

BENEDICK   I have the toothache.[1]

DON PEDRO   Draw° it.   *Extract*

20 BENEDICK   Hang it.

CLAUDIO   You must hang it first and draw it afterwards.[2]

DON PEDRO   What? Sigh for the toothache?

LEONATO   Where is but a humour[3] or a worm.

BENEDICK   Well, everyone can master a grief but he that has it.

25 CLAUDIO   Yet say I he is in love.

DON PEDRO   There is no appearance of fancy° in him, unless it   *love*
be a fancy that he hath to strange disguises, as to be a Dutchman today, a Frenchman tomorrow, or in the shape of two
countries at once, as a German from the waist downward, all
30 slops,° and a Spaniard from the hip upward, no doublet.[4]   *baggy breeches*
Unless he have a fancy to this foolery, as it appears he hath, he
is no fool for fancy, as you would have it appear he is.

CLAUDIO   If he be not in love with some woman there is no
believing old° signs. A° brushes his hat o' mornings, what should *time-honored / He*
35 that bode?

DON PEDRO   Hath any man seen him at the barber's?

CLAUDIO   No, but the barber's man hath been seen with him,
and the old ornament of his cheek hath already stuffed tennis balls.[5]

40 LEONATO   Indeed, he looks younger than he did by the loss of a
beard.

DON PEDRO   Nay, a rubs himself with civet.° Can you smell him   *perfume*
out[6] by that?

CLAUDIO   That's as much as to say the sweet youth's in love.

45 DON PEDRO   The greatest note of it is his melancholy.

CLAUDIO   And when was he wont to wash[7] his face?

DON PEDRO   Yea, or to paint himself?—for the which I hear what
they say of him.

CLAUDIO   Nay, but his jesting spirit, which is now crept into a
50 lute-string, and now governed by stops.[8]

DON PEDRO   Indeed, that tells a heavy tale for him. Conclude,
conclude, he is in love.

CLAUDIO   Nay, but I know who loves him.

DON PEDRO   That would I know, too. I warrant, one that knows
55 him not.

CLAUDIO   Yes, and his ill conditions,° and in despite of all, dies   *qualities*
for him.

DON PEDRO   She shall be buried with her face upwards.[9]

BENEDICK   Yet is this no charm for the toothache. Old signor,
60 walk aside with me. I have studied eight or nine wise words to
speak to you which these hobby-horses° must not hear.   *clowns*

                    [*Exeunt* BENEDICK *and* LEONATO]

DON PEDRO   For° my life, to break° with him about Beatrice.   *Upon / speak*

---

1. Toothaches supposedly plagued lovers.
2. *hang it*: a mild expletive (like "darn it"). Claudio
plays on the notion of hanging criminals, who were
then cut down and "drawn" (disemboweled).
3. Poisonous fluid in the body (which, along with
worms, was thought to be the cause of toothache).
4. His doublet is covered with a Spanish cloak.
5. Benedick has shaved off his beard. Tennis balls were
stuffed with hair.
6. Detect his secret (with play on literal "smell").

7. When was he accustomed to use cosmetics on (compare "paint" in following line).
8. Frets on a lute's fingerboard; restraints. (Lutes were
associated with lovers' serenades.)
9. That is, in Benedick's arms, where she will die (Elizabethan slang for "orgasm") in the act of love; perhaps a
joking reversal of the idea that as one responsible for
her own fate, she should be buried, like a suicide, with
her face downward.

CLAUDIO 'Tis even so. Hero and Margaret[1] have by this° played   *now*
    their parts with Beatrice, and then the two bears will not bite
65 one another when they meet.

       Enter [DON] JOHN *the bastard*

DON JOHN My lord, and brother, God save you.
DON PEDRO Good-e'en,° brother.   *Good evening*
DON JOHN If your leisure served I would speak with you.
DON PEDRO In private?
70 DON JOHN If it please you. Yet Count Claudio may hear, for
    what I would speak of concerns him.
DON PEDRO What's the matter?
DON JOHN [*to* CLAUDIO] Means your lordship to be married
    tomorrow?
75 DON PEDRO You know he does.
DON JOHN I know not that when he knows what I know.
CLAUDIO If there be any impediment, I pray you discover° it.   *reveal*
DON JOHN You may think I love you not. Let that appear here-
    after, and aim better at° me by that I now will manifest. For my   *think better of*
80 brother, I think he holds you well° and in dearness° of heart   *in high respect / affection*
    hath holp° to effect your ensuing marriage—surely suit ill   *helped*
    spent, and labour ill bestowed.
DON PEDRO Why, what's the matter?
DON JOHN I came hither to tell you, and, circumstances short-
85 ened°—for she has been too long a-talking of[2]—the lady is   *put simply*
    disloyal.°   *unfaithful*
CLAUDIO Who, Hero?
DON JOHN Even she. Leonato's Hero, your Hero, every man's
    Hero.
90 CLAUDIO Disloyal?
DON JOHN The word is too good to paint out° her wickedness. I   *fully describe*
    could say she were worse. Think you of a worse title, and I will
    fit her to it. Wonder not till further warrant.° Go but with me   *evidence*
    tonight, you shall see her chamber window entered, even the
95 night before her wedding day. If you love her then, tomorrow
    wed her. But it would better fit your honour to change your
    mind.
CLAUDIO May this be so?
DON PEDRO I will not think it.
100 DON JOHN If you dare not trust that you see, confess not that you
    know.[3] If you will follow me I will show you enough, and when
    you have seen more and heard more, proceed accordingly.
CLAUDIO If I see anything tonight why I should not marry her,
    tomorrow, in the congregation where I should wed, there will
105 I shame her.
DON PEDRO And as I wooed for thee to obtain her, I will join
    with thee to disgrace her.
DON JOHN I will disparage her no farther till you are my wit-
    nesses. Bear it coldly° but till midnight, and let the issue show   *calmly*
110 itself.
DON PEDRO O day untowardly turned!°   *miserably changed*
CLAUDIO O mischief strangely thwarting!

---

1. Ursula and Hero played the trick on Beatrice with
help from Margaret.
2. For we have already talked about her too much.

3. If you won't risk seeing for yourself, don't claim to
know.

DON JOHN   O plague right well prevented!—So will you say
when you have seen the sequel.   *Exeunt*

3.3

Enter DOGBERRY *and his compartner* [VERGES], *with the*
WATCH[1]

DOGBERRY   Are you good men and true?

VERGES   Yea, or else it were pity but they should suffer salvation,[2]
body and soul.

DOGBERRY   Nay, that were a punishment too good for them if
5   they should have any allegiance° in them, being chosen for the   *(for "disloyalty")*
Prince's watch.

VERGES   Well, give them their charge,° neighbour Dogberry.   *instructions*

DOGBERRY   First, who think you the most desertless° man to be   *(for "deserving")*
constable?[3]

10   SECOND WATCHMAN   Hugh Oatcake, sir, or George Seacoal, for
they can write and read.

DOGBERRY   Come hither, neighbour Seacoal, God hath blest
you with a good name.[4] To be a well-favoured° man is the gift   *good-looking*
of fortune, but to write and read comes by nature.

15   FIRST WATCHMAN   Both which, Master Constable—

DOGBERRY   You have. I knew it would be your answer. Well, for
your favour,° sir, why, give God thanks, and make no boast of   *looks*
it. And for your writing and reading, let that appear when there
is no need of such vanity. You are thought here to be the most
20   senseless° and fit man for the constable of the watch, therefore   *(for "sensible")*
bear you the lantern. This is your charge: you shall compre-
hend all vagrom[5] men. You are to bid any man stand,° in the   *stop*
Prince's name.

FIRST WATCHMAN   How if a will not stand?

25   DOGBERRY   Why then take no note of him, but let him go, and
presently° call the rest of the watch together, and thank God   *immediately*
you are rid of a knave.

VERGES   If he will not stand when he is bidden he is none of the
Prince's subjects.

30   DOGBERRY   True, and they are to meddle with none but the
Prince's subjects.—You shall also make no noise in the streets,
for for the watch to babble and to talk is most tolerable° and   *(for "intolerable")*
not to be endured.

A WATCHMAN   We will rather sleep than talk. We know what
35   belongs° to a watch.   *is appropriate*

DOGBERRY   Why, you speak like an ancient° and most quiet   *experienced*
watchman, for I cannot see how sleeping should offend. Only
have a care that your bills[6] be not stolen. Well, you are to call
at all the alehouses and bid those that are drunk get them to
40   bed.

A WATCHMAN   How if they will not?

DOGBERRY   Why then, let them alone till they are sober. If they

---

3.3   Location: A street.
1. Watchmen who patrolled the streets, proclaiming the
hour and performing police duties. "Verges" probably
alludes to a "verge," or wand of office, carried by officials.
2. For "damnation." (Verges and Dogberry repeatedly
say the opposite of what they mean.)
3. The leader of the Watch. (Dogberry himself is the

parish constable.) Q's speech prefixes are confusing in
this scene, making it difficult to identify the leader of
the Watch; some of them have been rearranged.
4. Sea coal from Newcastle was known for its high
quality (thus the "good name").
5. For "vagrant." *comprehend*: for "apprehend."
6. Weapons (long shafts with blades or ax heads).

make you not then the better answer, you may say they are not
the men you took them for.

45 A WATCHMAN Well, sir.

DOGBERRY If you meet a thief you may suspect him, by virtue of
your office, to be no true° man; and for such kind of men, the
less you meddle or make° with them why, the more is° for your
honesty.

honest
have to do / better it is

50 A WATCHMAN If we know him to be a thief, shall we not lay
hands on him?

DOGBERRY Truly, by your office you may, but I think they that
touch pitch will be defiled.[7] The most peaceable way for you if
you do take a thief is to let him show himself what he is, and

55 steal out of your company.

VERGES You have been always called a merciful man, partner.

DOGBERRY Truly, I would not hang a dog by my will, much
more° a man who hath any honesty in him.

(for "less")

VERGES If you hear a child cry in the night you must call to the
60 nurse and bid her still° it.

calm

A WATCHMAN How if the nurse be asleep and will not hear us?

DOGBERRY Why then, depart in peace and let the child wake
her with crying, for the ewe that will not hear her lamb when
it baes will never answer a calf° when he bleats.

blockhead

65 VERGES 'Tis very true.

DOGBERRY This is the end of the charge. You, constable, are to
present° the Prince's own person.[8] If you meet the Prince in the
night you may stay° him.

represent
stop

VERGES Nay, by'r Lady, that I think a cannot.

70 DOGBERRY Five shillings to one on't with any man that knows
the statutes he may stay him. Marry, not without° the Prince
be willing, for indeed the watch ought to offend no man, and
it is an offence to stay a man against his will.

unless

VERGES By'r Lady, I think it be so.

75 DOGBERRY Ha ha ha! Well, masters, good night. An there be
any matter of weight chances,° call up me. Keep your fellows'
counsels, and your own, and good night. Come, neighbour.

that occurs

FIRST WATCHMAN Well, masters, we hear our charge. Let us go
sit here upon the church bench till two, and then all to bed.

80 DOGBERRY One word more, honest neighbours. I pray you
watch about Signor Leonato's door, for the wedding being
there tomorrow, there is a great coil° tonight. Adieu. Be vigi-
tant,° I beseech you.

to-do, bustle
(for "vigilant")

Exeunt [DOGBERRY *and* VERGES. *The* WATCH *sit*]
Enter BORACHIO *and* CONRAD

BORACHIO What, Conrad!

85 FIRST WATCHMAN [*aside*] Peace; stir not.

BORACHIO Conrad, I say.

CONRAD Here, man, I am at thy elbow.

BORACHIO Mass,° an my elbow itched,[9] I thought there would a
scab[1] follow.

By the mass

7. A proverbial saying, derived from the Apocryphal
book of Ecclesiasticus (13:1).
8. Dogberry presents a parodic version of the notion
that the monarch's authority was in theory separable
from his person (others could represent that authority

when he was physically absent).
9. Proverbially, itching elbows alerted you against
shady company.
1. Contemptible person; punning on a literal "scab."

90 CONRAD I will owe thee an answer for that. And now, forward
with thy tale.

BORACHIO Stand thee close, then, under this penthouse,° for it   *overhanging structure*
drizzles rain, and I will, like a true drunkard, utter[2] all to thee.

A WATCHMAN [*aside*] Some treason, masters. Yet stand close.°   *keep hidden*

95 BORACHIO Therefore, know I have earned of Don John a thousand ducats.

CONRAD Is it possible that any villainy should be so dear?°   *valuable*

BORACHIO Thou shouldst rather ask if it were possible any villainy should be so rich. For when rich villains have need of

100 poor ones, poor ones may make what price they will.

CONRAD I wonder at it.

BORACHIO That shows thou art unconfirmed.° Thou knowest   *inexperienced*
that the fashion of a doublet, or a hat, or a cloak is nothing to[3]
a man.

105 CONRAD Yes, it is apparel.

BORACHIO I mean the fashion.

CONRAD Yes, the fashion is the fashion.

BORACHIO Tush, I may as well say the fool's the fool. But seest
thou not what a deformed° thief[4] this fashion is?   *deforming*

110 A WATCHMAN [*aside*] I know that Deformed. A° has been a vile   *He*
thief this seven year. A goes up and down° like a gentleman. I   *struts here and there*
remember his name.

BORACHIO Didst thou not hear somebody?

CONRAD No, 'twas the vane on the house.

115 BORACHIO Seest thou not, I say, what a deformed thief this fashion is, how giddily a turns about all the hot-bloods° between   *dandies*
fourteen and five-and-thirty, sometimes fashioning them like
Pharaoh's soldiers in the reechy° painting,[5] sometime like god   *grimy*
Bel's[6] priests in the old church window, sometime like the

120 shaven Hercules[7] in the smirched, worm-eaten tapestry, where
his codpiece[8] seems as massy as his club?

CONRAD All this I see, and I see that the fashion wears out more
apparel than the man.[9] But art not thou thyself giddy with the
fashion, too, that thou hast shifted[1] out of thy tale into telling

125 me of the fashion?

BORACHIO Not so, neither. But know that I have tonight wooed
Margaret, the Lady Hero's gentlewoman, by the name of Hero.
She leans me° out at her mistress' chamber window, bids me a   *leans*
thousand times good night—I tell this tale vilely, I should first

130 tell thee how the Prince, Claudio, and my master, planted and
placed and possessed[2] by my master, Don John, saw afar off in
the orchard this amiable° encounter.   *loving*

CONRAD And thought they Margaret was Hero?

BORACHIO Two of them did, the Prince and Claudio, but the

135 devil my master knew she was Margaret, and partly by his oaths,

---

2. The drunken Borachio, whose name means "drunkard," alludes to the Latin tag *in vino veritas*.
3. Tells us nothing about (but Conrad takes him to
mean "means nothing to").
4. Used here to mean "rogue"—but also that keeping
up with fashion robs men of their money.
5. Perhaps refers to a painting of the fleeing Israelites
pursued by Pharaoh's army.
6. Bel (Baal) was a Babylonian god who had seventy
priests. His story, told in the biblical Apocrypha, is

sometimes depicted in stained-glass windows.
7. Probably referring to the story of Omphale (compare
2.1.220), or perhaps confusing Hercules with Samson.
8. Pouch, often stuffed and ornamented, worn over a
man's breeches, covering the genitals.
9. *fashion . . . man*: fashions change before clothes
wear out.
1. Punning on "changed clothes."
2. Informed; but, perhaps also, controlled (as by the
devil).

which first possessed them, partly by the dark night, which did
deceive them, but chiefly by my villainy, which did confirm
any slander that Don John had made, away went Claudio
enraged, swore he would meet her as he was appointed next
140   morning at the temple,° and there, before the whole congrega-   *church*
tion, shame her with what he saw o'ernight, and send her home
again without a husband.

FIRST WATCHMAN [*coming forward*]   We charge you in the
Prince's name. Stand.

145   A WATCHMAN   Call up the right³ Master Constable. We have here
recovered the most dangerous piece of lechery⁴ that ever was
known in the commonwealth.

FIRST WATCHMAN   And one Deformed is one of them. I know
him—a wears a lock.⁵

150   CONRAD   Masters, masters!

A WATCHMAN   You'll be made bring Deformed forth, I warrant
you.

CONRAD   Masters—

A WATCHMAN   Never speak. We charge you. Let us obey° you to   *(for "compel")*
155   go with us.

BORACHIO [*to* CONRAD]   We are like to prove a goodly° commod-   *fine (ironic)*
ity, being taken up of these men's bills.⁶

CONRAD   A commodity in question,⁷ I warrant you. Come, we'll
obey you.   *Exeunt*

3.4

Enter HERO, MARGARET, *and* URSULA

HERO   Good Ursula, wake my cousin Beatrice, and desire her to
rise.

URSULA   I will, lady.

HERO   And bid her come hither.

5   URSULA   Well.°   [*Exit*]   *Very well*

MARGARET   Troth, I think your other rebato° were better.   *stiffly wired ruff*

HERO   No, pray thee, good Meg, I'll wear this.

MARGARET   By my troth, 's° not so good, and I warrant° your   *it's / am sure*
cousin will say so.

10   HERO   My cousin's a fool, and thou art another: I'll wear none
but this.

MARGARET   I like the new tire° within excellently, if the hair were   *headdress with wig*
a thought browner. And your gown's a most rare fashion, i'faith.
I saw the Duchess of Milan's gown that they praise so.

15   HERO   O, that exceeds,° they say.   *surpasses all*

MARGARET   By my troth, 's but a night-gown° in respect of yours—   *dressing gown*
cloth o' gold, and cuts, and laced with silver, set with pearls,
down sleeves, side sleeves, and skirts round underborne with a
bluish tinsel.¹ But for a fine, quaint,° graceful, and excellent   *elegant*
20   fashion, yours is worth ten on't.

---

3. Respectfully, as in "right worshipful."
4. For "treachery." *recovered:* for "discovered."
5. A "lovelock," or curl of hair, worn by courtiers.
6. *being . . . bills:* a multiple pun: after we have been
hoisted on their halberds (weapons); been arrested on
their warrants; been obtained on credit ("taken up") in
exchange for their bonds ("bills").
7. Of doubtful value; about to be judicially interrogated.

3.4 Location: Leonato's house.
1. *cloth . . . tinsel:* made of silk or woolen cloth interwoven with gold thread, with ornamental slashes
("cuts") showing the fabric beneath, and decorated
with silver embroidery or lace and with pearls; with fitted ("down") sleeves and another pair that hung open
from the shoulder; trimmed at the hem or fully lined
("underborne") with another kind of metallic fabric.

HERO   God give me joy to wear it, for my heart is exceeding
   heavy.

MARGARET   'Twill be heavier soon by the weight of a man.

HERO   Fie upon thee, art not ashamed?

25 MARGARET   Of what, lady? Of speaking honourably? Is not marriage honourable in° a beggar? Is not your lord honourable   *even in*
   without marriage? I think you would have me say 'saving your
   reverence,² a husband'. An° bad thinking do not wrest° true   *If / pervert*
   speaking, I'll offend nobody. Is there any harm in 'the heavier
30   for a husband'? None, I think, an it be the right husband and
   the right wife—otherwise 'tis light° and not heavy. Ask my Lady   *licentious*
   Beatrice else. Here she comes.

      Enter BEATRICE

HERO   Good morrow, coz.

BEATRICE   Good morrow, sweet Hero.

35 HERO   Why, how now? Do you speak in the sick tune?

BEATRICE   I am out of all other tune, methinks.

MARGARET   Clap 's° into 'Light o' love'. That goes without a bur-   *Let us shift*
   den.³ Do you sing it, and I'll dance it.

BEATRICE   Ye light o' love with your heels.⁴ Then if your hus-
40   band have stables enough, you'll see he shall lack no barns.⁵

MARGARET   O illegitimate construction!⁶ I scorn that with my
   heels.⁷

BEATRICE [*to* HERO]   'Tis almost five o'clock, cousin. 'Tis time
   you were ready. By my troth, I am exceeding ill. Heigh-ho!

45 MARGARET   For a hawk, a horse,⁸ or a husband?

BEATRICE   For the letter that begins them all—h.⁹

MARGARET   Well, an you be not turned Turk,¹ there's no more
   sailing by the star.²

BEATRICE   What means the fool, trow?°   *I wonder*

50 MARGARET   Nothing, I. But God send everyone their heart's
   desire.

HERO   These gloves the Count sent me, they are an excellent
   perfume.³

BEATRICE   I am stuffed,⁴ cousin. I cannot smell.

55 MARGARET   A maid, and stuffed! There's goodly catching of cold.

BEATRICE   O, God help me, God help me. How long have you
   professed apprehension?°   *claimed to be witty*

MARGARET   Ever since you left it. Doth not my wit become me
   rarely?°   *excellently*

60 BEATRICE   It is not seen enough. You should wear it in your cap.⁵
   By my troth, I am sick.

MARGARET   Get you some of this distilled *carduus benedictus,*⁶
   and lay it to your heart. It is the only thing for a qualm.°   *sudden faintness*

HERO   There thou prickest her with a thistle.

2. A polite expression of apology (as if "husband" were
an offensive term).
3. Bass part (for a man's voice), with play on heavy
"weight of a man." "Light o' Love" was a popular tune.
4. *Ye . . . heels:* Your dancing toys with love ("light-
heeled" was slang for "promiscuous").
5. Punning on "bairns," children.
6. A multiple pun: forced interpretation; making of
bastards; illegal building (of stables and barns).
7. I kick that away (reject it).
8. Responding to Beatrice's ostentatious sigh as a
hunting cry.

9. Punningly: "ache" was pronounced in the same way.
1. If you have not reneged (on your vows against marriage). "To turn Turk" is, in the Christian proverb, to
become a renegade (by going over to the enemy, the
Muslim Turks).
2. No more navigating by the polestar. (No truths can
be trusted from now on.)
3. Perfumed gloves were fashionable.
4. In the nose; Margaret follows with an obscene pun.
5. Like the coxcomb of a professional fool.
6. Holy thistle, or blessed thistle (a medicinal herb
good for the heart).

65   BEATRICE   Benedictus—why Benedictus? You have some moral[7]
in this Benedictus.

MARGARET   Moral? No, by my troth, I have no moral meaning. I
meant plain holy-thistle. You may think perchance° that I think   *perhaps*
you are in love. Nay, by'r Lady, I am not such a fool to think
70   what I list,° nor I list not to think what I can, nor indeed I   *please*
cannot think, if I would think my heart out of thinking, that
you are in love, or that you will be in love, or that you can be in
love. Yet Benedick was such another,[8] and now is he become a
man. He swore he would never marry, and yet now in despite
75   of his heart he eats his meat without grudging.[9] And how you
may be converted I know not, but methinks you look with your
eyes, as other women do.

BEATRICE   What pace is this that thy tongue keeps?

MARGARET   Not a false gallop.[1]

Enter URSULA

80   URSULA [*to* HERO]   Madam, withdraw. The Prince, the Count,
Signor Benedick, Don John, and all the gallants of the town
are come to fetch you to church.

HERO   Help to dress me, good coz, good Meg, good Ursula.

Exeunt

3.5

Enter LEONATO, *and* [DOGBERRY] *the constable, and*
[VERGES] *the headborough*°   *local constable*

LEONATO   What would you with me, honest neighbour?

DOGBERRY   Marry, sir, I would have some confidence° with you   *(for "conference")*
that decerns° you nearly.   *(for "concerns")*

LEONATO   Brief° I pray you, for you see it is a busy time with me.   *Be brief*

5   DOGBERRY   Marry, this it is, sir.

VERGES   Yes, in truth it is, sir.

LEONATO   What is it, my good friends?

DOGBERRY   Goodman° Verges, sir, speaks a little off the mat-   *(commoner's title)*
ter°—an old man, sir, and his wits are not so blunt° as, God   *subject / (for "sharp")*
10   help, I would desire they were. But in faith, honest as the skin
between his brows.

VERGES   Yes, I thank God, I am as honest as any man living that
is an old man and no honester than I.

DOGBERRY   Comparisons are odorous.° Palabras,[1] neighbour   *(for "odious")*
15   Verges.

LEONATO   Neighbours, you are tedious.[2]

DOGBERRY   It pleases your worship to say so, but we are the poor
Duke's° officers. But truly, for mine own part, if I were as   *the Duke's poor*
tedious as a king I could find in my heart to bestow it all of
20   your worship.

LEONATO   All thy tediousness on me, ah?

DOGBERRY   Yea, an 'twere a thousand pound more than 'tis, for I
hear as good exclamation[3] on your worship as of any man in
the city, and though I be but a poor man, I am glad to hear it.

25   VERGES   And so am I.

---

7. Hidden meaning (with ensuing pun on "no moral"
as "immoral").
8. Benedick was once an enemy of love.
9. Nonetheless, he has a perfectly good appetite.
1. Not a canter. (I am not speaking at a false pace.)
3.5 Location: Leonato's house.

1. Be brief (from a Spanish expression, *pocas palabras:*
"few words").
2. Dogberry takes it to mean "rich."
3. Properly, "accusation"; but Dogberry probably
intends "acclamation."

LEONATO   I would fain° know what you have to say.   *gladly*

VERGES   Marry, sir, our watch tonight, excepting your worship's
presence,[4] ha' ta'en a couple of as arrant knaves as any in Messina.

30 DOGBERRY   A good old man, sir. He will be talking. As they say,
when the age is in, the wit is out.[5] God help us, it is a world to
see.[6] Well said, i'faith, neighbour Verges. Well, God's a good
man. An° two men ride of a horse, one must ride behind. An   *If*
honest soul, i'faith, sir, by my troth he is, as ever broke bread.[7]
35 But, God is to be worshipped, all men are not alike, alas, good
neighbour.

LEONATO   Indeed, neighbour, he comes too short of you.

DOGBERRY   Gifts that God gives!

LEONATO   I must leave you.

40 DOGBERRY   One word, sir. Our watch, sir, have indeed comprehended two auspicious[8] persons, and we would have them this
morning examined before your worship.

LEONATO   Take their examination yourself, and bring it me. I am
now in great haste, as it may appear unto you.

45 DOGBERRY   It shall be suffigance.°   *(for "sufficient")*

LEONATO   Drink some wine ere you go. Fare you well.

[Enter a MESSENGER*]*

MESSENGER   My lord, they stay° for you to give your daughter to   *wait*
her husband.

LEONATO   I'll wait upon them, I am ready.

[Exeunt LEONATO *and* MESSENGER*]*

50 DOGBERRY   Go, good partner, go get you to Francis Seacoal,[9]
bid him bring his pen and inkhorn to the jail. We are now to
examination° these men.   *(for "examine")*

VERGES   And we must do it wisely.

DOGBERRY   We will spare for no wit, I warrant you. Here's that°   *that which*
55 shall drive some of them to a non-com.[1] Only get the learned
writer to set down our excommunication,° and meet me at the   *(for "examination")*
jail.   *Exeunt*

4.1

Enter [DON PEDRO *the*] *Prince,* [DON JOHN *the*] *bastard,*
LEONATO, FRIAR [FRANCIS], CLAUDIO, BENEDICK,
HERO, *and* BEATRICE

LEONATO   Come, Friar Francis, be brief. Only to the plain form
of marriage, and you shall recount their particular duties
afterwards.

FRIAR [*to* CLAUDIO]   You come hither, my lord, to marry this
5 lady?

CLAUDIO   No.

LEONATO   To be married to her. Friar, you come to marry her.

FRIAR [*to* HERO]   Lady, you come hither to be married to this
count?

---

4. For "respecting your worship's presence": an apology
for speaking what might displease.
5. Dogberry's version of the proverb "When the wine is
in, the wit is out."
6. Dogberry seems to mean "a strange world"; the
expression normally meant "wonderful to behold."
7. Dogberry strings together three proverbial sentences,

all of which are remembered correctly but irrelevantly.
8. For "suspicious." *comprehended*: for "apprehended."
9. Refers to the Sexton in 4.2, not the George Seacoal
of the Watch in 3.3.
1. For "nonplus" (bewilderment); perhaps confused by
Dogberry with *non compos mentis* (insane).
4.1 Location: A church.

10   HERO   I do.

  FRIAR   If either of you know any inward° impediment why you   secret
should not be conjoined, I charge you on your souls to utter it.

  CLAUDIO   Know you any, Hero?

  HERO   None, my lord.

15   FRIAR   Know you any, Count?

  LEONATO   I dare make his answer—none.

  CLAUDIO   O, what men dare do! What men may do! What men
daily do, not knowing what they do!

  BENEDICK   How now! Interjections? Why then, some be of

20   laughing, as 'ah, ha, he!'[1]

  CLAUDIO   Stand thee by, Friar. Father, by your leave,
Will you with free and unconstrainèd soul
Give me this maid, your daughter?

  LEONATO   As freely, son, as God did give her me.

25   CLAUDIO   And what have I to give you back whose worth
May counterpoise° this rich and precious gift?   equal

  DON PEDRO   Nothing, unless you render her again.

  CLAUDIO   Sweet Prince, you learn° me noble thankfulness.   teach
There, Leonato, take her back again.

30   Give not this rotten orange to your friend.
She's but the sign° and semblance of her honour.   mere appearance
Behold how like a maid she blushes here!
O, what authority and show of truth
Can cunning sin cover itself withal!

35   Comes not that blood° as modest evidence   blush
To witness° simple virtue? Would you not swear,   testify to
All you that see her, that she were a maid,
By these exterior shows? But she is none.
She knows the heat of a luxurious° bed.   lustful

40   Her blush is guiltiness, not modesty.

  LEONATO   What do you mean, my lord?

  CLAUDIO   Not to be married,
Not to knit my soul to an approvèd° wanton.   a proven

  LEONATO   Dear my lord, if you in your own proof°   testing (of her)
Have vanquished the resistance of her youth

45   And made defeat of her virginity—

  CLAUDIO   I know what you would say. If I have known her,
You will say she did embrace me as a husband,
And so extenuate the forehand sin.[2]
No, Leonato,

50   I never tempted her with word too large,°   immodest
But as a brother to his sister showed
Bashful sincerity and comely love.

  HERO   And seemed I ever otherwise to you?

  CLAUDIO   Out on thee,[3] seeming! I will write against it.

55   You seem to me as Dian in her orb,[4]
As chaste as is the bud ere it be blown.°   blossom
But you are more intemperate in your blood°   passion

---

1. Benedick alludes to a passage in William Lily's Latin
grammar, used in all Elizabethan schools: "Some [inter-
jections] are of laughing; as Ha ha he" (1567 edition).
2. And so sin only in anticipation of marriage.

3. A curse; "thee" could refer to Hero or "seeming"
(putting on a false show).
4. Diana (Roman goddess of chastity and of the moon)
in her orbit, or sphere of activity.

Than Venus or those pampered animals
That rage in savage sensuality.
60 HERO   Is my lord well that he doth speak so wide?°   *wildly*
LEONATO   Sweet Prince, why speak not you?
DON PEDRO   What should I speak?
I stand dishonoured, that have gone about°   *have tried*
To link my dear friend to a common stale.°   *prostitute*
LEONATO   Are these things spoken, or do I but dream?
65 DON JOHN   Sir, they are spoken, and these things are true.
BENEDICK   This looks not like a nuptial.
HERO   'True'! O God!
CLAUDIO   Leonato, stand I here?
Is this the Prince? Is this the Prince's brother?
70 Is this face Hero's? Are our eyes our own?
LEONATO   All this is so. But what of this, my lord?
CLAUDIO   Let me but move° one question to your daughter,   *put*
And by that fatherly and kindly° power   *natural*
That you have in her, bid her answer truly.
75 LEONATO [*to* HERO]   I charge thee do so, as thou art my child.
HERO   O God defend me, how am I beset!
What kind of catechizing⁵ call you this?
CLAUDIO   To make you answer truly to your name.⁶
HERO   Is it not Hero? Who can blot that name
With any just reproach?
80 CLAUDIO   Marry, that can Hero.
Hero itself⁷ can blot out Hero's virtue.
What man was he talked with you yesternight
Out at your window betwixt twelve and one?
Now if you are a maid, answer to this.
85 HERO   I talked with no man at that hour, my lord.
DON PEDRO   Why, then are you no maiden. Leonato,
I am sorry you must hear. Upon mine honour,
Myself, my brother, and this grievèd° Count   *wronged*
Did see her, hear her, at that hour last night
90 Talk with a ruffian at her chamber window,
Who hath indeed, most like a liberal° villain,   *loose-tongued*
Confessed the vile encounters they have had
A thousand times in secret.
DON JOHN   Fie, fie, they are
Not to be named, my lord, not to be spoke of.
95 There is not chastity enough in language
Without offence to utter them. Thus, pretty lady,
I am sorry for thy much misgovernment.°   *ample misconduct*
CLAUDIO   O Hero! What a Hero hadst thou been
If half thy outward graces had been placed
100 About thy thoughts and counsels of thy heart!
But fare thee well, most foul, most fair, farewell
Thou pure impiety and impious purity.
For° thee I'll lock up all the gates of love,   *Because of*
And on my eyelids shall conjecture° hang   *suspicion*

5. A catechism was a set of formal questions and
answers used to teach church doctrine.
6. To make you admit that you are what you have been
called.
7. The name (or reputation) of Hero.

105　　To turn all beauty into thoughts of harm,
　　　And never shall it more be gracious.° *attractive*
　LEONATO　Hath no man's dagger here a point for me?
　　　[HERO *falls to the ground*]
　BEATRICE　Why, how now, cousin, wherefore sink you down?
　DON JOHN　Come. Let us go. These things come thus to light
110　　Smother her spirits° up. *vital forces*
　　　　　　　[*Exeunt* DON PEDRO, DON JOHN, *and* CLAUDIO]
　BENEDICK　How doth the lady?
　BEATRICE　　　　　　　　　Dead, I think. Help, uncle.
　　　Hero, why Hero! Uncle, Signor Benedick, Friar—
　LEONATO　O fate, take not away thy heavy hand.
　　　Death is the fairest cover for her shame
　　　That may be wished for.
115　BEATRICE　　　　　　　How now, cousin Hero?
　FRIAR　[*to* HERO]　Have comfort, lady.
　LEONATO　[*to* HERO]　Dost thou look up?
　FRIAR　Yea, wherefore should she not?
　LEONATO　Wherefore? Why, doth not every earthly thing
120　　Cry shame upon her? Could she here deny
　　　The story that is printed in her blood?° *blush*
　　　Do not live, Hero, do not ope thine eyes,
　　　For did I think thou wouldst not quickly die,
　　　Thought I thy spirits were stronger than thy shames,
125　　Myself would on the rearward° of reproaches *in the wake*
　　　Strike at thy life. Grieved I I had but one?
　　　Chid I for that at frugal nature's frame?° *plan*
　　　O one too much by thee! Why had I one?
　　　Why ever wast thou lovely in my eyes?
130　　Why had I not with charitable hand
　　　Took up a beggar's issue at my gates,
　　　Who smirchèd thus° and mired with infamy, *(as you are)*
　　　I might have said 'No part of it is mine,
　　　This shame derives itself from unknown loins.'
135　　But mine, and mine I loved, and mine I praised,
　　　And mine that I was proud on,° mine so much *of*
　　　That I myself was to myself not mine,[8]
　　　Valuing of her—why she, O she is fallen
　　　Into a pit of ink, that the wide sea
140　　Hath drops too few to wash her clean again,
　　　And salt too little which may season[9] give
　　　To her foul tainted flesh.
　BENEDICK　　　　　　　　Sir, sir, be patient.
　　　For my part, I am so attired in wonder
　　　I know not what to say.
145　BEATRICE　O, on my soul, my cousin is belied.° *slandered*
　BENEDICK　Lady, were you her bedfellow last night?
　BEATRICE　No, truly not, although until last night
　　　I have this twelvemonth been her bedfellow.
　LEONATO　Confirmed, confirmed. O, that is stronger made
150　　Which was before° barred up with ribs of iron. *already*
　　　Would the two princes lie? And Claudio lie,

---

8. That I cared nothing for myself in comparison.　　9. Give renewal. (Salt is a preservative for meat.)

Who loved her so that, speaking of her foulness,
Washed it with tears? Hence from her, let her die.
FRIAR   Hear me a little,
155 For I have only been silent so long
And given way unto this course of fortune[1]
By noting of the lady.[2] I have marked
A thousand blushing apparitions
To start into her face, a thousand innocent shames
160 In angel whiteness beat away those blushes,
And in her eye there hath appeared a fire
To burn the errors° that these princes hold   (like heretics)
Against her maiden truth. Call me a fool,
Trust not my reading nor my observations,
165 Which with experimental seal doth warrant
The tenor of my book.[3] Trust not my age,
My reverence, calling, nor divinity,
If this sweet lady lie not guiltless here
Under some biting error.
LEONATO   Friar, it cannot be.
170 Thou seest that all the grace that she hath left
Is that she will not add to her damnation
A sin of perjury. She not denies it.
Why seek'st thou then to cover with excuse
That which appears in proper° nakedness?   true
175 FRIAR [to HERO]   Lady, what man is he you are accused of?
HERO   They know that do accuse me. I know none.
If I know more of any man alive
Than that which maiden modesty doth warrant,
Let all my sins lack mercy. O my father,
180 Prove you that any man with me conversed
At hours unmeet,° or that I yesternight   improper
Maintained the change° of words with any creature,   exchange
Refuse° me, hate me, torture me to death.   Disown
FRIAR   There is some strange misprision° in the princes.   misunderstanding
185 BENEDICK   Two of them have the very bent of° honour,   are wholly devoted to
And if their wisdoms be misled in this
The practice° of it lives in John the bastard,   trickery
Whose spirits toil in frame of° villainies.   in plotting
LEONATO   I know not. If they speak but truth of her
190 These hands shall tear her. If they wrong her honour
The proudest of them shall well hear of it.
Time hath not yet so dried this blood of mine,
Nor age so eat up my invention,°   cleverness
Nor fortune made such havoc of my means,°   wealth
195 Nor my bad life reft me so much of friends,
But they shall find awaked in such a kind°   manner
Both strength of limb and policy° of mind,   cunning
Ability in means, and choice of friends,
To quit me of[4] them throughly.°   thoroughly
FRIAR   Pause awhile,

---

1. Q erroneously sets the beginning of the speech in cramped prose; some words seem to have been lost in the compression.
2. By . . . lady: So I could observe, or because I was observing, Hero.
3. Which . . . book: Which guarantees, with the confirmation of experience, the truth of the conclusions I have drawn from my study.
4. To be avenged upon.

200 And let my counsel sway you in this case.
Your daughter here the princes left for dead,
Let her a while be secretly kept in,
And publish° it that she is dead indeed.   announce
Maintain a mourning ostentation,°   formal display
205 And on your family's old monument°   burial vault
Hang mournful epitaphs, and do all rites
That appertain unto a burial.

LEONATO   What shall become of this? What will this do?

FRIAR   Marry, this, well carried,° shall on her behalf   managed
210 Change slander to remorse.° That is some good.   pity
But not for that dream I on this strange course,
But on° this travail look for greater birth.[5]   from
She—dying, as it must be so maintained,
Upon the instant that she was accused—
215 Shall be lamented, pitied, and excused
Of° every hearer. For it so falls out   By
That what we have, we prize not to the worth°   full value
Whiles we enjoy it, but, being lacked and lost,
Why then we rack[6] the value, then we find
220 The virtue that possession would not show us
Whiles it was ours. So will it fare with Claudio.
When he shall hear she died upon° his words,   as a result of
Th'idea° of her life shall sweetly creep   The image
Into his study of imagination,°   reverie
225 And every lovely organ° of her life   aspect
Shall come apparelled in more precious habit,
More moving-delicate, and full of life,
Into the eye and prospect° of his soul   vision
Than when she lived indeed. Then shall he mourn,
230 If ever love had interest in his liver,[7]
And wish he had not so accusèd her,
No, though he thought his accusation true.
Let this be so, and doubt not but success°   what follows
Will fashion the event° in better shape   result
235 Than I can lay it down in likelihood.
But if all aim but this be levelled false,[8]
The supposition of the lady's death
Will quench the wonder of her infamy.
And if it sort° not well, you may conceal her,   turn out
240 As best befits her wounded reputation,
In some reclusive° and religious life,   cloistered
Out of all eyes, tongues, minds, and injuries.°   calumny

BENEDICK   Signor Leonato, let the Friar advise you.
And though you know my inwardness° and love   intimacy
245 Is very much unto the Prince and Claudio,
Yet, by mine honour, I will deal in this
As secretly and justly as your soul
Should with your body.

LEONATO   Being that I flow in° grief,   Since I am flooded by
250 The smallest twine may lead me.

---

5. Look for a more important consequence (with pun
on "travail" as "labor pains" as well as "effort").
6. Stretch (as on a rack, an instrument of torture).

7. Thought of as the seat of passions, including love.
8. But if we miss our aim in all but this.

FRIAR 'Tis well consented. Presently away,
For to strange sores strangely they strain the cure.⁹
[*To* HERO] Come, lady, die to live. This wedding day
Perhaps is but prolonged.° Have patience, and endure.   *postponed*
       Exeunt [*all but* BEATRICE *and* BENEDICK]

255 BENEDICK Lady Beatrice, have you wept all this while?
BEATRICE Yea, and I will weep a while longer.
BENEDICK I will not desire that.
BEATRICE You have no reason, I do it freely.
BENEDICK Surely I do believe your fair cousin is wronged.
260 BEATRICE Ah, how much might the man deserve of me that
would right her!
BENEDICK Is there any way to show such friendship?
BEATRICE A very even° way, but no such friend.   *clear*
BENEDICK May a man do it?
265 BEATRICE It is a man's office, but not yours.
BENEDICK I do love nothing in the world so well as you. Is not
that strange?
BEATRICE As strange as the thing I know not. It were as possible
for me to say I loved nothing so well as you, but believe me
270 not, and yet I lie not. I confess nothing nor I deny nothing. I
am sorry for my cousin.
BENEDICK By my sword, Beatrice, thou lovest me.
BEATRICE Do not swear and eat it.¹
BENEDICK I will swear by it that you love me, and I will make
275 him eat it that says I love not you.
BEATRICE Will you not eat your word?
BENEDICK With no sauce that can be devised to it. I protest° I   *affirm*
love thee.
BEATRICE Why then, God forgive me.
280 BENEDICK What offence, sweet Beatrice?
BEATRICE You have stayed me in a happy hour.² I was about to
protest I loved you.
BENEDICK And do it with all thy heart.
BEATRICE I love you with so much of my heart that none is left
285 to protest.
BENEDICK Come, bid me do anything for thee.
BEATRICE Kill Claudio.
BENEDICK Ha! Not for the wide world.
BEATRICE You kill me to deny° it. Farewell.   *by refusing*
290 BENEDICK Tarry, sweet Beatrice.
BEATRICE I am gone though I am here. There is no love in
you.—Nay, I pray you, let me go.
BENEDICK Beatrice.
BEATRICE In faith, I will go.
295 BENEDICK We'll be friends first.
BEATRICE You dare easier be friends with me than fight with
mine enemy.
BENEDICK Is Claudio thine enemy?
BEATRICE Is a not approved in the height³ a villain, that hath
300 slandered, scorned, dishonoured my kinswoman? O that I were

9. Compare the proverb "A desperate disease must
have a desperate cure."
1. Eat your words, go back on your oath. Benedick takes

it to mean his sword (as does F: "swear by it and eat it").
2. You have stopped me at a fortunate moment.
3. Is he not proved in the highest degree.

a man! What, bear her in hand⁴ until they come to take hands, and then with public accusation, uncovered° slander, unmit-   *barefaced*
igated rancour—O God that I were a man! I would eat his heart
in the market place.

305   BENEDICK   Hear me, Beatrice.

    BEATRICE   Talk with a man out at a window—a proper saying!°   *a likely story*

    BENEDICK   Nay, but Beatrice.

    BEATRICE   Sweet Hero, she is wronged, she is slandered, she is
undone.

310   BENEDICK   Beat—

    BEATRICE   Princes and counties! Surely a princely testimony, a
goodly count,⁵ Count Comfit,° a sweet gallant, surely. O that I   *Sugarplum*
were a man for his sake! Or that I had any friend would be a
man for my sake! But manhood is melted into courtesies,
315   valour into compliment, and men are only turned into tongue,
and trim° ones, too. He is now as valiant as Hercules that° only   *fine (ironic) / who*
tells a lie and swears it. I cannot be a man with° wishing, there-   *by*
fore I will die a woman with grieving.

    BENEDICK   Tarry, good Beatrice. By this hand, I love thee.

320   BEATRICE   Use it for my love some other way than swearing by
it.

    BENEDICK   Think you in your soul the Count Claudio hath
wronged Hero?

    BEATRICE   Yea, as sure as I have a thought or a soul.

325   BENEDICK   Enough, I am engaged,° I will challenge him. I will   *pledged*
kiss your hand, and so I leave you. By this hand, Claudio shall
render me a dear account.° As you hear of me, so think of me.   *pay me dearly*
Go comfort your cousin. I must say she is dead. And so,
farewell.   [*Exeunt*]

4.2

Enter [DOGBERRY *and* VERGES] *the constables, and the
Town Clerk* [*the* SEXTON], *in gowns,*¹ [*and the* WATCH,
with] BORACHIO [*and* CONRAD]

  DOGBERRY   Is our whole dissembly° appeared?   *(for "assembly")*

    VERGES   O, a stool and a cushion for the Sexton.

    SEXTON [*sits*]   Which be the malefactors?²

    DOGBERRY   Marry, that am I, and my partner.

5   VERGES   Nay, that's certain, we have the exhibition° to examine.   *(for "commission")*

    SEXTON   But which are the offenders that are to be examined?
Let them come before Master Constable.

    DOGBERRY   Yea, marry, let them come before me. What is your
name, friend?

10   BORACHIO   Borachio.

    DOGBERRY [*to the* SEXTON]   Pray write down 'Borachio'. [*To* CON-
RAD] Yours, sirrah?³

    CONRAD   I am a gentleman, sir, and my name is Conrad.

    DOGBERRY   Write down 'Master Gentleman Conrad'.—Masters,
15   do you serve God?

---

4. *bear her in hand*: lead her on with false hopes.
5. Story, tale (with plays on "count" as a legal indictment and as Claudio's title).
4.2 Location: A prison or hearing room in Messina.
1. Constables wore black gowns. The Sexton is presumably Francis Seacoal (3.5.50). Q's direction calls
him the town clerk, an office more appropriate to his
function in the scene than sexton, with which, however,
it seems often to have been combined.
2. Dogberry seems to mistake "malefactors" for "factors," or agents.
3. Contemptuous, since "sirrah" is used to address
inferiors, provoking Conrad's claim to be a gentleman.

CONRAD *and* BORACHIO   Yea, sir, we hope.

DOGBERRY   Write down that they hope they serve God. And
write 'God' first, for God defend° but God should go before[4]   *forbid*
such villains. Masters, it is proved already that you are little
20   better than false knaves, and it will go near to be thought so
shortly. How answer you for yourselves?

CONRAD   Marry, sir, we say we are none.

DOGBERRY   A marvellous witty° fellow, I assure you, but I will go   *clever*
about with° him. Come you hither, sirrah. A word in your ear,   *will outwit*
25   sir. I say to you it is thought you are false knaves.

BORACHIO   Sir, I say to you we are none.

DOGBERRY   Well, stand aside. Fore God, they are both in a tale.°   *telling the same story*
Have you writ down that they are none?

SEXTON   Master Constable, you go not the way to examine. You
30   must call forth the watch that are their accusers.

DOGBERRY   Yea, marry, that's the eftest° way. Let the watch come   *(for "aptest")*
forth. Masters, I charge you in the Prince's name accuse these
men.

FIRST WATCHMAN   This man said, sir, that Don John, the Prince's
35   brother, was a villain.

DOGBERRY   Write down Prince John a villain. Why, this is flat
perjury,[5] to call a prince's brother villain.

BORACHIO   Master Constable.

DOGBERRY   Pray thee, fellow, peace. I do not like thy look, I
40   promise thee.

SEXTON   What heard you him say else?

SECOND WATCHMAN   Marry, that he had received a thousand
ducats of Don John for accusing the Lady Hero wrongfully.

DOGBERRY   Flat burglary, as ever was committed.

45   VERGES   Yea, by mass,[6] that it is.

SEXTON   What else, fellow?

FIRST WATCHMAN   And that Count Claudio did mean upon° his   *with*
words to disgrace Hero before the whole assembly, and not
marry her.

50   DOGBERRY   O villain! Thou wilt be condemned into everlasting
redemption° for this.   *(for "damnation")*

SEXTON   What else?

WATCH   This is all.

SEXTON   And this is more, masters, than you can deny. Prince
55   John is this morning secretly stolen away. Hero was in this manner accused, in this very manner refused, and upon the grief of
this suddenly died. Master Constable, let these men be bound
and brought to Leonato's. I will go before and show him their
examination.   [*Exit*]

60   DOGBERRY   Come, let them be opinioned.°   *(for "pinioned")*

VERGES   Let them be, in the hands—

CONRAD   Off, coxcomb![7]

DOGBERRY   God's° my life, where's the Sexton? Let him write   *God save*
down the Prince's officer coxcomb. Come, bind them. Thou
65   naughty varlet!°   *wicked knave*

CONRAD   Away, you are an ass, you are an ass.

---

4. (Punningly) take precedence over.
5. Perhaps a mistake for "treason" or "slander."
6. "By the mass," a common oath.

7. This is an emendation of a corrupt passage, given in
Q as part of the previous speech. These words could be
spoken by Borachio.

DOGBERRY   Dost thou not suspect° my place? Dost thou not sus-   *(for "respect")*
pect my years? O that he were here to write me down an ass!
But masters, remember that I am an ass. Though it be not
70   written down, yet forget not that I am an ass. No, thou villain,
thou art full of piety,° as shall be proved upon thee by good   *(for "impiety")*
witness. I am a wise fellow, and which is more, an officer, and
which is more, a householder, and which is more, as pretty a
piece of flesh[8] as any is in Messina, and one that knows the
75   law, go to, and a rich fellow enough, go to, and a fellow that
hath had losses,[9] and one that hath two gowns, and everything
handsome about him. Bring him away. O that I had been writ
down an ass!   *Exeunt*

5.1

Enter LEONATO *and* [ANTONIO] *his brother*

ANTONIO   If you go on thus, you will kill yourself,
And 'tis not wisdom thus to second° grief   *assist*
Against yourself.
LEONATO   I pray thee cease thy counsel,
Which falls into mine ears as profitless
5   As water in a sieve. Give not me counsel,
Nor let no comforter delight mine ear
But such a one whose wrongs do suit° with mine.   *match*
Bring me a father that so loved his child,
Whose joy of° her is overwhelmed like mine,   *in*
10   And bid him speak of patience.
Measure his woe the length and breadth of mine,
And let it answer every strain° for strain,   *strong feeling*
As thus for thus, and such a grief for such,
In every lineament, branch, shape, and form.
15   If such a one will smile and stroke his beard,
Bid sorrow wag,° cry 'hem'[1] when he should groan,   *be off*
Patch° grief with proverbs, make misfortune drunk°   *Mend / insensible*
With candle-wasters,[2] bring him yet to me,
And I of him will gather patience.
20   But there is no such man, for, brother, men
Can counsel and speak comfort to that grief
Which they themselves not feel, but tasting it
Their counsel turns to passion, which before
Would give preceptial° medicine to rage,   *precepts as*
25   Fetter strong madness in a silken thread,
Charm ache with air° and agony with words.   *breath*
No, no, 'tis all men's office° to speak patience   *business*
To those that wring° under the load of sorrow,   *writhe*
But no man's virtue nor sufficiency°   *ability*
30   To be so moral° when he shall endure   *moralizing*
The like himself. Therefore give me no counsel.
My griefs cry louder than advertisement.°   *advice*
ANTONIO   Therein do men from children nothing differ.
LEONATO   I pray thee peace, I will be flesh and blood,
35   For there was never yet philosopher

---

8. *as pretty . . . flesh:* as fine (or gallant) a mortal man.
9. *hath had losses:* was once richer.
5.1 Location: Near Leonato's house.

1. Clear his throat (as if about to make a speech).
2. Philosophers, burners of midnight oil (and their works).

That could endure the toothache patiently,
However they have writ the style of gods,
And made a pish at chance and sufferance.[3]

ANTONIO   Yet bend° not all the harm upon yourself.   direct
40   Make those that do offend you suffer, too.

LEONATO   There thou speak'st reason, nay I will do so.
My soul doth tell me Hero is belied,
And that shall Claudio know, so shall the Prince,
And all of them that thus dishonour her.

          Enter [DON PEDRO *the*] *Prince and* CLAUDIO

45   ANTONIO   Here comes the Prince and Claudio hastily.

DON PEDRO   Good e'en,° good e'en.   evening

CLAUDIO   Good day to both of you.

LEONATO   Hear you, my lords?

DON PEDRO   We have some haste, Leonato.

LEONATO   Some haste, my lord! Well, fare you well, my lord.
Are you so hasty now? Well, all is one.°   no matter
50   DON PEDRO   Nay, do not quarrel with us, good old man.

ANTONIO   If he could right himself with quarrelling,
Some of us° would lie low.   (Don Pedro and Claudio)

CLAUDIO   Who wrongs him?

LEONATO   Marry, thou dost wrong me, thou dissembler, thou.[4]
Nay, never lay thy hand upon thy sword,
I fear thee not.

55   CLAUDIO   Marry, beshrew° my hand   curse
If it should give your age such cause of fear.
In faith, my hand meant nothing to[5] my sword.

LEONATO   Tush, tush, man, never fleer° and jest at me.   sneer; mock
I speak not like a dotard nor a fool,
60   As under privilege of age to brag
What I have done being young, or what would do
Were I not old. Know Claudio to thy head,°   face
Thou hast so wronged mine innocent child and me
That I am forced to lay my reverence by
65   And with grey hairs and bruise of many days
Do challenge thee to trial of a man.°   of manhood
I say thou hast belied mine innocent child.
Thy slander hath gone through and through her heart,
And she lies buried with her ancestors,
70   O, in a tomb where never scandal slept
Save this of hers, framed° by thy villainy.   created

CLAUDIO   My villainy?

LEONATO   Thine, Claudio, thine I say.

DON PEDRO   You say not right, old man.

LEONATO   My lord, my lord,
I'll prove it on his body if he dare,
75   Despite his nice fence[6] and his active practice,
His May of youth and bloom of lustihood.°   virility

CLAUDIO   Away, I will not have to do with you.

LEONATO   Canst thou so doff me?° Thou hast killed my child.   brush me off
If thou kill'st me, boy, thou shalt kill a man.

---

3. *writ . . . sufferance:* written as if they transcended   4. "Thou" is used contemptuously here.
human passion, and expressed themselves scornfully   5. My hand had no designs upon.
about (said "pish" to) bad luck and suffering.   6. His nimble fencing (said contemptuously).

80 ANTONIO   He shall kill two of us, and men indeed.
       But that's no matter, let him kill one first.
       Win me and wear me.[7] Let him answer me.°   *(in a duel)*
       Come follow me boy, come sir boy, come follow me,
       Sir boy, I'll whip you from your foining fence.[8]
85   Nay, as I am a gentleman, I will.
LEONATO   Brother.
ANTONIO   Content yourself.° God knows, I loved my niece,   *Don't interfere*
       And she is dead, slandered to death by villains
       That dare as well answer a man indeed
90   As I dare take a serpent by the tongue.
       Boys, apes,° braggarts, jacks,° milksops!   *fools / knaves*
LEONATO   Brother Antony—
ANTONIO   Hold you content. What, man, I know them, yea
       And what they weigh, even to the utmost scruple.°   *¹⁄₂₄ ounce*
95   Scambling, outfacing, fashion-monging boys,[9]
       That lie, and cog,° and flout,° deprave,° and slander,   *cheat / mock / defame*
       Go anticly,° and show an outward hideousness,[1]   *outlandishly dressed*
       And speak off half a dozen dangerous words,
       How they might hurt their enemies, if they durst,
100   And this is all.
LEONATO   But brother Antony—
ANTONIO   Come, 'tis no matter,
       Do not you meddle, let me deal in this.
DON PEDRO   Gentlemen both, we will not wake° your patience.   *test*
105   My heart is sorry for your daughter's death,
       But on my honour she was charged with nothing
       But what was true and very full of proof.
LEONATO   My lord, my lord—
DON PEDRO   I will not hear you.
LEONATO   No? Come brother, away. I will be heard.
110 ANTONIO   And shall, or some of us will smart for it.
                  Exeunt [LEONATO *and* ANTONIO]
       Enter BENEDICK
DON PEDRO   See, see, here comes the man we went to seek.
CLAUDIO   Now signor, what news?
BENEDICK   [*to* DON PEDRO]   Good day, my lord.
DON PEDRO   Welcome, signor. You are almost come to part
115   almost a fray.
CLAUDIO   We had liked to have had° our two noses snapped off   *We nearly had*
       with° two old men without teeth.   *by*
DON PEDRO   Leonato and his brother. What thinkest thou? Had
       we fought, I doubt° we should have been too young for them.   *suspect*
120 BENEDICK   In a false quarrel there is no true valour. I came to
       seek you both.
CLAUDIO   We have been up and down to seek thee, for we are
       high-proof° melancholy and would fain have it beaten away.   *to a high degree*
       Wilt thou use thy wit?
125 BENEDICK   It is in my scabbard. Shall I draw it?
DON PEDRO   Dost thou wear thy wit by thy side?

---

7. A form of challenge: let him beat me and only then boast of it.
8. Thrusting position in fencing (Antonio probably means that he will compel Claudio to close with him in the duel, or that he will literally take a whip to him).
9. *Scambling . . . boys:* Quarrelsome, insolent, faddish boys.
1. A fearsome exterior.

CLAUDIO   Never any did so, though very many have been beside
     their wit.° I will bid thee draw as we do the minstrels,[2] draw to   *out of their minds*
     pleasure us.

130 DON PEDRO   As I am an honest man he looks pale. Art thou sick,
     or angry?

CLAUDIO   What, courage, man. What though care killed a cat,
     thou hast mettle° enough in thee to kill care.   *spirit; courage*

BENEDICK   Sir, I shall meet your wit in the career° an you   *at full gallop*
135 charge° it against me. I pray you choose another subject.   *aim*

CLAUDIO   Nay then, give him another staff.° This last was broke   *lance*
     cross.[3]

DON PEDRO   By this light, he changes° more and more. I think   *changes color*
     he be angry indeed.

140 CLAUDIO   If he be, he knows how to turn his girdle.[4]

BENEDICK   [*aside to* CLAUDIO]   Shall I speak a word in your ear?

CLAUDIO   God bless° me from a challenge.   *protect*

BENEDICK   You are a villain. I jest not. I will make it good how
     you dare, with what° you dare, and when you dare. Do me   *whatever weapon*
145 right,[5] or I will protest° your cowardice. You have killed a sweet   *proclaim*
     lady, and her death shall fall heavy on you. Let me hear from
     you.

CLAUDIO   Well, I will meet you, so I may have good cheer.

DON PEDRO   What, a feast, a feast?

150 CLAUDIO   I'faith, I thank him, he hath bid me to a calf's head
     and a capon, the which if I do not carve most curiously,° say   *daintily*
     my knife's naught.° Shall I not find a woodcock[6] too?   *useless*

BENEDICK   Sir, your wit ambles[7] well, it goes easily.

DON PEDRO   I'll tell thee how Beatrice praised thy wit the other
155 day. I said thou hadst a fine wit. 'True,' said she, 'a fine little
     one.' 'No,' said I, 'a great wit.' 'Right,' says she, 'a great gross
     one.' 'Nay,' said I, 'a good wit.' 'Just,' said she, 'it hurts nobody.'
     'Nay,' said I, 'the gentleman is wise.' 'Certain,' said she, 'a wise
     gentleman.'[8] 'Nay,' said I, 'he hath the tongues.'° That I   *knows several languages*
160 believe,' said she, 'for he swore a thing to me on Monday night
     which he forswore on Tuesday morning. There's a double
     tongue, there's two tongues.' Thus did she an hour together
     trans-shape° thy particular virtues, yet at last she concluded   *distort*
     with a sigh thou wast the properest° man in Italy.   *handsomest*

165 CLAUDIO   For the which she wept heartily and said she cared
     not.

DON PEDRO   Yea, that she did. But yet for all that, an if° she did   *an if=if*
     not hate him deadly she would love him dearly. The old man's
     daughter told us all.

170 CLAUDIO   All, all. And moreover, God saw him when he was hid
     in the garden.[9]

DON PEDRO   But when shall we set the savage bull's horns on the
     sensible Benedick's head?

---

2. *draw . . . minstrels:* draw a sword, the way a minstrel
is bidden to draw a bow across his musical instrument.
3. Was snapped in the middle, like a badly handled
lance. (Claudio is mocking Benedick's attempt at wit.)
4. A colloquialism of uncertain derivation, possibly
meaning "let him get on with it" or "that's his problem."
5. Give me satisfaction.
6. The calf's head, capon, and woodcock were varieties

of food that also symbolize stupidity.
7. Moves slowly (in other words, it does not gallop as a
quick wit would).
8. A phrase often used ironically to mean "an old fool."
9. Allusion to Genesis 3:8 (Adam attempting to hide
from God in the Garden of Eden); contains a half-
hidden reference to the trick played on Benedick in the
garden.

CLAUDIO   Yea, and text underneath, 'Here dwells Benedick the
175   married man'.[1]

BENEDICK   Fare you well, boy, you know my mind. I will leave
you now to your gossip-like° humour. You break° jests as brag-   old-womanish / crack
garts do their blades[2] which, God be thanked, hurt not. [To
DON PEDRO] My lord, for your many courtesies I thank you.

180   I must discontinue your company. Your brother the bastard is
fled from Messina. You have among you killed a sweet and
innocent lady. For my lord Lackbeard there, he and I shall
meet, and till then, peace be with him.   Exit

DON PEDRO   He is in earnest.

185   CLAUDIO   In most profound earnest, and, I'll warrant you, for the
love of Beatrice.

DON PEDRO   And hath challenged thee.

CLAUDIO   Most sincerely.

DON PEDRO   What a pretty thing man is when he goes in his
190   doublet and hose and leaves off his wit![3]

Enter [DOGBERRY and VERGES] the constables, [the
WATCH,] CONRAD, and BORACHIO

CLAUDIO   He is then a giant to an ape. But then is an ape a
doctor to such a man.[4]

DON PEDRO   But soft you,° let me be. Pluck up,° my heart, and   wait / Collect yourself
be sad. Did he not say my brother was fled?

195   DOGBERRY   Come you sir, if justice cannot tame you, she shall
ne'er weigh more reasons[5] in her balance.° Nay, an you be a   scales
cursing hypocrite once,° you must be looked to.   even once

DON PEDRO   How now, two of my brother's men bound? Borachio one.

200   CLAUDIO   Hearken after° their offence, my lord.   Inquire into

DON PEDRO   Officers, what offence have these men done?

DOGBERRY   Marry, sir, they have committed false report, more-
over they have spoken untruths, secondarily they are slanders,°   (for "slanderers")
sixth and lastly they have belied a lady, thirdly they have veri-
205   fied° unjust things, and to conclude, they are lying knaves.   affirmed as true

DON PEDRO   First I ask thee what they have done, thirdly I ask
thee what's their offence, sixth and lastly why they are commit-
ted,° and to conclude, what you lay to their charge.   held on arrest

CLAUDIO   Rightly reasoned, and in his own division.° And by my   logical organization
210   troth there's one meaning well suited.[6]

DON PEDRO   [to CONRAD and BORACHIO]   Who have you offended, masters, that you are thus bound to your answer?[7] This
learned constable is too cunning to be understood. What's your
offence?

215   BORACHIO   Sweet Prince, let me go no farther to mine answer.° trial; account
Do you hear me, and let this Count kill me. I have deceived
even your very eyes. What your wisdoms could not discover,
these shallow fools have brought to light, who in the night overheard me confessing to this man how Don John your brother

1. Claudio and Don Pedro recall that Benedick joked
that if he ever fell in love, his friends could set horns in
his forehead, have his picture painted, and title it
"Benedick, the married man" (1.1.215–19).
2. Braggarts secretly dent their swords to make it
appear that they have been dealing fierce blows.
3. When he puts on fine clothes but forgets to wear his
brain.

4. Such a man is much bigger than an ape, but an ape
is a learned man ("doctor") compared with him.
5. Legal cases. Also, "reason" was pronounced like
"raisin," producing a comic image here.
6. Dressed in several different costumes (with play on
legal "suit").
7. Required to respond (punning on "bound over for
trial" and "bound with ropes").

220   incensed° me to slander the Lady Hero, how you were brought   *incited*
into the orchard and saw me court Margaret in Hero's gar-
ments, how you disgraced her when you should marry her. My
villainy they have upon record, which I had rather seal° with   *confirm; end*
my death than repeat over to my shame. The lady is dead upon
225   mine and my master's false accusation, and briefly, I desire
nothing but the reward of a villain.

DON PEDRO [*to* CLAUDIO]   Runs not this speech like iron through
your blood?

CLAUDIO   I have drunk poison whiles he uttered it.

230 DON PEDRO [*to* BORACHIO]   But did my brother set thee on to
this?

BORACHIO   Yea, and paid me richly for the practice° of it.   *execution*

DON PEDRO   He is composed and framed° of treachery,   *made up*
And fled he is upon this villainy.

235 CLAUDIO   Sweet Hero, now thy image doth appear
In the rare semblance° that I loved it first.   *likeness*

DOGBERRY   Come, bring away the plaintiffs.° By this time our   *(for "defendants")*
Sexton hath reformed° Signor Leonato of the matter. And mas-   *(for "informed")*
ters, do not forget to specify, when time and place shall serve,
240   that I am an ass.

VERGES   Here, here comes Master Signor Leonato, and the Sexton, too.

             Enter LEONATO, [ANTONIO *his*] *brother, and the* SEXTON

LEONATO   Which is the villain? Let me see his eyes,
That when I note another man like him
245   I may avoid him. Which of these is he?

BORACHIO   If you would know your wronger, look on me.

LEONATO   Art thou the slave that with thy breath hast killed
Mine innocent child?

BORACHIO   Yea, even I alone.

LEONATO   No, not so, villain, thou beliest thyself.
250   Here stand a pair of honourable men.°   *men of rank*
A third is fled that had a hand in it.
I thank you, Princes, for my daughter's death.
Record it with your high and worthy deeds.
'Twas bravely done, if you bethink you of it.

255 CLAUDIO   I know not how to pray your patience,
Yet I must speak. Choose your revenge yourself,
Impose° me to what penance your invention   *Subject*
Can lay upon my sin. Yet sinned I not
But in mistaking.

DON PEDRO   By my soul, nor I,
260   And yet to satisfy this good old man
I would bend under any heavy weight
That he'll enjoin me to.

LEONATO   I cannot bid you bid my daughter live—
That were impossible—but I pray you both
265   Possess° the people in Messina here   *Inform*
How innocent she died, and if your love
Can labour aught in sad invention,[8]
Hang her an epitaph upon her tomb
And sing it to her bones, sing it tonight.

8. Can create any fruit from your sad imagination.

270   Tomorrow morning come you to my house,
     And since you could not be my son-in-law,
     Be yet my nephew. My brother hath a daughter,
     Almost the copy of my child that's dead,
     And she alone is heir to both of us.⁹
275   Give her the right you should have giv'n her cousin,
     And so dies my revenge.
    CLAUDIO   O noble sir!
     Your overkindness doth wring tears from me.
     I do embrace your offer; and dispose
     For henceforth° of poor Claudio.   *For the future*
280 LEONATO   Tomorrow then I will expect your coming.
     Tonight I take my leave. This naughty° man   *evil*
     Shall face to face be brought to Margaret,
     Who I believe was packed° in all this wrong,   *confederate*
     Hired to it by your brother.
    BORACHIO   No, by my soul, she was not,
285   Nor knew not what she did when she spoke to me,
     But always hath been just and virtuous
     In anything that I do know by° her.   *of*
    DOGBERRY [*to* LEONATO]   Moreover, sir, which indeed is not
     under white and black, this plaintiff¹ here, the offender, did
290   call me ass. I beseech you let it be remembered in his punish-
     ment. And also the watch heard them talk of one Deformed.
     They say he wears a key in his ear and a lock hanging by it,²
     and borrows money in God's name, the which he hath used°   *done habitually*
     so long and never paid that now men grow hard-hearted and
295   will lend nothing for God's sake.³ Pray you examine him upon
     that point.
    LEONATO   I thank thee for thy care and honest pains.
    DOGBERRY   Your worship speaks like a most thankful and rever-
     end youth, and I praise God for you.
300 LEONATO [*giving him money*]   There's for thy pains.
    DOGBERRY   God save the foundation.⁴
    LEONATO   Go. I discharge thee of thy prisoner, and I thank thee.
    DOGBERRY   I leave an arrant knave with your worship, which I
     beseech your worship to correct yourself,⁵ for the example of
305   others. God keep your worship, I wish your worship well. God
     restore you to health. I humbly give you leave to depart, and
     if a merry meeting may be wished, God prohibit° it. Come,   *(for "permit")*
     neighbour.   *Exeunt* [DOGBERRY *and* VERGES]
    LEONATO   Until tomorrow morning, lords, farewell.
310 ANTONIO   Farewell, my lords. We look for you tomorrow.
    DON PEDRO   We will not fail.
    CLAUDIO   Tonight I'll mourn with Hero.
    LEONATO [*to the* WATCH]   Bring you these fellows on.—We'll talk
       with Margaret
     How her acquaintance grew with this lewd° fellow. *Exeunt* *worthless*

---

9. Shakespeare (or Leonato) has apparently forgotten
Antonio's son mentioned at 1.2.1.
1. For "defendant." *under white and black:* in writing.
2. Dogberry's garbled recollection of the lovelock mentioned at 3.3.149.
3. "In God's name" and "for God's sake" were phrases

used by beggars.
4. A conventional response to alms from a charitable
foundation.
5. Dogberry wishes Leonato himself to punish ("correct") Borachio but accidentally says that Leonato
should be punished.

5.2

Enter BENEDICK *and* MARGARET

BENEDICK   Pray thee, sweet Mistress Margaret, deserve well at
my hands by helping me to the speech of Beatrice.

MARGARET   Will you then write me a sonnet in praise of my
beauty?

5   BENEDICK   In so high a style, Margaret, that no man living shall
come over[1] it, for in most comely truth, thou deservest it.

MARGARET   To have no man come over me—why, shall I always
keep below stairs?[2]

BENEDICK   Thy wit is as quick as the greyhound's mouth, it
10   catches.

MARGARET   And yours as blunt as the fencer's foils,[3] which hit
but hurt not.

BENEDICK   A most manly wit, Margaret, it will not hurt a
woman. And so I pray thee call Beatrice. I give thee the buck-
15   lers.[4]

MARGARET   Give us the swords. We have bucklers of our own.

BENEDICK   If you use them, Margaret, you must put in the pikes
with a vice°—and they are dangerous weapons for maids.   screw

MARGARET   Well, I will call Beatrice to you, who I think hath
20   legs.   *Exit*

BENEDICK   And therefore will come.[5]

        [*Sings*]   The god love
                        That sits above,
                        And knows me, and knows me,
25   How pitiful I deserve—[6]

I mean in singing; but in loving, Leander the good swimmer,
Troilus the first employer of panders,[7] and a whole book full
of these quondam carpet-mongers[8] whose names yet run
smoothly in the even road of a blank verse, why they were never
30   so truly turned over and over° as my poor self in love. Marry, I   head over heels
cannot show it in rhyme. I have tried. I can find out no rhyme
to 'lady' but 'baby', an innocent° rhyme; for 'scorn' 'horn', a   a childish
hard[9] rhyme; for 'school' 'fool', a babbling rhyme. Very omi-
nous endings. No, I was not born under a rhyming planet,[1] nor
35   I cannot woo in festival terms.°   in fancy rhetoric

        Enter BEATRICE

Sweet Beatrice, wouldst thou come when I called thee?

BEATRICE   Yea, signor, and depart when you bid me.

BENEDICK   O, stay but till then.

BEATRICE   'Then' is spoken. Fare you well now. And yet ere I go,

---

5.2 Location: Near Leonato's house or in his garden.
1. Surpass; climb over (punning on "stile": stairs over
a fence). Margaret humorously takes "come over" in a
sexual sense.
2. In the servants' quarters (and therefore never as a
"mistress").
3. Practice rapiers, capped at the tip.
4. Benedick offers to surrender by giving up the bucklers: shields with spikes ("pikes") in the center. Margaret bawdily interprets this as the female sexual organ.
5. A popular question and answer of the time was
"How came you hither?" "On my legs."
6. How greatly I deserve pity (but Benedick takes it as

"How pitifully small my deserts are"). These four lines
are the beginning of a popular sentimental ballad.
7. Troilus, loving Cressida, employed her uncle Pandarus as go-between. Leander swam the Hellespont
nightly to be with his love, Hero.
8. Knights of long ago ("quondam") who avoided military service and spent their time in ladies' carpeted
boudoirs.
9. Disagreeable, because horns were associated with
cuckoldry.
1. At a time when the stars would influence me to
become a poet.

40   let me go with that° I came for, which is with knowing what   *what*
     hath passed between you and Claudio.

BENEDICK   Only foul words, and thereupon I will kiss thee.

BEATRICE   Foul words is but foul wind, and foul wind is but foul
     breath, and foul breath is noisome,° therefore I will depart   *nauseating*
45   unkissed.

BENEDICK   Thou hast frighted the word out of his° right sense,°   *its / meaning; wits*
     so forcible is thy wit. But I must tell thee plainly, Claudio
     undergoes° my challenge, and either I must shortly hear from   *is subject to*
     him or I will subscribe° him a coward. And I pray thee now tell   *proclaim*
50   me, for which of my bad parts didst thou first fall in love with
     me?

BEATRICE   For them all together, which maintain so politic° a   *cunningly governed*
     state of evil that they will not admit any good part to intermin-
     gle with them. But for which of my good parts did you first
55   suffer° love for me?   *feel*

BENEDICK   Suffer love—a good epithet.° I do suffer° love indeed,   *expression / suffer from*
     for I love thee against my will.

BEATRICE   In spite of your heart, I think. Alas, poor heart. If you
     spite it for my sake I will spite it for yours, for I will never love
60   that which my friend hates.

BENEDICK   Thou and I are too wise to woo peaceably.

BEATRICE   It appears not in this confession.² There's not one
     wise man among twenty that will praise himself.

BENEDICK   An old, an old instance,° Beatrice, that lived in the   *proverb*
65   time of good neighbours.³ If a man do not erect in this age his
     own tomb ere he dies, he shall live no longer in monument°   *remembrance*
     than the bell rings and the widow weeps.

BEATRICE   And how long is that, think you?

BENEDICK   Question⁴—why, an hour in clamour° and a quarter   *ringing*
70   in rheum.° Therefore is it most expedient for the wise, if Don   *tears*
     Worm—his conscience⁵—find no impediment to the contrary,
     to be the trumpet of his own virtues, as I am to myself. So
     much for praising myself who, I myself will bear witness, is
     praiseworthy. And now tell me, how doth your cousin?

75 BEATRICE   Very ill.

BENEDICK   And how do you?

BEATRICE   Very ill too.

BENEDICK   Serve God, love me, and mend.° There will I leave   *recover*
     you too, for here comes one in haste.

          Enter URSULA

80 URSULA   Madam, you must come to your uncle. Yonder's old
     coil° at home. It is proved my lady Hero hath been falsely   *great disturbance*
     accused, the Prince and Claudio mightily abused,° and Don   *deceived*
     John is the author of all, who is fled and gone. Will you come
     presently?

85 BEATRICE   Will you go hear this news, signor?

BENEDICK   I will live in thy heart, die⁶ in thy lap, and be buried
     in thy eyes. And moreover, I will go with thee to thy uncle's.

          Exeunt

---

2. Since it is not wise to claim to be wise.
3. In the good old days, when neighbors praised each
other.
4. That is the question.

5. Facetious way of referring to the proverbial gnawing
"worm of conscience."
6. With the common Elizabethan connotation of
orgasm.

5.3

Enter CLAUDIO, [DON PEDRO *the*] *Prince, and three or*
four with tapers][1] *all in black.*

CLAUDIO   Is this the monument of Leonato?

A LORD   It is, my lord.

CLAUDIO[2]   [*reading from a scroll*]

    Done to death by slanderous tongues
    Was the Hero that here lies.

5   Death in guerdon° of her wrongs   *recompense*
    Gives her fame which never dies.
    So the life that died with° shame   *from*
    Lives in death with glorious fame.

[*He hangs the*] epitaph [*on the tomb*]

    Hang thou there upon the tomb,
10   Praising her when I am dumb.

Now music sound, and sing your solemn hymn.

       Song
    Pardon, goddess of the night,[3]
    Those that slew thy virgin knight,[4]
    For the which with songs of woe
15   Round about her tomb they go.
    Midnight, assist our moan,
    Help us to sigh and groan,
      Heavily, heavily.
    Graves yawn, and yield your dead
20   Till death be uttered,°   *fully lamented*
      Heavily, heavily.

CLAUDIO   Now, unto thy bones good night.
    Yearly will I do this rite.

DON PEDRO   Good morrow, masters, put your torches out.
25   The wolves have preyed,[5] and look, the gentle day
    Before the wheels of Phoebus[6] round about
    Dapples the drowsy east with spots of grey.
    Thanks to you all, and leave us. Fare you well.

CLAUDIO   Good morrow, masters. Each his several° way.   *separate*

DON PEDRO   Come, let us hence, and put on other weeds,°   *garments*
30   And then to Leonato's we will go.

CLAUDIO   And Hymen now with luckier issue speed 's[7]
    Than this° for whom we rendered up this woe.   *Exeunt*   *this woman*

5.4

Enter LEONATO, [ANTONIO,] BENEDICK, BEATRICE, MAR-
GARET, URSULA, FRIAR [FRANCIS], *and* HERO

FRIAR   Did I not tell you she was innocent?

LEONATO   So are the Prince and Claudio who accused her
    Upon° the error that you heard debated.   *Because of*

5.3 Location: A churchyard.
1. Candles or torches carried in token of penitence.
2. In Q, the poem is headed "Epitaph" and is not
ascribed to a particular speaker.
3. Diana, Roman goddess of the moon and patroness
of virgins.

4. Hero (imagined as a knight, or follower, of Diana).
5. Have finished preying (for the night has passed).
6. The sun god's chariot wheels.
7. And may Hymen (Greek god of marriage) grant us
more favorable results.
5.4 Location: Leonato's house.

But Margaret was in some fault for this,
5 Although against her will° as it appears   unintentionally
In the true course of all the question.°   investigation
ANTONIO Well, I am glad that all things sorts° so well.   turn out
BENEDICK And so am I, being else by faith° enforced   my pledge
To call young Claudio to a reckoning for it.
10 LEONATO Well, daughter, and you gentlewomen all,
Withdraw into a chamber by yourselves,
And when I send for you come hither masked.

            Exeunt [BEATRICE, HERO, MARGARET, *and* URSULA]

The Prince and Claudio promised by this hour
To visit me. You know your office,° brother,   task
15 You must be father to your brother's daughter,
And give her to young Claudio.
ANTONIO Which I will do with confirmed° countenance.   serious
BENEDICK Friar, I must entreat your pains, I think.
FRIAR To do what, signor?
20 BENEDICK To bind me or undo° me, one of them.   ruin; unbind
Signor Leonato, truth it is, good signor,
Your niece regards me with an eye of favour.
LEONATO That eye my daughter lent her, 'tis most true.
BENEDICK And I do with an eye of love requite her.
25 LEONATO The sight whereof I think you had from me,
From Claudio and the Prince. But what's your will?
BENEDICK Your answer, sir, is enigmatical.
But for my will, my will is° your good will   is that
May stand with ours this day to be conjoined
30 In the state of honourable marriage,
In which, good Friar, I shall desire your help.
LEONATO My heart is with your liking.
FRIAR   And my help.
Here comes the Prince and Claudio.

            Enter [DON PEDRO *the*] *Prince and* CLAUDIO *with attendants*

DON PEDRO Good morrow to this fair assembly.
35 LEONATO Good morrow, Prince. Good morrow, Claudio.
We here attend you. Are you yet° determined   still
Today to marry with my brother's daughter?
CLAUDIO I'll hold my mind,° were she an Ethiope.[1]   intention
LEONATO Call her forth, brother, here's the Friar ready.

            [*Exit* ANTONIO]

40 DON PEDRO Good morrow, Benedick. Why, what's the matter
That you have such a February face,
So full of frost, of storm and cloudiness?
CLAUDIO I think he thinks upon the savage bull.[2]
Tush, fear not, man, we'll tip thy horns with gold,
45 And all Europa° shall rejoice at thee   Europe
As once Europa did at lusty Jove
When he would play the noble beast in love.[3]
BENEDICK Bull Jove, sir, had an amiable° low,   amorous
And some such strange bull leapt your father's cow

---

1. In other words, black and therefore, according to the Elizabethan racist stereotype, ugly.
2. Continuing the teasing of 5.1.172.
3. In Greek mythology, Jove took the form of a bull to carry off the princess Europa, with whom he was in love.

50 And got a calf° in that same noble feat   *begot a blockhead*
    Much like to you, for you have just his bleat.
           Enter [ANTONIO *with*] HERO, BEATRICE, MARGARET, *and*
           URSULA [*masked*]
  CLAUDIO   For this I owe you.[4] Here comes other reck'nings.°   *accounts to settle*
    Which is the lady I must seize upon?
  ANTONIO   This same is she, and I do give you her.
55 CLAUDIO   Why then, she's mine. Sweet, let me see your face.
  LEONATO   No, that you shall not till you take her hand
    Before this Friar and swear to marry her.
  CLAUDIO   [*to* HERO]   Give me your hand before this holy friar.
    I am your husband if you like of me.°   *like me*
60 HERO   [*unmasking*]   And when I lived I was your other wife;
    And when you loved, you were my other husband.
  CLAUDIO   Another Hero!
  HERO   Nothing certainer.
    One Hero died defiled,° but I do live,   *slandered*
    And surely as I live, I am a maid.
65 DON PEDRO   The former Hero, Hero that is dead!
  LEONATO   She died, my lord, but whiles her slander lived.
  FRIAR   All this amazement can I qualify°   *lessen*
    When after that the holy rites are ended
    I'll tell you largely° of fair Hero's death.   *in full*
70   Meantime, let wonder° seem familiar,°   *marvels / commonplace*
    And to the chapel let us presently.
  BENEDICK   Soft and fair,° Friar, which is Beatrice?   *Wait a minute*
  BEATRICE   [*unmasking*]   I answer to that name, what is your will?
  BENEDICK   Do not you love me?
  BEATRICE   Why no, no more than reason.
75 BENEDICK   Why then, your uncle and the Prince and Claudio
    Have been deceived. They swore you did.
  BEATRICE   Do not you love me?
  BENEDICK   Troth no, no more than reason.
  BEATRICE   Why then, my cousin, Margaret, and Ursula
    Are much deceived, for they did swear you did.
80 BENEDICK   They swore that you were almost sick for me.
  BEATRICE   They swore that you were wellnigh dead for me.
  BENEDICK   'Tis no such matter. Then you do not love me?
  BEATRICE   No, truly, but in friendly recompense.
  LEONATO   Come, cousin, I am sure you love the gentleman.
85 CLAUDIO   And I'll be sworn upon't that he loves her,
    For here's a paper written in his hand,
    A halting sonnet of his own pure brain,
    Fashioned° to Beatrice.   *Addressed*
  HERO   And here's another,
    Writ in my cousin's hand, stol'n from her pocket,
90   Containing her affection unto Benedick.
  BENEDICK   A miracle! Here's our own hands against our hearts.[5]
    Come, I will have thee, but by this light, I take thee for pity.
  BEATRICE   I would not deny you, but by this good day, I yield
    upon great persuasion, and partly to save your life, for I was
95   told you were in a consumption.°   *wasting away ill*

---

4. I will pay you back later (for the insults).   indifference we claim to feel in our hearts (or proves
5. Our own handwritten testimony contradicts the   our hearts to be guilty of loving).

BENEDICK [*kissing her*]   Peace, I will stop your mouth.
DON PEDRO   How dost thou, Benedick the married man?
BENEDICK   I'll tell thee what, Prince: a college of wit-crackers
cannot flout° me out of my humour. Dost thou think I care for   *jeer*
a satire or an epigram? No, if a man will be beaten with brains,
a° shall wear nothing handsome about him.[6] In brief, since I   *he*
do purpose° to marry, I will think nothing to any purpose that   *intend*
the world can say against it, and therefore never flout at me for
what I have said against it. For man is a giddy thing, and this is
my conclusion. For thy part, Claudio, I did think to have
beaten thee, but in that thou art like° to be my kinsman, live   *likely*
unbruised, and love my cousin.
CLAUDIO   I had well hoped thou wouldst have denied Beatrice,
that I might have cudgelled thee out of thy single life to make
thee a double dealer,° which out of question thou wilt be, if   *married man; adulterer*
my cousin do not look exceeding narrowly° to thee.   *closely*
BENEDICK   Come, come, we are friends, let's have a dance ere
we are married, that we may lighten our own hearts and our
wives' heels.
LEONATO   We'll have dancing afterward.
BENEDICK   First, of my word. Therefore play, music. [*To* DON
PEDRO] Prince, thou art sad, get thee a wife, get thee a wife.
There is no staff more reverend than one tipped with horn.[7]
            Enter MESSENGER
MESSENGER   My lord, your brother John is ta'en in flight,
And brought with armèd men back to Messina.
BENEDICK   Think not on him till tomorrow, I'll devise thee
brave° punishments for him. Strike up, pipers.   *fine*
            Dance [*and exeunt*]

6. No, if a man is easily injured by ridicule, he will   attention).
never even dare to dress well (since that would provoke   7. A final allusion to the cuckold's horns.

Henry V

From a military point of view, Henry V was perhaps the most capable king England ever had. In 1414, reviving an English royal claim on the French throne, Henry invaded France. The following year, he won the Battle of Agincourt against impossible odds, forcing the King of France to declare him his heir and marry him to his daughter. Not surprisingly, Henry's story was a favorite with his English compatriots. It was lovingly chronicled by the historians Raphael Holinshed (died c. 1580) and Edward Hall (d. 1547), and probably dramatized once or more by other playwrights before Shakespeare brought his own version to the stage in 1599.

Shakespeare's *Henry V* is the last written of a set of eight plays on medieval English history. His first four history plays had dealt with the tumultuous years between 1422 and 1485, when England was first at war with France and then, after 1455, embroiled in a civil war—the Wars of the Roses. Shakespeare wrote another four plays several years later, presenting the events of 1398 to 1420 that led up to these long wars over the royal succession. *Richard II* depicts Henry Bolingbroke's successful rebellion against Richard II and his coronation as Henry IV. The next two plays describe the troubled reign of the usurper, whose former allies turn against him and whose son keeps company with thieves. At the end of *2 Henry IV,* the King dies and young Prince Hal ascends the throne as Henry V, quickly belying his wastrel reputation and proving himself an astute leader in the play that bears his name. In the final lines of *Henry V,* however, the Chorus foresees Henry's imminent death, after which civil strife will break out once again.

Henry V is, therefore, one of a group of plays rather than a freestanding work. It refers constantly to events before and after its own temporal limits, events familiar to Shakespeare's audience from plays they had already seen performed. These references complicate the play's tone considerably. The Chorus's final predictions, for instance, darken the otherwise straightforwardly triumphal conclusion. Surely our awareness of the internecine strife that precedes and follows Henry's reign reinforces our admiration for him—he prospers where others have failed and will again fail, miserably. At the same time, *Henry V* is haunted by problems merely deferred, not resolved; in the long view, its hero's success looks transitory, even futile.

In 1599, such complexities may have seemed especially pertinent. England was mobilizing for a major campaign against Ireland to be led by Elizabeth's dashing young favorite, the Earl of Essex. *Henry V* registers both the patriotic excitement generated by the prospect of a military venture in foreign parts and the dread of war in a notoriously difficult environment (in the event, Essex's expedition was a disaster). These acutely mixed feelings were symptomatic of more general disputes about England's foreign policy. For much of the sixteenth century, England had attempted merely to defend its borders, but as it became wealthier and more powerful, expansion seemed feasible again. Ireland and the Netherlands beckoned; so did the New World, where France and Spain had already established colonies. Henry V's foray into France typified the kind of aggressive enterprise some of Shakespeare's contemporaries wished their nation to underwrite and others denounced as wasteful and dangerous.

Given the circumstances in which *Henry V* was originally written, it is not surprising that it has generated striking interpretive disagreements or that the play continues to be viewed through the lens of contemporary events. In Laurence Olivier's film version, made during World War II, *Henry V* is a vindication of England's excellence, and the victory at Agincourt a hopeful precedent for success in a justified

Henricus v. From John Rastell, *The Pastyme of People* (1529).

European war. Kenneth Branagh's 1989 film, on the other hand, reflects the murkier experience of more recent conflicts: the American intervention in Vietnam, the British in the Falkland Islands. Did Shakespeare intend the play as a paeon to militarism or as an exposé of war's pointless brutality? Is Henry supposed to be a heroic or a repellent character? Is the war in France justified or purely expedient?

Henry's impressive leadership is repeatedly emphasized by the Chorus, by his followers, and even occasionally by his enemies. He not merely copes with, but triumphs over, the difficult circumstances bequeathed him: uniting his disputatious people against an external enemy, spending their aggressions abroad instead of at home, and gaining himself a kingdom to boot. He displays unshakeable personal courage in the campaign in France, in the smaller skirmishes as well as in the desperate moments before Agincourt. His "Once more unto the breach" speech (3.1.1–34) and his prophetic vision of aged veterans boasting to their compatriots on St. Crispin's Day (4.3.41ff.) have often been held up as models of inspirational eloquence.

On the other hand, *Henry V* clear-sightedly acknowledges, as had *Richard II* and *1* and *2 Henry IV*, that the factors that render someone an effective king are not necessarily morally admirable ones. Even while Shakespeare displays Henry's charisma to the full, he refuses to be entirely dazzled by his allure. In the early sixteenth century, Machiavelli had introduced Renaissance political thinkers to the notion that success as a ruler might be separable from, or even inimical to, what was conventionally considered virtuous behavior. A successful leader, he argued, needed the traits of both the fox and the lion: in other words, he had to know how to use deception and violence to achieve his ends. Shakespeare's Henry is certainly no monster of iniquity, but his career poses some of the same questions that Machiavelli raised in *The Prince*. What is the relationship of political success to personal goodness? Should princes be judged by moral rules different from those that apply to the rest of mankind?

A closer look at *Henry V* reveals a play not only deeply equivocal but self-consciously so. The capstone of Shakespeare's years of experimentation in the history play form, *Henry V* seems profoundly aware of the way generic constraints bear in upon its hero. Comedy and tragedy form themselves upon the rhythms of an individual life, ending in marriage or in death. History plays, by contrast, even when they seem to concentrate on the fortunes of a single character, dramatize the life of a nation, or at least its governing class. Characters in history plays are conceived as an endless generational succession, inheriting a political and historical situation from their ancestors and passing it down to their descendants. When one person dies, another steps into his place. The King's marriage represents not merely a natural culmination of his personal story, but one episode in a family's attempt to perpetuate a dynasty.

The young King Henry V is, therefore, both more and less than a talented and intelligent individual. One of a series, like the play that bears his name, he must come to terms with what it means to be part of a family line, what it means for one's "career" to begin before birth and end long after death. And Henry's family line is, of course, a tangled matter. His dubious title to the English throne reflects some of the instabilities in the concept of inheritance: what can it mean to acquire name and title "legitimately" from a man who stole the throne? The passing of property and title from one generation to the next might seem to reflect facts of nature, but it is also, as the Archbishop of Canterbury's discussion of "Salic law" reveals in 1.2, a matter of custom, a cultural construction. Inheritance can be altered as well by force or by negotiation: Henry IV compelled Richard to abdicate, and Henry V's victory at Agincourt requires the French King to recognize an English conqueror rather than his own son as heir to the French throne.

Troubles over the way proper generational sequence ought to be defined resonate throughout the play. War, in particular, seems intimately tied up with questions of lineage. Battlefield heroics can reinforce and clarify the relationship between fathers and sons. King Charles of France, for instance, describes Henry's belligerence as his birthright:

> The kindred of him hath been fleshed upon us,
> And he is bred out of that bloody strain
> That haunted us in our familiar paths.
> Witness our too-much-memorable shame
> When Crécy battle fatally was struck,
> And all our princes captived by the hand
> Of that black name, Edward, Black Prince of Wales,
> Whiles that his mountant sire, on mountain standing,
> Up in the air, crowned with the golden sun,
> Saw his heroical seed and smiled to see him
> Mangle the work of nature and deface
> The patterns that by God and by French fathers
> Had twenty years been made.
>
> (2.4.50–62)

Henry's great-uncle, Edward the Black Prince, butchers the French while the Prince's father, King Edward III, gladly looks on. There seem to be no mothers in this entirely male domain, merely God and fathers in alliance, so that Edward III himself seems rather improbably deified, "up in the air, crowned with the golden sun." Henry, in his stirring speech to his troops at Harfleur, evidences a similar pattern of assumptions:

> On, on, you noblest English,
> Whose blood is fet from fathers of war-proof,
> Fathers that like so many Alexanders
> Have in these parts from morn till even fought,
> And sheathed their swords for lack of argument.
> Dishonor not your mothers; now attest
> That those whom you called fathers did beget you.
>
> (3.1.17–23)

Mothers get a mention from Henry, as they did not from the French King, but they contribute nothing of their own nature to their offspring: their function is merely to duplicate the fathers in the next generation. Any discrepancy between the achievement of the fathers and the achievement of the sons, in fact, "dishonors" the mothers by implying that they must have slept with men other than their husbands, because the only explanation for such an inconsistency is that the biological father must be different from the acknowledged one. Once again, fathers set demanding precedents for sons eager to emulate their exploits but inevitably threatened by the possibility of falling short. The French King and Henry imagine inheritance, which might seem a passive process, as a strenuous endeavor.

If battle clarifies the pedigrees of winners, it simultaneously obscures those of the losers. In practical terms, of course, Henry's victory debars the Dauphin, the French heir apparent, from assuming his father's title. More generally, however, as both Henry and the French King insist, defeat in battle disrupts familial affinity, defacing paternal patterns, dishonoring mothers. Negotiating with Harfleur's governor, Henry predicts the consequences of the town's refusal to surrender quietly:

> why, in a moment look to see
> The blind and bloody soldier with foul hand
> Defile the locks of your shrill-shrieking daughters;
> Your fathers taken by the silver beards,
> And their most reverend heads dashed to the walls;
> Your naked infants spitted upon pikes,
> Whiles the mad mothers with their howls confused
> Do break the clouds, as did the wives of Jewry
> At Herod's bloody-hunting slaughtermen.
>
> (3.3.110–18)

On the face of it, it might seem surprising for a general to characterize his own troops as rapists and murderers, or implicitly to compare himself with the infanticidal King Herod, one of the Bible's wickedest villains. Yet Henry's rhetorical tactics are entirely deliberate: by describing his soldiers' potential victims as members of families—as daughters, fathers, infants, mothers—he heightens the impact of their violence. The rampaging army, he implies, will shatter not merely individuals but whole networks of affiliation. The speech effectively intimidates his auditors, who give up without a fight.

Soldiers using a battering ram. From Flavius Vegetius Renatus, *The Foure Bookes of Flavius Vegetius Renatus: Briefelye contayninge a plaine forme, and perfect knowledge of martiall policye . . .* (1572).

Unfortunately, even soldiers in the "winning" camp, insofar as they are vulnerable to the enemy, are liable to similar familial disasters. Exeter's description of war's misfortunes exempts neither side from calamity, from

> the widows' tears, the orphans' cries,
> The dead men's blood, the pining maidens' groans,
> For husbands, fathers, and betrothèd lovers . . . .
> (2.4.106–08)

Although Henry's invasion leaves the French more bloodied and tearful than the English, the English, too, suffer emotional and practical losses. Henry's soldiers are wasted by disease, hanged, occasionally even killed in battle. In 4.1, the common soldier worries, in an age without veteran's benefits, of dying with "wives left poor behind them" and "children rawly left" (lines 132–34). Henry's insistence on his inheritance rights, in other words, may disrupt not only his enemies' but his subordinates'. If infants are slaughtered, daughters raped, fathers torn from dependents, how can families be reconstituted? How can legitimate inheritance possibly be determined?

The difficulties of succession and inheritance are issues for Shakespeare the playwright as well as for his protagonist. Just as the character Henry V must strive to match and excel the patterns set by his ancestors, so the play *Henry V* must concern itself with what it means to be a sequel in two different senses: the way in which it represents actual historical events in a necessarily diminished theatrical form, and the way in which it must struggle to gratify an audience whose expectations had been formed by three exceedingly popular plays in the same series. At the beginning of every act, a Chorus pointedly emphasizes the play's self-conscious lack of realism:

> Can this cock-pit hold
> The vasty fields of France? Or may we cram
> Within this wooden O the very casques
> That did affright the air at Agincourt?
> (Prologue, lines 11–14)

Of course, *Henry V* is no more implausible than most other Renaissance plays. But in a sense, the theatrical anxieties of *Henry V* are cognate with the personal anxieties of its hero; the play is afraid of degenerating from its precursors, proving an inadequate replica of a distinguished original. And just as Henry V seems to overcompensate, not merely living up to his illustrious predecessors but going beyond them, so, too, *Henry V*, like many sequels, copes with its belatedness by a strategy of overstatement. It exaggerates some of the themes and issues of the earlier plays. In *1 Henry IV*, Hotspur, Prince Hal's valiant antagonist, epitomized many of the traditional ideals of chivalry—a word derived from the French *cheval*, "horse." In *Henry V*, Bourbon, one of Henry's new opponents, writes a sonnet to his horse that begins "Wonder of nature"—for, he says, "my horse is my mistress" (3.7.36–37, 40). Hotspur's chivalry, caricatured to the point of ridiculousness, degenerates in *Henry V* into bestiality jokes made at the expense of a blustering fop.

Shakespeare dramatizes Henry's success, in other words, not merely by magnifying his exploits but by minimizing the threat from possible competitors. Although the enemies of Henry's adulthood are technically more formidable than the enemies of his adolescence, they are characterized as bumbling and laughable, so that Henry's victory over them seems virtually preordained. Henry's allies seem similarly diminished. Falstaff, who dominated much of *1* and *2 Henry IV*, dies without reappearing in *Henry V*, leaving his cronies Bardolph, Nim, and Pistol to accompany Henry to France. They are joined by Fluellen, a Welsh soldier; MacMorris, an Irish one; Jamy, a Scots one; and Williams, a rural English one. This miscellany is proof of Henry's charisma; while in the previous plays the Irish, Scots, and Welsh were up in arms, Henry V successfully enlists them in his cause—not by homogenizing their differences, but by inspiring their allegiance to him even as they quarrel furiously with one another. Henry's triumph at Agincourt, Shakespeare claims, involves all the peoples of the British Isles. At the same time, these loyal adherents are given little of Falstaff's subversive wit, presumably because Falstaff's wholesale critique of military valor would undercut too thoroughly the premises of Henry's royal magnetism. Even the bluff yeoman Williams, who complains of the disproportionate suffering common people undergo to satisfy the ambitions of their betters, does not dissent from the fundamental principle of social and military hierarchy: to disobey one's superiors, he claims, "were against all proportion of subjection" (4.1.138). For better or worse, everyone seems to agree, the subject's life is at the ruler's disposal.

Shakespeare's excision of Falstaff's skeptical intelligence from *Henry V* means that there is no one within the play to point out the ironies of many of the turns of the plot. Presumably, though no one comments explicitly upon it, the venality of the clerics who finance Henry's expedition to France is sufficiently clear to the audience. Likewise, when Gower loyally remarks that Henry, unlike Alexander, never killed any of his friends, we are likely to think back to Falstaff's death, attributed earlier to Henry's neglect, and also to reflect that of Henry's other Eastcheap chums only Pistol has survived the "great victory" at Agincourt. Elsewhere it is unclear how or even whether the audience is expected to grasp an irony. In 1.1, Henry decides to press his claim on the French throne through the female line of descent. Shortly thereafter, he executes three erstwhile friends for conspiring against his life. In fact their plot was inspired by the conviction that Henry's title to the English throne was obstructed by the Earl of Mortimer's daughter, the Earl of Cambridge's wife. In other words, Henry employs against the French a principle that, if it were enforced against him, would strip him of both English and French kingdoms. Yet the point is made so obliquely that only a spectator cognizant of the tangled Plantagenet genealogy is likely to catch it.

As the stature of Henry's foes and associates diminishes, the ethical problems posed by his exploits are correspondingly aggravated. As we have already seen, Henry's self-assertion necessarily occurs at the expense of others, thereby raising the question of the extent to which his interests ought to take precedence over competing claims. Neither we nor Henry can be certain whether his exceptional situation and abilities exempt him from the criteria by which common persons are judged. In fact, Henry's unusual gifts as a leader render the uncertainty more pointed. Richard II disregarded common folk, and Henry IV deliberately avoided them; but Henry V inspires them by his capacity to immerse himself sympathetically in their lives. His insistence upon his ordinariness becomes a strategy of rule—part of what he is loved for during his lifetime and what becomes legendary after his death. But then, when he insists on seeing himself as a unique case nonetheless, he seems not merely to be asserting a King's usual prerogatives, but to be inconsistently or hypocritically making special allowances for himself.

This unresolved ambivalence becomes obvious in 4.1, when Henry disguises himself as a commoner and ventures among his rank and file. Initially, he argues for the essential similarity between himself and his followers.

> I think the King is but a man, as I am. The violet smells to him as it doth to me; the element shows to him as it doth to me. All his senses have but human conditions. His ceremonies laid by, in his nakedness he appears but a man, and though his affections are higher mounted than ours, yet when they stoop, they stoop with the like wing. (lines 99–104)

The ordinary soldiers, Williams and Bates, are unconvinced, pointing out that if they lose the battle, the King will be ransomed while they will be killed. On the other hand, they note, because they are required to obey the King under any circumstances, they need not concern themselves with the justice of the King's cause: their blood will be on Henry's head if he is waging an unjust war. The common soldiers see the King as unlike themselves, with special responsibilities that compensate for his special privileges. Henry responds indignantly:

> The King is not bound to answer the particular endings of his soldiers, the father of his son, nor the master of his servant, for they purpose not their deaths when they propose their services. Besides, there is no king, be his cause never so spotless, if it come to the arbitrament of swords, can try it out with all unspotted soldiers. Some, peradventure, have on them the guilt of premeditated and contrived murder; some, of beguiling virgins with the broken seals of perjury; some, making the wars their bulwark, that have before gored the gentle bosom of peace with pillage and robbery. (lines 146–55)

Henry resists accepting the extraordinary moral burden his followers would confer upon him. Yet his refusal is based not on his earlier assertion of the shared humanity of king and subject, but on a conviction of the king's special position. He distinguishes sharply and problematically between the king's "superior" violence—the violence of war—and the violence of individual subjects, which is merely criminal. After the soldiers leave, Henry exclaims bitterly:

> Upon the King.
> 'Let us our lives, our souls, our debts, our care-full wives,
> Our children, and our sins, lay on the King.'
> We must bear all. O hard condition,
> Twin-born with greatness: subject to the breath
> Of every fool, whose sense no more can feel
> But his own wringing. What infinite heartsease
> Must kings neglect that private men enjoy?
>
> (lines 212–19)

It is hard to take this self-pity seriously, given that Henry attempts to deflect all blame for his actions onto enemies and inferiors, even while accepting as his due the rewards that accrue to him by virtue of his exceptional status.

On the other hand, Shakespeare also shows effectively the King's genuine isolation from ordinary pleasures of work and play that normal people can take for granted. Though he repudiates Falstaff, the King retains a distinctly sportive quality; but the moral and practical gap that yawns between the ascendant Henry and his correspondingly diminished associates complicates the effect of his playfulness. In 2.2, with a typical flourish, he pretends to hand the traitors Scrope, Grey, and Cambridge their military commissions, after feigning to inquire about mercy for traitors. Actually, he gives them letters showing that he knows of their plot. This is splendid theater, but it is also quite chilling: Henry plays with his guilty victims as a cat plays with a mouse. His joke signifies not true contest, but absolute control.

Elsewhere, too, Henry's power tips the balance of hostility and affection that usually characterizes practical jokes in a markedly aggressive direction. In disguise on the eve of the Battle of Agincourt, he argues with the commoner Williams, as we have already seen, over the question of the king's responsibility for his subjects. He and Williams exchange gloves so they will be able to resume the quarrel after the battle. In 4.7, with victory assured, Henry gives Williams's glove to Fluellen to see what Williams will do when he sees it again. When Williams attacks Fluellen, Henry stops the fight, pretending to be angry at the insult to himself. Williams—technically guilty of the capital crime of mutiny—defends himself boldly enough, and Henry, thinking to be generous, returns Williams's glove to him filled with coins. Yet Williams fails to thank Henry, and when Fluellen attempts to add to the gift, he spurns it angrily. It is unclear from the script whether Williams eventually accepts the gold; either way, Henry's power contaminates what he wants to see as a game. While in the earlier plays Prince Hal always had the advantage of rank, it was still possible for Falstaff to give him almost as

Game of tennis. From Johann Amos Comenius, *Orbis Sensualium Pictus* (1659).

good as he got. Now that Henry is king and Falstaff is dead, Henry is always the winner, and so the game is no game at all. Arguably, in fact, Henry goes to war with France because he misses a sense of *competition*—because the fate of the effective king is that he cannot find real opposition at home.

Henry's wooing of Catherine in 5.2 is typified by the same dubious sense of fun. This scene, often quite endearing onstage, is also entirely beside the point. We hear from the Chorus in 3.0 that the French King offered Catherine to Henry before his forces arrived in France, but he rejected the offer because the suggested dowry—some "petty and unprofitable dukedoms"—did not suffice. Nonetheless, in 5.2, Henry calls Catherine his "capital demand" and presents himself to her as a wooer. He pretends that Catherine is free to reject him, even though the marriage is already arranged as part of the peace treaty. Rather like Williams, Catherine refuses to play along: when he asks, "Canst thou love me?" she replies, "I cannot tell." "Wilt thou have me?" "Dat is as it shall please de *roi mon père*" (lines 183ff.). Is Catherine being coy, or is she simply speaking the literal truth? In the game as Henry constructs it, Catherine's refusals can as easily be interpreted as coquettishness as real denial. In other words, even if she refuses to play Henry's game, she necessarily plays it anyhow. In *Henry V*, Shakespeare must cope with a knotty dramatic problem: how to interest an audience in a man who has, or wins, everything—whose life seems an unbroken series of successes. In the final scene as in the rest of the play, Shakespeare fascinates us by exhibiting the inevitably equivocal nature of kingly glory.

KATHARINE EISAMAN MAUS

TEXTUAL NOTE

Henry V exists in the 1623 First Folio (F) version and in a quarto version first issued in 1600 and reprinted in 1602 and 1619. The Folio version is generally accepted as the most authoritative text and was probably derived from Shakespeare's "foul papers," or manuscript, but there are also signs that the compositor consulted the 1619 Quarto

(Q3) when setting up the Folio text. F is not, however, a wholly reliable source; it contains a fairly large number of readings rejected by modern editors, probably the result of a compositor misreading a handwritten text. The Oxford editors argue that Q, although printed much earlier than F and obviously corrupt in some respects, actually represents a later stage of the text and may therefore incorporate some of Shakespeare's second thoughts and modifications. They believe that Q is based on memorial reconstruction by actors who played the parts of Exeter and Gower, for the text is far more reliable when these characters are onstage than for other scenes.

The quarto text also has a slightly different cast of characters than Folio's: F's Bedford is Q's Clarence, F's Westmoreland is Q's Warwick, and speeches assigned in F to Britain and to the Dauphin in the Agincourt scenes are given to Bourbon in Q. The most important substitution is the last, Bourbon's replacement of the Dauphin in 3.7, 4.2, and 4.5. In F, the Dauphin's substantial role sets him up as Henry's personal adversary, much as Hotspur was in *1 Henry IV*. Also in F, the Dauphin's amply demonstrated folly seems to warrant his eventual displacement by Henry. The quarto speech assignments, on the other hand, are consistent with King Charles's order in 3.5 that the Dauphin remain with him at Rouen. In Q, the Dauphin's absence from the battlefield, rather than his extravagantly frivolous presence, implies his unfitness for rule.

Although most editors accept the Folio speech assignments, Gary Taylor, editor of the Oxford text, argues that Shakespeare in fact vacillated about whether to include the Dauphin in the Agincourt scenes and that Q represents his final decision not to do so. In consequence, although F remains the Oxford control text, Taylor adopts many more readings from Q than do most editors. In this respect, the Oxford *Henry V* seems to depart from the editors' usual policy of not conflating distinctly different texts of the same play (the policy that produces the two *King Lear*s later in this volume). Taylor provides information on the tangled textual history of the play and a full explanation of his editorial choices in his single-volume edition of *Henry V* (Oxford: Clarendon, 1982).

SELECTED BIBLIOGRAPHY

Altman, Joel. "'Vile Participation': The Amplification of Violence in the Theatre of *Henry V*." *Shakespeare Quarterly* 42 (1991): 1–32. *Henry V* in the context of contemporary political and religious issues—in particular, the debate over the nature of Communion.

Barton, Anne. "The King Disguised: Shakespeare's *Henry V* and the Comical History." *The Triple Bond: Plays, Mainly Shakespearean, in Performance*. Ed. Joseph G. Price. University Park: Pennsylvania State University Press, 1975. 92–117. Sees *Henry V* in a tradition of Elizabethan plays that combine history and comedy.

Cormack, Bradin. "'If We Be Conquered': Legal Nationalism and the France of Shakespeare's English Histories." *A Power to Do Justice: Jurisdiction and Early English Literature*. Chicago: University of Chicago Press, 2007. Shakespeare's treatment of France and the French language in terms of sixteenth-century English anxieties about national identity.

Danson, Lawrence. "*Henry V*: King, Chorus, and Critics." *Shakespeare Quarterly* 34 (1983): 27–43. King Henry as an actor; the Chorus as a means of drawing attention to the relationship between history and theater.

Dollimore, Jonathan, and Alan Sinfield. "History and Ideology, Masculinity and Miscegenation." *Faultlines: Cultural Materialism and the Politics of Dissident Reading*. By Alan Sinfield. Berkeley: University of California Press, 1992. 109–42. Imperialist and masculinist attitudes reinforce one another in the play.

Greenblatt, Stephen. "Invisible Bullets: Renaissance Authority and Its Subversion, *Henry IV* and *Henry V*." *Political Shakespeare: New Essays in Cultural Materialism*. Ed. Jonathan Dollimore and Alan Sinfield. Manchester: Manchester University

Press, 1985. 18–47. Theater and the glamour of a royal power that incorporates what seems to undermine it.

Ornstein, Robert. *"Henry V." A Kingdom for a Stage: The Achievement of Shakespeare's History Plays.* Cambridge, Mass.: Harvard University Press, 1972. 175–202. *Henry V* as an equivocal celebration of the King's victories.

Quint, David. "Alexander the Pig: Shakespeare on History and Poetry." *Boundary* 2 10 (1982): 49–63. Shakespeare's relation to Renaissance humanists' conceptions of history.

Rabkin, Norman. "Rabbits, Ducks, and *Henry V*." *Shakespeare Quarterly* 28 (1977): 279–96. *Henry V* as an unresolvably ambiguous play.

Wells, Stanley, with Gary Taylor. *Modernizing Shakespeare's Spelling* [Wells], *with Three Studies in the Text of "Henry V"* [Taylor]. Oxford: Clarendon, 1979. Provides the scholarly rationale for the textual editing of the Oxford/Norton version of the play.

FILMS

Henry V. 1944. Dir. Laurence Olivier. UK. 137 min. Colorful, patriotic version made near the end of World War II, with Oliver as a very sympathetic king. Intelligently translates the play's theatrical self-consciousness to the film medium.

Henry V. 1979. Dir. David Giles. UK. 163 min. This BBC-TV production retains more features of a stage production than do the elaborate Olivier and Branagh versions. David Gwillim is a pleasant but resolute hero.

Henry V. 1989. Dir. Kenneth Branagh. UK. 137 min. Harsher and more violent than the Olivier version, with an elaborate reenactment of the Battle of Agincourt. Branagh stars as a grimly driven Henry.

The Life of Henry the Fifth

THE PERSONS OF THE PLAY

CHORUS
KING HARRY V of England, claimant to the French throne
Duke of GLOUCESTER }
Duke of CLARENCE } his brothers
Duke of EXETER, his uncle
Duke of YORK
SALISBURY
WESTMORLAND
WARWICK
Archbishop of CANTERBURY
Bishop of ELY
Richard, Earl of CAMBRIDGE }
Henry, Lord SCROPE of Masham } traitors
Sir Thomas GREY
PISTOL }
NIM } formerly Falstaff's companions
BARDOLPH
BOY, formerly Falstaff's page
HOSTESS, formerly Mistress Quickly, now Pistol's wife
Captain GOWER, an Englishman
Captain FLUELLEN, a Welshman
Captain MACMORRIS, an Irishman
Captain JAMY, a Scot
Sir Thomas ERPINGHAM
John BATES }
Alexander COURT } English soldiers
Michael WILLIAMS
HERALD
KING CHARLES VI of France
ISABEL, his wife and queen
The DAUPHIN, their son and heir
CATHERINE, their daughter
ALICE, an old gentlewoman
The CONSTABLE of France }
Duke of BOURBON
Duke of ORLÉANS
Duke of BERRI } French noblemen at Agincourt
Lord RAMBURES
Lord GRANDPRÉ
Duke of BURGUNDY
MONTJOY, the French Herald
GOVERNOR of Harfleur
French AMBASSADORS to England

Prologue

Enter [CHORUS as] Prologue

CHORUS   O for a muse of fire, that would ascend
The brightest heaven of invention:°   *imagination*
A kingdom for a stage, princes to act,
And monarchs to behold the swelling° scene.   *expansive; splendid*
5   Then should the warlike Harry, like himself,
Assume the port° of Mars,° and at his heels,   *bearing / god of war*
Leashed in like hounds, should famine, sword, and fire
Crouch for employment. But pardon, gentles° all,   *gentlefolk*
The flat unraisèd° spirits that hath dared   *uninspired*
10   On this unworthy scaffold° to bring forth   *platform*
So great an object. Can this cock-pit° hold   *small cockfighting arena*
The vasty fields of France? Or may we cram
Within this wooden O° the very casques°   *round theater / helmets*
That did affright the air at Agincourt?[1]
15   O pardon: since a crookèd figure[2] may
Attest° in little place a million,   *Represent*
And let us, ciphers° to this great account,°   *zeroes / sum; story*
On your imaginary forces° work.   *powers of imagination*
Suppose within the girdle of these walls
20   Are now confined two mighty monarchies,
Whose high uprearèd and abutting fronts°   *frontiers*
The perilous narrow ocean° parts asunder.   *(English Channel)*
Piece out our imperfections with your thoughts:
Into a thousand parts divide one man,
25   And make imaginary puissance.°   *power*
Think, when we talk of horses, that you see them,
Printing their proud hoofs i'th' receiving earth;
For 'tis your thoughts that now must deck° our kings,   *equip*
Carry them here and there, jumping o'er times,
30   Turning th'accomplishment of many years
Into an hourglass—for the which supply,°   *to supplement which*
Admit me Chorus to this history,
Who Prologue-like your humble patience pray
Gently to hear, kindly to judge, our play.   *Exit*

1.1

*Enter the [Archbishop] of CANTERBURY and [the Bishop
of] ELY*

CANTERBURY   My lord, I'll tell you. That self ° bill is urged   *same*
Which in th'eleventh year of the last king's reign
Was like,° and had indeed against us passed,   *likely*
But that the scrambling and unquiet time
5   Did push it out of farther question.°   *consideration*
ELY   But how, my lord, shall we resist it now?
CANTERBURY   It must be thought on. If it pass against us,
We lose the better half of our possession,
For all the temporal lands[1] which men devout
10   By testament have given to the Church
Would they strip from us—being valued thus:

---

1. Site of Henry's famous victory over the French in 1415.
2. A zero, which multiplies a digit's value by ten.

crookèd: curved.
1.1 Location: In Henry's court.
1. Land devoted to secular uses.

As much as would maintain, to the King's honour,
Full fifteen earls and fifteen hundred knights,
Six thousand and two hundred good esquires;[2]
15 And, to relief of lazars° and weak age,   *lepers*
Of indigent faint souls past corporal° toil,   *bodily*
A hundred almshouses right well supplied;
And to the coffers of the King beside
A thousand pounds by th' year. Thus runs the bill.
20 ELY   This would drink deep.
CANTERBURY   'Twould drink the cup and all.
ELY   But what prevention?
CANTERBURY   The King is full of grace and fair regard.°   *kindly inclination*
ELY   And a true lover of the holy Church.
25 CANTERBURY   The courses of his youth promised it not.
The breath no sooner left his father's body
But that his wildness, mortified° in him,   *struck dead*
Seemed to die too. Yea, at that very moment
Consideration° like an angel came   *Spiritual reflection*
30 And whipped th'offending Adam° out of him,   *innate depravity*
Leaving his body as a paradise
T'envelop and contain celestial spirits.
Never was such a sudden scholar made;
Never came reformation in a flood
35 With such a heady currance° scouring faults;   *headlong current*
Nor never Hydra-headed[3] wilfulness
So soon did lose his seat°—and all at once—   *throne*
As in this king.
ELY   We are blessèd in the change.
CANTERBURY   Hear him but reason in divinity°   *theology*
40 And, all-admiring, with an inward wish
You would desire the King were made a prelate;°   *an important clergyman*
Hear him debate of commonwealth affairs,
You would say it hath been all-in-all his study;
List° his discourse of war, and you shall hear   *Listen to*
45 A fearful battle rendered you in music;
Turn him to any cause of policy,°   *political issue*
The Gordian knot[4] of it he will unloose,
Familiar° as his garter—that when he speaks,   *Offhandedly*
The air, a chartered libertine,° is still,   *licensed freedman*
50 And the mute wonder lurketh in men's ears
To steal his sweet and honeyed sentences:
So that the art and practic part of life
Must be the mistress to this theoric.[5]
Which is a wonder how his grace should glean it,
55 Since his addiction° was to courses vain,   *inclination*
His companies° unlettered, rude, and shallow,   *companions*
His hours filled up with riots,° banquets, sports,   *reveling*
And never noted in him any study,
Any retirement, any sequestration°   *removal*
60 From open haunts and popularity.[6]

---

2. Gentlemen below knightly rank.
3. Many-headed (the Hydra was a monstrous snake, killed by Hercules).
4. It was foretold that whoever untied the intricate Gordian knot would rule Asia; Alexander the Great cut it with his sword.
5. *the art . . . theoric*: practical experience must have taught him the theory.
6. From public places and unrefined companions.

ELY   The strawberry grows underneath the nettle,
    And wholesome berries thrive and ripen best
    Neighboured by fruit of baser quality;
    And so the Prince obscured his contemplation
65   Under the veil of wildness—which, no doubt,
    Grew like the summer grass, fastest by night,
    Unseen, yet crescive in his faculty.[7]
CANTERBURY   It must be so, for miracles are ceased,[8]
    And therefore we must needs admit the means°   *natural causes*
    How things are perfected.
70 ELY   But, my good lord,
    How now for mitigation of this bill
    Urged by the Commons? Doth his majesty
    Incline to it, or no?
CANTERBURY   He seems indifferent,
    Or rather swaying more upon our part
75   Than cherishing th'exhibitors[9] against us;
    For I have made an offer to his majesty,
    Upon our spiritual convocation[1]
    And in regard of causes now in hand,
    Which I have opened° to his grace at large: *expounded*
80   As touching France, to give a greater sum
    Than ever at one time the clergy yet
    Did to his predecessors part withal.°   *with*
ELY   How did this offer seem received, my lord?
CANTERBURY   With good acceptance of his majesty,
85   Save that there was not time enough to hear,
    As I perceived his grace would fain° have done,   *gladly*
    The severals[2] and unhidden passages°   *channels of descent*
    Of his true titles to some certain dukedoms,
    And generally to the crown and seat of France,
90   Derived from Edward,° his great-grandfather.   *King Edward III*
ELY   What was th'impediment that broke this off?
CANTERBURY   The French ambassador upon that instant
    Craved audience—and the hour I think is come
    To give him hearing. Is it four o'clock?
95 ELY   It is.
CANTERBURY   Then go we in, to know his embassy°—   *message*
    Which I could with a ready guess declare
    Before the Frenchman speak a word of it.
ELY   I'll wait upon you, and I long to hear it.   *Exeunt*

1.2

Enter KING [HARRY, *the Dukes of* GLOUCESTER], CLARENCE, *and*
    EXETER, [*and the Earls of*] WARWICK [*and*] WESTMORLAND
KING HARRY   Where is my gracious lord of Canterbury?
EXETER   Not here in presence.
KING HARRY   Send for him, good uncle.
WESTMORLAND   Shall we call in th'ambassador, my liege?

---

7. Yet growing according to its natural ability.
8. Protestants believed that no miracles occurred after scriptural times (anachronistic in the mouth of a medieval archbishop).
9. Parliamentary sponsors of the bill.

1. On behalf of the assembled clergy.
2. Legal means by which land is conveyed in separate parts to different heirs.
1.2 Location: The royal court.

KING HARRY   Not yet, my cousin.[1] We would be resolved,
5   Before we hear him, of some things of weight
    That task° our thoughts, concerning us and France.   *exercise*
        Enter [Archbishop of CANTERBURY *and Bishop of* ELY]
CANTERBURY   God and his angels guard your sacred throne,
    And make you long become° it.   *adorn*
KING HARRY   Sure we thank you.
    My learnèd lord, we pray you to proceed,
10   And justly and religiously unfold
    Why the law Salic[2] that they have in France
    Or° should or should not bar us in our claim.   *Either*
    And God forbid, my dear and faithful lord,
    That you should fashion, wrest, or bow your reading,[3]
15   Or nicely charge° your understanding soul   *foolishly burden*
    With opening titles miscreate,[4] whose right
    Suits not in native colours° with the truth;   *Does not accord*
    For God doth know how many now in health
    Shall drop their blood in approbation°   *confirmation*
20   Of what your reverence shall incite us to.
    Therefore take heed how you impawn° our person,   *pledge*
    How you awake our sleeping sword of war;
    We charge you in the name of God take heed.
    For never two such kingdoms did contend
25   Without much fall of blood, whose guiltless drops
    Are every one a woe, a sore complaint
    'Gainst him whose wrongs gives edge unto the swords
    That makes such waste in brief mortality.°   *short-lived humankind*
    Under this conjuration° speak, my lord,   *injunction*
30   For we will hear, note, and believe in heart
    That what you speak is in your conscience washed
    As pure as sin with baptism.
CANTERBURY   Then hear me, gracious sovereign, and you peers
    That owe your selves, your lives, and services
35   To this imperial throne. There is no bar
    To make against your highness' claim to France
    But this, which they produce from Pharamond:°   *legendary French King*
    'In terram Salicam mulieres ne succedant'—
    'No woman shall succeed in Salic[5] land'—
40   Which 'Salic land' the French unjustly gloss°   *interpret*
    To be the realm of France, and Pharamond
    The founder of this law and female bar.[6]
    Yet their own authors faithfully affirm
    That the land Salic is in Germany,
45   Between the floods° of Saale and of Elbe,   *rivers*
    Where, Charles the Great having subdued the Saxons,
    There left behind and settled certain French
    Who, holding in disdain the German women
    For some dishonest° manners of their life,   *unchaste*
50   Established there this law: to wit, no female
    Should be inheritrix in Salic land—
    Which Salic, as I said, 'twixt Elbe and Saale,

---

1. Kinsman; complimentary form of address from King to nobles.
2. Explained below, lines 35ff.
3. Should shape, pervert, or bend your interpretation.
4. With explicating false property rights.
5. Referring to an ancient Frankish tribe that lived beside the Rhine River.
6. And prohibition of female inheritance.

Is at this day in Germany called Meissen.
Then doth it well appear the Salic Law
55   Was not devisèd for the realm of France.
Nor did the French possess the Salic land
Until four hundred one-and-twenty years
After defunction° of King Pharamond,   *death*
Idly° supposed the founder of this law,   *Foolishly*
60   Who died within the year of our redemption°   A.D.
Four hundred twenty-six; and Charles the Great°   *Charlemagne*
Subdued the Saxons, and did seat° the French   *establish*
Beyond the river Saale, in the year
Eight hundred five. Besides, their writers say,
65   King Pépin, which deposèd Childéric,
Did, as heir general[7]—being descended
Of Blithild, which was daughter to King Clotaire—
Make claim and title to the crown of France.
Hugh Capet also—who usurped the crown
70   Of Charles the Duke of Lorraine, sole heir male
Of the true line and stock of Charles the Great—
To fine° his title with some shows of truth,   *complete; purify*
Though in pure truth it was corrupt and naught,
Conveyed himself as heir to th' Lady Lingard,
75   Daughter to Charlemain, who was the son
To Louis the Emperor, and Louis the son
Of Charles the Great. Also, King Louis the Ninth,
Who was sole heir to the usurper Capet,
Could not keep quiet in his conscience,
80   Wearing the crown of France, till satisfied
That fair Queen Isabel, his grandmother,
Was lineal of ° the Lady Ermengarde,   *descended from*
Daughter to Charles, the foresaid Duke of Lorraine;
By the which marriage, the line of Charles the Great
85   Was reunited to the crown of France.
So that, as clear as is the summer's sun,
King Pépin's title and Hugh Capet's claim,
King Louis his° satisfaction, all appear   *(Louis's)*
To hold in right and title of the female;
90   So do the kings of France unto this day,
Howbeit they would hold up this Salic Law
To bar your highness claiming from the female,
And rather choose to hide them in a net°   *complexities*
Than amply to embar° their crookèd titles,   *frankly to rule out*
95   Usurped from you and your progenitors.
KING HARRY   May I with right and conscience make this claim?
CANTERBURY   The sin upon my head, dread sovereign.
For in the Book of Numbers° is it writ,   *Numbers 27:8*
'When the son dies, let the inheritance
100   Descend unto the daughter.' Gracious lord,
Stand for your own; unwind your bloody flag;
Look back into your mighty ancestors.
Go, my dread lord, to your great-grandsire's tomb,
From whom you claim;[8] invoke his warlike spirit,

7. One who inherits through either the male or female line.   8. Edward III claimed the French throne through his mother, Isabella.

105   And your great-uncle's, Edward the Black Prince,
        Who on the French ground played a tragedy,
        Making defeat° on the full power of France,   *(at Crécy, in 1346)*
        Whiles his most mighty father° on a hill   *(Edward III)*
        Stood smiling to behold his lion's whelp
110   Forage in blood of French nobility.
        O noble English, that could entertain°   *encounter*
        With half their forces the full pride of France,
        And let another half stand laughing by,
        All out of work, and cold for° action.   *for want of*
115 ELY   Awake remembrance of those valiant dead,
        And with your puissant° arm renew their feats.   *powerful*
        You are their heir, you sit upon their throne,
        The blood and courage that renownèd them°   *made them famous*
        Runs in your veins—and my thrice-puissant liege
120   Is in the very May-morn of his youth,
        Ripe for exploits and mighty enterprises.
    EXETER   Your brother kings and monarchs of the earth
        Do all expect that you should rouse yourself
        As did the former lions of your blood.
125 WESTMORLAND   They know your grace hath cause; and means and might,
        So hath your highness. Never king of England
        Had nobles richer and more loyal subjects,
        Whose hearts have left their bodies here in England
        And lie pavilioned° in the fields of France.   *encamped*
130 CANTERBURY   O let their bodies follow, my dear liege,
        With blood and sword and fire, to win your right.
        In aid whereof, we of the spiritualty°   *clergy*
        Will raise your highness such a mighty sum
        As never did the clergy at one time
135   Bring in to any of your ancestors.
    KING HARRY   We must not only arm t'invade the French,
        But lay down our proportions[9] to defend
        Against the Scot, who will make raid upon us
        With all advantages.°   *Given any opportunity*
140 CANTERBURY   They of those marches,° gracious sovereign,   *borderlands*
        Shall be a wall sufficient to defend
        Our inland from the pilfering borderers.
    KING HARRY   We do not mean the coursing snatchers° only,   *mounted raiders*
        But fear the main intendment° of the Scot,   *hostile intention*
145   Who hath been still a giddy° neighbour to us.   *always an unreliable*
        For you shall read that my great-grandfather
        Never unmasked his power unto France
        But that the Scot on his unfurnished° kingdom   *unprotected*
        Came pouring like the tide into a breach°   *gap in a dike*
150   With ample and brim fullness of his force
        Galling° the gleanèd° land with hot assays,°   *Hurting / depleted / attacks*
        Girding with grievous siege castles and towns,
        That England, being empty of defence,
        Hath shook and trembled at the bruit° thereof.   *noise*
155 CANTERBURY   She hath been then more feared than harmed, my liege.
        For hear her but exampled° by herself :   *given an example*
        When all her chivalry hath been in France

---

9. Decide the distribution of our forces.

And she a mourning widow of her nobles,
She hath herself not only well defended
160 But taken and impounded as a stray
The King of Scots,[1] whom she did send to France
To fill King Edward's fame with prisoner kings
And make your chronicle as rich with praise
As is the ooze and bottom of the sea
165 With sunken wrack° and sumless treasuries.[2]   shipwrecks
A LORD   But there's a saying very old and true:
            'If that you will France win,
            Then with Scotland first begin.'
For once the eagle England being in prey,°   out hunting
170 To her unguarded nest the weasel Scot
Comes sneaking, and so sucks her princely eggs,
Playing the mouse in absence of the cat,
To 'tame[3] and havoc° more than she can eat.   spoil
EXETER   It follows then the cat must stay at home.
175 Yet that is but a crushed° necessity,   forced
Since we have locks to safeguard necessaries
And pretty° traps to catch the petty thieves.   clever
While that the armèd hand doth fight abroad,
Th'advisèd° head defends itself at home.   well-advised
180 For government, though high and low and lower,[4]
Put into parts,[5] doth keep in one consent,°   harmony
Congreeing° in a full and natural close,°   Coming together / cadence
Like music.
CANTERBURY   True. Therefore doth heaven divide
The state of man in divers functions,
185 Setting endeavour in continual motion;
To which is fixèd, as an aim or butt,°   target
Obedience. For so work the honey-bees,
Creatures that by a rule in nature teach
The act of order to a peopled kingdom.
190 They have a king,[6] and officers of sorts,
Where some like magistrates correct at home;
Others like merchants venture trade abroad;
Others like soldiers, armèd in their stings,
Make boot upon° the summer's velvet buds,   Plunder
195 Which pillage they with merry march bring home
To the tent royal of their emperor,
Who busied in his majesty surveys
The singing masons building roofs of gold,
The civil citizens lading° up the honey,   weighing
200 The poor mechanic° porters crowding in   menial
Their heavy burdens at his narrow gate,
The sad-eyed justice with his surly hum
Delivering o'er to executors° pale   executioners
The lazy yawning drone. I this infer:
205 That many things, having full reference
To one consent,[7] may work contrariously.°   disparately

1. David II of Scotland, taken prisoner in 1346, when   4. That is, composed of three social classes.
Edward III was in France; actually, he was imprisoned   5. Divided into different functions.
in London.   6. The queen bee was thought to be male.
2. Incalculable riches.   7. *having . . . consent:* united by a common purpose.
3. Attame, or meddle with.

As many arrows, loosèd several ways,°   *from different places*
Fly to one mark, as many ways meet in one town,
As many fresh streams meet in one salt sea,
210   As many lines close in the dial's° centre,   *sundial's*
So may a thousand actions once afoot
End in one purpose, and be all well borne
Without defect. Therefore to France, my liege.
Divide your happy England into four,
215   Whereof take you one quarter into France,
And you withal shall make all Gallia° shake.   *France*
If we with thrice such powers left at home
Cannot defend our own doors from the dog,
Let us be worried,° and our nation lose   *savaged*
220   The name° of hardiness and policy.[8]   *reputation*
KING HARRY   Call in the messengers sent from the Dauphin.[9]
                         [Exit one or more]
Now are we well resolved, and by God's help
And yours, the noble sinews of our power,
France being ours we'll bend it to our awe,°   *make it submit to us*
225   Or break it all to pieces. Or° there we'll sit,   *Either*
Ruling in large and ample empery°   *sovereignty*
O'er France and all her almost kingly dukedoms,
Or lay these bones in an unworthy urn,
Tombless, with no remembrance over them.
230   Either our history shall with full mouth
Speak freely of our acts, or else our grave,
Like Turkish mute,[1] shall have a tongueless mouth,
Not worshipped with a waxen epitaph.[2]
      Enter AMBASSADORS *of France [with a tun]°*   *chest; barrel*
Now are we well prepared to know the pleasure
235   Of our fair cousin Dauphin, for we hear
Your greeting is from him, not from the King.
AMBASSADOR   May't please your majesty to give us leave
Freely to render what we have in charge,
Or shall we sparingly show you far off [3]
240   The Dauphin's meaning and our embassy?
KING HARRY   We are no tyrant, but a Christian king,
Unto whose grace our passion is as subject
As is our wretches fettered in our prisons.
Therefore with frank and with uncurbèd plainness
Tell us the Dauphin's mind.
245   AMBASSADOR   Thus then in few:°   *short*
Your highness lately sending into France
Did claim some certain dukedoms, in the right
Of your great predecessor, King Edward the Third.
In answer of which claim, the Prince our master
250   Says that you savour° too much of your youth,   *show traces*
And bids you be advised, there's naught in France
That can be with a nimble galliard° won: *lively dance*
You cannot revel into dukedoms there.
He therefore sends you, meeter° for your spirit,   *more appropriate*

---

8. Political discernment.
9. Title of the French heir apparent.
1. Turkish harem attendants were reportedly castrated

and deprived of speech.
2. Not dignified with (even) a perishable memorial.
3. Show you in an abridged and roundabout way.

255   This tun of treasure, and in lieu of this
      Desires you let the dukedoms that you claim
      Hear no more of you. This the Dauphin speaks.
      KING HARRY   What treasure, uncle?
      EXETER [*opening the tun*]   Tennis balls, my liege.
      KING HARRY   We are glad the Dauphin is so pleasant° with us.   *jocular*
260   His present and your pains we thank you for.
      When we have matched our rackets to these balls,
      We will in France, by God's grace, play a set
      Shall strike his father's crown° into the hazard.⁴   *royal crown; coin*
      Tell him he hath made a match with such a wrangler
265   That all the courts of France will be disturbed
      With chases.⁵ And we understand him well,
      How he comes o'er° us with our wilder days,   *taunts*
      Not measuring what use we made of them.
      We never valued this poor seat° of England,   *throne*
270   And therefore, living hence,° did give ourself   *away from court*
      To barbarous licence—as 'tis common
      That men are merriest when they are from home.
      But tell the Dauphin I will keep my state,°   *dignity; territory*
      Be like a king, and show my sail of greatness
275   When I do rouse me in° my throne of France.   *about*
      For that have I laid by my majesty
      And plodded like a man for working days,
      But I will rise there with so full a glory
      That I will dazzle all the eyes of France,
280   Yea strike the Dauphin blind to look on us.
      And tell the pleasant Prince this mock of his
      Hath turned his balls to gunstones,° and his soul   *cannonballs*
      Shall stand sore chargèd° for the wasteful vengeance   *heavily burdened*
      That shall fly from them—for many a thousand widows
285   Shall this his mock mock out of their dear husbands,
      Mock mothers from their sons, mock castles down;
      Ay, some are yet ungotten and unborn
      That shall have cause to curse the Dauphin's scorn.
      But this lies all within the will of God,
290   To whom I do appeal, and in whose name
      Tell you the Dauphin I am coming on
      To venge me° as I may, and to put forth   *avenge myself*
      My rightful hand in a well-hallowed cause.
      So get you hence in peace. And tell the Dauphin
295   His jest will savour but of shallow wit
      When thousands weep more than did laugh at it.—
      Convey them with safe conduct.—Fare you well.
                                          Exeunt AMBASSADORS
      EXETER   This was a merry message.
      KING HARRY   We hope to make the sender blush at it.
300   Therefore, my lords, omit no happy hour
      That may give furth'rance to our expedition;
      For we have now no thought in us but France,
      Save those to God, that run before our business.

---

4. Jeopardy; aperture in the back wall of an Elizabethan tennis court.
5. Military pursuit; in tennis, second impact of a

missed return, rated by its proximity to the back wall (a
disputable point, hence "wrangler" in line 264).

Therefore let our proportions for these wars
305　Be soon collected, and all things thought upon
That may with reasonable swiftness add
More feathers to our wings; for, God before,[6]
We'll chide this Dauphin at his father's door.
Therefore let every man now task his thought,
310　That this fair action may on foot be brought.

Exeunt. Flourish

2.0

Enter CHORUS

CHORUS　Now all the youth of England are on fire,
And silken° dalliance in the wardrobe lies;　　　　　*luxurious*
Now thrive the armourers, and honour's thought
Reigns solely in the breast of every man.
5　They sell the pasture now to buy the horse,
Following the mirror° of all Christian kings　　　　*exemplar*
With wingèd heels, as English Mercuries.[1]
For now sits expectation in the air
And hides a sword from hilts unto the point
10　With crowns imperial, crowns° and coronets,　　　*titles; coins*
Promised to Harry and his followers.
The French, advised by good intelligence°　　　　　*espionage*
Of this most dreadful preparation,
Shake in their fear, and with pale policy°　　　　　*feeble intrigue*
15　Seek to divert the English purposes.
O England!—model° to thy inward greatness,　　　*small replica*
Like little body with a mighty heart,
What mightst thou do, that honour would thee do,
Were all thy children kind and natural?
20　But see, thy fault France hath in thee found out:
A nest of hollow[2] bosoms, which he fills
With treacherous crowns; and three corrupted men—
One, Richard, Earl of Cambridge; and the second
Henry, Lord Scrope of Masham; and the third
25　Sir Thomas Grey, knight, of Northumberland—
Have, for the gilt[3] of France—O guilt indeed!—
Confirmed conspiracy with fearful° France;　　　　*frightened*
And by their hands this grace of kings must die,
If hell and treason hold° their promises,　　　　　*keep*
30　Ere he take ship for France, and in Southampton.
Linger your patience on, and we'll digest
Th'abuse of distance, force—perforce—a play.[4]
The sum is paid, the traitors are agreed,
The King is set from London, and the scene
35　Is now transported, gentles, to Southampton.
There is the playhouse now, there must you sit,
And thence to France shall we convey you safe,
And bring you back, charming the narrow seas
To give you gentle pass—for if we may
40　We'll not offend one stomach[5] with our play.

---

6. With God leading us; if God leads us.
2.0
1. Messenger of the gods; patron of thieves.
2. Hypocritical; empty (as receptacles for money).
3. Gold; gold leaf (suggesting superficiality).

4. *digest . . . play*: incorporate (and make acceptable) a violation of the unity of place, and stuff a play with events.
5. Offend anyone; make anyone seasick.

But till the King come forth, and not till then,
Unto Southampton do we shift our scene.   *Exit*

2.1

Enter Corporal NIM *and Lieutenant* BARDOLPH

BARDOLPH   Well met, Corporal Nim.

NIM   Good morrow, Lieutenant Bardolph.

BARDOLPH   What, are Ensign° Pistol and you friends yet?   *flag bearer*

NIM   For my part, I care not. I say little, but when time shall
5   serve, there shall be smiles—but that shall be as it may. I dare
not fight, but I will wink° and hold out mine iron.° It is a simple   *close my eyes / sword*
one, but what though?° It will toast cheese, and it will endure   *of that*
cold, as another man's sword will—and there's an end.

BARDOLPH   I will bestow a breakfast to make you friends, and
10   we'll be all three sworn brothers to France. Let't be so, good
Corporal Nim.

NIM   Faith, I will live so long as I may, that's the certain of it,
and when I cannot live any longer, I will do as I may. That is
my rest, that is the rendezvous° of it.   *last word?*

15   BARDOLPH   It is certain, corporal, that he is married to Nell
Quickly, and certainly she did you wrong, for you were troth-
plight° to her.   *betrothed*

NIM   I cannot tell. Things must be as they may. Men may sleep,
and they may have their throats about them at that time, and
20   some say knives have edges. It must be as it may. Though
Patience be a tired mare, yet she will plod. There must be conclusions. Well, I cannot tell.

Enter [Ensign] PISTOL *and* HOSTESS *Quickly*

BARDOLPH   Good morrow, Ensign Pistol.[1] *[To* NIM*]* Here comes
Ensign Pistol and his wife. Good Corporal, be patient here.

25   NIM   How now, mine host° Pistol?   *tavern keeper; pimp*

PISTOL   Base tick, call'st thou me host? Now by Gad's lugs°   *God's ears*
I swear I scorn the term. Nor shall my Nell keep lodgers.

HOSTESS   No, by my troth, not long, for we cannot lodge and
board a dozen or fourteen gentlewomen that live honestly by
30   the prick° of their needles, but it will be thought we keep a   *(unwittingly obscene)*
bawdy-house straight.

*[*NIM *draws his sword]*

O well-a-day,° Lady![2] If he be not hewn now, we shall see wilful   *alas*
adultery° and murder committed.   *(for "assault")*

*[*PISTOL *draws his sword]*

BARDOLPH   Good lieutenant, good corporal, offer nothing° here.   *don't fight*
35   NIM   Pish.

PISTOL   Pish for thee, Iceland dog.° Thou prick-eared cur of   *small, hairy breed*
Iceland.

HOSTESS   Good Corporal Nim, show thy valour, and put up°   *away*
your sword.

[They sheathe their swords]

NIM   Will you shog off ?° I would have you *solus*.[3]   *move along*
40   PISTOL   'Solus', egregious dog? O viper vile!
The *solus* in thy most marvellous face,

2.1 Location: Eastcheap, a slum section of London,
site of the tavern scenes in *1* and *2 Henry IV.* Bardolph,
Pistol, and Hostess Quickly were featured in the *Henry
IV* plays; Nim (slang for "thief") is a new character.

1. Sixteenth-century pistols were notoriously noisy and
inaccurate.
2. By our Lady, a mild oath.
3. Alone; unmarried.

The *solus* in thy teeth, and in thy throat,
And in thy hateful lungs, yea in thy maw pardie[4]—
And which is worse, within thy nasty mouth.
45   I do retort° the *solus* in thy bowels,   *send back*
For I can take,° and Pistol's cock is up,[5]   *take fire; strike*
And flashing fire will follow.

NIM   I am not Barbason,° you cannot conjure me.[6] I have an   *(the name of a devil)*
humour° to knock you indifferently well. If you grow foul with   *inclination*
50   me, Pistol, I will scour you with my rapier, as I may, in fair
terms.° If you would walk off, I would prick your guts a little,   *pretty thoroughly*
in good terms, as I may, and that's the humour of it.

PISTOL   O braggart vile, and damnèd furious wight!°   *creature*
The grave doth gape and doting death is near.
55   Therefore ex-hale.°   *draw (your sword)*
        [PISTOL *and* NIM] *draw* [*their swords*]
BARDOLPH   Hear me, hear me what I say.
        [*He draws his sword*]
He that strikes the first stroke, I'll run him up to the hilts, as I
am a soldier.

PISTOL   An oath of mickle° might, and fury shall abate.   *great*
        [*They sheathe their swords*]
60   [*To* NIM] Give me thy fist,° thy forefoot to me give.   *(i.e., hand)*
Thy spirits are most tall.°   *valiant*

NIM   I will cut thy throat one time or other, in fair terms, that is
the humour of it.

PISTOL   *Couple a gorge,*[7]
65   That is the word. I thee defy again.
O hound of Crete, think'st thou my spouse to get?
No, to the spital[8] go,
And from the powd'ring tub[9] of infamy
Fetch forth the lazar kite of Cressid's kind,[1]
70   Doll Tearsheet[2] she by name, and her espouse.
I have, and I will hold, the quondam° Quickly   *former*
For the only she, and—*pauca,*° there's enough. Go to.   *few (words)*
        Enter the BOY [*running*]
BOY   Mine host Pistol, you must come to my master,° and you,   *(Sir John Falstaff)*
hostess. He is very sick, and would to bed.—Good Bardolph,
75   put thy face between his sheets, and do the office of a warming-
pan.[3]—Faith, he's very ill.

BARDOLPH   Away, you rogue!

HOSTESS   By my troth, he'll yield the crow a pudding[4] one of
these days. The King has killed his heart.[5] Good husband,
80   come home presently.°   *Exit* [*with* BOY]   *right away*

BARDOLPH   Come, shall I make you two friends? We must to
France together. Why the devil should we keep knives to cut
one another's throats?

PISTOL   Let floods o'erswell,[6] and fiends for food howl on!

85   NIM   You'll pay me the eight shillings I won of you at betting?

---

4. *in thy maw pardie*: in your stomach, indeed (old-fashioned).
5. Pistol's trigger is cocked (unwittingly obscene).
6. Frighten me with big words.
7. Corrupt French for "Cut the throat."
8. Hospital; in Elizabethan times, a filthy, disease-ridden place occupied by indigents near death.
9. Sweat bath, used in treating syphilis.

1. The diseased, scavenging whore (Cressida, a faithless Trojan woman, was a pattern of female wickedness).
2. A prostitute who appears in *2 Henry IV*.
3. Referring to Bardolph's "fiery" complexion.
4. He'll feed the crows (after his death).
5. By rejecting him, in the last scene of *2 Henry IV*.
6. Let destruction reign (perhaps an unidentified quotation).

PISTOL   Base is the slave that pays.

NIM   That now I will have. That's the humour of it.

PISTOL   As manhood shall compound.° Push home.   *valor will determine*
          [PISTOL *and* NIM] *draw* [*their swords*]

90 BARDOLPH [*drawing his sword*]   By this sword, he that makes the
          first thrust, I'll kill him. By this sword, I will.

PISTOL   Sword is an oath,[7] and oaths must have their course.
          [*He sheathes his sword*]

BARDOLPH   Corporal Nim, an° thou wilt be friends, be friends.   *if*
          An thou wilt not, why then be enemies with me too. Prithee,
          put up.

95 NIM   I shall have my eight shillings?

PISTOL   A noble° shalt thou have, and present pay,[8]   *6 shillings 8 pence*
          And liquor likewise will I give to thee,
          And friendship shall combine, and brotherhood.
          I'll live by Nim, and Nim shall live by me.

100   Is not this just? For I shall sutler[9] be
          Unto the camp, and profits will accrue.
          Give me thy hand.

NIM   I shall have my noble?

PISTOL   In cash, most justly paid.

105 NIM   Well then, that's the humour of't.
          [NIM *and* BARDOLPH *sheathe their swords*]
          Enter HOSTESS [*Quickly*]

HOSTESS   As ever you come of women, come in quickly to Sir
          John. Ah, poor heart, he is so shaked of a burning quotidian-
          tertian,[1] that it is most lamentable to behold. Sweet men, come
          to him.   [*Exit*]

110 NIM   The King hath run bad humours on° the knight, that's the   *shows ill will toward*
          even° of it.   *truth*

PISTOL   Nim, thou hast spoke the right.
          His heart is fracted° and corroborate.[2]   *broken*

NIM   The King is a good king, but it must be as it may. He passes

115   some humours and careers.°   *behaves strangely*

PISTOL   Let us condole° the knight—for, lambkins, we will live.   *console*

                                        Exeunt

2.2

          Enter [*Duke of*] EXETER, [*Duke of* GLOUCESTER,] *and*
          [*Earl of*] WESTMORLAND

GLOUCESTER   Fore God, his grace is bold to trust these traitors.

EXETER   They shall be apprehended by and by.

WESTMORLAND   How smooth and even they do bear themselves,
          As if allegiance in their bosoms sat,

5   Crownèd with faith and constant loyalty.

GLOUCESTER   The King hath note of all that they intend,
          By interception which they dream not of.

EXETER   Nay, but the man that was his bedfellow,[1]
          Whom he hath dulled and cloyed° with gracious favours—   *tired and sated*

10   That he should for a foreign purse so sell
          His sovereign's life to death and treachery.

---

7. Punning on "'s word," by God's word.
8. And immediate payment.
9. Seller of provisions (notoriously dishonest).
1. Dangerous fever (the Hostess conflates quotidian
fever, which recurs daily, with tertian fever, which

recurs every third day).
2. Confirmed (error for "corrupted").
2.2 Location: Southampton, a port in the south of England.
1. It was common for men to share a bed.

Sound trumpets. Enter KING [HARRY, *Lord*] SCROPE,
[*Earl of*] CAMBRIDGE, *and* [*Sir Thomas*] GREY

KING HARRY   Now sits the wind fair, and we will aboard.
My lord of Cambridge, and my kind lord of Masham,
And you, my gentle knight, give me your thoughts.

15 Think you not that the powers we bear with us
Will cut their passage through the force of France,
Doing the execution° and the act   destruction
For which we have in head° assembled them?   an army

SCROPE   No doubt, my liege, if each man do his best.

20 KING HARRY   I doubt not that, since we are well persuaded
We carry not a heart with us from hence
That grows not in a fair consent with ours,
Nor leave not one behind that doth not wish
Success and conquest to attend on us.

25 CAMBRIDGE   Never was monarch better feared and loved
Than is your majesty. There's not, I think, a subject
That sits in heart-grief and uneasiness
Under the sweet shade of your government.

GREY   True. Those that were your father's enemies

30 Have steeped their galls° in honey, and do serve you   bitterness
With hearts create of duty and of zeal.

KING HARRY   We therefore have great cause of thankfulness,
And shall forget the office° of our hand   use
Sooner than quittance° of desert and merit,   payment

35 According to their weight and worthiness.

SCROPE   So service shall with steelèd sinews toil,
And labour shall refresh itself with hope,
To do your grace incessant services.

KING HARRY   We judge no less.—Uncle of Exeter,

40 Enlarge° the man committed° yesterday   Release / imprisoned
That railed against our person. We consider
It was excess of wine that set him on,
And on his more advice° we pardon him.   sober reconsideration

SCROPE   That's mercy, but too much security.°   complacency

45 Let him be punished, sovereign, lest example
Breed, by his sufferance,° more of such a kind.   by pardoning him

KING HARRY   O let us yet be merciful.

CAMBRIDGE   So may your highness, and yet punish too.

GREY   Sir, you show great mercy if you give him life,

50 After the taste of much correction.

KING HARRY   Alas, your too much love and care of me
Are heavy orisons° 'gainst this poor wretch.   weighty pleas
If little faults proceeding on distemper°   from drunkenness
Shall not be winked at,° how shall we stretch our eye   overlooked

55 When capital crimes, chewed, swallowed, and digested,[2]
Appear before us? We'll yet° enlarge that man,   nonetheless
Though Cambridge, Scrope, and Grey, in their dear° care   loving
And tender preservation of our person,
Would have him punished. And now to our French causes.
Who are the late[3] commissioners?

60 CAMBRIDGE   I one, my lord.
Your highness bade me ask for it° today.   (*the commission*)

---

2. That is, crimes thoroughly premeditated.   3. Newly appointed (to govern during Henry's absence).

SCROPE   So did you me, my liege.

GREY   And I, my royal sovereign.

KING HARRY   Then Richard, Earl of Cambridge, there is yours;
There yours, Lord Scrope of Masham, and sir knight,
65   Grey of Northumberland, this same is yours.
Read them, and know I know your worthiness.—
My lord of Westmorland, and Uncle Exeter,
We will aboard tonight.—Why, how now, gentlemen?
What see you in those papers, that you lose
70   So much complexion?—Look ye how they change:
Their cheeks are paper.—Why, what read you there   sight
That have so cowarded and chased your blood
Out of appearance?°   sight

CAMBRIDGE   I do confess my fault,
And do submit me to your highness' mercy.

75   GREY *and* SCROPE   To which we all appeal.

KING HARRY   The mercy that was quick° in us but late   alive
By your own counsel is suppressed and killed.
You must not dare, for shame, to talk of mercy,
For your own reasons turn into your bosoms,
80   As dogs upon their masters, worrying° you.—   tearing
See you, my princes and my noble peers,
These English monsters?⁴ My lord of Cambridge here,
You know how apt our love was to accord°   agree
To furnish him with all appurtenants°   privileges
85   Belonging to his honour; and this vile man
Hath for a few light crowns lightly conspired
And sworn unto the practices° of France   plots
To kill us here in Hampton. To the which
This knight,° no less for bounty bound to us   (Grey)
90   Than Cambridge is, hath likewise sworn. But O
What shall I say to thee, Lord Scrope, thou cruel,
Ingrateful, savage, and inhuman creature?
Thou that didst bear the key of all my counsels,
That knew'st the very bottom of my soul,
95   That almost mightst ha' coined me into gold
Wouldst thou ha' practised on° me for thy use: conspired against
May it be possible that foreign hire
Could out of thee extract one spark of evil
That might annoy my finger? 'Tis so strange
100   That though the truth of it stands off as gross°   clearly
As black on white, my eye will scarcely see it.
Treason and murder ever kept together,
As two yoke-devils sworn to either's purpose,
Working so grossly in a natural° cause   (for devils)
105   That admiration° did not whoop° at them;   astonishment / cry out
But thou, 'gainst all proportion,° didst bring in   natural order
Wonder to wait on° treason and on murder.   consort with
And whatsoever cunning fiend it was
That wrought upon thee so preposterously°   unnaturally
110   Hath got the voice° in hell for excellence.   vote
And other devils that suggest° by treasons   seduce
Do botch and bungle up° damnation   clumsily conceal

---

4. "Monsters" were usually imported freaks.

With patches, colours,° and with forms, being fetched°   *pretexts / derived*
From glist'ring semblances of piety;
115 But he that tempered° thee, bade thee stand up,°   *molded / rebel*
Gave thee no instance° why thou shouldst do treason,   *motive*
Unless to dub thee with the name[5] of traitor.
If that same demon that hath gulled° thee thus   *duped*
Should with his lion gait walk the whole world,
120 He might return to vasty Tartar° back   *to huge hell*
And tell the legions,° 'I can never win   *armies of devils*
A soul so easy as that Englishman's.'
O how hast thou with jealousy° infected   *suspicion*
The sweetness of affiance.° Show men dutiful?   *trust*
125 Why so didst thou. Seem they grave and learned?
Why so didst thou. Come they of noble family?
Why so didst thou. Seem they religious?
Why so didst thou. Or are they spare in diet,
Free from gross passion, or° of mirth or anger,   *either*
130 Constant in spirit, not swerving with the blood,°   *passion*
Garnished and decked in modest complement,°   *appearance*
Not working with the eye without the ear,
And but in purgèd° judgement trusting neither?   *purified*
Such, and so finely boulted,° didst thou seem.   *sifted*
135 And thus thy fall hath left a kind of blot
To mark the full-fraught° man, and best endowed,   *packed (with excellences)*
With some suspicion. I will weep for thee,
For this revolt of thine methinks is like
Another fall of man.—Their faults are open.°   *obvious*
140 Arrest them to the answer of the law,
And God acquit them of their practices.
EXETER   I arrest thee of high treason, by the name of Richard,
Earl of Cambridge.—I arrest thee of high treason, by the name
of Henry, Lord Scrope of Masham.—I arrest thee of high trea-
145 son, by the name of Thomas Grey, knight, of Northumberland.
SCROPE   Our purposes God justly hath discovered,°   *revealed*
And I repent my fault more than my death,
Which I beseech your highness to forgive
Although my body pay the price of it.
150 CAMBRIDGE   For me, the gold of France did not seduce,
Although I did admit it as a motive
The sooner to effect what I intended.[6]
But God be thankèd for prevention,
Which heartily in sufferance° will rejoice,   *suffering punishment*
155 Beseeching God and you to pardon me.
GREY   Never did faithful subject more rejoice
At the discovery of most dangerous treason
Than I do at this hour joy o'er myself,
Prevented from a damnèd enterprise.
160 My fault, but not my body, pardon, sovereign.
KING HARRY   God 'quit° you in his mercy. Hear your sentence.   *acquit*
You have conspired against our royal person,
Joined with an enemy proclaimed and fixed,

---

5. To knight you with the title.
6. The Earl of Cambridge was heir of Edmund Mortimer through his wife, Edmund's sister, and Mortimer

arguably had a better claim to the English throne than did Henry himself. Henry's adherence to a principle of inheritance "through the female line" is hardly absolute.

And from his coffers
165 Received the golden earnest of° our death,   *advance payment for*
Wherein you would have sold your king to slaughter,
His princes and his peers to servitude,
His subjects to oppression and contempt,
And his whole kingdom into desolation.
170 Touching our person seek we no revenge,
But we our kingdom's safety must so tender,°   *regard*
Whose ruin you have sought, that to her laws
We do deliver you. Get ye therefore hence,
Poor miserable wretches, to your death;
175 The taste whereof, God of his mercy give
You patience to endure, and true repentance
Of all your dear° offences.—Bear them hence.   *grievous*

Exeunt [the traitors, guarded]

Now lords for France, the enterprise whereof
Shall be to you, as us, like° glorious.   *equally*
180 We doubt not of a fair and lucky war,
Since God so graciously hath brought to light
This dangerous treason lurking in our way
To hinder our beginnings. We doubt not now
But every rub° is smoothèd on our way.   *obstacle*
185 Then forth, dear countrymen. Let us deliver
Our puissance° into the hand of God,   *power*
Putting it straight in expedition.°   *at once in action*
Cheerly to sea, the signs° of war advance: *flags*
No king of England, if not king of France.   *Flourish. Exeunt*

2.3

Enter [Ensign] PISTOL, *[Corporal]* NIM, *[Lieutenant]*
BARDOLPH, BOY, *and* HOSTESS *[Quickly]*

HOSTESS Prithee, honey, sweet husband, let me bring° thee to   *accompany*
Staines.[1]

PISTOL No, for my manly heart doth erne.° Bardolph,   *grieve*
Be blithe; Nim, rouse thy vaunting veins; boy, bristle
5 Thy courage up. For Falstaff he is dead,
And we must erne therefore.

BARDOLPH Would I were with him, wheresome'er he is, either
in heaven or in hell.

HOSTESS Nay, sure he's not in hell. He's in Arthur's bosom,[2] if
10 ever man went to Arthur's bosom. A° made a finer end, and   *He*
went away an° it had been any christom[3] child. A parted ev'n   *as if*
just between twelve and one, ev'n at the turning o'th' tide—for
after I saw him fumble with the sheets, and play with flowers,°   *(on the bedclothes)*
and smile upon his finger's end, I knew there was but one way.
15 For his nose was as sharp as a pen, and a babbled of green
fields.[4] 'How now, Sir John?' quoth I. 'What, man! Be o' good
cheer.' So a cried out, 'God, God, God', three or four times.
Now I, to comfort him, bid him a should not think of God; I
hoped there was no need to trouble himself with any such

2.3 Location: Eastcheap.
1. Town on the road to Southampton.
2. Mistake for "Abraham's bosom," heaven.
3. Error for "chrisom," just christened.
4. Falstaff was reciting the Twenty-third Psalm ("The

Lord is my shepherd"), but Hostess Quickly does not
recognize it. The text is corrupt at this point, reading "a
Table of green fields," and was corrected by the
eighteenth-century editor Lewis Theobald in a famous
emendation.

20   thoughts yet. So a bade me lay more clothes on his feet. I put
    my hand into the bed and felt them, and they were as cold as
    any stone. Then I felt to his knees, and so up'ard and up'ard,
    and all was as cold as any stone.

    NIM   They say he cried out of sack.[5]

25   HOSTESS   Ay, that a did.

    BARDOLPH   And of women.

    HOSTESS   Nay, that a did not.

    BOY   Yes, that a did, and said they were devils incarnate.

    HOSTESS   A could never abide carnation, 'twas a colour he never
30   liked.

    BOY   A said once the devil would have him about women.

    HOSTESS   A did in some sort, indeed, handle° women—but then   *discuss*
    he was rheumatic,[6] and talked of the Whore of Babylon.[7]

    BOY   Do you not remember, a saw a flea stick upon Bardolph's
35   nose, and a said it was a black soul burning in hell-fire.

    BARDOLPH   Well, the fuel[8] is gone that maintained that fire.
    That's all the riches I got in his service.

    NIM   Shall we shog?° The King will be gone from Southampton.   *be off*

    PISTOL   Come, let's away.—My love, give me thy lips.
        [*He kisses her*]

40   Look to my chattels and my movables.°   *personal property*
    Let senses rule. The word is 'Pitch and pay'.°   *Cash down, no credit*
    Trust none, for oaths are straws, men's faiths are wafer-cakes,°   *fragile*
    And Holdfast is the only dog,[9] my duck.°   *darling*
    Therefore *caveto*° be thy counsellor.   *beware*
45   Go, clear thy crystals.°—Yokefellows in arms,   *wipe your eyes*
    Let us to France, like horseleeches, my boys,
    To suck, to suck, the very blood to suck!

    BOY [*aside*]   And that's but unwholesome food, they say.

    PISTOL   Touch her soft mouth, and march.

50   BARDOLPH   Farewell, hostess.
        [*He kisses her*]

    NIM   I cannot kiss, that is the humour of it, but adieu.

    PISTOL [*to* HOSTESS]   Let housewifery appear. Keep close,° I   *Stay indoors; be thrifty*
    thee command.

    HOSTESS   Farewell! Adieu!   *Exeunt* [*severally*]°   *separately*

2.4

Flourish. Enter KING [CHARLES *the Sixth of France*]*, the*
DAUPHIN, [*the* CONSTABLE,] *and the Dukes of* BERRI *and*
[BOURBON]

    KING CHARLES   Thus comes the English with full power upon us,
    And more than carefully it us concerns
    To answer royally in our defences.
    Therefore the Dukes of Berri and of Bourbon,
5   Of Brabant and of Orléans shall make forth,
    And you Prince Dauphin, with all swift dispatch
    To line° and new-repair our towns of war   *garrison*

---

5. *of sack*: against wine, formerly one of Falstaff's great
indulgences.
6. Error for "lunatic," delirious.
7. The scarlet woman of Revelation, identified by
Protestants with the Catholic Church.

8. That is, Falstaff's liquor.
9. Alluding to the proverb "Brag is a good dog, but
Holdfast is better."
2.4 Location: France, where the remainder of the play
takes place. The King's court at Rouen.

With men of courage and with means defendant.°   *of defense*
For England° his approaches makes as fierce   *the King of England*
10 As waters to the sucking of a gulf.°   *whirlpool*
It fits us then to be as provident
As fear may teach us, out of late° examples   *recent*
Left by the fatal and neglected[1] English
Upon our fields.
DAUPHIN   My most redoubted° father,   *formidable*
15 It is most meet° we arm us 'gainst the foe,   *proper*
For peace itself should not so dull a kingdom—
Though war, nor no known quarrel, were in question—
But that defences, musters, preparations
Should be maintained, assembled, and collected
20 As° were a war in expectation.   *As if*
Therefore, I say, 'tis meet we all go forth
To view the sick and feeble parts of France.
And let us do it with no show of fear,
No, with no more than if we heard that England
25 Were busied with a Whitsun morris dance[2]
For, my good liege, she is so idly° kinged,   *frivolously*
Her sceptre so fantastically° borne   *irrationally*
By a vain, giddy, shallow, humorous° youth,   *capricious*
That fear attends her not.
CONSTABLE   O peace, Prince Dauphin.
30 You are too much mistaken in this king.
Question your grace the late° ambassadors   *recent*
With what great state he heard their embassy,
How well supplied with agèd counsellors,
How modest in exception,° and withal   *objecting*
35 How terrible° in constant resolution,   *fearsome*
And you shall find his vanities forespent°   *his former follies*
Were but the outside of the Roman Brutus,[3]
Covering discretion with a coat of folly,
As gardeners do with ordure° hide those roots   *manure*
40 That shall first spring and be most delicate.
DAUPHIN   Well, 'tis not so, my Lord High Constable.
But though° we think it so, it is no matter.   *if*
In cases of defence 'tis best to weigh°   *consider*
The enemy more mighty than he seems.
45 So the proportions of defence are filled[4]—
Which, of a weak and niggardly projection,°   *scale*
Doth like a miser spoil his coat with scanting°   *skimping*
A little cloth.
KING CHARLES   Think we King Harry strong.
And princes, look you strongly arm to meet him.
50 The kindred of him hath been fleshed[5] upon us,
And he is bred out of that bloody strain
That haunted us in our familiar paths.
Witness our too-much-memorable shame

---

1. The fatally underestimated, at the Battles of Crécy (1346) and Poitiers (1356).
2. Folk dance celebrating Whitsuntide, a summer holiday.
3. Lucius Junius Brutus pretended idiocy to disarm the tyrant Lucius Tarquinius Superbus, against whom he led a successful revolt.
4. A proper defense is mounted.
5. Have been given their first taste of blood.

When Crécy battle fatally was struck,°   *fought*
55 And all our princes captived by the hand
    Of that black name, Edward, Black Prince of Wales,
    Whiles that his mountant° sire, on mountain standing,   *ascendant*
    Up in the air, crowned with the golden sun,
    Saw his heroical seed and smiled to see him
60 Mangle the work of nature and deface
    The patterns that by God and by French fathers
    Had twenty years been made. This is a stem
    Of that victorious stock, and let us fear
    The native° mightiness and fate° of him.   *hereditary / fortune*
              Enter a MESSENGER
65 MESSENGER   Ambassadors from Harry, King of England,
    Do crave admittance to your majesty.
    KING CHARLES   We'll give them present audience. Go and bring them.
                                                    [*Exit* MESSENGER]
    You see this chase is hotly followed, friends.
    DAUPHIN   Turn head[6] and stop pursuit. For coward dogs
70 Most spend their mouths° when what they seem to threaten   *bark the loudest*
    Runs far before them. Good my sovereign,
    Take up the English short, and let them know
    Of what a monarchy you are the head.
    Self-love, my liege, is not so vile a sin
    As self-neglecting.
              Enter [*Duke of*] EXETER [*attended*]
75 KING CHARLES   From our brother England?
    EXETER   From him, and thus he greets your majesty:
    He wills you, in the name of God Almighty,
    That you divest yourself and lay apart°   *aside*
    The borrowed glories that by gift of heaven,
80 By law of nature and of nations, 'longs°   *belongs*
    To him and to his heirs, namely the crown,
    And all wide-stretchèd honours that pertain
    By custom and the ordinance of times°   *laws of ages*
    Unto the crown of France. That you may know
85 'Tis no sinister° nor no awkward° claim,   *illegitimate / oblique*
    Picked from the worm-holes of long-vanished days,
    Nor from the dust of old oblivion raked,
    He sends you this most memorable line,°   *pedigree*
    In every branch truly demonstrative,°   *conclusive*
90 Willing you over-look° this pedigree,   *Wishing you to look over*
    And when you find him evenly derived°   *directly descended*
    From his most famed of famous ancestors,
    Edward the Third, he bids you then resign
    Your crown and kingdom, indirectly° held   *unjustly*
95 From him, the native and true challenger.°   *claimant*
    KING CHARLES   Or else what follows?
    EXETER   Bloody constraint. For if you hide the crown
    Even in your hearts, there will he rake for it.
    Therefore in fierce tempest is he coming,
100 In thunder and in earthquake, like a Jove,
    That if requiring° fail, he will compel;   *requesting*

---

6. Make a stand (a hunting term).

And bids you, in the bowels° of the Lord,   compassion
Deliver up the crown, and to take mercy
On the poor souls for whom this hungry war
105   Opens his vasty jaws; and on your head
Turns he the widows' tears, the orphans' cries,
The dead men's blood, the pining maidens' groans,
For husbands, fathers, and betrothèd lovers
That shall be swallowed in this controversy.
110   This is his claim, his threat'ning, and my message—
Unless the Dauphin be in presence here,
To whom expressly I bring greeting too.
      KING CHARLES   For us, we will consider of this further.
Tomorrow shall you bear our full intent
Back to our brother England.
115   DAUPHIN   For the Dauphin,
I stand here for him. What to him from England?
      EXETER   Scorn and defiance, slight regard, contempt;
And anything that may not misbecome
The mighty sender, doth he prize° you at.   assess
120   Thus says my king: an if° your father's highness   an if = if
Do not, in grant° of all demands at large,°   concession / in full
Sweeten the bitter mock you sent his majesty,
He'll call you to so hot an answer for it
That caves and womby vaultages° of France   hollow caverns
125   Shall chide your trespass and return your mock
In second accent° of his ordinance.°   echo / artillery
      DAUPHIN   Say if my father render fair return
It is against my will, for I desire
Nothing but odds° with England. To that end,   strife
130   As matching to his youth and vanity,°   frivolity
I did present him with the Paris° balls.   tennis
      EXETER   He'll make your Paris Louvre° shake for it,   French royal palace
Were it the mistress° court of mighty Europe.   principal (in tennis)
And be assured, you'll find a diff'rence,
135   As we his subjects have in wonder found,
Between the promise of his greener° days   younger
And these he masters now: now he weighs time
Even to the utmost grain.° That you shall read   smallest unit
In your own losses, if he stay in France.
140   KING CHARLES [rising]   Tomorrow shall you know our mind at full.
      Flourish⁷
      EXETER   Dispatch us with all speed, lest that our king
Come here himself to question our delay—
For he is footed° in this land already.   come ashore
      KING CHARLES   You shall be soon dispatched with fair conditions.
145   A night is but small breath° and little pause   small time
To answer matters of this consequence.   Exeunt. Flourish

7. Fanfare (to signal the end of the interview; Exeter unceremoniously continues).

3.0

Enter CHORUS

CHORUS Thus with imagined wing° our swift scene flies *wings of imagination*
  In motion of no less celerity
  Than that of thought. Suppose that you have seen
  The well-appointed° king at Dover pier *well-equipped*
5 Embark his royalty, and his brave fleet
  With silken streamers the young Phoebus fanning.¹
  Play with your fancies,° and in them behold *imagination*
  Upon the hempen tackle ship-boys climbing;
  Hear the shrill whistle,° which doth order give *(of the ship's captain)*
10 To sounds confused; behold the threaden° sails, *woven of thread*
  Borne with th'invisible and creeping wind,
  Draw the huge bottoms° through the furrowed sea, *hulls*
  Breasting the lofty surge. O do but think
  You stand upon the rivage° and behold *shore*
15 A city on th'inconstant billows dancing—
  For so appears this fleet majestical,
  Holding due course to Harfleur.² Follow, follow!
  Grapple° your minds to sternage° of this navy, *Fasten / the sterns*
  And leave your England, as dead midnight still,
20 Guarded with grandsires, babies, and old women,
  Either past or not arrived to pith° and puissance. *strength*
  For who is he, whose chin is but enriched
  With one appearing hair, that will not follow
  These culled° and choice-drawn cavaliers to France? *select*
25 Work, work your thoughts, and therein see a siege.
  Behold the ordnance° on their carriages, *cannons*
  With fatal mouths gaping on girded° Harfleur. *encircled*
  Suppose th'ambassador from the French comes back,
  Tells Harry that the King doth offer him
30 Catherine his daughter, and with her, to° dowry, *as*
  Some petty and unprofitable dukedoms.
  The offer likes° not, and the nimble gunner *pleases*
  With linstock° now the devilish cannon touches, *lighting stick*
    Alarum, and chambers° go off *small cannon*
  And down goes all before them. Still be kind,
35 And eke out our performance with your mind. *Exit*

3.1

Alarum. Enter KING [HARRY *and the English army, with*]
  scaling ladders

KING HARRY Once more unto the breach,¹ dear friends, once more,
  Or close the wall up with our English dead.
  In peace there's nothing so becomes a man
  As modest stillness and humility,
5 But when the blast of war blows in our ears,
  Then imitate the action of the tiger.
  Stiffen the sinews, conjure up the blood,
  Disguise fair nature with hard-favoured rage.
  Then lend the eye a terrible aspect,

3.0
1. *the . . . fanning:* fluttering toward the rising sun.
2. French port on the mouth of the Seine.

3.1 Location: Before Harfleur.
1. Gap in the fortifications, created by artillery bombardment.

10 Let it pry° through the portage² of the head   *peer*
Like the brass cannon, let the brow o'erwhelm° it   *overhang*
As fearfully as doth a gallèd° rock   *worn*
O'erhang and jutty° his confounded° base,   *jut out over / ruined*
Swilled° with the wild and wasteful° ocean.   *Washed / destructive*
15 Now set the teeth and stretch the nostril wide,
Hold hard the breath, and bend up every spirit
To his full height. On, on, you noblest English,
Whose blood is fet° from fathers of war-proof,°   *fetched / proven in war*
Fathers that like so many Alexanders³
20 Have in these parts from morn till even fought,
And sheathed their swords for lack of argument.°   *opposition*
Dishonour not your mothers; now attest
That those whom you called fathers did beget you.
Be copy° now to men of grosser° blood,   *example / less noble*
25 And teach them how to war. And you, good yeomen,° *men below noble rank*
Whose limbs were made in England, show us here
The mettle° of your pasture; let us swear   *quality*
That you are worth your breeding—which I doubt not,
For there is none of you so mean and base
30 That hath not noble lustre in your eyes.
I see you stand like greyhounds in the slips,°   *leashes*
Straining upon the start. The game's afoot.
Follow your spirit, and upon this charge
Cry, 'God for Harry! England and Saint George!'° *patron saint of England*
           Alarum, and chambers go off. [Exeunt]

3.2

Enter NIM, BARDOLPH, [*Ensign*] PISTOL, *and* BOY

BARDOLPH   On, on, on, on, on! To the breach, to the breach!
NIM   Pray thee corporal, stay. The knocks are too hot, and for
    mine own part I have not a case° of lives. The humour of it is   *set*
    too hot, that is the very plainsong° of it.   *plain truth*
5 PISTOL   'The plainsong' is most just,° for humours do abound.   *apt*
    Knocks go and come, God's vassals drop and die,
    [*sings*]   And sword and shield
                    In bloody field
                    Doth win immortal fame.
10 BOY   Would I were in an alehouse in London. I would give all
    my fame for a pot of ale, and safety.
PISTOL [*sings*]   And I.
           If wishes would prevail with me°   *in my case*
           My purpose should not fail with me
15   But thither would I hie.°   *go*
BOY [*sings*]   As duly
           But not as truly
               As bird doth sing on bough.
         Enter [*Captain*] FLUELLEN *and beats them in*
FLUELLEN   God's plud!¹ Up to the breaches, you dogs! Avaunt,
20   you cullions!²
PISTOL   Be merciful, great duke, to men of mould.³

---

2. Portholes (that is, eye sockets).
3. Alexander the Great was said to have wept because
no worlds remained for him to conquer.
3.2 Scene continues.

1. Blood (Fluellen's Welsh accent substitutes "p" for
"b," and also "f" for "v" and "ch" for "j").
2. Be off, you wretches. *cullions:* testicles.
3. Earth (that is, mortal men).

Abate thy rage, abate thy manly rage,
Abate thy rage, great duke. Good bawcock,[4] bate
Thy rage. Use lenity,° sweet chuck.   *leniency*

25   NIM   These be good humours![5]
      [FLUELLEN *begins to beat* NIM]
      Your honour runs bad humours.°   *Exeunt [all but the* BOY]   *is ill tempered*
      BOY   As young as I am, I have observed these three swashers.° I   *swashbucklers*
      am boy to them all three, but all they three, though they should
      serve me, could not be man[6] to me, for indeed three such
30   antics° do not amount to a man. For Bardolph, he is white-   *buffoons*
      livered° and red-faced—by the means whereof a° faces it out,   *cowardly / he*
      but fights not. For Pistol, he hath a killing tongue and a quiet
      sword—by the means whereof a breaks words, and keeps whole
      weapons. For Nim, he hath heard that men of few words are
35   the best men, and therefore he scorns to say his prayers, lest a
      should be thought a coward. But his few bad words are
      matched with as few good deeds—for a never broke any man's
      head but his own, and that was against a post, when he was
      drunk. They will steal anything, and call it 'purchase'.[7] Bar-
40   dolph stole a lute case, bore it twelve leagues,° and sold it for   *about 36 miles*
      three halfpence. Nim and Bardolph are sworn brothers in
      filching,° and in Calais[8] they stole a fire shovel. I knew by that   *stealing*
      piece of service the men would carry coals.[9] They would have
      me as familiar with men's pockets as their gloves or their hand-
45   kerchiefs—which makes° much against my manhood, if I   *offends*
      should take from another's pocket to put into mine, for it is
      plain pocketing up of wrongs.[1] I must leave them, and seek
      some better service. Their villainy goes against my weak stom-
      ach, and therefore I must cast it up.°   *Exit*   *vomit it; leave it*

3.3

Enter [Captain] GOWER [*and Captain* FLUELLEN,
meeting]

      GOWER   Captain Fluellen, you must come presently° to the   *immediately*
      mines.[1] The Duke of Gloucester would speak with you.
      FLUELLEN   To the mines? Tell you the Duke it is not so good to
      come to the mines. For look you, the mines is not according to
5   the disciplines° of the war. The concavities° of it is not suffi-   *tactics; art / depth*
      cient. For look you, th'athversary, you may discuss unto the
      Duke, look you, is digt° himself, four yard under, the coun-   *digged (dug)*
      termines.[2] By Cheshu,° I think a will plow° up all, if there is not   *Jesu / blow*
      better directions.
10   GOWER   The Duke of Gloucester, to whom the order° of the   *supervision*
      siege is given, is altogether directed by an Irishman, a very val-
      iant gentleman, i'faith.
      FLUELLEN   It is Captain MacMorris, is it not?
      GOWER   I think it be.
15   FLUELLEN   By Cheshu, he is an ass, as[3] in the world. I will verify

---

4. Fine chap (French *beau coq*).
5. This is fine behavior (sarcastic).
6. Punning on the sense "personal servant."
7. Booty (seized in combat).
8. French port town.
9. Do dirty work; tolerate insults.

1. Pocketing stolen goods; putting up with insults (unmanly behavior).
3.3 Location: Outside Harfleur.
1. Tunnels dug to undermine a besieged fortress.
2. Tunnels dug to undermine enemy "mines."
3. *he is an ass, as:* he is as big an ass as there is.

as much in his beard.° He has no more directions in the true   *to his face*
disciplines of the wars, look you—of the *Roman* disciplines—
than is a puppy dog.

        Enter [Captain] MACMORRIS *and Captain* JAMY

GOWER   Here a comes, and the Scots captain, Captain Jamy,
20   with him.

FLUELLEN   Captain Jamy is a marvellous falorous° gentleman,   *valorous*
that is certain, and of great expedition° and knowledge in   *quick-wittedness*
th'ancient wars, upon my particular knowledge of his directions.
By Cheshu, he will maintain his argument as well as any mili-
25   tary man in the world, in the disciplines of the pristine wars of
the Romans.

JAMY   I say gud day, Captain Fluellen.

FLUELLEN   Good e'en to your worship, good Captain James.

GOWER   How now, Captain MacMorris, have you quit the
30   mines? Have the pioneers given o'er?°   *diggers stopped work*

MACMORRIS   By Chrish law,[4] 'tish ill done. The work ish give
over, the trumpet sound the retreat. By my hand I swear, and
my father's soul, the work ish ill done, it ish give over. I would
have blowed up the town, so Chrish save me law, in an hour.
35   O 'tish ill done, 'tish ill done, by my hand 'tish ill done.

FLUELLEN   Captain MacMorris, I beseech you now, will you
vouchsafe° me, look you, a few disputations with you, as partly   *allow*
touching or concerning the disciplines of the war, the Roman
wars, in the way of argument, look you, and friendly communi-
40   cation? Partly to satisfy my opinion and partly for the satisfaction, look you, of my mind. As touching the direction of the
military discipline, that is the point.

JAMY   It sall be vary gud, gud feith, gud captains bath,° and I sall   *both*
quite° you with gud leve, as I may pick occasion. That sall I,   *requite; answer*
45   marry.

MACMORRIS   It is no time to discourse, so Chrish save me. The
day is hot, and the weather and the wars and the King and the
dukes. It is no time to discourse. The town is besieched. An the
trumpet call us to the breach, and we talk and, be Chrish, do
50   nothing, 'tis shame for us all. So God sa'° me, 'tis shame to   *save*
stand still, it is shame by my hand. And there is throats to be
cut, and works to be done, and there ish nothing done, so
Christ sa' me law.

JAMY   By the mess,° ere these eyes of mine take themselves to   *By the mass (an oath)*
55   slumber, ay'll de gud service, or I'll lig° i'th' grund for it. Ay   *lie*
owe Got a death, and I'll pay't as valorously as I may, that sall I
suirely do, that is the brief and the long. Marry, I wad full fain
heard° some question 'tween you twae.°   *eagerly have heard / two*

FLUELLEN   Captain MacMorris, I think, look you, under your
60   correction, there is not many of your nation—

MACMORRIS   Of my nation? What ish my nation? Ish a villain
and a bastard and a knave and a rascal? What ish my nation?
Who talks of my nation?

FLUELLEN   Look you, if you take the matter otherwise than is
65   meant, Captain MacMorris, peradventure I shall think you do
not use me with that affability as in discretion you ought to use

---

4. La (adds force to an utterance).

me, look you, being as good a man as yourself, both in the
disciplines of war and in the derivation of my birth, and in
other particularities.

70 MACMORRIS I do not know you so good a man as myself. So
Chrish save me, I will cut off your head.

GOWER Gentlemen both, you will mistake each other.

JAMY Ah, that's a foul fault.

     A parley⁵ [is sounded]

GOWER The town sounds a parley.

75 FLUELLEN Captain MacMorris, when there is more better
opportunity to be required, look you, I will be so bold as to tell
you I know the disciplines of war. And there is an end. *Exit*

     [Flourish.] Enter KING *[*HARRY*] and all his train before
the gates*

KING HARRY How yet resolves the Governor of the town?

  This is the latest parle° we will admit.   *last parley*

80 Therefore to our best mercy give yourselves,

  Or like to men proud of° destruction   *glorying in*

  Defy us to our worst. For as I am a soldier,

  A name that in my thoughts becomes me best,

  If I begin the batt'ry° once again   *bombardment*

85 I will not leave the half-achievèd Harfleur

  Till in her ashes she lie burièd.

  The gates of mercy shall be all shut up,

  And the fleshed° soldier, rough and hard of heart,   *inflamed*

  In liberty of bloody hand shall range

90 With conscience wide° as hell, mowing like grass   *permissive*

  Your fresh fair virgins and your flow'ring infants.

  What is it then to me if impious war

  Arrayed in flames like to the prince of fiends

  Do with his smirched complexion all fell° feats   *cruel*

95 Enlinked to waste° and desolation?   *destruction*

  What is't to me, when you yourselves are cause,

  If your pure maidens fall into the hand

  Of hot and forcing violation?

  What rein can hold licentious wickedness

100 When down the hill he holds° his fierce career?°   *maintains / gallop*

  We may as bootless° spend our vain command   *unprofitably*

  Upon th'enragèd soldiers in their spoil

  As send precepts° to the leviathan°   *summons / sea monster*

  To come ashore. Therefore, you men of Harfleur,

105 Take pity of your town and of your people

  Whiles yet my soldiers are in my command,

  Whiles yet the cool and temperate wind of grace

  O'erblows° the filthy and contagious clouds⁶   *Disperses*

  Of heady° murder, spoil, and villainy.   *headstrong*

110 If not—why, in a moment look to see

  The blind and bloody soldier with foul hand

  Defile the locks of your shrill-shrieking daughters;

  Your fathers taken by the silver beards,

  And their most reverend heads dashed to the walls;

115 Your naked infants spitted° upon pikes,   *impaled*

  Whiles the mad mothers with their howls confused

---

5. Trumpet call requesting negotiation.   6. Pestilence was believed to drop from the sky.

Do break the clouds, as did the wives of Jewry[7]
At Herod's bloody-hunting slaughtermen.
What say you? Will you yield, and this avoid?
120   Or, guilty in defence, be thus destroyed?
          Enter GOVERNOR [*on the wall*]
GOVERNOR   Our expectation hath this day an end.
The Dauphin, whom of succours we entreated,
Returns° us that his powers are yet not ready   *Replies to*
To raise so great a siege. Therefore, dread King,
125   We yield our town and lives to thy soft mercy.
Enter our gates, dispose of us and ours,
For we no longer are defensible.
KING HARRY   Open your gates.   [*Exit* GOVERNOR]
          Come, Uncle Exeter,
Go you and enter Harfleur. There remain,
130   And fortify it strongly 'gainst the French.
Use mercy to them all. For us, dear uncle,
The winter coming on, and sickness growing
Upon our soldiers, we will retire to Calais.
Tonight in Harfleur will we be your guest;
135   Tomorrow for the march are we addressed.°   *ready*
        [*The gates are opened.*] *Flourish, and* [*they*] *enter the town*

3.4

Enter [*Princess*] CATHERINE *and* ALICE, *an old gentle-*
woman

CATHERINE   Alice, tu as été en Angleterre, et tu bien parles
le langage.[1]
ALICE   Un peu, madame.
CATHERINE   Je te prie, m'enseignez. Il faut que j'apprenne à
5   parler. Comment appelez-vous la main en anglais?
ALICE   La main? Elle est appelée *de hand*.
CATHERINE   *De hand*. Et les doigts?
ALICE   Les doigts? Ma foi, j'oublie les doigts, mais je me souviendrai. Les doigts—je pense qu'ils sont appelés *de fingres*. Oui, *de*
10   *fingres*.
CATHERINE   La main, *de hand*; les doigts, *de fingres*. Je pense que
je suis la bonne écolière; j'ai gagné deux mots d'anglais vite-
ment. Comment appelez-vous les ongles?
ALICE   Les ongles? Nous les appelons *de nails*.
15   CATHERINE   *De nails*. Écoutez—dites-moi si je parle bien: *de*
hand, de fingres, et de nails.

---

7. Judaea; see Matthew 2:16–18.
3.4 Location: The French King's palace.
1. A translation of this French scene follows, with editorial comments in brackets.

CATHERINE   Alice, you've been in England, and you speak the language well.
ALICE   A little, madam.
CATHERINE   Please teach me. I must learn to speak it. What do you call *la main* in English?
ALICE   *La main?* It is called "de hand."
CATHERINE   De hand. And *les doigts?*
ALICE   *Les doigts?* Faith, I forget *les doigts,* but I'll remember. *Les doigts*—I think they're called "de fingres." Yes, de
fingres.
CATHERINE   *Le main,* de hand; *les doigts,* de fingres. I think I'm a good scholar; I've learned two words of English
quickly. What do you call *les ongles?*
ALICE   *Les ongles?* We call them "de nails."
CATHERINE   De nails. Listen—tell me if I speak well: de hand, de fingres, and de nails.

ALICE   C'est bien dit, madame. Il est fort bon anglais.

CATHERINE   Dites-moi l'anglais pour le bras.

ALICE   *De arma,* madame.

20   CATHERINE   Et le coude?

ALICE   *D'elbow.*

CATHERINE   *D'elbow.* Je m'en fais la répétition de tous les mots que vous m'avez appris dès à présent.

ALICE   Il est trop difficile, madame, comme je pense.

25   CATHERINE   Excusez-moi, Alice. Écoutez: *d'hand, de fingre, de nails, d'arma, de bilbow.*

ALICE   *D'elbow,* madame.

CATHERINE   O Seigneur Dieu, je m'en oublie! *D'elbow.* Comment appelez-vous le col?

30   ALICE   *De nick,* madame.

CATHERINE   *De nick.* Et le menton?

ALICE   *De chin.*

CATHERINE   *De sin.* Le col, *de nick;* le menton, *de sin.*

ALICE   Oui. Sauf votre honneur, en vérité vous prononcez les

35   mots aussi droit que les natifs d'Angleterre.

CATHERINE   Je ne doute point d'apprendre, par la grâce de Dieu, et en peu de temps.

ALICE   N'avez-vous y déjà oublié ce que je vous ai enseigné?

CATHERINE   Non, et je réciterai à vous promptement: *d'hand, de*

40   *fingre, de mailès—*

ALICE   *De nails,* madame.

CATHERINE   *De nails, de arma, de ilbow—*

ALICE   Sauf votre honneur, *d'elbow.*

CATHERINE   Ainsi dis-je. *D'elbow, de nick, et de sin.* Comment

45   appelez-vous les pieds et la robe?

ALICE   *De foot,* madame, et *de cown.*

CATHERINE   *De foot* et *de cown?* O Seigneur Dieu! Ils sont les mots de son mauvais, corruptible, gros, et impudique, et non pour les dames d'honneur d'user. Je ne voudrais prononcer ces

50   mots devant les seigneurs de France pour tout le monde. Foh! *De foot* et *de cown!* Néanmoins, je réciterai une autre fois ma

ALICE   That's well said, madam. It is very good English.

CATHERINE   Tell me the English for *le bras.*

ALICE   "De arma," madam.

CATHERINE   And *le coude?*

ALICE   "D'elbow."

CATHERINE   D'elbow. I'll repeat all the words you have taught me so far.

ALICE   It is too difficult, madam, in my opinion.

CATHERINE   Excuse me, Alice. Listen: d'hand, de fingre, de nails, d'arma, de bilbow.

ALICE   D'elbow, madam.

CATHERINE   O Lord God, I forgot. D'elbow. What do you call *le col?*

ALICE   "De nick," madam.

CATHERINE   De nick. And *le menton?*

ALICE   "De chin."

CATHERINE   De sin. *Le col,* de nick; *le menton,* de sin.

ALICE   Yes. Saving your honor, to tell the truth you pronounce the words just as properly as the native English.

CATHERINE   I don't doubt that I'll learn, with God's help, and in a short time.

ALICE   Haven't you already forgotten what I have taught you?

CATHERINE   No, I shall recite to you right now: d'hand, de fingre, de mailès—

ALICE   De nails, madam.

CATHERINE   De nails, de arma, de ilbow—

ALICE   Saving your honor, d'elbow.

CATHERINE   That's what I said. D'elbow, de nick, and de sin. What do you call *les pieds* and *la robe?*

ALICE   "De foot," madam, and "de cown" [gown].

CATHERINE   De foot and de cown? O Lord God, those are evil-sounding words, easily misconstrued, vulgar, and immodest, and not for respectable ladies to use. [They sound like the French *foutre,* "fuck," and *con,* "cunt."] I wouldn't speak those words in front of French gentlemen for all the world. Ugh! de foot and de cown! Still, I shall

leçon ensemble. *D'hand, de fingre, de nails, d'arma, d'elbow,*
de nick, de sin, de foot, de cown.

ALICE   Excellent, madame!

55   CATHERINE   C'est assez pour une fois. Allons-nous à dîner.

Exeunt

3.5

Enter KING [CHARLES *the Sixth*] *of France,* DAUPHIN,
CONSTABLE, [DUKE *of*] BOURBON, *and others*

KING CHARLES   'Tis certain he hath passed the River Somme.

CONSTABLE   And if he be not fought withal,° my lord,   *with*
Let us not live in France; let us quit all
And give our vineyards to a barbarous people.

5   DAUPHIN   *O Dieu vivant!*° Shall a few sprays[1] of us,   *O living God*
The emptying of our fathers' luxury,[2]
Our scions,° put in wild and savage stock,   *grafts*
Spirt° up so suddenly into the clouds   *Sprout*
And over-look their grafters?

10   BOURBON   Normans, but bastard Normans, Norman bastards!
Mort de ma vie,° if they march along   *Death of my life*
Unfought withal, but I will sell my dukedom
To buy a slobb'ry° and a dirty farm   *muddy*
In that nook-shotten[3] isle of Albion.°   *England*

15   CONSTABLE   *Dieu de batailles!*° Where° have they this mettle?   *God of battles / Whence*
Is not their climate foggy, raw, and dull,
On whom as in despite° the sun looks pale,   *contempt*
Killing their fruit with frowns? Can sodden° water,   *boiled; to make ale*
A drench for sur-reined jades[4]—their barley-broth—

20   Decoct° their cold blood to such valiant heat?   *Boil, to purify*
And shall our quick blood, spirited with wine,
Seem frosty? O for honour of our land
Let us not hang like roping° icicles   *ropelike*
Upon our houses' thatch, whiles a more frosty people

25   Sweat drops of gallant youth in our rich fields—
'Poor' may we call them,° in their native lords.   *(the fields)*

DAUPHIN   By faith and honour,
Our madams mock at us and plainly say
Our mettle is bred out,° and they will give   *is exhausted*

30   Their bodies to the lust of English youth,
To new-store France with bastard warriors.

BOURBON   They bid us, 'To the English dancing-schools,
And teach lavoltas° high and swift corantos'[5]—   *leaping dance*
Saying our grace is only in our heels,

35   And that we are most lofty runaways.

KING CHARLES   Where is Montjoy the herald? Speed° him hence.   *Quickly send*
Let him greet England with our sharp defiance.
Up, princes, and with spirit of honour edged
More sharper than your swords, hie° to the field.   *go*

40   Charles Delabret, High Constable of France,
You Dukes of Orléans, Bourbon, and of Berri,
Alençon, Brabant, Bar, and Burgundy,

---

recite my entire lesson once more. D'hand, de fingre, de nails, d'arma, d'elbow, de nick, de sin, de foot, de cown.
ALICE   Excellent, madam!
CATHERINE   That's enough for one time. Let's go to dinner.
3.5 Location: The French King's court.
1. Offshoots (bastards).
2. The discharge ("emptying") of our forefathers' lust.
3. With an indented shore.
4. A tonic for overworked horses.
5. Running dance.

Jaques Châtillion, Rambures, Vaudemont,
Beaumont, Grandpré, Roussi, and Fauconbridge,
45 Foix, Lestrelles, Boucicault, and Charolais,
High dukes, great princes, barons, lords, and knights,
For your great seats now quit you⁶ of great shames.
Bar Harry England, that sweeps through our land
With pennons° painted in the blood of Harfleur;   *banners*
50 Rush on his host, as doth the melted snow
Upon the valleys, whose low vassal seat
The Alps doth spit and void his rheum° upon.   *empty its moisture*
Go down upon him, you have power enough,
And in a captive chariot into Rouen
Bring him our prisoner.
55 CONSTABLE   This becomes the great.°   *befits noblemen*
Sorry am I his numbers are so few,
His soldiers sick and famished in their march,
For I am sure when he shall see our army
He'll drop his heart into the sink° of fear   *pit*
60 And, fore achievement,° offer us his ransom.   *instead of battle*
KING CHARLES   Therefore, Lord Constable, haste on Montjoy,
And let him say to England that we send
To know what willing ransom he will give.—
Prince Dauphin, you shall stay with us in Rouen.
65 DAUPHIN   Not so, I do beseech your majesty.
KING CHARLES   Be patient, for you shall remain with us.—
Now forth, Lord Constable, and princes all,
And quickly bring us word of England's fall. *Exeunt* [*severally*]

3.6

Enter Captains GOWER *and* FLUELLEN [*meeting*]

GOWER   How now, Captain Fluellen, come you from the bridge?
FLUELLEN   I assure you there is very excellent services committed at the bridge.
GOWER   Is the Duke of Exeter safe?
5 FLUELLEN   The Duke of Exeter is as magnanimous as Agamemnon,¹ and a man that I love and honour with my soul and my
heart and my duty and my live and my living and my uttermost
power. He is not, God be praised and blessed, any hurt in the
world, but keeps the bridge most valiantly, with excellent disci-
10 pline. There is an ensign lieutenant there at the pridge, I think
in my very conscience he is as valiant a man as Mark Antony,
and he is a man of no estimation° in the world, but I did see   *fame*
him do as gallant service.
GOWER   What do you call him?
15 FLUELLEN   He is called Ensign Pistol.
GOWER   I know him not.

Enter Ensign PISTOL

FLUELLEN   Here is the man.
PISTOL   Captain, I thee beseech to do me favours.
The Duke of Exeter doth love thee well.
20 FLUELLEN   Ay, I praise God, and I have merited some love at his
hands.

---

6. *For . . . you*: In defense of your high ranks, now revenge
yourselves.

3.6 Location: The English camp.
1. Greek general in the Trojan War.

PISTOL   Bardolph, a soldier firm and sound of heart,
    Of buxom° valour, hath by cruel fate   *lively*
    And giddy Fortune's furious fickle wheel,
25   That goddess blind that stands upon the rolling restless stone—
FLUELLEN   By your patience, Ensign Pistol: Fortune is painted
    blind, with a muffler° afore her eyes, to signify to you that For-   *blindfold*
    tune is blind. And she is painted also with a wheel, to signify to
    you—which is the moral of it—that she is turning and incon-
30   stant and mutability and variation. And her foot, look you, is
    fixed upon a spherical stone, which rolls and rolls and rolls.
    In good truth, the poet makes a most excellent description of
    it; Fortune is an excellent moral.°   *symbolic emblem*
PISTOL   Fortune is Bardolph's foe and frowns on him,
35   For he hath stol'n a pax,[2] and hangèd must a° be.   *he*
    A damnèd death—
    Let gallows gape for dog, let man go free,
    And let not hemp[3] his windpipe suffocate.
    But Exeter hath given the doom° of death   *sentence*
40   For pax of little price.
    Therefore go speak, the Duke will hear thy voice,
    And let not Bardolph's vital thread be cut
    With edge of penny cord and vile reproach.
    Speak, captain, for his life, and I will thee requite.
45 FLUELLEN   Ensign Pistol, I do partly understand your meaning.
PISTOL   Why then rejoice therefor.
FLUELLEN   Certainly, ensign, it is not a thing to rejoice at. For
    if, look you, he were my brother, I would desire the Duke to
    use his good pleasure, and put him to executions. For disci-
50   pline ought to be used.
PISTOL   Die and be damned! and *fico*[4] for thy friendship.
FLUELLEN   It is well.
PISTOL   The fig of Spain.
FLUELLEN   Very good.
55 PISTOL   I say the fig within thy bowels and thy dirty maw.   *Exit*
FLUELLEN   Captain Gower, cannot you hear it lighten and
    thunder?
GOWER   Why, is this the ensign you told me of? I remember him
    now. A bawd, a cutpurse.°   *thief*
60 FLUELLEN   I'll assure you, a uttered as prave words at the pridge
    as you shall see in a summer's day. But it is very well. What he
    has spoke to me, that is well, I warrant you, when time is serve.
GOWER   Why 'tis a gull,° a fool, a rogue, that now and then goes   *simpleton*
    to the wars, to grace himself at his return into London under
65   the form of a soldier. And such fellows are perfect in the great
    commanders' names, and they will learn° you by rote where   *teach*
    services were done— at such and such a sconce,° at such a   *fortification*
    breach, at such a convoy, who came off bravely, who was shot,
    who disgraced, what terms the enemy stood on—and this they
70   con° perfectly in the phrase of war, which they trick up° with   *memorize / adorn*
    new-tuned° oaths. And what a beard of the General's cut and a   *newly coined*
    horrid suit of the camp[5] will do among foaming bottles and ale-

---

2. Small tablet with a crucifix stamped on it.
3. Of which ropes were made.
4. Spanish for "fig"; obscene gesture made by thrusting

the thumb between two fingers.
5. *horrid . . . camp*: frightening soldier's attire.

washed wits is wonderful to be thought on. But you must learn
to know such slanders° of the age, or else you may be marvel-   *disgraces*
75 lously mistook.

FLUELLEN   I tell you what, Captain Gower, I do perceive he is
not the man that he would gladly make show to the world he
is. If I find a hole in his coat,° I will tell him my mind.   *means of exposing him*
      [*A drum is heard*]
Hark you, the King is coming, and I must speak with him from
80 the pridge.
      Enter KING [HARRY] *and his poor soldiers,* [*with*] *drum*
        and colours°   *drummer and flag bearer*
God pless your majesty.

KING HARRY   How now, Fluellen, com'st thou from the bridge?

FLUELLEN   Ay, so please your majesty. The Duke of Exeter has
very gallantly maintained the pridge. The French is gone off,
85 look you, and there is gallant and most prave passages.° Marry,   *altercations*
th'athversary was have possession of the pridge, but he is
enforced to retire, and the Duke of Exeter is master of the
pridge. I can tell your majesty, the Duke is a prave man.

KING HARRY   What men have you lost, Fluellen?

90 FLUELLEN   The perdition° of th'athversary hath been very great,   *loss*
reasonable great. Marry, for my part I think the Duke hath lost
never a man, but one that is like to be executed for robbing a
church, one Bardolph, if your majesty know the man. His face
is all bubuncles and whelks° and knobs and flames o' fire, and   *abscesses and pimples*
95 his lips blows at his nose, and it is like a coal of fire, sometimes
plue and sometimes red. But his nose is executed,[6] and his
fire's out.

KING HARRY   We would have all such offenders so cut off, and
we here give express charge that in our marches through the
100 country there be nothing compelled from the villages, nothing
taken but° paid for, none of the French upbraided or abused in   *unless*
disdainful language. For when lenity° and cruelty play for a   *leniency*
kingdom, the gentler gamester is the soonest winner.
      Tucket.° *Enter* MONTJOY   *Trumpet call*

MONTJOY   You know me by my habit.°   *herald's coat*
105 KING HARRY   Well then, I know thee. What shall I know of thee?

MONTJOY   My master's mind.

KING HARRY   Unfold it.

MONTJOY   Thus says my King:
'Say thou to Harry of England, though we seemed dead, we did
but sleep. Advantage° is a better soldier than rashness. Tell   *Circumspection*
him, we could have rebuked him at Harfleur, but that we
110 thought not good to bruise an injury° till it were full ripe. Now   *squeeze a pimple*
we speak upon our cue,° and our voice is imperial. England   *at the proper time*
shall repent his folly, see his weakness, and admire our suffer-
ance.° Bid him therefore consider of his ransom, which must   *wonder at our patience*
proportion the losses we have borne, the subjects we have lost,
115 the disgrace we have digested°—which in weight to re-answer,°   *endured / compensate*
his pettiness would bow under. For our losses, his exchequer°   *King's treasury*
is too poor; for th'effusion of our blood, the muster[7] of his kingdom too faint a number; and for our disgrace, his own person
kneeling at our feet but a weak and worthless satisfaction. To
120 this add defiance, and tell him for conclusion he hath betrayed

---

6. Slit (in the pillory before he is hanged).   7. Entire population, assembled for military service.

his followers, whose condemnation is pronounced.'
So far my King and master; so much my office.
KING HARRY   What is thy name? I know thy quality.°   rank
MONTJOY   Montjoy.
125 KING HARRY   Thou dost thy office fairly. Turn thee back
And tell thy king I do not seek him now,
But could be willing to march on to Calais
Without impeachment,° for to say the sooth°—   hindrance / truth
Though 'tis no wisdom to confess so much
130 Unto an enemy of craft and vantage°—   cunning and superiority
My people are with sickness much enfeebled,
My numbers lessened, and those few I have
Almost no better than so many French;
Who when they were in health—I tell thee herald,
135 I thought upon one pair of English legs
Did march three Frenchmen. Yet forgive me, God,
That I do brag thus. This your air of France
Hath blown that vice in me. I must repent.
Go, therefore, tell thy master here I am;
140 My ransom is this frail and worthless trunk,°   body
My army but a weak and sickly guard.
Yet, God before, tell him we will come on,
Though France himself and such another neighbour
Stand in our way. There's for thy labour, Montjoy.[8]
145 Go bid thy master well advise himself.
If we may pass, we will; if we be hindered,
We shall your tawny ground with your red blood
Discolour. And so, Montjoy, fare you well.
The sum of all our answer is but this:
150 We would not seek a battle as we are,
Nor as we are we say we will not shun it.
So tell your master.
MONTJOY   I shall deliver so. Thanks to your highness.   *Exit*
GLOUCESTER   I hope they will not come upon us now.
155 KING HARRY   We are in God's hand, brother, not in theirs.
March to the bridge. It now draws toward night.
Beyond the river we'll encamp ourselves,
And on tomorrow bid them march away.   *Exeunt*

3.7

Enter the CONSTABLE, *Lord* RAMBURES, [*Dukes of*]
ORLÉANS [*and*] BOURBON,[1] *with others*

CONSTABLE   Tut, I have the best armour of the world. Would it
were day.
ORLÉANS   You have an excellent armour. But let my horse have
his due.
5 CONSTABLE   It is the best horse of Europe.
ORLÉANS   Will it never be morning?
BOURBON   My lord of Orléans and my Lord High Constable, you
talk of horse and armour?
ORLÉANS   You are as well provided of both as any prince in the
10 world.
BOURBON   What a long night is this! I will not change my horse

8. Henry generously "tips" the enemy herald.   1. As in Q; F has "Dauphin" in this scene and in 4.2
3.7 Location: The French camp near Agincourt.   and 4.5. See Textual Note.

with any that treads but on four pasterns.° Ah ha! He bounds   *hooves*
from the earth as if his entrails were hares—*le cheval volant,*
the Pegasus, *qui a les narines de feu!*[2] When I bestride him, I
15 soar, I am a hawk; he trots the air, the earth sings when he
touches it,[3] the basest horn° of his hoof is more musical than   *lowest part (with pun)*
the pipe of Hermes.[4]

ORLÉANS   He's of the colour of the nutmeg.

BOURBON   And of the heat of the ginger.[5] It is a beast for Per-
20 seus. He is pure air and fire, and the dull elements of earth and
water never appear in him, but only in patient stillness while
his rider mounts him. He is indeed a horse, and all other jades°   *nags*
you may call beasts.

CONSTABLE   Indeed, my lord, it is a most absolute° and excellent   *perfect*
25 horse.

BOURBON   It is the prince of palfreys.° His neigh is the bidding   *warhorses*
of a monarch, and his countenance enforces homage.

ORLÉANS   No more, cousin.

BOURBON   Nay, the man hath no wit, that cannot from the ris-
30 ing of the lark to the lodging of the lamb vary deserved praise
on my palfrey. It is a theme as fluent° as the sea. Turn the sands   *flowing; abundant*
into eloquent tongues, and my horse is argument° for them all.   *subject*
'Tis a subject for a sovereign to reason on, and for a sovereign's
sovereign to ride on, and for the world, familiar to us and
35 unknown, to lay apart their particular functions, and wonder at
him. I once writ a sonnet in his praise, and began thus: 'Wonder of nature!—'

ORLÉANS   I have heard a sonnet begin so to one's mistress.

BOURBON   Then did they imitate that which I composed to my
40 courser, for my horse is my mistress.

ORLÉANS   Your mistress bears well.[6]

BOURBON   *Me* well, which is the prescribed praise and perfection
of a good and particular° mistress.   *private*

CONSTABLE   Nay, for methought yesterday your mistress
45 shrewdly° shook your back.   *severely*

BOURBON   So perhaps did yours.

CONSTABLE   Mine was not bridled.

BOURBON   O then belike she was old and gentle, and you rode
like a kern° of Ireland, your French hose° off, and in your strait   *soldier / wide breeches*
50 strossers.°   *tights*

CONSTABLE   You have good judgement in horsemanship.

BOURBON   Be warned by me then: they that ride so, and ride not
warily, fall into foul bogs. I had rather have my horse to my
mistress.

55 CONSTABLE   I had as lief have my mistress a jade.°   *horse; whore*

BOURBON   I tell thee, Constable, my mistress wears his own
hair.[7]

CONSTABLE   I could make as true a boast as that, if I had a sow
to my mistress.

60 BOURBON   *'Le chien est retourné à son propre vomissement, et la*

---

2. The flying horse . . . with nostrils of fire. Pegasus was
a mythological flying horse, ridden by the hero Perseus.
3. When Pegasus struck Mount Helicon with his hoof,
the fountain of the Muses sprang forth.
4. Greek messenger god, whose sweet playing on the
pipe charmed the many-eyed guard Argus, allowing the
imprisoned Io to escape.

5. Horses' colors supposedly suggested their dispositions: "nutmeg" meant "pleasant and nimble"; "ginger"
meant "hot and skittish."
6. Carries weight (with obscene innuendo).
7. Implying that the constable's mistress does not, having lost it to syphilis.

truie lavée au bourbier.[8] Thou makest use of anything.

CONSTABLE   Yet do I not use my horse for my mistress, or any such proverb so little kin to the purpose.

RAMBURES   My Lord Constable, the armour that I saw in your
65   tent tonight, are those stars or suns upon it?

CONSTABLE   Stars, my lord.

BOURBON   Some of them will fall tomorrow, I hope.

CONSTABLE   And yet my sky shall not want.

BOURBON   That may be, for you bear a many superfluously,
70   and 'twere more honour some were away.

CONSTABLE   Even as your horse bears your praises, who would trot as well were some of your brags dismounted.

BOURBON   Would I were able to load him with his desert! Will it never be day? I will trot tomorrow a mile, and my way shall
75   be paved with English faces.

CONSTABLE   I will not say so, for fear I should be faced out of my way.° But I would it were morning, for I would fain° be about   turned aside / gladly
the ears of the English.

RAMBURES   Who will go to hazard° with me for twenty prisoners?   wager

80   CONSTABLE   You must first go yourself to hazard, ere you have them.

BOURBON   'Tis midnight. I'll go arm myself.   *Exit*

ORLÉANS   The Duke of Bourbon longs for morning.

RAMBURES   He longs to eat the English.

85   CONSTABLE   I think he will eat all he kills.

ORLÉANS   By the white hand of my lady, he's a gallant prince.

CONSTABLE   Swear by her foot, that she may tread out° the oath.   erase with her foot

ORLÉANS   He is simply the most active gentleman of France.

CONSTABLE   Doing is activity, and he will still be doing.

90   ORLÉANS   He never did harm that I heard of.

CONSTABLE   Nor will do none tomorrow. He will keep that good name still.

ORLÉANS   I know him to be valiant.

CONSTABLE   I was told that by one that knows him better than
95   you.

ORLÉANS   What's he?

CONSTABLE   Marry, he told me so himself, and he said he cared not who knew it.

ORLÉANS   He needs not; it is no hidden virtue in him.

100   CONSTABLE   By my faith, sir, but it is. Never anybody saw it but his lackey.[9] 'Tis a hooded valour, and when it appears it will bate.[1]

ORLÉANS   'Ill will never said well.'

CONSTABLE   I will cap that proverb with 'There is flattery in
105   friendship.'

ORLÉANS   And I will take up that with 'Give the devil his due.'

CONSTABLE   Well placed! There stands your friend for the devil. Have at the very eye° of that proverb with 'A pox of the devil!'   bull's-eye

ORLÉANS   You are the better at proverbs by how much 'a fool's
110   bolt° is soon shot'.   short, blunt arrow

---

8. "The dog is turned to his own vomit again and the sow that was washed to her wallowing in the mire" (quoting 2 Peter 2:22).
9. That is, the only person he is brave enough to beat

is his servant.
1. Beat its wings (like a hawk, which was kept "hooded" until prey was sighted); also, abate.

CONSTABLE   You have shot over.°   *overshot the target*

ORLÉANS   'Tis not the first time you were overshot.°   *defeated*

Enter a MESSENGER

MESSENGER   My Lord High Constable, the English lie within
fifteen hundred paces of your tents.

115 CONSTABLE   Who hath measured the ground?

MESSENGER   The Lord Grandpré.

CONSTABLE   A valiant and most expert gentleman.

[*Exit* MESSENGER]

Would it were day! Alas, poor Harry of England. He longs not
for the dawning as we do.

120 ORLÉANS   What a wretched and peevish fellow is this King of
England, to mope° with his fat-brained followers so far out of   *wander*
his knowledge.

CONSTABLE   If the English had any apprehension,° they would   *sense*
run away.

125 ORLÉANS   That they lack—for if their heads had any intellectual
armour, they could never wear such heavy headpieces.

RAMBURES   That island of England breeds very valiant creatures.
Their mastiffs are of unmatchable courage.

ORLÉANS   Foolish curs, that run winking° into the mouth of a   *with closed eyes*
130 Russian bear², and have their heads crushed like rotten apples.
You may as well say, 'That's a valiant flea that dare eat his
breakfast on the lip of a lion.'

CONSTABLE   Just,° just. And the men do sympathize with the   *True*
mastiffs in robustious and rough coming on, leaving their wits
135 with their wives. And then, give them great meals of beef,³ and
iron and steel, they will eat like wolves and fight like devils.

ORLÉANS   Ay, but these English are shrewdly° out of beef.   *badly*

CONSTABLE   Then shall we find tomorrow they have only stom-
achs° to eat, and none to fight. Now is it time to arm. Come,   *appetite*
140 shall we about it?

ORLÉANS   It is now two o'clock. But let me see—by ten
We shall have each a hundred Englishmen.   *Exeunt*

4.0

[*Enter*] CHORUS

CHORUS   Now entertain conjecture of° a time   *imagine*
When creeping murmur and the poring° dark   *pouring; eye-straining*
Fills the wide vessel of the universe.
From camp to camp through the foul womb of night
5   The hum of either army stilly sounds,
That° the fixed sentinels almost receive   *So that*
The secret whispers of each other's watch.
Fire answers fire, and through their paly° flames   *pale*
Each battle sees the other's umbered° face.   *shadowed*
10   Steed threatens steed, in high and boastful neighs
Piercing the night's dull ear, and from the tents
The armourers, accomplishing° the knights,   *equipping*
With busy hammers closing rivets up,
Give dreadful note of preparation.
15   The country cocks do crow, the clocks do toll

---

2. Referring to the sport of bearbaiting, in which dogs
were set upon bears chained to a post.

3. A traditional English food.
4.0

And the third hour of drowsy morning name.
Proud of their numbers and secure in soul,
The confident and overlusty French
Do the low-rated° English play at dice,[1]   underrated
20 And chide the cripple tardy-gaited night,
Who like a foul and ugly witch doth limp
So tediously away. The poor condemnèd English,
Like sacrifices, by their watchful fires
Sit patiently and inly° ruminate   inwardly
25 The morning's danger; and their gesture sad,
Investing° lank lean cheeks and war-worn coats,   Accompanying
Presented them unto the gazing moon
So many horrid ghosts. O now, who will behold
The royal captain of this ruined band
30 Walking from watch to watch, from tent to tent,
Let him cry, 'Praise and glory on his head!'
For forth he goes and visits all his host,°   army
Bids them good morrow with a modest smile
And calls them brothers, friends, and countrymen.
35 Upon his royal face there is no note°   sign
How dread an army hath enrounded° him;   encircled
Nor doth he dedicate° one jot of colour   lose
Unto the weary and all-watchèd night,
But freshly looks and overbears attaint[2]
40 With cheerful semblance and sweet majesty,
That every wretch, pining and pale before,
Beholding him, plucks comfort from his looks.
A largess universal,° like the sun,   wealth available to all
His liberal eye doth give to everyone,
45 Thawing cold fear, that mean and gentle° all   lowborn and noble
Behold, as may unworthiness define,[3]
A little touch of Harry in the night.
And so our scene must to the battle fly,
Where O for pity, we shall much disgrace,
50 With four or five most vile and ragged foils,°   swords
Right ill-disposed in brawl ridiculous,
The name of Agincourt. Yet sit and see,
Minding° true things by what their mock'ries be.   Exit   Imagining

4.1

Enter KING [HARRY] *and* [*Duke of*] GLOUCESTER [*then*
the Duke of CLARENCE]

KING HARRY   Gloucester, 'tis true that we are in great danger;
The greater therefore should our courage be.
Good morrow, brother Clarence. God Almighty!
There is some soul of goodness in things evil,
5   Would men observingly distil it out—
For our bad neighbour makes us early stirrers,
Which is both healthful and good husbandry.°   economy
Besides, they are our outward consciences,
And preachers to us all, admonishing
10 That we should dress us fairly° for our end.   prepare adequately

---

1. See 3.7.79.
2. And suppresses signs of exhaustion.
3. As far as their limited capacities permit.
4.1 Location: The English camp at Agincourt.

Thus may we gather honey from the weed
And make a moral of the devil himself.

Enter [Sir Thomas] ERPINGHAM

Good morrow, old Sir Thomas Erpingham.
A good soft pillow for that good white head

15   Were better than a churlish turf of France.

ERPINGHAM   Not so, my liege. This lodging likes° me better,   *pleases*
Since I may say, 'Now lie I like a king.'

KING HARRY   'Tis good for men to love their present pains
Upon example.[1] So the spirit is eased,

20   And when the mind is quickened, out of doubt
The organs, though defunct and dead before,
Break up their drowsy grave and newly move
With casted slough[2] and fresh legerity.°   *nimbleness*
Lend me thy cloak, Sir Thomas.

[He puts on Erpingham's cloak]
                                        Brothers both,

25   Commend me to the princes in our camp.
Do my good morrow° to them, and anon   *Say good morning*
Desire them all to my pavilion.

GLOUCESTER   We shall, my liege.

ERPINGHAM   Shall I attend your grace?

30   KING HARRY   No, my good knight.
Go with my brothers to my lords of England.
I and my bosom must debate awhile,
And then I would no other company.

ERPINGHAM   The Lord in heaven bless thee, noble Harry.

35   KING HARRY   God-a-mercy,° old heart, thou speak'st cheerfully.   *Thank you*

Exeunt [all but KING HARRY]

Enter PISTOL *[to him]*

PISTOL   *Qui vous là?*°   *Who goes there*

KING HARRY   A friend.

PISTOL   Discuss unto me: art thou officer,
Or art thou base, common, and popular?°   *plebeian*

40   KING HARRY   I am a gentleman of a company.

PISTOL   Trail'st thou the puissant pike?°   *Are you an infantryman*

KING HARRY   Even so. What are you?

PISTOL   As good a gentleman as the Emperor.

KING HARRY   Then you are a better than the King.

45   PISTOL   The King's a bawcock and a heart-of-gold,
A lad of life, an imp of fame,°   *a scion of noble stock*
Of parents good, of fist most valiant.
I kiss his dirty shoe, and from heartstring
I love the lovely bully.° What is thy name?   *lovable swashbuckler*

50   KING HARRY   Harry *le roi*.°   *the King*

PISTOL   Leroi? A Cornish name. Art thou of Cornish crew?

KING HARRY   No, I am a Welshman.

PISTOL   Know'st thou Fluellen?

KING HARRY   Yes.

55   PISTOL   Tell him I'll knock his leek about his pate
Upon Saint Davy's day.[3]

KING HARRY   Do not you wear your dagger in your cap that day,
lest he knock that about yours.

---

1. By the pattern provided by others.
2. Old skin having been cast off (like a snake).

3. March 1, Welsh national holiday celebrating St. David's victory over the Saxons.

PISTOL   Art thou his friend?

60 KING HARRY   And his kinsman too.

PISTOL   The *fico*⁴ for thee then.

KING HARRY   I thank you. God be with you.

PISTOL   My name is Pistol called.

KING HARRY   It sorts° well with your fierceness.   *Exit* [PISTOL]   agrees
    Enter [*Captains*] FLUELLEN *and* GOWER [*severally.* KING
    HARRY *stands apart*]

65 GOWER   Captain Fluellen!

FLUELLEN   So! In the name of Jesu Christ, speak fewer. It is the
    greatest admiration° in the universal° world, when the true and   wonder / whole
    ancient prerogatifs and laws of the wars is not kept. If you
    would take the pains but to examine the wars of Pompey the
70 Great,⁵ you shall find, I warrant you, that there is no tiddle-
    taddle nor pibble-babble° in Pompey's camp. I warrant you,   chattering
    you shall find the ceremonies of the wars, and the cares of it,
    and the forms of it, and the sobriety of it, and the modesty of
    it, to be otherwise.

75 GOWER   Why, the enemy is loud. You hear him all night.

FLUELLEN   If the enemy is an ass and a fool and a prating cox-
    comb,° is it meet,° think you, that we should also, look you, be   yammering fool / proper
    an ass and a fool and a prating coxcomb? In your own con-
    science now?

80 GOWER   I will speak lower.

FLUELLEN   I pray you and beseech you that you will.
                    Exeunt [FLUELLEN *and* GOWER]

KING HARRY   Though it appear a little out of fashion,°   unconventional
    There is much care and valour in this Welshman.
        Enter three soldiers: John BATES, *Alexander* COURT, *and*
        Michael WILLIAMS

COURT   Brother John Bates, is not that the morning which breaks
85 yonder?

BATES   I think it be. But we have no great cause to desire the
    approach of day.

WILLIAMS   We see yonder the beginning of the day, but I think
    we shall never see the end of it.—Who goes there?

90 KING HARRY   A friend.

WILLIAMS   Under what captain serve you?

KING HARRY   Under Sir Thomas Erpingham.

WILLIAMS   A good old commander and a most kind gentleman.
    I pray you, what thinks he of our estate?°   situation

95 KING HARRY   Even as men wrecked upon a sand, that look to be
    washed off the next tide.

BATES   He hath not told his thought to the King?

KING HARRY   No, nor it is not meet he should. For though I speak
    it to you, I think the King is but a man, as I am. The violet
100 smells to him as it doth to me; the element shows° to him as it   the sky appears
    doth to me. All his senses have but human conditions.° His   limitations
    ceremonies laid by, in his nakedness he appears but a man,
    and though his affections° are higher mounted than ours, yet   desires
    when they stoop,⁶ they stoop with the like wing. Therefore,
105 when he sees reason of fears,° as we do, his fears, out of doubt,   to fear

---

4. See 3.6.51.   6. Plummet down (term from falconry).
5. Roman general, defeated by Julius Caesar.

be of the same relish° as ours are. Yet, in reason, no man should   *taste; kind*
possess him with⁷ any appearance of fear, lest he, by showing
it, should dishearten his army.

BATES   He may show what outward courage he will, but I
110   believe, as cold a night as 'tis, he could wish himself in Thames
up to the neck. And so I would he were, and I by him, at all
adventures,⁸ so we were quit° here.   *away from*

KING HARRY   By my troth,° I will speak my conscience of the   *oath*
King. I think he would not wish himself anywhere but where
115   he is.

BATES   Then I would he were here alone. So should he be sure
to be ransomed, and a many poor men's lives saved.

KING HARRY   I dare say you love him not so ill to wish him here
alone, howsoever you speak this to feel° other men's minds.   *test*
120   Methinks I could not die anywhere so contented as in the
King's company, his cause being just and his quarrel honourable.

WILLIAMS   That's more than we know.

BATES   Ay, or more than we should seek after. For we know
125   enough if we know we are the King's subjects. If his cause be
wrong, our obedience to the King wipes the crime of it out of
us.

WILLIAMS   But if the cause be not good, the King himself hath a
heavy reckoning to make, when all those legs and arms and
130   heads chopped off in a battle shall join together at the latter
day,⁹ and cry all, 'We died at such a place'—some swearing,
some crying for a surgeon, some upon their wives left poor
behind them, some upon the debts they owe, some upon their
children rawly° left. I am afeard there are few die well that die   *abruptly; poorly*
135   in a battle, for how can they charitably dispose of anything,
when blood is their argument?° Now, if these men do not die   *business*
well, it will be a black matter for the King that led them to it—
who° to disobey were against all proportion of subjection.¹   *whom*

KING HARRY   So, if a son that is by his father sent about merchan-
140   dise do sinfully miscarry upon the sea, the imputation of° his   *blame for*
wickedness, by your rule, should be imposed upon his father,
that sent him. Or if a servant, under his master's command
transporting a sum of money, be assailed by robbers, and die in
many irreconciled iniquities,° you may call the business of the   *unatoned sins*
145   master the author of the servant's damnation. But this is not so.
The King is not bound to answer the particular endings of his
soldiers, the father of his son, nor the master of his servant, for
they purpose not their deaths when they propose their services.
Besides, there is no king, be his cause never so spotless, if it
150   come to the arbitrament° of swords, can try it out with all   *settlement*
unspotted° soldiers. Some, peradventure,° have on them the   *unblemished / perhaps*
guilt of premeditated and contrived murder; some, of beguiling
virgins with the broken seals of perjury; some, making the wars
their bulwark,° that have before gored the gentle bosom of   *defense (against the law)*
155   peace with pillage and robbery. Now, if these men have

---

7. Induce him to experience.
8. Whatever might happen.
9. Last Judgment, when human beings are to be resurrected in the body.
1. *against . . . subjection*: to defy all proper relation-ships of authority and subordination.

defeated the law and outrun native° punishment, though they _at home_
can outstrip men, they have no wings to fly from God. War is
his beadle.° War is his vengeance. So that here men are pun- _police officer_
ished for before-breach° of the King's laws, in now the King's _earlier breaking_
160 quarrel. Where they feared the death, they have borne life
away; and where they would be safe, they perish. Then if they
die unprovided,° no more is the King guilty of their damnation _unprepared_
than he was before guilty of those impieties for the which they
are now visited.° Every subject's duty is the King's, but every _punished_
165 subject's soul is his own. Therefore should every soldier in the
wars do as every sick man in his bed: wash every mote° out of _speck_
his conscience. And dying so, death is to him advantage;° or _profit_
not dying, the time was blessedly lost wherein such preparation
was gained. And in him that escapes, it were not sin to think
170 that, making God so free an offer, he° let him outlive that day _(God)_
to see his greatness and to teach others how they should prepare.

BATES   'Tis certain, every man that dies ill,° the ill upon his own _in sin_
head. The King is not to answer it. I do not desire he
175 should answer for me, and yet I determine to fight lustily for
him.

KING HARRY   I myself heard the King say he would not be ransomed.

WILLIAMS   Ay, he said so, to make us fight cheerfully, but when
180 our throats are cut he may be ransomed, and we ne'er the
wiser.

KING HARRY   If I live to see it, I will never trust his word after.

WILLIAMS   You pay him then! That's a perilous shot out of an
elder-gun,° that a poor and a private displeasure can do against _a popgun_
185 a monarch. You may as well go about to turn the sun to ice
with fanning in his face with a peacock's feather. You'll never
trust his word after! Come, 'tis a foolish saying.

KING HARRY   Your reproof is something too round.° I should be _blunt_
angry with you, if the time were convenient.

190 WILLIAMS   Let it be a quarrel between us, if you live.

KING HARRY   I embrace it.

WILLIAMS   How shall I know thee again?

KING HARRY   Give me any gage° of thine, and I will wear it in my _token_
bonnet. Then if ever thou darest acknowledge it, I will make it
195 my quarrel.

WILLIAMS   Here's my glove. Give me another of thine.

KING HARRY   There.
        [_They exchange gloves_]

WILLIAMS   This will I also wear in my cap. If ever thou come to
me and say, after tomorrow, 'This is my glove', by this hand I
200 will take thee a box on the ear.

KING HARRY   If ever I live to see it, I will challenge it.

WILLIAMS   Thou darest as well be hanged.

KING HARRY   Well, I will do it, though I take thee in the King's
company.

205 WILLIAMS   Keep thy word. Fare thee well.

BATES   Be friends, you English fools, be friends. We have
French quarrels enough, if you could tell how to reckon.° _count_

KING HARRY   Indeed, the French may lay twenty French crowns° _coins; heads_
to one they will beat us, for they bear them on their shoulders.

210   But it is no English treason to cut French crowns,[2] and tomor-
        row the King himself will be a clipper.   *Exeunt soldiers*
        Upon the King.
        'Let us our lives, our souls, our debts, our care-full wives,
        Our children, and our sins, lay on the King.'
215   We must bear all. O hard condition,
        Twin-born with greatness: subject to the breath
        Of every fool, whose sense no more can feel
        But his own wringing.° What infinite heartsease   *pain*
        Must kings neglect that private men enjoy?
220   And what have kings that privates have not too,
        Save ceremony, save general ceremony?
        And what art thou, thou idol ceremony?
        What kind of god art thou, that suffer'st more
        Of mortal griefs than do thy worshippers?
225   What are thy rents?° What are thy comings-in?°   *revenues / income*
        O ceremony, show me but thy worth.
        What is thy soul of adoration?[3]
        Art thou aught° else but place, degree, and form,   *anything*
        Creating awe and fear in other men?
230   Wherein thou art less happy, being feared,
        Than they in fearing.
        What drink'st thou oft, instead of homage sweet,
        But poisoned flattery? O be sick, great greatness,
        And bid thy ceremony give thee cure.
235   Think'st thou the fiery fever will go out
        With titles blown from adulation?
        Will it give place to flexure° and low bending?   *bowing*
        Canst thou, when thou command'st the beggar's knee,
        Command the health of it? No, thou proud dream
240   That play'st so subtly with a king's repose;
        I am a king that find° thee, and I know   *expose*
        'Tis not the balm, the sceptre, and the ball,°   *orb (royal accessory)*
        The sword, the mace, the crown imperial,
        The intertissued robe of gold and pearl,
245   The farcèd° title running fore the king,   *stuffed*
        The throne he sits on, nor the tide of pomp
        That beats upon the high shore of this world—
        No, not all these, thrice-gorgeous ceremony,
        Not all these, laid in bed majestical,
250   Can sleep so soundly as the wretched slave
        Who with a body filled and vacant mind
        Gets him to rest, crammed with distressful bread;
        Never sees horrid night, the child of hell,
        But like a lackey° from the rise to set   *servant*
255   Sweats in the eye of Phoebus,° and all night   *the sun*
        Sleeps in Elysium;° next day, after dawn   *classical paradise*
        Doth rise and help Hyperion° to his horse,   *the sun's charioteer*
        And follows so the ever-running year
        With profitable labour to his grave.
260   And but for ceremony such a wretch,
        Winding up days with toil and nights with sleep,

---

2. "Clipping" (line 211), or shaving, precious metal off   3. What is the secret of the adoration you inspire?
coins was punishable as treason.

Had the forehand° and vantage of a king.   advantage
The slave, a member of the country's peace,
Enjoys it, but in gross brain little wots°   thinks
265   What watch the King keeps to maintain the peace,
Whose hours the peasant best advantages.°   profits most from

Enter [Sir Thomas] ERPINGHAM

ERPINGHAM   My lord, your nobles, jealous of° your absence,   concerned about
Seek through your camp to find you.

KING HARRY   Good old knight,
Collect them all together at my tent.
I'll be before thee.

270   ERPINGHAM   I shall do't, my lord.   *Exit*

KING HARRY   O God of battles, steel my soldiers' hearts.
Possess them not with fear. Take from them now
The sense of reck'ning,° ere th'opposèd numbers   ability to count
Pluck their hearts from them. Not today, O Lord,
275   O not today, think not upon the fault
My father made in compassing the crown.[4]
I Richard's body have interrèd new,°   buried anew
And on it have bestowed more contrite tears
Than from it issued forcèd drops of blood.
280   Five hundred poor have I in yearly pay
Who twice a day their withered hands hold up°   (in prayer)
Toward heaven to pardon blood. And I have built
Two chantries,[5] where the sad and solemn priests
Sing still for Richard's soul. More will I do,
285   Though all that I can do is nothing worth,
Since that my penitence comes after ill,°   sin
Imploring pardon.

Enter the [Duke of] GLOUCESTER

GLOUCESTER   My liege.

KING HARRY   My brother Gloucester's voice? Ay.
290   I know thy errand, I will go with thee.
The day, my friends, and all things stay° for me.   *Exeunt*   wait

4.2

Enter [Dukes of BOURBON *and]* ORLÉANS, *and [Lord]*
RAMBURES

ORLÉANS   The sun doth gild our armour. Up, my lords!
BOURBON   *Monte cheval!*° My horse! *Varlet, lacquais!*° Ha!   To horse / valet
ORLÉANS   O brave spirit!
BOURBON   *Via les eaux et terre!*
5   ORLÉANS   *Rien plus? L'air et feu!*[1]
BOURBON   *Cieux,*° Cousin Orléans!   To the heavens

Enter CONSTABLE

Now, my Lord constable!
CONSTABLE   Hark how our steeds for present° service neigh.   immediate
BOURBON   Mount them and make incision in their hides,
10   That their hot blood may spin in English eyes
And dout° them with superfluous courage. Ha!   extinguish
RAMBURES   What, will you have them weep our horses' blood?

---

4. Henry's father usurped the throne from its rightful
possessor, Richard II.
5. Chapels where Masses for the dead were sung.
4.2. Location: The French camp.

1. Away over water and earth!
No more? Air and fire! (Playing on the four elements,
of which fire was the highest.)

How shall we then behold their natural tears?

    Enter MESSENGER

MESSENGER The English are embattled,[2] you French peers.

15 CONSTABLE To horse, you gallant princes, straight to horse!
   Do but behold yon poor and starvèd band,
   And your fair show° shall suck away their souls,   *appearance*
   Leaving them but the shells and husks of men.
   There is not work enough for all our hands,
20 Scarce blood enough in all their sickly veins
   To give each naked curtal-axe° a stain   *cutlass*
   That our French gallants shall today draw out
   And sheathe for lack of sport. Let us but blow on them,
   The vapour of our valour will o'erturn them.
25 'Tis positive 'gainst all exceptions,° lords,   *'Tis definitely true*
   That our superfluous lackeys and our peasants,
   Who in unnecessary action swarm
   About our squares of battle, were enough
   To purge this field of such a hilding° foe,   *worthless*
30 Though we upon this mountain's basis by°   *foot nearby*
   Took stand° for idle speculation,   *Stood still*
   But that our honours must not. What's to say?
   A very little little let us do
   And all is done. Then let the trumpets sound
35 The tucket sonance° and the note to mount,   *trumpet signal*
   For our approach shall so much dare the field
   That England shall couch down in fear and yield.

    Enter [Lord] GRANDPRÉ

GRANDPRÉ Why do you stay so long, my lords of France?
   Yon island carrions,° desperate of their bones,   *cadavers*
40 Ill-favouredly become the morning field.
   Their ragged curtains° poorly are let loose   *banners*
   And our air shakes them passing scornfully.
   Big Mars° seems bankrupt in their beggared host   *god of war*
   And faintly through a rusty beaver° peeps.   *visor*
45 The horsemen sit like fixèd candlesticks
   With torchstaves° in their hands, and their poor jades *tapers*
   Lob° down their heads, drooping the hides and hips,   *Hang*
   The gum down-roping° from their pale dead eyes, *mucus dripping*
   And in their palled° dull mouths the gimmaled° bit *pale / jointed*
50 Lies foul with chewed grass, still and motionless.
   And their executors,[3] the knavish crows,
   Fly o'er them all impatient for their hour.
   Description cannot suit itself in words
   To demonstrate the life of° such a battle   *depict realistically*
55 In life so lifeless as it shows itself.

CONSTABLE They have said their prayers, and they stay° for death. *wait*

BOURBON Shall we go send them dinners and fresh suits
   And give their fasting horses provender,°   *food*
   And after° fight with them?   *afterward*

60 CONSTABLE I stay but for my guidon.° To the field!   *pennant*
   I will the banner from a trumpet° take   *trumpeter*
   And use it for my haste. Come, come away!
   The sun is high, and we outwear° the day.   *Exeunt* *waste*

---

2. Drawn into lines of battle.

3. Administrators of wills (who dispose of the remains of the dead).

4.3

Enter [Dukes of] GLOUCESTER, [CLARENCE, *and*] EXE-
TER, [*Earls of*] SALISBURY *and* [WARWICK, *and Sir*
Thomas] ERPINGHAM, *with all [the] host*

GLOUCESTER   Where is the King?

CLARENCE   The King himself is rode to view their battle.°   army

WARWICK   Of fighting men they have full threescore thousand.°   60,000

EXETER   There's five to one. Besides, they all are fresh.

5   SALISBURY   God's arm strike with us! 'Tis a fearful odds.
God b'wi' you, princes all. I'll to my charge.°   command post
If we no more meet till we meet in heaven,
Then joyfully, my noble Lord of Clarence,
My dear Lord Gloucester, and my good Lord Exeter,
10   And [*to* WARWICK] my kind kinsman, warriors all, adieu.

CLARENCE   Farewell, good Salisbury, and good luck go with thee.

EXETER   Farewell, kind lord. Fight valiantly today—
And yet I do thee wrong to mind° thee of it,   remind
For thou art framed of the firm truth of valour.

[*Exit* SALISBURY]

15   CLARENCE   He is as full of valour as of kindness,
Princely in both.

Enter KING; [HARRY, *behind*]

WARWICK   O that we now had here
But one ten thousand of those men in England
That do no work today.

KING HARRY   What's he that wishes so?
My cousin Warwick? No, my fair cousin.
20   If we are marked to die, we are enough
To do our country loss;° and if to live,   For our country to lose
The fewer men, the greater share of honour.
God's will, I pray thee wish not one man more.
By Jove, I am not covetous for gold,
25   Nor care I who doth feed upon my cost;
It ernes° me not if men my garments wear;   grieves
Such outward things dwell not in my desires.
But if it be a sin to covet honour
I am the most offending soul alive.
30   No, faith, my coz,° wish not a man from England.   kinsman
God's peace, I would not lose so great an honour
As one man more methinks would share° from me   deprive
For the best hope I have. O do not wish one more.
Rather proclaim it presently° through my host°   immediately / army
35   That he which hath no stomach° to this fight,   appetite; courage
Let him depart. His passport shall be made
And crowns for convoy° put into his purse.   money for transport
We would not die in that man's company
That fears his fellowship° to die with us.   duty as our companion
40   This day is called the Feast of Crispian.[1]
He that outlives this day and comes safe home
Will stand a-tiptoe when this day is named
And rouse him at the name of Crispian.
He that shall see this day and live t'old age

4.3 Location: The English camp.
1. October 25, dedicated to the martyred brothers Crispin and Crispianus (or Crispinian).

45	Will yearly on the vigil° feast his neighbours
	eve of the saint's day

45 Will yearly on the vigil° feast his neighbours   *eve of the saint's day*
   And say, 'Tomorrow is Saint Crispian.'
   Then will he strip his sleeve and show his scars
   And say, 'These wounds I had on Crispin's day.'
   Old men forget; yet all shall be forgot,
50 But he'll remember, with advantages,°   *embellishments*
   What feats he did that day. Then shall our names,
   Familiar in his mouth as household words—
   Harry the King, Bedford and Exeter,
   Warwick and Talbot, Salisbury and Gloucester—
55 Be in their flowing cups freshly remembered.
   This story shall the good man teach his son,
   And Crispin Crispian shall ne'er go by
   From this day to the ending of the world
   But we in it shall be rememberèd,
60 We few, we happy few, we band of brothers.
   For he today that sheds his blood with me
   Shall be my brother; be he ne'er so vile,°   *lowborn*
   This day shall gentle his condition.[2]
   And gentlemen in England now abed
65 Shall think themselves accursed they were not here,
   And hold their manhoods cheap whiles any speaks
   That fought with us upon Saint Crispin's day.

   Enter [Earl of] SALISBURY

SALISBURY My sovereign lord, bestow yourself° with speed.   *take your positions*
   The French are bravely in their battles° set   *battle lines*
70 And will with all expedience° charge on us.   *speed*
KING HARRY All things are ready if our minds be so.
WARWICK Perish the man whose mind is backward now.
KING HARRY Thou dost not wish more help from England, coz?
WARWICK God's will, my liege, would you and I alone,
75 Without more help, could fight this royal battle.
KING HARRY Why now thou hast unwished five thousand men,
   Which likes° me better than to wish us one.—   *pleases*
   You know your places. God be with you all.

   Tucket. Enter MONTJOY

MONTJOY Once more I come to know of thee, King Harry,
80 If for thy ransom thou wilt now compound°   *make terms*
   Before thy most assurèd overthrow.
   For certainly thou art so near the gulf
   Thou needs must be englutted.° Besides, in mercy   *swallowed*
   The Constable desires thee thou wilt mind°   *remind*
85 Thy followers of repentance, that their souls
   May make a peaceful and a sweet retire
   From off these fields where, wretches, their poor bodies
   Must lie and fester.
KING HARRY   Who hath sent thee now?
90 MONTJOY The Constable of France.
KING HARRY   I pray thee bear my former answer back.
   Bid them achieve° me, and then sell my bones.   *get*
   Good God, why should they mock poor fellows thus?
   The man that once did sell the lion's skin
95 While the beast lived, was killed with hunting him.[3]

---

2. Shall raise him to gentlemanly rank.   3. *The man . . . him*: alluding to one of Aesop's fables.

A many of our bodies shall no doubt
Find native° graves, upon the which, I trust,   *(English)*
Shall witness live in brass of this day's work.
And those that leave their valiant bones in France,
100 Dying like men, though buried in your dunghills
They shall be famed. For there the sun shall greet them
And draw their honours reeking° up to heaven,   *steaming; stinking*
Leaving their earthly parts to choke your clime,
The smell whereof shall breed a plague in France.
105 Mark then abounding valour in our English,
That, being dead, like to the bullets grazing°   *ricocheting*
Break out into a second course of mischief,
Killing in relapse of mortality.°   *another fatal outbreak*
Let me speak proudly. Tell the Constable
110 We are but warriors for the working day.°   *workaday warriors*
Our gayness and our gilt are all besmirched
With rainy marching in the painful field.
There's not a piece of feather° in our host—   *decorative plume*
Good argument, I hope, we will not fly—
115 And time hath worn us into slovenry.°   *filth*
But by the mass, our hearts are in the trim.°   *fine shape*
And my poor soldiers tell me, yet ere night
They'll be in fresher robes, as they will pluck
The gay new coats o'er your French soldiers' heads,
120 And turn them out of service.[4] If they do this—
As if God please, they shall—my ransom then
Will soon be levied.[5] Herald, save thou thy labour.
Come thou no more for ransom, gentle herald.
They shall have none, I swear, but these my joints—
125 Which if they have as I will leave 'em them,
Shall yield them little. Tell the Constable.
MONTJOY   I shall, King Harry. And so fare thee well.
Thou never shalt hear herald any more.
KING HARRY   I fear thou wilt once more come for a ransom.

                              Exit [MONTJOY]

          Enter [*Duke of* YORK]

130 YORK   My lord, most humbly on my knee I beg
The leading of the vanguard.
KING HARRY   Take it, brave York.—Now soldiers, march away,
And how thou pleasest, God, dispose the day.   *Exeunt*

4.4

Alarum. Excursions.° Enter PISTOL, [*a*] FRENCH SOL-   *Skirmishes*
DIER, [*and the*] BOY
PISTOL   Yield, cur.
FRENCH SOLDIER   *Je pense que vous êtes le gentilhomme de bon
qualité.*[1]
PISTOL   *Qualité? 'Calin o custure me!*[2]
5   Art thou a gentleman? What is thy name? Discuss.
FRENCH SOLDIER   *O Seigneur Dieu!*°   *O Lord God*
PISTOL [*aside*]   O Seigneur Dew should be a gentleman.—

---

4. Dismiss them, stripped of their servant's uniforms.   1. I think you are a gentleman of high rank.
5. Collected (from the French themselves).   2. The Irish refrain of a popular ballad, meaning "I am
4.4. Location: The battlefield.   a girl from beside the Suir."

Perpend° my words, O Seigneur Dew, and mark: *Weigh*

O Seigneur Dew, thou diest, on point of fox,°   *sword*

10 Except, O Seigneur, thou do give to me

Egregious° ransom.   *Extraordinary*

FRENCH SOLDIER *O prenez miséricorde! Ayez pitié de moi!*[3]

PISTOL 'Moy' shall not serve, I will have forty 'moys',[4]

Or I will fetch thy rim° out at thy throat   *stomach lining*

15 In drops of crimson blood.

FRENCH SOLDIER *Est-il impossible d'échapper la force de ton bras?*[5]

PISTOL Brass, cur? Thou damnèd and luxurious° mountain goat, *lecherous*

Offer'st me brass?

FRENCH SOLDIER *O pardonne-moi!*

20 PISTOL Sayst thou me so? Is that a ton of moys?—

Come hither boy. Ask me this slave in French

What is his name.

BOY *Écoutez: comment êtes-vous appelé?*[6]

FRENCH SOLDIER *Monsieur le Fer.*

25 BOY He says his name is Master Fer.

PISTOL Master Fer? I'll fer him, and firk° him, and ferret° him. *beat / savage*

Discuss the same in French unto him.

BOY I do not know the French for fer and ferret and firk.

PISTOL Bid him prepare, for I will cut his throat.

30 FRENCH SOLDIER *Que dit-il, monsieur?*°   *What does he say, sir*

BOY *Il me commande à vous dire que vous faites vous prêt, car ce*

soldat ici est disposé tout à cette heure de couper votre gorge.° *(translates Pistol)*

PISTOL *Oui, couper la gorge, par ma foi,*[7]

Peasant, unless thou give me crowns, brave crowns;

35 Or mangled shalt thou be by this my sword.

FRENCH SOLDIER *O je vous supplie, pour l'amour de Dieu, me*

pardonner. Je suis le gentilhomme de bonne maison. Gardez ma

vie, et je vous donnerai deux cents écus° *(translated by the boy)*

PISTOL What are his words?

40 BOY He prays you to save his life. He is a gentleman of a good

house, and for his ransom he will give you two hundred

crowns.

PISTOL Tell him, my fury shall abate, and I the crowns will take.

FRENCH SOLDIER *Petit monsieur, que dit-il?*[8]

45 BOY *Encore qu'il est contre son jurement de pardonner aucun*

prisonnier; néanmoins, pour les écus que vous lui ci promettez, il

est content à vous donner la liberté, le franchisement.

FRENCH SOLDIER [*kneeling to* PISTOL] *Sur mes genoux je vous*

donne mille remerciements, et je m'estime heureux que j'ai

50 *tombé entre les mains d'un chevalier, comme je pense, le plus*

brave, vaillant, et treis-distingué seigneur d'Angleterre.° *(translated by the boy)*

PISTOL Expound unto me, boy.

BOY He gives you upon his knees a thousand thanks, and he

esteems himself happy that he hath fallen into the hands of

55 one, as he thinks, the most brave, valorous, and thrice-worthy

seigneur of England.

PISTOL As I suck blood, I will some mercy show.

Follow me.

---

3. O take pity! Have pity on me!
4. Pistol mistakes *moi* for the name of a coin.
5. Is it impossible to escape the strength of your arm?
6. Listen: what's your name?
7. Yes, cut your throat, by my faith.
8. Little sir, what says he?

BOY   *Suivez-vous le grand capitaine.*[9]

               [*Exeunt* PISTOL *and* FRENCH SOLDIER]

60 I did never know so full a voice issue from so empty a heart.
But the saying is true: 'The empty vessel makes the greatest
sound.' Bardolph and Nim had ten times more valour than this
roaring devil i'th' old play, that everyone may pare his nails
with a wooden dagger,[1] and they are both hanged, and so

65 would this be, if he durst steal anything adventurously.° I must   recklessly
stay with the lackeys with the luggage of our camp. The French
might have a good prey of us, if he knew of it, for there is none
to guard it but boys.   *Exit*

4.5

    Enter CONSTABLE, [*Dukes of*] ORLÉANS [*and*] BOURBON,
      and [*Lord*] RAMBURES

CONSTABLE   *O diable!*

ORLÉANS   *O Seigneur! Le jour est perdu, tout est perdu!*

BOURBON   *Mort de ma vie!*[1] All is confounded,° all.   *lost*
Reproach and everlasting shame

5 Sits mocking in our plumes.
    A short alarum
    O méchante fortune!°—[*To* RAMBURES] Do not run away.   *evil fate*

ORLÉANS   We are enough yet living in the field
To smother up the English in our throngs,
If any order might be thought upon.

10 BOURBON   The devil take order. Once more back again!
And he that will not follow Bourbon now,
Let him go home, and with his cap in hand
Like a base leno° hold the chamber door   *pimp*
Whilst by a slave no gentler° than my dog   *better born*

15 His fairest daughter is contaminated.

CONSTABLE   Disorder that hath spoiled° us friend° us now.   *ruined / befriend*
Let us on heaps go offer up our lives.

BOURBON   I'll to the throng.
Let life be short, else shame will be too long.[2]   *Exeunt*

4.6

    Alarum. Enter KING [HARRY] *and his train,*° *with pris-*   *followers*
      oners

KING HARRY   Well have we done, thrice-valiant countrymen.
But all's not done; yet keep the French the field.
    [*Enter the Duke of* EXETER]

EXETER   The Duke of York commends him to your majesty.

KING HARRY   Lives he, good uncle? Thrice within this hour

5 I saw him down, thrice up again and fighting.
From helmet to the spur, all blood he was.

EXETER   In which array, brave soldier, doth he lie,
Larding° the plain. And by his bloody side,   *Moistening*
Yokefellow to his honour-owing° wounds,   *honorable*

10 The noble Earl of Suffolk also lies.

---

9. Follow the great captain.
1. Allegorical "Vice" characters in old-fashioned morality plays were typically armed with wooden daggers.
4.5 Location: The battlefield.
1. O the devil!

O God! The day is lost, all is lost!
    Death of my life!
2. See Additional Passages at end of play for the Folio
and quarto versions of this scene.
4.6 Location: The battlefield.

    Suffolk first died, and York, all haggled over,°   *hacked up*
    Comes to him, where in gore he lay insteeped,°   *soaked*
    And takes him by the beard, kisses the gashes
    That bloodily did yawn upon his face,
15   And cries aloud, "Tarry, dear cousin Suffolk.
    My soul shall thine keep company to heaven.
    Tarry, sweet soul, for mine, then fly abreast,
    As in this glorious and well-foughten field
    We kept together in our chivalry.'
20   Upon these words I came and cheered him up.
    He smiled me in the face, raught° me his hand,   *reached*
    And with a feeble grip says, 'Dear my lord,
    Commend my service to my sovereign.'
    So did he turn, and over Suffolk's neck
25   He threw his wounded arm, and kissed his lips,
    And so espoused to death, with blood he sealed
    A testament of noble-ending love.
    The pretty and sweet manner of it forced
    Those waters from me which I would have stopped.
30   But I had not so much of man in me,
    And all my mother° came into mine eyes   *(feminine) tenderness*
    And gave me up to tears.
KING HARRY   I blame you not,
    For hearing this I must perforce compound°   *come to terms*
    With mistful eyes, or they will issue° too.   *weep*
        Alarum
35   But hark, what new alarum is this same?
    The French have reinforced their scattered men.
    Then every soldier kill his prisoners.
    [*The soldiers kill their prisoners*][1]
    Give the word through.
PISTOL   *Coup' la gorge.*°   *Exeunt*   *Cut the throat*

4.7

    Enter [Captains] FLUELLEN *and* GOWER

FLUELLEN   Kill the poys and the luggage! 'Tis expressly against
    the law of arms. 'Tis as arrant a piece of knavery, mark you
    now, as can be offert. In your conscience now, is it not?
GOWER   'Tis certain there's not a boy left alive. And the cowardly
5   rascals that ran from the battle ha' done this slaughter. Besides,
    they have burned and carried away all that was in the King's
    tent; wherefore the King most worthily hath caused every sol-
    dier to cut his prisoner's throat. O 'tis a gallant king.
FLUELLEN   Ay, he was porn at Monmouth.° Captain Gower,   *(in Wales)*
10   what call you the town's name where Alexander the Pig was
    born?
GOWER   Alexander the Great.
FLUELLEN   Why I pray you, is not 'pig' great? The pig or the
    great or the mighty or the huge or the magnanimous are all
15   one reckonings, save the phrase is a little variations.°   *(for "varied")*
GOWER   I think Alexander the Great was born in Macedon. His
    father was called Philip of Macedon, as I take it.
FLUELLEN   I think it is e'en Macedon where Alexander is porn.

---

1. This may or may not be done onstage.   4.7 Location: Before Henry's pavilion.

I tell you, captain, if you look in the maps of the world I warrant
20   you sall find, in the comparisons between Macedon and Monmouth, that the situations, look you, is both alike. There is a
river in Macedon, and there is also moreover a river at Monmouth. It is called Wye at Monmouth, but it is out of my prains
what is the name of the other river—but 'tis all one, 'tis alike as
25   my fingers is to my fingers, and there is salmons in both. If you
mark Alexander's life well, Harry of Monmouth's life is come
after it indifferent well.[1] For there is figures° in all things. Alex-   comparisons
ander, God knows, and you know, in his rages and his furies
and his wraths and his cholers° and his moods and his displea-   angers
30   sures and his indignations, and also being a little intoxicates in
his prains, did in his ales and his angers, look you, kill his best
friend Cleitus—

GOWER   Our King is not like him in that. He never killed any of
his friends.

35   FLUELLEN   It is not well done, mark you now, to take the tales
out of my mouth ere it is made an end and finished. I speak
but in the figures and comparisons of it. As Alexander killed his
friend Cleitus, being in his ales and his cups, so also Harry
Monmouth, being in his right wits and his good judgements,
40   turned away the fat knight with the great-belly doublet—he was
full of jests and gipes° and knaveries and mocks—I have forgot   gibes
his name.

GOWER   Sir John Falstaff.

FLUELLEN   That is he. I'll tell you, there is good men porn at
45   Monmouth.

GOWER   Here comes his majesty.

   Alarum. Enter KING HARRY *and* [*the English army*], *with*
   [*Duke of*] BOURBON, [*Duke of* ORLÉANS, *and other*] *pris-*
   oners.[2] *Flourish*

KING HARRY   I was not angry since I came to France
Until this instant. Take a trumpet, herald;
Ride thou unto the horsemen on yon hill.
50   If they will fight with us, bid them come down,
Or void° the field: they do offend our sight.   leave
If they'll do neither, we will come to them,
And make them skirr° away as swift as stones   scurry
Enforcèd° from the old Assyrian slings.   Driven
55   Besides, we'll cut the throats of those we have,
And not a man of them that we shall take
Shall taste our mercy. Go and tell them so.
   Enter MONTJOY

EXETER   Here comes the herald of the French, my liege.

GLOUCESTER   His eyes are humbler than they used to be.

60   KING HARRY   How now, what means this, herald? Know'st thou not
That I have fined° these bones of mine for ransom?   pledged
Com'st thou again for ransom?

MONTJOY   No, great King.
I come to thee for charitable licence,°   permission
That we may wander o'er this bloody field
65   To book° our dead and then to bury them,   register

1. *is . . . well*: resembles it fairly well.
2. This is a second batch of prisoners, captured after the French counterattack.

To sort our nobles from our common men—
For many of our princes, woe the while,
Lie drowned and soaked in mercenary blood.[3]
So do our vulgar° drench their peasant limbs   *common people*
70   In blood of princes, and our wounded steeds
Fret fetlock°-deep in gore, and with wild rage   *ankle*
Jerk out their armèd heels at their dead masters,
Killing them twice. O give us leave, great King,
To view the field in safety, and dispose
Of their dead bodies.
75   KING HARRY   I tell thee truly, herald,
I know not if the day be ours or no,
For yet a many of your horsemen peer°   *appear*
And gallop o'er the field.
MONTJOY   The day is yours.
KING HARRY   Praisèd be God, and not our strength, for it.
80   What is this castle called that stands hard by?
MONTJOY   They call it Agincourt.
KING HARRY   Then call we this the field of Agincourt,
Fought on the day of Crispin Crispian.
FLUELLEN   Your grandfather of famous memory, an't° please   *if it*
85   your majesty, and your great-uncle Edward the Plack Prince of
Wales, as I have read in the chronicles, fought a most prave
pattle here in France.
KING HARRY   They did, Fluellen.
FLUELLEN   Your majesty says very true. If your majesties is
90   remembered of it, the Welshmen did good service in a garden
where leeks did grow, wearing leeks in their Monmouth caps,[4]
which your majesty know to this hour is an honourable badge
of the service. And I do believe your majesty takes no scorn to
wear the leek upon Saint Tavy's day.
95   KING HARRY   I wear it for a memorable honour,
For I am Welsh, you know, good countryman.
FLUELLEN   All the water in Wye° cannot wash your majesty's   *Welsh river*
Welsh plood out of your pody, I can tell you that. God pless it
and preserve it, as long as it pleases his grace, and his majesty
100   too.
KING HARRY   Thanks, good my countryman.
FLUELLEN   By Jeshu, I am your majesty's countryman. I care not
who know it, I will confess it to all the world. I need not to be
ashamed of your majesty, praised be God, so long as your maj-
105   esty is an honest man.
KING HARRY   God keep me so.
          Enter WILLIAMS [*with a glove in his cap*]
                    Our heralds go with him.
Bring me just notice° of the numbers dead   *accurate record*
On both our parts.
          Exeunt [MONTJOY, GOWER, *and English*] *heralds*
            Call yonder fellow hither.
EXETER [*to* WILLIAMS]   Soldier, you must come to the King.
110   KING HARRY   Soldier, why wearest thou that glove in thy cap?
WILLIAMS   An't please your majesty, 'tis the gage° of one that I   *token*
should fight withal, if he be alive.

---

3. Common soldiers, unlike noblemen, fought for pay.   4. Tall, tapering caps without brims.

KING HARRY   An Englishman?

WILLIAMS   An't please your majesty, a rascal, that swaggered with
115   me last night—who, if a live, and ever dare to challenge this
glove, I have sworn to take him a box o'th' ear; or if I can see
my glove in his cap—which he swore, as he was a soldier, he
would wear if a lived—I will strike it out soundly.

KING HARRY   What think you, Captain Fluellen? Is it fit this sol-
120   dier keep his oath?

FLUELLEN   He is a craven° and a villain else, an't please your   coward
majesty, in my conscience.

KING HARRY   It may be his enemy is a gentleman of great sort,
quite from the answer of his degree.⁵

125   FLUELLEN   Though he be as good a gentleman as the devil is,
as Lucifer and Beelzebub° himself, it is necessary, look your   Satan
grace, that he keep his vow and his oath. If he be perjured, see
you now, his reputation is as arrant a villain and a Jack-sauce°   saucy knave
as ever his black shoe trod upon God's ground and his earth,
130   in my conscience, law.

KING HARRY   Then keep thy vow, sirrah, when thou meetest the
fellow.

WILLIAMS   So I will, my liege, as I live.

KING HARRY   Who serv'st thou under?

135   WILLIAMS   Under Captain Gower, my liege.

FLUELLEN   Gower is a good captain, and is good knowledge and
literatured° in the wars.   well read

KING HARRY   Call him hither to me, soldier.

WILLIAMS   I will, my liege.   *Exit*

140   KING HARRY [*giving him Williams's other glove*]   Here, Fluellen,
wear thou this favour for me and stick it in thy cap. When
Alençon and myself were down together, I plucked this glove
from his helm. If any man challenge this, he is a friend to
Alençon and an enemy to our person. If thou encounter any
145   such, apprehend° him, an° thou dost me love.   arrest / if

FLUELLEN   Your grace does me as great honours as can be
desired in the hearts of his subjects. I would fain° see the man   gladly
that has but two legs that shall find himself aggriefed at this
glove, that is all; but I would fain see it once. An't please God
150   of his grace, that I would see.

KING HARRY   Know'st thou Gower?

FLUELLEN   He is my dear friend, an't please you.

KING HARRY   Pray thee, go seek him and bring him to my tent.

FLUELLEN   I will fetch him.   *Exit*

155   KING HARRY   My lord of Warwick and my brother Gloucester,
Follow Fluellen closely at the heels.
The glove which I have given him for a favour
May haply purchase him a box o'th' ear.
It is the soldier's. I by bargain should
160   Wear it myself. Follow, good cousin Warwick.
If that the soldier strike him, as I judge
By his blunt bearing he will keep his word,
Some sudden mischief may arise of it,
For I do know Fluellen valiant
165   And touched with choler,° hot as gunpowder,   made angry

5. Quite above responding to a challenge from one of Williams's rank.

And quickly will return an injury.°   *insult*
Follow, and see there be no harm between them.
Go you with me, uncle of Exeter.   *Exeunt* [*severally*]

4.8

Enter [*Captain*] GOWER *and* WILLIAMS

WILLIAMS   I warrant° it is to knight you, captain.   *I'm sure*

Enter [*Captain*] FLUELLEN

FLUELLEN   God's will and his pleasure, captain, I beseech you
now, come apace° to the King. There is more good toward you,   *quickly*
peradventure,° than is in your knowledge to dream of.   *perhaps*

5   WILLIAMS   Sir, know you this glove?

FLUELLEN   Know the glove? I know the glove is a glove.

WILLIAMS [*plucking the glove from Fluellen's cap*]   I know this,
and thus I challenge it.

[*He*] *strikes* [FLUELLEN]

FLUELLEN   God's plood, and his! An arrant traitor as any's in the
10   universal world, or in France, or in England.

GOWER [*to* WILLIAMS]   How now, sir? You villain!

WILLIAMS   Do you think I'll be forsworn?

FLUELLEN   Stand away, Captain Gower. I will give treason his
payment into plows, I warrant you.

15   WILLIAMS   I am no traitor.

FLUELLEN   That's a lie in thy throat. I charge you in his majesty's
name, apprehend him. He's a friend of the Duke Alençon's.

Enter [*Earl of*] WARWICK *and* [*Duke of*] GLOUCESTER

WARWICK   How now, how now, what's the matter?

FLUELLEN   My lord of Warwick, here is—praised be God for it—
20   a most contagious° treason come to light, look you, as you shall   *noxious*
desire in a summer's day.

Enter KING [HARRY] *and* [*Duke of*] EXETER

Here is his majesty.

KING HARRY   How now, what is the matter?

FLUELLEN   My liege, here is a villain and a traitor that, look your
25   grace, has struck the glove which your majesty is take out of
the helmet of Alençon.

WILLIAMS   My liege, this was my glove—here is the fellow° of   *mate*
it—and he that I gave it to in change promised to wear it in his
cap. I promised to strike him, if he did. I met this man with my
30   glove in his cap, and I have been as good as my word.

FLUELLEN   Your majesty hear now, saving your majesty's manhood, what an arrant rascally beggarly lousy knave it is. I hope
your majesty is pear° me testimony and witness, and will   *(for "will bear")*
avouchment° that this is the glove of Alençon that your maj-   *(for "vouch")*
35   esty is give me, in your conscience now.

KING HARRY   Give me thy glove, soldier.
Look, here is the fellow of it.
'Twas I indeed thou promisèd'st to strike,
And thou hast given me most bitter terms.°   *words*

40   FLUELLEN   An't please your majesty, let his neck answer for it, if
there is any martial law in the world.

KING HARRY   How canst thou make me satisfaction?

WILLIAMS   All offences, my lord, come from the heart. Never
came any from mine that might offend your majesty.

4.8 Location: Before Henry's pavilion.

45 KING HARRY   It was ourself thou didst abuse.
WILLIAMS   Your majesty came not like yourself. You appeared to
    me but as a common man. Witness the night, your garments,
    your lowliness. And what your highness suffered under that
    shape, I beseech you take it for your own fault, and not mine,
50   for had you been as I took you for, I made no offence. There-
    fore I beseech your highness pardon me.
KING HARRY   Here, Uncle Exeter, fill this glove with crowns
    And give it to this fellow.—Keep it, fellow,
    And wear it for an honour in thy cap
55   Till I do challenge it.—Give him the crowns.
    —And captain, you must needs be friends with him.
FLUELLEN   By this day and this light, the fellow has mettle
    enough in his belly.—Hold, there is twelve pence for you, and
    I pray you to serve God, and keep you out of prawls and prab-
60   bles and quarrels and dissensions, and I warrant you it is the
    better for you.
WILLIAMS   I will none of your money.
FLUELLEN   It is with a good will. I can tell you, it will serve you
    to mend your shoes. Come, wherefore should you be so pash-
65   ful? Your shoes is not so good. 'Tis a good shilling, I warrant
    you, or I will change it.[1]
              Enter [an English] HERALD
KING HARRY   Now, herald, are the dead numbered?
HERALD   Here is the number of the slaughtered French.
KING HARRY   What prisoners of good sort° are taken, uncle?   high rank
70 EXETER   Charles, Duke of Orléans, nephew to the King;
    Jean, Duke of Bourbon, and Lord Boucicault;
    Of other lords and barons, knights and squires,
    Full fifteen hundred, besides common men.
KING HARRY   This note doth tell me of ten thousand French
75   That in the field lie slain. Of princes in this number
    And nobles bearing banners,° there lie dead   coats of arms
    One hundred twenty-six; added to these,
    Of knights, esquires, and gallant gentlemen,
    Eight thousand and four hundred, of the which
80   Five hundred were but yesterday dubbed knights.
    So that in these ten thousand they have lost
    There are but sixteen hundred mercenaries;
    The rest are princes, barons, lords, knights, squires,
    And gentlemen of blood and quality.
85   The names of those their nobles that lie dead:
    Charles Delabret, High Constable of France;
    Jaques of Châtillion, Admiral of France;
    The Master of the Crossbows, Lord Rambures;
    Great-Master of France, the brave Sir Guiscard Dauphin;
90   Jean, Duke of Alençon; Antony, Duke of Brabant,
    The brother to the Duke of Burgundy;
    And Édouard, Duke of Bar; of lusty earls,
    Grandpré and Roussi, Fauconbridge and Foix,
    Beaumont and Marle, Vaudemont and Lestrelles.
95   Here was a royal fellowship of death.

1. Williams may or may not take the money.

Where is the number of our English dead?

[*He is given another paper*]

Edward the Duke of York, the Earl of Suffolk,
Sir Richard Keighley, Davy Gam Esquire;
None else of name,° and of all other men   high rank
100 But five-and-twenty. O God, thy arm was here,
And not to us, but to thy arm alone
Ascribe we all. When, without stratagem,
But in plain shock° and even play of battle,   confrontation
Was ever known so great and little loss
105 On one part and on th'other? Take it God,
For it is none but thine.

EXETER   'Tis wonderful.

KING HARRY   Come, go we in procession to the village,
And be it death proclaimèd through our host
To boast of this, or take that praise from God
110 Which is his only.

FLUELLEN   Is it not lawful, an't please your majesty, to tell how
many is killed?

KING HARRY   Yes, captain, but with this acknowledgement,
That God fought for us.

115 FLUELLEN   Yes, in my conscience, he did us great good.

KING HARRY   Do we all holy rites:
Let there be sung *Non nobis* and *Te Deum*,[2]
The dead with charity enclosed in clay;°   buried with pious love
And then to Calais, and to England then,
120 Where ne'er from France arrived more-happy° men.   *Exeunt*   more fortunate

5.0

Enter CHORUS

CHORUS   Vouchsafe° to those that have not read the story   Allow
That I may prompt them—and of such as have,
I humbly pray them to admit th'excuse
Of time, of numbers, and due course of things,
5 Which cannot in their huge and proper life
Be here presented. Now we bear the King
Toward Calais. Grant him there; there seen,
Heave him away upon your wingèd thoughts
Athwart the sea. Behold, the English beach
10 Pales-in° the flood, with men, maids, wives, and boys,   Fences in
Whose shouts and claps out-voice the deep-mouthed sea,
Which like a mighty whiffler[1] fore the King
Seems to prepare his way. So let him land,
And solemnly see him set on to London.
15 So swift a pace hath thought, that even now
You may imagine him upon Blackheath,[2]
Where that his lords desire him to have borne
His bruisèd helmet and his bended sword
Before him through the city; he forbids it,
20 Being free from vainness and self-glorious pride,
Giving full trophy, signal, and ostent°   honor for the victory

2. *Non nobis* is Psalm 115, beginning "Not unto us, O
Lord, not unto us, but unto thy name give the glory." *Te
Deum* is a canticle of thanks beginning "We praise thee,
O God."

5.0
1. Official who cleared the way for a procession.
2. Open space outside London.

Quite from himself, to God. But now behold,
In the quick forge and working-house of thought,
How London doth pour out her citizens.
25 The Mayor and all his brethren, in best sort,°   clothing
Like to the senators of th'antique Rome
With the plebeians° swarming at their heels,   commoners
Go forth and fetch their conqu'ring Caesar in—
As, by a lower but high-loving likelihood,[3]
30 Were now the General of our gracious Empress[4]—
As in good time he may—from Ireland coming,
Bringing rebellion broachèd° on his sword,   impaled
How many would the peaceful city quit
To welcome him! Much more, and much more cause,
35 Did they this Harry. Now in London place him;
As yet the lamentation of the French
Invites the King of England's stay at home.
The Emperor's coming[5] in behalf of France,
To order peace between them [
40   ][6] and omit
All the occurrences, whatever chanced,
Till Harry's back-return again to France.[7]
There must we bring him, and myself have played
The interim by rememb'ring° you 'tis past.   reminding
45 Then brook° abridgement, and your eyes advance,   tolerate
After your thoughts, straight back again to France.   *Exit*

5.1

Enter [Captain] GOWER *and [Captain]* FLUELLEN *[with
a leek in his cap and a cudgel]*

GOWER   Nay, that's right. But why wear you your leek today?
Saint Davy's day is past.
FLUELLEN   There is occasions and causes why and wherefore in
all things. I will tell you, ass my friend, Captain Gower. The
5 rascally scald° beggarly lousy pragging knave Pistol—which you   scabby
and yourself and all the world know to be no petter than a
fellow, look you now, of no merits—he is come to me, and
prings me pread and salt yesterday,° look you, and bid me eat   (on St. Davy's Day)
my leek. It was in a place where I could not breed no con-
10 tention with him, but I will be so bold as to wear it in my cap
till I see him once again, and then I will tell him a little piece
of my desires.
Enter [Ensign] PISTOL
GOWER   Why, here a° comes, swelling like a turkey-cock.   he
FLUELLEN   'Tis no matter for his swellings nor his turkey-
15 cocks.—God pless you Ensign Pistol, you scurvy lousy knave,
God pless you.
PISTOL   Ha, art thou bedlam?° Dost thou thirst, base Trojan,°   crazy/villain
To have me fold up Parca's[1] fatal web?
Hence! I am qualmish° at the smell of leek.   nauseated

---

3. Lovingly anticipated probability.
4. *General . . . Empress:* Earl of Essex (see Introduction).
5. Sigismund; the Holy Roman Emperor, attempted, and failed, to negotiate a peace between France and England.
6. A line is evidently missing here.
7. Henry invaded France a second and third time, in 1417 and 1421; Act 5 begins in the latter year.
5.1 Location: The English camp.
1. The Parcae were the mythological Fates who spun and cut the thread of life.

20 FLUELLEN   I peseech you heartily, scurvy lousy knave, at my
desires and my requests and my petitions, to eat, look you, this
leek. Because, look you, you do not love it, nor your affections
and your appetites and your digestions does not agree with it, I
would desire you to eat it.

25 PISTOL   Not for Cadwallader° and all his goats.   *last Welsh king*
FLUELLEN   There is one goat for you. [*He*] *strikes* [PISTOL] Will
you be so good, scald° knave, as eat it?   *worthless*
PISTOL   Base Trojan, thou shalt die.
FLUELLEN   You say very true, scald knave, when God's will is. I
30 will desire you to live in the mean time, and eat your victuals.°   *food*
Come, there is sauce for it. [*He strikes him*] You called me
yesterday 'mountain-squire',° but I will make you today a   *(Wales is moutainous)*
'squire of low degree'. I pray you, fall to. If you can mock a leek
you can eat a leek.
          [*He strikes him*]
35 GOWER   Enough, captain, you have astonished° him.   *stunned*
FLUELLEN   By Jesu, I will make him eat some part of my leek, or
I will peat his pate° four days and four nights.—Bite, I pray you. *head*
It is good for your green° wound and your ploody coxcomb.° *fresh / head*
PISTOL   Must I bite?
40 FLUELLEN   Yes, certainly, and out of doubt and out of question
too, and ambiguities.
PISTOL   By this leek, I will most horribly revenge—
          [FLUELLEN *threatens him*]
I eat and eat—I swear—
FLUELLEN   Eat, I pray you. Will you have some more sauce to
45 your leek? There is not enough leek to swear by.
PISTOL   Quiet thy cudgel,° thou dost see I eat.   *wooden club*
FLUELLEN   Much good do you, scald knave, heartily. Nay, pray
you throw none away. The skin is good for your broken cox-
comb. When you take occasions to see leeks hereafter, I pray
50 you mock at 'em, that is all.
PISTOL   Good.
FLUELLEN   Ay, leeks is good. Hold you, there is a groat° to heal   *fourpence*
your pate.
PISTOL   Me, a groat?
55 FLUELLEN   Yes, verily,° and in truth you shall take it, or I have   *truly*
another leek in my pocket which you shall eat.
PISTOL   I take thy groat in earnest° of revenge.   *advance payment*
FLUELLEN   If I owe you anything, I will pay you in cudgels. You
shall be a woodmonger, and buy nothing of me but cudgels.
60 God b'wi' you, and keep you, and heal your pate.   *Exit*
PISTOL   All hell shall stir for this.
GOWER   Go, go, you are a counterfeit cowardly knave. Will you
mock at an ancient tradition, begun upon an honourable
respect and worn as a memorable trophy of predeceased
65 valour, and dare not avouch° in your deeds any of your words?   *prove*
I have seen you gleeking and galling° at this gentleman twice   *jesting and annoying*
or thrice. You thought, because he could not speak English in
the native garb, he could not therefore handle an English cudgel. You find it otherwise. And henceforth let a Welsh correc-
70 tion teach you a good English condition. Fare ye well.   *Exit*
PISTOL   Doth Fortune play the hussy° with me now?   *whore*
News have I that my Nell is dead

I'th' spital of a malady of France,°   *venereal disease*
And there my rendezvous° is quite cut off.   *refuge*
75   Old I do wax, and from my weary limbs
Honour is cudgelled. Well, bawd° I'll turn,   *pimp*
And something lean to cutpurse of quick hand.
To England will I steal, and there I'll steal,
And patches will I get unto these cudgelled scars,
80   And swear I got them in the Gallia° wars.   *Exit*   *French*

5.2

Enter at one door KING [HARRY, *Dukes of*] EXETER [*and*
CLARENCE, *Earl of*] WARWICK, *and other lords; at*
another, KING [CHARLES *the Sixth*] *of France,* QUEEN ISA-
BEL, *the Duke of* BURGUNDY, *and other French,* [*among*
them Princess] CATHERINE [*and* ALICE]

KING HARRY   Peace to this meeting, wherefor° we are met.   *for which*
Unto our brother France and to our sister,
Health and fair time of day. Joy and good wishes
To our most fair and princely cousin Catherine;
5   And as a branch and member of this royalty,
By whom this great assembly is contrived,
We do salute you, Duke of Burgundy.
And princes French, and peers, health to you all.
KING CHARLES   Right joyous are we to behold your face.
10   Most worthy brother England, fairly met.
So are you, princes English, every one.
QUEEN ISABEL   So happy be the issue,° brother England,   *outcome*
Of this good day and of this gracious meeting,
As we are now glad to behold your eyes—
15   Your eyes which hitherto have borne in them,
Against the French that met them in their bent,°   *glance*
The fatal balls° of murdering basilisks.[1]   *eyeballs; cannonballs*
The venom of such looks we fairly hope
Have lost their quality,° and that this day   *nature*
20   Shall change all griefs and quarrels into love.
KING HARRY   To cry amen to that, thus we appear.
QUEEN ISABEL   You English princes all, I do salute you.
BURGUNDY   My duty to you both, on equal love,
Great Kings of France and England. That I have laboured
25   With all my wits, my pains, and strong endeavours,
To bring your most imperial majesties
Unto this bar° and royal interview,   *court*
Your mightiness on both parts best can witness.
Since, then, my office hath so far prevailed
30   That face to face and royal eye to eye
You have congreeted,° let it not disgrace me   *met*
If I demand, before this royal view,
What rub° or what impediment there is   *hindrance*
Why that the naked, poor, and mangled peace,
35   Dear nurse of arts, plenties, and joyful births,
Should not in this best garden of the world,
Our fertile France, put up her lovely visage?
Alas, she hath from France too long been chased,

5.2 Location: The French court.   1. Fabulous animals able to kill with a glance.

40	And all her husbandry° doth lie on heaps,	*agriculture*
	Corrupting in it° own fertility.	*its*
	Her vine, the merry cheerer of the heart,	
	Unprunèd dies; her hedges even-plashed°	*interwoven*
	Like prisoners wildly overgrown with hair	
	Put forth disordered twigs; her fallow leas°	*unplanted fields*
45	The darnel, hemlock, and rank fumitory°	*kinds of weeds*
	Doth root upon, while that the coulter° rusts	*plow*
	That should deracinate° such savagery.	*root out*
	The even mead°—that erst brought sweetly forth	*meadow*
	The freckled cowslip, burnet, and green clover—	
50	Wanting the scythe, all uncorrected, rank,	
	Conceives by idleness,° and nothing teems	*Breeds worthless things*
	But hateful docks, rough thistles, kecksies, burs,°	*(all are weeds)*
	Losing both beauty and utility.	
	An° all our vineyards, fallows, meads, and hedges,	*And if*
55	Defective in their natures, grow to wildness,	
	Even so our houses and ourselves and children	
	Have lost, or do not learn for want of time,	
	The sciences° that should become° our country,	*knowledge/adorn*
	But grow like savages—as soldiers will	
60	That nothing do but meditate on blood—	
	To swearing and stern looks, diffused° attire,	*disordered*
	And everything that seems unnatural.	
	Which to reduce into our former favour[2]	
	You are assembled, and my speech entreats	
65	That I may know the let° why gentle peace	*impediment*
	Should not expel these inconveniences	
	And bless us with her former qualities.	
	KING HARRY If, Duke of Burgundy, you would the peace	
	Whose want gives growth to th'imperfections	
70	Which you have cited, you must buy that peace	
	With full accord to all our just demands,	
	Whose tenors° and particular effects	*general principles*
	You have enscheduled briefly in your hands.	
	BURGUNDY The King hath heard them, to the which as yet	
	There is no answer made.	
75	KING HARRY Well then, the peace,	
	Which you before so urged, lies in his answer.	
	KING CHARLES I have but with a cursitory° eye	*cursory*
	O'erglanced the articles. Pleaseth your grace	
	To appoint some of your council presently	
80	To sit with us once more, with better heed	
	To re-survey them, we will suddenly	
	Pass our accept and peremptory° answer.	*approved and definite*
	KING HARRY Brother, we shall.—Go, Uncle Exeter	
	And brother Clarence, and you, brother Gloucester;	
85	Warwick and Huntingdon, go with the King,	
	And take with you free power to ratify,	
	Augment, or alter, as your wisdoms best	
	Shall see advantageable for our dignity,	
	Anything in or out of our demands,	
90	And we'll consign° thereto.—Will you, fair sister,	*agree*

2. To revert to our old appearance.

Go with the princes, or stay here with us?

QUEEN   Our gracious brother, I will go with them.
Haply° a woman's voice may do some good   *Perhaps*
When articles too nicely° urged be stood on.   *punctiliously*

95   KING HARRY   Yet leave our cousin Catherine here with us.
She is our capital° demand, comprised   *chief*
Within the fore-rank of our articles.

QUEEN   She hath good leave.

*Exeunt [all but] KING HARRY, CATHERINE, and [ALICE]
the gentlewoman*

KING HARRY   Fair Catherine, and most fair,
Will you vouchsafe to teach a soldier terms
100   Such as will enter at a lady's ear
And plead his love-suit to her gentle heart?

CATHERINE   Your majesty shall mock at me. I cannot speak your
England.

KING HARRY   O fair Catherine, if you will love me soundly with
105   your French heart, I will be glad to hear you confess it brokenly
with your English tongue. Do you like me, Kate?

CATHERINE *Pardonnez-moi,*° I cannot tell vat is 'like me'.   *Excuse me*

KING HARRY   An angel is like you, Kate, and you are like an
angel.

110   CATHERINE [*to* ALICE]   *Que dit-il?—que je suis semblable à les
anges?*

ALICE   *Oui, vraiment—sauf votre grâce—ainsi dit-il.*[3]

KING HARRY   I said so, dear Catherine, and I must not blush to
affirm it.

115   CATHERINE   *O bon Dieu!*° *Les langues des hommes sont pleines*   *O good God*
de tromperies.°   *(translated below)*

KING HARRY   What says she, fair one? That the tongues of men
are full of deceits?

ALICE   *Oui,* dat de tongeus of de mans is be full of deceits—dat
120   is de Princess.

KING HARRY   The Princess is the better Englishwoman. I'faith,
Kate, my wooing is fit for thy understanding. I am glad thou
canst speak no better English, for if thou couldst, thou wouldst
find me such a plain king that thou wouldst think I had sold
125   my farm to buy my crown. I know no ways to mince it in love,
but directly to say, 'I love you'; then if you urge me farther than
to say, 'Do you in faith?', I wear out my suit. Give me your
answer, i'faith do, and so clap° hands and a bargain. How say   *shake*
you, lady?

130   CATHERINE   *Sauf votre honneur,*° me understand well.   *Save your honor*

KING HARRY   Marry, if you would put me to verses, or to dance
for your sake, Kate, why, you undid me. For the one I have
neither words nor measure,° and for the other I have no   *meter*
strength in measure°—yet a reasonable measure in strength. If   *talent for dancing*
135   I could win a lady at leap-frog, or by vaulting into my saddle
with my armour on my back, under the correction of bragging
be it spoken, I should quickly leap into a wife. Or if I might
buffet° for my love, or bound my horse for her favours, I could   *box*
lay on like a butcher, and sit like a jackanapes,° never off. But   *monkey*
140   before God, Kate, I cannot look greenly,° nor gasp out my elo-   *abashed*

---

3. What does he say? That I am like an angel? Yes, truly, save your grace, he says that.

quence, nor I have no cunning in protestation—only downright oaths, which I never use till urged, nor never break for
urging. If thou canst love a fellow of this temper,° Kate, whose   *makeup*
face is not worth sunburning, that never looks in his glass° for   *mirror*
145   love of anything he sees there, let thine eye be thy cook. I speak
to thee plain soldier: if thou canst love me for this, take me. If
not, to say to thee that I shall die, is true—but for thy love, by
the Lord, no. Yet I love thee, too. And while thou livest, dear
Kate, take a fellow of plain and uncoined° constancy, for he   *not in common use*
150   perforce must do thee right, because he hath not the gift to
woo in other places. For these fellows of infinite tongue, that
can rhyme themselves into ladies' favours, they do always reason themselves out again. What! A speaker is but a prater,° a   *chatterer*
rhyme is but a ballad; a good leg will fall, a straight back will
155   stoop, a black beard will turn white, a curled pate will grow
bald, a fair face will wither, a full eye will wax° hollow, but a   *become*
good heart, Kate, is the sun and the moon—or rather the sun
and not the moon, for it shines bright and never changes, but
keeps his course truly. If thou would have such a one, take me;
160   and take me, take a soldier; take a soldier, take a king. And
what sayst thou then to my love? Speak, my fair—and fairly, I
pray thee.

CATHERINE   Is it possible dat I sould love de *ennemi* of France?

KING HARRY   No, it is not possible you should love the enemy of
165   France, Kate. But in loving me, you should love the friend of
France, for I love France so well that I will not part with a
village of it, I will have it all mine; and Kate, when France is
mine, and I am yours, then yours is France, and you are mine.

CATHERINE   I cannot tell vat is dat.

170   KING HARRY   No, Kate? I will tell thee in French—which I am
sure will hang upon my tongue like a new-married wife about
her husband's neck, hardly to be shook off. *Je quand suis le
possesseur de France, et quand vous avez le possession de moi*—
let me see, what then? Saint Denis be my speed!—*donc vôtre
175   est France, et vous êtes mienne.*[4] It is as easy for me, Kate, to
conquer the kingdom as to speak so much more French. I shall
never move° thee in French, unless it be to laugh at me.   *persuade*

CATHERINE *Sauf votre honneur, le français que vous parlez, il est
meilleur que l'anglais lequel je parle.*[5]

180   KING HARRY   No, faith, is't not, Kate. But thy speaking of my
tongue, and I thine, most truly-falsely, must needs be granted
to be much at one.° But Kate, dost thou understand thus much   *alike; united*
English? Canst thou love me?

CATHERINE I cannot tell.

185   KING HARRY   Can any of your neighbours tell, Kate? I'll ask them.
Come, I know thou lovest me, and at night when you come
into your closet° you'll question this gentlewoman about me,   *bedchamber*
and I know, Kate, you will to her dispraise those parts° in me   *qualities*
that you love with your heart. But good Kate, mock me merci-
190   fully—the rather, gentle princess, because I love thee cruelly.
If ever thou be'st mine, Kate—as I have a saving faith within
me tells me thou shalt—I get thee with scrambling,° and thou   *fighting*

4. Translation of the last part of his previous speech.
5. Saving your honor, the French you speak is better than the English I speak.

must therefore needs prove a good soldier-breeder. Shall not
thou and I, between Saint Denis and Saint George,[6] com-
195 pound a boy, half-French half-English, that shall go to Constantinople and take the Turk by the beard? Shall we not? What
sayst thou, my fair flower-de-luce?[7]

CATHERINE   I do not know dat.

KING HARRY   No, 'tis hereafter to know, but now to promise. Do
200 but now promise, Kate, you will endeavour for your French
part of such a boy, and for my English moiety° take the word   *half*
of a king and a bachelor. How answer you, *la plus belle Cather-*
ine du monde, mon très chère et divine déesse?[8]

CATHERINE   Your *majesté 'ave faux°* French enough to deceive   *false*
205 de most *sage demoiselle°* dat is *en France.*   *maiden*

KING HARRY   Now fie upon my false French! By mine honour,
in true English, I love thee, Kate. By which honour I dare not
swear thou lovest me, yet my blood° begins to flatter me that   *instinct*
thou dost, notwithstanding the poor and untempering° effect of   *uningratiating*
210 my visage. Now beshrew° my father's ambition! He was think-   *curse*
ing of civil wars when he got me; therefore was I created with
a stubborn outside, with an aspect° of iron, that when I come   *a face*
to woo ladies I fright them. But in faith, Kate, the elder I wax
the better I shall appear. My comfort is that old age, that ill
215 layer-up° of beauty, can do no more spoil upon my face. Thou   *preserver*
hast me, if thou hast me, at the worst, and thou shalt wear me,
if thou wear me, better and better; and therefore tell me, most
fair Catherine, will you have me? Put off your maiden blushes,
avouch the thoughts of your heart with the looks of an empress,
220 take me by the hand and say, 'Harry of England, I am thine'—
which word thou shalt no sooner bless mine ear withal, but I
will tell thee aloud, 'England is thine, Ireland is thine, France
is thine, and Henry Plantagenet is thine'—who, though I speak
it before his face, if he be not fellow° with the best king; thou   *equal*
225 shalt find the best king of good fellows. Come, your answer in
broken music°—for thy voice is music and thy English broken.   *music in parts*
Therefore, queen of all, Catherine, break thy mind to me in
broken English: wilt thou have me?

CATHERINE   Dat is as it shall please de *roi mon père.°*   *King my father*

230 KING HARRY   Nay, it will please him well, Kate. It shall please
him, Kate.

CATHERINE   Den it sall also content me.

KING HARRY   Upon that I kiss your hand, and I call you my
queen.

235 CATHERINE *Laissez, mon seigneur, laissez, laissez! Ma foi, je ne*
veux point que vous abbaissez votre grandeur en baisant la main
d'une de votre seigneurie indigne serviteur. Excusez-moi, je vous
supplie, mon treis-puissant seigneur.[9]

KING HARRY   Then I will kiss your lips, Kate.

240 CATHERINE   *Les dames et demoiselles pour être baisées devant*
leurs noces, il n'est pas la coutume de France.°   *(translated below)*

KING HARRY [*to* ALICE]   Madam my interpreter, what says she?

ALICE   Dat it is not be de *façon pour les°* ladies of France—I   *fashion for the*
cannot tell vat is *baiser en°* Anglish.   *"kiss" in*

---

6. Patron saints of France and England.
7. Fleur-de-lis, French national emblem.
8. The most beautiful Catherine in the world, my very
dear and divine goddess.

9. Stop, my lord, stop, stop! My faith, I do not want you
to lower your grandeur by kissing the hand of one of
your humble servants. Excuse me, I beseech you, my
very powerful lord.

245   KING HARRY   To kiss.

     ALICE   Your *majesté entend* bettre *que moi*.[1]

     KING HARRY   It is not a fashion for the maids in France to kiss
before they are married, would she say?

     ALICE   *Oui, vraiment.*°   *Yes, truly*

250   KING HARRY   O Kate, nice° customs curtsy to great kings. Dear   *fastidious*
Kate, you and I cannot be confined within the weak list° of a   *barrier*
country's fashion. We are the makers of manners, Kate, and the
liberty that follows our places stops the mouth of all find-faults,
as I will do yours, for upholding the nice fashion of your coun-

255   try in denying me a kiss. Therefore, patiently and yielding. [*He
kisses her*] You have witchcraft in your lips, Kate. There is more
eloquence in a sugar touch of them than in the tongues of the
French Council, and they should sooner persuade Harry of
England than a general petition of monarchs. Here comes

260   your father.

         Enter KING [CHARLES, QUEEN ISABEL, *the Duke of* BUR-
         GUNDY,] *and the French* [*and*] *English lords*

     BURGUNDY   God save your majesty. My royal cousin, teach you
our princess English?

     KING HARRY   I would have her learn, my fair cousin, how per-
fectly I love her, and that is good English.

265   BURGUNDY   Is she not apt?

     KING HARRY   Our tongue is rough, coz,° and my condition is not   *kinsman*
smooth, so that having neither the voice nor the heart of flattery
about me I cannot so conjure up the spirit of love in her that
he will appear in his true likeness.

270   BURGUNDY   Pardon the frankness of my mirth, if I answer you for
that. If you would conjure in her, you must make a circle;[2] if
conjure up love in her in his true likeness, he must appear
naked and blind.° Can you blame her then, being a maid yet   *(like Cupid, god of love)*
rosed over with the virgin crimson of modesty, if she deny the

275   appearance of a naked blind boy in her naked seeing self? It
were, my lord, a hard condition for a maid to consign to.

     KING HARRY   Yet they do wink° and yield, as love is blind and   *close their eyes*
enforces.

     BURGUNDY   They are then excused, my lord, when they see not

280   what they do.

     KING HARRY   Then, good my lord, teach your cousin to consent
winking.

     BURGUNDY   I will wink on her to consent, my lord, if you will
teach her to know my meaning. For maids, well summered

285   and warm kept, are like flies at Bartholomew-tide:° blind,   *August 24*
though they have their eyes. And then they will endure han-
dling, which before would not abide looking on.

     KING HARRY   This moral ties me over to time and a hot summer,
and so I shall catch the fly, your cousin, in the latter end,[3] and

290   she must be blind too.

     BURGUNDY   As love is, my lord, before that it loves.

     KING HARRY   It is so. And you may, some of you, thank love for
my blindness, who cannot see many a fair French city for one
fair French maid that stands in my way.

---

1. Your majesty understands better than I.   devils).
2. By embracing her (sorcerers drew circles to call up   3. At last; in the backside.

295   KING CHARLES   Yes, my lord, you see them perspectively,[4] the
cities turned into a maid—for they are all girdled with maiden
walls that war hath never entered.

KING HARRY   Shall Kate be my wife?

KING CHARLES   So please you.

300   KING HARRY   I am content, so the maiden° cities you talk of may   *unconquered*
wait on her: so the maid that stood in the way for my wish shall
show me the way to my will.

KING CHARLES   We have consented to all terms of reason.

KING HARRY   Is't so, my lords of England?

305   WARWICK   The King hath granted every article:
His daughter first, and so in sequel all,
According to their firm proposèd natures.

EXETER   Only he hath not yet subscribèd° this: *signed to*
where your majesty demands that the King of France, having

310   any occasion to write for matter of grant,° shall name your high-   *in formal documents*
ness in this form and with this addition: [*reads*] in French,
Notre très cher fils Henri, Roi d'Angleterre, Héritier de France,
and thus in Latin, *Praeclarissimus filius noster Henricus, Rex
Angliae et Haeres Franciae.*[5]

315   KING CHARLES   Nor this I have not, brother, so denied,
But your request shall make me let it pass.

KING HARRY   I pray you then, in love and dear alliance,
Let that one article rank with the rest,
And thereupon give me your daughter.

320   KING CHARLES   Take her, fair son, and from her blood raise up
Issue° to me, that the contending kingdoms   *Offspring*
Of France and England, whose very shores look pale
With envy of each other's happiness,
May cease their hatred, and this dear conjunction°   *loving union*

325   Plant neighbourhood° and Christian-like accord   *neighborliness*
In their sweet bosoms, that never war advance
His bleeding sword 'twixt England and fair France.

ALL   Amen.

KING HARRY   Now welcome, Kate, and bear me witness all

330   That here I kiss her as my sovereign Queen.
     Flourish

QUEEN ISABEL   God, the best maker of all marriages,
Combine your hearts in one, your realms in one.
As man and wife, being two, are one in love,
So be there 'twixt your kingdoms such a spousal

335   That never may ill office° or fell° jealousy,   *bad action / cruel*
Which troubles oft the bed of blessèd marriage,
Thrust in between the paction° of these kingdoms   *agreement*
To make divorce of their incorporate league;
That English may as French, French Englishmen,

340   Receive each other, God speak this 'Amen'.

ALL   Amen.

KING HARRY   Prepare we for our marriage. On which day,
My lord of Burgundy, we'll take your oath,
And all the peers', for surety of our leagues.

---

4. In a lens that produces optical illusions.
5. Our very dear son Henry, King of England, heir of France.

345   Then shall I swear to Kate, and you to me,
       And may our oaths well kept and prosp'rous be.

                             Sennet.° *Exeunt*   *Ceremonial trumpet call*

Epilogue

       Enter CHORUS[1]

CHORUS   Thus far with rough and all-unable pen
       Our bending° author hath pursued the story,   *(over a desk)*
       In little room confining mighty men,
         Mangling by starts the full course of their glory.
5   Small time, but in that small most greatly lived
         This star of England. Fortune made his sword,
       By which the world's best garden he achieved,
         And of it left his son imperial lord.
       Henry the Sixth, in infant bands° crowned king   *swaddling clothes*
10   Of France and England, did this king succeed,
       Whose state so many had the managing
         That they lost France and made his England bleed,
       Which oft our stage hath shown[2]—and, for their sake,
       In your fair minds let this acceptance take.°   *[Exit]*   *this play find favor*

Additional Passages

The Dauphin / Bourbon variant, which usually involves only the speech prefixes,
has several consequences for the dialogue and structure of 4.5. Following are the
edited Folio and quarto versions of this scene.

A. Folio

       Enter CONSTABLE, ORLÉANS, BOURBON, DAUPHIN, *and*
       RAMBURES

CONSTABLE   *O diable!*
ORLÉANS   *O Seigneur! Le jour est perdu, tout est perdu.*
DAUPHIN   *Mort de ma vie!* All is confounded, all.
     Reproach and everlasting shame
5   Sits mocking in our plumes.
       A short alarum
     O méchante fortune! Do not run away.   *[Exit* RAMBURES]
CONSTABLE   Why, all our ranks are broke.
DAUPHIN   O perdurable shame! Let's stab ourselves:
     Be these the wretches that we played at dice for?
10   ORLÉANS   Is this the king we sent to for his ransom?
BOURBON   Shame, an eternall shame, nothing but shame!
     Let us die in pride. In once more, back again!
     And he that will not follow Bourbon now,
     Let him go home, and with his cap in hand
15   Like a base leno hold the chamber door,
     Whilst by a slave no gentler than my dog
     His fairest daughter is contaminated.
CONSTABLE   Disorder that hath spoiled us, friend us now,
     Let us on heaps go offer up our lives.
20   ORLÉANS   We are enough yet living in the field
     To smother up the English in our throngs,

---

1. The following lines form a sonnet.
2. In *1 Henry VI*, *The First Part of the Contention* (2   *Henry VI*), *Richard Duke of York* (*3 Henry VI*), and *Richard III*.

If any order might be thought upon.
BOURBON   The devil take order now. I'll to the throng.
Let life be short, else shame will be too long.   *Exeunt*

B. Quarto

Enter the four French lords: [*the* CONSTABLE, ORLÉANS,
        BOURBON, *and* GEBON]
GEBON   *O diabello!*°   devil
CONSTABLE   *Mort de ma vie!*
ORLÉANS   O what a day is this!
BOURBON   *O jour de honte,*° all is gone, all is lost.   day of shame
5   CONSTABLE   We are enough yet living in the field
To smother up the English,
If any order might be thought upon.
BOURBON   A plague of order! Once more to the field!
And he that will not follow Bourbon now,
10   Let him go home, and with his cap in hand,
Like a base leno hold the chamber door,
Whilst by a slave no gentler than my dog
His fairest daughter is contaminated.
CONSTABLE   Disorder that hath spoiled us, right us now.
15   Come we in heaps, we'll offer up our lives
Unto these English, or else die with fame.
BOURBON   Come, come along.
Let's die with honour, our shame doth last too long.   *Exeunt*

Julius Caesar

In *Julius Caesar,* Shakespeare dramatizes incidents that seem not merely locally momentous but of world-historical significance. Indeed, one of the protagonists of his play, Caius Cassius, eagerly anticipates his own impersonated presence on Shakespeare's stage:

> How many ages hence
> Shall this our lofty scene be acted over,
> In states unborn and accents yet unknown!
> (3.1.112–14)

Cassius correctly predicts that his own actions, although they will eventually become ancient history, will nonetheless remain compelling to people far removed in time and place from the original events. When Shakespeare imagines ancient Romans, he imagines not people famous by accident, but people constantly aware that the eyes of the world are upon them, and will remain upon them for centuries to come.

The Romans' unbridled sense of self-importance results from the unprecedented scope of their political and military power. By 44 B.C.E., an astonishing sequence of conquests had made Rome, once an unremarkable Italian town, the center of an empire that stretched from North Africa to Britain, from Persia to Spain. The vastness of these domains magnifies the exploits of Rome's central political figures, because the consequences of their actions resonate across continents and down the centuries.

Yet as *Julius Caesar* opens, Rome's outsized ambitions are threatening to destroy it. For centuries, Rome had been governed not by a king or a dictator, but by elected officers, and its republican traditions had been a source of fierce civic pride. Yet as the city's military endeavors grow increasingly ambitious, its generals, with the might of their armies behind them, wield more power than the factionalized senate to which they supposedly owe allegiance. Of these generals, the charismatic and enterprising Julius Caesar, who had subdued much of northwest Europe even while consolidating his popularity among the poorer classes at home, seems particularly dangerous. When legal and military attempts to curb Caesar's growing power fail, a group of conspirators led by Caius Cassius and Marcus Brutus assassinate him. Yet the death of Caesar does not, as his killers had hoped, restore Rome to its tradition of republican government. Instead, civil war ensues, in which Caesar's friend Mark Antony and Caesar's adopted heir, Octavius, defeat the forces of the conspirators. Eventually, after a power struggle among the victors (recounted in Shakespeare's *Antony and Cleopatra*), Octavius is enthroned as the emperor Augustus. His ascendancy, consolidating immense power in a single individual, completes the political transformation that Julius Caesar's assassins had tried to prevent.

Even though these consequences took years to unfold, the assassination of Julius Caesar is historically important because it seems to mark the end of one epoch and the beginning of another. Similarly, Shakespeare's *Julius Caesar,* first performed in 1599, marks a watershed in his career as a playwright. On the one hand, it returns to, and reworks, some of the central political concerns of the series of eight English history plays that Shakespeare wrote in the 1590s. The questions with which the play grapples include: Who constitutes a political community—everybody in the state, both rich and poor, or only the elite and powerful among them? What limits can a community appropriately set on the activities of its most remarkable members? Are citizens allowed, or even obliged, to defend the rule of law against an exceptionally powerful individual by resorting to extralegal violence? When the demands of civic responsibility apparently conflict with those of personal loyalty, which ought to prevail? Ultimately, these are questions not about individual choices and behaviors, but about the future of a society: Does Rome's success as a military power eventually doom the republican political system that made that success possible in the first place?

The English history plays, especially the "second tetralogy" consisting of *Richard II, 1* and *2 Henry IV,* and *Henry V,* dramatize political change in a way that highlights the significance of individual characters. In *Julius Caesar,* the problem of character figures even more profoundly. In the conflicted, highly self-conscious Brutus, Shakespeare invents a kind of hero that resembles those of the tragedies that he will begin to write at the turn of the seventeenth century: the brooding Hamlet, the self-destructive Othello, the murderous but self-analytical Macbeth. Of course, distinctions between "personal" and "political" matters tend to be fuzzy and suspect, and, in a play about an assassination, are likely to be impossible to disentangle. Nonetheless, for all its acute analysis of human beings in groups, *Julius Caesar* turns on a question that seems more individual than social: What brings a man to destroy what he claims to love?

Shakespeare's source materials in *Julius Caesar* may well have encouraged this simultaneous attention to political dilemmas and psychological complexity. Virtually from the moment the conspirators pulled their swords from Caesar's bleeding corpse, the events that Shakespeare treats in *Julius Caesar* were amply documented and their rationale debated. Different commentators from antiquity to the Renaissance, depending on their own political convictions, viewed the assassination as an act of heroism or villainy and celebrated or denounced its perpetrators accordingly. While Michelangelo and Milton idealize Brutus as a selfless defender of human liberty, Dante plunges him, with Cassius, into the deepest pit of hell. It is not surprising that Shakespeare, ever alive to the dramatic possibilities inherent in multiple, conflicting perspectives, should choose to stage an incident that had been provoking debate for more than sixteen hundred years.

For Shakespeare's contemporaries, the political questions raised by Caesar's career were not merely of antiquarian interest. Throughout early modern Europe, strong monarchs were attempting, with varying degrees of success, to consolidate their power. In England, these efforts threatened the traditional prerogatives of the aristocracy and of elected representatives in the House of Commons. For thinkers and writers saturated by their classical education in the antique past, it was easy to see the shift toward strong monarchy as replaying the shift from republican to imperial Rome. In England in 1599, moreover, concerns over this general trend were exacerbated by more specific anxieties. Queen Elizabeth I had proven a remarkably durable queen—she had already survived several attempts on her life—but at sixty-six, she was a very old woman by Renaissance standards, and her reign was clearly soon to come to an end. Since, however, she had never begotten children or named an heir, it was unclear who would succeed her or how the new monarch would be selected. Conceivably, England would revert, upon her death, to the kind of civil chaos through which it had suffered in the fifteenth century. In a state in which censorship made direct commentary on contemporary political affairs virtually impossible, the story of Caesar's death and its calamitous aftermath provided an opportunity to reflect, at a suitably prudent distance, upon what might happen when accepted methods of allocating and transferring sovereign power disintegrated.

Julius Caesar. From Plutarch, *The Lives of the Noble Grecians and Romanes* (1595).

The most important source for Shakespeare's *Julius Caesar* is not, however, a political treatise but the biographies of Caesar and Brutus in Plutarch's *Lives of the Noble Grecians and Romanes,* translated into English by Thomas North. Writing in the first century C.E., Plutarch had construed the biographer's task as inextricable from the historian's, since in his view history recorded the achievements of great men. Shakespeare followed Plutarch in stressing the decisive roles played by the acknowledged leaders of Roman society, rather than dwelling on the frictions among larger social groups. Not that he was unaware of the latter: the testiness of *Julius Caesar*'s opening scene makes the internal divisions in Roman society abundantly clear. But throughout the play, commoners are largely imagined from an upper-class perspective—as a politically unsophisticated mob that hardly seems to deserve the scrupulous civic responsibility of its betters. The capacity for conscious and reflective political decision making rests in the hands of a small elite.

Plutarch's "great man" view of history conduces to compelling dramas involving a manageable number of psychologically complex characters. And Shakespeare's drastic condensation of narrative time frame in *Julius Caesar* has the effect of exaggerating Plutarch's emphases. In Plutarch, Caesar's triumph over Pompey's sons occurs in October, but Shakespeare makes it coincide with the Lupercalia in February, so that the assassination on the ides of March seems a direct response to a specific display of arrogance. Likewise, in Plutarch, Brutus and Cassius withdraw from Rome more than a year after Caesar's funeral, but in Shakespeare, their flight follows immediately upon Antony's brilliant incitement of the Roman mob. The effect is not only to escalate dramatic momentum but also to make the personal strengths and weaknesses of Rome's leaders seem matters of titanic consequence.

In the Roman Republic, Plutarch claimed, there was always more than one powerful person, but rarely more than a few. Shakespeare depicts the last days of the Republic in a drama that no single protagonist appropriates wholly to himself. Instead, *Julius Caesar* divides its attention among several characters, setting them off against one another, while the titular hero makes less claim upon the audience's attention than might be expected. Plutarch's biography emphasizes Caesar's military genius, his ruthless executive skill, and his astonishing capacity to rescue himself repeatedly from crushing adversity. Shakespeare's Caesar seems less outsized. His accomplishments are not shown or much alluded to, and much of what we do hear is filtered through the hostile reports of resentful observers. He wants supremacy less, apparently, because he has any particular vision for the Roman polity than because he yearns for the unqualified homage of others. His egotism seems ridiculous: despite his physical frailties, he imagines himself as embodying a godlike permanence, "unshaked of motion" (3.1.70):

> . . . I am constant as the Northern Star,
> Of whose true fixed and resting quality
> There is no fellow in the firmament.
> (3.1.60–62)

Shakespeare loads this moment of self-description with dramatic irony: even as Caesar speaks these lines, the conspirators encircle him, daggers in hand. Yet Caesar's weaknesses also make the conspirators' fears seem less plausible. Deaf, epileptic, doting over his wife, he seems an unlikely aspirant to tyrannical power.

Brutus, Caesar's friend and killer, is far more fully elaborated, and in fact the originality of Shakespeare's play lies in its concentration of attention on Brutus instead of upon the play's titular hero. Unlike the other characters, Brutus appears to us in several guises: as a public figure, a husband, a master of servants, a military leader. Thus he experiences painfully in his own person the value conflicts that are elsewhere dispersed among various antagonists. How is Brutus—and how are we—to reconcile his tender regard for his wife and servant with his willingness to commit political murder? Does Brutus's intimacy with Caesar make his decision to assassinate him truly noble, since it cannot be said to stem from self-interest? Or does it suggest a troubling insensitivity to the claims of friendship and to Caesar's genuinely exceptional character?

The soliloquies in which Brutus carefully deliberates upon his reasons for, and the possible consequences of, his actions provide abundant insight into his turbulent inner life. Yet the soliloquies raise as many questions about his motives as they resolve. They force the audience to wonder how Brutus's idealism and his commitment to principle is to be evaluated. Surely his habit of appealing to abstract moral and political tenets is an admirable trait, especially in a city in which selfishness seems the dominant passion. But repeatedly, this practice leads him to commit disastrous tactical errors. Concerned to minimize bloodshed, he refuses to countenance Cassius's suggestion that Antony be killed along with Caesar. Then—once again ignoring Cassius's advice—he permits Antony to deliver an unsupervised eulogy at Caesar's funeral, thus losing the "spin" on Caesar's death and unleashing the rage of the crowd against himself and his allies. Later, his indignation at what he believes to be Cassius's corrupt practices seriously endangers their alliance.

In all these cases, Brutus tries to diminish the extent to which any of his actions might conceivably serve his own self-interested ends, even though by doing so he risks and eventually dooms the cause he is attempting to serve. Brutus shares Caesar's admiration for the Stoic virtue of "constancy," framing it, however, less in terms of power over others than in terms of personal self-control. By behaving according to immovable principles, he tries to give his life a stern but reassuring fixity. Like Caesar, Brutus ends up paying for this aspiration with his life, and even before he does so, the desire to be, in Caesar's words, "constant as the Northern star" seems misplaced in a play in which character seems complex and highly mutable.

In comparison, the impulsive, unscrupulous Cassius is far more alert to the way the world really works, willingly stooping to expediency to get what he wants and what his cause needs. The contrast with Antony likewise clarifies the way in which Brutus's principles incapacitate him. Antony emerges as a formidable opponent not despite but because of traits that Brutus can see only as weaknesses: love of sensual indulgence, lack of principle, a tendency to live in the present without sufficient care for past or future. Antony's uninhibited, improvisatory nature suits him beautifully for swaying the plebeians. A marvelous actor, Antony exploits gestures, cunning rhetoric, props, and any other means that fully serve the particular moment in which he finds himself. In fact, his political astuteness seems to arise directly from his personal familiarity with passion, since much of politics is, as Brutus never quite realizes, a matter of assessing and responding to group desire. While Brutus naively believes that Caesar's death simply restores the Republic to its status quo ante, Antony immediately understands that the future of Rome and its institutions rests in the hands of Rome's populace and, thus—since that populace is fickle and violent—ultimately in the hands of whoever can sway that populace to his will.

Even while Shakespeare vividly differentiates his characters, he shows clearly how they derive from the particular social and intellectual culture they inhabit. Shakespeare was no antiquarian: he imagines the characters of *Julius Caesar* wearing Elizabethan doublet and hose, and he notoriously equips ancient Rome with a medieval invention, the mechanical clock. Nonetheless, his Romans share a set of distinctive values, ideals, and assumptions. When Antony, at the end of the play, calls Brutus "the noblest Roman of them all," he is not simply praising Brutus as an individual. Instead, he is locating Brutus in a tradition of specifically "Roman" virtue, a virtue associated with the particular strengths of the republican form of government that Brutus died attempting to defend.

Marc Antony. From Plutarch, *The Lives of the Noble Grecians and Romanes* (1595).

What does this virtue entail? Brutus's willingness to identify his abstract principles with the common good, as well as his intense suspicion of anyone who appears self-aggrandizing, is wholly characteristic of an ethos that distinguishes sharply between duty and pleasure, between public good and private self-enrichment. The heroes of the Roman Republic had always been celebrated for their incorruptibility and for their preference for public service, however thankless, over private goods such as marriage, friendship, sensual pleasure, and personal enrichment. Many of them adhered to a Stoic code of personal conduct that mandated emotional self-control and self-sacrifice. At the same time, Rome was in fact a hotbed of nepotism and unscrupulousness, and its venality grew along with its power. Thus, pillars of the Roman Republic like Lucius Junius Brutus, Marcus Cato, Scipio Africanus, and Marcus Brutus himself were admired not merely because their civic-mindedness was socially valuable, but because such exemplars were rarer and more surprising than Romans liked to admit.

The sharp distinction that Roman culture made between public and private domains has important consequences in *Julius Caesar*. The public world is an all-male affair: bonds and rivalries provide both the glue that holds the Roman Republic together and a competitive petulancy that ordinarily precludes a single individual's gaining too much power. We are given a vivid picture of this complex interpersonal dynamic in Cassius's account of his swimming contest with Caesar. In this incident of pure bravado, friends test their toughness against one another, and one ends up saving the other's life; but because all neediness is imagined to be shameful, what seems like generosity or charity is shot through with contempt. The same rivalrous intensity characterizes the almost erotically charged quarrel and reconciliation between Brutus and Cassius in 4.2. These are people who will kill each other while loving them and, after killing them, will generously eulogize them.

Beside the fraught intensity of such relationships, the heterosexual connections in the play are rather pallid. Although Brutus is deeply attached to Portia, it does not occur to him to take her into his confidence until she struggles mightily for the privilege on the eve of the assassination; even then, all she requests is information, not permission to offer advice. Similarly, Decius easily shames Caesar into ignoring Calpurnia's foreboding dream:

> it were a mock
> Apt to be rendered for someone to say
> 'Break up the Senate till another time,
> When Caesar's wife shall meet with better dreams.'
> (2.2.96–99)

Even the most powerful man in the Roman Empire, apparently, cannot risk being seen to be influenced by a mere wife. Most tellingly, in what is perhaps a sign of textual corruption but more probably an instance of Shakespearean skill in delineating character, we are given two successive accounts of the way Brutus learns of Portia's suicide. In the first, Brutus divulges the loss himself to Cassius, expressing his grief in solitary conference with an old friend. Shortly thereafter, however, he tells his military subordinates that he has not received any news of Portia at all. Once informed that she has died "in strange manner," he affects a studied indifference, insisting that the tidings merely interfere with more important matters at hand. His ability to sequester domestic concerns from public and military ones elicits the admiration of those around him: for true "Romans" are willing to incur huge emotional costs for what they imagine is the greater good.

Since honor, in this conceptual system, is imagined to involve fierce commitment to the public sphere, and since that sphere is exclusively the domain of men, the women in *Julius Caesar* are weak and marginalized. Even within the confines of the household, they seem unable to cultivate an alternative form of social value. Maternity, for instance, is not a source of power here: Calpurnia is barren, and Portia, too, is apparently childless. The "feminine intuition" that both women possess in abundance has no practical effect. Their "nobility" requires them to internalize values that for them have little use. Portia proves what she calls her masculine courage to her husband by the bizarre means of stabbing herself deliberately in the thigh, a gesture that suggests a self-castration, as if a woman were at best a slashed man. For the virtue that she claims to possess is not truly her own possession; rather, it is a quality reflected from her male

Brutus falling on his sword. From Geffrey Whitney, *A Choice of Emblemes* (1586).

relatives that makes her superior to ordinary women. "Think you I am no stronger than my sex, / Being so fathered and so husbanded?" (2.1.295–96). Portia kills herself, typically, in an exceptionally painful way, by swallowing hot coals. While the fabled hardihood of Portia's father, Cato, or her husband, Brutus, has at least some military rationale, Portia's imitation of their fortitude seems pointlessly self-punishing, serving neither their ends nor her own.

The pressure of Roman values on the characters of *Julius Caesar* suggests that its protagonists are not entirely free to invent themselves; they are limited to the cultural materials at hand. Moreover the complexity of the situation in which they find themselves makes it difficult for them to know exactly why they behave as they do. Often in *Julius Caesar*, the same scene provides a character with a variety of motives, permitting alternative descriptions of a single action. Thus, when Brutus decides to participate in the conspiracy to kill Caesar, he believes that he has carefully sequestered his self-interest from his convictions about the common good. But Cassius has meanwhile been tossing flattering messages through his window, so the theater audience must consider the possibility that Brutus's appeal to principle is a rationalization, and that he is swayed by a personal ambition of which he may not be entirely aware.

Elsewhere, Shakespeare complicates his portraits by what might be called a technique of gradual release. By slowly making details available to the audience, he forces it to revise its previous impressions to take account of new information. For instance, Antony's bravura eulogy reaches a climax when he reads Caesar's will, thus harnessing the plebeians' greed to the end of revenging Caesar's death. A mere two scenes later, he is shown in conference with Lepidus and Octavius, giving brisk orders to minimize the cost of Caesar's generosity. The incongruity between the first scene and the second makes Antony's original celebration of his friend's magnanimity seem, in retrospect, less sincere or spontaneous. Nonetheless, the two scenes do not force the audience to a single obvious conclusion. Does Antony's later parsimony indicate that he was simply hypocritical when he used Caesar's will to provoke a riot? Perhaps, but not necessarily; he could simply have been caught up in a wave of loyalty to Caesar and in the pathos of the situation, or he could have had vaguely ambitious but not yet fully articulated plans. In such cases, Shakespeare's cunning dramatic presentation enhances the complexity of his characterizations. The realistic illusion depends as much on what he withholds from the audience as on what he provides it.

On other grounds, too, a reading focusing purely on character seems finally inadequate. In oft-cited lines, Cassius pronounces: "The fault, dear Brutus, is not in our stars, / But in ourselves, that we are underlings" (1.2.141–42). It is not at all clear, however, that he is right. Plutarch emphasizes how the fates of his biographical subjects fail to reflect their virtues. Caesar, who had miraculously survived so many strange adventures in hostile foreign lands, can be dispatched in a few minutes by his erstwhile friends just moments after leaving his own house. Cicero, whose oratory had held sway in Rome for so many years, is obliterated by Antony and Octavius practically as an afterthought. The gifted and honorable Brutus meets death after a military defeat that seems almost accidental. Cassius's suicide is even more haphazard. The inscrutable workings of fate play at least as great a role as personality does in determining the outcome of the action.

For this reason, virtually all the characters find it impossible to achieve a reliable perspective on events in which they are immersed. In the play's most literal case of limited vision, the "thick-sighted" Cassius misinterprets victory as defeat and kills himself moments before his triumphant soldiers arrive, hoping to congratulate him. Here and elsewhere, Shakespeare drums home the difference between the perspective of the theater audience, for whom the killing of Julius Caesar is an act centuries old, now replayed for its entertainment value, and the perspective of the characters within the play, for whom it is unfolding in the present moment, its consequences both dire and unknown. From our point of view, ironies are everywhere. Caesar pronounces upon his immovable constancy moments before being dispatched; his murderers, attempting to eliminate a potential tyrant, open the way for centuries of despotism. As Antony plots with Octavius to eliminate Lepidus, the audience knows as Antony cannot that the cold, noncommittal Octavius will ultimately annihilate both his triumviral associates.

To be alive to such ironies, the characters would need to be able to look into the future. Struggling to understand their own place in history, they continually resort to augury, attempting—usually incorrectly—to comprehend the omens that shadow forth their fates. In *Julius Caesar*, omens are always telling, but they are rarely intelligible except in retrospect. No one knows what to make of the lions loose in the streets; the soothsayer arrives too late; Caesar's dream is misinterpreted; Cassius notices carrion birds on his standards but decides to disregard them. By emphasizing the analogies among personal, political, and natural forms of disruption, omens on the one hand intensify the significance of the play's characters: their decisions, quirks, and flaws affect the structure of the universe itself. They are indeed, as they have imagined themselves, persons of unprecedented and enormous significance. On the other hand, the reliability of omens challenges the notion that history is the product of personal effort, since augury implies restrictions on free will, suggesting that individuals are caught in the toils of a historical process they cannot possibly control or understand. Undergirding the other questions of authority, responsibility, and agency in *Julius Caesar* are unanswerable questions about who creates history, and what that history can possibly mean.

KATHARINE EISAMAN MAUS

TEXTUAL NOTE

The 1623 First Folio (F) provides the only authoritative text for *Julius Caesar*. The fullness of the stage directions, which specify sound effects as well as actors' exits and entrances, and the absence of Shakespearean spellings suggest that the Folio text was derived from the theater company's official promptbook rather than from Shakespeare's manuscript.

Despite the general reliability of the Folio *Julius Caesar*, there are a few editorial puzzles. In Act 4, there is some confusion about the parts played by the minor characters Titinius, Lucillius, and Lucius, leading some scholars to believe that Shakespeare revised these scenes. Two conundrums have more significant consequences for the play's characterizations. In 1614 and again in 1625, Shakespeare's contemporary Ben Jonson ridiculed a line in 3.1 in which Caesar supposedly proclaims: "Know Caesar doth not wrong but with just cause." F omits the last four words, but the currency of Jonson's joke even after the publication of the Folio suggests that they were retained in performance. Indeed, the apparent illogic of Caesar's utterance (how can a wrong have a just cause?) seems to testify powerfully to the speaker's megalomaniac sense that he transcends the rules ordinary mortals must obey. The Oxford text restores the line as reported by Jonson rather than emending it to some more "reasonable" possibility. Some textual scholars see a similar lapse of logic in 4.2, in which Brutus's account of Portia's death to Cassius seems to contradict his claim, moments later, that he is ignorant of that death. Possibly Shakespeare revised the scene and forgot to cancel the rejected lines. However, as in 3.1, the seeming inconsistency might be justified as revealing an interesting aspect of Brutus's character or of Roman attitudes toward the difference between domestic and public domains.

SELECTED BIBLIOGRAPHY

Bloom, Harold, ed. *William Shakespeare's "Julius Caesar."* New York: Chelsea House, 1988. Anthology of critical essays.

Burckhardt, Sigurd. "How Not to Murder Caesar." *Shakespearean Meanings.* Princeton: Princeton University Press, 1968. 3–21. *Julius Caesar* and historical change.

Knights, L. C. "Shakespeare and Political Wisdom: A Note on the Personalism of *Julius Caesar* and *Coriolanus.*" *Sewanee Review* 61 (1953): 43–55. Politics and individual character.

Miles, Gary B. "How Roman Are Shakespeare's 'Romans'?" *Shakespeare Quarterly* 40 (1989): 257–83. Shakespeare's adaptation and revision of his classical sources.

Miola, Robert S. "*Julius Caesar* and the Tyrannicide Debate." *Renaissance Quarterly* 38 (1985): 271–89. Renaissance political theorists disagreed over whether the killing of a king was ever justified; *Julius Caesar* shows Shakespeare's knowledge of this dispute.

Paster, Gail Kern. "'In the Spirit of Men There Is No Blood': Blood as a Trope of Gender in *Julius Caesar.*" *Shakespeare Quarterly* 40 (1989): 284–98. Manliness and bloody bodies in the play.

Rebhorn, Wayne. "The Crisis of the Aristocracy in *Julius Caesar.*" *Renaissance Quarterly* 43 (1990): 75–111. Shakespeare's Romans resemble sixteenth-century English aristocrats in their desire for self-mastery and competitiveness with one another.

Visser, Nicholas. "Plebeian Politics in Julius Caesar." *Shakespeare in Southern Africa* 7 (1994): 22–31. Contemporary South African performances offer insights into the play's concept of class relations and of the mob.

Wilson, Richard, ed. *Julius Caesar.* New York: Palgrave, 2002. Collection of recent essays on the play.

FILMS

Julius Caesar. 1953. Dir. Joseph L. Mankiewicz. USA. 120 min. This black-and-white Hollywood production features James Mason as a brooding, intense Brutus, John Gielgud as Cassius, and the young Marlon Brando, in an Oscar-nominated performance, as a charismatic Antony.

Julius Caesar. 1970. Dir. Stuart Burge. UK. 117 min. A brisk production, enlivened by colorful street and battle scenes. Jason Robards Plays Brutus, Charlton Heston is Antony, John Gielgud is Caesar, and Diana Rigg is Portia.

Julius Caesar. 1979. Dir. Herbert Wise. UK. 161 min. A BBC-TV production. Textually faithful but blandly acted. David Collings is, however, effective as Cassius.

The Tragedy of Julius Caesar

The Persons of the Play

Julius CAESAR
CALPURNIA, his wife
Marcus BRUTUS, a noble Roman, opposed to Caesar
PORTIA, his wife
LUCIUS, his servant

Caius CASSIUS
CASCA
TREBONIUS
DECIUS Brutus } opposed to Caesar
METELLUS Cimber
CINNA
Caius LIGARIUS

Mark ANTONY
OCTAVIUS Caesar } rulers of Rome after Caesar's death
LEPIDUS

FLAVIUS
MURELLUS } tribunes of the people

CICERO
PUBLIUS } senators
POPILLIUS Laena

A SOOTHSAYER
ARTEMIDORUS
CINNA the Poet
PINDARUS, Cassius' bondman
TITINIUS, an officer in Cassius' army

LUCILLIUS
MESSALA
VARRUS
CLAUDIO
YOUNG CATO } officers and soldiers in Brutus' army
STRATO
VOLUMNIUS
FLAVIUS
DARDANIUS
CLITUS

A POET
A GHOST of Caesar
A COBBLER
A CARPENTER
Other PLEBEIANS
A MESSENGER
SERVANTS
Senators, soldiers, and attendants

1.1

Enter FLAVIUS, MURELLUS, *and certain commoners over*
the stage

FLAVIUS   Hence, home, you idle creatures, get you home!
Is this a holiday? What, know you not,
Being mechanical,° you ought not walk   *of the artisan class*
Upon a labouring day without the sign°   *tools and garments*
5   Of your profession?—Speak, what trade art thou?
CARPENTER   Why, sir, a carpenter.
MURELLUS   Where is thy leather apron and thy rule?
What dost thou with thy best apparel on?—
You, sir, what trade are you?
10 COBBLER   Truly, sir, in respect of° a fine workman I am but, as   *in comparison with*
you would say, a cobbler.[1]
MURELLUS   But what trade art thou? Answer me directly.
COBBLER   A trade, sir, that I hope I may use with a safe con-
science, which is indeed, sir, a mender of bad soles.°   *(punning on "souls")*
15 FLAVIUS   What trade, thou knave? Thou naughty° knave, what trade?   *wicked*
COBBLER   Nay, I beseech you, sir, be not out[2] with me. Yet if
you be out, sir, I can mend you.
MURELLUS   What mean'st thou by that? Mend me, thou saucy fellow?
COBBLER   Why, sir, cobble you.
20 FLAVIUS   Thou art a cobbler, art thou?
COBBLER   Truly, sir, all that I live by is with the awl. I meddle
with no tradesman's matters, nor women's matters,° but withal[3]   *(a bawdy joke)*
I am indeed, sir, a surgeon to old shoes: when they are in great
danger I recover° them. As proper° men as ever trod upon   *resole; cure / fine*
25 neat's leather° have gone° upon my handiwork.   *cowhide / walked*
FLAVIUS   But wherefore art not in thy shop today?
Why dost thou lead these men about the streets?
COBBLER   Truly, sir, to wear out their shoes to get myself into
more work. But indeed, sir, we make holiday to see Caesar, and
30 to rejoice in his triumph.[4]
MURELLUS   Wherefore rejoice? What conquest brings he home?
What tributaries° follow him to Rome   *ransom payers*
To grace in captive bonds his chariot wheels?[5]
You blocks, you stones, you worse than senseless° things!   *inanimate*
35 O, you hard hearts, you cruel men of Rome,
Knew you not Pompey?[6] Many a time and oft
Have you climbed up to walls and battlements,
To towers and windows, yea to chimney-tops,
Your infants in your arms, and there have sat
40 The livelong day with patient expectation
To see great Pompey pass the streets of Rome.
And when you saw his chariot but appear,
Have you not made an universal shout,
That Tiber[7] trembled underneath her banks
45 To hear the replication° of your sounds   *echo*
Made in her concave shores?

1.1 Location: A street in Rome.
1. Mender of shoes; bungler (the sense Murellus
understands).
2. Angry; worn out, like shoes.
3. Nevertheless; punning on "awl."
4. Triumphal procession in honor of victory (by Roman
custom, over foreign enemies, but here over Caesar's

political adversaries, Pompey's sons).
5. Captives were tied to their conquerors' chariots.
6. Pompey the Great, who had shared rule of Rome with
Caesar and Crassus; he was defeated by Caesar after
their alliance disintegrated and was later assassinated.
7. River that flows through Rome.

And do you now put on your best attire?
And do you now cull out° a holiday?   *choose*
And do you now strew flowers in his way
50   That comes in triumph over Pompey's blood?°   *offspring*
Be gone!
Run to your houses, fall upon your knees,
Pray to the gods to intermit[8] the plague
That needs must light on this ingratitude.
55   FLAVIUS   Go, go, good countrymen, and for this fault
Assemble all the poor men of your sort;°   *rank*
Draw them to Tiber banks, and weep your tears
Into the channel, till the lowest stream
Do kiss the most exalted shores of all.°   *tops of the riverbanks*
Exeunt all the commoners
60   See whe'er° their basest mettle be not moved.   *whether*
They vanish tongue-tied in their guiltiness.
Go you down that way towards the Capitol;[9]
This way will I. Disrobe the images
If you do find them decked with ceremonies.[1]
65   MURELLUS   May we do so?
You know it is the Feast of Lupercal.[2]
FLAVIUS   It is no matter. Let no images
Be hung with Caesar's trophies.° I'll about,   *ornaments*
And drive away the vulgar° from the streets;   *commoners*
70   So do you too where you perceive them thick.
These growing feathers plucked from Caesar's wing
Will make him fly an ordinary pitch,[3]
Who else° would soar above the view of men   *otherwise*
And keep us all in servile fearfulness.   *Exeunt*

1.2

[Loud music.] Enter CAESAR, ANTONY *[stripped] for the*
course,[1] CALPURNIA, PORTIA, DECIUS, CICERO, BRUTUS,
CASSIUS, CASCA, *a* SOOTHSAYER[, *a throng of citizens];*
after them, MURELLUS *and* FLAVIUS

CAESAR   Calpurnia.
CASCA   Peace, ho! Caesar speaks.
[Music ceases]
CAESAR   Calpurnia.
CALPURNIA   Here, my lord.
5   CAESAR   Stand you directly in Antonio's way
When he doth run his course.—Antonio.
ANTONY   Caesar, my lord.
CAESAR   Forget not in your speed, Antonio,
To touch Calpurnia, for our elders say
10   The barren, touchèd in this holy chase,
Shake off their sterile curse.
ANTONY   I shall remember:
When Caesar says 'Do this', it is performed.

8. Withhold (plague was considered a divine punishment).
9. Hill on whose top was the Temple of Jupiter, where
victorious generals in a triumph offered sacrifice.
1. Caesar's followers had put imperial crowns ("ceremonies") on his statues.
2. Lupercalia, a festival celebrated February 15. His-

torically, Caesar's triumph took place in October.
3. At a medium height (an image from falconry).
1.2 Location: A public place in Rome.
1. During the Lupercalia, two celebrants ran naked
through Rome, striking those they met with goatskin
thongs.

CAESAR   Set on,° and leave no ceremony out.   *Proceed*
     [*Music*]
SOOTHSAYER   Caesar!
15   CAESAR   Ha! Who calls?
CASCA   Bid every noise be still. Peace yet again.
     [*Music ceases*]
CAESAR   Who is it in the press° that calls on me?   *crowd*
     I hear a tongue shriller than all the music
     Cry 'Caesar!' Speak. Caesar is turned to hear.
SOOTHSAYER   Beware the ides[2] of March.
20   CAESAR   What man is that?
BRUTUS   A soothsayer bids you beware the ides of March.
CAESAR   Set him before me; let me see his face.
CASSIUS   Fellow, come from the throng; look upon Caesar.
     [*The* SOOTHSAYER *comes forward*]
CAESAR   What sayst thou to me now? Speak once again.
25   SOOTHSAYER   Beware the ides of March.
CAESAR   He is a dreamer. Let us leave him. Pass!°   *Onward*
             Sennet.° Exeunt. Manent° BRUTUS *and* CASSIUS | *Trumpet flourish / Remain*
CASSIUS   Will you go see the order of the course?°   *running of the race*
BRUTUS   Not I.
CASSIUS   I pray you, do.
30   BRUTUS   I am not gamesome;° I do lack some part   *fond of sport*
     Of that quick° spirit that is in Antony.   *lively*
     Let me not hinder, Cassius, your desires.
     I'll leave you.
CASSIUS   Brutus, I do observe you now of late.
35   I have not from your eyes that gentleness
     And show of love as I was wont° to have.   *accustomed*
     You bear too stubborn and too strange° a hand[3] *unfriendly*
     Over your friend that loves you.
BRUTUS   Cassius,
     Be not deceived. If I have veiled my look,°   *seemed less outgoing*
40   I turn the trouble of my countenance°   *my troubled looks*
     Merely° upon myself. Vexèd I am   *Wholly*
     Of late with passions of some difference,°   *conflicting kinds*
     Conceptions only proper° to myself,   *suitable*
     Which give some soil,° perhaps, to my behaviours. *blemish*
45   But let not therefore my good friends be grieved—
     Among which number, Cassius, be you one—
     Nor construe any further° my neglect   *make any more of*
     Than that poor Brutus, with himself at war,
     Forgets the shows of love to other men.
50   CASSIUS   Then, Brutus, I have much mistook your passion,° *feelings*
     By means whereof[4] this breast of mine hath buried° *concealed*
     Thoughts of great value, worthy cogitations.
     Tell me, good Brutus, can you see your face?
BRUTUS   No, Cassius, for the eye sees not itself
55   But by reflection, by some other things.
CASSIUS   'Tis just;°   *true*
     And it is very much lamented, Brutus,

---

2. The ides marked roughly the midpoint of every Roman month (usually the thirteenth); in March, the fifteenth.

3. Management of horse's reins (figurative).
4. In consequence of which mistake.

That you have no such mirrors as will turn
Your hidden worthiness into your eye,

60   That you might see your shadow.° I have heard   *reflection*
     Where many of the best respect° in Rome—   *repute*
     Except immortal Caesar—speaking of Brutus,
     And groaning underneath this age's yoke,
     Have wished that noble Brutus had his eyes.⁵

65   BRUTUS   Into what dangers would you lead me, Cassius,
     That you would have me seek into myself
     For that which is not in me?

     CASSIUS   Therefor,° good Brutus, be prepared to hear.   *As to that*
     And since you know you cannot see yourself

70   So well as by reflection, I, your glass,°   *mirror*
     Will modestly discover° to yourself   *reveal*
     That of yourself which you yet know not of.
     And be not jealous on° me, gentle Brutus.   *suspicious of*
     Were I a common laughter,° or did use   *object of ridicule*

75   To stale° with ordinary° oaths my love   *debase / cheap*
     To every new protester;° if you know   *declarer of friendship*
     That I do fawn on men and hug them hard,
     And after scandal° them; or if you know   *defame*
     That I profess myself° in banqueting   *declare friendship*

80   To all the rout:° then hold me dangerous.   *mob*

            Flourish, and shout [within]

     BRUTUS   What means this shouting? I do fear the people
     Choose Caesar for their king.

     CASSIUS   Ay, do you fear it?
     Then must I think you would not have it so.

     BRUTUS   I would not, Cassius; yet I love him well.

85   But wherefore do you hold me here so long?
     What is it that you would impart to me?
     If it be aught toward the general good,
     Set honour in one eye and death i'th' other,
     And I will look on both indifferently;°   *impartially*

90   For let the gods so speed me as⁶ I love
     The name of honour more than I fear death.

     CASSIUS   I know that virtue to be in you, Brutus,
     As well as I do know your outward favour.°   *appearance*
     Well, honour is the subject of my story.

95   I cannot tell what you and other men
     Think of this life; but for my single self,
     I had as lief not be,° as live to be   *I had rather be dead*
     In awe of such a thing as I myself.
     I was born free as Caesar, so were you.

100 We both have fed as well, and we can both
     Endure the winter's cold as well as he.
     For once upon a raw and gusty day,
     The troubled Tiber chafing with° her shores,   *raging against*
     Said Caesar to me 'Dar'st thou, Cassius, now

105 Leap in with me into this angry flood,
     And swim to yonder point?'° Upon the word,   *promontory*
     Accoutred° as I was I plungèd in,   *Dressed in armor*
     And bade him follow. So indeed he did.

---

5. That is, could see properly.   6. Make me fortunate insofar as.

The torrent roared, and we did buffet it
110   With lusty sinews, throwing it aside,
And stemming° it with hearts of controversy.°   *confronting / rivalry*
But ere we could arrive° the point proposed,   *reach*
Caesar cried 'Help me, Cassius, or I sink!'
Ay, as Aeneas[7] our great ancestor
115   Did from the flames of Troy upon his shoulder
The old Anchises bear, so from the waves of Tiber
Did I the tirèd Caesar. And this man
Is now become a god, and Cassius is
A wretched creature, and must bend his body°   *(must bow)*
120   If Caesar carelessly but nod on him.
He had a fever when he was in Spain,
And when the fit was on him, I did mark
How he did shake. 'Tis true, this god did shake.
His coward lips did from their colour fly;[8]
125   And that same eye whose bend° doth awe the world   *glance*
Did lose his° lustre. I did hear him groan,   *its*
Ay, and that tongue of his that bade the Romans
Mark him and write his speeches in their books,
'Alas!' it cried, 'Give me some drink, Titinius',
130   As a sick girl. Ye gods, it doth amaze me
A man of such a feeble temper° should   *constitution*
So get the start of° the majestic world,   *advantage over*
And bear the palm° alone!   *be victor*
          Shout [*within*]. *Flourish*
BRUTUS   Another general shout!
I do believe that these applauses are
135   For some new honours that are heaped on Caesar.
CASSIUS   Why, man, he doth bestride the narrow world
Like a Colossus,[9] and we petty men
Walk under his huge legs, and peep about
To find ourselves dishonourable graves.
140   Men at sometime° were masters of their fates.   *formerly*
The fault, dear Brutus, is not in our stars,
But in ourselves, that we are underlings.
Brutus and Caesar: what should be in that 'Caesar'?
Why should that name be sounded more than yours?
145   Write them together: yours is as fair a name.
Sound them: it doth become the mouth as well.
Weigh them: it is as heavy. Conjure with 'em:
'Brutus' will start[1] a spirit as soon as 'Caesar'.
Now in the names of all the gods at once,
150   Upon what meat° doth this our Caesar feed   *food*
That he is grown so great? Age, thou art shamed.
Rome, thou hast lost the breed of noble bloods.
When went there by an age since the great flood,[2]
But it was famed with° more than with one man?   *renowned for*
155   When could they say till now, that talked of Rome,

7. Legendary Trojan warrior and founder of Rome; when the Greeks burned Troy, he carried his father, Anchises, out on his back.
8. Did turn pale; did desert their flag (Caesar suffered epileptic seizures).
9. Giant statue of Apollo, which straddled the harbor of Rhodes.
1. Raise (only the names of the gods were thought to be able to raise the dead).
2. A great flood was recorded in classical as well as biblical accounts.

That her wide walls encompassed but one man?
Now is it Rome indeed, and room° enough   *(pronounced like "Rome")*
When there is in it but one only man.
O, you and I have heard our fathers say
160   There was a Brutus once³ that would have brooked°   *endured*
Th'eternal devil to keep his state° in Rome   *hold court*
As easily as a king.
BRUTUS   That you do love me I am nothing jealous.°   *not at all uncertain*
What you would work° me to I have some aim.°   *persuade / idea*
165   How I have thought of this and of these times
I shall recount hereafter. For this present,°   *present time*
I would not, so with love° I might entreat you,   *if in friendship*
Be any further moved.° What you have said   *persuaded*
I will consider. What you have to say
170   I will with patience hear, and find a time
Both meet° to hear and answer such high things.   *Fitting both*
Till then, my noble friend, chew upon this:
Brutus had rather be a villager
Than to repute himself a son of Rome
175   Under these hard conditions as this time
Is like to lay upon us.
CASSIUS   I am glad
That my weak words have struck but thus much show
Of fire from Brutus.
        [*Music.*] *Enter* CAESAR *and his train*°   *retinue*
BRUTUS   The games are done, and Caesar is returning.
180 CASSIUS   As they pass by, pluck Casca by the sleeve,⁴
And he will, after his sour fashion, tell you
What hath proceeded worthy° note today.   *worthy of*
BRUTUS   I will do so. But look you, Cassius,
The angry spot doth glow on Caesar's brow,
185   And all the rest look like a chidden° train.   *scolded*
Calpurnia's cheek is pale, and Cicero
Looks with such ferret⁵ and such fiery eyes
As we have seen him in the Capitol
Being crossed in conference° by some senators.   *opposed in debate*
190 CASSIUS   Casca will tell us what the matter is.
CAESAR   Antonio.
ANTONY   Caesar.
CAESAR   Let me have men about me that are fat,
Sleek-headed men, and such as sleep a-nights.
195   Yon Cassius has a lean and hungry look.
He thinks too much. Such men are dangerous.
ANTONY   Fear him not, Caesar, he's not dangerous.
He is a noble Roman, and well given.°   *well disposed*
CAESAR   Would he were fatter! But I fear him not.
200   Yet if my name⁶ were liable to fear,
I do not know the man I should avoid
So soon as that spare Cassius. He reads much,
He is a great observer, and he looks

---

3. Lucius Junius Brutus, an ancestor of Marcus Brutus and a founder of the Roman Republic, famed for his role in expelling the Tarquins, who had ruled Rome as Kings.
4. Like "cloak" (line 216), "doublet" (line 262), and

"unbracèd" (1.3.48), this suggests a performance in Elizabethan dress.
5. Ferretlike (red and darting).
6. One of my name (that is, myself).

Quite through[7] the deeds of men. He loves no plays,
205 As thou dost, Antony; he hears no music.[8]
Seldom he smiles, and smiles in such a sort°   *manner*
As if he mocked himself, and scorned his spirit
That could be moved to smile at anything.
Such men as he be never at heart's ease
210 Whiles they behold a greater than themselves,
And therefore are they very dangerous.
I rather tell thee what is to be feared
Than what I fear, for always I am Caesar.
Come on my right hand, for this ear is deaf,
215 And tell me truly what thou think'st of him.

         Sennet. Exeunt CAESAR *and his train.* [BRUTUS,
                CASSIUS, *and* CASCA *remain*]

CASCA [*to* BRUTUS]   You pulled me by the cloak.° Would you   *pulled me aside*
     speak with me?
BRUTUS   Ay, Casca. Tell us what hath chanced today,
     That Caesar looks so sad.°   *serious*
220 CASCA   Why, you were with him, were you not?
BRUTUS   I should not then ask Casca what had chanced.
CASCA   Why, there was a crown offered him; and being offered
     him, he put it by with the back of his hand, thus; and then the
     people fell a-shouting.
225 BRUTUS   What was the second noise for?
CASCA   Why, for that too.
CASSIUS   They shouted thrice. What was the last cry for?
CASCA   Why, for that too.
BRUTUS   Was the crown offered him thrice?
230 CASCA   Ay, marry,° was't; and he put it by thrice, every time   *indeed*
     gentler than other; and at every putting by, mine honest°   *(sarcastic)*
     neighbours shouted.
CASSIUS   Who offered him the crown?
CASCA   Why, Antony.
BRUTUS   Tell us the manner of it, gentle° Casca.   *noble*
235 CASCA   I can as well be hanged as tell the manner of it. It was
     mere foolery,° I did not mark it. I saw Mark Antony offer him   *utter absurdity*
     a crown—yet 'twas not a crown neither, 'twas one of these coro-
     nets—and as I told you he put it by once; but for all that, to my
     thinking he would fain° have had it. Then he offered it to him   *gladly*
240   again; then he put it by again—but to my thinking he was very
     loath to lay his fingers off it. And then he offered it the third
     time; he put it the third time by. And still° as he refused it,   *continually*
     the rabblement hooted, and clapped their chapped hands, and
     threw up their sweaty nightcaps,[9] and uttered such a deal of
245   stinking breath because Caesar refused the crown that it had
     almost choked Caesar; for he swooned and fell down at it. And
     for mine own part, I durst not laugh for fear of opening my lips
     and receiving the bad air.
CASSIUS   But soft, I pray you. What, did Caesar swoon?
250 CASCA   He fell down in the market-place, and foamed at mouth,
     and was speechless.

7. Completely into the motives of.   *Merchant of Venice.*
8. This was regarded as a sign of wickedness; see *The*   9. Artisans wore felt hats on holidays.

BRUTUS 'Tis very like: he hath the falling sickness.[1]

CASSIUS   No, Caesar hath it not; but you and I
And honest Casca, we have the falling sickness.

255   CASCA   I know not what you mean by that, but I am sure Caesar
fell down. If the tag-rag people° did not clap him and hiss him,   *riffraff*
according as he pleased and displeased them, as they use° to   *are accustomed*
do the players in the theatre, I am no true man.

BRUTUS   What said he when he came unto himself?

260   CASCA   Marry, before he fell down, when he perceived the common herd was glad he refused the crown, he plucked me ope[2]
his doublet° and offered them his throat to cut. An° I had been   *jacket / If*
a man of any occupation, if I would not have taken him at a°   *his*
word, I would I might go to hell among the rogues. And so he

265   fell. When he came to himself again, he said, if he had done
or said anything amiss, he desired their worships to think it was
his infirmity. Three or four wenches where I stood cried 'Alas,
good soul!' and forgave him with all their hearts. But there's no
heed to be taken of them: if Caesar had stabbed[3] their mothers

270   they would have done no less.

BRUTUS   And after that he came thus sad away?

CASCA   Ay.

CASSIUS   Did Cicero say anything?

CASCA   Ay, he spoke Greek.

275   CASSIUS   To what effect?

CASCA   Nay, an I tell you that, I'll ne'er look you i'th' face again.
But those that understood him smiled at one another, and
shook their heads. But for mine own part, it was Greek to me.
I could tell you more news, too. Murellus and Flavius, for pull-

280   ing scarves[4] off Caesar's images, are put to silence.° Fare you   *deprived of office*
well. There was more foolery yet, if I could remember it.

CASSIUS   Will you sup with me tonight, Casca?

CASCA   No, I am promised forth.°   *elsewhere*

CASSIUS   Will you dine with me tomorrow?

285   CASCA   Ay, if I be alive, and your mind hold,° and your dinner   *does not change*
worth the eating.

CASSIUS   Good; I will expect you.

CASCA   Do so. Farewell both.   *Exit*

BRUTUS   What a blunt fellow is this grown to be!

290   He was quick mettle° when he went to school.   *of energetic spirit*

CASSIUS   So is he now, in execution
Of any bold or noble enterprise,
However he puts on this tardy form.[5]
This rudeness° is a sauce to his good wit,°   *harshness / intelligence*

295   Which gives men stomach° to digest his words   *relish*
With better appetite.

BRUTUS   And so it is. For this time I will leave you.
Tomorrow, if you please to speak with me,
I will come home to you; or if you will,

300   Come home to me and I will wait for you.

CASSIUS   I will do so. Till then, think of the world.°   *Exit* BRUTUS   *state of affairs*
Well, Brutus, thou art noble; yet I see

---

1. Epilepsy (Cassius puns on "collapse from power").   4. Decorations (see 1.1.63–64).
2. Pulled open ("me" is colloquial).   5. Although he feigns this indolent manner.
3. Playing on "sexually penetrated."

Thy honourable mettle may be wrought
From that it is disposed.⁶ Therefore it is meet°   *fitting*
305   That noble minds keep ever with their likes;
For who so firm that cannot be seduced?
Caesar doth bear me hard,° but he loves Brutus.   *ill will*
If I were Brutus now, and he were Cassius,
He should not humour° me. I will this night   *influence*
310   In several hands° in at his windows throw—   *various handwritings*
As if they came from several citizens—
Writings, all tending to° the great opinion   *intimating*
That Rome holds of his name, wherein obscurely°   *cryptically*
Caesar's ambition shall be glancèd° at.   *hinted*
315   And after this, let Caesar seat him sure,⁷
For we will shake him, or worse days endure.   *Exit*

1.3

Thunder and lightning. Enter CASCA, [*at one door, with
his sword drawn,*] *and* CICERO [*at another*]

CICERO   Good even, Casca. Brought° you Caesar home?   *Escorted*
Why are you breathless, and why stare you so?
CASCA   Are not you moved, when all the sway° of earth   *realm*
Shakes like a thing unfirm? O Cicero,
5   I have seen tempests when the scolding winds
Have rived° the knotty oaks, and I have seen   *split*
Th'ambitious ocean swell and rage and foam
To be exalted with° the threat'ning clouds;   *raised as high as*
But never till tonight, never till now,
10   Did I go through a tempest dropping fire.
Either there is a civil strife in heaven,
Or else the world, too saucy° with the gods,   *insolent*
Incenses them to send destruction.
CICERO   Why, saw you anything more° wonderful?   *else*
15   CASCA   A common slave—you know him well by sight—
Held up his left hand, which did flame and burn
Like twenty torches joined; and yet his hand,
Not sensible of° fire, remained unscorched.   *Not feeling*
Besides—I ha' not since put up° my sword—   *sheathed*
20   Against° the Capitol I met a lion   *Next to*
Who glazed° upon me, and went surly by   *stared*
Without annoying° me. And there were drawn   *harming*
Upon a heap¹ a hundred ghastly° women,   *pallid*
Transformèd with their fear, who swore they saw
25   Men all in fire walk up and down the streets.
And yesterday the bird of night° did sit   *screech owl*
Even at noonday upon the market-place,
Hooting and shrieking. When these prodigies°   *abnormalities*
Do so conjointly meet,° let not men say   *happen together*
30   'These are their reasons', 'they are natural',
For I believe they are portentous things
Unto the climate° that they point upon.   *region*
CICERO   Indeed it is a strange-disposèd time;

---

6. *wrought . . . disposed*: changed from its natural prop-   1.3 Location: A street in Rome.
erty (alluding to the alchemical transmutation of metals).   1. Huddled in a crowd.
7. Establish himself securely.

But men may construe things after their fashion,°   *in their own way*
35   Clean° from the purpose of the things themselves.   *Completely different*
     Comes Caesar to the Capitol tomorrow?
    CASCA   He doth, for he did bid Antonio
     Send word to you he would be there tomorrow.
    CICERO   Good night then, Casca. This disturbèd sky
     Is not to walk in.
40   CASCA   Farewell, Cicero.   *Exit* CICERO
         Enter CASSIUS [*unbraced*]°   *with open doublet*
    CASSIUS   Who's there?
    CASCA   A Roman.
    CASSIUS   Casca, by your voice.
    CASCA   Your ear is good. Cassius, what night is this?
    CASSIUS   A very pleasing night to honest men.
    CASCA   Who ever knew the heavens menace so?
45   CASSIUS   Those that have known the earth so full of faults.
     For my part, I have walked about the streets,
     Submitting me unto the perilous night;
     And thus unbracèd, Casca, as you see,
     Have bared my bosom to the thunder-stone;°   *thunderbolt*
50   And when the cross° blue lightning seemed to open   *forked; hostile*
     The breast of heaven, I did present myself
     Even° in the aim and very flash of it.   *Exactly*
    CASCA   But wherefore did you so much tempt the heavens?
     It is the part of men to fear and tremble
55   When the most mighty gods by tokens° send   *signs*
     Such dreadful heralds to astonish° us.   *dismay*
    CASSIUS   You are dull, Casca, and those sparks of life
     That should be in a Roman you do want,°   *lack*
     Or else you use not. You look pale, and gaze,
60   And put on fear, and cast yourself in wonder,
     To see the strange impatience of the heavens;
     But if you would consider the true cause
     Why all these fires, why all these gliding ghosts,
     Why birds and beasts from quality and kind[2]—
65   Why old men, fools, and children calculate°—   *prophesy*
     Why all these things change from their ordinance,°—   *usual order*
     Their natures, and preformèd faculties,
     To monstrous° quality—why, you shall find   *unnatural*
     That heaven hath infused them with these spirits
70   To make them instruments of fear and warning
     Unto some monstrous state.[3] Now could I, Casca,
     Name to thee a man most like this dreadful night,
     That thunders, lightens, opens graves, and roars
     As doth the lion in the Capitol;
75   A man no mightier than thyself or me
     In personal action, yet prodigious° grown,   *ominous*
     And fearful,° as these strange eruptions° are.   *terrifying / upheavals*
    CASCA   'Tis Caesar that you mean, is it not, Cassius?
    CASSIUS   Let it be who it is; for Romans now
80   Have thews° and limbs like to their ancestors.   *sinews*
     But woe the while!° Our fathers' minds are dead,   *alas for these times*

---

2. *from quality and kind*: behaving contrary to their   3. Abnormal situation; atrocious government.
nature.

And we are governed with our mothers' spirits.
Our yoke and sufferance° show us womanish.   *servitude and patience*

CASCA   Indeed they say the senators tomorrow
85   Mean to establish Caesar as a king,
And he shall wear his crown by sea and land
In every place save here in Italy.

CASSIUS [*drawing his dagger*]   I know where I will wear this dagger then:
Cassius from bondage will deliver Cassius.
90   Therein, ye gods, you make the weak most strong;
Therein, ye gods, you tyrants do defeat.
Nor stony tower, nor walls of beaten brass,
Nor airless dungeon, nor strong links of iron,
Can be retentive to° the strength of spirit;   *Can imprison*
95   But life, being weary of these worldly bars,°   *hindrances*
Never lacks power to dismiss itself.
If I know this, know all the world besides,
That part of tyranny that I do bear
I can shake off at pleasure.

        Thunder still

CASCA   So can I.
100   So every bondman in his own hand bears
The power to cancel his captivity.

CASSIUS   And why should Caesar be a tyrant then?
Poor man, I know he would not be a wolf
But that he sees the Romans are but sheep.
105   He were no lion, were not Romans hinds.°   *female deer; servants*
Those that with haste will make a mighty fire
Begin it with weak straws. What trash is Rome,
What rubbish, and what offal,° when it serves   *wood chips; refuse*
For the base° matter to illuminate   *underlying; despicable*
110   So vile a thing as Caesar! But, O grief,
Where hast thou led me? I perhaps speak this
Before a willing bondman; then I know
My answer must be made.⁴ But I am armed,°   *(physically and morally)*
And dangers are to me indifferent.°   *insignificant*
115 CASCA   You speak to Casca, and to such a man
That is no fleering° tell-tale. Hold.° My hand.   *sneering / Enough*
Be factious° for redress of all these griefs,   *Form a group*
And I will set this foot of mine as far
As who° goes farthest.   *whoever*
       [*They join hands*]

CASSIUS   There's a bargain made.
120   Now know you, Casca, I have moved° already   *persuaded*
Some certain of the noblest-minded Romans
To undergo° with me an enterprise   *undertake*
Of honourable-dangerous consequence.
And I do know by this° they stay° for me   *this time / wait*
125   In Pompey's Porch;⁵ for now, this fearful night,
There is no stir or walking in the streets,
And the complexion of the element°   *disposition of the sky*
In favour's° like the work we have in hand,   *In appearance is*
Most bloody, fiery, and most terrible.

       Enter CINNA

---

4. I must pay the penalty.   5. Portico of a theater commissioned by Pompey.

130 CASCA   Stand close° a while, for here comes one in haste.   *concealed*
CASSIUS   'Tis Cinna; I do know him by his gait.
He is a friend.—Cinna, where haste you so?
CINNA   To find out you. Who's that? Metellus Cimber?
CASSIUS   No, it is Casca, one incorporate°   *a party*
135 To our attempts. Am I not stayed for,° Cinna?   *awaited*
CINNA   I am glad on't.⁶ What a fearful night is this!
There's two or three of us have seen strange sights.
CASSIUS   Am I not stayed for? Tell me.
CINNA   Yes, you are.
140 O Cassius, if you could
But win the noble Brutus to our party—
CASSIUS   Be you content. Good Cinna, take this paper,
[*He gives* CINNA *letters*]
And look you lay it in the Praetor's⁷ Chair,
Where Brutus may but° find it; and throw this   *must surely*
145 In at his window. Set this up with wax
Upon old Brutus'° statue. All this done,   *Lucius Junius Brutus's*
Repair° to Pompey's Porch where you shall find us.   *Proceed*
Is Decius Brutus and Trebonius there?
CINNA   All but Metellus Cimber, and he's gone
150 To seek you at your house. Well, I will hie,°   *hasten*
And so bestow these papers as you bade me.
CASSIUS   That done, repair to Pompey's Theatre.   *Exit* CINNA
Come, Casca, you and I will yet ere day
See Brutus at his house. Three parts° of him   *quarters*
155 Is ours already, and the man entire
Upon the next encounter yields him ours.
CASCA   O, he sits high in all the people's hearts,
And that which would appear offence in us
His countenance, like richest alchemy,⁸
160 Will change to virtue and to worthiness.
CASSIUS   Him and his worth, and our great need of him,
You have right well conceited.° Let us go,   *understood*
For it is after midnight, and ere day
We will awake him and be sure of him.   *Exeunt*

2.1
Enter BRUTUS *in his orchard*
BRUTUS   What, Lucius, ho!—
I cannot by the progress of the stars
Give guess how near to day.—Lucius, I say!—
I would it were my fault to sleep so soundly.—
5 When, Lucius, when?° Awake, I say! What, Lucius!   *(expressing impatience)*
Enter LUCIUS
LUCIUS   Called you, my lord?
BRUTUS   Get me a taper° in my study, Lucius.   *candle*
When it is lighted, come and call me here.
LUCIUS   I will, my lord.   *Exit*
10 BRUTUS   It must be by his° death. And for my part   *(Caesar's)*
I know no personal cause to spurn° at him,   *kick*

6. Cinna is responding to Cassius's information about Casca.
7. Brutus was one of sixteen praetors, or chief magistrates, subordinate only to the two consuls.
8. Alchemy attempted to change base metals into gold. *countenance:* approval; noble appearance.
2.1 Location: Outside Brutus's house.

But for the general.° He would be crowned.   *common good*
How that might change his nature, there's the question.
It is the bright day that brings forth the adder,
15   And that craves° wary walking. Crown him: that!   *calls for*
And then I grant we put a sting in him
That at his will he may do danger with.
Th'abuse of greatness is when it disjoins
Remorse° from power. And to speak truth of Caesar,   *Conscience*
20   I have not known when his affections swayed°   *passions ruled*
More than his reason. But 'tis a common proof°   *experience*
That lowliness° is young ambition's ladder,   *humility*
Whereto the climber-upward turns his face;
But when he once attains the upmost round,°   *rung*
25   He then unto the ladder turns his back,
Looks in the clouds, scorning the base degrees[1]
By which he did ascend. So Caesar may.
Then lest he may, prevent. And since the quarrel
Will bear no colour for the thing he is,[2]
30   Fashion° it thus: that what he is, augmented,   *Describe*
Would run to these and these extremities;
And therefore think him as a serpent's egg,
Which, hatched, would as his kind° grow mischievous,°   *by its nature / harmful*
And kill him in the shell.
           Enter LUCIUS [*with a letter*]
35   LUCIUS   The taper burneth in your closet,° sir.   *private room*
Searching the window for a flint, I found
This paper, thus sealed up, and I am sure
It did not lie there when I went to bed.
           [*He*] *gives him the letter*
BRUTUS   Get you to bed again; it is not day.
40   Is not tomorrow, boy, the ides of March?
LUCIUS   I know not, sir.
BRUTUS   Look in the calendar and bring me word.
LUCIUS   I will, sir.   *Exit*
BRUTUS   The exhalations° whizzing in the air   *meteors*
45   Give so much light that I may read by them.
           [*He*] *opens the letter and reads*
'Brutus, thou sleep'st. Awake, and see thyself.
Shall Rome, et cetera? Speak, strike, redress.'—
'Brutus, thou sleep'st. Awake.'
Such instigations have been often dropped
50   Where I have took them up.
'Shall Rome, et cetera?' Thus must I piece it out:
Shall Rome stand under one man's awe? What, Rome?
My ancestors did from the streets of Rome
The Tarquin drive when he was called a king.[3]
55   'Speak, strike, redress.' Am I entreated
To speak and strike? O Rome, I make thee promise,
If the redress will follow,[4] thou receivest
Thy full petition at the hand of Brutus.
           Enter LUCIUS
LUCIUS   Sir, March is wasted fifteen days.

---

1. Low rungs; contemptible means; lowly social ranks.
2. Will find no plausible pretext in his conduct so far.
3. See note to 1.2.160.
4. That is, if killing Caesar will restore the Republic.

Knock within

60 BRUTUS 'Tis good. Go to the gate; somebody knocks. [*Exit* LUCIUS]
Since Cassius first did whet° me against Caesar   incite
I have not slept.
Between the acting of a dreadful thing
And the first motion,° all the interim is   impulse
65 Like a phantasma° or a hideous dream.   nightmare
The genius° and the mortal instruments[5]   immortal spirit
Are then in counsel, and the state of man,
Like to a little kingdom, suffers then
The nature of an insurrection.[6]

Enter LUCIUS

70 LUCIUS Sir, 'tis your brother Cassius[7] at the door,
Who doth desire to see you.
BRUTUS   Is he alone?
LUCIUS No, sir, there are more with him.
BRUTUS   Do you know them?
LUCIUS No, sir; their hats are plucked about their ears,
And half their faces buried in their cloaks,
75 That by no means I may discover° them   identify
By any mark of favour.°   distinctive feature
BRUTUS   Let 'em enter.   [*Exit* LUCIUS]
They are the faction. O conspiracy,
Sham'st thou to show thy dang'rous brow by night,
When evils are most free?° O then by day   uninhibited
80 Where wilt thou find a cavern dark enough
To mask thy monstrous visage? Seek none, conspiracy.
Hide it in smiles and affability;
For if thou put thy native semblance on,[8]
Not Erebus° itself were dim enough   dark underworld region
85 To hide thee from prevention.[9]

Enter the conspirators [*muffled*]: CASSIUS, CASCA,
DECIUS, CINNA, METELLUS, *and* TREBONIUS

CASSIUS I think we are too bold[1] upon your rest.
Good morrow, Brutus. Do we trouble you?
BRUTUS I have been up this hour, awake all night.
Know I these men that come along with you?
90 CASSIUS Yes, every man of them; and no man here
But honours you; and every one doth wish
You had but that opinion of yourself
Which every noble Roman bears of you.
This is Trebonius.
BRUTUS   He is welcome hither.
CASSIUS This, Decius Brutus.
95 BRUTUS   He is welcome too.
CASSIUS This, Casca; Cinna, this; and this, Metellus Cimber.
BRUTUS They are all welcome.
What watchful° cares do interpose themselves   sleep-preventing
Betwixt your eyes and night?
CASSIUS   Shall I entreat a word?

[CASSIUS *and* BRUTUS *stand aside and*] *whisper*

---

5. Bodily powers.
6. *the state . . . insurrection:* referring to a common-place analogy between disorder in man, in the body politic, and in nature.

7. Cassius was married to Brutus's sister.
8. Display your natural appearance.
9. From being recognized and thwarted.
1. We intrude too presumptuously.

100   DECIUS   Here lies the east. Doth not the day break here?
     CASCA   No.
     CINNA   O pardon, sir, it doth; and yon grey lines
      That fret° the clouds are messengers of day.   *interlace*
     CASCA   You shall confess that you are both deceived.
      [*He points his sword*]
105   Here, as I point my sword, the sun arises,
      Which is a great way growing° on the south,   *encroaching*
      Weighing° the youthful season of the year.   *On account of*
      Some two months hence up higher toward the north
      He first presents his fire, and the high° east   *due*
110   Stands, as the Capitol, directly here.
      [*He points his sword*]
      [BRUTUS *and* CASSIUS *join the other conspirators*]
     BRUTUS   Give me your hands all over, one by one.
      [*He shakes their hands*]
     CASSIUS   And let us swear our resolution.
     BRUTUS   No, not an oath. If not the face° of men,   *(grave) expressions*
      The sufferance° of our souls, the time's abuse²—   *suffering*
115   If these be motives weak, break off betimes,°   *at once*
      And every man hence to his idle° bed.   *unused; lazy*
      So let high-sighted° tyranny range on   *arrogant*
      Till each man drop by lottery.³ But if these,°   *these reasons*
      As I am sure they do, bear fire enough
120   To kindle cowards and to steel with valour
      The melting spirits of women, then, countrymen,
      What need we any spur but our own cause
      To prick us to redress? What other bond
      Than secret Romans,⁴ that have spoke the word
125   And will not palter?° And what other oath   *equivocate*
      Than honesty° to honesty engaged   *integrity*
      That this shall be or we will fall for it?
      Swear° priests and cowards and men cautelous,°   *Let swear / crafty; wary*
      Old feeble carrions,° and such suffering souls   *corpselike men*
130   That welcome wrongs;⁵ unto bad causes swear
      Such creatures as men doubt;° but do not stain   *suspect*
      The even° virtue of our enterprise,   *just; straightforward*
      Nor th'insuppressive° mettle of our spirits,   *the indomitable*
      To think that or° our cause or our performance   *either*
135   Did need an oath, when every drop of blood
      That every Roman bears, and nobly bears,
      Is guilty of a several bastardy⁶
      If he do break the smallest particle
      Of any promise that hath passed from him.
140   CASSIUS   But what of Cicero? Shall we sound him?°   *find out his thoughts*
      I think he will stand very strong with us.
     CASCA   Let us not leave him out.
     CINNA   No, by no means.
     METELLUS   O, let us have him, for his silver hairs
      Will purchase us a good opinion,°   *reputation*

---

2. The corruption of the present time.   5. That gladly submit to oppression.
3. Chance (the tyrant's caprice).   6. Will show itself individually to be adulterated by
4. Than that we are Romans capable of secrecy.   non-Roman blood.

145	And buy men's voices to commend our deeds.	
	It shall be said his judgement ruled our hands.	
	Our youths and wildness shall no whit appear,	
	But all be buried in his gravity.	
	BRUTUS O, name him not! Let us not break with° him,	*disclose our plans to*
150	For he will never follow anything	
	That other men begin.	
	CASSIUS Then leave him out.	
	CASCA Indeed he is not fit.	
	DECIUS Shall no man else be touched, but only Caesar?	
155	CASSIUS Decius, well urged.° I think it is not meet°	*suggested / proper*
	Mark Antony, so well beloved of Caesar,	
	Should outlive Caesar. We shall find of him	
	A shrewd° contriver. And you know his means,	*malicious*
	If he improve° them, may well stretch so far	*make the most of*
160	As to annoy° us all; which to prevent,	*harm*
	Let Antony and Caesar fall together.	
	BRUTUS Our course[7] will seem too bloody, Caius Cassius,	
	To cut the head off and then hack the limbs,	
	Like wrath in death and envy° afterwards—	*malice*
165	For Antony is but a limb of Caesar.	
	Let's be sacrificers, but not butchers, Caius.	
	We all stand up against the spirit of Caesar,	
	And in the spirit of men there is no blood.	
	O, that we then could come by° Caesar's spirit,	*obtain*
170	And not dismember Caesar! But, alas,	
	Caesar must bleed for it. And, gentle friends,	
	Let's kill him boldly, but not wrathfully.	
	Let's carve him as a dish fit for the gods,	
	Not hew him as a carcass fit for hounds.	
175	And let our hearts, as subtle° masters do,	*cunning*
	Stir up their servants° to an act of rage,	*(that is, our hands)*
	And after seem to chide 'em. This shall make	
	Our purpose necessary, and not envious;°	*malicious*
	Which so appearing to the common eyes,	
180	We shall be called purgers,° not murderers.	*purifiers*
	And for Mark Antony, think not of him,	
	For he can do no more than Caesar's arm	
	When Caesar's head is off.	
	CASSIUS Yet I fear him;	
	For in the engrafted° love he bears to Caesar—	*deep-rooted*
185	BRUTUS Alas, good Cassius, do not think of him.	
	If he love Caesar, all that he can do	
	Is to himself: take thought,° and die for Caesar.	*succumb to melancholy*
	And that were much he should,[8] for he is given	
	To sports, to wildness, and much company.	
190	TREBONIUS There is no fear° in him. Let him not die;	*nothing to fear*
	For he will live, and laugh at this hereafter.	
	Clock strikes	
	BRUTUS Peace, count the clock.[9]	
	CASSIUS The clock hath stricken three.	

---

7. Punning on "corse," meaning "corpse."
8. And that is more than he is likely to do.

9. The clock is an anachronism, like sleeves and doublets.

TREBONIUS   'Tis time to part.

CASSIUS   But it is doubtful yet
Whether Caesar will come forth today or no;
195   For he is superstitious grown of late,
Quite from the main° opinion he held once   *Contrary to the strong*
Of fantasy, of dreams and ceremonies.
It may be these apparent° prodigies,   *manifest*
The unaccustomed terror of this night,
200   And the persuasion of his augurers,[1]
May hold him from the Capitol today.

DECIUS   Never fear that. If he be so resolved
I can o'ersway° him; for he loves to hear   *prevail upon*
That unicorns may be betrayed with trees,[2]
205   And bears with glasses,[3] elephants with holes,°   *pits*
Lions with toils,° and men with flatterers;   *nets*
But when I tell him he hates flatterers;
He says he does, being then most flattered. Let me work,
For I can give his humour the true bent,[4]
210   And I will bring him to the Capitol.

CASSIUS   Nay, we will all of us be there to fetch him.

BRUTUS   By the eighth hour. Is that the uttermost?°   *latest*

CINNA   Be that the uttermost, and fail not then.

METELLUS   Caius Ligarius doth bear Caesar hard,°   *ill will*
215   Who rated° him for speaking well of Pompey.   *rebuked*
I wonder none of you have thought of him.

BRUTUS   Now good Metellus, go along by him.°   *to his house*
He loves me well, and I have given him reasons.
Send him but hither, and I'll fashion° him.   *work upon*
220   CASSIUS   The morning comes upon's. We'll leave you, Brutus.
And, friends, disperse yourselves; but all remember
What you have said, and show yourselves true Romans.

BRUTUS   Good gentlemen, look fresh and merrily.
Let not our looks put on° our purposes;   *display*
225   But bear it as our Roman actors do,
With untired spirits and formal constancy.°   *decorous self-possession*
And so good morrow to you every one.

                          Exeunt. Manet° BRUTUS   *Remains*
Boy, Lucius!—Fast asleep? It is no matter.
Enjoy the honey-heavy dew of slumber.
230   Thou hast no figures° nor no fantasies   *imaginings*
Which busy care draws in the brains of men;
Therefore thou sleep'st so sound.

                  Enter PORTIA

PORTIA   Brutus, my lord.

BRUTUS   Portia, what mean you? Wherefore rise you now?
It is not for° your health thus to commit   *good for*
235   Your weak condition to the raw cold morning.

PORTIA   Nor for yours neither. You've ungently,° Brutus,   *unkindly*
Stole from my bed; and yesternight at supper
You suddenly arose, and walked about

---

1. Priests who interpreted "auguries," or omens.
2. The unicorn could supposedly be caught by tricking
it into impaling its horn on a tree.

3. Mirrors (imagined to bewilder bears).
4. Give his disposition the right direction.

Musing and sighing, with your arms across;[5]
240 And when I asked you what the matter was,
You stared upon me with ungentle looks.
I urged you further; then you scratched your head,
And too impatiently stamped with your foot.
Yet I insisted; yet you answered not,
245 But with an angry wafture° of your hand *gesture*
Gave sign for me to leave you. So I did,
Fearing to strengthen that impatience
Which seemed too much enkindled, and withal° *besides*
Hoping it was but an effect of humour,° *moodiness*
250 Which sometime hath his° hour with every man. *its*
It will not let you eat, nor talk, nor sleep;
And could it work so much upon your shape
As it hath much prevailed on your condition,° *disposition*
I should not know you° Brutus. Dear my lord, *recognize you as*
255 Make me acquainted with your cause of grief.
BRUTUS I am not well in health, and that is all.
PORTIA Brutus is wise, and were he not in health
He would embrace the means to come by it.
BRUTUS Why, so I do. Good Portia, go to bed.
260 PORTIA Is Brutus sick? And is it physical° *curative*
To walk unbracèd° and suck up the humours[6] *with open doublet*
Of the dank morning? What, is Brutus sick?
And will he steal out of his wholesome bed
To dare the vile contagion of the night,
265 And tempt the rheumy and unpurgèd° air *moist and impure*
To add unto his sickness? No, my Brutus,
You have some sick offence° within your mind, *disturbance*
Which by the right and virtue° of my place° *prerogative / (as a wife)*
I ought to know of. [*Kneeling*] And upon my knees,
270 I charm° you by my once-commended beauty, *conjure*
By all your vows of love, and that great vow
Which did incorporate and make us one,
That you unfold to me, your self, your half,
Why you are heavy,° and what men tonight *dejected*
275 Have had resort to you—for here have been
Some six or seven, who did hide their faces
Even from darkness.
BRUTUS   Kneel not, gentle Portia.
PORTIA [*rising*] I should not need if you were gentle Brutus.
Within the bond of marriage, tell me, Brutus,
280 Is it excepted[7] I should know no secrets
That appertain to you? Am I your self
But as it were in sort or limitation?[8]
To keep with you at meals, comfort your bed,
And talk to you sometimes? Dwell I but in the suburbs[9]
285 Of your good pleasure? If it be no more,
Portia is Brutus' harlot, not his wife.
BRUTUS You are my true and honourable wife,

---

5. Crossed (a sign of melancholy).
6. Inhale the mists.
7. Is it stipulated as a qualification that.
8. *in sort or limitation*: after a fashion or with restric-

tions (like "excepted," "limited" is a legal term).
9. Outlying areas (where brothels were located in Shakespeare's time).

As dear to me as are the ruddy drops
That visit° my sad heart.   *afflict; come to*

290 PORTIA If this were true, then should I know this secret.
I grant I am a woman, but withal°   *still*
A woman that Lord Brutus took to wife.
I grant I am a woman, but withal
A woman well reputed, Cato's daughter.[1]
295 Think you I am no stronger than my sex,
Being so fathered and so husbanded?
Tell me your counsels;° I will not disclose 'em.   *secrets*
I have made strong proof of my constancy,
Giving myself a voluntary wound
300 Here in the thigh. Can I bear that with patience,
And not my husband's secrets?
BRUTUS   O ye gods,
Render me worthy of this noble wife!
                    Knock[ing within]
Hark, hark, one knocks. Portia, go in a while,
And by and by thy bosom shall partake
305 The secrets of my heart.
All my engagements° I will construe° to thee,   *commitments / explain*
All the charactery[2] of my sad brows.
Leave me with haste.
                                                  Exit PORTIA
            Lucius, who's that knocks?
            Enter LUCIUS, and LIGARIUS [with a kerchief round his
            head][3]
LUCIUS Here is a sick man that would speak with you.
310 BRUTUS Caius Ligarius, that Metellus spake of.—
Boy, stand aside.   *[Exit LUCIUS]*
            Caius Ligarius, how?°   *how are you*
LIGARIUS Vouchsafe° good morrow from a feeble tongue.   *Deign to accept*
BRUTUS O, what a time have you chose out, brave Caius,
To wear a kerchief! Would you were not sick!
315 LIGARIUS I am not sick if Brutus have in hand
Any exploit worthy the name of honour.
BRUTUS Such an exploit have I in hand, Ligarius,
Had you a healthful ear to hear of it.
LIGARIUS By all the gods that Romans bow before,
I here discard my sickness.
            [He pulls off his kerchief]
320   Soul of Rome,
Brave son derived from honourable loins,
Thou like an exorcist° hast conjured up   *a magician*
My mortifièd° spirit. Now bid me run,   *deadened*
And I will strive with things impossible,
325 Yea, get the better of them. What's to do?
BRUTUS A piece of work that will make sick men whole.°   *healthy*
LIGARIUS But are not some whole that we must make sick?
BRUTUS That must we also. What it is, my Caius,
I shall unfold to thee as we are going
To whom it must be done.

---

1. Marcus Porcius Cato was renowned for his strict
moral integrity; after Caesar's victory over Pompey, he
killed himself rather than submit to Caesar's rule.
2. Handwriting (the lines of care "inscribed" on his

forehead).
3. Kerchiefs were commonly worn by the sick in
Elizabethan England.

330 LIGARIUS   Set on° your foot,   *Advance*
      And with a heart new-fired I follow you
      To do I know not what; but it sufficeth
      That Brutus leads me on.

BRUTUS   Follow me then.   *Exeunt*

2.2

Thunder and lightning.
Enter Julius CAESAR *in his nightgown°*   *dressing gown*

CAESAR   Nor heaven nor earth have been at peace tonight.
      Thrice hath Calpurnia in her sleep cried out
      'Help, ho! They murder Caesar!'—Who's within?
            Enter a SERVANT

SERVANT   My lord.

5   CAESAR   Go bid the priests do present° sacrifice,   *immediate*
      And bring me their opinions of success.[1]

SERVANT   I will, my lord.   *Exit*
            Enter CALPURNIA

CALPURNIA   What mean you, Caesar? Think you to walk forth?
      You shall not stir out of your house today.

10 CAESAR   Caesar shall forth. The things that threatened me
      Ne'er looked but on my back; when they shall see
      The face of Caesar, they are vanishèd.

CALPURNIA   Caesar, I never stood on ceremonies,°   *heeded omens*
      Yet now they fright me. There is one within,
15   Besides the things that we have heard and seen,
      Recounts most horrid sights seen by the watch.[2]
      A lioness hath whelpèd in the streets,
      And graves have yawned and yielded up their dead.
      Fierce fiery warriors fight upon the clouds,
20   In ranks and squadrons and right form of war,°   *regular battle formation*
      Which drizzled blood upon the Capitol.
      The noise of battle hurtled in the air.
      Horses do neigh, and dying men did groan,
      And ghosts did shriek and squeal about the streets.
25   O Caesar, these things are beyond all use,°   *all normal experience*
      And I do fear them.

CAESAR   What can be avoided
      Whose end is purposed by the mighty gods?
      Yet Caesar shall go forth, for these predictions
      Are to° the world in general as to Caesar.   *Are as applicable to*

30 CALPURNIA   When beggars die there are no comets seen;
      The heavens themselves blaze forth° the death of princes.   *flame out; proclaim*

CAESAR   Cowards die many times before their deaths;
      The valiant never taste of death but once.
      Of all the wonders that I yet have heard,
35   It seems to me most strange that men should fear,
      Seeing that death, a necessary end,
      Will come when it will come.
            Enter SERVANT
                         What say the augurers?

SERVANT   They would not have you to stir forth today.

2.2 Location: Caesar's house.   reading the entrails of the sacrificial animals.
1. Of the outcome (good or bad), as determined by   2. Night watchmen (another anachronism).

Plucking the entrails of an offering forth,
40 They could not find a heart within the beast.
CAESAR The gods do this in shame of cowardice.°   *to put cowardice to shame*
Caesar should be a beast without a heart
If he should stay at home today for fear.
No, Caesar shall not. Danger knows full well
45 That Caesar is more dangerous than he.
We are two lions littered in one day,
And I the elder and more terrible.
And Caesar shall go forth.
CALPURNIA   Alas, my lord,
Your wisdom is consumed in confidence.°   *overconfidence*
50 Do not go forth today. Call it my fear
That keeps you in the house, and not your own.
We'll send Mark Antony to the Senate House,
And he shall say you are not well today.
Let me upon my knee prevail in this.
[*She kneels*]
55 CAESAR Mark Antony shall say I am not well,
And for thy humour° I will stay at home.   *whim*
                Enter DECIUS
Here's Decius Brutus; he shall tell them so.
[CALPURNIA *rises*]
DECIUS Caesar, all hail! Good morrow, worthy Caesar.
I come to fetch you to the Senate House.
60 CAESAR And you are come in very happy° time   *opportune*
To bear my greeting to the senators
And tell them that I will not come today.
Cannot is false, and that I dare not, falser.
I will not come today; tell them so, Decius.
CALPURNIA Say he is sick.
65 CAESAR   Shall Caesar send a lie?
Have I in conquest stretched mine arm so far,
To be afeard to tell greybeards the truth?
Decius, go tell them Caesar will not come.
DECIUS Most mighty Caesar, let me know some cause,
70 Lest I be laughed at when I tell them so.
CAESAR The cause is in my will; I will not come.
That is enough to satisfy the Senate.
But for your private satisfaction,
Because I love you, I will let you know.
75 Calpurnia here, my wife, stays° me at home.   *keeps*
She dreamt tonight° she saw my statue,   *last night*
Which like a fountain with an hundred spouts
Did run pure blood; and many lusty° Romans   *joyful*
Came smiling and did bathe their hands in it.
80 And these does she apply° for warnings and portents   *interpret*
Of evils imminent, and on her knee
Hath begged that I will stay at home today.
DECIUS This dream is all amiss interpreted.
It was a vision fair and fortunate.
85 Your statue spouting blood in many pipes,
In which so many smiling Romans bathed,
Signifies that from you great Rome shall suck
Reviving blood, and that great men shall press

For tinctures, stains, relics, and cognizance.[3]
90   This by Calpurnia's dream is signified.
CAESAR   And this way have you well expounded it.
DECIUS   I have, when you have heard what I can say.
    And know it now: the Senate have concluded
    To give this day a crown to mighty Caesar.
95   If you shall send them word you will not come,
    Their minds may change. Besides, it were a mock
    Apt to be rendered[4] for someone to say
    'Break up the Senate till another time,
    When Caesar's wife shall meet with better dreams.'
100   If Caesar hide himself, shall they not whisper
    'Lo, Caesar is afraid'?
    Pardon me, Caesar; for my dear dear love
    To your proceeding° bids me tell you this,   *advancement*
    And reason to my love is liable.[5]
105 CAESAR   How foolish do your fears seem now, Calpurnia!
    I am ashamèd I did yield to them.
    Give me my robe, for I will go.
        Enter [CASSIUS,] BRUTUS, LIGARIUS, METELLUS, CASCA,
        TREBONIUS, *and* CINNA
    And look where Cassius is come to fetch me.
CASSIUS   Good morrow, Caesar.
CAESAR   Welcome, Cassius.—
110   What, Brutus, are you stirred so early too?—
    Good morrow, Casca.—Caius Ligarius,
    Caesar was ne'er so much your enemy
    As that same ague° which hath made you lean.   *fever*
    What is't o'clock?
BRUTUS   Caesar, 'tis strucken eight.
115 CAESAR   I thank you for your pains and courtesy.
        Enter ANTONY
    See, Antony that revels long a-nights
    Is notwithstanding up. Good morrow, Antony.
ANTONY   So to most noble Caesar.
CAESAR [*to* CALPURNIA]   Bid them prepare within.
    I am to blame to be thus waited for.   [*Exit* CALPURNIA]
120   Now, Cinna.—Now, Metellus.—What, Trebonius!
    I have an hour's talk in store for you.
    Remember that you call on me today.
    Be near me, that I may remember you.
TREBONIUS   Caesar, I will, [*aside*] and so near will I be
125   That your best friends shall wish I had been further.
CAESAR   Good friends, go in and taste some wine with me,
    And we, like[6] friends, will straightway go together.
BRUTUS [*aside*]   That every like is not the same, O Caesar,
    The heart of Brutus ernes° to think upon.   *Exeunt*   *grieves*

2.3
    Enter ARTEMIDORUS, *reading a letter*
ARTEMIDORUS   'Caesar, beware of Brutus. Take heed of Cassius.

---

3. Heraldic colors and emblems ("tinctures," "stains," and "cognizance"); venerated properties of saints ("tinctures," "stains," and "relics").
4. *a mock . . . rendered*: a sarcastic reply likely to be made.

5. And prudence is subordinate to my affection.
6. As becomes (but Brutus plays on the senses "resembling" and "equal to").
2.3 Location: A street near the Capitol.

Come not near Casca. Have an eye to Cinna. Trust not Trebonius. Mark well Metellus Cimber. Decius Brutus loves thee
not. Thou hast wronged Caius Ligarius. There is but one mind

5   in all these men, and it is bent against Caesar. If thou beest not
immortal, look about you. Security gives way to° conspiracy.   *Overconfidence permits*
The mighty gods defend thee!
                                              Thy lover,°   *friend*
                                              Artemidorus.'

10   Here will I stand till Caesar pass along,
And as a suitor° will I give him this.   *petitioner*
My heart laments that virtue cannot live
Out of the teeth of emulation.[1]
If thou read this, O Caesar, thou mayst live.

15   If not, the fates with traitors do contrive.°   *Exit*   *conspire*

2.4

Enter PORTIA *and* LUCIUS

PORTIA   I prithee, boy, run to the Senate House.
Stay not to answer me, but get thee gone.—
Why dost thou stay?

LUCIUS   To know my errand, madam.

PORTIA   I would have had thee there and here again

5   Ere I can tell thee what thou shouldst do there.
[*Aside*] O constancy, be strong upon my side;
Set a huge mountain 'tween my heart and tongue.
I have a man's mind, but a woman's might.
How hard it is for women to keep counsel!°   *a secret*
[*To* LUCIUS] Art thou here yet?

10   LUCIUS   Madam, what should I do?
Run to the Capitol, and nothing else?
And so return to you, and nothing else?

PORTIA   Yes, bring me word, boy, if thy lord look well,
For he went sickly forth; and take good note

15   What Caesar doth, what suitors press to him.
Hark, boy, what noise is that?

LUCIUS   I hear none, madam.

PORTIA   Prithee, listen well.
I heard a bustling rumour,° like a fray,   *disturbed clamor*

20   And the wind brings it from the Capitol.

LUCIUS   Sooth,° madam, I hear nothing.   *In truth*
Enter the SOOTHSAYER

PORTIA   Come hither, fellow. Which way hast thou been?

SOOTHSAYER   At mine own house, good lady.

PORTIA   What is't o'clock?

25   SOOTHSAYER   About the ninth hour, lady.

PORTIA   Is Caesar yet gone to the Capitol?

SOOTHSAYER   Madam, not yet. I go to take my stand
To see him pass on to the Capitol.

PORTIA   Thou hast some suit to Caesar, hast thou not?

30   SOOTHSAYER   That I have, lady. If it will please Caesar
To be so good to Caesar as to hear me,
I shall beseech him to befriend himself.

PORTIA   Why, know'st thou any harms intended towards him?

---

1. Beyond the danger of ambitious envy.   **2.4** Location: Brutus's house.

SOOTHSAYER   None that I know will be; much that I fear may chance.
Good morrow to you.
  [*He moves away*]
35   Here the street is narrow.
The throng that follows Caesar at the heels,
Of senators, of praetors, common suitors,
Will crowd a feeble man almost to death.
I'll get me to a place more void,° and there   *empty*
40   Speak to great Caesar as he comes along.   *Exit*
PORTIA [*aside*]   I must go in. Ay me! How weak a thing
The heart of woman is! O Brutus,
The heavens speed thee in thine enterprise!—
Sure the boy heard me. [*To* LUCIUS] Brutus hath a suit
45   That Caesar will not grant. [*Aside*] O, I grow faint!
[*To* LUCIUS] Run, Lucius, and commend me to my lord.
Say I am merry.° Come to me again,   *in good spirits*
And bring me word what he doth say to thee.
                              Exeunt [*severally*]°   *separately*

3.1

Enter [*at one door*] ARTEMIDORUS, *the* SOOTHSAYER [*and
citizens*]. *Flourish. Enter* [*at another door*] CAESAR, BRUTUS,
CASSIUS, CASCA, DECIUS, METELLUS, TREBONIUS, CINNA,
[LIGARIUS,] ANTONY, LEPIDUS, PUBLIUS[, POPILLIUS,
and other senators]

CAESAR [*to the* SOOTHSAYER]   The ides of March are come.
SOOTHSAYER   Ay, Caesar, but not gone.
ARTEMIDORUS   Hail, Caesar! Read this schedule.°   *document*
DECIUS [*to* CAESAR]   Trebonius doth desire you to o'er-read
5   At your best leisure this his humble suit.
ARTEMIDORUS   O Caesar, read mine first, for mine's a suit
That touches° Caesar nearer. Read it, great Caesar.   *concerns*
CAESAR   What touches us ourself shall be last served.°   *attended to*
ARTEMIDORUS   Delay not, Caesar, read it instantly.
CAESAR   What, is the fellow mad?
10   PUBLIUS [*to* ARTEMIDORUS]   Sirrah, give place.
CASSIUS [*to* ARTEMIDORUS]   What, urge you your petitions in the street?
Come to the Capitol.
  [*They walk about the stage*]¹
POPILLIUS [*aside to* CASSIUS]   I wish your enterprise today may thrive.
CASSIUS   What enterprise, Popillius?
POPILLIUS   Fare you well.
  [*He leaves* CASSIUS, *and makes to*° CAESAR]   *goes toward*
15   BRUTUS   What said Popillius Laena?
CASSIUS   He wished today our enterprise might thrive.
I fear our purpose is discoverèd.
BRUTUS   Look how he makes to Caesar. Mark him.
CASSIUS   Casca, be sudden,° for we fear prevention.°—   *swift / being thwarted*
20   Brutus, what shall be done? If this be known,
Cassius or Caesar never shall turn back,°   *return alive*
For I will slay myself.
BRUTUS   Cassius, be constant.°   *resolute*

3.1 Location: At the Capitol.
1. Indicating a movement from the street outside to the interior of the Capitol.

Popillius Laena speaks not of our purposes,
For look, he smiles, and Caesar doth not change.

25 CASSIUS   Trebonius knows his time, for look you, Brutus,
He draws Mark Antony out of the way. [*Exeunt* TREBONIUS *and* ANTONY]

DECIUS   Where is Metellus Cimber? Let him go
And presently prefer° his suit to Caesar.   at once present
[CAESAR *sits*]

BRUTUS   He is addressed.° Press near, and second him.   ready

30 CINNA   Casca, you are the first that rears your hand.
[*The conspirators and the other senators
take their places*]

CAESAR   Are we all ready? What is now amiss
That Caesar and his Senate must redress?

METELLUS [*coming forward and kneeling*]   Most high, most
mighty, and most puissant Caesar,
Metellus Cimber throws before thy seat
An humble heart.

35 CAESAR   I must prevent° thee, Cimber.   thwart
These couchings° and these lowly courtesies°   stoopings / bows
Might fire the blood° of ordinary men,   passions
And turn preordinance and first decree²
Into the law of children.° Be not fond³   childish whims
40 To think that Caesar bears such rebel° blood   lawless
That will be thawed from the true quality°   proper constancy
With that which melteth fools: I mean sweet words,
Low-crookèd° curtsies, and base spaniel fawning.   Obsequious; dishonest
Thy brother by decree is banishèd.
45 If thou dost bend and pray and fawn for him,
I spurn thee like a cur out of my way.
Know Caesar doth not wrong but with just cause,⁴
Nor without cause will he be satisfied.

METELLUS   Is there no voice more worthy than my own
50 To sound more sweetly in great Caesar's ear
For the repealing of my banished brother?

BRUTUS [*coming forward and kneeling*]   I kiss thy hand, but not
in flattery, Caesar,
Desiring thee that Publius Cimber may
Have an immediate freedom of repeal.°   release from banishment

CAESAR   What, Brutus?

CASSIUS [*coming forward and kneeling*]
                    Pardon, Caesar; Caesar, pardon.
55 As low as to thy foot doth Cassius fall
To beg enfranchisement° for Publius Cimber.   liberation

CAESAR   I could be well moved if I were as you.
If I could pray to move,° prayers would move me.   make pleas
60 But I am constant as the Northern Star,°   polestar
Of whose true fixed and resting° quality   stationary
There is no fellow° in the firmament.   equal
The skies are painted with unnumbered sparks;
They are all fire, and every one doth shine;
65 But there's but one in all doth hold his place.
So in the world: 'tis furnished well with men,

---

2. Established precedent and original rulings.   4. F reads merely, "Know Caesar doth not wrong." See
3. Do not be so foolish as.   Textual Note.

And men are flesh and blood, and apprehensive;°   *capable of understanding*
Yet in the number I do know but one
That unassailable holds on his rank,°   *maintains his place*
70   Unshaked of motion;[5] and that I am he
Let me a little show it even in this—
That I was constant° Cimber should be banished,   *resolute*
And constant do remain to keep him so.
CINNA [*coming forward and kneeling*]
    O Caesar!
CAESAR   Hence! Wilt thou lift up Olympus?[6]
DECIUS [*coming forward with* LIGARIUS *and kneeling*]
    Great Caesar!
75   CAESAR   Doth not Brutus bootless° kneel?   *in vain*
CASCA [*coming forward and kneeling*]
    Speak hands for me.[7]
    They stab CAESAR [CASCA *first*, BRUTUS *last*]
CAESAR   *Et tu, Bruté?*[8]—Then fall Caesar.
                              [*He*] *dies*
CINNA   Liberty! Freedom! Tyranny is dead!
    Run hence, proclaim, cry it about the streets.
CASSIUS   Some to the common pulpits,° and cry out   *public platforms (rostra)*
80   'Liberty, freedom, and enfranchisement!'
BRUTUS   People and senators, be not affrighted.
    [*Exeunt in a tumult* LEPIDUS, POPILLIUS, *other senators*,
               ARTEMIDORUS, SOOTHSAYER, *and citizens*]
    Fly not! Stand still! Ambition's debt is paid.
CASCA   Go to the pulpit, Brutus.
DECIUS   And Cassius too.
85   BRUTUS   Where's Publius?°
CINNA   Here, quite confounded° with this mutiny.°   *confused / tumult*
METELLUS   Stand fast together, lest some friend of Caesar's
    Should chance—
BRUTUS   Talk not of standing.—Publius, good cheer!
90   There is no harm intended to your person,
    Nor to no Roman else—so tell them, Publius.
CASSIUS   And leave us, Publius, lest that the people,
    Rushing on us, should do your age some mischief.°   *injury*
BRUTUS   Do so; and let no man abide° this deed   *pay the penalty for*
95   But we the doers.   [*Exit* PUBLIUS]
    Enter TREBONIUS
CASSIUS   Where is Antony?
TREBONIUS   Fled to his house, amazed.
    Men, wives, and children stare, cry out, and run,
    As° it were doomsday.   *As if*
BRUTUS   Fates, we will know your pleasures.
100   That we shall die, we know; 'tis but the time
    And drawing days out that men stand upon.[9]
CASCA   Why, he that cuts off twenty years of life
    Cuts off so many years of fearing death.

---

5. Completely steady; unmoved by persuasion.
6. High mountain in Greece where the gods were supposed to dwell.
7. Let my hands beseech in prayer; let violent action take over where speech has failed.
8. Latin: And you, Brutus? According to Plutarch, Cae-

sar spoke these words in Greek and stopped defending himself when he saw Brutus among the conspirators.
9. *'tis . . . upon:* it is but the specific time of death and the possibility of extending their lives with which men concern themselves.

BRUTUS Grant that, and then is death a benefit.
105   So are we Caesar's friends, that have abridged
His time of fearing death. Stoop, Romans, stoop,
And let us bathe our hands in Caesar's blood
Up to the elbows, and besmear our swords;
Then walk we forth even to the market-place,°   *the Roman Forum*
110   And, waving our red weapons o'er our heads,
Let's all cry 'peace, freedom, and liberty!'
CASSIUS Stoop, then, and wash.
      [*They smear their hands with Caesar's blood*]
                      How many ages hence
Shall this our lofty scene be acted over,
In states unborn and accents° yet unknown!   *languages*
115 BRUTUS How many times shall Caesar bleed in sport,°   *for entertainment*
That now on Pompey's basis lies along,[1]
No worthier than the dust!
CASSIUS   So oft as that shall be,
So often shall the knot° of us be called   *group*
The men that gave their country liberty.
DECIUS What, shall we forth?
120 CASSIUS   Ay, every man away.
Brutus shall lead, and we will grace° his heels   *honor*
With the most boldest and best hearts of Rome.
      Enter [*Antony's*] SERVANT
BRUTUS Soft;° who comes here? A friend of Antony's.   *Wait*
SERVANT [*kneeling and falling prostrate*] Thus, Brutus, did my master
    bid me kneel.
125   Thus did Mark Antony bid me fall down,
And, being prostrate, thus he bade me say.
'Brutus is noble, wise, valiant, and honest.°   *honorable*
Caesar was mighty, bold, royal, and loving.
Say I love Brutus, and I honour him.
130   Say I feared Caesar, honoured him, and loved him.
If Brutus will vouchsafe that Antony
May safely come to him and be resolved°   *learn for certain*
How Caesar hath deserved to lie in death,
Mark Antony shall not love Caesar dead
135   So well as Brutus living, but will follow
The fortunes and affairs of noble Brutus
Thorough° the hazards of this untrod state[2]   *Through*
With all true faith.' So says my master Antony.
BRUTUS Thy master is a wise and valiant Roman.
140   I never thought him worse.
Tell him, so° please him come unto this place,   *if it should*
He shall be satisfied, and, by my honour,
Depart untouched.
SERVANT [*rising*]   I'll fetch him presently.°   *Exit*   *at once*
BRUTUS I know that we shall have him well to friend.°   *as a friend*
145 CASSIUS I wish we may. But yet have I a mind
That fears him much; and my misgiving still
Falls shrewdly to the purpose.[3]
      Enter ANTONY

---

1. Lies stretched out on the pedestal ("basis") of Pompey's statue.
2. These unprecedented circumstances.
3. *my . . . purpose:* my suspicions always turn out to be unfortunately pertinent.

BRUTUS   But here comes Antony.—Welcome, Mark Antony.

ANTONY   O mighty Caesar! Dost thou lie so low?

150   Are all thy conquests, glories, triumphs, spoils,
    Shrunk to this little measure? Fare thee well.—
    I know not, gentlemen, what you intend—
    Who else must be let blood, who else is rank.[4]
    If I myself, there is no hour so fit

155   As Caesar's death's hour, nor no instrument
    Of half that worth as those your swords, made rich
    With the most noble blood of all this world.
    I do beseech ye, if you bear me hard,°   *bear me ill will*
    Now, whilst your purpled° hands do reek° and smoke,   *bloody / steam*

160   Fulfil your pleasure. Live° a thousand years,   *If I live*
    I shall not find myself so apt° to die.   *ready*
    No place will please me so, no mean° of death,   *manner*
    As here by Caesar, and by you cut off,
    The choice° and master spirits of this age.   *most select*

165 BRUTUS   O Antony, beg not your death of us!
    Though now we must appear bloody and cruel,
    As by our hands and this our present act
    You see we do, yet see you but our hands,
    And this the bleeding business they have done.

170   Our hearts you see not; they are pitiful;°   *full of pity*
    And pity to the general wrong of Rome—
    As fire drives out fire, so pity pity[5]—
    Hath done this deed on Caesar. For your part,°   *As for you*
    To you our swords have leaden° points, Mark Antony.   *blunt*

175   Our arms, unstrung of malice,[6] and our hearts
    Of brothers' temper,° do receive you in   *disposition*
    With all kind love, good thoughts, and reverence.

CASSIUS   Your voice° shall be as strong as any man's   *opinion*
    In the disposing of new dignities.[7]

180 BRUTUS   Only be patient till we have appeased°   *calmed*
    The multitude, beside themselves with fear,
    And then we will deliver you the cause
    Why I, that did love Caesar when I struck him,
    Have thus proceeded.

ANTONY   I doubt not of your wisdom.

185   Let each man render me his bloody hand.

        He shakes hands with the conspirators

    First, Marcus Brutus, will I shake with you.—
    Next, Caius Cassius, do I take your hand.—
    Now, Decius Brutus, yours;—now yours, Metellus;—
    Yours, Cinna;—and my valiant Casca, yours;—

190   Though last, not least in love, yours, good Trebonius.
    Gentlemen all—alas, what shall I say?
    My credit° now stands on such slippery ground   *credibility*
    That one of two bad ways you must conceit° me: *judge*
    Either a coward or a flatterer.

195   That I did love thee, Caesar, O, 'tis true.
    If then thy spirit look upon us now,

4. Festering with disease; overgrown. *let blood*: have blood drawn off medically (that is, killed).
5. That is, pity for the state has driven out pity for Caesar.
6. Having given up their power to harm. (The image is of a bow with its string loosened or removed.)
7. Conferring new offices of state.

Shall it not grieve thee dearer° than thy death   *more keenly*
To see thy Antony making his peace,
Shaking the bloody fingers of thy foes—
200 Most noble!—in the presence of thy corpse?
Had I as many eyes as thou hast wounds,
Weeping as fast as they stream forth thy blood,
It would become me better than to close°   *agree*
In terms of friendship with thine enemies.
205 Pardon me, Julius. Here wast thou bayed,° brave hart;[8]   *brought to bay*
Here didst thou fall, and here thy hunters stand
Signed° in thy spoil° and crimsoned in thy lethe.[9]   *Marked / slaughter*
O world, thou wast the forest to this hart;
And this indeed, O world, the heart of thee.
210 How like a deer strucken by many princes
Dost thou here lie!
CASSIUS   Mark Antony.
ANTONY   Pardon me, Caius Cassius.
The enemies of Caesar shall say this;
215 Then in a friend it is cold modesty.°   *moderation*
CASSIUS   I blame you not for praising Caesar so;
But what compact° mean you to have with us?   *agreement*
Will you be pricked in number of° our friends,   *be counted among*
Or shall we on,° and not depend on you?   *proceed*
220 ANTONY   Therefore I took your hands, but was indeed
Swayed from the point by looking down on Caesar.
Friends am I with you all, and love you all
Upon this hope: that you shall give me reasons
Why and wherein Caesar was dangerous.
225 BRUTUS   Or else were this a savage spectacle.
Our reasons are so full of good regard,°   *sound considerations*
That were you, Antony, the son of Caesar,
You should be satisfied.
ANTONY   That's all I seek;
And am, moreover, suitor° that I may   *petitioner*
230 Produce° his body to the market-place,   *Bring out*
And in the pulpit,° as becomes a friend,   *rostrum*
Speak in the order° of his funeral.   *ceremony*
BRUTUS   You shall, Mark Antony.
CASSIUS   Brutus, a word with you.
[*Aside to* BRUTUS] You know not what you do. Do not consent
235 That Antony speak in his funeral.
Know you how much the people may be moved
By that which he will utter?
BRUTUS [*aside to* CASSIUS]   By your pardon,°   *With your permission*
I will myself into the pulpit first,
And show the reason of our Caesar's death.
240 What Antony shall speak I will protest°   *proclaim*
He speaks by leave and by permission;
And that we are contented Caesar shall
Have all true° rites and lawful ceremonies,   *proper*
It shall advantage° more than do us wrong.   *benefit*
245 CASSIUS [*aside to* BRUTUS]   I know not what may fall.° I like it not.   *happen*

8. Stag (punning on "heart").
9. Lost lifeblood (Lethe was the river of forgetfulness in the classical underworld).

BRUTUS Mark Antony, here, take you Caesar's body.
　　　You shall not in your funeral speech blame us;
　　　But speak all good you can devise of Caesar,
　　　And say you do't by our permission;
250　　　Else shall you not have any hand at all
　　　About° his funeral. And you shall speak　　　　　　　　　*In*
　　　In the same pulpit whereto I am going,
　　　After my speech is ended.
BRUTUS Be it so;
255　　　I do desire no more.
BRUTUS Prepare the body then, and follow us.
　　　　　　　　　　　Exeunt. Manet ANTONY
ANTONY O pardon me, thou bleeding piece of earth,
　　　That I am meek and gentle with these butchers.
　　　Thou art the ruins of the noblest man
260　　　That ever livèd in the tide of times.°　　　　　*flow of history*
　　　Woe to the hand that shed this costly° blood!　　　*precious*
　　　Over thy wounds now do I prophesy—
　　　Which like dumb mouths do ope their ruby lips
　　　To beg the voice and utterance of my tongue—
265　　　A curse shall light upon the limbs of men;
　　　Domestic fury and fierce civil strife
　　　Shall cumber° all the parts of Italy;　　　　　　　*oppress*
　　　Blood and destruction shall be so in use,°　　　*so customary*
　　　And dreadful objects so familiar,
270　　　That mothers shall but smile when they behold
　　　Their infants quartered° with the hands of war,　　*cut in pieces*
　　　All pity choked with custom of fell° deeds;　　*familiarity with cruel*
　　　And Caesar's spirit, ranging° for revenge,　　*roving like a wild beast*
　　　With Ate° by his side come hot from hell,　　*goddess of discord*
275　　　Shall in these confines° with a monarch's voice　　*regions*
　　　Cry 'havoc!'[1] and let slip° the dogs of war,　　*unleash*
　　　That this foul deed shall smell above the earth
　　　With carrion men, groaning for burial.
　　　　　　　　Enter Octavius' SERVANT
　　　You serve Octavius Caesar, do you not?
280　SERVANT I do, Mark Antony.
ANTONY Caesar did write for him to come to Rome.
SERVANT He did receive his letters, and is coming,
　　　And bid me say to you by word of mouth—
　　　[*Seeing the body*] O Caesar!
285　ANTONY Thy heart is big.° Get thee apart and weep.　　*swollen with grief*
　　　Passion,° I see, is catching, for mine eyes,　　　*Sorrow*
　　　Seeing those beads of sorrow stand in thine,
　　　Began to water. Is thy master coming?
SERVANT He lies° tonight within seven leagues° of Rome.　*stays / 20 miles*
290　ANTONY Post° back with speed and tell him what hath chanced.　*Ride quickly*
　　　Here is a mourning Rome, a dangerous Rome,
　　　No Rome of safety for Octavius yet.
　　　Hie° hence and tell him so.—Yet stay awhile.　　*Hasten*
　　　Thou shalt not back till I have borne this corpse
295　　　Into the market-place. There shall I try°　　*test*
　　　In my oration how the people take

---

1. Military order for slaughter and pillage.

The cruel issue° of these bloody men;   *deed*
According to the which thou shalt discourse
To young Octavius of the state of things.
300   Lend me your hand.   *Exeunt [with Caesar's body]*

3.2

Enter BRUTUS *and* CASSIUS, *with the* PLEBEIANS

ALL THE PLEBEIANS   We will be satisfied!° Let us be satisfied!   *given an explanation*
BRUTUS   Then follow me, and give me audience, friends.
  [*Aside to* CASSIUS] Cassius, go you into the other street,
  And part the numbers.°   *divide the multitude*
5   [*To the* PLEBEIANS] Those that will hear me speak, let 'em stay here;
  Those that will follow Cassius, go with him;
  And public reasons shall be renderèd
  Of Caesar's death.
        BRUTUS [*ascends to*] *the pulpit*
FIRST PLEBEIAN   I will hear Brutus speak.
SECOND PLEBEIAN   I will hear Cassius, and compare their reasons
10   When severally° we hear them renderèd.   *separately*
        [*Exit* CASSIUS, *with some* PLEBEIANS]
        [*Enter* BRUTUS *above in the pulpit*]
THIRD PLEBEIAN   The noble Brutus is ascended. Silence.
BRUTUS   Be patient till the last.°   *end of my address*
  Romans, countrymen, and lovers,° hear me for my cause, and   *dear friends*
  be silent that you may hear. Believe me for° mine honour, and   *on account of*
15   have respect to° mine honour, that you may believe. Censure°   *regard for / Judge*
  me in your wisdom, and awake your senses,° that you may the   *understanding*
  better judge. If there be any in this assembly, any dear friend
  of Caesar's, to him I say that Brutus' love to Caesar was no less
  than his. If then that friend demand why Brutus rose against
20   Caesar, this is my answer: not that I loved Caesar less, but that
  I loved Rome more. Had you rather Caesar were living, and
  die all slaves, than that Caesar were dead, to live all free men?
  As Caesar loved me, I weep for him. As he was fortunate, I
  rejoice at it. As he was valiant, I honour him. But as he was
25   ambitious, I slew him. There is tears for his love, joy for his
  fortune, honour for his valour, and death for his ambition. Who
  is here so base that would be a bondman? If any, speak, for him
  have I offended.° Who is here so rude° that would not be a   *wronged / barbarous*
  Roman? If any, speak, for him have I offended. Who is here so
30   vile that will not love his country? If any, speak, for him have I
  offended. I pause for a reply.
ALL THE PLEBEIANS   None, Brutus, none.
BRUTUS   Then none have I offended. I have done no more to
  Caesar than you shall do¹ to Brutus. The question of° his   *reasons for*
35   death is enrolled° in the Capitol, his glory not extenuated°   *recorded / diminished*
  wherein he was worthy, nor his offences enforced° for which   *unduly stressed*
  he suffered death.
      Enter Mark ANTONY, *with [others bearing] Caesar's*
      body [in a coffin]
  Here comes his body, mourned by Mark Antony, who, though
  he had no hand in his death, shall receive the benefit of his
40   dying: a place in the commonwealth—as which of you shall

---

3.2 Location: The Forum.   1. Should do (in such circumstances).

not? With this I depart: that as I slew my best lover° for the   *friend*
good of Rome, I have the same dagger for myself when it shall
please my country to need my death.

ALL THE PLEBEIANS   Live, Brutus, live, live!

45   FIRST PLEBEIAN   Bring him with triumph home unto his house.

FOURTH PLEBEIAN   Give him a statue with his ancestors.

THIRD PLEBEIAN   Let him be Caesar.

FIFTH PLEBEIAN   Caesar's better parts°   *faculties*
Shall be crowned in Brutus.

FIRST PLEBEIAN   We'll bring him to his house with shouts and clamours.

BRUTUS   My countrymen.

50   FOURTH PLEBEIAN   Peace, silence. Brutus speaks.

FIRST PLEBEIAN   Peace, ho!

BRUTUS   Good countrymen, let me depart alone,
And, for my sake, stay here with Antony.
Do grace° to Caesar's corpse, and grace² his speech   *Pay respect*
55   Tending° to Caesar's glories, which Mark Antony,   *Relating*
By our permission, is allowed to make.
I do entreat you, not a man depart
Save I alone till Antony have spoke.   *Exit*

FIRST PLEBEIAN   Stay, ho, and let us hear Mark Antony.

60   THIRD PLEBEIAN   Let him go up into the public chair.
We'll hear him. Noble Antony, go up.

ANTONY   For Brutus' sake I am beholden to you.
          [ANTONY *ascends to the pulpit*]

FIFTH PLEBEIAN   What does he say of Brutus?

THIRD PLEBEIAN   He says, for Brutus' sake
He finds himself beholden to us all.

65   FIFTH PLEBEIAN   'Twere best he speak no harm of Brutus here!

FIRST PLEBEIAN   This Caesar was a tyrant.

THIRD PLEBEIAN   Nay, that's certain.
We are blessed that Rome is rid of him.
          [*Enter* ANTONY *in the pulpit*]

FOURTH PLEBEIAN   Peace, let us hear what Antony can say.

ANTONY   You gentle Romans.

ALL THE PLEBEIANS   Peace, ho! Let us hear him.

70   ANTONY   Friends, Romans, countrymen, lend me your ears.
I come to bury Caesar, not to praise him.
The evil that men do lives after them;
The good is oft interrèd with their bones.
So let it be with Caesar. The noble Brutus
75   Hath told you Caesar was ambitious.
If it were so, it was a grievous fault,
And grievously hath Caesar answered° it.   *paid the penalty for*
Here, under leave° of Brutus and the rest—   *by permission*
For Brutus is an honourable man,
80   So are they all, all honourable men—
Come I to speak in Caesar's funeral.
He was my friend, faithful and just to me.
But Brutus says he was ambitious,
And Brutus is an honourable man.
85   He hath brought many captives home to Rome,

2. Courteously hear.

Whose ransoms did the general coffers° fill.   *public treasury*
Did this in Caesar seem ambitious?
When that the poor have cried, Caesar hath wept.
Ambition should be made of sterner stuff.
90   Yet Brutus says he was ambitious,
And Brutus is an honourable man.
You all did see that on the Lupercal
I thrice presented him a kingly crown,
Which he did thrice refuse. Was this ambition?
95   Yet Brutus says he was ambitious,
And sure he is an honourable man.
I speak not to disprove what Brutus spoke,
But here I am to speak what I do know.
You all did love him once, not without cause.
100   What cause withholds you then to mourn for him?
O judgement, thou art fled to brutish beasts,
And men have lost their reason!
      [*He weeps*]
                  Bear with me.
My heart is in the coffin there with Caesar,
And I must pause till it come back to me.
105 FIRST PLEBEIAN   Methinks there is much reason in his sayings.
FOURTH PLEBEIAN   If thou consider rightly of the matter,
  Caesar has had great wrong.
THIRD PLEBEIAN   Has he not, masters?
  I fear there will a worse come in his place.
FIFTH PLEBEIAN   Marked ye his words? He would not take the crown,
110   Therefore 'tis certain he was not ambitious.
FIRST PLEBEIAN   If it be found so, some will dear abide° it.   *pay dearly for*
FOURTH PLEBEIAN   Poor soul, his eyes are red as fire with weeping.
THIRD PLEBEIAN   There's not a nobler man in Rome than Antony.
FIFTH PLEBEIAN   Now mark him; he begins again to speak.
115 ANTONY   But° yesterday the word of Caesar might   *Only*
Have stood against the world. Now lies he there,
And none so poor to do him reverence.[3]
O masters, if I were disposed to stir
Your hearts and minds to mutiny° and rage,   *rebellion*
120   I should do Brutus wrong, and Cassius wrong,
Who, you all know, are honourable men.
I will not do them wrong. I rather choose
To wrong the dead, to wrong myself and you,
Than I will wrong such honourable men.
125   But here's a parchment with the seal of Caesar.
I found it in his closet.° 'Tis his will.   *study*
Let but the commons° hear this testament—   *commoners*
Which, pardon me, I do not mean to read—
And they would go and kiss dead Caesar's wounds,
130   And dip their napkins[4] in his sacred blood,
Yea, beg a hair of him for memory,
And, dying, mention it within their wills,
Bequeathing it as a rich legacy
Unto their issue.°   *children*

---

3. And no one is so lowly as to owe obeisance to him.
4. Handkerchiefs (implying that Caesar is a martyr whose bloody relics should be regarded as holy).

135 FIFTH PLEBEIAN We'll hear the will. Read it, Mark Antony.
ALL THE PLEBEIANS The will, the will! We will hear Caesar's will.
ANTONY Have patience, gentle friends, I must not read it.
It is not meet° you know how Caesar loved you.   *fitting*
You are not wood, you are not stones, but men;
140 And, being men, hearing the will of Caesar,
It will inflame you, it will make you mad.
'Tis good you know not that you are his heirs,
For if you should, O what would come of it?
FIFTH PLEBEIAN Read the will. We'll hear it, Antony.
145 You shall read us the will, Caesar's will.
ANTONY Will you be patient? Will you stay a while?
I have o'ershot myself⁵ to tell you of it.
I fear I wrong the honourable men
Whose daggers have stabbed Caesar; I do fear it.
150 FIFTH PLEBEIAN They were traitors. Honourable men?
ALL THE PLEBEIANS The will, the testament!
FOURTH PLEBEIAN They were villains, murderers. The will, read
    the will!
ANTONY You will compel me then to read the will?
155 Then make a ring about the corpse of Caesar,
And let me show you him that made the will.
Shall I descend? And will you give me leave?
ALL THE PLEBEIANS
    Come down.
FOURTH PLEBEIAN Descend.
THIRD PLEBEIAN   You shall have leave.
    [ANTONY *descends from the pulpit*]
FIFTH PLEBEIAN   A ring.
    Stand round.
FIRST PLEBEIAN Stand from the hearse.° Stand from the body.   *bier*
160 FOURTH PLEBEIAN Room for Antony, most noble Antony!
    [*Enter* ANTONY *below*]
ANTONY Nay, press not so upon me. Stand farre° off.   *farther*
ALL THE PLEBEIANS Stand back! Room! Bear back!
ANTONY If you have tears, prepare to shed them now.
You all do know this mantle. I remember
165 The first time ever Caesar put it on.
'Twas on a summer's evening in his tent,
That day he overcame the Nervii.⁶
Look, in this place ran Cassius' dagger through.
See what a rent the envious° Casca made.   *spiteful*
170 Through this the well-belovèd Brutus stabbed;
And as he plucked his cursèd steel away,
Mark how the blood of Caesar followed it,
As° rushing out of doors to be resolved⁷   *As if*
If Brutus so unkindly° knocked or no—   *cruelly; unnaturally*
175 For Brutus, as you know, was Caesar's angel.⁸
Judge, O you gods, how dearly Caesar loved him!
This was the most unkindest cut of all.
For when the noble Caesar saw him stab,

5. I have gone too far (an image from archery).   7. To find out for sure.
6. Gallic tribe conquered by Caesar in 57 B.C.E.; it was   8. Attendant spirit (that is, dearest friend).
an important victory, extravagantly celebrated in Rome.

Ingratitude, more strong than traitors' arms,
180 Quite vanquished him. Then burst his mighty heart,
And in his mantle muffling up his face,
Even at the base of Pompey's statue,
Which all the while ran blood, great Caesar fell.
O, what a fall was there, my countrymen!
185 Then I, and you, and all of us fell down,
Whilst bloody treason flourished° over us.
O now you weep, and I perceive you feel
The dint° of pity. These are gracious drops.   impression
Kind souls, what, weep you when you but behold
190 Our Caesar's vesture° wounded? Look you here.   garment
Here is himself, marred, as you see, with traitors.
        [*He uncovers Caesar's body*]
FIRST PLEBEIAN   O piteous spectacle!
FOURTH PLEBEIAN   O noble Caesar!
THIRD PLEBEIAN   O woeful day!
FIFTH PLEBEIAN   O traitors, villains!
FIRST PLEBEIAN   O most bloody sight!
195 FOURTH PLEBEIAN   We will be revenged.
ALL THE PLEBEIANS   Revenge! About!° Seek! Burn! Fire! Kill! Slay!   To work
    Let not a traitor live!
ANTONY   Stay, countrymen.
FIRST PLEBEIAN   Peace there, hear the noble Antony.
FOURTH PLEBEIAN   We'll hear him, we'll follow him, we'll die
200   with him!
ANTONY   Good friends, sweet friends, let me not stir you up
    To such a sudden flood of mutiny.
    They that have done this deed are honourable.
    What private griefs° they have, alas, I know not,   personal grievances
205   That made them do it. They are wise and honourable,
    And will no doubt with reasons answer you.
    I come not, friends, to steal away your hearts.
    I am no orator as Brutus is,
    But, as you know me all, a plain blunt man
210   That love my friend; and that they know full well
    That gave me public leave to speak¹ of him.
    For I have neither wit,° nor words, nor worth,°   intelligence / stature
    Action,° nor utterance, nor the power of speech,   Gesture
    To stir men's blood. I only speak right on.°   straightforwardly
215   I tell you that which you yourselves do know,
    Show you sweet Caesar's wounds, poor poor dumb mouths,
    And bid them speak for me. But were I Brutus,
    And Brutus Antony, there were an Antony
    Would ruffle° up your spirits, and put a tongue   stir
220   In every wound of Caesar that should move
    The stones of Rome to rise and mutiny.°   riot
ALL THE PLEBEIANS   We'll mutiny.
FIRST PLEBEIAN   We'll burn the house of Brutus.
THIRD PLEBEIAN   Away then! Come, seek the conspirators.
ANTONY   Yet hear me, countrymen, yet hear me speak.
225 ALL THE PLEBEIANS   Peace, ho! Hear Antony, most noble Antony.
ANTONY   Why, friends, you go to do you know not what.

9. Shook its sword; triumphed.   1. Permission to speak in public.

Wherein hath Caesar thus deserved your loves?
Alas, you know not. I must tell you then.
You have forgot the will I told you of.

230 ALL THE PLEBEIANS   Most true. The will. Let's stay and hear the will.

ANTONY   Here is the will, and under Caesar's seal.
To every Roman citizen he gives—
To every several° man—seventy-five drachmas.²   °individual

FOURTH PLEBEIAN   Most noble Caesar! We'll revenge his death.

THIRD PLEBEIAN   O royal Caesar!

ANTONY   Hear me with patience.

235 ALL THE PLEBEIANS   Peace,° ho!   °Silence

ANTONY   Moreover he hath left you all his walks,
His private arbours, and new-planted orchards,°   °gardens
On this side Tiber. He hath left them you,
And to your heirs for ever—common pleasures°   °public parks

240 To walk abroad and recreate yourselves.
Here was a Caesar. When comes such another?

FIRST PLEBEIAN   Never, never! Come, away, away!
We'll burn his body in the holy place,
And with the brands fire the traitors' houses.

245 Take up the body.

FOURTH PLEBEIAN   Go, fetch fire!

THIRD PLEBEIAN   Pluck down benches!

FIFTH PLEBEIAN   Pluck down forms,° windows,° anything!   °benches / shutters

                    Exeunt PLEBEIANS [*with Caesar's body*]

ANTONY   Now let it work. Mischief, thou art afoot.
Take thou what course thou wilt.

                    Enter [*Octavius'*] SERVANT

250   How now, fellow?

SERVANT   Sir, Octavius is already come to Rome.

ANTONY   Where is he?

SERVANT   He and Lepidus are at Caesar's house.

ANTONY   And thither will I straight° to visit him.   °at once

255 He comes upon a wish.° Fortune is merry,   °just as I wished
And in this mood will give us anything.

SERVANT   I heard him say Brutus and Cassius
Are rid° like madmen through the gates of Rome.   °Have ridden

ANTONY   Belike° they had some notice° of the people,   °Probably / warning

260 How I had moved them. Bring me to Octavius.   *Exeunt*

3.3

            Enter CINNA *the poet*

CINNA   I dreamt tonight° that I did feast with Caesar,   °last night
And things unlucky charge my fantasy.¹
I have no will to wander forth of doors,
Yet something leads me forth.

            [*Enter*] *the* PLEBEIANS

5 FIRST PLEBEIAN   What is your name?

SECOND PLEBEIAN   Whither are you going?

THIRD PLEBEIAN   Where do you dwell?

FOURTH PLEBEIAN   Are you a married man or a bachelor?

SECOND PLEBEIAN   Answer every man directly.²

---

2. Greek silver coins.   1. And bad omens oppress my imagination.
3.3 Location: A street in Rome.   2. At once; speaking straightforwardly.

10 FIRST PLEBEIAN Ay, and briefly.
    FOURTH PLEBEIAN Ay, and wisely.
    THIRD PLEBEIAN Ay, and truly, you were best.°   *you'd better*
    CINNA What is my name? Whither am I going? Where do I
        dwell? Am I a married man or a bachelor? Then to answer
15   every man directly and briefly, wisely and truly: wisely, I say, I
        am a bachelor.
    SECOND PLEBEIAN That's as much as to say they are fools that
        marry. You'll bear me a bang° for that, I fear. Proceed directly.   *get a blow from me*
    CINNA Directly I am going to Caesar's funeral.
20 FIRST PLEBEIAN As a friend or an enemy?
    CINNA As a friend.
    SECOND PLEBEIAN That matter is answered directly.
    FOURTH PLEBEIAN For your dwelling—briefly.
    CINNA Briefly, I dwell by the Capitol.
25 THIRD PLEBEIAN Your name, sir, truly.
    CINNA Truly, my name is Cinna.
    FIRST PLEBEIAN Tear him to pieces! He's a conspirator.
    CINNA I am Cinna the poet, I am Cinna the poet.
    FOURTH PLEBEIAN Tear him for his bad verses, tear him for his
30   bad verses.
    CINNA I am not Cinna the conspirator.
    FOURTH PLEBEIAN It is no matter, his name's Cinna. Pluck but
        his name out of his heart, and turn him going.°   *send him packing*
    THIRD PLEBEIAN Tear him, tear him!
                    [*They set upon* CINNA]
35   Come, brands, ho! Firebrands! To Brutus', to Cassius'! Burn
        all! Some to Decius' house, and some to Casca's; some to Liga-
        rius'. Away, go!
                    Exeunt all the PLEBEIANS [*with* CINNA]

4.1

                Enter ANTONY [*with papers*], OCTAVIUS, *and* LEPIDUS
    ANTONY These many, then, shall die; their names are pricked.°   *marked down*
    OCTAVIUS [*to* LEPIDUS] Your brother too must die. Consent you, Lepidus?
    LEPIDUS I do consent.
    OCTAVIUS   Prick him down, Antony.
    LEPIDUS Upon condition° Publius shall not live,   *Provided that*
5   Who is your sister's son, Mark Antony.
    ANTONY He shall not live. Look, with a spot I damn him.[1]
        But Lepidus, go you to Caesar's house;
        Fetch the will hither, and we shall determine
        How to cut off some charge in legacies.[2]
10 LEPIDUS What, shall I find you here?
    OCTAVIUS Or° here or at the Capitol.   *Exit* LEPIDUS   *Either*
    ANTONY This is a slight, unmeritable° man,   *undeserving*
        Meet° to be sent on errands. Is it fit,   *Fit*
        The three-fold world divided,[3] he should stand
        One of the three to share it?
15 OCTAVIUS   So you thought him,
        And took his voice° who should be pricked to die   *accepted his opinion*

4.1 Location: Antony's house in Rome.
1. With a mark I condemn him to death.
2. Reduce the amount paid out to beneficiaries of
Caesar's will.

3. Antony, Octavius, and Lepidus, in the second triumvirate, or joint rule of three, parceled out rule of
Rome's empire among themselves.

In our black° sentence and proscription.[4]   death

ANTONY   Octavius, I have seen more days than you,
And though we lay these honours on this man
20   To ease ourselves of divers sland'rous loads,°   burdens of reproach
He shall but bear them as the ass bears gold,
To groan and sweat under the business,
Either led or driven as we point the way;
And having brought our treasure where we will,
25   Then take we down his load, and turn him off,
Like to the empty° ass, to shake his ears   unladen
And graze in commons.[5]

OCTAVIUS   You may do your will;
But he's a tried and valiant soldier.

ANTONY   So is my horse, Octavius, and for that
30   I do appoint° him store of provender.   provide
It is a creature that I teach to fight,
To wind,° to stop, to run directly on,   turn
His corporal° motion governed by my spirit;   bodily
And in some taste° is Lepidus but so.   measure
35   He must be taught, and trained, and bid go forth—
A barren-spirited fellow, one that feeds
On objects, arts, and imitations,[6]
Which, out of use and staled° by other men,   made uninteresting
Begin his fashion.[7] Do not talk of him
40   But as a property.° And now, Octavius,   tool
Listen° great things. Brutus and Cassius   Give ear to
Are levying powers.° We must straight make head.[8]   armies
Therefore let our alliance be combined,
Our best friends made,° our meinies stretched,[9]   mustered
45   And let us presently go sit in council,
How covert matters° may be best disclosed,   dangers
And open perils surest answerèd.°   most safely confronted

OCTAVIUS   Let us do so, for we are at the stake[1]
And bayed about with many enemies;
50   And some that smile have in their hearts, I fear,
Millions of mischiefs.°   evils

                                        Exeunt

                            4.2
      Drum. Enter BRUTUS, [LUCIUS,] *and the army.* LUCIL-
      LIUS, TITINIUS, *and* PINDARUS *meet them*

BRUTUS   Stand, ho!°   Halt

SOLDIER   Give the word 'ho', and stand.[1]

BRUTUS   What now, Lucillius: is Cassius near?

LUCILLIUS   He is at hand, and Pindarus is come
5   To do you salutation from his master.

BRUTUS   He greets me well.° Your master, Pindarus,   with a worthy man
In his own change or by ill officers,[2]

4. A "proscribed" person had a price on his head, his
property was confiscated, and his children were prevented from holding office.
5. In the public pasture; among the common people.
6. On curiosities, contrivances, and counterfeits.
7. He then takes up as fashionable.
8. We must raise an army at once.
9. Our bands of followers augmented.

1. That is, like bears in the sport of bearbaiting, tied to
a stake and surrounded by baying hounds.
4.2 Location: Sardis, in what is now western Turkey.
Brutus's tent in his army's camp.
1. Pass the word, and halt.
2. By his own altered feelings or through the actions of
bad subordinates.

Hath given me some worthy° cause to wish   *justifiable*
Things done undone. But if he be at hand,
I shall be satisfied.³

10 PINDARUS   I do not doubt
But that my noble master will appear
Such as he is, full of regard⁴ and honour.

BRUTUS   He is not doubted.—A word, Lucillius.

        BRUTUS *and* LUCILLIUS *speak apart*

How he received you let me be resolved.°   *informed*

15 LUCILLIUS   With courtesy and with respect enough,
But not with such familiar instances,°   *tokens of friendship*
Nor with such free and friendly conference,°   *conversation*
As he hath used of old.

BRUTUS   Thou hast described
A hot friend cooling. Ever note, Lucillius:

20 When love begins to sicken and decay
It useth an enforcèd ceremony.°   *a strained formality*
There are no tricks° in plain and simple faith;   *artifices*
But hollow° men, like horses hot at hand,⁵   *insincere*
Make gallant show and promise of their mettle;

        *Low march*⁶ *within*

25 But when they should endure the bloody spur,
They fall their crests° and, like deceitful jades,°   *lower their necks / nags*
Sink° in the trial. Comes his army on?   *Fail*

LUCILLIUS   They mean this night in Sardis to be quartered.
The greater part, the horse in general,°   *all the cavalry*
Are come with Cassius.

        Enter CASSIUS *and his powers*°   *armies*

30 BRUTUS   Hark, he is arrived.
March gently° on to meet him.   *slowly*

        [*The armies march*]

CASSIUS   Stand, ho!

BRUTUS   Stand, ho! Speak the word along.

FIRST SOLDIER   Stand!

35 SECOND SOLDIER   Stand!

THIRD SOLDIER   Stand!

CASSIUS   Most noble brother, you have done me wrong.

BRUTUS   Judge me, you gods: wrong I mine enemies?
And if not so, how should I wrong a brother?

40 CASSIUS   Brutus, this sober form of yours hides wrongs,
And when you do them—

BRUTUS   Cassius, be content.°   *keep calm*
Speak your griefs° softly. I do know you well.   *grievances*
Before the eyes of both our armies here,
Which should perceive nothing but love from us,

45 Let us not wrangle. Bid them move away,
Then in my tent, Cassius, enlarge° your griefs,   *express fully*
And I will give you audience.

CASSIUS   Pindarus,
Bid our commanders lead their charges° off   *troops*
A little from this ground.

---

3. I shall receive a full explanation.
4. Respect for you; renown (for his own abilities).
5. Eager at the outset.

6. Soft drumbeat (as from a distance; the sound becomes louder as the army enters).

50 BRUTUS Lucillius, do you the like; and let no man
　　　　　Come to our tent till we have done our conference.
　　　　　Let Lucius and Titinius guard our door. *Exeunt [the armies]*
　　　　　　Manent BRUTUS *and* CASSIUS [*with* TITINIUS *and*
　　　　　　LUCIUS *guarding the door*][7]
　　CASSIUS That you have wronged me doth appear in this:
　　　　　You have condemned and noted° Lucius Pella　　　　　　*publicly disgraced*
55　　　　For taking bribes here of the Sardians,
　　　　　Wherein my letters praying on his side,
　　　　　Because I knew the man, was slighted off.°　　*contemptuously ignored*
　　BRUTUS You wronged yourself to write in such a case.
　　CASSIUS In such a time as this it is not meet°　　　　　　　　*appropriate*
60　　　　That every nice° offence should bear his comment.°　*trivial / be criticized*
　　BRUTUS Let me tell you, Cassius, you yourself
　　　　　Are much condemned to have° an itching palm,　　　　　*for having*
　　　　　To sell and mart° your offices for gold　　　　　　　　　*traffic in*
　　　　　To undeservers.
　　CASSIUS　　　　　　　　I, an itching palm?
65　　　　You know that you are Brutus that speaks this,
　　　　　Or, by the gods, this speech were else° your last.　　　*otherwise*
　　BRUTUS The name of Cassius honours this corruption,[8]
　　　　　And chastisement doth therefore hide his head.
　　CASSIUS Chastisement?
70 BRUTUS Remember March, the ides of March, remember.
　　　　　Did not great Julius bleed for justice' sake?
　　　　　What villain touched his body, that did stab,
　　　　　And not for justice?[9] What, shall one of us,
　　　　　That struck the foremost man of all this world
75　　　　But for supporting robbers,[1] shall we now
　　　　　Contaminate our fingers with base bribes,
　　　　　And sell the mighty space of our large honours°　　*impressive reputations*
　　　　　For so much trash° as may be graspèd thus?　　　*money (contemptuous)*
　　　　　I had rather be a dog and bay° the moon　　　　　　　　*howl at*
　　　　　Than such a Roman.
80 CASSIUS　　　　　　　　Brutus, bay° not me.　　　*howl at; hold at bay*
　　　　　I'll not endure it. You forget yourself
　　　　　To hedge me in.° I am a soldier, I,　　　　　　　*limit my authority*
　　　　　Older in practice, abler than yourself
　　　　　To make conditions.°　　　　　　　　　　　　　　　　*manage affairs*
85 BRUTUS Go to, you are not, Cassius.
　　CASSIUS I am.
　　BRUTUS I say you are not.
　　CASSIUS Urge° me no more, I shall forget myself.　　　　　*Provoke*
　　　　　Have mind upon your health. Tempt me no farther.
90 BRUTUS Away, slight man.
　　CASSIUS Is't possible?
　　BRUTUS Hear me, for I will speak.
　　　　　Must I give way and room to your rash choler?[2]
　　　　　Shall I be frighted when a madman stares?
95 CASSIUS O ye gods, ye gods! Must I endure all this?
　　BRUTUS All this? Ay, more. Fret till your proud heart break.

---

7. Some editors begin a new scene at this point.
8. Makes this corruption appear honorable.
9. *What . . . justice?*: Who was so villainous as to stab
Caesar for any motive other than justice?

1. Caesar was accused of permitting, even encouraging, corruption among his subordinates.
2. Must I allow free passage to your rash anger?

Go show your slaves how choleric° you are,   *enraged*
And make your bondmen tremble. Must I budge?°   *flinch*
Must I observe° you? Must I stand and crouch°   *defer to / cringe*
100   Under your testy humour?° By the gods,   *irritable temper*
You shall digest³ the venom of your spleen,°   *anger*
Though it do split you. For from this day forth
I'll use you for my mirth, yea for my laughter,
When you are waspish.
CASSIUS   Is it come to this?
105   BRUTUS   You say you are a better soldier.
Let it appear so, make your vaunting° true,   *boasting*
And it shall please me well. For mine own part,
I shall be glad to learn of° noble men.   *from*
CASSIUS   You wrong me every way, you wrong me, Brutus.
110   I said an elder soldier, not a better.
Did I say better?
BRUTUS   If you did, I care not.
CASSIUS   When Caesar lived he durst not thus have moved° me.   *angered*
BRUTUS   Peace, peace; you durst not so have tempted him.
CASSIUS   I durst not?
115   BRUTUS   No.
CASSIUS   What, durst not tempt him?
BRUTUS   For your life you durst not.
CASSIUS   Do not presume too much upon my love.
I may do that I shall be sorry for.
120   BRUTUS   You have done that you should be sorry for.
There is no terror, Cassius, in your threats,
For I am armed so strong in honesty°   *rectitude*
That they pass by me as the idle wind,
Which I respect not.° I did send to you   *pay no attention to*
125   For certain sums of gold, which you denied me;
For I can raise no money by vile means.
By heaven, I had rather coin my heart
And drop my blood for drachmas than to wring
From the hard hands of peasants their vile trash
130   By any indirection.° I did send   *devious means*
To you for gold to pay my legions,
Which you denied me. Was that done like Cassius?
Should I have answered Caius Cassius so?
When Marcus Brutus grows so covetous
135   To lock such rascal counters from his friends,
Be ready, gods, with all your thunderbolts;
Dash him to pieces.
CASSIUS   I denied you not.
BRUTUS   You did.
CASSIUS   I did not. He was but a fool
That brought my answer back. Brutus hath rived° my heart.   *broken*
140   A friend should bear his friend's infirmities,
But Brutus makes mine greater than they are.
BRUTUS   I do not, till you practise them on me.
CASSIUS   You love me not.
BRUTUS   I do not like your faults.
CASSIUS   A friendly eye could never see such faults.

---

3. Swallow (not give vent to).

145 BRUTUS A flatterer's would not, though they do appear
    As huge as high Olympus.
    CASSIUS Come, Antony and young Octavius, come,
    Revenge yourselves alone on Cassius;
    For Cassius is aweary of the world,
150   Hated by one he loves, braved° by his brother,   *defied*
    Checked° like a bondman; all his faults observed,   *Rebuked*
    Set in a notebook, learned and conned by rote,°   *memorized*
    To cast into my teeth. O, I could weep
    My spirit from mine eyes! There is my dagger,
155   And here my naked breast; within, a heart
    Dearer° than Pluto's⁴ mine, richer than gold.   *More valuable*
    If that thou beest a Roman, take it forth.
    I that denied thee gold will give my heart.
    Strike as thou didst at Caesar; for I know
160   When thou didst hate him worst, thou loved'st him better
    Than ever thou loved'st Cassius.
    BRUTUS   Sheathe your dagger.
    Be angry when you will; it shall have scope.°   *room for exercise*
    Do what you will; dishonour shall be humour.⁵
    O Cassius, you are yokèd° with a lamb   *allied*
165   That carries anger as the flint bears fire,
    Who, much enforcèd,° shows a hasty spark   *struck*
    And straight° is cold again.   *immediately*
    CASSIUS   Hath Cassius lived
    To be but mirth and laughter to his Brutus
    When grief and blood ill-tempered⁶ vexeth him?
170 BRUTUS When I spoke that, I was ill-tempered too.
    CASSIUS Do you confess so much? Give me your hand.
    BRUTUS And my heart too.
          [*They embrace*]
    CASSIUS   O Brutus!
    BRUTUS   What's the matter?
    CASSIUS Have not you love enough to bear with me
    When that rash humour° which my mother gave me   *temperament*
    Makes me forgetful?
175 BRUTUS   Yes, Cassius, and from henceforth,
    When you are over-earnest with your Brutus,
    He'll think your mother chides, and leave you so.°   *let you alone*
         Enter [LUCILLIUS *and*] *a* POET
    POET Let me go in to see the generals.
    There is some grudge between 'em; 'tis not meet
    They be alone.
180 LUCILLIUS   You shall not come to them.
    POET Nothing but death shall stay me.
    CASSIUS   How now! What's the matter?
    POET For shame, you generals, what do you mean?
    Love and be friends, as two such men should be,
    For I have seen more years, I'm sure, than ye.
185 CASSIUS Ha, ha! How vilely doth this cynic⁷ rhyme!

---

4. Roman god of riches (Plutus; often conflated with Pluto, god of the underworld).
5. Dishonorable actions shall be ascribed to moodiness.

6. Literally, badly mixed blood (thought to produce anger and melancholy).
7. Member of a philosophical school that refused to respect differences in social class.

BRUTUS [*to the* POET]   Get you hence, sirrah;° saucy fellow,   (*contemptuous address*)
Not hence!

CASSIUS   Bear with him, Brutus, 'tis his fashion.

BRUTUS   I'll know his humour when he knows his time.[8]
What should the wars do with these jigging° fools?   *incompetently versifying*
[*To the* POET] Companion,° hence!   (*contemptuous*)

190 CASSIUS [*to the* POET]   Away, away, be gone!

Exit POET

BRUTUS   Lucillius and Titinius, bid the commanders
Prepare to lodge their companies tonight.

CASSIUS   And come yourselves, and bring Messala with you
Immediately to us.   [*Exeunt* LUCILLIUS *and* TITINIUS]

BRUTUS   Lucius, a bowl of wine.   [*Exit* LUCIUS]

195 CASSIUS   I did not think you could have been so angry.

BRUTUS   O Cassius, I am sick of° many griefs.   *suffering from*

CASSIUS   Of your philosophy you make no use,
If you give place to accidental evils.[9]

BRUTUS   No man bears sorrow better. Portia is dead.

200 CASSIUS   Ha! Portia?

BRUTUS   She is dead.

CASSIUS   How scaped I killing° when I crossed you so?   *being killed*
O insupportable and touching loss!
Upon what sickness?

BRUTUS   Impatience of° my absence,   *Inability to tolerate*

205 And grief that young Octavius with Mark Antony
Have made themselves so strong—for with° her death   *with the news of*
That tidings came. With this, she fell distraught,
And, her attendants absent, swallowed fire.[1]

CASSIUS   And died so?

BRUTUS   Even so.

CASSIUS   O ye immortal gods!

Enter [LUCIUS] *with wine and tapers*°   *candles*

210 BRUTUS   Speak no more of her. [*To* LUCIUS] Give me a bowl of wine.
[*To* CASSIUS] In this I bury all unkindness, Cassius.
[*He*] *drinks*

CASSIUS   My heart is thirsty for that noble pledge.
Fill, Lucius, till the wine o'erswell° the cup.   *overflow*
I cannot drink too much of Brutus' love.
[*He drinks*]   [*Exit* LUCIUS]

Enter TITINIUS *and* MESSALA[2]

215 BRUTUS   Come in, Titinius; welcome, good Messala.
Now sit we close about this taper here,
And call in question° our necessities.   *discuss*

CASSIUS [*aside*]   Portia, art thou gone?

BRUTUS   No more, I pray you.
[*They sit*]
Messala, I have here receivèd letters

220 That young Octavius and Mark Antony
Come down upon us with a mighty power,
Bending their expedition° toward Philippi.[3]   *Pressing hastily*

---

8. I'll tolerate his eccentricity when he finds an appropriate time for it.
9. Brutus admired the Stoics, who taught that the wise man should remain unaffected by circumstances outside himself. *evils:* misfortunes.

1. Portia committed suicide by swallowing live embers.
2. Lucillius, who ought logically to return at this point (see lines 193–94), is not mentioned, an inconsistency that suggests Shakespearean revision of this scene.
3. City in northeastern Greece.

MESSALA   Myself have letters of the selfsame tenor.

BRUTUS   With what addition?

225   MESSALA   That by proscription[4] and bills of outlawry
Octavius, Antony, and Lepidus
Have put to death an hundred senators.

BRUTUS   Therein our letters do not well agree.
Mine speak of seventy senators that died

230   By their proscriptions, Cicero being one.

CASSIUS   Cicero one?

MESSALA   Ay, Cicero is dead,
And by that order of proscription.
[*To* BRUTUS] Had you your letters from your wife, my lord?

BRUTUS   No, Messala.

235   MESSALA   Nor nothing in your letters writ of her?

BRUTUS   Nothing, Messala.

MESSALA   That methinks is strange.

BRUTUS   Why ask you? Hear you aught of her in yours?

MESSALA   No, my lord.

BRUTUS   Now as you are a Roman, tell me true.

240   MESSALA   Then like a Roman bear the truth I tell;
For certain she is dead, and by strange manner.

BRUTUS   Why, farewell, Portia.[5] We must die, Messala.
With meditating that she must die once,°   *at some time*
I have the patience to endure it now.

245   MESSALA   Even so great men great losses should endure.

CASSIUS   I have as much of this in art[6] as you,
But yet my nature could not bear it so.

BRUTUS   Well, to our work alive.[7] What do you think
Of marching to Philippi presently?°   *at once*

CASSIUS   I do not think it good.

BRUTUS   Your reason?

250   CASSIUS   This it is:
'Tis better that the enemy seek us;
So shall he waste his means, weary his soldiers,
Doing himself offence; whilst we, lying still,
Are full of rest, defence, and nimbleness.

255   BRUTUS   Good reasons must of force° give place to better.   *of necessity*
The people 'twixt Philippi and this ground
Do stand but in a forced affection,
For they have grudged us contribution.[8]
The enemy marching along by them

260   By them shall make a fuller number up,
Come on refreshed, new added,° and encouraged;   *reinforced*
From which advantage shall we cut him off,
If at Philippi we do face him there,
These people at our back.

CASSIUS   Hear me, good brother.

265   BRUTUS   Under your pardon.° You must note beside   *Allow me to continue*
That we have tried the utmost of our friends;
Our legions are brim-full, our cause is ripe.
The enemy increaseth every day;

4. See note to 4.1.17.
5. On the apparent conflict between this passage and
lines 199–210, see the Introduction and the Textual
Note.

6. I have learned as much of this philosophy.
7. *alive:* of concern to those now living.
8. Money to support the army.

We at the height are ready to decline.

270 There is a tide in the affairs of men
Which, taken at the flood, leads on to fortune;
Omitted,° all the voyage of their life   *Once missed*
Is bound in° shallows and in miseries.   *confined to*
On such a full sea are we now afloat,

275 And we must take the current when it serves,
Or lose our ventures.[9]

CASSIUS   Then, with your will,° go on.   *as you wish*
We'll along ourselves, and meet them at Philippi.

BRUTUS   The deep of night is crept upon our talk,
And nature must obey necessity,

280 Which we will niggard° with a little rest.   *stint*
There is no more to say.

CASSIUS   No more. Good night.
Early tomorrow will we rise and hence.°   *depart*

BRUTUS   Lucius.

         Enter LUCIUS

            My gown.°   [*Exit* LUCIUS]   *dressing gown*
              Farewell, good Messala.
Good night, Titinius. Noble, noble, Cassius,
Good night and good repose.

285 CASSIUS   O my dear brother,
This was an ill beginning of the night!
Never come such division 'tween our souls.
Let it not, Brutus.

         Enter LUCIUS *with the gown*

BRUTUS   Everything is well.

CASSIUS   Good night, my lord.

BRUTUS   Good night, good brother.

TITINIUS *and* MESSALA   Good night, Lord Brutus.

290 BRUTUS   Farewell, every one.

            Exeunt [CASSIUS, TITINIUS, *and* MESSALA]

Give me the gown.

      [*He puts on the gown*]

            Where is thy instrument?°   *(probably a lute)*

LUCIUS   Here in the tent.

BRUTUS   What, thou speak'st drowsily.
Poor knave,° I blame thee not; thou art o'erwatched.[1]   *lad*
Call Claudio and some other of my men.

295 I'll have them sleep on cushions in my tent.

LUCIUS   Varrus and Claudio!

         Enter VARRUS *and* CLAUDIO

VARRUS   Calls my lord?

BRUTUS   I pray you, sirs, lie in my tent and sleep.
It may be I shall raise you° by and by   *get you up*
On business to my brother Cassius.

300 VARRUS   So please you, we will stand and watch your pleasure.[2]

BRUTUS   I will not have it so. Lie down, good sirs.
It may be I shall otherwise bethink me.°   *change my mind*

      [VARRUS *and* CLAUDIO *lie down to sleep*]

Look, Lucius, here's the book I sought for so.

---

9. Investments (in trading voyages).   2. And stay awake to attend to your wishes.
1. You have stayed up too long.

I put it in the pocket of my gown.
305 LUCIUS I was sure your lordship did not give it me.
BRUTUS Bear with me, good boy, I am much forgetful.
Canst thou hold up thy heavy eyes a while,
And touch thy instrument a strain or two?
LUCIUS Ay, my lord, an't° please you.   if it
BRUTUS   It does, my boy.
310 I trouble thee too much, but thou art willing.
LUCIUS It is my duty, sir.
BRUTUS I should not urge thy duty past thy might.
I know young bloods° look for a time of rest.   youthful spirits
LUCIUS I have slept, my lord, already.
315 BRUTUS It was well done, and thou shalt sleep again.
I will not hold thee long. If I do live,
I will be good to thee.
   [LUCIUS plays] music and [sings] a song [and so falls
   asleep]
This is a sleepy tune. O murd'rous slumber,
Lay'st thou thy leaden mace° upon my boy   heavy staff of office
320 That plays thee music?—Gentle knave, good night.
I will not do thee so much wrong to wake thee.
If thou dost nod thou break'st thy instrument;
I'll take it from thee, and, good boy, good night.
   [He takes away Lucius' instrument, then opens the book]
Let me see, let me see, is not the leaf turned down
325 Where I left reading? Here it is, I think.
   Enter the GHOST of Caesar
How ill this taper burns![3] Ha! Who comes here?
I think it is the weakness of mine eyes
That shapes this monstrous apparition.
It comes upon° me. Art thou any thing?   toward
330 Art thou some god, some angel, or some devil,
That mak'st my blood cold and my hair to stare?°   stand on end
Speak to me what thou art.
GHOST Thy evil spirit, Brutus.
BRUTUS Why com'st thou?
335 GHOST To tell thee thou shalt see me at Philippi.
BRUTUS Well; then I shall see thee again?
GHOST   Ay, at Philippi.
BRUTUS Why, I will see thee at Philippi then.   Exit GHOST
Now I have taken heart, thou vanishest.
Ill spirit, I would hold more talk with thee.—
340 Boy, Lucius, Varrus, Claudio, sirs, awake!
Claudio!
LUCIUS   The strings, my lord, are false.°   out of tune
BRUTUS He thinks he still is at his instrument.—
Lucius, awake!
LUCIUS My lord.
345 BRUTUS Didst thou dream, Lucius, that thou so cried'st out?
LUCIUS My lord, I do not know that I did cry.
BRUTUS Yes, that thou didst. Didst thou see anything?
LUCIUS Nothing, my lord.
BRUTUS Sleep again, Lucius.—Sirrah Claudio!

3. The dimming of a flame was held to indicate a ghost's presence.

[*To* VARRUS]   Fellow,
350   Thou, awake!
VARRUS   My lord.
CLAUDIO   My lord.
BRUTUS   Why did you so cry out, sirs, in your sleep?
BOTH   Did we, my lord?
BRUTUS   Ay. Saw you anything?
VARRUS   No, my lord, I saw nothing.
355   CLAUDIO   Nor I, my lord.
BRUTUS   Go and commend me° to my brother Cassius.   *send my regards*
Bid him set on his powers betimes before,⁴
And we will follow.
BOTH   It shall be done, my lord.
                     Exeunt [VARRUS *and* CLAUDIO *at one door,* BRUTUS
                                and LUCIUS *at another door*]

5.1

                Enter OCTAVIUS, ANTONY, *and their army*
OCTAVIUS   Now, Antony, our hopes are answerèd.
You said the enemy would not come down,
But keep the hills and upper regions.
It proves not so; their battles° are at hand.   *forces*
5   They mean to warn° us at Philippi here,   *challenge*
Answering before we do demand of them.
ANTONY   Tut, I am in their bosoms,¹ and I know
Wherefore they do it. They could be content
To visit other places;° and come down   *To go elsewhere*
10   With fearful bravery,² thinking by this face°   *pretense; defiance*
To fasten in our thoughts that they have courage;
But 'tis not so.
                Enter a MESSENGER
MESSENGER   Prepare you, generals.
The enemy comes on in gallant show.
Their bloody sign° of battle is hung out,   *red flag*
15   And something to° be done immediately.   *is to*
ANTONY   Octavius, lead your battle softly° on   *your army warily*
Upon the left hand of the even field.
OCTAVIUS   Upon the right hand, I; keep thou the left.
ANTONY   Why do you cross° me in this exigent?°   *thwart / critical moment*
20   OCTAVIUS   I do not cross you,³ but I will do so.
                [*Drum.* ANTONY *and* OCTAVIUS] *march* [*with their army*].
                Drum [*within*]. *Enter* [*marching*] BRUTUS, CASSIUS, *and*
                their army [*amongst them* TITINIUS, LUCILLIUS, *and* MES-
                SALA]
                [*Octavius' and Antony's army makes a stand*]
BRUTUS   They stand, and would have parley.
CASSIUS   Stand fast, Titinius. We must out° and talk.   *go forward*
                [*Brutus' and Cassius' army makes a stand*]
OCTAVIUS   Mark Antony, shall we give sign of battle?
ANTONY   No, Caesar, we will answer on their charge.⁴

---

4. March off with his army before me.   terrifying display.
5.1 Location: The remainder of the play takes place on   3. March on the right side; dispute with you in the
the battlefield near Philippi.   future.
1. I know their secret thoughts.   4. We will meet them when they attack.
2. With a show of courage that conceals fear; with a

25   Make forth,° the generals would have some words.   *Go forward*
       OCTAVIUS [*to his army*]   Stir not until the signal.
               [ANTONY *and* OCTAVIUS *meet* BRUTUS *and* CASSIUS]
       BRUTUS   Words before blows: is it so, countrymen?
       OCTAVIUS   Not that we love words better, as you do.
       BRUTUS   Good words are better than bad strokes, Octavius.
30   ANTONY   In your° bad strokes, Brutus, you give good words.   *As you deliver*
          Witness the hole you made in Caesar's heart,
          Crying 'Long live, hail Caesar'.
       CASSIUS   Antony,
          The posture° of your blows are yet unknown;   *quality*
          But for your words, they rob the Hybla⁵ bees,
35   And leave them honeyless.
       ANTONY   Not stingless too.
       BRUTUS   O yes, and soundless too,
          For you have stolen their buzzing, Antony,
          And very wisely threat before you sting.
40   ANTONY   Villains, you did not so when your vile daggers
          Hacked one another in the sides of Caesar.
          You showed your teeth like apes,° and fawned like hounds,   *You imitated smiles*
          And bowed like bondmen, kissing Caesar's feet,
          Whilst damnèd Casca, like a cur, behind,
45   Struck Caesar on the neck. O you flatterers!
       CASSIUS   Flatterers? Now, Brutus, thank yourself.
          This tongue had not offended so today
          If Cassius might have ruled.°   *had his way*
       OCTAVIUS   Come, come, the cause.° If arguing make us sweat,   *matter in hand*
50   The proof° of it will turn to redder drops.   *testing*
              [*He draws*]
          Look, I draw a sword against conspirators.
          When think you that the sword goes up again?
          Never till Caesar's three and thirty wounds
          Be well avenged, or till another Caesar⁶
55   Have added slaughter to⁷ the swords of traitors.
       BRUTUS   Caesar, thou canst not die by traitors' hands,
          Unless thou bring'st them with thee.°   *(Unless by your hand)*
       OCTAVIUS   So I hope.
          I was not born to die on Brutus' sword.
       BRUTUS   O, if thou wert the noblest of thy strain,°   *family*
60   Young man, thou couldst not die more honourable.
       CASSIUS   A peevish° schoolboy, worthless of such honour,   *silly*
          Joined with a masquer and a reveller!⁸
       ANTONY   Old Cassius still.
       OCTAVIUS   Come, Antony, away.
          Defiance, traitors, hurl we in your teeth.
65   If you dare fight today, come to the field.
          If not, when you have stomachs.°   *inclination; courage*
              Exeunt OCTAVIUS, ANTONY, *and* [*their*] *army*
       CASSIUS   Why, now blow wind, swell billow, and swim bark.°   *ship*
          The storm is up, and all is on the hazard.°   *at risk*
       BRUTUS   Ho, Lucillius! Hark, a word with you.

---

5. Sicilian town famous for honey.   8. That is, Antony, who was noted for his love of extrav-
6. That is, Octavius Caesar himself.   agant entertainments and banquets.
7. Has increased the slaughter committed by.

LUCILLIUS   My lord.
   [He] stand[s] forth° *[and speaks with* BRUTUS]   *comes forward*
CASSIUS Messala.
MESSALA *[standing forth]* What says my general?
70 CASSIUS   Messala,
  This is my birthday; as° this very day   *on*
  Was Cassius born. Give me thy hand, Messala.
  Be thou my witness that, against my will,
  As Pompey was, am I compelled to set
75 Upon one battle all our liberties.
  You know that I held Epicurus strong,
  And his opinion.[9] Now I change my mind,
  And partly credit things that do presage.
  Coming from Sardis, on our former ensigns°   *foremost banners*
80 Two mighty eagles fell,° and there they perched,   *alighted*
  Gorging and feeding from our soldiers' hands,
  Who to Philippi here consorted° us.   *accompanied*
  This morning are they fled away and gone,
  And in their steads do ravens, crows, and kites[1]
85 Fly o'er our heads and downward look on us,
  As° we were sickly prey. Their shadows seem   *As if*
  A canopy most fatal,° under which   *ominous*
  Our army lies ready to give° the ghost.   *give up*
MESSALA Believe not so.
CASSIUS   I but believe it partly,
90 For I am fresh of spirit, and resolved
  To meet all perils very constantly.°   *resolutely*
BRUTUS Even so, Lucillius.
CASSIUS *[joining* BRUTUS] Now, most noble Brutus,
  The gods° today stand friendly, that we may,   *May the gods*
  Lovers° in peace, lead on our days to age.   *Close friends*
95 But since the affairs of men rest still° incertain, *always remain*
  Let's reason with° the worst that may befall. *consider*
  If we do lose this battle, then is this
  The very last time we shall speak together.
  What are you then determinèd to do?
100 BRUTUS Even by the rule of that philosophy[2]
  By which I did blame Cato[3] for the death
  Which he did give himself—I know not how,
  But I do find it cowardly and vile
  For fear of what might fall° so to prevent° *happen / anticipate*
105 The time° of life—arming myself with patience *natural limit*
  To stay° the providence of some high powers *await*
  That govern us below.
CASSIUS   Then if we lose this battle,
  You are contented to be led in triumph[4]
  Thorough° the streets of Rome?   *Through*
110 BRUTUS No, Cassius, no.
  Think not, thou noble Roman,
  That ever Brutus will go bound to Rome.

9. Epicurus, a Greek philosopher, thought the gods indifferent to human affairs and therefore disbelieved omens.
1. These are all scavenger birds, considered bad omens.

2. Brutus admired Plato, who rejected suicide.
3. See note to 2.1.294.
4. As a captive in a triumphal procession; see note to 1.1.30.

He bears too great a mind. But this same day
Must end that work the ides of March begun;
115 And whether we shall meet again I know not.
Therefore our everlasting farewell take.
For ever and for ever farewell, Cassius.
If we do meet again, why, we shall smile.
If not, why then, this parting was well made.
120 CASSIUS   For ever and for ever farewell, Brutus.
If we do meet again, we'll smile indeed.
If not, 'tis true this parting was well made.
BRUTUS   Why then, lead on. O that a man might know
The end of this day's business ere it come!
125 But it sufficeth that the day will end,
And then the end is known.—Come, ho, away!   *Exeunt*

5.2

Alarum.° Enter BRUTUS *and* MESSALA   *Offstage call to battle*
BRUTUS   Ride, ride, Messala, ride, and give these bills°   *written orders*
Unto the legions on the other side.°   *(Cassius's wing)*
Loud alarum
Let them set on° at once, for I perceive   *advance*
But cold demeanour° in Octavio's wing,   *lack of fighting spirit*
5 And sudden push gives them the overthrow.
Ride, ride, Messala; let them all come down.
                                              Exeunt [*severally*]

5.3

Alarums. Enter CASSIUS [*with an ensign,°*] *and* TITINIUS   *a banner*
CASSIUS   O look, Titinius, look: the villains° fly.   *(Cassius's own men)*
Myself have to mine own turned enemy:
This ensign° here of mine was turning back;   *standard-bearer*
I slew the coward, and did take it° from him.   *(the standard)*
5 TITINIUS   O Cassius, Brutus gave the word too early,
Who, having some advantage on Octavius,
Took it too eagerly. His soldiers fell to spoil,°   *looting*
Whilst we by Antony are all enclosed.
Enter PINDARUS
PINDARUS   Fly further off, my lord, fly further off!
10 Mark Antony is in your tents, my lord;
Fly therefore, noble Cassius, fly farre° off.   *farther*
CASSIUS   This hill is far enough. Look, look, Titinius,
Are those my tents where I perceive the fire?
TITINIUS   They are, my lord.
CASSIUS   Titinius, if thou lovest me,
15 Mount thou my horse, and hide thy spurs in him
Till he have brought thee up to yonder troops
And here again, that I may rest assured
Whether yon troops are friend or enemy.
TITINIUS   I will be here again even with° a thought.   *Exit*   *as fast as*
20 CASSIUS   Go, Pindarus, get higher on that hill.
My sight was ever thick.° Regard, Titinius,   *dim*
And tell me what thou not'st about the field.   [*Exit* PINDARUS]
This day I breathèd first. Time is come round,

And where I did begin, there shall I end.
My life is run his compass.°   *its circuit*
     [Enter PINDARUS *above]°*   *(on the stage balcony)*
25   Sirrah, what news?
PINDARUS   O my lord!
CASSIUS   What news?
PINDARUS   Titinius is enclosèd round about
    With horsemen, that make to him on the spur.¹
30   Yet he spurs on. Now they are almost on him.
    Now Titinius. Now some light.° O, he lights too.   *alight*
    He's ta'en.°   *taken*
       Shout [within]
    And hark, they shout for joy.
CASSIUS   Come down; behold no more.
                    [Exit PINDARUS*]*
    O coward that I am, to live so long
35   To see my best friend ta'en before my face!
       Enter PINDARUS *[below]*
    Come hither, sirrah. In Parthia° did I take thee prisoner,   *(modern Iran)*
    And then I swore thee, saving of² thy life,
    That whatsoever I did bid thee do
    Thou shouldst attempt it. Come now, keep thine oath.
40   Now be a freeman, and, with this good sword
    That ran through Caesar's bowels, search° this bosom.   *penetrate*
    Stand° not to answer. Here, take thou the hilts,°   *Delay / sword handle*
       *[*PINDARUS *takes the sword]*
    And when my face is covered, as 'tis now,
    Guide thou the sword.
       *[*PINDARUS *stabs him]*
                Caesar, thou art revenged,
45   Even with the sword that killed thee.   *[He dies]*
PINDARUS   So, I am free, yet would not so have been
    Durst° I have done my will. O Cassius!   *Dared*
    Far from this country Pindarus shall run,
    Where never Roman shall take note of him.   *Exit*
       Enter TITINIUS *[wearing a wreath of victory°] and* MES-   *(made of laurel leaves)*
       SALA
50 MESSALA   It is but change,° Titinius, for Octavius   *an even exchange*
    Is overthrown by noble Brutus' power,
    As Cassius' legions are by Antony.
TITINIUS   These tidings will well comfort Cassius.
MESSALA   Where did you leave him?
TITINIUS   All disconsolate,
55   With Pindarus his bondman, on this hill.
MESSALA   Is not that he that lies upon the ground?
TITINIUS   He lies not like the living.—O my heart!
MESSALA   Is not that he?
TITINIUS   No, this was he, Messala;
    But Cassius is no more. O setting sun,
60   As in thy red rays thou dost sink tonight,
    So in his red blood Cassius' day is set.
    The sun of Rome is set. Our day is gone.

5.3
1. Who approach him at a gallop.   2. I made you swear, when I spared.

Clouds, dews, and dangers come. Our deeds are done.
Mistrust of my success³ hath done this deed.
65 MESSALA   Mistrust of good success hath done this deed.
O hateful Error, Melancholy's child,⁴
Why dost thou show to the apt° thoughts of men   *impressionable*
The things that are not? O Error, soon conceived,
Thou never com'st unto a happy birth,
70 But kill'st the mother° that engendered thee.   *(the melancholy person)*
TITINIUS   What, Pindarus! Where art thou, Pindarus?
MESSALA   Seek him, Titinius, whilst I go to meet
The noble Brutus, thrusting this report
Into his ears. I may say 'thrusting' it,
75 For piercing steel and darts° envenomèd   *spears*
Shall be as welcome to the ears of Brutus
As tidings of this sight.
TITINIUS   Hie you, Messala,
And I will seek for Pindarus the while.   [*Exit* MESSALA]
Why didst thou send me forth, brave Cassius?
80 Did I not meet thy friends, and did not they
Put on my brows this wreath of victory,
And bid me give it thee? Didst thou not hear their shouts?
Alas, thou hast misconstrued everything.
But hold thee, take this garland on thy brow.
85 Thy Brutus bid me give it thee, and I
Will do his bidding. Brutus, come apace,°   *quickly*
And see how I regarded° Caius Cassius.   *esteemed*
By your leave, gods, this is a Roman's part:
Come Cassius' sword, and find Titinius' heart.
                              [*He stabs himself, and*] *dies*
        Alarum. Enter BRUTUS, MESSALA, YOUNG CATO,⁵ STRATO,
              VOLUMNIUS, LUCILLIUS[, LABIO, *and* FLAVIO]
90 BRUTUS   Where, where, Messala, doth his body lie?
MESSALA   Lo yonder, and Titinius mourning it.
BRUTUS   Titinius' face is upward.
CATO   He is slain.
BRUTUS   O Julius Caesar, thou art mighty yet.
Thy spirit walks abroad, and turns our swords
In our own proper° entrails.   *our very own*
        Low° Alarums   *Soft*
95 CATO   Brave Titinius,
Look whe'er° he have not crowned dead Cassius.   *whether*
BRUTUS   Are yet two Romans living such as these?
The last of all the Romans, fare thee well.
It is impossible that ever Rome
100 Should breed thy fellow. Friends, I owe more tears
To this dead man than you shall see me pay.—
I shall find time, Cassius, I shall find time.—
Come, therefore, and to Thasos° send his body.   *an island near Philippi*
His funerals shall not be in our camp,
105 Lest it discomfort° us. Lucillius, come;   *dishearten*
And come, young Cato. Let us to the field.
Labio and Flavio, set our battles° on.   *forces*

---

3. Doubt about the outcome of my mission.   5. The son of Marcus Portius Cato.
4. That is, bred from melancholy thoughts.

'Tis three o'clock, and, Romans, yet ere night
We shall try fortune in a second fight.

Exeunt [with the bodies]

5.4

Alarum. Enter BRUTUS, MESSALA, YOUNG CATO, LUCIL-
LIUS, *and* FLAVIUS

BRUTUS   Yet, countrymen, O yet hold up your heads.

[Exit with MESSALA *and* FLAVIUS]

CATO   What bastard° doth not? Who will go with me?   *untrue Roman*
I will proclaim my name about the field.
I am the son of Marcus Cato, ho!
5   A foe to tyrants, and my country's friend.
I am the son of Marcus Cato, ho!

Enter SOLDIERS, *and fight*

LUCILLIUS   And I am Brutus, Marcus Brutus, I,
Brutus, my country's friend. Know me for Brutus.

*[*SOLDIERS *kill* CATO]

O young and noble Cato, art thou down?
10   Why, now thou diest as bravely as Titinius,
And mayst be honoured, being Cato's son.

FIRST SOLDIER   Yield, or thou diest.

LUCILLIUS   Only I yield to die.[1]
There is so much,[2] that thou wilt kill me straight:°   *immediately*
Kill Brutus, and be honoured in his death.

15   FIRST SOLDIER   We must not.—A noble prisoner.

SECOND SOLDIER   Room, ho! Tell Antony Brutus is ta'en.

Enter ANTONY

FIRST SOLDIER   I'll tell the news. Here comes the general.—
[To ANTONY] Brutus is ta'en, Brutus is ta'en, my lord.

ANTONY   Where is he?

20   LUCILLIUS   Safe, Antony, Brutus is safe enough.
I dare assure thee that no enemy
Shall ever take alive the noble Brutus.
The gods defend him from so great a shame.
When you do find him, or° alive or dead,   *either*
25   He will be found like Brutus, like himself.°   *true to his noble nature*

ANTONY *[to* FIRST SOLDIER]   This is not Brutus, friend, but, I assure you,
A prize no less in worth. Keep this man safe.
Give him all kindness. I had rather have
Such men my friends than enemies.
[To another SOLDIER]   Go on,
30   And see whe'er Brutus be alive or dead,
And bring us word unto Octavius' tent
How everything is chanced.°   *has happened*

Exeunt [the SOLDIER *at one door,* ANTONY,
LUCILLIUS *and other* SOLDIERS, *some bearing
Cato's body, at another door]*

5.4
1. I yield only so that I may die.   2. There is enough inducement.

5.5

Enter BRUTUS, DARDANIUS, CLITUS, STRATO, *and*
VOLUMNIUS

BRUTUS   Come, poor remains of friends, rest on this rock.
  [*He sits.* STRATO *rests and falls asleep*]
CLITUS   Statillius[1] showed the torchlight, but, my lord,
  He came not back. He is or ta'en° or slain.   *either captured*
BRUTUS   Sit thee down, Clitus. Slaying is the word:
5   It is a deed in fashion. Hark thee, Clitus.
  [*He whispers*]
CLITUS   What I, my lord? No, not for all the world.
BRUTUS   Peace, then, no words.
CLITUS   I'll rather kill myself.
  [*He stands apart*]
BRUTUS   Hark thee, Dardanius.
  [*He whispers*]
DARDANIUS   Shall I do such a deed?
  [*He joins* CLITUS]
CLITUS   O Dardanius!
10   DARDANIUS   O Clitus!
CLITUS   What ill request did Brutus make to thee?
DARDANIUS   To kill him, Clitus. Look, he meditates.
CLITUS   Now is that noble vessel full of grief,
  That it runs over even at his eyes.
15   BRUTUS   Come hither, good Volumnius. List° a word.   *Listen to*
VOLUMNIUS   What says my lord?
BRUTUS   Why this, Volumnius.
  The ghost of Caesar hath appeared to me
  Two several° times by night—at Sardis once,   *different*
  And this last night, here in Philippi fields.
  I know my hour is come.
20   VOLUMNIUS   Not so, my lord.
BRUTUS   Nay, I am sure it is, Volumnius.
  Thou seest the world, Volumnius, how it goes.
  Our enemies have beat° us to the pit,[2]   *driven*
    Low alarums
  It is more worthy to leap in ourselves
25   Than tarry till they push us. Good Volumnius,
  Thou know'st that we two went to school together.
  Even for that, our love of old, I prithee,
  Hold thou my sword hilts whilst I run on it.
VOLUMNIUS   That's not an office for a friend, my lord.
    Alarum still
30   CLITUS   Fly, fly, my lord! There is no tarrying here.
BRUTUS   Farewell to you, and you, and you, Volumnius.—
  Strato, thou hast been all this while asleep.
  [STRATO *wakes*]
  Farewell to thee too, Strato. Countrymen,
  My heart doth joy that yet in all my life
35   I found no man but he was true to me.

5.5
1. A soldier sent ahead with instructions to signal by torchlight if all is well.
2. Animal trap; grave.

I shall have glory by this losing day,
More than Octavius and Mark Antony
By this vile conquest shall attain unto.
So fare you well at once, for Brutus' tongue
40 Hath almost ended his life's history.
Night hangs upon mine eyes. My bones would rest,
That have but laboured³ to attain this hour.
          Alarum. Cry within: 'Fly, fly, fly!'
CLITUS Fly, my lord, fly!
BRUTUS   Hence; I will follow.
          [*Exeunt* CLITUS, DARDANIUS, *and* VOLUMNIUS]
I prithee, Strato, stay thou by thy lord.
45 Thou art a fellow of a good respect.°   reputation
Thy life hath had some smatch° of honour in it.   relish
Hold then my sword, and turn away thy face
While I do run upon it. Wilt thou, Strato?
STRATO Give me your hand first. Fare you well, my lord.
BRUTUS Farewell, good Strato.
          [STRATO *holds the sword, while* BRUTUS *runs on it*]
50   Caesar, now be still.
I killed not thee with half so good a will.   [*He*] *dies*
          *Alarum. Retreat.*⁴ *Enter* ANTONY, OCTAVIUS, MESSALA,
          LUCILLIUS, *and the army*
OCTAVIUS What man is that?
MESSALA My master's man. Strato, where is thy master?
STRATO Free from the bondage you are in, Messala.
55 The conquerors can but make a fire of him,°   burn his body
For Brutus only overcame himself,⁵
And no man else hath honour by his death.
LUCILLIUS So Brutus should be found. I thank thee, Brutus,
That thou hast proved Lucillius' saying true.
60 OCTAVIUS All that served Brutus, I will entertain them.°   take them into service
[*To* STRATO] Fellow, wilt thou bestow° thy time with me?   spend
STRATO Ay, if Messala will prefer° me to you.   recommend
OCTAVIUS Do so, good Messala.
MESSALA   How died my master, Strato?
STRATO I held the sword, and he did run on it.
65 MESSALA Octavius, then take him to follow° thee,   serve
That did the latest° service to my master.   last
ANTONY This was the noblest Roman of them all.
All the conspirators save only he
Did that° they did in envy of great Caesar.   what
70 He only in a general honest thought⁶
And common good to all⁷ made one of them.
His life was gentle,° and the elements⁸   noble
So mixed in him that nature might stand up
And say to all the world 'This was a man'.
75 OCTAVIUS According° to his virtue let us use him,   In accordance with
With all respect and rites of burial.
Within my tent his bones tonight shall lie,
Most like a soldier, ordered° honourably.   treated

---

3. Labored for no other purpose than.
4. Trumpet signal to cease pursuit.
5. For only Brutus conquered Brutus.
6. With a virtuous, principled conviction.

7. And desire for the common good.
8. The four bodily humors, different combinations of
which supposedly affected temperament; in the ideal
individual, no single humor predominated.

So call the field to rest, and let's away
80 To part° the glories of this happy day.   *share*

Exeunt [with Brutus' body]

As You Like It

Much of *As You Like It* takes place in a forest, where characters in flight from treachery at court and injustice in the family take refuge. The play thus participates in the rich tradition of Renaissance pastoral literature in which the rustic world of forest and field offers an alternative to and a sanctuary from the urban or courtly milieu to which it is contrasted. The pastoral mode had its origins in ancient Greece, where the poet Theocritus used rural settings and rustic shepherds to explore the sorrows of love and the harsh injustices of daily life. The Roman poet Virgil expanded this tradition, elaborating in particular the opposition between city and country life that in the Renaissance was often transmuted into an opposition between court and country. In England, many of Shakespeare's contemporaries worked in pastoral forms, particularly Edmund Spenser, whose *Shepheardes Calendar* (1579) was modeled on Virgil's *Eclogues,* and Sir Philip Sidney, whose vast prose romance *The Countess of Pembrokes Arcadia* was first published in revised form in 1590.

As a literary mode, pastoral can take many forms. There can be pastoral lyrics, dialogues, prose romances, and dramas. Certain topics and situations, however, are common features of many kinds of pastoral. Often, for example, exiles from urban or courtly life temporarily take up residence in the country where they live and converse with shepherds, often disguising *themselves* as shepherds before an eventual return to the life from which they had fled. In their rural retreat, they hold singing contests and discuss the relative merits of country and court life, whether nature is improved or spoiled by art, and whether "gentleness" (meaning both "nobility" and "a virtuous nature") is a condition one can achieve or to which one must be born.

Fundamental to pastoral debates is a concern about the relationship of what is "natural" to what is "artificial," that is, about whether what human beings have made—cities, gardens, or systems of social hierarchy—is preferable to the simplicity and lack of artifice supposedly found in rural settings and communities. This preoccupation makes pastoral particularly suited to social criticism. Pastoral figures often dissect the evils of various ways of life—the cruelty of hard-hearted mistresses, the greed of landlords, the deceit of courtiers, and the venality of the clergy. But while pastoral frequently celebrates simplicity, it does so in a highly artful manner, drawing on conventions that have been part of the Western literary tradition for at least two thousand years. Pastoral is therefore not so much a spontaneous expression of "natural" simplicity as the artful imitation of such simplicity by characters exiled from more sophisticated realms who for a time assume the guise of shepherds and play an elaborate game of "Let's pretend." Hence the many disguises found in pastoral, where courtiers pose as rustic shepherds, men as women, women as men, and dukes as forest outlaws. To minds of a stolidly serious cast, pastoral can appear to be a silly, escapist genre. To those less dismissive of the world of "Let's pretend," it offers an opportunity to see more clearly—and perhaps then to change—the world in which one ordinarily lives by entering for a time the playful, meditative, and artificial realm of imaginary shepherds.

In *As You Like It,* Shakespeare gave himself over to the pleasures and the seriousness of pastoral without seeming to find them antithetical. In the main action, a good ruler, Duke Senior, has been ousted from his throne by a usurping younger brother, Duke Frederick. The banished Duke takes refuge in the Forest of Ardenne, where he lives like Robin Hood with a band of loyal followers. When his daughter, Rosalind, companion to Frederick's daughter, Celia, is likewise banished, she disguises herself as a

First page of the *Gest of Robin Hood*, one of the most important sixteenth-century renditions of the Robin Hood legend.

young man named Ganymede and also journeys to Ardenne. Celia, posing as a lowborn woman named Aliena, goes with her, as does Touchstone the clown. A second line of action concerns two other brothers: Orlando, the youngest son, and Oliver, the oldest son of Sir Rowland de Bois. The inheritor of his father's estate, Oliver treats Orlando cruelly, denying him the education befitting a gentleman. In danger both from Duke Frederick and from his brother, Orlando also flees to the forest, accompanied by Adam, his dead father's eighty-year-old servant. By Act 2, all of these refugees from court life find themselves in a natural world, which, in spite of its considerable hardships, they prefer to the treachery of court. Ardenne is not Edenic. There are lions and snakes in this pastoral retreat and real shepherds like Corin who speak matter-of-factly about the hard and dirty labor that tending real sheep entails. But in Ardenne, there is also room for courtship games, for brotherly kindness, and for music. In fact, this play contains more songs than any other Shakespearean drama. In their song-filled green world, the characters hunt deer, tend sheep, and converse endlessly about love, exile, and the relative merits of court and country. Eventually, their chief troubles resolved, most return to court, leaving the forest once more to its native inhabitants and to those few courtiers who permanently embrace it.

The broad outlines of this story are taken from Thomas Lodge's enormously popular prose romance *Rosalynde,* written in 1586–87 and published in 1590, although Shakespeare changes many details and points of emphasis. In Lodge, for example, the Duke Senior and Duke Frederick characters are not brothers, but in both the ducal and the Orlando-Oliver plots, Shakespeare makes the enmity of brothers the principal sign of the corruption of "civilized" life. In Lodge, moreover, the father in the Orlando-Oliver plot does not follow the English custom of primogeniture, by which all property is settled on the oldest son; instead, he divides his property among his male offspring according to their merits. By having Oliver inherit almost everything, Shakespeare evokes an English social practice that caused great hardship to many younger brothers. The court women are handled differently as well by Shakespeare: he reduces the Celia character's centrality and instead emphasizes Rosalind and her love affair with Orlando. Shakespeare also tempers the violence of Lodge's resolution and adds to his cast of characters. In *Rosalynde,* the exiled Duke defeats the usurper in battle, but Shakespeare's Frederick has a religious conversion and voluntarily relinquishes the dukedom. Oliver Martext, William, Audrey, Touchstone the clown, and Jaques the melancholy satirist are all Shakespeare's creations. Jaques, in particular, adds a touch of caustic salt and Touchstone a dash of earthy realism to the play's exploration of competing value systems.

In fact, *As You Like It* is poised carefully on the razor's edge separating fantasy from harsh reality. Shakespeare's use of place is a case in point. Lodge's romance is set in the Forest of Ardenne, an ancient woodland comprising part of what is now France, Belgium, and Luxembourg. Shakespeare also uses a French setting, and this edition emphasizes that fact by giving the French spelling, "Ardenne," to the forest. But in the First Folio (1623), this woodland is called the Forest of Arden, an anglicized spelling that also happens to be the name of an English forest near Shakespeare's birthplace in Warwickshire. This fortuitous overlapping of French and English place-names is indicative of the play's double vision. Overtly set in a fantastical foreign kingdom, *As You Like It* nonetheless alludes to places (such as the Forest of Arden), people (such as Robin Hood), and practices (such as primogeniture) native to Shakespeare's own England. Through the distancing artifice of pastoral, the play deals with problems close to home.

Lodge's prose romance is not the only source for *As You Like It*. The play also draws upon *The Tale of Gamelyn*, a violent Middle English narrative in which a younger brother seeks revenge upon an older brother who mistreats him, and which explicitly evokes the name of Robin Hood, the popular English hero whose deeds were celebrated in countless ballads and stories. In the opening scene of *As You Like It*, Charles the wrestler reports that the banished Duke is "already in the forest of Ardenne, and a many merry men with him; and there they live like the old Robin Hood of England. They say many young gentlemen flock to him every day, and fleet the time carelessly, as they did in the golden world" (1.1.99–103). Shakespeare could count on his audience to know the story of Robin Hood, and its evocation carried certain associations. The legendary figure and his band of men stood not only for the community and brotherhood characteristic of the Golden Age and absent in modern life, but also for resistance to tyranny. The great forests of England were the King's own preserves. To kill the deer in those forests was a crime against the monarch. Yet Robin Hood lived in the forest, dined on the King's deer, and opposed King John's unjust reign. In the 1590s, many of those resisting the enclosure of farmland for sheep grazing took refuge in forest areas, and poaching the King's deer had long been one way the poor defied the law to feed themselves when food was short, as it often was because of bad food harvests in the late 1590s.

As You Like It only obliquely alludes to this immediate social context, but Act 1 depicts a world of injustice and social disorder that both motivates the flight to Ardenne and evokes the tradition of opposition to injustice associated with Robin Hood. Orlando's situation speaks to the peculiarly English plight of younger brothers who, under the system of primogeniture, inherited little from their fathers and were often at the mercy of elder siblings. Oliver is a nightmare version of an eldest son: he deprives Orlando of a gentleman's education, connives with the Duke's professional wrestler to have his brother injured, and throws his father's old servant, Adam, out of the house. His cruelty is echoed by the tyranny of Duke Frederick. The play's opening thus clearly underscores the existence of inhumanity and tyrannical willfulness in the court and in the household of old Sir Rowland's eldest son. Less clear is whether this corruption stems from human institutions, particularly the system of primogeniture, or from the "naturally" evil natures of Frederick and Oliver. The play does not answer this or other thorny questions directly. In fact, it seems organized to provoke thought rather than urge conclusions, and the ending does not so much lay out a plan for social reform as indulge the fantasy that all desires, however contradictory, can be fulfilled through marriage and the renewal of brotherly affection. The play's most sustained examination of human folly focuses on the behavior of those who succumb to Cupid's arrows. There are many lovers in Ardenne, and for almost none does the course of love run smooth. Lovesickness was a recognized malady in early modern culture, a condition that so disordered those who endured it that it could cause paleness, sighing, tears, fainting, melancholy, palpitations, and a host of other symptoms. The play represents all lovers as slightly mad and approaches their tribulations with a mixture of sympathy, detached amusement, and analytical curiosity. In part, Shakespeare draws on the critical capacities of pastoral to explore the causes of lovers' unhappiness and to probe the surprisingly complex issue of what is natural in matters of love and sexual desire. In this regard, the play takes little for granted—neither the stability of gender difference nor the naturalness of heterosexuality nor the invariant nature of being in love.

Rosalind and Orlando are the play's most prominent lovers, and through their courtship the play begins its exploration of the problems of loving well. Orlando, for example, loves by the book—that is, in imitation of the conventions employed by the fourteenth-century Italian poet Petrarch, whose love poems to a woman named Laura established one of the paradigmatic love rhetorics of Renaissance culture. Conventionally, the Petrarchan lover worships and idealizes a woman who is inaccessible to him, either because of her rank or because of her cold heart. He burns with passion; he wastes from despair; she does not respond. Orlando, rushing through the forest pinning bad love poems on trees, is a sendup of a Petrarchan lover. Touchstone makes fun of his verses; Rosalind, dressed as a man but pretending to be "Rosalind" in order to cure Orlando of his lovesickness, delights in showing how exaggerated and unrealistic are the Petrarchan lover's claims for the perfection of his mistress and the vastness of his suffering. As she caustically says to him, when he protests that he will die for his passion: "Men have died from time to time, and worms have eaten them, but not for love" (4.1.91–92). She is equally hard on the idealization of women, insisting that real women can be fickle and bad-tempered as easily as they can be goddesses. One way to interpret Orlando and Rosalind's interactions is to see her slowly educating him in a more realistic and egalitarian approach to the relationship of man to woman than that offered by the Petrarchan tradition. Yet the self-mockery, realism, and genuine regard for the other that come to characterize their relationship are hardly in themselves natural behaviors, but ones in which Orlando must be tutored.

Rosalind and Orlando, however, are not the only lovers in the forest. There is also the mooning shepherd, Silvius, who believes no one has ever loved with his intensity, and his proud mistress, Phoebe, who thinks much too well of her own limited charms and throws herself quite inappropriately into the part of the disdainful Petrarchan mistress. As Rosalind informs her: "I must tell you friendly in your ear, / Sell when you can. You are not for all markets" (3.5.60–61). Even Touchstone, ever ready to puncture the romantic ravings of Orlando and Rosalind, Silvius and Phoebe, cannot escape love's call. Functioning as the clown figure often does, to provide a detached commentary on the action around him, Touchstone is nonetheless a participant as well as an observer. His "love" is about as natural—in the sense of urgently physical—and as far removed from Petrarchan idealizations as can be imagined. His intended, Audrey, does not know what "poetical" means, and Touchstone laments that she has such a rudimentary command of language that she often cannot understand what he says to her. And yet, as he confides to Jaques, "As the ox hath his bow, sir, the horse his curb, and the falcon her bells, so man hath his desires" (3.3.65–66)—that is, as each creature has some restraint placed on his movement, so a man's sexual desires constrain him to accommodate himself to a woman, even one like Audrey, and to the marriage yoke. If Orlando and Silvius live too much in the thrall of poetic idealizations, Touchstone and Audrey starkly reveal what love looks like when it is reduced to a matter of pure desire, and all artfulness, all poetry, and all sweet amorous delay are eschewed.

The figure who instigates much of the play's talk about love is Rosalind, one of Shakespeare's liveliest heroines. Her attractiveness stems partly from the fact that she is at once an observer and critic of others and herself a full participant in the whirligig of love. In this, she resembles Touchstone and differs from the melancholy Jaques, who persistently catalogs the follies of others but holds back from full participation in the life around him. (Fittingly, Jaques remains in the forest at the end of the play, when most of the others return to their lives outside the pastoral retreat.) Rosalind is at the center of nearly everything that happens in As You Like It, and the complexity of her role is enhanced by the fact that for much of four acts she dresses like a man and successfully passes for one. In the 1590s, Shakespeare wrote a number of other comedies (Two Gentlemen of Verona, The Merchant of Venice, Twelfth Night) in which women dress as men to protect themselves from danger, to pursue a lover, or temporarily to acquire the prerogatives of the socially dominant gender. Rosalind's is arguably the most complicated of these cases of cross-dressing because she not only passes as a man, but while in her male disguise plays the role of Rosalind in her forest encounters with Orlando. A woman disguised as a man thus makes her own identity into a fiction she performs!

Rosalind's complex cross-dressing has many consequences. For one thing, it makes problematic how natural are the gender distinctions that supposedly separate man from woman. In a literal sense, clothes here make the man—or woman. A doublet and hose and a swaggering demeanor effectively create the illusion of masculinity, and Rosalind uses her disguise to try on the privileges of the supposedly superior sex. Far from a passive object of Petrarchan adoration, she takes charge of her escape from Frederick's court and her encounters with Orlando in the forest. Typically, Renaissance women remained under the control of their fathers and mothers until marriage bequeathed them to the care of a husband. Rosalind's special circumstances—a father banished, an uncle who wants her gone from court—put her in an unusual situation. Her decision to cross-dress further sets her apart. Mobile, loquacious, and bossy, Rosalind confutes the idea that women are by nature passive, silent, and in need of masculine supervision. At the same time, she exhibits certain stereotypically "female" behavior: to Celia she confesses how much she is in love with Orlando, and when he is wounded, she faints when she sees his blood on a cloth. Perhaps the point is that the figure of the cross-dressed Rosalind keeps open the question of what a woman (or a man) "really" is.

To the question of how men and women differ, Renaissance anatomical theory gave some answers dissimilar to those we now take for granted. According to Galen, an ancient Greek anatomist whose work on the body was widely influential in the early modern period, men and woman had the same anatomical structures; women were simply less perfect than men, there having been less heat present when they were conceived. This meant, among other things, that women's genitalia were just like a man's—with the vagina and ovaries corresponding to the penis and scrotum—except that they had not been pushed outside the body as a man's had been. Because by this account male-female difference was less grounded in ideas of absolute bodily difference than is typical today, much emphasis was placed on behavioral differences and on distinctions of dress. Preachers enjoined women to be chaste, silent, and obedient, and forbade them to wear the clothes of the opposite sex. In such a context, female cross-dressing, however playfully undertaken, always threatened to expose the artifice of gender distinctions by showing how easily one sex could assume the clothes and ape the behavior of the other.

The particularities of Rosalind's disguise, moreover, complicate her representation

Typical sixteenth-century anatomy-book illustration of the female organs of generation. *Left:* the vagina and uterus are almost indistinguishable from the male penis and scrotum. *Right:* they have been cut open to reveal a tiny fetus in the uterus. From Fritz Weindler, *Geschichte der Gynäkologisch-anatomischen Abbildung* (1908). (Originally appeared in George Bartisch, *Kunstbuch,* 1575.)

even further. In disguise, Rosalind calls herself Ganymede, a name that had long-standing and unmistakable associations with homoerotic love. In Greek mythology, Ganymede was a beautiful boy whom Jove desired and whom he seized and carried to Mount Olympus to be cupbearer to the gods. A number of early modern paintings, woodcuts, and engravings depict the moment when Jove, in the form of an eagle, sweeps the boy away from earth and into the heavens. In Shakespeare's day, the word "Ganymede" commonly signified a young boy who was the lover of another (usually older) man. Shakespeare could hardly have been unaware of these associations when he had Rosalind choose this name as her alias. Consequently, when the cross-dressed heroine commands Orlando to woo his "Rosalind," he woos a figure who is dressed like a man and who bears a name signifying his status as a homoerotic love object. In performance, what the audience *sees* is one "man" flirting with another, even while the audience *knows* that one of these "men" is a woman. Provocatively, Shakespeare uses Orlando and Rosalind's encounters to overlay a story of male-female desire with traces of another tale of a man's love for a boy.

Long before *As You Like It* was penned, pastoral had been used to depict the beauty of both male friendship and homoerotic love. Edmund Spenser, in the January Eclogue of *The Shepheardes Calendar,* describes the passion of Hobbinol for Colin Cloute, who in turn loves an unresponsive woman named Rosalind. Commenting on this passage, E. K., the anonymous annotator of *The Shepheardes Calendar,* drew on classical precedent to defend pederastic love (love of an older man for a younger boy) as less dangerous than gynerastic love (love of man for woman). Since women were generally considered men's intellectual and moral inferiors, love for a woman was—so the argument went—less likely to be a rational passion than was love for a boy or a man. In the 1580s, Richard Barnfield wrote a pastoral work called *The Affectionate Shepherd,* in which the male speaker celebrates his love for a beautiful young man named Ganymede.

Ganymede being abducted by Jupiter in the form of an eagle. Woodcut by Virgil Solis. From *Metamorphosis Ovidii . . .* (1563).

Shakespeare is therefore not unique in introducing a Ganymede figure into the pastoral landscape, though he does so with a difference. In *As You Like It,* Ganymede is a disguise, a persona assumed and eventually discarded by Rosalind. As with much else in this play, Shakespeare thus has things at least two ways at once. For several acts, Orlando seems to pursue in one person both a boy and a woman, but in the final scene Rosalind reassumes her female clothes and Ganymede disappears, thus ending the play with an emphasis on the culmination of male-female love in marriage. But even this is not quite the whole story. On the Renaissance stage, women's parts were played by boy actors. In the Epilogue, which she speaks, Rosalind calls attention to this fact, making it clear that if Orlando has finally won his Rosalind, the two players who enact this union are a young boy and a man.

In *As You Like It,* the erotic possibilities never seem to stop. The friendship between Rosalind and Celia, for example, is remarkably close. Charles the wrestler says, "Never two ladies loved as they do" (1.1.97). Celia readily gives up her father, her fortune, and her position at the court to follow Rosalind to Ardenne, where the two women in effect set up household together. Although they are yoked in love like Juno's swans, from the beginning Celia is afraid that Rosalind does not love her as much as she loves Rosalind (1.2.6–11). Quite quickly, Rosalind's primary interest does become her pursuit of Orlando. Yet in the midst of her love games with him, Rosalind also dallies with the ambitious and amorous Phoebe, who has taken the disguised Rosalind for a man. Overtly, Rosalind scorns Phoebe and directs her to love Silvius, but she also takes care to tell Phoebe where she lives (3.5.75–76) and encourages her attentions even as she denies them. As with other relationships in the play, it is not altogether clear whom Phoebe really desires: is it the man she thinks she sees or the woman beneath? Though the play eventually deposits Rosalind, Celia, and Phoebe all within Hymen's circle, it does so only after raising the possibility of other erotic conjunctions, including woman's love for woman.

In part, *As You Like It* can play so freely with various erotic possibilities because in the early modern period people were not assumed, as they often are today, to have a fixed sexual identity, to *be,* that is, a lesbian or a heterosexual. Often, one could engage in a range of sexual practices without contradiction. Depending on life stage and social circumstance, a man might have sex with a dependent man, such as a servant, and with a woman, such as his wife. The point is that performing a specific sexual act did not presume—or guarantee—a particular sexual identity. And yet Shakespeare's comedy, like many others, also acknowledges the social weight that the early modern period placed on marriage, the institution through which political alliances were forged, property passed, and lineage established. *As You Like It* both celebrates and pokes fun at the social inevitability of marriage by having Hymen, god of marriage, appear onstage in the last act to preside over a veritable spate of betrothals—four, to be exact. As Jaques suggests (5.4.35–36), it is indeed as if the beasts were proceeding, two by two, into Noah's ark.

Besides yoking individual man to individual woman, marriage in this play also helps to resolve seemingly intractable social problems. For example, Orlando's situation as younger brother is miraculously ameliorated through his marriage to Rosalind. As her husband, he becomes Duke Senior's heir, thus achieving a fortune equal to his gentle nature. Again, the play has things two ways at once. Duke Senior is restored to his dukedom, which confirms the prerogatives of older brothers, but Orlando does not have to suffer permanently the disadvantages of being a younger son. Primogeniture is simultaneously affirmed and circumvented. Moreover, when Oliver reforms, that reformation is sealed by his marriage to Celia, an indication that he now takes part in the communal life of his culture without the willful displays of indifference and selfishness that marked his earlier behavior.

Yet as this comedy celebrates marriage, it also registers a certain resistance to it and persistently maps alternative routings of desire. Rosalind registers that resistance when she complains of how avidly men court women before marriage and how indifferently they treat them afterward: "Men are April when they woo, December when they wed" (4.1.124–25). Marriage, she implies, can dull a man's desire and lessen a woman's emotional power over him. It also, of course, made women legally subject to their husbands. When Rosalind doffs her man's disguise to become a wife, she relinquishes many kinds of freedom. But the play also records *men's* resistance to marriage, partly through its many cuckold jokes. These jokes acknowledge that marriage may not fully circumscribe or satisfy a woman's sexual desires, that a man's control of his wife's sexuality may be more fiction than fact, leaving him vulnerable to public mockery. As the Duke's men sing as they bring home a slaughtered deer:

> Take thou no scorn to wear the horn;
> It was a crest ere thou wast born.
> Thy father's father wore it,
> And thy father bore it.

> (4.2.14–17)

The song transforms cuckold anxiety into entertainment, but it cannot erase that anxiety.

Consider, as well, the strange moment when Orlando comes across his brother Oliver lying asleep under an old oak. As Oliver sleeps, a female snake approaches his open mouth, threatening his life. Though the snake is frightened off, it is immediately replaced in this fantastic, dreamlike scenario by a hungry female lion with whom Orlando fights in order to save his brother's life (4.3.97–131). Twice, danger is represented in female form, and the reconciliation of the two brothers occurs only when Orlando spills his blood to beat back these threats. In *As You Like It,* as marriage is both desired and feared, so the feminine is represented as both an attraction and a source of danger.

In pastoral, little is immune from critique; the world men and women have made is an imperfect world. Yet the remarkable thing about *As You Like It* is that critique does not cancel affirmation. The play anatomizes court life and exposes its treachery, but many leave Ardenne to journey back to the court when Frederick has repented and the benevolent Duke Senior has returned to power. The play likewise dissects the problems of marriage, yet many marry at the end. Pastoral has a utopian as well as a critical dimension. The green world of shepherds holds traces of the simplicity of a lost Golden Age, and a sojourn in that world can prompt transformations in the everyday world to which the sojourners return. *As You Like It* is to a remarkable degree open to the infinite malleability of human beings and their social practices. A duke can become a forest outlaw and embrace the change; a tyrannical usurper can be touched by the words of a holy man, relinquish his power, and retire from the world. What men and women have marred, they may also mend.

It is with the heroine, however, that *As You Like It* offers its richest dramatization of a figure who plays endlessly with the limits and possibilities of her circumstances. This is true even in the Epilogue, when Rosalind, now in woman's clothing, steps forward to address the audience and solicit their applause. The persona of Ganymede cast aside, the heroine appears as the woman she "really is." But it is precisely at this moment of closure that she breaks the dramatic frame to remind the audience of *another* reality: that "she" is played by a "he." Dressed like a woman but declaring she is not, this unpredictable figure, this he/she, continues to the end to defy the fixed identities and the exclusionary choices of the everyday world, offering instead a world of multiple possibilities and transformable identities, a world as perhaps we might come to like it.

JEAN E. HOWARD

TEXTUAL NOTE

As You Like It was probably written between 1598 and 1600. It was entered in the Stationers' Register on August 4, 1600, but no edition followed this entry. Francis Meres, one of Shakespeare's contemporaries, in September of 1598 published a list of the Shakespeare plays known to him. It did not include *As You Like It,* suggesting that the play was performed sometime after that date but prior to its entry in the Stationers' Register. Two topical references suggest 1599 as the likely time of composition. At one point, Jaques, the play's cynical satirist, opines, "All the world's a stage" (2.7.138), perhaps an allusion to the motto *Totus mundus agit histrionem* (All the world plays the actor), of the Globe Theater, to which Shakespeare's company moved in the summer of 1599. Elsewhere, Touchstone, the play's clown, refers to the time "since the little wit that fools have was silenced" (1.2.74–75), a possible reference to the banning and burning of satirical books in June of 1599 by order of the Bishop of London.

The play was first published in the First Folio of 1623 (F) either from a promptbook or, less probably, from a literary transcript of either the promptbook or Shakespeare's foul papers. The present edition follows the act and scene divisions of F.

SELECTED BIBLIOGRAPHY

Colie, Rosalie L. "Perspectives on Pastoral: Romance, Comic and Tragic." *Shakespeare's Living Art*. Princeton: Princeton University Press, 1974. 243–83. Analyzes the many pastoral conventions found in *As You Like It* and how they contribute to the play's perspectivism—that is, its juxtaposition of competing viewpoints.

Crane, Mary. "Theatrical Practice and the Ideologies of Status in *As You Like It*." *Shakespeare's Brain: Reading with Cognitive Theory*. Princeton: Princeton University Press, 2001. 67–93. Examines how, through its emphasis on words like *villain* and *clown, As You Like It* explores possibilities for upward and downward mobility in the world of the play and in the social world at large, including the theatrical community of which Shakespeare was a part.

Elam, Keir. "As They Did in the Golden World: Romantic Rapture and Semantic Rupture in *As You Like It*." *Reading the Renaissance: Culture, Poetics, and Drama*. Ed. Jonathan Hart. New York: Garland, 1996. 163–76. Focuses on the way Shakespeare rewrites pastoral in *As You Like It* to banish nostalgia and linguistic earnestness in favor of the magical, forward-looking affirmations of romance.

Erickson, Peter. "Sexual Politics and Social Structure in *As You Like It*." *Patriarchal Structures in Shakespeare's Drama*. Berkeley: University of California Press, 1985. 15–38. Argues that the play advocates a benevolent patriarchy that ultimately subordinates women to men while allowing men to assume nurturing functions.

Howard, Jean E. "Power and Eros: Crossdressing in Dramatic Representation and Theatrical Practice." *The Stage and Social Struggle in Early Modern England*. London: Routledge, 1994. 93–128. Examines cross-dressing as a convention through which *As You Like It* and other comedies explore the politics of early modern gender relations and the fluidity of sexual desire.

Marshall, Cynthia. "The Doubled Jaques and Constructions of Negation in *As You Like It*." *Shakespeare Quarterly* 49 (1998): 375–92. Argues that in *As You Like It* the repression of melancholia, registered as a trace in the figure of Jaques, allows for the release of the high spirits and verbal fireworks proper to comedy.

Montrose, Louis. " 'The Place of a Brother' in *As You Like It*: Social Process and Comic Form." *Shakespeare Quarterly* 32 (1981): 28–54. Argues that in *As You Like It* the process of comedy repairs the negative consequences of primogeniture for younger sons as Orlando finds a surrogate father in Duke Senior and a fortune through marriage.

Neely, Carol Thomas. "Destabilizing Lovesickness, Gender, and Sexuality: *Twelfth Night* and *As You Like It*." *Distracted Subjects: Madness and Gender in Shakespeare and Early Modern Culture*. Ithaca, N.Y.: Cornell University Press, 2004. 99–135. Details the increasingly strong link between lovesickness and women in the Renaissance and compares its representation in *Twelfth Night* and *As You Like It*.

Traub, Valerie. "The Homoerotics of Shakespearean Comedy." *Desire and Anxiety: Circulations of Sexuality in Shakespearean Drama*. London: Routledge, 1992. 117–44. Explores the role of the boy actor in the production and circulation of homoerotic desire and argues that *As You Like It* playfully refuses the binary distinction between the heteroerotic and the homoerotic.

Wilson, Richard. "Like the Old Robin Hood: *As You Like It* and the Enclosure Riots." *Will Power: Essays on Shakespearean Authority*. London: Harvester Wheatsheaf, 1993. 63–82. Connects *As You Like It* to the social disturbances and food shortages of the 1590s but argues that the play pulls back from lodging a radical critique of social injustice.

FILMS

As You Like It. 1936. Dir. Paul Czinner. UK. 96 min. This black-and-white film features Laurence Olivier, in his first Shakespeare performance on film, as the dashing but moody Orlando with Elisabeth Bergner as an insipid Rosalind. Charming woodland scenes in a significantly cut production.

As You Like It. 1978. Dir. Basil Coleman. UK. 150 min. Traditional BBC-TV production with lively performances by Helen Mirren as Rosalind, Angharad Rees as Celia, and Victoria Plucknett as Phoebe. Playing Jaques, Richard Pasco brings poignant understatement to the famous "seven ages of man" speech.

As You Like It. 2006. Dir. Kenneth Branagh. UK. 127 min. In this gorgeous production, the action is relocated from medieval France to nineteenth-century Japan. With Bryce Dallas Howard (Rosalind), David Oyelowo (Orlando), Rowola Garai (Celia), Brian Blessed (Duke Senior and Duke Frederick), and Alfred Molina (Touchstone).

As You Like It

THE PERSONS OF THE PLAY

DUKE SENIOR, living in banishment
ROSALIND, his daughter, later disguised as Ganymede
AMIENS ⎱ Lords attending on him
JAQUES ⎰
TWO PAGES
DUKE FREDERICK
CELIA, his daughter, later disguised as Aliena
LE BEAU, a courtier attending on him
CHARLES, Duke Frederick's wrestler
TOUCHSTONE, a clown
OLIVER, eldest son of Sir Rowland de Bois
JAQUES ⎱ his younger brothers
ORLANDO ⎰
ADAM, a former servant of Sir Rowland
DENIS, Oliver's servant
SIR OLIVER MARTEXT, a country clergyman
CORIN, an old shepherd
SILVIUS, a young shepherd, in love with Phoebe
PHOEBE, a shepherdess
WILLIAM, a countryman, in love with Audrey
AUDREY, a goatherd, betrothed to Touchstone
HYMEN, god of marriage
Lords, pages, and other attendants

1.1

Enter ORLANDO *and* ADAM

ORLANDO As I remember, Adam, it was upon this fashion bequeathed me by will but poor° a thousand crowns,[1] and, as thou sayst, charged° my brother on his blessing[2] to breed me well—and there begins my sadness. My brother Jaques he
5 keeps at school,° and report speaks goldenly of his profit. For my part, he keeps me rustically at home—or, to speak more properly, stays° me here at home unkept;° for call you that keeping for a gentleman of my birth, that differs not from the stalling of an ox? His horses are bred better, for besides that
10 they are fair with° their feeding, they are taught their manège,[3] and to that end riders dearly° hired. But I, his brother, gain nothing under him but growth, for the which his animals on his dunghills are as much bound to him as I. Besides this nothing that he so plentifully gives me, the something that nature
15 gave me his countenance° seems to take from me. He lets me feed with his hinds,° bars me[4] the place of a brother, and as much as in him lies, mines my gentility with my education.[5]

only
he (my father) charged

university

detains / uncared for

handsome because of
expensively

conduct
farmworkers

1.1 Location: The orchard of Oliver's house, in the vicinity of Duke Frederick's court in France.
1. Equivalent to about 250 English pounds. Orlando's inheritance is worth twice as much as Adam's life savings (see 2.3.39).
2. On pain of losing his blessing.
3. Paces and actions of a trained horse.
4. Excludes me from.
5. Undermines my gentility by my (poor) education.

This is it, Adam, that grieves me; and the spirit of my father,
which I think is within me, begins to mutiny against this servi-
20 tude. I will no longer endure it, though yet I know no wise
remedy how to avoid it.

    Enter OLIVER

ADAM Yonder comes my master, your brother.

ORLANDO Go apart, Adam, and thou shalt hear how he will
shake me up.°   *insult me*

    [ADAM *stands aside*]

25 OLIVER Now, sir, what make you° here?   *are you doing*

ORLANDO Nothing. I am not taught to make anything.

OLIVER What mar you then, sir?

ORLANDO Marry,[6] sir, I am helping you to mar that which God
made, a poor unworthy brother of yours, with idleness.

30 OLIVER Marry, sir, be better employed, and be nought° awhile.   *get lost*

ORLANDO Shall I keep your hogs, and eat husks with them?
What prodigal portion have I spent, that I should come to such
penury?[7]

OLIVER Know you where you are, sir?

35 ORLANDO O sir, very well; here in your orchard.

OLIVER Know you before whom, sir?

ORLANDO Ay, better than him I am before knows me. I know
you are my eldest brother, and in the gentle condition of blood
you should so know me.[8] The courtesy of nations[9] allows you
40 my better, in that you are the first-born; but the same tradition
takes not away my blood, were there twenty brothers betwixt
us. I have as much of my father in me as you, albeit I confess
your coming before me is nearer to his reverence.[1]

OLIVER [*assailing him*] What, boy!

45 ORLANDO [*seizing him by the throat*] Come, come, elder
brother, you are too young° in this.   *inexperienced*

OLIVER Wilt thou lay hands on me, villain?°   *lowborn man; scoundrel*

ORLANDO I am no villein.° I am the youngest son of Sir Rowland *serf (pun on "villain")*
de Bois. He was my father, and he is thrice a villain that says
50 such a father begot villeins. Wert thou not my brother, I would
not take this hand from thy throat till this other had pulled out
thy tongue for saying so. Thou hast railed on° thyself.   *abused*

ADAM [*coming forward*] Sweet masters, be patient. For your
father's remembrance, be at accord.

55 OLIVER [*to* ORLANDO] Let me go, I say.

ORLANDO I will not till I please. You shall hear me. My father
charged you in his will to give me good education. You have
trained me like a peasant, obscuring and hiding from me all
gentleman-like qualities.° The spirit of my father grows strong *accomplishments*
60 in me, and I will no longer endure it. Therefore allow me such
exercises° as may become a gentleman, or give me the poor *pursuits*
allottery° my father left me by testament. With that I will go *portion*
buy my fortunes.

OLIVER And what wilt thou do—beg when that is spent? Well,

---

6. An oath, derived from the name of the Virgin Mary.
7. Alluding to the biblical parable of the prodigal son
(Luke 15:11–32), who after squandering his share of
his father's fortune envied the swine he tended and
wished to eat their fodder.
8. And because of the noble blood that we share, you

should acknowledge me as a brother.
9. Customs of civil society. Referring to the English
system of primogeniture, which allowed for the transmission of all property to the eldest son.
1. Your being older than I makes you more worthy of
the respect that he commanded.

65   sir, get you in. I will not long be troubled with you. You shall
       have some part of your will. I pray you, leave me.

ORLANDO   I will no further offend you than becomes me for my
       good.

OLIVER [*to* ADAM]   Get you with him, you old dog.

70 ADAM   Is 'old dog' my reward? Most true, I have lost my teeth in
       your service. God be with my old master, he would not have
       spoke such a word.   *Exeunt* ORLANDO [*and*] ADAM

OLIVER   Is it even so? Begin you to grow upon me?[2] I will physic°   *give medicine to*
       your rankness,[3] and yet give no thousand crowns neither.

75   Holla, Denis!

               Enter DENIS

DENIS   Calls your worship?

OLIVER   Was not Charles, the Duke's wrestler, here to speak with
       me?

DENIS   So please you, he is here at the door, and importunes
80   access to you.

OLIVER   Call him in.   [*Exit* DENIS]
       'Twill be a good way. And tomorrow the wrestling is.

               Enter CHARLES

CHARLES   Good morrow to your worship.

OLIVER   Good Monsieur Charles—what's the new news at the
85   new court?

CHARLES   There's no news at the court, sir, but the old news: that
       is, the old Duke is banished by his younger brother, the new
       Duke, and three or four loving lords have put themselves into
       voluntary exile with him, whose lands and revenues enrich the
90   new Duke; therefore he gives them good leave° to wander.   *full permission*

OLIVER   Can you tell if Rosalind, the Duke's daughter, be ban-
       ished with her father?

CHARLES   O no; for the Duke's daughter her cousin so loves her,
       being ever from their cradles bred° together, that she would   *brought up*
95   have followed her exile, or have died to stay behind her. She is
       at the court, and no less beloved of her uncle than his own
       daughter; and never two ladies loved as they do.

OLIVER   Where will the old Duke live?

CHARLES   They say he is already in the forest of Ardenne,[4] and a
100   many merry men with him; and there they live like the old
       Robin Hood[5] of England. They say many young gentlemen
       flock to him every day, and fleet° the time carelessly,° as they   *pass / without worries*
       did in the golden world.[6]

OLIVER   What, you wrestle tomorrow before the new Duke?

105 CHARLES   Marry do I, sir, and I came to acquaint you with a
       matter. I am given, sir, secretly to understand that your younger
       brother, Orlando, hath a disposition to come in disguised
       against me to try a fall.° Tomorrow, sir, I wrestle for my credit,°   *bout / reputation*
       and he that escapes me without some broken limb, shall acquit
110   him well. Your brother is but young and tender, and for your
       love I would be loath to foil° him, as I must for my own honour   *defeat*

---

2. To grow so big you crowd upon me.
3. Overgrown vegetation; diseased blood.
4. The name of an ancient forest encompassing parts
of France, Belgium, and Luxembourg. F uses the anglicized spelling "Arden," evoking the English forest of
Arden near Shakespeare's birthplace in Warwickshire.
5. A legendary English outlaw, associated with
Nottingham's Sherwood Forest, who robbed from the
rich and gave his plunder to the poor.
6. Alluding to the classical myth of an earlier world of
perpetual spring, abundance, and ease from which
humankind had degenerated (Ovid, *Metamorphoses* 1).
This golden world was often identified with a pastoral life.

if he come in. Therefore out of my love to you I came hither
to acquaint you withal,° that either you might stay° him from
his intendment,° or brook° such disgrace well as he shall run

— with this / keep
intent / endure

115   into, in that it is a thing of his own search,° and altogether
against my will.

— seeking

OLIVER   Charles, I thank thee for thy love to me, which thou
shalt find I will most kindly requite. I had myself notice of my
brother's purpose herein, and have by underhand° means

120   laboured to dissuade him from it; but he is resolute. I'll tell

— subtle

thee, Charles, it is the stubbornest young fellow of France, full
of ambition, an envious emulator of every man's good parts,° a
secret and villainous contriver against me his natural brother.

— qualities

Therefore use thy discretion. I had as lief° thou didst break his

— willingly

125   neck as his finger. And thou wert best look to't; for if thou dost
him any slight disgrace, or if he do not mightily grace° himself

— win credit for

on thee, he will practise° against thee by poison, entrap thee by

— plot

some treacherous device, and never leave thee till he hath ta'en
thy life by some indirect means or other. For I assure thee—

130   and almost with tears I speak it—there is not one so young and
so villainous this day living. I speak but brotherly[7] of him, but
should I anatomize° him to thee as he is, I must blush and

— dissect; fully open

weep, and thou must look pale and wonder.
CHARLES   I am heartily glad I came hither to you. If he come

135   tomorrow I'll give him his payment. If ever he go alone° again,

— walk without aid

I'll never wrestle for prize more. And so God keep your wor-
ship.
OLIVER   Farewell, good Charles.   *Exit* [CHARLES]
Now will I stir this gamester.° I hope I shall see an end of him,

— (Orlando)

140   for my soul—yet I know not why—hates nothing more than
he. Yet he's gentle;° never schooled, and yet learned; full of

— of noble character

noble device;° of all sorts enchantingly beloved;[8] and, indeed,

— purposes

so much in the heart of the world, and especially of my own
people, who best know him, that I am altogether misprized.°

— despised

145   But it shall not be so long. This wrestler shall clear all.° Noth-

— fix everything

ing remains but that I kindle° the boy thither,° which now I'll

— urge / (to the court)

go about.   *Exit*

1.2

Enter ROSALIND *and* CELIA
CELIA   I pray thee Rosalind, sweet my coz,° be merry.

— cousin

ROSALIND   Dear Celia, I show more mirth than I am mistress of;
and would you yet I were merrier? Unless you could teach me
to forget a banished father you must not learn° me how to

— teach

5   remember any extraordinary pleasure.
CELIA   Herein I see thou lovest me not with the full weight that
I love thee. If my uncle, thy banished father, had banished thy
uncle, the Duke my father, so° thou hadst been still with me I

— provided

could have taught my love to take thy father for mine. So
10   wouldst thou, if the truth of thy love to me were so righteously
tempered° as mine is to thee.

— properly constituted

ROSALIND   Well, I will forget the condition of my estate° to

— circumstances

rejoice in yours.

7. In a manner proper to a brother.   1.2 Location: The grounds of Duke Frederick's court.
8. Beloved of all ranks as if by enchantment.

CELIA   You know my father hath no child but I, nor none is like
15   to have. And truly, when he dies thou shalt be his heir; for what
        he hath taken away from thy father perforce,° I will render thee   °by force
        again in affection. By mine honour I will, and when I break
        that oath, let me turn monster. Therefore, my sweet Rose, my
        dear Rose, be merry.
20 ROSALIND   From henceforth I will, coz, and devise sports.° Let   °entertainments
        me see, what think you of falling in love?
    CELIA   Marry, I prithee do, to make sport withal;° but love no   °to provide amusement
        man in good earnest, nor no further in sport neither than with
        safety of a pure blush thou mayst in honour come off again.[1]
25 ROSALIND   What shall be our sport, then?
    CELIA   Let us sit and mock the good housewife Fortune[2] from
        her wheel, that her gifts may henceforth be bestowed equally.
    ROSALIND   I would we could do so, for her benefits are mightily
        misplaced; and the bountiful blind woman° doth most mistake   °(Fortune)
30   in her gifts to women.
    CELIA   'Tis true; for those that she makes fair she scarce makes
        honest,° and those that she makes honest she makes very ill-   °chaste
        favouredly.°   °ugly
    ROSALIND   Nay, now thou goest from Fortune's office° to   °function
35   Nature's. Fortune reigns in° gifts of the world, not in the linea-   °presides over
        ments of nature.°   °one's natural features
                    Enter [TOUCHSTONE[3] the] clown
    CELIA   No. When Nature hath made a fair creature, may she not
        by Fortune fall into the fire? Though Nature hath given us wit
        to flout at Fortune, hath not Fortune sent in this fool to cut off
40   the argument?
    ROSALIND   Indeed, there is Fortune too hard for Nature, when
        Fortune makes Nature's natural° the cutter-off of Nature's wit.   °fool
    CELIA   Peradventure° this is not Fortune's work, neither, but   °Perhaps
        Nature's, who perceiveth our natural wits too dull to reason of
45   such goddesses, and hath sent this natural for our whetstone;°   °stone to sharpen tools
        for always the dullness of the fool is the whetstone of the wits.
        How now, wit: whither wander you?[4]
    TOUCHSTONE   Mistress, you must come away to your father.
    CELIA   Were you made the messenger?
50 TOUCHSTONE   No, by mine honour, but I was bid to come for
        you.
    ROSALIND   Where learned you that oath, fool?
    TOUCHSTONE   Of a certain knight that swore 'by his honour' they
        were good pancakes, and swore 'by his honour' the mustard
55   was naught.° Now I'll stand to it° the pancakes were naught and   °worthless / affirm
        the mustard was good, and yet was not the knight forsworn.°   °perjured
    CELIA   How prove you that in the great heap of your knowledge?
    ROSALIND   Ay, marry, now unmuzzle your wisdom.
    TOUCHSTONE   Stand you both forth now. Stroke your chins, and
60   swear by your beards that I am a knave.
    CELIA   By our beards—if we had them—thou art.

---

1. Than, with the protection afforded by your innocence ("pure blush"), you may honorably escape
("come off again").
2. Referring to the blind goddess of classical mythology
who directed human destiny with the movements of her
wheel, here likened to the mistress of a household with
a spinning wheel.
3. A touchstone was a black mineral used to test the
purity of gold and silver. Touchstone, the fool, tests the
wit of those he encounters.
4. Alluding to the catchphrase "wandering wits."

TOUCHSTONE   By my knavery—if I had it—then I were; but if
you swear by that that is not, you are not forsworn. No more
was this knight, swearing by his honour, for he never had any;
65   or if he had, he had sworn it away before ever he saw those
pancakes or that mustard.

CELIA   Prithee, who is't that thou meanest?

TOUCHSTONE   One that old Frederick, your father, loves.

CELIA[5]   My father's love is enough to honour him. Enough,
70   speak no more of him; you'll be whipped for taxation° one of   *slander*
these days.

TOUCHSTONE   The more pity that fools may not speak wisely
what wise men do foolishly.

CELIA   By my troth, thou sayst true; for since the little wit that
75   fools have was silenced,[6] the little foolery that wise men have
makes a great show. Here comes Monsieur Le Beau.

Enter LE BEAU

ROSALIND   With his mouth full of news.

CELIA   Which he will put on° us as pigeons feed their young.   *force upon*

ROSALIND   Then shall we be news-crammed.[7]

80   CELIA   All the better: we shall be the more marketable. *Bonjour*,°   *Good day*
Monsieur Le Beau, what's the news?

LE BEAU   Fair princess, you have lost much good sport.

CELIA   Sport? Of what colour?°   *kind*

LE BEAU   What colour, madam? How shall I answer you?

85   ROSALIND   As wit and fortune will.°   *desire*

TOUCHSTONE   Or as the destinies decrees.

CELIA   Well said. That was laid on with a trowel.[8]

TOUCHSTONE   Nay, if I keep not my rank[9]—

ROSALIND   Thou losest thy old smell.

90   LE BEAU   You amaze° me, ladies. I would have told you of good   *confuse*
wrestling, which you have lost the sight of.

ROSALIND   Yet tell us the manner of the wrestling.

LE BEAU   I will tell you the beginning, and if it please your lady-
ships you may see the end, for the best is yet to do,° and here,   *to come*
95   where you are, they are coming to perform it.

CELIA   Well, the beginning that is dead and buried.

LE BEAU   There comes an old man and his three sons—

CELIA   I could match this beginning with an old tale.[1]

LE BEAU   Three proper° young men, of excellent growth and   *handsome*
100   presence.

ROSALIND   With bills° on their necks: 'Be it known unto all men   *proclamations*
by these presents'[2]—

LE BEAU   The eldest of the three wrestled with Charles, the
Duke's wrestler, which Charles in a moment threw him, and
105   broke three of his ribs, that there is little hope of life in him.
So he served the second, and so the third. Yonder they lie, the

---

5. F attributes this speech to Rosalind, but most editors
assign it to Celia on the grounds that she asked the
question to which Touchstone has just responded. It is
unlikely that Rosalind would insert herself here or insist
on the preeminence of her father's love over Frederick's.
6. This is a possible allusion to the Bishop of London's
order for the burning of satirical books in June 1599.
7. Forced to digest news, with a pun on "mews" as
meaning the cages in which pigeons were kept before
being fattened, or "crammed," for the table.

8. Bluntly; excessively. With a reference to a builder's
heavy application of mortar.
9. My status (as a jester). Rosalind then puns on the
meaning of "rank" as "foul smelling."
1. *Old tale:* Celia suggests that the motif of a father and
his three sons is the starting point for many familiar
folktales.
2. That is, by these legal documents. A legal phrase
that appears at the start of formal documents, with a
pun on "presence."

poor old man their father making such pitiful dole° over them   *mourning*
that all the beholders take his part with weeping.

ROSALIND   Alas!

110 TOUCHSTONE   But what is the sport, monsieur, that the ladies
have lost?

LE BEAU   Why, this that I speak of.

TOUCHSTONE   Thus men may grow wiser every day. It is the first
time that ever I heard breaking of ribs was sport for ladies.

115 CELIA   Or I, I promise thee.

ROSALIND   But is there any else° longs to see this broken music³   *anyone else who*
in his sides? Is there yet another dotes upon rib-breaking? Shall
we see this wrestling, cousin?

LE BEAU   You must if you stay here, for here is the place
120 appointed for the wrestling, and they are ready to perform it.

CELIA   Yonder sure they are coming. Let us now stay and see it.

*Flourish.*⁴ *Enter* DUKE [FREDERICK], *Lords,* ORLANDO,
CHARLES, *and attendants*

DUKE FREDERICK   Come on. Since the youth will not be
entreated,° his own peril on his forwardness.⁵   *persuaded (to desist)*

ROSALIND   Is yonder the man?

125 LE BEAU   Even he, madam.

CELIA   Alas, he is too young. Yet he looks successfully.°   *as if he would do well*

DUKE FREDERICK   How now, daughter and cousin;⁶ are you
crept hither to see the wrestling?

ROSALIND   Ay, my liege, so please you give us leave.

130 DUKE FREDERICK   You will take little delight in it, I can tell you,
there is such odds° in the man. In pity of the challenger's youth   *superiority*
I would fain° dissuade him, but he will not be entreated. Speak   *willingly*
to him, ladies; see if you can move him.

CELIA   Call him hither, good Monsieur Le Beau.

135 DUKE FREDERICK   Do so. I'll not be by.

[*He stands aside*]

LE BEAU   [*to* ORLANDO]   Monsieur the challenger, the Princess
calls for you.

ORLANDO   I attend them with all respect and duty.

ROSALIND   Young man, have you challenged Charles the wres-
140 tler?

ORLANDO   No, fair Princess. He is the general challenger; I come
but in as others do, to try with him the strength of my youth.

CELIA   Young gentleman, your spirits are too bold for your years.
You have seen cruel proof of this man's strength. If you saw
145 yourself with your eyes, or knew yourself with your judgement,⁷
the fear° of your adventure would counsel you to a more equal   *danger*
enterprise. We pray you for your own sake to embrace your
own safety and give over this attempt.

ROSALIND   Do, young sir. Your reputation shall not therefore be
150 misprized.° We will make it our suit to the Duke that the wres-   *undervalued*
tling might not go forward.

ORLANDO   I beseech you, punish me not with your hard
thoughts,° wherein I confess me much guilty to deny so fair   *displeasure*

---

3. Literally, a musical composition for a variety of
instruments; here referring to the labored breathing
caused by the broken ribs.
4. The sounding of horns or trumpets to signal the
arrival of an important person.

5. *his own . . . forwardness:* let the danger he encounters be blamed on his own rashness.
6. *cousin:* a term used to signify many kinship relations.
7. If you used your discernment and judgment upon
yourself.

and excellent ladies anything. But let your fair eyes and gentle
155   wishes go with me to my trial, wherein if I be foiled,° there is   *defeated*
but one shamed that was never gracious,° if killed, but one   *in favor*
dead that is willing to be so. I shall do my friends no wrong, for
I have none to lament me; the world no injury, for in it I have
nothing. Only in the world I fill up a place which may be better
160   supplied when I have made it empty.

ROSALIND   The little strength that I have, I would it were with
you.

CELIA   And mine, to eke out hers.

ROSALIND   Fare you well. Pray heaven I be deceived in you.

165   CELIA   Your heart's desires be with you.

CHARLES   Come, where is this young gallant that is so desirous
to lie with his mother earth?[8]

ORLANDO   Ready, sir; but his will° hath in it a more modest   *(sexual) desire*
working.°   *undertaking*

170   DUKE FREDERICK   You shall try but one fall.

CHARLES   No, I warrant your grace you shall not entreat him to
a second that have so mightily persuaded him from a first.

ORLANDO   You mean to mock me after; you should not have
mocked me before. But come your ways.°   *let's begin*

175   ROSALIND [*to* ORLANDO]   Now Hercules be thy speed,[9] young
man!

CELIA   I would I were invisible, to catch the strong fellow by the
leg.

[CHARLES *and* ORLANDO] *wrestle*

ROSALIND   O excellent young man!

180   CELIA   If I had a thunderbolt in mine eye, I can tell who should
down.

[ORLANDO *throws* CHARLES.] *Shout*

DUKE FREDERICK   No more, no more.

ORLANDO   Yes, I beseech your grace.
I am not yet well breathed.°   *exercised*

DUKE FREDERICK   How dost thou, Charles?

185   LE BEAU   He cannot speak, my lord.

DUKE FREDERICK   Bear him away.

[*Attendants carry* CHARLES *off*]

What is thy name, young man?

ORLANDO   Orlando, my liege, the youngest son of Sir Rowland
de Bois.

190   DUKE FREDERICK   I would thou hadst been son to some man else.
The world esteemed thy father honourable,
But I did find him still° mine enemy.   *always*
Thou shouldst have better pleased me with this deed
Hadst thou descended from another house.
195   But fare thee well, thou art a gallant youth.
I would thou hadst told me of another father.

Exeunt DUKE [FREDERICK, LE BEAU, TOUCHSTONE,[1]
Lords, and attendants]

CELIA [*to* ROSALIND]   Were I my father, coz, would I do this?

8. To fall to the ground. Echoing biblical descriptions
of the body's return to earth at death and punning on
"lie with" as slang for "have sexual relations with."
9. May Hercules bring you luck. Alluding to a mythological wrestling match in which Hercules, whose name was

synonymous with physical strength, vanquished Antaeus.
1. Although F does not indicate an exit for Touchstone,
many editors assume that he leaves the stage with the
Duke's party and does not reappear until 2.4.

ORLANDO   I am more proud to be Sir Rowland's son,
His youngest son, and would not change that calling°   *title*
200 To be adopted heir to Frederick.
ROSALIND   My father loved Sir Rowland as his soul,
And all the world was of my father's mind.
Had I before known this young man his son
I should have given him tears unto° entreaties   *as well as*
Ere he should thus have ventured.
205 CELIA   Gentle° cousin,   *Noble; kind*
Let us go thank him, and encourage him.
My father's rough and envious° disposition   *spiteful*
Sticks° me at heart.—Sir, you have well deserved.   *Stabs*
If you do keep your promises in love
210 But justly,° as you have exceeded all promise,   *to the same degree*
Your mistress shall be happy.
ROSALIND [*giving him a chain from her neck*]   Gentleman,
Wear this for me—one out of suits° with fortune,   *favor*
That could° give more but that her hand lacks means.   *would*
Shall we go, coz?
CELIA   Ay. Fare you well, fair gentleman.
[ROSALIND *and* CELIA *turn to go*]
215 ORLANDO [*aside*]   Can I not say 'I thank you'? My better parts
Are all thrown down, and that which here stands up
Is but a quintain,[2] a mere lifeless block.
ROSALIND [*to* CELIA]   He calls us back. My pride fell with my fortunes,
I'll ask him what he would.—Did you call, sir?
220 Sir, you have wrestled well, and overthrown
More than your enemies.
CELIA   Will you go, coz?
ROSALIND   Have with you.° [*To* ORLANDO] Fare you well.   *I'll go with you*
Exeunt [ROSALIND *and* CELIA][3]
ORLANDO   What passion hangs these weights upon my tongue?
225 I cannot speak to her, yet she urged conference.°   *conversation*
Enter LE BEAU
O poor Orlando! Thou art overthrown.
Or° Charles or something weaker masters thee.   *Either*
LE BEAU   Good sir, I do in friendship counsel you
To leave this place. Albeit you have deserved
230 High commendation, true applause, and love,
Yet such is now the Duke's condition°   *state of mind*
That he misconsters° all that you have done.   *misconstrues*
The Duke is humorous.[4] What he is indeed
More suits you to conceive than I to speak of.
235 ORLANDO   I thank you, sir. And pray you tell me this,
Which of the two was daughter of the Duke
That here was at the wrestling?
LE BEAU   Neither his daughter, if we judge by manners—
But yet indeed the shorter[5] is his daughter.

---

2. A wooden post used as a target in jousts and other aristocratic sports. Orlando suggests that his reason and speech (his "better parts") have been "thrown down," or defeated, in his encounter with Rosalind, leaving him standing speechless, like a post.
3. F marks only a single exit for Rosalind here, but Celia almost certainly accompanies her offstage.
4. Moody. The term derives from Renaissance medical

theory, which held that good mental and physical health depended on the proper balance of four bodily fluids, or humors.
5. F reads "taller," but see 1.3.109, where Rosalind declares that she is "more than common tall" and will therefore disguise herself as a man. Shakespeare may not have been consistent in determining who was to be the taller woman.

240 The other is daughter to the banished Duke,
And here detained by her usurping uncle
To keep his daughter company, whose loves
Are dearer than the natural bond of sisters.
But I can tell you that of late this Duke
245 Hath ta'en displeasure 'gainst his gentle niece,
Grounded upon no other argument°   *reason*
But that the people praise her for her virtues
And pity her for her good father's sake.
And, on my life, his malice 'gainst the lady
250 Will suddenly break forth. Sir, fare you well.
Hereafter, in a better world than this,
I shall desire more love and knowledge of you.
ORLANDO   I rest much bounden° to you. Fare you well.   *obliged*
[*Exit* LE BEAU]
Thus must I from the smoke into the smother,⁶
255 From tyrant Duke unto a tyrant brother.—
But heavenly Rosalind!   *Exit*

1.3

Enter CELIA *and* ROSALIND
CELIA   Why cousin, why Rosalind—Cupid have mercy,¹ not a
   word?
ROSALIND   Not one to throw at a dog.
CELIA   No, thy words are too precious to be cast away upon curs.
5   Throw some of them at me. Come, lame me with reasons.²
ROSALIND   Then there were two cousins laid up, when the one
   should be lamed with reasons and the other mad without any.
CELIA   But is all this for your father?
ROSALIND   No, some of it is for my child's father.³ O how full of
10   briers is this working-day world!
CELIA   They are but burs, cousin, thrown upon thee in holiday
   foolery. If we walk not in the trodden paths our very petticoats
   will catch them.
ROSALIND   I could shake them off my coat. These burs are in my
15   heart.
CELIA   Hem⁴ them away.
ROSALIND   I would try, if I could cry 'hem' and have him.
CELIA   Come, come, wrestle with thy affections.
ROSALIND   O, they take the part of a better wrestler than myself.
20 CELIA   O, a good wish upon you!° You will try in time, in despite   *good luck to you*
   of a fall.⁵ But turning these jests out of service,° let us talk in   *dismissing these jokes*
   good earnest. Is it possible on such a sudden you should fall
   into so strong a liking with old Sir Rowland's youngest son?
ROSALIND   The Duke my father loved his father dearly.
25 CELIA   Doth it therefore ensue that you should love his son
   dearly? By this kind of chase° I should hate him, for my father   *logic*
   hated his father dearly; yet I hate not Orlando.
ROSALIND   No, faith, hate him not, for my sake.

---

6. Out of the frying pan into the fire. *smother:* thick,
suffocating smoke.
1.3 Location: Duke Frederick's court.
1. May Cupid (god of love) be compassionate.
2. Throw so many reasons (for your silence) at me that
if they were stones, I would be made lame.

3. That is, for one who will be father to my child.
4. Cough, with a pun on "bur" (line 14) as meaning
"something that sticks in your throat."
5. You are destined to wrestle with him eventually even
though it will cause you to fall, with a pun on "fall" as
"lapse from chastity."

CELIA   Why should I not? Doth he not deserve well?

Enter DUKE [FREDERICK], *with Lords*

30   ROSALIND   Let me love him for that, and do you love him
because I do. Look, here comes the Duke.

CELIA   With his eyes full of anger.

DUKE FREDERICK [*to* ROSALIND]   Mistress, dispatch you with your safest haste,[6]
And get you from our court.

35   ROSALIND   Me, uncle?

DUKE FREDERICK   You, cousin.
Within these ten days if that thou beest found
So near our public court as twenty miles,
Thou diest for it.

ROSALIND   I do beseech your grace

40   Let me the knowledge of my fault bear with me.
If with myself I hold intelligence,°   *I communicate*
Or have acquaintance with mine own desires,
If that I do not dream, or be not frantic°—   *insane*
As I do trust I am not—then, dear uncle,

45   Never so much as in a thought unborn
Did I offend your highness.

DUKE FREDERICK   Thus do all traitors.
If their purgation° did consist in words   *exoneration*
They are as innocent as grace itself.
Let it suffice thee that I trust thee not.

50   ROSALIND   Yet your mistrust cannot make me a traitor.
Tell me whereon the likelihood depends?

DUKE FREDERICK   Thou art thy father's daughter—there's enough.

ROSALIND   So was I when your highness took his dukedom;
So was I when your highness banished him.

55   Treason is not inherited, my lord,
Or if we did derive it from our friends,°   *relatives*
What's that to me? My father was no traitor.
Then, good my liege, mistake me not so much
To think my poverty is treacherous.

60   CELIA   Dear sovereign, hear me speak.

DUKE FREDERICK   Ay, Celia, we stayed° her for your sake,   *detained*
Else had she with her father ranged° along.   *roamed*

CELIA   I did not then entreat to have her stay.
It was your pleasure, and your own remorse.°   *pity; sense of guilt*

65   I was too young that time to value her,
But now I know her. If she be a traitor,
Why, so am I. We still° have slept together,   *always*
Rose at an instant,° learned, played, eat together, *at the same moment*
And wheresoe'er we went, like Juno's swans

70   Still we went coupled and inseparable.[7]

DUKE FREDERICK   She is too subtle° for thee, and her smoothness,   *cunning*
Her very silence, and her patience
Speak to the people, and they pity her.
Thou art a fool. She robs thee of thy name,°   *reputation*

75   And thou wilt show more bright and seem more virtuous
When she is gone. Then open not thy lips.

---

6. Leave quickly, which is your best safety.
7. That is, yoked together inseparably like the swans
that draw the chariot of Juno (queen of the gods).

According to Ovid, swans were associated with Venus
(goddess of love), not with Juno.

Firm and irrevocable is my doom°   judgment
Which I have passed upon her. She is banished.
CELIA   Pronounce that sentence then on me, my liege.
80   I cannot live out of her company.
DUKE FREDERICK   You are a fool.—You, niece, provide yourself.°   make preparation
If you outstay the time, upon mine honour
And in the greatness of my word,[8] you die.

                Exit DUKE [FREDERICK, *with Lords*]

CELIA   O my poor Rosalind, whither wilt thou go?
85   Wilt thou change° fathers? I will give thee mine.   exchange
I charge thee, be not thou more grieved than I am.
ROSALIND   I have more cause.
CELIA   Thou hast not, cousin.
Prithee, be cheerful. Know'st thou not the Duke
Hath banished me, his daughter?
ROSALIND   That he hath not.
90   CELIA   No, hath not? Rosalind, lack'st thou then the love
Which teacheth thee that thou and I am one?
Shall we be sundered? Shall we part, sweet girl?
No. Let my father seek another heir.
Therefore devise with me how we may fly,
95   Whither to go, and what to bear with us,
And do not seek to take your change upon you,[9]
To bear your griefs yourself, and leave me out.
For by this heaven, now at our sorrows pale,
Say what thou canst, I'll go along with thee.
100   ROSALIND   Why, whither shall we go?
CELIA   To seek my uncle in the forest of Ardenne.
ROSALIND   Alas, what danger will it be to us,
Maids as we are, to travel forth so far!
Beauty provoketh thieves sooner than gold.
105   CELIA   I'll put myself in poor and mean° attire,   lowly
And with a kind of umber[1] smirch my face.
The like do you, so shall we pass along
And never stir° assailants.   provoke
ROSALIND   Were it not better,
Because that I am more than common tall,
110   That I did suit° me all points° like a man,   dress / ways
A gallant curtal-axe° upon my thigh,   short sword
A boar-spear[2] in my hand, and in my heart,
Lie there what hidden woman's fear there will.
We'll have a swashing° and a martial outside,   swaggering
115   As many other mannish cowards have,
That do outface it with their semblances.[3]
CELIA   What shall I call thee when thou art a man?
ROSALIND   I'll have no worse a name than Jove's own page,
And therefore look you call me Ganymede.[4]
120   But what will you be called?

8. And in accordance with the power of my decree as
Duke.
9. To bear alone the burden of your change of fortunes.
1. Brown pigment. By rubbing it on their faces, Rosalind and Celia take on the dark or sunburned complexion that in Elizabethan society marked the low
social status of those who labored outside. Ladies wore
masks to keep their complexions white.

2. A long-bladed spear used to impale boar.
3. Who brazenly defy the world with the mere appearance of bravery.
4. The name of a beautiful young man who, according
to classical mythology, was so beloved by Jove (king of the
gods) that Jove carried him off to heaven and made him
his cupbearer. Also a slang term for a young man who
sold his sexual services to or was kept by an older man.

CELIA   Something that hath a reference to my state.
No longer Celia, but Aliena.°   *"the estranged one"*
ROSALIND   But cousin, what if we essayed° to steal   *tried*
The clownish fool out of your father's court.
125   Would he not be a comfort to our travel?
CELIA   He'll go along o'er the wide world with me.
Leave me alone to woo him. Let's away,
And get our jewels and our wealth together,
Devise the fittest time and safest way
130   To hide us from pursuit that will be made
After my flight. Now go we in content,
To liberty, and not to banishment.   *Exeunt*

2.1

Enter DUKE SENIOR, AMIENS,[1] *and two or three* LORDS
like° foresters   *dressed as*

DUKE SENIOR   Now, my co-mates and brothers in exile,
Hath not old custom° made this life more sweet   *long acquaintance*
Than that of painted pomp?° Are not these woods   *artificial splendor*
More free from peril than the envious court?
5   Here feel we not the penalty of Adam,[2]
The seasons' difference,° as° the icy fang   *change / such as*
And churlish° chiding of the winter's wind,   *rough*
Which when it bites and blows upon my body
Even till I shrink with cold, I smile, and say
10   'This is no flattery. These are counsellors
That feelingly° persuade me what I am.'   *through my senses*
Sweet are the uses° of adversity   *benefits*
Which, like the toad, ugly and venomous,
Wears yet a precious jewel in his head;[3]
15   And this our life, exempt from public haunt,°   *free from crowds*
Finds tongues in trees, books in the running brooks,
Sermons in stones, and good in everything.
AMIENS   I would not change it. Happy is your grace
That can translate the stubbornness of fortune
20   Into so quiet and so sweet a style.
DUKE SENIOR   Come, shall we go and kill us venison?
And yet it irks me the poor dappled fools,°   *innocent creatures*
Being native burghers° of this desert° city,   *citizens / unpeopled*
Should in their own confines with forkèd heads°   *two-pronged arrows*
Have their round haunches gored.
25   FIRST LORD   Indeed, my lord,
The melancholy Jaques[4] grieves at that,
And in that kind° swears you do more usurp   *vein*
Than doth your brother that hath banished you.
Today my lord of Amiens and myself
30   Did steal behind him as he lay along°   *stretched out*
Under an oak, whose antic° root peeps out   *old; oddly shaped*
Upon the brook that brawls° along this wood,   *loudly flows*

2.1 Location: The Forest of Ardenne.
1. The name of a town in northern France with which
this character is perhaps associated.
2. In Genesis 3, Adam's punishment for disobeying God
involved expulsion from Eden and the laying of a curse
upon the earth. This was frequently interpreted as the
end of the temperate climate associated with paradise.

3. The toad was popularly believed to be poisonous and
to have in its head a jewel, the toadstone.
4. Jaques's name, usually pronounced with two syllables, puns on "jakes," the word for "privy" (toilet). He is
a stock figure of the melancholic man prone to solitude
and black thoughts because of an excess of black bile,
one of the four humors.

To the which place a poor sequestered° stag   *cut off from the herd*
That from the hunter's aim had ta'en a hurt
35   Did come to languish. And indeed, my lord,
The wretched animal heaved forth such groans
That their discharge did stretch his leathern coat
Almost to bursting, and the big round tears
Coursed° one another down his innocent nose   *Pursued*
40   In piteous chase. And thus the hairy fool,
Much markèd of° the melancholy Jaques,   *observed by*
Stood on th'extremest verge° of the swift brook,   *farthest edge*
Augmenting it with tears.

DUKE SENIOR   But what said Jaques?
Did he not moralize° this spectacle?   *draw a moral from*
45   FIRST LORD   O yes, into a thousand similes.
First, for his weeping into the needless° stream;   *needing no more water*
'Poor deer,' quoth he, 'thou mak'st a testament
As worldlings do, giving thy sum of more°   *your supplement*
To that which had too much.' Then being there alone,
50   Left and abandoned of° his velvet friend,[5]   *by*
'Tis right,' quoth he, 'thus misery doth part°   *separate from*
The flux° of company.' Anon a careless[6] herd   *flow*
Full of the pasture° jumps along by him   *Full from grazing*
And never stays to greet him. 'Ay,' quoth Jaques,
55   'Sweep on, you fat and greasy citizens,
'Tis just the fashion. Wherefore should you look
Upon that poor and broken bankrupt there?'
Thus most invectively he pierceth through
The body of the country, city, court,
60   Yea, and of this our life, swearing that we
Are mere usurpers, tyrants, and what's worse,°   *whatever is worse*
To fright the animals and to kill them up°   *off*
In their assigned and native dwelling place.

DUKE SENIOR   And did you leave him in this contemplation?
65   SECOND LORD   We did, my lord, weeping and commenting
Upon the sobbing deer.

DUKE SENIOR   Show me the place.
I love to cope° him in these sullen fits,   *contend with*
For then he's full of matter.°   *material for thought; pus*

FIRST LORD   I'll bring you to him straight.°   *immediately*

Exeunt

2.2

Enter DUKE [FREDERICK], *with* LORDS

DUKE FREDERICK   Can it be possible that no man saw them?
It cannot be. Some villains of my court
Are of consent and sufferance in this.[1]

FIRST LORD   I cannot hear of any that did see her.
5   The ladies her attendants of her chamber
Saw her abed, and in the morning early
They found the bed untreasured of their mistress.

SECOND LORD   My lord, the roynish° clown at whom so oft   *vulgar*

---

5. Smooth-coated companion. Alluding both to the velvet covering the male deer's antlers and to an expensive fabric worn by the prosperous.
6. Just then a carefree.
2.2 Location: Duke Frederick's court.
1. Have agreed to and tolerated this.

Your grace was wont° to laugh is also missing.   *accustomed*
10   Hisperia, the Princess' gentlewoman,
Confesses that she secretly o'erheard
Your daughter and her cousin much commend
The parts° and graces of the wrestler   *qualities*
That did but lately foil the sinewy Charles,
15   And she believes wherever they are gone
That youth is surely in their company.
DUKE FREDERICK   Send to his brother;° fetch that gallant hither.   *(Oliver)*
If he° be absent, bring his brother to me,   *(Orlando)*
I'll make him find him. Do this suddenly,
20   And let not search and inquisition quail°   *fail*
To bring again° these foolish runaways.   *Exeunt [severally]°*   *back / separately*

2.3

Enter ORLANDO *and* ADAM [*meeting*]

ORLANDO   Who's there?
ADAM   What, my young master, O my gentle master,
O my sweet master, O you memory
Of old Sir Rowland, why, what make you° here!   *what are you doing*
5   Why are you virtuous? Why do people love you?
And wherefore° are you gentle, strong, and valiant?   *why*
Why would you be so fond° to overcome   *foolish*
The bonny prizer° of the humorous° Duke?   *robust champion / moody*
Your praise is come too swiftly home before you.
10   Know you not, master, to some kind of men
Their graces° serve them but as enemies?   *virtues*
No more° do yours. Your virtues, gentle master,   *No better*
Are sanctified and holy traitors to you.
O, what a world is this, when what is comely
15   Envenoms° him that bears it!   *Poisons*
ORLANDO   Why, what's the matter?
ADAM   O, unhappy youth,
Come not within these doors. Within this roof
The enemy of all your graces lives,
20   Your brother—no, no brother—yet the son—
Yet not the son, I will not call him son—
Of him I was about to call his father,
Hath heard your praises, and this night he means
To burn the lodging where you use° to lie,   *are accustomed*
25   And you within it. If he fail of that,
He will have other means to cut you off.
I overheard him and his practices.°   *plots*
This is no place,° this house is but a butchery.°   *home / slaughterhouse*
Abhor it, fear it, do not enter it.
30   ORLANDO   Why, whither, Adam, wouldst thou have me go?
ADAM   No matter whither, so you come not here.
ORLANDO   What, wouldst thou have me go and beg my food,
Or with a base and boisterous° sword enforce   *violent*
A thievish living on the common road?
35   This I must do, or know not what to do.
Yet this I will not do, do how I can.

2.3 Location: Oliver's house.

I rather will subject me to the malice
Of a diverted blood[1] and bloody° brother.   *murderous*
ADAM   But do not so. I have five hundred crowns,[2]
40   The thrifty hire I saved[3] under your father,
Which I did store to be my foster-nurse[4]
When service should in my old limbs lie lame,°   *be lamely performed*
And unregarded age in corners thrown.°   *be thrown*
Take that, and he that doth the ravens feed,
45   Yea providently caters for the sparrow,[5]
Be comfort to my age. Here is the gold.
All this I give you. Let me be your servant.
Though I look old, yet I am strong and lusty,°   *robust*
For in my youth I never did apply
50   Hot and rebellious° liquors in my blood,   *unhealthful*
Nor did not with unbashful forehead° woo   *bold countenance*
The means of weakness and debility.
Therefore my age is as a lusty winter,
Frosty but kindly.° Let me go with you,   *pleasant; natural*
55   I'll do the service of a younger man
In all your business and necessities.
ORLANDO   O good old man, how well in thee appears
The constant° service of the antique world,   *faithful*
When service sweat° for duty, not for meed!°   *labored / reward*
60   Thou art not for the fashion of these times,
Where none will sweat but for promotion,
And having that do choke their service up°   *cease service*
Even with the having. It is not so with thee.
But, poor old man, thou prun'st a rotten tree,
65   That cannot so much as a blossom yield
In lieu of° all thy pains and husbandry.°   *return for / gardening*
But come thy ways. We'll go along together,
And ere we have thy youthful wages spent,
We'll light upon some settled low content.°   *humble contentment*
70   ADAM   Master, go on, and I will follow thee
To the last gasp with truth and loyalty.
From seventeen years till now almost fourscore
Here livèd I, but now live here no more.
At seventeen years, many their fortunes seek,
75   But at fourscore, it is too late a week.°   *a time*
Yet fortune cannot recompense me better
Than to die well, and not my master's debtor.   *Exeunt*

2.4

Enter ROSALIND *[in man's clothes] for*° Ganymede;   *as*
CELIA *for* Aliena, *[a shepherdess;] and* TOUCHSTONE
[the] clown

ROSALIND   O Jupiter,[1] how weary are my spirits!
TOUCHSTONE   I care not for my spirits, if my legs were not weary.
ROSALIND   I could find in my heart to disgrace my man's apparel

---

1. Of a kinship diverted from its natural course.
2. Approximately 125 English pounds.
3. The wages I thriftily saved.
4. Caretaker. A foster nurse was a woman hired to breast-feed and care for other people's children.
5. Alluding to various biblical passages (especially

Luke 12:6 and 22–24 and Psalm 147:9) that characterize God as the caretaker of all creatures.
2.4 Location: The remainder of Act 2 takes place in the Forest of Ardenne.
1. Another name for Jove, king of the gods in classical mythology and Ganymede's master.

and to cry like a woman. But I must comfort the weaker vessel,°   *woman*
5   as doublet and hose² ought to show itself courageous to petticoat; therefore, courage, good Aliena!

CELIA   I pray you, bear with me. I cannot go no further.

TOUCHSTONE   For my part, I had rather bear with you than bear
you. Yet I should bear no cross³ if I did bear you, for I think
10   you have no money in your purse.

ROSALIND   Well, this is the forest of Ardenne.

TOUCHSTONE   Ay, now am I in Ardenne; the more fool I. When
I was at home I was in a better place; but travellers must be
content.

        Enter CORIN *and* SILVIUS

15   ROSALIND   Ay, be so, good Touchstone. Look you, who comes
here—a young man and an old in solemn talk.

CORIN [*to* SILVIUS]   That is the way to make her scorn you still.

SILVIUS   O Corin, that thou knew'st how I do love her!

CORIN   I partly guess; for I have loved ere now.

20   SILVIUS   No, Corin, being old thou canst not guess,
Though in thy youth thou wast as true a lover
As ever sighed upon a midnight pillow.
But if thy love were ever like to mine—
As sure I think did never man love so—
25   How many actions most ridiculous
Hast thou been drawn to by thy fantasy?°   *imagination*

CORIN   Into a thousand that I have forgotten.

SILVIUS   O, thou didst then never love so heartily.
If thou rememberest not the slightest folly
30   That ever love did make thee run into,
Thou hast not loved.
Or if thou hast not sat as I do now,
Wearing° thy hearer in thy mistress' praise,   *Wearying*
Thou hast not loved.
35   Or if thou hast not broke from company
Abruptly, as my passion now makes me,
Thou hast not loved.
O, Phoebe, Phoebe, Phoebe!   *Exit*

ROSALIND   Alas, poor shepherd, searching of° thy wound,   *probing*
40   I have by hard adventure° found mine own.   *unlucky chance*

TOUCHSTONE   And I mine. I remember when I was in love I
broke my sword upon a stone and bid him take that for coming
a-night to Jane Smile,⁴ and I remember the kissing of her batlet,⁵ and the cow's dugs° that her pretty chapped hands had   *udder*
45   milked; and I remember the wooing of a peascod instead of
her, from whom I took two cods, and giving her them again,
said with weeping tears, 'Wear these for my sake.'⁶ We that are
true lovers run into strange capers. But as all is mortal in
nature, so is all nature in love mortal in folly.⁷

---

2. That is, as manhood (signified by male attire, close-fitting jacket and breeches).
3. Trouble; money, specifically Elizabethan coins stamped with the image of a cross.
4. *I broke . . . Smile*: I struck a stone as though it were a rival to me in my nocturnal visits to Jane Smile.
5. A wooden bat for beating clothes while washing them.

6. *wooing . . . sake'*: referring to English country courtship rituals in which a pea pod ("peascod") and its husks ("cods") were considered lucky gifts. "Peascod" and "cods" were also slang terms for "male genitalia," suggesting the implicit sexual import of these gifts.
7. So all lovers show their humanity in their foolishness.

50 ROSALIND   Thou speak'st wiser than thou art ware° of.   *aware*
TOUCHSTONE   Nay, I shall ne'er be ware° of mine own wit till I   *wary*
break my shins against it.
ROSALIND   Jove, Jove, this shepherd's passion
Is much upon my fashion.°   *of my sort*
55 TOUCHSTONE   And mine, but it grows something° stale with me.   *somewhat*
CELIA   I pray you, one of you question yon man
If he for gold will give us any food.
I faint almost to death.
TOUCHSTONE [*to* CORIN]   Holla, you clown!°   *peasant; yokel*
60 ROSALIND   Peace, fool, he's not thy kinsman.
CORIN   Who calls?
TOUCHSTONE   Your betters, sir.
CORIN   Else are they very wretched.
ROSALIND [*to* TOUCHSTONE]   Peace, I say. [*To* CORIN]   Good
even° to you, friend.   *evening*
65 CORIN   And to you, gentle sir, and to you all.
ROSALIND   I prithee, shepherd, if that love or gold
Can in this desert place buy entertainment,°   *accommodation*
Bring us where we may rest ourselves, and feed.
Here's a young maid with travel much oppressed,
And faints for succour.°   *for lack of aid (food)*
70 CORIN   Fair sir, I pity her,
And wish, for her sake more than for mine own,
My fortunes were more able to relieve her.
But I am shepherd to another man,
And do not shear the fleeces that I graze.
75 My master is of churlish° disposition,   *miserly*
And little recks° to find the way to heaven   *thinks*
By doing deeds of hospitality.
Besides, his cot,° his flocks, and bounds of feed°   *cottage / grazing rights*
Are now on sale, and at our sheepcote° now   *cottage*
80 By reason of his absence there is nothing
That you will feed on. But what is, come see,
And in my voice[8] most welcome shall you be.
ROSALIND   What° is he that shall buy his flock and pasture?   *Who*
CORIN   That young swain that you saw here but erewhile,°   *just now*
85 That little cares for buying anything.
ROSALIND   I pray thee, if it stand with honesty,
Buy thou the cottage, pasture, and the flock,
And thou shalt have to pay° for it of us.   *the money to pay*
CELIA   And we will mend° thy wages. I like this place,   *improve*
90 And willingly could waste° my time in it.   *spend*
CORIN   Assuredly the thing is to be sold.
Go with me. If you like upon report
The soil, the profit, and this kind of life,
I will your very faithful feeder° be,   *servant*
95 And buy it with your gold right suddenly.   *Exeunt*

8. And insofar as my authority stretches.

2.5

Enter AMIENS, JAQUES, *and other* [*Lords dressed as foresters*]

AMIENS [*sings*][1]   Under the greenwood tree
           Who loves to lie with me,
           And turn° his merry note   *tune*
           Unto the sweet bird's throat,°   *voice*
5   Come hither, come hither, come hither.
              Here shall he see
                No enemy
           But winter and rough weather.

JAQUES   More, more, I prithee, more.

10 AMIENS   It will make you melancholy, Monsieur Jaques.

JAQUES   I thank it. More, I prithee, more. I can suck melancholy
out of a song as a weasel sucks eggs. More, I prithee, more.

AMIENS   My voice is ragged,° I know I cannot please you.   *harsh*

JAQUES   I do not desire you to please me, I do desire you to sing.
15 Come, more; another stanza. Call you 'em stanzas?[2]

AMIENS   What you will, Monsieur Jaques.

JAQUES   Nay, I care not for their names,[3] they owe me nothing.
Will you sing?

AMIENS   More at your request than to please myself.

20 JAQUES   Well then, if ever I thank any man, I'll thank you. But
that° they call compliment is like th'encounter of two dog- *what*
apes,° and when a man thanks me heartily methinks I have *dog-faced baboons*
given him a penny and he renders me the beggarly thanks.[4]
Come, sing; and you that will not, hold your tongues.

25 AMIENS   Well, I'll end the song.—Sirs, cover the while.[5]
    [*Lords prepare food and drink*]
The Duke will drink under this tree. [*To* JAQUES] He hath been
all this day to look° you.   *searching for*

JAQUES   And I have been all this day to avoid him. He is too
disputable° for my company. I think of as many matters as he, *argumentative*
30 but I give heaven thanks, and make no boast of them. Come,
warble, come.

ALL [*sing*][6]   Who doth ambition shun,
           And loves to live i'th' sun,
           Seeking the food he eats,
35   And pleased with what he gets,
           Come hither, come hither, come hither.
              Here shall he see
                No enemy
           But winter and rough weather.

40 JAQUES   I'll give you a verse to this note° that I made yesterday in *tune*
despite of my invention.[7]

AMIENS   And I'll sing it.

JAQUES   Thus it goes:
           If it do come to pass
45   That any man turn ass,

2.5

1. F does not indicate who sings this song. Traditionally it has been assigned to Amiens, whose part may have been played by Robert Armin, a clown who joined Shakespeare's company in 1599 and who was known for his fine singing voice.
2. A relatively new, and Italianate, word at the time of the play's composition.
3. Punning on the legal sense of "names" as "signatures of borrowers."
4. Excessive thanks, like that given by a beggar.
5. Set the table in the meantime.
6. F's direction before this song reads: "Song. Altogether here."
7. Even though I have little power of creativity.

                    Leaving his wealth and ease
                    A stubborn will to please,
                  Ducdame,[8] ducdame, ducdame.
                    Here shall he see
50   Gross fools as he,
                  An if° he will come to me.   *If only*

AMIENS   What's that 'ducdame'?

JAQUES   'Tis a Greek[9] invocation to call fools into a circle. I'll go
    sleep if I can. If I cannot, I'll rail against all the firstborn of
55 Egypt.[1]

AMIENS   And I'll go seek the Duke; his banquet[2] is prepared.

                                                              Exeunt

                              2.6

          Enter ORLANDO *and* ADAM

ADAM   Dear master, I can go no further. O, I die for food. Here
    lie I down and measure out my grave. Farewell, kind master.

ORLANDO   Why, how now, Adam? No greater heart in thee? Live
    a little, comfort° a little, cheer thyself a little. If this uncouth°   *be comforted / wild*
5   forest yield anything savage I will either be food for it or bring it
    for food to thee. Thy conceit° is nearer death than thy powers.   *imagination*
    For my sake be comfortable. Hold death awhile at the arm's
    end. I will here be with thee presently,° and if I bring thee not   *soon*
    something to eat, I will give thee leave to die. But if thou diest
10 before I come, thou art a mocker of my labour. Well said. Thou
    lookest cheerly,° and I'll be with thee quickly. Yet thou liest in   *cheerfully*
    the bleak air. Come, I will bear thee to some shelter, and thou
    shalt not die for lack of a dinner if there live anything in this
    desert.° Cheerly, good Adam.   [ORLANDO *carries* ADAM *off*]   *uninhabited place*

                              2.7

          Enter DUKE SENIOR *and* LORD[S] *like*° *outlaws*   *dressed as*

DUKE SENIOR   I think he be transformed into a beast,
    For I can nowhere find him like° a man.   *in the shape of*

FIRST LORD   My lord, he is but even now gone hence.
    Here was he merry, hearing of a song.

5 DUKE SENIOR   If he, compact of jars,° grow musical   *made up of discords*
    We shall have shortly discord in the spheres.[1]
    Go seek him. Tell him I would speak with him.

          Enter JAQUES

FIRST LORD   He saves my labour by his own approach.

DUKE SENIOR   Why, how now, monsieur, what a life is this,
10 That your poor friends must woo your company!
    What, you look merrily.

JAQUES   A fool, a fool, I met a fool i'th' forest,
    A motley fool[2]—a miserable world!—
    As I do live by food, I met a fool,

---

8. A word of unknown meaning. Possibly a variation on
a Welsh phrase meaning "Come hither" or on a Gypsy
phrase meaning "I foretell."
9. "Greek" was used to signify anything unintelligible.
1. According to Exodus 11 and 12, the Hebrew God
caused the deaths of all firstborn Egyptian children
after Pharaoh would not let the Israelites leave his
country. Jaques may be vowing to denounce all firstborn
sons, which would include Duke Senior.

2. A light meal of sweetmeats and wine.
2.7
1. Alluding to the Pythagorean belief that the earth
was the center of eight concentric spheres whose movements created a heavenly harmony (the music of the
spheres) inaudible to humans.
2. Someone wearing "motley," the multicolored costume conventionally associated with fools and jesters.

15 Who laid him down and basked him in the sun,
And railed on Lady Fortune in good terms,
In good set° terms, and yet a motley fool.   *outspoken; rhetorical*
'Good morrow, fool,' quoth I. 'No, sir,' quoth he,
'Call me not fool till heaven hath sent me fortune.'³
20 And then he drew a dial⁴ from his poke,°   *pocket; pouch*
And looking on it with lack-lustre eye
Says very wisely 'It is ten o'clock.'
'Thus we may see', quoth he, 'how the world wags.°   *moves on*
'Tis but an hour ago since it was nine,
25 And after one hour more 'twill be eleven.
And so from hour to hour we ripe and ripe,
And then from hour to hour we rot and rot;
And thereby hangs a tale.'⁵ When I did hear
The motley fool thus moral on the time
30 My lungs began to crow like chanticleer,°   *a rooster*
That fools should be so deep°-contemplative,   *profoundly*
And I did laugh sans° intermission   *without*
An hour by his dial. O noble fool,
A worthy fool—motley's the only wear.°   *garb worth wearing*
35 DUKE SENIOR   What fool is this?
JAQUES   O worthy fool!—One that hath been a courtier,
And says 'If ladies be but young and fair
They have the gift to know it.' And in his brain,
Which is as dry⁶ as the remainder° biscuit   *last*
40 After a voyage, he hath strange places° crammed   *sites; commonplaces*
With observation, the which he vents
In mangled forms. O that I were a fool,
I am ambitious for a motley coat.
DUKE SENIOR   Thou shalt have one.
JAQUES   It is my only suit,°   *request; costume*
45 Provided that you weed your better judgements
Of all opinion that grows rank° in them   *wild*
That I am wise. I must have liberty
Withal, as large a charter° as the wind,   *license*
To blow on whom I please, for so fools have;
50 And they that are most gallèd° with my folly,   *vexed*
They most must laugh. And why, sir, must they so?
The why is plain as way to parish church:
He that a fool doth very wisely hit
Doth very foolishly, although he smart,
55 Seem aught but senseless of the bob.° If not,   *unaware of the taunt*
The wise man's folly is anatomized°   *dissected; laid open*
Even by the squandering glances° of the fool.   *random hits*
Invest me in my motley. Give me leave
To speak my mind, and I will through and through
60 Cleanse the foul body of th'infected world,
If they will patiently receive my medicine.
DUKE SENIOR   Fie on thee, I can tell what thou wouldst do.

3. Referring to the proverbial notion that fortune favored fools.
4. Probably a portable sundial about the size of a napkin ring.
5. *Tis . . . tale*: the puns and sexual wordplay in these lines suggest a story of male sexual activity leading to debility: "hour" puns on "whore" (they were pronounced similarly); "ripe" means "to come of age sexually"; "rot" puns on "rut," which means "to have sex in an animal-like state of excitement"; and "tale" puns on "tail," slang for "penis." "And thereby hangs a tale" was an Elizabethan commonplace.
6. According to Renaissance medical theory, dry brains signified slow wits and strong memories.

JAQUES   What, for a counter,[7] would I do but good?
DUKE SENIOR   Most mischievous foul sin, in chiding sin;
65   For thou thyself hast been a libertine,
     As sensual as the brutish sting° itself,   *lust*
     And all th'embossèd sores and headed evils[8]
     That thou with licence of free foot° hast caught   *travel*
     Wouldst thou disgorge° into the general world.   *vomit*
70   JAQUES   Why, who cries out on pride°   *extravagance*
     That can therein tax° any private party?   *blame*
     Doth it not flow as hugely as the sea,
     Till that the weary very means° do ebb?   *source itself*
     What woman in the city do I name
75   When that I say the city-woman bears
     The cost° of princes on unworthy shoulders?   *costly attire*
     Who can come in and say that I mean her
     When such a one as she, such is her neighbour?
     Or what is he of basest function,°   *lowliest social status*
80   That says his bravery° is not on° my cost,   *fine attire / at*
     Thinking that I mean him, but therein suits
     His folly to the mettle° of my speech?   *spirit*
     There then, how then, what then, let me see wherein
     My tongue hath wronged him. If it do him right,°   *describe him justly*
85   Then he hath wronged himself. If he be free,°   *virtuous*
     Why then my taxing° like a wild goose flies,   *reproof*
     Unclaimed of any man. But who comes here?
                    Enter ORLANDO [*with sword drawn*]
     ORLANDO   Forbear, and eat no more!
     JAQUES   Why, I have eat° none yet.   *eaten*
     ORLANDO   Nor shalt not till necessity be served.
90   JAQUES   Of what kind° should this cock come of?   *lineage; stock*
     DUKE SENIOR   Art thou thus boldened, man, by thy distress?
     Or else a rude despiser of good manners,
     That in civility thou seem'st so empty?
     ORLANDO   You touched my vein° at first. The thorny point   *assessed my condition*
95   Of bare distress hath ta'en from me the show
     Of smooth civility. Yet am I inland bred,[9]
     And know some nurture. But forbear, I say.
     He dies that touches any of this fruit
     Till I and my affairs are answerèd.°   *satisfied*
100 JAQUES   An° you will not be answered with reason, I must die.   *If*
     DUKE SENIOR   What would you have? Your gentleness° shall   *gentility; kindness*
     force
     More than your force move us to gentleness.
     ORLANDO   I almost die for food; and let me have it.
     DUKE SENIOR   Sit down and feed, and welcome to our table.
105 ORLANDO   Speak you so gently? Pardon me, I pray you.
     I thought that all things had been savage here,
     And therefore put I on the countenance
     Of stern commandment. But whate'er you are
     That in this desert inaccessible,
110 Under the shade of melancholy boughs,

---

7. In return for a coin of no value (normally used for reckoning sums).
8. Swollen sores and boils that have come to a head. Both were symptoms of venereal disease.

9. Brought up in a civilized way—that is, raised in the country's interior regions rather than near its supposedly savage borders.

Lose and neglect the creeping hours of time,
If ever you have looked on better days,
If ever been where bells have knolled° to church,   summoned
If ever sat at any good man's feast,
115 If ever from your eyelids wiped a tear,
And know what 'tis to pity, and be pitied,
Let gentleness my strong enforcement be,[1]
In the which hope I blush, and hide my sword.

DUKE SENIOR   True is it that we have seen better days,
120 And have with holy bell been knolled to church,
And sat at good men's feasts, and wiped our eyes
Of drops that sacred pity hath engendered.
And therefore sit you down in gentleness,
And take upon command° what help we have   at your will
125 That to your wanting may be ministered.

ORLANDO   Then but forbear your food a little while
Whiles, like a doe, I go to find my fawn
And give it food. There is an old poor man
Who after me hath many a weary step
130 Limped in pure love. Till he be first sufficed,°   satisfied
Oppressed with two weak° evils, age and hunger,   enfeebling
I will not touch a bit.

DUKE SENIOR   Go find him out,
And we will nothing waste° till you return.   consume

ORLANDO   I thank ye; and be blessed for your good comfort!
                                                            [Exit]

135 DUKE SENIOR   Thou seest we are not all alone unhappy.
This wide and universal theatre
Presents more woeful pageants° than the scene   spectacles
Wherein we play in.

JAQUES   All the world's a stage,
And all the men and women merely players.
140 They have their exits and their entrances,
And one man in his time plays many parts,
His acts being seven ages. At first the infant,
Mewling° and puking in the nurse's arms.   Crying
Then the whining schoolboy with his satchel
145 And shining morning face, creeping like snail
Unwillingly to school. And then the lover,
Sighing like furnace,[2] with a woeful ballad
Made to his mistress' eyebrow. Then, a soldier,
Full of strange oaths, and bearded like the pard,[3]
150 Jealous in honour,[4] sudden, and quick in quarrel,
Seeking the bubble reputation
Even in the cannon's mouth. And then the justice,
In fair round belly with good capon[5] lined,°   filled; stuffed
With eyes severe and beard of formal cut,
155 Full of wise saws° and modern° instances;   sayings / trite
And so he plays his part. The sixth age shifts

1. Let natural kindness or gentility be what compels your compassion.
2. Emitting sighs as a furnace emits smoke.
3. Leopard. The soldier's bristling mustache is being compared to the leopard's whiskers.
4. Vigilant in matters of honor.
5. A cock, castrated and fattened as a delicacy (proverbially, a bribe for magistrates).

Into the lean and slippered pantaloon,[6]
With spectacles on nose and pouch on side,
His youthful hose, well saved, a world too wide
160 For his shrunk shank,° and his big, manly voice,   calf
Turning again toward childish treble, pipes
And whistles in his° sound. Last scene of all,   its
That ends this strange, eventful history,
Is second childishness and mere° oblivion,   complete
165 Sans° teeth, sans eyes, sans taste, sans everything.   Without

      Enter ORLANDO [*bearing*] ADAM

DUKE SENIOR   Welcome. Set down your venerable burden
   And let him feed.
ORLANDO   I thank you most for him.
ADAM   So had you need;
170   I scarce can speak to thank you for myself.
DUKE SENIOR   Welcome. Fall to. I will not trouble you
   As yet to question you about your fortunes.
   Give us some music, and, good cousin, sing.
AMIENS [*sings*][7]   Blow, blow, thou winter wind,
175   Thou art not so unkind
              As man's ingratitude.
           Thy tooth is not so keen,
           Because thou art not seen,
              Although thy breath be rude.°   rough
180   Hey-ho, sing hey-ho, unto the green holly.[8]
        Most friendship is feigning, most loving, mere folly.
           Then hey-ho, the holly;
           This life is most jolly.

           Freeze, freeze, thou bitter sky,
185   That dost not bite so nigh°   closely
              As benefits forgot.
           Though thou the waters warp,°   cause to contract; freeze
           Thy sting is not so sharp
              As friend remembered not.
190   Hey-ho, sing hey-ho, unto the green holly.
        Most friendship is feigning, most loving, mere folly.
           Then hey-ho, the holly;
           This life is most jolly.
DUKE SENIOR [*to* ORLANDO]   If that you were the good Sir Rowland's son,
195   As you have whispered faithfully you were,
   And as mine eye doth his effigies° witness   likeness
   Most truly limned° and living in your face,   portrayed
   Be truly welcome hither. I am the Duke
   That loved your father. The residue of your fortune,
200   Go to my cave and tell me. [*To* ADAM] Good old man,
   Thou art right welcome, as thy master is.—
   [*To* LORDS] Support him by the arm. [*To* ORLANDO] Give me your hand,
   And let me all your fortunes understand.   *Exeunt*

---

6. A foolish old man named after a figure in *commedia*
dell'arte, Italian popular comedy.
7. Again, F does not indicate who sings this song. It is

usually assigned to Amiens.
8. The evergreen associated with English holiday festivities.

3.1

Enter DUKE [FREDERICK], *Lords, and* OLIVER

DUKE FREDERICK   Not see him since? Sir, sir, that cannot be.
But were I not the better part made° mercy,   *composed of*
I should not seek an absent argument°   *subject*
Of my revenge, thou present. But look to it:
5 Find out thy brother wheresoe'er he is.
Seek him with candle.° Bring him, dead or living,   *diligently*
Within this twelvemonth, or turn° thou no more   *return*
To seek a living in our territory.
Thy lands, and all things that thou dost call thine
10 Worth seizure, do we seize into our hands
Till thou canst quit° thee by thy brother's mouth   *acquit*
Of what we think against thee.
OLIVER   O that your highness knew my heart in this.
I never loved my brother in my life.
DUKE FREDERICK   More villain thou. [*To Lords*] Well, push
15 him out of doors,
And let my officers of such a nature°   *whose job it is*
Make an extent° upon his house and lands.   *a writ of seizure*
Do this expediently,° and turn° him going. *Exeunt* [*severally*] *quickly / set*

3.2

Enter ORLANDO [*with a paper*]

ORLANDO   Hang there, my verse, in witness of my love;
 And thou thrice-crownèd queen of night,[1] survey
With thy chaste eye, from thy pale sphere above,
 Thy huntress' name° that my full life doth sway.° *(Rosalind) / rule*
5 O Rosalind, these trees shall be my books,
 And in their barks my thoughts I'll character°   *inscribe*
That every eye which in this forest looks
 Shall see thy virtue witnessed everywhere.
Run, run, Orlando; carve on every tree
10 The fair, the chaste, and unexpressive° she. *Exit*[2] *inexpressible*

Enter CORIN *and* [TOUCHSTONE *the*] *clown*

CORIN   And how like you this shepherd's life, Master Touchstone?
TOUCHSTONE   Truly, shepherd, in respect of° itself, it is a good *with regard to*
life; but in respect that it is a shepherd's life, it is naught.° In *worthless*
respect that it is solitary, I like it very well; but in respect that it
15 is private, it is a very vile life. Now in respect it is in the fields,
it pleaseth me well; but in respect it is not in the court, it is
tedious. As it is a spare° life, look you, it fits my humour° well; *frugal / temperament*
but as there is no more plenty in it, it goes much against my
stomach.° Hast any philosophy in thee, shepherd?   *inclination*
20 CORIN   No more but that I know the more one sickens, the worse
at ease he is, and that he that wants° money, means, and con- *lacks*
tent is without three good friends; that the property of rain is to

---

3.1 Location: Duke Frederick's court.
3.2 Location: The remaining scenes of the play take place in the Forest of Ardenne.
1. The goddess who ruled on earth as Diana, patron of chastity and of the hunt; in the heavens as Cynthia, Phoebe, or Luna, goddess of the moon; and in the underworld as Hecate.

2. Orlando's appearance at lines 1–10 is self-contained and could form a separate scene. However, the ensuing conversation between Corin and Touchstone appears to take place on the same spot where Orlando has just stood, making the action continuous. This edition, like F, makes Orlando's lines part of the longer scene involving Corin, Touchstone, and eventually Rosalind and others.

wet, and fire to burn; that good pasture makes fat sheep; and
that a great cause of the night is lack of the sun; that he that
25   hath learned no wit by nature nor art may complain° of good   *lament his lack*
breeding or comes of a very dull kindred.

TOUCHSTONE   Such a one is a natural philosopher.[3] Wast ever in
court, shepherd?

CORIN   No, truly.

30   TOUCHSTONE   Then thou art damned.

CORIN   Nay, I hope.

TOUCHSTONE   Truly thou art damned, like an ill-roasted egg, all
on one side.

CORIN   For not being at court? Your reason?

35   TOUCHSTONE   Why, if thou never wast at court thou never sawest
good manners.° If thou never sawest good manners, then thy   *etiquette; morals*
manners must be wicked, and wickedness is sin, and sin is dam-
nation. Thou art in a parlous° state, shepherd.   *perilous*

CORIN   Not a whit, Touchstone. Those that are good manners at
40   the court are as ridiculous in the country as the behaviour of
the country is most mockable at the court. You told me you
salute not at the court but° you kiss your hands. That courtesy   *unless*
would be uncleanly if courtiers were shepherds.

TOUCHSTONE   Instance,° briefly; come, instance.   *An example*

45   CORIN   Why, we are still° handling our ewes, and their fells,° you   *constantly / skins*
know, are greasy.

TOUCHSTONE   Why, do not your courtier's hands sweat? And is
not the grease of a mutton as wholesome as the sweat of a man?
Shallow, shallow. A better instance, I say. Come.

50   CORIN   Besides, our hands are hard.

TOUCHSTONE   Your lips will feel them the sooner. Shallow again.
A more sounder instance. Come.

CORIN   And they are often tarred over with the surgery of our
sheep;[4] and would you have us kiss tar? The courtier's hands
55   are perfumed with civet.[5]

TOUCHSTONE   Most shallow, man. Thou worms' meat in respect
of° a good piece of flesh indeed, learn of the wise, and per-   *in comparison with*
pend:° civet is of a baser birth than tar, the very uncleanly flux°   *consider / discharge*
of a cat. Mend° the instance, shepherd.   *Improve*

60   CORIN   You have too courtly a wit for me. I'll rest.

TOUCHSTONE   Wilt thou rest damned? God help thee, shallow
man. God make incision in thee, thou art raw.[6]

CORIN   Sir, I am a true labourer. I earn that° I eat, get° that I   *what / make*
wear; owe no man hate, envy no man's happiness; glad of other
65   men's good, content with my harm;° and the greatest of my   *misfortune*
pride is to see my ewes graze and my lambs suck.

TOUCHSTONE   That is another simple° sin in you, to bring the   *simpleminded*
ewes and the rams together, and to offer° to get your living by   *undertake*
the copulation of cattle; to be bawd to a bell-wether,[7] and to
70   betray a she-lamb of a twelve-month to a crooked-pated old

---

3. A born philosopher; a philosopher who studies natural phenomena; a fool.
4. Referring to the practice of treating sheep wounds
with tar.
5. A musk-scented substance obtained from the anal
glands of certain cats.

6. Make a cut to let blood (and thus cure you of your
"raw"ness, or inexperience); make a cut to score you, as
raw meat was scored in preparation for cooking.
7. The leading sheep of a flock, who usually wore a
bell.

cuckoldly ram,[8] out of all reasonable match. If thou beest not
damned for this, the devil himself will have no shepherds.[9] I
cannot see else how thou shouldst scape.

CORIN   Here comes young Master Ganymede, my new mistress's
75   brother.

Enter ROSALIND [*as Ganymede*]

ROSALIND [*reads*]   'From the east to western Ind°   *Indies*
No jewel is like Rosalind.
Her worth being mounted on the wind
Through all the world bears Rosalind.
80   All the pictures fairest lined°   *drawn*
Are but black to° Rosalind.   *compared to*
Let no face be kept in mind
But the fair of Rosalind.'

TOUCHSTONE   I'll rhyme you so eight years together, dinners, and
85   suppers, and sleeping-hours excepted. It is the right butter-
women's rank to market.[1]

ROSALIND   Out, fool.

TOUCHSTONE   For a taste:
If a hart° do lack a hind,°   *male deer / female deer*
90   Let him seek out Rosalind.
If the cat will after kind,°   *act naturally; mate*
So, be sure, will Rosalind.
Wintered garments must be lined,[2]
So must slender Rosalind.
95   They that reap must sheaf and bind,
Then to cart[3] with Rosalind.
'Sweetest nut hath sourest rind',
Such a nut is Rosalind.
He that sweetest rose will find
100   Must find love's prick,° and Rosalind.   *thorn; penis*
This is the very false gallop of verses.° Why do you infect your-   *way verses canter on*
self with them?

ROSALIND   Peace, you dull fool, I found them on a tree.

TOUCHSTONE   Truly, the tree yields bad fruit.

105   ROSALIND   I'll graft it with you,° and then I shall graft it with a   *(punning on "yew")*
medlar;[4] then it will be the earliest fruit i'th' country, for you'll
be rotten ere you be half-ripe, and that's the right° virtue of the   *true*
medlar.

TOUCHSTONE   You have said; but whether wisely or no, let the
110   forest judge.

Enter CELIA [*as Aliena*], *with a writing*

ROSALIND   Peace, here comes my sister, reading. Stand aside.

CELIA [*reads*]   'Why should this a desert be?
For it is unpeopled? No.
Tongues I'll hang on every tree,
115   That shall civil° sayings show.   *civilized*

---

8. Cuckolds, men whose wives were sexually unfaithful, supposedly wore horns to signify their shame. The
ram may *make* cuckolds—that is, be lecherous.
crooked-pated: with crooked horns.
9. It will be because the devil refuses to admit shepherds into hell.
1. *It . . . market*: The rhymes are truly like a stream of
dairywomen going to market at the same time. Such
women were proverbially talkative.

2. Clothes worn in winter must be stuffed with material, with a pun on "lined" as meaning "mated," used
especially of female animals.
3. A cart on which harvests were transported to the
market; a cart on which women accused of prostitution
or other forms of disorderly conduct were transported
and exposed to public abuse.
4. A tree whose fruit was not ripe until it was so soft as
to be rotten, with a pun on "meddler," one who meddles.

Some, how brief the life of man
  Runs his erring° pilgrimage,   *wandering*
That the stretching of a span
  Buckles in his sum of age.⁵
120 Some of violated vows
  'Twixt the souls of friend and friend.
But upon the fairest boughs,
  Or at every sentence end,
Will I 'Rosalinda' write,
125   Teaching all that read to know
The quintessence of every sprite°   *spirit; soul*
  Heaven would in little show.⁶
Therefore heaven nature charged
  That one body should be filled
130 With all graces wide-enlarged.⁷
  Nature presently° distilled   *at once*
Helen's cheek, but not her heart,⁸
  Cleopatra's⁹ majesty,
Atalanta's better part,¹
135   Sad Lucretia's modesty.²
Thus Rosalind of many parts
  By heavenly synod° was devised   *assembly*
Of many faces, eyes, and hearts
  To have the touches° dearest prized.   *traits*
140 Heaven would that she these gifts should have
And I to live and die her slave.'

ROSALIND   O most gentle Jupiter! What tedious homily of love
  have you wearied your parishioners withal, and never cried
  'Have patience, good people.'

145 CELIA   How now, back, friends. Shepherd, go off a little. Go with
  him, sirrah.

TOUCHSTONE   Come, shepherd, let us make an honourable
  retreat, though not with bag and baggage, yet with scrip and
  scrippage.³   *Exit [with* CORIN]

150 CELIA   Didst thou hear these verses?

ROSALIND   O yes, I heard them all, and more, too, for some of
  them had in them more feet° than the verses would bear.   *metrical units*

CELIA   That's no matter; the feet might bear° the verses.   *carry*

ROSALIND   Ay, but the feet were lame, and could not bear them-
155   selves without° the verse, and therefore stood lamely in the   *out of*
  verse.

CELIA   But didst thou hear without wondering how thy name
  should be° hanged and carved upon these trees?   *came to be*

---

5. *the stretching . . . age:* the width of an open hand (a
"span") encompasses an entire lifetime. A comparison
derived from verses appearing in Elizabethan prayer
books.
6. Which heaven would portray in miniature, or
through one individual (Rosalind).
7. Graces that otherwise have been widely distributed.
8. The features, but not the false heart, of Helen of
Troy. Supposedly Helen's abduction by Paris from her
husband, Menelaus, was the event that precipitated the
Trojan War. In some accounts, Helen is blamed for her
abduction and so could be said to have a false heart.
9. Queen of Egypt and the tragic heroine of Shake-

speare's *Antony and Cleopatra.*
1. In Greek myth, Atalanta was a fleet-footed and
chaste hunter who challenged her suitors to a race. She
was only defeated when one of them dropped three
golden apples, which she stopped to pick up. The reference here is possibly to her beauty or her speed,
rather than her greed.
2. Lucretia killed herself to save her honor after being
raped by Tarquin (a story told by Shakespeare in *The
Rape of Lucrece*).
3. Though not with the belongings retained by an army
in retreat, yet with a shepherd's pouch and its contents.

ROSALIND   I was seven of the nine days out of the wonder[4] before
you came; for look here what I found on a palm-tree; [*showing*
CELIA *the verses*] I was never so berhymed since Pythagoras'
time that I was an Irish rat,[5] which I can hardly remember.

CELIA   Trow you° who hath done this?   *Can you imagine*

ROSALIND   Is it a man?

CELIA   And a chain that you once wore about his neck. Change
you colour?

ROSALIND   I prithee, who?

CELIA   O Lord, Lord, it is a hard matter for friends to meet. But
mountains may be removed with° earthquakes, and so   *moved by*
encounter.

ROSALIND   Nay, but who is it?

CELIA   Is it possible?

ROSALIND   Nay, I prithee now with most petitionary vehemence,
tell me who it is.

CELIA   O wonderful, wonderful, and most wonderful-wonderful,
and yet again wonderful, and after that out of all whooping![6]

ROSALIND   Good my complexion![7] Dost thou think, though I am
caparisoned° like a man, I have a doublet and hose in my dispo-   *dressed*
sition? One inch of delay more is a South Sea of discovery.[8] I
prithee tell me who is it quickly, and speak apace.° I would   *at once*
thou couldst stammer, that thou mightst pour this concealed
man out of thy mouth as wine comes out of a narrow-mouthed
bottle—either too much at once, or none at all. I prithee, take
the cork out of thy mouth, that I may drink thy tidings.

CELIA   So you may put a man in your belly.°   *stomach; womb*

ROSALIND   Is he of God's making? What manner of man? Is his
head worth a hat? Or his chin worth a beard?

CELIA   Nay, he hath but a little beard.

ROSALIND   Why, God will send more, if the man will be thank-
ful. Let me stay° the growth of his beard, if thou delay me not   *wait for*
the knowledge of his chin.

CELIA   It is young Orlando, that tripped up the wrestler's heels
and your heart both in an instant.

ROSALIND   Nay, but the devil take mocking. Speak sad brow and
true maid.[9]

CELIA   I'faith, coz, 'tis he.

ROSALIND   Orlando?

CELIA   Orlando.

ROSALIND   Alas the day, what shall I do with my doublet and
hose! What did he when thou sawest him? What said he? How
looked he? Wherein went he?° What makes he here? Did he   *What was he wearing*
ask for me? Where remains he? How parted he with thee? And
when shalt thou see him again? Answer me in one word.

CELIA   You must borrow me Gargantua's[1] mouth first, 'tis a word

---

4. Referring to the proverbial "nine days' wonder," a novelty that caused amazement.
5. I was never so overwhelmed with rhyme since the days of the ancient Greeks, when I was an Irish rat. Alluding to Pythagoras's doctrine of the transmigration of souls and to the popular belief in England that Irish bards were capable of rhyming rats to death.
6. After that, beyond what all shouts of astonishment can express.
7. An expression of impatience. "Complexion" means

"temperament," believed to be caused by the particular mixture of the four humors in one's body. Her meaning seems to be: Pay attention to my womanly temperament (which is impatient)!
8. More delay will seem as infinite as a voyage of discovery to the South Seas.
9. Speak seriously and as a virtuous woman or on your honor as a virgin.
1. A voracious giant famous in French folklore and from the writings of Rabelais.

205 too great for any mouth of this age's size. To say ay and no to
these particulars is more than to answer in a catechism.[2]

ROSALIND   But doth he know that I am in this forest, and in
man's apparel? Looks he as freshly as he did the day he wrestled?

210 CELIA   It is as easy to count atomies° as to resolve the proposi-   specks (of dust)
tions° of a lover; but take a taste of my finding him, and relish   answer the questions
it with good observance.[3] I found him under a tree, like a
dropped acorn—

ROSALIND   It may well be called Jove's tree[4] when it drops forth
215 such fruit.

CELIA   Give me audience, good madam.

ROSALIND   Proceed.

CELIA   There lay he, stretched along like a wounded knight—

ROSALIND   Though it be pity to see such a sight, it well becomes
220 the ground.

CELIA   Cry 'holla'° to thy tongue, I prithee: it curvets° unseason-   hold / leaps about
ably.—He was furnished° like a hunter—   dressed

ROSALIND   O ominous—he comes to kill my heart.

CELIA   I would sing my song without a burden;° thou bringest   refrain
225 me out of tune.

ROSALIND   Do you not know I am a woman? When I think, I
must speak.—Sweet, say on.

          Enter ORLANDO *and* JAQUES

CELIA   You bring me out.° Soft, comes he not here?   make me lose the tune

ROSALIND   'Tis he. Slink by, and note him.

230   [ROSALIND *and* CELIA *stand aside*]

JAQUES [*to* ORLANDO] I thank you for your company, but, good
faith, I had as lief° have been myself alone.   as willingly

ORLANDO   And so had I. But yet for fashion' sake, I thank you too
for your society.

JAQUES   God b'wi'you;° let's meet as little as we can.   Good-bye

235 ORLANDO   I do desire we may be better strangers.

JAQUES   I pray you mar no more trees with writing love-songs in
their barks.

ORLANDO   I pray you mar no more of my verses with reading
them ill-favouredly.°   unsympathetically

240 JAQUES   Rosalind is your love's name?

ORLANDO   Yes, just.

JAQUES   I do not like her name.

ORLANDO   There was no thought of pleasing you when she was
christened.

245 JAQUES   What stature is she of?

ORLANDO   Just as high as my heart.

JAQUES   You are full of pretty answers. Have you not been
acquainted with goldsmiths' wives, and conned them out of
rings?[5]

250 ORLANDO   Not so; but I answer you right painted cloth,[6] from
whence you have studied your questions.

---

2. A summary, in question-and-answer form, of basic
tenets of religious doctrine. In Shakespeare's time, all
members of the Church of England learned to recite
such a catechism.
3. And enhance its flavor by paying careful attention.
4. The oak was traditionally viewed as sacred to Jove, the
god of thunder, and was said therefore to be often struck

by lightning.
5. Romantic verses were often inscribed on rings sold
in shops managed by the wives of goldsmiths; with a
pun on "rings" as a slang term for "vaginas."
6. I answer you in the style of the pithy sayings issuing
from the mouths of figures in painted wall hangings (a
popular and inexpensive form of interior decoration).

JAQUES   You have a nimble wit; I think 'twas made of Atalanta's heels.[7] Will you sit down with me, and we two will rail against our mistress the world, and all our misery?

255   ORLANDO   I will chide no breather° in the world but myself,   *person*
against whom I know most faults.

JAQUES   The worst fault you have is to be in love.

ORLANDO   'Tis a fault I will not change for your best virtue. I am weary of you.

260   JAQUES   By my troth, I was seeking for a fool when I found you.

ORLANDO   He is drowned in the brook. Look but in, and you shall see him.

JAQUES   There I shall see mine own figure.

ORLANDO   Which I take to be either a fool or a cipher.[8]

265   JAQUES   I'll tarry no longer with you. Farewell, good Signor Love.

ORLANDO   I am glad of your departure. Adieu, good Monsieur Melancholy.   [*Exit* JAQUES][9]

ROSALIND [*to* CELIA]   I will speak to him like a saucy lackey, and
270   under that habit° play the knave with him. [*To* ORLANDO] Do   *guise; disguise*
you hear, forester?

ORLANDO   Very well. What would you?

ROSALIND   I pray you, what is't o'clock?

ORLANDO   You should ask me what time o' day. There's no clock
275   in the forest.

ROSALIND   Then there is no true lover in the forest, else sighing
every minute and groaning every hour would detect° the lazy   *reveal*
foot of time as well as a clock.

ORLANDO   And why not the swift foot of time? Had not that been
280   as proper?

ROSALIND   By no means, sir. Time travels in divers paces with
divers persons. I'll tell you who time ambles withal,° who time   *with*
trots withal, who time gallops withal, and who he stands still
withal.

285   ORLANDO   I prithee, who doth he trot withal?

ROSALIND   Marry, he trots hard° with a young maid between the   *uncomfortably*
contract of her marriage and the day it is solemnized. If the
interim be but a se'nnight,° time's pace is so hard that it seems   *week*
the length of seven year.

290   ORLANDO   Who ambles time withal?

ROSALIND   With a priest that lacks Latin, and a rich man that
hath not the gout; for the one sleeps easily because he cannot
study, and the other lives merrily because he feels no pain, the
one lacking the burden of lean and wasteful° learning, the   *weakening*
295   other knowing no burden of heavy tedious penury.° These time   *poverty*
ambles withal.

ORLANDO   Who doth he gallop withal?

ROSALIND   With a thief to the gallows; for though he go as softly°   *slowly*
as foot can fall, he thinks himself too soon there.

300   ORLANDO   Who stays it still withal?

---

7. See note to 3.2.134.
8. A zero; punning on "figure" (line 263) as meaning "numeral."
9. Editors usually give Jaques an exit here, although none is indicated in F. It would not be out of character,

however, for Jaques to remain onstage in the background during Orlando and Rosalind's exchange (as he does during Touchstone's courting of Audrey in 3.3) and to exit with them at the end of the scene.

ROSALIND   With lawyers in the vacation; for they sleep between
term[1] and term, and then they perceive not how time moves.

ORLANDO   Where dwell you, pretty youth?

ROSALIND   With this shepherdess, my sister, here in the skirts° of   *edges*
305   the forest, like fringe upon a petticoat.

ORLANDO   Are you native of this place?

ROSALIND   As the coney° that you see dwell where she is kin-   *rabbit*
dled.°   *born*

ORLANDO   Your accent is something finer than you could pur-
310   chase° in so removed° a dwelling.   *acquire / remote*

ROSALIND   I have been told so of many; but indeed an old religious uncle of mine taught me to speak, who was in his youth
an inland man; one that knew courtship° too well, for there he   *court life; wooing*
fell in love. I have heard him read many lectures against it, and
315   I thank God I am not a woman, to be touched with so many
giddy offences as he hath generally taxed their whole sex
withal.

ORLANDO   Can you remember any of the principal evils that he
laid to the charge of women?

320   ROSALIND   There were none principal; they were all like one
another as halfpence are, every one fault seeming monstrous
till his fellow-fault came to match it.

ORLANDO   I prithee, recount some of them.

ROSALIND   No. I will not cast away my physic but° on those that   *my medicine except*
325   are sick. There is a man haunts the forest that abuses our young
plants with carving Rosalind on their barks; hangs odes upon
hawthorns and elegies on brambles; all, forsooth, deifying the
name of Rosalind. If I could meet that fancy-monger,° I would   *dealer in love*
give him some good counsel, for he seems to have the quotid-
330   ian[2] of love upon him.

ORLANDO   I am he that is so love-shaked. I pray you, tell me your
remedy.

ROSALIND   There is none of my uncle's marks upon you. He
taught me how to know a man in love, in which cage of rushes[3]
335   I am sure you are not prisoner.

ORLANDO   What were his marks?

ROSALIND   A lean cheek, which you have not; a blue eye[4] and
sunken, which you have not; an unquestionable° spirit, which   *a taciturn*
you have not; a beard neglected, which you have not—but I
340   pardon you for that, for simply your having in beard° is a   *such beard as you have*
younger brother's revenue.[5] Then your hose should be ungar-
tered, your bonnet unbanded,° your sleeve unbuttoned, your   *lacking a band*
shoe untied, and everything about you demonstrating a careless
desolation. But you are no such man. You are rather point-
345   device° in your accoutrements, as loving yourself than seeming   *extremely precise*
the lover of any other.

ORLANDO   Fair youth, I would I could make thee believe I love.

ROSALIND   Me believe it? You may as soon make her that you love
believe it, which I warrant she is apter to do than to confess
350   she does. That is one of the points in the which women still°   *always*

1. *terms:* limited periods of time in which the courts
were in session and when lawyers were therefore busy.
Vacation came between terms.
2. Daily recurring fever said to be a sign of love.
3. A prison easy to escape from.

4. An eye ringed with dark circles (suggesting insomnia).
5. Younger brothers traditionally received small inher-
itances, here suggesting that Orlando's beard is likewise
thin or small.

give the lie to their consciences. But in good sooth,° are you   truth
he that hangs the verses on the trees wherein Rosalind is so
admired?

ORLANDO   I swear to thee, youth, by the white hand of Rosalind,
355   I am that he, that unfortunate he.

ROSALIND   But are you so much in love as your rhymes speak?

ORLANDO   Neither rhyme nor reason can express how much.

ROSALIND   Love is merely a madness, and I tell you, deserves as
well a dark house and a whip as madmen do;[6] and the rea-
360   son why they° are not so punished and cured is that the lunacy   (lovers)
is so ordinary that the whippers are in love too. Yet I profess
curing it by counsel.

ORLANDO   Did you ever cure any so?

ROSALIND   Yes, one; and in this manner. He was to imagine me
365   his love, his mistress; and I set him every day to woo me. At
which time would I, being but a moonish° youth, grieve, be   changeable
effeminate,[7] changeable, longing and liking, proud, fantasti-
cal,° apish,° shallow, inconstant, full of tears, full of smiles; for   capricious / affected
every passion something, and for no passion truly anything, as
370   boys and women are for the most part cattle of this colour—
would now like him, now loathe him; then entertain him,°   treat him kindly
then forswear him; now weep for him, then spit at him, that I
drave° my suitor from his mad humour of love to a living   drove
humour° of madness, which was to forswear the full stream of   an actual condition
375   the world and to live in a nook merely monastic.° And thus I   as a hermit
cured him, and this way will I take upon me to wash your liver[8]
as clean as a sound sheep's heart, that there shall not be one
spot of love in't.

ORLANDO   I would not be cured, youth.
380   ROSALIND   I would cure you if you would but call me Rosalind
and come every day to my cot,° and woo me.   cottage

ORLANDO   Now by the faith of my love, I will. Tell me where it
is.

ROSALIND   Go with me to it, and I'll show it you. And by the way
385   you shall tell me where in the forest you live. Will you go?

ORLANDO   With all my heart, good youth.

ROSALIND   Nay, you must call me Rosalind.—Come, sister. Will
you go?   Exeunt

3.3

Enter [TOUCHSTONE the] clown and AUDREY, [followed
by] JAQUES

TOUCHSTONE   Come apace, good Audrey. I will fetch up your
goats, Audrey. And how, Audrey, am I the man yet? Doth my
simple feature° content you?   appearance

AUDREY   Your features, Lord warrant° us—what features?   defend
5   TOUCHSTONE   I am here with thee and thy goats as the most
capricious° poet honest Ovid was among the Goths.[1]   witty; lascivious

---

6. Confinement in a dark room and whipping, common
treatments for insanity, were believed to rid the insane
of the devils that possessed them.
7. Like a woman; sensual or self-indulgent; a term
often used to deride men perceived as excessive in their
sexual interest in women.

8. In Renaissance medical theory, the seat of the passions.
3.3
1. Punning on "goats / Goths," which were similarly
pronounced, and referring to the Roman poet's exile
among the Goths.

JAQUES [*aside*]   O knowledge ill-inhabited; worse than Jove in a
thatched house.[2]

10 TOUCHSTONE   When a man's verses cannot be understood, nor a
man's good wit seconded with° the forward child, understand-   *supported by*
ing, it strikes a man more dead than a great reckoning° in a   *tavern bill*
little room.[3] Truly, I would the gods had made thee poetical.

AUDREY   I do not know what 'poetical' is. Is it honest in deed
and word? Is it a true thing?

15 TOUCHSTONE   No, truly; for the truest poetry is the most
feigning,° and lovers are given to poetry; and what they swear   *imaginative; false*
in poetry it may be said, as lovers, they do feign.

AUDREY   Do you wish, then, that the gods had made me poetical?

TOUCHSTONE   I do, truly; for thou swearest to me thou art hon-
20 est.° Now if thou wert a poet, I might have some hope thou   *chaste*
didst feign.

AUDREY   Would you not have me honest?

TOUCHSTONE   No, truly, unless thou wert hard-favoured;° for   *ugly*
honesty coupled to beauty is to have honey a sauce to sugar.

25 JAQUES [*aside*]   A material° fool.   *full of matter or sense*

AUDREY   Well, I am not fair, and therefore I pray the gods make
me honest.

TOUCHSTONE   Truly, and to cast away honesty upon a foul slut
were to put good meat into an unclean dish.

30 AUDREY   I am not a slut, though I thank the gods I am foul.[4]

TOUCHSTONE   Well, praised be the gods for thy foulness. Sluttishness may come hereafter. But be it as it may be, I will marry
thee; and to that end I have been with Sir Oliver Martext, the
vicar of the next village, who hath promised to meet me in this
35 place of the forest, and to couple us.

JAQUES [*aside*]   I would fain° see this meeting.   *gladly*

AUDREY   Well, the gods give us joy.

TOUCHSTONE   Amen.—A man may, if he were of a fearful heart,
stagger° in this attempt; for here we have no temple but the   *hesitate*
40 wood, no assembly but horn-beasts.[5] But what though? Courage. As horns are odious, they are necessary. It is said many a
man knows no end of his goods.[6] Right: many a man has good
horns, and knows no end of them. Well, that is the dowry of
his wife, 'tis none of his own getting.[7] Horns? Even so. Poor
45 men alone? No, no; the noblest deer hath them as huge as the
rascal.° Is the single man therefore blessed? No. As a walled   *young or lean deer*
town is more worthier than a village, so is the forehead of a
married man more honourable than the bare brow of a bache-
lor. And by how much defence° is better than no skill, by so   *skill in self-defense*
50 much is a horn more precious than to want.°   *to lack (one)*

Enter SIR OLIVER MARTEXT

Here comes Sir Oliver.—Sir Oliver Martext, you are well met.
Will you dispatch us here under this tree, or shall we go with
you to your chapel?

---

2. In *Metamorphoses* 8, Ovid tells how the king of the
gods was given shelter for a time in the humble
dwelling of Philemon and Baucis.

3. These lines have been taken to refer to the death in
1593 of Christopher Marlowe, a contemporary playwright, in a quarrel in a tavern over a bill.

4. Ugly. Audrey apparently takes "foul" as a term of
praise.

5. Horned beasts such as deer, goats, and the like that
inhabited the forest, with an allusion to the horns of the
cuckolded husband.

6. A proverbial expression suggesting a man so wealthy
he can't count all his money.

7. *'tis . . . getting:* he is not responsible for the horns;
he is not responsible for conceiving his children (since
his wife has been sexually unfaithful).

SIR OLIVER MARTEXT   Is there none here to give the woman?

55   TOUCHSTONE   I will not take her on gift of any man.

SIR OLIVER MARTEXT   Truly she must be given, or the marriage
is not lawful.

JAQUES   [*coming forward*]   Proceed, proceed. I'll give her.

TOUCHSTONE   Good even, good Monsieur What-ye-call't. How

60   do you, sir? You are very well met. God'ield you for your last
company.[8] I am very glad to see you. Even a toy° in hand here,   *trifling matter*
sir.

[JAQUES *removes his hat*]
Nay, pray be covered.°   *replace your hat*

JAQUES   Will you be married, motley?

65   TOUCHSTONE   As the ox hath his bow,° sir, the horse his curb,[9]   *yoke*
and the falcon her bells,[1] so man hath his desires; and as
pigeons bill,° so wedlock would be nibbling.   *rub bill to bill*

JAQUES   And will you, being a man of your breeding, be married
under a bush, like a beggar? Get you to church, and have a

70   good priest that can tell you what marriage is. This fellow will
but join you together as they join wainscot;° then one of you   *wood paneling*
will prove a shrunk panel and, like green timber, warp,° warp.   *go wrong; shrink*

TOUCHSTONE   I am not in the mind but° I were better to be mar-   *not sure but that*
ried of° him than of another, for he is not like to marry me   *by*

75   well, and not being well married, it will be a good excuse for
me hereafter to leave my wife.

JAQUES   Go thou with me, and let me counsel thee.

TOUCHSTONE   Come, sweet Audrey.
We must be married,° or we must live in bawdry.°   *(properly wed) / in sin*

80   Farewell, good Master Oliver. Not
         O, sweet Oliver,
         O, brave Oliver,
         Leave me not behind thee[2]
but

85   Wind° away,   *Go*
         Begone, I say,
         I will not to wedding with thee.

SIR OLIVER MARTEXT [*aside*]   'Tis no matter. Ne'er a fantastical
knave of them all shall flout me out of my calling.

Exeunt

3.4

Enter ROSALIND [*as Ganymede*] *and* CELIA [*as Aliena*]

ROSALIND   Never talk to me. I will weep.

CELIA   Do, I prithee, but yet have the grace to consider that tears
do not become a man.

ROSALIND   But have I not cause to weep?

5   CELIA   As good cause as one would desire; therefore weep.

ROSALIND   His very hair is of the dissembling colour.[1]

CELIA   Something° browner than Judas's. Marry, his kisses are   *Somewhat*
Judas's own children.

ROSALIND   I'faith, his hair is of a good colour.

---

8. God yield you (a salutation meaning "May God
reward you") for your recent companionship.
9. A bit placed in the horse's mouth to control its
movements.
1. Bells attached to a falcon's legs before releasing it for

the hunt so that it might be easily reclaimed afterward.
2. Lines from a popular Elizabethan ballad.
3.4
1. Alluding to the tradition that Judas, the disciple who
betrayed Jesus, had red hair.

10   CELIA   An excellent colour. Your chestnut was ever the only
        colour.

        ROSALIND   And his kissing is as full of sanctity as the touch of
        holy bread.[2]

        CELIA   He hath bought a pair of cast° lips of Diana.[3] A nun of   *cast-off; sculpted*

15   winter's sisterhood° kisses not more religiously. The very ice of   *devoted to coldness*
        chastity is in them.

        ROSALIND   But why did he swear he would come this morning,
        and comes not?

        CELIA   Nay, certainly, there is no truth in him.

20   ROSALIND   Do you think so?

        CELIA   Yes. I think he is not a pick-purse, nor a horse-stealer; but
        for his verity° in love, I do think him as concave° as a covered   *truthfulness / hollow*
        goblet, or a worm-eaten nut.

        ROSALIND   Not true in love?

25   CELIA   Yes, when he is in. But I think he is not in.

        ROSALIND   You have heard him swear downright he was.

        CELIA   'Was' is not 'is'. Besides, the oath of a lover is no stronger
        than the word of a tapster. They are both the confirmer of false
        reckonings. He attends° here in the forest on the Duke your   *waits*

30   father.

        ROSALIND   I met the Duke yesterday, and had much question°   *conversation*
        with him. He asked me of what parentage I was. I told him, of
        as good as he, so he laughed and let me go. But what talk we
        of fathers when there is such a man as Orlando?

35   CELIA   O that's a brave° man. He writes brave verses, speaks   *splendid*
        brave words, swears brave oaths, and breaks them bravely, quite
        traverse,[4] athwart the heart of his lover, as a puny° tilter that   *an unskilled*
        spurs his horse but° on one side breaks his staff, like a noble   *only*
        goose.° But all's brave that youth mounts, and folly guides.   *fool*

40   Who comes here?

              Enter CORIN

        CORIN   Mistress and master, you have oft enquired
        After the shepherd that complained of love
        Who you saw sitting by me on the turf,
        Praising the proud disdainful shepherdess
        That was his mistress.

45   CELIA   Well, and what of him?

        CORIN   If you will see a pageant truly played
        Between the pale complexion of true love
        And the red glow of scorn and proud disdain,[5]
        Go hence a little, and I shall conduct you,
        If you will mark° it.   *observe*

50   ROSALIND [*to* CELIA]   O come, let us remove.
        The sight of lovers feedeth those in love.
        [*To* CORIN] Bring us to this sight, and you shall say
        I'll prove a busy actor in their play.   *Exeunt*

---

2. Referring to bread blessed after the Eucharist during Christian religious services and distributed to those who did not take Communion.

3. The goddess of chastity. See note to 3.2.2.

4. Crossways. A term from jousting used to designate the dishonorable practice of breaking one's lance across, rather than directly against, an opponent's shield.

5. Referring to the paleness of Silvius, the true lover, and the red cheeks of the disdainful Phoebe.

3.5

Enter SILVIUS *and* PHOEBE

SILVIUS   Sweet Phoebe, do not scorn me, do not, Phoebe.
Say that you love me not, but say not so
In bitterness. The common executioner,
Whose heart th'accustomed sight of death makes hard,

5   Falls not° the axe upon the humbled neck   *Does not let fall*
But first begs° pardon. Will you sterner be   *Without first begging*
Than he that dies and lives by bloody drops?

Enter ROSALIND [*as Ganymede*], CELIA [*as Aliena*], *and*
    CORIN [*and stand aside*]

PHOEBE [*to* SILVIUS]   I would not be thy executioner.
I fly thee for I would not injure thee.

10   Thou tell'st me there is murder in mine eye.
'Tis pretty, sure, and very probable
That eyes, that are the frail'st and softest things,
Who shut their coward gates on atomies,°   *dust motes*
Should be called tyrants, butchers, murderers.

15   Now I do frown on thee with all my heart,
And if mine eyes can wound, now let them kill thee.
Now counterfeit to swoon, why now fall down;
Or if thou canst not, O, for shame, for shame,
Lie not, to say mine eyes are murderers.

20   Now show the wound mine eye hath made in thee.
Scratch thee but with a pin, and there remains
Some scar of it. Lean upon a rush,
The cicatrice and capable impressure[1]
Thy palm some moment keeps. But now mine eyes,

25   Which I have darted at thee, hurt thee not;
Nor I am sure there is no force in eyes
That can do hurt.

SILVIUS   O dear Phoebe,
If ever—as that ever may be near—

30   You meet in some fresh cheek the power of fancy,°   *love*
Then shall you know the wounds invisible
That love's keen arrows make.

PHOEBE   But till that time
Come not thou near me. And when that time comes,
Afflict me with thy mocks, pity me not,

35   As till that time I shall not pity thee.

ROSALIND [*coming forward*]   And why, I pray you? Who might
    be your mother,
That you insult, exult, and all at once,°   *all in one breath*
Over the wretched? What though you have no beauty—
As, by my faith, I see no more in you

40   Than without candle may go dark to bed[2]—
Must you be therefore proud and pitiless?
Why, what means this? Why do you look on me?
I see no more in you than in the ordinary°   *common run*
Of nature's sale-work.°—'Od's my little life,[3]   *ready-made goods*

45   I think she means to tangle° my eyes, too.   *entrap*
No, faith, proud mistress, hope not after it.

3.5
1. The scarlike mark and the impression that the skin
receives.

2. *I see . . . bed:* I see you have not enough beauty to
light your way to bed without a candle.
3. An abbreviated version of the oath "God save my life."

'Tis not your inky brows, your black silk hair,   *like black glass beads*
Your bugle° eyeballs, nor your cheek of cream,   *the worship of you*
That can entame my spirits to your worship.°
50   [*To* SILVIUS] You, foolish shepherd, wherefore do you follow her
Like foggy south,° puffing with wind and rain?[4]   *south wind*
You are a thousand times a properer° man   *more attractive*
Than she a woman. 'Tis such fools as you
That makes the world full of ill-favoured° children.   *ugly*
55   'Tis not her glass° but you that flatters her,   *mirror*
And out of you° she sees herself more proper   *from you (as mirror)*
Than any of her lineaments can show her.
[*To* PHOEBE] But, mistress, know yourself; down on your knees
And thank heaven, fasting, for a good man's love;
60   For I must tell you friendly in your ear,
Sell when you can. You are not for all markets.
Cry the man mercy,° love him, take his offer;   *Beg his pardon*
Foul is most foul, being foul to be a scoffer.[5]—
So, take her to thee, shepherd. Fare you well.
65 PHOEBE   Sweet youth, I pray you chide a year together.°   *without interruption*
   I had rather hear you chide than this man woo.
ROSALIND [*to* PHOEBE]   He's fallen in love with your foulness, [*to*
   SILVIUS] and she'll fall in love with my anger. If it be so, as fast
   as she answers thee with frowning looks, I'll sauce° her   *sharply rebuke*
70   with bitter words.
   [*To* PHOEBE] Why look you so upon me?
PHOEBE   For no ill will I bear you.
ROSALIND   I pray you do not fall in love with me,
   For I am falser than vows made in wine.°   *when drinking*
75   Besides, I like you not. If you will know my house,
   'Tis at the tuft of olives,° here hard by.   *olive trees*
   [*To* CELIA] Will you go, sister? [*To* SILVIUS] Shepherd, ply her
     hard.°—   *assail her vigorously*
   Come, sister. [*To* PHOEBE] Shepherdess, look on him better,
   And be not proud. Though all the world could see,
80   None could be so abused in sight as he.—
   Come, to our flock.   *Exeunt* [ROSALIND, CELIA, *and* CORIN][6]
PHOEBE [*aside*]   Dead shepherd,[7] now I find thy saw of might:°   *your saying powerful*
   'Who ever loved that loved not at first sight?'
SILVIUS   Sweet Phoebe—
PHOEBE   Ha, what sayst thou, Silvius?
85 SILVIUS   Sweet Phoebe, pity me.
PHOEBE   Why, I am sorry for thee, gentle Silvius.
SILVIUS   Wherever sorrow is, relief would be.
   If you do sorrow at my grief in love,
   By giving love your sorrow and my grief
90   Were both exterminèd.°   *Would both be ended*
PHOEBE   Thou hast my love, is not that neighbourly?[8]
SILVIUS   I would have you.
PHOEBE   Why, that were covetousness.[9]

---

4. That is, with sighs and tears.
5. The ugly seem most ugly when they are abusive.
6. F marks a single exit for Rosalind here, but it is unlikely that Celia and Corin remain.
7. Referring to Christopher Marlowe, poet and playwright who died in 1593. Line 83 is taken from his poem *Hero and Leander*.

8. With a reference to Romans 13:9: "Thou shalt love thy neighbour as thyself."
9. With a reference to Exodus 20:17: "Thou shalt not covet thy neighbour's house, thou shalt not covet thy neighbour's wife, nor his manservant, nor his maid servant, nor his ox, nor his ass, nor any thing that is thy neighbour's."

Silvius, the time was that I hated thee;
And yet it is not° that I bear thee love.   *it has not yet happened*
95   But since that thou canst talk of love so well,
Thy company, which erst° was irksome to me,   *formerly*
I will endure; and I'll employ thee, too.
But do not look for further recompense
Than thine own gladness that thou art employed.
100 SILVIUS   So holy and so perfect is my love,
And I in such a poverty of grace,[1]
That I shall think it a most plenteous crop
To glean the broken ears° after the man   *(of corn)*
That the main harvest reaps. Loose now and then
105   A scattered° smile, and that I'll live upon.   *stray*
  PHOEBE   Know'st thou the youth that spoke to me erewhile?
  SILVIUS   Not very well, but I have met him oft,
And he hath bought the cottage and the bounds°   *pastures*
That the old Carlot once was master of.
110 PHOEBE   Think not I love him, though I ask for him.
'Tis but a peevish boy. Yet he talks well.
But what care I for words? Yet words do well
When he that speaks them pleases those that hear.
It is a pretty youth—not very pretty—
115   But sure he's proud; and yet his pride becomes him.
He'll make a proper° man. The best thing in him   *handsome*
Is his complexion; and faster than his tongue
Did make offence, his eye did heal it up.
He is not very tall; yet for his years he's tall.
120   His leg is but so-so; and yet 'tis well.
There was a pretty redness in his lip,
A little riper and more lusty-red
Than that mixed in his cheek. 'Twas just the difference
Betwixt the constant red and mingled damask.[2]
125   There be some women, Silvius, had they marked him
In parcels° as I did, would have gone near   *Item by item*
To fall in love with him; but for my part,
I love him not, nor hate him not. And yet
Have I more cause to hate him than to love him,
130   For what had he to do to chide at me?
He said mine eyes were black, and my hair black,
And now I am remembered, scorned at me.
I marvel why I answered not again.
But that's all one. Omittance is no quittance.[3]
135   I'll write to him a very taunting letter,
And thou shalt bear it. Wilt thou, Silvius?
  SILVIUS   Phoebe, with all my heart.
  PHOEBE   I'll write it straight.°   *immediately*
The matter's in my head and in my heart.
I will be bitter with him, and passing° short.   *extremely*
140   Go with me, Silvius.   *Exeunt*

---

1. And I so lacking in (your) favor.
2. *constant . . . damask:* uniform red and a mixture of red and white characteristic of certain kinds of roses.

3. A proverbial expression meaning that a debt is not canceled simply because one fails ("omits") to exact it.

4.1

Enter ROSALIND [*as Ganymede*], CELIA [*as Aliena*], *and*
JAQUES

JAQUES   I prithee, pretty youth, let me be better acquainted with
thee.

ROSALIND   They say you are a melancholy fellow.

JAQUES   I am so. I do love it better than laughing.

5   ROSALIND   Those that are in extremity of either are abominable
fellows, and betray themselves to every modern censure worse
than drunkards.

JAQUES   Why, 'tis good to be sad° and say nothing.   *serious*

ROSALIND   Why then, 'tis good to be a post.

10   JAQUES   I have neither the scholar's melancholy, which is emulation,° nor the musician's, which is fantastical,° nor the court-   *envy / overly fanciful*
ier's, which is proud, nor the soldier's, which is ambitious, nor
the lawyer's, which is politic, nor the lady's, which is nice,° nor   *fastidious*
the lover's, which is all these; but it is a melancholy of mine
15   own, compounded of many simples,° extracted from many   *ingredients*
objects,° and indeed the sundry contemplation of my travels,[1]   *sights*
in° which my often° rumination wraps me in a most humor-   *upon / frequent*
ous° sadness.   *moody*

ROSALIND   A traveller! By my faith, you have great reason to be
20   sad. I fear you have sold your own lands to see other men's.
Then to have seen much and to have nothing is to have rich
eyes and poor hands.

JAQUES   Yes, I have gained my experience.

Enter ORLANDO

ROSALIND   And your experience makes you sad. I had rather have
25   a fool to make me merry than experience to make me sad—
and to travel for it too!

ORLANDO   Good day and happiness, dear Rosalind.

JAQUES   Nay then, God b'wi'you an° you talk in blank verse.   *if*

ROSALIND   Farewell, Monsieur Traveller. Look you lisp,[2] and
30   wear strange° suits; disable° all the benefits of your own coun-   *foreign / disparage*
try; be out of love with your nativity,° and almost chide God for   *birthplace*
making you that countenance you are, or I will scarce think
you have swam in a gondola.[3]   [*Exit* JAQUES][4]
Why, how now, Orlando? Where have you been all this while?
35   You a lover? An you serve me such another trick, never come
in my sight more.

ORLANDO   My fair Rosalind, I come within an hour of my
promise.

ROSALIND   Break an hour's promise in love! He that will divide a
40   minute into a thousand parts and break but a part of the thousand part of a minute in the affairs of love, it may be said of
him that Cupid hath clapped him o'th' shoulder, but I'll warrant him heartwhole.[5]

ORLANDO   Pardon me, dear Rosalind.

4.1
1. The various thoughts arising during my travels, with
a pun on "travails," meaning "labors."
2. Speak with an affected (foreign) accent.
3. Ridden in a gondola—that is, seen Venice, a popular destination for English travelers.

4. F marks no exit for Jaques here, but he and Rosalind
have formally parted, and Jaques enters with a new
group of characters at the beginning of 4.2.
5. Cupid has tapped him (as in an arrest) or wounded
him (with his arrow), but I'll guarantee he left his heart
intact.

45 ROSALIND   Nay, an you be so tardy, come no more in my sight.
    I had as lief be wooed of a snail.

    ORLANDO   Of a snail?

    ROSALIND   Ay, of a snail; for though he comes slowly, he carries
    his house on his head—a better jointure,° I think, than you   marriage settlement
50 make a woman. Besides, he brings his destiny with him.

    ORLANDO   What's that?

    ROSALIND   Why, horns, which such as you are fain to be
    beholden to your wives for.[6] But he comes armed in his for-
    tune,[7] and prevents the slander of his wife.

55 ORLANDO   Virtue is no hornmaker, and my Rosalind is virtuous.

    ROSALIND   And I am your Rosalind.

    CELIA   It pleases him to call you so; but he hath a Rosalind of a
    better leer° than you.   more attractive

    ROSALIND   Come, woo me, woo me, for now I am in a holiday
60 humour, and like enough to consent. What would you say to
    me now an I were your very, very Rosalind?

    ORLANDO   I would kiss before I spoke.

    ROSALIND   Nay, you were better speak first, and when you were
    gravelled° for lack of matter you might take occasion to kiss.   at a loss
65 Very good orators, when they are out,° they will spit; and for   speechless
    lovers, lacking—God warr'nt° us— matter, the cleanliest shift°   defend / cleverest device
    is to kiss.

    ORLANDO   How if the kiss be denied?

    ROSALIND   Then she puts you to entreaty, and there begins new
70 matter.

    ORLANDO   Who could be out, being before his beloved mistress?

    ROSALIND   Marry, that should you if I were your mistress, or I
    should think my honesty ranker than my wit.[8]

    ORLANDO   What, of my suit?[9]

75 ROSALIND   Not out of your apparel, and yet out of your suit. Am
    not I your Rosalind?

    ORLANDO   I take some joy to say you are because I would be
    talking of her.

    ROSALIND   Well, in her person I say I will not have you.

80 ORLANDO   Then in mine own person I die.

    ROSALIND   No, faith; die by attorney.° The poor world is almost   proxy
    six thousand years old,[1] and in all this time there was not any
    man died in his own person, videlicet,° in a love-cause. Troi-   namely
    lus[2] had his brains dashed out with a Grecian club, yet he did
85 what he could to die before, and he is one of the patterns of
    love. Leander,[3] he would have lived many a fair year though
    Hero had turned nun if it had not been for a hot midsummer
    night, for, good youth, he went but forth to wash him in the
    Hellespont and, being taken with the cramp, was drowned; and
90 the foolish chroniclers of that age found° it was Hero of Sestos.   claimed
    But these are all lies. Men have died from time to time, and
    worms have eaten them, but not for love.

---

6. An allusion to the cuckold's horns.
7. Equipped with the insignia of his destined future.
8. I would think my chastity was fouler than my intelligence; with a pun on "out" (lines 65, 71) as meaning
"not permitted sexual entrance."
9. My petition. Orlando asks if he will be at a loss for
words ("out") in furthering his courtship ("suit"). Ros-

alind puns on "suit" as meaning "clothing."
1. Elizabethan divines generally dated the world's creation somewhere around 4000 B.C.E.
2. The forsaken Trojan lover of Cressida, killed by the
Greek warrior Achilles.
3. In Greek mythology, the lover of Hero; he swam the
Hellespont nightly to visit her and was drowned.

ORLANDO I would not have my right° Rosalind of this mind, for
I protest her frown might kill me.   *true*

95   ROSALIND By this hand, it will not kill a fly. But come, now I
will be your Rosalind in a more coming-on° disposition; and   *agreeable*
ask me what you will, I will grant it.

ORLANDO Then love me, Rosalind.

ROSALIND Yes, faith, will I, Fridays and Saturdays and all.

100 ORLANDO And wilt thou have me?

ROSALIND Ay, and twenty such.

ORLANDO What sayst thou?

ROSALIND Are you not good?

ORLANDO I hope so.

105 ROSALIND Why then, can one desire too much of a good thing?
[*To* CELIA] Come, sister, you shall be the priest and marry us.—
Give me your hand, Orlando.—What do you say, sister?

ORLANDO [*to* CELIA] Pray thee, marry us.

CELIA I cannot say the words.

110 ROSALIND You must begin, 'Will you, Orlando'—

CELIA Go to.[4] Will you, Orlando, have to wife this Rosalind?

ORLANDO I will.

ROSALIND Ay, but when?

ORLANDO Why now, as fast as she can marry us.

115 ROSALIND Then you must say, 'I take thee, Rosalind, for wife.'

ORLANDO I take thee, Rosalind, for wife.

ROSALIND I might ask you for your commission;° but I do take   *authority*
thee, Orlando, for my husband. There's a girl goes before° the   *who anticipates*
priest; and certainly a woman's thought runs before her actions.

120 ORLANDO So do all thoughts; they are winged.

ROSALIND Now tell me how long you would have her after you
have possessed her?

ORLANDO For ever and a day.

ROSALIND Say a day without the ever. No, no, Orlando; men are
125 April when they woo, December when they wed. Maids are
May when they are maids, but the sky changes when they are
wives. I will be more jealous of thee than a Barbary cock-
pigeon[5] over his hen, more clamorous than a parrot against°   *in expectation of*
rain, more new-fangled° than an ape, more giddy in my desires   *in love with novelty*
130 than a monkey. I will weep for nothing, like Diana in the fountain,[6] and I will do that when you are disposed to be merry. I
will laugh like a hyena, and that when thou art inclined to
sleep.

ORLANDO But will my Rosalind do so?

135 ROSALIND By my life, she will do as I do.

ORLANDO O, but she is wise.

ROSALIND Or else she could not have the wit to do this. The
wiser, the waywarder. Make° the doors upon a woman's wit,   *Close*
and it will out at the casement. Shut that, and 'twill out at the
140 key-hole. Stop that, 'twill fly with the smoke out at the
chimney.

---

4. An expression of mild impatience.
5. An ornamental bird, traditionally an emblem of jealousy. It was introduced into Europe from Asia by Turks, whom Elizabethans associated with North Africa's Barbary Coast. Turkish husbands were imagined by the English to be excessively vigilant about the sexual fidelity of their wives.
6. Referring to the figures of the goddess Diana used as centerpieces for ornamental fountains in London and elsewhere.

ORLANDO   A man that had a wife with such a wit, he might say
'Wit, whither wilt?'[7]

ROSALIND   Nay, you might keep that check° for it till you met   *rebuke*
145   your wife's wit going to your neighbour's bed.

ORLANDO   And what wit could wit have to excuse that?

ROSALIND   Marry, to say she came to seek you there. You shall
never take her without her answer unless you take her without
her tongue. O, that woman that cannot make her fault her
150   husband's occasion,[8] let her never nurse her child herself, for
she will breed it like a fool.

ORLANDO   For these two hours, Rosalind, I will leave thee.

ROSALIND   Alas, dear love, I cannot lack thee two hours.

ORLANDO   I must attend the Duke at dinner. By two o'clock I
155   will be with thee again.

ROSALIND   Ay, go your ways, go your ways. I knew what you
would prove;° my friends told me as much, and I thought no   *turn out to be*
less. That flattering tongue of yours won me. 'Tis but one cast
away,° and so, come, death! Two o'clock is your hour?   *one lover jilted*
160   ORLANDO   Ay, sweet Rosalind.

ROSALIND   By my troth, and in good earnest, and so God mend
me, and by all pretty oaths that are not dangerous, if you break
one jot of your promise or come one minute behind your hour,
I will think you the most pathetical° break-promise, and the   *pathetic*
165   most hollow lover, and the most unworthy of her you call Rosalind that may be chosen out of the gross° band of the unfaith-   *entire*
ful. Therefore beware my censure, and keep your promise.

ORLANDO   With no less religion° than if thou wert indeed my   *faith*
Rosalind. So, adieu.

170   ROSALIND   Well, Time is the old justice that examines all such
offenders; and let Time try.° Adieu.   *Exit* [ORLANDO]   *determine*

CELIA   You have simply misused° our sex in your love-prate. We   *completely slandered*
must have your doublet and hose plucked over your head, and
show the world what the bird hath done to her own nest.

175   ROSALIND   O coz, coz, coz, my pretty little coz, that thou didst
know how many fathom deep I am in love. But it cannot be
sounded. My affection hath an unknown bottom, like the Bay
of Portugal.

CELIA   Or rather bottomless, that° as fast as you pour affection   *so that*
180   in, it runs out.

ROSALIND   No, that same wicked bastard of Venus,[9] that was
begot of thought, conceived of spleen,° and born of madness,   *caprice*
that blind rascally boy that abuses° everyone's eyes because his   *deceives*
own are out, let him be judge how deep I am in love. I'll tell
185   thee, Aliena, I cannot be out of the sight of Orlando. I'll go
find a shadow° and sigh till he come.   *shady place*

CELIA   And I'll sleep.   *Exeunt*

---

7. Wit, where would you go? A catchphrase addressed
to one who talks too much.
8. Who cannot make her error a means of putting her
husband in the wrong.
9. Cupid, the son of Venus by her lover Mercury, not by
her husband, Vulcan.

4.2

Enter JAQUES *and* LORDS [*dressed as*] *foresters*[1]

JAQUES   Which is he that killed the deer?

FIRST LORD   Sir, it was I.

JAQUES [*to the others*]   Let's present him to the Duke like a
Roman conqueror. And it would do well to set the deer's horns
5   upon his head for a branch° of victory. Have you no song, for-   wreath
ester, for this purpose?

SECOND LORD   Yes, sir.

JAQUES   Sing it. 'Tis no matter how it be in tune, so it make
noise enough.

10   LORDS [*sing*][2]   What shall he have that killed the deer?
His leather skin and horns to wear.
Then sing him home; the rest shall bear°   carry; sing
This burden.°   (the deer); refrain
Take thou no scorn° to wear the horn;   Do not disdain
15   It was a crest[3] ere thou wast born.
Thy father's father wore it,
And thy father bore it.
The horn, the horn, the lusty horn
Is not a thing to laugh to scorn.   *Exeunt*

4.3

Enter ROSALIND [*as Ganymede*] *and* CELIA [*as Aliena*]

ROSALIND   How say you now? Is it not past two o'clock? And
here much Orlando.

CELIA   I warrant you, with pure love and troubled brain he hath
ta'en his bow and arrows and is gone forth to sleep.

Enter SILVIUS

5   Look who comes here.

SILVIUS [*to* ROSALIND]   My errand is to you, fair youth.
My gentle Phoebe did bid me give you this.
[*He offers* ROSALIND *a letter, which she takes and reads*]
I know not the contents, but as I guess
By the stern brow and waspish action
10   Which she did use as she was writing of it,
It bears an angry tenor. Pardon me;
I am but as a guiltless messenger.

ROSALIND   Patience herself would startle at this letter,
And play the swaggerer. Bear this, bear all.
15   She says I am not fair, that I lack manners;
She calls me proud, and that she could not love me
Were man as rare as Phoenix.[1] 'Od's° my will,   God's
Her love is not the hare that I do hunt.
Why writes she so to me? Well, shepherd, well,
20   This is a letter of your own device.

SILVIUS   No, I protest; I know not the contents.
Phoebe did write it.

ROSALIND   Come, come, you are a fool,

4.2
1. F's stage direction—"Enter Jaques and Lords,
Foresters"—leaves ambiguous whether Jaques and the
lords are dressed as foresters or are accompanied by
them.
2. F does not assign this song to anyone. The stage

direction reads: "Music, Song."
3. Coat of arms; head ornament.
4.3
1. A legendary bird of Arabia, supposedly unique,
which lived five hundred years, died in flames, and was
reborn from its own ashes.

And turned° into the extremity of love.   *brought*
I saw her hand. She has a leathern hand,
25   A free-stone° coloured hand. I verily did think   *yellow-brown limestone*
That her old gloves were on; but 'twas her hands.
She has a housewife's hand—but that's no matter.
I say she never did invent this letter.
This is a man's invention, and his hand.
30 SILVIUS   Sure, it is hers.
ROSALIND   Why, 'tis a boisterous and a cruel style,
A style for challengers. Why, she defies me,
Like Turk to Christian.[2] Women's gentle brain
Could not drop forth such giant-rude invention,
35   Such Ethiop[3] words, blacker in their effect
Than in their countenance. Will you hear the letter?
SILVIUS   So please you, for I never heard it yet,
Yet heard too much of Phoebe's cruelty.
ROSALIND   She Phoebes me.[4] Mark how the tyrant writes:
40   *Read*[s]   'Art thou god to shepherd turned,
        That a maiden's heart hath burned?'
Can a woman rail thus?
SILVIUS   Call you this railing?
ROSALIND *read*[s]   'Why, thy godhead laid apart,°   *set aside*
45   Warr'st thou with a woman's heart?'
Did you ever hear such railing?
      'Whiles the eye of man did woo me
      That could do no vengeance° to me.'—   *harm*
Meaning me a beast.
50   'If the scorn of your bright eyne°   *eyes*
      Have power to raise such love in mine,
      Alack, in me what strange effect
      Would they work in mild aspect?°   *if they looked kindly*
      Whiles you chid me I did love;
55   How then might your prayers move?
      He that brings this love to thee
      Little knows this love in me,
      And by him seal up thy mind[5]
      Whether that thy youth and kind°   *nature*
60   Will the faithful offer take
      Of me, and all that I can make,°   *offer you*
      Or else by him my love deny,
      And then I'll study how to die.'
SILVIUS   Call you this chiding?
65 CELIA   Alas, poor shepherd.
ROSALIND   Do you pity him? No, he deserves no pity. [*To* SIL-
VIUS] Wilt thou love such a woman? What, to make thee an
instrument,[6] and play false strains upon thee?—not to be
endured. Well, go your way to her—for I see love hath made
70 thee a tame snake—and say this to her: that if she love me, I

---

2. Alluding to medieval plays in which Turks and
Christians appeared as bitter enemies or to a common
Elizabethan perception of the Turk as an enemy to the
Christian countries of western Europe.
3. Ethiopian. In Elizabethan racial discourse, the term
signified blackness and evil.

4. Addresses me as Phoebe would—that is, in a disdainful manner.
5. And by means of him (Silvius), send your thoughts
to me (in a letter).
6. Tool; musical instrument.

charge her to love thee. If she will not, I will never have her
unless thou entreat for her. If you be a true lover, hence, and
not a word; for here comes more company. _Exit_ SILVIUS
Enter OLIVER

OLIVER Good morrow, fair ones. Pray you, if you know,
75 Where in the purlieus° of this forest stands   outskirts
A sheepcote fenced about with olive trees?
CELIA West of this place, down in the neighbour bottom.°   next valley
The rank of osiers° by the murmuring stream   row of willows
Left on your right hand brings you to the place.
80 But at this hour the house doth keep itself.
There's none within.
OLIVER If that an eye may profit by a tongue,
Then should I know you by description:
Such garments, and such years. 'The boy is fair,
85 Of female favour,° and bestows° himself   appearance / behaves
Like a ripe° sister. The woman low°   mature / short
And browner than her brother.' Are not you
The owner of the house I did enquire for?
CELIA It is no boast, being asked, to say we are.
90 OLIVER Orlando doth commend him to you both,
And to that youth he calls his Rosalind
He sends this bloody napkin.° Are you he?   handkerchief
ROSALIND I am. What must we understand by this?
OLIVER Some of my shame, if you will know of me
95 What man I am, and how, and why, and where
This handkerchief was stained.
CELIA   I pray you tell it.
OLIVER When last the young Orlando parted from you,
He left a promise to return again
Within an hour, and pacing through the forest,
100 Chewing the food of sweet and bitter fancy,
Lo what befell. He threw his eye aside,
And mark what object° did present itself.   what a spectacle
Under an old oak, whose boughs were mossed with age
And high top bald with dry antiquity,
105 A wretched, ragged man, o'ergrown with hair,
Lay sleeping on his back. About his neck
A green and gilded snake had wreathed itself,
Who with her head, nimble in threats, approached
The opening of his mouth. But suddenly
110 Seeing Orlando, it unlinked° itself,   uncoiled
And with indented° glides did slip away   undulating
Into a bush, under which bush's shade
A lioness, with udders all drawn dry,[7]
Lay couching, head on ground, with catlike watch
115 When that° the sleeping man should stir. For 'tis   In readiness for when
The royal disposition of that beast
To prey on nothing that doth seem as dead.
This seen, Orlando did approach the man
And found it was his brother, his elder brother.
120 CELIA O, I have heard him speak of that same brother,
And he did render him the most unnatural

---

7. Having been nursed dry, the lion would be ferociously hungry.

That lived amongst men.

OLIVER   And well he might so do,
For well I know he was unnatural.

ROSALIND   But to Orlando. Did he leave him there,
125   Food to the sucked and hungry lioness?

OLIVER   Twice did he turn his back, and purposed so.
But kindness, nobler ever than revenge,
And nature, stronger than his just occasion,°   *fair opportunity*
Made him give battle to the lioness,
130   Who quickly fell before him; in which hurtling°   *conflict*
From miserable slumber I awaked.

CELIA   Are you his brother?

ROSALIND   Was't you he rescued?

CELIA   Was't you that did so oft contrive° to kill him?   *plot*

OLIVER   'Twas I, but 'tis not I. I do not shame
135   To tell you what I was, since my conversion
So sweetly tastes, being the thing I am.

ROSALIND   But for° the bloody napkin?   *What about*

OLIVER   By and by.
When from the first to last betwixt us two
Tears our recountments° had most kindly bathed—   *narratives*
140   As how I came into that desert place—
I' brief, he led me to the gentle Duke,
Who gave me fresh array, and entertainment,°   *hospitality*
Committing me unto my brother's love,
Who led me instantly unto his cave,
145   There stripped himself, and here upon his arm
The lioness had torn some flesh away,
Which all this while had bled. And now he fainted,
And cried in fainting upon Rosalind.
Brief, I recovered° him, bound up his wound,   *revived*
150   And after some small space, being strong at heart,
He sent me hither, stranger as I am,
To tell this story, that you might excuse
His broken promise, and to give this napkin,
Dyed in his blood, unto the shepherd youth
155   That he in sport doth call his Rosalind.
[ROSALIND *faints*]

CELIA   Why, how now, Ganymede, sweet Ganymede!

OLIVER   Many will swoon when they do look on blood.

CELIA   There is more in it. Cousin Ganymede!

OLIVER   Look, he recovers.
160   ROSALIND   I would I were at home.

CELIA   We'll lead you thither.
[*To* OLIVER] I pray you, will you take him by the arm?

OLIVER   Be of good cheer, youth. You a man? You lack a man's
heart.
165   ROSALIND   I do so, I confess it. Ah, sirrah, a body would think
this was well counterfeited. I pray you, tell your brother how
well I counterfeited. Heigh-ho!

OLIVER   This was not counterfeit. There is too great testimony in
your complexion that it was a passion of earnest.°   *a genuine fit*
170   ROSALIND   Counterfeit, I assure you.

OLIVER   Well then, take a good heart, and counterfeit to be a
man.

ROSALIND So I do; but, i'faith, I should have been a woman by right.

175 CELIA Come, you look paler and paler. Pray you, draw homewards. Good sir, go with us.

OLIVER That will I, for I must bear answer back
How you excuse my brother, Rosalind.

ROSALIND I shall devise something. But I pray you commend
180 my counterfeiting to him. Will you go?   *Exeunt*

5.1

Enter [TOUCHSTONE *the*] *clown and* AUDREY

TOUCHSTONE We shall find a time, Audrey. Patience, gentle Audrey.

AUDREY Faith, the priest was good enough, for all the old gentleman's° saying.   *(Jaques's)*

5 TOUCHSTONE A most wicked Sir Oliver, Audrey, a most vile Martext. But, Audrey, there is a youth here in the forest lays claim to you.

AUDREY Ay, I know who 'tis. He hath no interest in me° in the   *no right to me*
world. Here comes the man you mean.

Enter WILLIAM

10 TOUCHSTONE It is meat and drink to me to see a clown.° By my   *peasant; yokel*
troth, we that have good wits have much to answer for. We
shall be flouting; we cannot hold.°   *refrain*

WILLIAM Good ev'n, Audrey.

AUDREY God ye° good ev'n, William.   *God give you*

15 WILLIAM [*to* TOUCHSTONE] And good ev'n to you, sir.

TOUCHSTONE Good ev'n, gentle friend. Cover thy head,[1] cover
thy head. Nay, prithee, be covered. How old are you, friend?

WILLIAM Five-and-twenty, sir.

TOUCHSTONE A ripe age. Is thy name William?

20 WILLIAM William, sir.

TOUCHSTONE A fair name. Wast born i'th' forest here?

WILLIAM Ay, sir, I thank God.

TOUCHSTONE Thank God—a good answer. Art rich?

WILLIAM Faith, sir, so-so.

25 TOUCHSTONE So-so is good, very good, very excellent good. And
yet it is not, it is but so-so. Art thou wise?

WILLIAM Ay, sir, I have a pretty wit.

TOUCHSTONE Why, thou sayst well. I do now remember a saying: 'The fool doth think he is wise, but the wise man knows
30 himself to be a fool.' The heathen philosopher, when he had a
desire to eat a grape, would open his lips when he put it into
his mouth, meaning thereby that grapes were made to eat, and
lips to open.[2] You do love this maid?

WILLIAM I do, sir.

35 TOUCHSTONE Give me your hand. Art thou learned?

WILLIAM No, sir.

TOUCHSTONE Then learn this of me: to have is to have. For it is
a figure in rhetoric° that drink, being poured out of a cup into   *rhetorical commonplace*
a glass, by filling the one doth empty the other. For all your

---

5.1
1. Evidently William has taken off his hat in a gesture
of deference.

2. Touchstone's speech may be a response to William's
gaping mouth.

40 writers do consent that *ipse* is he.[3] Now you are not *ipse*, for I
am he.

WILLIAM   Which he, sir?

TOUCHSTONE   He, sir, that must marry this woman. Therefore,
you clown, abandon—which is in the vulgar, leave—the soci-
45 ety—which in the boorish is company—of this female—which
in the common is woman; which together is, abandon the society of this female, or, clown, thou perishest; or, to thy better
understanding, diest; or, to wit, I kill thee, make thee away,
translate thy life into death, thy liberty into bondage. I will deal
50 in poison with thee, or in bastinado,° or in steel. I will bandy   *beating with a club*
with thee in faction, I will o'errun thee with policy.[4] I will kill
thee a hundred and fifty ways. Therefore tremble, and depart.

AUDREY   Do, good William.

WILLIAM   God rest you merry, sir.   *Exit*

            Enter CORIN

55 CORIN   Our master and mistress seeks you. Come, away, away.

TOUCHSTONE   Trip, Audrey, trip, Audrey. [*To* CORIN] I attend, I
attend.   *Exeunt*

5.2

            Enter ORLANDO *and* OLIVER

ORLANDO   Is't possible that on so little acquaintance you should
like her? That but seeing, you should love her? And loving,
woo? And wooing, she should grant? And will you persevere to
enjoy her?

5 OLIVER   Neither call the giddiness° of it in question, the poverty   *foolish haste*
of her, the small acquaintance, my sudden wooing, nor her
sudden consenting; but say with me, 'I love Aliena'; say with
her, that she loves me; consent with both that we may enjoy
each other. It shall be to your good, for my father's house and
10 all the revenue that was old Sir Rowland's will I estate° upon   *settle*
you, and here live and die a shepherd.

            Enter ROSALIND [*as Ganymede*]

ORLANDO   You have my consent. Let your wedding be tomorrow.
Thither will I invite the Duke and all's contented followers. Go
you, and prepare Aliena; for look you, here comes my Rosalind.

15 ROSALIND   God save you, brother.

OLIVER   And you, fair sister.   [*Exit*]

ROSALIND   O, my dear Orlando, how it grieves me to see thee
wear thy heart in a scarf.°   *sling*

ORLANDO   It is my arm.

20 ROSALIND   I thought thy heart had been wounded with the claws
of a lion.

ORLANDO   Wounded it is, but with the eyes of a lady.

ROSALIND   Did your brother tell you how I counterfeited to
swoon when he showed me your handkerchief?

25 ORLANDO   Ay, and greater wonders than that.

ROSALIND   O, I know where you are. Nay, 'tis true. There was
never anything so sudden but the fight of two rams, and Cae-

---

3. For all authorities agree that *ipse* is translated as "he
himself." The Latin word was proverbially applied to
successful lovers.

4. I will contend ("bandy") with you in argument, I will
overwhelm you with craftiness.
5.2

sar's thrasonical° brag of 'I came, saw, and overcame',[1] for your   *boastful*
brother and my sister no sooner met but they looked; no sooner
30 looked but they loved; no sooner loved but they sighed; no
sooner sighed but they asked one another the reason; no sooner
knew the reason but they sought the remedy; and in these
degrees have they made a pair° of stairs to marriage, which they   *flight*
will climb incontinent,° or else be incontinent[2] before mar-   *hastily*
35 riage. They are in the very wrath of love,° and they will together.   *heat of passion*
Clubs cannot part them.

ORLANDO   They shall be married tomorrow, and I will bid the
Duke to the nuptial. But O, how bitter a thing it is to look into
happiness through another man's eyes. By so much the more
40 shall I tomorrow be at the height of heart-heaviness by how
much I shall think my brother happy in having what he wishes
for.

ROSALIND   Why, then, tomorrow I cannot serve your turn[3] for
Rosalind?

45 ORLANDO   I can live no longer by thinking.

ROSALIND   I will weary you then no longer with idle talking.
Know of me then—for now I speak to some purpose—that I
know you are a gentleman of good conceit.° I speak not this   *understanding*
that you should bear a good opinion of my knowledge, inso-
50 much° I say I know you are; neither do I labour for a greater   *inasmuch as*
esteem than may in some little measure draw a belief from you
to do yourself good,[4] and not to grace me. Believe then, if you
please, that I can do strange things. I have since I was three
year old conversed° with a magician, most profound in his art,   *associated*
55 and yet not damnable.[5] If you do love Rosalind so near the
heart as your gesture° cries it out, when your brother marries   *behavior*
Aliena shall you marry her. I know into what straits of fortune
she is driven, and it is not impossible to me, if it appear not
inconvenient to you, to set her before your eyes tomorrow,
60 human as she is, and without any danger.

ORLANDO   Speakest thou in sober meanings?

ROSALIND   By my life, I do, which I tender° dearly, though I say   *value*
I am a magician. Therefore put you in your best array, bid°   *invite*
your friends: for if you will be married tomorrow, you shall;
65 and to Rosalind if you will.

Enter SILVIUS *and* PHOEBE

Look, here comes a lover of mine and a lover of hers.

PHOEBE [*to* ROSALIND]   Youth, you have done me much ungentleness,°   *discourtesy*
To show the letter that I writ to you.

ROSALIND   I care not if I have. It is my study
70 To seem despiteful° and ungentle to you.   *contemptuous*
You are there followed by a faithful shepherd.
Look upon him; love him. He worships you.

PHOEBE [*to* SILVIUS]   Good shepherd, tell this youth what 'tis to love.

SILVIUS   It is to be all made of sighs and tears,
75 And so am I for Phoebe.

---

1. Caesar's well-known announcement of military victory, quoted as it appears in Thomas North's translation
of Plutarch's *Lives* (1579).
2. Be sexually unrestrained.
3. Substitute for Rosalind; satisfy you sexually in Rosalind's place.

4. *neither . . . good*: nor am I attempting to enhance my
reputation more than is necessary to persuade you to do
yourself some good.
5. That is, not meriting execution for heresy. Elizabethan statutes made certain forms of witchcraft and
black magic punishable by death.

PHOEBE   And I for Ganymede.

ORLANDO   And I for Rosalind.

ROSALIND   And I for no woman.

SILVIUS   It is to be all made of faith and service,

80   And so am I for Phoebe.

PHOEBE   And I for Ganymede.

ORLANDO   And I for Rosalind.

ROSALIND   And I for no woman.

SILVIUS   It is to be all made of fantasy,

85   All made of passion, and all made of wishes,

All adoration, duty, and observance,°   *devotion*

All humbleness, all patience and impatience,

All purity, all trial, all obedience,

And so am I for Phoebe.

90   PHOEBE   And so am I for Ganymede.

ORLANDO   And so am I for Rosalind.

ROSALIND   And so am I for no woman.

PHOEBE [*to* ROSALIND]   If this be so, why blame you me to love you?

95   SILVIUS [*to* PHOEBE]   If this be so, why blame you me to love you?

ORLANDO   If this be so, why blame you me to love you?

ROSALIND   Why do you speak too, 'Why blame you me to love you?'

100   ORLANDO   To her that is not here nor doth not hear.

ROSALIND   Pray you, no more of this, 'tis like the howling of Irish wolves against the moon.[6]   [*To* SILVIUS] I will help you if I can. [*To* PHOEBE] I would love you if I could.—Tomorrow meet me all together. [*To* PHOEBE] I will marry you if ever I

105   marry woman, and I'll be married tomorrow. [*To* ORLANDO] I will satisfy you if ever I satisfy man, and you shall be married tomorrow. [*To* SILVIUS] I will content you if what pleases you contents you, and you shall be married tomorrow. [*To* ORLANDO] As you love Rosalind, meet. [*To* SILVIUS] As you

110   love Phoebe, meet. And as I love no woman, I'll meet. So fare you well. I have left you commands.

SILVIUS   I'll not fail, if I live.

PHOEBE   Nor I.

ORLANDO   Nor I.   *Exeunt* [*severally*]

5.3

Enter [TOUCHSTONE *the*] *clown and* AUDREY

TOUCHSTONE   Tomorrow is the joyful day, Audrey, tomorrow will we be married.

AUDREY   I do desire it with all my heart; and I hope it is no dishonest° desire to desire to be a woman of the world.° Here   *unchaste / married*

5   come two of the banished Duke's pages.

Enter two PAGES

FIRST PAGE   Well met, honest gentleman.

TOUCHSTONE   By my troth, well met. Come, sit, sit, and a song.

---

6. That is, it is barbaric. The howling of wolves at the moon was a proverbial way of referring to an irrational or futile course of action. Irish wolves might be perceived as especially disorderly, for Ireland's abundance of wolves was for many Elizabethan writers a mark of that country's lack of civility.

5.3

SECOND PAGE   We are for you.° Sit i'th' middle.   *That suits us*

FIRST PAGE   Shall we clap into't roundly, without hawking[1], or
10   spitting, or saying we are hoarse, which are the only° prologues   *proper*
        to a bad voice?

SECOND PAGE   I'faith, i'faith, and both in a tune,° like two gipsies   *in unison*
        on a horse.

BOTH PAGES [*sing*][2]   It was a lover and his lass,
15   With a hey, and a ho, and a hey-nonny-no,
                  That o'er the green cornfield° did pass   *field of wheat*
                      In spring-time, the only pretty ring-time,°   *time for weddings*
                  When birds do sing, hey ding-a-ding ding,
                  Sweet lovers love the spring.

20   Between the acres of the rye,
                      With a hey, and a ho, and a hey-nonny-no,
                  These pretty country folks would lie,
                      In spring-time, the only pretty ring-time,
                  When birds do sing, hey ding-a-ding ding,
25   Sweet lovers love the spring.

                  This carol they began that hour,
                      With a hey, and a ho, and a hey-nonny-no,
                  How that a life was but a flower,
                      In spring-time, the only pretty ring-time,
30   When birds do sing, hey ding-a-ding ding,
                  Sweet lovers love the spring.

                  And therefore take° the present time,   *seize*
                      With a hey, and a ho, and a hey-nonny-no,
                  For love is crownèd with the prime,°   *spring; perfection*
35   In spring time, the only pretty ring-time,
                  When birds do sing, hey ding-a-ding ding,
                  Sweet lovers love the spring.

TOUCHSTONE   Truly, young gentlemen, though there was no
        great matter° in the ditty, yet the note[3] was very untunable.   *sense*
40 FIRST PAGE   You are deceived, sir, we kept time, we lost not our
        time.

TOUCHSTONE   By my troth, yes, I count it but time lost to hear
        such a foolish song. God b'wi'you, and God mend your voices.
        Come, Audrey.   *Exeunt [severally]*

5.4

Enter DUKE SENIOR, AMIENS, JAQUES, ORLANDO, OLIVER,
[*and*] CELIA [*as Aliena*]

DUKE SENIOR   Dost thou believe, Orlando, that the boy
        Can do all this that he hath promisèd?

ORLANDO   I sometimes do believe, and sometimes do not,
        As those that fear they hope,[1] and know they fear.

Enter ROSALIND [*as Ganymede*], [*with*] SILVIUS *and*
        PHOEBE

---

1. Shall we begin energetically and at once, without
clearing our throats?
2. F does not include this speech prefix, simply the
world "song." This is one of the few Shakespeare songs
for which contemporary music survives. It is set for a

single voice with lute accompaniment in Thomas Morley's *First Booke of Ayres* (1600).
3. Yet the music was disagreeable.
5.4
1. Fear that their hope will not be fulfilled.

5   ROSALIND   Patience once more, whiles our compact is urged.°   *declared*
    [*To the* DUKE] You say if I bring in your Rosalind
    You will bestow her on Orlando here?
    DUKE SENIOR   That would I, had I° kingdoms to give with her.   *even if I had*
    ROSALIND [*to* ORLANDO]   And you say you will have her when I
        bring her?
10 ORLANDO   That would I, were I of all kingdoms king.
    ROSALIND [*to* PHOEBE]   You say you'll marry me if I be willing?
    PHOEBE   That will I, should I die the hour after.
    ROSALIND   But if you do refuse to marry me
        You'll give yourself to this most faithful shepherd?
15 PHOEBE   So is the bargain.
    ROSALIND [*to* SILVIUS]   You say that you'll have Phoebe if she will.
    SILVIUS   Though to have her and death were both one thing.
    ROSALIND   I have promised to make all this matter even.°   *smooth*
        Keep you your word, O Duke, to give your daughter.
20   You yours, Orlando, to receive his daughter.
        Keep your word, Phoebe, that you'll marry me,
        Or else refusing me to wed this shepherd.
        Keep your word, Silvius, that you'll marry her
        If she refuse me; and from hence I go
25   To make these doubts all even.   *Exeunt* ROSALIND *and* CELIA
    DUKE SENIOR   I do remember in this shepherd boy
        Some lively° touches of my daughter's favour.°   *vivid / appearance*
    ORLANDO   My lord, the first time that I ever saw him,
        Methought he was a brother to your daughter.
30   But, my good lord, this boy is forest-born,
        And hath been tutored in the rudiments
        Of many desperate° studies by his uncle,   *dangerous*
        Whom he reports to be a great magician
        Obscurèd in the circle of this forest.[2]
        Enter [TOUCHSTONE *the*] *clown and* AUDREY
35 JAQUES   There is sure another flood toward,° and these couples   *at hand*
        are coming to the ark.[3] Here comes a pair of very strange
        beasts, which in all tongues are called fools.
    TOUCHSTONE   Salutation and greeting to you all.
    JAQUES [*to the* DUKE]   Good my lord, bid him welcome. This is
40   the motley-minded° gentleman that I have so often met in the   *foolish-brained*
        forest. He hath been a courtier, he swears.
    TOUCHSTONE   If any man doubt that, let him put me to my pur-
        gation.[4] I have trod a measure,° I have flattered a lady, I have   *danced*
        been politic with my friend, smooth with mine enemy, I have
45   undone° three tailors, I have had four quarrels, and like to have   *made bankrupt*
        fought° one.   *came close to fighting*
    JAQUES   And how was that ta'en up?°   *settled*
    TOUCHSTONE   Faith, we met, and found the quarrel was upon
        the seventh cause.
50 JAQUES   How, seventh cause?—Good my lord, like this fellow.
    DUKE SENIOR   I like him very well.
    TOUCHSTONE   God'ield you, sir, I desire you of the like. I press

---

2. Concealed within the boundaries of this forest. Perhaps a reference to the magic circle within which magi-
cians were supposed to be able to practice their art safely.
3. Alluding to a biblical account in Genesis 7:2 in
which pairs of male and female animals shelter on
Noah's ark to escape the flood that covers the earth.
4. Let me be put to trial to clear myself (of the charge
of lying).

in here, sir, amongst the rest of the country copulatives,[5] to
swear, and to forswear, according as marriage binds and blood
55   breaks.° A poor virgin, sir, an ill-favoured thing, sir, but mine   *passion rebels*
own. A poor humour° of mine, sir, to take that that no man else   *whim*
will. Rich honesty° dwells like a miser, sir, in a poor house, as   *chastity*
your pearl in your foul oyster.

DUKE SENIOR   By my faith, he is very swift and sententious.°   *witty and wise*
60 TOUCHSTONE   According to the fool's bolt,[6] sir, and such dulcet
diseases.°   *sweet afflictions*

JAQUES   But for the seventh cause. How did you find the quarrel on the seventh cause?

TOUCHSTONE   Upon a lie seven times removed.—Bear your body
65 more seeming,° Audrey.—As thus, sir: I did dislike[7] the cut of   *becomingly*
a certain courtier's beard. He sent me word if I said his beard
was not cut well, he was in the mind it was. This is called the
Retort Courteous. If I sent him word again it was not well cut,
he would send me word he cut it to please himself. This is
70 called the Quip Modest. If again it was not well cut, he disa-
bled° my judgement. This is called the Reply Churlish. If again   *disparaged*
it was not well cut, he would answer I spake not true. This is
called the Reproof Valiant. If again it was not well cut, he
would say I lie. This is called the Countercheck° Quarrelsome.   *rebuff*
75 And so to the Lie Circumstantial,° and the Lie Direct.   *indirect*

JAQUES   And how oft did you say his beard was not well cut?

TOUCHSTONE   I durst go no further than the Lie Circumstantial,
nor he durst not give me the Lie Direct; and so we measured
swords,[8] and parted.

80 JAQUES   Can you nominate° in order now the degrees of the lie?   *name*

TOUCHSTONE   O sir, we quarrel in print, by the book,[9] as you
have books for good manners.[1] I will name you the degrees.
The first, the Retort Courteous; the second, the Quip Modest;
the third, the Reply Churlish; the fourth, the Reproof Valiant;
85 the fifth, the Countercheck Quarrelsome; the sixth, the Lie
with Circumstance; the seventh, the Lie Direct. All these you
may avoid but the Lie Direct; and you may avoid that, too, with
an 'if'. I knew when seven justices could not take up° a quarrel,   *settle*
but when the parties were met themselves, one of them
90 thought but of an 'if', as 'If you said so, then I said so', and they
shook hands and swore brothers.° Your 'if' is the only peace   *became sworn brothers*
maker; much virtue in 'if'.

JAQUES [*to the* DUKE]   Is not this a rare fellow, my lord? He's as
good at anything, and yet a fool.

95 DUKE SENIOR   He uses his folly like a stalking-horse,[2] and under
the presentation° of that he shoots his wit.   *appearance*

        Still° music. Enter HYMEN[3] [*with*] ROSALIND *and* CELIA   *Soft*
        [*as themselves*]

HYMEN   Then is there mirth in heaven

---

5. People about to copulate.
6. And his wittiness quickly disappears. Alluding to the
proverb "A fool's bolt (or arrow) is soon shot."
7. Show my dislike of.
8. Checked that our swords were of the same length
(as was usual prior to a duel).
9. According to the rules as set down in books on the
etiquette of dueling. Touchstone's speech exposes the
absurd aspects of the elaborate codes of behavior set

forth in such books.
1. Elizabethan England witnessed an outpouring of
courtesy literature aimed at both social aspirants and
established courtiers.
2. A real or imitation horse used as a means of camou-
flage in hunting.
3. The god of marriage in classical mythology, conventionally depicted as a young man who carried a veil and
a bridal torch.

When earthly things made even°   *set right*
Atone° together.   *Are at one; unite*
100   Good Duke, receive thy daughter;
Hymen from heaven brought her,
    Yea, brought her hither,
That thou mightst join her hand with his
Whose heart within his bosom is.
105   ROSALIND [*to the* DUKE]   To you I give myself, for I am yours.
    [*To* ORLANDO] To you I give myself, for I am yours.
  DUKE SENIOR   If there be truth in sight, you are my daughter.
  ORLANDO   If there be truth in sight, you are my Rosalind.
  PHOEBE   If sight and shape be true,
110   Why then, my love adieu!
  ROSALIND [*to the* DUKE]   I'll have no father if you be not he.
    [*To* ORLANDO]   I'll have no husband if you be not he,
    [*To* PHOEBE]   Nor ne'er wed woman if you be not she.
  HYMEN   Peace, ho, I bar° confusion.   *forbid*
115   'Tis I must make conclusion
        Of these most strange events.
        Here's eight that must take hands
        To join in Hymen's bands,°   *bonds of marriage*
        If truth holds true contents.⁴
    [*To* ORLANDO *and* ROSALIND]
120   You and you no cross° shall part.   *adversity*
    [*To* OLIVER *and* CELIA]
     You and you are heart in heart.
    [*To* PHOEBE]
     You to his love must accord,°   *consent*
     Or have a woman to° your lord.   *as*
    [*To* TOUCHSTONE *and* AUDREY]
     You and you are sure together°   *tightly bound*
125   As the winter to foul weather.—
     Whiles a wedlock hymn we sing,
     Feed° yourselves with questioning,   *Satisfy*
     That reason wonder may diminish
     How thus we met, and these things finish.

Song

130   Wedding is great Juno's° crown,   *goddess of marriage*
        O blessèd bond of board and bed.
     'Tis Hymen peoples every town.
        High° wedlock then be honourèd.   *Solemn*
     Honour, high honour and renown
135   To Hymen, god of every town.
  DUKE SENIOR [*to* CELIA]   O my dear niece, welcome thou art to me,
  Even daughter; welcome in no less degree.⁵
  PHOEBE [*to* SILVIUS]   I will not eat my word. Now thou art mine,
  Thy faith my fancy° to thee doth combine.   *love*
    Enter [JAQUES DE BOIS, *the*] *second brother*
140   JAQUES DE BOIS   Let me have audience for a word or two.
  I am the second son of old Sir Rowland,

---

4. If truth is true; if truth please you.   5. You are no less welcome than a daughter.

That bring these tidings to this fair assembly.
Duke Frederick, hearing how that every day
Men of great worth resorted to this forest,
145 Addressed a mighty power,° which were on foot,   army
In his own conduct,° purposely to take   Under his command
His brother here, and put him to the sword.
And to the skirts° of this wild wood he came   outskirts
Where, meeting with an old religious man,
150 After some question° with him was converted   conversation
Both from his enterprise and from the world,
His crown bequeathing to his banished brother,
And all their lands restored to them again
That were with him exiled. This to be true
I do engage° my life.   pledge
155 DUKE SENIOR   Welcome, young man.
Thou offer'st fairly° to thy brothers' wedding: You bring fine gifts
To one° his lands withheld, and to the other°   (Oliver) / (Orlando)
A land itself at large,⁶ a potent° dukedom.   powerful
First, in this forest let us do° those ends   accomplish
160 That here were well begun, and well begot.°   conceived
And after, every° of this happy number   every one
That have endured shrewd° days and nights with us   evil
Shall share the good of our returnèd fortune
According to the measure of their states.°   ranks
165 Meantime, forget this new-fallen° dignity   newly acquired
And fall into our rustic revelry.
Play, music, and you brides and bridegrooms all,
With measure heaped in joy to th' measures fall.⁷
JAQUES   Sir, by your patience.° [To JAQUES DE BOIS] If I heard   with your permission
          you rightly
170 The Duke hath put on a religious life
And thrown into neglect the pompous° court.   ceremonious
JAQUES DE BOIS   He hath.
JAQUES   To him will I. Out of these convertites°   converts
There is much matter to be heard and learned.
[To the DUKE]
175 You to your former honour I bequeath;
Your patience and your virtue well deserves it.
[To ORLANDO]
You to a love that your true faith doth merit;
[To OLIVER]
You to your land, and love, and great allies;°   relatives
[To SILVIUS]
You to a long and well-deservèd bed;
[To TOUCHSTONE]
180 And you to wrangling, for thy loving voyage
Is but for two months victualled.°—So, to your pleasures;   supplied with food
I am for other than for dancing measures.
DUKE SENIOR   Stay, Jaques, stay.
JAQUES   To see no pastime, I. What you would have°   like (from me)
185 I'll stay to know at your abandoned cave.   *Exit*

---

6. An entire country. As Rosalind's husband, Orlando is heir to the dukedom returned to Duke Senior.

7. With a measure of overflowing joy, begin your dances ("measures").

DUKE SENIOR   Proceed, proceed. We'll so begin these rites
As we do trust they'll end, in true delights.
        [*They dance; then*] *exeunt* [*all but* ROSALIND]⁸

[Epilogue]

ROSALIND [*to the audience*]   It is not the fashion to see the lady
the epilogue;¹ but it is no more unhandsome than to see the
lord the prologue. If it be true that good wine needs no bush,²
'tis true that a good play needs no epilogue. Yet to good wine
5   they do use good bushes, and good plays prove the better by
the help of good epilogues. What a case° am I in then, that am   *plight; costume*
neither a good epilogue nor cannot insinuate° with you in the   *ingratiate myself*
behalf of a good play! I am not furnished like a beggar, there-
fore to beg will not become me. My way is to conjure° you;   *charge; bewitch*
10   and I'll begin with the women. I charge you, O women, for the
love you bear to men, to like as much of this play as please you.
And I charge you, O men, for the love you bear to women—as
I perceive by your simpering none of you hates them—that
between you and the women the play° may please. If I were a   *drama; love play*
15   woman³ I would kiss as many of you as had beards that pleased
me, complexions that liked° me, and breaths that I defied° not.   *pleased / disdained*
And I am sure, as many as have good beards, or good faces, or
sweet breaths will for my kind offer, when I make curtsy, bid
me farewell.°   *Exit*   *(with applause)*

---

8. F indicates only a single exit for Duke Senior, but
most editors assume that Rosalind remains alone
onstage to deliver the Epilogue.
Epilogue
1. In the vast majority of Elizabethan plays, the Epilogue is spoken by a male character.

2. Advertisement. A proverb derived from the practice
of hanging a branch of ivy in tavern windows to indicate
that wine was for sale.
3. A pointed reference to the fact that women's roles in
the Elizabethan theater were played by boys.

Hamlet

"Who's there?" Shakespeare's most famous play begins. The question, turned back on the tragedy itself, has haunted actors, audiences and readers for centuries. *Hamlet* is an enigma. Mountains of feverish speculation have only deepened the interlocking mysteries: Why does Hamlet delay avenging the murder of his father by Claudius, his father's brother? How much guilt does Hamlet's mother, Gertrude, who has since married Claudius, bear in this crime? How trustworthy is the ghost of Hamlet's father, who has returned from the grave to demand that Hamlet avenge his murder? Is vengeance morally justifiable in this play, or is it to be condemned? What exactly *is* the ghost, and where has it come from? Why is the ghost, visible to everyone in the first act, visible only to Hamlet in Act 3? Is Hamlet's madness feigned or true, a strategy masquerading as a reality or a reality masquerading as a strategy? Does Hamlet, who once loved Ophelia, continue to love her in spite of his apparent cruelty? Does Ophelia, crushed by that cruelty and driven mad by Hamlet's murder of her father, Polonius, actually intend to drown herself, or does she die accidentally? What enables Hamlet to pass from thoughts of suicide to faith in God's providence, from "To be, or not to be" to "Let be"? What was Hamlet trying to say before death stopped his speech at the close?

Shakespeare probably wrote *Hamlet* in 1600 (shortly after *Julius Caesar,* to which Polonius seems to allude at 3.2.93), but the precise date of composition is uncertain, and this uncertainty is compounded by the exceptionally complex state of the text. *The Tragedie of Hamlet, Prince of Denmarke* is included in the First Folio of 1623, but most editions of the play since the eighteenth century have incorporated passages that appear only in an earlier text, the Second Quarto, dated 1604 and entitled *The Tragicall Historie of Hamlet, Prince of Denmarke*. In the present edition of the play, based on the Folio text, lines that appear only in the Second Quarto are indented and numbered separately, so that readers will be able to assess the difference between the two versions. (Further information on these texts and on the First or so-called Bad Quarto is given in the Textual Note.) *Hamlet* is a monument of world literature, but it is a monument built on shifting sands.

With a text so fraught with uncertainty, it is tempting to think that our unresolved questions are largely the result of the perplexities that must inevitably come with the passage of time and the vagaries of editors. Yet the play in all its versions seems designed to provoke such perplexities. "What art thou?" Horatio asks the Ghost, and the question, unanswered, is echoed again and again until it seems to touch on everything: "Is it not like the King?" (1.1.57); "Why seems it so particular with thee?" (1.2.75); "What does this mean, my lord?" (1.4.8); "Whither wilt thou lead me?" (1.5.1); "What's Hecuba to him, or he to Hecuba, / That he should weep for her?" (2.2.536–37); "Why wouldst thou be a breeder of sinners?" (3.1.122–23); "What should such fellows as I do crawling between heaven and earth?" (3.1.127–28); "Do you see nothing there?" (3.4.122); "What is it ye would see?" (5.2.306). The dream of getting answers to such questions tantalizes many of the play's characters and drives them to scrutinize one another. But the task is maddeningly difficult. When Hamlet repeatedly asks Guildenstern, one of the school friends whom his uncle has set to spy on him, to play the recorder, Guildenstern protests that he does not know how. "You would play upon me," Hamlet returns, "you would seem to know my stops, you would pluck out the heart of my mystery. . . . do you think I am easier to be played on than a pipe?" (3.2.335–40).

Hamlet at once invites and resists interrogation. He is, more than any theatrical

A man may not marrie his

Mother. Stepmother. Wiues mother.	} The right afcending line, and firſt degree.
Sonnes daughter. Daughters daughter. Wiues ſonnes daughter. Wiues daughters daughter.	} The right defcéding line and ſecond degree.
Daughter. Wiues daughter. Sonnes wife.	} The right defcending line and firſt degree.
Siſter. Wiues ſiſter. Brothers wife.	} The equall collaterall line, and firſt degree.
Fathers ſiſter. Mothers ſiſter. Fathers brothers wife.	} The vnequall collaterall line, and ſecond degree.

30 Therfore ſhall ye keepe mine ordinances, that ye doe not any of the abhominable cuſtomes, which haue been done before you.

Table of prohibited marriages. From William Clerke, *The Triall of Bastardie* (London, 1594).

character before and perhaps since, a figure constructed around an unseen or secret core. Such a figure in the theater is something of a paradox, since all that exists of any character onstage is what is seen and heard there. But from his place onstage at the center of a courtly world in which he is "the observed of all observers" and hence a person allowed virtually no privacy, Hamlet insists that he has "that within which passeth show" (1.2.85). What is it that he has "within"? In the nineteenth century, following a suggestion by the German poet Johann Wolfgang von Goethe, critics frequently argued that Hamlet has within him the soul of a poet, too sensitive, delicate, and complex to endure the cruel pressures of a coarse world. In the twentieth century, following a suggestion by the founder of psychoanalysis, Sigmund Freud, many critics have speculated that Hamlet has within him an unresolved Oedipus complex, a sexual desire for his mother that prevents him from taking decisive action against the man who has done in reality the thing that Hamlet unconsciously desires to do: kill his father and marry his mother. On occasion, this psychological speculation has been challenged by a political one: Hamlet hides within himself a spirit of political resistance, a subversive challenge to a corrupt, illegitimate regime shored up by lies, spies, and treachery.

These recurrent attempts to pluck out the heart of Hamlet's mystery are a modern continuation of an interpretive activity that goes on throughout the play itself. Attempting to solve the riddle of Hamlet's strange behavior, Polonius speculates that the Prince is desperately lovesick for his daughter, but Claudius concludes, after spying on Hamlet's conversation with Ophelia, that "his affections do not that way tend" (3.1.161). Rosencrantz and Guildenstern propose that Hamlet is suffering from ambition—after all, though Denmark is an elective monarchy, the Prince could have hoped to succeed his father on the throne—but Hamlet vehemently refutes the charge: "O God, I could be bounded in a nutshell and count myself a king of infinite space, were it not that I have bad dreams" (2.2.248–50). Claudius doubts that Hamlet is mad and, even though he never directly articulates this suspicion, seems to fear that the Prince somehow knows of his secret crime. But Hamlet's painful interiority, his melancholy insistence that he has something "within," is already clear from his first appearance, before the Ghost's revelation. Gertrude therefore seems wiser to argue that her son's distemper at least originates in "his father's death and our o'er-hasty marriage" (2.2.57).

As we first encounter him, Hamlet is a young man in deep mourning, which his mother and uncle both urge him to cease. The death of fathers is natural and inevitable, they point out, and while it is customary to grieve, it is unreasonable to persist obstinately in sorrow. Hamlet responds that his grief is not a theatrical performance, a mere costume to be put on and then discarded. When he is alone onstage a few moments later, he discloses, in the first of his famous soliloquies, a near-suicidal despair and a corrosive bitterness centered on the haste with which his mother has remarried. This bitterness is intensified by Hamlet's idealized image of his father and by painful memories of what had seemed to him his parents' perfect mutual love. As he broods on the brief time between his father's death and his mother's remarriage, Hamlet's mind convulsively shortens the interval: "two months," "nay, not so much, not two," "within a month."

At such moments—and there are many in the play—the audience seems to have direct access to the protagonist's tormented inner life. That life appears startlingly raw and unscripted, but the impression is actually the consequence of Shakespeare's sophisticated poetic skills. Hamlet's soliloquies are carefully crafted rhetorical performances. Thus, for example, the celebrated lines that begin "To be, or not to be; that is the question" (3.1.58ff.) have the structure of a formal academic debate on the subject of suicide: prudently considering both sides of the question and rehearsing venerable commonplaces, Hamlet does not once use the words "I" or "me." Yet here and elsewhere his words manage with astonishing vividness to convey the spontaneous rhythms of a mind in motion. Shakespeare had anticipated this achievement in such plays as *Richard II, 1 Henry IV,* and *Julius Caesar*: King Richard, Prince Hal, and Brutus all have intimate moments in which they seem to disclose the troubled faces that are normally hidden behind expressionless social masks. But in its moral complexity, psychological depth, and philosophical power, *Hamlet* seems to mark an epochal shift not only in Shakespeare's own career but in Western drama; it is as if the play were giving birth to a whole new kind of literary subjectivity. This subjectivity—the sense of being inside a character's psyche and following its twists and turns—is to a large degree an effect of language, the product of dramatic poetry and prose of unprecedented intensity. In order to convey a traumatized mind struggling to articulate perceptions of a shattered world, Shakespeare developed a complex syntax and a remarkably expanded diction. Take the moment, for example, in which Hamlet broods about the spectacle of Fortinbras's army marching off to fight to the death for a worthless piece of ground. Hamlet is struck by the absurd waste of lives and wealth, but then his agonized consciousness of his failure to act more quickly to avenge his father's death begins to transform his thinking. The strain in the syntax reflects the strain of a mind queasily in motion:

> Rightly to be great
> Is not to stir without great argument,
> But greatly to find quarrel in a straw
> When honour's at the stake.
>
> (4.4.9.43–9.46)

So, too, by one scholar's count, Shakespeare introduced over six hundred words in *Hamlet* that he had not used before. Many of these words—"self-slaughter," "unweeded," "fanged," "malefaction," "unpolluted," "compulsive," and so on—do not appear, at least in the form or with the meaning they have here, in any previous English text. The innovative inwardness is not restricted to scenes in which Hamlet is alone onstage, nor is it restricted to the Prince himself; indeed, many of the deepest psychic revelations in the play are conveyed not in moments of isolation but in disturbing exchanges, intimate encounters in which love and poison are intertwined.

These innovations are not called for by the story itself. In *Hamlet,* as in so many of his plays, Shakespeare was recycling narratives long in circulation. The legendary tale of Hamlet (Amleth) was already recounted at length in the late twelfth-century *Danish History* compiled in Latin by Saxo the Grammarian. (The tale was retold in French in François de Belleforest's 1570 collection *Histoires Tragiques*.) In Saxo's version, the unscrupulous Feng ambushes and kills his brother Horwendil and marries Horwendil's wife, Gerutha. Horwendil and Gerutha had a son, Amleth, who undertakes to avenge his father. In doing so, the son suffers no pangs of conscience, since in pre-Christian Denmark revenge was not a violation of the moral or religious law but a filial obligation. And he needs no ghost to inform him of what happened and experiences no sickening uncertainty about his uncle's guilt, since the murder is public knowledge. Amleth's problem is survival: young and surrounded by Feng's henchmen, his every move is carefully watched. In order to avert suspicion and buy time, the cunning avenger pretends to be feebleminded. His strategy works: with the active assistance of his mother, Amleth eventually succeeds in killing his uncle, along with the uncle's followers, and is enthusiastically proclaimed King of Denmark.

This is the rough outline of the story that Shakespeare inherited, along, it seems, with at least one other version about which we know tantalizingly little: by 1589, English audiences had evidently seen a play, now lost, on the theme of Hamlet. Apparently, this play—which scholars call the Ur (original)-*Hamlet*—featured a ghost who cried, "Hamlet, revenge!" On the basis of the barest shreds of contemporary evidence, scholars have constructed elaborate theories about this supposed source play, but there is little agreement among them. Assuming that there was an Elizabethan staging of the story that preceded Shakespeare's, its author remains unknown. Many scholars have assigned it to Thomas Kyd, who wrote *The Spanish Tragedy* (c. 1587), one of the most successful and enduring Elizabethan plays. *The Spanish Tragedy* itself has features that strikingly anticipate Shakespeare's tragedy, including a ghost impatient for revenge, a secret crime, a hero tormented by uncertainty and self-reproach, the strategic feigning of a madness that seems disturbingly close to the real thing, a woman who goes mad from grief and commits suicide, a play within the play, and a final slaughter that wipes out much of the royal family and court, along with the avenger himself. Kyd's play is entirely structured around the problem of revenge—"wild justice," in Francis Bacon's haunting phrase—and gave rise to a whole genre of revenge plays in which *Hamlet* participates.

These plays generally share certain conventional assumptions. First, revenge is an individual response to an intolerable wrong or a public insult. It is an unauthorized, violent action in a world whose institutions seem unable or unwilling to satisfy a craving for justice. Second, since institutional channels are closed and since the criminal is usually either hidden or well protected, revenge almost always follows a devious path toward its violent end. Third, the revenger is in the grip of an inner compulsion: his course of action may be motivated by institutional failure—for example, the mechanisms of justice are in the hands of the criminals themselves—but even if these mechanisms were operating perfectly, they would not allow the psychic satisfactions of revenge. Fourth, revengers generally need their victims to know what is happening and why: satisfaction depends on a moment of declaration and vindication. And fifth, revenge is a universal imperative more powerful than the pious injunctions of any particular belief system, including Christianity itself.

Shakespeare had already produced a sensationally violent version of these conventions in *Titus Andronicus*. In *Hamlet*, he at once reproduces them and calls them into question. The audience knows for certain—from Claudius's tortured attempt to pray in Act 3—that there has been a "foul murder," a fratricide successfully covered over by the story that a serpent stung the sleeping King. But Hamlet does not overhear Claudius's confession and has only the questionable testimony of the Ghost. That testimony is open to question because the nature of the Ghost is open to question. The Ghost speaks as if he were condemned to a term of suffering in the realm Catholics called purgatory:

> Doomed for a certain term to walk the night,
> And for the day confined to fast in fires
> Till the foul crimes done in my days of nature
> Are burnt and purged away.
>
> (1.5.10–13)

But Protestant theologians vehemently denied that purgatory existed and argued that spirits thought to be ghosts were in fact devils sent to lure humans into sinful actions. Hamlet responds at first as if he believes the Ghost to be the authentic spirit of his

The man in prayer. By Mair von Landshut (1499).

father returned from the dead, but he subsequently expresses serious doubts—"The spirit that I have seen / May be the devil" (2.2.575–76)—and in the play's most famous soliloquy he speaks of death as "the undiscovered country from whose bourn / No traveller returns" (3.1.81–82).

The theatrical test Hamlet devises to authenticate the Ghost's accusation—carefully watching the reaction of his uncle to *The Mousetrap*—appears to resolve any doubts: "I'll take the Ghost's word," Hamlet exults, after the King has stormed out in a rage, "for a thousand pound" (3.2.263–64). Yet even here Shakespeare introduces an occasion for uncertainty: after all, the murderer in the play within the play is "one Lucianus, nephew to the King" (3.2.223). Claudius's anger could have arisen from the spectacle of the player-nephew killing his player-uncle and not from the spectacle of his own hidden crime. The effect on the audience is not so much to cast doubt on the Ghost's word as to uncouple Hamlet's inner life once again from the external world, even at the moment that he himself thinks they are at last securely linked.

This uncoupling, this sense of inward thoughts and feelings painfully cut off from the world around him, haunts virtually all of Hamlet's relationships. When he speaks with his old school friends Rosencrantz and Guildenstern, with the courtier Osric, or with Polonius, he is deliberately evasive, but his exchanges with Ophelia are equally oblique and baffling. Even with his intimate friend Horatio, there is some gap across which Hamlet struggles to speak: "There are more things in heaven and earth, Hora-tio," Hamlet says after his first encounter with the Ghost, "than are dreamt of in our philosophy" (1.5.168–69). (The quarto variant—"in your philosophy"—marks the gap between them still more sharply.) When Hamlet directly confronts his mother with the charge of murder, she reacts with astonishment. The painful words that follow, Ham-let's weird, tormented admonition to his mother to shun her husband's bed, do indeed seem to strike home: "These words like daggers," Gertrude exclaims, "enter in mine ears" (3.4.85). But the Ghost's sudden reappearance, visible this time only to Hamlet (and, of course, to the audience), convinces his mother that her son is mad. "Do you see nothing there?" asks Hamlet, to which his mother, certain that her son is halluci-nating, replies steadfastly, "Nothing at all, yet all that is I see" (3.4.122–23).

Ironically, the distance between what Hamlet sees and what those around him see is smallest in the case of Claudius, since both share a knowledge of the secret crime that has poisoned the kingdom, and each maneuvers against the other throughout the play. But their fatal opposition never rises to full, open view until the final violent sec-onds, nor does Hamlet ever establish unequivocal, unambiguous public confirmation of his uncle's guilt. It would have been easy for Shakespeare to provide such confirmation—for example, in a last speech by the mortally wounded usurper—but he chooses instead to leave what Horatio calls "th' yet unknowing world" (5.2.323) in the dark. Until the explosion of treason and murder, the horrified bystanders know only a court in which the loving Claudius appeals to Hamlet as his "son" and wagers on his skill in fencing. Hamlet begins an explanation—"O I could tell you"—but he is cut short by death. The effect is to extend Hamlet's tragic isolation, his gnawing inward pain, all the way to his final silence.

What would it take to get rid of this pain? The possibility of cleansing, definitive action at once continually tantalizes and eludes the Prince. Such action is embodied in the soldier Fortinbras, but if Hamlet finds some way of easing his mental anguish, it is not through any comparable martial exploit, nor is it through the secret plotting undertaken by Laertes. The fact that both Fortinbras and Laertes are also attempting

Swordsmen. From *Vincentio Saviolo his Practise* (London, 1595).

to avenge the deaths of fathers underscores the shared crisis of dynastic succession but only intensifies the contrast with Hamlet's spiritual journey. The calm to which he gives voice near the play's close—"There's a special providence in the fall of a sparrow. If it be now, 'tis not to come. If it be not to come, it will be now. If it be not now, yet it will come. The readiness is all" (5.2.157–60)—descends upon him *before*, not as a result of, his revenge. The act of revenge itself happens in a flash of rage, without planning, without any self-vindicating declaration by Hamlet to Claudius, and without any public confession of guilt by the usurper. Revenge leaves the Prince not with inner satisfaction but with intense anxiety over his "wounded name."

Standing on a stage littered with corpses, Horatio promises to fulfill Hamlet's dying request to tell his story, but his account of "carnal, bloody, and unnatural acts," though it may be accurate, must be inadequate to the play we have just witnessed. For *Hamlet* situates the need for revenge in a context that goes beyond any crime, however heinous, and that seems resistant to violent solutions. Before the Ghost disclosed his uncle's villainy, Hamlet was suffering from the traumas of mortality: the searing pain of his father's death, a troubled recognition of his mother's sexuality, a sickening awareness of the vulnerability and corruptibility of the flesh. There was a time, the play implies, when Hamlet embodied all the hopes and aspirations of his age and his own vision of human possibility was unbounded—"What a piece of work is a man!"—but that vision has given way to bitter disillusionment: "And yet to me what is this quintessence of dust?" (2.2.293–94, 297–98).

Renaissance psychologists had a word for Hamlet's condition: melancholy, a state of spiritual desolation akin to madness but also to the literary and artistic genius. In Hamlet's melancholy consciousness, human existence has been reduced to dust at its dustiest. Although Claudius's secret crime is a political act that has poisoned the public sphere, the roots of Hamlet's despair seem to lie in a more intractably inward place, a place perhaps less consonant with revenge than with suicide. If there were only the evil usurper to depose, Hamlet might compass a straightforward course of action, but his soul-sickness has receding layers: beyond political corruption, there is the time-serving shallowness of his friends Rosencrantz and Guildenstern, and beyond this there is Ophelia's dismayingly compliant obedience to her father, and beyond this there is his mother's disturbing carnality, and beyond this there is the ongoing, endlessly transformative, morally indifferent cycle of life itself. For Hamlet, the quintessence of dust is not only the cold, inert matter produced by the nauseating triumph of death—the flesh of Alexander the Great metamorphosed into a plug of dirt stopping up a beer barrel—but also living matter pullulating with tenacious, meaningless vitality, produced by the equally nauseating triumph of life. "We fat all creatures else to fat us," Hamlet tells Claudius, "and we fat ourselves for maggots" (4.3.22–23).

In a world pervaded by decay, the process of natural renewal has come to seem grotesque and disgusting:

> 'Tis an unweeded garden
> That grows to seed; things rank and gross in nature
> Possess it merely.
>
> (1.2.135–37)

These lines immediately give way to bitter reflections on his mother's sexual appetite: in Hamlet's diseased consciousness, the spectacle of nature run riot, of uncontrolled breeding and feeding, centers on the body of woman. His bitterness at his mother's remarriage spreads like a stain to include all women, including the woman he had once ardently courted. "Get thee to a nunnery," Hamlet urges Ophelia, as if the only virtuous course of action were renunciation of the flesh. "Why wouldst thou be a breeder of sinners?" (3.1.122–23) Even this desperate advice seems to be undermined by Hamlet's obsessive sense of rampant female sexuality and of his own corruption, since in Elizabethan slang "nunnery" could also be a term for "brothel."

The fragile Ophelia begins to crack under the strain of Hamlet's misogynistic revulsion. Gertrude, who takes the full force of this revulsion, does not lose her wits, but when confronted alone by her son, she fears for her life. Both women sense the violence and despair seething in Hamlet beneath what he calls his "antic disposition" (1.5.173). That disposition, manifested in his disordered dress and in the "wild and whirling words" (1.5.137) that he begins to speak after encountering the Ghost, casts Hamlet in the strange role of jester in the court in which he is the mourning son and the heir apparent. Of all Shakespeare's tragic heroes, he is at once the saddest and the funniest. His blend of sarcasm, riddling, and sly wordplay initially strikes those around him as folly, but this first impression continually gives way to an uneasy awareness of hidden meanings: Claudius, alert to danger, notes that "there's something in his soul / O'er which his melancholy sits on brood" (3.1.163–64). The "something" Claudius senses is in part the murderous design of the revenger, but it is also the philosophical meditation on life and death that haunts Hamlet throughout the play. This meditation reaches a climax in the graveyard, where Hamlet, trading zany quibbles with one of the gravediggers, directly confronts the corruption and decay that had obsessed him ever since his father's death. If there is any release for Hamlet from this obsession—and it is not clear that there is—it comes from an unflinching gaze at a skull, the skull of the jester Yorick, but also, by extension, his father's skull and his own.

STEPHEN GREENBLATT

TEXTUAL NOTE

Hamlet exists in three distinct early texts. The relationship among these texts, along with a mountain of speculation about an earlier theatrical version of the story, now lost, have occupied scholars for decades. These are some of the bare facts. A printer named James Roberts placed an entry in the Stationers' Register on July 26, 1602, for "A booke called the Revenge of Hamlett Prince Denmarke as yt was latelie Acted by the Lord Chamberleyne his servantes." The first known edition (Q1) is a Quarto dated 1603, printed not by Roberts but by Nicholas Ling and John Trundell. This edition, "*The Tragicall Historie of* HAMLET *Prince of Denmarke By William Shake-speare*," is a text markedly inferior, except for a few details, to the others and, at 2,200 type lines long, markedly shorter. Generally regarded as a highly suspect version of the play, it is often referred to as the "bad Quarto"—often differing markedly even when it overlaps with the other versions. (The Prince's most famous soliloquy, for example, begins "To be or not to be, ay there's the point.") Only two copies of this Quarto, first identified in 1823, are known to exist; one is in the British Library in London, the other in the Huntington Library in San Marino, California.

A second edition (Q2), dated 1604, was printed by James Roberts. The title page advertises itself as "Newly imprinted and enlarged to almost as much againe as it was, according to the true and perfect Coppie." At 3,800 type lines, Q2 makes good on its claim to substantial enlargement, and scholars tend to agree that the printer's shop set the text from the playwright's own handwritten draft, or "foul papers," occasionally supplemented by consultation with Q1. Q2 was reprinted once, without significant alteration, during Shakespeare's lifetime.

If Shakespeare's manuscript is behind Q2, what is the source of the substantially different Q1? The most widely accepted theory, first proposed in 1941 by G. I. Duthie (*The 'Bad' Quarto of Hamlet*), is that Q1 is the product of memorial reconstruction. That is, one or more actors in the play reported what they remembered to a scribe, who prepared copy for the printer. Scholars have conjectured that the principal reporter was the actor who played Marcellus and probably doubled as Valtemand and Lucianus, since the accuracy of the text, as measured by the subsequent editions, greatly improves whenever those characters are onstage. Along with virtually every other aspect of the textual history of *Hamlet,* this appeal to memorial reconstruction is a subject of continuing scholarly debate.

The third major version of the play appeared in 1623 in the First Folio (F), where it is entitled *The Tragedie of Hamlet, Prince of Denmarke.* This edition differs in important ways from Q2: there are a great many small changes, along with some substantial cuts and additions. Most recent editors believe that F was set not from the author's own draft but from a scribal transcript, possibly from a promptbook prepared while Shakespeare was still active in the company. Such a promptbook would normally have been made by annotating a fair copy of the author's foul papers. In other words, the text of *Hamlet* in F is probably closer than Q2 to the play as it was performed in the theater when Shakespeare was alive.

Traditionally, many editors regarded any changes introduced in the passage from the author's own draft to the transcript prepared for the prompter (and thus in the case of *Hamlet* from Q2 to F) as corruptions of the text. Their goal, then, was to remove the corruptions and restore the play to its original state, the text as the author had conceived it. But most if not all of the passages that appear in F and not in Q2 seem unmistakably by Shakespeare himself, while the passages that appear in Q2 and not in F seem equally authentic. Consequently, editors were forced to conjecture that the compositors of Q2 had in 1604 unaccountably omitted the passages that appear in F, while the compositors of the Folio had similarly omitted those passages that only appear in Q2. As early as the eighteenth century, *Hamlet's* editors routinely conflated Q2 and F, incorporating in a single text as much as possible of both versions of the play.

The Oxford editors broke with this tradition. They observed that since Shakespeare was an active member of his company, the passage from foul papers to promptbook was not necessarily a corruption of his text. Rather, it could as easily have been the occasion for deliberate authorial revision, drawing upon his own second thoughts as well as the suggestions of his trusted professional colleagues. Close study of the differences between Q2 and F suggests the strong possibility of such revision, reflecting a coherent strategy. The Oxford editors hypothesized that Shakespeare himself prepared a fair copy of the foul papers from which Q2 was set, that in making that fair copy he revised the text in a number of ways, and that F derives, at one or possibly more removes, from that fair copy. Therefore, since the Oxford editors concluded that Shakespeare's own revisions are reflected in F, they adopted F as the control text.

In keeping with this decision, the *Oxford Shakespeare* relegated passages from Q2 that do not appear in F to an appendix. This format enables readers to imagine more readily the version of *Hamlet* thought to have been revised for performance during Shakespeare's own lifetime, but it has certain disadvantages, the principal of which is that only a reader extremely familiar with the play can easily imagine exactly how the Q2 passages functioned in what everyone agrees was a version of the play also written by Shakespeare. Moreover, since several of these passages have long been regarded as integral parts of the play, their relegation to an appendix makes it difficult for readers to participate fully in the great cultural conversation about *Hamlet* that has occupied artists, critics, and scholars for generations. Accordingly, the *Norton Shakespeare,* while following the Oxford text, has moved the Q2 passages from the appendix to the body of the play. But in order not to once again produce a conflated text, the Q2 passages are indented, printed in a different typeface, and numbered in such a way as to make clear their provenance. Also, at the points where the Folio and the Q2 passages directly overlap (3.4.70, 3.4.151, and 5.2.154), the overlapping lines are repeated. Those who wish to read the Folio version of *Hamlet* can thus simply skip over the offset Q2 passages, while at the same time it is possible for readers to see clearly the place that the Q2 passages occupy.

The First Quarto (Q1) of *Hamlet,* published in 1603, was evidently cobbled together from the memory of one or more of the actors in a production of Shakespeare's play. The text is notoriously defective, as its version of Hamlet's most famous soliloquy suggests:*

Q1 [cf. 3.1.58ff.]

To be, or not to be; ay, there's the point.
To die, to sleep: is that all? Ay all.
No, to sleep, to dream; ay marry, there it goes.
For in that dream of death, when we awake
And borne before an everlasting judge
From whence no passenger ever returned,
The undiscovered country at whose sight
The happy smile and the accursed damned—
But for this, the joyful hope of this,
Who'd bear the scorns and flattery of the world,
Scorned by the right rich, the rich cursed of the poor,
The widow being oppressed, the orphan wronged,
The taste of hunger or a tyrant's reign,
And thousand more calamities besides,
To grunt and sweat under this weary life,
When that he may his full quietus make
With a bare bodkin? Who would this endure,
But for a hope of something after death,
Which puzzles the brain and doth confound the sense,
Which makes us rather bear those evils we have
Than fly to others that we know not of?
Ay that. O, this conscience makes cowards of us all.—
Lady, in thy orisons be all my sins remembered.

Between the two authoritative versions of the play, the Second Quarto (Q2: 1604) and the Folio (F: 1623), there are many substantial differences, most notably the Q2-only passages that this edition indents and prints in a different typeface. In addition to these major alterations, apparently the consequence of Shakespeare's own revision of his play, there are many other small but suggestive differences between Q2 and F that also seem to reflect shifting authorial intentions. A sampling of these follows:

2.2.212ff.

Q2:

HAMLET You cannot take from me anything that I will not more willingly part withal: except my life, except my life, except my life.

F:

HAMLET You cannot, sir, take from me anything that I will more willingly part withal: except my life, my life.

5.1.166ff.

Q2:

FIRST CLOWN This same skull, sir, was sir Yorick's skull, the King's jester.

F:

FIRST CLOWN This same skull, sir, this same skull, sir, was Yorick's skull, the King's jester.

*Modernization from Kathleen O. Irace, ed., *The First Quarto of Hamlet* (New York: Cambridge University Press, 1998).

HAMLET   This?

FIRST CLOWN   E'en that.

HAMLET   Alas, poor Yorick. I knew him, Horatio—a fellow of infinite jest, of most excellent fancy. He hath bore me on his back a thousand times; and now how abhorred in my imagination it is! My gorge rises at it. Here hung those lips that I have kissed I know not how oft. Where be your gibes now, your gambols, your songs, your flashes of merriment that were wont to set the table on a roar? Not one now to mock your own grinning?

HAMLET   This?

FIRST CLOWN   E'en that.

HAMLET   Let me see. Alas, poor Yorick. I knew him, Horatio—a fellow of infinite jest, of most excellent fancy. He hath borne me on his back a thousand times; and how abhorred my imagination is! My gorge rises at it. Here hung those lips that I have kissed I know not how oft. Where be your gibes now, your gambols, your songs, your flashes of merriment that were wont to set the table on a roar? No one now to mock your own jeering?

5.1.196ff.

Q2:

HAMLET   Imperious Caesar, dead and turned to clay,
Might stop a hole to keep the wind away.
O, that the earth which kept the world in awe
Should patch a wall t'expel the water's flaw.
But soft, but soft, awhile. Here comes the King.

F:

HAMLET   Imperial Caesar, dead and turned to clay,
Might stop a hole to keep the wind away.
O, that the earth which kept the world in awe
Should patch a wall t'expel the winter's flaw.
But soft, but soft; aside. Here comes the King.

5.2.297ff.

Q2:

HAMLET   But I do prophecy th'election lights
On Fortinbras. He has my dying voice.
So tell him, with th'occurants, more and less,
Which have solicited. The rest is silence.

HORATIO   Now cracks a noble heart.

F:

HAMLET   But I do prophecy th'election lights
On Fortinbras. He has mydying voice.
So tell him, with th'occurants, more and less,
Which have solicited. The rest is silence.

O, O, O, O!

HORATIO   Now crack a noble heart.

SELECTED BIBLIOGRAPHY

Adelman, Janet. "Man and His Wife Is One Flesh: *Hamlet* and the Confrontation with the Maternal Body." *Suffocating Mothers: Fantasies of Maternal Origin in Shakespeare's Plays, "Hamlet" to "The Tempest."* New York: Routledge, 1992. 11–37. For Shakespeare, fully realized female sexuality (in the form of Gertrude) gives birth not only to fallen and contaminated man, but also to tragedy itself.

Bradley, A. C. *Shakespearean Tragedy: Lectures on "Hamlet," "Othello," "King Lear," "Macbeth."* 1904. 3rd ed. Basingstoke, Eng.: Macmillan, 1992. Hamlet's character—at the center of the tragedy that bears his name—is dominated by a morbid melancholy that weakens his ability to love and impedes his ability to act.

De Grazia, Margreta. *"Hamlet" Without Hamlet.* Cambridge, Mass.: Cambridge University Press, 2007. The elusiveness of Hamlet's inner life is a largely modern critical invention, obscuring the dispossession that Renaissance audiences would have seen as the tragedy's central crisis.

Eliot, T. S. "Hamlet and His Problems." *The Sacred Wood: Essays on Poetry and Criticism*. London: Methuen, 1920. *Hamlet* proves deficient as a work of art: the prince's disproportionate confusion about his condition reflects Shakespeare's own confusion concerning the proper assembly of his diverse literary materials.

Garber, Marjorie. "*Hamlet:* Giving Up the Ghost." *Shakespeare's Ghost Writers: Literature as Uncanny Causality.* New York: Methuen, 1987. 124–76. Simultaneously constituting and dissolving the self, the Ghost haunts the unstable relationship between action and memory; Shakespeare himself has a similarly haunting purchase on the modern imagination.

Greenblatt, Stephen. *Hamlet in Purgatory.* Princeton: Princeton University Press, 2001. *Hamlet* exploits and transforms into theatrical ritual the fears and desires generated by the Catholic cult of purgatory, a cult banned by Tudor Protestantism.

Maguire, Laurie. "'Actions that a man might play': Mourning, Memory, Editing." *Performance Research* 7 (2002): 66–76. Editors of Shakespeare searching for one "true" text of the play should take a hint from Hamlet himself: single viewpoints (whether ontological or editorial) ultimately bow to the daunting yet rich reality of multiplicity.

McGee, Arthur. *The Elizabethan Hamlet.* New Haven: Yale University Press, 1987. Hamlet emerges as a sophisticated manifestation of Vice from the medieval morality-play tradition.

Showalter, Elaine. "Representing Ophelia: Women, Madness, and the Responsibilities of Feminist Criticism." *Shakespeare and the Question of Theory.* Ed. Patricia Parker and Geoffrey Hartman. New York: Methuen, 1985. 77–94. A survey of shifting cultural attitudes toward the representation of Ophelia serves as a barometer of ideological conflict and as a contribution to the evolving discourse of feminist criticism.

Targoff, Ramie. "The Performance of Prayer: Sincerity and Theatricality in Early Modern England." *Representations* 60 (1997): 49–69. Hamlet's misreading of Claudius's prayer is neither accidental nor further evidence of his inability to act; rather, it is symptomatic of early modern Protestant anxieties over how to determine sincerity and hypocrisy.

Wilson, J. Dover. *What Happens in "Hamlet."* 3rd ed. Cambridge, Mass.: Cambridge University Press, 1951. In grappling with the play's dramatic difficulties, especially the problematic "Mouse-trap" scene, we more nearly approach "the secret of Hamlet's character."

See also the creative uses of *Hamlet* in Johann Wolfgang von Goethe's *Wilhelm Meister's Apprenticeship* (1796); James Joyce's *Ulysses* (1922); Tom Stoppard's *Rosencrantz and Guildenstern Are Dead* (1967); Heiner Müller's *Die Hamletmaschine* (1978); and John Updike's *Gertrude and Claudius* (2000).

FILMS

Hamlet. 1948. Dir. Laurence Olivier. UK. 155 min. In this black-and-white film, Olivier's Hamlet is an oedipal prince, tormented by a desire to kill his father and sleep with his mother (played in the film by an actress only two years older than Olivier).

Gamlet. 1964. Dir. Grigori Kozintsev and Iosif Shapiro. Soviet Union. 148 min. A black-and-white Cold-war *Hamlet,* in Russian, set in a prisonlike Elsinore.

Hamlet. 1990. Dir. Franco Zeffirelli. UK. 130 min. Naturalistic medieval scenes, with Glenn Close's strong Gertrude in an oedipally charged relationship with Mel Gibson's Hamlet.

Hamlet. 1996. Dir. Kenneth Branagh. UK. 242 min. (cut version 150 min.). Opulent, full-text epic rendered in the mirrored halls of a palatial nineteenth-century Austrian court.

Hamlet. 2000. Dir. Michael Almereyda. USA. 112 min. Inspired by director Akira Kurosawa, Almereyda updates the play to modern New York and draws on communications technologies such as videocameras, fax machines, and computers.

The Tragedy of Hamlet, Prince of Denmark

THE PERSONS OF THE PLAY

GHOST of Hamlet, the late King of Denmark
KING CLAUDIUS, his brother
QUEEN GERTRUDE of Denmark, widow of King Hamlet, now
    wife of Claudius
Prince HAMLET, son of King Hamlet and Queen Gertrude
POLONIUS, a lord
LAERTES, son of Polonius
OPHELIA, daughter of Polonius
REYNALDO, servant of Polonius
HORATIO ⎫
ROSENCRANTZ ⎬ friends of Prince Hamlet
GUILDENSTERN ⎭
FRANCISCO ⎫
BARNARDO ⎬ soldiers
MARCELLUS ⎭
VALTEMAND ⎫
CORNELIUS ⎪
OSRIC ⎬ courtiers
GENTLEMEN ⎭
A SAILOR
Two CLOWNS, a gravedigger and his companion
A PRIEST
FORTINBRAS, Prince of Norway
A CAPTAIN in his army
AMBASSADORS from England
PLAYERS, who play the parts of the PROLOGUE, PLAYER KING,
    PLAYER QUEEN, and LUCIANUS, in *The Mousetrap*
Lords, messengers, attendants, guards, soldiers, followers of
    Laertes, sailors

1.1

Enter BARNARDO *and* FRANCISCO, *two sentinels* [*at several*° *doors*]   *separate*

BARNARDO   Who's there?
FRANCISCO   Nay, answer me.[1] Stand and unfold° yourself.   *identify*
BARNARDO   Long live the King!
FRANCISCO   Barnardo?
BARNARDO   He.
FRANCISCO   You come most carefully° upon your hour.   *dutifully; cautiously*
5 BARNARDO   'Tis now struck twelve. Get thee to bed, Francisco.
FRANCISCO   For this relief much thanks. 'Tis bitter cold,
  And I am sick at heart.

1.1 Location: A guard platform at Elsinore Castle, Denmark.

1. Francisco, as sentry on duty, is responsible for challenging anyone who appears.

BARNARDO	Have you had quiet guard?	
FRANCISCO	Not a mouse stirring.	
BARNARDO	Well, good night.	

If you do meet Horatio and Marcellus,
10 The rivals° of my watch, bid them make haste.   *partners*

Enter HORATIO *and* MARCELLUS

FRANCISCO   I think I hear them—Stand! Who's there?
HORATIO   Friends to this ground.°   *country*
MARCELLUS   And liegemen° to the Dane.[2]   *sworn servants*
FRANCISCO   Give° you good night.   *God give*
MARCELLUS   O farewell, honest soldier. Who hath relieved you?
FRANCISCO   Barnardo has my place. Give you good night.   *Exit*
15 MARCELLUS   Holla, Barnardo!
BARNARDO   Say—what, is Horatio there?
HORATIO   A piece of him.
BARNARDO   Welcome, Horatio. Welcome, good Marcellus.
MARCELLUS[3]   What, has this thing appeared again tonight?
20 BARNARDO   I have seen nothing.
MARCELLUS   Horatio says 'tis but our fantasy,
And will not let belief take hold of him
Touching this dreaded sight twice seen of us.
Therefore I have entreated him along
25 With us to watch the minutes of this night,
That if again this apparition come
He may approve° our eyes and speak to it.[4]   *verify the evidence of*
HORATIO   Tush, tush, 'twill not appear.
BARNARDO   Sit down a while,
And let us once again assail your ears,
30 That are so fortified against our story,
What we two nights have seen.
HORATIO   Well, sit we down,
And let us hear Barnardo speak of this.
BARNARDO   Last night of all,°   *Just last night*
When yon same star that's westward from the pole°   *polestar*
35 Had made his° course t'illume that part of heaven   *its*
Where now it burns, Marcellus and myself,
The bell then beating one—

Enter the GHOST [*in complete armour, holding a truncheon, with his beaver up*][5]

MARCELLUS   Peace, break thee off. Look where it comes again.
BARNARDO   In the same figure like the King that's dead.
40 MARCELLUS [*to* HORATIO]   Thou art a scholar—speak to it, Horatio.
BARNARDO   Looks it not like the King?—Mark it, Horatio.
HORATIO   Most like. It harrows me with fear and wonder.
BARNARDO   It would° be spoke to.   *wishes to*
MARCELLUS   Question it, Horatio.
HORATIO   [*to the* GHOST]   What art thou that usurp'st[6] this time of night,
45 Together with that fair and warlike form
In which the majesty of buried Denmark°   *the buried King*

2. King of Denmark.
3. Q2 gives this line to Horatio.
4. A ghost was believed to speak only when spoken to. As a precaution, the experiment will be conducted by an educated man (Horatio) who knows Latin (the language effective for exorcising demonic spirits).
5. Holding a baton (military commander's sign of office), with his visor ("beaver") raised.
6. Wrongfully seize (both the night and the shape of the King). The familiar "thou" would be an inappropriate form of address for a real King.

Did sometimes° march? By heaven, I charge thee speak.   *formerly*

MARCELLUS   It is offended.

BARNARDO   See, it stalks away.

HORATIO [*to the* GHOST]   Stay, speak, speak, I charge thee speak.

                                                Exit GHOST

50   MARCELLUS   'Tis gone, and will not answer.

BARNARDO   How now, Horatio? You tremble and look pale.
Is not this something more than fantasy?
What think you on't?°   *of it*

HORATIO   Before my God, I might not this believe

55   Without the sensible° and true avouch°   *sensory / testimony*
Of mine own eyes.

MARCELLUS   Is it not like the King?

HORATIO   As thou art to thyself.
Such was the very armour he had on

60   When he th'ambitious Norway° combated.   *King of Norway*
So frowned he once when in an angry parley°   *debate*
He smote the sledded Polacks⁷ on the ice.
'Tis strange.

MARCELLUS   Thus twice before, and just at this dead hour,

65   With martial stalk hath he gone by our watch.

HORATIO   In what particular thought to work⁸ I know not,
But in the gross and scope of my opinion⁹
This bodes some strange eruption° to our state.   *calamity*

MARCELLUS   Good now,° sit down, and tell me, he that knows,   *(an entreaty: Good sir, now)*

70   Why this same strict and most observant watch
So nightly toils the subject of the land,¹
And why such daily cast° of brazen cannon,   *production*
And foreign mart° for implements of war,   *trade*
Why such impress° of shipwrights, whose sore task   *drafting*

75   Does not divide the Sunday from the week:
What might be toward° that this sweaty haste   *impending*
Doth make the night joint-labourer with the day,
Who is't that can inform me?

HORATIO   That can I—
At least the whisper goes so: our last king,

80   Whose image even but now appeared to us,
Was as you know by Fortinbras of Norway,
Thereto pricked° on by a most emulate° pride,   *spurred / rivalrous*
Dared to the combat; in which our valiant Hamlet—
For so this side of our known world esteemed him—

85   Did slay this Fortinbras, who by a sealed compact²
Well ratified by law and heraldry³
Did forfeit with his life all those his lands
Which he stood seized on° to the conqueror;   *held possession of*
Against the which a moiety competent°   *an equal portion*

90   Was gagèd° by our King, which had returned⁴   *staked*
To the inheritance° of Fortinbras   *ownership*
Had he been vanquisher, as by the same cov'nant
And carriage of the article designed⁵

---

7. Poles who traveled by sled.
8. *In . . . work:* What precise theory to follow.
9. But in my general opinion.
1. *So . . . land:* Requires the country's subjects to toil every night.
2. A mutually agreed-upon contract ("compact") to

which each set his seal.
3. Properly ratified in accordance with civil law and the law of arms.
4. Which would have gone.
5. And execution of the contract's provision.

95 His fell to Hamlet. Now sir, young Fortinbras,
Of unimprovèd° mettle hot and full,   *untested; untrained*
Hath in the skirts° of Norway here and there   *outlying parts*
Sharked up a list⁶ of landless⁷ resolutes
For food and diet to some enterprise
That hath a stomach in't,⁸ which is no other—
100 And it doth well° appear unto our state—   *obviously*
But to recover of us by strong hand⁹
And terms compulsative° those foresaid lands   *forcible*
So by his father lost. And this, I take it,
Is the main motive of our preparations,
105 The source of this our watch, and the chief head°   *source*
Of this post-haste and rummage¹ in the land.²

106.1 BARNARDO   *I think it be no other but e'en so.*
Well may it sort° that this portentous figure   *be fitting*
Comes armèd through our watch so like the king
That was and is the question° of these wars.   *cause*
106.5 HORATIO   *A mote° it is to trouble the mind's eye.*   *speck of dust*
In the most high and palmy° state of Rome,   *flourishing*
A little ere the mightiest Julius fell,
The graves stood tenantless, and the sheeted° dead   *shrouded*
Did squeak and gibber in the Roman streets
106.10 *At stars with trains of fire,³ and dews of blood,*
Disasters⁴ in the sun; and the moist star,⁵
Upon whose influence Neptune's empire stands,°   *depends*
Was sick almost to doomsday with eclipse.⁶
And even the like precurse° of feared events,   *forerunner*
106.15 *As harbingers preceding still° the fates,*   *always*
And prologue to the omen°coming on,   *disastrous event*
Have heaven and earth together demonstrated
Unto our climature° and countrymen.   *region*
Enter the GHOST *[as before]*
But soft,° behold—lo where it comes again!   *hush*
I'll cross⁷ it though it blast° me.—Stay, illusion.   *wither*
    [The GHOST*] spreads his arms*
If thou hast any sound or use of voice,
110 Speak to me.
If there be any good thing to be done
That may to thee do ease and grace to me,
Speak to me.
If thou art privy to thy country's fate
115 Which happily° foreknowing may avoid,   *perhaps; fortunately*
O speak!
Or if thou hast uphoarded in thy life
Extorted treasure in the womb of earth—

6. Gathered together indiscriminately (as a shark takes prey) a band ("list").
7. Q1, Q2 print "lawless," which accurately conveys Horatio's view of these men; F's "landless," however, provides a more specific motive for their enlistment.
8. *For . . . in't:* The men will "feed" his enterprise; they are fed in return for their service. *stomach:* courageous action; challenge to the pride (of both the Prince and his men).
9. By main force (punning on the name "Fortinbras," literally "strong arm").
1. Of this feverish activity and commotion.

2. After this line, Q2 contains the following passage, 106.1–106.18, omitted in F.
3. "At" is emended from Q2's "As," which would require another verb.
4. Malevolent influences (astrological term).
5. The moon, thought to control tides by drawing water out of the sea ("Neptune's empire," line 106.12).
6. Eclipses of sun and moon would accompany Christ's return to earth on Judgment Day (see Revelation 6:12).
7. Confront, cross its path; also, make the sign of the cross (to counter its evil influence).

For which, they say, you spirits oft walk in death—
The cock crows

120 Speak of it, stay and speak.—Stop it, Marcellus.
MARCELLUS Shall I strike at it with my partisan?° *spear-handled blade*
HORATIO Do, if it will not stand.
BARNARDO   'Tis here.
HORATIO   'Tis here.

Exit GHOST

MARCELLUS 'Tis gone.
We do it wrong, being so majestical,
125 To offer it the show of violence,
For it is as the air invulnerable,
And our vain blows malicious mockery.
BARNARDO It was about to speak when the cock crew.
HORATIO And then it started like a guilty thing
130 Upon a fearful summons. I have heard
The cock, that is the trumpet to the morn,
Doth with his lofty and shrill-sounding throat
Awake the god of day,⁸ and at his warning,
Whether in sea or fire, in earth or air,
135 Th'extravagant and erring⁹ spirit hies° *hurries*
To his confine;° and of the truth herein *enclosure*
This present object° made probation.° *example / proof*
MARCELLUS It faded on the crowing of the cock.
Some say that ever 'gainst° that season comes *always when*
140 Wherein our saviour's birth is celebrated
The bird of dawning singeth all night long;
And then, they say, no spirit can walk abroad,
The nights are wholesome; then no planets strike,¹
No fairy takes,° nor witch hath power to charm, *bewitches*
145 So hallowed and so gracious° is the time. *full of God's grace*
HORATIO So have I heard, and do in part believe it.
But look, the morn in russet mantle clad
Walks o'er the dew of yon high eastern hill.
Break we our watch up, and by my advice
150 Let us impart what we have seen tonight
Unto young Hamlet; for upon my life,
This spirit, dumb to us, will speak to him.
Do you consent we shall acquaint him with it,
As needful in our loves,² fitting our duty?
155 MARCELLUS Let's do't, I pray; and I this morning know
Where we shall find him most conveniently. *Exeunt*

1.2

Flourish. Enter CLAUDIUS, *King of Denmark,* GERTRUDE
the Queen, [*members of the*] *Council,* [*such*] *as* POLON-
IUS, *his son* LAERTES *and* [*daughter*] OPHELIA, [*Prince*]
HAMLET [*dressed in black*], *cum aliis*° *with others*
KING CLAUDIUS Though yet of Hamlet our¹ dear brother's death
The memory be green, and that it us befitted

---

8. The sun god, Phoebus Apollo.
9. Wandering out of its boundaries.
1. When they were in certain unfavorable astrological positions, heavenly bodies were thought to exercise a negative influence on earthly events.

2. As necessary because of the love we have for him.
1.2 Location: The castle.
1. My. (Kings often referred to themselves in the plural, the royal "we," although in the lines that follow, Claudius may also be talking about Danes in general.)

To bear our hearts in grief and our whole kingdom
To be contracted in one brow of woe,[2]
5 Yet so far hath discretion fought with nature°   *natural love*
That we with wisest sorrow think on him
Together with remembrance of ourselves.[3]
Therefore our sometime° sister, now our queen,[4]   *former*
Th'imperial jointress° of this warlike state,   *joint possessor*
10 Have we as 'twere with a defeated joy,
With one auspicious and one dropping eye,[5]
With mirth in funeral and with dirge in marriage,
In equal scale weighing delight and dole,°   *sorrow*
Taken to wife. Nor have we herein barred°   *excluded; contradicted*
15 Your better wisdoms, which have freely gone
With this affair along. For all, our thanks.
Now follows that you know° young Fortinbras,   *should be informed that*
Holding a weak supposal° of our worth,   *a poor opinion*
Or thinking by our late dear brother's death
20 Our state to be disjoint° and out of frame,°   *fractured / order*
Co-leaguèd with the dream of his advantage,[6]
He hath not failed to pester us with message
Importing° the surrender of those lands   *Concerning*
Lost by his father, with all bonds° of law,   *legal procedures*
25 To our most valiant brother. So much for him.
      Enter VALTEMAND *and* CORNELIUS
Now for ourself, and for this time of meeting,
Thus much the business is: we have here writ
To Norway, uncle of young Fortinbras—
Who, impotent and bed-rid, scarcely hears
30 Of this his nephew's purpose—to suppress
His further gait° herein, in that the levies,   *progress*
The lists, and full proportions are all made
Out of his subject;[7] and we here dispatch
You, good Cornelius, and you, Valtemand,
35 For bearers of this greeting to old Norway,
Giving to you no further personal power
To business with the King more than the scope
Of these dilated° articles allow.   *lengthy*
Farewell, and let your haste commend your duty.[8]
40 VALTEMAND   In that and all things will we show our duty.
KING CLAUDIUS   We doubt it nothing,° heartily farewell.   *not at all*
      Exeunt VALTEMAND *and* CORNELIUS
And now, Laertes, what's the news with you?
You told us of some suit. What is't, Laertes?
You cannot speak of reason to the Dane°   *the Danish King*
45 And lose your voice. What wouldst thou beg, Laertes,

---

2. To be drawn together into a collective expression of mourning (playing on "the frowning brow of a mourner").

3. *we . . . ourselves:* "He is not wise that is not wise for himself" was proverbial.

4. English canon law forbade marriage between former brother- and sister-in-law (Leviticus 18:16; Book of Common Prayer); it was on this ground that Henry VIII annulled his marriage to his brother's widow and married Anne Boleyn, Queen Elizabeth's mother. The relationship between Claudius and Gertrude could thus be regarded as incestuous. In some early Germanic soci-

eties, however, a new King customarily married the late King's widow.

5. One eye looking hopefully, the other downcast, or "dropping" tears.

6. Reinforced by the illusion of his own advantageous position.

7. *in that . . . subject:* since the moneys, enlistments, and forces are made up of his (the King of Norway's) subjects.

8. Let your swift departure (rather than elaborate speeches) show your loyalty.

That shall not be my offer, not thy asking?[9]
The head is not more native[1] to the heart,
The hand more instrumental to the mouth,
Than is the throne of Denmark to thy father.
What wouldst thou have, Laertes?

50 LAERTES   Dread my° lord,   *My revered*
Your leave° and favour° to return to France,   *permission / approval*
From whence though willingly I came to Denmark
To show my duty in your coronation,
Yet now I must confess, that duty done,
55 My thoughts and wishes bend again towards France
And bow them to your gracious leave and pardon.[2]
KING CLAUDIUS   Have you your father's leave? What says Polonius?
POLONIUS   He hath, my lord, wrung from me my slow leave
By laboursome petition, and at last
60 Upon his will° I sealed my hard° consent.   *desire / reluctant*
I do beseech you give him leave to go.
KING CLAUDIUS   Take thy fair hour,[3] Laertes. Time be thine,
And thy best graces spend it at thy will.[4]
But now, my cousin[5] Hamlet, and my son—
65 HAMLET   A little more than kin and less than kind[6]
KING CLAUDIUS   How is it that the clouds still hang on you?
HAMLET   Not so, my lord, I am too much i'th' sun.[7]
QUEEN GERTRUDE   Good Hamlet, cast thy nightly colour[8] off,
And let thine eye look like a friend on Denmark.[9]
70 Do not for ever with thy vailèd lids°   *downcast eyes*
Seek for thy noble father in the dust.
Thou know'st 'tis common—all that lives must die,
Passing through nature to eternity.
HAMLET   Ay, madam, it is common.[1]
QUEEN GERTRUDE   If it be,
75 Why seems it so particular° with thee?   *personal*
HAMLET   Seems, madam? Nay, it *is*. I know not 'seems'.
'Tis not alone my inky cloak, good-mother,[2]
Nor customary suits of solemn black,
Nor windy suspiration° of forced breath,   *sighs*
80 No, nor the fruitful° river in the eye,   *copious*
Nor the dejected haviour° of the visage,   *expression*
Together with all forms, moods, shows of grief
That can denote me truly. These indeed 'seem',
For they are actions that a man might play;
85 But I have that within which passeth show—
These but the trappings and the suits of woe.

9. *What wouldst . . . asking:* What could you ask of me that I would not offer before you asked?
1. Naturally connected; an allusion to the "body politic," headed by the King and having as its heart the King's council.
2. And humbly ask you to grant permission to depart.
3. Opportunity (while you are young).
4. *Time . . . will:* Your time is your own; use it in accordance with your best qualities.
5. Kinsman (outside one's immediate family).
6. "The nearer in kin the less in kindness" was proverbial. Hamlet's riddling comment indicates first that there is little warmth in their new, only nominally closer

relationship. Playing on "kind" in the sense of natural type or offspring, however, he also refers to the incestuousness of the marriage that has produced their unnatural kinship.
7. In the sunshine of Claudius's favor; also, punning on "son."
8. Black mourning garments and melancholic behavior.
9. Both the King of Denmark and the country.
1. Commonplace (?); crude (?).
2. Stepmother. The hyphen, an editorial addition to F's "good Mother," calls attention to the ironic implication of Hamlet's words.

KING CLAUDIUS   'Tis sweet and commendable in your nature, Hamlet,
To give these mourning duties to your father;
But you must know your father lost a father;
90   That father lost, lost his; and the survivor bound
In filial obligation for some term
To do obsequious sorrow.[3] But to persever
In obstinate condolement° is a course   *lamenting*
Of impious stubbornness, 'tis unmanly grief,
95   It shows a will most incorrect° to heaven,   *unsubmissive*
A heart unfortified, a mind impatient,[4]
An understanding simple° and unschooled;   *childish*
For what we know must be, and is as common
As any the most vulgar thing to sense,[5]
100   Why should we in our peevish opposition
Take it to heart? Fie, 'tis a fault to heaven,
A fault against the dead, a fault to nature,
To reason most absurd, whose common theme
Is death of fathers, and who still° hath cried   *always*
105   From the first corpse[6] till he that died today,
'This must be so'. We pray you throw to earth
This unprevailing° woe, and think of us   *unavailing*
As of a father; for let the world take note
You are the most immediate° to our throne,   *next in succession*
110   And with no less nobility° of love   *purity; generosity*
Than that which dearest father bears his son
Do I impart towards you. For your intent
In going back to school in Wittenberg,[7]
It is most retrograde° to our desire,   *contrary*
115   And we beseech you bend you° to remain   *yield; agree*
Here in the cheer and comfort of our eye,
Our chiefest courtier, cousin, and our son.
QUEEN GERTRUDE   Let not thy mother lose her prayers, Hamlet.
I pray thee stay with us, go not to Wittenberg.
120   HAMLET   I shall in all my best obey you, madam.
KING CLAUDIUS   Why, 'tis a loving and a fair reply.
Be as ourself in Denmark. [*To* GERTRUDE] Madam, come.
This gentle and unforced accord of Hamlet
Sits smiling to° my heart; in grace° whereof,   *Pleases / honor*
125   No jocund health that Denmark° drinks today   *the King*
But the great cannon to the clouds shall tell,°   *sound*
And the King's rouse[8] the heavens shall bruit again,°   *loudly echo*
Re-speaking earthly thunder. Come, away.
                     Flourish. Exeunt all but HAMLET
HAMLET   O that this too too solid[9] flesh would melt,
130   Thaw, and resolve° itself into a dew,   *dissolve*
Or that the Everlasting had not fixed
His canon° 'gainst self-slaughter! O God, O God,   *law*
How weary, stale, flat, and unprofitable

---

3. To mourn as befits obsequies, or funeral ceremonies.
4. A heart not strengthened (against emotion or misfortune), a mind unprepared to suffer.
5. As the most obvious and ordinary thing we perceive
using our senses.
6. That of Abel, the first human to die, murdered by his
brother, Cain.

7. The birthplace of Protestantism, the university of
Luther and Faustus; many Danes studied there.
8. Bout of drinking.
9. F's reading; Q2 has "sallied," a possible spelling of
"sullied." Editors have seen wordplay on "sallied,"
assailed, or, alternatively, salty, tear-soaked (salting was
a method of preserving meat), and "sullied," or contaminated, ill used. "Solid" accords best with "melt."

	Seem to me all the uses° of this world!	*customs; business*
135	Fie on't, ah fie, fie! 'Tis an unweeded garden	
	That grows to seed; things rank and gross in nature	
	Possess it merely.° That it should come to this—	*entirely*
	But two months dead—nay, not so much, not two—	
	So excellent a king, that was to this	
140	Hyperion to a satyr,[1] so loving to my mother	
	That he might not beteem° the winds of heaven	*permit*
	Visit her face too roughly! Heaven and earth,	
	Must I remember? Why, she would hang on him	
	As if increase of appetite had grown	
145	By what it fed on, and yet within a month—	
	Let me not think on't; frailty, thy name is woman—	
	A little month, or ere° those shoes were old	*before*
	With which she followed my poor father's body,	
	Like Niobe, all tears,[2] why she, even she—	
150	O God, a beast that wants discourse of reason[3]	
	Would have mourned longer!—married with mine uncle,	
	My father's brother, but no more like my father	
	Than I to Hercules; within a month,	
	Ere yet the salt of most unrighteous tears	
155	Had left the flushing of her gallèd° eyes,	*inflamed*
	She married. O most wicked speed, to post°	*hurry*
	With such dexterity to incestuous sheets!	
	It is not, nor it cannot come to good.	
	But break, my heart, for I must hold my tongue.	

Enter HORATIO, MARCELLUS, *and* BARNARDO

HORATIO   Hail to your lordship.

160 HAMLET   I am glad to see you well.
    Horatio—or I do forget myself.

HORATIO   The same, my lord, and your poor servant ever.

HAMLET   Sir, my good friend; I'll change° that name with you.   *exchange*
    And what make you from[4] Wittenberg, Horatio?—
    Marcellus.

165 MARCELLUS   My good lord.

HAMLET   I am very glad to see you. [*To* BARNARDO]   Good even, sir.—
    But what in faith make you from Wittenberg?

HORATIO   A truant disposition, good my lord.

HAMLET   I would not have your enemy say so,
170   Nor shall you do mine ear that violence
    To make it truster° of your own report   *believer*
    Against yourself. I know you are no truant.
    But what is your affair in Elsinore?
    We'll teach you to drink deep ere you depart.

175 HORATIO   My lord, I came to see your father's funeral.

HAMLET   I prithee do not mock me, fellow-student;
    I think it was to see my mother's wedding.

HORATIO   Indeed, my lord, it followed hard upon.

HAMLET   Thrift, thrift, Horatio. The funeral baked meats°   *meat pies and pastries*
180   Did coldly° furnish forth the marriage tables.   *when cold*
    Would I had met my dearest° foe in heaven   *most hated*

---

1. *So . . . satyr:* That King was to this as the sun god (Hyperion, a Titan) is to a lustful half goat (mythological companion of the wine god, Bacchus).
2. Niobe's fourteen children were killed by Apollo and Artemis to punish her for boasting about them. She continued to weep bitterly even after she was turned to stone.
3. That lacks the faculty of rational thought.
4. What are you doing away from.

Ere I had ever seen that day, Horatio.
My father—methinks I see my father.
HORATIO   O where, my lord?
HAMLET   In my mind's eye, Horatio.
185 HORATIO   I saw him once. A° was a goodly king.   *He*
HAMLET   A was a man. Take him for all in all,
I shall not look upon his like again.
HORATIO   My lord, I think I saw him yesternight.
HAMLET   Saw? Who?
190 HORATIO   My lord, the King your father.
HAMLET   The King my father?
HORATIO   Season° your admiration° for a while   *Moderate / amazement*
With an attent° ear till I may deliver,   *attentive*
Upon the witness of these gentlemen,
This marvel to you.
195 HAMLET   For God's love let me hear!
HORATIO   Two nights together had these gentlemen,
Marcellus and Barnardo, on their watch,
In the dead waste° and middle of the night,   *stillness*
Been thus encountered. A figure like your father,
200 Armed at all points° exactly, cap-à-pie,°   *details / head to foot*
Appears before them, and with solemn march
Goes slow and stately by them. Thrice he walked
By their oppressed and fear-surprisèd eyes
Within his truncheon's⁵ length, whilst they distilled°   *dissolved*
205 Almost to jelly with the act° of fear   *effect*
Stand dumb and speak not to him. This to me
In dreadful secrecy impart they did,
And I with them the third night kept the watch,
Where, as they had delivered, both in time,
210 Form of the thing, each word made true and good,
The apparition comes. I knew your father;
These hands are not more like.⁶
HAMLET   But where was this?
MARCELLUS   My lord, upon the platform where we watched.
HAMLET   Did you not speak to it?
HORATIO   My lord, I did,
215 But answer made it none; yet once methought
It lifted up it° head and did address   *its*
Itself to motion like as it would speak,⁷
But even° then the morning cock crew loud,   *just*
And at the sound it shrunk in haste away
And vanished from our sight.
220 HAMLET   'Tis very strange.
HORATIO   As I do live, my honoured lord, 'tis true,
And we did think it writ down° in our duty   *prescribed*
To let you know of it.
HAMLET   Indeed, indeed, sirs; but this troubles me.—
Hold you the watch tonight?
225 BARNARDO *and* MARCELLUS   We do, my lord.
HAMLET   Armed, say you?
BARNARDO *and* MARCELLUS   Armed, my lord.

5. Officer's baton (see stage direction at 1.1.37).   7. *address . . . speak:* start to move as though it wished
6. These hands are not more like each other than the   to speak.
apparition was like King Hamlet.

HAMLET   From top to toe?

BARNARDO *and* MARCELLUS   My lord, from head to foot.

HAMLET   Then saw you not his
       face.

HORATIO   O yes, my lord, he wore his beaver up.

HAMLET   What° looked he? Frowningly?   *How*

HORATIO   A countenance more
       In sorrow than in anger.

230   HAMLET   Pale or red?

HORATIO   Nay, very pale.

HAMLET   And fixed his eyes upon you?

HORATIO   Most constantly.

HAMLET   I would I had been there.

HORATIO   It would have much amazed you.

235   HAMLET   Very like, very like. Stayed it long?

HORATIO   While one with moderate haste might tell° a hundred.   *count*

BARNARDO *and* MARCELLUS   Longer, longer.

HORATIO   Not when I saw't.

HAMLET   His beard was grizzly,° no?   *gray*

240   HORATIO   It was as I have seen it in his life,
       A sable silvered.[8]

HAMLET   I'll watch tonight. Perchance
       'Twill walk[9] again.

HORATIO   I warrant° you it will.   *guarantee*

HAMLET   If it assume my noble father's person
       I'll speak to it though hell itself should gape

245   And bid me hold my peace. I pray you all,
       If you have hitherto concealed this sight,
       Let it be treble[1] in your silence still,
       And whatsoever else shall hap° tonight,   *occur*
       Give it an understanding but no tongue.

250   I will requite your loves. So fare ye well.
       Upon the platform 'twixt eleven and twelve
       I'll visit you.

ALL THREE   Our duty to your honour.

HAMLET   Your love, as mine to you. Farewell.

                          Exeunt [*all but* HAMLET]
       My father's spirit in arms! All is not well.

255   I doubt° some foul play. Would the night were come.   *suspect*
       Till then, sit still, my soul. Foul deeds will rise,
       Though all the earth o'erwhelm them, to men's eyes.   *Exit*

1.3

         Enter LAERTES *and* OPHELIA, *his sister*

LAERTES   My necessaries are inbarqued.° Farewell.   *aboard ship*
       And, sister, as the winds give benefit
       And convoy is assistant,[1] do not sleep
       But let me hear from you.

OPHELIA   Do you doubt that?

5   LAERTES   For Hamlet and the trifling of his favour,

---

8. Black sprinkled with white.
9. "Wake," F's reading, suggests a return to consciousness.
1. Triply (F's reading); most editors follow Q2's "ten-

able" (that is, able to be held).
1.3 Location: Polonius's apartments in the castle.
1. And means of transport is available.

Hold it a fashion and a toy in blood,
A violet in the youth of primy nature,
Forward² not permanent, sweet not lasting,
The perfume and suppliance° of a minute,   *diversion*
No more.

OPHELIA   No more but so?

10 LAERTES   Think it no more.
For nature crescent° does not grow alone   *growing*
In thews° and bulk, but as his temple° waxes   *muscles / body*
The inward service° of the mind and soul   *responsibility*
Grows wide withal.° Perhaps he loves you now,   *along with it*
15 And now no soil° nor cautel° doth besmirch   *stain / deception*
The virtue of his will;° but you must fear,   *intentions; desires*
His greatness weighed,³ his will is not his own,
For he himself is subject to his birth.
He may not, as unvalued° persons do,   *common*
20 Carve for himself,⁴ for on his choice depends
The sanity⁵ and health of the whole state;
And therefore must his choice be circumscribed
Unto the voice° and yielding° of that body⁶   *vote / consent*
Whereof he is the head. Then if he says he loves you,
25 It fits° your wisdom so far to believe it   *befits*
As he in his peculiar sect and force⁷
May give his saying deed,⁸ which is no further
Than the main° voice of Denmark goes withal.   *collective*
Then weigh what loss your honour may sustain
30 If with too credent° ear you list° his songs,   *trusting / listen to*
Or lose your heart, or your chaste treasure open
To his unmastered° importunity.   *uncontrolled*
Fear it, Ophelia, fear it, my dear sister,
And keep within the rear of your affection,⁹
35 Out of the shot and danger of desire.
The chariest° maid is prodigal enough   *most careful; modest*
If she unmask her beauty to the moon.¹
Virtue itself scapes not calumnious strokes.
The canker galls the infants² of the spring
40 Too oft before their buttons be disclosed,°   *buds are open*
And in the morn and liquid dew of youth
Contagious blastments° are most imminent.   *blights*
Be wary then; best safety lies in fear;
Youth to itself rebels, though none else near.³
45 OPHELIA   I shall th'effect of this good lesson keep
As watchman to my heart; but, good my brother,
Do not, as some ungracious° pastors do,   *ungodly*
Show me the steep and thorny way to heaven
Whilst like a puffed° and reckless libertine   *proud*

---

2. *a toy . . . / Forward:* a passing sexual fancy, a flower of his natural impulses in their prime, early blooming ("forward").
3. When his high rank is considered.
4. Help himself to his own choice of the roast (proverbially, to choose for himself).
5. Well-being, emended from F's "sanctity"; Q2 prints "safety."
6. Body politic; nation.
7. His special rank and power (F). Q2 (and most editors) give "particular act and place," which has been interpreted as "power of action and social position."

8. May act on his promise.
9. And be restrained, despite the forward march of your feelings.
1. *prodigal . . . moon:* risk-taking enough if she exposes herself to the chaste moon. (Upper-class women wore masks to screen their complexions from the sun.) Q2 introduces lines 36, 38, and 39 with quotation marks, identifying these sentences as proverbial or noteworthy.
2. The cankerworm injures the shoots.
3. Young people are naturally rebellious, even without provocation.

50 Himself the primrose path of dalliance treads
And recks° not his own rede.° — heeds / advice
LAERTES   O fear me not.° — fear not for me
Enter POLONIUS
I stay too long—but here my father comes.
A double blessing is a double grace;
Occasion smiles upon a second leave.[4]
55 POLONIUS   Yet here, Laertes? Aboard, aboard, for shame!
The wind sits in the shoulder° of your sail, — at the back
And you are stayed° for. There—my blessing with thee, — waited
And these few precepts in thy memory
See thou character.° Give thy thoughts no tongue, — inscribe
60 Nor any unproportioned° thought his act. — unruly
Be thou familiar° but by no means vulgar.[5] — friendly
The friends thou hast, and their adoption tried,° — their friendship tested
Grapple them to thy soul with hoops of steel,
But do not dull° thy palm with entertainment[6] — callous
65 Of each new-hatched unfledged comrade. Beware
Of entrance to a quarrel, but being in,
Bear't° that th'opposèd may beware of thee. — Manage it so
Give every man thine ear but few thy voice.
Take each man's censure,° but reserve thy judgement. — opinion
70 Costly thy habit° as thy purse can buy, — dress
But not expressed in fancy;° rich not gaudy; — bizarre excess
For the apparel oft proclaims the man,
And they in France of the best rank and station
Are of all most select and generous chief in that.[7]
75 Neither a borrower nor a lender be,
For loan oft loses both itself and friend,
And borrowing dulls the edge of husbandry.° — economy
This above all—to thine own self be true,
And it must follow, as the night the day,
80 Thou canst not then be false to any man.
Farewell—my blessing season° this in thee. — mature
LAERTES   Most humbly do I take my leave, my lord.
POLONIUS   The time invites you. Go; your servants tend.° — wait
LAERTES   Farewell, Ophelia, and remember well
What I have said to you.
85 OPHELIA   'Tis in my memory locked,
And you yourself shall keep the key of it.
LAERTES   Farewell.   *Exit*
POLONIUS   What is't, Ophelia, he hath said to you?
OPHELIA   So please you, something touching the Lord Hamlet.
90 POLONIUS   Marry,[8] well bethought.
'Tis told me he hath very oft of late
Given private time to you, and you yourself
Have of your audience° been most free and bounteous. — attention
If it be so—as so 'tis put on° me, — suggested to
95 And that in way of caution—I must tell you
You do not understand yourself so clearly

4. Favorable circumstances provide us with a second farewell.
5. Indiscriminately social.
6. Greeting (handshaking).

7. Are of all people the most adept at displaying rank in fine appearance.
8. By the Virgin Mary, a mild oath.

As it behoves my daughter and your honour.
What is between you? Give me up the truth.

OPHELIA   He hath, my lord, of late made many tenders°   *offers*
100   Of his affection to me.

POLONIUS   Affection, pooh! You speak like a green girl
Unsifted° in such perilous circumstance.   *Inexperienced*
Do you believe his 'tenders' as you call them?

OPHELIA   I do not know, my lord, what I should think.

105   POLONIUS   Marry, I'll teach you: think yourself a baby
That you have ta'en his tenders for true pay,
Which are not sterling.⁹ Tender° yourself more dearly,   *Value; protect*
Or—not to crack the wind of the poor phrase,
Running it thus¹—you'll tender me a fool.²

110   OPHELIA   My lord, he hath importuned me with love
In honourable fashion—

POLONIUS   Ay, fashion° you may call it. Go to,³ go to.   *conventional flattery*

OPHELIA   And hath given countenance° to his speech, my lord,   *authority*
With all the vows of heaven.

115   POLONIUS   Ay, springes to catch woodcocks.⁴ I do know
When the blood burns how prodigal° the soul   *lavishly*
Lends the tongue vows. These blazes, daughter,
Giving more light than heat, extinct° in both   *extinguished*
Even in their promise as it is a-making,
120   You must not take for fire. From this time, daughter,
Be somewhat scanter of your maiden presence.
Set your entreatments at a higher rate
Than a command to parley.⁵ For Lord Hamlet,
Believe so much in° him, that he is young,   *concerning*
125   And with a larger tether may he walk
Than may be given you. In few,° Ophelia,   *brief*
Do not believe his vows, for they are brokers,°   *go-betweens*
Not of the dye which their investments° show,   *clerical vestments*
But mere imploratators° of unholy suits,   *solicitors*
130   Breathing° like sanctified and pious bawds   *Speaking*
The better to beguile. This is for all—
I would not, in plain terms, from this time forth
Have you so slander° any moment leisure   *disgrace*
As to give words or talk with the Lord Hamlet.
135   Look to't, I charge you. Come your ways.°   *Come along*

OPHELIA   I shall obey, my lord.   *Exeunt*

1.4

Enter [Prince] HAMLET, HORATIO, *and* MARCELLUS

HAMLET   The air bites shrewdly,° it is very cold.   *sharply*

HORATIO   It is a nipping and an eager° air.   *a bitter*

HAMLET   What hour now?

HORATIO   I think it lacks of twelve.

5   MARCELLUS   No, it is struck.

HORATIO   Indeed? I heard it not. Then it draws near the season°   *time*
Wherein the spirit held his wont° to walk.   *was accustomed*

---

9. Genuine currency.
1. *crack . . . thus*: ruin the phrase with overworking (like a "broken-winded" horse).
2. A multiple pun: make me look foolish; seem yourself a fool; show me a baby (idiomatically, a "fool").

3. That's enough; come, come.
4. (Obvious) traps for proverbially gullible birds.
5. *Set . . . parley*: Do not negotiate a surrender (of your chastity) just because he asks to speak with you.
1.4 Location: The castle's battlements.

A flourish of trumpets, and two pieces [of ordnance]°   cannons
goes off

What does this mean, my lord?

HAMLET   The King doth wake tonight and takes his rouse,
10   Keeps wassail, and the swagg'ring upspring reels,¹
And as he drains his draughts of Rhenish° down   Rhine wine
The kettle-drum and trumpet thus bray out
The triumph of his pledge.²

HORATIO   Is it a custom?

15   HAMLET   Ay, marry is't,
And to my mind, though I am native here
And to the manner° born, it is a custom   custom
More honoured in the breach than the observance.³

18.1   *This heavy-headed revel east and west*
Makes us traduced and taxed of other nations.
They clepe° us drunkards, and with swinish phrase   call
Soil our addition;° and indeed it takes   reputation
18.5   *From our achievements, though performed at height,°*   excellently
The pith° and marrow of our attribute.°   heart / attributed glory
So, oft it chances in particular men
That, for some vicious mole of nature⁴ in them—
As in their birth,° wherein they are not guilty,   parentage
18.10   *Since nature cannot choose his° origin,*   its
By the o'ergrowth of some complexion,⁵
Oft breaking down the pales° and forts of reason,   fences; boundaries
Or by some habit that too much o'erleavens
The form of plausive manners⁶—that these men,
18.15   *Carrying, I say, the stamp of one defect,*
Being nature's livery or fortune's star,⁷
His virtues else be they as pure as grace,
As infinite as man may undergo,°   sustain
Shall in the general censure° take corruption   the public opinion
18.20   *From that particular fault. The dram of evil⁸*
Doth all the noble substance over-daub⁹
To his own scandal.°   shame

Enter GHOST [*as before*]

HORATIO   Look, my lord, it comes.

20   HAMLET   Angels and ministers of grace defend us!
Be thou a spirit of health or goblin° damned,   demon
Bring with thee airs° from heaven or blasts¹ from hell,   gentle breezes
Be thy intents wicked or charitable,
Thou com'st in such a questionable shape
25   That I will speak to thee. I'll call thee Hamlet,
King, father, royal Dane. O answer me!

1. *The King . . . reels:* The King revels and carouses rather than sleeping, has a drinking party ("wassail"), and staggers ("reels") through a wild German dance.
2. His success in draining his cup upon making a toast.
3. Which is more honored in being broken than in being observed. After this line, Q2 has the following passage, 18.1–18.22, omitted in F (possibly in deference to the English Queen, Anne of Denmark).
4. Natural blemish that tends to vice.
5. By the disproportionate amount of one humor (see note to 2.2.310–11), and thus an unbalanced personality.
6. *o'erleavens . . . manners:* changes the whole effect of otherwise pleasing ("plausive") manners for the worse (as

too much yeast ruins a batch of bread).
7. Being a congenital defect (the "livery," or clothing, given by nature) or a blemish caused by fortune (the influence of chance astrological events).
8. Tiny amount (eighth of an ounce) of bad qualities. This is a conjectural emendation of Q2's "eale," although there is no consensus on the correct reading.
9. *Doth . . . over-daub:* Obscures the virtuous essence with adhering dirt. Emended from Q2's "of a doubt," an incomplete thought; "often dout" (extinguish) is another plausible correction.
1. Pestilent gusts.

Let me not burst in ignorance, but tell
Why thy canonized° bones, hearsèd° in death,   *consecrated / coffined*
Have burst their cerements,° why the sepulchre   *grave clothes*
30   Wherein we saw thee quietly enurned°   *entombed*
Hath oped his ponderous and marble jaws
To cast thee up again. What may this mean,
That thou, dead corpse, again in complete steel,°   *armor*
Revisitst thus the glimpses of the moon,[2]
35   Making night hideous, and we fools of nature[3]
So horridly to shake our disposition°   *mental foundations*
With thoughts beyond the reaches of our souls?
Say, why is this? Wherefore? What should we do?
            GHOST *beckons* HAMLET
HORATIO   It beckons you to go away with it
40   As if it some impartment° did desire   *communication*
To you alone.
MARCELLUS [*to* HAMLET]   Look with what courteous action
It wafts° you to a more removèd ground.   *beckons*
But do not go with it.
HORATIO [*to* HAMLET]   No, by no means.
HAMLET   It will not speak. Then will I follow it.
HORATIO   Do not, my lord.
45   HAMLET   Why, what should be the fear?
I do not set my life at a pin's fee,°   *value*
And for my soul, what can it do to that,
Being a thing immortal as itself?
         [GHOST *beckons* HAMLET]
It waves me forth again. I'll follow it.
50   HORATIO   What if it tempt you toward the flood,° my lord,   *sea*
Or to the dreadful summit of the cliff
That beetles o'er° his base into the sea,   *overhangs*
And there assume some other horrible form
Which might deprive your sovereignty of reason
55   And draw you into madness? Think of it.[4]
55.1   *The very place puts toys of desperation,*[5]
         Without more motive,° into every brain   *cause*
         That looks so many fathoms to the sea
         And hears it roar beneath.
         [GHOST *beckons* HAMLET]
HAMLET   It wafts me still. [*To* GHOST] Go on, I'll follow thee.
MARCELLUS   You shall not go, my lord.
HAMLET   Hold off your hand.
HORATIO   Be ruled. You shall not go.
HAMLET   My fate cries out,
And makes each petty artere° in this body   *artery*
60   As hardy as the Nemean lion's[6] nerve.
         [GHOST *beckons* HAMLET]
Still am I called. Unhand me, gentlemen.
By heav'n, I'll make a ghost of him that lets° me.   *hinders*
I say, away! [*To* GHOST] Go on, I'll follow thee.
          Exeunt GHOST *and* HAMLET

---

2. *glimpses of the moon:* (earth lit by) flickering moonlight.

3. Mere mortals (terrified by encounters with the supernatural).

4. After this line, Q2 has the following passage, 55.1–55.4, omitted in F.

5. Imaginings of despair and suicide.

6. A ferocious beast killed by Hercules.

HORATIO   He waxes desperate with imagination.
65   MARCELLUS   Let's follow. 'Tis not fit thus to obey him.
HORATIO   Have after.° To what issue° will this come?   *Go on / end*
MARCELLUS   Something is rotten in the state of Denmark.
HORATIO   Heaven will direct it.
MARCELLUS   Nay, let's follow him.   *Exeunt*

1.5

Enter GHOST, *and* [*Prince*] HAMLET [*following*]

HAMLET   Whither wilt thou lead me? Speak. I'll go no further.
GHOST   Mark me.
HAMLET   I will.
GHOST   My hour is almost come
When I to sulph'rous and tormenting flames
Must render up myself.
HAMLET   Alas, poor ghost!
5   GHOST   Pity me not, but lend thy serious hearing
To what I shall unfold.
HAMLET   Speak, I am bound to hear.
GHOST   So art thou to revenge when thou shalt hear.
HAMLET   What?
GHOST   I am thy father's spirit,
10   Doomed for a certain term to walk the night,
And for the day confined to fast° in fires   *do penance*
Till the foul crimes done in my days of nature°   *my natural life*
Are burnt and purged away. But that I am forbid
To tell the secrets of my prison-house
15   I could a tale unfold whose lightest word
Would harrow up thy soul, freeze thy young blood,
Make thy two eyes like stars start from their spheres,
Thy knotty and combinèd locks to part,
And each particular hair to stand on end
20   Like quills upon the fretful porcupine.
But this eternal blazon¹ must not be
To ears of flesh and blood. List,° Hamlet, list, O list!   *Listen*
If thou didst ever thy dear father love—
HAMLET   O God!
25   GHOST   Revenge his foul and most unnatural murder.
HAMLET   Murder?
GHOST   Murder most foul, as in the best it is,
But this most foul, strange, and unnatural.
HAMLET   Haste, haste me to know it, that with wings as swift
30   As meditation or the thoughts of love
May sweep to my revenge.
GHOST   I find thee apt,
And duller shouldst thou be than the fat° weed   *gross*
That rots itself² in ease on Lethe wharf³
Wouldst thou not stir in this. Now, Hamlet, hear.
35   'Tis given out that, sleeping in mine orchard,
A serpent stung me. So the whole ear of Denmark
Is by a forgèd process° of my death   *a fabricated account*

1.5 Location: Scene continues.
1. Catalogue or display of the afterlife's mysteries.
2. Decays under its own excessive growth (F). Q1, Q2
print "roots itself," another possible reading.
3. In classical mythology, Lethe was the river of forgetfulness in Hades.

Rankly abused.° But know, thou noble youth,   *deceived*
The serpent that did sting thy father's life
40 Now wears his crown.

HAMLET   O my prophetic soul! Mine uncle?

GHOST   Ay, that incestuous, that adulterate° beast,   *adulterous*
With witchcraft of his wit, with traitorous gifts°—   *abilities; presents*
O wicked wit and gifts, that have the power
45 So to seduce!—won to his shameful lust
The will of my most seeming-virtuous queen.
O Hamlet, what a falling off was there!—
From me, whose love was of that dignity
That it went hand-in-hand even with the vow
50 I made to her in marriage, and to decline
Upon a wretch whose natural gifts were poor
To° those of mine.   *Compared to*
But virtue, as it never will be moved,
Though lewdness court it in a shape of heaven,
55 So lust, though to a radiant angel linked,
Will sate itself[4] in a celestial bed,
And prey on garbage.
But soft, methinks I scent the morning's air.
Brief let me be. Sleeping within mine orchard,
60 My custom always in the afternoon,
Upon my secure hour thy uncle stole
With juice of cursèd hebenon[5] in a vial,
And in the porches° of mine ears did pour   *entranceways*
The leperous distilment,[6] whose effect
65 Holds such an enmity with blood of man
That swift as quicksilver it courses through
The natural gates and alleys of the body,
And with a sudden vigour it doth posset°   *curdle*
And curd, like eager° droppings into milk,   *acid (like wine)*
70 The thin and wholesome blood. So did it mine;
And a most instant tetter° barked about,[7]   *scaly rash*
Most lazar-like,° with vile and loathsome crust,   *leperlike*
All my smooth body.
Thus was I, sleeping, by a brother's hand
75 Of life, of crown, of queen at once dispatched,°   *deprived*
Cut off even in the blossoms of my sin,[8]
Unhouseled, dis-appointed, unaneled,[9]
No reck'ning made, but sent to my account
With all my imperfections on my head.[1]
80 O horrible, O horrible, most horrible!
If thou hast nature° in thee, bear it not.   *natural feeling*
Let not the royal bed of Denmark be
A couch for luxury° and damnèd incest.   *lechery*
But howsoever thou pursuest this act,
85 Taint not thy mind,[2] nor let thy soul contrive
Against thy mother aught.° Leave her to heaven,   *any punishment*

---

4. Will become satiated (and unable to find further pleasure).
5. A poison, possibly henbane.
6. Distillation causing skin to become scaly (as in leprosy, a disease familiar in Elizabethan England).
7. Covered the body like bark.
8. Cut off when my sins were full-blown, flourishing.

9. Without the sacrament of the Eucharist, without death-bed confession and absolution, and without extreme unction, the ritual anointing of those who are close to death.
1. *No . . . head:* Without having made restitution for my sins, but sent to the Last Judgment liable for all my faults.
2. Do not let yourself be corrupted.

And to those thorns that in her bosom lodge
To prick and sting her. Fare thee well at once.
The glow-worm shows the matin° to be near,   *morning*
90   And gins° to pale his uneffectual fire.   *begins*
Adieu, adieu, Hamlet. Remember me.   *Exit*
HAMLET   O all you host of heaven! O earth! What else?
And shall I couple° hell? O fie! Hold, hold, my heart,   *add*
And you, my sinews, grow not instant old,
95   But bear me stiffly up. Remember thee?
Ay, thou poor ghost, while memory holds a seat
In this distracted globe.³ Remember thee?
Yea, from the table° of my memory   *tablet; book*
I'll wipe away all trivial fond° records,   *foolish*
100   All saws of books, all forms, all pressures past,⁴
That youth and observation copied there,
And thy commandment all alone shall live
Within the book and volume of my brain
Unmixed with baser matter. Yes, yes, by heaven.
105   O most pernicious woman!
O villain, villain, smiling, damnèd villain!
My tables,⁵
My tables—meet it is I set it down
That one may smile and smile and be a villain.
110   At least I'm sure it may be so in Denmark.
      [*He writes*]
So, uncle, there you are. Now to my word:°   *watchword; motto*
It is 'Adieu, adieu, remember me'.
I have sworn't.
HORATIO *and* MARCELLUS [*within*]   My lord, my lord.
      Enter HORATIO *and* MARCELLUS
115   MARCELLUS [*calling*]   Lord Hamlet!
HORATIO   Heaven secure him.
HAMLET   So be it.
HORATIO [*calling*]   Illo, ho, ho, my lord.
HAMLET   Hillo, ho, ho, boy; come, bird, come.⁶
120   MARCELLUS   How is't, my noble lord?
HORATIO [*to* HAMLET]   What news, my lord?
HAMLET   O wonderful!
HORATIO   Good my lord, tell it.
HAMLET   No, you'll reveal it.
HORATIO   Not I, my lord, by heaven.
MARCELLUS   Nor I, my lord.
125   HAMLET   How say you then, would heart of man once think it?
But you'll be secret?
HORATIO *and* MARCELLUS   Ay, by heav'n, my lord.
HAMLET   There's ne'er a villain dwelling in all Denmark
But he's an arrant° knave.   *a downright*
HORATIO   There needs no ghost, my lord, come from the grave
To tell us this.
130   HAMLET   Why, right, you are i'th' right,
And so without more circumstance° at all   *elaborate speech*

3. Confused head; disordered world; often also taken as
a reference to the Globe Theatre and the audience.
4. All adages from books, all images or customs, all past
impressions.

5. Scholars and others might carry two writing tables
hinged together, as a notebook.
6. Hamlet parodies a falconer's call.

I hold it fit that we shake hands and part,
You as your business and desires shall point you—
For every man has business and desire,
135 Such as it is—and for mine own poor part,
Look you, I'll go pray.

HORATIO These are but wild and whirling words, my lord.

HAMLET I'm sorry they offend you, heartily,
Yes, faith, heartily.

HORATIO   There's no offence, my lord.

140 HAMLET Yes, by Saint Patrick,[7] but there is, Horatio,
And much offence, too. Touching this vision here,
It is an honest° ghost, that let me tell you.   *a reliable; a genuine*
For your desire to know what is between us,
O'ermaster't as you may. And now, good friends,
145 As you are friends, scholars, and soldiers,
Give me one poor request.

HORATIO   What is't, my lord? We will.

HAMLET Never make known what you have seen tonight.

HORATIO *and* MARCELLUS My lord, we will not.

HAMLET   Nay, but swear't.

HORATIO In faith, my lord, not I.[8]

MARCELLUS   Nor I, my lord, in faith.

HAMLET Upon my sword.[9]

150 MARCELLUS   We have sworn, my lord, already.

HAMLET Indeed, upon my sword, indeed.

                    GHOST *cries under the stage*

GHOST   Swear.

HAMLET Ah ha, boy, sayst thou so? Art thou there, truepenny?°—   *trusty fellow*
Come on. You hear this fellow in the cellarage.
Consent to swear.

HORATIO   Propose the oath, my lord.

155 HAMLET Never to speak of this that you have seen,
Swear by my sword.

GHOST [*under the stage*]   Swear.
                    [*They swear*]

HAMLET *Hic et ubique?*[1] Then we'll shift our ground.—
Come hither, gentlemen,
160 And lay your hands again upon my sword.
Never to speak of this that you have heard,
Swear by my sword.

GHOST [*under the stage*]   Swear.
                    [*They swear*]

HAMLET Well said, old mole. Canst work i'th' earth so fast?
165 A worthy pioneer.[2]—Once more remove,° good friends.   *move*

HORATIO O day and night, but this is wondrous strange!

HAMLET And therefore as a stranger give it welcome.[3]
There are more things in heaven and earth, Horatio,
Than are dreamt of in our philosophy.[4] But come,

---

7. Perhaps because Patrick was thought to be keeper of purgatory.
8. I will indeed not reveal it.
9. Swearing on a sword was a fairly common practice because the hilt and blade form a cross.
1. Here and everywhere (Latin).

2. Army trench digger.
3. As if it had a guest's right to courteous hospitality.
4. Human speculative knowledge. Q2 and most editors print "your philosophy"; F's "our" shows Hamlet himself still trying to reconcile his own understanding with the supernatural revelations.

170 Here as before, never, so help you mercy,
How strange or odd soe'er I bear myself—
As I perchance hereafter shall think meet
To put an antic disposition on⁵—
That you at such time seeing me never shall,
175 With arms encumbered° thus, or this headshake,   folded
Or by pronouncing of some doubtful° phrase   ambiguous
As 'Well, we know' or 'We could an if° we would',   an if=if
Or 'If we list° to speak', or 'There be, an if they might',⁶   liked
Or such ambiguous giving out, to note
180 That you know aught° of me—this not to do,   anything
So grace and mercy at your most need help you, swear.
GHOST [*under the stage*]   Swear.
[*They swear*]
HAMLET   Rest, rest, perturbèd spirit.—So, gentlemen,
With all my love I do commend me to you,
185 And what so poor a man as Hamlet is
May do t'express his love and friending° to you,   friendship
God willing, shall not lack.° Let us go in together,   be left undone
And still° your fingers on your lips, I pray.   always
The time is out of joint.° O cursèd spite   dislocated; disordered
190 That ever I was born to set it right!
Nay, come,⁷ let's go together.
                                                Exeunt

2.1

Enter old POLONIUS *with his man* REYNALDO
POLONIUS   Give him this money and these notes, Reynaldo.
REYNALDO   I will, my lord.
POLONIUS   You shall do marv'lous wisely, good Reynaldo,
Before you visit him to make enquire
Of his behaviour.
5 REYNALDO   My lord, I did intend it.
POLONIUS   Marry, well said, very well said. Look you, sir,
Enquire me° first what Danskers° are in Paris,   for me / Danes
And how, and who, what means,° and where they keep,°   wealth; income / lodge
What company, at what expense; and finding
10 By this encompassment and drift of question¹
That they do know my son, come you more nearer
Than your particular demands will touch it.²
Take you,° as 'twere, some distant knowledge of him,   Pretend
As thus: 'I know his father and his friends,
15 And in part him'—do you mark this, Reynaldo?
REYNALDO   Ay, very well, my lord.
POLONIUS   'And in part him, but', you may say, 'not well,
But if 't be he I mean, he's very wild,
Addicted so and so'; and there put on him°   attribute to him
20 What forgeries° you please—marry, none so rank³   made-up tales
As may dishonour him, take heed of that—
But, sir, such wanton,° wild, and usual slips   unrestrained

---

5. To assume the behavior of a madman.
6. There are those who would speak if they were allowed.
7. The others are politely waiting for Hamlet, the Prince,
to lead the way; he insists on informality.
2.1 Location: Polonius's apartments in the castle.

1. By this roundabout and indirect way of inquiry.
2. *come . . . it*: you will come closer to the truth than by
direct questions.
3. Excessive; foul.

As are companions noted and most known
To youth and liberty.

25 REYNALDO   As gaming, my lord?

POLONIUS   Ay, or drinking, fencing, swearing,
Quarrelling, drabbing°—you may go so far.   *whoring*

REYNALDO   My lord, that would dishonour him.

POLONIUS   Faith, no, as you may season° it in the charge.   *mitigate*

30 You must not put another scandal on him,
That he is open° to incontinency.°   *inclined / sexual excess*
That's not my meaning—but breathe his faults so quaintly
That they may seem the taints of liberty,[4]
The flash and outbreak of a fiery mind,

35 A savageness in unreclaimèd° blood,   *unchecked*
Of general assault.[5]

REYNALDO   But, my good lord—

POLONIUS   Wherefore should you do this?

REYNALDO   Ay, my lord.
I would know that.

POLONIUS   Marry, sir, here's my drift,
And I believe it is a fetch of warrant:[6]

40 You laying these slight sullies on my son,
As 'twere a thing a little soiled i'th' working,[7]
Mark you, your party° in converse, him you would sound,°   *partner / sound out*
Having° ever seen in the prenominate crimes[8]   *If he has*
The youth you breathe of guilty, be assured

45 He closes° with you in this consequence:[9]   *confides*
'Good sir', or so, or 'friend', or 'gentleman',
According to the phrase° and the addition[1]   *expression*
Of man and country.

REYNALDO   Very good, my lord.

POLONIUS   And then, sir, does a° this—a does—   *he*

50 what was I about to say? By the mass, I was about to say something. Where did I leave?

REYNALDO   At 'closes in the consequence', at 'friend,
Or so', and 'gentleman'.

POLONIUS   At 'closes in the consequence'—ay, marry,

55 He closes with you thus: 'I know the gentleman,
I saw him yesterday'—or t'other day,
Or then, or then—'with such and such, and, as you say,
There was a° gaming, there o'ertook in 's rouse,   *he*
There falling out° at tennis', or perchance   *quarrelling*

60 'I saw him enter such a house of sale',
Videlicet,° a brothel, or so forth. See you now,   *That is to say*
Your bait of falsehood takes this carp of truth;
And thus do we of wisdom and of reach°   *wide understanding*
With windlasses and with assays of bias[2]

65 By indirections find directions° out.   *real tendencies*
So, by my former° lecture and advice,   *preceding*
Shall you my son. You have me,° have you not?   *my meaning*

---

4. Faults resulting from freedom of action.
5. Which afflicts all young men.
6. *fetch of warrant*: justifiable trick (F). Q2 has "fetch of wit" (clever scheme).
7. Stained by education in the ways of the world, "shop soiled."

8. Aforesaid faults.
9. To the following effect.
1. Title of address.
2. And with indirect tests, like the curved line, or "bias," that a weighted bowling ball describes. *windlasses*: round-about paths (a hunter's circuit to intercept game).

REYNALDO   My lord, I have.

POLONIUS   God b'wi' ye. Fare ye well.

70   REYNALDO   Good my lord.

POLONIUS   Observe his inclination in° yourself.   *for*

REYNALDO   I shall, my lord.

POLONIUS   And let him ply° his music.   *work at*

REYNALDO   Well, my lord.

        Enter OPHELIA

POLONIUS   Farewell.   *Exit* REYNALDO

75   How now, Ophelia, what's the matter?

OPHELIA   Alas, my lord, I have been so affrighted.

POLONIUS   With what, i'th' name of God?

OPHELIA   My lord, as I was sewing in my chamber,

    Lord Hamlet, with his doublet all unbraced,°   *jacket all unfastened*

80   No hat upon his head, his stockings fouled,

    Ungartered, and down-gyvèd to his ankle,³

    Pale as his shirt, his knees knocking each other,

    And with a look so piteous in purport

    As if he had been loosèd out of hell

85   To speak of horrors, he comes before me.

POLONIUS   Mad for thy love?

OPHELIA   My lord, I do not know,

    But truly I do fear it.

POLONIUS   What said he?

OPHELIA   He took me by the wrist and held me hard,

    Then goes he to the length of all his arm,

90   And with his other hand thus o'er his brow

    He falls to such perusal of my face

    As a° would draw it. Long stayed he so.   *As if he*

    At last, a little shaking of mine arm,

    And thrice his head thus waving up and down,

95   He raised a sigh so piteous and profound

    That it did seem to shatter all his bulk

    And end his being. That done, he lets me go,

    And, with his head over his shoulder turned,

    He seemed to find his way without his eyes,

100   For out o' doors he went without their help,

    And to the last bended their light⁴ on me.

POLONIUS   Come, go with me. I will go seek the King.

    This is the very ecstasy° of love,   *insanity*

    Whose violent property fordoes° itself   *nature destroys*

105   And leads the will to desperate undertakings

    As oft as any passion under heaven

    That does afflict our natures. I am sorry—

    What, have you given him any hard words of late?

OPHELIA   No, my good lord, but as you did command

110   I did repel his letters and denied

    His access to me.

POLONIUS   That hath made him mad.

    I am sorry that with better speed and judgement

    I had not quoted° him. I feared he did but trifle   *observed*

---

3. Fallen round his ankles, like a prisoner's fetters, or "gyves."

4. Sight was thought to result from both sending light out and taking it in through the eyes.

And meant to wreck thee.⁵ But beshrew my jealousy!°   *curse my suspicion*
115 By heaven, it is as proper to our age
To cast beyond ourselves⁶ in our opinions
As it is common for the younger sort
To lack discretion. Come, go we to the King.
This must be known, which, being kept close, might move
120 More grief to hide than hate to utter love.⁷   *Exeunt*

2.2

Flourish. Enter KING [CLAUDIUS] *and* QUEEN [GER-
TRUDE], ROSENCRANTZ *and* GUILDENSTERN,¹ *cum aliis*

KING CLAUDIUS   Welcome, dear Rosencrantz and Guildenstern.
Moreover° that we much did long to see you,   *Beyond the fact*
The need we have to use you did provoke
Our hasty sending.° Something have you heard   *summons*
5 Of Hamlet's transformation—so I call it,
Since not th'exterior nor the inward man
Resembles that° it was. What it should be,   *what*
More than his father's death, that thus hath put him
So much from th'understanding of himself,
10 I cannot deem of.² I entreat you both
That, being of so young days³ brought up with him,
And since so neighboured° to his youth and humour,°   *familiar / temperament*
That you vouchsafe your rest⁴ here in our court
Some little time, so by your companies
15 To draw him on to pleasures, and to gather,
So much as from occasions° you may glean,   *opportunities*
Whether aught to us unknown afflicts him thus
That, opened,° lies within our remedy.   *if disclosed*
QUEEN GERTRUDE   Good gentlemen, he hath much talked of you,
20 And sure I am two men there is not living
To whom he more adheres.⁵ If it will please you
To show us so much gentry° and good will   *courtesy*
As to expend your time with us a while
For the supply and profit of our hope,⁶
25 Your visitation shall receive such thanks
As fits a king's remembrance.
ROSENCRANTZ   Both your majesties
Might, by the sovereign power you have of° us,   *over*
Put your dread° pleasures more into command   *reverend*
Than to entreaty.
GUILDENSTERN   But we both obey,
30 And here give up ourselves in the full bent⁷
To lay our service freely at your feet
To be commanded.
KING CLAUDIUS   Thanks, Rosencrantz and gentle Guildenstern.

---

5. To ruin you through seduction.
6. *as proper . . . ourselves*: as natural to us old men to go
too far and (like hunting dogs) lose the scent, thus erring
out of caution.
7. *which . . . love*: we may incur hatred by revealing
(Hamlet's) love, but to conceal it may cause greater suffering. *close*: secret.
2.2 Location: A stateroom in the castle.
1. Historical figures with these names are mentioned

in an ambassador's report to Queen Elizabeth sent from
Elsinore in 1588.
2. Judge (F). Q2 prints "dream."
3. From such an early age.
4. That you agree to stay.
5. To whom he is more attached.
6. *For . . . hope*: To provide support for and furtherance
of our hope.
7. To the fullest extent (like an archer's bow, fully drawn).

QUEEN GERTRUDE   Thanks, Guildenstern and gentle Rosencrantz.

35   And I beseech you instantly to visit
My too-much changèd son.—Go, some of ye,
And bring the gentlemen where Hamlet is.

GUILDENSTERN   Heavens make our presence and our practices
Pleasant and helpful to him.

QUEEN GERTRUDE   Ay, amen!

         Exeunt ROSENCRANTZ *and* GUILDENSTERN [*with others*]
         Enter POLONIUS

40   POLONIUS   Th'ambassadors from Norway, my good lord,
Are joyfully returned.

KING CLAUDIUS   Thou still° hast been the father of good news.   *always*

POLONIUS   Have I, my lord? Assure you, my good liege,
I hold my duty, as I hold my soul,

45   Both to my God and to my gracious King.
And I do think—or else this brain of mine
Hunts not the trail of policy° so sure   *cleverness*
As it hath used to do—that I have found
The very cause of Hamlet's lunacy.

50   KING CLAUDIUS   O speak of that, that I do long to hear!

POLONIUS   Give first admittance to th'ambassadors.
My news shall be the fruit° to that great feast.   *dessert*

KING CLAUDIUS   Thyself do grace to them, and bring them in.

                            [*Exit* POLONIUS]

He tells me, my sweet queen, that he hath found

55   The head° and source of all your son's distemper.   *origin; chief part*

QUEEN GERTRUDE   I doubt[8] it is no other but the main°—   *main matter*
His father's death and our o'er-hasty marriage.

KING CLAUDIUS   Well, we shall sift him.°   *interrogate (Polonius)*

         Enter POLONIUS, VALTEMAND, *and* CORNELIUS
                   Welcome, my good friends.
Say, Valtemand, what from our brother° Norway?   *fellow monarch*

60   VALTEMAND   Most fair return of greetings and desires.°   *good wishes*
Upon our first[9] he sent out to suppress
His nephew's levies, which to him appeared
To be a preparation 'gainst the Polack;°   *King of Poland*
But better looked into, he truly found

65   It was against your highness; whereat grieved
That so his sickness, age, and impotence
Was falsely borne in hand,[1] sends out arrests
On Fortinbras,[2] which he, in brief, obeys,
Receives rebuke from Norway, and, in fine,°   *conclusion*

70   Makes vow before his uncle never more
To give th'essay of arms[3] against your majesty;
Whereon old Norway, overcome with joy,
Gives him three thousand crowns in annual fee°   *income*
And his commission to employ those soldiers

75   So levied as before, against the Polack,
With an entreaty herein further shown,

        [*He gives a letter to* CLAUDIUS]

That it might please you to give quiet pass

---

8. Fear, suspect. *distemper*: unbalanced mind.
9. When we first raised the matter.
1. Disloyally taken advantage of, tricked.
2. *arrests / On Fortinbras*: orders commanding Fortin-

bras to stop his preparations and (presumably) present
himself to explain them.
3. To mount a military challenge.

Through your dominions for his enterprise
On such regards of safety and allowance[4]
As therein are set down.

80 KING CLAUDIUS   It likes° us well,   *pleases*
And at our more considered° time we'll read,   *suitable for thought*
Answer, and think upon this business.
Meantime we thank you for your well-took labour.
Go to your rest; at night we'll feast together.
85 Most welcome home.

              Exeunt [VALTEMAND *and* CORNELIUS]

POLONIUS   This business is very well ended.
My liege, and madam, to expostulate°   *debate*
What majesty should be, what duty is,
Why day is day, night night, and time is time,
90 Were nothing but to waste night, day, and time.
Therefore, since brevity is the soul of wit,
And tediousness the limbs and outward flourishes,°   *rhetorical devices*
I will be brief. Your noble son is mad—
'Mad' call I it, for to define true madness,
95 What is't but to be nothing else but mad?
But let that go.

QUEEN GERTRUDE   More matter with less art.
POLONIUS   Madam, I swear I use no art at all.
That he is mad, 'tis true; 'tis true 'tis pity,
And pity 'tis 'tis true—a foolish figure,°   *figure of speech*
100 But farewell it, for I will use no art.
Mad let us grant him, then; and now remains
That we find out the cause of this effect—
Or rather say 'the cause of this *defect*',
For this effect defective[5] comes by cause.
105 Thus it remains, and the remainder thus.
Perpend.°   *Consider*
I have a daughter—have whilst she is mine°—   *until she marries*
Who in her duty and obedience, mark,
Hath given me this. Now gather and surmise.
           [*He reads a*] *letter*
110 'To the celestial and my soul's idol, the most beautified Ophe-
lia'—that's an ill phrase, a vile phrase, 'beautified' is a vile
phrase. But you shall hear—'these in° her excellent white   *these words unto*
bosom, these'.

QUEEN GERTRUDE   Came this from Hamlet to her?
115 POLONIUS   Good madam, stay° a while. I will be faithful.[6]   *wait*
     'Doubt thou the stars are fire,
       Doubt that the sun doth move,
     Doubt° truth to be a liar,   *Suspect*
       But never doubt I love.
120 O dear Ophelia, I am ill at these numbers.[7] I have not art to
reckon my groans.[8] But that I love thee best, O most best,
believe it. Adieu.
      Thine evermore, most dear lady, whilst this
       machine is° to him,   *this body belongs*

---

4. *On . . . allowance*: Conditions regarding your realm's safety, subject to your approval.
5. This consequence showing a lack of something (Hamlet's reason).
6. I will accurately read out the letter's contents.
7. Hamlet is both bad at writing verse and lovesick while he is writing.
8. Count my groans; also, number my groans metrically.

Hamlet.'

125 This in obedience hath my daughter showed me,
And more above° hath his solicitings,   in addition
As they fell out° by time, by means, and place,   occurred
All given to mine ear.
KING CLAUDIUS   But how hath she
Received his love?
POLONIUS   What do you think of me?
130 KING CLAUDIUS As of a man faithful and honourable.
POLONIUS I would fain° prove so. But what might you think,   be glad to
When I had seen this hot love on the wing,
As I perceived it—I must tell you that—
Before my daughter told me, what might you,
135 Or my dear majesty your queen here, think,
If I had played the desk or table-book,[9]
Or given my heart a winking mute and dumb,[1]
Or looked upon this love with idle sight—
What might you think? No, I went round° to work,   directly
140 And my young mistress thus I did bespeak:°   address
'Lord Hamlet is a prince out of thy star.°   above your sphere
This must not be'. And then I precepts gave her,
That she should lock herself from his resort,°   visits
Admit no messengers, receive no tokens;
145 Which done, she took the fruits of my advice,
And he, repulsèd—a short tale to make—
Fell into a sadness, then into a fast,
Thence to a watch,° thence into a weakness,   an insomnia
Thence to a lightness,° and, by this declension,°   dizziness / decline
150 Into the madness wherein now he raves,
And all we° wail for.   of us
KING CLAUDIUS [to GERTRUDE] Do you think 'tis this?
QUEEN GERTRUDE It may be; very likely.
POLONIUS Hath there been such a time—I'd fain know that—
155 That I have positively said ''Tis so'
When it proved otherwise?
KING CLAUDIUS   Not that I know.
POLONIUS [touching his head, then his shoulder]
Take this from this if this be otherwise.
If circumstances lead me I will find
Where truth is hid, though it were hid indeed
Within the centre.°   middle of the earth
160 KING CLAUDIUS   How may we try° it further?   test
POLONIUS You know sometimes he walks four hours together
Here in the lobby.
QUEEN GERTRUDE So he does indeed.
POLONIUS At such a time I'll loose my daughter to him.
[To CLAUDIUS] Be you and I behind an arras° then.   a tapestry
165 Mark the encounter. If he love her not,
And be not from his reason fall'n thereon,°   on that account

9. If I had recorded the perception (in my memory) but   1. Or made my heart close its eyes and remain silent.
kept it hidden.

Let me be no assistant for a state,
But keep a farm and carters.°   *wagon drivers*

KING CLAUDIUS   We will try it.

*Enter [Prince] HAMLET, [madly attired,] reading on a
book²*

QUEEN GERTRUDE   But look where sadly° the poor wretch comes   *gravely*
reading.

170   POLONIUS   Away, I do beseech you both, away.
I'll board him presently.° O give me leave.³   *accost him immediately*

Exit KING *and* QUEEN

How does my good Lord Hamlet?

HAMLET   Well, God-'a'-mercy.⁴

POLONIUS   Do you know me, my lord?

175   HAMLET   Excellent, excellent well. You're a fishmonger.

POLONIUS   Not I, my lord.

HAMLET   Then I would you were so honest a man.

POLONIUS   Honest, my lord?

HAMLET   Ay, sir. To be honest, as this world goes, is to be one

180   man picked out of ten thousand.

POLONIUS   That's very true, my lord.

HAMLET   For if the sun breed maggots in a dead dog, being a
good kissing carrion⁵—have you a daughter?

POLONIUS   I have, my lord.

185   HAMLET   Let her not walk i'th' sun.⁶ Conception⁷ is a blessing,
but not as your daughter may conceive. Friend, look to't.°   *take care*

POLONIUS   [*aside*]   How say you by that? Still harping on my
daughter. Yet he knew me not at first—a° said I was a fish-   *he*
monger. A is far gone, far gone, and truly, in my youth I suf-

190   fered much extremity for love, very near this. I'll speak to him
again.—What do you read, my lord?

HAMLET   Words, words, words.

POLONIUS   What is the matter,⁸ my lord?

HAMLET   Between who?

195   POLONIUS   I mean the matter you read, my lord.

HAMLET   Slanders, sir; for the satirical slave° says here that old   *scoundrel*
men have grey beards, that their faces are wrinkled, their eyes
purging° thick amber° or plum-tree gum, and that they have a   *discharging / resin*
plentiful lack of wit,° together with most weak hams.° All which,   *intellect / thighs*

200   sir, though I most powerfully and potently believe, yet I hold
it not honesty° to have it thus set down; for you yourself, sir,   *honorable*
should be old as I am—if, like a crab, you could go backward.

POLONIUS   [*aside*]   Though this be madness, yet there is method
in't.—Will you walk out of the air,⁹ my lord?

205   HAMLET   Into my grave.

POLONIUS   Indeed, that is out o'th' air. [*Aside*] How pregnant°   *meaningful*
sometimes his replies are! A happiness° that often madness hits   *An appropriateness*

---

2. Hamlet possibly has two entrances here, the first at
the inner stage ("lobby," line 162) and the second at the
outer stage representing the audience chamber, where
Claudius, Gertrude, and Polonius are talking. Hamlet
would thus have overheard Polonius's plan before they
notice him reading (line 169). (See 2.1.79–82 for
Ophelia's description of Hamlet's attire.)
3. Excuse me (politely asking the King and Queen to
leave).
4. Thank you (used with inferiors).

5. Piece of flesh good for kissing. Dead matter was
thought to breed maggots, especially in sunlight.
6. Walk out in public or (as in 1.2.67) expose herself too
much to a Prince's (or son's) love.
7. The ability to form ideas; pregnancy.
8. Content, although Hamlet deliberately takes it as
"subject of a quarrel."
9. Outdoor air was regarded as a hazard for the sick;
Polonius may mean "out of the draughts," since the
scene seems to be set indoors.

on, which reason and sanity could not so prosperously° be   *successfully*
delivered of. I will leave him, and suddenly° contrive the means   *immediately*
210   of meeting between him and my daughter.—My lord, I will
take my leave of you.

HAMLET   You cannot, sir, take from me anything that I will more
willingly part withal°—except my life, my life, my life.   *with*

POLONIUS [*going*]   Fare you well, my lord.

215   HAMLET   These tedious old fools!

             Enter GUILDENSTERN *and* ROSENCRANTZ[1]

POLONIUS   You go to seek the Lord Hamlet. There he is.

ROSENCRANTZ   God save you, sir.

GUILDENSTERN [*to* POLONIUS]   Mine honoured lord.

                              [*Exit* POLONIUS]

ROSENCRANTZ [*to* HAMLET]   My most dear lord.

220   HAMLET   My ex'llent good friends. How dost thou, Guildenstern? Ah, Rosencrantz—good lads, how do ye both?

ROSENCRANTZ   As the indifferent° children of the earth.   *ordinary*

GUILDENSTERN   Happy° in that we are not over-happy,   *Fortunate*
On Fortune's cap we are not the very button.°   *highest point*

225   HAMLET   Nor the soles of her shoe?

ROSENCRANTZ   Neither, my lord.

HAMLET   Then you live about her waist, or in the middle of her
favour?

GUILDENSTERN   Faith, her privates[2] we.

230   HAMLET   In the secret parts of Fortune? O, most true, she is a
strumpet.° What's the news?   *whore*

ROSENCRANTZ   None, my lord, but that the world's grown
honest.

HAMLET   Then is doomsday near. But your news is not true. Let
235   me question more in particular. What have you, my good
friends, deserved at the hands of Fortune that she sends you to
prison hither?

GUILDENSTERN   Prison, my lord?

HAMLET   Denmark's a prison.

240   ROSENCRANTZ   Then is the world one.

HAMLET   A goodly[3] one, in which there are many confines,°   *enclosures*
wards,° and dungeons, Denmark being one o'th' worst.   *cells*

ROSENCRANTZ   We think not so, my lord.

HAMLET   Why, then 'tis none to you, for there is nothing either
245   good or bad but thinking makes it so. To me it is a prison.

ROSENCRANTZ   Why, then your ambition makes it one; 'tis too
narrow for your mind.

HAMLET   O God, I could be bounded in a nutshell and count
myself a king of infinite space, were it not that I have bad
250   dreams.

GUILDENSTERN   Which dreams indeed are ambition; for the very
substance of the ambitious is merely the shadow of a dream.

HAMLET   A dream itself is but a shadow.

ROSENCRANTZ   Truly, and I hold ambition of so airy and light a
255   quality that it is but a shadow's shadow.

---

1. In F, Rosencrantz and Guildenstern enter after line
215; in Q1, after line 211; in Q2, after line 213. Because
Polonius addresses them at line 216, this seems the best
place for their entry.

2. A triple pun: private persons holding no office; intimate friends; private parts, genitalia.
3. Spacious; fine.

HAMLET Then are our beggars bodies, and our monarchs and outstretched heroes the beggars' shadows.[4] Shall we to th' court? For, by my fay,° I cannot reason.   *faith*

ROSENCRANTZ *and* GUILDENSTERN We'll wait upon° you.   *accompany*

260 HAMLET No such matter.° I will not sort° you with the rest of my   *Certainly not / class* servants, for, to speak to you like an honest man, I am most dreadfully attended.° But in the beaten way[5] of friendship, what   *waited upon* make you° at Elsinore?   *are you doing*

ROSENCRANTZ To visit you, my lord, no other occasion.

265 HAMLET Beggar that I am, I am even poor in thanks, but I thank you; and sure, dear friends, my thanks are too dear a half-penny.[6] Were you not sent for? Is it your own inclining? Is it a free° visitation? Come, deal justly with me. Come, come. Nay,   *voluntary* speak.

270 GUILDENSTERN What should we say, my lord?

HAMLET Why, anything—but to th' purpose. You were sent for, and there is a kind of confession in your looks which your modesties[7] have not craft enough to colour.° I know the good King   *disguise* and Queen have sent for you.

275 ROSENCRANTZ To what end, my lord?

HAMLET That you must teach me. But let me conjure° you by   *solemnly request* the rights of our fellowship, by the consonancy° of our youth,   *harmonious friendship* by the obligation of our ever-preserved love, and by what more dear a better proposer could charge you withal, be even° and   *level*
280 direct with me whether you were sent for or no.

ROSENCRANTZ [*to* GUILDENSTERN] What say you?

HAMLET Nay then, I have an eye of° you—if you love me, hold   *on* not off.

GUILDENSTERN My lord, we were sent for.

285 HAMLET I will tell you why. So shall my anticipation prevent°   *forestall* your discovery, and your secrecy to the King and Queen moult no feather.[8] I have of late—but wherefore I know not—lost all my mirth, forgone all custom of exercise; and indeed it goes so heavily with my disposition[9] that this goodly frame,° the earth,   *structure*
290 seems to me a sterile promontory. This most excellent canopy the air, look you, this brave o'erhanging,[1] this majestical roof fretted° with golden fire—why, it appears no other thing to me   *adorned* than a foul and pestilent congregation° of vapours. What a   *mass* piece of work is a man! How noble in reason, how infinite in
295 faculty,° in form and moving how express[2] and admirable, in   *natural powers* action how like an angel, in apprehension how like a god—the beauty of the world, the paragon of animals! And yet to me what is this quintessence of dust?[3] Man delights not me—no,

---

4. *Then . . . shadows:* Then beggars, being without ambition, are not shadows but have substance; if monarchs and heroes (who ambitiously "stretch" too far) are shadows and only substantial bodies can cast shadows, they must be the beggars' shadows.
5. Well-worn track (plain words).
6. Too expensive at a halfpenny (not worth a halfpenny); perhaps also, too expensive by a halfpenny for me to give in return for such worthless information.
7. Senses of decency.
8. Remain unimpaired. To pull the feathers off a reputation meant to detract from it.
9. *it goes . . . disposition:* I am so heavy with melancholy.

F, however, prints "heavenly" for Q2's "heavily," which, if accepted, gives a startling image of Hamlet's impatient world-weariness.
1. This splendid overhang (F). Most editions give Q2's "o'erhanging firmament" (heavens). In either case, the image may refer to the "heavens," the roof overhanging the Elizabethan stage, which was decorated with stars.
2. Precise; expressive.
3. It was thought that the heavenly bodies were composed of a fifth element ("quintessence"), superior to the other four (earth, air, fire, and water) and also the purest distillation of earthly objects. Hamlet thinks of humanity as dust at its dustiest.

nor woman neither, though by your smiling you seem to say
300   so.

ROSENCRANTZ   My lord, there was no such stuff in my thoughts.

HAMLET   Why did you laugh, then, when I said 'Man delights
not me'?

ROSENCRANTZ   To think, my lord, if you delight not in man what
305   lenten entertainment[4] the players shall receive from you. We
coted° them on the way, and hither are they coming to offer   *passed*
you service.

HAMLET   He that plays the King shall be welcome; his majesty
shall have tribute of me. The adventurous Knight shall use his
310   foil° and target,° the Lover shall not sigh gratis,° the Humorous   *sword / shield / for free*
Man shall end his part in peace,[5] the Clown shall make those
laugh whose lungs are tickled o'th' sear,[6] and the Lady shall say
her mind freely, or the blank verse shall halt for't.[7] What players are they?

315 ROSENCRANTZ   Even those you were wont to take delight in, the
tragedians° of the city.   *actors*

HAMLET   How chances it they travel? Their residence° both in   *(in the city)*
reputation and profit was better both ways.

ROSENCRANTZ   I think their inhibition comes by the means of
320   the late innovation.[8]

HAMLET   Do they hold the same estimation° they did when I was   *esteem*
in the city? Are they so followed?

ROSENCRANTZ   No, indeed, they are not.

HAMLET   How comes it? Do they grow rusty?

325 ROSENCRANTZ   Nay, their endeavour keeps° in the wonted° pace.   *continues / accustomed*
But there is, sir, an eyrie of children, little eyases,[9] that cry out
on the top of question[1] and are most tyrannically° clapped for't.   *outrageously*
These are now the fashion, and so berattle° the common   *noisily abuse*
stages[2]—so they call them—that many wearing rapiers are
330   afraid of goose-quills,[3] and dare scarce come thither.

HAMLET   What, are they children? Who maintains 'em? How are
they escoted?° Will they pursue the quality° no longer than   *provided for / profession*
they can sing?[4] Will they not say afterwards, if they should grow
themselves to common players—as it is like° most will, if their   *likely*
335   means° are not better—their writers do them wrong to make   *financial options*
them exclaim against their own succession?°   *later employment*

ROSENCRANTZ   Faith, there has been much to-do on both sides,
and the nation° holds it no sin to tarre° them to controversy.   *populace / goad*
There was for a while no money bid for argument unless the
340   poet and the player went to cuffs in the question.[5]

HAMLET   Is't possible?

---

4. Welcome. Lent was a period of penitence and fasting (when London theaters were closed).
5. *the Humorous . . . peace*: the eccentric (governed by
excess of one humor, or mood-influencing bodily fluid)
should be allowed to rant on without disturbance.
6. Whose lungs are primed to laugh. (The "sear" is the
part of a gun holding back the hammer until the trigger
releases it.)
7. *and the Lady . . . for't*: if the lady is not allowed to
speak all her part, the poetry will "halt," or limp (fail to
scan).
8. Comes from recent fashion (probably the rage for boy-
acting companies). An "inhibition" could be either a hindrance or an official prohibition. (Elizabethan theaters

were commonly closed at signs of political instability.)
9. Young hawks. A company of boy actors flourished at
the private Blackfriars Theatre, leased from the
Burbages, from 1600 to 1608. *eyrie*: nest for a bird of
prey.
1. That yell over their critics' voices.
2. Public theaters (such as the Globe).
3. That gentlemen are afraid of the poet's satirical pen.
4. Only until their voices break.
5. *no money . . . question*: nothing offered for the plot (or
draft) of a play unless it added to the dispute between the
children's dramatists and the public theater companies.
went to cuffs: came to blows.

GUILDENSTERN O, there has been much throwing about of brains.[6]

HAMLET Do the boys carry it° away? *(the victory)*

345 ROSENCRANTZ Ay, that they do, my lord, Hercules and his load too.[7]

HAMLET It is not strange; for mine uncle is King of Denmark, and those that would make mows° at him while my father lived *grimaces* give twenty, forty, an hundred ducats apiece for his picture in

350 little.° 'Sblood,[8] there is something in this more than natural, *miniature* if philosophy could find it out.

A *flourish*[9] *for the* PLAYERS

GUILDENSTERN There are the players.

HAMLET Gentlemen, you are welcome to Elsinore. Your hands, come. Th'appurtenance° of welcome is fashion and ceremony. *fitting accompaniment*

355 Let me comply with you in the garb,[1] lest my extent° to the *offering (of welcome)* players—which, I tell you, must show fairly° outward—should *courteously* more appear like entertainment° than yours. *(warm) welcome*

[*He shakes hands with them*]

You are welcome. But my uncle-father and aunt-mother are deceived.

360 GUILDENSTERN In what, my dear lord?

HAMLET I am but mad north-north-west;[2] when the wind is southerly, I know a hawk from a handsaw.[3]

Enter POLONIUS

POLONIUS Well be with you, gentlemen.

HAMLET [*aside*] Hark you, Guildenstern, and you too—at each

365 ear a hearer—that great baby you see there is not yet out of his swathing-clouts.° *swaddling clothes*

ROSENCRANTZ [*aside*] Haply° he's the second time come to *Perhaps* them, for they say an old man is twice a child.

HAMLET [*aside*] I will prophesy he comes to tell me of the play-

370 ers. Mark it.—You say right, sir, for o' Monday morning, 'twas so indeed.

POLONIUS My lord, I have news to tell you.

HAMLET My lord, I have news to tell you. When Roscius[4] was an actor in Rome—

375 POLONIUS The actors are come hither, my lord.

HAMLET Buzz, buzz.[5]

POLONIUS Upon mine honour—

HAMLET Then came each actor on his ass.

POLONIUS The best actors in the world, either for tragedy, com-

380 edy, history, pastoral, pastorical-comical, historical-pastoral, tragical-historical, tragical-comical-historical-pastoral, scene individable[6] or poem unlimited.[7] Seneca cannot be too heavy,

---

6. A great battle of wits.
7. In the course of one of his labors, Hercules held up the world on his shoulders while Atlas (its usual support) ran an errand; Hercules bearing the world was the sign of the Globe.
8. By God's blood.
9. Trumpet flourishes often heralded dramatic performances.
1. Let me follow accepted forms in the recognized manner (by shaking hands).
2. The smallest compass point away from true north, and thus not far from sane; or possibly, only mad on

occasions when the wind blows from the north-northwest.
3. A small saw, and possibly a variant of "heronshaw" (heron).
4. The most famous ancient Roman actor, a rather dated news item.
5. A response to stale news.
6. Probably, play with no breaks in performance, or play observing the unity of place (and presumably the other classical unities). Shakespeare parodies the classifications of contemporary dramatic theorists.
7. (Dramatic) poem unrestricted by classical rules.

nor Plautus too light.[8] For the law of writ and the liberty,[9] these
are the only men.

385 HAMLET   O Jephthah, judge of Israel, what a treasure hadst
thou![1]

POLONIUS   What a treasure had he, my lord?

HAMLET   Why,
'One fair daughter and no more,

390 The which he loved passing° well'.   surpassingly

POLONIUS [aside]   Still on my daughter.

HAMLET   Am I not i'th' right, old Jephthah?

POLONIUS   If you call me Jephthah, my lord, I have a daughter
that I love passing well.

395 HAMLET   Nay, that follows not.[2]

POLONIUS   What follows then, my lord?

HAMLET   Why
'As by lot°   chance
God wot',°   knows

400 and then you know
'It came to pass
As most like° it was'—   probable
the first row° of the pious chanson° will show you more, for   stanza / ballad
look where my abridgements[3] come.

Enter four or five PLAYERS

405 You're welcome, masters, welcome all.—I am glad to see thee
well.—Welcome, good friends.—O, my old friend! Thy face is
valanced° since I saw thee last. Com'st thou to beard° me in   fringed (with beard) / defy
Denmark?—What, my young lady and mistress.[4] By'r Lady,
your ladyship is nearer heaven than when I saw you last by the

410 altitude of a chopine.° Pray God your voice, like a piece of   high platform shoe
uncurrent gold, be not cracked within the ring.[5]—Masters, you
are all welcome. We'll e'en to't like French falc'ners,[6] fly at
anything we see. We'll have a speech straight.° Come, give us   right away
a taste of your quality.° Come, a passionate speech.   professional skill

415 FIRST PLAYER   What speech, my good lord?

HAMLET   I heard thee speak me a speech once, but it was never
acted, or, if it was, not above once; for the play, I remember,
pleased not the million. 'Twas caviare to the general.° But it   populace
was—as I received it, and others whose judgements in such

420 matters cried in the top of[7] mine—an excellent play, well
digested° in the scenes, set down with as much modesty° as   organized / restraint
cunning. I remember one said there was no sallets[8] in the lines
to make the matter savoury, nor no matter in the phrase that
might indict the author of affectation, but called it an honest

425 method, as wholesome as sweet, and by very much more handsome than fine.[9] One speech in it I chiefly loved, 'twas Aeneas'
tale to Dido, and thereabout of it especially where he speaks of

---

8. The best-known Roman playwrights, masters of
tragedy and comedy, respectively.
9. For plays where classical rules are either observed or
abandoned.
1. Jephthah vowed that if he defeated the Ammonites,
he would sacrifice the first living thing he saw on his
return. He won, and his daughter became the sacrificial
victim (Judges 11). "Jephthah, Judge of Israel" was the
title of a popular ballad, the "pious chanson" from
which Hamlet subsequently quotes or sings.
2. Polonius's having a daughter is not a logical consequence of Hamlet's calling him Jephthah.

3. Those who cut me short; also, entertainments.
4. The boy who played female roles.
5. A coin was no longer legal tender if the circle or ring
enclosing the monarch's head was broken (by "clipping," or trimming off small amounts of gold).
6. We'll go to work at once. (French falconers seem to
have been regarded as experts, willing to try any potential
prey.)
7. *cried . . . of:* outweighed.
8. Literally, salads (seasoned dishes); highly flavored, or
"salty" (lecherous).
9. Beautifully crafted rather than showy.

Priam's slaughter.[1] If it live in your memory, begin at this
line—let me see, let me see:

430 'The rugged° Pyrrhus,[2] like th'Hyrcanian beast'°—   *savage / tiger*
'tis not so. It begins with Pyrrhus—
'The rugged Pyrrhus, he whose sable° arms,   *black*
Black as his purpose, did the night resemble
When he lay couchèd° in the ominous horse,[3]   *hidden*
435 Hath now this dread and black complexion° smeared   *appearance*
With heraldry° more dismal. Head to foot   *heraldic colors*
Now is he total gules,° horridly tricked°   *all red / inked over*
With blood of fathers, mothers, daughters, sons,
Baked and impasted with° the parching° streets,   *encrusted by / fiery*
440 That lend a tyranous and damnèd light
To their vile murders. Roasted in wrath and fire,
And thus o'er-sizèd[4] with coagulate gore,
With eyes like carbuncles[5] the hellish Pyrrhus
Old grandsire Priam seeks.'
445 So, proceed you.

POLONIUS Fore God, my lord, well spoken, with good accent
and good discretion.

FIRST PLAYER   'Anon° he finds him,   *Soon*
Striking too short at Greeks. His antique sword,
450 Rebellious to his arm, lies where it falls,
Repugnant° to command. Unequal match,   *Resistant*
Pyrrhus at Priam drives, in rage strikes wide;
But with the whiff and wind of his fell° sword   *fierce*
Th'unnervèd° father falls. Then senseless Ilium,[6]   *strengthless*
455 Seeming to feel his blow, with flaming top
Stoops to his° base, and with a hideous crash   *its*
Takes prisoner Pyrrhus' ear. For lo, his sword,
Which was declining° on the milky° head   *descending / white*
Of reverend Priam, seemed i'th' air to stick.
460 So, as a painted tyrant,[7] Pyrrhus stood,
And, like a neutral to his will and matter,[8]
Did nothing.
But as we often see against° some storm   *before*
A silence in the heavens, the rack° stand still,   *cloud banks*
465 The bold winds speechless, and the orb° below   *earth*
As hush as death, anon the dreadful thunder
Doth rend the region:° so, after Pyrrhus' pause,   *sky*
A rousèd vengeance sets him new a-work;
And never did the Cyclops'[9] hammers fall
470 On Mars his° armour, forged for proof eterne,[1]   *(Mars's)*
With less remorse° than Pyrrhus' bleeding sword   *pity; hesitation*
Now falls on Priam.
Out, out, thou strumpet Fortune! All you gods,
In general synod, take away her power,

1. The murder of the Trojan King Priam, at the end of
the Trojan War; adapted from Virgil's *Aeneid*, possibly
via Christopher Marlowe's *Dido, Queen of Carthage*.
Aeneas recounts the story of Priam's slaughter to his
beloved, Dido.
2. Also known as Neoptolemus, he came to Troy to
avenge the death of his father, the Greek hero Achilles.
3. The Trojan horse, full of Greek warriors.
4. As though coated with sizing, the thick liquid used
to prepare a canvas for painting.

5. Gems supposed to glow with their own light.
6. The citadel of Troy.
7. Tyrant depicted in a painting and so incapable of
moving.
8. And as one indifferent toward his intention and the
action at hand.
9. The three one-eyed giants who served as armorers to
the classical gods and heroes.
1. To remain impenetrable forever.

475 Break all the spokes and fellies from her wheel,[2]
And bowl the round nave° down the hill of heaven,°   *wheel hub / Mt. Olympus*
As low as to the fiends!'

POLONIUS   This is too long.

HAMLET   It shall to the barber's, with your beard.°   [*To* FIRST   *It shall be cut short*
480   PLAYER] Prithee, say on. He's for a jig[3] or a tale of bawdry, or
he sleeps. Say on, come to Hecuba.

FIRST PLAYER   'But who, O who had seen the mobbled°   *veiled; muffled*
queen'—

HAMLET   'The mobbled queen'?

POLONIUS   That's good; 'mobbled queen' is good.

485 FIRST PLAYER   'Run barefoot up and down, threat'ning the flames
With bisson rheum;° a clout° upon that head   *blinding tears / cloth*
Where late the diadem stood, and for a robe,
About her lank and all o'er-teemèd[4] loins,
A blanket in th'alarm of fear caught up—
490 Who this had seen, with tongue in venom steeped,
'Gainst Fortune's state° would treason have pronounced.   *rule*
But if the gods themselves did see her then,
When she saw Pyrrhus make malicious sport
In mincing with his sword her husband's limbs,
495 The instant burst of clamour that she made—
Unless things mortal move them not at all—
Would have made milch° the burning eyes of heaven,   *milky; moist*
And passion° in the gods.'   *suffering; pity*

POLONIUS   Look whe'er° he has not turned his colour, and has   *whether*
500 tears in 's eyes. [*To* FIRST PLAYER] Prithee, no more.

HAMLET [*to* FIRST PLAYER]   'Tis well. I'll have thee speak out the
rest soon. [*To* POLONIUS] Good my lord, will you see the players well bestowed?° Do ye hear?—let them be well used,° for   *lodged / treated*
they are the abstracts° and brief chronicles of the time. After   *summaries*
505 your death you were better have a bad epitaph than their ill
report while you live.

POLONIUS   My lord, I will use them according to their desert.

HAMLET   God's bodykins,° man, much better. Use every man   *By God's dear body*
after° his desert, and who should scape whipping? Use them   *according to*
510 after your own honour and dignity—the less they deserve, the
more merit is in your bounty. Take them in.

POLONIUS [*to* PLAYERS]   Come, sirs.   *Exit*

HAMLET [*to* PLAYERS]   Follow him, friends. We'll hear a play
tomorrow. Dost thou hear me, old friend? Can you play the
515 murder of Gonzago?

PLAYERS   Ay, my lord.

HAMLET   We'll ha't° tomorrow night. You could for a need° study   *have it / if necessary*
a speech of some dozen or sixteen lines which I would set down
and insert in't, could ye not?

520 PLAYERS   Ay, my lord.

HAMLET   Very well. Follow that lord, and look you mock him
not.

Exeunt PLAYERS[5]

---

2. The power of Fortune's ever-turning wheel, raising
and lowering men in succession, was proverbial. *fellies:*
curved sections of a wooden wheel rim.
3. A ridiculous piece of poetry, or the dance that followed
many plays (unrelated to the drama).
4. Completely worn out with childbearing. (Hecuba was

supposed to have borne seventeen or more children.)
5. In F and Q1, the players leave after line 524. In Q2,
they leave with Polonius after line 512. Their exit has
been relocated here to coincide with Hamlet's command
that they follow Polonius.

My good friends, I'll leave you till night. You are welcome to
Elsinore.
525 ROSENCRANTZ   Good my lord.
HAMLET   Ay, so. God b'wi'° ye.   *Exeunt [all but]* HAMLET   *be with*
Now I am alone.
O, what a rogue and peasant slave am I!
Is it not monstrous that this player here,
But° in a fiction, in a dream of passion,   *Merely*
530 Could force his soul so to his whole conceit⁶
That from her° working all his visage wanned,°   *(the soul's)* / *grew pale*
Tears in his eyes, distraction in 's aspect,
A broken voice, and his whole function suiting
With forms to his conceit?⁷ And all for nothing.
535 For Hecuba!
What's Hecuba to him, or he to Hecuba,
That he should weep for her? What would he do
Had he the motive and the cue for passion
That I have? He would drown the stage with tears,
540 And cleave the general ear⁸ with horrid speech,
Make mad the guilty and appal the free,°   *innocent*
Confound the ignorant, and amaze° indeed   *bewilder*
The very faculty of eyes and ears. Yet I,
A dull and muddy-mettled° rascal, peak°   *dull-spirited* / *mope*
545 Like John-a-dreams,° unpregnant of⁹ my cause,   *a sleepy idler*
And can say nothing—no, not for a king
Upon whose property° and most dear life   *rightful sovereignty*
A damned defeat¹ was made. Am I a coward?
Who calls me villain, breaks my pate° across,   *head*
550 Plucks off my beard and blows it in my face,
Tweaks me by th' nose, gives me the lie i'th' throat
As deep as to the lungs?² Who does me this?
Ha? 'Swounds,° I should take it; for it cannot be   *By God's wounds*
But I am pigeon-livered and lack gall³
555 To make oppression bitter, or ere this
I should 'a' fatted all the region kites⁴
With this slave's offal. Bloody, bawdy villain!
Remorseless, treacherous, lecherous, kindless villain!
O, vengeance!—
560 Why, what an ass am I? Ay, sure, this is most brave,°   *fine*
That I, the son of the dear murderèd,°   *the dear murdered man*
Prompted to my revenge by heaven and hell,
Must, like a whore, unpack my heart with words
And fall a-cursing like a very drab,°   *whore*
565 A scullion!⁵ Fie upon't, foh!—About,° my brain.   *Into action*
I have heard that guilty creatures sitting at a play
Have by the very cunning° of the scene   *artfulness*
Been struck so to the soul that presently°   *immediately*
They have proclaimed their malefactions;
570 For murder, though it have no tongue, will speak

6. Could make his innermost being conform so well with
his imagined situation.
7. *his whole . . . conceit:* the action of his whole body in
outward accord with his imagination.
8. The ears of people generally.
9. Not quickened into action by.

1. An act of overthrow worthy of damnation.
2. *gives . . . lungs:* calls me a thoroughgoing liar.
3. Pigeons were thought not to secrete gall, a bitter fluid
produced by the liver and the supposed source of anger.
4. All the kites (birds of prey) in the sky ("region").
5. Kitchen servant.

With most miraculous organ. I'll have these players
Play something like the murder of my father
Before mine uncle. I'll observe his looks,
I'll tent° him to the quick. If a° but blench,   probe (a wound) / he
575   I know my course. The spirit that I have seen
May be the devil, and the devil hath power
T'assume a pleasing shape; yea, and perhaps,
Out of my weakness and my melancholy—
As he is very potent with such spirits⁶—
580   Abuses° me to damn me. I'll have grounds   Deceives
More relative° than this. The play's the thing   relevant
Wherein I'll catch the conscience of the King.   *Exit*

3.1

Enter KING [CLAUDIUS], QUEEN [GERTRUDE], POLONIUS,
OPHELIA, ROSENCRANTZ, GUILDENSTERN, *and lords*

KING CLAUDIUS   [*to* ROSENCRANTZ *and* GUILDENSTERN]
And can you by no drift of circumstance¹
Get from him why he puts on this confusion,
Grating so harshly all his days of quiet
With turbulent and dangerous lunacy?
5   ROSENCRANTZ   He does confess he feels himself distracted,°   confused; agitated
But from what cause a will by no means speak.
GUILDENSTERN   Nor do we find him forward° to be sounded,°   eager / probed
But with a crafty madness keeps aloof
When we would bring him on to some confession
10   Of his true state.
QUEEN GERTRUDE   Did he receive you well?
ROSENCRANTZ   Most like a gentleman.
GUILDENSTERN   But with much forcing of his disposition.°   mood
ROSENCRANTZ   Niggard of question,² but of° our demands   to
Most free in his reply.
15   QUEEN GERTRUDE   Did you assay° him   try to persuade
To any pastime?
ROSENCRANTZ   Madam, it so fell out that certain players
We o'er-raught° on the way. Of these we told him,   passed
And there did seem in him a kind of joy
20   To hear of it. They are about the court,
And, as I think, they have already order
This night to play before him.
POLONIUS   'Tis most true,
And he beseeched me to entreat your majesties
To hear and see the matter.
25   KING CLAUDIUS   With all my heart; and it doth much content me
To hear him so inclined.—Good gentlemen,
Give him a further edge,° and drive his purpose on   stimulus; appetite
To these delights.
ROSENCRANTZ   We shall, my lord.

Exeunt ROSENCRANTZ *and* GUILDENSTERN

30   KING CLAUDIUS   Sweet Gertrude, leave us too,
For we have closely° sent for Hamlet hither,   privately

6. *Out of . . . spirits:* It was thought that those afflicted
with too much black bile, a humor (fluid), or "spirit"
(distillation) became melancholy and subject to halluci-
nations, which in turn made them easily tricked by the

devil. *potent with:* powerful over.
3.1 Location: The castle.
1. By no carefully directed conversation.
2. Reluctant to offer conversation.

That he, as 'twere by accident, may here
Affront° Ophelia.   *Confront*
Her father and myself, lawful espials,°   *spies*
35   Will so bestow ourselves that, seeing unseen,
We may of their encounter frankly judge,
And gather by him, as he is behaved,
If't be th'affliction of his love or no
That thus he suffers for.
QUEEN GERTRUDE   I shall obey you.
40   And for your part, Ophelia, I do wish
That your good beauties be the happy cause
Of Hamlet's wildness; so shall I hope your virtues
Will bring him to his wonted° way again,   *customary*
To both your honours.
OPHELIA   Madam, I wish it may.

                                                     [Exit GERTRUDE]
45   POLONIUS   Ophelia, walk you here.—Gracious,° so please you,   *Your Grace*
We will bestow ourselves.—Read on this book,
That show of such an exercise may colour
Your loneliness.[3] We are oft to blame in this:
'Tis too much proved° that with devotion's visage   *true in experience*
50   And pious action we do sugar o'er
The devil himself.
KING CLAUDIUS   O, 'tis too true.
[*Aside*] How smart° a lash that speech doth give my conscience.   *sharp*
The harlot's cheek, beautied with plast'ring° art,   *cosmetic; healing*
Is not more ugly to the thing that helps it[4]
55   Than is my deed to my most painted word.
O heavy burden!
POLONIUS   I hear him coming. Let's withdraw, my lord.
                         Exeunt [CLAUDIUS *and* POLONIUS]
                    Enter [*Prince*] HAMLET
HAMLET   To be, or not to be; that is the question:
Whether 'tis nobler in the mind to suffer
60   The slings and arrows of outrageous fortune,
Or to take arms against a sea of troubles,
And, by opposing, end them. To die, to sleep—
No more, and by a sleep to say we end
The heartache and the thousand natural shocks
65   That flesh is heir to—'tis a consummation
Devoutly to be wished. To die, to sleep.
To sleep, perchance to dream. Ay, there's the rub,[5]
For in that sleep of death what dreams may come
When we have shuffled° off this mortal coil°   *cast / turmoil; flesh*
70   Must give us pause. There's the respect°   *consideration*
That makes calamity of so long life,[6]
For who would bear the whips and scorns of time,
Th'oppressor's wrong, the proud man's contumely,°   *scornful abuse*
The pangs of disprized° love, the law's delay,   *unvalued*
75   The insolence of office,° and the spurns[7]   *bureaucrats*

---

3. *may . . . loneliness:* may explain your solitude, and also give it a virtuous or pious look. The "book" is a prayer book or devotional text.
4. *to . . . it:* compared to the artificially beautiful surface that covers it.

5. Obstacle in the game of bowls, an impediment to the ball's intended path.
6. Makes adversity so long-lived (as opposed to quickly ended in suicide).
7. Kicks, insults.

That patient merit of th'unworthy takes,[8]
When he himself might his quietus make[9]
With a bare bodkin?° Who would these fardels° bear, *mere dagger / burdens*
To grunt and sweat under a weary life,
80 But that the dread of something after death,
The undiscovered country from whose bourn° *border*
No traveller returns, puzzles the will,
And makes us rather bear those ills we have
Than fly to others that we know not of?
85 Thus conscience[1] does make cowards of us all,
And thus the native hue° of resolution *ruddy complexion*
Is sicklied o'er with the pale cast° of thought, *tint*
And enterprises of great pith and moment[2]
With this regard° their currents turn awry, *consideration*
90 And lose the name of action. Soft you, now,[3]
The fair Ophelia!—Nymph, in thy orisons° *prayers*
Be all my sins remembered.

OPHELIA   Good my lord,
How does your honour for this many a day?

HAMLET   I humbly thank you, well, well, well.

95 OPHELIA   My lord, I have remembrances of yours
That I have longèd long to redeliver.
I pray you now receive them.

HAMLET   No, no, I never gave you aught.

OPHELIA   My honoured lord, you know right well you did,
100 And with them words of so sweet breath composed
As made the things more rich. Their perfume lost,
Take these again; for to the noble mind
Rich gifts wax° poor when givers prove unkind. *grow*
There, my lord.

105 HAMLET   Ha, ha? Are you honest?° *chaste; truthful*

OPHELIA   My lord.

HAMLET   Are you fair?

OPHELIA   What means your lordship?

HAMLET   That if you be honest and fair, your honesty should
110 admit no discourse to[4] your beauty.

OPHELIA   Could beauty, my lord, have better commerce° than *dealings*
with honesty?

HAMLET   Ay, truly, for the power of beauty will sooner transform
honesty from what it is to a bawd than the force of honesty can
115 translate beauty into his° likeness. This was sometime a par- *its (honesty's)*
adox, but now the time[5] gives it proof. I did love you once.

OPHELIA   Indeed, my lord, you made me believe so.

HAMLET   You should not have believed me, for virtue cannot so
inoculate our old stock but we shall relish of it.[6] I loved you
120 not.

OPHELIA   I was the more deceived.

HAMLET   Get thee to a nunnery.[7] Why wouldst thou be a breeder

8. That the deserving has to accept patiently from the unworthy.
9. A paid-off account was marked "Quietus est" ("laid to rest").
1. Both consciousness (introspective knowledge) and moral conscience.
2. Of profundity and importance (F). Q2 gives "pitch," meaning "height" (in the context of a falcon's flight).
3. Wait a moment (an expression of surprise).

4. No familiar conversation with.
5. This was formerly an uncredited opinion, but now the present age.
6. *You . . . it:* Virtue grafted onto fallen human nature cannot eradicate completely the taste ("relish") of original sin.
7. By entering a nunnery, Ophelia will take a vow of life-long chastity. But in Elizabethan slang, "nunnery" could also mean "brothel."

of sinners? I am myself indifferent honest,° but yet I could   *moderately virtuous*
accuse me of such things that it were better my mother had not
125 borne me. I am very proud, revengeful, ambitious, with more
offences at my beck° than I have thoughts to put them in, imag-   *command*
ination to give them shape, or time to act them in. What should
such fellows as I do crawling between heaven and earth? We
are arrant° knaves, all. Believe none of us. Go thy ways to a   *downright*
130 nunnery. Where's your father?

OPHELIA   At home, my lord.

HAMLET   Let the doors be shut upon him, that he may play the
fool nowhere but in 's own house. Farewell.

OPHELIA   O help him, you sweet heavens!

135 HAMLET   If thou dost marry, I'll give thee this plague for thy
dowry: be thou as chaste as ice, as pure as snow, thou shalt not
escape calumny. Get thee to a nunnery, go, farewell. Or if thou
wilt needs marry, marry a fool; for wise men know well enough
what monsters[8] you° make of them. To a nunnery, go, and   *you women*
140 quickly, too. Farewell.

OPHELIA   O heavenly powers, restore him!

HAMLET   I have heard of your paintings,° too, well enough. God   *cosmetics*
hath given you one face, and you make yourselves another. You
jig, you amble, and you lisp,[9] and nickname God's creatures,[1]
145 and make your wantonness your ignorance.[2] Go to, I'll no
more on't.° It hath made me mad. I say we will have no more   *of it*
marriages. Those that are married already—all but one—shall
live. The rest shall keep as they are. To a nunnery, go.   *Exit*

OPHELIA   O what a noble mind is here o'erthrown!
150 The courtier's, soldier's, scholar's eye, tongue, sword,
Th'expectancy and rose of the fair state,
The glass° of fashion and the mould of form,[3]   *mirror image*
Th'observed of all observers, quite, quite, down!
And I, of ladies most deject and wretched,
155 That sucked the honey of his music vows,
Now see that noble and most sovereign reason
Like sweet bells jangled out of tune and harsh;
That unmatched form and feature of blown° youth   *fully blossoming*
Blasted° with ecstasy.° O woe is me,   *Withered / madness*
160 T'have seen what I have seen, see what I see!

Enter KING [CLAUDIUS] *and* POLONIUS

KING CLAUDIUS   Love? His affections° do not that way tend,   *emotions*
Nor what he spake, though it lacked form a little,
Was not like madness. There's something in his soul
O'er which his melancholy sits on brood,
165 And I do doubt° the hatch and the disclose[4]   *fear*
Will be some danger; which to prevent
I have in quick determination
Thus set it down:° he shall with speed to England   *resolved it*
For the demand of our neglected tribute.[5]

---

8. Alluding to the belief that cuckolds grew horns, but Hamlet may mean a more spiritual or psychological transformation as well.
9. *You jig . . . lisp:* You dance (or sing), walk with an affectedly easy gait, and speak artificially.
1. Use new and fashionable names instead of the God-given ones.

2. *make . . . ignorance:* "play dumb" to excuse your (seductive) affectations.
3. Pattern of decorum.
4. Public disclosure.
5. Although the play is set in a Renaissance world, Claudius's words invoke a distant medieval past, when England paid tribute to Denmark.

170   Haply° the seas and countries different,   *Perhaps; with luck*
        With variable objects,⁶ shall expel
        This something-settled° matter in his heart,   *somewhat rooted*
        Whereon his brains still° beating puts him thus   *constantly*
        From fashion of himself.⁷ What think you on't?
175   POLONIUS   It shall do well. But yet do I believe
        The origin and commencement of this grief
        Sprung from neglected° love.—How now, Ophelia?   *unrequited*
        You need not tell us what Lord Hamlet said;
        We heard it all.—My lord, do as you please,
180   But, if you hold it fit, after the play
        Let his queen mother all alone entreat him
        To show his griefs. Let her be round° with him,   *blunt*
        And I'll be placed, so please you, in the ear°   *within earshot*
        Of all their conference. If she find him not,⁸
185   To England send him, or confine him where
        Your wisdom best shall think.
        KING CLAUDIUS   It shall be so.
        Madness in great ones must not unwatched go.   *Exeunt*

3.2

Enter [Prince] HAMLET *and two or three of the* PLAYERS

        HAMLET   Speak the speech, I pray you, as I pronounced it to
        you—trippingly on the tongue; but if you mouth it,¹ as many
        of your players do, I had as lief° the town-crier had spoke my   *willingly*
        lines. Nor do not saw the air too much with your hand, thus,
5   but use all gently; for in the very torrent, tempest, and as I may
        say the whirlwind of your passion, you must acquire and beget
        a temperance that may give it smoothness. O, it offends me to
        the soul to hear a robustious,° periwig-pated° fellow tear a pas-   *bombastic / wig-wearing*
        sion to tatters, to very rags, to split the ears of the groundlings,²
10   who for the most part are capable of nothing but inexplicable
        dumb shows³ and noise. I would have such a fellow whipped
        for o'erdoing Termagant. It out-Herods Herod.⁴ Pray you avoid
        it.
        A PLAYER   I warrant your honour.⁵
15   HAMLET   Be not too tame, neither; but let your own discretion
        be your tutor. Suit the action to the word, the word to the
        action, with this special observance: that you o'erstep not the
        modesty° of nature. For anything so overdone is from° the pur-   *moderation / opposed to*
        pose of playing, whose end, both at the first and now, was and
20   is to hold as 'twere the mirror up to nature, to show virtue her
        own feature, scorn her own image, and the very age and body
        of the time his form and pressure.⁶ Now this overdone, or come
        tardy° off, though it make the unskilful⁷ laugh, cannot but   *faultily*
        make the judicious grieve; the censure of the which one⁸ must

6. With different sights or interests.
7. *puts . . . himself*: makes him unlike his normal self.
8. If she fails to discover his secret.
3.2 Location: A stateroom of the castle.
1. If you speak exaggeratedly.
2. Spectators standing on the ground before the stage (the cheapest area).
3. Brief mimed scenes giving the plot of the scene to follow (see 3.2.122ff.). By Shakespeare's time, this once-common device was out of fashion.
4. It surpasses the excesses of Herod, who, as a char-

acter in medieval cycle plays, was famous for his ranting. Termagant, an imaginary deity supposedly worshipped by Muslims, takes the form of a violent speaking idol in medieval drama.
5. I assure your Honor (that we will avoid it).
6. *the very . . . pressure*: the true state of things at present, in shape ("form") and likeness (as a stamp pressed in wax).
7. Undiscriminating.
8. The judgment of one of whom (judicious persons).

25   in your allowance o'erweigh a whole theatre of others. O, there
      be players that I have seen play, and heard others praise, and
      that highly, not to speak it profanely,[9] that neither having the
      accent of Christians nor the gait of Christian, pagan, nor no
      man, have so strutted and bellowed that I have thought some
30   of nature's journeymen[1] had made men, and not made them
      well, they imitated humanity so abominably.

A PLAYER   I hope we have reformed that indifferently° with us,   *moderately well*
      sir.

HAMLET   O, reform it altogether. And let those that play your
35   clowns speak no more than is set down for them; for there be
      of° them that will themselves laugh to set° on some quantity of   *some of / urge*
      barren° spectators to laugh too, though in the mean time some   *unthinking*
      necessary question of the play be then to be considered. That's
      villainous, and shows a most pitiful ambition in the fool that
40   uses it. Go make you ready.   *Exeunt* PLAYERS
                  Enter POLONIUS, GUILDENSTERN, *and* ROSENCRANTZ
      [*To* POLONIUS] How now, my lord? Will the King hear this
      piece of work?

POLONIUS   And the Queen too, and that presently.°   *immediately*

HAMLET   Bid the players make haste.   *Exit* POLONIUS
      Will you two help to hasten them?

45 ROSENCRANTZ *and* GUILDENSTERN   We will, my lord.   *Exeunt*

HAMLET   What ho, Horatio!
                        Enter HORATIO

HORATIO   Here, sweet lord, at your service.

HAMLET   Horatio, thou art e'en as just° a man   *honest; balanced*
      As e'er my conversation coped withal.[2]

HORATIO   O my dear lord—

HAMLET   Nay, do not think I flatter;
50   For what advancement° may I hope from thee,   *political favors*
      That no revenue hast but thy good spirits
      To feed and clothe thee? Why should the poor be flattered?
      No, let the candied° tongue lick absurd pomp,   *flattering*
      And crook the pregnant° hinges of the knee   *ready (to bow)*
55   Where thrift may follow feigning.[3] Dost thou hear?—
      Since my dear soul was mistress of her choice
      And could of° men distinguish, her election   *between*
      Hath sealed thee for herself;[4] for thou hast been
      As one in suff'ring all that suffers nothing,
60   A man that Fortune's buffets and rewards
      Hath ta'en with equal thanks; and blest are those
      Whose blood° and judgement are so well commingled   *passion*
      That they are not a pipe for Fortune's finger
      To sound what stop° she please. Give me that man   *finger holes; notes*
65   That is not passion's slave, and I will wear him
      In my heart's core, ay, in my heart of heart,
      As I do thee. Something too much of this.
      There is a play tonight before the King.
      One scene of it comes near the circumstance

9. Meaning no blasphemy (by implying as he goes on
to do that some humans were not created by God).
1. Hired assistants to the master craftsmen, still learning their trade.
2. As I ever encountered in my dealings with men.

3. Where prosperity may result from (flattering) lies.
Most editions follow Q2's "fawning."
4. Has marked you as her own (on a document, a legal
sign of possession).

70 Which I have told thee of my father's death.
I prithee, when thou seest that act afoot,
Even with the very comment of thy soul[5]
Observe mine uncle. If his occulted° guilt   hidden
Do not itself unkennel in one speech,
75 It is a damnèd ghost that we have seen,
And my imaginations are as foul
As Vulcan's stithy.[6] Give him heedful note,
For I mine eyes will rivet to his face,
And after, we will both our judgements join
To censure of his seeming.[7]
80 HORATIO   Well, my lord.
If a° steal aught the whilst this play is playing   he
And scape detecting, I will pay the theft.

Enter trumpets and kettle drums. Sound a flourish

HAMLET   They are coming to the play. I must be idle.°   mad; unoccupied
Get you a place.

Danish march. Enter KING [CLAUDIUS], QUEEN [GER-
TRUDE], POLONIUS, OPHELIA, ROSENCRANTZ, GUILDEN-
STERN, *and other lords attendant, with* [*the King's*]
guard carrying torches

KING CLAUDIUS   How fares[8] our cousin° Hamlet?   kinsman
85 HAMLET   Excellent, i'faith, of the chameleon's dish. I eat the air,
promise-crammed.[9] You cannot feed capons[1] so.
KING CLAUDIUS   I have nothing with this answer, Hamlet. These
words are not mine.
HAMLET   No, nor mine now. [*To* POLONIUS] My lord, you played
90 once i'th' university, you say.
POLONIUS   That I did, my lord, and was accounted a good actor.
HAMLET   And what did you enact?
POLONIUS   I did enact Julius Caesar. I was killed i'th' Capitol.[2]
Brutus killed me.
95 HAMLET   It was a brute part of him to kill so capital a calf°   such a prize fool
there.—Be the players ready?
ROSENCRANTZ   Ay, my lord, they stay° upon your patience.   wait
QUEEN GERTRUDE   Come hither, my good Hamlet. Sit by me.
HAMLET   No, good-mother,° here's mettle[3] more attractive.   stepmother
[*He sits by* OPHELIA]
100 POLONIUS [*aside*]   O ho, do you mark that?
HAMLET [*to* OPHELIA]   Lady, shall I lie in your lap?
OPHELIA   No, my lord.
HAMLET   I mean my head upon your lap?
OPHELIA   Ay, my lord.
105 HAMLET   Do you think I meant country matters?[4]
OPHELIA   I think nothing, my lord.
HAMLET   That's a fair thought to lie between maids' legs.

5. With your utmost critical faculty.
6. Smithy, or forge, of Vulcan, the Roman blacksmith god.
7. To judge by his outward reaction.
8. How does; Hamlet's response puns on "fare" as food and drink.
9. The chameleon was supposed to live on air. Hamlet puns on "heir," referring to Claudius's insubstantial promise of the succession.
1. Castrated cocks, crammed or fattened for the table (and a term for a fool).
2. Perhaps an allusion to Shakespeare's own *Julius Caesar*; the actor who first played Polonius may also have played the part of Caesar.
3. A disposition (punning on magnetically attractive "metal").
4. Rustic doings (with an obscene pun on "cunt"). The punning continues in the following lines, where "nothing" suggests the female genitals (often linked to the shape of a zero), and "thing" the male genitals.

OPHELIA   What is, my lord?

HAMLET   No thing.

110   OPHELIA   You are merry, my lord.

HAMLET   Who, I?

OPHELIA   Ay, my lord.

HAMLET   O God, your only jig-maker![5] What should a man do
but be merry? For look you how cheerfully my mother looks,
115   and my father died within 's° two hours.   *these*

OPHELIA   Nay, 'tis twice two months, my lord.

HAMLET   So long? Nay then, let the devil wear black, for I'll have
a suit of sables.[6] O heavens, die two months ago and not forgotten yet! Then there's hope a great man's memory may outlive
120   his life half a year. But, by'r Lady, a must build churches then,
or else shall a suffer not thinking on,[7] with the hobby-horse,
whose epitaph is 'For O, for O, the hobby-horse is forgot.'[8]

Hautboys° play. The dumb show enters. Enter a KING   *Oboes*
and a QUEEN *very lovingly, the* QUEEN *embracing him.*
She kneels and makes show of protestation unto him. He
takes her up and declines° his head upon her neck. He   *leans*
lays him down upon a bank of flowers. She, seeing him
asleep, leaves him. Anon comes in a fellow, takes off his
crown, kisses it, and pours poison in the King's ears, and
exits. The QUEEN *returns, finds the* KING *dead, and*
makes passionate action. The poisoner, with some two or
three mutes,° comes in again, seeming to lament with   *nonspeaking actors*
her. The dead body is carried away. The poisoner woos
the QUEEN *with gifts. She seems loath and unwilling a*
while, but in the end accepts his love. Exeunt [the
PLAYERS]

OPHELIA   What means this, my lord?

HAMLET   Marry, this is miching *malhecho.*° That means mis-   *sneaking wrongdoing*
125   chief.

OPHELIA   Belike this show imports the argument° of the play.   *plot*

Enter PROLOGUE

HAMLET   We shall know by this fellow. The players cannot keep
counsel,° they'll tell all.   *a secret*

OPHELIA   Will a tell us what this show meant?

130   HAMLET   Ay, or any show that you'll show him. Be not you
ashamed to show, he'll not shame to tell you what it means.

OPHELIA   You are naught,° you are naught. I'll mark the play.   *indecent*

PROLOGUE   For us and for our tragedy
Here stooping to your clemency,
135   We beg your hearing patiently.   *[Exit]*

HAMLET   Is this a prologue, or the posy of a ring?[9]

OPHELIA   'Tis brief, my lord.

HAMLET   As woman's love.

*Enter the [*PLAYER*]* KING *and his* QUEEN

PLAYER KING   Full thirty times hath Phoebus' cart[1] gone round

---

5. The leading comic actor often devised and performed
the farcical song and dance concluding a play. *only:* unri-
valed.
6. Sable is both an expensive fur for cloaks and trim and
the heraldic term for "black"; Hamlet simultaneously for-
swears his ascetic mourning and vows to continue it.
7. He shall have to endure being forgotten.

8. The hobbyhorse, a man with a mock horse's body
strapped round his waist, was a figure in May Day morris dances (under attack in Shakespeare's time by religious reformers). "The hobby horse is forgot" seems to
have been a ballad refrain.
9. The motto engraved in a ring.
1. Apollo's chariot (the sun).

140   Neptune's salt wash and Tellus' orbèd ground,[2]
       And thirty dozen moons with borrowed sheen°   *reflected light*
       About the world have times twelve thirties been
       Since love our hearts and Hymen° did our hands   *goddess of marriage*
       Unite commutual in most sacred bands.
145   PLAYER QUEEN   So many journeys may the sun and moon
       Make us again count o'er ere love be done.
       But woe is me, you are so sick of late,
       So far from cheer and from your former state,
       That I distrust° you. Yet, though I distrust,   *am worried about*
150   Discomfort° you my lord it nothing must.   *Sadden*
       For women's fear and love holds quantity,[3]
       In neither aught, or in extremity.[4]
       Now what my love is, proof° hath made you know,   *experience*
       And as my love is sized,° my fear is so.[5]   *in quantity*
154.1   *Where love is great, the littlest doubts are fear:*
           Where little fears grow great, great love grows there.
155   PLAYER KING   Faith, I must leave thee, love, and shortly too.
       My operant° powers their functions leave° to do,   *vital / cease*
       And thou shalt live in this fair world behind,
       Honoured, beloved; and haply° one as kind   *perhaps*
       For husband shalt thou—
       PLAYER QUEEN   O, confound the rest!
160   Such love must needs be treason in my breast.
       In second husband let me be accurst;
       None wed the second but who killed the first.
       HAMLET   Wormwood,[6] wormwood.
       PLAYER QUEEN   The instances° that second marriage move°   *motives / prompt*
165   Are base respects of thrift,° but none of love.   *considerations of profit*
       A second time I kill my husband dead
       When second husband kisses me in bed.
       PLAYER KING   I do believe you think what now you speak;
       But what we do determine oft we break.
170   Purpose is but the slave to[7] memory,
       Of violent birth but poor validity,°   *enduring strength*
       Which now like fruit unripe sticks on the tree,
       But fall unshaken when they mellow be.
       Most necessary 'tis that we forget
175   To pay ourselves what to ourselves is debt.[8]
       What to ourselves in passion we propose,
       The passion ending, doth the purpose lose.
       The violence of either grief or joy
       Their own enactures with themselves destroy.[9]
180   Where joy most revels, grief doth most lament;
       Grief joys, joy grieves, on slender accident.[1]
       This world is not for aye,° nor 'tis not strange   *eternity*
       That even our loves should with our fortunes change;

2. *Neptune's . . . ground:* The salty flood of the sea god and the round foundation of Tellus (the earth).
3. Are in equal proportions. Q2 includes one other line before this one: "For women fear too much, even as they love / And women's fear . . ."
4. *In . . . extremity:* Either love and fear are both absent, or both are extremely strong.
5. After this line, Q2 has a couplet, 154.1–154.2, omitted in F.
6. A bitter herb taken medicinally (hence, "a bitter pill to swallow").
7. Our intentions serve and depend on.
8. *Most . . . debt:* It is inevitable (or necessary for our well-being) that we neglect to fulfill those promises made to ourselves.
9. *The violence . . . destroy:* Extreme grief and joy destroy themselves, and the motive for action vanishes with them.
1. On account of a small, unforeseen event.

For 'tis a question left us yet to prove

185   Whether love lead fortune or else fortune love.

The great man down, you mark his favourite flies;

The poor advanced° makes friends of enemies.   *promoted*

And hitherto° doth love on fortune tend,°   *to this extent / attend*

For who not needs shall never lack a friend,

190   And who in want a hollow friend doth try°   *test*

Directly seasons him² his enemy.

But orderly to end where I begun,

Our wills and fates do so contrary run³

That our devices still° are overthrown;   *our plans always*

195   Our thoughts are ours, their ends° none of our own.   *results*

So think thou wilt no second husband wed;

But die thy thoughts when thy first lord is dead.

PLAYER QUEEN   Nor earth to me give food, nor heaven light,

Sport and repose lock from me day and night,⁴

199.1   *To desperation turn my trust and hope;*

An anchor's cheer⁵ in prison be my scope.°   *extent (of good)*

200   Each opposite⁶ that blanks° the face of joy   *makes pale*

Meet what I would have well and it destroy,

Both here and hence pursue me lasting strife

If, once a widow, ever I be wife.

HAMLET   If she should break it now!

PLAYER KING [*to* PLAYER QUEEN]

205   'Tis deeply sworn. Sweet, leave me here a while.

My spirits grow dull, and fain° I would beguile   *gladly*

The tedious day with sleep.

PLAYER QUEEN   Sleep rock thy brain,

And never come mischance between us twain.

[PLAYER KING] sleeps. Exit [PLAYER QUEEN]

HAMLET [*to* GERTRUDE]   Madam, how like you this play?

210   QUEEN GERTRUDE   The lady protests too much, methinks.

HAMLET   O, but she'll keep her word.

KING CLAUDIUS   Have you heard the argument?° Is there no   *plot*
offence in't?

HAMLET   No, no, they do but jest, poison in jest. No offence i'th'

215   world.

KING CLAUDIUS   What do you call the play?

HAMLET   *The Mousetrap.* Marry, how? Tropically.⁷ This play is
the image of a murder done in Vienna. Gonzago is the Duke's
name, his wife Baptista.⁸ You shall see anon. 'Tis a knavish

220   piece of work; but what o' that? Your majesty, and we that have
free° souls, it touches⁹ us not. Let the galled jade wince, our   *guiltless*
withers are unwrung.¹

Enter [PLAYER] LUCIANUS

This is one Lucianus, nephew to the King.

---

2. Immediately hardens him, as timber is seasoned for
use.

3. What we desire and what is destined to happen are so
opposed.

4. After this line, Q2 has a couplet omitted in F, 199.1–
199.2.

5. Food for an anchorite (ascetic religious hermit).

6. Each adverse force.

7. As a trope, or rhetorical figure (perhaps punning on

"trap").

8. That is, the Player King and Queen (called "Duke"
and "Duchess" throughout Q1). Shakespeare seems to
base *The Mousetrap* on an extremely muddled version
of the Duke of Urbino's alleged 1538 murder by Luigi
Gonzaga.

9. Wounds; concerns.

1. Let the chafed horse wince, our shoulders are not
rubbed sore.

OPHELIA   You are as good as a chorus,[2] my lord.

225 HAMLET   I could interpret between you and your love if I could
see the puppets dallying.[3]

OPHELIA   You are keen,° my lord, you are keen.   *sharply satirical*

HAMLET   It would cost you a groaning to take off mine edge.[4]

OPHELIA   Still better, and worse.[5]

230 HAMLET   So you mis-take your husbands.[6] [*To* LUCIANUS] Begin,
murderer. Pox, leave thy damnable° faces and begin. Come: *grimacing*
'the croaking raven doth bellow for revenge'.[7]

PLAYER LUCIANUS   Thoughts black, hands apt, drugs fit, and time
agreeing,

Confederate° season, else no creature seeing;   *Complicit*

235 Thou mixture rank° of midnight weeds collected,   *foul*
With Hecate's ban[8] thrice blasted, thrice infected,
Thy natural magic and dire property°   *quality*
On wholesome life usurp immediately.

[*He*] *pours the poison in* [*the Player King's*] *ears*

HAMLET   A poisons him i'th' garden for 's estate.° His name's   *position; state*

240 Gonzago. The story is extant, and writ in choice Italian. You
shall see anon how the murderer gets the love of Gonzago's
wife.

OPHELIA   The King rises.

HAMLET   What, frighted with false fire?[9]

245 QUEEN GERTRUDE [*to* CLAUDIUS]   How fares my lord?

POLONIUS   Give o'er the play.

KING CLAUDIUS   Give me some light. Away.

COURTIERS   Lights, lights, lights![1]

Exeunt all but HAMLET *and* HORATIO

HAMLET   Why, let the stricken deer go weep,[2]

250 The hart ungallèd° play,   *unafflicted*
For some must watch,° while some must sleep,   *stay awake*
So runs the world away.[3]

Would not this,° sir, and a forest of feathers,[4] if the rest of my (The Mousetrap)
fortunes turn Turk° with me, with two Provençal roses on my   *renegade*

255 razed[5] shoes, get me a fellowship in a cry of players,[6] sir?

HORATIO   Half a share.

HAMLET   A whole one, I.

For thou dost know, O Damon[7] dear,
This realm dismantled° was   *deprived*

260 Of Jove himself, and now reigns here
A very, very—pajock.[8]

---

2. The Chorus explained the forthcoming action. In puppet shows, a choric narrator, or "interpreter," announced the characters' names and spoke the dialogue.

3. Flirting. Hamlet uses "interpret" here in the sense of acting as the go-between, or pander, for two lovers.

4. To satisfy my sexual appetite (leading to groaning in either sexual intercourse or childbirth).

5. Wittier, and more obscene.

6. With these false promises ("for better and for worse"), you take your husbands in marriage and cheat on them.

7. Misquoted from *The True Tragedy of Richard III* (c. 1591; not to be confused with Shakespeare's own *Richard III*).

8. Curse by the goddess of witchcraft.

9. Fireworks or blank cartridges.

1. This line is spoken by Polonius in Q2 and by "All"

in F.

2. A deer was thought to weep when mortally wounded. These four lines are probably from a lost ballad.

3. That's the way of the world.

4. Plumes, worn often onstage.

5. Decorated with slashes. *Provençal roses:* large rosettes concealing shoelaces.

6. *a fellowship . . . players:* a profit-sharing partnership in a pack ("cry") of actors (such as Shakespeare had in the Lord Chamberlain's Men).

7. Damon and Pythias were legendary ideals of friendship.

8. "Patchock" (rare, meaning something like "oaf"), or "peacock," emblem of the sin of pride. (The expected rhyme word would be "ass.")

HORATIO   You might have rhymed.

HAMLET   O good Horatio, I'll take the Ghost's word for a thousand pound. Didst perceive?

265   HORATIO   Very well, my lord.

HAMLET   Upon the talk of the pois'ning?

HORATIO   I did very well note him.

Enter ROSENCRANTZ *and* GUILDENSTERN

HAMLET   Ah ha! Come, some music, come, the recorders,
        For if the King like not the comedy,

270   Why then, belike he likes it not, pardie.°   indeed (pardieu)
        Come, some music.

GUILDENSTERN   Good my lord, vouchsafe me a word with you.

HAMLET   Sir, a whole history.

GUILDENSTERN   The King, sir—

275   HAMLET   Ay, sir, what of him?

GUILDENSTERN   Is in his retirement° marvellous distempered.   withdrawal

HAMLET   With drink, sir?

GUILDENSTERN   No, my lord, rather with choler.[9]

HAMLET   Your wisdom should show itself more richer° to signify   resourceful

280   this to his doctor, for for me to put him to his purgation[1] would
        perhaps plunge him into far more choler.

GUILDENSTERN   Good my lord, put your discourse into some
        frame,° and start° not so wildly from my affair.   order / jump away

HAMLET   I am tame, sir. Pronounce.

285   GUILDENSTERN   The Queen your mother, in most great affliction of spirit, hath sent me to you.

HAMLET   You are welcome.

GUILDENSTERN   Nay, good my lord, this courtesy is not of the
        right breed.° If it shall please you to make me a wholesome°   kind; nobility / sane

290   answer, I will do your mother's commandment; if not, your
        pardon° and my return shall be the end of my business.   permission to go

HAMLET   Sir, I cannot.

GUILDENSTERN   What, my lord?

HAMLET   Make you a wholesome answer. My wit's diseased. But,

295   sir, such answers as I can make, you shall command; or rather,
        as you say, my mother. Therefore no more, but to the matter.
        My mother, you say?

ROSENCRANTZ   Then thus she says: your behaviour hath struck
        her into amazement and admiration.°   bewilderment

300   HAMLET   O wonderful son, that can so astonish a mother! But is
        there no sequel at the heels of this mother's admiration?

ROSENCRANTZ   She desires to speak with you in her closet° ere   private chamber
        you go to bed.

HAMLET   We shall obey, were she ten times our mother. Have

305   you any further trade with us?

ROSENCRANTZ   My lord, you once did love me.

HAMLET   So I do still, by these pickers and stealers.[2]

ROSENCRANTZ   Good my lord, what is your cause of distemper?

9. Both anger (Guildenstern's meaning) and indigestion (Hamlet's). In Renaissance medical psychology, each was a symptom of too much yellow bile—an imbalance ("distemper") of the bodily fluids (humors).
1. A complicated pun: bloodletting; spiritual purging (confession and absolution); legal purging (clearing oneself of a crime).
2. Hands. (The catechism in the Book of Common Prayer includes a promise to "keep my hands from picking and stealing, and my tongue from evil speaking, lying, and slandering.")

You do freely° bar the door of your own liberty if you deny your   *voluntarily*
310   griefs to your friend.
HAMLET   Sir, I lack advancement.
ROSENCRANTZ   How can that be when you have the voice of the
King himself for your succession in Denmark?
HAMLET   Ay, but 'while the grass grows . . .'³—the proverb is
315   something° musty.   *somewhat*

     *Enter one with a recorder*⁴

O, the recorder. Let me see. [*To* ROSENCRANTZ *and* GUILDEN-
STERN, *taking them aside*] To withdraw° with you, why do you   *speak privately*
go about to recover the wind of me as if you would drive me
into a toil?⁵
320   GUILDENSTERN   O my lord, if my duty be too bold, my love is
too unmannerly.⁶
HAMLET   I do not well understand that. Will you play upon this
pipe?
GUILDENSTERN   My lord, I cannot.
325   HAMLET   I pray you.
GUILDENSTERN   Believe me, I cannot.
HAMLET   I do beseech you.
GUILDENSTERN   I know no touch of it, my lord.
HAMLET   'Tis as easy as lying. Govern these ventages° with your   *finger holes*
330   fingers and thumb, give it breath with your mouth, and it will
discourse most excellent music. Look you, these are the stops.°   *finger holes; notes*
GUILDENSTERN   But these cannot I command to any utterance
of harmony. I have not the skill.
HAMLET   Why, look you now, how unworthy a thing you make
335   of me! You would play upon me, you would seem to know my
stops, you would pluck out the heart of my mystery, you would
sound° me from my lowest note to the top of my compass;° and   *fathom; play on / range*
there is much music, excellent voice in this little organ,° yet   *musical instrument*
cannot you make it speak. 'Sblood, do you think I am easier to
340   be played on than a pipe? Call me what instrument you will,
though you can fret⁷ me, you cannot play upon me.

     Enter POLONIUS

God bless you, sir.
POLONIUS   My lord, the Queen would speak with you, and pres-
ently.
345   HAMLET   Do you see yonder cloud that's almost in shape of a
camel?
POLONIUS   By th' mass, and 'tis: like a camel, indeed.
HAMLET   Methinks it is like a weasel.
POLONIUS   It is backed like a weasel.
350   HAMLET   Or like a whale.
POLONIUS   Very like a whale.
HAMLET   Then will I come to my mother by and by. [*Aside*]
They fool me to the top of my bent.⁸ [*To* POLONIUS] I will come
by and by.
355   POLONIUS   I will say so.
HAMLET   'By and by' is easily said.   *Exit* [POLONIUS]

---

3. "While the grass grows, the horse starves."
4. Q2 has "Enter the Players with Recorders."
5. *go . . . toil:* both conspire and take a roundabout
course in order to get to the windward (like a hunter
using his own smell to drive quarry to a waiting snare,
or "toil").

6. If I have been discourteous in pursuing what is my
duty, my love for you is to blame.
7. Irritate, punning on "frets of stringed instruments,"
which regulate fingering and pitch.
8. They go along with my foolishness to its limit, or to
the limit of my endurance.

Leave me, friends. [*Exeunt* ROSENCRANTZ *and* GUILDENSTERN]
'Tis now the very witching time of night,
When churchyards yawn, and hell itself breathes out
360   Contagion to this world. Now could I drink hot blood,
And do such bitter business as the day
Would quake to look on. Soft, now to my mother.
O heart, lose not thy nature!° Let not ever   *natural affection*
The soul of Nero⁹ enter this firm° bosom.   *resolved*
365   Let me be cruel, not unnatural.
I will speak daggers to her, but use none.
My tongue and soul in this be hypocrites¹—
How in my words somever² she be shent,°   *rebuked*
To give them seals³ never my soul consent.   *Exit*

3.3

Enter KING [CLAUDIUS], ROSENCRANTZ, *and* GUILDEN-
    STERN

KING CLAUDIUS   I like him not, nor stands it safe with us
To let his madness range. Therefore prepare you.
I your commission will forthwith dispatch,
And he to England shall along with you.
5   The terms of our estate¹ may not endure
Hazard so dangerous as doth hourly grow
Out of his lunacies.²

GUILDENSTERN   We will ourselves provide.
Most holy and religious fear° it is   *care*
To keep those many many bodies safe
10   That live and feed upon your majesty.

ROSENCRANTZ   The single° and peculiar° life is bound   *individual / private*
With all the strength and armour of the mind
To keep itself from noyance;° but much more   *harm*
That spirit upon whose weal° depends and rests   *well-being*
15   The lives of many. The cease° of majesty   *decease*
Dies not alone, but like a gulf° doth draw   *whirlpool*
What's near it with it. It is a massy° wheel   *massive*
Fixed on the summit of the highest mount,
To whose huge spokes ten thousand lesser things
20   Are mortised° and adjoined, which° when it falls   *affixed / so that*
Each small annexment, petty consequence,
Attends° the boist'rous ruin. Never alone   *Accompanies*
Did the King sigh, but with a general groan.

KING CLAUDIUS   Arm° you, I pray you, to this speedy voyage,   *Prepare*
25   For we will fetters put upon this fear
Which now goes too free-footed.

ROSENCRANTZ *and* GUILDENSTERN   We will haste us.
                              Exeunt [*both*]

    Enter POLONIUS

POLONIUS   My lord, he's going to his mother's closet.
Behind the arras° I'll convey myself   *wall tapestry*
To hear the process.° I'll warrant she'll tax him home.³   *proceedings*

---

9. The Roman Emperor Nero reputedly murdered his
mother, in one account, by cutting open her womb.
1. Let me appear and speak as if I intended violence
(though I do not).
2. However much by my words.
3. To confirm them with visible deeds.

3.3 Location: The castle.
1. The responsibilities of our position.
2. Mad actions, apparently a revision in F of Q2's
"browes" (an ambiguous term suggesting "brain,"
"expressions," or "effrontery").
3. I'm sure she will rebuke him thoroughly.

30   And, as you said—and wisely was it said—
        'Tis meet° that some more audience than a mother,   *fitting*
        Since nature makes them partial, should o'erhear
        The speech of vantage.° Fare you well, my liege.   *in addition*
        I'll call upon you ere you go to bed,
        And tell you what I know.

35   KING CLAUDIUS   Thanks, dear my lord.

                                Exit [POLONIUS]

        O, my offence is rank! It smells to heaven.
        It hath the primal eldest curse⁴ upon't,
        A brother's murder. Pray can I not.
        Though inclination be as sharp as will,⁵
40   My stronger guilt defeats my strong intent,
        And like a man to double business bound⁶
        I stand in pause where I shall first begin,
        And both neglect. What if this cursèd hand
        Were thicker than itself with brother's blood,⁷
45   Is there not rain enough in the sweet heavens
        To wash it white as snow?⁸ Whereto serves mercy
        But to confront the visage of offence?⁹
        And what's in prayer but this twofold force,
        To be forestallèd° ere we come to fall,   *prevented*
50   Or pardoned being down? Then I'll look up.
        My fault is past—but O, what form of prayer
        Can serve my turn? 'Forgive me my foul murder'?
        That cannot be, since I am still possessed
        Of those effects for which I did the murder—
55   My crown, mine own ambition, and my queen.
        May one be pardoned and retain th'offence?¹
        In the corrupted currents of this world
        Offence's gilded° hand may shove by justice,   *bribing*
        And oft 'tis seen the wicked prize² itself
60   Buys out the law. But 'tis not so above.
        There is no shuffling,° there the action lies   *evasion*
        In his true nature,³ and we ourselves compelled
        Even to the teeth and forehead of⁴ our faults
        To give in evidence.⁵ What then? What rests?°   *remains to be done*
65   Try what repentance can. What can it not?
        Yet what can it when one cannot repent?
        O wretched state, O bosom black as death,
        O limèd⁶ soul that, struggling to be free,
        Art more engaged!° Help, angels! Make assay.° *entangled / some attempt*
70   Bow, stubborn knees; and heart with strings of steel,

---

4. The first, oldest curse (God's curse on Cain for murdering his brother, Abel; see Genesis 4:10–12).
5. Though my desire (to pray) is as strong as my determination to do so.
6. Committed to two different goals.
7. Were covered with a layer of brother's blood deeper than the hand's thickness.
8. Compare Isaiah 1:15–18: "And though ye make many prayers, I will not hear: for your hands are full of blood. Wash you, make you clean; take away the evil of your works from before mine eyes. . . . though your sins were as crimson, they shall be made white as snow."

9. *Whereto . . . offence:* What purpose has mercy if not to oppose sin face to face?
1. And keep what was gained from the crime.
2. The profits from wickedness.
3. *the action . . . nature:* the deed appears in its true form; legal proceedings are properly conducted.
4. *Even . . . of:* Even face to face with. (English law provided for the confrontation of the accused and the witnesses.)
5. To testify. In English law, one cannot be forced to give evidence against oneself; heavenly justice is different.
6. Caught as if in birdlime, a sticky substance smeared on twigs to catch birds.

Be soft as sinews of the new-born babe.
All may be well.
    [He kneels.]
    Enter [Prince] HAMLET *[behind him]*
HAMLET   Now might I do it pat,° now a° is praying,   *neatly / he*
And now I'll do't,
    [He draws his sword]
        and so a goes to heaven,
75 And so am I revenged. That would be scanned.[7]
A villain kills my father, and for that
I, his sole son, do this same villain send
To heaven.
O, this is hire and salary, not revenge!
80 A took my father grossly, full of bread,[8]
With all his crimes broad blown,[9] as flush° as May;   *vigorously thriving*
And how his audit° stands, who knows save heaven?   *spiritual account*
But in our circumstance and course of thought[1]
'Tis heavy with him. And am I then revenged
85 To take him in the purging of his soul,
When he is fit and seasoned° for his passage?   *made ready*
No.
    [He sheathes his sword]
Up, sword, and know thou a more horrid hint.°   *occasion*
When he is drunk asleep, or in his rage,
90 Or in th'incestuous pleasure of his bed,
At gaming, swearing, or about some act
That has no relish° of salvation in't,   *trace*
Then trip him that his heels may kick at heaven,
And that his soul may be as damned and black
95 As hell whereto it goes. My mother stays.°   *waits*
This physic[2] but prolongs thy sickly days.   *Exit*
KING CLAUDIUS   My words fly up, my thoughts remain below.
Words without thoughts never to heaven go.   *Exit*

3.4

Enter QUEEN GERTRUDE *and* POLONIUS
POLONIUS   A will come straight.° Look you lay home to him.[1]   *immediately*
Tell him his pranks have been too broad° to bear with,   *outrageous*
And that your grace hath screened and stood between
Much heat and him. I'll silence me e'en here.
5 Pray you be round° with him.   *blunt*
HAMLET *(within)*   Mother, mother, mother!
QUEEN GERTRUDE   I'll warr'nt you. Fear° me not. Withdraw; I   *Doubt*
    hear him coming.
    *[*POLONIUS *hides behind the arras.]*
    Enter [Prince] HAMLET
HAMLET   Now, mother, what's the matter?
QUEEN GERTRUDE   Hamlet, thou hast thy father much offended.
10 HAMLET   Mother, you have my father much offended.

7. That needs careful evaluation.
8. Not spiritually prepared. Compare Ezekiel 16:49: "Behold, this was the iniquity of thy sister Sodom, pride, fullness of bread, and abundance of idleness."
9. With all his sins in full bloom.
1. But in our indirect and limited way of knowing on earth.
2. Medicine (both Claudius's prayer and Hamlet's postponement of the revenge).
3.4 Location: The Queen's private chamber.
1. Be sure to rebuke him thoroughly.

QUEEN GERTRUDE   Come, come, you answer with an idle tongue.

HAMLET   Go, go, you question with a wicked tongue.

QUEEN GERTRUDE   Why, how now,° Hamlet?   *what's this*

HAMLET   What's the matter now?

QUEEN GERTRUDE   Have you forgot me?[2]

HAMLET   No, by the rood,° not so.   *Cross of Christ*

15   You are the Queen, your husband's brother's wife.

    But—would you were not so—you are my mother.

QUEEN GERTRUDE   Nay, then, I'll set those to you that can speak.[3]

HAMLET   Come, come, and sit you down. You shall not budge.

    You go not till I set you up a glass°   *mirror*

20   Where you may see the inmost part of you.

QUEEN GERTRUDE   What wilt thou do? Thou wilt not murder me?

    Help, help, ho!

POLONIUS [*behind the arras*]   What ho! Help, help, help!

HAMLET   How now, a rat? Dead for a ducat, dead.[4]

    [*He thrusts his sword through the arras.*] *Kills* POLONIUS

POLONIUS   O, I am slain!

QUEEN GERTRUDE [*to* HAMLET]   O me, what hast thou done?

25   HAMLET   Nay, I know not. Is it the King?

QUEEN GERTRUDE   O, what a rash and bloody deed is this!

HAMLET   A bloody deed—almost as bad, good-mother,°   *stepmother*

    As kill a king and marry with his brother.

QUEEN GERTRUDE   As kill a king?

HAMLET   Ay, lady, 'twas my word.

30   [*To* POLONIUS] Thou wretched, rash, intruding fool, farewell.

    I took thee for thy better. Take thy fortune.

    Thou find'st to be too busy° is some danger.—   *nosy*

    Leave wringing of your hands. Peace, sit you down,

    And let me wring your heart; for so I shall

35   If it be made of penetrable stuff,

    If damnèd custom° have not brassed it so   *sinful habit*

    That it is proof and bulwark against sense.[5]

QUEEN GERTRUDE   What have I done, that thou dar'st wag thy tongue

    In noise so rude against me?

HAMLET   Such an act

40   That blurs the grace and blush of modesty,

    Calls virtue hypocrite, takes off the rose

    From the fair forehead of an innocent love

    And sets a blister there,[6] makes marriage vows

    As false as dicers' oaths—O, such a deed

45   As from the body of contraction° plucks   *marriage contract*

    The very soul, and sweet religion makes

    A rhapsody[7] of words. Heaven's face doth glow,°   *blush*

    Yea, this solidity and compound mass[8]

    With tristful° visage, as against the doom,[9]   *sad*

    Is thought-sick at the act.

50   QUEEN GERTRUDE   Ay me, what act,

2. Forgotten the respect you owe to me as your mother.
3. *that can speak*: who can deal with someone as impossibly rude as you.
4. I bet a ducat I have killed it.
5. *brassed . . . sense*: made it so brasslike (or brazen) that it is impenetrably fortified against natural feeling ("sense").

6. Prostitutes, among other criminals, were branded on the forehead during the sixteenth and seventeenth centuries.
7. Meaningless jumble.
8. Solid earth (a compound of the four elements).
9. As if preparing for the Last Judgment.

That roars so loud and thunders in the index?[1]

HAMLET   Look here upon this picture, and on this,
The counterfeit presentment° of two brothers. *painted portrayal*
See what a grace was seated on this brow—
55 Hyperion's° curls, the front° of Jove himself, *The sun god's / forehead*
An eye like Mars,° to threaten or command, *the god of war*
A station like the herald Mercury[2]
New lighted° on a heaven-kissing hill; *alighted*
A combination and a form indeed
60 Where every god did seem to set his seal
To give the world assurance of a man.
This *was* your husband. Look you now what follows.
Here *is* your husband, like a mildewed ear° *ear of grain*
Blasting° his wholesome brother. Have you eyes? *Infesting*
65 Could you on this fair mountain leave° to feed, *cease*
And batten on this moor?[3] Ha, have you eyes?
You cannot call it love, for at your age
The heyday in the blood[4] is tame, it's humble,
And waits° upon the judgement; and what judgement *follows*
70 Would step from this to this?[5]
70.1 *Sense[6] sure you have,*
Else could you not have motion; but sure that sense
Is apoplexed,° for madness would not err, *paralyzed*
Nor sense to ecstasy was ne'er so thralled
70.5 *But it reserved some quantity of choice*
To serve in such a difference.[7] What devil was't
That thus hath cozened you at hoodman-blind?[8]
Eyes without feeling, feeling without sight,
Ears without hands or eyes, smelling sans all,[9]
70.10 *Or but a sickly part of one true sense*
Could not so mope.[1]
What devil was't
That thus hath cozened you at hood-man blind?[2]
O shame, where is thy blush? Rebellious hell,
If thou canst mutine° in a matron's bones, *mutiny*
To flaming youth let virtue be as wax
75 And melt in her° own fire. Proclaim no shame *(youth's)*
When the compulsive ardour gives the charge,° *order to attack*
Since frost itself as actively doth burn,
And reason panders will.[3]

QUEEN GERTRUDE   O Hamlet, speak no more!
Thou turn'st mine eyes into my very soul,
80 And there I see such black and grainèd° spots *engrained*
As will not leave their tinct.° *lose their color*

HAMLET   Nay, but to live
In the rank sweat of an enseamèd° bed, *a greasy*

---

1. Table of contents; preface.
2. A stance like the winged herald of the gods.
3. And glut yourself on this poor pastureland (possibly punning on "blackamoor").
4. The excitement of sexual passion.
5. After "this?" Q2 has a longer version, 70.1–70.11, of Hamlet's subsequent one and a half lines.
6. Sensation; the five senses (sight, smell, hearing, taste, and touch).
7. *ne'er . . . difference:* never so enslaved by madness that it did not retain some ability to choose between such different men ("sense" connoting "reason").

8. See note to line 71.
9. *sans all:* without any other sense. Cf. Psalm 115:5–6 on idolaters: "Eyes have they, but they see not: They have ears but they hear not: noses have they, but they smell not."
1. Could not be so obtuse.
2. That in this way has cheated you in blindman's buff (as if her second husband had been put in her way while she was groping blindfolded).
3. And mature reason abets lust (rather than restraining it).

Stewed in corruption, honeying and making love
Over the nasty sty—

QUEEN GERTRUDE   O, speak to me no more!
85   These words like daggers enter in mine ears.
No more, sweet Hamlet.

HAMLET   A murderer and a villain,
A slave that is not twenti'th part the tithe°   one-tenth
Of your precedent° lord, a vice⁴ of kings,   previous
A cutpurse° of the empire and the rule,   pickpocket
90   That from a shelf the precious diadem stole
And put it in his pocket—

QUEEN GERTRUDE   No more.

HAMLET   A king of shreds and patches⁵—
                  Enter GHOST *in his nightgown⁶*
Save me and hover o'er me with your wings,
95   You heavenly guards! [*To* GHOST] What would you, gracious figure?

QUEEN GERTRUDE   Alas, he's mad.

HAMLET [*to* GHOST]   Do you not come your tardy son to chide,
That, lapsed in time and passion,⁷ lets go by
Th'important° acting of your dread command?   urgent
O, say!

100   GHOST   Do not forget. This visitation
Is but to whet thy almost blunted purpose.
But look, amazement on thy mother sits.
O, step between her and her fighting soul.
Conceit° in weakest bodies strongest works.   Imagination
105   Speak to her, Hamlet.

HAMLET   How is it with you, lady?

QUEEN GERTRUDE   Alas, how is't with you,
That you do bend your eye on vacancy,
And with th'incorporal° air do hold discourse?   bodiless
110   Forth at your eyes your spirits wildly peep,
And, as the sleeping soldiers in th'alarm,°   call to arms
Your bedded hair, like life in excrements,⁸
Start up and stand on end. O gentle son,
Upon the heat and flame of thy distemper°   unbalanced mind
115   Sprinkle cool patience! Whereon do you look?

HAMLET   On him, on him. Look you how pale he glares.
His form and cause conjoined,⁹ preaching to stones,
Would make them capable. [*To* GHOST] Do not look
            upon me,
Lest with this piteous action you convert°   change (to mercy)
120   My stern effects.° Then what I have to do   intended acts
Will want true colour¹—tears perchance° for blood.   perhaps

QUEEN GERTRUDE   To whom do you speak this?

HAMLET   Do you see nothing there?

QUEEN GERTRUDE   Nothing at all, yet all that is I see.

HAMLET   Nor did you nothing hear?

QUEEN GERTRUDE   No, nothing but ourselves.

---

4. In morality plays, the buffoon who personified evil.
5. *shreds and patches:* motley, the costume of a jester.
6. The nightgown is specified only in Q1; Q2 and F
leave open the possibility that the Ghost is appearing
again in his armor.
7. *lapsed . . . passion:* having allowed time to pass and

passionate dedication (to revenge) to fade.
8. In insensate outgrowths (used of nails and hair).
bedded: (formerly) flat and inert.
9. His appearance joined with his reason for appearing.
1. Will not be as it should (since he cries colorless tears
instead of shedding red blood).

125   HAMLET   Why, look you there. Look how it steals away.
My father, in his habit[2] as° he lived.   *when; as if*
Look where he goes even now out at the portal.

                                 Exit GHOST

     QUEEN GERTRUDE   This is the very coinage of your brain.
This bodiless creation ecstasy
Is very cunning in.[3]

130   HAMLET   Ecstasy?
My pulse as yours doth temperately keep time,
And makes as healthful music. It is not madness
That I have uttered. Bring me to the test,
And I the matter will reword,° which madness   *repeat exactly*

135   Would gambol° from. Mother, for love of grace   *skitter away*
Lay not a flattering unction[4] to your soul
That not your trespass but my madness speaks.
It will but skin° and film the ulcerous place   *cover*
Whilst rank corruption, mining° all within,   *undermining*

140   Infects unseen. Confess yourself to heaven;
Repent what's past, avoid what is to come,
And do not spread the compost o'er the weeds
To make them ranker. Forgive me this my virtue,°   *virtuous exhortation*
For in the fatness° of these pursy° times   *grossness / flatulent*

145   Virtue itself of vice must pardon beg,
Yea, curb° and woo for leave° to do him good.   *bow / permission*

     QUEEN GERTRUDE   O Hamlet, thou hast cleft my heart in twain!

     HAMLET   O, throw away the worser part of it,
And live the purer with the other half!

150   Good night—but go not to mine uncle's bed.
Assume° a virtue if you have it not.[5]   *Put on (actions of)*

151.1   *That monster custom, who all sense doth eat,*
Of habits devilish,[6] is angel yet in this:
That to the use° of actions fair and good   *habitual practice*
He likewise gives a frock or livery

151.5   *That aptly° is put on. Refrain tonight,*   *quickly*
And that shall lend a kind of easiness
To the next abstinence, the next more easy—
For use almost can change the stamp of nature—
And either in° the devil, or throw him out   *let in*

151.10   *With wondrous potency.*
Refrain tonight,
And that shall lend a kind of easiness
To the next abstinence. Once more, good night;

155   And when you are desirous to be blest,
I'll blessing beg of you. For this same lord,
I do repent. But heaven hath pleased it so
To punish me with this, and this with me,
That I must be their scourge and minister.[7]

160   I will bestow° him, and will answer well[8]   *dispose of*
The death I gave him. So, again, good night.

---

2. Dress and bearing.
3. *This bodiless . . . in:* This type of hallucination is a particular skill ("cunning") of madness.
4. Do not apply an ointment that relieves pain but does not heal (contrasted to a sacramental unction that blesses the soul).

5. Q2 has the following longer version (151.1–151.10) of lines 152–54 (*Refrain . . . abstinence*).
6. Emended from Q2's "devil," apparently in compressed opposition to "angel."
7. Heaven's agent of punishment.
8. Will take responsibility for.

I must be cruel only to be kind.
Thus bad begins, and worse remains behind.⁹

QUEEN GERTRUDE   What shall I do?

165   HAMLET   Not this, by no means, that I bid you do:
Let the bloat King tempt you again to bed,
Pinch wanton on your cheek, call you his mouse,
And let him for a pair of reechy° kisses,   *filthy*
Or paddling° in your neck with his damned fingers,   *fondly fingering*
170   Make you to ravel° all this matter out,   *disclose*
That I essentially am not in madness,
But mad in craft.° 'Twere good you let him know,   *cunning*
For who that's but° a queen, fair, sober, wise,   *only*
Would from a paddock,° from a bat, a gib,°   *toad / tomcat*
175   Such dear concernings° hide? Who would do so?   *Such vital affairs*
No, in despite of sense and secrecy,
Unpeg the basket on the house's top,
Let the birds fly, and, like the famous ape,
To try conclusions in the basket creep,
180   And break your own neck down.¹

QUEEN GERTRUDE   Be thou assured, if words be made of breath,
And breath of life, I have no life to breathe
What thou hast said to me.

HAMLET   I must to England.
You know that?

QUEEN GERTRUDE   Alack, I had forgot.
185   'Tis so concluded on.²

185.1   HAMLET   *There's letters sealed, and my two schoolfellows—*
Whom I will trust as I will adders fanged—
They bear the mandate, they must sweep my way
And marshal me to knavery³ Let it work,°   *proceed*
185.5   *For 'tis the sport to have the engineer⁴*
Hoised with his own petard;⁵ and't shall go hard
But I will delve one yard below their mines°   *military tunnels*
And blow them at the moon. O, 'tis most sweet
When in one line two crafts directly meet.⁶

HAMLET   This man shall set me packing.
I'll lug the guts into the neighbour room.
Mother, good night indeed. This counsellor
Is now most still, most secret, and most grave,
Who was in life a foolish prating knave.—
190   Come, sir, to draw toward an end with you.⁷—
Good night, mother.   *Exit, tugging in* POLONIUS

---

9. To follow. Q2 here adds, "One word more good
Lady."
1. *like . . . down:* a tale presumably involving an ape who
opened a wicker cage full of birds and released them from
the rooftop; after climbing into the basket, he tried to imitate their flight to freedom but died in the fall. *try con-*
clusions: test the results.
2. Q2 contains the following additional passage.
3. *sweep . . . knavery:* prepare my path and escort me

into a trap (also, and provoke me to crime).
4. Designer and builder of "engines" (military devices).
5. Blown skyward by his own bomb (for breaching
enemy fortifications).
6. That is, when two devious plots ("crafts") meet along
the same path of tunneling (a standard technique in siege
warfare).
7. To conclude my dealings with you (punning on
"draw" as "drag").

4.1

Enter KING CLAUDIUS *to* QUEEN GERTRUDE[1]

KING CLAUDIUS There's matter in these sighs, these profound heaves;
    You must translate. 'Tis fit we understand them.
    Where is your son?[2]

3.1   QUEEN GERTRUDE *Bestow this place on us a little while*
            Exeunt [ROSENCRANTZ *and* GUILDENSTERN]
    Ah, my good lord, what have I seen tonight!

5 KING CLAUDIUS What, Gertrude? How does Hamlet?

QUEEN GERTRUDE Mad as the sea and wind when both contend
    Which is the mightier. In his lawless fit,
    Behind the arras hearing something stir,
    He whips his rapier out and cries 'A rat, a rat!',

10   And in his brainish apprehension° kills   *brain-sick notion*
    The unseen good old man.

KING CLAUDIUS   O heavy deed!
    It had been so with us° had we been there.   *me (royal "we")*
    His liberty is full of threats to all—
    To you yourself, to us, to everyone.

15   Alas, how shall this bloody deed be answered?°   *accounted for*
    It will be laid to° us, whose providence°   *blamed on / foresight*
    Should have kept short,° restrained, and out of haunt[3] *closely tethered*
    This mad young man. But so much was our love,
    We would not understand what was most fit,

20   But, like the owner° of a foul disease,   *victim*
    To keep it from divulging,° let it feed   *being seen*
    Even on the pith of life. Where is he gone?

QUEEN GERTRUDE To draw apart the body he hath killed,
    O'er whom—his very madness, like some ore°   *vein of gold*

25   Among a mineral° of metals base,   *mine*
    Shows itself pure—a° weeps for what is done.   *he*

KING CLAUDIUS O Gertrude, come away!
    The sun no sooner shall the mountains touch
    But we will ship him hence; and this vile deed

30   We must with all our majesty and skill
    Both countenance° and excuse.—Ho, Guildenstern! *condone*
        Enter ROSENCRANTZ *and* GUILDENSTERN
    Friends both, go join you with some further aid.
    Hamlet in madness hath Polonius slain,
    And from his mother's closet hath he dragged him.

35   Go seek him out, speak fair, and bring the body
    Into the chapel. I pray you haste in this.
            Exeunt [ROSENCRANTZ *and* GUILDENSTERN]
    Come, Gertrude, we'll call up our wisest friends
    To let them know both what we mean to do
    And what's untimely done.[4]

39.1   *So envious slander,*[5]
        Whose whisper o'er the world's diameter,°   *whole extent*

4.1 Location: The castle.
1. The action continues, Gertrude remaining onstage. (Act divisions in the play are not authorial.) In Q2, Rosencrantz and Guildenstern enter with Claudius.
2. In Q2, Rosencrantz and Guildenstern, having entered with Claudius and Gertrude, can exit here (see line 3.1).
3. Public gatherings.
4. After "done," Q2 has the following passage, 39.1–39.5, omitted in F.
5. The phrase is conjectural. Q2 is missing a half line that contains the subject of the sentence.

As level as the cannon to his blank,[6]
Transports his poisoned shot, may miss our name
39.5   And hit the woundless° air.   *invulnerable*
                       O, come away!
40   My soul is full of discord and dismay.   *Exeunt*

4.2

Enter [Prince] HAMLET

HAMLET   Safely stowed.
ROSENCRANTZ *and* GUILDENSTERN (*within*) Hamlet, Lord Hamlet!
HAMLET   What noise? Who calls on Hamlet?

Enter ROSENCRANTZ *and* GUILDENSTERN

                       O, here they come.

ROSENCRANTZ   What have you done, my lord, with the dead body?
5   HAMLET   Compounded° it with dust, whereto 'tis kin.   *Mixed*
ROSENCRANTZ   Tell us where 'tis, that we may take it thence
  And bear it to the chapel.
HAMLET   Do not believe it.
ROSENCRANTZ   Believe what?
10   HAMLET   That I can keep your counsel and not mine own.[1]
  Besides, to be demanded of° a sponge—what replication°   *questioned by / reply*
  should be made by the son of a king?
ROSENCRANTZ   Take you me for a sponge, my lord?
HAMLET   Ay, sir, that soaks up the King's countenance,° his   *favor*
15   rewards, his authorities. But such officers do the King best service in the end. He keeps them, like an ape an apple in the
  corner of his jaw, first mouthed to be last swallowed. When he
  needs what you have gleaned, it is but squeezing you, and,
  sponge, you shall be dry again.
20   ROSENCRANTZ   I understand you not, my lord.
HAMLET   I am glad of it. A knavish speech sleeps in a foolish
  ear.[2]
ROSENCRANTZ   My lord, you must tell us where the body is, and
  go with us to the King.
25   HAMLET   The body is with the King, but the King is not with the
  body.[3] The King is a thing—
GUILDENSTERN   A thing, my lord?
HAMLET   Of nothing. Bring me to him. Hide fox, and all after.[4]
                [Exit running, pursued by the others]

4.3

Enter KING [CLAUDIUS][1]

KING CLAUDIUS   I have sent to seek him, and to find the body.
  How dangerous is it that this man goes loose!
  Yet must not we put the strong law on him.
  He's loved of° the distracted° multitude,   *by / unreasonable*

---

6. As straight as the cannon at a target at point-blank range. (The cannon would be tilted to aim at a distant target.)
4.2 Location: Scene continues.
1. Hamlet plays on two senses of "counsel": That I can follow your advice and not keep my secret.
2. An insulting remark is not perceived by a fool.
3. A riddle. Hamlet may mean that Polonius is gone to the afterlife with King Hamlet but Claudius is still alive; or he may refer to the legal theory of the "king's two bod-

ies" (one the king's natural body, the other the immortal abstract body of the state).
4. From the children's game fox-and-hounds, similar to hide-and-seek.
4.3 Location: Scene continues.
1. Q2 reads, "Enter King and two or three," thus allowing the ensuing lines to be spoken to other characters rather than treating them as a soliloquy or directed to the audience.

5   Who like not in their judgement but their eyes,[2]

And where 'tis so, th'offender's scourge° is weighed,   *punishment*

But never the offence. To bear° all smooth and even,   *manage*

This sudden sending him away must seem

Deliberate pause.° Diseases desperate grown   *Careful planning*

10   By desperate appliance° are relieved,   *remedy*

Or not at all.

       Enter ROSENCRANTZ

               How now, what hath befall'n?

ROSENCRANTZ   Where the dead body is bestowed, my lord,

We cannot get from him.

KING CLAUDIUS   But where is he?

ROSENCRANTZ   Without, my lord, guarded to know your pleasure.

15   KING CLAUDIUS   Bring him before us.

ROSENCRANTZ   Ho, Guildenstern! Bring in my lord.

       Enter [Prince] HAMLET *and* GUILDENSTERN

KING CLAUDIUS   Now, Hamlet, where's Polonius?

HAMLET   At supper.

KING CLAUDIUS   At supper? Where?

20   HAMLET   Not where he eats, but where a is eaten.[3] A certain

convocation of politic° worms are e'en° at him. Your worm is   *cunning / now*

your only emperor for diet.[4] We fat all creatures else° to fat us,   *besides ourselves*

and we fat ourselves for maggots. Your fat king and your lean

beggar is but variable service°—two dishes, but to one table.   *different courses*

25   That's the end.

KING CLAUDIUS   Alas, alas!

HAMLET   A man may fish with the worm that hath eat of a king,

and eat of the fish that hath fed of that worm.

KING CLAUDIUS   What dost thou mean by this?

30   HAMLET   Nothing but to show you how a king may go a progress°   *royal journey*

through the guts of a beggar.

KING CLAUDIUS   Where is Polonius?

HAMLET   In heaven. Send thither to see. If your messenger find

him not there, seek him i'th' other place yourself. But indeed,

35   if you find him not this month, you shall nose him as you go

up the stairs into the lobby.

KING CLAUDIUS [*to* ROSENCRANTZ]   Go seek him there.

HAMLET [*to* ROSENCRANTZ]   A will stay till ye come.

             [*Exit* ROSENCRANTZ]

KING CLAUDIUS   Hamlet, this deed of thine, for thine especial safety—

40   Which we do tender° as we dearly grieve   *value*

For that which thou hast done—must send thee hence

With fiery quickness. Therefore prepare thyself.

The barque is ready, and the wind at help,

Th'associates tend,° and everything is bent°   *companions wait / poised*

45   For England.

HAMLET   For England?

KING CLAUDIUS   Ay, Hamlet.

---

2. Who choose not by reason but by external appearance.
3. Possibly an allusion to the Eucharist (Lord's Supper), in which the body of Christ is consumed in the form of bread.
4. *Your worm . . . diet:* The average worm is the only creature with a diet superior to a King's. The Diet

(Council) of Emperor Charles V at Worms in 1521 called on Luther to defend his new doctrine. A scholar at Hamlet's university at Wittenberg, Luther maintained that faith alone, rather than sacramental ritual, was the basis of salvation.

HAMLET   Good.

KING CLAUDIUS   So is it if thou knew'st our purposes.

50   HAMLET   I see a cherub⁵ that sees them. But come, for England.
    Farewell, dear mother.

KING CLAUDIUS   Thy loving father, Hamlet.

HAMLET   My mother. Father and mother is man and wife, man
    and wife is one flesh,⁶ and so my mother. Come, for England.
                                     Exit

55   KING CLAUDIUS [*to* GUILDENSTERN]   Follow him at foot.° Tempt   *his heel*
    him with speed aboard.
    Delay it not. I'll have him hence tonight.
    Away, for everything is sealed and done
    That else leans° on th'affair. Pray you, make haste.   *bears*
                         [*Exit* GUILDENSTERN]
    And, England,⁷ if my love thou hold'st at aught°—   *any value*

60   As my great power thereof may give thee sense,⁸
    Since yet thy cicatrice° looks raw and red   *scar*
    After the Danish sword, and thy free awe⁹
    Pays homage to us—thou mayst not coldly set°   *indifferently view*
    Our sovereign process, which imports at full,¹

65   By letters conjuring to that effect,
    The present° death of Hamlet. Do it, England,   *immediate*
    For like the hectic° in my blood he rages,   *fever*
    And thou must cure me. Till I know 'tis done,
    Howe'er my haps,° my joys were ne'er begun.   *Exit*   *fortunes*

4.4

Enter FORTINBRAS *with a drum and his army over the*
stage

FORTINBRAS   Go, captain, from me greet the Danish king.
    Tell him that by his licence° Fortinbras   *permission*
    Claims the conveyance of° a promised march   *escort for*
    Over his kingdom. You know the rendezvous.

5   If that his majesty would aught with us,
    We shall express our duty in his eye,°   *presence*
    And let him know so.

CAPTAIN   I will do't, my lord.   [*Exit*]

FORTINBRAS   Go safely¹ on.   *Exeunt* [*marching*]

Enter [*Prince*] HAMLET, ROSENCRANTZ, [GUILDENSTERN,] *etc.*

9.1   HAMLET [*to the* CAPTAIN]   *Good sir, whose powers° are these?*   *forces*

CAPTAIN   *They are of Norway, sir.*

HAMLET   *How purposed, sir, I pray you?*

CAPTAIN   *Against some part of Poland.*

HAMLET   *Who commands them, sir?*

CAPTAIN   *The nephew to old Norway, Fortinbras.*

9.5   HAMLET   *Goes it against the main° of Poland, sir,*   *heart*
    Or for some frontier?

CAPTAIN   *Truly to speak, and with no addition,°*   *exaggeration*

---

5. The keen-sighted second order of angels, cherubim
symbolized heavenly knowledge.
6. As stated in Genesis 2:23 and the marriage rite of
the Book of Common Prayer.
7. King of England.
8. May give you a reason to feel the value of that love.
9. Your respect unconstrained (by an army of occupation).
1. Our sovereign command, which signifies in detailed
instructions.
4.4 Location: The Danish coast.
1. In Q2, "softly" (that is, slowly, circumspectly). In Q2,
the captain remains onstage, and the scene continues
with the following passage, 9.1–9.56.

We go to gain a little patch of ground
That hath in it no profit but the name.

9.10   To pay five ducats, five, I would not farm° it,   *lease*
Nor will it yield to Norway or the Pole
A ranker rate, should it be sold in fee.[2]

CAPTAIN   Yes, it is already garrisoned.
HAMLET   Why then, the Polack never will defend it.

9.15   HAMLET   Two thousand souls and twenty thousand ducats
Will now[3] debate the question of this straw.°   *trifle*
This is th'imposthume° of much wealth and peace,   *abscess*
That inward breaks and shows no cause without[4]
Why the man dies. I humbly thank you, sir.

CAPTAIN   God buy° you, sir.   [*Exit*]   *be with*

9.20   ROSENCRANTZ   *Will't please you go, my lord?*
HAMLET   I'll be with you straight. Go a little before

                         [*Exeunt all but* HAMLET]

How all occasions do inform against° me   *accuse*
And spur my dull revenge! What is a man
If his chief good and market° of his time   *profit*
9.25   Be but to sleep and feed?—a beast, no more.
Sure, he that made us with such large discourse,°   *reasoning faculty*
Looking before and after,[5] gave us not
That capability° and god-like reason   *intelligence*
To fust° in us unused. Now whether it be   *grow moldy*
9.30   Bestial oblivion,[6] or some craven scruple
Of thinking too precisely on th'event—
A thought which, quartered, hath but one part wisdom
And ever three parts coward—I do not know
Why yet I live to say 'This thing's to do',
9.35   Sith° I have cause, and will, and strength, and means,   *Since*
To do't. Examples gross as earth exhort me,
Witness this army of such mass and charge,°   *cost*
Led by a delicate and tender° prince,   *young*
Whose spirit with divine ambition puffed°   *inspired*
9.40   Makes mouths at the invisible event,[7]
Exposing what is mortal and unsure
To all that fortune, death, and danger dare,
Even for an eggshell. Rightly to be great
Is not to stir without great argument,
9.45   But greatly to find quarrel in a straw
When honour's at the stake.[8] How stand I, then,
That have a father killed, a mother stained,
Excitements° of my reason and my blood,   *Urgings*
And let all sleep while, to my shame, I see
9.50   The imminent death of twenty thousand men
That, for a fantasy and trick° of fame,   *fragile trifle*
Go to their graves like beds, fight for a plot
Whereon the numbers cannot try the cause,[9]

---

2. Sold outright as a freehold. *ranker rate*: more generous return.
3. Oxford's emendation of Q2's "Will not."
4. That ruptures internally without external symptom.
5. Able to see past and future.
6. Animal-like inability to remember.

7. Shows a scornful face to unforeseeable outcomes.
8. *Rightly . . . stake*: These lines, syntactically ambiguous, seem to mean that true greatness lies not in rational restraint but in noble action. *the stake*: post to which a bull or bear was fastened for baiting.
9. Which is not big enough for the armies to fight on.

Which is not tomb enough and continent°   *container*
9.55   To hide the slain. O, from this time forth
My thoughts be bloody or be nothing worth!   *Exit*

4.5

Enter QUEEN GERTRUDE *and* HORATIO

QUEEN GERTRUDE   I will not speak with her.

HORATIO[1]   She is importunate,
  Indeed distraught. Her mood will needs be pitied.

QUEEN GERTRUDE   What would she have?

HORATIO   She speaks much of her father, says she hears
5   There's tricks i'th' world, and hems, and beats her heart,
    Spurns enviously at straws,[2] speaks things in doubt°   *obscurely*
    That carry but half sense. Her speech is nothing,
    Yet the unshapèd use° of it doth move   *incoherent manner*
    The hearers to collection.° They aim° at it,   *inference / guess*
10   And botch° the words up fit to° their own thoughts,   *patch / to match*
    Which,° as her winks and nods and gestures yield them,   *(words)*
    Indeed would make one think there might be thought,
    Though nothing sure, yet much unhappily.[3]

QUEEN GERTRUDE   'Twere good she were spoken with, for she may strew
15   Dangerous conjectures in ill-breeding minds.
    Let her come in.

          [HORATIO *withdraws to admit* OPHELIA]

QUEEN GERTRUDE   To my sick soul, as sin's true nature is,
    Each toy° seems prologue to some great amiss.°   *triviality / calamity*
    So full of artless jealousy° is guilt,   *uncontrolled suspicion*
20   It spills itself in fearing to be spilt.

    Enter OPHELIA *distracted, playing on a lute, and her
    hair down, singing*[4]

OPHELIA   Where is the beauteous majesty of Denmark?

QUEEN GERTRUDE   How now,° Ophelia?   *What's this*

OPHELIA *(sings)* How should I your true love know
                From another one?—
25   By his cockle hat and staff,
           And his sandal shoon.[5]

QUEEN GERTRUDE   Alas, sweet lady, what imports° this song?   *means*

OPHELIA   Say you? Nay, pray you, mark.°   *listen*
  (Song)   He is dead and gone, lady,
30   He is dead and gone.
        At his head a grass-green turf,
        At his heels a stone.

QUEEN GERTRUDE   Nay, but Ophelia—

OPHELIA   Pray you, mark.
35   *(Song)*   White his shroud as the mountain snow—

    Enter KING [CLAUDIUS]

QUEEN GERTRUDE   Alas, look here, my lord.

4.5 Location: A public room of the castle.
1. As in F. In Q2, lines 1–2 and 4–13 are spoken by a "Gent.," while Horatio comments on them in lines 14–15 (assigned in F to Gertrude).
2. Kicks bitterly (takes offense) at the slightest thing.
3. Though they reveal nothing for certain, her words

could lead to unfortunate impressions.
4. F simply notes that Ophelia enters distracted; the additional details are taken from Q1.
5. Shoes. *cockle hat:* a cockle-shell badge worn in the hat was a pilgrim's memento of St. James's shrine at Compostela in Spain.

OPHELIA (*Song*)   Larded° with sweet flowers,   *Garnished*
                   Which bewept to the grave did—not⁶—go
                   With true-love showers.°   *tears*

40   KING CLAUDIUS   How do ye, pretty lady?

OPHELIA   Well, God'ield° you. They say the owl was a baker's   *God yield (reward)*
daughter.⁷ Lord, we know what we are, but know not what we
may be. God be at your table!

KING CLAUDIUS [*to* GERTRUDE]   Conceit° upon her father.   *Brooding imagination*

45   OPHELIA   Pray you, let's have no words of this, but when they ask
you what it means, say you this.
        (*Song*)   Tomorrow is Saint Valentine's day,
                    All in the morning betime,°   *early*
                    And I a maid at your window
50   To be your Valentine.
                    Then up he rose, and donned his clothes,
                    And dupped° the chamber door;   *unlatched*
                    Let in the maid, that out a maid
                    Never departed more.

55   KING CLAUDIUS   Pretty Ophelia—

OPHELIA   Indeed, la? Without an oath, I'll make an end on't.°   *of it*
        (*Song*)   By Gis,° and by Saint Charity,   *Jesus*
                    Alack, and fie for shame!
                    Young men will do't if they come to't,
60   By Cock,⁸ they are to blame.
                    Quoth she 'Before you tumbled me,
                    You promised me to wed.'
                    So would I 'a' done, by yonder sun,
                    An° thou hadst not come to my bed.   *If*

65   KING CLAUDIUS [*to* GERTRUDE]   How long hath she been thus?

OPHELIA   I hope all will be well. We must be patient. But I cannot choose but weep to think they should lay him i'th' cold
ground. My brother shall know of it. And so I thank you for
your good counsel. Come, my coach! Good night, ladies, good
70   night, sweet ladies, good night, good night.   *Exit*

KING CLAUDIUS [*to* HORATIO]   Follow her close. Give her good
watch, I pray you.   [*Exit* HORATIO]
O, this is the poison of deep grief! It springs
All from her father's death. O Gertrude, Gertrude,
When sorrows come they come not single spies,°   *scouts*
75   But in battalions. First, her father slain;
Next, your son gone, and he most violent author
Of his own just remove; the people muddied,°   *confused*
Thick and unwholesome in their thoughts and whispers
For good Polonius' death; and we have done but greenly°   *naively*
80   In hugger-mugger° to inter him; poor Ophelia   *secrecy*
Divided from herself and her fair judgement,
Without the which we are pictures or mere beasts;
Last, and as much containing° as all these,   *and as important*
Her brother is in secret come from France,

---

6. By adding "not," Ophelia changes the song's words
and meter to fit the circumstances of Polonius's burial
(see lines 79–80).
7. A folktale: Christ turned a baker's daughter into an

owl because when he asked for food, she would give
him only a small loaf.
8. A corruption of "God" in very mild swearing (playing
on "penis").

85   Feeds on this wonder, keeps himself in clouds,°   *unverified suspicion*
       And wants° not buzzers° to infect his ear   *lacks / scandal mongers*
       With pestilent speeches of his father's death;
       Wherein necessity, of matter beggared,
       Will nothing stick our persons to arraign
90   In ear and ear.[9] O my dear Gertrude, this,
       Like to a murd'ring-piece,[1] in many places
       Gives me superfluous° death.   *redundant*
          A noise within

QUEEN GERTRUDE   Alack, what noise is this?
KING CLAUDIUS   Where is my Switzers?[2] Let them guard the door.
         Enter a MESSENGER
       What is the matter?
MESSENGER   Save yourself, my lord.
95   The ocean, overpeering of his list,[3]
       Eats not the flats with more impetuous[4] haste
       Than young Laertes, in a riotous head,°   *insurrection; tidal wave*
       O'erbears your officers. The rabble call him lord,
       And, as° the world were now but° to begin,   *as if / only now*
100   Antiquity forgot, custom not known,
       The ratifiers and props of every word,[5]
       They cry 'Choose we! Laertes shall be king.'
       Caps, hands, and tongues applaud it to the clouds,
       'Laertes shall be king, Laertes king.'
105 QUEEN GERTRUDE   How cheerfully on the false trail they cry![6]
         A noise within
       O, this is counter,[7] you false Danish dogs!
KING CLAUDIUS   The doors are broke.
         Enter LAERTES *with [his* FOLLOWERS *at the door]*
LAERTES   Where is the King?—Sirs, stand you all without.
ALL HIS FOLLOWERS   No, let's come in.
110 LAERTES   I pray you, give me leave.
ALL HIS FOLLOWERS   We will, we will.
LAERTES   I thank you. Keep the door.   *[Exeunt* FOLLOWERS*]*
           O thou vile king,
       Give me my father.
QUEEN GERTRUDE   Calmly, good Laertes.
LAERTES   That drop of blood that's calm proclaims me bastard,
115   Cries cuckold to my father, brands the harlot
       Even here between the chaste unsmirchèd brow
       Of my true mother.
KING CLAUDIUS   What is the cause, Laertes,
       That thy rebellion looks so giant-like?—
       Let him go, Gertrude. Do not fear° our person.   *fear for*
120   There's such divinity doth hedge a king

---

9. *Wherein . . . ear*: In which affair, because they have no real information and need to give some account, they will not hesitate to whisper accusations against us.
1. Small cannon that fired shrapnel.
2. Company of Swiss mercenaries (employed as royal bodyguards in many European countries).
3. Rising over its boundary at the shore.
4. Spelled "impittious" in F and "impitious" in Q2, probably meaning "merciless" as well as "rash." *flats:* low-

lying countryside.
5. *Antiquity . . . word:* Ignoring history and traditional precedents, which give meaning, order, and stability to society by fixing the agreed-upon meaning of political contracts (and of any truth expressed in language).
6. How enthusiastically they run after the wrong scent (like a pack of hounds hunting the murderer of Polonius).
7. This is following the quarry's trail, but in the wrong direction.

That treason can but peep to what it would,[8]
Acts little of his will.—Tell me, Laertes,
Why thou art thus incensed.—Let him go, Gertrude.—
Speak, man.

LAERTES Where is my father?

KING CLAUDIUS Dead.

QUEEN GERTRUDE [*to* LAERTES] But not by him.

125 KING CLAUDIUS Let him demand his fill.

LAERTES How came he dead? I'll not be juggled with.°   deceived
To hell, allegiance! Vows to the blackest devil!
Conscience and grace to the profoundest pit!
I dare damnation. To this point° I stand,   resolve
130 That both the worlds I give to negligence,[9]
Let come what comes. Only I'll be revenged
Most throughly° for my father.   thoroughly

KING CLAUDIUS Who shall stay° you?   prevent

LAERTES My will, not all the world;
135 And for my means, I'll husband them so well
They shall go far with little.

KING CLAUDIUS Good Laertes,
If you desire to know the certainty
Of your dear father's death, is't writ in your revenge
That, sweepstake,[1] you will draw° both friend and foe,   take from
140 Winner and loser?

LAERTES None but his enemies.

KING CLAUDIUS Will you know them then?

LAERTES To his good friends thus wide I'll ope my arms,
And, like the kind life-rend'ring pelican,
Repast them with my blood.[2]

145 KING CLAUDIUS Why, now you speak
Like a good child and a true gentleman.
That I am guiltless of your father's death,
And am most sensibly° in grief for it,   sympathetically
It shall as level° to your judgement pierce   directly
150 As day does to your eye.

A noise within

VOICES [*within*] Let her come in.[3]

LAERTES How now, what noise is that?

Enter OPHELIA [*as before*]

O heat dry up my brains! Tears seven times salt
Burn out the sense and virtue° of mine eye!   natural power
155 By heaven, thy madness shall be paid by weight
Till our scale turns the beam.[4] O rose of May,
Dear maid, kind sister, sweet Ophelia!
O heavens, is't possible a young maid's wits
Should be as mortal as an old man's life?
160 Nature is fine in love, and where 'tis fine

---

8. That treason can only glance furtively at what it would
like to do.
9. That both this world and the next do not matter to me.
1. Indiscriminately. (The winner of a sweepstake gained
the stakes of all other players.)
2. The female pelican was supposed to feed, and even
revive, its young with blood from a wound it pecked in its

own breast. *Repast:* Feed.
3. This line is assigned to no one in F but rather appears
in italic following the stage direction "A noise within."
Q2 gives the line to Laertes.
4. *shall . . . beam:* shall be atoned for until vengeance
outweighs the injury of madness (thus tilting the "scale"
of justice).

It sends some precious instance of itself
After the thing it loves.[5]

OPHELIA (*Song*)   They bore him barefaced on the bier,
                   Hey non nony, nony, hey nony,
165   And on his grave rained many a tear—
Fare you well, my dove.

LAERTES   Hadst thou thy wits and didst persuade° revenge,   argue for
It could not move thus.

OPHELIA   You must sing 'Down, a-down', and you, 'Call him a
170   down-a'. O, how the wheel[6] becomes it! It is the false steward
that stole his master's daughter.[7]

LAERTES   This nothing's more than matter.[8]

OPHELIA   There's rosemary, that's for remembrance. Pray, love,
remember. And there is pansies; that's for thoughts.[9]

175   LAERTES   A document in madness—thoughts and remembrance
fitted.

OPHELIA   There's fennel for you, and columbines.[1] There's rue
for you, and here's some for me. We may call it herb-grace o'
Sundays. O, you must wear your rue with a difference.[2] There's
180   a daisy. I would give you some violets,[3] but they withered all
when my father died. They say a made a good end.
(*Song*)   For bonny sweet Robin is all my joy.

LAERTES   Thought and affliction, passion, hell itself
She turns to favour° and to prettiness.   beauty

185   OPHELIA (*Song*)   And will a not come again,
                   And will a not come again?
                   No, no, he is dead,
                   Go to thy death-bed,
                   He never will come again.

190   His beard as white as snow,
                   All flaxen° was his poll.°   white / head
                   He is gone, he is gone,
                   And we cast away moan.
                   God 'a' mercy on his soul.
195   And of all Christian souls, I pray God. God b'wi' ye.

                           Exeunt OPHELIA [*and* GERTRUDE]

LAERTES   Do you see this, O God?

KING CLAUDIUS   Laertes, I must commune with your grief,
Or you deny me right. Go but apart,
Make choice of whom° your wisest friends you will,   whichever of
200   And they shall hear and judge 'twixt you and me.
If by direct or by collateral° hand   an agent's
They find us touched,° we will our kingdom give,   involved in guilt

---

5. *Nature . . . loves*: Human nature is made most ethere-
ally pure by love and sends a precious token ("instance")
of itself after the object of its love. Laertes struggles to say
that because of Ophelia's great love for her father, her
sanity departed with him.
6. Probably refrain, although possibly spinning wheel (at
which women sang ballads) or Fortune's wheel. "Down,
a-down" resembles the refrain of recorded ballads.
7. *false . . . daughter*: the tale is unknown; Laertes seems
to recognize it.
8. This nonsense signifies more than coherent speech.
9. *There's . . . thoughts*: Ophelia, recalling the flowers'

symbolic significance, distributes them to Laertes,
Gertrude, and Claudius.
1. Columbines were associated with ingratitude or
marital infidelity, fennel with flattery.
2. In heraldry, minor branches of a family were distinguished by a "difference," a variation or addition to the
coat of arms. Ophelia probably means "for a different
reason." Rue is associated with repentance, and Ophelia
identifies it with the "herb of grace" (wormwood), since
penitence depended on and enabled God's blessing.
3. Representing faithfulness; daisies could symbolize
dissembling seduction.

Our crown, our life, and all that we call ours,   *recompense*
To you in satisfaction.° But if not,
205 Be you content to lend your patience to us,
And we shall jointly labour with your soul
To give it due content.
LAERTES   Let this be so.
His means of death, his obscure burial—
No trophy, sword, nor hatchment⁴ o'er his bones,
210 No noble rite nor formal ostentation°—   *rite of grief*
Cry to be heard, as 'twere from heaven to earth,
That I must call't in question.⁵
KING CLAUDIUS   So you shall;
And where th'offence is, let the great axe fall.
I pray you go with me.   *Exeunt*

4.6

Enter HORATIO *with* [*a* SERVANT]
HORATIO What are they that would speak with me?
SERVANT Sailors, sir. They say they have letters for you.
HORATIO Let them come in.   [*Exit* SERVANT]
I do not know from what part of the world
5 I should be greeted if not from Lord Hamlet.
Enter SAILOR[S]
A SAILOR God bless you, sir.
HORATIO Let him bless thee too.
A SAILOR A shall, sir, an't° please him. There's a letter for you,   *if it*
sir. It comes from th'ambassador that was bound for England—
10 if your name be Horatio, as I am let to know it is.
HORATIO (*reads*) 'Horatio, when thou shalt have overlooked°   *read*
this, give these fellows some means° to the King. They have   *access*
letters for him. Ere we were two days old at sea, a pirate of very
warlike appointment° gave us chase. Finding ourselves too slow   *equipment*
15 of sail, we put on a compelled valour, and in the grapple I
boarded them. On the instant they got clear of our ship, so I
alone became their prisoner. They have dealt with me like
thieves of mercy; but they knew what they did:¹ I am to do a
good turn for them. Let the King have the letters I have sent,
20 and repair thou° to me with as much haste as thou wouldst fly   *come*
death. I have words to speak in thine ear will make thee dumb,
yet are they much too light for the bore° of the matter. These   *caliber; size*
good fellows will bring thee where I am. Rosencrantz and
Guildenstern hold their course for England. Of them I have
25 much to tell thee. Farewell.
He that thou knowest thine,
Hamlet.'
Come, I will give you way° for these your letters,   *means of delivery*
And do't the speedier that you may direct me
30 To him from whom you brought them.   *Exeunt*

---

4. Lozenge-shaped tablet bearing a coat of arms, carried in funeral processions and deposited near the tomb. *trophy:* memorial (often consisting of real or symbolic weapons and armor).
5. I must demand an explanation of it.
4.6 Location: The castle.

1. *They have . . . did:* They have been merciful, but with the expectation of a return. Hamlet recalls the thieves crucified next to Christ (one of whom he blessed) and Christ's plea of forgiveness for those who "know not what they do" (Luke 23:34–43).

4.7

Enter KING [CLAUDIUS] *and* LAERTES

KING CLAUDIUS   Now must your conscience my acquittance seal,[1]
And you must put me in your heart for friend,
Sith° you have heard, and with a knowing ear,   *Since*
That he which hath your noble father slain
Pursued my life.

5   LAERTES   It well appears. But tell me
Why you proceeded not against these feats,°   *acts*
So crimeful and so capital° in nature,   *punishable by death*
As by your safety, wisdom, all things else,
You mainly° were stirred up.   *greatly*

KING CLAUDIUS   O, for two special reasons,
10   Which may to you perhaps seem much unsinewed,°   *uncompelling*
And yet to me they're strong. The Queen his mother
Lives almost by his looks; and for myself—
My virtue or my plague, be it either which—
She's so conjunctive to my life and soul
15   That, as the star moves not but in his sphere,[2]
I could not but by her. The other motive
Why to a public count° I might not go   *accounting*
Is the great love the general gender° bear him,   *the common people*
Who, dipping all his faults in their affection,
20   Would, like the spring that turneth wood to stone,[3]
Convert his guilts to graces; so that my arrows,
Too slightly timbered for so loud a wind,
Would have reverted to my bow again,
And not where I had aimed them.

25   LAERTES   And so have I a noble father lost,
A sister driven into desp'rate terms,
Who has, if praises may go back again,[4]
Stood challenger, on mount, of all the age
For her perfections.[5] But my revenge will come.

30   KING CLAUDIUS   Break not your sleeps for that. You must not think
That we are made of stuff so flat and dull
That we can let our beard be shook with danger,[6]
And think it pastime. You shortly shall hear more.
I loved your father, and we love ourself.
35   And that, I hope, will teach you to imagine—

Enter a MESSENGER *with letters*

How now? What news?

MESSENGER   Letters, my lord, from Hamlet.
This to your majesty; this to the Queen.

KING CLAUDIUS   From Hamlet? Who brought them?

MESSENGER   Sailors, my lord, they say. I saw them not.
40   They were given me by Claudio. He received them.

KING CLAUDIUS   Laertes, you shall hear them.—Leave us.

Exit MESSENGER

4.7 Location: Claudius's private apartments.
1. *my acquittance seal:* affirm my innocence (of Polonius's death).
2. According to Ptolemaic astronomy, heavenly bodies moved in hollow spheres. *conjunctive* (line 14): closely united (as two planets were said astronomically to be "in conjunction" when they appeared close).
3. In limestone-rich areas (such as south Warwickshire),

concentrations in spring water may be great enough to petrify absorbent objects.
4. May refer to what was (but is no longer).
5. *Stood . . . perfections:* Conspicuously challenged the world to match her perfections.
6. That I can allow anyone to endanger me with contemptuous behavior.

[*Reads*] 'High and mighty, you shall know I am set naked° on   *destitute*
your kingdom. Tomorrow shall I beg leave to see your kingly
eyes, when I shall, first asking your pardon,° thereunto recount   *permission*
45   th'occasions of my sudden and more strange return.
                                  Hamlet.'
What should this mean? Are all the rest come back?
Or is it some abuse,° and no such thing?   *deception*

LAERTES   Know you the hand?

KING CLAUDIUS   'Tis Hamlet's character.°   *handwriting*
50   'Naked'—and in a postscript here he says
'Alone'. Can you advise me?

LAERTES   I'm lost in it, my lord. But let him come.
It warms the very sickness in my heart
That I shall live and tell him to his teeth,
'Thus diddest thou'.[7]

55 KING CLAUDIUS   If it be so, Laertes—
As how should it be so, how otherwise?[8]—
Will you be ruled by me?

LAERTES   If so° you'll not o'errule me to a peace.   *Provided that*

KING CLAUDIUS   To thine own peace. If he be now returned,
60   As checking at[9] his voyage, and that he means
No more to undertake it, I will work him
To an exploit, now ripe in my device,°   *planning*
Under the which he shall not choose but fall;
And for his death no wind of blame shall breathe;
65   But even his mother shall uncharge° the practice°   *not accuse / connivance*
And call it accident.[1]

66.1   LAERTES   *My lord, I will be ruled,*
        The rather if you could devise it so
        That I might be the organ.°   *agent*

    KING CLAUDIUS   *It falls right.*
        You have been talked of, since your travel, much,
66.5   *And that in Hamlet's hearing, for a quality*
        Wherein they say you shine. Your sum of parts°   *abilities*
        Did not together pluck such envy from him
        As did that one, and that, in my regard,
        Of the unworthiest siege.°   *lowest rank*

    LAERTES   *What part is that, my lord?*

66.10   KING CLAUDIUS   *A very ribbon in the cap of youth,*
        Yet needful too, for youth no less becomes°   *is suited by*
        The light and careless livery that it wears
        Than settled age his sables and his weeds
        Importing health and graveness.[2]
                         Some two months since
Here was a gentleman of Normandy.
I've seen myself, and served against, the French,
And they can well° on horseback; but this gallant   *are skilled*
70   Had witchcraft in't. He grew into his seat,
And to such wondrous doing brought his horse

---

7. This which I do now to you, you did to my father.
8. *As . . . otherwise:* How could Hamlet be returning, and yet how else could he have sent this letter?
9. As one who has been diverted from ("checking at" is a term from falconry).

1. After "accident," Q2 has the following passage, 66.1–66.14, omitted in F.
2. *his . . . graveness:* its rich gowns trimmed with sable, garments ("weeds") signifying concern for prosperity and dignity.

As had he been incorpsed and demi-natured[3]
With the brave beast. So far he passed my thought
That I in forgery of shapes and tricks[4]
Come short of what he did.

75   LAERTES   A Norman was't?

KING CLAUDIUS   A Norman.

LAERTES   Upon my life, Lamord.

KING CLAUDIUS   The very same.

LAERTES   I know him well. He is the brooch° indeed,   ornament
And gem, of all the nation.

KING CLAUDIUS   He made confession° of you,   testimonial
80   And gave you such a masterly report
For art and exercise in your defence,
And for your rapier most especially,
That he cried out 'twould be a sight indeed
If one could match you.[5]

84.1   *Th'escrimers° of their nation*   fencers
He swore had neither motion, guard, nor eye
If you opposed them.

KING CLAUDIUS   Sir, this report of his
85   Did Hamlet so envenom with his envy
That he could nothing do but wish and beg
Your sudden° coming o'er to play with him.   immediate
Now, out of this—

LAERTES   What out of this, my lord?

KING CLAUDIUS   Laertes, was your father dear to you?
90   Or are you like the painting of a sorrow,
A face without a heart?

LAERTES   Why ask you this?

KING CLAUDIUS   Not that I think you did not love your father,
But that I know love is begun by time,°   circumstance
And that I see, in passages of proof,[6]
95   Time qualifies° the spark and fire of it.[7]   moderates
95.1   *There lives within the very flame of love*
A kind of wick or snuff[8] that will abate it,
And nothing is at a like° goodness still,°   an equal / always
For goodness, growing to a plurisy,[9]
95.5   *Dies in his own too much.° That we would do*   overabundance
We should do when we would, for this 'would' changes,
And hath abatements and delays as many
As there are tongues, are hands, are accidents;
And then this 'should' is like a spendthrift's sigh,
95.10   *That hurts by easing.[1] But to the quick° of th'ulcer—*   center
Hamlet comes back. What would you undertake
To show yourself your father's son in deed
More than in words?

LAERTES   To cut his throat i'th' church.

---

3. As if he had been in the same body and had half the
nature of (the image of a centaur).
4. That I in my very imagination ("forgery") of figures
and skillful feats of horsemanship.
5. After "you," Q2 has the following passage, 84.1–84.3,
omitted in F.
6. From experiences that have tested this.
7. After this line, Q2 has the following passage, 95.1–

95.10, omitted in F.
8. Burned part of the wick (which causes smoke and
reduces light if not removed).
9. A chest inflammation, metaphorically like a fire in the
heart; thought to take its name from the Latin for "more"
(*plus*) and to be caused by an excess of humors (and so
playing on "excess").
1. A sigh was thought to use up a drop of blood.

KING CLAUDIUS   No place indeed should murder sanctuarize.[2]

100   Revenge should have no bounds. But, good Laertes,
    Will you do this?—keep close within your chamber.
    Hamlet returned shall know you are come home.
    We'll put on those shall[3] praise your excellence,
    And set a double varnish on the fame

105   The Frenchman gave you; bring you, in fine,° together,   *conclusion*
    And wager on your heads. He, being remiss,°   *unwary*
    Most generous,° and free from all contriving,   *noble*
    Will not peruse the foils; so that with ease,
    Or with a little shuffling, you may choose

110   A sword unbated, and, in a pass of practice,[4]
    Requite him for your father.

LAERTES   I will do't,
    And for that purpose I'll anoint my sword.
    I bought an unction° of a mountebank°   *ointment / quack*
    So mortal that, but dip a knife in it,

115   Where it draws blood no cataplasm° so rare,   *poultice*
    Collected from all simples° that have virtue°   *herbs / potency*
    Under the moon, can save the thing from death
    That is but scratched withal.° I'll touch my point   *with it*
    With this contagion, that if I gall° him slightly,   *prick*
    It may be death.

120 KING CLAUDIUS   Let's further think of this;
    Weigh what convenience both of time and means
    May fit us to our shape.[5] If this should fail,
    And that our drift look° through our bad performance,   *our intention be seen*
    'Twere better not essayed. Therefore this project

125   Should have a back or second[6] that might hold
    If this should blast in proof.[7] Soft, let me see.
    We'll make a solemn wager on your cunnings . . .°   *skills*
    I ha't! When in your motion° you are hot and dry—   *exercise*
    As make your bouts more violent to that end—

130   And that he calls for drink, I'll have prepared him
    A chalice for the nonce,° whereon but sipping,   *occasion*
    If he by chance escape your venomed stuck,°   *thrust*
    Our purpose may hold there.—

        Enter QUEEN [GERTRUDE]

                   How now, sweet Queen?

QUEEN GERTRUDE   One woe doth tread upon another's heel,

135   So fast they follow. Your sister's drowned, Laertes.

LAERTES   Drowned? O, where?

QUEEN GERTRUDE   There is a willow grows aslant a brook
    That shows his hoar leaves[8] in the glassy stream.
    Therewith fantastic garlands did she make

140   Of crow-flowers, nettles, daisies, and long purples,[9]

---

2. Give sanctuary to a murderer. In English tradition, a criminal remained invulnerable to secular authority for most crimes (save sacrilege and treason) as long as he took refuge in a church.

3. *We'll . . . shall:* I shall incite some people to.

4. In a treacherous thrust. *unbated:* unblunted (as recreational or practice foils were).

5. May make us ready to put into effect our plot and to assume the roles we are to play.

6. Should have reserve soldiers (military metaphor for

the plotting).

7. Should blow up in our faces when put to the test (like a cannon).

8. The willow leaf is gray-white ("hoar") on the undersides (reflected from below by the water). The willow was an emblem of mourning and of forsaken love.

9. Early purple orchises. *crow-flowers:* common name for several wildflowers, including Ragged Robin and bluebells (often appearing beside long purples in woodland and sharing their association with fertility).

That liberal shepherds give a grosser[1] name,
But our cold° maids do dead men's fingers call them.   *chaste*
There on the pendent boughs her crownet° weeds   *garlanded*
Clamb'ring to hang,[2] an envious sliver° broke,   *a malicious twig*
145 When down the weedy trophies and herself
Fell in the weeping brook. Her clothes spread wide,
And mermaid-like a while they bore her up;
Which time she chanted snatches of old tunes,
As one incapable° of her own distress,   *uncomprehending*
150 Or like a creature native and endued
Unto that element.[3] But long it could not be
Till that her garments, heavy with their drink,
Pulled the poor wretch from her melodious lay°   *song*
To muddy death.
155 LAERTES   Alas, then is she drowned.
QUEEN GERTRUDE   Drowned, drowned.
LAERTES   Too much of water hast thou, poor Ophelia,
And therefore I forbid my tears. But yet
It is our trick;° nature her custom holds,   *characteristic way*
Let shame say what it will.
              [*He weeps*]
160   When these are gone,
The woman will be out.[4] Adieu, my lord.
I have a speech of fire that fain° would blaze,   *gladly*
But that this folly douts° it.   *extinguishes*
                                            Exit
KING CLAUDIUS   Let's follow, Gertrude.
How much I had to do to calm his rage!
165 Now fear I this will give it start again;
Therefore let's follow.
                                            Exeunt

5.1

Enter two CLOWNS° *carrying a spade and a pickaxe*   *rustics; peasants*

FIRST CLOWN   Is she to be buried in Christian burial that wilfully
    seeks her own salvation?[1]
SECOND CLOWN   I tell thee she is, and therefore make her grave
    straight.° The coroner hath sat on her,[2] and finds it Christian   *right away*
5   burial.[3]
FIRST CLOWN   How can that be unless she drowned herself in
    her own defence?
SECOND CLOWN   Why, 'tis found so.
FIRST CLOWN   It must be *se offendendo*,[4] it cannot be else; for
10   here lies the point: if I drown myself wittingly, it argues an act;
    and an act hath three branches: it is to act, to do, and to per-
    form. Argal[5] she drowned herself wittingly.

---

1. More indecent. Among the recorded names for the purple orchis are "priest's-pintle" (penis), "dog's cullions" (testicles), "goat's cullions," and "fool's ballochs." *liberal*: free-spoken.
2. Deserted lovers proverbially hung garlands on willows.
3. *native . . . element*: naturally fit to live in water.
4. *When . . . out*: When I have cried my tears, the feminine side of my nature will be gone with them.
5.1 Location: A churchyard.
1. Probably a mistake for "damnation"; suicide was a mortal sin. Ordinarily, suicides would not receive a "Christian burial" (in consecrated ground with the

church's blessing and ritual).
2. Conducted an inquest on the cause of her death.
3. And has given the verdict that she is eligible for a Christian burial (in effect, a decision that Ophelia did not drown herself).
4. A mangled version of *se defendendo*, the term for "killing in self-defense."
5. For "ergo," or "therefore." The argument parodies a famous law case of 1554 concerning suicide by drowning, in which the act was said to have three parts: imagination, resolution, and perfection (accomplishment).

SECOND CLOWN   Nay, but hear you, Goodman Delver.[6]

FIRST CLOWN   Give me leave. Here lies the water—good. Here
15   stands the man—good. If the man go to this water and drown
himself, it is, will he nill he,° he goes. Mark you that. But if the   *willy-nilly*
water come to him and drown him, he drowns not himself;
argal he that is not guilty of his own death shortens not his own
life.

20   SECOND CLOWN   But is this law?

FIRST CLOWN   Ay, marry, is't: coroner's quest° law.   *inquest*

SECOND CLOWN   Will you ha' the truth on't? If this had not been
a gentlewoman, she should have been buried out o' Christian
burial.

25   FIRST CLOWN   Why, there thou sayst,° and the more pity that   *how right you are*
great folk should have count'nance° in this world to drown or   *privilege*
hang themselves more than their even° Christian. Come, my   *fellow*
spade. There is no ancient gentlemen but gardeners, ditchers,
and gravemakers; they hold up° Adam's profession.   *carry on*

[FIRST CLOWN *digs*]

30   SECOND CLOWN   Was he a gentleman?

FIRST CLOWN   A was the first that ever bore arms.[7]

SECOND CLOWN   Why, he had none.

FIRST CLOWN   What, art a heathen? How dost thou understand
the Scripture? The Scripture says Adam digged. Could he dig
35   without arms? I'll put another question to thee. If thou answer-
est me not to the purpose, confess thyself[8]—

SECOND CLOWN   Go to.[9]

FIRST CLOWN   What is he that builds stronger than either the
mason, the shipwright, or the carpenter?

40   SECOND CLOWN   The gallows-maker; for that frame° outlives a   *structure*
thousand tenants.

FIRST CLOWN   I like thy wit well, in good faith. The gallows does°   *serves*
well. But how does it well? It does well to those that do ill. Now
thou dost ill to say the gallows is built stronger than the church,
45   argal the gallows may do well to thee. To't again, come.

SECOND CLOWN   'Who builds stronger than a mason, a shipwright, or a carpenter?'

FIRST CLOWN   Ay, tell me that, and unyoke.[1]

SECOND CLOWN   Marry, now I can tell.

50   FIRST CLOWN   To't.

SECOND CLOWN   Mass,° I cannot tell.   *By the Mass*

Enter [*Prince*] HAMLET *and* HORATIO *afar off*

FIRST CLOWN   Cudgel thy brains no more about it, for your dull
ass will not mend° his pace with beating; and when you are   *improve*
asked this question next, say 'a grave-maker'; the houses that he
55   makes lasts till doomsday. Go, get thee to Johan.[2] Fetch me a
stoup° of liquor.   [*Exit* SECOND CLOWN]   *flagon*

(*Sings*) In youth when I did love, did love,
          Methought it was very sweet

---

6. Master Digger ("Goodman" was the ordinary title in
addressing a man by his occupation).
7. Those bearing a family coat of arms were officially
recognized as gentlemen; playing on "limbs."
8. "Confess thyself and be hanged" was proverbial.

9. An expression of impatience.
1. Rest your wits from work (like draft animals).
2. *Johan:* unknown (presumably a neighborhood alehouse keeper).

To contract°-O-the time for-a-my behove,°   shorten / advantage
60   O methought there-a-was nothing-a-meet.³

HAMLET   Has this fellow no feeling of his business that a sings at
grave-making?

HORATIO   Custom hath made it in him a property of easiness.⁴

HAMLET   'Tis e'en so; the hand of little employment hath the
65   daintier sense.⁵

FIRST CLOWN (sings) But age with his stealing steps
Hath caught me in his clutch,
And hath shipped me intil the land,°   into the earth
As if I had never been such.
[He throws up a skull]

70 HAMLET   That skull had a tongue in it and could sing once. How
the knave jowls° it to th' ground as if 'twere Cain's jawbone,   slams
that did the first murder! This might be the pate of a politician
which this ass o'er-offices,⁶ one that would circumvent God,
might it not?

75 HORATIO   It might, my lord.

HAMLET   Or of a courtier, which could say 'Good morrow, sweet
lord. How dost thou, good lord?' This might be my lord such a
one, that praised my lord such a one's horse when a meant to
beg it, might it not?

80 HORATIO   Ay, my lord.

HAMLET   Why, e'en so, and now my lady Worm's, chapless,° and   lacking a lower jaw
knocked about the mazard° with a sexton's spade. Here's fine   head
revolution,⁷ an° we had the trick° to see't. Did these bones cost   if / ability
no more the breeding but to play at loggats with 'em?⁸ Mine
85   ache to think on't.

FIRST CLOWN (sings) A pickaxe and a spade, a spade,
For and° a shrouding-sheet;   And also
O, a pit of clay for to be made
For such a guest is meet.
[He throws up another skull]

90 HAMLET   There's another. Why might not that be the skull of a
lawyer? Where be his quiddits⁹ now, his quillets,° his cases, his   quibbles
tenures,° and his tricks? Why does he suffer this rude knave   property titles
now to knock him about the sconce° with a dirty shovel, and   head
will not tell him of his action of battery?¹ H'm! This fellow
95   might be in 's time a great buyer of land, with his statutes, his
recognizances, his fines, his double vouchers, his recoveries.²
Is this the fine° of his fines and the recovery° of his recoveries,   end / profit
to have his fine° pate full of fine° dirt? Will his vouchers vouch³   subtle / fine-grained
him no more of his purchases, and double ones too, than the

---

3. *meet*: suitable. The Clown sings garbled snatches of Thomas Lord Vaux's poem "The Aged Lover Renounceth Love," printed in *Tottel's Miscellany* (1557). The extrametrical "O"s and "A"s are probably grunts while digging.
4. *a property of easiness*: something he can do without distress.
5. Has more delicate feeling (because not hardened by callouses).
6. *o'er-offices*: lords it over because of his position, pulls rank on. A "politician" was a schemer for political advantage.
7. Reversal of fortune (literally, the turning of Fortune's wheel).
8. Was it so inexpensive and easy to bring these bones to maturity that they can be treated as loggats (small wooden clubs thrown at a stake)?
9. Subtle distinctions.
1. Legal prosecution for assault.
2. Fines and recoveries were both kinds of lawsuits brought to make legal an agreement to transfer land ownership. The "double voucher" summoned two witnesses to attest to the land's ownership in these cases. *statutes*: mortgages on land, often linked with "recognizances" (bonds acknowledging a particular debt).
3. Guarantee.

100   length and breadth of a pair of indentures?[4] The very convey-
        ances° of his lands will hardly lie in this box;° and must th'in-   *deeds / deed box; coffin*
        heritor° himself have no more, ha?   *owner*

HORATIO   Not a jot more, my lord.

HAMLET   Is not parchment made of sheepskins?

105 HORATIO   Ay, my lord, and of calf-skins too.

HAMLET   They are sheep and calves° that seek out assurance[5] in   *simpletons and fools*
        that. I will speak to this fellow. [*To the* FIRST CLOWN] Whose
        grave's this, sirrah?[6]

FIRST CLOWN   Mine, sir.

110 (*Sings*)   O, a pit of clay for to be made
                    For such a guest is meet.

HAMLET   I think it be thine indeed, for thou liest in't.

FIRST CLOWN   You lie out on't, sir, and therefore it is not yours.
        For my part, I do not lie in't, and yet it is mine.

115 HAMLET   Thou dost lie in't, to be in't and say 'tis thine. 'Tis for
        the dead, not for the quick;° therefore thou liest.   *living*

FIRST CLOWN   'Tis a quick° lie, sir, 'twill away again from me to   *nimble*
        you.

HAMLET   What man dost thou dig it for?

120 FIRST CLOWN   For no man, sir.

HAMLET   What woman, then?

FIRST CLOWN   For none, neither.

HAMLET   Who is to be buried in't?

FIRST CLOWN   One that was a woman, sir; but, rest her soul, she's
125   dead.

HAMLET   How absolute° the knave is! We must speak by the   *precise*
        card,[7] or equivocation will undo us. By the Lord, Horatio, these
        three years I have taken note of it. The age is grown so picked°   *punctilious*
        that the toe of the peasant comes so near the heel of the court-
130   ier he galls his kibe.° [*To the* FIRST CLOWN] How long hast thou   *chafes his heel sore*
        been a grave-maker?

FIRST CLOWN   Of all the days i'th' year I came to't that day that
        our last King Hamlet o'ercame Fortinbras.

HAMLET   How long is that since?

135 FIRST CLOWN   Cannot you tell that? Every fool can tell that. It
        was the very day that young Hamlet was born—he that was
        mad and sent into England.

HAMLET   Ay, marry, why was he sent into England?

FIRST CLOWN   Why, because a was mad. A shall recover his wits
140   there; or if a do not, 'tis no great matter there.

HAMLET   Why?

FIRST CLOWN   'Twill not be seen in him there. There the men
        are as mad as he.

HAMLET   How came he mad?

145 FIRST CLOWN   Very strangely, they say.

HAMLET   How strangely?

FIRST CLOWN   Faith, e'en with losing his wits.

HAMLET   Upon what ground?[8]

---

4. The two copies of a document (written on one sheet
and separated by an irregular cut so that they could later
be proved to be part of one transaction). The dead man's
property (his grave) is hardly bigger than these elaborate
papers.
5. Security, playing on the legal conveyance of a property

title.
6. An address used with inferiors.
7. With precisely defined meanings (literally, by the
directions marked on a mariner's compass card).
8. From what cause? (The Clown takes him to mean "In
what country?")

FIRST CLOWN   Why, here in Denmark. I have been sexton here,
150   man and boy, thirty years.

HAMLET   How long will a man lie i'th' earth ere he rot?

FIRST CLOWN   I'faith, if a be not rotten before a die—as we have
      many pocky corpses nowadays, that will scarce hold the laying
      in⁹—a will last you some eight year or nine year. A tanner will
155   last you nine year.

HAMLET   Why he more than another?

FIRST CLOWN   Why, sir, his hide is so tanned with his trade that
      a will keep out water a great while, and your water is a sore
      decayer of your whoreson° dead body. Here's a skull, now. This   *vile*
160   skull has lain in the earth three-and-twenty years.

HAMLET   Whose was it?

FIRST CLOWN   A whoreson mad fellow's it was. Whose do you
      think it was?

HAMLET   Nay, I know not.

165   FIRST CLOWN   A pestilence on him for a mad rogue—a poured a
      flagon of Rhenish° on my head once! This same skull, sir, was   *Rhine wine*
      Yorick's skull, the King's jester.

HAMLET   This?

FIRST CLOWN   E'en that.

170   HAMLET   Let me see.
      [*He takes the skull*]
      Alas, poor Yorick. I knew him, Horatio—a fellow of infinite
      jest, of most excellent fancy. He hath borne me on his back a
      thousand times; and now, how abhorred my imagination is! My
      gorge rises at it. Here hung those lips that I have kissed I know
175   not how oft. Where be your gibes now, your gambols, your
      songs, your flashes of merriment that were wont to set the table
      on a roar? Not one now to mock your own grinning? Quite
      chop-fallen?¹ Now get you to my lady's chamber and tell her,
      let her paint an inch thick, to this favour° she must come. Make   *appearance*
180   her laugh at that. Prithee, Horatio, tell me one thing.

HORATIO   What's that, my lord?

HAMLET   Dost thou think Alexander looked o' this fashion i'th'
      earth?

HORATIO   E'en so.

185   HAMLET   And smelt so? Pah!
      [*He throws the skull down*]

HORATIO   E'en so, my lord.

HAMLET   To what base uses we may return, Horatio! Why may
      not imagination trace the noble dust of Alexander till a find it
      stopping a bung-hole?°   *opening of a cask*

190   HORATIO   'Twere to consider too curiously° to consider so.   *oversubtly*

HAMLET   No, faith, not a jot; but to follow him thither with mod-
      esty° enough, and likelihood to lead it, as thus: Alexander died,   *reasonable speculation*
      Alexander was buried, Alexander returneth into dust, the dust
      is earth, of earth we make loam,² and why of that loam whereto
195   he was converted might they not stop a beer-barrel?
      Imperial Caesar, dead and turned to clay,
      Might stop a hole to keep the wind away.
      O, that that earth which kept the world in awe

---

9. *pocky . . . in:* bodies riddled with venereal disease that
hardly keep from disintegrating during their burial rites.

1. Dejected; also, with a dropped or lost lower jaw.
2. A mix of clay and straw used as plaster.

Should patch a wall t'expel the winter's flaw!°   *violent wind*
But soft, but soft; aside.
    [HAMLET *and* HORATIO *stand aside.*] *Enter* KING [CLAU-
    DIUS], QUEEN [GERTRUDE], LAERTES, *and a coffin, with*
    [*a* PRIEST *and*] *lords attendant*

200   Here comes the King,
The Queen, the courtiers—who is that they follow,
And with such maimèd rites?³ This doth betoken
The corpse they follow did with desp'rate hand
Fordo it° own life. 'Twas of some estate.°   *Bring down its / rank*
Couch we° a while, and mark.   *Let's lie low*

205 LAERTES   What ceremony else?
HAMLET [*aside to* HORATIO]   That is Laertes, a very noble youth. Mark.
LAERTES   What ceremony else?
PRIEST   Her obsequies have been as far enlarged
As we have warrantise.° Her death was doubtful,⁴   *proper sanction*
210 And but that great command o'ersways the order⁵
She should in ground unsanctified have lodged
Till the last trumpet. For° charitable prayers,   *Rather than*
Shards, flints, and pebbles should be thrown on her,
Yet here she is allowed her virgin rites,
215 Her maiden strewments,⁶ and the bringing home
Of bell and burial.⁷
LAERTES   Must there no more be done?
PRIEST   No more be done.
We should profane the service of the dead
220 To sing sage° requiem and such rest to her   *solemn*
As to peace-parted° souls.   *peacefully deceased*
LAERTES   Lay her i'th' earth,
And from her fair and unpolluted flesh
May violets spring. I tell thee, churlish priest,
A minist'ring angel shall my sister be
225 When thou liest howling.°   *(in hell)*
HAMLET [*aside*]   What, the fair Ophelia!
QUEEN GERTRUDE [*scattering flowers*]   Sweets to the sweet. Farewell.
I hoped thou shouldst have been my Hamlet's wife.
I thought thy bride-bed to have decked, sweet maid,
And not t'have strewed thy grave.
230 LAERTES   O, treble woe
Fall ten times treble on that cursèd head
Whose wicked deed thy most ingenious sense⁸
Deprived thee of!—Hold off the earth a while,
Till I have caught her once more in mine arms.
    [LAERTES] *leaps into the grave*
235 Now pile your dust upon the quick and dead
Till of this flat a mountain you have made
To o'ertop old Pelion, or the skyish head
Of blue Olympus.⁹

---

3. Truncated ceremonies (ordinarily grand for a court funeral).
4. That is, possibly suicide.
5. And if royal authority had not prevailed over the usual ecclesiastical procedure.
6. Flowers strewed over the casket or grave. Throughout northern Europe, funerary flowers of an unmarried girl often included a special wreath that was sometimes afterward hung in the church. (Q2's "crants" [garlands] for F's "rites" specifically evokes this practice.)
7. *the bringing . . . burial:* the taking her to her resting place with the ritual passing bells and funeral service.
8. Quick, perceptive intelligence.
9. In Greek mythology, giants piled Pelion (a mountain in Thessaly) on top of Mount Ossa in an attempt to climb Mount Olympus.

HAMLET [*coming forward*]   What is he whose grief
 Bears such an emphasis,[1] whose phrase° of sorrow   *rhetoric*
240 Conjures the wand'ring stars° and makes them stand   *planets*
 Like wonder-wounded° hearers? This is I,   *awestruck*
 Hamlet the Dane.[2]
   HAMLET *leaps in after* LAERTES
LAERTES The devil take thy soul.
HAMLET Thou pray'st not well.
245 I prithee take thy fingers from my throat,
 For though I am not splenative° and rash,   *quick-tempered*
 Yet have I something in me dangerous,
 Which let thy wiseness fear. Away thy hand.
KING CLAUDIUS [*to* LORDS] Pluck them asunder.
QUEEN GERTRUDE   Hamlet, Hamlet!
ALL THE LORDS Gentlemen!
250 HORATIO [*to* HAMLET]   Good my lord, be quiet.
HAMLET Why, I will fight with him upon this theme
 Until my eyelids will no longer wag.°   *blink*
QUEEN GERTRUDE O my son, what theme?
HAMLET I loved Ophelia. Forty thousand brothers
255 Could not, with all their quantity of love,
 Make up my sum.—What wilt thou do for her?
KING CLAUDIUS O, he is mad, Laertes.
QUEEN GERTRUDE [*to* LAERTES] For love of God, forbear him.°   *let him alone*
HAMLET [*to* LAERTES] 'Swounds,° show me what thou'lt do.   *By Christ's wounds*
260 Woot° weep, woot fight, woot fast, woot tear thyself,   *Wilt thou*
 Woot drink up eisel,° eat a crocodile?   *vinegar*
 I'll do't. Dost thou come here to whine,
 To outface me with leaping in her grave?
 Be buried quick with her, and so will I.
265 And if thou prate of mountains, let them throw
 Millions of acres on us, till our ground,
 Singeing his pate° against the burning zone,°   *his head / sun's sphere*
 Make Ossa[3] like a wart. Nay, an° thou'lt mouth,°   *if / speak excessively*
 I'll rant as well as thou.
KING CLAUDIUS [*to* LAERTES] This is mere madness,
270 And thus a while the fit will work on him.
 Anon,° as patient as the female dove   *Soon*
 When that her golden couplets are disclosed,°   *chicks are hatched*
 His silence will sit drooping.
HAMLET [*to* LAERTES]   Hear you, sir,
 What is the reason that you use me thus?
275 I loved you ever. But it is no matter.
 Let Hercules himself do what he may,
 The cat will mew, and dog will have his day.[4]   *Exit*
KING CLAUDIUS I pray you, good Horatio, wait upon him.
          [*Exit*] HORATIO
[*To* LAERTES] Strengthen your patience in° our last night's   *with*
  speech.
280 We'll put the matter to the present push.°—   *the immediate trial*
 Good Gertrude, set some watch over your son.—

---

1. A violent expression.
2. Normally the title of the King of Denmark.
3. Greek mountain (see note to line 238).

4. *Let . . . day:* Despite Laertes' Herculean ranting, my
day will come.

This grave shall have a living monument.[5]
An hour of quiet shortly shall we see;
Till then, in patience our proceeding be.   *Exeunt*

5.2

Enter [Prince] HAMLET *and* HORATIO

HAMLET   So much for this, sir. Now, let me see, the other.°   *other matter*
You do remember all the circumstance?°   *state of things then*
HORATIO   Remember it, my lord!
HAMLET   Sir, in my heart there was a kind of fighting
5   That would not let me sleep. Methought I lay
Worse than the mutines in the bilboes.[1] Rashly°—   *Impulsively*
And praised be rashness for it: let us know°   *acknowledge*
Our indiscretion° sometime serves us well   *unreasoned action*
When our dear plots do pall,° and that should teach us   *grow weak*
10   There's a divinity that shapes our ends,
Rough-hew them° how we will—   *Form them roughly*
HORATIO   That is most certain.
HAMLET   Up from my cabin,
My sea-gown scarfed about me in the dark,
15   Groped I to find out them, had my desire,
Fingered° their packet, and in fine° withdrew   *Stole / finally*
To mine own room again, making so bold,
My fears forgetting manners, to unseal
Their grand commission; where I found, Horatio—
20   O royal knavery!—an exact command,
Larded° with many several° sorts of reasons   *Elaborated / different*
Importing° Denmark's health, and England's, too,   *Concerning*
With ho! such bugs and goblins in my life,[2]
That on the supervise,° no leisure bated,°   *reading / allowed*
25   No, not to stay° the grinding of the axe,   *await*
My head should be struck off.
HORATIO   Is't possible?
HAMLET [*giving it to him*]   Here's the commission. Read it at more leisure.
But wilt thou hear me how I did proceed?
HORATIO   I beseech you.
30   HAMLET   Being thus benetted round with villainies—
Ere I could make a prologue to my brains,
They had begun the play[3]—I sat me down,
Devised a new commission, wrote it fair.[4]
I once did hold it, as our statists° do,   *statesmen*
35   A baseness to write fair, and laboured much
How to forget that learning;[5] but, sir, now
It did me yeoman's service.[6] Wilt thou know
Th'effect of what I wrote?
HORATIO   Ay, good my lord.

---

5. A lasting memorial; hinting that Hamlet, now "living,"
will soon be sacrificed to Ophelia's memory.
5.2 Location: A stateroom of the castle.
1. Worse than the mutineers in the ankle fetters.
2. Such fanciful horrors that would result were I to
remain alive. *bugs*: bugbears.
3. *Ere . . . play*: Hamlet's brains "acted" before he consciously thought out a plan.
4. In the professional handwriting of finished (published) documents.

5. *I once . . . learning*: In the sixteenth century, the upper
echelons of government became increasingly profes-
sionalized; Hamlet implies that these newly elevated
officials are prone to snobbish pretensions, covering up
their education as common clerks, and he confesses
that he once shared their snobbery.
6. It served me valiantly. English yeomen (free landhold-
ers) were famous for military strength, supposedly
because they fought for their national interest rather than
for base pay.

HAMLET · An earnest conjuration° from the King,   *appeal*
40 As England was his faithful tributary,
As love between them like the palm should flourish,
As peace should still her wheaten garland[7] wear
And stand a comma[8] 'tween their amities,
And many such like 'as'es of great charge,[9]
45 That on the view and know of these contents,
Without debatement further more or less,
He should the bearers put to sudden death,
Not shriving-time[1] allowed.
HORATIO   How was this sealed?
HAMLET Why, even in that was heaven ordinant.°   *guiding*
50 I had my father's signet in my purse,
Which was the model of that Danish seal;
Folded the writ up in the form of th'other,
Subscribed° it, gave't th'impression,° placed it safely, *Signed / seal (in wax)*
The changeling[2] never known. Now the next day
55 Was our sea-fight; and what to this was sequent°   *subsequent*
Thou know'st already.
HORATIO So Guildenstern and Rosencrantz go to't.
HAMLET Why, man, they did make love to this employment.
They are not near my conscience. Their defeat°   *destruction*
60 Doth by their own insinuation grow.
'Tis dangerous when the baser nature comes
Between the pass and fell incensèd points[3]
Of mighty opposites.°   *opponents*
HORATIO   Why, what a king is this!
HAMLET Does it not, think'st thee, stand me now upon[4]—
65 He that hath killed my king and whored my mother,
Popped in between th'election and my hopes,
Thrown out his angle° for my proper° life,   *fishhook/own*
And with such coz'nage°—is't not perfect conscience *trickery*
To quit° him with this arm? And is't not to be damned *requite*
70 To let this canker° of our nature come   *cancerous sore*
In° further evil?   *Into*
HORATIO It must be shortly known to him from England
What is the issue° of the business there.   *result*
HAMLET It will be short. The interim's mine,
75 And a man's life's no more than to say 'one'.[5]
But I am very sorry, good Horatio,
That to Laertes I forgot myself;
For by the image° of my cause I see   *mirror's reflection*
The portraiture of his. I'll court his favours.
80 But sure, the bravery° of his grief did put me *ostentation*
Into a tow'ring passion.
HORATIO   Peace, who comes here?
  Enter young OSRIC, *a courtier [taking off his hat]*

---

7. Like the palm tree, an emblem of peace and prosperity.
8. And hold their interests separate but still connected (unlike a period, which would cut off "amity").
9. Weighty clauses beginning with "as"; asses bearing heavy loads.
1. Time for final confession and absolution, a part of the state ritual of legal executions.

2. A malicious elf child substituted for an infant, as Hamlet swaps his counterfeit letter for their authentic one.
3. *the pass . . . points:* fencing language; the thrust ("pass") and fiercely angry ("fell") rapiers.
4. Rest incumbent upon me.
5. And life lasts no longer than it takes to pronounce ("say") the monosyllable "one."

OSRIC   Your lordship is right welcome back to Denmark.

HAMLET   I humbly thank you, sir. [*To* HORATIO] Dost know this
water-fly?

85   HORATIO   No, my good lord.

HAMLET   Thy state is the more gracious,° for 'tis a vice to know   *blessed*
him. He hath much land, and fertile. Let a beast be lord of
beasts, and his crib shall stand at the king's mess.[6] 'Tis a chuff,°   *rich boor; jackdaw*
but, as I say, spacious in the possession of dirt.

90   OSRIC   Sweet lord, if your friendship were at leisure I should
impart a thing to you from his majesty.

HAMLET   I will receive it, sir, with all diligence of spirit. Put your
bonnet° to his right use; 'tis for the head.   *hat*

OSRIC   I thank your lordship, 'tis very hot.

95   HAMLET   No, believe me, 'tis very cold. The wind is northerly.

OSRIC   It is indifferent° cold, my lord, indeed.   *rather*

HAMLET   Methinks it is very sultry and hot for my complexion.°   *constitution*

OSRIC   Exceedingly, my lord. It is very sultry, as 'twere—I cannot
tell how. But, my lord, his majesty bade me signify to you that

100   a° has laid a great wager on your head. Sir, this is the matter.   *he*

HAMLET   I beseech you, remember.[7]

OSRIC   Nay, good my lord, for mine ease, in good faith.[8]

102.1   *Sir here is newly come to court Laertes, believe me, an*
absolute gentleman, full of most excellent differences,°   *superior qualities*
of very soft° society and great showing.° Indeed, to speak   *pleasing / appearance*
feelingly° of him, he is the card or calendar of gentry,[9]   *appreciatively*

102.5   *for you shall find in him the continent of what part[1] a*
gentleman would see.

HAMLET   *Sir, his definement suffers no perdition in you,[2]*
though I know to divide him inventorially would dizzy
th'arithmetic of memory, and yet but yaw neither in

102.10   *respect of his quick sail.[3] But in the verity of extolment,°*   *in truthful praise*
I take him to be a soul of great article,[4] and his infusion°   *inborn essence*
of such dearth° and rareness as, to make true diction[5] of   *preciousness*
him, his semblable° is his mirror, and who else would   *likeness*
trace him his umbrage, nothing more.[6]

102.15   OSRIC   *Your lordship speaks most infallibly of him.*

HAMLET   *The concernancy,° sir? Why do we wrap the gen-*   *relevance (to us)*
tleman in our more rawer breath?[7]

OSRIC   *Sir?*

HORATIO   *Is't not possible to understand in another*
102.20   *tongue? You will to't, sir, rarely.[8]*

HAMLET   *What imports the nomination° of this gentleman?*   *mention*

OSRIC   *Of Laertes?*

---

6. *Let . . . mess:* If an animal owned enough herds, even
it might find a place at the King's table. *crib:* manger.
7. "Remember your courtesy," the conventional expression inviting a subordinate to put his hat back on.
8. A conventional expression declining Hamlet's invitation. Q2 adds the following passage, lines 102.1–102.34,
in place of lines 103–4, placing a comma instead of a
period after "faith."
9. The model of gentlemanly behavior. *card:* chart or
map. *calendar:* account book, directory.
1. Attribute or quality, playing on "region" (to which
Laertes is the "card"). *continent:* embodiment, continuing the geographical pun.
2. Your picture of him ("definement") loses none of the
man's real excellence.

3. *to divide . . . sail:* to list his qualities individually would
confuse the memory's reckoning up (through recount-
ing vast numbers), and yet only steer erratically ("yaw")
around Laertes' skills—that is, the description would
only approximate his virtues.
4. Large scope (?); excellent qualities (?).
5. To speak truly.
6. And whoever imitates him is like his shadow
("umbrage"), not the real thing at all.
7. Our less refined words (since we are so much inferior to Laertes).
8. *Is't . . . rarely:* Can't he understand his words in
another man's mouth? You will have your joke, sir, splendidly.

HORATIO [*aside to* HAMLET]   *His purse is empty already; all*
　　's golden words are spent.

102.25　HAMLET [*to* OSRIC]   *Of him, sir.*

OSRIC   *I know you are not ignorant—*

HAMLET   *I would you did, sir; yet, in faith, if you did it*
　　would not much approve° me. Well, sir?　　　　　　commend

OSRIC   *You are not ignorant of what excellence Laertes is.*

102.30　HAMLET   *I dare not confess that, lest I should compare*
　　with him in excellence.[9] *But to know a man well were*
　　to know himself.[1]

OSRIC   *I mean, sir, for his weapon. But in the imputation*
　　laid on him by them, in his meed° he's unfellowed.°　　merit / unmatched
Sir, you are not ignorant of what excellence Laertes is at his
weapon.

105　HAMLET   What's his weapon?

OSRIC   Rapier and dagger.

HAMLET   That's two of his weapons. But well.

OSRIC   The King, sir, hath wagered with him six Barbary horses,
against the which he imponed,° as I take it, six French rapiers　　staked
110　and poniards, with their assigns° as girdle,° hanger,[2] or so.　accessories / sword belt
Three of the carriages, in faith, are very dear to fancy, very
responsive to the hilts, most delicate carriages, and of very liberal conceit.[3]

HAMLET   What call you the carriages?[4]

114.1　HORATIO   [*aside to* HAMLET]   *I know you must be edified*
　　by the margin[5] *ere you had done.*

115　OSRIC   The carriages, sir, are the hangers.

HAMLET   The phrase would be more germane to the matter if we
could carry cannon by our sides. I would it might be hangers
till then. But on: six Barbary horses against six French swords,
their assigns, and three liberal-conceited carriages—that's the
120　French bet against the Danish. Why is this 'imponed', as you
call it?

OSRIC   The King, sir, hath laid,° sir, that in a dozen passes　　placed his bet
between you and him he shall not exceed you three hits.[6] He
hath on't twelve for nine,[7] and it would come to immediate
125　trial if your lordship would vouchsafe the answer.[8]

HAMLET   How if I answer no?

OSRIC   I mean, my lord, the opposition of your person in trial.

HAMLET   Sir, I will walk here in the hall. If it please his majesty,
'tis the breathing° time of day with me. Let the foils be brought;　exercising
130　the gentleman willing, an° the King hold his purpose, I will　　　if
win for him an I can. If not, I'll gain nothing but my shame
and the odd hits.

OSRIC   Shall I re-deliver you e'en so?

HAMLET   To this effect, sir; after what flourish your nature will.

9. Claim to match him (since, proverbially, only excellence recognizes excellence).
1. For in order to know another man truly, one must
know oneself.
2. Attaching straps.
3. *are . . . conceit*: capture the imagination ("fancy")
and match or echo ("respond to") the ornamentation on
the rapiers' hilts; further, they are finely wrought ("delicate") and of an elaborate ("liberal") design.
4. Osric's inflated term for "hangers," or straps. Here Q2
adds the following aside by Horatio, lines 114.1–114.2.

5. Must be informed by an explanatory note (from the
margin of a book).
6. Laertes must score three more "hits" than Hamlet
out of twelve bouts of swordplay to win the wager.
7. If "he" is Laertes, Osric may mean "He has bet twelve
passes for nine hits" (a greater challenge than the King's
terms, by which he would only need eight hits to win).
8. Would accept the challenge (Osric's meaning, and the
only honorable response). In the next line, Hamlet
deliberately misunderstands "answer" as "(any) reply."

135 OSRIC I commend my duty° to your lordship.   *dedicate my service*

HAMLET Yours, yours.   [*Exit* OSRIC]
He does well to commend° it himself; there are no tongues   *recommend*
else for 's turn.°   *purpose*

HORATIO This lapwing runs away with the shell on his head.[9]

140 HAMLET A did comply with his dug[1] before a sucked it. Thus
has he—and many more of the same bevy that I know the
drossy° age dotes on—only got the tune of the time and out-   *worthless*
ward habit of encounter,[2] a kind of yeasty collection which
carries them through and through the most fanned and win-
145 nowed opinions;[3] and do but blow them to their trial, the
bubbles are out.[4]

Enter a LORD

146.1 LORD [*to* HAMLET] *My lord, his majesty commended him
to you by young Osric, who brings back to him that you
attend him in the hall. He sends to know if your pleasure
hold to play with Laertes, or that you will take longer*
146.5 *time.*

HAMLET *I am constant to my purposes; they follow the
King's pleasure. If his fitness speaks, mine is ready, now
or whensoever, provided I be so able as now.*

LORD *The King and Queen and all are coming down.*

146.10 HAMLET *In happy time.*

LORD *The Queen desires you to use some gentle entertainment[5] to Laertes before you fall to play.*

HAMLET *She well instructs me.*   [*Exit* LORD]

HORATIO *You will lose, my lord.*

HORATIO You will lose this wager, my lord.

HAMLET I do not think so. Since he went into France, I have
been in continual practice. I shall win at the odds. But thou
150 wouldst not think how all here about my heart—but it is no
matter.

HORATIO Nay, good my lord—

HAMLET It is but foolery, but it is such a kind of gain-giving° as   *misgiving*
would perhaps trouble a woman.

155 HORATIO If your mind dislike anything, obey it. I will forestall
their repair° hither, and say you are not fit.   *coming*

HAMLET Not a whit. We defy augury. There's a special providence[6] in the fall of a sparrow. If it be now, 'tis not to come.
If it be not to come, it will be now. If it be not now, yet it will
160 come. The readiness is all. Since no man has aught of what he
leaves, what is't to leave betimes?[7]

---

9. The newly hatched chicks of the plover ("lapwing")
were supposed to scurry about still wearing their
eggshells, a reference to the bonnet that Osric has finally
put back on as well as to the courtier's brainless chirping.
1. He bowed politely to his mother's breast.
2. *the tune . . . encounter:* the fashionable turns of
speech ("tune of the time") and the formulas ('habit')
of courteous conversation ("encounter").
3. *a kind of . . . opinions:* their empty clichés get them
through or pass for the most carefully considered wisdom (which is "fanned and winnowed" like wheat separated from chaff during threshing). *yeasty collection:* a
frothy and inflated repertoire of speech and behavior.
4. And if you test them by blowing on them—as Hamlet does by speaking to Osric—they pop and dissolve. In
Q2, the following passage, lines 146.1–146.14, replaces
Horatio's line in F, "You will lose this wager, my lord."

5. To behave with conciliatory courtesy. Shakespeare
seems to have considered two alternative explanations
for Hamlet's final graciousness toward Laertes; here, in
Q2, the Queen's maternal guidance nudges him to it,
while F instead supplies Hamlet's own regret for his
graveside brawling in 5.2.76–81.
6. God's direction for a specific event (over and above
"general providence," the whole shape of God's design).
Compare Matthew 10:29. The specifically Protestant
theology of God's predestinating power is more explicit
in Q1's version of this line: "There's a predestinate providence / In the fall of a sparrow."
7. Since man does not truly possess what he must leave
behind him (worldly things and earthly flesh), why does
it matter to leave them sooner ("betimes")? Q2 reads
"Since no man of ought he leaves, knows what is't to
leave betimes, let be."

Enter KING [CLAUDIUS], QUEEN [GERTRUDE], LAERTES,
and lords, with [OSRIC *and*] *other attendants with trum-*
pets, drums, cushions, foils, and gauntlets; a table, and
flagons of wine on it

KING CLAUDIUS   Come, Hamlet, come, and take this hand from me.

HAMLET [*to* LAERTES]   Give me your pardon, sir. I've done you wrong;
But pardon't as you are a gentleman.

165 This presence° knows,   *royal company*
And you must needs have heard, how I am punished
With sore distraction.° What I have done   *agitation; insanity*
That might your nature, honour, and exception°   *disapproval*
Roughly awake, I here proclaim was madness.

170 Was't Hamlet wronged Laertes? Never Hamlet.
If Hamlet from himself be ta'en away,
And when he's not himself does wrong Laertes,
Then Hamlet does it not, Hamlet denies it.
Who does it then? His madness. If't be so,

175 Hamlet is of the faction that is wronged.
His madness is poor Hamlet's enemy.
Sir, in this audience
Let my disclaiming from a purposed evil[8]
Free me so far in your most generous thoughts

180 That I have shot mine arrow o'er the house
And hurt my brother.[9]

LAERTES   I am satisfied in nature,
Whose motive in this case should stir me most
To my revenge. But in my terms of honour[1]
I stand aloof, and will no reconcilement

185 Till by some elder masters of known honour
I have a voice and precedent of peace[2]
To keep my name ungored;° but till that time   *my reputation intact*
I do receive your offered love like love,
And will not wrong it.

HAMLET   I do embrace it freely,

190 And will this brothers' wager frankly° play.—   *freely*
[*To attendants*]   Give us the foils. Come on.

LAERTES [*to attendants*]   Come, one for me.

HAMLET   I'll be your foil,[3] Laertes. In mine ignorance
Your skill shall, like a star i'th' darkest night,
Stick° fiery off indeed.   *Sparkle; jab*

195 LAERTES   You mock me, sir.

HAMLET   No, by this hand.

KING CLAUDIUS   Give them the foils, young Osric. Cousin Hamlet,
You know the wager?

HAMLET   Very well, my lord.
Your grace hath laid the odds o'th' weaker side.

200 KING CLAUDIUS   I do not fear it; I have seen you both.
But since he is bettered,° we have therefore odds.°   *favored / handicapping*

LAERTES   [*taking a foil*]   This is too heavy; let me see another.

---

8. Let my disavowal of evil intention.
9. F's reading is "mother."
1. But where my social standing as a man of honor is
concerned.
2. *Till . . . peace:* Until the consensus of men of author-

itative standing, judging by the standards of tradition
(precedent), holds that I can make an honorable peace.
3. Flattering contrast. Jewels were often set with a
piece of metal foil under them to increase their glitter.

HAMLET [*taking a foil*]   This likes° me well. These foils have all   *pleases*
      a° length?   *the same*
OSRIC   Ay, my good lord.
      [HAMLET *and* LAERTES] *prepare to play*
KING CLAUDIUS [*to attendants*]   Set me the stoups° of wine upon   *flagons*
205   that table.
      If Hamlet give the first or second hit,
      Or quit in answer of the third exchange,[4]
      Let all the battlements their ordnance° fire.   *canons*
      The King shall drink to Hamlet's better breath,°   *energy*
210   And in the cup an union[5] shall he throw
      Richer than that which four successive kings
      In Denmark's crown have worn. Give me the cups,
      And let the kettle° to the trumpet speak,   *kettledrum*
      The trumpet to the cannoneer without,
215   The cannons to the heavens, the heaven to earth,
      'Now the King drinks to Hamlet'.
           Trumpets the while [*he drinks*]
                              Come, begin.
      And you, the judges, bear a wary eye.
HAMLET [*to* LAERTES]   Come on, sir.
LAERTES   Come, my lord.
           They play
220 HAMLET   One.
      LAERTES   No.
      HAMLET [*to* OSRIC]   Judgement.
      OSRIC   A hit, a very palpable hit.
      LAERTES   Well, again.
225 KING CLAUDIUS   Stay.° Give me drink. Hamlet, this pearl is thine.   *Stop*
      Here's to thy health.—
           Drum [*and*] *trumpets sound, and shot goes off*
                        Give him the cup.
HAMLET   I'll play this bout first. Set it by a while.—
      Come.
           They play again
            Another hit. What say you?
LAERTES   A touch, a touch, I do confess.
KING CLAUDIUS   Our son shall win.
230 QUEEN GERTRUDE   He's fat° and scant of breath.—   *sweaty*
      Here, Hamlet, take my napkin.° Rub thy brows.   *handkerchief*
      The Queen carouses to thy fortune, Hamlet.
HAMLET   Good madam.
KING CLAUDIUS   Gertrude, do not drink.
QUEEN GERTRUDE   I will, my lord, I pray you pardon me.
           She drinks [*then offers the cup to* HAMLET]
235 KING CLAUDIUS [*aside*]   It is the poisoned cup; it is too late.
      HAMLET   I dare not drink yet, madam; by and by.
      QUEEN GERTRUDE [*to* HAMLET]   Come, let me wipe thy face.
      LAERTES [*aside to* CLAUDIUS]   My lord, I'll hit him now.
      KING CLAUDIUS [*aside to* LAERTES]   I do not think't.
240 LAERTES [*aside*]   And yet 'tis almost 'gainst my conscience.

---

4. Or repay Laertes' victories by winning the third bout.

5. A pearl, of exceptional quality. Claudius is perhaps proposing to dissolve the gem, as Cleopatra did in a much-repeated legend.

HAMLET   Come for the third, Laertes, you but dally.
I pray you pass° with your best violence.   *thrust*
I am afeard you make a wanton° of me.   *spoiled child*
LAERTES   Say you so? Come on.
        [*They*] *play*
OSRIC   Nothing neither way.
LAERTES [*to* HAMLET]   Have at you now!
        [LAERTES *wounds* HAMLET.] *In scuffling, they change*
        rapiers[6] [*and* HAMLET *wounds* LAERTES]
245   KING CLAUDIUS [*to attendants*]   Part them, they are incensed.
HAMLET [*to* LAERTES]   Nay, come again.
        The QUEEN *falls down*[7]
OSRIC   Look to the Queen there, ho!
HORATIO   They bleed on both sides. [*To* HAMLET] How is't, my lord?
OSRIC   How is't, Laertes?
LAERTES   Why, as a woodcock to mine own springe,° Osric.   *snare*
250   I am justly killed with mine own treachery.
HAMLET   How does the Queen?
KING CLAUDIUS   She swoons to see them bleed.
QUEEN GERTRUDE   No, no, the drink, the drink! O my dear Hamlet,
The drink, the drink—I am poisoned.   [*She dies*]
HAMLET   O villainy! Ho! Let the door be locked!   [*Exit* OSRIC]
255   Treachery, seek it out.
LAERTES   It is here, Hamlet. Hamlet, thou art slain.
No med'cine in the world can do thee good.
In thee there is not half an hour of life.
The treacherous instrument is in thy hand,
260   Unbated° and envenomed. The foul practice   *Not blunted*
Hath turned itself on me. Lo, here I lie,
Never to rise again. Thy mother's poisoned.
I can no more. The King, the King's to blame.
HAMLET   The point envenomed too? Then, venom, to thy work.
        [*He*] *hurts* KING [CLAUDIUS]
265   ALL THE COURTIERS   Treason, treason!
KING CLAUDIUS   O yet defend me, friends! I am but hurt.
HAMLET   Here, thou incestuous, murd'rous, damnèd Dane,
Drink off this potion. Is thy union[8] here?
Follow my mother.   KING [CLAUDIUS] *dies*
LAERTES   He is justly served.
270   It is a poison tempered° by himself.   *mixed*
Exchange forgiveness with me, noble Hamlet.
Mine and my father's death come not upon thee,[9]
Nor thine on me.   LAERTES *dies*
HAMLET   Heaven make thee free of it! I follow thee.
275   I am dead, Horatio. Wretched Queen, adieu!
You that look pale and tremble at this chance,
That are but mutes° or audience to this act,   *nonspeaking actors*
Had I but time—as this fell sergeant[1] Death
Is strict in his arrest—O, I could tell you—

6. *In . . . rapiers*: from F. While Q2 lacks any stage direction here, Q1 has "They catch one another's Rapiers," suggesting that each combatant is trying to disarm the other with his free hand. Q1 also supplies daggers at line 161; these would presumably have been dropped so that each man would have a free hand.
7. This stage direction and the one at line 253 are taken

from Q1, where they occur together.
8. Referring to both the pearl and his incestuous marriage to Gertrude.
9. May your soul not be judged accountable for our murders.
1. As this fierce sheriff's officer.

280   But let it be. Horatio, I am dead,
         Thou liv'st. Report me and my cause aright
         To the unsatisfied.

HORATIO   Never believe it.
         I am more an antique Roman than a Dane.²
         Here's yet some liquor left.

HAMLET   As thou'rt a man,

285   Give me the cup. Let go. By heaven, I'll ha't.
         O God, Horatio, what a wounded name,
         Things standing thus unknown, shall live behind me!
         If thou didst ever hold me in thy heart,
         Absent thee from felicity a while,

290   And in this harsh world draw thy breath in pain
         To tell my story.

             March afar off, and shout within
                    What warlike noise is this?

         Enter OSRIC

OSRIC   Young Fortinbras, with conquest come from Poland,
         To th'ambassadors of England gives
         This warlike volley.°   *military salute*

HAMLET   O, I die, Horatio!

295   The potent poison quite o'ercrows³ my spirit.
         I cannot live to hear the news from England,
         But I do prophesy th'election lights
         On Fortinbras. He has my dying voice.⁴
         So tell him, with th'occurrents,° more and less,   *events*

300   Which have solicited.⁵ The rest is silence.
         O, O, O, O!⁶   *HAMLET dies*

HORATIO   Now cracks a noble heart. Good night, sweet prince,
         And flights of angels sing thee to thy rest.—
         Why does the drum come hither?

         Enter FORTINBRAS *with the English* AMBASSADORS, *with*
         drumme[r], colours, and attendants

305 FORTINBRAS   Where is this sight?

HORATIO   What is it ye would see?
         If aught of woe or wonder, cease your search.

FORTINBRAS   This quarry cries on havoc.⁷ O proud death,
         What feast is toward° in thine eternal cell   *preparing*

310   That thou so many princes at a shot
         So bloodily hast struck!

AMBASSADOR   The sight is dismal,
         And our affairs from England come too late.
         The ears are senseless that should give us hearing
         To tell him° his commandment is fulfilled,   *(Claudius)*

315   That Rosencrantz and Guildenstern are dead.
         Where should we have our thanks?

HORATIO   Not from his mouth,
         Had it th'ability of life to thank you.

---

2. Ancient ("antique") Romans generally regarded suicide as preferable to dishonor; in particular, they believed that servants or retainers should not outlive their master's overthrow.

3. Announces triumph over, like the victorious rooster in a cockfight.

4. Vote. Because Denmark is an elective monarchy, Fortinbras can only become King by receiving the "voice," or vote, of electors like Hamlet.

5. Some editors assume that the sentence is grammatically incomplete, broken off by death. Hamlet seems to refer to the events that have moved ("solicited") him to have his story told and to give his support to Fortinbras.

6. These exclamations, omitted from Q2, might be suggestive stage directions for death throes, rather than scripted cries.

7. All this slaughtered game ("quarry") proclaims a massacre.

He never gave commandment for their death.
But since so jump° upon this bloody question°   *immediately / matter*
320   You from the Polack wars, and you from England,
Are here arrived, give order that these bodies
High on a stage be placèd to the view;
And let me speak to th' yet unknowing world
How these things came about. So shall you hear
325   Of carnal, bloody, and unnatural acts,
Of accidental judgements,° casual° slaughters,   *retributions / chance*
Of deaths put on° by cunning and forced cause;   *instigated*
And, in this upshot, purposes mistook
Fall'n on th'inventors' heads. All this can I
330   Truly deliver.
FORTINBRAS   Let us haste to hear it,
And call the noblest to the audience.
For me, with sorrow I embrace my fortune.
I have some rights of memory[8] in this kingdom,
Which now to claim my vantage° doth invite me.   *favorable opportunity*
335   HORATIO   Of that I shall have also cause to speak,
And from his mouth whose voice will draw on more.[9]
But let this same be presently performed,
Even whiles men's minds are wild, lest more mischance
On° plots and errors happen.   *On top of*
FORTINBRAS   Let four captains
340   Bear Hamlet like a soldier to the stage,
For he was likely, had he been put on,°   *put to the test*
To have proved° most royally; and for his passage,   *shown himself; acted*
The soldiers' music and the rites of war
Speak loudly for him.
345   Take up the body. Such a sight as this
Becomes the field,[1] but here shows° much amiss.   *appears*
Go, bid the soldiers shoot.

                    Exeunt, marching [with the bodies]; after
                    the which, a peal of ordnance are shot off

---

8. *of memory:* unforgotten; traditional.
9. Whose choice will induce more votes of support.

1. Is most appropriate to a battlefield.

Twelfth Night

Shakespeare's contemporary Thomas Coryat wrote that he witnessed something quite remarkable when he went to the theater in Venice: "I saw women act, a thing that I never saw before." That an Englishman had to travel abroad to see women actors for the first time is not surprising. All the great women's roles in Elizabethan and Jacobean plays were written to be performed by trained adolescent boys, and boys played the female parts as well in all grammar school and university productions. But what struck Coryat in Venice was neither the gratifying naturalness of finally seeing women play women's parts nor the comparative inadequacy of English boy actors. Rather, he was impressed that the women actors managed to hold their own in representing the female sex: "They performed it," he writes, "with as good a grace, as ever I saw any masculine Actor."

Recent scholars have observed that there were in fact occasions in which audiences in England could have seen women performing: troupes from abroad, including women actors, occasionally toured England, and English women performed in the theatrical spectacles known as masques and in other entertainments. But in England, women did not perform on the public stage (the word "actress" had not yet entered the English language), and the remarks of Coryat and others suggest that their absence was rarely if ever lamented. The boy actors were evidently extraordinarily skillful, and the audiences were sufficiently immersed in the conventions both of theater and of social life in general to accept gesture, makeup, and above all dress as a convincing representation of femininity.

Twelfth Night, or What You Will, written for Shakespeare's all-male company, plays brilliantly with these conventions. The comedy depends on an actor's ability to transform himself, through costume, voice, and gesture, into a young noblewoman, Viola, who transforms herself, through costume, voice, and gesture, into a young man, Cesario. The play's delicious complications follow from the emotional crosscurrents that Viola's transformation engenders. Shipwrecked on a strange coast and bereft of her twin brother, the disguised Viola finds a place in the service of the powerful Duke Orsino, with whom she promptly falls in love. Orsino is in love with Lady Olivia, a wealthy aristocrat whose household includes, among its servants and dependents, a steward or house manager, a waiting-gentlewoman, a professional entertainer, and a down-at-the-heels, perpetually drunken uncle. When Orsino sends Cesario to help him woo the proud Olivia, Olivia not only rejects the Duke's suit but falls in love with his messenger. Discomfited to learn that she is the object of Olivia's love, Viola reflects on the plot's impassioned triangle:

> My master loves her dearly,
> And I, poor monster, fond as much on him,
> And she, mistaken, seems to dote on me.
> What will become of this?
>
> (2.2.31–34)

"Poor monster": in *Twelfth Night,* clothes do not simply reveal or disguise identity; they partly constitute identity—or so Viola playfully imagines—making her a strange, hybrid creature. To be sure, she understands perfectly well the narrow biological definition of her sex (though in the characteristically male-centered language of Shakespeare's culture, she phrases that definition in terms of what she "lacks" [3.4.269]). Yet there is something almost magical in this play about costume, so that even at the close, when identities have been sorted out and the couples happily matched, Orsino cannot bring himself to call his bride-to-be by her rightful name or to address her as a woman:

Cesario, come—
For so you shall be while you are a man;
But when in other habits you are seen,
Orsino's mistress, and his fancy's queen.
(5.1.372–75)

It would have been simple for Shakespeare to devise a concluding scene in which Viola appears in women's "habits," but he goes out of his way to leave her in men's clothes and hence to disrupt with a delicate comic touch the return to the "normal." The transforming power of costume unsettles fixed categories of gender and social class, and allows characters to explore emotional territory that a culture officially hostile to same-sex desire and cross-class marriage would ordinarily have ruled out of bounds. In *Twelfth Night,* conventional expectations repeatedly give way to a different way of perceiving the world.

Shakespeare wrote *Twelfth Night* around 1601. He had already written such comedies as *A Midsummer Night's Dream, Much Ado About Nothing,* and *As You Like It,* with their playful, subtly ironic investigations of the ways in which heterosexual couples are produced out of the murkier crosscurrents of male and female friendships; as interesting, perhaps, he had probably just recently completed *Hamlet,* with its unprecedented exploration of mourning, betrayal, antic humor, and tragic isolation. *Twelfth Night* would prove to be, in the view of many critics, both the most perfect and in some sense the last of the great festive comedies. Shakespeare returned to comedy later in his career, but always with more insistent overtones of bitterness, loss, and grief. There are dark notes in *Twelfth Night* as well: Olivia is in mourning for her brother, Viola thinks that her brother, too, is dead, Antonio believes that he has been betrayed by the man he loves, Orsino threatens to kill Cesario. Desire is repeatedly linked to frustration and loss. But these notes are swept up in the current of sweet music that pervades the play, and the characters are all drawn into a giddy, carnivalesque dance of illusion, disguise, folly, and clowning.

The play's subtitle, *What You Will,* underscores the celebratory spirit associated with Twelfth Night, the Feast of the Epiphany (January 6), which in Elizabethan England marked the culminating night of the traditional Christmas revels. On Twelfth Night 1601, the queen's guest of honor was a twenty-eight-year-old Italian nobleman, Don Virginio Orsino, Duke of Bracciano. Orsino wrote to his wife that he was entertained that night with "a mingled comedy, with pieces of music and dances." Since the company that performed was the Lord Chamberlain's Men—Shakespeare's company—it has been argued that the comedy was *Twelfth Night,* but there is no scholarly consensus on this hypothesis. The title, in any case, would for Shakespeare's contemporaries have conjured up a whole series of time-honored festivities associated with the midwinter season. A rigidly hierarchical social order that ordinarily demanded deference, sobriety, and strict obedience to authority temporarily gave way to raucous rituals of inversion: young boys were crowned for a day as bishops and carried through the streets in mock religious processions; abstemiousness was toppled by bouts of heavy drinking and feasting; the spirit of parody, folly, and misrule reigned briefly in places normally reserved for stern-faced moralists and sober judges.

The fact that these festivities were associated with Christian holidays—the Epiphany marked the visit of the Three Kings to Bethlehem to worship the Christ child—did not altogether obscure the continuities with pagan winter rituals such as the Roman Saturnalia, with its comparably explosive release from everyday discipline into a disorderly realm of belly laughter and belly cheer. Puritans emphasized these continuities in launching a fierce attack on the Elizabethan festive calendar and its whole ethos, just as they attacked the theater for what they saw as its links with paganism, idleness, and sexual license. Elizabethan and Jacobean authorities in the church and the state had their own concerns about idleness and subversion, but they generally protected and patronized both festive ritual and theater on the grounds that these provided a valuable release from tensions that might otherwise prove dangerous. Sobriety, piety, and discipline were no doubt admirable virtues, but most human beings were not saints. "Dost thou think because thou art virtuous," the drunken Sir Toby asks the censorious steward Malvolio, "there shall be no more cakes and ale?" (2.3.103–04).

Fittingly, the earliest firm record of a performance of *Twelfth Night*, as noted in the diary of John Manningham, was "at our feast" in the Middle Temple (one of London's law schools) in February 1602. Manningham wrote observantly that the play was "much like the *Comedy of Errors*, or *Menaechmi* in Plautus, but most like and near to that in Italian called *Inganni*." That is, *Twelfth Night* resembles Shakespeare's own earlier play on identical twins (along with that play's Roman source) and still more resembles a series of sixteenth-century Italian comedies built around the intertwining themes of love, fraud *(inganno)*, and mistaken identity. Several of these comedies feature the plot device of a female twin who takes service as a page with the man she loves. Closest of these to Shakespeare's comedy is *Gl'Ingannati* (The Deceived), written for performance at Carnival time in Siena in 1531 and translated into French in 1543. It seems likely that Shakespeare knew this play or one that derived from it, and may have picked up several details in addition to the overall plot line. But the tone of *Gl'Ingannati*, with its bawdy jokes about nuns and old men, its sly, sardonic servants, and its farcical intrigues, is far from *Twelfth Night*'s mingled melancholy and delight, its bittersweet play of divided and contradictory desires. Tellingly, in the Italian comedy, the heroine is all along plotting to win the love of the man she serves; she has disguised herself in order to dissuade him from wooing elsewhere. Viola's predicament—her attempt to serve Orsino even at the cost of her own deepest longings—represents a wholly different emotional register.

That predicament is not Shakespeare's invention; he found it, with many other elements of his plot, in an English story, Barnabe Riche's tale "Apollonius and Silla" in *Riche His Farewell to Militarie Profession* (1581), which was in turn based on French and Italian sources. Riche is too addicted to moralizing to explore his heroine's character with much subtlety, but he does underscore how painful it is for her to hide her feelings while acting as go-between, and hence he anticipates, if only woodenly, the mood that Shakespeare exquisitely captures in Viola's lines about one who "sat like patience on a monument, / Smiling at grief" (2.4.113–14). There is less precedent, in Riche or in any of the known sources, for the aspect of *Twelfth Night* that Manningham

Gentlemen drinking and smoking. From Phillip Stubbes, *The Anatomie of Abuses* (1583).

found particularly memorable and that has continued to delight audiences: the gulling of Malvolio.

Malvolio (*mal volio*, "ill will") is explicitly linked to those among Shakespeare's contemporaries most hostile to the theater and to such holidays as Twelfth Night: "Sometimes," says Lady Olivia's waiting-gentlewoman Maria, "he is a kind of puritan" (2.3.125). When we first see Malvolio, he is harshly critical of Feste the clown, who is attempting to win back Olivia's favor. "Unless you laugh and minister occasion to him," Malvolio sourly observes, "he is gagged" (1.5.74–75). Though ungenerous, the observation is canny, for comedy does seem to depend on a collaborative spirit from which Malvolio conspicuously excludes himself. He is a man without friends. More dangerously, he is a man in a socially dependent position with a gift for acquiring enemies, as he does when he tries to silence the noisy revelry of that classic carnivalesque threesome a drunkard, a blockhead, and a professional fool: Olivia's uncle Sir Toby, his boon companion Sir Andrew Aguecheek, and Feste.

Olivia remarks to Malvolio that he is "sick of self-love" (1.5.77), and it is this narcissism that his enemies exploit to undo him. When Malvolio finds Maria's forged letter, he is in the midst of a deliciously self-gratifying fantasy that he has married Olivia, a fantasy less of erotic bliss than of social domination. The dream of rising above his station fuels his credulous eagerness to interpret the letter according to his fondest wishes and to comply with its absurd suggestions for his festive dress and demeanor. This compliance, by making it seem to Olivia that he has gone mad, renders Malvolio vulnerable to a further humiliation. In a parody of the age's brutal "therapy" for insanity, he is clapped into a dark room and subjected to a mock exorcism. Finally, he suffers what is perhaps the cruelest punishment for someone who dreams that greatness will be thrust upon him: he is simply forgotten. When in the play's final moments he is released, Malvolio is in no mood to join in the general air of communal wonder and rejoicing. More alone than ever, he introduces into the comedy's resolution an extraordinary note of vindictive bitterness: "I'll be revenged on the whole pack of you!" (5.1.365). Shakespeare does not hide the cruelty of the treatment to which Malvolio has been subjected—"He hath been most notoriously abused" (5.1.366), says Olivia— nor does he shrink from showing the audience other disagreeable qualities in Sir Toby and his companions. But while the close of the comedy seems to embrace these failings in a tolerant, bemused, aristocratic recognition of human folly, it can find no place for Malvolio's blend of puritanism and social climbing.

Malvolio is scapegoated for indulging in a fantasy that colors several of the key relationships in *Twelfth Night*: the fantasy of winning the hand of one of the noble and enormously wealthy aristocrats who reign over the social world of the play. The beautiful heiress Olivia, mistress of a great house, is a glittering prize that lures not only Malvolio but also the foolish Sir Andrew and the elegant, imperious Duke Orsino. In falling in love with the Duke's graceful messenger (and, as she thinks she has done, in marrying him), Olivia seems to have made precisely the kind of match that had fueled Malvolio's social-climbing imagination. As it turns out, the match is not between unequals: "Be not amazed," the Duke tells her when she realizes that she has married someone she

Lutenist. By Jost Amman.

scarcely knows. "Right noble is his blood" (5.1.257). The social order, then, has not been overturned: as in a carnival, when the disguises are removed, the revelers resume their "proper," socially and sexually approved positions.

Yet there is something decidedly improper about the perverse erotic excitement that the play discovers in disguise, displacement, indirection, and deferral and something irreducibly strange about the marriages with which *Twelfth Night* ends. Sir Toby has married Maria as a reward for devising the plot against Malvolio. Olivia has entered into a "contract of eternal bond of love" (5.1.152) with someone whose actual identity is only revealed to her after the marriage ceremony. (In Riche's version of the story, she is pregnant and her marriage saves her from social disgrace, but Shakespeare omits this plot twist, thereby raising the tone but heightening the irrationality of the finale.) The strangeness of the bond between virtual strangers is matched by the strangeness of Orsino's instantaneous decision to marry Cesario—as soon as "he" can become Viola by changing into women's clothes. Only a few minutes earlier, in a fit of jealous rage at Olivia's love for Cesario, Orsino had threatened to kill "the lamb that I do love" (5.1.126); now he will wed that lamb.

The sudden transformation is prepared for in part by Orsino's passionate insistence that he loves the boy he intends to kill and in part by the earlier signs of intimacy between them: "I have," he tells Cesario, "unclasped / To thee the book even of my secret soul" (1.4.12–13). But this intimacy has been formed around Orsino's grand passion for Olivia, a passion that is reiterated through virtually the entire play. The revelation at the play's climax—"One face, one voice, one habit, and two persons" (5.1.208)—forces a realignment of all the relationships. With Sebastian married to Olivia, Viola becomes Olivia's "sister" (or, as we would say, sister-in-law); and by marrying Viola, Orsino likewise makes Olivia his "sweet sister" (5.1.371). Orsino then will continue in a sense to "love" Olivia but only through the bond of kinship formed by the linked twins: a strangely appropriate fate for someone who tried to woo by proxy!

That this solution does not seem entirely zany—that it seems a fit ending for a romantic comedy—depends on several key features in *Twelfth Night*'s emotional landscape. It is significant that Orsino's love for Olivia, though poetically intense, is detached from any direct personal encounter. Not only does her vow of a seven-year seclusion compel Orsino to delegate his passion to a messenger, this passion seems largely self-regarding and self-indulgent. His famous opening lines on the paradoxes of love—its close intertwining of fulfillment and decline, stealing and giving, freshness and decay—revolve around the contemplation less of the lady than of his own solitary, self-gratifying imagination: "So full of shapes is fancy / That it alone is high fantastical" (1.1.14–15). The play does not ridicule Orsino's aristocratic reveries, although they seem at moments like elegant versions of what is cruelly mocked in Malvolio, but it does invite the audience to treat them with a certain ironic detachment.

Orsino's love seems to circle all too readily back upon himself: he is fascinated by his role as melancholy lover. That self-absorption is not the only shape of passion is made clear by several contrasting figures of whom the most selfless is the sea captain Antonio, consumed with desire for his friend Sebastian. In a play full of coy allusions to same-sex desire, Antonio's "willing love" (3.3.11) is the most explicit representation of passion as absolute devotion, a willingness to sacrifice everything in the service of the beloved. The mistaken belief that this devotion has been callously betrayed is one of the play's most poignant moments, a moment perhaps only partially redeemed by the manifest relief and joy with which the newly wed Sebastian greets his friend in the last act.

Intense, intimate bonding between men is a recurrent theme in Shakespeare's culture. (A comparable interest in female friendship is reflected in the love between Hermia and Helena in *A Midsummer Night's Dream* and Rosalind and Celia in *As You Like It.*) Shakespeare explores the pleasures and perils of male friendship in such plays as *The Two Gentlemen of Verona*, *The Merchant of Venice*, and *Much Ado About Nothing* and, most famously, in the sonnets to the fair young man whom he calls "the master-mistress of my passion" (sonnet 20). Orsino expresses doubt that a woman can love with an intensity equal to a man's:

> There is no woman's sides
> Can bide the beating of so strong a passion
> As love doth give my heart; no woman's heart
> So big, to hold so much. They lack retention.
>
> (2.4.91–94)

It is perhaps this belief (which the play proves to be utterly wrong) that conditions the only authentic emotional bond that we see Orsino forge, the bond with his devoted young servant Cesario. In conversation with Cesario, the haughty Duke manages for a few moments at least to escape from his languid self-absorption and express interest in someone else's thoughts and feelings: "What dost thou know?"; "And what's her history?"; "But died thy sister of her love, my boy?" (2.4.103, 108, 118). These simple questions, modest in themselves, are sufficiently distinct from Orsino's usual manner of speech to signal both a curiosity and a responsiveness that he does not manifest with anyone else. Part of the quirky delight of the play's resolution is to give to the union between Orsino and Viola something of the intimacy that had only seemed possible between men.

This resolution depends principally on the remarkable qualities of the play's central character, Viola. Like Antonio, Viola is prepared to sacrifice herself for her beloved: "And I most jocund, apt, and willingly," she tells Orsino, "to do you rest a thousand deaths would die" (5.1.128–29). But where Antonio experiences passion as tragic compulsion—he speaks of Sebastian's beauty as "witchcraft" drawing him into danger—Viola's spirit, as her word "jocund" suggests, is extraordinarily resilient. No sooner does she sadly observe that her brother must have perished in the shipwreck than she remarks, "Perchance he is not drowned" (1.2.4); no sooner does she find herself isolated and unprotected than she determines to serve Lady Olivia, and then, learning that this route is blocked, she at once resolves to disguise herself as a man and serve Orsino instead. Here and throughout the play, Viola seems to draw on an inward principle of hope. That principle, along with an improvisational boldness, an eloquent tongue, and a keen wit, enables her to keep afloat in an increasingly mad swirl of misunderstandings and cross-purposes.

Those misunderstandings, of course, are largely her creation in the sense that they mainly derive from a disguise that confounds the distinction between male and female. "They shall yet belie thy happy years / That say thou art a man," Orsino says to Cesario (1.4.29–30). The description that follows seems to imagine that boys begin almost as girls and only subsequently become males:

> Diana's lip
> Is not more smooth and rubious; thy small pipe
> Is as the maiden's organ, shrill and sound,
> And all is semblative a woman's part.
>
> (1.4.30–33)

This perception of ambiguity, rooted in early modern ideas about sexuality and gender, is one of the elements that enabled a boy actor in this period convincingly to mime "a woman's part." According to an ancient anatomical tradition, still highly influential in Shakespeare's time, sexual difference is not absolute: males and females share a single physiological structure whose differentiation only occurs over time. Such a theory implies a prolonged period of indistinction upon which *Twelfth Night* continually plays, and that helps to account for the emotional tangle that the cross-dressed Viola inspires.

Having, in her role as intermediary, aroused Olivia's love, Viola does not see how to disabuse the enamored Countess without abandoning the disguise. For all her lively resolution, she is passive in the face of the complexities she has engendered, counting on time and chance to sort out what she cannot: "O time, thou must untangle this, not

I. / It is too hard a knot for me t'untie" (2.2.38–39). Perhaps this passivity, or more accurately this trust in time, is a form of wisdom in a world where everything seems topsy-turvy. If so, it is a wisdom that links Viola to the fool Feste, who exults at the play's close in what he calls "the whirligig of time" (5.1.364).

Feste does not have a major part in the comedy's plot, but he shares with Viola a place at its imaginative center. A few years before the creation of *Twelfth Night,* the famous, boisterous clown Will Kempe quit Shakespeare's company in a huff and was replaced by Robert Armin, a comic actor of unusual sensitivity and subtlety. In paying handsome tribute to Feste's intelligence, Viola seems to acknowledge Armin's special gift: "This fellow is wise enough to play the fool, / And to do that well craves a kind of wit" (3.1.53–54). His wit often takes the form of a perverse literalism that slyly calls attention to the play's repeated confounding of such simple binaries as male and female, outside and inside, role and reality. The paradox of the wise fool, celebrated by Erasmus in his famous *Praise of Folly* (1509), is one that fascinated Shakespeare, who returned to it in plays as diverse as *As You Like It* and *King Lear.* In *Twelfth Night,* Feste is irresponsible, vulnerable, and dependent, but he also understands, as he teasingly shows Olivia, that it is foolish to bewail forever a loss that cannot be recovered. And he understands that it is important to take such pleasures as life offers and not to wait: "In delay there lies no plenty," he sings. "Then come kiss me, sweet and twenty. / Youth's a stuff will not endure" (2.3.46–48). There is in this wonderful song, as in all of his jests, a current of sadness. Feste knows, as the refrain of the last of his songs puts it, that "the rain it raineth every day" (5.1.379). His counsel is for "present mirth" and "present laughter" (2.3.44). This is, of course, the advice of a fool. But do the Malvolios of the world have anything wiser to suggest?

STEPHEN GREENBLATT

TEXTUAL NOTE

The text of *Twelfth Night* is mercifully straightforward: the play first appeared in the 1623 First Folio (F), and the text is unusually clean, including careful act and scene divisions. Contemporary or near-contemporary musical settings survive for several of the songs in the play. For example, "O mistress mine" (2.3.35ff.) appears in three early versions, including Thomas Morley's *First Book of Consort Lessons* (1599). "Hold thy peace" (2.3.59) appears in a manuscript book of rounds collected by Thomas Lant (1580), as well as a version printed in 1609. The well-known setting for Feste's epilogue, "When that I was and a little tiny boy" (5.1.376), was first printed in Joseph Vernon's 1772 volume *The New Songs in the Pantomime of the Witches: The Celebrated Epilogue in the Comedy of Twelfth Night . . . Sung by Mr. Vernon at Vaux Hall, Composed by J. Vernon.* It is not entirely clear whether this setting was composed by Vernon (as the title page seems to suggest) or arranged from a traditional tune.

SELECTED BIBLIOGRAPHY

Auden, W. H. "Music in Shakespeare." *The Dyer's Hand, and Other Essays.* New York: Random House, 1948. Analyzing songs from the plays, Auden reflects on music as a social exercise, dramatic convention, and supernatural signifier.

Bloom, Harold, ed. *William Shakespeare's "Twelfth Night."* Modern Critical Interpretation series. New York: Chelsea House, 1987. Essays written since the 1960s, treating the representation of character, music, class ideology, gender, and role-playing.

Booth, Stephen. *"Twelfth Night* 1.1: The Audience as Malvolio." *Shakespeare's "Rough Magic": Essays in Honor of C. L. Barber.* Ed. Peter Erickson and Coppélia Kahn.

Newark: University of Delaware Press, 1985. 149–67. An otherwise nonsensical play makes sense only when audiences ignore the textual evidence in favor of contextual probability.

Callaghan, Dympna. "'And all is semblative a woman's part': Body Politics and *Twelfth Night*." *Shakespeare Without Women: Representing Gender and Race on the Renaissance Stage*. New York: Routledge, 2000. 26–48. The misogynistic ridicule of Olivia's genitals in the Malvolio letter is an assertion of male control over the female body.

Gay, Penny. "*Twelfth Night*: Desire and Its Discontents." *As She Likes It: Shakespeare's Unruly Women*. London: Routledge, 1994. 17–47. Describes key postwar English stage productions.

Greenblatt, Stephen. "Fiction and Friction." *Shakespearean Negotiations: The Circulation of Social Energy in Renaissance England*. Berkeley: University of California Press, 1988. 66–93. In light of contemporary anatomical theories, relates sexual chafing to verbal sparring and the generation of identity.

Hollander, John. "*Twelfth Night* and the Morality of Indulgence." *Sewanee Review* 67 (1959): 220–38. In *Twelfth Night*'s intense moral vision, the surfeit of appetite through indulgence leads to the rebirth of the unencumbered self.

Neely, Carol Thomas. *Distracted Subjects: Madness and Gender in Shakespeare and Early Modern Culture*. Ithaca: Cornell University Press, 2004. *Twelfth Night*'s displaced erotic choices cohere with changing medical discourse about pathological female lovesickness.

Orgel, Stephen. *Impersonations: The Performance of Gender in Shakespeare's England*. Cambridge, Mass.: Cambridge University Press, 1996. Approaches paradoxes in English playacting practice through contemporary notions of gender construction and sexual desire.

Wells, Stanley, ed. *"Twelfth Night": Critical Essays*. New York: Garland, 1986. Twenty essays from the nineteenth century onward, treating mainly formal and structural aspects and early twentieth-century productions.

FILM

Twelfth Night. 1996. Dir. Trevor Nunn. UK. 134 min. Romantic Celtic coastlines combine with a poignant musical score, a stuffy Malvolio, and a gravely wise Feste. With Ben Kingsley, Helena Bonham Carter, and Nigel Hawthorne.

Twelfth Night, or What You Will

The Persons of the Play

ORSINO, Duke of Illyria

VALENTINE
CURIO } attending on Orsino

FIRST OFFICER

SECOND OFFICER

VIOLA, a lady, later disguised as Cesario

A CAPTAIN

SEBASTIAN, her twin brother

ANTONIO, another sea-captain

OLIVIA, a Countess

MARIA, her waiting-gentlewoman

SIR TOBY Belch, Olivia's kinsman

SIR ANDREW Aguecheek, companion of Sir Toby

MALVOLIO, Olivia's steward

FABIAN, a member of Olivia's household

FESTE the clown, her jester

A PRIEST

A SERVANT of Olivia

Musicians, sailors, lords, attendants

1.1

Music. Enter ORSINO *Duke of Illyria,* CURIO, *and other lords*

ORSINO If music be the food of love, play on,
    Give me excess of it that, surfeiting,
    The appetite may sicken and so die.
    That strain again, it had a dying fall.°   *cadence*
5 O, it came o'er my ear like the sweet sound
    That breathes upon a bank of violets,
    Stealing and giving odour. Enough, no more,
    'Tis not so sweet now as it was before.
        [*Music ceases*]
    O spirit of love, how quick and fresh° art thou   *lively and eager*
10 That, notwithstanding thy capacity
    Receiveth as the sea,° naught enters there,   *Receives without limit*
    Of what validity° and pitch° so e'er,   *value / height; excellence*
    But falls into abatement° and low price   *lesser value*
    Even in a minute! So full of shapes is fancy°   *love; desire*
15 That it alone is high fantastical.°   *uniquely imaginative*

CURIO Will you go hunt, my lord?

ORSINO   What, Curio?

CURIO   The hart.

ORSINO Why so I do, the noblest that I have.[1]
    O, when mine eyes did see Olivia first
    Methought she purged the air of pestilence;[2]

1.1 Location: Illyria, Greek and Roman name for the eastern Adriatic coast; probably not suggesting a real country to Shakespeare's audience.

1. Orsino plays on "hart/heart."
2. Plague and other illnesses were thought to be caused by bad air.

20 That instant was I turned into a hart,
And my desires, like fell° and cruel hounds,   *savage*
E'er since pursue me.³
            Enter VALENTINE
            How now, what news from her?
VALENTINE   So please my lord, I might not be admitted,
But from her handmaid do return this answer:
25 The element itself till seven years' heat⁴
Shall not behold her face at ample° view,   *full*
But like a cloistress° she will veilèd walk   *nun*
And water once a day her chamber round
With eye-offending brine°—all this to season   *stinging tears*
30 A brother's dead love,⁵ which she would keep fresh
And lasting in her sad remembrance.
ORSINO   O, she that hath a heart of that fine° frame   *exquisitely made*
To pay this debt of love but to a brother,
How will she love when the rich golden shaft⁶
35 Hath killed the flock of all affections else°   *other emotions*
That live in her—when liver, brain, and heart,⁷
These sovereign thrones, are all supplied, and filled
Her sweet perfections⁸ with one self° king!   *one and the same*
Away before me to sweet beds of flowers.
40 Love-thoughts lie rich when canopied with bowers.
                                    Exeunt

1.2

            Enter VIOLA, *a* CAPTAIN, *and sailors*
VIOLA¹   What country, friends, is this?
CAPTAIN   This is Illyria, lady.
VIOLA   And what should I do in Illyria?
My brother, he is in Elysium.²
Perchance° he is not drowned. What think you sailors?   *Perhaps*
5 CAPTAIN   It is perchance° that you yourself were saved.   *by chance*
VIOLA   O my poor brother!—and so perchance may he be.
CAPTAIN   True, madam, and to comfort you with chance,³
Assure yourself, after our ship did split,
When you and those poor number savèd with you
10 Hung on our driving boat,⁴ I saw your brother,
Most provident in peril, bind himself—
Courage and hope both teaching him the practice—
To a strong mast that lived° upon the sea,   *remained afloat*
Where, like Arion⁵ on the dolphin's back,
15 I saw him hold acquaintance with the waves
So long as I could see.
VIOLA [*giving money*]   For saying so, there's gold.

---

3. Alluding to the classical legend of Actaeon, who was turned into a stag and hunted by his own hounds for having seen Artemis naked.
4. The sky itself / for seven hot summers.
5. *all . . . love:* all this to preserve (by the salt of the tears) the love of a dead brother.
6. Of Cupid's golden-tipped arrow, which caused desire.
7. In Elizabethan psychology, these were the seats of passion, intellect, and feeling.
8. *and filled . . . perfections:* and all her flawless qualities

are governed by.
1.2 Location: The coast of Illyria.
1. Viola is not named in the dialogue until 5.1.237.
2. The heaven of classical mythology.
3. With what may have happened.
4. The ship's boat. *driving:* being driven by the wind.
5. A legendary Greek musician who, in order to save himself from being murdered on a voyage, jumped overboard and was carried to land by a dolphin.

Mine own escape unfoldeth to° my hope,   *encourages*
Whereto thy speech serves for authority,°   *support*
The like of him.[6] Know'st thou this country?

20 CAPTAIN   Ay, madam, well, for I was bred and born
Not three hours' travel from this very place.

VIOLA   Who governs here?

CAPTAIN   A noble duke, in nature
As in name.

VIOLA   What is his name?

CAPTAIN   Orsino.

VIOLA   Orsino. I have heard my father name him.
25 He was a bachelor then.

CAPTAIN   And so is now, or was so very late,°   *lately*
For but a month ago I went from hence,
And then 'twas fresh in murmur°—as, you know,   *newly rumored*
What great ones do the less will prattle of—
30 That he did seek the love of fair Olivia.

VIOLA   What's she?

CAPTAIN   A virtuous maid, the daughter of a count
That died some twelvemonth since, then leaving her
In the protection of his son, her brother,
35 Who shortly also died, for whose dear love,
They say, she hath abjured the sight
And company of men.

VIOLA   O that I served that lady,
And might not be delivered° to the world   *revealed*
Till I had made mine own occasion mellow,°   *ripe (to be revealed)*
What my estate° is.   *social rank*

40 CAPTAIN   That were hard to compass,°   *achieve*
Because she will admit no kind of suit,°   *petition*
No, not the Duke's.

VIOLA   There is a fair behaviour[7] in thee, captain,
And though that nature with a beauteous wall
45 Doth oft close in pollution, yet of thee
I will believe thou hast a mind that suits
With this thy fair and outward character.[8]
I pray thee—and I'll pay thee bounteously—
Conceal me what I am, and be my aid
50 For such disguise as haply shall become
The form of my intent.[9] I'll serve this duke.
Thou shalt present me as an eunuch[1] to him.
It may be worth thy pains, for I can sing,
And speak to him in many sorts of music
55 That will allow° me very worth his service.   *prove*
What else may hap, to time I will commit.
Only shape thou thy silence to my wit.°   *imagination; plan*

CAPTAIN   Be you his eunuch, and your mute[2] I'll be.
When my tongue blabs, then let mine eyes not see.

60 VIOLA   I thank thee. Lead me on.   *Exeunt*

---

6. That he too has survived.
7. Outward appearance; conduct.
8. Appearance (suggesting moral qualities).
9. *as . . . intent*: that perhaps may be fitting to my purpose. *form*: shape.
1. Castrati (hence, "eunuchs") were prized as male sopranos; the disguise would have explained Viola's

feminine voice. Viola (or perhaps Shakespeare) seems to have changed plans: she presents herself instead as a young page.
2. In Turkish harems, eunuchs served as guards and were assisted by "mutes" (usually servants whose tongues had been cut out).

1.3

Enter SIR TOBY [*Belch*] *and* MARIA

SIR TOBY What a plague means my niece to take the death of
her brother thus? I am sure care's an enemy to life.

MARIA By my troth, Sir Toby, you must come in earlier o' nights.
Your cousin,[1] my lady, takes great exceptions to your ill hours.

5 SIR TOBY Why, let her except, before excepted.[2]

MARIA Ay, but you must confine yourself within the modest°   *moderate*
limits of order.

SIR TOBY Confine? I'll confine myself no finer[3] than I am. These
clothes are good enough to drink in, and so be these boots too;

10 an° they be not, let them hang themselves in their own straps.   *if*

MARIA That quaffing and drinking will undo you. I heard my
lady talk of it yesterday, and of a foolish knight that you brought
in one night here to be her wooer.

SIR TOBY Who, Sir Andrew Aguecheek?

15 MARIA Ay, he.

SIR TOBY He's as tall a man as any's[4] in Illyria.

MARIA What's that to th' purpose?

SIR TOBY Why, he has three thousand ducats a year.

MARIA Ay, but he'll have but a year in all these ducats.[5] He's a

20 very° fool, and a prodigal.   *an absolute*

SIR TOBY Fie that you'll say so! He plays o'th' viol-de-gamboys,[6]
and speaks three or four languages word for word without
book,° and hath all the good gifts of nature.   *from memory*

MARIA He hath indeed, almost natural,[7] for besides that he's a

25 fool, he's a great quarreller, and but that he hath the gift° of a   *talent; present*
coward to allay the gust° he hath in quarrelling, 'tis thought   *gusto*
among the prudent he would quickly have the gift of a grave.

SIR TOBY By this hand, they are scoundrels and substractors[8] that
say so of him. Who are they?

30 MARIA They that add, moreover, he's drunk nightly in your
company.

SIR TOBY With drinking healths to my niece. I'll drink to her as
long as there is a passage in my throat and drink in Illyria. He's
a coward and a coistrel° that will not drink to my niece till his   *horse groom; lout*

35 brains turn o'th' toe, like a parish top. What wench, *Castiliano,*
vulgo,[9] for here comes Sir Andrew Agueface.

Enter SIR ANDREW [*Aguecheek*]

SIR ANDREW Sir Toby Belch! How now, Sir Toby Belch?

SIR TOBY Sweet Sir Andrew.

SIR ANDREW [*to* MARIA] Bless you, fair shrew.[1]

40 MARIA And you too, sir.

SIR TOBY Accost, Sir Andrew, accost.[2]

SIR ANDREW What's that?

1.3 Location: The Countess Olivia's house.
1. Term used generally of kinsfolk.
2. Playing on the legal jargon *exceptis excipiendis,* "with
the previously stated exceptions." Sir Toby refuses to take
Olivia's displeasure seriously.
3. Suggesting both "a refined manner of dress" and
"narrowly" (referring to his girth).
4. Any (man who) is. *tall:* brave; worthy. (Maria takes it
in the modern sense of height.)
5. He'll spend his fortune in a year.
6. A facetious corruption of "viola da gamba," a bass viol
held between the knees.

7. Idiots and fools were called "naturals."
8. Corruption of "detractors." (In reply, Maria puns on
"substract" as "subtract.")
9. Variously interpreted, but may mean "Speak of the
devil," since Castilians were considered devilish, and
vulgo refers to the common tongue (?). *parish top:* parishes kept large tops that were spun by whipping them,
for the parishioners' amusement and exercise.
1. Andrew possibly confuses "shrew" (ill-tempered
woman) with "mouse," an endearment.
2. Address (her); originally a naval term meaning "go
alongside; greet."

SIR TOBY My niece's chambermaid.[3]

SIR ANDREW Good Mistress Accost, I desire better acquaintance.

45 MARIA My name is Mary, sir.

SIR ANDREW Good Mistress Mary Accost.

SIR TOBY You mistake, knight. 'Accost' is front° her, board her,   °confront
woo her, assail[4] her.

SIR ANDREW By my troth, I would not undertake[5] her in this
50 company.° Is that the meaning of 'accost'?   °the audience

MARIA Fare you well, gentlemen.

SIR TOBY An thou let part so,[6] Sir Andrew, would thou mightst
never draw sword again.

SIR ANDREW An you part so, mistress, I would I might never draw
55 sword again. Fair lady, do you think you have fools in hand?°   °to deal with

MARIA Sir, I have not you by th' hand.

SIR ANDREW Marry, but you shall have, and here's my hand.

MARIA [taking his hand] Now sir, thought is free.[7] I pray you,
bring your hand to th' buttery-bar,[8] and let it drink.

60 SIR ANDREW Wherefore, sweetheart? What's your metaphor?

MARIA It's dry,[9] sir.

SIR ANDREW Why, I think so. I am not such an ass but I can
keep my hand dry.[1] But what's your jest?

MARIA A dry jest,[2] sir.

65 SIR ANDREW Are you full of them?

MARIA Ay, sir, I have them at my fingers' ends.[3] Marry, now I let
go your hand I am barren.°   Exit   °empty of jokes

SIR TOBY O knight, thou lackest a cup of canary.[4] When did I
see thee so put down?[5]

70 SIR ANDREW Never in your life, I think, unless you see canary
put me down. Methinks sometimes I have no more wit than a
Christian° or an ordinary man has; but I am a great eater of   °an average man
beef,[6] and I believe that does harm to my wit.

SIR TOBY No question.

75 SIR ANDREW An I thought that, I'd forswear it. I'll ride home
tomorrow, Sir Toby.

SIR TOBY Pourquoi,° my dear knight?   °Why

SIR ANDREW What is 'Pourquoi'? Do, or not do? I would I had
bestowed that time in the tongues[7] that I have in fencing, danc-
80 ing, and bear-baiting. O, had I but followed the arts!

SIR TOBY Then hadst thou had an excellent head of hair.

SIR ANDREW Why, would that have mended° my hair?   °improved

SIR TOBY Past question, for thou seest it will not curl by nature.[8]

SIR ANDREW But it becomes me well enough, does't not?

85 SIR TOBY Excellent, it hangs like flax on a distaff,[9] and I hope to
see a housewife[1] take thee between her legs and spin it off.[2]

---

3. Lady-in-waiting; not a menial servant, but a gentle-woman in attendance on a great lady.
4. board: speak to; tackle. assail: greet (also nautical).
5. Take her on (with sexual implication).
6. If you let her go without protest or without bidding her farewell.
7. The customary retort to "Do you think I am a fool?"
8. Ledge on the half door to a buttery or a wine cellar on which drinks were served.
9. Thirsty; but also thought to be a sign of impotence.
1. Alluding to the proverb "Even fools have enough wit to come in out of the rain."
2. A stupid joke (referring to Andrew's stupidity); an ironic quip; a joke about dryness.

3. Always ready; or "by th' hand" (line 56).
4. A sweet wine, like sherry, originally from the Canary Islands.
5. Defeated in repartee; "put down" with drink.
6. Contemporary medicine held that beef dulled the intellect.
7. Foreign languages; Toby takes him to mean "curling tongs."
8. To contrast with Andrew's "arts" (line 80).
9. In spinning, flax would hang in long, thin, yellowish strings on the "distaff," a pole held between the knees.
1. Housewives spun flax; the pronunciation, "huswife," also suggests the meaning "prostitute."
2. Make him bald (as a result of venereal disease).

SIR ANDREW Faith, I'll home tomorrow, Sir Toby. Your niece
will not be seen, or if she be, it's four to one she'll none of me.
The Count himself here hard by woos her.

90 SIR TOBY She'll none o'th' Count. She'll not match above her
degree,° neither in estate,[3] years, nor wit, I have heard her   social rank
swear't. Tut, there's life in't,[4] man.

SIR ANDREW I'll stay a month longer. I am a fellow o'th' strangest
mind i'th' world. I delight in masques and revels sometimes
95 altogether.

SIR TOBY Art thou good at these kickshawses,[5] knight?

SIR ANDREW As any man in Illyria, whatsoever he be, under the
degree of my betters; and yet I will not compare with an old
man.[6]

100 SIR TOBY What is thy excellence in a galliard,[7] knight?

SIR ANDREW Faith, I can cut a caper.[8]

SIR TOBY And I can cut the mutton to't.

SIR ANDREW And I think I have the back-trick[9] simply as strong
as any man in Illyria.

105 SIR TOBY Wherefore are these things hid? Wherefore have these
gifts a curtain[1] before 'em? Are they like to take dust, like Mistress Mall's[2] picture? Why dost thou not go to church in a galliard, and come home in a coranto?[3] My very walk should be a
jig. I would not so much as make water but in a cinquepace.[4]
110 What dost thou mean? Is it a world to hide virtues in? I did
think by the excellent constitution of thy leg it was formed
under the star of a galliard.[5]

SIR ANDREW Ay, 'tis strong, and it does indifferent° well in a   moderately
divers-coloured stock.° Shall we set about some revels?   stocking

115 SIR TOBY What shall we do else—were we not born under
Taurus?[6]

SIR ANDREW Taurus? That's sides and heart.

SIR TOBY No, sir, it is legs and thighs: let me see thee caper.

[SIR ANDREW capers]
Ha, higher! Ha ha, excellent.   Exeunt

1.4

Enter VALENTINE, and VIOLA [as Cesario] in man's attire

VALENTINE If the Duke continue these favours towards you,
Cesario, you are like to be much advanced. He hath known
you but three days, and already you are no stranger.

VIOLA You either fear his humour° or my negligence, that you   moodiness
5 call in question the continuance of his love. Is he inconstant,
sir, in his favours?

VALENTINE No, believe me.

Enter DUKE, CURIO, and attendants

---

3. Status; possession.
4. Proverbial: "While there's life, there's hope."
5. Trifles; trivialities (from the French quelque chose).
6. Expert (perhaps a backhanded compliment).
7. A lively, complex dance, including the caper.
8. Leap. (Toby puns on the pickled flower buds used in
a sauce of mutton.)
9. Probably a dance movement, a kick of the foot behind
the body (also suggesting sexual prowess, with later reference to "mutton" as "prostitute").

1. Used to protect paintings from dust.
2. Like "Moll[y]," "Mall" was a nickname for "Mary."
3. An even more rapid dance than the galliard.
4. Galliard, or, more properly, the steps joining the figures of the dance; punning on "sink," as in "sewer."
5. Astrological influences favorable to dancing.
6. The astrological sign of the bull was usually thought
to govern the neck and throat (appropriate to heavy
drinkers).
1.4 Location: Orsino's palace.

VIOLA   I thank you. Here comes the Count.

ORSINO   Who saw Cesario, ho?

10   VIOLA   On your attendance,° my lord, here.   *Waiting at your service*

ORSINO [*to* CURIO *and attendants*]   Stand you a while aloof.° [*To*   *aside*
    VIOLA] Cesario,
Thou know'st no less but all.° I have unclasped   *than everything*
To thee the book even of my secret soul.
Therefore, good youth, address thy gait° unto her,   *go*

15   Be not denied access, stand at her doors,
And tell them there thy fixèd foot shall grow°   *take root*
Till thou have audience.

VIOLA   Sure, my noble lord,
If she be so abandoned to her sorrow
As it is spoke, she never will admit me.

20   ORSINO   Be clamorous, and leap all civil bounds,[1]
Rather than make unprofited° return.   *unsuccessful*

VIOLA   Say I do speak with her, my lord, what then?

ORSINO   O then unfold the passion of my love,
Surprise[2] her with discourse of my dear° faith.   *heartfelt*

25   It shall become thee well to act my woes—
She will attend it better in thy youth
Than in a nuncio's° of more grave aspect.°   *messenger's / appearance*

VIOLA   I think not so, my lord.

ORSINO   Dear lad, believe it;
For they shall yet belie thy happy years

30   That say thou art a man. Diana's lip
Is not more smooth and rubious;° thy small pipe°   *ruby red / voice*
Is as the maiden's organ, shrill and sound,[3]
And all is semblative° a woman's part.   *like*
I know thy constellation[4] is right apt

35   For this affair. [*To* CURIO *and attendants*] Some four or five attend him.
All if you will, for I myself am best
When least in company. [*To* VIOLA] Prosper well in this
And thou shalt live as freely as thy lord,
To call his fortunes thine.

VIOLA   I'll do my best

40   To woo your lady—[*aside*] yet a barful strife[5]—
Whoe'er I woo, myself would be his wife.   *Exeunt*

1.5

Enter MARIA, *and* [FESTE,[1] *the*] *clown*

MARIA   Nay, either tell me where thou hast been or I will not
open my lips so wide as a bristle may enter in° way of thy   *by*
excuse. My lady will hang thee for thy absence.

FESTE   Let her hang me. He that is well hanged in this world
5   needs to fear no colours.[2]

MARIA   Make that good.°   *Explain that*

FESTE   He shall see none to fear.

---

1. All constraints of polite behavior.
2. Capture by unexpected attack (of military origin).
3. High-pitched and uncracked.
4. Nature and abilities (as supposedly determined by the stars).

5. An undertaking full of impediments.
1.5 Location: Olivia's house.
1. The name is used only once, at 2.4.11.
2. Proverbial for "fear nothing." *colours*: worldly deceptions, with a pun on "collars" as "hangman's noose."

MARIA   A good lenten³ answer. I can tell thee where that saying
was born, of 'I fear no colours'.

10   FESTE   Where, good Mistress Mary?

MARIA   In the wars,⁴ and that may you be bold to say in your
foolery.

FESTE   Well, God give them wisdom that have it; and those that
are fools, let them use their talents.⁵

15   MARIA   Yet you will be hanged for being so long absent, or to be
turned away⁶—is not that as good as a hanging to you?

FESTE   Many a good hanging prevents a bad marriage;⁷ and for
turning away, let summer bear it out.°   make it endurable

MARIA   You are resolute then?

20   FESTE   Not so neither, but I am resolved on two points.°   matters; laces

MARIA   That if one break, the other will hold; or if both break,
your gaskins° fall.   wide breeches

FESTE   Apt, in good faith, very apt. Well, go thy way. If Sir Toby
would leave drinking thou wert as witty a piece of Eve's flesh⁸

25   as any in Illyria.

MARIA   Peace, you rogue, no more o' that. Here comes my lady.
Make your excuse wisely, you were best.°   [Exit]   you had better

Enter Lady OLIVIA, _with_ MALVOLIO° [_and attendants_]   "ill will"

FESTE [_aside_]   Wit,⁹ an't° be thy will, put me into good fooling!   if it
Those wits that think they have thee do very oft prove fools,

30   and I that am sure I lack thee may pass for a wise man. For
what says Quinapalus?¹—'Better a witty fool than a foolish wit.'
[_To_ OLIVIA] God bless thee, lady.

OLIVIA [_to attendants_]   Take the fool away.

FESTE   Do you not hear, fellows? Take away the lady.

35   OLIVIA   Go to, you're a dry² fool. I'll no more of you. Besides,
you grow dishonest.°   unreliable

FESTE   Two faults, madonna,° that drink and good counsel will   my lady
amend, for give the dry fool drink, then is the fool not dry; bid
the dishonest man mend° himself : if he mend, he is no longer   reform

40   dishonest; if he cannot, let the botcher° mend him. Anything   tailor; cobbler
that's mended is but patched. Virtue that transgresses is but
patched with sin, and sin that amends is but patched with virtue. If that this simple syllogism will serve, so. If it will not, what
remedy? As there is no true cuckold but calamity, so beauty's a

45   flower.³ The lady bade take away the fool, therefore I say again,
take her away.

OLIVIA   Sir, I bade them take away you.

FESTE   Misprision⁴ in the highest degree! Lady, '_Cucullus non
facit monachum_'⁵—that's as much to say as I wear not motley⁶

50   in my brain. Good madonna, give me leave to prove you a fool.

---

3. Thin or meager (like Lenten fare).
4. _In the wars:_ "colours" in line 9 refers to military flags.
5. Alluding to the parable of the talents, Matthew 25.
The comic implication is that a fool should strive to
increase his measure of folly. Since "fool" and "fowl" had
similar pronunciations, there may also be a play on
"talents/talons."
6. Dismissed; also, perhaps, turned off or hanged.
7. _Many . . . marriage:_ Proverbial. _hanging:_ execution;
sexual prowess.
8. Woman. Feste may imply both that Maria and Toby
would make a good match and that Maria is as witty as

Toby is sober.
9. Intelligence, which is often contrasted with will.
1. Feste frequently invents his own authorities.
2. Dull, but Feste interprets as "thirsty." _Go to:_ an
expression of impatience.
3. _As . . . flower:_ In taking her vow (1.2.36–37), Olivia
has wedded herself to calamity but must be unfaithful,
or let pass her moment of beauty.
4. Misapprehension; wrongful arrest.
5. The cowl does not make the monk (a Latin proverb).
6. The multicolored costume of a fool.

OLIVIA	Can you do it?	
FESTE	Dexteriously,° good madonna.	*Dexterously*
OLIVIA	Make your proof.	
FESTE	I must catechize[7] you for it, madonna. Good my mouse	
55	of virtue,° answer me.	*My good virtuous mouse*
OLIVIA	Well, sir, for want of other idleness° I'll bide° your proof.	*pastime / await*
FESTE	Good madonna, why mournest thou?	
OLIVIA	Good fool, for my brother's death.	
FESTE	I think his soul is in hell, madonna.	
60 OLIVIA	I know his soul is in heaven, fool.	
FESTE	The more fool, madonna, to mourn for your brother's	
	soul, being in heaven. Take away the fool, gentlemen.	
OLIVIA	What think you of this fool, Malvolio? Doth he not	
	mend?[8]	
65 MALVOLIO	Yes, and shall do till the pangs of death shake him.	
	Infirmity,° that decays the wise, doth ever make the better fool.[9]	*(Old) age*
FESTE	God send you, sir, a speedy infirmity for the better	
	increasing your folly. Sir Toby will be sworn that I am no fox,	
	but he will not pass his word for twopence that you are no fool.	
70 OLIVIA	How say you to that, Malvolio?	
MALVOLIO	I marvel your ladyship takes delight in such a barren	
	rascal. I saw him put down° the other day with an ordinary fool	*defeated in repartee*
	that has no more brain than a stone. Look you now, he's out of	
	his guard° already. Unless you laugh and minister occasion[1] to	*defenseless*
75	him, he is gagged. I protest I take these wise men that crow so	
	at these set° kind of fools no better than the fools' zanies.°	*artificial / "straight men"*
OLIVIA	O, you are sick of self-love, Malvolio, and taste with a	
	distempered[2] appetite. To be generous, guiltless, and of free°	*magnanimous*
	disposition is to take those things for birdbolts[3] that you deem	
80	cannon bullets. There is no slander in an allowed fool, though	
	he do nothing but rail; nor no railing in a known discreet man,	
	though he do nothing but reprove.	
FESTE	Now Mercury indue thee with leasing,[4] for thou speakest	
	well of fools.	
	Enter MARIA	
85 MARIA	Madam, there is at the gate a young gentleman much	
	desires to speak with you.	
OLIVIA	From the Count Orsino, is it?	
MARIA	I know not, madam. 'Tis a fair young man, and well	
	attended.	
90 OLIVIA	Who of my people hold him in delay?	
MARIA	Sir Toby, madam, your kinsman.	
OLIVIA	Fetch him off, I pray you, he speaks nothing but mad-	
	man.° Fie on him. Go you, Malvolio. If it be a suit from the	*madman's talk*
	Count, I am sick, or not at home—what you will to dismiss it.	
	Exit MALVOLIO	
95	Now you see, sir, how your fooling grows old,° and people dis-	*stale*
	like it.	
FESTE	Thou hast spoke for us, madonna, as if thy eldest son	

---

7. Question (as in catechism, which tests the orthodoxy of belief).
8. Improve, but Malvolio takes "mend" to mean "grow
more foolish."
9. Make the fool more foolish.

1. And give opportunity.
2. An unbalanced; a sick.
3. Blunt arrows for shooting birds.
4. May Mercury, the god of deception, endow you with
the talent of tactful lying.

should be a fool, whose skull Jove cram with brains, for—here
he comes—

     Enter SIR TOBY

100   one of thy kin has a most weak *pia mater*.[5]

OLIVIA   By mine honour, half-drunk. What is he at the gate,
     cousin?°   *kinsman*

SIR TOBY   A gentleman.

OLIVIA   A gentleman? What gentleman?

105 SIR TOBY   'Tis a gentleman here. [*He belches*] A plague o' these
     pickle herring! [*To* FESTE] How now, sot?°   *fool; drunkard*

FESTE   Good Sir Toby.

OLIVIA   Cousin, cousin, how have you come so early by this
     lethargy?

110 SIR TOBY   Lechery? I defy lechery. There's one° at the gate.   *someone*

OLIVIA   Ay, marry, what is he?

SIR TOBY   Let him be the devil an° he will, I care not. Give me   *if*
     faith,[6] say I. Well, it's all one.°   *Exit*   *it doesn't matter*

OLIVIA   What's a drunken man like, fool?

115 FESTE   Like a drowned man, a fool, and a madman—one
     draught above heat[7] makes him a fool, the second mads him,
     and a third drowns him.

OLIVIA   Go thou and seek the coroner, and let him sit o'° my   *hold an inquest for*
     coz,° for he's in the third degree of drink, he's drowned. Go   *cousin; uncle*

120   look after him.

FESTE   He is but mad yet, madonna, and the fool shall look to
     the madman.   [*Exit*]

     Enter MALVOLIO

MALVOLIO   Madam, yon young fellow swears he will speak with
     you. I told him you were sick—he takes on him to understand

125   so much, and therefore° comes to speak with you. I told him   *for that very reason*
     you were asleep—he seems to have a foreknowledge of that
     too, and therefore comes to speak with you. What is to be said
     to him, lady? He's fortified against any denial.

OLIVIA   Tell him he shall not speak with me.

130 MALVOLIO   He's been told so, and he says he'll stand at your door
     like a sheriff's post,[8] and be the supporter to a bench, but he'll
     speak with you.

OLIVIA   What kind o' man is he?

MALVOLIO   Why, of mankind.°   *like any other*

135 OLIVIA   What manner of man?

MALVOLIO   Of very ill manner: he'll speak with you, will you or
     no.

OLIVIA   Of what personage° and years is he?   *appearance*

MALVOLIO   Not yet old enough for a man, nor young enough for

140   a boy; as a squash[9] is before 'tis a peascod, or a codling° when   *an unripe apple*
     'tis almost an apple. 'Tis with him in standing water° between   *at the turn of the tide*
     boy and man. He is very well-favoured,° and he speaks very   *handsome*
     shrewishly.° One would think his mother's milk were scarce   *sharply*
     out of him.

145 OLIVIA   Let him approach. Call in my gentlewoman.

MALVOLIO   Gentlewoman, my lady calls.   *Exit*

---

5. Brain; or literally, the membrane enclosing it.
6. To defy the devil by faith alone.
7. One drink ("draught")/beyond the quantity necessary
to warm him.

8. A decorative post set before a sheriff's door, as a sign
of authority.
9. An undeveloped pea pod.

Enter MARIA

OLIVIA   Give me my veil. Come, throw it o'er my face.
We'll once more hear Orsino's embassy.

Enter VIOLA *[as Cesario]*

VIOLA   The honourable lady of the house, which is she?

150 OLIVIA   Speak to me, I shall answer for her. Your will.

VIOLA   Most radiant, exquisite, and unmatchable beauty.—I pray
you, tell me if this be the lady of the house, for I never saw
her. I would be loath to cast away° my speech, for besides that   *waste*
it is excellently well penned, I have taken great pains to

155 con° it. Good beauties, let me sustain° no scorn; I am very   *memorize / suffer*
'countable,° even to the least sinister usage.[1]   *sensitive*

OLIVIA   Whence came you, sir?

VIOLA   I can say little more than I have studied,[2] and that question's out of my part. Good gentle one, give me modest° assur-   *adequate*

160 ance if you be the lady of the house, that I may proceed in my
speech.

OLIVIA   Are you a comedian?°   *an actor*

VIOLA   No, my profound heart;[3] and yet—by the very fangs of
malice I swear—I am not that I play. Are you the lady of the

165 house?

OLIVIA   If I do not usurp[4] myself, I am.

VIOLA   Most certain if you are she you do usurp yourself, for what
is yours to bestow is not yours to reserve. But this is from my
commission.° I will on with my speech in your praise, and then   *beyond my instructions*

170 show you the heart of my message.

OLIVIA   Come to what is important in't, I forgive you° the praise.   *excuse you from*

VIOLA   Alas, I took great pains to study it, and 'tis poetical.

OLIVIA   It is the more like to be feigned, I pray you keep it in. I
heard you were saucy° at my gates, and allowed your approach   *impertinent*

175 rather to wonder at you than to hear you. If you be not mad,°   *utterly mad*
be gone. If you have reason,° be brief. 'Tis not that time of   *any sanity*
moon with me to make one in so skipping a dialogue.[5]

MARIA   Will you hoist sail, sir? Here lies your way.

VIOLA   No, good swabber, I am to hull[6] here a little longer.

180 *[To* OLIVIA*]* Some mollification for your giant,[7] sweet lady. Tell
me your mind, I am a messenger.[8]

OLIVIA   Sure, you have some hideous matter to deliver when the
courtesy° of it is so fearful. Speak your office.°   *introduction / business*

VIOLA   It alone concerns your ear. I bring no overture° of war,   *declaration*

185 no taxation of homage.[9] I hold the olive[1] in my hand. My words
are as full of peace as matter.°   *meaning*

OLIVIA   Yet you began rudely. What are you? What would you?

VIOLA   The rudeness that hath appeared in me have I learned
from my entertainment.° What I am and what I would are as   *reception*

190 secret as maidenhead;° to your ears, divinity; to any others',   *virginity*
profanation.

1. To the slightest discourteous treatment.
2. Learned by heart (a theatrical term).
3. My most wise lady; upon my soul.
4. Counterfeit; misappropriate.
5. *'Tis . . . dialogue:* I am not lunatic enough to take part
in so flighty a conversation. (Lunacy was thought to be
influenced by the phases of the moon.)
6. To lie unanchored with lowered sails. *swabber:* a
cleaner of boat decks.
7. Mythical giants guarded ladies; here, also mocking
Maria's diminutive size. *Some . . . for:* Please pacify.
8. From Orsino; Olivia pretends she understands her to
mean a king's messenger, or a messenger-at-arms,
employed on important state affairs.
9. Demand for dues paid to a superior.
1. Olive branch (as a symbol of peace).

OLIVIA [*to* MARIA *and attendants*]   Give us the place alone, we
will hear this divinity.°   [*Exeunt* MARIA *and attendants*]   *religious discourse*
Now sir, what is your text?²

195 VIOLA   Most sweet lady—
OLIVIA   A comfortable° doctrine, and much may be said of it.   *comforting*
Where lies your text?
VIOLA   In Orsino's bosom.
OLIVIA   In his bosom? In what chapter of his bosom?
200 VIOLA   To answer by the method,° in the first of his heart.   *in the same style*
OLIVIA   O, I have read it. It is heresy. Have you no more to say?
VIOLA   Good madam, let me see your face.
OLIVIA   Have you any commission from your lord to negotiate
with my face? You are now out of° your text. But we will draw   *straying from*
205 the curtain and show you the picture.
       [*She unveils*]
Look you, sir, such a one I was this present.³ Is't not well done?
VIOLA   Excellently done, if God did all.⁴
OLIVIA   'Tis in grain,° sir, 'twill endure wind and weather.   *The dye is fast*
VIOLA   'Tis beauty truly blent,⁵ whose red and white
210 Nature's own sweet and cunning° hand laid on.   *skillful*
Lady, you are the cruell'st she° alive   *woman*
If you will lead these graces to the grave
And leave the world no copy.⁶
OLIVIA   O sir, I will not be so hard-hearted. I will give out divers
215 schedules° of my beauty. It shall be inventoried and every parti-   *various inventories*
cle and utensil labelled⁷ to my will, as, *item*, two lips, indiffer-
ent° red; *item*, two grey eyes, with lids⁸ to them; *item*, one neck,   *moderate*
one chin, and so forth. Were you sent hither to praise° me?   *appraise; flatter*
VIOLA   I see you what you are, you are too proud,
220 But if° you were the devil, you are fair.   *Even if*
My lord and master loves you. O, such love
Could be but recompensed though⁹ you were crowned
The nonpareil of beauty.°   *An unequaled beauty*
OLIVIA   How does he love me?
VIOLA   With adorations, fertile° tears,   *ever-flowing*
225 With groans that thunder love, with sighs of fire.
OLIVIA   Your lord does know my mind, I cannot love him.
Yet I suppose him virtuous, know him noble,
Of great estate, of fresh and stainless youth,
In voices well divulged,° free,° learned, and valiant,   *spoken of / generous*
230 And in dimension and the shape of nature¹
A gracious person; but yet I cannot love him.
He might have took his answer long ago.
VIOLA   If I did love you in° my master's flame,°   *with / passion*
With such a suff'ring, such a deadly° life,   *deathlike*
235 In your denial I would find no sense,
I would not understand it.

2. Quotation (as a theme of a sermon, in keeping with
"divinity," "doctrine," "heresy," etc.).
3. Portraits usually gave the year of painting. "This
present" was a term used to date letters.
4. If it is natural (without the use of cosmetics).
5. Blended, or mixed (of paints). Shakespeare uses the
same metaphor in sonnet 20, lines 1–2, and Viola's next
lines recall sonnet 11, lines 13–14. As Cesario, Viola is
playing with established conventions of poetic courtship.

6. Viola means "child"; Olivia takes her to mean "list" or
"inventory."
7. Every single part and article added as a codicil (parodying the legal language of a last will and testament).
8. Eyelids, but also punning on "pot lids" (punning on
"utensil" as a household implement).
9. *Could . . . though:* Would have to be requited even if.
1. *dimension . . . shape of nature:* the two terms are
synonymous, meaning "bodily form."

OLIVIA   Why, what would you?

VIOLA   Make me a willow² cabin at your gate

And call upon my soul° within the house,   *(Olivia)*

Write loyal cantons of contemnèd° love,   *songs of rejected*

240   And sing them loud even in the dead of night;

Halloo³ your name to the reverberate° hills,   *echoing*

And make the babbling gossip of the air⁴

Cry out 'Olivia!' O, you should not rest

Between the elements of air and earth

245   But you should pity me.

OLIVIA   You might do much.

What is your parentage?

VIOLA   Above my fortunes, yet my state° is well.   *social status*

I am a gentleman.

OLIVIA   Get you to your lord.

250   I cannot love him. Let him send no more,

Unless, perchance, you come to me again

To tell me how he takes it. Fare you well.

I thank you for your pains. [*Offering a purse*] Spend this for me.

VIOLA   I am no fee'd post,° lady. Keep your purse.   *hired messenger*

255   My master, not myself, lacks recompense.

Love make his heart of flint that you shall love,⁵

And let your fervour, like my master's, be

Placed in contempt. Farewell, fair cruelty.   *Exit*

OLIVIA   'What is your parentage?'

260   'Above my fortunes, yet my state is well.

I am a gentleman.' I'll be sworn thou art.

Thy tongue, thy face, thy limbs, actions, and spirit

Do give thee five-fold blazon.⁶ Not too fast. Soft,° soft—   *Wait*

Unless the master were the man.⁷ How now?

265   Even so quickly may one catch the plague?

Methinks I feel this youth's perfections

With an invisible and subtle stealth

To creep in at mine eyes. Well, let it be.

What ho, Malvolio.

              Enter MALVOLIO

MALVOLIO   Here, madam, at your service.

270   OLIVIA   Run after that same peevish messenger

The County's° man. He left this ring behind him,   *Count's*

Would I° or not. Tell him I'll none of it.   *Whether I wished it*

Desire him not to flatter with° his lord,   *encourage*

Nor hold him up with hopes. I am not for him.

275   If that the youth will come this way tomorrow,

I'll give him reasons for't. Hie thee,° Malvolio.   *Hurry*

MALVOLIO   Madam, I will.   *Exit* [*at one door*]

OLIVIA   I do I know not what, and fear to find

Mine eye too great a flatterer for my mind.⁸

---

2. Traditional symbol of rejected love.
3. Shout; or perhaps "hallow," as in "bless."
4. For the love of Narcissus, the nymph Echo wasted away to a mere voice, only able to repeat whatever she heard spoken.
5. *Love . . . love:* May love make the heart of the man you

love as hard as flint.
6. Formal description of a gentleman's coat of arms.
7. If Orsino were Cesario (*man:* servant).
8. My eye (through which love has entered my heart) has seduced my reason.

280 Fate, show thy force. Ourselves we do not owe.°   *own*
What is decreed must be; and be this so.

[*Exit at another door*]

2.1

Enter ANTONIO *and* SEBASTIAN

ANTONIO   Will you stay no longer, nor will° you not that I go   *wish*
with you?

SEBASTIAN   By your patience, no. My stars shine darkly over me.
The malignancy of my fate[1] might perhaps distemper° yours,   *infect*
5   therefore I shall crave of you your leave that I may bear my
evils alone. It were a bad recompense for your love to lay any
of them on you.

ANTONIO   Let me yet know of you whither you are bound.

SEBASTIAN   No, sooth,° sir. My determinate° voyage is mere   *truly / destined*
10   extravagancy.° But I perceive in you so excellent a touch of   *idle wandering*
modesty° that you will not extort from me what I am willing to   *politeness*
keep in. Therefore it charges me in manners[2] the rather to
express° myself. You must know of me then, Antonio, my name   *reveal*
is Sebastian, which I called Roderigo. My father was that Sebas-
15   tian of Messaline[3] whom I know you have heard of. He left
behind him myself and a sister, both born in an° hour. If the   *within the same*
heavens had been pleased, would we had so ended. But you,
sir, altered that, for some hour before you took me from the
breach° of the sea was my sister drowned.   *surf*
20   ANTONIO   Alas the day!

SEBASTIAN   A lady, sir, though it was said she much resembled
me, was yet of many accounted beautiful. But though I could
not with such estimable° wonder over-far believe that, yet   *appreciative*
thus far I will boldly publish° her: she bore a mind that   *proclaim*
25   envy° could not but call fair. She is drowned already, sir, with   *malice*
salt water, though I seem to drown her remembrance again
with more.

ANTONIO   Pardon me, sir, your bad entertainment.[4]

SEBASTIAN   O good Antonio, forgive me your trouble.

30   ANTONIO   If you will not murder me[5] for my love, let me be your
servant.

SEBASTIAN   If you will not undo what you have done—that is,
kill him whom you have recovered°—desire it not. Fare ye well   *rescued*
at once. My bosom is full of kindness,° and I am yet° so near   *tender emotion / still*
35   the manners of my mother[6] that upon the least occasion more
mine eyes will tell tales of me.° I am bound to the Count   *betray my feelings*
Orsino's court. Farewell.   *Exit*

ANTONIO   The gentleness° of all the gods go with thee!   *favor*
I have many enemies in Orsino's court,
40   Else would I very shortly see thee there.
But come what may, I do adore thee so
That danger shall seem sport, and I will go.   *Exit*

2.1 Location: Near the coast of Illyria.   3. Possibly Messina, Sicily.
1. Evil influence of the stars; "malignancy" also signifies   4. Your poor reception; your inhospitality.
a deadly disease.   5. Murder him by insisting that they part.
2. Therefore courtesy requires.   6. So near woman's readiness to weep.

2.2

Enter VIOLA *as Cesario, and* MALVOLIO, *at several° doors*   separate

MALVOLIO   Were not you ev'n° now with the Countess Olivia?   just

VIOLA   Even now, sir, on° a moderate pace, I have since arrived   at
but hither.°   come only this far

MALVOLIO [*offering a ring*]   She returns this ring to you, sir.

5   You might have saved me my pains to have taken° it away your-   by taking
self. She adds, moreover, that you should put your lord into a
desperate assurance° she will none of him. And one thing   hopeless certainty
more: that you be never so hardy° to come again in his affairs,   bold
unless it be to report your lord's taking of this.[1] Receive it so.

10   VIOLA   She took the ring of me.[2] I'll none of it.

MALVOLIO   Come, sir, you peevishly threw it to her, and her will
is it should be so returned.
[*He throws the ring down*]
If it be worth stooping for, there it lies, in your eye;° if not, be   sight
it his that finds it.   *Exit*

15   VIOLA [*picking up the ring*]   I left no ring with her. What means this lady?
Fortune forbid my outside° have not charmed her.   appearance
She made good view of° me, indeed so much   looked carefully at
That straight methought her eyes had lost° her tongue,   made her lose
For she did speak in starts, distractedly.

20   She loves me, sure. The cunning of her passion
Invites me in° this churlish messenger.   by means of
None of my lord's ring! Why, he sent her none.
I am the man.[3] If it be so—as 'tis—
Poor lady, she were better love a dream!

25   Disguise, I see thou art a wickedness
Wherein the pregnant enemy[4] does much.
How easy is it for the proper false[5]
In women's waxen hearts to set their forms![6]
Alas, our frailty is the cause, not we,

30   For such as we are made of, such we be.[7]
How will this fadge?° My master loves her dearly,   turn out
And I, poor monster,[8] fond° as much on him,   dote
And she, mistaken, seems to dote on me.
What will become of this? As I am man,

35   My state is desperate° for my master's love.   hopeless
As I am woman, now, alas the day,
What thriftless° sighs shall poor Olivia breathe!   unprofitable
O time, thou must untangle this, not I.
It is too hard a knot for me t'untie.   [*Exit*]

2.3

Enter SIR TOBY *and* SIR ANDREW

SIR TOBY   Approach, Sir Andrew. Not to be abed after midnight
is to be up betimes,° and *diliculo surgere*,[1] thou knowest.   early

---

2.2 Location: Between Olivia's house and Orsino's
palace.
1. Reception of this rejection.
2. Viola pretends to believe Olivia's story. *of*: from.
3. The man with whom she has fallen in love.
4. The devil, who is always quick and ready (to deceive).
5. Handsome, but deceitful (men).

6. *In . . . forms:* To impress their images on women's
affections (as a seal stamps its image in wax).
7. For being made of frail flesh, we are frail.
8. Since she is both man and woman.
2.3 Location: Olivia's house.
1. Part of a Latin proverb, meaning "to rise at dawn (is
most healthy)."

SIR ANDREW   Nay, by my troth,° I know not; but I know to be up   *faith*
late is to be up late.

5 SIR TOBY   A false conclusion. I hate it as an unfilled can.° To be   *tankard*
up after midnight and to go to bed then is early; so that to go
to bed after midnight is to go to bed betimes. Does not our lives
consist of the four elements?[2]

SIR ANDREW   Faith, so they say, but I think it rather consists of
10 eating and drinking.

SIR TOBY   Thou'rt a scholar; let us therefore eat and drink. Marian, I say, a stoup° of wine.   *two-pint tankard*

Enter [FESTE, *the*] *clown*

SIR ANDREW   Here comes the fool, i'faith.

FESTE   How now, my hearts. Did you never see the picture of
15 'we three'?[3]

SIR TOBY   Welcome, ass. Now let's have a catch.[4]

SIR ANDREW   By my troth, the fool has an excellent breast.° I had   *singing voice*
rather than forty shillings I had such a leg,° and so sweet a   *(for dancing)*
breath to sing, as the fool has. In sooth, thou wast in very gra-
20 cious fooling last night, when thou spokest of Pigrogromitus, of
the Vapians passing the equinoctial of Queubus.[5] 'Twas very
good, i'faith. I sent thee sixpence for thy leman.° Hadst it?   *sweetheart*

FESTE   I did impeticos thy gratility;[6] for Malvolio's nose is no
whipstock. My lady has a white hand, and the Myrmidons are
25 no bottle-ale houses.[7]

SIR ANDREW   Excellent! Why, this is the best fooling, when all is
done. Now a song.

SIR TOBY [*to* FESTE]   Come on, there is sixpence for you. Let's
have a song.

30 SIR ANDREW [*to* FESTE]   There's a testril[8] of me, too. If one knight
give a—[9]

FESTE   Would you have a love-song, or a song of good life?

SIR TOBY   A love song, a love-song.

SIR ANDREW   Ay, ay. I care not for good life.

FESTE (*sings*)

35   O mistress mine, where are you roaming?
           O stay and hear, your true love's coming,
              That can sing both high and low.
           Trip° no further, pretty sweeting.   *Go*
           Journeys end in lovers meeting,
40   Every wise man's son doth know.[1]

SIR ANDREW   Excellent good, i'faith.

SIR TOBY   Good, good.

FESTE   What is love? 'Tis not hereafter,
           Present mirth hath present laughter.
45   What's to come is still° unsure.   *always*
           In delay there lies no plenty,

2. The four elements, thought to make up all matter,
were earth, air, fire, and water.
3. A trick picture portraying two fools' or asses' heads, the
third being the viewer.
4. Round: a simple song for several voices.
5. *Pigrogromitus . . . Queubus:* Feste's mock learning.
equinoctial: equator of the astronomical heavens.
6. Comic jargon for "impocket (or impetticoat) your gra-
tuity."
7. *for . . . houses:* perhaps it is the sheer inscrutability of
Feste's foolery that so impresses Sir Andrew (line 26).

whipstock: handle of a whip. *bottle-ale houses:* cheap
taverns.
8. Sir Andrew's version of "tester" (sixpence).
9. In F, "give a" appears at the end of a justified line; an
omission is possible.
1. *O mistress . . . know:* the words are not certainly
Shakespeare's; they fit the tune of an instrumental piece
printed in Thomas Morley's *First Book of Consort Lessons* (1599). *wise man's son:* wise men were thought to
have foolish sons.

Then come kiss me, sweet and twenty.°   *twenty times sweet*
    Youth's a stuff will not endure.

SIR ANDREW   A mellifluous voice, as I am true knight.

50   SIR TOBY   A contagious breath.[2]

SIR ANDREW   Very sweet and contagious, i'faith.

SIR TOBY   To hear by the nose, it is dulcet in contagion.[3] But
shall we make the welkin° dance indeed? Shall we rouse the   *sky*
night-owl in a catch that will draw three souls out of one

55   weaver?[4] Shall we do that?

SIR ANDREW   An° you love me, let's do't. I am dog° at a catch.   *If / clever*

FESTE   By'r Lady, sir, and some dogs will catch well.

SIR ANDREW   Most certain. Let our catch be 'Thou knave'.

FESTE   'Hold thy peace, thou knave',[5] knight. I shall be con-

60   strained in't to call thee knave, knight.

SIR ANDREW   'Tis not the first time I have constrained one to call
me knave. Begin, fool. It begins 'Hold thy peace'.

FESTE   I shall never begin if I hold my peace.

SIR ANDREW   Good, i'faith. Come, begin.

    [*They sing the*] *catch.*

    Enter MARIA

65   MARIA   What a caterwauling do you keep here! If my lady have
not called up her steward Malvolio and bid him turn you out
of doors, never trust me.

SIR TOBY   My lady's a Cathayan,[6] we are politicians,° Malvolio's   *schemers*
a Peg-o'-Ramsey,[7] and 'Three merry men be we'. Am not I con-

70   sanguineous?[8] Am I not of her blood? Tilly-vally°—'lady'!   *Fiddlesticks*
'There dwelt a man in Babylon, lady, lady.'[9]

FESTE   Beshrew° me, the knight's in admirable fooling.   *Curse*

SIR ANDREW   Ay, he does well enough if he be disposed, and so
do I, too. He does it with a better grace, but I do it more

75   natural.[1]

SIR TOBY   'O' the twelfth day of December'[2]—

MARIA   For the love o' God, peace.

    Enter MALVOLIO

MALVOLIO   My masters, are you mad? Or what are you? Have
you no wit,° manners, nor honesty,° but to gabble like tinkers   *sense / decency*

80   at this time of night? Do ye make an alehouse of my lady's
house, that ye squeak out your coziers' catches without any
mitigation or remorse[3] of voice? Is there no respect of place,
persons, nor time in you?

SIR TOBY   We did keep time, sir, in our catches. Sneck up!°   *Go hang yourself*

85   MALVOLIO   Sir Toby, I must be round° with you. My lady bade   *plainspoken*
me tell you that though she harbours you as her kinsman she's
nothing allied to your disorders. If you can separate yourself
and your misdemeanours you are welcome to the house. If not,

---

2. Catchy voice; with a play on "disease-causing air."
3. If one could hear through the nose, the sound would
be sweetly ("dulcet") infectious.
4. Weavers were traditionally addicted to psalm singing,
so to move them with popular catches would be a great
triumph. Music was said to be able to draw the soul from
the body.
5. The words of the catch are "Hold thy peace, I prithee
hold thy peace, thou knave" (see Textual Note). Each
singer repeatedly calls the others knaves and tells them
to stop singing.
6. Chinese; but also ethnocentric slang for "trickster" or

"cheat."
7. Name of a dance and popular song; here, used
contemptuously.
8. A blood relative of Olivia's. *'Three . . . we':* a refrain
from a popular song.
9. The opening and refrain of a popular song called
"Constant Susanna."
1. Effortlessly; but unconsciously playing on "fool" or
"idiot."
2. Snatch of a ballad; or possibly a drunken version of
"twelfth day of Christmas"—that is, Twelfth Night.
3. Without any abating or softening.

an it would please you to take leave of her she is very willing to
90 bid you farewell.
SIR TOBY 'Farewell, dear heart, since I must needs be gone.'⁴
MARIA Nay, good Sir Toby.
FESTE 'His eyes do show his days are almost done.'
MALVOLIO Is't even so?
95 SIR TOBY 'But I will never die.'
FESTE 'Sir Toby, there you lie.'
MALVOLIO This is much credit to you.
SIR TOBY 'Shall I bid him go?'
FESTE 'What an if° you do?'   *an if* = if
100 SIR TOBY 'Shall I bid him go, and spare not?'
FESTE 'O no, no, no, no, you dare not.'
SIR TOBY Out o' tune, sir, ye lie. [*To* MALVOLIO] Art any more
than a steward? Dost thou think because thou art virtuous there
shall be no more cakes and ale?⁵
105 FESTE Yes, by Saint Anne, and ginger⁶ shall be hot i'th' mouth,
too.
SIR TOBY Thou'rt i'th' right. [*To* MALVOLIO] Go, sir, rub your
chain with crumbs.⁷ [*To* MARIA] A stoup of wine, Maria.
MALVOLIO Mistress Mary, if you prized my lady's favour at any-
110 thing more than contempt you would not give means° for this   *drink*
uncivil rule.° She shall know of it, by this hand.   *Exit*⁸   *behavior*
MARIA Go shake your ears.°   *(like an ass)*
SIR ANDREW 'Twere as good a deed as to drink when a man's a-
hungry to challenge him the field° and then to break promise   *to a duel*
115 with him, and make a fool of him.
SIR TOBY Do't, knight. I'll write thee a challenge, or I'll deliver
thy indignation to him by word of mouth.
MARIA Sweet Sir Toby, be patient for tonight. Since the youth
of the Count's was today with my lady she is much out of quiet.
120 For Monsieur Malvolio, let me alone with him. If I do not gull
him into a nayword⁹ and make him a common recreation,° do   *sport; jest*
not think I have wit enough to lie straight in my bed. I know I
can do it.
SIR TOBY Possess° us, possess us, tell us something of him.   *Inform*
125 MARIA Marry, sir, sometimes he is a kind of puritan.¹
SIR ANDREW O, if I thought that I'd beat him like a dog.
SIR TOBY What, for being a puritan? Thy exquisite° reason, dear   *ingenious*
knight.
SIR ANDREW I have no exquisite reason for't, but I have reason
130 good enough.
MARIA The dev'l a puritan that he is, or anything constantly but
a time-pleaser,° an affectioned° ass that cons state without book   *boot licker / affected*
and utters it by great swathes;² the best persuaded of himself,³
so crammed, as he thinks, with excellencies, that it is his

---

4. Part of another song that Sir Toby and Feste adapt for
the occasion.
5. *cakes and ale*: traditionally associated with church
festivals, and therefore disliked by Puritans.
6. Used to spice ale. *Saint Anne*: mother of the Virgin;
the oath would be offensive to Puritans who attacked her
cult.
7. Clean your steward's chain; mind your own business.
8. Feste plays no further part in this scene, and he seems
not to be present by line 153. This is the suggested exit

for him.
9. If I do not trick ("gull") him into a byword (for
"dupe").
1. Could mean "morally strict and censorious," as well as
"a follower of the Puritan religious faith."
2. *cons . . . swathes*: memorizes dignified and high-flown
language and utters it in great sweeps (like hay falling
under a scythe).
3. Having the highest opinion of himself.

135 grounds of faith° that all that look on him love him; and on   *his creed*
that vice in him will my revenge find notable cause to work.

SIR TOBY   What wilt thou do?

MARIA   I will drop in his way some obscure epistles of love,
wherein by the colour of his beard, the shape of his leg, the

140 manner of his gait, the expressure° of his eye, forehead, and   *expression*
complexion, he shall find himself most feelingly personated.° I   *represented*
can write very like my lady your niece; on a forgotten° matter   *bygone*
we can hardly make distinction of our hands.°   *handwriting*

SIR TOBY   Excellent, I smell a device.

145 SIR ANDREW   I have't in my nose too.

SIR TOBY   He shall think by the letters that thou wilt drop that
they come from my niece, and that she's in love with him.

MARIA   My purpose is indeed a horse of that colour.

SIR ANDREW   And your horse now would make him an ass.

150 MARIA   Ass° I doubt not.   *(punning on "as")*

SIR ANDREW   O, 'twill be admirable.

MARIA   Sport royal, I warrant you. I know my physic° will work   *medicine*
with him. I will plant you two—and let the fool make a third—
where he shall find the letter. Observe his construction° of it.   *interpretation*

155 For this night, to bed, and dream on the event.° Farewell.   *outcome*

                              Exit

SIR TOBY   Good night, Penthesilea.[4]

SIR ANDREW   Before me,[5] she's a good wench.

SIR TOBY   She's a beagle true bred, and one that adores me. What
o' that?

160 SIR ANDREW   I was adored once, too.

SIR TOBY   Let's to bed, knight. Thou hadst need send for more
money.

SIR ANDREW   If I cannot recover° your niece, I am a foul way   *win*
out.°   *out of money*

165 SIR TOBY   Send for money, knight. If thou hast her not i'th' end,
call me cut.[6]

SIR ANDREW   If I do not, never trust me, take it how you will.

SIR TOBY   Come, come, I'll go burn some sack,[7] 'tis too late to
go to bed now. Come knight, come knight.   *Exeunt*

2.4

Enter Duke, VIOLA *[as Cesario],* CURIO, *and others*

ORSINO   Give me some music. Now good morrow,° friends.   *morning*
Now good Cesario, but° that piece of song,   *just*
That old and antic° song we heard last night.   *quaint*
Methought it did relieve my passion° much,   *suffering*

5 More than light airs and recollected° terms   *studied; artificial*
Of these most brisk and giddy-pacèd times.
Come, but one verse.

CURIO   He is not here, so please your lordship, that should sing
it.

10 ORSINO   Who was it?

---

4. Queen of the Amazons (a joke about Maria's small size).
5. On my soul (a mild oath).
6. A dock-tailed horse; also, slang for "gelding" or for

"female genitals."
7. I'll go warm and spice some Spanish wine.
2.4 Location: Orsino's palace.

CURIO Feste the jester, my lord, a fool that the lady Olivia's father took much delight in. He is about the house.

ORSINO Seek him out, and play the tune the while.

[*Exit* CURIO]

Music plays

[*To* VIOLA] Come hither, boy. If ever thou shalt love,
15   In the sweet pangs of it remember me;
For such as I am, all true lovers are,
Unstaid° and skittish in all motions° else   Unstable / emotions
Save in the constant image of the creature
That is beloved. How dost thou like this tune?

20 VIOLA It gives a very echo to the seat
Where love is throned.[1]

ORSINO   Thou dost speak masterly.°   expertly
My life upon't, young though thou art thine eye
Hath stayed upon some favour° that it loves.   face
Hath it not, boy?

VIOLA   A little, by your favour.°   leave; face

ORSINO What kind of woman is't?

25 VIOLA   Of your complexion.

ORSINO She is not worth thee then. What years, i'faith?

VIOLA About your years, my lord.

ORSINO Too old, by heaven. Let still° the woman take   always
An elder than herself. So wears° she to him;   adapts
30 So sways she level[2] in her husband's heart.
For, boy, however we do praise ourselves,
Our fancies° are more giddy and unfirm,   affections
More longing, wavering, sooner lost and worn,°   exhausted
Than women's are.

VIOLA   I think° it well, my lord.   believe

35 ORSINO Then let thy love be younger than thyself,
Or thy affection cannot hold the bent;[3]
For women are as roses, whose fair flower
Being once displayed,° doth fall that very hour.   opened

VIOLA And so they are. Alas that they are so:
40   To die even° when they to perfection grow.   just

Enter CURIO *and* [FESTE, *the*] *clown*

ORSINO [*to* FESTE] O fellow, come, the song we had last night.
Mark it, Cesario, it is old and plain.
The spinsters,° and the knitters in the sun,   spinners
And the free° maids that weave their thread with bones,[4]   carefree
45   Do use to chant it. It is silly sooth,°   simple truth
And dallies with° the innocence of love,   lingers lovingly on
Like the old° age.   golden

FESTE Are you ready, sir?

ORSINO I prithee, sing.

Music

50 FESTE [*sings*] Come away,° come away death,   Come hither
          And in sad cypress[5] let me be laid.
       Fie away, fie away breath,
          I am slain by a fair cruel maid.

---

1. *It . . . throned:* It reflects back to the heart.
2. So does she balance influence and affection.
3. Cannot remain at full stretch (like the tautness of a bowstring).
4. Spools made from bone on which lace (called "bone lace") was woven.
5. Cypress-wood coffin. Like yews, cypresses were emblematic of mourning.

My shroud of white, stuck all with yew,°   *yew sprigs*
55   O prepare it.
My part of death no one so true
          Did share it.[6]
Not a flower, not a flower sweet

          On my black coffin let there be strewn.
60   Not a friend, not a friend greet
          My poor corpse, where my bones shall be thrown.
     A thousand thousand sighs to save,
          Lay me O where
     Sad true lover never find my grave,
65   To weep there.

ORSINO [*giving money*]   There's for thy pains.

FESTE   No pains, sir. I take pleasure in singing, sir.

ORSINO   I'll pay thy pleasure then.

FESTE   Truly, sir, and pleasure will be paid,°   one time or   *paid for*
70   another.

ORSINO   Give me now leave° to leave° thee.   *permission / dismiss*

FESTE   Now the melancholy god[7] protect thee, and the tailor
     make thy doublet of changeable taffeta,[8] for thy mind is a very
     opal.[9] I would have men of such constancy put to sea, that their
75   business might be everything, and their intent° everywhere, for   *destination*
     that's it that always makes a good voyage of nothing.[1] Farewell.

Exit

ORSINO   Let all the rest give place:°   [*Exeunt* CURIO *and others*]   *withdraw*
          Once more, Cesario,
     Get thee to yon same sovereign cruelty.
     Tell her my love, more noble than the world,
80   Prizes not quantity of dirty lands.
     The parts° that fortune hath bestowed upon her   *possessions*
     Tell her I hold as giddily[2] as fortune;
     But 'tis that miracle and queen of gems
     That nature pranks° her in attracts my soul.   *adorns*
85 VIOLA   But if she cannot love you, sir?

ORSINO   I cannot be so answered.

VIOLA   Sooth,° but you must.   *In truth*
     Say that some lady, as perhaps there is,
     Hath for your love as great a pang of heart
     As you have for Olivia. You cannot love her.
90   You tell her so. Must she not then be answered?

ORSINO   There is no woman's sides
     Can bide° the beating of so strong a passion   *withstand*
     As love doth give my heart; no woman's heart
     So big, to hold so much. They lack retention.°   *constancy*
95   Alas, their love may be called appetite,
     No motion of the liver, but the palate,[3]
     That suffer surfeit, cloyment,° and revolt.°   *satiety / revulsion*
     But mine is all as hungry as the sea,

---

6. *My part . . . it:* No one has died so true to love as I.
7. Saturn (thought to control the melancholic).
8. Shot silk, whose color changes with the angle of vision. *doublet:* close-fitting jacket.
9. An iridescent gemstone that changes color depending on the angle from which it is seen.
1. *that's . . . nothing:* this fickle lack of direction can

make a voyage in the notoriously changeful sea carefree and consonant with one's desires.
2. Lightly (fortune being fickle).
3. *appetite . . . palate:* appetite, like the palate, is easily sated, and thus lacks the emotional depth and complexity of real love, whose seat is the liver. *motion:* impulse.

And can digest as much. Make no compare
100   Between that love a woman can bear me
And that I owe° Olivia.   *have for*
VIOLA   Ay, but I know—
ORSINO   What dost thou know?
VIOLA   Too well what love women to men may owe.
105   In faith, they are as true of heart as we.
My father had a daughter loved a man
As it might be, perhaps, were I a woman
I should your lordship.
ORSINO   And what's her history?
VIOLA   A blank, my lord. She never told her love,
110   But let concealment, like a worm i'th' bud,
Feed on her damask⁴ cheek. She pined in thought,
And with a green and yellow° melancholy   *pale and sallow*
She sat like patience on a monument,⁵
Smiling at grief. Was not this love indeed?
115   We men may say more, swear more, but indeed
Our shows are more than will;⁶ for still° we prove   *always*
Much in our vows, but little in our love.
ORSINO   But died thy sister of her love, my boy?
VIOLA   I am all the daughters of my father's house,
120   And all the brothers too; and yet I know not.
Sir, shall I to this lady?
ORSINO   Ay, that's the theme,
To her in haste. Give her this jewel. Say
My love can give no place, bide no denay.⁷   *Exeunt [severally]*

2.5

Enter SIR TOBY, SIR ANDREW, *and* FABIAN
SIR TOBY   Come thy ways,° Signor Fabian.   *Come along*
FABIAN   Nay, I'll come. If I lose a scruple° of this sport let me be   *miss a scrap*
boiled to death with melancholy.¹
SIR TOBY   Wouldst thou not be glad to have the niggardly rascally
5   sheep-biter² come by some notable shame?
FABIAN   I would exult, man. You know he brought me out o'
favour with my lady about a bear-baiting³ here.
SIR TOBY   To anger him we'll have the bear again, and we will
fool° him black and blue, shall we not, Sir Andrew?   *mock*
10   SIR ANDREW   An° we do not, it is pity of our lives.   *If*
Enter MARIA [*with a letter*]
SIR TOBY   Here comes the little villain. How now, my metal of
India?⁴
MARIA   Get ye all three into the box-tree.° Malvolio's coming   *hedge of boxwood*
down this walk. He has been yonder i' the sun practising behav-
15   iour to his own shadow this half-hour. Observe him, for the
love of mockery, for I know this letter will make a contempla-
tive° idiot of him. Close,° in the name of jesting!   *vacuous / Keep close; hide*

---

4. Pink and white, like a damask rose.
5. A memorial statue symbolizing patience.
6. Our displays of love are greater than our actual feelings.
7. My love cannot be bated, nor tolerate refusal.
2.5 Location: Olivia's garden.

1. Melancholy was a cold humor; "boiled" puns on
"bile," the surplus of which produced melancholy.
2. Literally, a dog that attacks sheep; here, a malicious
sneak.
3. Puritans disapproved of blood sports like bearbaiting.
4. A woman worth her weight in gold.

[The men hide. MARIA *places the letter]*
Lie thou there, for here comes the trout that must be caught
with tickling.⁵   *Exit*

Enter MALVOLIO

20 MALVOLIO 'Tis but fortune, all is fortune. Maria once told me
she° did affect° me, and I have heard herself come thus near,   *(Olivia) / care for*
that should she fancy° it should be one of my complexion.   *fall in love*
Besides, she uses me with a more exalted respect than anyone
else that follows her. What should I think on't?

25 SIR TOBY Here's an overweening rogue.

SIR TOBY O, peace! Contemplation makes a rare turkeycock⁶ of
him—how he jets° under his advanced° plumes!   *struts / raised*

SIR ANDREW 'Slight,⁷ I could so beat the rogue.

SIR TOBY Peace, I say.

30 MALVOLIO To be Count Malvolio!

SIR TOBY Ah, rogue.

SIR ANDREW Pistol him, pistol him.

SIR TOBY Peace, peace.

MALVOLIO There is example° for't: the Lady of the Strachey mar-   *precedent*
35 ried the yeoman of the wardrobe.⁸

SIR ANDREW Fie on him, Jezebel.⁹

FABIAN O peace, now he's deeply in. Look how imagination
blows him.°   *puffs him up*

MALVOLIO Having been three months married to her, sitting in
40 my state°—   *chair of state*

SIR TOBY O for a stone-bow¹ to hit him in the eye!

MALVOLIO Calling my officers° about me, in my branched² vel-   *household attendants*
vet gown, having come from a day-bed° where I have left Olivia   *couch*
sleeping—

45 SIR TOBY Fire and brimstone!

FABIAN O peace, peace.

MALVOLIO And then to have the humour of state³ and—after a
demure travel of regard,⁴ telling them I know my place, as I
would they should do theirs—to ask for my kinsman Toby.

50 SIR TOBY Bolts and shackles!

FABIAN O peace, peace, peace, now, now.

MALVOLIO Seven of my people with an obedient start make° out   *go*
for him. I frown the while, and perchance wind up my watch,
or play with my—*[touching his chain]*⁵ some rich jewel. Toby
55 approaches; curtsies° there to me.   *bows*

SIR TOBY Shall this fellow live?

FABIAN Though our silence be drawn from us with cars,⁶ yet
peace.

MALVOLIO I extend my hand to him thus, quenching my famil-
60 iar smile with an austere regard of control—

SIR TOBY And does not Toby take° you a blow o' the lips, then?   *give*

5. Flattery; trout can be caught by stroking them under
the gills.
6. Proverbially proud; they display their feathers like
peacocks.
7. By God's light (an oath).
8. Perhaps an allusion to a noblewoman who had married her manservant, but there is no certain identification. *yeoman of the wardrobe:* keeper of clothes and linen.
9. Biblical allusion to the proud wife of Ahab, King of
Israel.

1. Catapult, or crossbow for stones.
2. Embroidered with branch patterns.
3. To adopt the grand air of exalted greatness.
4. After casting my eyes gravely about the room.
5. Malvolio momentarily forgets that he will have abandoned his steward's chain; watches were an expensive
luxury at this time.
6. A prisoner might be tied to two carts or chariots
("cars") and pulled by horses in opposite directions to
extort information.

MALVOLIO   Saying 'Cousin Toby, my fortunes, having cast me
　　on your niece, give me this prerogative of speech'—
SIR TOBY   What, what!
65　MALVOLIO   'You must amend your drunkenness.'
SIR TOBY   Out, scab.
FABIAN   Nay, patience, or we break the sinews of our plot.
MALVOLIO   'Besides, you waste the treasure of your time with a
　　foolish knight'—
70　SIR ANDREW   That's me, I warrant you.
MALVOLIO   'One Sir Andrew.'
SIR ANDREW   I knew 'twas I, for many do call me fool.
MALVOLIO [*seeing the letter*]   What employment° have we here?　　*business*
FABIAN   Now is the woodcock near the gin.[7]
75　SIR TOBY   O peace, and the spirit of humours intimate[8] reading
　　aloud to him.
MALVOLIO [*taking up the letter*]   By my life, this is my lady's
　　hand. These be her very c's, her u's, and her t's,[9] and thus
　　makes she her great P's. It is in contempt of° question her　　*beyond*
80　hand.
SIR ANDREW   Her c's, her u's, and her t's? Why that?
MALVOLIO [*reads*]   'To the unknown beloved, this, and my good
　　wishes.' Her very phrases! [*Opening the letter*] By your leave,
　　wax[1]—soft,° and the impressure her Lucrece,[2] with which she　　*wait*
85　uses to seal° —'tis my lady. To whom should this be?　　*habitually seals*
FABIAN   This wins him, liver and all.
MALVOLIO　　　　　'Jove knows I love,
　　　　　　　　But who?
　　　　　　　　Lips do not move,
90　　　　　　　　No man must know.'
　　'No man must know.' What follows? The numbers altered.°　　*meter changed*
　　'No man must know.' If this should be thee, Malvolio?
SIR TOBY   Marry, hang thee, brock.[3]
MALVOLIO   'I may command where I adore,
95　　　　　　　But silence like a Lucrece knife
　　　　　　　With bloodless stroke my heart doth gore.
　　　　　　　M.O.A.I. doth sway my life.'
FABIAN   A fustian° riddle.　　*bombastic*
SIR TOBY   Excellent wench, say I.
100　MALVOLIO   'M.O.A.I. doth sway my life.' Nay, but first let me
　　see, let me see, let me see.
FABIAN   What dish o' poison has she dressed° him!　　*prepared*
SIR TOBY   And with what wing the staniel checks at it![4]
MALVOLIO   'I may command where I adore.' Why, she may com-
105　mand me. I serve her, she is my lady. Why, this is evident to
　　any formal capacity.° There is no obstruction in this. And the　　*normal intelligence*
　　end—what should that alphabetical position° portend? If I　　*arrangement*
　　could make that resemble something in me. Softly—'M.O.A.I.'
SIR TOBY   O ay,[5] make up that, he is now at a cold scent.

---

7. Snare. *woodcock*: a proverbially foolish bird.
8. And may a capricious impulse suggest.
9. Malvolio unwittingly spells out "cut," slang for "female genitals"; the meaning is compounded by "great P's." In fact, these letters do not appear on the outside of the letter.

1. *By . . . wax*: addressed to the sealing wax.
2. The figure of Lucrece, Roman model of chastity, is the device ("impressure") imprinted on the seal.
3. Badger (proverbially stinking).
4. And with what alacrity the sparrow hawk goes after it.
5. *O, ay*: playing on "O.I."

110 FABIAN   Sowter will cry upon't for all this, though it be as rank
as a fox.[6]

MALVOLIO   'M.' Malvolio—'M'—why, that begins my name.

FABIAN   Did not I say he would work it out? The cur is excellent
at faults.[7]

115 MALVOLIO   'M.' But then there is no consonancy in the sequel.[8]
That suffers under probation.[9] 'A' should follow, but 'O' does.

FABIAN   And 'O'[1] shall end, I hope.

SIR TOBY   Ay, or I'll cudgel him, and make him cry 'O!'

MALVOLIO   And then 'I' comes behind.

120 FABIAN   Ay, an you had any eye behind you you might see more
detraction° at your heels than fortunes before you.   defamation

MALVOLIO   'M.O.A.I.' This simulation° is not as the former; and   disguise; riddle
yet to crush° this a little, it would bow° to me, for every one of   force / yield; point
these letters are in my name. Soft, here follows prose: 'If this
125 fall into thy hand, revolve.° In my stars° I am above thee, but   consider / fortunes
be not afraid of greatness. Some are born great, some achieve
greatness, and some have greatness thrust upon 'em. Thy fates
open their hands,° let thy blood and spirit embrace them, and   bestow gifts
to inure° thyself to what thou art like° to be, cast thy humble   accustom / likely
130 slough,[2] and appear fresh. Be opposite° with a kinsman, surly   contrary
with servants. Let thy tongue tang arguments of state;[3] put thy-
self into the trick of singularity.° She thus advises thee that sighs   cultivate eccentricity
for thee. Remember who commended thy yellow stockings,
and wished to see thee ever cross-gartered.[4] I say remember, go
135 to,[5] thou art made if thou desirest to be so; if not, let me see
thee a steward still, the fellow of servants, and not worthy to
touch Fortune's fingers. Farewell. She that would alter services[6] with thee,

The Fortunate-Unhappy.'

140 Daylight and champaign discovers[7] not more. This is open.° I   clear
will be proud, I will read politic° authors, I will baffle[8] Sir   political
Toby, I will wash off gross acquaintance, I will be point-device
the very man.[9] I do not now fool myself, to let imagination
jade° me; for every reason excites to this, that my lady loves me.   trick
145 She did commend my yellow stockings of late, she did praise
my leg, being cross-gartered, and in this she manifests herself
to my love, and with a kind of injunction drives me to these
habits° of her liking. I thank my stars, I am happy. I will be   clothes
strange,° stout,° in yellow stockings, and cross-gartered, even   aloof / proud
150 with the swiftness of putting on. Jove and my stars be praised.
Here is yet a postscript. 'Thou canst not choose but know who
I am. If thou entertainest° my love, let it appear in thy smiling,   accept
thy smiles become thee well. Therefore in my presence still°   constantly
smile, dear my sweet, I prithee.' Jove, I thank thee. I will smile,
155 I will do everything that thou wilt have me.   *Exit*

---

6. "Sowter" (the name of a hound), having lost the scent,
will start to bay loudly as he picks up the new, rank (stinking) smell of the fox. *though:* as though.

7. At picking up a scent after it is momentarily lost. A
"fault" is a "cold scent" (line 109).

8. There is no consistency in what follows.

9. That weakens upon being put to the test.

1. As in the hangman's noose; the last letter of Malvolio's
name; or "O" as a lamentation.

2. A snake's old skin, which peels away.

3. Let your tongue ring out arguments of statecraft or

politics.

4. An antiquated way of adjusting a garter—going once
below the knee, crossing behind it, and knotting above
the knee at the side.

5. An emphatic expression, like "I tell you."

6. Change places (of servant and mistress or master).

7. *champaign discovers:* open countryside reveals.

8. Term used to describe the formal unmaking of a
knight; hence, "disgrace."

9. I will be in every detail the identical man (described
in the letter).

[SIR TOBY, SIR ANDREW, *and* FABIAN *come from hiding*]

FABIAN   I will not give my part of this sport for a pension of
thousands to be paid from the Sophy.°   *Shah of Persia*

SIR TOBY   I could marry this wench for this device.

SIR ANDREW   So could I, too.

160   SIR TOBY   And ask no other dowry with her but such another jest.

Enter MARIA

SIR ANDREW   Nor I neither.

FABIAN   Here comes my noble gull-catcher.°   *trickster*

SIR TOBY [*to* MARIA]   Wilt thou set thy foot o' my neck?

SIR ANDREW [*to* MARIA]   Or o' mine either?

165   SIR TOBY [*to* MARIA]   Shall I play my freedom at tray-trip,[1] and
become thy bondslave?

SIR ANDREW [*to* MARIA]   I'faith, or I either?

SIR TOBY [*to* MARIA]   Why, thou hast put him in such a dream
that when the image of it leaves him, he must run mad.

170   MARIA   Nay, but say true, does it work upon him?

SIR TOBY   Like aqua vitae° with a midwife.   *spirits; liquor*

MARIA   If you will then see the fruits of the sport, mark his first
approach before my lady. He will come to her in yellow stockings, and 'tis a colour she abhors, and cross-gartered, a fashion
175   she detests; and he will smile upon her, which will now be so
unsuitable to her disposition, being addicted to a melancholy
as she is, that it cannot but turn him into a notable contempt.[2]
If you will see it, follow me.

SIR TOBY   To the gates of Tartar,° thou most excellent devil of   *hell*
180   wit.

SIR ANDREW   I'll make one,° too.   *Exeunt*   *go along*

3.1

Enter VIOLA [*as Cesario*] *and* [FESTE, *the*] *clown* [*with
pipe and tabor*][1]

VIOLA   Save° thee, friend, and thy music. Dost thou live by thy   *God save*
tabor?

FESTE   No, sir, I live by° the church.   *near*

VIOLA   Art thou a churchman?

5   FESTE   No such matter, sir. I do live by[2] the church for I do live
at my house, and my house doth stand by the church.

VIOLA   So thou mayst say the king lies by[3] a beggar if a beggar
dwell near him, or the church stands° by thy tabor if thy tabor   *is maintained*
stand by the church.

10   FESTE   You have said, sir. To see this age!—A sentence° is but a   *saying*
cheverel° glove to a good wit, how quickly the wrong side may   *kidskin*
be turned outward.

VIOLA   Nay, that's certain. They that dally nicely° with words   *play subtly*
may quickly make them wanton.[4]

15   FESTE   I would therefore my sister had had no name, sir.

VIOLA   Why, man?

FESTE   Why, sir, her name's a word, and to dally with that word

---

1. A game of dice in which the winner throws a three
("tray" is from the Spanish *tres*). *play:* wager.
2. A notorious object of contempt.
3.1 Location: Olivia's garden.
1. The dialogue demands only a tabor, but jesters com-

monly played a pipe with one hand while tapping a tabor
(small drum, hanging from the neck) with the other.
2. I do earn my keep with.
3. Lives near; punning on "goes to bed with."
4. Equivocal; Feste puns on the sense "unchaste."

might make my sister wanton. But indeed, words are very rascals since bonds disgraced them.[5]

20 VIOLA   Thy reason, man?

FESTE   Troth, sir, I can yield you none without words, and words
are grown so false I am loath to prove reason with them.

VIOLA   I warrant thou art a merry fellow, and carest for nothing.

FESTE   Not so, sir, I do care for something; but in my con-
25 science, sir, I do not care for you. If that be to care for nothing,
sir, I would it would make you invisible.

VIOLA   Art not thou the Lady Olivia's fool?

FESTE   No indeed, sir, the Lady Olivia has no folly, she will keep
no fool, sir, till she be married, and fools are as like husbands
30 as pilchards[6] are to herrings—the husband's the bigger. I am
indeed not her fool, but her corrupter of words.

VIOLA   I saw thee late° at the Count Orsino's.   *lately*

FESTE   Foolery, sir, does walk about the orb[7] like the sun, it
shines everywhere. I would be sorry, sir, but the fool should be
35 as oft with your master as with my mistress.[8] I think I saw your
wisdom[9] there.

VIOLA   Nay, an thou pass upon[1] me, I'll no more with thee. [*Giving money*] Hold, there's expenses for thee.

FESTE   Now Jove in his next commodity° of hair send thee a   *shipment*
40 beard.

VIOLA   By my troth I'll tell thee, I am almost sick for one,[2]
though I would not have it grow on *my* chin. Is thy lady within?

FESTE   Would not a pair of these have bred,[3] sir?

VIOLA   Yes, being kept together and put to use.[4]

45 FESTE   I would play Lord Pandarus[5] of Phrygia, sir, to bring a
Cressida to this Troilus.

VIOLA [*giving money*]   I understand you, sir, 'tis well begged.

FESTE   The matter I hope is not great, sir; begging but a beggar—Cressida was a beggar.[6] My lady is within, sir. I will con-
50 ster° to them whence you come. Who you are and what you   *explain*
would are out of my welkin—I might say 'element', but the
word is over-worn.[7]   *Exit*

VIOLA   This fellow is wise enough to play the fool,
And to do that well craves a kind of wit.°   *intelligence*
55 He must observe their mood on whom he jests,
The quality of persons, and the time,
And, like the haggard, check at every feather
That comes before his eye.[8] This is a practice°   *skill*
As full of labour as a wise man's art,
60 For folly that he wisely shows is fit,[9]

5. Since legal contracts replaced a man's word of honor.
("Bonds" plays on "sworn statements" and "fetters," beto-
kening criminality.)
6. Small fish similar to herring.
7. World; the sun was still believed to circle the earth.
8. I, Feste, should visit master and mistress alike;
Orsino should be called "fool" as often as Olivia.
9. *your wisdom*: a mocking title for Cesario.
1. If you express an opinion of; if you joke about.
2. Almost eager for a beard; almost pining for a man
(Orsino).
3. Would not a pair of coins such as these have multiplied (with possible pun on "be enough to buy bread").

4. *put to use*: invested to produce interest.
5. Go-between, or "pander," since Feste needs a "mate"
for his coin(s). Shakespeare dramatizes the story in
Troilus and Cressida.
6. In asking for the "mate" to his Troilus coin, Feste
draws on a version of the story of Troilus and Cressida in
which Cressida became a beggar.
7. "Welkin" (sky or air) is synonymous with one meaning
of "element," used in what Feste regards as the overworn
phrase "out of my element."
8. *And . . . eye*: As a wild hawk ("haggard") must be sensitive to its prey's disposition.
9. For folly that he skillfully displays is proper.

But wise men, folly-fall'n, quite taint[1] their wit.
    Enter SIR TOBY *and* [SIR] ANDREW

SIR TOBY Save you, gentleman.

VIOLA And you, sir.

SIR ANDREW *Dieu vous garde,*[2] *monsieur.*

65 VIOLA *Et vous aussi, votre serviteur.*[3]

SIR ANDREW I hope, sir, you are, and I am yours.

SIR TOBY Will you encounter[4] the house? My niece is desirous
    you should enter if your trade be to her.

VIOLA I am bound to° your niece, sir: I mean she is the list° of   *for / destination*
70   my voyage.

SIR TOBY Taste° your legs, sir, put them to motion.   *Try*

VIOLA My legs do better understand° me, sir, than I understand   *stand under*
    what you mean by bidding me taste my legs.

SIR TOBY I mean to go, sir, to enter.

75 VIOLA I will answer you with gait and entrance.
    Enter OLIVIA, *and* [MARIA, *her*] *gentlewoman*
    But we are prevented.° [*To* OLIVIA] Most excellent accom-   *anticipated*
    plished lady, the heavens rain odours on you.

SIR ANDREW [*to* SIR TOBY] That youth's a rare° courtier; 'rain   *an excellent*
    odours'—well.°   *well put*

80 VIOLA My matter hath no voice,° lady, but to your own most   *must not be spoken*
    pregnant° and vouchsafed° ear.   *receptive / proffered*

SIR ANDREW [*to* SIR TOBY] 'Odours', 'pregnant', and 'vouch-
    safed'—I'll get 'em all three all ready.[5]

OLIVIA Let the garden door be shut, and leave me to my
85   hearing.   [*Exeunt* SIR TOBY, SIR ANDREW, *and* MARIA]
    Give me your hand, sir.

VIOLA My duty, madam, and most humble service.

OLIVIA What is your name?

VIOLA Cesario is your servant's name, fair princess.

90 OLIVIA My servant, sir? 'Twas never merry world[6]
    Since lowly feigning° was called compliment.   *pretended humility*
    You're servant to the Count Orsino, youth.

VIOLA And he is yours, and his must needs be yours.
    Your servant's servant is *your* servant, madam.

95 OLIVIA For° him, I think not on him. For his thoughts,   *As for*
    Would they were blanks rather than filled with me.

VIOLA Madam, I come to whet your gentle thoughts
    On his behalf.

OLIVIA   O by your leave,[7] I pray you.
    I bade you never speak again of him;
100   But would you undertake another suit,
    I had rather hear you to solicit that
    Than music from the spheres.[8]

VIOLA   Dear lady—

OLIVIA Give me leave, beseech you. I did send,
    After the last enchantment you did here,
105   A ring in chase of you. So did I abuse°   *deceive; dishonor*

---

1. Discredit; spoil. *folly-fall'n:* fallen into folly.
2. God protect you (French).
3. And you also, (I am) your servant. (Sir Andrew's awkward reply demonstrates that his French is limited.)
4. Pedantry for "enter" (Toby mocks Viola's courtly language).
5. *I'll . . . ready:* to commit to memory for later use.
6. *'Twas . . . world:* the proverbial "Things have never been the same."
7. Permit me to interrupt (polite expression).
8. Exquisite music thought to be made by the planets as they moved, but inaudible to mortal ears.

Myself, my servant, and I fear me you.°   *and, as I fear, you*
Under your hard construction⁹ must I sit,
To force° that on you in a shameful cunning   *For forcing*
Which you knew none of yours. What might you think?
110 Have you not set mine honour at the stake
And baited it with all th'unmuzzled thoughts¹
That tyrannous heart can think? To one of your receiving°   *perception*
Enough is shown. A cypress,² not a bosom,
Hides my heart. So let me hear you speak.

VIOLA   I pity you.

115 OLIVIA   That's a degree to° love.   *toward*

VIOLA   No, not a grece,° for 'tis a vulgar proof°   *step / common experience*
That very oft we pity enemies.

OLIVIA   Why then, methinks 'tis time to smile again.³
O world, how apt° the poor are to be proud!   *ready*
120 If one should be a prey, how much the better
To fall before the lion than the wolf!⁴

    Clock strikes

The clock upbraids me with the waste of time.
Be not afraid, good youth, I will not have you;
And yet when wit and youth is come to harvest
125 Your wife is like to reap a proper° man.   *handsome; worthy*
There lies your way, due west.

VIOLA   Then westward ho!⁵
Grace and good disposition° attend your ladyship.   *peace of mind*
You'll nothing, madam, to my lord by me?

OLIVIA   Stay. I prithee tell me what thou⁶ think'st of me.

130 VIOLA   That you do think you are not what you are.⁷

OLIVIA   If I think so, I think the same of you.⁸

VIOLA   Then think you right, I am not what I am.

OLIVIA   I would you were as I would have you be.

VIOLA   Would it be better, madam, than I am?
135 I wish it might, for now I am your fool.⁹

OLIVIA [*aside*]   O, what a deal of scorn looks beautiful
In the contempt and anger of his lip!
A murd'rous guilt shows not itself more soon
Than love that would seem hid. Love's night is noon.¹
140 [*To* VIOLA] Cesario, by the roses of the spring,
By maidhood, honour, truth, and everything,
I love thee so that, maugre° all thy pride,   *despite*
Nor° wit nor reason can my passion hide.   *Neither*
Do not extort thy reasons from this clause,²
145 For that° I woo, thou therefore hast no cause.   *That because*
But rather reason thus with reason fetter:³
Love sought is good, but given unsought, is better.

---

9. Your unfavorable interpretation (of my behavior).
1. *set . . . thoughts*: as bears that were tied up at the stake and baited with dogs.
2. Veil of transparent silken gauze; the cypress tree was also emblematic of mourning.
3. Time to discard love's melancholy.
4. *If . . . wolf*: If I had to fall prey to love, it would have been better to succumb to the noble Orsino than to the hardhearted Cesario.
5. Thames watermen's cry to attract passengers for the court at Westminster from London.
6. Olivia changes from "you" to the familiar "thou."

7. That you think you are in love with a man, but you are mistaken.
8. Olivia may think that Cesario has suggested that she is mad; or she may imply that she thinks that Cesario, despite his subordinate position, is noble.
9. You have made a fool of me.
1. Love, though attempting secrecy, still shines out as bright as day.
2. Do not take the position that just because I woo you, you are under no obligation to reciprocate.
3. But instead constrain your reasoning with this argument.

VIOLA   By innocence I swear, and by my youth,
 I have one heart, one bosom, and one truth,
150 And that no woman has, nor never none
 Shall mistress be of it save I alone.
 And so adieu, good madam. Never more
 Will I my master's tears to you deplore.°   lament
OLIVIA   Yet come again, for thou perhaps mayst move
155 That heart which now abhors, to like his love.

                                      Exeunt [*severally*]

3.2

            Enter SIR TOBY, SIR ANDREW, *and* FABIAN
SIR ANDREW   No, faith, I'll not stay a jot longer.
SIR TOBY   Thy reason, dear venom,° give thy reason.   venomous one
FABIAN   You must needs yield your reason, Sir Andrew.
SIR ANDREW   Marry, I saw your niece do more favours to the
5   Count's servingman than ever she bestowed upon me. I saw't
 i'th' orchard.°   garden
SIR TOBY   Did she see thee the while, old boy? Tell me that.
SIR ANDREW   As plain as I see you now.
FABIAN   This was a great argument° of love in her toward you.   proof
10 SIR ANDREW   'Slight,° will you make an ass o' me?   By God's light
FABIAN   I will prove it legitimate, sir, upon the oaths of judgement and reason.
SIR TOBY   And they have been grand-jurymen[1] since before
 Noah was a sailor.
15 FABIAN   She did show favour to the youth in your sight only to
 exasperate you, to awake your dormouse° valour, to put fire in   meek; timid
 your heart and brimstone in your liver. You should then have
 accosted her, and with some excellent jests, fire-new from the
 mint,° you should have banged the youth into dumbness. This   newly minted
20 was looked for at your hand, and this was balked.° The double   neglected
 gilt[2] of this opportunity you let time wash off, and you are now
 sailed into the north of my lady's opinion,[3] where you will hang
 like an icicle on a Dutchman's[4] beard unless you do redeem it
 by some laudable attempt either of valour or policy.°   cunning
25 SIR ANDREW   An't° be any way, it must be with valour, for policy   If it
 I hate. I had as lief° be a Brownist as a politician.[5]   as soon
SIR TOBY   Why then, build me thy fortunes upon the basis of
 valour. Challenge me° the Count's youth to fight with him,   for me
 hurt him in eleven places. My niece shall take note of it; and
30 assure thyself, there is no love-broker in the world can more
 prevail in man's commendation with woman than report of
 valour.
FABIAN   There is no way but this, Sir Andrew.
SIR ANDREW   Will either of you bear me a challenge to him?
35 SIR TOBY   Go, write it in a martial hand, be curst° and brief. It is   sharp
 no matter how witty so it be eloquent and full of invention.° imagination; untruth

---

3.2 Location: Olivia's house.
1. Grand jurymen were supposed to be good judges of
evidence.
2. Twice gilded, and as such, Sir Andrew's "golden
opportunity" to prove both love and valor.

3. Into Olivia's cold disfavor.
4. Perhaps an allusion to navigator Willem Barents, who
led an expedition to the Arctic in 1596–97.
5. Schemer. A Brownist was a member of the Puritan
sect founded in 1581 by Robert Browne.

Taunt him with the licence of ink.[6] If thou 'thou'st'[7] him some
thrice, it shall not be amiss, and as many lies° as will lie in thy   *accusations of lying*
sheet of paper, although the sheet were big enough for the bed
40   of Ware,[8] in England, set 'em down, go about it. Let there be
gall[9] enough in thy ink; though thou write with a goose-pen,[1]
no matter. About it.

SIR ANDREW   Where shall I find you?

SIR TOBY   We'll call thee at the cubiculo.° Go.   *little chamber*

Exit SIR ANDREW

45   FABIAN   This is a dear manikin° to you, Sir Toby.   *puppet*

SIR TOBY   I have been dear° to him, lad, some two thousand   *costly*
strong or so.

FABIAN   We shall have a rare letter from him; but you'll not
deliver't.

50   SIR TOBY   Never trust me then; and by all means stir on the youth
to an answer. I think oxen and wain-ropes[2] cannot hale° them   *drag*
together. For Andrew, if he were opened and you find so much
blood in his liver[3] as will clog° the foot of a flea, I'll eat the rest   *weigh down*
of th'anatomy.°   *cadaver*

55   FABIAN   And his opposite,° the youth, bears in his visage no great   *adversary*
presage of cruelty.

Enter MARIA

SIR TOBY   Look where the youngest wren of nine[4] comes.

MARIA   If you desire the spleen,° and will laugh yourselves into   *a laughing fit*
stitches, follow me. Yon gull° Malvolio is turned heathen, a   *fool*
60   very renegado,[5] for there is no Christian that means to be saved
by believing rightly can ever believe such impossible passages
of grossness.[6] He's in yellow stockings.

SIR TOBY   And cross-gartered?

MARIA   Most villainously,° like a pedant° that keeps a school i'th'   *abominably / teacher*
65   church.[7] I have dogged him like his murderer. He does obey
every point of the letter that I dropped to betray him. He does
smile his face into more lines than is in the new map with the
augmentation of the Indies.[8] You have not seen such a thing as
'tis. I can hardly forbear hurling things at him. I know my lady
70   will strike him. If she do, he'll smile, and take't for a great
favour.

SIR TOBY   Come bring us, bring us where he is.   *Exeunt*

3.3

Enter SEBASTIAN *and* ANTONIO

SEBASTIAN   I would not by my will have troubled you,
But since you make your pleasure of your pains
I will no further chide you.

ANTONIO   I could not stay behind you. My desire,

---

6. *licence of ink:* freedom taken in writing, but not risked
in conversation.
7. Call him "thou" (an insult to a stranger).
8. Famous Elizabethan bedstead, nearly eleven feet
square, now in the Victoria and Albert Museum, London.
9. Oak gall, an ingredient in ink; bitterness or rancor.
1. Quill made of a goose feather. (The goose was proverbially cowardly and foolish.)
2. Wagon ropes pulled by oxen.
3. Supposed to be the source of blood, which engendered courage.

4. The smallest of small birds; the smallest wren in a
family of nine.
5. Renegade (Spanish); a Christian converted to Islam.
6. Such patent absurdities (in the letter).
7. Because no schoolroom is available in a small rustic
community.
8. Possibly refers to a map published in 1599 showing
the East Indies more fully than in earlier maps and
crisscrossed by many rhumb lines.
3.3 Location: A street scene.

5   More sharp than filèd steel, did spur me forth,
And not all° love to see you—though so much   *only*
As might have drawn one to a longer voyage—
But jealousy° what might befall your travel,   *apprehension*
Being skilless in° these parts, which to a stranger,   *unfamiliar to*
10   Unguided and unfriended, often prove
Rough and unhospitable. My willing love
The rather° by these arguments of fear   *more willingly*
Set forth in your pursuit.

SEBASTIAN   My kind Antonio,
I can no other answer make but thanks,
15   And thanks; and ever oft° good turns   *very often*
Are shuffled off° with such uncurrent[1] pay.   *shrugged off*
But were my worth as is my conscience° firm,   *sense of indebtedness*
You should find better dealing. What's to do?
Shall we go see the relics° of this town?   *sights*
20 ANTONIO   Tomorrow, sir. Best first go see your lodging.

SEBASTIAN   I am not weary, and 'tis long to night.
I pray you let us satisfy our eyes
With the memorials and the things of fame
That do renown this city.

ANTONIO   Would you'd pardon me.
25 I do not without danger walk these streets.
Once in a sea-fight 'gainst the Count his° galleys   *(the Count's)*
I did some service, of such note indeed
That were I ta'en° here it would scarce be answered.[2]   *captured*

SEBASTIAN   Belike° you slew great number of his people.   *Perhaps*
30 ANTONIO   Th'offence is not of such a bloody nature,
Albeit the quality° of the time and quarrel   *circumstances*
Might well have given us bloody argument.°   *cause for bloodshed*
It might have since been answered in repaying
What we took from them, which for traffic's° sake   *trade's*
35 Most of our city did. Only myself stood out,
For which if I be latchèd° in this place   *caught*
I shall pay dear.

SEBASTIAN   Do not then walk too open.

ANTONIO   It doth not fit me. Hold, sir, here's my purse.
In the south suburbs at the Elephant°   *name of an inn*
40 Is best to lodge. I will bespeak our diet°   *order our meals*
Whiles you beguile° the time and feed your knowledge   *pass*
With viewing of the town. There shall you have me.

SEBASTIAN   Why I your purse?

ANTONIO   Haply° your eye shall light upon some toy°   *Perhaps / trifle*
45 You have desire to purchase; and your store°   *resources*
I think is not for idle markets,[3] sir.

SEBASTIAN   I'll be your purse-bearer, and leave you
For an hour.

ANTONIO   To th' Elephant.

SEBASTIAN   I do remember.

Exeunt [*severally*]

---

1. Out of currency; worthless.
2. It would be difficult for me to make reparation (and
thus my life would be in danger).
3. Not large enough to spend on luxuries.

3.4

Enter OLIVIA *and* MARIA

OLIVIA [*aside*]   I have sent after him, he says he'll come.
How shall I feast him? What bestow of° him?   on
For youth is bought more oft than begged or borrowed.[1]
I speak too loud.
5   [*To* MARIA] Where's Malvolio? He is sad° and civil,°   sober / respectful
And suits well for a servant with my fortunes.
Where is Malvolio?

MARIA   He's coming, madam, but in very strange manner. He is
sure possessed,° madam.   (by the devil); insane

10 OLIVIA   Why, what's the matter? Does he rave?

MARIA   No, madam, he does nothing but smile. Your ladyship
were best to have some guard about you if he come, for sure
the man is tainted in's wits.

OLIVIA   Go call him hither.   [*Exit* MARIA]
I am as mad as he,
15   If sad and merry madness equal be.
Enter MALVOLIO [*cross-gartered and wearing yellow
stockings, with* MARIA]
How now, Malvolio?

MALVOLIO   Sweet lady, ho, ho!

OLIVIA   Smil'st thou? I sent for thee upon a sad occasion.°   about a serious matter

MALVOLIO   Sad, lady? I could be sad. This does make some
20   obstruction in the blood, this cross-gartering, but what of that?
If it please the eye of one, it is with me as the very true sonnet°   song
is, 'Please one, and please all'.[2]

OLIVIA   Why, how dost thou, man? What is the matter with thee?

MALVOLIO   Not black in my mind, though yellow[3] in my legs. It
25   did come to his hands, and commands shall be executed. I
think we do know the sweet roman hand.°   italic calligraphy

OLIVIA   Wilt thou go to bed,[4] Malvolio?

MALVOLIO [*kissing his hand*]   To bed? 'Ay, sweetheart, and I'll
come to thee.'[5]

30 OLIVIA   God comfort thee. Why dost thou smile so, and kiss thy
hand so oft?

MARIA   How do you, Malvolio?

MALVOLIO   At your request?—yes, nightingales answer daws.[6]

MARIA   Why appear you with this ridiculous boldness before my
35   lady?

MALVOLIO   'Be not afraid of greatness'—'twas well writ.

OLIVIA   What meanest thou by that, Malvolio?

MALVOLIO   'Some are born great'—

OLIVIA   Ha?

40 MALVOLIO   'Some achieve greatness'—

OLIVIA   What sayst thou?

MALVOLIO   'And some have greatness thrust upon them.'

OLIVIA   Heaven restore thee.

3.4 Location: The garden of Olivia's house.
1. "Better to buy than to beg or borrow" was proverbial.
2. If I please one, I please all I care to please (words of a popular bawdy ballad).
3. Black and yellow biles indicated choleric and melancholic dispositions, respectively. "Black and yellow" was

the name of a popular song; to "wear yellow hose" was to be jealous.
4. In order to cure his madness with sleep.
5. A line from a popular song.
6. Shall I deign to reply to you? Yes, since even the nightingale sings in response to the crowing of the jackdaw.

MALVOLIO 'Remember who commended thy yellow
45 stockings'—
OLIVIA 'Thy yellow stockings'?
MALVOLIO 'And wished to see thee cross-gartered.'
OLIVIA 'Cross-gartered'?
MALVOLIO 'Go to, thou art made, if thou desirest to be so.'
50 OLIVIA Am I made?
MALVOLIO 'If not, let me see thee a servant still.'
OLIVIA Why, this is very midsummer madness.
      Enter a SERVANT
SERVANT Madam, the young gentleman of the Count Orsino's
      is returned. I could hardly entreat him back. He attends your
55   ladyship's pleasure.
OLIVIA I'll come to him.   [*Exit* SERVANT]
      Good Maria, let this fellow be looked to. Where's my cousin
      Toby? Let some of my people have a special care of him, I
      would not have him miscarry° for the half of my dowry.   come to harm
      Exeunt [OLIVIA *and* MARIA, *severally*]
60 MALVOLIO O ho, do you come near° me now? No worse man   appreciate
      than Sir Toby to look to me. This concurs directly with the
      letter, she sends him on purpose, that I may appear stubborn to
      him, for she incites me to that in the letter. 'Cast thy humble
      slough,' says she, 'be opposite with a kinsman, surly with ser-
65   vants, let thy tongue tang arguments of state, put thyself into
      the trick of singularity', and consequently° sets down the man-   subsequently
      ner how, as a sad face, a reverend carriage, a slow tongue, in
      the habit of some sir of note,° and so forth. I have limed[7] her,   gentleman
      but it is Jove's doing, and Jove make me thankful. And when
70   she went away now, 'let this fellow be looked to'. Fellow![8]—not
      'Malvolio', nor after my degree, but 'fellow'. Why, everything
      adheres together that no dram of a scruple, no scruple of a
      scruple,[9] no obstacle, no incredulous or unsafe circumstance—
      what can be said?—nothing that can be can come between me
75   and the full prospect of my hopes. Well, Jove, not I, is the doer
      of this, and he is to be thanked.
      Enter [SIR] TOBY, FABIAN, *and* MARIA
SIR TOBY Which way is he, in the name of sanctity? If all the
      devils of hell be drawn in little,[1] and Legion[2] himself possessed
      him, yet I'll speak to him.
80 FABIAN Here he is, here he is. [*To* MALVOLIO] How is't with you,
      sir? How is't with you, man?
MALVOLIO Go off, I discard you. Let me enjoy my private.° Go   privacy
      off.
MARIA Lo, how hollow° the fiend speaks within him. Did not I   resonantly
85   tell you? Sir Toby, my lady prays you to have a care of him.
MALVOLIO Aha, does she so?
SIR TOBY Go to, go to. Peace, peace, we must deal gently with
      him. Let me alone.° How do you, Malvolio? How is't with you?   Leave him to me

7. Birds were caught by smearing sticky birdlime on
branches.
8. Malvolio takes the word to mean "companion."
9. *no dram . . . scruple:* both phrases mean "no scrap of
a doubt." *dram:* one-eighth of a fluid ounce. *scruple:* one-
third of a dram.
1. Be contracted into a small space (punning on

"painted in miniature").
2. Alluding to a scene of exorcism in Mark 5:8–9: "For
he [Jesus] said unto him, Come out of the man, thou
unclean spirit. And he asked him, What is thy name? And
he answered saying, My name is Legion: for we are
many."

What, man, defy the devil. Consider, he's an enemy to man-
90   kind.

MALVOLIO   Do you know what you say?

MARIA   La° you, an you speak ill of the devil, how he takes it at   *Look*
heart. Pray God he be not bewitched.

FABIAN   Carry his water to th' wise woman.[3]

95 MARIA   Marry, and it shall be done tomorrow morning, if I live.
My lady would not lose him for more than I'll say.

MALVOLIO   How now, mistress?

MARIA   O Lord!

SIR TOBY   Prithee hold thy peace, this is not the way. Do you not
100   see you move° him? Let me alone with him.   *anger*

FABIAN   No way but gentleness, gently, gently. The fiend is
rough,° and will not be roughly used.   *violent*

SIR TOBY   Why how now, my bawcock?[4] How dost thou, chuck?

MALVOLIO   Sir!

105 SIR TOBY   Ay, biddy,° come with me. What man, 'tis not for grav-   *hen*
ity° to play at cherry-pit[5] with Satan. Hang him, foul collier.[6]   *for a man of dignity*

MARIA   Get him to say his prayers. Good Sir Toby, get him to
pray.

MALVOLIO   My prayers, minx?°   *impertinent girl*

110 MARIA   No, I warrant you, he will not hear of godliness.

MALVOLIO   Go hang yourselves, all. You are idle° shallow things,   *foolish*
I am not of your element.° You shall know more hereafter.   *social sphere*

                                                  Exit

SIR TOBY   Is't possible?

FABIAN   If this were played upon a stage, now, I could condemn
115   it as an improbable fiction.

SIR TOBY   His very genius° hath taken the infection of the   *spirit*
device,° man.   *trick*

MARIA   Nay, pursue him now, lest the device take air and taint.[7]

FABIAN   Why, we shall make him mad indeed.

120 MARIA   The house will be the quieter.

SIR TOBY   Come, we'll have him in a dark room and bound.[8] My
niece is already in the belief that he's mad. We may carry it
thus° for our pleasure and his penance till our very pastime,   *continue the pretense*
tired out of breath, prompt us to have mercy on him, at which
125   time we will bring the device to the bar[9] and crown thee for a
finder of madmen.[1] But see, but see.

                Enter SIR ANDREW [*with a paper*]

FABIAN   More matter for a May morning.[2]

SIR ANDREW   Here's the challenge, read it. I warrant there's vinegar and pepper in't.

130 FABIAN   Is't so saucy?

SIR ANDREW   Ay—is't? I warrant him. Do but read.

SIR TOBY   Give me.

      [*Reads*] 'Youth, whatsoever thou art, thou art but a scurvy
fellow.'

---

3. *water*: urine (for medical diagnosis). *wise woman*: local
healer, "good witch."
4. Fine fellow (from the French *beau coq,* "fine bird").
5. A children's game in which cherrystones were thrown
into a hole.
6. Dirty coal man (the devil was supposed to be black).
7. Spoil (like leftover food) by exposure to air; become

known (and thus ruined).
8. Customary treatments for madness.
9. Into the open court (to be judged).
1. *finder of madmen*: one of a jury "finding," or declaring,
a man to be mad.
2. More pastime fit for a holiday.

135   FABIAN   Good, and valiant.

     SIR TOBY 'Wonder not, nor admire° not in thy mind why I do   *marvel*
     call thee so, for I will show thee no reason for't.'

     FABIAN   A good note, that keeps you from the blow of the law.[3]

     SIR TOBY 'Thou comest to the Lady Olivia, and in my sight she
140   uses thee kindly; but thou liest in thy throat,° that is not the   *deeply*
     matter I challenge thee for.'

     FABIAN   Very brief, and to exceeding good sense [*aside*] -less.[4]

     SIR TOBY 'I will waylay thee going home, where if it be thy
     chance to kill me'—

145   FABIAN   Good.

     SIR TOBY 'Thou killest me like a rogue and a villain.'

     FABIAN   Still you keep o'th' windy side[5] of the law—good.

     SIR TOBY 'Fare thee well, and God have mercy upon one of our
     souls. He may have mercy upon mine, but my hope is better,[6]
150   and so look to thyself.

     Thy friend as thou usest him, and thy sworn enemy,

                             Andrew Aguecheek.'

     If this letter move° him not, his legs cannot. I'll give't him.   *provoke*

     MARIA   You may have very fit occasion for't. He is now in some
155   commerce° with my lady, and will by and by depart.   *conversation*

     SIR TOBY Go, Sir Andrew. Scout me° for him at the corner of   *Look out*
     the orchard like a bum-baily.[7] So soon as ever thou seest him,
     draw, and as thou drawest, swear horrible, for it comes to pass
     oft that a terrible oath, with a swaggering accent sharply
160   twanged off, gives manhood more approbation° than ever   *credit*
     proof° itself would have earned him. Away.   *trial*

     SIR ANDREW   Nay, let me alone for swearing.[8]   *Exit*

     SIR TOBY Now will not I deliver his letter, for the behaviour of
     the young gentleman gives him out to be of good capacity° and   *ability*
165   breeding. His employment between his lord and my niece
     confirms no less. Therefore this letter, being so excellently
     ignorant, will breed no terror in the youth. He will find it
     comes from a clodpoll.° But, sir, I will deliver his challenge by   *blockhead*
     word of mouth, set upon Aguecheek a notable report of valour,
170   and drive the gentleman—as I know his youth will aptly receive
     it[9]—into a most hideous opinion of his rage, skill, fury, and
     impetuosity. This will so fright them both that they will kill one
     another by the look, like cockatrices.[1]

           Enter OLIVIA, *and* VIOLA [*as Cesario*]

     FABIAN   Here he comes with your niece. Give them way° till he   *Stand aside*
175   take leave, and presently after him.

     SIR TOBY I will meditate the while upon some horrid message
     for a challenge.   [*Exeunt* SIR TOBY, FABIAN, *and* MARIA]

     OLIVIA   I have said too much unto a heart of stone,
     And laid mine honour too unchary° out.   *carelessly*
180   There's something in me that reproves my fault,
     But such a headstrong potent fault it is
     That it but mocks reproof.

---

3. That protects you from a charge of a breach of peace.
4. F's "sence-lesse" appears to use the hyphen to signal an aside.
5. To windward (and therefore safe, not exposed to the law's blasts).
6. *my hope is better*: Andrew means he expects to survive, but he ineptly implies that he expects to be damned.

7. Petty sheriff's officer employed to arrest debtors.
8. Have no doubts as to my swearing ability.
9. As I know his inexperience will readily believe the report.
1. Basilisks; mythical creatures supposed to kill at a glance.

VIOLA   With the same 'haviour[2] So
That your passion bears[2] goes on my master's griefs.

OLIVIA [*giving a jewel*]   Here, wear this jewel[3] for me, 'tis my picture—
185   Refuse it not, it hath no tongue to vex you—
And I beseech you come again tomorrow.
What shall you ask of me that I'll deny,
That honour, saved, may upon asking give?[4]

VIOLA   Nothing but this: your true love for my master.

190   OLIVIA   How with mine honour may I give him that
Which I have given to you?

VIOLA   I will acquit you.[5]

OLIVIA   Well, come again tomorrow. Fare thee well.
A fiend like thee might bear my soul to hell.   *Exit*

Enter [SIR] TOBY *and* FABIAN

SIR TOBY   Gentleman, God save thee.

195   VIOLA   And you, sir.

SIR TOBY   That defence thou hast, betake thee to't. Of what
nature the wrongs are thou hast done him, I know not, but thy
interceptor, full of despite,° bloody as the hunter, attends° thee   *defiance / awaits*
at the orchard end. Dismount thy tuck,[6] be yare° in thy prepara-   *prompt*
200   tion, for thy assailant is quick, skilful, and deadly.

VIOLA   You mistake, sir, I am sure no man hath any quarrel to
me. My remembrance° is very free and clear from any image   *memory*
of offence done to any man.

SIR TOBY   You'll find it otherwise, I assure you. Therefore, if you
205   hold your life at any price, betake you to your guard, for your
opposite° hath in him what youth, strength, skill, and wrath can   *opponent*
furnish man withal.

VIOLA   I pray you, sir, what is he?

SIR TOBY   He is knight dubbed with unhatched[7] rapier and on
210   carpet consideration,[8] but he is a devil in private brawl. Souls
and bodies hath he divorced three, and his incensement at this
moment is so implacable that satisfaction can be none but by
pangs of death and sepulchre. Hob nob[9] is his word,° give't or   *motto*
take't.

215   VIOLA   I will return again into the house and desire some con-
duct° of the lady. I am no fighter. I have heard of some kind of   *escort*
men that put quarrels purposely on others, to taste° their   *test*
valour. Belike this is a man of that quirk.

SIR TOBY   Sir, no. His indignation derives itself out of a very com-
220   petent° injury, therefore get you on, and give him his desire.   *sufficient*
Back you shall not to the house unless you undertake that° with   *(a duel)*
me which with as much safety you might answer him. There-
fore on, or strip your sword stark naked, for meddle° you must,   *engage in a duel*
that's certain, or forswear to wear iron about you.[1]

225   VIOLA   This is as uncivil as strange. I beseech you do me this
courteous office, as to know of° the knight what my offence   *ascertain from*
to him is. It is something of my negligence, nothing of my
purpose.

---

2. *'haviour . . . bears:* behavior that characterizes your
lovesickness.
3. Jeweled ornament, here a brooch or a locket with
Olivia's picture.
4. That honor may grant without compromising itself.
5. I will release you from your promise.

6. Draw your rapier.
7. Unhacked, or undented; never used in battle.
8. A "carpet knight" obtained his title through connections at court rather than valor on the battlefield.
9. Have or have not ("all or nothing").
1. Or forfeit your right to wear a sword.

SIR TOBY   I will do so. Signor Fabian, stay you by this gentleman
230   till my return.   *Exit*

VIOLA   Pray you, sir, do you know of this matter?

FABIAN   I know the knight is incensed against you even to a mortal arbitrement,° but nothing of the circumstance more.   *deadly duel*

VIOLA   I beseech you, what manner of man is he?

235   FABIAN   Nothing of that wonderful promise to read him by his
form² as you are like to find him in the proof of his valour. He
is indeed, sir, the most skilful, bloody, and fatal opposite that
you could possibly have found in any part of Illyria. Will you°   *If you will*
walk towards him, I will make your peace with him if I can.

240   VIOLA   I shall be much bound to you for't. I am one that had
rather go with Sir Priest³ than Sir Knight—I care not who
knows so much of my mettle.°   *Exeunt*   *disposition*

          Enter [SIR] TOBY *and* [SIR] ANDREW

SIR TOBY   Why, man, he's a very devil, I have not seen such a
virago.⁴ I had a pass° with him, rapier, scabbard, and all, and   *fencing bout*
245   he gives me the stuck-in⁵ with such a mortal motion that it is
inevitable, and on the answer,° he pays you as surely as your   *return hit*
feet hits the ground they step on. They say he has been fencer
to the Sophy.°   *Shah of Persia*

SIR ANDREW   Pox on't, I'll not meddle with him.

250   SIR TOBY   Ay, but he will not now be pacified, Fabian can scarce
hold him yonder.

SIR ANDREW   Plague on't, an° I thought he had been valiant and   *if*
so cunning in fence I'd have seen him damned ere I'd have
challenged him. Let him let the matter slip and I'll give him
255   my horse, grey Capulet.

SIR TOBY   I'll make the motion.° Stand here, make a good show   *offer*
on't—this shall end without the perdition of souls.°   *loss of lives*
[*Aside*] Marry, I'll ride your horse as well as I ride you.

          Enter FABIAN, *and* VIOLA [*as Cesario*]

[*Aside to* FABIAN] I have his horse to take up° the quarrel, I have   *settle*
260   persuaded him the youth's a devil.

FABIAN [*aside to* SIR TOBY]   He is as horribly conceited⁶ of him,
and pants and looks pale as if a bear were at his heels.

SIR TOBY [*to* VIOLA]   There's no remedy, sir, he will fight with
you for's oath' sake. Marry, he hath better bethought him of his
265   quarrel, and he finds that now scarce to be worth talking of.
Therefore draw for the supportance of his vow, he protests he
will not hurt you.

VIOLA [*aside*]   Pray God defend me. A little thing would make
me tell them how much I lack of a man.

270   FABIAN [*to* SIR ANDREW]   Give ground if you see him furious.

SIR TOBY   Come, Sir Andrew, there's no remedy, the gentleman
will for his honour's sake have one bout with you, he cannot
by the duello° avoid it, but he has promised me, as he is a   *code of dueling*
gentleman and a soldier, he will not hurt you. Come on, to't.

275   SIR ANDREW   Pray God he keep his oath.

          Enter ANTONIO

2. *Nothing . . . form:* From his outward appearance,
you cannot perceive him to be as remarkable.
3. Priests were often addressed as "sir."
4. Woman warrior (suggesting great ferocity with a
feminine appearance).
5. Thrust (from the Italian *stoccata*).
6. He has as terrifying an idea.

VIOLA I do assure you 'tis against my will.
  [SIR ANDREW *and* VIOLA *draw their swords*]

ANTONIO [*drawing his sword, to* SIR ANDREW] Put up your sword.
  If this young gentleman
  Have done offence, I take the fault on me.
  If you offend him, I for him defy you.

280 SIR TOBY You, sir? Why, what are you?

ANTONIO One, sir, that for his love dares yet do more
  Than you have heard him brag to you he will.

SIR TOBY [*drawing his sword*] Nay, if you be an undertaker,[7] I
  am for you.

  Enter OFFICERS

285 FABIAN O, good Sir Toby, hold. Here come the officers.

SIR TOBY [*to* ANTONIO] I'll be with you anon.

VIOLA [*to* SIR ANDREW] Pray, sir, put your sword up if you please.

SIR ANDREW Marry will I, sir, and for that° I promised you I'll be   *as for that*
  as good as my word. He will bear you easily, and reins well.
  [SIR ANDREW *and* VIOLA *put up their swords*]

290 FIRST OFFICER This is the man, do thy office.

SECOND OFFICER Antonio, I arrest thee at the suit of Count
  Orsino.

ANTONIO You do mistake me, sir.

FIRST OFFICER No, sir, no jot. I know your favour° well,   *face*
295 Though now you have no seacap on your head.
  [*To* SECOND OFFICER] Take him away, he knows I know him well.

ANTONIO I must obey. [*To* VIOLA] This comes with seeking you.
  But there's no remedy, I shall answer° it.   *answer for*
  What will you do now my necessity
300 Makes me to ask you for my purse? It grieves me
  Much more for what I cannot do for you
  Than what befalls myself. You stand amazed,
  But be of comfort.

SECOND OFFICER   Come, sir, away.

ANTONIO [*to* VIOLA] I must entreat of you some of that money.

305 VIOLA What money, sir?
  For the fair kindness you have showed me here,
  And part° being prompted by your present trouble,   *in part*
  Out of my lean and low ability
  I'll lend you something. My having is not much.
310 I'll make division of my present° with you.   *ready money*
  Hold, [*offering money*] there's half my coffer.

ANTONIO   Will you deny me now?
  Is't possible that my deserts to you
  Can lack persuasion?[8] Do not tempt my misery,
  Lest that it make me so unsound° a man   *morally weak*
315 As to upbraid you with those kindnesses
  That I have done for you.

VIOLA   I know of none,
  Nor know I you by voice, or any feature.
  I hate ingratitude more in a man
  Than lying, vainness, babbling drunkenness,

---

7. One who would take upon himself a task (here, a
challenge).

8. *Is't . . . persuasion:* Is it possible my past kindness
can fail to persuade you?

320 Or any taint of vice whose strong corruption
Inhabits our frail blood.
ANTONIO   O heavens themselves!
SECOND OFFICER   Come, sir, I pray you go.
ANTONIO   Let me speak a little. This youth that you see here
I snatched one half out of the jaws of death,
325 Relieved him with such sanctity° of love,   *great devotion*
And to his image,⁹ which methought did promise
Most venerable worth,¹ did I devotion.
FIRST OFFICER   What's that to us? The time goes by, away.
ANTONIO   But O, how vile an idol proves this god!
330 Thou hast, Sebastian, done good feature° shame.   *physical beauty*
In nature there's no blemish but the mind.
None can be called deformed but the unkind.
Virtue is beauty, but the beauteous evil
Are empty trunks o'er-flourished² by the devil.
335 FIRST OFFICER   The man grows mad, away with him. Come, come, sir.
ANTONIO   Lead me on.   *Exit [with* OFFICERS]
VIOLA [*aside*]   Methinks his words do from such passion fly
That he believes himself. So do not I.³
Prove true, imagination, O prove true,
340 That I, dear brother, be now ta'en for you!
SIR TOBY   Come hither, knight. Come hither, Fabian. We'll
whisper o'er a couplet or two of most sage saws.°   *sayings; maxims*
[*They stand aside*]
VIOLA   He named Sebastian. I my brother know
Yet living in my glass.° Even such and so   *mirror*
345 In favour° was my brother, and he went   *appearance*
Still° in this fashion, colour, ornament,   *Always*
For him I imitate. O, if it prove,
Tempests are kind, and salt waves fresh in love!   *Exit*
SIR TOBY [*to* SIR ANDREW]   A very dishonest,° paltry boy, and   *dishonorable*
350 more a coward than a hare. His dishonesty appears in leaving
his friend here in necessity, and denying him; and for his cow-
ardship, ask Fabian.
FABIAN   A coward, a most devout coward, religious in it.
SIR ANDREW   'Slid,° I'll after him again, and beat him.   *By God's eyelid*
355 SIR TOBY   Do, cuff him soundly, but never draw thy sword.
SIR ANDREW   An I do not—   [*Exit*]
FABIAN   Come, let's see the event.°   *outcome*
SIR TOBY   I dare lay any money 'twill be nothing yet.°   *Exeunt*   *after all*

4.1

Enter SEBASTIAN *and* [FESTE, *the*] *clown*

FESTE   Will you° make me believe that I am not sent for you?   *Are you trying to*
SEBASTIAN   Go to, go to, thou art a foolish fellow,
Let me be clear° of thee.   *rid*
FESTE   Well held out,° i'faith! No, I do not know you, nor I am   *kept up*
5 not sent to you by my lady to bid you come speak with her, nor

---

9. Appearance (with a play on "religious icon").
1. *did . . . worth:* was worthy of veneration.
2. Chests decorated with carving or painting; beautified
bodies.

3. *So do not I:* I do not entirely believe the passionate
hope (for my brother's rescue) that is arising in me.
4.1 Location: Near Olivia's house.

your name is not Master Cesario, nor this is not my nose, neither. Nothing that is so, is so.

SEBASTIAN I prithee vent° thy folly somewhere else,   *utter; excrete*
    Thou know'st not me.

10 FESTE Vent my folly! He has heard that word of some great
man, and now applies it to a fool. Vent my folly—I am afraid
this great lubber° the world will prove a cockney.° I prithee   *lout / sissy*
now ungird thy strangeness,¹ and tell me what I shall 'vent' to
my lady? Shall I 'vent' to her that thou art coming?

15 SEBASTIAN I prithee, foolish Greek,° depart from me.   *buffoon*
There's money for thee. If you tarry longer
I shall give worse payment.

FESTE By my troth, thou hast an open hand. These wise men
that give fools money get themselves a good report,° after four-   *reputation*
20 teen years' purchase.²

        Enter [SIR] ANDREW, [SIR] TOBY, *and* FABIAN

SIR ANDREW [*to* SEBASTIAN] Now, sir, have I met you again?
[*Striking him*] There's for you.

SEBASTIAN [*striking* SIR ANDREW *with his dagger*] Why, there's
for thee, and there, and there.
Are all the people mad?

25 SIR TOBY [*to* SEBASTIAN, *holding him back*] Hold, sir, or I'll throw
your dagger o'er the house.

FESTE This will I tell my lady straight,° I would not be in some   *straightaway*
of your coats for twopence.   [*Exit*]

SIR TOBY Come on, sir, hold.

30 SIR ANDREW Nay, let him alone, I'll go another way to work with
him. I'll have an action of battery° against him if there be any   *a lawsuit for assault*
law in Illyria. Though I struck him first, yet it's no matter for
that.

SEBASTIAN Let go thy hand.

35 SIR TOBY Come, sir, I will not let you go. Come, my young soldier, put up your iron. You are well fleshed.³ Come on.

SEBASTIAN [*freeing himself*] I will be free from thee. What wouldst thou now?
If thou dar'st tempt me further, draw thy sword.

SIR TOBY What, what? Nay then, I must have an ounce or two
40 of this malapert° blood from you.   *impudent*

    [SIR TOBY *and* SEBASTIAN *draw their swords.*]
        Enter OLIVIA

OLIVIA Hold, Toby, on thy life I charge thee hold.

SIR TOBY Madam.

OLIVIA Will it be ever thus? Ungracious wretch,
Fit for the mountains and the barbarous caves,
45 Where manners ne'er were preached—out of my sight!
Be not offended, dear Cesario.
[*To* SIR TOBY] Rudesby,° be gone.   *Ruffian*
    [*Exeunt* SIR TOBY, SIR ANDREW, *and* FABIAN]
        I prithee, gentle friend,
Let thy fair wisdom, not thy passion sway
In this uncivil and unjust extent°   *assault*

---

1. *I . . . strangeness:* Stop pretending not to know me.
(Feste mocks Sebastian's affected language.)
2. *after . . . purchase:* at a high price. The purchase price

of land was normally twelve times its annual rent.
3. Experienced in combat. Hunting hounds were said to
be "fleshed" after being fed part of their first kill.

50 Against thy peace. Go with me to my house,
And hear thou there how many fruitless pranks
This ruffian hath botched up,° that thou thereby   clumsily contrived
Mayst smile at this. Thou shalt not choose but go.
Do not deny. Beshrew° his soul for me,   Curse
55 He started one poor heart of mine in thee.[4]
SEBASTIAN   What relish° is in this? How runs the stream?
Or° I am mad, or else this is a dream.   Either
Let fancy° still my sense in Lethe[5] steep.   imagination
If it be thus to dream, still let me sleep.
60 OLIVIA   Nay, come, I prithee, would thou'dst be ruled by me.
SEBASTIAN   Madam, I will.
OLIVIA   O, say so, and so be.   *Exeunt*

4.2

Enter MARIA [*carrying a gown and false beard, and*
FESTE, *the*] *clown*

MARIA   Nay, I prithee put on this gown and this beard, make
him believe thou art Sir Topas[1] the curate. Do it quickly. I'll
call Sir Toby the whilst.°   *Exit*   in the meantime
FESTE   Well, I'll put it on, and I will dissemble[2] myself in't, and
5 I would I were the first that ever dissembled in such a gown.
[*He disguises himself*]
I am not tall enough to become the function well,[3] nor lean
enough to be thought a good student,° but to be said° 'an hon-   (of divinity) / reputed
est man and a good housekeeper'° goes as fairly as[4] to say 'a   host
careful man and a great scholar'. The competitors° enter.   associates
Enter [SIR] TOBY [*and* MARIA]
10 SIR TOBY   Jove bless thee, Master Parson.
FESTE   *Bonos dies,*[5] Sir Toby, for, as the old hermit of Prague,[6]
that never saw pen and ink, very wittily° said to a niece of King   intelligently
Gorboduc,° 'That that is, is.' So I, being Master Parson, am   legendary British king
Master Parson; for what is 'that' but 'that', and 'is' but 'is'?
15 SIR TOBY   To him, Sir Topas.
FESTE   What ho, I say, peace in this prison.
SIR TOBY   The knave counterfeits well—a good knave.
                    MALVOLIO *within*
MALVOLIO   Who calls there?
FESTE   Sir Topas the curate, who comes to visit Malvolio the
20 lunatic.
MALVOLIO   Sir Topas, Sir Topas, good Sir Topas, go to my lady.
FESTE   Out, hyperbolical fiend,[7] how vexest thou this man! Talk-
est thou nothing but of ladies?
SIR TOBY   Well said, Master Parson.
25 MALVOLIO   Sir Topas, never was man thus wronged. Good Sir

---

4. *He . . . thee:* By attacking Sebastian, Sir Toby frightened Olivia, who has exchanged hearts with Sebastian.
started: an allusion to hunting, creating a pun on "hart /
heart."
5. The mythical river of oblivion.
4.2 Location: Olivia's house, where Malvolio will be
found (offstage) "in a dark room and bound" (3.4.121).
1. The comical hero of Chaucer's *Rime of Sir Topas.*
Also alluding to the mineral topaz, which was thought to

have special curative qualities for insanity.
2. Disguise; with subsequent play on "lie."
3. Grace the priestly office. *tall:* stout, rather than of
great height.
4. *goes as fairly as:* sounds as well as.
5. Good day (false Latin).
6. Probably an invented authority.
7. Feste treats Malvolio as a man possessed by vehement
("hyperbolical") evil spirits.

Topas, do not think I am mad. They have laid me here in hideous darkness.

FESTE   Fie, thou dishonest Satan—I call thee by the most mod- est° terms, for I am one of those gentle ones that will use the
30   devil himself with courtesy. Sayst thou that house° is dark?

MALVOLIO   As hell, Sir Topas.

FESTE   Why, it hath bay windows transparent as barricadoes, and the clerestories[8] toward the south-north are as lustrous as ebony,[9] and yet complainest thou of obstruction?

35   MALVOLIO   I am not mad, Sir Topas; I say to you this house is dark.

FESTE   Madman, thou errest. I say there is no darkness but igno- rance, in which thou art more puzzled than the Egyptians in their fog.[1]

40   MALVOLIO   I say this house is as dark as ignorance, though igno- rance were as dark as hell; and I say there was never man thus abused. I am no more mad than you are. Make the trial of it in any constant question.°

FESTE   What is the opinion of Pythagoras[2] concerning wildfowl?

45   MALVOLIO   That the soul of our grandam might haply° inhabit a bird.

FESTE   What thinkest thou of his opinion?

MALVOLIO   I think nobly of the soul, and no way approve his opinion.

50   FESTE   Fare thee well. Remain thou still in darkness. Thou shalt hold th'opinion of Pythagoras ere I will allow of thy wits,° and fear to kill a woodcock[3] lest thou dispossess the soul of thy gran- dam. Fare thee well.

MALVOLIO   Sir Topas, Sir Topas!

55   SIR TOBY   My most exquisite Sir Topas.

FESTE   Nay, I am for all waters.[4]

MARIA   Thou mightst have done this without thy beard and gown, he sees thee not.

SIR TOBY   [to FESTE]   To him in thine own voice, and bring me
60   word how thou findest him. I would we were well rid of this knavery. If he may be conveniently delivered, I would he were, for I am now so far in offence with my niece that I cannot pursue with any safety this sport to the upshot. [To MARIA] Come by and by to my chamber.   Exit [with MARIA]

65   FESTE   [sings][5]   'Hey Robin, jolly Robin,
                      Tell me how thy lady does.'

MALVOLIO   Fool!

FESTE   'My lady is unkind, pardie.'[6]

MALVOLIO   Fool!

70   FESTE   'Alas, why is she so?'

MALVOLIO   Fool, I say!

FESTE   'She loves another.'
Who calls, ha?

mildest

room

logical discussion

perhaps

certify your sanity

---

8. Upper windows, usually in a church or great hall. *bar- ricadoes:* barricades (subsequent paradoxes are equiva- lent to "as clear as mud").
9. A dense and naturally dull black wood.
1. One of the plagues of Egypt was a "black darkness" lasting for three days (Exodus 10:21–23).
2. An ancient Greek philosopher who held that the same

soul could successively inhabit different creatures.
3. A traditionally stupid bird.
4. I am able to turn my hand to anything.
5. Feste's song, which makes Malvolio aware of his pres- ence, is traditional. There is a version by Sir Thomas Wyatt.
6. A corruption of the French *pardieu,* "by God."

MALVOLIO   Good fool, as ever thou wilt deserve well at my hand,
75   help me to a candle and pen, ink, and paper. As I am a gentle-
      man, I will live to be thankful to thee for't.

FESTE   Master Malvolio?

MALVOLIO   Ay, good fool.

FESTE   Alas, sir, how fell you besides° your five wits?[7]   *out of*

80 MALVOLIO   Fool, there was never man so notoriously° abused. I   *outrageously*
      am as well in my wits, fool, as thou art.

FESTE   But as well? Then you are mad indeed, if you be no bet-
      ter in your wits than a fool.

MALVOLIO   They have here propertied me,[8] keep me in darkness,
85   send ministers to me, asses, and do all they can to face me[9] out
      of my wits.

FESTE   Advise you° what you say, the minister is here.   *Be careful*
      [*As Sir Topas*] Malvolio, Malvolio, thy wits the heavens restore.
      Endeavour thyself to sleep, and leave thy vain bibble-babble.

90 MALVOLIO   Sir Topas.

FESTE   [*as Sir Topas*]   Maintain no words with him, good fellow.
      [*As himself*] Who I, sir? Not I, sir. God b'wi' you,° good Sir   *God be with you*
      Topas. [*As Sir Topas*] Marry, amen. [*As himself*] I will, sir, I
      will.

95 MALVOLIO   Fool, fool, fool, I say.

FESTE   Alas, sir, be patient. What say you, sir? I am shent° for   *scolded*
      speaking to you.

MALVOLIO   Good fool, help me to some light and some paper. I
      tell thee I am as well in my wits as any man in Illyria.

100 FESTE   Well-a-day° that you were, sir.   *Alas*

MALVOLIO   By this hand, I am. Good fool, some ink, paper, and
      light, and convey what I will set down to my lady. It shall advan-
      tage thee more than ever the bearing of letter did.

FESTE   I will help you to't. But tell me true, are you not mad
105   indeed, or do you but counterfeit?

MALVOLIO   Believe me, I am not, I tell thee true.

FESTE   Nay, I'll ne'er believe a madman till I see his brains. I
      will fetch you light, and paper, and ink.

MALVOLIO   Fool, I'll requite it in the highest degree. I prithee,
110   be gone.

FESTE   I am gone, sir,
                         And anon, sir,
                              I'll be with you again,
                         In a trice,
115   Like to the old Vice,[1]
                              Your need to sustain,
                         Who with dagger of lath
                         In his rage and his wrath
                              Cries 'Aha,' to the devil,
120   Like a mad lad,
                         'Pare thy nails, dad,
                              Adieu, goodman[2] devil.'   *Exit*

---

7. Usually regarded as common sense, fantasy, memory, judgment, and imagination.
8. Treated me as a piece of property.
9. *face me*: brazenly construe me as.

1. A stock comic figure in the old morality plays; the Vice often carried a wooden dagger.
2. Yeoman; a title given to one not of gentle birth, hence a parting insult to Malvolio.

4.3

Enter SEBASTIAN

SEBASTIAN   This is the air, that is the glorious sun.
This pearl she gave me, I do feel't and see't,
And though 'tis wonder that enwraps me thus,
Yet 'tis not madness. Where's Antonio then?
5   I could not find him at the Elephant,
Yet there he was,° and there I found this credit,°   *had been / report*
That he did range the town to seek me out.
His counsel now might do me golden service,
For though my soul disputes well with my sense[1]
10   That this may be some error but no madness,
Yet doth this accident and flood of fortune
So far exceed all instance,° all discourse,°   *precedent / reasoning*
That I am ready to distrust mine eyes
And wrangle with my reason that persuades me
15   To any other trust° but that I am mad,   *belief*
Or else the lady's mad. Yet if 'twere so
She could not sway° her house, command her followers,   *rule*
Take and give back affairs and their dispatch[2]
With such a smooth, discreet, and stable bearing
20   As I perceive she does. There's something in't
That is deceivable.° But here the lady comes.   *deceptive*

Enter OLIVIA *and* PRIEST

OLIVIA   Blame not this haste of mine. If you mean well
Now go with me, and with this holy man,
Into the chantry by.° There before him,   *nearby chapel*
25   And underneath that consecrated roof,
Plight me the full assurance of your faith,[3]
That my most jealous° and too doubtful soul   *anxious*
May live at peace. He shall conceal it
Whiles° you are willing it shall come to note,   *Until*
30   What° time we will our celebration keep   *At which*
According to my birth.° What do you say?   *rank*
SEBASTIAN   I'll follow this good man, and go with you,
And having sworn truth, ever will be true.
OLIVIA   Then lead the way, good father, and heavens so shine
35   That they may fairly note° this act of mine.   *Exeunt*   *look favorably upon*

5.1

Enter [FESTE, *the*] *clown and* FABIAN

FABIAN   Now, as thou lovest me, let me see his letter.
FESTE   Good Master Fabian, grant me another request.
FABIAN   Anything.
FESTE   Do not desire to see this letter.
5   FABIAN   This is to give a dog, and in recompense desire my dog
      again.[1]

Enter Duke, VIOLA [*as Cesario*], CURIO, *and lords*

ORSINO   Belong you to the Lady Olivia, friends?

4.3 Location: Near Olivia's house.
1. For though my reason and my sense both concur.
2. Undertake business, and ensure that it is carried
out.
3. Enter into the solemn contract of betrothal.
5.1 Location: Before Olivia's house.

1. Perhaps a reference to an anecdote, recorded in
John Manningham's diary, in which Queen Elizabeth
requested a dog, and the donor, when granted a wish in
return, asked for the dog back.

FESTE Ay, sir, we are some of her trappings.°　　　　　　　　　*ornaments*

ORSINO I know thee well. How dost thou, my good fellow?

10　FESTE Truly, sir, the better for my foes and the worse for my
friends.

ORSINO Just the contrary—the better for thy friends.

FESTE No, sir, the worse.

ORSINO How can that be?

15　FESTE Marry, sir, they praise me, and make an ass of me. Now
my foes tell me plainly I am an ass, so that by my foes, sir, I
profit in the knowledge of myself, and by my friends I am
abused;° so that, conclusions to be as kisses, if your four nega-　　*deceived*
tives make your two affirmatives,[2] why then the worse for my

20　friends and the better for my foes.

ORSINO Why, this is excellent.

FESTE By my troth, sir, no, though it please you to be one of my
friends.

ORSINO [*giving money*] Thou shalt not be the worse for me.

25　There's gold.

FESTE But° that it would be double-dealing,[3] sir, I would you　　*Except for the fact*
could make it another.

ORSINO O, you give me ill counsel.

FESTE Put your grace in your pocket,[4] sir, for this once, and let

30　your flesh and blood obey it.[5]

ORSINO Well, I will be so much a sinner to° be a double-dealer.　　*as to*
[*Giving money*] There's another.

FESTE *Primo, secundo, tertio*[6] is a good play,° and the old saying　　*game*
is 'The third pays for all'.[7] The triplex,° sir, is a good tripping　　*triple time in music*

35　measure, or the bells of Saint Bennet,[8] sir, may put you in
mind—'one, two, three'.

ORSINO You can fool no more money out of me at this throw.°　　*throw of the dice*
If you will let your lady know I am here to speak with her, and
bring her along with you, it may awake my bounty further.

40　FESTE Marry, sir, lullaby to your bounty till I come again. I go,
sir, but I would not have you to think that my desire of having
is the sin of covetousness. But as you say, sir, let your bounty
take a nap, I will awake it anon.　　　　　　　　　　*Exit*

　　　　Enter ANTONIO *and* OFFICERS

VIOLA Here comes the man, sir, that did rescue me.

45　ORSINO That face of his I do remember well,
Yet when I saw it last it was besmeared
As black as Vulcan[9] in the smoke of war.
A baubling° vessel was he captain of,　　　　　　　　　　*trifling*
For shallow draught and bulk unprizable,[1]

50　With which such scatheful° grapple did he make　　　　*destructive*
With the most noble bottom° of our fleet　　　　　　　　*ship*

2. *conclusions . . affirmatives*: as in grammar, a double
negative can make an affirmative (and therefore four neg-
atives can make two affirmatives); so when a coy girl is
asked for a kiss, her four refusals can be construed as
"yes, yes."
3. A duplicity; a double donation.
4. Set aside (pocket up) your virtue; also (with a play on
the customary form of address for a duke, "your grace"),
reach into your pocket and grace me with another coin.
5. Let your normal human instincts (as opposed to

grace) follow the "ill counsel" (line 28).
6. First, second, third (Latin); perhaps an allusion to a
dice throw or a child's game.
7. Third time lucky (proverbial).
8. A London church, across the Thames from the Globe,
was known as St. Bennet Hithe.
9. Blacksmith of the Roman gods.
1. Of no value because of its small size. *draught*: water
displaced by a vessel.

That very envy° and the tongue of loss°   *even enmity / the losers*
Cried fame and honour on him. What's the matter?

FIRST OFFICER   Orsino, this is that Antonio
55   That took the *Phoenix* and her freight from Candy,²
And this is he that did the *Tiger* board
When your young nephew Titus lost his leg.
Here in the streets, desperate of shame and state,³
In private brabble° did we apprehend him.   *brawl*

60 VIOLA   He did me kindness, sir, drew on my side,⁴
But in conclusion put strange speech upon° me.   *spoke strangely to*
I know not what 'twas but distraction.°   *if not insanity*

ORSINO [*to* ANTONIO]   Notable° pirate, thou salt-water thief,   *Notorious*
What foolish boldness brought thee to their mercies
65   Whom thou in terms so bloody and so dear°   *dire*
Hast made thine enemies?

ANTONIO   Orsino, noble sir,
Be pleased that I shake off these names you give me.
Antonio never yet was thief or pirate,
Though, I confess, on base° and ground enough   *foundation*
70   Orsino's enemy. A witchcraft drew me hither.
That most ingrateful boy there by your side
From the rude sea's enragèd and foamy mouth
Did I redeem. A wreck past hope he was.
His life I gave him, and did thereto add
75   My love without retention° or restraint,   *reservation*
All his in dedication. For his sake
Did I expose myself, pure° for his love,   *only*
Into the danger of this adverse° town,   *hostile*
Drew to defend him when he was beset,
80   Where being apprehended, his false cunning—
Not meaning to partake with me in danger—
Taught him to face me out of his acquaintance,⁵
And grew a twenty years' removèd thing
While one would wink,⁶ denied me mine own purse,
85   Which I had recommended° to his use   *consigned*
Not half an hour before.

VIOLA   How can this be?

ORSINO   When came he to this town?

ANTONIO   Today, my lord, and for three months before,
90   No int'rim, not a minute's vacancy,°   *interval*
Both day and night did we keep company.

         Enter OLIVIA *and attendants*

ORSINO   Here comes the Countess. Now heaven walks on earth.
But for thee, fellow—fellow, thy words are madness.
Three months this youth hath tended upon me.
95   But more of that anon. Take him aside.

OLIVIA   What would my lord, but that he may not have,⁷
Wherein Olivia may seem serviceable?
Cesario, you do not keep promise with me.

VIOLA   Madam—

---

2. Candia, capital of Crete.
3. *desperate . . . state*: recklessly oblivious of the danger to his honor and his position (as a free man and public enemy).
4. Drew his sword in my defense.

5. To brazenly deny my acquaintance.
6. *And . . . wink*: In the wink of an eye, pretended we had been estranged for twenty years.
7. Except that which he may not have (my love).

100   ORSINO   Gracious Olivia—
     OLIVIA   What do you say, Cesario? Good my lord—
     VIOLA   My lord would speak, my duty hushes me.
     OLIVIA   If it be aught° to the old tune, my lord,   *anything*
     It is as fat and fulsome° to mine ear   *gross and offensive*
105   As howling after music.
     ORSINO   Still so cruel?
     OLIVIA   Still so constant, lord.
     ORSINO   What, to perverseness? You uncivil lady,
     To whose ingrate and unauspicious° altars   *unfavorable*
110   My soul the faithfull'st off 'rings hath breathed out
     That e'er devotion tendered—what shall I do?
     OLIVIA   Even what it please my lord that shall become° him.   *be fitting for*
     ORSINO   Why should I not, had I the heart to do it,
     Like to th' Egyptian thief, at point of death
115   Kill what I love[8]—a savage jealousy
     That sometime savours nobly.° But hear me this: *of nobility*
     Since you to non-regardance° cast my faith,   *oblivion*
     And that I partly know the instrument
     That screws° me from my true place in your favour,   *wrenches*
120   Live you the marble-breasted tyrant still.
     But this your minion,° whom I know you love,   *darling*
     And whom, by heaven I swear, I tender° dearly,   *regard*
     Him will I tear out of that cruel eye
     Where he sits crownèd in his master's spite.[9]
125   [*To* VIOLA] Come, boy, with me. My thoughts are ripe in mischief.
     I'll sacrifice the lamb that I do love
     To spite a raven's heart within a dove.
     VIOLA   And I most jocund,° apt,° and willingly   *cheerfully / ready*
     To do you rest a thousand deaths would die.
     OLIVIA   Where goes Cesario?
130   VIOLA   After him I love
     More than I love these eyes, more than my life,
     More by all mores[1] than e'er I shall love wife.
     If I do feign, you witnesses above,
     Punish my life for tainting of my love.
135   OLIVIA   Ay me detested, how am I beguiled!
     VIOLA   Who does beguile you? Who does do you wrong?
     OLIVIA   Hast thou forgot thyself? Is it so long?
     Call forth the holy father.   [*Exit an attendant*]
     ORSINO [*to* VIOLA]   Come, away.
     OLIVIA   Whither, my lord? Cesario, husband, stay.
     ORSINO   Husband?
140   OLIVIA   Ay, husband. Can he that deny?
     ORSINO [*to* VIOLA]   Her husband, sirrah?[2]
     VIOLA   No, my lord, not I.
     OLIVIA   Alas, it is the baseness of thy fear
     That makes thee strangle thy propriety.[3]
     Fear not, Cesario, take thy fortunes up,

---

8. In Heliodorus of Emesa's *Ethiopica*, a Greek prose
romance translated into English in 1569 and popular in
Shakespeare's day, the Egyptian robber chief Thyamis
tries to kill his captive Chariclea, whom he loves, when he
is in danger from a rival band.

9. To the mortification of his master.
1. More beyond all comparison.
2. Contemptuous form of address to an inferior.
3. That makes you deny your identity (as my husband).

145 Be that thou know'st thou art, and then thou art
As great as that° thou fear'st.   *him whom*

Enter PRIEST

O welcome, father.
Father, I charge thee by thy reverence
Here to unfold—though lately we intended
To keep in darkness what occasion° now   *necessity*
150 Reveals before 'tis ripe—what thou dost know
Hath newly passed between this youth and me.

PRIEST   A contract of eternal bond of love,
Confirmed by mutual joinder° of your hands,   *joining*
Attested by the holy close° of lips,   *meeting*
155 Strengthened by interchangement of your rings,
And all the ceremony of this compact
Sealed in my function,⁴ by my testimony;
Since when, my watch hath told me, toward my grave
I have travelled but two hours.

160 ORSINO [*to* VIOLA]   O thou dissembling cub, what wilt thou be
When time hath sowed a grizzle on thy case?⁵
Or will not else thy craft° so quickly grow   *craftiness*
That thine own trip shall be thine overthrow?⁶
Farewell, and take her, but direct thy feet
165 Where thou and I henceforth may never meet.

VIOLA   My lord, I do protest.

OLIVIA   O, do not swear!
Hold little° faith, though thou hast too much fear.   *Preserve some*

Enter SIR ANDREW

SIR ANDREW   For the love of God, a surgeon—send one pres-
ently° to Sir Toby.   *immediately*

170 OLIVIA   What's the matter?

SIR ANDREW   He's broke° my head across, and has given Sir Toby   *cut*
a bloody coxcomb,⁷ too. For the love of God, your help! I had
rather than forty pound I were at home.

OLIVIA   Who has done this, Sir Andrew?

175 SIR ANDREW   The Count's gentleman, one Cesario. We took him
for a coward, but he's the very devil incardinate.⁸

ORSINO   My gentleman, Cesario?

SIR ANDREW   'Od's lifelings,° here he is. [*To* VIOLA] You broke   *By God's little lives*
my head for nothing, and that that I did I was set on to do't by
180 Sir Toby.

VIOLA   Why do you speak to me? I never hurt you.
You drew your sword upon me without cause,
But I bespake you fair,⁹ and hurt you not.

Enter [SIR] TOBY *and* [FESTE, *the*] *clown*

SIR ANDREW   If a bloody coxcomb be a hurt you have hurt me. I
185 think you set nothing by° a bloody coxcomb. Here comes Sir   *think nothing of*
Toby, halting.° You shall hear more; but if ° he had not been   *limping / if only*
in drink he would have tickled° you othergates° than he did.   *chastised / in other ways*

ORSINO [*to* SIR TOBY]   How now, gentleman? How is't with you?

---

4. Ratified by priestly authority.
5. A gray hair ("grizzle") on your hide (sustaining the metaphor of "cub").
6. That your attempt to trip someone else will be the cause of your downfall.

7. Head; also, a fool's cap, which resembles the crest of a cock.
8. Sir Andrew's blunder for "incarnate" (in the flesh).
9. But I spoke courteously to you.

SIR TOBY   That's all one,° he's hurt me, and there's th'end on't.   *No matter*

190   [*To* FESTE] Sot,° didst see Dick Surgeon, sot?   *Fool; drunkard*

FESTE   O, he's drunk, Sir Toby, an hour agone. His eyes were
set[1] at eight i'th' morning.

SIR TOBY   Then he's a rogue, and a passy-measures pavan.[2] I hate
a drunken rogue.

195   OLIVIA   Away with him! Who hath made this havoc with them?

SIR ANDREW   I'll help you, Sir Toby, because we'll be dressed[3]
together.

SIR TOBY   Will *you* help—an ass-head, and a coxcomb,° and a   *fool*
knave; a thin-faced knave, a gull?°   *dupe*

200   OLIVIA   Get him to bed, and let his hurt be looked to.

[*Exeunt* SIR TOBY, SIR ANDREW, FESTE, *and* FABIAN]

Enter SEBASTIAN

SEBASTIAN [*to* OLIVIA]   I am sorry, madam, I have hurt your kinsman,
But had it been the brother of my blood
I must have done no less with wit and safety.[4]
You throw a strange regard upon me,° and by that   *regard me strangely*
205   I do perceive it hath offended you.
Pardon me, sweet one, even for the vows
We made each other but so late ago.

ORSINO   One face, one voice, one habit, and two persons,
A natural perspective,[5] that is and is not.

210   SEBASTIAN   Antonio! O, my dear Antonio,
How have the hours racked and tortured me
Since I have lost thee!

ANTONIO   Sebastian are you?

SEBASTIAN   Fear'st thou° that, Antonio?   *Do you doubt*

215   ANTONIO   How have you made division of yourself ?
An apple cleft in two is not more twin
Than these two creatures. Which is Sebastian?

OLIVIA   Most wonderful!°   *full of wonder*

SEBASTIAN [*seeing* VIOLA]   Do I stand there? I never had a brother,
220   Nor can there be that deity° in my nature   *divine power*
Of here and everywhere.° I had a sister,   *Of omnipresence*
Whom the blind waves and surges have devoured.
Of charity,° what kin are you to me?   *Please*
What countryman? What name? What parentage?

225   VIOLA   Of Messaline. Sebastian was my father.
Such a Sebastian was my brother, too.
So went he suited° to his watery tomb.   *in appearance; clad*
If spirits can assume both form and suit
You come to fright us.

SEBASTIAN   A spirit I am indeed,
230   But am in that dimension grossly clad
Which from the womb I did participate.[6]
Were you a woman, as the rest goes even,°   *the rest suggests*
I should my tears let fall upon your cheek
And say 'Thrice welcome, drownèd Viola.'

235   VIOLA   My father had a mole upon his brow.

---

1. Closed (as the sun sets).
2. A variety of the slow dance known as "pavane" (from the Italian *passamezzo pavana*). Sir Toby may think its swaying movements suggest drunkenness.
3. We'll have our wounds dressed.

4. With any sense of my welfare.
5. An optical illusion produced by nature (rather than by a mirror).
6. *But . . . participate*: I am glad, like all mortals, in the flesh in which I was born.

SEBASTIAN   And so had mine.

VIOLA   And died that day when Viola from her birth
　　Had numbered thirteen years.

SEBASTIAN   O, that record is lively° in my soul.

240　He finishèd indeed his mortal act
　　That day that made my sister thirteen years.

VIOLA   If nothing lets° to make us happy both   *hinders*
　　But this my masculine usurped attire,
　　Do not embrace me till each circumstance

245　Of place, time, fortune do cohere and jump°   *agree*
　　That I am Viola, which to confirm
　　I'll bring you to a captain in this town
　　Where lie my maiden weeds,° by whose gentle help   *clothes*
　　I was preserved to serve this noble count.

250　All the occurrence of my fortune since
　　Hath been between this lady and this lord.

SEBASTIAN [*to* OLIVIA]   So comes it, lady, you have been mistook.
　　But nature to her bias drew in that.[8]
　　You would have been contracted° to a maid,   *betrothed*

255　Nor are you therein, by my life, deceived.
　　You are betrothed both to a maid and man.[9]

ORSINO [*to* OLIVIA]   Be not amazed. Right noble is his blood.
　　If this be so, as yet the glass seems true,[1]
　　I shall have share in this most happy wreck.

260　[*To* VIOLA] Boy, thou hast said to me a thousand times
　　Thou never shouldst love woman like to me.

VIOLA   And all those sayings will I overswear,°   *swear again*
　　And all those swearings keep as true in soul
　　As doth that orbèd continent[2] the fire

　　That severs day from night.

265　ORSINO   Give me thy hand,
　　And let me see thee in thy woman's weeds.

VIOLA   The captain that did bring me first on shore
　　Hath my maid's garments. He upon some action°   *legal charge*
　　Is now in durance,° at Malvolio's suit,   *prison*

270　A gentleman and follower of my lady's.

OLIVIA   He shall enlarge° him. Fetch Malvolio hither—   *release*
　　And yet, alas, now I remember me,
　　They say, poor gentleman, he's much distraught.

　　Enter [FESTE, *the*] *clown with a letter, and* FABIAN

　　A most extracting° frenzy of mine own   *distracting*

275　From my remembrance clearly banished his.
　　How does he, sirrah?

FESTE   Truly, madam, he holds Beelzebub at the stave's end[3] as
　　well as a man in his case may do. He's here writ a letter to you.
　　I should have given't you today morning. But as a madman's

280　epistles are no gospels,[4] so it skills° not much when they are   *matters*
　　delivered.

OLIVIA   Open't and read it.

---

7. The memory of that is vivid.
8. But nature followed her inclination. (The image is from the game of bowls, which uses a ball with an off-centered weight that causes it to curve away from a straight course.)
9. *maid and man*: a man who is a virgin.
1. *the glass seems true*: the "natural perspective" (line

209) continues to seem real.
2. Referring to either the sun or the sphere within which the sun was thought to be fixed.
3. He holds the devil (who threatens to possess him) at a distance (proverbial).
4. Gospel truths. *epistles*: letters (playing on the sense of apostolic accounts of Christ in the New Testament).

FESTE   Look then to be well edified when the fool delivers° the

speaks the words of

madman. [*Reads*] 'By the Lord, madam'—

285 OLIVIA   How now, art thou mad?

FESTE   No, madam, I do but read madness. An your ladyship
will have it as it ought to be you must allow *vox*.[5]

OLIVIA   Prithee, read i'thy right wits.

FESTE   So I do, madonna, but to read his right wits[6] is to read

290 thus. Therefore perpend,° my princess, and give ear.

pay attention

OLIVIA [*to* FABIAN]   Read it you, sirrah.

[FESTE *gives the letter to* FABIAN]

FABIAN (*reads*)   'By the Lord, madam, you wrong me, and the
world shall know it. Though you have put me into darkness
and given your drunken cousin rule over me, yet have I the

295 benefit of my senses as well as your ladyship. I have your own
letter that induced me to the semblance I put on, with the
which I doubt not but to do myself much right or you much
shame. Think of me as you please. I leave my duty a little
unthought of, and speak out of my injury.[7]

300   The madly-used Malvolio.

OLIVIA   Did he write this?

FESTE   Ay, madam.

ORSINO   This savours not much of distraction.°

insanity

OLIVIA   See him delivered,° Fabian, bring him hither.

released

305 My lord, so please you—these things further thought on—
To think me as well a sister as a wife,[8]
One day shall crown th'alliance[9] on't, so please you,
Here at my house and at my proper cost.°

own expense

ORSINO   Madam, I am most apt° t'embrace your offer.

ready

310 [*To* VIOLA] Your master quits° you, and for your service done him

releases

So much against the mettle° of your sex,

disposition

So far beneath your soft and tender breeding,
And since you called me master for so long,
Here is my hand. You shall from this time be
Your master's mistress.

315 OLIVIA [*to* VIOLA]   A sister, you are she.

Enter MALVOLIO

ORSINO   Is this the madman?

OLIVIA   Ay, my lord, this same.
How now, Malvolio?

MALVOLIO   Madam, you have done me wrong,
Notorious wrong.

OLIVIA   Have I, Malvolio? No.

MALVOLIO [*showing a letter*]   Lady, you have. Pray you peruse that letter.

320 You must not now deny it is your hand.°

handwriting

Write from° it if you can, in hand or phrase,

differently from

Or say 'tis not your seal, not your invention.°

composition

You can say none of this. Well, grant it then,
And tell me in the modesty of honour[1]

325 Why you have given me such clear lights° of favour,

signs

5. The appropriate voice (Latin).
6. To accurately represent his mental state.
7. I neglect the formality I owe you as your servant and speak as an injured person.
8. To think as well of me as a sister-in-law as you would

have thought of me as a wife.
9. The impending double-marriage ceremony.
1. Tell me with the propriety that becomes a noble-woman.

Bade me come smiling and cross-gartered to you,
To put on yellow stockings, and to frown
Upon Sir Toby and the lighter° people,   lesser
And acting° this in an obedient hope,   Upon doing
330   Why have you suffered me to be imprisoned,
Kept in a dark house, visited by the priest,
And made the most notorious geck° and gull   fool
That e'er invention° played on? Tell me why?   trickery
OLIVIA   Alas, Malvolio, this is not my writing,
335   Though I confess much like the character,°   handwriting
But out of question, 'tis Maria's hand.
And now I do bethink me, it was she
First told me thou wast mad; then cam'st° in smiling,   you came
And in such forms which here were presupposed°   previously suggested
340   Upon thee in the letter. Prithee be content;
This practice hath most shrewdly passed² upon thee,
But when we know the grounds and authors of it
Thou shalt be both the plaintiff and the judge
Of thine own cause.
FABIAN   Good madam, hear me speak,
345   And let no quarrel nor no brawl to come
Taint the condition of this present hour,
Which I have wondered° at. In hope it shall not,   marveled
Most freely I confess myself and Toby
Set this device against Malvolio here
350   Upon° some stubborn and uncourteous parts°   Because / behavior
We had conceived against him.³ Maria writ
The letter, at Sir Toby's great importance,°   importunity
In recompense whereof he hath married her.
How with a sportful malice it was followed°   followed through
355   May rather pluck on° laughter than revenge   incite
If that the injuries be justly weighed
That have on both sides passed.
OLIVIA [to MALVOLIO]   Alas, poor fool, how have they baffled° thee!   disgraced
FESTE   Why, 'Some are born great, some achieve greatness, and
360   some have greatness thrown upon them.' I was one, sir, in this
interlude,° one Sir Topas, sir; but that's all one. 'By the Lord,   comedy
fool, I am not mad'—but do you remember, 'Madam, why
laugh you at such a barren rascal, an you smile not, he's
gagged'—and thus the whirligig° of time brings in his revenges.   spinning top
365 MALVOLIO   I'll be revenged on the whole pack of you.   [Exit]
OLIVIA   He hath been most notoriously abused.
ORSINO   Pursue him, and entreat him to a peace.
He hath not told us of the captain yet.   [Exit one or more]
When that is known, and golden time convents,°   summons; is convenient
370   A solemn combination shall be made
Of our dear souls. Meantime, sweet sister,
We will not part from hence.° Cesario, come—   (Olivia's house)
For so you shall be while you are a man;
But when in other habits you are seen,
375   Orsino's mistress, and his fancy's° queen.   love's; imagination's
                 Exeunt [all but FESTE]

---

2. This trick has most mischievously played.   3. *We . . . him:* To which we took exception.

FESTE (*sings*)   When that I was and a little tiny boy,
      With hey, ho, the wind and the rain,
  A foolish thing was but a toy,
      For the rain it raineth every day.

380   But when I came to man's estate,
      With hey, ho, the wind and the rain,
  'Gainst knaves and thieves men shut their gate,
      For the rain it raineth every day.

  But when I came, alas, to wive,
385   With hey, ho, the wind and the rain,
  By swaggering° could I never thrive,   *bullying*
      For the rain it raineth every day.

  But when I came unto my beds,
      With hey, ho, the wind and the rain,
390   With tosspots° still had drunken heads,   *drunkards*
      For the rain it raineth every day.

  A great while ago the world begun,
      With hey, ho, the wind and the rain,
  But that's all one, our play is done,
395   And we'll strive to please you every day.   *Exit*

Troilus and Cressida

Audiences or readers who come to *Troilus and Cressida* (1601–02) from the *Iliad* are in for a shock. Where Homer sings of heroic conflict culminating in the epic battle between Hector and Achilles, Shakespeare gives center stage to a love story that, like the events of the Trojan War itself, he treats in skeptical, arguably cynical, fashion. Where Homer finds tragic grandeur in the events he portrays, Shakespeare finds only carnage, a carnage not relieved by a romantic plot that ends in disillusionment. This unfamiliar recasting of traditional material produces a darkly ironic view of sexuality and politics that feels radically modern.

Shakespeare knew Homer through George Chapman's *Seaven Bookes of the Iliades of Homere* (1598) and perhaps through earlier English and French translations. (The frontispiece from Chapman's *Homer* suggests the standard view of the Trojan War at the time.) More generally, the English monarchy had long traced its lineage back to Troy. For the titular figures—and, hence, for his core narrative—Shakespeare almost certainly drew on Geoffrey Chaucer's *Troilus and Criseyde* (1380s), which views the central relationship through the code of courtly love and produces an aristocratic medieval tragedy from the failure of that love. Shakespeare was also indebted to a range of other texts: classical (Virgil's *Aeneid*, Ovid's *Metamorphoses,* perhaps several plays of Euripides), medieval (John Lydgate's *Troy Book,* early fifteenth century), and Renaissance (probably including Robert Greene's *Euphues His Censure to Philautus,* 1587). In *Doctor Faustus* (1592), a tragedy that broadly influenced Shakespeare, Christopher Marlowe's titular figure lovingly apostrophizes Helen of Troy: "Was this the face that launched a thousand ships, / And burned the topless towers of Ilium?" And in 1599, a London theatrical company apparently performed Thomas Dekker and Henry Chettle's *Troyelles and Cresseda,* but only a fragmentary list of little more than stage entrances and exits survives today. The lost drama may have covered the same territory as *Troilus and Cressida* from an epic, didactic, and sentimental perspective to which Shakespeare and his company, perceiving the commercial opportunities of a rival work on the topic, stingingly replied.

Less speculative is the ironic effect *Troilus and Cressida* achieves by self-consciously retelling a familiar story. The lovers swear oaths of fidelity that, as the audience but not the characters realize, anticipate their quite different literary reputations. Cressida's uncle, the go-between Pandarus, provides a summary: "If ever you prove false one to another, . . . let all pitiful goers-between be called to the world's end after my name: call them all panders. Let all constant men be Troiluses, all false women Cressids, and all brokers-between panders" (3.2.185–90). Here Pandarus's initial neutrality ("If ever you prove false one to another") reverts to the traditional sexual double standard, a shift predictive of the outcome and already voiced in the lovers' immediately preceding speeches, where only Cressida's faithfulness is open to question. Similarly, the military plot calls attention to the very different Homeric version of its tale. Achilles is outfought by Hector and must avail himself of the Trojan's chivalric generosity: "Pause, if thou wilt" (5.6.14). Achilles then treacherously employs his soldiers, the Myrmidons, to ambush and kill Hector:

> HECTOR   I am unarmed. Forgo this vantage, Greek.
> ACHILLES   Strike, fellows, strike! This is the man I seek.
> . . . .
> On, Myrmidons, and cry you all amain,
> 'Achilles hath the mighty Hector slain!'
>   (5.9.9–14)

In addition to deflating the epic account, the passage explains how that false account arose in the first place. Such literary self-consciousness reconciles conflicting interpretations while helping to produce a movement toward increasing bitterness.

The play breaks in equally startling fashion with the drama Shakespeare composed in the first half of his career. The romantic comedies from *Two Gentlemen of Verona* (1590–91) to *Twelfth Night* (1601) generally focus on romantic attachment and conclude in marriage. By contrast, *Troilus and Cressida* moves from extramarital sex to infidelity, recriminations, deception, self-deception, venereal disease, and despair. The English history plays from *The First Part of the Contention of the Two Famous Houses of York and Lancaster* (2 *Henry VI*; 1591) to *Henry V* (1599) usually turn on martial action

Title page of the *Iliad* of Homer in George Chapman's translation (1611?). Shakespeare probably used the less complete 1598 edition.

in defense of the state. Again in contrast, *Troilus and Cressida* casts doubt on the moral legitimacy of war, increasingly seen as an arena of mindless brutality.

Nonetheless, the play hardly emerges from nowhere. First, its negativity is partly anticipated in the sources, beginning with the *Iliad*. That poem's nostalgic admiration for warrior culture is tinged with an awareness of human suffering. Robert Henryson's *Testament of Cresseid* (late fifteenth century) moralistically punishes Cressida's infidelity by the infliction of leprosy, and William Caxton's *Recuyell of the Historyes of Troye* (the first English printed book, about 1474) has a jaundiced view of the Trojan War. Similarly, Shakespeare's earlier comedies and histories hint at the dyspeptic vision of *Troilus and Cressida*. More important, London stage practice of the period provides a suggestive context. The children's theaters that reopened in 1599 popularized misogynistic dramatic satire, to which *Troilus and Cressida* responds. The play arguably participates in the battle of rival playwrights at the turn of the century, known as the Poets' War. The ridiculous figure of Ajax may satirize Ben Jonson, whose own drama had criticized Shakespeare's works. And the railing Thersites perhaps points to John Marston, the most vituperative of the satiric playwrights. Within Shakespeare's own oeuvre, *Troilus and Cressida*'s tone anticipates the so-called problem plays, *Measure for Measure* and *All's Well That Ends Well*. Further, beginning in 1599 with *Julius Caesar*, Shakespeare initiated a decade-long appropriation of classical history in which—to oversimplify—Rome is the subject of tragedy and Greece of satire. But a satiric streak and especially a loathing of women, sexuality, and the diseased body are major strands within Shakespeare's tragic period as a whole (1599–1608), appearing at least as early as *Hamlet* (1600), with which *Troilus and Cressida* has much in common.

Finally, because the play is hardly homogeneous in tone, it sometimes connects with less bitter motifs in Shakespeare's earlier work. Troilus's initial state echoes the comically extravagant romantic excess in which Duke Orsino begins *Twelfth Night*. When asked by an attendant whether he will hunt the "hart" (deer, with a pun on "heart," line 16), the Duke explains that when he first saw Olivia, he was

> . . . turned into a hart,
> And my desires, like fell and cruel hounds,
> E'er since pursue me.
>
> (1.1.20–22)

Lovesick Troilus also renounces the hunt:

> Why should I war without the walls of Troy
> That find such cruel battle here within?
> Each Trojan that is master of his heart,
> Let him to field—Troilus, alas, hath none.
>
> (1.1.2–5)

This opening succeeds the military exposition of the Prologue and is followed by scenes of sexual comedy, cynical politics, satiric abuse, and perverse idealism. By the time any of these perspectives is repeated, one-third of the play is over. *Troilus and Cressida* thus entertains a dizzying multiplicity of views: one of its salient features is its generic hybridity.

Hence, even though ironic disillusionment becomes increasingly pervasive, it does not subsume all other perspectives. As a result, the nature of the work has always provoked disagreement. Early seventeenth-century references label it variously a history, a comedy, and a tragedy. By adding satire to the list, twentieth-century critics intensified the uncertainty of their predecessors. Although Shakespeare's entire career is marked by the mixing of genres and by the consequent violation of neoclassical norms that separated comedy sharply from tragedy, *Troilus and Cressida* represents an extreme. The play never adopts a consistent outlook in its dismantling of the leading aristocratic narrative forms—medieval chivalric romance and classical epic.

This disorientation is also produced within particular scenes. Even with the general darkening of tone, the play eschews a homogenized outlook. In Act 5, Scene 2, one of Shakespeare's most celebrated forays into eavesdropping, Diomedes and Cressida have an assignation, Troilus and Ulysses secretly watch them, Thersites covertly observes both pairs of figures, and the audience sees all five characters. Cressida's behavior elicits judgments from Diomedes and especially from Cressida herself; it also produces the following commentary.

> ULYSSES   . . . Cressid was here but now.
> TROILUS   Let it not be believed, for womanhood.

A neuer writer, to an euer reader. Newes.

Ternall reader, you haue heere a new play, neuer stal'd with the Stage, neuer clapper-clawd with the palmes of the vulger, and yet passing full of the palme comicall; for it is a birth of your braine, that neuer vnder-tooke any thing commicall, vainely: And were but the vaine names of commedies changde for the titles of Commodities, or of Playes for Pleas; you should see all those grand censors, that now stile them such vanities, flock to them for the maine grace of their grauities: especially this authors Commedies, that are so fram'd to the life, that they serue for the most common Commentaries, of all the actions of our liues. shewing such a dexteritie, and power of witte, that the most displeased with Playes, are pleasd with his Commedies. And all such dull and heauy-witted worldlings, as were neuer capable of the witte of a Commedie, comming by report of them to his representations, haue found that witte there, that they neuer found in them-selues, and haue parted better wittied then they came: feeling an edge of witte set vpon them, more then euer they dreamd they had braine to grinde it on. So much and such sauored salt of witte is in his Commedies, that they seeme (for their height of pleasure) to be borne in that sea that brought forth Venus. Amongst all there is none more witty then this: And had I time I would comment vpon it, though I know it needs not, (for so

¶ 2   much

This prefatory epistle (continued on the facing page) was added to the second state of the 1609 Quarto of *Troilus and Cressida* (Qb). It is not found in the first state (Qa) or in the First Folio (F) and is not included in the present edition. See the Textual Note.

Think: we had mothers. Do not give advantage
To stubborn critics, apt without a theme
For depravation to square the general sex
By Cressid's rule. Rather, think this not Cressid.
ULYSSES   What hath she done, Prince, that can soil our mothers?
TROILUS   Nothing at all, unless that this were she.
THERSITES [aside]   Will a swagger himself out on's own eyes?

(5.2.128–36)

Troilus oscillates between misogynistic generalization and idealistic denial of Cressida's
infidelity, Ulysses rejects extrapolation from individual to gender, and Thersites ridicules
Troilus's willful blindness. This pattern suggests that the play's view is broader than Thersites'. What that view is, however, is another matter. Although the audience apparently

THE EPISTLE.

much as will make you thinke your testerne well be-
stowd) but for so much worth, as euen poore I know to be
stuft in it. It deserues such a labour, as well as the best
Commedy in Terence or Plautus. And beleeue this,
that when hee is gone, and his Commedies out of sale,
you will scramble for them, and set vp a new English
Inquestion. Take this for a warning, and at the perrill
of your pleasures losse, and Iudgements, refuse not, nor
like this the lesse, for not being sullied, with the smoaky
breath of the multitude; but thinke fortune for the
scape it hath made amongst you. Since by the grand
possessors wills I beleeue you should haue prayd for them
rather then beene prayd. And so I leaue all such to bee
prayd for (for the states of their wits healths)
that will not praise it
Vale.

occupies a privileged position, it must synthesize incompatible perspectives and recognize that its privilege cannot guarantee comprehensive judgment. Rather, multiple eavesdropping onstage opens up an infinite regress that extends to the spectators, thereby undermining interpretive certainty. This uncertainty holds throughout *Troilus and Cressida*.

The play's urge to provide philosophical rationales for even the most trivial actions intensifies this effect. The characters disagree with each other and with themselves in the sense that their words bear little relation to their deeds. If this discrepancy had a casual feel to it, it might be easy to overlook. But the linkage of policy questions to foundational principles highlights the practical irrelevance of those principles. Further, since the military story remains almost devoid of combat until Act 5, the play sustains interest by relying on talk and on decisions about how—or even whether—to prosecute the war. In the meeting of the Greek leaders (1.3), Ulysses considers Achilles' defection from the war an illustration of the disruption of "degree" (1.3.82)—of a hierarchically ordered world—by mere power. His is the most famous speech in the play, and it is often read as Shakespeare's own orthodox credo. The dramatic context undermines this judgment, however. Ulysses' humanely conservative political vision sits oddly with the manipulative scheme that he immediately proposes in the same scene to return Achilles to the fray. Similarly, Ulysses complains that Patroclus amuses Achilles by satirically impersonating the other Greek leaders. To illustrate, he reproduces Patroclus's performances, in the process ridiculing Agamemnon and Nestor. And his own satiric voice is repeatedly heard, most often on the subject of Ajax.

A similar slippage from lofty precept to dubious behavior marks the corresponding Trojan council (2.2), hence establishing a parallel between the contending camps. In debating with Troilus the merits of fighting for Helen, Hector asserts, "Every tithe-soul, 'mongst many thousand dimes [souls], / Hath been as dear as Helen" (2.2.18–19). He continues:

> HECTOR Brother, she [Helen] is not worth what she doth cost
>   The holding.
> TROILUS   What's aught but as 'tis valued?
> HECTOR But value dwells not in particular will.
>   It holds his estimate and dignity
>   As well wherein 'tis precious of itself
>   As in the prizer.
>
>   (2.2.50–55)

In response to Troilus's subjective view, then, Hector offers an objective standard that, he insists, must carry equal weight.

Undeterred, Troilus argues against returning Helen to end the war by appealing to constancy of purpose.

> I take today a wife, and my election
> Is led on in the conduct of my will;
>
> . . . .
> . . . How may I avoid—
> Although my will distaste what it elected—
> The wife I chose? There can be no evasion
> To blench from this and to stand firm by honour.
>   (2.2.60–67)

Troilus's defense of marital commitment unwittingly militates against his own position, however. Helen is Menelaus's wife, not Paris's, and Troilus himself gives no thought to marrying Cressida. Even Hector, the noblest character in the play, cannot make good on his words. Claiming that to keep Helen is both self-destructive and immoral, he wins the debate with Troilus (and Paris). But partly inspired by the desire for chivalric glory, he collapses intellectually, agreeing to continue fighting for the Trojans' "dignities," the very aristocratic honor he had just seen through.

The friendly chivalric combat between two noble kinsmen, Hector and Ajax. From Geffrey Whitney, *A Choice of Emblemes* (1586).

The Trojan council of war is echoed at least twice. Hector's disabused view of Helen is more bitterly refracted when Paris asks who deserves her more, "myself or Menelaus" (4.1.56). Diomedes replies,

> He merits well to have her that doth seek her,
> Not making any scruple of her soilure,
> With such a hell of pain and world of charge;
> And you as well to keep her that defend her,
> Not palating the taste of her dishonour,
> With such a costly loss of wealth and friends.
> (4.1.57–62)

In addition, Helen is branded a "whore" by both Thersites and Diomedes (2.3.65, 4.1.68) before that term comes to be attached to Cressida. Misogyny thus informs antiwar sentiment—the play's dominant position. Second, however, when the Greek leaders earlier snub Achilles to get him to fight, Ulysses tells the shaken warrior that value consists not in merit but in reputation—almost the opposite of Hector's position. And the play provides no resolution to this argument.

The romantic plot also holds contradictory outlooks in tension. Reacting against earlier twentieth-century criticism that identified with Troilus, recent discussions have looked skeptically at the male lover and sympathetically at the woman who apparently betrays him. Troilus has a mundane goal: "Her bed is India; there she lies, a pearl" (1.1.96). This sensual motivation turns Cressida into an object of exchange. The idealized image of love he articulates elsewhere is not simply ironized by this jarring juxtaposition: the metaphor parallels the businesslike enterprise of seduction in which Pandarus is so instrumental. When Troilus calls himself as "skilless as unpractised infancy" and "simpler than the infancy of truth" (1.1.12, 3.2.157), he continues his self-regarding rhetoric in a different vein, distances himself from his own sexually aggressive behavior, and arguably imagines sexual intercourse between adults as the relationship between infant and mother. Troilus also fears a subsequent letdown: he worries "that the will is infinite and the execution confined; that the desire is boundless and the act a slave to limit" (3.2.76–77).

Disappointment is Cressida's anxiety as well, although her concern is male inconstancy: "Yet hold I off. Women are angels, wooing; / Things won are done. Joy's soul lies in the doing" (1.2.264–65). Cressida's ambivalence turns on the conviction, deeply embedded in gender inequality, that female sexual surrender cools male ardor. She seems to act out of multiple motives—love and sexual desire, vulnerability, fear of betrayal, the possibility of the self-betrayal of her feelings out of the need to protect herself, and the tendency to understand herself as others define her. The play validates this ambivalence. She has been abandoned by her father, and her remaining relative seeks only to send her to bed with Troilus. Following their first and only night together, the lovers' common fear is realized. Troilus cheerfully gets up to leave, over Cressida's objections. The news that she will be swapped for Antenor—will literally become an object of exchange—elicits passionate refusal from her but immediate resignation from him. Although her reference to "the merry Greeks" (4.5.55) arouses Troilus's jealousy, Cressida interprets his renewed passion as further devaluation of her. Upon her arrival in the enemy camp, she is kissed by the Greek leaders in a scene that has been taken to reveal everything from her wantonness to a near gang rape. Reunited with a father who delivers her to Diomedes, she acts with characteristic ambiguity, perhaps combining ambivalence, a sense of entrapment, desperation, weakness, desire, and manipulation.

But one should not simply reverse Troilus's self-understanding, seeing him as victimizer and Cressida as victim. The play provides the material for competing interpretations without privileging any of them. In a way, this uncertainty does not matter. Troilus and Cressida's relationship is a zero-sum game in that however one explains their behavior, the effect is to undermine ideals that prove to have been overrated all along. Ambiguity and degradation also mark the military climax, in which Hector compounds his failure in the Trojan council by disastrous chivalric generosity. Driven by honor, he insists on fighting, although he is warned not to, and the fate of Troy hangs on his health. Ulysses, Ajax, and Troilus all remark on his habit of sparing a defeated foe. This habit is accompanied by the assumption, despite clear evidence to the contrary, that others operate similarly. Thus, when Hector disarms before Achilles comes upon him, he becomes an easy target. With this implicit judgment of Hector, the play universalizes its critique. The result is a near moral vacuum. Although aristocratic norms retain a vestige of their former appeal, the struggle to live—and die—by them is scarcely worth the effort. The play may thus gesture toward the political crisis at the end of Elizabeth's reign, highlighted by the execution of the Earl of Essex, whose ambitious factionalism (perhaps echoed in Achilles) and chivalric competitiveness (perhaps exemplified by Hector) more generally marked the behavior of competing groups of courtiers who had long sought the queen's favor.

The systematic ambiguity of *Troilus and Cressida*, though perhaps not its movement toward disillusionment, is intensified by the early publishing history of the play. (See the Textual Note.) The First Quarto emphasizes Troilus, Cressida, and Pandarus on the title page and is prefaced by an anonymous prose epistle that defines the work as a comedy. (See the facsimile reproduction of the epistle on pages 1850–51.) The version in the First Folio (1623) is called a tragedy and lacks the epistle, instead introducing the play by a verse Prologue that says nothing of the lovers while focusing on the Trojan War itself, which it treats in heroic terms. In other words, the two texts set up antithetical expectations for their readers. The Quarto closes much as it opens—with Pandarus's lewd and satiric identification with the audience. (See the indented text after 5.11.31.) Although the Folio provides the same conclusion, perhaps it was meant to end with Troilus's despairing, vengeful response to Hector's death. That hypothesis governs the present edition, which views the Folio as the revised and, hence, more authoritative text. Although beginnings and endings cannot determine the meaning of a play, they have disproportionate weight. The modified Folio printed here, like the Quarto, provides a consistent frame around the play, with the difference that the frame is heroic rather than satiric. But the present text does not convert satire into tragedy; in any version, there is satire as well as tragedy. The present text, then, slightly reduces the likelihood that tragic elements will be drowned in a sea of bitter irony.

The Quarto's satiric thrust and the claim in its epistle that the work was never performed in a public theater have given rise to the theory that it was composed for, or even limited to, elite private performance—possibly at one of the Inns of Court (law schools) or at Cambridge. This view, often supported by emphasis on the play's Latinate language, legal references, and penchant for philosophical argument, is contradicted by contemporary documents and is certainly at odds with Shakespeare's normal practice. Possibly, however, *Troilus and Cressida* was relatively unsuccessful at the Globe; probably, it was influenced by the Inns of Court; possibly it was performed there, at Cambridge, or in both locales. Whatever the truth, the debate about the nature and location of the early audience reproduces the ambivalence about the genre of *Troilus and Cressida*: coterie performance implies satire; the public stage, tragedy.

This uncertainty did not sit well with neoclassical writers. In 1679, John Dryden removed "that heap of rubbish" which prevented the play from being a proper tragedy. He has Cressida remain true to Troilus but commit suicide, and he uses Achilles to kill off Troilus. Dryden's radical adaptation was occasionally staged between 1679 and 1734. Thereafter, *Troilus and Cressida* went unperformed until 1898, perhaps because of its grim outlook. Especially in the last fifty years, however, its unsettling proliferation of incompatible meanings and bitter view of love and war have made it extremely popular. Just as Shakespeare's history plays were mobilized to support patriotic sentiment, *Troilus and Cressida* has given expression to antiwar views—on the eve of both world wars, repeatedly during the Vietnam War in the 1960s and 1970s, and recently with reference to the Balkans. Consequently, Thersites sometimes becomes the central spokesman of the play; Ulysses, advocate of traditional hierarchy, accordingly is ironized. Similarly, increased sympathy for Cressida inspired by feminism has led to a complementary depreciation of Troilus.

But does the play offer an alternative system of positive values, even if those values cannot be openly articulated? In this explicitly sexual work, the best place to look may be moments with only an implicitly sexual undertone. The ceremonial exchanges between the leaders of the rival armies suggest the lure of homosocial coupling, which simultaneously excludes women and drives the men back to battle. Performances since the 1960s have frequently been sensitive to this motif. Hector challenges "the fair'st of Greece," by which he means not a woman but a man, and indeed a man who will "dare avow her [his mistress's] beauty and her worth / In other arms than hers" (1.3.262, 268–69). Ulysses resorts to similar wordplay when trying to persuade Achilles to overcome the scruples of heterosexual love: "Better would it fit Achilles much / To throw down Hector than Polyxena" (3.3.200–01).

But one cannot consistently link either misogyny to antiwar views or same-sex bonding to a warrior ethos. Everything has a flip side. An ambivalent imagistic pattern connecting women, effeminacy, and sexual deviation comes closest to providing a countervision to the heroic ethos. Cassandra interrupts the Trojan council with prophecies of doom, a tactic she repeats with equal lack of success in seconding Andromache's efforts to prevent Hector from entering battle near the end of the play. Priam sums up the primarily female forces urging inaction when he tells Hector, "Go back. / Thy wife hath dreamt, thy mother hath had visions, / Cassandra doth foresee" (5.3.64–66). Paris reports, "I would fain have armed today, but my Nell [Helen] would not have it so" (3.1.127–28). And Achilles' not-so-secret love for Polyxena keeps him out of the war entirely: "Fall, Greeks; fail, fame; honour, or go or stay. / My major vow lies here; this I'll obey" (5.1.38–39). More strikingly, the warriors internalize the female perspective. Achilles has "a woman's longing, / . . . To see great Hector in his weeds of peace" (3.3.230–32). Troilus cannot fight because his love for Cressida makes him "weaker than a woman's tear, / . . . Less valiant than the virgin in the night" (1.1.9–11). Hector echoes the sentiment in opening his attack on the war: "There is no lady . . . / More ready to cry out, 'Who knows what follows?' / Than Hector is" (2.2.10–13). Ajax calls the play's leading satirist "Mistress Thersites" (2.1.34), and when faced with "a bastard son of Priam's" (5.8.7) on the battlefield, Thersites makes an illogical, if life-saving, argument: "I am a bastard, too. I love bastards. . . . Take heed: the quarrel's most ominous to us. If the son of a whore fight for a whore, he tempts judgement" (5.8.8–13). Here, Thersites' cowardice conjures up a brotherhood of sexual illegitimacy opposed to meaningless slaughter. Finally, Patroclus complains to Achilles that their enforced leisure makes him loathed as "an effeminate man" (3.3.211):

> . . . I stand condemned for this.
> They think my little stomach to the war
> And your great love to me restrains you thus.
> (3.3.212–14)

What "they think" may be true. Thersites calls Patroclus "Achilles' brach" (bitch hound, 2.1.109), later describing him as "Achilles' male varlet . . . his masculine whore" (5.1.14–16). The death of "my sweet Patroclus" (5.1.32) causes Achilles to break his vow and seek revenge, just as the loss of Cressida turns Troilus toward savagery. In a play about the most famous war in Western literature, opposition to battle brings disgrace. But in such moments—moments of sexual, romantic, or familial intimacy rooted in female or homoerotic experience—an alternative to both aristocratic values and their ironic deflation can be glimpsed.

WALTER COHEN

TEXTUAL NOTE

The textual history of *Troilus and Cressida* (1601–02) poses complex problems of potential interpretive significance. In early 1603, "The booke of Troilus and Cresseda as yt is acted by my lo: Chamberlens Men" was listed in the Stationers' Register—a necessary prelude to authorized publication. In fact, the play was not published; a second entry in the Stationers' Register, this one from 1609, now refers to "THE history of Troylus and Cressida," but with no mention of theatrical performance. The First Quarto (Q) appeared the same year in two distinct states. The earlier version, like the 1609 Stationers' Register, calls it "THE Historie of Troylus and Cresseida" but echoes the 1603 Stationers' Register in evoking stage history—"*As it was acted by the Kings Maiesties seruants at the Globe.*" (Shakespeare's acting company, the Lord Chamberlain's Men, became the King's Men after James succeeded Elizabeth on the throne in 1603.) The second version's title page announces "THE Famous Historie of Troylus *and* Cresseid," goes on to emphasize their love and Pandarus's role, and omits any mention of performance. That omission is developed in a new prefatory epistle, which calls the play a comedy, appeals to elite literary taste by saying that it was never acted in the public theater, and implies—correctly, it seems—that publication is unauthorized.

Moreover, when the First Folio (F) was being prepared for publication in 1623, *Troilus and Cressida* was originally intended to follow *Romeo and Juliet* in the tragedy section. But after only three pages of it were set, printing was discontinued. The play was finally incorporated at the last minute, too late to be mentioned in the Catalogue (table of contents). It excluded the epistle but included a new Prologue, a reset version of its Folio first page, the remaining two pages of the original and incomplete Folio printing, and newly set type for the remainder of the play. It was placed between *All Is True (Henry VIII)*, the last of the histories, and *Coriolanus*, which was meant to be the first of the tragedies. In this intermediate zone, the work in effect became the initial tragedy of the volume, bearing the title "THE TRAGEDIE OF Troylus and Cressida."

Beyond revealing an uncertainty about genre that has continued to the present day, this twenty-year sequence leaves a number of issues obscure. Why was the play not published in 1603: lack of authorization, fear of political reprisals, or, most likely, no real intention to publish? Was it performed at the Globe (probably) or just for an elite audience at the law schools known as the Inns of Court or Cambridge (perhaps in addition to, less likely instead of, the Globe)? Why did the printer of Q change the title page and insert the prefatory epistle in midstream: access to new information, discovery of the epistle at the end of the play manuscript, desire to distance the work from the King's Men, or, most likely, hope of selling more copies? When was the epistle written: 1603 or, more likely, 1609? None of these questions admits of a definitive answer. The delay in printing the Folio version, however, is perhaps less mysterious: it may have been necessitated by copyright troubles that were subsequently resolved.

Equally contentious are the questions about Q and F—their nature, the texts that stand behind them, their relationship to each other. Both, scholars agree, are authoritative in the sense of ultimately deriving from authorial manuscripts. After that, there is less agreement. Q appears to derive from a copy of Shakespeare's draft that has been revised, probably—but not certainly—by Shakespeare. The three pages of the false start in printing the F version are based exclusively on Q, and presumably the initial intention was to follow this procedure throughout the play. But most of the actual F text relies on a substantively different manuscript of *Troilus and Cressida* that usually, but not always, seems to represent an earlier Shakespearean version than the one behind Q. This version has been annotated for performance and hence is a promptbook. In addition, after the first three pages F intermittently relies on Q. It is likely, then, that the F *Troilus* derives from both the manuscript and Q. (Alternatively, it may depend solely on the promptbook manuscript after the first three pages, but that manuscript then would have been influenced by Q.) Accordingly, neither Q nor F has clear priority. The Oxford editors, however, believe that only F incorporates Shakespeare's revisions. Thus, except in a few long passages (1.1.0–1.2.215, 2.2.103–209, 3.3.1–95, and 4.6.0–64), this edition tends to follow F.

For the most part, the consequences of this decision are modest. Both Q and F end with an epilogue spoken by Pandarus, introduced by a three-line exchange between him and Troilus in which Troilus angrily dismisses him. Only F, however, includes almost the identical three lines at the end of Act 5, Scene 3. Both locations cannot be correct. But since this earlier placement occurs only in F and hence is viewed by the Oxford editors as Shakespeare's final judgment on the matter, it is retained in the present edition while Pandarus's epilogue is cut and printed as an indented passage. This excision, the exclusion of the epistle as well as other (very brief) passages found in Q but not F, and the inclusion of the Prologue as well as other (somewhat longer) passages found in F but not Q all point in the same direction. They slightly reduce the satiric elements in the portrayal of Troilus, Cressida, and Pandarus and, more important, downplay the central love affair and shift the focus to the Trojan War itself. These thematic matters are treated in greater detail in the Introduction.

Neither Q nor F has act or scene divisions, with the exception of the first scene in F, which is labeled *"Actus Primus. Scœna Prima."* Editors have supplied these divisions since the early eighteenth century. This edition, unlike most of its predecessors, begins a new scene each time the stage is cleared. Accordingly, Act 4 includes a new Scene 3 after 4.2.75 and a new Scene 7 after 4.6.119, for a total of seven scenes rather than the conventional five. Similarly, Act 5 has a new Scene 8 after 5.7.8, for a total of eleven rather than ten scenes. These changes are discussed in the footnotes.

SELECTED BIBLIOGRAPHY

Bednarz, James P. *Shakespeare and the Poets' War.* New York: Columbia University Press, 2001. 32–52, 257–64. Links the play to the satirical Poets' War of about 1599–1602, with Ajax representing Ben Jonson and Thersites John Marston.

Bredbeck, Gregory W. *Sodomy and Interpretation: Marlowe to Milton.* Ithaca, N.Y.: Cornell University Press, 1991. 33–47. Satire and statecraft joined in the (unjustified) charge of sodomy against Patroclus, a strategy that serves Greek political ends in a chaotic world.

Charnes, Linda. " 'So Unsecret to Ourselves': Notorious Identity and the Material Subject in Shakespeare's *Troilus and Cressida.*" *Shakespeare Quarterly* 40 (1989): 413–40. The characters' literary reputation as fixed identities against which they struggle in the effort to assert their own subjectivity.

Girard, René. "The Politics of Desire in *Troilus and Cressida.*" *Shakespeare and the Question of Theory.* Ed. Patricia Parker and Geoffrey Hartman. New York: Methuen, 1985. 188–209. The love plot and the war plot as instances of mimetic desire (desire inspired by emulous rivalry); generally sympathetic to Cressida and unsympathetic to Troilus.

Grady, Hugh. *Shakespeare's Universal Wolf: Studies in Early Modern Reification.* Oxford: Clarendon, 1996. 58–94. Argues that, philosophically, the play negates all value, seeing a world, from which it dissents, dominated by desire, power, capital, and instrumental reason unlinked to ethics.

James, Heather. *Shakespeare's Troy: Drama, Politics, and the Translation of Empire.* New York: Cambridge University Press, 1997. 85–118. Shakespeare's refusal to choose among alternative versions of the Troy legend, some of which trace a direct lineage from the Trojan to the English monarchy, the result being a conflicted play rooted in the late Elizabethan crisis.

Mallin, Eric S. "Emulous Factions and the Collapse of Chivalry: *Troilus and Cressida.*" *Representations* 29 (1990): 145–79. Links the play to the nostalgic chivalry of the Essex faction at court, in tension with the actual reality of self-interested greed.

Martin, Priscilla, ed. *Shakespeare, "Troilus and Cressida": A Casebook.* London: Macmillan, 1976. Three hundred years of criticism beginning in 1679, concentrating on 1945–1975.

Shirley, Frances A., ed. *Troilus and Cressida.* New York: Cambridge University Press, 2005. Performance history, followed by a text of the play with notes on staging from various productions.

Yachnin, Paul. "The Perfection of Ten": Populuxe Art and Artisanal Value in *Troilus and Cressida.*" *Shakespeare Quarterly* 56 (2005): 306–28. *Troilus and Cressida* as an upscale, deluxe satire performed by a popular, artisan acting company whose need to win audience approval informs the play's debates about value and reputation.

FILM

Troilus & Cressida. 1981. Dir. Jonathan Miller. UK. 190 min. Relatively conservative BBC production that steers clear of homoeroticism but that offers a spirited, rather than a debased, Cressida and makes use of TV's resources by utilizing both broad background shots and intimate close-ups.

Troilus and Cressida

THE PERSONS OF THE PLAY

PROLOGUE

Trojans

PRIAM, King of Troy
HECTOR ⎫
DEIPHOBUS ⎪
HELENUS, a priest ⎪
PARIS ⎬ his sons
TROILUS ⎪
MARGARETON, a bastard ⎭
CASSANDRA, Priam's daughter, a prophetess
ANDROMACHE, wife of Hector
AENEAS ⎫
ANTENOR ⎬ commanders
PANDARUS, a lord
CRESSIDA, his niece
CALCHAS, her father, who has joined the Greeks
HELEN, wife of Menelaus, now living with Paris
ALEXANDER, servant of Cressida
Servants of Troilus, musicians, soldiers, attendants

Greeks

AGAMEMNON, Commander-in-Chief
MENELAUS, his brother
NESTOR
ULYSSES
ACHILLES
PATROCLUS, his companion
DIOMEDES
AJAX
THERSITES
MYRMIDONS, soldiers of Achilles
Servants of Diomedes, soldiers

Prologue

[*Enter the* PROLOGUE *armed*][1]
PROLOGUE   In Troy there lies the scene. From isles of Greece
  The princes orgulous, their high blood chafed,[2]
  Have to the port of Athens sent their ships,
  Fraught° with the ministers and instruments   *Weighted down*
5 Of cruel war. Sixty-and-nine, that wore

Prologue
1. In armor (see line 23); perhaps referring to Ben Jonson's prologue to *Poetaster* (1601), in which an armed figure appears to defend Jonson's embattled reputation among playwrights. *Troilus and Cressida*'s Ajax is sometimes seen as a further jab at Jonson's warlike posturing. The Prologue first appeared in F. Modern editions tend

to include an epistle to the reader either before the opening list of characters, in the notes, or in an appendix. The epistle prefaced the second state of Q and was probably not written by Shakespeare. It is excluded here, but a photograph of it as it appeared in Q is provided. See the Textual Note and Introduction.
2. The princes proud, their noble blood heated.

Their crownets° regal, from th'Athenian bay   *coronets*
Put forth toward Phrygia,[3] and their vow is made
To ransack Troy, within whose strong immures°   *fortifications*
The ravished° Helen, Menelaus' queen,   *kidnapped (sexual)*
10   With wanton Paris sleeps—and that's the quarrel.
To Tenedos° they come,   *island near Troy*
And the deep-drawing barques[4] do there disgorge
Their warlike freightage; now on Dardan[5] plains
The fresh and yet unbruisèd Greeks do pitch
15   Their brave pavilions.° Priam's six-gated city—   *finely arrayed tents*
Dardan and Timbria, Helias, Chetas, Troien,
And Antenorides—with massy staples°   *bolt holes*
And corresponsive and full-filling bolts
Spar up the sons of Troy.[6]
20   Now expectation, tickling skittish° spirits   *excitable*
On one and other side, Trojan and Greek,
Sets all on hazard.° And hither am I come,   *at stake*
A Prologue armed—but not in confidence
Of author's pen or actor's voice,[7] but suited
25   In like conditions as our argument[8]—
To tell you, fair beholders, that our play
Leaps o'er the vaunt° and firstlings of those broils,   *preliminaries*
Beginning in the middle,[9] starting thence away
To what may be digested in a play.
30   Like or find fault; do as your pleasures are;
Now, good or bad, 'tis but the chance of war.   [*Exit*]

1.1

Enter PANDARUS, *and* TROILUS [*armed*]

TROILUS   Call here my varlet.° I'll unarm again.   *page (of genteel birth)*
Why should I war without° the walls of Troy   *outside*
That° find such cruel battle here within?°   *Who / in myself*
Each Trojan that is master of his heart,
5   Let him to field—Troilus, alas, hath none.[1]
PANDARUS   Will this gear° ne'er be mended?   *affair*
TROILUS   The Greeks are strong, and skilful to their strength,[2]
Fierce to their skill, and to their fierceness valiant.
But I am weaker than a woman's tear,
10   Tamer than sleep, fonder° than ignorance,   *sillier*
Less valiant than the virgin in the night,
And skilless as unpractised infancy.
PANDARUS   Well, I have told you enough of this. For my part, I'll

---

3. The region around Troy (now northwestern Turkey).
4. Boats riding deeply in the water (because they are heavily laden).
5. Trojan. Dardanus was the mythical founder of the city.
6. The sons of Troy shut up the six-gated city. (But the inverted syntax also suggests that the city, whose six gates the Prologue has just named, shuts in "the sons of Troy.")
7. *not . . . voice*: not confident of success at writing or acting.
8. *suited . . . argument*: dressed appropriately for our subject (unlike Jonson's).
9. On the model of epic poetry in the Homeric tradition and as recommended by the ancient Latin poet Horace

in his *Art of Poetry*. Despite the play's classical subject matter, the double plot and generic hybridity deviate from what Renaissance critics understood to be classical dramatic norms. But the play comes close to observing two of the three supposedly Aristotelian unities (of time, place, and action) by compressing events after Act 1, Scene 2, into little more than forty-eight hours and by restricting the scene to Troy and its immediate surroundings.

1.1 Location: Troy.
1. Has no heart for battle (having lost his heart to Cressida).
2. And as skilled as they are strong.

not meddle nor make° no farther. He that will have a cake out   *be involved (proverbial)*
15 of the wheat must tarry° the grinding.   *wait for*

TROILUS   Have I not tarried?

PANDARUS   Ay, the grinding; but you must tarry the boulting.°   *sifting*

TROILUS   Have I not tarried?

PANDARUS   Ay, the boulting; but you must tarry the leavening.

20 TROILUS   Still have I tarried.

PANDARUS   Ay, to the leavening; but here's yet in the word 'hereafter' the kneading, the making of the cake, the heating the
oven, and the baking—nay, you must stay the cooling too, or
ye may chance burn your lips.

25 TROILUS   Patience herself, what goddess e'er she be,
Doth lesser blench at suff'rance³ than I do.
At Priam's royal table do I sit
And when fair Cressid comes into my thoughts—
So, traitor!⁴ 'When she comes'? When is she thence?

30 PANDARUS   Well, she looked yesternight fairer than ever I saw
her look, or any woman else.

TROILUS   I was about to tell thee: when my heart,
As wedged° with a sigh, would rive° in twain,   *divided / tear apart*
Lest Hector or my father should perceive me
35 I have, as when the sun doth light askance,°   *obliquely*
Buried this sigh in wrinkle of a smile.
But sorrow that is couched° in seeming gladness   *concealed*
Is like that mirth fate turns to sudden sadness.

PANDARUS   An° her hair were not somewhat darker than Hel-   *If*
40 en's⁵—well, go to,° there were no more comparison between   *say no more*
the women. But, for my part, she is my kinswoman; I would
not, as they term it, 'praise'° her. But I would somebody had   *compliment; appraise*
heard her talk yesterday, as I did. I will not dispraise your sister
Cassandra's wit, but—

45 TROILUS   O Pandarus! I tell thee, Pandarus,
When I do tell thee 'There my hopes lie drowned',
Reply not in how many fathoms deep
They lie endrenched. I tell thee I am mad
In Cressid's love; thou answer'st 'She is fair',
50 Pourest in the open ulcer of my heart
Her eyes, her hair, her cheek, her gait, her voice;
Handlest in thy discourse, O, that her hand,⁶
In whose comparison all whites are ink
Writing their own reproach, to° whose soft seizure°   *compared to / grasp*
55 The cygnet's down is harsh, and spirit of sense⁷
Hard as the palm of ploughman. This thou tell'st me—
As true thou tell'st me—when I say I love her.
But saying thus, instead of oil and balm
Thou lay'st in every gash that love hath given me
60 The knife that made it.

PANDARUS   I speak no more than truth.

---

3. Shies away less from suffering. (Shakespeare presumably means more, not "lesser.")

4. Troilus considers himself a "traitor" to Cressida for ever forgetting her.

5. Pandarus shows the standard Elizabethan hostility to dark hair or a dark complexion.

6. *Handlest . . . hand:* You treat in your discussion, O, that hand of hers. (Troilus's use of "handlest" reminds him of Cressida's hand.)

7. The quintessential medium of feeling or touch that conveyed sense impressions from body to mind.

TROILUS Thou dost not speak so much.

PANDARUS Faith, I'll not meddle in it. Let her be as she is. If she
be fair, 'tis the better for her; an she be not, she has the mends°   *cure (cosmetics)*
65 in her own hands.

TROILUS Good Pandarus, how now, Pandarus!

PANDARUS I have had my labour for my travail.° Ill thought on   *my pains as payment*
of her and ill thought on of you. Gone between and between,
but small thanks for my labour.

70 TROILUS What, art thou angry, Pandarus? What, with me?

PANDARUS Because she's kin to me, therefore she's not so fair as
Helen. An she were not kin to me, she would be as fair o'
Friday as Helen is on Sunday.[8] But what care I? I care not an
she were a blackamoor. 'Tis all one to me.

75 TROILUS Say I she is not fair?

PANDARUS I do not care whether you do or no. She's a fool to
stay behind her father.[9] Let her to the Greeks—and so I'll tell
her the next time I see her. For my part, I'll meddle nor make
no more i'th' matter.

80 TROILUS Pandarus—

PANDARUS Not I.

TROILUS Sweet Pandarus—

PANDARUS Pray you, speak no more to me. I will leave all as I
found it. And there an end.   *Exit*

        Alarum°   *Trumpet call to arms*

85 TROILUS Peace, you ungracious clamours! Peace, rude sounds!
Fools on both sides. Helen must needs be fair
When with your blood you daily paint° her thus.   *daub (as with rouge)*
I cannot fight upon this argument.°   *on these grounds*
It is too starved a subject° for my sword.   *too weak a reason*
90 But Pandarus—O gods, how do you plague me!
I cannot come to Cressid but by Pandar,
And he's as tetchy to be° wooed to woo   *touchy about being*
As she is stubborn-chaste against all suit.
Tell me, Apollo, for thy Daphne's love,[1]
95 What Cressid is, what Pandar, and what we?
Her bed is India;[2] there she lies, a pearl.
Between our Ilium° and where she resides   *Priam's palace*
Let it be called the wild and wand'ring flood,
Ourself the merchant, and this sailing Pandar
100 Our doubtful° hope, our convoy,° and our barque.   *uncertain / escort*

        Alarum. Enter AENEAS

AENEAS How now, Prince Troilus? Wherefore not afield?

TROILUS Because not there. This woman's answer sorts,°   *is fitting*
For womanish it is to be from thence.
What news, Aeneas, from the field today?

105 AENEAS That Paris is returnèd home, and hurt.

TROILUS By whom, Aeneas?

AENEAS   Troilus, by Menelaus.

---

8. *An . . . Sunday:* If she weren't my kinswoman (with the
result that my praise seems biased), she'd be as beautiful
in everyday dress as Helen is in her finest clothes.
9. She's a fool not to leave with her father, Calchas, a
prophet who deserted to the Greeks, having foreseen
their victory.

1. For your love of Daphne. Daphne was a nymph who
prayed (successfully) to be turned into a bay tree to escape
the advances of Apollo, god of poetry.
2. Source of jewels, precious metals, exotic spices, and
rich fabrics.

TROILUS   Let Paris bleed, 'tis but a scar to scorn:
Paris is gored with Menelaus' horn.[3]
    Alarum

AENEAS   Hark what good sport is out of town° today.   *outside Troy*

110 TROILUS   Better at home, if 'would I might' were 'may'.
But to the sport abroad—are you bound thither?

AENEAS   In all swift haste.

TROILUS   Come, go we then together.   *Exeunt*

1.2

Enter [above] CRESSIDA *and her [servant* ALEXANDER]

CRESSIDA   Who were those went by?

ALEXANDER   Queen Hecuba and Helen.

CRESSIDA   And whither go they?

ALEXANDER   Up to the eastern tower,
Whose height commands as subject all the vale,°   *valley*
To see the battle. Hector, whose patience

5 Is as a virtue fixed,° today was moved.°   *unwavering / angry*
He chid Andromache and struck his armourer
And, like as there were husbandry in war,
Before the sun rose[1] he was harnessed light,°   *in lightweight armor*
And to the field goes he, where every flower

10 Did as a prophet weep° what it foresaw   *Was wet with dew at*
In Hector's wrath.

CRESSIDA   What was his cause of anger?

ALEXANDER   The noise° goes this: there is among the Greeks   *rumor*
A lord of Trojan blood, nephew° to Hector;   *relation*
They call him Ajax.

CRESSIDA   Good,° and what of him?   *Well*

15 ALEXANDER   They say he is a very man *per se,*°   *unique man*
And stands alone.°   *is preeminent*

CRESSIDA   So do all men
Unless they are drunk, sick, or have no legs.

ALEXANDER   This man, lady, hath robbed many beasts of their
particular additions:° he is as valiant as the lion, churlish as the   *characteristics*

20 bear, slow as the elephant—a man into whom nature hath so
crowded humours[2] that his valour is crushed into folly, his folly
farced° with discretion. There is no man hath a virtue that he   *stuffed*
hath not a glimpse° of, nor any man an attaint° but he carries   *hint / flaw*
some stain of it. He is melancholy without cause and merry

25 against the hair;° he hath the joints of everything, but every-   *against the grain*
thing so out of joint that he is a gouty Briareus, many hands
and no use, or purblind Argus, all eyes and no sight.[3]

CRESSIDA   But how should this man that makes me smile make
Hector angry?

30 ALEXANDER   They say he yesterday coped° Hector in the battle   *engaged*
and struck him down, the disdain° and shame whereof hath   *indignation*
ever since kept Hector fasting and waking.

---

3. *'tis . . . horn:* it's just a trivial wound (or a wound given in return for Paris's scorn of Menelaus): Paris is wounded by the emblem of the cuckold (having seduced Helen, Menelaus's wife).
1.2 Location: Troy.
1. *Like . . . rose:* as if there were prudent management in war as in agriculture, where the conscientious laborer

gets up before dawn. The comparison continues with "field" and "flower" (line 9).
2. Peculiarities. Humors were the four main bodily fluids and were believed to determine a person's temperament.
3. He is a giant (Briareus), whose hundred hands are ruined by gout, or totally blind Argus, whose hundred eyes Juno deprived of sight because he fell asleep guarding Io.

CRESSIDA Who comes here?

ALEXANDER Madam, your uncle Pandarus.

       Enter PANDARUS [*above*]

35 CRESSIDA Hector's a gallant man.

ALEXANDER As may be in the world, lady.

PANDARUS What's that? What's that?

CRESSIDA Good morrow, uncle Pandarus.

PANDARUS Good morrow, cousin° Cressid. What do you talk   *relation*
40 of?— Good morrow, Alexander.—How do you, cousin? When
were you at Ilium?

CRESSIDA This morning, uncle.

PANDARUS What were you talking of when I came? Was Hector
armed and gone ere ye came to Ilium? Helen was not up, was
45 she?

CRESSIDA Hector was gone but Helen was not up?

PANDARUS E'en so. Hector was stirring early.

CRESSIDA That were we talking of, and of his anger.

PANDARUS Was he angry?

50 CRESSIDA So he° says here.   *Alexander*

PANDARUS True, he was so. I know the cause too. He'll lay about
him today, I can tell them that. And there's Troilus will not
come far behind him. Let them take heed of Troilus, I can tell
them that too.

55 CRESSIDA What, is he angry too?

PANDARUS Who, Troilus? Troilus is the better man of the two.

CRESSIDA O Jupiter! There's no comparison.

PANDARUS What, not between Troilus and Hector? Do you
know a man if you see him?

60 CRESSIDA Ay, if I ever saw him before and knew him.[4]

PANDARUS Well, I say Troilus is Troilus.°   *(that special man)*

CRESSIDA Then you say as I say, for I am sure
He is not Hector.

PANDARUS No, nor Hector is not Troilus, in some degrees.°   *respects*
65 CRESSIDA 'Tis just to each of them: he is himself.

PANDARUS Himself? Alas, poor Troilus, I would he were.

CRESSIDA So he is.

PANDARUS Condition I had gone barefoot to India.[5]

CRESSIDA He is not Hector.

70 PANDARUS Himself? No, he's not himself. Would a° were him-   *he*
self! Well, the gods are above, time must friend or end.° Well, *befriend or kill him*
Troilus, well, I would my heart were in her body. No, Hector
is not a better man than Troilus.

CRESSIDA Excuse me.[6]

75 PANDARUS He is elder.

CRESSIDA Pardon me, pardon me.

PANDARUS Th'other's not come to't.° You shall tell me another *his prime; intercourse*
tale when th'other's come to't. Hector shall not have his will[7]
this year.

80 CRESSIDA He shall not need it if he have his own.

PANDARUS Nor his qualities.

---

4. Here and in the following lines, Cressida obstinately
takes Pandarus's figurative language literally. Recognized
him; met an ideal man; saw him from the front ("before")
and had sexual intercourse with ("knew") him.

5. If I'd gone barefoot (on pilgrimage) to India—an
impossibility.
6. Cressida disagrees, as in line 76.
7. Troilus's resolve; Troilus's sexual desire.

CRESSIDA   No matter.

PANDARUS   Nor his beauty.

CRESSIDA   'Twould not become him; his own's better.

85 PANDARUS   You have no judgement, niece. Helen herself swore
th'other day that Troilus for a brown favour,[8] for so 'tis, I must
confess—not brown neither—

CRESSIDA   No, but brown.

PANDARUS   Faith, to say truth, brown and not brown.

90 CRESSIDA   To say the truth, true and not true.

PANDARUS   She praised his complexion above Paris'.

CRESSIDA   Why, Paris hath colour enough.

PANDARUS   So he has.

CRESSIDA   Then Troilus should° have too much. If she praised   *must therefore*
95 him above, his° complexion is higher than his;° he having col-   *Troilus's / Paris's*
our enough, and the other higher, is too flaming a praise for
a good complexion. I had as lief Helen's golden tongue had
commended Troilus for a copper nose.[9]

PANDARUS   I swear to you, I think Helen loves him better than
100 Paris.

CRESSIDA   Then she's a merry Greek[1] indeed.

PANDARUS   Nay, I am sure she does. She came to him th'other
day into the compassed° window, and you know he has not past   *bay*
three or four hairs on his chin—

105 CRESSIDA   Indeed, a tapster's° arithmetic may soon bring his par-   *the simplest*
ticulars therein to a total.

PANDARUS   Why, he is very young—and yet will he within three
pound lift as much as his brother Hector.

CRESSIDA   Is he so young a man and so old a lifter?°   *so practiced a thief*
110 PANDARUS   But to prove to you that Helen loves him: she came
and puts me° her white hand to his cloven chin.   *puts me = puts*

CRESSIDA   Juno have mercy! How came it cloven?

PANDARUS   Why, you know, 'tis dimpled. I think his smiling
becomes him better than any man in all Phrygia.

115 CRESSIDA   O he smiles valiantly.

PANDARUS   Does he not?

CRESSIDA   O yes, an't were a cloud in autumn.[2]

PANDARUS   Why, go to then. But to prove to you that Helen loves
Troilus—

120 CRESSIDA   Troilus will stand to the proof[3] if you'll prove it so.

PANDARUS   Troilus? Why, he esteems her no more than I esteem
an addle° egg.   *rotten*

CRESSIDA   If you love an addle egg as well as you love an idle
head you would eat chickens i'th' shell.[4]

125 PANDARUS   I cannot choose but laugh to think how she tickled
his chin. Indeed, she has a marvellous white hand, I must
needs confess—

CRESSIDA   Without the rack.°   *being tortured*

PANDARUS   And she takes upon her to spy a white hair on his
130 chin.

---

8. Notwithstanding his (unfashionably) dark or tanned
face.
9. Red nose, caused by drinking; perhaps also an artificial
nose, made necessary by syphilis.
1. Slang for a reveler or wanton, implying good
fellowship and superficiality; here, appropriately applied

to Helen and more generally to the Greeks, at least as
they treat Cressida.
2. As if he were a rain cloud.
3. Will uphold the proof; will have an erection.
4. An addled egg often resulted from the chick dying
during hatching.

CRESSIDA   Alas, poor chin! Many a wart is richer.°   *(in hairs)*

PANDARUS   But there was such laughing! Queen Hecuba laughed
    that° her eyes ran o'er.   *so much that*

CRESSIDA   With millstones.⁵

135   PANDARUS   And Cassandra laughed.

CRESSIDA   But there was a more temperate fire under the pot of
    her eyes⁶—or did her eyes run o'er too?

PANDARUS   And Hector laughed.

CRESSIDA   At what was all this laughing?

140   PANDARUS   Marry,⁷ at the white hair that Helen spied on Troilus'
    chin.

CRESSIDA   An't had been a green hair I should have laughed too.

PANDARUS   They laughed not so much at the hair as at his pretty°   *witty*
    answer.

145   CRESSIDA   What was his answer?

PANDARUS   Quoth she, 'Here's but two-and-fifty hairs on your
    chin, and one of them is white.'

CRESSIDA   This is her question.

PANDARUS   That's true, make no question of that. 'Two-and-fifty

150   hairs,' quoth he, 'and one white? That white hair is my father,
    and all the rest are his sons.'⁸ 'Jupiter!' quoth she, 'which of
    these hairs° is Paris my husband?' 'The forked⁹ one,' quoth he,   *pun on "heirs"*
    'pluck't out and give it him.' But there was such laughing, and
    Helen so blushed and Paris so chafed° and all the rest so   *(was) so irritated*

155   laughed, that it passed.°   *surpassed description*

CRESSIDA   So let it now, for it has been a great while going by.

PANDARUS   Well, cousin, I told you a thing yesterday. Think on't.

CRESSIDA   So I do.

PANDARUS   I'll be sworn 'tis true. He will weep you an't° were a   *for you as if he*

160   man born in April.°   *month of showers*

CRESSIDA   And I'll spring up in his tears an't° were a nettle   *as if I*
    against° May.   *in anticipation of*

    A retreat [is] sound[ed]

PANDARUS   Hark, they are coming from the field. Shall we stand
    up here and see them as they pass toward Ilium? Good niece,

165   do, sweet niece Cressida.

CRESSIDA   At your pleasure.

PANDARUS   Here, here, here's an excellent place, here we may
    see most bravely.° I'll tell you them all by their names as they   *very finely*
    pass by, but mark Troilus above the rest.

    Enter AENEAS *[passing by below]*

170   CRESSIDA   Speak not so loud.

PANDARUS   That's Aeneas. Is not that a brave° man? He's one of   *splendid; courageous*
    the flowers° of Troy, I can tell you. But mark Troilus; you shall   *finest men*
    see anon.

    Enter ANTENOR *[passing by below]*

CRESSIDA   Who's that?

175   PANDARUS   That's Antenor. He has a shrewd wit, I can tell you,

---

5. A hard-hearted person was proverbially said to weep
millstones rather than tears. Cressida doesn't think the
story is particularly funny.
6. Cassandra's tears are "more temperate" because she
was associated with mournful, doom-laden prophecy.
Cressida imagines tears of laughter as a pot boiling over.

7. An oath based on the name of the Virgin Mary, here
meaning "Why," elsewhere "Indeed."
8. Priam reputedly had fifty sons. The "forked" hair (line
152) apparently counts as two.
9. Like a cuckold's horns, thereby suggesting Helen's
unfaithfulness to Paris.

and he's a man good enough. He's° one o'th' soundest judge-   *He has*
ments in Troy whosoever,° and a proper man of person.[1] When   *of any man*
comes Troilus? I'll show you Troilus anon. If he see me you
shall see him nod at me.
180 CRESSIDA   Will he give you the nod?
PANDARUS   You shall see.
CRESSIDA   If he do, the rich shall have more.[2]

    Enter HECTOR [*passing by below*]

PANDARUS   That's Hector, that, that, look you, that. There's a
fellow!— Go thy way, Hector!—There's a brave man, niece. O
185 brave Hector! Look how he looks. There's a countenance. Is't
not a brave man?
CRESSIDA   O a brave man.
PANDARUS   Is a° not? It does a man's heart good. Look you what   *he*
hacks are on his helmet. Look you yonder, do you see? Look
190 you there. There's no jesting. There's laying on, take't off who
will,[3] as they say. There be hacks.
CRESSIDA   Be those with swords?

    Enter PARIS [*passing by below*]

PANDARUS   Swords, anything, he cares not. An the devil come to
him it's all one.° By God's lid° it does one's heart good. Yonder   *the same / eyelid*
195 comes Paris, yonder comes Paris. Look ye yonder, niece. Is't
not a gallant° man too? Is't not? Why, this is brave now. Who   *fine*
said he came hurt home today? He's not hurt. Why, this will
do Helen's heart good now, ha! Would I could see Troilus now.
You shall see Troilus anon.

    Enter HELENUS [*passing by below*]

200 CRESSIDA   Who's that?
PANDARUS   That's Helenus. I marvel where Troilus is. That's
Helenus. I think he went not forth today. That's Helenus.
CRESSIDA   Can Helenus fight, uncle?
PANDARUS   Helenus? No—yes, he'll fight indifferent° well. I mar-   *fairly*
205 vel where Troilus is.

    [*A Shout*]

Hark, do you not hear the people cry 'Troilus'? Helenus is a
priest.

    Enter TROILUS [*passing by below*]

CRESSIDA   What sneaking fellow comes yonder?
PANDARUS   Where? Yonder? That's Deiphobus.—'Tis Troilus!
210 There's a man, niece, h'm? Brave Troilus, the prince of chivalry!
CRESSIDA   Peace, for shame, peace.
PANDARUS   Mark him, note him. O brave Troilus! Look well
upon him, niece. Look you how his sword is bloodied and
215 his helm more hacked than Hector's, and how he looks and
how he goes.° O admirable youth! He ne'er saw three-and-   *walks*
twenty. —Go thy way, Troilus, go thy way!—Had I a sister were
a grace,[4] or a daughter a goddess, he should take his choice. O
admirable man! Paris? Paris is dirt to him, and I warrant Helen
220 to change° would give an eye to boot.   *exchange*

    Enter common soldiers [*passing by below*]

---

1. Good-looking man.
2. If Troilus acknowledges Pandarus with a nod, this will
make Pandarus even more of a noddy, a fool.

3. There's hard fighting, denials notwithstanding (with
wordplay: "laying on" versus "take't off").
4. The three Graces were goddesses of beauty and charm.

CRESSIDA　Here comes more.

PANDARUS　Asses, fools, dolts. Chaff and bran, chaff and bran.
Porridge° after meat. I could live and die i'th' eyes of Troilus.　　　　*Soup*
Ne'er look, ne'er look, the eagles are gone. Crows and daws,°　　　　*jackdaws; fools*
225　crows and daws. I had rather be such a man as Troilus than
Agamemnon and all Greece.

CRESSIDA　There is among the Greeks Achilles, a better man
than Troilus.

PANDARUS　Achilles? A drayman,° a porter, a very camel.　　　　*cart driver*
230　CRESSIDA　Well, well.

PANDARUS　Well, well? Why, have you any discretion? Have you
any eyes? Do you know what a man is? Is not birth,° beauty,　　　　*lineage*
good shape, discourse,° manhood, learning, gentleness,° virtue,　　　　*eloquence / gentility*
youth, liberality, and so forth, the spice and salt that season a
235　man?

CRESSIDA　Ay, a minced⁵ man—and then to be baked with no
date in the pie, for then the man's date is out.⁶

PANDARUS　You are such another woman!° One knows not at　　　　*like other women*
what ward you lie.⁷

240　CRESSIDA　Upon my back to defend my belly,⁸ upon my wit to
defend my wiles, upon my secrecy° to defend mine honesty,⁹　　　　*privacy; genitals*
my mask to defend my beauty,° and you to defend all these—　　　　*(from sun)*
and at all these wards I lie at a thousand watches.¹

PANDARUS　Say one of your watches.

245　CRESSIDA　'Nay, I'll watch you for that'—and that's one of the
chiefest of them too.² If I cannot ward what I would not have
hit,° I can watch you for° telling how I took the blow— unless　　　　*(sexually) / from*
it swell past hiding,° and then it's past watching.　　　　*(from pregnancy)*

PANDARUS　You are such another!

Enter BOY

250　BOY　Sir, my lord would instantly speak with you.

PANDARUS　Where?

BOY　At your own house.

PANDARUS　Good boy, tell him I come.　　　　[*Exit* BOY]
I doubt° he be hurt. Fare ye well, good niece.　　　　*fear*

255　CRESSIDA　Adieu, uncle.

PANDARUS　I'll be with you, niece, by and by.

CRESSIDA　To bring, uncle?

PANDARUS　Ay, a token from Troilus.

CRESSIDA　By the same token, you are a bawd.°　　　　*pander; pimp*

Exeunt PANDARUS [*and* ALEXANDER]

260　Words, vows, gifts, tears, and love's full sacrifice
He offers in another's enterprise;
But more in Troilus thousandfold I see
Than in the glass° of Pandar's praise may be.　　　　*mirror*
Yet hold I off. Women are angels, wooing;³

---

5. Affected (punning on "mincemeat" to suggest the
multiple ingredients of Troilus and thus beginning to
develop Pandarus's "spice and salt" metaphor).
6. The man is flavorless; out of date; not in female genitalia.
7. A man doesn't know what position of defense in fencing ("ward") you adopt. (A man doesn't know how to deal
with you.)
8. Vagina. Lying on one's back is not, of course, the obvious way to defend one's virginity.

9. Reputation.
1. Ways of guarding; hours of the night; the duties of a
watchman (playing on "watch" and "ward," line 243);
devotional exercises (line 244). "Watch" as a verb is also
implied: observe (line 245); prevent (line 246); worry
(line 247).
2. Presumably the immediately preceding phrase is one
of her chief devotional exercises.
3. Men call women angels only while wooing them.

265 Things won are done. Joy's soul lies in the doing.
That she beloved knows naught that knows not this:
Men price the thing ungained more than it is.°   *is worth*
That she was never yet that ever knew
Love got so sweet as when desire did sue.[4]
270 Therefore this maxim out of° love I teach: *taken from*
Achievement is command; ungained, beseech.[5]
Then though my heart's contents[6] firm love doth bear,
Nothing of that shall from mine eyes appear.   *Exit*

1.3

Sennet.° Enter AGAMEMNON, NESTOR, ULYSSES, DIO-   *Fanfare*
MEDES, [*and*] MENELAUS, *with others*

AGAMEMNON   Princes, what grief hath set the jaundice° on your cheeks?   *sickliness*
The ample proposition that hope makes
In all designs begun on earth below
Fails in the promised largeness. Checks° and disasters   *Obstacles*
5 Grow in the veins[1] of actions highest reared,
As knots, by the conflux° of meeting sap,   *confluence*
Infects the sound pine and diverts his° grain   *its*
Tortive° and errant° from his course of growth.   *Contorted / straying*
Nor, princes, is it matter new to us
10 That we come short of our suppose° so far   *intention*
That after seven years' siege yet Troy walls stand,
Sith° every action that hath gone before,   *Since*
Whereof we have record, trial did draw
Bias and thwart,[2] not answering° the aim   *living up to*
15 And that unbodied figure° of the thought   *theoretical design*
That gave't surmisèd shape. Why then, you princes,
Do you with cheeks abashed behold our works,
And think them shames, which are indeed naught else
But the protractive trials of great Jove
20 To find persistive constancy in men?
The fineness of which mettle° is not found   *temperament; metal*
In fortune's love—for then the bold and coward,
The wise and fool, the artist° and unread,   *learned*
The hard and soft, seem all affined° and kin.   *related*
25 But in the wind and tempest of her frown
Distinction with a loud and powerful fan,
Puffing at all, winnows the light away,[3]
And what hath mass or matter by itself
Lies rich in virtue and unmingled.
30 NESTOR   With due observance of° thy godly seat,°   *respect to / throne*
Great Agamemnon, Nestor shall apply°   *gloss*
Thy latest words. In the reproof of° chance   *rebuff by; rebuttal of*
Lies the true proof of men. The sea being smooth,
How many shallow bauble°-boats dare sail   *toy*
35 Upon her patient breast, making their way

---

4. *That . . . sue:* No woman has ever known making love with a man to be as sweet as when it is still desired for the first time.
5. Once a woman yields, the man controls her; what the man doesn't have he must plead for.
6. *contents':* happiness; *con'tents:* substance.
1.3 Location: The Greek camp outside Troy.

1. It is assumed that trees have veins through which sap flows.
2. *trial . . . thwart:* attempting the deed ("action") called it into being crookedly and in a manner at odds with the purpose.
3. The comparison is to light, dry chaff blown away from grain.

With those of nobler bulk!

But let the ruffian Boreas° once enrage   *North wind*

The gentle Thetis,[4] and anon behold

The strong-ribbed barque through liquid mountains cut,

40   Bounding between the two moist elements°   *(water and air)*

Like Perseus' horse.° Where's then the saucy° boat   *(winged Pegasus) / bold*

Whose weak untimbered sides but even° now   *just*

Co-rivalled greatness? Either to harbour fled,

Or made a toast for Neptune.[5] Even so

45   Doth valour's show and valour's worth divide

In storms of fortune. For in her° ray and brightness   *(fortune's)*

The herd hath more annoyance by the breese°   *gadfly*

Than by the tiger; but when the splitting wind

Makes flexible the knees° of knotted° oaks   *tough timber / gnarled*

50   And flies flee under shade, why then the thing of courage,°   *brave person*

As roused with rage, with rage doth sympathize,[6]

And with an accent tuned in selfsame key

Retorts to chiding fortune.

ULYSSES   Agamemnon,

Thou great commander, nerve° and bone of Greece,   *sinew*

55   Heart of our numbers,° soul and only spirit   *troops*

In whom the tempers and the minds of all

Should be shut up,° hear what Ulysses speaks.   *encapsulated*

Besides th'applause° and approbation   *approval*

The which, [*to* AGAMEMNON] most mighty for thy place and

sway,°   *position and power*

60   And thou, [*to* NESTOR] most reverend for thy stretched-out life,

I give to both your speeches—which were such

As, Agamemnon, every hand of Greece

Should hold up high in brass,° and such again   *record permanently*

As, venerable Nestor, hatched[7] in silver,

65   Should with a bond of air, strong as the axle-tree[8]

On which the heavens ride, knit all Greeks' ears

To his experienced tongue—yet let it please both,

Thou [*to* AGAMEMNON] great, and [*to* NESTOR] wise, to hear Ulysses speak.

AGAMEMNON   Speak, Prince of Ithaca, and be't of less expect°   *likelihood*

70   That matter needless, of importless burden,°   *irrelevant meaning*

Divide thy lips, than we are confident

When rank° Thersites opes his mastic° jaws   *rancid / abusive*

We shall hear music, wit, and oracle.

ULYSSES   Troy, yet upon his basis,° had been down   *still standing*

75   And the great Hector's sword had lacked a master

But for these instances:°   *causes*

The specialty° of rule hath been neglected.   *rights and duties*

And look how many° Grecian tents do stand   *however many*

Hollow° upon this plain: so many hollow° factions.   *Empty / false*

80   When that the general is not like the hive

To whom the foragers° shall all repair,   *food collectors*

What honey is expected? Degree° being vizarded,°   *Rank / concealed*

---

4. Sea goddess (mother of Achilles), here standing for the sea.

5. Morsel of toasted bread, floated in wine, for the god of the sea.

6. Himself enraged, behaves like the raging storm.

7. Etched with parallel lines, as if inlaid with precious metal (alluding to Nestor's white hair and beard, or his wrinkled face).

8. *bond of air:* persuasive rhetoric. *axle-tree:* the axis on which the universe was imagined to revolve, earth being at the center.

Th'unworthiest shows as fairly in the masque
[   ].⁹
85 The heavens themselves, the planets, and this centre°   *(the earth)*
Observe degree, priority, and place,
Infixture,° course, proportion, season, form,   *Fixity*
Office° and custom, in all line of order.   *Function*
And therefore is the glorious planet Sol¹
90 In noble eminence enthroned and sphered°   *placed in orbit*
Amidst the other,° whose med'cinable² eye   *rest*
Corrects the ill aspects° of planets evil   *astrological influence*
And posts° like the commandment of a king,   *hastens*
Sans° check, to good and bad. But when the planets   *Without*
95 In evil mixture to disorder wander,³
What plagues and what portents, what mutiny?
What raging of the sea, shaking of earth?
Commotion in the winds, frights, changes,° horrors   *political strife*
Divert and crack, rend and deracinate°   *uproot*
100 The unity and married calm of states
Quite from their fixture. O when degree is shaked,
Which is the ladder to all high designs,
The enterprise is sick. How could communities,
Degrees in schools,° and brotherhoods° in cities,   *Academic rank / guilds*
105 Peaceful commerce from dividable° shores,   *isolated*
The primogenity° and due of birth,   *primogeniture*
Prerogative of age, crowns, sceptres, laurels,
But by degree stand in authentic place?
Take but degree away, untune that string,
110 And hark what discord follows. Each thing meets
In mere oppugnancy.° The bounded waters   *total antagonism*
Should lift their bosoms higher than the shores
And make a sop° of all this solid globe;   *lump of soaked bread*
Strength should be lord of imbecility,°   *weakness*
115 And the rude son should strike his father dead.
Force should be right—or rather, right and wrong,
Between whose endless jar justice resides,⁴
Should lose their names, and so should justice too.
Then everything includes itself in° power,   *comes down to*
120 Power into will,° will into appetite;   *egotism; lust*
And appetite, an universal wolf,
So doubly seconded with will and power,
Must make perforce an universal prey,°   *seizing*
And last eat up himself. Great Agamemnon,
125 This chaos, when degree is suffocate,
Follows the choking.
And this neglection of degree it is
That by a pace goes backward in a purpose
It hath to climb.⁵ The general's disdained
130 By him one step below; he, by the next;
That next, by him beneath. So every step,

9. A line providing the contrast to "Th'unworthiest" may be lost.
1. In the Ptolemaic system, the sun was thought to be a planet revolving round the earth.
2. Curative. The eyes were thought to see by emitting rays—like the sun. Kings sometimes claimed a similar ability to cure.

3. The word "planets" means "wanderers," referring to their apparently erratic course, as seen from earth. *evil mixture*: wicked coupling.
4. Justice stands between the clashing ("jar") of the opposing contenders.
5. *That . . . climb*: That drops back step by step when it intends to climb.

Exampled by the first pace that is sick
Of his superior, grows to an envious fever
Of pale and bloodless emulation.°   sick rivalry
135   And 'tis this fever that keeps Troy on foot,°   standing
Not her own sinews. To end a tale of length:
Troy in our weakness lives, not in her strength.
NESTOR   Most wisely hath Ulysses here discovered°   revealed
The fever whereof all our power is sick.
140   AGAMEMNON   The nature of the sickness found, Ulysses,
What is the remedy?
ULYSSES   The great Achilles, whom opinion° crowns   consensus
The sinew and the forehand° of our host,°   strongest / army
Having his ear full of his airy° fame   lofty; insubstantial
145   Grows dainty of° his worth, and in his tent   too conscious of
Lies mocking our designs. With him Patroclus
Upon a lazy bed the livelong day
Breaks scurrile° jests   scurrilous
And, with ridiculous and awkward action°   gesture
150   Which, slanderer, he 'imitation' calls,
He pageants° us. Sometime, great Agamemnon,   mimics
Thy topless deputation° he puts on,   supreme rank
And like a strutting player, whose conceit
Lies in his hamstring[6] and doth think it rich
155   To hear the wooden dialogue and sound
'Twixt his stretched footing and the scaffoldage,[7]
Such to-be-pitied and o'er-wrested seeming°   pitiful imitation
He acts thy greatness in. And when he speaks
'Tis like a chime a-mending, with terms unsquared[8]
160   Which from the tongue of roaring Typhon[9] dropped
Would seem hyperboles. At this fusty° stuff   stale; bombastic
The large Achilles on his pressed[1] bed lolling
From his deep chest laughs out a loud applause,
Cries 'Excellent! 'Tis Agamemnon just.'°   exactly
165   Now play me Nestor, hem° and stroke thy beard,   (as in "ahem")
As he being dressed to° some oration.'   preparing for
That's done as near as the extremest ends
Of parallels, as like as Vulcan and his wife.[2]
Yet god° Achilles still cries, 'Excellent!   semidivine (ironic)
170   'Tis Nestor right. Now play him me, Patroclus,
Arming to answer in° a night alarm'.   respond to
And then forsooth the faint° defects of age   weak
Must be the scene of mirth: to cough and spit,
And with a palsy, fumbling on his gorget,°   throat armor
175   Shake in and out the rivet.° And at this sport   fastening bolt
Sir Valour dies,° cries, 'O enough, Patroclus!   (laughing)
Or give me ribs of steel. I shall split all
In pleasure of my spleen.'° And in this fashion   (seat of mirth)
All our abilities, gifts, natures, shapes,

6. *whose . . . hamstring*: whose brains are in his thighs.
7. *To hear . . . scaffoldage*: To hear the sound of his long, powerful strides (and dull speech?) on the platform stage.
8. Like bells being repaired (or tuned?), with ill-fitting expressions.
9. Monster with a hundred heads, each uttering the cry of a different beast; eventually buried by Jupiter under (and so associated with) a volcano.

1. Weighed down (by Achilles).
2. *as near . . . wife*: as closely as the ends of parallel lines (which, since they are equidistant, never meet), and as the ugly, limping god Vulcan, the smith, resembles his beautiful wife Venus. Ulysses is stressing how bad the acting is, while at the same time covertly belittling Agamemnon and Nestor.

180 Severals and generals of grace exact,³
Achievements, plots, orders, preventions,°   *precautions*
Excitements° to the field or speech for truce,   *Urgings*
Success or loss, what is or is not, serves
As stuff for these two to make paradoxes.°   *absurdities*

185 NESTOR   And in the imitation of these twain
Who, as Ulysses says, opinion crowns
With an imperial voice, many are infect.°   *infected*
Ajax is grown self-willed and bears his head
In such a rein,° in full as proud a place   *So high*

190 As broad Achilles, and keeps° his tent like him,   *stays within*
Makes factious feasts, rails on° our state of war   *complains about*
Bold as an oracle, and sets Thersites,
A slave whose gall° coins slanders like a mint,   *rancor*
To match us in comparisons with dirt,

195 To weaken and discredit our exposure,°   *exposed position*
How rank° so ever rounded in with° danger.   *densely / hemmed in by*
ULYSSES   They tax° our policy and call it cowardice,   *criticize*
Count wisdom as no member of the war,
Forestall prescience° and esteem no act   *advance planning*

200 But that of hand. The still and mental parts
That do contrive how many hands shall strike
When fitness° calls them on, and know by measure   *the right moment*
Of their observant toil the enemy's weight,°   *power*
Why, this hath not a finger's dignity.

205 They call this 'bed-work', 'mapp'ry',° 'closet war'.   *mere mapping; planning*
So that the ram that batters down the wall,
For the great swing and rudeness of his poise⁴
They place before° his hand that made the engine,°   *exalt above / (the ram)*
Or those that with the finesse° of their souls   *subtlety*

210 By reason guide his execution.°   *the ram's use*
NESTOR   Let this be granted, and Achilles' horse
Makes many Thetis' sons.⁵
             Tucket°   *Trumpet call*
AGAMEMNON   What trumpet?
Look, Menelaus.
MENELAUS   From Troy.
            Enter AENEAS [*and a trumpeter*]
AGAMEMNON   What would you fore° our tent?   *before*

215 AENEAS   Is this great Agamemnon's tent I pray you?
AGAMEMNON   Even this.
AENEAS   May one that is a herald and a prince
Do a fair message to his kingly ears?
AGAMEMNON   With surety° stronger than Achilles' arm,   *security*

220 Fore all the Greekish heads, which with one voice
Call Agamemnon heart and general.
AENEAS   Fair leave and large° security. How may   *generous*
A stranger to those most imperial looks
Know them from eyes of other mortals?
AGAMEMNON   How?

225 AENEAS   Ay, I ask that I might waken reverence

---

3. Supreme merits, possessed individually and in common.

4. Because of the impetus and violence of its impact.

5. *Let . . . sons*: If this is true, then Achilles' horse is worth many Achilleses. Thetis was the mother of Achilles.

And on the cheek be ready with a blush
Modest as morning when she coldly eyes
The youthful Phoebus.[6]
Which is that god in office, guiding men?
230   Which is the high and mighty Agamemnon?
  AGAMEMNON [to the Greeks] This Trojan scorns us, or the men of Troy
    Are ceremonious courtiers.
  AENEAS Courtiers as free,° as debonair,° unarmed,   *generous / gracious*
    As bending° angels—that's their fame in peace.   *ministering*
235   But when they would seem soldiers they have galls,[7]
    Good arms, strong joints, true swords—and great Jove's acorn[8]
    Nothing so full of heart.° But peace, Aeneas,   *courage; nutmeat*
    Peace, Trojan; lay thy finger on thy lips.
    The worthiness of praise distains° his worth,   *stains*
240   If that the praised himself bring the praise forth.
    But what, repining,° the enemy commends,   *grudging(ly)*
    That breath fame blows; that praise, sole pure, transcends.
  AGAMEMNON Sir, you of Troy, call you yourself Aeneas?
  AENEAS Ay, Greek,° that is my name.   *cheater (slang)*
  AGAMEMNON   What's your affair, I pray you?
245   AENEAS Sir, pardon, 'tis for Agamemnon's ears.
  AGAMEMNON He hears naught privately that comes from Troy.
  AENEAS Nor I from Troy come not to whisper him.
    I bring a trumpet to awake his ear,
    To set his sense on the attentive bent,
    And then to speak.
250   AGAMEMNON   Speak frankly° as the wind.   *freely*
    It is not Agamemnon's sleeping hour.
    That thou shalt know, Trojan, he is awake,
    He tells thee so himself.
  AENEAS   Trumpet,° blow loud.   *Trumpeter*
    Send thy brass voice through all these lazy tents,
255   And every Greek of mettle let him know
    What Troy means fairly shall be spoke aloud.
    The trumpet sound[s]
    We have, great Agamemnon, here in Troy
    A prince called Hector—Priam is his father—
    Who in this dull and long-continued truce
260   Is resty° grown. He bade me take a trumpet   *lazy*
    And to this purpose speak: 'Kings, princes, lords,
    If there be one among the fair'st of Greece
    That holds his honour higher than his ease,
    That seeks his praise more than he fears his peril,
265   That knows his valour and knows not his fear,
    That loves his mistress more than in confession
    With truant vows to her own lips he loves,[9]
    And dare avow her beauty and her worth
    In other arms than hers°—to him this challenge.   *armor; Hector's arms*
270   Hector in view of Trojans and of Greeks
    Shall make it good, or do his best to do it:
    He hath a lady wiser, fairer, truer,
    Than ever Greek did compass° in his arms,   *hold*

---

6. *Modest . . . Phoebus:* Modest as Aurora, the blushing dawn personified, when she coldly eyes Apollo, the sun god ("youthful" because it is early morning).
7. But when it is time for them to be warriors, their courageous tempers do not tolerate mistreatment.
8. The oak was Jupiter's tree.
9. *That . . . loves:* Who will declare his love with stronger proof (deeds) than unreliable, private promises.

275	And will tomorrow with his trumpet call
	Midway between your tents and walls of Troy
	To rouse a Grecian that is true in love.
	If any come, Hector shall honour him.
	If none, he'll say in Troy when he retires

And will tomorrow with his trumpet call
275 Midway between your tents and walls of Troy
To rouse a Grecian that is true in love.
If any come, Hector shall honour him.
If none, he'll say in Troy when he retires
The Grecian dames are sunburnt° and not worth   *not fair*
280 The splinter° of a lance.' Even so much.   *breaking; fragment*
AGAMEMNON   This shall be told our lovers, Lord Aeneas.
If none of them have soul in such a kind,
We left them all at home. But we are soldiers,
And may that soldier a mere recreant prove
285 That means not, hath not,[1] or is not in love.
If then one is, or hath, or means to be,
That one meets Hector. If none else, I'll be he.
NESTOR [*to* AENEAS]   Tell him of Nestor, one that was a man
When Hector's grandsire sucked. He is old now,
290 But if there be not in our Grecian mould°   *character; model*
One noble man that hath one spark of fire
To answer for his love, tell him from me
I'll hide my silver beard in a gold beaver°   *helmet's face guard*
And in my vambrace° put this withered brawn,°   *forearm armor / arm*
295 And meeting him will tell him that my lady
Was fairer than his grandam, and as chaste
As may be in the world. His youth in flood,°   *Despite his youth*
I'll prove this truth with my three drops of blood.
AENEAS   Now heavens forbid such scarcity of youth.
300 ULYSSES   Amen.
AGAMEMNON   Fair Lord Aeneas, let me touch° your hand.   *shake*
To our pavilion shall I lead you first.
Achilles shall have word of this intent;
So shall each lord of Greece, from tent to tent.
305 Yourself shall feast with us before you go,
And find the welcome of a noble foe.
                                    Exeunt. Manent° ULYSSES *and* NESTOR   *Remain*
ULYSSES   Nestor!
NESTOR   What says Ulysses?
ULYSSES   I have a young
Conception in my brain; be you my time[2]
To bring it to some shape.
NESTOR   What is't?
ULYSSES   This 'tis:
310 Blunt wedges rive° hard knots. The seeded pride   *split*
That hath to this maturity blown° up   *swelled*
In rank° Achilles must or° now be cropped   *overgrown / either*
Or, shedding,° breed a nursery of like evil   *dropping its seed*
To overbulk° us all.   *overrun*
NESTOR   Well, and how?
315 ULYSSES   This challenge that the gallant Hector sends,
However it is spread in general name,
Relates in purpose only to Achilles.
NESTOR   The purpose is perspicuous,° even as substance°   *easy to see / wealth*
Whose grossness little characters sum up.[3]

---

1. Who does not aim (to be), has never been.
2. *Conception . . . time*: The primary meaning (unfolding of a plan) metaphorically extended to pregnancy's onset and gestation period, the latter associated with the male and aged Nestor, who is oddly associated with this female and ordinarily youthful activity, presumably because he embodies the passage of time.
3. Whose size is reckoned by small figures (on paper).

320 And, in the publication, make no strain[4]
But that Achilles, were his brain as barren
As banks of Libya°—though, Apollo knows,   *the Sahara desert*
'Tis dry° enough—will with great speed of judgement,   *infertile; empty*
Ay with celerity, find Hector's purpose
325 Pointing on him.°   *himself*

ULYSSES And wake him to the answer, think you?

NESTOR Yes, 'tis most meet.° Who may you else oppose,   *fitting*
That can from Hector bring his honour off,
If not Achilles? Though't be a sportful combat,
330 Yet in this trial much opinion° dwells,   *reputation*
For here the Trojans taste our dear'st repute
With their fin'st palate. And trust to me, Ulysses,
Our imputation° shall be oddly poised[5]   *reputation*
In this wild° action: for the success,   *uncontrollable*
335 Although particular, shall give a scantling
Of good or bad unto the general[6]—
And in such indices,° although small pricks   *tables of contents*
To° their subsequent volumes, there is seen   *Compared to*
The baby figure of the giant mass
340 Of things to come at large. It is supposed
He that meets Hector issues from our choice,
And choice, being mutual act of all our souls,
Makes merit her election,° and doth boil,   *grounds of choice*
As 'twere, from forth us all a man distilled
345 Out of our virtues—who miscarrying,°   *should he lose*
What heart from hence receives the conqu'ring part
To steel a strong opinion to themselves?[7]
Which entertained, limbs are e'en his instruments,
In no less working than are swords and bows
Directive by the limbs.[8]

350 ULYSSES   Give pardon to my speech:
Therefore 'tis meet° Achilles meet not Hector.   *appropriate*
Let us like merchants show our foulest wares
And think perchance they'll sell. If not,
The lustre of the better yet to show°   *not yet shown*
355 Shall show the better. Do not consent
That ever Hector and Achilles meet,
For both our honour and our shame in this
Are dogged with two strange followers.°   *surprising results*

NESTOR I see them not with my old eyes. What are they?

360 ULYSSES What glory our Achilles shares° from Hector,   *gains*
Were he not proud we all should wear° with him.   *share*
But he already is too insolent,
And we were better parch in Afric sun
Than in the pride and salt° scorn of his eyes,   *bitter*
365 Should he scape Hector fair. If he were foiled,
Why then we did our main opinion° crush   *common reputation*
In taint of° our best man. No, make a lott'ry,   *In the dishonor of*

---

4. And, with the announcement, do not doubt.
5. Disproportionately judged.
6. *the success . . . general:* the outcome, although relating only to one person, shall serve as an example of the whole army's abilities.
7. *What . . . themselves:* What (Greek) warriors could possibly get a sense of victory from this that would make

them feel more confident?; what motivation will the Trojans get from this to make them feel more confident?
8. *Which . . . limbs:* Assuming that this confidence ("strong opinion") is received from the victory, the soldiers' limbs become the mechanisms ("instruments") of that confidence in the same way that swords and bows are subject to direction by the limbs themselves.

And by device let blockish° Ajax draw   *blockheaded*
The sort° to fight with Hector. Among ourselves   *lot*
370   Give him allowance° as the worthier man—   *acknowledgment*
For that will physic the great Myrmidon,[9]
Who broils in° loud applause, and make him fall°   *is excited by / lower*
His crest, that prouder than blue Iris[1] bends.
If the dull brainless Ajax come safe off,
375   We'll dress him up in voices;° if he fail,   *sing his praises*
Yet go we under our opinion still
That we have better men. But hit or miss,
Our project's life° this shape of sense° assumes: *success / rationale*
Ajax employed plucks down Achilles' plumes.
380   NESTOR   Now, Ulysses, I begin to relish thy advice,
And I will give a taste of it forthwith
To Agamemnon. Go we to him straight.°   *immediately*
Two curs shall tame each other; pride alone
Must tarre the mastiffs on,[2] as 'twere° their bone.   *Exeunt*   *if it were*

2.1

Enter AJAX *and* THERSITES

AJAX   Thersites.
THERSITES   Agamemnon—how if he had boils, full,° all over,   *(of pus)*
generally?
AJAX   Thersites.
5   THERSITES   And those boils did run? Say so, did not the General
run then? Were not that a botchy core?°   *ulcerous center*
AJAX   Dog.
THERSITES   Then there would come some matter° from him. I   *pus; sense*
see none now.
10   AJAX   Thou bitch-wolf's son, canst thou not hear? Feel then.
*[He] strikes [*THERSITES*]*
THERSITES   The plague of Greece upon thee, thou mongrel[1]
beef-witted° lord!   *dumb as an ox*
AJAX   Speak then, thou unsifted leaven,° speak! I will beat[2] thee   *dough*
into handsomeness.°   *decency; good looks*
15   THERSITES   I shall sooner rail thee into wit and holiness. But I
think thy horse will sooner con° an oration than thou learn a   *memorize*
prayer without book.°   *by heart*
*[*AJAX *strikes him]*
Thou canst strike, canst thou? A red murrain° o' thy jade's[3]   *bloody plague*
tricks.
20   AJAX   Toad's stool![4]
[He strikes THERSITES*]*
Learn me° the proclamation.   *Instruct me (about)*
THERSITES   Dost thou think I have no sense,° thou strikest me   *feeling*
thus?
AJAX   The proclamation.
25   THERSITES   Thou art proclaimed a fool, I think.
AJAX   Do not, porcupine,[5] do not. My fingers itch.°   *(to hit you)*

---

9. Will give medicine to (purge) Achilles, who led the
Myrmidons.
1. Goddess of the rainbow; blue flower.
2. Must incite these large, aggressive dogs.
2.1 Location: The Greek camp.
1. Ajax's mother was Trojan; hence, he was of mixed

breed, "mongrel."
2. Punning on the pounding of bread dough.
3. Temperamental horse's.
4. Toadstools were once thought to be a toad's poisonous
excrement (stool).

THERSITES   I would thou didst itch from head to foot. An° I had   *If*
the scratching of thee, I would make thee the loathsomest
scab in Greece.

30   AJAX   I say, the proclamation.

THERSITES   Thou grumblest and railest every hour on Achilles,
and thou art as full of envy at his greatness as Cerberus is at
Proserpina's[6] beauty, ay, that thou barkest at him.

AJAX   Mistress[7] Thersites.

35   THERSITES   Thou shouldst strike him.

AJAX   Cobloaf.°   *Small crusty loaf*

THERSITES   He would pun° thee into shivers° with his fist, as a   *pound / pieces*
sailor breaks a biscuit.

AJAX   You whoreson cur.
       [*He strikes* THERSITES]

40   THERSITES   Do! Do!°   *Go on*

AJAX   Thou stool° for a witch.   *privy*
       [*He strikes* THERSITES]

THERSITES   Ay, do, do! Thou sodden-witted° lord, thou hast in   *boiled-brained*
thy skull no more brain than I have in mine elbows. An *asnico*°   *little ass*
may tutor thee. Thou scurvy valiant ass, thou art here but to
45   thrash Trojans, and thou art bought and sold[8] among those of
any wit like a barbarian slave. If thou use° to beat me, I will   *continue*
begin at thy heel and tell what thou art by inches, thou thing
of no bowels,° thou.   *with no pity*

AJAX   You dog.

50   THERSITES   You scurvy lord.

AJAX   You cur.
       [*He strikes* THERSITES]

THERSITES   Mars his idiot!° Do, rudeness! Do, camel, do, do!   *God of war's jester*
       Enter ACHILLES *and* PATROCLUS

ACHILLES   Why, how now, Ajax? Wherefore do ye thus?
How now, Thersites? What's the matter, man?

55   THERSITES   You see him there? Do you?

ACHILLES   Ay. What's the matter?

THERSITES   Nay, look upon him.

ACHILLES   So I do. What's the matter?

THERSITES   Nay, but regard him well.

60   ACHILLES   'Well'? Why, I do so.

THERSITES   But yet you look not well upon him.[9] For whoso-
mever you take him to be, he is Ajax.°   *a jakes = toilet*

ACHILLES   I know that, fool.

THERSITES   Ay, but 'that fool' knows not himself.[1]

65   AJAX   Therefore I beat thee.[2]

THERSITES   Lo,° lo, lo, lo, what modicums of wit he utters. His   *Behold (sarcastic)*
evasions have ears thus long.[3] I have bobbed° his brain more   *thumped*

---

5. The porcupine's sharp quills were emblematic of the satirist (here, Thersites).

6. Cerberus was the monstrous three-headed dog who guarded the gate of Hades. Proserpina was Queen of Hades and wife of Pluto, god of the underworld.

7. Because a woman's only weapon was thought to be her tongue, because Thersites is a coward, or because he is believed to be homosexual.

8. You are traded like goods—hence, treated as an object, treated contemptuously.

9. Thersites is probably feigning amazement that Achil-

les can look at Ajax and yet not see what a fool he is; but he may also mean that Achilles does not do well to favor ("look . . . upon") him.

1. Thersites deliberately understands Achilles' line without the intended comma: "I know that fool" (Ajax), rather than "I know that [fact], fool."

2. Ajax thinks Thersites is calling himself (rather than Ajax) a "fool" who does not know himself.

3. His efforts to dodge witty rejoinders are like an ass's—hence asinine.

than he has beat my bones. I will° buy nine sparrows for a   *can*
penny, and his *pia mater*° is not worth the ninth part of a spar-   *brain*
70   row. This lord, Achilles—Ajax, who wears his wit in his belly
and his guts in his head—I'll tell you what I say of him.

ACHILLES   What?

THERSITES   I say, this Ajax—

    [AJAX *threatens to strike him*]

ACHILLES   Nay, good Ajax.

75 THERSITES   Has not so much wit—

    [AJAX *threatens to strike him*]

ACHILLES [*to* AJAX]   Nay, I must hold° you.   *restrain*

THERSITES   As will stop the eye of Helen's needle,⁴ for whom he
comes to fight.

ACHILLES   Peace, fool.

80 THERSITES   I would have peace and quietness, but the fool° will   *Ajax*
not. He, there, that he, look you there.

AJAX   O thou damned cur I shall—

ACHILLES [*to* AJAX]   Will you set your wit to° a fool's?   *against*

THERSITES   No, I warrant you, for a fool's will shame it.

85 PATROCLUS   Good words,° Thersites.   *Speak with restraint*

ACHILLES [*to* AJAX]   What's the quarrel?

AJAX   I bade the vile owl⁵ go learn me the tenor of the proclamation, and he rails upon me.

THERSITES   I serve thee not.

90 AJAX   Well, go to, go to.

THERSITES   I serve here voluntary.°   *as a volunteer*

ACHILLES   Your last service was sufferance. 'Twas not voluntary:
no man is beaten voluntary. Ajax was here the voluntary, and
you as under an impress.⁶

95 THERSITES   E'en so. A great deal of your wit, too, lies in your
sinews, or else there be liars. Hector shall have a great catch an
a° knock out either of your brains. A were as good° crack a   *if he / might as well*
fusty° nut with no kernel.   *rotten*

ACHILLES   What, with me too, Thersites?

100 THERSITES   There's Ulysses and old Nestor, whose wit was
mouldy ere your grandsires had nails on their toes, yoke you
like draught oxen and make you plough up the war.°   *(pun on ware = crops)*

ACHILLES   What? What?

THERSITES   Yes, good sooth. To° Achilles! To, Ajax, to—   *(urging on the oxen)*

105 AJAX   I shall cut out your tongue.

THERSITES   'Tis no matter. I shall speak as much wit as thou
afterwards.

PATROCLUS   No more words, Thersites, peace.

THERSITES   I will hold my peace when Achilles' brach° bids me,   *bitch*
110 shall I?

ACHILLES   There's for you, Patroclus.

THERSITES   I will see you hanged like clodpolls° ere I come any   *blockheads*
more to your tents. I will keep where there is wit stirring, and
leave the faction of fools.   *Exit*

115 PATROCLUS   A good riddance.

---

4. "Eye" perhaps alludes to "vagina"; "needle" is also obscene. *stop*: fill.
5. The owl is associated with evil portent.
6. As a conscript; being hit as though with a stamp (by Ajax).

ACHILLES [*to* AJAX] Marry, this, sir, is proclaimed through all our host:
That Hector, by the fifth hour° of the sun,   11 A.M.
Will with a trumpet 'twixt our tents and Troy
Tomorrow morning call some knight to arms
120 That hath a stomach,° and such a one that dare   *appetite for combat*
Maintain—I know not what. 'Tis trash. Farewell.
AJAX Farewell. Who shall answer him?
ACHILLES I know not. 'Tis put to lott'ry. Otherwise,
He knew his man.   [*Exeunt* ACHILLES *and* PATROCLUS]
125 AJAX O, meaning you? I will go learn more of it.   *Exit*

2.2

[*Sennet.*] *Enter* [*King*] PRIAM, HECTOR, TROILUS, PARIS,
and HELENUS

PRIAM After so many hours, lives, speeches spent,
Thus once again says Nestor from the Greeks:
'Deliver Helen, and all damage else—
As honour, loss of time, travail,° expense,   *hard labor*
5 Wounds, friends, and what else dear° that is consumed   *beloved; costly*
In hot digestion of this cormorant° war—   *rapacious*
Shall be struck off.'° Hector, what say you to't?   *expunged*
HECTOR Though no man lesser fears the Greeks than I,
As far as toucheth my particular,° yet, dread Priam,   *own concerns*
10 There is no lady of more softer bowels,°   *compassion*
More spongy to suck in° the sense of fear,   *able to absorb*
More ready to cry out, 'Who knows what follows?'
Than Hector is. The wound of peace is surety,[1]
Surety secure; but modest doubt is called
15 The beacon° of the wise, the tent[2] that searches   *lighthouse*
To th' bottom of the worst. Let Helen go.
Since the first sword was drawn about this question,
Every tithe-soul, 'mongst many thousand dimes,
Hath been as dear as Helen[3]—I mean, of ours.
20 If we have lost so many tenths of ours
To guard a thing not ours—nor worth to us,
Had it our name, the value of one ten[4]—
What merit's in that reason which denies
The yielding of her up?
TROILUS   Fie, fie, my brother!
25 Weigh you the worth and honour of a king
So great as our dread father in a scale
Of common ounces? Will you with counters° sum   *worthless chips*
The past-proportion of his infinite,[5]
And buckle in a waist most fathomless[6]
30 With spans° and inches so diminutive   *nine inches*
As fears and reasons?° Fie, for godly shame!   (*pun on "raisins"*)
HELENUS No marvel though you bite so sharp at reasons,

2.2 Location: The palace in Troy.
1. (Overconfident) sense of security.
2. Surgeon's probe.
3. *Every . . . Helen:* Every soul taken to pay the tithe (a tenth of one's goods, paid as a tax), among many thousand "dimes" (tenths; tithes paid, through soldiers' deaths), has been as valuable as Helen.
4. Even if Helen were Trojan, the value of one-tenth (one

of the men lost).
5. Add up the infinitude of his measurelessness.
6. Most immeasurable even in fathoms (6 foot lengths, used in calculating sea depths). "Waist" puns on "waste" as uninhabited expanse, especially the ocean, and as the squandering of resources (the second unintended by Troilus).

You are so empty of them. Should not our father
Bear the great sway of his affairs with reason
35 Because your speech hath none that tells him so?
TROILUS You are for dreams and slumbers, brother priest.
You fur your gloves with 'reason'.[7] Here are your reasons:
You know an enemy intends you harm,
You know a sword employed is perilous,
40 And reason flies the object of all harm.°   *any sight of danger*
Who marvels then, when Helenus beholds
A Grecian and his sword, if he do set
The very wings of reason to his heels
And fly like chidden Mercury[8] from Jove,
45 Or like a star disorbed?° Nay, if we talk of reason,   *a shooting star*
Let's shut our gates and sleep. Manhood and honour
Should have hare° hearts, would they but fat their thoughts   *timid*
With this crammed° reason. Reason and respect°   *fattened / deliberation*
Make livers° pale and lustihood° deject.   *courage / energy*
50 HECTOR Brother, she is not worth what she doth cost
The holding.°   *To keep*
TROILUS   What's aught but as 'tis valued?[9]
HECTOR But value dwells not in particular will.°   *individual desire*
It holds his° estimate and dignity   *its*
As well wherein 'tis precious of itself
55 As in the prizer. 'Tis mad idolatry
To make the service° greater than the god;   *the devotion paid*
And the will dotes that is inclinable
To what infectiously itself affects
Without some image of th'affected merit.[1]
60 TROILUS I take today a wife, and my election°   *choice*
Is led on in the conduct° of my will;   *under the guidance*
My will enkindled by mine eyes and ears,
Two traded° pilots 'twixt the dangerous shores   *experienced*
Of will and judgement. How may I avoid—
65 Although my will distaste what it elected—
The wife I chose? There can be no evasion
To blench° from this and to stand firm by honour.   *shy away*
We turn not back° the silks upon° the merchant   *don't return / to*
When we have spoiled them; nor the remainder viands°   *uneaten food*
70 We do not throw in unrespective° sewer   *undiscriminating*
Because we now are full. It was thought meet°   *appropriate that*
Paris should do some vengeance on the Greeks.
Your breath of full consent bellied° his sails;   *swelled*
The seas and winds, old wranglers,° took a truce   *opponents*
75 And did him service. He touched the ports desired,
And for an old aunt whom the Greeks held captive[2]
He brought a Grecian queen,° whose youth and freshness   *pun on quean = whore?*

7. You rationalize your desire for comfort.
8. Messenger of the gods, usually pictured with wings on his heels. Mercury was once arraigned before Jove for stealing cattle and was ordered to go and return them.
9. That is, no absolute measure of value exists; there is only the esteem granted to an object by particular individuals.
1. *the will . . . merit:* the will is foolishly obsessed that is committed to what it likes in a sick way (having caught this desire like a disease), without some conception of that object's real value. The point is related to Jesus' attack on the scribes and Pharisees in Matthew 23, for instance verse 19: "whether is greater, the offering, or the altar which sanctifieth the offering?"
2. Hesione, Priam's sister, kidnapped by the Greeks; "aunt" is also slang for "whore." The "vengeance" (line 72) is for the kidnapping.

Wrinkles Apollo's and makes stale the morning.[3]
Why keep we her? The Grecians keep our aunt.
80 Is she worth keeping? Why, she is a pearl
Whose price hath launched above a thousand ships[4]
And turned crowned kings to merchants.
If you'll avouch 'twas wisdom Paris went—
As you must needs, for you all cried, 'Go, go!';
85 If you'll confess he brought home noble prize—
As you must needs, for you all clapped your hands
And cried, 'Inestimable!'—why do you now
The issue° of your proper° wisdoms rate,°   *result / own / berate*
And do a deed that never fortune did:[5]
90 Beggar the estimation[6] which you prized
Richer than sea and land? O theft most base,
That we have stol'n what we do fear to keep!
But thieves unworthy of a thing so stol'n,
That in their country did them that disgrace
95 We fear to warrant in our native place.[7]
CASSANDRA [*within*]
     Cry, Trojans, cry!
PRIAM   What noise? What shriek is this?
TROILUS   'Tis our mad sister. I do know her voice.
CASSANDRA [*within*]   Cry, Trojans!
HECTOR   It is Cassandra.
     Enter CASSANDRA[8] *raving, with her hair about her ears*
100 CASSANDRA   Cry, Trojans, cry! Lend me ten thousand eyes
And I will fill them with prophetic tears.
HECTOR   Peace, sister, peace.
CASSANDRA   Virgins and boys, mid-age, and wrinkled old,°   *old people*
Soft infancy that nothing canst° but cry,   *can do*
105 Add to my clamours. Let us pay betimes°   *in advance*
A moiety° of that mass° of moan to come.   *portion / sum*
Cry, Trojans, cry! Practise your eyes with tears.°   *Learn to weep*
Troy must not be, nor goodly Ilium stand.
Our firebrand[9] brother, Paris, burns us all.
110 Cry, Trojans, cry! Ah Helen, and ah woe!
Cry, cry 'Troy burns!'—or else let Helen go.   *Exit*
HECTOR   Now, youthful Troilus, do not these high strains
Of divination in our sister work
Some touches of remorse? Or is your blood
115 So madly hot that no discourse of reason,
Nor fear of bad success° in a bad cause,   *outcome*
Can qualify° the same?   *moderate*
TROILUS   Why, brother Hector,
We may not think the justness of each act
Such and no other than the event doth form it,[1]

---

3. Helen's "youth and freshness" by comparison make Apollo's (hence also the sun's) "youth and freshness" seem old and rosy dawn seem dried out (but also, unintentionally on Troilus's part, sluttish).
4. A well-worn phrase even when Marlowe used it in *Doctor Faustus*: "Was this the face that launched a thousand ships?" Here given a mercantile turn.
5. And act more erratically than fortune.
6. Deem worthless the valued object.
7. *That . . . place:* (We Trojans) who in Greece dishonored the Greeks but back home are afraid to stand up for what we did.
8. Apollo gave Cassandra the gift of prophecy to win her love, but because she rejected his wooing, he cursed her by causing her prophecies to be disregarded.
9. When pregnant with Paris, Hecuba dreamed of giving birth to a firebrand.
1. *We . . . it:* We must not judge the "justness" of our cause only by the results.

120	Nor once deject° the courage of our minds	reduce
	Because Cassandra's mad. Her brainsick raptures
	Cannot distaste° the goodness of a quarrel	make distasteful
	Which hath our several honours all engaged
	To make it gracious.° For my private part,	righteous; successful
125	I am no more touched° than all Priam's sons.	implicated
	And Jove forbid there should be done amongst us
	Such things as might offend the weakest spleen
	To fight for and maintain.²

PARIS   Else might the world convince° of levity   *convict*
As well my undertakings as your counsels.
But I attest° the gods, your full consent   *call to witness*
Gave wings to my propension° and cut off   *leaning*
All fears attending on so dire a project.
For what, alas, can these my single arms?°   *can my arms do alone*
What propugnation° is in one man's valour   *defense*
To stand the push° and enmity of those   *thrust*
This quarrel would excite?° Yet I protest,   *incite to battle*
Were I alone to pass° the difficulties   *endure*
And had as ample power as I have will,
Paris should ne'er retract what he hath done
Nor faint in the pursuit.

PRIAM   Paris, you speak
Like one besotted° on your sweet delights.   *drunk*
You have the honey still, but these the gall.
So° to be valiant is no praise at all.   *In such circumstances*

PARIS   Sir, I propose not merely to myself°   *for my own benefit*
The pleasures such a beauty brings with it,
But I would have the soil of her fair rape³
Wiped off in honourable keeping her.
What treason were it to the ransacked° queen,   *carried off as plunder*
Disgrace to your great worths, and shame to me,
Now to deliver her possession up
On terms of base compulsion? Can it be
That so degenerate a strain° as this   *impulse*
Should once set footing in your generous° bosoms?   *noble*
There's not the meanest spirit on our party
Without a heart to dare or sword to draw
When Helen is defended; nor none so noble
Whose life were ill bestowed or death unfamed
Where Helen is the subject. Then I say:
Well may we fight for her whom we know well
The world's large spaces cannot parallel.

HECTOR   Paris and Troilus, you have both said well,
But on the cause and question now in hand
Have glossed° but superficially—not much   *commented*
Unlike young men, whom Aristotle thought
Unfit to hear moral philosophy.⁴
The reasons you allege do more conduce
To the hot passion of distempered blood
Than to make up a free determination

Line numbers: 130, 135, 140, 145, 150, 155, 160, 165 appear in the left margin.

---

2. *And Jove . . . maintain*: We ("Priam's sons") shouldn't undertake something unless even the least courageous of us is willing to fight to defend it.
3. The defilement (of Helen or Paris, or both) resulting from her proper (also, beautiful) abduction (also, sexual violation).
4. Political philosophy. This is an anachronistic reference to Aristotle's *Nicomachean Ethics* 1.3.

170 'Twixt right and wrong; for pleasure and revenge
Have ears more deaf than adders[5] to the voice
Of any true decision. Nature craves
All dues be rendered to their owners. Now,
What nearer debt in all humanity
175 Than wife is to the husband? If this law
Of nature be corrupted through affection,°   lust
And that great minds, of partial° indulgence   though prejudiced
To their benumbèd° wills, resist the same,   dulled
There is a law in each well-ordered nation
180 To curb those raging appetites that are
Most disobedient and refractory.°   stubborn
If Helen then be wife to Sparta's king,
As it is known she is, these moral laws
Of nature and of nations speak aloud
185 To have her back returned. Thus to persist
In doing wrong extenuates not wrong,
But makes it much more heavy. Hector's opinion
Is this in way of° truth—yet ne'ertheless,   with respect to
My sprightly° brethren, I propend° to you   spirited / incline
190 In resolution to keep Helen still;
For 'tis a cause that hath no mean dependence
Upon our joint and several° dignities.   separate
TROILUS   Why, there you touched the life of our design.
Were it not glory that we more affected°   desired
195 Than the performance of our heaving spleens,°   acting on our anger
I would not wish a drop of Trojan blood
Spent more in her defence. But, worthy Hector,
She is a theme of honour and renown,
A spur to valiant and magnanimous° deeds,   noble
200 Whose present courage may beat down our foes,
And fame in time to come canonize° us—   glorify
For I presume brave Hector would not lose
So rich advantage of a promised glory
As smiles upon the forehead° of this action   countenance
For the wide world's revenue.
205 HECTOR   I am yours,
You valiant offspring of great Priamus.
I have a roisting° challenge sent amongst   boisterous
The dull and factious nobles of the Greeks
Will shriek amazement to their drowsy spirits.
210 I was advertised their great general[6] slept
Whilst emulation° in the army crept;   jealous rivalry
This I presume will wake him.   [Flourish.] Exeunt

2.3

Enter THERSITES

THERSITES   How now, Thersites? What, lost in the labyrinth of
thy fury? Shall the elephant Ajax carry it° thus? He beats me   get away with it
and I rail at him. O worthy satisfaction! Would it were other-

---

5. Adders were proverbially deaf. See Psalms 58:4–5:   in charming."
"like the deaf adder that stoppeth his ear. Which heareth   6. I was told that Achilles (Agamemnon?) slept.
not the voice of the enchanter, though he be most expert   2.3 Location: The Greek camp, outside Achilles' tent.

wise: that I could beat him whilst he railed at me. 'Sfoot,° I'll   *God's foot*
5 learn to conjure and raise devils but I'll see some issue of my
spiteful execrations.[1] Then there's Achilles: a rare engineer.[2] If
Troy be not taken till these two undermine it, the walls will
stand till they fall of themselves. O thou great thunder-darter of
Olympus, forget that thou art Jove, the king of gods; and Mer-
10 cury, lose all the serpentine craft of thy caduceus,[3] if ye take
not that little, little, less than little wit from them that they
have—which short-armed ignorance[4] itself knows is so abun-
dant—scarce it will not in circumvention° deliver a fly from a   *craftiness*
spider without drawing their massy irons° and cutting the web.   *swords*
15 After this, the vengeance on the whole camp—or rather, the
Neapolitan bone-ache,° for that methinks is the curse depen-   *syphilis*
dent° on those that war for a placket.[5] I have said my prayers,   *impending*
and devil Envy say 'Amen'.—What ho! My lord Achilles!

    Enter PATROCLUS [*at the door to the tent*]

PATROCLUS   Who's there? Thersites? Good Thersites, come in
20   and rail.   [*Exit*]

THERSITES   If I could ha' remembered a gilt counterfeit, thou
wouldst not have slipped out of my contemplation;[6] but it is no
matter. Thyself upon thyself![7] The common curse of mankind,
folly and ignorance, be thine in great revenue!° Heaven bless°   *amounts / save*
25   thee from a tutor, and discipline come not near thee! Let thy
blood° be thy direction° till thy death! Then if she that lays thee   *lust / guide*
out says thou art a fair corpse, I'll be sworn and sworn upon't
she never shrouded any but lazars.°   *lepers; sick bodies*

    [*Enter* PATROCLUS]

Amen.—Where's Achilles?
30 PATROCLUS   What, art thou devout? Wast thou in prayer?

THERSITES   Ay. The heavens hear me!

PATROCLUS   Amen.

    Enter ACHILLES

ACHILLES   Who's there?

PATROCLUS   Thersites, my lord.
35 ACHILLES   Where? Where? O where?—Art thou come? Why,
my cheese,° my digestion, why hast thou not served thyself   *digestive aid*
into my table so many meals? Come: what's Agamemnon?

THERSITES   Thy commander, Achilles.—Then tell me, Patroclus, what's Achilles?
40 PATROCLUS   Thy lord, Thersites. Then tell me, I pray thee,
what's Thersites?

THERSITES   Thy knower, Patroclus. Then tell me, Patroclus,
what art thou?

PATROCLUS   Thou mayst tell, that knowest.
45 ACHILLES   O tell, tell.

THERSITES   I'll decline the whole question.[8] Agamemnon com-

---

1. *but I'll . . . execrations:* if I must, in order to get tangible results from my contemptuous curses. "Spiteful"
keeps its unintended sense of "malicious."
2. Constructor of military earthworks and machines.
3. Mercury's emblem, a rod entwined by snakes.
Known for "craft," Mercury was the patron of thieves.
4. Ignorance is "short-armed" because most things are
beyond its grasp.
5. Petticoat; woman; woman's genitalia (obscene).

6. If I could have remembered a fake gold coin (worthless
Patroclus), you wouldn't have been forgotten (punning on
"slip," a counterfeit coin) in my devout meditation (which
focused on Ajax and Achilles, but only to curse them).
7. To be Patroclus is the worst possible fate—hence,
Thersites' curse on him is to be himself.
8. I'll recite in order the entire subject under investigation. "Decline," "Derive" (line 55), and "positive" (line
58) are all grammatical terms.

mands Achilles, Achilles is my lord, I am Patroclus' knower,
and Patroclus is a fool.

PATROCLUS You rascal.

50 THERSITES Peace, fool, I have not done.

ACHILLES [*to* PATROCLUS] He is a privileged man.[9]—Proceed,
Thersites.

THERSITES Agamemnon is a fool, Achilles is a fool, Thersites is
a fool, and as aforesaid Patroclus is a fool.

55 ACHILLES Derive this.° Come.   *Show your reasoning*

THERSITES Agamemnon is a fool to offer to command Achilles;
Achilles is a fool to be commanded of Agamemnon; Thersites
is a fool to serve such a fool; and Patroclus is a fool positive.° *absolute*

PATROCLUS Why am I a fool?

60 THERSITES Make that demand to the Creator. It suffices me
thou art. Look you, who comes here?

Enter AGAMEMNON, ULYSSES, NESTOR, DIOMEDES, AJAX,
and CALCHAS

ACHILLES Patroclus, I'll speak with nobody.—Come in with me,
Thersites.   *Exit*

THERSITES Here is such patchery,° such juggling° and such *foolery / deception*
65 knavery. All the argument is a whore and a cuckold. A good
quarrel to draw[1] emulous° factions and bleed to death upon. *envious*
Now the dry serpigo° on the subject, and war and lechery con- *skin disease*
found all.   [*Exit*]

AGAMEMNON [*to* PATROCLUS] Where is Achilles?

70 PATROCLUS Within his tent; but ill-disposed,° my lord. *unwell; bad-tempered*

AGAMEMNON Let it be known to him that we are here.
He faced° our messengers, and we lay by   *bullied*
Our appertainments,° visiting of him.   *rights of rank*
Let him be told so, lest perchance he think
75 We dare not move the question of our place,°   *assert our authority*
Or know not what we are.

PATROCLUS   I shall so say to him.   [*Exit*]

ULYSSES We saw him at the opening of his tent.
He is not sick.

AJAX Yes, lion-sick:° sick of proud heart. You may call it 'melan- *sick with pride*
80 choly'[2] if you will favour the man, but by my head 'tis pride.
But why? Why? Let him show us the cause. [*To* AGAMEMNON]
A word, my lord.

[AJAX *and* AGAMEMNON *talk apart*]

NESTOR What moves Ajax thus to bay at him?

ULYSSES Achilles hath inveigled° his fool from him.   *enticed away*

85 NESTOR Who? Thersites?

ULYSSES He.

NESTOR Then will Ajax lack matter,[3] if he have lost his argument.°   *subject matter*

ULYSSES No, you see, he *is* his argument that *has* his argument:[4]
90 Achilles.

NESTOR All the better—their fraction° is more our wish than *division*

9. An acknowledged fool could speak with impunity.
1. Attract to itself, like a magnet; extract, like a sword;
tear to pieces; drag to execution.
2. A fashionable philosophical malady.
3. Something to say; sense; pus.

4. Achilles is the person who is Ajax's argument. Since
Achilles has taken Thersites (who used to be Ajax's object
of derision) as the object of his derision, Ajax has transferred his scorn from Thersites to Achilles.

their faction.° But it was a strong council that a fool could dis-   *union in rebellion*
unite.°   *(ironic)*

ULYSSES   The amity that wisdom knits not, folly may easily untie.

       Enter PATROCLUS

95 Here comes Patroclus.

NESTOR   No Achilles with him.

ULYSSES   The elephant hath joints, but none for courtesy:[5] his
legs are legs for necessity, not for flexure.°   *bending*

PATROCLUS [*to* AGAMEMNON]   Achilles bids me say he is much sorry
100 If anything more than your sport and pleasure
Did move your greatness and this noble state°   *company*
To call upon him. He hopes it is no other
But for your health and your digestion's sake:
An after-dinner's breath.°   *exercise*

AGAMEMNON   Hear you, Patroclus.
105 We are too well acquainted with these answers.
But his evasion, winged thus swift with scorn,
Cannot outfly° our apprehensions.°   *escape / understanding*
Much attribute° he hath, and much the reason   *reputation*
Why we ascribe it to him. Yet all his virtues,
110 Not virtuously on his own part beheld,
Do in our eyes begin to lose their gloss,
Yea, and like fair fruit in an unwholesome dish
Are like to rot untasted. Go and tell him
We come to speak with him—and you shall not sin
115 If you do say we think him over-proud
And under-honest, in self-assumption° greater   *his own opinion*
Than in the note of judgement. And worthier than himself
Here tend° the savage strangeness° he puts on,   *wait on / aloofness*
Disguise the holy strength of their command,
120 And underwrite in an observing kind°   *submit compliantly to*
His humorous predominance[6]—yea, watch
His pettish lunes,[7] his ebbs, his flows, as if
The passage and whole carriage° of this action   *means and ends*
Rode on his tide. Go tell him this, and add
125 That if he overhold° his price so much   *overestimate*
We'll none of him, but let him, like an engine
Not portable, lie under this report:
'Bring action hither, this cannot go to war.'
A stirring° dwarf we do allowance give   *bustling*
130 Before a sleeping giant. Tell him so.

PATROCLUS   I shall, and bring his answer presently.°   *immediately*

AGAMEMNON   In second voice° we'll not be satisfied;   *By proxy (Patroclus)*
We come to speak with him.—Ulysses, enter you.

       Exit ULYSSES [*with* PATROCLUS]

AJAX   What is he more than another?
135 AGAMEMNON   No more than what he thinks he is.[8]

AJAX   Is he so much? Do you not think he thinks himself a better
man than I am?

AGAMEMNON   No question.

---

5. The elephant's supposed lack of knee joints made it resemble a proud, unbowing man.
6. His idiosyncratic assumption of superiority; the domination of one particular "humor" (temperament)—pride.
7. His fits of madness (caused by the moon's changing

phases; as the moon also produces sea tides, hence "ebbs," "flows," and "tide," lines 122, 124). "Lunes" is an editorial emendation of F's "lines."
8. He's the only one with a high opinion of him; he's worth as much as he thinks he is.

AJAX Will you subscribe his thought, and say he is?

140 AGAMEMNON No, noble Ajax. You are as strong, as valiant, as
wise, no less noble, much more gentle, and altogether more
tractable.

AJAX Why should a man be proud? How doth pride grow? I
know not what it is.

145 AGAMEMNON Your mind is the clearer, Ajax, and your virtues
the fairer. He that is proud eats up himself. Pride is his own
glass,° his own trumpet, his own chronicle—and whatever *its own mirror*
praises itself but in the deed devours the deed in the praise.⁹

  Enter ULYSSES

AJAX I do hate a proud man as I hate the engendering° of toads. *mating*

150 NESTOR [*aside*] Yet he loves himself. Is't not strange?

ULYSSES Achilles will not to the field tomorrow.

AGAMEMNON What's his excuse?

ULYSSES   He doth rely on none,
But carries on the stream of his dispose° *disposition*
Without observance or respect of any,
155 In will peculiar and in self-admission.¹

AGAMEMNON Why, will he not, upon our fair request,
Untent his person and share the air with us?

ULYSSES Things small as nothing, for request's sake only,²
He makes important. Possessed° he is with greatness, *Bewitched*
160 And speaks not to himself but with a pride
That quarrels at self-breath.³ Imagined worth
Holds in his blood such swoll'n and hot discourse
That 'twixt his mental and his active parts
Kingdomed Achilles⁴ in commotion° rages *insurrection*
165 And batters 'gainst himself. What should I say?
He is so plaguy proud that the death tokens of it⁵
Cry 'No recovery'.

AGAMEMNON   Let Ajax go to him.
[*To* AJAX] Dear lord, go you and greet him in his tent.
'Tis said he holds you well and will be led,
170 At your request, a little from himself.° *from his self-conceit*

ULYSSES O Agamemnon, let it not be so.
We'll consecrate the steps that Ajax makes
When they go from Achilles. Shall the proud lord
That bastes his arrogance with his own seam⁶
175 And never suffers matter° of the world *the affairs*
Enter his thoughts, save° such as do revolve *except*
And ruminate° himself—shall he be worshipped *turn on*
Of that° we hold an idol more than he? *By one who*
No, this thrice-worthy and right valiant lord
180 Must not so stale his palm,° nobly acquired, *sully his honor*
Nor by my will assubjugate° his merit, *reduce to subjection*
As amply titled as Achilles' is,
By going to Achilles—
That were to enlard his fat-already pride

9. Whatever self-praise arises except from silently performing the noble deed itself destroys the deed by the act
of praising it.
1. In self-will and in acknowledgment of only his own
authority.
2. Merely because they are asked for.
3. *And . . . self-breath:* Achilles is not even satisfied with

what he himself has to say in praise of his merits; he is too
proud to talk even to himself.
4. Achilles' body is imagined as a state at civil war.
5. He is so annoyingly (diseasedly) proud that the fatal
signs of plague.
6. Fat; appearance. Achilles is accused of feeding self-
flattery to his already inflated arrogance.

185	And add more coals to Cancer[7] when he burns	
	With entertaining great Hyperion.°	*the sun*
	This lord go to him? Jupiter forbid,	
	And say in thunder 'Achilles, go to him'.	
	NESTOR [*aside to* DIOMEDES] O this is well. He rubs the vein of him.°	*stirs up Ajax*
190	DIOMEDES [*aside to* NESTOR] And how his silence drinks up this applause.	
	AJAX If I go to him, with my armèd fist	
	I'll pash° him o'er the face.	*smash*
	AGAMEMNON O no, you shall not go.	
	AJAX An a° be proud with me, I'll feeze° his pride.	*If he / take care of*
	Let me go to him.	
195	ULYSSES Not for the worth that hangs upon our quarrel.°	*(with Troy)*
	AJAX A paltry insolent fellow.	
	NESTOR [*aside*] How he describes himself!	
	AJAX Can he not be sociable?	
	ULYSSES [*aside*] The raven chides blackness.	
200	AJAX I'll let his humour's blood.[8]	
	AGAMEMNON [*aside*] He will be the physician that should be the	
	patient.	
	AJAX An all men were o' my mind—	
	ULYSSES [*aside*] Wit would be out of fashion.	
205	AJAX A should not bear it so. A should eat swords[9] first. Shall	
	pride carry it?	
	NESTOR [*aside*] An't would, you'd carry half.	
	AJAX A would have ten shares.[1]	
	ULYSSES [*aside*] I will knead him; I'll make him supple.° He's	*compliant*
210	not yet through warm.[2]	
	NESTOR [*aside*] Farce° him with praises. Pour in, pour in! His	*Stuff; sauce*
	ambition is dry.°	*thirsty*
	ULYSSES [*to* AGAMEMNON] My lord, you feed too much on this dislike.	
	NESTOR [*to* AGAMEMNON] Our noble general, do not do so.	
215	DIOMEDES [*to* AGAMEMNON] You must prepare to fight without Achilles.	
	ULYSSES Why, 'tis this naming of him° does him harm.	*(as our sole hope)*
	Here is a man°—but 'tis before his face.	*Ajax*
	I will be silent.	
	NESTOR Wherefore should you so?	
	He is not emulous,° as Achilles is.	*hungry for praise*
220	ULYSSES Know the whole world he is as valiant—	
	AJAX A whoreson dog, that shall palter° thus with us—would he	*deal evasively*
	were a Trojan!	
	NESTOR What a vice were it in Ajax now—	
	ULYSSES If he were proud—	
	DIOMEDES Or covetous of praise—	
	ULYSSES Ay, or surly borne—	
225	DIOMEDES Or strange,° or self-affected.°	*aloof / egotistical*
	ULYSSES [*to* AJAX] Thank the heavens, lord, thou art of sweet	
	composure.°	*temperament*

7. And add fuel to the fire. Cancer is the sign of the
Zodiac that begins on June 21—hence, a symbol of summer heat.
8. I'll cure his illness (pride) by bloodletting, as a doctor
would to get rid of surplus humors.
9. He wouldn't carry on so. He would be defeated in
combat (eat his words).
1. Probably alluding to the ten shares into which the
Lord Chamberlain's Men's assets were divided—hence,

everything.
2. Warm all through. In F, the speech prefixes for lines
208–09 are reversed. In the arrangement printed here,
Ajax's line refers to Achilles and Ulysses' to Ajax, whom
Ulysses says he plans to manipulate further. In F's version,
Ulysses gets the first line, which refers to Ajax, who in the
next two lines describes what he'll do to Achilles. Q has
still another approach, and additional variations are found
in modern editions.

Praise him that got thee, she that gave thee suck.
Famed be thy tutor, and thy parts of nature°   *natural attributes*
Thrice famed beyond, beyond all erudition.³
230   But he that disciplined thine arms to fight—
Let Mars divide eternity in twain,
And give him half. And for thy vigour,
Bull-bearing Milo⁴ his addition° yield   *reputation*
To sinewy Ajax. I will not praise thy wisdom,
235   Which like a bourn, a pale, a shore confines⁵
Thy spacious and dilated° parts. Here's Nestor,   *ample; famous*
Instructed by the antiquary° times: *ancient*
He must, he is, he cannot but be, wise.
But pardon, father Nestor: were your days
240   As green⁶ as Ajax', and your brain so tempered,°   *composed*
You should not have the eminence of° him,   *be superior to*
But be as° Ajax.   *equal to*
AJAX   Shall I call you father?°   *guide*
ULYSSES   Ay, my good son.
DIOMEDES   Be ruled by him, Lord Ajax.
ULYSSES [*to* AGAMEMNON]   There is no tarrying here: the hart Achilles
245   Keeps thicket.° Please it our great general°   *stays home / Agamemnon*
To call together all his state° of war.   *council*
Fresh kings° are come today to Troy; tomorrow   *Reinforcements*
We must with all our main of power° stand fast.   *utmost strength*
And here's a lord, come knights from east to west°   *the whole world*
250   And cull their flower,⁷ Ajax shall cope° the best.   *match*
AGAMEMNON   Go we to counsel. Let Achilles sleep.
Light boats sail swift, though greater hulks draw deep.⁸ *Exeunt*

3.1

Music sounds within. Enter PANDARUS [*at one door*] *and
a* SERVANT [*at another door*]

PANDARUS   Friend? You. Pray you, a word. Do not you follow the
young Lord Paris?
SERVANT   Ay, sir, when he goes before me.
PANDARUS   You depend upon him,° I mean.   *serve him*
5   SERVANT   Sir, I do depend upon the Lord.°   *God; Paris*
PANDARUS   You depend upon a notable gentleman; I must needs
praise him.
SERVANT   The Lord be praised!
PANDARUS   You know me—do you not?
10   SERVANT   Faith, sir, superficially.
PANDARUS   Friend, know me better. I am the Lord Pandarus.
SERVANT   I hope I shall know your honour better.¹
PANDARUS   I do desire it.

---

3. Ajax's glory exceeds anything scholars might say
about it. Also ironic: learning constitutes no part of it.
4. Famous Greek athlete who bore a four-year-old bull
on his shoulders.
5. Which like a boundary, a fence, a shore limits the
uses of (probably ironic).
6. Young, fresh; immature; gullible.
7. And choose their best men.
8. We will progress more swiftly without Achilles (perhaps alluding to the famous success of "light" English
ships against the "greater hulks" of the Spanish

Armada). This line is doubly ironic: on the one hand,
Ajax can hardly be called a "light boat"; on the other, the
Greeks as a whole have already been associated with
"deep-drawing" boats in the Prologue (line 12).
3.1 Location: Troy's palace.
1. I hope to get to know you better. I hope to learn of
an improvement in your spiritual health. The double
meaning here is typical of the servant's playful mockery
of Pandarus, which partly contrasts Pandarus' secular
concerns with more important, albeit anachronistic,
Christian ones.

SERVANT	You are in the state of grace?[2]	
15	PANDARUS Grace? Not so, friend. 'Honour' and 'lordship' are my titles. What music is this?	
	SERVANT I do but partly know, sir. It is music in parts.	
	PANDARUS Know you the musicians?	
	SERVANT Wholly, sir.	
20	PANDARUS Who play they to?	
	SERVANT To the hearers, sir.	
	PANDARUS At whose pleasure, friend?	
	SERVANT At mine, sir, and theirs that love music.	
	PANDARUS 'Command' I mean, friend.	
25	SERVANT Who shall I command, sir?	
	PANDARUS Friend, we understand not one another. I am too courtly and thou too cunning. At whose request do these men play?	
30	SERVANT That's to't° indeed, sir. Marry, sir, at the request of Paris my lord, who's there in person; with him, the mortal° Venus, the heart-blood of beauty, love's visible soul°—	*to the point* *living; fatal* *love incarnate*
	PANDARUS Who, my cousin Cressida?	
	SERVANT No, sir, Helen. Could not you find out that by her attributes?	
35	PANDARUS It should seem, fellow, that thou hast not seen the Lady Cressid. I come to speak with Paris from the Prince Troilus. I will make a complimental° assault upon him, for my business seethes.°	*courteous* *boils; is pressing*
	SERVANT Sodden business! There's a stewed[3] phrase, indeed.	

Enter PARIS *and* HELEN [*attended by musicians*]

40	PANDARUS Fair be to you, my lord, and to all this fair company. Fair desires in all fair measure fairly guide them—especially to you, fair Queen. Fair thoughts be your fair pillow.	
	HELEN Dear lord, you are full of fair words.	
	PANDARUS You speak your fair pleasure, sweet Queen. [*To* PARIS]	
45	Fair prince, here is good broken music.[4]	
	PARIS You have broke° it, cousin,[5] and by my life you shall make it whole again. You shall piece it out° with a piece of your performance.° —Nell, he is full of harmony.	*interrupted* *repair it* *performed by you*
	PANDARUS Truly, lady, no.	
50	HELEN O sir.	
	[*She tickles him*]	
	PANDARUS Rude,° in sooth, in good sooth very rude.	*Unskilled; unmusical*
	PARIS Well said, my lord. Will you say so in fits?[6]	
	PANDARUS I have business to my lord, dear Queen.—My lord, will you vouchsafe me a word?	
55	HELEN Nay, this shall not hedge° us out. We'll hear you sing, certainly.	*keep*
	PANDARUS Well, sweet Queen, you are pleasant with° me.—But marry, thus, my lord: my dear lord and most esteemed friend, your brother Troilus—	*teasing*

---

2. Theologically (deliberately misunderstanding Pandarus's "desire" in line 13 as a wish for moral improvement rather than social acquaintance). Pandarus proceeds to misunderstand "grace" as the status of being called "your grace" (a Duke's title).
3. "Stewed" (overdone, literally and metaphorically; associated with stews, or brothels) puns on "sodden," which means "boiled" (picking up on "seethes," line 38);

is stupid; is drunk; is being treated for venereal disease.
4. Music for instruments of different kinds—for example, strings and woodwind.
5. Kinsman (used especially by sovereigns to noblemen, whether or not related).
6. Would you please say (do you insist on saying) so in sections of songs or music (fits and starts; spasms of laughter)?

60 HELEN   My lord Pandarus, honey-sweet lord.

PANDARUS   Go to, sweet Queen, go to!—commends himself
most affectionately to you.

HELEN   You shall not bob° us out of our melody. If you do, our   *swindle*
melancholy[7] upon your head.

65 PANDARUS   Sweet Queen, sweet Queen, that's a sweet Queen.
Ay, faith—

HELEN   And to make a sweet lady sad is a sour offence.

PANDARUS   Nay, that shall not serve your turn; that shall it not,
in truth, la. Nay, I care not for such words. No, no.—And, my
70 lord, he desires you that, if the King call for him at supper, you
will make his excuse.

HELEN   My lord Pandarus.

PANDARUS   What says my sweet Queen, my very very sweet
Queen?

75 PARIS   What exploit's in hand? Where sups he tonight?

HELEN   Nay, but my lord—

PANDARUS   What says my sweet Queen? My cousin will fall out
with you.[8]

HELEN   [*to* PARIS]   You must not° know where he sups.   *are not supposed to*

80 PARIS   I'll lay my life, with my dispenser[9] Cressida.

PANDARUS   No, no! No such matter. You are wide.° Come, your   *way off target*
dispenser is sick.

PARIS   Well, I'll make 's° excuse.   *his*

PANDARUS   Ay, good my lord. Why should you say Cressida? No,
85 your poor dispenser's sick.

PARIS   'I spy.'[1]

PANDARUS   You spy? What do you spy?—[*To a musician*] Come,
give me an instrument.—Now, sweet Queen.

HELEN   Why, this is kindly done!

90 PANDARUS   My niece is horrible° in love with a thing you have,   *horribly*
sweet Queen.

HELEN   She shall have it, my lord—if it be not my lord Paris.

PANDARUS   He? No, she'll none of him. They two are twain.°   *estranged*

HELEN   Falling in,[2] after falling out,° may make them three.   *arguing*

95 PANDARUS   Come, come, I'll hear no more of this. I'll sing you a
song now.

HELEN   Ay, ay, prithee. Now by my troth, sweet lord, thou hast a
fine forehead.[3]

[*She strokes his forehead*]

PANDARUS   Ay, you may, you may.°   *(go on)*

100 HELEN   Let thy song be love. 'This love will undo us all.' O
Cupid, Cupid, Cupid!

PANDARUS   Love? Ay, that it shall,° i'faith.   *(be); (undo us)*

PARIS   Ay, good now,° 'Love, love, nothing but love'.   *please*

PANDARUS   In good truth, it° begins so.   *the song; love*

---

7. May our "melancholy" mood (supposedly cured by
music) be.
8. *What . . . you:* If you (Helen) keep interrupting, my
"cousin" Paris (as in line 46) will be angry with you; if
you keep inquiring about private affairs, my "cousin"
Cressida will be angry with you.
9. Excuser (of Troilus's failure to attend dinner); pro-
visioner (again, of dinner); bestower of (sexual) favors;
dispenser of cures (with "sick," lines 82, 85, a remedy

for Troilus's lovesickness). Here and in lines 82 and 85,
"dispenser" is an editorial emendation for "disposer," of
uncertain meaning but perhaps suggesting that Cressida can do what she likes with Troilus and Paris.
1. I understand (alluding to a child's game).
2. "Falling in" sexually, so as to produce a child.
3. Impudence; modesty; sign of male beauty; hint of
cuckoldry.

105 [*Sings*] Love, love, nothing but love, still° love, still more!   *always*
  For O love's bow
  Shoots buck and doe.°   *male and female*
  The shaft° confounds   *arrow; penis*
  Not that it wounds
110 But tickles still the sore.⁴

  These lovers cry 'O! O!', they die.°   *perish; have an orgasm*
  Yet that which seems the wound to kill°   *mortal wound*
  Doth turn 'O! O!' to 'ha ha he!'⁵
  So dying love lives still.
115   'O! O!' a while, but 'ha ha ha!'
     'O! O!' groans out for 'ha ha ha!'—

Heigh-ho.

HELEN   In love—ay, faith, to the very tip of the nose.

PARIS   He eats nothing but doves,° love, and that breeds hot   *emblem of true love*
120 blood, and hot blood begets hot thoughts, and hot thoughts
  beget hot deeds, and hot deeds is love.

PANDARUS   Is this the generation° of love: hot blood, hot thoughts,   *genealogy*
  and hot deeds? Why, they are vipers. Is love a generation of
  vipers?⁶
  [*Alarum*]
125 Sweet lord, who's afield today?

PARIS   Hector, Deiphobus, Helenus, Antenor, and all the gal-
  lantry of Troy. I would fain have° armed today, but my Nell   *like to have*
  would not have it so. How chance my brother Troilus went
  not?

130 HELEN   He hangs the lip° at something. You know all, Lord Pan-   *looks despondent*
  darus.

PANDARUS   Not I, honey-sweet Queen. I long to hear how they
  sped today.— You'll remember your brother's excuse?

PARIS   To a hair.°   *Exactly*

135 PANDARUS   Farewell, sweet Queen.

HELEN   Commend me to your niece.

PANDARUS   I will, sweet Queen.   [*Exit*]
  Sound a retreat

PARIS   They're come from field. Let us to Priam's hall
  To greet the warriors. Sweet Helen, I must woo you
140 To help unarm our Hector. His stubborn buckles,
  With these your white enchanting fingers touched,
  Shall more obey than to the edge of steel°   *sword blade*
  Or force of Greekish sinews. You shall do more
  Than all the island kings:° disarm great Hector.   *Greek lords*

145 HELEN   'Twill make us proud to be his servant, Paris;
  Yea, what he shall receive of us in duty
  Gives us more palm in° beauty than we have—   *fame for*
  Yea, overshines ourself.

PARIS   Sweet above thought, I love thee!
                                    Exeunt

---

4. Wound; four-year-old buck.
5. Turns pain to joy; turns ecstasy to derision.
6. Anachronistic allusion, not intended by Pandarus,
to a biblical phrase—for instance, the "generation of
vipers" in Matthew 23:33, promising damnation.

3.2

Enter PANDARUS [*at one door*] *and Troilus'* MAN [*at another door*]

PANDARUS How now, where's thy master? At my cousin
Cressida's?

MAN No, sir, he stays for you to conduct him thither.

Enter TROILUS

PANDARUS O here he comes.—How now, how now?

5   TROILUS Sirrah, walk off.   [*Exit* MAN]

PANDARUS Have you seen my cousin?

TROILUS No, Pandarus, I stalk about her door
Like a strange° soul upon the Stygian banks   newly arrived
Staying for waftage.[1] O be thou my Charon,

10   And give me swift transportance to those fields[2]
Where I may wallow° in the lily beds   roll around
Proposed for° the deserver. O gentle Pandar,[3]   Promised to
From Cupid's shoulder pluck his painted° wings   brightly colored
And fly with me to Cressid.

15   PANDARUS Walk here i'th' orchard.° I'll bring her straight. *Exit*   garden

TROILUS I am giddy. Expectation whirls me round.
Th'imaginary relish° is so sweet   pleasant anticipation
That it enchants my sense. What will it be
When that the wat'ry° palates taste indeed   watering

20   Love's thrice-repurèd nectar?[4] Death, I fear me,
Swooning destruction, or some joy too fine,°   exquisite
Too subtle-potent, tuned too sharp in sweetness°   (musically)
For the capacity of my ruder powers.
I fear it much, and I do fear besides

25   That I shall lose distinction° in my joys,   power to discriminate
As doth a battle° when they charge on heaps   army
The enemy flying.

Enter PANDARUS

PANDARUS She's making her ready. She'll come straight.° You   immediately
must be witty now. She does so blush, and fetches her wind° so   breath

30   short as if she were frayed with a spirit.[5] I'll fetch her. It is the
prettiest villain!° She fetches her breath as short as a new-ta'en[6]   (affectionate)
sparrow.   *Exit*

TROILUS Even such a passion doth embrace my bosom.
My heart beats thicker° than a feverous pulse,   faster

35   And all my powers do their bestowing° lose,   function
Like vassalage at unawares° encount'ring   vassals unexpectedly
The eye of majesty.

Enter PANDARUS, [*with*] CRESSIDA [*veiled*]

PANDARUS [*to* CRESSIDA] Come, come, what need you blush?
Shame's a baby. [*To* TROILUS] Here she is now. Swear the oaths

40   now to her that you have sworn to me. [*To* CRESSIDA] What,
are you gone again? You must be watched ere you be made
tame,[7] must you? Come your ways, come your ways. An you
draw backward, we'll put you i'th' thills.[8] [*To* TROILUS] Why do

---

3.2 Location: Cressida's garden.
1. Waiting to be ferried across. The dead were carried across the river Styx into the underworld by the ferryman Charon.
2. The Elysian Fields, which were reserved for the blessed dead ("the deserver" line 12).
3. The shortened form of the name here helps define

Pandarus as a pander.
4. Thrice-purified drink of the gods (giving immortality).
5. Frightened by a ghost.
6. Just captured.
7. Hawks were kept awake at night to tame them.
8. If you back away, we'll back you, like a horse, into the shafts of a cart.

you not speak to her? [*To* CRESSIDA] Come, draw this curtain,
45 and let's see your picture.[9] [*He unveils her*] Alas the day! How
    loath you are to offend daylight! An't were dark, you'd close°   *agree; unite*
    sooner. So, so. [*To* TROILUS] Rub on, and kiss the mistress.[1]
    [*They kiss*] How now, a kiss in fee farm!° Build there, carpenter,   *perpetual land tenure*
    the air° is sweet. Nay, you shall fight your hearts out ere I part   *her breath*
50 you. The falcon as the tercel,[2] for° all the ducks i'th' river. Go   *I'd bet*
    to, go to.
    TROILUS   You have bereft me of all words, lady.
    PANDARUS   Words pay no debts; give her deeds. But she'll
    bereave you o'th' deeds° too, if she call your activity° in ques-   *wear you out / virility*
55 tion. [*They kiss*] What, billing° again? Here's 'in witness   *kissing*
    whereof the parties interchangeably'.[3] Come in, come in. I'll
    go get a fire.°   [*Exit*]   *(for the bedroom)*
    CRESSIDA   Will you walk in, my lord?
    TROILUS   O Cressida, how often have I wished me thus.
60 CRESSIDA   Wished, my lord? The gods grant—O, my lord!
    TROILUS   What should they grant? What makes this pretty abrup-
    tion?° What too-curious dreg° espies my sweet lady in the foun-   *pause / speck of dirt*
    tain of our love?
    CRESSIDA   More dregs than water, if my fears have eyes.
65 TROILUS   Fears make devils of cherubims;° they never see truly.   *predict the worst*
    CRESSIDA   Blind fear, that seeing° reason leads, finds safer foot-   *clear-sighted*
    ing than blind reason, stumbling without fear. To fear the worst
    oft cures the worse.
    TROILUS   O let my lady apprehend no fear. In all Cupid's pag-
70 eant there is presented no monster.
    CRESSIDA   Nor nothing monstrous neither?
    TROILUS   Nothing but our undertakings,° when we vow to weep   *promises*
    seas, live in fire, eat rocks, tame tigers, thinking it harder for
    our mistress to devise imposition enough° than for us to   *a big enough challenge*
75 undergo any difficulty imposed. This is the monstruosity in
    love, lady—that the will is infinite and the execution confined;
    that the desire is boundless and the act° a slave to limit.   *(sex) act*
    CRESSIDA   They say all lovers swear more performance than they
    are able, and yet reserve an ability that they never perform:
80 vowing more than the perfection of ten,° and discharging less   *(lovers)*
    than the tenth part of one. They that have the voice of lions
    and the act of hares, are they not monsters?
    TROILUS   Are there such? Such are not we. Praise us as we are
    tasted;° allow° us as we prove. Our head shall go bare till merit   *tested / praise*
85 crown it. No perfection in reversion[4] shall have a praise in
    present. We will not name desert° before his° birth, and being   *mention merit / its*
    born his addition° shall be humble. Few words to fair faith.[5]   *title*
    Troilus shall be such to Cressid as what envy can say worst
    shall be a mock for his truth;[6] and what truth can speak truest,
90 not truer[7] than Troilus.
    CRESSIDA   Will you walk in, my lord?

---

9. Cressida's face is veiled. Pictures were curtained for
protection against light and dust.
1. Metaphor from the game of bowls: keep on course,
and touch gently the master ball (a small ball at which
bowls were aimed).
2. The female hawk as (eagerly) the male.
3. A garbled version of a betrothal; also a contractual
legal formula completed by the words "have set their

hands and seals."
4. No perfection by right of eventual succession (like
lands or title)—hence, in the future.
5. Brevity goes with honesty (proverbial).
6. *as . . . truth*: that envy's most malicious comment on
Troilus can only be to mock him for constancy.
7. *not truer*: could not be more reliable.

Enter PANDARUS

PANDARUS   What, blushing still? Have you not done talking yet?

CRESSIDA   Well, uncle, what folly° I commit I dedicate to you.   *whatever indiscretion*

PANDARUS   I thank you for that. If my lord get a boy of you, you'll

95   give him me. Be true to my lord. If he flinch,° chide me for it.   *(sexually)*

TROILUS [*to* CRESSIDA]   You know now your hostages:° your uncle's   *pledges*
        word and my firm faith.

PANDARUS   Nay, I'll give my word for her too. Our kindred,
        though they be long ere they are wooed, they are constant

100   being won. They are burrs, I can tell you: they'll stick where
        they are thrown.°   *laid (sexual)*

CRESSIDA   Boldness comes to me now, and brings me heart.
        Prince Troilus, I have loved you night and day
        For many weary months.

105 TROILUS   Why was my Cressid then so hard to win?

CRESSIDA   Hard to seem won; but I was won, my lord,
        With the first glance that ever—pardon me:
        If I confess much, you will play the tyrant.
        I love you now, but till now not so much

110   But I might master it. In faith, I lie:
        My thoughts were like unbridled children, grown
        Too headstrong for their mother. See, we fools!
        Why have I blabbed? Who shall be true to us,°   *women*
        When we are so unsecret to ourselves?°   *betray ourselves*

115   But though I loved you well, I wooed you not—
        And yet, good faith, I wished myself a man,
        Or that we women had men's privilege
        Of speaking first. Sweet, bid me hold my tongue,
        For in this rapture I shall surely speak

120   The thing I shall repent. See, see, your silence,
        Cunning in dumbness, in my weakness draws
        My soul of counsel° from me. Stop my mouth.   *most secret thoughts*

TROILUS   And shall, albeit sweet music issues thence.
        [*He kisses her*]

PANDARUS   Pretty, i' faith.

125 CRESSIDA [*to* TROILUS]   My lord, I do beseech you pardon me.
        'Twas not my purpose thus to beg a kiss.
        I am ashamed. O heavens, what have I done?
        For this time will I take my leave, my lord.

TROILUS   Your leave, sweet Cressid?

130 PANDARUS   Leave? An you take leave till tomorrow morning—

CRESSIDA   Pray you, content you.°   *be quiet*

TROILUS   What offends you, lady?

CRESSIDA   Sir, mine own company.

TROILUS   You cannot shun yourself.

CRESSIDA   Let me go and try.

135   I have a kind of self resides with you—
        But an unkind° self, that itself will leave   *unnatural*
        To be another's fool. Where is my wit?
        I would be gone. I speak I know not what.

TROILUS   Well know they what they speak that speak so wisely.

140 CRESSIDA   Perchance, my lord, I show more craft° than love,   *cunning*
        And fell so roundly° to a large° confession   *openly / full*
        To angle for° your thoughts. But you are wise,   *fish for*

Or else you love not[8]—for to be wise and love
Exceeds man's might: that dwells with gods above.

145 TROILUS   O that I thought it could be in a woman—
As, if it can, I will presume in° you—   *it to be in*
To feed for aye° her lamp and flames of love,   *forever*
To keep her constancy in plight° and youth,   *health*
Outliving beauty's outward,° with a mind   *exterior*
150 That doth renew swifter than blood° decays;   *passion*
Or that persuasion could but thus convince me
That my integrity and truth to you
Might be affronted° with the match and weight°   *met / same amount*
Of such a winnowed[9] purity in love.
155 How were I then uplifted! But alas,
I am as true as truth's simplicity,°   *truth itself*
And simpler° than the infancy of truth.   *more naive*
CRESSIDA   In that I'll war° with you.   *compete*
TROILUS   O virtuous fight,
When right with right wars who shall be most right.
160 True swains in love shall in the world to come
Approve° their truth by Troilus. When their rhymes,   *Attest*
Full of protest,° of oath and big compare,[1]   *protestation*
Wants° similes, truth tired with iteration°—   *Lack / repetition*
'As true as steel, as plantage to the moon,[2]
165 As sun to day, as turtle° to her mate,   *turtledove*
As iron to adamant,° as earth to th' centre'[3]—   *a magnet*
Yet, after all comparisons of truth,
As truth's authentic author to be cited,
'As true as Troilus' shall crown up the verse
And sanctify the numbers.°   *verses*
170 CRESSIDA   Prophet may you be!
If I be false, or swerve a hair from truth,
When time is old and hath forgot itself,
When water drops have worn the stones of Troy
And blind oblivion swallowed cities up,
175 And mighty states characterless are grated[4]
To dusty nothing, yet let memory
From false° to false among false maids in love   *falsehood*
Upbraid my falsehood. When they've said, 'as false
As air, as water, wind or sandy earth,
180 As fox to lamb, or wolf to heifer's calf,
Pard° to the hind, or stepdame to her son',   *Panther; leopard*
Yea, let them say, to stick the heart° of falsehood,   *hit the bullseye*
'As false as Cressid'.
PANDARUS   Go to, a bargain made. Seal it, seal it. I'll be the wit-
185 ness. Here I hold your hand; here, my cousin's.[5] If ever you
prove false one to another, since I have taken such pain to
bring you together, let all pitiful goers-between be called to the
world's end after my name: call them all panders. Let all con-

---

8. Alternative explanations for why he has made no "large confession" (line 141).
9. Grain is "winnowed" (separated from worthless light chaff).
1. Exaggerated comparisons.
2. Plants were supposed to be affected in growth by the moon.
3. The earth's surface to the earth's center, or axis.
4. Are ground up unrecorded.
5. Taking hands before a witness could be regarded as a (civil) marriage.

stant men be Troiluses, all false women Cressids, and all
190   brokers-between° panders. Say 'Amen'.   *pimps*
  TROILUS   Amen.
  CRESSIDA   Amen.
  PANDARUS   Amen. Whereupon I will show you a chamber with
  a bed—which bed, because it shall not speak of your pretty
195   encounters, press it to death.[6] Away!
                       Exeunt [TROILUS *and* CRESSIDA]
  And Cupid grant all tongue-tied maidens° here   *male or female virgins*
  Bed, chamber, pander to provide this gear.°   *Exit*   *equipment*

3.3

Flourish. Enter ULYSSES, DIOMEDES, NESTOR, AGAMEM-
NON, MENELAUS, [AJAX,] *and* CALCHAS[1]

  CALCHAS   Now, princes, for the service I have done you,
  Th'advantage° of the time prompts me aloud   *opportunity*
  To call for recompense. Appear° it to your mind   *Let it appear*
  That through the sight I bear in things to come
5   I have abandoned Troy, left my profession,°   *priestly role*
  Incurred a traitor's name, exposed myself
  From certain and possessed conveniences
  To doubtful fortunes, sequest'ring° from me all   *divorcing*
  That time, acquaintance, custom, and condition°   *position*
10   Made tame° and most familiar to my nature,   *accustomed*
  And here to do you service am become
  As new into the world, strange, unacquainted.
  I do beseech you, as in way of taste,°   *a foretaste*
  To give me now a little benefit
15   Out of those many registered in promise°   *many promised things*
  Which you say live to come° in my behalf.   *wait to be fulfilled*
  AGAMEMNON   What wouldst thou of us, Trojan? Make demand.
  CALCHAS   You have a Trojan prisoner called Antenor,
  Yesterday took. Troy holds him very dear.
20   Oft have you—often have you thanks therefor°—   *for it*
  Desired my Cressid in right great exchange,[2]
  Whom Troy hath still denied. But this Antenor
  I know is such a wrest[3] in their affairs
  That their negotiations° all must slack,   *affairs of state*
25   Wanting his manage,° and they will almost   *guidance*
  Give us a prince of blood,° a son of Priam,   *a royal prince*
  In change of° him. Let him be sent, great princes, *exchange for*
  And he shall buy my daughter, and her presence
  Shall quite strike off° all service I have done   *annul*
  In most accepted° pain.   *willingly undertaken*
30   AGAMEMNON   Let Diomedes bear him,
  And bring us Cressid hither; Calchas shall have
  What he requests of us. Good Diomed,
  Furnish you fairly° for this interchange;   *completely ready yourself*
  Withal° bring word if Hector will tomorrow   *At the same time*
35   Be answered in his challenge. Ajax is ready.

---

6. Customary punishment for an accused person who
remained silent and would not plead.
3.3 Location: The Greek camp.
1. Calchas is Cressida's father, a Trojan priest siding
with the Greeks.

2. In return for someone important.
3. Tuning key for a stringed instrument (hence probably related to "slack," line 24); peg for tightening a sur-
gical ligature.

DIOMEDES   This shall I undertake, and 'tis a burden
Which I am proud to bear.   *Exit* [*with* CALCHAS]
   Enter ACHILLES *and* PATROCLUS *in their tent*
ULYSSES   Achilles stands i'th' entrance of his tent.
Please it our general pass strangely° by him,   *aloofly*
40 As if he were forgot; and, princes all,
Lay negligent and loose° regard upon him.   *casual*
I will come last. 'Tis like he'll question me
Why such unplausive° eyes are bent, why turned on him. *unapproving*
If so, I have derision medicinable°   *health-giving scorn*
45 To use° between your strangeness and his pride, *act as intermediary*
Which his own will shall have desire to drink.
It may do good. Pride hath no other glass
To show itself but pride;[4] for supple knees° *bowing and scraping*
Feed arrogance and are the proud man's fees.° *expected reward*
50 AGAMEMNON   We'll execute your purpose and put on
A form° of strangeness as we pass along.   *appearance*
So do each lord, and either greet him not
Or else disdainfully, which shall shake him more
Than if not looked on. I will lead the way.
    [*They pass by the tent, in turn*]
55 ACHILLES   What, comes the general to speak with me?
You know my mind: I'll fight no more 'gainst Troy.
AGAMEMNON [*to* NESTOR]   What says Achilles? Would he aught with us?
NESTOR [*to* ACHILLES]   Would you, my lord, aught with the general?
ACHILLES   No.
NESTOR [*to* AGAMEMNON]   Nothing, my lord.
AGAMEMNON   The better.
    [*Exeunt* AGAMEMNON *and* NESTOR]
ACHILLES [*to* MENELAUS]   Good day, good day.
60 MENELAUS   How do you? How do you?   [*Exit*]
ACHILLES [*to* PATROCLUS]
 What, does the cuckold scorn me?
AJAX   How now, Patroclus?
ACHILLES   Good morrow, Ajax.
AJAX   Ha?
ACHILLES   Good morrow.
AJAX   Ay, and good next day too.   *Exit*
ACHILLES [*to* PATROCLUS]   What mean these fellows? Know they
65 not Achilles?
PATROCLUS   They pass by strangely. They were used to bend,
To send their smiles before them to Achilles,
To come as humbly as they use° to creep   *are accustomed*
To holy altars.
ACHILLES   What, am I poor° of late?   *insignificant*
'Tis certain, greatness once fall'n out with fortune
70 Must fall out with men too. What the declined is
He shall as soon read in the eyes of others
As feel in his own fall; for men, like butterflies,
Show not their mealy° wings but to the summer, *powdery*
And not a man, for being simply man,
75 Hath any honour, but° honour for those honours *but instead has*
That are without° him—as place, riches, and favour: *external to*

---

4. *Pride . . . pride:* A proud person recognizes excessive pride only when shown it in others.

Prizes of accident° as oft as merit;   *that come by chance*
Which, when they fall, as being slippery standers° —   *on an uncertain base*
The love that leaned on them, as slippery too—
80   Doth one° pluck down another, and together   *The one doth*
Die in the fall. But 'tis not so with me.
Fortune and I are friends. I do enjoy
At ample point° all that I did possess,   *Fully*
Save° these men's looks—who do methinks find out   *Except*
85   Something not worth in me such rich beholding°   *attention*
As they have often given. Here is Ulysses;
I'll interrupt his reading. How now, Ulysses?

ULYSSES   Now, great Thetis' son.

ACHILLES   What are you reading?

90   ULYSSES   A strange fellow here
Writes me that man, how dearly ever parted,°   *however valuably endowed*
How much in having, or without or in,[5]
Cannot make boast to have that which he hath,
Nor feels not what he owes,° but by reflection—   *owns*
95   As when his virtues, shining upon others,
Heat them, and they retort° that heat again   *cast back*
To the first givers.

ACHILLES   This is not strange, Ulysses.
The beauty that is borne here in the face
The bearer knows not, but commends itself
100   To others' eyes. Nor doth the eye itself,
That most pure spirit of sense,° behold itself,   *of the five senses*
Not going from itself; but eye to eye opposed
Salutes each other with each other's form.[6]
For speculation° turns not to itself   *sight*
105   Till it hath travelled and is mirrored there
Where it may see itself. This is not strange at all.

ULYSSES   I do not strain at° the position° —   *question / thesis*
It is familiar—but at the author's drift;
Who in his circumstance expressly° proves   *in detail explicitly*
110   That no man is the lord of anything,
Though in and of him there be much consisting,°   *value*
Till he communicate his parts° to others.   *qualities*
Nor doth he of himself know them for aught°   *as valuable*
Till he behold them formèd in th'applause
115   Where they're extended—who,° like an arch,° reverb'rate   *(the applauders) / vault*
The voice again; or, like a gate of steel
Fronting° the sun, receives and renders back   *Facing*
His figure° and his heat. I was much rapt in this,   *Its appearance*
And apprehended here immediately
120   The unknown Ajax.
Heavens, what a man is there! A very horse,
That has he knows not what.° Nature, what things there are,   *doesn't know himself*
Most abject in regard and dear in use.°   *Despised but useful*
What things again, most dear in the esteem
125   And poor in worth. Now shall we see tomorrow
An act that very° chance doth throw upon him.   *pure*

---

5. However much he possesses, either externally or   two eyes (in two people), looking at each other, can
internally.   show both people their images.
6. *Not going . . . form:* Being unable to leave itself; but

Ajax renowned? O heavens, what some men do,
While some men leave to do.°   *leave undone*
How some men creep in skittish Fortune's hall
130   Whiles others play the idiots in her eyes;[7]
How one man eats into another's pride
While pride is fasting in his wantonness.[8]
To see these Grecian lords! Why, even already
They clap the lubber° Ajax on the shoulder,   *lout*
135   As if his foot were on brave Hector's breast
And great Troy shrinking.°   *cowering; declining*

ACHILLES   I do believe it,
For they passed by me as misers do by beggars,
Neither gave to me good word nor look.
What, are my deeds forgot?

ULYSSES   Time hath, my lord,
140   A wallet° at his back, wherein he puts   *satchel*
Alms for oblivion, a great-sized monster[9]
Of ingratitudes. Those scraps are good deeds past,
Which are devoured as fast as they are made,
Forgot as soon as done. Perseverance, dear my lord,
145   Keeps honour bright. To have done° is to hang   *rely on past deeds*
Quite out of fashion, like a rusty mail°   *coat of armor*
In monumental mock'ry.° Take the instant way,   *a useless monument*
For honour travels in a strait so narrow,
Where one but goes abreast.° Keep then the path,   *must go single file*
150   For emulation hath a thousand sons
That one by one pursue: if you give way,
Or hedge aside from the direct forthright,°   *straightforward path*
Like to an entered tide they all rush by
And leave you hindmost;
155   Or, like a gallant horse fall'n in first rank,
Lie there for pavement to the abject rear,°   *worthless rearguard*
O'errun and trampled on. Then what they do in present,
Though less than yours in past, must o'ertop yours.
For Time is like a fashionable host,
160   That slightly shakes his parting guest by th' hand
And, with his arms outstretched as he would° fly,   *as if he wanted to*
Grasps in the comer. Welcome ever smiles,
And Farewell goes out sighing. O let not virtue seek
Remuneration for the thing it was;
165   For beauty, wit,
High birth, vigour of bone,° desert in service,°   *strength / worthiness*
Love, friendship, charity, are subjects all
To envious and calumniating time.
One touch of nature° makes the whole world kin°—   *natural fault / similar*
170   That all with one consent praise new-born gauds,°   *toys*
Though they are made and moulded of things past,
And give to dust that is a little gilt°   *gilded*
More laud than gilt o'er-dusted.°   *older treasures*
The present eye praises the present object.
175   Then marvel not, thou great and complete man,

---

7. While others act like fools to get Fortune's attention; do nothing to get Fortune's attention.
8. While the second man in effect starves his pride, and hence his reputation, through his odd behavior.
9. *Alms for oblivion:* Feats that won't be remembered. Traditionally, if you wore your satchel behind you, it contained your vices, which you in this way forgot. *monster:* time or, more likely, oblivion.

That all the Greeks begin to worship Ajax,
Since things in motion sooner catch the eye
Than what not stirs. The cry° went once on thee,   *approval*
And still it might, and yet it may again,
180   If thou wouldst not entomb thyself alive
And case° thy reputation in thy tent,   *shut up*
Whose glorious deeds but in these fields of late
Made emulous missions 'mongst the gods themselves,[1]
And drove great Mars to faction.°   *to take sides*

ACHILLES   Of this my privacy
  I have strong reasons.
185   ULYSSES   But 'gainst your privacy
  The reasons are more potent and heroical.
  'Tis known, Achilles, that you are in love
  With one of Priam's daughters.°   *Polyxena*

ACHILLES   Ha? Known?
ULYSSES   Is that a wonder?
  The providence that's in a watchful state[2]
190   Knows almost every grain of Pluto's[3] gold,
  Finds bottom in th'uncomprehensive° deeps,   *unimaginable*
  Keeps place with aught,[4] and almost like the gods
  Do infant thoughts unveil in their dumb cradles.[5]
  There is a mystery, with whom relation°   *report*
195   Durst never meddle, in the soul of state,
  Which hath an operation more divine
  Than breath or pen can give expressure° to.   *expression*
  All the commerce° that you have had with Troy   *dealings*
  As perfectly is ours as yours,[6] my lord;
200   And better would it fit Achilles much
  To throw down° Hector than Polyxena.   *(in war); (in love)*
  But it must grieve young Pyrrhus° now at home,   *Achilles' son*
  When fame shall in his island sound her trump
  And all the Greekish girls shall tripping sing,
205   'Great Hector's sister did Achilles win,
  But our great Ajax bravely beat down *him*'.°   *(Hector)*
  Farewell, my lord. I as your lover° speak.   *good friend*
  The fool slides o'er the ice that you should break.[7]   *[Exit]*

PATROCLUS   To this effect, Achilles, have I moved you.
210   A woman impudent° and mannish grown   *immodest*
  Is not more loathed than an effeminate° man   *cowardly*
  In time of action. I stand condemned for this.
  They think my little stomach to° the war   *appetite for*
  And your great love to me restrains you thus.
215   Sweet, rouse yourself, and the weak wanton Cupid
  Shall from your neck unloose his amorous fold°   *embrace*
  And like a dew-drop from the lion's mane
  Be shook to air.

ACHILLES   Shall Ajax fight with Hector?
PATROCLUS   Ay, and perhaps receive much honour by him.

---

1. Caused the gods to join the fight on both sides in an effort to match Achilles.
2. Government foresight is compared to divine "providence"—perhaps ironically.
3. God of the underworld (regularly identified with Plutus, god of wealth).
4. Stays abreast of everything.

5. Do . . . cradles: Discovers thoughts before they are spoken.
6. Is as well known to us (the other Greek leaders) as to you.
7. Perhaps: Ajax (the fool) is engaged in superficial action, whereas only you can initiate real combat.

220 ACHILLES   I see my reputation is at stake.
My fame is shrewdly gored.°   *severely wounded*

PATROCLUS   O then beware:
Those wounds heal ill that men do give themselves.
Omission to do what is necessary
Seals a commission to a blank of danger,[8]
225 And danger like an ague subtly taints
Even then when we sit idly in the sun.[9]

ACHILLES   Go call Thersites hither, sweet Patroclus.
I'll send the fool to Ajax, and desire him
T'invite the Trojan lords after the combat
230 To see us here unarmed. I have a woman's longing,
An appetite that I am sick withal,°   *with*
To see great Hector in his weeds° of peace,   *garments*
       Enter THERSITES
To talk with him and to behold his visage
Even to my full of view.°—A labour saved.   *in full view*

235 THERSITES   A wonder!

ACHILLES   What?

THERSITES   Ajax goes up and down the field, as° asking for him- *as if*
self.[1]

ACHILLES   How so?

240 THERSITES   He must° fight singly tomorrow with Hector, and is   *is to*
so prophetically proud of an heroical cudgelling° that he raves *(by Hector)*
in saying nothing.

ACHILLES   How can that be?

THERSITES   Why, a° stalks up and down like a peacock—a stride   *he*
245 and a stand; ruminates like an hostess that hath no arithmetic
but her brain to set down her reckoning;[2] bites his lip with a
politic regard,° as who should say 'There were wit in this head, *judicious expression*
an't would out'°—and so there is; but it lies as coldly in him as *if it would come out*
fire in a flint, which will not show without knocking.° The   *striking (into flame)*
250 man's undone for ever, for if Hector break not his neck i'th'
combat he'll break't himself in vainglory. He knows not me. I
said, 'Good morrow, Ajax', and he replies, 'Thanks, Agamemnon'. What think you of this man that takes me for the Gen-
eral? He's grown a very land-fish,° languageless, a monster. A   *unnatural creature*
255 plague of opinion! A man may wear it on both sides like a
leather jerkin.[3]

ACHILLES   Thou must be my ambassador to him, Thersites.

THERSITES   Who, I? Why, he'll answer nobody. He professes not
answering.° Speaking is for beggars. He wears his tongue in's   *refuses to respond*
260 arms. I will put on° his presence. Let Patroclus make demands   *imitate*
to me. You shall see the pageant of Ajax.

ACHILLES   To him, Patroclus. Tell him I humbly desire the valiant Ajax to invite the most valorous Hector to come unarmed
to my tent, and to procure safe-conduct for his person of the
265 magnanimous and most illustrious six-or-seven-times-honoured
captain-general of the Grecian army, Agamemnon; et cetera.
Do this.

---

8. Gives danger free rein (literally, provides danger
with a blank warrant to fill in as it pleases).
9. *danger . . . sun:* danger, like a fever, insidiously weakens (causes shivering) even when one is sitting in the sun.
1. Punning on "Ajax" and "a jakes" (a toilet), the point
presumably being that Ajax is so terrified by battle, he

cannot help relieving himself.
2. Like the hostess at an inn whose mathematical ineptitude makes it hard for her to work out the bill.
3. A plague on conceit (or reputation)! One can wear it
either way (conceit or reputation) like a reversible
jacket (but it's still the same pride).

PATROCLUS [*to* THERSITES]   Jove bless great Ajax!
THERSITES   H'm.
270   PATROCLUS   I come from the worthy Achilles—
THERSITES   Ha?
PATROCLUS   Who most humbly desires you to invite Hector to
his tent—
THERSITES   H'm!
275   PATROCLUS   And to procure safe-conduct from Agamemnon.
THERSITES   Agamemnon?
PATROCLUS   Ay, my lord.
THERSITES   Ha!
PATROCLUS   What say you to't?
280   THERSITES   God b'wi' you,° with all my heart.   (*dismissive*)
PATROCLUS   Your answer, sir?
THERSITES   If tomorrow be a fair day, by eleven o'clock it will go
one way or other. Howsoever, he shall pay for me ere° he has   *pay dearly before*
me.
285   PATROCLUS   Your answer, sir?
THERSITES   Fare ye well, with all my heart.
ACHILLES   Why, but he is not in this tune,° is he?   *mood*
THERSITES   No, but he's out o' tune thus. What music will be in
him when Hector has knocked out his brains, I know not. But
290   I am feared° none, unless the fiddler Apollo get his sinews to   *afraid*
make catlings⁴ on.
ACHILLES   Come, thou shalt bear a letter to him straight.
THERSITES   Let me carry another to his horse, for that's the more
capable° creature.   *intelligent*
295   ACHILLES   My mind is troubled like a fountain stirred,
And I myself see not the bottom of it.   [*Exit with* PATROCLUS]
THERSITES   Would the fountain of your mind were clear again,
that I might water an ass at it. I had rather be a tick in a sheep
than such a valiant ignorance.°   *Exit*   *puffed-up fool*

4.1

Enter at one door AENEAS *with a torch; at another* PARIS,
DEIPHOBUS, ANTENOR, [*and*] DIOMEDES *the Grecian,*
with torch[*-bearers*]

PARIS   See, ho! Who is that there?
DEIPHOBUS   It is the Lord Aeneas.
AENEAS   Is the Prince there in person?
Had I so good occasion to lie long
5   As you, Prince Paris, nothing but heavenly business
Should rob my bed-mate of my company.
DIOMEDES   That's my mind too. Good morrow, Lord Aeneas.
PARIS   A valiant Greek, Aeneas, take his hand.
Witness the process of your speech,¹ wherein
10   You told how Diomed e'en a whole week by days°   *every day*
Did haunt you in the field.
AENEAS [*to* DIOMEDES]   Health to you, valiant sir,
During all question of° the gentle truce.   *conversations during*
But when I meet you armed, as black defiance

---

4. Instrument strings made of catgut.
4.1 Location: A street in Troy.

1. *Witness . . . speech:* As the thrust of your narrative
made clear (that he is valiant).

As heart can think or courage execute.
15 DIOMEDES   The one and other Diomed embraces.
Our bloods are now in calm; and so long, health.
But when contention and occasion meet,°   *it's time to fight*
By Jove I'll play the hunter for thy life
With all my force, pursuit, and policy.°   *cunning*
20 AENEAS   And thou shalt hunt a lion that will fly
With his face backward.² In humane gentleness,
Welcome to Troy. Now by Anchises' life,
Welcome indeed! By Venus'³ hand I swear
No man alive can love in such a sort°   *to such an extent*
25 The thing he means to kill more excellently.
DIOMEDES   We sympathize.° Jove, let Aeneas live—   *feel the same*
If to my sword his fate be not the glory—
A thousand complete courses of the sun;
But, in mine emulous honour,⁴ let him die
30 With every joint a wound—and that, tomorrow.
AENEAS   We know each other well.
DIOMEDES   We do, and long to know each other worse.
PARIS   This is the most despitefull'st gentle greeting,
The noblest hateful love, that e'er I heard of.
35 What business, lord, so early?
AENEAS   I was sent for to the King; but why, I know not.
PARIS   His purpose meets you:° 'twas to bring this Greek   *I'll tell you why*
To Calchas' house, and there to render him,
For the enfreed Antenor, the fair Cressid.
40 Let's have your company, or if you please
Haste there before us. [*Aside*] I constantly° do think—   *firmly*
Or rather, call my thought a certain knowledge—
My brother Troilus lodges there tonight.
Rouse him and give him note of our approach,
45 With the whole quality° wherefore. I fear   *cause*
We shall be much unwelcome.
AENEAS [*aside*]   That I assure you.
Troilus had rather Troy were borne to Greece
Than Cressid borne from Troy.
PARIS [*aside*]   There is no help.
The bitter disposition of the time
50 Will have it so.
[*Aloud*] On, lord, we'll follow you.
AENEAS   Good morrow all.   *Exit*
PARIS   And tell me, noble Diomed—faith, tell me true,
Even in the soul of sound good-fellowship—
55 Who in your thoughts merits fair Helen most,
Myself or Menelaus?
DIOMEDES   Both alike.
He merits well to have her that doth seek her,
Not making any scruple of her soilure,°   *issue of her dishonor*
With such a hell of pain and world of charge;°   *expense*
60 And you as well to keep her that defend her,
Not palating the taste of° her dishonour,   *Not even tasting*

---

2. In the imagery of heraldry for chivalric combat, a
lion walking and looking back over his shoulder; also,
Aeneas will still fight even as he retreats.

3. Anchises and Venus, the goddess of love, were
Aeneas's parents.
4. If his death will increase my honor.

With such a costly loss of wealth and friends.
He like a puling° cuckold would drink up   °whining
The lees and dregs of a flat 'tamèd piece;⁵
65 You like a lecher out of whorish loins
Are pleased to breed out your inheritors.
Both merits poised,° each weighs nor less nor more,   °weighed in the scales
But he as he: which heavier for a whore?⁶
PARIS   You are too bitter to your countrywoman.
70 DIOMEDES   She's bitter to her country. Hear me, Paris.
For every false drop in her bawdy veins
A Grecian's life hath sunk; for every scruple°   °tiny unit of weight
Of her contaminated carrion° weight   °putrid
A Trojan hath been slain. Since she could speak
75 She hath not given so many good words breath
As, for her, Greeks and Trojans suffered death.
PARIS   Fair Diomed, you do as chapmen° do: °merchants
Dispraise the thing that you desire to buy.
But we in silence hold this virtue well:°   °act similarly
80 We'll but commend what we intend to sell.⁷—
Here lies our way.   *Exeunt*

4.2

Enter TROILUS *and* CRESSIDA

TROILUS   Dear, trouble not yourself. The morn is cold.
CRESSIDA   Then, sweet my lord, I'll call mine uncle down.
He shall unbolt the gates.
TROILUS   Trouble him not.
To bed, to bed! Sleep lull those pretty eyes
5 And give as soft attachment° to thy senses   °imprisonment
As to infants empty of all thought.
CRESSIDA   Good morrow, then.
TROILUS   I prithee now, to bed.
CRESSIDA   Are you aweary of me?
10 TROILUS   O Cressida! But that the busy day,
Waked by the lark, hath roused the ribald° crows,   °offensively noisy
And dreaming night will hide our joys no longer,
I would not from thee.
CRESSIDA   Night hath been too brief.
TROILUS   Beshrew the witch! With venomous wights¹ she stays
15 As hideously as hell, but flies° the grasps of love   °flees
With wings more momentary-swift than thought.
You will catch cold and curse me.
CRESSIDA   Prithee, tarry. You men will never tarry.
O foolish Cressid! I might have still held off,
20 And then you would have tarried.—Hark, there's one up.
[*She veils herself*]
PANDARUS [*within*]   What's° all the doors open here?   °Why are
TROILUS   It is your uncle.
CRESSIDA   A pestilence on him! Now will he be mocking.
I shall have such a life.

---

5. Of a stale insipid (penetrated) cask of wine (woman).
6. But one the same as the other: which more deserves
(is made sadder by) the whore?
7. We'll praise only what we're trying to sell. (But we

don't intend to bargain for Helen and so won't praise her.)
4.2 Location: Cressida's house.
1. Curse the night! With evil people (who are hateful to
each other).

	Enter PANDARUS	
25	PANDARUS How now, how now, how go° maidenheads?	*what's the price of*
	[*To* CRESSIDA] Here, you, maid! Where's my cousin Cressid?²	
	CRESSIDA [*unveiling*] Go hang yourself. You naughty, mocking uncle!	
	You bring me to do°—and then you flout me too.	*have sex*
	PANDARUS To do what? To do what?—Let her say what.—What	
30	have I brought you to do?	
	CRESSIDA Come, come, beshrew° your heart. You'll ne'er be good,	*curses on*
	Nor suffer others.°	*let others be good*
	PANDARUS Ha ha! Alas, poor wretch. Ah, poor *capocchia*,° hast	*simpleton; foreskin*
	not slept tonight? Would he not—a naughty man—let it sleep?	
35	A bugbear° take him.	*goblin*
	CRESSIDA [*to* TROILUS] Did not I tell you? Would he were	
	knocked i'th' head.°	*killed*
	One knocks [*within*]	
	Who's that at door?—Good uncle, go and see.—	
	My lord, come you again into my chamber.	
	You smile and mock me, as if I meant naughtily.	
40	TROILUS Ha ha!	
	CRESSIDA Come, you are deceived, I think of no such thing.	
	[*One*] knock[*s within*]	
	How earnestly they knock! Pray you come in.	
	I would not for half Troy have you seen here.	
	Exeunt [TROILUS *and* CRESSIDA]	
	PANDARUS Who's there? What's the matter? Will you beat down	
45	the door?	
	[*He opens the door. Enter* AENEAS]	
	How now, what's the matter?	
	AENEAS Good morrow, lord, good morrow.	
	PANDARUS Who's there? My Lord Aeneas? By my troth,	
	I knew you not. What news with you so early?	
	AENEAS Is not Prince Troilus here?	
50	PANDARUS Here? What should he do here?	
	AENEAS Come, he is here, my lord. Do not deny him.	
	It doth import° him much to speak with me.	*concern*
	PANDARUS Is he here, say you? It's more than I know, I'll be	
	sworn. For my own part, I came in late. What should he do	
55	here?	
	AENEAS Whoa! Nay, then. Come, come, you'll do him wrong	
	Ere you are ware.° You'll be so true to him	*aware*
	To be false to him.° Do not you know of him,	*As to harm him*
	But yet go fetch him hither. Go.	
	[*Exit* PANDARUS]³	
	Enter TROILUS	
60	TROILUS How now, what's the matter?	
	AENEAS My lord, I scarce have leisure to salute you,	
	My matter is so rash.° There is at hand	*urgent*
	Paris your brother and Deiphobus,	
	The Grecian Diomed, and our Antenor	

---

2. Pandarus pretends not to recognize Cressida, now that she is no longer a virgin. It is possible that he addresses her as "maid" (line 26) because she is wearing a veil, which suggests a modesty appropriate to virgins. 3. Editors usually keep him on and have Cressida enter alone at what is the beginning of 4.3 in this edition.

65   Delivered to us—and for him° forthwith,   *(Antenor)*
        Ere the first sacrifice, within this hour,
        We must give up to Diomedes' hand
        The Lady Cressida.
TROILUS   Is it so concluded?
AENEAS   By Priam and the general state° of Troy.   *council*
70   They are at hand, and ready to effect it.
TROILUS   How my achievements mock me.
        I will go meet them—and, my Lord Aeneas,
        We° met by chance: you did not find me here.   *(Pretend that) we*
AENEAS   Good, good, my lord: the untold secrecies° of nature   *untold secrets*
75   Have not more gift in taciturnity.   *Exeunt*

<h2 style="text-align:center">4.3</h2>

Enter PANDARUS *and* CRESSIDA[1]

PANDARUS   Is't possible? No sooner got but lost. The devil take
        Antenor! The young prince will go mad. A plague upon Ante-
        nor! I would they had broke 's neck.
CRESSIDA   How now? What's the matter? Who was here?
5   PANDARUS   Ah, ah!
CRESSIDA   Why sigh you so profoundly? Where's my lord?
        Gone? Tell me, sweet uncle, what's the matter?
PANDARUS   Would I were as deep under the earth as I am above.
CRESSIDA   O the gods! What's the matter?
10 PANDARUS   Pray thee, get thee in. Would thou hadst ne'er been
        born. I knew thou wouldst be his death. O poor gentleman! A
        plague upon Antenor!
CRESSIDA   Good uncle, I beseech you on my knees; I beseech
        you, what's the matter?
15 PANDARUS   Thou must be gone, wench, thou must be gone.
        Thou art changed° for Antenor. Thou must to thy father, and   *exchanged*
        be gone from Troilus. 'Twill be his death. 'Twill be his bane.
        He cannot bear it.
CRESSIDA   O you immortal gods! I will not go.
20 PANDARUS   Thou must.
CRESSIDA   I will not, uncle. I have forgot my father.
        I know no touch of consanguinity,
        No kin, no love, no blood, no soul, so near me
        As the sweet Troilus. O you gods divine,
25   Make Cressid's name the very crown° of falsehood   *height*
        If ever she leave Troilus. Time, force, and death
        Do to this body what extremity you can,
        But the strong base and building of my love
        Is as the very centre of the earth,
30   Drawing all things to it. I'll go in and weep—
PANDARUS   Do, do.
CRESSIDA   Tear my bright hair, and scratch my praisèd cheeks,
        Crack my clear voice with sobs, and break my heart
        With sounding 'Troilus'. I will not go from Troy.   *Exeunt*

4.3 Location: Scene continues.   this affects the numbering of the following lines and
1. Most modern editions do not mark a scene break here;   scenes. See note to 4.2.59 and Textual Note.

4.4

Enter PARIS, TROILUS, AENEAS, DEIPHOBUS, ANTENOR,
    and DIOMEDES

PARIS It is great morning,° and the hour prefixed°   *daylight / arranged*
    Of her delivery to this valiant Greek
    Comes fast upon us. Good my brother Troilus,
    Tell you the lady what she is to do,
    And haste her to the purpose.
5 TROILUS   Walk into her house.
    I'll bring her to the Grecian presently°—   *immediately*
    And to his hand when I deliver her,
    Think it an altar, and thy brother Troilus
    A priest, there off'ring to it his own heart.
10 PARIS I know what 'tis to love,
    And would,° as I shall pity, I could help.—   *wish*
    Please you walk in, my lords?   *Exeunt*

4.5

Enter PANDARUS *and* CRESSIDA

PANDARUS Be moderate, be moderate.
CRESSIDA Why tell you me of moderation?
    The grief is fine,° full, perfect that I taste,   *undiluted*
    And violenteth° in a sense° as strong   *rages / manner*
5   As that which causeth it.° How can I moderate it?   *(her love)*
    If I could temporize with° my affection   *adjust to*
    Or brew° it to a weak and colder palate,°   *dilute / taste*
    The like allayment° could I give my grief.   *dilution*
    My love admits no qualifying dross;°   *modifying impurity*
10   No more° my grief, in such a precious loss.   *Any more than does*

Enter TROILUS

PANDARUS Here, here, here he comes. Ah, sweet ducks!
CRESSIDA [*embracing him*] O Troilus, Troilus!
PANDARUS What a pair of spectacles° is here! Let me embrace   *sights*
    you too. 'O heart', as the goodly saying is,
15   'O heart, heavy heart,
          Why sigh'st thou without breaking?'
    where he answers again
       'Because thou canst not ease thy smart
         By friendship nor by speaking.'
20   There was never a truer rhyme. Let us cast away nothing, for
    we may live to have need of such a verse. We see it, we see it.
    How now, lambs?
TROILUS Cressid, I love thee in so strained° a purity   *refined*
    That the blest gods, as° angry with my fancy°—   *as if / love*
25   More bright in zeal than the devotion which
    Cold lips blow to their deities—take thee from me.
CRESSIDA Have the gods envy?
PANDARUS Ay, ay, ay, ay, 'tis too plain a case.
CRESSIDA And is it true that I must go from Troy?
TROILUS A hateful truth.
30 CRESSIDA   What, and from Troilus too?
TROILUS From Troy and Troilus.

4.4 Location: Outside Cressida's house.   **4.5** Location: Inside Cressida's house.

CRESSIDA   Is't possible?

TROILUS   And suddenly°—where injury of° chance   *immediately / injurious*
    Puts back° leave-taking, jostles roughly by   *Prevents*
    All time of pause, rudely beguiles° our lips   *deprives*
35   Of all rejoindure,° forcibly prevents   *joining again*
    Our locked embrasures, strangles our dear vows
    Even in the birth of our own labouring breath.°   *(as in childbirth)*
    We two, that with so many thousand sighs
    Did buy each other, must poorly sell ourselves
40   With the rude brevity and discharge of one.°   *(sigh)*
    Injurious Time now with a robber's haste
    Crams his rich thiev'ry up, he knows not how.[1]
    As many farewells as be stars in heaven,
    With distinct breath and consigned° kisses to them,   *ratifying*
45   He fumbles up° into a loose adieu   *clumsily combines*
    And scants us with a single famished kiss,
    Distasted[2] with the salt of broken° tears.   *interrupted*

       Enter AENEAS

AENEAS   My lord, is the lady ready?

TROILUS [*to* CRESSIDA]   Hark, you are called. Some say the *genius*° so   *guardian spirit*
50   Cries 'Come!' to him that instantly must die.
    [*To* PANDARUS] Bid them have patience. She shall come anon.

PANDARUS   Where are my tears? Rain, to lay this wind,° or my   *allay my sighs*
    heart will be blown up by the root.   [*Exit with* AENEAS]

CRESSIDA   I must then to the Grecians.

TROILUS   No remedy.

55 CRESSIDA   A woeful Cressid 'mongst the merry Greeks![3]
    When shall we see again?

TROILUS   Hear me, my love: be thou but true of heart—

CRESSIDA   I true? How now! What wicked deem° is this?   *thought*

TROILUS   Nay, we must use expostulation° kindly,   *conversation*
60   For it° is parting from us.   *the opportunity*
    I speak not 'Be thou true' as fearing thee—
    For I will throw my glove to° Death himself   *challenge*
    That there's no maculation° in thy heart—   *stain of infidelity*
    But 'Be thou true' say I, to fashion in°   *introduce*
65   My sequent° protestation: 'Be thou true,   *following*
    And I will see thee'.

CRESSIDA   O you shall be exposed, my lord, to dangers
    As infinite as imminent. But I'll be true.

TROILUS   And I'll grow friend with danger. Wear this sleeve.[4]

70 CRESSIDA   And you this glove. When shall I see you?

TROILUS   I will corrupt the Grecian sentinels
    To° give thee nightly visitation.   *In order that I may*
    But yet, be true.

CRESSIDA   O heavens! 'Be true' again!

75 TROILUS   Hear why I speak it, love.
    The Grecian youths are full of quality,
    Their loving well composed, with gifts of nature flowing,
    And swelling o'er with arts° and exercise.°   *education / practice*
    How novelty may move, and parts with person,°   *talent and good looks*
80   Alas, a kind of godly° jealousy—   *divinely sanctioned*

---

1. Compresses his stolen goods (farewell kisses) into a short period, distractedly.
2. Made distasteful.

3. Common phrase for licentious revelers, here also meant literally.
4. Often detachable in Elizabethan dress.

Which I beseech you call a virtuous sin—
Makes me afeard.

CRESSIDA   O heavens, you love me not!

TROILUS   Die I a villain then!

85　In this I do not call your faith° in question　　　　　　　*fidelity*
So mainly° as my merit.⁵ I cannot sing,　　　　　　　　　　*much*
Nor heel the high lavolt, nor sweeten talk,⁶
Nor play at subtle games—fair virtues all,
To which the Grecians are most prompt and pregnant.°　　　*ready*

90　But I can tell that in each grace of these
There lurks a still and dumb-discoursive° devil　　*silently communicating*
That tempts most cunningly. But be not tempted.

CRESSIDA   Do you think I will?

TROILUS   No, but something may be done that we will not,°　　*do not will*

95　And sometimes we are devils to ourselves,
When we will tempt the frailty of our powers,
Presuming on their changeful potency.°　　　*unreliable strength*

AENEAS (*within*)   Nay, good my lord!

TROILUS　　　　　　　　　　Come, kiss, and let us part.

PARIS [*at the door*]   Brother Troilus?

TROILUS　　　　　　　　　　Good brother, come you hither,

100　And bring Aeneas and the Grecian with you. *Exit* [PARIS]

CRESSIDA   My lord, will you be true?

TROILUS   Who, I? Alas, it is my vice, my fault.
Whiles others fish with craft° for great opinion,°　　*guile / reputation*
I with great truth catch mere simplicity;⁷

105　Whilst some with cunning gild their copper crowns,°　　*coins; heads*
With truth and plainness I do wear° mine bare.　　　*dress; erode*

　　　Enter [PARIS, AENEAS, ANTENOR, DEIPHOBUS, *and* DIO-
　　　MEDES]

Fear not my truth. The moral° of my wit　　　　　　　　*maxim*
Is 'plain and true!'; there's all the reach of it.—
Welcome, Sir Diomed. Here is the lady

110　Which for Antenor we deliver you.
At the port,° lord, I'll give her to thy hand,　　　　*gate of the city*
And by the way possess° thee what she is.　　　　　　　*instruct*
Entreat° her fair, and by my soul, fair Greek,　　　　　*Treat*
If e'er thou stand at mercy of my sword,

115　Name Cressid, and thy life shall be as safe
As Priam is in Ilium.

DIOMEDES　　　　　　　　Fair Lady Cressid,
So please you, save the thanks this prince expects.⁸
The lustre in your eye, heaven in your cheek,
Pleads your fair usage;° and to Diomed　　　　　　　　*treatment*

120　You shall be mistress, and command him wholly.

TROILUS   Grecian, thou dost not use me courteously,
To shame the zeal of my petition towards thee
In praising her. I tell thee, lord of Greece,
She is as far high-soaring o'er thy praises

---

5. Deserts; good works, deserving of salvation (picking up the religious language of the preceding lines, especially "faith," line 85).
6. Nor dance the "lavolt" (which involved spectacular jumps), nor flatter.
7. Absolute rusticity (sincerity).
8. *save . . . expects:* you won't need to thank Troilus for the good treatment I will give you.

125   As thou unworthy to be called her servant.[9]
    I charge thee use her well, even for my charge;°   *simply at my command*
    For, by the dreadful Pluto, if thou dost not,
    Though the great bulk Achilles be thy guard
    I'll cut thy throat.
    DIOMEDES   O be not moved,° Prince Troilus.   *angry*
130   Let me be privileged by my place and message
    To be a speaker free. When I am hence
    I'll answer to my lust.° And know you, lord,   *do as I please*
    I'll nothing do on charge.° To her own worth   *command*
    She shall be prized; but that° you say 'Be't so',   *simply because*
135   I'll speak it in my spirit and honour 'No!'
    TROILUS   Come, to the port.—I'll tell thee, Diomed,
    This brave° shall oft make thee to hide thy head.—   *boast*
    Lady, give me your hand, and as we walk
    To our own selves bend we our needful talk.

          [Exeunt TROILUS, CRESSIDA, *and* DIOMEDES*]*
        [A] trumpet sound[s]
    PARIS   Hark, Hector's trumpet.
140   AENEAS   How have we spent this morning?
    The Prince must think me tardy and remiss,
    That swore to ride before him in the field.
    PARIS   'Tis Troilus' fault. Come, come to field with him.
    DEIPHOBUS   Let us make ready straight.
145   AENEAS   Yea, with a bridegroom's fresh alacrity
    Let us address° to tend on Hector's heels.   *prepare*
    The glory of our Troy doth this day lie
    On his fair worth and single chivalry.   *Exeunt*

4.6

Enter AJAX *armed,* ACHILLES, PATROCLUS, AGAMEMNON,
MENELAUS, ULYSSES, NESTOR[*, a trumpeter, and others*]

    AGAMEMNON   Here art thou in appointment° fresh and fair,   *equipment*
    Anticipating time[1] with starting° courage.   *bounding*
    Give with thy trumpet a loud note to Troy,
    Thou dreadful° Ajax, that the appallèd air   *causing fear*
5   May pierce the head of the great combatant
    And hale° him hither.   *draw*
    AJAX   Thou trumpet,° there's my purse.   *trumpeter*
        [He gives him money]
    Now crack thy lungs and split thy brazen pipe.°   *trumpet; windpipe*
    Blow, villain,° till thy spherèd bias° cheek   *servant / puffed-out*
    Outswell the colic of puffed Aquilon.[2]
10   Come, stretch thy chest and let thy eyes spout blood;
    Thou blow'st for Hector.
        [The trumpet sounds]
    ULYSSES   No trumpet answers.
    ACHILLES   'Tis but early days.
    AGAMEMNON   Is not yond Diomed with Calchas' daughter?
15   ULYSSES   'Tis he. I ken° the manner of his gait.   *recognize*

---

9. Like "mistress" (line 120), a cliché of courtly love.
4.6 Location: Between the Greek camp and Troy.
1. Ajax has not waited for Hector to appear with his challenge.

2. Outswells the intestinal pain (from bloating) of the north wind (Aquilon). (Winds on contemporary maps were represented as human heads blowing.)

He rises on the toe: that spirit of his
In aspiration lifts him from the earth.
      [*Enter* DIOMEDES *and* CRESSIDA]
AGAMEMNON [*to* DIOMEDES]   Is this the Lady Cressid?
DIOMEDES   Even she.
AGAMEMNON   Most dearly welcome to the Greeks, sweet lady.
      [*He kisses her*]
20 NESTOR [*to* CRESSIDA]   Our General doth salute you with a kiss.
ULYSSES   Yet is the kindness but particular;°   *from only one of us*
      'Twere better she were kissed in general.
NESTOR   And very courtly counsel. I'll begin.
      [*He kisses her*]
      So much for Nestor.
25 ACHILLES   I'll take that winter° from your lips, fair lady.   *Nestor's old age*
      [*He kisses her*]
      Achilles bids you welcome.
MENELAUS [*to* CRESSIDA]   I had good argument° for kissing once.   *Helen*
PATROCLUS   But that's no argument for kissing now;
      For thus [*stepping between them*] popped° Paris in his   *thrust in*
            hardiment,°   *boldness; hardness*
30 And parted thus you and your argument.
      [*He kisses her*]
ULYSSES [*aside*]   O deadly gall, and theme of all our scorns!
      For which we lose our heads to gild his horns.°   *cuckold's horns*
PATROCLUS [*to* CRESSIDA]   The first was Menelaus' kiss; this, mine.
      Patroclus kisses you.
      [*He kisses her again*]
MENELAUS   O this is trim.°   *excellent*
35 PATROCLUS [*to* CRESSIDA]   Paris and I kiss evermore° for him.   *always*
MENELAUS   I'll have my kiss, sir.—Lady, by your leave.
CRESSIDA   In kissing do you render or receive?
MENELAUS   Both take and give.
CRESSIDA   I'll make my match to live,°   *bet my life*
      The kiss you take is better than you give.
40 Therefore no kiss.
MENELAUS   I'll give you boot:° I'll give you three for one.   *profit*
CRESSIDA   You are an odd³ man: give even or give none.
MENELAUS   An odd man, lady? Every man is odd.
CRESSIDA   No, Paris is not—for you know 'tis true
45 That you are odd, and he is even° with you.   *has gotten even*
MENELAUS   You fillip me o'th' head.⁴
CRESSIDA   No, I'll be sworn.
ULYSSES   It were no match, your nail against his horn.⁵
      May I, sweet lady, beg a kiss of you?
CRESSIDA   You may.
ULYSSES   I do desire it.
CRESSIDA   Why, beg too.
50 ULYSSES   Why then, for Venus' sake, give me a kiss,
      When Helen is a maid again, and his°—   *Menelaus's*
CRESSIDA   I am your debtor; claim it when 'tis due.

---

3. *odd* (lines 42–45): strange; unique; left out; single (lacking a partner); opposite of "even" (line 45).
4. You tease me about being a cuckold (literally, flick your fingernail on my head).
5. No contest, Cressida's fingernail against Menelaus's cuckold's horn (which is far harder).

ULYSSES   Never's my day,° and then a kiss of you.   *the due date*
DIOMEDES   Lady, a word. I'll bring you to your father.
    [*They talk apart*]
NESTOR   A woman of quick sense.°   *intelligence; sexuality*
55   ULYSSES   Fie, fie upon her!
    There's language in her eye, her cheek, her lip;
    Nay, her foot speaks. Her wanton spirits look out°   *are exposed*
    At every joint and motive° of her body.   *moving limb*
    O these encounterers so glib of tongue,
60   That give accosting° welcome ere it comes,   *an approach*
    And wide unclasp the tables° of their thoughts   *tablets*
    To every ticklish° reader, set them down°   *lustful / mark them*
    For sluttish spoils of opportunity°   *As easy sexual prey*
    And daughters of the game.°   *prostitutes*
                Exeunt [DIOMEDES *and* CRESSIDA]
    Flourish
65   ALL   The Trojans' trumpet.°   *(Trojan strumpet)*
    Enter all of Troy: HECTOR [*armed*], PARIS, AENEAS, HELE-
    NUS, *and attendants* [*among them* TROILUS]
AGAMEMNON   Yonder comes the troop.
AENEAS [*coming forward*]   Hail, all you state° of Greece! What   *noblemen*
    shall be done°   *rewarded*
    To him that victory commands? Or do you purpose
    A victor shall be known? Will you° the knights   *Do you wish that*
70   Shall to the edge of all extremity°   *the death*
    Pursue each other, or shall they be divided
    By any voice or order of the field?[6]
    Hector bade ask.
AGAMEMNON   Which way would Hector have it?
AENEAS   He cares not; he'll obey conditions.°   *your choice*
75   ACHILLES   'Tis done like Hector—but securely° done,   *too boldly*
    A little proudly, and great deal disprising°   *underestimating*
    The knight opposed.
AENEAS   If not Achilles, sir,
    What is your name?
ACHILLES   If not Achilles, nothing.
AENEAS   Therefore Achilles. But whate'er, know this:
80   In the extremity of great and little,
    Valour and pride excel themselves in Hector,
    The one° almost as infinite as all,   *(valor)*
    The other° blank as nothing. Weigh him well,   *(pride)*
    And that which looks like pride is courtesy.
85   This Ajax is half made of Hector's blood,[7]
    In love whereof half Hector stays at home.
    Half heart, half hand, half Hector comes to seek
    This blended knight, half Trojan and half Greek.
ACHILLES   A maiden° battle, then? O I perceive you.   *bloodless*
    [*Enter* DIOMEDES]
90   AGAMEMNON   Here is Sir Diomed.—Go, gentle knight,
    Stand by our Ajax. As you and Lord Aeneas
    Consent° upon the order° of their fight,   *Decide / terms*

6. By any umpire or rules of combat?   7. Ajax was Priam's nephew.

So be it: either to the uttermost
Or else a breath.°   *bout of exercise*

[*Exeunt* AJAX, DIOMEDES, HECTOR, *and* AENEAS][8]

The combatants being kin
95 Half stints their strife before their strokes begin.
ULYSSES   They are opposed already.
AGAMEMNON   What Trojan is that same that looks so heavy?°   *sorrowful*
ULYSSES   The youngest son of Priam, a true knight:
   They call him Troilus.
100 Not yet mature, yet matchless-firm of word,
   Speaking in deeds and deedless in his tongue;°   *not boastful*
   Not soon provoked, nor being provoked soon calmed;
   His heart and hand both open and both free.°   *generous*
   For what he has he gives; what thinks, he shows;
105 Yet gives he not till judgement guide his bounty,°   *generosity*
   Nor dignifies an impare° thought with breath.   *unworthy*
   Manly as Hector but more dangerous,
   For Hector in his blaze of wrath subscribes°   *relents*
   To tender objects, but he in heat of action
110 Is more vindicative° than jealous love.   *vindictive*
   They call him Troilus, and on him erect
   A second hope as fairly built as Hector.
   Thus says Aeneas, one that knows the youth
   Even to his inches, and with private soul[9]
115 Did in great Ilium thus translate° him to me.   *describe*
      Alarum
AGAMEMNON   They are in action.
NESTOR   Now, Ajax, hold thine own!
TROILUS   Hector, thou sleep'st! Awake thee!
AGAMEMNON   His blows are well disposed. There, Ajax!   [*Exeunt*]

4.7

[*Enter* HECTOR *and* AJAX *fighting, and* AENEAS *and* DIO-
MEDES *interposing.*] *Trumpets cease*[1]

DIOMEDES   You must no more.
AENEAS   Princes, enough, so please you.
AJAX   I am not warm yet. Let us fight again.
DIOMEDES   As Hector pleases.
HECTOR   Why then will I no more.—
   Thou art, great lord, my father's sister's son,
5   A cousin-german° to great Priam's seed.   *first cousin*
   The obligation of our blood forbids
   A gory emulation° 'twixt us twain.   *competition*
   Were thy commixtion° Greek and Trojan so°   *blending / such*
   That thou couldst say 'This hand is Grecian all,
10 And this is Trojan; the sinews of this leg
   All Greek, and this all Troy; my mother's blood
   Runs on the dexter° cheek, and this sinister°   *right / left*
   Bounds in my father's,' by Jove multipotent°   *most powerful*
   Thou shouldst not bear from me a Greekish member°   *part of the body*

---

8. The combat might take place onstage.
9. *Even . . . soul:* In utmost detail, and in confidence.
4.7 Location: Scene continues.

1. Most modern editions do not mark a scene break
here; this affects the numbering of the following lines
as well as the following scenes. See Textual Note.

15   Wherein my sword had not impressure made
      Of our rank° feud. But the just gods gainsay°   heated / prohibit
      That any drop thou borrowed'st from thy mother,
      My sacred aunt, should by my mortal sword
      Be drained. Let me embrace thee, Ajax.
20   By him that thunders,° thou hast lusty arms.   Jupiter
      Hector would have them fall upon him thus.°   in an embrace
      Cousin, all honour to thee.
AJAX   I thank thee, Hector.
      Thou art too gentle and too free a man.
      I came to kill thee, cousin, and bear hence
25   A great addition° earnèd in thy death.   title
HECTOR   Not Neoptolemus² so mirable,°   wonderful
      On whose bright crest° Fame with her loud'st oyez°   helmet / hear ye
      Cries 'This is he!', could promise to himself
      A thought of added honour torn from Hector.
30 AENEAS   There is expectance here from both the sides
      What further you will do.
HECTOR   We'll answer it:
      The issue° is embracement.—Ajax, farewell.   conclusion
AJAX   If I might in entreaties find success,
      As seld° I have the chance, I would desire   seldom
35   My famous cousin to our Grecian tents.
DIOMEDES   'Tis Agamemnon's wish—and great Achilles
      Doth long to see unarmed the valiant Hector.
HECTOR   Aeneas, call my brother Troilus to me,
      And signify this loving interview
40   To the expecters of our Trojan part.°   awaiting Trojans
      Desire them home.°   [Exit AENEAS]   to go home
                     Give me thy hand, my cousin.
      I will go eat with thee, and see your knights.
           Enter AGAMEMNON and the rest [AENEAS, ULYSSES,
           MENELAUS, NESTOR, ACHILLES, PATROCLUS, TROILUS,
           and others]
AJAX   Great Agamemnon comes to meet us here.
HECTOR [to AENEAS]   The worthiest of them,° tell me name by name.   the Greeks
45   But for Achilles, mine own searching eyes
      Shall find him by his large and portly size.
AGAMEMNON [embracing him]   Worthy of arms, as welcome as to° one   as you can be to
      That would be rid of such an enemy.
      But that's no welcome. Understand more clear:
50   What's past and what's to come is strewed with husks
      And formless ruin of oblivion,
      But in this extant° moment faith and troth,   present
      Strained purely from all hollow bias-drawing,³
      Bids thee with most divine integrity
55   From heart of very heart, 'Great Hector, welcome!'
HECTOR   I thank thee, most imperious° Agamemnon.   imperial
AGAMEMNON [to TROILUS]   My well-famed lord of Troy, no less to you.
MENELAUS   Let me confirm my princely brother's greeting.
      You brace° of warlike brothers, welcome hither.   pair
           [He embraces HECTOR and TROILUS]

---

2. Achilles' son Pyrrhus (but Shakespeare may have   3. Freed from all insincerity and indirectness.
thought Neoptolemus was Achilles' surname).

HECTOR [*to* AENEAS]   Who must we answer?

60   AENEAS   The noble Menelaus.

HECTOR   O, you, my lord! By Mars his° gauntlet, thanks.   *Mars's*
Mock not that I affect° th'untraded° oath.   *choose / unfamiliar*
Your quondam° wife swears still by Venus' glove.[4]   *former*
She's well, but bade me not commend her to you.

65   MENELAUS   Name her not now, sir. She's a deadly theme.

HECTOR   O, pardon. I offend.

NESTOR   I have, thou gallant Trojan, seen thee oft,
Labouring for destiny,[5] make cruel way
Through ranks of Greekish youth, and I have seen thee

70   As hot as Perseus° spur thy Phrygian steed,   *(on winged Pegasus)*
And seen thee scorning forfeits and subduements,[6]
When thou hast hung° th'advancèd sword i'th' air,   *kept high*
Not letting it decline° on the declined,°   *fall / fallen*
That I have said unto my standers-by,

75   'Lo, Jupiter is yonder, dealing life'.[7]
And I have seen thee pause and take thy breath,
When that a ring of Greeks have hemmed thee in,
Like an Olympian,° wrestling. This have I seen;   *a god*
But this thy countenance, still° locked in steel,   *always*

80   I never saw till now. I knew thy grandsire[8]
And once fought with him. He was a soldier good,
But—by great Mars, the captain of us all—
Never like thee. Let an old man embrace thee;
And, worthy warrior, welcome to our tents.

[*He embraces* HECTOR]

85   AENEAS [*to* HECTOR]   'Tis the old Nestor.

HECTOR   Let me embrace thee, good old chronicle,°   *record of history*
That hast so long walked hand in hand with time.
Most reverend Nestor, I am glad to clasp thee.

NESTOR   I would my arms could match thee in contention°   *in battle*

90   As they contend with thee in courtesy.

HECTOR   I would they could.

NESTOR   Ha! By this white beard I'd fight with thee tomorrow.
Well, welcome, welcome! I have seen the time.[9]

ULYSSES   I wonder now how yonder city stands

95   When we have here her base and pillar by us?

HECTOR   I know your favour,° Lord Ulysses, well.   *face*
Ah, sir, there's many a Greek and Trojan dead
Since first I saw yourself and Diomed
In Ilium on your Greekish embassy.

100   ULYSSES   Sir, I foretold you then what would ensue.
My prophecy is but half his journey yet;
For yonder walls that pertly front your town,
Yon towers whose wanton° tops do buss° the clouds,   *reckless / kiss*
Must kiss their own feet.

HECTOR   I must not believe you.

105   There they stand yet, and modestly I think
The fall of every Phrygian stone will cost

---

4. *Venus' glove*: contrasting with Mars's gauntlet and alluding to Venus's adultery with Mars; possibly with an obscene innuendo.
5. Doing the Fates' work for them.
6. Scorning those whose lives might have been forfeit

and (possible) conquests.
7. Giving life being the gods' prerogative.
8. Laomedon, builder of Troy's walls.
9. That is, the time when I could have met you in combat.

A drop of Grecian blood. The end crowns all,
And that old common arbitrator Time
Will one day end it.
ULYSSES   So to him we leave it.
110 Most gentle and most valiant Hector, welcome.
       [*He embraces him*]
     After the General, I beseech you next
     To feast with me and see me at my tent.
ACHILLES   I shall forestall thee, Lord Ulysses. [*To* HECTOR] Thou!°   (*insulting*)
     Now, Hector, I have fed mine eyes on thee.
115 I have with exact view perused° thee, Hector,   *minutely looked over*
     And quoted° joint by joint.   *taken note*
HECTOR   Is this Achilles?
ACHILLES   I am Achilles.
HECTOR   Stand fair,° I pray thee, let me look on thee.   *open to view*
ACHILLES   Behold thy fill.
120 HECTOR   Nay, I have done already.
ACHILLES   Thou art too brief. I will the second time,
     As° I would buy thee, view thee limb by limb.   *As though*
HECTOR   O, like a book of sport° thou'lt read me o'er.   *hunting manual*
     But there's more in me than thou understand'st.
125 Why dost thou so oppress[1] me with thine eye?
ACHILLES   Tell me, you heavens, in which part of his body
     Shall I destroy him—whether there, or there, or there—
     That I may give the local wound a name,
     And make distinct the very breach whereout
130 Hector's great spirit flew? Answer me, heavens.
HECTOR   It would discredit the blest gods, proud man,
     To answer such a question. Stand again.°   *Let me look again*
     Think'st thou to catch my life so pleasantly°   *easily*
     As to prenominate° in nice° conjecture   *name in advance / exact*
     Where thou wilt hit me dead?
135 ACHILLES   I tell thee, yea.
HECTOR   Wert thou the oracle to tell me so,
     I'd not believe thee. Henceforth guard thee well.
     For I'll not kill thee there, nor there, nor there,
     But, by the forge that stithied° Mars his helm,   *forged*
140 I'll kill thee everywhere, yea, o'er and o'er.—
     You wisest Grecians, pardon me this brag:
     His insolence draws folly from my lips.
     But I'll endeavour deeds to match these words,
     Or may I never—
AJAX   Do not chafe thee,° cousin.—   *get angry*
145 And you, Achilles, let these threats alone,
     Till accident or purpose bring you to't.
     You may have every day enough of Hector,
     If you have stomach.° The general state,° I fear,   *appetite / Greek lords*
     Can scarce entreat you to be odd° with him.   *at odds*
150 HECTOR [*to* ACHILLES]   I pray you, let us see you in the field.
     We have had pelting° wars since you refused   *paltry*
     The Grecians' cause.
ACHILLES   Dost thou entreat me, Hector?

---

1. Molest; in heraldry, place a perpendicular or diagonal stripe across an animal (continuing the metaphor of Hector as a hunted animal from "book of sport," line 123).

Tomorrow do I meet thee, fell as death;
Tonight, all friends.

HECTOR   Thy hand upon that match.

155 AGAMEMNON   First, all you peers of Greece, go to my tent.
There in the full convive you.° Afterwards,   *feast together*
As Hector's leisure and your bounties shall
Concur together, severally entreat° him.   *individually invite*
Beat loud the taborins,° let the trumpets blow,   *small drums*
160 That this great soldier may his welcome know.
    [*Flourish.*] *Exeunt* [*all but* TROILUS *and* ULYSSES]

TROILUS   My Lord Ulysses, tell me, I beseech you,
In what place of the field doth Calchas keep?°   *reside*

ULYSSES   At Menelaus' tent, most princely Troilus.
There Diomed doth feast with him tonight—
165 Who neither looks on heaven nor on earth,
But gives all gaze and bent° of amorous view   *inclination*
On the fair Cressid.

TROILUS   Shall I, sweet lord, be bound to you so much,
After we part from Agamemnon's tent,
To bring me thither?

170 ULYSSES   You shall command me, sir.
As gentle° tell me, of what honour was   *courteously*
This Cressida in Troy? Had she no lover there
That wails her absence?

TROILUS   O sir, to such as boasting show their scars°   *brag of past wounds*
175 A mock is due. Will you walk on, my lord?
She was beloved, she loved; she is, and doth.
But still sweet love is food for fortune's tooth.   *Exeunt*

5.1

Enter ACHILLES *and* PATROCLUS

ACHILLES   I'll heat his blood with Greekish wine tonight,
Which with my scimitar I'll cool° tomorrow.   *expose to air*
Patroclus, let us feast him to the height.

PATROCLUS   Here comes Thersites.

Enter THERSITES

ACHILLES   How now, thou core° of envy,   *(of an ulcer)*
5 Thou crusty botch[1] of nature, what's the news?

THERSITES   Why, thou picture° of what thou seemest, and idol   *mere image*
of idiot-worshippers, here's a letter for thee.

ACHILLES   From whence, fragment?°   *scrap of leftovers*

THERSITES   Why, thou full dish of fool,[2] from Troy.
    [ACHILLES *reads the letter*]

10 PATROCLUS   Who keeps the tent now?[3]

THERSITES   The surgeon's box or the patient's wound.

PATROCLUS   Well said, adversity.° And what need these tricks?   *perversity*

THERSITES   Prithee be silent, boy. I profit not by thy talk. Thou
art thought to be Achilles' male varlet.°   *servant; concubine?*

15 PATROCLUS   'Male varlet', you rogue? What's that?

THERSITES   Why, his masculine whore. Now the rotten diseases

---

5.1. Location: The Greek camp, near Achilles' tent.
1. You scab-encrusted (bad-tempered) boil.
2. Punning on the name of a dessert, probably clotted cream or egg custard.

3. Who stays in the tent now? Thersites can no longer taunt Achilles for remaining indoors. But Thersites deliberately mistakes Patroclus to mean the surgeon's probe or lint used to clean a wound.

of the south, guts-griping, ruptures, catarrhs, loads o' gravel
i'th' back, lethargies, cold palsies, and the like,[4] take and take
again such preposterous discoveries!°   *revealed perversion*

19.1   THERSITES   *Why, his masculine whore. Now the rotten*
diseases of the south, the guts-griping, ruptures, loads
o' gravel in the back, lethargies, cold palsies, raw eyes,
dirt-rotten livers, wheezing lungs, bladders full of
19.5   *impostume,° sciaticas, lime-kilns° i'th' palm, incur-*   *abscess / burning*
able bone-ache, and the rivelled fee-simple of the
tetter,[5] take and take again such preposterous dis-
coveries.

20   PATROCLUS   Why, thou damnable box of envy thou, what
mean'st thou to curse thus?

THERSITES   Do I curse thee?

PATROCLUS   Why, no, you ruinous butt,° you whoreson indistin-   *leaky tub*
guishable cur,° no.   *formless beast*

25   THERSITES   No? Why art thou then exasperate?° Thou idle   *irritated*
immaterial skein of sleave-silk, thou green sarsenet flap[6] for a
sore eye,[7] thou tassel of a prodigal's purse, thou! Ah, how the
poor world is pestered with such waterflies!° Diminutives of   *tiny, flashy insects*
nature.

30   PATROCLUS   Out, gall!

THERSITES   Finch egg!°   *(small, gaudy egg)*

ACHILLES   My sweet Patroclus, I am thwarted quite
From my great purpose in tomorrow's battle.
Here is a letter from Queen Hecuba,

35   A token from her daughter, my fair love,
Both taxing° me, and gaging° me to keep   *reproving / binding*
An oath that I have sworn. I will not break it.
Fall, Greeks; fail, fame; honour, or° go or stay.   *either*
My major vow lies here; this I'll obey.—

40   Come, come, Thersites, help to trim° my tent.   *decorate*
This night in banqueting must all be spent.—
Away, Patroclus.   *Exeunt* [ACHILLES *and* PATROCLUS]

THERSITES   With too much blood° and too little brain these two   *passion*
may run mad, but if with too much brain and too little blood

45   they do, I'll be a curer of madmen.[8] Here's° Agamemnon: an   *Take*
honest fellow enough, and one that loves quails,° but he has   *(as food); prostitutes*
not so much brain as ear-wax. And the goodly transformation
of Jupiter there, his brother the bull,[9] the primitive° statue and   *archetypal*
oblique° memorial of cuckolds, a thrifty shoeing-horn in a   *perverse*

50   chain, hanging at his brother's leg:[1] to what form but that he is
should wit larded with malice and malice farced° with wit turn   *stuffed*
him to? To an ass were nothing: he is both ass and ox. To an
ox were nothing: he is both ox and ass. To be a dog, a mule, a
cat, a fitchew,[2] a toad, a lizard, an owl, a puttock,° or a herring   *kite*

4. These may be separate diseases, but they can nearly
all be symptoms of venereal disease. *south:* referring to
the arrival of venereal disease in Europe after the Crusades and its association with Italy, particularly Naples.
loads . . . back: kidney stones. *lethargies:* inertia. *palsies:*
paralysis. *and the like:* for the additional diseases listed
in Q's more elaborate version of this speech, see the
indented passage following (lines 19.1–19.8).
5. Incurable syphilis, and the shriveled absolute possession (as of property) of skin disease.
6. *Thou idle . . . flaps:* You insubstantial fine silk

thread, you immature patch of silk fabric.
7. Possible symptom of venereal disease.
8. A paradox and distinct improbability: a fool curing a
madman.
9. Jupiter made himself into a bull to rape Europa; but
Menelaus is bull-like for almost the opposite reason—
he has the horns of a cuckold.
1. A convenient tool (the shoehorn, suggested by the
cuckold's horn, was sometimes worn on "a chain")
available to serve Agamemnon; also, always underfoot.
2. Polecat (proverbially lecherous and stinking).

55 without a roe,° I would not care; but to be Menelaus!—I would   *(of no value)*
conspire against destiny. Ask me not what I would be if I were
not Thersites, for I care not to be° the louse of a lazar, so³ I   *wouldn't mind being*
were not Menelaus.—Hey-day, sprites and fires.⁴

    Enter HECTOR, AJAX, AGAMEMNON, ULYSSES, NESTOR,
    [MENELAUS, TROILUS,] *and* DIOMEDES, *with lights*

AGAMEMNON   We go wrong, we go wrong.

AJAX   No, yonder 'tis:
There, where we see the light.

60 HECTOR   I trouble you.

AJAX   No, not a whit.

    Enter ACHILLES

ULYSSES   Here comes himself° to guide you.   *the man himself*

ACHILLES   Welcome, brave Hector. Welcome, princes all.

AGAMEMNON [*to* HECTOR]   So now, fair prince of Troy, I bid good night.
Ajax commands the guard to tend on you.

65 HECTOR   Thanks and good night to the Greeks' general.

MENELAUS   Good night, my lord.

HECTOR   Good night, sweet Lord Menelaus.

THERSITES [*aside*]   Sweet draught!⁵ 'Sweet', quoth a?° Sweet   *he*
sink,° sweet sewer.   *cesspool*

ACHILLES   Good night and welcome both at once, to those
70 That go or tarry.

AGAMEMNON   Good night.

    Exeunt AGAMEMNON [*and*] MENELAUS

ACHILLES   Old Nestor tarries, and you too, Diomed.
Keep Hector company an hour or two.

DIOMEDES   I cannot, lord. I have important business
75 The tide° whereof is now.—Good night, great Hector.   *time*

HECTOR   Give me your hand.

ULYSSES [*aside to* TROILUS]   Follow his torch, he goes to Calchas' tent.
I'll keep you company.

TROILUS [*aside*]   Sweet sir, you honour me.

HECTOR [*to* DIOMEDES]   And so good night.

ACHILLES   Come, come, enter my tent.

    Exeunt [DIOMEDES, *followed by* ULYSSES *and* TROILUS,
    at one door; and ACHILLES, HECTOR, AJAX, *and* NESTOR
    at another door]

80 THERSITES   That same Diomed's a false-hearted rogue, a most
unjust knave. I will no more trust him when he leers° than I   *smiles*
will a serpent when he hisses. He will spend his mouth and
promise like Brabbler the hound, but when he performs astronomers foretell it: that is prodigious, there will come some
85 change.⁶ The sun borrows of the moon⁷ when Diomed keeps
his word. I will rather leave to see Hector than not to dog him.⁸
They say he keeps a Trojan drab,° and uses the traitor Calchas   *whore*
his tent. I'll after.—Nothing but lechery! All incontinent varlets!   *Exit*

---

3. The louse of a leper, as long as.
4. The Greeks approach with torches, suggesting night;
Thersites imagines them to be light-bearing spirits.
5. Drink; team of beasts used for pulling wagons;
cesspool, toilet.
6. *He will . . . change:* He will bark and "promise" (that
there is prey) like a hound that is noisy (quarrelsome),
even when off the scent, but when he actually "per-

forms" (acts in good faith, keeps his word), astronomers
make predictions on that basis: it is such a rare event that
they consider it an ominous warning of a cosmic happening (often indicative of massive political upheaval).
7. It was well known that the moon's light was merely
a reflection of the sun's.
8. I'll stop seeing Hector rather than give up tailing
Diomedes.

5.2

Enter DIOMEDES

DIOMEDES   What, are you up here? Ho! Speak!

CALCHAS [*at the door*]   Who calls?

DIOMEDES   Diomed. Calchas, I think. Where's your daughter?

CALCHAS [*at the door*]   She comes to you.

Enter TROILUS *and* ULYSSES [*unseen*]

5   ULYSSES [*aside*]   Stand where the torch may not discover° us.   disclose

TROILUS [*aside*]   Cressid comes forth to him.

Enter CRESSIDA

DIOMEDES   How now, my charge?

CRESSIDA   Now, my sweet guardian. Hark, a word with you.

[*She whispers to him.*]

[*Enter* THERSITES, *unseen*]

TROILUS [*aside*]   Yea, so familiar?

ULYSSES [*aside*]   She will sing any man at first sight.¹

10   THERSITES [*aside*]   And any man may sing her, if he can take her

clef. She's noted.²

DIOMEDES   Will you remember?

CRESSIDA   Remember? Yes.

DIOMEDES   Nay, but do then,

15   And let your mind be coupled with your words.

TROILUS [*aside*]   What should she remember?

ULYSSES [*aside*]   List!°   Listen

CRESSIDA   Sweet honey Greek, tempt me no more to folly.°   promiscuity

THERSITES [*aside*]   Roguery.

20   DIOMEDES   Nay, then!

CRESSIDA   I'll tell you what—

DIOMEDES   Fo, fo! Come, tell a pin.° You are forsworn.   tell me nothing

CRESSIDA   In faith, I cannot.° What would you have me do?   do as I promised

THERSITES [*aside*]   A juggling trick: to be secretly open.³

25   DIOMEDES   What did you swear you would bestow on me?

CRESSIDA   I prithee, do not hold me to mine oath.

Bid me do anything but that, sweet Greek.

DIOMEDES   Good night.

TROILUS [*aside*]   Hold, patience!

ULYSSES [*aside*]   How now, Trojan?

CRESSIDA   Diomed.

30   DIOMEDES   No, no, good night. I'll be your fool no more.

TROILUS [*aside*]   Thy better must.°   (be Cressida's fool)

CRESSIDA   Hark, one word in your ear.

[*She whispers to him*]

TROILUS [*aside*]   O plague and madness!

ULYSSES [*aside*]   You are movèd, Prince. Let us depart, I pray you,

35   Lest your displeasure should enlarge itself

To wrathful terms. This place is dangerous,

The time right deadly. I beseech you go.

TROILUS [*aside*]   Behold, I pray you.

ULYSSES [*aside*]   Nay, good my lord, go off.

You flow° to great distraction. Come, my lord.   rise; flood

TROILUS [*aside*]   I prithee, stay.

5.2 Location: Outside Calchas's tent.
1. As in sight reading of music; Cressida does not need
to know the man beforehand to play (upon) him.
2. *if . . . noted:* if he can take her musical key (also, her

cleft, or pudenda). She's like music written down; she's
notorious.
3. *juggling:* often meant sexual dexterity. *open:* public;
available for sexual intercourse.

40 ULYSSES [*aside*]   You have not patience. Come.

TROILUS [*aside*]   I pray you, stay. By hell and all hell's torments,
   I will not speak a word.

DIOMEDES   And so good night.

CRESSIDA   Nay, but you part in anger.

TROILUS [*aside*]   Doth that grieve thee?
   O withered truth!

ULYSSES [*aside*]   Why, how now, lord?

TROILUS [*aside*]   By Jove,
45   I will be patient.

       [DIOMEDES *starts to go*]

CRESSIDA   Guardian! Why, Greek!

DIOMEDES   Fo, fo! Adieu. You palter.°   *equivocate*

CRESSIDA   In faith, I do not. Come hither once again.

ULYSSES [*aside*]   You shake, my lord, at something. Will you go?
   You will break out.

TROILUS [*aside*]   She strokes his cheek.

50 ULYSSES [*aside*]   Come, come.

TROILUS [*aside*]   Nay, stay. By Jove, I will not speak a word.
   There is between my will and all offences°   *any bad deeds*
   A guard° of patience. Stay a little while.   *barrier*

THERSITES [*aside*]   How the devil Luxury° with his fat rump and   *lust*
55   potato[4] finger tickles these together! Fry, lechery, fry.[5]

DIOMEDES   But will you then?

CRESSIDA   In faith, I will, la. Never trust me else.

DIOMEDES   Give me some token for the surety of it.

CRESSIDA   I'll fetch you one.   *Exit*

60 ULYSSES [*aside*]   You have sworn patience.

TROILUS [*aside*]   Fear me not, sweet lord.
   I will not be myself, nor have cognition°   *awareness*
   Of what I feel. I am all patience.

       Enter CRESSIDA [*with Troilus' sleeve*]

THERSITES [*aside*]   Now the pledge! Now, now, now.

65 CRESSIDA   Here Diomed, keep this sleeve.

TROILUS [*aside*]   O beauty, where is thy faith?

ULYSSES [*aside*]   My lord.

TROILUS [*aside*]   I will be patient; outwardly I will.

CRESSIDA   You look upon that sleeve. Behold it well.
70   He loved me—O false wench!—give't me again.

       [*She takes it back*]

DIOMEDES   Whose was't?

CRESSIDA   It is no matter, now I ha't again.
   I will not meet with you tomorrow night.
   I prithee, Diomed, visit me no more.

75 THERSITES [*aside*]   Now she sharpens.[6] Well said, whetstone.

DIOMEDES   I shall have it.

CRESSIDA   What, this?

DIOMEDES   Ay, that.

CRESSIDA   O all you gods! O pretty pretty pledge!
80   Thy master now lies thinking on his bed
   Of thee and me, and sighs, and takes my glove
   And gives memorial° dainty kisses to it—   *in remembrance*

---

4. The Spanish, or sweet, potato was thought to be an aphrodisiac.

5. In the fires of lust and of hell.

6. Becomes harsh; whets his desire.

DIOMEDES   As I kiss thee.

    [*He snatches the sleeve*]

CRESSIDA   Nay, do not snatch it from me.
He that takes that doth take my heart withal.

85 DIOMEDES   I had your heart before; this follows it.

TROILUS [*aside*]   I did swear patience.

CRESSIDA   You shall not have it, Diomed. Faith, you shall not.
I'll give you something else.

DIOMEDES   I will have this. Whose was it?

CRESSIDA   It is no matter.

DIOMEDES   Come, tell me whose it was?

90 CRESSIDA   'Twas one's that loved me better than you will.
But now you have it, take it.

DIOMEDES   Whose was it?

CRESSIDA   By all Diana's waiting-women[7] yond,
And by herself, I will not tell you whose.

DIOMEDES   Tomorrow will I wear it on my helm,

95 And grieve° his spirit that dares not challenge it.   *afflict*

TROILUS [*aside*]   Wert thou the devil and wor'st it on thy horn,
It should be challenged.

CRESSIDA   Well, well, 'tis done, 'tis past—and yet it is not.
I will not keep my word.

DIOMEDES   Why then, farewell.

100 Thou never shalt mock Diomed again.

CRESSIDA   You shall not go. One cannot speak a word
But it straight starts you.°   *makes you run off*

DIOMEDES   I do not like this fooling.

TROILUS [*aside*]   Nor I, by Pluto—but that that likes° not you   *pleases*
Pleases me best.

DIOMEDES   What, shall I come? The hour—

105 CRESSIDA   Ay, come. O Jove, do come. I shall be plagued.[8]

DIOMEDES   Farewell till then.

CRESSIDA   Good night. I prithee, come.

    Exit [DIOMEDES]

Troilus, farewell. One eye yet looks on thee,
But with my heart the other eye doth see.
Ah, poor our° sex! This fault in us I find: *our poor*

110 The error of our eye directs our mind.
What error° leads must err. O then conclude: *wandering*
Minds swayed by eyes are full of turpitude.   *Exit*

THERSITES [*aside*]   A proof of strength she could not publish more[9]
Unless she said, 'My mind is now turned whore'.

ULYSSES   All's done, my lord.

TROILUS   It is.

115 ULYSSES   Why stay we then?

TROILUS   To make a recordation to my soul
Of every syllable that here was spoke.
But if I tell how these two did co-act,
Shall I not lie in publishing a truth?

120 Sith yet there is a credence in my heart,
An esperance° so obstinately strong,   *hope*

---

7. The stars (Diana being the goddess of the moon and, ironically, of chastity).
8. Vexed; teased (but also alluding to her eventual fate in late medieval narrative, as a leper). See the Introduction.
9. She could not make a strong proof known more clearly.

	That doth invert th'attest° of eyes and ears,	*reverse the testimony*
	As if those organs had deceptious° functions	*deceptive*
	Created only to calumniate.	
	Was Cressid here?	
125	ULYSSES I cannot conjure,° Trojan.	*produce a ghost*
	TROILUS She was not, sure.	
	ULYSSES Most sure, she was.	
	TROILUS Why, my negation hath no taste of madness.	
	ULYSSES Nor mine, my lord. Cressid was here but now.	
	TROILUS Let it not be believed, for° womanhood.	*for the sake of*
130	Think: we had mothers. Do not give advantage	
	To stubborn critics, apt without a theme	
	For depravation° to square the general sex	*denigration*
	By Cressid's rule.[1] Rather, think this not Cressid.	
	ULYSSES What hath she done, Prince, that can soil our mothers?	
135	TROILUS Nothing at all, unless that this were she.	
	THERSITES [aside] Will a swagger himself out on's own eyes?[2]	
	TROILUS This, she? No, this is Diomed's Cressida.	
	If beauty have a soul, this is not she.	
	If souls guide vows, if vows be sanctimonies,°	*sacred things*
140	If sanctimony° be the gods' delight,	*sanctity*
	If there be rule in unity itself,°	*unity is indivisible*
	This is not she. O madness of discourse,°	*reason*
	That cause[3] sets up with and against thyself!	
	Bifold authority, where reason can revolt	
145	Without perdition, and loss assume all reason	
	Without revolt![4] This is and is not Cressid.	
	Within my soul there doth conduce° a fight	*come together*
	Of this strange nature, that a thing inseparate°	*indivisible*
	Divides more wider than the sky and earth,	
150	And yet the spacious breadth of this division	
	Admits no orifex° for a point as subtle°	*orifice / fine*
	As Ariachne's[5] broken woof° to enter.	*weaving thread*
	Instance,° O instance, strong as Pluto's gates:	*Evidence*
	Cressid is mine, tied with the bonds of heaven.	
155	Instance, O instance, strong as heaven itself:	
	The bonds of heaven are slipped, dissolved, and loosed,	
	And with another knot, five-finger-tied,[6]	
	The fractions° of her faith, orts° of her love,	*pieces / leftover scraps*
	The fragments, scraps, the bits and greasy relics	
160	Of her o'er-eaten° faith, are bound to Diomed.	*eaten-away; surfeited*
	ULYSSES May worthy Troilus e'en be half attached	
	With that which here his passion doth express?[7]	
	TROILUS Ay, Greek, and that shall be divulgèd well	

1. to square . . . rule: to measure all women by the standard of Cressida.
2. Will he bluster himself out of (the evidence of) his own eyes?
3. Case; plea (where, here, defendant and plaintiff are one).
4. Bifold . . . revolt: The meaning is obscure. Perhaps: Divided authority, where reason (belief in the testimony of the senses) can revolt against itself (by claiming that this is not in fact Cressida) without being accused of loss of reason ("perdition"); and where loss of reason (inability to trust the senses), without rebelling against reason, can lay claim to being the highest form of reason precisely

because the sensual evidence, which ought to be the highest form of reason, lies (because this cannot be Cressida).
5. A conflation of Arachne the weaver, turned into a spider by Athena for overweening pride in her work, and Ariadne, who gave Theseus a ball of thread to mark his way out of the Labyrinth of her father.
6. United by human hands (Cressida's and Diomedes'), as opposed to "the bonds of heaven" (line 156); evilly consummated (alluding to the devil's five fingers, symbolizing the steps to lechery).
7. May . . . express: Can worthy Troilus be even half as affected as he seems to be?

In characters as red as Mars his° heart   Mars's
165   Inflamed with Venus. Never did young man fancy°   love
With so eternal and so fixed a soul.
Hark, Greek: as much as I do Cressid love,
So much by weight hate I her Diomed.
That sleeve is mine that he'll bear in his helm.
170   Were it a casque° composed by Vulcan's[8] skill,   helmet
My sword should bite it. Not the dreadful spout
Which shipmen do the hurricano° call,   waterspout
Constringed° in mass by the almighty sun,   Drawn together
Shall dizzy° with more clamour Neptune's ear   stun
175   In his descent, than shall my prompted° sword   eager
Falling on Diomed.
THERSITES [aside]   He'll tickle it for his concupy.[9]
TROILUS   O Cressid, O false Cressid! False, false, false.
Let all untruths stand by° thy stainèd name,   be compared with
And they'll seem glorious.
180   ULYSSES   O contain yourself.
Your passion draws ears hither.
            Enter AENEAS
AENEAS [to TROILUS]   I have been seeking you this hour, my lord.
Hector by this° is arming him in Troy.   by this time
Ajax your guard stays to conduct you home.
185   TROILUS   Have° with you, Prince.—My courteous lord, adieu.—   I shall come
Farewell, revolted fair; and Diomed,
Stand fast and wear a castle° on thy head.   strong defense
ULYSSES   I'll bring you to the gates.
TROILUS   Accept distracted thanks.
            Exeunt TROILUS, AENEAS, and ULYSSES
THERSITES   Would I could meet that rogue Diomed! I would
190   croak like a raven.[1] I would bode,° I would bode. Patroclus will   foretell evil
give me anything for the intelligence° of this whore. The parrot   secret information
will not do more for an almond[2] than he for a commodious
drab.° Lechery, lechery, still wars and lechery! Nothing else   willing whore
holds fashion. A burning devil° take them!   Exit   venereal disease

5.3

            Enter HECTOR [armed] and ANDROMACHE
ANDROMACHE   When was my lord so much ungently tempered
To stop his ears against admonishment?
Unarm, unarm, and do not fight today.
HECTOR   You train° me to offend you. Get you in.   teach
5   By all the everlasting gods, I'll go.
ANDROMACHE   My dreams will sure prove ominous to the day.°   true omens of the day
HECTOR   No more, I say.
            Enter CASSANDRA
CASSANDRA   Where is my brother Hector?
ANDROMACHE   Here, sister, armed and bloody in intent.
Consort° with me in loud and dear° petition,   Join / earnest

---

8. Smith of the gods, Vulcan made armor for various | 1. Proverbially birds of ill omen.
classical heroes, most notably Achilles. | 2. *The parrot . . . almond:* Proverbial for a brainless
9. (Probably) Troilus will "tickle" (beat [ironic]) | passion for a trivial delicacy.
Diomedes' helmet for his lust (his concubine). | 5.3 Location: Priam's palace.

10 Pursue we him on knees—for I have dreamed
Of bloody turbulence, and this whole night
Hath nothing been but shapes and forms of slaughter.
CASSANDRA   O 'tis true.
HECTOR   Ho! Bid my trumpet sound.
CASSANDRA   No notes of sally, for the heavens, sweet brother.
15 HECTOR   Begone, I say. The gods have heard me swear.
CASSANDRA   The gods are deaf to hot and peevish° vows.   *headstrong*
They° are polluted off'rings, more abhorred   *Rash vows*
Than spotted livers° in the sacrifice.   *ruined offerings*
ANDROMACHE [*to* HECTOR]   O, be persuaded. Do not count it holy
20 To hurt by being just.° It is as lawful,   *true to your vow*
For we would° give much, to use violent thefts,   *Because we want to*
And rob in the behalf of charity.
CASSANDRA   It is the purpose that makes strong the vow,
But vows to every purpose must not° hold.   *do not have to*
Unarm, sweet Hector.
25 HECTOR   Hold you still,° I say.   *Stop it*
Mine honour keeps the weather[1] of my fate.
Life every man holds dear, but the dear° man   *worthy*
Holds honour far more precious-dear than life.
   Enter TROILUS [*armed*]
How now, young man, mean'st thou to fight today?
30 ANDROMACHE [*aside*]   Cassandra, call my father° to persuade.   *father-in-law*
   Exit CASSANDRA
HECTOR   No, faith, young Troilus. Doff thy harness,° youth.   *Disarm*
I am today i'th' vein of° chivalry.   *mood for*
Let grow thy sinews till their knots be strong,
And tempt not yet the brushes° of the war.   *encounters*
35 Unarm thee, go—and doubt thou not, brave boy,
I'll stand today for thee and me and Troy.
TROILUS   Brother, you have a vice of mercy in you,
Which better fits a lion[2] than a man.
HECTOR   What vice is that? Good Troilus, chide me for it.
40 TROILUS   When many times the captive° Grecian falls   *miserable*
Even in the fan and wind of your fair sword,[3]
You bid them rise and live.
HECTOR   O 'tis fair play.
TROILUS   Fool's play, by heaven, Hector.
45 HECTOR   How now! How now!
TROILUS   For th' love of all the gods,
Let's leave the hermit pity with our mother
And, when we have our armours buckled on,
The venomed vengeance ride upon our swords,
50 Spur them to ruthful° work, rein them from ruth.°   *woeful / pity*
HECTOR   Fie, savage, fie!
TROILUS   Hector, then 'tis wars.°   *then it's a true war*
HECTOR   Troilus, I would not have you fight today.
TROILUS   Who should withhold me?
Not fate, obedience, nor the hand of Mars

---

1. My honor stays to windward (in sailing, a ship windward of another takes its wind, and so gets the better of it).
2. Lions were said not to attack any animal that submitted to them.
3. The rapidly moving sword is like a fan, blowing his enemies down before he reaches them.

55 Beck'ning with fiery truncheon⁴ my retire,
Not Priamus and Hecuba on knees,
Their eyes o'er-gallèd° with recourse° of tears,   sore / repeated flow
Nor you, my brother, with your true sword drawn
Opposed to hinder me, should stop my way
60 But by my ruin.

Enter PRIAM *and* CASSANDRA

CASSANDRA Lay hold upon him, Priam, hold him fast.
He is thy crutch: now if thou loose thy stay,°   prop
Thou on him leaning and all Troy on thee,
Fall all together.

PRIAM   Come, Hector, come. Go back.
65 Thy wife hath dreamt, thy mother hath had visions,
Cassandra doth foresee, and I myself
Am like a prophet suddenly enrapt°   inspired
To tell thee that this day is ominous.
Therefore come back.

HECTOR   Aeneas is afield,
70 And I do stand engaged to many Greeks,
Even in the faith of valour,° to appear   warrior's honor
This morning to them.

PRIAM Ay, but thou shalt not go.

HECTOR [*kneeling*] I must not break my faith.
75 You know me dutiful; therefore, dear sire,
Let me not shame respect,° but give me leave   duty to a parent
To take that course, by your consent and voice,
Which you do here forbid me, royal Priam.

CASSANDRA O Priam, yield not to him.

ANDROMACHE   Do not, dear father.
80 HECTOR Andromache, I am offended with you.
Upon the love you bear me, get you in.   *Exit* ANDROMACHE

TROILUS This foolish, dreaming, superstitious girl
Makes all these bodements.°   warnings

CASSANDRA   O farewell, dear Hector.
Look how thou diest; look how thy eye turns pale;
85 Look how thy wounds do bleed at many vents.
Hark how Troy roars, how Hecuba cries out,
How poor Andromache shrills her dolours forth.
Behold: distraction, frenzy, and amazement
Like witless antics° one another meet,   buffoons
90 And all cry 'Hector, Hector's dead, O Hector!'

TROILUS Away, away!

CASSANDRA Farewell. Yet soft:° Hector, I take my leave.   wait a moment
Thou dost thyself and all our Troy deceive.   *Exit*

HECTOR [*to* PRIAM] You are amazed, my liege, at her exclaim.°   outcry
95 Go in and cheer the town. We'll forth and fight,
Do deeds of praise, and tell you them at night.

PRIAM Farewell. The gods with safety stand about thee.
[*Exeunt* PRIAM *and* HECTOR *severally.*°] *Alarum*   separately

TROILUS They are at it, hark! Proud Diomed, believe
I come to lose my arm or win my sleeve.

Enter PANDARUS

100 PANDARUS Do you hear, my lord, do you hear?

---

4. Staff of office (carried by the marshal of a formal combat).

TROILUS What now?

PANDARUS Here's a letter come from yon poor girl.

TROILUS Let me read.

       [TROILUS *reads the letter*]

PANDARUS A whoreson phthisic,° a whoreson rascally phthisic so   *consumptive cough*
105 troubles me, and the foolish fortune of this girl, and what one
thing, what another, that I shall leave you one o' these days.
And I have a rheum° in mine eyes too, and such an ache in my   *watery discharge*
bones° that unless a man were cursed I cannot tell what to   *(suggesting syphilis)*
think on't.—What says she there?

TROILUS [*tearing the letter*] Words, words, mere words, no mat-
110 ter from the heart.

Th'effect° doth operate another way.   *Her action*

Go, wind, to wind: there turn and change together.[5]

My love with words and errors° still she feeds,   *lies*

But edifies another with her deeds.

115 PANDARUS Why, but hear you—

TROILUS Hence, broker-lackey!° Ignomy° and shame   *pimp / Ignominy*

Pursue thy life, and live aye with thy name. *Exeunt* [*severally*][6]

5.4

Alarum. Enter THERSITES [*in*] *excursions*°   *advancing troops*

THERSITES Now they are clapper-clawing° one another. I'll go   *thrashing*
look on. That dissembling abominable varlet Diomed has got
that same scurvy doting foolish young knave's sleeve of Troy°   *Trojan knave's sleeve*
there in his helm. I would fain see them meet, that that same
5 young Trojan ass that loves the whore there might send that
Greekish whoremasterly villain with the sleeve back to the dissembling luxurious drab of a sleeveless errand.[1] O'th' t'other
side, the policy° of those crafty swearing rascals—that stale old   *statecraft; scheming*
mouse-eaten dry cheese Nestor and that same dog-fox° Ulys-   *crafty one*
10 ses—is proved not worth a blackberry.° They set me up° in   *proved worthless / set up*
policy that mongrel cur Ajax against that dog of as bad a kind
Achilles. And now is the cur Ajax prouder than the cur Achilles, and will not arm today—whereupon the Grecians began
to proclaim barbarism,[2] and policy grows into an ill opinion.°   *gets a bad reputation*

    Enter DIOMEDES, [*followed by*] TROILUS

15 Soft, here comes sleeve and t'other.

TROILUS [*to* DIOMEDES] Fly not, for shouldst thou take the river Styx[3]
I would swim after.

DIOMEDES   Thou dost miscall retire.°   *mistake my retreat*

I do not fly, but advantageous care°   *tactical caution*

Withdrew me from the odds of multitude. Have at thee!

    [*They fight*]

20 THERSITES Hold thy whore, Grecian! Now for thy whore, Trojan! Now the sleeve, now the sleeve!

        [*Exit* DIOMEDES, *driving in* TROILUS]

    Enter HECTOR [*behind*]

---

5. Go, empty words, into the breeze: there, along with
the air, toss about ("turn" was often used of sexual infidelity).

6. The last three lines of this scene are not in Q. A similar exchange occurs at the end of the play in both Q and
F. See indented passage after 5.11.31 and Textual Note.

5.4 Location: The rest of the play takes place on the
battlefield.

1. To the lying, lecherous slut on a pointless errand
(punning on the actual sleeve).

2. Began to set up whim and ignorance in authority
("barbarism" being normally contrasted with "Greek").

3. Even if you should enter the river of the underworld
(as prey hoping to make the hunter lose the scent).

HECTOR   What art thou, Greek? Art thou for Hector's match?
Art thou of blood° and honour?   *nobility*
THERSITES   No, no, I am a rascal, a scurvy railing knave, a very
25   filthy rogue.
HECTOR   I do believe thee: live.[4]
THERSITES   God-a-mercy,° that thou wilt believe me—   *Thank God*
                                                              [*Exit* HECTOR]
but a plague break thy neck for frighting me. What's become
of the wenching rogues? I think they have swallowed one
30   another. I would laugh at that miracle—yet in a sort lechery
eats itself. I'll seek them.   *Exit*

5.5

Enter DIOMEDES *and* SERVANTS

DIOMEDES   Go, go, my servant, take thou Troilus' horse.
Present the fair steed to my Lady Cressid.
Fellow, commend my service to her beauty.
Tell her I have chastised the amorous Trojan,
And am her knight by proof.°   *(of deeds)*
5   SERVANT   I go, my lord.   [*Exit*]
Enter AGAMEMNON

AGAMEMNON   Renew, renew! The fierce Polydamas
Hath beat down Menon; bastard Margareton
Hath Doreus prisoner,
And stands colossus-wise waving his beam°   *spearshaft*
10   Upon the pashèd° corpses of the kings   *smashed*
Epistropus and Cedius; Polixenes is slain,
Amphimacus and Thoas deadly hurt,
Patroclus ta'en or slain, and Palamedes
Sore hurt and bruised; the dreadful sagittary[1]
15   Appals our numbers.° Haste we, Diomed,   *soldiers*
To reinforcement, or we perish all.
Enter NESTOR [*with Patroclus' body*]

NESTOR   Go, bear Patroclus' body to Achilles,
And bid the snail-paced Ajax arm for shame.
                                [*Exit one or more with the body*]
There is a thousand Hectors in the field.
20   Now here he fights on Galathe his horse,
And there lacks work; anon he's there afoot,
And there they fly or die, like scalèd schools[2]
Before the belching° whale. Then is he yonder,   *spouting*
And there the strawy Greeks, ripe for his edge,°   *sword blade*
25   Fall down before him like the mower's swath.
Here, there, and everywhere he leaves and takes,[3]
Dexterity so obeying appetite
That what he will he does, and does so much
That proof° is called impossibility.   *his achievement*
Enter ULYSSES

30   ULYSSES   O courage, courage, princes! Great Achilles
Is arming, weeping, cursing, vowing vengeance.

---

4. Here Hector is at once contemptuous and merciful.   2. Scaly (armor-clad) schools of fish.
5.5   3. He spares and kills; possibly, he "leaves" the dead
1. A legendary centaurlike beast, armed with bow and   and "takes" on the living.
arrows.

Patroclus' wounds have roused his drowsy blood,
Together with his mangled Myrmidons,
That noseless, handless, hacked and chipped come to him

35 Crying on° Hector. Ajax hath lost a friend   *Complaining of*
And foams at mouth, and he is armed and at it,
Roaring for Troilus—who hath done today
Mad and fantastic execution,
Engaging and redeeming of° himself   *Risking and saving*

40 With such a careless force and forceless care°   *effortless diligence*
As if that luck, in very spite of cunning,°   *his foes' skill*
Bade him win all.

        Enter AJAX

AJAX   Troilus, thou coward Troilus!   *Exit*
DIOMEDES   Ay, there, there!   *Exit*

45 NESTOR   So, so, we draw together.°   *join forces*

        Enter ACHILLES

ACHILLES   Where is this Hector?
Come, come, thou brave boy-queller, show thy face.
Know what it is to meet Achilles angry.
Hector! Where's Hector? I will none but Hector.   *Exeunt*

5.6

        Enter AJAX

AJAX   Troilus, thou coward Troilus! Show thy head!

        Enter DIOMEDES

DIOMEDES   Troilus, I say! Where's Troilus?
AJAX   What wouldst thou?
DIOMEDES   I would correct° him.   *chastise*
AJAX   Were I the general, thou shouldst have my office

5 Ere° that correction.—Troilus, I say! What, Troilus!   *Before you should have*

        Enter TROILUS

TROILUS   O traitor Diomed! Turn thy false face, thou traitor,
And pay the life thou ow'st me for my horse.
DIOMEDES   Ha, art thou there?
AJAX   I'll fight with him alone. Stand, Diomed.

10 DIOMEDES   He is my prize; I will not look upon.°   *be a spectator*
TROILUS   Come, both you cogging° Greeks, have at you both!   *cheating*
    [*They fight.*]

        Enter HECTOR

HECTOR   Yea, Troilus? O well fought, my youngest brother!

        Exit TROILUS [*driving* DIOMEDES *and* AJAX *in*]
        Enter ACHILLES [*behind*]

ACHILLES   Now do I see thee.—Ha! Have at thee, Hector.
    [*They fight.* ACHILLES *is bested*]
HECTOR   Pause, if thou wilt.

15 ACHILLES   I do disdain thy courtesy, proud Trojan.
Be happy that my arms are out of use.°   *practice*
My rest and negligence befriends thee now;
But thou anon shalt hear of me again.
Till when, go seek thy fortune.   *Exit*
HECTOR   Fare thee well.

20 I would have been much more a fresher man
Had I expected thee.

        Enter TROILUS [*in haste*]

How now, my brother?

TROILUS Ajax hath ta'en° Aeneas. Shall it be?   *taken captive*
No, by the flame of yonder glorious heaven,
He shall not carry him. I'll be ta'en too,
25 Or bring him off.° Fate, hear me what I say: *rescue Aeneas*
I reck° not though thou end my life today.   *Exit*   *care*

Enter one in [sumptuous] armour

HECTOR Stand, stand, thou Greek! Thou art a goodly mark.°   *target*
No? Wilt thou not? I like thy armour well.
I'll frush° it and unlock the rivets all,   *smash*
But I'll be master of it.   *[Exit one in armour]*
30   Wilt thou not, beast, abide?
Why then, fly on; I'll hunt thee for thy hide.   *Exit*

5.7

Enter ACHILLES with Myrmidons

ACHILLES Come here about me, you my Myrmidons.
Mark what I say. Attend me where I wheel;°   *range*
Strike not a stroke, but keep yourselves in breath,
And when I have the bloody Hector found,
5 Empale° him with your weapons round about.   *Fence in*
In fellest° manner execute your arms.   *fiercest*
Follow me, sirs, and my proceedings eye.
It is decreed Hector the great must die.   *Exeunt*

5.8

Enter MENELAUS and PARIS, [fighting, then] THERSITES[1]

THERSITES The cuckold and the cuckold-maker are at it.—
Now, bull! Now, dog! 'Loo,[2] Paris, 'loo! Now, my double-
horned[3] Spartan! 'Loo, Paris, 'loo! The bull has the game.°   *is winning*
Ware° horns, ho!   *Exit MENELAUS, [driving in] PARIS*   *Beware*

Enter BASTARD [behind]

5 BASTARD Turn, slave, and fight.
THERSITES What art thou?
BASTARD A bastard son of Priam's.
THERSITES I am a bastard, too. I love bastards. I am bastard
begot, bastard instructed, bastard in mind, bastard in valour,
10 in everything illegitimate. One bear will not bite another, and
wherefore should one bastard? Take heed: the quarrel's most
ominous to us. If the son of a whore fight for a whore, he tempts
judgement. Farewell, bastard.   *[Exit]*
BASTARD The devil take thee, coward.   *Exit*

5.9

Enter HECTOR [dragging the one in sumptuous armour]

HECTOR *[taking off the helmet]* Most putrefièd core, so fair without,
Thy goodly armour thus hath cost thy life.
Now is my day's work done. I'll take good breath.
Rest, sword: thou hast thy fill of blood and death.

5.8
1. Most modern editions do not mark a scene break
here; this affects the numbering of the following lines
and scenes. See Textual Note.

2. Halloo (shout to encourage dogs chasing game or in
bullbaiting).
3 Two-horned, like a bull; horned because a cuckold.
5.9

[*He disarms.*]
Enter ACHILLES *and his Myrmidons* [*surrounding*
HECTOR]

5 ACHILLES   Look, Hector, how the sun begins to set,
How ugly night comes breathing at his heels.
Even with the veil¹ and dark'ning of the sun
To close the day up, Hector's life is done.
HECTOR   I am unarmed. Forgo this vantage, Greek.
10 ACHILLES   Strike, fellows, strike! This is the man I seek.
[*The Myrmidons kill* HECTOR]
So, Ilium, fall thou. Now, Troy, sink down.
Here lies thy heart, thy sinews, and thy bone.—
On, Myrmidons, and cry you all amain,°   *with full force*
'Achilles hath the mighty Hector slain!'
[*A*] *retreat* [*is sounded*]
15 Hark, a retire upon our Grecian part.
[*Another retreat is sounded*]
A MYRMIDON   The Trojan trumpets sound the like, my lord.
ACHILLES   The dragon wing of night o'erspreads the earth
And, stickler°-like, the armies separates.   *referee (in combat)*
My half-supped° sword, that frankly° would have fed,   *half-satisfied / freely*
20 Pleased with this dainty bait,° thus goes to bed.   *snack*
[*He sheathes his sword*]
Come, tie his body to my horse's tail.
Along the field I will the Trojan trail.   *Exeunt* [*dragging the bodies*]

5.10

[*A*] *retreat* [*is*] *sound*[*ed*]. *Enter* AGAMEMNON, AJAX,
MENELAUS, NESTOR, DIOMEDES, *and the rest, marching.*
[*A*] *shout* [*within*]
AGAMEMNON   Hark, hark! What shout is that?
NESTOR   Peace, drums.
MYRMIDONS (*within*)   Achilles!
Achilles! Hector's slain! Achilles!
DIOMEDES   The bruit° is: Hector's slain, and by Achilles.   *report*
AJAX   If it be so, yet bragless let it be.
5 Great Hector was a man as good as he.
AGAMEMNON   March patiently along. Let one be sent
To pray Achilles see us at our tent.
If in his death the gods have us befriended,
Great Troy is ours, and our sharp° wars are ended.   *fierce*
Exeunt [*marching*]

5.11

Enter AENEAS, PARIS, ANTENOR, *and* DEIPHOBUS
AENEAS   Stand, ho! Yet are we masters of the field.
Never go home; here starve¹ we out the night.
Enter TROILUS
TROILUS   Hector is slain.
ALL THE OTHERS   Hector? The gods forbid.

---

1. At the same time as the setting.
5.11

1. Wait in discomfort; outlast, kill by starvation (the
night being imagined as a city under siege).

TROILUS He's dead, and at the murderer's horse's tail
5   In beastly sort° dragged through the shameful field.   *manner*
       Frown on, you heavens; effect your rage with speed;
       Sit, gods, upon your thrones, and smite at Troy.
       I say, at once: let your brief plagues be mercy,[2]
       And linger not our sure destructions on.
10 AENEAS My lord, you do discomfort all the host.°   *army*
    TROILUS You understand me not that tell me so.
       I do not speak of flight, of fear of death,
       But dare all imminence that gods and men
       Address their dangers in.[3] Hector is gone.
15   Who shall tell Priam so, or Hecuba?
       Let him that will a screech-owl aye° be called   *voice of doom always*
       Go into Troy and say their Hector's dead.
       There is a word° will Priam turn to stone,   *sentence*
       Make wells and Niobes[4] of the maids and wives,
20   Cold statues of the youth, and in a word
       Scare Troy out of itself. But march away.
       Hector is dead; there is no more to say.
       Stay yet.—You vile abominable tents
       Thus proudly pitched upon our Phrygian plains,
25   Let Titan° rise as early as he dare,   *sun god Hyperion*
       I'll through and through you! And thou great-sized coward,°   *Achilles*
       No space of earth shall sunder our two hates.
       I'll haunt thee like a wicked conscience still,
       That mouldeth goblins swift as frenzy's thoughts.
30   Strike a free march! To Troy with comfort° go: *this one comfort*
       Hope of revenge shall hide our inward woe.   [*Exeunt marching*][5]
          [*Enter* PANDARUS]
31.1   PANDARUS But hear you, hear you.
       TROILUS Hence, broker-lackey. [*Strikes him*] Ignomy and shame
          Pursue thy like, and live aye with thy name.   Exeunt [*all but* PANDARUS]
       PANDARUS A goodly medicine for my aching bones. O
31.5   world, world, world!—thus is the poor agent despised.
          O traitors and bawds, how earnestly are you set a° work,   *to*
          and how ill requited! Why should our endeavour be so
          desired and the performance so loathed? What verse
          for it? What instance° for it? Let me see,   *traditional saying*
31.10   Full merrily the humble-bee doth sing
             Till he hath lost his honey and his sting,
             And being once subdued in armèd tail,[6]
             Sweet honey and sweet notes together fail.
          Good traders in the flesh, set this in your painted cloths:[7]
31.15   As many as be here of Pandar's hall,°   *guild hall*
             Your eyes, half out,[8] weep out at Pandar's fall.
             Or if you cannot weep, yet give some groans,
             Though not for me, yet for your aching bones.°   *(from syphilis)*
             Brethren and sisters of the hold-door trade,°   *Pimps and bawds*

2. Be mercifully quick in destruction.
3. *But . . . in:* But dare all impending danger that gods
and men prepare for me.
4. Mythical Queen of Thebes, who wept so much at
the murder of her children by the gods that the gods
turned her into a statue that flowed with water.
5. For the extended conclusion with Pandarus's epilogue, see indented passage below (lines 31.1–31.24).

The exit marked here is deferred until line 31.3. For discussion, see the Textual Note and Introduction.
6. And having lost his sting: alluding to impotence
caused by venereal disease.
7. Inexpensive substitutes for tapestries, often including moralistic inscriptions.
8. Half-blinded by venereal disease.

31.20 *Some two months hence my will shall here be made.*[9]
It should be now, but that my fear is this:
Some gallèd goose of Winchester would hiss.[1]
Till then I'll sweat[2] *and seek about for eases,*
And at that time bequeath you my diseases.   Exit

9. "Here" is possibly a reference to the stage of the Globe and hence the promise of a sequel that never materialized; it has also been taken to refer to an Inn of Court, where young men studied law, a plausible place to make a "will" and thus hypothesized by some scholars to be the location of the first performance. See the Introduction.

1. A prostitute or customer afflicted with venereal disease, from the diocese of Winchester (which had jurisdiction over Southwark, home of both the brothels and the Globe), would disapprove—of the will and/or the play.
2. Usual treatment for venereal disease.

The Sonnets and
"A Lover's Complaint"

Shakespeare's plays often seem indifferent to high-cultural rules of construction. His sonnets (composed from about 1591 to 1604, possibly revised thereafter, and published in 1609) are the opposite: they faithfully adhere to the norms of an international tradition inspired by the fourteenth-century Italian poet Petrarch. Paradoxically, the very strictness of sonnet structure is the condition of possibility for Shakespeare's originality. The rigor of the form encourages a logical, rationalist approach to the standard topic of the Renaissance sonnet—love and its attendant emotions (desire, jealousy, and the like). The conflict between passionate feelings and a mobile intellect often skeptical of those feelings accordingly becomes a central theme of the poems. And that mobility is conveyed through a linguistic virtuosity marked by metaphors and puns that can work either with or against the larger structure of the sonnet.

Thematically, the sonnets are equally distinctive. The typical object of love—the unapproachable, exalted lady—is displaced so as to make room for a daring representation of homoerotic and adulterous passions. Almost the entire sequence can be divided along these lines. Sonnets 1–126 recount the speaker's idealized, sometimes painful love for a femininely beautiful, well-born male youth; 127–52 his unidealized, ultimately bitter affair with a darkly attractive, unaristocratic "mistress"—where this term invokes, however ironically, the vocabulary of courtly love rather than the derogatory modern meaning. The two love relationships are complicated by a lovers' triangle (40–42, 133–34, 144) and a poetic rival for the youth's affections (78–80, 82–86). These topics provide the occasion for a complex meditation upon a range of issues—time, nature, human mortality, economics, perhaps class and race, and, not least, an artistic immortality. And this self-referential reflection upon the sonnets' very composition is heightened by the reader's intense proximity to a speaker who is and is not Shakespeare.

The poems are best approached by locating their formal specificity against the background of two artistic practices through which Shakespeare came to the poems: his work in the theater, and the prior tradition of the sonnet. The standard verse line of Shakespearean drama and Shakespearean sonnet alike is iambic pentameter. But there the similarity ends. Roughly two-thirds of all lines in the plays are composed in unrhymed iambic pentameter, or blank verse; less than 10 percent employ rhyme. By contrast, Shakespeare's sonnets almost always consist of fourteen rhyming iambic-pentameter lines. Blank verse easily accommodates enjambment, the runover of sense from one line to the next. Rhyme encourages congruence between syntax and verse line: a unit of meaning ends when the line does. Blank verse supports the narrative logic of Shakespearean drama, rhyme the lyric impulse of the Shakespearean sonnet. You watch a play to see what happens next; you read a sonnet to discover the original expression of feelings and thoughts. Language is thus more obtrusively part of meaning in poetry than in drama.

It is easy to find exceptions to these claims. The crucial consideration, however, is the significance for Shakespeare of inherited conventions. The sonnet originated in Italy a century before Petrarch. Petrarch's decisive poetic sequence chronicles the author's passionately complex emotions in relation to his beloved Laura. The Petrarchan sonnet is divided into two frequently contrasting units, an octave (eight lines) and a sestet (six lines), by its rhyme scheme—*abbaabba cdecde,* where each letter represents a line and a repeated letter indicates a rhyme. The Petrarchan mode reached England by the early sixteenth century in the works of Wyatt and Surrey, whose modified rhyme scheme (*abab cdcd efef gg*), later taken over by Shakespeare, divides the sonnet into three quatrains (four-line groupings) and a couplet. This organization offers greater conceptual range than does the Petrarchan model. The quatrains can operate in parallel, represent steps in a logical argument, or contradict each other. They may be grouped into larger units of eight-and-four lines or eight-and-six lines (if the couplet is included) that are set against each other, with the result in the latter case that the Petrarchan octave-sestet structure is approximated. In turn, the epigrammatic concluding couplet, whose analytical tendencies contrast with the more experiential approach of at least the first two quatrains, can summarize the preceding lines, generalize from them, draw appropriate inferences, contribute a new thought, or even reverse the preceding argument.

Sonnet structure often guides Shakespeare's pervasive use of imagery and metaphor. In Sonnet 73, each quatrain pursues a different metaphor as part of a single argument:

> That time of year thou mayst in me behold
> When yellow leaves, or none, or few, do hang
> Upon those boughs which shake against the cold,
> Bare ruined choirs where late the sweet birds sang.
> In me thou seest the twilight of such day
> As after sunset fadeth in the west,
> Which by and by black night doth take away,
> Death's second self, that seals up all in rest.
> In me thou seest the glowing of such fire
> That on the ashes of his youth doth lie
> As the death-bed whereon it must expire,
> Consumed with that which it was nourished by.
>   This thou perceiv'st, which makes thy love more strong,
>   To love that well which thou must leave ere long.

The evocation of fall in the opening quatrain nostalgically communicates the sadness of aging. Enjambment supports the imagistic pattern: it causes meaning to "hang" in the balance at the end of the line, just as "yellow leaves . . . do hang / Upon those boughs." The "yellow leaves" are also leaves of a book, "bare ruined choirs," or quires (manuscript gatherings). Similarly, the birds' former song, together with the primary meaning of "choirs" (the part of a church where the choir sings), may refer to the speaker's own voice and hence to a lost poetic creativity. In short, the experience of aging is compared to the annual movement toward colder seasons and to the decline of artistic inspiration. In the second quatrain, the unit of time constricts: "That time of year" is replaced by "the twilight of such day." Although, like autumn, sunset is a natural process, it is not an organic one. Emphasis accordingly shifts away from bodily degeneration. These lines also look forward in a way the first quatrain does not. Twilight is taken away by "black night . . . , / Death's second self, that seals up all in rest." The rest that night brings is a source of comfort, but night is compared with death, and the syntax, at odds with the literal meaning, suggests that it is death rather than night "that seals up all in [eternal] rest."

The third quatrain opens like the second, with "In me thou seest," a phrase also partly anticipated in the first line of the poem. This repetition reinforces the parallelism among the quatrains and suggests that the poem proceeds less by narrative progression than by thematic variation. Yet this quatrain, while highlighting the transition from aging to mortality, narrows time further, to the "glowing" fire, in effect abandoning the temporal model of the first two quatrains for a spatial metaphor. Only the ashes remain from the fire's and, by implication, the speaker's "youth" (line 10); they are also the fire's and the speaker's "death-bed" (line 11). The earlier idealization of youth, now reduced to "ashes," has disappeared; conversely, although the fire of old age no longer rages, it is still "glowing"—it still gives off heat. The present is thus a continuation of the past. Furthermore, the metaphorical relationship is reversed. The dying fire is a metaphor for human aging, but that aging becomes a metaphor for the dying fire.

Paradoxically, the fire is "Consumed with that which it was nourished by"; it is "consumed" (or choked) by—and along with—the very ashes that, as fuel, previously "nourished" it. Normally, the fire consumes the fuel, not the other way around. Both "consumed" and "nourished" metaphorically explain the already metaphorical fire, which they connect back to humanity through their allusions to eating. The speaker's fiery passion for the youth he addresses nourished him when he was young but consumes him now. Indeed, the line structurally enacts the tacit thematic rejection of a temporal model of decline. It is an example of chiasmus, in which the elements of the first half ("Consumed . . . that") are repeated in reverse order in the second half ("which . . . nourished"), thus producing an *abba* semantic pattern. Accordingly, this quatrain has no equivalent to the earlier "cold" or "night," which are metaphorically responsible for the approach of death. Life and death have the same source.

All three quatrains employ cyclical metaphors of life, death, and rebirth. But the cycle remains incomplete. Autumn does not lead to spring or night to day. The "long-lived phoenix" (19.4), the legendary self-resurrecting bird that dies in flames and is reborn from the ashes, doesn't quite appear. Perhaps these suppressed allusions to cyclical patterns raise and then frustrate expectations, denying the consolation of the future. The concluding couplet, which moves away from metaphor and toward a new idea, suggests this interpretation. Recognizing the speaker's literally consuming passion makes the youth's "love more strong" (line 13). The youth, therefore, loves well what he "must leave ere long" (line 14)—explicitly, the speaker; implicitly, his own life, partly because that leaving recalls the "yellow leaves" with which the poem opened. There is no answer to the destructive power of time, but that power is partly counteracted by love.

Sonnet 73 suggests how conformity to sonnet convention can enable a thoughtful interplay among time, love, death, and art. Sonnet 81, on the other hand, offers a radical disjunction of syntax and rhyme scheme: almost any two consecutive lines can produce a complete sentence, depending on how you punctuate:

> And toungs to be, your beeing shall rehearse,
> When all the breathers of this world are dead,
> You still shall liue (such vertue hath my Pen).
> (81.11–13)

This three-line sequence, presented as it appears in the first edition of 1609, runs over the end of a quatrain but nonetheless produces two possible sentences that are grammatically correct and semantically effective (lines 11 and 12 or 12 and 13). Conceptually, the unorthodox move here is the implicit equation of the speaker with his social superior, the youth. The poet's literary prowess promises enduring renown for both the writer and his subject. Or does it? If you take lines 11 and 12 together, as modern editions do, the emphasis falls on "dead." But if you instead take lines 12 and 13 as a unit, the center of interest becomes "liue" and "my Pen." The poem thus promises both death and immortality, just as the wordplay on "rehearse" (line 11) predicts a future in which the youth is both still spoken about and literally re-hearsed.

The relationship between formal and thematic innovation can also be approached by considering the sonnets as a sequence. English enthusiasm for such sequences was triggered by the posthumous printing of Sir Philip Sidney's collection *Astrophel and Stella* (1591). Sonnets also circulated in manuscript form, since print culture was often considered beneath the dignity of (would-be) gentlemen or courtier-poets. The vogue for sonnet sequences responded to poets' ambitions as well as to the gender politics of the late Elizabethan court. Middle-class writers, for instance, sought financial assistance for their work by praising their aristocratic patrons. Expressions of love in this hierarchical relationship may be less indications of deep feeling than competitive strategies of advancement. Shakespeare's rival poet sonnets seem to convert this competition into literary theme. In general, then, it is often hard to determine where authentic sentiment ends and professional calculation begins.

The sonnet sequence itself is not the only larger formal category, however. When Shakespeare's sonnets first appeared in print, they were immediately followed in the same collection by "A Lover's Complaint." This work belongs to the genre of complaint poetry in which a woman laments her (usually) sexual ruin amid doleful reflections on life. Between 1593 and 1596, six poets published works consisting of a sonnet sequence, a brief intermediate piece usually based on ancient Greek form or subject matter (Cupid, for example), and a concluding complaint. The sonnets section of one such work, from which Shakespeare probably borrowed, is addressed to an attractive male youth. Another poet anticipates Shakespeare's sequence in dividing his sonnets into two main groups. It would be wrong to overstate the homogeneity of this mini-tradition. Nonetheless, the 1609 Quarto—a sonnet sequence divided into two parts, the first concerning a beautiful male youth and the second a woman; two concluding sonnets on Cupid; and a poetic complaint—is less miscellaneous collection than multi-generic form. Recent critics have had no trouble in demonstrating such connections between Shakespeare's sonnets and "A Lover's Complaint"—voyeurism, seduction, abandonment, and a similar cast of characters, among others. Nonetheless, the differences are obvious—for instance, the longer poem's ornamental, archaic diction and lack of emotional intensity. More important, the most detailed scholarship on the subject argues powerfully that not Shakespeare but John Davies of Hereford wrote "A Lover's Complaint." If so, as seems likely, Shakespeare could not have authorized the publication of the 1609 Quarto.

This line of reasoning raises questions about the internal organization of the sonnets as well (although not about their authorship). It has been suggested that the division of the sequence into two main groups is unwarranted. Most of the poems are not explicitly about either the youth or the mistress and do not even designate the sex of the person discussed. Only their relative position in the collection has produced the standard simplification adopted here. Furthermore, the sequence as a whole is relatively uninterested in plot. The poems to the mistress in particular show little sign of organization or process, combining occasional affection with chaos, bitterness, self-abasement, shame, unwilling sexual desire, and self-loathing. Perhaps, in 1609, they had not yet been placed in a particular order; perhaps they were intended for a separate collection. But the first 126 sonnets, too, evince only intermittent interest in linear movement, emphasizing longing, jealousy, and a fear of separation, while anticipating both the desire and the anguish of the subsequent poems.

Nonetheless, many of the sonnets are carefully ordered in pairs or longer groups. More important, the two main sections of the sequence are of compelling thematic interest. For the two centuries ending about a generation ago, the homoerotic attachment to the youth, now a routine part of critical discussion, provoked revulsion or denial. Sonnet 20 was—and still is—at the center of the debate:

> A woman's face with nature's own hand painted
> Hast thou, the master-mistress of my passion;
> A woman's gentle heart, but not acquainted
> With shifting change as is false women's fashion;
> An eye more bright than theirs, less false in rolling,
> Gilding the object whereupon it gazeth;
> A man in hue, all hues in his controlling,
> Which steals men's eyes and women's souls amazeth.

> And for a woman wert thou first created,
> Till nature as she wrought thee fell a-doting,
> And by addition me of thee defeated
> By adding one thing to my purpose nothing. [one thing=a penis]
>   But since she pricked thee out for women's pleasure,
>   Mine be thy love and thy love's use their treasure.

Nature originally intended the youth to be a woman (the octave). But she fell in love with her creation and hence turned him into a male, a change that benefited her but forced the speaker to limit his relationship to the youth to love without sexual consummation (the sestet). Thus, the poem wittily plays with gender boundaries—"master-mistress," "A woman's face," "one thing," "A man in hue" (with a further sexual reference if "hue" was pronounced like "you"; lines 2, 1, 12, 7). "Acquainted" and "controlling" pun on "cunt"; "nothing" and "treasure" refer to the female sexual organ as well (lines 3, 7, 12, 14). As someone "pricked . . . out for women's pleasure" (line 13), the youth is equipped to give women pleasure but also to be "pricked" and hence experience women's pleasure.

"Thy beauty's form in table of my heart" (24.2). Here a man is holding a "table" (tablet) in front of his heart while another man engraves the first man's portrait on it. From Geffrey Whitney, *A Choice of Emblems* (1586).

Even the form gets into the act: this is the only sonnet where all the rhymes have "feminine" endings—the term since the Renaissance for a two-syllable rhyme with the second syllable unstressed. Finally, the misogyny of the poem's complaint about "false" women (lines 4, 5) is consistent with its homoeroticism. Women are to be resented because the speaker prefers males, or at least the youth, and also because they get to enjoy "love's use," while he must content himself merely with "love" (line 14)—where the contrast suggests that "love" carries both its Renaissance meaning of "friendship" and its modern sense of romantic and sexual desire.

Sonnet 20 looks forward to poems that express passionate, erotic love for the youth, apparently without sexual fulfillment. But they also look back to the opening seventeen sonnets, in which the speaker urges the youth to marry and produce an heir. Hence, the speaker solicits the youth's love for someone else, since the point is procreation and, therefore, an immortality comparable to the artistic immortality promised later in the sequence. The exhortation cuts against both the conventional aspiration of the love sonnet and the speaker's unconventional aim of winning the youth. But this is because the multiple possible meanings of "love" in Sonnet 20 characterize the poems to the youth more generally.

How the case for marriage is argued is instructive. Shakespeare's reversal of the metaphorical relationship in sonnet 73, it will be recalled, removes any fixed point of reference. A comparable reversal also marks economic imagery of the first seventeen sonnets. As in Sonnet 20 (line 14), that imagery frequently turns on usury. Long subject to denunciation, usury in Renaissance England was just beginning its conversion into the respectable financial category of interest. Shakespeare shared the prevailing repugnance at the idea of making money out of money. Thus, the speaker condemns his mistress for her affair with the young man, represented as collecting a debt:

> The statute of thy beauty thou wilt take,
> Thou usurer that putt'st forth all to use.
>   (134.9–10)

She will "take" the full amount owed to her financially (sexually) because, like a "usurer," she employs "all" her wealth (her body) for profit ("use" means both "engage in usury" and "engage in sexual activity"). Elsewhere, more ambivalently, the youth is criticized for being, paradoxically, both "unthrifty" and a "niggard" (4.1, 5):

> Profitless usurer, why dost thou use
> So great a sum of sums yet canst not live?
>
> (4.7–8)

Here, "use" antithetically means both "use up" and "lend at interest." Literally, how can the youth lend vast "sums" for profit and be unable to support himself? Metaphorically, he acts in a "profitless" manner in wasting his endowments. Hence, he cannot "live" on in his children. By implication, a usurer is always without value.

But the lines also imagine the opposite. If there is a profitless usurer, there might be a profitable one. This good usurer predominates in the sonnets:

> That use is not forbidden usury
> Which happies those that pay the willing loan.
>
> (6.5–6)

Is "forbidden" an attribute of all, or just unallowable, usury? Keeping one's "treasure" to oneself merits only "thriftless praise"; "beauty's use" deserves "much more praise" if a child results (2.6–9). At least "an unthrift" allows the world to enjoy his wealth; "beauty's waste" is indefensible—"kept unused, the user so destroys it" (9.9–12). And sonnet 20 ends, as we've seen, with the speaker declaring, as if to console himself: "Mine be thy love and thy love's use their treasure" (line 14). The speaker gets the youth's love, whereas the "treasure" women get is merely the "use" (metaphorically, children) of that love. He obtains the principal, they the interest. These passages activate metaphorical meanings of "use" to promote marriage and family. But in so doing, they connect the proper use of beauty with usury, which comes to be understood as the economic equivalent of human reproduction, the early sonnet's highest ideal. The neo-feudal celebration of tradition as lineage smuggles in a defense of economic behavior destructive of tradition. Usury is transformed into a potentially noble activity. Through metaphor, then, Shakespeare entertains ideas that might have been less accessible as bald statements.

The poems to the speaker's mistress are also scandalously unconventional—in their focus on a sordid, adulterous affair with an unfaithful woman that is marked by passionate desire and equally passionate recrimination. Even the relatively serene sonnets in this section self-consciously undermine convention:

> My mistress' eyes are nothing like the sun;
> . . . .
> And yet, by heaven, I think my love as rare
> As any she belied with false compare.
>
> (130.1, 13–14)

Here the target is the standard Petrarchan mode of praise. More generally, the aim is to dismantle falsely idealizing rhetoric:

> When my love swears that she is made of truth
> I do believe her though I know she lies,
> . . . .
> Therefore I lie with her, and she with me,
> And in our faults by lies we flattered be.
>
> (138.1–2, 13–14)

In Sonnet 130, true love requires the speaker to reject "false compare." In Sonnet 138, love paradoxically requires the speaker to "credit . . . false-speaking," to suppress "simple truth" (lines 7–8), and to embrace "lies." The sequence ends, however, with the bitter deployment of the same rhetoric against speaker and woman alike:

> For I have sworn thee fair—more perjured eye
> To swear against the truth so foul a lie.
>
> (152.13–14)

This concluding couplet recalls the opening of the sequence on the mistress:

> In the old age black was not counted fair,
> . . . .
> But now is black beauty's successive heir.
>
> (127.1, 3)

Black is the color of the woman's eyes, eyebrows, breasts, hair (127.9–10, 132.3, 130.3–4), and skin:

> Then I will swear beauty herself is black,
> And all they foul that thy complexion lack.
>
> (132.13–14)

As in other poetry of the time, this paradoxical, anticonventional praise of blackness echoes the biblical Song of Songs as well as sixteenth-century Continental and English poetry, including Sidney's. The praise is often inseparable from a misogynistic denunciation of the use of cosmetics to produce artificial beauty (127.4–12). Black hair and eyes gained prestige in the 1590s through a shift in fashion from blond hair to dark. Thus the speaker's personal views accord with broader social change.

The mistress's color may or may not be racialized, however, since even dark skin might merely distinguish her from falsely idealized women or aristocratic ladies able to avoid the sun. Nonetheless, *Titus Andronicus, Othello, Antony and Cleopatra*, and *The Tempest* feature actual or threatened interracial coupling. The mistress's combination of blackness and promiscuity may provoke both desire and fear of powerfully exotic female sexuality. The valence of blackness accordingly moves from the paradoxical to the conventional: "In nothing art thou black save in thy deeds" (131.13); "For I have sworn thee fair, and thought thee bright, / Who art as black as hell, and dark as night" (147.13–14). Like usury, then, blackness oscillates between conventional norms and radical innovation. Such is the case with the sonnets more generally.

Finally, the intense emotion here and elsewhere, the psychological complexity with which it is scrutinized, the unconventional subject matter, the sense that one is overhearing snatches of conversation, the first-person speaker, that speaker's self-conscious identification with Shakespeare (135–136)—all encourage a biographical interpretation of the sonnets. For two centuries, such interpretation has proven risky either to undertake or to avoid. There has been a major but unsuccessful scholarly effort to discover the real people whom Shakespeare discusses but does not name. The youth has most often been identified with Henry Wriothesley, Earl of Southampton, or William Herbert, Earl of Pembroke. The sonnets' dedication is to "Mr. W. H.," Pembroke's initials and the reverse of Southampton's. But neither is likely to have been addressed as "Mr." Proposals about the identity of the mistress are much shakier. Christopher Marlowe and George Chapman are among those suggested as the rival poet—on the basis of no real evidence. This inconclusiveness led mid-twentieth-century critics to focus on formal concerns. But the resulting advances often entailed evading the disconcerting biographical material that the poems do seem to provide. Shakespeare's sonnets, like his plays, combine verbal artistry and conceptual unorthodoxy with psychological exploration. Their special fascination, however, is that the soul they examine is apparently Shakespeare's own.

WALTER COHEN

TEXTUAL NOTE

The sonnets and "A Lover's Complaint" were printed for the first time in "SHAKESPEARES SONNETS," a Quarto that appeared in 1609. The type for the volume was set by two compositors, who probably worked from a scribal transcript of an authorial manuscript. It is likely that the arrangement of the sonnets is primarily, or perhaps entirely, Shakespearean. But since the compositors punctuated in different ways, the Quarto's punctuation cannot be regarded as authorial. Indeed, it is unlikely that Shakespeare had anything to do with the printing of the Quarto; it is also unlikely that this was an authorized edition—although the second point is more controversial than the first. Finally, it now appears that "A Lover's Complaint" was written not by Shakespeare but by John Davies. (See Vickers in the Selected Bibliography.)

The Quarto was reprinted in *Poems: Written by W. Shakespeare, Gent.* (1640), in which the sonnets (with eight omitted) and "A Lover's Complaint" were joined by additional poetry of Shakespeare and other writers, individual sonnets were run together to produce longer works, the sonnets were titled, their order was rearranged, and a few pronouns were changed or (in the titles) invented. This collection has no independent textual value. *The Passionate Pilgrim* (first edition, 1599 or earlier; second edition, 1599–1600), an unauthorized volume attributed to Shakespeare by its publisher, is a different matter. The second edition includes twenty poems—three from *Love's Labour's Lost* (the 1598 Quarto of which presumably had already appeared in print), four others more reliably attributed to other writers, eleven pieces by unknown authors, and versions of sonnets 138 and 144 that seem to be both erroneous and unrevised.

Another dozen sonnets survive in various manuscripts, all from 1620 or later. Although many derive from the Quarto, a few may preserve—amid mistakes in transcription—authentically Shakespearean phrasing from versions earlier than those in the 1609 edition. It is possible that one or more of these transcripts derive directly from an authorial manuscript and in that sense are closer to what Shakespeare wrote than is the Quarto. The Alternative Versions, printed after "A Lover's Complaint" in this edition, include manuscript renditions of sonnets 2 (the most popular, judging by the number of extant copies) and 106, as well as sonnets 138 and 144 as they appeared in *The Passionate Pilgrim*. Sonnets 8 and 128, for which additional versions are not included here, could also possibly derive from authorial manuscripts. From the four included in the Alternative Versions, one may perhaps learn something of Shakespeare's process of revision.

The poems were probably composed over more than a decade. *The Passionate Pilgrim* and, more inferentially, some of the manuscripts show that Shakespeare wrote a number of the sonnets in the 1590s at the latest. So, too, does Francis Meres's reference in 1598 to Shakespeare's "sugred Sonnets among his priuate friends." The circulation of manuscripts was a common form of "publication" at the time. It should be noted, however, that a "sonnet" could be any short lyric poem. The best candidate for early composition is probably 145, on the basis of its vocabulary, its use of tetrameters rather than pentameters, and the words "hate away" (line 13)—a possible pun on the name of the poet's wife, Anne Hathaway. Further chronological hints are provided by the boom in love-sonnet sequences during the 1590s as well as by Shakespeare's own plays from 1594 to 1596—*Love's Labour's Lost, A Midsummer Night's Dream, Romeo and Juliet*, and *Richard II*—plays that, despite belonging to a variety of genres, are all linked to the sonnets in vocabulary, lyrical feel, and (by the standards of Shakespearean drama) high incidence of rhyme.

Recent scholarship, however, has suggested a later composition or revision for a considerable number of the sonnets. Although no consensus currently exists, a plausible recent estimate is as follows:

1–60:	c. 1595–1596 (later revised?)
61–103:	c. 1594–1595
104–26:	c. 1598–1604
127–54:	c. 1591–1595

Even if this dating is only roughly accurate, it indicates that the sequence of the sonnets as published in 1609 sharply deviates from the chronology of composition. Beyond revealing that Shakespeare—and perhaps not Shakespeare alone—rearranged the sonnets according to other criteria, this conclusion also implies a disconnect between autobiographical impulse and chronological narrative (unless the sonnets that were composed later uniformly refer back to an earlier time). If the poems are in fact autobiographical, they cannot provide a linear account of events. This nonnarrative hypothesis is supported by internal evidence, specifically the references to the love triangle involving the speaker, the youth, and the mistress both early and late in the sequence (40–42, 133–34, 144). Alternatively, if the sequence does provide a linear narrative, it cannot be autobiographical. And, of course, the sequence may offer neither chronological narrative nor actual autobiography.

SELECTED BIBLIOGRAPHY

Bloom, Harold, ed. *Shakespeare's Sonnets*. New York: Chelsea House, 1987. Five leading critical essays from 1960 to 1985.

Booth, Stephen. *An Essay on Shakespeare's Sonnets*. New Haven: Yale University Press, 1969. Detailed evidence for multiple overlapping structures within individual sonnets, structures that expand possible meaning without cohering into a unified whole.

———, ed. *Shakespeare's Sonnets*. New Haven: Yale University Press, 1977. Same argument as above, but in the form of a detailed poem-by-poem commentary, together with both the 1609 Quarto of the sonnets and a modernized version.

Fineman, Joel. *Shakespeare's Perjured Eye: The Invention of Poetic Subjectivity in the Sonnets*. Berkeley: University of California Press, 1986. Psychoanalytical study that distinguishes the narcissistic, homosexual visual identification of sonnets 1–126 from the misogynistic heterosexual desire and conflict of 127–52, the latter being the founding moment of modern subjectivity.

Halpern, Richard. *Shakespeare's Perfume: Sodomy and Sublimity in the Sonnets, Wilde, Freud, and Lacan*. Philadelphia: University of Pennsylvania Press, 2002. 11–31. Links sodomy, aesthetics, sublimation, and the sublime.

Hernstein, Barbara, ed. *Discussions of Shakespeare's Sonnets*. Boston: Heath, 1964. Brief pre-twentieth-century accounts plus thirteen important essays from 1930 to 1960.

Schoenfeldt, Michael, ed. *A Companion to Shakespeare's Sonnets*. Malden, Mass.: Blackwell, 2007. The sonnets and "A Lover's Complaint" together with twenty-three essays from the current century plus contributions from Booth (1969) and Vendler (1997).

Vendler, Helen. *The Art of Shakespeare's Sonnets*. Cambridge, Mass.: Belknap Press, 1997. Detailed sonnet-by-sonnet interpretation, focusing on formal considerations, together with the 1609 Quarto and a modernized version of the text, as well as a CD-ROM of Vendler reading the poems.

Vickers, Brian. *Shakespeare, "A Lover's Complaint," and John Davies of Hereford*. New York: Cambridge University Press, 2007. Argues that Davies, not Shakespeare, wrote "A Lover's Complaint."

Willen, Gerald, and Victor B. Reed, eds. *A Casebook on Shakespeare's Sonnets*. New York: Crowell, 1964. Annotated modern edition of the sonnets together with six major critical essays from the 1930s to the early 1950s and very brief explications of a few individual sonnets.

Sonnets

1

From fairest creatures we desire increase,°   *offspring*
That thereby beauty's rose[1] might never die,
But as the riper should by time decease,
His tender[2] heir might bear his memory;
5 But thou, contracted° to thine own bright eyes,   *engaged; reduced*
Feed'st thy light's flame with self-substantial fuel,[3]
Making a famine where abundance lies,
Thyself thy foe, to thy sweet self too cruel.
Thou that art now the world's fresh ornament
10 And only herald to the gaudy° spring   *brilliant*
Within thine own bud buriest thy content,°   *substance; happiness*
And, tender churl,° mak'st waste in niggarding.   *young old miser*
    Pity the world, or else this glutton be:
    To eat the world's due, by the grave and thee.[4]

Dedication
1. The identity of W. H. has generated much speculation. As "the only begetter of these ensuing sonnets," "W. H." is probably a misprint for "W. S." or "W. SH." (William Shakespeare). Other candidates include the person who obtained the manuscript for the publisher and the youth who apparently inspired most of the poems. For biographical speculation about the sonnets, see the Introduction.
2. God, literally "ever-living," who promises eternity to Shakespeare (if, as suggested in the previous note, "W.H." refers to Shakespeare); or, less probably, Shakespeare, who promises "eternity" to the young man.
3. Thomas Thorpe, the printer, is the "well-wishing adventurer."
Sonnet 1
1. In Q, "rose," unlike most other nouns, is always capitalized (35.2; 54.3, 6, 11; 67.8; 95.2; 98.10; 99.8; 109.14; and 130.5, 6). Here, it is also italicized. These printing

conventions, combined with the placement of the word near the beginning of the first sonnet and its frequent repetition thereafter, suggest that "rose" is the poet's name for the object of his desire, on the model of, for instance, Stella in Sir Philip Sidney's influential sonnet sequence *Astrophel and Stella* (published 1591). The rose had long been associated with female genitalia, most notably in the thirteenth-century French narrative poem *The Romance of the Rose,* by Guillaume de Lorris and Jean de Meun. In Shakespeare's case, however, the object of desire is male. He is most frequently referred to as "youth," almost never as "boy" or "man." Shakespeare's "mistress" in the later sonnets is contrasted with "roses" (130.5, 6).
2. The rose's (the youth's) young.
3. Are consuming yourself like a candle.
4. *this . . . thee:* be a glutton by causing what is due to the world (your posterity) to be consumed both by the grave and within yourself.

2[1]

When forty winters shall besiege thy brow
And dig deep trenches in thy beauty's field,
Thy youth's proud livery,° so gazed on now,   *uniform; appearance*
Will be a tattered weed,° of small worth held.   *clothing; plant*
5   Then being asked where all thy beauty lies,
Where all the treasure of thy lusty days,
To say within thine own deep-sunken eyes
Were an all-eating shame and thriftless praise.[2]
How much more praise deserved thy beauty's use[3]
10 If thou couldst answer 'This fair child of mine
Shall sum my count, and make my old excuse',[4]
Proving his beauty by succession thine.°   *inherited from you*
      This were° to be new made when thou art old,   *would be*
      And see thy blood warm when thou feel'st it cold.

3

Look in thy glass,° and tell the face thou viewest   *mirror*
Now is the time that face should form another,
Whose fresh repair° if now thou not renewest   *state*
Thou dost beguile° the world, unbless° some mother.   *swindle / leave childless*
5   For where is she so fair whose uneared° womb   *unplowed*
Disdains the tillage of thy husbandry?[1]
Or who is he so fond will be the tomb
Of his self-love to stop posterity?[2]
Thou art thy mother's glass, and she in thee
10 Calls back the lovely April of her prime;
So thou through windows of thine age[3] shalt see,
Despite of wrinkles, this thy golden time.
      But if thou live remembered not to be,[4]
      Die single, and thine image dies with thee.

4

Unthrifty loveliness, why dost thou spend
Upon thyself thy beauty's legacy?
Nature's bequest gives nothing, but doth lend,
And being frank, she lends to those are free.[1]
5   Then, beauteous niggard, why dost thou abuse
The bounteous largess given thee to give?
Profitless usurer, why dost thou use°   *lend for profit; spend*
So great a sum of sums yet canst not live?[2]
For having traffic° with thyself alone,   *(commercial); (sexual)*
10 Thou of thyself thy sweet self dost deceive.°   *defraud*
Then how when nature calls thee to be gone:
What acceptable audit canst thou leave?
      Thy unused[3] beauty must be tombed with thee,
      Which usèd, lives th'executor to be.

Sonnet 2
1. See *Spes Altera* in the Alternative Versions.
2. Would be a shameful admission of gluttony and boast
of excessive expenditure.
3. How much more would the use (employment;
investment or usurious lending) of your beauty merit.
4. Shall make my accounts balance and defend (absolve)
me in my age.
Sonnet 3
1. Cultivation; acting as a husband.

2. *who . . . posterity:* who is so foolish that he will selfishly
deny posterity a child?
3. Eyes weakened by old age; your children.
4. But if you live to be forgotten.
Sonnet 4
1. And being generous, she lends to those who (also) are
generous.
2. Make a living; live on in your children.
3. Not put to use; not interest-bearing.

5

Those hours that with gentle work did frame°   *form*
The lovely gaze° where every eye doth dwell   *face*
Will play the tyrants to the very same,
And that unfair which fairly doth excel;[1]
5 For never-resting time leads summer on
To hideous winter, and confounds° him there,   *destroys*
Sap checked with frost, and lusty leaves quite gone,
Beauty o'er-snowed, and bareness everywhere.
Then were not summer's distillation left
10 A liquid prisoner pent in walls of glass,
Beauty's effect with beauty were bereft,[2]
Nor° it nor no remembrance what it was.   *Neither*
  But flowers distilled, though they with winter meet,
  Lose[3] but their show; their substance still lives sweet.

6[1]

Then let not winter's ragged° hand deface   *rough*
In thee thy summer ere thou be distilled.
Make sweet some vial,° treasure° thou some place *womb / enrich*
With beauty's treasure ere it be self-killed.
5 That use° is not forbidden usury   *lending for profit*
Which happies those that pay the willing loan;[2]
That's for thyself° to breed another thee,   *So you would do*
Or ten times happier, be it ten for one;°   *1,000% interest*
Ten times thyself were happier than thou art,
10 If ten of thine ten times refigured° thee.   *copied*
Then what could death do if thou shouldst depart,
Leaving thee living in posterity?
  Be not self-willed,[3] for thou art much too fair
  To be death's conquest and make worms thine heir.

7

Lo, in the orient° when the gracious light°   *east / sun*
Lifts up his burning head, each under° eye   *earthly*
Doth homage to his new-appearing sight,
Serving with looks his sacred majesty,
5 And having climbed the steep-up heavenly hill,
Resembling strong youth in his middle age,°   *noon*
Yet mortal looks adore his beauty still,
Attending on his golden pilgrimage.
But when from highmost pitch, with weary car,° *sun god's chariot*
10 Like feeble age he reeleth from the day,
The eyes, 'fore duteous, now converted° are   *turned*
From his low tract,° and look another way.   *path*
  So thou, thyself outgoing in thy noon,
  Unlooked on diest unless thou get° a son.° *beget / (sun)*

Sonnet 5
1. Will make unattractive that which now excels in beauty.
2. *Then . . . bereft:* Then if there were no perfume distilled from flowers bottled in glass vials, both beauty and its effect would be lost.
3. Q has "Leese," understood in this edition as a cognate of "lose." This is Shakespeare's only use of "Leese," which

allows a pun on "lease." See 13.5.
Sonnet 6
1. This sonnet links with 5.
2. Which makes happy those who willingly lend, or who willingly repay the loan with interest (in the form of children).
3. Stubborn; leaving everything in a will to yourself alone.

8

Music to hear,[1] why hear'st thou music sadly?
Sweets° with sweets war not, joy delights in joy. *Sweet things*
Why lov'st thou that which thou receiv'st not gladly,
Or else receiv'st with pleasure thine annoy?
5 If the true concord of well-tunèd sounds
By unions° married do offend thine ear, *harmony*
They do but sweetly chide thee, who confounds° *destroys*
In singleness the parts[2] that thou shouldst bear.
Mark how one string, sweet husband to another,
10 Strikes each in each° by mutual ordering, *Resonates*
Resembling sire and child and happy mother,
Who all in one one pleasing note do sing;
  Whose speechless° song, being many, seeming one, *The strings' wordless*
  Sings this to thee: 'Thou single wilt prove none.'[3]

9

Is it for fear to wet a widow's eye
That thou consum'st thyself in single life?
Ah, if thou issueless° shalt hap to die, *childless*
The world will wail thee like a makeless° wife. *widowed*
5 The world will be thy widow, and still° weep *continually*
That thou no form of thee hast left behind,
When every private° widow well may keep *individual*
By children's eyes her husband's shape in mind.
Look what° an unthrift in the world doth spend *Whatever*
10 Shifts but his° place, for still the world enjoys it; *its*
But beauty's waste hath in the world an end,
And kept unused, the user° so destroys it. *spender; lender*
  No love toward others in that bosom sits
  That on himself such murd'rous shame commits.

10

For shame deny that thou bear'st love to any,
Who for thyself art so unprovident.
Grant, if thou wilt, thou art beloved of many,
But that thou none lov'st is most evident;
5 For thou art so possessed with murd'rous hate
That 'gainst thyself thou stick'st not to conspire,° *don't balk at conspiring*
Seeking that beauteous roof to ruinate
Which to repair should be thy chief desire.
O, change thy thought, that I may change my mind!° *judgment*
10 Shall hate be fairer lodged than gentle love?
Be as thy presence° is, gracious and kind, *appearance*
Or to thyself at least kind-hearted prove.
  Make thee another self for love of me,
  That beauty still may live in thine or thee.

Sonnet 8
1. You whose voice is music.
2. Musical parts; roles as husband and father.

3. Without an heir, death will render you nothing (alluding to the proverb "One is no number").

11

As fast as thou shalt wane, so fast thou grow'st
In one of thine from that which thou departest,[1]
And that fresh blood which youngly thou bestow'st
Thou mayst call thine when thou from youth convertest.°   *turn away*
5 Herein lives wisdom, beauty, and increase;
Without this, folly, age, and cold decay.
If all were minded so, the times should cease,
And threescore year would make the world away.
Let those whom nature hath not made for store,°   *breeding*
10 Harsh,° featureless,° and rude,° barrenly perish.   *ugly (all three words)*
Look whom she best endowed she gave the more,[2]
Which bounteous gift thou shouldst in bounty° cherish.   *by using bountifully*
    She carved thee for her seal,[3] and meant thereby
    Thou shouldst print more, not let that copy die.

12

When I do count the clock° that tells the time,   *hours as they strike*
And see the brave° day sunk in hideous night;   *fine*
When I behold the violet past prime,
And sable° curls ensilvered o'er with white;   *black*
5 When lofty trees I see barren of leaves,
Which erst° from heat did canopy the herd,   *once*
And summer's green all girded up in sheaves
Borne on the bier with white and bristly beard:[1]
Then of thy beauty do I question make
10 That thou among the wastes of time must go,
Since sweets° and beauties do themselves forsake,   *sweet things*
And die as fast as they see others grow;
    And nothing 'gainst time's scythe can make defence
    Save breed to brave him° when he takes thee hence.   *children to defy time*

13

O that you were yourself![1] But, love, you are
No longer yours than you yourself here live.
Against° this coming end you should prepare,   *For*
And your sweet semblance to some other give.
5 So should that beauty which you hold in lease
Find no determination;° then you were°   *never end / would be*
Yourself again after your self's decease,
When your sweet issue your sweet form should bear.
Who lets so fair a house fall to decay,
10 Which husbandry[2] in honour might uphold
Against the stormy gusts of winter's day,
And barren rage of death's eternal cold?
    O, none but unthrifts,° dear my love, you know.   *spendthrifts*
    You had a father; let your son say so.

Sonnet 11
1. In a child begotten in youth (with suggestions of sexual intercourse and of death).
2. To whomever nature gave most (made best-looking) she gave even more (extra reproductive abilities). The near circularity of "best endowed" and "more" alludes to Matthew 25:29, the paradoxical parable of the talents: "For unto every man that hath, it shall be given."

3. Literally, a stamp of authority.
Sonnet 12
1. *An . . . beard*: And sheaves of mature ("bearded") grain carried away on the harvest cart; old man borne on a funeral bier.
Sonnet 13
1. If only you could remain your (eternal) self.
2. Stewardship; being a husband.

14

Not from the stars do I my judgement pluck,
And yet methinks I have astronomy;°   *astrological knowledge*
But not to tell of good or evil luck,
Of plagues, of dearths, or seasons' quality.
5 Nor can I fortune to brief minutes° tell,   *precisely*
'Pointing to each his thunder, rain, and wind,
Or say with princes if it shall go well
By oft predict° that I in heaven find;   *numerous signs*
But from thine eyes my knowledge I derive,
10 And, constant stars, in them I read such art
As[1] truth and beauty shall together thrive
If from thyself to store thou wouldst convert.[2]
     Or else of thee this I prognosticate:
     Thy end is truth's and beauty's doom and date.°   *final judgment and end*

15

When I consider every thing that grows
Holds° in perfection but a little moment,   *Remains*
That this huge stage presenteth naught but shows
Whereon the stars in secret influence° comment;   *(astrologically)*
5 When I perceive that men as plants increase,
Cheerèd and checked even by the selfsame sky;
Vaunt° in their youthful sap,° at height decrease,   *Gloat / strength*
And wear their brave state out of memory:[1]
Then the conceit° of this inconstant stay°   *imagination / (on earth)*
10 Sets you most rich in youth before my sight,
Where wasteful time debateth° with decay   *competes*
To change your day of youth to sullied night;
     And all in war with time for love of you,
     As he takes from you, I engraft you new.[2]

16[1]

But wherefore do not you a mightier way
Make war upon this bloody tyrant, time,
And fortify yourself in your decay
With means more blessèd than my barren rhyme?
5 Now stand you on the top of happy hours,°   *in your prime*
And many maiden gardens yet unset°   *unplanted*
With virtuous wish would bear your living flowers,
Much liker than your painted counterfeit.°   *image in art or poetry*
So should the lines of life[2] that life repair°   *restore*
10 Which this time's pencil or my pupil pen[3]
Neither in inward worth nor outward fair
Can make you live yourself° in eyes of men.   *as yourself*
     To give away yourself keeps yourself still,°   *(as children)*
     And you must live drawn by your own sweet skill.

Sonnet 14
1. *such art* / *As*: such predictions as that.
2. If you would provide for the future.
Sonnet: 15
1. Wear their splendid clothing until they are forgotten (with a sense of "wearing out").
2. *And . . . new*: And I, in competition with time because

I love you, restore you with my verse.
Sonnet 16
1. This sonnet links with 15.
2. Lineage; living lines (unlike those of poet or painter).
3. Neither today's painters ("pencil" means "paintbrush") nor I, who imitate painting in my verse.

17

Who will believe my verse in time to come
If it were filled with your most high deserts?—
Though yet, heaven knows, it is but as a tomb
Which hides your life, and shows not half your parts.°   *attributes*
5 If I could write the beauty of your eyes
And in fresh numbers° number all your graces,   *lively verses*
The age to come would say 'This poet lies;
Such heavenly touches ne'er touched earthly faces.'
So should my papers, yellowed with their age,
10 Be scorned, like old men of less truth than tongue,
And your true rights° be termed a poet's rage°   *praises / hyperbole*
And stretchèd metre° of an antique song.   *overwrought poetry*
    But were some child of yours alive that time,
    You should live twice: in it, and in my rhyme.

18

Shall I compare thee to a summer's day?
Thou art more lovely and more temperate.
Rough winds do shake the darling buds of May,
And summer's lease° hath all too short a date.   *fixed span of time*
5 Sometime too hot the eye of heaven shines,
And often is his gold complexion dimmed,
And every fair from fair¹ sometime declines,
By chance or nature's changing course untrimmed;°   *rendered ordinary*
But thy eternal summer shall not fade
10 Nor lose possession of that fair thou ow'st,°   *own*
Nor shall death brag thou wander'st in his shade
When in eternal lines to time thou grow'st.²
    So long as men can breathe or eyes can see,
    So long lives this, and this gives life to thee.

19

Devouring time, blunt thou the lion's paws,
And make the earth devour her own sweet brood;
Pluck the keen teeth from the fierce tiger's jaws,
And burn the long-lived phoenix¹ in her blood.°   *alive*
5 Make glad and sorry seasons as thou fleet'st,
And do whate'er thou wilt, swift-footed time,
To the wide world and all her fading sweets.°   *sweet things*
But I forbid thee one most heinous crime:
O, carve not with thy hours my love's fair brow,
10 Nor draw no lines there with thine antique° pen.   *old; capricious*
Him in thy course untainted do allow
For beauty's pattern to succeeding men.
    Yet do thy worst, old time; despite thy wrong
    My love shall in my verse ever live young.

Sonnet 18
1. Lovely thing from loveliness.
2. When in immortal poetry you become engrafted to time.

Sonnet 19
1. Legendary, self-resurrecting bird believed to live in cycles of several centuries, dying in flames and reborn from the ashes. See also 73.9–12.

20

A woman's face with nature's own hand° painted   *(without cosmetics)*
Hast thou, the master-mistress[1] of my passion;[2]
A woman's gentle heart, but not acquainted°   *(pun on "quaint," "cunt")*
With shifting change as is false women's fashion;
5 An eye more bright than theirs, less false in rolling,°   *wandering (sexually)*
Gilding the object whereupon it gazeth;
A man in hue, all hues in his controlling,[3]
Which steals men's eyes and women's souls amazeth.°   *overwhelms*
And for° a woman wert thou first created,   *to be; to be with*
10 Till nature as she wrought thee fell a-doting,°   *behaved foolishly*
And by addition me of thee defeated°   *cheated me of you*
By adding one thing to my purpose nothing.[4]
    But since she pricked° thee out for women's pleasure,[5]   *chose; (sexual)*
    Mine be thy love and thy love's use their treasure.[6]

21

So is it not with me as with that muse°   *poet*
Stirred by a painted° beauty to his verse,   *(with cosmetics)*
Who heaven itself for ornament° doth use,   *poetic imagery*
And every fair with his fair doth rehearse,[1]
5 Making a couplement of proud compare[2]
With sun and moon, with earth, and sea's rich gems,
With April's first-born flowers, and all things rare
That heaven's air in this huge rondure hems.°   *globe surrounds*
O let me, true in love, but truly write,
10 And then believe me my love is as fair
As any mother's child, though not so bright
As those gold candles° fixed in heaven's air.   *(the stars)*
    Let them say more that like of hearsay° well;   *clichés*
    I will not praise that purpose not° to sell.   *since I don't intend*

22

My glass° shall not persuade me I am old   *mirror*
So long as youth and thou are of one date;°   *While you're young*
But when in thee time's furrows I behold,
Then look I° death my days should expiate.°   *I expect / conclude*
5 For all that beauty that doth cover thee
Is but the seemly° raiment of my heart,   *fitting*
Which in thy breast doth live, as thine in me;
How can I then be elder than thou art?
O therefore, love, be of thyself so wary
10 As I, not for myself, but for thee will,
Bearing thy heart, which I will keep so chary°   *cautiously*
As tender nurse her babe from faring ill.

Sonnet 20
1. Both patron and sexual mistress (hence, homoerotic); referring to the youth's feminine looks.
2. Object of my love; controller of my feelings; controller of my passionate poetry.
3. A man whose looks enable him to attract and dominate all others; a man whose looks encompass all other appearances (both male and female). "Hue" may pun on "you" with possible sexual connotations. "Hues" may pun on "use"; see line 14 and note. "Controlling" puns on "cunt."
4. *one . . . nothing*: something (a penis) of no use to me;

"thing" meant sexual organ; "nothing" meant female sexual organ.
5. To give women pleasure; to have the pleasure women have.
6. I'll have the main part of your love (the capital or principal), while women get just the "use" (interest; pleasure; children) of it (or, while you use women sexually).
Sonnet 21
1. And compares every beautiful thing with his beloved.
2. Making a link in proud comparison.

Presume not on[1] thy heart when mine is slain:
Thou gav'st me thine not to give back again.

23

As an unperfect actor on the stage
Who with his fear is put besides° his part,   *forgets*
Or some fierce thing replete with too much rage
Whose strength's abundance weakens his own heart,
5 So I, for fear of trust,° forget to say   *lack of confidence*
 The perfect ceremony of love's rite,[1]
And in mine own love's strength seem to decay,
O'er-charged with burden of mine own love's might.
O let my books be then the eloquence
10 And dumb presagers° of my speaking breast,   *mute presenters*
Who plead for love, and look for recompense
More than that tongue that more hath more expressed.[2]
  O learn to read what silent love hath writ;
  To hear with eyes belongs to love's fine wit.

24

Mine eye hath played the painter,[1] and hath steeled[2]
Thy beauty's form in table° of my heart.   *the painted tablet*
My body is the frame wherein 'tis held,
And perspective[3] it is best painter's art;
5 For through the painter must you see his skill
To find where your true image pictured lies,
Which in my bosom's shop° is hanging still,   *heart's workshop*
That hath his windows glazèd with thine eyes.[4]
Now see what good turns eyes for eyes have done:
10 Mine eyes have drawn thy shape, and thine for me
Are windows to my breast, wherethrough the sun
Delights to peep, to gaze therein on thee.
  Yet eyes this cunning want° to grace their art: *lack this talent*
  They draw but what they see, know not the heart.

25

Let those who are in favour with their stars
Of public honour and proud titles boast,
Whilst I, whom fortune of such triumph bars,
Unlooked-for joy in that I honour most.[1]
5 Great princes' favourites their fair leaves spread°   *bloom*
But as the marigold at the sun's eye,[2]
And in themselves their pride lies° burièd,   *will lie*
For at a frown they in their glory die.
The painful warrior famousèd for might,

Sonnet 22
1. Do not expect to get back.
Sonnet 23
1. Q reads "right," suggesting love's due as well as ritual.
2. More than that (rival) speaker who has more often said more.
Sonnet 24
1. The running conceit is of the speaker and addressee looking into one another's eyes, seeing both the other and himself reflected.
2. Engraved. Editors often emend Q's "steeld" to "stell'd" (fixed, placed) for a better fit with "painter."
3. Seen from the proper angle, through the painter's

eyes. A "perspective" was a distorted painting that looked right only if viewed from the correct angle.
4. The addressee looks into the speaker's eyes ("windows"), which seem fitted with glass ("glazèd") by the reflection there of the addressee's own eyes. The eyes are the heart's ("his" [its], referring to "bosom's," line 7) windows, through which the addressee can therefore see his own image in the speaker's heart.
Sonnet 25
1. Unexpectedly (privately) take pleasure in what I most esteem (the youth).
2. Only at the prince's pleasure or whim.

10 After a thousand victories once foiled
Is from the book of honour razèd° quite,   *deleted*
And all the rest forgot for which he toiled.
    Then happy I, that love and am beloved
    Where I may not remove nor be removed.

26

Lord of my love, to whom in vassalage°   *feudal allegiance*
Thy merit hath my duty strongly knit,
To thee I send this written embassage°   *missive*
To witness duty, not to show my wit;
5 Duty so great which wit so poor as mine
May make seem bare in wanting° words to show it,   *lacking*
But that I hope some good conceit° of thine   *opinion*
In thy soul's thought, all naked,[1] will bestow° it,   *provide a place for*
Till whatsoever star that guides my moving°   *actions*
10 Points on me graciously with fair aspect,°   *astrological influence*
And puts apparel on my tattered loving
To show me worthy of thy sweet respect.
    Then may I dare to boast how I do love thee;
    Till then, not show my head where thou mayst prove° me.   *test*

27

Weary with toil I haste me to my bed,
The dear repose for limbs with travel° tired;   *work; journeying*
But then begins a journey in my head
To work my mind when body's work's expired;
5 For then my thoughts, from far where I abide,
Intend a zealous pilgrimage to thee,
And keep my drooping eyelids open wide,
Looking on darkness which the blind do see:
Save that my soul's imaginary sight
10 Presents thy shadow° to my sightless view,   *picture*
Which like a jewel hung in ghastly night
Makes black night beauteous and her old face new.
    Lo, thus by day my limbs, by night my mind,
    For° thee, and for myself, no quiet find.   *Because of*

28[1]

How can I then return in happy plight,°   *condition*
That am debarred the benefit of rest,
When day's oppression is not eased by night,
But day by night and night by day oppressed,
5 And each, though enemies to either's° reign,   *each other's*
Do in consent shake hands to torture me,
The one by toil, the other to complain[2]
How far I toil, still farther off from thee?
I tell the day to please him thou art bright,
10 And do'st him grace when clouds do blot the heaven;[3]
So flatter I the swart°-complexioned night   *dark*
When sparkling stars twire not thou gild'st the even.[4]

Sonnet 26
1. Refers to his "bare"-seeming "duty."
Sonnet 28
1. This sonnet links with 27.

2. *one:* day. *other:* night, making me "complain."
3. And confer beauty on him as a substitute for the sun.
4. By saying that when stars aren't twinkling, you brighten the evening.

But day doth daily draw my sorrows longer,
And night doth nightly make grief's strength seem stronger.

29

When, in disgrace with fortune and men's eyes,
I all alone beweep my outcast state,
And trouble deaf heaven with my bootless° cries,   unavailing
And look upon myself and curse my fate,
5   Wishing me like to one more rich in hope,
Featured like him, like him with friends possessed,[1]
Desiring this man's art° and that man's scope,°   skill / range
With what I most enjoy° contented least: like; own
Yet in these thoughts myself almost despising,
10 Haply[2] I think on thee, and then my state,°   mood; fortunes
Like to the lark at break of day arising
From sullen earth, sings hymns at heaven's gate;
    For thy sweet love remembered such wealth brings
    That then I scorn to change my state with kings'.

30

When to the sessions° of sweet silent thought   court sittings
I summon up remembrance of things past,
I sigh° the lack of many a thing I sought,   mourn
And with old woes new wail my dear time's waste.[1]
5   Then can I drown an eye unused to flow
For precious friends hid in death's dateless° night,   endless
And weep afresh love's long-since-cancelled° woe,   repaid (with sorrow)
And moan th'expense° of many a vanished sight.   passing
Then can I grieve at grievances foregone,°   bygone
10 And heavily° from woe to woe tell° o'er   sadly / say; count
The sad account° of fore-bemoanèd moan,   story; finances
Which I new pay as if not paid before.
    But if the while I think on thee, dear friend,
    All losses are restored, and sorrows end.

31

Thy bosom is endearèd with° all hearts   loved by; enriched by
Which I by lacking have supposèd dead,
And there reigns love, and all love's loving parts,
And all those friends which I thought burièd.
5   How many a holy and obsequious° tear   dutifullly mourning
Hath dear religious° love stol'n from mine eye   devoted
As interest of° the dead, which° now appear   due payment to / who
But things removed° that hidden in thee lie!   absent
Thou art the grave where buried love doth live,
10 Hung with the trophies° of my lovers gone,   memorials
Who all their parts° of me to thee did give: shares
    That due of many[1] now is thine alone.

Sonnet 29
1. *Wishing . . . possessed:* Three people he wants to be
like—"like to one" with better prospects, better looking
"like him," and having friends "like him."
2. By chance; also, pun on "happily."

Sonnet 30
1. *my . . . waste:* the frittering or wasting away of my
precious time.
Sonnet 31
1. What was owed to many (myself).

Their images I loved I view in thee,
And thou, all they,[2] hast all the all of me.

32

If thou survive my well-contented day[1]
When that churl death my bones with dust shall cover,
And shalt by fortune° once more resurvey   *chance*
These poor rude° lines of thy deceasèd lover,   *rough*
5 Compare them with the bett'ring° of the time,   *progress; better art*
And though they be outstripped by every pen,
Reserve them for my love, not for their rhyme
Exceeded by the height of happier men.[2]
O then vouchsafe me but this loving thought:
10 'Had my friend's muse grown with this growing age,
A dearer birth° than this his love had brought   *worthier poem*
To march in ranks of better equipage;°   *poems*
   But since he died, and poets better prove,°   *have improved*
   Theirs for their style I'll read, his for his love.'

33

Full many a glorious morning have I seen
Flatter the mountain tops with sovereign eye,°   *sunlight*
Kissing with golden face the meadows green,
Gilding pale streams with heavenly alchemy;
5 Anon° permit the basest° clouds to ride   *(But) soon / darkest*
With ugly rack° on his celestial face,   *cloudy mask*
And from the forlorn world his visage hide,
Stealing unseen to west with this disgrace.
Even so my sun one early morn did shine
10 With all triumphant splendour on my brow;
But out, alack,° he was but one hour mine;   *alas*
The region° cloud hath masked him from me now.   *high*
   Yet him for this my love no whit disdaineth:
   Suns of the world may stain° when heaven's sun staineth.   *darken*

34[1]

Why didst thou promise such a beauteous day
And make me travel forth without my cloak,
To let base clouds o'ertake me in my way,
Hiding thy brav'ry° in their rotten smoke?°   *finery / noxious mists*
5 'Tis not enough that through the cloud thou break
To dry the rain on my storm-beaten face,
For no man well of such a salve can speak
That heals the wound and cures not the disgrace.[2]
Nor can thy shame° give physic to° my grief;   *remorse / cure*
10 Though thou repent, yet I have still the loss.
Th'offender's sorrow lends but weak relief
To him that bears the strong offence's cross.°   *consequences*

2. And you, who are made up of all of them.
Sonnet 32
1. Day of my death, which I shall willingly accept.
2. *Reserve . . . men*: Keep them because you love me, not for their value as poetry, which is surpassed by poets more fortunate in their talent than I.
Sonnet 34
1. This sonnet links with 33.
2. Disfigurement; dishonor done the poet by the youth's neglect.

Ah, but those tears are pearl which thy love sheds,
And they are rich, and ransom° all ill deeds.   *atone for*

35

No more be grieved at that which thou hast done:
Roses have thorns, and silver fountains mud.
Clouds and eclipses stain° both moon and sun,   *darken*
And loathsome canker° lives in sweetest bud.   *(worm)*
5   All men make faults, and even I in this,
Authorizing thy trespass with compare,[1]
Myself corrupting salving thy amiss,[2]
Excusing thy sins more than thy sins are;[3]
For to thy sensual fault I bring in sense[4]—
10 Thy adverse party is thy advocate—
And 'gainst myself a lawful plea commence.
Such civil war is in my love and hate
    That I an accessory needs must be
    To that sweet thief which sourly robs from me.

36

Let me confess that we two must be twain[1]
Although our undivided loves are one;
So shall those blots° that do with me remain   *flaws; sources of shame*
Without thy help by me be borne alone.
5   In our two loves there is but one respect,°   *focus of attention*
Though in our lives a separable spite[2]
Which, though it alter not love's sole° effect,   *single-minded*
Yet doth it steal sweet hours from love's delight.
I may not evermore acknowledge thee
10 Lest my bewailèd guilt should do thee shame,
Nor thou with public kindness honour me
Unless thou take° that honour from thy name.   *lose*
    But do not so. I love thee in such sort°   *such a way*
    As, thou being mine, mine is thy good report.[3]

37

As a decrepit father takes delight
To see his active child do deeds of youth,
So I, made lame by fortune's dearest° spite,   *direst*
Take all my comfort of° thy worth and truth;   *in*
5   For whether beauty, birth, or wealth, or wit,
Or any of these all, or all, or more,
Entitled in thy parts[1] do crownèd sit,
I make my love engrafted to this store.[2]
So then I am not lame, poor, nor despised,
10 Whilst that this shadow° doth such substance give   *idea*
That I in thy abundance am sufficed

Sonnet 35
1. Justifying your offense with comparisons.
2. Corrupting myself in minimizing your transgression.
3. Excusing you (overindulgently) from worse sins than the ones you've committed.
4. I use reason to defend your sensual offense.
Sonnet 36
1. Separated; but also, paradoxically, two of a kind or bound together.

2. Separation that causes vexation; vexation that causes separation.
3. Reputation. This couplet also ends 96.
Sonnet 37
1. Enrolled among your good qualities.
2. I engraft my love onto this abundance (of good qualities).

And by a part of all thy glory live.
Look what° is best, that best I wish in thee;   *whatever*
This° wish I have, then ten times happy me.   *When this*

38

How can my muse want subject to invent°   *lack subject matter*
While thou dost breathe, that pour'st into my verse
Thine own sweet argument,° too excellent   *theme*
For every vulgar paper to rehearse?¹
5 O, give thyself the thanks if aught in me
Worthy perusal stand against thy sight;²
For who's so dumb that cannot write to thee,
When thou thyself dost give invention light?
Be thou the tenth muse, ten times more in worth
10 Than those old nine which rhymers invocate;
And he that calls on thee, let him bring forth
Eternal numbers° to outlive long° date.   *verses / a distant*
   If my slight muse do please these curious° days,   *finicky*
   The pain° be mine, but thine shall be the praise.   *pains; effort*

39

O, how thy worth with manners° may I sing   *modesty*
When thou art all the better part of me?
What can mine own praise to mine own self bring,
And what is't but mine own when I praise thee?
5 Even for° this let us divided live,   *Because of*
And our dear love lose name of single one,°   *the reputation of unity*
That by this separation I may give
That due to thee which thou deserv'st alone.
O absence, what a torment wouldst thou prove
10 Were it not thy sour leisure gave sweet leave
To entertain° the time with thoughts of love,   *enliven*
Which time and thoughts so sweetly doth deceive,
   And that thou teachest how to make one twain
   By praising him here° who doth hence remain!   *in this poem*

40¹

Take all my loves, my love, yea, take them all:
What hast thou then more than thou hadst before?
No love, my love, that thou mayst true love call—
All mine was thine before thou hadst this more.
5 Then if for my love thou my love receivest,²
I cannot blame thee for my love thou usest;³
But yet be blamed if thou this self⁴ deceivest
By wilful taste of what thyself° refusest.   *your better nature*
I do forgive thy robb'ry, gentle thief,
10 Although thou steal thee all my poverty;°   *what little I own*
And yet love knows it is a greater grief

Sonnet 38
1. Every ordinary, commonplace piece of writing to set forth.
2. *if . . . sight:* if you see anything in my writing worth reading.
Sonnet 40
1. Sonnets 40–42 concern a situation that may be identi-

cal to the love triangle described in 133–34 and 144.
2. Then if for love of me you take my beloved.
3. *for . . . usest:* because you use my beloved (sexually).
4. The poet (often emended, perhaps rightly, to "thyself").

To bear love's wrong than hate's known injury.
    Lascivious grace,° in whom all ill well shows,   *Charming wanton*
    Kill me with spites,° yet we must not be foes.   *offenses*

41

Those pretty° wrongs that liberty° commits   *minor / licentiousness*
When I am sometime absent from thy heart
Thy beauty and thy years full well befits,
For still° temptation follows where thou art.   *continually*
5 Gentle° thou art, and therefore to be won;   *Tender; upper-class*
Beauteous thou art, therefore to be assailed;
And when a woman woos, what woman's son
Will sourly leave her till he have prevailed?[1]
Ay me, but yet thou mightst my seat[2] forbear,
10 And chide thy beauty and thy straying youth
Who lead thee in their riot° even there   *depraved conduct*
Where thou art forced to break a two-fold troth:
    Hers, by thy beauty tempting her to thee,
    Thine, by thy beauty being false to me.

42

That thou hast her, it is not all my grief,
And yet it may be said I loved her dearly;
That she hath thee is of my wailing chief,°   *chief reason*
A loss in love that touches me more nearly.
5 Loving offenders, thus I will excuse ye:
Thou dost love her because thou know'st I love her,
And for my sake even so doth she abuse° me,   *mistreat*
Suff'ring my friend for my sake to approve her.[1]
If I lose thee, my loss is my love's gain,
10 And losing° her, my friend hath found that loss: *I losing*
Both find each other, and I lose both twain,
And both for my sake lay on me this cross.°   *affliction*
    But here's the joy: my friend and I are one.
    Sweet flattery!° Then she loves but me alone.   *Pleasing delusion*

43

When most I wink,° then do mine eyes best see,   *shut my eyes*
For all the day they view things unrespected;°   *unheeded; unworthy*
But when I sleep, in dreams they look on thee,
And, darkly bright, are bright in dark directed.[1]
5 Then thou, whose shadow shadows doth make bright,[2]
How would thy shadow's form° form happy show°   *substance / sight*
To the clear day with thy much clearer light,
When to unseeing eyes[3] thy shade shines so!
How would, I say, mine eyes be blessèd made
10 By looking on thee in the living day,
When in dead night thy fair imperfect° shade   *incorporeal*

Sonnet 41
1. Until he has had his way. But Q's "he" could easily be a misprint for "she."
2. Rightful place (my mistress).
Sonnet 42
1. To put her to the test (sexually).

Sonnet 43
1. (My eyes) seeing in the dark turn toward your bright eyes in the dark.
2. Whose image lightens darkness.
3. Because closed in sleep.

Through heavy sleep on sightless eyes doth stay!
    All days are nights to see till I see thee,
    And nights bright days when dreams do show thee me.°   *to me*

44

If the dull° substance of my flesh were thought,   *heavy*
Injurious distance should not stop my way;
For then, despite of space, I would be brought
From limits° far remote where° thou dost stay.   *places / to where*
5 No matter then although my foot did stand
Upon the farthest earth removed from thee;
For nimble thought can jump both sea and land
As soon as think the place where he° would be.   *(thought)*
But ah, thought kills me that I am not thought,
10 To leap large lengths of miles when thou art gone,
But that, so much of earth and water wrought,[1]
I must attend time's leisure[2] with my moan,
    Receiving naught by elements so slow
    But heavy tears, badges of either's woe.[3]

45[1]

The other two,[2] slight° air and purging fire,   *light*
Are both with thee wherever I abide;
The first my thought, the other my desire,
These present-absent[3] with swift motion slide;
5 For when these quicker° elements are gone   *livelier*
In tender embassy of love to thee,
My life, being made of four, with two alone
Sinks down to death, oppressed with melancholy,
Until life's composition be recured°   *renewed*
10 By those swift messengers returned from thee,
Who even but now come back again assured
Of thy fair health, recounting it to me.
    This told, I joy; but then no longer glad,
    I send them back again and straight° grow sad.   *suddenly*

46

Mine eye and heart are at a mortal° war   *lethal*
How to divide the conquest of thy sight.[1]
Mine eye my heart thy picture's sight would bar,
My heart, mine eye the freedom° of that right.   *free enjoyment*
5 My heart doth plead that thou in him dost lie,
A closet° never pierced with crystal eyes;   *room*
But the defendant doth that plea deny,
And says in him thy fair appearance lies.
To 'cide° this title is empanellèd°   *decide / enrolled*
10 A quest° of thoughts, all tenants to the heart,

Sonnet 44
1. Being compounded of so much earth and water (the heavy elements).
2. I must wait humbly (as if on a great man) for time to reunite us.
3. Emblems of the grief of each of the poet's elements (of earth because heavy [sad], of water because wet).
Sonnet 45
1. This sonnet links with 44.

2. Of the poet's four elements. See 44.11.
3. Now present, now absent; constantly coming and going.
Sonnet 46
1. The spoils of the sight of you (possibly in a painting; see 47.5–14).

And by their verdict is determinèd   *jury*
The clear eye's moiety° and the dear heart's part,   *share*
    As thus: mine eye's due is thy outward part,
    And my heart's right thy inward love of heart.

47[1]

Betwixt mine eye and heart a league is took,°   *truce is made*
And each doth good turns now unto the other.
When that mine eye is famished for a look,
Or heart in love with sighs himself doth smother,[2]
5   With my love's picture then my eye doth feast,
And to the painted banquet bids my heart.
Another time mine eye is my heart's guest
And in his thoughts of love doth share a part.
So either by thy picture or my love,
10 Thyself away art present still with me;
For thou no farther than my thoughts canst move,
And I am still° with them, and they with thee;   *constantly*
    Or if they sleep, thy picture in my sight
    Awakes my heart to heart's and eye's delight.

48

How careful was I when I took my way°   *set off*
Each trifle under truest° bars to thrust,   *most reliable*
That to my use° it might unusèd stay   *benefit*
From hands of falsehood, in sure wards° of trust.   *safe places*
5   But thou, to° whom my jewels trifles are,   *compared to*
Most worthy comfort, now my greatest grief,[1]
Thou best of dearest and mine only care
Art left the prey of every vulgar thief.
Thee have I not locked up in any chest
10 Save where thou art not, though I feel thou art—
Within the gentle closure of my breast,
From whence at pleasure thou mayst come and part;°   *go*
    And even thence thou wilt be stol'n, I fear,
    For truth° proves thievish for a prize so dear.   *even honesty*

49

Against° that time—if ever that time come—   *In preparation for*
When I shall see thee frown on my defects,
Whenas thy love hath cast his utmost sum,[1]
Called to that audit by advisèd respects;°   *judicious reasons*
5   Against that time when thou shalt strangely° pass   *as a stranger*
And scarcely greet me with that sun, thine eye,
When love converted from the thing it was
Shall reasons find of settled gravity:[2]
Against that time do I ensconce me° here   *secure myself*
10 Within the knowledge of mine own desert,[3]
And this my hand against myself uprear°   *testify against myself*

Sonnet 47
1. This sonnet links with 46.
2. Or when my loving heart smothers itself with sighs.
Sonnet 48
1. Because absent and in danger of being stolen.

Sonnet 49
1. When your love has calculated the bottom line.
2. Shall find reasons for a dignified reserve; shall find reasons of well-established seriousness (for leaving me).
3. My (lack of?) worthiness to be loved.

To guard the lawful reasons on thy part.°   *defend your case*
  To leave poor me thou hast the strength of laws,
  Since why to love° I can allege no cause.   *why you should love*

50

How heavy° do I journey on the way,   *wearily*
When what I seek—my weary travel's end—
Doth teach that ease and that repose to say[1]
'Thus far the miles are measured from thy friend.'
5 The beast that bears me, tired with my woe,
Plods dully on to bear° that weight in me,   *while bearing*
As if by some instinct the wretch did know
His rider loved not speed, being made[2] from thee.
The bloody spur cannot provoke him on
10 That sometimes anger thrusts into his hide,
Which heavily he answers with a groan
More sharp to me than spurring to his side;
  For that same groan doth put this in my mind:
  My grief lies onward and my joy behind.

51[1]

Thus can my love excuse the slow offence°   *offense of slowness*
Of my dull bearer when from thee I speed:
From where thou art why should I haste me thence?
Till I return, of posting° is no need.   *riding quickly*
5 O what excuse will my poor beast then find
When swift extremity° can seem but slow?   *extreme (return) speed*
Then should I spur, though mounted on the wind;
In wingèd speed no motion shall I know.[2]
Then can no horse with my desire keep pace;
10 Therefore desire, of perfect'st love being made,
Shall rein° no dull flesh in his fiery race;   *curb*
But love, for love,° thus shall excuse my jade: *on love's behalf*
  Since from thee going he went wilful-slow,
  Towards thee I'll run and give him leave to go.°   *walk*

52

So am I as the rich° whose blessèd key   *rich man*
Can bring him to his sweet up-lockèd treasure,
The which he will not ev'ry hour survey,
For° blunting the fine point of seldom° pleasure.   *To avoid / occasional*
5 Therefore are feasts° so solemn° and so rare   *feast days / dignified*
Since, seldom coming, in the long year set
Like stones of worth they thinly placèd are,
Or captain° jewels in the carcanet.°   *chief / jeweled collar*
So is the time that keeps you as° my chest,°   *like / jewel case*
10 Or as the wardrobe which the robe doth hide,
To make some special instant special blest

Sonnet 50
1. Teach the comforts at the end of the road to remind me that.
2. *speed, being made:* hastening away; haste, when and because it is.
Sonnet 51
1. This sonnet links with 50.

2. I will feel no motion when desire carries me back through the air. See line 11 and sonnets 44–45 for the association of fire and air with desire and thought, and of earth and water with dull, slow flesh.

By new unfolding his imprisoned pride.
    Blessèd are you whose worthiness gives scope,
    Being had, to triumph; being lacked, to hope.[1]

53

What is your substance, whereof are you made,
That millions of strange shadows on you tend?°   *attend*
Since every one hath, every one, one shade,[1]
And you, but one, can every shadow lend.[2]
5 Describe° Adonis, and the counterfeit°   *Draw / likeness*
Is poorly imitated after you.
On Helen's cheek all art of beauty set,
And you in Grecian tires are painted new.[3]
Speak of the spring and foison° of the year: *harvest time*
10 The one doth shadow of your beauty show,
The other as your bounty doth appear;
And you in every blessèd shape we know.°   *recognize*
    In all external grace you have some part,
    But you like none, none you, for constant heart.

54

O how much more doth beauty beauteous seem
By° that sweet ornament which truth doth give!   *Because of*
The rose looks fair, but fairer we it deem
For that sweet odour which doth in it live.
5 The canker blooms[1] have full as deep a dye
As the perfumèd tincture° of the roses,   *color*
Hang on such thorns, and play as wantonly°   *flatter as playfully*
When summer's breath their maskèd buds discloses;
But for° their virtue only is° their show   *since / lies wholly in*
10 They live unwooed and unrespected° fade,   *unappreciated*
Die to themselves.° Sweet roses do not so;   *alone; without influence*
Of their sweet deaths are sweetest odours made:
    And so of you, beauteous and lovely youth,
    When that° shall fade, by verse distils your truth.[2]   *beauty*

55

Not marble nor the gilded monuments
Of princes shall outlive this powerful rhyme,
But you shall shine more bright in these contents
Than unswept stone besmeared with sluttish° time.   *slovenly*
5 When wasteful war shall statues overturn,
And broils° root out the work of masonry,   *battles*
Nor Mars his° sword nor war's quick fire shall burn   *Neither Mars's*
The living record of your memory.
'Gainst death and all oblivious enmity
10 Shall you pace forth; your praise shall still find room

Sonnet 52
1. *gives . . . hope:* allows me to exult when with you and to hope when not with you.
Sonnet 53
1. Since each person has an individual shadow.
2. Can cast all shadows (are visible in every image).
3. *On . . . new:* If one were to use every art to reproduce the beauty of Helen of Troy (or use artful cosmetics on Helen's cheek) it would look like you in Grecian headgear.
Sonnet 54
1. Dog roses (having little scent).
2. See sonnet 5. Q's "vade" is a variant of "fade," the reading adopted here, but it probably has the secondary meaning of "depart," from the Latin *vadere*.

Even in the eyes of all posterity
That wear this world out to the ending doom.[1]
  So, till the judgement that yourself arise,
  You live in this, and dwell in lovers' eyes.

56

Sweet love,[1] renew thy force. Be it not said
Thy edge should blunter be than appetite,
Which but° today by feeding is allayed,   *merely for*
Tomorrow sharpened in his former might.
5   So, love, be thou; although today thou fill
Thy hungry eyes even till they wink° with fullness,   *close (to sleep)*
Tomorrow see again, and do not kill
The spirit of love with a perpetual dullness.
Let this sad int'rim like the ocean be
10 Which parts the shore where two contracted new
Come daily to the banks, that when they see
Return of love, more blessed may be the view;[2]
  Or call it winter, which, being full of care,
  Makes summer's welcome, thrice more wished, more rare.°   *valuable*

57

Being your slave, what should I do but tend°   *wait*
Upon the hours and times of your desire?
I have no precious time at all to spend,
Nor services to do, till you require;
5   Nor dare I chide the world-without-end° hour   *endless*
Whilst I, my sovereign, watch the clock for you,
Nor think the bitterness of absence sour
When you have bid your servant once adieu.
Nor dare I question with my jealous thought
10 Where you may be, or your affairs suppose,°   *speculate on*
But like a sad slave stay and think of naught
Save, where you are, how happy you make those.
  So true a fool is love that in your will,[1]
  Though you do anything, he thinks no ill.

58[1]

That god forbid, that made me first your slave,
I should in thought control your times of pleasure,
Or at your hand th'account of hours to crave,[2]
Being your vassal° bound to stay° your leisure.   *slave / wait upon*
5   O let me suffer, being at your beck,
Th'imprisoned absence of your liberty,[3]
And patience, tame to sufferance, bide each check,[4]
Without accusing you of injury.

Sonnet 55
1. Doomsday: in Christianity, the Day of Judgment, when dead bodies are supposed to "arise" (line 13) from the grave and be united with their souls.
Sonnet 56
1. The feeling (not the beloved).
2. *Let . . . view*: The "sad" interval between periods of feeling love is like an ocean dividing shores where two lovers come daily hoping for the (emotionally renewing) sight of a boat bringing the other. *contracted new*: newly betrothed.

Sonnet 57
1. Desire (including sexual desire); capitalized in Q, perhaps punning on Shakespeare's name. See 135–36.
Sonnet 58
1. This sonnet links with 57.
2. Or should seek an account of how you pass your time.
3. The imprisoned feeling caused by your licentiousness when you're away.
4. And (let me) patient, acquiescent in suffering, endure each setback.

Be where you list,° your charter° is so strong   *wish / freedom*
10 That you yourself may privilege° your time   *allocate*
    To what you will; to you it doth belong
    Yourself to pardon of self-doing° crime.   *commited by you*
       I am to wait, though waiting so be hell,
       Not blame your pleasure, be it ill or well.

59

    If there be nothing new, but that which is
    Hath been before, how are our brains beguiled,°   *cheated*
    Which, labouring° for invention, bear amiss   *working; giving birth*
    The second burden of a former child![1]
5 O that record° could with a backward look   *recollection*
    Even of five hundred courses of the sun
    Show me your image in some antique book
    Since mind at first in character was done,[2]
    That I might see what the old world could say
10 To this composèd wonder of your frame;[3]
    Whether we are mended° or whe'er better they,   *improved*
    Or whether revolution be the same.[4]
       O, sure I am the wits° of former days   *clever writers*
       To subjects worse have given admiring praise.

60

    Like as the waves make towards the pebbled shore,
    So do our minutes hasten to their end,
    Each changing place with that which goes before;
    In sequent toil all forwards do contend.[1]
5 Nativity,° once in the main of light,°   *A newborn / in the world*
    Crawls to maturity, wherewith being crowned
    Crookèd° eclipses 'gainst his glory fight,   *Pernicious*
    And time that gave doth now his gift confound.°   *ruin*
    Time doth transfix the flourish[2] set on youth,
10 And delves the parallels° in beauty's brow;   *carves the wrinkles*
    Feeds on the rarities of nature's truth,[3]
    And nothing stands but for his scythe to mow.
       And yet to times in hope° my verse shall stand,   *future days*
       Praising thy worth despite his cruel hand.

61

    Is it thy will thy image should keep open
    My heavy eyelids to the weary night?
    Dost thou desire my slumbers should be broken
    While shadows° like to thee do mock my sight?   *visions*
5 Is it thy spirit that thou send'st from thee
    So far from home into my deeds to pry,
    To find out shames and idle hours in me,
    The scope and tenor of thy jealousy?[1]
    O no; thy love, though much, is not so great.

Sonnet 59
1. *bear . . . child:* mistakenly ("amiss") give birth for a second time to a child that has already been born.
2. Since writing was invented.
3. To the wonderful composition of your form (perhaps referring to the sonnet itself as well).
4. Whether the revolving of the ages makes no difference.

Sonnet 60
1. Toiling one after the other, all seek to move forward.
2. Time pierces and destroys the ornament (beauty).
3. On the most precious products of nature's perfection.
Sonnet 61
1. The object and intent of your distrust (that is, "shames and idle hours," line 7).

10　It is my love that keeps mine eye awake,
　　Mine own true love that doth my rest defeat,
　　To play the watchman ever for thy sake.
　　　　For thee watch I° whilst thou dost wake elsewhere,　　　　*I remain awake*
　　　　From me far off, with others all too near.

62

　　Sin of self-love possesseth all mine eye,
　　And all my soul, and all my every part;
　　And for this sin there is no remedy,
　　It is so grounded inward in my heart.
5　Methinks no face so gracious is as mine,
　　No shape so true,° no truth of such account,　　　　　　*perfect*
　　And for myself mine own worth do define
　　As° I all other° in all worths surmount.　　　　　　*As if / others*
　　But when my glass° shows me myself indeed,　　　　　*mirror*
10　Beated and chapped with tanned antiquity,
　　Mine own self-love quite contrary I read;
　　Self so self-loving were iniquity.
　　　　'Tis thee, my self,° that for° myself I praise,　　*you, my other self / as*
　　　　Painting my age with beauty of thy days.

63

　　Against° my love shall be as I am now,　　　　　　*Preparing for when*
　　With time's injurious hand crushed and o'erworn;
　　When hours have drained his blood and filled his brow
　　With lines and wrinkles; when his youthful morn
5　Hath travelled° on to age's steepy¹ night,　　　　　*progressed; toiled*
　　And all those beauties whereof now he's king
　　Are vanishing, or vanished out of sight,
　　Stealing away the treasure of his spring:
　　For such a time do I now fortify
10　Against confounding° age's cruel knife,　　　　　　*devastating*
　　That he shall never cut from memory
　　My sweet love's beauty, though° my lover's life.　　　*though he will sever*
　　　　His beauty shall in these black lines be seen,
　　　　And they shall live, and he in them still green.°　　*perpetually youthful*

64

　　When I have seen by time's fell° hand defaced　　　　　*fierce*
　　The rich proud cost° of outworn buried age;　　　　　*expense*
　　When sometime°-lofty towers I see down razed,　　　　　*once*
　　And brass eternal slave to mortal rage;¹
5　When I have seen the hungry ocean gain
　　Advantage on the kingdom of the shore,
　　And the firm soil win of° the wat'ry main,　　　　　　*win ground from*
　　Increasing store with loss and loss with store;²
　　When I have seen such interchange of state,
10　Or state³ itself confounded to decay,°　　　　　　　*reduced to ruins*
　　Ruin hath taught me thus to ruminate:

Sonnet 63
1. Precipitous (like the path of the setting sun).
Sonnet 64
1. And eternal brass forever succumbs to death's violence.

2. Adding to the stock of one by loss of the other, and vice versa.
3. *state* (line 9): condition; sovereign territory. *state* (line 10): pomp.

That time will come and take my love away.
  This thought is as a death, which° cannot choose   *since thought*
  But weep to have° that which it fears to lose.   *at having*

65

Since° brass, nor stone, nor earth, nor boundless sea,   *Since there is neither*
But sad mortality o'ersways their power,
How with this rage shall beauty hold a plea,[1]
Whose action is no stronger than a flower?
5 O how shall summer's honey breath hold out
Against the wrackful° siege of battering days   *damaging*
When rocks impregnable are not so stout,
Nor gates of steel so strong, but time decays?°   *decays them*
O fearful meditation! Where, alack,
10 Shall time's best jewel° from time's chest[2] lie hid,   *(the beloved)*
Or what strong hand can hold his swift foot back,
Or who his spoil° of beauty can forbid?   *destruction*
  O none, unless this miracle have might:
  That in black ink my love may still shine bright.

66

Tired with all these°, for restful death I cry: *(the ensuing wrongs)*
As,° to behold desert° a beggar born,   *For example / merit*
And needy nothing trimmed in jollity,[1]
And purest faith unhappily forsworn,°   *betrayed; perjured*
5 And gilded honour shamefully misplaced,
And maiden virtue rudely strumpeted,
And right perfection wrongfully disgraced,
And strength by limping sway° disablèd,   *feeble leaders*
And art made tongue-tied° by authority,   *learning silenced*
10 And folly, doctor-like, controlling skill,[2]
And simple truth miscalled simplicity,°   *naïveté*
And captive good attending° captain ill.   *serving*
  Tired with all these, from these would I be gone,
  Save that to die I leave my love alone.

67

Ah, wherefore with infection[1] should he live
And with his presence grace impiety,
That° sin by him advantage should achieve   *So that*
And lace° itself with his society?   *decorate*
5 Why should false painting imitate his cheek,
And steal dead seeming of[2] his living hue?
Why should poor° beauty indirectly seek   *lesser*
Roses of shadow,° since his rose is true?   *Cosmetic beauty*
Why should he live now nature bankrupt is,
10 Beggared of blood to blush through lively veins,
For she hath no exchequer° now but his,   *treasury*

Sonnet 65
1. How can beauty make a (legal) case against such a power to destroy?
2. Treasure chest; coffin.
Sonnet 66
1. And ungifted (or impoverished) worthlessness adorned with finery.

2. And folly, feigning erudition, dominating true wisdom or ability. Before modern medicine, doctors were often portrayed as fools or con artists.
Sonnet 67
1. The world's ills (as in 66).
2. *dead seeming of*: an inanimate outward resemblance from.

And proud of many, lives upon his gains?³
    O, him she stores° to show what wealth she had   *keeps*
In days long since, before these last so bad.

68¹

Thus is his cheek the map° of days outworn,   *image*
When beauty lived and died as flowers do now,
5 Before these bastard signs of fair° were borne°   *cosmetics / worn; born*
Or durst inhabit on a living brow;
Before the golden tresses of the dead,
The right of sepulchres,² were shorn away
To live a second life on second head;
Ere beauty's dead fleece made another gay.
In him those holy antique hours° are seen   *good old days*
10 Without all ornament, itself and true,
Making no summer of another's green,
Robbing no old to dress his beauty new;
    And him as for a map doth nature store,°   *keep*
    To show false art what beauty was of yore.

69

Those parts of thee that the world's eye doth view
Want° nothing that the thought of hearts can mend.°   *Lack / imagine better*
All tongues, the voice of souls, give thee that due,
Utt'ring bare truth even so as foes commend.¹
5 Thy outward thus with outward praise is crowned,
But those same tongues that give thee so thine own°   *your due*
In other accents° do this praise confound°   *words / undermine*
By seeing farther than the eye hath shown.
They look into the beauty of thy mind,
10 And that in guess they measure by thy deeds.
Then, churls, their thoughts—although their eyes were kind—
To thy fair flower add the rank smell of weeds.
    But why thy odour matcheth not thy show,°   *appearance*
    The soil is this: that thou dost common grow.²

70¹

That thou are blamed shall not be thy defect,
For slander's mark° was ever yet the fair.   *target*
The ornament of beauty is suspect,°   *suspicion*
A crow that flies in heaven's sweetest air.
5 So° thou be good, slander doth but approve   *So long as*
Thy worth the greater, being wooed of time;²
For canker vice³ the sweetest buds doth love,
And thou present'st a pure unstainèd prime.°   *youth*
Thou hast passed by the ambush of young days
10 Either not assailed, or victor being charged;

3. Though (falsely) taking pride in her abundance (of off-spring?), lives off the interest he earns (from his endow-ment of beauty).
Sonnet 68
1. This sonnet links with 67.
2. Properly belonging to tombs (wigs were made from the hair of corpses).
Sonnet 69
1. Uttering minimal truth, in the way that enemies

praise.
2. The ground (reason; also, stain) is this: you are becom-ing low (promiscuous).
Sonnet 70
1. This sonnet links with 69.
2. *slander . . . time:* the gossip merely proves that you're so popular ("wooed of time") that you're worth even more.
3. Slander, like a cankerworm.

Yet this thy praise cannot be so° thy praise   *enough*
To tie up envy, evermore enlarged.°   *forever at large*
  If some suspect of ill masked not thy show,°   *appearance*
  Then thou alone kingdoms of hearts shouldst owe.°   *own*

71

No longer mourn for me when I am dead
Than you shall hear the surly sullen bell
Give warning to the world that I am fled
From this vile world with vilest[1] worms to dwell.
5 Nay, if you read this line, remember not
The hand that writ it; for I love you so
That I in your sweet thoughts would be forgot
If thinking on me then should make you woe.
O, if, I say, you look upon this verse
10 When I perhaps compounded am° with clay,   *am mixed*
Do not so much as my poor name rehearse,°   *repeat; rebury*
But let your love even with my life decay,
  Lest the wise world should look into your moan
  And mock you with me° after I am gone.   *for loving me*

72

O, lest the world should task you to recite
What merit lived in me that you should love,
After my death, dear love, forget me quite;
For you in me can nothing worthy prove—
5 Unless you would devise some virtuous lie
To do more for me than mine own desert,
And hang more praise upon deceasèd I
Than niggard truth would willingly impart.
O, lest your true love may seem false in this,
10 That you for love speak well of me untrue,°   *untruthfully*
My° name be buried where my body is,   *Let my*
And live no more to shame nor me nor you;
  For I am shamed by that which I bring forth,[1]
  And so should you,° to love things nothing worth.   *you be*

73

That time of year thou mayst in me behold
When yellow leaves, or none, or few, do hang
Upon those boughs which shake against the cold,
Bare ruined choirs where late the sweet birds sang.[1]
5 In me thou seest the twilight of such day
As after sunset fadeth in the west,
Which by and by black night doth take away,
Death's second self, that seals up all in rest.
In me thou seest the glowing of such fire
10 That° on the ashes of his youth[2] doth lie   *As*

Sonnet 71
1. Q's "vildest" is an archaic form of "vilest" that may also
carry the connotation of "most reviled."
Sonnet 72
1. Presumably alluding to the writer's poems or to his
profession as actor and playwright.
Sonnet 73
1. *choirs:* the area in a church where the choir ("sweet

birds") sings; gatherings of manuscript "leaves" (line 2),
or quires ("quiers" in Q).
2. Perhaps referring to the phoenix, a legendary self-
resurrecting bird believed to live in cycles of several centuries, dying in flames and being reborn from the ashes.
See also 19.4.

As the death-bed whereon it must expire,
Consumed with that which it was nourished by.³
  This thou perceiv'st, which makes thy love more strong,
  To love that° well which thou must leave ere long.   *(the speaker); (life)*

74¹

But be contented when that fell arrest°   *fearful death*
Without all bail shall carry me away.
My life hath in this line° some interest,°   *verse / legal claim*
Which for memorial still with thee shall stay.
5 When thou reviewest° this, thou dost review   *reread*
The very part° was consecrate to thee.   *part of me that*
The earth can have but earth, which is his due;
My spirit is thine, the better part of me.
So then thou hast but lost the dregs of life,
10 The prey of worms, my body being dead,
The coward conquest of a wretch's knife,²
Too base of° thee to be rememberèd.   *by*
  The worth of that° is that which it contains,   *(the body)*
  And that is this,° and this with thee remains.   *this spirit (his poetry)*

75

So are you to my thoughts as food to life,
Or as sweet-seasoned° showers are to the ground;   *spring*
And for the peace of you° I hold such strife   *you provide*
As 'twixt a miser and his wealth is found:
5 Now proud as an enjoyer, and anon
Doubting the filching age¹ will steal his treasure;
Now counting° best to be with you alone,   *estimating*
Then bettered° that the world may see my pleasure;   *better contented*
Sometime all full with feasting on your sight,
10 And by and by clean° starvèd for a look;   *wholly*
Possessing or pursuing no delight
Save what is had or must from you be took.
  Thus do I pine and surfeit day by day,
  Or° gluttoning on all, or all away.°   *Either / having nothing*

76

Why is my verse so barren of new pride,°   *adornments*
So far from variation or quick° change?   *lively*
Why, with the time,° do I not glance aside   *following the fashion*
To new-found methods and to compounds¹ strange?
5 Why write I still all one, ever the same,
And keep invention in a noted weed,²
That every word doth almost tell my name,
Showing their birth and where° they did proceed?   *whence*
O know, sweet love, I always write of you,

---

3. Ironically, the fire is choked ("consumed") by (along with) the ashes, which are the residue of the fuel that the fire previously fed upon ("was nourished by").
Sonnet 74
1. This sonnet links with 73.
2. The cowardly conquest of a wretch such as Death (who was thought to carry a scythe).

Sonnet 75
1. Fearing that these dishonest times.
Sonnet 76
1. *compounds*: stylistic or formal mixtures; compound words; elaborate medicines (with "methods," which also refers to both literary and medical treatments).
2. And keep literary creativity in such familiar clothing.

10 And you and love are still my argument;°   *always my topic*
    So all my best is dressing old words new,
    Spending again what is already spent;
      For as the sun is daily new and old,
      So is my love, still telling what is told.

77[1]

    Thy glass° will show thee how thy beauties wear,[2]   *mirror*
    Thy dial° how thy precious minutes waste,   *sundial*
    The vacant leaves thy mind's imprint° will bear,   *written ideas*
    And of this book this learning mayst thou taste:
5   The wrinkles which thy glass will truly show
    Of mouthèd° graves will give thee memory;°   *gaping / remind you*
    Thou by thy dial's shady stealth° mayst know   *stealing shadow*
    Time's thievish progress to eternity;
    Look what° thy memory cannot contain   *Whatever*
10 Commit to these waste blanks,° and thou shalt find   *empty pages*
    Those children nursed,° delivered from thy brain,   *preserved*
    To take a new acquaintance of thy mind.°   *strike you afresh*
      These offices° so oft as thou wilt look   *functions*
      Shall profit thee and much enrich thy book.

78[1]

    So oft have I invoked thee for my muse
    And found such fair assistance in my verse
    As every alien pen hath got my use,[2]
    And under thee° their poesy disperse.   *with you as patron*
5   Thine eyes, that taught the dumb on high° to sing   *aloud*
    And heavy ignorance aloft to fly,
    Have added feathers to the learned's wing[3]
    And given grace° a double majesty.   *excellence*
    Yet be most proud of that which I compile,°   *write*
10 Whose influence° is thine and born of thee.   *power to move*
    In others' works thou dost but mend° the style,   *improve*
    And arts° with thy sweet graces gracèd be;   *(their) artistry*
      But thou art all my art, and dost advance
      As high as learning my rude ignorance.

79

    Whilst I alone did call upon thy aid
    My verse alone had all thy gentle grace;
    But now my gracious numbers are decayed,
    And my sick muse doth give another place.°   *way to another poet*
5   I grant, sweet love, thy lovely argument[1]
    Deserves the travail° of a worthier pen,   *labor*
    Yet what of thee thy poet doth invent
    He robs thee of, and pays it thee again.
    He lends thee virtue, and he stole that word
10 From thy behaviour; beauty doth he give,
    And found it in thy cheek: he can afford°   *extend*

Sonnet 77
1. This sonnet appears to have accompanied the gift of a notebook.
2. Last; wear away; "were" (Q's spelling).
Sonnet 78
1. This sonnet begins the rival poet sequence (78–80,

82–86).
2. That every other poet imitates me.
3. Have improved the poetic "flights" of even accomplished poets.
Sonnet 79
1. The subject of your loveliness.

No praise to thee but what in thee doth live.
Then thank him not for that which he doth say,
Since what he owes thee thou thyself dost pay.

80

O, how I faint° when I of you do write,   *get discouraged*
Knowing a better spirit° doth use your name,   *(the rival poet)*
And in the praise thereof spends all his might,
To make me tongue-tied, speaking of your fame!
5 But since your worth, wide as the ocean is,
The humble as° the proudest sail doth bear,   *as well as*
My saucy barque,° inferior far to his,   *impudent boat*
On your broad main° doth wilfully appear.   *waters*
Your shallowest help will hold me up afloat
10 Whilst he upon your soundless° deep doth ride;   *bottomless*
Or, being wrecked, I am a worthless boat,
He of tall building[1] and of goodly pride.°   *magnificence*
    Then if he thrive and I be cast away,
    The worst was this: my love was my decay.

81[1]

Or° I shall live your epitaph to make,   *Either*
Or you survive when I in earth am rotten.
From hence° your memory death cannot take,   *the world; my poetry*
Although in me each part° will be forgotten.   *each of my attributes*
5 Your name from hence° immortal life shall have,   *henceforth; my poetry*
Though I, once gone, to all the world must die.
The earth can yield me but a common grave
When you entombèd in men's eyes shall lie.
Your monument shall be my gentle verse,
10 Which eyes not yet created shall o'er-read,
And tongues to be° your being shall rehearse°   *future tongues / recite*
When all the breathers of this world are dead.
    You still shall live—such virtue° hath my pen—   *power*
    Where breath most breathes, even in° the mouths of men.   *right in*

82

I grant thou wert not married to my muse,
And therefore mayst without attaint o'erlook°   *dishonor read*
The dedicated[1] words which writers° use   *other writers*
Of their fair subject, blessing every book.
5 Thou art as fair in knowledge as in hue,°   *appearance*
Finding thy worth a limit° past my praise,   *region*
And therefore art enforced to seek anew
Some fresher stamp of these time-bettering days.[2]
And do so, love; yet when they have devised
10 What strainèd touches rhetoric can lend,
Thou, truly fair, wert truly sympathized[3]
In true plain words by thy true-telling friend;

Sonnet 80
1. Tall, strong build.
Sonnet 81
1. Except for lines 2–3 and 10–11, any two consecutive lines in this sonnet form a complete sentence.

Sonnet 82
1. Devoted; referring to a prefatory dedication.
2. Some more recent imprint (commendation) of these culturally progressive times.
3. Would be accurately represented.

And their gross painting° might be better used   cosmetics; flattery
Where cheeks need blood: in thee it is abused.°   used wrongly

83

I never saw that you did painting° need,   cosmetics
And therefore to your fair° no painting set.   beauty
I found—or thought I found—you did exceed
The barren tender° of a poet's debt;   payment
5   And therefore have I slept in your report:[1]
That° you yourself, being extant, well might show   So that
How far a modern° quill doth come too short,   trite; fashionable
Speaking of worth, what worth[2] in you doth grow.
This silence for° my sin you did impute,   to be
10   Which shall be most my glory, being dumb;
For I impair not beauty, being mute,
When others would give life, and bring a tomb.[3]
There lives more life in one of your fair eyes
Than both your poets can in praise devise.

84

Who is it that says most which[1] can say more
Than this rich praise: that you alone are you,[2]
In whose confine immurèd is the store
Which should example where your equal grew?[3]
5   Lean penury within that pen doth dwell
That to his subject lends not some small glory;
But he that writes of you, if he can tell
That you are you, so dignifies his story.
Let him but copy what in you is writ,
10   Not making worse what nature made so clear,°   purely excellent
And such a counterpart shall fame° his wit,   copy will make famous
Making his style admirèd everywhere.
You to your beauteous blessings add a curse,[4]
Being fond on praise, which makes your praises worse.[5]

85

My tongue-tied muse in manners holds her still°   tactfully says nothing
While comments of° your praise, richly compiled,   commentaries in
Reserve thy character° with golden quill   Hoard up your features
And precious phrase by all the muses filed.°   polished
5   I think good thoughts whilst other° write good words,   others
And like unlettered clerk still cry 'Amen'
To every hymn[1] that able spirit affords°   offers
In polished form of well-refinèd pen.
Hearing you praised I say ' 'Tis so, 'tis true,'

Sonnet 83
1. Neglected to sing your praises.
2. In speaking of value of the worth that.
3. When others who try to make you live in their writings
only end up burying you.
Sonnet 84
1. *Who . . . which:* What hyperbolical enthusiast.
2. The line is a poetical in-joke, echoing a passage in
Gervase Markham's *Devoreux* (published 1597) that
addresses and praises Penelope Rich, a famous beauty of
the Elizabethan court. Like *Devoreux*, Q has *"Rich"*
rather than "rich." See also 85.2.

3. *In . . . grew:* Within whom is contained the stock that
would be needed to produce your equal?
4. Personality flaw; vexation (for those who would praise
you).
5. Being (too) fond of praise, which makes the praise
seem like flattery; being (too) fond of the sort of praise
that detracts from you.
Sonnet 85
1. *like . . . hymn:* like an illiterate parish clerk reflexively
approve ("cry 'Amen'" after) every poem ("hymn") of
praise.

10 And to the most° of praise add something more; *highest*
But that is in my thought,° whose love to you, *unspoken*
Though words come hindmost, holds his rank before.° *before all others*
   Then others for the breath of words respect,° *regard*
   Me for my dumb thoughts, speaking in effect.° *in reality*

86

Was it the proud full sail of his° great verse *(a rival poet's)*
Bound for the prize° of all-too-precious you *pirate's spoils*
That did my ripe thoughts in my brain inhearse,° *bury*
Making their tomb the womb wherein they grew?
5 Was it his spirit, by spirits taught to write
Above a mortal pitch,° that struck me dead? *height*
No, neither he nor his compeers[1] by night
Giving him aid my verse astonishèd.° *made silent*
He nor that affable familiar ghost° *spirit*
10 Which nightly gulls° him with intelligence,° *fools / ideas*
As victors, of my silence cannot boast;
I was not sick of any fear from thence.
   But when your countenance filled up[2] his line,
   Then lacked I matter; that enfeebled mine.

87

Farewell—thou art too dear° for my possessing, *costly*
And like° enough thou know'st thy estimate.° *it is likely / value*
The charter of thy worth gives thee releasing;[1]
My bonds in thee are all determinate.° *terminated*
5 For how do I hold thee but by thy granting,
And for that riches where is my deserving?
The cause of this fair gift in me is wanting,
And so my patent back again is swerving.[2]
Thyself thou gav'st, thy own worth then not knowing,
10 Or me to whom thou gav'st it else mistaking;° *overestimating*
So thy great gift, upon misprision growing,° *based on error*
Comes home again, on better judgement making.[3]
   Thus have I had thee as a dream doth flatter:° *creates an illusion*
   In sleep a king, but waking no such matter.

88

When thou shalt be disposed to set me light° *value me little*
And place my merit in the eye of scorn,
Upon thy side against myself I'll fight,
And prove thee virtuous though thou art forsworn.
5 With mine own weakness being best acquainted,
Upon thy part I can set down a story
Of faults concealed wherein I am attainted,
That thou in losing me shall win much glory;
And I by this will be a gainer too;
10 For bending all my loving thoughts on thee,
The injuries that to myself I do,
Doing thee vantage, double vantage me.

Sonnet 86
1. Colleagues (the "spirits" in line 5).
2. Your features gave subject matter to; your approval made up for any lack in.

Sonnet 87
1. The privilege you derive from your worth releases you from love's bonds.
2. My rights of possession revert to you.
3. *on . . . making:* when you realize your error.

Such is my love, to thee I so belong,
That for thy right myself will bear all wrong.

89

Say that thou didst forsake me for some fault,
And I will comment° upon that offence;   *elaborate*
Speak of my lameness, and I straight will halt,[1]
Against thy reasons making no defence.
5   Thou canst not, love, disgrace me half so ill,
To set a form upon desirèd change,[2]
As I'll myself disgrace, knowing thy will.
I will acquaintance strangle and look strange,[3]
Be absent from thy walks,° and in my tongue   *familiar places*
10 Thy sweet belovèd name no more shall dwell,
Lest I, too much profane, should do it wrong,
And haply° of our old acquaintance tell.   *by chance*
    For thee, against myself I'll vow debate;°   *combat*
    For I must ne'er love him whom thou dost hate.

90[1]

Then hate me when thou wilt, if ever, now,
Now while the world is bent my deeds to cross,°   *foil*
Join with the spite of fortune, make me bow,
And do not drop in for an after-loss.[2]
5   Ah do not, when my heart hath scaped this sorrow,
Come in the rearward of a conquered woe;[3]
Give not a windy night a rainy morrow
To linger out a purposed overthrow.[4]
If thou wilt leave me, do not leave me last,
10 When other petty griefs have done their spite,
But in the onset come; so shall I taste
At first the very worst of fortune's might,
    And other strains° of woe, which now seem woe,   *types; burdens*
    Compared with loss of thee will not seem so.

91

Some glory in their birth, some in their skill,
Some in their wealth, some in their body's force,
Some in their garments (though new-fangled ill),°   *fashionably ugly*
Some in their hawks and hounds, some in their horse,°   *horses*
5   And every humour hath his° adjunct pleasure   *temperament has its*
Wherein it finds a joy above the rest.
But these particulars are not my measure;°   *(of joy)*
All these I better° in one general best.   *exceed*
Thy love is better than high birth to me,
10 Richer than wealth, prouder than garments' cost,
Of more delight than hawks or horses be,
And having thee of all men's pride[1] I boast,

Sonnet 89
1. Talk of my disability (perhaps alluding to the lame meter of line 2), and I at once will limp (stop objecting).
2. To lend justification to the change you seek.
3. I will end our familiarity and act like a stranger.
Sonnet 90
1. This sonnet links with 89.

2. Do not fall upon me to inflict a later disaster.
3. Assault me again after I have overcome my present grief.
4. *To . . . overthrow:* By protracting or delaying your intended assault.
Sonnet 91
1. Of everything in which others take pride.

Wretched in this alone: that thou mayst take
All this away, and me most wretched make.

92[1]

But do thy worst to steal thyself away,
For term of° life thou art assurèd mine,   *the duration of my*
And life no longer than thy love will stay,
For it depends upon that love of thine.
5   Then need I not to fear the worst of wrongs
When in the least of them[2] my life hath end.
I see a better state to me belongs
Than that which on thy humour doth depend.
Thou canst not vex me with inconstant mind,
10 Since that my life on thy revolt doth lie.[3]
O, what a happy title[4] do I find—
Happy to have thy love, happy to die!
    But what's so blessèd fair that fears no blot?
    Thou mayst be false, and yet I know it not.

93[1]

So shall I live supposing thou art true
Like a deceivèd husband; so love's face°   *appearance*
May still seem love to me, though altered new—
Thy looks with me, thy heart in other place.
5   For there can live no hatred in thine eye,
Therefore in that I cannot know thy change.
In many's looks the false heart's history
Is writ in moods and frowns and wrinkles strange,[2]
But heaven in thy creation did decree
10 That in thy face sweet love should ever dwell;
Whate'er thy thoughts or thy heart's workings be,
Thy looks should nothing thence but sweetness tell.
    How like Eve's apple doth thy beauty grow
    If thy sweet virtue answer not thy show![3]

94

They that have power to hurt and will do none,
That do not do the thing they most do show,[1]
Who moving others are themselves as stone,
Unmovèd, cold,° and to temptation slow—   *composed*
5   They rightly° do inherit heaven's graces,   *truly*
And husband nature's riches from expense;[2]
They are the lords and owners of their faces,
Others but stewards° of their excellence.   *hired managers*
The summer's flower is to the summer sweet
10 Though to itself it only live and die,[3]
But if that flower with base infection meet

Sonnet 92
1. This sonnet links with 91.
2. In the slightest sign of your displeasure.
3. Since change in your affections would kill me.
4. What a claim to be considered happy.
Sonnet 93
1. This sonnet links with 92.
2. In signs of anger and frowns and displeased expressions.
3. Does not correspond to your looks.
Sonnet 94
1. *they most do show:* that their appearance implies.
2. And protect nature's rich endowment from waste.
3. *is . . . die:* emits its sweetness to others even though it lives and dies in apparent isolation (unpollinated: compare 54.5–11).

The basest weed outbraves his dignity;[4]
  For sweetest things turn sourest by their deeds:
  Lilies that fester smell far worse than weeds.[5]

95

How sweet and lovely dost thou make the shame
Which, like a canker° in the fragrant rose,   *cankerworm*
Doth spot the beauty of thy budding name!°   *fame*
O, in what sweets dost thou thy sins enclose!
5 That tongue that tells the story of thy days,
Making lascivious comments on thy sport,°   *amorous adventures*
Cannot dispraise, but in a kind of praise,
Naming thy name, blesses° an ill report.   *makes positive*
O, what a mansion have those vices got
10 Which for their habitation chose out thee,
Where beauty's veil doth cover every blot
And all things turns to fair that eyes can see!
  Take heed, dear heart, of this large privilege:
  The hardest knife ill used doth lose his° edge.   *its*

96

Some say thy fault is youth, some wantonness;°   *promiscuity; frivolity*
Some say thy grace is youth and gentle sport.[1]
Both grace and faults are loved of more and less;°   *by people of all ranks*
Thou mak'st faults graces that to thee resort.
5 As on the finger of a thronèd queen
The basest jewel will be well esteemed,
So are those errors that in thee are seen
To truths translated° and for true things deemed.   *converted*
How many lambs might the stern° wolf betray   *vicious*
10 If like° a lamb he could his looks translate!   *into*
How many gazers mightst thou lead away
If thou wouldst use the strength of all thy state!°   *power*
  But do not so: I love thee in such sort°   *such a way*
  As, thou being mine, mine is thy good report.[2]

97

How like a winter hath my absence been
From thee, the pleasure of the fleeting year!
What freezings have I felt, what dark days seen,
What old December's bareness everywhere!
5 And yet this time removed° was summer's time,   *away*
The teeming autumn big° with rich increase,   *pregnant*
Bearing the wanton burden of the prime°   *harvest of wanton spring*
Like widowed wombs after their lords' decease.
Yet this abundant issue seemed[1] to me
10 But hope of orphans and unfathered fruit,
For summer and his pleasures wait° on thee,   *attend*
And thou away, the very birds are mute;

---

4. Exceeds the flower in magnificence.
5. This line also occurs in *The Reign of King Edward III*,
a play printed anonymously in 1596 and sometimes attributed, in whole or in part, to Shakespeare.

Sonnet 96
1. A gentleman's sexual prerogative.
2. Reputation. The same couplet ends 36.
Sonnet 97
1. Offspring seemed in prospect, before the beloved's
absence.

Or if they sing, 'tis with so dull a cheer°   *such a dismal mood*
That leaves look pale, dreading the winter's near.

98

From you have I been absent in the spring
When proud-pied° April, dressed in all his trim,°   *multicolored / finery*
Hath put a spirit of youth in everything,
That heavy Saturn[1] laughed and leapt with him.
5   Yet nor the lays° of birds nor the sweet smell   *not the songs*
Of different flowers° in odour and in hue   *flowers differing*
Could make me any summer's story tell,°   *speak (write) happily*
Or from their proud lap° pluck them where they grew;   *(the ground)*
Nor did I wonder at the lily's white,
10 Nor praise the deep vermilion in the rose.
They were but sweet, but figures° of delight   *merely emblems*
Drawn after you, you pattern of all those;
   Yet seemed it winter still, and, you away,
   As with your shadow I with these did play.[2]

99[1]

The forward° violet thus did I chide: *early*
Sweet thief, whence didst thou steal thy sweet° that smells,   *perfume*
If not from my love's breath? The purple pride°   *beauty*
Which on thy soft cheek for complexion dwells
5   In my love's veins thou hast too grossly° dyed.   *obviously*
The lily I condemnèd for thy hand,[2]
And buds of marjoram[3] had stol'n thy hair;
The roses fearfully on thorns did stand,
One blushing shame, another white despair;
10 A third, nor red nor white, had stol'n of both,°   *(making it pink)*
And to° his robb'ry had annexed thy breath;   *in addition to*
But for his theft in pride of all his growth
A vengeful canker° ate him up to death.   *cankerworm*
   More flowers I noted, yet I none could see
   But sweet° or colour it had stol'n from thee.   *perfume*

100

Where are thou, muse, that thou forget'st so long
To speak of that which gives thee all thy might?
Spend'st thou thy fury[1] on some worthless song,
Dark'ning° thy power to lend base subjects light?   *Debasing*
5   Return, forgetful muse, and straight° redeem   *immediately*
In gentle numbers° time so idly spent;   *noble poetry*
Sing to the ear that doth thy lays esteem
And gives thy pen both skill and argument.°   *substance*
Rise, resty° muse, my love's sweet face survey   *lazy*
10 If° time have any wrinkle graven there.   *To see if*
If any, be a satire to° decay   *satirist of*
And make time's spoils despisèd everywhere.

Sonnet 98
1. The planet Saturn was regarded as cold and slow, exerting a melancholy influence.
2. As if with your image I played with these flowers.
Sonnet 99
1. This sonnet has an extra opening line.

2. For stealing whiteness from your (the beloved's) hand.
3. The herb, sweet of scent and auburn in color.
Sonnet 100
1. Inspiration (the "poet's rage" of 17.11).

Give my love fame faster than time wastes life;
So, thou prevene'st° his scythe and crookèd knife.   *impede*

101[1]

O truant muse, what shall be thy amends
For thy neglect of truth in beauty dyed?
Both truth and beauty on my love depends;
So dost thou too, and therein° dignified.   *therein are you*
5   Make answer, muse. Wilt thou not haply° say   *perhaps*
'Truth needs no colour with his colour fixed,[2]
Beauty no pencil beauty's truth to lay,[3]
But best is best if never intermixed'?°   *(with cosmetics)*
Because he needs no praise wilt thou be dumb?
10   Excuse not silence so, for't lies in thee
To make him much outlive a gilded tomb,
And to be praised of° ages yet to be.   *by*
     Then do thy office,° muse; I teach thee how   *duty*
     To make him seem long° hence as he shows° now.   *a long time / appears*

102

My love is strengthened, though more weak in seeming.°   *appearance*
I love not less, though less the show appear.
That love is merchandized[1] whose rich esteeming°   *appraisal*
The owner's tongue doth publish everywhere.
5   Our love was new and then but in the spring°   *just beginning*
When I was wont to greet it with my lays,
As Philomel[2] in summer's front° doth sing,   *beginning*
And stops her pipe in growth of riper days—
Not that the summer is less pleasant now
10   Than when her mournful hymns did hush the night,
But that wild music burdens[3] every bough,
And sweets grown common lose their dear delight.
     Therefore like her I sometime hold my tongue,
     Because I would not dull° you with my song.   *overfeed*

103

Alack, what poverty my muse brings forth
That, having such a scope to show her pride,[1]
The argument all bare° is of more worth   *subject by itself*
Than when it hath my added praise beside!
5   O blame me not if I no more can write!
Look in your glass° and there appears a face   *mirror*
That overgoes my blunt invention[2] quite,
Dulling° my lines and doing me disgrace.   *(by contrast)*
Were it not sinful then, striving to mend,°   *improve*
10   To mar the subject that before was well?—
For to no other pass° my verses tend   *end*

Sonnet 101
1. This sonnet links with 100.
2. Truth needs no artificial color to be added to his natural coloring.
3. True beauty need apply no (cosmetic) brush.
Sonnet 102
1. (Debased by being) turned into merchandise for sale.
2. Nightingale; with ambiguous hints of the myth of Philomel, whose brother-in-law raped her and ripped out her

tongue to ensure her silence. See Book 6 of Ovid's *Metamorphoses*.
3. Loads; provides a musical refrain (probably from many other poets) on.
Sonnet 103
1. Considering that she has such opportunity (in you) to display her skill (her pride in you).
2. That surpasses my dull powers of invention.

Than of your graces and your gifts to tell;
    And more, much more, than in my verse can sit
    Your own glass shows you when you look in it.

104

To me, fair friend, you never can be old;
For as you were when first your eye I eyed,
Such seems your beauty still. Three winters cold
Have from the forests shook three summers' pride;°   *splendor*
5 Three beauteous springs to yellow autumn turned
In process° of the seasons have I seen,   *the progress*
Three April perfumes in three hot Junes burned
Since first I saw you fresh, which yet° are green.   *who still*
Ah yet doth beauty, like a dial hand,
10 Steal from his figure and no pace perceived;[1]
So your sweet hue,° which methinks still doth stand,   *appearance*
Hath motion, and mine eye may be deceived.
    For fear of which, hear this, thou age unbred:°   *future age*
    Ere you were born was beauty's summer dead.

105

Let not my love be called idolatry,
Nor my belovèd as an idol show,
Since all alike my songs and praises be
To one, of one, still° such, and ever so.   *continually*
5 Kind is my love today, tomorrow kind,
Still constant in a wondrous excellence.
Therefore my verse, to constancy confined,
One thing expressing, leaves out difference.°   *diversity (of theme)*
'Fair, kind, and true' is all my argument,
10 'Fair, kind, and true' varying to other words,
And in this change is my invention spent,[1]
Three themes in one, which wonderous scope affords.
    Fair, kind, and true have often lived alone,°   *separately*
    Which three till now never kept seat° in one.   *dwelt permanently*

106[1]

When in the chronicle of wasted° time   *past*
I see descriptions of the fairest wights,°   *people*
And beauty making beautiful old rhyme
In praise of ladies dead and lovely knights;
5 Then in the blazon[2] of sweet beauty's best,
Of hand, of foot, of lip, of eye, of brow,
I see their antique pen would have expressed
Even such a beauty as you master° now.   *possess*
So all their praises are but prophecies
10 Of this our time, all you prefiguring,
And for° they looked but with divining° eyes   *as / prophetic*
They had not skill enough your worth to sing;   *want to*

Sonnet 104
1. *doth . . . perceived*: beauty imperceptibly "steals" (departs stealthily from; robs from) the youthful appearance ("figure") of the beloved as the hand of the watch ("dial") stealthily progresses ("steals") away from the number ("figure") on the watch face.

Sonnet 105
1. And in varying the words alone my inventiveness is expended.

Sonnet 106
1. See "On his Mistress' Beauty" in the Alternative Versions.
2. Poetic catalog of virtues.

For we° which now behold these present days   *even we*
Have eyes to wonder, but lack tongues to praise.

107

Not mine own fears nor the prophetic soul
Of the wide world dreaming on things to come
Can yet the lease° of my true love control,   *allotted term*
Supposed as forfeit to a confined doom.[1]
5 The mortal moon hath her eclipse endured,[2]
And the sad augurs mock their own presage;[3]
Incertainties now crown themselves assured,[4]
And peace proclaims olives of endless age.[5]
Now with the drops[6] of this most balmy time
10 My love looks fresh, and death to me subscribes,°   *submits*
Since spite of him I'll live in this poor rhyme
While he insults° o'er dull and speechless tribes,[7]   *prevails*
    And thou in this shalt find thy monument
    When tyrants' crests and tombs of brass are spent.°   *ruined*

108

What's in the brain that ink may character°   *express*
Which hath not figured° to thee my true spirit?   *shown*
What's new to speak, what now to register,°   *record*
That may express my love or thy dear merit?
5 Nothing, sweet boy; but yet like prayers divine
I must each day say o'er the very same,
Counting no old thing old, thou mine, I thine,
Even as when first I hallowed thy fair name.
So that eternal love in love's fresh case°   *covering*
10 Weighs not° the dust and injury of age,   *Overlooks*
Nor gives to necessary° wrinkles place,°   *inevitable / priority*
But makes antiquity for aye his page,[1]
    Finding the first conceit of love there bred[2]
    Where time and outward form would° show it dead.   *want to*

109

O never say that I was false of heart,
Though absence seemed my flame to qualify°—   *reduce*
As easy might I from myself depart
As from my soul, which in thy breast doth lie.
5 That is my home of love. If I have ranged,
Like him that travels I return again,
Just to the time,° not with the time exchanged,°   *Punctually / changed*
So that myself bring water for my stain.[1]

Sonnet 107
1. Imagined as limited to a finite term.
2. Survived. The line is variously taken to refer to an eclipse of the moon, to an event in the life (or, more likely, to the death in 1603) of Queen Elizabeth (often known as Diana, the moon goddess), or, less probably, to the defeat of the Spanish Armada (1588).
3. And prophets of doom now ridicule their own prophecies.
4. Desired but doubtful possibilities now celebrate their realization; uncertainty is now unavoidable.
5. And peace declares the olive branches that symbolize it to be everlasting. Perhaps a reference to the peace treaty

with Spain signed by King James, who succeeded Elizabeth.
6. Soothing drops of dew, rain, or balm. Balm was used in the coronation ceremony.
7. Over those legions of dead who have no poetic legacy.
Sonnet 108
1. But makes (old) age forever the (youthful) servant to love; perhaps referring to the pages of poetry written when the "sweet boy" (line 5) was still young.
2. The first feeling (poetic expression) of love generated in that place (the beloved; the poem).
Sonnet 109
1. *for my stain:* to cleanse the stain of my absence.

Never believe, though in my nature reigned
10 All frailties that besiege all kinds of blood,°   *disposition*
That it could so preposterously be stained
To leave for° nothing all thy sum of good;   *exchange for*
    For nothing this wide universe I call
    Save thou my rose; in it thou art my all.

110

Alas, 'tis true, I have gone here and there
And made myself a motley to the view,°   *clown to the world*
Gored° mine own thoughts, sold cheap what is most dear,   *Injured*
Made old offences of affections new.¹
5 Most true it is that I have looked on truth°   *fidelity*
Askance and strangely.° But, by all above,   *coldly*
These blenches° gave my heart another youth,   *alterations*
And worse essays° proved thee my best of love   *experiments*
Now all is done, have what shall have no end;²
10 Mine appetite I never more will grind
On newer proof to try³ an older friend,
A god in love, to whom I am confined.
    Then give me welcome, next my heaven the best,° *next best to heaven*
    Even to thy pure and most most loving breast.

111

O, for my sake do you with¹ fortune chide,
The guilty goddess of my harmful deeds,
That did not better for my life provide
Than public means which public manners breeds.²
5 Thence comes it that my name receives a brand,°   *stigma*
And almost thence my nature is subdued
To what it works in, like the dyer's hand.
Pity me then, and wish I were renewed,°   *cured*
Whilst like a willing patient I will drink
10 Potions of eisel° 'gainst my strong infection; *medicinal vinegar*
No° bitterness that I will bitter think,   *There is no*
Nor double penance to correct correction.° *correct me twice over*
    Pity me then, dear friend, and I assure ye
    Even that your pity is enough to cure me.

112¹

Your love and pity doth th'impression fill°   *eliminates the scar*
Which vulgar° scandal stamped upon my brow;   *public*
For what care I who calls me well or ill,
So you o'er-green my bad, my good allow?²
5 You are my all the world, and I must strive
To know my shames and praises from your tongue—
None else to me, nor I to none alive,

Sonnet 110
1. Repeated traditional misbehavior (infidelity)—or offended old friends—in (my treatment of) new attachments.
2. *have . . . end:* take that (my love) which will not expire.
3. *grind . . . try:* sharpen with new experience to test.
Sonnet 111
1. Q has "wish," which gives a more problematic array of

alternative meanings.
2. Probably: Than employment as an actor, which requires one to curry favor with the public.
Sonnet 112
1. This sonnet links with 111.
2. So long as you allow new growth to cover what is bad in me, and give credit for what is good.

That my steeled sense or changes, right or wrong.[3]
In so profound abyss I throw all care
10   Of others' voices that my adder's sense°   *deaf ears*
To critic and to flatterer stoppèd are.
Mark how with my neglect I do dispense:[4]
   You are so strongly in my purpose bred[5]
   That all the world besides, methinks, they're dead.

113

Since I left you mine eye is in my mind,[1]
And that which governs me to go about°   *And my real sight*
Doth part his° function and is partly blind,   *Divides its*
Seems seeing, but effectually is out;°   *blind*
5   For it no form delivers to the heart
Of bird, of flower, or shape which it doth latch.°   *catch sight of*
Of his quick objects° hath the mind no part,   *fleeting impressions*
Nor his own vision holds[2] what it doth catch;
For if it see the rud'st or gentlest° sight,   *coarsest or noblest*
10   The most sweet favour[3] or deformèd'st creature,
The mountain or the sea, the day or night,
The crow or dove, it shapes them to your feature.[4]
   Incapable of more, replete with you,
   My most true mind thus makes mine eye untrue.

114[1]

Or whether doth my mind, being crowned with you,[2]
Drink up the monarch's plague, this flattery,
Or whether shall I say mine eye saith true,
And that your love taught it this alchemy,[3]
5   To make of monsters and things indigest°   *chaotic*
Such cherubins° as your sweet self resemble,   *angels*
Creating every° bad a perfect best   *from every*
As fast as objects to his beams assemble?[4]
O, 'tis the first, 'tis flatt'ry in my seeing,
10   And my great° mind most kingly drinks it up.   *pompous*
Mine eye well knows what with his gust is 'greeing,[5]
And to his palate doth prepare the cup.
   If it be poisoned, 'tis the lesser sin
   That mine eye loves it and doth first begin.[6]

115

Those lines that I before have writ do lie,
Even those that said I could not love you dearer;
Yet then my judgement knew no reason why

3. *None . . . wrong*: perhaps, There being no one else to
influence me, and no one else's influence being capable
of positively or negatively affecting my hardened disposition.
4. How I excuse my neglect (of "other's voices," line 10).
5. Nurtured in all my plans.
Sonnet 113
1. I see with my mind's eye.
2. Nor does the eye's vision hold on to.
3. Face; perhaps Q's "sweet-favor" means "sweet-
favored," or "good-looking."
4. It makes them look like you.

Sonnet 114
1. This sonnet links with 113.
2. Being made a King by having you. "Or whether" introduces alternatives.
3. And that love of you taught my eye how thus to transform things.
4. As fast as objects come before its gaze. (The eye was
thought to emit beams of light.)
5. What pleases the mind's appetite.
6. And drinks first (like a King's taster).

My most full flame should afterwards burn clearer.
5 But reckoning time,[1] whose millioned accidents
Creep in 'twixt vows° and change decrees of kings,   *(and their performance)*
Tan° sacred beauty, blunt the sharp'st intents,   *Darken*
Divert strong minds to th' course of alt'ring things—
Alas, why, fearing of time's tyranny,
10 Might I not then say[2] 'Now I love you best',
When I was certain o'er° incertainty,   *beyond*
Crowning° the present, doubting of the rest?   *°Exalting*
    Love is a babe; then might I not say so,[3]
    To give° full growth to that which still doth grow.   *Thereby giving*

116

Let me not to the marriage of true minds
Admit impediments.° Love is not love   *legal barriers to marriage*
Which alters when it alteration finds,
Or bends with the remover to remove.[1]
5 O no, it is an ever fixèd mark[2]
That looks on tempests and is never shaken;
It is the star to every wand'ring barque,
Whose worth's unknown although his height be taken.[3]
Love's not time's fool,° though rosy lips and cheeks   *plaything*
10 Within his bending sickle's compass[4] come;
Love alters not with his brief hours and weeks,
But bears it out even to the edge of doom.[5]
    If this be error and upon° me proved,   *against*
    I never writ, nor no man ever loved.

117

Accuse me thus: that I have scanted° all   *neglected*
Wherein I should your great deserts repay,
Forgot upon your dearest love to call
Whereto all bonds do tie me day by day;
5 That I have frequent° been with unknown minds,°   *friendly / strangers*
And given to time your own dear-purchased right;[1]
That I have hoisted sail to all the winds
Which should° transport me farthest from your sight.   *were likely to*
Book both my wilfulness and errors down,
10 And on just proof surmise accumulate;[2]
Bring me within the level° of your frown,   *aim*
But shoot not at me in your wakened hate,
    Since my appeal says I did strive to prove[3]
    The constancy and virtue of your love.

Sonnet 115
1. But taking time into account; but time, which settles accounts.
2. Was I not then right to have said.
3. Thus I shouldn't say, "Now I love you best" (line 10).

Sonnet 116
1. Or abandons the relationship when the loved one is unfaithful or has departed or died, or when time ("the remover") alters things for the worse.
2. An unmoving sea mark, such as a lighthouse or a beacon, which provides a constant reference point for sailors.
3. *Whose . . . taken:* The star's (great) intrinsic value cannot be assessed, although navigators at sea can measure height above the horizon.
4. Within range of time's curved (and hostile) scythe. "Compass" also recalls the imagery of the second quatrain.
5. But endures until the eve of doomsday.

Sonnet 117
1. And wasted idly what should have been your right (rite) because acquired by your great worth and affection (because acquired at your great cost).
2. And pile suspicion on top of your proof.
3. Since my defense is that I was trying to test.

118

Like° as, to make our appetites more keen,   *Just*
With eager° compounds we our palate urge;°   *sharp / stimulate*
As to prevent° our maladies unseen   *forestall*
We sicken to shun sickness when we purge:[1]
5   Even so, being full of your ne'er cloying sweetness,
To bitter sauces did I frame° my feeding,   *adjust*
And, sick of welfare,[2] found a kind of meetness°   *suitability*
To be diseased ere that there was true needing.
Thus policy° in love, t'anticipate   *strategy*
10   The ills that were not, grew to faults assured,
And brought to[3] medicine a healthful state
Which, rank of goodness, would by ill be cured.[4]
     But thence I learn, and find the lesson true:
     Drugs poison him that so° fell sick of you.   *thus; so badly*

119

What potions have I drunk of siren[1] tears
Distilled from limbecks° foul as hell within,   *stills*
Applying° fears to hopes and hopes to fears,   *(as a medicine)*
Still° losing when I saw myself° to win!   *Always / expected*
5   What wretched errors hath my heart committed
Whilst it hath thought itself so blessèd never!
How have mine eyes out of their spheres been fitted[2]
In the distraction° of this madding° fever!   *delirium / fit-inducing*
O benefit of ill! Now I find true
10   That better is by evil still made better,
And ruined love when it is built anew
Grows fairer than at first, more strong, far greater.
     So I return rebuked to my content,
     And gain by ills thrice more than I have spent.

120

That you were once unkind befriends me now,
And for° that sorrow which I then did feel   *because of*
Needs must I under my transgression bow,
Unless my nerves° were brass or hammered steel.   *sinews*
5   For if you were by my unkindness shaken
As I by yours, you've past a hell of time,
And I, a tyrant, have no leisure taken
To weigh° how once I suffered in° your crime.   *contemplate / from*
O that our night of woe[1] might have remembered°   *reminded*
10   My deepest sense how hard true sorrow hits,
And soon to you as you to me then tendered°   *offered*
The humble salve which wounded bosoms fits![2]

Sonnet 118
1. We make ourselves sick with medicine that causes vomiting or bowel movements so as to prevent greater illness.
2. Made ill by good food.
3. Treated with; brought to the need of.
4. Overfull with goodness (health, the beloved), sought to be cured by disease (evil).
Sonnet 119
1. Deceitfully and dangerously alluring. Sirens were mythological creatures, part bird, part woman, said to lure sailors to their death with their irresistible songs.
2. Been driven convulsively out of their sockets.
Sonnet 120
1. Our earlier time of suffering (caused by the youth's unfaithfulness).
2. The salve of apology that is just the thing for an injured heart.

But that your trespass° now becomes a fee;°   *offense / compensation*
Mine ransoms° yours, and yours must ransom me.   *absolves*

121

'Tis better to be vile than vile esteemed°   *reputed vile*
When not to be receives reproach of being,°   *being so (vile)*
And the just pleasure lost, which is so deemed
Not by our feeling but by others' seeing.[1]
5 For why should others' false adulterate° eyes   *corrupted*
Give salutation to my sportive blood?[2]
Or on my frailties why are frailer spies,
Which in their wills[3] count bad what I think good?
No, I am that I am, and they that level°   *aim*
10 At my abuses reckon up their own.
I may be straight, though they themselves be bevel;°   *crooked*
By their rank° thoughts my deeds must not be shown,°   *foul / measured*
    Unless this general evil they maintain:
    All men are bad and in their badness reign.°   *thrive*

122

Thy gift, thy tables,° are within my brain   *notebook*
Full charactered° with lasting memory,   *written*
Which shall above that idle rank[1] remain
Beyond all date, even to eternity;
5 Or at the least so long as brain and heart
Have faculty° by nature to subsist,   *power*
Till each to razed° oblivion yield his part   *destroying*
Of thee, thy record never can be missed.°   *lost*
That poor retention[2] could not so much hold,
10 Nor need I tallies thy dear love to score;[3]
Therefore to give them° from me was I bold,   *(the "tables")*
To trust those tables° that receive thee more.   *memory*
    To keep an adjunct° to remember thee   *aid*
    Were to import° forgetfulness in me.   *imply*

123

No, time, thou shalt not boast that I do change!
Thy pyramids built up with newer might[1]
To me are nothing° novel, nothing strange,   *in no way*
They are but dressings of a former sight.[2]
5 Our dates° are brief, and therefore we admire   *lives*
What thou dost foist upon us that is old,
And rather make them born to our desire[3]

Sonnet 121

1. *And . . . seeing*: And we are denied the appropriate, innocent pleasure (or, we don't even get to enjoy the sin we've supposedly committed), which is considered sinful not by us but by others.

2. Wink knowingly at my lustful behavior.

3. *Or . . . wills*: Why should my failings be pried into by even more culpable people, who wilfully (who licentiously; who in Will Shakespeare).

Sonnet 122

1. Trivial status (of the "tables" as opposed to "memory").

2. That inadequate container (the "tables"); that faulty memory.

3. Nor do I need the notched sticks used in calculating sums (to which the "tables" are contemptuously compared) to reckon up your precious love.

Sonnet 123

1. Grand buildings constructed by more modern means. Possibly referring to structures erected in Rome in 1586 or in London in 1603 (for James's coronation), but retaining a sense of almost timeless Egyptian antiquity.

2. Replicas of what's been seen before.

3. And consider them made just for us.

Than think that we before have heard them told.°   described
Thy registers° and thee I both defy,   records
10   Not wond'ring at the present nor the past;
For thy records and what we see doth lie,
Made more or less by thy continual haste.[4]
This I do vow, and this shall ever be:
I will be true despite thy scythe and thee.

124

If my dear love° were but the child of state[1]   (for you)
It might for fortune's bastard be unfathered,[2]
As subject to time's love or to time's hate,
Weeds among weeds or flowers with flowers gathered.[3]
5   No, it was builded far from accident;°   chance
It suffers° not in smiling pomp, nor falls   changes
Under the blow of thrallèd° discontent   captive
Whereto th'inviting time our fashion calls.[4]
It fears not policy,° that heretic   expediency
10   Which works on leases of short-numbered hours,°   short-term contracts
But all alone stands hugely politic,°   prudent
That it nor° grows with heat° nor drowns with showers.   neither / prosperity
To this I witness call the fools of time,
Which die for goodness, who have lived for crime.[5]

125

Were't aught to me I bore the canopy,[1]
With my extern° the outward honouring,   exterior action
Or laid great bases for eternity[2]
Which proves more short than waste° or ruining?   decay
5   Have I not seen dwellers on form and favour[3]
Lose all and more by paying too much rent,°   overdoing homage
For compound sweet forgoing simple savour,[4]
Pitiful thrivers in their gazing spent?[5]
No, let me be obsequious° in thy heart,   dutiful
10   And take thou my oblation,° poor but free,°   offering / freely given
Which is not mixed with seconds,[6] knows no art°   artifice
But mutual render,° only me for thee.   exchange
Hence, thou suborned informer![7] A true soul
When most impeached° stands least in thy control.   accused

4. Raised and destroyed by time's swift passage; made to seem more or less majestic by virtue of newness or antiquity and the tastes of the times.
Sonnet 124
1. Were simply the result of circumstances; of your high position.
2. It might be disinherited as a passing fancy, a product of fortune (chance, wealth).
3. *As . . . gathered:* Regarded as useless or valuable as time and fortune decide.
4. To which ("pomp" and "discontent") we are driven by the latest trend ("fashion").
5. *To . . . crime:* I call as witness those playthings of time

who, having lived wicked lives, reform or repent at death.
Sonnet 125
1. Would I care if I enhanced my status by carrying a ceremonial canopy for a royal person?
2. Laid foundations for eternal monuments.
3. Seen those who depend (linger) on ceremony and appearance.
4. For obsequious praise giving up plain candor.
5. Pitiful in their empty achievements, ruined by love of show.
6. The second-rate.
7. Paid spy: jealousy or the detractor whose charges the poem answers.

126¹

O thou my lovely boy, who in thy power
Dost hold time's fickle glass,² his sickle-hour;³
Who hast by waning grown,⁴ and therein show'st
Thy lovers withering as thy sweet self grow'st—
5 If nature, sovereign mistress over wrack,°   *decay*
As thou goest onwards still° will pluck thee back,   *constantly*
She keeps thee to this purpose: that her skill
May time disgrace, and wretched minutes kill.
Yet fear her, O thou minion° of her pleasure!   *darling*
10 She may detain but not still keep her treasure.
　　　Her audit,° though delayed, answered° must be,   *debt (to time) / paid*
　　　And her quietus° is to render° thee.   *settlement / relinquish*

127¹

In the old age° black was not counted fair,²   *old days*
Or if it were, it bore not beauty's name;
But now is black beauty's successive heir,°   *heir by succession*
And beauty slandered with a bastard shame:³
5 For since each hand hath put on° nature's power,   *usurped*
Fairing° the foul with art's false borrowed face,   *Beautifying*
Sweet beauty hath no name, no holy bower,
But is profaned, if not lives in disgrace.
Therefore my mistress' eyes are raven-black,
10 Her brow so suited,⁴ and they mourners seem
At such who, not born fair, no beauty lack,
Sland'ring creation with a false esteem.⁵
　　　Yet so° they mourn, becoming of° their woe,   *in such a way / adorning*
　　　That every tongue says beauty should look so.

128

How oft, when thou, my music, music play'st
Upon that blessèd wood whose motion° sounds   *mechanism*
With thy sweet fingers when thou gently sway'st°   *govern*
The wiry concord that mine ear confounds,°   *amazes (with delight)*
5 Do I envy those jacks¹ that nimble leap
To kiss the tender inward of thy hand
Whilst my poor lips, which should that harvest reap,
At the wood's boldness by thee blushing stand!
To be so tickled they would change their state
10 And situation with those dancing chips

Sonnet 126

1. This "sonnet" or envoi, of six couplets, concludes the part of the sequence apparently addressed to the youth and formally signals a change in tone and subject matter in the remaining sonnets.
2. Capricious, treacherous hourglass (?); mirror showing changing images (?).
3. Reaping time. "Sickle-hour" emends Q's "sickle, hower," which may be an error for "sickle o'er." A familiar emblem for time placed the hourglass below and the sickle above.
4. Become more beautiful with age. As the sand in the top half of an hourglass wanes, the sand in the bottom part grows.

Sonnet 127

1. Sonnets 127–52 have been traditionally known as the "dark lady" group, although their subject matter is not uniform and their object is only once called "dark" (147.14)

and never a "lady." She is referred to as the poet's "mistress" (127.9; 130.1, 8, 12), however, and often described as "black" (127.1, 3, 9; 130.4; 131.12, 13; 132.3, 13; 147.14). The celebration of black beauty goes back to the biblical Song of Songs, 1:4: "I am blacke . . . but comelie." See the Introduction.
2. Beautiful; light-colored.
3. And (fair) beauty accused of illegitimacy (by use of cosmetics).
4. Her brow dressed (matched) in an eyebrow black like her eyes (and for the same reason).
5. *At . . . esteem:* Because of those who, not being fair, make up for it with cosmetics, so that even natural beauty is presumed artificial.

Sonnet 128

1. Keys of the virginal, a harpsichordlike instrument; fellows.

O'er whom thy fingers walk with gentle gait,
Making dead wood more blessed than living lips.
    Since saucy° jacks so happy are in this,   *impudent*
    Give them thy fingers, me thy lips to kiss.

129

Th'expense of spirit in a waste of shame
Is lust in action;[1] and till action, lust
Is perjured, murd'rous, bloody, full of blame,
Savage, extreme, rude,° cruel, not to trust,°   *harsh / be trusted*
5 Enjoyed no sooner but despisèd straight,°   *immediately*
Past reason° hunted, and no sooner had   *Madly*
Past reason hated as a swallowed bait
On purpose laid to make the taker mad;
Mad in pursuit and in possession so,°   *(mad)*
10 Had, having, and in quest to have, extreme;
A bliss in proof and proved,[2] a very woe;
Before, a joy proposed; behind, a dream.
    All this the world well knows, yet none knows well
    To shun the heaven that leads men to this hell.

130

My mistress' eyes are nothing like the sun;
Coral is far more red than her lips' red.
If snow be white, why then her breasts are dun;°   *grayish brown*
If hairs be wires,[1] black wires grow on her head.
5 I have seen roses damasked,° red and white,   *dappled*
But no such roses see I in her cheeks;
And in some perfumes is there more delight
Than in the breath that from my mistress reeks.°   *issues; smells*
I love to hear her speak, yet well I know
10 That music hath a far more pleasing sound.
I grant I never saw a goddess go:°   *walk*
My mistress when she walks treads on the ground.
    And yet, by heaven, I think my love as rare
    As any she belied with false compare.[2]

131

Thou art as tyrannous so as thou art[1]
As those whose beauties proudly make them cruel,
For well thou know'st to my dear° doting heart   *fond(ly)*
Thou art the fairest and most precious jewel.
5 Yet, in good faith, some say that thee behold
Thy face hath not the power to make love groan.
To say they err I dare not be so bold,
Although I swear it to myself alone;
And, to be sure° that is not false I swear,   *for proof; surely*
10 A thousand groans but thinking on° thy face   *just thinking about*
One on another's neck° do witness bear   *In quick succession*

Sonnet 129
1. *Th'expense . . . action:* The expenditure of vital energy (semen) in a shameful waste (waist) is consummated lust.
2. *in proof:* while being experienced. *proved:* having been experienced.
Sonnet 130
1. Elizabethan poets often compared women's hair to golden wires.
2. As any woman misrepresented by false comparison.
Sonnet 131
1. As cruel as you are dark (hence not conventionally beautiful).

Thy black° is fairest in my judgment's place.²   *dark appearance*
  In nothing art thou black° save in thy deeds,   *ugly*
  And thence this slander,³ as I think, proceeds.

132

Thine eyes I love, and they, as° pitying me—   *as if*
Knowing thy heart torment° me with disdain—   *to torment*
Have put on black, and loving mourners be,
Looking with pretty ruth° upon my pain;   *pity*
5 And truly, not the morning sun of heaven
Better becomes° the gray cheeks° of the east,   *beautifies / clouds*
Nor that full star that ushers in the even°   (*Venus, the evening star*)
Doth° half that glory to the sober west,   *Imparts*
As those two mourning° eyes become thy face.   (*pun on "morning"*)
10 O, let it then as well beseem° thy heart   *become*
To mourn for me, since mourning doth thee grace,
And suit thy pity like in every part.¹
    Then will I swear beauty herself is black,
    And all they foul° that thy complexion lack.   *ugly*

133

Beshrew° that heart that makes my heart to groan   *Curse (a mild term)*
For that deep wound it gives my friend and me!
Is't not enough to torture me alone,
But slave to slavery° my sweet'st friend must be?   *utterly enslaved*
5 Me from myself thy cruel eye hath taken,
And my next self thou harder hast engrossed.¹
Of him, myself, and thee I am forsaken—
A torment thrice threefold thus to be crossed.°   *afflicted*
Prison° my heart in thy steel bosom's ward,°   *Imprison / cell*
10 But then my friend's heart let my poor heart bail;
Whoe'er keeps° me, let my heart be his guard;²   *guards*
Thou canst not then use rigour° in my jail.   *severity*
    And yet thou wilt; for I, being pent° in thee,   *locked up*
    Perforce am thine, and° all that is in me.   *as is*

134¹

So, now° I have confessed that he is thine,   *now that*
And I myself am mortgaged to thy will,°   *intent; sexual desire*
Myself I'll forfeit, so that other mine²
Thou wilt restore to be my comfort still.
5 But thou wilt not, nor he will not° be free,   *doesn't want to*
For thou art covetous, and he is kind.
He learned but surety-like° to write° for me   *as guarantor / sign*
Under that bond° that him as fast³ doth bind.   (*of infatuation*)
The statute⁴ of thy beauty thou wilt take,
10 Thou usurer that putt'st forth all to use,°   *at interest; for sex*
And sue a friend came° debtor for my sake;   *who became*

2. In my opinion.
3. See line 6 for "this slander."
Sonnet 132
1. And dress your pity similarly, in heart as well as eyes.
Sonnet 133
1. And my second self, or closest friend, you have even more cruelly monopolized.

2. My friend's prison.
Sonnet 134
1. This sonnet links with 133.
2. So long as my other self.
3. As firmly as myself.
4. The total guaranteed by the bond.

So him I lose through my unkind abuse.[5]
  Him have I lost; thou hast both him and me;
  He pays the whole,° and yet am I not free.   *(pun on "hole")*

135[1]

Whoever hath her wish, thou hast thy Will,
And Will to boot,° and Will in overplus.   *in addition*
More than enough am I that vex thee still,°   *always (by wooing)*
To thy sweet will making addition thus.
5 Wilt thou, whose will is large and spacious,
Not once vouchsafe to hide my will in thine?
Shall will in others° seem right gracious,   *others' wills*
And in my will no fair acceptance shine?[2]
The sea, all water, yet receives rain still,
10 And in abundance addeth to his° store;   *its*
So thou, being rich in Will, add to thy Will
One will of mine to make thy large Will more.
  Let no unkind no fair beseechers kill;[3]
  Think all but one,° and me in that one Will.   *one suitor*

136[1]

If thy soul check° thee that I come so near,[2]   *chide*
Swear to thy blind soul that I was thy Will,[3]
And will, thy soul knows, is admitted there;
Thus far for love my love-suit, sweet, fulfil.°   *grant*
5 Will will fulfill the treasure° of thy love,   *fill up the treasury*
Ay, fill it full with wills, and my will one.°   *one of them*
In things of great receipt° with ease we prove   *volume*
Among a number one is reckoned none.[4]
Then in the number let me pass untold,°   *uncounted*
10 Though in thy store's account° I one must be;   *tally (of lovers)*
For nothing hold me, so it please thee hold
That nothing me a something, sweet, to thee.[5]
  Make but my name thy love,[6] and love that still,°   *always*
  And then thou lov'st me for my name is Will.

137

Thou blind fool love, what dost thou to mine eyes
That they behold and see not what they see?
They know what beauty is, see where it lies,
Yet what the best is take the worst to be.[1]
5 If eyes corrupt° by over-partial° looks   *corrupted / overly doting*

---

5. Through your ill treatment of me; through my ill-treatment of the youth.
Sonnet 135
1. This sonnet, as well as 136, 143, and "A Lover's Complaint," lines 126–33, puns elaborately on different senses of "will": wishes, sexual desire, futurity, testament, the name "Will" (applied to one or more persons, including Shakespeare, and capitalized and sometimes italicized in Q), and the male and female sexual organs. See also 57.13 and note.
2. And my will not be greeted with a kind reception.
3. Let no unkindness of yours kill any of your worthy suitors.

Sonnet 136
1. This sonnet links with 135.
2. I am so forthright; I am so physically close.
3. See sonnet 135, note 1.
4. Proverbially, one is no number.
5. *For . . . thee:* Think me worthless so long as, my darling, you treasure worthless me. Q's punctuation, "something sweet to thee," emphasizes the sexual implications.
6. Love only my name, "Will"; that is, act on your desire.
Sonnet 137
1. Yet take the worst to be the best.

Be anchored in the bay where all men ride,[2]
Why of eyes' falsehood hast thou forgèd hooks
Whereto the judgement of my heart is tied?
Why should my heart think that a several plot°   *private land*
Which my heart knows the wide world's common place?[3]—
Or° mine eyes, seeing this, say this is not,   *Or why should*
To put fair truth upon so foul a face?
    In things right true my heart and eyes have erred,
    And to this false plague[4] are they now transferred.

10 (line 10 marker)

138[1]

When my love swears that she is made of truth
I do believe her though I know she lies,
That° she might think me some untutored youth   *So that*
Unlearnèd in the world's false subtleties.
Thus vainly° thinking that she thinks me young,   *in vain; with vanity*
Although she knows my days are past the best,
Simply I credit[2] her false-speaking tongue;
On both sides thus is simple truth suppressed.
But wherefore says she not she is unjust,°   *unfaithful*
And wherefore say not I that I am old?
O, love's best habit is in seeming trust,[3]
And age in love loves not to have years told.°   *counted*
    Therefore I lie° with her, and she with me,   *tell lies; lie down*
    And in our faults by lies we flattered be.

139

O, call° not me to justify° the wrong   *ask / approve*
That thy unkindness° lays upon my heart.   *infidelity*
Wound me not with thine eye[1] but with thy tongue;
Use power with power,[2] and slay me not by art.°   *by deceit*
Tell me thou lov'st elsewhere, but in my sight,
Dear heart, forbear to glance thine eye aside.
What° need'st thou wound with cunning when thy might   *Why*
Is more than my o'erpressed defence can bide?°   *endure*
Let me excuse thee: 'Ah, my love well knows
Her pretty looks have been mine enemies,
And therefore from my face she turns my foes
That they elsewhere might dart their injuries.'
    Yet do not so; but since I am near slain,
    Kill me outright with looks, and rid° my pain.   *put an end to*

140

Be wise as thou art cruel; do not press
My tongue-tied patience with too much disdain,
Lest sorrow lend me words, and words express

---

2. Harbor for general use (suggesting a promiscuous woman).
3. *the wide . . . place:* common land, open to all (suggesting promiscuity); a commonplace known by all.
4. This plague of false perception; this deceitful woman.
Sonnet 138
1. Another version of this sonnet appears in *The Passionate Pilgrim.* See the Textual Note and the Alternative Ver-

sions.
2. Naively (foolishly; giving the appearance of folly) I (pretend to) believe.
3. Love is best dressed in apparent fidelity (apparent trust).
Sonnet 139
1. By looking elsewhere, at other men (see line 6).
2. Use power frankly; fairly.

The manner of my pity-wanting[1] pain.
5 If I might teach thee wit,° better it were,　　　　　　*wisdom*
Though not to love, yet, love, to tell me so—
As testy sick men when their deaths be near
No news but health from their physicians know.°　　　*learn*
For if I should despair I should grow mad,
10 And in my madness might speak ill of thee.
Now this ill-wresting world[2] is grown so bad
Mad slanderers by mad ears believèd be.
　　That I may not be so, nor thou belied,°　　　　　*maligned*
　　Bear thine eyes straight,[3] though thy proud heart go wide.°　*astray*

141

In faith, I do not love thee with mine eyes,
For they in thee a thousand errors note;
But 'tis my heart that loves what they despise,
Who in despite of view° is pleased to dote.　　　*despite what it sees*
5 Nor are mine ears with thy tongue's tune delighted,
Nor tender feeling to base touches prone;[1]
Nor taste nor smell desire to be invited
To any sensual feast with thee alone;
But my five wits[2] nor my five senses can
10 Dissuade one foolish heart from serving thee,
Who leaves unswayed the likeness of a man.[3]
Thy proud heart's slave and vassal-wretch to be.
　　Only my plague thus far° I count my gain:　　　*to this extent*
　　That she that makes me sin awards me pain.[4]

142[1]

Love is my sin, and thy dear virtue hate,
Hate of my sin grounded on sinful loving.[2]
O, but with mine compare thou thine own state,
And thou shalt find it° merits not reproving;　　　*(my state)*
5 Or if it do, not from those lips of thine
That have profaned their scarlet ornaments[3]
And sealed[4] false bonds of love as oft as mine,
Robbed others' beds' revenues of their rents.[5]
Be it lawful° I love thee as thou lov'st those　　　*let it be lawful that*
10 Whom thine eyes woo as mine importune thee.
Root pity in thy heart, that when it grows
Thy pity may deserve to pitied be.°　　　*make you pitiable*
　　If thou dost seek to have what thou dost hide,°　　　*(pity)*
　　By self example mayst thou be denied!

Sonnet 140
1. Unpitied; desiring pity; pitiable.
2. Now this world, that tends to interpret in the worst light.
3. Keep looking only at me (see 139).
Sonnet 141
1. Nor is my keen sense of touch susceptible to "base" sexual contact.
2. Mental faculties (common sense, imagination, fancy, judgment, memory).
3. Which (the heart, serving you) leaves without a commander the mere semblance of a man.
4. By making me sin, she causes me to suffer punitive penance, which will reduce my sufferings after death.

Sonnet 142
1. This sonnet links with 141.
2. *Love . . . loving:* My only sin is love, and your most valuable virtue is hatred, hatred of my sin in loving you (but also, your most valuable virtue is the haughty rejection of my wooing) based on (your) immoral sexual affairs.
3. Lips, which are scarlet, like a cardinal's robe.
4. "Sealed" with a kiss: comparing the mistress's lips to the red wax used to seal official documents.
5. Stolen the sexual and emotional intimacy ("rents" paid by a tenant) from others' marriages by committing adultery, thus reducing the possibility that these marriages will result in children ("revenues," estates that yield income).

143

Lo, as a care-full° housewife runs to catch   *busy*
One of her feathered creatures broke away,
Sets down her babe and makes all swift dispatch°   *hurries*
In pursuit of the thing she would have stay,
5   Whilst her neglected child holds her in chase,
Cries to catch her whose busy care is bent
To follow that which flies before her face,
Not prizing° her poor infant's discontent: *regarding*
So runn'st thou after that which flies from thee,
10 Whilst I, thy babe, chase thee afar behind;
But if thou catch thy hope, turn back to me
And play the mother's part: kiss me, be kind.
    So will I pray that thou mayst have thy Will[1]
    If thou turn back and my loud crying still.

144[1]

Two loves I have, of comfort and despair,
Which like two spirits do suggest° me still.   *entice*
The better angel is a man right fair,
The worser spirit a woman coloured ill.°   *darkly*
5   To win me soon to hell my female evil
Tempteth my better angel from my side,
And would corrupt my saint to be a devil,
Wooing his purity with her foul pride;
And whether that my angel be turned fiend
10 Suspect I may, yet not directly tell;
But being both from me, both to each friend,[2]
I guess one angel in another's hell.[3]
    Yet this shall I ne'er know, but live in doubt
    Till my bad angel fire my good one out.[4]

145[1]

Those lips that love's own hand did make
Breathed forth the sound that said 'I hate'
To me that languished for her sake;
But when she saw my woeful state,
5   Straight in her heart did mercy come,
Chiding that tongue that ever sweet
Was used in giving gentle doom,°   *judgment*
And taught it thus anew to greet:
'I hate' she altered with an end
10 That followed it as gentle day
Doth follow night who, like a fiend,
From heaven to hell is flown away.
    'I hate' from hate away she threw,[2]
    And saved my life, saying 'not you.'

Sonnet 143
1. A pun; see sonnet 135, note 1.
Sonnet 144
1. Another version of this sonnet appears in *The Passionate Pilgrim*. See Textual Note and Alternative Versions.
2. Both away from me and lovers to one another.
3. Each torments the other; they are in the "hell," or middle den, of a (sexual) game called barley-break; the man occupies the sex organ ("hell") of the woman.
4. Until my bad angel expels my good one, who has become an animal to be smoked out of a burrow; until my bad angel infects my good one with venereal disease; until bad money ("angel" = gold coin) drives out good.
Sonnet 145
1. Unlike the other sonnets, which are in iambic pentameter, 145 is composed of eight-syllable (iambic tetrameter) lines.
2. She converted the normal meaning of the phrase "I hate" away from "hate." A pun on "hate away" and "(Anne) Hathaway," Shakespeare's wife, is possible.

146

Poor soul, the centre of my sinful earth,
[   ] these rebel powers that thee array;[1]
Why dost thou pine within and suffer dearth,
Painting thy outward walls so costly gay?
5 Why so large cost, having so short a lease,
Dost thou upon thy fading mansion° spend?   *(the body)*
Shall worms, inheritors of this excess,
Eat up thy charge?° Is this thy body's end?   *expense*
Then, soul, live thou upon thy servant's° loss,   *(the body's)*
10 And let that pine to aggravate thy store.[2]
Buy terms divine° in selling hours of dross;°   *eternal life / waste*
Within be fed, without be rich no more.
    So shalt thou feed on death, that feeds on men,
    And death once dead, there's no more dying then.

147

My love is as a fever, longing still°   *continually*
For that which longer nurseth° the disease,   *nourishes*
Feeding on that which doth preserve° the ill,   *prolong*
Th'uncertain° sickly appetite to please.   *capricious*
5 My reason, the physician to my love,
Angry that his prescriptions are not kept,
Hath left me, and I desperate now approve
Desire is death, which physic did except.[1]
Past cure I am, now reason is past care,[2]
10 And frantic mad with evermore° unrest.   *constant*
My thoughts and my discourse as madmen's are,
At random from° the truth vainly° expressed;   *unconnected to / idly*
    For I have sworn thee fair, and thought thee bright,
    Who art as black as hell, as dark as night.

148

O me, what eyes hath love put in my head,
Which have no correspondence with true sight!
Or if they have, where is my judgement fled,
That censures falsely[1] what they see aright?
5 If that be fair whereon my false eyes dote,
What means the world to say it is not so?
If it be not, then love doth well denote[2]
Love's eye is not so true as all men's. No,[3]
How can it, O, how can love's eye be true,
10 That is so vexed with watching° and with tears?   *staying awake*

Sonnet 146
1. This rebellious body in which you are clothed. At the beginning of the line, Q repeats "My sinful earth" from the previous line. There is no way of discovering what Shakespeare wrote; among the guesses are "Starved by," "Foiled by," "Spoiled by," and "Feeding."
2. And let the body dwindle to add to your wealth.
Sonnet 147
1. *now . . . except:* now discover that desire, which rejected medicine, is fatal.
2. Medical care: inverting the proverb "Past cure, past

care" (don't worry about what you can't control). In the proverb, you don't care because you can't cure; here, because you don't care, you can't cure.
Sonnet 148
1. That judges inaccurately (dishonestly). "False" (line 5) has similar meanings.
2. Then my self-delusion in love proves that.
3. Not so true as all other men's eye. On the contrary. Q's "all men's, no" is often emended to "all men's 'No,'" suggesting a pun on "eye/aye" (yes).

No marvel then though I° mistake my view: *that I (eye)*
The sun itself sees not till heaven clears.
    O cunning love, with tears thou keep'st me blind
    Lest eyes, well seeing, thy foul faults should find!

149

Canst thou, O cruel, say I love thee not
When I against myself with thee partake?°   *take sides*
Do I not think on thee when I forgot
Am of myself, all-tyrant,[1] for thy sake?
5 Who hateth thee that I do call my friend?
On whom frown'st thou that I do fawn upon?
Nay, if thou lour'st° on me, do I not spend°   *scowl / wreak*
Revenge upon myself with present moan?°   *instant anguish*
What merit do I in myself respect°   *value; note*
10 That is so proud thy service to despise,[2]
When all my best° doth worship thy defect,°   *best qualities / flaws*
Commanded by the motion of thine eyes?
    But, love, hate on; for now I know thy mind.
    Those that can see thou lov'st, and I am blind.[3]

150

O, from what power hast thou this powerful might
With insufficiency° my heart to sway,   *By your flaws*
To make me give the lie to my true sight
And swear that brightness doth not grace the day?[1]
5 Whence hast thou this becoming of things ill,[2]
That in the very refuse of thy deeds°   *your basest behavior*
There is such strength and warrantise° of skill   *guarantee*
That in my mind thy worst all best exceeds?
Who taught thee how to make me love thee more
10 The more I hear and see just cause of hate?
O, though I love what others do abhor,
With others thou shouldst not abhor my state.
    If thy unworthiness raised love in me,
    More worthy I to be beloved of thee.

151

Love is too young° to know what conscience is,   *(Cupid being a boy)*
Yet who knows not conscience[1] is born of love?
Then, gentle cheater, urge° not my amiss,°   *stress / fault*
Lest guilty of my faults thy sweet self prove.
5 For, thou betraying me, I do betray
My nobler part° to my gross body's treason.   *soul*
My soul doth tell my body that he may
Triumph in love; flesh stays no farther reason,[2]

Sonnet 149
1. *when . . . all-tyrant*: when I tyrannically neglect myself.
2. So proud as to scorn to serve you.
3. You love those who see you accurately and thus admire you, but I am blinded (by love and thus, from your point of view, unworthy of being loved). The first clause may have the opposite sense, however: you love those who see your defects well enough not to love you.
Sonnet 150
1. *To . . . day*: the speaker is so blindly in love that he finds beauty only in the blackness he associates with his mistress.
2. This capacity to render the ugly attractive.
Sonnet 151
1. Moral sense; carnal knowledge.
2. Flesh, specifically the sexual organ, needs no further encouragement.

10 But rising at thy name doth point out thee
    As his triumphant prize. Proud of this pride,[3]
    He is contented thy poor drudge to be,
    To stand° in thy affairs, fall by thy side.   assist; be erect
        No want of conscience hold it that I call
        Her 'love' for whose dear love I rise and fall.

152

    In loving thee thou know'st I am forsworn,[1]
    But thou art twice forsworn to me love swearing°   in swearing love to me
    In act thy bed-vow° broke, and new faith torn   to husband (or lover)
5   In vowing new hate after new love bearing.[2]
    But why of two oaths' breach do I accuse thee
    When I break twenty? I am perjured most,
    For all my vows are oaths but to misuse° thee,   deceive
    And all my honest faith in thee is lost.
10 For I have sworn deep oaths of thy deep kindness,
    Oaths of thy love, thy truth, thy constancy,
    And to enlighten thee gave eyes to blindness,[3]
    Or made them swear against the thing they see.
        For I have sworn thee fair—more perjured eye°   (punning on "I")
        To swear against the truth so foul a lie.

153[1]

    Cupid laid by his brand° and fell asleep.   torch
    A maid of Dian's[2] this advantage found,°   seized
    And his love-kindling fire did quickly steep
5   In a cold valley-fountain of that ground,
    Which borrowed from this holy fire of love
    A dateless° lively heat, still° to endure,   An endless / always
    And grew a seething bath which yet men prove
    Against strange maladies a sovereign cure.[3]
10 But at my mistress' eye love's brand new fired,°   being newly lit
    The boy for trial° needs would touch my breast.   to test it
    I, sick withal,° the help of bath desired,   from it
    And thither hied, a sad distempered° guest,   seriously ill
        But found no cure; the bath for my help lies
        Where Cupid got new fire: my mistress' eyes.

3. Swelling with pride (and lust).
Sonnet 152
1. Forsworn presumably in breaking loving vows—perhaps to his wife, to the youth to whom he promised
unswerving devotion in earlier sonnets, or to both.
2. *new faith . . . bearing*: the "new faith" followed by
"new hate" may be addressed either to the speaker's
young friend or to the speaker himself.
3. And to make you fair (give you insight), I looked
blindly on your failings (pretended to see what I
couldn't).

Sonnet 153
1. This and the following sonnet derive indirectly from
classical fifth-century Greek epigrams.
2. Diana, goddess of chastity.
3. *And grew . . . cure*: And became a boiling-hot medicinal bath (used, among other purposes, for the treatment
of venereal disease), which men still find to be an outstanding remedy for foreign illnesses (venereal diseases
were associated with foreigners). There may be an allusion here and in 154 to the town of Bath, which became
a famous health spa in the eighteenth century.

154[1]

  5   The little love-god lying once asleep

Laid by his side his heart-inflaming brand,°   *torch*

Whilst many nymphs that vowed chaste life to keep

Came tripping by; but in her maiden hand

The fairest votary took up that fire

10   Which many legions of true hearts had warmed,

And so the general° of hot desire   *commander (Cupid)*

Was sleeping by a virgin hand disarmed.

This brand she quenchèd in a cool well by,°   *close by*

Which from love's fire took heat perpetual,

Growing a bath and healthful remedy

For men diseased; but I, my mistress' thrall,°   *slave*

    Came there for cure; and this° by that I prove: *the following*

    Love's fire heats water, water cools not love.

Sonnet 154

1. This sonnet varies the topic of 153.

A Lover's Complaint

From off a hill whose concave womb re-worded°   *hollow side echoed*
A plaintful story from a sist'ring° vale,   *nearby*
My spirits t'attend° this double voice accorded,°   *hear / agreed*
And down I laid to list° the sad-tuned tale;   *listen to*
5 Ere long espied a fickle° maid full pale,   *a disturbed*
Tearing of papers, breaking rings a-twain,°   *in two*
Storming her world with sorrow's wind and rain.

Upon her head a plaited hive° of straw   *hat*
Which fortified° her visage from the sun,   *protected*
10 Whereon the thought° might think sometime it saw   *imagination*
The carcass of a beauty spent and done.
Time had not scythèd all that youth begun,
Nor youth all quit; but spite° of heaven's fell° rage,   *in spite / fierce*
Some beauty peeped through lattice of seared° age.   *withered*

15 Oft did she heave her napkin to her eyne,[1]
Which on it had conceited characters,°   *imaginative designs*
Laund'ring the silken figures in the brine
That seasoned° woe had pelleted in tears,   *experienced; salted*
And often reading what contents it bears;
20 As often shrieking undistinguished° woe   *inarticulate*
In clamours of all size, both high and low.

Sometimes her levelled eyes their carriage ride[2]
As° they did batt'ry to the spheres° intend;   *As if / planets*
Sometime diverted their poor balls° are tied   *eyeballs; cannonballs*
25 To th'orbèd° earth; sometimes they do extend   *spherical*
Their view right on;° anon their gazes lend   *straight*
To every place at once, and nowhere fixed,
The mind and sight distractedly commixed.°   *confused*

Her hair, nor° loose nor tied in formal plait,   *neither*
30 Proclaimed in her a careless hand of pride;[3]
For some, untucked, descended her sheaved° hat,   *fell from her straw*
Hanging her pale and pinèd cheek beside.
Some in her threaden fillet° still did bide,   *headband*
And, true to bondage, would not break from thence,
35 Though slackly braided in loose negligence.

A thousand favours° from a maund° she drew   *love tokens / basket*
Of amber, crystal, and of beaded jet,°   *beads of black stone*
Which one by one she in a river threw
Upon whose weeping margin she was set;°   *seated*
40 Like usury applying wet to wet,[4]

---

1. Often did she raise her handkerchief to her eyes.
2. Sometimes her eyes, aimed (like a cannon), glare (are mounted on a swivel).
3. A hand careless of pride; a hand proud in its care-lessness (knowing that she could attract with no effort).
4. Like usury making wealth wealthier (by adding tears to the stream).

Or monarch's hands that lets not bounty fall
Where want cries some, but where excess begs all.[5]

Of folded schedules° had she many a one   °letters
Which she perused, sighed, tore, and gave the flood;
45 Cracked many a ring of posied gold and bone,[6]
Bidding them find their sepulchres in mud;
Found yet more letters sadly penned in blood,
With sleided silk feat and affectedly
Enswathed[7] and sealed to curious° secrecy.   °careful

50 These often bathed she in her fluxive° eyes,   °flowing
And often kissed, and often 'gan to tear;
Cried 'O false blood, thou register° of lies,   °record
What unapprovèd° witness dost thou bear!   °unreliable
Ink would have seemed more black and damnèd here!'
55 This said, in top of rage the lines she rents,°   °rips
Big° discontent so breaking their contents.   °Powerful

A reverend man that grazed his cattle nigh
Sometime a blusterer that the ruffle knew[8]
Of court, of city, and had let go by
60 The swiftest hours observèd as they flew,[9]
Towards this afflicted fancy fastly[1] drew,
And, privileged by age, desires to know
In brief the grounds and motives of her woe.

So slides he down upon his grainèd bat,[2]
65 And comely° distant sits he by her side,   °politely
When he again desires her, being sat,
Her grievance with his hearing to divide.°   °share
If that from him there may be aught applied
Which may her suffering ecstasy° assuage,   °grief
70 'Tis promised in the charity of age.

'Father,' she says, 'though in me you behold
The injury of many a blasting° hour,   °disfiguring
Let it not tell your judgement I am old;
Not age, but sorrow over me hath power.
75 I might as yet have been a spreading° flower,   °blooming
Fresh to myself, if I had self-applied
Love to myself, and to no love beside.

'But, woe is me, too early I attended
A youthful suit—it was° to gain my grace°—   °was designed / favor
80 O, one by nature's outwards° so commended   °external appearance
That maidens' eyes stuck over all° his face.   °were glued to
Love lacked a dwelling and made him her place,

---

5. Or . . . all: Or like the monarch who, rather than give
a little to the truly needy, gives a great deal to those who
already have plenty.
6. A ring of gold and ivory inscribed with messages (of
love).
7. With . . . / Enswathed: Delicately and affectionately
wrapped in strands of separated ("sleided") silk.

8. Once a man of the world who was accustomed to the
busier life.
9. had . . . flew: was past the prime of life, but had
learned from experience.
1. Toward this person afflicted by love rapidly (close by).
2. So he comes down the bank with the help of his
forked herdsman's staff.

And when in his fair parts she did abide
She was new-lodged and newly deified.

85 'His browny locks did hang in crookèd curls,
And every light occasion° of the wind   *chance stirring*
Upon his lips their silken parcels° hurls.   *(of hair)*
What's sweet to do, to do will aptly find.[3]
Each eye that saw him did enchant the mind,
90 For on his visage was in little° drawn   *miniature*
What largeness thinks in paradise was sawn.[4]

'Small show of man was yet upon his chin;
His phoenix° down began but to appear,   *singularly lovely*
Like unshorn velvet, on that termless skin[5]
95 Whose bare outbragged the web[6] it seemed to wear;
Yet showed his visage by that cost more dear,[7]
And nice affections° wavering stood in doubt   *discriminating tastes*
If best were as it was, or best without.°   *(shaven)*

'His qualities were beauteous as his form,
100 For maiden-tongued° he was, and thereof free.° *modest / well spoken*
Yet if men moved° him, was he such a storm   *angered*
As oft twixt May and April is to see
When winds breathe sweet, unruly though they be.
His rudeness so with his authorized youth
105 Did livery falseness in a pride of truth.[8]

'Well could he ride, and often men would say
"That horse his mettle from his rider takes;
Proud of subjection, noble by the sway,°   *control*
What rounds, what bounds, what course,° what stop he makes!" *gallop*
110 And controversy hence a question takes,
Whether the horse by him became his deed,
Or he his manège by th' well-doing steed.[9]

'But quickly on this side the verdict went:
His real habitude° gave life and grace   *disposition*
115 To appertainings° and to ornament,   *external attributes*
Accomplished in himself, not in his case.°   *mere appearance*
All aids, themselves made fairer by their place,
Came for additions;[1] yet their purposed trim
Pieced not[2] his grace, but were all graced by him.

120 'So on the tip of his subduing tongue
All kind of arguments and question deep,
All replication prompt,° and reason strong,   *quick reply*

---

3. Ways are easily found to do pleasant things (look, love).
4. What one would imagine seeing on a larger scale in paradise.
5. Like velvet with its nap unclipped, on that indescribable (invulnerable to time) skin.
6. Whose naked surface showed more beautiful than the down covering.
7. Yet his face looked more precious (attractive) because

of its rich clothing.
8. *His . . . truth:* His roughness, sanctioned by his "youth," employed falseness in truth's uniform.
9. *Whether . . . steed:* Whether he performed so well because of his horsemanship or because his grace in horsemanship (French: *manège*) was a result of the horse's skill.
1. Attempted to increase his worth.
2. *their . . . not:* their anticipated decorative effect did not increase.

For his advantage still did wake and sleep.[3]
To make the weeper laugh, the laugher weep,
125 He had the dialect and different skill,[4]
Catching all passions in his craft of will,[5]

'That° he did in the general bosom reign   So that
Of young, of old, and sexes both enchanted,
To dwell with him in thoughts, or to remain
130 In personal duty, following where he haunted.°   often went
Consents[6] bewitched, ere he desire,° have granted,   before he asks
And dialogued for him what he would say,
Asked their own wills, and made their wills obey.

'Many there were that did his picture get
135 To serve their eyes, and in it put their mind,
Like fools that in th'imagination set
The goodly objects° which abroad° they find   sights / traveling
Of lands and mansions, theirs in thought assigned,
And labour in more pleasures to bestow them[7]
140 Than the true gouty landlord which doth owe° them.   own

'So many have, that never touched his hand,
Sweetly supposed them mistress of his heart.
My woeful self, that did in freedom stand,
And was my own fee-simple,[8] not in part,
145 What with his art in youth, and youth in art,
Threw my affections in his charmèd° power,   magical
Reserved the stalk and gave him all my flower.

'Yet did I not, as some my equals° did,   young girls of my rank
Demand of him, nor being desired yielded.°   yielded sexual favors
150 Finding myself in honour so forbid,
With safest distance I mine honour° shielded.   chastity
Experience° for me many bulwarks builded   (of "my equals")
Of proofs new bleeding, which remained the foil[9]
Of this false jewel and his amorous spoil.

155 'But ah, who ever shunned by precedent
The destined ill she must herself assay,°   try out
Or forced examples 'gainst her own content
To put the by-past perils in her way?[1]
Counsel may stop a while what will not stay,°   stop for good
160 For when we rage,° advice is often seen,   (with lust)
By blunting° us, to make our wills more keen.   repressing

---

3. For . . . sleep: (Like servants) adjusted their waking
and sleeping hours for the benefit of their master.
4. The manner of speech and versatile skill.
5. His faculty of persuasion. Here and in the next stanza,
there are suggestions of other senses of "will." See sonnets
135–36.
6. Powers of (sexual) consent; consenting people.
7. theirs . . . them: imagining the "lands and mansions"
their own, they try harder to use them pleasurably.
8. And had absolute control of myself (as of land in freehold).

9. Of . . . foil: Fresh examples of seduction, which
remained the defense (or sword—picking up the military,
specifically fencing, imagery of "distance," "shielded,"
"bulwarks," "bleeding," lines 151–53). But "foil" as the
dark material in which gems are set to make them look
more brilliant also works with "false jewel" in the following line, to suggest that the young man's sexual escapades
made him more attractive.
1. Or . . . way: Or reminded herself, to counter her present inclinations, of bygone dangers. forced: urged.

'Nor gives it satisfaction to our blood°   *sexuality*
That we must curb it upon others' proof,°   *experience*
To be forbod° the sweets that seems so good   *forbidden*
165 For fear of harms that preach in our behoof.°   *for our benefit*
O appetite, from judgement stand aloof!
The one a palate hath that needs will taste,
Though reason weep, and cry it is thy last.

'For further I could say this man's untrue,[2]
170 And knew the patterns° of his foul beguiling;   *instances*
Heard where his plants in others' orchards° grew,   *(wombs)*
Saw how deceits were gilded in his smiling,
Knew vows were ever brokers° to defiling,   *go-betweens*
Thought characters and words merely but art,[3]
175 And bastards of his foul adulterate heart.

'And long upon these terms I held my city°   *chastity*
Till thus he gan° besiege me: "Gentle maid,   *began to*
Have of my suffering youth some feeling pity,
And be not of my holy vows afraid.
180 That's° to ye sworn to none was ever said;   *What is*
For feasts of love I have been called unto,
Till now did ne'er invite nor never woo.

'"All my offences that abroad° you see°   *in the world / learn of*
Are errors of the blood,° none of the mind.   *sexual passion*
185 Love made them not; with acture they may be,[4]
Where neither party is nor true nor kind.°   *faithful or loving*
They sought their shame that so their shame did find,
And so much less of shame in me remains
By how much of me their reproach contains.[5]

190 '"Among the many that mine eyes have seen,
Not° one whose flame my heart so much as warmèd   *There is not*
Or my affection put to th' smallest teen,°   *pain*
Or any of my leisures° ever charmèd.   *hours of leisure*
Harm have I done to them, but ne'er was harmèd;
195 Kept hearts in liveries,° but mine own was free,   *in uniform (service)*
And reigned commanding in his monarchy.

'"Look here what tributes wounded fancies° sent me   *lovers*
Of pallid pearls and rubies red as blood,
Figuring° that they their passions likewise lent me   *Showing*
200 Of grief and blushes, aptly understood
In bloodless white and the encrimsoned mood°—   *form (of rubies)*
Effects of terror and dear modesty,
Encamped in hearts, but fighting outwardly.[6]

2. I am able to say more about this man's perfidy.
3. Written and spoken words were merely instruments of
skill (in seduction).
4. with . . . be: by a mere physical act they may be performed.

5. By . . . contains: The more they name me in their
reproaches (thus revealing that they are unchaste and,
hence, by this logic, to blame).
6. Effects . . . outwardly: White ("terror") and red (blushing "modesty") fighting on their faces.

'"And lo, behold, these talents° of their hair,   *riches*
205 With twisted mettle amorously impleached,[7]
I have received from many a several fair,°   *a different beauty*
Their kind acceptance weepingly beseeched,
With th'annexations° of fair gems enriched,   *additions*
And deep-brained sonnets that did amplify°   *expound; increase*
210 Each stone's dear nature, worth, and quality.

'"The diamond?—why, 'twas beautiful and hard,
Whereto his invised[8] properties did tend;
The deep-green em'rald, in whose fresh regard
Weak sights their sickly radiance do amend;[9]
215 The heaven-hued sapphire and the opal blend[1]
With objects manifold; each several° stone,   *distinct*
With wit well blazoned,° smiled or made some moan.   *described*

'"Lo, all these trophies of affections° hot,   *passions*
Of pensived° and subdued desires the tender,°   *saddened / gifts*
220 Nature hath charged me that I hoard them not,
But yield them up where I myself must render—
That is to you, my origin and ender;°   *alpha and omega; all*
For these of force must your oblations[2] be,
Since I their altar, you enpatron me.[3]

225 '"O then advance of yours that phraseless° hand   *beyond description*
Whose white weighs down the airy scale of praise.[4]
Take all these similes[5] to your own command,
Hallowed with sighs that burning° lungs did raise.   *(with love)*
What me, your minister for you, obeys,
230 Works under you,[6] and to your audit° comes   *account*
Their distract parcels° in combinèd sums.   *component parts*

'"Lo, this device was sent me from a nun,
A sister sanctified of holiest note,°   *reputation*
Which late her noble suit° in court did shun,   *attendance; suitors*
235 Whose rarest havings° made the blossoms° dote;   *qualities / young nobles*
For she was sought by spirits of richest coat,°   *coat of arms*
But kept cold distance, and did thence remove
To spend her living° in eternal love.°   *life / (of God)*

'"But O, my sweet, what labour is't to leave
240 The thing we have not, mast'ring what not strives,°   *does not resist*
Planing° the place which did no form[7] receive,   *Smoothing*
Playing patient sports in unconstrainèd gyves![8]
She that her fame so to herself contrives[9]

---

7. With misdirected courage (confused spirit?) lovingly intertwined. Many editors emend "mettle" to "metal."
8. Its unseen—referring to the diamond but also, perhaps, to the equally "beautiful and hard" young man.
9. *in . . . amend:* which, when looked at, can heal weak vision.
1. Blended: many-colored; accompanying other "objects" (line 216).
2. For these necessarily must be offerings at your altar.
3. Since I am the altar (on which they were offered), you must necessarily be the patron saint of the altar (me).

4. Whose white exceeds any measure of praise.
5. These emblematic gifts and the sonnets that explain them.
6. *What . . . under you:* Whatever pays homage to me, your agent, serves you.
7. No impression (of love, on the heart).
8. Patiently enduring shackles ("gyves") that have not been forced upon one and that can be removed (or that do not constrain). (The entire sentence is ironic.)
9. She who thus contrives for herself the reputation of disinterest in love.

The scars of battle scapeth by the flight,
245 And makes her absence valiant, not her might.[1]

'"O, pardon me, in that my boast is true!
The accident which brought me to her eye
Upon the moment° did her force° subdue,   *Immediately / resolve*
And now she would the cagèd cloister fly.
250 Religious° love put out religion's eye.   *Devoted (sexual)*
Not to be tempted would she be immured,°   *walled up*
And now, to tempt, all liberty procured.

'"How mighty then you are, O hear me tell!
The broken bosoms° that to me belong   *hearts*
255 Have emptied all their fountains in my well,
And mine I pour° your ocean all among.   *pour into*
I strong o'er them, and you o'er me being strong,
Must for your victory us all congest,°   *gather*
As compound° love to physic° your cold breast.   *medicinal / treat*

260 '"My parts° had power to charm a sacred nun,   *attributes*
Who disciplined, ay dieted in° grace,   *sustained by*
Believed her eyes when they t' assail begun,[2]
All vows and consecrations giving place.°   *yielding*
O most potential love: vow, bond, nor space
265 In thee hath neither sting, knot, nor confine,[3]
For thou art all, and all things else are thine.

'"When thou impressest,[4] what are precepts worth
Of stale example? When thou wilt inflame,
How coldly those impediments stand forth
270 Of wealth, of filial fear, law, kindred, fame.
Love's arms are° peace, 'gainst rule, 'gainst sense, 'gainst shame;   *Love's power compels*
And° sweetens in the suff'ring pangs it bears   *And love*
The aloes° of all forces, shocks, and fears.   *bitterness*

'"Now all these hearts that do on mine depend,
275 Feeling it break, with bleeding groans they pine,[5]
And supplicant° their sighs to you extend   *as supplicants*
To leave° the batt'ry that you make 'gainst mine,   *cease*
Lending soft audience to my sweet design,[6]
And credent° soul to that strong-bonded oath   *trustful*
280 That shall prefer and undertake° my troth."   *advance and guarantee*

'This said, his wat'ry eyes he did dismount,°   *lower (military)*
Whose sights till then were levelled° on my face.   *aimed*
Each cheek a river running from a fount
With brinish current downward flowed apace.
285 O, how the channel° to the stream° gave grace,   *cheeks / tears*

---

1. And achieves a reputation for valor by avoiding the temptation of love, not by strongly resisting it.
2. When my attributes ("parts") began to assail her heart.
3. *potential . . . confine*: powerful love: a "vow" has no force ("sting"), a "bond" does not tie ("knot"), and "space" does not restrain ("confine").
4. When you draft someone into your (military) service; make an impression on the heart.
5. Because each sigh supposedly robbed the heart of a drop of blood.
6. Looking favorably on my intentions.

Who glazed with crystal gate the glowing roses
That flame through water which their hue encloses.[7]

'O father, what a hell of witchcraft lies
In the small orb of one particular° tear!   *single*
290   But with the inundation of the eyes
What rocky heart to water will not wear?°   *wear away*
What breast so cold that is not warmèd here?
O cleft° effect! Cold modesty, hot wrath,°   *divided / passion*
Both fire from hence and chill extincture hath.[8]

295   'For lo, his passion,° but an art of craft,   *passionate speech*
Even there resolved° my reason into tears.   *dissolved*
There my white stole of chastity I daffed,°   *took off*
Shook off my sober guards and civil° fears;   *seemly*
Appear to him as he to me appears,
300   All melting, though our drops this diff'rence bore:
His poisoned me, and mine did him restore.

'In him a plenitude of subtle matter,°   *raw material; cunning*
Applied to cautels,° all strange forms receives,[9]   *tricky devices*
Of burning blushes or of weeping water,
305   Or swooning paleness; and he takes and leaves,°   *uses this and shuns that*
In either's aptness,° as it best deceives,   *As each is appropriate*
To blush at speeches rank,° to weep at woes,   *offensive*
Or to turn white and swoon at tragic shows,

'That not a heart which in his level° came   *range (of fire)*
310   Could scape the hail of his all-hurting aim,
Showing fair nature is[1] both kind and tame,
And, veiled in them,° did win whom he would maim.   *(kindness and tameness)*
Against the thing he sought he would exclaim;
When he most burned in heart-wished luxury,°   *lust*
315   He preached pure maid° and praised cold chastity.   *virginal purity*

'Thus merely with the garment of a grace°   *with external appeal*
The naked and concealèd fiend he covered,
That th'unexperient° gave the tempter place,°   *inexperienced / entry*
Which like a cherubin above them hovered.°   *(as if protectively)*
320   Who, young and simple, would not be so lovered?[2]
Ay me, I fell, and yet do question make°   *wonder*
What I should do again for such a sake.°   *person; pleasure*

'O that infected° moisture of his eye,   *tainted*
O that false fire which in his cheek so glowed,
325   O that forced thunder from° his heart did fly,   *that from*
O that sad breath his spongy lungs bestowed,°   *emitted*
O all that borrowed motion seeming owed[3]
Would yet again betray the fore-betrayed,
And new pervert a reconcilèd° maid.'   *penitent*

---

7. *Who . . . encloses*: The river is seen as a kind of glass covering ("crystal gate") over the cheeks ("roses"), whose color shines through the "water," like a jewel enclosed in glass. *Who*: (the stream).
8. *Both . . . hath*: Tears heat up cold modesty and extin-guish hot passion (as the following stanza elaborates).
9. *all . . . receives*: is shaped into novel forms.
1. Pretending his nature is.
2. Would not desire such a lover.
3. That emotion apparently his own.

Alternative Versions

Each of the four sonnets below exists in an alternative version. The text on top is the version as it appeared in the 1609 Quarto. *"Spes Altera"* and *"On his Mistress' Beauty"* derive from seventeenth-century manuscripts. The alternative versions of sonnets 138 and 144 are from *The Passionate Pilgrim* (1599).

2

When forty winters shall besiege thy brow
And dig deep trenches in thy beauty's field,
Thy youth's proud livery, so gazed on now,
Will be a tattered weed, of small worth held.
5   Then being asked where all thy beauty lies,
Where all the treasure of thy lusty days,
To say within thine own deep-sunken eyes
Were an all-eating shame and thriftless praise.
How much more praise deserved thy beauty's use
10   If thou couldst answer 'This fair child of mine
Shall sum my count, and make my old excuse',
Proving his beauty by succession thine.
This were to be new made when thou art old,
And see thy blood warm when thou feel'st it cold.

Spes Altera°   *Another Hope*

When forty winters shall besiege thy brow
And trench deep furrows in that lovely field,
Thy youth's fair liv'ry, so accounted° now,   *esteemed*
Shall be like rotten weeds of no worth held.
5   Then being asked where all thy beauty lies,
Where all the lustre of thy youthful days,
To say 'Within these hollow sunken eyes'
Were an all-eaten truth[1] and worthless praise.
O how much better were thy beauty's use
10   If thou couldst say 'This pretty child of mine
Saves my account[2] and makes my old excuse',
Making his beauty by succession thine.
This were to be new born when thou art old,
And see thy blood warm when thou feel'st it cold.

106

When in the chronicle of wasted time
I see description of the fairest wights,
And beauty making beautiful old rhyme
In praise of ladies dead and lovely knights;
5   Then in the blazon of sweet beauty's best,
Of hand, of foot, of lip, of eye, of brow,
I see their antique pen would have expressed
Even such a beauty as you master now.
So all their praises are but prophecies
10   Of this our time, all you prefiguring,
And for they looked but with divining eyes
They had not skill enough your worth to sing;

Spes Altera
1. An accurate statement that you had been gluttonous.   2. Preserves (increases) my wealth (my moral record).

For we which now behold these present days
Have eyes to wonder, but lack tongues to praise.

On his Mistress' Beauty

When in the annals of all-wasting time
I see descriptions of the fairest wights,
And beauty making beautiful old rhyme
In praise of ladies dead and lovely knights;
5   Then in the blazon of sweet beauty's best,
Of face, of hand, of lip, of eye, or brow,
I see their antique pen would have expressed
E'en such a beauty as you master now.
So all their praises were but prophecies
10 Of these our days, all you prefiguring,
And for they saw but with divining eyes
They had not skill enough your worth to sing;
  For we which now behold these present days
  Have eyes to wonder, but no tongues to praise.

138

When my love swears that she is made of truth
I do believe her though I know she lies,
That she might think me some untutored youth
Unlearnèd in the world's false subtleties.
5   Thus vainly thinking that she thinks me young,
Although she knows my days are past the best,
Simply I credit her false-speaking tongue;
On both sides thus is simple truth suppressed.
But wherefore says she not she is unjust,
10 And wherefore say not I that I am old?
O, love's best habit is in seeming trust,
And age in love loves not to have years told.
  Therefore I lie with her, and she with me,
  And in our faults by lies we flattered be.

138

When my love swears that she is made of truth
I do believe her though I know she lies,
That she might think me some untutored youth
Unskilful in the world's false forgeries.
5   Thus vainly thinking that she thinks me young,
Although I know my years be past the best,
I, smiling, credit her false-speaking tongue,
Outfacing° faults in love with love's ill rest.[1]   *Defying*
But wherefore says my love that she is young,
10 And wherefore say not I that I am old?
O, love's best habit's in a soothing tongue,
And age in love loves not to have years told.
  Therefore I'll lie with love,° and love with me,   *my lover; lovingly*
  Since that our faults in love thus smothered be.

Sonnet 138
1. With the "rest" of what's bad in love; restlessness.

144

Two loves I have, of comfort and despair,
Which like two spirits do suggest me still.
The better angel is a man right fair,
The worser spirit a woman coloured ill.
5   To win me soon to hell my female evil
Tempteth my better angel from my side,
And would corrupt my saint to be a devil,
Wooing his purity with her foul pride;
And whether that my angel be turned fiend
10 Suspect I may, yet not directly tell;
But being both from me, both to each friend,
I guess one angel in another's hell.
    Yet this shall I ne'er know, but live in doubt
    Till my bad angel fire my good one out.

144

Two loves I have, of comfort and despair,
That like two spirits do suggest me still.
My better angel is a man right fair,
My worser spirit a woman coloured ill.
5   To win me soon to hell my female evil
Tempteth my better angel from my side,
And would corrupt my saint to be a devil,
Wooing his purity with her fair pride;
And whether that my angel be turned fiend,
10 Suspect I may, yet not directly tell;
For being both to me, both to each friend,
I guess one angel in another's hell.
    The truth I shall not know, but live in doubt
    Till my bad angel fire my good one out.

Various Poems

The short poems included here are occasional pieces. That is, they were written not as part of a longer work by a single author but for specific occasions. They are arranged in the order in which Shakespeare might have written them from the early 1590s until shortly before his death, if in fact he wrote them all—an extremely unlikely supposition. (See the Textual Note.) Unlike the sonnets, which collectively possess considerable coherence, these poems employ a number of meters, line lengths, rhyme schemes, and stanzaic forms. Until very recently, scholarly discussion generally focused on the relationship of the poems to Shakespeare's biography and on the question of whether Shakespeare actually wrote them.

"A Song," one of the two longer poems printed here, is noteworthy mainly as a virtuoso display of rhyming: there are usually eight pairs of rhyme words in each ten-line stanza, with the rhymes occurring as often as every three syllables and on occasion every two syllables ("Being set, lips met," line 39). *The Passionate Pilgrim* appeared under Shakespeare's name in 1599, apparently without his approval. Of its twenty poems, five are lifted from Shakespeare's other works and hence appear elsewhere in this volume, four are clearly by other writers, and eleven remain unattributed and are accordingly printed here. Numbers 4, 6, and 9—all sonnets—are noteworthy for their focus on the theme of *Venus and Adonis*, to which they may be a response. By 1599, Shakespeare's name had considerable cachet. *The Passionate Pilgrim* very possibly seeks to exploit that cachet, interweaving a few pieces by Shakespeare with other poems so as to produce a thematically resonant sequence that obscures the homoeroticism of some of the sonnets and in effect becomes a testament to poetic artifice.

Several of the other poems are elegies—compositions in memory of the dead, though sometimes written while the subject was still alive. The first of the two epitaphs on the usurer John Combe reveals a conventional hostility to usury. The second, however, deploys the complex, sometimes positive, metaphorical relationship between usury and breeding characteristic of the early sonnets. Combe

> did gather [wealth from usury]
> To make the poor his issue [heirs]; he, their father,
> . . . [made] record of his tilth and seed.
>
> (lines 3–5)

Urging marriage and a family, sonnet 3 speaks of "the tillage of thy husbandry" (line 6). And sonnet 6 argues:

> That use is not forbidden usury
> Which happies those that pay the willing loan:
> That's for thyself to breed another thee,
> Or ten times happier, be it ten for one.
>
> (lines 5–8)

Thus, in the sonnets, the language of usury helps clarify paternity, whereas in the second epitaph, the language of paternity helps clarify usury. In both, however, the two terms are mutually illuminating. The last line quoted from sonnet 6 is also reminiscent of the opening of the first epitaph: "Ten in the hundred here lies engraved; / A hundred to ten his soul is not saved." Both refer to the highest legal interest rate—ten in a hundred, or 10 percent—although only the sonnet converts the allusion into a positive image.

Similarly, "Verses upon the Stanley Tomb at Tong" closely parallels the language of some of Shakespeare's sonnets concerned with the destructive power of time. The "register" of the first of the two poems (1.3) and the "sky-aspiring pyramids" of the second (2.2) also appear in sonnet 123 ("pyramids built up," "registers," lines 2, 9). Closer still is the connection to sonnet 55: "Not marble nor the gilded monuments / Of princes shall outlive this powerful rhyme" (lines 1–2). Stanley's "fame is more perpetual than these stones" (1.4); "Not monumental stone preserves our fame" (2.1). Stanley's "memory," however, "shall outlive marble and defacers' hands" as well as "time's consumption" (2.3, 4, 5), just as "memory" need not worry that "war shall statues overturn" and is not dependent on "unswept stone besmeared with sluttish time" in sonnet 55 (lines 8, 5, 4). Although the guarantee of immortality seems to be Stanley's life rather than the "powerful rhyme" of the sonnet (line 2), the end is the same: Stanley "is not dead; he doth but sleep" (1.2), while in the sonnet, "'gainst death and all oblivious enmity / Shall you pace forth" (lines 9–10). Ultimately, poetic fame in the sonnet lasts only "till the judgement that yourself arise" (on Judgment Day; line 13); analogously, "Stanley for whom this stands shall stand in heaven" (2.6). The pun on the name in this concluding line ("Stanley/stands/stand") is similar to the sign of the author's hand left in "Upon a pair of gloves that master sent to his mistress," where "the will is all" recalls Shakespeare's emphatic references to his first name in sonnets 135 and 136.

"Upon a pair of gloves" seems to reveal the poet intruding himself into a composition ostensibly from Alexander Aspinall to his (future?) wife; the "Epitaph on Himself" is strikingly impersonal. The lack of specificity may in this case be a poetic signature, however. By 1616, perhaps only Shakespeare could have written about Shakespeare without reference to his theatrical or literary career. This modesty coincides with an open threat: "cursed be he that moves my bones" (line 4). The apparently conventional warning was designed to forestall the very real danger of his body being dug up to make room for fresh corpses; in this case, it proved successful.

The second relatively long occasional poem, "The Phoenix and Turtle," is another matter. The one work in this section whose literary quality has been widely admired, it was one of several poems—others were by George Chapman, Ben Jonson, and John Marston—appended to Robert Chester's *Loves Martyr* (1601). An abstruse philosophical composition, "The Phoenix and Turtle" may represent Shakespeare's effort to refashion himself as a different kind of poet from the one who appeared two years earlier in unauthorized form in *The Passionate Pilgrim*. Literary innovation here may also have an element of poetic competition with his three fellow contributors to Chester's volume, all of whom were also dramatists. With two of them, Johnson and Marston, Shakespeare was then probably engaged in the satirical Poets' War, a battle of rival playwrights.

"The Phoenix and Turtle" is divided into three sections and composed in trochaic tetrameter, an atypical meter for Shakespeare. In the first five quatrains, which may be indebted to Chaucer's *Parliament of Fowls*, a language of elaborate circumlocution merely calls the birds together to mourn the deaths of two remarkably constant lovers—the proverbially faithful turtledove (here, male) and the legendary phoenix (here, female). Supposedly, only one phoenix was alive at any given moment, and the bird died only to be reborn from its own ashes. Neither of the two birds is named yet, however. The anthem, which constitutes the next eight stanzas, is presumably intoned by the birds. In a reversal of the procedure of the opening twenty lines, this epithalamion, or marriage hymn, turns to a deceptively simple vocabulary that conceals dense argumentation. Behind the emphasis on the paradoxical unity of two separate beings lies the mystery of the Christian Trinity as understood in Scholastic theology—medieval Europe's assimilation of the recently translated writings of Aristotle, which began in the twelfth century. The ideal love of the two birds ultimately defies the efforts at comprehension by Reason, which cannot understand how

> . . . love in twain
> Had the essence but in one,
> Two distincts, division none,

or how

> . . . the self was not the same.
> Single nature's double name
> Neither two nor one was called.
> (lines 25–27, 38–40)

In other words, the rationalist vocabulary of this section ultimately undermines its own legitimacy. Perhaps the lines vindicate the more mystical understanding of ideal love that Renaissance thought derived from Plato, whose doctrines Aristotle had sought to answer. In any case, the heterosexual love praised in this self-contradictory fashion parallels the celebration of homoerotic love in the sonnets to the young man: "Let me confess that we two must be twain / Although our undivided loves are one" (36.1–2). Following the anthem, Reason delivers the concluding section of the poem, the *threnos*, or mourning song, in which Shakespeare returns to the central genre of his occasional poetry—the elegy. Retaining the straightforwardly abstract diction of the anthem and the trochaic-tetrameter meter of both of the first two parts but abandoning quatrains (rhyming *abba*) for tercets (rhyming *aaa*), the last five stanzas emphasize the finality of the death of the couple, which apparently excludes both rebirth (even on the part of the immortal phoenix) and "posterity"—the latter as a result of a "married chastity" (lines 59, 61) that has the same (lack of) consequences as the love for the young man in the sonnets. The result is the diminution of life: the only authentic or perhaps ideal "truth and beauty buried be" (line 64).

"The Phoenix and Turtle" raises all sorts of interpretive problems. Since the *threnos* is spoken by Reason, who has been defeated by the phoenix and turtle, should the concluding stanzas be seen not as authorial statement but as the position of a fallible character who lets fly a crow of triumph at the couple's death? Moreover, the concluding summons of all "that are either true or fair" (line 66) sits oddly with the immediately preceding insistence that genuine truth and beauty no longer exist: perhaps now they exist only separately. And why does Shakespeare, through Reason, insist on the lack of offspring and, apparently rejecting a central feature of the legend, on the mortality of the phoenix? This last question is only emphasized by the occasion of publication. All of the poems with which "The Phoenix and Turtle" were printed are on the subject of the phoenix and turtle, and all but Shakespeare's deny the finality of the phoenix's death. "The Phoenix and Turtle" alone forgoes the possibility of exploiting the standard treatment of the phoenix as the intersection of the temporal and the timeless.

The title page of the volume advertises Chester's long poem as "allegorically shadowing the truth of Love, in the constant Fate of the Phoenix and Turtle." This claim, the abstract language of "The Phoenix and Turtle," and the avowed purpose of the volume—to honor Sir John Salusbury of Lleweni, knighted by the Queen in June 1601—have all encouraged a search in Shakespeare's poem for allegorical meaning (beyond the praise of ideal human union through a tale of two birds). The marriage of phoenix and turtle has been seen as the joining of the literal and the metaphorical in poetry, so that the poem self-referentially becomes a metaphor for metaphor itself. Historical readings have found candidates for the parts of the turtle and the phoenix in Salusbury and his wife, as well as in the Earl of Essex, Salusbury, or the English people in relation to Queen Elizabeth. Although none of these theories is convincing, in part because of a failure to explain what real "tragic scene" is being allegorically represented by the couple's deaths (line 52), all testify to the poem's ability to hint at hidden meanings. Perhaps it is safer to explain the poem's suggestiveness simply by saying that "The Phoenix and Turtle" labors to construct an ideal image of love while simultaneously circumscribing the real utility of that ideal. Marriage and funeral, celebration and dirge, ideal affirmation and pragmatic denial, the poem is a characteristically Shakespearean venture in having it both ways.

WALTER COHEN

TEXTUAL NOTE

"A Song" survives in two related manuscript collections of poetry by different authors, dating from 1637 and 1639. It is untitled in both manuscripts, unattributed in the later collection, and ascribed to Shakespeare in the earlier one. The text printed here is based on the earlier version, although the choice between the two is not very important. Both manuscripts of "A Song" derive from a scribal transcript of the writer's original version, but it is impossible to determine how many intermediate copies there may have been. The poem was first assigned in print to Shakespeare in 1985, a claim that has aroused considerable skepticism. The name in the 1637 manuscript and the independent analysis of the poem's language carried out by statisticians make attribution to Shakespeare possible (c. 1592–95) though unlikely. It probably dates from 1613–30.

"Upon a pair of gloves" is found in a manuscript compiled around 1629 by Sir Francis Fane of Bulbeck (1611–80). The poem supposedly accompanied gloves presented by Alexander Aspinall, a Stratford schoolmaster, to his second wife, whom he married in 1594. The poem's second line, "The will is all," could refer to Shakespeare or to William Shaw, a glover who was the son of Aspinall's second wife. Hence, the attribution to Shakespeare is conjectural.

The eleven poems from *The Passionate Pilgrim* (1599) printed here are of uncertain authorship, although probably not by Shakespeare. This collection of twenty lyrics published under Shakespeare's name includes five pieces that are clearly his. Three come from *Love's Labour's Lost;* the other two are sonnets 138 and 144, and are included in this edition as Alternative Versions at the end of the section on the sonnets and "A Lover's Complaint." Four poems are apparently by other writers—Richard Barnfield, Bartholomew Griffin, and Christopher Marlowe. "The Phoenix and Turtle" was printed in 1601, untitled and ascribed to Shakespeare, among the "Poeticall Essaies" that follow Robert Chester's *Loves Martyr: or Rosalins Complaint.* The ascription is widely accepted.

The remaining poems are about specific people, and in each instance, as in "Upon a pair of gloves," there is a plausible London or Stratford connection between Shakespeare and the person(s) in question. The "Verses upon the Stanley Tomb at Tong," perhaps by Shakespeare (c. 1600–03) even though there are possible chronological difficulties, are first attributed to him in a manuscript from around 1630. It is not clear whether the lines constitute one poem or two, whether they are addressed to one member of the Stanley family or two, and which member or members are referred to. If they are intended as a single poem, it is not certain which group of six lines should come first. "On Ben Jonson" is first attributed to Shakespeare, improbably, in a manuscript from roughly 1650. "An Epitaph on Elias James," published in the 1633 edition of John Stow's *Survey of London*, is more likely to be Shakespeare's. James died in 1610. "An extemporary epitaph on John Combe," who died in 1614, employs a joke about usurers that became popular starting in 1608. The earliest manuscripts do not assign the poem to Shakespeare. There is an ambiguous attribution to Shakespeare in 1634 and an unambiguous ascription of the last one and a half lines in a manuscript from around 1650. On balance, Shakespeare probably did not write the poem. "Another Epitaph on John Combe" is first attributed to Shakespeare in the same manuscript (c. 1650); the case for Shakespearean authorship of this poem is stronger, however. "Upon the King" was printed, unattributed, beneath an engraving of King James that was the frontispiece to the 1616 edition of the King's *Works*. The earliest ascription is found in a

manuscript of about 1633–34, where the poem is entitled "Shakespeare on the King."
Again, late attribution following earlier lack of attribution casts doubt on Shakespearean
authorship. "Epitaph on Himself" appears on Shakespeare's gravestone in Stratford.
The earliest other attribution occurs in a manuscript compiled by Sir Francis Fane,
about 1655–56. The lines may be Shakespearean.

SELECTED BIBLIOGRAPHY

Adams, Joseph Quincy. "Shakespeare as a Writer of Epitaphs." *The Manly Anniversary
Studies in Language and Literature*. 1923; repr.: Freeport, N.Y.: Books for Libraries
Press, 1968. 78–89. Defends Shakespeare's authorship.

Bednarz, James P. "*The Passionate Pilgrim* and 'The Phoenix and Turtle.'" *The Cambridge Companion to Shakespeare's Poetry*. Ed. Patrick Cheney. New York: Cambridge University Press, 2007. 108–24. Locates these works in the context of late
Elizabethan poetic publication and literary and theatrical competition.

Cunningham, V. J. "'Essence' and 'The Phoenix and Turtle.'" *English Literary History*
19 (1952): 265–76. Discusses the theological language of the poem.

Hobday, C. H. "Shakespeare's Venus and Adonis Sonnets." *Shakespeare Survey* 26
(1973): 103–09. Discussion of the poems on this topic in *The Passionate Pilgrim*.

Honigmann, E. A. J. *Shakespeare: The Lost Years*. Totowa, N.J.: Barnes & Noble, 1985.
77–83, 90–113. "The Phoenix and Turtle" as a celebration of Salusbury's marriage
in 1586; briefer comments on Shakespeare's elegies.

Hyland, Peter. *An Introduction to Shakespeare's Poems*. Houndmills, Basingstoke: Palgrave Macmillan, 2002. 194–213. Survey of Shakespeare's occasional poetry, with
special attention paid to "The Phoenix and Turtle."

Hume, Anthea. "*Love's Martyr*, 'The Phoenix and Turtle,' and the Aftermath of the Essex
Rebellion." *Review of English Studies* n.s., 40 (1989): 48–71. Reads the poem as an
allegory of Essex's relationship to Elizabeth.

Kay, Dennis. *William Shakespeare: Sonnets and Poems*. New York: Twayne, 1998.
77–95. Surveys the occasional poems.

Roberts, Sasha. *Reading Shakespeare's Poems in Early Modern England*. Houndmills,
Basingstoke: Palgrave Macmillan, 2003. 154–58, 177–90. *The Passionate Pilgrim*,
both in print form and in manuscript transcription of individual poems, seen as suppressing the homoeroticism of Shakespeare's sonnets, contributing to misogynistic
literature, and celebrating erotic poetic art. Emphasis on the various interpretive
contexts generated by different collections.

Underwood, Richard Allan. *Shakespeare's "The Phoenix and Turtle": A Survey of Scholarship*. Salzburg Studies in English Literature 15. Salzburg: Institut für Englische
Sprache und Literatur, Universität Salzburg, 1974. Overview of previous criticism
of the poem.

Various Poems

A Song[1]

1

Shall I die? Shall I fly
Lovers' baits and deceits,
   sorrow breeding?
Shall I tend?° Shall I send?   *wait passively*
5 Shall I sue, and not rue
   my proceeding?[2]
In all duty her beauty
Binds me her servant for ever.
  If she scorn, I mourn,
10 I retire to despair, joining° never.   *(sexually; militarily)*

2

Yet I must vent my lust
And explain inward pain
   by my love conceiving.[3]
If she smiles, she exiles
15 All my moan; if she frown,
   all my hopes deceiving—
Suspicious doubt,° O keep out,   *fear (of rejection)*
For thou art my tormentor.
  Fie away, pack away;
20 I will love, for hope bids me venture.

3

'Twere abuse to accuse
My fair love, ere I prove°   *test*
   her affection.
Therefore try! Her reply
25 Gives thee joy—or annoy,
   or affliction.[4]
Yet howe'er, I will bear
Her pleasure with patience, for beauty
  Sure will not seem to blot
30 Her deserts, wronging him doth her duty.[5]

4

In a dream it did seem—
But alas, dreams do pass
   as do shadows—
I did walk, I did talk
35 With my love, with my dove,

---

1. This poem may or may not have been set to music.
2. Both "sue" (line 5) and "proceeding" refer to lawsuits.
3. Yet I must give expression to my lust by explaining (in poetry) the pain caused by my love. "Conceiving" may also refer to conceiving a child (line 13).

4. "Affliction" may also suggest a sexually transmitted disease.
5. *for beauty . . . duty:* for true beauty will not allow her reputation to appear tarnished by wronging him who serves her faithfully.

through fair meadows.
Still° we passed till at last   *Continually*
We sat to repose us for pleasure.
    Being set, lips met,
40   Arms twined, and did bind my heart's treasure.

5

    Gentle wind sport did find
Wantonly° to make fly   *Capriciously*
    her gold tresses.
    As they shook I did look,
45   But her fair° did impair   *beauty*
    all my senses.
    As amazed, I gazed
On more than a mortal complexion.
    You that love can prove[6]
50   Such force in beauty's inflection.°   *bending*

6

    Next° her hair, forehead fair,   *Next to*
Smooth and high; neat doth lie
    without wrinkle,
    Her fair brows;° under those,   *forehead*
55   Star-like eyes win love's prize
    when they twinkle.
    In her cheeks who° seeks   *whoever*
Shall find there displayed beauty's banner;°   *(a blush)*
    O admiring desiring
60   Breeds, as I look still upon her.

7

    Thin lips red, fancy's[7] fed
With all sweets when he meets,
    and is granted
There to trade,[8] and is made
65   Happy, sure, to endure
    still undaunted.
    Pretty chin doth win
Of all their culled commendations;[9]
    Fairest neck, no speck;
70   All her parts merit high admirations.

8

    Pretty bare, past compare,
Parts those plots which besots
    still asunder.[1]
It is meet naught but sweet
75   Should come near that so rare
    'tis a wonder.[2]
    No mis-shape, no scape°   *transgression*

---

6. You who are in love are able to test.
7. Affection is; imagination is.
8. *granted / There to trade:* allowed to kiss there.
9. Wins from all people their specially chosen praises.
1. *Pretty . . . asunder:* Incomparably pretty "bare" skin

and breasts (exposed above a low neckline) separate the nipples ("plots") that, always separated, (always) cause infatuation.
2. It is proper that nothing but good should come near that which is so wonderfully valuable.

Inferior to nature's perfection;
   No blot, no spot:
80 She's beauty's queen in election.

9

   Whilst I dreamt, I exempt
   From all care, seemed to share
      pleasure's plenty;
   But awake, care take—
85 For I find to my mind
      pleasures scanty.
   Therefore I will try
   To compass° my heart's chief contenting.   *accomplish*
   To delay, some say,
90 In such a case causeth repenting.

'Upon a pair of gloves that master sent to his mistress'

    The gift is small,
    The will is all:[3]
    Alexander Aspinall[4]

Poems from *The Passionate Pilgrim*

4

  Sweet Cytherea,[5] sitting by a brook
  With young Adonis, lovely, fresh, and green,°   *young; inexperienced*
  Did court the lad with many a lovely° look,   *amorous*
  Such looks as none could look but beauty's queen.
5 She told him stories to delight his ear,
  She showed him favours to allure his eye;
  To win his heart she touched him here and there—
  Touches so soft still° conquer chastity.   *always*
  But whether unripe years did want conceit,°   *lack understanding*
10 Or he refused to take her figured° proffer,   *implied*
  The tender nibbler would not touch the bait,
  But smile and jest at every gentle offer.
    Then fell she on her back, fair queen and toward:°   *ready*
    He rose and ran away—ah, fool too froward!°   *obstinate*

6

  Scarce had the sun dried up the dewy morn,
  And scarce the herd gone to the hedge for shade,
  When Cytherea, all in love forlorn,
  A longing tarriance° for Adonis made   *waiting*
5 Under an osier° growing by a brook,   *a willow*
  A brook where Adon used to cool his spleen.°   *hot temper*
  Hot was the day, she hotter, that did look
  For his approach that often there had been.
  Anon he comes and throws his mantle by,

---

3. With a characteristic pun on the poet's name: the goodwill behind the gift is all-encompassing; it's the thought that counts.
4. Stratford schoolmaster from 1582 to 1624.

5. Sonnets 4, 6, and 9 all treat the unsuccessful wooing of the beautiful but unresponsive young man Adonis by Venus ("Cytherea"), the goddess of love.

10 And stood stark naked on the brook's green brim.
   The sun looked on the world with glorious eye,
   Yet not so wistly° as this queen on him.   *eagerly; longingly*
     He, spying her, bounced in whereas he stood.[6]
     'O Jove,' quoth she, 'why was not I a flood?'°   *body of water*

7

   Fair is my love, but not so fair as fickle,
   Mild as a dove, but neither true nor trusty,°   *trustworthy*
   Brighter than glass, and yet, as glass is, brittle;
   Softer than wax, and yet as iron rusty;°   *corrupt (morally)*
5   A lily pale, with damask° dye to grace her,   *red*
     None fairer, nor none falser to deface her.[7]

   Her lips to mine how often hath she joined,
   Between each kiss her oaths of true love swearing.
   How many tales to please me hath she coined,°   *invented*
10 Dreading my love, the loss whereof still fearing.[8]
     Yet in the midst of all her pure protestings
     Her faith, her oaths, her tears, and all were jestings.

   She burnt with love as straw with fire flameth,
   She burnt out love as soon as straw out burneth.
15 She framed° the love, and yet she foiled° the framing,   *built / ruined*
   She bade love last, and yet she fell a-turning.°   *(to another lover)*
     Was this a lover or a lecher whether,°   *which of the two*
     Bad in the best, though excellent in neither?[9]

9

   Fair was the morn when the fair queen of love,°   *Venus*
   [   ]¹
   Paler for sorrow than her milk-white dove,
   For Adon's sake, a youngster proud and wild,
5   Her stand she takes upon a steep-up hill.
   Anon° Adonis comes with horn and hounds.   *Soon*
   She, seely° queen, with more than love's good will   *foolish*
   Forbade the boy he should not pass those grounds.°   *cross those valleys*
   'Once,' quoth she, 'did I see a fair sweet youth
10 Here in these brakes° deep-wounded with° a boar,   *thickets / by*
   Deep in the thigh, a spectacle of ruth.°   *pity*
   See in my thigh,' quoth she, 'here was the sore.'
     She showèd hers; he saw more wounds than one,°   *(sexual)*
     And blushing fled, and left her all alone.

10

   Sweet rose, fair flower, untimely plucked, soon faded—
   Plucked in the bud and faded in the spring;
   Bright orient pearl, alack, too timely shaded;²
   Fair creature, killed too soon by death's sharp sting,

---

6. Jumped in from where he stood.
7. Nor is anyone more false, to her discredit; with a possible reference to cosmetics in "falser" and "deface."
8. Continually being anxious about losing my love.
9. Bad in romance, but not outstanding merely as a sex-

ual partner either.
1. A line is missing here in the original edition.
2. Darkened too soon. "Orient" pearls were valued as more lustrous than their European counterparts.

5   Like a green plum that hangs upon a tree
       And falls through wind before the fall should be.

       I weep for thee, and yet no cause I have,
       For why:° thou left'st me nothing in thy will,   *Because*
       And yet thou left'st me more than I did crave,
10   For why: I cravèd nothing of thee still.³
       O yes, dear friend, I pardon crave of thee:⁴
       Thy discontent° thou didst bequeath to me.   *unhappiness*

12

       Crabbèd° age and youth cannot live together: *Ill-tempered*
       Youth is full of pleasance, age is full of care;
       Youth like summer morn, age like winter weather;
       Youth like summer brave,° age like winter bare.   *well dressed*
5   Youth is full of sport, age's breath is short.
       Youth is nimble, age is lame.
       Youth is hot and bold, age is weak and cold.
       Youth is wild and age is tame.
       Age, I do abhor thee; youth, I do adore thee.
10   O my love, my love is young.
       Age, I do defy thee. O sweet shepherd, hie thee,°   *hurry up*
       For methinks thou stay'st° too long.   *delay*

13

       Beauty is but a vain and doubtful good,
       A shining gloss that fadeth suddenly,
       A flower that dies when first it 'gins to bud,
       A brittle glass that's broken presently.°   *immediately*
5   A doubtful good, a gloss, a glass, a flower,
       Lost, faded, broken, dead within an hour.
       And as goods lost are seld° or never found,   *seldom*
       As faded gloss no rubbing will refresh,
       As flowers dead lie withered on the ground,
10   As broken glass no cement can redress,°   *repair*
           So beauty blemished once, for ever lost,
       In spite of physic,° painting, pain,° and cost.   *medicine / labor*

14

       Good night, good rest—ah, neither be my share.
       She bade good night that kept my rest away,
       And daffed° me to a cabin hanged° with care   *dismissed / adorned*
       To descant on the doubts° of my decay.   *expand upon the fears*
5   'Farewell,' quoth she, 'and come again tomorrow.'
       Fare well I could not, for I supped with sorrow.

       Yet at my parting sweetly did she smile,
       In scorn or friendship nill I conster whether.⁵
       'Tmay be she joyed to jest at my exile

---

3. "Nothing" (lines 8, 10) evokes the tangibility of absence caused by death. But "nothing" also may denote female sexual organs. In line 8, it would go with "will" (testament; lust) to suggest that the dead woman's desire (formerly) made her sexually available to the speaker. In line 10, the speaker would be saying that he always ("still") desired her.
4. This line seems to contradict the previous one by claiming that the speaker did, after all, "crave" something—"pardon."
5. I will not guess which of the two.

10   'Tmay be, again to make me wander thither.
      'Wander'—a word for shadows like myself,
      As take the pain but cannot pluck the pelf.°   *reward*

    Lord, how mine eyes throw gazes to the east!
    My heart doth charge the watch, the morning rise[6]
15   Doth cite° each moving° sense from idle rest,   *summon / living*
    Not daring trust the office of mine eyes.
      While Philomela° sings I sit and mark,°   *the nightingale / listen*
      And wish her lays were tunèd like the lark.[7]

    For she doth welcome daylight with her dite,°   *song*
20   And daylight drives away dark dreaming night.
    The night so packed,° I post° unto my pretty;   *sent off / hasten*
    Heart hath his hope, and eyes their wishèd sight,
      Sorrow changed to solace, and solace mixed with sorrow,
      Forwhy° she sighed and bade me come tomorrow.   *Because*

25   Were I with her, the night would post too soon,
    But now are minutes added to the hours.
    To spite me now each minute seems a moon,
    Yet not for me, shine sun[8] to succour flowers!
      Pack night, peep day; good day, of night now borrow;
30   Short night tonight, and length thyself tomorrow.[9]

Sonnets
to Sundry Notes of Music

15

    It was a lording's° daughter, the fairest one of three,   *lord's*
    That likèd of her master° as well as well might be,   *tutor*
    Till looking on an Englishman, the fairest that eye could see,
      Her fancy fell a-turning.°   *(to another lover)*

5   Long was the combat doubtful° that love with love did fight: *uncertain*
    To leave the master loveless, or kill the gallant knight.
    To put in practice either, alas, it was a spite°   *would be a vexation*
      Unto the seely° damsel.   *helpless*
    But one must be refusèd, more mickle° was the pain   *great*
10   That nothing could be usèd° to turn them both to gain.   *done*
    For of the two the trusty knight was wounded with disdain—
      Alas, she could not help it.

    Thus art° with arms contending was victor of the day,   *learning*
    Which by a gift of learning did bear the maid away.
15   Then lullaby, the learned man hath got the lady gay;
      For now my song is ended.

---

6. My heart blames those on watch, the break of day.
Or, perhaps: My heart orders the "eyes" (line 13) to
watch for morning; my heart urges the night watch to
hurry or proclaim morning.
7. And wish her (nighttime) songs were the songs of

the (morning) lark.
8. Let the sun shine, not for my sake, but.
9. The speaker is asking night to shorten now and to
lengthen tomorrow, when he's with his mistress.

17

My flocks feed not, my ewes breed not,
   My rams speed° not, all is amiss.   *thrive*
Love is dying, faith's defying,[1]
   Heart's denying causer of this.
5 All my merry jigs are quite forgot,
   All my lady's love is lost, God wot.°   *knows*
Where her faith was firmly fixed in love,
   There a nay is placed without remove.°   *immovably*
    One seely cross° wrought all my loss—   *foolish mishap*
10   O frowning fortune, cursèd fickle dame!
    For now I see inconstancy
    More in women than in men remain.

    In black mourn I, all fears scorn I,
    Love hath forlorn me, living in thrall.°   *enslaved (to love)*
15 Heart is bleeding, all help needing—
    O cruel speeding,° freighted with gall.   *fortune*
My shepherd's pipe can sound no deal,°   *not at all*
My wether's[2] bell rings doleful knell,
My curtal dog[3] that wont to° have played *formerly liked to*
20 Plays not at all, but seems afraid,
    With sighs so deep procures to weep
    In howling wise° to see my doleful plight.   *fashion*
How sighs resound through heartless ground,
Like a thousand vanquished men in bloody fight!

25 Clear wells spring not, sweet birds sing not,
    Green plants bring not forth their dye.
Herd stands weeping, flocks all sleeping,
    Nymphs back peeping fearfully.
All our pleasure known to us poor swains,
30 All our merry meetings on the plains,
All our evening sport from us is fled,
All our love is lost, for love is dead.
    Farewell, sweet lass, thy like ne'er was
    For as sweet content, the cause of all my moan.
35 Poor Corydon[4] must live alone,
    Other help for him I see that there is none.

18

Whenas° thine eye hath chose the dame   *When*
And stalled° the deer that thou shouldst strike, *entrapped*
Let reason rule things worthy blame
As well as fancy, partial might.[5]
5   Take counsel of some wiser head,
    Neither too young nor yet unwed,
And when thou com'st thy tale to tell,
Smooth not thy tongue with filèd° talk   *rehearsed; scheming*

---

1. Faith's rejection; "de-fying" means de-faithing.
2. A male sheep castrated while still immature. The "bell-wether" is the lead sheep of the flock.
3. Dog with a cut tail.
4. Conventional name for a shepherd (from one of

Virgil's *Eclogues*, which were pastoral poems).
5. Let reason as well as desire (fancy), which is biased and by itself inadequate, govern your potentially blame-worthy love affairs.

Lest she some subtle practice° smell:—   *deception*
10 A cripple soon can find a halt.⁶
    But plainly say thou lov'st her well,
    And set her person forth to sale,⁷

And to her will° frame all thy ways.°   *desire / habits*
Spare not to spend, and chiefly there
15 Where thy desert may merit praise
By ringing in thy lady's ear.⁸
    The strongest castle, tower, and town,
    The golden bullet° beats it down.   *words; money*

Serve always with assurèd trust,°   *reliability*
20 And in thy suit be humble-true;
Unless thy lady prove unjust,°   *unfaithful*
Press never thou to choose anew.⁹
    When time° shall serve, be thou not slack   *occasion*
    To proffer, though she put thee back.¹

25 What though° her frowning brows be bent,   *Although*
Her cloudy looks will calm ere night,
And then too late she will repent
That thus dissembled her delight,²
    And twice desire,° ere it be day,   *(sexual gratification)*
30   That which with scorn she put away.° *rejected*

What though she strive to try her strength,
And ban,° and brawl,° and say thee nay,   *curse / shout*
Her feeble force will yield at length
When craft° hath taught her thus to say: *craftiness*
35   'Had women been so strong as men,
    In faith you had not had it then.'

The wiles and guiles that women work,°   *employ*
Dissembled with an outward show,
The tricks and toys° that in them lurk   *whims*
40 The cock that treads them³ shall not know.
    Have you not heard it said full oft
    A woman's nay doth stand for nought?⁴

Think women still to strive with men,
To sin and never for to saint.⁵
45 There is no heaven; be holy then
When time with age shall them attaint.⁶
    Were kisses all the joys in bed,
    One woman would another wed.

6. Those practiced in deceit can easily sense deception. *find a halt:* detect a limp.

7. Like a salesman, start praising her qualities. One of the manuscript versions of this poem has "& set thy body forth to sale."

8. Don't be stingy about spending your money in ways that will draw your lady's attention to your merit.

9. Don't make attempts to choose someone else (?)

1. Even if she resists you. The "proffer," at first an offer, becomes outright rape here and in the following stanzas.

2. She who in this way concealed her desire.

3. The man who copulates with them.

4. Nothing; (sexual) naughtiness; a vulva.

5. Expect women always to engage (compete) with men in sin but not in saintliness, or chastity.

6. There is no thought of heaven (purity) in women seeking sexual pleasure. Let them be holy when they're old and unattractive.

But soft, enough—too much, I fear,
50 Lest that my mistress hear my song
She will not stick to round me on th'ear[7]
To teach my tongue to be so long.
    Yet will she blush (here be it said)
    To hear her secrets so bewrayed.°   revealed

The Phoenix and Turtle[8]

Let the bird of loudest lay[9]
On the sole Arabian tree[1]
Herald sad and trumpet be,
To whose sound chaste wings° obey.   virtuous birds

5 But thou shrieking harbinger,°   the screech owl
Foul precurrer of the fiend,[2]
Augur of the fever's end°—   Prophet of death or cure
To this troupe[3] come thou not near.

From this session° interdict°   (of a court) / forbid
10 Every fowl of tyrant wing°   bird of prey
Save the eagle, feathered king.
Keep the obsequy° so strict.   funeral rite

Let the priest in surplice white[4]
That defunctive music can,[5]
15 Be the death-divining swan,
Lest the requiem lack his right.°   its due; its rite

And thou treble-dated° crow,   long-lived
That thy sable gender mak'st
With the breath thou giv'st and tak'st,[6]
20 'Mongst our mourners shalt thou go.

Here the anthem doth commence:
Love and constancy is dead,
Phoenix and the turtle fled
In a mutual flame from hence.

25 So they loved as° love in twain   that
Had the essence but in one,
Two distincts, division none.
Number there in love was slain.[7]

---

7. She won't refrain from scolding me (boxing me) on the ear.
8. *Phoenix:* a legendary, self-resurrecting bird believed to live in cycles of several centuries, dying in flames and reborn from its own ashes—here, regarded as female. *Turtle:* turtledove, symbol of constancy—here, regarded as male.
9. Song. It is unclear which bird this refers to—possibly the phoenix, unless one reads "Death is now the phoenix' nest" (line 56) not as part of a cycle but as a final resting place. Alternately, it is some other bird (the rooster?) known for its loud voice.
1. Supposedly, a unique tree on which sits the phoenix, which is similarly unique: only one exists at any given time.
2. Precursor of the devil: screech owls were thought to

foretell death.
3. The troupe of mourning birds called forth by "the bird of loudest lay" (line 1).
4. The swan. A "surplice" is a loose clerical outer garment.
5. That is skilled in funereal music. Swans were thought to sing beautifully just before (their own) death (hence the phrase "swan song").
6. *That . . . tak'st:* crows were believed to conceive by billing (kissing)—hence, "With the breath." *sable gender:* black offspring.
7. The stanza toys with the commonplace paradox of lovers' simultaneous unity and separateness, ending with the hyperbolic claim that being neither one nor two, the love of the phoenix and the turtle killed the very notion of "number" (line 28).

Hearts remote° yet not asunder,   *separate*
30   Distance and no space was seen
'Twixt this turtle and his queen.
But in them it were a wonder.[8]

So° between them love did shine   *So much*
That the turtle saw his right°   *due; possession; nature*
35   Flaming in the Phoenix' sight.°   *eyesight; appearance*
Either was the other's mine.°   *self; wealth*

Property was thus appalled
That the self was not the same.[9]
Single nature's double name[1]
40   Neither two nor one was called.

Reason, in itself confounded,°   *thoroughly destroyed*
Saw division° grow together   *things divided*
To themselves, yet either neither,[2]
Simple were so well compounded[3]

45   That it cried 'How true° a twain   *faithful; truly*
Seemeth this concordant one!
Love hath reason, reason none,
If what parts can so remain.'[4]

Whereupon it made this threne[5]
50   To the phoenix and the dove,
Co-supremes° and stars of love,   *Joint rulers*
As chorus to their tragic scene.

Threnos

Beauty, truth,° and rarity,   *fidelity*
Grace in all simplicity,
55   Here enclosed in cinders lie.

Death is now the phoenix' nest,[6]
And the turtle's loyal breast
To eternity doth rest.[7]

Leaving no posterity,
60   'Twas not their infirmity,°   *sterility*
It was married chastity.

Truth may seem but cannot be,
Beauty brag, but 'tis not she.[8]
Truth and beauty buried be.

---

8. It would have seemed extraordinary in any creatures but them.
9. The notion of an essential self was thus weakened by the fact that the self was not identical to itself.
1. An indivisible essence with two separate names.
2. Saw separate entities paradoxically become one, but each one was neither single nor united.
3. Single elements were so perfectly combined (appearing to remain "simple" rather than "compounded").
4. Love represents a higher reason than reason itself

because of this embodiment of the paradox of unity of separate elements.
5. Reason made this threnody (a mourning song or epitaph).
6. The phoenix's nest, ordinarily a site of regeneration, is finally a place of death; alternatively, the regenerative qualities of the phoenix's nest will overcome death.
7. Rests eternally; endures forever.
8. Any appearances of fidelity or beauty will only be illusions.

65 To this urn let those repair°   go
That are either true or fair.
For these dead birds sigh a prayer.

Verses upon the Stanley Tomb⁹ at Tong

Written upon the east end of the tomb

Ask who lies here, but do not weep.
He is not dead; he doth but sleep.
This stony register° is for his bones;   record
His fame is more perpetual than these stones,
5   And his own goodness, with himself being gone,
Shall live when earthly monument is none.

Written upon the west end thereof

Not monumental stone preserves our fame,
Nor sky-aspiring pyramids¹ our name.
The memory of him for whom this stands
Shall outlive marble and defacers' hands.
5   When all to time's consumption shall be given,
Stanley for whom this stands shall stand in heaven.

On Ben Jonson²

Master Ben Jonson and master William Shakespeare being merry
at a tavern, Master Jonson having begun this for his epitaph:

Here lies Ben Jonson
That was once one,°   alive

he gives it to Master Shakespeare to make up who presently
writes:

Who while he lived was a slow thing,³
And now, being dead, is nothing.

An Epitaph on Elias James⁴

When God was pleased, the world unwilling yet,⁵
Elias James to nature paid his debt,
And here reposeth. As he lived, he died,
The saying strongly in him verified:
5   'Such life, such death'.° Then, a known truth to tell,   One dies as one lives
He lived a godly life, and died as well.

---

9. Shakespeare had various connections to the Stanley family. It is unclear whether these verses, still visible on the tombstone, memorialize Sir Edward Stanley, Sir Thomas Stanley, or both (with one verse devoted to each).
1. Grand buildings constructed by more modern means. Possibly referring to structures erected in Rome in 1586 or in London in 1603 (for James's coronation), but retaining from their association with Egypt a sense of almost timeless antiquity.

2. One of the best-known of Shakespeare's fellow playwrights (1572–1637).
3. Jonson was a notoriously slow writer.
4. A London brewer of Shakespeare's acquaintance who gave 10 pounds to the parish poor when he died. His tomb was destroyed in the Great Fire of London (1666).
5. Though the world was still unwilling.

An extemporary epitaph on John Combe,[6] a noted usurer

Ten in the hundred[7] here lies engraved;
A hundred to ten° his soul is not saved.   *(odds)*
If anyone ask who lies in this tomb,
'O ho!' quoth the devil, ''tis my John-a-Combe.'

Another Epitaph on John Combe

He being dead, and making the poor his heirs,[8] William
Shakespeare after writes this for his epitaph:

Howe'er he livèd judge not,
John Combe shall never be forgot
While poor hath memory, for he did gather[9]
To make the poor his issue;° he, their father,   *offspring; heirs*
5 As record of his tilth and seed[1]
Did crown him° in his latter deed.   *himself*

Upon the King
At the foot of the effigy of King James I, before his *Works*
(1616)[2]

Crowns have their compass;° length of days, their date;°   *boundaries / limit*
Triumphs, their tombs; felicity, her fate.
Of more than earth can earth make none partaker,[3]
But knowledge makes the king most like his maker.

Epitaph on Himself[4]

Good friend, for Jesus' sake forbear
To dig the dust enclosèd here.
Blessed be the man that spares these stones,
And cursed be he that moves my bones.

---

6. Combe, a wealthy Stratford bachelor, left Shakespeare 5 pounds—a fairly generous sum—in his will.
7. A slang term for "usurer," suggesting one who lends money at 10-percent interest.
8. Combe left generous bequests to the poor of Stratford in his will, including a provision that 100 pounds continue to be lent out, with the interest given as alms.

9. Accumulate wealth (through usury).
1. Tillage and planting (offspring).
2. These lines appear below a picture of James that was the frontispiece to the 1616 edition of his works.
3. No earthly power (not even a King) has power over the afterlife.
4. Carved above Shakespeare's grave in Stratford.

Sir Thomas More: *Passages Attributed to Shakespeare*

The play *Sir Thomas More* was originally composed between late 1592 and mid-1595, probably in 1592–93, by Anthony Munday, Henry Chettle, and perhaps a third writer (Thomas Dekker?). Sometime later, perhaps in 1593–94 or 1603–04, Shakespeare seems to have participated in its revision. The original version was designed for Lord Strange's Men, who presumably intended to stage it at their regular theater, the Rose. Drawing on Raphael Holinshed's *Chronicles of England, Scotland, and Ireland* (1587), Nicholas Harpsfield's *Life and Death of Sir Thomas Moore,* and Thomas Stapleton's Latin biography *Vita Thomae Mori,* the play conforms to the popular tragic model known in Latin as *de casibus virorum illustrium* (on the fall of illustrious men). It follows the career of More—leading English Renaissance humanist and author of *Utopia,* Lord Chancellor of England and persecutor of Protestants, and, finally, Catholic martyr when the religious tide turned. The work focuses on his success as sheriff in peacefully quelling the anti-alien London riots of May Day 1517; his elevation to the post of Lord Chancellor; and his eventual execution for refusing to subscribe to certain of the King's articles. Throughout and especially at the end, the witty and wise protagonist is treated with almost uncritical admiration.

Strange's Men specialized in plays on English subjects with a loosely nationalist appeal; they also liked to live dangerously. *Sir Thomas More* was doubly dangerous. First, even though it carefully converts the issue that led to More's death (papal versus royal supremacy of the church) into a less concrete conflict between worldly authority and individual conscience that would appeal to a Puritan-leaning audience, it sympathetically dramatizes the life of a Catholic martyr killed by Henry VIII, the father of the ruling Protestant monarch, Queen Elizabeth. Second, although it shows More successfully preventing popular protest that historically he was unable to control, the play exploits contemporary antiforeign resentment, which was noticeable by late 1592 and led to rioting and harsh government reprisals between 1593 and 1595. On neither issue does the absolute monarch end up looking particularly good. Before the first performance, however, the censor, Sir Edmund Tilney, Master of the Revels, demanded substantial rewriting, in particular a toning down of the attack on foreigners and the elimination of the scene dramatizing the 1517 rebellion against them. Apparently before the manuscript could be revised, an outbreak of plague closed the theaters for most of the period from mid-1592 to mid-1594, and the actors abandoned the play.

Early in the seventeenth century, the text was revised for performance—possibly at the Fortune, the regular theater of Lord Admiral's Men/Prince Henry's Men, conceivably at the Globe by Shakespeare's company, the Lord Chamberlain's Men/King's Men. (On James I's accession in 1603, Prince Henry and his father, the King, assumed the patronage of the Lord Admiral's and Lord Chamberlain's companies.) The play fit the strategy of the Lord Admiral's Men in the years immediately after 1600, when they specialized in revivals from the Strange's repertory of the early 1590s and the Admiral's own of 1594–97. Also, during the same period, both the Lord Admiral's and the Lord Chamberlain's Men mounted a number of plays set during the reign of Henry VIII. A new monarch and the absence of the dangerous political context of the 1590s allowed the revisers to imagine how they might take account of the censor's earlier concerns. But they could not disregard the fact that the play as originally written required more actors than were in either company, and they adapted the text accordingly. No record of performance exists.

For the original version, Anthony Munday (manuscript Hand S) had copied out the entire text, modifying the work of his collaborator(s). The revision, which also significantly improved the quality of the play, was undertaken by Henry Chettle (Hand A), Thomas Dekker (Hand E), probably Thomas Heywood (Hand B), a playhouse scribe (Hand C), and very probably Shakespeare (Hand D). The result, "The Booke of Sir Thomas Moore" (British Library, MS Harleian 7368)—where "Booke" means theatrical promptbook—is arguably the messiest and most extensively revised dramatic manuscript

From Anthony Munday and others, "The Booke of Sir Thomas Moore" (British Library MS Harleian 7368), fol. 9a. This is the most legible of the pages believed to be in Shakespeare's hand.

of the age. It was not printed until the nineteenth century. It is worth emphasizing the existence of other possible explanations—three in particular—of the text besides the one offered here. The revisions may have occurred immediately following the initial composition of the play, either before or after Tilney's censorship. Second, a small minority denies that Shakespeare is Hand D. Third and most striking, it has been argued that Hand D, whatever his identity, was one of the original playwrights rather than a reviser.

Hand D is present in the first of the two passages printed here, Add.II.D (Addition II, Hand D; 8^r, 8^v, 9^r), which was subsequently edited by Hand C, partly to make it conform to the other revisions. If Add.II.D is Shakespearean, it is by far the longest extant specimen of Shakespeare's handwriting and as such is of considerable scholarly, as well as theatrical and literary, value. It shows what a Shakespearean first draft looks like and, hence, some of the challenges a scribe or printer had to contend with. The attribution to Shakespeare is based on resemblances to his other extant handwriting (almost exclusively signatures), spelling similarities to printed texts that probably are directly based on manuscripts in Shakespeare's hand, and stylistic affinities. The text printed here excludes the emendations that Hand C made to Add.II.D. Normally, this edition opts for the theatrical, rather than the authorial, version of a play on the grounds that Shakespeare was aware of and accepted the revisions introduced by his acting company when preparing his manuscript for the stage. In this instance, however, his involvement in rehearsal and performance is less likely than usual. The second passage included here, Add.III (folio 11^{*b}), is in Hand C and is attributed to Shakespeare, with somewhat less confidence, on stylistic grounds. Normally, as well, this edition prints an entire play rather than a fragment. Here, however, Shakespeare's contribution is small and his involvement probably late—long after the play had been conceptualized and, indeed, written. The entire play is available, however, online at the *Norton Shakespeare* Web site.

Add.II.D constitutes almost the first two-thirds of what one modern edition calls Scene 6 and another Act 2, Scene 3. Earlier in the play, the citizens of London, angered by the high-handed, legally protected behavior of foreigners, prepare to take bloody revenge. Here, More, acting on behalf of a state otherwise prepared to meet force with force, talks the assembled crowd out of violence and into submission to the King. Shakespeare's revision belittles the protesters, depriving them of an individuality they possessed earlier in the play and reducing them to the idiotic fear of disease-causing foreign vegetables (the parsnip and the pumpkin, lines 10–19). Although the rhetoric of More's arguments for obedience is clever and even arresting in its evocation of "the wretched strangers" leaving England (line 81), the claims are orthodox and traditional. They may represent changes from the original manuscript and, like the imagery, certainly have parallels in Shakespeare's other plays, most tellingly in Ulysses' speech on degree in 1.3 of *Troilus and Cressida* (probably from 1602). Even though the lines seem at least partly designed to reassure the censor, their political implications also point in a different direction. Once the crowd has listened to More, whom they already trust and respect, they willingly submit to royal authority. The text demonstrates the fundamental decency of the common folk. And More's brilliant success provides a plausible, if historically inaccurate, explanation of his appointment as Lord Chancellor.

Like Ulysses' speech, however, More's is undermined by the rest of the play. The passage also engages in powerfully ironic foreshadowing at the expense of the monarchy. More promises,

> Submit you to these noble gentlemen,
> Entreat their mediation to the King,
> Give up yourself to form, obey the magistrate,
> And there's no doubt but mercy may be found,
> If you so seek it.

(lines 157–61)

There is, however, a "doubt": Lincoln goes to the scaffold, his noble death anticipating More's own fate. More also insists that

> . . . to the King God hath his office lent
> . . . .
> . . . What do you then,
> Rising 'gainst him that God himself installs,
> But rise 'gainst God?
>
> (lines 107, 113–15)

The equation of God and King, the divine sanction for royal authority—these are the principles that More repudiates at the cost of his life. A similar effect is achieved in Add.III, which opens Scene 8 of one modern edition and Act 3, Scene 1, of another. Newly named Lord Chancellor, More soliloquizes on the suddenness of his ascent, in which he sees evidence of a providential force at odds with explanations based on "our fortunes" (line 2; Fortune is usually represented in *de casibus* tragedy by the image of the turning wheel). This view leads him to predict, accurately, that "to be great / Is" to be "greatly undone" (lines 19–21)—where the greatness of the undoing can refer both to the height from which he falls and to the stature of the cause for which he goes to his death.

WALTER COHEN

SELECTED BIBLIOGRAPHY

Fox, Alistair. "The Paradoxical Design of *The Book of Sir Thomas More.*" *Renaissance and Reformation/Renaissance et Réforme* n.s. 5 (1981): 162–73. Includes discussion of the symbolic resonance of the dramatic interlude that More puts on for the Lord Mayor (Scene 9).

Gabrieli, Vittorio. "*Sir Thomas More*: Sources, Characters, Ideas." *Moreana* 23 (June 1986): 17–43. The central study of the play's sources.

Howard-Hill, T. H., ed. *Shakespeare and "Sir Thomas More": Essays on the Play and Its Shakespearian Interest.* Cambridge, Eng.: Cambridge University Press, 1989. A collection of articles dealing with both authorship issues and critical interpretation.

Levine, Nina S. "Citizens' Games: Differentiating Collaboration and *Sir Thomas More.*" *Shakespeare Quarterly* 58 (2007): 31–64. Investigates the analogy between collaborative authorship and the subject of that collaboration, rebellious citizen solidarity.

Masten, Jeffrey. "More or Less: Editing the Collaborative." *Shakespeare Studies* 29 (2001): 109–31. Argues for including the full play, rather than just the Shakespearean portions, in editions of Shakespeare, thus avoiding a practice that underemphasizes the unity of the work.

McMillin, Scott. *The Elizabethan Theatre and "The Book of Sir Thomas More."* Ithaca, N.Y.: Cornell University Press, 1987. Interprets the play in the context of theatrical practice at the time, arguing that Shakespeare was part of the collaboration that originally composed the play rather than one of its revisers.

Munday, Anthony, and others. Revised by Henry Chettle, Thomas Dekker, Thomas Heywood, and William Shakespeare. *Sir Thomas More: A Play.* Ed. Vittorio Gabrieli and Giorgio Melchiori. The Revels Plays series. Manchester: Manchester University Press, 1990. Annotated modern edition of the play.

Wentersdorf, Karl P. "On 'Momtanish Inhumanyty' in *Sir Thomas More.*" *Studies in Philology* 103 (2006): 178–85. Argues that More criticizes the citizens' hostility to foreigners as Muslim inhumanity.

Sir Thomas More: *Passages Attributed*
to Shakespeare

Add.II.D

[*John*] LINCOLN [*a broker*],° DOLL, BETTS, [SHERWIN (*a*   *buying and selling agent*
goldsmith), *and prentices*° *armed; Thomas* MORE (*sheriff*   *apprentices*
of the City of London), *the other sheriff, Sir Thomas*
PALMER, *Sir Roger* CHOLMELEY,] *and a* SERJEANT-*at-*
arms [*stand aloof*]

LINCOLN [*to the prentices*]   Peace, hear me! He that will not see°   *tolerate*
   a red herring at a Harry groat,° butter at eleven pence a pound,   *cost of fourpence*
   meal at nine shillings a bushel, and beef at four nobles a stone,
   list[1] to me.

5   OTHER   It will come to that pass if strangers be suffered.[2] Mark
   him.

LINCOLN   Our country is a great eating country; argo,[3] they eat
   more in our country than they do in their own.

OTHER   By a halfpenny loaf a day, troy weight.°   *standard measure*

10   LINCOLN   They bring in strange roots,[4] which is merely° to the   *entirely*
   undoing of poor prentices, for what's a sorry parsnip[5] to a good
   heart?

OTHER   Trash, trash. They breed sore eyes, and 'tis enough to
   infect the city with the palsy.

15   LINCOLN   Nay, it has infected it with the palsy, for these bastards
   of dung[6]—as you know, they grow in dung—have infected us,
   and it is our infection will make the city shake, which partly
   comes through the eating of parsnips.

OTHER   True, and pumpions° together.   *pumpkins*

SERJEANT [*coming forward*]   What say you to the mercy of the
20   King?
   Do you refuse it?

LINCOLN   You would have us upon th'hip,° would you? No,   *at a disadvantage*
   marry, do we not. We accept of the King's mercy; but we will
   show no mercy upon the strangers.

25   SERJEANT   You are the simplest things
   That ever stood in such a question.[7]

LINCOLN   How say you now? Prentices 'simple'? [*To the pren-*
   tices] Down with him!

ALL   Prentices simple! Prentices simple!

Add.II.D Location: St. Martin's Lane, London; May Day
1517.
1. *noble:* gold coin worth 6 shillings 8 pence. *stone:* 14
pounds. *list:* listen. These prices would have seemed high
to a contemporary audience.
2. If foreigners ("strangers" means "foreigners" throughout the scene) are allowed (to remain in London).
3. As Lincoln says, England had a reputation for gluttony. *argo:* for Latin *ergo* (therefore).

4. Foreign vegetables.
5. Lincoln confuses parsnips with potatoes, which were
introduced to England from the Americas in the 1580s
and were rumored to cause disease.
6. Illegitimate growths made still more repugnant by
their association with excrement; perhaps merely abusive.
7. Stood their ground in such circumstances (against
the King's wishes).

Enter the Lord MAYOR, [*the Earl of*] SURREY, [*and the*
Earl of] SHREWSBURY

30   SHERIFF [*to the prentices*]   Hold in the King's name! Hold!
   SURREY [*to the prentices*]   Friends, masters, countrymen—
   MAYOR [*to the prentices*]   Peace ho, peace! I charge you, keep
      the peace!
   SHREWSBURY [*to the prentices*]   My masters, countrymen—
   SHERWIN   The noble Earl of Shrewsbury, let's hear him.
35   BETTS   We'll hear the Earl of Surrey.
   LINCOLN   The Earl of Shrewsbury.
   BETTS   We'll hear both.
   ALL   Both, both, both, both!
   LINCOLN   Peace, I say peace! Are you men of wisdom, or what
40   are you?
   SURREY   What you will have them,° but not men of wisdom.   *Whatever you call them*
   SOME   We'll not hear my Lord of Surrey.
   OTHERS   No, no, no, no, no! Shrewsbury, Shrewsbury!
   MORE [*to the nobles and officers*]   Whiles they are o'er the bank
      of their obedience,
45   Thus will they bear down all things.[8]
   LINCOLN [*to the prentices*]   Sheriff More speaks. Shall we hear
      Sheriff More speak?
   DOLL   Let's hear him. A keeps a plentiful shrievalty,[9] and a
      made my brother Arthur Watchins Sergeant Safe's yeoman.°   *assistant*
50   Let's hear Sheriff More.
   ALL   Sheriff More, More, More, Sheriff More!
   MORE   Even by the rule you have among yourselves,
      Command still audience.°   *quiet hearing*
   SOME   Surrey, Surrey!
55   OTHERS   More, More!
   LINCOLN *and* BETTS   Peace, peace, silence, peace!
   MORE   You that have voice and credit with the number,°   *the crowd*
      Command them to a stillness.
   LINCOLN   A plague on them! They will not hold their peace.
60   The devil cannot rule them.
   MORE   Then what a rough and riotous charge° have you,   *people in your care; duty*
      To lead those that the devil cannot rule.
      [*To the prentices*] Good masters, hear me speak.
   DOLL   Ay, by th' mass, will we. More, thou'rt a good house-
65   keeper,[1] and I thank thy good worship for my brother Arthur
      Watchins.
   ALL   Peace, peace!
   MORE   Look, what you do offend you cry upon,[2]
      That is the peace. Not one of you here present,
70   Had there such fellows lived when you were babes
      That could have topped the peace as now you would,
      The peace wherein you have till now grown up
      Had been ta'en from you, and the bloody times
      Could not have brought you to the state of men.[3]

8. The image is of water flooding over the banks (of obedience), destroying everything in its path.
9. He ("A") is a generous sheriff.
1. Patron; head of a well-to-do household.
2. By yelling "peace" (though you call for peace), you
break the peace. More's speeches to the crowd, especially
lines 79–94, echo Ulysses' speech on degree in *Troilus*

and Cressida 1.3.74–137, in particular lines 110–24. Both
of these sincere expositions of orthodoxy are ironized by
the ensuing events.
3. *Not one . . . men:* If such peace breakers as you had
been around when you were children, you wouldn't have
had peaceful times to grow up in, and you wouldn't have
lived to become men.

75 Alas, poor things, what is it you have got,
    Although we grant you get the thing you seek?
BETTS Marry, the removing of the strangers, which cannot
    choose but much advantage the poor handicrafts° of the city. *craftspeople*
MORE Grant them removed, and grant that this your noise
80 Hath chid down all the majesty of England.[4]
    Imagine that you see the wretched strangers,
    Their babies at their backs, with their poor luggage
    Plodding to th' ports and coasts for transportation,
    And that you sit as kings in your desires,[5]
85 Authority quite silenced by your brawl
    And you in ruff of your opinions clothed:[6]
    What had you got? I'll tell you. You had taught
    How insolence and strong hand° should prevail, *force*
    How order should be quelled—and by this pattern
90 Not one of you should live an agèd man,
    For other ruffians as their fancies wrought
    With selfsame hand, self reasons, and self right
    Would shark° on you, and men like ravenous fishes *prey*
    Would feed on one another.
95 DOLL Before God, that's as true as the gospel.
BETTS Nay, this'° a sound fellow, I tell you. Let's mark° him. *this is / listen to*
MORE Let me set up before your thoughts, good friends,
    One supposition,° which if you will mark *proposition*
    You shall perceive how horrible a shape
100 Your innovation° bears. First, 'tis a sin *rebellion*
    Which oft th'apostle° did forewarn us of, *Paul (Romans 13:1–5)*
    Urging obedience to authority;
    And 'twere no error if I told you all
    You were in arms 'gainst God.
105 ALL Marry, God forbid that!
MORE Nay, certainly you are.
    For to the King God hath his office lent
    Of dread,° of justice, power and command, *fearful respect*
    Hath bid him rule and willed you to obey;
110 And to add ampler majesty to this,
    He hath not only lent the King his figure,
    His throne and sword, but given him his own name,
    Calls him a god on earth. What do you then,
    Rising 'gainst him that God himself installs,
115 But rise 'gainst God?[7] What do you to your souls
    In doing this? O desperate as you are,
    Wash your foul minds with tears, and those same hands
    That you like rebels lift against the peace
    Lift up for peace; and your unreverent knees,
120 Make them your feet. To kneel to be forgiven
    Is safer wars than ever you can make,
    Whose discipline is riot.[8]

---

4. *grant that . . . England:* suppose your action overthrew
the state.
5. You get what you want; your wishes are obeyed.
6. And you wearing the clothes ("ruff" was a fancy
starched collar; also, the highest pride) befitting the rank
and authority you think you deserve (alluding to Elizabethan sumptuary laws, which determined, according to

rank and income, the clothes one was permitted to wear).
7. More argues in this speech that the monarch's authority has divine sanction—ironically, a position that, as the
end of the play reveals, he later repudiated at the cost of
his life.
8. *Is . . . riot:* Is a safer means of fighting (for your goals)
than your rebellion.

In, in, to your obedience!⁹ Why, even your hurly°   *riot*
Cannot proceed but by obedience.
125   What rebel captain,
As mut'nies are incident,° by his name   *about to happen*
Can still the rout?° Who will obey a traitor?   *quiet the rabble*
Or how can well that proclamation sound,
When there is no addition° but 'a rebel'   *title of rank*
130   To qualify° a rebel? You'll put down strangers,   *signify*
Kill them, cut their throats, possess their houses,
And lead the majesty of law in lyam°   *on a leash*
To slip° him like a hound—alas, alas!   *release*
Say now the King,
135   As he is clement° if th'offender mourn,°   *merciful / repent*
Should so much come too short of your great trespass¹
As but to banish you: whither would you go?
What country, by° the nature of your error,   *in light of*
Should give you harbour? Go you to France or Flanders,
140   To any German province, Spain or Portugal,
Nay, anywhere that not adheres² to England—
Why, you must needs° be strangers. Would you be pleased   *necessarily*
To find a nation of such barbarous temper
That breaking out in hideous violence
145   Would not afford you an abode on earth,
Whet° their detested knives against your throats,   *But would whet*
Spurn you like dogs, and like as if that God
Owed° not nor made not you, nor that the elements   *Owned*
Were not all appropriate° to your comforts   *suitable*
150   But chartered unto° them, what would you think   *reserved only for*
To be thus used? This is the strangers' case,
And this your mountainish³ inhumanity.
ONE [*to the others*]   Faith, a° says true. Let's do as we may be   *he*
done by.⁴
155   ANOTHER [*to* MORE]   We'll be ruled by you, Master More, if
you'll stand our friend to procure our pardon.
    MORE   Submit you to these noble gentlemen,
Entreat their mediation to the King,
Give up yourself to form,° obey the magistrate,   *correct behavior*
160   And there's no doubt but mercy may be found,
If you so seek it.⁵

Add.III

Enter [Sir Thomas] MORE

    MORE   It is in heaven that I am thus and thus,¹
And that which we profanely term our fortunes
Is the provision of the power above,
Fitted and shaped just to that strength of nature
5   Which we are born withal.° Good God, good God,   *with*
That I from such an humble bench² of birth

---

9. Get back within the boundaries of your obedience.
1. Should reduce by so much the punishment for your great offense.
2. Anywhere whose customs don't conform.
3. Gross, coarse. Possibly a contraction of Mahometanish, or Muslim.
4. Proverbial. From the Sermon on the Mount (Matthew 7:12 and Luke 6:31).

5. In the event, More's intercession is unable to save Lincoln, whose noble death on the scaffold foreshadows More's own and, like his, reflects badly on the King—the dying men's loyal words notwithstanding.
Add.III Location: The chancery staterooms in Westminster.
1. It is up to heaven that I am one thing and then another.
2. Legal position; foot of the table: hence, origin.

Should step as 'twere up to my country's head
And give the law out there; ay, in my father's life
To take prerogative and tithe of knees[3]
10   From elder kinsmen, and him bind by my place
To give the smooth and dexter way to me[4]
That owe it him by nature!° Sure these things,   by birth
Not physicked° by respect, might turn our blood   regulated
To much corruption. But More, the more thou hast
15   Either of honour, office, wealth and calling,
Which might accite° thee to embrace and hug them,   entice
The more do thou e'en° serpents' natures think them: even
Fear their gay skins, with thought of their sharp stings,
And let this be thy maxim: to be great
20   Is, when the thread of hazard is once spun,
A bottom great wound up, greatly undone.[5]

---

3. *To . . . knees:* To have preeminence and the deference of having others curtsy.
4. *and him . . . me:* and for my rank to force ("bind") someone ("him") to yield the right-hand side and the smooth part of the road.
5. *to be great . . . undone:* worldly power, when the thread that Fortune ("hazard") allots has been all wound up onto a big spool ("bottom"; or, when the hazards of reaching a high position have been surmounted), simply means a greater fall (or, falling only for something important). In Greek mythology, the end of a life occurred when the Fates cut a person's thread. Regardless of the exact interpretation of the passage, it accurately predicts More's fate.

Measure for Measure

A young man is in grave trouble with the law, and his beautiful sister goes to the magistrate to plead for mercy. The magistrate offers to remit the penalty if the sister will sleep with him. It is an old story in more ways than one. Shakespeare knew several sixteenth-century versions: the Italian Giovanbattista Giraldi Cinthio produced both prose and dramatic renderings, and in 1578 the English playwright George Whetstone published *Promos and Cassandra,* the most important source for *Measure for Measure.* Shakespeare took the title of his play from Jesus' Sermon on the Mount: "Judge not, that ye be not judged. For with what judgment ye judge, ye shall be judged: and with what measure ye mete, it shall be measured to you again" (Matthew 7:1–2). Jesus' advice combines threat with promise: a prudent fear of heavenly retaliation persuades believers not to pass judgment themselves, while at the same time, an apparent abdication of equity is folded into an overall scheme of just compensation. As we shall see, the passage in all its complexity complements the intricacies of Shakespeare's treatment of the ancient tale.

Measure for Measure was performed in 1604 at a pivotal moment in Shakespeare's career. The play is the last in a long series of comedies that explore complex issues of sex, marriage, and personal identity. Its tone, themes, and methods of characterization, however, veer close to tragedy, the genre that largely, though not exclusively, preoccupied Shakespeare in the years immediately following. Many critics, therefore, classify *Measure for Measure* as a "problem" comedy. The designation attests both to the difficult moral issues that the play confronts and to the boldness with which it stretches—some would say shatters—the normal limits of comic form.

The play's distinctiveness becomes evident almost immediately. In Act 1, Scene 2, Claudio and his pregnant lover, Juliet, appear in the custody of the Provost, being led away to prison. Their crime is premarital sex; the penalty, for Claudio at least, is death. The seriousness of their situation is not in itself unusual: "The course of true love never did run smooth," Lysander remarks in *A Midsummer Night's Dream,* and if it did, it would hardly make an engrossing dramatic subject. Nonetheless, Claudio's initial description of his plight is quite remarkable:

> LUCIO   Why, how now, Claudio? Whence comes this restraint?
> CLAUDIO   From too much liberty, my Lucio, liberty.
> As surfeit is the father of much fast,
> So every scope, by the immoderate use,
> Turns to restraint. Our natures do pursue,
> Like rats that raven down their proper bane,
> A thirsty evil; and when we drink, we die.
>
> (1.2.104–10)

Claudio likens his passion for his beloved to a rat's craving for poison: compulsive, irrational, and self-destructive. Excessive indulgence, or "surfeit," inevitably brings regret and punishment in its train. Claudio sounds as if he is describing the most arrant kind of lust, although, as he will subsequently explain, he is actually "precontracted" to Juliet, bound by a promise of marriage that many in Renaissance England saw as providing conjugal privileges. (Shakespeare himself may have subscribed to this view, since his wife gave birth to their daughter five months after their wedding. More pertinently, the Duke, in his guise as a friar, affirms that the precontract sanctions Mariana's intimacy with Angelo later in the play.) Interestingly, however, neither Claudio nor Juliet is inclined to argue that their devotion to one another mitigates their guilt. Instead, they admit that they have committed "fornication," a severely condemnatory term that conflates all kinds of sex outside of marriage under the same rubric, recognizing no difference between long-term relationships and sheerest promiscuity.

As the play continues, it becomes clear that Claudio's imagery of suicidal animalism, havoc, and pollution is not merely the consequence of his immediate agitation, but expresses a profound assumption of the society in which he lives. For his sister, Isabella, sexual intercourse is "what I abhor to name" (3.1.100); the Duke deplores Pompey's "filthy vice" and Juliet's "most offenseful act"; the wise Escalus acknowledges Claudio's "error" even as he attempts to alleviate his punishment. Few doubt that human sexuality is an essentially sordid matter, a sign of degradation rather than a means of creativity or love. Occasional glimpses of an alternative vision—Lucio's brief, radiant analogy between Juliet's pregnancy and agricultural fertility, for instance—by their very rarity reinforce the prevailing pessimism.

Such austere views of human sexuality have ancient roots. When the Duke calls Vienna's sex laws "needful bits and curbs to headstrong weeds" (1.3.20), he recalls an image from Plato, who compared the desiring part of the soul to a useful but refractory horse, which the rational part of the soul needs to keep strictly bridled and under firm control. When Isabella refers to erotic desire as a "natural guiltiness" (2.2.142), she draws upon a traditional Christian connection between sexuality and original sin, the disobedience committed by Adam and Eve in the Garden of Eden and passed on to all their offspring as a kind of intrinsic pollution.

To say that a view is traditional, however, is not to say that it is inevitable. What makes sexuality so troublesome in this particular play? In Shakespeare's earlier, more optimistic comedies, the prospect of heterosexual consummation usually seems automatically to entail marriage, so that the weddings with which the plays conclude seem to follow spontaneously from the eroticism that fuels the plot. By marrying and establishing a family, the young couples simultaneously satisfy their mutual yearning for one another, and their community's demand for clear kinship structures and for orderly means of transferring property to "legitimate" members of a new generation. In *Measure for Measure*, however, the link between heterosexual desire and marriage seems to have snapped. Claudio and Juliet defer their wedding day; Angelo abandons Mariana; Lucio refuses to support his child or marry its mother. Prostitution flourishes. Rampant promiscuity makes syphilis a familiar ailment and a standard topic for nervous jokes.

Once carnal desire comes unhinged from the institution of marriage, it begins to seem subversive of personal and civic order. And if one believes, rightly or wrongly, that one's sexuality is intrinsically antisocial and depraved, then complete sexual renunication might seem the wisest course. In *Measure for Measure*, the morally ambitious characters—the Duke, Angelo, and Isabella—initially assume that their virtue is tied up with, perhaps even identical with, their chastity. "Believe not that the dribbling dart of love / Can pierce a complete bosom," the Duke boasts to the Friar (1.3.2–3). Angelo attempts to

Charioteer with two galloping horses. From Geffrey Whitney, *A Choice of Emblemes* (1586).

protect his reputation for austerity even as he hopelessly compromises his scruples in secret. Isabella believes that sleeping with Angelo will defile her forever, even if she does so in order to save her brother's life.

The value of celibacy is endorsed by characters who do not themselves aspire to such high standards of conduct. Lucio is a libertine, but he believes that Isabella's intention to enter a nunnery renders her "a thing enskied and sainted" (1.4.33). Likewise, Pompey admits that his life as a pimp "does stink in some sort, sir" (3.1.283). A few of those who cannot be chaste themselves are, like Claudio, capable of moments of shame or self-loathing; others, like Lucio, shruggingly accept their lack of saintliness. The Vienna of *Measure for Measure* is full of people unlikely to be enlisted for projects of social or spiritual improvement: the moronic Elbow, the impenitent Pompey, the unregenerate Mistress Overdone, the "gravel-hearted" Barnardine, the heedless First and Second Gentlemen, the gullible Froth. These people are part of the commonwealth, subject to the law, and willy-nilly part, too, of a Catholic church that aspires—unlike some of the Protestant sects of Shakespeare's time—to include the entire community. Should the laws of this community reflect its stringent ideals or the actual behavior of most of its members? Throughout the play, those who aspire to belong to a principled moral elite deplore the weaknesses of the reprobate. At the same time, because the rascals in *Measure for Measure* are so vividly memorable, the play also suggests that moral "failure" is often at least as humanly compelling as moral excellence is—at least moral excellence defined in the narrow, self-denying terms that prevail in Vienna.

For the intransigent majority unable or unwilling to control the horses of lust, the "needful bits and curbs" of which the Duke speaks impose an external system of repression. Such a system would not have been unfamiliar to Shakespeare's original audience. Courts administered by the Church of England prosecuted many sexual infractions: among them fathering or giving birth to a bastard, committing adultery or bigamy, deserting a spouse, reneging on a wedding engagement, or groundlessly accusing others of such transgressions. Convicted individuals could be fined, whipped, displayed in the marketplace, or made to announce their sins in church. (Thus Claudio and Juliet are paraded about the streets of Vienna before being taken to prison, to humiliate them and to serve as an example for others.) Repeat offenders were excommunicated, or cast out of the church.

Underlying such proceedings was the assumption, as in *Measure for Measure*, that morality could and should be legislated; that the sexual conduct of individuals was the business of the entire community. Indeed, in the early seventeenth century, when Shakespeare was writing *Measure for Measure*, an increasingly powerful group of Puritans, or "precisians," argued that the church courts' punishments were far too mild. Threats of disgrace and excommunication failed to deter the most egregious offenders, who had no reputation to lose and were unlikely to fret at their exclusion from church. Moreover, shaming punishments worked less well in the increasingly busy, heterogeneous neighborhoods of Jacobean London than they had in the smaller rural communities for which they had originally been designed.

In *Measure for Measure,* the repeated characterization of Angelo as "precise" associates him with the rigorists of Shakespeare's time; and since Viennese justice treats Claudio more strictly than it does professionals in the sex trade, the question of what constitutes adequate severity is certainly at issue. Perhaps, then, the play comprises Shakespeare's reflection on an issue of contemporary concern: what would happen if, as some argued, sexual misconduct could be punished with death? At the same time, Shakespeare carefully distinguishes the world of his play from seventeenth-century England, most obviously by making Vienna a Catholic city peopled with the nuns and friars who had been eliminated from Protestant England over half a century earlier. For despite obvious connections between *Measure for Measure* and some of the issues of its own day, Shakespeare's play hardly constitutes a clear policy recommendation. He is more deeply attentive to general issues about the often-vexed relationship between civic life and human passion, and between religious commitment and the conduct of secular affairs. What happens to individuals and a community when sexuality is viewed as transgressive, when it becomes the subject of public discipline? Is it possible or advisable to regulate sexual behavior through the courts? How do religious convictions affect the experience of sexual desire? These concerns resonate in an era like our own, characterized by a lack of consensus in religion and in sexual mores, by widespread transformations in the institution of marriage, and by debates over the extent to which the state ought to monitor the sexual behavior of citizens.

In *Measure for Measure,* Angelo's disastrous career suggests one possible effect of strict sexual self-denial: that the habits of restraint can themselves provoke sexual excitement. Rigid and self-righteous, Angelo seems not to have experienced the violence of desire until Isabella's first visit on behalf of her brother awakens his appetite:

> What's this? What's this? Is this her fault or mine?
> The tempter or the tempted, who sins most, ha?
> Not she; nor doth she tempt; but it is I
> That, lying by the violet in the sun,
> Do, as the carrion does, not as the flower,
> Corrupt with virtuous season.
>
> (2.2.167–72)

Like Claudio, Angelo thinks of passion in terms of death and decay, but the resemblance between the two men ends there. Angelo imagines himself as tainted meat rotting all the

Jost Amman, Poor Clare nun, from *Cleri totius Romanae ecclesiae subjecti* (1585).

faster under the very sun that gives life to innocent, lovely things. What ought to improve Angelo—his keen appreciation for the presence of virtue—makes him worse.

Angelo is sexually aroused by prohibition. Mariana loves him, and his relationship with her breaches no social norms; he discards her. Isabella is ostentatiously pristine, and her nun's habit marks her as taboo; he finds her irresistible. In order to extract pleasure from the encounter, however, Angelo must force himself to remain aware of the principles he attempts so flagrantly to violate. If he rationalized his behavior or blamed it on Isabella, he would lose the nearly sensual luxury of self-hatred. Therefore, the lucidity with which Angelo analyzes his own motives leads not to penitence but to an increasing moral recklessness. His inclination to categorize all sexual conduct as transgressive actually makes his offense easier to commit. Propositioning Isabella in their second meeting together, he tells her: "I have begun, / And now I give my sensual race the rein" (2.4.159–60). Angelo explains why he cannot govern himself with the same image the Duke used to underscore the necessity of control. Once embarked on the "sensual race," he imagines, there is no alternative to utter abandon.

For Isabella, however, sleeping with Angelo is out of the question. Some modern critics have found her defiance heroic, others chilling or selfish. Doubtless in Shakespeare's time, she elicited a similarly mixed response. Shakespeare alters his source story considerably to expand Isabella's role and specify its implications more exactly. In Whetstone's *Promos and Cassandra*, the sister has no plans to enter a convent, and she eventually goes to bed with the deputy in order to save her brother's life. For Isabella, by contrast, virginity is a principled choice, not an accident of youth. The vow of lifelong, religiously dedicated chastity she plans to take is a matter about which Shakespeare's contemporaries had conflicting feelings. One effect of England's break with the Catholic Church had been a spectacular change in official attitudes toward celibacy. While Catholics honored sexual renunciation and demanded that their clergy remain chaste, Protestants discouraged veneration of the Virgin Mary, abolished convents and monasteries, and urged clergy to marry. Despite these alterations, however, a powerful appreciation for virginity and belief in its semimagical powers persisted in Reformation England, cut loose from its explicitly religious moorings. The effect of Shakespeare's innovations on Whetstone, then, is both to heighten the ambivalence of the story and to focus the moral spotlight on Isabella's convictions and the choices that follow from them.

Isabella believes that she would damn herself by sleeping with Angelo.

> Better it were a brother died at once
> Than that a sister, by redeeming him,
> Should die for ever.
>
> (2.4.107–9)

Is she right? St. Augustine, the most influential Christian writer on sexual morality, insists that since sin is a property of the will, not a physical state, persons who are forced to perform sexual acts are blameless. If chastity is a state of mind, then the fate of Isabella's body is possibly independent of, and irrelevant to, the fate of her soul. Perhaps, in fact, by acquiescing to Angelo, Isabella would perform an act of charity, generously sacrificing her own preferences for Claudio's benefit. On the other hand, female "virtue" has traditionally been defined in physical as well as mental terms, so that chastity, the spiritual attitude, is hard to separate from virginity, the bodily condition. Moreover, Isabella is not exactly a rape victim; she must, as Angelo says, "fit her consent" to his proposal. Does that consent, however reluctant, contaminate her with his sin? Quite possibly. Would it permanently unsuit her for her religious vocation? Quite possibly. Clearly it is reasonable, then, for Isabella to be cautious; and no one, says Augustine, is obliged to put him- or herself in eternal peril merely in order to save the life of another person.

Since, however, Shakespeare characteristically translates sweeping moral questions into scrupulously personal terms, apparently reasonable general maxims do not entirely suffice to explain Isabella's motives. On one hand, her obstinacy seems justified after the fact, when Angelo decides to execute Claudio, because clearly her capitulation would not have saved her brother's life. On the other hand, Isabella's obsession with her own purity seems excessive, especially in 3.1, when it manifests itself in gross insensitivity to her plaintive, terrified brother. Moreover, her fervent yearning for constraint, like Angelo's, seems luridly imbued with sadomasochism.

> were I under the terms of death,
> Th'impression of keen whips I'd wear as rubies,
> And strip myself to death as to a bed
> That longing have been sick for, ere I'd yield
> My body up to shame.
>
> (2.4.100–04)

At such moments, Isabella seems not to be exterminating or transcending her own sexuality, but redirecting it in ways of which she is not entirely conscious. She not only shares Angelo's assumption that the sexual act is a defilement, but like him she finds discipline exciting. With all our disapproval of Angelo's abuse of power and our sympathy with Isabella's indignation, we can still see how their conflict arises as much from their similarities as from their differences.

Isabella's difficulty is hard to resolve because it is unclear how much her chastity is worth. Is it more valuable than her brother's life? Is it more valuable than her own life, which she would throw down for Claudio, she claims, "as frankly as a pin" (3.1.105)? Is it only fair, as Angelo claims, to yield him her body as compensation for overlooking Claudio's offense, or is "lawful mercy . . . nothing kin to foul redemption" (2.4.113–14)? Shakespeare provides no answer to these questions, but the conflict they produce yields the play's most vividly realized interactions. As the title suggests, *Measure for Measure* is obsessed with problems of substitution and commensurability—from the opening scene in which Angelo takes over as the Duke's deputy to Angelo's proposal that Isabella vindicate Claudio by committing his sin herself, to the bed trick that replaces Isabella with Mariana, to the Provost's exchange of Ragusine's head for Claudio's. Even the most apparently trivial comic interchanges persistently echo the concern with equivalence, proportionality, and relative priority: the Gentlemen argue about whether they are cut from lists or velvet; Pompey and Abhorson debate the relative standing of bawd and hangman.

Questions of equivalence seem to underlie the very possibility of justice, even the possibility of any ethical thinking. When a person commits a misdeed, restoring the status quo ante is usually impossible. Thus the wrongdoer ought, we feel, either to make adequate restitution or to suffer in rough proportion to the anguish he or she has caused, rendering, in the biblical phrase, measure for measure. In sexual matters, however, such problems of equivalence are murky, because there is no consensus regarding how apparently straightforward bodily acts ought to be interpreted. Angelo compares Claudio's offense to murder and counterfeiting; Lucio thinks it is trivial, "a game of tick-tack" (1.2.167). What seem to be the same actions can be evaluated in wildly different ways, depending on one's frame of reference: to the abstemious Angelo, Claudio's behavior looks like gross debauchery, while to Mistress Overdone's dissolute patrons, it looks positively restrained. Motives alter what seem to be the same actions, so that we are inclined to regard Claudio more leniently than Lucio, who abandoned his mistress after making her pregnant. So do outcomes: the bed trick means that Angelo, intending to commit an impermissible act, in fact performs a licit one, unknowingly laying the groundwork for his pardon in the final scene.

The commitment of several characters to a Christian religious vocation further complicates the possibility of establishing some kind of commensurability. Isabella, especially, assumes that spiritual goods like honor and purity are infinitely more important than secular, visible possessions. In her system of values, a promise of ardent prayer constitutes the most potent bribe she can offer Angelo, beside which gold is barren and trivial. The counterintuitive otherworldliness of Isabella's concept of commensurability is central to Christianity, a religion founded on the spectacularly lopsided substitution of the blameless Christ for sinful humanity in the system of God's justice. But since such religious convictions are not subject to the verification of the senses, they are open to challenge by those more firmly attached to the things of this world. For Claudio, any fate seems better than death. His hierarchy of priorities is different from Isabella's, and so, therefore, are his conceptions of commensurability.

How are such drastic discrepancies between the various characters' moral and social outlooks to be reconciled? The agent for bringing order and justice is Duke Vincentio, a concealed authority who learns everybody's secrets in the course of the play. Far from providing an authoritative solution to the play's ethical impasse, however, the Duke has elicited almost as much controversy as Isabella. Some critics see him as a version of God, "like power divine," as Angelo declares in the final scene. Some have suggested that the Duke was meant to compliment the diffident King James I, who at the time of the play's first performance had just ascended the English throne, after the death of his extroverted predecessor, Elizabeth I. More skeptical critics see the Duke as a schemer who foists his dirty work onto political subordinates and meddles impudently, even sacrilegiously, with the lives of his subjects.

The Duke's function as clergyman reflects the fact that the problems of *Measure for Measure* can only be solved by someone who can obtain access to the concealed realm of motives and intentions, a privilege usually reserved for a confessor. But merely knowing such information will not bring practical redress of injustice. So at the same time, unlike a clergyman, he must retain the secular ruler's ability to mandate changes in the world in order to bring matters to a satisfactory conclusion. A prince disguised as a friar, the Duke bridges, however unsteadily, the gap between knowledge and power. An actual sovereign with such prerogatives would approach tyranny—for that reason, the functions of priest and lay magistrate were ordinarily separated even in Shakespeare's time, when church and state were far more closely allied than they are today. In the play's fictional Vienna, however, the Duke's sweeping authority conveniently allows him to impose a resolution.

There are limits to Vincentio's power. Not even a Duke can sequester erotic fervor from the cruelty and disorder with which it has proven to be so intimately and insidiously allied. Not even a Duke can make passion tractable. The best he can manage is to introduce his subjects to some socially sanctioned medium between celibacy and abandon. Marriage in *Measure for Measure* is thus patently not a happy aspiration but a stopgap measure imposed on reluctant or noncommittal individuals, for whom the alternative in several cases is death. Indeed, Lucio, forthright as usual, complains that marriage is a worse fate than hanging; the others are distinctly muted in their response to the Duke's nuptial stratagems. Claudio and Juliet are given no lines in which to celebrate their reunion; nor do we hear that Angelo, who claims to "crave death more willingly than mercy" (5.1.470), is grateful to be preserved as Mariana's husband. Isabella remains silent in the face of the Duke's unexpected proposal of marriage, leaving it an open question whether she is overwhelmed with joy or gripped with horror, whether the Duke provides her with a socially and personally satisfying alternative to the cloister or merely recapitulates Angelo's harassment.

The pro forma quality of the coupling with which *Measure for Measure* concludes suggests that marital union is not, finally, the resolution toward which the play most convincingly moves. Most of the last scene is devoted to finding a way out of the difficulties posed by the radical moral incommensurabilities described above. In quick succession, the Duke's trial rehearses the normal outcome of Isabella's complaint—her condemnation and Angelo's exoneration—and then demonstrates that in this instance, almost miraculously, Angelo's secret vice will be made manifest after all. But this disclosure does not end the play, for the Duke's plan demands that Isabella plead for Angelo's life "against all sense," as the Sermon on the Mount commands her to do. The simple asceticism of the flesh with which *Measure for Measure* begins is displaced at last by a more subtle and exacting asceticism of the spirit, as Isabella renounces the hunger for vengeance in favor of a forgiveness that goes very much against the grain. Only this principled willingness to overlook injury and tolerate difference, the play seems to imply, can still the jostling among heterogeneous moral perspectives that endlessly complicate life in Vienna.

KATHARINE EISAMAN MAUS

TEXTUAL NOTE

The First Folio (1623, F) is the only authoritative text for most of *Measure for Measure,* and the *Norton Shakespeare* in general follows F closely. This text has some puzzling features. In F's 1.2, Claudio's imprisonment is first announced by Mistress Overdone, then shortly thereafter described by Pompey to Mistress Overdone, who seems unaware of the situation she has just related. The Oxford editors believe that *Measure for Measure* was adapted by Thomas Middleton for a performance after Shakespeare's death. In this scene, they argue, F reproduces in succession both the adapted text and the passage it was designed to replace. The same theory would explain some curious features of the action at the end of Act 3 and the beginning of Act 4: Mariana's song seems to have been taken from *The Bloody Brother,* a play first performed around 1617, and the Duke's soliloquy during the absence of Mariana and Isabella is irrelevant to its context. The adapter, in the course of rewriting the beginning of Act 4, probably switched this soliloquy with the one at the end of Act 3.

Because the line between adapted and original material is impossible to recover with any certainty, this edition does not attempt to restore a supposedly "Shakespearean" version of the play, but instead reconstructs the version presumably performed by the King's Men a few years before the printing of the Folio. This reconstruction departs from F only in omitting the short, redundant Shakespearean passage. The omitted passage is reproduced as an appendix, as is the soliloquy at the end of Act 3 as the Oxford editors believe Shakespeare originally wrote it (see Additional Passages). Mariana's song at the beginning of Act 4 has been collated with the authoritative manuscript originally belonging to John Wilson, the composer who set the lyric to music; as a result, F's "but" in line 6 has been emended to "though."

SELECTED BIBLIOGRAPHY

Adelman, Janet. "Bed Tricks: On Marriage as the End of Comedy in *All's Well That Ends Well* and *Measure for Measure.*" *Shakespeare's Personality.* Ed. Norman H. Holland, Sidney Homan, and Bernard J. Paris. Berkeley: University of California Press, 1989. 151–74. Sexuality as defilement and marriage as punishment in *Measure for Measure.*

Baines, Barbara. "Assaying the Power of Chastity in *Measure for Measure.*" *Studies in English Literature* 30 (1990): 248–98. Isabella's chastity as an active virtue in the Vienna of *Measure for Measure.*

Bennett, Josephine Waters. *"Measure for Measure" as Royal Entertainment.* New York: Columbia University Press, 1966. The play as it reflects James I's court, political philosophy, and royal persona.

Bloom, Harold, ed. *William Shakespeare's "Measure for Measure."* New York: Chelsea House, 1987. Anthology of critical essays.

Dollimore, Jonathan. "Transgression and Surveillance in *Measure for Measure.*" *Political Shakespeare: New Essays in Cultural Materialism.* Ed. Jonathan Dollimore and Alan Sinfield. Ithaca, N.Y.: Cornell University Press, 1985. 72–87.

Engle, Lars. "*Measure for Measure* and Modernity: The Problem of the Skeptic's Authority." *Shakespeare and Modernity: Early Modern to Millennium.* Ed. Hugh Grady. New York: Routledge, 2000. 85–104. Ethical relativism and difficulties of judgment.

Hawkins, Harriett. *Measure for Measure*. Boston: Twayne, 1987. Chapters on stage history, critical reception, and the play's major interpretive cruxes.

Knight, G. Wilson. "*Measure for Measure* and the Gospels." *The Wheel of Fire: Essays in Interpretation of Shakespeare's Sombre Tragedies*. London: Oxford University Press, 1930. 80–106. Duke Vincentio as godlike: *Measure for Measure* as a Christian play.

Maus, Katharine Eisaman. "Sexual Secrecy in *Measure for Measure*." *Inwardness and Theater in the English Renaissance*. Chicago: University of Chicago Press, 1995. 157–81. Sexual privacy as a challenge for legal supervision and as the grounds for character in *Measure for Measure*.

Shell, Marc. *The End of Kinship: "Measure for Measure," Incest, and the Ideal of Universal Siblinghood*. Stanford: Stanford University Press, 1988. Proper and improper exchanges in the Christian world of *Measure for Measure*, in which everyone is a brother or sister to everyone else.

Shuger, Debora Kuller. *Political Theologies in Shakespeare's England: The Sacred and the State in "Measure for Measure."* New York: Palgrave, 2001. *Measure for Measure* shows the intimate connection between problems of governance and religion in early modern Europe.

Wheeler, Richard P. *Shakespeare's Development* and the *Problem Comedies: Turn and Counter-Turn*. Berkeley: University of California Press, 1981. 1–33, 92–153. Detailed psychoanalytic interpretation.

FILM

Measure for Measure. 1979. Dir. Desmond Davis. UK. BBC-TV production. Nuanced performances from the entire ensemble, particularly Tim Pigott-Smith (Angelo), Kenneth Colley (Duke), Kate Nelligan (Isabella), and Frank Middlemass (Pompey).

Measure for Measure

The Persons of the Play

VINCENTIO, the DUKE of Vienna
ANGELO, appointed his deputy
ESCALUS, an old lord, appointed Angelo's secondary
CLAUDIO, a young gentleman
JULIET, betrothed to Claudio
ISABELLA, Claudio's sister, novice to a sisterhood of nuns
LUCIO, a 'fantastic'
Two other such GENTLEMEN
FROTH, a foolish gentleman
MISTRESS OVERDONE, a bawd
POMPEY, her clownish servant
A PROVOST
ELBOW, a simple constable
A JUSTICE
ABHORSON, an executioner
BARNARDINE, a dissolute condemned prisoner
MARIANA, betrothed to Angelo
A BOY, attendant on Mariana
FRIAR PETER
FRANCESCA, a nun
VARRIUS, a lord, friend to the Duke
Lords, officers, citizens, servants

1.1

Enter DUKE, ESCALUS, [*and other*] lords

DUKE   Escalus.

ESCALUS   My lord.

DUKE   Of government the properties to unfold°   *explain*
    Would seem in me t'affect° speech and discourse,   *love; show off*
5   Since I am put° to know that your own science°   *obliged / knowledge*
    Exceeds in that the lists° of all advice   *limits*
    My strength can give you. Then no more remains
    But this: to° your sufficiency,° as your worth is able,   *rely on / ability*
    And let them[1] work. The nature of our people,
10   Our city's institutions and the terms°   *procedures*
    For common justice, you're as pregnant° in   *expert*
    As art° and practice hath enrichèd any   *learning*
    That we remember.
           [*He gives* ESCALUS *papers*]
                There is our commission,
    From which we would not have you warp.°   *deviate*
    [*To a lord*]   Call hither,
15   I say bid come before us, Angelo.   [*Exit lord*]

1.1 Location: The play takes place in Vienna. Some scene locations can merely be inferred. This scene may be set in the Duke's palace.

1. The referent of "them" is unclear. Perhaps a line is missing.

[*To* ESCALUS] What figure of us think you he will bear?[2]
For you must know we have with special soul°   *deliberation*
Elected° him our absence to supply,°   *Chosen / make up for*
Lent him our terror, dressed him with our love,
20   And given his deputation° all the organs°   *deputyship / instruments*
Of our own power. What think you of it?

ESCALUS   If any in Vienna be of worth
To undergo° such ample grace° and honour,   *sustain / favor*
It is Lord Angelo.

Enter ANGELO

DUKE   Look where he comes.
25   ANGELO   Always obedient to your grace's will,
I come to know your pleasure.

DUKE   Angelo,
There is a kind of character[3] in thy life
That to th'observer doth thy history°   *life story*
Fully unfold. Thyself and thy belongings°   *endowments*
30   Are not thine own so proper° as to waste   *exclusively*
Thyself upon thy virtues, they on thee.
Heaven doth with us as we with torches do,
Not light them for themselves; for if our virtues
Did not go forth of° us, 'twere all alike   *from*
35   As if we had them not.[4] Spirits are not finely touched
But to fine issues;[5] nor nature never lends
The smallest scruple° of her excellence   *bit*
But, like a thrifty goddess, she determines°   *ordains*
Herself the glory of a creditor,
40   Both thanks and use.° But I do bend° my speech   *interest / direct*
To one that can my part in him advertise.°   *make known*
Hold[6] therefore, Angelo.
In our remove be thou at full ourself.
Mortality° and mercy in Vienna   *Power to kill*
45   Live in thy tongue and heart. Old Escalus,
Though first in question, is thy secondary.[7]
Take thy commission.

ANGELO   Now good my lord,
Let there be some more test made of my metal°   *(variant of "mettle")*
Before so noble and so great a figure
Be stamped upon it.

50   DUKE   No more evasion.
We have with leavened° and preparèd choice   *fermented (mature)*
Proceeded to you; therefore take your honours.

[ANGELO *takes his commission*]

Our haste from hence is of so quick condition
That it prefers itself, and leaves unquestioned[8]
55   Matters of needful value. We shall write to you
As time and our concernings° shall importune,°   *affairs / demand*
How it goes with us; and do look° to know   *expect*
What doth befall you here. So fare you well.

---

2. How do you think he will represent me (with the royal plural)? Angelo is imagined bearing his ruler's image like a coin; compare "metal" in line 48.
3. Handwriting; engraved pattern.
4. *Heaven . . . not*: similarly, Jesus, in Matthew 5:14–16, tells his followers not to hide their light under a bushel.

5. *Spirits . . . issues*: Spirits are not made fine except to do fine deeds.
6. Silence; take (this commission).
7. Though first to be addressed, is your subordinate.
8. That it takes precedence, and leaves unconsidered.

To th' hopeful execution do I leave you
Of your commissions.

60 ANGELO   Yet give leave, my lord,
That we may bring you something° on the way.   *some distance*
DUKE   My haste may not admit° it;   *permit*
Nor need you, on mine honour, have to do
With⁹ any scruple. Your scope is as mine own,
65 So to enforce or qualify° the laws   *mitigate*
As to your soul seems good. Give me your hand.
I'll privily away. I love the people,
But do not like to stage me° to their eyes.   *display myself*
Though it do well,° I do not relish well   *is politically useful*
70 Their loud applause and *aves*° vehement;   *salutations*
Nor do I think the man of safe discretion°   *sound judgment*
That does affect° it. Once more, fare you well.   *desire*
ANGELO   The heavens give safety to your purposes!
ESCALUS   Lead forth and bring you back in happiness!
75 DUKE   I thank you. Fare you well.   *Exit*
ESCALUS   I shall desire you, sir, to give me leave
To have free° speech with you; and it concerns me   *frank*
To look into the bottom of my place.¹
A power I have, but of what strength and nature
80 I am not yet instructed.°   *informed*
ANGELO   'Tis so with me. Let us withdraw together,
And we may soon our satisfaction have
Touching that point.
ESCALUS   I'll wait upon° your honour.   *Exeunt*   *accompany*

<h2 style="text-align:center">1.2</h2>

Enter LUCIO, *and two other* GENTLEMEN

LUCIO   If the Duke with the other dukes come not to composi-
tion° with the King of Hungary, why then, all the dukes fall   *agreement*
upon° the King.   *attack*
FIRST GENTLEMAN   Heaven grant us its peace, but not the King
5   of Hungary's!
SECOND GENTLEMAN   Amen.
LUCIO   Thou concludest like the sanctimonious pirate, that went
to sea with the Ten Commandments, but scraped° one out of   *erased*
the table.°   *tablet*
10 SECOND GENTLEMAN   'Thou shalt not steal'?
LUCIO   Ay, that he razed.
FIRST GENTLEMAN   Why, 'twas a commandment to command
the captain and all the rest from their functions: they put forth
to steal. There's not a soldier of us all that in the thanksgiving
15   before meat° do relish the petition well that prays for peace.   *food*
SECOND GENTLEMAN   I never heard any soldier dislike° it.   *express aversion to*
LUCIO   I believe thee, for I think thou never wast where grace
was said.
SECOND GENTLEMAN   No? A dozen times at least.
20 FIRST GENTLEMAN   What, in metre?
LUCIO   In any proportion,° or in any language.   *meter*

---

9. *have to do / With*: worry about.
1. To examine my duties thoroughly.
1.2. Location: A street or public place. In F, as here, the
scene begins with what is evidently an interpolation

introduced after Shakespeare's death. A reconstruction
of the original opening appears at the end of the play as
Additional Passage A.

FIRST GENTLEMAN I think, or in any religion.

LUCIO Ay, why not? Grace is grace despite of all controversy;[1] as
for example, thou thyself art a wicked villain despite of all
25 grace.

FIRST GENTLEMAN Well, there went but a pair of shears between us.[2]

LUCIO I grant—as there may between the lists° and the velvet.   *selvages*
Thou art the list.

FIRST GENTLEMAN And thou the velvet. Thou art good velvet,
30 thou'rt a three-piled[3] piece, I warrant thee. I had as lief° be a   *had rather*
list of an English kersey° as be piled as thou art pilled,[4] for a   *wool cloth*
French velvet. Do I speak feelingly° now?   *to the point; painfully*

LUCIO I think thou dost, and indeed with most painful feeling°   *conviction*
of thy speech. I will out of thine own confession learn to begin°   *drink to*
35 thy health, but whilst I live forget to drink after thee.°   *(to avoid infection)*

FIRST GENTLEMAN I think I have done myself wrong,° have I   *laid myself open to that*
not?

SECOND GENTLEMAN Yes, that thou hast, whether thou art
tainted or free.°   *sick or well*

Enter [MISTRESS OVERDONE]

40 LUCIO Behold, behold, where Madam Mitigation° comes! I   *(of sexual desire)*
have purchased as many diseases under her roof as come to—

SECOND GENTLEMAN To what, I pray?

LUCIO Judge.°   *Guess*

SECOND GENTLEMAN To three thousand dolours° a year?   *pains; dollars*

45 FIRST GENTLEMAN Ay, and more.

LUCIO A French crown° more.   *coin; syphilitic sore*

FIRST GENTLEMAN Thou art always figuring° diseases in me, but   *imagining*
thou art full of error—I am sound.°   *healthy*

LUCIO Nay not, as one would say, healthy, but so sound° as   *resounding*
50 things that are hollow—thy bones are hollow,[5] impiety° has   *wickedness*
made a feast of thee.

FIRST GENTLEMAN [*to* MISTRESS OVERDONE] How now, which of
your hips has the most profound sciatica?[6]

MISTRESS OVERDONE Well, well! There's one yonder arrested
55 and carried to prison was worth five thousand of you all.

SECOND GENTLEMAN Who's that, I pray thee?

MISTRESS OVERDONE Marry° sir, that's Claudio, Signor Claudio.   *By the Virgin Mary*

FIRST GENTLEMAN Claudio to prison? 'Tis not so.

MISTRESS OVERDONE Nay, but I know 'tis so. I saw him arrested,
60 saw him carried away; and, which is more, within these three
days his head to be chopped off.

LUCIO But after° all this fooling, I would not have it so. Art thou   *despite*
sure of this?

MISTRESS OVERDONE I am too sure of it, and it is for getting
65 Madame Julietta with child.

LUCIO Believe me, this may be. He promised to meet me two
hours since and he was ever precise in promise-keeping.

---

1. Referring to the religious controversy over whether
human beings are saved by divine grace or by good works.
grace: divine favor; prayer before a meal.
2. We are cut from the same cloth.
3. Very plush; full of rectal sores (a symptom of syphilis).
Lucio accuses the First Gentleman of being a "list," a
selvage or edging of inferior cloth; the Gentleman retorts
that he'd rather be a plain selvage than an expensively

"piled" velvet like Lucio. Lucio then uses the Gentleman's knowledge of "piles" to score a point against him.
4. Ruined; made bald (a sign of syphilis, the "French
pox"). Syphilitic sores were covered with velvet patches.
5. Syphilis causes bones to become brittle.
6. Ache in the sciatic vein of the hip, associated with
venereal disease.

SECOND GENTLEMAN Besides, you know, it draws° something   *approaches*
near to the speech we had to such a purpose.

70 FIRST GENTLEMAN But most of all agreeing with the proclamation.

LUCIO Away; let's go learn the truth of it.

    Exeunt [LUCIO *and* GENTLEMEN]

MISTRESS OVERDONE Thus, what with the war, what with the
sweat,° what with the gallows, and what with poverty, I am cus-   *plague*
tom-shrunk.°   *short on customers*

    Enter [POMPEY *the*] *Clown*

75 How now, what's the news with you?

POMPEY You have not heard of the proclamation, have you?

MISTRESS OVERDONE What proclamation, man?

POMPEY All houses in the suburbs[7] of Vienna must be plucked° down.   *torn*

MISTRESS OVERDONE And what shall become of those in the city?

80 POMPEY They shall stand for seed.[8] They had gone down too,
but that a wise burgher put in° for them.   *citizen interceded*

MISTRESS OVERDONE But shall all our houses of resort in the
suburbs be pulled down?

POMPEY To the ground, mistress.

85 MISTRESS OVERDONE Why, here's a change indeed in the commonwealth. What shall become of me?

POMPEY Come, fear not you. Good counsellors° lack no clients.   *attorneys*
Though you change your place, you need not change your
trade. I'll be your tapster still. Courage, there will be pity taken

90 on you. You that have worn your eyes almost out in the service,[9] you will be considered.°   *recompensed*

    [*A noise within*]

MISTRESS OVERDONE What's to do° here, Thomas Tapster?[1]   *the matter*
Let's withdraw!

    Enter PROVOST,° CLAUDIO, JULIET,[2] [*and*] *officers;* LUCIO   *jailer*
    and [*the*] *two* GENTLEMEN

POMPEY Here comes Signor Claudio, led by the Provost to
95 prison; and there's Madame Juliet.

    Exeunt [MISTRESS OVERDONE *and* POMPEY]

CLAUDIO [*to the* PROVOST] Fellow, why dost thou show me thus
to th' world?
Bear me to prison, where I am committed.

PROVOST I do it not in evil disposition,
But from Lord Angelo by special charge.

100 CLAUDIO Thus can the demigod Authority
Make us pay down for our offence, by weight,°   *fully*
The bonds of ° heaven. On whom it will, it will;[3]   *obligations to*
On whom it will not, so; yet still 'tis just.

LUCIO Why, how now, Claudio? Whence comes this restraint?

105 CLAUDIO From too much liberty,° my Lucio, liberty.   *looseness*
As surfeit is the father of much fast,°   *gluttony precedes fasting*
So every scope,° by the immoderate use,   *freedom*
Turns to restraint. Our natures do pursue,

---

7. London brothels ("houses") were located outside the
city walls, where civic authorities had difficulty controlling them.
8. Grain for the next crop; semen.
9. "Eye" was slang for "female genital"; blindness is
another symptom of syphilis.
1. Stock name for a tapster (bartender).

2. Claudio and Juliet are perhaps wearing white sheets of
penance; such public humiliations were common punishments for sexual transgressions.
3. Paul has God say in Romans 9:15: "I will have mercy
on him, to whom I will show mercy: and I will have compassion on him, on whom I will have compassion."

Like rats that raven° down their proper bane,°   *devour / poison*
110 A thirsty evil; and when we drink, we die.

LUCIO If I could speak so wisely under an arrest, I would send
for certain of my creditors.[4] And yet, to say the truth, I had as
lief have the foppery° of freedom as the morality of imprison-   *folly*
ment. What's thy offence, Claudio?

115 CLAUDIO What but to speak of would offend again.

LUCIO What, is't murder?

CLAUDIO   No.

LUCIO   Lechery?

CLAUDIO   Call it so.

PROVOST Away, sir; you must go.

CLAUDIO One word, good friend.

[*The* PROVOST *shows assent*]
Lucio, a word with you.

120 LUCIO A hundred, if they'll do you any good.

[CLAUDIO *and* LUCIO *speak apart*]
Is lechery so looked after?

CLAUDIO Thus stands it with me. Upon a true contract,[5]
I got possession of Julietta's bed.
You know the lady; she is fast° my wife,   *nearly; entirely*
125 Save that we do the denunciation° lack   *declaration*
Of outward order.° This we came not to   *public ceremony*
Only for propagation° of a dower   *enlargement*
Remaining in the coffer of her friends,°   *relatives*
From whom we thought it meet° to hide our love   *appropriate*
130 Till time had made them for° us. But it chances   *favorably disposed to*
The stealth of our most mutual° entertainment   *reciprocal; intimate*
With character too gross° is writ on Juliet.   *writing too large*

LUCIO With child, perhaps?

CLAUDIO   Unhapp'ly even so.
And the new deputy now for the Duke—
135 Whether it be the fault and glimpse° of newness,   *glitter*
Or whether that the body public be
A horse whereon the governor doth ride,
Who, newly in the seat, that it may know
He can command, lets it straight° feel the spur—   *immediately*
140 Whether the tyranny be in his place,°   *office*
Or in his eminence that fills it up—
I stagger in.° But this new governor   *hesitate to say*
Awakes me all the enrollèd° penalties   *recorded*
Which have, like unscoured armour, hung by th' wall
145 So long that fourteen zodiacs° have gone round,   *years*
And none of them been worn; and, for a name,°   *reputation*
Now puts the drowsy and neglected act
Freshly on me. 'Tis surely for a name.

LUCIO I warrant° it is; and thy head stands so tickle° on thy   *I'm sure / insecurely*
150 shoulders that a milkmaid, if she be in love, may sigh it off.[6]
Send after the Duke, and appeal to him.

---

4. Who, Lucio implies, would have him arrested for nonpayment of debts.
5. A secret plighting of troth, as opposed to public nuptials; in seventeenth-century England, such a contract could constitute legal marriage if made in the present tense ("I marry you" rather than "I will marry you") and followed by sexual consummation. The nature of the contract between Claudio and Juliet is unclear.
6. That a milkmaid's lovesick sigh may blow it off (with wordplay on "maidenhead").

CLAUDIO   I have done so, but he's not to be found.
 I prithee, Lucio, do me this kind service.
 This day my sister should the cloister enter,
155 And there receive her approbation.°   *become a novice*
 Acquaint her with the danger of my state.
 Implore her in my voice that she make friends
 To the strict deputy. Bid herself assay° him.   *try*
 I have great hope in that, for in her youth
160 There is a prone° and speechless dialect   *eager; submissive*
 Such as move men; beside, she hath prosperous art° *skill*
 When she will play with reason and discourse,
 And well she can persuade.
LUCIO   I pray she may—as well for the encouragement of thy
165 like,° which else would stand under grievous imposition,° as for *those like you / burden*
 the enjoying of thy life, who I would be sorry should be thus
 foolishly lost at a game of tick-tack.[7] I'll to her.
CLAUDIO   I thank you, good friend Lucio.
LUCIO   Within two hours.
170   CLAUDIO   Come, officer; away.

    Exeunt [LUCIO *and* GENTLEMEN *at one door;*
    CLAUDIO, JULIET, PROVOST, *and officers at another*]

1.3

Enter DUKE *and* [a] FRIAR

DUKE   No, holy father, throw away that thought.
 Believe not that the dribbling[1] dart of love
 Can pierce a complete° bosom. Why I desire thee *an invulnerable*
 To give me secret harbour hath a purpose
5 More grave and wrinkled° than the aims and ends *(suggesting aged wisdom)*
 Of burning youth.
FRIAR   May your grace speak of it?
DUKE   My holy sir, none better knows than you
 How I have ever loved the life removed,°   *retired*
 And held in idle price° to haunt assemblies *thought it frivolous*
10 Where youth and cost a witless bravery° keeps. *pointless ostentation*
 I have delivered to Lord Angelo—
 A man of stricture° and firm abstinence— *self-restraint*
 My absolute power and place here in Vienna;
 And he supposes me travelled to Poland—
15 For so I have strewed it in the common ear,° *ears of common people*
 And so it is received.° Now, pious sir,   *believed*
 You will demand of me why I do this.
FRIAR   Gladly, my lord.
DUKE   We have strict statutes and most biting laws,
20 The needful bits and curbs to headstrong weeds,[2]
 Which for this fourteen years we have let slip;° *slide*
 Even like an o'ergrown lion in a cave
 That goes not out to prey. Now, as fond° fathers, *doting*
 Having bound up the threat'ning twigs of birch
25 Only to stick it in their children's sight
 For terror, not to use, in time the rod

---

7. A kind of backgammon scored by placing pegs into holes; with sexual innuendo.
1.3 Location: A Friar's cell.
1. Inadequate, like an arrow shot without sufficient force.

2. Since "bits and curbs" are parts of bridles, many editors emend "weeds" to "jades" or "steeds," but the Oxford English Dictionary records several instances of "weed" as a slang term for a worthless horse.

More mocked becomes than feared: so our decrees,
Dead to infliction,° to themselves are dead;   *Never inflicted*
And Liberty plucks Justice by the nose,[3]
30   The baby beats the nurse, and quite athwart
Goes all decorum.

FRIAR   It rested in° your grace   *remained possible for*
To unloose this tied-up Justice when you pleased,
And it in you more dreadful would have seemed
Than in Lord Angelo.

DUKE   I do fear, too dreadful.
35   Sith° 'twas my fault to give the people scope,   *Since*
'Twould be my tyranny to strike and gall° them   *chafe*
For what I bid them do—for we bid this be done
When evil deeds have their permissive pass,°   *unhindered passage*
And not the punishment. Therefore indeed, my father,
40   I have on Angelo imposed the office,
Who may in th'ambush° of my name strike home,   *under cover*
And yet my nature never in the fight
T'allow in slander.° And to behold his sway,°   *To permit slander / rule*
I will as 'twere a brother of your order
45   Visit both prince° and people. Therefore, I prithee,   *ruler*
Supply me with the habit, and instruct me
How I may formally in person bear°   *behave in character*
Like a true friar. More reasons for this action
At our more leisure shall I render you.
50   Only this one: Lord Angelo is precise,°   *puritanical*
Stands at a guard with envy,° scarce confesses   *on guard against desire*
That his blood flows, or that his appetite
Is more to bread than stone. Hence shall we see
If power change purpose, what our seemers be.   *Exeunt*

1.4

Enter ISABELLA, *and* FRANCESCA, *a nun*

ISABELLA   And have you nuns no farther privileges?
FRANCESCA   Are not these large° enough?   *generous*
ISABELLA   Yes, truly. I speak not as desiring more,
But rather wishing a more strict restraint
5   Upon the sisterhood, the votarists of Saint Clare.
LUCIO (*within*)   Ho, peace be in this place!
ISABELLA [*to* FRANCESCA]   Who's that which calls?
FRANCESCA   It is a man's voice. Gentle Isabella.
Turn you the key, and know° his business of° him.   *find out / from*
You may, I may not; you are yet unsworn.
10   When you have vowed, you must not speak with men
But in the presence of the prioress.
Then if you speak, you must not show your face;
Or if you show your face, you must not speak.
[LUCIO *calls within*]
He calls again. I pray you answer him.
[*She stands aside*][1]
15   ISABELLA   Peace and prosperity! Who is't that calls?
[*She opens the door*]

3. Licentiousness insults the administration of law.   austere discipline.
1.4 Location: A convent of St. Clare, an order known for   1. Or Francesca may exit here.

[*Enter* LUCIO] ~ Cludio fried

LUCIO   Hail, virgin, if you be—as those cheek-roses°   *glowing cheeks*
    Proclaim you are no less. Can you so stead° me   *help*
    As bring me to the sight of Isabella,
    A novice of this place, and the fair sister
20   To her unhappy° brother Claudio?   *unfortunate*
ISABELLA   Why her unhappy brother? Let me ask,
    The rather for I now must make you know
    I am that Isabella, and his sister.
LUCIO   Gentle and fair, your brother kindly greets you.
25   Not to be weary° with you, he's in prison.   *tedious*
ISABELLA   Woe me! For what?
LUCIO   For that which, if myself might be his judge,
    He should receive his punishment in thanks.
    He hath got his friend° with child.   *lover*
ISABELLA   Sir, make me not your story.°   *don't tell me tales*
30 LUCIO   'Tis true. I would not—though 'tis my familiar° sin   *habitual*
    With maids to seem the lapwing,[2] and to jest
    Tongue far from heart—play with all virgins so.
    I hold you as a thing enskied° and sainted   *placed in heaven*
    By your renouncement, an immortal spirit,
35   And to be talked with in sincerity
    As with a saint.
ISABELLA   You do blaspheme the good in mocking me.
LUCIO   Do not believe it. Fewness° and truth, 'tis thus: *In few words*
    Your brother and his lover have embraced.
40   As those that feed grow full, as blossoming time
    That from the seedness° the bare fallow° brings   *sowing / plowland*
    To teeming foison,° even so her plenteous womb   *abundance*
    Expresseth his full tilth° and husbandry.[3]   *tillage*
ISABELLA   Someone with child by him? My cousin Juliet?
45 LUCIO   Is she your cousin?
ISABELLA   Adoptedly,° as schoolmaids change° their names   *By choice / exchange*
    By vain° though apt affection.   *foolish*
LUCIO   She it is.
ISABELLA   O, let him marry her!
LUCIO   This is the point.
    The Duke is very strangely gone from hence;
50   Bore many gentlemen—myself being one—
    In hand and hope of action;[4] but we do learn,
    By those that know the very nerves° of state,   *sinews (inward secrets)*
    His giving out° were of an infinite distance   *What he proclaimed*
    From his true-meant design. Upon° his place,   *In*
55   And with full line° of his authority,   *extent*
    Governs Lord Angelo—a man whose blood
    Is very snow-broth;° one who never feels   *melted snow*
    The wanton stings and motions° of the sense,   *stimulants and impulses*
    But doth rebate° and blunt his natural edge   *dull*
60   With profits of the mind, study, and fast.
    He, to give fear to use° and liberty,   *custom*
    Which have for long run by the hideous law

2. Bird that cries alarm when far from its nest, a common figure for deception.
3. Cultivation (punning on "husband").
4. *Bore . . . action:* Deceived us into hoping for some military action.

	As mice by lions, hath picked out an act°	*a statute*
	Under whose heavy° sense your brother's life	*oppressive*
65	Falls into forfeit. He arrests him on it,	
	And follows close the rigour of the statute	
	To make him an example. All hope is gone,	
	Unless you have the grace by your fair prayer	
	To soften Angelo. And that's my pith°	*essence*
70	Of business 'twixt you and your poor brother.	

ISABELLA   Doth he so seek his life?

LUCIO   Has censured° him already,   *sentenced*
And, as I hear, the Provost hath a warrant
For's execution.

ISABELLA   Alas, what poor
Ability's in me to do him good?

75 LUCIO   Assay the power you have.

ISABELLA   My power? Alas, I doubt.

LUCIO   Our doubts are traitors,
And makes us lose the good we oft might win,
By fearing to attempt. Go to Lord Angelo;
80 And let him learn to know, when maidens sue,
Men give like gods, but when they weep and kneel,
All their petitions are as freely theirs
As° they themselves would owe° them.   *As if / were to own*

ISABELLA   I'll see what I can do.

LUCIO   But speedily.

ISABELLA   I will about it straight,°   *immediately*
85 No longer staying but to give the Mother°   *Mother Superior*
Notice of my affair.° I humbly thank you.   *business*
Commend me to my brother. Soon at night
I'll send him certain word of my success.°   *fortune (good or bad)*

LUCIO   I take my leave of you.

ISABELLA   Good sir, adieu.

Exeunt [ISABELLA *and* FRANCESCA *at one door,*
LUCIO *at another door*]

2.1

Enter ANGELO, ESCALUS, *and servants;* [*a*] JUSTICE

ANGELO   We must not make a scarecrow of the law,
Setting it up to fear° the birds of prey,   *frighten*
And let it keep one shape till custom make it
Their perch, and not their terror.

ESCALUS   Ay, but yet
5 Let us be keen, and rather cut a little
Than fall and bruise to death. Alas, this gentleman
Whom I would save had a most noble father.
Let but your honour know—
Whom I believe to be most strait° in virtue—   *rigorous*
10 That in the working of your own affections,°   *passions*
Had time cohered with place, or place with wishing,
Or that the resolute acting of your blood°   *desire*
Could have attained th'effect° of your own purpose—   *fulfillment*
Whether you had not sometime in your life

2.1 Location: The court of justice.

15   Erred in this point which now you censure° him,   condemn in
        And pulled the law upon you.
ANGELO   'Tis one thing to be tempted, Escalus,
        Another thing to fall. I not° deny   do not
        The jury passing on the prisoner's life
20   May in the sworn twelve have a thief or two
        Guiltier than him they try. What knows the law[1]
        That thieves do pass on thieves? What's open° made to justice,   evident
        That justice seizes. 'Tis very pregnant:°   clear
        The jewel that we find, we stoop and take't
25   Because we see it, but what we do not see
        We tread upon and never think of it.
        You may not so extenuate his offence
        For° I have had such faults; but rather tell me,   Because
        When I that censure him do so offend,
30   Let mine own judgement pattern out° my death,   give precedent for
        And nothing come in partial.° Sir, he must die.   no allowances be made
ESCALUS   Be it as your wisdom will.
ANGELO   Where is the Provost?
                Enter PROVOST
PROVOST   Here, if it like your honour.
ANGELO   See that Claudio
        Be execute by nine tomorrow morning.
35   Bring him his confessor, let him be prepared,
        For that's the utmost of his pilgrimage.°   [Exit PROVOST]   life's journey
ESCALUS   Well, heaven forgive him, and forgive us all!
        Some rise by sin, and some by virtue fall.
        Some run from brakes of vice,[2] and answer none;°   not at all
40   And some condemnèd for a fault alone.°   single imperfection
                Enter ELBOW, FROTH, POMPEY, and officers
ELBOW   Come, bring them away. If these be good people in a
        commonweal, that do nothing but use their abuses° in com-   do their bad deeds
        mon houses,° I know no law. Bring them away.   brothels
ANGELO   How now, sir? What's your name? And what's the matter?
45 ELBOW   If it please your honour, I am the poor Duke's constable,
        and my name is Elbow. I do lean° upon justice, sir; and do   depend
        bring in here before your good honour two notorious benefactors.[3]
ANGELO   Benefactors? Well! What benefactors are they?
        Are they not malefactors?
50 ELBOW   If it please your honour, I know not well what they are;
        but precise[4] villains they are, that I am sure of, and void of all
        profanation° in the world that good Christians ought to have.   (for "reverence")
ESCALUS [to ANGELO]   This comes off° well; here's a wise officer!   turns out
ANGELO   Go to, what quality° are they of ? Elbow is your name?   rank
55   Why dost thou not speak, Elbow?
POMPEY   He cannot, sir; he's out at elbow.[5]
ANGELO   What are you, sir?
ELBOW   He, sir? A tapster, sir, parcel bawd;° one that serves a bad   part-time pimp

---

1. What does the law know; who knows what law.
2. F has "brakes of ice," a famous crux; often amended as here. *brakes*: thickets.
3. Elbow comically misuses words; here he means "malefactors," criminals.
4. Elbow means "precious"; "precise" (morally scrupulous) is elsewhere applied to Angelo.
5. Ragged; perplexed at the sound of his name. Pompey loves to play on the double meanings of words.

woman whose house, sir, was, as they say, plucked down in the
60 suburbs; and now she professes a hot-house,° which I think is *pretends to run a sauna*
    a very ill house too.

ESCALUS How know you that?

ELBOW My wife, sir, whom I detest° before heaven and your *(for "protest")*
    honour—

65 ESCALUS How, thy wife?

ELBOW Ay, sir, whom I thank heaven is an honest woman—

ESCALUS Dost thou detest her therefor?

ELBOW I say, sir, I will detest myself also, as well as she, that this
    house, if it be not a bawd's house, it is pity of her life,° for it is *a great pity*
70 a naughty° house. *wicked*

ESCALUS How dost thou know that, constable?

ELBOW Marry, sir, by my wife, who, if she had been a woman
    cardinally° given, might have been accused in fornication, *(for "carnally")*
    adultery, and all uncleanliness there.

75 ESCALUS By the woman's means?

ELBOW Ay, sir, by Mistress Overdone's means. But as she° spit *(Elbow's wife)*
    in his° face, so she defied him. *(Pompey's)*

POMPEY [*to* ESCALUS] Sir, if it please your honour, this is not so.

ELBOW Prove it before these varlets° here, thou honourable *villains*
80 man, prove it.

ESCALUS [*to* ANGELO] Do you hear how he misplaces?° *confuses his words*

POMPEY Sir, she came in great with child, and longing—saving
    your honour's reverence°—for stewed prunes.[6] Sir, we had but *excuse the expression*
    two in the house, which at that very distant° time stood, as it *(for "instant")*
85 were, in a fruit dish[7]—a dish of some threepence; your honours
    have seen such dishes; they are not china dishes, but very good
    dishes.

ESCALUS Go to, go to, no matter for the dish, sir.

POMPEY No, indeed, sir, not of° a pin; you are therein in the *worth*
90 right. But to the point. As I say, this Mistress Elbow, being, as I
    say, with child, and being great-bellied, and longing, as I said,
    for prunes; and having but two in the dish, as I said, Master
    Froth here, this very man, having eaten the rest, as I said, and,
    as I say, paying for them very honestly; for, as you know, Master
95 Froth, I could not give you threepence again.° *in change*

FROTH No, indeed.

POMPEY Very well. You being, then, if you be remembered,
    cracking the stones of the foresaid prunes—

FROTH Ay, so I did indeed.

100 POMPEY Why, very well.—I telling you then, if you be remem-
    bered, that such a one and such a one were past cure of the
    thing you wot of,[8] unless they kept very good diet, as I told
    you—

FROTH All this is true.

105 POMPEY Why, very well then—

ESCALUS Come, you are a tedious fool. To the purpose. What
    was done to Elbow's wife that he hath cause to complain of?
    Come me° to what was done to her. *Get*

POMPEY Sir, your honour cannot come to that yet.[9]

---

6. Commonly served in brothels; also suggesting "testicles" in the series of double entendres that follows.
7. Slang term for "female genital."

8. Euphemism for syphilis. *wot:* know.
9. Taking "done" in the sexual sense, Pompey pretends
shock at Escalus's salaciousness.

110 ESCALUS No, sir, nor I mean it not.°   *I don't mean that*
    POMPEY Sir, but you shall come to it, by your honour's leave.
        And I beseech you, look into° Master Froth here, sir, a man of   *consider*
        fourscore pound a year,[1] whose father died at Hallowmas°—   *Nov. 1, All Saint's Day*
        was't not at Hallowmas, Master Froth?
115 FROTH All Hallow Eve.°   *Halloween*
    POMPEY Why, very well. I hope here be truths. He, sir, sitting,
        as I say, in a lower° chair, sir—'twas in the Bunch of Grapes,[2]   *reclining?*
        where indeed you have a delight to sit, have you not?
    FROTH I have so, because it is an open room,[3] and good for
120   winter.
    POMPEY Why, very well then. I hope here be truths.
    ANGELO This will last out a night in Russia,
        When nights are longest there. [*To* ESCALUS] I'll take my leave,
        And leave you to the hearing of the cause,°   *case*
125   Hoping you'll find good cause to whip them all.
    ESCALUS I think no less. Good morrow to your lordship.
                             Exit [ANGELO]
    Now, sir, come on, what was done to Elbow's wife, once more?
    POMPEY Once, sir? There was nothing done to her once.
    ELBOW I beseech you, sir, ask him what this man did to my wife.
130 POMPEY I beseech your honour, ask me.
    ESCALUS Well, sir, what did this gentleman to her?
    POMPEY I beseech you, sir, look in this gentleman's face. Good
        Master Froth, look upon his honour. 'Tis for a good purpose.
        Doth your honour mark° his face?   *note*
135 ESCALUS Ay, sir, very well.
    POMPEY Nay, I beseech you, mark it well.
    ESCALUS Well, I do so.
    POMPEY Doth your honour see any harm in his face?
    ESCALUS Why, no.
140 POMPEY I'll be supposed° upon a book° his face is the worst   *(for "deposed") / Bible*
        thing about him. Good, then—if his face be the worst thing
        about him, how could Master Froth do the constable's wife any
        harm? I would know that of your honour.
    ESCALUS He's in the right, constable; what say you to it?
145 ELBOW First, an it like° you, the house is a respected[4] house;   *if it please*
        next, this is a respected fellow; and his mistress is a respected
        woman.
    POMPEY [*to* ESCALUS] By this hand, sir, his wife is a more
        respected person than any of us all.
150 ELBOW Varlet, thou liest; thou liest, wicked varlet. The time is
        yet to come that she was ever respected with man, woman, or
        child.
    POMPEY Sir, she was respected with him before he married with her.
    ESCALUS Which is the wiser here, justice or iniquity? [*To*
155   ELBOW] Is this true?
    ELBOW [*to* POMPEY] O thou caitiff, O thou varlet, O thou wicked
        Hannibal![5] I respected with her before I was married to her?
        [*To* ESCALUS] If ever I was respected with her, or she with

---

1. Eighty pounds was a low income for a gentleman. The
father's recent death means that Froth has just come into
his inheritance.
2. A room in a tavern.
3. A public room (where fires were kept burning).
4. For "suspected."
5. Blunder for "cannibal"; also, both Hannibal and Pompey were famous generals of ancient times.

me, let not your worship think me the poor Duke's officer. [*To*

160 POMPEY] Prove this, thou wicked Hannibal, or I'll have mine
action of battery° on thee. *(for "slander")*

ESCALUS If he took° you a box o'th' ear you might have your   *struck*
action of slander too.

ELBOW Marry, I thank your good worship for it. What is't your

165 worship's pleasure I shall do with this wicked caitiff?°   *knave*

ESCALUS Truly, officer, because he hath some offences in him
that thou wouldst discover° if thou couldst, let him continue in   *expose*
his courses° till thou knowest what they are.   *conduct*

ELBOW Marry, I thank your worship for it.—Thou seest, thou

170 wicked varlet now, what's come upon thee. Thou art to continue now, thou varlet, thou art to continue.

ESCALUS [*to* FROTH] Where were you born, friend?

FROTH Here in Vienna, sir.

ESCALUS Are you of fourscore pounds a year?

175 FROTH Yes, an't please you, sir.

ESCALUS So. [*To* POMPEY] What trade are you of, sir?

POMPEY A tapster, a poor widow's tapster.

ESCALUS Your mistress's name?

POMPEY Mistress Overdone.

180 ESCALUS Hath she had any more than one husband?

POMPEY Nine, sir—Overdone by the last.[6]

ESCALUS Nine?—Come hither to me, Master Froth. Master
Froth, I would not have you acquainted with tapsters. They will
draw you,[7] Master Froth, and you will hang them.° Get you   *get them hanged*

185 gone, and let me hear no more of you.

FROTH I thank your worship. For mine own part, I never come
into any room in a tap-house but I am drawn in.

ESCALUS Well, no more of it, Master Froth. Farewell.

[*Exit* FROTH]

Come you hither to me, Master Tapster. What's your name,

190 Master Tapster?

POMPEY Pompey.

ESCALUS What else?

POMPEY Bum, sir.

ESCALUS Troth, and your bum is the greatest thing about you;

195 so that, in the beastliest sense, you are Pompey the Great.[8]
Pompey, you are partly a bawd, Pompey, howsoever you colour
it in being a tapster, are you not? Come, tell me true; it shall
be the better for you.

POMPEY Truly, sir, I am a poor fellow that would live.

200 ESCALUS How would you live, Pompey? By being a bawd? What
do you think of the trade, Pompey? Is it a lawful trade?

POMPEY If the law would allow it, sir.

ESCALUS But the law will not allow it, Pompey; nor it shall not°   *nor shall it*
be allowed in Vienna.

205 POMPEY Does your worship mean to geld and spay all the youth
of the city?

ESCALUS No, Pompey.

6. She takes her name from Overdone, her last husband; her last husband wore her out.
7. Get you beer; steal your substance; convey you to execution.
8. The Roman general Pompey was surnamed "the
Great."

POMPEY   Truly, sir, in my poor opinion they will to't then. If your
worship will take order° for the drabs° and the knaves, you need   *measures / whores*
210   not to fear the bawds.

ESCALUS   There is pretty orders beginning, I can tell you. It is
but heading° and hanging.   *beheading*

POMPEY   If you head and hang all that offend that way but for
ten year together, you'll be glad to give out a commission° for   *an order*
215   more heads. If this law hold° in Vienna ten year, I'll rent the   *remain*
fairest house in it after threepence a bay.⁹ If you live to see this
come to pass, say Pompey told you so.

ESCALUS   Thank you, good Pompey; and in requital of° your   *return for*
prophecy, hark you. I advise you, let me not find you before
220   me again upon any complaint whatsoever; no, not for° dwelling   *even for*
where you do. If I do, Pompey, I shall beat you to your tent,
and prove a shrewd Caesar to you;¹ in plain dealing, Pompey,
I shall have you whipped. So for this time, Pompey, fare you well.

POMPEY   I thank your worship for your good counsel; [*aside*] but
225   I shall follow it as the flesh and fortune shall better determine.
Whip me? No, no; let carman° whip his jade.°   *cart driver / horse*
The valiant heart's not whipped out of his trade.   *Exit*

ESCALUS   Come hither to me, Master Elbow; come hither, Master Constable. How long have you been in this place of con-
230   stable?

ELBOW   Seven year and a half, sir.

ESCALUS   I thought, by the readiness in the office, you had continued in it some time. You say seven years together?

ELBOW   And a half, sir.

235   ESCALUS   Alas, it hath been great pains to you. They do you
wrong to put you so oft upon't. Are there not men in your ward
sufficient° to serve it?   *fit*

ELBOW   Faith, sir, few of any wit in such matters. As they are
chosen, they are glad to choose me for them. I do it for some
240   piece of money, and go through with all.

ESCALUS   Look° you bring me in the names of some six or seven,   *See that*
the most sufficient of your parish.

ELBOW   To your worship's house, sir?

ESCALUS   To my house. Fare you well.

       [*Exit* ELBOW *with officers*]

245   What's o'clock, think you?

JUSTICE   Eleven, sir.

ESCALUS   I pray you home to dinner with me.²

JUSTICE   I humbly thank you.

ESCALUS   It grieves me for the death of Claudio,
250   But there's no remedy.

JUSTICE   Lord Angelo is severe.

ESCALUS   It is but needful.
Mercy is not itself that oft looks so.
Pardon is still° the nurse of second woe.   *always*
255   But yet, poor Claudio! There is no remedy.
Come, sir.   *Exeunt*

---

9. Townhouse rental was based on the number of front   harsh.
windows ("bays").   2. Dinner was served at midday. *pray:* ask.
1. Julius Caesar defeated Pompey in 48 B.C.E. *shrewd:*

2.2

Enter PROVOST [*and a*] SERVANT

SERVANT He's hearing of a cause;° he will come straight.°   *case / right away*
    I'll tell him of you.

PROVOST   Pray you do.   [*Exit* SERVANT]
                     I'll know
    His pleasure; maybe he will relent. Alas,
    He° hath but as offended in a dream.   *(Claudio)*
5   All sects,° all ages, smack° of this vice; and he   *kinds of people / partake*
    To die for't!

Enter ANGELO

ANGELO   Now, what's the matter, Provost?

PROVOST   Is it your will Claudio shall die tomorrow?

ANGELO   Did not I tell thee yea? Hadst thou not order?
    Why dost thou ask again?

PROVOST   Lest I might be too rash.

10 Under your good correction, I have seen
    When after execution judgement hath
    Repented o'er his doom.°   *sentence*

ANGELO   Go to; let that be mine.°   *my concern*
    Do you your office, or give up your place,
    And you shall well be spared.°   *easily be done without*

PROVOST   I crave your honour's pardon.

15 What shall be done, sir, with the groaning Juliet?
    She's very near her hour.°   *(of childbirth)*

ANGELO   Dispose of her
    To some more fitter place, and that with speed.

[*Enter* SERVANT]

SERVANT   Here is the sister of the man condemned
    Desires access to you.

ANGELO   Hath he a sister?

20 PROVOST   Ay, my good lord; a very virtuous maid,
    And to be shortly of a sisterhood,
    If not already.

ANGELO   Well, let her be admitted.   [*Exit* SERVANT]
    See you the fornicatress be removed.
    Let her have needful but not lavish means.
    There shall be order° for't.   *written direction*

Enter LUCIO *and* ISABELLA

25 PROVOST   God save your honour.

ANGELO   Stay a little while. [*To* ISABELLA] You're welcome.
    What's your will?

ISABELLA   I am a woeful suitor to your honour.
    Please° but your honour hear me.   *If it please*

ANGELO   Well, what's your suit?

ISABELLA   There is a vice that most I do abhor,
30 And most desire should meet the blow of justice,
    For which I would not plead, but that I must;
    For which I must not plead, but that I am
    At war 'twixt will and will not.

ANGELO   Well, the matter?

ISABELLA   I have a brother is condemned to die.

2.2 Location: A room in the court of justice.

35   I do beseech you, let it be his fault,°   his fault be condemned
      And not my brother.
      PROVOST [*aside*]   Heaven give thee moving graces!°   the gift of persuasion
      ANGELO   Condemn the fault, and not the actor° of it?   doer
      Why, every fault's condemned ere it be done.
      Mine were the very cipher of a function,
40   To fine° the faults whose fine° stands in record,   condemn / penalty
      And let go by° the actor.   leave unpunished
      ISABELLA   O just but severe law!
      I had a brother, then. Heaven keep your honour.
      LUCIO [*aside to* ISABELLA]   Give't not o'er° so. To him again;   Don't give up
          entreat him.
      Kneel down before him; hang upon° his gown.   ┌ *clings up*   cling to
45   You are too cold. If you should need a pin,
      You could not with more tame a tongue desire it.
      To him, I say!
      ISABELLA [*to* ANGELO]   Must he needs° die?   necessarily
      ANGELO   Maiden, no remedy.
50   ISABELLA   Yes, I do think that you might pardon him,
      And neither heaven nor man grieve at the mercy.
      ANGELO   I will not do't.
      ISABELLA   But can you if you would?
      ANGELO   Look what° I will not, that I cannot do.   Whatever
      ISABELLA   But might you do't, and do the world no wrong,
55   If so your heart were touched with that remorse°   pity
      As mine is to him?
      ANGELO   He's sentenced; 'tis too late.
      LUCIO [*aside to* ISABELLA]   You are too cold.
      ISABELLA   Too late? Why, no; I that do speak a word
60   May call° it again. Well, believe this,   retract
      No ceremony° that to great ones 'longs,   symbolic accessory
      Not the king's crown, nor the deputed sword,
      The marshal's truncheon, nor the judge's robe,
      Become them with one half so good a grace
65   As mercy does.
      If he had been as you and you as he,
      You would have slipped like him, but he, like you,
      Would not have been so stern.
      ANGELO   Pray you be gone.
      ISABELLA   I would to heaven I had your potency,°   power
70   And you were Isabel! Should it then be thus?
      No; I would tell what 'twere to be a judge,
      And what a prisoner.
      LUCIO [*aside to* ISABELLA]   Ay, touch him;[1] there's the vein.°   that's the style
      ANGELO   Your brother is a forfeit of the law,
      And you but waste your words.
      ISABELLA   Alas, alas!
75   Why, all the souls that were were forfeit[2] once,
      And He that might the vantage° best have took   advantage
      Found out° the remedy.[3] How would you be   Procured
      If He which is the top° of judgement should   highest pattern or source
      But judge you as you are? O, think on that,

---

1. Influence him; but perhaps Isabella touches Angelo's   2. Lost (as a result of Adam and Eve's disobedience).
arm or garment here.   3. By saving all mankind in the person of Christ.

80 And mercy then will breathe within your lips,
Like man new made.° *renewed by faith*
(with play on "new made")
ANGELO   Be you content, fair maid.°
It is the law, not I, condemn your brother.
Were he my kinsman, brother, or my son,
It should be thus with him. He must die tomorrow.
85 ISABELLA   Tomorrow? O, that's sudden! Spare him, spare him!
He's not prepared for death. Even for our kitchens
We kill the fowl of season.° Shall we serve heaven *at the proper time*
With less respect than we do minister
To our gross selves? Good good my lord, bethink you:
90 Who is it that hath died for this offence?
There's many have committed it.
LUCIO [*aside*]   Ay, well said.
ANGELO   The law hath not been dead, though it hath slept.
Those many had not dared to do that evil
If the first that did th'edict infringe
95 Had answered for his deed. Now 'tis awake,
Takes note of what is done, and, like a prophet,
Looks in a glass° that shows what future evils, *mirror*
Either raw,° or by remissness new conceived *unripe*
And so in progress to be hatched and born,
100 Are now to have no successive degrees,[4]
But ere they live, to end.
ISABELLA   Yet show some pity.
ANGELO   I show it most of all when I show justice,
For then I pity those I do not know
Which a dismissed° offence would after gall,° *Whom a pardoned / hurt*
105 And do him right that, answering° one foul wrong, *paying for*
Lives not to act another. Be satisfied.
Your brother dies tomorrow. Be content.
ISABELLA   So you must be the first that gives this sentence,
And he that suffers. O, it is excellent
110 To have a giant's strength, but it is tyrannous
To use it like a giant.
LUCIO [*aside to* ISABELLA]   That's well said.
ISABELLA   Could great men thunder
As Jove[5] himself does, Jove would never be quiet,
115 For every pelting° petty officer *paltry*
Would use his heaven for thunder, nothing but thunder.
Merciful heaven,
Thou rather with thy sharp and sulphurous° bolt *fiery*
Split'st the unwedgeable and gnarlèd oak
120 Than the soft myrtle. But man, proud man,
Dressed in a little brief authority,
Most ignorant of what he's most assured,
His glassy° essence, like an angry ape[6] *fragile; illusory*
Plays such fantastic tricks before high heaven
125 As makes the angels weep, who, with our spleens,[7]
Would all themselves laugh mortal.

---

4. Future stages of development.
5. King of the Roman gods, whose weapon was the thunderbolt.
6. A figure of grotesque mimicry.
7. Thought to be the seat of laughter.

LUCIO [*aside to* ISABELLA]   O, to him, to him, wench!° He will   *girl*
    relent.
    He's coming;° I perceive't.   *yielding*
PROVOST [*aside*]   Pray heaven she win him!
ISABELLA   We cannot weigh our brother with ourself.[8]
130   Great men may jest with saints; 'tis wit in them,
    But in the less,° foul profanation.   *ordinary people*
LUCIO [*aside to* ISABELLA]   Thou'rt i'th' right, girl. More o' that.
ISABELLA   That in the captain's but a choleric word,
    Which in the soldier is flat blasphemy.
135 LUCIO [*aside to* ISABELLA]   Art advised o' that?° More on't.   *So you know about that*
ANGELO   Why do you put° these sayings upon me?   *impose*
ISABELLA   Because authority, though it err like others,
    Hath yet a kind of medicine in itself
    That skins the vice o'th' top.[9] Go to your bosom;
140   Knock there, and ask your heart what it doth know
    That's like my brother's fault. If it confess
    A natural guiltiness, such as is his,
    Let it not sound a thought upon your tongue
    Against my brother's life.
ANGELO [*aside*]   She speaks, and 'tis such sense°   *sound advice*
145   That my sense breeds° with it. [*To* ISABELLA] Fare you well.   *desire increases*
ISABELLA   Gentle my° lord, turn back.   *My gracious*
ANGELO   I will bethink me.° Come again tomorrow.   *consider*
ISABELLA   Hark how I'll bribe you; good my lord, turn back.
ANGELO   How, bribe me?
150 ISABELLA   Ay, with such gifts that° heaven shall share with° you.   *as / apportion to*
LUCIO [*aside to* ISABELLA]   You had marred all else.
ISABELLA   Not with fond° shekels of the tested° gold,   *foolish / refined*
    Or stones,° whose rate° are either rich or poor   *jewels / value*
    As fancy values them; but with true prayers,
155   That shall be up at heaven and enter there
    Ere sunrise, prayers from preservèd° souls,   *protected*
    From fasting maids whose minds are dedicate
    To nothing temporal.
ANGELO   Well, come to me tomorrow.
160 LUCIO [*aside to* ISABELLA]   Go to;° 'tis well; away.   *Come on*
ISABELLA   Heaven keep your honour[1] safe.
ANGELO [*aside*]   Amen;
    For I am that way going to temptation,
    Where prayer is crossed.°   *corrupted; frustrated*
ISABELLA   At what hour tomorrow
    Shall I attend your lordship?
165 ANGELO   At any time fore noon.
ISABELLA   God save your honour.
ANGELO [*aside*]   From thee; even from thy virtue.
        [*Exeunt* ISABELLA, LUCIO, *and* PROVOST]
    What's this? What's this? Is this her fault or mine?
    The tempter or the tempted, who sins most, ha?
    Not she; nor doth she tempt; but it is I
170   That, lying by the violet in the sun,
    Do, as the carrion does, not as the flower,

---

8. We cannot judge others as we judge ourselves.
9. That causes a skin to grow over the sore.

1. Isabella calls Angelo "your honor" as a term of respect;
    Angelo understands the phrase as referring to his virtue.

Corrupt with virtuous season.° Can it be   *Rot in fine weather*
That modesty may more betray our sense°   *seduce our appetite*
Than woman's lightness?° Having waste ground enough,   *licentiousness*
175   Shall we desire to raze the sanctuary,
And pitch° our evils there? O, fie, fie, fie!   *hurl; set up*
What dost thou, or what art thou, Angelo?
Dost thou desire her foully for those things
That make her good? O, let her brother live!
180   Thieves for their robbery have authority,
When judges steal themselves. What, do I love her,
That I desire to hear her speak again,
And feast upon her eyes? What is't I dream on?
O cunning enemy,° that, to catch a saint,°   *(Satan) / holy person*
185   With saints dost bait thy hook! Most dangerous
Is that temptation that doth goad us on
To sin in loving virtue. Never could the strumpet,
With all her double vigour°—art and nature—   *twofold power*
Once stir my temper;° but this virtuous maid   *excite me*
190   Subdues me quite. Ever till now
When men were fond,° I smiled, and wondered how.   *Exit*   *infatuated*

2.3

Enter [at one door] the DUKE, *[disguised as a friar,] and*
[at another door, the] PROVOST

DUKE   Hail to you, Provost!—so I think you are.
PROVOST   I am the Provost. What's your will, good friar?
DUKE   Bound by my charity and my blest order,
    I come to visit the afflicted spirits
5   Here in the prison.[1] Do me the common right°   *right of all clerics*
    To let me see them, and to make me know
    The nature of their crimes, that I may minister
    To them accordingly.
PROVOST   I would do more than that, if more were needful.

    Enter JULIET

10   Look, here comes one, a gentlewoman of mine,°   *in my care*
    Who, falling in the flaws° of her own youth,   *faults; gusts of passion*
    Hath blistered her report.° She is with child,   *reputation*
    And he that got° it, sentenced—a young man   *begot*
    More fit to do another such offence
15   Than die for this.
DUKE   When must he die?
PROVOST   As I do think, tomorrow.
    [*To* JULIET] I have provided for you. Stay a while,
    And you shall be conducted.
20   DUKE   Repent you, fair one, of the sin you carry?
JULIET   I do, and bear the shame most patiently.
DUKE   I'll teach you how you shall arraign° your conscience,   *accuse*
    And try your penitence if it be sound
    Or hollowly put on.
25   JULIET   I'll gladly learn.
DUKE   Love you the man that wronged you?
JULIET   Yes, as I love the woman that wronged him.

2.3 Location: The prison.
1. Echoing 1 Peter 3:19: "He . . . went, and preached unto the spirits that were in prison."

DUKE   So then it seems your most offenceful act
    Was mutually committed?

JULIET   Mutually.

30 DUKE   Then was your sin of heavier° kind than his.   *graver*

JULIET   I do confess it and repent it, father.

DUKE   'Tis meet° so, daughter. But lest you do repent   *appropriate*
    As that° the sin hath brought you to this shame—   *Because*
    Which sorrow is always toward ourselves, not heaven,

35   Showing we would not spare heaven[2] as we love it,
    But as we stand in fear—

JULIET   I do repent me as it is an evil,
    And take the shame with joy.

DUKE   There rest.°   *remain*
    Your partner, as I hear, must die tomorrow,

40   And I am going with instruction to him.
    Grace go with you. *Benedicite!*°   *Exit*   *Bless you*

JULIET   Must die tomorrow? O injurious law,
    That respites me a life[3] whose very comfort
    Is still a dying horror!

PROVOST   'Tis pity of° him.   *Exeunt*   *for*

2.4

Enter ANGELO

ANGELO   When I would pray and think, I think and pray
    To several° subjects: heaven hath my empty words,   *different*
    Whilst my invention,° hearing not my tongue,   *imagination*
    Anchors on Isabel; God in my mouth,

5   As if I did but only chew his name,
    And in my heart the strong and swelling evil
    Of my conception.[1] The state° whereon I studied   *statecraft; dignity*
    Is like a good thing, being often read,
    Grown seared° and tedious. Yea, my gravity,   *arid*

10   Wherein—let no man hear me—I take pride,
    Could I with boot° change for an idle plume[2]   *advantage*
    Which the air beats in vain. O place,° O form,°   *rank / formality*
    How often dost thou with thy case,° thy habit,°   *appearance / dress*
    Wrench awe from fools, and tie the wiser souls

15   To thy false seeming! Blood, thou art blood.[3]
    Let's write 'good angel'[4] on the devil's horn—
    'Tis now the devil's crest.°   *heraldic device*

Enter SERVANT

             How now? Who's there?

SERVANT   One Isabel, a sister, desires access to you.

ANGELO   Teach her the way.   *[Exit* SERVANT]
           O heavens,

20   Why does my blood thus muster° to my heart,   *crowd*
    Making both it unable° for itself,   *weak*
    And dispossessing all my other parts
    Of necessary fitness?
    So play° the foolish throngs with one that swoons—   *act*

---

2. Relieve heaven from distress.
3. Pregnant women were spared the death penalty, at
least until after childbirth.
2.4 Location: A room in the court of justice.
1. *the strong . . . conception:* the wickedness of my idea;
original sin, inherited through the parents.

2. A frivolous feather, as worn in the hats of rakish
youths.
3. That is, basic passions cannot be eradicated (contrasts
with 1.4.56–58).
4. With pun on Angelo's name.

25 Come all to help him, and so stop the air
By which he should revive—and even so
The general subject° to a well-wished king   *common people*
Quit their own part° and, in obsequious fondness,°   *place / foolish love*
Crowd to his presence, where their untaught° love   *ignorant*
Must needs appear offence.

         Enter ISABELLA

30   How now, fair maid?

ISABELLA   I am come to know your pleasure.

ANGELO   [*aside*]   That you might know[5] it would much better
    please me
      Than to demand° what 'tis. [*To* ISABELLA] Your brother cannot live.   *ask*

ISABELLA   Even so.° Heaven keep your honour.[6]   *So be it*

35 ANGELO   Yet may he live a while, and it may be
    As long as you or I. Yet he must die.

ISABELLA   Under your sentence?

ANGELO   Yea.

ISABELLA   When, I beseech you?—that in his reprieve,
40   Longer or shorter, he may be so fitted°   *prepared*
    That his soul sicken not.

ANGELO   Ha, fie, these filthy vices! It were as good
    To pardon him that hath from nature stolen
    A man already made,[7] as to remit°   *excuse*
45   Their saucy sweetness that do coin God's image
    In stamps that are forbid.[8] 'Tis all as easy
    Falsely° to take away a life true° made   *Wrongly / legitimately*
    As to put metal[9] in restrainèd° moulds,   *forbidden*
    To make a false one.

50 ISABELLA   'Tis set down so in heaven, but not in earth.

ANGELO   Say you so? Then I shall pose° you quickly.   *ask*
    Which had you rather: that the most just law
    Now took your brother's life, or, to redeem him,
    Give up your body to such sweet uncleanness
    As she that he hath stained?

55 ISABELLA   Sir, believe this.
    I had rather give my body than my soul.

ANGELO   I talk not of your soul. Our compelled sins
    Stand more for number than for account.[1]

ISABELLA   How say you?

ANGELO   Nay, I'll not warrant that,[2] for I can speak
60   Against the thing I say. Answer to this.
    I now, the voice of the recorded law,
    Pronounce a sentence on your brother's life.
    Might there not be a charity in sin
    To save this brother's life?

ISABELLA   Please° you to do't,   *If it please*
65   I'll take it as a peril to my soul
    It is no sin at all, but charity.

ANGELO   Pleased you to do't at peril of your soul
    Were equal poise° of sin and charity.   *balance*

---

5. With pun on "carnal knowledge."
6. A form of farewell.
7. *hath . . . made*: has committed murder.
8. *coin . . . forbid*: counterfeit God's image (by begetting illegitimate children).
9. Variant spelling of "mettle" (spirit). Some thought the child's spirit was conveyed in its father's semen.
1. *Our . . . account*: Sins we are forced to commit fill out the list but are not held against us.
2. I'll not guarantee that to be true.

ISABELLA   That I do beg his life, if it be sin,
70   Heaven let me bear it. You granting° of my suit,   *Supposing you grant*
If that be sin, I'll make it my morn prayer
To have it added to the faults of mine,
And nothing of your answer.

ANGELO   Nay, but hear me.
Your sense pursues not mine.³ Either you are ignorant,
75   Or seem so craftily, and that's not good.

ISABELLA   Let me be ignorant, and in nothing good
But graciously° to know I am no better.   *by God's grace*

ANGELO   Thus wisdom wishes to appear most bright
When it doth tax° itself: as these black masks⁴   *reprove*
80   Proclaim an enshield° beauty ten times louder   *a shielded*
Than beauty could, displayed. But mark me.
To be received° plain, I'll speak more gross.°   *understood / clearly*
Your brother is to die.

ISABELLA   So.°   *Yes*

85   ANGELO   And his offence is so, as it appears,
Accountant° to the law upon that pain.°   *Accountable / penalty*

ISABELLA   True.

ANGELO   Admit° no other way to save his life—   *Suppose*
As I subscribe not° that nor any other—   *agree to neither*
90   But, in the loss of question,⁵ that you his sister,
Finding yourself desired of such a person
Whose credit with the judge, or own great place,°   *rank*
Could fetch your brother from the manacles
Of the all-binding law, and that there were
95   No earthly mean to save him, but that either
You must lay down the treasures of your body
To this supposed,° or else to let him suffer—   *supposed man*
What would you do?

ISABELLA   As much for my poor brother as myself.
100   That is, were I under the terms° of death,   *sentence*
Th'impression of keen whips I'd wear as rubies,
And strip myself to death as to a bed
That longing have been sick for, ere I'd yield
My body up to shame.

105   ANGELO   Then must your brother die.

ISABELLA   And 'twere the cheaper way.
Better it were a brother died at once
Than that a sister, by redeeming him,
Should die for ever.°   *be eternally damned*

110   ANGELO   Were not you then as cruel as the sentence
That you have slandered so?

ISABELLA   Ignominy in ransom and free pardon
Are of two houses;° lawful mercy   *different families*
Is nothing kin to foul redemption.

115   ANGELO   You seemed of late to make the law a tyrant,
And rather proved° the sliding of your brother   *argued*
A merriment than a vice.

ISABELLA   O pardon me, my lord. It oft falls out
To have what we would° have, we speak not what we mean.   *wish to*

---

3. You don't follow my meaning; your desire is not
aroused by mine.

4. Worn at court entertainments.
5. For the sake of discussion.

120   I something° do excuse the thing I hate   *to some extent*
          For his advantage that I dearly love.

ANGELO   We are all frail.[6]

ISABELLA   Else° let my brother die—   *Otherwise*
          If not a federy,° but only he,   *confederate*
          Owe and succeed thy weakness.[7]

ANGELO   Nay, women are frail too.

125   ISABELLA   Ay, as the glasses° where they view themselves,   *mirrors*
          Which are as easy broke as they make forms.
          Women? Help, heaven! Men their creation° mar   *origin*
          In profiting by them. Nay, call us ten times frail,
          For we are soft as our complexions are,
          And credulous to false prints.[8]

130   ANGELO   I think it well,°   *agree completely*
          And from this testimony of your own sex,
          Since I suppose we are made to be no stronger
          Than faults may shake our frames, let me be bold.°   *presumptuous*
          I do arrest° your words. Be that you are;   *seize upon*
135   That is, a woman. If you be more,° you're none.   *(that is, better)*
          If you be one, as you are well expressed°   *shown to be*
          By all external warrants,° show it now,   *evidence*
          By putting on the destined livery.[9]

ISABELLA   I have no tongue° but one. Gentle my lord,   *speech*
140   Let me entreat you speak the former language.

ANGELO   Plainly conceive, I love you.

ISABELLA   My brother did love Juliet,
          And you tell me that he shall die for it.

ANGELO   He shall not, Isabel, if you give me love.

145   ISABELLA   I know your virtue hath a licence[1] in't,
          Which seems a little fouler than it is,
          To pluck on° others.   *test; mislead*

ANGELO   Believe me, on mine honour,
          My words express my purpose.

ISABELLA   Ha, little honour to be much believed,
150   And most pernicious purpose! Seeming, seeming!
          I will proclaim° thee, Angelo; look for't.   *denounce*
          Sign me a present° pardon for my brother,   *an immediate*
          Or with an outstretched throat I'll tell the world aloud
          What man thou art.

ANGELO   Who will believe thee, Isabel?
155   My unsoiled name, th'austereness of my life,
          My vouch° against you, and my place i'th' state,   *attestation*
          Will so your accusation overweigh
          That you shall stifle in your own report,°   *story; reputation*
          And smell of calumny. I have begun,
160   And now I give my sensual race the rein.
          Fit thy consent to my sharp appetite.
          Lay by all nicety and prolixious° blushes   *coyness and excessive*
          That banish what they sue for. Redeem thy brother
          By yielding up thy body to my will,

---

6. Echoing Ecclesiasticus 8:5: "We are all worthy blame."
7. Own and inherit the weakness under discussion, or the weakness that you possess.
8. And receptive to false impressions; referring to Angelo's counterfeiting imagery, lines 45ff.
9. That is, by accepting women's sexual destiny and subjection to men. *livery:* servant's uniform.
1. Liberty to seem licentious.

165 Or else he must not only die the death,
But thy unkindness° shall his death draw out   *unnaturalness*
To ling'ring sufferance.° Answer me tomorrow,   *torment*
Or by the affection° that now guides me most,   *passion*
I'll prove a tyrant to him. As for you,
170 Say what you can, my false o'erweighs your true.   *Exit*
ISABELLA   To whom should I complain? Did I tell this,
Who would believe me? O perilous mouths,
That bear in them one and the selfsame tongue
Either of condemnation or approof,°   *approval*
175 Bidding the law make curtsy° to their will,   *submit*
Hooking both right and wrong to th'appetite,
To follow as it draws! I'll to my brother.
Though he hath fall'n by prompture° of the blood,   *instigation*
Yet hath he in him such a mind of honour
180 That had he twenty heads to tender° down   *pay*
On twenty bloody blocks, he'd yield them up
Before his sister should her body stoop
To such abhorred pollution.
Then Isabel live chaste, and brother die:
185 More than our brother is our chastity.
I'll tell him yet of Angelo's request,
And fit his mind to death, for his soul's rest.   *Exit*

3.1

Enter DUKE *[disguised as a friar],* CLAUDIO, *and* PROVOST
DUKE   So then you hope of pardon from Lord Angelo?
CLAUDIO   The miserable have no other medicine
But only hope.
I've hope to live, and am prepared to die.
5 DUKE   Be absolute° for death. Either death or life   *resolved*
Shall thereby be the sweeter. Reason thus with life.
If I do lose thee, I do lose a thing
That none but fools would keep. A breath thou art,
Servile to all the skyey influences[1]
10 That dost this habitation where thou keep'st°   *live*
Hourly afflict. Merely° thou art death's fool,°   *Utterly / dupe*
For him thou labour'st by thy flight to shun,
And yet runn'st toward him still.° Thou art not noble,   *always*
For all th'accommodations° that thou bear'st   *material comforts*
15 Are nursed by baseness.[2] Thou'rt by no means valiant,
For thou dost fear the soft and tender fork°   *forked tongue*
Of a poor worm.° Thy best of rest is sleep,   *snake*
And that thou oft provok'st,° yet grossly fear'st   *summon*
Thy death, which is no more. Thou art not thyself,°   *self-contained*
20 For thou exist'st on many a thousand grains
That issue out of dust.° Happy thou art not,   *grow from the ground*
For what thou hast not, still thou striv'st to get,
And what thou hast, forget'st. Thou art not certain,°   *stable*
For thy complexion° shifts to strange effects   *temperament*
25 After° the moon. If thou art rich, thou'rt poor,[3]   *Following*

3.1 Location: The prison.
1. Subject to all the influences of the heavenly bodies.
2. Are grown from plants and animals; made by lower-class people.

3. From Revelation 3:17: "For thou sayest, I am rich and increased with goods, and have need of nothing, and knowest not how thou art wretched and miserable, and poor, and blind, and naked."

For like an ass whose back with ingots bows,
Thou bear'st thy heavy riches but a journey,
And death unloads thee. Friend hast thou none,
For thine own bowels,° which do call thee sire,   *offspring*
30   The mere effusion° of thy proper° loins,   *very emission / own*
Do curse the gout, serpigo,° and the rheum,°   *skin disease / congestion*
For ending thee no sooner. Thou hast nor youth nor age,
But as it were an after-dinner's sleep
Dreaming on both; for all thy blessèd youth
35   Becomes as agèd,° and doth beg the alms°   *as if old / for money*
Of palsied eld;° and when thou art old and rich,   *old people*
Thou hast neither heat,° affection, limb,° nor beauty,   *desire / strength*
To make thy riches pleasant. What's in this
That bears the name of life? Yet in this life
40   Lie hid more thousand° deaths; yet death we fear   *a thousand more*
That makes these odds° all even.   *irregularities*

CLAUDIO   I humbly thank you.
To sue° to live, I find I seek to die,   *ask*
And seeking death, find life.[4] Let it come on.

ISABELLA [*within*]   What ho! Peace here, grace, and good company!
45 PROVOST   Who's there? Come in; the wish deserves a welcome.

DUKE [*to* CLAUDIO]   Dear sir, ere long I'll visit you again.

CLAUDIO   Most holy sir, I thank you.

Enter ISABELLA

ISABELLA   My business is a word or two with Claudio.

PROVOST   And very welcome. Look, signor, here's your sister.

DUKE   Provost, a word with you.

50 PROVOST   As many as you please.

[*The* DUKE *and* PROVOST *draw aside*]

DUKE   Bring me to hear them speak where I may be concealed.

[*They conceal themselves*]

CLAUDIO   Now sister, what's the comfort?

ISABELLA   Why, as all comforts are: most good, most good indeed.
Lord Angelo, having affairs to heaven,
55   Intends you for his swift ambassador,
Where you shall be an everlasting leiger.°   *resident ambassador*
Therefore your best appointment° make with speed.   *preparation*
Tomorrow you set on.°   *forward*

CLAUDIO   Is there no remedy?

ISABELLA   None but such remedy as, to save a head,
60   To cleave a heart in twain.

CLAUDIO   But is there any?

ISABELLA   Yes, brother, you may live.
There is a devilish mercy in the judge,
If you'll implore it, that will free your life,
But fetter you till death.

65 CLAUDIO   Perpetual durance?°   *imprisonment*

ISABELLA   Ay, just,° perpetual durance; a restraint,   *exactly so*
Though all the world's vastidity° you had,   *vastness*
To a determined scope.[5]

CLAUDIO   But in what nature?

---

4. Echoing Matthew 16:25: "For whosoever will save his life, shall lose it: and whosoever shall lose his life for my sake, shall find it."

5. Constricted space (by the awareness of the means by which he had been saved).

ISABELLA   In such a one as you consenting to't

70   Would bark[6] your honour from that trunk° you bear,   *body; tree trunk*
      And leave you naked.

CLAUDIO   Let me know the point.

ISABELLA   O, I do fear thee, Claudio, and I quake
      Lest thou a feverous° life shouldst entertain,°   *feverish / cherish*
      And six or seven winters more respect°   *esteem*

75   Than a perpetual honour. Dar'st thou die?
      The sense° of death is most in apprehension,°   *awareness / anticipation*
      And the poor beetle that we tread upon
      In corporal sufferance° finds a pang as great   *bodily suffering*
      As when a giant dies.

CLAUDIO   Why give you me this shame?

80   Think you I can a resolution fetch°   *derive*
      From flow'ry° tenderness? If I must die,   *florid*
      I will encounter darkness as a bride,
      And hug it in mine arms.

ISABELLA   There spake my brother; there my father's grave

85   Did utter forth a voice. Yes, thou must die.
      Thou art too noble to conserve a life
      In base appliances.° This outward-sainted deputy,   *ignoble means*
      Whose settled° visage and deliberate word   *composed*
      Nips youth i'th' head[7] and follies doth enew°   *drive into hiding*

90   As falcon doth the fowl, is yet a devil.
      His filth within being cast,[8] he would appear
      A pond as deep as hell.

CLAUDIO   The precise[9] Angelo?

ISABELLA   O, 'tis the cunning livery of hell
      The damnedest body to invest° and cover   *dress*

95   In precise guards!° Dost thou think, Claudio: *trimmings*
      If I would yield him my virginity,
      Thou might'st be freed!

CLAUDIO   O heavens, it cannot be!

ISABELLA   Yes, he would give't thee, from this rank offence,
      So to offend him still.[1] This night's the time

100   That I should do what I abhor to name,
      Or else thou diest tomorrow.

CLAUDIO   Thou shalt not do't.

ISABELLA   O, were it but my life,
      I'd throw it down for your deliverance
      As frankly° as a pin.   *freely*

105 CLAUDIO   Thanks, dear Isabel.

ISABELLA   Be ready, Claudio, for your death tomorrow.

CLAUDIO   Yes. Has he affections in him
      That thus can make him bite the law by th' nose°   *flout the law*
      When he would force it? Sure it is no sin,

110   Or of the deadly seven[2] it is the least.

ISABELLA   Which is the least?

CLAUDIO   If it were damnable, he being so wise,
      Why would he for the momentary trick°   *trifle*

---

6. Strip off, like bark from a tree.
7. As a hawk kills a bird.
8. Cleaned out; measured; vomited.
9. F has "prenzie" here and in line 95; some editors emend (as here) to "precise," others to "princely."

1. *give't thee . . . still:* grant you freedom in return for his foul sin, so that you might continue offending him.
2. Seven deadly sins (pride, lechery, envy, anger, covetousness, gluttony, and sloth).

Be perdurably fined?° O Isabel!   *eternally punished*
115 ISABELLA What says my brother?
    CLAUDIO Death is a fearful thing.
    ISABELLA And shamèd life a hateful.
    CLAUDIO Ay, but to die, and go we know not where;
      To lie in cold obstruction,° and to rot;   *congealment*
120   This sensible warm motion° to become   *conscious warm body*
      A kneaded clod, and the dilated° spirit   *expansive; released*
      To bath in fiery floods, or to reside
      In thrilling° region of thick-ribbèd ice;   *bitterly cold*
      To be imprisoned in the viewless° winds,   *unseeing; invisible*
125   And blown with restless violence round about
      The pendent° world; or to be worse than worst   *hanging in space*
      Of those that lawless and incertain thought³
      Imagine howling—'tis too horrible!
      The weariest and most loathèd worldly life
130   That age, ache, penury, and imprisonment
      Can lay on nature is a paradise
      To what we fear of death.
    ISABELLA Alas, alas!
    CLAUDIO Sweet sister, let me live.
135   What sin you do to save a brother's life,
      Nature dispenses with° the deed so far   *excuses*
      That it becomes a virtue.
    ISABELLA   O, you beast!
      O faithless coward, O dishonest wretch,
      Wilt thou be made a man° out of my vice?   *given life*
140   Is't not a kind of incest to take life
      From thine own sister's shame? What should I think?
      Heaven shield° my mother played my father fair,   *forbid*
      For such a warpèd slip of wilderness°   *shoot of wild stock*
      Ne'er issued from his blood. Take my defiance,°   *rejection*
145   Die, perish! Might but my bending down
      Reprieve thee from thy fate, it should proceed.
      I'll pray a thousand prayers for thy death,
      No word to save thee.
    CLAUDIO Nay, hear me, Isabel.
150 ISABELLA O fie, fie, fie!
      Thy sin's not accidental,° but a trade.°   *casual / habit*
      Mercy to thee would prove itself a bawd.⁴
      'Tis best that thou diest quickly.
              [*She parts from* CLAUDIO]
    CLAUDIO O hear me, Isabella.
    DUKE [*coming forward to* ISABELLA] Vouchsafe a word, young
155   sister, but one word.
    ISABELLA What is your will?
    DUKE Might you dispense with your leisure,° I would by and by   *spare the time*
      have some speech with you. The satisfaction I would require
      is likewise your own benefit.
160 ISABELLA I have no superfluous leisure; my stay must be stolen
      out of other affairs; but I will attend° you a while.   *await*
    DUKE [*standing aside with* CLAUDIO] Son, I have overheard what
      hath passed between you and your sister. Angelo had never the

---

3. Of those whom unbridled and dubious conjecture.   4. By facilitating sinful behavior.

	purpose to corrupt her; only he hath made an assay°	*a trial*
165	of her virtue, to practise his judgement with the disposition of	
	natures. She, having the truth of honour° in her, hath made	*chastity*
	him that gracious° denial which he is most glad to receive. I	*virtuous*
	am confessor to Angelo, and I know this to be true. Therefore	
	prepare yourself to death. Do not falsify° your resolution with	*corrupt*
170	hopes that are fallible. Tomorrow you must die. Go to your	
	knees and make ready.	

CLAUDIO Let me ask my sister pardon. I am so out of love with
life that I will sue to be rid of it.

DUKE Hold you there.° Farewell.   *Remain so resolved*

    [CLAUDIO *joins* ISABELLA][5]

175   Provost, a word with you.

PROVOST [*coming forward*] What's your will, father?

DUKE That now you are come, you will be gone. Leave me a
while with the maid. My mind° promises with my habit° no   *intention / friar's gown*
loss shall touch her by my company.

180 PROVOST In good time.°   *Exit* [*with* CLAUDIO]   *Very well*

DUKE The hand that hath made you fair hath made you good.
The goodness that is cheap in beauty makes beauty brief in
goodness;[6] but grace,° being the soul of your complexion,° shall   *virtue / constitution*
keep the body of it ever fair. The assault that Angelo hath made
185 to you fortune hath conveyed to my understanding; and but
that frailty hath examples° for his falling, I should wonder at   *precedents*
Angelo. How will you do to content this substitute,° and to save   *deputy*
your brother?

ISABELLA I am now going to resolve him. I had rather my
190 brother die by the law than my son should be unlawfully born.
But O, how much is the good Duke deceived in Angelo! If ever
he return and I can speak to him, I will open my lips in vain,
or discover° his government.[7]   *expose*

DUKE That shall not be much amiss. Yet as the matter now
195 stands, he will avoid° your accusation: he made trial of you   *quash*
only. Therefore fasten your ear on my advisings. To the love I
have in doing good, a remedy presents itself. I do make myself
believe that you may most uprighteously do a poor wronged
lady a merited benefit, redeem your brother from the angry
200 law, do no stain to your own gracious person, and much please
the absent Duke, if peradventure he shall ever return to have
hearing of this business.

ISABELLA Let me hear you speak farther. I have spirit to do anything that appears not foul in the truth of my spirit.

205 DUKE Virtue is bold, and goodness never fearful. Have you not
heard speak of Mariana, the sister of Frederick, the great soldier
who miscarried° at sea?   *perished*

ISABELLA I have heard of the lady, and good words went with
her name.

210 DUKE She should this Angelo have married, was affianced to her
oath, and the nuptial appointed;° between which time of the   *wedding day set*
contract and limit° of the solemnity, her brother Frederick was   *date*
wrecked at sea, having in that perished vessel the dowry of his

---

5. The Duke's conversation with the Provost provides an
opportunity for a silent reconciliation.
6. The goodness that is little valued by the beautiful

makes beauty short-lived.
7. Conduct; mode of governing.

sister. But mark how heavily this befell to the poor gentle-
215   woman. There she lost a noble and renowned brother, in his
love toward her ever most kind and natural; with him, the portion and sinew° of her fortune, her marriage dowry; with both,   *mainstay*
her combinate° husband, this well-seeming Angelo.   *betrothed*

ISABELLA   Can this be so? Did Angelo so leave her?

220 DUKE   Left her in her tears, and dried not one of them with his
comfort; swallowed° his vows whole, pretending° in her discov-   *retracted / alleging*
eries of dishonour;° in few, bestowed her on her own lamenta-   *unchastity*
tion, which she yet wears for his sake; and he, a marble° to her   *impervious*
tears, is washed with them, but relents not.

225 ISABELLA   What a merit were it in death to take this poor maid
from the world! What corruption in this life, that it will let this
man live! But how out of this can she avail?°   *profit*

DUKE   It is a rupture that you may easily heal, and the cure of it
not only saves your brother, but keeps you from dishonour in
230 doing it.

ISABELLA   Show me how, good father.

DUKE   This forenamed maid hath yet in her the continuance of
her first affection.° His unjust unkindness, that in all reason   *passion*
should have quenched her love, hath, like an impediment in
235 the current, made it more violent and unruly. Go you to
Angelo, answer his requiring with a plausible obedience, agree
with his demands to the point;° only refer yourself to this advan-   *exactly*
tage: first, that your stay with him may not be long; that the
time may have all shadow° and silence in it; and the place   *darkness*
240 answer to convenience. This being granted in course, and now
follows all. We shall advise this wronged maid to stead up° your   *fulfill*
appointment, go in your place. If the encounter acknowledge
itself° hereafter, it may compel him to her recompense; and   *becomes known*
hear, by this is your brother saved, your honour untainted, the
245 poor Mariana advantaged, and the corrupt deputy scaled.[8] The
maid will I frame° and make fit for his attempt. If you think   *prepare*
well to carry this, as you may, the doubleness of the benefit
defends the deceit from reproof. What think you of it?

ISABELLA   The image of it gives me content already, and I trust
250 it will grow to a most prosperous perfection.°   *completion*

DUKE   It lies much in your holding up. Haste you speedily to
Angelo. If for this night he entreat you to his bed, give him
promise of satisfaction. I will presently to Saint Luke's; there
at the moated grange° resides this dejected[9] Mariana. At that   *country house*
255 place call upon me; and dispatch° with Angelo, that it may be   *settle*
quickly.

ISABELLA   I thank you for this comfort. Fare you well, good
father.   *Exit*

Enter ELBOW, [POMPEY *the*] *Clown, and officers*[1]

ELBOW   Nay, if there be no remedy for it but that you will needs°   *you must*
260 buy and sell men and women like beasts, we shall have all the
world drink brown and white bastard.°   *sweet wine (with pun)*

DUKE   O heavens, what stuff is here?

POMPEY   'Twas never merry world since, of two usuries,[2] the

---

8. Overreached; weighed (and found wanting).
9. Depressed; rejected.
1. The rest of the scene takes place on the street. Some

editors begin a new scene here, though the Duke remains
onstage.
2. Lending of money at interest; prostitution.

merriest was put down, and the worser allowed by order of law,³
265   a furred gown° to keep him warm—and furred with fox on   *(worn by usurers)*
    lambskins too, to signify that craft,° being richer than inno-   *cunning*
    cency, stands for the facing.⁴

ELBOW   Come your way, sir.—Bless you, good father friar.⁵

DUKE   And you, good brother father. What offence hath this man
270   made you, sir?

ELBOW   Marry, sir, he hath offended the law; and, sir, we take
    him to be a thief, too, sir, for we have found upon him, sir, a
    strange picklock,° which we have sent to the deputy.   *skeleton key*

DUKE [*to* POMPEY]   Fie, sirrah, a bawd,° a wicked bawd!   *pimp*
275   The evil that thou causest to be done,
    That is thy means to live. Do thou but think
    What 'tis to cram a maw or clothe a back
    From such a filthy vice. Say to thyself,
    'From their abominable and beastly touches
280   I drink, I eat, array° myself, and live'.   *dress*
    Canst thou believe thy living is a life,
    So stinkingly depending?° Go mend, go mend.   *dependent*

POMPEY   Indeed it does stink in some sort, sir. But yet, sir, I
    would prove—

285 DUKE   Nay, if the devil have given thee proofs for sin,
    Thou wilt prove° his.—Take him to prison, officer.   *prove to be*
    Correction° and instruction must both work   *Punishment*
    Ere this rude° beast will profit.°   *barbarous / improve*

ELBOW   He must before the deputy, sir; he has given him warn-
290   ing. The deputy cannot abide a whoremaster. If he be a whore-
    monger and comes before him, he were as good go a mile on
    his errand.⁶

DUKE   That° we were all as some would seem to be—   *Would that*
    Free from our faults, or faults from seeming free.°   *free from seeming*
295 ELBOW   His neck will come to° your waist: a cord,⁷ sir.   *end up like*

        Enter LUCIO

POMPEY   I spy comfort, I cry bail. Here's a gentleman, and a
    friend of mine.

LUCIO   How now, noble Pompey? What, at the wheels of Cae-
    sar? Art thou led in triumph?⁸ What, is there none of Pygmali-
300   on's images⁹ newly made woman to be had now, for putting
    the hand in the pocket and extracting clutched?¹ What reply,
    ha? What sayst thou to this tune, matter, and method?² Is't not
    drowned i'th' last rain,³ ha? What sayst thou, trot?° Is the world   *bawd*
    as it was, man? Which is the way? Is it sad and few words? Or
305   how? The trick° of it?   *style*

DUKE   Still° thus and thus; still worse!   *Always*

LUCIO   How doth my dear morsel thy mistress? Procures she still, ha?

---

3. A statute of 1570 allowed interest of 10 percent or less.
4. Is used to trim the garment; displays itself to the world.
5. Absurd, since "friar" means "brother"; hence the Duke's reply.
6. *he were . . . errand:* he would be better doing anything rather than that.
7. Encircled by a rope, as the friar's cord encircles his waist.

8. After Roman victories, vanquished generals were paraded behind the chariot wheels of their conquerors.
9. In classical legend, the sculptor Pygmalion fell in love with one of his statues, who was given life by Venus, the goddess of love; with a play on "become a woman" (lose one's virginity).
1. Clenched, with money for bail.
2. This style, topic, and sequence of thought.
3. Overwhelmed with recent misfortune.

POMPEY Troth, sir, she hath eaten up° all her beef,° and she is   *worn out / prostitutes*
herself in the tub.[4]

310 LUCIO Why, 'tis good, it is the right of it, it must be so. Ever
your fresh whore and your powdered[5] bawd; an unshunned°   *unavoidable*
consequence, it must be so. Art going to prison, Pompey?

POMPEY Yes, faith, sir.

LUCIO Why 'tis not amiss, Pompey. Farewell. Go; say I sent thee
315 thither. For debt, Pompey, or how?

ELBOW For being a bawd, for being a bawd.

LUCIO Well then, imprison him. If imprisonment be the due of
a bawd, why, 'tis his right. Bawd is he doubtless, and of antiq-
uity° too—bawd born.° Farewell, good Pompey. Commend me   *long standing / at birth*
320 to the prison, Pompey. You will turn good husband° now, Pom-   *householder*
pey; you will keep the house.

POMPEY I hope, sir, your good worship will be my bail?

LUCIO No, indeed, will I not, Pompey; it is not the wear.° I will   *fashion*
pray, Pompey, to increase your bondage. If you take it not
325 patiently, why, your mettle° is the more. Adieu, trusty Pom-   *spirit; shackles*
pey.— Bless you, friar.

DUKE And you.

LUCIO Does Bridget paint° still, Pompey, ha?   *use cosmetics*

ELBOW [to POMPEY] Come your ways, sir, come.

330 POMPEY [to LUCIO] You will not bail me then, sir?

LUCIO Then, Pompey, nor now.—What news abroad,° friar,   *in the world*
what news?

ELBOW [to POMPEY] Come your ways, sir, come.

LUCIO Go to kennel, Pompey,[6] go.

[Exeunt ELBOW, POMPEY, and officers]

335 What news, friar, of the Duke?

DUKE I know none. Can you tell me of any?

LUCIO Some say he is with the Emperor of Russia; other some,°   *some others*
he is in Rome. But where is he, think you?

DUKE I know not where; but wheresoever, I wish him well.

340 LUCIO It was a mad, fantastical trick° of him to steal from the   *eccentric caprice*
state, and usurp the beggary he was never born to. Lord Angelo
dukes it° well in his absence; he puts transgression to't.[7]   *plays the Duke*

DUKE He does well in't.

LUCIO A little more lenity to lechery would do no harm in him.
345 Something too crabbed° that way, friar.   *Somewhat too harsh*

DUKE It is too general a vice, and severity must cure it.

LUCIO Yes, in good sooth, the vice is of a great° kindred, it is   *an extensive; powerful*
well allied.° But it is impossible to extirp° it quite, friar, till   *connected / extirpate*
eating and drinking be put down. They say this Angelo was not
350 made by man and woman, after this downright[8] way of creation. Is it true, think you?

DUKE How should he be made, then?

LUCIO Some report a sea-maid° spawned him, some that he was   *mermaid*
begot between two stockfishes.° But it is certain that when he   *dried fish*
355 makes water his urine is congealed ice; that I know to be true.
And he is a motion ungenerative;[9] that's infallible.°   *certain*

DUKE You are pleasant,° sir, and speak apace.°   *merry / unrestrainedly*

---

4. Pickling tub for preserving ("powdering") beef; sweating tub for curing venereal disease.
5. Pickled; covered with cosmetic powder.
6. "Pompey" was a common dog's name.

7. He prosecutes lawbreaking vigorously.
8. In accordance with this straightforward.
9. An impotent puppet.

LUCIO   Why, what a ruthless thing is this in him, for the rebellion of a codpiece[1] to take away the life of a man! Would the
360   Duke that is absent have done this? Ere he would have hanged
a man for the getting° a hundred bastards, he would have paid   begetting
for the nursing a thousand. He had some feeling of the sport,
he knew the service,° and that instructed him to mercy.   (of prostitution)
DUKE   I never heard the absent Duke much detected° for   accused
365   women; he was not inclined that way.
LUCIO   O sir, you are deceived.
DUKE   'Tis not possible.
LUCIO   Who, not the Duke? Yes, your beggar of fifty; and his
use° was to put a ducat in her clack-dish.[2] The Duke had cro-   custom
370   chets° in him. He would be drunk too, that let me inform you.   odd notions
DUKE   You do him wrong, surely.
LUCIO   Sir, I was an inward° of his. A shy fellow was the Duke,   intimate
and I believe I know the cause of his withdrawing.
DUKE   What, I prithee, might be the cause?
375   LUCIO   No, pardon, 'tis a secret must be locked within the teeth
and the lips. But this I can let you understand. The greater file
of the subject° held the Duke to be wise.   majority of the people
DUKE   Wise? Why, no question but he was.
LUCIO   A very superficial, ignorant, unweighing° fellow.   injudicious
380   DUKE   Either this is envy° in you, folly, or mistaking. The very   malice
stream° of his life, and the business he hath helmed,° must,   course / steered
upon a warranted need,° give him a better proclamation.° Let   necessarily / reputation
him be but testimonied° in his own bringings-forth,° and he   proven / public actions
shall appear to the envious a scholar, a statesman, and a soldier.
385   Therefore you speak unskilfully,° or, if your knowledge be   ignorantly
more, it is much darkened in your malice.
LUCIO   Sir, I know him and I love him.
DUKE   Love talks with better knowledge, and knowledge with
dearer love.
390   LUCIO   Come, sir, I know what I know.
DUKE   I can hardly believe that, since you know not what you
speak. But if ever the Duke return, as our prayers are he may,
let me desire you to make your answer before him. If it be
honest you have spoke, you have courage to maintain it. I am
395   bound to call upon° you; and I pray you, your name?   accuse
LUCIO   Sir, my name is Lucio, well known to the Duke.
DUKE   He shall know you better, sir, if I may live to report you.
LUCIO   I fear you not.
DUKE   O, you hope the Duke will return no more, or you imag-
400   ine me too unhurtful an opposite.° But indeed I can do you   adversary
little harm; you'll forswear this again.°   at another time
LUCIO   I'll be hanged first. Thou art deceived in me, friar. But
no more of this. Canst thou tell if Claudio die tomorrow or no?
DUKE   Why should he die, sir?
405   LUCIO   Why? For filling a bottle with a tundish.° I would the   funnel (with innuendo)
Duke we talk of were returned again; this ungenitured agent°   sexless deputy
will unpeople the province with continency. Sparrows° must   (proverbially lustful)
not build in his house-eaves, because they are lecherous. The
Duke yet would have dark deeds darkly answered:° he would   secretly requited
410   never bring them to light. Would he were returned. Marry, this

---

1. Padded pouch worn over a man's breeches.   2. Begging bowl (with sexual innuendo).

Claudio is condemned for untrussing.° Farewell, good friar. I   *undoing his leggings*
prithee pray for me. The Duke, I say to thee again, would eat
mutton on Fridays.[3] He's not past it yet, and, I say to thee, he
would mouth° with a beggar, though she smelt° brown bread   *kiss / smelled of*
415   and garlic.[4] Say that I said so. Farewell.   *Exit*

DUKE   No might nor greatness in mortality°   *mortal existence*
Can censure scape;° back-wounding calumny[5]   *escape censure*
The whitest virtue strikes. What king so strong
Can tie the gall° up in the slanderous tongue?   *rancor*
       Enter ESCALUS, PROVOST, *and* [MISTRESS OVERDONE]
But who comes here?

420   ESCALUS [*to the* PROVOST]   Go, away with her to prison.

MISTRESS OVERDONE   Good my lord, be good to me. Your honour is accounted a merciful man, good my lord.

ESCALUS   Double and treble admonition,[6] and still forfeit in the
same kind!° This would make mercy swear[7] and play the tyrant.   *way*

425   PROVOST   A bawd of eleven years' continuance, may it please
your honour.

MISTRESS OVERDONE   My lord, this is one Lucio's information°   *accusation*
against me. Mistress Kate Keepdown was with child by him in
the Duke's time; he promised her marriage. His child is a year

430   and a quarter old come Philip and Jacob.[8] I have kept it myself;
and see how he goes about° to abuse° me.   *out of his way / injure*

ESCALUS   That fellow is a fellow of much licence. Let him be
called before us. Away with her to prison. Go to, no more
words. Provost, my brother° Angelo will not be altered; Claudio   *colleague*

435   must die tomorrow. Let him be furnished with divines, and
have all charitable preparation.[9] If my brother wrought by° my   *acted according to*
pity, it should not be so with him.

PROVOST   So please you, this friar hath been with him and
advised him for th'entertainment° of death.   *acceptance*
        [*Exeunt* PROVOST *and* MISTRESS OVERDONE]

440   ESCALUS   Good even, good father.

DUKE   Bliss and goodness on you.

ESCALUS   Of whence are you?

DUKE   Not of this country, though my chance° is now   *fortune*
To use it for my time.° I am a brother   *dwell here at present*

445   Of gracious order, late come from the See°   *Vatican*
In special business from his Holiness.

ESCALUS   What news abroad i'th' world?

DUKE   None, but that there is so great a fever on goodness that
the dissolution of it must cure it.[1] Novelty is only in request,°   *alone in demand*

450   and it is as dangerous to be aged in° any kind of course as it is   *habituated to*
virtuous to be inconstant in any undertaking. There is scarce
truth° enough alive to make societies secure, but security[2]   *honesty; loyalty*
enough to make fellowships° accursed. Much upon° this riddle   *partnerships / According to*
runs the wisdom of the world. This news is old enough, yet it

---

3. *mutton:* prostitute (slang); it was forbidden to eat meat
on Fridays.
4. The food of the poor.
5. *back-wounding calumny:* slander ("calumny") is cowardly because it is not done to the victim's face.
6. Exceeding that recommended by Paul in Titus 3:10:
"Reject him that is an heretic, after once or twice admonition."
7. Varying the proverbial "make a saint swear."

8. May 1 was the Feast of St. Philip and St. James
(Jacob), but also the time of sexually licentious May Day
festivities, when the child was presumably conceived.
9. Spiritual preparation enjoined by Christian charity.
1. *there is . . . it:* that is, goodness is so sick that only
death will "cure" it.
2. Financial bonds liable to forfeit; blind trustfulness.
societies: association with others.

455   is every day's news. I pray you, sir, of what disposition was the Duke?

ESCALUS   One that, above all other strifes, contended especially
to know himself.[3]

DUKE   What pleasure was he given to?

ESCALUS   Rather rejoicing to see another merry than merry at
460   anything which professed° to make him rejoice; a gentleman   attempted
of all temperance. But leave we him to his events,° with a   affairs
prayer they may prove prosperous, and let me desire to know°   ask
how you find Claudio prepared. I am made to understand that
you have lent him visitation.°   visited him

465   DUKE   He professes to have received no sinister measure° from   unjust treatment
his judge, but most willingly humbles himself to the determi-
nation° of justice. Yet had he framed° to himself, by the instruc-   sentence / imagined
tion of his frailty, many deceiving promises of life, which I, by
my good leisure,° have discredited to him; and now is he   gradually
470   resolved to die.

ESCALUS   You have paid the heavens your function, and the prisoner the very debt of your calling.[4] I have laboured for the
poor gentleman to the extremest shore° of my modesty, but my   utmost limit
brother-justice have I found so severe that he hath forced me
475   to tell him he is indeed Justice.[5]

DUKE   If his own life answer° the straitness° of his proceeding, it   correspond to / strictness
shall become him well; wherein if he chance to fail, he hath
sentenced° himself.   condemned

ESCALUS   I am going to visit the prisoner. Fare you well.

480   DUKE   Peace be with you.   [*Exit* ESCALUS][6]
He who the sword of heaven[7] will bear
Should be as holy as severe,
Pattern in himself to know,
Grace to stand, and virtue go,[8]
485   More nor less to others paying
Than by self-offences° weighing.   his own offenses
Shame to him whose cruel striking
Kills for faults of his own liking!
Twice treble shame on Angelo,
490   To weed my vice,[9] and let his grow!
O, what may man within him hide,
Though angel on the outward side!
How may likeness made in crimes[1]
Make my practice on the times
495   To draw with idle spiders' strings
Most ponderous and substantial things?[2]
Craft against vice I must apply.
With Angelo tonight shall lie
His old betrothèd but despisèd.
500   So disguise shall, by th' disguisèd,[3]
Pay with falsehood false exacting,
And perform an old contracting.   *Exit*

---

3. "Know thyself" was proverbial advice.
4. You have repaid the heavens for giving you your vocation, and given the prisoner all he can expect of a friar.
5. Absolute justice personified.
6. For a reconstruction of the following episodes as they
were originally written, see Additional Passage B.
7. The authority of a ruler, conferred by God.
8. When to stand firm, and when to take action (?).

9. The Duke speaks as a representative sinner.
1. How can the similarity between Claudio's and
Angelo's offenses.
2. *To draw . . . things:* the law was proverbially compared
to a spider's web, which caught small insects but which
large insects could break through. *idle:* ineffectual.
3. Mariana, "disguised" as Isabella.

4.1

MARIANA [*discovered with a*] BOY *singing*

BOY   Take, O take those lips away
        That so sweetly were forsworn,°   *perjured*
        And those eyes, the break of day
        Lights° that do mislead° the morn;   *Suns / guide falsely*
5   But my kisses bring again, bring again,°   *return*
        Seals of love, though sealed in vain, sealed in vain.

Enter DUKE [*disguised as a friar*]

MARIANA   Break off thy song, and haste thee quick away.
    Here comes a man of comfort, whose advice
    Hath often stilled my brawling° discontent.   [*Exit* BOY]   *clamorous*
10   I cry you mercy,° sir, and well could wish   *beg your pardon*
    You had not found me here so musical.
    Let me excuse me, and believe me so:°   *in this*
    My mirth it much displeased, but pleased my woe.[1]
DUKE   'Tis good; though music oft hath such a charm°   *magic spell*
15   To make bad good,° and good provoke to harm. I pray you tell   *bad appear good*
    me, hath anybody enquired for me here today? Much upon°   *at about*
    this time have I promised here to meet.
MARIANA   You have not been enquired after; I have sat here all day.

Enter ISABELLA

DUKE   I do constantly° believe you; the time is come even now.   *assuredly*
20   I shall crave your forbearance° a little. Maybe I will call upon   *departure; patience*
    you anon, for some advantage to yourself.
MARIANA   I am always bound to you.   *Exit*
DUKE   Very well met, and welcome.
    What is the news from this good deputy?
25 ISABELLA   He hath a garden circummured° with brick,   *walled about*
    Whose western side is with a vineyard backed;
    And to that vineyard is a planckèd° gate,   *made of planks*
    That makes his opening with this bigger key.
    This other doth command a little door
30   Which from the vineyard to the garden leads.
    There have I made my promise
    Upon the heavy° middle of the night   *In the gloomy*
    To call upon him.
DUKE   But shall you on your knowledge° find this way?   *with this information*
35 ISABELLA   I have ta'en a due and wary note upon't.
    With whispering and most guilty diligence,
    In action all of precept,° he did show me   *With explanatory gestures*
    The way twice o'er.
DUKE   Are there no other tokens°   *signs*
    Between you 'greed concerning her observance?[2]
40 ISABELLA   No, none, but only a repair° i'th' dark,   *journey to the place*
    And that I have possessed° him my most° stay   *informed / longest*
    Can be but brief, for I have made him know
    I have a servant comes with me along
    That stays upon° me, whose persuasion is   *waits for*
    I come about my brother.
45 DUKE   'Tis well borne up.°   *maintained*

4.1 Location: Mariana's house. Probably Mariana and the Boy are "discovered" by drawing back a curtain to reveal the characters within an alcove at the back of the stage.

1. The music drove away mirth but nurtured melancholy.
2. That she (Mariana) must observe.

I have not yet made known to Mariana
A word of this.—What ho, within! Come forth!

Enter MARIANA

[*To* MARIANA] I pray you be acquainted with this maid.
She comes to do you good.

ISABELLA   I do desire the like.

50   DUKE [*to* MARIANA]   Do you persuade yourself° that I respect you?   *believe*
MARIANA   Good friar, I know you do, and so have found it.
DUKE   Take then this your companion° by the hand,   *partner*
Who hath a story ready for your ear.
I shall attend your leisure;° but make haste,   *wait until you are ready*
The vaporous night approaches.

55   MARIANA [*to* ISABELLA]   Will't please you walk aside?

Exeunt [MARIANA *and* ISABELLA]

DUKE[3]   O place° and greatness, millions of false° eyes   *rank / misjudging*
Are stuck° upon thee; volumes of report°   *fixed / rumors*
Run with their false and most contrarious quest°   *misguided inquiry*
Upon thy doings; thousand escapes° of wit   *sallies*
60   Make thee the father° of their idle dream,°   *subject / fantasy*
And rack[4] thee in their fancies.

Enter MARIANA *and* ISABELLA

Welcome. How agreed?

ISABELLA   She'll take the enterprise upon her, father,
If you advise it.

DUKE   It is not my consent,
But my entreaty too.

ISABELLA [*to* MARIANA]   Little have you to say
65   When you depart from him but, soft and low,
'Remember now my brother'.

MARIANA   Fear me not.[5]

DUKE   Nor, gentle daughter, fear you not at all.
He is your husband on a pre-contract.°   *formal betrothal*
To bring you thus together 'tis no sin,
70   Sith that° the justice of your title to him   *Since*
Doth flourish° the deceit. Come, let us go.   *give propriety to*
Our corn's to reap, for yet our tilth's° to sow.   *Exeunt*   *tilled land*

4.2

Enter PROVOST *and* [POMPEY]

PROVOST   Come hither, sirrah. Can you cut off a man's head?
POMPEY   If the man be a bachelor, sir, I can; but if he be a married man, he's his wife's head,[1] and I can never cut off a woman's head.[2]
5   PROVOST   Come, sir, leave me° your snatches,° and yield me a   *stop / quips*
direct answer. Tomorrow morning are to die Claudio and Bar-
nardine. Here is in our prison a common executioner, who in
his office lacks a helper. If you will take it on you to assist him,
it shall redeem you from your gyves;° if not, you shall have   *fetters*

---

3. The following lines, which seem out of context, may
have originally been part of the Duke's soliloquy at the
end of Act 3.
4. Misrepresent (literally, "torture by stretching").
5. Rely upon me; but the Duke takes "fear" in its modern
sense.

4.2 Location: The prison.
1. Alluding to Paul's doctrine "the husband is the wife's
head," Ephesians 5:23.
2. Playing on "married woman's maidenhead," an
improbability.

10   your full time of imprisonment, and your deliverance with an
    unpitied° whipping; for you have been a notorious bawd.   *unmerciful*

POMPEY   Sir, I have been an unlawful bawd time out of mind,
    but yet I will be content to be a lawful hangman. I would be
    glad to receive some instruction from my fellow partner.

15 PROVOST   What ho, Abhorson! Where's Abhorson there?

        Enter ABHORSON

ABHORSON   Do you call, sir?

PROVOST   Sirrah, here's a fellow will help you tomorrow in your
    execution. If you think it meet, compound with him by the
    year,[3] and let him abide here with you; if not, use him for the

20   present, and dismiss him. He cannot plead his estimation° with   *reputation*
    you; he hath been a bawd.

ABHORSON   A bawd, sir? Fie upon him, he will discredit our mystery.[4]

PROVOST   Go to, sir, you weigh equally; a feather will turn the scale.

                        Exit

POMPEY   Pray, sir, by your good favour°—for surely, sir, a good   *permission*

25   favour° you have, but that you have a hanging look[5]—do you   *face*
    call, sir, your occupation a mystery?

ABHORSON   Ay, sir, a mystery.

POMPEY   Painting,[6] sir, I have heard say is a mystery; and your
    whores, sir, being members of my occupation, using painting,

30   do prove my occupation a mystery. But what mystery there
    should be in hanging, if I should be hanged I cannot imagine.

ABHORSON   Sir, it is a mystery.

POMPEY   Proof.

ABHORSON   Every true man's apparel fits your thief[7]—

35 POMPEY   If it be too little for your thief, your true man thinks it
    big enough.° If it be too big for your thief, your thief thinks it   *a big enough loss*
    little enough.° So every true man's apparel fits your thief.   *a small enough gain*

        Enter PROVOST

PROVOST   Are you agreed?

POMPEY   Sir, I will serve him, for I do find your hangman is

40   a more penitent trade than your bawd—he doth oftener ask
    forgiveness.[8]

PROVOST [*to* ABHORSON]   You, sirrah, provide your block and
    your axe tomorrow, four o'clock.

ABHORSON [*to* POMPEY]   Come on, bawd, I will instruct thee in

45   my trade. Follow.

POMPEY   I do desire to learn, sir, and I hope, if you have occasion
    to use me for your own turn, you shall find me yare.° For truly,   *skillful; eager*
    sir, for your kindness I owe you a good turn.[9]

PROVOST   Call hither Barnardine and Claudio.

        Exeunt [ABHORSON *and* POMPEY]

50   Th'one has my pity; not a jot the other,
    Being a murderer, though he were my brother.

        Enter CLAUDIO

    Look, here's the warrant, Claudio, for thy death.
    'Tis now dead midnight, and by eight tomorrow
    Thou must be made immortal. Where's Barnardine?

---

3. Settle regular terms of employment with him.
4. Profession, requiring specialized skills and training.
5. Downcast expression; hangman's face.
6. Artist's occupation; use of cosmetics.
7. Abhorson implies that the thief assumes the character of an honest man by stealing his clothing; he also

suggests an analogy between the thief and the hangman, who was awarded the clothes of his victims.
8. Executioners customarily asked forgiveness of their
victims before killing them.
9. Favor; turning off the scaffold.

55 CLAUDIO   As fast locked up in sleep as guiltless labour
When it lies starkly° in the travailer's° bones.   *stiffly / worker's*
He will not wake.
PROVOST   Who can do good on him?
Well, go prepare yourself.
          [*Knocking within*]
                              But hark, what noise?
Heaven give your spirits comfort!   [*Exit* CLAUDIO]
          [*Knocking again*]
                              By and by!
60 I hope it is some pardon or reprieve
For the most gentle Claudio.
                    Enter DUKE [*disguised as a friar*]
                              Welcome, father.
DUKE   The best and wholesom'st spirits of the night
Envelop you, good Provost! Who called here of late?
PROVOST   None since the curfew[1] rung.
65 DUKE   Not Isabel?
PROVOST   No.
DUKE   They will then, ere't be long.
PROVOST   What comfort is for Claudio?
DUKE   There's some in hope.
70 PROVOST   It is a bitter° deputy.   *cruel*
DUKE   Not so, not so; his life is paralleled
Even with the stroke and line[2] of his great justice.
He doth with holy abstinence subdue
That in himself which he spurs on his power
75 To qualify° in others. Were he mealed° with that   *moderate / stained*
Which he corrects, then were he tyrannous;
But this being so, he's just.
          [*Knocking within*]
                              Now are they come.
          [*The* PROVOST *goes to a door*]
This is a gentle Provost. Seldom when°   *Rarely*
The steelèd° jailer is the friend of men.   *hard-hearted*
          [*Knocking within*]
[*To* PROVOST] How now, what noise? That spirit's possessed
80   with haste
That wounds th'unlisting postern° with these strokes.   *unyielding door*
PROVOST   There he° must stay until the officer   *(the messenger)*
Arise to let him in. He° is called up.   *(the officer)*
DUKE   Have you no countermand for Claudio yet,
But he must die tomorrow?
85 PROVOST   None, sir, none.
DUKE   As near the dawning, Provost, as it is,
You shall hear more ere morning.
PROVOST   Happily°   *Perhaps*
You something know, yet I believe there comes
No countermand. No such example° have we;   *precedent*
90 Besides, upon the very siege° of justice   *seat*
Lord Angelo hath to the public ear
Professed the contrary.

---

1. Evening bell, rung at 9:00 P.M.
2. Exact course; also suggesting ax blows and hanging ropes.

Enter a MESSENGER

This is his lordship's man.

DUKE   And here comes Claudio's pardon.

95 MESSENGER [*giving a paper to* PROVOST]   My lord hath sent you
this note, and by me this further charge: that you swerve not
from the smallest article of it, neither in time, matter, or other
circumstance. Good morrow; for, as I take it, it is almost day.

PROVOST   I shall obey him.   [*Exit* MESSENGER]

100 DUKE [*aside*]   This is his pardon, purchased by such sin
For which the pardoner himself is in.
Hence hath offence his° quick celerity,   *its*
When it is borne in high authority.
When vice makes mercy, mercy's so extended

105 That for the fault's love³ is th'offender friended.°—   *befriended*
Now sir, what news?

PROVOST   I told you: Lord Angelo, belike thinking me remiss in
mine office, awakens me with this unwonted putting-on;°   *urging*
methinks strangely, for he hath not used° it before.   *practiced*

110 DUKE   Pray you let's hear.

PROVOST [*reading the letter*]   'Whatsoever you may hear to the
contrary, let Claudio be executed by four of the clock, and in
the afternoon Barnardine. For my better satisfaction, let me
have Claudio's head sent me by five. Let this be duly per-

115 formed, with a thought that more depends on it than we must
yet deliver.° Thus fail not to do your office, as you will answer   *make known*
it at your peril.'
What say you to this, sir?

DUKE   What is that Barnardine, who is to be executed in th'afternoon?

120 PROVOST   A Bohemian born, but here nursed up and bred; one
that is a prisoner nine years old.°   *nine years a prisoner*

DUKE   How came it that the absent Duke had not either delivered him to his liberty or executed him? I have heard it was
ever his manner to do so.

125 PROVOST   His friends still° wrought reprieves for him; and indeed   *continually*
his fact,° till now in the government of Lord Angelo, came not   *crime*
to an undoubtful° proof.   *a certain*

DUKE   It is now apparent?

PROVOST   Most manifest, and not denied by himself.

130 DUKE   Hath he borne himself penitently in prison? How seems
he to be touched?°   *affected*

PROVOST   A man that apprehends death no more dreadfully but as
a drunken sleep; careless, reckless, and fearless of what's past,
present, or to come; insensible of mortality, and desperately

135 mortal.⁴

DUKE   He wants° advice.   *needs*

PROVOST   He will hear none. He hath evermore had the liberty
of the prison. Give him leave to escape hence, he would not.
Drunk many times a day, if not many days entirely° drunk. We   *continuously*

140 have very oft awaked him as if to carry him to execution, and
showed him a seeming warrant for it; it hath not moved him at all.

DUKE   More of him anon. There is written in your brow, Provost,
honesty and constancy. If I read it not truly, my ancient skill

3. For love of the fault.   4. Reckless of death, and in a state of mortal sin.

beguiles me. But in the boldness° of my cunning,° I will lay   confidence / skill
145 myself in hazard.⁵ Claudio, whom here you have warrant to
execute, is no greater forfeit to the law than Angelo who hath
sentenced him. To make you understand this in a manifested
effect,° I crave but four days' respite, for the which you are to   clear demonstration
do me both a present° and a dangerous courtesy.°   an immediate / favor
150 PROVOST Pray sir, in what?
DUKE In the delaying death.
PROVOST Alack, how may I do it, having the hour limited, and
an express command under penalty to deliver his head in the
view of Angelo? I may make my case as Claudio's to cross° this   oppose
155 in the smallest.
DUKE By the vow of mine order, I warrant you, if my instructions
may be your guide, let this Barnardine be this morning executed, and his head borne to Angelo.
PROVOST Angelo hath seen them both, and will discover° the   discern
160 favour.
DUKE O, death's a great disguiser, and you may add to it. Shave
the head and tie the beard, and say it was the desire of the
penitent to be so bared before his death; you know the course
is common. If anything fall to you upon° this more than thanks   as a result of
165 and good fortune, by the saint whom I profess,⁶ I will plead
against it with my life.
PROVOST Pardon me, good father, it is against my oath.
DUKE Were you sworn to the Duke or to the deputy?
PROVOST To him and to his substitutes.
170 DUKE You will think you have made no offence if the Duke
avouch° the justice of your dealing?   vouch for
PROVOST But what likelihood is in that?
DUKE Not a resemblance,° but a certainty. Yet since I see you   likelihood
fearful, that neither my coat,° integrity, nor persuasion can with   religious garb
175 ease attempt you,° I will go further than I meant, to pluck all   win you over
fears out of you. [Showing a letter] Look you, sir, here is the
hand and seal of the Duke. You know the character,° I doubt   handwriting
not, and the signet is not strange to you?
PROVOST I know them both.
180 DUKE The contents of this is the return of the Duke. You shall
anon° over-read it at your pleasure, where you shall find within   right away
these two days he will be here. This is a thing that Angelo
knows not, for he this very day receives letters of strange tenor,
perchance of the Duke's death, perchance entering into some
185 monastery; but by chance nothing of what is writ.° Look, th'un-   written here
folding star⁷ calls up the shepherd. Put not yourself into amaze-
ment° how these things should be. All difficulties are but easy   perplexity
when they are known. Call your executioner, and off with Bar-
nardine's head. I will give him a present shrift,° and advise him   an immediate confession
190 for a better place. Yet° you are amazed; but this° shall abso-   Still / (the letter)
lutely resolve you.° Come away, it is almost clear dawn.   free you from doubt

Exeunt

---

5. I will bet on it; I will put myself in peril.   7. Morning star (which tells the shepherd he may
6. The patron saint of my order.   safely release the sheep from the fold).

4.3

Enter [POMPEY]

POMPEY I am as well acquainted here as I was in our house of
profession.[1] One would think it were Mistress Overdone's own
house, for here be many of her old customers. First, here's
young Master Rash; he's in for a commodity[2] of brown paper
and old ginger, nine score and seventeen pounds, of which he
made five marks ready money.[3] Marry, then ginger[4] was not
much in request, for the old women were all dead.[5] Then is
there here one Master Caper,° at the suit of Master Threepile[6]   *fashionable dance*
the mercer,° for some four suits of peach-coloured satin, which   *cloth dealer*
now peaches° him a beggar. Then have we here young Dizzy,   *impeaches; declares*
and young Master Deepvow, and Master Copperspur and Mas-
ter Starve-lackey[7] the rapier and dagger man,[8] and young Drop-
hair[9] that killed lusty Pudding,° and Master Forthright the   *stuffed guts*
tilter,° and brave Master Shoe-tie the great traveller,[1] and wild   *fencer*
Half-can that stabbed Pots,[2] and I think forty more, all great
doers in our trade, and are now 'for the Lord's sake'.[3]

Enter ABHORSON

ABHORSON Sirrah, bring Barnardine hither.

POMPEY Master Barnardine! You must rise[4] and be hanged,
Master Barnardine!

ABHORSON What ho, Barnardine!

BARNARDINE [*within*] A pox o' your throats! Who makes that
noise there? What are you?

POMPEY Your friends, sir; the hangman. You must be so good,
sir, to rise and be put to death.

BARNARDINE Away, you rogue, away! I am sleepy.

ABHORSON Tell him he must awake, and that quickly too.

POMPEY Pray, Master Barnardine, awake till you are executed,
and sleep afterwards.

ABHORSON Go in to him and fetch him out.

POMPEY He is coming, sir, he is coming. I hear his straw rustle.

ABHORSON Is the axe upon the block, sirrah?

POMPEY Very ready, sir.

Enter BARNARDINE

BARNARDINE How now, Abhorson, what's the news with you?

ABHORSON Truly, sir, I would desire you to clap into[5] your prayers, for, look you, the warrant's come.

BARNARDINE You rogue, I have been drinking all night. I am not
fitted for't.

POMPEY O, the better, sir; for he that drinks all night, and is
hanged betimes° in the morning, may sleep the sounder all the   *early*
next day.

Enter DUKE [*disguised as a friar*]

4.3 Location: Scene continues.
1. Religious house ("nunnery" was slang for "brothel").
2. To evade the statutory limit on interest, usurers would
give borrowers part of their loan in practically worthless
"commodities," which they were supposed to sell for
ready money. *he's in for:* he's in for falling into debt here.
3. Rash paid 197 pounds for the "commodity," a very
large sum, and sold it for about 3.3 pounds.
4. Used to make warming tonics.
5. Presumably victims of the 1603 plague, mentioned
earlier by Mistress Overdone.

6. Richest sort of velvet.
7. One who fails to feed his servants.
8. Suggesting a reputation for brawling.
9. Premature baldness was a sign of syphilis.
1. Observer of foreign fashions (probably ironic).
2. Suggesting drinking cups.
3. The cry of prisoners begging from the prison grate.
Prisoners had to pay for their own food and lodging.
4. Get out of bed; mount the scaffold.
5. Immediately begin; join your hands for.

ABHORSON [*to* BARNARDINE]   Look you, sir, here comes your
ghostly° father. Do we jest now, think you?   spiritual
DUKE [*to* BARNARDINE]   Sir, induced by my charity, and hearing
how hastily you are to depart, I am come to advise you, comfort
45   you, and pray with you.
BARNARDINE   Friar, not I. I have been drinking hard all night,
and I will have more time to prepare me, or they shall beat out
my brains with billets.° I will not consent to die this day, that's   thick sticks
certain.
50   DUKE   O sir, you must; and therefore, I beseech you,
Look forward on the journey you shall go.
BARNARDINE   I swear I will not die today, for any man's persuasion.
DUKE   But hear you—
BARNARDINE   Not a word. If you have anything to say to me,
55   come to my ward,° for thence will not I today.   *Exit*   cell
DUKE   Unfit to live or die. O gravel° heart!   (*i.e., hard*)
After him, fellows; bring him to the block.
                    [*Exeunt* ABHORSON *and* POMPEY]
            Enter PROVOST
PROVOST   Now, sir, how do you find the prisoner?
DUKE   A creature unprepared, unmeet° for death;   unfit
60   And to transport° him in the mind he is   execute (euphemistic)
Were damnable.
PROVOST   Here in the prison, father,
There died this morning of a cruel fever
One Ragusine, a most notorious pirate,
A man of Claudio's years, his beard and head
65   Just of his colour. What if we do omit°   disregard
This reprobate till he were well inclined,
And satisfy the deputy with the visage
Of Ragusine, more like to Claudio?
DUKE   O, 'tis an accident that heaven provides.
70   Dispatch it presently; the hour draws on
Prefixed° by Angelo. See this be done,   Fixed in advance
And sent according to command, whiles I
Persuade this rude° wretch willingly to die.   uncivilized
PROVOST   This shall be done, good father, presently.
75   But Barnardine must die this afternoon;
And how shall we continue° Claudio,   maintain
To save me from the danger that might come
If he were known alive?
DUKE   Let this be done:
Put them in secret holds,° both Barnardine and Claudio.   cells
80   Ere twice the sun hath made his journal° greeting   daily
To yonder generation,[6] you shall find
Your safety manifested.
PROVOST   I am your free dependant.°   willing servant
DUKE   Quick, dispatch, and send the head to Angelo.
                    Exit [PROVOST]
Now will I write letters to Angelo[7]—
85   The Provost, he shall bear them—whose contents
Shall witness to him I am near at home,

6. That is, the people outside the prison.
7. "Angelo" may be an error for "Varrius," whom the Duke meets outside the city in 4.5.

And that by great injunctions° I am bound   *for compelling reasons*
To enter publicly. Him I'll desire
To meet me at the consecrated fount
90   A league below the city, and from thence,
By cold gradation° and well-balanced form,   *deliberate degrees*
We shall proceed with Angelo.

       Enter PROVOST [*with Ragusine's head*]

PROVOST   Here is the head; I'll carry it myself.
DUKE   Convenient° is it. Make a swift return,   *Suitable*
95   For I would commune° with you of such things   *confer*
That want no ear but yours.
PROVOST   I'll make all speed.   *Exit*
ISABELLA [*within*]   Peace, ho, be here!
DUKE   The tongue of Isabel. She's come to know
100   If yet her brother's pardon be come hither;
But I will keep her ignorant of her good,
To make her heavenly comforts of° despair   *out of*
When it is least expected.
ISABELLA [*within*]   Ho, by your leave!

       Enter ISABELLA

DUKE   Good morning to you, fair and gracious daughter.
105 ISABELLA   The better, given me° by so holy a man.   *so greeted*
Hath yet the deputy sent my brother's pardon?
DUKE   He hath released him, Isabel, from the world.
His head is off and sent to Angelo.
ISABELLA   Nay, but it is not so.
DUKE   It is no other.
110   Show your wisdom, daughter, in your close° patience.   *silent*
ISABELLA   O, I will to° him and pluck out his eyes!   *will go to*
DUKE   You shall not be admitted to his sight.
ISABELLA [*weeping*]   Unhappy Claudio! Wretched Isabel!
Injurious world! Most damnèd Angelo!
115 DUKE   This nor° hurts him, nor profits you a jot.   *neither*
Forbear it, therefore; give your cause° to heaven.   *grievance*
Mark what I say, which you shall find
By every syllable a faithful verity.
The Duke comes home tomorrow—nay, dry your eyes—
120   One of our convent, and his confessor,
Gives me this instance.° Already he hath carried   *indication*
Notice to Escalus and Angelo,
Who do prepare to meet him at the gates,
There to give up their power. If you can pace° your wisdom   *train to walk*
125   In that good path that I would wish it go,
And you shall have your bosom° on this wretch,   *desire*
Grace° of the Duke, revenges to your heart,   *Favor*
And general honour.
ISABELLA   I am directed by you.
DUKE   This letter, then, to Friar Peter give.
130   'Tis that he sent me of the Duke's return.
Say by this token I desire his company
At Mariana's house tonight. Her cause and yours
I'll perfect° him withal, and he shall bring you   *fully instruct*
Before the Duke, and to the head of° Angelo   *and directly to*
135   Accuse him home and home.° For my poor self,   *to the utmost*
I am combinèd° by a sacred vow,   *bound*

And shall be absent. [*Giving the letter*] Wend you° with this letter.   *Depart*
Command these fretting° waters from your eyes   *agitated; corrosive*
With a light heart. Trust not my holy order
If I pervert° your course.   *lead astray*

Enter LUCIO

Who's here?

140 LUCIO   Good even.°   *evening*
Friar, where's the Provost?

DUKE   Not within, sir.

LUCIO   O pretty Isabella, I am pale at mine heart to see thine
eyes so red. Thou must be patient. I am fain to dine and sup
with water and bran;[8] I dare not for my head fill my belly; one
145   fruitful° meal would set me to't.[9] But they say the Duke will be   *plentiful*
here tomorrow. By my troth, Isabel, I loved thy brother. If the
old fantastical° Duke of dark corners° had been at home, he   *capricious/secret places*
had lived.   [*Exit* ISABELLA]

DUKE   Sir, the Duke is marvellous° little beholden to your   *remarkably*
150   reports; but the best is, he lives not° in them.   *is not to be found*

LUCIO   Friar, thou knowest not the Duke so well as I do. He's a
better woodman[1] than thou tak'st him for.

DUKE   Well, you'll answer° this one day. Fare ye well.   *account for*

LUCIO   Nay, tarry, I'll go along with thee. I can tell thee pretty
155   tales of the Duke.

DUKE   You have told me too many of him already, sir, if they be
true; if not true, none were enough.

LUCIO   I was once before him for getting a wench with child.

DUKE   Did you such a thing?

160 LUCIO   Yes, marry, did I; but I was fain to forswear it. They would
else° have married me to the rotten medlar.[2]   *otherwise*

DUKE   Sir, your company is fairer° than honest. Rest you well.   *more speciously pleasant*

LUCIO   By my troth, I'll go with thee to the lane's end. If bawdy
talk offend you, we'll have very little of it. Nay, friar, I am a
165   kind of burr; I shall stick.   *Exeunt*

4.4

Enter ANGELO *and* ESCALUS

ESCALUS   Every letter he hath writ hath disvouched other.°   *repudiated the others*

ANGELO   In most uneven and distracted manner. His actions
show much like to madness. Pray heaven his wisdom be not
tainted.° And why meet him at the gates, and redeliver our   *impaired*
5   authorities there?

ESCALUS   I guess not.

ANGELO   And why should we proclaim it in an hour before his
entering, that if any crave redress of injustice, they should
exhibit° their petitions in the street?   *present*

10 ESCALUS   He shows his reason for that—to have a dispatch° of   *prompt settlement*
complaints, and to deliver us from devices° hereafter, which   *contrivances*
shall then have no power to stand against us.

ANGELO   Well, I beseech you let it be proclaimed.
Betimes° i'th' morn I'll call you at your house.   *Early*

---

8. Diet thought to suppress lust.
9. Would incite me to lechery.
1. Hunter (literally, of game; here, of women).

2. Kind of pear eaten when rotten; slang for "prostitute."
4.4 Location: Vienna.

15   Give notice to such men of sort and suit°   *rank and retinue*
          As are to meet him.

ESCALUS   I shall, sir. Fare you well.

ANGELO   Good night.   *Exit* [ESCALUS]

          This deed unshapes° me quite, makes me unpregnant°   *destroys/unready*
20   And dull to all proceedings. A deflowered maid,
          And by an eminent body[1] that enforced°   *exerted; raped*
          The law against it! But that her tender shame
          Will not proclaim against her maiden loss,°   *loss of virginity*
          How might she tongue° me! Yet reason dares her no,[2]   *reproach*
25   For my authority bears off a credent bulk,[3]
          That no particular° scandal once can touch   *private; single*
          But it confounds° the breather. He should have lived, *confutes; overthrows*
          Save that his riotous youth, with dangerous sense,° *sensibility; sensuality*
          Might in the times to come have ta'en revenge
30   By° so receiving a dishonoured life   *Because of*
          With ransom of such shame. Would yet he had lived.
          Alack, when once our grace we have forgot,
          Nothing goes right; we would, and we would not.   *Exit*

4.5

Enter DUKE, [*in his own habit*] *and* FRIAR PETER

DUKE   These letters at fit time deliver me.
          The Provost knows our purpose and our plot.
          The matter being afoot, keep° your instruction,   *observe*
          And hold you ever to our special drift,°   *purpose*
5   Though sometimes you do blench° from this to that   *swerve*
          As cause doth minister.° Go call at Flavio's house,   *serve*
          And tell him where I stay. Give the like notice
          To Valentinus, Rowland, and to Crassus,
          And bid them bring the trumpets° to the gate.   *trumpeters*
          But send me Flavius first.
10 FRIAR PETER   It shall be speeded well.°   [*Exit*]   *quickly done*

Enter VARRIUS

DUKE   I thank thee, Varrius; thou hast made good haste.
          Come, we will walk.° There's other of our friends   *withdraw*
          Will greet us here anon. My gentle° Varrius!   *Exeunt*   *noble*

4.6

Enter ISABELLA *and* MARIANA

ISABELLA   To speak so indirectly° I am loath—   *evasively*
          I would say the truth, but to accuse him so,
          That is your part—yet I am advised to do it,
          He says, to veil full purpose.

MARIANA   Be ruled by him.

5 ISABELLA   Besides, he tells me that if peradventure
          He speak against me on the adverse side,
          I should not think it strange, for 'tis a physic°   *medicine*
          That's bitter to sweet end.

Enter [FRIAR] PETER

MARIANA   I would Friar Peter—

---

1. Person (also suggesting the physical body).
2. Makes her dare not.
3. Sustains such massive credibility.

4.5 Location: Outside the city.
4.6 Location: A street near the city gates.

10 ISABELLA   O, peace; the friar is come.
FRIAR PETER   Come, I have found you out a stand° most fit,   *place*
Where you may have such vantage° on the Duke   *advantageous position*
He shall not pass you. Twice have the trumpets sounded.[1]
The generous° and gravest citizens   *noble*
15 Have hent° the gates, and very near upon   *reached*
The Duke is ent'ring; therefore hence, away.   *Exeunt*

5.1

Enter [at one door] DUKE, VARRIUS, [*and*] *lords;* [*at
another door*] ANGELO, ESCALUS, LUCIO, *citizens* [*and
officers*]

DUKE [*to* ANGELO]   My very worthy cousin,° fairly met.   *fellow nobleman*
[*To* ESCALUS] Our old and faithful friend, we are glad to see you.
ANGELO *and* ESCALUS   Happy return be to your royal grace.
DUKE   Many and hearty thankings to you both.
5 We have made enquiry of you, and we hear
Such goodness of your justice that our soul
Cannot but yield you forth to public thanks,
Forerunning more requital.°   *greater reward*
ANGELO   You make my bonds° still greater.   *obligations*
DUKE   O, your desert speaks loud, and I should wrong it
10 To lock it in the wards° of covert bosom,   *prison cells*
When it deserves with characters° of brass   *letters*
A forted° residence 'gainst the tooth of time   *fortified*
And razure° of oblivion. Give me your hand,   *erasure*
And let the subject° see, to make them know   *people*
15 That outward courtesies would fain proclaim
Favours that keep° within. Come, Escalus,   *dwell*
You must walk by us on our other hand,
And good supporters[1] are you.
[*They walk forward*]
Enter [FRIAR] PETER *and* ISABELLA
FRIAR PETER   Now is your time. Speak loud, and kneel before him.
20 ISABELLA [*kneeling*]   Justice, O royal Duke! Vail your regard°   *Look down*
Upon a wronged—I would fain° have said, a maid.   *like to*
O worthy prince, dishonour not your eye
By throwing it on any other object,
Till you have heard me in my true complaint,
25 And given me justice, justice, justice, justice!
DUKE   Relate your wrongs. In what? By whom? Be brief.
Here is Lord Angelo shall give you justice.
Reveal yourself° to him.   *(your complaint)*
ISABELLA   O worthy Duke,
You bid me seek redemption of the devil.
30 Hear me yourself, for that which I must speak
Must either punish me, not being believed,
Or wring redress from you. Hear me, O hear me, hear!
ANGELO   My lord, her wits, I fear me, are not firm.
She hath been a suitor to me for her brother,
Cut off° by course of justice.   *Executed*
35 ISABELLA [*standing*]   By course of justice!

---

1. The third flourish will signal the Duke's arrival.
5.1 Location: The city gates.

1. Attendants; in heraldry, "supporters" are figures
depicted beside a shield, holding it up.

ANGELO   And she will speak most bitterly and strange.

ISABELLA   Most strange, but yet most truly, will I speak.

 That Angelo's forsworn, is it not strange?

 That Angelo's a murderer, is't not strange?

40 That Angelo is an adulterous thief,

 An hypocrite, a virgin-violator,

 Is it not strange, and strange?

DUKE   Nay, it is ten times strange!

ISABELLA   It is not truer he is Angelo

 Than this is all as true as it is strange.

45 Nay, it is ten times true, for truth is truth

 To th'end of reck'ning.[2]

DUKE   Away with her. Poor soul,

 She speaks this in th'infirmity of sense.

ISABELLA   O prince, I conjure° thee, as thou believ'st   *appeal to*

 There is another comfort than this world,

50 That thou neglect me not with that opinion

 That I am touched with madness. Make not impossible

 That which but seems unlike.° 'Tis not impossible   *unlikely*

 But° one, the wicked'st caitiff° on the ground,   *That/villain*

 May seem as shy,° as grave, as just, as absolute,°   *reserved/perfect*

55 As Angelo; even so may Angelo,

 In all his dressings, characts,[3] titles, forms,°   *formalities*

 Be an arch-villain. Believe it, royal prince,

 If he be less, he's nothing; but he's more,

 Had I more name for badness.

DUKE   By mine honesty,

60 If she be mad, as I believe no other,

 Her madness hath the oddest frame° of sense,   *shape*

 Such a dependency° of thing on thing   *connected sequence*

 As e'er I heard in madness.

ISABELLA   O gracious Duke,

 Harp not on that, nor do not banish reason

65 For inequality;[4] but let your reason serve

 To make the truth appear where it seems hid,

 And hide the false seems° true.   *that seems*

DUKE   Many that are not mad

 Have sure more lack of reason. What would you say?

ISABELLA   I am the sister of one Claudio,

70 Condemned upon the act of° fornication   *decree against*

 To lose his head, condemned by Angelo.

 I, in probation of a sisterhood,

 Was sent to by my brother, one Lucio

 As° then the messenger.   *Being*

LUCIO   That's I, an't like your grace.

75 I came to her from Claudio, and desired her

 To try her gracious fortune with Lord Angelo

 For her poor brother's pardon.

ISABELLA   That's he indeed.

DUKE [*to* LUCIO]   You were not bid to speak.

---

2. *for truth . . . reck'ning*: echoing 1 Esdras 4:38: "But
truth doth abide, and is strong forever, and liveth and
reigneth for ever and ever." *reck'ning*: day of reckoning.

3. Signs (of office).

4. Difference in rank (between Isabella and Angelo); discrepancy (between my report and what seems true).

LUCIO   No, my good lord,
    Nor wished to hold my peace.
80   DUKE   I wish you now, then. Pray you take note of it;
    And when you have a business for yourself,
    Pray heaven you then be perfect.
LUCIO   I warrant° your honour.   *assure*
    DUKE   The warrant's[5] for yourself; take heed to't.
ISABELLA   This gentleman told somewhat of my tale—
85   LUCIO   Right.
    DUKE   It may be right, but you are i'the wrong
    To speak before your time. [*To* ISABELLA] Proceed.
ISABELLA   I went
    To this pernicious caitiff deputy—
    DUKE   That's somewhat madly spoken.
ISABELLA   Pardon it;
    The phrase is to the matter.°   *appropriate*
90   DUKE   Mended again.
    The matter; proceed.
ISABELLA   In brief, to set the needless process by,[6]
    How I persuaded, how I prayed and kneeled,
    How he refelled° me, and how I replied—   *repelled*
95   For this was of much length—the vile conclusion
    I now begin with grief and shame to utter.
    He would not, but by gift of my chaste body
    To his concupiscible° intemperate lust,   *desirous*
    Release my brother; and after much debatement,
100   My sisterly remorse confutes° mine honour,   *overcomes*
    And I did yield to him. But the next morn betimes,
    His purpose surfeiting,° he sends a warrant   *satisfied*
    For my poor brother's head.
    DUKE   This is most likely!
ISABELLA   O, that it were as like° as it is true!   *probable*
105   DUKE   By heaven, fond° wretch, thou knows't not what thou speak'st,   *foolish*
    Or else thou art suborned against his honour
    In hateful practice.° First, his integrity   *conspiracy*
    Stands without blemish. Next, it imports no reason°   *makes no sense*
    That with such vehemency he should pursue
110   Faults proper° to himself. If he had so offended,   *belonging*
    He would have weighed thy brother by himself,
    And not have cut him off. Someone hath set you on.°   *incited you*
    Confess the truth, and say by whose advice
    Thou cam'st here to complain.
ISABELLA   And is this all?
115   Then, O you blessèd ministers° above,   *angels*
    Keep me in patience, and with ripened time
    Unfold the evil which is here wrapped up
    In countenance![7] Heaven shield your grace from woe,
    As I, thus wronged, hence unbelievèd go.
120   DUKE   I know you'd fain be gone. An officer!
    To prison with her.
             [*An officer guards* ISABELLA]
                    Shall we thus permit

5. That is, for arrest, punning on the verb in line 83.   7. In false appearance; in royal favor.
6. To skip unnecessary parts of the story.

A blasting° and a scandalous breath to fall   *blighting*
On him so near us? This needs must be a practice.°   *conspiracy*
Who knew of your intent and coming hither?

125 ISABELLA   One that I would were here, Friar Lodowick.⁸

[*Exit, guarded*]

DUKE   A ghostly father, belike. Who knows that Lodowick?

LUCIO   My lord, I know him. 'Tis a meddling friar;
I do not like the man. Had he been lay, my lord,
For certain words he spake against your grace
130 In your retirement, I had swinged° him soundly.   *beat*

DUKE   Words against me? This'° a good friar, belike!   *This is*
And to set on this wretched woman here
Against our substitute! Let this friar be found.

[*Exit one or more*]

LUCIO   But yesternight, my lord, she and that friar,
135 I saw them at the prison. A saucy friar,
A very scurvy fellow.

FRIAR PETER   Blessed be your royal grace!
I have stood by, my lord, and I have heard
Your royal ear abused. First hath this woman
Most wrongfully accused your substitute,
140 Who is as free from touch or soil with her
As she from one ungot.°   *not yet begotten*

DUKE   We did believe no less.
Know you that Friar Lodowick that she speaks of?

FRIAR PETER   I know him for a man divine and holy,
Not scurvy, nor a temporary meddler,⁹
145 As he's reported by this gentleman;
And, on my trust, a man that never yet
Did, as he vouches,° misreport your grace.   *asserts*

LUCIO   My lord, most villainously; believe it.

FRIAR PETER   Well, he in time may come to clear himself;
150 But at this instant he is sick, my lord,
Of a strange fever. Upon his mere° request,   *Solely at his*
Being come to knowledge that there was complaint
Intended 'gainst Lord Angelo, came I hither
To speak, as from his mouth, what he doth know
155 Is true and false, and what he with his oath
And all probation° will make up full clear   *proof*
Whensoever he's convented.° First, for this woman: *summoned*
To justify° this worthy nobleman,   *vindicate*
So vulgarly and personally accused,
160 Her shall you hear disprovèd to her eyes,
Till she herself confess it.

DUKE   Good friar, let's hear it.

[*Exit FRIAR PETER*]

Do you not smile at this, Lord Angelo?
O heaven, the vanity of wretched fools!
Give us some seats.

[*Seats are brought in*]

Come, cousin Angelo,

---

8. Evidently the Duke's name when in disguise.   9. Meddler in temporal matters.

165 In this I'll be impartial; be you judge
Of your own cause.[1]
[*The* DUKE *and* ANGELO *sit*]
Enter [FRIAR PETER *and*] MARIANA [*veiled*]
Is this the witness, friar?
First let her show her face, and after speak.
MARIANA Pardon, my lord, I will not show my face
Until my husband bid me.
170 DUKE What, are you married?
MARIANA No, my lord.
DUKE Are you a maid?°   unmarried woman; virgin
MARIANA No, my lord.
DUKE A widow then?
175 MARIANA Neither, my lord.
DUKE Why, you are nothing then; neither maid, widow, nor wife!
LUCIO My lord, she may be a punk,° for many of them are nei-   prostitute
ther maid, widow, nor wife.
DUKE Silence that fellow. I would° he had some cause to prattle   wish
180 for himself.°   (in his own defense)
LUCIO Well, my lord.
MARIANA My lord, I do confess I ne'er was married,
And I confess besides, I am no maid.
I have known[2] my husband, yet my husband
185 Knows not that ever he knew me.
LUCIO He was drunk then, my lord, it can be no better.
DUKE For the benefit of silence, would thou wert so too.
LUCIO Well, my lord.
DUKE This is no witness for Lord Angelo.
190 MARIANA Now I come to't, my lord.
She that accuses him of fornication
In self-same manner doth accuse my husband,
And charges him, my lord, with such a time
When I'll depose° I had him in mine arms   testify
With all th'effect° of love.   manifestations
195 ANGELO   Charges she more than me?
MARIANA Not that I know.
DUKE   No? You say your husband.
MARIANA Why just,° my lord, and that is Angelo,   just so
Who thinks he knows that he ne'er knew my body,
But knows, he thinks, that he knows Isabel's.
200 ANGELO This is a strange abuse.° Let's see thy face.   imposture
MARIANA [*unveiling*] My husband bids me; now I will unmask.
This is that face, thou cruel Angelo,
Which once thou swor'st was worth the looking on.
This is the hand which, with a vowed contract,
205 Was fast belocked in thine. This is the body
That took away the match° from Isabel,   assignation
And did supply° thee at thy garden-house   satisfy
In her imagined person.
DUKE [*to* ANGELO] Know you this woman?
210 LUCIO Carnally, she says.
DUKE Sirrah, no more!

---

1. Ironically recalling the principle that no one ought   2. Had sexual intercourse with.
to judge his or her own cause.

LUCIO   Enough, my lord.

ANGELO   My lord, I must confess I know this woman;
And five years since there was some speech of marriage
215   Betwixt myself and her, which was broke off,
Partly for that her promisèd proportions°   *dowry*
Came short of composition,° but in chief   *the agreed sum*
For that her reputation was disvalued°   *discredited*
In levity;° since which time of five years   *For wantonness*
220   I never spake with her, saw her, nor heard from her,
Upon my faith and honour.

MARIANA [*kneeling before the* DUKE]   Noble prince,
As there comes light from heaven, and words from breath,
As there is sense° in truth, and truth in virtue,   *significance*
I am affianced this man's wife, as strongly
225   As words could make up vows. And, my good lord,
But Tuesday night last gone, in's garden-house,
He knew me as a wife. As this is true,
Let me in safety raise me from my knees,
Or else forever be confixèd° here,   *fixed firmly*
A marble monument.

230 ANGELO   I did but smile till now.
Now, good my lord, give me the scope° of justice.   *extent*
My patience here is touched.° I do perceive   *irritated*
These poor informal° women are no more   *disorderly*
But instruments° of some more mightier member° *agents/power*
235   That sets them on. Let me have way, my lord,
To find this practice out.

DUKE [*standing*]   Ay, with my heart,
And punish them even to your height of pleasure.—
Thou foolish friar, and thou pernicious woman
Compact with° her that's gone, think'st thou thy oaths, *In league with*
240   Though they would swear down each particular saint,
Were testimonies against his worth and credit
That's sealed in approbation?° You, Lord Escalus, *ratified by proof*
Sit with my cousin; lend him your kind pains
To find out this abuse, whence 'tis derived.
245   There is another friar that set them on.
Let him be sent for.
         [ESCALUS *sits*]

FRIAR PETER   Would he were here, my lord, for he indeed
Hath set the women on to this complaint.
Your Provost knows the place where he abides,
And he may fetch him.

250 DUKE [*to one or more*]   Go, do it instantly. [*Exit one or more*]
    [*To* ANGELO] And you, my noble and well-warranted cousin,
Whom it concerns to hear this matter forth,°   *out*
Do with your injuries as seems you best
In any chastisement. I for a while will leave you,
255   But stir not you till you have well determined° *passed judgment*
Upon these slanderers.

ESCALUS   My lord, we'll do it throughly.° *thoroughly*
                         Exit [DUKE]
Signor Lucio, did not you say you knew that Friar Lodowick to
be a dishonest person?

LUCIO *Cucullus non facit monachum:*[3] honest in nothing but in
260 his clothes; and one that hath spoke most villainous speeches
of the Duke.

ESCALUS We shall entreat you to abide here till he come, and
enforce° them against him. We shall find this friar a notable   urge
fellow.

265 LUCIO As any in Vienna, on my word.

ESCALUS Call that same Isabel here once again; I would speak
with her.   [*Exit one or more*]
[*To* ANGELO] Pray you, my lord, give me leave to question. You
shall see how I'll handle her.

270 LUCIO Not better than he, by her own report.

ESCALUS Say you?

LUCIO Marry, sir, I think if you handled her privately, she would
sooner confess; perchance publicly she'll be ashamed.

ESCALUS I will go darkly° to work with her.   privately; soberly

275 LUCIO That's the way, for women are light[4] at midnight.

Enter ISABELLA [*guarded*]

ESCALUS [*to* ISABELLA] Come on, mistress, here's a gentlewoman denies all that you have said.

Enter DUKE [*disguised as a friar, hooded, and*] PROVOST

LUCIO My lord, here comes the rascal I spoke of, here with the
Provost.

280 ESCALUS In very good time. Speak not you to him till we call
upon you.

LUCIO Mum.

ESCALUS [*to the* DUKE] Come, sir, did you set these women on
to slander Lord Angelo? They have confessed you did.

285 DUKE 'Tis false.

ESCALUS How! Know you where you are?

DUKE Respect to your great place, and let the devil
Be sometime honoured fore his burning throne.[5]
Where is the Duke? 'Tis he should hear me speak.

290 ESCALUS The Duke's in° us, and we will hear you speak.   power is vested in
Look you speak justly.°   accurately

DUKE   Boldly at least.
[*To* ISABELLA *and* MARIANA]   But O, poor souls,
Come you to seek the lamb here of the fox,
Good night to your redress! Is the Duke gone?
Then is your cause gone too. The Duke's unjust

295 Thus to retort° your manifest appeal,°   cast back / accusation
And put your trial in the villain's mouth
Which here you come to accuse.

LUCIO This is the rascal, this is he I spoke of.

ESCALUS Why, thou unreverend and unhallowed° friar,   impious
300 Is't not enough thou hast suborned these women
To accuse this worthy man but, in foul mouth,
And in the witness of his proper° ear,   own
To call him villain, and then to glance° from him   ricochet
To th' Duke himself, to tax° him with injustice?   reproach

3. The hood does not make the monk (proverbial).
4. Licentious; exploiting the unintentional sexual suggestion of Escalus's "go darkly to work."

5. *let . . . throne:* that is, the devil, too, seated on his
throne in hell, seems a figure of honor. *fore:* before.

305 Take him hence; to th' rack with him. We'll touse° you   *tear*
Joint by joint—but we will know his⁶ purpose.
What, 'unjust'?

DUKE   Be not so hot. The Duke
Dare no more stretch this finger of mine than he
Dare rack his own. His subject am I not,
310 Nor here provincial.⁷ My business in this state
Made me a looker-on here in Vienna,
Where I have seen corruption boil and bubble
Till it o'errun the stew;° laws for all faults,   *cauldron; brothel*
But faults so countenanced that the strong statutes
315 Stand like the forfeits⁸ in a barber's shop,
As much in mock as mark.

ESCALUS   Slander to th' state!
Away with him to prison.

ANGELO   What can you vouch against him, Signor Lucio?
320 Is this the man that you did tell us of?

LUCIO   'Tis he, my lord.—Come hither, goodman Bald-pate.⁹
Do you know me?

DUKE   I remember you, sir, by the sound of your voice.¹ I met
you at the prison, in the absence of the Duke.

325 LUCIO   O, did you so? And do you remember what you said of
the Duke?

DUKE   Most notedly, sir.

LUCIO   Do you so, sir? And was the Duke a fleshmonger,° a fool,   *whoremaster*
and a coward, as you then reported him to be?

330 DUKE   You must, sir, change persons with me ere you make that
my report. You indeed spoke so of him, and much more, much
worse.

LUCIO   O, thou damnable fellow! Did not I pluck thee by the
nose° for thy speeches?   *(gesture of contempt)*
335 DUKE   I protest I love the Duke as I love myself.

ANGELO   Hark how the villain would close² now, after his treasonable abuses.

ESCALUS   Such a fellow is not to be talked withal. Away with him
to prison. Where is the Provost? Away with him to prison. Lay
340 bolts° enough upon him. Let him speak no more. Away with   *fetters*
those giglets° too, and with the other confederate companion.³   *strumpets*

       [MARIANA *is raised to her feet, and is guarded.*
       The PROVOST *makes to seize the* DUKE]

DUKE   Stay, sir, stay a while.

ANGELO   What, resists he? Help him, Lucio.

LUCIO [*to the* DUKE]   Come, sir; come, sir; come, sir! Foh,° sir!   *(expression of disgust)*
345 Why, you bald-pated lying rascal, you must be hooded, must
you? Show your knave's visage, with a pox to you! Show your
sheep-biting face,⁴ and be hanged an hour!⁵ Will't not off?

       [*He pulls off the friar's hood, and discovers the* DUKE.
       ANGELO *and* ESCALUS *rise*]

---

6. The friar's; the confusion of pronouns suggests Escalus's fury.
7. Subject to local ecclesiastical authorities.
8. Jocular list of penalties for minor infractions.
9. Mr. Bald-head: "goodman" was a form of address for
a man below the rank of gentleman; friars shaved their
heads.
1. The friar's hood presumably covers his face so that he

cannot see Lucio.
2. Conclude; hide himself; come to a settlement.
3. Fellow (contemptuous).
4. Like the wolf in sheep's clothing.
5. Jocular way of saying "be hanged." Animals were
sometimes executed like human beings for destroying life
or property.

DUKE   Thou art the first knave that e'er madest a duke.
        First, Provost, let me bail these gentle three.
350   [*To* LUCIO] Sneak not away, sir, for the friar and you
        Must have a word anon. [*To one or more*] Lay hold on him.
LUCIO   This may prove worse than hanging.
DUKE [*to* ESCALUS] What you have spoke, I pardon. Sit you down.
        We'll borrow place° of him.   seat; office
                [ESCALUS *sits*]
        [*To* ANGELO]   Sir, by your leave.
                [*He takes Angelo's seat*]
355   Hast thou or° word or wit or impudence   either
        That yet can do thee office?° If thou hast,   service
        Rely upon it till my tale be heard,
        And hold no longer out.
ANGELO   O my dread lord,
        I should be guiltier than my guiltiness
360   To think I can be undiscernible,
        When I perceive your grace, like power divine,
        Hath looked upon my passes.[6] Then, good prince,
        No longer session° hold upon my shame,   inquiry
        But let my trial be mine own confession.
365   Immediate sentence then, and sequent° death,   thereafter
        Is all the grace I beg.
DUKE   Come hither, Mariana.
        [*To* ANGELO] Say, wast thou e'er contracted to this woman?
ANGELO   I was, my lord.
DUKE   Go, take her hence and marry her instantly.
370   Do you the office, friar; which consummate,°   finished
        Return him here again. Go with him, Provost.
                Exeunt [ANGELO, MARIANA, FRIAR PETER, *and the* PROVOST]
ESCALUS   My lord, I am more amazed at his dishonour
        Than at the strangeness of it.°   (the situation)
DUKE   Come hither, Isabel.
        Your friar is now your prince. As I was then
375   Advertising° and holy to your business,   Attentive
        Not changing heart with habit I am still
        Attorneyed° at your service.   Engaged as advocate
ISABELLA   O, give me pardon,
        That I, your vassal, have employed and pained°   troubled
        Your unknown sovereignty.
DUKE   You are pardoned, Isabel.
380   And now, dear maid, be you as free° to us.   generous
        Your brother's death I know sits at your heart,
        And you may marvel why I obscured myself,
        Labouring to save his life, and would not rather
        Make rash remonstrance° of my hidden power   demonstration
385   Than let him so be lost. O most kind maid,
        It was the swift celerity of his death,
        Which I did think with slower foot came on,
        That brained° my purpose. But peace be with him!   killed
        That life is better life, past fearing death,
390   Than that which lives to fear. Make it your comfort,
        So happy is your brother.

---

6. Actions, trespasses; recalling Job 34:21: "For his eyes are upon the ways of man, and he seeth all his goings."

ISABELLA   I do, my lord.

       Enter ANGELO, MARIANA, [FRIAR] PETER, [*and*] PROVOST

DUKE   For this new-married man approaching here,

     Whose salt° imagination yet hath wronged   *salacious*

     Your well-defended honour, you must pardon

395   For Mariana's sake; but as he adjudged° your brother—   *condemned*

     Being criminal in double violation

     Of sacred chastity and of promise-breach,

     Thereon dependent, for your brother's life—

     The very mercy° of the law cries out   *Even the merciful aspect*

400   Most audible, even from his proper° tongue,   *its own*

     'An Angelo for Claudio, death for death'.

     Haste still° pays haste, and leisure° answers leisure;   *always / deliberation*

     Like doth quit° like, and measure still for measure.   *requite*

     Then, Angelo, thy fault's thus manifested,

405   Which, though° thou wouldst deny, denies thee vantage.°   *even if / (i.e., clemency)*

     We do condemn thee to the very block

     Where Claudio stooped to death, and with like haste.

     Away with him.

MARIANA   O my most gracious lord,

     I hope you will not mock me with a husband!

410 DUKE   It is your husband mocked you with a husband.

     Consenting to the safeguard of your honour,

     I thought your marriage fit; else imputation,°   *censure*

     For that he knew you, might reproach your life,

     And choke your good to come.° For his possessions,   *ruin your prospects*

415   Although by confiscation they are ours,[7]

     We do enstate and widow you° with all,   *give you widow's rights*

     To buy you a better husband.

MARIANA   O my dear lord,

     I crave no other, nor no better man.

DUKE   Never crave him; we are definitive.°   *resolute*

MARIANA   Gentle my liege—

420 DUKE   You do but lose your labour.—

     Away with him to death. [*To* LUCIO] Now, sir, to you.

MARIANA [*kneeling*]   O my good lord!—Sweet Isabel, take my part;

     Lend me your knees, and all my life to come

     I'll lend you all my life to do you service.

425 DUKE   Against all sense you do importune her.

     Should she kneel down in mercy of this fact,°   *crime*

     Her brother's ghost his pavèd bed° would break,   *stone-covered grave*

     And take her hence in horror.

MARIANA   Isabel,

     Sweet Isabel, do yet but kneel by me.

430   Hold up your hands; say nothing; I'll speak all.

     They say best men are moulded out of faults,

     And, for the most,° become much more the better   *most part*

     For being a little bad. So may my husband.

     O Isabel, will you not lend a knee?

DUKE   He dies for Claudio's death.

435 ISABELLA [*kneeling*]   Most bounteous sir,

     Look, if it please you, on this man condemned

     As if my brother lived. I partly think

---

7. Because a felon's property was forfeit to the crown.

A due sincerity governed his deeds,
Till he did look on me. Since it is so,
440　　Let him not die. My brother had but justice,
In that he did the thing for which he died.
For Angelo,
His act did not o'ertake his bad intent,
And must be buried° but as an intent　　　　　　　　　　　(i.e., forgotten)
445　　That perished by the way. Thoughts are no subjects,[8]
Intents but merely thoughts.

MARIANA　　　　　　　　　　　　　Merely, my lord.
　　　　DUKE　Your suit's unprofitable. Stand up, I say.
　　　　　　　[MARIANA and ISABELLA stand]
I have bethought me of another fault.
Provost, how came it Claudio was beheaded
At an unusual hour?
450　　PROVOST　　　　　　　　　　It was commanded so.
　　　　DUKE　Had you a special warrant for the deed?
　　　　PROVOST　No, my good lord, it was by private message.
　　　　DUKE　For which I do discharge you of your office.
Give up your keys.
　　　　PROVOST　　　　　　　　Pardon me, noble lord.
455　　I thought it was a fault, but knew it not,
Yet did repent me after more advice;°　　　　　　　　　　deliberation
For° testimony whereof one in the prison　　　　　　　　As
That should by private order else° have died　　　　　　otherwise
I have reserved alive.
460　　DUKE　What's he?
　　　　PROVOST　His name is Barnardine.
　　　　DUKE　I would thou hadst done so by Claudio.
Go fetch him hither. Let me look upon him.　　[Exit PROVOST]
　　　　ESCALUS　I am sorry one so learned and so wise
465　　As you, Lord Angelo, have still° appeared,　　　　　　always
Should slip so grossly, both in the heat of blood
And lack of tempered judgement afterward.
　　　　ANGELO　I am sorry that such sorrow I procure,°　　　　cause
And so deep sticks it in my penitent heart
470　　That I crave death more willingly than mercy.
'Tis my deserving, and I do entreat it.
　　　　　　　Enter BARNARDINE and PROVOST; CLAUDIO, [muffled,°　　with his face wrapped
　　　　　　　and] JULIET
　　　　DUKE　Which is that Barnardine?
　　　　PROVOST　　　　　　　　This, my lord.
　　　　DUKE　There was a friar told me of this man.
　　　　　　　[To BARNARDINE] Sirrah, thou art said to have a stubborn soul
475　　That apprehends no further than this world,
And squar'st° thy life according. Thou'rt condemned;　　frames
But, for those earthly faults,[9] I quit° them all,　　　　pardon
And pray thee take this mercy to provide
For better times to come.—Friar, advise him.
480　　I leave him to your hand. [To PROVOST] What muffled fellow's that?
　　　　PROVOST　This is another prisoner that I saved,
Who should have died when Claudio lost his head,
As like almost to Claudio as himself.

---

8. Thoughts are not subject to prosecution.　　　　9. Offenses subject to earthly punishment.

[*He unmuffles* CLAUDIO]

DUKE [*to* ISABELLA]   If he be like your brother, for his sake
485   Is he pardoned; and for your lovely sake
Give me your hand, and say you will be mine.[1]
He is my brother° too. But fitter time for that.   (*as a brother-in-law*)
By this Lord Angelo perceives he's safe.
Methinks I see a quick'ning in his eye.
490   Well, Angelo, your evil quits° you well.   *recompenses*
Look that you love your wife, her worth worth° yours.   *being equal to*
I find an apt remission° in myself;   *inclination to mercy*
And yet here's one in place° I cannot pardon.   *present*
[*To* LUCIO] You, sirrah, that knew me for a fool, a coward,
495   One all of luxury,° an ass, a madman,   *lasciviousness*
Wherein have I so deserved of you
That you extol me thus?
LUCIO   Faith, my lord, I spoke it but according to the trick.° If   *fashion*
you will hang me for it, you may; but I had rather it would
500   please you I might be whipped.
DUKE   Whipped first, sir, and hanged after.
Proclaim it, Provost, round about the city,
If any woman wronged by this lewd fellow,
As I have heard him swear himself there's one
505   Whom he begot with child, let her appear,
And he shall marry her. The nuptial finished,
Let him be whipped and hanged.
LUCIO   I beseech your highness, do not marry me to a whore.
Your highness said even now I made you a duke; good my lord,
510   do not recompense me in making me a cuckold.
DUKE   Upon mine honour, thou shalt marry her.
Thy slanders I forgive, and therewithal
Remit thy other forfeits.°—Take him to prison,   *punishments*
And see our pleasure herein executed.
515   LUCIO   Marrying a punk, my lord, is pressing to death,[2] whip-
ping, and hanging.
DUKE   Slandering a prince deserves it.   [*Exit* LUCIO *guarded*]
She, Claudio, that you wronged, look you restore.[3]
Joy to you, Mariana. Love her, Angelo.
520   I have confessed her,° and I know her virtue.   *been her confessor*
Thanks, good friend Escalus, for thy much goodness.
There's more behind° that is more gratulate.°   *to come / gratifying*
Thanks, Provost, for thy care and secrecy.
We shall employ thee in a worthier place.
525   Forgive him, Angelo, that brought you home
The head of Ragusine for Claudio's.
Th'offence pardons itself. Dear Isabel,
I have a motion° much imports your good,   *proposal*
Whereto, if you'll a willing ear incline,
530   What's mine is yours, and what is yours is mine.
[*To all*] So bring° us to our palace, where we'll show   *accompany*
What's yet behind that's meet you all should know.   [*Exeunt*]

---

1. It is not clear how Isabella responds to the Duke's pro-   2. Executing by crushing under heavy weights.
posal of marriage.   3. To her good name, by marrying her.

Additional Passages

The text of *Measure for Measure* given in this edition is probably that of an adapted version made for Shakespeare's company after his death. Adaptation seems to have affected two passages, printed below as the Oxford editors believe Shakespeare to have written them.

A. 1.2.0.1–104

The passage begins with seven lines that the adapter (believed to be Thomas Middleton) intended to be replaced by 1.2.52–71 of the play as printed here. The adapter must have contributed all of 1.2.0.1–74, which in the earliest and subsequent printed texts precede the discussion between the clown (Pompey) and the bawd (Mistress Overdone) about Claudio's arrest. Lucio's entry alone at line 36 below, some eleven lines after his reentry with the two Gentlemen and the Provost's party in the adapted text, probably represents Shakespeare's original intention. In his version, Juliet, present but silent in the adapted text both in 1.2 and 5.1, probably did not appear in either scene; accordingly, the words "and there's Madam Juliet" (1.2.95) must also be the reviser's work, and do not appear below.

> *Enter* POMPEY *and* MISTRESS OVERDONE, *meeting*
> MISTRESS OVERDONE   How now, what's the news with you?
> POMPEY   Yonder man is carried to prison.
> MISTRESS OVERDONE   Well! What has he done?
> POMPEY   A woman.
> 5 MISTRESS OVERDONE   But what's his offence?
> POMPEY   Groping for trouts[1] in a peculiar° river.   private
> MISTRESS OVERDONE   What, is there a maid[2] with child by him?
> POMPEY   No, but there's a woman with maid[3] by him: you have
>   not heard of the proclamation, have you?
> 10 MISTRESS OVERDONE   What proclamation, man?
> POMPEY   All houses in the suburbs of Vienna must be plucked down.
> MISTRESS OVERDONE   And what shall become of those in the city?
> POMPEY   They shall stand for seed. They had gone down too, but
>   that a wise burgher put in for them.
> 15 MISTRESS OVERDONE   But shall all our houses of resort in the
>   suburbs be pulled down?
> POMPEY   To the ground, mistress.
> MISTRESS OVERDONE   Why, here's a change indeed in the com-
>   monwealth. What shall become of me?
> 20 POMPEY   Come, fear not you. Good counsellors lack no clients.
>   Though you change your place, you need not change your
>   trade. I'll be your tapster still. Courage, there will be pity taken
>   on you. You that have worn your eyes almost out in the service,
>   you will be considered.
>   *A noise within*
> 25 MISTRESS OVERDONE   What's to do here, Thomas Tapster?
>   Let's withdraw!
>   *Enter the* PROVOST *and* CLAUDIO
> POMPEY   Here comes Signor Claudio, led by the Provost to
>   prison.   *Exeunt* MISTRESS OVERDONE *and* POMPEY
> CLAUDIO   Fellow, why dost thou show me thus to th' world?
> 30 Bear me to prison, where I am committed.
> PROVOST   I do it not in evil disposition,

---

1. Literally, a way of catching trout by tickling their bellies.
2. Young woman (but Pompey understands "virgin").
3. Pregnant with a baby girl.

But from Lord Angelo by special charge.

CLAUDIO   Thus can the demigod Authority
    Make us pay down for our offence, by weight,
35   The bonds of heaven. On whom it will, it will;
    On whom it will not, so; yet still 'tis just.

      Enter LUCIO

LUCIO   Why, how now, Claudio? Whence comes this restraint?

B. 3.1.479–4.1.65

Before revision, there would have been no act break and no song; the lines immediately following the song would also have been absent. The Duke's soliloquies "He who the sword of heaven will bear" and "O place and greatness" have evidently been transposed in revision; in the original, the end of "O place and greatness" would have led straight on to the Duke's meeting with Isabella and then Mariana.

ESCALUS   I am going to visit the prisoner. Fare you well.
DUKE   Peace be with you.   *Exit* ESCALUS
    O place and greatness, millions of false eyes
    Are stuck upon thee; volumes of report
5   Run with their false and most contrarious quest
    Upon thy doings; thousand escapes of wit
    Make thee the father of their idle dream,
    And rack thee in their fancies.

      Enter ISABELLA

DUKE   Very well met.
    What is the news from this good deputy?
10 ISABELLA   He hath a garden circummured with brick,
    Whose western side is with a vineyard backed;
    And to that vineyard is a planckèd gate,
    That makes his opening with this bigger key.
    This other doth command a little door
15   Which from the vineyard to the garden leads.
    There have I made my promise
    Upon the heavy middle of the night
    To call upon him.
DUKE   But shall you on your knowledge find this way?
20 ISABELLA   I have ta'en a due and wary note upon't.
    With whispering and most guilty diligence,
    In action all of precept, he did show me
    The way twice o'er.
DUKE   Are there no other tokens
    Between you 'greed concerning her observance?
25 ISABELLA   No, none, but only a repair i'th' dark,
    And that I have possessed him my most stay
    Can be but brief, for I have made him know
    I have a servant comes with me along
    That stays upon me, whose persuasion is
    I come about my brother.
30 DUKE   'Tis well borne up.
    I have not yet made known to Mariana
    A word of this.—What ho, within! Come forth!

      Enter MARIANA

    [*To* MARIANA] I pray you be acquainted with this maid.
    She comes to do you good.

ISABELLA   I do desire the like.

35   DUKE [to MARIANA]   Do you persuade yourself that I respect you?

MARIANA   Good friar, I know you do, and so have found it.

DUKE   Take then this your companion by the hand,
     Who hath a story ready for your ear.
     I shall attend your leisure; but make haste,
     The vaporous night approaches.

40   MARIANA   Will't please you walk aside.

                     Exeunt MARIANA *and* ISABELLA

DUKE   He who the sword of heaven will bear
     Should be as holy as severe,
     Pattern in himself to know,
     Grace to stand, and virtue go,
45   More nor less to others paying
     Than by self-offences weighing.
     Shame to him whose cruel striking
     Kills for faults of his own liking!
     Twice treble shame on Angelo,
50   To weed my vice, and let his grow!
     O, what may man within him hide,
     Though angel on the outward side!
     How may likeness made in crimes
     Make my practice on the times
55   To draw with idle spiders' strings
     Most ponderous and substantial things?
     Craft against vice I must apply.
     With Angelo tonight shall lie
     His old betrothèd but despisèd.
60   So disguise shall, by th' disguisèd,
     Pay with falsehood false exacting,
     And perform an old contracting.

        Enter MARIANA *and* ISABELLA

     Welcome. How agreed?

ISABELLA   She'll take the enterprise upon her, father,
65   If you advise it.

Othello

"The problem of the twentieth century is the problem of the color-line." So prophesied the African American intellectual and activist W. E. B. Du Bois in his classic study *The Souls of Black Folk* (1903) just as the century began. Du Bois's prediction may have been premature with respect to Shakespearean tragedy, where *Hamlet, King Lear,* and *Macbeth* continued to dominate critical attention throughout most of the twentieth century. But today, *Othello* (1602–03) speaks to readers and audiences alike with unusual power, largely because it explores race and racism in unsettling fashion. Does this emphasis, centered on the dark skin of the title character, belatedly recognize a crucial issue previously neglected or misconstrued? Alternatively, does the recent preoccupation with race impose contemporary concerns on material with a different orientation?

Yes, to both questions. Interpretation is always influenced by both past and present—here by the play itself, together with its theatrical and critical heritage, and by the current preoccupations of contemporary audiences and readers. A complex work elicits different responses in different times or places: in *Othello,* to oversimplify, one issue (jealousy) was formerly more prominent, while another (race) has emerged—or reemerged—only recently. Neither race nor jealousy is the play's sole concern. *Othello* provocatively investigates gender and sexuality. It is preoccupied with class conflict, morality, and metaphysics. And it sets its central domestic disaster against the international conflict between Venetians and Turks over the island of Cyprus—a religious, political, and military antagonism that subtly informs the characters' catastrophic personal relationships.

This thematic range can be investigated by looking at Shakespeare's handling of his sources, at his unusual manipulation of dramatic genres and, hence, of audience expectations, at the psychology of Iago and Othello as well as their interaction, and, finally, at race itself. Much of *Othello's* plot—but little of its outlook, characterization, or language—derives from Giovanbattista Giraldi Cinthio's *De gli hecatommithi* ("Hundred Tales," third decade, seventh story, 1565). In Shakespeare's version, racial issues are more persistent. The play here draws primarily on the 1600 translation of *A Geographical Historie of Africa* by Leo Africanus, a Moroccan Muslim who had been captured by Christian pirates and brought to Rome, where he converted to Catholicism. The public world of Venetian-Turkish affairs, absent from Cinthio, probably derives from Richard Knolles's *Generall Historie of the Turkes* (1603). Minor characters are given interesting twists. For instance, Emilia, the wife of Iago, the story's villain, is passive in Cinthio but in Shakespeare speaks for the rights of women, stands by Desdemona, Othello's wife, and ultimately brings her own husband down—at the cost of her life. The changes to Iago and Othello are even more consequential. Unlike *De gli hecatommithi*'s malefactor, who is motivated by unrequited lust for Desdemona and anger that she has refused his advances, Shakespeare's Iago loathes Othello and is determined to destroy him. His manipulative mastery is given greater scope, thereby enhancing a sense of his power as well as his fathomless viciousness. Similarly, by making Othello Desdemona's killer (Iago's job in Cinthio) and by having him publicly acknowledge his responsibility for the act, Shakespeare increases the character's guilt as well as his grandeur—the latter further enhanced by an elevation in social status from his position in the source. Thus *Othello,* unlike *De gli hecatommithi,* ties everything to the central murder.

The manipulation of generic expectations in *Othello* produces multiple perspectives on the plot. Though familiar with the classical dramatic genres of comedy and tragedy, Shakespeare was also influenced by late medieval–early Renaissance morality plays and

Two views of "the Moor" (one Arab or Berber, the other sub-Saharan), suggesting the range of images Shakespeare may have had in mind. Left: the Moroccan ambassador to Queen Elizabeth I (1600); right: "a Moor," from Cesare Vecellio, *De gli habiti antichi et moderni* (1590).

by Renaissance experimentation with hybrid forms. Hence, all of his plays are mixtures. The distinctiveness of *Othello*, however, lies not in the copresence of comic and tragic elements—a common feature in Shakespearean drama—but in the work's daring experiments with shifting generic frameworks. Its opening act, probably Shakespeare's invention, employs a strategy of studied indirection. It is night in a city—Venice, we are later told (1.1.107). Plot and character are presented in nonspecific terms: Roderigo is irritated that Iago "shouldst know of this," "of such a matter"—a matter concerning a "him" (1.1.3, 5, 6), an unnamed personage invoked only by pronouns until the snide reference to "his Moorship" (1.1.32). The play's first audiences might have connected this character with the titular figure, even though Othello himself does not appear on stage until scene 2 and is not named until scene 3. Iago tells Roderigo to "call up her father" (1.1.67), again without identifying "her" or "her father." The two men provoke Brabanzio, "her father," in similarly oblique fashion, only gradually revealing that Roderigo's "this" is a sexual relationship and, still later, that it is a marriage. Their imprecision about "this" encourages the audience to wonder what kind of play they are watching. It turns out to be a romantic comedy. Iago and Roderigo's strategy is aimed at persuading Brabanzio to nullify the union. They do get Brabanzio's aid, but they do not get what they want. Against the cultural norms of Shakespeare's time and subsequent centuries, the play celebrates Othello's grandeur, Desdemona's assertive autonomy (she wooed him), and the result—marriage between Moor and Venetian, old and young, black and white. The initial suppression of the names of the lovers renders them as character types to which stylized attributes, however misleading, can be attached before their individuality emerges. The darkness and the urban setting point to romantic concerns. The villain's machinations fail; the opposition of the old father, a standard blocking figure in stage comedy, proves ineffectual; the Duke, the play's highest ranking character, ratifies the marriage. It has all been so easy. Midway through the third scene, the story is over.

Except, of course, that it isn't. A new obstacle to marital bliss has arisen—the Turkish fleet's threat to Cyprus. The Venetian Senate dispatches Othello there to defend the interests of the state. To these vicissitudes of war the play adds the trial of separation. Although Desdemona will join Othello, she travels separately—with Iago. Before Venetian ships reach Cyprus, however, a storm destroys the Turkish armada. But by removing one danger, the storm creates two others. Will Desdemona be safe at sea? Will Othello? Romantic comedy has modulated into romance in the manner of late antique Greek and Roman prose fiction: faithful lovers, separated by storms, must undergo prolonged suffering before their final reunion. But Desdemona soon arrives unharmed; Othello promptly follows. By early in the second act, the play has apparently resolved issues of race and ethnicity, love and sexuality, religious and military hostilities. But less than halfway through the play, romantic comedy and romance both give way to domestic tragedy, a popular dramatic form of the time, usually set in England, in which female marital infidelity leads to disaster. Since there is no adultery, however, this third generic movement does not automatically occur. Iago must fabricate pretexts for Othello's sexual jealousy, a sensibility often associated on the Renaissance English stage with modern Italy and the Mediterranean. Accordingly, as we'll later see, neither comedy nor romance is ever definitively rejected.

These multiple formal perspectives—comedy, romance, domestic tragedy—help generate a correspondingly complex treatment of the characters and their interaction. The play begins with Iago. We quickly learn that "his Moorship," presumably a foreigner to Venice, has chosen as his lieutenant Cassio, an unproven gentleman from Florence and, hence, also a foreigner. Iago, the battle-tested, homegrown common soldier, deeply resents the slight. Out for himself and passed over for promotion, Iago is a young man on the make driven by class, regional, and ethnic resentment and willing to use others as means to his ends. Moreover, he has no illusions about those means. For instance, he anticipates that Brabanzio's opposition to his daughter's marriage will fail because of Othello's military importance to Venice (1.1.145–160). But Iago is more than a cool calculator; he is also tortured by a superheated sexual jealousy. Although he lacks any evidence, he believes that Othello has become Emilia's lover. He invents the sexual liaison between Cassio and Desdemona in order to supplant Cassio as lieutenant and make Othello jealous, arguing to himself that the charge of adultery he knows he has simply made up is actually real. Here, perhaps, we glimpse Iago's own sexual anxieties. Thus, he acknowledges his lust for Desdemona, explaining, however, that it is motivated by a desire to do to Othello what he assumes Othello has already done to him. And he converts his careerist resentment of Cassio into a fear that Cassio, too, will become Emilia's lover (2.1.273–299).

Furthermore, Iago enjoys the sport of ruining Othello's life. In this respect, he descends from a key figure of the earlier English morality plays—the Vice, a semisecularized devil who employs his comic verve to try to destroy his virtuous antagonists and whose colloquial intimacy with the audience often half-succeeds in winning that audience over. His diabolism is emphasized throughout the play. As he explains,

> When devils will the blackest sins put on,
> They do suggest at first with heavenly shows,
> As I do now.
>
> (2.3.325–27)

Similarly, Othello concludes:

> OTHELLO I look down towards his feet, but that's a fable.
> [*To* IAGO] If that thou beest a devil I cannot kill thee.
> [*He wounds* IAGO]
> . . . .
> IAGO   I bleed, sir, but not killed.
>
> (5.2.292–94)

The "fable" is that the devil's feet are cloven hooves. If Iago is the devil, he cannot die, a point he mockingly makes by insisting he is "not killed."

For more than a century, *Othello* in performance has often been Iago's show, partly because he wittily speaks to—not just before—the audience. Iago is also extremely talkative, uttering two hundred more lines than Othello himself—indeed, more than any other Shakespearean character except Hamlet. Thus, he potentially dominates a play that deploys the smallest cast in Shakespearean tragedy and that, after the first act, conforms to the Aristotelian unities of time, place, and action that Shakespeare normally ignores. As a matter of fact, his prominence has proven a recurrent problem, since it runs the risk of belittling Othello.

On the other hand, Iago's various motives help the play offer multiple accounts of Othello as well. Why does Othello move from nobly loving husband to insanely jealous murderer? If Iago is driven by resentment and jealousy, Othello is a savage fool. But if Iago is devilish, the play acquires a religious cast. Othello's soul hangs in the balance; in repudiating his good "angel" (5.2.140) and succumbing to temptation, he reenacts the fall. Faced with a supernatural adversary, Othello is less culpable. Hence, the long-standing debate about the protagonist's character cannot be resolved: Othello is noble victim and barbaric dupe.

Indeed, the disastrous outcome partly results from Iago's ability to turn Desdemona's and Othello's very nobility against them. Desdemona's bold, generous spirit becomes evidence of her affair with Cassio. Othello's "free and open nature" enables him to "be led by th' nose" (1.3.381, 383). Iago can also count on Othello's military resoluteness. Before Othello becomes jealous, he has staked everything on Desdemona: "My life upon her faith" (1.3.293). His grief at Desdemona's supposed betrayal, combining the martial and the marital, is at first moving in its stately repetitions:

> Farewell the tranquil mind, farewell content,
> Farewell the plumèd troops and the big wars
> That makes ambition virtue! O, farewell,
> Farewell the neighing steed and the shrill trump.
> (3.3.353–56)

But as Othello's psyche breaks down, incoherent prose supplants measured verse: "Handkerchief—confessions—handkerchief. . . . Pish! Noses, ears, and lips! Is't possible? Confess? Handkerchief? O devil! *He falls down in a trance*" (4.1.36–41, s.d.).

Put another way, Othello is out of his element. A soldier since childhood, he knows little of peacetime urban existence. He should feel at home on Cyprus, a military prize. But when the Turkish threat dissipates, the island becomes the typical other world of Shakespearean drama, where all characters are displaced and fundamental change occurs. In particular, Cyprus's ancient association with sexual license emerges. Although this seems antithetical to republican Venice's sobriety, we come to suspect that Venice is no better. As a result, Othello is more vulnerable to Iago's influence than he would be on the battlefield. He accepts narratives about himself and Desdemona composed from the repugnant sexual—and especially misogynist—stereotypes of European society that also torment Iago. Brabanzio warns Othello: "She has deceived her father, and may thee" (1.3.292). Iago retrieves the thought:

> IAGO She did deceive her father, marrying you.
> . . . .
> OTHELLO   And so she did.
>   (3.3.210–12)

As Iago's thinking has revealed, sexual guilt need be merely plausible. "'Tis probable, and palpable to thinking," Brabanzio argues, that Othello used magic on Desdemona (1.2.77). The Duke rejects mere assertion and "poor likelihoods" (1.3.108). But Iago gets away with "imputation, and strong circumstances" (3.3.411) rather than "ocular proof" (3.3.365), because Othello cannot challenge Iago's cynical view of sexuality:

"In Venice they do let God see the pranks / They dare not show their husbands" (3.3.206–07). Hence, Iago's description of Cassio and Desdemona in the play's recurrent animal imagery—"as prime as goats, as hot as monkeys" (3.3.408)—returns in Othello's "Goats and monkeys!" (4.1.260). This outcome seems to depend, however, on Iago's ability to elicit Othello's own sexual anxieties.

The sexual loathing Othello reveals here may also be inspired by Desdemona's directness:

> That I did love the Moor to live with him,
> My downright violence and storm of fortunes
> May trumpet to the world.
> (1.3.247–49)

Othello registers the allure and the threat of such erotic boldness when he and Desdemona are reunited on Cyprus: "If it were now to die / 'Twere now to be most happy," where "to die" also means to have an orgasm (2.1.186–87). Christian doctrine sometimes considered excessive marital sexual pleasure a form of adultery. Earlier, Iago plots "after some time to abuse Othello's ears / That he is too familiar with his wife" (1.3.377–78). "He" is presumably Cassio, to whom Iago has recently referred. But the nearer mention of Othello and the pronoun confusion—since "his" must refer to Othello—suggest that Othello experiences his own sexual desire as adulterous, that following sexual consummation of his marriage (if that actually occurs) he projects this desire onto Cassio, and that he punishes his sexual feelings by killing Desdemona.

Not surprisingly, the conclusion also encourages an ambivalent view of Othello. Shakespeare emphasizes Desdemona's innocent victimization by dramatizing her obedience to her husband.

DESDEMONA O, falsely, falsely murdered!

. . . .

A guiltless death I die.

EMILIA   O, who hath done this deed?

DESDEMONA Nobody, I myself. Farewell.
Commend me to my kind lord. O, farewell!
(5.2.126–34)

A loyally subordinate Desdemona is more conventionally reassuring than the Desdemona who flouted convention to marry Othello. This diminution of female autonomy retreats from Desdemona's bolder position early in the play, which is itself echoed by Emilia's brave, principled defiance at the end. Yet Desdemona's final words may indicate a masochistic submissiveness as unsettling as her previous behavior or perhaps, taken from a Christian perspective, a paradox—the simultaneous assertion of suicide (a mortal sin) and guiltlessness. Her words also increase Othello's guilt and underscore the mistreatment of women that we see as well in both Iago's relationship with Emilia and Cassio's with Bianca, the courtesan who loves him.

Othello himself believes he is administering secular justice or performing a religious ritual in killing Desdemona. But his rage forces him to "call what I intend to do / A murder, which I thought a sacrifice" (5.2.69–70). Confronted with Desdemona's innocence, he assumes the same role—this time, however, executing himself. But suicide evokes Christian despair and certainty of damnation as well as disinterested justice and ancient Stoic heroism. Similarly, one may disagree with Othello's conviction that he is "an honourable murderer," "one not easily jealous" (5.2.300, 354).

The persistence of a comic outlook further complicates our judgment. As in Shakespeare's earlier romantic comedy *Much Ado About Nothing* (1598), information sufficient to unmask the villain's slandering of female sexual propriety has always been available. Further, Othello speculates that Desdemona's infidelity arises because "I am declined / Into the vale of years" (3.3.269–70), thereby invoking farce's standard cuckolding of old man by young woman, of January by May. Similarly, Emilia oxymoronically calls Othello a "murderous coxcomb" (fool) and asks a familiar comic question: "What should such a fool / Do with so good a wife?" (5.2.240–41). The play then concludes by literalizing the metaphorical destination of romantic comedy—the marriage bed, here present in grimly parodic form.

A pervasive association between sex and death also promotes ambivalence. The fatal "napkin," or handkerchief, indicative of aristocratic privilege but important because of its very triviality, symbolically captures these feelings. Presented, according to Othello, to his mother by "an Egyptian . . . charmer," the handkerchief combines the magic and ethnic exoticism Othello earlier repudiates in defending his marriage to Desdemona. It enabled his mother to "subdue my father / Entirely to her love" (3.4.57–58). Or per- haps not. Othello ultimately offers a more prosaic account: "It was a handkerchief, an antique token / My father gave my mother" (5.2.223–24). "Spotted with strawberries" (3.3.440), it may evoke the blood Desdemona loses with her virginity on the marriage bed. Desdemona has Emilia "lay on my bed my wedding sheets" (4.2.108); Othello anticipates that "thy bed, lust-stained, shall with lust's blood be spotted" (5.1.37). This association between sexual pleasure and death is then enacted. Attracted by his sleep- ing wife, Othello cannot resist kissing her: "Be thus when thou art dead, and I will kill thee / And love thee after" (5.2.18–19). He recalls this necrophilic perversity at his own death: "I kissed thee ere I killed thee. No way but this: / Killing myself, to die upon a kiss" (5.2.368–69), where "die" once again carries a secondary sexual sense. Romance's movement toward reuniting long-separated lovers takes the form of a postmortem embrace. Furthermore, this concluding tableau includes not only Othello and Desde- mona but perhaps Emilia as well, whose dying wish is to "lay me by my mistress' side!" (5.2.244). If so, we witness the very ménage à trois or intimate bedroom relationship between Emilia and Othello that Iago invoked to motivate his revenge.

What, then, of race? It is there from the start. Iago warns Brabanzio that "an old black ram / Is tupping your white ewe" (1.1.88–89). The arousal of Bra- banzio's fear of miscegenation works. The old man cannot believe that his daughter would ever "run . . . to the sooty bosom / Of such a thing as thou" (1.2.71–72). He is wrong, however, not just about Desdemona but also about the sympathies of the Venetian Senate. As the Duke explains, "Your son-in-law is far more fair than black" (1.3.289). Yet this vic- tory is uncomfortable: the praise arises from the negative connota- tions of blackness. Hence, when Othello seeks to understand his wife's betrayal, he adopts these connotations literally—"Haply for I am black" (3.3.267)—and meta- phorically—"My name . . . is now begrimed and black / As mine own face" (3.3.391–93).

The manner of Tur-
kiſh tyrannie over
Chriſtian ſlaves.

Compare Othello's last speech before killing himself (5.2.361–65). Woodcut, from F. Knight, *A Relation of Seavan Yeares Slaverie Under the Turkes of Argeire* . . . (1640).

The language of color in the play draws on the biblical associ- ation of blackness and evil, Eliza- bethan prejudice toward black Africans resident in England, ethnographic accounts of passionately jealous Africans, and the early stages of the slave trade. Yet it lacks the full racist import it subsequently acquired. Renaissance thought was innocent of the biological view of ethnic difference that triumphed in the nineteenth century. Othello's mention of being "sold to slavery" (1.3.137), given its Mediterranean context, has more to do with social hierarchy and religious difference than skin color. Until the late seventeenth century, *Othello*'s commentators make little of Othello's appearance, although they assume, in line with most of the play's language, that he is black—a position rejected in the nineteenth century and still sometimes challenged today. (See the two renderings of Moors on page 2110.) Shakespeare also followed less prominent, more sympathetic accounts of Moors, deriving from subordinate strains in both travel literature and the religious tradition. The racial issues of *Othello* are, therefore, both like and unlike those of the present, with which they are connected partly by the unbroken influence of the play itself.

These issues have produced powerful contradictory reactions on the stage, where *Othello* has always been one of Shakespeare's most popular works. Well into the twentieth century, audiences and critics often agreed with Brabanzio, seeing in the conclusion the triumph of Othello's barbaric African essence over his civilized European surface. When they defended his nobility, they denied he was black. "Othello *was* a *white* man," Mary Preston of Baltimore wrote in 1869. A compromise resolution offered by the actor Herbert Beerbohm Tree in 1912 suggests the underlying racist agreement between antithetical conclusions about Othello's skin color: "Othello was an Oriental, not a Negro: a stately Arab of the best caste."

But especially when Othello is played by an actor of sub-Saharan descent, performances have seemed to strike a blow for freedom—on the Continent following the revolutions of 1848, in czarist Russia on the eve of the liberation of the serfs, after 1863 and the emancipation of American slaves, in World War II America, and in the final years of South African apartheid. The 1943 American *Othello,* featuring what may have been the American theater's first kiss between a black actor (Paul Robeson) and a white actress, was at the time the longest-running production of any Shakespearean play in the United States. Yet commentators of African descent have sometimes taken the opposite view—that a black actor as Othello runs the risk of reinforcing racial stereotypes. The problem for a white actor is even graver. With the recent return on the stage to the pre-1800 conviction that Othello is black, productions have steered away from white performers in the part, fearing that they would produce minstrel-show figures in blackface reminiscent of nineteenth-century burlesques of the play—precisely the charge sometimes made against Laurence Olivier's 1965 portrayal.

This history inevitably affects contemporary understanding of the conclusion of the play, when race seems to return literally with a vengeance. The alien connotations of the handkerchief are echoed by the ethnic rhetoric of Othello's last long speech, in which the conflict of civilizations reemerges in the Moor's identification with the exotic non-European, non-Christian world. In the quarto version (see the Textual Note), Othello is "like the base Indian" who "threw a pearl away / Richer than all his tribe" (5.2.356–57). But the Folio reads "base Iudean" (Judean) and hence may allude to Judas, betrayer of Christ, or to Herod the Great, murderer of his wife, Mariamne, out of jealousy. Othello "drops tears as fast as the Arabian trees / Their medicinable gum" (5.2.359–60). He asks his listeners to remind the Venetian state

> that in Aleppo once,
> Where a malignant and a turbaned Turk
> Beat a Venetian and traduced the state,
> I took by th' throat the circumcisèd dog
> And smote him thus.
> *He stabs himself*
> (5.2.361–65, s.d.)

In Act 1, Othello, an orthodox Christian and loyal servant of the state, agrees to defend Venice from the Turks—to protect Christianity from a Muslim people with whom Moors were linked on religious, political, and military grounds. By having Venice send Othello to that island to protect Christian interests from the forces of Islam, Shakespeare inserts his protagonist into a defining struggle of the age. In Act 5, Othello remembers that he defended Venice from the Turks once before. This recollection is the occasion for his suicide, a deed that splits him in two. Othello is agent and object of justice, servant and enemy of the Christian state. As a "base Iudean" and "circumcisèd dog," he is a Jew. Circumcision also makes him a Turk. The external military conflict returns as internal division within Othello's soul. Othello half assumes an ethnic and religious otherness to exorcise his guilt. The development of the plot both undermines and validates ethnocentric and racist stereotypes. But is this conclusion really about race, or does it turn instead on religious—and, hence, cultural—antagonism? The question resonates in today's world, where the "problem of the color-line" seems both related to and distinct from the persistence, in the eastern Mediterranean and beyond, of the very religious and military conflicts evoked by *Othello*. Hence, the uneasiness of the ending, where the unwarranted projection of guilt entirely beyond the confines of Europe is the precondition of that noble acceptance of responsibility with which Othello so memorably leaves the world and the play.

WALTER COHEN

TEXTUAL NOTE

The Tragedy of Othello, the Moore of Venice survives in two early authoritative versions—the First Quarto of 1622 (Q) and the First Folio of the following year (F). Extensive study of the background and relationship of the two texts has yet to produce anything close to a consensus. The Oxford editors hypothesize that F uses a scribal copy of Shakespeare's own revision of his earlier manuscript preserved in Q. On the other hand, Q more accurately preserves Shakespeare's characteristic spelling and punctuation, its stage directions are fuller and more authorial (although some were probably added later), and it contains more than fifty oaths excluded from F presumably in response to the Profanity Act of 1606. It is also the only Shakespearean Quarto with act divisions. In order to capture these features, the version printed here uses Q for these details. But it includes the roughly 160 lines from F not found in Q, and it usually prefers F to Q in the over one thousand places where their wording differs. In general, then, F is the primary source for the language, whereas Q provides the spelling, punctuation, oaths, and to some extent stage directions. Act divisions are the same in the two versions. Other modern editions of the play, although differing in their assumptions and in many details, produce broadly similar texts.

The passages unique to F fall into three main categories. In Act 1, Roderigo's and Brabanzio's accusations against Othello are longer. Second, beginning in Act 3, F provides Othello with greater opportunity to express his anguish. Finally and most important, the last two acts of F provide fuller parts for Desdemona (mainly by giving her the willow song in 4.3) and Emilia. These passages tend to place F further away from cynicism and disillusionment than is Q. Some of the more extensive or striking differences from Q are mentioned in the notes. By contrast, differences in Iago's role between Q and F are minor and incidental. The excision of oaths places the scribal transcript for F after 1606. Perhaps the Profanity Act necessitated certain limited revisions for a revival in 1606 or later. Perhaps then or at another time, the Oxford editors hypothesize, Shakespeare introduced more substantive changes—occasionally in the oaths, more often in the characters themselves.

Various alternatives to this approach appear in the scholarly literature on the play. One recent explanation is worthy of particular note, however. According to this argument, the 160 lines found only in F are part of the original text. Q represents an abridgment designed for performance and, for the most part, dictated to a scribe by the actors who initially played the parts. If this is so (and it currently seems the most persuasive hypothesis), the thematic differences between Q and F suggested above would represent not two distinct stages in Shakespeare's career but two different versions of the same play—the *Othello* performed for some or all audiences in the early seventeenth century and the version available to readers and potentially to spectators at least from 1623 on, though perhaps earlier as well.

SELECTED BIBLIOGRAPHY

Barthelemy, Anthony Gerard, ed. *Critical Essays on Shakespeare's "Othello."* New York: Hall, 1994. A collection of important essays (including Boose, Fineman, Loomba, Neely, Neill, Newman), mainly from the 1970s and 1980s, focusing on race and gender.

Danson, Lawrence. "England, Islam, and the Mediterranean Drama: *Othello* and Others." *Journal for Early Modern Cultural Studies* 2.2 (2002): 1–25. Contextual study of East and West, showing the instability of standard distinctions among Moor, Turk, Jew, and Christian.

Greenblatt, Stephen. *Renaissance Self-Fashioning: From More to Shakespeare.* Chicago: University of Chicago Press, 1980. 222–54. Othello's narrative self-fashioning and its subversion by Desdemona's submission and Iago's malice; a central essay for modern *Othello* scholarship and for New Historicist criticism generally.

Hankey, Julie, ed. *Othello.* 2nd ed. New York: Cambridge University Press, 2005. History of performance (stage, film, and television), with an extensive list of productions over 400 years and a text of the play with theatrical annotations.

Neill, Michael, ed. *Othello, the Moor of Venice.* Oxford: Clarendon, 2006. Outstanding scholarly edition with a book-length critical introduction.

Nostbakken, Faith, ed. *Understanding "Othello": A Student Casebook to Issues, Sources, and Historical Documents.* Westport, Conn.: Greenwood Press, 2000. Extensive excerpts from Renaissance sources, including Cinthio and Knowles; briefer selections from literary and performance criticism; suggestions of contemporary relevance (O.J. Simpson, Bill Clinton, etc.).

Orlin, Lena Cowen, ed. *Othello.* New York: Palgrave Macmillan, 2004. Leading essays since 1990, mostly on gender and marriage (Berger, Bristol, Sinfield) or race and reception (Bartels, Singh, Hodgdon, Albanese).

Pechter, Edward. *"Othello" and Interpretive Traditions.* Iowa City: University of Iowa Press, 1999. Relatively traditional account of the play's power that recognizes the inextricable link between text and interpretation while arguing for the continuing influence of earlier critical debates on current scholarship.

Potter, Lois. *Othello.* Shakespeare in Performance series. Manchester: Manchester University Press, 2002. Manchester: Manchester University Press, 2002. Focus on recent stagings, live or electronic, seeing Paul Robeson's performances from the 1930s to the 1950s as the defining events in modern productions of the play.

Wain, John, ed. *Shakespeare, "Othello": A Casebook.* London: Macmillan, 1971. Classic essays by Rymer, Johnson, Coleridge, Bradley, Eliot, Knight, Empson, Leavis, Gardner, Bayley, Auden, Coghill.

FILMS

Othello. 1952. Dir. Orson Welles. USA. 93 min. This black-and-white film stars Welles as Othello. Famous for its innovative and disorienting camera work more than for its acting.

Othello. 1965. Dir. Stuart Burge and John Dexter. UK. 165 min. Film of a stage performance, with Laurence Olivier as Othello and Maggie Smith as Desdemona. Notable not only for the white actor's effort fully to impersonate a black African—seen at the time as both troubling and moving—but also for Smith's spirited Desdemona, a break with the prior stage tradition of representing the character as a passive victim.

Othello. 1988. Dir. Janet Suzman. South Africa/UK. 187 min. Film of the controversial South African stage performance (the first with a black African actor and a white actress) that became a form of antiapartheid protest.

Othello. 1995. Dir. Oliver Parker. USA/UK. 123 min. First version made for film with an African American, Laurence Fishburne, as Othello. Kenneth Branagh as Iago dominates the play (as often happens with Iago). Ironically, racial issues are muted.

O. 2001. Dir. Tim Blake Nelson. USA. 95 min. Set in a contemporary high school, centered on a basketball player, Odin (Mekhi Phifer), in love with Desi (Julia Stiles), undone by Hugo (Josh Hartnett); also with Martin Sheen.

The Tragedy of Othello, the Moor of Venice

THE PERSONS OF THE PLAY

OTHELLO, the Moor of Venice
DESDEMONA, his wife
Michael CASSIO, his lieutenant
BIANCA, a courtesan, in love with Cassio
IAGO, the Moor's ensign
EMILIA, Iago's wife
A CLOWN, a servant of Othello
The DUKE of Venice
BRABANZIO, Desdemona's father, a senator of Venice
GRAZIANO, Brabanzio's brother
LODOVICO, kinsman of Brabanzio
SENATORS of Venice
RODERIGO, a Venetian gentleman, in love with Desdemona
MONTANO, Governor of Cyprus
A HERALD
A MESSENGER
Attendants, officers, sailors, gentlemen of Cyprus, musicians

1.1

Enter IAGO[1] *and* RODERIGO

RODERIGO   Tush, never tell me!° I take it much unkindly   *(Annoyance; disbelief)*
That thou, Iago, who hast had my purse
As if the strings were thine, shouldst know of this.

IAGO   'Sblood,° but you'll not hear me!   *By Christ's blood*
5   If ever I did dream of such a matter, abhor me.

RODERIGO   Thou told'st me thou didst hold him in thy hate.

IAGO   Despise me
If I do not. Three great ones of the city,
In personal suit to make me his lieutenant,
10   Off-capped° to him; and by the faith of man   *Took off their caps*
I know my price, I am worth no worse a place.
But he, as loving his own pride and purposes,
Evades them with a bombast circumstance[2]
Horribly stuffed with epithets of war,°   *military jargon*
15   Nonsuits° my mediators; for 'Certes,'° says he,   *Denies / Certainly*
'I have already chose my officer.'
And what was he?
Forsooth, a great arithmetician,[3]
One Michael Cassio, a Florentine,

1.1   Location: A street in Venice.
1. Iago's name may be related to Santiago Matamoros, St. James the Moor Slayer, the patron saint of Spain.
2. With an inflated circumlocution. *bombast:* cotton padding in clothes, a metaphor picked up by "stuffed" (line 14) and possibly "suit" (line 9) and "Nonsuits" (line 15).
3. Implying that Cassio's knowledge of war is purely theoretical.

20   A fellow almost damned in a fair wife,[4]
     That° never set a squadron in the field   *Who*
     Nor the division° of a battle° knows   *ordering / battalion*
     More than a spinster°—unless the bookish theoric,°   *housewife / learning*
     Wherein the togaed consuls can propose[5]
25   As masterly as he. Mere prattle without practice
     Is all his soldiership; but he, sir, had th'election,
     And I—of whom his eyes had seen the proof
     At Rhodes, at Cyprus, and on other grounds
     Christened and heathen—must be beleed° and calmed°   *without wind / becalmed*
30   By debitor and creditor. This counter-caster,[6]
     He in good time° must his lieutenant be,   *indeed (scornful)*
     And I—God bless the mark!°—his Moorship's ensign.[7]   *God help us*
     RODERIGO   By heaven, I rather would have been his hangman.
     IAGO   Why, there's no remedy. 'Tis the curse of service.
35   Preferment goes by letter and affection,[8]
     And not by old gradation,° where each second   *traditional seniority*
     Stood heir to th' first. Now, sir, be judge yourself
     Whether I in any just term am affined°   *am bound in any just way*
     To love the Moor.[9]
40   RODERIGO   I would not follow him then.
     IAGO   O sir, content you.°   *be content*
     I follow him to serve my turn upon him.
     We cannot all be masters, nor all masters
     Cannot be truly followed. You shall mark
45   Many a duteous and knee-crooking knave
     That, doting on his own obsequious bondage,
     Wears out his time much like his master's ass
     For naught but provender,° and when he's old, cashiered.°   *animal feed / fired*
     Whip me° such honest knaves. Others there are   *The hell with*
50   Who, trimmed° in forms and visages of duty,   *outwardly decorated*
     Keep yet their hearts attending on themselves,
     And, throwing but shows of service on their lords,
     Do well thrive by 'em, and when they have lined their coats,
     Do themselves homage. These fellows have some soul,
55   And such a one do I profess myself—for, sir,
     It is as sure as you are Roderigo,
     Were I the Moor I would not be Iago.
     In following him I follow but myself.
     Heaven is my judge, not I for° love and duty,   *I am not driven by*
60   But seeming so for my peculiar° end.   *personal*
     For when my outward action doth demonstrate
     The native act and figure[1] of my heart

4. Obscure. Cassio has not yet met Bianca and is unmarried, although in Shakespeare's source he is. Perhaps Shakespeare's error, a reference to Cassio as a ladies' man, or an oblique, debatable anticipation of the main plot.
5. In which the toga-wearing senators can debate.
6. *debitor and creditor, counter-caster:* pejorative terms for an accountant (Cassio).
7. As "ensign," Iago is something like a standard-bearer or third-in-command. He clearly ranks below "lieutenant" Cassio, the second-in-command. This reference to "his Moorship" is also the first indication about whom Iago has been complaining.

8. Promotion comes through connections and favoritism.
9. A Moor was a Muslim of the mixed Berber and Arab people inhabiting northwest Africa. This term, like the comparison of Othello to a "Barbary horse" (an Arab, line 113), formerly led to the denial of Othello's blackness. But the passages describing Othello's appearance—"thick-lips," "black ram," "sooty bosom," "black Othello," "I am black," "black / As mine own face" (1.1.66, 1.1.88, 1.2.71, 2.3.27–28, 3.3.267, 3.3.392–93)—seem to have greater weight. "Moor" often meant sub-Saharan African in the Renaissance.
1. The innate operation (or motivation) and shape (or nature).

In compliment extern,° 'tis not long after   *outward appearance*
But I will wear my heart upon my sleeve
65   For daws° to peck at. I am not what I am.   *crowlike birds*
RODERIGO   What a full fortune does the thick-lips owe°   *own*
     If he can carry't thus!
IAGO   Call up her father,
     Rouse him, make after him, poison his delight,
     Proclaim him in the streets; incense her kinsmen,
70   And, though he in a fertile climate dwell,
     Plague him with flies. Though that his joy be joy,
     Yet throw such chances of vexation on't
     As it may lose some colour.
RODERIGO   Here is her father's house. I'll call aloud.
75   IAGO   Do, with like timorous accent° and dire yell   *frightening tone*
     As when, by night and negligence, the fire
     Is spied in populous cities.
RODERIGO [*calling*]   What ho, Brabanzio, Signor Brabanzio, ho!
IAGO [*calling*]   Awake, what ho, Brabanzio, thieves, thieves, thieves!
80   Look to your house, your daughter, and your bags.
     Thieves, thieves!

          [*Enter*] BRABANZIO [*in his nightgown*] *at a window
          above*

BRABANZIO   What is the reason of this terrible summons?
     What is the matter there?
RODERIGO   Signor, is all your family within?
IAGO   Are your doors locked?
85   BRABANZIO   Why, wherefore ask you this?
IAGO   'Swounds,° sir, you're robbed. For shame, put on your   *By Christ's wounds*
          gown.
     Your heart is burst, you have lost half your soul.
     Even now, now, very now, an old black ram
     Is tupping° your white ewe. Arise, arise!   *copulating with*
90   Awake the snorting° citizens with the bell,   *snoring*
     Or else the devil will make a grandsire of you.
     Arise, I say.
BRABANZIO   What, have you lost your wits?
RODERIGO   Most reverend signor, do you know my voice?
BRABANZIO   Not I. What are you?
95   RODERIGO   My name is Roderigo.
BRABANZIO   The worser welcome.
     I have charged thee not to haunt about my doors.
     In honest plainness thou hast heard me say
     My daughter is not for thee, and now in madness,
100 Being full of supper and distempering° draughts,   *destabilizing*
     Upon malicious bravery° dost thou come   *defiance*
     To start° my quiet.   *upset*
RODERIGO   Sir, sir, sir.
BRABANZIO   But thou must needs be sure
105 My spirits and my place° have in their power   *rank*
     To make this bitter to thee.
RODERIGO   Patience, good sir.
BRABANZIO   What tell'st thou me of robbing? This is Venice.
     My house is not a grange.°   *country house*
RODERIGO   Most grave Brabanzio,

In simple and pure soul I come to you.

110 IAGO [*to* BRABANZIO]   'Swounds, sir, you are one of those that will
not serve God if the devil bid you. Because we come to do you
service and you think we are ruffians, you'll have your daughter
covered with a Barbary horse,[2] you'll have your nephews° neigh   grandsons
to you, you'll have coursers for cousins and jennets for ger-
115 mans.[3]

BRABANZIO   What profane wretch art thou?

IAGO   I am one, sir, that comes to tell you your daughter and the
Moor are now making the beast with two backs.°   copulating

BRABANZIO   Thou art a villain.

IAGO   You are a senator.

120 BRABANZIO   This thou shalt answer.° I know thee, Roderigo.   account for

RODERIGO   Sir, I will answer anything. But I beseech you,
If't be your pleasure and most wise consent[4]—
As partly I find it is—that your fair daughter,
At this odd-even° and dull watch o'th' night,   late (around midnight)
125 Transported with no worse nor better guard
But with a knave of common° hire, a gondolier,   public
To the gross clasps of a lascivious Moor—
If this be known to you, and your allowance,°   allowed by you
We then have done you bold and saucy wrongs.
130 But if you know not this, my manners tell me
We have your wrong rebuke. Do not believe
That, from° the sense of all civility,   in opposition to
I thus would play and trifle with your reverence.
Your daughter, if you have not given her leave,
135 I say again hath made a gross revolt,
Tying her duty, beauty, wit, and fortunes
In an extravagant and wheeling stranger[5]
Of here and everywhere. Straight° satisfy yourself.   Immediately
If she be in her chamber or your house,
140 Let loose on me the justice of the state
For thus deluding you.

BRABANZIO [*calling*]   Strike on the tinder,° ho!   A light
Give me a taper,° call up all my people.   candle
This accident° is not unlike my dream;   event
Belief of it oppresses me already.
Light, I say, light!   *Exit*

145 IAGO   Farewell, for I must leave you.
It seems not meet° nor wholesome to my place   proper
To be produced°—as, if I stay, I shall—   presented as witness
Against the Moor, for I do know the state,
However this may gall him with some check,°   reprimand
150 Cannot with safety cast° him, for he's embarked°   dismiss / committed
With such loud reason° to the Cyprus wars,   vociferous, just support
Which even now stands in act,° that, for their souls,   are taking place
Another of his fathom° they have none   caliber
To lead their business, in which regard—

---

2. Horse from northwest coastal Africa; an Arab; suggesting barbarism.
3. *coursers:* strong horses. *cousins:* kinsmen. *jennets:*
small Spanish horses. *germans:* close relatives.

4. Lines 122–138 do not appear in Q.
5. In a vagrant and vagabond foreigner (perhaps suggesting a planet wandering off course).

155   Though I do hate him as I do hell pains—
       Yet for necessity of present life
       I must show out a flag and sign of love,
       Which is indeed but sign. That you shall surely find him,
       Lead to the Sagittary⁶ the raisèd search,°   *awakened searchers*
160   And there will I be with him. So farewell.   *Exit*

       Enter [below] BRABANZIO *in his nightgown, and servants*
       with torches

BRABANZIO   It is too true an evil. Gone she is,
       And what's to come of my despisèd time°   *lifetime*
       Is naught but bitterness. Now, Roderigo,
       Where didst thou see her?—O unhappy girl!—
165   With the Moor, sayst thou?—Who would be a father?—
       How didst thou know 'twas she?—O, she deceives me
       Past thought!—What said she to you? [*To servants*] Get more tapers,
       Raise all my kindred.   [*Exit one or more*]
       [*To* RODERIGO]   Are they married, think you?
RODERIGO   Truly, I think they are.
170 BRABANZIO   O heaven, how got she out? O, treason of the blood!
       Fathers, from hence trust not your daughters' minds
       By what you see them act. Is there not charms°   *magic*
       By which the property° of youth and maidhood°   *attribute / virginity*
       May be abused? Have you not read, Roderigo,
       Of some such thing?
175 RODERIGO   Yes, sir, I have indeed.
BRABANZIO [*to servants*]   Call up my brother. [*To* RODERIGO] O,
         would you had had her.
       [*To servants*] Some one way, some another.   [*Exit one or more*]
       [*To* RODERIGO]   Do you know
       Where we may apprehend her and the Moor?
RODERIGO   I think I can discover him, if you please
180   To get good guard and go along with me.
BRABANZIO   Pray you lead on. At every house I'll call;
       I may command° at most. [*Calling*] Get weapons, ho,   *demand help*
       And raise some special officers of night.
       On, good Roderigo. I will deserve° your pains.   *Exeunt*   *reward*

1.2

       Enter OTHELLO, IAGO, *and attendants with torches*
IAGO   Though in the trade of war I have slain men,
       Yet do I hold it very stuff ° o'th' conscience   *essence*
       To do no contrived° murder. I lack iniquity,   *premeditated*
       Sometime, to do me service. Nine or ten times
5   I had thought to've yerked him° here, under the ribs.   *stabbed (Roderigo)*
OTHELLO   'Tis better as it is.
IAGO   Nay, but he prated,
       And spoke such scurvy and provoking terms
       Against your honour
       That, with the little godliness I have,

---

6. Perhaps indicating an inn named for the astrological sign Sagitarius, where Othello and Desdemona are staying. It may also suggest Othello himself, since Sagitarius is depicted as a centaur (a mythological being part man, part horse), and Iago has already likened Othello to a "Barbary horse."

1.2 Location: Another street in Venice, before Othello's lodgings.

10 I did full hard forbear him.[1] But I pray you, sir,
Are you fast° married? Be assured of this: *legitimately*
That the magnifico° is much beloved,   *(Brabanzio)*
And hath in his effect a voice potential°   *powerful*
As double as the Duke's. He will divorce you,
15 Or put upon you what restraint or grievance
The law, with all his might to enforce it on,
Will give him cable.°   *scope*
OTHELLO   Let him do his spite.
My services which I have done the signory°   *Venetian government*
Shall out-tongue his complaints. 'Tis yet to know°—   *not publicly known*
20 Which, when I know that boasting is an honour,
I shall promulgate—I fetch my life and being
From men of royal siege,° and my demerits°   *rank / deserts*
May speak unbonneted[2] to as proud a fortune
As this that I have reached. For know, Iago,
25 But that I love the gentle Desdemona
I would not my unhousèd° free condition   *unconfined*
Put into circumscription and confine
For the seas' worth.
              Enter CASSIO *and officers, with torches*
                   But look, what lights come yond?
IAGO   Those are the raisèd father and his friends.
You were best go in.
30 OTHELLO   Not I. I must be found.
My parts,° my title, and my perfect soul[3]   *qualities*
Shall manifest me rightly. Is it they?
IAGO   By Janus,° I think no.   *two-faced Roman god*
OTHELLO   The servants of the Duke, and my lieutenant!
35 The goodness of the night upon you, friends.
What is the news?
CASSIO   The Duke does greet you, general,
And he requires your haste-post-haste appearance
Even on the instant.
OTHELLO   What is the matter, think you?
CASSIO   Something from Cyprus, as I may divine;
40 It is a business of some heat.° The galleys   *urgency*
Have sent a dozen sequent° messengers   *successive*
This very night at one another's heels,
And many of the consuls, raised and met,
Are at the Duke's already. You have been hotly called for,
45 When, being not at your lodging to be found,
The senate sent about three several quests
To search you out.
OTHELLO   'Tis well I am found by you.
I will but spend a word here in the house
And go with you.   *[Exit]*
CASSIO   Ensign, what makes he here?
50 IAGO   Faith, he tonight hath boarded a land-carrack.°   *large merchant ship*
If it prove lawful prize, he's made for ever.
CASSIO   I do not understand.

---

1. I barely restrained myself from attacking him.   3. My clear conscience.
2. Without deference; modestly.

IAGO	He's married.	
CASSIO	To who?	

Enter BRABANZIO, RODERIGO, *and* OFFICERS, *with lights and weapons*

IAGO   Marry,° to—   *By Mary (mild oath)*
   [*Enter* OTHELLO]
   [*To* OTHELLO] Come, captain, will you go?

OTHELLO   Have with you.°   *Let's go*

55   CASSIO   Here comes another troop to seek for you.
   IAGO   It is Brabanzio. General, be advised.
      He comes to bad intent.

OTHELLO   Holla, stand, there!

RODERIGO [*to* BRABANZIO]   Signor, it is the Moor.

BRABANZIO   Down with him, thief!

IAGO [*drawing his sword*]   You, Roderigo? Come, sir, I am for you.

60   OTHELLO   Keep up° your bright swords, for the dew will rust 'em.   *Put away*
      [*To* BRABANZIO] Good signor, you shall more command with years
      Than with your weapons.

BRABANZIO   O thou foul thief, where hast thou stowed my daughter?
      Damned as thou art, thou hast enchanted her,
65   For I'll refer me to all things of sense,[4]
      If she in chains of magic were not bound,
      Whether a maid so tender, fair, and happy,
      So opposite to marriage that she shunned
      The wealthy curlèd darlings of our nation,
70   Would ever have, t'incur a general mock,
      Run from her guardage to the sooty bosom
      Of such a thing as thou—to fear, not to delight.
      Judge me the world if 'tis not gross in sense[5]
      That thou hast practised on her with foul charms,
75   Abused her delicate youth with drugs or minerals
      That weakens motion. I'll have't disputed on.°   *argued by experts*
      'Tis probable, and palpable to thinking.
      I therefore apprehend and do attach° thee   *arrest*
      For an abuser of the world, a practiser
80   Of arts inhibited and out of warrant.°   *prohibited and illegal*
      [*To* OFFICERS] Lay hold upon him. If he do resist,
      Subdue him at his peril.

OTHELLO   Hold your hands,
      Both you of my inclining° and the rest.   *following*
      Were it my cue to fight, I should have known it
85   Without a prompter. Whither will you that I go
      To answer this your charge?

BRABANZIO   To prison, till fit time
      Of law and course of direct session
      Call thee to answer.

OTHELLO   What if I do obey?
      How may the Duke be therewith satisfied,
90   Whose messengers are here about my side
      Upon some present business of the state
      To bring me to him?

OFFICER [*to* BRABANZIO]   'Tis true, most worthy signor.

4. For I'll ask, relying on common sense.
5. If it is not patently obvious. Lines 73–78 do not appear in Q.

The Duke's in council, and your noble self,
I am sure, is sent for.
BRABANZIO   How, the Duke in council?
95   In this time of the night? Bring him away.°   along
Mine's not an idle cause. The Duke himself,
Or any of my brothers of the state,
Cannot but feel this wrong as 'twere their own;
For if such actions may have passage free,
100 Bondslaves and pagans shall our statesmen be.   *Exeunt*

1.3

Enter [the] DUKE *and* SENATORS *set at a table, with
lights and* OFFICERS
DUKE   There is no composition in these news
That gives them credit.[1]
FIRST SENATOR   Indeed, they are disproportioned.°   inconsistent
My letters say a hundred and seven galleys.
DUKE   And mine a hundred-forty.
SECOND SENATOR   And mine two hundred.
5   But though they jump not on a just account°—   don't exactly agree
As, in these cases, where the aim reports
'Tis oft with difference[2]—yet do they all confirm
A Turkish fleet, and bearing up to Cyprus.
DUKE   Nay, it is possible enough to judgement.
10   I do not so secure me in the error,
But the main article I do approve
In fearful sense.[3]
SAILOR *(within)*   What ho, what ho, what ho!
          Enter [a] SAILOR
OFFICER   A messenger from the galleys.
DUKE   Now, what's the business?
SAILOR   The Turkish preparation° makes for Rhodes.   battle-ready fleet
15   So was I bid report here to the state
By Signor Angelo.[4]
DUKE [*to* SENATORS]   How say you by this change?
FIRST SENATOR   This cannot be,
By no assay° of reason—'tis a pageant   test
20   To keep us in false gaze. When we consider
The importancy of Cyprus to the Turk,
And let ourselves again but understand
That, as it more concerns the Turk than Rhodes,
So may he with more facile question bear it,[5]
25   For that it stands not in such warlike brace,
But altogether lacks th'abilities
That Rhodes is dressed in—if we make thought of this,
We must not think the Turk is so unskilful
To leave that latest° which concerns him first,   last
30   Neglecting an attempt of ease and gain
To wake and wage° a danger profitless.   risk

1.3 Location: A Venetian council room.
1. *There . . . credit:* The reports lack the consistency
that would make them believable.
2. *where . . . difference:* where the reports are esti-
mates, there are often discrepancies among them.
3. *I do not . . . sense:* I am not so reassured by the discrepancies as to dismiss the main concern—the

approach of the Turkish fleet.
4. Not mentioned elsewhere in the play, Angelus Sori-
anus was a Venetian sea captain who received the Venetian ambassador bearing from Constantinople the
Turkish ultimatum to surrender Cyprus shortly before
its capture by the Turks in 1571.
5. So also can the Turkish fleet more easily win it.

DUKE Nay, in all confidence, he's not for Rhodes.

OFFICER Here is more news.

Enter a MESSENGER

MESSENGER The Ottomites,° reverend and gracious, °*Ottoman Turks*
35 Steering with due course toward the Isle of Rhodes,
Have there injointed them with an after° fleet. °*joined with another*

FIRST SENATOR Ay, so I thought. How many, as you guess?

MESSENGER Of thirty sail, and now they do restem° °*retrace*
Their backward course, bearing with frank appearance
40 Their purposes toward Cyprus. Signor Montano,
Your trusty and most valiant servitor,
With his free duty recommends you thus,[6]
And prays you to believe him.

DUKE 'Tis certain then for Cyprus.
Marcus Luccicos,[7] is not he in town?

45 FIRST SENATOR He's now in Florence.

DUKE Write from us to him post-post-haste. Dispatch.

Enter BRABANZIO, OTHELLO, RODERIGO, IAGO, CASSIO,
and officers

FIRST SENATOR Here comes Brabanzio and the valiant Moor.

DUKE Valiant Othello, we must straight° employ you °*immediately*
Against the general enemy° Ottoman. °*(of all Christendom)*
50 [*To* BRABANZIO] I did not see you. Welcome, gentle° signor. °*noble*
We lacked your counsel and your help tonight.

BRABANZIO So did I yours. Good your grace, pardon me.
Neither my place,° nor aught I heard of business, °*official duty*
Hath raised me from my bed, nor doth the general care
55 Take hold on me; for my particular grief
Is of so floodgate and o'erbearing nature
That it engluts and swallows other sorrows,
And it is still itself.[8]

DUKE Why, what's the matter?

BRABANZIO My daughter, O, my daughter!

SENATORS Dead?

BRABANZIO Ay, to me.
60 She is abused,° stol'n from me, and corrupted °*deluded*
By spells and medicines bought of mountebanks.° °*quacks*
For nature so preposterously to err,
Being not deficient, blind, or lame of sense,
Sans° witchcraft could not. °*Without*

65 DUKE Whoe'er he be that in this foul proceeding
Hath thus beguiled your daughter of herself
And you of her, the bloody book of law
You shall yourself read in the bitter letter
After your own sense, yea, though our proper son
70 Stood in your action.[9]

BRABANZIO Humbly I thank your grace.
Here is the man, this Moor, whom now it seems
Your special mandate for the state affairs
Hath hither brought.

SENATORS We are very sorry for't.

---

6. With his freely given loyalty reports to you thus.
7. Not mentioned elsewhere in the play.
8. *That . . . itself:* That my "grief" can incorporate other "sorrows" without being affected.

9. *You shall . . . action:* You yourself shall interpret the law as you see fit even if my own son is the one you accuse.

DUKE [*to* OTHELLO]   What in your own part can you say to this?
75 BRABANZIO   Nothing but this is so.
OTHELLO   Most potent, grave, and reverend signors,
My very noble and approved good masters,
That I have ta'en away this old man's daughter,
It is most true, true I have married her.
80 The very head and front° of my offending   *height and breadth*
Hath this extent, no more. Rude° am I in my speech,   *Unpolished*
And little blessed with the soft phrase of peace,
For since these arms of mine had seven years' pith°   *strength*
Till now some nine moons wasted,° they have used   *Nine months ago*
85 Their dearest° action in the tented field,   *most valued*
And little of this great world can I speak
More than pertains to feats of broils° and battle.   *combats*
And therefore little shall I grace my cause
In speaking for myself. Yet, by your gracious patience,
90 I will a round° unvarnished tale deliver   *plain*
Of my whole course of love, what drugs, what charms,
What conjuration and what mighty magic—
For such proceeding I am charged withal°—   *with*
I won his daughter.
BRABANZIO   A maiden never bold,
95 Of spirit so still and quiet that her motion
Blushed at herself[1]—and she in spite of nature,
Of years, of country, credit,° everything,   *reputation*
To fall in love with what she feared to look on!
It is a judgement maimed and most imperfect
100 That will confess perfection so could err
Against all rules of nature, and must° be driven   *(we therefore) must*
To find out practices of cunning hell
Why this should be. I therefore vouch again
That with some mixtures powerful o'er the blood,°   *passions*
105 Or with some dram conjured° to this effect,   *enchanted dose*
He wrought upon her.
DUKE   To vouch this is no proof
Without more wider and more overt test
Than these thin habits and poor likelihoods
Of modern seeming do prefer against him.[2]
110 A SENATOR   But Othello, speak.
Did you by indirect and forcèd courses°   *means*
Subdue and poison this young maid's affections,
Or came it by request and such fair question°   *conversation*
As soul to soul affordeth?
OTHELLO   I do beseech you,
115 Send for the lady to the Sagittary,
And let her speak of me before her father.
If you do find me foul in her report,
The trust, the office I do hold of you
Not only take away, but let your sentence
Even fall upon my life.
120 DUKE [*to* OFFICERS]   Fetch Desdemona hither.

1. *her . . . herself*: she blushed at herself at the slightest provocation.
2. *Without . . . him*: Without fuller and more direct
testimony than mere appearances and conjecture based
on currently popular beliefs against him.

OTHELLO   Ensign, conduct them. You best know the place.

Exit [IAGO *with*] *two or three* [*officers*]

    And till she come, as truly as to heaven

    I do confess the vices of my blood,°   *sins of passion*

    So justly to your grave ears I'll present

125   How I did thrive in this fair lady's love,

    And she in mine.

DUKE   Say it, Othello.

OTHELLO   Her father loved me, oft invited me,

    Still° questioned me the story of my life   *Constantly*

    From year to year, the battles, sieges, fortunes

130   That I have passed.

    I ran it through even from my boyish days

    To th' very moment that he bade me tell it,

    Wherein I spoke of most disastrous chances,°   *events*

    Of moving accidents° by flood and field,   *events*

135   Of hair-breadth scapes i'th' imminent deadly breach,[3]

    Of being taken by the insolent foe

    And sold to slavery, of my redemption thence,

    And portance° in my traveller's history,   *conduct*

    Wherein of antres° vast and deserts idle,   *caves*

140   Rough quarries, rocks, and hills whose heads touch heaven,

    It was my hint° to speak. Such was my process,°   *occasion / story*

    And of the cannibals that each other eat,

    The Anthropophagi,[4] and men whose heads

    Do grow beneath their shoulders. These things to hear

145   Would Desdemona seriously incline,

    But still the house affairs would draw her thence,

    Which ever as° she could with haste dispatch   *Whenever*

    She'd come again, and with a greedy ear

    Devour up my discourse; which I observing,

150   Took once a pliant° hour, and found good means   *convenient*

    To draw from her a prayer of earnest heart

    That I would all my pilgrimage dilate,°   *relate*

    Whereof by parcels she had something heard,

    But not intentively.° I did consent,   *continuously*

155   And often did beguile her of her tears

    When I did speak of some distressful stroke

    That my youth suffered. My story being done,

    She gave me for my pains a world of kisses.[5]

    She swore in faith 'twas strange, 'twas passing° strange,   *exceptionally*

160   'Twas pitiful, 'twas wondrous pitiful.

    She wished she had not heard it, yet she wished

    That heaven had made her such a man.[6] She thankèd me,

    And bade me, if I had a friend that loved her,

    I should but teach him how to tell my story,

165   And that would woo her. Upon this hint I spake.

    She loved me for the dangers I had passed,

    And I loved her that she did pity them.

    This only is the witchcraft I have used.

---

3. In the deadly gaps in a fortification.

4. Man-eaters. The term is from the ancient Roman writer Pliny the Elder. Shakespeare was also indebted to the travel literature of the Middle Ages (*Mandeville's Travels*) and the Renaissance (Hakluyt's *Principal Navigations,* among others).

5. F reads "kisses," Q "sighs." It is hard to explain "kisses" as a textual error.

6. Made such a man for her; made her into such a man.

Enter DESDEMONA, IAGO, *and attendants*

Here comes the lady. Let her witness it.

170   DUKE   I think this tale would win my daughter, too.—
Good Brabanzio,
Take up this mangled matter at the best.°   *Make the best of this*
Men do their broken weapons rather use
Than their bare hands.

  BRABANZIO   I pray you hear her speak.

175   If she confess that she was half the wooer,
Destruction on my head if my bad blame
Light on the man! Come hither, gentle mistress.
Do you perceive in all this noble company
Where most you owe obedience?

  DESDEMONA   My noble father,

180   I do perceive here a divided duty.
To you I am bound for life and education.
My life and education both do learn° me   *teach*
How to respect you. You are the lord of duty,
I am hitherto your daughter. But here's my husband,

185   And so much duty as my mother showed
To you, preferring you before her father,
So much I challenge° that I may profess   *assert*
Due to the Moor my lord.

  BRABANZIO   God b'wi'you, I ha' done.
Please it your grace, on to the state affairs.

190   I had rather to adopt a child than get° it.   *beget*
Come hither, Moor.
I here do give thee that° with all my heart   *that which*
Which, but° thou hast already, with all my heart   *except that*
I would keep from thee. [*To* DESDEMONA] For your sake, jewel,

195   I am glad at soul I have no other child,
For thy escape would teach me tyranny,
To hang clogs[7] on 'em. I have done, my lord.

  DUKE   Let me speak like yourself, and lay a sentence°   *draw a moral*
Which, as a grece° or step, may help these lovers   *step*

200   Into your favour.
When remedies are past, the griefs are ended
By seeing the worst which late on hopes depended.[8]
To mourn a mischief that is past and gone
Is the next way to draw new mischief on.

205   What cannot be preserved when fortune takes,
Patience her injury a mockery makes.[9]
The robbed that smiles steals something from the thief;
He robs himself that spends a bootless° grief.   *pointless*

  BRABANZIO   So let the Turk of Cyprus us beguile,

210   We lose it not so long as we can smile.
He bears the sentence° well that nothing bears   *saying; judgment*
But the free comfort which from thence he hears,
But he bears both the sentence and the sorrow
That, to pay grief, must of poor patience borrow.

215   These sentences, to sugar or to gall,°   *both sweet and bitter*

---

7. Blocks of wood tied to criminals' legs to keep them from escaping.
8. By seeing those things come to pass that caused grief in anticipation. The Duke paints the moral in rhyming couplets, to which Brabanzio replies in kind.
9. Patience laughs at what cannot be helped (and thus reduces the "injury").

Being strong on both sides, are equivocal.
But words are words. I never yet did hear
That the bruisèd heart was piercèd[1] through the ear. I humbly
beseech you proceed to th'affairs of state.

220 DUKE   The Turk with a most mighty preparation makes for
Cyprus. Othello, the fortitude of the place is best known to
you, and though we have there a substitute of most allowed
sufficiency,° yet opinion, a more sovereign mistress of effects,   *known ability*
throws a more safer voice on you.[2] You must therefore be con-
225 tent to slubber° the gloss of your new fortunes with this more   *soil*
stubborn° and boisterous expedition.   *rougher*

OTHELLO   The tyrant custom, most grave senators,
Hath made the flinty and steel couch of war
My thrice-driven° bed of down. I do agnize°   *sifted / acknowledge*
230 A natural and prompt alacrity
I find in hardness,° and do undertake   *hardship*
This present wars against the Ottomites.
Most humbly therefore bending to your state,°   *authority*
I crave fit disposition for my wife,
235 Due reference of place and exhibition,[3]
With such accommodation and besort°   *suitable attendance*
As levels with her breeding.

DUKE   Why, at her father's!

BRABANZIO   I will not have it so.

240 OTHELLO   Nor I.

DESDEMONA   Nor would I there reside,
To put my father in impatient thoughts
By being in his eye. Most gracious Duke,
To my unfolding° lend your prosperous° ear,   *proposal / receptive*
245 And let me find a charter° in your voice   *an authorization*
T'assist my simpleness.

DUKE   What would you, Desdemona?

DESDEMONA   That I did love the Moor to live with him,
My downright violence and storm of fortunes[4]
May trumpet to the world. My heart's subdued
250 Even to the very quality of my lord.[5]
I saw Othello's visage in his mind,
And to his honours and his valiant parts°   *qualities*
Did I my soul and fortunes consecrate;
So that, dear lords, if I be left behind,
255 A moth of peace, and he go to the war,
The rites° for why I love him are bereft me,   *(of love); (of war?)*
And I a heavy interim shall support
By his dear absence. Let me go with him.

OTHELLO [to the DUKE]   Let her have your voice.
260 Vouch with me heaven, I therefor beg it not
To please the palate of my appetite,
Nor to comply with heat°—the young affects[6]   *sexual passion*
In me defunct—and proper° satisfaction,   *personal; fitting*

---

1. Surgically lanced (and presumably cured).
2. *opinion . . . you:* public opinion, which determines
what gets done, finds greater security with you.
3. Proper accommodation and maintenance.
4. My outright defiance of custom.
5. *My heart's . . . lord:* I love him for what he is (military,

adventurous). Q reads "utmost pleasure" for "very
quality"—an openly sexual formulation that makes
Desdemona's response one of subordination rather
than of identification, sexual and otherwise.
6. The youthful desires.

But to be free° and bounteous to her mind;   *liberal*
265   And heaven defend your good souls that you think
        I will your serious and great business scant
        When she is with me. No, when light-winged toys°   *diversions*
        Of feathered Cupid seel° with wanton dullness   *blind*
        My speculative and officed instruments,[7]
270   That my disports° corrupt and taint my business,   *sexual pleasures*
        Let housewives make a skillet of my helm,
        And all indign° and base adversities   *undignified*
        Make head against my estimation.[8]
DUKE   Be it as you shall privately determine,
275   Either for her stay or going. Th'affair cries haste,
        And speed must answer it.
A SENATOR [*to* OTHELLO]   You must away tonight.
DESDEMONA   Tonight, my lord?
DUKE   This night.
OTHELLO   With all my heart.
DUKE   At nine i'th' morning here we'll meet again.
        Othello, leave some officer behind,
280   And he shall our commission bring to you,
        And such things else of quality and respect°   *weight and importance*
        As doth import° you.   *concern*
OTHELLO   So please your grace, my ensign.
        A man he is of honesty[9] and trust.
        To his conveyance I assign my wife,
285   With what else needful your good grace shall think
        To be sent after me.
DUKE   Let it be so.
        Good night to everyone. [*To* BRABANZIO] And, noble signor,
        If virtue no delighted° beauty lack,   *delightful*
        Your son-in-law is far more fair than black.
290   A SENATOR   Adieu, brave Moor. Use Desdemona well.
BRABANZIO   Look to her,° Moor, if thou hast eyes to see.   *Watch her carefully*
        She has deceived her father, and may thee.
              Exeunt [DUKE, BRABANZIO, CASSIO, SENATORS,
                                      and officers]
OTHELLO   My life upon her faith. Honest Iago,
        My Desdemona must I leave to thee.
295   I prithee let thy wife attend on her,
        And bring them after in the best advantage.[1]
        Come, Desdemona. I have but an hour
        Of love, of worldly matter and direction
        To spend with thee. We must obey the time.
              Exeunt [OTHELLO *the*] *Moor and* DESDEMONA
300   RODERIGO   Iago.
IAGO   What sayst thou, noble heart?
RODERIGO   What will I do, think'st thou?
IAGO   Why, go to bed and sleep.
RODERIGO   I will incontinently° drown myself.   *immediately*
305   IAGO   If thou dost, I shall never love thee after. Why, thou silly
        gentleman!

---

7. My duty-bound faculties of sense.   of them deeply ironic, some unwittingly so.
8. Raise an army against my good reputation.   1. And bring them along at the most favorable moment.
9. The first of many references to Iago's "honesty," all

RODERIGO　It is silliness to live when to live is torment; and then
have we a prescription° to die when death is our physician.　*right; doctor's order*

IAGO　O, villainous!° I ha' looked upon the world for four times　*absurd; immoral?*
310　seven years, and since I could distinguish betwixt a benefit and
an injury I never found man that knew how to love himself.
Ere I would say I would drown myself for the love of a guinea-
hen,° I would change my humanity with a baboon.　*woman*

RODERIGO　What should I do? I confess it is my shame to be so
315　fond, but it is not in my virtue° to amend it.　*native ability*

IAGO　Virtue? A fig!° 'Tis in ourselves that we are thus or thus.　*(an obscenity)*
Our bodies are our gardens, to the which our wills are garden-
ers; so that if we will plant nettles or sow lettuce, set hyssop° and　*mint herb*
weed up thyme, supply it with one gender of herbs or distract it
320　with many, either to have it sterile with idleness° or manured　*noncultivation*
with industry, why, the power and corrigible authority° of this　*ability to decide*
lies in our wills. If the beam° of our lives had not one scale of　*(as on a scale)*
reason to peise° another of sensuality, the blood and baseness　*counterweigh*
of our natures would conduct us to most preposterous conclu-
325　sions. But we have reason to cool our raging motions,° our car-　*appetites*
nal stings, our unbitted° lusts; whereof I take this that you call　*unrestrained*
love to be a sect or scion.°　*offshoot*

RODERIGO　It cannot be.

IAGO　It is merely a lust of the blood and a permission of the will.
330　Come, be a man. Drown thyself? Drown cats and blind puppies. I have professed me thy friend, and I confess me knit to
thy deserving with cables of perdurable° toughness. I could　*durable*
never better stead° thee than now. Put money in thy purse.　*help*
Follow thou the wars, defeat thy favour with an usurped beard.²
335　I say, put money in thy purse. It cannot be long that Desdemona should continue her love to the Moor—put money in
thy purse—nor he his to her. It was a violent commencement°　*an abruptly begun affair*
in her, and thou shalt see an answerable sequestration³—put
but money in thy purse. These Moors are changeable in their
340　wills—fill thy purse with money. The food that to him now
is as luscious as locusts⁴ shall be to him shortly as bitter as
coloquintida.⁵ She must change for youth. When she is sated
with his body, she will find the error of her choice. Therefore
put money in thy purse. If thou wilt needs° damn thyself, do it　*If you must*
345　a more delicate way than drowning. Make all the money thou
canst. If sanctimony° and a frail vow betwixt an erring° barbar-　*holy rite / a wandering*
ian and a super-subtle° Venetian be not too hard for my wits　*highly sensitive*
and all the tribe of hell, thou shalt enjoy her; therefore make
money. A pox o' drowning thyself—it is clean out of the way.°　*of no use*
350　Seek thou rather to be hanged in compassing° thy joy than to　*encompassing*
be drowned and go without her.

RODERIGO　Wilt thou be fast° to my hopes if I depend on the　*duty bound*
issue?°　*outcome*

IAGO　Thou art sure of me. Go, make money. I have told thee
355　often, and I re-tell thee again and again, I hate the Moor. My
cause is hearted,° thine hath no less reason. Let us be conjunc-　*heartfelt*
tive° in our revenge against him. If thou canst cuckold him,　*joined*

2. Disguise your appearance with a fake beard.
3. A correspondingly abrupt separation.
4. A sweet, exotic fruit, perhaps carob or honeysuckle.

5. Colocynth, a purgative—one of Iago's many references to the digestive tract.

thou dost thyself a pleasure, me a sport. There are many events
in the womb of time, which will be delivered. Traverse,° go,   Go (to arms)
360   provide thy money. We will have more of this tomorrow.
Adieu.

RODERIGO   Where shall we meet i'th' morning?

IAGO   At my lodging.

RODERIGO   I'll be with thee betimes.°   early

IAGO   Go to, farewell—
Do you hear, Roderigo?

RODERIGO   I'll sell all my land.   Exit

365 IAGO   Thus do I make my fool my purse—
For I mine own gained knowledge should profane
If I would time expend with such a snipe°   fool
But for my sport and profit. I hate the Moor,
And it is thought abroad° that 'twixt my sheets   rumored
370   He has done my office. I know not if't be true,
But I, for mere suspicion in that kind,
Will do° as if for surety. He holds° me well: act / esteems
The better shall my purpose work on him.
Cassio's a proper° man. Let me see now,   handsome
375   To get his place, and to plume up° my will   gratify
In double knavery—how, how? Let's see.
After some time to abuse Othello's ears
That he is too familiar with his wife;[6]
He hath a person and a smooth dispose°   manner
380   To be suspected, framed to make women false.
The Moor is of a free° and open nature,   liberal
That thinks men honest that but seem to be so,
And will as tenderly° be led by th' nose   easily
As asses are.
385   I ha't. It is ingendered. Hell and night
Must bring this monstrous birth to the world's light.   Exit

2.1

Enter [below] MONTANO, *Governor of Cyprus; two other*
GENTLEMEN [*above*]

MONTANO   What from the cape can you discern at sea?

FIRST GENTLEMEN   Nothing at all. It is a high-wrought flood.°   very rough sea
I cannot 'twixt the heaven and the main°   sea
Descry° a sail.   Discern

5 MONTANO   Methinks the wind hath spoke aloud at land.
A fuller blast ne'er shook our battlements.
If it ha' ruffianed° so upon the sea,   raged
What ribs of oak, when mountains melt on them,
Can hold the mortise?[1] What shall we hear of this?

10 SECOND GENTLEMEN   A segregation° of the Turkish fleet;   separation
For do but stand upon the foaming shore,
The chidden billow[2] seems to pelt the clouds,
The wind-shaked surge with high and monstrous mane

---

6. "He" is Cassio (as in line 379), but "his" refers to
Othello—a potential confusion of pronouns.
2.1 Location: A seaport in Cyprus; outdoors near the
harbor.
1. *What . . . mortise:* What ship (with "ribs of oak")

can hold its joints ("mortise") together when "mountains" of water pour on it?
2. The surging ocean, rebuked ("chidden") by the wind
(or repulsed by the land).

Seems to cast water on the burning Bear
15 And quench the guards of th'ever-fixèd Pole.[3]
I never did like molestation view°   *see such a tumult*
On the enchafèd flood.

MONTANO   If that the Turkish fleet
Be not ensheltered and embayed, they are drowned.
It is impossible to bear it out.

Enter a THIRD GENTLEMEN

20 THIRD GENTLEMEN   News, lads! Our wars are done.
The desperate tempest hath so banged the Turks
That their designment° halts. A noble ship of Venice   *plan*
Hath seen a grievous wrack and sufferance
On most part of their fleet.

25 MONTANO   How, is this true?

THIRD GENTLEMEN   The ship is here put in,
A Veronessa.[4] Michael Cassio,
Lieutenant to the warlike Moor Othello,
Is come on shore; the Moor himself at sea,
30 And is in full commission here for Cyprus.

MONTANO   I am glad on't; 'tis a worthy governor.

THIRD GENTLEMEN   But this same Cassio, though he speak of comfort
Touching the Turkish loss, yet he looks sadly,°   *seriously*
And prays the Moor be safe, for they were parted
With foul and violent tempest.

35 MONTANO   Pray heavens he be,
For I have served him, and the man commands
Like a full soldier. Let's to the sea-side, ho!—
As well to see the vessel that's come in
As to throw out our eyes for brave Othello,
40 Even till we make the main and th'aerial blue
An indistinct regard.[5]

THIRD GENTLEMEN   Come, let's do so,
For every minute is expectancy
Of more arrivance.

Enter CASSIO

CASSIO   Thanks, you the valiant of this warlike isle
45 That so approve the Moor! O, let the heavens
Give him defence against the elements,
For I have lost him on a dangerous sea.

MONTANO   Is he well shipped?

CASSIO   His barque is stoutly timbered, and his pilot
50 Of very expert and approved allowance.°   *known ability*
Therefore my hopes, not surfeited to death,°   *not excessive*
Stand in bold cure.°   *likely to be rewarded*

VOICES (*within*)   A sail, a sail, a sail!

CASSIO   What noise?

A GENTLEMAN   The town is empty. On the brow° o'th' sea   *cliff at the edge*
55 Stand ranks of people, and they cry 'A sail!'

CASSIO   My hopes do shape him° for the governor.   *make it out to be*
A *shot*

---

3. *burning Bear:* the constellation Ursa Minor. *guards:* probably two stars in the constellation that point in a line to the polestar, also in Ursa Minor.
4. Meaning unclear: originally from Verona, though now used by the Venetians; a cutter; possibly meant to modify not "ship" but Cassio, although he is Florentine (1.1.19).
5. *Even . . . regard:* Until we can't distinguish sea from sky.

A GENTLEMAN   They do discharge their shot of courtesy—
    Our friends, at least.
CASSIO   I pray you, sir, go forth,
    And give us truth who 'tis that is arrived.
60 A GENTLEMAN   I shall.   *Exit*
MONTANO   But, good lieutenant, is your general wived?
CASSIO   Most fortunately. He hath achieved a maid
    That paragons° description and wild fame,   *stands above*
    One that excels the quirks of blazoning° pens,   *praise-giving*
65 And in th'essential vesture of creation
    Does tire the engineer.⁶
          Enter GENTLEMAN
               How now, who has put in?
GENTLEMAN   'Tis one Iago, ensign to the general.
CASSIO   He's had most favourable and happy speed.
    Tempests themselves, high seas, and howling winds,
70 The guttered° rocks and congregated° sands, *jagged / accumulated*
    Traitors ensteeped° to enclog the guiltless keel,   *underwater*
    As having sense of beauty do omit°   *forgo*
    Their mortal° natures, letting go safely by   *deadly*
    The divine Desdemona.
MONTANO   What is she?
75 CASSIO   She that I spake of, our great captain's captain,
    Left in the conduct of the bold Iago,
    Whose footing here anticipates our thoughts
    A sennight's speed.⁷ Great Jove, Othello guard,
    And swell his sail with thine own powerful breath,
80 That he may bless this bay with his tall ship,
    Make love's quick pants in Desdemona's arms,
    Give renewed fire to our extincted spirits,
    And bring all Cyprus comfort.
          Enter DESDEMONA, IAGO, EMILIA, *and* RODERIGO
               O, behold,
    The riches of the ship is come on shore!
85 You men of Cyprus, let her have your knees.
    [MONTANO *and the* GENTLEMEN *make curtsy to*
    DESDEMONA]
    Hail to thee, lady, and the grace of heaven
    Before, behind thee, and on every hand
    Enwheel thee round!
DESDEMONA   I thank you, valiant Cassio.
    What tidings can you tell me of my lord?
90 CASSIO   He is not yet arrived, nor know I aught
    But that he's well and will be shortly here.
DESDEMONA   O, but I fear—how lost you company?
CASSIO   The great contention of the sea and skies
    Parted our fellowship.
95 VOICES (*within*)   A sail, a sail!
CASSIO   But hark, a sail.
    [*A shot*]
A GENTLEMAN   They give their greeting to the citadel.
    This likewise is a friend.

---

6. *in . . . engineer:* whose natural beauty exhausts the
poet's capacity to invent praise.

7. *Whose . . . speed:* Whose arrival predates our expectations by a week.

CASSIO   See for the news. [*Exit* GENTLEMAN].

    Good ensign, you are welcome. [*Kissing* EMILIA] Welcome, mistress.

100   Let it not gall your patience, good Iago,

    That I extend my manners. 'Tis my breeding

    That gives me this bold show of courtesy.

IAGO   Sir, would she give you so much of her lips

    As of her tongue she oft bestows on me,

105   You would have enough.

DESDEMONA   Alas, she has no speech!⁸

IAGO   In faith, too much.

    I find it still when I ha' leave to sleep.

    Marry, before your ladyship, I grant,

110   She puts her tongue a little in her heart,⁹

    And chides with thinking.

EMILIA   You ha' little cause to say so.

IAGO   Come on, come on. You are pictures out of door,

    Bells in your parlours; wildcats in your kitchens,

    Saints in your injuries; devils being offended,

115   Players in your housewifery, and hussies in your beds.¹

DESDEMONA   O, fie upon thee, slanderer!

IAGO   Nay, it is true, or else I am a Turk.

    You rise to play and go to bed to work.

EMILIA   You shall not write my praise.

IAGO   No, let me not.

120 DESDEMONA   What wouldst write of me, if thou shouldst praise me?

IAGO   O, gentle lady, do not put me to't,

    For I am nothing if not critical.

DESDEMONA   Come on, essay°—there's one gone to the harbour?   *try*

IAGO   Ay, madam.

125 DESDEMONA   I am not merry, but I do beguile°   *disguise*

    The thing I am° by seeming otherwise.   (*worried for Othello*)

    Come, how wouldst thou praise me?

IAGO   I am about it, but indeed my invention

    Comes from my pate as birdlime² does from frieze°—   *coarse wool cloth*

130   It plucks out brains and all. But my muse labours,°   (*in childbirth*)

    And thus she is delivered:

    If she be fair and wise, fairness and wit,

    The one's for use, the other useth it.³

DESDEMONA   Well praised! How if she be black and witty?

135 IAGO   If she be black and thereto have a wit,

    She'll find a white that shall her blackness fit.⁴

DESDEMONA   Worse and worse.

EMILIA   How if fair and foolish?

IAGO   She never yet was foolish that was fair,

    For even her folly° helped her to an heir.   *foolishness; lechery*

140 DESDEMONA   These are old fond° paradoxes, to make fools laugh   *foolish*

    i'th' alehouse.

---

8. Perhaps: Alas, the accused scolding chatterbox is not even rising to her own defense (both a defense of Emilia and a prod for her to speak).
9. She keeps her (critical) thoughts to herself.
1. *You are . . . beds:* Iago shifts from Emilia to women generally in this speech. *pictures:* models of silent propriety. *Bells:* Noisy. *kitchens:* perhaps domestic affairs generally, rather than a specific room. *Saints:* Martyrs.

Players in your housewifery: Deceptive in managing household expenses. *hussies:* wanton (perhaps businesslike, or sparing of sexual favors).
2. Sticky substance used to trap small birds.
3. *The one's . . . it:* Intelligence makes use of beauty.
4. *black:* dark-haired or dark-complexioned. *white:* fair-skinned person ("wight" means "person"). *fit:* (sexual).

What miserable praise hast thou for her
That's foul° and foolish?   *ugly*
IAGO   There's none so foul and foolish thereunto,°   *to boot*
145 But does foul° pranks which fair and wise ones do.   *lascivious*
DESDEMONA   O heavy ignorance! Thou praisest the worst best.
But what praise couldst thou bestow on a deserving woman
indeed—one that, in the authority of her merit, did justly put
on the vouch° of very malice itself?   *compel the approval*
150 IAGO   She that was ever fair and never proud,
Had tongue at will and yet was never loud,
Never lacked gold and yet went never gay,°   *lavishly clothed*
Fled from her wish, and yet said 'Now I may';[5]
She that, being angered, her revenge being nigh,
155 Bade her wrong stay° and her displeasure fly;   *sense of injury end*
She that in wisdom never was so frail
To change the cod's head for the salmon's tail;[6]
She that could think and ne'er disclose her mind,
See suitors following, and not look behind—
160 She was a wight, if ever such wights were—
DESDEMONA   To do what?
IAGO   To suckle fools, and chronicle small beer.[7]
DESDEMONA   O most lame and impotent conclusion! Do not
learn of him, Emilia, though he be thy husband. How say you,
165 Cassio, is he not a most profane and liberal° counsellor?   *outspoken*
CASSIO   He speaks home, madam. You may relish him more in°   *as*
the soldier than in the scholar.
           [CASSIO *and* DESDEMONA *talk apart*]
IAGO [*aside*]   He takes her by the palm. Ay, well said°—whisper.   *well done*
With as little a web as this will I ensnare as great a fly as Cassio.
170 Ay, smile upon her, do. I will gyve° thee in thine own court-   *shackle*
ship.° You say true, 'tis so indeed. If such tricks as these strip   *courtliness*
you out of your lieutenantry, it had been better you had not
kissed your three fingers[8] so oft, which now again you are most
apt to play the sir° in. Very good, well kissed, an excellent   *gentleman*
175 curtsy, 'tis so indeed; yet again your fingers to your lips? Would
they were clyster-pipes° for your sake.   *enema tubes*
           Trumpets within
[*Aloud*] The Moor—I know his trumpet.
CASSIO   'Tis truly so.
DESDEMONA   Let's meet him and receive him.
CASSIO   Lo where he comes!
           Enter OTHELLO *and attendants*
OTHELLO [*to* DESDEMONA]   O my fair warrior!
DESDEMONA   My dear Othello.
180 OTHELLO   It gives me wonder great as my content
To see you here before me. O my soul's joy,
If after every tempest come such calms,
May the winds blow till they have wakened death,
And let the labouring barque° climb hills of seas   *small ship*

5. Voluntarily withstood temptation even when given the choice.
6. To make an unworthy exchange. Probably also suggesting sexual infidelity: "cod" means "penis," and "tail" equals "vulva."
7. To breast-feed babies and keep track of trivial domestic goods. That is, such perfect virtue suits only a dull, complacent, decidedly ungenteel housewife.
8. Kissing one's own hand was a common courtly gesture from a gentleman to a lady.

185   Olympus-high,[9] and duck again as low
         As hell's from heaven. If it were now to die[1]
         'Twere now to be most happy, for I fear
         My soul hath her content so absolute
         That not another comfort like to this
         Succeeds° in unknown fate.°   *will follow / future*

190 DESDEMONA   The heavens forbid
         But that our loves and comforts should increase
         Even as our days do grow.

OTHELLO   Amen to that, sweet powers!
         I cannot speak enough of this content.
         It stops me here, it is too much of joy.
195   And this, *(they kiss)* and this, the greatest discords be
         That e'er our hearts shall make.

IAGO [*aside*]   O, you are well tuned now,
         But I'll set down the pegs that make this music,[2]
         As honest as I am.

OTHELLO   Come, let us to the castle.
         News, friends: our wars are done, the Turks are drowned.
200   How does my old acquaintance of this isle?—
         Honey, you shall be well desired° in Cyprus,   *welcomed*
         I have found great love amongst them. O my sweet,
         I prattle out of fashion, and I dote
         In mine own comforts. I prithee, good Iago,
205   Go to the bay and disembark my coffers.
         Bring thou the master° to the citadel.   *captain*
         He is a good one, and his worthiness
         Does challenge° much respect. Come, Desdemona.—   *deserve*
         Once more, well met at Cyprus!

                     Exeunt OTHELLO *and* DESDEMONA
                     [*with all but* IAGO *and* RODERIGO]

210 IAGO [*to an attendant as he goes out*]   Do thou meet me pres-
         ently at the harbour.   [*To* RODERIGO] Come hither. If thou beest
         valiant—as they say base° men being in love have then a nobil-   *lowly born*
         ity in their natures more than is native to them—list° me. The   *listen to*
         lieutenant tonight watches on the court of guard.[3] First, I
215   must tell thee this: Desdemona is directly in love with him.

RODERIGO   With him? Why, 'tis not possible!

IAGO   Lay thy finger thus,° and let thy soul be instructed. Mark   *Be silent*
         me with what violence she first loved the Moor, but for brag-
         ging and telling her fantastical lies. To love him still for prat-
220   ing?—let not thy discreet heart think it. Her eye must be fed,
         and what delight shall she have to look on the devil? When the
         blood is made dull with the act of sport, there should be again
         to inflame it, and to give satiety a fresh appetite, loveliness in
         favour,° sympathy in years, manners, and beauties, all which   *looks*
225   the Moor is defective in. Now, for want of these required con-
         veniences,° her delicate tenderness will find itself abused,°   *compatibilities / revolted*
         begin to heave the gorge,° disrelish and abhor the Moor. Very   *feel nausea*
         nature will instruct her in it and compel her to some second
         choice. Now, sir, this granted—as it is a most pregnant° and   *obvious; (sexual)*

---

9. Mt. Olympus, home of the Greek gods and hence
too high for mortals.
1. To perish; to have an orgasm.

2. I'll untune (by loosening) the "pegs" that hold the
strings of a musical instrument taut.
3. Cassio is in charge of the watch at the guardhouse.

230   unforced position—who stands so eminent in the degree of°[4]
        this fortune as Cassio does?—a knave very voluble,° no further   *facile*
        conscionable° than in putting on the mere form of civil and   *no more ethical*
        humane seeming for the better compass° of his salt° and most *achievement / lewd*
        hidden loose affection. Why, none; why, none—a slipper° and   *slippery*

235   subtle knave, a finder of occasion, that has an eye can stamp
        and counterfeit advantages,[5] though true advantage never pre-
        sent itself, a devilish knave! Besides, the knave is handsome,
        young, and hath all those requisites in him that folly° and green   *wantonness*
        minds look after. A pestilent° complete knave, and the woman   *damnably*

240   hath found him already.

      RODERIGO   I cannot believe that in her. She's full of most blessed
      condition.

      IAGO   Blessed fig's end!° The wine she drinks is made of grapes.   *(obscene)*
      If she had been blessed, she would never have loved the Moor.

245   Blessed pudding!° Didst thou not see her paddle with the palm   *sausage*
      of his hand? Didst not mark that?

      RODERIGO   Yes, that I did, but that was but courtesy.

      IAGO   Lechery, by this hand; an index and obscure prologue to
      the history of lust and foul thoughts.[6] They met so near with

250   their lips that their breaths embraced together. Villainous
      thoughts, Roderigo! When these mutualities so marshal the
      way, hard at hand comes the master and main exercise,[7] th'in-
      corporate° conclusion. Pish! But, sir, be you ruled by me. I have   *in the flesh*
      brought you from Venice. Watch you tonight. For the com-

255   mand, I'll lay't upon you.[8] Cassio knows you not; I'll not be far
      from you. Do you find some occasion to anger Cassio, either
      by speaking too loud, or tainting° his discipline, or from what   *insulting*
      other course you please, which the time shall more favourably
      minister.°   *provide*

260   RODERIGO   Well.

      IAGO   Sir, he's rash and very sudden in choler, and haply° may   *perhaps*
      strike at you. Provoke him that he may, for even out of that will
      I cause these of Cyprus to mutiny, whose qualification shall
      come into no true taste again[9] but by the displanting of Cassio.

265   So shall you have a shorter journey to your desires by the means
      I shall then have to prefer° them, and the impediment most   *promote*
      profitably removed, without the which there were no expecta-
      tion of our prosperity.

      RODERIGO   I will do this, if you can bring it to any opportunity.

270   IAGO   I warrant thee. Meet me by and by at the citadel. I must
      fetch his necessaries° ashore. Farewell.   *Othello's possessions*

      RODERIGO   Adieu.   *Exit*

      IAGO   That Cassio loves her, I do well believe it.
      That she loves him, 'tis apt and of great credit.°   *likely and believable*

275   The Moor—howbe't that I endure him not—
      Is of a constant, loving, noble nature,
      And I dare think he'll prove to Desdemona
      A most dear° husband. Now I do love her too,   *affectionate; costly*
      Not out of absolute lust—though peradventure

---

4. *in the degree of*: as next in line for.
5. Who can (like a counterfeiter) create his own opportunities.
6. *an . . . thoughts*: the analogy is to a dirty book. *index*:
table of contents. *obscure*: encoded. *history*: story.

7. When these intimacies have cleared the way, the
main event follows close behind. Here, the analogy is to
an official procession.
8. Stand watch tonight. I'll see that you receive orders.
9. *whose . . . again*: who will not be adequately appeased.

280	I stand accountant° for as great a sin—
	But partly led to diet° my revenge
	For that I do suspect the lusty Moor
	Hath leapt into my seat,° the thought whereof
	Doth, like a poisonous mineral, gnaw my inwards;°
285	And nothing can or shall content my soul
	Till I am evened with him, wife for wife—
	Or failing so, yet that I put the Moor
	At least into a jealousy so strong
	That judgement cannot cure, which thing to do,
290	If this poor trash of Venice whom I trace
	For his quick hunting stand the putting on,[1]
	I'll have our Michael Cassio on the hip,°
	Abuse° him to the Moor in the rank garb°—
	For I fear Cassio with my nightcap,° too—
295	Make the Moor thank me, love me, and reward me
	For making him egregiously an ass,
	And practising upon° his peace and quiet
	Even to madness. 'Tis here,° but yet confused.
	Knavery's plain face is never seen till used. *Exit*

Right-margin glosses:
- accountable
- feed
- slept with my wife
- innards
- at my mercy
- Slander / "hot" manner
- (as sexual rival)
- undermining
- My plan is here

2.2

Enter Othello's HERALD *reading a proclamation*

HERALD   It is Othello's pleasure—our noble and valiant general—that, upon certain tidings now arrived importing the
mere perdition° of the Turkish fleet, every man put himself
into triumph: some to dance, some to make bonfires, each man
5   to what sport and revels his addiction° leads him; for besides
these beneficial news, it is the celebration of his nuptial. So
much was his pleasure should be proclaimed. All offices° are
open, and there is full liberty of feasting from this present hour
of five till the bell have told eleven. Heaven bless the isle of
10   Cyprus and our noble general, Othello!   *Exit*

Right-margin glosses:
- entire loss
- inclination
- storehouses

2.3

Enter OTHELLO, DESDEMONA, CASSIO, *and attendants*

OTHELLO   Good Michael, look you to the guard tonight.
Let's teach ourselves that honourable stop°
Not to outsport° discretion.
CASSIO   Iago hath direction what to do,
5   But notwithstanding, with my personal eye
Will I look to't.
OTHELLO   Iago is most honest.
Michael, good night. Tomorrow with your earliest
Let me have speech with you. [*To* DESDEMONA] Come, my dear love,
The purchase made, the fruits are to ensue.
10   That profit's yet to come 'tween me and you.[1]
[*To* CASSIO] Good night.
          Exeunt OTHELLO, DESDEMONA [*and attendants*]
          Enter IAGO

Right-margin glosses:
- self-restraint
- pass the limits of

---

1. *If . . . on:* If Roderigo, whom I follow (?), train (?),
put weights on to slow him down (?), is successfully set
on the hunt when incited.

2.2   Location: A street in Cyprus.
2.3   Location: The citadel at Cyprus.
1. We haven't yet consummated our marriage.

CASSIO   Welcome, Iago. We must to the watch.

IAGO   Not this hour, lieutenant; 'tis not yet ten o'th' clock. Our
general cast° us thus early for the love of his Desdemona, who   *dismissed*
15   let us not therefore blame. He hath not yet made wanton the
night with her, and she is sport for Jove.

CASSIO   She's a most exquisite lady.

IAGO   And I'll warrant her full of game.

CASSIO   Indeed, she's a most fresh and delicate creature.

20   IAGO   What an eye she has! Methinks it sounds a parley° to prov-   *(military) call*
ocation.

CASSIO   An inviting eye, and yet, methinks, right modest.

IAGO   And when she speaks, is it not an alarum° to love?   *a call (to arms)*

CASSIO   She is indeed perfection.

25   IAGO   Well, happiness to their sheets. Come, lieutenant. I have
a stoup° of wine, and here without are a brace° of Cyprus gal-   *two quarts / pair*
lants that would fain have a measure° to the health of black   *would like to drink*
Othello.

CASSIO   Not tonight, good Iago. I have very poor and unhappy
30   brains for drinking. I could well wish courtesy would invent
some other custom of entertainment.

IAGO   O, they are our friends! But one cup. I'll drink for you.

CASSIO   I ha' drunk but one cup tonight, and that was craftily
qualified,° too, and behold what innovation° it makes here! I   *well diluted / disorder*
35   am infortunate in the infirmity, and dare not task my weakness
with any more.

IAGO   What, man, 'tis a night of revels, the gallants desire it!

CASSIO   Where are they?

IAGO   Here at the door. I pray you call them in.

40   CASSIO   I'll do't, but it dislikes me.°   *Exit*   *I don't like doing it*

IAGO   If I can fasten but one cup upon him,
With that which he hath drunk tonight already
He'll be as full of quarrel and offence
As my young mistress' dog. Now my sick fool Roderigo,
45   Whom love hath turned almost the wrong side out,
To Desdemona hath tonight caroused
Potations pottle-deep, and he's to watch.²
Three else of Cyprus—noble swelling° spirits   *proud*
That hold their honours in a wary distance,³
50   The very elements° of this warlike isle—   *typical residents*
Have I tonight flustered with flowing cups,
And they watch too. Now 'mongst this flock of drunkards
Am I to put our Cassio in some action
That may offend the isle.

Enter MONTANO, CASSIO, GENTLEMEN, *and* [*servants
with wine*]

But here they come.
55   If consequence do but approve my dream,⁴
My boat sails freely both with wind and stream.°   *current*

CASSIO   Fore God, they have given me a rouse° already.   *full draft*

MONTANO   Good faith, a little one; not past a pint,
As I am a soldier.

IAGO   Some wine, ho!

2. *caroused . . . watch:* consumed drink to the bottom   3. Who are touchy about their honor.
of the tankard, and he's assigned guard duty.   4. If events turn out as I hope.

60 [*Sings*] And let me the cannikin° clink, clink, *drinking vessel*
　　　　　　And let me the cannikin clink.
　　　　　　　　A soldier's a man,
　　　　　　　　O, man's life's but a span,
　　　　　　　Why then, let a soldier drink.
65 　Some wine, boys!
CASSIO　Fore God, an excellent song.
IAGO　I learned it in England, where indeed they are most potent
　　in potting.⁵ Your Dane, your German, and your swag°-bellied *hanging*
　　Hollander—drink, ho!—are nothing to your English.
70 CASSIO　Is your Englishman so exquisite in his drinking?
IAGO　Why, he drinks you with facility your Dane dead drunk.
　　He sweats not to overthrow your Almain.° He gives your Hol- *German*
　　lander a vomit ere the next pottle° can be filled. *tankard*
CASSIO　To the health of our general!
75 MONTANO　I am for it, lieutenant, and I'll do you justice.° *match your drinking*
IAGO　O sweet England!
　　[*Sings*]　King Stephen was and a worthy peer,
　　　　　　　His breeches cost him but a crown;
　　　　　　　He held them sixpence all too dear,
80 　　　　　　　With that he called the tailor lown.° *lout*
　　　　　　　He was a wight of high renown,
　　　　　　　And thou art but of low degree.
　　　　　　　'Tis pride° that pulls the country down, *ostentatious clothing*
　　　　　　　Then take thy auld cloak about thee.
85 　Some wine, ho!
CASSIO　Fore God, this is a more exquisite song than the other.
IAGO　Will you hear't again?
CASSIO　No, for I hold him to be unworthy of his place that does
　　those things. Well, God's above all, and there be souls must be
90 　saved, and there be souls must not be saved.⁶
IAGO　It's true, good lieutenant.
CASSIO　For mine own part—no offence to the general, nor any
　　man of quality°—I hope to be saved. *rank*
IAGO　And so do I too, lieutenant.
95 CASSIO　Ay, but, by your leave, not before me. The lieutenant is
　　to be saved before the ensign. Let's ha' no more of this. Let's to
　　our affairs. God forgive us our sins. Gentlemen, let's look to
　　our business. Do not think, gentlemen, I am drunk. This is my
　　ensign, this is my right hand, and this is my left. I am not drunk
100 　now. I can stand well enough, and I speak well enough.
GENTLEMEN　Excellent well.
CASSIO　Why, very well then. You must not think then that I am
　　drunk. *Exit*
MONTANO　To th' platform, masters. Come, let's set the watch.
　　　　　　　　　　　　　　　　　　　[*Exeunt* GENTLEMEN]
105 IAGO　You see this fellow that is gone before—
　　He's a soldier fit to stand by Caesar
　　And give direction; and do but see his vice.
　　'Tis to his virtue a just equinox,° *of equal size*
　　The one as long as th'other. 'Tis pity of him.
110 　I fear the trust Othello puts him in,

---

5. Most adept at drinking.
6. Referring to the idea of predestination, the belief
held by Calvinist Protestants that some souls are destined from the outset to be saved and others damned.

On some odd time of his infirmity,
Will shake this island.
MONTANO   But is he often thus?
IAGO 'Tis evermore his prologue to his sleep.
He'll watch the horologe a double set[7]
If drink rock not his cradle.
115 MONTANO   It were well
The general were put in mind of it.
Perhaps he sees it not, or his good nature
Prizes the virtue that appears in Cassio,
And looks not on his evils. Is not this true?
                Enter RODERIGO
120 IAGO [*aside*] How now, Roderigo!
I pray you after the lieutenant, go.   *Exit* RODERIGO
MONTANO And 'tis great pity that the noble Moor
Should hazard such a place as his own second
With one of an engraffed° infirmity.   ingrained
125 It were an honest action to say so
To the Moor.
IAGO   Not I, for this fair island!
I do love Cassio well, and would do much
To cure him of this evil.
VOICES (*within*) Help, help!
IAGO   But hark, what noise?
                Enter CASSIO, *driving in* RODERIGO
130 CASSIO 'Swounds, you rogue, you rascal!
MONTANO What's the matter, lieutenant?
CASSIO A knave teach me my duty?—I'll beat the knave into a
twiggen° bottle.   wicker-cased
RODERIGO Beat me?
135 CASSIO Dost thou prate, rogue?
MONTANO Nay, good lieutenant, I pray you, sir, hold your hand.
CASSIO Let me go, sir, or I'll knock you o'er the mazard.°   head
MONTANO Come, come, you're drunk.
CASSIO Drunk?
                They fight
140 IAGO [*to* RODERIGO] Away, I say. Go out and cry a mutiny.
                                                        [*Exit* RODERIGO]
Nay, good lieutenant. God's will, gentlemen!
Help, ho! Lieutenant! Sir! Montano! Sir!
Help, masters. Here's a goodly watch indeed.
                A bell rung
Who's that which rings the bell? Diablo,° ho!   The devil
145 The town will rise. God's will, lieutenant, hold.
You'll be ashamed for ever.
                Enter OTHELLO *and attendants, with weapons*
OTHELLO   What is the matter here?
MONTANO 'Swounds, I bleed still. I am hurt to th' death.
                [*Attacking* CASSIO] He dies.
OTHELLO Hold, for your lives!
IAGO Hold, ho, lieutenant, sir, Montano, gentlemen!
150 Have you forgot all place of sense and duty?
Hold, the general speaks to you. Hold, hold, for shame.

7. He'll stay up twice around the clock.

OTHELLO   Why, how now, ho? From whence ariseth this?
Are we turned Turks, and to ourselves do that
Which heaven hath forbid the Ottomites?°   *(by raising a storm)*
155   For Christian shame, put by this barbarous brawl.
He that stirs next to carve for his own rage°   *draw a sword in anger*
Holds his soul light. He dies upon his motion.
Silence that dreadful bell—it frights the isle
From her propriety.
          [*Bell stops*]
                  What is the matter, masters?
160   Honest Iago, that looks dead with grieving,
Speak. Who began this? On thy love I charge thee.
IAGO   I do not know. Friends all but now, even now,
In quarter° and in terms like bride and groom   *Under control*
Devesting them° for bed; and then but now—   *Getting undressed*
165   As if some planet° had unwitted men—   *astrological influence*
Swords out, and tilting one at others' breasts
In opposition bloody. I cannot speak
Any beginning to this peevish odds,°   *silly quarrel*
And would in action glorious I had lost
170   Those legs that brought me to a part of it.
OTHELLO   How comes it, Michael, you are thus forgot?
CASSIO   I pray you pardon me. I cannot speak.
OTHELLO   Worthy Montano, you were wont be° civil.   *you used to be*
The gravity and stillness of your youth
175   The world hath noted, and your name is great
In mouths of wisest censure.° What's the matter,   *judgment*
That you unlace your reputation thus,
And spend your rich opinion° for the name   *reputation*
Of a night-brawler? Give me answer to it.
180 MONTANO   Worthy Othello, I am hurt to danger.
Your officer Iago can inform you,
While I spare speech—which something now offends me°—   *somewhat now pains me*
Of all that I do know; nor know I aught
By me that's said or done amiss this night,
185   Unless self-charity° be sometimes a vice,   *care of oneself*
And to defend ourselves it be a sin
When violence assails us.
OTHELLO   Now, by heaven,
My blood begins my safer guides to rule,
And passion, having my best judgement collied,°   *darkened*
190   Essays to lead the way. 'Swounds, if I stir,
Or do but lift this arm, the best of you
Shall sink in my rebuke. Give me to know
How this foul rout began, who set it on,
And he that is approved in this offence,
195   Though he had twinned with me, both at a birth,
Shall lose me. What, in a town of war
Yet° wild, the people's hearts brimful of fear,   *Still*
To manage° private and domestic quarrel   *carry on*
In night, and on the court and guard of safety!8
200   'Tis monstrous. Iago, who began't?
MONTANO   [*to* IAGO]   If partially affined° or leagued in office   *biased (for Cassio)*

---

8. And at the place where safety and security are at stake (on the night watch).

Thou dost deliver more or less than truth,
Thou art no soldier.
IAGO   Touch me not so near.
I had rather ha' this tongue cut from my mouth
205   Than it should do offence to Michael Cassio.
Yet I persuade myself to speak the truth
Shall nothing wrong him. This it is, general.
Montano and myself being in speech,
There comes a fellow crying out for help,
210   And Cassio following him with determined sword
To execute upon° him. Sir, this gentleman   *To attack*
Steps in to Cassio, and entreats his pause.
Myself the crying fellow did pursue,
Lest by his clamour, as it so fell out,
215   The town might fall in fright. He, swift of foot,
Outran my purpose, and I returned, the rather
For that I heard the clink and fall of swords
And Cassio high in oath, which till tonight
I ne'er might say before. When I came back—
220   For this was brief—I found them close together
At blow and thrust, even as again they were
When you yourself did part them.
More of this matter cannot I report,
But men are men. The best sometimes forget.
225   Though Cassio did some little wrong to him,
As men in rage strike those that wish them best,
Yet surely Cassio, I believe, received
From him that fled some strange indignity
Which patience could not pass.°   *let pass*
OTHELLO   I know, Iago,
230   Thy honesty and love doth mince° this matter,   *minimize*
Making it light to Cassio. Cassio, I love thee,
But never more be officer of mine.
            Enter DESDEMONA, *attended*
Look if my gentle love be not raised up.
I'll make thee an example.
235   DESDEMONA   What is the matter, dear?
OTHELLO   All's well now, sweeting.
Come away to bed. [*To* MONTANO] Sir, for your hurts
Myself will be your surgeon. [*To attendants*] Lead him off.
            [*Exeunt attendants with* MONTANO]
Iago, look with care about the town,
240   And silence those whom this vile brawl distracted.
Come, Desdemona. 'Tis the soldier's life
To have their balmy slumbers waked with strife.
            Exeunt [OTHELLO *the*] *Moor,* DESDEMONA,
                                    and attendants
IAGO   What, are you hurt, lieutenant?
CASSIO   Ay, past all surgery.
245   IAGO   Marry, God forbid.
CASSIO   Reputation, reputation, reputation—O, I ha' lost my rep-
    utation, I ha' lost the immortal part of myself, and what remains
    is bestial! My reputation, Iago, my reputation.
IAGO   As I am an honest man, I thought you had received some
250   bodily wound. There is more sense in that than in reputation.

Reputation is an idle and most false imposition,° oft got without   *artificial notion*
merit and lost without deserving. You have lost no reputation
at all unless you repute yourself such a loser. What, man, there
are more ways to recover the general again. You are but now
255   cast in his mood—a punishment more in policy[9] than in malice, even so as one would beat his offenceless dog to affright an
imperious lion. Sue to° him again, and he's yours.   *Petition*

CASSIO   I will rather sue to be despised than to deceive so good
      a commander with so slight, so drunken, and so indiscreet an
260   officer. Drunk, and speak parrot,° and squabble? Swagger,   *rant on*
      swear, and discourse fustian° with one's own shadow? O thou   *nonsense*
      invisible spirit of wine, if thou hast no name to be known by,
      let us call thee devil.

IAGO   What was he that you followed with your sword? What had
265   he done to you?

CASSIO   I know not.

IAGO   Is't possible?

CASSIO   I remember a mass of things, but nothing distinctly; a
      quarrel, but nothing wherefore.° O God, that men should put   *but not why*
270   an enemy in their mouths° to steal away their brains! That we   *should drink*
      should with joy, pleasance, revel, and applause transform our-
      selves into beasts!

IAGO   Why, but you are now well enough. How came you thus
      recovered?

275 CASSIO   It hath pleased the devil drunkenness to give place to
      the devil wrath. One unperfectness shows me another, to make
      me frankly despise myself.

IAGO   Come, you are too severe a moraller. As the time, the
      place, and the condition of this country stands, I could heartily
280   wish this had not befallen; but since it is as it is, mend it for
      your own good.

CASSIO   I will ask him for my place again. He shall tell me I am
      a drunkard. Had I as many mouths as Hydra,[1] such an answer
      would stop them all. To be now a sensible man, by and by a
285   fool, and presently a beast! O, strange! Every inordinate cup is
      unblessed, and the ingredient is a devil.

IAGO   Come, come. Good wine is a good familiar creature, if it
      be well used. Exclaim no more against it. And, good lieutenant,
      I think you think I love you.

290 CASSIO   I have well approved° it, sir—I drunk?   *tested*

IAGO   You or any man living may be drunk at a time, man. I'll
      tell you what you shall do. Our general's wife is now the gen-
      eral. I may say so in this respect, for that he hath devoted and
      given up himself to the contemplation, mark, and denotement°   *observation*
295   of her parts° and graces. Confess yourself freely to her. Impor-   *qualities*
      tune her help to put you in your place again. She is of so free,°   *generous*
      so kind, so apt, so blessed a disposition, she holds it a vice in
      her goodness not to do more than she is requested. This broken
      joint between you and her husband entreat her to splinter,°   *heal with a splint*
300   and, my fortunes against any lay° worth naming, this crack of   *wager*
      your love shall grow stronger than it was before.

CASSIO   You advise me well.

---

9. *cast . . . policy*: dismissed in anger—a matter of
policy (of public example).

1. A mythical serpent with many heads who grew two
more when one was cut off.

IAGO   I protest,° in the sincerity of love and honest kindness.   *insist*
CASSIO   I think it freely, and betimes° in the morning I will   *early*
305   beseech the virtuous Desdemona to undertake for me. I am
desperate of my fortunes if they check° me here.   *stop*
IAGO   You are in the right. Good night, lieutenant. I must to the
watch.
CASSIO   Good night, honest Iago.   *Exit*
310   IAGO   And what's he then that says I play the villain,
When this advice is free I give, and honest,
Probal° to thinking, and indeed the course   *Wise*
To win the Moor again? For 'tis most easy
Th'inclining° Desdemona to subdue   *The well-disposed*
315   In any honest suit. She's framed as fruitful°   *generous*
As the free elements; and then for her
To win the Moor, were't to renounce his baptism,
All seals and symbols of redeemèd sin,
His soul is so enfettered to her love
320   That she may make, unmake, do what she list,
Even as her appetite° shall play the god   *wishes*
With his weak function.° How am I then a villain,   *faculties*
To counsel Cassio to this parallel° course   *suitable*
Directly to his good? Divinity° of hell: *Theology*
325   When devils will the blackest sins put on,
They do suggest at first with heavenly shows,
As I do now; for whiles this honest fool
Plies Desdemona to repair his fortune,
And she for him pleads strongly to the Moor,
330   I'll pour this pestilence into his ear:
That she repeals him° for her body's lust,   *appeals for him*
And by how much she strives to do him good
She shall undo her credit with the Moor.
So will I turn her virtue into pitch,[2]
335   And out of her own goodness make the net
That shall enmesh them all.
                          Enter RODERIGO
                  How now, Roderigo?
RODERIGO   I do follow here in the chase, not like a hound that
hunts, but one that fills up the cry.° My money is almost spent,   *a pack follower*
I ha' been tonight exceedingly well cudgelled, and I think the
340   issue will be I shall have so much° experience for my pains: *only so much*
and so, with no money at all and a little more wit, return again
to Venice.
IAGO   How poor are they that ha' not patience!
What wound did ever heal but by degrees?
345   Thou know'st we work by wit and not by witchcraft,
And wit depends on dilatory° time.   *drawn-out*
Does't not go well? Cassio hath beaten thee,
And thou by that small hurt hast cashiered° Cassio.   *dismissed*
Though other things grow fair against the sun,
350   Yet fruits that blossom first will first be ripe.[3]
Content thyself a while. By the mass,° 'tis morning.   *(a mild oath)*

2. Black, sticky substance used as a snare. The more the thing caught in it tries to escape, the more stuck it becomes.

3. *Though . . . ripe:* Although others may appear to be prospering, your plan will be successful soonest because started first.

Pleasure and action make the hours seem short.
Retire thee. Go where thou art billeted.
Away, I say. Thou shalt know more hereafter.
Nay, get thee gone.   *Exit* RODERIGO

355   Two things are to be done.
My wife must move for Cassio to her mistress.
I'll set her on.
Myself a while to draw the Moor apart,
And bring him jump° when he may Cassio find   *exactly*
360 Soliciting his wife. Ay, that's the way.
Dull not device by coldness and delay.[4]   *Exit*

3.1

Enter CASSIO *with* MUSICIANS

CASSIO   Masters, play here—I will content° your pains—   *reward*
Something that's brief, and bid 'Good morrow, general'.
     [*Music.*] *Enter* CLOWN

CLOWN   Why, masters, ha' your instruments been in Naples,
that they speak i'th' nose thus?[1]

5 MUSICIAN   How, sir, how?

CLOWN   Are these, I pray you, wind instruments?[2]

MUSICIAN   Ay, marry are they, sir.

CLOWN   O, thereby hangs a tail.

MUSICIAN   Whereby hangs a tale, sir?

10 CLOWN   Marry, sir, by many a wind instrument that I know. But
masters, here's money for you, and the general so likes your
music that he desires you, for love's sake, to make no more
noise with it.

MUSICIAN   Well, sir, we will not.

15 CLOWN   If you have any music that may not° be heard, to't again;   *cannot*
but, as they say, to hear music the general does not greatly care.

MUSICIAN   We ha' none such, sir.

CLOWN   Then put up your pipes in your bag, for I'll away. Go,
vanish into air, away.   *Exeunt* MUSICIANS

20 CASSIO   Dost thou hear, my honest friend?

CLOWN   No, I hear not your honest friend, I hear you.

CASSIO   Prithee, keep up thy quillets.° There's a poor piece of   *pack up your puns*
gold for thee. If the gentlewoman that attends the general's wife
be stirring, tell her there's one Cassio entreats her a little favour
25 of speech. Wilt thou do this?

CLOWN   She is stirring, sir. If she will stir hither, I shall seem° to   *arrange*
notify unto her.

CASSIO   Do, good my friend.   *Exit* CLOWN
     Enter IAGO
               In happy time,° Iago.   *Well met*

IAGO   You ha' not been abed, then.

CASSIO   Why, no. The day had broke
30 Before we parted. I ha' made bold, Iago,
To send in to your wife. My suit to her

---

4. Don't let sluggishness and slowness to act weaken
the plot.
3.1 Location: Outside Othello and Desdemona's room.
1. That they sound so nasal; perhaps a reference to
venereal disease, often associated with Naples, or a

phallic or anal joke.
2. The exchange that follows depends on the connections between wind instruments, flatulence, and
"tale/tail."

Is that she will to virtuous Desdemona
Procure me some access.

IAGO   I'll send her to you presently,°   *immediately*
35   And I'll devise a mean to draw the Moor
Out of the way, that your converse and business
May be more free.

CASSIO   I humbly thank you for't.   *Exit* IAGO
I never knew a Florentine more kind and honest.

        Enter EMILIA

EMILIA   Good morrow, good lieutenant. I am sorry
40   For your displeasure, but all will sure be well.
The general and his wife are talking of it,
And she speaks for you stoutly. The Moor replies
That he you hurt is of great fame in Cyprus,
And great affinity,° and that in wholesome wisdom   *well connected*
45   He might not but refuse you. But he protests he loves you,
And needs no other suitor but his likings
To take the saf'st occasion by the front°   *forelock*
To bring you in again.

CASSIO   Yet I beseech you,
If you think fit, or that it may be done,
50   Give me advantage of some brief discourse
With Desdemon alone.

EMILIA   Pray you come in.
I will bestow you where you shall have time
To speak your bosom° freely.   *heart*

CASSIO   I am much bound to you.

                                        Exeunt

3.2

        Enter OTHELLO, IAGO, *and* GENTLEMEN

OTHELLO   These letters give, Iago, to the pilot,
And by him do my duties° to the senate.   *send my respects*
That done, I will be walking on the works.°   *fortifications*
Repair there to me.

IAGO   Well, my good lord, I'll do't.   *[Exit]*
5   OTHELLO   This fortification, gentlemen—shall we see't?

A GENTLEMAN   We'll wait upon your lordship.   *Exeunt*

3.3

        Enter DESDEMONA, CASSIO, *and* EMILIA

DESDEMONA   Be thou assured, good Cassio, I will do
All my abilities in thy behalf.

EMILIA   Good madam, do. I warrant it grieves my husband
As if the cause were his.

5   DESDEMONA   O, that's an honest fellow. Do not doubt, Cassio,
But I will have my lord and you again
As friendly as you were.

CASSIO   Bounteous madam,
Whatever shall become of Michael Cassio
He's never anything but your true servant.

10   DESDEMONA   I know't. I thank you. You do love my lord.
You have known him long, and be you well assured

3.2 Location: The citadel.   3.3 Location: The citadel's garden.

He shall in strangeness stand no farther off
Than in a politic distance.[1]

CASSIO   Ay, but, lady,
That policy may either last so long,

15   Or feed upon such nice and wat'rish diet,
Or breed itself so out of circumstance,[2]
That, I being absent and my place supplied,°   *filled*
My general will forget my love and service.

DESDEMONA   Do not doubt° that. Before Emilia here   *fear*

20   I give thee warrant° of thy place. Assure thee,   *assurance*
If I do vow a friendship I'll perform it
To the last article. My lord shall never rest.
I'll watch him tame, and talk him out of patience.[3]
His bed shall seem a school, his board a shrift.°   *confessional*

25   I'll intermingle everything he does
With Cassio's suit. Therefore be merry, Cassio,
For thy solicitor° shall rather die   *advocate*
Than give thy cause away.°   *up*

         Enter OTHELLO *and* IAGO

EMILIA   Madam, here comes my lord.

CASSIO   Madam, I'll take my leave.

DESDEMONA   Why, stay, and hear me speak.

30   CASSIO   Madam, not now. I am very ill at ease,
Unfit for mine own purposes.

DESDEMONA   Well, do your discretion.   *Exit* CASSIO

IAGO   Ha! I like not that.

OTHELLO   What dost thou say?

35   IAGO   Nothing, my lord. Or if, I know not what.

OTHELLO   Was not that Cassio parted from my wife?

IAGO   Cassio, my lord? No, sure, I cannot think it,
That he would steal away so guilty-like
Seeing your coming.

40   OTHELLO   I do believe 'twas he.

DESDEMONA   How now, my lord?
I have been talking with a suitor here,
A man that languishes in your displeasure.

OTHELLO   Who is't you mean?

45   DESDEMONA   Why, your lieutenant, Cassio; good my lord,
If I have any grace or power to move you,
His present reconciliation take;°   *Accept him now*
For if he be not one that truly loves you,
That errs in ignorance and not in cunning,°   *not knowingly*

50   I have no judgement in an honest face.
I prithee call him back.

OTHELLO   Went he hence now?

DESDEMONA   Yes, faith, so humbled
That he hath left part of his grief with me

55   To suffer with him. Good love, call him back.

OTHELLO   Not now, sweet Desdemon. Some other time.

DESDEMONA   But shall't be shortly?

OTHELLO   The sooner, sweet, for you.

---

1. *He . . . distance:* He will distance himself from you
only as much as good diplomacy requires.
2. *Or feed . . . circumstance:* Or persist based on such
unimportant and poor justifications, or continue by
chance.
3. I'll keep him awake until he obeys me, and talk to
him beyond his endurance.

DESDEMONA Shall't be tonight at supper?
OTHELLO   No, not tonight.
DESDEMONA Tomorrow dinner,° then?   *midday meal*
OTHELLO   I shall not dine at home.
60 I meet the captains at the citadel.
DESDEMONA Why then, tomorrow night, or Tuesday morn,
    On Tuesday noon, or night, on Wednesday morn—
    I prithee name the time, but let it not
    Exceed three days. In faith, he's penitent,
65 And yet his trespass, in our common reason°—   *normal judgment*
    Save that, they say, the wars must make example
    Out of her° best—is not almost a fault   *(war's)*
    T'incur a private check.⁴ When shall he come?
    Tell me, Othello. I wonder in my soul
70 What you would ask me that I should deny,
    Or stand so mamm'ring° on? What, Michael Cassio,   *hesitating*
    That came a-wooing with you, and so many a time
    When I have spoke of you dispraisingly
    Hath ta'en your part—to have so much to-do
75 To bring him in?° By'r Lady, I could do much.⁵   *into favor*
OTHELLO Prithee, no more. Let him come when he will.
    I will deny thee nothing.
DESDEMONA   Why, this is not a boon.
    'Tis as I should entreat you wear your gloves,
    Or feed on nourishing dishes, or keep you warm,
80 Or sue to you to do a peculiar° profit   *particular*
    To your own person. Nay, when I have a suit
    Wherein I mean to touch your love indeed,
    It shall be full of poise° and difficult weight,   *balanced judgment*
    And fearful to be granted.
OTHELLO   I will deny thee nothing,
85 Whereon I do beseech thee grant me this:
    To leave me but a little to myself.
DESDEMONA Shall I deny you? No. Farewell, my lord.
OTHELLO Farewell, my Desdemona. I'll come to thee straight.°   *immediately*
DESDEMONA Emilia, come. [*To* OTHELLO] Be as your fancies
    teach° you.   *as your whims lead*
90 Whate'er you be, I am obedient.
                    Exeunt DESDEMONA *and* EMILIA
OTHELLO Excellent wretch!° Perdition catch my soul   *(affectionate)*
    But I do love thee, and when I love thee not,
    Chaos is come again.
IAGO My noble lord.
95 OTHELLO What dost thou say, Iago?
IAGO Did Michael Cassio, when you wooed my lady,
    Know of your love?
OTHELLO He did, from first to last. Why dost thou ask?
IAGO But for a satisfaction of my thought,
    No further harm.
100 OTHELLO   Why of thy thought, Iago?
IAGO I did not think he had been acquainted with her.
OTHELLO O yes, and went between us very oft.
IAGO Indeed?

---

4. *is . . . check:* is barely worth even private criticism.   5. Do much to make you regret your reluctance (?).

OTHELLO   Indeed? Ay, indeed. Discern'st thou aught in that?
105   Is he not honest?
IAGO   Honest, my lord?
OTHELLO   Honest? Ay, honest.
IAGO   My lord, for aught I know.
OTHELLO   What dost thou think?
IAGO   Think, my lord?
110   OTHELLO   'Think, my lord?' By heaven, thou echo'st me
        As if there were some monster in thy thought
        Too hideous to be shown! Thou dost mean something.
        I heard thee say even now thou liked'st not that,
        When Cassio left my wife. What didst not like?
115   And when I told thee he was of my counsel°   in my confidence
        In my whole course of wooing, thou cried'st 'Indeed?'
        And didst contract and purse thy brow together
        As if thou then hadst shut up in thy brain
        Some horrible conceit.° If thou dost love me,   thought
120   Show me thy thought.
IAGO   My lord, you know I love you.
OTHELLO   I think thou dost,
        And for° I know thou'rt full of love and honesty,   since
        And weigh'st thy words before thou giv'st them breath,
125   Therefore these stops° of thine fright me the more;   reluctances
        For such things in a false disloyal knave
        Are tricks of custom,° but in a man that's just,   habitual
        They're close dilations,[6] working from the heart
        That passion cannot rule.°   control
IAGO   For Michael Cassio,
130   I dare be sworn I think that he is honest.
OTHELLO   I think so too.
IAGO   Men should be what they seem,
        Or those that be not, would they might seem none.[7]
OTHELLO   Certain, men should be what they seem.
IAGO   Why then, I think Cassio's an honest man.
135   OTHELLO   Nay, yet there's more in this.
        I prithee speak to me as to thy thinkings,
        As thou dost ruminate, and give thy worst of thoughts
        The worst of words.
IAGO   Good my lord, pardon me.
        Though I am bound to every act of duty,
140   I am not bound to that all slaves are free to.[8]
        Utter my thoughts? Why, say they are vile and false,
        As where's that palace whereinto foul things
        Sometimes intrude not? Who has that breast so pure
        But some uncleanly apprehensions
145   Keep leets and law-days, and in sessions sit
        With meditations lawful?[9]
OTHELLO   Thou dost conspire against thy friend,° Iago,   (Othello)
        If thou but think'st him wronged and mak'st his ear
        A stranger to thy thoughts.
IAGO   I do beseech you,

---

6. Involuntary revelations of interior, close-kept secrets.
7. Or . . . none: If only those who are not what they
seem didn't seem to be what they are not.
8. I am not obligated to reveal my inner thoughts,

something about which even slaves have a choice.
9. uncleanly . . . lawful: illegitimate thoughts meet in
court ("leets") from time to time (on "law-days") and
debate (in court "sessions") with legitimate ones.

150 Though I perchance am vicious° in my guess—   *mistaken*
As I confess it is my nature's plague
To spy into abuses, and oft my jealousy
Shapes faults that are not—that your wisdom then,
From one that so imperfectly conceits,°   *imagines*
155 Would take no notice, nor build yourself a trouble
Out of his scattering° and unsure observance.   *incoherent*
It were not for your quiet nor your good,
Nor for my manhood, honesty, and wisdom,
To let you know my thoughts.

OTHELLO   What dost thou mean?

160 IAGO   Good name in man and woman, dear my lord,
Is the immediate jewel of their souls.
Who steals my purse steals trash; 'tis something, nothing;
'Twas mine, 'tis his, and has been slave to thousands.
But he that filches from me my good name
165 Robs me of that which not enriches him
And makes me poor indeed.

OTHELLO   By heaven, I'll know thy thoughts.

IAGO   You cannot, if my heart were in your hand;
Nor shall not whilst 'tis in my custody.

OTHELLO   Ha!

IAGO   O, beware, my lord, of jealousy.
170 It is the green-eyed monster which doth mock
The meat it feeds on.[1] That cuckold lives in bliss
Who, certain of his fate, loves not his wronger.[2]
But O, what damnèd minutes tells he o'er
Who dotes yet doubts, suspects yet fondly loves!

175 OTHELLO   O misery!

IAGO   Poor and content is rich, and rich enough,
But riches fineless° is as poor as winter   *boundless*
To him that ever fears he shall be poor.
Good God the souls of all my tribe defend
From jealousy!

180 OTHELLO   Why, why is this?
Think'st thou I'd make a life of jealousy,
To follow still the changes of the moon°   *To renew endlessly*
With fresh suspicions? No, to be once in doubt
Is once to be resolved.° Exchange me for a goat   *to be finally settled*
185 When I shall turn the business of my soul
To such exsufflicate and blowed° surmises   *inflated and blown-up*
Matching thy inference. 'Tis not to make me jealous
To say my wife is fair, feeds well, loves company,
Is free of speech, sings, plays, and dances well.
190 Where virtue is, these are more virtuous,
Nor from mine own weak merits will I draw
The smallest fear or doubt of her revolt,°   *or fear of her betrayal*
For she had eyes and chose me. No, Iago,
I'll see before I doubt; when I doubt, prove;
195 And on the proof, there is no more but this:
Away at once with love or jealousy.

---

1. *which . . . on:* that tortures, as it consumes, the heart of the jealous person.

2. Who, knowing it is his fate to be cuckolded, doesn't love his wife.

IAGO   I am glad of this, for now I shall have reason
　　　To show the love and duty that I bear you
　　　With franker spirit. Therefore, as I am bound,
200　Receive it from me. I speak not yet of proof.
　　　Look to your wife. Observe her well with Cassio.
　　　Wear your eyes thus: not jealous, nor secure.
　　　I would not have your free and noble nature
　　　Out of self-bounty be abused.³ Look to't.
205　I know our country disposition well.
　　　In Venice they do let God see the pranks
　　　They dare not show their husbands; their best conscience
　　　Is not to leave't undone, but keep't unknown.
OTHELLO　Dost thou say so?
210　IAGO　She did deceive her father, marrying you,
　　　And when she seemed to shake and fear your looks
　　　She loved them most.
OTHELLO　　　　　　　　And so she did.
IAGO　　　　　　　　　　　Why, go to,° then.　　　　*that's it*
　　　She that so young could give out such a seeming,
　　　To seel her father's eyes up close as oak,⁴
215　He thought 'twas witchcraft! But I am much to blame.
　　　I humbly do beseech you of your pardon
　　　For too much loving you.
OTHELLO　　　　　　　　I am bound to thee for ever.
IAGO　I see this hath a little dashed your spirits.
OTHELLO　Not a jot, not a jot.
IAGO　　　　　　　　I'faith, I fear it has.
220　I hope you will consider what is spoke
　　　Comes from my love. But I do see you're moved.
　　　I am to pray you not to strain my speech
　　　To grosser issues,° nor to larger reach　　　*greater conclusions*
　　　Than to suspicion.
225　OTHELLO　I will not.
IAGO　　　Should you do so, my lord,
　　　My speech should fall into such vile success
　　　Which my thoughts aimed not. Cassio's my worthy friend.
　　　My lord, I see you're moved.
OTHELLO　　　　　　　　No, not much moved.
230　I do not think but Desdemona's honest.
IAGO　Long live she so, and long live you to think so!
OTHELLO　And yet how nature, erring from itself—
IAGO　Ay, there's the point; as, to be bold with you,
　　　Not to affect° many proposèd matches　　　*desire*
235　Of her own clime, complexion, and degree,
　　　Whereto we see in all things nature tends.
　　　Foh, one may smell in such a will most rank,
　　　Foul disproportions, thoughts unnatural!
　　　But pardon me. I do not in position°　　　*argument*
240　Distinctly speak of her, though I may fear
　　　Her will,° recoiling° to her better judgement,　　　*desire / submitting*
　　　May fall to match you with her country forms⁵
　　　And happily° repent.　　　*perhaps*

3. Be deceived on account of your own goodness.　　father's eyes as tightly as oak (a fine-grained wood).
4. Perhaps: To cover ("seel" means "to blind") her　5. May happen to compare you with Venetian standards.

OTHELLO   Farewell, farewell.
If more thou dost perceive, let me know more.
245   Set on thy wife to observe. Leave me, Iago.

IAGO [*going*]   My lord, I take my leave.

OTHELLO   Why did I marry? This honest creature doubtless
Sees and knows more, much more, than he unfolds.

IAGO [*returning*]   My lord, I would I might entreat your honour
250   To scan this thing no farther. Leave it to time.
Although 'tis fit that Cassio have his place—
For sure he fills it up with great ability—
Yet, if you please to hold him off a while,
You shall by that perceive him and his means.[6]
255   Note if your lady strain his entertainment°   urge his reception
With any strong or vehement importunity.
Much will be seen in that. In the mean time,
Let me be thought too busy° in my fears—   meddlesome
As worthy cause I have to fear I am—
260   And hold her free,° I do beseech your honour.   believe her innocent

OTHELLO   Fear not my government.°   self-conduct

IAGO   I once more take my leave.
                                                                Exit

OTHELLO   This fellow's of exceeding honesty,
And knows all qualities° with a learned spirit   (human) types
Of human dealings. If I do prove her haggard,°   wild (falconry)
265   Though that her jesses were my dear heart-strings
I'd whistle her off and let her down the wind
To prey at fortune.[7] Haply for° I am black,   Perhaps because
And have not those soft parts of conversation°   easy manners
That chamberers° have; or for I am declined   gallants
270   Into the vale of years—yet that's not much—
She's gone. I am abused,° and my relief   deceived
Must be to loathe her. O curse of marriage,
That we can call these delicate creatures ours
And not their appetites! I had rather be a toad
275   And live upon the vapour of a dungeon
Than keep a corner in the thing I love
For others' uses. Yet 'tis the plague of great ones;
Prerogatived° are they less than the base.°   Privileged / lowborn
'Tis destiny unshunnable, like death.
280   Even then this forkèd plague is fated to us
When we do quicken.[8]
                Enter DESDEMONA *and* EMILIA
                                Look where she comes.
If she be false, O then heaven mocks itself !
I'll not believe't.

DESDEMONA   How now, my dear Othello?
Your dinner, and the generous° islanders   noble
285   By you invited, do attend° your presence.   wait for

OTHELLO   I am to blame.

DESDEMONA   Why do you speak so faintly? Are you not well?

OTHELLO   I have a pain upon my forehead here.°   (from cuckold's horns)

---

6. Method (for restoring himself to favor).
7. *Though . . . fortune:* Even if what tied her ("jesses"
were leg straps put on a hawk) were my own heartstrings,
I'd set her loose downwind forever to hunt on her own.

8. *Even . . . quicken:* The "plague" of horns (imagined
to grow from the forehead of a cuckold) is our fate as
soon as we live.

DESDEMONA   Faith, that's with watching.° 'Twill away again. *from lack of sleep*
290   Let me but bind it hard, within this hour
      It will be well.
OTHELLO   Your napkin° is too little. *handkerchief*
      [*He puts the napkin from him. It drops*]
      Let it alone. Come, I'll go in with you.
DESDEMONA   I am very sorry that you are not well.
                  Exeunt OTHELLO *and* DESDEMONA
EMILIA [*taking up the napkin*]   I am glad I have found this napkin.
295   This was her first remembrance from the Moor.
      My wayward husband hath a hundred times
      Wooed me to steal it, but she so loves the token—
      For he conjured her[9] she should ever keep it—
      That she reserves it evermore about her
300   To kiss and talk to. I'll ha' the work ta'en out,° *embroidery copied*
      And give't Iago. What he will do with it,
      Heaven knows, not I.
      I nothing,° but to please his fantasy. *intend nothing*
          Enter IAGO
IAGO   How now, what do you here alone?
305 EMILIA   Do not you chide. I have a thing for you.
IAGO   You have a thing for me? It is a common thing.[1]
EMILIA   Ha?
IAGO   To have a foolish wife.
EMILIA   O, is that all? What will you give me now
310   For that same handkerchief?
IAGO   What handkerchief?
EMILIA   What handkerchief?
      Why, that the Moor first gave to Desdemona,
      That which so often you did bid me steal.
315 IAGO   Hast stol'n it from her?
EMILIA   No, faith, she let it drop by negligence,
      And to th'advantage° I, being here, took't up. *taking the occasion*
      Look, here 'tis.
IAGO   A good wench! Give it me.
EMILIA   What will you do with it, that you have been so earnest
      To have me filch it?
320 IAGO   Why, what is that to you?
      [*He takes the napkin*]
EMILIA   If it be not for some purpose of import,
      Give't me again. Poor lady, she'll run mad
      When she shall lack it.
IAGO   Be not acknown on't.° I have use for it. Go, leave me. *Don't let it be known*
                  Exit EMILIA
325   I will in Cassio's lodging lose this napkin,
      And let him find it. Trifles light as air
      Are to the jealous confirmations strong
      As proofs of holy writ. This may do something.
      The Moor already changes with my poison.
330   Dangerous conceits° are in their natures poisons, *ideas*
      Which at the first are scarce found to distaste,
      But, with a little act° upon the blood, *effect*

9. Made her swear; perhaps also an unwitting backward glance at Brabanzio's charge in 1.3 that Othello
employed witchcraft to win Desdemona.
1. It is a vagina ("thing") available to all.

Burn like the mines of sulphur.²

Enter OTHELLO

I did say so.

Look where he comes. Not poppy nor mandragora³
335   Nor all the drowsy syrups of the world
Shall ever medicine thee to that sweet sleep
Which thou owedst° yesterday.   *owned*

OTHELLO   Ha, ha, false to me?

IAGO   Why, how now, general? No more of that.

340 OTHELLO   Avaunt, be gone. Thou hast set me on the rack.
I swear 'tis better to be much abused°   *mistreated; deceived*
Than but to know't a little.

IAGO   How now, my lord?

OTHELLO   What sense had I of her stol'n hours of lust?
I saw't not, thought it not; it harmed not me.
345   I slept the next night well, fed well, was free and merry.
I found not Cassio's kisses on her lips.
He that is robbed, not wanting° what is stol'n,   *missing*
Let him not know't and he's not robbed at all.

IAGO   I am sorry to hear this.

350 OTHELLO   I had been happy if the general camp,
Pioneers° and all, had tasted her sweet body,   *Manual laborers*
So° I had nothing known. O, now for ever   *If*
Farewell the tranquil mind, farewell content,
Farewell the plumèd troops and the big wars
355   That makes ambition virtue! O, farewell,
Farewell the neighing steed and the shrill trump,
The spirit-stirring drum, th'ear-piercing fife,
The royal banner, and all quality,°   *aspects*
Pride,° pomp, and circumstance° of glorious war!   *Magnificence / ceremony*
360   And O, you mortal engines° whose rude throats   *deadly cannons*
Th'immortal Jove's dread clamours° counterfeit,   *thunderclaps*
Farewell! Othello's occupation's gone.

IAGO   Is't possible, my lord?

OTHELLO [*taking* IAGO *by the throat*]   Villain, be sure thou prove
        my love a whore.
365   Be sure of it. Give me the ocular proof,
Or, by the worth of mine eternal soul,
Thou hadst been better have been born a dog
Than answer my waked wrath.

IAGO   Is't come to this?

OTHELLO   Make me to see't, or at the least so prove it
370   That the probation° bear no hinge nor loop   *proof*
To hang a doubt on, or woe upon thy life.

IAGO   My noble lord.

OTHELLO   If thou dost slander her and torture me,
Never pray more; abandon all remorse,
375   On horror's head horrors accumulate,
Do deeds to make heaven weep, all earth amazed,
For nothing canst thou to damnation add
Greater than that.

---

2. Pliny the Elder describes two islands of sulfur between mainland Italy and Sicily that were rumored to be always on fire.   3. A sleep-inducing substance made from the mandrake root.

IAGO   O grace, O heaven forgive me!
       Are you a man? Have you a soul or sense?

380   God buy you, take mine office.[4] O wretched fool,°   *(to himself)*
       That lov'st to make thine honesty a vice!°   *fault*
       O monstrous world, take note, take note, O world,
       To be direct and honest is not safe!
       I thank you for this profit,° and from hence   *profitable lesson*
385   I'll love no friend, sith° love breeds such offence.   *since*

OTHELLO   Nay, stay. Thou shouldst be honest.

IAGO   I should be wise, for honesty's a fool,
       And loses that° it works for.   *what*

OTHELLO   By the world,[5]
       I think my wife be honest, and think she is not.
390   I think that thou art just, and think thou art not.
       I'll have some proof. My name, that was as fresh
       As Dian's[6] visage, is now begrimed and black
       As mine own face. If there be cords, or knives,
       Poison, or fire, or suffocating streams,
395   I'll not endure it. Would I were satisfied!

IAGO   I see, sir, you are eaten up with passion.
       I do repent me that I put it to you.
       You would be satisfied?

OTHELLO   Would? Nay, and I will.

IAGO   And may. But how, how satisfied, my lord?
400   Would you, the supervisor,° grossly gape on,   *observer*
       Behold her topped?

OTHELLO   Death and damnation! O!

IAGO   It were a tedious° difficulty, I think,   *painful*
       To bring them to that prospect. Damn them then
       If ever mortal eyes do see them bolster°   *share a pillow*
405   More° than their own!° What then, how then?   *Other / own eyes*
       What shall I say? Where's satisfaction?
       It is impossible you should see this,
       Were they as prime° as goats, as hot as monkeys,   *lustful*
       As salt as wolves in pride,[7] and fools as gross
410   As ignorance made drunk. But yet I say,
       If imputation, and strong circumstances[8]
       Which lead directly to the door of truth,
       Will give you satisfaction, you might ha't.

OTHELLO   Give me a living reason she's disloyal.

415 IAGO   I do not like the office,
       But sith I am entered in this cause so far,
       Pricked to't° by foolish honesty and love,   *Prodded on*
       I will go on. I lay with Cassio lately,
       And being troubled with a raging tooth,
420   I could not sleep. There are a kind of men
       So loose of soul that in their sleeps
       Will mutter their affairs. One of this kind is Cassio.
       In sleep I heard him say 'Sweet Desdemona,
       Let us be wary, let us hide our loves',
425   And then, sir, would he grip and wring my hand,

---

4. Good-bye, I resign my official position (ensign).
5. Othello's speech (lines 388–95) does not appear in Q.
6. Diana, goddess of chastity and of the (pale) moon.
The Second Quarto (1630) replaces "My" (line 391)

with "Her," a plausible but arguably less powerful reading that lacks textual authority.
7. As lecherous as wolves in heat.
8. If inference and strong circumstantial evidence.

Cry 'O, sweet creature!', then kiss me hard,
As if he plucked up kisses by the roots,
That grew upon my lips, lay his leg o'er my thigh,
And sigh, and kiss, and then cry 'Cursèd fate,
430   That gave thee to the Moor!'
OTHELLO   O, monstrous, monstrous!
IAGO   Nay, this was but his dream.
OTHELLO   But this denoted a foregone conclusion.°   *an earlier event*
IAGO   'Tis a shrewd doubt,° though it be but a dream,   *reasonable fear*
435   And this may help to thicken other proofs
That do demonstrate thinly.
OTHELLO   I'll tear her all to pieces.
IAGO   Nay, yet be wise; yet we see nothing done.
She may be honest yet. Tell me but this:
Have you not sometimes seen a handkerchief
440   Spotted with strawberries in your wife's hand?
OTHELLO   I gave her such a one. 'Twas my first gift.
IAGO   I know not that, but such a handkerchief—
I am sure it was your wife's—did I today
See Cassio wipe his beard with.
OTHELLO   If it be that—
445 IAGO   If it be that, or any that was hers,
It speaks against her with the other proofs.
OTHELLO   O that the slave° had forty thousand lives!   *(Cassio)*
One is too poor, too weak for my revenge.
Now do I see 'tis true. Look here, Iago.
450   All my fond love thus do I blow to heaven—'tis gone.
Arise, black vengeance, from the hollow hell.
Yield up, O love, thy crown and hearted throne°   *rule of the heart*
To tyrannous hate! Swell, bosom, with thy freight,°   *burden*
For 'tis of aspics'° tongues.   *poison snakes'*
IAGO   Yet be content.
OTHELLO   O, blood, blood, blood!
455 IAGO   Patience, I say. Your mind may change.
OTHELLO   Never, Iago. Like to the Pontic Sea,°   *Black Sea*
Whose icy current and compulsive course
Ne'er knows retiring ebb, but keeps due on
To the Propontic and the Hellespont,⁹
460   Even so my bloody thoughts with violent pace
Shall ne'er look back, ne'er ebb to humble love,
Till that a capable° and wide revenge   *capacious*
Swallow them up.
     [*He kneels*]
                         Now, by yon marble heaven,
In the due reverence of a sacred vow
I here engage my words.
465 IAGO   Do not rise yet.
     IAGO *kneels*¹
Witness you ever-burning lights above,
You elements that clip° us round about,   *embrace (sexual?)*
Witness that here Iago doth give up

---

9. The Propontic was the body of water bounded by the
straits of Bosphorus and the Dardanelles (Hellespont),
the latter strait leading to the Aegean.
1. Parody of the marriage ceremony.

The execution° of his wit, hands, heart   *command*

470   To wrongèd Othello's service. Let him command,

And to obey shall be in me remorse,°   *pity (for Othello)*

What bloody business ever.°   *soever*

      [*They rise*]

OTHELLO   I greet thy love,

Not with vain thanks, but with acceptance bounteous,

And will upon the instant put thee to't.°   *immediately test it*

475   Within these three days let me hear thee say

That Cassio's not alive.

IAGO   My friend is dead.

'Tis done at your request; but let her live.

OTHELLO   Damn her, lewd minx!° O, damn her, damn her!   *wanton*

Come, go with me apart. I will withdraw

480   To furnish me with some swift means of death

For the fair devil. Now art thou my lieutenant.

IAGO   I am your own for ever.   *Exeunt*

3.4

Enter DESDEMONA, EMILIA, *and the* CLOWN

DESDEMONA   Do you know, sirrah,[1] where Lieutenant Cassio lies?

CLOWN   I dare not say he lies anywhere.

DESDEMONA   Why, man?

5   CLOWN   He's a soldier, and for me to say a soldier lies, 'tis stabbing.

DESDEMONA   Go to. Where lodges he?

CLOWN   To tell you where he lodges is to tell you where I lie.

DESDEMONA   Can anything be made of this?

10   CLOWN   I know not where he lodges, and for me to devise a lodging and say he lies here, or he lies there, were to lie in mine own throat.°   *lie outrageously*

DESDEMONA   Can you enquire him out, and be edified by report?

15   CLOWN   I will catechize the world for him; that is, make questions, and by them answer.

DESDEMONA   Seek him, bid him come hither, tell him I have moved° my lord on his behalf, and hope all will be well.   *petitioned*

CLOWN   To do this is within the compass° of man's wit, and   *scope*

20   therefore I will attempt the doing it.   *Exit*

DESDEMONA   Where should° I lose the handkerchief, Emilia?   *did*

EMILIA   I know not, madam.

DESDEMONA   Believe me, I had rather have lost my purse

Full of crusadoes,° and but° my noble Moor   *gold coins / but that*

25   Is true of mind, and made of no such baseness

As jealous creatures are, it were enough

To put him to ill thinking.

EMILIA   Is he not jealous?

DESDEMONA   Who, he? I think the sun where he was born

Drew all such humours from him.

      Enter OTHELLO

EMILIA   Look where he comes.

30   DESDEMONA   I will not leave him now till Cassio

3.4 Location: Before the citadel.   1. A form of address to an inferior.

Be called to him. How is't with you, my lord?

OTHELLO   Well, my good lady. [*Aside*] O hardness to dissemble!—
How do you, Desdemona?

DESDEMONA   Well, my good lord.

OTHELLO   Give me your hand. This hand is moist, my lady.

35 DESDEMONA   It hath felt no age, nor known no sorrow.

OTHELLO   This argues fruitfulness and liberal heart.[2]
Hot, hot and moist—this hand of yours requires
A sequester from liberty; fasting, and prayer,
Much castigation, exercise devout,

40 For here's a young and sweating devil here
That commonly rebels. 'Tis a good hand,
A frank° one.   (sexually) open

DESDEMONA   You may indeed say so,
For 'twas that hand that gave away my heart.

OTHELLO   A liberal hand. The hearts of old gave hands,

45 But our new heraldry is hands, not hearts.[3]

DESDEMONA   I cannot speak of this. Come now, your promise.

OTHELLO   What promise, chuck?°   woodchuck (affectionate)

DESDEMONA   I have sent to bid Cassio come speak with you.

OTHELLO   I have a salt and sorry rheum° offends me.   badly watering eyes
Lend me thy handkerchief.

50 DESDEMONA [*offering a handkerchief*]   Here, my lord.

OTHELLO   That which I gave you.

DESDEMONA   I have it not about me.

OTHELLO   Not?

DESDEMONA   No, faith, my lord.

OTHELLO   That's a fault. That handkerchief
Did an Egyptian to my mother give.

55 She was a charmer,° and could almost read   sorceress
The thoughts of people. She told her, while she kept it
'Twould make her amiable,° and subdue my father   desirable
Entirely to her love; but if she lost it,
Or made a gift of it, my father's eye

60 Should hold her loathèd, and his spirits should hunt
After new fancies. She, dying, gave it me,
And bid me, when my fate would have me wived,
To give it her.° I did so, and take heed on't.   to my wife
Make it a darling, like your precious eye.

65 To lose't or give't away were such perdition°   loss; damnation
As nothing else could match.

DESDEMONA   Is't possible?

OTHELLO   'Tis true. There's magic in the web of it.
A sibyl° that had numbered in the world   female prophet
The sun to course two hundred compasses[4]

70 In her prophetic fury sewed the work.
The worms were hallowed that did breed the silk,
And it was dyed in mummy,[5] which the skilful
Conserved of° maidens' hearts.   Preserved out of

DESDEMONA   I'faith, is't true?

---

2. This demonstrates fertility (perhaps, by implication, lust) and a generous (loose) heart. A moist hand was thought to be a sign of active desire.
3. These days the joining of hands doesn't signify the

joining of hearts.
4. *that . . . compasses*: who was two hundred years old.
5. Fluid drained from mummified bodies, supposedly magical.

OTHELLO	Most veritable. Therefore look to't well.	
75 DESDEMONA	Then would to God that I had never seen it!	
OTHELLO	Ha, wherefore?	
DESDEMONA	Why do you speak so startingly and rash?	
OTHELLO	Is't lost? Is't gone? Speak, is't out o'th' way?	
DESDEMONA	Heaven bless us!	
80 OTHELLO	Say you?	
DESDEMONA	It is not lost, but what an if° it were?	*an if=if*
OTHELLO	How?	
DESDEMONA	I say it is not lost.	
OTHELLO	Fetch't, let me see't.	
DESDEMONA	Why, so I can, sir, but I will not now.	
85	This is a trick to put me from my suit.	
	Pray you let Cassio be received again.	
OTHELLO	Fetch me the handkerchief. My mind misgives.	
DESDEMONA	Come, come, you'll never meet a more sufficient° man.	*complete*
OTHELLO	The handkerchief.	
DESDEMONA	I pray, talk me of Cassio.	
OTHELLO	The handkerchief.	
90 DESDEMONA	A man that all his time	
	Hath founded his good fortunes on your love,	
	Shared dangers with you—	
OTHELLO	The handkerchief.	
DESDEMONA	I'faith, you are to blame.	
95 OTHELLO	'Swounds!	*Exit*
EMILIA	Is not this man jealous?	
DESDEMONA	I ne'er saw this before.	
	Sure there's some wonder in this handkerchief.	
	I am most unhappy in the loss of it.	
EMILIA	'Tis not a year or two shows us a man.[6]	
100	They are all but° stomachs, and we all but food.	*nothing but*
	They eat us hungrily, and when they are full,	
	They belch us.	
	Enter IAGO *and* CASSIO	
	Look you, Cassio and my husband.	
IAGO [*to* CASSIO]	There is no other way. 'Tis she must do't,	
	And lo, the happiness![7] Go and importune her.	
105 DESDEMONA	How now, good Cassio? What's the news with you?	
CASSIO	Madam, my former suit. I do beseech you	
	That by your virtuous means I may again	
	Exist and be a member of his love	
	Whom I, with all the office of my heart,	
110	Entirely honour. I would not be delayed.	
	If my offence be of such mortal° kind	*deadly*
	That nor° my service past, nor present sorrows,	*neither*
	Nor purposed merit in futurity	
	Can ransom me into his love again,	
115	But to know so° must be my benefit.	*Even to know this*
	So° shall I clothe me in a forced content,	*If so*
	And shut° myself up in some other course	*give*
	To fortune's alms.	
DESDEMONA	Alas, thrice-gentle Cassio!	

6. Probably: It doesn't take long to see what men are made of.   7. What a happy coincidence (seeing Desdemona).

My advocation is not now in tune.[8]
120 My lord is not my lord, nor should I know him
Were he in favour° as in humour altered.   *appearance*
So help me every spirit sanctified
As I have spoken for you all my best,
And stood within the blank of° his displeasure   *in the aim of*
125 For my free speech! You must a while be patient.
What I can do I will, and more I will
Than for myself I dare. Let that suffice you.

IAGO   Is my lord angry?

EMILIA   He went hence but now,
And certainly in strange unquietness.

130 IAGO   Can he be angry? I have seen the cannon
When it hath blown his ranks into the air,
And, like the devil, from his very arm
Puffed his own brother;[9] and is he angry?
Something of moment then. I will go meet him.
135 There's matter in't indeed, if he be angry.

DESDEMONA   I prithee do so.   *Exit* IAGO
                        Something sure of state,[1]
Either from Venice or some unhatched practice°   *unfinished plot*
Made demonstrable here in Cyprus to him,
Hath puddled his clear spirit; and in such cases
140 Men's natures wrangle with inferior things,
Though great ones are their object. 'Tis even so;
For let our finger ache and it indues°   *induces*
Our other, healthful members even to a sense
Of pain. Nay, we must think men are not gods,
145 Nor of them look for such observancy°   *careful attention*
As fits the bridal.° Beshrew me° much, Emilia,   *wedding / (mild curse)*
I was—unhandsome° warrior as I am—   *unskilled*
Arraigning his unkindness with my soul;
But now I find I had suborned the witness,
And he's indicted falsely.[2]

150 EMILIA   Pray heaven it be
State matters, as you think, and no conception
Nor no jealous toy° concerning you.   *whim*

DESDEMONA   Alas the day, I never gave him cause.

EMILIA   But jealous souls will not be answered so.
155 They are not ever jealous for the cause,
But jealous for they're jealous. It is a monster
Begot upon itself, born on itself.

DESDEMONA   Heaven keep the monster from Othello's mind.

EMILIA   Lady, amen.

160 DESDEMONA   I will go seek him. Cassio, walk here about.
If I do find him fit I'll move your suit,
And seek to effect it to my uttermost.

CASSIO   I humbly thank your ladyship.

                        Exeunt DESDEMONA *and* EMILIA

---

8. My advocacy isn't working properly.
9. Blew up his own brother (and Othello wasn't angry
even then).

1. Surely some official business.
2. *suborned . . . falsely:* made the witness lie and so
accused Othello falsely.

Enter BIANCA[3]

BIANCA Save you,° friend Cassio.   *God save you*

CASSIO   What make° you from home?   *brings*

165 How is't with you, my most fair Bianca?
I'faith, sweet love, I was coming to your house.

BIANCA And I was going to your lodging, Cassio.
What, keep a week away? Seven days and nights,
Eightscore-eight hours, and lovers' absent hours

170 More tedious than the dial eightscore times![4]
O weary reckoning!°   *calculating*

CASSIO   Pardon me, Bianca,
I have this while with leaden thoughts been pressed,
But I shall in a more continuate° time   *opportune*
Strike off° this score of absence. Sweet Bianca,   *Make up*
Take me this work out.°   *Copy this embroidery*

[*He gives her Desdemona's napkin*]

175 BIANCA   O Cassio, whence came this?
This is some token from a newer friend.
To the felt absence now I feel a cause.
Is't come to this? Well, well.

CASSIO   Go to,° woman.   *Stop it*
Throw your vile guesses in the devil's teeth,

180 From whence you have them. You are jealous now
That this is from some mistress, some remembrance.
No, by my faith, Bianca.

BIANCA   Why, whose is it?

CASSIO I know not, neither. I found it in my chamber.
I like the work well. Ere it be demanded°—   *sought out*

185 As like° enough it will—I would have it copied.   *likely*
Take it, and do't, and leave me for this time.

BIANCA Leave you? Wherefore?

CASSIO I do attend here on the general,
And think it no addition,° nor my wish,   *(to my cause)*
To have him see me womaned.

190 BIANCA   Why, I pray you?

CASSIO Not that I love you not.

BIANCA   But that you do not love me.
I pray you bring me on the way a little,
And say if I shall see you soon at night.

CASSIO 'Tis but a little way that I can bring you,

195 For I attend here; but I'll see you soon.

BIANCA 'Tis very good. I must be circumstanced.[5]

Exeunt

4.1

Enter IAGO *and* OTHELLO

IAGO Will you think so?

OTHELLO   Think so, Iago?

IAGO What, to kiss in private?

OTHELLO   An unauthorized kiss.

3. "Bianca" means "white" in Italian—perhaps part of the play's ironic reversal of conventional color imagery, given that Bianca is a "customer" (courtesan, 4.1.117).
4. *lovers' . . . times:* each hour lovers are parted is eight

score (160) times more tedious than normal clock time.
5. Content with what circumstances offer.
4.1 Location: Before the citadel.

IAGO   Or to be naked with her friend in bed
         An hour or more, not meaning any harm?
5   OTHELLO   Naked in bed, Iago, and not mean harm?
         It is hypocrisy against the devil.¹
         They that mean virtuously and yet do so,
         The devil their virtue tempts, and they tempt heaven.²
     IAGO   If they do nothing, 'tis a venial slip.°   *an excusable sin*
10   But if I give my wife a handkerchief—
     OTHELLO   What then?
     IAGO   Why then, 'tis hers, my lord, and being hers,
         She may, I think, bestow't on any man.
     OTHELLO   She is protectress of her honour, too.
15   May she give that?
     IAGO   Her honour is an essence that's not seen.
         They° have it very oft that have it not.   *They are reputed to*
         But for the handkerchief—
     OTHELLO   By heaven, I would most gladly have forgot it.
20   Thou said'st—O, it comes o'er my memory
         As doth the raven o'er the infectious house,³
         Boding to all!—he had my handkerchief.
     IAGO   Ay, what of that?
     OTHELLO   That's not so good now.
     IAGO   What if I had said I had seen him do you wrong,
25   Or heard him say—as knaves be such abroad,⁴
         Who having by their own importunate suit
         Or voluntary dotage of some mistress
         Convincèd or supplied° them, cannot choose   *Seduced or satisfied*
         But they must blab—
     OTHELLO   Hath he said anything?
30   IAGO   He hath, my lord. But, be you well assured,
         No more than he'll unswear.
     OTHELLO   What hath he said?
     IAGO   Faith, that he did—I know not what he did.
     OTHELLO   What, what?
     IAGO   Lie—
     OTHELLO   With her?
     IAGO   With her, on her, what
         you will.
     OTHELLO   Lie with her? Lie on her? We say 'lie on her' when
35   they belie° her. Lie with her? 'Swounds, that's fulsome!°   *slander / nauseating*
         Handkerchief—confessions—handkerchief. To⁵ confess and be
         hanged for his labour. First to be hanged and then to confess!
         I tremble at it. Nature would not invest herself in such shadow-
         ing passion without some instruction.⁶ It is not words that
40   shakes me thus. Pish! Noses, ears, and lips! Is't possible? Con-
         fess? Handkerchief? O devil!

         He falls down in a trance

---

1. *Naked . . . devil*: By showing every sign of committing adultery but then stopping just in time, they deliberately mislead the devil, who wrongly takes their
apparent intention to sin at face value (just as an ordinary hypocrite deceives by professing virtue).
2. *They . . . heaven*: Those who mean well ("virtuously")
but act in this lascivious fashion ("so") make it easy for the
devil successfully to tempt them, and they push heaven to
the point where it may not be able to forgive them (?).
3. The raven was thought to be an ill omen and a carrier of plague. *infectious*: plague-infested.
4. As such knaves do exist in the world.
5. Lines 36–41 do not appear in Q. Arguably, these
lines provide more time for Othello to drive himself to
distraction and hence make his collapse more plausible.
6. *Nature . . . instruction*: It isn't natural that I would
feel such overwhelming ("shadowing") emotion (jealousy) unless there were some cause for it.

IAGO   Work on; my medicine works. Thus credulous fools are caught,
     And many worthy and chaste dames even thus,
     All guiltless, meet reproach. What ho, my lord!
     My lord, I say. Othello!

                    Enter CASSIO

45   How now, Cassio?
CASSIO   What's the matter?
IAGO   My lord is fall'n into an epilepsy.
     This is his second fit. He had one yesterday.
CASSIO   Rub him about the temples.
IAGO   No, forbear.
50   The lethargy° must have his° quiet course.   *trance / its*
     If not, he foams at mouth, and by and by
     Breaks out to savage madness. Look, he stirs.
     Do you withdraw yourself a little while,
     He will recover straight.° When he is gone   *immediately*
55   I would on great occasion° speak with you. [*Exit* CASSIO]   *important matters*
     How is it, general? Have you not hurt your head?[7]
OTHELLO   Dost thou mock me?
IAGO   I mock you not, by heaven.
     Would you would bear your fortune like a man.
OTHELLO   A hornèd man's a monster and a beast.
60   IAGO   There's many a beast then in a populous city,
     And many a civil° monster.   *city-dwelling*
OTHELLO   Did he confess it?
IAGO   Good sir, be a man.
     Think every bearded fellow that's but yoked
65   May draw with you.[8] There's millions now alive
     That nightly lie in those unproper beds
     Which they dare swear peculiar.[9] Your case is better.
     O, 'tis the spite of hell, the fiend's arch-mock,°   *devil's greatest mock*
     To lip° a wanton in a secure° couch   *kiss / an unsuspected*
70   And to suppose her chaste! No, let me know,
     And knowing what I am,° I know what she shall be.   *(a cuckold)*
OTHELLO   O, thou art wise, 'tis certain.
IAGO   Stand you a while apart.
     Confine yourself but in a patient list.°   *boundary*
     Whilst you were here, o'erwhelmèd with your grief—
75   A passion most unsuiting such a man—
     Cassio came hither. I shifted him away,
     And laid good 'scuse upon your ecstasy,°   *for your fit*
     Bade him anon return and here speak with me,
     The which he promised. Do but encave° yourself,   *hide*
80   And mark the fleers,° the gibes and notable scorns   *sneers*
     That dwell in every region of his face.
     For I will make him tell the tale anew,
     Where, how, how oft, how long ago, and when
     He hath and is again to cope° your wife.   *copulate with*
85   I say, but mark his gesture. Marry, patience,
     Or I shall say you're all-in-all in spleen,°   *completely impulsive*
     And nothing of a man.

---

7. Othello takes this as suggesting that he has grown
cuckold's horns.
8. *every . . . you:* every married man ("yoked," like an
ox, to his wife and hence to cuckoldry) labors ("draws")
under the same fate.
9. *That . . . peculiar:* Who lie in beds that don't belong
entirely to them but that they would swear are exclusively their own.

OTHELLO   Dost thou hear, Iago?
I will be found most cunning in my patience,
But—dost thou hear?—most bloody.

IAGO   That's not amiss,

90   But yet keep time° in all. Will you withdraw?   *maintain control*
         [OTHELLO *stands apart*]
Now will I question Cassio of Bianca,
A hussy that by selling her desires
Buys herself bread and cloth. It is a creature
That dotes on Cassio—as 'tis the strumpet's plague

95   To beguile many and be beguiled by one.
He, when he hears of her, cannot restrain
From the excess of laughter.
         Enter CASSIO
                 Here he comes.
As he shall smile, Othello shall go mad;
And his unbookish° jealousy must conster°   *ignorant / construe*

100   Poor Cassio's smiles, gestures, and light behaviours
Quite in the wrong. How do you now, lieutenant?

CASSIO   The worser that you give me the addition
Whose want even kills me.

IAGO   Ply Desdemona well and you are sure on't.

105   Now, if this suit lay in Bianca's power,
How quickly should you speed!

CASSIO [*laughing*]   Alas, poor caitiff!°   *wretch*

OTHELLO [*aside*]   Look how he laughs already.

IAGO   I never knew a woman love man so.

110   CASSIO   Alas, poor rogue! I think i'faith she loves me.

OTHELLO [*aside*]   Now he denies it faintly, and laughs it out.

IAGO   Do you hear, Cassio?

OTHELLO [*aside*]   Now he importunes him
To tell it o'er. Go to, well said, well said.

IAGO   She gives it out that you shall marry her.
Do you intend it?

115   CASSIO   Ha, ha, ha!

OTHELLO [*aside*]   Do ye triumph, Roman,[1] do you triumph?

CASSIO   I marry! What, a customer?° Prithee, bear some charity   *courtesan*
to my wit°—do not think it so unwholesome. Ha, ha, ha!   *sense*

OTHELLO [*aside*]   So, so, so, so. They laugh that wins.

120   IAGO   Faith, the cry goes that you marry her.

CASSIO   Prithee, say true.

IAGO   I am a very villain else.°   *if it's not true*

OTHELLO [*aside*]   Ha' you scored° me? Well.   *scored off*

CASSIO   This is the monkey's own giving out.° She is persuaded   *Bianca's own story*

125   I will marry her out of her own love and flattery, not out of my
promise.

OTHELLO [*aside*]   Iago beckons me. Now he begins the story.
         [OTHELLO *draws closer*]

CASSIO   She was here even now. She haunts me in every place.
I was the other day talking on the sea-bank with certain Vene-

130   tians, and thither comes the bauble,° and falls me thus about   *toy*
my neck.

---

1. Perhaps Othello draws on associations either with Rome's imperial successes (and subsequent collapse) or with the
Roman practice of holding celebratory processions.

OTHELLO [*aside*]   Crying 'O dear Cassio!' as it were. His gesture
　　imports° it.　　　　　　　　　　　　　　　　　　　　　　　　*indicates*

CASSIO   So hangs and lolls and weeps upon me, so shakes and
135　pulls me—ha, ha, ha!

OTHELLO [*aside*]   Now he tells how she plucked him to my
　　chamber. O, I see that nose of yours, but not that dog I shall
　　throw it to!²

CASSIO   Well, I must leave her company.

　　　　　Enter BIANCA

140　IAGO   Before me, look where she comes.

CASSIO   'Tis such another fitchew!³ Marry, a perfumed one. [*To*
　　BIANCA] What do you mean by this haunting of me?

BIANCA   Let the devil and his dam° haunt you. What did you　　*mother*
　　mean by that same handkerchief you gave me even now? I was
145　a fine fool to take it. I must take out° the whole work—a likely　*copy*
　　piece of work,° that you should find it in your chamber and　*an implausible story*
　　know not who left it there. This is some minx's token, and I
　　must take out the work. There, give it your hobby-horse.° [*Giv-*　*loose woman*
　　ing CASSIO *the napkin*] Wheresoever you had it, I'll take out
150　no work on't.

CASSIO   How now, my sweet Bianca, how now, how now?

OTHELLO [*aside*]   By heaven, that should° be my handkerchief.　*must*

BIANCA   An° you'll come to supper tonight, you may. An you will　*If*
　　not, come when you are next prepared for.⁴　　　　　　　*Exit*

155　IAGO   After her, after her.

CASSIO   Faith, I must, she'll rail in the streets else.

IAGO   Will you sup there?

CASSIO   Faith, I intend so.

IAGO   Well, I may chance to see you, for I would very fain speak
160　with you.

CASSIO   Prithee, come, will you?

IAGO   Go to, say no more.　　　　　　　　　　　*Exit* CASSIO

OTHELLO   How shall I murder him, Iago?

IAGO   Did you perceive how he laughed at his vice?

165　OTHELLO   O Iago!

IAGO   And did you see the handkerchief?

OTHELLO   Was that mine?

IAGO   Yours, by this hand. And to see how he prizes the foolish
　　woman your wife. She gave it him, and he hath given it his
170　whore.

OTHELLO   I would have him nine years a-killing.⁵ A fine woman,
　　a fair woman, a sweet woman.

IAGO   Nay, you must forget that.

OTHELLO   Ay, let her rot and perish, and be damned tonight, for
175　she shall not live. No, my heart is turned to stone; I strike it,
　　and it hurts my hand. O, the world hath not a sweeter creature!
　　She might lie by an emperor's side, and command him tasks.

IAGO   Nay, that's not your way.°　　　　　　　　　　*(the way to think)*

OTHELLO   Hang her, I do but say what she is—so delicate with
180　her needle, an admirable musician. O, she will sing the savage-
　　ness out of a bear! Of so high and plenteous wit and invention.°　*imagination*

2. *I see . . . to:* I'm envisioning my revenge, but the time
is not yet quite right. Cutting off the enemy's nose was
understood as a form of retribution.
3. Polecat, associated with prostitutes because of its

bad smell and presumed lecherousness.
4. Come next time I prepare for you (never).
5. I would spend nine years killing him.

IAGO   She's the worse for all this.

OTHELLO   O, a thousand, a thousand times! And then of so gen-
tle° a condition.   *highly born*

185 IAGO   Ay, too gentle.°   *generous (sexually)*

OTHELLO   Nay, that's certain. But yet the pity of it, Iago. O, Iago,
the pity of it, Iago!

IAGO   If you are so fond° over her iniquity, give her patent° to   *foolish / license*
offend; for if it touch not you, it comes near nobody.

190 OTHELLO   I will chop her into messes.° Cuckold me!   *pieces of food*

IAGO   O, 'tis foul in her.

OTHELLO   With mine officer.

IAGO   That's fouler.

OTHELLO   Get me some poison, Iago, this night. I'll not expostu-
195 late with her, lest her body and beauty unprovide my mind°   *weaken my resolve*
again. This night, Iago.

IAGO   Do it not with poison. Strangle her in her bed, even the
bed she hath contaminated.

OTHELLO   Good, good, the justice of it pleases, very good.

200 IAGO   And for Cassio, let me be his undertaker.° You shall hear   *murderer*
more by midnight.

OTHELLO   Excellent good.

        A trumpet
What trumpet is that same?

IAGO   I warrant, something from Venice.

        Enter LODOVICO, DESDEMONA, *and attendants*

205 'Tis Lodovico. This comes from the Duke. See, your wife's with
him.

LODOVICO   God save the worthy general.

OTHELLO   With all my heart,° sir.   *Thank you*

LODOVICO [*giving* OTHELLO *a letter*]   The Duke and the senators
210 of Venice greet you.

OTHELLO   I kiss the instrument° of their pleasures.°   *bearer / commands*
        [*He reads the letter*]

DESDEMONA   And what's the news, good cousin Lodovico?

IAGO [*to* LODOVICO]   I am very glad to see you, signor. Welcome
to Cyprus.

215 LODOVICO   I thank you. How does Lieutenant Cassio?

IAGO   Lives, sir.

DESDEMONA   Cousin, there's fall'n between him and my lord
An unkind° breach. But you shall make all well.   *unnatural*

OTHELLO   Are you sure of that?

220 DESDEMONA   My lord.

OTHELLO [*reads*]   'This fail you not to do as you will'—

LODOVICO   He did not call, he's busy in the paper.
Is there division 'twixt my lord and Cassio?

DESDEMONA   A most unhappy one. I would do much
225 T'atone° them, for the love I bear to Cassio.   *To reconcile*

OTHELLO   Fire and brimstone!

DESDEMONA   My lord?

OTHELLO   Are you wise?

DESDEMONA   What, is he angry?

LODOVICO   Maybe the letter moved him,
For, as I think, they do command him home,
Deputing Cassio in his government.°   *official position*

230 DESDEMONA   By my troth, I am glad on't.

OTHELLO   Indeed!

DESDEMONA   My lord?

OTHELLO [*to* DESDEMONA]   I am glad to see you mad.[6]

DESDEMONA   Why, sweet Othello!

235   OTHELLO   Devil!

[*He strikes her*]

DESDEMONA   I have not deserved this.

LODOVICO   My lord, this would not be believed in Venice,

Though I should swear I saw't. 'Tis very much.°   *going too far*

Make her amends, she weeps.

OTHELLO   O, devil, devil!

240   If that the earth could teem with° woman's tears,   *become pregnant by*

Each drop she falls would prove a crocodile.[7]

Out of my sight!

DESDEMONA [*going*]   I will not stay to offend you.

LODOVICO   Truly, an obedient lady.

I do beseech your lordship call her back.

245   OTHELLO   Mistress!

DESDEMONA [*returning*]   My lord?

OTHELLO [*to* LODOVICO]   What would you° with her, sir?   *do you wish*

LODOVICO   Who, I, my lord?

OTHELLO   Ay, you did wish that I would make her turn.°   *return*

250   Sir, she can turn and turn,° and yet go on   *(sexually)*

And turn again, and she can weep, sir, weep,

And she's obedient, as you say, obedient,

Very obedient. [*To* DESDEMONA] Proceed you in your tears.

[*To* LODOVICO] Concerning this, sir—[*To* DESDEMONA] O well

painted passion!

[*To* LODOVICO] I am commanded home. [*To* DESDEMONA] Get

255   you away.

I'll send for you anon. [*To* LODOVICO] Sir, I obey the mandate,

And will return to Venice. [*To* DESDEMONA] Hence, avaunt!°   *begone*

[*Exit* DESDEMONA]

[*To* LODOVICO] Cassio shall have my place, and, sir, tonight

I do entreat that we may sup together.

260   You are welcome, sir, to Cyprus. Goats and monkeys![8]   *Exit*

LODOVICO   Is this the noble Moor whom our full senate

Call all-in-all sufficient? Is this the nature

Whom passion could not shake, whose solid virtue

The shot of accident nor dart of chance

Could neither graze nor pierce?

265   IAGO   He is much changed.

LODOVICO   Are his wits safe? Is he not light of brain?

IAGO   He's that he is. I may not breathe my censure

What he might be. If what he might he is not,

I would to heaven he were.[9]

LODOVICO   What, strike his wife!

270   IAGO   Faith, that was not so well. Yet would I knew

---

6. Perhaps Othello is pleased that she's rejoicing in Cassio's promotion and hence revealing their adulterous affair, which she would be "mad" to do in public and in front of him.

7. Each drop would cause the earth to conceive a crocodile (crocodiles proverbially wept false tears for their victims).

8. Symbols of lust.

9. *I may . . . were:* I won't express my judgment on whether he is sane. If he is sane, I wish he were insane (because only that would excuse his bad behavior); if he is not sane, I wish he were.

That stroke would prove the worst.

LODOVICO   Is it his use,°   custom
Or did the letters work upon his blood°   passions
And new-create his fault?

IAGO   Alas, alas.
It is not honesty in me to speak

275   What I have seen and known. You shall observe him,
And his own courses° will denote him so   actions
That I may save my speech. Do but go after,
And mark how he continues.

LODOVICO   I am sorry that I am deceived in him.   *Exeunt*

4.2

Enter OTHELLO *and* EMILIA

OTHELLO   You have seen nothing then?

EMILIA   Nor ever heard, nor ever did suspect.

OTHELLO   Yes, you have seen Cassio and she together.

EMILIA   But then I saw no harm, and then I heard

5   Each syllable that breath made up between 'em.

OTHELLO   What, did they never whisper?

EMILIA   Never, my lord.

OTHELLO   Nor send you out o'th' way?

EMILIA   Never.

10   OTHELLO   To fetch her fan, her gloves, her mask, nor nothing?

EMILIA   Never, my lord.

OTHELLO   That's strange.

EMILIA   I durst, my lord, to wager she is honest,
Lay down my soul at stake. If you think other,

15   Remove your thought; it doth abuse your bosom.
If any wretch ha' put this in your head,
Let heaven requite it with the serpent's curse,[1]
For if she be not honest, chaste, and true,
There's no man happy; the purest of their wives
Is foul as slander.

20   OTHELLO   Bid her come hither. Go.   *Exit* EMILIA
She says enough, yet she's a simple bawd
That cannot say as much.[2] This is a subtle whore,
A closet lock and key° of villainous secrets,   A hider
And yet she'll kneel and pray—I ha' seen her do't.

Enter DESDEMONA *and* EMILIA

DESDEMONA   My lord, what is your will?

25   OTHELLO   Pray you, chuck, come hither.

DESDEMONA   What is your pleasure?

OTHELLO   Let me see your eyes.
Look in my face.

DESDEMONA   What horrible fancy's this?

OTHELLO [*to* EMILIA]   Some of your function,[3] mistress.

30   Leave procreants° alone, and shut the door,   copulators
Cough or cry 'Hem' if anybody come.
Your mystery, your mystery°—nay, dispatch.   *Exit* EMILIA   profession

DESDEMONA   Upon my knees, what doth your speech import?

4.2 Location: The citadel.   2. yet . . . much: yet it would be a simpleminded go-
1. In Genesis, the curse that God laid on the serpent   between who can't say as much as she did.
who deceived Eve.   3. Fulfill your bawd's function by guarding the door.

I understand a fury in your words,
But not the words.

35 OTHELLO   Why, what art thou?

DESDEMONA   Your wife, my lord, your true and loyal wife.

OTHELLO   Come, swear it, damn thyself,
Lest, being° like one of heaven, the devils themselves   *appearing*
Should fear to seize thee. Therefore be double-damned:
Swear thou art honest.

40 DESDEMONA   Heaven doth truly know it.

OTHELLO   Heaven truly knows that thou art false as hell.

DESDEMONA   To whom, my lord? With whom? How am I false?

OTHELLO [*weeping*]   Ah, Desdemon, away, away, away!

DESDEMONA   Alas, the heavy day! Why do you weep?
45 Am I the motive of these tears, my lord?
If haply° you my father do suspect   *perhaps*
An instrument of this your calling back,
Lay not your blame on me. If you have lost him,
I have lost him too.

OTHELLO   Had it pleased God
50 To try me with affliction; had He rained
All kind of sores and shames on my bare head,
Steeped me in poverty to the very lips,
Given to captivity me and my utmost hopes,
I should have found in some place of my soul
55 A drop of patience. But, alas, to make me
The fixèd figure for the time of scorn
To point his slow and moving finger at[4]—
Yet could I bear that too, well, very well.
But there where I have garnered° up my heart,   *stored*
60 Where either I must live or bear no life,
The fountain[5] from the which my current runs
Or else dries up—to be discarded thence,
Or keep it as a cistern for foul toads
To knot and gender° in! Turn thy complexion there,   *To couple and engender*
65 Patience,[6] thou young and rose-lipped cherubin,
Ay, here look grim as hell.

DESDEMONA   I hope my noble lord esteems me honest.

OTHELLO   O, ay—as summer flies are in the shambles,°   *slaughterhouse*
That quicken even with blowing.[7] O thou weed,
70 Who art so lovely fair, and smell'st so sweet,
That the sense aches at thee—would thou hadst ne'er been born!

DESDEMONA   Alas, what ignorant sin have I committed?

OTHELLO   Was this fair paper, this most goodly book,
Made to write 'whore' upon? What committed?
75 Committed?[8] O thou public commoner,°   *prostitute*
I should make very forges of my cheeks,
That would to cinders burn up modesty,
Did I but speak thy deeds. What committed?

---

4. *The fixed . . . at:* The designated object of scorn for this scornful time to point (as on a clock face) its slowly moving hand at.

5. Spring. The language here imagines Desdemona as the source of Othello's potential offspring.

6. *Turn . . . / Patience:* Change color at the thought of that, Patience. Or perhaps Patience and the "cherubin"

(end of line) are Desdemona, whom Othello directs to gaze at his own face or a mirror.

7. Who come to life (or bring their offspring to life and hence make the meat foul) as soon as the eggs are deposited. The point seems to be the speed of breeding, inferred from Desdemona's supposed infidelity.

8. Lines 75–78 do not appear in Q.

Heaven stops the nose at it, and the moon winks;°   *closes its eyes*
80   The bawdy° wind, that kisses all it meets,   *promiscuous*
     Is hushed within the hollow mine of earth°   *within a cave*
     And will not hear't. What committed?
DESDEMONA   By heaven, you do me wrong.
OTHELLO   Are not you a strumpet?
85 DESDEMONA   No, as I am a Christian.
     If to preserve this vessel for my lord
     From any other foul unlawful touch
     Be not to be a strumpet, I am none.
OTHELLO   What, not a whore?
DESDEMONA   No, as I shall be saved.
90 OTHELLO   Is't possible?
DESDEMONA   O heaven forgive us!
OTHELLO   I cry you mercy° then.   *I beg your pardon*
     I took you for that cunning whore of Venice
     That married with Othello. [*Calling*] You, mistress,
95   That have the office opposite to Saint Peter
     And keeps the gate of hell,
            Enter EMILIA
                   you, you, ay, you.
     We ha' done our course.° [*Giving money*] There's money for your pains.   *business*
     I pray you, turn the key and keep our counsel.   *Exit*
EMILIA   Alas, what does this gentleman conceive?°   *believe*
100   How do you, madam? How do you, my good lady?
DESDEMONA   Faith, half asleep.
EMILIA   Good madam, what's the matter with my lord?
DESDEMONA   With who?
EMILIA   Why, with my lord, madam.
DESDEMONA   Who is thy lord?
EMILIA   He that is yours, sweet lady.
105 DESDEMONA   I ha' none. Do not talk to me, Emilia.
     I cannot weep, nor answers have I none
     But what should go by water.° Prithee tonight   *appear in tears*
     Lay on my bed my wedding sheets, remember.
     And call thy husband hither.
EMILIA   Here's a change indeed.   *Exit*
110 DESDEMONA   'Tis meet° I should be used so, very meet.   *fitting*
     How have I been behaved, that he might stick
     The small'st opinion on my least misuse?[9]
            Enter IAGO *and* EMILIA
IAGO   What is your pleasure, madam? How is't with you?
DESDEMONA   I cannot tell. Those that do teach young babes
115   Do it with gentle means and easy tasks.
     He might ha' chid me so, for, in good faith,
     I am a child to chiding.
IAGO   What is the matter, lady?
EMILIA   Alas, Iago, my lord hath so bewhored her,°   *called her whore*
     Thrown such despite° and heavy terms upon her,   *spite*
120   That true hearts cannot bear it.
DESDEMONA   Am I that name, Iago?
IAGO   What name, fair lady?
DESDEMONA   Such as she said my lord did say I was.

---

9. *that . . . misuse*: perhaps, which would cause him to suspect even slightly the least fault.

EMILIA   He called her whore. A beggar in his drink
125   Could not have laid such terms upon his callet.°   *whore*
IAGO   Why did he so?
DESDEMONA   I do not know. I am sure I am none such.
IAGO   Do not weep, do not weep. Alas the day!
EMILIA   Hath she forsook so many noble matches,
130   Her father and her country and her friends,
To be called whore? Would it not make one weep?
DESDEMONA   It is my wretched fortune.
IAGO   Beshrew° him for't.   *Curse*
How comes this trick° upon him?   *behavior*
DESDEMONA   Nay, heaven doth know.
EMILIA   I will be hanged if some eternal villain,
135   Some busy° and insinuating rogue,   *meddling*
Some cogging,° cozening° slave, to get some office,   *deceiving / cheating*
Have not devised this slander. I will be hanged else.
IAGO   Fie, there is no such man. It is impossible.
DESDEMONA   If any such there be, heaven pardon him.
140   EMILIA   A halter° pardon him, and hell gnaw his bones!   *hangman's noose*
Why should he call her whore? Who keeps her company?
What place, what time, what form, what likelihood?
The Moor's abused by some most villainous knave,
Some base, notorious knave, some scurvy fellow.
145   O heaven, that such companions thou'dst unfold,°   *reveal*
And put in every honest hand a whip
To lash the rascals naked through the world,
Even from the east to th' west!
IAGO   Speak within door.°   *more softly*
EMILIA   O, fie upon them. Some such squire° he was   *fellow*
150   That turned your wit the seamy side without,°   *wrong side out*
And made you to suspect me with the Moor.
IAGO   You are a fool. Go to.
DESDEMONA   O God, Iago,
What shall I do to win my lord again?
Good friend, go to him; for by this light of heaven,
I know not how I lost him.
      [*She kneels*]
155   Here I kneel.[1]
If e'er my will did trespass 'gainst his love,
Either in discourse of thought or actual deed,
Or that mine eyes, mine ears, or any sense
Delighted them in any other form,[2]
160   Or that I do not yet,° and ever did,   *still*
And ever will—though he do shake me off
To beggarly divorcement—love him dearly,
Comfort forswear me.° Unkindness may do much,   *Deny me divine solace*
And his unkindness may defeat my life,
But never taint my love.
      [*She rises*]
165   I cannot say 'whore'.
It does abhor me[3] now I speak the word.

---

1. Lines 155–68 (beginning with "Here") do not
appear in Q.
2. Took pleasure in anyone but him.

3. Fill me with abhorrence; make me abhorrent, with a
pun on "ab-whore."

To do the act that might the addition° earn,   *label*
Not the world's mass of vanity° could make me.   *all worldly splendor*

IAGO   I pray you, be content. 'Tis but his humour.°   *mood*
170   The business of the state does him offence,
And he does chide with you.

DESDEMONA   If 'twere no other!

IAGO   It is but so, I warrant.
        [*Flourish within*]
Hark how these instruments summon you to supper.
175   The messengers of Venice stays the meat.°   *are waiting to eat*
Go in, and weep not. All things shall be well.
        Exeunt DESDEMONA *and* EMILIA
    Enter RODERIGO
How now, Roderigo?

RODERIGO   I do not find that thou deal'st justly with me.

IAGO   What in the contrary?

180   RODERIGO   Every day thou daff'st me with some device,[4] Iago,
and rather, as it seems to me now, keep'st from me all conve-
niency° than suppliest me with the least advantage of hope. I   *opportunity*
will indeed no longer endure it, nor am I yet persuaded to put
up in peace what already I have foolishly suffered.

185   IAGO   Will you hear me, Roderigo?

RODERIGO   Faith, I have heard too much, for your words and
performances are no kin together.

IAGO   You charge me most unjustly.

RODERIGO   With naught but truth. I have wasted myself out of
190   my means. The jewels you have had from me to deliver Desdemona would half have corrupted a votarist.° You have told me   *nun*
she hath received 'em, and returned me expectations and comforts of sudden respect and acquaintance, but I find none.

IAGO   Well, go to,° very well.   *(expresses remonstrance)*

195   RODERIGO   'Very well', 'go to'! I cannot go to,° man, nor 'tis not   *succeed sexually*
very well. Nay, I think it is scurvy, and begin to find myself
fopped° in it.   *made a fool*

IAGO   Very well.

RODERIGO   I tell you 'tis not very well. I will make myself known
200   to Desdemona. If she will return me my jewels, I will give
over my suit and repent my unlawful solicitation. If not, assure
yourself I will seek satisfaction of you.

IAGO   You have said° now.   *finished*

RODERIGO   Ay, and said nothing but what I protest intendment
205   of doing.

IAGO   Why, now I see there's mettle in thee, and even from this
instant do build on thee a better opinion than ever before. Give
me thy hand, Roderigo. Thou hast taken against me a most just
exception, but yet I protest I have dealt most directly in thy
210   affair.

RODERIGO   It hath not appeared.

IAGO   I grant, indeed, it hath not appeared, and your suspicion
is not without wit and judgement. But, Roderigo, if thou hast
that in thee indeed which I have greater reason to believe now
215   than ever—I mean purpose, courage, and valour—this night
show it. If thou the next night following enjoy not Desdemona,

---

4. You put me off with some trick.

take me from this world with treachery, and devise engines
for° my life.

plots against

RODERIGO   Well, what is it? Is it within reason and compass?°

possibility

220 IAGO   Sir, there is especial commission come from Venice to
depute Cassio in Othello's place.

RODERIGO   Is that true? Why then, Othello and Desdemona
return again to Venice.

IAGO   O no, he goes into Mauritania,⁵ and takes away with him
225 the fair Desdemona, unless his abode be lingered here by some
accident, wherein none can be so determinate° as the remov-

effectual

ing of Cassio.

RODERIGO   How do you mean 'removing' of him?

IAGO   Why, by making him uncapable of Othello's place—
230 knocking out his brains.

RODERIGO   And that you would have me to do.

IAGO   Ay, if you dare do yourself a profit and a right. He sups
tonight with a harlotry, and thither will I go to him. He knows
not yet of his honourable fortune.° If you will watch his going

his promotion

235 thence, which I will fashion° to fall out between twelve and

arrange

one, you may take him at your pleasure. I will be near, to second your attempt, and he shall fall between us. Come, stand
not amazed at it, but go along with me. I will show you such a
necessity in his death that you shall think yourself bound to put
240 it on him. It is now high supper-time, and the night grows to
waste. About it.

RODERIGO   I will hear further reason for this.

IAGO   And you shall be satisfied.   *Exeunt*

4.3

Enter OTHELLO, DESDEMONA, LODOVICO, EMILIA, *and*
attendants

LODOVICO   I do beseech you, sir, trouble yourself no further.

OTHELLO   O, pardon me, 'twill do me good to walk.

LODOVICO [*to* DESDEMONA]   Madam, good night. I humbly thank
your ladyship.

DESDEMONA   Your honour is most welcome.

OTHELLO   Will you walk, sir?
5 O, Desdemona!

DESDEMONA   My lord?

OTHELLO   Get you to bed on th'instant. I will be returned forthwith. Dismiss your attendant there. Look't be done.

DESDEMONA   I will, my lord.

                    Exeunt [OTHELLO, LODOVICO, *and attendants*]

10 EMILIA   How goes it now? He looks gentler than he did.

DESDEMONA   He says he will return incontinent.°

immediately

He hath commanded me to go to bed,
And bid me to dismiss you.

EMILIA   Dismiss me?

DESDEMONA   It was his bidding. Therefore, good Emilia,
15 Give me my nightly wearing, and adieu.
We must not now displease him.

EMILIA   I would you had never seen him.

DESDEMONA   So would not I. My love doth so approve him

---

5. Country in the western Sahara.   4.3 Location: Scene continues.

That even his stubbornness, his checks, his frowns—
20   Prithee unpin me—have grace and favour in them.
        [EMILIA *helps* DESDEMONA *to undress*]
    EMILIA   I have laid those sheets you bade me on the bed.
    DESDEMONA   All's one.° Good faith, how foolish are our minds!   *It doesn't matter*
    If I do die before thee, prithee shroud me
    In one of these same sheets.
    EMILIA   Come, come, you talk.
25   DESDEMONA   My mother had a maid called Barbary.[1]
    She was in love, and he she loved proved mad
    And did forsake her. She had a song of willow.
    An old thing 'twas, but it expressed her fortune,
    And she died singing it. That song tonight
30   Will not go from my mind. I[2] have much to do
    But to[3] go hang my head all at one side
    And sing it, like poor Barbary. Prithee, dispatch.
    EMILIA   Shall I go fetch your nightgown?
    DESDEMONA   No. Unpin me here.
    This Lodovico is a proper man.
    EMILIA   A very handsome man.
35   DESDEMONA   He speaks well.
    EMILIA   I know a lady in Venice would have walked barefoot to
    Palestine for a touch of his nether lip.
    DESDEMONA [*sings*]   'The poor soul sat sighing by a sycamore tree,
    Sing all a green willow.[4]
40   Her hand on her bosom, her head on her knee,
    Sing willow, willow, willow.
    The fresh streams ran by her and murmured her moans,
    Sing willow, willow, willow.
    Her salt tears fell from her and softened the stones,
45   Sing willow'—
    Lay by these.—
                     'willow, willow.'
    Prithee, hie thee.° He'll come anon.   *hurry*
    'Sing all a green willow must be my garland.
50   Let nobody blame him, his scorn I approve'—
    Nay, that's not next. Hark, who is't that knocks?
    EMILIA   It's the wind.
    DESDEMONA [*sings*]   'I called my love false love, but what said he then?[5]
    Sing willow, willow, willow.
55   If I court more women, you'll couch with more men.'
    So, get thee gone. Good night. Mine eyes do itch.
    Doth that bode weeping?
    EMILIA   'Tis neither here nor there.
    DESDEMONA   I have heard it said so. O, these men, these men![6]
    Dost thou in conscience think—tell me, Emilia—
60   That there be women do abuse their husbands
    In such gross kind?°   *fashion*
    EMILIA   There be some such, no question.
    DESDEMONA   Wouldst thou do such a deed for all the world?
    EMILIA   Why, would not you?

---

1. Iago compares Othello to a "Barbary horse" in 1.1.113.
2. Lines 30–51 ("I . . . next") do not appear in Q.
3. I can barely bring myself not to.
4. A conventional symbol of disappointed love.
5. Lines 53–55 do not appear in Q.
6. Lines 58–61 do not appear in Q.

DESABLEMONA No, by this heavenly light.

EMILIA Nor I neither, by this heavenly light. I might do't as well

65 i'th' dark.

DESDEMONA Wouldst thou do such a deed for all the world?

EMILIA The world's a huge thing. It is a great price for a small
vice.

DESDEMONA In truth, I think thou wouldst not.

70 EMILIA In truth, I think I should, and undo't when I had done.
Marry, I would not do such a thing for a joint ring,[7] nor for
measures of lawn,° nor for gowns, petticoats, nor caps, nor any   *linen*
petty exhibition;° but for all the whole world? Ud's° pity, who   *gift / God's*
would not make her husband a cuckold to make him a mon-

75 arch? I should venture purgatory for't.

DESDEMONA Beshrew me if I would do such a wrong
For the whole world.

EMILIA Why, the wrong is but a wrong i'th' world, and having
the world for your labour, 'tis a wrong in your own world, and

80 you might quickly make it right.

DESDEMONA I do not think there is any such woman.

EMILIA Yes, a dozen, and as many
To th' vantage as would store the world they played for.[8]
But I do think it is their husbands' faults[9]

85 If wives do fall. Say that they slack their duties,°   *marital duties*
And pour our treasures into foreign laps,[1]
Or else break out in peevish jealousies,
Throwing restraint upon us; or say they strike us,
Or scant our former having in despite:[2]

90 Why, we have galls;° and though we have some grace,   *tempers*
Yet have we some revenge. Let husbands know
Their wives have sense like them. They see, and smell,
And have their palates both for sweet and sour,
As husbands have. What is it that they do

95 When they change us for others? Is it sport?
I think it is. And doth affection° breed it?   *lust*
I think it doth. Is't frailty that thus errs?
It is so, too. And have not we affections,
Desires for sport, and frailty, as men have?

100 Then let them use us well, else let them know
The ills we do, their ills instruct us so.

DESDEMONA Good night, good night. God me such uses° send   *habits*
Not to pick bad from bad, but by bad mend![3]   *Exeunt*

5.1

Enter IAGO *and* RODERIGO

IAGO Here, stand behind this bulk.° Straight° will he come.   *shop stall / Right away*
Wear thy good rapier bare, and put it home.°   *drive it into him*
Quick, quick, fear nothing. I'll be at thy elbow.
It makes us or it mars us. Think on that,

5 And fix most firm thy resolution.

RODERIGO Be near at hand. I may miscarry in't.

---

7. A cheap ring in separable halves.
8. *and . . . for:* and as many more as it would take to
populate the world they gained by doing it.
9. Lines 84–101 do not appear in Q.
1. And give the semen that belongs to us to other women.

2. Or reduce our allowances out of spite.
3. Not to take bad behavior as an example, but to know
what to avoid.
5.1 Location: A street in Cyprus.

IAGO   Here at thy hand. Be bold, and take thy stand.

RODERIGO [*aside*]   I have no great devotion to the deed,
   And yet he hath given me satisfying reasons.

10   'Tis but a man gone. Forth my sword—he dies!

IAGO [*aside*]   I have rubbed this young quat° almost to the sense,°   *pimple / to the quick*
   And he grows angry. Now, whether he kill Cassio
   Or Cassio him, or each do kill the other,
   Every way makes my gain. Live Roderigo,°   *If Roderigo lives*

15   He calls me to a restitution large
   Of gold and jewels that I bobbed from him°   *defrauded him of*
   As gifts to Desdemona.
   It must not be. If Cassio do remain,
   He hath a daily beauty in his life

20   That makes me ugly; and besides, the Moor
   May unfold° me to him—there stand I in much peril.   *reveal*
   No, he must die. But so, I hear him coming.

       Enter CASSIO

RODERIGO   I know his gait, 'tis he. [*Attacking* CASSIO] Villain, thou diest.

CASSIO   That thrust had been mine enemy indeed,

25   But that my coat is better° than thou know'st.   *thicker; more armored*
   I will make proof of° thine.   *test*

       [*He stabs* RODERIGO, *who falls*]

RODERIGO   O, I am slain!

       [IAGO *wounds* CASSIO *in the leg from behind. Exit* IAGO]

CASSIO [*falling*]   I am maimed for ever. Help, ho, murder, murder!

       Enter OTHELLO [*above*]

OTHELLO   The voice of Cassio. Iago keeps his word.

RODERIGO   O, villain that I am!

30   OTHELLO   It is even so.

CASSIO   O, help, ho! Light, a surgeon!

OTHELLO   'Tis he. O brave Iago, honest and just,
   That hast such noble sense of thy friend's wrong—
   Thou teachest me. Minion,° your dear lies dead,   *Hussy*

35   And your unblessed fate hies.° Strumpet, I come.   *damnation hurries on*
   Forth of° my heart those charms, thine eyes, are blotted.   *Out of*
   Thy bed, lust-stained, shall with lust's blood be spotted.   *Exit*

       Enter LODOVICO *and* GRAZIANO

CASSIO   What ho, no watch, no passage?° Murder, murder!   *passersby*

GRAZIANO   'Tis some mischance. The voice is very direful.

40   CASSIO   O, help!

LODOVICO   Hark.

RODERIGO   O wretched villain!

LODOVICO   Two or three groan. 'Tis heavy° night.   *dark*
   These may be counterfeits. Let's think't unsafe

45   To come into° the cry without more help.   *go near*

RODERIGO   Nobody come? Then shall I bleed to death.

       Enter IAGO *with a light*

LODOVICO   Hark.

GRAZIANO   Here's one comes in his shirt, with light and weapons.

IAGO   Who's there? Whose noise is this that cries on murder?

LODOVICO   We do not know.

50   IAGO   Do not you hear a cry?

CASSIO   Here, here. For heaven's sake, help me.

IAGO   What's the matter?

GRAZIANO [*to* LODOVICO]   This is Othello's ensign, as I take it.

LODOVICO   The same indeed, a very valiant fellow.

IAGO [*to* CASSIO]   What are you here that cry so grievously?

55   CASSIO   Iago—O, I am spoiled, undone by villains.
　　　Give me some help.

IAGO   O me, lieutenant, what villains have done this?

CASSIO   I think that one of them is hereabout
　　　And cannot make away.

IAGO   O treacherous villains!
　　　[*To* LODOVICO *and* GRAZIANO]   What are you there? Come in

60   　　　and give some help.

RODERIGO   O, help me there!

CASSIO   That's one of 'em.

IAGO [*stabbing* RODERIGO]   O murderous slave! O villain!

RODERIGO   O damned Iago! O inhuman dog!

65   IAGO   Kill men i'th' dark? Where be these bloody thieves?
　　　How silent is this town! Ho, murder, murder!
　　　[*To* LODOVICO *and* GRAZIANO]   What may you be? Are you of
　　　　good or evil?

LODOVICO   As you shall prove us, praise us.

IAGO   Signor Lodovico.

LODOVICO   He, sir.

70   IAGO   I cry you mercy. Here's Cassio hurt by villains.

GRAZIANO   Cassio?

IAGO   How is't, brother?

CASSIO   My leg is cut in two.

IAGO   Marry, heaven forbid!

75   　　　Light, gentlemen. I'll bind it with my shirt.
　　　　　　　　Enter BIANCA

BIANCA   What is the matter, ho? Who is't that cried?

IAGO   Who is't that cried?

BIANCA   O my dear Cassio,
　　　My sweet Cassio, O, Cassio, Cassio!

IAGO   O notable strumpet! Cassio, may you suspect

80   　　　Who they should be that have thus mangled you?

CASSIO   No.

GRAZIANO   I am sorry to find you thus. I have been to seek you.

IAGO   Lend me a garter. So. O for a chair,°   *litter*
　　　To bear him easily hence!

85   BIANCA   Alas, he faints. O, Cassio, Cassio, Cassio!

IAGO   Gentlemen all, I do suspect this trash
　　　To be a party in this injury.
　　　Patience a while, good Cassio. Come, come,
　　　Lend me a light. [*Going to* RODERIGO]   Know we this face or no?

90   　　　Alas, my friend, and my dear countryman.
　　　Roderigo? No—yes, sure—O heaven, Roderigo!

GRAZIANO   What, of Venice?

IAGO   Even he, sir. Did you know him?

GRAZIANO   Know him? Ay.

95   IAGO   Signor Graziano, I cry your gentle pardon.
　　　These bloody accidents must excuse my manners
　　　That so neglected you.

GRAZIANO   I am glad to see you.

IAGO   How do you, Cassio? O, a chair, a chair!

GRAZIANO   Roderigo.

IAGO   He, he, 'tis he.

[*Enter attendants with a chair*]

100 O, that's well said, the chair!
Some good man bear him carefully from hence.
I'll fetch the general's surgeon. [*To* BIANCA] For you, mistress,
Save you your labour. He that lies slain here, Cassio,
Was my dear friend. What malice was between you?

105 CASSIO None in the world, nor do I know the man.
IAGO [*to* BIANCA] What, look you pale? [*To attendants*] O, bear
        him out o'th' air.[1]
[*To* LODOVICO *and* GRAZIANO] Stay you, good gentlemen.
        [*Exeunt attendants with* CASSIO *in the chair*
          and with Roderigo's body]
[*To* BIANCA]   Look you pale, mistress?
[*To* LODOVICO *and* GRAZIANO] Do you perceive the ghastness° of her eye?   terror
[*To* BIANCA] Nay, an° you stare we shall hear more anon.   if
110 [*To* LODOVICO *and* GRAZIANO] Behold her well; I pray you look upon her.
Do you see, gentlemen? Nay, guiltiness
Will speak, though tongues were out of use.
        Enter EMILIA
EMILIA Alas, what is the matter? What is the matter, husband?
IAGO Cassio hath here been set on in the dark
115 By Roderigo and fellows that are scaped.
He's almost slain, and Roderigo dead.
EMILIA Alas, good gentleman! Alas, good Cassio!
IAGO This is the fruits of whoring. Prithee, Emilia,
Go know of Cassio where he supped tonight.
120 [*To* BIANCA] What, do you shake at that?
BIANCA He supped at my house, but I therefore shake not.
IAGO O, did he so? I charge you go with me.
EMILIA [*to* BIANCA] O, fie upon thee, strumpet!
BIANCA I am no strumpet, but of life as honest
As you that thus abuse me.
125 EMILIA   As I? Fough, fie upon thee!
IAGO Kind gentlemen, let's go see poor Cassio dressed.
[*To* BIANCA] Come, mistress, you must tell's another tale.
Emilia, run you to the citadel
And tell my lord and lady what hath happed.
Will you go on afore?   [*Exit* EMILIA]
130 [*Aside*]   This is the night
That either makes me or fordoes° me quite.   *Exeunt*   undoes

5.2
Enter OTHELLO *with a light.* [*He draws back a curtain,*
revealing] DESDEMONA [*asleep*] *in her bed*
OTHELLO It is the cause,[1] it is the cause, my soul.
Let me not name it to you, you chaste stars.
It is the cause. Yet I'll not shed her blood,
Nor scar that whiter skin of hers than snow,
5 And smooth as monumental alabaster.°   *stone used in tombs*
Yet she must die, else she'll betray more men.
Put out the light, and then put out the light.[2]

1. Out of the open air (thought to be bad for wounds).
5.2 Location: Desdemona and Othello's bedroom.
1. What matters is Desdemona's infidelity; the "cause"
of justice, which Othello sees himself defending, as in
the subsequent lines.
2. This and the following lines compare the light of
Othello's lamp or torch to Desdemona's "light" of life.

If I quench thee, thou flaming minister,°   *light that serves me*

I can again thy former light restore

10   Should I repent me; but once put out thy light,

Thou cunning'st pattern of excelling nature,[3]

I know not where is that Promethean heat[4]

That can thy light relume.° When I have plucked thy rose   *relight*

I cannot give it vital growth again.

15   It needs must wither. I'll smell thee on the tree.

     [*He kisses her*]

O balmy breath, that dost almost persuade

Justice to break her sword! One more, one more.

Be thus when thou art dead, and I will kill thee

And love thee after. One more, and that's the last.

     He kisses her

20   So sweet was ne'er so fatal. I must weep,

But they are cruel tears. This sorrow's heavenly,

It strikes where it doth love.[5] She wakes.

DESDEMONA   Who's there? Othello?

OTHELLO   Ay, Desdemona.

25 DESDEMONA   Will you come to bed, my lord?

OTHELLO   Have you prayed tonight, Desdemon?

DESDEMONA   Ay, my lord.

OTHELLO   If you bethink yourself of any crime

Unreconciled as yet to heaven and grace,

30   Solicit° for it straight.   *Ask forgiveness*

DESDEMONA   Alack, my lord, what may you mean by that?

OTHELLO   Well, do it, and be brief. I will walk by.

I would not kill thy unpreparèd spirit.

No, heavens forfend! I would not kill thy soul.

DESDEMONA   Talk you of killing?

OTHELLO   Ay, I do.

35 DESDEMONA   Then heaven

Have mercy on me.

OTHELLO   Amen, with all my heart.

DESDEMONA   If you say so, I hope you will not kill me.

OTHELLO   Hum!

DESDEMONA   And yet I fear you, for you're fatal then

40   When your eyes roll so. Why I should fear I know not,

Since guiltiness I know not, but yet I feel I fear.

OTHELLO   Think on thy sins.

DESDEMONA   They are loves I bear to you.

OTHELLO   Ay, and for that thou diest.

45 DESDEMONA   That death's unnatural that kills for loving.

Alas, why gnaw you so your nether lip?

Some bloody passion shakes your very frame.

These are portents, but yet I hope, I hope

They do not point on me.

OTHELLO   Peace, and be still.

DESDEMONA   I will so. What's the matter?

50 OTHELLO   That handkerchief

Which I so loved and gave thee, thou gav'st to Cassio.

---

3. You most cleverly wrought example of nature's work.
4. Life-giving fire. In Greek mythology, Prometheus stole fire from heaven to give it to humankind; in a different tradition, he is credited with animating humankind from clay.

5. See Hebrews 12:6: "For whom the Lord loveth, he chasteneth."

DESDEMONA   No, by my life and soul. Send for the man
        And ask him.
OTHELLO   Sweet soul, take heed, take heed of perjury.
55   Thou art on thy deathbed.
DESDEMONA   Ay, but not yet to die.
OTHELLO   Presently.°   *Immediately*
        Therefore confess thee freely of thy sin,
        For to deny each article with oath
60   Cannot remove nor choke the strong conception
        That I do groan withal.⁶ Thou art to die.
DESDEMONA   Then Lord have mercy on me.
OTHELLO   I say amen.
DESDEMONA   And have you mercy, too. I never did
        Offend you in my life, never loved Cassio
65   But with such general warranty of heaven
        As I might love. I never gave him token.
OTHELLO   By heaven, I saw my handkerchief in's hand.
        O perjured woman! Thou dost stone° my heart,   *harden*
        And makes me call what I intend to do
70   A murder, which I thought a sacrifice.
        I saw the handkerchief.
DESDEMONA   He found it, then.
        I never gave it him. Send for him hither.
        Let him confess a truth.
OTHELLO   He hath confessed.
DESDEMONA   What, my lord?
OTHELLO   That he hath usèd thee.
75 DESDEMONA   How, unlawfully?
OTHELLO   Ay.
DESDEMONA   He will not say so.
OTHELLO   No, his mouth is stopped.
        Honest Iago hath ta'en order for't.
80 DESDEMONA   O, my fear interprets! What, is he dead?
OTHELLO   Had all his hairs been lives, my great revenge
        Had stomach for 'em all.
DESDEMONA [*weeping*]   Alas, he is betrayed, and I undone.
OTHELLO   Out, strumpet! Weep'st thou for him to my face?
85 DESDEMONA   O, banish me, my lord, but kill me not.
OTHELLO [*attacking her*]   Down, strumpet.
DESDEMONA   Kill me tomorrow; let me live tonight.
OTHELLO   Nay, an you strive—
DESDEMONA   But half an hour.
90 OTHELLO   Being done, there is no pause.⁷
DESDEMONA   But while I say one prayer.
OTHELLO   It is too late.
                He smothers her
DESDEMONA   O Lord, Lord, Lord!
                EMILIA *at the door*
EMILIA (*within*)   My lord, my lord, what ho, my lord, my lord!
95 OTHELLO   What noise is this? Not dead? Not yet quite dead?
        I that am cruel am yet merciful.

---

6. *Cannot . . . withal:* Cannot stop the strong conviction
I have in your guilt (or the firm plan to kill you), which
makes me groan so. The metaphor is from childbirth.
7. Now that I've started, there's no stopping.

I would not have thee linger in thy pain.
So, so.

EMILIA [*within*]   What ho, my lord, my lord!

OTHELLO   Who's there?

EMILIA [*within*]   O, good my lord, I would speak a word with you.

OTHELLO [*calling*]   Yes.—'Tis Emilia. [*Calling*] By

100   and by!—She's dead.
'Tis like she comes to speak of Cassio's death.
The noise was high.° Ha! No more moving.   *commotion was loud*
Still as the grave. Shall she come in? Were't good?
I think she stirs again. No. What's best to do?

105   If she come in, she'll sure speak to my wife.
My wife, my wife! What wife? I ha' no wife.
O insupportable, O heavy hour!
Methinks it should be now a huge eclipse
Of sun and moon, and that th'affrighted globe
Should yawn at alteration.[8]

110   EMILIA [*within*]   I do beseech you
That I may speak with you. O, good my lord!

OTHELLO   I had forgot thee.—O, come in, Emilia.—
Soft,° by and by. Let me the curtains draw.   *Quiet*
            [*He closes the bed-curtains*]
Where art thou?
            [*He opens the door.*] *Enter* EMILIA
                          What's the matter with thee now?

115   EMILIA   O my good lord, yonder's foul murder's done.

OTHELLO   What, now?

EMILIA   But° now, my lord.   *Just*

OTHELLO   It is the very error° of the moon,   *deviation*
She comes more nearer earth than she was wont,

120   And makes men mad.

EMILIA   Cassio, my lord, hath killed a young Venetian
Called Roderigo.

OTHELLO   Roderigo killed
And Cassio killed?

EMILIA   No, Cassio is not killed.

OTHELLO   Not Cassio killed? Then murder's out of tune,

125   And sweet revenge grows harsh.

DESDEMONA   O, falsely, falsely murdered!

EMILIA   O Lord, what cry is that?

OTHELLO   That? What?

EMILIA   Out and alas, that was my lady's voice!
            [*She opens the bed-curtains*]

130   Help, help, ho, help! O lady, speak again!
Sweet Desdemona, O sweet mistress, speak!

DESDEMONA   A guiltless death I die.

EMILIA   O, who hath done this deed?

DESDEMONA   Nobody, I myself. Farewell.
Commend me to my kind lord. O, farewell!   *She dies*

OTHELLO   Why, how should she be murdered?

135   EMILIA   Alas, who knows?

OTHELLO   You heard her say herself it was not I.

EMILIA   She said so, I must needs report the truth.

---

8. Should gape at the change. Earthquakes were associated with eclipses.

OTHELLO   She's like a liar gone to burning hell.
   'Twas I that killed her.
140   EMILIA   O, the more angel she, and you the blacker devil!
OTHELLO   She turned to folly,° and she was a whore.   *wantonness*
EMILIA   Thou dost belie her, and thou art a devil.
OTHELLO   She was false as water.
EMILIA   Thou art rash as fire
   To say that she was false. O, she was heavenly true!
145   OTHELLO   Cassio did top her. Ask thy husband else.°   *if you doubt it*
   O, I were damned beneath all depth in hell
   But that I did proceed upon just grounds
   To this extremity! Thy husband knew it all.
EMILIA   My husband?
OTHELLO   Thy husband.
EMILIA   That she was false to wedlock?
150   OTHELLO   Ay, with Cassio. Had she been true,
   If heaven would make me such another world
   Of one entire and perfect chrysolite°   *topaz*
   I'd not have sold her for it.
EMILIA   My husband?
OTHELLO   Ay, 'twas he that told me on her first.
155   An honest man he is, and hates the slime
   That sticks on filthy deeds.
EMILIA   My husband?
OTHELLO   What needs this iterance?° Woman, I say thy husband.   *repetition*
EMILIA   O mistress, villainy hath made mocks with° love.⁹   *at*
   My husband say she was false?
OTHELLO   He, woman.
160   I say thy husband. Dost understand the word?
   My friend, thy husband, honest, honest Iago.
EMILIA   If he say so, may his pernicious soul
   Rot half a grain a day. He lies to th' heart.
   She was too fond of her most filthy bargain.
165   OTHELLO   Ha?
EMILIA   Do thy worst.
   This deed of thine is no more worthy heaven
   Than thou wast worthy her.
OTHELLO   Peace, you were best.°   *it would be best for you*
EMILIA   Thou hast not half that power to do me harm
170   As I have to be hurt. O gull,° O dolt,   *fool*
   As ignorant as dirt! Thou hast done a deed—
   I care not for thy sword, I'll make thee known
   Though I lost twenty lives. Help, help, ho! Help!
   The Moor hath killed my mistress. Murder, murder!
       Enter MONTANO, GRAZIANO, *and* IAGO
175   MONTANO   What is the matter? How now, general?
EMILIA   O, are you come, Iago? You have done well,
   That men must lay their murders on your neck.
GRAZIANO   What is the matter?
EMILIA [*to* IAGO]   Disprove this villain if thou beest a man.
180   He says thou told'st him that his wife was false.
   I know thou didst not. Thou'rt not such a villain.
   Speak, for my heart is full.

9. Lines 158–61 do not appear in Q.

IAGO   I told him what I thought, and told no more
Than what he found himself was apt and true.

185　EMILIA   But did you ever tell him she was false?

IAGO   I did.

EMILIA   You told a lie, an odious, damnèd lie,
Upon my soul a lie, a wicked lie.
She false with Cassio? Did you say with Cassio?

190　IAGO   With Cassio, mistress. Go to, charm° your tongue.　　　　　*silence*

EMILIA   I will not charm my tongue. I am bound to speak.
My mistress here lies murdered in her bed.[1]

MONTANO *and* GRAZIANO   O heavens forfend!

EMILIA [*to* IAGO]   And your reports have set the murder on.

195　OTHELLO   Nay, stare not, masters. It is true indeed.

GRAZIANO   'Tis a strange truth.

MONTANO　　　　　　　　　　O monstrous act!

EMILIA   Villainy, villainy, villainy!
I think upon't, I think. I smell't. O villainy!
I thought so then. I'll kill myself for grief.

200　O villainy, villainy!

IAGO   What, are you mad? I charge you get you home.

EMILIA   Good gentlemen, let me have leave to speak.
'Tis proper I obey him, but not now.
Perchance, Iago, I will ne'er go home.

OTHELLO   O, O, O!

　　　　　　OTHELLO *falls on the bed*

205　EMILIA　　　　　　　　Nay, lay thee down and roar,
For thou hast killed the sweetest innocent
That e'er did lift up eye.°　　　　　　　　　　*(to heaven)*

OTHELLO [*rising*]　　　　　O, she was foul!
[*To* GRAZIANO] I scarce did know you, uncle. There lies your niece,
Whose breath indeed these hands have newly stopped.

210　I know this act shows° horrible and grim.　　　　　*appears*

GRAZIANO   Poor Desdemon, I am glad thy father's dead.
Thy match was mortal to him, and pure grief
Shore his old thread in twain.[2] Did he live now
This sight would make him do a desperate turn,°　　　*act*

215　Yea, curse his better angel from his side,
And fall to reprobance.[3]

OTHELLO　　'Tis pitiful. But yet Iago knows
That she with Cassio hath the act of shame
A thousand times committed. Cassio confessed it,

220　And she did gratify his amorous works
With that recognizance° and pledge of love　　　　　*token*
Which I first gave her. I saw it in his hand.
It was a handkerchief, an antique token
My father gave my mother.

EMILIA　　　　　　　　O God! O heavenly God!

IAGO   'Swounds, hold your peace!

225　EMILIA　　　　　　　　'Twill out, 'twill out. I peace?
No, I will speak as liberal as the north.[4]
Let heaven, and men, and devils, let 'em all,
All, all cry shame against me, yet I'll speak.

---

1. Lines 192–200 do not appear in Q.
2. Cut the thread of his life.
3. Suicide, the unforgivably sinful act of despair.
4. As freely as the north wind.

IAGO   Be wise and get you home.

230   EMILIA   I will not.
                [IAGO *draws his sword*]

GRAZIANO [*to* IAGO]   Fie, your sword upon a woman?

EMILIA   O thou dull Moor, that handkerchief thou speak'st of
        I found by fortune and did give my husband,
        For often, with a solemn earnestness—
235   More than indeed belonged to such a trifle—
        He begged of me to steal't.

IAGO   Villainous whore!

EMILIA   She give it Cassio? No, alas, I found it,
        And I did give't my husband.

IAGO   Filth, thou liest.

EMILIA   By heaven I do not, I do not, gentlemen.
240   O murderous coxcomb!° What should such a fool   *fool*
        Do with so good a wife?

OTHELLO   Are there no stones° in heaven   *thunderbolts*
        But what serves for the thunder? Precious° villain!   *Absolute*
                The Moor runs at IAGO. [MONTANO *disarms* OTHELLO.]
                IAGO [*wounds*] *his wife*

GRAZIANO   The woman falls. Sure he hath killed his wife.

EMILIA   Ay, ay. O, lay me by my mistress' side!   *Exit* IAGO

245   GRAZIANO   He's gone, but his wife's killed.

MONTANO   'Tis a notorious villain. Take you this weapon
        Which I have here recovered from the Moor.
        Come, guard the door without. Let him not pass,
        But kill him rather. I'll after that same villain,
        For 'tis a damnèd slave.   *Exeunt* MONTANO *and* GRAZIANO

250   OTHELLO   I am not valiant neither,
        But every puny whipster° gets my sword.   *insignificant person*
        But why should honour outlive honesty?[5]
        Let it go all.

EMILIA   What did thy song bode, lady?[6]
        Hark, canst thou hear me? I will play the swan,
255   And die in music. [*Sings*] 'Willow, willow, willow.'—
        Moor, she was chaste. She loved thee, cruel Moor.
        So come my soul to bliss as I speak true.
        So, speaking as I think, alas, I die.   *She dies*

OTHELLO   I have another weapon in this chamber.
260   It was a sword of Spain, the ice-brook's temper.°   *tempered in icy water*
        O, here it is. [*Calling*] Uncle, I must come forth.

GRAZIANO (*within*)   If thou attempt it, it will cost thee dear.
        Thou hast no weapon, and perforce must suffer.

OTHELLO   Look in upon me then, and speak with me,
265   Or, naked° as I am, I will assault thee.   *unarmed*
                [*Enter* GRAZIANO]

GRAZIANO   What is the matter?

OTHELLO   Behold, I have a weapon;
        A better never did itself sustain
        Upon a soldier's thigh. I have seen the day
        That, with this little arm and this good sword,
270   I have made my way through more impediments

---

5. Why should military reputation outlive integrity?
6. Lines 253–55 ("What . . . willow.'—") do not appear in Q.

Than twenty times your stop.° But O, vain boast! *power to stop*
Who can control his fate? 'Tis not so now.
Be not afraid, though you do see me weaponed.
Here is my journey's end, here is my butt[7]

275 And very sea-mark° of my utmost sail. *beacon*
Do you go back dismayed? 'Tis a lost° fear. *an unnecessary*
Man but a rush° against Othello's breast *Aim even a reed*
And he retires. Where should Othello go?
[*To* DESDEMONA] Now, how dost thou look now? O ill-starred wench,

280 Pale as thy smock! When we shall meet at count° *Judgment Day*
This look of thine will hurl my soul from heaven,
And fiends will snatch at it.
      [*He touches her*]
                        Cold, cold, my girl,
Even like thy chastity. O cursèd, cursèd slave!
Whip me, ye devils,

285 From the possession of this heavenly sight.
Blow me about in winds, roast me in sulphur,
Wash me in steep-down gulfs of liquid fire!
O Desdemon! Dead Desdemon! Dead! O! O!
      Enter LODOVICO, MONTANO, IAGO [*guarded by*] *officers,*
      with CASSIO *in a chair*
LODOVICO   Where is this rash and most unfortunate man?

290 OTHELLO   That's he that was Othello. Here I am.
LODOVICO   Where is that viper? Bring the villain forth.
OTHELLO   I look down towards his feet,[8] but that's a fable.
    [*To* IAGO] If that thou beest a devil I cannot kill thee.
      [*He wounds* IAGO]
LODOVICO   Wrench his sword from him.
      [*Officers disarm* OTHELLO]
IAGO   I bleed, sir, but not killed.

295 OTHELLO   I am not sorry, neither. I'd have thee live,
For in my sense° 'tis happiness to die. *state of feeling*
LODOVICO   O thou Othello, that was once so good,
Fall'n in the practice° of a cursèd slave, *plot*
What shall be said to thee?
OTHELLO   Why, anything;

300 An honourable murderer, if you will,
For naught I did in hate, but all in honour.
LODOVICO   This wretch hath part confessed his villainy.
Did you and he consent in Cassio's death?
OTHELLO   Ay.

305 CASSIO   Dear general, I never gave you cause.
OTHELLO   I do believe it, and I ask your pardon.
Will you, I pray, demand that demi-devil
Why he hath thus ensnared my soul and body?
IAGO   Demand me nothing. What you know, you know.

310 From this time forth I never will speak word.
LODOVICO [*to* IAGO]   What, not to pray?
GRAZIANO [*to* IAGO]   Torments° will ope your lips. *Tortures*
OTHELLO   Well, thou dost best.
LODOVICO   Sir, you shall understand what hath befall'n,

315 Which as, I think, you know not. Here is a letter,

---

7. Goal. Lines 273–79 do not appear in Q.   8. To look for the devil's cloven feet.

Found in the pocket of the slain Roderigo,
And here another. The one of them imports
The death of Cassio, to be undertook
By Roderigo.
320 OTHELLO   O villain!
CASSIO   Most heathenish and most gross.°   monstrous
LODOVICO   Now here's another discontented paper
Found in his pocket too, and this it seems
Roderigo meant to've sent this damnèd villain,
325 But that, belike,° Iago in the interim   most likely
Came in and satisfied him.
OTHELLO [to IAGO]   O thou pernicious caitiff!°   wretch
How came you, Cassio, by that handkerchief
That was my wife's?
CASSIO   I found it in my chamber,
330 And he himself confessed it, but even now,
That there he dropped it for a special purpose
Which wrought to his desire.
OTHELLO   O fool, fool, fool!
CASSIO   There is besides in Roderigo's letter
How he upbraids Iago, that he made him
335 Brave° me upon the watch, whereon it came   Defy
That I was cast;° and even but now he spake   dismissed
After long seeming dead, Iago hurt him,
Iago set him on.
LODOVICO [to OTHELLO]   You must forsake this room and go with us.
340 Your power and your command is taken off,
And Cassio rules in Cyprus. For this slave,
If there be any cunning cruelty
That can torment him much and hold him° long,   (alive)
It shall be his. You shall close° prisoner rest   tightly confined
345 Till that the nature of your fault be known
To the Venetian state. [To officers] Come, bring away.
OTHELLO   Soft you,° a word or two before you go.   Wait
I have done the state some service, and they know't.
No more of that. I pray you, in your letters,
350 When you shall these unlucky deeds relate,
Speak of me as I am. Nothing extenuate,
Nor set down aught in malice. Then must you speak
Of one that loved not wisely but too well,
Of one not easily jealous but, being wrought,
355 Perplexed in the extreme; of one whose hand,
Like the base Indian, threw a pearl away
Richer than all his tribe;⁹ of one whose subdued° eyes,   (by grief)
Albeit unusèd to the melting mood,
Drops tears as fast as the Arabian trees
360 Their medicinable gum.° Set you down this,   myrrh
And say besides that in Aleppo once,
Where a malignant and a turbaned Turk
Beat a Venetian and traduced the state,
I took by th' throat the circumcisèd dog

9. Othello supposes an uncivilized "Indian" unaware of the value of a pearl. Compare this reading from Q with F's "Judean," which may suggest malice rather than ignorance by alluding to Judas (betrayer of Christ) or perhaps Herod (who killed his wife Mariamne out of jealousy). "Judean" also anticipates "circumcisèd" (line 364) and hence an identification of Othello with Jews.

365   And smote him thus.
          He stabs himself
LODOVICO   O bloody period!°   *conclusion; sentence*
GRAZIANO   All that is spoke is marred.
OTHELLO [*to* DESDEMONA]   I kissed thee ere I killed thee. No way but this:
    Killing myself, to die upon a kiss.[1]   *He* [*kisses* DESDEMONA *and*] *dies*
370   CASSIO   This did I fear, but thought he had no weapon,
    For he was great of heart.
LODOVICO [*to* IAGO]   O Spartan dog,°   *notoriously savage*
    More fell° than anguish, hunger, or the sea,   *cruel*
    Look on the tragic loading of this bed.
    This is thy work. The object poisons sight.
    Let it be hid.
          [*They close the bed-curtains*]
375   Graziano, keep the house,
    And seize upon the fortunes of the Moor,
    For they succeed on you. [*To* CASSIO] To you, Lord Governor,
    Remains the censure° of this hellish villain.   *sentence*
    The time, the place, the torture, O, enforce it!
380   Myself will straight aboard, and to the state
    This heavy act with heavy heart relate.   *Exeunt* [*with Emilia's body*]

---

1. At 5.2.244, the dying Emilia says, "O, lay me by my mistress' side!" She then addresses Desdemona in a way that suggests that her wish has been granted. If it has, however, the presence of her body intrudes upon the concluding tableau of the dead Desdemona being kissed by the dying Othello, where "die" in line 369, as earlier, has the secondary sense of "orgasm."

All's Well That Ends Well

In innumerable old folktales, an unknown or lowborn young man of great courage, intelligence, or expertise addresses himself to a serious peril: a dragon no one can slay, a riddle no one can solve, a wound no one can cure. The grateful recipient of his aid— a king or mighty duke—rewards the youth with marriage to a princess who would ordinarily be far above his station. *All's Well That Ends Well* retells this popular tale of fantastic upward mobility but with the genders reversed: the resourceful young quester is female, the marital prize male. Shakespeare did not invent the reversal; he adapted his plot from a story in Boccaccio's *Decameron* that is itself a retelling of a traditional tale. But *All's Well That Ends Well* considerably heightens the heroine's risk-taking initiative, making Helen's adventures in the first two acts correspond more precisely, in sexually transposed form, to the masculine quest-romance pattern.

Even today, this reversal makes the story seem problematic. In the customary masculine version, no one inquires into the feelings of the noblewoman who is the champion's prize. But in *All's Well*, when a man becomes a reward, he reacts with astonished anger:

> BERTRAM My wife, my liege? I shall beseech your highness,
> In such a business give me leave to use
> The help of mine own eyes.
> KING   Know'st thou not, Bertram,
> What she has done for me?
> BERTRAM   Yes, my good lord,
> But never hope to know why I should marry her.
>
> (2.3.102–6)

After the wedding ceremony, Bertram flees without consummating the union. He leaves behind a letter detailing for Helen two apparently impossible conditions she must satisfy before he will consider her his wife: "When thou canst get the ring upon my finger, which never shall come off, and show me a child begotten of thy body that I am father to, then call me husband" (3.2.55–57).

Folklorists have traced the second part of the play, in which Helen ingeniously fulfills Bertram's stipulations, to yet another old tale, that of the "clever wench" who ultimately wins a reluctant husband's affection by turning his recalcitrance to her own benefit. In Helen's case, however, her "unfeminine" audacity both before and after her wedding has repelled some commentators. Others have expressed doubts about Helen's bed trick, wherein she secretly substitutes herself for another woman and becomes pregnant by the spouse who thinks he loathes her. How, they wonder, could such a maneuver possibly convert anyone, much less Bertram, into a loving husband?

By rewriting the comic plot, then, Shakespeare makes the difference in conventional expectations for men and women vividly clear. His revisions implicitly challenge those conventions, making them seem artificial and restrictive. At the same time, the deviations from comic norms in *All's Well* also might be taken as reflecting badly on the hero and heroine. The generic uneasiness of the play has led some critics to classify it as a "problem comedy," a category that also includes *Measure for Measure* and sometimes *Troilus and Cressida*. Editors conjecture that all three plays were written between 1602 and 1606, a period in which Shakespeare was largely preoccupied with tragedy: *Hamlet, Othello, King Lear, Timon of Athens, Macbeth*, and *Antony and Cleopatra* are roughly contemporaneous compositions. The "problem comedies" often seem closer in theme and tone to these tragedies than to the sunnier romantic comedies Shakespeare wrote in the 1590s.

Nonetheless, *All's Well* has obvious connections to Shakespeare's earlier achievements. In *The Merchant of Venice, As You Like It,* and *Much Ado About Nothing,* Shakespeare had gradually developed the dramatic possibilities of an articulate, assertive, and sympathetic heroine—a kind of character virtually without precedent in the Western tradition. Helen is recognizably one of this company: generally beloved by those around her, premaritally chaste but intensely sexual, tenacious in pursuit of the man she desires. Bertram is likewise a version of a standard Shakespearean type: the immature youth who finds aggressively "masculine" enterprises like hunting or war emotionally easier to negotiate than the complications of heterosexual intimacy. Bertram's predecessors include the unwilling Adonis in *Venus and Adonis,* the naive Claudio in *Much Ado About Nothing,* the edgily unself-conscious Hotspur of *1 Henry IV,* and the narcissistic young man of the sonnets. Both Helen and Bertram, however, "push the envelop" of their generic type. No previous comic heroine finds herself, as Helen does, publicly repudiated by the man she loves, and thus none need show herself as relentless as Helen in seeking a remedy. And Bertram is surely the most perfidious, and the most thoroughly disgraced, of Shakespeare's callow males.

In its portrayal of older characters, too, *All's Well* seems to develop out of Shakespeare's previous romantic plays. In much Greek and Roman comedy, parents or parent surrogates attempt to hinder their children's sexual happiness, and as a young playwright Shakespeare adhered to this ancient convention. In *A Midsummer Night's Dream* and *Romeo and Juliet,* written in the mid-1590s, parents are killjoys who block the glorious passions of youth out of mere peevishness. But in *The Merchant of Venice,* written a year or two later, Shylock's paternal possessiveness contrasts with the wise policy of Portia's father, whose strict constraints upon his daughter's marital options in fact ensure her happiness. In *Much Ado About Nothing* (1598), the sexually anxious young couples seem incapable of forming heterosexual pairs without the intervention of elders and friends. In *All's Well That Ends Well,* the marriage between Helen and Bertram is unthinkable without the support of the Countess and the King; the match is also roundly endorsed by the elderly courtier Lafeu. If the oldsters are culpable, it is for pushing the young people together prematurely, not for keeping them apart.

Arguably this change in perspective is a consequence of Shakespeare's own aging. By the time he wrote *All's Well,* he was the father of two marriageable daughters, and surviving records indicate that he had strong opinions about the men they wed. At any rate, the role of family members in Shakespeare's romantic plays becomes more benign, even essential for the pairing-off with which the comedies conclude; by the time of the late romances, in fact, the primary dramatic emphasis tends to be less on the young couple than on their parents. Seen in such a light, *All's Well* marks an important transition in the generational dynamics of Shakespearean comedy.

At the same time, the expanded role of family and friends in "making a match" seems to reflect an increasing pessimism about sex. In both *All's Well* and *Measure for Measure,* mutual desire fails to flower spontaneously between eligible bachelors and maidens. Moreover, even when desire is somehow kindled, its relationship to the institution of lifelong monogamy seems difficult. In *All's Well,* erotic passion burns hottest not when it is gratified but when its goal is still unattained. Bertram wants Diana only so long as she rebuffs him:

> Madding my eagerness with her restraint,
> As all impediments in fancy's course
> Are motives of more fancy.
>
> (5.3.215–17)

Once he imagines he has deflowered her, he deserts her without compunction. Bertram behaves reprehensibly, and yet Helen's more steadfast love, too, seems at least in part an effect of distance and difficulty. In Act 1, she declares Bertram to be a "bright particular star," fascinating although inaccessible, and perhaps *because* inaccessible. The obstacles Bertram places in the way of their union seem to make him all the more precious in Helen's eyes and to stimulate her extraordinary efforts to win his affections. But the more resolutely she strives to catch him, the more difficult it becomes to imagine her content with him once he is caught.

In sexual matters, apparently, as soon as one gets what one thinks one wants, it no longer seems so intensely appealing. "Success" brings disillusion in its train. In *All's Well,* this unfortunate arrangement is reflected in passages and episodes that oscillate painfully between imagined extremes of distance and intimacy. In Act 2, Helen frets about the social gap that separates her from Bertram: he seems too alien for her. But when the Countess pleads that Helen consider her a "mother," Helen suffers a paroxysm of anxiety on the opposite count: that she and Bertram may be all too closely allied. "God's mercy, maiden!" exclaims the Countess. "Does it curd thy blood / To say I am thy mother?" (1.3.133–34). Helen's hysterical overreaction suggests that she fears being "too close" at the same time she fears being "too remote." Later in *All's Well,* the bed trick rehearses, in another key, a similar paradox of intimacy and distance. Fleeing his home and a spouse closely associated with his upbringing, Bertram lusts after a foreign woman. But this foreigner turns out, unbeknownst to him, to be his own wife.

Thus the fundamental structure of sexual desire seems inimical to a durably happy marriage, but marriage nonetheless remains the only socially approved arena for sexual expression. Caught in this dilemma, lovers simply cannot be trusted to make proper arrangements among themselves. The community therefore assumes a new prominence in initiating and regulating marriages. In *All's Well,* two means of such regulation are central to the plot. The first is the institution of wardship, a remnant of the feudal system. Minors who inherited estates automatically fell into the care of their feudal superiors: the King in Bertram's case, the Countess in Helen's. Once the guardian chose a marriage partner of suitable social rank for the "ward," the ward could not refuse the match except by forfeiting much of his property; thus the tense exchange in 2.3 between Bertram and the King about Helen's qualifications in this respect.

Another form of external pressure is brought to bear upon Bertram at the end of the play, when Helen once again appeals to the King to enforce her claim. The hearing that ensues resembles those of the ecclesiastical courts, judicial bodies that settled complaints of sexual misconduct in early modern England. The conflicting testimony of Diana and Bertram painfully recalls the proceedings of the "bawdy courts," as they were popularly known: interminable prosecutions and counterprosecutions for premarital fornication, breach of promise, adultery, child support, and sexual slander—cases in which, as here, evidence was often hard to come by and truth difficult to unearth.

In the early seventeenth century, both wardship and the judicial regulation of sexual conduct were topics of considerable controversy. Some people fiercely resented any meddling in their domestic and sexual affairs, but others wanted the courts to monitor such behavior even more aggressively. Likewise, some attacked wardship on the grounds that guardians often trampled on the

Drummers before an encampment. From Geffrey Whitney, *A Choice of Emblemes* (1586).

personal inclinations of the ward, while others argued that young heirs and heiresses required supervision to prevent their seduction by unscrupulous gold diggers. In both cases, the point at issue is whether sexual conduct is an essentially personal matter or a matter for public concern. By making both the custom of wardship and the procedures of the bawdy courts crucial to the plot of *All's Well,* Shakespeare seems to endorse the assumption upon which both institutions are premised: that individuals are not competent to manage their own sexual lives, and that stern legal measures are required to coerce the likes of Bertram into matrimony.

A comedy normally depicts the progress of young lovers toward marriage, and in *All's Well,* Bertram's stubborn resistance to his generically mandated fate has important consequences. The protagonists of almost all comedies undergo some kind of suffering in the middle acts of the play, but that suffering is overcome. The happy ending retrospectively makes the hardships that preceded it seem worthwhile; conversely, pain validates and gives an appropriate significance to the concluding felicities. Despite its cheerful once-and-for-all title, *All's Well That Ends Well* does not conform to this timeworn pattern. Instead, the play constantly derails narrative expectations and promises endings that turn out to be mirages. Helen cures the King and weds Bertram, but the story is not yet over. She must then encounter Bertram somehow (whether by accident or design is unclear) and arrange to bed him. Then she must make sure she is pregnant; then she must return to France to beg justice of the King. The action continues past the point where one would expect it to terminate, again and again requiring the expenditure of additional effort and ingenuity on Helen's part: early in Act 5, even the King's court turns out to be surprisingly difficult to locate.

Helen's stamina is not demanded of the other characters, but they, too, persist willynilly after one might have expected them to subside, and they resurface after one might have expected them to vanish. The King is preparing for his own death when Helen's arrival returns him to the life he had resigned himself to losing. Later, Bertram believes that by fleeing Italy for France he has left Helen behind; similarly, he forsakes Diana. But the two women decline to evaporate. They reappear together in a scene that begins with the King announcing that "the nature of [Bertram's] great offence is dead" (5.3.23), then revives and exacerbates his offense, then declares it buried once more.

Occasion with her forelock. From Geffrey Whitney, *A Choice of Emblemes* (1586). She must be "taken by the forelock"—that is, at the moment when she presents herself; the back of her head is bald to signify that once she is past, she can no longer be grasped. See *All's Well That Ends Well* 5.3.40.

These aborted endings, continual deferrals, unanticipated reemergences, and surprising persistences inevitably make the actual end of the play seem rather arbitrary. Eventually it becomes hard to credit the permanence of any resolution, any happy ending. When, in the play's final lines, the King blithely promises Diana her choice of husbands from among his stable of remaining wards, *All's Well* may seem not to be drawing to a close, but merely to be forecasting its own reiteration. The play's open-endedness has generated both dismay and appreciation, depending on the temperament of the critic and, often, on his or her convictions about literary form. Those who prefer celebratory and romantic modes often find the play's lack of convincing closure a disturbing flaw. Those who find the happy endings of most comedies wishful and unrealistic tend to applaud Shakespeare's eschewal of easy answers.

Once again, *All's Well's* apparent noncompliance with "normal" comic practice implicitly suggests limitations inherent in the comic forms it forsakes. In 2.4, when Helen asks Lavatch whether the Countess is well, Lavatch replies that "she is not well," despite the fact that "she's very well and wants nothing i'th' world." To the baffled Helen, Lavatch goes on to explain that he does not consider the Countess well because "she's not in heaven, whither God send her quickly" (lines 2ff.). In Lavatch's mind, only the dead are happy, a notion that gives a distinctly uncomical twist to the concept of ending well. Consciously or not, Lavatch echoes a long tradition of classical and Christian thought that emphasizes the misery of this world and defers true happiness until after death. In 4.3, the first Lord Dumaine relates this apparently inevitable misery to the intransigence of human passions, an intransigence imagined in the Christian tradition in terms of original sin. "As we are ourselves, what things are we" (lines 19–20). Only divine grace can remedy the defects of human nature in general and of human sexuality in particular. Only another world can offer the prospect of true, lasting felicity. But comedy is a secular mode, lacking the means to represent heaven or divine intervention, and to that extent its happy endings must be illusory or partial. *All's Well* is not unique among Shakespearean comedies in gesturing beyond the mundane, imperfect world with which plays are necessarily concerned, to an ideal world that cannot be directly represented in the theater. Lorenzo's discussion of the music of the spheres in *The Merchant of Venice* and Isabella's acute conviction of divine mentorship in *Measure for Measure* likewise have the effect of implicitly contrasting the limited bliss of comic endings with an unlimited, indescribable counterpart.

But although absolute fulfillment may be impossible in this world, relative improvements are surely feasible. In *All's Well,* it seems that a community can constructively intervene to correct, at least provisionally, some of the grosser imperfections of individuals. In Act 4, Bertram acknowledges that he has misjudged Paroles and at the end of the play begs pardon for his behavior, finally promising to love his wife "ever ever dearly." These apparent changes of heart are not motivated by an instinctive sense of regret for his past actions or by a spontaneous upwelling of love for Helen. Rather, the vigorous efforts of his mother, his king, his friends, and his wife force him onto the path that seems best for him whether he likes it or not. Those critics who find his apparent reformation at the end of the play unconvincing are often those skeptical of whether this kind of social pressure will suffice to rescue Bertram from himself. If, however, we are to believe that Bertram is salvageable, as the play implies, then we must acknowledge the effectiveness of the community's efforts to rectify him.

Obviously a society can have these beneficial effects on its more wayward members only if its moral intuitions are fundamentally sound, and only if its coercive resources have the potential to induce heartfelt, lasting change. The King can force Bertram to marry Helen and to acknowledge the legitimacy of the child in her womb. But such decrees will ensure Bertram's *love* of Helen only if his inner convictions somehow follow from, or develop out of, his external submission to the King's commands. How actual—not merely apparent—compliance might be achieved is suggested in a speech in which the King warmly remembers Bertram's father, the late Count of Roussillon. The old Count, according to the King, adhered to a traditional aristocratic code: he was careful to speak no more than he was willing to defend with his sword. Thought, word, and deed were thus inextricable. The King characterizes this inextricability as "honor," for honor and its corollary, shame, bridge the gap between external behavior and private states of mind, internalizing social scruples so that the aristocrat behaves well even in the absence of obvious incentives or punishments. At best, honor is thus a "clock to itself," a self-regulating mechanism. Only when that clock fails to function properly— as it fails in Bertram's case—must the same results be compelled by clumsier, more obviously extrinsic means.

In his comments on the old Count, the King claims that the up-and-coming generation has an insufficiently vivid conception of honor and its importance:

> Such a man
> Might be a copy to these younger times,
> Which followed well would demonstrate them now
> But goers-backward.
>
> (1.2.45–48)

The danger of such a regression is embodied in Paroles, whose name means "words." Paroles exhibits all the superficial signs of courtiership—wit, lavish dress, a familiarity with military and courtly jargons—without any of the real skills or virtues those signs are supposed to indicate. Paroles endangers the social processes by which the world of *All's Well* is imagined to operate, estranging externals from inner substance and subversively demonstrating limitations in the courtly code of honor. He is tightly connected to Bertram, not merely through their friendship but by similarities in their circumstances. The staged drum trick on Paroles coincides temporally with the unstageable bed trick on Bertram, and there are clear thematic parallels as well: both victims are blind, morally as well as literally, to plots perpetrated by close acquaintances masquerading as strangers.

Still, Paroles's menace should not be overestimated. Everyone except Bertram sees through him instantly, and Bertram's inability to discern Paroles's pretenses is a telling mark of his immaturity. Once Bertram finally recognizes that Paroles is a "counterfeit module," moreover, he recoils violently from his former friend and adviser. Bertram may be gauche and inattentive, but he recognizes gross cowardice when he sees it, and in that rudimentary recognition of the difference between honorable and dishonorable conduct will lie the possibility of his reform.

Foppish camp follower. Peter Flötner (mid-sixteenth century).

Paroles, then, both incarnates Bertram's flaws and diminishes Bertram's culpability. "Your son was misled with a snipped-taffeta fellow there," opines Lafeu indignantly to the Countess, "whose villainous saffron would have made all the unbaked and doughy youth of a nation in his colour" (4.5.1–3). If, in the world of *All's Well,* good associates and benign forms of institutional duress can maneuver Bertram in the right direction, then bad associates and bad customs likewise have the power to exacerbate his worst impulses. On the other hand, unlike a sterner and more principled character, the "unbaked" Bertram retains the capacity to be reformed, like a lump of dough, despite his unpromising shape.

In less obvious ways, Paroles's presence in *All's Well* also deflects criticism from Helen. Helen's marital plans involve, as she herself admits, quite startling social ambitions. Marrying Bertram will elevate her from the relatively large gentry class to a tiny elite at the pinnacle of the social pyramid. In a hierarchically stratified society where people are supposed to "know their places," such aspirations might well seem disruptive. But Paroles, a cruder and less principled social climber, helps clarify the actually *conservative* nature of Helen's desires. In marked contrast to the craven Paroles, Helen is willing to certify her words with her body as honorable aristocrats are supposed to do, proposing to sacrifice life and reputation if her promises to cure the King prove empty. Helen's conviction that words must suit actions, that her tongue must obey her hand, marks her as "noble" despite her lack of material resources, and gain her the respect of the older members of the nobility, such as the King, the Countess, and Lafeu. Thus marriage to Bertram seems to remedy an unaccountable lapse in the proper social order, rather than to create a breach in that order.

Left deliberately vague is what relationship, if any, merit really has with birth. On the one hand, Helen's excellence seems to belie her humble origins; on the other hand, although both Helen and Diana are poor, it is carefully specified that they are not "base" persons of artisan or peasant stock. Their gentility, however modest, seems to lend their upward mobility a respectability that Paroles's attempts at self-promotion can never possess. Paroles thus draws off criticism that Helen might otherwise attract for violating class boundaries. Similarly, his presence in the play serves partially to allay criticism of Helen's sexual transgressiveness: his boastful inaction is so obviously worse than Helen's vigorous but possibly "unfeminine" enterprise that once again he seems an instructive example that tells in Helen's favor.

Although Paroles functions as a scapegoat of sorts, at the end of the play he does not suffer the scapegoat's usual cruel fate. After his disgrace, his dramatic function as corrupter of Bertram and foil to Helen is evidently complete, and we might imagine that we have seen the last of him. But like so many other characters in *All's Well*, good and bad, Paroles has a surprising durability. "Simply the thing I am," he declares, "shall make me live" (4.3.310–11). Like Helen and Diana, he reappears in the final scenes, reinserting himself, in a reduced capacity, into a world that had scorned him. The partial, incremental improvement promised by the conclusion of *All's Well That Ends Well* may from some points of view seem disappointing. But its pessimism inspires a certain tolerance, a forbearance that allows even the ridiculous or debased to find a home.

KATHARINE EISAMAN MAUS

TEXTUAL NOTE

All's Well That Ends Well was first printed in the Folio of 1623 (F), and all subsequent editions have relied on that text. The presence in F of some stage directions that explain rather than merely indicate the action, as well as variant speech prefixes in different scenes (for instance, "Countess," "Mother," "Old Countess"), suggests that the printed text was prepared directly from Shakespeare's "foul papers," or manuscript draft. Some textual scholars believe that before printing, this manuscript must have been further annotated by the King's Men's bookkeeper, the person who prepared play texts for performance. Unfortunately, perhaps because of difficulties reading the foul papers, the compositors did a poor job of setting up the text, forcing later editors to make an unusual number of conjectural emendations.

The Oxford edition preserves the Folio act divisions and the traditional editorial (that is, non-Shakespearean) scene divisions. For those familiar with other editions of the play, the primary novelty of the Oxford text will be its decision to use "Helen" instead of "Hellena" to designate the heroine. In fact, the latter form occurs only four times in the play and only once in dialogue, so the Oxford editors argue that Shakespeare's preference was clearly for the two-syllable name.

SELECTED BIBLIOGRAPHY

Bradbrook, Muriel. "Virtue Is the True Nobility: A Study of the Structure of *All's Well That Ends Well*." *Review of English Studies* n.s. 1 (1950): 289–301. True nobility of virtue, as exemplified by Helen, versus the false nobility of birth, as exemplified by Bertram.

Calderwood, James L. "Styles of Knowing in *All's Well*." *Modern Language Quarterly* 25 (1964): 272–94. Sexuality and honor for Helen and Bertram.

Donaldson, Ian. "*All's Well That Ends Well*: Shakespeare's Play of Endings." *Essays in Criticism* 27 (1977): 34–55. Discusses the play's preoccupation with endings and its problematic final scene.

Engle, Lars. "Shakespeare Normativity in *All's Well That Ends Well*." *Shakespeare Studies Today*. Ed. Graham Bradshaw, Tom Bishop, and Mark Turner. Shakespeare International Yearbook 4. Burlington, Vt.: Ashgate, 2004. 264–79. The establishment and violation of norms in *All's Well That Ends Well*.

Frye, Northrop. *The Myth of Deliverance: Reflections on Shakespeare's Problem Comedies*. Toronto: University of Toronto Press, 1983. General discussion of patterns of reversal in the problem comedies.

Hodgdon, Barbara. "The Making of Virgins and Mothers: Sexual Signs, Substitute Scenes, and Doubled Presences in *All's Well That Ends Well*." *Philological Quarterly* 66 (1987): 47–72. The character of Helen, as Shakespeare develops it from the source story in Boccaccio's *Decameron*.

Huston, J. Dennis. "'Some Stain of Soldier': The Functions of Paroles in *All's Well That Ends Well*." *Shakespeare Quarterly* 21 (1970): 431–38. Paroles compared with Helen.

Muir, Kenneth, and Stanley Wells, eds. *Aspects of Shakespeare's "Problem Plays": Articles Reprinted from Shakespeare Survey*. New York: Cambridge University Press, 1982. Essays on *Measure for Measure, All's Well That Ends Well*, and *Troilus and Cressida*, with selected reviews of theater productions from 1953 to 1976.

Parker, Patricia. "*All's Well That Ends Well*: Increase and Multiply." *Creative Imitation: New Essays on Renaissance Literature in Honor of Thomas M. Greene*. Ed. David Quint, Margaret Ferguson, G. W. Pigman, and Wayne Rebhorn. Binghamton, N.Y.: Medieval & Renaissance Texts & Studies, 1992. 355–90. Linguistic and sexual deferral and displacement as the key to abundance in *All's Well That Ends Well*.

Traister, Barbara Howard. "'Doctor She': Healing and Sex in *All's Well That Ends Well*." *A Companion to Shakespeare Works, IV: Poems, Problem Comedies, Late Plays*. Blackwell Companions to Literature and Culture 20. Ed. Richard Dutton and Jean E. Howard. Malden, Mass.: Blackwell, 2003. 333–47. Helen as lovesick physician.

Wheeler, Richard P. "Imperial Love and the Dark House: *All's Well That Ends Well*." *Shakespeare's Development and the Problem Comedies: Turn and Counter-Turn*. Berkeley: University of California Press, 1981. 35–91. Detailed psychoanalytic reading.

Zitner, Sheldon P. *All's Well That Ends Well*. Boston: Twayne, 1989. Stage and reception histories as well as critical commentary on the play.

FILM

All's Well That Ends Well. 1981. Dir. Elijah Moshinsky. UK. 142 min. From BBC-TV. An elegant production, with sets and lighting that recall the paintings of Vermeer and Caravaggio. Compelling performances from Angela Down (Helen), Celia Johnson (Countess), Donald Sinden (King), and Ian Charleson (Bertram).

All's Well That Ends Well

THE PERSONS OF THE PLAY

The Dowager COUNTESS of Roussillon
BERTRAM, Count of Roussillon, her son
HELEN, an orphan, attending on the Countess
LAVATCH, a Clown, the Countess's servant
REYNALDO, the Countess's steward
PAROLES, Bertram's companion
The KING of France
LAFEU, an old lord
FIRST LORD DUMAINE
SECOND LORD DUMAINE } brothers
INTERPRETER, a French soldier
A GENTLEMAN Austringer
The DUKE of Florence
WIDOW Capilet
DIANA, her daughter
MARIANA, a friend of the Widow
Lords, attendants, soldiers, citizens

1.1

Enter young BERTRAM *Count of Roussillon, his mother*
[*the* COUNTESS], HELEN, [*and*] *Lord* LAFEU, *all in black*

COUNTESS In delivering my son from me I bury a second husband.[1]

BERTRAM And I in going, madam, weep o'er my father's death anew; but I must attend° his majesty's command, to whom I   *heed*
5 am now in ward,[2] evermore in subjection.

LAFEU You shall find of the King a husband,° madam; you, sir,   *patron*
a father. He that so generally° is at all times good must of neces-   *universally*
sity hold° his virtue to you, whose worthiness would stir it up   *uphold*
where it wanted° rather than lack it where there is such abun-   *was lacking*
10 dance.

COUNTESS What hope is there of his majesty's amendment?°   *improvement*

LAFEU He hath abandoned his physicians,[3] madam, under whose practices he hath persecuted time with hope,[4] and finds no other advantage in the process but only the losing of hope
15 by time.

COUNTESS This young gentlewoman had a father—O that 'had': how sad a passage° 'tis!—whose skill was almost as great as his   *expression; passing away*
honesty;° had it° stretched so far, would have made nature   *integrity / (his skill)*
immortal, and death should have play for lack of work. Would
20 for the King's sake he were living. I think it would be the death of the King's disease.

1.1 Location: Bertram's palace in Roussillon, in southwest France.
1. Giving up my son grieves me as much as my husband's death (playing on "deliver" as "give birth").
2. Upon the old Count's death, the King becomes guardian of Bertram's estate until he comes of age. A guardian

could arrange his ward's marriage, provided the match was with a social equal.
3. Playing on the usual "His physicians have abandoned him" (given up hope of his cure).
4. Afflicted his days by hoping for a cure.

LAFEU How called you the man you speak of, madam?

COUNTESS He was famous, sir, in his profession, and it was his
great right to be so: Gérard de Narbonne.⁵

25 LAFEU He was excellent indeed, madam. The King very lately
spoke of him, admiringly and mourningly. He was skilful
enough to have lived still, if knowledge could be set up against
mortality.

BERTRAM What is it, my good lord, the King languishes of?

30 LAFEU A fistula,° my lord.   *abscess (often anal)*

BERTRAM I heard not of it before.

LAFEU I would it were not notorious.°—Was this gentlewoman   *known to everyone*
the daughter of Gérard de Narbonne?

COUNTESS His sole child, my lord, and bequeathed to my over-

35 looking.⁶ I have those hopes of her good that her education°   *upbringing*
promises; her dispositions she inherits, which makes fair gifts°   *abilities*
fairer—for where an unclean mind carries virtuous qualities,°   *acquired skills*
there commendations go with pity:° they are virtues and traitors   *mingle with regret*
too.⁷ In her they are the better for their simpleness.° She   *purity*

40 derives° her honesty and achieves her goodness.   *inherits*

LAFEU Your commendations, madam, get from her tears.

COUNTESS 'Tis the best brine a maiden can season° her praise   *preserve (as with salt)*
in. The remembrance of her father never approaches her heart
but the tyranny of her sorrows takes all livelihood° from her   *liveliness*

45 cheek.—No more of this, Helen. Go to, no more, lest it be
rather thought you affect° a sorrow than to have—   *make a show of*

HELEN I do affect a sorrow indeed, but I have it too.

LAFEU Moderate lamentation is the right of the dead, excessive
grief the enemy to the living.

50 COUNTESS If the living be not enemy to the grief, the excess
makes it soon mortal.°   *fatal*

BERTRAM [*kneeling*] Madam, I desire your holy wishes.°   *blessing*

LAFEU How understand we that?⁸

COUNTESS Be thou blessed, Bertram, and succeed thy father

55 In manners° as in shape. Thy blood and virtue⁹   *behavior*
Contend for empire in thee, and thy goodness
Share with thy birthright. Love all, trust a few,
Do wrong to none. Be able° for thine enemy   *a match for*
Rather in power than use,¹ and keep thy friend

60 Under thy own life's key.² Be checked° for silence   *criticized*
But never taxed for speech.° What heaven more will   *rebuked for chatter*
That thee may furnish° and my prayers pluck down,   *embellish*
Fall on thy head. Farewell. [*To* LAFEU] My lord,
'Tis an unseasoned° courtier. Good my lord,   *immature*
Advise him.

65 LAFEU   He cannot want the best
That shall attend his love.³

COUNTESS Heaven bless him!—Farewell, Bertram.

BERTRAM [*rising*] The best wishes that can be forged° in your   *fashioned*
thoughts be servants to you.°   [*Exit* COUNTESS]   *assist you*

---

5. Town just north of Roussillon.
6. Guardianship (Helen is the Countess's ward, as
Bertram is the King's).
7. Because the skills are used for evil purposes.
8. Possibly a misplaced line; possibly Lafeu thinks
Bertram's interruption discourteous.

9. (May) your noble birth and acquired goodness.
1. By having power, rather than using it.
2. *keep . . . key*: safeguard your friend's life as you do
your own.
3. *He . . . love*: He will not lack the best advice my
affection for him can supply.

70   [*To* HELEN] Be comfortable° to my mother, your mistress, and   *comforting*
        make much of her.
    LAFEU   Farewell, pretty lady. You must hold the credit° of your   *uphold the reputation*
        father.   *Exeunt* BERTRAM *and* LAFEU
    HELEN   O were that all! I think not on my father,
75   And these great tears grace his remembrance more
        Than those I shed for him.[4] What was he like?
        I have forgot him. My imagination
        Carries no favour° in't but Bertram's.   *face; liking; love token*
        I am undone. There is no living, none,
80   If Bertram be away. 'Twere all one
        That° I should love a bright particular star   *It is just as if*
        And think to wed it, he is so above me.
        In his bright radiance and collateral[5] light
        Must I be comforted, not in his sphere.
85   Th'ambition in my love thus plagues itself.
        The hind° that would be mated by the lion   *doe*
        Must die for love. 'Twas pretty, though a plague,
        To see him every hour, to sit and draw
        His archèd brows, his hawking° eye, his curls,   *sharp*
90   In our heart's table°—heart too capable°   *drawing table / receptive*
        Of every line and trick° of his sweet favour.°   *trait / face*
        But now he's gone, and my idolatrous fancy°   *love*
        Must sanctify his relics.[6] Who comes here?
             Enter PAROLES
        One that goes with him. I love him for his sake—
95   And yet I know him a notorious liar,
        Think him a great way° fool, solely° a coward.   *mostly a / completely*
        Yet these fixed evils sit so fit in him°   *fit him so well*
        That they take place[7] when virtue's steely bones°   *rigid severity*
        Looks bleak i'th' cold wind. Withal, full oft we see
100   Cold wisdom waiting on superfluous folly.
    PAROLES   Save° you, fair queen.   *God save*
    HELEN   And you, monarch.
    PAROLES   No.
    HELEN   And no.
105   PAROLES   Are you meditating on virginity?
    HELEN   Ay. You have some stain° of soldier in you, let me ask   *tinge*
        you a question. Man is enemy to virginity: how may we barri-
        cado° it against him?   *barricade*
    PAROLES   Keep him out.
110   HELEN   But he assails, and our virginity, though valiant in the
        defence, yet is weak. Unfold to us some warlike resistance.
    PAROLES   There is none. Man, setting down before° you, will   *laying siege to*
        undermine you and blow you up.[8]
    HELEN   Bless our poor virginity from underminers and blowers-
115   up. Is there no military policy° how virgins might blow up   *strategy*
        men?
    PAROLES   Virginity being blown down, man will quicklier be
        blown up.° Marry,[9] in blowing him down again, with the *have an erection*

---

4. *grace . . . him:* are a better tribute to my father than those (few) tears I actually shed for him.
5. Rotating in a separate orbit (in Ptolomaic astronomy).
6. Must worship what reminds me of him.
7. Take precedence.

8. *undermine you:* dig tunnels under you (to plant explosives). *blow you up:* punning on "inflate," "make you pregnant."
9. By Mary (a mild oath).

breach yourselves made you lose your city. It is not politic° in   *expedient*
120 the commonwealth of nature to preserve virginity. Loss of virginity is rational increase,[1] and there was never virgin got° till   *begotten*
virginity was first lost. That° you were made of is mettle° to   *What / substance*
make virgins. Virginity by being once lost may be ten times
found;° by being ever kept it is ever lost. 'Tis too cold a com-   *reproduced tenfold*
125 panion, away with't.

HELEN   I will stand for't° a little, though therefore I die a virgin.   *defend it*

PAROLES   There's little can be said in't.° 'Tis against the rule of   *for it*
nature. To speak on the part of virginity is to accuse your mothers, which is most infallible disobedience. He that hangs him-
130 self is a virgin:[2] virginity murders itself, and should be buried
in highways, out of all sanctified limit,[3] as a desperate
offendress against nature. Virginity breeds mites, much like a
cheese;[4] consumes itself to the very paring, and so dies with
feeding his own stomach.° Besides, virginity is peevish, proud,   *pride*
135 idle, made of self-love—which is the most inhibited° sin in the   *prohibited*
canon.° Keep it not, you cannot choose but lose by't. Out   *scriptures*
with't![5] Within t'one year it will make itself two, which is a
goodly increase, and the principal[6] itself not much the worse.
Away with't.

140 HELEN   How might one do, sir, to lose it to her own liking?

PAROLES   Let me see. Marry, ill, to like him that ne'er it likes.[7]
'Tis a commodity will lose the gloss with lying:° the longer kept,   *remaining idle*
the less worth. Off with't while 'tis vendible.° Answer the time   *salable*
of request.[8] Virginity like an old courtier wears her cap out of
145 fashion, richly suited° but unsuitable,° just like the brooch and   *dressed / inappropriate*
the toothpick, which wear not now.[9] Your date° is better in   *fruit; age*
your pie and your porridge than in your cheek, and your virginity, your old virginity, is like one of our French withered pears:[1]
it looks ill, it eats drily, marry, 'tis a withered pear—it was for-
150 merly better, marry, yet 'tis a withered pear. Will you anything
with it?

HELEN   Not my virginity, yet . . .[2]
There° shall your master have a thousand loves,   *(At court)*
A mother and a mistress and a friend,
155 A phoenix,[3] captain, and an enemy,
A guide, a goddess, and a sovereign,
A counsellor, a traitress, and a dear:
His humble ambition, proud humility,
His jarring concord and his discord dulcet,[4]
160 His faith, his sweet disaster, with a world
Of pretty fond adoptious christendoms
That blinking Cupid gossips.[5] Now shall he—
I know not what he shall. God send him well.
The court's a learning place, and he is one—

1. *rational increase:* judicious growth in the human
("rational") population.
2. A suicide, like a virgin, is a self-destroyer.
3. Consecrated ground (in which suicides were denied
burial).
4. Cheese was thought to generate spontaneously the
mites that fed on it.
5. Get rid of it; put it out at interest.
6. Original investment (the woman's body).
7. To please him who doesn't appreciate virginity.

8. Respond to demand (greatest in youth).
9. Which are no longer in fashion.
1. Dried pears (suggesting aged female genitals).
2. Not with *my* virginity: not my virginity *yet* (but soon).
3. The mythical phoenix was a one-of-a-kind bird; hence,
marvelous, unique being.
4. Harmonious (all these oxymorons were typical of
courtly love poetry).
5. *pretty . . . gossips:* foolish nicknames given when blind
Cupid is godfather at a christening.

165   PAROLES   What one, i'faith?

        HELEN   That I wish well. 'Tis pity.

        PAROLES   What's pity?

        HELEN   That wishing well had not a body in't

        Which might be felt,° that we, the poorer born,   *perceived*

170   Whose baser stars do shut us up in wishes,[6]

        Might with effects of them follow our friends

        And show what we alone must° think, which never   *must only*

        Returns us thanks.°   *wins us gratitude*

            Enter [a] PAGE

        PAGE   Monsieur Paroles, my lord calls for you.   *[Exit]*

175   PAROLES   Little Helen, farewell. If I can remember thee I will

        think of thee at court.

        HELEN   Monsieur Paroles, you were born under a charitable star.

        PAROLES   Under Mars,[7] I.

        HELEN   I especially think *under* Mars.

180   PAROLES   Why '*under* Mars'?

        HELEN   The wars hath so kept you under that you must needs be

        born under Mars.

        PAROLES   When he was predominant.°   *in the ascendant*

        HELEN   When he was retrograde,[8] I think rather.

185   PAROLES   Why think you so?

        HELEN   You go so much backward when you fight.

        PAROLES   That's for advantage.°   *tactical gain*

        HELEN   So is running away, when fear proposes the safety. But

        the composition° that your valour and fear makes in you is a   *truce; mixture*

190   virtue of a good wing,[9] and I like the wear° well.   *habit; fashion*

        PAROLES   I am so full of businesses I cannot answer thee acutely.

        I will return perfect courtier, in the which my instruction shall

        serve to naturalize° thee, so thou wilt be capable of a courtier's   *familiarize*

        counsel and understand what advice shall thrust upon thee;

195   else thou diest in thine unthankfulness, and thine ignorance

        makes thee away.° Farewell. When thou hast leisure say thy   *puts an end to you*

        prayers; when thou hast none remember thy friends.[1] Get thee

        a good husband and use° him as he uses thee. So farewell.   *treat*

                                                 [Exit]

        HELEN   Our remedies oft in ourselves do lie

200   Which we ascribe to heaven. The fated° sky   *destiny-ordaining*

        Gives us free scope, only doth backward pull

        Our slow designs when we ourselves are dull.°   *sluggish*

        What power is it which mounts my love so high,[2]

        That makes me see and cannot feed mine eye?

205   The mightiest space in fortune nature brings

        To join like likes and kiss like native things.[3]

        Impossible be strange° attempts to those   *unusual*

        That weigh their pains in sense[4] and do suppose

        What hath been cannot be. Who ever strove

210   To show her merit that did miss° her love?   *fail to achieve*

---

6. Whose less elevated destinies confine us merely to wishing.

7. The planet was identified with the god of war.

8. Retreating (said of a planet's apparent movement relative to the zodiac).

9. *of a good wing*: that is, rapid in flight; also, with large shoulder flaps. Paroles is foppishly dressed.

1. Unclear: perhaps, Say your prayers when you have the chance, and when you're too busy, rely on your friends instead.

2. Which elevates my love to so lofty an object.

3. *The mightiest . . . things*: Natural affect brings persons greatly distant in rank together as if they were similar and conjoins them as if they had a common origin.

4. Who vividly imagine the difficulties.

The King's disease—my project may deceive me,
But my intents are fixed and will not leave me.   *Exit*

1.2

A flourish of cornetts.° Enter the KING *of France with let-*   horn fanfare
ters, [*the two* LORDS DUMAINE,] *and divers attendants*

KING   The Florentines and Sienese are by th'ears,°   quarreling
Have fought with equal fortune, and continue
A braving° war.   defiant; gallant

FIRST LORD DUMAINE   So 'tis reported, sir.

KING   Nay, 'tis most credible: we here receive it
5   A certainty vouched from our cousin° Austria,   fellow sovereign
With caution that the Florentine will move° us   entreat
For speedy aid—wherein our dearest friend°   (the Duke of Austria)
Prejudicates° the business, and would seem   Prejudges
To have us make denial.

FIRST LORD DUMAINE   His love and wisdom
10   Approved° so to your majesty may plead   Proven
For amplest credence.

KING   He hath armed° our answer,   hardened
And Florence is denied before he comes.
Yet for our gentlemen that mean to see
The Tuscan service, freely have they leave
To stand on either part.°   fight on either side

15   SECOND LORD DUMAINE   It well may serve
A nursery to[1] our gentry, who are sick°   pining
For breathing° and exploit.   exercise

KING   What's he comes here?

Enter BERTRAM, LAFEU, *and* PAROLES

FIRST LORD DUMAINE   It is the Count Roussillon, my good lord,
Young Bertram.

KING [*to* BERTRAM]   Youth, thou bear'st thy father's face.
20   Frank° nature, rather curious° than in haste,   generous / meticulous
Hath well composed thee. Thy father's moral parts°   qualities
Mayst thou inherit, too. Welcome to Paris.

BERTRAM   My thanks and duty are your majesty's.

KING   I would I had that corporal soundness now
25   As when thy father and myself in friendship
First tried our soldiership. He did look far°   see deeply
Into the service° of the time, and was   military service
Discipled of° the bravest. He lasted long,   Followed by; taught by
But on us both did haggish° age steal on,   witchlike; malevolent
30   And wore us out of act.° It much repairs me   action
To talk of your good father. In his youth
He had the wit which I can well observe
Today in our young lords, but they may jest
Till their own scorn return to them unnoted[2]
35   Ere they can hide their levity in honour.[3]
So like a courtier,° contempt nor bitterness   paradigm of courtesy
Were in his pride° or sharpness;[4] if they were   self-esteem

---

1.2 Location: The King's court at Paris.
1. As a training school for.
2. *they may . . . unnoted:* their ridicule merely rebounds
upon them, ignored by others.

3. Before they can compensate for their frivolity with
noble acts.
4. Keenness of wit.

His equal had awaked them,[5] and his honour—
Clock to itself°—knew the true minute when   *Self-regulating*
40 Exception° bid him speak, and at this time   *Disapproval*
His tongue obeyed his hand.[6] Who were below him
He used as creatures of another place,[7]
And bowed his eminent top° to their low ranks,   *head*
Making them proud of his humility,
45 In their poor praise he humbled.[8] Such a man
Might be a copy° to these younger times,   *model*
Which followed well would demonstrate them now
But goers-backward.°   *backsliders*

BERTRAM   His good remembrance, sir,
Lies richer in your thoughts than on his tomb.
50 So in approof° lives not his epitaph   *confirmation*
As in your royal speech.

KING   Would I were with him! He would always say—
Methinks I hear him now; his plausive° words   *praiseworthy*
He scattered not in ears, but grafted them[9]
55 To grow there and to bear. 'Let me not live'—
This his good melancholy oft began
On the catastrophe° and heel of pastime,   *end*
When it was out°—'Let me not live', quoth he,   *finished*
'After my flame lacks oil, to be the snuff[1]
60 Of younger spirits, whose apprehensive° senses   *quick*
All but new things disdain, whose judgements are
Mere fathers of their garments,[2] whose constancies°   *loyalties*
Expire before their fashions.' This he wished.
I after him do after° him wish too,   *in harmony with*
65 Since I nor wax nor honey can bring home,
I quickly were dissolvèd° from my hive   *removed*
To give some labourers room.

SECOND LORD DUMAINE   You're lovèd, sir.
They that least lend it you° shall lack° you first.   *grant you love / miss*

KING   I fill a place, I know't.—How long is't, Count,
70 Since the physician at your father's died?
He was much famed.

BERTRAM   Some six months since, my lord.

KING   If he were living I would try him yet.—
Lend me an arm.—The rest have worn me out
With several applications.° Nature and sickness   *various treatments*
75 Debate it at their leisure.[3] Welcome, Count.
My son's no dearer.

BERTRAM   Thank your majesty. *[Flourish.] Exeunt*

1.3

Enter the COUNTESS, [REYNALDO *her*] *steward, and*
[*behind*, LAVATCH *her*] *clown*

COUNTESS   I will now hear. What say you of this gentlewoman?

---

5. *if they were . . . them*: if ever he spoke bitterly or contemptuously, it was to a social equal.
6. He said no more than he would back up with action.
7. He treated as people of a higher station.
8. He willingly humbled himself to praise their poor selves.
9. He did not strew (words) superficially among his hearers (like seed), but planted them permanently (as twigs

of fruit trees are grafted to a tree trunk).
1. Burned upper wick, which if not trimmed keeps the lower part from burning properly.
2. *whose judgements . . . garments*: whose mental prowess creates only new clothes.
3. Argue over my condition at length.
1.3 Location: Roussillon.

REYNALDO　Madam, the care I have had to even your content[1] I
wish might be found in the calendar° of my past endeavours,　　　　　*record*
for then we wound our modesty and make foul the clearness of
5　our deservings, when of ourselves we publish° them.　　　　　*advertise*

COUNTESS　What does this knave here? [*To* LAVATCH] Get you
gone, sirrah. The complaints I have heard of you I do not all
believe. 'Tis my slowness that I do not, for I know you lack not
folly to commit them and have ability enough to make such
10　knaveries yours.

LAVATCH　'Tis not unknown to you, madam, I am a poor fellow.

COUNTESS　Well, sir?

LAVATCH　No, madam, 'tis not so well that I am poor, though
many of the rich are damned. But if I may have your ladyship's
15　good will to go to the world,° Isbel the woman° and I will do as　　*marry / maidservant*
we may.[2]

COUNTESS　Wilt thou needs be a beggar?

LAVATCH　I do beg your good will in this case.

COUNTESS　In what case?

20　LAVATCH　In Isbel's case and mine own. Service is no heritage,[3]
and I think I shall never have the blessing of God till I have
issue o' my body, for they say bairns° are blessings.　　　　　*children*

COUNTESS　Tell me thy reason why thou wilt marry.

LAVATCH　My poor body, madam, requires it. I am driven on by
25　the flesh, and he must needs go that the devil drives.

COUNTESS　Is this all your worship's reason?

LAVATCH　Faith, madam, I have other holy reasons,[4] such as they
are.

COUNTESS　May the world know them?

30　LAVATCH　I have been, madam, a wicked creature, as you—and
all flesh and blood—are, and indeed I do marry that I may
repent.[5]

COUNTESS　Thy marriage sooner than thy wickedness.

LAVATCH　I am out o' friends, madam, and I hope to have friends
35　for my wife's sake.

COUNTESS　Such friends are thine enemies, knave.

LAVATCH　You're shallow,° madam—in great friends, for the　　*a superficial judge*
knaves come to do that for me which I am aweary of. He that
ears° my land spares my team, and gives me leave to in° the　　*plows / harvest*
40　crop. If I be his cuckold, he's my drudge. He that comforts my
wife is the cherisher of my flesh and blood; he that cherishes
my flesh and blood loves my flesh and blood; he that loves my
flesh and blood is my friend; *ergo,* he that kisses my wife is my
friend. If men could be contented to be what they are,° there　　*(cuckolds)*
45　were no fear in marriage. For young Chairbonne the puritan
and old Poisson the papist,[6] howsome'er their hearts are severed in religion, their heads are both one:° they may jowl°　　*identical / bump*
horns together like any deer i'th' herd.[7]

COUNTESS　Wilt thou ever be a foul-mouthed and calumnious
50　knave?

1. To meet your desires.
2. Will do our best (with sexual pun on "do").
3. A servant has little to leave his children (proverbial;
with sexual pun on "service").
4. Other motives sanctified by the marriage ceremony;
with puns on "holy" ("hole-y") and "reasons" ("raisings").
5. That I may make my illicit sexual activity lawful (but

alluding to the proverb "Marry in haste and repent at leisure").
6. *chair bonne:* good meat (French). *poisson:* fish. Catholics ate fish on fast days, but Puritans rejected the custom.
7. Cuckolds were supposed to have horns in their foreheads.

LAVATCH   A prophet? Ay, madam, and I speak the truth the next°   *most direct*
way.
[*He sings*]   For I the ballad will repeat,
                       Which men full true shall find:
55   Your marriage comes by destiny,
                       Your cuckoo sings by kind.⁸

COUNTESS   Get you gone, sir. I'll talk with you more anon.

REYNALDO   May it please you, madam, that he bid Helen come
to you? Of her I am to speak.

60   COUNTESS [*to* LAVATCH]   Sirrah, tell my gentlewoman I would
speak with her. Helen, I mean.

LAVATCH   [*sings*]
            'Was this fair face the cause', quoth she,⁹
            'Why the Grecians sackèd Troy?
            Fond° done, done fond. Was this¹ King Priam's joy?'   *Foolishly; lovingly*
65   With that she sighèd as she stood,
            With that she sighèd as she stood,
            And gave this sentence° then: *maxim*
            'Among nine bad if one be good,
            Among nine bad if one be good,
70   There's yet one good in ten.'

COUNTESS   What, 'one good in ten'? You corrupt² the song,
sirrah.

LAVATCH   One good *woman* in ten, madam, which is a purifying
o'th' song. Would God would serve the world so all the year!
75   We'd find no fault with the tithe-woman³ if I were the parson.
One in ten, quoth a?° An° we might have a good woman born   *did he say / If*
but ere every blazing star,° or at an earthquake, 'twould mend   *comet*
the lottery° well. A man may draw his heart out ere a pluck⁴   *improve the odds*
one.

80   COUNTESS   You'll be gone, sir knave, and do as I command you.

LAVATCH   That man should be at woman's command, and yet
no hurt done! Though honesty be no puritan,⁵ yet it will do no
hurt;° it will wear the surplice of humility over the black gown   *harm*
of a big heart.⁶ I am going, forsooth. The business is for Helen
85   to come hither.   *Exit*

COUNTESS   Well now.

REYNALDO   I know, madam, you love your gentlewoman
entirely.

COUNTESS   Faith, I do. Her father bequeathed her to me, and
90   she herself without other advantage⁷ may lawfully make title
to° as much love as she finds. There is more owing her than is   *claim*
paid, and more shall be paid her than she'll demand.

REYNALDO   Madam, I was very late° more near her than I think   *recently*
she wished me. Alone she was, and did communicate to her
95   self, her own words to her own ears; she thought, I dare vow for

8. *by kind*: according to its nature (the cuckoo's song was supposed to mock cuckolds).
9. Lavatch is reminded of the "fair face" of Helen of Troy, the most famous cuckold maker. *she*: probably Hecuba, wife of Priam and mother of Paris, Helen's lover.
1. *this*: probably refers to Paris.
2. Debase (the original presumably had "one bad in ten," referring to Paris, Priam's only bad son).
3. One-tenth of the parish produce was tithed to the church.

4. Before he draw (as from a lottery).
5. Though my honest self is not morally strict.
6. *it will wear . . . heart*: that is, Lavatch will conceal his pride under apparent meekness. Some Puritan ministers obeyed English ecclesiastical law by wearing the surplice, or priestly garment, but with a black Calvinist gown underneath.
7. Even without any interest accrued (Helen being regarded as the "principal" bequeathed by her father).

her, they touched not any stranger sense.[8] Her matter° was, she   *subject*
loved your son. Fortune, she said, was no goddess, that had put
such difference betwixt their two estates;° Love no god, that   *social stations*
would not extend his might only where qualities were level;[9]
100 Dian° no queen of virgins, that would suffer her poor knight   *goddess of chastity*
surprised[1] without rescue in the first assault or ransom after-
ward. This she delivered in the most bitter touch° of sorrow that   *strain*
e'er I heard virgin exclaim in; which I held my duty speedily to
acquaint you withal, sithence° in the loss that may happen it   *since*
105 concerns you something to know it.
    COUNTESS   You have discharged this honestly. Keep it to your-
self. Many likelihoods informed me of this before, which hung
so tott'ring in the balance that I could neither believe nor misdoubt.° Pray you, leave me. Stall° this in your bosom, and I   *doubt / Enclose*
110 thank you for your honest care. I will speak with you further
anon.   *Exit steward*
        Enter HELEN
    COUNTESS [*aside*]   Even so it was with me when I was young.
      If ever we are nature's, these° are ours: this thorn   *(love pangs)*
    Doth to our rose of youth rightly belong.
115   Our blood° to us, this to our blood is born;   *passions*
    It is the show° and seal of nature's truth,   *sign*
    Where love's strong passion is impressed in youth.
    By our remembrances of days foregone,
    Such were our faults—or° then we thought them none.   *although*
120   Her eye is sick on't.° I observe her now.   *with it*
    HELEN   What is your pleasure, madam?
    COUNTESS   You know, Helen,
    I am a mother to you.
    HELEN   Mine honourable mistress.
    COUNTESS   Nay, a mother.
    Why not a mother? When I said 'a mother',
125   Methought you saw a serpent. What's in 'mother'
    That you start at it? I say I am your mother,
    And put you in the catalogue of those
    That were enwombèd mine. 'Tis often seen
    Adoption strives with nature, and choice breeds
130   A native slip to us from foreign seeds.[2]
    You ne'er oppressed me with a mother's groan,°   *(in childbirth)*
    Yet I express to you a mother's care.
    God's mercy, maiden! Does it curd thy blood
    To say I am thy mother? What's the matter,
135   That this distempered° messenger of wet,°   *disturbed / rain; tears*
    The many-coloured Iris,[3] rounds thine eye?
    Why, that you are my daughter?
    HELEN   That I am not.
    COUNTESS   I say I am your mother.
    HELEN   Pardon, madam.
    The Count Roussillon cannot be my brother.
140   I am from humble, he from honoured name;
    No note° upon my parents, his all noble.   *distinction*

---

8. Any other persons' hearing.
9. Would not exercise his power except where rank was
equal.
1. Would allow her poor devotee to be captured.

2. *choice . . . seeds:* a twig chosen from foreign seed
becomes, once engrafted, part of our plant.
3. Goddess of rainbows (Helen's tear-filled eyes are iridescent).

My master, my dear lord he is, and I
His servant live and will his vassal die.
He must not be my brother.

COUNTESS   Nor I your mother?

145 HELEN   You are my mother, madam. Would you were—
So° that my lord your son were not my brother—   *Provided*
Indeed my mother! Or were you both our mothers°   *mother of us both*
I care no more for than I do for heaven,
So I were not his sister. Can 't no other

150 But, I, your daughter, he must be my brother?

COUNTESS   Yes, Helen, you might be my daughter-in-law.
God shield you mean it not! 'Daughter' and 'mother'
So strive upon your pulse. What, pale again?
My fear hath catched your fondness.° Now I see   *love; folly*

155 The myst'ry of your loneliness, and find
Your salt tears' head.° Now to all sense 'tis gross:°   *source / obvious*
You love my son. Invention[4] is ashamed
Against° the proclamation of thy passion   *In the face of*
To say thou dost not. Therefore tell me true,

160 But tell me then 'tis so—for look, thy cheeks
Confess it t'one to th'other, and thine eyes
See it so grossly shown in thy behaviours
That in their kind° they speak it. Only sin   *after their fashion*
And hellish obstinacy tie thy tongue,

165 That truth should be suspected.° Speak, is't so?   *doubted*
If it be so you have wound a goodly clew;[5]
If it be not, forswear't.° Howe'er,° I charge thee,   *deny it / In any case*
As heaven shall work in me for thine avail,°   *benefit*
To tell me truly.

HELEN   Good madam, pardon me.

COUNTESS   Do you love my son?

170 HELEN   Your pardon, noble mistress.

COUNTESS   Love you my son?

HELEN   Do not you love him, madam?

COUNTESS   Go not about.[6] My love hath in't a bond
Whereof the world takes note.° Come, come, disclose   *society recognizes*
The state of your affection, for your passions
Have to the full appeached.°   *informed against you*

175 HELEN   Then I confess,
Here on my knee, before high heaven and you,
That before you° and next unto high heaven   *even more than I love you*
I love your son.
My friends° were poor but honest; so's my love.   *relatives*

180 Be not offended, for it hurts not him
That he is loved of me. I follow him not
By any token° of presumptuous suit,°   *manifestations / wooing*
Nor would I have him till I do deserve him,
Yet never know how that desert should be.

185 I know I love in vain, strive against hope;
Yet in this captious° and intenable° sieve   *receptive / unretentive*
I still° pour in the waters of my love   *continually*
And lack not to lose still.° Thus, Indian-like,   *And keep losing it*

4. (Your) capacity to invent excuses.   6. Don't beat around the bush.
5. You have made a fine tangle of thread (mess).

Religious in mine error, I adore
190 The sun that looks upon his worshipper
     But knows of him no more. My dearest madam,
     Let not your hate encounter with° my love   oppose
     For loving where you do; but if yourself,
     Whose agèd honour cites° a virtuous youth,   testifies to
195 Did ever in so true a flame of liking
     Wish chastely and love dearly, that your Dian
     Was both herself and Love,⁷ then give pity
     To her whose state is such that cannot choose
     But lend and give where she is sure to lose,
200 That seeks to find not that° her search implies,   what
     But riddle-like⁸ lives sweetly where she dies.
     COUNTESS Had you not lately an intent—speak truly—
     To go to Paris?
     HELEN Madam, I had.
205 COUNTESS Wherefore? Tell true.
     HELEN I will tell truth, by grace itself I swear.
     You know my father left me some prescriptions
     Of rare and proved effects, such as his reading
     And manifest° experience had collected   obvious
210 For general sovereignty,° and that he willed me   effectiveness
     In heedfull'st reservation° to bestow them,   With most sparing care
     As notes whose faculties inclusive were
     More than they were in note.⁹ Amongst the rest
     There is a remedy, approved,° set down,   tested
215 To cure the desperate languishings whereof
     The King is rendered lost.°   held to be dying
     COUNTESS   This was your motive
     For Paris, was it? Speak.
     HELEN My lord your son made me to think of this,
     Else Paris and the medicine and the King
220 Had from the conversation of my thoughts
     Haply° been absent then.   Perhaps
     COUNTESS   But think you, Helen,
     If you should tender° your supposèd aid,   offer
     He would receive it? He and his physicians
     Are of a° mind: he, that they cannot help him;   one
225 They, that they cannot help. How shall they credit
     A poor unlearnèd virgin, when the schools,
     Embowelled° of their doctrine, have left off   Emptied
     The danger to itself?
     HELEN   There's something in't
     More than my father's skill, which was the great'st
230 Of his profession, that his good receipt°   prescription
     Shall for my legacy be sanctified
     By th' luckiest stars in heaven, and would your honour
     But give me leave to try success,° I'd venture   test the outcome
     The well-lost life of mine on his grace's cure
235 By such a day, an hour.
     COUNTESS Dost thou believe't?

---

7. Venus, goddess of erotic love, is usually the antagonist
of Diana, goddess of chastity; Helen's love reconciles
them.

8. Paradoxically; retaining her secret.
9. As . . . note: As prescriptions of greater powers than
were recognized.

HELEN Ay, madam, knowingly.[1]

COUNTESS Why, Helen, thou shalt have my leave and love,
Means and attendants, and my loving greetings
240 To those of mine in court. I'll stay at home
And pray God's blessing into thy attempt.
Be gone tomorrow, and be sure of this:
What I can help thee to, thou shalt not miss.°   *Exeunt*   lack

2.1

Flourish cornetts. Enter the KING [*carried in a chair*],
with [*the two* LORDS DUMAINE,] *divers young lords tak-*
ing leave for the Florentine war, [*and* BERTRAM] *and*
PAROLES

KING Farewell, young lords. These warlike principles°   military precepts
Do not throw from you. And you, my lords,[1] farewell.
Share the advice betwixt you; if both gain all,
The gift doth stretch itself as 'tis received,
And is enough for both.

5 FIRST LORD DUMAINE   'Tis our hope, sir,
After well-entered soldiers,[2] to return
And find your grace in health.

KING No, no, it cannot be—and yet my heart
Will not confess he owes° the malady   it owns
10 That doth my life besiege. Farewell, young lords.
Whether I live or die, be you the sons
Of worthy Frenchmen; let higher° Italy—   northern
Those bated° that inherit but the fall   dwindled peoples
Of the last monarchy[3]—see that you come
15 Not to woo honour but to wed it. When
The bravest questant° shrinks, find what you seek,   seeker
That fame may cry you loud.° I say farewell.   acclaim you loudly

FIRST LORD DUMAINE Health at your bidding serve your majesty.

KING Those girls of Italy, take heed of them.
20 They say our French lack language to deny
If they demand.° Beware of being captives[4]   request
Before you serve.°   (militarily)

BOTH LORDS DUMAINE Our hearts receive your warnings.

KING Farewell.—Come hither to me.
[*Some lords stand aside with the* KING]

FIRST LORD DUMAINE [*to* BERTRAM] O my sweet lord, that you
will stay behind us.

PAROLES 'Tis not his fault, the spark.°   spirited person

25 SECOND LORD DUMAINE   O 'tis brave° wars.   splendid

PAROLES Most admirable! I have seen those wars.

BERTRAM I am commanded° here, and kept a coil° with   (to stay) / fussed over
'Too young' and 'the next year' and ''tis too early'.

PAROLES An° thy mind stand to't, boy, steal away bravely.   If

30 BERTRAM I shall stay here the forehorse to a smock,[5]
Creaking my shoes on the plain masonry,[6]

---

1. Fully aware of what I am doing.
2.1 Location: The King's palace.
1. Presumably leaving to take the opposite side in the war.
2. After we are well initiated as soldiers.
3. Perhaps the Holy Roman Empire, the Medici, or the

papacy.
4. Of your mistresses.
5. Lead horse of a team driven by a woman (figuratively, part of a dancing couple).
6. Level stonework (of the palace floors, in contrast to the rough battlefield).

Till honour be bought up,° and no sword worn   *all acquired (by others)*
But one to dance with. By heaven, I'll steal away.
FIRST LORD DUMAINE   There's honour in the theft.
PAROLES   Commit it, Count.
35 SECOND LORD DUMAINE   I am your accessary.° And so, farewell.   *accomplice*
BERTRAM   I grow° to you,   *am deeply attached*
And our parting is a tortured body.
FIRST LORD DUMAINE   Farewell, captain.
SECOND LORD DUMAINE   Sweet Monsieur Paroles.
PAROLES   Noble heroes, my sword and yours are kin. Good
40 sparks and lustrous, a word, good mettles.° You shall find in the   *spirits; sword blades*
regiment of the Spinii one Captain Spurio, with his cicatrice,°   *scar*
an emblem of war, here on his sinister° cheek. It was this very   *left*
sword entrenched it. Say to him I live, and observe his reports°   *note his reply*
for me.
45 FIRST LORD DUMAINE   We shall, noble captain.
PAROLES   Mars dote on you for his novices.
               [Exeunt both LORDS DUMAINE*]*
     [To BERTRAM*]* What will ye do?
BERTRAM   Stay° the King.   *Await*
PAROLES   Use a more spacious ceremony° to the noble lords.   *expansive courtesy*
50 You have restrained yourself within the list° of too cold an   *limit*
adieu. Be more expressive to them, for they wear themselves
in the cap of the time,[7] there do muster true gait;[8] eat, speak,
and move under the influence of the most received° star—and   *fashionable*
though the devil lead the measure,° such are to be followed.   *dance*
55 After them, and take a more dilated° farewell.   *extended*
BERTRAM   And I will do so.
PAROLES   Worthy fellows, and like to prove most sinewy sword-
men.   *Exeunt* [BERTRAM *and* PAROLES]
     Enter LAFEU [*to the* KING]
LAFEU [*kneeling*]   Pardon, my lord, for me and for my tidings.
60 KING   I'll fee[9] thee to stand up.
LAFEU [*rising*]   Then here's a man stands that has bought his pardon.
I would you had kneeled, my lord, to ask me mercy,
And that at my bidding you could so stand up.
KING   I would I had, so I had broke thy pate°   *head*
And asked thee mercy for't.
65 LAFEU   Good faith, across![1]
But my good lord, 'tis thus: will you be cured
Of your infirmity?
KING   No.
LAFEU   O will you eat
No grapes, my royal fox?[2] Yes, but you will,
My noble grapes, an if° my royal fox   *an if=if*
70 Could reach them. I have seen a medicine°   *physician; remedy*
That's able to breathe life into a stone,
Quicken° a rock, and make you dance canary°   *Animate / a lively dance*
With sprightly fire and motion; whose simple° touch   *mere; medicinal herb*
Is powerful to araise King Pépin,[3] nay,

---

7. Are ornaments of fashion.
8. Display grace of movement.
9. Pay (not merely "pardon").
1. A weak jest: in tilting, a blow "across" is a bad hit.

2. In Aesop, a fox pretends not to want a bunch of grapes he cannot reach.
3. Eighth-century French King.

75 To give great Charlemagne[4] a pen in's hand,
And write to her a love-line.

KING   What 'her' is this?

LAFEU   Why, Doctor She. My lord, there's one arrived,
If you will see her. Now by my faith and honour,
If seriously I may convey my thoughts

80 In this my light deliverance,° I have spoke   *mode of speaking*
With one that in her sex, her years, profession,°   *claims of skill*
Wisdom and constancy, hath amazed me more
Than I dare blame my weakness.° Will you see her—   *(as an old man)*
For that is her demand—and know her business?
That done, laugh well at me.

85 KING   Now, good Lafeu,
Bring in the admiration,° that we with thee   *marvel*
May spend our wonder too, or take off thine
By wond'ring how thou took'st° it.   *came by*

LAFEU   Nay, I'll fit° you,   *satisfy*
And not be all day neither.
        [*He goes to the door*]

90 KING   Thus he his special nothing° ever prologues.   *trifles*

LAFEU [*to* HELEN, *within*]   Nay, come your ways.°   *come along*
        Enter HELEN

KING   This haste hath wings indeed.

LAFEU [*to* HELEN]   Nay, come your ways.
This is his majesty. Say your mind to him.

95 A traitor[5] you do look like, but such traitors
His majesty seldom fears. I am Cressid's uncle,[6]
That dare leave two together. Fare you well.
        Exeunt [all but the KING *and* HELEN]

KING   Now, fair one, does your business follow us?

HELEN   Ay, my good lord. Gérard de Narbonne was my father;
In what he did profess, well found.°   *found to be good*

100 KING   I knew him.

HELEN   The rather will I spare my praises towards him;
Knowing him is enough. On's° bed of death   *On his*
Many receipts he gave me, chiefly one
Which, as the dearest issue[7] of his practice,

105 And of his old experience th'only darling,
He bade me store up as a triple° eye   *third*
Safer than mine own two, more dear. I have so,
And hearing your high majesty is touched
With that malignant cause wherein the honour

110 Of my dear father's gift stands chief in power,[8]
I come to tender it and my appliance°   *treatment*
With all bound° humbleness.   *dutiful*

KING   We thank you, maiden,
But may not be so credulous of cure,
When our most learnèd doctors leave us, and

115 The congregated College[9] have concluded
That labouring art° can never ransom nature   *medical skill*
From her inaidable estate.° I say we must not   *condition*

---

4. Pépin's son, founder of the Holy Roman Empire.
5. Because she avoids the King's gaze.
6. Pandarus, the go-between for Troilus and Cressida and archetypal pimp.
7. Best product; favorite child.
8. *malignant . . . power*: disease for which my father's honored gift is most effective.
9. Assembled College of Physicians.

So stain our judgement or corrupt our hope,
To prostitute° our past-cure malady   *submit*
120 To empirics,[1] or to dissever so
Our great self and our credit,[2] to esteem
A senseless help,° when help past sense we deem.   *An unbelievable cure*
HELEN   My duty then shall pay me for my pains.
I will no more enforce mine office° on you,   *service*
125 Humbly entreating from your royal thoughts
A modest one[3] to bear me back again.
KING   I cannot give thee less, to be called grateful.
Thou thought'st to help me, and such thanks I give
As one near death to those that wish him live.
130 But what at full I know, thou know'st no part;°   *not at all*
I knowing all my peril, thou no art.
HELEN   What I can do can do no hurt to try,
Since you set up your rest° 'gainst remedy.   *stake everything*
He that of greatest works is finisher
135 Oft does them by the weakest minister.
So holy writ in babes hath judgement shown
When judges have been babes;[4] great floods have flow'n
From simple sources, and great seas have dried.
When miracles have by th' great'st been denied
140 [   ][5]
Oft expectation fails, and most oft there
Where most it promises, and oft it hits°   *succeeds*
Where hope is coldest and despair most fits.
KING   I must not hear thee. Fare thee well, kind maid.
145 Thy pains, not used, must by thyself be paid:
Proffers not took reap thanks° for their reward.   *only thanks*
HELEN   Inspirèd merit so by breath is barred.[6]
It is not so with him that all things knows
As 'tis with us that square our guess by shows;[7]
150 But most it is presumption in us when
The help of heaven we count the act of men.
Dear sir, to my endeavours give consent.
Of heaven, not me, make an experiment.
I am not an impostor, that proclaim
155 Myself against the level of mine aim,[8]
But know I think, and think I know most sure,
My art is not past° power, nor you past cure.   *without*
KING   Art thou so confident? Within what space
Hop'st thou my cure?
HELEN   The great'st grace lending grace,
160 Ere twice the horses of the sun shall bring
Their fiery coacher his diurnal ring,°   *daily round*
Ere twice in murk and occidental damp

1. Physicians whose methods were based on experience
rather than on medical theory. In early modern Europe,
"theoretical" practitioners, like the members of the
French College of Physicians, often considered their
"empirical" colleagues mere quacks; the "empirics" usually hailed from lower social classes and had less formal
education.
2. *to dissever . . . credit:* to open such a gap between my
royal station and my gullibility.
3. A favorable thought appropriate to a woman and a
subject.
4. *So . . . babes:* "Thou hast hid these things from the
wise and men of understanding, and hast opened them
unto babes" (Matthew 11:25).
5. The Oxford editors conjecture a lost line here.
6. Divinely inspired virtue is thus denied by human
speech.
7. Who base our conjectures on appearances.
8. *proclaim . . . aim:* boast in advance of the accuracy of
my aim; declare myself to be different from what I am.

Moist Hesperus° hath quenched her sleepy lamp,   *the evening star*
Or four-and-twenty times the pilot's glass°   *hourglass*
165   Hath told the thievish minutes how they pass,
What is infirm from your sound parts shall fly,
Health shall live free, and sickness freely die.

KING   Upon thy certainty and confidence
What dar'st thou venture?°   *risk*

HELEN   Tax° of impudence,   *Accusation*
170   A strumpet's boldness, a divulgèd shame;
Traduced by odious ballads, my maiden's name
Seared[9] otherwise, nay—worse of worst—extended[1]
With vilest torture, let my life be ended.

KING   Methinks in thee some blessèd spirit doth speak,
175   His powerful sound within an organ weak;
And what impossibility would slay
In common sense, sense saves another way.[2]
Thy life is dear, for all that life can rate
Worth name of life in thee hath estimate:°   *is present*
180   Youth, beauty, wisdom, courage, all
That happiness and prime[3] can happy call.
Thou this to hazard needs must intimate[4]
Skill infinite, or monstrous desperate.
Sweet practiser,° thy physic I will try,   *practitioner; schemer*
185   That ministers thine own death if I die.

HELEN   If I break time, or flinch in property[5]
Of what I spoke, unpitied let me die,
And well deserved. Not helping, death's my fee.
But if I help, what do you promise me?

KING   Make thy demand.

190   HELEN   But will you make it even?°   *satisfy it*

KING   Ay, by my sceptre and my hopes of heaven.

HELEN   Then shalt thou give me with thy kingly hand
What husband in thy power I will command.
Exempted be from me the arrogance
195   To choose from forth the royal blood of France,
My low and humble name to propagate
With any branch or image of thy state;°   *royal place*
But such a one, thy vassal, whom I know
Is free for me to ask, thee to bestow.

200   KING   Here is my hand. The premises observed,°   *conditions fulfilled*
Thy will by my performance shall be served.
So make the choice of thy own time, for I,
Thy resolved patient, on thee still° rely.   *always*
More should I question thee, and more I must,
205   Though more to know could not be more to trust:
From whence thou cam'st, how tended on°—but rest   *attended*
Unquestioned[6] welcome, and undoubted blessed.—
Give me some help here, ho! If thou proceed
As high as word, my deed shall match thy deed.

Flourish. Exeut [the KING, *carried, and* HELEN]

---

9. Branded (like a criminal).
1. Prolonged; stretched on the rack.
2. sense . . . way: makes sense in another, uncommon way.
3. That good fortune and the springtime of life.

4. For you to risk this must suggest.
5. If I fail to meet the deadline or fall short in the particulars.
6. Not having been asked; unquestionably.

2.2

Enter the COUNTESS *and* [LAVATCH] *the clown*

COUNTESS   Come on, sir. I shall now put you to the height¹ of
your breeding.

LAVATCH   I will show myself highly fed and lowly taught.² I know
my business is but to the court.

5 COUNTESS   'To the court'? Why, what place make you special,
when you put off° that with such contempt? 'But to the court'!   °dismiss

LAVATCH   Truly, madam, if God have lent a man any manners
he may easily put it off° at court. He that cannot make a leg,°   °lose it; take it off / bow
put off's cap, kiss his hand, and say nothing, has neither leg,

10 hands, lip, nor cap, and indeed such a fellow, to say precisely,
were not for the court. But for me, I have an answer will serve
all men.

COUNTESS   Marry, that's a bountiful answer that fits all questions.

LAVATCH   It is like a barber's chair that fits all buttocks: the pin°-   °pointed

15 buttock, the quatch°-buttock, the brawn-buttock, or any but-   °fat
tock.

COUNTESS   Will your answer serve fit to all questions?

LAVATCH   As fit as ten groats is for the hand of an attorney, as
your French crown³ for your taffeta punk,° as Tib's rush⁴ for   °prostitute

20 Tom's forefinger, as a pancake⁵ for Shrove Tuesday, a morris°   °morris dance
for May Day, as the nail to his hole, the cuckold to his horn, as
a scolding quean° to a wrangling knave, as the nun's lip to the   °whore
friar's mouth, nay as the pudding° to his skin.   °sausage

COUNTESS   Have you, I say, an answer of such fitness for all ques-

25 tions?

LAVATCH   From beyond your duke to beneath your constable, it
will fit any question.

COUNTESS   It must be an answer of most monstrous size that
must fit all demands.

30 LAVATCH   But a trifle neither,° in good faith, if the learned   °No, just a trifle
should speak truth of it. Here it is, and all that belongs to't. Ask
me if I am a courtier. It shall do you no harm to learn.

COUNTESS   To be young again, if we could! I will be a fool in
question, hoping to be the wiser by your answer. I pray you, sir,

35 are you a courtier?

LAVATCH   O Lord, sir!⁶—There's a simple putting off. More,
more, a hundred of them.

COUNTESS   Sir, I am a poor friend of yours that loves you.

LAVATCH   O Lord, sir!—Thick,° thick, spare not me.   °Quick

40 COUNTESS   I think, sir, you can eat none of this homely° meat.   °plain

LAVATCH   O Lord, sir!—Nay, put me to't, I warrant you.

COUNTESS   You were lately whipped, sir, as I think.

LAVATCH   O Lord, sir!—Spare not me.

COUNTESS   Do you cry 'O Lord, sir!' at your whipping, and 'spare

45 not me'? Indeed, your 'O Lord, sir!' is very sequent⁷ to your
whipping. You would answer very well⁸ to a whipping, if you
were but bound to't.⁹

2.2 Location: Bertram's palace.
1. Make you display your best manners.
2. Spoiled children were called "better fed than taught."
3. Coin; bald head (from syphilis, the "French disease").
4. Reed twisted into a ring for use in folk marriage, with
sexual innuendo.
5. Traditionally eaten on Shrove Tuesday, the day before

the beginning of Lent.
6. A voguish catchphrase that evades an answer by
appearing to wonder at the question. *putting off*: evasion.
7. Follows naturally upon (as a plea for mercy).
8. Reply cleverly to; be a fitting recipient of.
9. Required to answer; tied to a whipping post.

LAVATCH   I ne'er had worse luck in my life in my 'O Lord, sir!' I
see things may serve long, but not serve ever.

50 COUNTESS   I play the noble housewife° with the time, to enter-   good steward (ironic)
tain it so merrily with a fool.

LAVATCH   O Lord, sir!—Why, there't serves well again.

COUNTESS   An end, sir! To your business: give Helen this,
[She gives him a letter]
And urge her to a present° answer back.   immediate

55 Commend me to my kinsmen and my son.
This is not much.

LAVATCH   Not much commendation to them?

COUNTESS   Not much employment for you. You understand me.

LAVATCH   Most fruitfully. I am there before my legs.

60 COUNTESS   Haste you again.°   Exeunt [severally]   back again

2.3

Enter [BERTRAM,] LAFEU [*with a ballad*], *and* PAROLES

LAFEU   They say miracles are past, and we have our philosophical persons to make modern and familiar things supernatural
and causeless.[1] Hence is it that we make trifles of terrors,
ensconcing ourselves into° seeming knowledge when we   sheltering ourselves with

5   should submit ourselves to an unknown fear.°   awe of the unknown

PAROLES   Why, 'tis the rarest argument° of wonder that hath   best instance
shot out in our latter° times.   recent

BERTRAM   And so 'tis.

LAFEU   To be relinquished of the artists[2]—

10 PAROLES   So I say—both of Galen and Paracelsus.[3]

LAFEU   Of all the learned and authentic Fellows[4]—

PAROLES   Right, so I say.

LAFEU   That gave him out incurable—

PAROLES   Why, there 'tis, so say I too.

15 LAFEU   Not to be helped.

PAROLES   Right, as 'twere a man assured of a—

LAFEU   Uncertain life and sure death.

PAROLES   Just,° you say well, so would I have said.   Exactly

LAFEU   I may truly say it is a novelty to the world.

20 PAROLES   It is indeed. If you will have it in showing,° you shall   demonstrated
read it in [*pointing to the ballad*] what-do-ye-call there.

LAFEU [*reads*]   'A showing of a heavenly effect in an earthly
actor.'

PAROLES   That's it, I would have said the very same.

25 LAFEU   Why, your dolphin[5] is not lustier.° Fore me, I speak in   more sportive
respect°—   respectfully

PAROLES   Nay, 'tis strange, 'tis very strange, that is the brief ° and   short
the tedious° of it, and he's of a most facinorous° spirit that will   long / wicked
not acknowledge it to be the—

30 LAFEU   Very hand of heaven.

PAROLES   Ay, so I say.

LAFEU   In a most weak—

PAROLES   And debile minister° great power, great transcendence,   feeble agent

---

2.3 Location: The King's palace.
1. To make supernatural things, without apparent cause,
seem commonplace and easily explained.
2. Abandoned by the scholars.
3. Galen was a second-century Greek physician, the tra-

ditional medical authority; Paracelsus was a sixteenth-
century Swiss physician who tried to reform Galen's
teachings.
4. Accredited members of the College of Physicians.
5. Punning on "dauphin," heir to the French throne.

which should indeed give us a further use to be made than
35   alone the recov'ry of the king, as to be—
LAFEU   Generally° thankful.   *Universally*
                    Enter the KING, HELEN, *and attendants*
PAROLES   I would have said it, you say well. Here comes the King.
LAFEU   *Lustig,*° as the Dutchman says. I'll like a maid the better   *Frolicsome*
          whilst I have a tooth in my head.[6]
                    [*The* KING *and* HELEN *dance*]
40   Why, he's able to lead her a coranto.°   *running dance*
PAROLES   *Mort du vinaigre,*[7] is not this Helen?
LAFEU   Fore God, I think so.
KING   Go call before me all the lords in court.
                                                    [*Exit one or more*]
          Sit, my preserver, by thy patient's side,
                    [*The* KING *and* HELEN *sit*]
45   And with this healthful hand whose banished sense°   *sense of feeling*
          Thou hast repealed,° a second time receive   *restored*
          The confirmation of my promised gift,
          Which but attends° thy naming.   *awaits*
                    Enter four LORDS
          Fair maid, send forth thine eye. This youthful parcel°   *group*
50   Of noble bachelors stand at my bestowing,[8]
          O'er whom both sovereign power and father's voice
          I have to use. Thy frank election° make.   *free choice*
          Thou hast power to choose, and they none to forsake.
HELEN   To each of you one fair and virtuous mistress
55   Fall[9] when love please. Marry, to each but one.
LAFEU [*aside*]   I'd give bay Curtal and his furniture[1]
          My mouth no more were broken[2] than these boys',
          And writ° as little beard.   *laid claim to*
KING [*to* HELEN]   Peruse them well.
          Not one of these but had a noble father.
60   HELEN   Gentlemen,
          Heaven hath through me restored the King to health.
ALL [*but* HELEN]   We understand it, and thank heaven for you.
HELEN   I am a simple maid, and therein wealthiest
          That I protest I simply am a maid.—
65   Please it your majesty, I have done already.
          The blushes in my cheeks thus whisper me:
          'We blush that thou shouldst choose; but, be° refused,   *if you are*
          Let the white death sit on thy cheek for ever,
          We'll ne'er come there again.'
KING   Make choice and see.
70   Who shuns thy love shuns all his love in me.
HELEN [*rising*]   Now, Dian, from thy altar do I fly,
          And to imperial Love, that god most high,
          Do my sighs stream.
                    [*She addresses her to a* LORD]
                                        Sir, will you hear my suit?
FIRST LORD   And grant it.

---

6. *whilst . . . head:* so long as I have a taste for pleasure
("sweet tooth"); until I've degenerated into complete
senility.
7. Death of the vinegar—a pseudo-French oath.
8. Are in my power to bestow (because they are his

wards).
9. Befall, with the suggestion of a sexual "fall."
1. I'd give my dock-tailed bay horse and his trappings.
2. Contained broken teeth; of a boy's voice, "broken" at
puberty; of a horse, "broken" to the bit.

HELEN	Thanks, sir. All the rest is mute.°	*I will say no more*

75 LAFEU [*aside*] I had rather be in this choice than throw
ambs-ace[3] for my life.

HELEN [*to another* LORD] The honour, sir, that flames in your fair eyes,[4]
Before I speak, too threat'ningly replies.
Love make your fortunes twenty times above
Her that so wishes,° and her humble love.   *makes this wish*

SECOND LORD No better, if you please.

80 HELEN   My wish receive,
Which great Love grant. And so I take my leave.

LAFEU [*aside*] Do all they deny her?[5] An they were sons of mine
I'd have them whipped, or I would send them to th' Turk to
make eunuchs of.

85 HELEN [*to another* LORD] Be not afraid that I your hand should take;
I'll never do you wrong for your own sake.
Blessing upon your vows,° and in your bed   *marriage vows*
Find fairer fortune, if you ever wed.

LAFEU [*aside*] These boys are boys of ice, they'll none have her.

90 Sure they are bastards to the English, the French ne'er got°   *begot*
'em.

HELEN [*to another* LORD] You are too young, too happy, and too good
To make yourself a son out of my blood.

FOURTH LORD Fair one, I think not so.

95 LAFEU [*aside*] There's one grape° yet. I am sure thy father drunk   *fruit of a noble stock*
wine,[6] but if thou beest not an ass I am a youth of fourteen. I
have known° thee already.   *found out*

HELEN [*to* BERTRAM] I dare not say I take you, but I give
Me and my service ever whilst I live

100 Into your guiding power.—This is the man.

KING Why then, young Bertram, take her, she's thy wife.

BERTRAM My wife, my liege? I shall beseech your highness,
In such a business give me leave to use
The help of mine own eyes.

KING   Know'st thou not, Bertram,
What she has done for me?

105 BERTRAM   Yes, my good lord,
But never hope° to know why I should marry her.   *expect*

KING Thou know'st she has raised me from my sickly bed.

BERTRAM But follows it, my lord, to bring me down
Must answer for your raising? I know her well:

110 She had her breeding° at my father's charge.   *upbringing*
A poor physician's daughter, my wife? Disdain
Rather corrupt° me ever.   *ruin*

KING   'Tis only title° thou disdain'st in her, the which   *rank*
I can build up. Strange is it that our bloods,

115 Of colour, weight, and heat, poured all together,
Would quite confound distinction,[7] yet stands off °   *separated*
In differences so mighty. If she be
All that is virtuous, save what thou dislik'st—
'A poor physician's daughter'—thou dislik'st

---

3. Two aces (the lowest throw in dice); a joking understatement.
4. The pride of rank that shows in your look.
5. Either Lafeu, standing apart, misunderstands what is
happening, or (less probably) the lords' polite replies are

belied by their evident relief when Helen rejects them.
6. Was red-blooded (wine was supposed to turn directly
into blood).
7. Confuse the effort to distinguish.

120   Of virtue for the name.° But do not so.   *(lack of) a title*
    From lowest place when virtuous things proceed,
    The place is dignified by th' doer's deed.
    Where great additions° swell's, and virtue none,   *titles*
    It is a dropsied[8] honour. Good alone°   *in itself*
125   Is good without a name, vileness is so:
    The property° by what it is should go,   *quality*
    Not by the title. She is young, wise, fair.
    In these to nature she's immediate heir,
    And these breed honour. That is honour's scorn
130   Which challenges° itself as honour's born   *makes claims for*
    And is not like the sire; honours thrive
    When rather from our acts we them derive
    Than our foregoers. The mere word's a slave,
    Debauched° on every tomb, on every grave   *Debased*
135   A lying trophy,° and as oft is dumb   *memorial*
    Where dust and dammed° oblivion is the tomb   *stopped-up*
    Of honoured bones indeed. What should be said?
    If thou canst like this creature as a maid,
    I can create the rest. Virtue and she
140   Is her own dower;[9] honour and wealth from me.
    BERTRAM   I cannot love her, nor will strive° to do't.   *attempt*
    KING   Thou wrong'st thyself. If thou shouldst strive to choose—
    HELEN   That you are well restored, my lord, I'm glad.
    Let the rest go.
145   KING   My honour's at the stake, which to defeat
    I must produce my power. Here, take her hand,
    Proud, scornful boy, unworthy this good gift,
    That dost in vile misprision° shackle up   *wrongful disdain*
    My love and her desert; that canst not dream
150   We, poising us in her defective scale,
    Shall weigh thee to the beam;[1] that wilt not know
    It is in us° to plant thine honour where   *in our power*
    We please to have it grow. Check° thy contempt;   *Restrain*
    Obey our will, which travails in° thy good;   *labors for*
155   Believe not thy disdain, but presently
    Do thine own fortunes that obedient right
    Which both thy duty owes and our power claims,
    Or I will throw thee from my care for ever
    Into the staggers[2] and the careless lapse°   *fall; ruin*
160   Of youth and ignorance, both my revenge and hate
    Loosing upon thee in the name of justice
    Without all terms of° pity. Speak. Thine answer.   *any concessions to*
    BERTRAM [*kneeling*]   Pardon, my gracious lord, for I submit
    My fancy° to your eyes. When I consider   *perceptions; affection*
165   What great creation[3] and what dole° of honour   *portion*
    Flies where you bid it, I find that she, which late
    Was in my nobler thoughts most base, is now
    The praisèd of the King; who, so ennobled,
    Is as 'twere born so.

---

8. Unhealthily swollen.
9. *Virtue . . . dower:* Her own marriage gift is virtue and herself.
1. *We . . . beam:* Adding my weight to her deficient side

of the balance shall raise your (lighter) side. (The King uses the royal plural.)
2. Confusion (literally, a horse disease).
3. Creating of greatness.

KING   Take her by the hand
170   And tell her she is thine; to whom I promise
       A counterpoise, if not to thy estate
       A balance more replete.[4]
BERTRAM [*rising*]   I take her hand.
KING   Good fortune and the favour of the King
       Smile upon this contract, whose ceremony
175   Shall seem expedient on the now-born brief,[5]
       And be performed tonight. The solemn feast
       Shall more attend upon the coming space,
       Expecting absent friends.[6] As thou lov'st her
       Thy love's to me religious;° else, does err.   *properly devoted*
                 [*Flourish.*] *Exeunt* [*all but*] PAROLES *and* LAFEU,
                 [*who*] *stay behind, commenting on this wedding*
180 LAFEU   Do you hear, monsieur? A word with you.
     PAROLES   Your pleasure, sir.
     LAFEU   Your lord and master did well to make his recantation.
     PAROLES   Recantation? My lord? My master?
     LAFEU   Ay. Is it not a language I speak?
185 PAROLES   A most harsh one, and not to be understood without
          bloody succeeding.° My master?   *consequences*
     LAFEU   Are you companion to the Count Roussillon?
     PAROLES   To any count, to all counts, to what is man.°   *whatever is manly*
     LAFEU   To what is count's man;° count's master is of another   *servant*
190   style.
     PAROLES   You are too old, sir. Let it satisfy you,[7] you are too old.
     LAFEU   I must tell thee, sirrah, I write 'Man',[8] to which title age
          cannot bring thee.
     PAROLES   What I dare too well do I dare not do.[9]
195 LAFEU   I did think thee for two ordinaries° to be a pretty wise   *meals*
          fellow. Thou didst make tolerable vent° of thy travel; it might   *talk passibly*
          pass. Yet the scarves and the bannerets[1] about thee did mani-
          foldly dissuade me from believing thee a vessel of too great a
          burden.° I have now found thee;[2] when I lose thee again I care   *tonnage*
200   not. Yet art thou good for nothing but taking up,[3] and that
          thou'rt scarce worth.
     PAROLES   Hadst thou not the privilege of antiquity[4] upon thee—
     LAFEU   Do not plunge thyself too far in anger, lest thou hasten
          thy trial, which if—Lord have mercy on thee for a hen! So, my
205   good window of lattice,[5] fare thee well. Thy casement I need
          not open, for I look through thee. Give me thy hand.
     PAROLES   My lord, you give me most egregious indignity.
     LAFEU   Ay, with all my heart, and thou art worthy of it.
     PAROLES   I have not, my lord, deserved it.
210 LAFEU   Yes, good faith, every dram° of it, and I will not bate°   *one-eighth ounce / remit*
          thee a scruple.°   *one-third dram*
     PAROLES   Well, I shall be wiser.
     LAFEU   E'en as soon as thou canst, for thou hast to pull at a

---

4. *A counterpoise . . . replete*: A dowry equal to, if not
greater than, your own estate.
5. Shall expedite this newly made decree.
6. *The solemn . . . friends*: The wedding reception will be
postponed until relatives and friends can arrive.
7. Don't force me to avenge your insult.
8. I claim myself to be a man.
9. What I have the courage for (fighting), your age

prevents me from doing.
1. Streamers (which remind Lafeu of a ship's pennants).
2. Discovered what you are.
3. Rebuking; arresting; drafting as a soldier.
4. Exemption (from combat) because of age.
5. Paroles is easily seen through despite his affectation;
his fancy "latticework" of scarves suggests a lattice
window.

smack o'th' contrary.[6] If ever thou beest bound in thy scarf and
215   beaten thou shall find what it is to be proud of thy bondage. I
have a desire to hold° my acquaintance with thee, or rather my   maintain
knowledge, that I may say in the default,° 'He is a man I know'.   in the event

PAROLES   My lord, you do me most insupportable vexation.

LAFEU   I would it were hell-pains for thy sake, and my poor
220   doing[7] eternal; for doing[8] I am past, as I will by thee, in what
motion age will give me leave.   *Exit*

PAROLES   Well, thou hast a son shall take this disgrace off me.
Scurvy, old, filthy, scurvy lord. Well, I must be patient. There
is no fettering of authority. I'll beat him, by my life, if I can
225   meet him with any convenience, an° he were double and dou-   if
ble a lord. I'll have no more pity of his age than I would have
of—I'll beat him, an if I could but meet him again.

          Enter LAFEU

LAFEU   Sirrah, your lord and master's married. There's news for
you: you have a new mistress.

230   PAROLES   I most unfeignedly beseech your lordship to make
some reservation of your wrongs.° He is my good lord; whom I   restrain your abuse
serve above is my master.

LAFEU   Who? God?

PAROLES   Ay, sir.

235   LAFEU   The devil it is that's thy master. Why dost thou garter up[9]
thy arms o' this fashion? Dost make hose of thy sleeves? Do
other servants so? Thou wert best set thy lower part where thy
nose stands. By mine honour, if I were but two hours younger
I'd beat thee. Methink'st thou art a general offence° and every   public nuisance
240   man should beat thee. I think thou wast created for men to
breathe° themselves upon thee.   exercise

PAROLES   This is hard and undeserved measure, my lord.

LAFEU   Go to, sir. You were beaten in Italy for picking a kernel
out of a pomegranate,[1] you are a vagabond and no true travel-
245   ler, you are more saucy with lords and honourable personages
than the commission° of your birth and virtue gives you her-   warrant
aldry.° You are not worth another word, else I'd call you knave.   entitles you
I leave you.   *Exit*

PAROLES   Good, very good, it is so then. Good, very good, let it
250   be concealed awhile.

          [*Enter* BERTRAM]

BERTRAM   Undone and forfeited to cares for ever.

PAROLES   What's the matter, sweetheart?

BERTRAM   Although before the solemn priest I have sworn,
I will not bed her.

255   PAROLES   What, what, sweetheart?

BERTRAM   O my Paroles, they have married me.
I'll to the Tuscan wars and never bed her.

PAROLES   France is a dog-hole, and it no more merits
The tread of a man's foot. To th' wars!

260   BERTRAM   There's letters from my mother. What th'import is
I know not yet.

PAROLES   Ay, that would be known. To th' wars, my boy, to th' wars!

---

6. *pull . . . contrary:* drink a quantity of the opposite
quality.
7. My poor attempt to vex you.

8. Activity (with sexual suggestion).
9. Tie up (commenting again on Paroles's outfit).
1. *for picking . . . pomegranate:* on the slightest pretext.

He wears his honour in a box unseen°   (*with sexual innuendo*)
That hugs his kicky-wicky° here at home,   *darling*
265 Spending his manly marrow in her arms,
Which should sustain the bound and high curvet°   *leap*
Of Mars's fiery steed. To other regions!
France is a stable, we that dwell in't jades.[2]
Therefore to th' war.
270 BERTRAM   It shall be so. I'll send her to my house,
Acquaint my mother with my hate to her,
And wherefore I am fled, write to the King
That which I durst not speak. His present gift[3]
Shall furnish me to° those Italian fields   *equip me for*
275 Where noble fellows strike. Wars is no strife
To° the dark house and the detested wife.   *Compared to*
PAROLES   Will this *capriccio*° hold in thee? Art sure?   *caprice*
BERTRAM   Go with me to my chamber and advise me.
I'll send her straight away. Tomorrow
280 I'll to the wars, she to her single sorrow.
PAROLES   Why, these balls bound,[4] there's noise in it. 'Tis hard:
A young man married is a man that's marred.
Therefore away, and leave her bravely. Go.
The King has done you wrong, but hush 'tis so.°   *Exeunt*   *but don't say so*

2.4

Enter HELEN *reading a letter, and* [LAVATCH *the*] *clown*

HELEN   My mother greets me kindly. Is she well?
LAVATCH   She is not well,[1] but yet she has her health. She's very
merry, but yet she is not well. But thanks be given she's very
well and wants° nothing i'th' world. But yet she is not well.   *lacks*
5 HELEN   If she be very well, what does she ail
That she's not very well?
LAVATCH   Truly, she's very well indeed, but for two things.
HELEN   What two things?
LAVATCH   One, that she's not in heaven, whither God send her
10 quickly. The other, that she's in earth, from whence God send
her quickly.

Enter PAROLES

PAROLES   Bless you, my fortunate lady.
HELEN   I hope, sir, I have your good will to have
Mine own good fortunes.
15 PAROLES   You had my prayers to lead them° on, and to keep   *(your good fortunes)*
them on have them still.—O my knave, how does my old lady?
LAVATCH   So that you had her wrinkles and I her money, I
would she did[2] as you say.
PAROLES   Why, I say nothing.
20 LAVATCH   Marry, you are the wiser man, for many a man's°   *servant's*
tongue shakes out[3] his master's undoing. To say nothing, to do
nothing, to know nothing, and to have nothing, is to be a great
part of your title,[4] which is within a very little of nothing.
PAROLES   Away, thou'rt a knave.

---

2. Worthless horses; sluts. Paroles considers staying in
France effeminating.
3. Wedding present just bestowed.
4. Are bouncing now (from tennis); that is, that's how it
should be done.

2.4 Location: The King's palace.
1. The dead were said to be well, because in heaven.
2. Perhaps playing on "died."
3. Inadvertently tumbles out.
4. Status; playing on "tittle," "tiny amount."

25   LAVATCH   You should have said, sir, 'Before[5] a knave, thou'rt a
      knave'—that's 'Before me,[6] thou'rt a knave'. This had been
      truth, sir.

      PAROLES   Go to, thou art a witty fool. I have found° thee.   *seen through*

      LAVATCH   Did you find me in yourself, sir, or were you taught to
30   find me?

      PAROLES   In[7] myself, knave.

      LAVATCH   The search, sir, was profitable, and much fool may you
      find in you, even to the world's pleasure and the increase of
      laughter.

35   PAROLES [*to* HELEN]   A good knave, i'faith, and well fed.°   *"better fed than taught"*
      Madam, my lord will go away tonight.
      A very serious business calls on him.
      The great prerogative and rite of love,
      Which as your due time claims, he does acknowledge,
40   But puts it off to a compelled restraint:
      Whose want and whose delay is strewed with sweets,
      Which they distil now in the curbèd time,[8]
      To make the coming hour o'erflow with joy,
      And pleasure drown the brim.

      HELEN   What's his will else?

45   PAROLES   That you will take your instant leave o'th' King,
      And make° this haste as your own good proceeding,   *represent*
      Strengthened with what apology you think
      May make it probable need.[9]

      HELEN   What more commands he?

      PAROLES   That having this obtained, you presently
      Attend° his further pleasure.°   *Await / command*

50   HELEN   In everything
      I wait upon his will.

      PAROLES   I shall report it so.

      HELEN   I pray you.   *Exit* PAROLES [*at one door*]
      Come, sirrah.

                     Exeunt [*at another door*]

2.5

      Enter LAFEU *and* BERTRAM

      LAFEU   But I hope your lordship thinks not him a soldier.

      BERTRAM   Yes, my lord, and of very valiant approof.°   *proven valor*

      LAFEU   You have it from his own deliverance.°   *report*

      BERTRAM   And by other warranted testimony.

5   LAFEU   Then my dial° goes not true. I took this lark for a   *clock*
      bunting.[1]

      BERTRAM   I do assure you, my lord, he is very great in knowledge,
      and accordingly° valiant.   *correspondingly*

      LAFEU   I have then sinned against his experience and trans-
10   gressed against his valour—and my state that way is dangerous,[2]
      since I cannot yet find in my heart to repent. Here he comes. I
      pray you make us friends. I will pursue the amity.

---

5. Even in comparison with; in the presence of.
6. An expression like "Upon my soul"; Lavatch insinuates that Paroles is another knave.
7. By (reinterpreted in lines 31–33 by Lavatch). This
speech is not in F, but clearly some such reply should go
here.
8. *whose delay . . . time:* the delay of which multiplies its

sweetness, as distillation intensifies perfumes.
9. May make the need for haste probable.
2.5 Location: The King's palace.
1. I underestimated him (since the bunting looks like a
lark but does not sing).
2. In that respect risks damnation.

Enter PAROLES

PAROLES [*to* BERTRAM]   These things shall be done, sir.

LAFEU [*to* BERTRAM]   Pray you, sir, who's his tailor?[3]

15   PAROLES   Sir!

LAFEU   O, I know him well.[4] Ay, 'Sir', he; 'Sir''s a good workman,
       a very good tailor.

BERTRAM [*aside to* PAROLES]   Is she gone to the King?

PAROLES   She is.

20   BERTRAM   Will she away tonight?

PAROLES   As you'll have her.

BERTRAM   I have writ my letters, casketed my treasure,
       Given order for our horses, and tonight,
       When I should take possession of the bride,
25   End ere I do begin.

LAFEU [*aside*]   A good traveller is something° at the latter end of   *an asset*
       a dinner,[5] but one that lies three-thirds and uses a known truth
       to pass a thousand nothings with, should be once heard and
       thrice beaten. [*To* PAROLES]   God save you, captain.

30   BERTRAM [*to* PAROLES]   Is there any unkindness between my
       lord and you, monsieur?

PAROLES   I know not how I have deserved to run into my lord's
       displeasure.

LAFEU   You have made shift° to run into't, boots and spurs and   *arranged*
35   all, like him that leaped into the custard,[6] and out of it you'll
       run again, rather than suffer question for your residence.[7]

BERTRAM   It may be you have mistaken him, my lord.

LAFEU   And shall do so ever, though I took him at's prayers. Fare
       you well, my lord, and believe this of me: there can be no
40   kernel in this light nut. The soul of this man is his clothes.
       Trust him not in matter of heavy° consequence. I have kept of   *serious*
       them tame,[8] and know their natures.—Farewell, monsieur. I
       have spoken better of you than you have wit or will[9] to deserve
       at my hand, but we must do good against evil.   *Exit*

45   PAROLES   An idle lord, I swear.

BERTRAM   I think not so.

PAROLES   Why, do you not know him?

BERTRAM   Yes, I do know him well, and common speech
       Gives him a worthy pass.° Here comes my clog.[1]   *report*

Enter HELEN[, *attended*]

50   HELEN   I have, sir, as I was commanded from you,
       Spoke with the King, and have procured his leave
       For present parting; only he desires
       Some private speech with you.

BERTRAM   I shall obey his will.
       You must not marvel, Helen, at my course;
55   Which holds not colour° with the time, nor does   *is not in keeping*
       The ministration and requirèd office
       On my particular.[2] Prepared I was not
       For such a business, therefore am I found

---

3. Mocking Paroles's clothes.
4. Lafeu pretends "Sir" is the tailor's name.
5. When stories are welcome.
6. At the annual Lord Mayor's feast in London, a jester
leaped into an enormous custard pie.
7. Rather than explain how you got there.

8. These kinds of tame animals.
9. The intelligence or intention.
1. Weighty fetter, "ball and chain."
2. *The ministration . . . particular:* The particular duty
incumbent on me (as a husband).

So much unsettled. This drives me to entreat you
60 That presently you take your way for home,
And rather muse° than ask why I entreat you,   *wonder*
For my respects° are better than they seem,   *reasons*
And my appointments° have in them a need   *purposes*
Greater than shows itself at the first view
65 To you that know them not. This to my mother.
　　　　　[*He gives her a letter*]
'Twill be two days ere I shall see you, so
I leave you to your wisdom.
HELEN　　　　　　　　　Sir, I can nothing say
But that I am your most obedient servant.
BERTRAM　Come, come, no more of that.
HELEN　　　　　　　　　　　And ever shall
70 With true observance° seek to eke out that   *dutiful service*
Wherein toward me my homely stars° have failed   *humble birth*
To equal my great fortune.
BERTRAM　　　　　　　Let that go.
My haste is very great. Farewell. Hie° home.   *Hurry*
HELEN　Pray sir, your pardon.
BERTRAM　　　　　　　Well, what would you say?
75 HELEN　I am not worthy of the wealth I owe,°   *own*
Nor dare I say 'tis mine—and yet it is—
But like a timorous thief most fain° would steal   *gladly*
What law does vouch mine own.
BERTRAM　　　　　　　　What would you have?
HELEN　Something, and scarce so much: nothing indeed.
80 I would not tell you what I would, my lord. Faith, yes:
Strangers and foes do sunder° and not kiss.   *separate*
BERTRAM　I pray you, stay° not, but in haste to horse.   *delay*
HELEN　I shall not break your bidding, good my lord.—
Where are my other men?—Monsieur, farewell.
　　　　　Exeunt HELEN [*and attendants at one door*]
85 BERTRAM　Go thou toward home, where I will never come
Whilst I can shake my sword or hear the drum.—
Away, and for our flight.
PAROLES　　　　　　　Bravely. *Coraggio!*°   *Courage*
　　　　　Exeunt [*at another door*]

3.1

Flourish of trumpets. Enter the DUKE *of Florence* [*and
the*] *two* [LORDS DUMAINE], *with a troop of soldiers*
DUKE　So that from point to point now have you heard
The fundamental reasons of this war,
Whose great decision° hath much blood let forth,   *process of resolution*
And more thirsts after.
FIRST LORD DUMAINE　　　Holy seems the quarrel
5 Upon your grace's part; black and fearful
On the opposer.
DUKE　Therefore we marvel much our cousin France
Would in so just a business shut his bosom
Against our borrowing prayers.°   *entreaties for aid*
SECOND LORD DUMAINE　　Good my lord,
10 The reasons of our state I cannot yield

3.1 Location: Florence.

But° like a common and an outward man°	*Except / an outsider*
That the great figure° of a council frames	*image*
By self-unable motion;° therefore dare not	*inadequate guess*
Say what I think of it, since I have found	
15 Myself in my incertain grounds° to fail	*conjectures*
As often as I guessed.	

DUKE   Be it his pleasure.

FIRST LORD DUMAINE   But I am sure the younger of our nation,

That surfeit on° their ease, will day by day   *have had too much of*
Come here for physic.[1]

DUKE   Welcome shall they be,

20 And all the honours that can fly° from us   *proceed*
Shall on them settle. You know your places well;
When better fall,[2] for your avails they fell.
Tomorrow to the field.   *Flourish. [Exeunt]*

3.2

Enter the COUNTESS [*with a letter,*] *and* [LAVATCH *the*]
        clown

COUNTESS   It hath happened all as I would have had it, save that
he comes not along with her.

LAVATCH   By my troth, I take my young lord to be a very melancholy man.

5 COUNTESS   By what observance, I pray you?

LAVATCH   Why, he will look upon his boot and sing, mend° the   *adjust*
ruff° and sing, ask questions and sing, pick his teeth and sing.   *boot's cuff*
I know a man that had this trick of melancholy sold a goodly
manor for a song.

10 COUNTESS   Let me see what he writes, and when he means to
come.

        [*She opens the letter and reads*]

LAVATCH [*aside*]   I have no mind to Isbel since I was at court.
Our old lings[1] and our Isbels o'th' country are nothing like your
old ling and your Isbels o'th' court. The brains of my Cupid's
15 knocked out, and I begin to love as an old man loves money:
with no stomach.°   *appetite*

COUNTESS   What have we here?

LAVATCH   E'en that you have there.   *Exit*

COUNTESS [*reads the letter aloud*]   'I have sent you a daughter-in-
20 law. She hath recovered° the King and undone me. I have wed-   *cured*
ded her, not bedded her, and sworn to make the "not"° eternal.   *punning on "knot"*
You shall hear I am run away; know it before the report come.
If there be breadth enough in the world I will hold a long
distance. My duty to you.

25   Your unfortunate son,
                                             Bertram.'

This is not well, rash and unbridled boy,
To fly the favours of so good a King,
To pluck° his indignation on thy head   *pull down*
30 By the misprizing° of a maid too virtuous   *undervaluing*
For the contempt of empire.°   *an emperor*

---

1. Cure (through bloodletting).
2. When better places fall vacant.

3.2 Location: Roussillon, Bertram's palace.
1. Salt cod (slang for "penis").

Enter [LAVATCH *the*] *clown*

LAVATCH O madam, yonder is heavy° news within, between two   *sad*
soldiers and my young lady.

COUNTESS What is the matter?

35 LAVATCH Nay, there is some comfort in the news, some comfort.
Your son will not be killed so soon as I thought he would.

COUNTESS Why should he be killed?

LAVATCH So say I, madam—if he run away, as I hear he does.
The danger is in standing to't;² that's the loss of men, though it
40 be the getting° of children. Here they come will tell you more.   *begetting*
For my part, I only heard your son was run away.   [*Exit*]

Enter HELEN [*with a letter,*] *and* [*the*] *two* [LORDS
DUMAINE]

SECOND LORD DUMAINE [*to the* COUNTESS] Save you, good
madam.

HELEN Madam, my lord is gone, for ever gone.

45 FIRST LORD DUMAINE Do not say so.

COUNTESS [*to* HELEN] Think upon patience.—Pray you, gentlemen,
I have felt so many quirks of joy and grief
That the first face° of neither on the start°   *appearance / suddenly*
Can woman me unto't.³ Where is my son, I pray you?

FIRST LORD DUMAINE Madam, he's gone to serve the Duke of
50 Florence.
We met him thitherward,° for thence we came,   *going there*
And, after some dispatch° in hand at court,   *business*
Thither we bend again.

HELEN Look on his letter, madam: here's my passport.°   *vagabond's license*
[*She reads aloud*]

55 'When thou canst get the ring upon my finger, which never
shall come off, and show me a child begotten of thy body that
I am father to, then call me husband; but in such a "then" I
write a "never".'
This is a dreadful sentence.

COUNTESS Brought you this letter, gentlemen?

60 FIRST LORD DUMAINE   Ay, madam,
And for the contents' sake are sorry for our pains.

COUNTESS I prithee, lady, have a better cheer.
If thou engrossest° all the griefs are thine   *monopolize*
Thou robb'st me of a moiety.° He was my son,   *share*
65 But I do wash his name out of my blood,
And thou art all my° child.—Towards Florence is he?   *my only*

FIRST LORD DUMAINE Ay, madam.

COUNTESS   And to be a soldier?

FIRST LORD DUMAINE Such is his noble purpose, and—believe't—
The Duke will lay upon him all the honour
That good convenience claims.°   *That is suitable*

70 COUNTESS   Return you thither?

SECOND LORD DUMAINE Ay, madam, with the swiftest wing of speed.

HELEN 'Till I have no wife, I have nothing in France.'
'Tis bitter.

COUNTESS Find you that there?

75 HELEN Ay, madam.

---

2. In standing one's ground (in love and war).   3. Can make me weep like a woman.

SECOND LORD DUMAINE   'Tis but the boldness of his hand,
    Haply,° which his heart was not consenting to.   *Perhaps*
COUNTESS   Nothing in France until he have no wife?
    There's nothing here that is too good for him
80   But only she, and she deserves a lord
    That twenty such rude boys might tend upon
    And call her, hourly, mistress. Who was with him?
SECOND LORD DUMAINE   A servant only, and a gentleman
    Which I have sometime known.
85 COUNTESS   Paroles, was it not?
SECOND LORD DUMAINE   Ay, my good lady, he.
COUNTESS   A very tainted fellow, and full of wickedness.
    My son corrupts a well-derivèd° nature   *nobly born*
    With his inducement.
SECOND LORD DUMAINE   Indeed, good lady,
90   The fellow has a deal of that too much,
    Which holds him much to have.[4]
COUNTESS   You're welcome, gentlemen.
    I will entreat you when you see my son
    To tell him that his sword can never win
    The honour that he loses. More I'll entreat you
    Written to bear along.
95 FIRST LORD DUMAINE   We serve you, madam,
    In that and all your worthiest affairs.
COUNTESS   Not so, but° as we change° our courtesies.   *except / exchange*
    Will you draw near?   *Exeunt [all but* HELEN]
HELEN   'Till I have no wife I have nothing in France.'
100 Nothing in France until he has no wife.
    Thou shalt have none, Roussillon, none in France;
    Then hast thou all again. Poor lord, is't I
    That chase thee from thy country and expose
    Those tender limbs of thine to the event°   *outcome*
105 Of the none-sparing war? And is it I
    That drive thee from the sportive court, where thou
    Wast shot at with fair eyes, to be the mark
    Of smoky muskets? O you leaden messengers°   *(bullets)*
    That ride upon the violent speed of fire,
110 Fly with false aim, cleave the still-piecing air[5]
    That sings with piercing, do not touch my lord.
    Whoever shoots at him, I set him there.
    Whoever charges on his forward° breast,   *brave; proud; advancing*
    I am the caitiff° that do hold him to't,   *wretch*
115 And though I kill him not, I am the cause
    His death was so effected. Better 'twere
    I met the ravin° lion when he roared   *ravenous*
    With sharp constraint of hunger; better 'twere
    That all the miseries which nature owes°   *human nature possesses*
120 Were mine at once. No, come thou home, Roussillon,
    Whence honour but of danger wins a scar,[6]
    As oft it loses all. I will be gone;
    My being here it is that holds thee hence.

---

4. Has all too much persuasive power, which greatly
profits him.
5. Air that is constantly repairing itself.

6. *Whence . . . scar:* From where honor at best can win a
scar.

Shall I stay here to do't? No, no, although
125 The air of paradise did fan the house
And angels officed all.[7] I will be gone,
That pitiful° rumour may report my flight   *pitying*
To consolate° thine ear. Come night, end day;   *console*
For with the dark, poor thief, I'll steal away.   *Exit*

3.3

Flourish. Enter the DUKE *of Florence,* [BERTRAM,] *a
drum[mer] and trumpet[ers], soldiers, and* PAROLES

DUKE [*to* BERTRAM]   The general of our horse° thou art, and we,   *cavalry*
Great in our hope, lay° our best love and credence°   *wager / trust*
Upon thy promising fortune.

BERTRAM   Sir, it is
A charge° too heavy for my strength, but yet   *load*
5 We'll strive to bear it for your worthy sake
To th'extreme edge of hazard.°   *limit of danger*

DUKE   Then go thou forth,
And Fortune play upon thy prosperous helm
As thy auspicious mistress.

BERTRAM   This very day,
Great Mars, I put myself into thy file.°   *line of soldiers*
10 Make me but like my thoughts, and I shall prove
A lover of thy drum, hater of love.   *Exeunt*

3.4

Enter the COUNTESS *and* [REYNALDO *her*] *steward* [*with
a letter*]

COUNTESS   Alas! And would you take the letter of her?
Might you not know she would do as she has done,
By sending me a letter? Read it again.

REYNALDO [*reads the*] *letter*[1]   'I am Saint Jaques' pilgrim,[2] thither gone.
5   Ambitious love hath so in me offended
That barefoot plod I the cold ground upon
     With sainted vow my faults to have amended.
Write, write, that from the bloody course of war
     My dearest master, your dear son, may hie.°   *hurry*
10 Bless him at home in peace, whilst I from far
     His name with zealous fervour sanctify.°   *(in prayer)*
His taken° labours bid him me forgive;   *undertaken*
     I, his despiteful Juno,[3] sent him forth
From courtly friends, with camping foes to live,
15   Where death and danger dogs the heels of worth.
He is too good and fair for death and me;
     Whom[4] I myself embrace to set him free.'

COUNTESS   Ah, what sharp stings are in her mildest words!
Reynaldo, you did never lack advice° so much   *discretion*
20 As letting her pass so. Had I spoke with her,
I could have well diverted her intents,
Which thus she hath prevented.

---

7. Performed all household tasks.
3.3 Location: Florence.
3.4 Location: Roussillon, Bertram's palace.
1. The letter forms a sonnet.
2. A pilgrim to the shrine of St. James (presumably in

Compostella in Spain).
3. Cruel goddess of marriage (who oppressed Hercules
by assigning him twelve supposedly impossible tasks).
4. Death (but the suggestion "Bertram" may be deliberate).

REYNALDO   Pardon me, madam.
      If I had given you this at over-night°   *last night*
      She might have been o'erta'en—and yet she writes
      Pursuit would be but vain.
25   COUNTESS   What angel shall
      Bless this unworthy husband? He cannot thrive
      Unless her prayers, whom heaven delights to hear
      And loves to grant, reprieve him from the wrath
      Of greatest justice. Write, write, Reynaldo,
30   To this unworthy husband of his wife.
      Let every word weigh heavy of° her worth,   *emphasize*
      That he does weigh too light; my greatest grief,
      Though little he do feel it, set down sharply.
      Dispatch the most convenient messenger.
35   When haply° he shall hear that she is gone,   *Perhaps when*
      He will return, and hope I may that she,
      Hearing so much, will speed her foot again,
      Led hither by pure love. Which of them both
      Is dearest to me I have no skill in sense
40   To make distinction. Provide° this messenger.   *Make ready*
      My heart is heavy and mine age is weak;
      Grief would have tears, and sorrow bids me speak.   *Exeunt*

3.5

A tucket° afar off. Enter [an] old WIDOW *of Florence, her*   *trumpet call*
*daughter [*DIANA*], and* MARIANA, *with other citizens*
WIDOW   Nay, come, for if they do approach the city we shall
      lose° all the sight.   *miss*
DIANA   They say the French Count has done most honourable
      service.
5   WIDOW   It is reported that he has taken their° greatest com-   *(the Sienese)*
      mander, and that with his own hand he slew the Duke's
      brother. [*Tucket*] We have lost our labour; they are gone a con-
      trary way. Hark. You may know by their trumpets.
MARIANA   Come, let's return° again, and suffice ourselves with   *go home*
10   the report of it.—Well, Diana, take heed of this French earl.
      The honour of a maid is her name,° and no legacy is so rich as   *reputation*
      honesty.°   *chastity*
WIDOW [*to* DIANA]   I have told my neighbour how you have been
      solicited by a gentleman, his companion.
15   MARIANA   I know that knave, hang him! One Paroles. A filthy
      officer° he is in those suggestions° for the young earl. Beware   *agent / solicitings*
      of them, Diana; their promises, enticements, oaths, tokens, and
      all their engines° of lust, are not the things they go[1] under.   *devices*
      Many a maid hath been seduced by them; and the misery is,
20   example, that so terrible shows in the wreck of maidenhood,
      cannot for all that dissuade succession,° but that they are limed   *prevent it recurring*
      with the twigs[2] that threatens them. I hope I need not to advise
      you further, but I hope your own grace° will keep you where   *virtue*
      you are, though there were no further danger° known but the   *(pregnancy)*
25   modesty which is so lost.
DIANA   You shall not need to fear° me.   *fear for*

3.5 Location: Florence.   2. *they . . . twigs:* other virgins are entrapped (sticky
1. Concealed themselves.   lime was applied to twigs to catch birds).

Enter HELEN [*dressed as a pilgrim*]

WIDOW   I hope so. Look, here comes a pilgrim. I know she will
lie at my house; thither they send one another. I'll question
her.

30   God save you, pilgrim. Whither are you bound?

HELEN   To Saint Jaques le Grand.
Where do the palmers° lodge, I do beseech you?   pilgrims

WIDOW   At the 'Saint Francis' here beside the port.°   city gate

HELEN   Is this the way?

WIDOW   Ay, marry, is't.
[*Sound of*] *a march, far off*

35   Hark you, they come this way. If you will tarry,
Holy pilgrim, but till the troops come by,
I will conduct you where you shall be lodged,
The rather for I think I know your hostess
As ample° as myself.   well

40   HELEN   Is it yourself ?

WIDOW   If you shall please so, pilgrim.

HELEN   I thank you, and will stay upon° your leisure.   await

WIDOW   You came, I think, from France?

HELEN   I did so.

WIDOW   Here you shall see a countryman of yours
That has done worthy service.

45   HELEN   His name, I pray you?

DIANA   The Count Roussillon. Know you such a one?

HELEN   But by the ear, that hears most nobly of him;
His face I know not.

DIANA   Whatsome'er° he is,   Whatever kind of man
He's bravely taken° here. He stole from France,   highly regarded

50   As 'tis reported; for the King had married him
Against his liking. Think you it is so?

HELEN   Ay, surely, mere° the truth. I know his lady.   simply

DIANA   There is a gentleman that serves the Count
Reports but coarsely of her.

HELEN   What's his name?

DIANA   Monsieur Paroles.

55   HELEN   O, I believe with him:
In argument of praise,³ or to° the worth   compared to
Of the great Count himself, she is too mean°   lowly
To have her name repeated. All her deserving°   Her only merit
Is a reservèd honesty,° and that   preserved chastity
I have not heard examined.°   questioned

60   DIANA   Alas, poor lady.
'Tis a hard bondage to become the wife
Of a detesting lord.

WIDOW   I warr'nt, good creature, wheresoe'er she is
Her heart weighs sadly. This young maid might do her
A shrewd turn° if she pleased.   nasty trick

65   HELEN   How do you mean?
Maybe the amorous Count solicits her
In the unlawful purpose.

WIDOW   He does indeed,
And brokes° with all that can in such a suit   bargains

---

3. As a topic of praise.

Corrupt the tender honour of a maid.
70 But she is armed for him, and keeps her guard
In honestest defence.
MARIANA   The gods forbid else.

Enter, [with] drum and colours, [BERTRAM,] PAROLES,
and the whole army

WIDOW   So, now they come.
That is Antonio, the Duke's eldest son;
That, Escalus.
HELEN   Which is the Frenchman?
75 DIANA   He—
That with the plume. 'Tis a most gallant fellow.
I would he loved his wife. If he were honester[4]
He were much goodlier. Is't not
A handsome gentleman?
80 HELEN   I like him well.
DIANA   'Tis pity he is not honest.
Yond's that same knave that leads him to those places.
Were I his lady, I would poison
That vile rascal.
HELEN   Which is he?
DIANA   That jackanapes°   *monkey*
85 With scarves. Why is he melancholy?
HELEN   Perchance he's hurt i'th' battle.
PAROLES [*aside*]   Lose our drum?[5] Well.
MARIANA   He's shrewdly° vexed at something.   *badly*
Look, he has spied us.
WIDOW [*to* PAROLES]   Marry, hang you!
90 MARIANA [*to* PAROLES]   And your courtesy,° for a ring-carrier.°   *bow / go-between*

Exeunt [BERTRAM, PAROLES, and the army]

WIDOW   The troop is past. Come, pilgrim, I will bring you
Where you shall host.° Of enjoined penitents[6]   *lodge*
There's four or five to great Saint Jaques bound
Already at my house.
HELEN   I humbly thank you.
95 Please it° this matron and this gentle maid   *If it please*
To eat with us tonight, the charge and thanking
Shall be for me. And to requite you further,
I will bestow some precepts of° this virgin   *advice on*
Worthy the note.
WIDOW *and* MARIANA   We'll take your offer kindly.°   *Exeunt*   *gratefully*

3.6

Enter [BERTRAM] and the [two Captains DUMAINE]

SECOND LORD DUMAINE [*to* BERTRAM]   Nay, good my lord, put
him to't.° Let him have his way.   *(to the test)*
FIRST LORD DUMAINE [*to* BERTRAM]   If your lordship find him not
a hilding,° hold me no more in your respect.   *worthless wretch*
5 SECOND LORD DUMAINE [*to* BERTRAM]   On my life, my lord, a
bubble.
BERTRAM   Do you think I am so far deceived in him?
SECOND LORD DUMAINE   Believe it, my lord. In mine own direct

---

4. More honorable (and chaste).
5. A military disgrace.

6. Those sworn to a penitential pilgrimage.
3.6 Location: The Florentine camp.

knowledge—without any malice, but to speak of him as° my   *as if he were*
10   kinsman—he's a most notable coward, an infinite and endless
liar, an hourly promise-breaker, the owner of no one good
quality worthy your lordship's entertainment.°   *patronage*
   FIRST LORD DUMAINE [*to* BERTRAM] It were fit you knew him,
lest reposing° too far in his virtue, which he hath not, he might   *trusting*
15   at some great and trusty business, in a main danger, fail you.
   BERTRAM   I would I knew in what particular action to try him.
   FIRST LORD DUMAINE   None better than to let him fetch off° his   *back*
drum, which you hear him so confidently undertake to do.
   SECOND LORD DUMAINE [*to* BERTRAM]   I, with a troop of Floren-
20   tines, will suddenly surprise° him. Such I will have whom I am   *ambush*
sure he knows not from the enemy; we will bind and hood-
wink° him so, that he shall suppose no other but that he is   *blindfold*
carried into the laager° of the adversary's when we bring him   *camp*
to our own tents. Be but your lordship present at his examina-
25   tion: if he do not, for the promise of his life and in the highest
compulsion of base fear, offer to betray you, and deliver all the
intelligence° in his power against you, and that with the divine   *information*
forfeit of his soul upon oath, never trust my judgement in anything.
30   FIRST LORD DUMAINE [*to* BERTRAM]   O, for the love of laughter,
let him fetch his drum. He says he has a stratagem for't. When
your lordship sees the bottom° of his success in't, and to what   *entirety*
metal this counterfeit lump of ore will be melted, if you give
him not John Drum's entertainment,[1] your inclining° cannot   *partiality*
35   be removed. Here he comes.
        Enter PAROLES
   SECOND LORD DUMAINE   O [*aside*] for the love of laughter
[*aloud*] hinder not the honour of his design; let him fetch off
his drum in any hand.°   *case*
   BERTRAM [*to* PAROLES]   How now, monsieur? This drum sticks
40   sorely in your disposition.°   *troubles you sorely*
   FIRST LORD DUMAINE   A pox on't, let it go. 'Tis but a drum.
   PAROLES   But a drum? Is't but a drum? A drum so lost! There
was excellent command: to charge in with our horse° upon our   *cavalry*
own wings° and to rend our own soldiers!   *flank units*
45   FIRST LORD DUMAINE   That was not to be blamed in the command
of the service. It was a disaster° of war that Caesar himself   *an accident*
could not have prevented, if he had been there to command.
   BERTRAM   Well, we cannot greatly condemn our success.[2] Some
dishonour we had in the loss of that drum, but it is not to be
50   recovered.
   PAROLES   It might have been recovered.
   BERTRAM   It might, but it is not now.
   PAROLES   It *is* to be recovered. But that the merit of service is
seldom attributed to the true and exact performer, I would have
55   that drum or another, or '*hic iacet*'.[3]
   BERTRAM   Why, if you have a stomach,° to't, monsieur. If you   *an inclination*
think your mystery in stratagem° can bring this instrument of   *tactical skill*
honour again into his native quarter,° be magnanimous° in the   *back home / valiant*

---

1. *John Drum's entertainment*: ignominious dismissal
(proverbial).
2. The general success of the battle.

3. Here lies (Latin): Paroles imagines himself dying in an
attempt to recover the drum.

enterprise and go on. I will grace° the attempt for a worthy   *honor*
60   exploit. If you speed° well in it, the Duke shall both speak of it   *succeed*
and extend to you what further becomes his greatness, even to
the utmost syllable of your worthiness.

PAROLES   By the hand of a soldier, I will undertake it.

BERTRAM   But you must not now slumber in it.

65 PAROLES   I'll about it this evening, and I will presently pen down
my dilemmas,[4] encourage myself in my certainty, put myself
into my mortal preparation;[5] and by midnight look to hear further from me.

BERTRAM   May I be bold to acquaint his grace you are gone
70   about it?

PAROLES   I know not what the success will be, my lord, but the
attempt I vow.

BERTRAM   I know thou'rt valiant, and to the possibility° of thy   *utmost capacity*
soldiership will subscribe° for thee. Farewell.   *vouch*

75 PAROLES   I love not many words.   *Exit*

SECOND LORD DUMAINE   No more than a fish loves water. [*To*
BERTRAM] Is not this a strange fellow, my lord, that so confidently seems to undertake this business, which he knows is not
to be done? Damns himself to do, and dares better be damned
80   than to do't.

FIRST LORD DUMAINE [*to* BERTRAM]   You do not know him, my
lord, as we do. Certain it is that he will steal himself into a
man's favour, and for a week escape a great deal of discoveries,[6]
but when you find him out, you have° him ever after.   *understand*

85 BERTRAM   Why, do you think he will make no deed° at all of this   *endeavor*
that so seriously he does address himself unto?

SECOND LORD DUMAINE   None in the world, but return with an
invention,° and clap upon you two or three probable° lies. But   *tall tale / plausible*
we have almost embosked[7] him. You shall see his fall tonight;
90   for indeed he is not for your lordship's respect.

FIRST LORD DUMAINE [*to* BERTRAM]   We'll make you some sport
with the fox ere we case° him. He was first smoked[8] by the old   *skin*
Lord Lafeu. When his disguise and he is parted, tell me what
a sprat° you shall find him, which you shall see this very night.   *tiny fish*

95 SECOND LORD DUMAINE   I must go look my twigs.° He shall be   *see to my bird trap*
caught.

BERTRAM   Your brother, he shall go along with me.

SECOND LORD DUMAINE   As't please your lordship. I'll leave you.
                                                [*Exit*]

BERTRAM   Now will I lead you to the house, and show you
100   The lass I spoke of.

FIRST LORD DUMAINE   But you say she's honest.°   *chaste*

BERTRAM   That's all the fault. I spoke with her but once
And found her wondrous cold, but I sent to her
By this same coxcomb that we have i'th' wind°   *are stalking*
105   Tokens and letters, which she did re-send,°   *return*
And this is all I have done. She's a fair creature.
Will you go see her?

FIRST LORD DUMAINE   With all my heart, my lord.   *Exeunt*

---

4. I will immediately reflect on my difficulties.
5. Spiritual preparation for death; readying of fatal
weapons.

6. *escape . . . discoveries:* largely get away with it.
7. Cornered; run to exhaustion (hunting term).
8. Forced into the open, like a fox smoked from its hole.

3.7

Enter HELEN *and the* WIDOW

HELEN   If you misdoubt° me that I am not she,   *doubt*
    I know not how I shall assure you further
    But I shall lose the grounds I work upon.[1]
WIDOW   Though my estate° be fall'n, I was well born,   *fortune*
5   Nothing acquainted with these businesses,
    And would not put my reputation now
    In any staining act.
HELEN   Nor would I wish you.
    First give me trust° the Count he is my husband,   *trust me that*
    And what to your sworn counsel° I have spoken   *secrecy*
10   Is so° from word to word, and then you cannot,   *true*
    By° the good aid that I of you shall borrow,   *With respect to*
    Err in bestowing it.
WIDOW   I should believe you,
    For you have showed me that which well approves°   *confirms*
    You're great in fortune.
HELEN   Take this purse of gold,
15   And let me buy your friendly help thus far,
    Which I will over-pay, and pay again
    When I have found it.° The Count he woos your daughter,   *succeeded*
    Lays down his wanton siege before her beauty,
    Resolved to carry° her. Let her in fine° consent,   *conquer / the end*
20   As we'll direct her how 'tis best to bear° it.   *manage*
    Now his important blood° will naught deny   *importunate passion*
    That she'll demand. A ring the County° wears,   *Count*
    That downward hath succeeded in his house
    From son to son some four or five descents°   *generations*
25   Since the first father wore it. This ring he holds
    In most rich choice;° yet in his idle° fire   *estimation / crazy*
    To buy his will° it would not seem too dear,   *lust*
    Howe'er repented after.
WIDOW   Now I see the bottom of your purpose.
30 HELEN   You see it lawful then. It is no more
    But that your daughter ere she seems as won
    Desires this ring; appoints him an encounter;
    In fine, delivers me to fill the time,°   *keep the appointment*
    Herself most chastely absent. After,
35   To marry her° I'll add three thousand crowns   *As her dowry*
    To what is passed already.
WIDOW   I have yielded.
    Instruct my daughter how she shall persever,
    That time and place with this deceit so lawful
    May prove coherent.° Every night he comes   *fitting*
40   With musics of all sorts, and songs composed
    To her unworthiness.[2] It nothing steads° us   *avails*
    To chide him from our eaves, for he persists
    As if his life lay on't.
HELEN   Why then tonight
    Let us essay° our plot, which if it speed°   *attempt / succeed*

3.7 Location: The widow's house, Florence.
1. *But . . . upon:* Unless I give up what my plot depends
upon (and reveal my identity to Bertram).

2. To my humble daughter; to persuade my daughter to
unworthy deeds.

45   Is wicked meaning° in a lawful deed   *intention (Bertram's)*
    And lawful meaning° in a wicked act,   *intention (Helen's)*
    Where both not sin, and yet a sinful fact.³
    But let's about it.   [*Exeunt*]

4.1

Enter [SECOND LORD DUMAINE], *with five or six other
soldiers, in ambush*

SECOND LORD DUMAINE   He can come no other way but by this
    hedge corner. When you sally° upon him, speak what terrible°   *rush / ferocious*
    language you will. Though you understand it not yourselves,
    no matter, for we must not seem to understand him, unless°   *except*
5   some one among us, whom we must produce for an interpreter.
INTERPRETER   Good captain, let me be th'interpreter.
SECOND LORD DUMAINE   Art not acquainted with him? Knows he
    not thy voice?
INTERPRETER   No, sir, I warrant you.
10 SECOND LORD DUMAINE   But what linsey-woolsey¹ hast thou to
    speak to us again?
INTERPRETER   E'en such as you speak to me.
SECOND LORD DUMAINE   He must think us some band of strang-
    ers° i'th' adversary's entertainment.° Now he hath a smack² of   *foreigners / service*
15   all neighbouring languages, therefore we must every one be a
    man of his own fancy. Not to know what we speak one to
    another, so° we seem to know, is to know straight° our purpose: *provided / suffices for*
    choughs'° language, gabble enough and good enough. As for   *crows*
    you, interpreter, you must seem very politic.° But couch,° ho!   *cunning / hide*
20   Here he comes, to beguile° two hours in a sleep, and then to   *while away*
    return and swear the lies he forges.
            [*They hide.*] *Enter* PAROLES. [*Clock strikes*]
PAROLES   Ten o'clock. Within these three hours 'twill be time
    enough to go home. What shall I say I have done? It must be a
    very plausive° invention that carries it. They begin to smoke°   *plausible / suspect*
25   me, and disgraces have of late knocked too often at my door. I
    find my tongue is too foolhardy, but my heart hath the fear of
    Mars before it, and of his creatures, not daring the reports of
    my tongue.³
SECOND LORD DUMAINE [*aside*]   This is the first truth that e'er
30   thine own tongue was guilty of.
PAROLES   What the devil should move me to undertake the
    recovery of this drum, being not ignorant of the impossibility,
    and knowing I had no such purpose? I must give myself some
    hurts, and say I got them in exploit. Yet slight ones will not
35   carry it. They will say, 'Came you off with so little?' And great
    ones I dare not give. Wherefore, what's the instance?° Tongue,   *evidence*
    I must put you into a butter-woman's⁴ mouth, and buy myself
    another of Bajazet's mute,⁵ if you prattle me into these perils.
SECOND LORD DUMAINE [*aside*]   Is it possible he should know
40   what he is, and be that he is?

---

3. Deed (as Bertram intends it).
4.1 Location: Outside the Florentine camp.
1. Hodgepodge (literally, cloth of mixed linen and wool
fibers).
2. Smattering.

3. *my heart . . . tongue:* I am frightened by the god of war
and his followers, not daring to do what I have boasted.
4. Proverbially talkative.
5. *of . . . mute:* from the Turkish sultan's servant (whose
tongue was cut off to ensure his discretion).

PAROLES I would the cutting of my garments would serve the
turn, or the breaking of my Spanish sword.

SECOND LORD DUMAINE [*aside*] We cannot afford° you so.   *accommodate*

PAROLES Or the baring° of my beard, and to say it was in strat-   *shaving*
45 agem.

SECOND LORD DUMAINE [*aside*] 'Twould not do.

PAROLES Or to drown my clothes, and say I was stripped.

SECOND LORD DUMAINE [*aside*] Hardly serve.

PAROLES Though I swore I leapt from the window of the citadel?

50 SECOND LORD DUMAINE [*aside*] How deep?

PAROLES Thirty fathom.°   *fathom = 6 feet*

SECOND LORD DUMAINE [*aside*] Three great oaths would scarce
make that be believed.

PAROLES I would I had any drum of the enemy's. I would swear
55 I recovered it.

SECOND LORD DUMAINE [*aside*] You shall hear one anon.°   *immediately*

PAROLES A drum now of the enemy's—
        Alarum° within. [*The ambush rushes forth*]   *Call to arms*

SECOND LORD DUMAINE *Throca movousus, cargo, cargo, cargo.*

SOLDIERS [*severally*] *Cargo, cargo, cargo, villianda par corbo,*
60 *cargo.*

        [*They seize and blindfold him*]

PAROLES O ransom, ransom, do not hide mine eyes.

INTERPRETER *Boskos thromuldo boskos.*

PAROLES I know you are the Moscows° regiment,   *Russian*
And I shall lose my life for want of language.
65 If there be here German or Dane, Low Dutch,
Italian, or French, let him speak to me,
I'll discover° that which shall undo the Florentine.   *reveal*

INTERPRETER *Boskos vauvado.*—
I understand thee, and can speak thy tongue.—
70 *Kerelybonto.*—Sir,
Betake thee to thy faith,° for seventeen poniards   *Say your prayers*
Are at thy bosom.

PAROLES   O!

INTERPRETER   O pray, pray, pray!—
Manka revania dulche?

SECOND LORD DUMAINE *Oscorbidulchos volivorco.*

75 INTERPRETER The general is content to spare thee yet,
And, hoodwinked[6] as thou art, will lead thee on[7]
To gather from thee. Haply° thou mayst inform   *Perhaps*
Something to save thy life.

PAROLES   O let me live,
And all the secrets of our camp I'll show,
80 Their force, their purposes; nay, I'll speak that
Which you will wonder at.

INTERPRETER   But wilt thou faithfully?[8]

PAROLES If I do not, damn me.

INTERPRETER   *Acordo linta.*—
Come on, thou art granted space.°   *breathing space*
        Exeunt [*all but* SECOND LORD DUMAINE *and a* SOLDIER]
        A short alarum within

6. Blindfolded; punning on "deceived."   8. Truthfully; loyally (ironic).
7. Will take you elsewhere; will deceive you further.

SECOND LORD DUMAINE   Go tell the Count Roussillon and my brother
85   We have caught the woodcock,[9] and will keep him muffled°   blindfolded
    Till we do hear from them.
SOLDIER   Captain, I will.
SECOND LORD DUMAINE   A° will betray us all unto ourselves.   He
    Inform on° that.   Report
SOLDIER   So I will, sir.
SECOND LORD DUMAINE   Till then I'll keep him dark and safely
90   locked.

                            Exeunt [severally]

                    4.2
    Enter BERTRAM and the maid called DIANA
BERTRAM   They told me that your name was Fontibel.
DIANA   No, my good lord, Diana.
BERTRAM   Titled° goddess,   Called
    And worth it, with addition.[1] But, fair soul,
    In your fine frame hath love no quality?
5   If the quick° fire of youth light not your mind,   vital
    You are no maiden but a monument.°   statue
    When you are dead you should be such a one
    As you are now, for you are cold and stern,
    And now you should be as your mother was
10   When your sweet self was got.°   begotten
DIANA   She then was honest.
BERTRAM   So should you be.
DIANA   No.
    My mother did but duty; such, my lord,
    As you owe to your wife.
BERTRAM   No more o' that.
15   I prithee do not strive against my vows.[2]
    I was compelled to her, but I love thee
    By love's own sweet constraint, and will for ever
    Do thee all rights of service.
DIANA   Ay, so you serve us
    Till we serve you.° But when you have our roses,   (sexually)
20   You barely° leave our thorns to prick ourselves,   only; exposed
    And mock us with our bareness.
BERTRAM   How have I sworn!
DIANA   'Tis not the many oaths that makes the truth,
    But the plain single vow that is vowed true.
    What is not holy, that we swear not by,
25   But take the high'st to witness; then pray you, tell me,
    If I should swear by Jove's great attributes
    I loved you dearly, would you believe my oaths
    When I did love you ill?° This has no holding,[3]   poorly; irreligiously
    To swear by him whom I protest to love
30   That I will work against him. Therefore your oaths
    Are words and poor conditions but unsealed,[4]
    At least in my opinion.

9. Proverbially stupid bird.
4.2 Location: The widow's house, Florence.
1. *worth it, with addition*: you more than deserve to be
called a goddess; with wordplay on "addition" as an honorific title. The goddess Diana was the patroness of chas-

tity, an "addition" that hardly bodes well for Bertram.
2. Do not quarrel with me about my wedding vows.
3. Consistency; binding power.
4. *words . . . unsealed*: contracts without the validating
seal.

BERTRAM   Change it, change it.
Be not so holy-cruel. Love is holy,
And my integrity ne'er knew the crafts°   *deceptive plays*
35   That you do charge men with. Stand no more off,
But give thyself unto my sick desires,
Who then recovers. Say thou art mine, and ever
My love as it begins shall so persever.

DIANA   I see that men make toys e'en such a surance⁵
40   That we'll forsake ourselves. Give me that ring.

BERTRAM   I'll lend it thee, my dear, but have no power
To give it from me.

DIANA   Will you not, my lord?

BERTRAM   It is an honour 'longing to our house,°   *family line*
Bequeathèd down from many ancestors,
45   Which were the greatest obloquy° i'th' world   *disgrace*
In me to lose.

DIANA   Mine honour's such a ring.
My chastity's the jewel of our house,
Bequeathèd down from many ancestors,
Which were the greatest obloquy i'th' world
50   In me to lose. Thus your own proper wisdom⁶
Brings in the champion Honour on my part°   *side*
Against your vain assault.

BERTRAM   Here, take my ring.
My house, mine honour, yea my life be thine,
And I'll be bid° by thee.   *commanded*
55 DIANA   When midnight comes, knock at my chamber window.
I'll order take my mother shall not hear.
Now will I charge you in the bond of truth,
When you have conquered my yet maiden bed,
Remain there but an hour, nor speak to me—
60   My reasons are most strong, and you shall know them
When back again this ring shall be delivered—
And on your finger in the night I'll put
Another ring that, what° in time proceeds,   *whatever*
May token° to the future our past deeds.   *betoken*
65   Adieu till then; then, fail not. You have won
A wife of° me, though there my hope be done.⁷   *in; through*

BERTRAM   A heaven on earth I have won by wooing thee.

DIANA   For which live long to thank both heaven and me.
You may so in the end.   [*Exit* BERTRAM]
70   My mother told me just how he would woo,
As if she sat in's heart. She says all men
Have the like oaths. He had sworn to marry me
When his wife's dead; therefore I'll lie with him
When I am buried. Since Frenchmen are so braid,°   *deceitful*
75   Marry° that will; I live and die a maid.   *Let those marry*
Only, in this disguise I think't no sin
To cozen° him that would unjustly win.   *Exit*   *cheat*

---

5. Men treat trifles as if they were such guarantees of good faith.
6. Wisdom in your own affairs.

7. My marriage hopes are ruined; my hope of aiding Helen is accomplished.

4.3

*Enter the two Captains [*DUMAINE*] and some two or three soldiers*

FIRST LORD DUMAINE   You have not given him his mother's letter?

SECOND LORD DUMAINE   I have delivered it an hour since. There is something in't that stings his nature, for on the reading it
5 he changed almost into another man.

FIRST LORD DUMAINE   He has much worthy° blame laid upon   deserved
him for shaking off so good a wife and so sweet a lady.

SECOND LORD DUMAINE   Especially he hath incurred the ever-lasting displeasure of the King, who had even tuned his bounty
10 to sing happiness to him.[1] I will tell you a thing, but you shall let it dwell darkly° with you.   secretly

FIRST LORD DUMAINE   When you have spoken it 'tis dead, and I am the grave of it.

SECOND LORD DUMAINE   He hath perverted a young gentle-
15 woman here in Florence of a most chaste renown,° and this   reputation
night he fleshes his will[2] in the spoil of her honour. He hath given her his monumental° ring, and thinks himself made in   memorial
the unchaste composition.°   bargain

FIRST LORD DUMAINE   Now God delay our rebellion!° As we are   stifle our unruliness
20 ourselves,° what things are we.   without divine aid

SECOND LORD DUMAINE   Merely° our own traitors. And as in the   Absolutely
common course of all treasons we still° see them reveal them-   always
selves° till they attain to their abhorred ends, so he that in this   (their true nature)
action contrives° against his own nobility, in his proper stream   plots
25 o'erflows himself.[3]

FIRST LORD DUMAINE   Is it not meant damnable° in us to be   meant to be mortal sin
trumpeters of our unlawful intents? We shall not then have his company tonight?

SECOND LORD DUMAINE   Not till after midnight, for he is dieted°   restricted
30 to his hour.

FIRST LORD DUMAINE   That approaches apace. I would gladly have him see his company anatomized,° that he might take a   companion exposed
measure of his own judgements, wherein so curiously° he had   carefully
set this counterfeit.[4]

35 SECOND LORD DUMAINE   We will not meddle with him° till he°   (Paroles) / (Bertram)
come, for his presence must be the whip of the other.

FIRST LORD DUMAINE   In the mean time, what hear you of these wars?

SECOND LORD DUMAINE   I hear there is an overture of peace.

40 FIRST LORD DUMAINE   Nay, I assure you, a peace concluded.

SECOND LORD DUMAINE   What will Count Roussillon do then? Will he travel higher,° or return again into France?   further

FIRST LORD DUMAINE   I perceive by this demand you are not alto-gether of his council.°   in his confidence

45 SECOND LORD DUMAINE   Let it be forbid, sir; so should I be a great deal of his act.[5]

FIRST LORD DUMAINE   Sir, his wife some two months since fled

---

4.3 Location: The Florentine camp.
1. Who had previously readied his generosity to make him happy (with musical metaphor).
2. He feeds his lust (hounds were "fleshed," or rewarded, with a piece of meat from their prey, or "spoil").

3. *in his . . . himself*: dissipates himself outside his appro-priate channel.
4. False jewel (Paroles).
5. An accessory to his deeds.

from his house. Her pretence° is a pilgrimage to Saint Jaques   *purpose*
le Grand, which holy undertaking with most austere sancti-
50   mony° she accomplished, and there residing, the tenderness of   *piety*
her nature became as a prey to her grief : in fine,° made a groan   *conclusion*
of her last breath, and now she sings in heaven.

SECOND LORD DUMAINE   How is this justified?°   *verified*

FIRST LORD DUMAINE   The stronger part of it by her own letters,
55   which makes her story true even to the point of her death. Her
death itself, which could not be her office to say is come, was
faithfully confirmed by the rector of the place.

SECOND LORD DUMAINE   Hath the Count all this intelligence?

FIRST LORD DUMAINE   Ay, and the particular confirmations,
60   point from point, to the full arming° of the verity.°   *corroboration / truth*

SECOND LORD DUMAINE   I am heartily sorry that he'll be glad of
this.

FIRST LORD DUMAINE   How mightily sometimes we make us
comforts of our losses.

65   SECOND LORD DUMAINE   And how mightily some other times we
drown our gain in tears. The great dignity that his valour hath
here acquired for him shall at home be encountered° with a   *opposed*
shame as ample.

FIRST LORD DUMAINE   The web° of our life is of a mingled yarn,   *fabric*
70   good and ill together. Our virtues would be proud if our faults
whipped them not, and our crimes would despair if they were
not cherished by our virtues.

           Enter a [SERVANT]
How now? Where's your master?

SERVANT   He met the Duke in the street, sir, of whom he hath
75   taken a solemn leave. His lordship will° next morning for   *intends to leave*
France. The Duke hath offered him letters of commendations
to the King.

SECOND LORD DUMAINE   They shall be no more than needful
there, if they were more than they can commend.⁶

           Enter [BERTRAM]
80   FIRST LORD DUMAINE   They cannot be too sweet for the King's
tartness. Here's his lordship now. How now, my lord, is't not
after midnight?

BERTRAM   I have tonight dispatched sixteen businesses, a
month's length apiece. By an abstract of success:° I have *con-*   *list of items*
géd with° the Duke, done my adieu with his nearest, buried a   *taken leave of*
85   wife, mourned for her, writ to my lady mother I am returning,
entertained my convoy,° and between these main parcels of dis-   *arranged my transport*
patch° affected many nicer° needs. The last was the greatest,   *business / more delicate*
but that I have not ended yet.

90   SECOND LORD DUMAINE   If the business be of any difficulty, and
this morning your departure hence, it requires haste of your
lordship.

BERTRAM   I mean the business is not ended, as fearing to hear of
it hereafter. But shall we have this dialogue between the Fool
95   and the Soldier? Come, bring forth this counterfeit model,° has   *image (of soldiership)*
deceived me like a double-meaning° prophesier.   *ambiguous*

SECOND LORD DUMAINE   Bring him forth.   [*Exit one or more*]
He's sat i'th' stocks all night, poor gallant knave.

---

6. Even if they were more commendatory than they possibly could be.

BERTRAM   No matter, his heels have deserved it in usurping his
100   spurs[7] so long. How does he carry himself ?
SECOND LORD DUMAINE   I have told your lordship already, the
      stocks carry him. But to answer you as you would be under-
      stood, he weeps like a wench that had shed° her milk. He hath   *spilled*
      confessed himself to Morgan, whom he supposes to be a friar,
105   from the time of his remembrance[8] to this very instant° disaster   *present*
      of his setting i'th' stocks. And what think you he hath con-
      fessed?
BERTRAM   Nothing of me, has a?°   *he*
SECOND LORD DUMAINE   His confession is taken, and it shall be
110   read to his face. If your lordship be in't, as I believe you are,
      you must have the patience to hear it.
            Enter PAROLES [*guarded and*] *blindfolded, with* [*his*]
            Interpreter
BERTRAM   A plague upon him! Muffled!° He can say nothing of   *Blindfolded*
      me.
FIRST LORD DUMAINE [*aside to* BERTRAM]   Hush, hush.
115   SECOND LORD DUMAINE [*aside to* BERTRAM]   Hoodman[9] comes.
      [*Aloud*] *Porto tartarossa.*
INTERPRETER [*to* PAROLES]   He calls for the tortures. What will
      you say without 'em?
PAROLES   I will confess what I know without constraint. If ye
120   pinch me like a pasty° I can say no more.   *piecrust*
INTERPRETER   *Bosko chimurcho.*
SECOND LORD DUMAINE   *Boblibindo chicurmurco.*
INTERPRETER   You are a merciful general.—Our general bids
      you answer to what I shall ask you out of a note.
125   PAROLES   And truly, as I hope to live.
INTERPRETER [*reads*]   'First demand of him how many horse° the   *horsemen*
      Duke is strong.'—What say you to that?
PAROLES   Five or six thousand, but very weak and unserviceable.
      The troops are all scattered and the commanders very poor
130   rogues, upon my reputation and credit, and as I hope to live.
INTERPRETER   Shall I set down your answer so?
PAROLES   Do. I'll take the sacrament on't, how and which way
      you will.[1]
FIRST LORD DUMAINE[2] [*aside*]   All's one to him.
135   BERTRAM [*aside*]   What a past-saving slave is this!
FIRST LORD DUMAINE [*aside*]   You're deceived, my lord. This is
      Monsieur Paroles, the 'gallant militarist'—that was his own
      phrase—that had the whole theoric° of war in the knot of his   *theory*
      scarf, and the practice in the chape° of his dagger.   *scabbard tip*
140   SECOND LORD DUMAINE [*aside*]   I will never trust a man again for
      keeping his sword clean, nor believe he can have everything in
      him by wearing his apparel neatly.
INTERPRETER [*to* PAROLES]   Well, that's set down.
PAROLES   'Five or six thousand horse,' I said—I will say true—'or
145   thereabouts' set down, for I'll speak truth.
FIRST LORD DUMAINE [*aside*]   He's very near the truth in this.

---

7. Symbolic of knightly valor.   1. According to whatever rite you prefer.
8. As far back as he can recall.   2. F attributes this remark to Bertram.
9. The blindfold player in blindman's buff.

BERTRAM [*aside*] But I con him no thanks° for't in the   *feel no gratitude*
   nature° he delivers it.   *manner*

PAROLES 'Poor rogues', I pray you say.

150 INTERPRETER Well, that's set down.

PAROLES I humbly thank you, sir. A truth's a truth. The rogues
   are marvellous poor.

INTERPRETER [*reads*] 'Demand of him of what strength they are
   a-foot.'—What say you to that?

155 PAROLES By my troth, sir, if I were to die this present hour, I will
   tell true. Let me see, Spurio a hundred and fifty; Sebastian so
   many;° Corambus so many; Jaques so many; Guillaume,   *the same number*
   Cosmo, Lodowick, and Gratii, two hundred fifty each; mine
   own company, Chitopher, Vaumond, Bentii, two hundred fifty
160   each. So that the muster file, rotten and sound,³ upon my life
   amounts not to fifteen thousand poll,° half of the which dare   *heads*
   not shake the snow from off their cassocks° lest they shake   *cloaks*
   themselves to pieces.

BERTRAM [*aside*] What shall be done to him?

165 FIRST LORD DUMAINE [*aside*] Nothing, but let him have thanks.
   [*To* INTERPRETER] Demand of him my condition, and what
   credit I have with the Duke.

INTERPRETER [*to* PAROLES] Well, that's set down. [*Reads*] 'You
   shall demand of him, whether one Captain Dumaine be i'th'
170   camp, a Frenchman; what his reputation is with the Duke;
   what his valour, honesty, and expertness in wars; or whether he
   thinks it were not possible with well-weighing° sums of gold to   *heavy; persuasive*
   corrupt him to a revolt.'—What say you to this? What do you
   know of it?

175 PAROLES I beseech you let me answer to the particular of the
   inter'gatories.° Demand them singly.   *judicial questions*

INTERPRETER Do you know this Captain Dumaine?

PAROLES I know him. A was a botcher's° prentice in Paris, from   *clothes mender*
   whence he was whipped for getting the sheriff's fool⁴ with
180   child—a dumb innocent° that could not say him nay.   *idiot*

BERTRAM [*aside to* FIRST LORD DUMAINE] Nay, by your leave,
   hold your hands, though I know his brains are forfeit to the
   next tile that falls.⁵

INTERPRETER Well, is this captain in the Duke of Florence's
185   camp?

PAROLES Upon my knowledge he is, and lousy.

FIRST LORD DUMAINE [*aside*] Nay, look not so upon me: we shall
   hear of your lordship anon.

INTERPRETER What is his reputation with the Duke?

190 PAROLES The Duke knows him for no other but a poor officer
   of mine, and writ to me this other day to turn him out o'th'
   band. I think I have his letter in my pocket.

INTERPRETER Marry, we'll search.

PAROLES In good sadness,° I do not know. Either it is there, or it   *all seriousness*
195   is upon a file with the Duke's other letters in my tent.

INTERPRETER Here 'tis, here's a paper. Shall I read it to you?

PAROLES I do not know if it be it or no.

BERTRAM [*aside*] Our interpreter does it well.

---

3. The total roll, sick and able-bodied.   5. I know he's close to sudden death.
4. Mentally retarded girl.

FIRST LORD DUMAINE [*aside*]   Excellently.

200   INTERPRETER [*reads the letter*]   'Dian, the Count's a fool, and full of gold.'

PAROLES   That is not the Duke's letter, sir. That is an advertise-
ment° to a proper maid in Florence, one Diana, to take heed   *admonition*
of the allurement of one Count Roussillon, a foolish idle boy,
but for all that very ruttish.° I pray you, sir, put it up again.   *lecherous*

205   INTERPRETER   Nay, I'll read it first, by your favour.

PAROLES   My meaning in't, I protest, was very honest in the
behalf of the maid, for I knew the young Count to be a dangerous and lascivious boy, who is a whale to virginity, and devours
up all the fry° it finds.   *tiny fish*

210   BERTRAM [*aside*]   Damnable both-sides rogue.

INTERPRETER [*reads*]   'When he swears oaths, bid him drop gold,
   and take it.
After he scores he never pays the score.°   *bill*
Half-won is match well made; match, and well make it.[6]
He ne'er pays after-debts,[7] take it before.

215   And say a soldier, Dian, told thee this:
Men are to mell° with, boys are not to kiss.   *meddle (sexually)*
For count° of this, the Count's a fool, I know it,   *on account*
Who pays before,° but not when he does owe it.   *in advance*
      Thine, as he vowed to thee in thine ear,

220   Paroles.'

BERTRAM [*aside*]   He shall be whipped through the army with
this rhyme in's[8] forehead.

SECOND LORD DUMAINE [*aside*]   This is your devoted friend, sir,
the manifold linguist and the armipotent° soldier.   *mighty-in-arms*

225   BERTRAM [*aside*]   I could endure anything before but a cat,[9] and
now he's a cat to me.

INTERPRETER   I perceive, sir, by the general's looks, we shall be
fain° to hang you.   *obliged*

PAROLES   My life, sir, in any case! Not that I am afraid to die,

230   but that, my offences being many, I would repent out the
remainder of nature.° Let me live, sir, in a dungeon, i'th' stocks,   *my natural life*
or anywhere, so I may live.

INTERPRETER   We'll see what may be done, so you confess freely.
Therefore once more to this Captain Dumaine. You have

235   answered to his reputation with the Duke, and to his valour.
What is his honesty?

PAROLES   He will steal, sir, an egg out of a cloister. For rapes and
ravishments he parallels Nessus.[1] He professes° not keeping of   *makes a practice of*
oaths; in breaking 'em he is stronger than Hercules. He will lie,

240   sir, with such volubility that you would think truth were a fool.
Drunkenness is his best virtue, for he will be swine-drunk, and
in his sleep he does little harm, save to his bedclothes; but they
about him know his conditions,° and lay him in straw. I have   *habits*
but little more to say, sir, of his honesty. He has everything that

245   an honest man should not have; what an honest man should
have, he has nothing.

FIRST LORD DUMAINE [*aside*]   I begin to love him for this.

---

6. Negotiating a good bargain is half the battle, so be
sure to bargain well.
7. Debts payable after receipt of goods.
8. On his (whores and their customers, when punished
by public whipping, were often made to wear signs indi-

cating their transgressions).
9. A common phobia, but "cat" is also a term of contempt, usually referring to a spiteful or sluttish woman.
1. Centaur who attempted to rape Hercules' wife.

BERTRAM [*aside*]   For this description of thine honesty? A pox
upon him! For me, he's more and more a cat.

250 INTERPRETER   What say you to his expertness in war?

PAROLES   Faith, sir, he's led the drum before the English tragedians.[2] To belie him I will not, and more of his soldiership I
know not, except in that country he had the honour to be the
officer at a place there called Mile End,[3] to instruct for the
255 doubling of files.[4] I would do the man what honour I can, but
of this I am not certain.

FIRST LORD DUMAINE [*aside*]   He hath out-villained villainy so far
that the rarity° redeems him.   *uniqueness*

BERTRAM [*aside*]   A pox on him! He's a cat still.

260 INTERPRETER   His qualities being at this poor price, I need not
to ask you if gold will corrupt him to revolt.

PAROLES   Sir, for a *quart d'écu*[5] he will sell the fee-simple° of   *absolute ownership*
his salvation, the inheritance of it, and cut th'entail from all
remainders,[6] and a perpetual succession for it perpetually.

265 INTERPRETER   What's his brother, the other Captain Dumaine?

SECOND LORD DUMAINE [*aside*]   Why does he ask him of me?

INTERPRETER   What's he?

PAROLES   E'en a crow o'th' same nest. Not altogether so great as
the first in goodness, but greater a great deal in evil. He excels
270 his brother for a coward, yet his brother is reputed one of the
best that is. In a retreat he outruns any lackey;[7] marry, in coming on° he has the cramp.   *advancing*

INTERPRETER   If your life be saved will you undertake to betray
the Florentine?

275 PAROLES   Ay, and the captain of his horse, Count Roussillon.

INTERPRETER   I'll whisper with the general and know his pleasure.

PAROLES   I'll no more drumming. A plague of all drums! Only
to seem to deserve well, and to beguile the supposition° of that   *judgment*
280 lascivious young boy, the Count, have I run into this danger.
Yet who would have suspected an ambush where I was taken?

INTERPRETER   There is no remedy, sir, but you must die. The
general says you that have so traitorously discovered° the secrets   *revealed*
of your army, and made such pestiferous reports of men very
285 nobly held,° can serve the world for no honest use; therefore   *regarded*
you must die.—Come, headsman, off with his head.

PAROLES   O Lord, sir!—Let me live, or let me see my death!

INTERPRETER   That shall you, and take your leave of all your
friends.
        [*He unmuffles* PAROLES]

290 So, look about you. Know you any here?

BERTRAM   Good morrow, noble captain.

SECOND LORD DUMAINE   God bless you, Captain Paroles.

FIRST LORD DUMAINE   God save you, noble captain.

SECOND LORD DUMAINE   Captain, what greeting will you° to my   *do you desire*
295 Lord Lafeu? I am for° France.   *off to*

FIRST LORD DUMAINE   Good captain, will you give me a copy of
the sonnet you writ to Diana in behalf of the Count Roussillon?

---

2. He's banged the drum to help advertise plays.
3. Where the London citizen militia drilled.
4. Simple drill exercise, in which the men stand in two
rows.

5. Quarter-crown, French coin of small value.
6. Prevent its succession to any future heirs.
7. Footman who runs before his master's coach.

An° I were not a very coward I'd compel it of you. But fare you   *If*
well.   *Exeunt [all but* PAROLES *and the* INTERPRETER]

300 INTERPRETER   You are undone, captain—all but your scarf; that
has a knot on't yet.

PAROLES   Who cannot be crushed with a plot?

INTERPRETER   If you could find out a country where but women
were that had received so much shame, you might begin an
305 impudent° nation. Fare ye well, sir. I am for France too. We   *a shameless*
shall speak of you there.   *Exit*

PAROLES   Yet am I thankful. If my heart were great
'Twould burst at this. Captain I'll be no more,
But I will eat and drink and sleep as soft
310 As captain shall. Simply the thing I am
Shall make me live.° Who knows himself a braggart,   *sustain me*
Let him fear this, for it will come to pass
That every braggart shall be found an ass.
Rust, sword; cool, blushes; and Paroles live
315 Safest in shame; being fooled, by fool'ry thrive.
There's place and means for every man alive.
I'll after them.   *Exit*

4.4

Enter HELEN, WIDOW, *and* DIANA

HELEN   That you may well perceive I have not wronged you,
One of the greatest in the Christian world
Shall be my surety;° fore whose throne 'tis needful,   *guarantee*
Ere I can perfect mine intents, to kneel.
5 Time was, I did him a desirèd office
Dear almost as his life; which gratitude
Through flinty Tartar's bosom[1] would peep forth
And answer 'Thanks'. I duly am informed
His grace is at Marseilles, to which place
10 We have convenient convoy.° You must know   *suitable transport*
I am supposèd dead. The army breaking,°   *disbanding*
My husband hies him home, where, heaven aiding,
And by the leave of my good lord the King,
We'll be before our welcome.°   *before we're expected*

WIDOW   Gentle madam,
15 You never had a servant to whose trust
Your business was more welcome.

HELEN   Nor you, mistress,
Ever a friend whose thoughts more truly labour
To recompense your love. Doubt not but heaven
Hath brought me up to be your daughter's dower,
20 As it hath fated her to be my motive°   *means*
And helper to a husband. But O, strange men,
That can such sweet use make of what they hate,
When saucy trusting of the cozened° thoughts   *deceived*
Defiles the pitchy night;[2] so lust doth play
25 With what it loathes, for° that which is away.   *in the place of*
But more of this hereafter. You, Diana,

4.4 Location: The widow's house, Florence.
1. Even from a savage's stony heart (Tartars, residents of
central Asia, were considered barbaric by western Euro-

peans).
2. *When . . . night:* When lascivious yielding to deceit
defiles even the black night.

Under my poor instructions yet must suffer
Something in my behalf.

DIANA   Let death and honesty°   *chastity*
Go with your impositions, I am yours,
Upon° your will to suffer.   *At*

30 HELEN   Yet,° I pray you.—   *A little longer*
But with that word° the time will bring on summer,   *("Yet")*
When briers shall have leaves as well as thorns
And be as sweet° as sharp. We must away,   *fragrant*
Our wagon is prepared, and time revives us.
35 All's well that ends well; still the fine's° the crown.   *end*
Whate'er the course, the end is the renown.°   *Exeunt*   *what is remembered*

4.5

Enter [LAVATCH *the*] *clown, old* [COUNTESS], *and* LAFEU

LAFEU   No, no, no, your son was misled with a snipped-taffeta[1]
fellow there, whose villainous saffron[2] would have made all the
unbaked and doughy youth of a nation in his colour. Else, your
daughter-in-law had been alive at this hour, and your son here
5   at home, more advanced by the King than by that red-tailed
humble-bee[3] I speak of.

COUNTESS   I would a° had not known him. It was the death of   *he*
the most virtuous gentlewoman that ever nature had praise for
creating. If she had partaken of my flesh and cost me the
10   dearest groans of a mother I could not have owed her a more
rooted love.

LAFEU   'Twas a good lady, 'twas a good lady. We may pick a
thousand salads ere we light on such another herb.

LAVATCH   Indeed, sir, she was the sweet marjoram of the salad,
15   or rather the herb of grace.°   *rue*

LAFEU   They are not grass,[4] you knave, they are nose-herbs.°   *fragrant plants*

LAVATCH   I am no great Nebuchadnezzar,[5] sir, I have not much
skill in grace.

LAFEU   Whether° dost thou profess thyself, a knave or a fool?   *Which*
20 LAVATCH   A fool, sir, at a woman's service, and a knave at a
man's.

LAFEU   Your distinction?

LAVATCH   I would cozen° the man of his wife and do his service.   *cheat*

LAFEU   So you were a knave at his service indeed.

25 LAVATCH   And I would give his wife my bauble,[6] sir, to do her
service.

LAFEU   I will subscribe° for thee, thou art both knave and fool.   *vouch*

LAVATCH   At your service.

LAFEU   No, no, no.

30 LAVATCH   Why, sir, if I cannot serve you I can serve as great a
prince as you are.

LAFEU   Who's that? A Frenchman?

LAVATCH   Faith, sir, a has an English name, but his phys'namy[7]
is more hotter in France than there.

35 LAFEU   What prince is that?

4.5 Location: Bertram's palace.
1. Silk slashed to show a contrasting lining.
2. Yellow dye, used for pastry; the coward's color.
3. Bumblebee (noisy, colorful, and useless).
4. Misconstruing "grace."

5. In Daniel 4:28–34, the King of Babylon who, lacking
spiritual "grace," went mad and ate "grass."
6. Fool's rod (suggesting "penis").
7. Physiognomy, face (in Elizabethan pronunciation,
punning on "name").

LAVATCH   The Black Prince,[8] sir, alias the prince of darkness,
alias the devil.

LAFEU   Hold thee, there's my purse. I give thee not this to sug-
gest° thee from thy master thou talk'st of; serve him still.   *lure*

40   LAVATCH   I am a woodland fellow, sir, that always loved a great
fire, and the master I speak of ever keeps a good fire. But since
he is the prince of the world, let the nobility remain in's court;
I am for the house with the narrow gate,[9] which I take to be
too little for pomp to enter. Some that humble themselves may,

45   but the many will be too chill and tender,[1] and they'll be for
the flow'ry way that leads to the broad gate and the great fire.

LAFEU   Go thy ways. I begin to be aweary of thee, and I tell thee
so before,° because I would not fall out with thee. Go thy ways.   *in advance*
Let my horses be well looked to, without any tricks.

50   LAVATCH   If I put any tricks upon 'em, sir, they shall be jades'
tricks,[2] which are their own right by the law of nature.   *Exit*

LAFEU   A shrewd° knave and an unhappy.   *bitter*

COUNTESS   So a is. My lord that's gone made himself much sport
out of him; by his authority he remains here, which he thinks

55   is a patent° for his sauciness, and indeed he has no pace,° but   *license / restraint*
runs where he will.

LAFEU   I like him well, 'tis not amiss. And I was about to tell you,
since I heard of the good lady's death and that my lord your
son was upon his return home, I moved the King my master to

60   speak in the behalf of my daughter; which, in the minority of
them both, his majesty out of a self-gracious remembrance[3] did
first propose. His highness hath promised me to do it; and to
stop up the displeasure he hath conceived against your son,
there is no fitter matter. How does your ladyship like it?

65   COUNTESS   With very much content, my lord, and I wish it happily effected.

LAFEU   His highness comes post° from Marseilles, of as able   *speedily*
body as when he numbered thirty. A will be here tomorrow, or
I am deceived by him° that in such intelligence° hath seldom   *someone / information*

70   failed.

COUNTESS   It rejoices me that I hope I shall see him ere I die. I
have letters that my son will be here tonight. I shall beseech
your lordship to remain with me till they meet together.

LAFEU   Madam, I was thinking with what manners I might safely

75   be admitted.°   *invited to be present*

COUNTESS   You need but plead your honourable privilege.[4]

LAFEU   Lady, of that I have made a bold charter,[5] but, I thank
my God, it holds yet.

Enter [LAVATCH *the*] *clown*

LAVATCH   O madam, yonder's my lord your son with a patch of

80   velvet[6] on's face. Whether there be a scar under't or no, the
velvet knows; but 'tis a goodly patch of velvet. His left cheek is

---

8. Punning on the nickname of Edward III's eldest son, who conquered the French.
9. "Enter in at the strait gate; for it is the wide gate, and broad way that leadeth to destruction, and many there be which go in thereat. Because the gate is strait and the way narrow that leadeth unto life, and few there be that find it" (Matthew 7:13–14; see also Luke 13:24). The devil is called the "prince of this world" in John 12:31 and else-where.

1. Fainthearted and self-indulgent.
2. Contemptible tricks; playing on the sense "tricks played on horses."
3. Recollection prompted by his own graciousness.
4. Privilege due your honor.
5. Made as bold a claim as I dare.
6. Used to cover a battle wound or a facial sore from syphilis.

a cheek of two pile and a half,[7] but his right cheek is worn bare.

LAFEU   A scar nobly got, or a noble scar, is a good liv'ry° of hon-
our. So belike° is that.   *uniform*
                                                                                              probably

85 LAVATCH   But it is your carbonadoed[8] face.

LAFEU [*to the* COUNTESS]   Let us go see your son, I pray you. I
long to talk with the young noble soldier.

LAVATCH   Faith, there's a dozen of 'em, with delicate fine hats,
and most courteous feathers, which bow the head and nod at
90 every man.   *Exeunt*

5.1

Enter HELEN, WIDOW, *and* DIANA, *with two attendants*

HELEN   But this exceeding posting° day and night   *this hasty riding*
Must wear your spirits low. We cannot help it.
But since you have made the days and nights as one
To wear° your gentle limbs in my affairs,   *tire*
5 Be bold° you do so grow in my requital°   *confident / repayment*
As nothing can unroot you.

                    Enter a GENTLE[MAN] *Austringer*°   *keeper of hawks*
                         In happy time!°   *Just at the right time*
This man may help me to his majesty's ear,
If he would spend his power.—God save you, sir.

GENTLEMAN   And you.

10 HELEN   Sir, I have seen you in the court of France.

GENTLEMAN   I have been sometimes there.

HELEN   I do presume, sir, that you are not fall'n
From the report that goes upon your goodness,
And therefore, goaded with most sharp occasions°   *urgent circumstances*
15 Which lay nice° manners by, I put° you to   *scrupulous / urge*
The use of your own virtues, for the which
I shall continue thankful.

GENTLEMAN   What's your will?

HELEN   That it will please you
To give this poor petition to the King,
20 And aid me with that store of power you have
To come into his presence.

GENTLEMAN   The King's not here.

HELEN   Not here, sir?

GENTLEMAN   Not indeed.
He hence removed° last night, and with more haste   *departed*
25 Than is his use.°   *custom*

WIDOW   Lord, how we lose our pains.

HELEN   All's well that ends well yet,
Though time seem so adverse, and means unfit.—
I do beseech you, whither is he gone?

30 GENTLEMAN   Marry, as I take it, to Roussillon,
Whither I am going.

HELEN   I do beseech you, sir,
Since you are like to see the King before me,
Commend° the paper to his gracious hand,   *Present*
Which I presume shall render you no blame,

___

7. The thickest velvet was three-piled; Lavatch invents
an imaginary next best.
8. Slashed (like meat for broiling) in battle or by a surgeon, to treat a syphilitic eruption.
5.1 Location: Marseilles.

35　But rather make you thank your pains for it.
　　I will come after you with what good speed
　　Our means will make us means.°　　　　　　　　　*resources will permit*

GENTLEMAN [*taking the paper*]　　This I'll do for you.

HELEN　And you shall find yourself to be well thanked,
　　Whate'er falls more. We must to horse again.—

40　Go, go, provide.　　　　　　　　　　[*Exeunt severally*]

5.2

Enter [LAVATCH] *and* PAROLES[, *with a letter*]

PAROLES　Good Master Lavatch, give my Lord Lafeu this letter.
　　I have ere now, sir, been better known to you, when I have held
　　familiarity with fresher clothes. But I am now, sir, muddied in
　　Fortune's mood, and smell somewhat strong of her strong

5　displeasure.

LAVATCH　Truly, Fortune's displeasure is but sluttish if it smell
　　so strongly as thou speakest of. I will henceforth eat no fish of
　　Fortune's butt'ring.° Prithee allow the wind.[1]　　　　*prepared by Fortune*

PAROLES　Nay, you need not to stop your nose, sir, I spake but by

10　a metaphor.

LAVATCH　Indeed, sir, if your metaphor stink I will stop my nose,
　　or against any man's metaphor. Prithee get thee further.

PAROLES　Pray you, sir, deliver me this paper.

LAVATCH　Foh, prithee stand away. A paper from Fortune's close-

15　stool° to give to a nobleman! Look, here he comes himself.　　*toilet*

Enter LAFEU

　　Here is a pur[2] of Fortune's, sir, or of Fortune's cat—but not a
　　musk-cat[3]—that has fallen into the unclean fish-pond of her
　　displeasure and, as he says, is muddied withal. Pray you, sir,
　　use the carp[4] as you may, for he looks like a poor, decayed,

20　ingenious, foolish, rascally knave. I do pity his distress in my
　　similes of comfort, and leave him to your lordship.　　*Exit*

PAROLES　My lord, I am a man whom Fortune hath cruelly
　　scratched.

LAFEU　And what would you have me to do? 'Tis too late to pare

25　her nails now. Wherein have you played the knave with For-
　　tune that she should scratch you, who of herself is a good lady
　　and would not have knaves thrive long under her? There's a
　　quart d'écu for you. Let the justices[5] make you and Fortune
　　friends; I am for other business.

30　PAROLES　I beseech your honour to hear me one single word—

LAFEU　You beg a single penny more. Come, you shall ha't. Save
　　your word.°　　　　　　　　　　　　　　　　　　　*breath*

PAROLES　My name, my good lord, is Paroles.

LAFEU　You beg more than one word[6] then. Cox my passion!°　　*By God's passion*

35　Give me your hand. How does your drum?

PAROLES　O my good lord, you were the first that found me.

LAFEU　Was I, in sooth? And I was the first that lost thee.

PAROLES　It lies in you, my lord, to bring me in some grace,[7] for
　　you did bring me out.°　　　　　　　　　　　　　　*out of favor*

5.2　Location: Roussillon.
1.　Stand downwind of me.
2.　Piece of dung; cat's purr; knave (in the card game post and pair).
3.　Civet cat, a source of perfume.

4.　Fish often bred in mud ponds; chatterbox.
5.　Of the peace, responsible for beggars.
6.　Playing on "Paroles," "words."
7.　Into some favor (but Lafeu takes "grace" in its religious sense).

40   LAFEU   Out upon thee, knave! Dost thou put upon me at once
        both the office of God and the devil? One brings thee in grace,
        and the other brings thee out.
            [*Trumpets sound*]
        The King's coming; I know by his trumpets. Sirrah, enquire
        further after me. I had talk of you last night. Though you are a
45   fool and a knave, you shall eat. Go to, follow.
    PAROLES   I praise God for you.   [*Exeunt*]

5.3

Flourish. Enter KING, *old* [COUNTESS], LAFEU, *and attendants*

  KING   We lost a jewel of° her, and our esteem°   *in / (own) worth*
      Was made much poorer by it. But your son,
      As mad in folly, lacked the sense to know
      Her estimation home.°   *value to the full*
  COUNTESS   'Tis past, my liege,
5   And I beseech your majesty to make° it   *consider*
      Natural rebellion done i'th' blade° of youth,   *greenness*
      When oil and fire, too strong for reason's force,
      O'erbears it and burns on.
  KING   My honoured lady,
      I have forgiven and forgotten all,
10   Though my revenges were high[1] bent upon him
      And watched° the time to shoot.   *vigilantly waited*
  LAFEU   This I must say—
      But first I beg my pardon—the young lord
      Did to his majesty, his mother, and his lady
      Offence of mighty note, but to himself
15   The greatest wrong of all. He lost a wife
      Whose beauty did astonish the survey°   *observation*
      Of richest° eyes, whose words all ears took captive,   *most experienced*
      Whose dear perfection hearts that scorned to serve
      Humbly called mistress.
  KING   Praising what is lost
20   Makes the remembrance dear. Well, call him hither.
      We are reconciled, and the first view shall kill
      All repetition.[2] Let him not ask our pardon.
      The nature of his great offence is dead,
      And deeper than oblivion we do bury
25   Th'incensing relics° of it. Let him approach   *infuriating reminders*
      A stranger, no offender; and inform him
      So 'tis our will he should.
  ATTENDANT   I shall, my liege.   [*Exit*]
  KING [*to* LAFEU]   What says he to your daughter? Have you spoke?
  LAFEU   All that he is hath reference° to your highness.   *is submitted*
30   KING   Then shall we have a match. I have letters sent me
      That sets him high in fame.
           Enter BERTRAM [*with a patch of velvet on his left cheek,*
           and kneels]
  LAFEU   He looks well on't.
  KING [*to* BERTRAM]   I am not a day of season,°   *constant weather*
      For thou mayst see a sunshine and a hail

5.3 Location: Roussillon.   2. Rehearsal of past grievances.
1. To the utmost (like a taut bow).

35   In me at once. But to the brightest beams
        Distracted° clouds give way; so stand thou forth.   *Agitated; broken*
        The time is fair again.
        BERTRAM   My high-repented blames,°   *much-repented faults*
        Dear sovereign, pardon to me.
        KING   All is whole.°   *healed*
        Not one word more of the consumèd time.
40   Let's take the instant by the forward top,[3]
        For we are old, and on our quick'st decrees
        Th'inaudible and noiseless foot of time
        Steals ere we can effect them. You remember
        The daughter of this lord?
45   BERTRAM   Admiringly, my liege. At first
        I stuck° my choice upon her, ere my heart   *fixed*
        Durst make too bold a herald of my tongue;
        Where, the impression of mine eye enfixing,[4]
        Contempt his scornful perspective[5] did lend me,
50   Which warped the line of every other favour,°   *face*
        Stained a fair colour° or expressed it stolen,[6]   *complexion*
        Extended or contracted all proportions
        To a most hideous object. Thence it came
        That she° whom all men praised and whom myself,   *(Helen)*
55   Since I have lost, have loved, was in mine eye
        The dust that did offend it.
        KING   Well excused.
        That thou didst love her strikes some scores° away   *debits*
        From the great count.° But love that comes too late,   *reckoning*
        Like a remorseful° pardon slowly carried,   *compassionate; regretful*
60   To the grace-sender turns a sour offence,
        Crying, 'That's good that's gone.' Our rash faults
        Make trivial price of° serious things we have,   *Underestimate*
        Not knowing them until we know their grave.°   *lose them forever*
        Oft our displeasures, to ourselves unjust,
65   Destroy our friends and after weep° their dust.   *mourn over*
        Our own love waking° cries to see what's done,   *coming to its senses*
        While shameful hate sleeps out the afternoon.
        Be this sweet Helen's knell, and now forget her.
        Send forth your amorous token for fair Maudlin.°   *Lafeu's daughter*
70   The main consents are had, and here we'll stay
        To see our widower's second marriage day.
        COUNTESS[7]   Which better than the first, O dear heaven, bless!
        Or ere they meet, in me, O nature, cease.[8]
        LAFEU [*to* BERTRAM]   Come on, my son, in whom my house's name
75   Must be digested,[9] give a favour from you
        To sparkle in the spirits of my daughter,
        That she may quickly come.
        [BERTRAM *gives* LAFEU *a ring*]
                      By my old beard
        And ev'ry hair that's on't, Helen that's dead
        Was a sweet creature. Such a ring as this,

---

3. Let's seize time by the forelock; proverbial for "taking a present opportunity."
4. Once the impression of Lafeu's daughter was implanted in my heart.
5. Distorting optical glass.

6. Declared it artificial.
7. In F, the King speaks these lines.
8. Before they come to resemble one another, let me die.
9. Absorbed (because Maudlin is his only child and will take Bertram's name).

80 The last° that ere I took her leave at court,   *last time*
I saw upon her finger.¹

BERTRAM   Hers it was not.

KING Now pray you let me see it; for mine eye,
While I was speaking, oft was fastened to't.
[LAFEU *gives him the ring*]
This ring was mine, and when I gave it Helen

85 I bade her, if her fortunes ever stood
Necessitied to° help, that by this token   *In need of*
I would relieve her. Had you that craft to reave° her   *deprive*
Of what should stead° her most?   *aid*

BERTRAM   My gracious sovereign,
Howe'er it pleases you to take it so,
The ring was never hers.

90 COUNTESS   Son, on my life
I have seen her wear it, and she reckoned it
At her life's rate.°   *value*

LAFEU   I am sure I saw her wear it.

BERTRAM You are deceived, my lord, she never saw it.
In Florence was it from a casement thrown me,

95 Wrapped in a paper which contained the name
Of her that threw it. Noble she was, and thought
I stood ingaged.² But when I had subscribed
To mine own fortune,° and informed her fully   *admitted my situation*
I could not answer in that course of honour

100 As she had made the overture, she ceased
In heavy satisfaction,° and would never   *sad acceptance*
Receive the ring again.

KING   Plutus° himself,   *god of riches*
That knows the tinct and multiplying med'cine,³
Hath not in nature's mystery more science°   *expertise*

105 Than I have in this ring. 'Twas mine, 'twas Helen's,
Whoever gave it you. Then if you know
That you are well acquainted with yourself,⁴
Confess 'twas hers, and by what rough enforcement
You got it from her. She called the saints to surety°   *guarantee*

110 That she would never put it from her finger
Unless she gave it to yourself in bed,
Where you have never come, or sent it us
Upon° her great disaster.   *On the occasion of*

BERTRAM   She never saw it.

KING Thou speak'st it falsely, as I love mine honour,

115 And mak'st conjectural fears to come into me
Which I would fain° shut out. If it should prove   *gladly*
That thou art so inhuman—'twill not prove so.
And yet I know not. Thou didst hate her deadly,
And she is dead, which nothing but to close

120 Her eyes myself could win me to believe,
More than to see this ring.—Take him away.
My fore-past proofs,⁵ howe'er the matter fall,°   *befalls*

---

1. See 4.2.60–64.
2. Pledged to her (alternatively, "ungaged," not promised to anyone else).
3. Alchemical elixir for turning other metals into gold.

4. That you know who you are; that you are willing to admit your actions.
5. My evidence already in hand.

Shall tax° my fears of little vanity,°   *accuse / foolishness*
Having vainly feared too little. Away with him.
We'll sift this matter further.

125 BERTRAM   If you shall prove
This ring was ever hers, you shall as easy
Prove that I husbanded her bed in Florence,
Where yet she never was.   *[Exit guarded]*

Enter the GENTLEMAN *[Austringer with a paper]*

KING   I am wrapped in dismal thinkings.

130 GENTLEMAN   Gracious sovereign,
Whether I have been to blame or no, I know not.
Here's a petition from a Florentine
Who hath for four or five removes come short
To tender it herself.[6] I undertook it,

135 Vanquished thereto by the fair grace and speech
Of the poor suppliant, who by this° I know   *now*
Is here attending. Her business looks° in her   *shows itself*
With an importing° visage, and she told me   *urgent*
In a sweet verbal brief° it did concern   *summary*

140 Your highness with herself.

KING *[reads] a letter* 'Upon his many protestations to marry me
when his wife was dead, I blush to say it, he won me. Now is
the Count Roussillon a widower, his vows are forfeited to me,[7]
and my honour's paid to him. He stole from Florence, taking

145 no leave, and I follow him to his country for justice. Grant it
me, O King! In you it best lies; otherwise a seducer flourishes
and a poor maid is undone.

                         Diana Capilet.'

LAFEU   I will buy me a son-in-law in a fair,[8] and toll or this.[9] I'll

150 none of him.

KING   The heavens have thought well on thee, Lafeu,
To bring forth this discov'ry.—Seek these suitors.
Go speedily and bring again the Count.   *Exit one or more*
I am afeard the life of Helen, lady,
Was foully snatched.

Enter BERTRAM *[guarded]*

155 COUNTESS   Now justice on the doers!

KING *[to* BERTRAM*]* I wonder, sir, since wives are monsters to you,
And that° you fly them as you swear them lordship,[1]   *since*
Yet you desire to marry.

Enter WIDOW *and* DIANA

                What woman's that?

DIANA   I am, my lord, a wretched Florentine,

160 Derivèd° from the ancient Capilet.   *Descended*
My suit, as I do understand, you know,
And therefore know how far I may be pitied.

WIDOW *[to the* KING*]* I am her mother, sir, whose age and
      honour
Both suffer under this complaint we bring,

165 And both° shall cease without your remedy.   *(life and honor)*

KING   Come hither, Count. Do you know these women?

---

6. *Who . . . herself:* Who has for four or five changes of
royal residence failed to arrive in time to deliver it herself.
7. His promises have fallen due.

8. Notorious for unreliable merchandise.
9. Pay a tax for the privilege of selling this one (Bertram).
1. As soon as you vow to wed them.

BERTRAM My lord, I neither can nor will deny
    But that I know them. Do they charge me further?
DIANA Why do you look so strange upon your wife?
BERTRAM [*to the* KING] She's none of mine, my lord.
170 DIANA   If you shall marry
    You give away this° hand, and that is mine;   *(Bertram's)*
    You give away heaven's vows, and those are mine;
    You give away myself, which is known mine,
    For I by vow am so embodied yours
175   That she which marries you must marry me,
    Either both or none.
LAFEU [*to* BERTRAM] Your reputation comes too short for my
    daughter, you are no husband for her.
BERTRAM [*to the* KING] My lord, this is a fond° and desp'rate   *foolish*
    creature
180   Whom sometime I have laughed with. Let your highness
    Lay a more noble thought upon mine honour
    Than for to think that I would sink it here.
KING Sir, for my thoughts, you have them ill to friend[2]
    Till your deeds gain them. Fairer prove your honour
    Than in my thought it lies.
185 DIANA   Good my lord,
    Ask him upon his oath if he does think
    He had not my virginity.
KING What sayst thou to her?
BERTRAM She's impudent, my lord,
190   And was a common gamester° to the camp.   *prostitute*
DIANA [*to the* KING] He does me wrong, my lord. If I were so
    He might have bought me at a common price.
    Do not believe him. O behold this ring,
    Whose high respect° and rich validity°   *worth / value*
195   Did lack a parallel; yet for all that
    He gave it to a commoner o'th' camp,
    If I be one.
COUNTESS He blushes and 'tis hit.°   *that hit the mark*
    Of six preceding ancestors, that gem;
    Conferred by testament to th' sequent issue°   *following generation*
200   Hath it been owed° and worn. This is his wife.   *owned*
    That ring's a thousand proofs.
KING [*to* DIANA]   Methought you said°   *(perhaps in the letter)*
    You saw one here in court could witness it.
DIANA I did, my lord, but loath am to produce
    So bad an instrument. His name's Paroles.
205 LAFEU I saw the man today, if man he be.
KING Find him and bring him hither.   [*Exit one*]
BERTRAM   What of him?
    He's quoted° for a most perfidious slave   *noted*
    With all the spots o'th' world taxed and debauched,
    Whose nature sickens but to speak a truth.
210   Am I or° that or this for what he'll utter,   *either*
    That will speak anything?
KING   She hath that ring of yours.
BERTRAM I think she has. Certain it is I liked her

2. *you . . . friend:* they are no friends of yours.

And boarded° her i'th' wanton way of youth.   *made advances to*
She knew her distance and did angle for me,
215   Madding° my eagerness with her restraint,   *Maddening*
As all impediments in fancy's° course   *love's*
Are motives° of more fancy; and in fine°   *causes / the end*
Her inf'nite cunning with her modern° grace   *commonplace*
Subdued me to her rate.° She got the ring,   *price*
220   And I had that which my inferior might
At market price have bought.

DIANA   I must be patient.
You that have turned off a first so noble wife
May justly diet° me. I pray you yet—   *starve (of favor)*
Since you lack virtue I will lose a husband—
225   Send for your ring, I will return it home,
And give me mine again.

BERTRAM   I have it not.

KING   [*to* DIANA]   What ring was yours, I pray you?

DIANA   Sir, much like the same upon your finger.

230   KING   Know you this ring? This ring was his of late.

DIANA   And this was it I gave him being abed.

KING   The story then goes false you threw it him
Out of a casement?

DIANA   I have spoke the truth.

            Enter PAROLES

BERTRAM   [*to the* KING]   My lord, I do confess the ring was hers.

235   KING   You boggle shrewdly;³ every feather starts° you.—   *startles*
Is this the man you speak of?

DIANA   Ay, my lord.

KING   [*to* PAROLES]   Tell me, sirrah—but tell me true, I charge you,
Not fearing the displeasure of your master,
Which on your just proceeding I'll keep off—
240   By° him and by this woman here what know you?   *About*

PAROLES   So please your majesty, my master hath been an honourable gentleman. Tricks he hath had in him which gentlemen have.

KING   Come, come, to th' purpose. Did he love this woman?

245   PAROLES   Faith, sir, he did love her, but how?

KING   How, I pray you?

PAROLES   He did love her, sir, as a gentleman loves a woman.

KING   How is that?

PAROLES   He loved her, sir, and loved her not.

250   KING   As thou art a knave and no knave. What an equivocal companion is this!

PAROLES   I am a poor man, and at your majesty's command.

LAFEU   [*to the* KING]   He's a good drum,⁴ my lord, but a
naughty° orator.   *bad*

DIANA   [*to* PAROLES]   Do you know he promised me marriage?

255   PAROLES   Faith, I know more than I'll speak.

KING   But wilt thou not speak all thou know'st?

PAROLES   Yes, so please your majesty. I did go between them, as
I said; but more than that, he loved her, for indeed he was mad
for her and talked of Satan and of limbo and of Furies and I

_____

3. You take fright violently; you attempt to evade the   4. Capable only of noise; Lafeu probably also refers to
point wickedly (or incompetently).   Paroles's earlier adventures.

260   know not what. Yet I was in that° credit with them at that time   *so much*
    that I knew of their going to bed and of other motions,° as   *proposals*
    promising her marriage and things which would derive me ill
    will to speak of. Therefore I will not speak what I know.

    KING   Thou hast spoken all already, unless thou canst say they

265   are married. But thou art too fine° in thy evidence, therefore   *hairsplitting*
    stand aside.—
    This ring you say was yours.

    DIANA   Ay, my good lord.

    KING   Where did you buy it? Or who gave it you?

    DIANA   It was not given me, nor I did not buy it.

    KING   Who lent it you?

270   DIANA   It was not lent me neither.

    KING   Where did you find it then?

    DIANA   I found it not.

    KING   If it were yours by none of all these ways,
    How could you give it him?

    DIANA   I never gave it him.

    LAFEU [*to the* KING]   This woman's an easy glove, my lord, she

275   goes off and on at pleasure.

    KING [*to* DIANA]   This ring was mine. I gave it his first wife.

    DIANA   It might be yours or hers for aught I know.

    KING [*to attendants*]   Take her away, I do not like her now.
    To prison with her. And away with him.—

280   Unless thou tell'st me where thou hadst this ring
    Thou diest within this hour.

    DIANA   I'll never tell you.

    KING [*to attendants*]   Take her away.

    DIANA   I'll put in bail, my liege.

    KING   I think thee now some common customer.°   *prostitute*

    DIANA   By Jove, if ever I knew° man 'twas you.   *(carnally)*

285   KING   Wherefore hast thou accused him all this while?

    DIANA   Because he's guilty, and he is not guilty.
    He knows I am no maid, and he'll swear to't;
    I'll swear I am a maid, and he knows not.
    Great King, I am no strumpet; by my life,

290   I am either maid or else this old man's° wife.   *(Lafeu's)*

    KING [*to attendants*]   She does abuse our ears. To prison with her.

    DIANA   Good mother, fetch my bail.   [*Exit* WIDOW]
                           Stay, royal sir.
    The jeweller that owes° the ring is sent for,   *owns*
    And he shall surety me.° But for this lord,   *be my security*

295   Who hath abused me as he knows himself,
    Though yet he never harmed me, here I quit° him.   *acquit; repay; leave*
    He knows himself my bed he hath defiled,
    And at that time he got his wife with child.
    Dead though she be she feels her young one kick.

300   So there's my riddle; one that's dead is quick.°   *alive; pregnant*
    And now behold the meaning.
               Enter HELEN *and* WIDOW

    KING   Is there no exorcist°   *conjurer*
    Beguiles the truer office° of mine eyes?   *function*
    Is't real that I see?

    HELEN   No, my good lord,

'Tis but the shadow° of a wife you see,   *ghost; imitation*
The name and not the thing.

305   BERTRAM   Both, both. O, pardon!

HELEN   O, my good lord, when I was like° this maid   *in the place of*
I found you wondrous kind. There is your ring.
And, look you, here's your letter. This it says:
'When from my finger you can get this ring,
310   And are by me with child,' et cetera. This is done.
Will you be mine now you are doubly won?

BERTRAM [*to the* KING]   If she, my liege, can make me know this clearly
I'll love her dearly, ever ever dearly.

HELEN   If it appear not plain and prove untrue,
315   Deadly divorce step between me and you.—
O my dear mother, do I see you living?

LAFEU   Mine eyes smell onions, I shall weep anon.
[*To* PAROLES] Good Tom Drum, lend me a handkerchief. So,
I thank thee. Wait on me home, I'll make sport with thee. Let
320   thy curtsies alone, they are scurvy ones.

KING [*to* HELEN]   Let us from point to point this story know
To make the even° truth in pleasure flow.   *plain*
[*To* DIANA] If thou be'st yet a fresh uncroppèd flower,
Choose thou thy husband and I'll pay thy dower.
325   For I can guess that by thy honest aid
Thou kept'st a wife herself, thyself a maid.
Of that and all the progress more and less⁵
Resolvèdly° more leisure shall express.   *So questions are resolved*
All yet seems well; and if it end so meet,°   *properly*
330   The bitter past, more welcome is the sweet.
            Flourish

                                        Epilogue

The King's a beggar now the play is done.
All is well ended if this suit be won:
That you express content,° which we will pay   *(by applause)*
With strife° to please you, day exceeding° day.   *trying / after*
5   Ours be your patience then, and yours our parts:¹
Your gentle hands lend us, and take our hearts.   *Exeunt*

---

5. The course of events, great and small.

Epilogue
1. *Ours . . . parts:* We will wait patiently, like an audience, while you take the active part.

The Life of Timon of Athens

In a jewelry advertisement, a handsome man and a beautiful woman share a rapturous embrace. A large diamond sparkles on the woman's finger; apparently, the impressive ring symbolizes a love equally magnificent. Although the deliberate confusion of emotional and financial investments seems crass once it is explicitly recognized, the ad can only be effective at selling jewelry if it captures something people know, or wish, to be true. What does love have to do with money? How closely entwined are friendship and material self-interest? Are persons esteemed for intrinsic personal characteristics or for the glamour of their possessions? Are affluent communities or prosperous individuals especially likely to confuse sheer wealth with other forms of value?

Timon of Athens asks such questions with a relentlessness unusual for Shakespeare. To many readers and audiences, the play has seemed uncharacteristic in other respects as well: its schematic plot and vivid but static characters evoke the morality drama of Shakespeare's predecessors or the satiric drama of his contemporaries more closely than the other tragedies that Shakespeare was writing around this time. Some argue that *Timon of Athens* was never finished; others suggest that the play is a collaborative work, about a third of which was written by Shakespeare's fellow dramatist Thomas Middleton. Nonetheless, some connections between *Timon* and Shakespeare's other plays are clear enough. The plot derives from that Shakespearean favorite, Plutarch's *Lives,* which also provided the sources for *Julius Caesar, Antony and Cleopatra,* and *Coriolanus. Timon* has strong affinities to *The Merchant of Venice* in its concern with the connections between affectional and monetary bonds, and between material and intangible goods. The play's jaundiced view of ancient Greece recalls *Troilus and Cressida,* as does its evasion of ordinary generic categories: although its protagonist dies at the end, its title does not promise a tragedy but merely a "life." The hero's sensational degradation from preeminence to utter penury, and his ferociously misanthropic reaction to that humiliation, has often prompted comparison with *King Lear.*

Timon opens on a panorama of glittering abundance. Purveyors of luxury goods— art, poems, jewels, textiles—flock to Timon's palace in hope of reward. Like advertisers today, they claim that their goods have a symbolic significance that goes beyond their obvious beauty or utility: these items give concrete expression to the ineffable virtues of their possessor. "Things of like value differing in the owners / Are prizèd by their masters," fawns the Jeweller. "You mend the jewel by the wearing it" (1.1.174–75, 176). The guests at Timon's sumptuous banquet are likewise loud in their admiration for their host. Their conversation turns almost obsessively upon Timon's apparently inexhaustible fortune.

And no wonder—for Timon seems not merely rich but unique. His generosity is characterized by what the Poet calls "magic of bounty," an outflow uncannily unbalanced by any apparent countereffort at acquisition. While ordinary owners have the power merely to transfer, not actually to generate, new goods, Timon seems freed from such basic material laws. He dispenses his "bounty" as if he were a god empowered to create wealth from nothing. But Timon's "magic" relies on a trick that he himself resolutely ignores. Using his lands as collateral, he borrows the money he needs to buy rich presents and keep a lavish table. The recipients of his hospitality are often the same men to whom he is indebted.

To Timon's surprise but hardly to the audience's, his elaborate charade collapses in the play's second act. Why has he behaved so self-destructively? We are given clues to his motives when, in the course of his banquet, he and his guests explicitly and implicitly offer several theories about the relationship of his "bounty" both to the social weal and to his own self-conception. Timon desires love and admiration, and in Athenian society, as in many others, money proves a potent way of getting both. The adjectives "good," "worthy," "free," "kind," "gentle," and "noble" echo through the first act—their simultaneously economic and moral significance tending to break down any difference between the two domains. When Ventidius offers to return the large sum that Timon has spent releasing him from prison, Timon refuses:

> You mistake my love.
> I gave it freely ever, and there's none
> Can truly say he gives if he receives.
> (1.2.8–10)

Typically, love and money are here almost inextricable. Is the "it" that Timon freely gives the love to which he refers in the previous line or the money he has bestowed upon Ventidius? Moreover, Timon's generosity is entangled with pride and with a desire for mastery. By always giving, never receiving, Timon attempts to force his beneficiaries into an endlessly grateful and therefore subordinate role. His conduct recalls that of the chiefs of the native American tribes of the Pacific Northwest, who consolidated their status by "potlatches," great parties at which they would give away virtually all their possessions, thus compelling their guests to serve them in the future. In such a system, divesting oneself of wealth, not accumulating it, is the primary mode of acquiring status.

In the socioeconomic world of the potlatch, in which the recipient of a gift is profoundly obliged to the donor, Timon might well escape serious financial danger. His "courtiers" would attempt to repay him, in kind or in service. Timon briefly imagines such a system when he rhapsodizes at his dinner party: "We are born to do benefits; and what better or properer can we call our own than the riches of our friends? O, what a precious comfort 'tis to have so many like brothers commanding one another's fortunes!" (1.2.95–98). Unfortunately, not only is this communitarian vision at odds with Timon's insistence on entirely unilateral gift-giving, but it is grossly out of kilter with the covetous society in which he actually lives. When Timon pays Ventidius's debt, Ventidius's messenger declares that "your lordship ever binds him" (1.1.106); likewise the First Lord claims to be "virtuously bound" by Timon's generosity (1.2.221). Yet by the middle of Act 2, they have already lost any sense of commitment to their erstwhile benefactor. Timon's "bonds," the legal instruments that enable his lenders to seize his lands when he forfeits cash repayment, turn out to be more "binding" than the unwritten ties of gratitude. In Athens, tangible goods are considered more real than intangible ones, legal commitments more real than obligations informally imposed.

Apemantus, the Cynic philosopher, hovering on the margins of Timon's dinner party, introduces an alternative economic language early in the play: the audience's perception of the entire banquet extravaganza is filtered through his commentary. For Timon, magnanimity apparently comes naturally, and gifts express sociability. For Apemantus, by contrast, people are naturally greedy and antisocial: protestations of friendship and gratitude hypocritically conceal an impulse to accumulate wealth at the expense of another, just as lavishness hypocritically conceals a desire for adulation. In such circumstances, the Cynic philosopher preserves his safety and integrity by repudiating his need both for property and for other people:

> Immortal gods, I crave no pelf.
> I pray for no man but myself.
> Grant I may never prove so fond
> To trust a man on his oath or bond,

> Or a harlot for her weeping,
> Or a dog that seems a-sleeping,
> Or a keeper with my freedom,
> Or my friends if I should need 'em.
> (1.2.61–68)

To Timon's generous trustfulness, Apemantus counterpoises a self-protective suspicion. The difference in the way the two men conceive of human nature correlates with a difference in the way they imagine the material world. Timon believes that wealth is endlessly renewable and thus endlessly sharable without decrease. Apemantus believes that resources are strictly limited and that one person's gain must entail another person's loss. Thus what Timon sees as banquet pleasantries amount, in Apemantus's view, to a form of cannibalism. "O you gods, what a number of men eats Timon, and he sees 'em not! It grieves me to see so many dip their meat in one man's blood" (1.2.38–40). Both of these apparently opposite attitudes, however—Timon's romanticism and Apemantus's reductiveness—are actually rooted in a conviction that one's possessions, or the lack of them, centrally determine the way one thinks of oneself and interacts with other people. Arguably, Apemantus's cannibal imagery makes the shared materialism of the two men's attitudes especially obvious to a Christian audience; for that vision of Timon's banquet parodies, in grotesquely literal terms, the dispersal of Christ's spiritual body in the communion ceremony.

Most scholars believe that *Timon of Athens* was written between 1605 and 1608, several years after the accession of James I to the English throne. There are good reasons why Timon's particular economic dilemma would interest dramatists observing the contemporary scene in these years. If the play was, as many argue, left unfinished and unproduced, perhaps it was too incendiary to be safely performed in Jacobean England: although most of Shakespeare's plays reflect to some extent the time in which they were written, *Timon* is unusual in its brutally direct topical relevance. In the first decade of the seventeenth century, the traditional aristocratic virtues of openhanded generosity and carelessness of expense were coming into increasingly acute conflict with the limited means upon which the great nobles could actually draw. As England became an international trading power, luxuries once unheard of became available to people with the money to buy them. As tastes grew more sophisticated, noblemen who wished to impress peers and subordinates with the splendor of their

Penthesilea, Queen of the Amazons. Drawing by Inigo Jones. From *The Masque of Queenes,* by Ben Jonson.

"bounty" were forced into ever greater expenditures. The result was an extraordinary expansion in the credit markets. The worst offender in this respect was King James, who—like Timon—showered his favorites with expensive gifts, a habit that created staggering deficits in the Royal Exchequer. By 1608, royal indebtedness had reached crisis proportions, and other members of the upper aristocracy were likewise floating on a sea of debt and credit.

Shakespeare, or Shakespeare and Middleton, thus bear witness to a society in the process of a crucial economic transition—a transition that affects more than financial matters narrowly defined. In the first act, Timon assumes that his money transactions are accompanied by affection on the part of the giver and gratitude on the part of the recipient. In an informal, small-scale credit system, the difference between love and money, and between loans and gifts, may indeed become blurred, for friends may help one another financially on occasion. In Jacobean England, however, the inability of the upper classes to live within their means overstrained the limits of "friendly understanding": for few people then or now lend really substantial sums of money out of sheer amiability. Borrowing and lending thus increasingly became business matters transacted between relative strangers, divorced from rather than continuous with friendship and patronage relationships. Usury, a practice traditionally deplored and even illegal, was nonetheless widespread and increasingly accepted as a necessary fact of life.

A fiscally prudent, hardworking businessman, Shakespeare may well have been shocked on occasion at the profligacy of the patrons upon whose expansiveness he and his theater company partly depended. Certainly he recognized acutely that the motives of the Poet and the Painter do not differ from the motives of the other courtiers: "artists" in Athens are as venal as everybody else. What seems to have intrigued him most, however, is the way in which an apparently rather limited social phenomenon—aristocratic reliance on credit—necessarily affects social and even biological relations that seem far removed from money lending. Uniquely among Shakespeare's plays, *Timon* is nearly bereft of women. The few who do briefly appear—the Amazons of Act 1, Alcibiades' whores in Act 4—are pointedly excluded from the "normal" marital relationships in which most socially useful reproductive activity traditionally takes place. In this nearly all-male world, the language of erotic intimacy is reserved for interactions among men. Exchanges of money and commodities take over some of the functions of procreative sexual intimacy, an appropriation that can easily be construed as perverse or depraved. Lending money at interest seems especially corrupt: *Timon of Athens* draws upon an ancient tradition of imagining usury to be a form of unnatural "breeding." After his disillusionment, Timon continually and deliberately conflates lust with greed, the venereal with the venal. Syphilis and its symptoms are not merely analogies for, but are perhaps even the consequences of, economic iniquity.

Despite the virtual absence of actual women, allegorical representations of female power play an important rhetorical role in *Timon of Athens*. The first half of the play is dominated by the allegorical figure of Dame Fortune. The Poet describes her as a "sovereign lady . . . upon a high and pleasant hill" (1.1.69, 64), huge, omnipotent, and whimsical, raising and crushing her struggling male subjects for no apparent reason. In the second half of the play, "Mother Earth" has some of the same threatening demeanor. The ruined Timon forsakes Athens for the wilderness outside it, rather as Shakespeare's lovers had done in that drastically different play *A Midsummer Night's Dream*. In *Dream*, the woods outside Athens are a lushly sexual place, but in *Timon*, roughly the same geographical locale is unusually harsh and minimalist. Like the whores to whom Timon compares her, Mother Earth is barren, refusing to surrender the roots for which Timon digs and instead yielding only the gold he had hoped to flee. Thus, for all the energy spent exposing the "unnaturalness" of Athenians' economic relations, a potentially restorative "natural" alternative is wholly lacking.

In many respects, Timon's disillusioned ferocity simply inverts, recoils from, the generous courtesy he had manifested throughout Act 1. Yet not everything changes: there is a clear continuity to Timon's personality in the first and second half of the play. Initially, as a wealthy patron and benefactor, Timon isolates himself from others by making himself a god of generosity. Later, as an indigent, he similarly sets himself apart, cursing mankind with all the immoderation with which he once blessed it. Shakespeare was fascinated throughout his career by self-absorbed, almost solipsistic characters: Adonis in *Venus and Adonis,* the young man of the sonnets, Malvolio in *Twelfth Night* "sick of self love." Timon exemplifies an extreme version of this egocentrism, his sense of his own separateness untouched even after his conception of human nature has been poisoned at its source. He not only dies alone, but mysteriously manages to bury himself and engrave his own epitaph: an epitaph that typically, and perversely, both demands that passersby remember him and orders them to "seek not my name" (5.5.73).

The necessarily social medium of the drama finds true hermits impossible to accommodate. For most of Acts 4 and 5, various acquaintances crowd to Timon's cave as they once crowded to his palace, some to commiserate or to offer advice, some to investigate rumors that Timon had discovered gold while digging for roots to eat. The disillusioned Timon no longer wants gold, because it has value only insofar as it can be exchanged, and thus requires that its users form relationships with other human beings. So, ironically, the man who once blessed his "friends" with treasure once again gives it away to them, this time with his curses. The sense of separateness Timon has always possessed makes satiric alienation congenial to him; but, like many satirists, he is an ambiguous figure. The satirist can tell truths about society because his disengagement gives him the standing to criticize practices he regards as corrupt. At the same time, his observational acuteness—his refusal to accept the complacencies of the majority—bespeaks a certain imbalance. The satirist's misanthropy coexists curiously with an inability to mind his own business. The tone of the play's latter acts thus becomes profoundly equivocal. Are we supposed to agree with Timon that virtually all human values and activities can be plausibly reduced to money and the greed for it? Certainly, the action of the play gives us ample reason to share his disgust at his erstwhile friends. Or is his rage disproportionate to the adversities he endures? Just as the Timon of the early acts can be variously characterized as noble and foolish, the later Timon has seemed to some critics a sublimely disappointed idealist, to others a petulant whiner.

A few characters suggest that Timon's unmitigated misanthropy is too simple and incomplete. The steward Flavius's loyalty to his former master defies the terms of Timon's blanket condemnation of all humankind, as Timon reluctantly acknowledges. Throughout *Timon,* low-ranking characters—having less to gain from greed—display an acute sense of gratitude and obligation sadly lacking in their "betters." All Timon's servants, not merely Flavius, seem dismayed by their master's ruin; and in 3.4, the usurers' servants, talking among themselves, freely condemn the commands they are forced to carry out. But Timon prefers to believe that rapacity is a universal human trait, not a more limited, class-linked phenomenon. Reduced to rags and roots though he is, Timon cannot help being a snob. And to some extent, his status consciousness seems justified: for if the servants are kindhearted, they are also ineffectual, disqualified by low rank from remedying the social problems they witness.

Alcibiades provides a more formidable alternative to the Athenian usurers, although the connection between this subplot and the main action is sketchy. Certainly he does not escape, or seek to disentangle, the interconnections between love and money that eventually seem so poisonous to Timon: when he visits Timon in the cave, he comes with a prostitute on each arm. Nonetheless, in his brief appearances, Alcibiades testifies to the existence of a less restricted, more complex sociopolitical world than the one we witness for most of the play. Whereas, for instance, Timon's function in Athens seems mainly to give expensive dinner parties, Alcibiades insists that Timon has performed important military services for the state: that his "bounty" has had a political and executive, as well as a sheerly economic, aspect. Unfortunately, the relationship between Timon and Alcibiades, as well as the relationship between the city's politics and its social organization, is left largely undeveloped in the text of the play as it has

Dame Fortune, blind, standing on a ball with wings (to show how quickly her favors may fly away). From George Wither, *A Collection of Emblemes* (1635).

come down to us. The soldier, pursuing his vocation in the bleak world beyond the city walls, is imagined as partly outside the economic system in which other characters are enmeshed. Like the hermit-satirist, he has the special credibility that comes with distance. But whereas Timon's detachment is the product of a merely negative disgust, Alcibiades' involves allegiance to a different set of positive values. In 3.6, not only does he risk himself to defend a friend, but the terms of his defense hint at a code of behavior divorced from cash rewards and penalties.

At the end of the play, after Timon's death, the Athenian senators invite Alcibiades and his army back into the city. He will, they hope, "approach the fold and cull th'infected forth" (5.5.43), as a shepherd kills the sick animals of his flock in order to keep disease from spreading to the remainder. The senators argue that greed is merely the failing of a degenerate few, not the universal human trait Timon had believed it to be. Alcibiades seems to accept this claim, agreeing to renounce the indiscriminate violence of a war against all Athens in favor of the more targeted punishment of particular offenders. But the play entertains this alternative view of Timon's plight too late and too hastily to carry much conviction, and the apparent optimism of the conclusion thus seems unearned. How Alcibiades' invasion will reform Athens is hard to imagine.

KATHARINE EISAMAN MAUS

TEXTUAL NOTE

The only source for *Timon* is the First Folio of 1623 (F), and the circumstances of its publication seem to have been unusual. Evidently the decision to include *Timon* in

Shakespeare's collected works was made quite late; it was inserted into a space early in F that had been originally designated for the longer *Troilus and Cressida,* a play for which the printer initially had trouble obtaining copyright. This peculiarity, especially when viewed in light of the play's many rough edges and inconsistencies, has led scholars to speculate that *Timon* seemed, to the Folio compilers, to be marginal to Shakespeare's oeuvre. Some scholars believe, on the basis of analyzing vocabulary, stage directions, spelling, and style, that *Timon* is a collaborative text jointly authored by Shakespeare and Thomas Middleton. Others suggest that whatever its authorship, the play was abandoned before it reached the final stages of revision. There is no evidence that the play was ever performed, but such firm evidence is often lacking in the scanty surviving documents: the record is similarly silent on such plays as *As You Like It, Troilus and Cressida, All's Well That Ends Well,* and *Antony and Cleopatra.*

SELECTED BIBLIOGRAPHY

Chorost, Michael. "Biological Finance in Shakespeare's *Timon of Athens*." *English Literary Renaissance* 21 (1991): 349–70. Gift and money economies in *Timon,* and the language of biological reproduction in which they are described.

Empson, William. "Timon's Dog." *The Structure of Complex Words.* London: Chatto & Windus, 1951. The dog as an icon of both flattery and cynicism in *Timon.*

Jowett, John. "Middleton and Debt in *Timon of Athens*." *Money and the Age of Shakespeare: Essays in New Economic Criticism.* Ed. Linda Woodbridge. New York: Palgrave Macmillan, 2003. The play reflects the economic attitudes of Thomas Middleton, Shakespeare's probable collaborator.

Kahn, Coppélia. "'Magic of Bounty': *Timon of Athens,* Jacobean Patronage, and Maternal Power." *Shakespeare Quarterly* 38 (1987): 34–57. *Timon's* links to the contradictory practices of Jacobean court patronage.

Nuttall, A. D. *Timon of Athens.* Harvester New Critical Introductions to Shakespeare. Hemel Hempstead, Eng.: Harvester Wheatsheaf, 1989. Chapters on stage history and critical reception, followed by a detailed commentary on the play.

Paster, Gail Kern. *The Idea of the City in the Age of Shakespeare.* Athens: University of Georgia Press, 1985. 99–108. *Timon's* bleak vision of urban life, as enacted in the hero's transformation from philanthropist to misanthrope.

Scott, Alison V. *Selfish Gifts: The Politics of Exchange and English Courtly Literature, 1580–1628.* Madison, N.J.: Fairleigh Dickinson University Press, 2005. Describes the culture of patronage and self-seeking upon which *Timon* comments.

FILM

Timon of Athens. 1981. Dir. Jonathan Miller. UK. 128 min. Sepia-toned BBC-TV production featuring Athenians in Jacobean dress. Jonathan Pryce stars as an initially clueless and eventually very battered Timon. Effectively slimy performances in the subsidiary roles.

The Life of Timon of Athens

THE PERSONS OF THE PLAY

TIMON of Athens
A POET
A PAINTER
A JEWELLER
A MERCHANT
A mercer
LUCILIUS, one of Timon's servants
An OLD ATHENIAN
LORDS and SENATORS of Athens
VENTIDIUS, one of Timon's false friends
ALCIBIADES, an Athenian captain
APEMANTUS, a churlish philosopher
One dressed as CUPID in the masque
LADIES dressed as Amazons in the masque
FLAVIUS, Timon's steward
FLAMINIUS }
SERVILIUS } Timon's servants
Other SERVANTS of Timon
A FOOL
A PAGE
CAPHIS
ISIDORE'S SERVANT }
Two of VARRO'S SERVANTS } servants to Timon's creditors
LUCULLUS }
LUCIUS } flattering lords
SEMPRONIUS }
LUCULLUS' SERVANT
LUCIUS' SERVANT
Three STRANGERS, one called Hostillius
TITUS' SERVANT
HORTENSIUS' SERVANT } other servants to Timon's creditors
PHILOTUS' SERVANT }
PHRYNIA }
TIMANDRA } whores with Alcibiades
The banditti, THIEVES
SOLDIER of Alcibiades' army
Messengers, attendants, soldiers

1.1

Enter POET [*at one door*], PAINTER [*carrying a picture at
another door, followed by*] JEWELLER, MERCHANT, *and
Mercer, at several doors*

POET Good day, sir.
PAINTER   I am glad you're well.
POET I have not seen you long. How goes the world?

1.1 Location: Timon's house, Athens.

2270

PAINTER   It wears,° sir, as it grows.°   *wears out / ages*

POET   Ay, that's well known.
But what particular rarity, what strange,

5   Which manifold record° not matches?—See,   *all recorded history*
Magic of bounty,° all these spirits thy power   *generosity*
Hath conjured to attend.

[MERCHANT *and* JEWELLER *meet. Mercer passes over the
stage, and exits*]

                            I know the merchant.

PAINTER   I know them both. Th'other's a jeweller.

MERCHANT [*to* JEWELLER]   O, 'tis a worthy lord!°   *(Timon)*

JEWELLER   Nay, that's most fixed.°   *definite*

10   MERCHANT   A most incomparable man, breathed,° as it were,   *trained; inspired*
To an untirable and continuate° goodness.   *habitual*
He passes.°   *excels*

JEWELLER [*showing a jewel*]   I have a jewel here.

MERCHANT   O, pray, let's see't. For the Lord Timon, sir?

JEWELLER   If he will touch the estimate.° But for that—   *meet the price*

15   POET [*to himself*]   'When we for recompense have praised the vile,
It stains the glory in that happy° verse   *appropriate*
Which aptly sings the good.'

MERCHANT [*to* JEWELLER]   'Tis a good form.°   *shape*

JEWELLER   And rich. Here is a water,° look ye.   *luster*

PAINTER [*to* POET]   You are rapt, sir, in some work, some dedication
To the great lord.[1]

20   POET   A thing slipped idly from me.
Our poesy is as a gum° which oozes   *sap*
From whence 'tis nourished. The fire i'th' flint
Shows not till it be struck; our gentle flame
Provokes° itself, and like the current flies   *Generates*

25   Each bound it chafes.[2] What have you there?

PAINTER   A picture, sir. When comes your book forth?

POET   Upon the heels of my presentment,[3] sir.
Let's see your piece.

PAINTER [*showing the picture*]   'Tis a good piece.

POET   So 'tis. This comes off well and excellent.

PAINTER   Indifferent.°   *So-so*

30   POET   Admirable. How this grace
Speaks his own standing![4] What a mental power
This eye shoots forth! How big imagination
Moves in this lip! To th' dumbness° of the gesture   *muteness*
One might interpret.°   *supply words*

35   PAINTER   It is a pretty mocking° of the life.   *imitation*
Here is a touch; is't good?

POET   I will say of it,
It tutors nature. Artificial strife°   *The striving of art*
Lives in these touches livelier than life.

           Enter certain Senators

PAINTER   How this lord is followed!

40   POET   The senators of Athens. Happy man!

PAINTER   Look, more.

---

1. Poets dedicated their volumes to wealthy patrons in
hopes of financial reward.
2. *like . . . chafes:* like the river overflows restricting

banks.
3. As soon as I have presented it formally (to Timon).
4. Imparts the dignity of his estate.

[*The Senators pass over the stage, and exeunt*]

POET   You see this confluence, this great flood of visitors.
    I have in this rough work shaped out a man
    Whom this beneath[5] world doth embrace and hug
45   With amplest entertainment.° My free drift°   *hospitality / meaning*
    Halts not particularly,[6] but moves itself
    In a wide sea of tax.[7] No levelled malice
    Infects one comma in the course I hold,
    But flies an eagle flight, bold and forth° on,   *straight*
50   Leaving no tract° behind.   *trace*
PAINTER   How shall I understand you?
POET   I will unbolt° to you.   *disclose*
    You see how all conditions, how all minds,
    As well of glib and slipp'ry creatures as
55   Of grave and austere quality, tender° down   *give*
    Their service to Lord Timon. His large fortune,
    Upon his good and gracious nature hanging,
    Subdues and properties° to his love and tendance°   *appropriates / attendance*
    All sorts of hearts; yea, from the glass-faced[8] flatterer
60   To Apemantus, that few things loves better
    Than to abhor himself; even he drops down
    The knee before him, and returns° in peace,   *leaves*
    Most rich in Timon's nod.
PAINTER   I saw them speak together.
POET   Sir, I have upon a high and pleasant hill
65   Feigned° Fortune to be throned. The base o'th' mount   *Imagined*
    Is ranked with all deserts,[9] all kind of natures
    That labour on the bosom of this sphere
    To propagate their states.° Amongst them all   *improve their fortunes*
    Whose eyes are on this sovereign lady fixed
70   One do I personate of Lord Timon's frame,
    Whom Fortune with her ivory hand wafts° to her,   *beckons*
    Whose present grace° to present slaves and servants   *graciousness*
    Translates his rivals.[1]
PAINTER   'Tis conceived to scope.°   *correctly*
    This throne, this Fortune, and this hill, methinks,
75   With one man beckoned from the rest below,
    Bowing his head against the steepy mount
    To climb his happiness,° would be well expressed   *good fortune*
    In our condition.[2]
POET   Nay, sir, but hear me on.
    All those which were his fellows° but of late,   *equals*
80   Some better than his value, on the moment
    Follow his strides, his lobbies fill with tendance,[3]
    Rain sacrificial° whisperings in his ear,   *respectful*
    Make sacred even his stirrup,[4] and through him
    Drink the free air.

---

5. Sublunar (in Ptolomaic astronomy, the earth was the center of the universe and the moon its closest satellite; things beyond the moon were eternally fixed, but things in the sublunar "sphere" died or changed).
6. Does not criticize individuals.
7. In general satire (the Oxford editors substitute "tax" [criticism] for F's "wax"). *levelled:* aimed (at a particular person).
8. Reflecting his patron's moods.

9. Is lined with people of all degrees of virtue.
1. *to present . . . rivals:* instantly converts Timon's rivals to his slaves and servants.
2. *would . . . condition:* would be a good expression of the human condition; would make a good design for a painter.
3. *his . . . tendance:* crowd his rooms to visit him.
4. By holding it reverently as he mounts.

	PAINTER	Ay, marry, what of these?	
85	POET	When Fortune in her shift and change of mood	
		Spurns° down her late belovèd, all his dependants,	*Kicks*
		Which laboured after him to the mountain's top	
		Even on their knees and hands, let him fall down,	
		Not one accompanying his declining foot.	
90	PAINTER	'Tis common.	

A thousand moral paintings I can show
That shall demonstrate these quick blows of Fortune's
More pregnantly° than words. Yet you do well   *forcibly*
To show Lord Timon that mean° eyes have seen   *base people's*
95 The foot above the head.

> *Trumpets sound. Enter* TIMON [*wearing a rich jewel*],
> *with a* MESSENGER *from Ventidius;* LUCILIUS *and other*
> *Servants attending.* TIMON *address[es] himself courte-*
> *ously to every suitor* [*then speaks to the* MESSENGER]

TIMON   Imprisoned is he, say you?
MESSENGER   Ay, my good lord. Five talents[5] is his debt,
His means most short, his creditors most strait.°   *severe*
Your honourable letter he desires
100 To those° have shut him up, which failing,   *those who*
Periods° his comfort.   *Ends*
TIMON   Noble Ventidius! Well,
I am not of that feather° to shake off   *sort*
My friend when he must need me. I do know him
A gentleman that well deserves a help,
105 Which he shall have. I'll pay the debt and free him.
MESSENGER   Your lordship ever binds° him.   *obligates*
TIMON   Commend me to him. I will send his ransom;
And, being enfranchised,° bid him come to me.   *set free*
'Tis not enough to help the feeble up,
110 But to support him after. Fare you well.
MESSENGER   All happiness to your honour.   *Exit*
> *Enter an* OLD ATHENIAN
OLD ATHENIAN   Lord Timon, hear me speak.
TIMON   Freely, good father.
OLD ATHENIAN   Thou hast a servant named Lucilius.
TIMON   I have so. What of him?
115 OLD ATHENIAN   Most noble Timon, call the man before thee.
TIMON   Attends he here or no? Lucilius!
LUCILIUS [*coming forward*]   Here at your lordship's service.
OLD ATHENIAN   This fellow here, Lord Timon, this thy creature,
By night frequents my house. I am a man
120 That from my first have been inclined to thrift,
And my estate deserves an heir more raised°   *exalted*
Than one which holds a trencher.[6]
TIMON   Well, what further?
OLD ATHENIAN   One only daughter have I, no kin else
On whom I may confer what I have got.
125 The maid is fair, o'th' youngest for a bride,
And I have bred her° at my dearest cost   *brought her up*

---

5. A large unit of money, usually taken as equivalent to several thousand dollars. Shakespeare seems undecided about how much a "talent" is worth in *Timon*, and his inconsistencies are often cited as evidence for incomplete revision of the text.
6. Platter (one who waits on table).

In qualities of the best. This man of thine
Attempts her love. I prithee, noble lord,
Join with me to forbid him her resort.°   *company*
130   Myself have spoke in vain.
    TIMON   The man is honest.
    OLD ATHENIAN   Therefore he will be,[7] Timon.
His honesty rewards him in itself;
It must not bear° my daughter.   *carry off*
135   TIMON   Does she love him?
    OLD ATHENIAN   She is young and apt.°   *impressionable*
Our own precedent° passions do instruct us   *former*
What levity's in youth.
    TIMON [*to* LUCILIUS]   Love you the maid?
    LUCILIUS   Ay, my good lord, and she accepts of it.
140   OLD ATHENIAN   If in her marriage my consent be missing,
I call the gods to witness, I will choose
Mine heir from forth the beggars of the world,
And dispossess her all.
    TIMON   How shall she be endowed°   *What dowry will she have*
If she be mated with an equal husband?
145   OLD ATHENIAN   Three talents on the present; in future, all.
    TIMON   This gentleman of mine hath served me long.
To build his fortune I will strain a little,
For 'tis a bond° in men. Give him thy daughter.   *duty of friendship*
What you bestow in him I'll counterpoise,
And make him weigh with her.
150   OLD ATHENIAN   Most noble lord,
Pawn me to this your honour,[8] she is his.
    TIMON   My hand to thee; mine honour on my promise.
    LUCILIUS   Humbly I thank your lordship. Never may
That state or fortune fall into my keeping
155   Which is not owed to you.

                Exeunt [LUCILIUS *and* OLD ATHENIAN]
    POET [*presenting a poem to* TIMON]   Vouchsafe° my labour, and   *Accept*
      long live your lordship!
    TIMON   I thank you. You shall hear from me anon.°   *soon*
Go not away. [*To* PAINTER] What have you there, my friend?
    PAINTER   A piece of painting, which I do beseech
Your lordship to accept.
160   TIMON   Painting is welcome.
The painting is almost the natural° man;   *actual*
For since dishonour traffics° with man's nature,   *has dealings*
He is but outside;° these pencilled figures are   *only superficial*
Even such as they give out.[9] I like your work,
165   And you shall find I like it. Wait attendance
Till you hear further from me.
    PAINTER   The gods preserve ye!
    TIMON   Well fare you, gentleman. Give me your hand.
We must needs dine together. [*To* JEWELLER] Sir, your jewel
Hath suffered under[1] praise.
    JEWELLER   What, my lord, dispraise?

---

7. He will behave honorably (and chastely).
8. If you pledge your honor to do this.
9. Just what they profess to be.

1. Has been inundated by (but the Jeweller misunderstands).

170 TIMON A mere° satiety of commendations.   *An utter*
     If I should pay you for't as 'tis extolled
     It would unclew° me quite.   *ruin*
     JEWELLER   My lord, 'tis rated
     As those which sell would give;[2] but you well know
     Things of like value differing in the owners
175 Are prizèd by their masters.[3] Believe't, dear lord,
     You mend° the jewel by the wearing it.   *improve*
     TIMON Well mocked.°   *You're kidding*
     MERCHANT No, my good lord, he speaks the common tongue°   *general opinion*
     Which all men speak with him.
               Enter APEMANTUS
     TIMON   Look who comes here.
180 Will you be chid?
     JEWELLER We will bear,° with your lordship.   *suffer*
     MERCHANT He'll spare none.
     TIMON Good morrow to thee, gentle Apemantus.
     APEMANTUS Till I be gentle, stay thou for thy good morrow—
185 When thou art Timon's dog, and these knaves honest.[4]
     TIMON Why dost thou call them knaves? Thou know'st them not.
     APEMANTUS Are they not Athenians?
     TIMON Yes.
     APEMANTUS Then I repent not.
190 JEWELLER You know me, Apemantus?
     APEMANTUS Thou know'st I do. I called thee by thy name.
     TIMON Thou art proud, Apemantus!
     APEMANTUS Of nothing so much as that I am not like Timon.
     TIMON Whither art going?
195 APEMANTUS To knock out an honest Athenian's brains.
     TIMON That's a deed thou'lt die for.
     APEMANTUS Right, if doing nothing[5] be death by th' law.
     TIMON How likest thou this picture, Apemantus?
     APEMANTUS The best for the innocence.[6]
200 TIMON Wrought he not well that painted it?
     APEMANTUS He wrought better that made the painter, and yet
     he's but a filthy piece of work.
     PAINTER You're a dog.[7]
     APEMANTUS Thy mother's of my generation. What's she, if I be a dog?
205 TIMON Wilt dine with me, Apemantus?
     APEMANTUS No, I eat not[8] lords.
     TIMON An° thou shouldst, thou'dst anger ladies.   *If*
     APEMANTUS O, they eat lords. So they come by great bellies.
     TIMON That's a lascivious apprehension.[9]
210 APEMANTUS So thou apprehend'st it; take it for thy labour.
     TIMON How dost thou like this jewel, Apemantus?
     APEMANTUS Not so well as plain dealing, which will not cost a
     man a doit.°   *tiny coin*
     TIMON What dost thou think 'tis worth?

---

2. At what a merchant would pay (the wholesale price).
3. Are valued as their owners are valued.
4. *stay . . . honest:* wait for a polite greeting until you are
changed into your own dog or (an equally likely prospect)
these crooks become honest.
5. Since there are no honest Athenians.

6. For its inability to harm anyone.
7. "Dog" is not merely a term of contempt; Apemantus
was a Cynic philosopher, a school whose name derived
from the Greek *kynē,* "dog."
8. I do not devour the substance of.
9. Interpretation; grasping.

APEMANTUS   Not worth my thinking.

215   How now, poet?

POET   How now, philosopher?

APEMANTUS   Thou liest.

POET   Art not one?

APEMANTUS   Yes.

220 POET   Then I lie not.

APEMANTUS   Art not a poet?

POET   Yes.

APEMANTUS   Then thou liest. Look in thy last work, where thou
hast feigned him° a worthy fellow.   *(Timon)*

225 POET   That's not feigned, he is so.

APEMANTUS   Yes, he is worthy of thee, and to pay thee for thy
labour. He that loves to be flattered is worthy o'th' flatterer.
Heavens, that I were a lord!

TIMON   What wouldst do then, Apemantus?

230 APEMANTUS   E'en as Apemantus does now: hate a lord with my heart.

TIMON   What, thyself?

APEMANTUS   Ay.

TIMON   Wherefore?

APEMANTUS   That I had no augury[1] but to be a lord.—Art not

235 thou a merchant?

MERCHANT   Ay, Apemantus.

APEMANTUS   Traffic confound° thee, if the gods will not!   *May business ruin*

MERCHANT   If traffic do it, the gods do it.

APEMANTUS   Traffic's thy god, and thy god confound thee!

      Trumpet sounds. Enter a MESSENGER

240 TIMON   What trumpet's that?

MESSENGER   'Tis Alcibiades, and some twenty horse°   *horsemen*
All of companionship.°   *in one group*

TIMON [*to Servants*]   Pray entertain them. Give them guide to us.

                   [*Exit one or more Servants*]

[*To* JEWELLER] You must needs dine with me.

[*To* POET]   Go not you hence

245 Till I have thanked you. [*To* PAINTER] When dinner's done
Show me this piece. [*To all*] I am joyful of your sights.°   *to see you*

      Enter ALCIBIADES *with* [*his horsemen*]

Most welcome, sir!

APEMANTUS [*aside*]   So, so, there.
Aches contract and starve° your supple joints!   *ruin*

250 That there should be small love 'mongst these sweet knaves,
And all this courtesy! The strain of man's bred out°   *degenerated*
Into baboon and monkey.

ALCIBIADES [*to* TIMON]   Sir, you have saved my longing,° and I   *anticipated my desire*
feed
Most hungrily on your sight.

TIMON   Right welcome, sir!

255 Ere we depart, we'll share a bounteous time
In different pleasures. Pray you, let us in.

               Exeunt [*all but* APEMANTUS]

      Enter two LORDS

FIRST LORD   What time o' day is't, Apemantus?

APEMANTUS   Time to be honest.

---

1. Foresight (so I could avoid it).

	FIRST LORD That time serves still.°	*always*
	APEMANTUS The most accursèd thou, that still omitt'st° it.	*do not take advantage of*
260	SECOND LORD Thou art going to Lord Timon's feast?	
	APEMANTUS Ay, to see meat fill knaves, and wine heat fools.	
	SECOND LORD Fare thee well, fare thee well.	
	APEMANTUS Thou art a fool to bid me farewell twice.	
	SECOND LORD Why, Apemantus?	
265	APEMANTUS Shouldst have kept one to thyself, for I mean to give	
	thee none.	
	FIRST LORD Hang thyself!	
	APEMANTUS No, I will do nothing at thy bidding. Make thy	
	requests to thy friend.	
270	SECOND LORD Away, unpeaceable dog, or I'll spurn° thee hence.	*kick*
	APEMANTUS I will fly, like a dog, the heels o'th' ass. *Exit*	
	FIRST LORD He's opposite° to humanity. Come, shall we in,	*antagonistic*
	And taste Lord Timon's bounty? He outgoes°	*surpasses*
	The very heart° of kindness.	*essence*
275	SECOND LORD He pours it out. Plutus the god of gold	
	Is but his steward; no meed° but he repays	*gift*
	Sevenfold above itself; no gift to him	
	But breeds the giver a return exceeding	
	All use of quittance.°	*customary interest rates*
	FIRST LORD The noblest mind he carries	
280	That ever governed man.	
	SECOND LORD Long may he live in fortunes! Shall we in?	
	FIRST LORD I'll keep you company. *Exeunt*	

1.2

Hautboys° playing loud music. A great banquet served in **Oboes**
[FLAVIUS and Servants attending]; and then enter
TIMON, [ALCIBIADES,] the [SENATORS], the Athenian
LORDS, [and] VENTIDIUS which TIMON redeemed from
prison. Then comes, dropping° after all, APEMANTUS, dis- **entering casually**
contentedly, like himself° **in everyday clothes**

	VENTIDIUS Most honoured Timon, it hath pleased the gods to	
	remember	
	My father's age and call him to long peace.°	*eternal rest*
	He is gone happy, and has left me rich.	
	Then, as in grateful virtue I am bound	
5	To your free° heart, I do return those talents,	*generous*
	Doubled with thanks and service, from whose help	
	I derived liberty.	
	TIMON O, by no means,	
	Honest Ventidius. You mistake my love.	
	I gave it freely ever, and there's none	
10	Can truly say he gives if he receives.	
	If our betters play at that game,° we must not dare	*pretend generosity*
	To imitate them. Faults that are rich° are fair.	*of rich people*
	VENTIDIUS A noble spirit!	
	[The LORDS stand with ceremony]	
	TIMON Nay, my lords,	
	Ceremony was but devised at first	
15	To set a gloss on¹ faint deeds, hollow welcomes,	

1.2 Location: Timon's banqueting room. 1. To give a fine appearance to.

Recanting goodness,[2] sorry ere 'tis shown;
But where there is true friendship, there needs none.°   *no ceremony*
Pray sit. More welcome are ye to my fortunes
Than my fortunes to me.
                        [*They sit*]

20 FIRST LORD   My lord, we always have confessed it.

APEMANTUS   Ho, ho, confessed it? Hanged it, have you not?

TIMON   O, Apemantus! You are welcome.

APEMANTUS   No,
You shall not make me welcome.
I come to have thee° thrust me out of doors.   *provoke you to*

25 TIMON   Fie, thou'rt a churl.° Ye've got a humour there   *rude one*
Does not become a man; 'tis much to blame.
They say, my lords, *Ira furor brevis est*,[3]
But yon man is ever angry.
Go, let him have a table by himself,
30 For he does neither affect° company   *like*
Nor is he fit for't, indeed.

APEMANTUS   Let me stay at thine apperil,° Timon.   *risk*
I come to observe, I give thee warning on't.

TIMON   I take no heed of thee; thou'rt an Athenian,
35 Therefore welcome. I myself would have no power:[4]
Prithee, let my meat make thee silent.

APEMANTUS   I scorn thy meat. 'Twould choke me, for I should
ne'er flatter thee. O you gods, what a number of men eats
Timon, and he sees 'em not! It grieves me to see so many dip
40 their meat in one man's blood; and all° the madness is, he   *the height of*
cheers them up,° too.   *encourages them*
I wonder men dare trust themselves with men.
Methinks they should invite them without knives:[5]
Good for their meat, and safer for their lives.
45 There's much example for't. The fellow that sits next him, now
parts° bread with him, pledges the breath of him in a divided   *shares*
draught,[6] is the readiest man to kill him. 'T'as been proved. If
I were a huge° man, I should fear to drink at meals,   *great*
Lest they should spy my windpipe's dangerous notes.[7]
50 Great men should drink with harness° on their throats.   *armor*

TIMON [*drinking to a* LORD]   My lord, in heart; and let the
health° go round.   *shared cup*

SECOND LORD   Let it flow° this way, my good lord.   *circulate*

APEMANTUS   'Flow this way'? A brave° fellow; he keeps his tides[8]   *fine (ironic)*
55 well. Those healths will make thee and thy state look ill,
Timon.
Here's that which is too weak to be a sinner:
Honest water, which ne'er left man i'th' mire.
This and my food are equals; there's no odds.
60 Feasts are too proud to give thanks to the gods.
          Apemantus' grace
Immortal gods, I crave no pelf.°   *property (contemptuous)*

---

2. Generosity that demands repayment or that is immediately revoked.
3. Anger is brief insanity (Latin).
4. Wish no power to silence you.
5. Renaissance dinner guests brought their own silver-
ware.

6. *pledges . . . draught*: toasts his health in a shared cup.
7. *my . . . notes*: the indications, when I drink, of where
my windpipe is (so they can cut my throat).
8. He observes his opportunity (joking, with wordplay on
"flow," that the Second Lord is ensuring that he gets
plenty to drink).

I pray for no man but myself.
Grant I may never prove so fond°   foolish
To trust man on his oath or bond,
65   Or a harlot for her weeping,
Or a dog that seems a-sleeping,
Or a keeper° with my freedom,   jailer
Or my friends if I should need 'em.
Amen. So fall to't.
70   Rich men sin, and I eat root.
     [*He eats*]
Much good dich° thy good heart, Apemantus.   may it do
TIMON   Captain Alcibiades, your heart's in the field° now.   battlefield
ALCIBIADES   My heart is ever at your service, my lord.
TIMON   You had rather be at a breakfast of enemies° than a din-   (at a battle)
75   ner of friends.
ALCIBIADES   So they were bleeding new, my lord; there's no
meat like 'em. I could wish my best friend at such a feast.
APEMANTUS   Would all those flatterers were thine enemies then,
That thou mightst kill 'em and bid me to 'em.
80   FIRST LORD [*to* TIMON]   Might we but have that happiness, my
lord, that you would once use our hearts,⁹ whereby we might
express some part of our zeals,° we should think ourselves for   love
ever perfect.°   happy
TIMON   O, no doubt, my good friends, but the gods themselves
85   have provided that I shall have much help from you. How had
you been my friends else? Why have you that charitable title°   loving name
from thousands, did not you chiefly belong to my heart? I have
told more of you to myself than you can with modesty speak in
your own behalf; and thus far I confirm you.¹ 'O you gods,'
90   think I, 'what need we have any friends if we should ne'er have
need of 'em? They were the most needless creatures living,
should we ne'er have use for 'em, and would most resemble
sweet instruments hung up in cases, that keeps their sounds to
themselves.' Why, I have often wished myself poorer, that I
95   might come nearer to you. We are born to do benefits; and
what better or properer° can we call our own than the riches of   more suitably
our friends? O, what a precious comfort 'tis to have so many
like brothers commanding° one another's fortunes! O, joy's   having at their command
e'en made away° ere't can be born: mine eyes cannot hold out   destroyed (by tears)
100 water, methinks. To forget their° faults, I drink to you.   (my eyes')
APEMANTUS   Thou weep'st to make them drink, Timon.
SECOND LORD [*to* TIMON]   Joy had the like° conception in our eyes,   some kind of
And at that instant like a babe sprung up.
APEMANTUS   Ho, ho, I laugh to think that babe a bastard.²
105 THIRD LORD [*to* TIMON]   I promise you, my lord, you moved me much.
APEMANTUS   Much!
     [*A*] tucket° sound[*s within*]   trumpet flourish
TIMON   What means that trump?
     Enter SERVANT
How now?
SERVANT   Please you, my lord, there are certain ladies most desir-
110 ous of admittance.

9. Would make trial of our affection.   2. That is, the guests' tears are illegitimate.
1. In your claim to be my friends.

TIMON	Ladies? What are their wills?	
SERVANT	There comes with them a forerunner, my lord, which	
	bears that office° to signify their pleasures.°	*function / desires*
TIMON	I pray let them be admitted.	

Enter [one as] CUPID

115 CUPID   Hail to thee, worthy Timon, and to all
That of his bounties taste! The five best senses
Acknowledge thee their patron, and come freely
To gratulate° thy plenteous bosom.° Th'ear,   *greet / generous heart*
Taste, touch, smell, all, pleased from thy table rise.
120 They° only now come but to feast thine eyes.   *(the masques)*

TIMON   They're welcome all. Let 'em have kind admittance.
Music make their welcome!   [*Exit* CUPID]

FIRST LORD   You see, my lord, how ample you're beloved.

[*Music.*] *Enter a masque of* LADIES [*as*] *Amazons, with
lutes in their hands, dancing and playing*

APEMANTUS   Hey-day, what a sweep of vanity comes this way!
125 They dance? They are madwomen.
Like madness is the glory° of this life   *vainglory*
As this pomp shows to a little oil and root.[3]
We make ourselves fools to disport° ourselves,   *amuse*
And spend our flatteries to drink° those men   *toast; drink up*
130 Upon whose age we void° it up again   *old age we spit*
With poisonous spite and envy.
Who lives that's not depravèd or depraves?
Who dies that bears not one spurn° to their graves   *insult*
Of their friends' gift?°   *giving*
135 I should fear those that dance before me now
Would one day stamp upon me. 'T'as been done.
Men shut their doors against a setting sun.

The LORDS *rise from table with much adoring of* TIMON;
*and to show their loves each singles out an Amazon, and
all dance, men with women, a lofty strain or two to the
hautboys, and cease*

TIMON   You have done our pleasures much grace, fair ladies,
Set a fair fashion on° our entertainment,   *Made elegant*
140 Which was not half so beautiful and kind.
You have added worth unto't and lustre,
And entertained me with mine own device.[4]
I am to thank you for't.

FIRST LADY   My lord, you take us even at the best.[5]
145 APEMANTUS   Faith; for the worst is filthy, and would not hold
taking,[6] I doubt me.

TIMON   Ladies, there is an idle° banquet 'tends you.   *a trifling*
Please you to dispose° yourselves.   *seat*

ALL LADIES   Most thankfully, my lord.   *Exeunt* [LADIES]
150 TIMON   Flavius.

FLAVIUS   My lord.

TIMON   The little casket bring me hither.

FLAVIUS   Yes, my lord. [*Aside*] More jewels yet?
There is no crossing him in's humour,°   *whim*

---

3. As this feast compares to a meager meal.
4. Plan. Timon may be implying that he himself arranged the entertainment or merely that it was designed for him by his admirers.

5. You consider our efforts in the best possible light.
6. Would not be worth noting; would not endure sexual penetration (because of venereal disease).

155   Else I should tell him well, i'faith I should.
          When all's spent, he'd be crossed[7] then, an° he could.   *if*
          'Tis pity bounty had not eyes behind,[8]
          That man might ne'er be wretched for his mind.[9]   *Exit*
    FIRST LORD   Where be our men?
160   SERVANT   Here, my lord, in readiness.
    SECOND LORD   Our horses.   *[Exit* SERVANT*]*
        [Enter FLAVIUS *with the casket. He gives it to* TIMON *and*
        exits]
    TIMON   O my friends, I have one word to say to you.
          Look you, my good lord,
          I must entreat you honour me so much
165   As to advance° this jewel. Accept and wear it,   *improve (by your worth)*
          Kind my lord.
    FIRST LORD   I am so far already in your gifts.
    ALL LORDS   So are we all.
        *[*TIMON *gives them jewels.]*
        Enter a SERVANT
    FIRST SERVANT   My lord, there are certain nobles of the senate
170   newly alighted and come to visit you.
    TIMON   They are fairly° welcome.   *[Exit* SERVANT*]*   *graciously*
        Enter FLAVIUS
    FLAVIUS   I beseech your honour, vouchsafe me a word; it does
          concern you near.
    TIMON   Near? Why then, another time I'll hear thee. I prithee,
175   let's be provided to show them entertainment.
    FLAVIUS   I scarce know how.
        Enter a [SECOND SERVANT]
    SECOND SERVANT   May it please your honour, Lord Lucius
          Out of his free love hath presented to you
          Four milk-white horses trapped° in silver.   *bedecked*
180   TIMON   I shall accept them fairly. Let the presents
          Be worthily entertained.°   *[Exit* SERVANT*]*   *accepted*
        Enter a [THIRD SERVANT]
               How now, what news?
    THIRD SERVANT   Please you, my lord, that honourable gentleman
          Lord Lucullus entreats your company tomorrow to hunt with
          him, and has sent your honour two brace° of greyhounds.   *pairs*
185   TIMON   I'll hunt with him, and let them be received
          Not without fair reward.   *[Exit* SERVANT*]*
    FLAVIUS *[aside]*   What will this come to?
          He commands us to provide and give great gifts,
          And all out of an empty coffer;
          Nor will he know his purse, or yield° me this: *allow*
190   To show him what a beggar his heart is,
          Being of no power to make his wishes good.
          His promises fly so beyond his state°   *estate*
          That what he speaks is all in debt, he owes
          For every word. He is so kind that he now
195   Pays interest for't. His land's put to their books.°   *mortgaged*
          Well, would I were gently put out of office
          Before I were forced out.

---

7. He'd want to have his debts canceled.   9. *for his mind:* because of his (generous) intentions.
8. 'Tis a pity generosity is not more careful.

Happier is he that has no friend to feed
Than such that do e'en enemies exceed.[1]
I bleed inwardly for my lord.   *Exit*

200 TIMON [*to the* LORDS]   You do yourselves
Much wrong, you bate° too much of your own merits.   *undervalue*
[*To* SECOND LORD] Here, my lord, a trifle of our love.

SECOND LORD   With more than common thanks I will receive it.

THIRD LORD   O, he's the very soul of bounty!

205 TIMON [*to* FIRST LORD]   And now I remember, my lord, you gave
good words the other day of a bay courser I rode on. 'Tis yours,
because you liked it.

FIRST LORD   O I beseech you pardon me, my lord, in that.[2]

TIMON   You may take my word, my lord, I know no man
210 Can justly praise but what he does affect.°   *desire*
I weigh my friends' affection with mine own.
I'll tell you true, I'll call to° you.   *on*

ALL LORDS   O, none so welcome.

TIMON   I take all and your several visitations
So kind to heart, 'tis not enough to give.
215 Methinks I could deal kingdoms to my friends,
And ne'er be weary. Alcibiades,
Thou art a soldier, therefore seldom rich.
[*Giving a present*] It comes in charity to thee, for all thy living
Is 'mongst the dead, and all the lands thou hast
Lie in a pitched field.

220 ALCIBIADES   Ay, defiled[3] land, my lord.

FIRST LORD   We are so virtuously bound—

TIMON   And so am I to you.

SECOND LORD   So infinitely endeared°—   *obliged*

TIMON   All to you. Lights, more lights!

225 FIRST LORD   The best of happiness, honour, and fortunes
Keep with you, Lord Timon.

TIMON   Ready for his friends.

               Exeunt [*all but* TIMON *and* APEMANTUS]

APEMANTUS   What a coil's° here,   *commotion is*
Serving of becks° and jutting-out of bums!   *bowing*
230 I doubt whether their legs° be worth the sums   *curtsies*
That are given for 'em. Friendship's full of dregs.
Methinks false hearts should never have sound legs.
Thus honest fools lay out their wealth on curtseys.

TIMON   Now, Apemantus, if thou wert not sullen
235 I would be good to thee.

APEMANTUS   No, I'll nothing; for if I should be bribed too, there
would be none left to rail upon thee, and then thou wouldst
sin the faster. Thou giv'st so long, Timon, I fear me thou wilt
give away thyself in paper° shortly. What needs these feasts,   *promissory notes*
240 pomps, and vainglories?

TIMON   Nay, an you begin to rail on society once, I am sworn
not to give regard° to you.   *pay attention*
Farewell, and come with better music.   *Exit*

---

1. Who ruin themselves faster than enemies could.
2. That is, I wasn't hinting for the horse.
3. Lined with ranks of soldiers; punning on Ecclesiasticus 13:1, "He that toucheth pitch, shall be defiled with
it."

APEMANTUS   So.
      Thou wilt not hear me now, thou shalt not then.
245   I'll lock thy heaven° from thee. O, that men's ears should be   *(my redemptive guidance)*
      To counsel deaf, but not to flattery!   *Exit*

                              2.1
                Enter a SENATOR *[with bonds]*

SENATOR   And late five thousand. To Varro and to Isidore
      He owes nine thousand, besides my former sum,
      Which makes it five-and-twenty. Still in motion
      Of raging waste!¹ It cannot hold,° it will not.   *last*
5   If I want gold, steal but a beggar's dog
      And give it Timon, why, the dog coins gold.
      If I would sell my horse and buy twenty more
      Better than he, why, give my horse to Timon—
      Ask nothing, give it him—it foals me straight,²
10   And able horses. No porter³ at his gate,
      But rather one that smiles and still invites
      All that pass by. It cannot hold. No reason
      Can sound his state in safety.⁴ Caphis ho!
      Caphis, I say!
                Enter CAPHIS
CAPHIS   Here, sir. What is your pleasure?
15 SENATOR   Get on your cloak and haste you to Lord Timon.
      Importune him for my moneys. Be not ceased°   *put off*
      With slight denial, nor then silenced when
      'Commend me to your master', and the cap
      Plays in the right hand,⁵ thus; but tell him
20   My uses cry to me, I must serve my turn
      Out of mine own,⁶ his days and times are past,
      And my reliances on his fracted° dates   *broken*
      Have smit° my credit. I love and honour him,   *hurt*
      But must not break my back to heal his finger.
25   Immediate are my needs, and my relief
      Must not be tossed and turned⁷ to me in words,
      But find supply immediate. Get you gone.
      Put on a most importunate aspect,
      A visage of demand, for I do fear
30   When every feather sticks in his own wing⁸
      Lord Timon will be left a naked gull,°   *an unfledged bird; dupe*
      Which flashes now a phoenix. Get you gone.
CAPHIS   I go, sir.
SENATOR *[giving him bonds]* Take the bonds along with you,
      And have the dates in count.°   *reckoned up*
CAPHIS   I will, sir.
SENATOR   Go.
                              Exeunt [severally]°   *separately*

2.1 Location: A Senator's house.
1. *Still . . . waste:* Still keeping up unending extravagance.
2. It immediately gives birth.
3. Gatekeeper (who restricts entrance). *able horses:* full-
grown horses (not "foals," baby horses).
4. *No reason . . . safety:* No rational person can investigate his financial situation and believe it safe.
5. *when . . . hand:* that is, with friendly speech and gestures.
6. *serve . . . own:* pay for my needs with my own money.
7. Returned (like a tennis ball).
8. When everything is returned to its proper owner.

2.2

Enter [FLAVIUS the] Steward, with many bills in his hand

FLAVIUS No care, no stop; so senseless of expense
    That he will neither know how to maintain it
    Nor cease his flow of riot,° takes no account   *his wastefulness*
    How things go from him, nor resumes° no care   *takes*
5   Of what is to continue. Never mind
    Was to be so unwise to be so kind.[1]
    What shall be done? He will not hear till feel.°   *he suffers*
    [A sound of horns within]
    I must be round° with him, now he comes from hunting.   *frank*
    Fie, fie, fie, fie!

          Enter CAPHIS *[at one door] and* [SERVANTS *of*] *Isidore and Varro [at another door]*

10 CAPHIS Good even, Varro. What, you come for money?

VARRO'S SERVANT Is't not your business too?

CAPHIS It is; and yours too, Isidore?

ISIDORE'S SERVANT   It is so.

CAPHIS Would we were all discharged.

VARRO'S SERVANT   I fear it.

CAPHIS   Here comes the lord.

          Enter TIMON *and his train [amongst them* ALCIBIADES, *as from hunting]*

TIMON So soon as dinner's done we'll forth again,
    My Alcibiades.
          [CAPHIS meets TIMON]
15   With me? What is your will?

CAPHIS My lord, here is a note of certain dues.°   *debts*

TIMON Dues? Whence are you?

CAPHIS Of Athens here, my lord.

TIMON Go to my steward.

20 CAPHIS Please it your lordship, he hath put me off,
    To the succession of new days, this month.°   *every day for a month*
    My master is awaked° by great occasion°   *driven / need*
    To call upon his own,° and humbly prays you   *own money*
    That with your other noble parts you'll suit[2]
    In giving him his right.

25 TIMON   Mine honest friend,
    I prithee but repair° to me next morning.   *come back*

CAPHIS Nay, good my lord.

TIMON   Contain thyself, good friend.

VARRO'S SERVANT One Varro's servant, my good lord.

ISIDORE'S SERVANT *[to* TIMON] From Isidore. He humbly prays
    your speedy payment.

30 CAPHIS *[to* TIMON] If you did know, my lord, my master's wants—

VARRO'S SERVANT *[to* TIMON] 'Twas due on forfeiture,[3] my lord,
    six weeks and past.

ISIDORE'S SERVANT *[to* TIMON] Your steward puts me off, my lord, and I
    Am sent expressly to your lordship.

2.2 Location: Before Timon's house.
1. *Never . . . kind:* Never was anyone so idiotically generous.

2. That you'll act in accordance with your noble qualities.
3. On penalty of forfeiting the security.

TIMON   Give me breath.—
    I do beseech you, good my lords, keep on.°   *go ahead*
    I'll wait upon you instantly.
            [*Exeunt* ALCIBIADES *and Timon's train*]
35   [*To* FLAVIUS]   Come hither. Pray you,
    How goes the world, that I am thus encountered
    With clamorous demands of broken bonds
    And the detention of° long-since-due debts,   *failure to pay*
    Against my honour?
FLAVIUS [*to* SERVANTS]   Please you, gentlemen,
40   The time is unagreeable to this business;
    Your importunacy cease till after dinner,
    That I may make his lordship understand
    Wherefore you are not paid.
TIMON [*to* SERVANTS]   Do so, my friends.
    [*To* FLAVIUS] See them well entertained.   *Exit*
FLAVIUS   Pray draw near. *Exit*
       Enter APEMANTUS *and* FOOL
45 CAPHIS   Stay, stay, here comes the fool with Apemantus.
    Let's ha' some sport with 'em.
VARRO'S SERVANT   Hang him, he'll abuse us.
ISIDORE'S SERVANT   A plague upon him, dog!
VARRO'S SERVANT   How dost, fool?
50 APEMANTUS   Dost dialogue with thy shadow?[4]
VARRO'S SERVANT   I speak not to thee.
APEMANTUS   No, 'tis to thyself. [*To* FOOL] Come away.
ISIDORE'S SERVANT [*to* VARRO'S SERVANT]   There's the fool[5] hangs
    on your back already.
55 APEMANTUS   No, thou stand'st single:° thou'rt not on him yet.   *alone (in being a fool)*
CAPHIS [*to* ISIDORE'S SERVANT]   Where's the fool now?
APEMANTUS   He last asked the question. Poor rogues' and usu-
    rers' men, bawds between gold and want.[6]
ALL SERVANTS   What are we, Apemantus?
60 APEMANTUS   Asses.
ALL SERVANTS   Why?
APEMANTUS   That you ask me what you are, and do not know
    yourselves. Speak to 'em, fool.
FOOL   How do you, gentlemen?
65 ALL SERVANTS   Gramercies,° good fool. How does your mistress?   *Many thanks*
FOOL   She's e'en° setting on water to scald such chickens[7] as you   *just now*
    are. Would we could see you at Corinth.[8]
APEMANTUS   Good; gramercy.
       Enter PAGE [*with two letters*]
FOOL   Look you, here comes my mistress' page.
70 PAGE   Why, how now, captain? What do you in this wise com-
    pany? How dost thou, Apemantus?
APEMANTUS   Would I had a rod[9] in my mouth, that I might
    answer thee profitably.

---

4. With your reflection (implying that Varro's servant is also a fool).

5. The name "fool." In Renaissance England, wrong-doers were punished by being made to wear signs declaring their offenses.

6. *bawds . . . want:* go-betweens making deals between moneylenders and those who need loans.

7. In order to remove the feathers (a "plucked bird" was

a hoodwinked fool; compare 2.1.31); also, syphilitics were "sweated" in tubs of very hot water.

8. Greek city famous for prostitution.

9. From Proverbs 26:3–4: "Unto the horse belongeth a whip, to the ass a bridle, and a rod to the fool's back. Answer not a fool according to his foolishness, lest thou also be like him."

PAGE Prithee, Apemantus, read me the superscription° of these °address
75   letters. I know not which is which.

APEMANTUS Canst not read?

PAGE No.

APEMANTUS There will little learning die then that day thou art
  hanged. This is to Lord Timon, this to Alcibiades. Go, thou
80   wast born a bastard, and thou'lt die a bawd.

PAGE Thou wast whelped a dog, and thou shalt famish° a dog's °die
  death. Answer not; I am gone. _Exit_

APEMANTUS E'en so thou outrunn'st grace.[1] Fool, I will go with
  you to Lord Timon's.

85 FOOL Will you leave me there?

APEMANTUS If Timon stay at home.[2] [_To_ SERVANTS] You three
  serve three usurers?

ALL SERVANTS Ay. Would they served us.° °treated us well

APEMANTUS So would I: as good a trick as ever hangman served
90   thief.

FOOL Are you three usurers' men?

ALL SERVANTS Ay, fool.

FOOL I think no usurer but has a fool to his servant. My mistress
  is one,[3] and I am her fool. When men come to borrow of your
95   masters they approach sadly and go away merry, but they enter
  my mistress's house merrily and go away sadly.[4] The reason of
  this?

VARRO'S SERVANT I could render one.

APEMANTUS Do it then, that we may account thee a whore-
100   master and a knave, which notwithstanding thou shalt be no
  less esteemed.

VARRO'S SERVANT What is a whoremaster, fool?

FOOL A fool in good clothes, and something like thee. 'Tis a
  spirit; sometime 't appears like a lord, sometime like a lawyer,
105   sometime like a philosopher with two stones[5] more than's° arti- °than his
  ficial one. He is very often like a knight; and generally in all
  shapes that man goes up and down in from fourscore to thirteen, this spirit walks in.

VARRO'S SERVANT Thou art not altogether a fool.

110 FOOL Nor thou altogether a wise man. As much foolery as I
  have, so much wit thou lack'st.

APEMANTUS That answer might have become° Apemantus. °suited
       Enter TIMON _and_ [FLAVIUS _the_] _Steward_

ALL SERVANTS Aside, aside, here comes Lord Timon.

APEMANTUS Come with me, fool, come.

115 FOOL I do not always follow lover, elder brother, and woman:[6]
  sometime the philosopher   [_Exeunt_ APEMANTUS _and_ FOOL]

FLAVIUS [_to_ SERVANTS] Pray you, walk near. I'll speak with you
  anon.   _Exeunt_ [SERVANTS]

TIMON You make me marvel wherefore ere this time
120   Had you not fully laid my state before me,[7]
  That I might so have rated° my expense °regulated
  As I had leave of means.° °As means permitted

---

1. You run away from profitable instruction.
2. There will be a fool at Timon's house as long as he is at home.
3. She is a "usurer" in the sense that she lends her body for financial gain; the connection between usury and prostitution was traditional.
4. According to Aristotle, all creatures are sad after sexual intercourse.
5. Testicles. In alchemy, the "philosopher's stone" was thought to turn base metals into gold.
6. All figures associated with folly.
7. Described my financial status.

FLAVIUS   You would not hear me.
 At many leisures I proposed—
TIMON   Go to.°   *(impatient exclamation)*
 Perchance some single vantages° you took, *isolated opportunities*
125 When my indisposition° put you back,   *disinclination*
 And that unaptness made your minister°   *allowed you*
 Thus to excuse yourself.
FLAVIUS   O my good lord,
 At many times I brought in my accounts,
 Laid them before you; you would throw them off
130 And say you summed them in mine honesty.[8]
 When for some trifling present you have bid me
 Return so much,° I have shook my head and wept, *a large sum*
 Yea, 'gainst th'authority of manners° prayed you *with rude bluntness*
 To hold your hand more close. I did endure
135 Not seldom nor no slight checks° when I have *rebukes*
 Prompted you in° the ebb of your estate   *Urged you to note*
 And your great flow of debts. My lovèd lord—
 Though you hear now too late, yet now's a time°— *better late than never*
 The greatest of your having[9] lacks a half
 To pay your present debts.
140 TIMON   Let all my land be sold.
FLAVIUS 'Tis all engaged,° some forfeited and gone, *mortgaged*
 And what remains will hardly stop the mouth
 Of present dues.° The future comes apace.   *debts*
 What shall defend the interim, and at length° *in the long term*
145 How goes our reck'ning?
TIMON To Lacedaemon° did my land extend. *Sparta*
FLAVIUS O my good lord, the world is but a word.
 Were it all yours to give it in a breath,
 How quickly were it gone.
TIMON   You tell me true.
150 FLAVIUS If you suspect my husbandry° or falsehood, *household management*
 Call me before th'exactest auditors
 And set me on the proof. So the gods bless me,
 When all our offices° have been oppressed *kitchens and workrooms*
 With riotous feeders, when our vaults have wept
155 With drunken spilth° of wine, when every room *spilling*
 Hath blazed with lights and brayed with minstrelsy,
 I have retired me to a wasteful cock,[1]
 And set mine eyes at flow.
TIMON   Prithee, no more.
FLAVIUS 'Heavens,' have I said, 'the bounty of this lord!
160 How many prodigal bits° have slaves and peasants *extravagant morsels*
 This night englutted! Who is not Timon's?° *devoted to Timon*
 What heart, head, sword, force, means, but is Lord Timon's?
 Great Timon, noble, worthy, royal Timon!
 Ah, when the means are gone that buy this praise,
165 The breath is gone whereof this praise is made.
 Feast won, fast° lost; one cloud of winter show'rs, *quickly; while fasting*
 These flies are couched.'°   *lying unseen*
TIMON   Come, sermon me no further.

---

8. You gauged their accuracy by my honesty.
9. The most generous estimate of your wealth.

1. I have sat down beside a wine spout, left wastefully
flowing.

No villainous° bounty yet hath passed my heart.   *shameful*
Unwisely, not ignobly, have I given.
170 Why dost thou weep? Canst thou the conscience° lack   *conviction*
To think I shall lack friends? Secure thy heart.
If I would broach° the vessels of my love   *tap (like a wine barrel)*
And try the argument° of hearts by borrowing,   *test the contents*
Men and men's fortunes could I frankly° use   *as freely*
As I can bid thee speak.

175 FLAVIUS   Assurance bless your thoughts!²
TIMON   And in some sort° these wants of mine are crowned°   *respect / exalted*
That I account them blessings, for by these
Shall I try friends. You shall perceive how you
Mistake my fortunes. I am wealthy in my friends.—
180 Within there, Flaminius, Servilius!

Enter [FLAMINIUS, SERVILIUS, *and a* THIRD] SERVANT

ALL SERVANTS   My lord, my lord.
TIMON   I will dispatch you severally,°   *separately*
[*To* SERVILIUS] You to Lord Lucius,
[*To* FLAMINIUS]   to Lord Lucullus you—
I hunted with his honour today—
[*To* THIRD SERVANT] You to Sempronius. Commend me to
    their loves,
185 And I am proud, say, that my occasions° have   *needs*
Found time° to use 'em toward a supply of money.   *occasion*
Let the request be fifty talents.°   *(a huge sum)*
FLAMINIUS   As you have said, my lord.   [*Exeunt* SERVANTS]
FLAVIUS   Lord Lucius and Lucullus? Hmh!
190 TIMON   Go you, sir, to the senators,
Of whom, even to the state's best health,³ I have
Deserved this hearing. Bid 'em send o'th' instant
A thousand talents to me.
FLAVIUS   I have been bold,
For that I knew it the most general° way,   *usual*
195 To them, to use your signet⁴ and your name;
But they do shake their heads, and I am here
No richer in return.
TIMON   Is't true? Can't be?
FLAVIUS   They answer in a joint and corporate voice
That now they are at fall,° want° treasure, cannot   *low ebb / lack*
200 Do what they would, are sorry, you are honourable,
But yet they could have wished—they know not—
Something hath been amiss—a noble nature
May catch a wrench°—would all were well—'tis pity;   *suffer a misfortune*
And so, intending° other serious matters,   *pretending; attending to*
205 After distasteful looks and these hard fractions,°   *phrases*
With certain half-caps° and cold moving nods   *reluctant salutations*
They froze me into silence.
TIMON   You gods reward them!
Prithee, man, look cheerly.° These old fellows   *cheerful*
Have their ingratitude in them hereditary.
210 Their blood is caked, 'tis cold, it seldom flows.
'Tis lack of kindly⁵ warmth they are not kind;

---

2. May your hopes be well founded.
3. Greatest welfare (see 4.3.92–95).

4. Signet ring (token of authorization).
5. Natural (punning on "caring").

And nature as it grows again toward earth°   *the grave*
Is fashioned for the journey dull and heavy.
Go to Ventidius. Prithee, be not sad.
215   Thou art true and honest—ingenuously° I speak—   *candidly*
No blame belongs to thee. Ventidius lately
Buried his father, by whose death he's stepped
Into a great estate. When he was poor,
Imprisoned, and in scarcity of friends,
220   I cleared him with five talents. Greet him from me.
Bid him suppose some good° necessity   *urgent*
Touches his friend, which craves to be remembered
With° those five talents. That had, give't these fellows   *By return of*
To whom 'tis instant due. Ne'er speak or think
225   That Timon's fortunes 'mong his friends can sink.
FLAVIUS   I would I could not think it. That thought is bounty's foe:
Being free° itself, it thinks all others so.   *Exeunt [severally]*   *generous*

3.1

[Enter] FLAMINIUS, *[with a box under his cloak,] waiting
to speak with* [LUCULLUS]. *From his master, enters a* SER-
VANT *to him*

LUCULLUS' SERVANT   I have told my lord of you. He is coming
down to you.
FLAMINIUS   I thank you, sir.
    Enter LUCULLUS
LUCULLUS' SERVANT   Here's my lord.
5   LUCULLUS *[aside]*   One of Lord Timon's men? A gift, I warrant.
Why, this hits right; I dreamt of a silver basin and ewer°   *pitcher*
tonight.—Flaminius, honest Flaminius, you are very respec-
tively° welcome, sir. *[To his* SERVANT] Fill me some wine.   *respectfully*
    [Exit SERVANT]
And how does that honourable, complete, free-hearted gentle-
10   man of Athens, thy very bountiful good lord and master?
FLAMINIUS   His health is well, sir.
LUCULLUS   I am right glad that his health is well, sir. And what
hast thou there under thy cloak, pretty Flaminius?
FLAMINIUS   Faith, nothing but an empty box, sir, which in my
15   lord's behalf I come to entreat your honour to supply, who,
having great and instant° occasion to use fifty talents, hath sent   *urgent*
to your lordship to furnish him, nothing doubting your present°   *immediate*
assistance therein.
LUCULLUS   La, la, la, la, 'nothing doubting' says he? Alas, good
20   lord! A noble gentleman 'tis, if he would not keep so good a
house.° Many a time and often I ha' dined with him and told   *such lavish hospitality*
him on't, and come again to supper to him of purpose to have
him¹ spend less; and yet he would embrace no counsel, take
no warning by my coming. Every man has his fault, and hon-
25   esty° is his. I ha' told him on't, but I could ne'er get him from't.   *generosity*
    Enter SERVANT, *with wine*
SERVANT   Please your lordship, here is the wine.
LUCULLUS   Flaminius, I have noted thee always wise.
    [Drinking]   Here's to thee!
FLAMINIUS   Your lordship speaks your pleasure.°   *It pleases you to say so*

3.1 Location: Lucullus's house.   **1.** *of . . . him:* in order to persuade him to.

30   LUCULLUS   I have observed thee always for a towardly° prompt   *promising*
    spirit, give thee thy due, and one that knows what belongs to
    reason;° and canst use the time well if the time use thee well.[2]   *is reasonable*
    [*Drinking*] Good parts in thee![3]
    [*To his* SERVANT] Get you gone, sirrah.   [*Exit* SERVANT]
35   Draw nearer, honest Flaminius. Thy lord's a bountiful gentle-
    man; but thou art wise, and thou know'st well enough,
    although thou com'st to me, that this is no time to lend money,
    especially upon bare° friendship without security. [*Giving*   *mere*
    coins] Here's three solidares° for thee. Good boy, wink at me,[4]   *shillings*
40   and say thou saw'st me not. Fare thee well.
  FLAMINIUS   Is't possible the world should so much differ,°   *alter*
    And we alive that lived?
                [*He throws the coins at* LUCULLUS]
                        Fly, damnèd baseness,
    To him that worships thee.
  LUCULLUS   Ha! Now I see thou art a fool, and fit for thy master.
                                        Exit
45   FLAMINIUS   May these add to the number that may scald thee.°   *(in hell)*
    Let molten coin be thy damnation,
    Thou disease of a friend, and not himself.°   *not a true friend*
    Has friendship such a faint and milky heart
    It turns° in less than two nights? O you gods,   *curdles*
50   I feel my master's passion!° This slave   *suffering*
    Unto this hour has my lord's meat in him.
    Why should it thrive and turn to nutriment,
    When he is turned to poison?
    O, may diseases only work upon't;
55   And when he's sick to death, let not that part of nature
    Which my lord paid for be of any power
    To expel sickness, but prolong his hour.°   *Exit*   *(of suffering)*

3.2

      Enter LUCIUS, *with three* STRANGERS
  LUCIUS   Who, the Lord Timon? He is my very good friend, and
    an honourable gentleman.
  FIRST STRANGER   We know him for no less, though we are but
    strangers to him. But I can tell you one thing, my lord, and
5   which I hear from common rumours: now Lord Timon's happy
    hours are done and past, and his estate shrinks from him.
  LUCIUS   Fie, no, do not believe it. He cannot want for money.
  SECOND STRANGER   But believe you this, my lord, that not long
    ago one of his men was with the Lord Lucullus to borrow so
10   many talents—nay, urged extremely for't, and showed what
    necessity belonged to't, and yet was denied.
  LUCIUS   How?
  SECOND STRANGER   I tell you, denied, my lord.
  LUCIUS   What a strange case was that! Now before the gods, I am
15   ashamed on't. Denied that honourable man? There was very
    little honour showed in't. For my own part, I must needs con-
    fess I have received some small kindnesses from him, as money,
    plate, jewels, and suchlike trifles—nothing comparing to his;

---

2. *canst . . . thee well*: know how to use an opportunity.   4. Close your eyes to me.
3. To your good qualities (a toast).   3.2 Location: A public place.

20 yet had he not mistook him[1] and sent to me, I should ne'er
have denied his occasion so many talents.

     Enter SERVILIUS

SERVILIUS [*aside*] See, by good hap yonder's my lord. I have
sweat° to see his honour. [*To* LUCIUS] My honoured lord!   *hurried*

LUCIUS Servilius! You are kindly met, sir. Fare thee well. Commend me to thy honourable virtuous lord, my very exquisite°   *extraordinary*
25 friend.

SERVILIUS May it please your honour, my lord hath sent—

LUCIUS Ha! What has he sent? I am so much endeared° to that   *obliged*
lord, he's ever sending. How shall I thank him, think'st thou?
And what has he sent now?

30 SERVILIUS He's only sent his present occasion now, my lord,
requesting your lordship to supply his instant use with so many
talents.

LUCIUS I know his lordship is but merry with me.
He cannot want fifty-five hundred[2] talents.

35 SERVILIUS But in the mean time he wants less, my lord.
If his occasion were not virtuous
I should not urge it half so faithfully.

LUCIUS Dost thou speak seriously, Servilius?

SERVILIUS Upon my soul, 'tis true, sir.

40 LUCIUS What a wicked beast was I to disfurnish myself against
such a good time[3] when I might ha' shown myself honourable!
How unluckily it happened that I should purchase the day
before a little part,° and undo a great deal of honour! Servilius,   *small investment*
now before the gods I am not able to do, the more beast I, I
45 say. I was sending to use° Lord Timon myself—these gentle-   *make use of*
men can witness—but I would not for the wealth of Athens I
had done't now. Commend me bountifully to his good lord-
ship; and I hope his honour will conceive the fairest° of me   *think the best*
because I have no power to be kind. And tell him this from me:
50 I count it one of my greatest afflictions, say, that I cannot plea-
sure° such an honourable gentleman. Good Servilius, will you   *gratify*
befriend me so far as to use mine own words to him?

SERVILIUS Yes, sir, I shall.

LUCIUS I'll look you out° a good turn, Servilius. *Exit* SERVILIUS   *seek to do you*
55 True as you said: Timon is shrunk indeed;
And he that's once denied will hardly speed.°   *Exit*   *prosper*

FIRST STRANGER Do you observe this, Hostilius?

SECOND STRANGER   Ay, too well.

FIRST STRANGER Why, this is the world's soul,° and just of the   *essence*
same piece°   *(of cloth)*
Is every flatterer's spirit. Who can call him his friend
60 That dips in the same dish?[4] For, in my knowing,
Timon has been this lord's father°   *patron*
And kept his° credit with his purse,   *sustained (Lucius's)*
Supported his estate; nay, Timon's money
Has paid his men their wages. He ne'er drinks,
65 But Timon's silver treads upon his lip;
And yet—O see the monstrousness of man

1. Not overestimated Lucullus's generosity.
2. This number possibly retains Shakespeare's revision
from "five hundred" to "fifty" or vice versa.
3. *disfurnish . . . time*: be unprepared for such a fine
occasion.
4. Alluding to Judas's betrayal of Christ after the Last
Supper.

When he looks out° in an ungrateful shape!—   *shows himself*
He does deny him, in respect of his,[5]
What charitable men afford to beggars.

THIRD STRANGER   Religion groans at it.

70 FIRST STRANGER   For mine own part,
I never tasted° Timon in my life,   *had experience of*
Nor came any of his bounties over me
To mark me for his friend; yet I protest,
For his right noble mind, illustrious virtue,
75 And honourable carriage,°   *conduct*
Had his necessity made use of me
I would have put my wealth into donation°   *given my wealth*
And the best half should have returned to him,
So much I love his heart. But I perceive
80 Men must learn now with pity to dispense,
For policy° sits above conscience.   *Exeunt*   *calculation*

3.3

Enter [Timon's] THIRD SERVANT, *with* SEMPRONIUS,
another of Timon's friends

SEMPRONIUS   Must he needs trouble me in't? Hmh! 'Bove all others?
He might have tried Lord Lucius or Lucullus;
And now Ventidius is wealthy too,
Whom he redeemed from prison. All these
Owes their estates unto him.

5 SERVANT   My lord,
They have all been touched° and found base metal,   *tested for purity*
For they have all denied him.

SEMPRONIUS   How, have they denied him?
Has Ventidius and Lucullus denied him,
And does he send to me? Three? Hmh!
10 It shows but little love or judgement in him.
Must I be his last refuge? His friends, like physicians,
Thrive, give him over;[1] must I take th' cure upon me?
He's much disgraced me in't. I'm angry at him,
That might have known my place.[2] I see no sense for't
15 But his occasions might have wooed me first,
For, in my conscience,° I was the first man   *on my word*
That e'er received gift from him.
And does he think so backwardly of me now
That I'll requite it last? No.
20 So it may prove an argument° of laughter   *a subject*
To th' rest, and I 'mongst lords be thought a fool.
I'd rather than the worth of thrice the sum
He'd sent to me first, but for my mind's sake.[3]
I'd such a courage to do him good. But now return,
25 And with their faint reply this answer join:
Who bates° mine honour shall not know my coin.   *Exit*   *undervalues*

SERVANT   Excellent. Your lordship's a goodly villain. The devil
knew not what he did when he made man politic°— he   *calculating*
crossed[4] himself by't, and I cannot think but in the end the

---

5. In proportion to what he owns.
3.3 Location: Sempronius's house.
1. Thrive, while abandoning him to death.
2. That is, his place in Timon's list of friends.

3. If only on account of my disposition to him.
4. Thwarted (by making men his equal); canceled from
the list of debtors.

30 villainies of man will set him clear.[5] How fairly° this lord strives   *fully; speciously*
to appear foul! Takes virtuous copies° to be wicked, like those[6]   *precepts*
that under hot ardent zeal would set whole realms on fire; of
such a nature is his politic love.
This was my lord's best hope. Now all are fled
35 Save only the gods. Now his friends are dead.
Doors that were ne'er acquainted with their wards°   *locks*
Many a bounteous year must be employed
Now to guard sure° their master;   *safely*
And this is all a liberal° course allows: *generous*
40 Who cannot keep his wealth must keep his house.[7]   *Exit*

3.4

Enter Varro's [two SERVANTS*], meeting others, all [*SER-
VANTS *of*] *Timon's creditors, to wait for his coming out.*
*Then enter [*SERVANTS *of*] *Lucius, [Titus,] and Horten-*
sius

VARRO'S FIRST SERVANT   Well met; good morrow, Titus and
Hortensius.
TITUS' SERVANT   The like to you, kind Varro.
HORTENSIUS' SERVANT   Lucius, what, do we meet together?
LUCIUS' SERVANT   Ay, and I think one business does command
us all,
For mine is money.
5 TITUS' SERVANT   So is theirs and ours.
Enter [a SERVANT *of*] *Philotus*
LUCIUS' SERVANT   And Sir Philotus too!
PHILOTUS' SERVANT   Good day at once.
LUCIUS' SERVANT   Welcome, good brother. What do you think
the hour?
PHILOTUS' SERVANT   Labouring for° nine.   *Approaching*
LUCIUS' SERVANT   So much?
10 PHILOTUS' SERVANT   Is not my lord seen yet?
LUCIUS' SERVANT   Not yet.
PHILOTUS' SERVANT   I wonder on't; he was wont to shine° at   *used to rise*
seven.
LUCIUS' SERVANT   Ay, but the days are waxed shorter with him.
You must consider that a prodigal course
15 Is like the sun's,[1]
But not, like his,° recoverable. I fear   *(the sun's)*
'Tis deepest winter in Lord Timon's purse; that is,
One may reach deep enough, and yet find little.
PHILOTUS' SERVANT   I am of° your fear for that.   *I share*
20 TITUS' SERVANT   I'll show you how t'observe a strange event.
Your lord sends now for money?
HORTENSIUS' SERVANT   Most true, he does.
TITUS' SERVANT   And he wears jewels now of Timon's gift,
For° which I wait for money.   *For the purchase of*
HORTENSIUS' SERVANT   It is against my heart.°   *desire*
25 LUCIUS' SERVANT   Mark how strange it shows.
Timon in this should pay more than he owes,

---

5. Will make him look innocent; will free him from debt.
6. Religious fanatics; perhaps alludes to the Catholic Gunpowder Plot to blow up King and Parliament.

7. Must stay indoors (for fear of arrest).
3.4 Location: Timon's house.
1. That is, waning after the summer solstice.

And e'en° as if your lord should wear rich jewels   *just*
And send for money for 'em.²

HORTENSIUS' SERVANT   I'm weary of this charge,° the gods can   *task*
    witness.
30   I know my lord hath spent of Timon's wealth,
    And now ingratitude makes it worse than stealth.°   *stealing*

VARRO'S FIRST SERVANT
    Yes; mine's three thousand crowns. What's yours?

LUCIUS' SERVANT   Five thousand, mine.

VARRO'S FIRST SERVANT   'Tis much° deep, and it should seem by th' sum   *very*
    Your master's confidence was above mine,°   *(my master's)*
    Else surely his° had equalled.   *(my master's loan)*

       Enter FLAMINIUS

35 TITUS' SERVANT   One of Lord Timon's men.

LUCIUS' SERVANT   Flaminius! Sir, a word. Pray, is my lord
    Ready to come forth?

FLAMINIUS   No, indeed he is not.

TITUS' SERVANT   We attend his lordship.
    Pray signify so much.

40 FLAMINIUS   I need not tell
    Him that; he knows you are too diligent.

       Enter [FLAVIUS *the*] *Steward, muffled in a cloak*

LUCIUS' SERVANT   Ha, is not that his steward muffled so?
    He goes away in a cloud.° Call him, call him.   *concealed; in trouble*

TITUS' SERVANT [*to* FLAVIUS]   Do you hear, sir?

45 VARRO'S SECOND SERVANT [*to* FLAVIUS]   By your leave, sir.

FLAVIUS   What do ye ask of me, my friend?

TITUS' SERVANT   We wait for certain money here, sir.

FLAVIUS   Ay,
    If money were as certain as your waiting,
    'Twere sure enough.

50   Why then preferred° you not your sums and bills   *brought forward*
    When your false masters ate of my lord's meat?
    Then they could smile and fawn upon his debts,
    And take down th'int'rest into their glutt'nous maws.
    You do yourselves but wrong to stir me up.
55   Let me pass quietly.
    Believe't, my lord and I have made an end.°   *finished with each other*
    I have no more to reckon, he to spend.

LUCIUS' SERVANT   Ay, but this answer will not serve.

FLAVIUS   If 'twill not serve³ 'tis not so base as you,
60   For you serve knaves.   *Exit*

VARRO'S FIRST SERVANT   How? What does his cashiered° worship   *dismissed*
    mutter?

VARRO'S SECOND SERVANT   No matter what; he's poor, and that's
    revenge enough. Who can speak broader⁴ than he that has no
65   house to put his head in? Such may rail against great buildings.

       Enter SERVILIUS

TITUS' SERVANT   O, here's Servilius. Now we shall know some
    answer.

SERVILIUS   If I might beseech you, gentlemen, to repair° some   *return*

---

2. And demand payment from Timon for supplying them.   4. More freely; more out of doors.
3. Suffice (but in line 60, "wait on").

other hour, I should derive° much from't; for, take't of my soul,   *gain*
70   my lord leans wondrously to discontent. His comfortable° tem-   *cheerful*
   per has forsook him. He's much out of health, and keeps his
   chamber.

LUCIUS' SERVANT   Many do keep their chambers are not sick,[5]
   And if it be so far beyond his health
75   Methinks he should the sooner pay his debts
   And make a clear way to the gods.

SERVILIUS   Good gods!

TITUS' SERVANT   We cannot take this for an answer, sir.

FLAMINIUS [*within*]   Servilius, help! My lord, my lord!

         Enter TIMON *in a rage*

TIMON   What, are my doors opposed against my passage?
80   Have I been ever free,° and must my house   *at liberty; generous*
   Be my retentive° enemy, my jail?   *confining; niggardly*
   The place which I have feasted, does it now,
   Like all mankind, show me an iron heart?

LUCIUS' SERVANT   Put in° now, Titus.   *Make your claim*

TITUS' SERVANT   My lord, here is my bill.

LUCIUS' SERVANT   Here's mine.

85 HORTENSIUS' SERVANT   And mine, my lord.

VARRO'S FIRST *and* SECOND SERVANTS   And ours, my lord.

PHILOTUS' SERVANT   All our bills.

TIMON   Knock me down with 'em, cleave me to the girdle.[6]

LUCIUS' SERVANT   Alas, my lord.

90 TIMON   Cut my heart in° sums.   *into*

TITUS' SERVANT   Mine fifty talents.

TIMON   Tell° out my blood.   *Count*

LUCIUS' SERVANT   Five thousand crowns, my lord.

TIMON   Five thousand drops pays that. What yours? And yours?

VARRO'S FIRST SERVANT   My lord—

95 VARRO'S SECOND SERVANT   My lord—

TIMON   Tear me, take me, and the gods fall upon you.   *Exit*

HORTENSIUS' SERVANT   Faith, I perceive our masters may throw
   their caps at° their money. These debts may well be called des-   *cease pursuing*
   perate° ones, for a madman owes 'em.   *Exeunt*   *hopeless; insane*

3.5

         Enter TIMON [*and* FLAVIUS]

TIMON   They have e'en put[1] my breath from me, the slaves.
   Creditors? Devils!

FLAVIUS   My dear lord—

TIMON   What if it should be so?[2]

5 FLAVIUS   My lord—

TIMON   I'll have it so. My steward!

FLAVIUS   Here, my lord.

TIMON   So fitly?° Go bid all my friends again: *conveniently*
   Lucius, Lucullus, and Sempronius—all luxors,° all.   *lechers*
   I'll once more feast the rascals.

FLAVIUS   O my lord,
10   You only speak from your distracted soul.

---

5. That is, they are avoiding arrest for debt.
6. Timon puns on "bills" (line 87) as weapons (halberds).
3.5 Location: Scene continues.

1. Have taken (referring to Timon's breathlessness and to the proverb "Air is free").
2. Timon is referring to a plan he has just thought of.

There is not so much left to furnish out
A moderate table.

TIMON   Be it not in thy care.°   *your responsibility*
Go, I charge thee, invite them all. Let in the tide
Of knaves once more. My cook and I'll provide.

Exeunt [severally]

3.6

Enter three SENATORS *at one door*

FIRST SENATOR   My lords, you have my voice to't.° The fault's°   *vote for it / crime is*
   bloody.
'Tis necessary he should die.
Nothing emboldens sin so much as mercy.

SECOND SENATOR   Most true; the law shall bruise 'im.

[Enter] ALCIBIADES *[at another door], with attendants*

5   ALCIBIADES   Honour, health, and compassion to the senate!

FIRST SENATOR   Now, captain.

ALCIBIADES   I am an humble suitor to your virtues;
   For pity is the virtue° of the law,   *essence*
   And none but tyrants use it cruelly.
10   It pleases time and fortune to lie heavy
   Upon a friend of mine, who in hot blood
   Hath stepped into° the law, which is past depth   *(as into quicksand)*
   To those that without heed do plunge into't.
   He is a man, setting his feat° aside,   *deed*
15   Of comely virtues;
   Nor did he soil the fact with cowardice—
   An honour in him which buys out his fault°—   *redeems his crime*
   But with a noble fury and fair spirit,
   Seeing his reputation touched to death,°   *fatally besmirched*
20   He did oppose his foe;
   And with such sober and unnoted[1] passion
   He did behave° his anger, ere 'twas spent,   *control*
   As if he had but proved an argument.

FIRST SENATOR   You undergo° too strict a paradox,   *undertake*
25   Striving to make an ugly deed look fair.
   Your words have took such pains as if they laboured
   To bring manslaughter into form,[2] and set quarrelling
   Upon the head° of valour—which indeed   *In the category of*
   Is valour misbegot, and came into the world
30   When sects and factions were newly born.
   He's truly valiant that can wisely suffer
   The worst that man can breathe,° and make his wrongs his   *utter*
      outsides°   *merely external things*
   To wear them like his raiment carelessly,
   And ne'er prefer° his injuries to his heart   *promote*
35   To bring it into danger.
   If wrongs be evils and enforce us kill,
   What folly 'tis to hazard life for ill!

ALCIBIADES   My lord—

FIRST SENATOR   You cannot make gross sins look clear.
   To revenge is no valour, but to bear.°   *endure (is valor)*

3.6 Location: The Senate house.   2. To make manslaughter legal.
1. Unnoticed (because moderate).

40 ALCIBIADES   My lords, then, under favour,° pardon me   *by your leave*
    If I speak like a captain.
    Why do fond° men expose themselves to battle,   *foolish*
    And not endure all threats, sleep upon't,
    And let the foes quietly cut their throats
45   Without repugnancy?° If there be   *resistance*
    Such valour in the bearing,° what make we   *enduring*
    Abroad?³ Why then, women are more valiant
    That stay at home if bearing carry it,°   *wins the day*
    And the ass more captain than the lion, the felon
50   Loaden with irons° wiser than the judge,   *shackles*
    If wisdom be in suffering. O my lords,
    As you are great, be pitifully good.°   *good in showing pity*
    Who cannot condemn rashness in cold blood?
    To kill, I grant, is sin's extremest gust,°   *outburst*
55   But in defence, by mercy,⁴ 'tis most just.
    To be in anger is impiety,
    But who is man that is not angry?
    Weigh but the crime with this.
SECOND SENATOR   You breathe in vain.
ALCIBIADES   In vain?
    His service done at Lacedaemon and Byzantium
60 Were a sufficient briber for his life.
FIRST SENATOR   What's that?
ALCIBIADES   Why, I say, my lords, he's done fair° service,   *fine*
    And slain in fight many of your enemies.
    How full of valour did he bear himself
    In the last conflict, and made plenteous wounds!
65 SECOND SENATOR   He has made too much plenty with 'em.
    He's a sworn rioter;° he has a sin   *committed reveler*
    That often drowns him and takes his valour prisoner.⁵
    If there were no foes, that were enough
    To overcome him. In that beastly fury
70   He has been known to commit outrages
    And cherish factions.° 'Tis inferred° to us   *foster dissension / alleged*
    His days are foul and his drink dangerous.
FIRST SENATOR   He dies.
ALCIBIADES   Hard fate! He might have died in war.
    My lords, if not for any parts° in him—   *good qualities*
75   Though his right arm might purchase his own time⁶
    And be in debt to none—yet more to move you,
    Take° my deserts to his and join 'em both.   *Combine*
    And for I know
    Your reverend ages love security,⁷
80   I'll pawn my victories, all my honour to you
    Upon his good returns.°   *repayment (of your trust)*
    If by this crime he owes the law his life,
    Why, let the war receive't in valiant gore,
    For law is strict, and war is nothing more.
85 FIRST SENATOR   We are for law; he dies. Urge it no more,
    On height of our° displeasure. Friend or brother,   *At risk of our highest*

---

3. *what make we / Abroad:* why do we (men) go outdoors?
4. But self-defense, considered mercifully.
5. *sin . . . prisoner:* that is, drunkenness.
6. Though performance in battle might redeem him for the duration of his life.
7. Collateral (as on a loan); safety.

He forfeits his own blood that spills another.
ALCIBIADES Must it be so? It must not be.
My lords, I do beseech you know me.
SECOND SENATOR   How?
ALCIBIADES Call me to your remembrances.
90 **THIRD SENATOR**   What?
ALCIBIADES I cannot think but your age has forgot me.
It could not else° be I should prove so base   *otherwise*
To sue and be denied such common grace.
My wounds ache at you.
FIRST SENATOR   Do you dare our anger?
95 'Tis in few words, but spacious° in effect: *great*
We banish thee for ever.
ALCIBIADES   Banish me?
Banish your dotage, banish usury
That makes the senate ugly.
FIRST SENATOR   If after two days' shine
Athens contain thee, attend our weightier judgement;
100 And, not to swell your spirit,° he shall be   *anger*
Executed presently.°   *Exeunt* [SENATORS *and attendants*]   *immediately*
ALCIBIADES Now the gods keep you old enough that you may live
Only in bone,° that none may look on you!   *as skeletons*
I'm worse than mad. I have kept back their foes
105 While they have told° their money and let out   *counted*
Their coin upon large interest—I myself,
Rich only in large hurts. All those for this?
Is this the balsam° that the usuring senate   *ointment*
Pours into captains' wounds? Banishment!
110 It comes not ill; I hate not to be banished.
It is a cause worthy my spleen and fury,
That I may strike at Athens. I'll cheer up
My discontented troops, and lay for hearts.°   *win their support*
'Tis honour with most lands° to be at odds.   *the richest*
115 Soldiers should brook° as little wrongs as gods.   *Exit*   *endure*

3.7

Enter divers [*of Timon's*] *friends,* [*amongst them* LUCUL-
LUS, LUCIUS, SEMPRONIUS, *and other* LORDS *and Senators,*] *at several doors*

FIRST LORD The good time of day to you, sir.
SECOND LORD I also wish it to you. I think this honourable lord
did but try° us this other day.   *test*
FIRST LORD Upon that were my thoughts tiring[1] when we
5 encountered.° I hope it is not so low with him as he made it   *met*
seem in the trial of his several friends.
SECOND LORD It should not be, by the persuasion° of his new *evidence*
feasting.
FIRST LORD I should think so. He hath sent me an earnest invit-
10 ing, which many my near occasions° did urge me to put off, but *my many urgent affairs*
he hath conjured me beyond them, and I must needs appear.
SECOND LORD In like manner was I in debt° to my importunate *I needed to attend*
business, but he would not hear my excuse. I am sorry when
he sent to borrow of me that my provision was out.

3.7 Location: Timon's house.   1. Feeding (as a hawk tears flesh).

15 FIRST LORD I am sick of that grief too, as I understand how all
   things go.²
   SECOND LORD Every man hears so. What would he have bor-
   rowed of you?
   FIRST LORD A thousand pieces.
20 SECOND LORD A thousand pieces?
   FIRST LORD What of you?
   SECOND LORD He sent to me, sir—
        [*Loud music.*] *Enter* TIMON *and attendants*
   Here he comes.
   TIMON With all my heart, gentlemen both; and how fare you?
25 FIRST LORD Ever at the best, hearing well of your lordship.
   SECOND LORD The swallow follows not summer more willing
   than we your lordship.
   TIMON [*aside*] Nor more willingly leaves winter, such summer
   birds are men.—Gentlemen, our dinner will not recompense
30 this long stay. Feast your ears with the music a while, if they
   will fare° so harshly o'th' trumpets' sound; we shall to't   *sustain themselves*
   presently.
   FIRST LORD I hope it remains not unkindly with your lordship
   that I returned you an empty messenger.
35 TIMON O sir, let it not trouble you.
   SECOND LORD My noble lord—
   TIMON Ah, my good friend, what cheer?
        [*A table and stools are*] *brought in*
   SECOND LORD My most honourable lord, I am e'en° sick of   *utterly*
   shame that when your lordship this other day sent to me I was
40 so unfortunate a beggar.
   TIMON Think not on't, sir.
   SECOND LORD If you had sent but two hours before—
   TIMON Let it not cumber° your better remembrance.—Come,   *burden*
   bring in all together.
        [*Enter Servants with covered dishes*]
45 SECOND LORD All covered dishes.
   FIRST LORD Royal cheer,° I warrant you.   *dining*
   THIRD LORD Doubt not that, if money and the season can yield it.
   FIRST LORD How do you? What's the news?
   THIRD LORD Alcibiades is banished. Hear you of it?
50 FIRST and SECOND LORDS Alcibiades banished?
   THIRD LORD 'Tis so, be sure of it.
   FIRST LORD How, how?
   SECOND LORD I pray you, upon what?°   *what grounds*
   TIMON My worthy friends, will you draw near?
55 THIRD LORD I'll tell you more anon. Here's a noble feast
   toward.°   *coming up*
   SECOND LORD This is the old³ man still.
   THIRD LORD Will't hold, will't hold?°   *last*
   SECOND LORD It does; but time will°—and so—   *"time will tell"*
60 THIRD LORD I do conceive.°   *understand*
   TIMON Each man to his stool with that spur° as he would to the   *speed*
   lip of his mistress. Your diet shall be in all places alike. Make

---

2. *as . . . go:* now that I understand the real situation.   3. Familiar (in his generosity).

not a city feast[4] of it, to let the meat cool ere we can agree
upon the first place.° Sit, sit. The gods require our thanks.   °place of honor
     They sit

65 You great benefactors, sprinkle our society with thankfulness.
For your own gifts make yourselves praised; but reserve still[5] to
give, lest your deities be despised. Lend to each man enough
that one need not lend to another; for were your godheads to
borrow of men, men would forsake the gods. Make the meat
70 be beloved more than the man that gives it. Let no assembly of
twenty be without a score of villains. If there sit twelve women
at the table, let a dozen of them be as they are. The rest of your
foes, O gods—the senators of Athens, together with the
common tag° of people—what is amiss in them, you gods,   °mob
75 make suitable for destruction. For these my present friends, as
they are to me nothing, so in nothing bless them; and to nothing are they welcome.—Uncover, dogs, and lap.
     [*The dishes are uncovered, and seen to be full of*
       steaming water and stones]

SOME LORDS   What does his lordship mean?
OTHER LORDS   I know not.
80 TIMON   May you a better feast never behold,
    You knot of mouth-friends.[6] Smoke and lukewarm water
    Is your perfection. This is Timon's last,
    Who, stuck and spangled with your flattery,
    Washes it off, and sprinkles in your faces
    Your reeking° villainy.   °steaming; stinking
     [*He throws water in their faces*]
85   Live loathed and long,
    Most smiling, smooth, detested parasites,
    Courteous destroyers, affable wolves, meek bears,
    You fools of fortune, trencher-friends,° time's flies,[7]   °mealtime friends
    Cap-and-knee° slaves, vapours, and minute-jacks![8]   °Sycophantic
90   Of man and beast the infinite malady[9]
    Crust you quite o'er.
     [*A* LORD *is going*]
                What, dost thou go?
    Soft,° take thy physic° first. Thou too, and thou.   °Wait / medicine
     [*He beats them*]
    Stay, I will lend thee money, borrow none.
     [*Exeunt* LORDS, *leaving caps and gowns*]
    What, all in motion? Henceforth be no feast
95   Whereat a villain's not a welcome guest.
    Burn house! Sink Athens! Henceforth hated be
    Of Timon man and all humanity!   *Exit*
     Enter the Senators [*and*] *other* LORDS
FIRST LORD   How now, my lords?
SECOND LORD   Know you the quality° of Lord Timon's fury?   °nature
THIRD LORD   Push!° Did you see my cap?   °(impatient expression)
100 FOURTH LORD   I have lost my gown.
FIRST LORD   He's but a mad lord, and naught but humours°   °unstable moods

---

4. Feast as given by London dignitaries, in which seating
arrangements were thought socially significant.
5. But always hold back something.
6. You group of insincere (or gluttonous) friends.

7. That is, vanishing in cold weather.
8. Mannekins that strike bells on medieval clocks; hence,
timeservers.
9. May every disease of man and beast.

sways him. He gave me a jewel th'other day, and now he has
beat it out of my hat.
Did you see my jewel?

THIRD LORD   Did you see my cap?
SECOND LORD   Here 'tis.
FOURTH LORD   Here lies my gown.
105 FIRST LORD   Let's make no stay.
SECOND LORD   Lord Timon's mad.
THIRD LORD   I feel't upon my bones.
FOURTH LORD   One day he gives us diamonds, next day stones.
                                                                Exeunt

4.1

          Enter TIMON
TIMON   Let me look back upon thee. O thou wall
        That girdles in those wolves, dive in the earth,
        And fence not Athens! Matrons, turn incontinent!°   *unchaste*
        Obedience fail in children! Slaves and fools,
5   Pluck the grave wrinkled senate from the bench
        And minister in their steads! To general filths°   *common whores*
        Convert o'th' instant, green¹ virginity!
        Do't in your parents' eyes. Bankrupts, hold fast!°   *refuse to pay*
        Rather than render back, out with your knives,
10   And cut your trusters'° throats. Bound° servants, steal!   *creditors'/Indentured*
        Large-handed robbers your grave masters are,
        And pill° by law. Maid, to thy master's bed!   *plunder*
        Thy mistress is o'th' brothel. Son of sixteen,
        Pluck the lined° crutch from thy old limping sire;   *padded*
15   With it beat out his brains! Piety and fear,
        Religion to the gods, peace, justice, truth,
        Domestic awe,² night rest, and neighbourhood,°   *neighborliness*
        Instruction, manners, mysteries,° and trades,   *crafts*
        Degrees,° observances,³ customs, and laws,   *Social ranks*
20   Decline to your confounding° contraries,   *destroying*
        And let confusion live! Plagues incident to men,
        Your potent and infectious fevers heap
        On Athens, ripe for stroke!° Thou cold sciatica,°   *to be struck/nerve pain*
        Cripple our senators, that their limbs may halt°   *limp*
25   As lamely as their manners! Lust and liberty,°   *licentiousness*
        Creep in the minds and marrows⁴ of our youth,
        That 'gainst the stream of virtue they may strive
        And drown themselves in riot!° Itches, blains,°   *debauchery/sores*
        Sow all th'Athenian bosoms, and their crop
30   Be general leprosy! Breath infect breath,
        That their society,° as their friendship, may   *company*
        Be merely° poison!   *wholly*
              He tears off his clothing
                        Nothing I'll bear from thee
        But nakedness, thou detestable town;
        Take thou that too, with multiplying bans.°   *curses*
35   Timon will to the woods, where he shall find

4.1 Location: Outside the walls of Athens.   2. Household government.
1. Young, newly menstruating girls often suffered ane-   3. Respectful customs.
mia, then called "greensickness" and thought to be cur-   4. Thought to be the site of vigor; proverbially melted by
able by sexual satisfaction.   lust.

Th'unkindest beast more kinder[5] than mankind.
The gods confound—hear me you good gods all—
Th'Athenians, both within and out that wall;
And grant, as Timon grows, his hate may grow
40   To the whole race of mankind, high and low.
Amen.   *Exit*

4.2

Enter [FLAVIUS *the*] *Steward, with two or three* SERVANTS

FIRST SERVANT   Hear you, master steward, where's our master?
Are we undone, cast off, nothing remaining?
FLAVIUS   Alack, my fellows, what should I say to you?
Let me be recorded: by the righteous gods,
I am as poor as you.
5   FIRST SERVANT   Such a house broke,
So noble a master fall'n? All gone, and not
One friend to take his° fortune by the arm   (Timon's)
And go along with him?
SECOND SERVANT   As we do turn our backs
From our companion thrown into his grave,
10   So his familiars to[1] his buried fortunes
Slink all away, leave their false vows with him
Like empty purses picked; and his poor self,
A dedicated° beggar to the air,   *Abandoned as a*
With his disease of all-shunned poverty,
Walks like contempt alone.
Enter other SERVANTS
15   More of our fellows.
FLAVIUS   All broken implements of a ruined house.
THIRD SERVANT   Yet do our hearts wear Timon's livery.°   *servants' uniforms*
That see I by our faces. We are fellows still,
Serving alike in sorrow. Leaked is our barque,°   *sailboat*
20   And we, poor mates, stand on the dying° deck   *sinking*
Hearing the surges'° threat. We must all part   *waves'*
Into this sea of air.
FLAVIUS   Good fellows all,
The latest° of my wealth I'll share amongst you.   *last bit*
Wherever we shall meet, for Timon's sake
25   Let's yet be fellows. Let's shake our heads and say,
As 'twere a knell unto our master's fortunes,
'We have seen better days.'
[*He gives them money*]
                           Let each take some.
Nay, put out all your hands. Not one word more.
Thus part we rich in sorrow, parting poor.
[*They*] *embrace, and* [*the* SERVANTS] *part several ways*
30   O, the fierce° wretchedness that glory brings us!   *excessive*
Who would not wish to be from wealth exempt,
Since riches point to misery and contempt?
Who would be so mocked with glory, or to live
But in a dream of friendship,

---

5. Gentler; more nearly akin.
4.2 Location: Timon's house.

1. So his intimate friends from (a "familiar" could also be a flattering devil).

35　　To have his pomp and all what state compounds[2]
　　　But only painted like his varnished friends?
　　　Poor honest lord, brought low by his own heart,
　　　Undone by goodness! Strange, unusual blood°　　　　　*disposition*
　　　When man's worst sin is he does too much good!
40　　Who then dares to be half so kind again?
　　　For bounty, that makes° gods, does still mar men.　　　*characterizes*
　　　My dearest lord, blessed to be most accursed,
　　　Rich only to be wretched, thy great fortunes
　　　Are made thy chief afflictions. Alas, kind lord!
45　　He's flung in rage from this ingrateful seat°　　　　　*residence*
　　　Of monstrous friends;
　　　Nor has he with him to supply° his life,　　　　　*resources to maintain*
　　　Or that° which can command it.　　　　　*(money)*
　　　I'll follow and enquire him out.
50　　I'll ever serve his mind with my best will.
　　　Whilst I have gold I'll be his steward still.　　　*Exit*

4.3

Enter TIMON [*from his cave*] *in the woods* [*half naked,
and with a spade*]

TIMON　　O blessèd breeding sun,[1] draw from the earth
　　　Rotten° humidity; below thy sister's[2] orb　　　　　*Putrid*
　　　Infect the air. Twinned brothers of one womb,
　　　Whose procreation, residence,° and birth　　　　　*time in the womb*
5　　Scarce is dividant,° touch them with several° fortunes,　　*separable / different*
　　　The greater scorns the lesser. Not nature,
　　　To whom all sores° lay siege, can bear great fortune　　*afflictions*
　　　But by contempt of nature.[3]
　　　It is the pasture lards[4] the brother's sides,
10　　The want that makes him lean.
　　　Raise me[5] this beggar and demit that lord,
　　　The senator shall bear contempt hereditary,°　　　*as if he had inherited it*
　　　The beggar native° honour. Who dares, who dares　　*inborn*
　　　In purity of manhood stand upright
15　　And say 'This man's a flatterer'? If one be,
　　　So are they all, for every grece° of fortune　　　*step on the staircase*
　　　Is smoothed by that below.[6] The learnèd pate°　　　*head*
　　　Ducks° to the golden fool. All's obliquy;°　　　*Bows / deviousness*
　　　There's nothing level° in our cursèd natures　　　*straight; consistent*
20　　But direct villainy. Therefore be abhorred
　　　All feasts, societies, and throngs of men.
　　　His semblable,° yea, himself, Timon disdains.　　　*His own image*
　　　Destruction fang° mankind. Earth, yield me roots.　　*seize*
　　　[*He digs*]
　　　Who seeks for better of thee, sauce his palate
　　　With thy most operant° poison.　　　*potent*
　　　[*He finds gold*]
25　　　　　　　　　　　　What is here?

---

2. And all that splendor is made of.
4.3 Location: Outside Athens.
1. The sun was supposed to be able to generate vermin spontaneously and to foment infection.
2. The moon's; see note to 1.1.44.
3. Without scorning those of like nature.

4. Fattens ("pasture" suggests both owning and eating from the land).
5. This "me" is an example of the so-called ethic dative (literally, "for me"), used to emphasize the verb. See also line 112.
6. By the people standing on the step below.

Gold? Yellow, glittering, precious gold?
No, gods, I am no idle° votarist: *frivolous*
Roots, you clear heavens. Thus much of this will make
Black white, foul fair, wrong right,
30   Base noble, old young, coward valiant.
Ha, you gods! Why this, what, this, you gods? Why, this
Will lug your priests and servants from your sides,
Pluck stout men's pillows from below their heads.°   *(to kill them)*
This yellow slave
35   Will knit and break religions, bless th'accursed,
Make the hoar° leprosy adored, place° thieves,   *gray / appoint to office*
And give them title, knee,° and approbation   *kneeling*
With senators on the bench. This is it
That makes the wappered° widow wed again.   *worn out*
40   She whom the spittle house° and ulcerous sores   *hospital*
Would cast the gorge° at, this embalms and spices   *vomit*
To th'April day⁷ again. Come, damnèd earth,°   *gold*
Thou common whore of mankind, that puts odds°   *quarrels*
Among the rout° of nations; I will make thee   *rabble*
Do⁸ thy right nature.
          March afar off
45   Ha, a drum! Thou'rt quick;⁹
But yet I'll bury thee.
          [*He buries gold*]
                    Thou'lt go, strong thief,
When gouty keepers of thee cannot stand.
          [*He keeps some gold*]
Nay, stay thou out for earnest.°   *as a pledge*
          Enter ALCIBIADES, *with* [*soldiers playing*] *drum and fife,*
          in warlike manner; and PHRYNIA *and* TIMANDRA
ALCIBIADES   What art thou there? Speak.
TIMON   A beast, as thou art. The canker¹ gnaw thy heart
50   For showing me again the eyes of man.
ALCIBIADES   What is thy name? Is man so hateful to thee
That art thyself a man?
TIMON   I am Misanthropos,° and hate mankind.   *man-hater (Greek)*
For thy part, I do wish thou wert a dog,
That I might love thee something.°   *somewhat*
55   ALCIBIADES   I know thee well,
But in thy fortunes am unlearned and strange.²
TIMON   I know thee too, and more than that I know thee
I not desire° to know. Follow thy drum.   *do not desire*
With man's blood paint the ground gules,° gules.   *red (heraldic term)*
60   Religious canons, civil laws, are cruel;
Then what should war be? This fell° whore of thine   *dreadful*
Hath in her more destruction than thy sword,
For all her cherubin look.
PHRYNIA   Thy lips rot off!°   *(as in syphilis)*
TIMON   I will not kiss thee; then the rot returns
65   To thine own lips again.
ALCIBIADES   How came the noble Timon to this change?

---

7. To youthful freshness.
8. Act according to (by concealing gold and yielding roots).
9. Swift to bring strife; alive.
1. Spreading ulcer; cankerworm.
2. Am ignorant and unacquainted.

TIMON   As the moon does, by wanting° light to give.   *lacking*
But then renew I could not like the moon;
There were no suns to borrow of.

70 ALCIBIADES   Noble Timon, what friendship may I do thee?

TIMON   None but to maintain my opinion.

ALCIBIADES   What is it, Timon?

TIMON   Promise me friendship, but perform none. If thou wilt
promise, the gods plague thee, for thou art a man. If thou dost

75 not perform, confound° thee, for thou art a man.   *damn*

ALCIBIADES   I have heard in some sort° of thy miseries.   *to some extent*

TIMON   Thou saw'st them when I had prosperity.

ALCIBIADES   I see them now; then was a blessèd time.

TIMON   As thine is now, held with a brace° of harlots.   *pair*

80 TIMANDRA   Is this th'Athenian minion,° whom the world   *favorite*
Voiced° so regardfully?   *Spoke of*

TIMON   Art thou Timandra?

TIMANDRA   Yes.

TIMON   Be a whore still. They love thee not that use thee.
Give them diseases, leaving with thee their lust.

85 Make use of thy salt° hours: season° the slaves   *lecherous / prepare*
For tubs and baths,³ bring down rose-cheeked youth
To the tub-fast and the diet.

TIMANDRA   Hang thee, monster!

ALCIBIADES   Pardon him, sweet Timandra, for his wits
Are drowned and lost in his calamities.

90 I have but little gold of late, brave Timon,
The want whereof doth daily make° revolt   *cause*
In my penurious band. I have heard and grieved
How cursèd Athens, mindless of thy worth,
Forgetting thy great deeds, when neighbour states

95 But for thy sword and fortune trod upon them⁴—

TIMON   I prithee, beat thy drum and get thee gone.

ALCIBIADES   I am thy friend, and pity thee, dear Timon.

TIMON   How dost thou pity him whom thou dost trouble?
I had rather be alone.

ALCIBIADES   Why, fare thee well.
Here is some gold for thee.

100 TIMON   Keep it. I cannot eat it.

ALCIBIADES   When I have laid proud Athens on a heap—

TIMON   Warr'st thou 'gainst Athens?

ALCIBIADES   Ay, Timon, and have cause.

TIMON   The gods confound them all in thy conquest,
And thee after, when thou hast conquerèd.

ALCIBIADES   Why me, Timon?

105 TIMON   That by killing of villains
Thou wast born to conquer my country.
Put up thy gold.
                [He gives ALCIBIADES gold]
                        Go on; here's gold; go on.
Be as a planetary plague⁵ when Jove
Will o'er some high-viced city hang his poison

---

3. Used, with "diet" (line 87), to treat venereal disease.
4. Alcibiades suggests that Timon's money and military
expertise saved Athens in the past.

5. Plagues were thought to be caused by the influence
of the other planets.

110　　　In the sick air. Let not thy sword skip one.
　　　　Pity not honoured age for his white beard;
　　　　He is an usurer. Strike me° the counterfeit matron;　　　　　　　　*Strike for me*
　　　　It is her habit° only that is honest,　　　　　　　　　　　　　　　　*attire*
　　　　Herself's a bawd. Let not the virgin's cheek
115　　　Make soft thy trenchant° sword; for those milk paps°　　　*cutting / breasts*
　　　　That through the window-bars° bore at men's eyes　　　*openwork bodice*
　　　　Are not within the leaf° of pity writ;　　　　　　　　　　　　　　　　*page*
　　　　But set them down horrible traitors. Spare not the babe
　　　　Whose dimpled smiles from fools exhaust° their mercy.　　　*draw out*
120　　　Think it a bastard whom the oracle
　　　　Hath doubtfully° pronounced thy throat shall cut,　　　　*ambiguously*
　　　　And mince it sans° remorse. Swear against objects.[6]　　　*without*
　　　　Put armour on thine ears and on thine eyes
　　　　Whose proof° nor yells of mothers, maids, nor babes,　　　*strength*
125　　　Nor sight of priests in holy vestments bleeding,
　　　　Shall pierce a jot. There's gold to pay thy soldiers.
　　　　Make large confusion, and, thy fury spent,
　　　　Confounded be thyself. Speak not. Be gone.
　　ALCIBIADES　　Hast thou gold yet? I'll take the gold thou giv'st me,
130　　Not all thy counsel.
　　TIMON　　Dost thou or dost thou not, heaven's curse upon thee!
　　PHRYNIA *and* TIMANDRA　　Give us some gold, good Timon. Hast
　　　　thou more?
　　TIMON　　Enough to make a whore forswear her trade,
　　　　And to make wholesomeness a bawd. Hold up, you sluts,
　　　　Your aprons mountant.[7]
　　　　　　　　　[*He throws gold into their aprons*]
135　　　　　　　　　　　　　You are not oathable,[8]
　　　　Although I know you'll swear, terribly swear,
　　　　Into strong shudders and to heavenly agues°　　　　　　　　　*fevers*
　　　　Th'immortal gods that hear you. Spare your oaths;
　　　　I'll trust to your conditions.° Be whores still,　　　*occupations; characters*
140　　　And he whose pious breath seeks to convert you,
　　　　Be strong in whore, allure him, burn him up.°　　　*inflame him; infect him*
　　　　Let your close° fire predominate his smoke;[9]　　　　　　　*secret*
　　　　And be no turncoats. Yet may your pain-sick months
　　　　Be quite contrary,° and thatch your poor thin roofs　　　*Make you suffer intensely*
145　　　With burdens of the dead[1]—some that were hanged,
　　　　No matter. Wear them, betray with them; whore still;
　　　　Paint° till a horse may mire° upon your face.　　　*Use cosmetics / get stuck*
　　　　A pox of wrinkles!
　　PHRYNIA *and* TIMANDRA　　Well, more gold; what then?
　　　　Believe't that we'll do anything for gold.
150　　TIMON　　Consumptions° sow　　　　　　　　　　　　　　　　　*Diseases*
　　　　In hollow bones of man, strike their sharp shins,[2]
　　　　And mar men's spurring.[3] Crack the lawyer's voice,
　　　　That he may never more false title plead
　　　　Nor sound his quillets° shrilly. Hoar the flamen[4]　　　*quibbles (wordplay)*

---

6. Vow not to listen to protests.
7. Your skirts lifted ("mountant," a heraldic term, puns on "sexual mounting").
8. Capable of being bound on oath.
9. Overcome his "pious breath" (line 140).
1. *thatch . . . dead:* wear wigs made of corpses' hair to cover your syphilitic baldness.
2. Syphilis causes bone degeneration.
3. Horseback riding; sexual intercourse. *Crack:* Ruin (an ulcerous larynx is an effect of syphilis).
4. Whiten the priest (with syphilis or leprosy).

155 That scolds against the quality° of flesh   *nature*
      And not believes himself. Down with the nose,
      Down with it flat;⁵ take the bridge quite away
      Of him that his particular° to foresee   *self-interest*
      Smells from the general weal.⁶ Make curled-pate ruffians bald,
160 And let the unscarred braggarts of the war
      Derive some pain from you. Plague all,
      That your activity may defeat and quell
      The source of all erection.⁷ There's more gold.
      Do you damn others, and let this damn you;
165 And ditches grave you all!⁸

PHRYNIA *and* TIMANDRA   More counsel with more money, boun-
      teous Timon.

TIMON   More whore, more mischief first; I have given you earnest.°   *a down payment*
ALCIBIADES   Strike up the drum towards Athens. Farewell, Timon.
      If I thrive well, I'll visit thee again.
170 TIMON   If I hope well, I'll never see thee more.
ALCIBIADES   I never did thee harm.
TIMON   Yes, thou spok'st well of me.
ALCIBIADES   Call'st thou that harm?
TIMON   Men daily find it.° Get thee away,   *discover it to be so*
      And take thy beagles° with thee.   *fawning curs (the whores)*
175 ALCIBIADES   We but offend him. Strike!
                      Exeunt [*to drum and fife, all but* TIMON]
TIMON   That nature, being sick of° man's unkindness,   *through excess of*
      Should yet be hungry!
                      [*He digs the earth*]
                      Common° mother—thou   *Universal*
      Whose womb unmeasurable and infinite breast
      Teems° and feeds all, whose selfsame mettle°   *Breeds / substance*
180 Whereof thy proud child, arrogant man, is puffed
      Engenders the black toad and adder blue,
      The gilded newt and eyeless venomed worm,
      With all th'abhorrèd births below crisp° heaven   *clear*
      Whereon Hyperion's quick'ning° fire doth shine—   *the sun's life-giving*
185 Yield him who all thy human sons do hate
      From forth thy plenteous bosom, one poor root.
      Ensear° thy fertile and conceptious womb;   *Dry up*
      Let it no more bring out ingrateful man.
      Go great° with tigers, dragons, wolves, and bears;   *pregnant*
190 Teem with new monsters whom thy upward° face   *upturned*
      Hath to the marbled mansion° all above   *heavens*
      Never presented.
                      [*He finds a root*]
                      O, a root! Dear thanks.
      Dry up thy marrows,° vines, and plough-torn leas,°   *pulpy fruits / fields*
      Whereof ingrateful man with liquorish draughts⁹
195 And morsels unctuous° greases his pure mind,   *oily*
      That from it all consideration° slips!—   *rationality*

---

5. Syphilis sometimes caused the bridge of the nose to
collapse.
6. The image suggests a dog leaving the pack to pursue
its own quarry.

7. Sexual erection; social advancement.
8. May you all suffer squalid deaths.
9. Sweet, lust-inducing drinks.

Enter APEMANTUS

More man? Plague, plague!

APEMANTUS   I was directed hither. Men report

    Thou dost affect° my manners, and dost use them.   *like; imitate*

200 TIMON   'Tis then because thou dost not keep a dog

    Whom I would imitate. Consumption catch thee!

APEMANTUS   This is in thee a nature but infected,[1]

    A poor unmanly melancholy, sprung

    From change of fortune. Why this spade, this place,

205   This slave-like habit,° and these looks of care?   *costume*

    Thy flatterers yet wear silk, drink wine, lie soft,

    Hug their diseased perfumes,° and have forgot   *perfumed women*

    That ever Timon was. Shame not these woods

    By putting on the cunning of a carper.[2]

210   Be thou a flatterer now, and seek to thrive

    By that which has undone thee. Hinge thy knee,

    And let his very breath whom thou'lt observe°   *pay court to*

    Blow off thy cap. Praise his most vicious strain,°   *trait*

    And call it excellent. Thou wast told thus.

215   Thou gav'st thine ears like tapsters° that bade welcome   *bartenders*

    To knaves and all approachers. 'Tis most just

    That thou turn rascal.° Hadst thou wealth again,   *knave; solitary deer*

    Rascals should have't. Do not assume my likeness.

TIMON   Were I like thee, I'd throw away myself.

220 APEMANTUS   Thou hast cast away thyself being like thyself—

    A madman so long, now a fool. What, think'st

    That the bleak air, thy boisterous chamberlain,°   *personal servant*

    Will put thy shirt on warm? Will these mossed trees

    That have outlived the eagle page° thy heels   *follow at*

225   And skip when thou point'st out?[3] Will the cold brook,

    Candied° with ice, caudle thy morning taste[4]   *Encrusted*

    To cure thy o'ernight's surfeit? Call the creatures

    Whose naked natures live in° all the spite   *exposed to*

    Of wreakful° heaven, whose bare unhousèd trunks°   *vengeful / bodies*

230   To the conflicting elements exposed

    Answer° mere nature; bid them flatter thee.   *Obey*

    O, thou shalt find—

TIMON   A fool of thee! Depart.

APEMANTUS   I love thee better now than e'er I did.

TIMON   I hate thee worse.

APEMANTUS   Why?

TIMON   Thou flatter'st misery.

235 APEMANTUS   I flatter not, but say thou art a caitiff.°   *wretch*

TIMON   Why dost thou seek me out?

APEMANTUS   To vex thee.

TIMON   Always a villain's office, or a fool's.

    Dost please thyself in't?

APEMANTUS   Ay.

TIMON   What, a knave too?

APEMANTUS   If thou didst put this sour cold habit° on   *dress; disposition*

240   To castigate thy pride, 'twere well; but thou

---

1. That is, not innately misanthropic or converted by   3. And jump to get whatever you indicate.
philosophical argument.   4. Give you a hot drink in the morning.
2. The knowledge of a faultfinder.

Dost it enforcèdly.° Thou'dst courtier be again   *by compulsion*
Wert thou not beggar. Willing misery
Outlives incertain° pomp, is crowned[5] before.   *insecure*
The one° is filling still,° never complete;   *("incertain pomp")/always*
245 The other at high wish.[6] Best state, contentless,[7]
Hath a distracted and most wretched being,
Worse than the worst, content.[8]
Thou shouldst desire to die, being miserable.

TIMON   Not by his breath that is more miserable.[9]
250 Thou art a slave whom fortune's tender arm
With favour never clasped, but bred a dog.
Hadst thou like us from our first swathe proceeded[1]
The sweet degrees[2] that this brief world affords
To such as° may the passive drudges of it   *To those who*
255 Freely command, thou wouldst have plunged thyself
In general riot,° melted down thy youth   *debauchery*
In different beds of lust, and never learned
The icy precepts of respect,° but followed   *restraint; judgment*
The sugared game° before thee. But myself,   *sweet quarry*
260 Who had the world as my confectionary,
The mouths, the tongues, the eyes and hearts of men
At duty,° more than I could frame° employment,   *my service/provide*
That numberless upon me stuck, as leaves
Do on the oak, have with one winter's brush
265 Fell from their boughs, and left me open, bare
For every storm that blows—I to bear this,
That never knew but better,° is some burden.   *anything but good fortune*
Thy nature did commence in sufferance,° time   *suffering*
Hath made thee hard° in't. Why shouldst thou hate men?   *hardened*
270 They never flattered thee. What hast thou given?
If thou wilt curse, thy father, that poor rag,°   *wretch*
Must be thy subject, who in spite put stuff
To[3] some she-beggar and compounded° thee   *constituted*
Poor rogue hereditary.° Hence, be gone.   *by birth*
275 If thou hadst not been born the worst of men
Thou hadst been a knave and flatterer.

APEMANTUS   Art thou proud yet?

TIMON   Ay, that I am not thee.

APEMANTUS   I that I was
No prodigal.

280 TIMON   I that I am one now.
Were all the wealth I have shut up° in thee   *contained*
I'd give thee leave to hang it. Get thee gone.
That° the whole life of Athens were in this!   *Would that*
Thus would I eat it.
    [*He bites the root*]

APEMANTUS [*offering food*]   Here, I will mend° thy feast.   *improve*

285 TIMON   First mend my company: take away thyself.

APEMANTUS   So I shall mend mine own by th' lack of thine.

---

5. Finds fulfillment.
6. (Misery) at the height of its wish.
7. The greatest prosperity, if not contented.
8. The least prosperity, living contented.
9. Not at the command of someone even unhappier
than I.
1. From our swaddling clothes mounted.
2. Social ranks; steps on Fortune's ladder.
3. *put stuff/To:* ejaculated into.

TIMON   'Tis not well mended so, it is but botched;[4]
If not, I would it were.

APEMANTUS   What wouldst thou have to[5] Athens?

TIMON   Thee thither in a whirlwind. If thou wilt,

290   Tell them there I have gold. Look, so I have.

APEMANTUS   Here is no use for gold.

TIMON   The best and truest,
For here it sleeps and does no hirèd harm.

APEMANTUS   Where liest a-nights, Timon?

TIMON   Under that's above me.°   Where feed'st thou a-days,   (the sky)

295   Apemantus?

APEMANTUS   Where my stomach finds meat;°   or rather, where I eat it.   food

TIMON   Would poison were obedient, and knew my mind!

APEMANTUS   Where wouldst thou send it?

TIMON   To sauce thy dishes.

300 APEMANTUS   The middle of humanity thou never knewest, but
the extremity of both ends. When thou wast in thy gilt and thy
perfume, they mocked thee for too much curiosity;° in thy rags   delicacy
thou know'st none, but art despised for the contrary. There's a
medlar[6] for thee; eat it.

305 TIMON   On what I hate I feed not.

APEMANTUS   Dost hate a medlar?

TIMON   Ay, though it look like thee.

APEMANTUS   An° thou'dst hated meddlers sooner, thou shouldst   If
have loved thyself better now. What man didst thou ever know

310   unthrift° that was beloved after[7] his means?   prodigal

TIMON   Who, without those means thou talk'st of, didst thou ever
know beloved?

APEMANTUS   Myself.

TIMON   I understand thee: thou hadst some means to keep a dog.[8]

315 APEMANTUS   What things in the world canst thou nearest compare to thy flatterers?

TIMON   Women nearest; but men, men are the things themselves. What wouldst thou do with the world, Apemantus, if it
lay in thy power?

320 APEMANTUS   Give it the beasts, to be rid of the men.

TIMON   Wouldst thou have thyself fall in the confusion° of men,   overthrow
and remain a beast with the beasts?

APEMANTUS   Ay, Timon.

TIMON   A beastly ambition, which the gods grant thee t'attain to.

325   If thou wert the lion, the fox would beguile thee. If thou wert
the lamb, the fox would eat thee. If thou wert the fox, the lion
would suspect thee when peradventure° thou wert accused by   perchance
the ass. If thou wert the ass, thy dullness would torment thee,
and still° thou lived'st but as a breakfast to the wolf. If thou wert   always

330   the wolf, thy greediness would afflict thee, and oft thou
shouldst hazard thy life for thy dinner. Wert thou the unicorn,
pride and wrath would confound thee, and make thine own
self the conquest of thy fury.[9] Wert thou a bear, thou wouldst

---

4. It is fixed badly (because Apemantus will still have to
endure himself).
5. Have conveyed to (but Timon changes the meaning).
6. A pear eaten when rotten; with puns in the following
lines on "lecher," "whore," and "interfering person."
7. In proportion to; after losing. *means:* money.

8. Which flattered its master for meager reward (or perhaps "dog" refers to Apemantus himself).
9. The legendary unicorn could be trapped by a hunter
who stood in front of a tree; when the unicorn charged,
the hunter stepped aside, and the unicorn's horn stuck
fast in the tree.

be killed by the horse.[1] Wert thou a horse, thou wouldst be
335   seized by the leopard. Wert thou a leopard, thou wert german°   *related*
to the lion, and the spots of thy kindred[2] were jurors on thy life;
all thy safety were remotion,° and thy defence absence. What   *remaining away*
beast couldst thou be that were not subject to a beast? And
what a beast art thou already, that seest not thy loss in transfor-
340   mation![3]

APEMANTUS   If thou couldst please me with speaking to me, thou
mightst have hit upon it here.[4] The commonwealth of Athens
is become a forest of beasts.

TIMON   How, has the ass broke the wall, that thou art out of the city?

345 APEMANTUS   Yonder comes a poet and a painter.[5] The plague of
company light upon thee! I will fear to catch it, and give way.°   *go away*
When I know not what else to do, I'll see thee again.

TIMON   When there is nothing living but thee, thou shalt be
welcome. I had rather be a beggar's dog than Apemantus.

350 APEMANTUS   Thou art the cap[6] of all the fools alive.

TIMON   Would thou wert clean enough to spit upon.

APEMANTUS   A plague on thee! Thou art too bad to curse.

TIMON   All villains that do stand by thee are pure.°   *(by comparison)*

APEMANTUS   There is no leprosy but what thou speak'st.

355 TIMON   If I name thee.
I'd beat thee, but I should infect my hands.

APEMANTUS   I would my tongue could rot them off.

TIMON   Away, thou issue° of a mangy dog!   *offspring; discharge*
Choler does kill me that thou art alive.

360 I swoon to see thee.

APEMANTUS   Would thou wouldst burst!

TIMON   Away, thou tedious rogue!
       [*He throws a stone at* APEMANTUS]
I am sorry I shall lose a stone by thee.

APEMANTUS   Beast!

365 TIMON   Slave!

APEMANTUS   Toad!

TIMON   Rogue, rogue, rogue!
I am sick of this false world, and will love naught
But even° the mere necessities upon't.   *Except*
370 Then, Timon, presently° prepare thy grave.   *at once*
Lie where the light foam of the sea may beat
Thy gravestone daily. Make thine epitaph,
That death in° me at others' lives may laugh.   *through*
       [*He looks on the gold*]
O, thou sweet king-killer, and dear divorce
375 'Twixt natural son and sire; thou bright defiler
Of Hymen's° purest bed; thou valiant Mars;[7]   *god of marriage*
Thou ever young, fresh, loved, and delicate wooer,
Whose blush° doth thaw the consecrated snow[8]   *glow*
That lies on Dian's lap; thou visible god,
380 That sold'rest close impossibilities[9]

---

1. Bears were supposedly hated by horses.
2. Lion's crimes; leopard's spots.
3. Being transformed to a beast.
4. *thou . . . here:* what you've just said would please me.
5. They do not appear until 5.1 (perhaps a sign of revision).
6. Supreme instance (with wordplay on "fool's cap").
7. Adulterous lover of Venus and the god of war.
8. The snow of chastity, of which the goddess Diana was patroness.
9. That tightly solders together incompatible things.

And mak'st them kiss, that speak'st with every tongue
To every purpose; O thou touch° of hearts: · · · · · · · · · · · · · · ·touchstone
Think thy slave man rebels, and by thy virtue° · · · · · · · · · · · · · ·power
Set them into confounding odds,° that beasts · · · · · · · · · ·men at ruinous strife
May have the world in empire.
385 APEMANTUS · · · · · · · · · · · · · · · · · · ·Would 'twere so,
But not till I am dead. I'll say thou'st gold.
Thou wilt be thronged to shortly.
TIMON ·Thronged to?
APEMANTUS ·Ay.
TIMON   Thy back,[1] I prithee.
APEMANTUS · · · · · · · · · · · · · · · · · ·Live, and love thy misery.
TIMON   Long live so, and so die. I am quit.° · · · · · · · · · · · · · ·rid of you
    Enter the Banditti [THIEVES]
390 APEMANTUS   More things like men. Eat, Timon, and abhor
them. ·*Exit*
FIRST THIEF   Where should he have° this gold? It is some poor · · · ·have obtained; have put
fragment, some slender ort° of his remainder. The mere want · · · · · · · · · ·scrap
of gold and the falling-from of his friends drove him into this
395 melancholy.
SECOND THIEF   It is noised° he hath a mass of treasure. · · · · · · · · · · ·rumored
THIRD THIEF   Let us make the assay° upon him. If he care not · · · · · ·test; assault
for't, he will supply us easily. If he covetously reserve it, how
shall 's get it?
400 SECOND THIEF   True, for he bears it not about him; 'tis hid.
FIRST THIEF   Is not this he?
OTHER THIEVES   Where?
SECOND THIEF   'Tis his description.
THIRD THIEF   He, I know him.
405 ALL THIEVES [*coming forward*]   Save° thee, Timon. · · · · · · · · · · ·God save
TIMON   Now, thieves.
ALL THIEVES   Soldiers, not thieves.
TIMON · · · · · · · · · · · · · · · · ·Both, too, and women's sons.
ALL THIEVES   We are not thieves, but men that much do want.° · · · · ·are very needy
TIMON   Your greatest want is, you want much of meat.° · · · · · · · · · · ·food
410 Why should you want? Behold, the earth hath roots.
Within this mile break forth a hundred springs.
The oaks bear mast,° the briars scarlet hips.[2] · · · · · · · · · ·acorns (fed to swine)
The bounteous housewife nature on each bush
Lays her full mess° before you. Want? Why want? · · · · · · · · · · · ·serving
415 FIRST THIEF   We cannot live on grass, on berries, water,
As beasts and birds and fishes.
TIMON   Nor on the beasts themselves, the birds and fishes;
You must eat men. Yet thanks I must you con° · · · · · · · · · · · · · ·render
That you are thieves professed, that you work not
420 In holier shapes; for there is boundless theft
In limited° professions. [*Giving gold*] Rascal thieves, · · · · · · · · · ·legitimate
Here's gold. Go suck the subtle° blood o'th' grape · · · · · · · ·delicate; deceptive
Till the high fever seethe° your blood to froth, · · · · · · ·boil (by drunkenness)
And so scape hanging.° Trust not the physician; · · · · · · ·(by dying of a fever)
425 His antidotes are poison, and he slays
More than you rob. Take wealth and lives together.
Do villainy; do, since you protest° to do't, · · · · · · · · · · · ·openly profess

1. Show me your back (go away). · · · · · · · · · · 2. Rose hips (sour fruit).

Like workmen.° I'll example you with[3] thievery.   *skilled artisans*
The sun's a thief, and with his great attraction°   *power to draw up*
430   Robs the vast sea. The moon's an arrant[4] thief,
And her pale fire she snatches from the sun.
The sea's a thief, whose liquid surge resolves°   *melts*
The moon into salt tears.[5] The earth's a thief,
That feeds and breeds by a composture° stol'n   *manure*
435   From gen'ral° excrement. Each thing's a thief.   *universal*
The laws, your curb and whip,° in their rough power   *restraint and punishment*
Has unchecked theft.[6] Love not yourselves. Away,
Rob one another. There's more gold. Cut throats;
All that you meet are thieves. To Athens go,
440   Break open shops; nothing can you steal
But thieves do lose it. Steal no less for° this I give you,   *because of*
And gold confound you howsoe'er.° Amen.   *whatever you do*

THIRD THIEF   He's almost charmed me from my profession by
persuading me to it.

445 FIRST THIEF   'Tis in the malice° of mankind that he thus advises   *out of hatred*
us, not to have us thrive in our mystery.°   *profession*

SECOND THIEF   I'll believe him as[7] an enemy, and give over my
trade.

FIRST THIEF   Let us first see peace in Athens.° There is no time   *(an unlikely prospect)*
450 so miserable but a man may be true.°   *Exeunt* THIEVES   *may repent*
Enter [FLAVIUS *the*] *Steward to* TIMON

FLAVIUS   O you gods!
Is yon despised and ruinous° man my lord,   *ruined*
Full of decay and failing? O monument
And wonder of good deeds evilly bestowed![8]
455   What an alteration of honour has desp'rate want made!
What viler thing upon the earth than friends,
Who can bring noblest minds to basest ends!
How rarely does it meet with this time's guise,
When man was wished to love his enemies![9]
460   Grant I may ever love and rather woo
Those that would mischief me than those that do![1]
    [TIMON *sees him*]
He's caught me in his eye. I will present
My honest grief unto him, and as my lord
Still serve him with my life.—My dearest master.

TIMON   Away! What art thou?
465 FLAVIUS   Have you forgot me, sir?

TIMON   Why dost ask that? I have forgot all men;
Then if thou grant'st thou'rt man, I have forgot thee.

FLAVIUS   An honest poor servant of yours.

TIMON   Then I know thee not. I never had
470   Honest man about me; ay, all I kept were knaves,
To serve in meat° to villains.   *serve food*

FLAVIUS   The gods are witness,
Ne'er did poor steward wear a truer grief

---

3. I'll give you precedents for.
4. Unmitigated; a wandering. The moon was considered auspicious to thieves.
5. Tides supposedly resulted from the sea drawing moisture from the moon.
6. Have unlimited power to steal.
7. As I would an enemy (that is, not at all).

8. Bestowed on ungrateful people.
9. *How . . . enemies:* How perfectly it accords with the customary exhortation to love one's enemies (since friends are one's undoing).
1. Those who would like to injure me, rather than those who really do so.

For his undone lord than mine eyes for you.

TIMON   What, dost thou weep? Come nearer then; I love thee

475 Because thou art a woman,° and disclaim'st   *(in weeping)*
Flinty mankind whose eyes do never give°   *succumb*
But thorough° lust and laughter. Pity's sleeping.   *through*
Strange times, that weep with laughing, not with weeping!

FLAVIUS   I beg of you to know me, good my lord,
T'accept my grief,
[*He offers his money*]

480   and whilst this poor wealth lasts
To entertain° me as your steward still.   *employ*

TIMON   Had I a steward
So true, so just, and now so comfortable?°   *comforting*
It almost turns my dangerous° nature mild.   *savage*

485 Let me behold thy face. Surely this man
Was born of woman.
Forgive my general and exceptless° rashness,   *indiscriminate*
You perpetual sober gods! I do proclaim
One honest man—mistake me not, but one,

490 No more, I pray—and he's a steward.
How fain° would I have hated all mankind,   *willingly*
And thou redeem'st thyself! But all save thee
I fell° with curses.   *cut down*
Methinks thou art more honest now than wise,

495 For by oppressing and betraying me
Thou mightst have sooner got another service;
For many so arrive at second masters
Upon° their first lord's neck. But tell me true—   *By stepping on*
For I must ever doubt, though ne'er so sure—

500 Is not thy kindness subtle,° covetous,   *treacherous*
A usuring kindness, and, as rich men deal gifts,
Expecting in return twenty for one?

FLAVIUS   No, my most worthy master, in whose breast
Doubt and suspect,° alas, are placed too late.   *suspicion*

505 You should have feared false times when you did feast.
Suspect still° comes where an estate is least.   *always*
That which I show, heaven knows, is merely love,
Duty and zeal to your unmatchèd mind,
Care of your food and living; and, believe it,

510 My most honoured lord,
For° any benefit that points to me,   *As for*
Either in hope° or present, I'd exchange   *the future*
For this one wish: that you had power and wealth
To requite° me by making rich yourself.   *repay*

515 TIMON   Look thee, 'tis so. Thou singly honest man,
[*He gives* FLAVIUS *gold*]
Here, take. The gods, out of my misery,
Has sent thee treasure. Go, live rich and happy,
But thus conditioned:[2] thou shalt build from° men,   *away from*
Hate all, curse all, show charity to none,

520 But let the famished flesh slide from the bone
Ere thou relieve the beggar. Give to dogs
What thou deniest to men. Let prisons swallow 'em,

---

2. But on this condition.

Debts wither 'em to nothing; be men° like blasted woods,   *let men be*
And may diseases lick up their false bloods.
And so farewell, and thrive.

525 FLAVIUS   O, let me stay
And comfort you, my master.

TIMON   If thou hat'st curses,
Stay not. Fly whilst thou art blest and free.
Ne'er see thou man, and let me ne'er see thee.

Exeunt [TIMON *into his cave,* FLAVIUS *another way*]

5.1

Enter POET *and* PAINTER

PAINTER   As I took note of the place, it cannot be far where he
abides.

POET   What's to be thought of him? Does the rumour hold for
true that he's so full of gold?

5 PAINTER   Certain. Alcibiades reports it. Phrynia and Timandra
had gold of him. He likewise enriched poor straggling soldiers
with great quantity. 'Tis said he gave unto his steward a mighty
sum.

POET   Then this breaking° of his has been but a try° for his   *bankruptcy / test*
10 friends?

PAINTER   Nothing else. You shall see him a palm[1] in Athens
again, and flourish with the highest. Therefore 'tis not amiss
we tender our loves to him in this supposed distress of his. It
will show honestly in us, and is very likely to load our purposes°   *to reward our efforts*
15 with what they travail° for, if it be a just and true report that   *labor; travel*
goes° of his having.°   *circulates / property*

POET   What have you now to present unto him?

PAINTER   Nothing at this time, but my visitation; only I will
promise him an excellent piece.

20 POET   I must serve him so too, tell him of an intent that's coming
toward him.

PAINTER   Good as the best.°   *That's excellent*

Enter TIMON *from his cave* [*unobserved*]

Promising is the very air° o'th' time; it opens the eyes of expec-   *fashion*
tation. Performance is ever the duller for his° act, and but in   *its*
25 the plainer and simpler kind of people the deed of saying° is   *doing what one says*
quite out of use. To promise is most courtly and fashionable.
Performance is a kind of will or testament which argues a great
sickness in his judgement that makes it.[2]

TIMON [*aside*]   Excellent workman, thou canst not paint a man
30 so bad as is thyself.

POET [*to* PAINTER]   I am thinking what I shall say I have provided
for him. It must be a personating° of himself, a satire against   *representation*
the softness of prosperity, with a discovery° of the infinite flat-   *revelation*
teries that follow youth and opulency.

35 TIMON [*aside*]   Must thou needs stand° for a villain in thine own   *model*
work? Wilt thou whip thine own faults in other men? Do so; I
have gold for thee.

POET [*to* PAINTER]   Nay, let's seek him.

5.1 Location: Outside Athens.
1. The highest tree: alluding to Psalm 92:12, "The righteous shall flourish like a palm tree."

2. That is, only those close to death worry about fulfilling their vows.

Then do we sin against our own estate°   *condition in life*
40   When we may profit meet° and come too late.   *make a profit*
    PAINTER   True.
    When the day serves,° before black-cornered night,   *allows*
    Find what thou want'st by free and offered light.
    Come.
45   TIMON [*aside*]   I'll meet you at the turn.³ What a god's gold,
    That he is worshipped in a baser temple
    Than where swine feed!
    'Tis thou that rigg'st the barque° and plough'st the foam,   *puts sails on the boat*
    Settlest admirèd reverence in a slave.⁴
50   To thee be worship, and thy saints for aye°   *ever*
    Be crowned with plagues, that thee alone obey.
    Fit° I meet them.   *It is fit*
        [*He comes forward to them*]
    POET   Hail, worthy Timon!
    PAINTER   Our late noble master!
    TIMON   Have I once° lived to see two honest men?   *really*
55   POET   Sir, having often of your open bounty tasted,
    Hearing you were retired,° your friends fall'n off,   *had gone away*
    Whose thankless natures, O abhorrèd spirits,
    Not all the whips of heaven are large enough—
    What, to you,
60   Whose star-like nobleness gave life and influence⁵
    To their whole being! I am rapt,° and cannot cover   *overwhelmed*
    The monstrous bulk of this ingratitude
    With any size⁶ of words.
    TIMON   Let it go naked; men may see't the better.
65   You that are honest, by being what you are
    Make them° best seen and known.   *(the "abhorrèd spirits")*
    PAINTER   He and myself
    Have travelled° in the great show'r of your gifts,   *walked*
    And sweetly felt it.
    TIMON   Ay, you are honest men.
    PAINTER   We are hither come to offer you our service.
70   TIMON   Most honest men. Why, how shall I requite you?
    Can you eat roots and drink cold water? No.
    POET *and* PAINTER   What we can do we'll do to do you service.
    TIMON   You're honest men. You've heard that I have gold,
    I am sure you have. Speak truth; you're honest men.
75   PAINTER   So it is said, my noble lord, but therefor
    Came not my friend nor I.
    TIMON   Good honest men. [*To* PAINTER] Thou draw'st a counterfeit°   *picture; fake*
    Best in all Athens; thou'rt indeed the best;
    Thou counterfeit'st most lively.
    PAINTER   So so, my lord.
80   TIMON   E'en so, sir, as I say. [*To* POET] And for thy fiction,°   *poetry; lying*
    Why, thy verse swells with stuff so fine and smooth
    That thou art even natural° in thine art.   *lifelike; idiotic*
    But for all this, my honest-natured friends,
    I must needs say you have a little fault.

---

3. I'll meet you when you come around the corner; I'll trick you in return.
4. Makes an unworthy person be revered.
5. Explained astrologically, "influence" was a substance

thought to stream forth from stars and affect events on earth.
6. Amount; sizing, a layer applied to walls prior to painting.

85   Marry, 'tis not monstrous in you, neither wish I
    You take much pains to mend.
POET *and* PAINTER   Beseech your honour
    To make it known to us.
TIMON   You'll take it ill.
POET *and* PAINTER   Most thankfully, my lord.
TIMON   Will you indeed?
90 POET *and* PAINTER   Doubt it not, worthy lord.
TIMON   There's never a one of you but trusts a knave
    That mightily deceives you.
POET *and* PAINTER   Do we, my lord?
TIMON   Ay, and you hear him cog,° see him dissemble,   *cheat*
    Know his gross patchery,° love him, feed him,   *roguery*
95   Keep° in your bosom; yet remain assured   *Keep him*
    That he's a made-up° villain.   *complete*
PAINTER   I know none such, my lord.
POET   Nor I.
TIMON   Look you, I love you well. I'll give you gold,
100   Rid me these villains from your companies.
    Hang them or stab them, drown them in a draught,°   *stream; cesspool*
    Confound° them by some course, and come to me,   *Destroy*
    I'll give you gold enough.
POET *and* PAINTER   Name them, my lord, let's know them.
TIMON   You that way and you this—but two in company—
105   Each man apart, all single and alone,
    Yet an arch-villain keeps him company.[7]
    [*To* PAINTER] If where thou art two villains shall not be,
    Come not near him. [*To* POET] If thou wouldst not reside
    But where one villain is, then him abandon.
110   Hence; pack!° [*Striking him*] There's gold. You came for gold,   *go away*
        ye slaves.
    [*Striking* PAINTER] You have work for me; there's payment.
        Hence!
    [*Striking* POET]   You are an alchemist;[8] make gold of that.
    Out, rascal dogs!   *Exeunt* [POET *and* PAINTER *one way,*
                              TIMON *into his cave*]

5.2

Enter [FLAVIUS *the*] *Steward and two* SENATORS
FLAVIUS   It is in vain that you would speak with Timon,
    For he is set so only to himself°   *so self-isolated*
    That nothing but himself which looks like man
    Is friendly with° him.   *congenial to*
FIRST SENATOR   Bring us to his cave.
5   It is our part and promise to th'Athenians
    To speak with Timon.
SECOND SENATOR   At all times alike
    Men are not still° the same. 'Twas time and griefs   *always*
    That framed him thus. Time with his fairer hand
    Offering the fortunes of his former days,
10   The former man may make him. Bring us to him,
    And chance it as it may.

---

7. That is, both of you are archvillains.
8. That is, one who can translate base metal (the beating)   into gold.
    5.2 Location: Scene continues.

FLAVIUS   Here is his cave.
[*Calling*] Peace and content be here! Lord Timon, Timon,
Look out and speak to friends. Th'Athenians
By two of their most reverend senate greet thee.
15   Speak to them, noble Timon.
            Enter TIMON *out of his cave*
TIMON   Thou sun that comforts, burn! Speak and be hanged.
For each true word a blister, and each false°   let each false word
Be as a cantherizing° to the root o'th' tongue,   cauterizing
Consuming it with speaking.
FIRST SENATOR   Worthy Timon—
20   TIMON   Of none but such as you, and you of Timon.[1]
FIRST SENATOR   The senators of Athens greet thee, Timon.
TIMON   I thank them, and would send them back the plague
Could I but catch it for them.
FIRST SENATOR   O, forget
What we are sorry for, ourselves in thee.[2]
25   The senators with one consent of° love   unanimous
Entreat thee back to Athens, who have thought
On special dignities° which vacant lie   titles; offices
For thy best use and wearing.
SECOND SENATOR   They confess
Toward thee forgetfulness too general-gross,°   obvious and extreme
30   Which now the public body,° which doth seldom   republic
Play the recanter,° feeling in itself   Change its mind
A lack of Timon's aid, hath sense withal
Of it own fail,° restraining° aid to Timon;   failure / withholding
And send forth us to make their sorrowed render,°   to apologize sadly
35   Together with a recompense more fruitful
Than their offence can weigh down by the dram;[3]
Ay, even such heaps and sums of love and wealth
As shall to thee blot out what wrongs were theirs,
And write in thee the figures[4] of their love,
Ever to read them thine.
40   TIMON   You witch° me in it,   bewitch
Surprise me to the very brink of tears.
Lend me a fool's heart and a woman's eyes,
And I'll beweep these comforts, worthy senators.
FIRST SENATOR   Therefore so please thee to return with us,
45   And of our Athens, thine and ours, to take
The captainship, thou shalt be met with thanks,
Allowed° with absolute power, and thy good name   Vested
Live with authority. So soon we shall drive back
Of Alcibiades th'approaches wild,
50   Who, like a boar too savage, doth root up
His country's peace.
SECOND SENATOR   And shakes his threat'ning sword
Against the walls of Athens.
FIRST SENATOR   Therefore, Timon—
TIMON   Well, sir, I will; therefore I will, sir, thus.
If Alcibiades kill my countrymen,
55   Let Alcibiades know this of Timon:

---

1. That is, we deserve each other.   3. Can outweigh even by painstaking calculation.
2. In the injuries we did you.   4. Distinctive marks; numbers in an account book.

That Timon cares not. But if he sack fair Athens,
And take our goodly agèd men by th' beards,
Giving our holy virgins to the stain°   (by rape)
Of contumelious,° beastly, mad-brained war,   insolent
60 Then let him know, and tell him Timon speaks it
In pity of our agèd and our youth,
I cannot choose but tell him that I care not;
And—let him take't at worst⁵—for their knives care not
While you have throats to answer.° For myself,   suitable for cutting
65 There's not a whittle° in th' unruly camp   pocket knife
But I do prize it at my love before
The reverend'st throat in Athens. So I leave you
To the protection of the prosperous gods,
As thieves to keepers.
FLAVIUS [to SENATORS]   Stay not; all's in vain.
70 TIMON   Why, I was writing of my epitaph.
It will be seen tomorrow. My long sickness
Of health and living now begins to mend,
And nothing° brings me all things. Go; live still.   oblivion
Be Alcibiades your plague, you his,
And last so long enough.
75 FIRST SENATOR   We speak in vain.
TIMON   But yet I love my country, and am not
One that rejoices in the common wrack°   ruin
As common bruit° doth put it.   rumor
FIRST SENATOR   That's well spoke.
TIMON   Commend me to my loving countrymen—
80 FIRST SENATOR   These words become your lips as they pass
      through them.
SECOND SENATOR   And enter in our ears like great triumphers⁶
In their applauding gates.⁷
TIMON   Commend me to them,
And tell them that to ease them of their griefs,
Their fears of hostile strokes, their aches, losses,
85 Their pangs of love, with other incident throes°   natural torments
That nature's fragile vessel doth sustain
In life's uncertain voyage, I will some kindness do them.
I'll teach them to prevent° wild Alcibiades' wrath.   forestall
FIRST SENATOR [aside]   I like this well; he will return again.
90 TIMON   I have a tree which grows here in my close°   enclosure
That mine own use° invites me to cut down,   purpose
And shortly must I fell it. Tell my friends,
Tell Athens, in the sequence of degree°   in order of rank
From high to low throughout, that whoso please
95 To stop affliction, let him take his haste,
Come hither ere my tree hath felt the axe,
And hang himself. I pray you do my greeting.
FLAVIUS [to SENATORS]   Trouble him no further. Thus you still
      shall find him.
TIMON   Come not to me again, but say to Athens,
100 Timon hath made his everlasting mansion°   (his grave)
Upon the beachèd verge° of the salt flood,°   edge / sea

5. Interpret what I say in the worst possible way.   7. Gates full of applauding fellow citizens.
6. Like conquerors returning home.

Who once a day with his embossèd° froth   *foaming*
The turbulent surge shall cover. Thither come,
And let my gravestone be your oracle.°   *source of revelation*
105 Lips, let four° words go by, and language end.   *(that is, few)*
What is amiss, plague and infection mend.
Graves only be men's works, and death their gain.
Sun, hide thy beams. Timon hath done his reign.

                                        Exit [into his cave]

FIRST SENATOR   His discontents are unremovably
110 Coupled to nature.°   *Intrinsic to his nature*
SECOND SENATOR   Our hope in him is dead. Let us return,
And strain what other means is left unto us
In our dear peril.
FIRST SENATOR   It requires swift foot.   *Exeunt*

5.3

Enter two other SENATORS, *with a* MESSENGER

THIRD SENATOR   Thou hast painfully discovered.[1] Are his files°   *troops*
As full as thy report?
MESSENGER   I have spoke the least.°   *estimated low*
Besides, his expedition° promises   *speed*
Present° approach.   *Immediate*
5 FOURTH SENATOR   We stand much hazard if they bring not Timon.
MESSENGER   I met a courier, one mine ancient friend,
Whom, though in general part° we were opposed,   *public matters*
Yet our old love made° a particular force   *exerted*
And made us speak like friends. This man was riding
10 From Alcibiades to Timon's cave
With letters of entreaty which imported°   *urged*
His fellowship i'th' cause against your city,
In part for his sake moved.
            Enter the other SENATORS
THIRD SENATOR   Here come our brothers.
FIRST SENATOR   No talk of Timon; nothing of him expect.
15 The enemy's drum is heard, and fearful scouring°   *hostile action*
Doth choke the air with dust. In, and prepare.
Ours is the fall, I fear, our foe's the snare.   *Exeunt*

5.4

Enter a SOLDIER, *in the woods, seeking* TIMON

SOLDIER   By all description, this should be the place.
Who's here? Speak, ho! No answer?
      [He discovers a gravestone]
                            What is this?
Dead, sure, and this his grave. What's on this tomb
I cannot read. The character I'll take with wax.[1]
5 Our captain hath in every figure° skill,   *kind of writing*
An aged° interpreter, though young in days.   *experienced*
Before proud Athens he's set down by this,°   *laid siege by this time*
Whose fall the mark° of his ambition is.   *Exit*   *goal*

5.3 Location: Outside the walls of Athens.   5.4 Location: Outside Athens.
1. Carefully reconnoitered; told us painful news.   1. By making an impression of the letters.

5.5

Trumpets sound. Enter ALCIBIADES *with his powers,°*   army
before Athens

ALCIBIADES   Sound° to this coward and lascivious town   *Proclaim*
Our terrible approach.
     A parley[1] *sound[s]. The* SENATORS *appear upon the*
     walls[2]
Till now you have gone on and filled the time
With all licentious measure,[3] making your wills
5   The scope of justice.[4] Till now myself and such
As slept° within the shadow of your power   *dwelled*
Have wandered with our traversed[5] arms, and breathed
Our sufferance[6] vainly. Now the time is flush
When crouching marrow,° in the bearer strong,   *latent vigor*
10   Cries of itself 'No more'; now breathless° wrong   *exhausted*
Shall sit and pant in your great chairs of ease,
And pursy° insolence shall break his wind°   *short-winded / pant; fart*
With fear and horrid° flight.   *terrified*
FIRST SENATOR   Noble and young,
When thy first griefs were but a mere conceit,°   *only merely imagined*
15   Ere thou hadst power or we had cause of fear,
We sent to thee to give thy rages balm,
To wipe out our ingratitude with loves
Above their quantity.[7]
SECOND SENATOR   So did we woo
Transformèd Timon to our city's love
20   By humble message and by promised means.°   *wealth*
We were not all unkind, nor all deserve
The common° stroke of war.   *indiscriminate*
FIRST SENATOR   These walls of ours
Were not erected by their hands from whom
You have received your grief; nor are they such
25   That these great tow'rs, trophies,° and schools[8] should fall   *monuments*
For private faults in them.°   *(the offenders)*
SECOND SENATOR   Nor are they living
Who were the motives that you first went out.[9]
Shame that they wanted° cunning, in excess,   *lacked*
Hath broke their hearts. March, noble lord,
30   Into our city with thy banners spread.
By decimation and a tithèd death,[1]
If thy revenges hunger for that food
Which nature loathes, take thou the destined tenth,
And by the hazard of the spotted die
35   Let die the spotted.[2]
FIRST SENATOR   All have not offended.
For those that were,° it is not square° to take,   *(living) / fair*
On those that are, revenges. Crimes like lands
Are not inherited. Then, dear countryman,
Bring in thy ranks, but leave without° thy rage.   *outside*

5.5 Location: Outside the walls of Athens.
1. Trumpet call to negotiate.
2. Probably on the upper gallery at stage rear.
3. All kinds of licentious conduct.
4. *making . . . justice:* making justice conform to your whims.
5. Crossed (as part of military training).

6. *breathed / Our sufferance:* voiced our grievances.
7. *loves . . . quantity:* friendly gestures greater than your grievances.
8. Public buildings.
9. Who were those who prompted your banishment.
1. Killing one of every ten person, chosen by lot.
2. Corrupt (punning on the spots of dice).

40   Spare thy Athenian cradle° and those kin   *birthplace*
        Which, in the bluster of thy wrath, must fall
        With those that have offended. Like a shepherd
        Approach the fold and cull th'infected forth,°   *pick out the corrupt*
        But kill not all together.
        SECOND SENATOR   What thou wilt,
45   Thou rather shalt enforce it with thy smile
        Than hew to't with thy sword.
        FIRST SENATOR   Set but thy foot
        Against our rampired° gates and they shall ope,   *barricaded*
        So° thou wilt send thy gentle heart before   *If*
        To say thou'lt enter friendly.
        SECOND SENATOR   Throw thy glove,
50   Or any token° of thine honour else,   *pledge*
        That thou wilt use the wars as thy redress,
        And not as our confusion.° All thy powers°   *ruin/army*
        Shall make their harbour° in our town till we   *lodging*
        Have sealed° thy full desire.   *satisfied*
        ALCIBIADES [*throwing up a glove*]   Then there's my glove.
55   Descend, and open your uncharged ports.°   *unattacked gates*
        Those enemies of Timon's and mine own
        Whom you yourselves shall set out for reproof°   *select for punishment*
        Fall, and no more; and to atone° your fears   *appease*
        With my more noble meaning, not a man°   *soldier*
60   Shall pass his quarter° or offend the stream   *leave his assigned place*
        Of regular justice[3] in your city's bounds
        But shall be remedied to° your public laws   *punished according to*
        At heaviest answer.°   *penalty*
        BOTH SENATORS   'Tis most nobly spoken.
65   ALCIBIADES   Descend, and keep your words.
           [*Trumpets sound. Exeunt* SENATORS *from the walls.*]
           Enter [SOLDIER, *with a tablet of wax*]
        SOLDIER   My noble general, Timon is dead,
        Entombed upon the very hem° o'th' sea;   *edge*
        And on his gravestone this insculpture,° which   *inscription*
        With wax I brought away, whose soft impression
70   Interprets for my poor ignorance.
           ALCIBIADES *reads the Epitaph*
        ALCIBIADES   'Here lies a wretched corpse,
           Of wretched soul bereft.
           Seek not my name. A plague consume
           You wicked caitiffs° left!   *wretches*
75   Here lie I, Timon, who alive
           All living men did hate.
           Pass by and curse thy fill, but pass
           And stay not here thy gait.'
        These well express in thee thy latter spirits.°   *sentiments*
80   Though thou abhorred'st in us our human griefs,
        Scorned'st our brains' flow[4] and those our droplets which
        From niggard[5] nature fall, yet rich conceit°   *imagination*
        Taught thee to make vast Neptune weep for aye°   *ever*
        On thy low grave, on faults forgiven. Dead

---

3. *offend . . . justice*: violate the ordinary laws.
4. Tears were thought to exude from the brain.

5. "Niggard" because teardrops are tiny compared with the sea, Neptune (line 83).

85　　Is noble Timon, of whose memory
　　　Hereafter more.
　　　　　　　[*Enter* SENATORS *through the gates*]
　　　　　　　　　Bring me into your city,
　　　And I will use the olive° with my sword,　　　　　　　　*(symbol of peace)*
　　　Make war breed peace, make peace stint° war, make each　　　*stop*
　　　Prescribe to other as each other's leech.[6]
90　　Let our drums strike.　　　[*Drums.*] *Exeunt* [*through the gates*]

---

6. Physician (because war purges peace of its decadence, and peace purges war of its violence).

King Lear

You have, King James told his eldest son a few years before Shakespeare wrote *King Lear,* a double obligation to love God: first because He made you a man, and second because He made you "a little God to sit on his Throne, and rule over other men." Whatever the realities of Renaissance kingship—realities that included the stern necessity of compromise, reciprocity, and restraint—the idea of sovereignty was closely linked to fantasies of divine omnipotence. From his exalted height, the sovereign looked down upon the tiny figures of the ordinary mortals below him. Their hopes, the material conditions of their miserable existence, their names, were of little interest, and yet the King knew that they too were looking back up at him. "For kings being public persons," James uneasily acknowledged, are set "upon a public stage, in the sight of all the people; where all the beholders' eyes are attentively bent to look and pry in the least circumstance of their secretist drifts." Under such circumstances, the sovereign's dream was to command, like God, not only unquestioning obedience but unqualified love.

In *King Lear,* Shakespeare explores the dark consequences of this dream not only in the state but also in the family, where the Renaissance father increasingly styled himself "a little God." If, as the play opens, the aged Lear, exercising his imperious will and demanding professions of devotion, is "every inch a king," he is also by the same token every inch a father, the absolute ruler of a family that conspicuously lacks the alternative authority of a mother. Shakespeare's play invokes this royal and paternal sovereignty only to chronicle its destruction in scenes of astonishing cruelty and power. The very words "every inch a king" are spoken not by the confident figure of supreme authority whom we glimpse in the first moments but by the ruined old man who perceives in his feverish rage and madness that the fantasy of omnipotence is a fraud: "When the rain came to wet me once, and the wind to make me chatter; when the thunder would not peace at my bidding, there I found 'em, there I smelt 'em out. Go to, they are not men o' their words. They told me I was everything; 'tis a lie, I am not ague-proof" (4.5.98–102; all quotations, except where noted, are from *The Tragedy of King Lear*).

"They told me I was everything": Shakespeare's culture continually staged public rituals of deference to authority. These rituals—kneeling, bowing, uncovering the head, and so forth—enacted respect for wealth, caste, power, and, at virtually every level of society, age. Jacobean England had a strong official regard for the rights and privileges of age. It told itself that, by the will of God and the natural order of things, authority gravitated to the old, particularly to old men, and it contrived to ensure that this proper, sanctified arrangement of society be everywhere respected.

" 'Tis a lie": Shakespeare's culture continually told itself at the same time that without the control of property and the threat of punishment, any claim to authority was chillingly vulnerable to the ruthless ambitions of the young, the restless, and the discontented. The incessant, ritualized spectacles of sovereignty have a nervous air, as if no one quite believed all the grand claims to divine sanction for the rule of Kings and fathers, as if those who ruled both states and families secretly feared that the elaborate hierarchical structure could vanish like a mirage, exposing their shivering, defenseless bodies. *King Lear* relentlessly stages this horrifying descent toward what the ruined King, contemplating the filthy, naked body of a mad beggar, calls "the thing itself": "Unaccommodated man is no more but such a poor, bare, forked animal as thou art" (3.4.95–97). Lear and the Earl of Gloucester, another old man whose terrible fate closely parallels Lear's, repeatedly look up at the heavens and call upon the gods for help, but the gods are silent. The despairing Gloucester concludes that the universe is actively malevolent—"As flies to wanton boys are we to th' gods; / They kill us for their sport" (4.1.37–38)—but the awful silence of the gods may equally be a sign of their indifference or their nonexistence.

The story of King Lear and his three daughters had been often told when Shakespeare undertook to make it the subject of a tragedy. The play, performed at court in December 1605, was probably written and first performed somewhat earlier, though not before 1603, since it contains allusions to a florid piece of anti-Catholic propaganda published in that year: Samuel Harsnett's *Declaration of Egregious Popish Imposture* (the source of the colorful names of the "foul fiends" by whom Shakespeare's mad beggar claims to be possessed). Thus scholars generally assign Shakespeare's composition of *King Lear* to 1604–05, shortly after *Othello* (c. 1603–04) and before *Macbeth* (c. 1606): an astounding succession of tragic masterpieces.

King Lear first appeared in print in a Quarto published in 1608 entitled *M. William Shak-speare: His True Chronicle Historie of the life and death of King Lear*; a substantially different text, entitled *The Tragedie of King Lear* and grouped with the other tragedies, was printed in the 1623 First Folio. From the eighteenth century, when the difference between the two texts was first noted, editors, assuming that they were imperfect versions of the identical play, customarily conflated them, blending together the approximately one hundred Folio lines not printed in the Quarto with the approximately three hundred quarto lines not printed in the Folio and selecting as best they could among the hundreds of particular alternative readings. But there is a growing scholarly consensus that the 1608 text of *Lear* represents the play as Shakespeare first wrote it and that the 1623 text represents a substantial revision. (See the Textual Note for further discussion.) Since this revision includes significant structural changes as well as many local details, the two texts provide a precious opportunity to glimpse Shakespeare's creative process as an artist and the collaborative work of his theater company. Accordingly, the *Norton Shakespeare* prints *The History of King Lear* and *The Tragedy of King Lear* on facing pages; in addition, a modern conflated version of the play follows, so that readers will be able to judge for themselves the effects of the familiar editorial practice of stitching together the two texts.

When *King Lear* was first performed, it may have struck contemporaries as strangely timely in the wake of a lawsuit that had occurred in late 1603. The two elder daughters of a doddering gentleman named Sir Brian Annesley attempted to get their father legally certified as insane, thereby enabling themselves to take over his estate, while his youngest daughter vehemently protested on her father's behalf. The youngest daughter's name happened to be Cordell, a name uncannily close to that of Lear's youngest daughter, Cordelia, who tries to save her father from the malevolent designs of her older sisters.

Cordeilla Queene. From Raphael Holinshed, *The Firste Volume of the Chronicles of England, Scotlande, and Irelande* (1577).

The Annesley case is worth invoking not only because it may have caught Shakespeare's attention but also because it directs our own attention to the ordinary family tensions and fears around which *King Lear,* for all of its wildness, violence, and strangeness, is constructed. Though the Lear story has the mythic quality of a folktale (specifically, it resembles both the tale of Cinderella and the tale told in many cultures of a daughter who falls into disfavor for telling her father she loves him as much as salt), it was rehearsed in Shakespeare's time as a piece of authentic British history from the very ancient past (c. 800

B.C.E.) and as an admonition to contemporary fathers not to put too much trust in the flattery of their children: "Remember what happened to old King Lear . . ." In some versions of the story, including Shakespeare's, the warning centers on a decision to retire.

Retirement has come to seem a routine event, but in the patriarchal, gerontocratic culture of Tudor and Stuart England, it was generally shunned. When through illness or extreme old age it became unavoidable, retirement put a severe strain on the politics and psychology of deference by driving a wedge between status—what Lear at society's pinnacle calls "the name and all th'addition to a king" (1.1.134)—and power. In both the state and the family, the strain could be somewhat eased by transferring power to the eldest legitimate male successor, but as the families of both the legendary Lear and the real Brian Annesley showed, such a successor did not always exist. In the absence of a male heir, the aged Lear, determined to "shake all cares and business" from himself and confer them on "younger strengths," attempts to divide his kingdom equally among his daughters so that, as he puts it, "future strife / May be prevented now" (1.1.37–38, 42–43). But this attempt is a disastrous failure. Critics have often argued that the roots of the failure lie in the division of the kingdom, that any parceling out of the land on a map would itself have provoked in the audience an ominous shudder, as it is clearly meant to do when the rebels spread out a map in anticipation of a comparable division in *1 Henry IV*. But the principal focus of Shakespeare's tragedy seems to lie elsewhere: Lear's folly is not (or not only) that he retires or even that he divides his kingdom—the play opens with the Earl of Gloucester and the Earl of Kent commenting without apparent disapproval on the scrupulous equality of the shares—but rather that he rashly disinherits the only child who truly loves him, his youngest daughter.

Shakespeare contrives moreover to show that the problem with which his characters are grappling does not simply result from the absence of a son and heir. In his most brilliant and complex use of a double plot, he intertwines the story of Lear and his three daughters with the story of Gloucester and his two sons, a tale he adapted from an episode in Philip Sidney's prose romance *Arcadia*. Gloucester has a legitimate heir, his elder son, Edgar, as well as an illegitimate son, Edmond, and in this family the tragic conflict originates not in an unusual manner of transferring property from one generation to another but rather in the reverse: Edmond seethes with murderous resentment at the disadvantage entirely customary for someone in his position, both as a younger son and as what was called a "base" or "natural" child. "Thou, nature, art my goddess," he declares:

> Wherefore should I
> Stand in the plague of custom and permit
> The curiosity of nations to deprive me
> For that I am some twelve or fourteen moonshines
> Lag of a brother? Why 'bastard'? Wherefore 'base'?
> (1.2.1–6)

For the seductive and ruthlessly ambitious Edmond, the social order and the language used to articulate it are merely arbitrary constraints, obstacles to the triumph of his will. He schemes to tear down the obstacles by playing on his father's fears, cleverly planting a forged letter in which his older brother appears to be plotting against his father's life. The letter's chilling sentences express Edmond's own impatience, his hatred of the confining power of custom, his disgusted observation of "the oppression of aged tyranny, who sways not as it hath power but as it is suffered" (1.2.48–49). Gloucester is predictably horrified and incensed; these are, as Edmond cunningly knows, the cold sentiments that the aged fear lie just beneath the surface of deference and flattery. The forged letter reflects back as well on the scene in which Gloucester himself has just participated: a scene in which everyone, with the exception of the Earl of Kent, has tamely suffered a tyrannical old man to banish his youngest daughter for her failure to flatter him.

Why does Lear, who has already drawn up the map dividing the kingdom, stage the love test? In Shakespeare's principal source, an anonymous play called *The True*

Stargazing. From John Cypriano, *A Most Strange and Wonderfull Prophesie* (1595). "I should have been that I am had the maidenliest star in the firmament twinkled on my bastardizing" (1.2.119–21).

Chronicle History of King Leir (published in 1605 but dating from 1594 or earlier), there is a gratifyingly clear answer. Leir's strong-willed daughter Cordella has vowed that she will only marry a man whom she herself loves; Leir wishes her to marry the man he chooses for his own dynastic purposes. He stages the love test, anticipating that in competing with her sisters Cordella will declare that she loves her father best, at which point Leir will demand that she prove her love by marrying the suitor of his choice. The stratagem backfires, but its purpose is clear.

By stripping his character of a comparable motive, Shakespeare makes Lear's act seem stranger, at once more arbitrary and more rooted in deep psychological needs. His Lear is a man who has determined to retire from power but who cannot endure dependence. Unwilling to lose his identity as an absolute authority both in the state and in the family, he arranges a public ritual—"Which of you shall we say doth love us most?" (1.1.49)—whose aim seems to be to allay his own anxiety by arousing it in his children. Since the shares have already been apportioned, Lear evidently wants his daughters to engage in a competition for his bounty without having to endure any of the actual consequences of such a competition; he wants, that is, to produce in them something like the effect of theater, where emotions run high and their practical effects are negligible. But in this absolutist theater Cordelia refuses to perform: "What shall Cordelia speak? Love and be silent" (1.1.60). When she says "Nothing," a word that echoes darkly throughout the play, Lear hears what he most dreads: emptiness, loss of respect, the extinction of identity. And when, under further interrogation, she declares that she loves her father "according to my bond" (1.1.91), Lear understands these words too to be the equivalent of "nothing."

As Cordelia's subsequent actions demonstrate, his youngest daughter's bond is in reality a sustaining, generous love, but it is a love that ultimately leads to her death. Here Shakespeare makes an even more startling departure not only from *The True Chronicle History of King Leir* but from all his known sources. The earliest of these, the account in Geoffrey of Monmouth's twelfth-century *Historia Regum Britanniae*, sets the pattern repeated in John Higgins's *Mirour for Magistrates* (1574 edition), William Warner's *Albions England* (1586), Raphael Holinshed's *Chronicles of England, Scotlande, and Irelande* (2nd ed., 1587), and Edmund Spenser's *Faerie Queene* (1590, 2.10.27–32): the aged Lear is overthrown by his wicked daughters and their husbands, but he is restored to the throne by the army of his good daughter's husband, the King of France. The story then is one of loss and restoration: Lear resumes his reign, and when, "made ripe for death" by old age, as Spenser puts it, he dies, he is succeeded by Cordelia. The conclusion is not unequivocally happy; in all of the known chronicles, Cordelia rules worthily for several years and then, after being deposed and imprisoned by her nephews, in despair commits suicide. But Shakespeare's ending is unprecedented in its tragic devastation. When in Act 5 Lear suddenly enters with the lifeless body of Cordelia in his arms, the original audience, secure in the expectation of a very different resolution, must have been doubly shocked, a shock cruelly reinforced when the signs that she might be reviving—"This feather stirs. She lives" (5.3.239)—all prove false. Lear apparently dies in the grip of the illusion that he detects some breath on his daughter's lips, but we know that Cordelia will, as he says a moment earlier, "come no more. / Never, never, never, never, never" (5.3.282–83).

Those five reiterated words, the bleakest pentameter line Shakespeare ever wrote, are the climax of an extraordinary poetics of despair that is set in motion when Lear disinherits Cordelia and when Gloucester credits Edmond's lies about Edgar. *King Lear* has seemed to many modern readers and audiences the greatest of Shakespeare's tragedies precisely because of its anguished look into the heart of darkness, but its vision of suffering and evil has not always commanded unequivocal admiration. In the eighteenth century, Samuel Johnson wrote, "I was many years ago so shocked by Cordelia's death that I know not whether I ever endured to read again the last scenes of the play till I undertook to revise them as an editor." Johnson's contemporaries preferred a revision of Shakespeare's tragedy undertaken in 1681 by Nahum Tate. Finding the play "a Heap of Jewels, unstrung, and unpolisht," Tate proceeded to restring them in order to save Cordelia's life and to produce the unambiguous and happy triumph of the forces of good.

Only in the nineteenth century was Shakespeare's deeply pessimistic ending—the old generation dead or dying, the survivors shaken to the core, the ruling families all broken with no impending marriage to promise renewal—generally restored to theatrical performance and the tragedy's immense power fully acknowledged. Even passionate admirers of *King Lear,* however, continued to express deep uneasiness, repeatedly noting not only its unbearably painful close but also what Johnson first called the "improbability of Lear's conduct" and Samuel Taylor Coleridge termed the plot's "glaring absurdity." Above all, critics questioned whether the tragedy was suitable for the stage. Coleridge compared the suffering Lear to one of Michelangelo's titanic figures, but the grandeur invoked by the comparison led his contemporary Charles Lamb to conclude flatly that "Lear is essentially impossible to be represented on stage." "To see Lear acted," Lamb wrote, "to see an old man tottering about the stage with a walking stick, turned out of doors by his daughters in a rainy night, has nothing in it but what is painful and disgusting." In such a view, *King Lear* could only be staged successfully in the imagination; there alone would Lear's passion be perceived not like ordinary human suffering but rather, in the marvelous characterization of another Romantic critic, William Hazlitt, "like a sea, swelling, chafing, raging, without bound, without hope, without beacon, or anchor." In the theater of the mind, Shakespeare's play could assume its true, stupendous proportions, enabling the reader to grasp its ultimate meaning. That meaning, the great early twentieth-century critic A. C. Bradley wrote, is that we must "renounce the world, hate it, and lose it gladly. The only real thing in it is the soul, with its courage, patience, devotion. And nothing outward can touch that." These are stirring words, but what about the body?

Brilliant modern stage performances and, more recently, films belying the view that *King Lear* is unactable have underscored not only the play's acute theatrical sophistication and self-awareness but also its emphasis on the body's inescapable centrality. If Shakespeare explores the extremes of the mind's anguish and the soul's devotion, he never forgets that his characters have bodies as well, bodies that have needs, cravings, and terrible vulnerabilities. When in this tragedy characters fall from high station, they plunge unprotected into a world of violent storms, murderous cruelty, and physical horror. The old King wanders raging on the heath, through a wild night of thunder and rain. Disguised as Poor Tom, a mad beggar possessed by demons, Gloucester's son Edgar enacts a life of utmost degradation: "Poor Tom, that eats the swimming frog, the toad, the tadpole, the wall-newt and the water; that in the fury of his heart, when the foul fiend rages, eats cowdung for salads, swallows the old rat and the ditch-dog, drinks the green mantle of the standing pool" (3.4.115–19). Gloucester's fate is even more terrible: betrayed by his son Edmond, he is seized in his own house by Lear's sadistic daughter Regan and her husband, Cornwall, tied to a chair, brutally interrogated, blinded, and then thrust bleeding out of doors.

Mental anguish in *King Lear,* then, is closely intertwined with physical anguish; the terrifying forces that are released by Lear's folly crash down upon both body and soul, just as the storm that rages on the heath seems at once an objective event and a symbolic representation of Lear's innermost being. The greatest expression of this intertwining in the play is Lear's madness, which brings together a devastating loss of identity, a relentless, radical assault on the hypocrisies of authority, and a demented, nauseated loathing of female sexuality. The loathing culminates in a fit of retching—"Fie, fie, fie; pah, pah!"—followed by Lear's delusional attempt to find a physical remedy for his psychic pain: "Give me an ounce of civet, good apothecary, sweeten my imagination" (4.5.123–24). In fact, relief from the chaotic rage of madness comes in the wake of a deep, restorative sleep and a change of garments.

The body in *King Lear* is a site not only of abject misery, nausea, and pain but of care and a nascent moral awareness. In the midst of his mad ravings, Lear turns to the shivering Fool and asks, "Art cold?" (3.2.67). The simple question anticipates his recognition a few moments later that there is more suffering in the world than his own:

> Poor naked wretches, wheresoe'er you are,
> That bide the pelting of this pitiless storm,
> How shall your houseless heads and unfed sides,
> Your looped and windowed raggedness, defend you
> From seasons such as these? O, I have ta'en
> Too little care of this.

> (3.4.28–33)

And if the world seems largely unjust and indifferent to human suffering, there are nonetheless throughout the play constant manifestations of generosity of body as well

Tom Durie (1614). By Marcus Gheeraerts the Younger. Durie was the jester of Anne of Denmark, who was married to James I.

as soul. "Help me, help me!" cries the frightened Fool, to which Kent (disguised in order to serve the King who has banished him) says simply, "Give me thy hand" (3.4.39–40). "What are you?" says the blind Gloucester to the son he has unjustly disinherited, to which the son, also in disguise, replies similarly, "Give me your hand" (4.5.213, 216). (In a moving moment from the *History of . . . King Lear,* absent from the Folio version, two of Gloucester's servants not only react with horror to their master's blinding but also resolve to assist him: "Go thou. I'll fetch some flax and whites of eggs / To apply to his bleeding face. Now heaven help him!" [14.103–04].) Such signs of goodness and empathy do not outweigh the harshness of the physical world of the play, let alone cancel out the vicious cruelty of certain of its inhabitants, but they do qualify its moral bleakness.

It is possible to detect in *King Lear* one of the great structural rhythms of Christianity: a passage through suffering, humiliation, and pain to a transcendent wisdom and love. Lear's initial actions were blind and selfish, but he comes to acknowledge his folly and, in an immensely poignant scene, to kneel down before the daughter he has wronged. Gloucester too learns that he was blind, even when his eyes could see, and he passes, by means of Edgar's strange deception at the imaginary cliff, from suicidal despair to patient resignation. "Men must endure / Their going hence even as their coming hither," Edgar wisely counsels his father. "Ripeness is all" (5.2.9–11). For a time, evil seems to flourish in the world, but the wicked do not ultimately triumph. The sadistic Duke of Cornwall is fatally wounded by his own morally upright servant, Edmond is killed by the brother he had tried to destroy, the loathsome Oswald is clubbed to death trying to murder Gloucester, one wicked sister poisons the other and then kills herself. Against self-interest and in the face of intolerable pressure, goodness shines forth. The Earl of Kent, banished by the rash Lear, dons a disguise in order to serve his King and master, and there are comparable acts of devoted service and self-sacrificing love from Edgar, Cordelia, and that remarkable figure the Fool. In one of the comic masterpieces of the sixteenth century, *The Praise of Folly,* the great Dutch humanist Erasmus used the fool as an emblem of the deepest Christian wisdom, revealed only when the pride, cruelty, and ambition of the world are shattered by a cleansing laughter. The shattering in *King Lear* is tragically violent and deadly, but the presence of the truth-telling Fool seems to point toward a comparable revelation.

Yet *King Lear,* set in a pagan world, resists the redemptive optimism that underlies the Christian vision (an optimism that led Dante to call his poem of damnation and salvation *The Divine Comedy*). The Fool's unnervingly perceptive observations sound far more corrosive than loving—he is, in Lear's words, "a bitter fool" (1.4.121)—and he disappears altogether in the third act. His moments of insight and those of all the other characters in the play are radically unstable, like brilliant flashes of lightning in a vast, dark landscape. Hence, for example, Lear's recognition of his folly in banishing Cordelia for her "most small fault" (1.4.228) is immediately followed by his hideous cursing of Goneril. His moving acknowledgment of the suffering of the poor, naked wretches is immediately followed by his inability to see the poor naked wretch before him in any terms but his own: "Didst thou give all to thy two daughters, / And art thou come to this?" (3.4.47–48). And his appeal to patient resignation—"When we are born, we cry that we are come / To this great stage of fools" (4.5.172–73)—is immediately followed by a mad fantasy of revenge: "Then kill, kill, kill, kill, kill, kill!" (4.5.177). Every time we seem to have reached firm moral ground, the ground shifts, and we are kept, as Johnson observed, in "a perpetual tumult of indignation, pity, and hope." There are moments of apparent resolution: "Let's away to prison," says Lear to the weeping Cordelia, when they are captured by the enemy. "We two alone will sing like birds i'th' cage" (5.3.8–9). But a more terrible fate lies before them. "Some good I mean to do," says the dying Edmond, "despite of mine own nature" (5.3.217–18). But his attempt to send a reprieve and therefore in some measure to redeem himself comes too late. The play's nightmarish events continually lurch ahead of intentions, and even efforts to say "I have seen the worst" are frustrated.

The tragedy is not only that the intervals of moral resolution, mental lucidity, and spiritual calm are so brief, continually giving way to feverish grief and rage, but also that the modest human understandings, moving in their simplicity, cost such an enormous amount of pain. Edgar saves his father from despair but also in some sense breaks his father's heart. Cordelia's steadfast honesty, her refusal to flatter the father she loves, may be admirable but has disastrous consequences, and her attempt to save Lear only leads to her own death. For a sublime moment, Lear actually *sees* his daughter, understands her separateness, acknowledges her existence—

> Do not laugh at me,
> For as I am a man, I think this lady
> To be my child, Cordelia—

but it has taken the destruction of virtually his whole world for him to reach this recognition (4.6.61–63).

An apocalyptic dream of last judgment and redemption hovers over the entire tragedy, but it is a dream forever deferred. At the sight of the howling Lear with the dead Cordelia in his arms, the bystanders can only ask a succession of stunned questions:

> KENT   Is this the promised end?
> EDGAR   Or image of that horror?
>
> (5.3.237–38)

Lear's own question a moment later seems the most terrible and the most important: "Why should a dog, a horse, a rat have life, / And thou no breath at all?" (5.3.281–82). It is a sign of *King Lear*'s astonishing freedom from orthodoxy that it refuses to offer any of the conventional answers to this question, answers that largely serve to conceal or deflect the mourner's anguish. Shakespeare's tragedy asks us not to turn away from evil, folly, and unbearable human pain but, seeing them face-to-face, to strengthen our capacity to speak the truth, to endure, and to love.

STEPHEN GREENBLATT

TEXTUAL NOTE

The textual traces of *King Lear* have probably given scholars more cause for debate than any of Shakespeare's other works. The debate centers on the relative authority of the two early texts of the tragedy, the First Quarto (Q1) and the First Folio (F), and the relationship between them. Q1 contains approximately three hundred lines that do not appear in F; F prints approximately one hundred lines that are not in Q1. There are also hundreds of individual variants, some apparently negligible but others highly significant. To take a single instance, the closing lines of the play—by convention assigned to the person who will now govern the state—are in Q1 spoken by Albany, in F spoken by Edgar.

Q1 was first printed in December and January of 1607–08 in the shop of Nicholas Okes, a London printer, under the following title:

> M. William Shak-speare: His True Chronicle Historie of the life and death of King Lear and his three Daughters. With the vnfortunate life of Edgar, sonne and heire to the Earle of Gloster, and his sullen and assumed humor of Tom of Bedlam: As it was played before the Kings Maiestie at Whitehall vpon S. Stephans night in Christmas Hollidayes. By his Maiesties seruants playing vsually at the Gloabe on the Bancke-side. London, Printed for Nathaniel Butter, and are to be sold at his shop in Pauls Church-yard at the signe of the Pide Bull neere St. Austins Gate. 1608.

Of the print run, only twelve copies have been found. Q1 was set, most scholars agree, from Shakespeare's own draft, his "foul papers." That Q1 was printed from such a draft and not from a scribe's copy or a promptbook promises strong authority. However, there are difficulties.

Peculiarities within the text and variations among the twelve copies suggest that

Okes's printing shop was not quite up to the task set by this long, complex play. *King Lear* appears indeed to have been the first play Okes attempted. There was clearly a shortage of typeface, particularly of full stops and colons: this may help to explain anomalous aspects of lineation and punctuation. Evidently, two compositors worked together on the play, one perhaps reading aloud while the other set the type; this may have caused what often appear to be aural errors in the text. And these errors, which may have been compounded by difficulties in reading the copy, might have been avoided had the printer's copy come from an experienced scribe rather than from Shakespeare's own handwriting, which appears at some points to have been illegible. The result is a text of great importance but tantalizing uncertainty. While no critics doubt that Q1 represents a legitimate early version of *King Lear*, it is a version whose authority is compromised by a succession of readings that are often confusing and sometimes nonsensical.

At a time when it was generally accepted that Q1 and F were, for all their differences, derived from one original text, now lost, these textual difficulties were relatively easily handled: the editor, positing a single ideal form of the play "behind" or "before" the versions that were printed, would conflate the two texts, weaving together the lines that appear in only one or the other version and correcting Q1 with reference to F or (in a much smaller number of instances) F with reference to Q1. The Oxford editors, upon whose work this edition is based, broke decisively with this tradition of conflation. Instead, they edited and printed Q1 and F as separate and distinct texts. In so doing, they gave up the luxury of editorial cross-referencing. As the principal Oxford editor of *King Lear*, Gary Taylor, points out, "The entire purpose of editing Q and F separately is to preserve the integrity of each, and such a purpose is not well served by importing revised readings into an unrevised fabric." Oxford therefore sought, insofar as possible, to emend Q1, where necessary, as if F did not exist.

Such emendation is almost unnecessary in the altogether more straightforward text of the First Folio, which appeared in 1623 as *The Tragedie of King Lear*. In contrast to Q1, F differentiates carefully between prose and verse, shows consistency in spelling, and offers detailed stage directions. The Folio also characteristically divides the play into acts and scenes. These differences, along with the cuts and the additional passages, are all the more striking if F is basically derived, as Oxford contends, from the text known as Q2. For this Second Quarto, printed in 1619 (three years after Shakespeare's death) although falsely dated 1608, is only a slightly improved copy of Q1. While spelling and punctuation were somewhat corrected and some attempts were made to emend difficult words and phrases, no independent manuscript was used to prepare Q2. Therefore, when the compositors sat down to print F, their copy of Q2, Oxford maintains, must have been annotated using an independent manuscript. What was the source of this manuscript? The Oxford editors think it likely that the manuscript was a scribal copy, perhaps a promptbook, that derived ultimately from Q1.

Though F is thus linked, if indirectly, to Q1, the fact remains that two quite different texts of the play exist. Efforts over the years to conflate them in the search for a hypothetical master text have been partly responsible for the neglect that Q1 has generally suffered and for the failure to explore fully the extraordinary opportunity that the survival of these distinct versions of the play presents. Each version has its own integrity; each contains passages intrinsically its own. In addition, the Quarto may give us a precious glimpse, as the Oxford editor notes, of the play "as Shakespeare first conceived it, probably before it was performed," while the Folio represents a revision made probably two or three years after the play had been first written and performed. The Folio, then, with its substantial cuts and its small additions, its streamlining and its subtle shifts in emphasis, is the more theatrical text.

The *Norton Shakespeare* presents Q1 and F on facing pages so that readers can compare them easily. In order to make it possible to read them independently of one another, both texts are glossed and footnoted. In addition, we offer a conflated version of *King Lear*, prepared by Barbara K. Lewalski, so that readers can encounter the tragedy in the form that it assumed in most editions from the eighteenth century until very recently.

SELECTED BIBLIOGRAPHY

Booth, Stephen. "On the Greatness of *King Lear*." *"King Lear," "Macbeth," Indefinition and Tragedy*. New Haven: Yale University Press, 1983. 1–57. Shakespeare's tragedy compels readers and audience through its power of indefiniteness: the play's characters, categories, and boundaries melt and blur, disclosing the instability of all attempts to impose order on the world.

Cavell, Stanley. "The Avoidance of Love: A Reading of *King Lear*." *Disowning Knowledge in Six Plays of Shakespeare*. Cambridge: Cambridge University Press, 1987. 39–124. To face the frightening isolation of all humans, to grasp the difference between the knowledge of love and the acknowledgment of love, to understand that in order to see one must also allow oneself to be seen, to endure the shame of exposure—these are among *King Lear*'s radical insights.

de Grazia, Margreta. "The Ideology of Superfluous Things: *King Lear* as Period Piece." *Subject and Object in Renaissance Culture*. Ed. Margreta de Grazia, Maureen Quilligan, and Peter Stallybrass. Cambridge: Cambridge University Press, 1996. 17–42. Far from being protomodern, the play depicts a world where persons and things cannot be separated and superfluity is a sign of apocalypse.

Greenblatt, Stephen. "Shakespeare and the Exorcists." *Shakespearean Negotiations: The Circulation of Social Energy in Renaissance England*. Berkeley: University of California Press, 1988. 94–128. Shakespeare draws theatrical energy from the contemporary practice of exorcism, a ritualized encounter with evil attacked by Protestant officials as a vicious, histrionic fraud.

Holland, Peter, ed. *King Lear and Its Afterlife: Shakespeare Survey* 55 (2002): 1–180. Treating four centuries of adaptations, appropriations, performances, and interpretations, this essay collection focuses on plays, songs, and novels that draw on *King Lear*.

Jones, John. *Shakespeare at Work*. Oxford: Oxford University Press, 1995. Close attention to the Folio revisions of the quarto text of the play discloses a cunning symbolic design that links Lear's craziness with an obsession with quantity.

Kronenfeld, Judy. *"King Lear" and the Naked Truth: Rethinking the Language of Religion and Resistance*. Durham, N.C.: Duke University Press, 1998. The play should be understood not through deconstruction or new historicism but through the common Christian culture that gave its terms meaning outside a polemical context.

Leggatt, Alexander. *King Lear*. 2nd ed. Manchester: Manchester University Press, 2004. Interpretive problems are explored through the history of twentieth-century stage and film productions.

Nuttall, A. D. "King Lear." *Why Does Tragedy Give Pleasure?* Oxford: Clarendon, 1996. 81–105. The play gives pleasure not by sealing off suffering in poetic form but by destroying the expected recognition and closure of tragedy.

Taylor, Gary, and Michael Warren, eds. *The Division of the Kingdoms: Shakespeare's Two Versions of "King Lear."* Oxford: Clarendon, 1983. This essay collection presents the case for the quarto and Folio texts as distinct works and explores the consequences for interpreting *King Lear*.

FILMS

Korol Lir. 1969. Dir. Grigori Kozintsev and Iosif Shapiro. Soviet Union. 139 min. This black-and-white film presents a wizened but childlike Lear in a peasant-filled wasteland; a romantic fable in the Christian Middle Ages.

King Lear. 1971. Dir. Peter Brook. UK. 137 min. Men in pelts wander in a primitive tundra. Breaks in cinematic realism signal Lear's decline. With Paul Scofield and Jack MacGowran.

King Lear. 1983. Dir. Michael Elliott. UK. 158 min. Laurence Olivier, nearly eighty, in his final *Lear*. A television production that opens at Stonehenge.

Ran. 1985. Dir. Akira Kurosawa. Japan. 160 min. Set in sixteenth-century feudal Japan, the story, loosely adapted from Shakespeare, is noted for its elegaic battle sequences and orgies of red. In Japanese. With Tatsuya Nakadai and Akira Terao.

King Lear. 1998. Dir. Richard Eyre. UK. 150 min. Garish hues and torch-lit interiors for an especially cruel Lear, with equally vicious Regan and Goneril. With Ian Holm and Victoria Hamilton.

The History of King Lear

THE PERSONS OF THE PLAY

LEAR, King of Britain
GONORIL, Lear's eldest daughter
Duke of ALBANY, her husband
REGAN, Lear's second daughter
Duke of CORNWALL, her husband
CORDELIA, Lear's youngest daughter
King of FRANCE } suitors of Cordelia
Duke of BURGUNDY
Earl of KENT, later disguised as Caius
Earl of GLOUCESTER
EDGAR, elder son of Gloucester, later disguised as Tom o' Bedlam
EDMUND, bastard son of Gloucester
OLD MAN, a tenant of Gloucester
CURAN, Gloucester's retainer
Lear's FOOL
OSWALD, Gonoril's steward
Three SERVANTS of Cornwall
DOCTOR, attendant on Cordelia
Three CAPTAINS
A HERALD
A KNIGHT
A MESSENGER
Gentlemen, servants, soldiers, followers, trumpeters, others

Scene 1

Enter [the Earl of] KENT, [the Earl of] GLOUCESTER,[1] and Bastard [EDMUND]

KENT I thought the King had more affected° the Duke of   *favored*
Albany° than Cornwall.   *Scotland*

GLOUCESTER It did always seem so to us, but now in the division
of the kingdoms it appears not° which of the Dukes he values   *is not clear*
5 most; for equalities° are so weighed° that curiosity in neither *shares / equal*
can make choice of either's moiety.[2]

KENT Is not this your son, my lord?

GLOUCESTER His breeding,° sir, hath been at my charge.[3] I have   *upbringing*
so often blushed to acknowledge him that now I am brazed° to   *hardened*
10 it.

KENT I cannot conceive° you.   *comprehend*

GLOUCESTER Sir, this young fellow's mother could,[4] whereupon
she grew round-wombed and had indeed, sir, a son for her cradle ere she had a husband for her bed. Do you smell a fault?[5]

Scene 1 Location: King Lear's court.
1. Pronounced "Gloster."
2. *that . . . moiety:* that careful scrutiny ("curiosity") of both parts cannot determine which portion ("moiety") is preferable.

3. My responsibility; at my cost.
4. Could conceive; punning on biological conception.
5. Sin, wrongdoing; female genitals.

The Tragedy of King Lear

THE PERSONS OF THE PLAY

LEAR, King of Britain
GONERIL, Lear's eldest daughter
Duke of ALBANY, her husband
REGAN, Lear's second daughter
Duke of CORNWALL, her husband
CORDELIA, Lear's youngest daughter
King of FRANCE } suitors of Cordelia
Duke of BURGUNDY
Earl of KENT, later disguised as Caius
Earl of GLOUCESTER
EDGAR, elder son of Gloucester, later disguised as Tom o' Bedlam
EDMOND, bastard son of Gloucester
OLD MAN, Gloucester's tenant
CURAN, Gloucester's retainer
Lear's FOOL
OSWALD, Goneril's steward
A SERVANT of Cornwall
A KNIGHT
A HERALD
A CAPTAIN
Gentlemen, servants, soldiers, attendants, messengers

1.1

Enter [the Earl of] KENT, *[the Earl of]* GLOUCESTER,[1]
and EDMOND

KENT I thought the King had more affected° the Duke of   *favored*
Albany° than Cornwall.   *Scotland*

GLOUCESTER It did always seem so to us, but now in the division of
the kingdom it appears not° which of the Dukes he values   *is not clear*
5 most; for qualities are so weighed that curiosity in neither can
make choice of either's moiety.[2]

KENT Is not this your son, my lord?

GLOUCESTER His breeding,° sir, hath been at my charge.[3] I have   *upbringing*
so often blushed to acknowledge him that now I am brazed°   *hardened*
10 to't.

KENT I cannot conceive° you.   *comprehend*

GLOUCESTER Sir, this young fellow's mother could,[4] whereupon
she grew round-wombed and had indeed, sir, a son for her
cradle ere she had a husband for her bed. Do you smell a fault?[5]

1.1 Location: King Lear's court.
1. Pronounced "Gloster."
2. *for . . . moiety:* because their qualities are so evenly
weighted that careful scrutiny ("curiosity") of both parts

cannot determine which portion ("moiety") is preferable.
3. My responsibility; at my cost.
4. Could conceive; punning on biological conception.
5. Sin, wrongdoing; female genitals.

15	KENT I cannot wish the fault undone, the issue° of it being so proper.°	offspring; result handsome; right
	GLOUCESTER But I have, sir, a son by order of law,° some year elder than this, who yet is no dearer in my account.° Though this knave° came something saucily⁶ into the world before he	legitimate son estimation scamp; fellow
20	was sent for, yet was his mother fair, there was good sport at his making, and the whoreson° must be acknowledged. [*To* EDMUND] Do you know this noble gentleman, Edmund?	rogue; bastard
	EDMUND No, my lord.	
	GLOUCESTER [*to* EDMUND] My lord of Kent. Remember him	
25	hereafter as my honourable friend.	
	EDMUND [*to* KENT] My services to your lordship.	
	KENT I must love you, and sue° to know you better.	seek
	EDMUND Sir, I shall study deserving.°	shall learn to deserve
	GLOUCESTER [*to* KENT] He hath been out° nine years, and away	away; abroad
30	he shall again.	

KENT   I cannot wish the fault undone, the issue° of it being so

Sound a sennet°　　　　　　　　　　　　　　　　*fanfare of trumpets*
The King is coming.
Enter one bearing a coronet, then [King] LEAR, *then the Dukes of* ALBANY *and* CORNWALL; *next* GONORIL, REGAN, CORDELIA, *with followers*

	LEAR Attend° my lords of France and Burgundy, Gloucester.	Attend upon; escort
	GLOUCESTER I shall, my liege.°　　　　　　　　　[*Exit*]	feudal superior
	LEAR Meantime we° will express our darker° purposes.	(royal "we") / more secret
35	The map there. Know we have divided	
	In three our kingdom, and 'tis our first intent	
	To shake all cares and business off our state,°	position (as King)
	Confirming them on younger years.	
	The two great princes, France and Burgundy—	
40	Great rivals in our youngest daughter's love—	
	Long in our court have made their amorous sojourn,	
	And here are to be answered. Tell me, my daughters,	
	Which of you shall we say doth love us most,	
	That° we our largest bounty° may extend	So that / generosity
45	Where merit doth most challenge it?°	best claims it
	Gonoril, our eldest born, speak first.	
	GONORIL Sir, I do love you more than words can wield° the matter;	convey
	Dearer than eyesight, space,° or liberty;	freedom of movement
	Beyond what can be valued, rich or rare;	
50	No less than life; with grace, health, beauty, honour;	
	As much as child e'er loved, or father, friend;°	or friend
	A love that makes breath° poor and speech unable.	language
	Beyond all manner of so much° I love you.	Beyond all comparison
	CORDELIA [*aside*] What shall Cordelia do? Love and be silent.	
55	LEAR [*to* GONORIL] Of all these bounds° even from this line to this,	regions
	With shady forests and wide skirted meads,°	broad meadows

6. Somewhat rudely; somewhat shamefully.

15	KENT I cannot wish the fault undone, the issue° of it being so proper.°	offspring; result / handsome; right
	GLOUCESTER But I have a son, sir, by order of law,° some year older than this, who yet is no dearer in my account.° Though this knave° came something saucily[6] to the world before he was sent for, yet was his mother fair, there was good sport at his making, and the whoreson° must be acknowledged. [*To* EDMOND*]* Do you know this noble gentleman, Edmond?	legitimate son / estimation / scamp; fellow / rogue; bastard
20		
	EDMOND No, my lord.	
	GLOUCESTER [*to* EDMOND] My lord of Kent. Remember him hereafter as my honourable friend.	
25		
	EDMOND [*to* KENT] My services to your lordship.	
	KENT I must love you, and sue° to know you better.	seek
	EDMOND Sir, I shall study deserving.°	shall learn to deserve
	GLOUCESTER [*to* KENT] He hath been out° nine years, and away he shall again.	away; abroad
30		
	Sennet°	Fanfare of trumpets
	The King is coming.	
	Enter King LEAR*, [the Dukes of]* CORNWALL *[and]*	
	ALBANY, GONERIL, REGAN, CORDELIA, *and attendants*	
	LEAR Attend° the lords of France and Burgundy, Gloucester.	Attend upon; escort
	GLOUCESTER I shall, my lord. *Exit*	
	LEAR Meantime we° shall express our darker° purpose.	(royal "we") / more secret
35	Give me the map there. Know that we have divided	
	In three our kingdom, and 'tis our fast° intent	fixed
	To shake all cares and business from our age,	
	Conferring them on younger strengths while we	
	Unburdened crawl toward death. Our son° of Cornwall,	son-in-law
40	And you, our no less loving son of Albany,	
	We have this hour a constant will to publish[7]	
	Our daughters' several dowers,° that future strife	individual dowries
	May be prevented now. The princes France and Burgundy—	
	Great rivals in our youngest daughter's love—	
45	Long in our court have made their amorous sojourn,	
	And here are to be answered. Tell me, my daughters—	
	Since now we will divest us both of rule,	
	Interest° of territory, cares of state—	Legal title
	Which of you shall we say doth love us most,	
50	That° we our largest bounty° may extend	So that / generosity
	Where nature doth with merit challenge?[8] Goneril,	
	Our eldest born, speak first.	
	GONERIL Sir, I love you more than words can wield° the matter;	convey
	Dearer than eyesight, space,° and liberty;	freedom of movement
55	Beyond what can be valued, rich or rare,	
	No less than life; with grace, health, beauty, honour;	
	As much as child e'er loved or father found;	
	A love that makes breath° poor and speech unable.	language
	Beyond all manner of so much° I love you.	Beyond all comparison
	CORDELIA [*aside*] What shall Cordelia speak? Love and be silent.	
60		
	LEAR [*to* GONERIL] Of all these bounds° even from this line to this,	regions
	With shadowy forests and with champaigns riched,°	enriched plains
	With plenteous rivers and wide-skirted meads,°	broad meadows

---

6. Somewhat rudely; somewhat shamefully.
7. A fixed determination to announce publicly.

8. *Where . . . challenge:* To the one whose natural love and deserving lay claim (to our generosity).

We make thee lady. To thine and Albany's issue°   *children; heirs*
Be this perpetual.—What says our second daughter?
Our dearest Regan, wife to Cornwall, speak.
60 REGAN Sir, I am made
Of the self-same mettle° that my sister is,   *spirit; substance*
And prize me at her worth.° In my true heart   *believe myself her equal*
I find she names my very deed of love—
Only she came short, that° I profess   *in that*
65 Myself an enemy to all other joys
Which the most precious square of sense possesses,[7]
And find I am alone felicitate°   *am only made happy*
In your dear highness' love.
CORDELIA [*aside*]   Then poor Cordelia—
And yet not so, since I am sure my love's
70 More richer than my tongue.
LEAR [*to* REGAN] To thee and thine hereditary ever
Remain this ample third of our fair kingdom,
No less in space, validity,° and pleasure   *value*
Than that confirmed° on Gonoril. [*To* CORDELIA] But now our joy, *fixed*
75 Although the last, not least in our dear love:
What can you say to win a third more opulent
Than your sisters?
CORDELIA Nothing, my lord.
LEAR How? Nothing can come of nothing.[8] Speak again.
80 CORDELIA Unhappy that I am, I cannot heave
My heart into my mouth. I love your majesty
According to my bond,° nor more nor less.   *filial duty*
LEAR Go to, go to, mend your speech a little
Lest it may mar your fortunes.
CORDELIA   Good my lord,
85 You have begot me, bred me, loved me.
I return those duties back as are right fit—
Obey you, love you, and most honour you.
Why have my sisters husbands if they say
They love you all°? Haply° when I shall wed *completely / Perhaps; if lucky*
90 That lord whose hand must take my plight° shall carry *marriage vow; condition*
Half my love with him, half my care and duty.
Sure, I shall never marry like my sisters,
To love my father all.
LEAR But goes this with thy heart?
95 CORDELIA Ay, good my lord.
LEAR So young and so untender?
CORDELIA So young, my lord, and true.°   *honest; faithful*
LEAR Well, let it be so. Thy truth then be thy dower;
For by the sacred radiance of the sun,
100 The mysteries of Hecate[9] and the night,
By all the operation of the orbs
From whom we do exist and cease to be,[1]

7. *Which . . . possesses*: That the body can enjoy. *precious square of sense*: measure of sensibility; or, perhaps, balanced and sensitive perception. The square may represent the even mixture of the body's four fluids, or humors.
8. *Ex nihilo nihil fit*, a maxim derived from Aristotle, was accepted by the Christian Middle Ages with the single exception of God having created the world out of nothing.

9. A classical goddess of the moon and the patron of witchcraft, she was associated with the underworld, Hades.
1. *By all . . . be*: Referring to the belief that the movements of stars and planets ("orbs") corresponded to physical and spiritual motions in a person and thus controlled his or her fate.

We make thee lady. To thine and Albany's issues°   *children; heirs*

65 Be this perpetual.—What says our second daughter?
Our dearest Regan, wife of Cornwall?

REGAN   I am made of that self° mettle° as my sister,   *same / spirit; substance*
And prize me at her worth.° In my true heart   *believe myself her equal*
I find she names my very deed of love—

70 Only she comes too short, that° I profess   *in that*
Myself an enemy to all other joys
Which the most precious square of sense possesses,[9]
And find I am alone felicitate°   *am only made happy*
In your dear highness' love.

CORDELIA [*aside*]   Then poor Cordelia—

75 And yet not so, since I am sure my love's
More ponderous° than my tongue.   *weighty*

LEAR [*to* REGAN]   To thee and thine hereditary ever
Remain this ample third of our fair kingdom,
No less in space, validity,° and pleasure   *value*

80 Than that conferred on Goneril. [*To* CORDELIA] Now our joy,
Although our last and least,° to whose young love   *youngest; smallest*
The vines of France and milk of Burgundy
Strive to be interested:° what can you say to draw   *admitted*
A third more opulent than your sisters? Speak.

85 CORDELIA   Nothing, my lord.

LEAR   Nothing?

CORDELIA   Nothing.

LEAR   Nothing will come of nothing.[1] Speak again.

CORDELIA   Unhappy that I am, I cannot heave

90 My heart into my mouth. I love your majesty
According to my bond,° no more nor less.   *filial duty*

LEAR   How, how, Cordelia? Mend your speech a little
Lest you may mar your fortunes.

CORDELIA   Good my lord,
You have begot me, bred me, loved me.

95 I return those duties back as are right fit—
Obey you, love you, and most honour you.
Why have my sisters husbands if they say
They love you all°? Haply° when I shall wed   *completely / Perhaps; if lucky*
That lord whose hand must take my plight° shall carry   *marriage vow; condition*

100 Half my love with him, half my care and duty.
Sure, I shall never marry like my sisters.

LEAR   But goes thy heart with this?

CORDELIA   Ay, my good lord.

LEAR   So young and so untender?

105 CORDELIA   So young, my lord, and true.°   *honest; faithful*

LEAR   Let it be so. Thy truth then be thy dower;
For by the sacred radiance of the sun,
The mysteries of Hecate[2] and the night,
By all the operation of the orbs

110 From whom we do exist and cease to be,[3]

---

9. *Which . . . possesses*: That the body can enjoy. *precious square of sense*: measure of sensibility; or, perhaps, balanced and sensitive perception. The square may represent the even mixture of the body's four fluids, or humors.
1. *Ex nihilo nihil fit*, a maxim derived from Aristotle, was accepted by the Christian Middle Ages with the single exception of God having created the world out of nothing.

2. A classical goddess of the moon and the patron of witchcraft, she was associated with the underworld, Hades.
3. *By all . . . be*: Referring to the belief that the movements of stars and planets ("orbs") corresponded to physical and spiritual motions in a person and thus controlled his or her fate.

Here I disclaim all my paternal care,
Propinquity,° and property of blood,°   *Closeness / kinship*
105 And as a stranger to my heart and me
Hold thee from this° for ever. The barbarous Scythian,[2]   *this time*
Or he that makes his generation
Messes[3] to gorge his appetite,
Shall be as well neighboured, pitied, and relieved
As thou, my sometime° daughter.   *former*
110 KENT   Good my liege—
LEAR   Peace, Kent. Come not between the dragon and his wrath.
I loved her most, and thought to set my rest[4]
On her kind nursery.° [*To* CORDELIA] Hence, and avoid my sight!—   *care*
So be my grave my peace[5] as here I give
115 Her father's heart from her. Call France. Who stirs?[6]
Call Burgundy.   [*Exit one or more*]
                        Cornwall and Albany,
With my two daughters' dowers digest° this third.   *incorporate*
Let pride, which she calls plainness,° marry her.   *directness*
I do invest you jointly in my power,
120 Pre-eminence, and all the large effects°   *outward shows; trappings*
That troop with° majesty. Ourself by monthly course,   *accompany*
With reservation of° an hundred knights   *legal right to retain*
By you to be sustained, shall our abode
Make with you by due turns. Only we still retain
125 The name and all the additions° to a king.   *prerogatives*
The sway,° revenue, execution of the rest,   *power*
Belovèd sons, be yours; which to confirm,
This crownet[7] part betwixt you.
KENT   Royal Lear,
Whom I have ever honoured as my king,
130 Loved as my father, as my master followed,
As my great patron thought on in my prayers—
LEAR   The bow is bent and drawn; make from° the shaft.   *get clear of*
KENT   Let it fall° rather, though the fork° invade   *strike here / arrowhead*
The region of my heart. Be Kent unmannerly
135 When Lear is mad. What wilt thou do, old man?
Think'st thou that duty shall have dread to speak
When power to flattery bows? To plainness° honour's bound   *plain speaking*
When majesty stoops to folly. Reverse thy doom,°   *Revoke your sentence*
And in thy best consideration check°   *halt*
140 This hideous rashness. Answer my life my judgement,[8]
Thy youngest daughter does not love thee least,
Nor are those empty-hearted whose low sound
Reverbs no hollowness.°   *Echoes no insincerity*
LEAR   Kent, on thy life, no more!
KENT   My life I never held but as a pawn°   *chess piece; stake*
145 To wage° against thy enemies, nor fear to lose it,   *wager*
Thy safety being the motive.

---

2. Notoriously savage Crimean nomads of classical antiquity.
3. *he . . . / Messes:* he who makes meals of his parents or his children.
4. To secure my repose; to stake my all, as in the card game known as primero.

5. So may I rest in peace (probably an oath).
6. Does nobody stir? An order, with the force of "Get moving."
7. Cordelia's crown, symbol of the endowment she has forsworn.
8. *Answer . . . judgement:* I'll stake my life on my opinion.

Here I disclaim all my paternal care,
Propinquity,° and property of blood,°   *Closeness / kinship*
And as a stranger to my heart and me
Hold thee from this° for ever. The barbarous Scythian,[4]   *this time*
115 Or he that makes his generation messes[5]
To gorge his appetite, shall to my bosom
Be as well neighboured, pitied, and relieved
As thou, my sometime° daughter.   *former*

KENT   Good my liege—
LEAR   Peace, Kent.
120 Come not between the dragon and his wrath.
I loved her most, and thought to set my rest[6]
On her kind nursery.° [*To* CORDELIA] Hence, and avoid my sight!—   *care*
So be my grave my peace[7] as here I give
Her father's heart from her. Call France. Who stirs?[8]
Call Burgundy.   [*Exit one or more*]
125   Cornwall and Albany,
With my two daughters' dowers digest° the third.   *incorporate*
Let pride, which she calls plainness,° marry her.   *directness*
I do invest you jointly with my power,
Pre-eminence, and all the large effects°   *outward shows; trappings*
130 That troop with° majesty. Ourself by monthly course,   *accompany*
With reservation of° an hundred knights   *legal right to retain*
By you to be sustained, shall our abode
Make with you by due turn. Only we shall retain
The name and all th'addition° to a king. The sway,°   *prerogatives / power*
135 Revenue, execution of the rest,
Belovèd sons, be yours; which to confirm,
This crownet[9] part between you.
KENT   Royal Lear,
Whom I have ever honoured as my king,
Loved as my father, as my master followed,
140 As my great patron thought on in my prayers—
LEAR   The bow is bent and drawn; make from° the shaft.   *get clear of*
KENT   Let it fall° rather, though the fork° invade   *strike here / arrowhead*
The region of my heart. Be Kent unmannerly
When Lear is mad. What wouldst thou do, old man?
145 Think'st thou that duty shall have dread to speak
When power to flattery bows? To plainness° honour's bound *plain speaking*
When majesty falls to folly. Reserve° thy state,°   *Retain / rule; position*
And in thy best consideration check°   *halt*
This hideous rashness. Answer my life my judgement,[1]
150 Thy youngest daughter does not love thee least,
Nor are those empty-hearted whose low sounds
Reverb no hollowness.°   *Echo no insincerity*
KENT   Kent, on thy life, no more!
KENT   My life I never held but as a pawn°   *chess piece; stake*
To wage° against thine enemies, ne'er feared to lose it,   *wager*
Thy safety being motive.°   *(my) motivation*

---

4. Notoriously savage Crimean nomads of classical
antiquity.
5. *he . . . messes:* he who makes meals of his parents or
his children.
6. To secure my repose; to stake my all, as in the card
game known as primero.

7. So may I rest in peace (probably an oath).
8. Does nobody stir? An order, with the force of "Get
moving."
9. Cordelia's crown, symbol of the endowment she has
forsworn.
1. *Answer . . . judgement:* I'll stake my life on my opinion.

LEAR   Out of my sight!

KENT   See better, Lear, and let me still° remain   *always*
The true blank° of thine eye.   *precise bull's-eye*

LEAR   Now, by Apollo—

KENT   Now, by Apollo, King, thou swear'st thy gods in vain.[9]

LEAR [*making to strike him*]   Vassal, recreant!°   *villain; unbeliever*

150   KENT   Do, kill thy physician,
And the fee bestow upon the foul disease.[1]
Revoke thy doom, or whilst I can vent clamour
From my throat I'll tell thee thou dost evil.

LEAR   Hear me; on thy allegiance hear me!

155   Since thou hast sought to make us break our vow,
Which we durst never yet, and with strayed° pride   *wayward; erring*
To come between our sentence and our power,
Which nor our nature nor our place[2] can bear,
Our potency made good° take thy reward: *demonstrated*

160   Four days we do allot thee for provision
To shield thee from dis-eases° of the world,   *discomforts*
And on the fifth to turn thy hated back
Upon our kingdom. If on the next day following
Thy banished trunk° be found in our dominions,   *body*

165   The moment is thy death. Away! By Jupiter,
This shall not be revoked.

KENT   Why, fare thee well, King; since thus thou wilt appear,
Friendship lives hence, and banishment is here.
[*To* CORDELIA] The gods to their protection take thee, maid,

170   That rightly thinks, and hast most justly said.
[*To* GONORIL *and* REGAN] And your large speeches may your deeds approve,[3]
That good effects may spring from words of love.
Thus Kent, O princes, bids you all adieu;
He'll shape his old course in a country new.   [*Exit*]

Enter [*the King of*] FRANCE *and* [*the Duke of*] BUR-
GUNDY, *with* GLOUCESTER

175   GLOUCESTER   Here's France and Burgundy, my noble lord.

LEAR   My lord of Burgundy,
We first address towards you, who with a king
Hath rivalled for our daughter: what in the least
Will you require in present dower with her
Or cease your quest of love?

180   BURGUNDY   Royal majesty,
I crave no more than what your highness offered;
Nor will you tender° less.   *offer*

LEAR   Right noble Burgundy,
When she was dear to us we did hold her so;
But now her price is fallen. Sir, there she stands.

185   If aught within that little seeming substance,[4]
Or all of it, with our displeasure pieced,°   *joined*
And nothing else, may fitly like° your grace,   *please*
She's there, and she is yours.

---

9. You invoke your gods falsely and without effect.
1. *kill . . . disease:* you would not only kill the doctor but hand his fee over to the disease.
2. Which neither my temperament nor my royal position.
3. And let your actions live up to your fine words.
4. *little seeming substance:* one who appears insubstantial; one who will not pretend.

155   LEAR   Out of my sight!

KENT   See better, Lear, and let me still° remain   *always*
The true blank° of thine eye.   *precise bull's-eye*

LEAR   Now, by Apollo—

KENT   Now, by Apollo, King, thou swear'st thy gods in vain.[2]

LEAR [*making to strike him*]   O vassal! Miscreant!°   *Villain; unbeliever*

ALBANY *and* CORDELIA   Dear sir, forbear.

160   KENT [*to* LEAR]   Kill thy physician, and thy fee bestow
Upon the foul disease.[3] Revoke thy gift,
Or whilst I can vent clamour from my throat
I'll tell thee thou dost evil.

LEAR   Hear me, recreant;° on thine allegiance hear me!   *traitor*

165   That thou hast sought to make us break our vows,
Which we durst never yet, and with strained° pride   *overblown*
To come betwixt our sentence and our power,
Which nor our nature nor our place[4] can bear,
Our potency made good° take thy reward: *demonstrated*

170   Five days we do allot thee for provision
To shield thee from disasters of the world,
And on the sixth to turn thy hated back
Upon our kingdom. If on the seventh day following
Thy banished trunk° be found in our dominions,   *body*

175   The moment is thy death. Away! By Jupiter,
This shall not be revoked.

KENT   Fare thee well, King; sith° thus thou wilt appear,   *since*
Freedom lives hence, and banishment is here.
[*To* CORDELIA] The gods to their dear shelter take thee, maid,

180   That justly think'st, and hast most rightly said.
[*To* GONERIL *and* REGAN] And your large speeches may your deeds approve,[5]
That good effects may spring from words of love.
Thus Kent, O princes, bids you all adieu;
He'll shape his old course in a country new.   *Exit*

          Flourish.° Enter GLOUCESTER *with* [*the King of*]   *Fanfare of trumpets*
          FRANCE, [*the Duke of*] BURGUNDY, *attendants*

185   CORDELIA   Here's France and Burgundy, my noble lord.

LEAR   My lord of Burgundy,
We first address toward you, who with this King
Hath rivalled for our daughter: what in the least
Will you require in present dower with her
Or cease your quest of love?

190   BURGUNDY   Most royal majesty,
I crave no more than hath your highness offered;
Nor will you tender° less.   *offer*

LEAR   Right noble Burgundy,
When she was dear to us we did hold her so;
But now her price is fallen. Sir, there she stands.

195   If aught within that little seeming substance,[6]
Or all of it, with our displeasure pieced,°   *joined*
And nothing more, may fitly like° your grace,   *please*
She's there, and she is yours.

2. You invoke your gods falsely and without effect.
3. *Kill . . . disease*: You would not only kill the doctor
but hand his fee over to the disease.
4. Which neither my temperament nor my royal position.

5. And let your actions live up to your fine words.
6. *little seeming substance*: one who appears insubstantial; one who will not pretend.

BURGUNDY   I know no answer.

LEAR   Sir, will you with those infirmities she owes,°   *owns*

190   Unfriended, new-adopted to our hate,

Covered with our curse and strangered° with our oath,   *estranged*

Take her or leave her?

BURGUNDY   Pardon me, royal sir.

Election makes not up on such conditions.[5]

LEAR   Then leave her, sir; for by the power that made me,

195   I tell you° all her wealth. [*To* FRANCE] For° you, great King,   *inform you of / As for*

I would not from your love make such a stray°   *stray so far*

To° match you where I hate, therefore beseech you   *As to*

To avert your liking° a more worthier way   *To turn your affections*

Than on a wretch whom nature is ashamed

200   Almost to acknowledge hers.

FRANCE   This is most strange, that she that even but now

Was your best object, the argument° of your praise,   *theme*

Balm of your age, most best, most dearest,

Should in this trice° of time commit a thing   *moment*

205   So monstrous to dismantle°   *as to strip off; disrobe*

So many folds of favour. Sure, her offence

Must be of such unnatural degree

That monsters it,° or your fore-vouched affections   *makes it monstrous*

Fall'n into taint;[6] which to believe of her

210   Must be a faith that reason without miracle

Could never plant in me.

CORDELIA [*to* LEAR]   I yet beseech your majesty,

If for I want° that glib and oily art   *because I lack*

To speak and purpose not°—since what I well intend,   *and not intend*

215   I'll do't before I speak—that you acknow°   *acknowledge*

It is no vicious blot, murder, or foulness,

No unclean action or dishonoured step

That hath deprived me of your grace and favour,

But even the want of that for which I am rich—

220   A still-soliciting° eye, and such a tongue   *An always-begging*

As I am glad I have not, though not to have it

Hath lost me in your liking.

LEAR   Go to, go to.

Better thou hadst not been born than not to have pleased me better.

FRANCE   Is it no more but this—a tardiness in nature,

225   That often leaves the history unspoke

That it intends to do?[7]—My lord of Burgundy,

What say you to the lady? Love is not love

When it is mingled with respects° that stands   *considerations*

Aloof from the entire point. Will you have her?

She is herself a dower.

230   BURGUNDY   Royal Lear,

Give but that portion which yourself proposed,

And here I take Cordelia by the hand,

Duchess of Burgundy—

LEAR   Nothing. I have sworn.

---

5. A choice cannot be made under those terms.

6. *or . . . taint:* or else the love you earlier swore for Cordelia must be regarded with suspicion. "Or" may also mean "before," in which case the phrase would

mean "before the love you once proclaimed could have decayed."

7. *a tardiness . . . do:* a natural reserve that inhibits voicing one's intentions.

BURGUNDY   I know no answer.

LEAR   Will you with those infirmities she owes,°   *owns*
200   Unfriended, new adopted to our hate,
       Dowered with our curse and strangered° with our oath,   *estranged*
       Take her or leave her?

BURGUNDY   Pardon me, royal sir.
       Election makes not up in such conditions.⁷

LEAR   Then leave her, sir; for by the power that made me,
205   I tell you° all her wealth. [*To* FRANCE] For° you, great King,   *inform you of / As for*
       I would not from your love make such a stray°   *stray so far*
       To° match you where I hate, therefore beseech you   *As to*
       T'avert your liking° a more worthier way   *To turn your affections*
       Than on a wretch whom nature is ashamed
       Almost t'acknowledge hers.

210 FRANCE   This is most strange,
       That she whom even but now was your best object,
       The argument° of your praise, balm of your age,   *theme*
       The best, the dear'st, should in this trice° of time   *moment*
       Commit a thing so monstrous to dismantle°   *as to strip off; disrobe*
215   So many folds of favour. Sure, her offence
       Must be of such unnatural degree
       That monsters it,° or your fore-vouched affection   *makes it monstrous*
       Fall into taint;⁸ which to believe of her
       Must be a faith that reason without miracle
220   Should never plant in me.

CORDELIA [*to* LEAR]   I yet beseech your majesty,
       If for I want° that glib and oily art   *because I lack*
       To speak and purpose not°—since what I well intend,   *and not intend*
       I'll do't before I speak—that you make known
225   It is no vicious blot, murder, or foulness,
       No unchaste action or dishonoured step
       That hath deprived me of your grace and favour,
       But even the want of that for which I am richer—
       A still-soliciting° eye, and such a tongue   *An always-begging*
230   That I am glad I have not, though not to have it
       Hath lost me in your liking.

LEAR   Better thou
       Hadst not been born than not t'have pleased me better.

FRANCE   Is it but this—a tardiness in nature,
       Which often leaves the history unspoke
235   That it intends to do?⁹—My lord of Burgundy,
       What say you to the lady? Love's not love
       When it is mingled with regards° that stands   *considerations*
       Aloof from th'entire point. Will you have her?
       She is herself a dowry.

BURGUNDY [*to* LEAR]   Royal King,
240   Give but that portion which yourself proposed,
       And here I take Cordelia by the hand,
       Duchess of Burgundy.

LEAR   Nothing. I have sworn. I am firm.

---

7. A choice cannot be made under those terms.
8. *or . . . taint:* or else the love you earlier swore for Cordelia must be regarded with suspicion. "Or" may also mean "before," in which case the phrase would mean "before the love you once proclaimed could have decayed."
9. *a tardiness . . . do:* a natural reserve that inhibits voicing one's intentions.

BURGUNDY [*to* CORDELIA]   I am sorry, then, you have so lost a father
235   That you must lose a husband.
CORDELIA   Peace be with Burgundy; since that respects
        Of fortune are his love, I shall not be his wife.
FRANCE   Fairest Cordelia, that art most rich, being poor;
        Most choice, forsaken; and most loved, despised:
240   Thee and thy virtues here I seize upon.
        Be it lawful, I take up what's cast away.
        Gods, gods! 'Tis strange that from their cold'st neglect
        My love should kindle to inflamed respect.°—   *ardent regard*
        Thy dowerless daughter, King, thrown to my chance,
245   Is queen of us, of ours, and our fair France.
        Not all the dukes in wat'rish° Burgundy   *irrigated; watery; weak*
        Shall buy this unprized° precious maid of me.—   *unappreciated*
        Bid them farewell, Cordelia, though unkind.°   *though they are unkind*
        Thou losest here,° a better where° to find.   *this place / place*
250 LEAR   Thou hast her, France. Let her be thine, for we
        Have no such daughter, nor shall ever see
        That face of hers again. Therefore be gone,
        Without our grace, our love, our benison.°—   *blessing*
        Come, noble Burgundy.
                    [*Flourish.*] *Exeunt* LEAR *and* BURGUNDY [*then*
                ALBANY, CORNWALL, GLOUCESTER, EDMUND,
                                and followers]
FRANCE [*to* CORDELIA]   Bid farewell to your sisters.
255 CORDELIA   Ye jewels of our father, with washed eyes
        Cordelia leaves you. I know you what you are,
        And like a sister am most loath to call
        Your faults as they are named.° Use well our father.   *are properly called*
        To your professèd bosoms° I commit him.   *publicly proclaimed love*
260   But yet, alas, stood I within his grace
        I would prefer° him to a better place.   *promote; recommend*
        So farewell to you both.
GONORIL   Prescribe not us our duties.
REGAN   Let your study
265   Be to content your lord, who hath received you
        At fortune's alms.[8] You have obedience scanted,°   *neglected*
        And well are worth the worst that you have wanted.[9]
CORDELIA   Time shall unfold what pleated cunning hides.
        Who covers faults, at last shame them derides.[1]
        Well may you prosper.
270 FRANCE   Come, fair Cordelia.
                        Exeunt FRANCE *and* CORDELIA
GONORIL   Sister, it is not a little I have to say of what most nearly
        appertains to us both. I think our father will hence tonight.
REGAN   That's most certain, and with you. Next month with us.
GONORIL   You see how full of changes° his age is. The observa-   *fickleness*
275   tion we have made of it hath not been little.[2] He always loved
        our sister most, and with what poor judgement he hath now
        cast her off appears too gross.°   *blatant*

---

8. As a charitable gift from Dame Fortune.
9. And you deserve to get no more love (from your husband) than you have given (to your father). "Want"
plays on its alternative meanings of "lack" and "desire."

1. *Who . . . derides:* Those who hide their faults will in
the end be put to shame.
2. We have observed it more than a little.

BURGUNDY [*to* CORDELIA]   I am sorry, then, you have so lost a father
    That you must lose a husband.
245 CORDELIA   Peace be with Burgundy;
    Since that respect and fortunes are his love,
    I shall not be his wife.
FRANCE   Fairest Cordelia, that art most rich, being poor;
    Most choice, forsaken; and most loved, despised:
250   Thee and thy virtues here I seize upon.
    Be it lawful, I take up what's cast away.
    Gods, gods! 'Tis strange that from their cold'st neglect
    My love should kindle to inflamed respect.° —   *ardent regard*
    Thy dowerless daughter, King, thrown to my chance,
255   Is queen of us, of ours, and our fair France.
    Not all the dukes of wat'rish° Burgundy   *irrigated; watery; weak*
    Can buy this unprized° precious maid of me. —   *unappreciated*
    Bid them farewell, Cordelia, though unkind.°   *though they are unkind*
    Thou losest here,° a better where° to find.   *this place / place*
260 LEAR   Thou hast her, France. Let her be thine, for we
    Have no such daughter, nor shall ever see
    That face of hers again. Therefore be gone,
    Without our grace, our love, our benison.° —   *blessing*
    Come, noble Burgundy.

                Flourish. Exeunt [*all but* FRANCE
                       and the sisters]

FRANCE   Bid farewell to your sisters.
265 CORDELIA   Ye jewels of our father, with washed eyes
    Cordelia leaves you. I know you what you are,
    And like a sister am most loath to call
    Your faults as they are named.° Love well our father.   *are properly called*
    To your professèd bosoms° I commit him.   *publicly proclaimed love*
270   But yet, alas, stood I within his grace
    I would prefer° him to a better place.   *promote; recommend*
    So farewell to you both.
REGAN   Prescribe not us our duty.
GONERIL   Let your study
275   Be to content your lord, who hath received you
    At fortune's alms.[1] You have obedience scanted,°   *neglected*
    And well are worth the want that you have wanted.[2]
CORDELIA   Time shall unfold what pleated cunning hides,
    Who covert faults at last with shame derides.[3]
    Well may you prosper.
280 FRANCE   Come, my fair Cordelia.

                  Exeunt FRANCE *and* CORDELIA

GONERIL   Sister, it is not little I have to say of what most nearly
    appertains to us both. I think our father will hence tonight.
REGAN   That's most certain, and with you. Next month with us.
GONERIL   You see how full of changes° his age is. The observa-   *fickleness*
285   tion we have made of it hath been little.° He always loved our   *meticulous*
    sister most, and with what poor judgement he hath now cast
    her off appears too grossly.°   *blatantly*

---

1. As a charitable gift from Dame Fortune.
2. And you deserve to get no more love (from your husband) than you have given (to your father). "Want"
plays on its alternative meanings of "lack" and "desire."
3. *Time . . . derides:* Time eventually exposes and shames all hidden faults.

REGAN   'Tis the infirmity of his age; yet he hath ever but slen-
derly known himself.

280   GONORIL   The best and soundest of his time hath been but rash;³   *therefore*
then° must we look to receive from his age not alone the imper-   *therefore*
fection of long-engrafted condition,° but therewithal unruly   *deep-rooted habit*
waywardness that infirm and choleric years bring with them.

REGAN   Such unconstant starts⁴ are we like° to have from him as   *likely*
285   this of Kent's banishment.

GONORIL   There is further compliment° of leave-taking between   *ceremony*
France and him. Pray, let's hit° together. If our father carry   *join; strike*
authority with such dispositions⁵ as he bears, this last surrender°   *abdication*
of his will but offend° us.   *harm*

290   REGAN   We shall further think on't.

GONORIL   We must do something, and i'th' heat.°   *Exeunt*   *quickly*

Scene 2

Enter Bastard [EDMUND]

EDMUND   Thou, nature, art my goddess. To thy law
My services are bound.¹ Wherefore° should I   *Why*
Stand in the plague of custom² and permit
The curiosity° of nations to deprive me   *legal niceties*
5   For that° I am some twelve or fourteen moonshines°   *Because / months*
Lag of° a brother? Why 'bastard'? Wherefore 'base',   *Younger than*
When my dimensions are as well compact,°   *composed*
My mind as generous,° and my shape as true   *noble*
As honest° madam's issue?   *married; chaste*
10   Why brand they us with 'base, base bastardy',
Who in the lusty stealth of nature take
More composition and fierce quality³
Than doth within a stale, dull-eyed bed go
To the creating a whole tribe of fops°   *fools*
15   Got° 'tween a sleep and wake? Well then,   *Begotten*
Legitimate Edgar, I must have your land.
Our father's love is to° the bastard Edmund   *as much to*
As to the legitimate. Well, my legitimate, if
This letter speed° and my invention° thrive,   *succeed / plot*
20   Edmund the base shall to° th' legitimate.   *match up to; usurp*
I grow, I prosper. Now gods, stand up for bastards!
Enter GLOUCESTER. [EDMUND *reads a letter*]

GLOUCESTER   Kent banished thus, and France in choler parted,°   *in anger departed*
And the King gone tonight,° subscribed° his power,   *last night / limited*
Confined to exhibition⁴—all this done
25   Upon the gad?°—Edmund, how now? What news?   *spur of the moment*

EDMUND   So please your lordship, none.

---

3. *The . . . rash:* Even in the prime of his life he was
impetuous.
4. Such impulsive outbursts.
5. Frame of mine.
Scene 2 Location: The Earl of Gloucester's house.
1. Edmund declares the raw force of unsocialized and
unregulated existence, as opposed to human law, to be
his ruler; ironically, "nature" also means "natural filial
affection." A "natural" was another word for "bastard"
(illegitimate child).
2. Submit to the imposition of inheritance law.

3. *Who . . . quality:* Whose begetting, by reason of its
furtiveness and heightened excitement, requires better
execution and more vigor. Alternatively (with "take"
meaning "give"), whose begetting produces (a person
of) more mixture and vigor. "Composition," or mixture,
may refer to the belief that the perfect offspring was
conceived from an equal quantity of male and female
essence and that physical and mental abnormalities
were caused by a predominance of one or the other.
4. Pension; mere show without force.

REGAN   'Tis the infirmity of his age; yet he hath ever but slen-
derly known himself.

290 GONERIL   The best and soundest of his time hath been but rash;[4]
then° must we look from his age to receive not alone the imper-   *therefore*
fections of long-engrafted condition,° but therewithal the   *deep-rooted habit*
unruly waywardness that infirm and choleric years bring with
them.

295 REGAN   Such unconstant starts[5] are we like° to have from him as   *likely*
this of Kent's banishment.

GONERIL   There is further compliment° of leave-taking between   *ceremony*
France and him. Pray you, let us sit together. If our father carry
authority with such disposition[6] as he bears, this last surrender°   *abdication*
300 of his will but offend° us.   *harm*

REGAN   We shall further think of it.

GONERIL   We must do something, and i'th' heat.°   *Exeunt*   *quickly*

1.2

Enter Bastard [EDMOND]

EDMOND   Thou, nature, art my goddess. To thy law
My services are bound.[1] Wherefore° should I   *Why*
Stand in the plague of custom[2] and permit
The curiosity° of nations to deprive me   *legal niceties*
5   For that° I am some twelve or fourteen moonshines°   *Because / months*
Lag of° a brother? Why 'bastard'? Wherefore 'base',   *Younger than*
When my dimensions are as well compact,°   *composed*
My mind as generous,° and my shape as true   *noble*
As honest° madam's issue? Why brand they us   *married; chaste*
10   With 'base', with 'baseness, bastardy—base, base'—
Who in the lusty stealth of nature take
More composition and fierce quality[3]
Than doth within a dull, stale, tirèd bed
Go to th' creating a whole tribe of fops°   *fools*
15   Got° 'tween a sleep and wake? Well then,   *Begotten*
Legitimate Edgar, I must have your land.
Our father's love is to° the bastard Edmond   *as much to*
As to th' legitimate. Fine word, 'legitimate'.
Well, my legitimate, if this letter speed°   *succeed*
20   And my invention° thrive, Edmond the base   *plot*
Shall to° th' legitimate. I grow, I prosper.   *match up to; usurp*
Now gods, stand up for bastards!

Enter GLOUCESTER. [EDMOND *reads a letter*]

GLOUCESTER   Kent banished thus, and France in choler parted,°   *in anger departed*
And the King gone tonight,° prescribed° his power,   *last night / limited*
25   Confined to exhibition[4]—all this done
Upon the gad?°—Edmond, how now? What news?   *spur of the moment*

EDMOND   So please your lordship, none.

---

4. *The . . . rash*: Even in the prime of his life he was
impetuous.
5. Such impulsive outbursts.
6. Frame of mind.
1.2 Location: The Earl of Gloucester's house.
1. Edmond declares the raw force of unsocialized and
unregulated existence, as opposed to human law, to be
his ruler; ironically, "nature" also means "natural filial
affection." A "natural" was another word for "bastard"
(illegitimate child).
2. Submit to the imposition of inheritance law.

3. *Who . . . quality*: Whose begetting, by reason of its
furtiveness and heightened excitement, requires better
execution and more vigor. Alternatively (with "take"
meaning "give"), whose begetting produces (a person
of) more mixture and vigor. "Composition," or mixture,
may refer to the belief that the perfect offspring was
conceived from an equal quantity of male and female
essence and that physical and mental abnormalities
were caused by a predominance of one or the other.
4. Pension; mere show without force.

GLOUCESTER   Why so earnestly seek you to put up that letter?

EDMUND   I know no news, my lord.

GLOUCESTER   What paper were you reading?

30   EDMUND   Nothing, my lord.

GLOUCESTER   No? What needs then that terrible dispatch° of it   *frightened haste*
into your pocket? The quality of nothing hath not such need
to hide itself. Let's see. Come, if it be nothing I shall not need
spectacles.

35   EDMUND   I beseech you, sir, pardon me. It is a letter from my
brother that I have not all o'er-read; for so much as I have
perused, I find it not fit for your liking.°   *pleasure*

GLOUCESTER   Give me the letter, sir.

EDMUND   I shall offend either to detain or give it. The contents,
40   as in part I understand them, are to blame.

GLOUCESTER   Let's see, let's see.

EDMUND   I hope for my brother's justification he wrote this but
as an assay or taste⁵ of my virtue.

[*He gives* GLOUCESTER] *a letter*

GLOUCESTER (*reads*)   'This policy of age makes the world bitter
45   to the best of our times,⁶ keeps our fortunes from us till our
oldness cannot relish them. I begin to find an idle and fond°   *a useless and foolish*
bondage in the oppression of aged tyranny, who sways not as
it hath power but as it is suffered.⁷ Come to me, that of this I
may speak more. If our father would sleep till I waked him, you
50   should enjoy half his revenue for ever and live the beloved of
your brother,
                                                                Edgar.'

Hum, conspiracy! 'Slept till I waked him, you should enjoy half
his revenue'—my son Edgar! Had he a hand to write this, a
55   heart and brain to breed it in? When came this to you? Who
brought it?

EDMUND   It was not brought me, my lord, there's the cunning
of it. I found it thrown in at the casement° of my closet.°   *window / private room*

60   GLOUCESTER   You know the character° to be your brother's?   *handwriting*

EDMUND   If the matter° were good, my lord, I durst swear it were   *content*
his; but in respect of that, I would fain° think it were not.   *gladly*

GLOUCESTER   It is his.

EDMUND   It is his hand, my lord, but I hope his heart is not in
the contents.

65   GLOUCESTER   Hath he never heretofore sounded you° in this   *sounded you out*
business?

EDMUND   Never, my lord; but I have often heard him maintain
it to be fit that, sons at perfect age° and fathers declining, his   *at maturity*
father should be as ward⁸ to the son, and the son manage the
70   revenue.

GLOUCESTER   O villain, villain—his very opinion in the letter!
Abhorred villain, unnatural, detested, brutish villain—worse
than brutish! Go, sir, seek him, ay, apprehend him. Abominable villain! Where is he?

---

5. *but . . . taste*: simply as a proof or test. Both terms
derive from metallurgy.
6. The established primacy of the elderly embitters us
at the prime of our lives. *policy*: statecraft; craftiness;
established order.

7. *who . . . suffered*: which rules not because it is powerful but because it is permitted to ("suffered").
8. A child under eighteen years who was legally dependent, often orphaned.

GLOUCESTER   Why so earnestly seek you to put up that letter?

EDMOND   I know no news, my lord.

30 GLOUCESTER   What paper were you reading?

EDMOND   Nothing, my lord.

GLOUCESTER   No? What needed then that terrible dispatch° of it   *frightened haste*
   into your pocket? The quality of nothing hath not such need
   to hide itself. Let's see. Come, if it be nothing I shall not need
35   spectacles.

EDMOND   I beseech you, sir, pardon me. It is a letter from my
   brother that I have not all o'er-read; and for so much as I have
   perused, I find it not fit for your o'erlooking.

GLOUCESTER   Give me the letter, sir.

40 EDMOND   I shall offend either to detain or give it. The contents,
   as in part I understand them, are to blame.

GLOUCESTER   Let's see, let's see.

EDMOND   I hope for my brother's justification he wrote this but
   as an assay or taste[5] of my virtue.

   [He gives GLOUCESTER *a letter]*

45 GLOUCESTER (*reads*)   'This policy and reverence of age makes
   the world bitter to the best of our times,[6] keeps our fortunes
   from us till our oldness cannot relish them. I begin to find an
   idle and fond° bondage in the oppression of aged tyranny, who   *a useless and foolish*
   sways not as it hath power but as it is suffered.[7] Come to me,
50   that of this I may speak more. If our father would sleep till I
   waked him, you should enjoy half his revenue for ever and live
   the beloved of your brother,
                                                    Edgar.'
   Hum, conspiracy! 'Sleep till I wake him, you should enjoy half
55   his revenue'—my son Edgar! Had he a hand to write this, a
   heart and brain to breed it in? When came you to this? Who
   brought it?

EDMOND   It was not brought me, my lord, there's the cunning
   of it. I found it thrown in at the casement° of my closet.°   *window / private room*

60 GLOUCESTER   You know the character° to be your brother's?   *handwriting*

EDMOND   If the matter° were good, my lord, I durst swear it were   *content*
   his; but in respect of that, I would fain° think it were not.   *gladly*

GLOUCESTER   It is his.

EDMOND   It is his hand, my lord, but I hope his heart is not in
65   the contents.

GLOUCESTER   Has he never before sounded° you in this   *sounded you out*
   business?

EDMOND   Never, my lord; but I have heard him oft maintain it
   to be fit that, sons at perfect age° and fathers declined, the   *at maturity*
70   father should be as ward[8] to the son, and the son manage his
   revenue.

GLOUCESTER   O villain, villain—his very opinion in the letter!
   Abhorred villain, unnatural, detested, brutish villain—worse
   than brutish! Go, sirrah,[9] seek him. I'll apprehend him. Abom-
75   inable villain! Where is he?

---

5. *but . . . taste:* simply as a proof or test. Both terms
derive from metallurgy.
6. The established primacy of the elderly embitters us
at the prime of our lives. *policy:* statecraft; craftiness;
established order.
7. *who . . . suffered:* which rules not because it is pow-

erful but because it is permitted to ("suffered").
8. A child under eighteen years who was legally dependent, often orphaned.
9. A form of address used with children or social inferiors.

75 EDMUND   I do not well know, my lord. If it shall please you to suspend your indignation against my brother till you can derive
from him better testimony of this intent, you should run a cer-
tain° course; where° if you violently proceed against him, mis-   *safe; reliable / whereas*
taking his purpose, it would make a great gap in your own
80 honour and shake in pieces the heart of his obedience. I dare
pawn down° my life for him he hath wrote this to feel° my   *I dare stake / feel out*
affection to your honour, and to no further pretence of danger.[9]
GLOUCESTER   Think you so?
EDMUND   If your honour judge it meet,° I will place you where   *appropriate*
85 you shall hear us confer of this, and by an auricular° assurance   *audible*
have your satisfaction, and that without any further delay
than this very evening.
GLOUCESTER   He cannot be such a monster.
EDMUND   Nor is not, sure.
90 GLOUCESTER   To his father, that so tenderly and entirely loves
him—heaven and earth! Edmund seek him out, wind me into
him.[1] I pray you, frame° your business after your own wisdom.   *arrange*
I would unstate myself to be in a due resolution.[2]
EDMUND   I shall seek him, sir, presently,° convey° the business   *immediately / carry out*
95 as I shall see means, and acquaint you withal.°   *therewith*
GLOUCESTER   These late° eclipses in the sun and moon portend   *recent*
no good to us.[3] Though the wisdom of nature can reason thus
and thus, yet nature finds itself scourged by the sequent
effects.[4] Love cools, friendship falls off, brothers divide; in cities
100 mutinies, in countries discords, palaces treason, the bond
cracked between son and father. Find out this villain,
Edmund; it shall lose thee nothing. Do it carefully. And the
noble and true-hearted Kent banished, his offence honesty!
Strange, strange!   *[Exit]*
105 EDMUND   This is the excellent foppery° of the world: that when   *foolishness*
we are sick in fortune—often the surfeit° of our own behav-   *excesses*
iour—we make guilty of° our disasters the sun, the moon, and   *we hold responsible for*
the stars, as if we were villains by necessity, fools by heavenly
compulsion, knaves, thieves, and treacherers° by spherical pre-   *traitors*
110 dominance,[5] drunkards, liars, and adulterers by an enforced
obedience of planetary influence, and all that we are evil in by
a divine thrusting on.° An admirable° evasion of whoremaster   *imposition / amazing*
man, to lay his goatish disposition to the charge of stars![6] My
father compounded° with my mother under the Dragon's tail   *coupled*
115 and my nativity was under Ursa Major,[7] so that it follows I am
rough and lecherous. Fut!° I should have been that° I am had   *By Christ's foot / what*
the maidenliest star of the firmament twinkled on my bastardy.
Edgar . . .

9. No further intention to do harm.
1. Worm your way into his confidence (with "me" as an
intensifier); worm your way into his confidence for me
("me" as a dative of respect).
2. I would give up everything to have my doubts resolved.
3. Lunar and solar eclipses that were recorded in London
about a year before the play's first recorded performance would have added spice to this superstitious
belief in the role of heavenly bodies as augurs of misfortune.
4. *Though . . . effects:* Though natural science may

explain the eclipses this way or that, nature (and family bonds) suffers in the effects that follow.
5. By the ascendancy of a particular planet. In the universe as conceived by Ptolemy, the planets revolved
about the earth on crystalline spheres.
6. *to lay . . . stars:* to hold the stars responsible for his
lustful desires. In Greek mythology, the satyr, a creature
with goatlike characteristics, was notoriously lecherous.
7. Constellations: *Dragon's tail* = Draco and *Ursa
Major* = Great Bear.

EDMOND   I do not well know, my lord. If it shall please you to
suspend your indignation against my brother till you can derive
from him better testimony of his intent, you should run a cer-
tain° course; where° if you violently proceed against him, mis-   *safe; reliable / whereas*
80 taking his purpose, it would make a great gap in your own
honour and shake in pieces the heart of his obedience. I dare
pawn down° my life for him that he hath writ this to feel° my   *I dare stake / feel out*
affection to your honour, and to no other pretence of danger.¹
GLOUCESTER   Think you so?
85 EDMOND   If your honour judge it meet,° I will place you where   *appropriate*
you shall hear us confer of this, and by an auricular° assurance   *audible*
have your satisfaction, and that without any further delay
than this very evening.
GLOUCESTER   He cannot be such a monster. Edmond, seek him
90 out, wind me into him,² I pray you. Frame° the business after   *Arrange*
your own wisdom. I would unstate myself to be in a due
resolution.³
EDMOND   I will seek him, sir, presently,° convey° the business as   *immediately / carry out*
I shall find means, and acquaint you withal.°   *therewith*
95 GLOUCESTER   These late° eclipses in the sun and moon portend   *recent*
no good to us.⁴ Though the wisdom of nature can reason it
thus and thus, yet nature finds itself scourged by the sequent
effects.⁵ Love cools, friendship falls off, brothers divide; in
cities, mutinies; in countries, discord; in palaces, treason; and
100 the bond cracked 'twixt son and father. This villain of mine
comes under the prediction: there's son against father. The
King falls from bias of nature:⁶ there's father against child. We
have seen the best of our time. Machinations, hollowness,°   *insincerity*
treachery, and all ruinous disorders follow us disquietly to our
105 graves. Find out this villain, Edmond; it shall lose thee nothing.
Do it carefully. And the noble and true-hearted Kent banished,
his offence honesty! 'Tis strange.   *Exit*
EDMOND   This is the excellent foppery° of the world: that when   *foolishness*
we are sick in fortune—often the surfeits° of our own behav-   *excesses*
110 iour—we make guilty of° our disasters the sun, the moon, and   *we hold responsible for*
stars, as if we were villains on necessity, fools by heavenly
compulsion, knaves, thieves, and treachers by spherical predominance,⁷ drunkards, liars, and adulterers by an enforced
obedience of planetary influence, and all that we are evil in by
115 a divine thrusting on.° An admirable° evasion of whoremaster   *imposition / amazing*
man, to lay his goatish disposition on the charge of a star!⁸ My
father compounded° with my mother under the Dragon's tail   *coupled*
and my nativity was under Ursa Major,⁹ so that it follows I
am rough and lecherous. Fut!° I should have been that° I am   *By Christ's foot / what*
120 had the maidenliest star in the firmament twinkled on my
bastardizing.

1. No other intention to do harm.
2. Worm your way into his confidence (with "me" as an
intensifier); worm your way into his confidence for me
("me" as a dative of respect).
3. I would give up everything to have my doubts resolved.
4. Lunar and solar eclipses that were seen in London
about a year before the play's first recorded performance
would have added spice to this superstitious belief in the
role of heavenly bodies as augurs of misfortune.
5. *Though . . . effects:* Though natural science may
explain the eclipses this way or that, nature (and family bonds) suffers in the effects that follow.

6. The King deviates from his natural inclination. In
the game of bowls, the "bias" ("course") is the eccentric
path taken by the weighted ball when thrown.
7. By the ascendancy of a particular planet. In the universe as conceived by Ptolemy, the planets revolved
about the earth on crystalline spheres.
8. *to lay . . . star:* to hold a star responsible for his lustful
desires. In Greek mythology, the satyr, a creature with
goatlike characteristics, was notoriously lecherous.
9. Constellations: *Dragon's tail* = Draco and *Ursa
Major* = Great Bear.

Enter EDGAR

and on's cue out he comes, like the catastrophe° of the old   *resolution*
120 comedy; mine° is villainous melancholy, with a sigh like them   *my cue; my role*
of Bedlam.[8]—O, these eclipses do portend these divisions.

EDGAR How now, brother Edmund, what serious contemplation
are you in?

EDMUND I am thinking, brother, of a prediction I read this
125 other day, what should follow these eclipses.

EDGAR Do you busy yourself about that?

EDMUND I promise you, the effects he writ of succeed° unhap-   *follow*
pily, as of unnaturalness between the child and the parent,
death, dearth, dissolutions of ancient amities, divisions in state,
130 menaces and maledictions against king and nobles, needless
diffidences,° banishment of friends, dissipation of cohorts,[9]   *baseless suspicions*
nuptial breaches, and I know not what.

EDGAR How long have you been a sectary astronomical?°   *a devotee of astrology*

EDMUND Come, come, when saw you my father last?

135 EDGAR Why, the night gone by.

EDMUND Spake you with him?

EDGAR Two hours together.

EDMUND Parted you in good terms? Found you no displeasure
in him by word or countenance?°   *appearance; demeanor*

140 EDGAR None at all.

EDMUND Bethink yourself wherein you may have offended him,
and at my entreaty forbear° his presence till some little time   *avoid*
hath qualified° the heat of his displeasure, which at this instant   *moderated*
so rageth in him that with the mischief of your person it would
145 scarce allay.[1]

EDGAR Some villain hath done me wrong.

EDMUND That's my fear, brother. I advise you to the best. Go
armed. I am no honest man if there be any good meaning
towards you. I have told you what I have seen and heard but
150 faintly, nothing like the image and horror of it. Pray you, away.

EDGAR Shall I hear from you anon?

EDMUND I do serve you in this business.   *Exit* EDGAR
A credulous father, and a brother noble,
Whose nature is so far from doing harms
155 That he suspects none; on whose foolish honesty
My practices° ride easy. I see the business.[2]   *plots*
Let me, if not by birth, have lands by wit.°   *intelligence*
All with me's meet that I can fashion fit.[3]   *Exit*

---

8. Like the inmates of Bedlam. "Bethlehem," shortened to "Bedlam," was the name of the oldest and best-
known London madhouse.
9. Scattering of forces.
1. *with . . . allay:* even harming you bodily would
hardly relieve his anger; alternatively, with the irritant

of your presence, it (Gloucester's anger) would not be
abated.
2. It is now clear to me what needs to be done.
3. Anything is fine by me as long as I can make it serve
my purpose. *meet:* justifiable; appropriate.

Enter EDGAR

Pat° he comes, like the catastrophe° of the old comedy. My cue   *On cue / resolution*
is villainous melancholy, with a sigh like Tom o' Bedlam.[1]
     [*He reads a book*]
—O, these eclipses do portend these divisions. Fa, so, la, mi.[2]

125 EDGAR How now, brother Edmond, what serious contemplation
     are you in?

     EDMOND I am thinking, brother, of a prediction I read this
     other day, what should follow these eclipses.

     EDGAR Do you busy yourself with that?

130 EDMOND I promise you, the effects he writes of succeed° unhap-   *follow*
     pily. When saw you my father last?

     EDGAR The night gone by.

     EDMOND Spake you with him?

     EDGAR Ay, two hours together.

135 EDMOND Parted you in good terms? Found you no displeasure
     in him by word nor countenance?°   *appearance; demeanor*

     EDGAR None at all.

     EDMOND Bethink yourself wherein you may have offended him,
     and at my entreaty forbear° his presence until some little time   *avoid*
140 hath qualified° the heat of his displeasure, which at this instant   *moderated*
     so rageth in him that with the mischief of your person it
     would scarcely allay.[3]

     EDGAR Some villain hath done me wrong.

     EDMOND That's my fear. I pray you have a continent forbear-
145 ance° till the speed of his rage goes slower; and, as I say, retire   *restrained absence*
     with me to my lodging, from whence I will fitly° bring you to   *when suitable*
     hear my lord speak. Pray ye, go. There's my key. If you do stir
     abroad, go armed.

     EDGAR Armed, brother?

150 EDMOND Brother, I advise you to the best. I am no honest man
     if there be any good meaning toward you. I have told you what
     I have seen and heard but faintly, nothing like the image and
     horror of it. Pray you, away.

     EDGAR Shall I hear from you anon?

155 EDMOND I do serve you in this business.   *Exit* [EDGAR]
     A credulous father, and a brother noble,
     Whose nature is so far from doing harms
     That he suspects none; on whose foolish honesty
     My practices° ride easy. I see the business.[4]   *plots*
160 Let me, if not by birth, have lands by wit.°   *intelligence*
     All with me's meet that I can fashion fit.[5]   *Exit*

---

1. The usual name for lunatic beggars; "Bethlehem,"
shortened to "Bedlam," was the name of the oldest and
best-known London madhouse.
2. The portion of the scale Edmund sings is an augmented fourth, an interval considered at this time very
discordant; it was sometimes referred to as "the devil in
music." *divisions:* social fractures; melodic embellishments.

3. *with . . . allay:* even harming you bodily ("mischief")
would hardly relieve his anger; alternatively, with the
irritant of your presence, it (Gloucester's anger) would
not be abated.
4. It is now clear to me what needs to be done.
5. Anything is fine by me as long as I can make it serve
my purpose. *meet:* justifiable; appropriate.

Scene 3

Enter GONORIL *and Gentleman* [OSWALD]

GONORIL   Did my father strike my gentleman
For chiding of his fool?

OSWALD   Yes, madam.

GONORIL   By day and night he wrongs me. Every hour
He flashes into one gross crime° or other   offense
5   That sets us all at odds. I'll not endure it.
His knights grow riotous, and himself upbraids us
On every trifle. When he returns from hunting
I will not speak with him. Say I am sick.
If you come slack of former services[1]
10   You shall do well; the fault of it I'll answer.°   answer for
      [*Hunting horns within*]

OSWALD   He's coming, madam. I hear him.

GONORIL   Put on what weary negligence you please,
You and your fellow servants. I'd have it come in° question.   into
If he dislike it, let him to our sister,
15   Whose mind and mine I know in that are one,
Not to be overruled. Idle° old man,   Foolish
That still would manage those authorities
That he hath given away! Now, by my life,
Old fools are babes again, and must be used
20   With checks as flatteries, when they are seen abused.[2]
Remember what I tell you.

OSWALD   Very well, madam.

GONORIL   And let his knights have colder looks among you.
What grows of it, no matter. Advise your fellows so.
I would breed from hence occasions, and I shall,
25   That I may speak.[3] I'll write straight° to my sister   straightaway
To hold my very° course. Go prepare for dinner.   exact
                                        Exeunt [*severally*]°   separately

Scene 4

Enter KENT [*disguised*]

KENT   If but as well[1] I other accents borrow
That can my speech diffuse,° my good intent   disguise
May carry through itself to that full issue°   result
For which I razed my likeness.[2] Now, banished Kent,
5   If thou canst serve where thou dost stand condemned,
Thy master, whom thou lov'st, shall find thee full of labour.° ready for work

Enter LEAR [*and servants from hunting*]

LEAR   Let me not stay° a jot for dinner. Go get it ready.   wait
                                        [*Exit one*]

[*To* KENT] How now, what° art thou?   who

KENT   A man, sir.

10   LEAR   What dost thou profess?[3] What wouldst thou with us?

KENT   I do profess to be no less than I seem, to serve him truly

---

Scene 3   Location: The Duke of Albany's castle.
1. If you offer him less service (and respect) than before.
2. *Old . . . abused:* When foolish old men act like children, rebukes are the kindest treatment when kind
treatment is abused.
3. *I would . . . speak:* I wish to foster situations, and I
shall, in which to speak my mind.

Scene 4   Location: As before.
1. As well as disguising my appearance.
2. Disguised my appearance; shaved off my beard (with
a pun on "razor").
3. What is your job (profession)? Kent, in reply, uses
"profess" punningly to mean "claim."

1.3

Enter GONERIL *and Steward* [OSWALD]

GONERIL   Did my father strike my gentleman
For chiding of his fool?

OSWALD   Ay, madam.

GONERIL   By day and night he wrongs me. Every hour
He flashes into one gross crime° or other   offense
5   That sets us all at odds. I'll not endure it.
His knights grow riotous, and himself upbraids us
On every trifle. When he returns from hunting
I will not speak with him. Say I am sick.
If you come slack of former services[1]
10   You shall do well; the fault of it I'll answer.°   answer for
     [*Horns within*]

OSWALD   He's coming, madam. I hear him.

GONERIL   Put on what weary negligence you please,
You and your fellows.° I'd have it come to question.   servants
If he distaste° it, let him to my sister,   dislike
15   Whose mind and mine I know in that are one.
Remember what I have said.

OSWALD   Well, madam.

GONERIL   And let his knights have colder looks among you.
What grows of it, no matter. Advise your fellows so.
I'll write straight° to my sister to hold my course.   straightaway
20   Prepare for dinner.   *Exeunt* [*severally*]°   separately

1.4

Enter KENT [*disguised*]

KENT   If but as well[1] I other accents borrow
That can my speech diffuse,° my good intent   disguise
May carry through itself to that full issue°   result
For which I razed my likeness.[2] Now, banished Kent,
5   If thou canst serve where thou dost stand condemned,
So may it come° thy master, whom thou lov'st,   come to pass
Shall find thee full of labours.°   helpful; keen
          Horns within.° Enter LEAR *and attendants* [*from*   Hunting horns offstage
          hunting][3]

LEAR   Let me not stay° a jot for dinner. Go get it ready.   wait
                                          [*Exit one*]

     [*To* KENT] How now, what° art thou?   who
10   KENT   A man, sir.

LEAR   What dost thou profess?[4] What wouldst thou with us?

KENT   I do profess to be no less than I seem, to serve him truly

---

1.3 Location: The Duke of Albany's castle.
1. If you offer him less service (and respect) than
before.
1.4 Location: As before.
1. As well as disguising my appearance.
2. Disguised my appearance; shaved off my beard (with
a pun on "razor").

3. The attendants include at least one knight. Critics of
James I complained that he devalued honors by granting too many knighthoods and that he squandered too
much time in hunting.
4. What is your job (profession)? Kent, in reply, uses
"profess" punningly to mean "claim."

that will put me in trust, to love him that is honest, to converse°   *associate*
with him that is wise and says little, to fear judgement, to fight
when I cannot choose,° and to eat no fish.[4]   *when I must*

15   LEAR   What art thou?

KENT   A very honest-hearted fellow, and as poor as the King.

LEAR   If thou be as poor for a subject as he is for a king, thou'rt
poor enough. What wouldst thou?

KENT   Service.

20   LEAR   Who wouldst thou serve?

KENT   You.

LEAR   Dost thou know me, fellow?

KENT   No, sir, but you have that in your countenance which I
would fain° call master.   *gladly*

25   LEAR   What's that?

KENT   Authority.

LEAR   What services canst do?

KENT   I can keep honest counsel,° ride, run, mar a curious tale   *keep secrets*
in telling it,[5] and deliver a plain message bluntly. That which
30   ordinary men are fit for I am qualified in; and the best of me
is diligence.

LEAR   How old art thou?

KENT   Not so young to love a woman for singing, nor so old to
dote on her for anything. I have years on my back forty-eight.

35   LEAR   Follow me. Thou shalt serve me, if I like thee no worse
after dinner. I will not part from thee yet.—Dinner, ho, dinner!
Where's my knave, my fool? Go you and call my fool hither.

                                        [Exit one]

        Enter steward [OSWALD]
You, sirrah, where's my daughter?

OSWALD   So please you—   *[Exit]*

40   LEAR   What says the fellow there? Call the clotpoll° back.   *blockhead*

                  [Exeunt SERVANT *and* KENT]
Where's my fool? Ho, I think the world's asleep.

        [*Enter* KENT *and a* SERVANT]
How now, where's that mongrel?

KENT   He says, my lord, your daughter is not well.

LEAR   Why came not the slave back to me when I called him?

45   SERVANT   Sir, he answered me in the roundest° manner he   *bluntest; rudest*
would not.

LEAR   A° would not?   *He*

SERVANT   My lord, I know not what the matter is, but to my
judgement your highness is not entertained with that ceremo-
50   nious affection as you were wont.° There's a great abatement   *accustomed to*
appears as well in the general dependants° as in the Duke him-   *servants*
self also, and your daughter.

LEAR   Ha, sayst thou so?

SERVANT   I beseech you pardon me, my lord, if I be mistaken, for
55   my duty cannot be silent when I think your highness wronged.

---

4. And not to be a Catholic or penitent (Catholics were obliged to eat fish on specified occasions and as penance); alternatively, to be a manly man, meat eater.

5. That is, Kent's plain, blunt speech would make him ill suited to tell a convoluted ("curious") tale.

that will put me in trust, to love him that is honest, to converse°   associate
with him that is wise and says little, to fear judgement, to fight
15   when I cannot choose,° and to eat no fish.⁵   when I must
LEAR   What art thou?
KENT   A very honest-hearted fellow, and as poor as the King.
LEAR   If thou be'st as poor for a subject as he's for a king, thou'rt
poor enough. What wouldst thou?
20   KENT   Service.
LEAR   Who wouldst thou serve?
KENT   You.
LEAR   Dost thou know me, fellow?
KENT   No, sir, but you have that in your countenance which I
25   would fain° call master.   gladly
LEAR   What's that?
KENT   Authority.
LEAR   What services canst do?
KENT   I can keep honest counsel,° ride, run, mar a curious tale   keep secrets
30   in telling it,⁶ and deliver a plain message bluntly. That which
ordinary men are fit for I am qualified in; and the best of me
is diligence.
LEAR   How old art thou?
KENT   Not so young, sir, to love a woman for singing, nor so old
35   to dote on her for anything. I have years on my back forty-eight.
LEAR   Follow me. Thou shalt serve me, if I like thee no worse
after dinner. I will not part from thee yet. Dinner, ho, dinner!
Where's my knave, my fool? Go you and call my fool hither.
                                        [Exit one]
            Enter Steward [OSWALD]
You, you, sirrah, where's my daughter?
40   OSWALD   So please you—
LEAR   What says the fellow there? Call the clotpoll° back.   Exit   blockhead
                                        [Exit a knight]
Where's my fool? Ho, I think the world's asleep.
            [Enter a KNIGHT]
How now? Where's that mongrel?
KNIGHT   He says, my lord, your daughter is not well.
45   LEAR   Why came not the slave back to me when I called him?
KNIGHT   Sir, he answered me in the roundest° manner he would   bluntest; rudest
not.
LEAR   A° would not?   He
KNIGHT   My lord, I know not what the matter is, but to my judge-
50   ment your highness is not entertained with that ceremonious
affection as you were wont.° There's a great abatement of kind-   accustomed to
ness appears as well in the general dependants° as in the   servants
Duke himself also, and your daughter.
LEAR   Ha, sayst thou so?
55   KNIGHT   I beseech you pardon me, my lord, if I be mistaken, for
my duty cannot be silent when I think your highness wronged.

---

5. And not to be a Catholic or penitent (Catholics were obliged to eat fish on specified occasions and as penance); alternatively, to be a manly man, meat eater.

6. That is, Kent's plain, blunt speech would make him ill suited to tell a convoluted ("curious") tale.

LEAR   Thou but rememberest° me of mine own conception.° I   remind / perception
have perceived a most faint neglect of late, which I have rather
blamed as mine own jealous curiosity⁶ than as a very pretence°   a true intention
and purport of unkindness. I will look further into't. But
60   where's this fool? I have not seen him these two days.

SERVANT   Since my young lady's going into France, sir, the fool
hath much pined away.

LEAR   No more of that, I have noted it. Go you and tell my
daughter I would speak with her.   [Exit one]
65   Go you, call hither my fool.   [Exit one]
            [Enter OSWALD crossing the stage]
O you, sir, you, sir, come you hither. Who am I, sir?

OSWALD   My lady's father.

LEAR   My lady's father? My lord's knave, you whoreson dog, you
slave, you cur!

70   OSWALD   I am none of this, my lord, I beseech you pardon me.

LEAR   Do you bandy looks with me, you rascal?
            [LEAR strikes him]

OSWALD   I'll not be struck, my lord—

KENT   [tripping him]   Nor tripped neither, you base football-
player.⁷

75   LEAR   [to KENT]   I thank thee, fellow. Thou serv'st me, and I'll
love thee.

KENT   [to OSWALD]   Come, sir, I'll teach you differences.° Away,   (of rank)
away. If you will measure your lubber's length again,⁸ tarry;
but away if you have wisdom.   [Exit OSWALD]

80   LEAR   Now, friendly knave, I thank thee.
            Enter [Lear's] FOOL
There's earnest of° thy service.   downpayment for
            [He gives KENT money]

FOOL   Let me hire him, too. [To KENT] Here's my coxcomb.°   fool's cap

LEAR   How now, my pretty knave, how dost thou?

FOOL   [to KENT]   Sirrah, you were best take my coxcomb.

85   KENT   Why, fool?

FOOL   Why, for taking one's part that's out of favour. Nay, an
thou canst not smile as the wind sits, thou'lt catch cold shortly.⁹
There, take my coxcomb. Why, this fellow hath banished two
on's daughters¹ and done the third a blessing against his will. If
90   thou follow him, thou must needs wear my coxcomb. [To
LEAR] How now, nuncle?° Would I had two coxcombs and two   (mine) uncle
daughters.

LEAR   Why, my boy?

FOOL   If I gave them my living° I'd keep my coxcombs myself.²   goods
95   There's mine; beg another off thy daughters.

LEAR   Take heed, sirrah—the whip.

---

6. jealous curiosity: paranoid concern with niceties.
7. Football was a rough street game played by the poor.
8. If you will be stretched out by me again. lubber:
clumsy oaf.
9. an . . . shortly: if you can't keep in favor with those in

power, you will soon find yourself left out in the cold.
1. By abdicating, Lear has in effect prevented his eldest daughters from any longer being his subjects, just
as if he had "banished" them.
2. I'd be twice as much a fool.

LEAR   Thou but rememberest° me of mine own conception.° I   *remind/perception*
have perceived a most faint neglect of late, which I have rather
blamed as mine own jealous curiosity[7] than as a very pretence°   *a true intention*
60   and purpose of unkindness. I will look further into't. But
where's my fool? I have not seen him these two days.

KNIGHT   Since my young lady's going into France, sir, the fool
hath much pined away.

LEAR   No more of that, I have noted it well. Go you and tell my
65   daughter I would speak with her.   [*Exit one*]
Go you, call hither my fool.   [*Exit one*]
Enter Steward [OSWALD *crossing the stage*]
O you, sir, you, come you hither, sir, who am I, sir?

OSWALD   My lady's father.

LEAR   My lady's father? My lord's knave, you whoreson dog, you
70   slave, you cur!

OSWALD   I am none of these, my lord, I beseech your pardon.

LEAR   Do you bandy looks with me, you rascal?
[LEAR *strikes him*]

OSWALD   I'll not be strucken, my lord.

KENT [*tripping him*]   Nor tripped neither, you base football
75   player.[8]

LEAR   [*to* KENT]   I thank thee, fellow. Thou serv'st me, and I'll
love thee.

KENT [*to* OSWALD]   Come, sir, arise, away. I'll teach you differences.° Away, away. If you will measure your lubber's length   *(of rank)*
80   again,[9] tarry; but away, go to. Have you wisdom? So.
[*Exit* OSWALD]

LEAR   Now, my friendly knave, I thank thee.
Enter [*Lear's*] FOOL
There's earnest of° thy service.   *downpayment for*
[*He gives* KENT *money*]

FOOL   Let me hire him, too. [*To* KENT] Here's my coxcomb.°   *fool's cap*

LEAR   How now, my pretty knave, how dost thou?

85   FOOL [*to* KENT]   Sirrah, you were best take my coxcomb.

LEAR   Why, my boy?

FOOL   Why? For taking one's part that's out of favour. [*To* KENT]
Nay, an thou canst not smile as the wind sits, thou'lt catch cold
shortly.[1] There, take my coxcomb. Why, this fellow has
90   banished two on's daughters[2] and did the third a blessing
against his will. If thou follow him, thou must needs wear my
coxcomb. [*To* LEAR] How now, nuncle?° Would I had two cox-   *(mine) uncle*
combs and two daughters.

LEAR   Why, my boy?

95   FOOL   If I gave them all my living° I'd keep my coxcombs   *goods*
myself.[3] There's mine; beg another off thy daughters.

LEAR   Take heed, sirrah—the whip.

---

7. *jealous curiosity:* paranoid concern with niceties.
8. Football was a rough street game played by the poor.
9. If you will be stretched out by me again. *lubber:* clumsy oaf.
1. *an . . . shortly:* if you can't keep in favor with those in

power, you will soon find yourself left out in the cold.
2. By abdicating, Lear has in effect prevented his eldest daughters from any longer being his subjects, just
as if he had "banished" them.
3. I'd be twice as much a fool.

FOOL   Truth is a dog that must to° kennel. He must be whipped   go to
out when Lady the brach³ may stand by the fire and stink.

LEAR   A pestilent gall° to me!   annoyance; bitterness

100 FOOL [to KENT]   Sirrah, I'll teach thee a speech.

LEAR   Do.

FOOL   Mark it, uncle.

       Have more than thou showest,

       Speak less than thou knowest,

105   Lend less than thou owest,°   own

       Ride more than thou goest,°   walk

       Learn° more than thou trowest,°   Hear / believe

       Set less than thou throwest,⁴

       Leave thy drink and thy whore,

110   And keep in-a-door,

       And thou shalt have more

       Than two tens to a score.⁵

LEAR   This is nothing, fool.

FOOL   Then, like the breath° of an unfee'd° lawyer, you gave me   speech / unpaid

115 nothing for't. Can you make no use of nothing, uncle?

LEAR   Why no, boy. Nothing can be made out of nothing.

FOOL [to KENT]   Prithee, tell him so much the rent of his land
comes to.⁶ He will not believe a fool.

LEAR   A bitter fool.

120 FOOL   Dost know the difference, my boy, between a bitter fool
and a sweet fool?

LEAR   No, lad. Teach me.

FOOL [sings]   That lord that counselled thee

       To give away thy land,

125   Come, place him here by me;

       Do thou for him stand.°   represent him

    The sweet and bitter fool

       Will presently appear,

    The one in motley⁷ here,

130   The other found out there.

LEAR   Dost thou call me fool, boy?

FOOL   All thy other titles thou hast given away. That thou wast
born with.

KENT [to LEAR]   This is not altogether fool,⁸ my lord.

135 FOOL   No, faith; lords and great men will not let me. If I had a
monopoly out, they would have part on't, and ladies too, they
will not let me have all the fool to myself—they'll be snatching. Give me an egg, nuncle, and I'll give thee two crowns.

LEAR   What two crowns shall they be?

140 FOOL   Why, after I have cut the egg in the middle and eat up
the meat,° the two crowns of the egg. When thou clovest° thy   edible part / cleaved
crown i'th' middle and gavest away both parts, thou borest° thy   you carried
ass o'th'° back o'er the dirt. Thou hadst little wit° in thy bald   on your / sense
crown when thou gavest thy golden one away. If I speak like
145 myself° in this, let him be whipped that first finds it so.⁹   (like a fool)

---

3. Lady the bitch. Pet dogs were often called "Lady"
such and such. The allusion is to Regan and Gonoril,
who are now being preferred to truthful Cordelia.
4. Don't gamble everything on a single cast of the dice.
5. *And thou . . . score:* And there will be more than two
tens in your twenty—that is, you will become richer.
6. Remind him that no land means no rent; with a pun

on "rent" meaning "torn," "divided."
7. Multicolored dress of a court jester.
8. Foolish, folly. In the next line, the Fool takes "altogether fool" to mean "one who has cornered the market
on folly."
9. *that . . . so:* who first discovers for himself that this
is true; who first considers this to be foolish.

FOOL   Truth's a dog must to° kennel. He must be whipped out   *go to*
     when the Lady Brach⁴ may stand by th' fire and stink.

100 LEAR   A pestilent gall° to me!   *annoyance; bitterness*

FOOL *[to* KENT]   Sirrah, I'll teach thee a speech.

LEAR   Do.

FOOL   Mark it, nuncle:
               Have more than thou showest,
105   Speak less than thou knowest,
               Lend less than thou owest,°   *own*
               Ride more than thou goest,°   *walk*
               Learn° more than thou trowest,°   *Hear / believe*
               Set less than thou throwest,⁵
110   Leave thy drink and thy whore,
               And keep in-a-door,
               And thou shalt have more
               Than two tens to a score.⁶

KENT   This is nothing, fool.

115 FOOL   Then 'tis like the breath° of an unfee'd° lawyer: you gave   *speech / unpaid*
     me nothing for't. *[To* LEAR] Can you make no use of nothing,
     nuncle?

LEAR   Why no, boy. Nothing can be made out of nothing.

FOOL *[to* KENT]   Prithee, tell him so much the rent of his land
120 comes to.⁷ He will not believe a fool.

LEAR   A bitter fool.

FOOL   Dost know the difference, my boy, between a bitter fool
     and a sweet one?

LEAR   No, lad. Teach me.

125 FOOL   Nuncle, give me an egg, and I'll give thee two crowns.

LEAR   What two crowns shall they be?

FOOL   Why, after I have cut the egg i'th' middle and eat up the
     meat,° the two crowns of the egg. When thou clovest° thy   *edible part / cleaved*
     crown i'th' middle and gavest away both parts, thou borest°   *you carried*
130 thine ass o'th'° back o'er the dirt. Thou hadst little wit° in thy   *on your / sense*
     bald crown when thou gavest thy golden one away. If I speak
     like myself° in this, let him be whipped that first finds it so.⁸   *(like a fool)*

4. Lady Bitch. Pet dogs were often called "Lady" such   tens in your twenty—that is, you will become richer.
and such. The allusion is to Regan and Goneril, who   7. Remind him that no land means no rent; with a pun
are now being preferred to truthful Cordelia.   on "rent" meaning "torn," "divided."
5. Don't gamble everything on a single cast of the dice.   8. *that . . . so:* who first discovers for himself that this
6. *And thou . . . score:* And there will be more than two   is true; who first considers this to be foolish.

[*Sings*]   Fools had ne'er less wit in a year,[1]
                    For wise men are grown foppish.[1]
                They know not how their wits do wear,
                    Their manners are so apish.°   stupid; imitative

150   LEAR   When were you wont° to be so full of songs, sirrah?   accustomed
       FOOL   I have used° it, nuncle, ever since thou madest thy daugh-   practiced
              ters thy mother; for when thou gavest them the rod and puttest
              down thine own breeches,
              [*Sings*]   Then they for sudden joy did weep,
155   And I for sorrow sung,
                          That such a king should play bo-peep°   a child's game
                          And go the fools among.
              Prithee, nuncle, keep a schoolmaster that can teach thy fool
              to lie. I would fain learn to lie.
160   LEAR   An° you lie, we'll have you whipped.   If
       FOOL   I marvel what kin° thou and thy daughters are. They'll   how alike
              have me whipped for speaking true, thou wilt have me
              whipped for lying, and sometime I am whipped for holding my
              peace. I had rather be any kind of thing than a fool; and yet I
165   would not be thee, nuncle. Thou hast pared thy wit o' both
              sides and left nothing in the middle.
                          Enter GONORIL
              Here comes one of the parings.
       LEAR   How now, daughter, what makes that frontlet[2] on?
              Methinks you are too much o' late i'th' frown.
170   FOOL   Thou wast a pretty fellow when thou hadst no need to
              care for her frown. Now thou art an O without a figure.[3] I am
              better than thou art, now. I am a fool; thou art nothing. [*To*
              GONORIL] Yes, forsooth, I will hold my tongue; so your face
              bids me, though you say nothing.
175   [*Sings*]   Mum, mum.
                          He that keeps neither crust nor crumb,
                          Weary of all, shall want° some.   lack; be in need of
              That's a shelled peascod.°   empty pea pod; nothing
       GONORIL [*to* LEAR]   Not only, sir, this your all-licensed° fool, unrestrained
180   But other of your insolent retinue
              Do hourly carp and quarrel, breaking forth
              In rank° and not-to-be-endurèd riots.   foul; spreading
              Sir, I had thought by making this well known unto you
              To have found a safe° redress, but now grow fearful,   sure
185   By what yourself too late° have spoke and done,   recently
              That you protect this course, and put it on°   encourage it
              By your allowance; which if you should, the fault
              Would not scape censure, nor the redress sleep
              Which in the tender of a wholesome weal
190   Might in their working do you that offence,
              That else were shame, that then necessity
              Must call discreet proceedings.[4]

---

1. *Fools . . . foppish*: Professional fools have never been as witless since wise men have lately outdone them in idiocy.
2. Band worn on the forehead; here, a metaphor for "frown."
3. A zero without a preceding digit; nothing.
4. *which if you . . . proceedings*: if you do approve (of your

attendants' behavior), you will not escape criticism, nor will it be without retribution, which for the common good will cause you pain. While this would otherwise be improper, it will be seen as a prudent ("discreet") action under the circumstances. *tender of:* concern for. *weal:* state, commonwealth. *then necessity:* the demands of the time.

[*Sings*] Fools had ne'er less grace in a year,
     For wise men are grown foppish,[9]
135   And know not how their wits to wear,
     Their manners are so apish.°   *stupid; imitative*

LEAR When were you wont° to be so full of songs, sirrah? *accustomed*

FOOL I have used° it, nuncle, e'er since thou madest thy daugh- *practiced*
ters thy mothers; for when thou gavest them the rod and
140 puttest down thine own breeches,

[*Sings*] Then they for sudden joy did weep,
     And I for sorrow sung,
     That such a king should play bo-peep°   *a child's game*
     And go the fools among.

145 Prithee, nuncle, keep a schoolmaster that can teach thy fool
to lie. I would fain learn to lie.

LEAR An° you lie, sirrah, we'll have you whipped.   *If*

FOOL I marvel what kin° thou and thy daughters are. They'll *how alike*
have me whipped for speaking true, thou'lt have me whipped
150 for lying, and sometimes I am whipped for holding my peace.
I had rather be any kind o' thing than a fool; and yet I would
not be thee, nuncle. Thou hast pared thy wit o' both sides and
left nothing i'th' middle.

Enter GONERIL

Here comes one o' the parings.

155 LEAR How now, daughter? What makes that frontlet[1] on?
You are too much of late i'th' frown.

FOOL Thou wast a pretty fellow when thou hadst no need to
care for her frowning. Now thou art an O without a figure.[2] I
am better than thou art, now. I am a fool; thou art nothing.
160 [*To* GONERIL] Yes, forsooth, I will hold my tongue; so your face
bids me, though you say nothing.

[*Sings*] Mum, mum.
     He that keeps nor crust nor crumb,
     Weary of all, shall want° some.   *lack; be in need of*
165 That's a shelled peascod.°   *empty pea pod; nothing*

GONERIL [*to* LEAR] Not only, sir, this your all-licensed° fool, *unrestrained*
But other of your insolent retinue
Do hourly carp and quarrel, breaking forth
In rank° and not-to-be-endurèd riots. Sir,   *foul; spreading*
170 I had thought by making this well known unto you
To have found a safe° redress, but now grow fearful, *sure*
By what yourself too late° have spoke and done,   *recently*
That you protect this course, and put it on°   *encourage it*
By your allowance; which if you should, the fault
175 Would not scape censure, nor the redresses sleep
Which in the tender of a wholesome weal
Might in their working do you that offence,
Which else were shame, that then necessity
Will call discreet proceeding.[3]

---

9. *Fools . . . foppish:* Professional fools have never been as witless since wise men have lately outdone them in idiocy.
1. Band worn on the forehead; here, a metaphor for "frown."
2. A zero without a preceding digit; nothing.
3. *which if you . . . proceeding:* if you do approve (of your attendants' behavior), you will not escape criticism, nor will it be without retribution, which for the common good will cause you pain. While this would otherwise be improper, it will be seen as a prudent ("discreet") action under the circumstances. *tender of:* concern for. *weal:* state, commonwealth. *then necessity:* the demands of the time.

FOOL [*to* LEAR]   For, you trow, nuncle,

    [*Sings*]   The hedge-sparrow fed the cuckoo⁵ so long

195   That it had it° head bit off by it young;°   *its / (the young cuckoo)*

    so out went the candle, and we were left darkling.°   *in the dark*

LEAR [*to* GONORIL]   Are you our daughter?

GONORIL   Come, sir, I would° you would make use of that good wisdom   *wish*

    Whereof I know you are fraught,° and put away   *full*

200   These dispositions° that of late transform you   *moods; attitudes*

    From what you rightly are.

FOOL   May not an ass know when the cart draws the horse?

    [*Sings*] 'Whoop, jug,⁶ I love thee!'

LEAR   Doth any here know me? Why, this is not Lear.

205   Doth Lear walk thus, speak thus? Where are his eyes?

    Either his notion° weakens, or his discernings   *intellect*

    Are lethargied. Sleeping or waking, ha?

    Sure, 'tis not so.

    Who is it that can tell me who I am?

210   Lear's shadow? I would° learn that, for by the marks°   *wish to / evidence*

    Of sovereignty, knowledge, and reason

    I should be false persuaded I had daughters.

FOOL   Which° they will make an obedient father.   *Whom*

LEAR [*to* GONORIL]   Your name, fair gentlewoman?

GONORIL   Come, sir,

215   This admiration° is much of the savour   *excessive amazement*

    Of other your new pranks. I do beseech you

    Understand my purposes aright,

    As you are old and reverend, should° be wise.   *you should*

    Here do you keep a hundred knights and squires,

220   Men so disordered,° so debauched and bold   *disorderly*

    That this our court, infected with their manners,

    Shows° like a riotous inn, epicurism°   *Appears / gluttony*

    And lust make more like to a tavern, or brothel,

    Than a great palace. The shame itself doth speak

225   For instant remedy. Be thou desired,

    By her that else will take the thing she begs,

    A little to disquantity your train,°   *to reduce your retinue*

    And the remainder that shall still depend°   *be retained*

    To be such men as may besort° your age,   *befit*

    That know themselves° and you.   *Who know their place*

230 LEAR   Darkness and devils!

    Saddle my horses, call my train together!—   [*Exit one or more*]

    Degenerate bastard, I'll not trouble thee.

    Yet° have I left a daughter.   *Still*

GONORIL   You strike my people, and your disordered rabble

235   Make servants of their betters.

           Enter Duke [*of* ALBANY]

---

5. The cuckoo lays its eggs in other birds' nests.   6. Nickname for "Joan"; sobriquet for a whore.

180   FOOL [*to* LEAR]   For, you know, nuncle,
          [*Sings*]   The hedge-sparrow fed the cuckoo⁴ so long
                That it's had it° head bit off by it young;°   *its / (the young cuckoo)*
      so out went the candle, and we were left darkling.°   *in the dark*
      LEAR [*to* GONERIL]   Are you our daughter?
185   GONERIL   I would° you would make use of your good wisdom,   *wish*
          Whereof I know you are fraught,° and put away   *full*
          These dispositions° which of late transport you   *moods; attitudes*
      From what you rightly are.
      FOOL   May not an ass know when the cart draws the horse?
190   [*Sings*] 'Whoop, jug,⁵ I love thee!'
      LEAR   Does any here know me? This is not Lear.
          Does Lear walk thus, speak thus? Where are his eyes?
          Either his notion° weakens, his discernings   *intellect*
          Are lethargied—ha, waking?° 'Tis not so.   *am I awake*
195   Who is it that can tell me who I am?
      FOOL   Lear's shadow.

      LEAR [*to* GONERIL]   Your name, fair gentlewoman?
      GONERIL   This admiration,° sir, is much o'th' savour   *excessive amazement*
          Of other your new pranks. I do beseech you
200   To understand my purposes aright,
          As you are old and reverend, should° be wise.   *you should*
          Here do you keep a hundred knights and squires,
          Men so disordered,° so debauched and bold   *disorderly*
          That this our court, infected with their manners,
205   Shows° like a riotous inn. Epicurism° and lust   *Appears / Gluttony*
          Makes it more like a tavern or a brothel
          Than a graced° palace. The shame itself doth speak   *an honored*
          For instant remedy. Be then desired,
          By her that else will take the thing she begs,
210   A little to disquantity your train,°   *to reduce your retinue*
          And the remainders that shall still depend°   *be retained*
          To be such men as may besort° your age,   *befit*
          Which know themselves° and you.   *Who know their place*
      LEAR   Darkness and devils!
          Saddle my horses, call my train together!—   [*Exit one or more*]
215   Degenerate bastard, I'll not trouble thee.
          Yet° have I left a daughter.   *Still*
      GONERIL   You strike my people, and your disordered rabble
          Make servants of their betters.
              Enter ALBANY

---

4. The cuckoo lays its eggs in other birds' nests.   5. Nickname for "Joan"; sobriquet for a whore.

LEAR We that too late repent's—O sir, are you come?
　　Is it your will that we—prepare my horses. [*Exit one or more*]
　　Ingratitude, thou marble-hearted fiend,
　　More hideous when thou show'st thee in a child
240　Than the sea-monster—[*to* GONORIL] detested kite,° thou liest.　　*carrion-eating hawk*
　　My train are men of choice and rarest parts,°　　　　　　　*qualities*
　　That all particulars of duty know,
　　And in the most exact regard support
　　The worships of° their name. O most small fault,　　*honor accorded*
245　How ugly didst thou in Cordelia show,
　　That, like an engine, wrenched my frame of nature
　　From the fixed place,⁷ drew from my heart all love,
　　And added to the gall! O Lear, Lear!
　　Beat at this gate° that let thy folly in　　　　　　　*(his head)*
250　And thy dear° judgement out.—Go, go, my people!　　*precious*
ALBANY　My lord, I am guiltless as I am ignorant.
LEAR　It may be so, my lord. Hark, nature, hear:
　　Dear goddess, suspend thy purpose if
　　Thou didst intend to make this creature fruitful.
255　Into her womb convey sterility.
　　Dry up in her the organs of increase,
　　And from her derogate° body never spring　　　　　　*debased*
　　A babe to honour her. If she must teem,°　　　　　　*breed*
　　Create her child of spleen,° that it may live　　　　　*malice*
260　And be a thwart disnatured° torment to her.　　*a perverse unnatural*
　　Let it stamp wrinkles in her brow of youth,
　　With cadent° tears fret° channels in her cheeks,　　*flowing / carve*
　　Turn all her mother's pains and benefits°　　*cares and kind actions*
　　To laughter and contempt, that she may feel—
265　That she may feel
　　How sharper than a serpent's tooth it is
　　To have a thankless child.—Go, go, my people!
　　　　　　[*Exeunt* LEAR, KENT, FOOL, *and servants*]
ALBANY　Now, gods that we adore, whereof comes this?
GONORIL　Never afflict yourself to know the cause,
270　But let his disposition have that scope
　　That dotage gives it.
　　　　　　[*Enter* LEAR *and* FOOL]
LEAR　What, fifty of my followers at a clap?
　　Within a fortnight?
ALBANY　　　　　　What is the matter, sir?
LEAR　I'll tell thee. [*To* GONORIL] Life and death! I am ashamed
275　That thou hast power to shake my manhood thus,
　　That these hot tears, that break from me perforce°　　*against my will*
　　And should make thee—worst blasts and fogs upon thee!
　　Untented woundings° of a father's curse　　　　*Undressed wounds*
　　Pierce every sense about thee! Old fond° eyes,　　*foolish*

---

7. *like . . . place:* as a machine (or lever) dislocated my natural affections from their proper foundations.

LEAR	Woe that° too late repents!	*Woe to him who*
	Is it your will? Speak, sir.—Prepare my horses.	

[*Exit one or more*]

220 Ingratitude, thou marble-hearted fiend,
More hideous when thou show'st thee in a child
Than the sea-monster—

ALBANY Pray sir, be patient.

LEAR [*to* GONERIL] Detested kite,° thou liest.   *carrion-eating hawk*

225 My train are men of choice and rarest parts,°   *qualities*
That all particulars of duty know,
And in the most exact regard support
The worships of° their name. O most small fault,   *honors accorded*
How ugly didst thou in Cordelia show,

230 Which, like an engine, wrenched my frame of nature
From the fixed place,[6] drew from my heart all love,
And added to the gall! O Lear, Lear, Lear!
Beat at this gate° that let thy folly in   *(his head)*
And thy dear° judgement out.—Go, go, my people!   *precious*

235 ALBANY My lord, I am guiltless, as I am ignorant
Of what hath moved you.

LEAR   It may be so, my lord.
Hear, nature; hear, dear goddess, hear:
Suspend thy purpose if thou didst intend
To make this creature fruitful.

240 Into her womb convey sterility.
Dry up in her the organs of increase,
And from her derogate° body never spring   *debased*
A babe to honour her. If she must teem,°   *breed*
Create her child of spleen,° that it may live   *malice*

245 And be a thwart disnatured° torment to her.   *a perverse unnatural*
Let it stamp wrinkles in her brow of youth,
With cadent° tears fret° channels in her cheeks,   *flowing / carve*
Turn all her mother's pains and benefits°   *cares and kind actions*
To laughter and contempt, that she may feel—

250 That she may feel
How sharper than a serpent's tooth it is
To have a thankless child. Away, away!

Exeunt [LEAR, KENT, *and attendants*]

ALBANY Now, gods that we adore, whereof comes this?

GONERIL Never afflict yourself to know more of it,

255 But let his disposition have that scope
As° dotage gives it.   *Which*

Enter LEAR

LEAR What, fifty of my followers at a clap?
Within a fortnight?

ALBANY   What's the matter, sir?

LEAR I'll tell thee. [*To* GONERIL] Life and death! I am ashamed

260 That thou hast power to shake my manhood thus,
That these hot tears, which break from me perforce,°   *against my will*
Should make thee worth them. Blasts and fogs upon thee!
Th'untented woundings° of a father's curse   *The undressed wounds*
Pierce every sense about thee! Old fond° eyes,   *foolish*

---

6. *like . . . place:* as a machine (or lever) dislocated my natural affections from their proper foundations.

280 Beweep° this cause again I'll pluck you out   *If you weep over*
     And cast you, with the waters that you make,
     To temper° clay. Yea,   *soften*
     Is't come to this? Yet have I left a daughter
     Whom, I am sure, is kind and comfortable.°   *comforting*
285 When she shall hear this of thee, with her nails
     She'll flay thy wolvish visage. Thou shalt find
     That I'll resume the shape which thou dost think
     I have cast off for ever; thou shalt, I warrant thee.   [*Exit*]
     GONORIL   Do you mark that, my lord?
290 ALBANY   I cannot be so partial,° Gonoril,   *biased*
     To° the great love I bear you—   *Because of*
     GONORIL   Come, sir, no more.—
     You, more knave than fool, after your master!
     FOOL   Nuncle Lear, nuncle Lear, tarry, and take the fool with
     thee.
295   A fox when one has caught her,
           And such a daughter,
           Should sure° to the slaughter,   *surely be sent*
           If my cap would buy a halter.°   *collar; noose*
           So, the fool follows after.   [*Exit*]

300 GONORIL   What, Oswald, ho!
     [*Enter* OSWALD]
     OSWALD   Here, madam.
     GONORIL   What, have you writ this letter to my sister?
     OSWALD   Yes, madam.
     GONORIL   Take you some company, and away to horse.
305 Inform her full of my particular fears,
     And thereto add such reasons of your own
     As may compact° it more. Get you gone,   *compound*
     And after, your retinue.   [*Exit* OSWALD]
                Now, my lord,
     This milky gentleness and course of yours,
310 Though I dislike not, yet under pardon°   *begging your pardon*
     You're much more ataxed° for want of wisdom   *taken to task; censured*
     Than praised for harmful mildness.
     ALBANY   How far your eyes may pierce° I cannot tell.   *foresee*
     Striving to better aught,° we mar what's well.   *anything*
315 GONORIL   Nay, then—
     ALBANY   Well, well, the event.°   *Exeunt*   *let's see the outcome*

265 Beweep° this cause again I'll pluck ye out   *If you weep over*
And cast you, with the waters that you loose,°   *let loose*
To temper° clay. Ha! Let it be so.   *soften*
I have another daughter
Who, I am sure, is kind and comfortable.°   *comforting*
270 When she shall hear this of thee, with her nails
She'll flay thy wolvish visage. Thou shalt find
That I'll resume the shape which thou dost think
I have cast off for ever.   *Exit*

GONERIL   Do you mark that?
ALBANY   I cannot be so partial,° Goneril,   *biased*
275 To° the great love I bear you—   *Because of*
GONERIL   Pray you, content.° What, Oswald, ho!—   *be quiet*
You, sir, more knave than fool, after your master.
FOOL   Nuncle Lear, nuncle Lear,
Tarry, take the fool with thee.
280 A fox when one has caught her,
And such a daughter,
Should sure° to the slaughter,   *surely be sent*
If my cap would buy a halter.°   *collar; noose*
So, the fool follows after.   *Exit*
285 GONERIL   This man hath had good counsel—a hundred knights?
'Tis politic° and safe to let him keep   *prudent*
At point° a hundred knights, yes, that on every dream,   *Armed*
Each buzz,° each fancy, each complaint, dislike,   *rumor*
He may enguard° his dotage with their powers   *protect*
290 And hold our lives in mercy.—Oswald, I say!
ALBANY   Well, you may fear too far.
GONERIL   Safer than trust too far.
Let me still° take away the harms I fear,   *always*
Not° fear still to be taken. I know his heart.   *Rather than*
What he hath uttered I have writ my sister.
295 If she sustain him and his hundred knights
When I have showed th'unfitness—
                    Enter Steward [OSWALD]
                                          How now, Oswald?
What, have you writ that letter to my sister?
OSWALD   Ay, madam.
GONERIL   Take you some company, and away to horse.
300 Inform her full of my particular fear,
And thereto add such reasons of your own
As may compact° it more. Get you gone,   *compound*
And hasten your return.   [*Exit* OSWALD]
                         No, no, my lord,
This milky gentleness and course of yours,
305 Though I condemn not, yet under pardon°   *begging your pardon*
You are much more attasked° for want of wisdom   *taken to task; censured*
Than praised for harmful mildness.
ALBANY   How far your eyes may pierce° I cannot tell.   *foresee*
Striving to better, oft we mar what's well.
310 GONERIL   Nay, then—
ALBANY   Well, well, th'event.°   *Exeunt*   *let's see the outcome*

Scene 5

Enter LEAR, KENT [*disguised, and* FOOL]

LEAR [*to* KENT]   Go you before° to Gloucester[1] with these letters.   *on ahead*
Acquaint my daughter no further with anything you know than
comes from her demand out of the letter.[2] If your diligence be
not speedy, I shall be there before you.

5   KENT   I will not sleep, my lord, till I have delivered your letter.

Exit

FOOL   If a man's brains were in his heels, were't not in danger of
kibes?°   *chilblains*

LEAR   Ay, boy.

FOOL   Then, I prithee, be merry: thy wit shall ne'er go slipshod.[3]

10   LEAR   Ha, ha, ha!

FOOL   Shalt° see thy other daughter will use thee kindly, for   *Thou shalt*
though she's as like this as a crab° is like an apple, yet I   *crab apple; sour apple*
con° what I can tell.   *know*

LEAR   Why, what canst thou tell, my boy?

15   FOOL   She'll taste as like this as a crab doth to a crab. Thou canst
not tell why one's nose stands in the middle of his face?

LEAR   No.

FOOL   Why, to keep his eyes on either side 's nose, that what a
man cannot smell out, a° may spy into.   *he*

20   LEAR   I did her wrong.

FOOL   Canst tell how an oyster makes his shell?

LEAR   No.

FOOL   Nor I neither; but I can tell why a snail has a house.

LEAR   Why?

25   FOOL   Why, to put his head in, not to give it away to his daughter
and leave his horns without a case.[4]

LEAR   I will forget my nature.[5] So kind a father!
Be my horses ready?

FOOL   Thy asses° are gone about them. The reason why the   *(servants)*
30   seven stars° are no more than seven is a pretty reason.   *the Pleiades*

LEAR   Because they are not eight.

FOOL   Yes. Thou wouldst make a good fool.

LEAR   To take't again perforce[6]—monster ingratitude!

FOOL   If thou wert my fool, nuncle, I'd have thee beaten for
35   being old before thy time.

LEAR   How's that?

FOOL   Thou shouldst not have been old before thou hadst been
wise.

LEAR   O, let me not be mad, sweet heaven!
40   I would not be mad.
Keep me in temper.° I would not be mad.   *sane*

Scene 5 Location: Before Albany's castle.
1. To Gloucestershire, where Cornwall and Regan
reside.
2. *than . . . letter*: other than such questions as are
prompted by the letter.
3. Literally, your brains will not wear slippers (to warm
feet that are afflicted with chilblains); feet of any intelligence would not walk toward Regan.

4. Protective covering for his head, or concealment for
his horns (horns were the conventional sign of a cuckold). The Fool reflects the cynical view, common in the
period, that all married men are inevitably cuckolded.
5. Lose my fatherly feelings. *nature*: character.
6. To take it back by force. Lear may refer to Gonoril's
treachery, or he may be contemplating resuming his
authority.

1.5

Enter LEAR, KENT [*disguised, the First*] GENTLEMAN, *and*
FOOL

LEAR [*to the* GENTLEMAN,[1] *giving him a letter*]   Go you before° to   on ahead
    Gloucester[2] with these letters.   [*Exit* GENTLEMAN]
    [*To* KENT, *giving him a letter*] Acquaint my daughter no fur-
    ther with anything you know than comes from her demand
5   out of the letter.[3] If your diligence be not speedy, I shall be
    there afore you.

KENT   I will not sleep, my lord, till I have delivered your letter.
                                                                Exit

FOOL   If a man's brains were in's heels, were't not in danger of
    kibes?°   *chilblains*

10 LEAR   Ay, boy.

FOOL   Then, I prithee, be merry: thy wit shall not go slipshod.[4]

LEAR   Ha, ha, ha!

FOOL   Shalt° see thy other daughter will use thee kindly, for   *Thou shalt*
    though she's as like this as a crab's° like an apple, yet I can tell *crab apple; sour apple*
15 what I can tell.

LEAR   What canst tell, boy?

FOOL   She will taste as like this as a crab does to a crab. Thou
    canst tell why one's nose stands i'th' middle on 's° face?   *of one's*

LEAR   No.

20 FOOL   Why, to keep one's eyes of either side 's nose, that what a
    man cannot smell out, a° may spy into.   *he*

LEAR   I did her wrong.

FOOL   Canst tell how an oyster makes his shell?

LEAR   No.

25 FOOL   Nor I neither; but I can tell why a snail has a house.

LEAR   Why?

FOOL   Why, to put 's head in, not to give it away to his daughters
    and leave his horns without a case.[5]

LEAR   I will forget my nature.[6] So kind a father!

30 Be my horses ready?

FOOL   Thy asses° are gone about 'em. The reason why the seven   *(servants)*
    stars° are no more than seven is a pretty reason.   *the Pleiades*

LEAR   Because they are not eight.

FOOL   Yes, indeed, thou wouldst make a good fool.

35 LEAR   To take't again perforce[7]—monster ingratitude!

FOOL   If thou wert my fool, nuncle, I'd have thee beaten for
    being old before thy time.

LEAR   How's that?

FOOL   Thou shouldst not have been old till thou hadst been
40 wise.

LEAR   O, let me not be mad, not mad, sweet heaven!
    Keep me in temper.° I would not be mad.   *sane*

1.5 Location: Before Albany's castle.
1. Most editors address this entire speech to Kent,
since in Q the first gentleman does not appear here.
2. To Gloucestershire, where Cornwall and Regan
reside.
3. *than . . . letter:* other than such questions as are
prompted by the letter.
4. Literally, your brains will not wear slippers (to warm
feet that are afflicted with chilblains); feet of any intel-

ligence would not walk toward Regan.
5. Protective covering for his head, or concealment for
his horns (horns were the conventional sign of a cuckold). The Fool reflects the cynical view, common in the
period, that all married men are inevitably cuckolded.
6. Lose my fatherly feelings. *nature:* character.
7. To take it back by force. Lear may refer to Goneril's
treachery, or he may be contemplating resuming his
authority.

[*Enter a* SERVANT]

Are the horses ready?

SERVANT   Ready, my lord.

LEAR [*to* FOOL]   Come, boy.   *Exeunt* [LEAR *and* SERVANT]

FOOL   She that is maid now, and laughs at my departure,

45   Shall not be a maid long, except things be cut shorter.[7]   *Exit*

Scene 6

Enter Bastard [EDMUND] *and* CURAN, *meeting*

EDMUND   Save° thee, Curan.   God save

CURAN   And you, sir. I have been with your father, and given
     him notice that the Duke of Cornwall and his duchess will be
     here with him tonight.

5   EDMUND   How comes that?

CURAN   Nay, I know not. You have heard of the news abroad?—
     I mean the whispered ones, for there are yet but ear-bussing
     arguments.[1]

EDMUND   Not. I pray you, what are they?

10   CURAN   Have you heard of no likely wars towards° twixt the two   impending
     Dukes of Cornwall and Albany?

EDMUND   Not a word.

CURAN   You may then in time. Fare you well, sir.   [*Exit*]

EDMUND   The Duke be here tonight! The better, best.

15   This weaves itself perforce° into my business.   necessarily

          Enter EDGAR [*at a window above*]

     My father hath set guard to take my brother,
     And I have one thing of a queasy question[2]
     Which must ask briefness. Wit and fortune help!—
     Brother, a word. Descend, brother, I say.

          [EDGAR *climbs down*]

20   My father watches. O, fly this place.
     Intelligence is given where you are hid.
     You have now the good advantage of the night.
     Have you not spoken 'gainst the Duke of Cornwall aught?°   anything
     He's coming hither now, in the night, i'th' haste,

25   And Regan with him. Have you nothing said
     Upon his party° against the Duke of Albany?   On his (Cornwall's) side
     Advise you°—   Consider carefully

EDGAR   I am sure on't,° not a word.   of it

EDMUND   I hear my father coming. Pardon me.
     In cunning I must draw my sword upon you.

30   Seem to defend yourself. Now, quit you° well.   acquit yourself
     [*Calling*]   Yield, come before my father. Light here, here!
     [*To* EDGAR] Fly, brother, fly! [*Calling*] Torches, torches! [*To*
          EDGAR] So, farewell.   [*Exit* EDGAR]
     Some blood drawn on me would beget opinion°   produce the impression
     Of my more fierce endeavour.

          He wounds his arm

---

7. *She . . . shorter:* A girl who would laugh at my leaving
would be so foolish that she could not remain a virgin for
long; "things" refers both to the unfolding event and to
penises.

Scene 6 Location: Gloucester's castle.
1. Barely whispered affairs. *bussing:* buzzing.
2. And I have a hazardous and delicate problem.

[*Enter the* FIRST GENTLEMAN]

How now, are the horses ready?

FIRST GENTLEMAN   Ready, my lord.

LEAR [*to* FOOL]   Come, boy.

45   FOOL   She that's a maid now, and laughs at my departure,
      Shall not be a maid long, unless things be cut shorter.[8]

Exeunt

2.1

Enter Bastard [EDMOND] *and* CURAN, *severally*

EDMOND   Save° thee, Curan.   *God save*

CURAN   And you, sir. I have been with your father, and given
      him notice that the Duke of Cornwall and Regan his duchess
      will be here with him this night.

5   EDMOND   How comes that?

CURAN   Nay, I know not. You have heard of the news abroad?—
      I mean the whispered ones, for they are yet but ear-kissing
      arguments.[1]

EDMOND   Not I. Pray you, what are they?

10   CURAN   Have you heard of no likely wars toward° twixt the Dukes   *impending*
      of Cornwall and Albany?

EDMOND   Not a word.

CURAN   You may do then in time. Fare you well, sir.   *Exit*

EDMOND   The Duke be here tonight! The better, best.

15   This weaves itself perforce° into my business.   *necessarily*

Enter EDGAR [*at a window above*]

My father hath set guard to take my brother,
And I have one thing of a queasy question[2]
Which I must act. Briefness and fortune work!°—   *be with me*
Brother, a word, descend. Brother, I say.

[EDGAR *climbs down*]

20   My father watches. O sir, fly this place.
Intelligence is given where you are hid.
You have now the good advantage of the night.
Have you not spoken 'gainst the Duke of Cornwall?
He's coming hither, now, i'th' night, i'th' haste,

25   And Regan with him. Have you nothing said
Upon his party° 'gainst the Duke of Albany?   *On his (Cornwall's) side*
Advise yourself.°   *Consider carefully*

EDGAR   I am sure on't,° not a word.   *of it*

EDMOND   I hear my father coming. Pardon me.
In cunning I must draw my sword upon you.

30   Draw. Seem to defend yourself. Now, quit you° well.   *acquit yourself*
[*Calling*] Yield, come before my father. Light ho, here!
[*To* EDGAR] Fly, brother! [*Calling*] Torches, torches!
[*To* EDGAR]   So, farewell.

Exit EDGAR

Some blood drawn on me would beget opinion°   *produce the impression*
Of my more fierce endeavour.

[*He wounds his arm*]

---

8. *She . . . shorter:* A girl who would laugh at my leaving would be so foolish that she could not remain a virgin for long; "things" refers both to the unfolding event
and to penises.

2.1 Location: Gloucester's castle.
1. Barely whispered affairs.
2. And I have a hazardous and delicate problem.

I have seen
35 Drunkards do more than this in sport. [*Calling*] Father, father!
Stop, stop! Ho, help!

Enter GLOUCESTER [*and others*]

GLOUCESTER   Now, Edmund, where is the villain?
EDMUND   Here stood he in the dark, his sharp sword out,
Warbling of wicked charms, conjuring the moon
To stand 's° auspicious mistress.   *To act as his*
GLOUCESTER   But where is he?
EDMUND   Look, sir, I bleed.
40 GLOUCESTER   Where is the villain, Edmund?
EDMUND   Fled this way, sir, when by no means he could—
GLOUCESTER   Pursue him, go after.   [*Exeunt others*]
By no means what?
EDMUND   Persuade me to the murder of your lordship,
But that° I told him the revengive gods   *In response to that*
45 'Gainst parricides did all their thunders bend,
Spoke with how manifold and strong a bond
The child was bound to the father. Sir, in fine,°   *finally*
Seeing how loathly opposite° I stood   *opposed*
To his unnatural purpose, with fell° motion,   *deadly*
50 With his preparèd sword he charges home°   *strikes to the heart of*
My unprovided° body, lanced° mine arm;   *unprotected / struck*
But when he saw my best alarumed spirits
Bold in the quarrel's rights,[3] roused to the encounter,
Or° whether ghasted° by the noise I made   *Either / frightened*
55 Or [   ] I know not,[4]
But suddenly he fled.
GLOUCESTER   Let him fly far,
Not in this land shall he remain uncaught,
And found, dispatch.° The noble Duke my master,   *And once found, killed*
My worthy arch° and patron, comes tonight.   *lord*
60 By his authority I will proclaim it
That he which finds him shall deserve our thanks,
Bringing the murderous caitiff° to the stake;[5]   *wretch*
He that conceals him, death.
EDMUND   When I dissuaded him from his intent
65 And found him pitched° to do it, with curst° speech   *resolved / bitter*
I threatened to discover° him. He replied,   *expose*
'Thou unpossessing bastard, dost thou think
If I would stand against thee, could the reposure°   *placing*
Of any trust, virtue, or worth in thee
70 Make thy words faithed?° No, what I should deny—   *credible*
As this I would, ay, though thou didst produce
My very character[6]—I'd turn it all
To[7] thy suggestion, plot, and damned pretence,°   *intent*
And thou must make a dullard of the world
75 If they not thought the profits of my death

I have seen drunkards
35   Do more than this in sport. [*Calling*] Father, father!
      Stop, stop! Ho, help!
          Enter GLOUCESTER, *and servants with torches*
GLOUCESTER   Now, Edmond, where's the villain?
EDMOND   Here stood he in the dark, his sharp sword out,
      Mumbling of wicked charms, conjuring the moon
      To stand 's° auspicious mistress.   *To act as his*
GLOUCESTER   But where is he?
EDMOND   Look, sir, I bleed.
40 GLOUCESTER   Where is the villain, Edmond?
EDMOND   Fled this way, sir, when by no means he could—
GLOUCESTER   Pursue him, ho! Go after.   [*Exeunt servants*]
                    By no means what?
EDMOND   Persuade me to the murder of your lordship,
      But that° I told him the revenging gods   *In response to that*
45   'Gainst parricides did all the thunder bend,
      Spoke with how manifold and strong a bond
      The child was bound to th' father. Sir, in fine,°   *finally*
      Seeing how loathly opposite° I stood   *opposed*
      To his unnatural purpose, in fell° motion   *deadly*
50   With his preparèd sword he charges home°   *strikes to the heart of*
      My unprovided° body, latched° mine arm;   *unprotected / struck*
      And when he saw my best alarumed spirits
      Bold in the quarrel's right,[3] roused to th'encounter,
      Or whether ghasted° by the noise I made,   *frightened*
      Full suddenly he fled.
55 GLOUCESTER   Let him fly far,
      Not in this land shall he remain uncaught,
      And found, dispatch.° The noble Duke my master,   *And once found, killed*
      My worthy arch° and patron, comes tonight.   *lord*
      By his authority I will proclaim it
60   That he which finds him shall deserve our thanks,
      Bringing the murderous coward to the stake;[4]
      He that conceals him, death.
EDMOND   When I dissuaded him from his intent
      And found him pitched° to do it, with curst° speech   *resolved / bitter*
65   I threatened to discover° him. He replied,   *expose*
      'Thou unpossessing bastard, dost thou think
      If I would stand against thee, would the reposal°   *placing*
      Of any trust, virtue, or worth in thee
      Make thy words faithed?° No, what I should deny—   *credible*
70   As this I would, ay, though thou didst produce
      My very character[5]—I'd turn it all
      To[6] thy suggestion, plot, and damnèd practice,°   *scheming*
      And thou must make a dullard of the world
      If they not thought the profits of my death

---

3. *my best . . . right:* that I was fully roused to action,   5. Handwriting; but also, a true summary of my char-
made brave by righteousness.   acter.
4. Treachery and rebellion were crimes for which one   6. *I'd . . . / To:* I'd blame it all on.
could be burned.

Were very pregnant and potential spurs

To make thee seek it.'[8]

GLOUCESTER   Strong° and fastened° villain!   *Flagrant / incorrigible*

Would he deny his letter? I never got° him.   *begot*

[*Trumpets within*]

Hark, the Duke's trumpets. I know not why he comes.

80   All ports° I'll bar. The villain shall not scape.   *seaports; exits*

The Duke must grant me that; besides, his picture

I will send far and near, that all the kingdom

May have note of him[9]—and of my land,

Loyal and natural° boy, I'll work the means   *loving; illegitimate*

85   To make thee capable.°   *legally able to inherit*

         Enter the Duke of CORNWALL [*and* REGAN]

CORNWALL   How now, my noble friend? Since I came hither,

Which I can call but now, I have heard strange news.

REGAN   If it be true, all vengeance comes too short

Which can pursue the offender. How dost, my lord?

90   GLOUCESTER   Madam, my old heart is cracked, is cracked.

REGAN   What, did my father's godson seek your life?

He whom my father named, your Edgar?

GLOUCESTER   Ay, lady, lady; shame would have it hid.

REGAN   Was he not companion with the riotous knights

95   That tend° upon my father?   *attend*

GLOUCESTER   I know not, madam. 'Tis too bad, too bad.

EDMUND   Yes, madam, he was.

REGAN   No marvel, then, though° he were ill affected.°   *that / ill disposed*

'Tis they have put him on° the old man's death,   *have urged him to seek*

100   To have the spoil and waste of his revenues.

I have this present evening from my sister

Been well informed of them, and with such cautions

That if they come to sojourn at my house

I'll not be there.

CORNWALL   Nor I, assure thee, Regan.

105   Edmund, I heard that you have shown your father

A childlike office.°   *filial service*

EDMUND   'Twas my duty, sir.

GLOUCESTER [*to* CORNWALL]   He did betray his practice,°   *uncover his (Edgar's) plot*

      and received

This hurt you see striving to apprehend him.

CORNWALL   Is he pursued?

GLOUCESTER   Ay, my good lord.

110   CORNWALL   If he be taken, he shall never more

Be feared of doing harm. Make your own purpose

How in my strength you please.[1] For you, Edmund,

Whose virtue and obedience doth this instant

So much commend itself, you shall be ours.

115   Natures of such deep trust we shall much need.

You we first seize on.

EDMUND   I shall serve you truly,

However else.°   *If nothing else*

GLOUCESTER [*to* CORNWALL]   For him I thank your grace.

---

8. *And thou . . . it:* And do you think the world so stupid that it could not see the benefit you would get from my death (and thus a motive for plotting to kill me)? *pregnant:* full. *potential spurs:* powerful temptations.
9. Likenesses of outlaws were drawn up, printed, and publicly displayed, sometimes with an offer of reward as in "Wanted" posters.
1. *Make . . . please:* Devise your plots making use of my forces and authority as you see fit.

75   Were very pregnant and potential spirits
      To make thee seek it.'[7]
GLOUCESTER   O strange° and fastened° villain!   *unnatural / incorrigible*
      Would he deny his letter, said he?
            Tucket° within   *Flourish of trumpets*
      Hark, the Duke's trumpets. I know not why he comes.
      All ports° I'll bar. The villain shall not scape.   *seaports; exits*
80   The Duke must grant me that; besides, his picture
      I will send far and near, that all the kingdom
      May have due note of him[8]—and of my land,
      Loyal and natural° boy, I'll work the means   *loving; illegitimate*
      To make thee capable.°   *legally able to inherit*
            Enter CORNWALL, REGAN, *and attendants*
85 CORNWALL   How now, my noble friend? Since I came hither,
      Which I can call but now, I have heard strange news.
REGAN   If it be true, all vengeance comes too short
      Which can pursue th'offender. How dost, my lord?
GLOUCESTER   O madam, my old heart is cracked, it's cracked.
90 REGAN   What, did my father's godson seek your life?
      He whom my father named, your Edgar?
GLOUCESTER   O lady, lady, shame would have it hid!
REGAN   Was he not companion with the riotous knights
      That tend° upon my father?   *attend*
95 GLOUCESTER   I know not, madam. 'Tis too bad, too bad.
EDMOND   Yes, madam, he was of that consort.°   *company*
REGAN   No marvel, then, though° he were ill affected.°   *that / ill disposed*
      'Tis they have put him on° the old man's death,   *have urged him to seek*
      To have th'expense° and spoil of his revenues.   *use*
100   I have this present evening from my sister
      Been well informed of them, and with such cautions
      That if they come to sojourn at my house
      I'll not be there.
CORNWALL   Nor I, assure thee, Regan.
      Edmond, I hear that you have shown your father
      A childlike office.°   *filial service*
105 EDMOND   It was my duty, sir.
GLOUCESTER [*to* CORNWALL]   He did bewray his practice,°   *uncover his (Edgar's) plot*
            and received
      This hurt you see striving to apprehend him.
CORNWALL   Is he pursued?
GLOUCESTER   Ay, my good lord.
CORNWALL   If he be taken, he shall never more
110   Be feared of doing harm. Make your own purpose
      How in my strength you please.[9] For you, Edmond,
      Whose virtue and obedience doth this instant
      So much commend itself, you shall be ours.
      Natures of such deep trust we shall much need.
      You we first seize on.
115 EDMOND   I shall serve you, sir,
      Truly, however else.°   *if nothing else*
GLOUCESTER [*to* CORNWALL]   For him I thank your grace.

---

7. *And thou . . . it:* And do you think the world so stupid that it could not see the benefit you would get from
my death (and thus a motive for plotting to kill me)?
pregnant: full. *potential spirits:* powerful temptations.
8. Likenesses of outlaws were drawn up, printed, and

publicly displayed, sometimes with an offer of reward
as in "Wanted" posters.
9. *Make . . . please:* Devise your plots making use of my
forces and authority as you see fit.

CORNWALL   You know not why we came to visit you—
REGAN   This out-of-season threat'ning dark-eyed night—
120   Occasions, noble Gloucester, of some poise,°   weight
Wherein we must have use of your advice.
Our father he hath writ, so hath our sister,
Of differences° which I least thought it fit   quarrels
To answer from our home. The several° messengers   various
125   From hence attend° dispatch. Our good old friend,   await
Lay comforts to your bosom, and bestow
Your needful° counsel to our business,   badly needed
Which craves the instant use.[2]
GLOUCESTER   I serve you, madam.
130   Your graces are right welcome.   *Exeunt*

Scene 7

Enter KENT, [*disguised, at one door,*] *and* Steward
[OSWALD *at another door*]

OSWALD   Good even° to thee, friend. Art° of the house?   evening / Are you a servant
KENT   Ay.
OSWALD   Where may we set our horses?
KENT   I'th' mire.
5   OSWALD   Prithee, if thou love me,° tell me.   if you will be so kind
KENT   I love thee not.
OSWALD   Why then, I care not for thee.
KENT   If I had thee in Lipsbury pinfold[1] I would make thee care
for me.
10   OSWALD   Why dost thou use° me thus? I know thee not.   treat
KENT   Fellow, I know thee.
OSWALD   What dost thou know me for?
KENT   A knave, a rascal, an eater of broken meats,° a base, proud,   scraps
shallow, beggarly, three-suited, hundred-pound, filthy worsted-
15   stocking knave;[2] a lily-livered, action-taking knave; a whoreson,
glass-gazing, superfinical rogue; one-trunk-inheriting slave;[3]
one that wouldst be a bawd in way of good service,[4] and art
nothing but the composition° of a knave, beggar, coward, pan-   combination
der, and the son and heir of a mongrel bitch, whom I will beat
20   into clamorous whining if thou deny the least syllable of the
addition.[5]
OSWALD   What a monstrous fellow art thou, thus to rail on one
that's neither known of° thee nor knows thee!   by
KENT   What a brazen-faced varlet° art thou, to deny thou   rascal
25   knowest me! Is it two days ago since I beat thee and tripped
up thy heels before the King? Draw, you rogue; for though it
be night, the moon shines.
[*He draws his sword*]

---

2. Which requires immediate attention.
Scene 7 Location: Before Gloucester's house.
1. If I had you in the enclosure of my mouth (gripped in my teeth). Lipsbury is probably an invented place-name. *pinfold:* pen, animal enclosure.
2. *three-suited . . . knave:* Oswald is being called a poor imitation of a gentleman. Servants were permitted three suits a year; one hundred pounds was the minimum qualification for the purchase of one of King James's knighthoods; a gentleman would wear silk, not

"worsted" (of thick woolen material), stockings.
3. *lily-livered:* cowardly. *action-taking:* litigious, one who would rather use the law than his fists. *glass-gazing:* mirror-gazing. *superfinical:* overly finicky, fastidious. *one-trunk-inheriting:* owning only what would fill one trunk.
4. *one that . . . service:* one who would even be a pimp if called upon.
5. Of the descriptions Kent has just applied to him. *addition:* title (used ironically).

CORNWALL   You know not why we came to visit you—

REGAN   Thus out of season, threading dark-eyed night—

120 Occasions, noble Gloucester, of some poise,° *weight*
Wherein we must have use of your advice.
Our father he hath writ, so hath our sister,
Of differences° which I least thought it fit *quarrels*
To answer from our home. The several° messengers *various*

125 From hence attend° dispatch. Our good old friend, *await*
Lay comforts to your bosom, and bestow
Your needful° counsel to our businesses, *badly needed*
Which craves the instant use.[1]

GLOUCESTER   I serve you, madam.

130 Your graces are right welcome. *Flourish. Exeunt*

2.2
Enter KENT, [*disguised,*] *and Steward* [OSWALD], *severally*

OSWALD   Good dawning to thee, friend. Art° of this house? *Are you a servant*

KENT   Ay.

OSWALD   Where may we set our horses?

KENT   I'th' mire.

5 OSWALD   Prithee, if thou lov'st me,° tell me. *if you will be so kind*

KENT   I love thee not.

OSWALD   Why then, I care not for thee.

KENT   If I had thee in Lipsbury pinfold[1] I would make thee care
for me.

10 OSWALD   Why dost thou use° me thus? I know thee not. *treat*

KENT   Fellow, I know thee.

OSWALD   What dost thou know me for?

KENT   A knave, a rascal, an eater of broken meats,° a base, proud, *scraps*
shallow, beggarly, three-suited, hundred-pound, filthy worsted-

15 stocking knave;[2] a lily-livered, action-taking, whoreson, glass-
gazing, super-serviceable, finical rogue; one-trunk-inheriting
slave;[3] one that wouldst be a bawd in way of good service,[4] and
art nothing but the composition° of a knave, beggar, coward, *combination*
pander, and the son and heir of a mongrel bitch, one whom I

20 will beat into clamorous whining if thou deniest the least syllable of thy addition.[5]

OSWALD   Why, what a monstrous fellow art thou, thus to rail on
one that is neither known of° thee nor knows thee! *by*

KENT   What a brazen-faced varlet° art thou, to deny thou *rascal*

25 knowest me! Is it two days since I tripped up thy heels and
beat thee before the King? Draw, you rogue; for though it be
night, yet the moon shines.
[*He draws his sword*]

---

1. Which require immediate attention.
2.2 Location: Before Gloucester's house.
1. If I had you in the enclosure of my mouth (gripped
in my teeth). Lipsbury is probably an invented place-
name. *pinfold:* pen, animal enclosure.
2. *three-suited . . . knave:* Oswald is being called a poor
imitation of a gentleman. Servants were permitted
three suits a year; one hundred pounds was the minimum qualification for the purchase of one of King
James's knighthoods; a gentleman would wear silk, not

"worsted" (of thick woolen material), stockings.
3. *lily-livered:* cowardly. *action-taking:* litigious, one who
would rather use the law than his fists. *glass-gazing:*
mirror-gazing. *super-serviceable:* overly officious, or too
ready to serve. *finical:* finicky, fastidious. *one-trunk-
inheriting:* owning only what would fill one trunk.
4. *one that . . . service:* one who would even be a pimp
if called upon.
5. Of the descriptions Kent has just applied to him.
addition: title (used ironically).

I'll make a sop of the moonshine[6] o'you. Draw, you whoreson,
cullionly barber-monger,[7] draw!

30 OSWALD   Away. I have nothing to do with thee.

KENT   Draw, you rascal. You bring letters against the King, and
take Vanity the puppet's part against the royalty of her father.[8]
Draw, you rogue, or I'll so carbonado[9] your shanks—draw, you
rascal, come your ways!°   come forward

35 OSWALD   Help, ho, murder, help!

KENT   Strike, you slave! Stand, rogue! Stand, you neat° slave,   elegant; foppish
strike!

OSWALD   Help, ho, murder, help!

Enter EDMUND *with his rapier drawn,* [*then*] GLOUCES-
TER, [*then*] *the Duke* [CORNWALL] *and Duchess*
[REGAN]

EDMUND [*parting them*]   How now, what's the matter?

40 KENT   With you, goodman boy. An° you please come, I'll flesh   If
you.[1] Come on, young master.

GLOUCESTER   Weapons? Arms? What's the matter here?

CORNWALL   Keep peace, upon your lives. He dies that strikes
again. What's the matter?

45 REGAN   The messengers from our sister and the King.

CORNWALL [*to* KENT *and* OSWALD]   What's your difference?°   quarrel
Speak.

OSWALD   I am scarce in breath, my lord.

KENT   No marvel, you have so bestirred your valour, you cow-
50 ardly rascal. Nature disclaims° in thee; a tailor[2] made thee.   disowns her part

CORNWALL   Thou art a strange fellow—a tailor make a man?

KENT   Ay, a tailor, sir. A stone-cutter or a painter could not have
made him so ill° though he had been but two hours at the   so badly
trade.

55 GLOUCESTER   Speak yet; how grew your quarrel?

OSWALD   This ancient ruffian, sir, whose life I have spared at
suit of° his grey beard—   on account of

KENT   Thou whoreson Z,[3] thou unnecessary letter—[*to* CORN-
WALL] my lord, if you'll give me leave I will tread this unboulted°   unsifted; coarse
60 villain into mortar and daub the walls of a jakes° with him. [*To*   privy; toilet
OSWALD] Spare my grey beard, you wagtail?[4]

CORNWALL   Peace, sir. You beastly knave, have you no
reverence?°   respect

KENT   Yes, sir, but anger has a privilege.

65 CORNWALL   Why art thou angry?

KENT   That such a slave as this should wear a sword,
That° wears no honesty. Such smiling rogues   Who
As these, like rats, oft bite those cords[5] in twain
Which are too entrenched° to unloose, smooth° every passion   intricate / flatter
70 That in the natures of their lords rebel,

---

6. Kent proposes so to skewer and pierce Oswald that
his body might soak up moonlight. *sop*: piece of bread
to be steeped or dunked in soup.
7. *cullionly barber-monger*: despicable frequenter of
hairdressers. *cullion*: testicle.
8. *and take . . . father*: and support Gonoril, here depicted as a dressed-up doll whose pride is contrasted
with Lear's kingliness.
9. Slash or score as one would the surface of meat in
preparation for broiling.

1. I'll initiate you into fighting, as a hunting dog is
given the taste of blood to rouse it for the chase.
2. Tailors, considered effeminate, were stock objects of
mockery.
3. The letter Z (zed) was considered superfluous and
omitted from many dictionaries.
4. A common English bird that takes its name from the
up-and-down flicking of its tail; this, and its characteristic hopping from foot to foot, causes it to appear nervous.
5. Bonds of kinship, affection, marriage, or rank.

I'll make a sop o'th' moonshine of you,[6] you whoreson, cullionly barber-monger,[7] draw!

30 OSWALD   Away. I have nothing to do with thee.

KENT   Draw, you rascal. You come with letters against the King, and
take Vanity the puppet's part against the royalty of her father.[8]
Draw, you rogue, or I'll so carbonado[9] your shanks—draw, you
rascal, come your ways!°   *come forward*

35 OSWALD   Help, ho, murder, help!

KENT   Strike, you slave! Stand, rogue! Stand, you neat° slave,   *elegant; foppish*
strike!

OSWALD   Help, ho, murder, murder!

     Enter Bastard [EDMOND], [*then*] CORNWALL, REGAN,
     GLOUCESTER, [*and*] *servants*

EDMOND   How now, what's the matter? Part.

40 KENT   With you, goodman boy. If you please, come, I'll flesh
ye.[1] Come on, young master.

GLOUCESTER   Weapons? Arms? What's the matter here?

CORNWALL   Keep peace, upon your lives. He dies that strikes
again. What is the matter?

45 REGAN   The messengers from our sister and the King.

CORNWALL [*to* KENT *and* OSWALD]   What is your difference?°   *quarrel*
Speak.

OSWALD   I am scarce in breath, my lord.

KENT   No marvel, you have so bestirred your valour, you cow-
50 ardly rascal. Nature disclaims° in thee; a tailor[2] made thee.   *disowns her part*

CORNWALL   Thou art a strange fellow—a tailor make a man?

KENT   A tailor, sir. A stone-cutter or a painter could not have
made him so ill° though they had been but two years o'th'°   *so badly / at the*
trade.

55 CORNWALL   Speak yet; how grew your quarrel?

OSWALD   This ancient ruffian, sir, whose life I have spared at suit
of° his grey beard—   *on account of*

KENT   Thou whoreson Z,[3] thou unnecessary letter—[*to* CORN-
WALL] my lord, if you'll give me leave I will tread this unbolted°   *unsifted; coarse*
60 villain into mortar and daub the wall of a jakes° with him. [*To*   *privy; toilet*
OSWALD] Spare my grey beard, you wagtail?[4]

CORNWALL   Peace, sirrah.
You beastly knave, know you no reverence?°   *respect*

KENT   Yes, sir, but anger hath a privilege.

65 CORNWALL   Why art thou angry?

KENT   That such a slave as this should wear a sword,
Who wears no honesty. Such smiling rogues as these,
Like rats, oft bite the holy cords[5] a-twain
Which are too intrince° t'unloose, smooth° every passion   *intricate / flatter*
70 That in the natures of their lords rebel;

---

6. Kent proposes so to skewer and pierce Oswald that
his body might soak up moonlight. *sop*: piece of bread
to be steeped or dunked in soup.
7. *cullionly barber-monger*: despicable frequenter of
hairdressers. *cullion*: testicle.
8. *and take . . . father*: and support Goneril, here
depicted as a dressed-up doll whose pride is contrasted
with Lear's kingliness.
9. Slash or score as one would the surface of meat in
preparation for broiling.

1. I'll initiate you into fighting, as a hunting dog is
given the taste of blood to rouse it for the chase.
2. Tailors, considered effeminate, were stock objects of
mockery.
3. The letter Z (zed) was considered superfluous and
omitted from many dictionaries.
4. A common English bird that takes its name from the
up-and-down flicking of its tail; this, and its characteristic hopping from foot to foot, causes it to appear nervous.
5. Bonds of kinship, affection, marriage, or rank.

Bring oil to fire, snow to their colder moods,
Renege,° affirm, and turn their halcyon beaks⁶   *Deny*
With every gale and vary° of their masters,   *mood*
Knowing naught, like dogs, but following.
75   [*To* OSWALD] A plague upon your epileptic° visage!   *distorted; grimacing*
Smile you° my speeches as° I were a fool?   *Do you smile at / as if*
Goose, an I had you upon Sarum Plain
I'd send you cackling home to Camelot.⁷

CORNWALL   What, art thou mad, old fellow?

GLOUCESTER [*to* KENT]   How fell you out?
80   Say that.

KENT   No contraries° hold more antipathy   *opposites*
Than I and such a knave.

CORNWALL   Why dost thou call him knave?
What's his offence?

KENT   His countenance likes° me not.   *pleases*

CORNWALL   No more perchance does mine, or his, or hers.
85   KENT   Sir, 'tis my occupation to be plain:
I have seen better faces in my time
Than stands on any shoulder that I see
Before me at this instant.

CORNWALL   This is a fellow
Who, having been praised for bluntness, doth affect
90   A saucy roughness, and constrains the garb
Quite from his nature.⁸ He cannot flatter, he.
He must be plain, he must speak truth.
An they will take't, so; if not, he's plain.⁹
These kind of knaves I know, which in this plainness
95   Harbour more craft and more corrupter ends
Than twenty silly-ducking observants
That stretch their duties nicely.¹

KENT   Sir, in good sooth, or in sincere verity,
Under the allowance of your grand aspect,²
100   Whose influence, like the wreath of radiant fire
In flickering Phoebus' front°—   *the sun god's forehead*

CORNWALL   What mean'st thou by this?

KENT   To go out of my dialect,° which you discommend so   *normal mode of speech*
much. I know, sir, I am no flatterer. He that beguiled you in a
plain accent was a plain knave, which for my part I will not
105   be, though I should win your displeasure to entreat me to't.³

CORNWALL [*to* OSWALD]   What's the offence you gave him?

6. It was believed that the kingfisher (in Greek, *halcyon*) could be used as a weather vane when dead: suspended by a fine thread, its beak would turn whatever way the wind blew.

7. *Goose . . . Camelot:* Comparing him to a cackling goose, Kent tells Oswald that if he had him on Salisbury Plain, he would drive him all the way to Camelot, legendary home of King Arthur.

8. *and constrains . . . nature:* and assumes the appearance though it is untrue to his real self. Alternatively (with "his" meaning "its"), and distorts the true shape of plainness from what it naturally is (by turning it into disrespect).

9. If they will accept (Kent's attitude), well and good;

if not, he is a plainspoken man (and does not care).

1. *Than . . . nicely:* Than twenty obsequious attendants who constantly bow idiotically, and who perform their functions with excessive diligence ("nicely").

2. With the permission of your great countenance. "Aspect" also refers to the astrological position of a planet; Kent's bombastic language here raises Cornwall to the mock-heroic proportions of a heavenly body.

3. *He that . . . to't:* The person who tried to hoodwink you with plain speaking was, indeed, a pure knave—something I won't be, even if you were to beg me to be one (a plain knave, or flatterer).

Being oil to fire, snow to the colder moods,
Renege,° affirm, and turn their halcyon beaks[6]   *Deny*
With every gall and vary° of their masters,   *irritation and mood*
Knowing naught, like dogs, but following.
75 [*To* OSWALD] A plague upon your epileptic° visage!   *distorted; grimacing*
Smile you° my speeches as° I were a fool?   *Do you smile at / as if*
Goose, an I had you upon Sarum Plain
I'd drive ye cackling home to Camelot.[7]

CORNWALL What, art thou mad, old fellow?
GLOUCESTER [*to* KENT]   How fell you out?
80 Say that.
KENT No contraries° hold more antipathy   *opposites*
Than I and such a knave.
CORNWALL   Why dost thou call him knave?
What is his fault?°   *offense*
KENT   His countenance likes° me not.   *pleases*
CORNWALL No more perchance does mine, nor his, nor hers.
85 KENT Sir, 'tis my occupation to be plain:
I have seen better faces in my time
Than stands on any shoulder that I see
Before me at this instant.
CORNWALL   This is some fellow
Who, having been praised for bluntness, doth affect
90 A saucy roughness, and constrains the garb
Quite from his nature.[8] He cannot flatter, he;
An honest mind and plain, he must speak truth.
An they will take't, so; if not, he's plain.[9]
These kind of knaves I know, which in this plainness
95 Harbour more craft and more corrupter ends
Than twenty silly-ducking observants
That stretch their duties nicely.[1]
KENT Sir, in good faith, in sincere verity,
Under th'allowance of your great aspect,[2]
100 Whose influence, like the wreath of radiant fire
On flick'ring Phoebus' front°—   *the sun god's forehead*
CORNWALL   What mean'st by this?
KENT To go out of my dialect,° which you discommend so   *normal mode of speech*
much. I know, sir, I am no flatterer. He that beguiled you in
a plain accent was a plain knave, which for my part I will not be,
105 though I should win your displeasure to entreat me to't.[3]
CORNWALL [*to* OSWALD] What was th'offence you gave him?

---

6. It was believed that the kingfisher (in Greek, *hal-cyon*) could be used as a weather vane when dead: sus-pended by a fine thread, its beak would turn whatever way the wind blew.
7. *Goose . . . Camelot*: Comparing him to a cackling goose, Kent tells Oswald that if he had him on Salisbury Plain, he would drive him all the way to Camelot, leg-endary home of King Arthur.
8. *and constrains . . . nature*: and assumes the appearance though it is untrue to his real self. Alternatively (with "his" meaning "its"), and distorts the true shape of plainness from what it naturally is (by turning it into disrespect).
9. If they will accept (Kent's attitude), well and good; if

not, he is a plainspoken man (and does not care).
1. *Than . . . nicely*: Than twenty obsequious atten-dants who constantly bow idiotically, and who perform their functions with excessive diligence ("nicely").
2. With the permission of your great countenance. "Aspect" also refers to the astrological position of a planet; Kent's bombastic language here raises Cornwall to the mock-heroic proportions of a heavenly body.
3. *He that . . . to't*: The person who tried to hoodwink you with plain speaking was, indeed, a pure knave—something I won't be, even if you were to beg me to be one (a plain knave, or flatterer).

OSWALD   I never gave him any.
It pleased the King his master very late°   *lately*
To strike at me upon his misconstruction,°   *misunderstanding (me)*
When he, conjunct,° and flattering his displeasure,   *in league with*
110   Tripped me behind; being down, insulted,° railed,   *I being down, he insulted*
And put upon him such a deal of man
That worthied him,⁴ got praises of the King
For him attempting who was self-subdued,⁵
And in the fleshment° of this dread exploit   *excitement; flush*
Drew on me here again.
115   KENT   None of these rogues and cowards
But Ajax is their fool.⁶
CORNWALL [*calling*]   Bring forth the stocks, ho!—
You stubborn, ancient knave, you reverend° braggart,   *old; revered*
We'll teach you.
KENT   I am too old to learn.
Call not your stocks for me. I serve the King,
120   On whose employments I was sent to you.
You should do small respect, show too bold malice
Against the grace° and person° of my master,   *majesty / personal honor*
Stocking° his messenger.   *By stocking*
CORNWALL [*calling*]   Fetch forth the stocks!—
As I have life and honour, there shall he sit till noon.
125   REGAN   Till noon?—till night, my lord, and all night too.
KENT   Why, madam, if I were your father's dog
You could not use me so.
REGAN   Sir, being° his knave, I will.   *since you are*
     [*Stocks brought out*]
CORNWALL   This is a fellow of the selfsame nature
Our sister° speaks of.—Come, bring away the stocks.   *sister-in-law*
130   GLOUCESTER   Let me beseech your grace not to do so.
His fault is much, and the good King his master
Will check° him for't. Your purposed° low correction   *reprimand / intended*
Is such as basest and contemnèd wretches
For pilf'rings and most common trespasses
135   Are punished with. The King must take it ill
That he's so slightly valued in his messenger,
Should have him thus restrained.
CORNWALL   I'll answer° that.   *be responsible for*
REGAN   My sister may receive it much more worse
To have her gentlemen abused, assaulted,
140   For following° her affairs. Put in his legs.   *carrying out*
     [*They put* KENT *in the stocks*]
Come, my good lord, away!
     [*Exeunt all but* GLOUCESTER *and* KENT]
GLOUCESTER   I am sorry for thee, friend. 'Tis the Duke's pleasure,
Whose disposition, all the world well knows,
Will not be rubbed° nor stopped. I'll entreat for thee.   *obstructed*

---

4. *And put . . . him*: And put on such a show of manliness that he was thought a worthy fellow.
5. For attacking a man who had already surrendered
(Kent attacking Oswald).

6. *None . . . fool*: Such rogues and cowards as these
talk as if they were greater warriors (and blusterers)
than Ajax; such rogues always make even mighty Ajax
out to be a fool.

OSWALD   I never gave him any.
It pleased the King his master very late°   *lately*
To strike at me upon his misconstruction,°   *misunderstanding (me)*
When he, compact,° and flattering his displeasure,   *in league with*
110   Tripped me behind; being down, insulted,° railed,   *I being down, he insulted*
And put upon him such a deal of man
That worthied him,[4] got praises of the King
For him attempting who was self-subdued,[5]
And in the fleshment° of this dread exploit   *excitement; flush*
Drew on me here again.
115   KENT   None of these rogues and cowards
But Ajax is their fool.[6]
CORNWALL   Fetch forth the stocks!
                               [Exeunt some servants]
You stubborn, ancient knave, you reverend° braggart,   *old; revered*
We'll teach you.
KENT   Sir, I am too old to learn.
Call not your stocks for me. I serve the King,
120   On whose employment I was sent to you.
You shall do small respect, show too bold malice
Against the grace° and person° of my master,   *majesty / personal honor*
Stocking° his messenger.   *By stocking*
CORNWALL *[calling]*   Fetch forth the stocks!—
As I have life and honour, there shall he sit till noon.
125   REGAN   Till noon?—till night, my lord, and all night too.
KENT   Why, madam, if I were your father's dog
You should not use me so.
REGAN   Sir, being° his knave, I will.   *since you are*
          [Stocks brought out]
CORNWALL   This is a fellow of the selfsame colour°   *character*
Our sister° speaks of.—Come, bring away the stocks.   *sister-in-law*
130   GLOUCESTER   Let me beseech your grace not to do so.
The King his master needs must take it ill
That he, so slightly valued in his messenger,
Should have him thus restrained.
CORNWALL   I'll answer° that.   *be responsible for*
          [They put KENT *in the stocks]*
REGAN   My sister may receive it much more worse
135   To have her gentlemen abused, assaulted.
CORNWALL   Come, my good lord, away!
              Exeunt [all but GLOUCESTER *and* KENT*]*
GLOUCESTER   I am sorry for thee, friend. 'Tis the Duke's pleasure,
Whose disposition, all the world well knows,
Will not be rubbed° nor stopped. I'll entreat for thee.   *obstructed*

---

4. *And put . . . him:* And put on such a show of manliness that he was thought a worthy fellow.
5. For attacking a man who had already surrendered (Kent attacking Oswald).

6. *None . . . fool:* Such rogues and cowards as these talk as if they were greater warriors (and blusterers) than Ajax; such rogues always make even mighty Ajax out to be a fool.

145   KENT   Pray you, do not, sir. I have watched° and travelled hard.   gone without sleep
                Some time I shall sleep out; the rest I'll whistle.
                A good man's fortune may grow out at heels.[7]
                Give° you good morrow.   God give
        GLOUCESTER   The Duke's to blame in this; 'twill be ill took.
                                                              [Exit]

150   KENT   Good King, that must approve° the common say:°   prove / saying
                Thou out of heaven's benediction com'st
                To the warm sun.[8]
                    [He takes out a letter]
                Approach, thou beacon[9] to this under globe,
                That by thy comfortable beams I may
155   Peruse this letter. Nothing almost sees miracles
                But misery.[1] I know 'tis from Cordelia,
                Who hath now fortunately been informed
                Of my obscurèd° course, and shall find time   hidden; disguised
                For this enormous state,° seeking to give   awful state of affairs
160   Losses their remedies. All weary and overwatched,°   too long awake
                Take vantage,° heavy eyes, not to behold   the opportunity
                This shameful lodging. Fortune, good night;
                Smile; once more turn thy wheel.[2]   Sleeps
                    Enter EDGAR
        EDGAR   I heard myself proclaimed,°   declared an outlaw
                And by the happy° hollow of a tree   opportune
165   Escaped the hunt. No port° is free, no place   seaport; exit
                That guard and most unusual vigilance
                Does not attend my taking.° While° I may scape   await my capture / Until
                I will preserve myself, and am bethought°   resolved
                To take the basest and most poorest shape
170   That ever penury in contempt of° man   for
                Brought near to beast. My face I'll grime with filth,
                Blanket my loins, elf all my hair with knots,[3]
                And with presented° nakedness outface   exposed
                The wind and persecution of the sky.
175   The country gives me proof and precedent
                Of Bedlam beggars who with roaring voices
                Strike° in their numbed and mortified° bare arms   Stick / deadened
                Pins, wooden pricks, nails, sprigs of rosemary,
                And with this horrible object° from low farms,   spectacle
180   Poor pelting° villages, sheep-cotes and mills   paltry; contemptible
                Sometime with lunatic bans,° sometime with prayers   curses
                Enforce their charity. 'Poor Tuelygod,[4] Poor Tom!'
                That's something yet. Edgar I nothing am.[5]   Exit
                    Enter King [LEAR, FOOL, and a KNIGHT]
        LEAR   'Tis strange that they should so depart from home
                And not send back my messenger.

7. The fortunes of even good men sometimes wear thin.
8. Thou . . . sun: You come from the blessing of heaven into the heat of the sun (go from good to bad).
9. It is arguable whether Kent here refers to the sun or the moon.
1. Nothing . . . misery: Only those suffering misery are granted miracles; any comfort seems miraculous to those who are miserable.

2. The goddess Fortune was traditionally depicted with a wheel to signify her mutability and caprice. She was believed to take pleasure in arbitrarily lowering those at the top of her wheel and raising those at the bottom.
3. Tangle the hair into "elf locks," supposed to be a favorite trick of malicious elves.
4. A word of unknown origin.
5. Edgar, I am nothing; I am no longer Edgar.

140   KENT   Pray do not, sir. I have watched° and travelled hard.   *gone without sleep*
       Some time I shall sleep out; the rest I'll whistle.
       A good man's fortune may grow out at heels.[7]
       Give° you good morrow.   *God give*
  GLOUCESTER   The Duke's to blame in this; 'twill be ill taken.
                                     Exit
145   KENT   Good King, that must approve° the common say:°   *prove / saying*
       Thou out of heaven's benediction com'st
       To the warm sun.[8]
       [*He takes out a letter*]
       Approach, thou beacon[9] to this under globe,
       That by thy comfortable beams I may
150   Peruse this letter. Nothing almost sees miracles
       But misery.[1] I know 'tis from Cordelia,
       Who hath now fortunately been informed
       Of my obscurèd° course, and shall find time   *hidden; disguised*
       For this enormous state,° seeking to give   *awful state of affairs*
155   Losses their remedies. All weary and o'erwatched,°   *too long awake*
       Take vantage,° heavy eyes, not to behold   *the opportunity*
       This shameful lodging. Fortune, good night;
       Smile once more; turn thy wheel.[2]   [*He sleeps*]
            Enter EDGAR

  EDGAR   I heard myself proclaimed,°   *declared an outlaw*
       And by the happy° hollow of a tree   *opportune*
160   Escaped the hunt. No port° is free, no place   *seaport; exit*
       That guard and most unusual vigilance
       Does not attend my taking.° Whiles° I may scape   *await my capture / Until*
       I will preserve myself, and am bethought°   *resolved*
       To take the basest and most poorest shape
165   That ever penury in contempt of° man   *for*
       Brought near to beast. My face I'll grime with filth,
       Blanket my loins, elf all my hairs in knots,[3]
       And with presented° nakedness outface   *exposed*
       The winds and persecutions of the sky.
170   The country gives me proof and precedent
       Of Bedlam beggars who with roaring voices
       Strike° in their numbed and mortified° arms   *Stick / deadened*
       Pins, wooden pricks, nails, sprigs of rosemary,
       And with this horrible object° from low farms,   *spectacle*
175   Poor pelting° villages, sheep-cotes and mills   *paltry; contemptible*
       Sometime with lunatic bans,° sometime with prayers   *curses*
       Enforce their charity. 'Poor Tuelygod,[4] Poor Tom.'
       That's something yet. Edgar I nothing am.[5]   *Exit*
        Enter LEAR, FOOL, *and* [*the* FIRST] GENTLEMAN[6]
  LEAR   'Tis strange that they should so depart from home
       And not send back my messenger.

---

7. The fortunes of even good men sometimes wear thin.
8. *Thou . . . sun:* You come from the blessing of heaven into the heat of the sun (go from good to bad).
9. It is arguable whether Kent here refers to the sun or the moon.
1. *Nothing . . . misery:* Only those suffering misery are granted miracles; any comfort seems miraculous to those who are miserable.
2. The goddess Fortune was traditionally depicted with a wheel to signify her mutability and caprice. She was

believed to take pleasure in arbitrarily lowering those at the top of her wheel and raising those at the bottom.
3. Tangle the hair into "elf locks," supposed to be a favorite trick of malicious elves.
4. A word of unknown origin.
5. Edgar, I am nothing; I am no longer Edgar.
6. F seems to reserve "a Gentleman" (referred to as "First Gentleman" in this edition) for this particular character, who returns in 5.3.

185 KNIGHT   As I learned,
The night before there was no purpose°   *intention*
Of his remove.°   *change of residence*
KENT [*waking*]   Hail to thee, noble master.
LEAR   How! Mak'st thou this shame thy pastime?
FOOL   Ha, ha, look, he wears cruel garters!⁶ Horses are tied by
190 the heads, dogs and bears by th' neck, monkeys by th' loins,
and men by th' legs. When a man's over-lusty at legs,⁷ then he
wears wooden nether-stocks.°   *knee socks*
LEAR [*to* KENT]   What's° he that hath so much thy place° mistook   *Who's / position*
To set thee here?
KENT   It is both he and she:
Your son° and daughter.   *son-in-law*
LEAR   No.
KENT   Yes.
195 LEAR   No, I say.
KENT   I say yea.
LEAR   No, no, they would not.
KENT   Yes, they have.
LEAR   By Jupiter, I swear no. They durst not do't,
They would not, could not do't. 'Tis worse than murder,
To do upon respect⁸ such violent outrage.
200 Resolve° me with all modest° haste which way   *Inform / reasonable*
Thou mayst deserve or they propose this usage,
Coming from us.
KENT   My lord, when at their home
I did commend° your highness' letters to them,   *deliver*
Ere I was risen from the place that showed
205 My duty kneeling, came there a reeking° post°   *steaming / messenger*
Stewed in his haste, half breathless, panting forth
From Gonoril, his mistress, salutations,
Delivered letters spite of intermission,⁹
Which presently° they read, on whose contents   *immediately*
210 They summoned up their meiny,° straight° took horse,   *retinue / straightaway*
Commanded me to follow and attend
The leisure of their answer, gave me cold looks;
And meeting here the other messenger,
Whose welcome I perceived had poisoned mine—
215 Being the very° fellow that of late   *same*
Displayed so saucily° against your highness—   *Acted so insolently*
Having more man° than wit° about me, drew.   *courage / sense*
He raised the house with loud and coward cries.
Your son and daughter found this trespass worth°   *deserving of*
220 This shame which here it suffers.

---

6. Worsted garters, punning on "crewel," a thin yarn.   8. To do to one who deserves respect.
The Fool is actually referring to the stocks in which   9. Regardless of interrupting me; despite the interrup-
Kent's feet are held.   tions in his account (as he gasped for breath).
7. When a man's liable to run away.

180   FIRST GENTLEMAN   As I learned,
        The night before there was no purpose in them°   *they had no intention*
        Of this remove.°   *change of residence*

     KENT [*waking*]   Hail to thee, noble master.

     LEAR   Ha! Mak'st thou this shame thy pastime?

     KENT   No, my lord.

     FOOL   Ha, ha, he wears cruel garters![7] Horses are tied by the
185   heads, dogs and bears by th' neck, monkeys by th' loins, and
        men by th' legs. When a man's overlusty at legs,[8] then he wears
        wooden nether-stocks.°   *knee socks*

     LEAR [*to* KENT]   What's° he that hath so much thy place° mistook   *Who's / position*
        To set thee here?

     KENT   It is both he and she:
        Your son° and daughter.   *son-in-law*

     LEAR   No.

     KENT   Yes.

190   LEAR   No, I say.

     KENT   I say yea.

     LEAR   By Jupiter, I swear no.

     KENT   By Juno,[9] I swear ay.

     LEAR   They durst not do't,
        They could not, would not do't. 'Tis worse than murder,
        To do upon respect[1] such violent outrage.
195   Resolve° me with all modest° haste which way   *Inform / reasonable*
        Thou mightst deserve or they impose this usage,
        Coming from us.

     KENT   My lord, when at their home
        I did commend° your highness' letters to them,   *deliver*
        Ere I was risen from the place that showed
200   My duty kneeling, came there a reeking° post°   *steaming / messenger*
        Stewed in his haste, half breathless, painting° forth   *panting*
        From Goneril, his mistress, salutations,
        Delivered letters spite of intermission,[2]
        Which presently° they read, on whose contents   *immediately*
205   They summoned up their meiny,° straight° took horse,   *retinue / straightaway*
        Commanded me to follow and attend
        The leisure of their answer, gave me cold looks;
        And meeting here the other messenger,
        Whose welcome I perceived had poisoned mine—
210   Being the very° fellow which of late   *same*
        Displayed so saucily° against your highness—   *Acted so insolently*
        Having more man° than wit° about me, drew.   *courage / sense*
        He raised the house with loud and coward cries.
        Your son and daughter found this trespass worth°   *deserving of*
215   The shame which here it suffers.

---

7. Worsted garters, punning on "crewel," a thin yarn.   whom she constantly quarreled.
The Fool is actually referring to the stocks in which   1. To do to one who deserves respect.
Kent's feet are held.   2. Regardless of interrupting me; despite the interrup-
8. When a man's liable to run away.   tions in his account (as he gasped for breath).
9. Queen of the Roman gods and wife of Jupiter, with

LEAR   O, how this mother° swells up toward my heart!   *hysteria*
    Histerica passio, down, thou climbing sorrow;[1]
    Thy element's° below.—Where is this daughter?   *natural place is*
KENT   With the Earl, sir, within.
LEAR   Follow me not; stay there.
                                     [Exit]
KNIGHT *[to* KENT*]*   Made you no more offence than what you
225   speak of?
KENT   No. How chance the King comes with so small a train?
FOOL   An° thou hadst been set in the stocks for that question,   *If*
    thou hadst well deserved it.
KENT   Why, fool?
230 FOOL   We'll set thee to school to an ant, to teach thee there's no
    labouring in the winter.[2] All that follow their noses are led by
    their eyes but blind men, and there's not a nose among a hun-
    dred but can smell him that's stinking.° Let go thy hold when   *(as his fortunes decay)*
    a great wheel runs down a hill, lest it break thy neck with fol-
235   lowing it; but the great one that goes up the hill,[3] let him draw
    thee after. When a wise man gives thee better counsel, give me
    mine again. I would have none but knaves follow it, since a
    fool gives it.
    [Sings]   That sir that serves for gain
240   And follows but for form,
              Will pack° when it begin to rain,   *pack up and go*
              And leave thee in the storm.

              But I will tarry, the fool will stay,
              And let the wise man fly.
245   The knave turns fool that runs away,[4]
              The fool no knave, pardie.°   *by God* (pardieu)
KENT   Where learnt you this, fool?
FOOL   Not in the stocks.
    Enter LEAR *and* GLOUCESTER
LEAR   Deny to speak with me? They're sick, they're weary?
250   They travelled hard tonight?—mere insolence,
    Ay, the images of revolt and flying off.[5]
    Fetch me a better answer.

---

1. Histerica . . . *sorrow: Hysterica passio* (a Latin expression originating in the Greek *steiros,* "suffering in the womb") was an inflammation of the senses. In Renaissance medicine, vapors from the abdomen were thought to rise up through the body, and in women, the uterus itself to wander around.
2. Ants, proverbially prudent, do not work in winter.

Implicitly, a wise person should know better than to look for sustenance to an old man who has fallen on wintry times.
3. A great wheel is a figure for Lear and of Fortune's wheel itself, which has swung downward.
4. The scoundrel who runs away is the real fool.
5. *images of:* signs of. *flying off:* desertion; insurrection.

FOOL   Winter's not gone yet if the wild geese fly that way.[3]

[*Sings*]   Fathers that wear rags
             Do make their children blind,[4]
        But fathers that bear bags
220   Shall see their children kind.
        Fortune, that arrant whore,
        Ne'er turns the key° to th' poor.   *opens the door*
But for all this thou shalt have as many dolours[5] for thy daughters as thou canst tell° in a year.   *count*

225   LEAR   O, how this mother° swells up toward my heart!   *hysteria*
Histerica passio down, thou climbing sorrow;[6]
Thy element's° below.—Where is this daughter?   *natural place is*

KENT   With the Earl, sir, here within.

LEAR   Follow me not; stay here.
                                    Exit

FIRST GENTLEMAN [*to* KENT]   Made you no more offence but
    what you speak of?

230   KENT   None.
How chance the King comes with so small a number?

FOOL   An° thou hadst been set i'th' stocks for that question,   *If*
thou'dst well deserved it.

KENT   Why, Fool?

235   FOOL   We'll set thee to school to an ant, to teach thee there's no
labouring i'th' winter.[7] All that follow their noses are led by
their eyes but blind men, and there's not a nose among twenty
but can smell him that's stinking.° Let go thy hold when a great   *(as his fortunes decay)*
wheel runs down a hill,[8] lest it break thy neck with follow-
240 ing; but the great one that goes upward, let him draw thee
after. When a wise man gives thee better counsel, give me
mine again. I would have none but knaves follow it, since a
fool gives it.

[*Sings*]   That sir which serves and seeks for gain
             And follows but for form,
245   Will pack° when it begin to rain,   *pack up and go*
             And leave thee in the storm.

             But I will tarry, the fool will stay,
             And let the wise man fly.
250   The knave turns fool that runs away,[9]
             The fool no knave, pardie.°   *by God* (pardieu)

KENT   Where learned you this, Fool?

FOOL   Not i'th' stocks, fool.

    Enter LEAR *and* GLOUCESTER

LEAR   Deny to speak with me? They are sick, they are weary,
255 They have travelled all the night?—mere fetches,°   *ruses; pretexts*
The images of revolt and flying off.[1]
Fetch me a better answer.

---

3. That is, things will get worse before they get better.
4. Blind to their father's needs.
5. Pain, sorrow; punning on "dollar," the English term for the German "thaler," a large silver coin.
6. Histerica . . . *sorrow*: *Histerica passio* (a Latin expression originating in the Greek *steiros*, "suffering in the womb") was an inflammation of the senses. In Renaissance medicine, vapors from the abdomen were thought to rise up through the body, and in women, the uterus itself to wander around.
7. Ants, proverbially prudent, do not work in winter. Implicitly, a wise person should know better than to look for sustenance to an old man who has fallen on wintry times.
8. A great wheel is a figure for Lear and of Fortune's wheel itself, which has swung downward.
9. The scoundrel who runs away is the real fool.
1. *images of*: signs of. *flying off*: desertion; insurrection.

GLOUCESTER   My dear lord,
        You know the fiery quality° of the Duke,   disposition
        How unremovable and fixed he is
        In his own course.
255 LEAR   Vengeance, death, plague, confusion!°   destruction
        What 'fiery quality'? Why, Gloucester, Gloucester, I'd
        Speak with the Duke of Cornwall and his wife.
        GLOUCESTER   Ay, my good lord.
        LEAR   The King would speak with Cornwall; the dear father
260   Would with his daughter speak, commands, tends° service.   awaits
        'Fiery'? The Duke?—tell the hot Duke that Lear—
        No, but not yet. Maybe he is not well.
        Infirmity doth still° neglect all office°   always / obligation
        Whereto our health is bound. We are not ourselves
265   When nature, being oppressed, commands the mind
        To suffer with the body. I'll forbear,
        And am fallen out with my more headier will,[6]
        To take° the indisposed and sickly fit   mistake
        For the sound man.—Death on my state,[7]
270   Wherefore° should he sit here? This act persuades me   Why
        That this remotion° of the Duke and her   remoteness; aloofness
        Is practice° only. Give me my servant forth.   trickery
        Tell the Duke and 's wife I'll speak with them,
        Now, presently.° Bid them come forth and hear me,   at once
275   Or at their chamber door I'll beat the drum
        Till it cry sleep to death.[8]
        GLOUCESTER   I would have all well
        Betwixt you.   [Exit]
        LEAR   O, my heart, my heart!
        FOOL   Cry to it, nuncle, as the cockney° did to the eels when she   Londoner (city woman)
        put 'em i'th' paste° alive. She rapped 'em o'th' coxcombs° with   pie; pastry / heads
280   a stick, and cried 'Down, wantons,° down!' 'Twas her brother   rogues
        that, in pure kindness to his horse, buttered his hay.[9]

        Enter Duke [of CORNWALL] and REGAN [GLOUCESTER,
            and others]

        LEAR   Good morrow to you both.
        CORNWALL   Hail to your grace.
            [KENT here set at liberty]
        REGAN   I am glad to see your highness.
285 LEAR   Regan, I think you are. I know what reason
        I have to think so. If thou shouldst not be glad
        I would divorce me from thy mother's shrine,
        Sepulchring° an adultress. [To KENT] Yea, are you free?   Because it entombed
        Some other time for that.—Belovèd Regan,
290   Thy sister is naught.° O, Regan, she hath tied   wicked; nothing
        Sharp-toothed unkindness like a vulture here.[1]
        I can scarce speak to thee. Thou'lt not believe
        Of how deplored a quality—O, Regan!

---

6. And disagree with my (earlier) more rash intention.
7. May my royal authority end (an oath). Ironically, this
has already happened.
8. Till the noise kills sleep.

9. Like that of his sister (who wanted to make eel pie
without killing the eels), his kindness was misplaced:
horses will not eat buttered hay.
1. Lear probably gestures to his heart.

GLOUCESTER   My dear lord,
  You know the fiery quality° of the Duke,   *disposition*
  How unremovable and fixed he is
  In his own course.
260 LEAR   Vengeance, plague, death, confusion!°   *destruction*
  'Fiery'? What 'quality'? Why, Gloucester, Gloucester,
  I'd speak with the Duke of Cornwall and his wife.
GLOUCESTER Well, my good lord, I have informed them so.
LEAR 'Informed them'? Dost thou understand me, man?
265 GLOUCESTER Ay, my good lord.
LEAR The King would speak with Cornwall; the dear father
  Would with his daughter speak, commands, tends° service.   *awaits*
  Are they 'informed' of this? My breath and blood—
  'Fiery'? The 'fiery' Duke—tell the hot Duke that—
270 No, but not yet. Maybe he is not well.
  Infirmity doth still° neglect all office°   *always / obligation*
  Whereto our health is bound. We are not ourselves
  When nature, being oppressed, commands the mind
  To suffer with the body. I'll forbear,
275 And am fallen out with my more headier will,[2]
  To take° the indisposed and sickly fit   *mistake*
  For the sound man.—Death on my state,[3] wherefore°   *why*
  Should he sit here? This act persuades me
  That this remotion° of the Duke and her   *remoteness; aloofness*
280 Is practice° only. Give me my servant forth.   *trickery*
  Go tell the Duke and 's wife I'd speak with them,
  Now, presently.° Bid them come forth and hear me,   *at once*
  Or at their chamber door I'll beat the drum
  Till it cry sleep to death.[4]
GLOUCESTER   I would have all well betwixt you.
                                            Exit
285 LEAR O me, my heart! My rising heart! But down.
FOOL Cry to it, nuncle, as the cockney° did to the eels when she   *Londoner (city woman)*
  put 'em i'th' paste° alive. She knapped 'em o'th' coxcombs°   *pie; pastry / heads*
  with a stick, and cried 'Down, wantons,° down!' 'Twas her   *rogues*
  brother that, in pure kindness to his horse, buttered his hay.[5]
        Enter CORNWALL, REGAN, GLOUCESTER, [*and*] *servants*
290 LEAR Good morrow to you both.
CORNWALL Hail to your grace.
        KENT *here set at liberty*
REGAN I am glad to see your highness.
LEAR Regan, I think you are. I know what reason
  I have to think so. If thou shouldst not be glad
295 I would divorce me from thy mother's shrine,
  Sepulchring° an adultress. [*To* KENT] O, are you free?   *Because it entombed*
  Some other time for that.   [*Exit* KENT]
                Belovèd Regan,
  Thy sister's naught.° O, Regan, she hath tied   *wicked; nothing*
  Sharp-toothed unkindness like a vulture here.[6]
300 I can scarce speak to thee. Thou'lt not believe
  With how depraved a quality—O, Regan!

---

2. And disagree with my (earlier) more rash intention.
3. May my royal authority end (an oath). Ironically, this has already happened.
4. Till the noise kills sleep.
5. Like that of his sister (who wanted to make eel pie without killing the eels), his kindness was misplaced: horses will not eat buttered hay.
6. Lear probably gestures to his heart.

REGAN I pray you, sir, take patience. I have hope
295 You less know how to value her desert
Than she to slack her duty.²

LEAR My curses on her.
REGAN O sir, you are old.
Nature° in you stands on the very verge   *Life*
300 Of her confine.° You should be ruled and led   *Of its limit*
By some discretion° that discerns your state   *discreet person*
Better than you yourself. Therefore I pray
That to our sister you do make return;
Say you have wronged her, sir.
LEAR   Ask her forgiveness?
305 Do you mark how this becomes the house?³
[*Kneeling*] 'Dear daughter, I confess that I am old.
Age° is unnecessary. On my knees I beg   *An old man*
That you'll vouchsafe me raiment,° bed, and food.'   *promise me clothing*
REGAN Good sir, no more. These are unsightly tricks.
Return you to my sister.
310 LEAR [*rising*]   No, Regan.
She hath abated° me of half my train,   *deprived*
Looked black upon me, struck me with her tongue
Most serpent-like upon the very heart.
All° the stored vengeances of heaven fall   *Let all*
315 On her ungrateful top!° Strike her young bones,   *head*
You taking° airs, with lameness!   *infectious; malignant*
CORNWALL   Fie, fie, sir.
LEAR You nimble lightnings, dart your blinding flames
Into her scornful eyes. Infect her beauty,
You fen-sucked fogs drawn by the pow'rful sun⁴
To fall and blast her pride.
320 REGAN   O, the blest gods!
So will you wish on me when the rash mood—
LEAR No, Regan. Thou shalt never have my curse.
Thy tender-hested° nature shall not give   *pledged to tenderness*
Thee o'er to harshness. Her eyes are fierce, but thine
325 Do comfort and not burn. 'Tis not in thee
To grudge my pleasures, to cut off my train,
To bandy hasty words, to scant my sizes,°   *reduce my allowances*
And, in conclusion, to oppose the bolt°   *to lock the door*
Against my coming in. Thou better know'st
330 The offices° of nature, bond of childhood,   *duties*
Effects° of courtesy, dues of gratitude.   *Actions*
Thy half of the kingdom hast thou not forgot,
Wherein I thee endowed.

---

2. *I have . . . duty:* I expect that you are worse at valu-
ing her deservings than she is at neglecting her duty.
The double negative here ("less," "scant") is acceptable
Jacobean usage.

3. Do you see how appropriate this is among members
of a family (spoken ironically)?
4. The sun was thought to suck poisonous vapors from
marshy ground.

REGAN   I pray you, sir, take patience. I have hope
You less know how to value her desert
Than she to scant her duty.[7]

LEAR   Say, how is that?

305   REGAN   I cannot think my sister in the least
Would fail her obligation. If, sir, perchance
She have restrained the riots of your followers,
'Tis on such ground and to such wholesome end
As clears her from all blame.

310   LEAR   My curses on her.

REGAN   O sir, you are old.
Nature° in you stands on the very verge   *Life*
Of his confine.° You should be ruled and led   *Of its limit*
By some discretion° that discerns your state   *discreet person*
315   Better than you yourself. Therefore I pray you
That to our sister you do make return;
Say you have wronged her.

LEAR   Ask her forgiveness?
Do you but mark how this becomes the house?[8]
[*Kneeling*] 'Dear daughter, I confess that I am old.
320   Age° is unnecessary. On my knees I beg   *An old man*
That you'll vouchsafe me raiment,° bed, and food.' *promise me clothing*

REGAN   Good sir, no more. These are unsightly tricks.
Return you to my sister.

LEAR [*rising*]   Never, Regan.
She hath abated° me of half my train,   *deprived*
325   Looked black upon me, struck me with her tongue
Most serpent-like upon the very heart.
All° the stored vengeances of heaven fall   *Let all*
On her ingrateful top!° Strike her young bones,   *head*
You taking° airs, with lameness!   *infectious; malignant*

CORNWALL   Fie, sir, fie.
330   LEAR   You nimble lightnings, dart your blinding flames
Into her scornful eyes. Infect her beauty,
You fen-sucked fogs drawn by the pow'rful sun[9]
To fall and blister.

REGAN   O, the blest gods!
So will you wish on me when the rash mood is on.

335   LEAR   No, Regan. Thou shalt never have my curse.
Thy tender-hafted[1] nature shall not give
Thee o'er to harshness. Her eyes are fierce, but thine
Do comfort and not burn. 'Tis not in thee
To grudge my pleasures, to cut off my train,
340   To bandy hasty words, to scant my sizes,°   *reduce my allowances*
And, in conclusion, to oppose the bolt°   *to lock the door*
Against my coming in. Thou better know'st
The offices° of nature, bond of childhood,   *duties*
Effects° of courtesy, dues of gratitude.   *Actions*
345   Thy half o'th' kingdom hast thou not forgot,
Wherein I thee endowed.

---

7. *I have . . . duty:* I expect that you are worse at valuing her deservings than she is at neglecting her duty. The double negative here ("less," "scant") is acceptable Jacobean usage.
8. Do you see how appropriate this is among members of a family (spoken ironically)?
9. The sun was thought to suck poisonous vapors from marshy ground.
1. Tender-handled; firmly set in a tender disposition (as a knife blade into its haft).

REGAN   Good sir, to th' purpose.°   *get to the point*

LEAR   Who put my man i'th' stocks?
　　　　　[*Trumpets within*]

CORNWALL   What trumpet's that?
　　　　　Enter Steward [OSWALD]

335   REGAN   I know't, my sister's. This approves° her letters   *confirms*
　　　　　That she would soon be here. [*To* OSWALD] Is your lady come?

LEAR   This is a slave whose easy-borrowed pride[5]
　　　　　Dwells in the fickle grace of her a° follows.   *he*
　　　　　[*He strikes* OSWALD]
　　　　　Out, varlet,° from my sight!   *wretch*

CORNWALL   What means your grace?
　　　　　Enter GONORIL

340   GONORIL   Who struck my servant? Regan, I have good hope
　　　　　Thou didst not know on't.°   *of it*

LEAR   Who comes here? O heavens,
　　　　　If you do love old men, if your sweet sway
　　　　　Allow obedience, if yourselves are old,
　　　　　Make it your cause! Send down and take my part.

345   [*To* GONORIL] Art not ashamed to look upon this beard?
　　　　　O Regan, wilt thou take her by the hand?

GONORIL   Why not by the hand, sir? How have I offended?
　　　　　All's not offence that indiscretion finds
　　　　　And dotage terms so.

LEAR   O sides,[6] you are too tough!

350   Will you yet hold?—How came my man i'th' stocks?

CORNWALL   I set him there, sir; but his own disorders°   *disorderly behavior*
　　　　　Deserved much less advancement.[7]

LEAR   You? Did you?

REGAN   I pray you, father, being weak, seem so.°   *behave so*
　　　　　If till the expiration of your month

355   You will return and sojourn with my sister,
　　　　　Dismissing half your train, come then to me.
　　　　　I am now from home, and out of that provision
　　　　　Which shall be needful for your entertainment.

LEAR   Return to her, and fifty men dismissed?

360   No, rather I abjure all roofs, and choose
　　　　　To be a comrade with the wolf and owl,
　　　　　To wage against the enmity of the air
　　　　　Necessity's sharp pinch.[8] Return with her?
　　　　　Why, the hot-blood in France that dowerless took

365   Our youngest born—I could as well be brought
　　　　　To knee° his throne and, squire-like, pension beg   *kneel to*
　　　　　To keep base life afoot. Return with her?
　　　　　Persuade me rather to be slave and sumpter°   *packhorse*
　　　　　To this detested groom.°   *(Oswald)*

GONORIL   At your choice, sir.

370   LEAR   Now I prithee, daughter, do not make me mad.
　　　　　I will not trouble thee, my child. Farewell.
　　　　　We'll no more meet, no more see one another.
　　　　　But yet thou art my flesh, my blood, my daughter—

5. Unmerited and unpaid-for arrogance; "pride" may also refer to Oswald's fine clothing received for his services to Gonoril.
6. Chest, where Lear's heart is swelling with emotion.
7. Deserved far worse treatment.

8. *To wage . . . pinch:* To counter the harshness of the elements with the hardness brought on by necessity. *pinch:* stress, pressure. Oxford has transposed lines 361 and 362.

REGAN   Good sir, to th' purpose.°   *get to the point*

LEAR   Who put my man i'th' stocks?

      Tucket within

CORNWALL   What trumpet's that?

      Enter Steward [OSWALD]

REGAN   I know't, my sister's. This approves° her letter   *confirms*

     That she would soon be here. [*To* OSWALD] Is your lady come?

350   LEAR   This is a slave whose easy-borrowed pride[2]

     Dwells in the sickly grace of her a° follows.   *he*

     [*To* OSWALD] Out, varlet,° from my sight!   *wretch*

CORNWALL   What means your grace?

      Enter GONERIL

LEAR   Who stocked my servant? Regan, I have good hope

     Thou didst not know on't.° Who comes here? O heavens,   *of it*

355   If you do love old men, if your sweet sway

     Allow obedience, if you yourselves are old,

     Make it your cause! Send down and take my part.

     [*To* GONERIL] Art not ashamed to look upon this beard?

     O Regan, will you take her by the hand?

360   GONERIL   Why not by th' hand, sir? How have I offended?

     All's not offence that indiscretion finds

     And dotage terms so.

LEAR   O sides,[3] you are too tough!

     Will you yet hold?—How came my man i'th' stocks?

CORNWALL   I set him there, sir; but his own disorders°   *disorderly behavior*

     Deserved much less advancement.[4]

365   LEAR   You? Did you?

REGAN   I pray you, father, being weak, seem so.°   *behave so*

     If till the expiration of your month

     You will return and sojourn with my sister,

     Dismissing half your train, come then to me.

370   I am now from home, and out of that provision

     Which shall be needful for your entertainment.

LEAR   Return to her, and fifty men dismissed?

     No, rather I abjure all roofs, and choose

     To be a comrade with the wolf and owl,

375   To wage against the enmity o'th' air

     Necessity's sharp pinch.[5] Return with her?

     Why, the hot-blooded France, that dowerless took

     Our youngest born—I could as well be brought

     To knee° his throne and, squire-like, pension beg   *kneel to*

380   To keep base life afoot. Return with her?

     Persuade me rather to be slave and sumpter°   *packhorse*

     To this detested groom.°   *(Oswald)*

GONERIL   At your choice, sir.

LEAR   I prithee, daughter, do not make me mad.

     I will not trouble thee, my child. Farewell.

385   We'll no more meet, no more see one another.

     But yet thou art my flesh, my blood, my daughter—

---

2. Unmerited and unpaid-for arrogance; "pride" may also refer to Oswald's fine clothing received for his services to Goneril.

3. Chest, where Lear's heart is swelled with emotion.

4. Deserved far worse treatment.

5. *To wage . . . pinch:* To counter the harshness of the elements with the hardness brought on by necessity. *pinch:* stress, pressure. Oxford has transposed lines 374 and 375.

Or rather a disease that lies within my flesh,
375 Which I must needs call mine. Thou art a boil,
A plague-sore, an embossèd° carbuncle   *a swollen*
In my corrupted blood. But I'll not chide thee.
Let shame come when it will, I do not call° it.   *call upon*
I do not bid the thunder-bearer° shoot,   *(Jove)*
380 Nor tell tales of thee to high-judging Jove.
Mend° when thou canst; be better at thy leisure.   *Make amends*
I can be patient, I can stay with Regan,
I and my hundred knights.
REGAN   Not altogether so, sir.
I look not for° you yet, nor am provided   *I did not expect*
385 For your fit welcome. Give ear, sir, to my sister;
For those that mingle reason with your passion[9]
Must be content to think you are old, and so—
But she knows what she does.
LEAR   Is this well° spoken now?   *earnestly*
REGAN   I dare avouch° it, sir. What, fifty followers?   *vouch for*
390 Is it not well? What should you need of more,
Yea, or so many, sith° that both charge° and danger   *since / expense*
Speaks 'gainst so great a number? How in a house
Should many people under two commands
Hold amity? 'Tis hard, almost impossible.
395 GONORIL   Why might not you, my lord, receive attendance
From those that she calls servants, or from mine?
REGAN   Why not, my lord? If then they chanced to slack° you,   *neglect*
We could control them. If you will come to me—
For now I spy a danger—I entreat you
400 To bring but five-and-twenty; to no more
Will I give place or notice.°   *acknowledgment*
LEAR   I gave you all.
REGAN   And in good time° you gave it.   *it was about time*
LEAR   Made you my guardians, my depositaries,°   *trustees*
405 But kept a reservation° to be followed   *reserved a right*
With such a number. What, must I come to you
With five-and-twenty, Regan? Said you so?
REGAN   And speak't again, my lord. No more with me.
LEAR   Those wicked creatures yet do seem well favoured°   *attractive*
410 When others are more wicked. Not being the worst
Stands in some rank of praise.[1] [*To* GONORIL] I'll go with thee.
Thy fifty yet doth double five-and-twenty,
And thou art twice her love.
GONORIL   Hear me, my lord.
What need you five-and-twenty, ten, or five,
415 To follow in a house where twice so many
Have a command to tend you?
REGAN   What needs one?
LEAR   O, reason not the need! Our basest beggars
Are in the poorest thing superfluous.[2]
Allow not° nature more than nature needs,   *If you don't allow*
420 Man's life is cheap as beast's. Thou art a lady.

9. For those who temper your passionate argument   2. *Our . . . superfluous:* Even the lowliest beggars have
with their own calm reasoning.   something more than the barest minimum.
1. Deserves some degree ("rank") of praise.

Or rather a disease that's in my flesh,
Which I must needs call mine. Thou art a boil,
A plague-sore or embossèd° carbuncle   *swollen*
390 In my corrupted blood. But I'll not chide thee.
Let shame come when it will, I do not call° it.   *call upon*
I do not bid the thunder-bearer° shoot,   *(Jove)*
Nor tell tales of thee to high-judging Jove.
Mend° when thou canst; be better at thy leisure.   *Make amends*
395 I can be patient, I can stay with Regan,
I and my hundred knights.
REGAN   Not altogether so.
I looked not for° you yet, nor am provided   *I did not expect*
For your fit welcome. Give ear, sir, to my sister;
For those that mingle reason with your passion[6]
400 Must be content to think you old, and so—
But she knows what she does.
LEAR   Is this well° spoken?   *earnestly*
REGAN   I dare avouch° it, sir. What, fifty followers?   *vouch for*
Is it not well? What should you need of more,
Yea, or so many, sith° that both charge° and danger   *since / expense*
405 Speak 'gainst so great a number? How in one house
Should many people under two commands
Hold amity? 'Tis hard, almost impossible.
GONERIL   Why might not you, my lord, receive attendance
From those that she calls servants, or from mine?
410 REGAN   Why not, my lord? If then they chanced to slack° ye,   *neglect*
We could control them. If you will come to me—
For now I spy a danger—I entreat you
To bring but five and twenty; to no more
Will I give place or notice.°   *acknowledgment*
415 LEAR   I gave you all.
REGAN   And in good time° you gave it.   *it was about time*
LEAR   Made you my guardians, my depositaries,°   *trustees*
But kept a reservation° to be followed   *reserved a right*
With such a number. What, must I come to you
420 With five and twenty? Regan, said you so?
REGAN   And speak't again, my lord. No more with me.
LEAR   Those wicked creatures yet do look well favoured°   *attractive*
When others are more wicked. Not being the worst
Stands in some rank of praise.[7] [*To* GONERIL] I'll go with thee.
425 Thy fifty yet doth double five and twenty,
And thou art twice her love.
GONERIL   Hear me, my lord.
What need you five and twenty, ten, or five,
To follow in a house where twice so many
Have a command to tend you?
REGAN   What need one?
430 LEAR   O, reason not the need! Our basest beggars
Are in the poorest thing superfluous.[8]
Allow not° nature more than nature needs,   *If you don't allow*
Man's life is cheap as beast's. Thou art a lady.

---

6. For those who temper your passionate argument   8. *Our . . . superfluous:* Even the lowliest beggars have
with their own calm reasoning.   something more than the barest minimum.
7. Deserves some degree ("rank") of praise.

If only to go warm were gorgeous,
Why, nature needs not what thou, gorgeous, wearest,
Which scarcely keeps thee warm.[3] But for true need—
You heavens, give me that patience,° patience I need.   endurance
425 You see me here, you gods, a poor old fellow,
As full of grief as age, wretchèd in both.
If it be you that stirs these daughters' hearts
Against their father, fool me not so much
To bear it tamely.[4] Touch me with noble anger.
430 O, let not women's weapons, water-drops,
Stain my man's cheeks! No, you unnatural hags,
I will have such revenges on you both
That all the world shall—I will do such things—
What they are, yet I know not; but they shall be
435 The terrors of the earth. You think I'll weep.
No, I'll not weep.
          [Storm within]
I have full cause of weeping, but this heart
Shall break into a hundred thousand flaws°   fragments
Or ere° I'll weep.—O fool, I shall go mad!   Before
          Exeunt LEAR, [GLOUCESTER,] KENT, [KNIGHT,] and FOOL
440 CORNWALL   Let us withdraw. 'Twill be a storm.
     REGAN   This house is little. The old man and his people
          Cannot be well bestowed.°   lodged
     GONORIL   'Tis his own blame;
          Hath put himself from° rest, and must needs taste his folly.   deprived himself of
     REGAN   For his particular° I'll receive him gladly,   single self
445 But not one follower.
     CORNWALL   So am I purposed. Where is my lord of Gloucester?
     REGAN   Followed the old man forth.
          Enter GLOUCESTER
                                         He is returned.
     GLOUCESTER   The King is in high rage, and will° I know not whither.   will go
     REGAN   'Tis good to give him way. He leads himself.
450 GONORIL [to GLOUCESTER]   My lord, entreat him by no means to stay.
     GLOUCESTER   Alack, the night comes on, and the bleak winds
          Do sorely rustle. For many miles about
          There's not a bush.
     REGAN   O sir, to wilful men
          The injuries that they themselves procure
455 Must be their schoolmasters. Shut up your doors.
          He is attended with a desperate° train,   violent
          And what they may incense° him to, being apt   incite
          To have his ear abused,° wisdom bids fear.   deceived
     CORNWALL   Shut up your doors, my lord. 'Tis a wild night.
460 My Regan counsels well. Come out o'th' storm.   Exeunt

---

3. *If . . . thee warm:* If gorgeousness in clothes is measured by the warmth they provide, your elaborate
clothes are superfluous, for they barely cover your body.

4. *fool . . . tamely:* do not make me so foolish as to
accept it meekly.

If only to go warm were gorgeous,
435 Why, nature needs not what thou, gorgeous, wear'st,
Which scarcely keeps thee warm.[9] But for true need—
You heavens, give me that patience,° patience I need.   endurance
You see me here, you gods, a poor old man,
As full of grief as age, wretchèd in both.
440 If it be you that stirs these daughters' hearts
Against their father, fool me not so much
To bear it tamely.[1] Touch me with noble anger,
And let not women's weapons, water-drops,
Stain my man's cheeks. No, you unnatural hags,
445 I will have such revenges on you both
That all the world shall—I will do such things—
What they are, yet I know not; but they shall be
The terrors of the earth. You think I'll weep.
No, I'll not weep. I have full cause of weeping,
          Storm and tempest
450 But this heart shall break into a hundred thousand flaws°   *fragments*
Or ere° I'll weep.—O Fool, I shall go mad!   *Before*
          Exeunt [LEAR, FOOL, GENTLEMAN, *and* GLOUCESTER]
CORNWALL   Let us withdraw. 'Twill be a storm.
REGAN   This house is little. The old man and 's people
          Cannot be well bestowed.°   *lodged*
GONERIL   'Tis his own blame;
455 Hath put himself from° rest, and must needs taste his folly.   *deprived himself of*
REGAN   For his particular° I'll receive him gladly,   *single self*
          But not one follower.
GONERIL   So am I purposed.
          Where is my lord of Gloucester?
CORNWALL   Followed the old man forth.
          Enter GLOUCESTER
                              He is returned.
GLOUCESTER   The King is in high rage.
460 CORNWALL   Whither is he going?
GLOUCESTER   He calls to horse, but will° I know not whither.   *will go*
CORNWALL   'Tis best to give him way. He leads himself.
GONERIL [*to* GLOUCESTER]   My lord, entreat him by no means to stay.
GLOUCESTER   Alack, the night comes on, and the high winds
465   Do sorely ruffle.° For many miles about   *bluster*
          There's scarce a bush.
REGAN   O sir, to wilful men
          The injuries that they themselves procure
          Must be their schoolmasters. Shut up your doors.
          He is attended with a desperate° train,   *violent*
470 And what they may incense° him to, being apt   *incite*
          To have his ear abused,° wisdom bids fear.   *deceived*
CORNWALL   Shut up your doors, my lord. 'Tis a wild night.
          My Regan counsels well. Come out o'th' storm.   *Exeunt*

---

9. *If . . . thee warm:* If gorgeousness in clothes is measured by the warmth they provide, your elaborate
clothes are superfluous, for they barely cover your body.

1. *fool . . . tamely:* do not make me so foolish as to
accept it meekly.

Scene 8

[*Storm.*] *Enter* KENT [*disguised,*] *and* [FIRST] GENTLE-
MAN, *at several° doors*   separate

KENT   What's here, beside foul weather?

FIRST GENTLEMAN   One minded like the weather,
Most unquietly.

KENT   I know you. Where's the King?

FIRST GENTLEMAN   Contending with the fretful element;
Bids the wind blow the earth into the sea
5   Or swell the curlèd waters 'bove the main,°   mainland
That things might change or cease; tears his white hair,
Which the impetuous blasts, with eyeless rage,
Catch in their fury and make nothing of;
Strives in his little world of man to outstorm
10   The to-and-fro-conflicting wind and rain.
This night, wherein the cub-drawn bear would couch,[1]
The lion and the belly-pinchèd wolf
Keep their fur dry, unbonneted° he runs,   hatless; uncrowned
And bids what will take all.

KENT   But who is with him?

15   FIRST GENTLEMAN   None but the fool, who labours to outjest
His heart-struck injuries.[2]

KENT   Sir, I do know you,
And dare upon the warrant of my art[3]
Commend a dear° thing to you. There is division,   Entrust a crucial
Although as yet the face of it be covered
20   With mutual cunning, 'twixt Albany and Cornwall;
But true it is. From France there comes a power
Into this scattered kingdom, who already,
Wise in° our negligence, have secret feet   Aware of
In some of our best ports, and are at point°   ready
25   To show their open banner. Now to you:
If on my credit you dare build° so far   If you trust me
To make your speed to Dover, you shall find
Some that will thank you, making just° report   accurate
Of how unnatural and bemadding° sorrow   maddening
30   The King hath cause to plain.°   complain
I am a gentleman of blood and breeding,
And from some knowledge and assurance offer
This office° to you.   role; duty

FIRST GENTLEMAN   I will talk farther with you.

35   KENT   No, do not.
For confirmation that I am much more
Than my out-wall,° open this purse, and take   outward appearance
What it contains. If you shall see Cordelia—
As fear not but you shall—show her this ring
40   And she will tell you who your fellow° is,   (Kent himself)

Scene 8 Location: Bare, open country.
1. In which even the bear, though starving, having been sucked dry ("drawn") by its cub, would not go out to forage.

2. *to outjest:* to relieve with laughter; to exorcise through ridicule. *heart-struck injuries:* injuries (from the betrayal of his paternal love) that penetrated to the heart.
3. On the basis of my skill (at judging people).

3.1

Storm still. Enter KENT *[disguised] and [the* FIRST] GEN-
TLEMAN, *severally*°   separately

KENT   Who's there, besides foul weather?

FIRST GENTLEMAN   One minded like the weather,
    Most unquietly.

KENT   I know you. Where's the King?

FIRST GENTLEMAN   Contending with the fretful elements;
    Bids the wind blow the earth into the sea

5   Or swell the curlèd waters 'bove the main,°   mainland
    That things might change or cease.

KENT   But who is with him?

FIRST GENTLEMAN   None but the Fool, who labours to outjest
    His heart-struck injuries.[1]

KENT   Sir, I do know you,
    And dare upon the warrant of my note[2]

10 Commend a dear° thing to you. There is division,   Entrust a crucial
    Although as yet the face of it is covered
    With mutual cunning, 'twixt Albany and Cornwall,
    Who have—as who have not that their great stars
    Throned and set high[3]—servants, who seem no less,°   who appear as such

15 Which are to France the spies and speculations°   observers
    Intelligent of[4] our state. What hath been seen,
    Either in snuffs and packings° of the Dukes,   quarrels and plots
    Or the hard rein° which both of them hath borne   treatment
    Against the old kind King; or something deeper,

20 Whereof perchance these are but furnishings°—   pretexts

FIRST GENTLEMAN   I will talk further with you.

KENT   No, do not.
    For confirmation that I am much more
    Than my out-wall,° open this purse, and take   outward appearance
    What it contains. If you shall see Cordelia—

25 As fear not but you shall—show her this ring
    And she will tell you who that fellow° is   (Kent himself)

3.1 Location: Bare, open country.
1. *to outjest:* to relieve with laughter; to exorcise through
ridicule. *heart-struck injuries:* injuries (from the betrayal
of his paternal love) that penetrated to the heart.

2. On the basis of my skill (at judging people).
3. *as . . . high:* as has everybody who has been favored
by destiny.
4. Supplying intelligence about; too well informed of.

That yet you do not know. Fie on this storm!
I will go seek the King.

FIRST GENTLEMAN   Give me your hand.
Have you no more to say?

KENT   Few words, but to effect°   *but in importance*
More than all yet: that when we have found the King—
45   In which endeavour I'll° this way, you that—   *I'll go*
He that first lights on him holla the other.   *Exeunt severally*

Scene 9

[*Storm.*] *Enter* LEAR *and* FOOL

LEAR   Blow, wind, and crack your cheeks! Rage, blow,
You cataracts and hurricanoes,[1] spout
Till you have drenched the steeples, drowned the cocks!°   *weather vanes*
You sulphurous and thought-executing fires,[2]
5   Vaunt-couriers° to oak-cleaving thunderbolts,   *Forerunners*
Singe my white head; and thou all-shaking thunder,
Smite flat the thick rotundity of the world,
Crack nature's mould, all germens° spill at once   *seeds*
That make ingrateful man.

FOOL   O nuncle, court holy water[3] in a dry house is better than
this rain-water out o' door. Good nuncle, in, and ask thy daughters blessing. Here's a night pities neither wise man nor fool.

LEAR   Rumble thy bellyful; spit, fire; spout, rain.
Nor rain, wind, thunder, fire are my daughters.
15   I tax° not you, you elements, with unkindness.   *blame*
I never gave you kingdom, called you children.
You owe me no subscription.° Why then, let fall   *obedience; allegiance*
Your horrible pleasure. Here I stand your slave,
A poor, infirm, weak and despised old man,
20   But yet I call you servile ministers,°   *agents*
That have with two pernicious daughters joined
Your high engendered battle° 'gainst a head   *heaven-bred forces*
So old and white as this. O, 'tis foul!

FOOL   He that has a house to put his head in has a good
25   headpiece.°   *hat; brain*
[*Sings*]   The codpiece that will house
Before the head has any,
The head and he shall louse,
So beggars marry many.[4]
30   The man that makes his toe
What he his heart should make
Shall have a corn cry woe,
And turn his sleep to wake[5]—
for there was never yet fair woman but she made mouths in a
35   glass.[6]

Scene 9 Location: As before.
1. *cataracts:* floodgates of the heavens. *hurricanoes:*
waterspouts (water from both sky and sea).
2. *thought-executing fires:* lightning that strikes as
swiftly as thought.
3. Sprinkled blessings of a courtier, flattery.
4. *The codpiece . . . many:* Whoever finds his penis a
lodging before providing shelter for his head will end up
in lice-infested poverty and live in married beggary. *cod-*

piece: a pouchlike covering for the male genitals, often
conspicuous, particularly in the costume of a fool.
5. *The man . . . wake:* The man who values an inferior
part of his body over the part that is truly valuable will
suffer from and lose sleep over that inferior part.
6. She practiced making pretty faces in a mirror. The
Fool probably refers to Regan's and Gonoril's vanity, or
the line may be thrown in to soften the harshness of his
satire.

That yet you do not know. Fie on this storm!
I will go seek the King.

FIRST GENTLEMAN   Give me your hand. Have you no more to say?

30   KENT   Few words, but to effect° more than all yet: *but in importance*
That when we have found the King—in which your pain
That way, I'll this[5]—he that first lights on him
Holla the other.   *Exeunt [severally]*

3.2

Storm still. Enter LEAR *and* FOOL

LEAR   Blow, winds, and crack your cheeks! Rage, blow,
You cataracts and hurricanoes,[1] spout
Till you have drenched our steeples, drowned the cocks!°   *weather vanes*
You sulph'rous and thought-executing fires,[2]
5   Vaunt-couriers° of oak-cleaving thunderbolts,   *Forerunners*
Singe my white head; and thou all-shaking thunder,
Strike flat the thick rotundity o'th' world,
Crack nature's moulds, all germens° spill at once   *seeds*
That makes ingrateful man.

10   FOOL   O nuncle, court holy water[3] in a dry house is better than
this rain-water out o' door. Good nuncle, in, ask thy daughters
blessing. Here's a night pities neither wise men nor fools.

LEAR   Rumble thy bellyful; spit, fire; spout, rain.
Nor rain, wind, thunder, fire are my daughters.
15   I tax° not you, you elements, with unkindness.   *blame*
I never gave you kingdom, called you children.
You owe me no subscription.° Then let fall   *obedience; allegiance*
Your horrible pleasure. Here I stand your slave,
A poor, infirm, weak and despised old man,
20   But yet I call you servile ministers,°   *agents*
That will with two pernicious daughters join
Your high-engendered battles° 'gainst a head   *heaven-bred forces*
So old and white as this. O, ho, 'tis foul!

FOOL   He that has a house to put 's head in has a good
25   headpiece.°   *hat; brain*
[*Sings*]   The codpiece that will house
                    Before the head has any,
                The head and he shall louse,
                    So beggars marry many.[4]
30   The man that makes his toe
                    What he his heart should make
                Shall of a corn cry woe,
                    And turn his sleep to wake[5]—
for there was never yet fair woman but she made mouths in a
35   glass.[6]

---

5. *in which . . . this:* in which effort you will go that
way and I this way.
3.2 Location: As before.
1. *cataracts:* floodgates of the heavens. *hurricanoes:*
waterspouts (water from both sky and sea).
2. *thought-executing fires:* lightning that strikes as
swiftly as thought.
3. Sprinkled blessings of a courtier; flattery.
4. *The codpiece . . . many:* Whoever finds his penis a
lodging before providing shelter for his head will end up
in lice-infested poverty and live in married beggary.

codpiece: a pouchlike covering for the male genitals,
often conspicuous, particularly in the costume of a
fool.
5. *The man . . . wake:* The man who values an inferior
part of his body over the part that is truly valuable will
suffer from and lose sleep over that inferior part.
6. She practiced making pretty faces in a mirror. The
Fool probably refers to Regan's and Goneril's vanity, or
the line may be thrown in to soften the harshness of his
satire.

LEAR   No, I will be the pattern of all patience.
      [*He sits.*] *Enter* KENT [*disguised*]
I will say nothing.

KENT   Who's there?

FOOL   Marry, here's grace and a codpiece—that's a wise man
40 and a fool.[7]

KENT [*to* LEAR]   Alas, sir, sit you here? Things that love night
Love not such nights as these. The wrathful skies
Gallow° the very wanderers of the dark   *Frighten*
And makes them keep° their caves. Since I was man   *keep inside*
45 Such sheets of fire, such bursts of horrid thunder,
Such groans of roaring wind and rain I ne'er
Remember to have heard. Man's nature cannot carry°   *bear*
The affliction nor the force.

LEAR   Let the great gods,
That keep this dreadful pother° o'er our heads,   *commotion*
50 Find out their enemies now. Tremble, thou wretch
That hast within thee undivulgèd crimes
Unwhipped of° justice; hide thee, thou bloody hand,   *Unpunished by*
Thou perjured and thou simular° man of virtue   *simulating; pretending*
That art incestuous; caitiff,° in pieces shake,   *wretch*
55 That under covert and convenient seeming°   *fitting hypocrisy*
Hast practisèd on° man's life;   *against*
Close° pent-up guilts, rive° your concealèd centres   *Secret / split open*
And cry these dreadful summoners grace.[8]
I am a man more sinned against than sinning.

60 KENT   Alack, bare-headed?
Gracious my lord, hard by here is a hovel.
Some friendship will it lend you 'gainst the tempest.
Repose you there whilst I to this hard house°—   *household*
More hard than is the stone whereof 'tis raised,
65 Which° even but now, demanding° after you,   *Who / I demanding*
Denied me to come in—return and force
Their scanted° courtesy.   *niggardly*

LEAR   My wit begins to turn.
[*To* FOOL] Come on, my boy. How dost, my boy? Art cold?
I am cold myself.—Where is this straw, my fellow?
70 The art° of our necessities is strange,   *skill; alchemy*
That can make vile things precious. Come, your hovel.—
Poor fool and knave, I have one part of my heart
That sorrows yet for thee.

FOOL [*sings*][9]   He that has a little tiny wit,°   *sense*
75   With heigh-ho, the wind and the rain,
           Must make content with his fortunes fit,
           For the rain it raineth every day.

LEAR   True, my good boy. [*To* KENT] Come, bring us to this hovel.
                            [*Exeunt*]

---

7. The supposedly wise King is symbolized by royal grace, the Fool by his codpiece (here, slang for "penis"). The Fool speaks ironically: the King, as he has pointed out, is now the foolish one. *Marry:* By the Virgin Mary (a mild oath).

8. And pray for mercy from these elements that bring you to justice.

9. The following song is an adaptation of one sung by Feste at the end of *Twelfth Night*.

Enter KENT [*disguised*]

LEAR No, I will be the pattern of all patience.
    I will say nothing.

KENT Who's there?

FOOL Marry, here's grace and a codpiece—that's a wise man
40 and a fool.[7]

KENT [*to* LEAR] Alas, sir, are you here? Things that love night
    Love not such nights as these. The wrathful skies
    Gallow° the very wanderers of the dark   *Frighten*
    And make them keep° their caves. Since I was man   *keep inside*
45 Such sheets of fire, such bursts of horrid thunder,
    Such groans of roaring wind and rain I never
    Remember to have heard. Man's nature cannot carry°   *bear*
    Th'affliction nor the fear.

LEAR   Let the great gods,
    That keep this dreadful pother° o'er our heads,   *commotion*
50 Find out their enemies now. Tremble, thou wretch
    That hast within thee undivulgèd crimes
    Unwhipped of° justice; hide thee, thou bloody hand,   *Unpunished by*
    Thou perjured and thou simular° of virtue   *simulator; pretender*
    That art incestuous; caitiff,° to pieces shake,   *wretch*
55 That under covert and convenient seeming°   *fitting hypocrisy*
    Has practised on° man's life; close° pent-up guilts,   *against / secret*
    Rive° your concealing continents° and cry   *Split open / coverings*
    These dreadful summoners grace.[8] I am a man
    More sinned against than sinning.

KENT   Alack, bare-headed?
60 Gracious my lord, hard by here is a hovel.
    Some friendship will it lend you 'gainst the tempest.
    Repose you there while I to this hard house°—   *household*
    More harder than the stones whereof 'tis raised,
    Which° even but now, demanding° after you,   *Who / I demanding*
65 Denied me to come in—return and force
    Their scanted° courtesy.   *niggardly*

LEAR   My wits begin to turn.
    [*To* FOOL] Come on, my boy. How dost, my boy? Art cold?
    I am cold myself.—Where is this straw, my fellow?
    The art° of our necessities is strange,   *skill; alchemy*
70 And can make vile things precious. Come, your hovel.—
    Poor fool and knave, I have one part in my heart
    That's sorry yet for thee.

FOOL [*Sings*][9] He that has and° a little tiny wit,°   *even / sense*
          With heigh-ho, the wind and the rain,
75   Must make content with his fortunes fit,
          Though the rain it raineth every day.

LEAR True, boy. [*To* KENT] Come, bring us to this hovel.

Exeunt [LEAR *and* KENT]

---

7. The supposedly wise King is symbolized by royal grace, the Fool by his codpiece (here, slang for "penis"). The Fool speaks ironically: the King, as he has pointed out, is now the foolish one. *Marry:* By the Virgin Mary (a mild oath).

8. *and cry . . . grace:* and pray for mercy from these elements that bring you to justice.

9. The following song is an adaptation of one sung by Feste at the end of *Twelfth Night*.

Scene 10

Enter GLOUCESTER *and the Bastard* [EDMUND], *with lights*

GLOUCESTER Alack, alack, Edmund, I like not this
Unnatural dealing. When I desired their leave
That I might pity° him, they took from me   relieve
The use of mine own house, charged me on pain
5   Of their displeasure neither to speak of him,
Entreat for him, nor any way sustain him.

EDMUND Most savage and unnatural!

GLOUCESTER Go to,° say you nothing. There's a division betwixt   (an expletive)
the Dukes, and a worse matter than that. I have received a
10   letter this night—'tis dangerous to be spoken—I have locked
the letter in my closet.° These injuries the King now bears will   private chamber
be revenged home.° There's part of a power° already landed.   to the hilt / an army
We must incline to¹ the King. I will seek him and privily°   secretly; privately
relieve him. Go you and maintain talk with the Duke, that my
15   charity be not of him perceived. If he ask for me, I am ill and
gone to bed. Though I die for't—as no less is threatened me—
the King my old master must be relieved. There is some
strange thing toward.° Edmund, pray you be careful.   *Exit*   coming

EDMUND This courtesy,° forbid° thee, shall the Duke   act of kindness / forbidden
20   Instantly know, and of that letter too.
This seems a fair deserving,² and must draw me
That which my father loses: no less than all.
The younger rises when the old do fall.   *Exit*

Scene 10 Location: At Gloucester's castle.   2. This seems an action that deserves to be rewarded.
1. We must take the side of.

FOOL   This is a brave night to cool a courtesan.[1] I'll speak a
        prophecy ere I go:[2]
80   When priests are more in word than matter;°   *real virtue*
        When brewers mar their malt with water;
        When nobles are their tailors' tutors,[3]
        No heretics burned, but wenches' suitors,[4]
        Then shall the realm of Albion°   *Britain*
85   Come to great confusion.°   *decay*

        When every case in law is right;°   *just*
        No squire in debt nor no poor knight;
        When slanders do not live in tongues,
        Nor cutpurses° come not to throngs;   *pickpockets*
90   When usurers tell their gold i'th' field,[5]
        And bawds and whores do churches build,
        Then comes the time, who lives to see't,
        That going° shall be used° with feet.   *walking / practiced*
This prophecy Merlin shall make; for I live before his time.[6]
                                                           Exit

3.3

Enter GLOUCESTER *and* EDMOND

GLOUCESTER   Alack, alack, Edmond, I like not this unnatural
        dealing. When I desired their leave that I might pity° him, they   *relieve*
        took from me the use of mine own house, charged me on pain
        of perpetual displeasure neither to speak of him, entreat for
5   him, or any way sustain him.
EDMOND   Most savage and unnatural!
GLOUCESTER   Go to,° say you nothing. There is division between   *(an expletive)*
        the Dukes, and a worse matter than that. I have received a let-
        ter this night—'tis dangerous to be spoken—I have locked
10   the letter in my closet.° These injuries the King now bears will   *private chamber*
        be revenged home.° There is part of a power already footed.[1]   *to the hilt*
        We must incline to[2] the King. I will look° him and privily°   *seek / secretly; privately*
        relieve him. Go you and maintain talk with the Duke, that my
        charity be not of him perceived. If he ask for me, I am ill and
15   gone to bed. If I die for't—as no less is threatened me—the
        King my old master must be relieved. There is strange things
        toward,° Edmond; pray you be careful.   *Exit*   *coming*
EDMOND   This courtesy,° forbid° thee, shall the Duke   *act of kindness / forbidden*
        Instantly know, and of that letter too.
20   This seems a fair deserving,[3] and must draw me
        That which my father loses: no less than all.
        The younger rises when the old doth fall.   *Exit*

---

1. To cool even the hot lusts of a prostitute.
2. What follows is a parody of the pseudo-Chaucerian
"Merlin's Prophecy" from *The Arte of English Poesie*. In
F, lines 84–85 follow line 91.
3. When noblemen follow fashion more closely than
their tailors do.
4. When the only heretics burned are faithless lovers,
who burn from venereal disease.
5. When usurers can count their profits openly (because

they have no shady dealings to hide).
6. Merlin was the great wizard at the legendary court
of King Arthur. Lear's Britain is set in an even more distant past.
3.3 Location: At Gloucester's castle.
1. Part of an army already landed.
2. We must take the side of.
3. This seems an action that deserves to be rewarded.

Scene 11

[*Storm.*] *Enter* LEAR, KENT [*disguised*], *and* FOOL

KENT   Here is the place, my lord. Good my lord, enter.
    The tyranny of the open night's too rough
    For nature° to endure.   *human weakness*

LEAR   Let me alone.

KENT   Good my lord, enter here.

LEAR   Wilt break my heart?

5 KENT   I had rather break mine own. Good my lord, enter.

LEAR   Thou think'st 'tis much that this contentious storm
    Invades us to the skin. So 'tis to thee;
    But where the greater malady is fixed,°   *rooted*
    The lesser is scarce felt. Thou'dst shun a bear,
10   But if thy flight lay toward the roaring sea
    Thou'dst meet the bear i'th' mouth. When the mind's free,°   *unburdened*
    The body's delicate.° This tempest in my mind   *sensitive*
    Doth from my senses take all feeling else
    Save° what beats there: filial ingratitude.   *Except*
15   Is it not as° this mouth should tear this hand   *as if*
    For lifting food to't? But I will punish sure.
    No, I will weep no more.—
    In such a night as this! O Regan, Gonoril,
    Your old kind father, whose frank heart gave you all—
20   O, that way madness lies. Let me shun that.
    No more of that.

KENT   Good my lord, enter.

LEAR   Prithee, go in thyself. Seek thy own ease.
    This tempest will not give me leave to° ponder   *allow me to*
    On things would hurt me more; but I'll go in.   [*Exit* FOOL]
25   Poor naked wretches, wheresoe'er you are,
    That bide° the pelting of this pitiless night,   *endure; dwell in*
    How shall your houseless heads and unfed sides,°   *starved ribs*
    Your looped and windowed[1] raggedness, defend you
    From seasons such as these? O, I have ta'en
30   Too little care of this. Take physic, pomp,[2]
    Expose thyself to feel what wretches feel,
    That thou mayst shake the superflux[3] to them
    And show the heavens more just.
                  [*Enter* FOOL]

FOOL   Come not in here, nuncle; here's a spirit. Help me, help
35 me!

KENT   Give me thy hand. Who's there?

FOOL   A spirit. He says his name's Poor Tom.

KENT   What art thou that dost grumble there in the straw?
    Come forth.

Scene 11 Location: Open country, before a cattle shed.
1. *looped and windowed:* full of holes and vents; "windowed" could also refer to cloth worn through to semi-transparency, like the oilcloth window "panes" of the poor.

2. Cure yourself, pompous person.
3. Superfluity; bodily discharge, suggested by "physic" (which also has the meaning of "purgative") in line 30. Excess here is also excess of wealth.

3.4

Enter LEAR, KENT [*disguised*], *and* FOOL

KENT   Here is the place, my lord. Good my lord, enter.
The tyranny of the open night's too rough
For nature° to endure.   *human weakness*

Storm still

LEAR   Let me alone.

KENT   Good my lord, enter here.

LEAR   Wilt break my heart?

5   KENT   I had rather break mine own. Good my lord, enter.

LEAR   Thou think'st 'tis much that this contentious storm
Invades us to the skin. So 'tis to thee;
But where the greater malady is fixed,°   *rooted*
The lesser is scarce felt. Thou'dst shun a bear,
10   But if thy flight lay toward the roaring sea
Thou'dst meet the bear i'th' mouth. When the mind's free,°   *unburdened*
The body's delicate.° This tempest in my mind   *sensitive*
Doth from my senses take all feeling else
Save° what beats there: filial ingratitude.   *Except*
15   Is it not as° this mouth should tear this hand   *as if*
For lifting food to't? But I will punish home.°   *thoroughly*
No, I will weep no more.—In such a night
To shut me out? Pour on, I will endure.
In such a night as this! O Regan, Goneril,
20   Your old kind father, whose frank heart gave all—
O, that way madness lies. Let me shun that.
No more of that.

KENT   Good my lord, enter here.

LEAR   Prithee, go in thyself. Seek thine own ease.
This tempest will not give me leave to° ponder   *allow me to*
25   On things would hurt me more; but I'll go in.
[*To* FOOL] In, boy; go first. [*Kneeling*] You houseless poverty°— *poor*
Nay, get thee in. I'll pray, and then I'll sleep.   *Exit* [FOOL]
Poor naked wretches, wheresoe'er you are,
That bide° the pelting of this pitiless storm,   *endure; dwell in*
30   How shall your houseless heads and unfed sides,°   *starved ribs*
Your looped and windowed[1] raggedness, defend you
From seasons such as these? O, I have ta'en
Too little care of this. Take physic, pomp,[2]
Expose thyself to feel what wretches feel,
35   That thou mayst shake the superflux[3] to them
And show the heavens more just.

Enter FOOL, *and* EDGAR [*as a Bedlam beggar in the
hovel*]

EDGAR   Fathom and half![4] Fathom and half! Poor Tom!

FOOL   Come not in here, nuncle. Here's a spirit. Help me, help
me!

40   KENT   Give me thy hand. Who's there?

FOOL   A spirit, a spirit. He says his name's Poor Tom.

KENT   What art thou that dost grumble there i'th' straw?
Come forth.

3.4 Location: Open country, before a cattle shed.
1. *looped and windowed*: full of holes and vents; "windowed" could also refer to cloth worn through to semitransparency, like the oilcloth window "panes" of the poor.
2. Cure yourself, pompous person.

3. Superfluity; bodily discharge, suggested by "physic" (which also has the meaning of "purgative") in line 33. Excess here is also excess of wealth.
4. "Nine feet," a sailor's cry when taking soundings to gauge the depth of water.

[*Enter* EDGAR *as a bedlam beggar*]

40 EDGAR   Away, the foul fiend follows me. Through the sharp
       hawthorn blows the cold wind.⁴ Go to thy cold bed and warm
       thee.⁵

    LEAR   Hast thou given all to thy two daughters,
       And art thou come to this?

45 EDGAR   Who gives anything to Poor Tom, whom the foul fiend
       hath led through fire and through ford and whirlypool, o'er bog
       and quagmire; that has laid knives under his pillow and halters
       in his pew, set ratsbane by his potage,⁶ made him proud of
       heart to ride on a bay trotting-horse over four-inched bridges,⁷

50 to course° his own shadow for° a traitor. Bless thy five wits,⁸   hunt / as
       Tom's a-cold! Bless thee from whirlwinds, star-blasting, and tak-
       ing.⁹ Do Poor Tom some charity, whom the foul fiend vexes.
       There could I have him, now, and there, and there again.¹

    LEAR   What, has his daughters brought him to this pass?

55 [*To* EDGAR] Couldst thou save nothing? Didst thou give them all?

    FOOL   Nay, he reserved a blanket, else we had been all shamed.

    LEAR [*to* EDGAR]   Now all the plagues that in the pendulous° air   overhanging; portentous
       Hang fated o'er men's faults fall on thy daughters!

    KENT   He hath no daughters, sir.

60 LEAR   Death, traitor! Nothing could have subdued nature
       To such a lowness but his unkind daughters.
       [*To* EDGAR] Is it the fashion that discarded fathers
       Should have thus little mercy on their flesh?
       Judicious punishment: 'twas this flesh begot

65 Those pelican² daughters.

    EDGAR   Pillicock sat on pillicock's hill; a lo, lo, lo.³

    FOOL   This cold night will turn us all to fools and madmen.

    EDGAR   Take heed o'th' foul fiend; obey thy parents; keep thy
       word justly; swear not; commit not with man's sworn spouse:

70 set not thy sweet heart on proud array.⁴ Tom's a-cold.

    LEAR   What hast thou been?

    EDGAR   A servingman, proud in heart and mind, that curled my
       hair, wore gloves in my cap,⁵ served the lust of my mistress'
       heart, and did the act of darkness with her; swore as many oaths

75 as I spake words, and broke them in the sweet face of heaven;
       one that slept in the contriving of lust, and waked to do it. Wine
       loved I deeply, dice dearly, and in woman out-paramoured the
       Turk.⁶ False of heart, light of ear,° bloody of hand; hog in sloth,   rumor-hungry
       fox in stealth, wolf in greediness, dog in madness, lion in prey.

80 Let not the creaking of shoes⁷ nor the rustlings of silks betray

---

4. *Through . . . wind:* Perhaps a fragment from a ballad.
5. *Go . . . thee:* This expression is also used by the
drunken beggar Christopher Sly in *The Taming of the
Shrew,* Induction 1.
6. *laid knives . . . potage:* these are all means by which
the foul fiend tempts Tom to commit suicide. *halters:*
nooses. *ratsbane:* rat poison. *potage:* soup.
7. Impossibly narrow, and probably suicidal to attempt
without diabolical help.
8. The five wits were common wit, imagination, fantasy, estimation, and memory (from medieval and Renaissance cognitive theory).
9. *whirlwinds, star-blasting:* malign astrological influences capable of causing sickness or death. *taking:*
infection; bewitchment.

1. As Edgar speaks this sentence, he might kill vermin
on his body as if they were devils.
2. Greedy. Young pelicans were reputed to feed on
blood from the wounds they made in their mother's
breast; in some versions, they first killed their father.
3. A fragment of an old rhyme, followed by hunting
cries or a ballad refrain; "Pillicock" was both a term of
endearment and a euphemism for "penis."
4. *obey . . . array:* these are fragments from the Ten
Commandments.
5. Favors from his mistress. In Petrarchan poetry, wooers are "servants" to their ladies.
6. And had more women than the sultan had in his
royal harem.
7. Creaking shoes were a fashionable affectation.

[EDGAR *comes forth*]

EDGAR   Away, the foul fiend follows me. Thorough the sharp
45   hawthorn blow the winds.[5] Hm! Go to thy cold bed and warm
thee.[6]

LEAR   Didst thou give all to thy two daughters,
And art thou come to this?

EDGAR   Who gives anything to Poor Tom, whom the foul fiend
50   hath led through fire and through flame, through ford and
whirlpool, o'er bog and quagmire; that hath laid knives under
his pillow and halters in his pew, set ratsbane by his porridge,[7]
made him proud of heart to ride on a bay trotting-horse over
four-inched[8] bridges, to course° his own shadow for° a traitor.   *hunt / as*
55   Bless thy five wits,[9] Tom's a-cold! O, do, de, do, de, do de. Bless
thee from whirlwinds, star-blasting, and taking.[1] Do Poor Tom
some charity, whom the foul fiend vexes. There could I have
him now, and there, and there again, and there.[2]

     Storm still

LEAR   Has his daughters brought him to this pass?
60 [*To* EDGAR] Couldst thou save nothing? Wouldst thou give 'em all?

FOOL   Nay, he reserved a blanket, else we had been all shamed.

LEAR [*to* EDGAR]   Now all the plagues that in the pendulous° air   *overhanging; portentous*
Hang fated o'er men's faults light on thy daughters!

KENT   He hath no daughters, sir.

65 LEAR   Death, traitor! Nothing could have subdued nature
To such a lowness but his unkind daughters.
[*To* EDGAR] Is it the fashion that discarded fathers
Should have thus little mercy on their flesh?
Judicious punishment: 'twas this flesh begot
70   Those pelican[3] daughters.

EDGAR   Pillicock sat on Pillicock Hill; alow, alow, loo, loo.[4]

FOOL   This cold night will turn us all to fools and madmen.

EDGAR   Take heed o'th' foul fiend; obey thy parents; keep thy
words' justice; swear not; commit not with man's sworn spouse;
75   set not thy sweet heart on proud array.[5] Tom's a-cold.

LEAR   What hast thou been?

EDGAR   A servingman, proud in heart and mind, that curled my
hair, wore gloves[6] in my cap, served the lust of my mistress'
heart, and did the act of darkness with her; swore as many oaths
80   as I spake words, and broke them in the sweet face of heaven;
one that slept in the contriving of lust, and waked to do it. Wine
loved I deeply, dice dearly, and in woman out-paramoured the
Turk.[7] False of heart, light of ear,° bloody of hand; hog in sloth,   *rumor-hungry*
fox in stealth, wolf in greediness, dog in madness, lion in prey.
85   Let not the creaking of shoes[8] nor the rustling of silks betray

5. *Thorough . . . winds:* Perhaps a fragment from a ballad.
6. *Go . . . thee:* This expression is also used by the
drunken beggar Christopher Sly in *The Taming of the
Shrew,* Induction 1.
7. *laid knives . . . porridge:* these are all means by
which the foul fiend tempts Tom to commit suicide.
halters: nooses. *ratsbane:* rat poison.
8. Impossibly narrow, and probably suicidal to attempt
without diabolical help.
9. The five wits were common wit, imagination, fantasy, estimation, and memory (from medieval and Renaissance cognitive theory).
1. *whirlwinds, star-blasting:* malign astrological influences capable of causing sickness or death. *taking:*
infection; bewitchment.

2. As Edgar speaks this sentence, he might kill vermin
on his body as if they were devils.
3. Greedy. Young pelicans were reputed to feed on
blood from the wounds they made in their mother's
breast; in some versions, they first killed their father.
4. A fragment of an old rhyme, followed by hunting
cries or a ballad refrain; "Pillicock" was both a term of
endearment and a euphemism for "penis."
5. *obey . . . array:* these are fragments from the Ten
Commandments.
6. Favors from his mistress. In Petrarchan poetry, wooers are "servants" to their ladies.
7. And had more women than the sultan had in his
royal harem.
8. Creaking shoes were a fashionable affectation

thy poor heart to women. Keep thy foot[8] out of brothel, thy
hand out of placket,[9] thy pen from lender's book, and defy
the foul fiend. Still through the hawthorn blows the cold
wind. Heigh no nonny. Dolphin, my boy, my boy! Cease, let
85   him trot by.[1]

LEAR   Why, thou wert better in thy grave than to answer° with   °encounter
thy uncovered body this extremity of the skies.° Is man no more   °violent weather
but this? Consider him well. Thou owest the worm no silk, the
beast no hide, the sheep no wool, the cat[2] no perfume. Here's
90   three on 's° are sophisticated; thou art the thing itself. Unac-   °of us
commodated[3] man is no more but such a poor, bare, forked°   °two-legged
animal as thou art. Off, off, you lendings!° Come on, be true.   °borrowed clothes

FOOL   Prithee, nuncle, be content. This is a naughty° night to   °foul
swim in. Now a little fire in a wild° field were like an old lech-   °barren; lustful
95   er's heart—a small spark, all the rest on 's° body cold. Look,   °of his
here comes a walking fire.

          Enter GLOUCESTER [*with a torch*]

EDGAR   This is the foul fiend Flibbertigibbet.[4] He begins at cur-
few° and walks till the first cock.° He gives the web and the   9:00 P.M. / midnight
pin,[5] squinies° the eye, and makes the harelip; mildews the   causes squints in
100   white° wheat, and hurts the poor creature of earth.   near-ripe
[*Sings*]   Swithin footed thrice the wold,[6]
          A met the night mare and her nine foal;[7]
          Bid her alight
          And her troth plight,°   °begone
105   And aroint thee,° witch, aroint thee!   °begone

KENT [*to* LEAR]   How fares your grace?

LEAR   What's° he?   °Who's

KENT [*to* GLOUCESTER]   Who's there? What is't you seek?

GLOUCESTER   What are you there? Your names?

EDGAR   Poor Tom, that eats the swimming frog, the toad, the
110   tadpole, the wall-newt and the water;° that in the fury of his   water newt
heart, when the foul fiend rages, eats cowdung for salads,° swal-   savories
lows the old rat and the ditch-dog,[8] drinks the green mantle° of   scum
the standing pool; who is whipped from tithing° to tithing, and   parish
stock-punished,° and imprisoned; who hath had three suits to   put in stocks
115   his back, six shirts to his body,
          Horse to ride, and weapon to wear.
          But mice and rats and such small deer[9]
          Hath been Tom's food for seven long year—
Beware my follower. Peace, Smolking;° peace, thou fiend!   a Harsnett devil
120 GLOUCESTER [*to* LEAR]   What, hath your grace no better company?

EDGAR   The Prince of Darkness is a gentleman;
          Modo he's called, and Mahu[1]—

---

8. Punning on the French *foutre* ("fuck").
9. Slits in skirts or petticoats.
1. These phrases are probably snatches from songs
and proverbs. "Dolphin" is an imagined animal or devil
or the heir to the French throne ("dauphin," which
Shakespeare usually Anglicizes), or all three.
2. Civet cat, in Shakespeare's time the major source of
musk for perfume.
3. Naked; without the trappings of civilization.
4. A devil drawn from folk beliefs but famous for his
prominent place in Samuel Harsnett's *Declaration
of Egregious Popish Impostures* (1603); the frequent
borrowings from Harsnett in *King Lear* set the earliest

possible composition date for the play.
5. *web and the pin:* cataract.
6. Swithin, an early English saint famous for healing,
traversed the hilly countryside three times.
7. *night mare:* a demon that is not necessarily in the
shape of a horse; "foal" can also signify the folds, or
coils, of a snake. *A:* He.
8. A dog found dead in a ditch.
9. *deer:* animals. These verses are adapted from a
romance popular in Shakespeare's time, *Bevis of Hampton.*
1. Modo and Mahu, more Harsnett devils, were commanding generals of the hellish troops.

thy poor heart to woman. Keep thy foot[9] out of brothels, thy
hand out of plackets,[1] thy pen from lenders' books, and defy
the foul fiend. Still through the hawthorn blows the cold wind,
says suum, mun, nonny. Dauphin, my boy! Boy, *cessez*;° let   *stop*
90   him trot by.[2]

          Storm still

LEAR   Thou wert better in a grave than to answer° with thy uncov-   *encounter*
ered body this extremity of the skies.° Is man no more than this?   *violent weather*
Consider him well. Thou owest the worm no silk, the beast
no hide, the sheep no wool, the cat[3] no perfume. Ha, here's
95   three on 's° are sophisticated; thou art the thing itself. Unac-   *of us*
commodated[4] man is no more but such a poor, bare, forked°   *two-legged*
animal as thou art. Off, off, you lendings!° Come, unbutton   *borrowed clothes*
here.

     Enter GLOUCESTER *with a torch*

FOOL   Prithee, nuncle, be contented. 'Tis a naughty° night to   *foul*
100   swim in. Now a little fire in a wild° field were like an old lech-   *barren; lustful*
er's heart—a small spark, all the rest on 's° body cold. Look,   *of his*
here comes a walking fire.

EDGAR   This is the foul fiend Flibbertigibbet.[5] He begins at cur-
few° and walks till the first cock.° He gives the web and the   *9:00 P.M./midnight*
105   pin,[6] squints the eye, and makes the harelip; mildews the
white° wheat, and hurts the poor creature of earth.   *near-ripe*
  [*Sings*]   Swithin footed thrice the wold,[7]
        A met the night mare and her nine foal,[8]
        Bid her alight
110   And her troth plight,°   *And gave her word*
        And aroint thee,° witch, aroint thee!   *begone*

KENT [*to* LEAR]   How fares your grace?

LEAR   What's° he?   *Who's*

KENT [*to* GLOUCESTER]   Who's there? What is't you seek?

GLOUCESTER   What are you there? Your names?

115 EDGAR   Poor Tom, that eats the swimming frog, the toad, the
tadpole, the wall-newt and the water;° that in the fury of his   *water newt*
heart, when the foul fiend rages, eats cowdung for salads,° swal-   *savories*
lows the old rat and the ditch-dog,[9] drinks the green mantle° of   *scum*
the standing pool; who is whipped from tithing° to tithing, and   *parish*
120   stocked,° punished, and imprisoned; who hath had three suits   *put in stocks*
to his back, six shirts to his body,
        Horse to ride, and weapon to wear;
        But mice and rats and such small deer[1]
        Have been Tom's food for seven long year.
125   Beware my follower. Peace, Smulkin;° peace, thou fiend!   *a Harsnett devil*

GLOUCESTER [*to* LEAR]   What, hath your grace no better company?

EDGAR   The Prince of Darkness is a gentleman.
Modo he's called, and Mahu.[2]

---

9. Punning on the French *foutre* ("fuck").
1. Slits in skirts or petticoats.
2. These phrases are probably snatches from songs and proverbs. *Dauphin*: the heir to the French throne, sometimes identified with the devil by the English.
3. Civet cat, in Shakespeare's time the major source of musk for perfume.
4. Naked; without the trappings of civilization.
5. A devil drawn from folk beliefs but famous for his prominent place in Samuel Harsnett's *Declaration of Egregious Popish Impostures* (1603); the frequent borrowings from Harsnett in *King Lear* set the earliest possible composition date for the play.

6. *web and the pin*: cataract.
7. Swithin, an early English saint famous for healing, traversed the hilly countryside three times.
8. *night mare*: a demon that is not necessarily in the shape of a horse; "foal" can also signify the folds, or coils, of a snake. A: He.
9. A dog found dead in a ditch.
1. *deer*: animals. These verses are adapted from a romance popular in Shakespeare's time, *Bevis of Hampton*.
2. Modo and Mahu, more Harsnett devils, were commanding generals of the hellish troops.

GLOUCESTER [*to* LEAR]   Our flesh and blood is grown so vile, my lord,
That it doth hate what gets° it.   *begets*
EDGAR   Poor Tom's a-cold.
125   GLOUCESTER [*to* LEAR]   Go in with me. My duty cannot suffer°   *permit me*
To obey in all your daughters' hard commands.
Though their injunction be to bar my doors
And let this tyrannous night take hold upon you,
Yet have I ventured to come seek you out
130   And bring you where both food and fire is ready.
LEAR   First let me talk with this philosopher.
[*To* EDGAR] What is the cause of thunder?
KENT   My good lord,
Take his offer; go into the house.
LEAR   I'll talk a word with this most learnèd Theban.°   *Greek sage*
135   [*To* EDGAR] What is your study?°   *field of expertise*
EDGAR   How to prevent the fiend, and to kill vermin.
LEAR   Let me ask you one word in private.
          [*They converse apart*]
KENT [*to* GLOUCESTER]   Importune him to go, my lord.
His wits begin to unsettle.
GLOUCESTER   Canst thou blame him?
140   His daughters seek his death. O, that good Kent,
He said it would be thus, poor banished man!
Thou sayst the King grows mad; I'll tell thee, friend,
I am almost mad myself. I had a son,
Now outlawed° from my blood; a° sought my life   *disowned / he*
145   But lately, very late.° I loved him, friend;   *recently*
No father his son dearer. True to tell thee,
The grief hath crazed my wits. What a night's this!
[*To* LEAR] I do beseech your grace—
LEAR   O, cry you mercy.°   *beg your pardon*
[*To* EDGAR] Noble philosopher, your company.
EDGAR   Tom's a-cold.
150   GLOUCESTER   In, fellow, there in t'hovel; keep thee warm.
LEAR   Come, let's in all.
KENT   This way, my lord.
LEAR   With him!
I will keep still with my philosopher.
KENT [*to* GLOUCESTER]   Good my lord, soothe° him; let him take   *humor*
the fellow.
155   GLOUCESTER   Take him you on.°   *on ahead*
KENT [*to* EDGAR]   Sirrah, come on. Go along with us.
LEAR [*to* EDGAR]   Come, good Athenian.°   *Greek philosopher*
GLOUCESTER   No words, no words. Hush.
EDGAR   Child Roland[2] to the dark tower come,
His word° was still° 'Fie, fo, and fum;   *motto / always*
160   I smell the blood of a British[3] man.'
                    [*Exeunt*]

---

2. *Child:* an aspirant to knighthood. Roland is the
famous hero of the Charlemagne legends.
3. "An Englishman" usually appears in this rhyme from

the cycle of tales of which "Jack and the Beanstalk" is
the best known. The alteration befits Lear's ancient
Britain.

GLOUCESTER [*to* LEAR] Our flesh and blood, my lord, is grown so vile
　　　　That it doth hate what gets° it.　　　　　　　　　　　*begets*
130　EDGAR　　　　　　　　　　Poor Tom's a-cold.
GLOUCESTER [*to* LEAR] Go in with me. My duty cannot suffer°　　*permit me*
　　　　T'obey in all your daughters' hard commands.
　　　　Though their injunction be to bar my doors
　　　　And let this tyrannous night take hold upon you,
135　　Yet have I ventured to come seek you out
　　　　And bring you where both fire and food is ready.
LEAR　　First let me talk with this philosopher.
　　　　[*To* EDGAR] What is the cause of thunder?
KENT　　Good my lord, take his offer; go into th' house.
140　LEAR　　I'll talk a word with this same learnèd Theban.°　　*Greek sage*
　　　　[*To* EDGAR] What is your study?°　　　　　　　　*field of expertise*
EDGAR　　How to prevent the fiend, and to kill vermin.
LEAR　　Let me ask you one word in private.
　　　　[*They converse apart*]
KENT [*to* GLOUCESTER] Importune him once more to go, my lord.
　　　　His wits begin t'unsettle.
145　GLOUCESTER　　　　　　　Canst thou blame him?
　　　　　　Storm still
　　　　His daughters seek his death. Ah, that good Kent,
　　　　He said it would be thus, poor banished man!
　　　　Thou sayst the King grows mad; I'll tell thee, friend,
　　　　I am almost mad myself. I had a son,
150　　Now outlawed° from my blood; a° sought my life　　*disowned / he*
　　　　But lately, very late.° I loved him, friend;　　　　*recently*
　　　　No father his son dearer. True to tell thee,
　　　　The grief hath crazed my wits. What a night's this!
　　　　[*To* LEAR] I do beseech your grace—
LEAR　　　　　　　　　　　O, cry you mercy,° sir!　　*beg your pardon*
　　　　[*To* EDGAR] Noble philosopher, your company.
155　EDGAR　　　　　　　　　　　　　Tom's a-cold.
GLOUCESTER　In, fellow, there in t'hovel; keep thee warm.
LEAR　　Come, let's in all.
KENT　　　　　　　　This way, my lord.
LEAR　　　　　　　　　　　　With him!
　　　　I will keep still with my philosopher.
KENT [*to* GLOUCESTER] Good my lord, soothe° him; let him take　　*humor*
　　　　the fellow.
160　GLOUCESTER　Take him you on.°　　　　　　　　　　*on ahead*
KENT [*to* EDGAR] Sirrah, come on. Go along with us.
LEAR [*to* EDGAR] Come, good Athenian.°　　　　　*Greek philosopher*
GLOUCESTER　　　　　　No words, no words. Hush.
EDGAR　　Child Roland[3] to the dark tower came,
　　　　His word° was still° 'Fie, fo, and fum;　　　　*motto / always*
165　　I smell the blood of a British[4] man.'　　　　*Exeunt*

---

3. *Child*: an aspirant to knighthood. Roland is the
famous hero of the Charlemagne legends.
4. "An Englishman" usually appears in this rhyme from

the cycle of tales of which "Jack and the Beanstalk" is
the best known. The alteration befits Lear's ancient
Britain.

Scene 12

Enter CORNWALL *and Bastard* [EDMUND]

CORNWALL   I will have my revenge ere I depart the house.

EDMUND   How, my lord, I may be censured,° that nature° thus   *judged / kinship*
    gives way to loyalty, something fears me° to think of.   *I am somewhat afraid*

CORNWALL   I now perceive it was not altogether your brother's

5   evil disposition made him seek his° death, but a provoking   *(Gloucester's)*
    merit set a-work by a reprovable badness in himself.[1]

EDMUND   How malicious is my fortune, that I must repent to be
    just! This is the letter he spoke of, which approves him an
    intelligent party to the advantages of France.[2] O heavens, that

10   his treason were not, or not I the detector!

CORNWALL   Go with me to the Duchess.

EDMUND   If the matter of this paper be certain, you have mighty
    business in hand.

CORNWALL   True or false, it hath made thee Earl of Gloucester.

15   Seek out where thy father is, that he may be ready for our
    apprehension.°   *arrest*

EDMUND [*aside*]   If I find him comforting the King, it will stuff
    his° suspicion more fully.   [*To* CORNWALL] I will persever in my   *(Cornwall's)*
    course of loyalty, though the conflict be sore between that and

20   my blood.°   *filial duty*

CORNWALL   I will lay trust upon thee, and thou shalt find a
    dearer father in my love.   *Exeunt*

Scene 13

Enter GLOUCESTER *and* LEAR, KENT [*disguised*], FOOL,
and EDGAR [*as a Bedlam beggar*]

GLOUCESTER   Here is better than the open air; take it thankfully.
    I will piece out° the comfort with what addition I can. I will   *augment*
    not be long from you.

KENT   All the power of his wits have given way to impatience;[1]

5   the gods° discern your kindness!   [*Exit* GLOUCESTER]   *may the gods*

EDGAR   Frateretto° calls me, and tells me Nero is an angler in   *a Harsnett devil*
    the lake of darkness.[2] Pray, innocent; beware the foul fiend.

FOOL [*to* LEAR]   Prithee, nuncle, tell me whether a madman be
    a gentleman or a yeoman.[3]

10 LEAR   A king, a king! To have a thousand
    With red burning spits come hissing in upon them!

EDGAR   The foul fiend bites my back.

FOOL [*to* LEAR]   He's mad that trusts in the tameness of a wolf, a
    horse's health, a boy's love, or a whore's oath.

15 LEAR   It shall be done. I will arraign° them straight.°   *prosecute / immediately*
    [*To* EDGAR] Come, sit thou here, most learnèd justicer.
    [*To* FOOL] Thou sapient sir, sit here.—No, you she-foxes—

EDGAR   Look where he stands and glares. Want'st thou eyes at
    troll-madam?[4]

Scene 12 Location: At Gloucester's castle.
1. *a provoking . . . himself*: Gloucester's own wickedness deservedly triggered the blameworthy evil in Edgar.
2. *which . . . France*: which proves him a spy and informer in the aid of France; "party," or faction, was usually a term of opprobrium in the Renaissance.
Scene 13 Location: Within an outbuilding of Gloucester's.
1. Rage; inability to bear more suffering.

2. In Chaucer's *Monk's Tale*, the infamously cruel Roman Emperor Nero is found fishing in hell (lines 485–86).
3. A free landowner but not a member of the gentry, lacking official family arms and the distinctions they confer. Shakespeare seems to have procured a coat of arms for his father in 1596.
4. *troll*: a board game using small balls. *eyes*: eyeballs (?). *to troll*: to fish; to sing.

3.5

Enter CORNWALL *and* EDMOND

CORNWALL   I will have my revenge ere I depart his house.

EDMOND   How, my lord, I may be censured,° that nature° thus   *judged / kinship*
gives way to loyalty, something fears me° to think of.   *I am somewhat afraid*

CORNWALL   I now perceive it was not altogether your brother's

5   evil disposition made him seek his° death, but a provoking   *(Gloucester's)*
merit set a-work by a reprovable badness in himself.¹

EDMOND   How malicious is my fortune, that I must repent to be
just! This is the letter which he spoke of, which approves him
an intelligent party to the advantages of France.² O heavens,

10   that this treason were not, or not I the detector!

CORNWALL   Go with me to the Duchess.

EDMOND   If the matter of this paper be certain, you have mighty
business in hand.

CORNWALL   True or false, it hath made thee Earl of Gloucester.

15   Seek out where thy father is, that he may be ready for our
apprehension.°   *arrest*

EDMOND [*aside*]   If I find him comforting the King, it will stuff
his° suspicion more fully. [*To* CORNWALL] I will persever in my   *(Cornwall's)*
course of loyalty, though the conflict be sore between that and

20   my blood.°   *filial duty*

CORNWALL   I will lay trust upon thee, and thou shalt find a
dearer father in my love.   *Exeunt*

3.6

Enter KENT [*disguised*]*, and* GLOUCESTER

GLOUCESTER   Here is better than the open air; take it thankfully.
I will piece out° the comfort with what addition I can. I will   *augment*
not be long from you.

KENT   All the power of his wits have given way to his impa-

5   tience;¹ the gods° reward your kindness!   Exit GLOUCESTER   *may the gods*

Enter LEAR, EDGAR [*as a Bedlam beggar*]*, and* FOOL

EDGAR   Frateretto° calls me, and tells me Nero is an angler in the   *a Harsnett devil*
lake of darkness.² Pray, innocent, and beware the foul fiend.

FOOL   Prithee, nuncle, tell me whether a madman be a gentleman or a yeoman.³

10   LEAR   A king, a king!

FOOL   No, he's a yeoman that has a gentleman to° his son; for   *for*
he's a mad yeoman that sees his son a gentleman before him.

LEAR   To have a thousand with red burning spits
Come hissing in upon 'em!

3.5 Location: At Gloucester's castle.

1. *a provoking . . . himself*: Gloucester's own wickedness deservedly triggered the blameworthy evil in Edgar.

2. *which . . . France*: which proves him a spy and informer in the aid of France; "party," or faction, was usually a term of opprobrium in the Renaissance.

3.6 Location: Within an outbuilding of Gloucester's.

1. Rage; inability to bear more suffering.

2. In Chaucer's *Monk's Tale,* the infamously cruel Roman Emperor Nero is found fishing in hell (lines 485–86).

3. A free landowner but not a member of the gentry, lacking official family arms and the distinctions they confer. Shakespeare seems to have procured a coat of arms for his father in 1596.

20   [*Sings*]   Come o'er the burn, Bessy, to me.⁵
         FOOL [*sings*]   Her boat hath a leak,⁶
                              And she must not speak
                              Why she dares not come over to thee.
         EDGAR   The foul fiend haunts Poor Tom in the voice of a night-
25   ingale. Hoppedance° cries in Tom's belly for two white° her-   *a demon / fresh*
         ring. Croak° not, black angel: I have no food for thee.   *Growl*
         KENT [*to* LEAR]   How do you, sir? Stand you not so amazed.
                  Will you lie down and rest upon the cushions?
         LEAR   I'll see their trial first. Bring in the evidence.
30   [*To* EDGAR] Thou robèd man of justice, take thy place;
         [*to* FOOL] And thou, his yokefellow of equity,°   *partner of law*
         Bench° by his side. [*To* KENT] You are o'th' commission,°   *Sit / judiciary*
         Sit you, too.
         EDGAR   Let us deal justly.
35   [*Sings*]   Sleepest or wakest thou, jolly shepherd?
                      Thy sheep be in the corn,°   *grain*
                      And for one blast of thy minikin° mouth   *dainty*
                      Thy sheep shall take no harm.
                  Purr, the cat⁷ is grey.
40   LEAR   Arraign her first. 'Tis Gonoril. I here take my oath before
         this honourable assembly she kicked the poor King her father.
         FOOL   Come hither, mistress. Is your name Gonoril?
         LEAR   She cannot deny it.
         FOOL   Cry you mercy, I took you for a join-stool.⁸
45   LEAR   And here's another, whose warped looks proclaim
         What store° her heart is made on.° Stop her there.   *material / of*
         Arms, arms, sword, fire, corruption in the place!
         False justicer, why hast thou let her scape?
——   EDGAR   Bless thy five wits.
50   KENT [*to* LEAR]   O pity! Sir, where is the patience now
         That you so oft have boasted to retain?
         EDGAR [*aside*]   My tears begin to take his part so much
         They'll mar my counterfeiting.
         LEAR   The little dogs and all,°   *Even the little dogs*
         Tray, Blanch, and Sweetheart—see, they bark at me.
55   EDGAR   Tom will throw his head at° them.—Avaunt,° you curs!   *will threaten? / Begone*
                  Be thy mouth or° black or white,   *either*
                  Tooth that poisons° if it bite,   *gives rabies*
                  Mastiff, greyhound, mongrel grim,
                  Hound or spaniel, brach° or him,   *bitch*
60   Bobtail tyke or trundle-tail,⁹
                  Tom will make them weep and wail;
                  For with throwing thus my head,
                  Dogs leap the hatch,¹ and all are fled.
                  Loudla, doodla! Come, march to wakes° and fairs   *parish festivals*
65   And market towns. Poor Tom, thy horn is dry.²

5. From an old song. *burn*: a small stream.
6. She has venereal disease; punning on "boat" as body
and "burn" as genital discomfort.
7. Purr the cat is another devil; such devils in the shape
of cats were the familiars of witches.
8. I beg your pardon, I mistook you for a stool. An
idiom of the day expressing annoyance at being

slighted. Here the part of Gonoril is actually being
played by a stool.
9. Short-tailed mongrel or long-tailed.
1. Dogs leap over the lower half of a divided door.
2. A begging formula that refers to the horn vessel that
vagabonds carried for drink; the covert sense is that
Edgar has run out of Bedlamite inspiration.

EDGAR   Bless thy five wits.

15   KENT [*to* LEAR]   O, pity! Sir, where is the patience now
That you so oft have boasted to retain?

EDGAR [*aside*]   My tears begin to take his part so much
They mar my counterfeiting.

LEAR   The little dogs and all,°   *Even the little dogs*
Tray, Blanch, and Sweetheart—see, they bark at me.

20   EDGAR   Tom will throw his head at° them.—Avaunt,° you curs!   *will threaten? / Begone*
Be thy mouth or° black or white,   *either*
Tooth that poisons° if it bite,   *gives rabies*
Mastiff, greyhound, mongrel grim,
Hound or spaniel, brach° or him,   *bitch*

25   Bobtail tyke or trundle-tail,[4]
Tom will make him weep and wail;
For with throwing thus my head,
Dogs leapt the hatch,[5] and all are fled.
Do, de, de, de. Sese![6] Come, march to wakes° and fairs   *parish festivals*

30   And market towns. Poor Tom, thy horn is dry.[7]

---

4. Short-tailed mongrel or long-tailed.
5. Dogs leaped over the lower half of a divided door.
6. Apparently nonsense, although "Sese" may be a version of the French *cessez* ("stop" or "hush").

7. A begging formula that refers to the horn vessel that vagabonds carried for drink; the covert sense is that Edgar has run out of Bedlamite inspiration.

LEAR   Then let them anatomize° Regan; see what breeds about   dissect
    her heart. Is there any cause in nature that makes this hardness?
    [*To* EDGAR] You, sir, I entertain° you for one of my hundred,   retain
    only I do not like the fashion of your garments. You'll say they
70 are Persian° attire; but let them be changed.   oriental; splendid
KENT   Now, good my lord, lie here a while.
LEAR   Make no noise, make no noise. Draw the curtains.° So, so,   bed curtains
    so. We'll go to supper i'th' morning. So, so, so.
            [*He sleeps.*] *Enter* GLOUCESTER
GLOUCESTER [*to* KENT]   Come hither, friend. Where is the King
75 my master?
KENT   Here, sir, but trouble him not; his wits are gone.
GLOUCESTER   Good friend, I prithee take him in thy arms.
    I have o'erheard a plot of death upon° him.   against
    There is a litter ready. Lay him in't
80 And drive towards Dover, friend, where thou shalt meet
    Both welcome and protection. Take up thy master.
    If thou shouldst dally half an hour, his life,
    With thine and all that offer to defend him,
    Stand in assurèd loss.° Take up, take up,   Are certainly doomed
85 And follow me, that will to some provision
    Give thee quick conduct.[3]
KENT [*to* LEAR]   Oppressèd nature sleeps.
    This rest might yet have balmed° thy broken sinews°   soothed / nerves
    Which, if convenience° will not allow,   circumstances
    Stand in hard cure.° [*To* FOOL] Come, help to bear thy   Will be hard to cure
    master.
    Thou must not stay behind.
90 GLOUCESTER   Come, come away.
                        Exeunt [*all but* EDGAR]
EDGAR   When we our betters see bearing our° woes,   our same
    We scarcely think our miseries our foes.
    Who alone suffers, suffers most i'th' mind,
    Leaving free° things and happy shows° behind.   carefree / scenes
95 But then the mind much sufferance doth o'erskip
    When grief hath mates, and bearing° fellowship.   pain; suffering
    How light and portable my pain seems now,
    When that which makes me bend, makes the King bow.
    He° childed as I fathered. Tom, away.   He is
100 Mark the high noises,° and thyself bewray°   important rumors / reveal
    When false opinion, whose wrong thoughts defile thee,
    In thy just proof repeals and reconciles thee.[4]
    What° will hap° more tonight, safe scape the King!   Whatever / chance
    Lurk, lurk.   [*Exit*]

---

3. *that . . . conduct:* who will quickly guide you to some   4. *In . . . thee:* When true evidence pardons you and
supplies.   reconciles you (with your father).

LEAR   Then let them anatomize° Regan; see what breeds about   dissect
    her heart. Is there any cause in nature that makes these hard-
    hearts? [*To* EDGAR] You, sir, I entertain° for one of my hundred,   retain
    only I do not like the fashion of your garments. You will say
35   they are Persian;° but let them be changed.   oriental; splendid
KENT   Now, good my lord, lie here and rest a while.
LEAR   Make no noise, make no noise. Draw the curtains.° So, so.   bed curtains
    We'll go to supper i'th' morning.
        [*He sleeps*]
FOOL   And I'll go to bed at noon.
        Enter GLOUCESTER
GLOUCESTER [*to* KENT]   Come hither, friend. Where is the King
40   my master?
KENT   Here, sir, but trouble him not; his wits are gone.
GLOUCESTER   Good friend, I prithee take him in thy arms.
    I have o'erheard a plot of death upon° him.   against
    There is a litter ready. Lay him in't
45   And drive toward Dover, friend, where thou shalt meet
    Both welcome and protection. Take up thy master.
    If thou shouldst dally half an hour, his life,
    With thine and all that offer to defend him,
    Stand in assurèd loss.° Take up, take up,   *Are certainly doomed*
50   And follow me, that will to some provision
    Give thee quick conduct.[8] Come, come away.
        Exeunt [KENT *carrying* LEAR *in his arms*]

---

8. *that . . . conduct*: who will quickly guide you to some supplies.

Scene 14

Enter CORNWALL *and* REGAN, *and* GONORIL *and Bastard*
[EDMUND, *and* SERVANTS]

CORNWALL [*to* GONORIL]   Post° speedily to my lord your husband.   *Ride*
Show him this letter. The army of France is landed.
[*To* SERVANTS] Seek out the villain Gloucester. [*Exeunt some*]

REGAN   Hang him instantly.

GONORIL   Pluck out his eyes.

CORNWALL   Leave him to my displeasure.—

5   Edmund, keep you our sister° company. The revenges we are   *sister-in-law*
    bound¹ to take upon your traitorous father are not fit for your
    beholding. Advise the Duke where you are going, to a most
    festinate preparation;² we are bound° to the like. Our posts°   *committed / messengers*
    shall be swift, and intelligence° betwixt us.—   *convey information*
10 Farewell, dear sister. Farewell, my lord of Gloucester.

Enter Steward [OSWALD]

    How now, where's the King?

OSWALD   My lord of Gloucester hath conveyed him hence.
    Some five- or six-and-thirty of his° knights,   *(Lear's)*
    Hot questants° after him, met him at gate,   *searchers*
15 Who, with some other of the lord's° dependants,   *(Gloucester's)*
    Are gone with him towards Dover, where they boast
    To have well-armèd friends.

CORNWALL   Get horses for your mistress.   [*Exit* OSWALD]

GONORIL   Farewell, sweet lord, and sister.

CORNWALL   Edmund, farewell.

Exeunt GONORIL *and Bastard* [EDMUND]

20 [*To* SERVANTS]   Go seek the traitor Gloucester.
    Pinion him° like a thief; bring him before us.   *Tie his arms*

[*Exeunt other* SERVANTS]

    Though we may not pass° upon his life   *pass sentence*
    Without the form° of justice, yet our power   *official proceedings*
    Shall do a curtsy³ to our wrath, which men
25 May blame but not control. Who's there—the traitor?

Enter GLOUCESTER *brought in by two or three*

REGAN   Ingrateful fox, 'tis he.

CORNWALL [*to* SERVANTS]   Bind fast his corky° arms.   *withered*

GLOUCESTER   What means your graces? Good my friends, consider
    You are my guests. Do me no foul play, friends.

CORNWALL [*to* SERVANTS]   Bind him, I say—

REGAN   Hard, hard! O filthy traitor!

30 GLOUCESTER   Unmerciful lady as you are, I am true.

CORNWALL [*to* SERVANTS]   To this chair bind him. [*To* GLOUCES-
    TER] Villain, thou shalt find—

    [REGAN *plucks Gloucester's beard*]°   *(an extreme insult)*

GLOUCESTER   By the kind gods, 'tis most ignobly done,
    To pluck me by the beard.

REGAN   So white,° and such a traitor!   *white-haired; venerable*

Scene 14 Location: At Gloucester's castle.   the Duke to prepare quickly.
1. Bound by duty; expected by destiny.   3. Shall allow a courtesy or indulgence; shall bow to.
2. *Advise . . . preparation:* When you reach Albany, tell

3.7

Enter CORNWALL, REGAN, GONERIL, *Bastard* [EDMOND],
and SERVANTS

CORNWALL [*to* GONERIL]   Post° speedily to my lord your husband.   *Ride*
show him this letter. the army of France is landed.
[*To* SERVANTS] Seek out the traitor Gloucester. [*Exeunt some*]

REGAN   Hang him instantly.

GONERIL   Pluck out his eyes.

CORNWALL   Leave him to my displeasure.

5   Edmond, keep you our sister° company.   *sister-in-law*
The revenges we are bound[1] to take upon your traitorous father
are not fit for your beholding. Advise the Duke where you are
going, to a most festinate preparation;[2] we are bound° to the   *committed*
like. Our posts° shall be swift and intelligent° betwixt us. [*To   *messengers / well informed*

10   GONERIL] Farewell, dear sister. [*To* EDMOND] Farewell, my lord
of Gloucester.

              Enter Steward [OSWALD]
How now, where's the King?

OSWALD   My lord of Gloucester hath conveyed him hence.
Some five or six and thirty of his° knights,   *(Lear's)*

15   Hot questrists° after him, met him at gate,   *searchers*
Who, with some other of the lord's° dependants,   *(Gloucester's)*
Are gone with him toward Dover, where they boast
To have well-armèd friends.

CORNWALL   Get horses for your mistress.   *Exit* [OSWALD]

20   GONERIL   Farewell, sweet lord, and sister.

CORNWALL   Edmond, farewell. [*Exeunt* GONERIL *and* EDMOND]
[*To* SERVANTS]   Go seek the traitor Gloucester.
Pinion him° like a thief; bring him before us.   *Tie his arms*
                                        [*Exeunt other* SERVANTS]
Though well we may not pass° upon his life   *pass sentence*
Without the form° of justice, yet our power   *official proceedings*

25   Shall do a curtsy[3] to our wrath, which men
May blame but not control.

              Enter GLOUCESTER *and* SERVANTS
                            Who's there—the traitor?

REGAN   Ingrateful fox, 'tis he.

CORNWALL [*to* SERVANTS]   Bind fast his corky° arms.   *withered*

GLOUCESTER   What means your graces? Good my friends, consider
You are my guests. Do me no foul play, friends.

CORNWALL [*to* SERVANTS]   Bind him, I say.

30   REGAN   Hard, hard! O filthy traitor!

GLOUCESTER   Unmerciful lady as you are, I'm none.

CORNWALL [*to* SERVANTS]   To this chair bind him. [*To* GLOUCES-
TER] Villain, thou shalt find—
              [REGAN *plucks Gloucester's beard*]°   *(an extreme insult)*

GLOUCESTER   By the kind gods, 'tis most ignobly done,
To pluck me by the beard.

35   REGAN   So white,° and such a traitor?   *white-haired; venerable*

3.7 Location: At Gloucester's castle.   the Duke to prepare quickly.
1. Bound by duty; expected by destiny.   3. Shall allow a courtesy or indulgence; shall bow to.
2. *Advise . . . preparation*: When you reach Albany, tell

35 GLOUCESTER   Naughty° lady,   *Wicked*
        These hairs which thou dost ravish from my chin
        Will quicken° and accuse thee. I am your host.   *come alive*
        With robbers' hands my hospitable favours°   *features*
        You should not ruffle° thus. What will you do?   *snatch at*
40 CORNWALL   Come, sir, what letters had you late° from France?   *lately*
    REGAN   Be simple,° answerer, for we know the truth.   *direct*
    CORNWALL   And what confederacy have you with the traitors
        Late footed° in the kingdom?   *landed*
    REGAN   To whose hands
        You have sent the lunatic King. Speak.
45 GLOUCESTER   I have a letter guessingly set down,[4]
        Which came from one that's of a neutral heart,
        And not from one opposed.
    CORNWALL   Cunning.
    REGAN   And false.
    CORNWALL   Where hast thou sent the King?
    GLOUCESTER   To Dover.
    REGAN   Wherefore° to Dover? Wast thou not charged° at peril—   *Why / commanded*
50 CORNWALL   Wherefore to Dover? Let him first answer that.
    GLOUCESTER   I am tied to th' stake, and I must stand the course.[5]
    REGAN   Wherefore to Dover, sir?
    GLOUCESTER   Because I would not see thy cruel nails
        Pluck out his poor old eyes, nor thy fierce sister
55   In his anointed[6] flesh rash° boarish fangs.   *slash; cut*
        The sea, with such a storm as his bowed head
        In hell-black night endured, would have buoyed° up   *risen*
        And quenched the stellèd° fires. Yet, poor old heart,   *stars'*
        He holped° the heavens to rage.   *helped*
60   If wolves had at thy gate howled that dern° time,   *dreary; dreadful*
        Thou shouldst have said 'Good porter, turn the key;°   *(to open the door)*
        All cruels I'll subscribe.'[7] But I shall see
        The wingèd vengeance[8] overtake such children.
    CORNWALL   See't shalt thou never.—Fellows,° hold the chair.—   *Servants*
65   Upon those eyes of thine I'll set my foot.
    GLOUCESTER   He that will think° to live till he be old   *Whoever hopes*
        Give me some help!—O cruel! O ye gods!
            [CORNWALL *pulls out one of* GLOUCESTER's *eyes and*
                stamps on it]
    REGAN [*to* CORNWALL]   One side will mock another; t'other, too.
    CORNWALL [*to* GLOUCESTER]   If you see vengeance—
    SERVANT   Hold your hand, my lord.
70   I have served you ever since I was a child,
        But better service have I never done you
        Than now to bid you hold.
    REGAN   How now, you dog!

---

4. Written without confirmation; speculative.
5. An image from bearbaiting, in which a bear on a short tether had to fight off the assault of dogs.
6. Consecrated with holy oils (as part of a King's coronation).
7. The cruelty of all creatures (but not yours) I can accept ("subscribe"). Oxford emends F ("else subscribe") and Q ("else subscrib'd"); the line is usually paraphrased "All other cruel beasts would have pity, but not you."
8. Swift or heaven-sent revenge; either an angel of God or the Furies, who were flying executors of divine vengeance in classical mythology.

GLOUCESTER   Naughty° lady,   *Wicked*
These hairs which thou dost ravish from my chin
Will quicken° and accuse thee. I am your host.   *come alive*
With robbers' hands my hospitable favours°   *features*
40   You should not ruffle° thus. What will you do?   *snatch at*
CORNWALL   Come, sir, what letters had you late° from France?   *lately*
REGAN   Be simple-answered,° for we know the truth.   *straightforward*
CORNWALL   And what confederacy have you with the traitors
Late footed° in the kingdom?   *landed*
REGAN   To whose hands
45   You have sent the lunatic King. Speak.
GLOUCESTER   I have a letter guessingly set down,[4]
Which came from one that's of a neutral heart,
And not from one opposed.
CORNWALL   Cunning.
REGAN   And false.
CORNWALL   Where hast thou sent the King?
GLOUCESTER   To Dover.
50   REGAN   Wherefore° to Dover? Wast thou not charged° at peril—   *Why / commanded*
CORNWALL   Wherefore to Dover?—Let him answer that.
GLOUCESTER   I am tied to th' stake, and I must stand the course.[5]
REGAN   Wherefore to Dover?
GLOUCESTER   Because I would not see thy cruel nails
55   Pluck out his poor old eyes, nor thy fierce sister
In his anointed[6] flesh stick boarish fangs.
The sea, with such a storm as his bare head
In hell-black night endured, would have buoyed° up   *risen*
And quenched the stellèd° fires.   *stars'*
60   Yet, poor old heart, he holp° the heavens to rain.   *helped*
If wolves had at thy gate howled that stern time,
Thou shouldst have said 'Good porter, turn the key;°   *(to open the door)*
All cruels I'll subscribe.'[7] But I shall see
The wingèd vengeance[8] overtake such children.
65   CORNWALL   See't shalt thou never.—Fellows,° hold the chair.—   *Servants*
Upon these eyes of thine I'll set my foot.
GLOUCESTER   He that will think° to live till he be old   *Whoever hopes*
Give me some help!—O cruel! O you gods!
        [CORNWALL *pulls out one of* GLOUCESTER'S *eyes and*
        stamps on it]
REGAN [*to* CORNWALL]   One side will mock another; th'other, too.
CORNWALL [*to* GLOUCESTER]   If you see vengeance—
70   SERVANT   Hold your hand, my lord.
I have served you ever since I was a child,
But better service have I never done you
Than now to bid you hold.
REGAN   How now, you dog!

4. Written without confirmation; speculative.
5. An image from bearbaiting, in which a bear on a short tether had to fight off the assault of dogs.
6. Consecrated with holy oils (as part of a King's coronation).
7. The cruelty of all creatures (but not yours) I can

accept ("subscribe"). Oxford emends F ("else subscribe") and Q ("else subscrib'd"); the line is usually paraphrased "All other cruel beasts would have pity, but not you."
8. Swift or heaven-sent revenge; either an angel of God or the Furies, who were flying executors of divine vengeance in classical mythology.

SERVANT   If you did wear a beard upon your chin
I'd shake it on this quarrel.⁹ [*To* CORNWALL] What do you mean?°   *intend*
75   CORNWALL   My villein!°   *servant; villain*
SERVANT   Why then, come on, and take the chance of anger.¹
           [*They*] *draw and fight*
REGAN [*to another* SERVANT]   Give me thy sword. A peasant stand up thus!
           She takes a sword and runs at him behind
SERVANT [*to* GLOUCESTER]   O, I am slain, my lord! Yet have you one eye left
To see some mischief° on him.   *injury*
           [REGAN *stabs him again*]
                         O!   [*He dies*]
80   CORNWALL   Lest it see more, prevent it. Out, vile jelly!
           [*He pulls out* GLOUCESTER's *other eye*]
Where is thy lustre now?
GLOUCESTER   All dark and comfortless. Where's my son Edmund?
Edmund, enkindle all the sparks of nature²
To quite° this horrid act.   *requite; avenge*
REGAN   Out, villain!
85   Thou call'st on him that hates thee. It was he
That made the overture° of thy treasons to us,   *revelation*
Who is too good to pity thee.
GLOUCESTER   O, my follies! Then Edgar was abused.°   *slandered*
Kind gods, forgive me that, and prosper him!
90   REGAN [*to* SERVANTS]   Go thrust him out at gates, and let him smell
His way to Dover. [*To* CORNWALL] How is't, my lord? How
           look you?°   *How do you feel*
CORNWALL   I have received a hurt. Follow me, lady.
[*To* SERVANTS] Turn out that eyeless villain. Throw this slave
Upon the dunghill.
           [*Exit one or more with* GLOUCESTER *and the body*]
                         Regan, I bleed apace.
95   Untimely comes this hurt. Give me your arm.
                         Exeunt [CORNWALL *and* REGAN]
SECOND SERVANT   I'll never care what wickedness I do
If this man come to good.³
THIRD SERVANT   If she live long
And in the end meet the old° course of death,   *usual*
Women will all turn monsters.
100   SECOND SERVANT   Let's follow the old Earl and get the bedlam°   *madman*
To lead him where he would. His roguish madness
Allows itself to anything.
THIRD SERVANT   Go thou. I'll fetch some flax and whites of eggs
To apply to his bleeding face. Now heaven help him!
                         Exeunt [*severally*]

9. I'd pluck it over this point; I'd issue a challenge.
1. Take the risk of fighting when angry; take the fortune of one who is governed by his anger.
2. All the warmth of filial love; all the anger that your

father has received such treatment.
3. *I'll . . . good:* Because this may be a sign that evil
goes unpunished. *this man:* Cornwall.

SERVANT   If you did wear a beard upon your chin
75   I'd shake it on this quarrel.[9] [*To* CORNWALL] What do you mean?°   *intend*
CORNWALL   My villein!°   *servant; villain*
SERVANT   Nay then, come on, and take the chance of anger.[1]
          [*They draw and fight*]
REGAN [*to another* SERVANT]   Give me thy sword. A peasant stand up thus!
          [*She*] *kills him*
SERVANT [*to* GLOUCESTER]   O, I am slain. My lord, you have one eye left
          To see some mischief° on him.   *injury*
          [REGAN *stabs him again*]
80   O!   [*He dies*]
CORNWALL   Lest it see more, prevent it. Out, vile jelly!
          [*He pulls out* GLOUCESTER's *other eye*]
          Where is thy lustre now?
GLOUCESTER   All dark and comfortless. Where's my son Edmond?
          Edmond, enkindle all the sparks of nature[2]
          To quite° this horrid act.   *requite; avenge*
85   REGAN   Out, treacherous villain!
          Thou call'st on him that hates thee. It was he
          That made the overture° of thy treasons to us,   *revelation*
          Who is too good to pity thee.
GLOUCESTER   O, my follies! Then Edgar was abused.°   *slandered*
90   Kind gods, forgive me that, and prosper him!
REGAN [*to* SERVANTS]   Go thrust him out at gates, and let him smell
          His way to Dover.   *Exit* [*one or more*] *with* GLOUCESTER
                         How is't, my lord? How look you?°   *How do you feel*
CORNWALL   I have received a hurt. Follow me, lady.
          [*To* SERVANTS] Turn out that eyeless villain. Throw this slave
95   Upon the dunghill. Regan, I bleed apace.
          Untimely comes this hurt. Give me your arm.
                                   Exeunt [*with the body*]

---

9. I'd pluck it over this point; I'd issue a challenge.   2. All the warmth of filial love; all the anger that your
1. Take the risk of fighting when angry; take the for-   father has received such treatment.
tune of one who is governed by his anger.

Scene 15

Enter EDGAR [*as a Bedlam beggar*]

EDGAR Yet better thus and known to be contemned°   despised
 Than still° contemned and flattered. To be worst,   always
 The low'st and most dejected thing of fortune,
 Stands still in esperance, lives not in fear.[1]
5 The lamentable change is from the best;
 The worst returns to laughter.[2]

Enter GLOUCESTER *led by an* OLD MAN

 Who's here? My father, parti-eyed?[3] World, world, O world!
 But that thy strange mutations make us hate thee,
 Life would not yield to age.[4]

 [EDGAR *stands aside*]

OLD MAN [*to* GLOUCESTER]   O my good lord,
10 I have been your tenant and your father's tenant
 This fourscore—
GLOUCESTER Away, get thee away, good friend, be gone.
 Thy comforts° can do me no good at all;   assistance
 Thee they may hurt.
15 OLD MAN Alack, sir, you cannot see your way.
GLOUCESTER I have no way, and therefore want no eyes.
 I stumbled when I saw. Full oft 'tis seen
 Our means secure us, and our mere defects
 Prove our commodities.[5] Ah dear son Edgar,
20 The food° of thy abusèd° father's wrath—   fuel; prey / deceived
 Might I but live to see thee in° my touch   through
 I'd say I had eyes again.
OLD MAN   How now? Who's there?
EDGAR [*aside*] O gods! Who is't can say 'I am at the worst'?
 I am worse than e'er I was.
OLD MAN   'Tis poor mad Tom.
25 EDGAR [*aside*] And worse I may be yet. The worst is not
 As long as we can say 'This is the worst.'
OLD MAN [*to* EDGAR] Fellow, where goest?
GLOUCESTER Is it a beggarman?
OLD MAN Madman and beggar too.
30 GLOUCESTER A° has some reason, else he could not beg.   He
 In the last night's storm I such a fellow saw,
 Which made me think a man a worm. My son
 Came then into my mind, and yet my mind
 Was then scarce friends with him. I have heard more since.
35 As flies to wanton° boys are we to th' gods;   playful; careless
 They kill us for their sport.

Scene 15 Location: Open country.
1. *Stands . . . fear*: Remains in hope ("esperance") because there is no fear of falling further.
2. *The lamentable . . . laughter*: The change to be lamented is one that alters the best of circumstances; the worst luck can only improve.
3. Multicolored like a fool's costume (red with blood under white dressings).
4. *But . . . age*: If there were no strange reversals of fortune to make the world hateful, we would not consent to aging and death.
5. *Our means . . . commodities*: Our wealth makes us overconfident, and our utter deprivation proves to be beneficial.

4.1

Enter EDGAR [*as a Bedlam beggar*]

EDGAR Yet better thus and known to be contemned°   *despised*
Than still° contemned and flattered. To be worst,   *always*
The low'st and most dejected thing of fortune,
Stands still in esperance, lives not in fear.[1]

5   The lamentable change is from the best;
The worst returns to laughter.[2] Welcome, then,
Thou unsubstantial air that I embrace.
The wretch that thou hast blown unto the worst
Owes nothing° to thy blasts.   *(because he can't pay)*

Enter GLOUCESTER [*led by*] *an* OLD MAN

         But who comes here?

10   My father, parti-eyed?[3] World, world, O world!
But that thy strange mutations make us hate thee,
Life would not yield to age.[4]

     [EDGAR *stands aside*]

OLD MAN [*to* GLOUCESTER]   O my good lord,
I have been your tenant and your father's tenant
These fourscore years.

15   GLOUCESTER   Away, get thee away, good friend, be gone.
Thy comforts° can do me no good at all;   *assistance*
Thee they may hurt.

OLD MAN   You cannot see your way.

GLOUCESTER   I have no way, and therefore want no eyes.
I stumbled when I saw. Full oft 'tis seen

20   Our means secure us, and our mere defects
Prove our commodities.[5] O dear son Edgar,
The food° of thy abusèd° father's wrath—   *fuel; prey / deceived*
Might I but live to see thee in° my touch   *through*
I'd say I had eyes again.

OLD MAN   How now? Who's there?

25   EDGAR [*aside*]   O gods! Who is't can say 'I am at the worst'?
I am worse than e'er I was.

OLD MAN [*to* GLOUCESTER]   'Tis poor mad Tom.

EDGAR [*aside*]   And worse I may be yet. The worst is not
So long as we can say 'This is the worst.'

OLD MAN [*to* EDGAR]   Fellow, where goest?

30   GLOUCESTER   Is it a beggarman?

OLD MAN   Madman and beggar too.

GLOUCESTER   A° has some reason, else he could not beg.   *He*
I'th' last night's storm I such a fellow saw,
Which made me think a man a worm. My son

35   Came then into my mind, and yet my mind
Was then scarce friends with him. I have heard more since.
As flies to wanton° boys are we to th' gods;   *playful; careless*
They kill us for their sport.

4.1 Location: Open country.
1. *Stands . . . fear*: Remains in hope ("esperance") because there is no fear of falling further.
2. *The lamentable . . . laughter*: The change to be lamented is one that alters the best of circumstances; the worst luck can only improve.
3. Multicolored like a fool's costume (red with blood under white dressings).
4. *But . . . age*: If there were no strange reversals of fortune to make the world hateful, we would not consent to aging and death.
5. *Our means . . . commodities*: Our wealth makes us overconfident, and our utter deprivation proves to be beneficial.

EDGAR [*aside*]   How should this be?
    Bad is the trade that must play fool to sorrow,[6]
    Ang'ring itself and others.
        [*He comes forward*]
                    Bless thee, master.

GLOUCESTER   Is that the naked fellow?

OLD MAN   Ay, my lord.

40 GLOUCESTER   Then prithee, get thee gone. If for my sake
    Thou wilt o'ertake us hence a mile or twain
    I'th' way toward Dover, do it for ancient love,[7]
    And bring some covering for this naked soul,
    Who I'll entreat to lead me.

OLD MAN   Alack, sir, he is mad.

45 GLOUCESTER   'Tis the time's plague when[8] madmen lead the blind.
    Do as I bid thee; or rather do thy pleasure.
    Above the rest, be gone.

OLD MAN   I'll bring him the best 'parel° that I have,   *apparel; clothing*
    Come on't what will.   [*Exit*]

GLOUCESTER   Sirrah, naked fellow!

50 EDGAR   Poor Tom's a-cold. I cannot dance it farther.[9]

GLOUCESTER   Come hither, fellow.

EDGAR   Bless thy sweet eyes, they bleed.

GLOUCESTER   Know'st thou the way to Dover?

EDGAR   Both stile and gate, horseway and footpath. Poor Tom
55 hath been scared out of his good wits. Bless thee, goodman,°   *commoner*
    from the foul fiend. Five fiends have been in Poor Tom at
    once, as Obidicut of lust, Hobbididence prince of dumbness,
    Mahu of stealing, Modo of murder, Flibbertigibbet of mocking
    and mowing,° who since possesses chambermaids and waiting-   *making faces*
60 women. So bless thee, master.

GLOUCESTER   Here, take this purse, thou whom the heavens' plagues
    Have humbled to all strokes.° That I am wretched   *to accept all blows*
    Makes thee the happier. Heavens deal so still.°   *always*
    Let the superfluous and lust-dieted man[1]
65 That stands° your ordinance,° that will not see   *resists / authority*
    Because he does not feel, feel your power quickly.
    So distribution should undo excess,
    And each man have enough. Dost thou know Dover?

EDGAR   Ay, master.

70 GLOUCESTER   There is a cliff whose high and bending° head   *overhanging*
    Looks saucily in the confinèd deep.[2]
    Bring me but to the very brim of it
    And I'll repair the misery thou dost bear
    With something rich about me. From that place
75 I shall no leading need.

EDGAR   Give me thy arm.
    Poor Tom shall lead thee.   [*Exit* EDGAR *guiding* GLOUCESTER]

---

6. It is a bad business to have to play the fool in the face of sorrow.

7. For the sake of our long and loyal relationship (as master and servant).

8. The time is truly sick when.

9. I cannot continue the charade.

1. Let the overprosperous man who indulges his appetite.

2. Looks fearsomely into the straits below.

EDGAR [*aside*]   How should this be?
Bad is the trade that must play fool to sorrow,[6]
Ang'ring itself and others.
    [*He comes forward*]

40   Bless thee, master.
GLOUCESTER   Is that the naked fellow?
OLD MAN   Ay, my lord.
GLOUCESTER   Get thee away. If for my sake
Thou wilt o'ertake us hence a mile or twain
I'th' way toward Dover, do it for ancient love,[7]

45   And bring some covering for this naked soul,
Which I'll entreat to lead me.
OLD MAN   Alack, sir, he is mad.
GLOUCESTER   'Tis the time's plague when[8] madmen lead the blind.
Do as I bid thee; or rather do thy pleasure.
Above the rest, be gone.

50 OLD MAN   I'll bring him the best 'parel° that I have,   *apparel; clothing*
Come on't what will.   *Exit*
GLOUCESTER   Sirrah, naked fellow!
EDGAR   Poor Tom's a-cold. [*Aside*] I cannot daub it further.[9]
GLOUCESTER   Come hither, fellow.
EDGAR   [*aside*]   And yet I must.
[*To* GLOUCESTER] Bless thy sweet eyes, they bleed.
GLOUCESTER   Know'st thou the way to Dover?

55 EDGAR   Both stile and gate, horseway and footpath. Poor Tom
hath been scared out of his good wits. Bless thee, goodman's°   *commoner's*
son, from the foul fiend.
GLOUCESTER   Here, take this purse, thou whom the heavens' plagues
Have humbled to all strokes.° That I am wretched   *to accept all blows*

60 Makes thee the happier. Heavens deal so still.°   *always*
Let the superfluous and lust-dieted man[1]
That slaves° your ordinance,° that will not see   *defers to / authority*
Because he does not feel, feel your power quickly.
So distribution should undo excess,

65 And each man have enough. Dost thou know Dover?
EDGAR   Ay, master.
GLOUCESTER   There is a cliff whose high and bending° head   *overhanging*
Looks fearfully in the confinèd deep.[2]
Bring me but to the very brim of it

70 And I'll repair the misery thou dost bear
With something rich about me. From that place
I shall no leading need.
EDGAR   Give me thy arm.
Poor Tom shall lead thee.   *Exit* [EDGAR *guiding* GLOUCESTER]

---

6. It is a bad business to have to play the fool in the face of sorrow.
7. For the sake of our long and loyal relationship (as master and servant).
8. The time is truly sick when.
9. I cannot continue the charade. *daub:* mask, plaster.
1. Let the overprosperous man who indulges his appetite.
2. Looks fearsomely into the straits below.

Scene 16

Enter [at one door] GONORIL and Bastard [EDMUND]

GONORIL   Welcome, my lord. I marvel our mild husband
 Not° met us on the way.   *Has not*

    Enter [at another door] Steward [OSWALD]

      Now, where's your master?

OSWALD   Madam, within; but never man so changed.
 I told him of the army that was landed;
5 He smiled at it. I told him you were coming;
 His answer was 'The worse.' Of Gloucester's treachery
 And of the loyal service of his son
 When I informed him, then he called me sot,°   *fool*
 And told me I had turned the wrong side out.[1]
10 What he should most defy seems pleasant to him;
 What like, offensive.

GONORIL [*to* EDMUND]   Then shall you go no further.
 It is the cowish° terror of his spirit   *cowardly*
 That dares not undertake. He'll not feel wrongs
 Which tie him to an answer.[2] Our wishes on the way
15 May prove effects.[3] Back, Edmund, to my brother.° *brother-in-law*
 Hasten his musters° and conduct his powers.° *call-up of troops / armies*
 I must change arms at home, and give the distaff[4]
 Into my husband's hands. This trusty servant
 Shall pass between us. Ere long you are like° to hear, *likely*
20 If you dare venture in your own behalf,
 A mistress's° command. Wear this. Spare speech. *(playing on "lover's")*
 Decline your head. This kiss, if it durst speak,
 Would stretch thy spirits up into the air.
   [*She kisses him*]
 Conceive,° and fare you well.   *Understand* (*my meaning*)
25 EDMUND   Yours in° the ranks of death.   *even in*

GONORIL   My most dear Gloucester.   [*Exit* EDMUND]
 To thee a woman's services are due;
 My foot usurps my body.[5]

OSWALD   Madam, here comes my lord. *Exit*
   [*Enter* ALBANY]

GONORIL   I have been worth the whistling.[6]

ALBANY   O Gonoril,
30 You are not worth the dust which the rude wind
 Blows in your face. I fear your disposition.
 That nature which contemns it° origin   *despises its*
 Cannot be bordered certain° in itself.   *be defended securely*
 She that herself will sliver and disbranch°   *split*
35 From her material sap perforce must wither,
 And come to deadly use.[7]

Scene 16 Location: Before Albany's castle.
1. I had reversed things (by mistaking loyalty for treachery).
2. *He'll . . . answer:* He'll ignore insults that would provoke him to retaliate.
3. May be put into action.
4. A device used in spinning and so emblematic of the female role. To "change arms," therefore, is to swap the insignia of male and female identity.
5. Continuing the inversion of roles, Albany, who should

be the head of the family, is seen by Gonoril as a subservient member with no right to control her.
6. At one time, you would have come to welcome me home; referring to the proverb "It is a poor dog that is not worth the whistling."
7. *She . . . use:* The allusion is probably biblical: "But that which beareth thorns and briers is reproved, and is near unto cursing; whose end is to be burned" (Hebrews 6:8). *come to deadly use:* be destroyed; be used for burning.

4.2

Enter GONERIL [*and*] *Bastard* [EDMOND *at one door*]
and Steward [OSWALD *at another*]

GONERIL Welcome, my lord. I marvel our mild husband
Not° met us on the way. [*To* OSWALD] Now, where's your master?   *Has not*
OSWALD Madam, within; but never man so changed.
I told him of the army that was landed;
5 He smiled at it. I told him you were coming;
His answer was 'The worse'. Of Gloucester's treachery
And of the loyal service of his son
When I informed him, then he called me sot,°   *fool*
And told me I had turned the wrong side out.¹
10 What most he should dislike seems pleasant to him;
What like, offensive.
GONERIL [*to* EDMOND] Then shall you go no further.
It is the cowish° terror of his spirit   *cowardly*
That dares not undertake. He'll not feel wrongs
Which tie him to an answer.² Our wishes on the way
15 May prove effects.³ Back, Edmond, to my brother.°   *brother-in-law*
Hasten his musters° and conduct his powers.°   *call-up of troops / armies*
I must change names° at home, and give the distaff⁴   *exchange roles*
Into my husband's hands. This trusty servant
Shall pass between us. Ere long you are like° to hear,   *likely*
20 If you dare venture in your own behalf,
A mistress's° command. Wear this. Spare speech.   *(playing on "lover's")*
Decline your head. This kiss, if it durst speak,
Would stretch thy spirits up into the air.
   [*She kisses him*]
Conceive,° and fare thee well.   *Understand (my meaning)*
25 EDMOND Yours in° the ranks of death.   *even in*
GONERIL My most dear Gloucester.   *Exit* [EDMOND]
O, the difference of man and man!
To thee a woman's services are due;
My fool usurps my body.⁵
OSWALD   Madam, here comes my lord.
   Enter ALBANY
GONERIL I have been worth the whistling.⁶
30 ALBANY   O Goneril,
You are not worth the dust which the rude wind
Blows in your face.

---

1. I had reversed things (by mistaking loyalty for treachery).
2. *He'll . . . answer*: He'll ignore insults that would provoke him to retaliate.
3. May be put into action.

4. Spinning staff, the female insignia that she wishes to exchange for Albany's manly sword.
5. My idiot husband presumes to possess me.
6. At one time, you would have come to welcome me home; referring to the proverb "It is a poor dog that is not worth the whistling."

GONORIL   No more. The text is foolish.
ALBANY Wisdom and goodness to the vile seem vile;
          Filths savour but themselves. What have you done?
          Tigers, not daughters, what have you performed?
40   A father, and a gracious, agèd man,
          Whose reverence even the head-lugged° bear would lick,   *dragged by the head*
          Most barbarous, most degenerate, have you madded.°   *driven mad*
          Could my good-brother° suffer you to do it—   *brother-in-law*
          A man, a prince by him so benefacted?
45   If that the heavens do not their visible spirits
          Send quickly down to tame these vile offences,
          It will come,
          Humanity must perforce° prey on itself,   *inevitably*
          Like monsters of the deep.
GONORIL   Milk-livered° man,   *Cowardly*
50   That bear'st a cheek for blows, a head for wrongs;[8]
          Who hast not in thy brows an eye discerning
          Thine honour from thy suffering;[9] that not know'st
          Fools do those villains pity who are punished
          Ere they have done their mischief: where's thy drum?°   *(to muster troops)*
55   France spreads his banners in our noiseless° land,   *peaceful*
          With plumèd helm thy flaxen biggin° threats,   *nightcap; child's cap*
          Whiles thou, a moral° fool, sits still and cries   *moralizing*
          'Alack, why does he so?'
ALBANY   See thyself, devil.
          Proper deformity shows not in the fiend
          So horrid as in woman.[1]
60 GONORIL   O vain° fool!   *useless*
ALBANY Thou changèd and self-covered[2] thing, for shame
          Bemonster not thy feature. Were't my fitness°   *If it were appropriate*
          To let these hands obey my blood,
          They are apt enough to dislocate and tear
65   Thy flesh and bones. Howe'er° thou art a fiend,   *Although*
          A woman's shape doth shield thee.
GONORIL Marry your manhood, mew[3]—
              Enter [SECOND] GENTLEMAN
ALBANY What news?
SECOND GENTLEMAN O my good lord, the Duke of Cornwall's dead,
          Slain by his servant going to put out
          The other eye of Gloucester.
70 ALBANY   Gloucester's eyes?
SECOND GENTLEMAN A servant that he bred, thralled with
              remorse,°   *shaken with pity*
          Opposed against the act, bending° his sword   *directing*
          To° his great master, who thereat enraged   *Against*

---

8. *for wrongs:* fit for abuse; ready for cuckold's horns.
9. *discerning . . . suffering:* that can distinguish
between an insult to your honor and something you
should patiently endure.
1. *Proper . . . woman:* Deformity (of morals) is appropriate in the devil and so less horrid than in woman, from
whom virtue is expected. Albany may hold a mirror in
front of Gonoril, since Jacobean women sometimes
wore small mirrors attached to their dresses.
2. Altered and with your true (womanly) self concealed.
3. Get control of your manhood—restrain ("mew") it.
Alternatively, assert your feeble masculinity (with a
derisive catcall, "mew").

GONERIL   Milk-livered° man,   *Cowardly*
That bear'st a cheek for blows, a head for wrongs;[7]
Who hast not in thy brows an eye discerning
Thine honour from thy suffering[8]—

35 ALBANY   See thyself, devil.
Proper deformity shows not in the fiend
So horrid as in woman.[9]
GONERIL   O vain° fool!   *useless*

Enter a MESSENGER

MESSENGER   O my good lord, the Duke of Cornwall's dead,
Slain by his servant going to put out
The other eye of Gloucester.
40 ALBANY   Gloucester's eyes?
MESSENGER   A servant that he bred, thrilled with remorse,°   *shaken with pity*
Opposed against the act, bending° his sword   *directing*
To° his great master, who thereat enraged   *Against*

---

7. *for wrongs:* fit for abuse; ready for cuckold's horns.
8. *discerning . . . suffering:* that can distinguish
between an insult to your honor and something you
should patiently endure.
9. *Proper . . . woman:* Deformity (of morals) is appropriate in the devil and so less horrid than in woman,
from whom virtue is expected. Albany may hold a mirror in front of Goneril, since Jacobean women sometimes wore small mirrors attached to their dresses.

Flew on him, and amongst them felled him dead,
75　But not without that harmful stroke which since
Hath plucked him after.[4]

ALBANY　　　　　　　　　This shows you are above,
You justicers,° that these our nether crimes[5]　　　　　　　　　*judges*
So speedily can venge. But O, poor Gloucester!
Lost he his other eye?

SECOND GENTLEMAN　　Both, both, my lord.
80　[*To* GONORIL] This letter, madam, craves a speedy answer.
'Tis from your sister.

GONORIL [*aside*]　　　　　One way I like this well;[6]
But being° widow, and my Gloucester with her,　　　　　　　　　*her being*
May all the building on my fancy pluck
Upon my hateful life.[7] Another way
85　The news is not so took.[8]—I'll read and answer.　　　*Exit*

ALBANY　Where was his son when they did take his eyes?

SECOND GENTLEMAN　Come with my lady hither.

ALBANY　　　　　　　　　　　　　　He is not here.

SECOND GENTLEMAN　No, my good lord; I met him back° again.　　　*returning*

ALBANY　Knows he the wickedness?
90　SECOND GENTLEMAN　Ay, my good lord; 'twas he informed against him,
And quit the house on purpose that their punishment
Might have the freer course.

ALBANY　　　　　　　　　　Gloucester, I live
To thank thee for the love thou showed'st the King,
And to revenge thy eyes.—Come hither, friend.
95　Tell me what more thou knowest.　　　　　　　*Exeunt*

Scene 17

Enter KENT [*disguised,*] *and* [FIRST] GENTLEMAN

KENT　Why the King of France is so suddenly gone back know
you no reason?

FIRST GENTLEMAN　Something he left imperfect° in the state　　　*unsettled*
Which, since his coming forth, is thought of;° which　　　　　*remembered*
5　Imports° to the kingdom so much fear and danger　　　　　　　*Portends*
That his personal return was most required
And necessary.

KENT　Who hath he left behind him general?

FIRST GENTLEMAN　The Maréchal° of France, Monsieur la Far.　　*Marshall*
10　KENT　Did your letters pierce the Queen to any demonstration
of grief?

FIRST GENTLEMAN　Ay, sir. She took them, read them in my presence,
And now and then an ample tear trilled down
Her delicate cheek. It seemed she was a queen
15　Over her passion who,° most rebel-like,　　　　　　　　　　　*which*
Sought to be king o'er her.

---

4. Has sent him to follow his servant into death.
5. Lower crimes, and so committed on earth, but also
suggesting that the deeds smack of the netherworld of
hell.
6. Because a political rival has been eliminated.

7. *May . . . life:* May pull down all of my built-up fantasies and thus make my life hateful.
8. The news may be taken otherwise.
Scene 17 Location: Near the French camp at Dover.

Flew on him, and amongst them felled him dead,
45 But not without that harmful stroke which since
Hath plucked him after.[1]

ALBANY   This shows you are above,
You justicers,° that these our nether crimes[2]   *judges*
So speedily can venge. But O, poor Gloucester!
Lost he his other eye?

MESSENGER   Both, both, my lord.—
50 This letter, madam, craves a speedy answer.
'Tis from your sister.

GONERIL [*aside*]   One way I like this well;[3]
But being° widow, and my Gloucester with her,   *her being*
May all the building in my fancy pluck
Upon my hateful life.[4] Another way
55 The news is not so tart.°—I'll read and answer.   *bitter*

[*Exit with* OSWALD]

ALBANY   Where was his son when they did take his eyes?

MESSENGER   Come with my lady hither.

ALBANY   He is not here.

MESSENGER   No, my good lord; I met him back° again.   *returning*

ALBANY   Knows he the wickedness?

60 MESSENGER   Ay, my good lord; 'twas he informed against him,
And quit the house on purpose that their punishment
Might have the freer course.

ALBANY   Gloucester, I live
To thank thee for the love thou showed'st the King,
And to revenge thine eyes.—Come hither, friend.
65 Tell me what more thou know'st.   *Exeunt*

---

1. Has sent him to follow his servant into death.
2. Lower crimes, and so committed on earth, but also suggesting that the deeds smack of the netherworld of hell.
3. Because a political rival has been eliminated.
4. *May . . . life:* May pull down all of my built-up fantasies and thus make my life hateful.

KENT   O, then it moved her.

FIRST GENTLEMAN   Not to a rage. Patience and sorrow strove
Who should express her goodliest.[1] You have seen
Sunshine and rain at once; her smiles and tears
20 Were like, a better way. Those happy smilets
That played on her ripe lip seemed not to know
What guests were in her eyes, which parted thence
As pearls from diamonds dropped. In brief,
Sorrow would be a rarity° most beloved   *gem*
If all could so become it.[2]

25 KENT   Made she no verbal question?

FIRST GENTLEMAN   Faith, once or twice she heaved the name of 'father'
Pantingly forth as if it pressed her heart,
Cried 'Sisters, sisters, shame of ladies, sisters,
Kent, father, sisters, what, i'th' storm, i'th' night,
30 Let piety not be believed!'[3] There she shook
The holy water from her heavenly eyes
And clamour° mastered, then away she started°   *crying / sprang*
To deal with grief alone.

KENT   It is the stars,
The stars above us govern our conditions,
35 Else one self mate and make[4] could not beget
Such different issues.° You spoke not with her since?   *offspring*

FIRST GENTLEMAN   No.

KENT   Was this before the King returned?

FIRST GENTLEMAN   No, since.

KENT   Well, sir, the poor distressèd Lear's i'th' town,
40 Who sometime in his better tune° remembers   *state of mind*
What we are come about, and by no means
Will yield° to see his daughter.   *consent*

FIRST GENTLEMAN   Why, good sir?

KENT   A sovereign shame so elbows° him: his own unkindness,   *prods; nudges*
That stripped her from his benediction, turned her
45 To foreign casualties,° gave her dear rights   *risks*
To his dog-hearted daughters—these things sting
His mind so venomously that burning shame
Detains him from Cordelia.

FIRST GENTLEMAN   Alack, poor gentleman!

KENT   Of Albany's and Cornwall's powers you heard not?

50 FIRST GENTLEMAN   'Tis so; they are afoot.

KENT   Well, sir, I'll bring you to our master Lear,
And leave you to attend him. Some dear cause°   *Some important reason*
Will in concealment wrap me up a while.
When I am known aright you shall not grieve°   *repent*
55 Lending me this acquaintance.° I pray you go   *news*
Along with me.   *Exeunt*

---

1. Which should best express her feelings.
2. If everyone wore it so beautifully.
3. Never believe in piety (pity, or filial respect); piety can-not exist.
4. Or else the same pair of spouses; "mate" and "make" may describe either partner.

Scene 18

Enter [Queen] CORDELIA, DOCTOR, *and others*

CORDELIA   Alack, 'tis he! Why, he was met even now,
As mad as the rackèd sea, singing aloud,
Crowned with rank fumitor and furrow-weeds,[1]
With burdocks, hemlock, nettles, cuckoo-flowers,
5   Darnel, and all the idle° weeds that grow   useless
In our sustaining corn. The centuries° send forth.   battalions
Search every acre in the high-grown field,
And bring him to our eye.   [*Exit one or more*]
                        What can man's wisdom
In the restoring° his bereavèd sense,   Do to restore
10 He that can help him
Take all my outward° worth.   material

DOCTOR   There is means, madam.
Our foster-nurse of nature[2] is repose,
The which he lacks. That to provoke in him
15 Are many simples operative,[3] whose power
Will close the eye of anguish.

CORDELIA   All blest secrets,
All you unpublished virtues° of the earth,   obscure healing plants
Spring with my tears, be aidant and remediate°   healing and remedial
In the good man's distress!—Seek, seek for him,
20 Lest his ungoverned rage dissolve the life
That wants° the means to lead it.   lacks
            Enter MESSENGER
MESSENGER   News, madam.
The British powers° are marching hitherward.   armies

CORDELIA   'Tis known before; our preparation stands
In expectation of them.—O dear father,
25 It is thy business that I go about;[4]
Therefore great France
My mourning and important° tears hath pitied.   urgent; solicitous
No blown° ambition doth our arms incite,   inflated
But love, dear love, and our aged father's right.[5]
30 Soon may I hear and see him!   *Exeunt*

Scene 18 Location: The French camp at Dover.
1. Fumitor was used against brain sickness. Furrow-weeds, like the other weeds in the following lines, grow in the furrows of plowed fields.
2. *Our . . . nature:* That which comforts and nourishes human nature.
3. *That . . . operative:* To induce that ("repose") in him,

there are many effective medicinal herbs.
4. The line echoes Christ's explanation of his mission in Luke 2:49, "I must go about my father's business."
5. *No . . . right:* 1 Corinthians 13:4–5 in the Bishops' Bible (1568) says that love "swelleth not, dealeth not dishonestly, seeketh not her own."

4.3

Enter with drum and colours, [Queen] CORDELIA, GEN-
TLEMEN, *and soldiers*

CORDELIA   Alack, 'tis he! Why, he was met even now,
As mad as the vexed sea, singing aloud,
Crowned with rank fumitor and furrow-weeds,[1]
With burdocks, hemlock, nettles, cuckoo-flowers,
5 Darnel, and all the idle° weeds that grow   *useless*
In our sustaining corn. A century° send forth.   *battalion (100 men)*
Search every acre in the high-grown field,
And bring him to our eye.   [*Exit one or more*]
                                What can man's wisdom
In the restoring° his bereavèd sense,   *Do to restore*
10 He that helps him take all my outward° worth.   *material*
FIRST GENTLEMAN   There is means, madam.
Our foster-nurse of nature[2] is repose,
The which he lacks. That to provoke in him
Are many simples operative,[3] whose power
Will close the eye of anguish.
15 CORDELIA   All blest secrets,
All you unpublished virtues° of the earth,   *obscure healing plants*
Spring with my tears, be aidant and remediate°   *healing and remedial*
In the good man's distress!—Seek, seek for him,
Lest his ungoverned rage dissolve the life
That wants° the means to lead it.   *lacks*
                Enter [a] MESSENGER
20 MESSENGER   News, madam.
The British powers° are marching hitherward.   *armies*
CORDELIA   'Tis known before; our preparation stands
In expectation of them.—O dear father,
It is thy business that I go about;[4]
25 Therefore great France
My mourning and importuned° tears hath pitied.   *importunate; solicitous*
No blown° ambition doth our arms incite,   *inflated*
But love, dear love, and our aged father's right.[5]
Soon may I hear and see him!   *Exeunt*

4.3 Location: The French camp at Dover.
1. Fumitor was used against brain sickness. Furrow-
weeds, like the other weeds in the following lines, grow
in the furrows of plowed fields.
2. *Our . . . nature:* That which comforts and nourishes
human nature.
3. *That . . . operative:* To induce that ("repose") in him,

there are many effective medicinal herbs.
4. The line echoes Christ's explanation of his mission in
Luke 2:49, "I must go about my father's business."
5. *No . . . right:* 1 Corinthians 13:4–5 in the Bishops'
Bible (1568) says that love "swelleth not, dealeth not dishonestly, seeketh not her own."

Scene 19

Enter REGAN *and Steward* [OSWALD]

REGAN   But are my brother's powers° set forth?   *(Albany's forces)*

OSWALD   Ay, madam.

REGAN   Himself in person?

OSWALD   Madam, with much ado.°   *trouble*
  Your sister is the better soldier.

REGAN   Lord Edmund spake not with your lord at home?

5   OSWALD   No, madam.

REGAN   What might import° my sister's letters to him?   *mean*

OSWALD   I know not, lady.

REGAN   Faith, he is posted° hence on serious matter.   *hurried*
  It was great ignorance, Gloucester's eyes being out,
10   To let him live. Where he arrives he moves
  All hearts against us. Edmund, I think, is gone,
  In pity of his misery,° to dispatch   *(ironic)*
  His 'nighted° life, moreover to descry°   *darkened / investigate*
  The strength o'th' army.

15   OSWALD   I must needs after° with my letters, madam.   *go after*

REGAN   Our troop sets forth tomorrow. Stay with us.
  The ways are dangerous.

OSWALD   I may not, madam.
  My lady charged° my duty in this business.   *commanded*

REGAN   Why should she write to Edmund? Might not you
20   Transport her purposes by word? Belike°—   *Perhaps*
  Something, I know not what. I'll love° thee much: *reward*
  Let me unseal the letter.

OSWALD   Madam, I'd rather—

REGAN   I know your lady does not love her husband.
  I am sure of that, and at her late° being here   *recently*
25   She gave strange oeillades° and most speaking looks   *amorous glances*
  To noble Edmund. I know you are of her bosom.°   *in her confidence*

OSWALD   I, madam?

REGAN   I speak in understanding,° for I know't.   *with certainty*
  Therefore I do advise you take this note.°   *take note of this*
30   My lord is dead. Edmund and I have talked,
  And more convenient° is he for my hand   *appropriate*
  Than for your lady's. You may gather° more.   *infer*
  If you do find him, pray you give him this,[1]
  And when your mistress hears thus much from you,
35   I pray desire her call her wisdom to her.[2]
  So, farewell.
  If you do chance to hear of that blind traitor,
  Preferment falls on him that cuts him off.°   *cuts his life short*

OSWALD   Would I could meet him, madam. I would show
  What lady I do follow.

40   REGAN   Fare thee well.   *Exeunt* [*severally*]

Scene 19 Location: At Gloucester's castle.   2. *desire . . . to her*: tell her to come to her senses.
1. This information, but possibly another letter or token.

4.4

Enter REGAN *and Steward* [OSWALD]

REGAN   But are my brother's powers° set forth?   (*Albany's forces*)

OSWALD   Ay, madam.

REGAN   Himself in person there?

OSWALD   Madam, with much ado.°   *trouble*
    Your sister is the better soldier.

REGAN   Lord Edmond spake not with your lord at home?

5 OSWALD   No, madam.

REGAN   What might import° my sister's letters to him?   *mean*

OSWALD   I know not, lady.

REGAN   Faith, he is posted° hence on serious matter.   *hurried*
    It was great ignorance, Gloucester's eyes being out,

10   To let him live. Where he arrives he moves
    All hearts against us. Edmond, I think, is gone,
    In pity of his misery,° to dispatch   (*ironic*)
    His 'nighted° life, moreover to descry°   *darkened / investigate*
    The strength o'th' enemy.

15 OSWALD   I must needs after,° madam, with my letter.   *go after*

REGAN   Our troops set forth tomorrow. Stay with us.
    The ways are dangerous.

OSWALD   I may not, madam.
    My lady charged° my duty in this business.   *commanded*

REGAN   Why should she write to Edmond? Might not you

20   Transport her purposes by word? Belike°—   *Perhaps*
    Some things—I know not what. I'll love° thee much: *reward*
    Let me unseal the letter.

OSWALD   Madam, I had rather—

REGAN   I know your lady does not love her husband.
    I am sure of that, and at her late° being here   *recently*

25   She gave strange oeillades° and most speaking looks   *amorous glances*
    To noble Edmond. I know you are of her bosom.°   *in her confidence*

OSWALD   I, madam?

REGAN   I speak in understanding.° Y'are, I know't.   *with certainty*
    Therefore I do advise you take this note.°   *take note of this*

30   My lord is dead. Edmond and I have talked,
    And more convenient° is he for my hand   *appropriate*
    Than for your lady's. You may gather° more.   *infer*
    If you do find him, pray you give him this,[1]
    And when your mistress hears thus much from you,

35   I pray desire her call her wisdom to her.[2]
    So, fare you well.
    If you do chance to hear of that blind traitor,
    Preferment falls on him that cuts him off.°   *cuts his life short*

OSWALD   Would I could meet him, madam. I should show
    What party I do follow.

40 REGAN   Fare thee well.   *Exeunt* [*severally*]

4.4 Location: At Gloucester's castle.   2. *desire . . . to her:* tell her to come to her senses.
1. This information, but possibly another letter or token.

Scene 20

Enter EDGAR *[disguised as a peasant, with a staff, guiding the blind]* GLOUCESTER

GLOUCESTER   When shall we come to th' top of that same° hill?   °agreed-upon

EDGAR   You do climb up it now. Look how we labour.

GLOUCESTER   Methinks the ground is even.

EDGAR   Horrible steep.
Hark, do you hear the sea?

GLOUCESTER   No, truly.

5   EDGAR   Why, then your other senses grow imperfect
By your eyes' anguish.

GLOUCESTER   So may it be indeed.
Methinks thy voice is altered, and thou speak'st
With better phrase and matter° than thou didst.   °sense

EDGAR   You're much deceived. In nothing am I changed
But in my garments.

10   GLOUCESTER   Methinks you're better spoken.

EDGAR   Come on, sir, here's the place. Stand still. How fearful
And dizzy 'tis to cast one's eyes so low!
The crows and choughs° that wing the midway air[1]   °jackdaws
Show° scarce so gross° as beetles. Halfway down   °Appear / big

15   Hangs one that gathers samphire,° dreadful trade!   °seaweed
Methinks he seems no bigger than his head.
The fishermen that walk upon the beach
Appear like mice, and yon tall anchoring barque°   °ship
Diminished to her cock,° her cock a buoy   °dinghy

20   Almost too small for sight. The murmuring surge
That on the unnumbered° idle pebble chafes   °innumerable
Cannot be heard, it's so high. I'll look no more,
Lest my brain turn and the° deficient sight   °my
Topple° down headlong.   °Topple me

GLOUCESTER   Set me where you stand.

25   EDGAR   Give me your hand. You are now within a foot
Of th'extreme verge. For all beneath the moon
Would I not leap upright.[2]

GLOUCESTER   Let go my hand.
Here, friend, 's another purse; in it a jewel
Well worth a poor man's taking. Fairies and gods

30   Prosper it[3] with thee! Go thou farther off.
Bid me farewell, and let me hear thee going.

EDGAR   Now fare you well, good sir.
[He stands aside]

GLOUCESTER   With all my heart.

EDGAR   *[aside]*   Why I do trifle thus with his despair
Is done to cure it.

GLOUCESTER   O you mighty gods,
He kneels

35   This world I do renounce, and in your sights
Shake patiently my great affliction off!

Scene 20   Location: Near Dover.
1. The air between cliff and sea.
2. I would not jump up and down (for fear of losing my
balance).
3. Make it increase. Fairies were sometimes held to
hoard and multiply treasure.

4.5

Enter EDGAR *[disguised as a peasant, with a staff, guiding the blind]* GLOUCESTER

GLOUCESTER   When shall I come to th' top of that same° hill?   agreed-upon
EDGAR   You do climb up it now. Look how we labour.
GLOUCESTER   Methinks the ground is even.
EDGAR   Horrible steep.
Hark, do you hear the sea?
GLOUCESTER   No, truly.
5   EDGAR   Why, then your other senses grow imperfect
By your eyes' anguish.
GLOUCESTER   So may it be indeed.
Methinks thy voice is altered, and thou speak'st
In better phrase and matter° than thou didst.   sense
EDGAR   You're much deceived. In nothing am I changed
But in my garments.
10   GLOUCESTER   Methinks you're better spoken.
EDGAR   Come on, sir, here's the place. Stand still. How fearful
And dizzy 'tis to cast one's eyes so low!
The crows and choughs° that wing the midway air[1]   jackdaws
Show° scarce so gross° as beetles. Halfway down   Appear / big
15   Hangs one that gathers samphire,° dreadful trade!   seaweed
Methinks he seems no bigger than his head.
The fishermen that walk upon the beach
Appear like mice, and yon tall anchoring barque°   ship
Diminished to her cock,° her cock a buoy   dinghy
20   Almost too small for sight. The murmuring surge
That on th'unnumbered° idle pebble chafes   innumerable
Cannot be heard so high. I'll look no more,
Lest my brain turn and the° deficient sight   my
Topple° down headlong.   Topple me
GLOUCESTER   Set me where you stand.
25   EDGAR   Give me your hand. You are now within a foot
Of th'extreme verge. For all beneath the moon
Would I not leap upright.[2]
GLOUCESTER   Let go my hand.
Here, friend, 's another purse; in it a jewel
Well worth a poor man's taking. Fairies and gods
30   Prosper it[3] with thee! Go thou further off.
Bid me farewell, and let me hear thee going.
EDGAR   Now fare ye well, good sir.
[He stands aside]
GLOUCESTER   With all my heart.
EDGAR [aside]   Why I do trifle thus with his despair
Is done to cure it.
GLOUCESTER [kneeling] O you mighty gods,
35   This world I do renounce, and in your sights
Shake patiently my great affliction off!

4.5 Location: Near Dover.
1. The air between cliff and sea.
2. I would not jump up and down (for fear of losing my
balance).
3. Make it increase. Fairies were sometimes held to
hoard and multiply treasure.

If I could bear it longer, and not fall
To quarrel° with your great opposeless wills,   *Into conflict*
My snuff and loathèd part of nature⁴ should
40 Burn itself out. If Edgar live, O bless him!—
Now, fellow, fare thee well.
EDGAR   Gone, sir. Farewell.
    [GLOUCESTER] *falls* [*forward*]
[*Aside*] And yet I know not how conceit may rob
The treasury of life, when life itself
Yields to the theft.⁵ Had he been where he thought,
45 By this° had thought been past.—Alive or dead?   *now*
[*To* GLOUCESTER] Ho you, sir; hear you, sir? Speak.
[*Aside*] Thus might he pass° indeed. Yet he revives.   *pass away*
[*To* GLOUCESTER] What are you, sir?
GLOUCESTER   Away, and let me die.
EDGAR   Hadst thou been aught° but goss'mer, feathers, air,   *anything*
50 So many fathom down precipitating°   *plunging*
Thou hadst shivered° like an egg. But thou dost breathe,   *shattered*
Hast heavy substance, bleed'st not, speak'st, art sound.
Ten masts a-length° make not the altitude   *end to end*
Which thou hast perpendicularly fell.
55 Thy life's a miracle. Speak yet again.
GLOUCESTER   But have I fallen, or no?
EDGAR   From the dread summit of this chalky bourn.⁶
Look up a-height. The shrill-gorged° lark so far   *shrill-throated*
Cannot be seen or heard. Do but look up.
60 GLOUCESTER   Alack, I have no eyes.
Is wretchedness deprived° that benefit   *deprived of*
To end itself by death? 'Twas yet some comfort
When misery could beguile° the tyrant's rage   *cheat*
And frustrate his proud will.
EDGAR   Give me your arm.
65 Up. So, how now? Feel you your legs? You stand.
GLOUCESTER   Too well, too well.
EDGAR   This is above all strangeness.
Upon the crown of the cliff what thing was that
Which parted from you?
GLOUCESTER   A poor unfortunate beggar.
EDGAR   As I stood here below, methoughts his eyes
70 Were two full moons. A had a thousand noses,
Horns whelked° and wavèd like the enridgèd sea.   *twisted*
It was some fiend. Therefore, thou happy father,°   *lucky old man*
Think that the clearest° gods, who made their honours   *purest; most illustrious*
Of men's impossibilities,⁷ have preserved thee.
75 GLOUCESTER   I do remember now. Henceforth I'll bear
Affliction till it do cry out itself
'Enough, enough,' and die. That thing you speak of,
I took it for a man. Often would it say

---

4. The scorched and hateful remnant of my lifetime.
snuff: end of a candlewick.
5. *And yet . . . theft*: Edgar worries that the imagined scenario ("conceit") he has invented may be enough to kill
his father, particularly as Gloucester wishes for ("yields

to") his own death.
6. The white chalk cliffs of Dover, which make a boundary ("bourn") between land and sea.
7. *who . . . impossibilities*: who attained honor for themselves by performing deeds impossible to men.

If I could bear it longer, and not fall
To quarrel° with your great opposeless wills,   *Into conflict*
My snuff and loathèd part of nature⁴ should
40 Burn itself out. If Edgar live, O bless him!—
Now, fellow, fare thee well.

EDGAR   Gone, sir. Farewell.
      [GLOUCESTER *falls forward*]
[*Aside*] And yet I know not how conceit may rob
The treasury of life, when life itself
Yields to the theft.⁵ Had he been where he thought,
45 By this° had thought been past.—Alive or dead?   *now*
[*To* GLOUCESTER] Ho, you, sir, friend; hear you, sir? Speak.
[*Aside*] Thus might he pass° indeed. Yet he revives.   *pass away*
[*To* GLOUCESTER] What are you, sir?

GLOUCESTER   Away, and let me die.

EDGAR Hadst thou been aught° but gossamer, feathers, air,   *anything*
50 So many fathom down precipitating°   *plunging*
Thou'dst shivered° like an egg. But thou dost breathe,   *shattered*
Hast heavy substance, bleed'st not, speak'st, art sound.
Ten masts a-length° make not the altitude   *end to end*
Which thou hast perpendicularly fell.
55 Thy life's a miracle. Speak yet again.

GLOUCESTER But have I fall'n, or no?

EDGAR From the dread summit of this chalky bourn.⁶
Look up a-height. The shrill-gorged° lark so far   *shrill-throated*
Cannot be seen or heard. Do but look up.

60 GLOUCESTER Alack, I have no eyes.
Is wretchedness deprived° that benefit   *deprived of*
To end itself by death? 'Twas yet some comfort
When misery could beguile° the tyrant's rage   *cheat*
And frustrate his proud will.

EDGAR   Give me your arm.
65 Up, so. How is't? Feel you your legs? You stand.

GLOUCESTER Too well, too well.

EDGAR   This is above all strangeness.
Upon the crown o'th' cliff what thing was that
Which parted from you?

GLOUCESTER   A poor unfortunate beggar.

EDGAR As I stood here below, methoughts his eyes
70 Were two full moons. He had a thousand noses,
Horns whelked° and wavèd like the enragèd sea.   *twisted*
It was some fiend. Therefore, thou happy father,°   *lucky old man*
Think that the clearest° gods, who make them honours   *purest; most illustrious*
Of men's impossibilities,⁷ have preserved thee.

75 GLOUCESTER I do remember now. Henceforth I'll bear
Affliction till it do cry out itself
'Enough, enough,' and die. That thing you speak of,
I took it for a man. Often 'twould say

4. The scorched and hateful remnant of my lifetime.   to") his own death.
snuff: end of a candlewick.   6. The white chalk cliffs of Dover, which make a bound-
5. *And yet . . . theft:* Edgar worries that the imagined sce-   ary ("bourn") between land and sea.
nario ("conceit") he has invented may be enough to kill   7. *who . . . impossibilities:* who attain honor for them-
his father, particularly as Gloucester wishes for ("yields   selves by performing deeds impossible to men.

'The fiend, the fiend!' He led me to that place.

EDGAR   Bear free and patient thoughts.

Enter LEAR *mad [crowned with weeds and flowers]*

80   But who comes here?
The safer sense will ne'er accommodate
His master thus.[8]

LEAR   No, they cannot touch me for coining.[9] I am the King
himself.

85   EDGAR   O thou side-piercing sight!

LEAR   Nature is above art in that respect.[1] There's your press-
money.[2] That fellow handles his bow like a crow-keeper.[3] Draw
me a clothier's yard.[4] Look, look, a mouse! Peace, peace, this
toasted cheese will do it.° There's my gauntlet. I'll prove it on   *(lure the mouse)*

90   a giant.[5] Bring up the brown bills.[6] O, well flown, bird,° in the   *arrow*
air. Ha! Give the word.°   *password*

EDGAR   Sweet marjoram.[7]

LEAR   Pass.

GLOUCESTER   I know that voice.

95   LEAR   Ha, Gonoril! Ha, Regan! They flattered me like a dog,°   *fawningly*
and told me I had white hairs in my beard ere the black ones
were there.[8] To say 'ay' and 'no' to everything I said 'ay' and
'no' to was no good divinity.[9] When the rain came to wet me
once, and the wind to make me chatter, when the thunder

100   would not peace at my bidding, there I found° them, there I   *understood*
smelt them out. Go to, they are not men of their words. They
told me I was everything; 'tis a lie, I am not ague-proof.°   *immune to illness*

GLOUCESTER   The trick° of that voice I do well remember.   *peculiarity*
Is't not the King?

LEAR   Ay, every inch a king.

[GLOUCESTER kneels]

105   When I do stare, see how the subject quakes!
I pardon that man's life. What was thy cause?°   *crime*
Adultery? Thou shalt not die for adultery.
No, the wren goes to't, and the small gilded fly
Does lecher in my sight.

110   Let copulation thrive, for Gloucester's bastard son
Was kinder to his father than my daughters
Got 'tween the lawful sheets. To't, luxury,° pell-mell,   *lechery*
For I lack soldiers. Behold yon simp'ring dame,
Whose face between her forks presageth snow,[1]

115   That minces° virtue, and does shake the head   *affects*
To hear of° pleasure's name: *even of*
The fitchew nor the soilèd horse[2] goes to't
With a more riotous appetite. Down from the waist

8. *The . . . thus:* A sane mind would never allow its possessor to dress up this way.
9. Because minting money was the prerogative of the
King, nobody could overtake or equal ("touch") him.
1. My true feelings will always outvalue others' hypocrisy;
my natural supremacy surpasses any attempt to create a
false new reign. This image may also be based on coining
(see note 9, above).
2. Fee paid to a soldier impressed, or forced, into the
army.
3. A person hired as a scarecrow, and thus unfit for anything else.
4. Draw the bowstring the full length of the arrow (a
standard English arrow was a cloth yard [37 inches]

long).
5. I'll defend my stand even against a giant. To throw
down an armored glove ("gauntlet") was to issue a challenge.
6. Brown painted pikes; the soldiers carrying them.
7. Used medicinally against madness.
8. Told me I had wisdom before age.
9. *no good divinity:* poor theology (because insincere);
from James 5:12, "Let your yea be yea; nay, nay."
1. Whose expression implies cold chastity. "Face" refers
to the area between her legs ("forks"), as well as to her
literal facial expression as framed by the aristocratic lady's
starched headpiece; also called a "fork."
2. Neither the polecat nor a horse full of fresh grass.

'The fiend, the fiend!' He led me to that place.

EDGAR   Bear free and patient thoughts.

Enter LEAR [*mad, crowned with weeds and flowers*]

80   But who comes here?
The safer sense will ne'er accommodate
His master thus.[8]

LEAR   No, they cannot touch me° for crying. I am the King   °lay hands on me
himself.

85 EDGAR   O thou side-piercing sight!

LEAR   Nature's above art in that respect.[9] There's your press-
money.[1] That fellow handles his bow like a crow-keeper.[2] Draw
me a clothier's yard.[3] Look, look, a mouse! Peace, peace, this
piece of toasted cheese will do't.° There's my gauntlet. I'll   °(*lure the mouse*)

90 prove it on a giant.[4] Bring up the brown bills.[5] O, well flown,
bird,° i'th' clout,° i'th' clout! Whew! Give the word.°   °*arrow* / *bull's-eye* / *password*

EDGAR   Sweet marjoram.[6]

LEAR   Pass.

GLOUCESTER   I know that voice.

95 LEAR   Ha! Goneril with a white beard? They flattered me like a
dog,° and told me I had the white hairs in my beard ere the   °*fawningly*
black ones were there.[7] To say 'ay' and 'no' to everything that I
said 'ay' and 'no' to was no good divinity.[8] When the rain came
to wet me once, and the wind to make me chatter; when the

100 thunder would not peace at my bidding, there I found° 'em,   °*understood*
there I smelt 'em out. Go to, they are not men o' their words.
They told me I was everything; 'tis a lie, I am not ague-proof.°   °*immune to illness*

GLOUCESTER   The trick° of that voice I do well remember.   °*peculiarity*
Is't not the King?

LEAR   Ay, every inch a king.
[GLOUCESTER *kneels*]

105 When I do stare, see how the subject quakes!
I pardon that man's life. What was thy cause?°   °*crime*
Adultery? Thou shalt not die. Die for adultery!
No, the wren goes to't, and the small gilded fly
Does lecher in my sight. Let copulation thrive,

110 For Gloucester's bastard son
Was kinder to his father than my daughters
Got 'tween the lawful sheets. To't, luxury,° pell-mell,   °*lechery*
For I lack soldiers. Behold yon simp'ring dame,
Whose face between her forks presages snow,[9]

115 That minces° virtue, and does shake the head   °*affects*
To hear of° pleasure's name.   °*even of*
The fitchew nor the soilèd horse[1] goes to't
With a more riotous appetite. Down from the waist

8. *The . . . thus:* A sane mind would never allow its possessor to dress up this way.
9. My true feelings will always outvalue others' hypocrisy;
my natural supremacy surpasses any attempt to create a
false new reign. This image may also be based on coining.
1. Fee paid to a soldier impressed, or forced, into the
army.
2. A person hired as a scarecrow, and thus unfit for anything else.
3. Draw the bowstring the full length of the arrow (a
standard English arrow was a cloth yard [37 inches]
long).
4. I'll defend my stand even against a giant. To throw

down an armored glove ("gauntlet") was to issue a challenge.
5. Brown painted pikes; the soldiers carrying them.
6. Used medicinally against madness.
7. Told me I had wisdom before age.
8. *no good divinity:* poor theology (because insincere);
from James 5:12, "Let your yea be yea; nay, nay."
9. Whose expression implies cold chastity. "Face"
refers to the area between her legs ("forks") as well as
to her literal facial expression as framed by the aristocratic lady's starched headpiece, also called a "fork."
1. Neither the polecat nor a horse full of fresh grass.

They're centaurs,[3] though women all above.
120 But° to the girdle° do the gods inherit;°   *Only / waist / own*
Beneath is all the fiend's. There's hell,[4] there's darkness,
There's the sulphury pit, burning, scalding,
Stench, consummation. Fie, fie, fie; pah, pah!
Give me an ounce of civet,[5] good apothecary,
125 To sweeten my imagination.
There's money for thee.
GLOUCESTER   O, let me kiss that hand!
LEAR   Here, wipe it first; it smells of mortality.
GLOUCESTER   O ruined piece° of nature! This great world   *masterpiece*
Shall so wear out to naught.[6] Do you know me?
130 LEAR   I remember thy eyes well enough. Dost thou squiny°   *squint*
on me?
No, do thy worst, blind Cupid, I'll not love.
Read thou that challenge. Mark the penning of 't.
GLOUCESTER   Were all the letters suns, I could not see one.
135 EDGAR [*aside*]   I would not take° this from report; it is,   *believe*
And my heart breaks at it.
LEAR [*to* GLOUCESTER]   Read.
GLOUCESTER   What—with the case° of eyes?   *sockets*
LEAR   O ho, are you there with me?[7] No eyes in your head, nor
140 no money in your purse? Your eyes are in a heavy case,[8] your
purse in a light; yet you see how this world goes.
GLOUCESTER   I see it feelingly.°   *by touch; painfully*
LEAR   What, art mad? A man may see how the world goes with
no eyes; look with thy ears. See how yon justice rails upon yon
145 simple° thief. Hark in thy ear: handy-dandy,[9] which is the thief,   *lowly; innocent*
which is the justice? Thou hast seen a farmer's dog bark at a
beggar?
GLOUCESTER   Ay, sir.
LEAR   An the creature° run from the cur, there thou mightst   *If the wretch*
150 behold the great image of authority. A dog's obeyed in office.
Thou rascal beadle,[1] hold° thy bloody hand.   *restrain*
Why dost thou lash that whore? Strip thine own back.
Thy blood as hotly lusts to use her in that kind°   *way*
For which thou whip'st her. The usurer hangs the cozener.[2]
155 Through tattered rags small vices do appear;
Robes and furred gowns hides all. Get thee glass eyes,
And, like a scurvy politician,[3] seem
To see the things thou dost not. No tears, now.
Pull off my boots. Harder, harder! So.
160 EDGAR [*aside*]   O, matter and impertinency° mixed—   *sense and nonsense*
Reason in madness!

---

3. Lecherous mythological creatures that have a human body to the waist and the legs and torso of a horse below.
4. Shakespeare's frequent term for female genitals.
5. Exotic perfume derived from the sex glands of the civet cat.
6. Shall decay to nothing in the same way. In Renaissance philosophy, humans were analogous to the cosmos, standing for the whole in miniature and as its masterpiece.

7. Is that what you are telling me?
8. In a sad condition; playing on "case" as "sockets."
9. Pick a hand, as in a child's game.
1. The parish officer responsible for whippings.
2. The ruinous moneylender, prosperous enough to be made a judge, convicts the ordinary cheat.
3. A vile schemer. In early modern England, "politician" meant an ambitious, even Machiavellian, upstart.

They're centaurs,[2] though women all above.

120 But° to the girdle° do the gods inherit;°   *Only / waist / own*
Beneath is all the fiend's. There's hell,[3] there's darkness, there
is the sulphurous pit, burning, scalding, stench, consumption.
Fie, fie, fie; pah, pah! Give me an ounce of civet,[4] good apothe-
cary, sweeten my imagination.
There's money for thee.

125 GLOUCESTER   O, let me kiss that hand!

LEAR   Let me wipe it first; it smells of mortality.

GLOUCESTER   O ruined piece° of nature! This great world   *masterpiece*
Shall so wear out to naught.[5] Dost thou know me?

LEAR   I remember thine eyes well enough. Dost thou squiny°   *squint*
130 at me?
No, do thy worst, blind Cupid, I'll not love.
Read thou this challenge. Mark but the penning of it.

GLOUCESTER   Were all thy letters suns, I could not see.

EDGAR [*aside*]   I would not take° this from report; it is,   *believe*
135 And my heart breaks at it.

LEAR [*to* GLOUCESTER]   Read.

GLOUCESTER   What—with the case° of eyes?   *socket*

LEAR   O ho, are you there with me?[6] No eyes in your head, nor
no money in your purse? Your eyes are in a heavy case,[7] your
140 purse in a light; yet you see how this world goes.

GLOUCESTER   I see it feelingly.°   *by touch; painfully*

LEAR   What, art mad? A man may see how this world goes with
no eyes; look with thine ears. See how yon justice rails upon
yon simple° thief. Hark in thine ear: change places, and handy-   *lowly; innocent*
145 dandy,[8] which is the justice, which is the thief? Thou hast seen
a farmer's dog bark at a beggar?

GLOUCESTER   Ay, sir.

LEAR   An the creature° run from the cur, there thou mightst   *If the wretch*
behold the great image of authority. A dog's obeyed in office.
150 Thou rascal beadle,[9] hold° thy bloody hand.   *restrain*
Why dost thou lash that whore? Strip thy own back.
Thou hotly lusts to use her in that kind°   *way*
For which thou whip'st her. The usurer hangs the cozener.[1]
Through tattered clothes great vices do appear;
155 Robes and furred gowns hide all. Plate° sin with gold,   *Armor; gild*
And the strong lance of justice hurtless° breaks;   *harmlessly*
Arm it in rags, a pygmy's straw does pierce it.
None does offend, none, I say none. I'll able° 'em.   *authorize*
Take that of me, my friend, who have the power
160 To seal th'accuser's lips. Get thee glass eyes,
And, like a scurvy politician,[2] seem
To see the things thou dost not. Now, now, now, now!
Pull off my boots. Harder, harder! So.

EDGAR [*aside*]   O, matter and impertinency° mixed—   *sense and nonsense*
165 Reason in madness!

---

2. Lecherous mythological creatures that have a human body to the waist and the legs and torso of a horse below.
3. Shakespeare's frequent term for female genitals.
4. Exotic perfume derived from the sex glands of the civet cat.
5. Shall decay to nothing in the same way. In Renaissance philosophy, humans were analogous to the cosmos, standing for the whole in miniature and as its masterpiece.

6. Is that what you are telling me?
7. In a sad condition; playing on "case" as "sockets."
8. Pick a hand, as in a child's game.
9. The parish officer responsible for whippings.
1. The ruinous moneylender, prosperous enough to be made a judge, convicts the ordinary cheat.
2. A vile schemer. In early modern England, "politician" meant an ambitious, even Machiavellian, upstart.

LEAR   If thou wilt weep my fortune, take my eyes.
I know thee well enough: thy name is Gloucester.
Thou must be patient. We came crying hither.
165 Thou know'st the first time that we smell the air
We wail and cry. I will preach to thee. Mark me.
GLOUCESTER   Alack, alack, the day!
LEAR [*removing his crown of weeds*]⁴   When we are born, we cry
that we are come
To this great stage of fools. This'° a good block.⁵   *This is*
170 It were a delicate° stratagem to shoe   *subtle*
A troop of horse with felt;⁶ and when I have stole upon
These son-in-laws, then kill, kill, kill, kill, kill, kill!
         Enter three GENTLEMEN
FIRST GENTLEMAN   O, here he is. Lay hands upon him, sirs.
[*To* LEAR] Your most dear—
175 LEAR   No rescue? What, a prisoner? I am e'en
The natural fool⁷ of fortune. Use° me well.   *Treat*
You shall have ransom. Let me have a surgeon;
I am cut to the brains.
FIRST GENTLEMAN   You shall have anything.
180 LEAR   No seconds?° All myself?   *supporters*
Why, this would make a man a man of salt,⁸
To use his eyes for garden water-pots,
Ay, and laying° autumn's dust.   *settling*
FIRST GENTLEMAN   Good sir—
LEAR   I will die bravely,⁹ like a bridegroom.
185 What, I will be jovial. Come, come,
I am a king, my masters, know you that?
FIRST GENTLEMAN   You are a royal one, and we obey you.
LEAR   Then there's life° in't. Nay, an° you get it, you shall get it   *hope / if*
with running. *Exit running [pursued by two* GENTLEMEN]
190 FIRST GENTLEMAN   A sight most pitiful in the meanest wretch,
Past speaking in a king. Thou hast one daughter
Who redeems nature from the general curse
Which twain hath brought her to.¹
EDGAR   Hail, gentle° sir.   *noble*
195 FIRST GENTLEMAN   Sir, speed you.° What's your will?   *God speed you*
EDGAR   Do you hear aught of a battle toward?°   *coming*
FIRST GENTLEMAN   Most sure and vulgar,° everyone hears that   *commonly known*
That can distinguish sense.°   *Who can understand*
EDGAR   But, by your favour,
200 How near's the other army?
FIRST GENTLEMAN   Near and on speedy foot, the main;°   *main army*
descriers°   *scouts*
Stands on the hourly thoughts.°   *Are expected forthwith*
EDGAR   I thank you, sir. That's all.

---

4. Like a preacher, removing his hat in the pulpit.
5. Stage (often called "scaffold" and hence linked to executioner's block); block used to shape a felt hat (such as
the hat removed by a preacher before a sermon); mounting block (such as the stump or stock Lear may have sat
on to remove his boots).
6. Hat material, to muffle the sound of the approaching
cavalry.
7. Born plaything; playing on "natural" as "mentally
deficient."

8. A man reduced to nothing but the salt his tears
deposit.
9. With courage; showily. "Die" plays on the Renaissance sense of "have an orgasm."
1. Who . . . to: Who restores proper meaning and order
to a universe plagued by the crimes of the other two
daughters; alluding to the fall of humankind and the natural world caused by the sin of Adam and Eve and to the
universal redemption brought about by Christ's sacrifice.

LEAR   If thou wilt weep my fortunes, take my eyes.
     I know thee well enough: thy name is Gloucester.
     Thou must be patient. We came crying hither.
     Thou know'st the first time that we smell the air
170   We waul and cry. I will preach to thee. Mark.

GLOUCESTER   Alack, alack the day!

LEAR [*removing his crown of weeds*]³   When we are born, we cry
        that we are come
     To this great stage of fools. This'° a good block.⁴   *This is*
     It were a delicate° stratagem to shoe   *subtle*
175   A troop of horse with felt.⁵ I'll put't in proof,°   *to the test*
     And when I have stol'n upon these son-in-laws,
     Then kill, kill, kill, kill, kill, kill!

            Enter a GENTLEMAN

FIRST GENTLEMAN   O, here he is. Lay hand upon him. [*To* LEAR] Sir,
     Your most dear daughter—

180   LEAR   No rescue? What, a prisoner? I am even
     The natural fool⁶ of fortune. Use° me well.   *Treat*
     You shall have ransom. Let me have surgeons;
     I am cut to th' brains.

FIRST GENTLEMAN   You shall have anything.

185   LEAR   No seconds?° All myself?   *supporters*
     Why, this would make a man a man of salt,⁷
     To use his eyes for garden water-pots.
     I will die bravely,⁸ like a smug° bridegroom. What,   *an elegant*
     I will be jovial. Come, come, I am a king.
190   Masters, know you that?

FIRST GENTLEMAN   You are a royal one, and we obey you.

LEAR   Then there's life° in't. Come, an° you get it, you shall get   *hope / if*
     it by running. Sa, sa, sa, sa!⁹

                                                           Exit [*running*]

FIRST GENTLEMAN   A sight most pitiful in the meanest wretch,
195   Past speaking in a king. Thou hast a daughter
     Who redeems nature from the general curse
     Which twain have brought her to.¹

EDGAR   Hail, gentle° sir.   *noble*

FIRST GENTLEMAN   Sir, speed you.° What's your will?   *God speed you*

200   EDGAR   Do you hear aught, sir, of a battle toward?°   *coming*

FIRST GENTLEMAN   Most sure and vulgar,° everyone hears that   *commonly known*
     That can distinguish sound.

EDGAR   But, by your favour,
     How near's the other army?

205   FIRST GENTLEMAN   Near and on speedy foot. The main descry°   *appearance*
     Stands in the hourly thought.°   *Is expected forthwith*

EDGAR   I thank you, sir. That's all.

---

3. Like a preacher removing his hat in the pulpit.
4. Stage (often called "scaffold" and hence linked to executioner's block); block used to shape a felt hat (such as the hat removed by a preacher before a sermon); mounting block (such as the stump or stock Lear may have sat on to remove his boots).
5. Hat material, to muffle the sound of the approaching cavalry.
6. Born plaything; playing on "natural" as "mentally deficient."

7. A man reduced to nothing but the salt his tears deposit.
8. With courage; showily. "Die" plays on the Renaissance sense of "have an orgasm."
9. A cry to encourage dogs in the hunt.
1. *Who . . . to:* Who restores proper meaning and order to a universe plagued by the crimes of the other two daughters; alluding to the fall of humankind and the natural world caused by the sin of Adam and Eve and to the universal redemption brought about by Christ's sacrifice.

FIRST GENTLEMAN Though that the Queen on° special cause°   *for / reason*
  is here,
    Her army is moved on.

EDGAR   I thank you, sir.   *Exit* GENTLEMAN

205 GLOUCESTER You ever gentle gods, take my breath from me.
    Let not my worser spirit² tempt me again
    To die before you please.

EDGAR   Well pray you, father.³

GLOUCESTER Now, good sir, what are you?

210 EDGAR A most poor man, made lame by fortune's blows,
    Who by the art of known and feeling° sorrows   *profound*
    Am pregnant to° good pity. Give me your hand,   *disposed to feel*
    I'll lead you to some biding.°   *resting place*

GLOUCESTER [*rising*]   Hearty thanks.
    The bounty and the benison of heaven
    To send thee boot to boot.⁴

        Enter Steward [OSWALD]

215 OSWALD   A proclaimed prize!⁵ Most happy!°   *lucky*
    That eyeless head of thine was first framed° flesh   *made of*
    To raise my fortunes. Thou most unhappy traitor,
    Briefly thyself remember.⁶ The sword is out
    That must destroy thee.

GLOUCESTER   Now let thy friendly hand
    Put strength enough to't.

220 OSWALD [*to* EDGAR]   Wherefore, bold peasant,
    Durst thou support a published° traitor? Hence,   *proclaimed*
    Lest the infection° of his fortune take   *(deathly) sickness*
    Like° hold on thee. Let go his arm.   *The same*

EDGAR 'Chill⁷ not let go, sir, without 'cagion.°   *occasion*

225 OSWALD Let go, slave, or thou diest.

EDGAR Good gentleman, go your gate.° Let poor volk pass. An   *be on your way*
    'chud° have been swaggered out of my life, it would not have   *If I could*
    been so long by a vortnight. Nay, come not near the old man.
    Keep out, 'che vor' ye, or I'll try whether your costard or my
230   baton be the harder;⁸ I'll be plain with you.

OSWALD Out, dunghill!

        They fight

EDGAR 'Chill pick your teeth, sir. Come, no matter for your
  foins.°   *sword thrusts*

        [EDGAR *knocks him down*]

OSWALD Slave, thou hast slain me. Villain, take my purse.
235 If ever thou wilt thrive, bury my body,
    And give the letters which thou find'st about me
    To Edmund, Earl of Gloucester. Seek him out
    Upon° the British party. O untimely death! Death!   *He dies*   *Within*

---

2. Wicked inclination; bad angel.
3. A term of respect for an elderly man.
4. To send you reward in addition (to my thanks).
5. A wanted man, with a bounty on his life.
6. Recollect and pray forgiveness for your sins.

7. I will; dialect from Somerset was a stage convention for peasant dialogue.
8. *'che vor' ye . . . harder:* I warrant you, or I'll test whether your head or my cudgel is harder. *costard:* a kind of apple.

FIRST GENTLEMAN   Though that the Queen on° special cause° is   °for / reason
        here,
    Her army is moved on.
EDGAR   I thank you, sir.   *Exit* [GENTLEMAN]
GLOUCESTER   You ever gentle gods, take my breath from me.
210   Let not my worser spirit² tempt me again
    To die before you please.
EDGAR   Well pray you, father.³
GLOUCESTER   Now, good sir, what are you?
EDGAR   A most poor man, made tame to fortune's blows,
215   Who by the art of known and feeling° sorrows   °profound
    Am pregnant to° good pity. Give me your hand,   °disposed to feel
    I'll lead you to some biding.°   °resting place
GLOUCESTER [*rising*]   Hearty thanks.
    The bounty and the benison of heaven
    To boot and boot.⁴
    Enter Steward [OSWALD]
OSWALD   A proclaimed prize!⁵ Most happy!°   °lucky
220   That eyeless head of thine was first framed° flesh   °made of
    To raise my fortunes. Thou old unhappy traitor,
    Briefly thyself remember.⁶ The sword is out
    That must destroy thee.
GLOUCESTER   Now let thy friendly hand
    Put strength enough to't.
OSWALD [*to* EDGAR]   Wherefore, bold peasant,
225   Durst thou support a published° traitor? Hence,   °proclaimed
    Lest that th'infection° of his fortune take   °(deathly) sickness
    Like° hold on thee. Let go his arm.   °The same
EDGAR   'Chill⁷ not let go, sir, without vurther 'cagion.°   °further occasion
OSWALD   Let go, slave, or thou diest.
230 EDGAR   Good gentleman, go your gate,° and let poor volk pass.   °be on your way
    An 'chud ha'° been swaggered out of my life, 'twould not ha'   °If I could have
    been so long as 'tis by a vortnight. Nay, come not near th'old
    man. Keep out, 'che vor' ye, or I's' try whether your costard or
    my baton be the harder;⁸ I'll be plain with you.
235 OSWALD   Out, dunghill!
EDGAR   'Chill pick your teeth, sir. Come, no matter vor your
        foins.°   °sword thrusts
    [EDGAR *knocks him down*]
OSWALD   Slave, thou hast slain me. Villain, take my purse.
    If ever thou wilt thrive, bury my body,
240   And give the letters which thou find'st about me
    To Edmond, Earl of Gloucester. Seek him out
    Upon° the English party. O untimely death! Death!   [*He dies*]   Within

---

2. Wicked inclination; bad angel.
3. A term of respect for an elderly man.
4. In addition to my thanks, and may it bring you some worldly reward.
5. A wanted man, with a bounty on his life.
6. Recollect and pray forgiveness for your sins.

7. I will; dialect from Somerset was a stage convention for peasant dialogue.
8. *'che vor' ye . . . harder:* I warrant you, or I shall test whether your head or my cudgel is harder. *costard:* a kind of apple.

EDGAR   I know thee well—a serviceable° villain,   *an officious*
240   As duteous to the vices of thy mistress
       As badness would desire.
GLOUCESTER   What, is he dead?
EDGAR   Sit you down, father. Rest you.
       [GLOUCESTER *sits*]
       Let's see his pockets. These letters that he speaks of
245   May be my friends. He's dead; I am only sorrow°   *sorry*
       He had no other deathsman.° Let us see.   *executioner*
       Leave,° gentle wax;⁹ and manners, blame us not.   *By your leave*
       To know our enemies' minds we'd rip their hearts;
       Their° papers is more lawful.   *To rip their*
       [*He reads*] *a letter*
250   'Let your reciprocal vows be remembered. You have many
       opportunities to cut him off. If your will want° not, time and   *lacks*
       place will be fruitfully offered. There is nothing done° if he   *accomplished*
       return the conqueror; then am I the prisoner, and his bed my
       jail, from the loathed warmth whereof, deliver me, and supply°   *fill*
255   the place for your labour.¹
              Your—wife, so I would say—your affectionate
                     servant, and for you her own for venture,²
                                                              Gonoril.'
       O indistinguished space of woman's wit³—
260   A plot upon her virtuous husband's life,
       And the exchange° my brother!—Here in the sands   *substitute*
       Thee I'll rake up,° the post unsanctified°   *cover up / unholy messenger*
       Of murderous lechers, and in the mature time°   *when the time is ripe*
       With this ungracious° paper strike the sight   *ungodly*
265   Of the death-practised Duke.⁴ For him 'tis well
       That of thy death and business I can tell.   [*Exit with the body*]
GLOUCESTER   The King is mad. How stiff is my vile sense,⁵
       That I stand up and have ingenious feeling⁶
       Of my huge sorrows! Better I were distraught;°   *mad*
270   So should my thoughts be fencèd from my griefs,
       And woes by wrong° imaginations lose   *false*
       The knowledge of themselves.
              A drum afar off. [*Enter* EDGAR]
EDGAR   Give me your hand.
       Far off methinks I hear the beaten drum.
       Come, father, I'll bestow° you with a friend.   *lodge*
                     Exit [EDGAR *guiding* GLOUCESTER]

9. The wax seal on the letter.
1. *for your labour*: as a reward for your endeavors, and
for further sexual exertion.
2. *for you . . . venture*: one willing to risk all for you; all
yours, if you dare be so bold.
3. Limitless extent of woman's cunning.

4. Of the Duke whose death is plotted.
5. How obstinate is my unwanted power of reason.
6. That I remain upright and firm in my sanity and
have rational perceptions.

EDGAR   I know thee well—a serviceable° villain,   *an officious*
    As duteous to the vices of thy mistress
245   As badness would desire.
    GLOUCESTER   What, is he dead?
    EDGAR   Sit you down, father. Rest you.
    [GLOUCESTER *sits*]
    Let's see these pockets. The letters that he speaks of
    May be my friends. He's dead; I am only sorrow°   *sorry*
250   He had no other deathsman.° Let us see.   *executioner*
    Leave,° gentle wax,[9] and manners; blame us not.   *By your leave*
    To know our enemies' minds we rip their hearts;
    Their° papers is more lawful.   *To rip their*
    Reads the letter
    'Let our reciprocal vows be remembered. You have many
255   opportunities to cut him off. If your will want° not, time and   *lacks*
    place will be fruitfully offered. There is nothing done° if he   *accomplished*
    return the conqueror; then am I the prisoner, and his bed my
    jail, from the loathed warmth whereof, deliver me, and supply°   *fill*
    the place for your labour.[1]
260   Your—wife, so I would say,—affectionate
                servant, and for you her own for venture,[2]
                      Goneril.'
    O indistinguished space of woman's will[3]—
    A plot upon her virtuous husband's life,
265   And the exchange° my brother!—Here in the sands   *substitute*
    Thee I'll rake up,° the post unsanctified°   *cover up / unholy messenger*
    Of murderous lechers, and in the mature time°   *when the time is ripe*
    With this ungracious° paper strike the sight   *ungodly*
    Of the death-practised Duke.[4] For him 'tis well
270   That of thy death and business I can tell.   [*Exit with the body*]
    GLOUCESTER   The King is mad. How stiff is my vile sense,[5]
    That I stand up and have ingenious feeling[6]
    Of my huge sorrows! Better I were distraught,°   *mad*
    So should my thoughts be severed from my griefs,
    Drum afar off
275   And woes by wrong° imaginations lose   *false*
    The knowledge of themselves.
    [*Enter* EDGAR]
    EDGAR   Give me your hand.
    Far off methinks I hear the beaten drum.
    Come, father, I'll bestow° you with a friend.   *lodge*
    Exit [EDGAR *guiding* GLOUCESTER]

---

9. The wax seal on the letter.

1. *for your labour:* as a reward for your endeavors, and for
further sexual exertion.

2. *for you . . . venture:* one willing to risk all for you; all
yours, if you dare be so bold.

3. Limitless extent of woman's willfulness. As with "hell"

in line 121, "will" might also refer to a woman's genitals.

4. Of the Duke whose death is plotted.

5. How obstinate is my unwanted power of reason.

6. That I remain upright and firm in my sanity and have
rational perceptions.

Scene 21

[*Soft music.*] *Enter* CORDELIA, *and* KENT [*disguised*]

CORDELIA   O thou good Kent,
How shall I live and work to match thy goodness?
My life will be too short, and every measure° fail me.   *attempt*

KENT   To be acknowledged, madam, is o'erpaid.°   *is more than enough*

5   All my reports go[1] with the modest truth,
Nor more, nor clipped, but so.[2]

CORDELIA   Be better suited.°   *attired*
These weeds° are memories of those worser hours.   *clothes*
I prithee put them off.

KENT   Pardon me, dear madam.
Yet to be known shortens my made intent.[3]

10   My boon I make it[4] that you know° me not   *acknowledge*
Till time and I think meet.°   *suitable*

CORDELIA   Then be't so, my good lord.

[*Enter* DOCTOR *and* FIRST GENTLEMAN]

How does the King?

DOCTOR   Madam, sleeps still.

CORDELIA   O you kind gods,
Cure this great breach in his abusèd nature;
The untuned and hurrying senses O wind up[5]
Of this child-changèd[6] father!

15   DOCTOR   So please your majesty
That we may wake the King? He hath slept long.

CORDELIA   Be governed by your knowledge, and proceed
I'th' sway° of your own will. Is he arrayed?°   *By the authority / clothed*

FIRST GENTLEMAN   Ay, madam. In the heaviness of his sleep

20   We put fresh garments on him.

DOCTOR   Good madam, be by when we do awake him.
I doubt not of his temperance.°   *calmness*

CORDELIA   Very well.

DOCTOR   Please you draw near. Louder the music there!

[LEAR *is discovered*° *asleep*]   *revealed*

CORDELIA   O my dear father, restoration hang

25   Thy medicine on my lips, and let this kiss
Repair those violent harms that my two sisters
Have in thy reverence° made!   *aged dignity*

KENT   Kind and dear princess!

CORDELIA   Had you not[7] been their father, these white flakes°   *locks of hair*
Had challenged° pity of them. Was this a face   *Would have provoked*

30   To be exposed against the warring winds,
To stand against the deep dread-bolted thunder
In the most terrible and nimble stroke
Of quick cross-lightning, to watch°—poor *perdu*[8]—   *to stand guard*

Scene 21 Location: The French camp at Dover.
1. May all accounts of me agree.
2. Not greater or less, but exactly the modest amount I
deserve.
3. Revealing myself now would abort my designs.
4. The reward I beg is.
5. *The . . . up*: Reorder his confused and delirious mind.

The image is of tightening the strings of a lute.
6. Changed by his children; changed into a child; playing on a musical key change.
7. Even if you had not.
8. Lost one; in military terms, a dangerously exposed
sentry.

4.6

Enter CORDELIA, KENT [*disguised*], *and* [*the* FIRST] GEN-
TLEMAN

CORDELIA   O thou good Kent, how shall I live and work
To match thy goodness? My life will be too short,
And every measure° fail me.   attempt

KENT   To be acknowledged, madam, is o'erpaid.°   is more than enough
5   All my reports go¹ with the modest truth,
Nor more, nor clipped, but so.²

CORDELIA   Be better suited.°   attired
These weeds° are memories of those worser hours.   clothes
I prithee put them off.

KENT   Pardon, dear madam.
Yet to be known shortens my made intent.³
10   My boon I make it⁴ that you know° me not   acknowledge
Till time and I think meet.°   suitable

CORDELIA   Then be't so, my good lord.—
How does the King?

FIRST GENTLEMAN   Madam, sleeps still.

CORDELIA   O you kind gods,
Cure this great breach in his abusèd nature;
Th'untuned and jarring senses O wind up⁵
Of this child-changèd⁶ father!

15   FIRST GENTLEMAN   So please your majesty
That we may wake the King? He hath slept long.

CORDELIA   Be governed by your knowledge, and proceed
I'th' sway° of your own will. Is he arrayed?°   By the authority / clothed

FIRST GENTLEMAN   Ay, madam. In the heaviness of sleep
20   We put fresh garments on him.

Enter LEAR [*asleep,*] *in a chair carried by servants*
Be by, good madam, when we do awake him.
I doubt not of his temperance.°   calmness

CORDELIA   O my dear father, restoration hang
Thy medicine on my lips, and let this kiss
25   Repair those violent harms that my two sisters
Have in thy reverence° made!   aged dignity

KENT   Kind and dear princess!

CORDELIA   Had you not⁷ been their father, these white flakes°   locks of hair
Did challenge° pity of them. Was this a face   Would have provoked
To be opposed against the warring winds?

4.6 Location: The French camp at Dover.
1. May all accounts of me agree.
2. Not greater or less, but exactly the modest amount I
deserve.
3. Revealing myself now would abort my designs.
4. The reward I beg is.

5. *Th'untuned . . . up:* Reorder his confused and delirious mind. The image is of tightening the strings of a lute.
6. Changed by his children; changed into a child; playing on a musical key change.
7. Even if you had not.

With this thin helm?° Mine injurer's mean'st dog,   *helmet (of hair)*
35   Though he had bit me, should have stood that night
Against my fire. And wast thou fain,° poor father,   *glad*
To hovel thee with swine and rogues forlorn
In short° and musty straw? Alack, alack,   *scant; broken*
'Tis wonder that thy life and wits at once
40   Had not concluded all!° [*To* DOCTOR] He wakes. Speak to him.   *altogether*
DOCTOR   Madam, do you; 'tis fittest.
CORDELIA [*to* LEAR]   How does my royal lord? How fares your majesty?
LEAR   You do me wrong to take me out o'th' grave.
Thou art a soul in bliss, but I am bound
45   Upon a wheel of fire, that mine own tears
Do scald like molten lead.[9]
CORDELIA   Sir, know me.
LEAR   You're a spirit, I know. Where did you die?
CORDELIA [*to the* DOCTOR]   Still, still far wide!°   *unbalanced*
DOCTOR   He's scarce awake. Let him alone a while.
50   LEAR   Where have I been? Where am I? Fair daylight?
I am mightily abused.° I should e'en die with pity   *wronged; deceived*
To see another thus. I know not what to say.
I will not swear these are my hands. Let's see:
I feel this pin prick. Would I were assured
Of my condition.
55   CORDELIA [*kneeling*]   O look upon me, sir,
And hold your hands in benediction o'er me.
No, sir, you must not kneel.
LEAR   Pray do not mock.
I am a very foolish, fond° old man,   *silly*
Fourscore and upward, and to deal plainly,
60   I fear I am not in my perfect mind.
Methinks I should know you, and know this man;
Yet I am doubtful, for I am mainly° ignorant   *entirely*
What place this is; and all the skill I have
Remembers not these garments; nor I know not
65   Where I did lodge last night. Do not laugh at me,
For as I am a man, I think this lady
To be my child, Cordelia.
CORDELIA   And so I am.
LEAR   Be your tears wet?[1] Yes, faith. I pray, weep not.
If you have poison for me, I will drink it.
70   I know you do not love me; for your sisters
Have, as I do remember, done me wrong.
You have some cause; they have not.
CORDELIA   No cause, no cause.

---

9. **but I . . . lead:** Lear puts himself in either hell or purgatory, both places of such punishment in medieval

accounts.
1. Are your tears real?; is this really happening?

30   Mine enemy's dog, though he had bit me, should have stood
        That night against my fire. And wast thou fain,° poor father,   glad
        To hovel thee with swine and rogues forlorn
        In short° and musty straw? Alack, alack,   scant; broken
        'Tis wonder that thy life and wits at once
35   Had not concluded all!° [*To the* GENTLEMAN] He wakes. Speak   altogether
            to him.
FIRST GENTLEMAN   Madam, do you; 'tis fittest.
CORDELIA [*to* LEAR]   How does my royal lord? How fares your majesty?
LEAR   You do me wrong to take me out o'th' grave.
        Thou art a soul in bliss, but I am bound
40   Upon a wheel of fire, that mine own tears
        Do scald like molten lead.[8]
CORDELIA   Sir, do you know me?
LEAR   You are a spirit, I know. Where did you die?
CORDELIA [*to the* GENTLEMAN]   Still, still far wide!°   unbalanced
FIRST GENTLEMAN   He's scarce awake. Let him alone a while.
45   LEAR   Where have I been? Where am I? Fair daylight?
        I am mightily abused.° I should ev'n die with pity   wronged; deceived
        To see another thus. I know not what to say.
        I will not swear these are my hands. Let's see:
        I feel this pin prick. Would I were assured
        Of my condition.
50   CORDELIA [*kneeling*]   O look upon me, sir,
        And hold your hands in benediction o'er me.
        You must not kneel.
LEAR   Pray do not mock.
        I am a very foolish, fond° old man,   silly
        Fourscore and upward,
55   Not an hour more nor less; and to deal plainly,
        I fear I am not in my perfect mind.
        Methinks I should know you, and know this man;
        Yet I am doubtful, for I am mainly° ignorant   entirely
        What place this is; and all the skill I have
60   Remembers not these garments; nor I know not
        Where I did lodge last night. Do not laugh at me,
        For as I am a man, I think this lady
        To be my child, Cordelia.
CORDELIA   And so I am, I am.
LEAR   Be your tears wet?[9] Yes, faith. I pray, weep not.
65   If you have poison for me, I will drink it.
        I know you do not love me; for your sisters
        Have, as I do remember, done me wrong.
        You have some cause; they have not.
CORDELIA   No cause, no cause.

---

8. *but I . . . lead:* Lear puts himself in either hell or purgatory, both places of such punishment in medieval

accounts.
9. Are your tears real?; is this really happening?

LEAR Am I in France?

KENT In your own kingdom, sir.

75 LEAR Do not abuse° me.   *deceive; mock*

DOCTOR Be comforted, good madam. The great rage
    You see is cured in him, and yet it is danger
    To make him even o'er° the time he has lost.   *go over*
    Desire him to go in; trouble him no more

80 Till further settling.°   *Until his mind eases*

CORDELIA [*to* LEAR] Will't please your highness walk?

LEAR You must bear with me.
    Pray now, forget and forgive. I am old
    And foolish. *Exeunt. Manent°* KENT *and* [FIRST] GENTLEMAN   *Remain*

FIRST GENTLEMAN Holds it true, sir, that the Duke
    Of Cornwall was so slain?

85 KENT   Most certain, sir.

FIRST GENTLEMAN Who is conductor° of his people?   *commander*

KENT   As 'tis said,
    The bastard son of Gloucester.

FIRST GENTLEMAN   They say Edgar,
    His banished son, is with the Earl of Kent
    In Germany.

KENT   Report° is changeable.   *Rumor*

90 'Tis time to look about.° The powers of the kingdom   *prepare defenses*
    Approach apace.

FIRST GENTLEMAN The arbitrement° is   *encounter*
    Like to be bloody. Fare you well, sir.   [*Exit*]

KENT My point and period² will be throughly wrought,
    Or° well or ill, as this day's battle's fought.   *Exit*   *For*

Scene 22

Enter EDMUND, REGAN, *and their powers*

EDMUND Know° of the Duke if his last purpose hold,¹   *Inquire*
    Or whether since he is advised by aught²
    To change the course. He's full of abdication³
    And self-reproving. Bring his constant pleasure.°   *his settled intent*
                                    [*Exit one or more*]

5 REGAN Our sister's man is certainly miscarried.⁴

EDMUND 'Tis to be doubted,° madam.   *feared*

REGAN   Now, sweet lord,
    You know the goodness I intend upon you.
    Tell me but truly—but then speak the truth—
    Do you not love my sister?

EDMUND   Ay: honoured° love.   *honorable*

10 REGAN But have you never found my brother's way
    To the forfended⁵ place?

---

2. The purpose and end of my life; literally, the full stop.
Scene 22 Location: The British camp near Dover.
1. If his previous intention (to wage war) remains firm.
2. Since then anything has persuaded him.

3. A tendency to give up his intentions or put aside his responsibilities.
4. Has surely come to grief by some accident.
5. Forbidden (to Edmund, because it is adulterous).

LEAR   Am I in France?

70   KENT   In your own kingdom, sir.

LEAR   Do not abuse° me.   *deceive; mock*

FIRST GENTLEMAN   Be comforted, good madam. The great rage
    You see is killed in him. Desire him to go in.
    Trouble him no more till further settling.°   *until his mind eases*

75   CORDELIA [*to* LEAR]   Will't please your highness walk?

LEAR   You must bear with me. Pray you now, forget
    And forgive. I am old and foolish.   *Exeunt*

5.1

Enter with drum and colours° EDMOND, REGAN, GENTLE-   *regimental flags*
MEN, *and soldiers*

EDMOND   Know° of the Duke if his last purpose hold,[1]   *Inquire*
    Or whether since he is advised by aught[2]
    To change the course. He's full of abdication[3]
    And self-reproving. Bring his constant pleasure.°   *his settled intent*
                          [*Exit one or more*]

5   REGAN   Our sister's man is certainly miscarried.[4]

EDMOND   'Tis to be doubted,° madam.   *feared*

REGAN   Now, sweet lord,
    You know the goodness I intend upon you.
    Tell me but truly—but then speak the truth—
    Do you not love my sister?

EDMOND   In honoured° love.   *honorable*

10   REGAN   But have you never found my brother's way
    To the forfended[5] place?

5.1 Location: The British camp near Dover.
1. If his previous intention (to wage war) remains firm.
2. Since then anything has persuaded him.
3. A tendency to give up his intentions or put aside his
responsibilities.
4. Has surely come to grief by some accident.
5. Forbidden (to Edmond, because it is adulterous).

EDMUND   That thought abuses° you.   *deceives*
REGAN   I am doubtful°   *suspicious*
That you have been conjunct° and bosomed with° her,   *complicit / enamored of*
As far as we call hers.⁶
15   EDMUND   No, by mine honour, madam.
REGAN   I never shall endure her. Dear my lord,
Be not familiar° with her.   *intimate*
EDMUND   Fear° me not.   *Doubt*
She and the Duke her husband—
        Enter ALBANY *and* GONORIL *with troops*
20   GONORIL [*aside*]   I had rather lose the battle than that sister
Should loosen° him and me.   *disunite*
ALBANY [*to* REGAN]   Our very loving sister, well bemet,°   *met*
For this I hear: the King is come to his daughter,
With others whom the rigour° of our state°   *harshness / government*
25   Forced to cry out. Where I could not be honest°   *honorable*
I never yet was valiant. For this business,
It touches° us as France invades our land;   *concerns*
Yet bold's the King, with others whom I fear.⁷
Most just and heavy causes make oppose.⁸
EDMUND   Sir, you speak nobly.
30   REGAN   Why is this reasoned?⁹
GONORIL   Combine together 'gainst the enemy;
For these domestic poor particulars°   *minor details*
Are not to° question here.   *the*
ALBANY   Let us then determine with the ensign° of war   *experienced officer(s)*
On our proceedings.
35   EDMUND   I shall attend you
Presently° at your tent.   [*Exit with his powers*]   *In a moment*
REGAN   Sister, you'll go with us?
GONORIL   No.
REGAN   'Tis most convenient.° Pray you go with us.¹   *suitable*
GONORIL [*aside*]   O ho, I know the riddle!° [*To* REGAN] I will go.   *disguised meaning*
        Enter EDGAR [*disguised as a peasant*]
40   EDGAR [*to* ALBANY]   If e'er your grace had speech with man so poor,
Hear me one word.
ALBANY [*to the others*]   I'll overtake you.
        Exeunt [*all but* ALBANY *and* EDGAR]
                    Speak.
EDGAR   Before you fight the battle, ope this letter.
If you have victory, let the trumpet sound
For him that brought it. Wretched though I seem,
45   I can produce a champion that will prove°   *defend*
What is avouchèd° there. If you miscarry,°   *asserted / perish*
Your business of the world hath so an end.
Fortune love you—
ALBANY   Stay till I have read the letter.

---

6. In total intimacy; all the way.
7. Albany expresses his ambivalence. The invasion concerns us insofar as we are facing a French army in our lands. On the other hand, King Lear, along with other powerful forces, is boldly claiming his own land.

8. Fair and serious causes are driven into opposition.
9. What is the point of this kind of speech?
1. Regan wants Gonoril to go with Albany and her, rather than with Edmund.

EDMOND   No, by mine honour, madam.

REGAN   I never shall endure her. Dear my lord,
Be not familiar° with her.   *intimate*

EDMOND   Fear° me not.   *Doubt*

15   She and the Duke her husband—

Enter with drum and colours ALBANY, GONERIL, [*and*]
soldiers

ALBANY [*to* REGAN]   Our very loving sister, well bemet.°   *met*
[*To* EDMOND] Sir, this I heard: the King is come to his daughter,
With others whom the rigour° of our state°   *harshness / government*
Forced to cry out.

REGAN   Why is this reasoned?[6]

20   GONERIL   Combine together 'gainst the enemy;
For these domestic and particular broils°   *minor details*
Are not the question here.

ALBANY   Let's then determine with th'ensign° of war   *experienced officer(s)*
On our proceeding.

REGAN   Sister, you'll go with us?[7]

25   GONERIL   No.

REGAN   'Tis most convenient.° Pray go with us.   *suitable*

GONERIL [*aside*]   O ho, I know the riddle!° [*To* REGAN] I will go.   *disguised meaning*

Enter EDGAR [*disguised as a peasant*]

EDGAR [*to* ALBANY]   If e'er your grace had speech with man so poor,
Hear me one word.

ALBANY [*to the others*]   I'll overtake you.   *Exeunt both the armies*
Speak.

30   EDGAR   Before you fight the battle, ope this letter.
If you have victory, let the trumpet sound
For him that brought it. Wretched though I seem,
I can produce a champion that will prove°   *defend*
What is avouchèd° there. If you miscarry,°   *asserted / perish*

35   Your business of the world hath so an end,
And machination° ceases. Fortune love you.   *plotting*

ALBANY   Stay till I have read the letter.

6. What is the point of this kind of speech?
7. Regan wants Goneril to go with Albany and her, rather than with Edmond.

50   EDGAR   I was forbid it.
      When time shall serve, let but the herald cry,
      And I'll appear again.
  ALBANY   Why, fare thee well.
      I will o'erlook the paper.   *Exit* [EDGAR]
      Enter EDMUND
55   EDMUND   The enemy's in view; draw up your powers.°   *troops*
      [*He offers* ALBANY *a paper*]
      Here is the guess° of their great strength and forces   *estimate*
      By diligent discovery;° but your haste   *spying*
      Is now urged on you.
  ALBANY   We will greet the time.[2]   *Exit*
  EDMUND   To both these sisters have I sworn my love,
60   Each jealous° of the other as the stung   *suspicious*
      Are of the adder. Which of them shall I take?—
      Both?—one?—or neither? Neither can be enjoyed
      If both remain alive. To take the widow
      Exasperates, makes mad, her sister Gonoril,
65   And hardly° shall I carry out my side,°   *with difficulty / plan*
      Her husband being alive. Now then, we'll use
      His countenance[3] for the battle, which being done,
      Let her that would be rid of him devise
      His speedy taking off. As for his mercy
70   Which he intends to Lear and to Cordelia,
      The battle done, and they within our power,
      Shall° never see his pardon; for my state°   *They shall / condition*
      Stands on° me to defend, not to debate.   *Exit*   *Obliges*

Scene 23

Alarum.[1] *Enter the powers of France over the stage* [*led
by*] CORDELIA *with her father in her hand.* [*Then*] *enter*
EDGAR [*disguised as a peasant, guiding*] GLOUCESTER
  EDGAR   Here, father,[2] take the shadow of this bush
      For your good host;° pray that the right may thrive.   *shelter*
      If ever I return to you again
      I'll bring you comfort.   *Exit*
  GLOUCESTER   Grace go with you, sir.
      Alarum and retreat.° [*Enter* EDGAR]   *trumpet signal*
5   EDGAR   Away, old man. Give me thy hand. Away.
      King Lear hath lost, he and his daughter ta'en.
      Give me thy hand. Come on.
  GLOUCESTER   No farther, sir. A man may rot even° here.   *right*
  EDGAR   What, in ill thoughts again? Men must endure
10   Their going hence even as their coming hither.
      Ripeness is all.[3] Come on.   [*Exit* EDGAR *guiding* GLOUCESTER]

---

2. We will be ready to meet the occasion.
3. Authority or backing; also suggesting "face," to be used like a mask for Edmund's ambition.
Scene 23 Location: The rest of the play takes place near the battlefield.
1. Trumpet call to battle.

2. See note to 20.208.
3. To await the destined time is the most important thing, as fruit falls only when ripe (playing on Gloucester's "rot," line 8); readiness for death is our only duty (compare *Hamlet* 5.2.160, "The readiness is all").

EDGAR   I was forbid it.

When time shall serve, let but the herald cry,

And I'll appear again.

40   ALBANY   Why, fare thee well.

I will o'erlook thy paper.   *Exit* [EDGAR]

          Enter EDMOND

EDMOND   The enemy's in view; draw up your powers.°   *troops*

          [*He offers* ALBANY *a paper*]

Here is the guess° of their true strength and forces   *estimate*

By diligent discovery;° but your haste   *spying*

Is now urged on you.

45   ALBANY   We will greet the time.[8]   *Exit*

EDMOND   To both these sisters have I sworn my love,

Each jealous° of the other as the stung   *suspicious*

Are of the adder. Which of them shall I take?—

Both?—one?—or neither? Neither can be enjoyed

50   If both remain alive. To take the widow

Exasperates, makes mad, her sister Goneril,

And hardly° shall I carry out my side,°   *with difficulty / plan*

Her husband being alive. Now then, we'll use

His countenance[9] for the battle, which being done,

55   Let her who would be rid of him devise

His speedy taking off. As for the mercy

Which he intends to Lear and to Cordelia,

The battle done, and they within our power,

Shall° never see his pardon; for my state°   *They shall / condition*

60   Stands on° me to defend, not to debate.   *Exit*   *Obliges*

5.2

Alarum within.[1] Enter with drum and colours LEAR, COR-
DELIA, *and soldiers over the stage; and exeunt. Enter*
EDGAR [*disguised as a peasant, guiding*] GLOUCESTER

EDGAR   Here, father,[2] take the shadow of this tree

For your good host;° pray that the right may thrive.   *shelter*

If ever I return to you again

I'll bring you comfort.

GLOUCESTER   Grace go with you, sir.   *Exit* [EDGAR]

          Alarum and retreat° *within. Enter* EDGAR   *trumpet signal*

5   EDGAR   Away, old man. Give me thy hand. Away.

King Lear hath lost, he and his daughter ta'en.

Give me thy hand. Come on.

GLOUCESTER   No further, sir. A man may rot even° here.   *right*

EDGAR   What, in ill thoughts again? Men must endure

10   Their going hence even as their coming hither.

Ripeness is all.[3] Come on.

GLOUCESTER   And that's true, too.

          [*Exit* EDGAR *guiding* GLOUCESTER]

---

8. We will be ready to meet the occasion.
9. Authority or backing; also suggesting "face," to be used like a mask for Edmond's ambition.
5.2 Location: The rest of the play takes place near the battlefield.
1. Trumpet call to battle (backstage).

2. See note to 4.5.212.
3 To await the destined time is the most important thing, as fruit falls only when ripe (playing on Gloucester's "rot," line 8); readiness for death is our only duty (compare *Hamlet* 5.2.160, "The readiness is all").

Scene 24

Enter EDMUND *with* LEAR *and* CORDELIA *prisoners*[, *a*
CAPTAIN, *and soldiers*]

EDMUND   Some officers take them away. Good guard
Until their greater pleasures[1] best be known
That are to censure° them.   judge

CORDELIA [*to* LEAR]   We are not the first
Who with best meaning° have incurred the worst.   intention
5   For thee, oppressèd King, am I cast down,°   (into unhappiness)
Myself could else outfrown false fortune's frown.[2]
Shall we not see these daughters and these sisters?

LEAR   No, no. Come, let's away to prison.
We two alone will sing like birds i'th' cage.
10   When thou dost ask me blessing, I'll kneel down
And ask of thee forgiveness; so we'll live,
And pray, and sing, and tell old tales, and laugh
At gilded butterflies,[3] and hear poor rogues
Talk of court news, and we'll talk with them too—
15   Who loses and who wins, who's in, who's out,
And take upon 's the mystery of things
As if we were God's spies; and we'll wear out°   outlast
In a walled prison packs and sects of great ones
That ebb and flow by th' moon.[4]

EDMUND [*to soldiers*]   Take them away.
20   LEAR [*to* CORDELIA]   Upon such sacrifices,[5] my Cordelia,
The gods themselves throw incense. Have I caught thee?
He that parts us shall bring a brand from heaven
And fire us hence like foxes.[6] Wipe thine eyes.
The goodyear shall devour 'em, flesh and fell,[7]
25   Ere they shall make us weep. We'll see 'em starve first. Come.

[*Exeunt all but* EDMUND *and* CAPTAIN]

EDMUND   Come hither, captain. Hark.
Take thou this note. Go follow them to prison.
One step I have advanced° thee; if thou dost   promoted
As this instructs thee, thou dost make thy way
30   To noble fortunes. Know thou this: that men
Are as the time is. To be tender-minded
Does not become a sword.° Thy great employment   befit a swordsman
Will not bear question.° Either say thou'lt do't,   discussion
Or thrive by other means.

CAPTAIN   I'll do't, my lord.
35   EDMUND   About it, and write 'happy' when thou hast done.[8]
Mark, I say, instantly, and carry it° so   carry it out
As I have set it down.

CAPTAIN   I cannot draw a cart,
Nor eat dried oats.° If it be man's work, I'll do't.   [*Exit*]   (like a horse)

Scene 24
1. *Good . . . pleasures:* Guard them well until the desires
of those greater persons.
2. Otherwise, I could be defiant in the face of bad fortune.
3. Gaudy courtiers.
4. *packs . . . moon:* followers and factions of important
people whose position at court varies as the tide.
5. Upon such sacrifices as we are or as you have made.

6. *shall . . . foxes:* must have divine aid to do so. The
image is of using a torch to smoke foxes out of their holes,
or, in the case of Lear and Cordelia, prison cells.
7. *flesh and fell:* meat and skin; entirely. The precise
meaning of "goodyear" has not been explained; it may
signify simply the passage of time or may suggest some
ominous, destructive power.
8. Go to it, and call yourself happy when you are done.

5.3

Enter in conquest with drum and colours EDMOND; LEAR
and CORDELIA *as prisoners; soldiers; a* CAPTAIN

EDMOND   Some officers take them away. Good guard
Until their greater pleasures[1] first be known
That are to censure° them.   *judge*
CORDELIA [*to* LEAR]   We are not the first
Who with best meaning° have incurred the worst.   *intention*
5   For thee, oppressèd King, I am cast down,°   *(into unhappiness)*
Myself could else outfrown false fortune's frown.[2]
Shall we not see these daughters and these sisters?
LEAR   No, no, no, no. Come, let's away to prison.
We two alone will sing like birds i'th' cage.
10   When thou dost ask me blessing, I'll kneel down
And ask of thee forgiveness; so we'll live,
And pray, and sing, and tell old tales, and laugh
At gilded butterflies,[3] and hear poor rogues
Talk of court news, and we'll talk with them too—
15   Who loses and who wins, who's in, who's out,
And take upon 's the mystery of things
As if we were God's spies; and we'll wear out°   *outlast*
In a walled prison packs and sects of great ones
That ebb and flow by th' moon.[4]
EDMOND [*to soldiers*]   Take them away.
20   LEAR   Upon such sacrifices,[5] my Cordelia,
The gods themselves throw incense. Have I caught thee?
He that parts us shall bring a brand from heaven
And fire us hence like foxes.[6] Wipe thine eyes.
The goodyear shall devour them, flesh and fell,[7]
25   Ere they shall make us weep. We'll see 'em starved first. Come.
Exeunt [*all but* EDMOND *and* CAPTAIN]
EDMOND   Come hither, captain. Hark.
Take thou this note. Go follow them to prison.
One step I have advanced° thee; if thou dost   *promoted*
As this instructs thee, thou dost make thy way
30   To noble fortunes. Know thou this: that men
Are as the time is. To be tender-minded
Does not become a sword.° Thy great employment   *befit a swordsman*
Will not bear question.° Either say thou'lt do't,   *discussion*
Or thrive by other means.
CAPTAIN   I'll do't, my lord.
35   EDMOND   About it, and write 'happy' when thou'st done.[8]
Mark, I say, instantly, and carry it° so   *carry it out*
As I have set it down.   *Exit* CAPTAIN

5.3
1. *Good . . . pleasures:* Guard them well until the desires of those greater persons.
2. Otherwise, I could be defiant in the face of bad fortune.
3. Gaudy courtiers.
4. *packs . . . moon:* followers and factions of important people whose position at court varies as the tide.
5. Upon such sacrifices as we are or as you have made.

6. *shall . . . foxes:* must have divine aid to do so. The image is of using a torch to smoke foxes out of their holes, or, in the case of Lear and Cordelia, prison cells.
7. *flesh and fell:* meat and skin; entirely. The precise meaning of "goodyear" has not been explained; it may signify simply the passage of time or may suggest some ominous, destructive power.
8. Go to it, and call yourself happy when you are done.

Enter Duke [*of* ALBANY], *the two ladies* [GONORIL *and*
REGAN, *another* CAPTAIN], *and others*

ALBANY [*to* EDMUND]   Sir, you have showed today your valiant
strain,°   *qualities; birth*
40 And fortune led you well. You have the captives
That were the opposites° of this day's strife.   *opponents*
We do require then of you, so to use° them   *treat*
As we shall find their merits and our safety
May equally determine.

EDMUND   Sir, I thought it fit
45 To send the old and miserable King
To some retention° and appointed guard,   *confinement*
Whose° age has charms in it, whose title more,   *(Lear's)*
To pluck the common bosom⁹ on his side
And turn our impressed lances° in our eyes   *conscripted lancers*
50 Which¹ do command them. With him I sent the Queen,
My reason all the same, and they are ready
Tomorrow, or at further space,° to appear   *at a future point*
Where you shall hold your session.° At this time   *court of judgment*
We sweat and bleed. The friend hath lost his friend,
55 And the best quarrels in the heat are cursed
By those that feel their sharpness.²
The question of Cordelia and her father
Requires a fitter place.

ALBANY   Sir, by your patience,
I hold you but a subject of° this war,   *in waging*
Not as a brother.

60 REGAN   That's as we list° to grace him.   *choose*
Methinks our pleasure should have been demanded³
Ere you had spoke so far. He led our powers,°   *armies*
Bore the commission of my place and person,
The which immediate° may well stand up   *close connection*
And call itself your brother.

65 GONORIL   Not so hot.°   *Not so fast*
In his own grace° he doth exalt himself   *merit*
More than in your advancement.⁴

REGAN   In my right
By me invested, he compeers° the best.   *equals*

GONORIL   That were the most⁵ if he should husband you.

REGAN   Jesters do oft prove prophets.

70 GONORIL   Holla, holla—
That eye that told you so looked but asquint.⁶

REGAN   Lady, I am not well, else I should answer
From a full-flowing stomach.° [*To* EDMUND] General,   *anger*
Take thou my soldiers, prisoners, patrimony.
75 Witness the world that I create thee here
My lord and master.

9. To garner the affection of the populace.
1. *in our eyes / Which:* in the eyes of us who.
2. *And . . . sharpness:* And in the heat of battle, even the
most just wars are cursed by those who must suffer the
fighting.
3. I think you should have inquired into my wishes.
4. In the honors you confer upon him.
5. That investiture would be complete.
6. Squinting was a proverbial effect of jealousy, because
of the tendency to look suspiciously at potential rivals.

Flourish. Enter ALBANY, GONERIL, REGAN, [*drummer,*
trumpeter and] *soldiers*

ALBANY   Sir, you have showed today your valiant strain,°   *qualities; birth*
And fortune led you well. You have the captives
40 Who were the opposites° of this day's strife.   *opponents*
I do require them of you, so to use° them   *treat*
As we shall find their merits and our safety
May equally determine.

EDMOND   Sir, I thought it fit
To send the old and miserable King
45 To some retention° and appointed guard,   *confinement*
Whose° age had charms in it, whose title more,   *(Lear's)*
To pluck the common bosom⁹ on his side
And turn our impressed lances° in our eyes   *conscripted lancers*
Which¹ do command them. With him I sent the Queen,
50 My reason all the same, and they are ready
Tomorrow, or at further space,° t'appear   *at a future point*
Where you shall hold your session.°   *court of judgment*

ALBANY   Sir, by your patience,
I hold you but a subject of° this war,   *in waging*
Not as a brother.

REGAN   That's as we list° to grace him.   *choose*
55 Methinks our pleasure might have been demanded²
Ere you had spoke so far. He led our powers,°   *armies*
Bore the commission of my place and person,
The which immediacy° may well stand up   *close connection*
And call itself your brother.

GONERIL   Not so hot.°   *Not so fast*
60 In his own grace° he doth exalt himself   *merit*
More than in your addition.³

REGAN   In my rights
By me invested, he compeers° the best.   *equals*

ALBANY   That were the most⁴ if he should husband you.

REGAN   Jesters do oft prove prophets.

GONERIL   Holla, holla—
65 That eye that told you so looked but asquint.⁵

REGAN   Lady, I am not well, else I should answer
From a full-flowing stomach.° [*To* EDMOND] General,   *anger*
Take thou my soldiers, prisoners, patrimony.
Dispose of them, of me. The walls° is thine.   *fortress of my heart*
70 Witness the world that I create thee here
My lord and master.

---

9. To garner the affection of the populace.
1. *in our eyes / Which*: in the eyes of us who.
2. I think you should have inquired into my wishes.
3. In the honors you confer upon him.

4. That investiture would be complete.
5. Squinting was a proverbial effect of jealousy, because
of the tendency to look suspiciously at potential rivals.

GONORIL   Mean you to enjoy him, then?

ALBANY   The let-alone° lies not in your good will.   veto

EDMUND   Nor in thine, lord.

ALBANY   Half-blooded° fellow, yes.   Bastard

EDMUND   Let the drum strike[7] and prove my title good.

80   ALBANY   Stay yet, hear reason. Edmund, I arrest thee
        On capital treason, and in thine attaint[8]
        This gilded serpent.   [To REGAN] For your claim, fair sister,°   sister-in-law
        I bar it in the interest of my wife.
        'Tis she is subcontracted to this lord,

85   And I, her husband, contradict the banns.°   announcement of marriage
        If you will marry, make your love to me.
        My lady is bespoke.—Thou art armed, Gloucester.
        If none appear to prove upon thy head
        Thy heinous, manifest, and many treasons,
            [He throws down a glove]

90   There is my pledge. I'll prove it on thy heart,
        Ere I taste bread, thou art in nothing less°   in no way less guilty
        Than I have here proclaimed thee.

REGAN   Sick, O sick!

GONORIL [aside]   If not, I'll ne'er trust poison.

EDMUND [to ALBANY, throwing down a glove]

95   There's my exchange. What° in the world he is   Whoever
        That names me traitor, villain-like he lies.
        Call by thy trumpet. He that dares, approach;
        On him, on you—who not?—I will maintain
        My truth and honour firmly.

100 ALBANY   A herald, ho!

EDMUND   A herald, ho, a herald!

ALBANY   Trust to thy single virtue,° for thy soldiers,   your unassisted power
        All levied in my name, have in my name
        Took their discharge.

REGAN   This sickness grows upon me.

105 ALBANY   She is not well. Convey her to my tent.
            [Exit one or more with REGAN]
        [Enter a HERALD and a trumpeter]
        Come hither, herald. Let the trumpet sound,
        And read out this.

---

7. Perhaps to announce the betrothal, or a challenge.
8. And in order to accuse you; and as one who shares your corruption or crime.

GONERIL	Mean you to enjoy him?	
ALBANY	The let-alone° lies not in your good will.	veto
EDMOND	Nor in thine, lord.	
ALBANY	Half-blooded° fellow, yes.	Bastard
REGAN [to EDMOND]	Let the drum strike⁶ and prove my title thine.	

75 ALBANY Stay yet, hear reason. Edmond, I arrest thee
On capital treason, and in thy attaint⁷
This gilded serpent. [*To* REGAN] For your claim, fair sister,°   *sister-in-law*
I bar it in the interest of my wife.
'Tis she is subcontracted to this lord,
80 And I, her husband, contradict your banns.°   *announcement of marriage*
If you will marry, make your loves to me.
My lady is bespoke.

GONERIL	An interlude!°	A farce

ALBANY Thou art armed, Gloucester. Let the trumpet sound.
If none appear to prove upon thy person
85 Thy heinous, manifest, and many treasons,
There is my pledge.
    [*He throws down a glove*]
                I'll make° it on thy heart,   *prove*
Ere I taste bread, thou art in nothing less°   *in no way less guilty*
Than I have here proclaimed thee.

REGAN	Sick, O sick!	

90 GONERIL [*aside*] If not, I'll ne'er trust medicine.°   *poison (euphemistic)*
EDMOND [*to* ALBANY, *throwing down a glove*] There's my
           exchange. What° in the world he is   *whoever*
That names me traitor, villain-like he lies.
Call by the trumpet. He that dares, approach;
On him, on you,—who not?—I will maintain
My truth and honour firmly.

ALBANY	A herald, ho!	

95   *Enter a* HERALD
[*To* EDMOND] Trust to thy single virtue,° for thy soldiers,   *your unassisted power*
All levied in my name, have in my name
Took their discharge.

REGAN	My sickness grows upon me.
ALBANY	She is not well. Convey her to my tent.

    [*Exit one or more with* REGAN]
100 Come hither, herald. Let the trumpet sound,
And read out this.

---

6. Perhaps to announce the betrothal, or a challenge.
7. And in order to accuse you; and as one who shares your corruption or crime.

SECOND CAPTAIN   Sound, trumpet!
    [*Trumpeter sounds*]
HERALD [*reads*]   'If any man of quality or degree in the host of
110   the army will maintain upon Edmund, supposed Earl of
    Gloucester, that he's a manifold traitor, let him appear at the
    third sound of the trumpet. He is bold in his defence.'
EDMUND   Sound! [*Trumpeter sounds*] Again!
    Enter EDGAR, [*armed,*] *at the third sound, a trumpet*
    before him
ALBANY [*to the* HERALD]   Ask him his purposes, why he appears
    Upon this call o'th' trumpet.
115 HERALD [*to* EDGAR]   What° are you?   *Who*
    Your name and quality,° and why you answer   *degree; rank*
    This present summons?
EDGAR   O, know my name is lost,
    By treason's tooth bare-gnawn and canker-bit.°   *worm-eaten*
    Yet ere I move't,° where is the adversary   *make my declaration*
    I come to cope withal?°   *to encounter with*
120 ALBANY   Which is that adversary?
EDGAR   What's he that speaks for Edmund, Earl of Gloucester?
EDMUND   Himself. What sayst thou to him?
EDGAR   Draw thy sword,
    That° if my speech offend a noble heart   *So that*
    Thy arm may do thee justice. Here is mine.
    [*He draws his sword*]
125 Behold, it is the privilege of my tongue,
    My oath, and my profession. I protest,
    Maugre° thy strength, youth, place, and eminence,   *Despite*
    Despite thy victor-sword and fire-new° fortune,   *newly minted*
    Thy valour and thy heart,° thou art a traitor,   *courage*
130 False to thy gods, thy brother, and thy father,
    Conspirant 'gainst this high illustrious prince,
    And from th'extremest upward° of thy head   *top*
    To the descent° and dust beneath thy feet   *lowest part; sole*
    A most toad-spotted⁹ traitor. Say thou no,
135 This sword, this arm, and my best spirits are bent°   *ready*
    To prove upon thy heart, whereto I speak,
    Thou liest.
EDMUND   In wisdom I should ask thy name,
    But since thy outside looks so fair and warlike,
    And that° thy tongue some say¹ of breeding breathes,   *since*
140 My right of knighthood° I disdain and spurn.   *(to ask your name)*
    Here do I toss those treasons to thy head,
    With the hell-hated° lie o'erturn thy heart,   *hated as much as hell*

---

9. Venomous, like a toad; spotted with disgrace.   1. Taste (from "assay"); utterance.

A trumpet sounds

HERALD [*reads*]   'If any man of quality or degree within the lists
of the army will maintain upon Edmond, supposed Earl of
Gloucester, that he is a manifold traitor, let him appear by the
105   third sound of the trumpet. He is bold in his defence.'

First trumpet

Again.

Second trumpet

Again.

Third trumpet

Trumpet answers within. Enter EDGAR, *armed*

ALBANY [*to the* HERALD]   Ask him his purposes, why he appears
Upon this call o'th' trumpet.

HERALD [*to* EDGAR]   What° are you?   *Who*
110   Your name, your quality,° and why you answer   *degree; rank*
This present summons?

EDGAR   Know, my name is lost,
By treason's tooth bare-gnawn and canker-bit.°   *worm-eaten*
Yet am I noble as the adversary
I come to cope.°   *to encounter*

ALBANY   Which is that adversary?

115   EDGAR   What's he that speaks for Edmond, Earl of Gloucester?

EDMOND   Himself. What sayst thou to him?

EDGAR   Draw thy sword,
That° if my speech offend a noble heart   *So that*
Thy arm may do thee justice. Here is mine.
[*He draws his sword*]
Behold, it is the privilege of mine honour,
120   My oath, and my profession. I protest,
Maugre° thy strength, place, youth, and eminence,   *Despite*
Despite thy victor-sword and fire-new° fortune,   *newly minted*
Thy valour and thy heart,° thou art a traitor,   *courage*
False to thy gods, thy brother, and thy father,
125   Conspirant 'gainst this high illustrious prince,
And from th'extremest upward° of thy head   *top*
To the descent° and dust below thy foot   *lowest part; sole*
A most toad-spotted[8] traitor. Say thou no,
This sword, this arm, and my best spirits are bent°   *ready*
130   To prove upon thy heart, whereto I speak,
Thou liest.

EDMOND   In wisdom I should ask thy name,
But since thy outside looks so fair and warlike,
And that° thy tongue some say[9] of breeding breathes,   *since*
What safe and nicely I might well demand
135   By rule of knighthood I disdain and spurn.[1]
Back do I toss those treasons to thy head,
With the hell-hated° lie o'erwhelm thy heart,   *hated as much as hell*

---

8. Venomous, like a toad; spotted with disgrace.
9. Taste (from "assay"); utterance.
1. *What . . . spurn:* What I have a right to know and what

would be prudent and technically correct to ask, I disdain to inquire about.

Which, for° they yet glance by and scarcely bruise,   *since*
This sword of mine shall give them instant way°   *access*
145 Where they shall rest for ever. Trumpets, speak!
        [*Flourish. They fight.* EDMUND *is vanquished*]
ALL[2]   Save° him, save him!   *Spare*
GONORIL   This is mere practice,° Gloucester.   *trickery*
By the law of arms thou art not bound to answer
An unknown opposite.° Thou art not vanquished,   *opponent*
But cozened and beguiled.°   *cheated and deceived*
ALBANY   Stop your mouth, dame,
150 Or with this paper shall I stopple° it.   *plug*
Thou worse than anything, read thine own evil.
Nay, no tearing, lady. I perceive you know't.
GONORIL   Say if I do, the laws are mine, not thine.
Who shall arraign° me for't?   *prosecute*
ALBANY   Most monstrous!
Know'st thou this paper?
155 GONORIL   Ask me not what I know.   *Exit*
ALBANY   Go after her. She's desperate. Govern° her.   *Restrain*
        [*Exit one or more*]
EDMUND   What you have charged me with, that have I done,
And more, much more. The time will bring it out.
'Tis past, and so am I.   [*To* EDGAR] But what art thou,
160 That hast this fortune on me?[3] If thou beest noble,
I do forgive thee.
EDGAR   Let's exchange charity.°   *forgiveness*
I am no less in blood than thou art, Edmund.
If more, the more ignobly thou hast wronged me.
        [*He takes off his helmet*]
My name is Edgar, and thy father's son.
165 The gods are just, and of our pleasant vices
Make instruments to scourge us.
The dark and vicious place where thee he got[4]
Cost him his eyes.
EDMUND   Thou hast spoken truth.
The wheel° is come full circled. I am here.[5]   *Fortune's wheel*
170 ALBANY [*to* EDGAR]   Methought thy very gait did prophesy
A royal nobleness. I must embrace thee.
Let sorrow split my heart if I did ever hate
Thee or thy father.
EDGAR   Worthy prince, I know't.
175 ALBANY   Where have you hid yourself?
How have you known the miseries of your father?
EDGAR   By nursing them, my lord. List° a brief tale,   *Listen to*
And when 'tis told, O that my heart would burst!
The bloody proclamation to escape[6]
180 That followed me so near—O, our lives' sweetness,

2. Both Q and F give this speech to "Alb." (for "Albany"), which may be a compositor's mistake for "All."
3. Who have this good fortune at my expense.
4. The adulterous bed in which you were born; or, possibly, the vagina. *got:* begot.
5. Back at the lowest point.
6. In order to escape the sentence of death.

Which, for° they yet glance by and scarcely bruise,   *since*
This sword of mine shall give them instant way°   *access*
140   Where they shall rest for ever. Trumpets, speak!
         Alarums. [They] fight. [EDMOND is vanquished]
ALL²   Save° him, save him!   *Spare*
GONERIL   This is practice,° Gloucester.   *trickery*
By th' law of arms thou wast not bound to answer
An unknown opposite.° Thou art not vanquished,   *opponent*
But cozened and beguiled.°   *cheated and deceived*
ALBANY   Shut your mouth, dame,
145   Or with this paper shall I stopple° it.   *plug*
   [*To* EDMOND] Hold,° sir, thou worse than any name: read   *Behold*
      thine own evil.
   [*To* GONERIL] No tearing, lady. I perceive you know it.
GONERIL   Say if I do, the laws are mine, not thine.
Who can arraign° me for't?   *Exit*   *prosecute*
ALBANY   Most monstrous!—
O, know'st thou this paper?
150   EDMOND   Ask me not what I know.
ALBANY   Go after her. She's desperate. Govern° her.   *Restrain*
                   [*Exit one or more*]
EDMOND   What you have charged me with, that have I done,
And more, much more. The time will bring it out.
'Tis past, and so am I.   [*To* EDGAR] But what art thou,
155   That hast this fortune on me?³ If thou'rt noble,
I do forgive thee.
EDGAR   Let's exchange charity.°   *forgiveness*
I am no less in blood than thou art, Edmond.
If more, the more thou'st wronged me.
                   [*He takes off his helmet*]
My name is Edgar, and thy father's son.
160   The gods are just, and of our pleasant vices
Make instruments to plague us.
The dark and vicious place where thee he got⁴
Cost him his eyes.
EDMOND   Thou'st spoken right. 'Tis true.
The wheel° is come full circle. I am here.⁵   *Fortune's wheel*
165   ALBANY [*to* EDGAR]   Methought thy very gait did prophesy
A royal nobleness. I must embrace thee.
Let sorrow split my heart if ever I
Did hate thee or thy father.
EDGAR   Worthy prince, I know't.
170   ALBANY   Where have you hid yourself?
How have you known the miseries of your father?
EDGAR   By nursing them, my lord. List° a brief tale,   *Listen to*
And when 'tis told, O that my heart would burst!
The bloody proclamation to escape⁶
175   That followed me so near—O, our lives' sweetness,

2. Both Q and F give this speech to "Alb." (for "Albany"), which may be a compositor's mistake for "All."
3. Who have this good fortune at my expense.
4. The adulterous bed in which you were born; or, possi-

bly, the vagina. *got*: begot.
5. Back at the lowest point.
6. In order to escape the sentence of death.

That with the pain of death would hourly die
Rather than die at once![7]—taught me to shift
Into a madman's rags, to assume a semblance
That very° dogs disdained; and in this habit   even
185   Met I my father with his bleeding rings,°   sockets
The precious stones° new-lost; became his guide,   eyes
Led him, begged for him, saved him from despair;
Never—O father!—revealed myself unto him
Until some half hour past, when I was armed.
190   Not sure, though hoping, of this good success,°   conclusion
I asked his blessing, and from first to last
Told him my pilgrimage; but his flawed° heart—   cracked
Alack, too weak the conflict to support—
'Twixt two extremes of passion, joy and grief,
Burst smilingly.
195   EDMUND   This speech of yours hath moved me,
And shall perchance do good. But speak you on—
You look as you had something more to say.
ALBANY   If there be more, more woeful, hold it in,
For I am almost ready to dissolve,°   melt into tears
Hearing of this.
200   EDGAR   This would have seemed a period°   conclusion
To such as love not sorrow; but another
To amplify,° too much would make much more,   enlarge; extend
And top extremity.
Whilst I was big in clamour° came there in a man   lamenting loudly
205   Who, having seen me in my worst estate,
Shunned my abhorred society; but then, finding
Who 'twas that so endured, with his strong arms
He fastened on my neck and bellowed out
As he'd burst heaven; threw him on my father,
210   Told the most piteous tale of Lear and him°   himself
That ever ear received, which in recounting
His grief grew puissant° and the strings of life   powerful
Began to crack. Twice then the trumpets sounded,
And there I left him tranced.
ALBANY   But who was this?
215   EDGAR   Kent, sir, the banished Kent, who in disguise
Followed his enemy king,[8] and did him service
Improper° for a slave.   Unfit even
        Enter [SECOND GENTLEMAN] *with a bloody knife*
SECOND GENTLEMAN   Help, help!
ALBANY   What kind of help?
What means that bloody knife?
SECOND GENTLEMAN   It's hot, it smokes.
It came even from the heart of—
ALBANY   Who, man? Speak.
220   SECOND GENTLEMAN   Your lady, sir, your lady; and her sister
By her is poisonèd—she hath confessed it.

---

7. *our . . . once:* how sweet must life be that we prefer
the constant pain of dying to death itself.

8. Because Lear had previously banished him. *enemy:*
hostile.

That we the pain of death would hourly die
Rather than die at once!⁷—taught me to shift
Into a madman's rags, t'assume a semblance
That very° dogs disdained; and in this habit   *even*
180   Met I my father with his bleeding rings,°   *sockets*
Their precious stones° new-lost; became his guide,   *eyes*
Led him, begged for him, saved him from despair;
Never—O fault!—revealed myself unto him
Until some half hour past, when I was armed.
185   Not sure, though hoping, of this good success,°   *conclusion*
I asked his blessing, and from first to last
Told him our pilgrimage; but his flawed° heart—   *cracked*
Alack, too weak the conflict to support—
'Twixt two extremes of passion, joy and grief,
Burst smilingly.
190   EDMOND   This speech of yours hath moved me,
And shall perchance do good. But speak you on—
You look as you had something more to say.
ALBANY   If there be more, more woeful, hold it in,
For I am almost ready to dissolve,°   *melt into tears*
195   Hearing of this.

Enter a GENTLEMAN [*with a bloody knife*]
GENTLEMAN   Help, help, O help!
EDGAR   What kind of help?
ALBANY   Speak, man.
EDGAR   What means this bloody knife?
GENTLEMAN   'Tis hot, it smokes.
It came even from the heart of—O, she's dead!
ALBANY   Who dead? Speak, man.
200   GENTLEMAN   Your lady, sir, your lady; and her sister
By her is poisoned. She confesses it.

---

7. *our . . . once:* how sweet must life be that we prefer the constant pain of dying to death itself.

EDMUND   I was contracted to them both; all three
        Now marry° in an instant.   *unite (in death)*
ALBANY   Produce their bodies, be they alive or dead.
225   This justice of the heavens, that makes us tremble,
        Touches us not with pity.
                        Enter KENT [*as himself*]
EDGAR   Here comes Kent, sir.
ALBANY   O, 'tis he; the time will not allow
        The compliment that very manners urges.[9]
KENT   I am come
230   To bid my king and master aye° good night.   *forever*
        Is he not here?
ALBANY   Great thing of° us forgot!—   *by*
        Speak, Edmund; where's the King, and where's Cordelia?
                The bodies of GONORIL *and* REGAN *are brought in*
        Seest thou this object,° Kent?   *spectacle*
KENT   Alack, why thus?
235   EDMUND   Yet° Edmund was beloved.   *Despite all*
        The one the other poisoned for my sake,
        And after slew herself.
ALBANY   Even so.—Cover their faces.
EDMUND   I pant for life. Some good I mean to do,
        Despite of my own nature. Quickly send,
240   Be brief° in't, to th' castle; for my writ[1]   *speedy*
        Is on the life of Lear and on Cordelia.
        Nay, send in time.
ALBANY   Run, run, O run!
EDGAR   To who, my lord? Who hath the office?° Send   *commission*
        Thy token of reprieve.
245   EDMUND   Well thought on! Take my sword. The captain,
        Give it the° captain.   *to the*
ALBANY   Haste thee for thy life.
                                [*Exit* SECOND CAPTAIN]
EDMUND   He hath commission from thy wife and me
        To hang Cordelia in the prison, and
        To lay the blame upon her own despair,
250   That she fordid herself.[2]
ALBANY   The gods defend her!—Bear him hence a while.
                                [*Exeunt some with* EDMUND]
                Enter LEAR *with* CORDELIA *in his arms* [*followed by the*
                SECOND CAPTAIN]
LEAR   Howl, howl, howl, howl! O, you are men of stones.
        Had I your tongues and eyes, I would use them so
        That heaven's vault should crack. She's gone for ever.
255   I know when one is dead and when one lives.
        She's dead as earth.

---

9. The ceremony that barest custom demands.
1. Order of execution.
2. Destroyed herself. In most of Shakespeare's source

texts for the play, Cordelia does in fact kill herself after
reigning for some years.

EDMOND   I was contracted to them both; all three
    Now marry° in an instant.   *unite (in death)*

EDGAR   Here comes Kent.
    Enter KENT [*as himself*]

ALBANY   Produce the bodies, be they alive or dead.
    Goneril's and Regan's bodies brought out

205   This judgement of the heavens, that makes us tremble,
    Touches us not with pity.—O, is this he?
    [*To* KENT] The time will not allow the compliment
    Which very manners urges.[8]

KENT   I am come
    To bid my king and master aye° good night.   *forever*
    Is he not here?

210   ALBANY   Great thing of° us forgot!—   *by*
    Speak, Edmond; where's the King, and where's Cordelia?—
    Seest thou this object,° Kent?   *spectacle*

KENT   Alack, why thus?

EDMOND   Yet° Edmond was beloved.   *Despite all*

215   The one the other poisoned for my sake,
    And after slew herself.

ALBANY   Even so.—Cover their faces.

EDMOND   I pant for life. Some good I mean to do,
    Despite of mine own nature. Quickly send,
    Be brief° in it, to th' castle; for my writ[9]   *speedy*

220   Is on the life of Lear and on Cordelia.
    Nay, send in time.

ALBANY   Run, run, O run!

EDGAR   To who, my lord?—Who has the office?° Send   *commission*
    Thy token of reprieve.

EDMOND   Well thought on! Take my sword. The captain,
    Give it the° captain.   *to the*

225   EDGAR   Haste thee for thy life.
                             [*Exit the* GENTLEMAN]

EDMOND [*to* ALBANY]   He hath commission from thy wife and me
    To hang Cordelia in the prison, and
    To lay the blame upon her own despair,
    That she fordid herself.[1]

230   ALBANY   The gods defend her!—Bear him hence a while.
                       [*Exeunt some with* EDMOND]
    Enter LEAR *with* CORDELIA *in his arms* [*followed by the*
    GENTLEMAN]

LEAR   Howl, howl, howl, howl! O, you are men of stones.
    Had I your tongues and eyes, I'd use them so
    That heaven's vault should crack. She's gone for ever.
    I know when one is dead and when one lives.
    She's dead as earth.

---

8. *the compliment . . . urges:* the ceremony that barest
custom demands.
9. Order of execution.

1. Destroyed herself. In most of Shakespeare's source
texts for the play, Cordelia does in fact kill herself after
reigning for some years.

[*He lays her down*]   Lend me a looking-glass.
If that her breath will mist or stain the stone,[3]
Why, then she lives.

KENT   Is this the promised end?[4]

EDGAR   Or image of that horror?

ALBANY   Fall and cease.[5]

260   LEAR   This feather stirs. She lives. If it be so,
It is a chance which does redeem all sorrows
That ever I have felt.

KENT [*kneeling*]   Ah, my good master!

LEAR   Prithee, away.

EDGAR   'Tis noble Kent, your friend.

LEAR   A plague upon you, murderous traitors all.

265   I might have saved her; now she's gone for ever.—
Cordelia, Cordelia: stay a little. Ha?
What is't thou sayst?—Her voice was ever soft,
Gentle, and low, an excellent thing in women.—
I killed the slave that was a-hanging thee.

SECOND CAPTAIN   'Tis true, my lords, he did.

270   LEAR   Did I not, fellow?
I have seen the day with my good biting falchion°   *light sword*
I would have made them skip. I am old now,
And these same crosses spoil me.[6] [*To* KENT] Who are you?
Mine eyes are not o' the best, I'll tell you straight.°   *recognize you soon*

275   KENT   If fortune bragged of two she loved or hated,[7]
One of them we behold.

LEAR   Are not you Kent?

KENT   The same, your servant Kent. Where is your servant
Caius?°   (*Kent's pseudonym*)

LEAR   He's a good fellow, I can tell you that.
He'll strike, and quickly too. He's dead and rotten.

280   KENT   No, my good lord, I am the very man—

LEAR   I'll see that straight.[8]

KENT   That from your first of difference and decay[9]
Have followed your sad steps.

LEAR   You're welcome hither.

KENT   Nor no man else.[1] All's cheerless, dark, and deadly.°   *deathly*

285   Your eldest daughters have fordone° themselves,   *destroyed*
And desperately° are dead.   *in despair*

LEAR   So think I, too.

---

3. Mica, or stone polished to a mirror finish.
4. Doomsday; expected end of the play. In no version of
the story previous to Shakespeare's does Cordelia die at
this point.
5. Let the world collapse and end.
6. And these recent adversities have weakened me;
and these parries I could once match would now
destroy me.
7. If Fortune bragged of two she treated only with good

or terrible extremes; "or" may be a variant of "ere," giving the meaning "loved before she hated."
8. I'll attend to that shortly; I'll comprehend that in a
moment.
9. Who from the beginning of your alteration and deterioration.
1. No, neither I nor anyone else is welcome. Alternatively, I am that man, not disguised as anyone else.

[*He lays her down*]

235   Lend me a looking-glass.
    If that her breath will mist or stain the stone,[2]
    Why, then she lives.

KENT   Is this the promised end?[3]

EDGAR   Or image of that horror?

ALBANY   Fall and cease.[4]

LEAR   This feather stirs. She lives. If it be so,

240   It is a chance which does redeem all sorrows
    That ever I have felt.

KENT [*kneeling*]   O, my good master!

LEAR   Prithee, away.

EDGAR   'Tis noble Kent, your friend.

LEAR   A plague upon you, murderers, traitors all.
    I might have saved her; now she's gone for ever.—

245   Cordelia, Cordelia: stay a little. Ha?
    What is't thou sayst?—Her voice was ever soft,
    Gentle, and low, an excellent thing in woman.—
    I killed the slave that was a-hanging thee.

GENTLEMAN   'Tis true, my lords, he did.

LEAR   Did I not, fellow?

250   I have seen the day with my good biting falchion°   *light sword*
    I would have made them skip. I am old now,
    And these same crosses spoil me.[5] [*To* KENT] Who are you?
    Mine eyes are not o'th' best, I'll tell you straight.°   *recognize you soon*

KENT   If fortune brag of two she loved and hated,
    One of them we behold.[6]

255 LEAR   This' a dull sight.[7]
    Are you not Kent?

KENT   The same, your servant Kent.
    Where is your servant Caius?°   (*Kent's pseudonym*)

LEAR   He's a good fellow, I can tell you that.

260   He'll strike, and quickly too. He's dead and rotten.

KENT   No, my good lord, I am the very man—

LEAR   I'll see that straight.[8]

KENT   That from your first of difference and decay[9]
    Have followed your sad steps.

LEAR   You're welcome hither.

265 KENT   Nor no man else.[1] All's cheerless, dark, and deadly.°   *deathly*
    Your eldest daughters have fordone° themselves,   *destroyed*
    And desperately° are dead.   *in despair*

LEAR   Ay, so think I.

---

2. Mica, or stone polished to a mirror finish.
3. Doomsday; expected end of the play. In no version of the story previous to Shakespeare's does Cordelia die at this point.
4. Let the world collapse and end.
5. And these recent adversities have weakened me; and these parries I could once match would now destroy me.
6. *If . . . behold:* If there were only two supreme examples in the world of Fortune's ability to raise up and

cast down, Lear would be one; alternatively, we are each of us one (Lear and Kent are here looking at each other).
7. This is a sad sight; my vision is failing.
8. I'll attend to that shortly; I'll comprehend that in a moment.
9. Who from the beginning of your alteration and deterioration.
1. No, neither I nor anyone else is welcome. Alternatively, I am that man, not disguised as anyone else.

ALBANY He knows not what he sees; and vain° it is   *in vain*
　　　　That we present us to him.

EDGAR 　　　　　　　　　　Very bootless.°   *futile*

Enter [another] CAPTAIN

THIRD CAPTAIN [*to* ALBANY] Edmund is dead, my lord.

ALBANY 　　　　　　　　　　That's but a trifle here.—
290　　　You lords and noble friends, know our intent.
　　　　What comfort to this great decay° may come   *ruin; destruction*
　　　　Shall be applied; for us, we will resign
　　　　During the life of this old majesty
　　　　To him our absolute power; [*to* EDGAR *and* KENT] you to your rights,
295　　　With boot° and such addition° as your honours   *reward / distinction*
　　　　Have more than merited. All friends shall taste
　　　　The wages of their virtue, and all foes
　　　　The cup of their deservings.—O see, see!

LEAR And my poor fool² is hanged. No, no life.
300　　　Why should a dog, a horse, a rat have life,
　　　　And thou no breath at all? O, thou wilt come no more.
　　　　Never, never, never.—Pray you, undo
　　　　This button. Thank you, sir. O, O, O, O!

EDGAR He faints. [*To* LEAR] My lord, my lord!

305 LEAR Break, heart, I prithee break.

EDGAR Look up, my lord.

KENT Vex not his ghost.³ O, let him pass. He hates him
　　　　That would upon the rack⁴ of this tough world
　　　　Stretch him out longer.
　　　　　　[LEAR *dies*]

EDGAR 　　　　　　　　　O, he is gone indeed.
310 KENT The wonder is he hath endured so long.
　　　　He but usurped his life.⁵

ALBANY [*to attendants*] Bear them from hence. Our present business
　　　　Is to general woe. [*To* KENT *and* EDGAR] Friends of my soul, you twain
　　　　Rule in this kingdom, and the gored° state sustain.   *wounded; bloody*

315 KENT I have a journey, sir, shortly to go:
　　　　My master calls, and I must not say no.

ALBANY The weight of this sad time we must obey,
　　　　Speak what we feel, not what we ought to say.
　　　　The oldest have borne most. We that are young
320　　　Shall never see so much, nor live so long.
　　　　　　　　　[*Exeunt carrying the bodies*]

---

2. A term of endearment, here used for Cordelia, though it also recalls the disappearance of Lear's Fool after Scene 13.

3. Do not disturb his departing soul.

4. Instrument of torture, used to stretch its victims.

5. From death, which already had a claim on it.

ALBANY   He knows not what he says; and vain° is it   *in vain*
    That we present us to him.
            Enter a MESSENGER
EDGAR   Very bootless.°   *futile*
MESSENGER [*to* ALBANY]   Edmond is dead, my lord.
270 ALBANY   That's but a trifle here.—
    You lords and noble friends, know our intent.
    What comfort to this great decay° may come   *ruin; destruction*
    Shall be applied; for us, we will resign
    During the life of this old majesty
    To him our absolute power;
275 [*To* EDGAR *and* KENT]   you to your rights,
    With boot° and such addition° as your honours   *reward / distinction*
    Have more than merited. All friends shall taste
    The wages of their virtue, and all foes
    The cup of their deservings.—O see, see!
280 LEAR   And my poor fool[2] is hanged. No, no, no life?
    Why should a dog, a horse, a rat have life,
    And thou no breath at all? Thou'lt come no more.
    Never, never, never, never, never.
    [*To* KENT] Pray you, undo this button. Thank you, sir.
285 Do you see this? Look on her. Look, her lips.
    Look there, look there.   *He dies*
EDGAR   He faints.   [*To* LEAR] My lord, my lord!
KENT [*to* LEAR]   Break, heart, I prithee break.
EDGAR [*to* LEAR]   Look up, my lord.
KENT   Vex not his ghost.[3] O, let him pass. He hates him
    That would upon the rack[4] of this tough world
    Stretch him out longer.
290 EDGAR   He is gone indeed.
KENT   The wonder is he hath endured so long.
    He but usurped his life.[5]
ALBANY   Bear them from hence. Our present business
    Is general woe. [*To* EDGAR *and* KENT] Friends of my soul, you twain
295 Rule in this realm, and the gored° state sustain.   *wounded; bloody*
KENT   I have a journey, sir, shortly to go:
    My master calls me; I must not say no.
EDGAR   The weight of this sad time we must obey,
    Speak what we feel, not what we ought to say.
300 The oldest hath borne most. We that are young
    Shall never see so much, nor live so long.
           Exeunt with a dead march [carrying the bodies]

---

2. A term of endearment, here used for Cordelia, though it also recalls the disappearance of Lear's Fool after 3.6.

3. Do not disturb his departing soul.
4. Instrument of torture, used to stretch its victims.
5. From death, which already had a claim on it.

King Lear

A CONFLATED TEXT

THE PERSONS OF THE PLAY

LEAR, King of Britain
GONERIL, Lear's eldest daughter
Duke of ALBANY, her husband
REGAN, Lear's second daughter
Duke of CORNWALL, her husband
CORDELIA, Lear's youngest daughter
King of FRANCE }
Duke of BURGUNDY } suitors of Cordelia
Earl of KENT, later disguised as Caius
Earl of GLOUCESTER
EDGAR, elder son of Gloucester, later disguised as Tom o' Bedlam
EDMUND, bastard son of Gloucester
OLD MAN, Gloucester's tenant
CURAN, Gloucester's retainer
Lear's FOOL
OSWALD, Goneril's steward
A DOCTOR
A CAPTAIN
A GENTLEMAN
A HERALD
SERVANTS to Cornwall
Knights, officers, messengers, soldiers, attendants

1.1

Enter KENT, GLOUCESTER,[1] *and* EDMUND

KENT I thought the king had more affected° the Duke of   *favored*
Albany° than Cornwall.   *Scotland*

GLOUCESTER It did always seem so to us; but now, in the division of the kingdom, it appears not° which of the dukes he   *is not clear*
5 values most; for equalities° are so weighed,° that curiosity in   *shares / equal*
neither can make choice of either's moiety.[2]

KENT Is not this your son, my lord?

GLOUCESTER His breeding,° sir, hath been at my charge.[3] I have   *upbringing*
so often blushed to acknowledge him, that now I am brazed°   *hardened*
10 to it.

KENT I cannot conceive° you.   *comprehend*

GLOUCESTER Sir, this young fellow's mother could;[4] whereupon
she grew round-wombed, and had, indeed, sir, a son for her
cradle ere she had a husband for her bed. Do you smell a
15 fault?[5]

1.1 Location: King Lear's court.
1. Pronounced "Gloster."
2. *that . . . moiety:* that careful scrutiny ("curiosity") of
both parts cannot determine which portion ("moiety") is

preferable.
3. My responsibility; at my cost.
4. Could conceive; punning on biological conception.
5. Sin, wrongdoing; female genitals.

KENT   I cannot wish the fault undone, the issue° of it being so   *offspring; result*
    proper.°   *handsome; right*

GLOUCESTER   But I have, sir, a son by order of law,° some year   *legitimate son*
    elder than this, who yet is no dearer in my account.° Though   *estimation*
20   this knave° came something saucily⁶ into the world before he   *scamp; fellow*
    was sent for, yet was his mother fair; there was good sport at his
    making, and the whoreson° must be acknowledged. Do you   *rogue; bastard*
    know this noble gentleman, Edmund?

EDMUND   No, my lord.

25 GLOUCESTER   My lord of Kent. Remember him hereafter as my
    honorable friend.

EDMUND   My services to your lordship.

KENT   I must love you, and sue° to know you better.   *seek*

EDMUND   Sir, I shall study deserving.°   *shall learn to deserve*

30 GLOUCESTER   He hath been out° nine years, and away he shall   *away; abroad*
    again. (*Sound a sennet*)° The king is coming.   *fanfare of trumpets*

        Enter one bearing a coronet, then King LEAR, CORN-
        WALL, ALBANY, GONERIL, REGAN, CORDELIA, *and atten-*
        dants

LEAR   Attend the lords of France and Burgundy, Gloucester.

GLOUCESTER   I shall, my liege.°   *feudal superior*

        Exeunt GLOUCESTER *and* EDMUND

LEAR   Meantime we° shall express our darker° purpose.   *(royal "we") / more secret*
35   Give me the map there. Know that we have divided
    In three our kingdom; and 'tis our fast° intent   *fixed*
    To shake all cares and business from our age,
    Conferring them on younger strengths, while we
    Unburthened crawl toward death. Our son° of Cornwall,   *son-in-law*
40   And you, our no less loving son of Albany,
    We have this hour a constant will to publish⁷
    Our daughters' several dowers,° that future strife   *individual dowries*
    May be prevented now. The princes, France and Burgundy,
    Great rivals in our youngest daughter's love,
45   Long in our court have made their amorous sojourn,
    And here are to be answered. Tell me, my daughters—
    Since now we will divest us, both of rule,
    Interest° of territory, cares of state—   *Legal title*
    Which of you shall we say doth love us most?
50   That° we our largest bounty° may extend   *So that / generosity*
    Where nature doth with merit challenge.⁸ Goneril,
    Our eldest-born, speak first.

GONERIL   Sir, I love you more than words can wield° the matter;   *convey*
    Dearer than eye-sight, space,° and liberty;   *freedom of movement*
55   Beyond what can be valued, rich or rare;
    No less than life, with grace, health, beauty, honor;
    As much as child e'er loved, or father found;
    A love that makes breath° poor, and speech unable;   *language*
    Beyond all manner of so much° I love you.   *Beyond all comparison*
60 CORDELIA (*aside*)   What shall Cordelia speak? Love, and be silent.

LEAR   Of all these bounds,° even from this line to this,   *regions*
    With shadowy forests and with champains riched,°   *enriched plains*
    With plenteous rivers and wide-skirted meads,°   *broad meadows*

---

6. Somewhat rudely; somewhat shamefully.
7. A fixed determination to announce publicly.

8. *Where . . . challenge*: To the one whose natural love
and deserving lay claim (to our generosity).

We make thee lady: to thine and Albany's issue°   *children; heirs*
65 Be this perpetual. What says our second daughter,
Our dearest Regan, wife to Cornwall? Speak.
REGAN   Sir, I am made
Of the self-same metal° that my sister is,   *spirit; substance*
And prize me at her worth.° In my true heart   *believe myself her equal*
70 I find she names my very deed of love;
Only she comes too short, that° I profess   *in that*
Myself an enemy to all other joys,
Which the most precious square of sense possesses,⁹
And find I am alone felicitate°   *am only made happy*
In your dear highness' love.
75 CORDELIA (*aside*)   Then poor Cordelia!
And yet not so; since, I am sure, my love's
More ponderous° than my tongue.   *weighty*
LEAR   To thee and thine hereditary ever
Remain this ample third of our fair kingdom;
80 No less in space, validity,° and pleasure,   *value*
Than that conferred on Goneril. Now, our joy,
Although our last and least;° to whose young love   *youngest; smallest*
The vines of France and milk of Burgundy
Strive to be interested,° what can you say to draw   *admitted*
85 A third more opulent than your sisters? Speak.
CORDELIA   Nothing, my lord.
LEAR   Nothing?
CORDELIA   Nothing.
LEAR   Nothing will come of nothing,¹ speak again.
90 CORDELIA   Unhappy that I am, I cannot heave
My heart into my mouth. I love your majesty
According to my bond;° nor more nor less.   *filial duty*
LEAR   How, how, Cordelia! mend your speech a little,
Lest it may mar your fortunes.
CORDELIA   Good my lord,
95 You have begot me, bred me, loved me; I
Return those duties back as are right fit,
Obey you, love you, and most honor you.
Why have my sisters husbands, if they say
They love you all°? Haply,° when I shall wed,   *completely / Perhaps; if lucky*
100 That lord whose hand must take my plight° shall carry   *marriage vow; condition*
Half my love with him, half my care and duty.
Sure, I shall never marry like my sisters,
To love my father all.
LEAR   But goes thy heart with this?
105 CORDELIA   Ay, good my lord.
LEAR   So young, and so untender?
CORDELIA   So young, my lord, and true.°   *honest; faithful*
LEAR   Let it be so! Thy truth, then, be thy dower!
For, by the sacred radiance of the sun,
110 The mysteries of Hecate,² and the night;

---

9. *Which . . . possesses:* That the body can enjoy. *precious square of sense:* measure of sensibility; or, perhaps, balanced and sensitive perception. The square may represent the even mixture of the body's four fluids, or humors.
1. *Ex nihilo nihil fit,* a maxim derived from Aristotle, was accepted by the Christian Middle Ages with the single exception of God having created the world out of nothing.
2. A classical goddess of the moon and the patron of witchcraft, she was associated with the underworld, Hades.

By all the operation of the orbs
From whom we do exist and cease to be;[3]
Here I disclaim all my paternal care,
Propinquity° and property of blood,°   *Closeness / kinship*
115 And as a stranger to my heart and me
Hold thee, from this,° for ever. The barbarous Scythian,[4]   *this time*
Or he that makes his generation messes[5]
To gorge his appetite, shall to my bosom
Be as well neighbored, pitied, and relieved,
As thou my sometime° daughter.   *former*
120 KENT   Good my liege—
LEAR   Peace, Kent!
Come not between the dragon and his wrath.
I loved her most, and thought to set my rest[6]
On her kind nursery.° Hence, and avoid my sight!   *care*
125 So be my grave my peace,[7] as here I give
Her father's heart from her! Call France; who stirs?[8]
Call Burgundy. Cornwall and Albany,
With my two daughters' dowers digest° this third: *incorporate*
Let pride, which she calls plainness,° marry her.   *directness*
130 I do invest you jointly with my power,
Pre-eminence, and all the large effects°   *outward shows; trappings*
That troop with° majesty. Ourself, by monthly course,   *accompany*
With reservation of° an hundred knights,   *legal right to retain*
By you to be sustained, shall our abode
135 Make with you by due turns. Only we still retain
The name, and all the additions° to a king;   *prerogatives*
The sway,° revenue, execution of the rest,   *power*
Beloved sons, be yours; which to confirm,
This coronet[9] part betwixt you.
KENT   Royal Lear,
140 Whom I have ever honored as my king,
Loved as my father, as my master followed,
As my great patron thought on in my prayers—
LEAR   The bow is bent and drawn, make from° the shaft.   *get clear of*
KENT   Let it fall° rather, though the fork° invade   *strike home / arrowhead*
145 The region of my heart: be Kent unmannerly,
When Lear is mad. What wilt thou do, old man?
Think'st thou that duty shall have dread to speak,
When power to flattery bows? To plainness° honor's bound,   *plain speaking*
When majesty stoops to folly. Reverse thy doom,°   *Revoke your sentence*
150 And, in thy best consideration, check°   *halt*
This hideous rashness. Answer my life my judgment,[1]
Thy youngest daughter does not love thee least;
Nor are those empty-hearted whose low sounds
Reverb no hollowness.°   *Echo no insincerity*
LEAR   Kent, on thy life, no more.
155 KENT   My life I never held but as a pawn°   *chess piece; stake*

---

3. *By all . . . be*: Referring to the belief that the movements of stars and planets ("orbs") corresponded to physical and spiritual motions in a person and thus controlled his or her fate.
4. Notoriously savage Crimean nomads of classical antiquity.
5. *he . . . messes*: he who makes meals of his parents or his children.

6. To secure my repose; to stake my all, as in the card game known as primero.
7. So may I rest in peace (probably an oath).
8. Does nobody stir? An order, with the force of "Get moving."
9. Cordelia's crown, symbol of the endowment she has forsworn.
1. *Answer . . . judgment*: I'll stake my life on my opinion.

To wage° against thy enemies; nor fear to lose it,   *wager*
Thy safety being the motive.

LEAR   Out of my sight!

KENT   See better, Lear; and let me still° remain   *always*
The true blank° of thine eye.   *precise bull's-eye*

LEAR   Now, by Apollo—

160   KENT   Now, by Apollo, king,
Thou swear'st thy gods in vain[2]

LEAR   O, vassal! miscreant!°   *villain; unbeliever*
Laying his hand on his sword

ALBANY   ⎱
CORNWALL ⎰ Dear sir, forbear.

KENT   Do;
Kill thy physician, and the fee bestow
165   Upon thy foul disease.[3] Revoke thy doom;
Or, whilst I can vent clamor from my throat,
I'll tell thee thou dost evil.

LEAR   Hear me, recreant!°   *traitor*
On thine allegiance, hear me!
Since thou hast sought to make us break our vow,
170   Which we durst never yet, and with strained° pride   *overblown*
To come between our sentence and our power,
Which nor our nature nor our place[4] can bear,
Our potency made good,° take thy reward.   *demonstrated*
Five days we do allot thee, for provision
175   To shield thee from diseases of the world;
And on the sixth to turn thy hated back
Upon our kingdom: if, on the tenth day following,
Thy banished trunk° be found in our dominions,   *body*
The moment is thy death. Away! by Jupiter,
180   This shall not be revoked.

KENT   Fare thee well, king. Sith° thus thou wilt appear,   *Since*
Freedom lives hence, and banishment is here.
(*To* CORDELIA) The gods to their dear shelter take thee, maid,
That justly think'st, and hast most rightly said!
185   (*To* REGAN *and* GONERIL) And your large speeches may your deeds approve,[5]
That good effects may spring from words of love.
Thus Kent, O princes, bids you all adieu;
He'll shape his old course in a country new.   *Exit*
Flourish.° *Re-enter* GLOUCESTER, *with* FRANCE, BUR-   *Fanfare of trumpets*
GUNDY, *and attendants*

GLOUCESTER   Here's France and Burgundy, my noble lord.
190   LEAR   My lord of Burgundy,
We first address towards you, who with this king
Hath rivaled for our daughter. What, in the least,
Will you require in present dower with her,
Or cease your quest of love?

BURGUNDY   Most royal majesty,
195   I crave no more than what your highness offered,
Nor will you tender° less.   *offer*

LEAR   Right noble Burgundy,

---

2. You invoke your gods falsely and without effect.
3. *Kill . . . disease:* You would not only kill the doctor but hand his fee over to the disease.
4. Which neither my temperament nor my royal position.
5. And let your actions live up to your fine words.

When she was dear to us, we did hold her so;
But now her price is fallen. Sir, there she stands;
If aught within that little seeming substance,[6]
200 Or all of it, with our displeasure pieced,°   joined
And nothing more, may fitly like° your grace,   please
She's there, and she is yours.

BURGUNDY   I know no answer.
LEAR   Will you, with those infirmities she owes,°   owns
Unfriended, new-adopted to our hate,
205 Dowered with our curse, and strangered° with our oath,   estranged
Take her, or leave her?

BURGUNDY   Pardon me, royal sir;
Election makes not up on such conditions.[7]

LEAR   Then leave her, sir; for, by the power that made me,
I tell you° all her wealth. (To FRANCE) For° you, great king,   inform you of / As for
210 I would not from your love make such a stray°   stray so far
To° match you where I hate; therefore beseech you   As to
To avert your liking° a more worthier way   To turn your affections
Than on a wretch whom nature is ashamed
Almost to acknowledge hers.

FRANCE   This is most strange,
215 That she, whom even but now was your best object,
The argument° of your praise, balm of your age,   theme
Most best, most dearest, should in this trice° of time   moment
Commit a thing so monstrous, to dismantle°   as to strip off; disrobe
So many folds of favor. Sure, her offense
220 Must be of such unnatural degree,
That monsters it,° or your fore-vouched affection   makes it monstrous
Fall'n into taint;[8] which to believe of her,
Must be a faith that reason without miracle
Could never plant in me.

CORDELIA   I yet beseech your majesty—
225 If for I want° that glib and oily art,   because I lack
To speak and purpose not°—since what I well intend,   and not intend
I'll do't before I speak—that you make known
It is no vicious blot, murder, or foulness,
No unchaste action, or dishonored step,
230 That hath deprived me of your grace and favor;
But even for want of that for which I am richer,
A still-soliciting° eye, and such a tongue   An always-begging
As I am glad I have not, though not to have it
Hath lost me in your liking.

LEAR   Better thou
235 Hadst not been born than not to have pleased me better.

FRANCE   Is it but this—a tardiness in nature
Which often leaves the history unspoke
That it intends to do?[9] My lord of Burgundy,
What say you to the lady? Love's not love
240 When it is mingled with regards° that stands   considerations

6. *little seeming substance:* one who appears insubstantial; one who will not pretend.
7. A choice cannot be made under those terms.
8. *or . . . taint:* or else the love you earlier swore for Cordelia must be regarded with suspicion. "Or" may also mean "before," in which case the phrase would mean "before the love you once proclaimed could have decayed."
9. *a tardiness . . . do:* a natural reserve that inhibits voicing one's intentions.

Aloof from th' entire point. Will you have her?
She is herself a dowry.

BURGUNDY   Royal Lear,
Give but that portion which yourself proposed,
And here I take Cordelia by the hand,
245   Duchess of Burgundy.

LEAR   Nothing! I have sworn; I am firm.

BURGUNDY   I am sorry, then, you have so lost a father
That you must lose a husband.

CORDELIA   Peace be with Burgundy!
Since that respects of fortune are his love,
250   I shall not be his wife.

FRANCE   Fairest Cordelia, that art most rich, being poor;
Most choice, forsaken; and most loved, despised!
Thee and thy virtues here I seize upon:
Be it lawful I take up what's cast away.
255   Gods, gods! 't is strange that from their cold'st neglect
My love should kindle to inflamed respect.°   *ardent regard*
Thy dowerless daughter, king, thrown to my chance,
Is queen of us, of ours, and our fair France.
Not all the dukes of waterish° Burgundy   *irrigated; watery; weak*
260   Can buy this unprized° precious maid of me.   *unappreciated*
Bid them farewell, Cordelia, though unkind;°   *though they are unkind*
Thou losest here,° a better where° to find.   *this place / place*

LEAR   Thou hast her, France; let her be thine; for we
Have no such daughter, nor shall ever see
265   That face of hers again. Therefore be gone
Without our grace, our love, our benison.°   *blessing*
Come, noble Burgundy.

Flourish. Exeunt all but FRANCE, GONERIL, REGAN, *and*
       CORDELIA

FRANCE   Bid farewell to your sisters.

CORDELIA   The jewels of our father, with washed eyes
270   Cordelia leaves you. I know you what you are,
And like a sister am most loath to call
Your faults as they are named.° Love well our father.   *are properly called*
To your professed bosoms° I commit him;   *publicly proclaimed love*
But yet, alas, stood I within his grace,
275   I would prefer° him to a better place.   *promote; recommend*
So, farewell to you both.

REGAN   Prescribe not us our duties.

GONERIL   Let your study
Be to content your lord, who hath received you
At fortune's alms.[1] You have obedience scanted,°   *neglected*
280   And well are worth the want that you have wanted.[2]

CORDELIA   Time shall unfold what pleated cunning hides:
Who cover faults, at last shame them derides.[3]
Well may you prosper!

FRANCE   Come, my fair Cordelia.
               Exeunt FRANCE *and* CORDELIA

---

1. As a charitable gift from Dame Fortune.
2. And you deserve to get no more love (from your husband) than you have given (to your father). "Want" plays

on its alternative meanings of "lack" and "desire."
3. Those who hide their faults will in the end be put to shame.

GONERIL   Sister, it is not a little I have to say of what most nearly
285   appertains to us both. I think our father will hence to-night.
REGAN   That's most certain, and with you; next month with us.
GONERIL   You see how full of changes° his age is; the observation   *fickleness*
we have made of it hath not been little:⁴ he always loved our
sister most; and with what poor judgment he hath now cast her
290   off appears too grossly.°   *blatantly*
REGAN   'Tis the infirmity of his age; yet he hath ever but slen-
derly known himself.
GONERIL   The best and soundest of his time hath been but rash;⁵
then° must we look to receive from his age, not alone the   *therefore*
295   imperfections of long-engraffed condition,° but therewithal the   *deep-rooted habit*
unruly waywardness that infirm and choleric years bring with
them.
REGAN   Such unconstant starts⁶ are we like° to have from him as   *likely*
this of Kent's banishment.
300   GONERIL   There is further compliment° of leave-taking between   *ceremony*
France and him. Pray you, let's hit° together: if our father carry   *join; strike*
authority with such dispositions⁷ as he bears, this last surren-
der° of his will but offend° us.   *abdication / harm*
REGAN   We shall further think on 't.
305   GONERIL   We must do something, and i' the heat.°   *Exeunt*   *quickly*

1.2

Enter EDMUND, *with a letter*

EDMUND   Thou, nature, art my goddess; to thy law
My services are bound.¹ Wherefore° should I   *Why*
Stand in the plague of custom,² and permit
The curiosity° of nations to deprive me,   *legal niceties*
5   For that° I am some twelve or fourteen moonshines°   *Because / months*
Lag of° a brother? Why bastard? wherefore base?   *Younger than*
When my dimensions are as well compact,°   *composed*
My mind as generous° and my shape as true,   *noble*
As honest° madam's issue? Why brand they us   *married; chaste*
10   With base? with baseness? bastardy? base, base?
Who, in the lusty stealth of nature, take
More composition and fierce quality³
Than doth, within a dull, stale, tired bed,
Go to creating a whole tribe of fops,°   *fools*
15   Got° 'tween asleep and wake? Well, then,   *Begotten*
Legitimate Edgar, I must have your land.
Our father's love is to° the bastard Edmund   *as much to*
As to the legitimate. Fine word—'legitimate'!
Well, my legitimate, if this letter speed,°   *succeed*
20   And my invention° thrive, Edmund the base   *plot*

---

4. We have observed it more than a little.
5. *The . . . rash*: Even in the prime of his life he was impetuous.
6. Such impulsive outbursts.
7. Frame of mind.
1.2 Location: The Earl of Gloucester's house.
1. Edmund declares the raw force of unsocialized and unregulated existence, as opposed to human law, to be his ruler; ironically, "nature" also means "natural filial affection." A "natural" was another word for "bastard" (illegitimate child).

2. Submit to the imposition of inheritance law.
3. *Who . . . quality*: Whose begetting, by reason of its furtiveness and heightened excitement, requires better execution and more vigor. Alternatively (with "take" meaning "give"), whose begetting produces (a person of) more mixture and vigor. "Composition," or mixture, may refer to the belief that the perfect offspring was conceived from an equal quantity of male and female essence and that physical and mental abnormalities were caused by a predominance of one or the other.

Shall top° the legitimate. I grow; I prosper.   *overcome; usurp*
Now, gods, stand up for bastards!
    Enter GLOUCESTER
GLOUCESTER   Kent banished thus? and France in choler
    parted?°   *in anger departed*
    And the king gone tonight?° subscribed° his power?   *last night / limited*
25   Confirmed to exhibition?⁴ All this done
    Upon the gad?° Edmund, how now! what news?   *spur of the moment*
EDMUND   So please your lordship, none.   *Putting up the letter*
GLOUCESTER   Why so earnestly seek you to put up that letter?
EDMUND   I know no news, my lord.
30   GLOUCESTER   What paper were you reading?
EDMUND   Nothing, my lord.
GLOUCESTER   No? What needed, then, that terrible dispatch° of   *frightened haste*
    it into your pocket? The quality of nothing hath not such need
    to hide itself. Let's see. Come, if it be nothing, I shall not need
35   spectacles.
EDMUND   I beseech you, sir, pardon me. It is a letter from my
    brother, that I have not all o'er-read; and for so much as I have
    perused, I find it not fit for your o'er-looking.
GLOUCESTER   Give me the letter, sir.
40   EDMUND   I shall offend, either to detain or give it. The contents,
    as in part I understand them, are to blame.
GLOUCESTER   Let's see, let's see.
EDMUND   I hope, for my brother's justification, he wrote this but
    as an essay or taste⁵ of my virtue.
45   GLOUCESTER (*reads*)   "This policy and reverence of age makes
    the world bitter to the best of our times;⁶ keeps our fortunes
    from us till our oldness cannot relish them. I begin to find an
    idle and fond° bondage in the oppression of aged tyranny; who   *a useless and foolish*
    sways, not as it hath power, but as it is suffered.⁷ Come to me,
50   that of this I may speak more. If our father would sleep till I
    waked him, you should enjoy half his revenue for ever, and live
    the beloved of your brother, Edgar."
    Hum—conspiracy!—"Sleep till I waked him—you should
    enjoy half his revenue"—My son Edgar! Had he a hand to
55   write this? a heart and brain to breed it in?—When came this
    to you? who brought it?
EDMUND   It was not brought me, my lord; there's the cunning of
    it; I found it thrown in at the casement° of my closet.°   *window / private room*
GLOUCESTER   You know the character° to be your brother's?   *handwriting*
60   EDMUND   If the matter° were good, my lord, I durst swear it were   *content*
    his; but, in respect of that, I would fain° think it were not.   *gladly*
GLOUCESTER   It is his.
EDMUND   It is his hand, my lord; but I hope his heart is not in
    the contents.
65   GLOUCESTER   Hath he never heretofore sounded you° in this   *sounded you out*
    business?
EDMUND   Never, my lord. But I have heard him oft maintain it
    to be fit, that, sons at perfect age,° and fathers declining, the   *at maturity*

---

4. Established as mere show; relegated to pension.
5. *but . . . taste:* simply as a proof or test. Both terms
derive from metallurgy.
6. The established primacy of the elderly embitters us at

the prime of our lives. *policy:* statecraft; craftiness;
established order.
7. *who . . . suffered:* which rules not because it is powerful but because it is permitted to ("suffered").

father should be as ward[8] to the son, and the son manage his
70   revenue.

GLOUCESTER   O villain, villain! His very opinion in the letter!
Abhorred villain! Unnatural, detested, brutish villain! worse
than brutish! Go, sirrah,[9] seek him. I'll apprehend him. Abominable villain! Where is he?

75 EDMUND   I do not well know, my lord. If it shall please you to
suspend your indignation against my brother till you can derive
from him better testimony of his intent, you shall run a certain°   *safe; reliable*
course; where,° if you violently proceed against him, mistaking   *whereas*
his purpose, it would make a great gap in your own honor and
80 shake in pieces the heart of his obedience. I dare pawn down°   *I dare stake*
my life for him that he hath wrote this to feel° my affection to   *feel out*
your honor, and to no further pretense of danger.[1]

GLOUCESTER   Think you so?

EDMUND   If your honor judge it meet,° I will place you where   *appropriate*
85 you shall hear us confer of this, and by an auricular° assurance   *audible*
have your satisfaction; and that without any further delay than
this very evening.

GLOUCESTER   He cannot be such a monster——

EDMUND   Nor is not, sure.

90 GLOUCESTER   To his father, that so tenderly and entirely loves
him. Heaven and earth! Edmund, seek him out; wind me into
him,[2] I pray you; frame° the business after your own wisdom. I   *arrange*
would unstate myself, to be in a due resolution.[3]

EDMUND   I will seek him, sir, presently;° convey° the business as   *immediately / carry out*
95 I shall find means, and acquaint you withal.°   *therewith*

GLOUCESTER   These late° eclipses in the sun and moon portend   *recent*
no good to us.[4] Though the wisdom of nature can reason it
thus and thus, yet nature finds itself scourged by the sequent
effects.[5] Love cools, friendship falls off, brothers divide; in
100 cities, mutinies; in countries, discord; in palaces, treason; and
the bond cracked 'twixt son and father. This villain of mine
comes under the prediction; there's son against father. The
king falls from bias of nature;[6] there's father against child. We
have seen the best of our time. Machinations, hollowness,°   *insincerity*
105 treachery, and all ruinous disorders, follow us disquietly to our
graves. Find out this villain, Edmund; it shall lose thee nothing; do it carefully. And the noble and true-hearted Kent banished! his offence, honesty! 'Tis strange.   *Exit*

EDMUND   This is the excellent foppery° of the world, that, when   *foolishness*
110 we are sick in fortune, often the surfeit° of our own behavior,   *excesses*
we make guilty of° our disasters the sun, the moon, and the   *we hold responsible for*
stars; as if we were villains by necessity; fools by heavenly compulsion; knaves, thieves, and treachers,° by spherical predomi-   *traitors*

---

8. A child under eighteen years who was legally dependent, often orphaned.
9. A form of address used with children or social inferiors.
1. No further intention to do harm.
2. Worm your way into his confidence (with "me" as an
intensifier); worm your way into his confidence for me
("me" as a term of respect).
3. I would give up everything to have my doubts resolved.
4. Lunar and solar eclipses that were seen in London

about a year before the play's first recorded performance
would have added spice to this superstitious belief in
the role of heavenly bodies as augurs of misfortune.
5. *Though . . . effects:* Though natural science may
explain the eclipses this way or that, nature (and family
bonds) suffers in the effects that follow.
6. The King deviates from his natural inclination. In the
game of bowls, the "bias" ("course") is the eccentric
path taken by the weighted ball when thrown.

nance;[7] drunkards, liars, and adulterers, by an enforced obe-
115 dience of planetary influence; and all that we are evil in, by a
divine thrusting on.° An admirable° evasion of whore-master   °imposition / amazing
man, to lay his goatish disposition to the charge of a star![8] My
father compounded° with my mother under the dragon's tail,   °coupled
and my nativity was under Ursa Major,[9] so that it follows, I am
120 rough and lecherous. Fut!° I should have been that° I am, had   °By Christ's foot / what
the maidenliest star in the firmament twinkled on my bas-
tardizing. Edgar—

    Enter EDGAR

and pat° he comes like the catastrophe° of the old comedy. My   °on cue / resolution
cue is villainous melancholy, with a sigh like Tom o' Bedlam.[1]
125 O, these eclipses do portend these divisions! Fa, sol, la, mi.[2]

EDGAR How now, brother Edmund? What serious contemplation are you in?

EDMUND I am thinking, brother, of a prediction I read this
other day, what should follow these eclipses.

130 EDGAR Do you busy yourself about that?

EDMUND I promise you, the effects he writes of succeed° unhap-   °follow
pily; as of unnaturalness between the child and the parent;
death, dearth, dissolutions of ancient amities; divisions in state,
menaces and maledictions against king and nobles; needless
135 diffidences,° banishment of friends, dissipation of cohorts,[3]   °baseless suspicions
nuptial breaches, and I know not what.

EDGAR How long have you been a sectary astronomical?°   °a devotee of astrology

EDMUND Come, come! When saw you my father last?

EDGAR Why, the night gone by.

140 EDMUND Spake you with him?

EDGAR Ay, two hours together.

EDMUND Parted you in good terms? Found you no displeasure
in him by word or countenance?°   °appearance; demeanor

EDGAR None at all.

145 EDMUND Bethink yourself wherein you may have offended him;
and at my entreaty forbear° his presence till some little time   °avoid
hath qualified° the heat of his displeasure; which at this instant   °moderated
so rageth in him, that with the mischief of your person it would
scarcely allay.[4]

150 EDGAR Some villain hath done me wrong.

EDMUND That's my fear. I pray you, have a continent forbear-
ance° till the speed of his rage goes slower; and, as I say, retire   °restrained absence
with me to my lodging, from whence I will fitly° bring you to   °when suitable
hear my lord speak. Pray ye, go! There's my key. If you do stir
155 abroad, go armed.

EDGAR Armed, brother?

EDMUND Brother, I advise you to the best. Go armed. I am no
honest man if there be any good meaning towards you. I have

---

7. By the ascendancy of a particular planet. In the universe as conceived by Ptolemy, the planets revolved about
the earth on crystalline spheres.
8. *to lay . . . star:* to hold a star responsible for his lustful
desires. In Greek mythology, the satyr, a creature with
goatlike characteristics, was notoriously lecherous.
9. Constellations: *Dragon's tail* = Draco and *Ursa
Major* = Great Bear.
1. The usual name for lunatic beggars; "Bethlehem,"
shortened to "Bedlam," was the name of the oldest and

best-known London madhouse.
2. The portion of the scale Edmund sings is an augmented fourth, an interval considered at this time very
discordant; it was sometimes referred to as "the devil in
music." *divisions:* social fractures; melodic embellishments.
3. Scattering of forces.
4. *with . . . allay:* even harming you bodily would hardly
relieve his anger; alternatively, with the irritant of your
presence, it (Gloucester's anger) would not be abated.

told you what I have seen and heard; but faintly, nothing like
160   the image and horror of it. Pray you, away!
  EDGAR   Shall I hear from you anon?
  EDMUND   I do serve you in this business.   *Exit* EDGAR
    A credulous father, and a brother noble,
    Whose nature is so far from doing harms,
165   That he suspects none; on whose foolish honesty
    My practices° ride easy! I see the business.[5]   *plots*
    Let me, if not by birth, have lands by wit:°   *intelligence*
    All with me's meet that I can fashion fit.[6]   *Exit*

1.3

Enter GONERIL, *and* OSWALD, *her steward*

  GONERIL   Did my father strike my gentleman for chiding of his fool?
  OSWALD   Yes, madam.
  GONERIL   By day and night he wrongs me; every hour
    He flashes into one gross crime° or other,   *offense*
5   That sets us all at odds. I'll not endure it.
    His knights grow riotous, and himself upbraids us
    On every trifle. When he returns from hunting,
    I will not speak with him. Say I am sick.
    If you come slack of former services,[1]
10   You shall do well; the fault of it I'll answer.°   *answer for*
  OSWALD   He's coming, madam; I hear him.
      Horns within°   *Hunting horns offstage*
  GONERIL   Put on what weary negligence you please,
    You and your fellows.° I'd have it come to question.   *servants*
    If he dislike it, let him to our sister,
15   Whose mind and mine, I know, in that are one,
    Not to be overruled. Idle° old man,   *Foolish*
    That still would manage those authorities
    That he hath given away! Now, by my life,
    Old fools are babes again, and must be used
20   With checks as flatteries, when they are seen abused.[2]
    Remember what I tell you.
  OSWALD   Well, madam.
  GONERIL   And let his knights have colder looks among you.
    What grows of it, no matter; advise your fellows so.
    I would breed from hence occasions, and I shall,
25   That I may speak.[3] I'll write straight° to my sister,   *straightaway*
    To hold my very° course. Prepare for dinner.   *Exeunt*   *exact*

1.4

Enter KENT, *disguised*

  KENT   If but as well[1] I other accents borrow,
    That can my speech defuse,° my good intent   *disguise*
    May carry through itself to that full issue°   *result*
    For which I razed my likeness.[2] Now, banished Kent,

---

5. It is now clear to me what needs to be done.
6. Anything is fine by me as long as I can make it serve my purpose. *meet*: justifiable; appropriate.
1.3 Location: The Duke of Albany's castle.
1. If you offer him less service (and respect) than before.
2. *Old . . . abused:* When foolish old men act like children, rebukes are the kindest treatment when kind treat-ment is abused.
3. *I would . . . speak:* I wish to foster situations, and I shall, in which to speak my mind.
1.4 Location: As before.
1. As well as disguising my appearance.
2. Disguised my appearance; shaved off my beard (with a pun on "razor").

5   If thou canst serve where thou dost stand condemned,

So may it come,° thy master, whom thou lovest,   *come to pass*

Shall find thee full of labors.°   *helpful; keen*

      Horns within. Enter LEAR, KNIGHTS, *and attendants*[3]

LEAR   Let me not stay° a jot for dinner; go get it ready.   *wait*

      Exit an attendant

   How now! What° art thou?   *Who*

10 KENT   A man, sir.

LEAR   What dost thou profess?[4] What wouldst thou with us?

KENT   I do profess to be no less than I seem; to serve him truly

that will put me in trust; to love him that is honest; to converse°   *associate*

with him that is wise and says little; to fear judgment; to fight

15   when I cannot choose;° and to eat no fish.[5]   *when I must*

LEAR   What art thou?

KENT   A very honest-hearted fellow, and as poor as the king.

LEAR   If thou be as poor for a subject as he is for a king, thou art

poor enough. What wouldst thou?

20 KENT   Service.

LEAR   Who wouldst thou serve?

KENT   You.

LEAR   Dost thou know me, fellow?

KENT   No, sir; but you have that in your countenance which I

25   would fain° call master.   *gladly*

LEAR   What's that?

KENT   Authority.

LEAR   What services canst thou do?

KENT   I can keep honest counsel,° ride, run, mar a curious tale   *keep secrets*

30   in telling it,[6] and deliver a plain message bluntly. That which

ordinary men are fit for, I am qualified in; and the best of me

is diligence.

LEAR   How old art thou?

KENT   Not so young, sir, to love a woman for singing, nor so old

35   to dote on her for anything. I have years on my back forty-eight.

LEAR   Follow me; thou shalt serve me. If I like thee no worse

after dinner, I will not part from thee yet. Dinner, ho dinner!

Where's my knave? my fool? Go you, and call my fool hither.

      Exit an attendant

      Enter OSWALD

   You, you, sirrah, where's my daughter?

40 OSWALD   So please you—   *Exit*

LEAR   What says the fellow there? Call the clotpoll° back. (*Exit*   *blockhead*

a KNIGHT) Where's my fool, ho? I think the world's asleep.

      Re-enter KNIGHT

   How now! where's that mongrel?

KNIGHT   He says, my lord, your daughter is not well.

45 LEAR   Why came not the slave back to me when I called him?

KNIGHT   Sir, he answered me in the roundest° manner, he would   *bluntest; rudest*

not.

LEAR   He would not!

KNIGHT   My lord, I know not what the matter is; but, to my judg-

---

3. Critics of James I complained that he devalued honors by granting too many knighthoods and that he squandered too much time in hunting.

4. What is your job (profession)? Kent, in reply, uses "profess" punningly to mean "claim."

5. And not to be a Catholic or penitent (Catholics were obliged to eat fish on specified occasions and as penance); alternatively, to be a manly man, a meat eater.

6. That is, Kent's plain, blunt speech would make him ill suited to tell a convoluted ("curious") tale.

50 ment, your highness is not entertained with that ceremonious
affection as you were wont,° there's a great abatement of kind-   *accustomed to*
ness appears as well in the general dependants° as in the duke   *servants*
himself also and your daughter.

LEAR Ha! sayest thou so?

55 KNIGHT I beseech you pardon me, my lord, if I be mistaken; for
my duty cannot be silent when I think your highness wronged.

LEAR Thou but rememberest° me of mine own conception.° I   *remind / perception*
have perceived a most faint neglect of late; which I have
rather blamed as mine own jealous curiosity[7] than as a very

60 pretense° and purpose of unkindness. I will look further into 't.   *a true intention*
But where's my fool? I have not seen him this two days.

KNIGHT Since my young lady's going into France, sir, the fool
hath much pined away.

LEAR No more of that; I have noted it well. Go you and tell my

65 daughter I would speak with her.   *Exit* KNIGHT
Go you, call hither my fool.   *Exit an attendant*
       Re-enter OSWALD
O, you sir, you! Come you hither, sir. Who am I, sir?

OSWALD My lady's father.

LEAR "My lady's father"! My lord's knave! You whoreson dog!

70 you slave! you cur!

OSWALD I am none of these, my lord; I beseech your pardon.

LEAR Do you bandy looks with me, you rascal? (*Striking him*)

OSWALD I'll not be struck, my lord.

KENT Nor tripped neither, you base foot-ball player.[8]
       Tripping up his heels

75 LEAR I thank thee, fellow; thou servest me, and I'll love thee.

KENT Come, sir, arise, away! I'll teach you differences.° Away,   *(of rank)*
away! If you will measure your lubber's length again,[9] tarry; but
away! Go to! Have you wisdom? so.   *Pushes* OSWALD *out*

LEAR Now, my friendly knave, I thank thee: there's earnest of°   *downpayment for*

80 thy service. (*Giving* KENT *money*)
       Enter FOOL

FOOL Let me hire him too. Here's my coxcomb.°   *fool's cap*
       Offering KENT *his cap*

LEAR How now, my pretty knave! How dost thou?

FOOL Sirrah, you were best take my coxcomb.

KENT Why, fool?

85 FOOL Why, for taking one's part that's out of favor. Nay, an thou
canst not smile as the wind sits, thou'lt catch cold shortly.[1]
There, take my coxcomb! Why, this fellow has banished two
on's daughters,[2] and did the third a blessing against his will. If
thou follow him, thou must needs wear my coxcomb. How

90 now, nuncle!° Would I had two coxcombs and two daughters!   *(mine) uncle*

LEAR Why, my boy?

FOOL If I gave them all my living,° I'd keep my coxcombs   *goods*
myself.[3] There's mine; beg another of thy daughters.

LEAR Take heed, sirrah; the whip.

95 FOOL Truth's a dog must to° kennel; he must be whipped out,   *go to*

---

7. *jealous curiosity:* paranoid concern with niceties.
8. Football was a rough street game played by the poor.
9. If you will be stretched out by me again. *lubber:*
clumsy oaf.
1. *an . . . shortly:* if you can't keep in favor with those

in power, you will soon find yourself left out in the cold.
2. By abdicating, Lear has in effect prevented his eldest daughters from any longer being his subjects, just
as if he had "banished" them.
3. I'd be twice as much a fool.

when Lady the brach⁴ may stand by the fire and stink.

LEAR   A pestilent gall° to me!   *annoyance; bitterness*

FOOL   Sirrah, I'll teach thee a speech.

LEAR   Do.

100   FOOL   Mark it, nuncle:

           Have more than thou showest,

           Speak less than thou knowest,

           Lend less than thou owest,°   *own*

           Ride more than thou goest,°   *walk*

105   Learn° more than thou trowest,°   *Hear / believe*

           Set less than thou throwest,⁵

           Leave thy drink and thy whore,

           And keep in-a-door,

           And thou shalt have more

110   Than two tens to a score.⁶

KENT   This is nothing, fool.

FOOL   Then 'tis like the breath° of an unfeed° lawyer; you gave   *speech / unpaid*
me nothing for 't. Can you make no use of nothing, nuncle?

LEAR   Why, no, boy; nothing can be made out of nothing.

115   FOOL   (*to* KENT)   Prithee, tell him, so much the rent of his land
comes to.⁷ He will not believe a fool.

LEAR   A bitter fool!

FOOL   Dost thou know the difference, my boy, between a bitter
fool and a sweet fool?

120   LEAR   No, lad; teach me.

FOOL   That lord that counseled thee

             To give away thy land,

             Come place him here by me,

             Do thou for him stand:°   *represent him*

125   The sweet and bitter fool

             Will presently appear;

           The one in motley⁸ here,

             The other found out there.

LEAR   Dost thou call me fool, boy?

130   FOOL   All thy other titles thou hast given away; that thou wast
born with.

KENT   This is not altogether fool,⁹ my lord.

FOOL   No, faith, lords and great men will not let me; if I had a
monopoly out, they would have part on 't: and ladies too, they

135   will not let me have all fool to myself; they'll be snatching.
Give me an egg, nuncle, and I'll give thee two crowns.

LEAR   What two crowns shall they be?

FOOL   Why, after I have cut the egg i' the middle, and eat up the
meat,° the two crowns of the egg. When thou clovest° thy   *edible part / cleaved*

140   crown i' the middle, and gavest away both parts, thou borest°   *you carried*
thy ass on thy back o'er the dirt. Thou hadst little wit° in thy   *sense*
bald crown, when thou gavest thy golden one away. If I speak
like myself° in this, let him be whipped that first finds it so.¹   *(like a fool)*

---

4. Lady the bitch. Pet dogs were often called "Lady"
such and such. The allusion is to Regan and Goneril,
who are now being preferred to truthful Cordelia.
5. Don't gamble everything on a single cast of the
dice.
6. *And thou . . . score:* And there will be more than two
tens in your twenty—that is, you will become richer.

7. Remind him that no land means no rent; with a pun
on "rent" meaning "torn," "divided."
8. Multicolored dress of a court jester.
9. Foolish, folly. In the next line, the Fool takes "altogether
fool" to mean "one who has cornered the market on folly."
1. *that . . . so:* who first discovers for himself that this
is true; who first considers this to be foolish.

Singing

    Fools had ne'er less wit in a year;
145   For wise men are grown foppish,[2]
    They know not how their wits to wear,
    Their manners are so apish.°   *stupid; imitative*

LEAR   When were you wont° to be so full of songs, sirrah?   *accustomed*

FOOL   I have used° it, nuncle, ever since thou madest thy daugh-   *practiced*
150 ters thy mother; for when thou gavest them the rod, and put'st
down thine own breeches,

    Singing

    Then they for sudden joy did weep,
    And I for sorrow sung,
    That such a king should play bo-peep,°   *a child's game*
155   And go the fools among.
Prithee, nuncle, keep a schoolmaster that can teach thy fool
to lie. I would fain learn to lie.

LEAR   An° you lie, sirrah, we'll have you whipped.   *If*

FOOL   I marvel what kin° thou and thy daughters are. They'll   *how alike*
160 have me whipped for speaking true, thou'lt have me whipped
for lying; and sometimes I am whipped for holding my peace.
I had rather be any kind o' thing than a fool; and yet I would
not be thee, nuncle; thou hast pared thy wit o' both sides, and
left nothing i' the middle. Here comes one o' the parings.

    Enter GONERIL

165 LEAR   How now, daughter! What makes that frontlet[3] on?
Methinks you are too much of late i' the frown.

FOOL   Thou wast a pretty fellow when thou hadst no need to
care for her frowning; now thou art an O without a figure.[4] I
am better than thou art now; I am a fool, thou art nothing. [*To*
170 GONERIL] Yes, forsooth, I will hold my tongue; so your face bids
me, though you say nothing. Mum, mum,

    He that keeps nor crust nor crum,
    Weary of all, shall want° some.   *lack; be in need of*
(*Pointing to* LEAR) That's a shealed peascod.°   *empty pea pod; nothing*

175 GONERIL   Not only, sir, this your all-licensed° fool,   *unrestrained*
But other of your insolent retinue
Do hourly carp and quarrel, breaking forth
In rank° and not-to-be-endured riots. Sir,   *foul; spreading*
I had thought, by making this well known unto you,
180 To have found a safe° redress; but now grow fearful,   *sure*
By what yourself too late° have spoke and done,   *recently*
That you protect this course, and put it on°   *encourage it*
By your allowance; which if you should, the fault
Would not 'scape censure, nor the redresses sleep,
185 Which, in the tender of a wholesome weal,
Might in their working do you that offense,
Which else were shame, that then necessity
Will call discreet proceeding.[5]

---

2. *Fools . . . foppish:* Professional fools have never been as witless since wise men have lately outdone them in idiocy.
3. Band worn on the forehead; here, a metaphor for "frown."
4. A zero without a preceding digit; nothing.
5. *which if you . . . proceeding:* if you do approve (of your attendants' behavior), you will not escape criticism, nor will it be without retribution, which for the common good will cause you pain. While this would otherwise be improper, it will be seen as a prudent ("discreet") action under the circumstances. *tender of:* concern for. *weal:* state, commonwealth. *then necessity:* the demands of the time.

FOOL   For, you know, nuncle,

190   The hedge-sparrow fed the cuckoo[6] so long,

       That it had it° head bit off by it young.°   *its / (the young cuckoo)*

       So, out went the candle, and we were left darkling.°   *in the dark*

LEAR   Are you our daughter?

GONERIL   Come, sir.

195   I would° you would make use of that good wisdom,   *wish*

       Whereof I know you are fraught,° and put away   *full*

       These dispositions,° that of late transform you   *moods; attitudes*

       From what you rightly are.

FOOL   May not an ass know when the cart draws the horse?

200   Whoop, Jug![7] I love thee.

LEAR   Doth any here know me? This is not Lear.

       Doth Lear walk thus? speak thus? Where are his eyes?

       Either his notion° weakens, his discernings   *intellect*

       Are lethargied—Ha! waking?° 'Tis not so.   *am I awake*

205   Who is it that can tell me who I am?

FOOL   Lear's shadow.

LEAR   I would° learn that; for, by the marks° of sovereignty,   *wish to / evidence*

       knowledge, and reason, I should be false persuaded I had

       daughters.

210 FOOL   Which° they will make an obedient father.   *Whom*

LEAR   Your name, fair gentlewoman?

GONERIL   This admiration,° sir, is much o' the savor   *excessive amazement*

       Of other your new pranks. I do beseech you

       To understand my purposes aright.

215   As you are old and reverend, you should be wise.

       Here do you keep a hundred knights and squires;

       Men so disordered,° so deboshed° and bold,   *disorderly / debauched*

       That this our court, infected with their manners,

       Shows° like a riotous inn. Epicurism° and lust   *Appears / Gluttony*

220   Make it more like a tavern or a brothel

       Than a graced° palace. The shame itself doth speak   *an honored*

       For instant remedy; be then desired

       By her, that else will take the thing she begs,

       A little to disquantity your train;°   *to reduce your retinue*

225   And the remainder that shall still depend,°   *be retained*

       To be such men as may besort° your age,   *befit*

       And know themselves° and you.   *know their place*

LEAR   Darkness and devils!

       Saddle my horses! call my train together!

       Degenerate bastard! I'll not trouble thee.

230   Yet° have I left a daughter.   *Still*

GONERIL   You strike my people, and your disordered rabble

       Make servants of their betters.

            Enter ALBANY

LEAR   Woe that° too late repents!—(*To* ALBANY)   *Woe to him who*

       O, sir, are you come?

235   Is it your will? Speak, sir. Prepare my horses!

       Ingratitude, thou marble-hearted fiend,

       More hideous when thou show'st thee in a child

       Than the sea-monster!

---

6. The cuckoo lays its eggs in other birds' nests.   7. Nickname for "Joan"; sobriquet for a whore.

ALBANY   Pray, sir, be patient.

LEAR (*to* GONERIL)   Detested kite!° thou liest: *carrion-eating hawk*

240   My train are men of choice and rarest parts,°   *qualities*

      That all particulars of duty know,

      And in the most exact regard support

      The worships of° their name. O most small fault,   *honors accorded*

      How ugly didst thou in Cordelia show!

245   That, like an engine, wrench'd my frame of nature

      From the fixed place;[8] drew from my heart all love,

      And added to the gall. O Lear, Lear, Lear!

      Beat at this gate, that let thy folly in, (*striking his head*)

      And thy dear° judgment out! Go, go, my people.   *precious*

250   ALBANY   My lord, I am guiltless, as I am ignorant

      Of what hath moved you.

LEAR   It may be so, my lord.

      Hear, Nature, hear! dear goddess, hear!

      Suspend thy purpose, if thou didst intend

      To make this creature fruitful!

255   Into her womb convey sterility!

      Dry up in her the organs of increase;

      And from her derogate° body never spring   *debased*

      A babe to honor her! If she must teem,°   *breed*

      Create her child of spleen,° that it may live   *malice*

260   And be a thwart, disnatured° torment to her!   *a perverse, unnatural*

      Let it stamp wrinkles in her brow of youth;

      With cadent° tears fret° channels in her cheeks;   *flowing / carve*

      Turn all her mother's pains and benefits°   *cares and kind actions*

      To laughter and contempt, that she may feel

265   How sharper than a serpent's tooth it is

      To have a thankless child! Away, away!   *Exit*

    ALBANY   Now, gods that we adore, whereof comes this?

    GONERIL   Never afflict yourself to know the cause;

      But let his disposition have that scope

270   That dotage gives it.

             Re-enter LEAR

    LEAR   What, fifty of my followers at a clap?

      Within a fortnight?

    ALBANY   What's the matter, sir?

    LEAR   I'll tell thee. (*To* GONERIL) Life and death! I am ashamed

      That thou hast power to shake my manhood thus;

275   That these hot tears, which break from me perforce,°   *against my will*

      Should make thee worth them. Blasts and fogs upon thee!

      The untented woundings° of a father's curse   *The undressed wounds*

      Pierce every sense about thee! Old fond° eyes,   *foolish*

      Beweep° this cause again, I'll pluck ye out,   *If you weep over*

280   And cast you, with the waters that you lose,

      To temper° clay. Yea, is it come to this?   *soften*

      Let it be so. Yet have I left a daughter,

      Who, I am sure, is kind and comfortable.°   *comforting*

      When she shall hear this of thee, with her nails

285   She'll flay thy wolvish visage. Thou shalt find

      That I'll resume the shape which thou dost think

      I have cast off for ever; thou shalt, I warrant thee.

---

8. *like . . . place:* as a machine (or lever) dislocated my natural affections from their proper foundations.

Exeunt LEAR, KENT, *and attendants*

GONERIL. Do you mark that, my lord?

ALBANY I cannot be so partial,° Goneril,   *biased*

290   To° the great love I bear you—   *Because of*

GONERIL Pray you, content.° What, Oswald, ho! (*To the* FOOL)   *be quiet*

You sir, more knave than fool, after your master!

FOOL Nuncle Lear, nuncle Lear, tarry and take the fool with
thee.

295   A fox, when one has caught her,

          And such a daughter,

          Should sure° to the slaughter,   *surely be sent*

          If my cap would buy a halter:°   *collar; noose*

          So the fool follows after.   *Exit*

GONERIL This man hath had good counsel!—a hundred

300   knights?

  'Tis politic° and safe to let him keep   *prudent*

  At point° a hundred knights? Yes, that on every dream,   *Armed*

  Each buzz,° each fancy, each complaint, dislike,   *rumor*

  He may enguard° his dotage with their powers,   *protect*

305   And hold our lives in mercy. Oswald, I say!

ALBANY Well, you may fear too far.

GONERIL   Safer than trust too far:

  Let me still° take away the harms I fear,   *always*

  Not° fear still to be taken. I know his heart.   *Rather than*

  What he hath uttered I have writ my sister.

310   If she sustain him and his hundred knights,

  When I have showed the unfitness—

     Re-enter OSWALD

                How now, Oswald!

  What, have you writ that letter to my sister?

OSWALD Yes, madam.

GONERIL Take you some company, and away to horse!

315   Inform her full of my particular fear,

  And thereto add such reasons of your own

  As may compact° it more. Get you gone,   *compound*

  And hasten your return.   *Exit* OSWALD

  No, no, my lord,

320   This milky gentleness and course of yours

  Though I condemn not, yet, under pardon,°   *begging your pardon*

  You are much more attaxed° for want of wisdom   *taken to task; censured*

  Than praised for harmful mildness.

ALBANY How far your eyes may pierce° I cannot tell: *foresee*

325   Striving to better, oft we mar what's well.

GONERIL Nay, then—

ALBANY Well, well; the event.°   *Exeunt*   *let's see the outcome*

1.5

Enter LEAR, KENT, *and* FOOL

LEAR Go you before° to Gloucester[1] with these letters. Acquaint   *on ahead*
  my daughter no further with any thing you know than comes
  from her demand out of the letter.[2] If your diligence be not
  speedy, I shall be there afore you.

5 KENT I will not sleep, my lord, till I have delivered your letter.

                                                          Exit

FOOL If a man's brains were in 's heels, were 't not in danger of
  kibes?°   *chilblains*

LEAR Ay, boy.

FOOL Then, I prithee, be merry; thy wit shall ne'er go slip-shod.[3]

10 LEAR Ha, ha, ha!

FOOL Shalt° see thy other daughter will use thee kindly; for   *Thou shalt*
  though she's as like this as a crab's° like an apple, yet I can tell   *crab apple; sour apple*
  what I can tell.

LEAR Why, what canst thou tell, my boy?

15 FOOL She will taste as like this as a crab does to a crab. Thou
  canst tell why one's nose stands i' the middle on's° face?   *of one's*

LEAR No.

FOOL Why, to keep one's eyes of either side's nose, that what a
  man cannot smell out, 'a° may spy into.   *he*

20 LEAR I did her wrong—

FOOL Canst tell how an oyster makes his shell?

LEAR No.

FOOL Nor I neither; but I can tell why a snail has a house.

LEAR Why?

25 FOOL Why, to put his head in; not to give it away to his daughters, and leave his horns without a case.[4]

LEAR I will forget my nature.[5] So kind a father! Be my horses
  ready?

FOOL Thy asses° are gone about 'em. The reason why the seven   *(servants)*
30 stars° are no more than seven is a pretty reason.   *the Pleiades*

LEAR Because they are not eight?

FOOL Yes, indeed. Thou wouldst make a good fool.

LEAR To take 't again perforce![6] Monster ingratitude!

FOOL If thou wert my fool, nuncle, I'd have thee beaten for
35 being old before thy time.

LEAR How's that?

FOOL Thou shouldst not have been old till thou hadst been wise.

LEAR O, let me not be mad, not mad, sweet heaven!
  Keep me in temper;° I would not be mad!   *sane*

      Enter GENTLEMEN

40 How now! Are the horses ready?

GENTLEMEN Ready, my lord.

LEAR Come, boy.

FOOL She that's a maid now, and laughs at my departure,

1.5 Location: Before Albany's castle.
1. To Gloucestershire, where Cornwall and Regan
reside.
2. *than . . . letter:* other than such questions as are
prompted by the letter.
3. Literally, your brains will not wear slippers (to warm
feet that are afflicted with chilblains); feet of any intelligence would not walk toward Regan.

4. Protective covering for his head or concealment for his
horns (horns were the conventional sign of a cuckold).
The Fool reflects the cynical view, common in the
period, that all married men are inevitably cuckolded.
5. Lose my fatherly feelings. *nature:* character.
6. To take it back by force. Lear may refer to Goneril's
treachery, or he may be contemplating resuming his
authority.

Shall not be a maid long, unless things be cut shorter.[7]

Exeunt

2.1

Enter EDMUND *and* CURAN *meeting*

EDMUND Save° thee, Curan.   *God save*

CURAN And you, sir. I have been with your father, and given
him notice that the Duke of Cornwall and Regan his duchess
will be here with him this night.

5 EDMUND How comes that?

CURAN Nay, I know not. You have heard of the news abroad—
I mean the whispered ones, for they are yet but ear-bussing
arguments?[1]

EDMUND Not I. Pray you, what are they?

10 CURAN Have you heard of no likely wars toward,° 'twixt the   *impending*
Dukes of Cornwall and Albany?

EDMUND Not a word.

CURAN You may do, then, in time. Fare you well, sir.   *Exit*

EDMUND The duke be here tonight? The better! best!

15 This weaves itself perforce° into my business.   *necessarily*
My father hath set guard to take my brother;
And I have one thing, of a queasy question,[2]
Which I must act. Briefness and fortune, work!°   *be with me*
Brother, a word! Descend! Brother, I say!

Enter EDGAR

20 My father watches. O sir, fly this place!
Intelligence is given where you are hid.
You have now the good advantage of the night.
Have you not spoken 'gainst the Duke of Cornwall?
He's coming hither; now, i' the night, i' the haste,

25 And Regan with him: have you nothing said
Upon his party° 'gainst the Duke of Albany?   *On his (Cornwall's) side*
Advise yourself.°   *Consider carefully*

EDGAR   I am sure on't,° not a word.   *of it*

EDMUND I hear my father coming. Pardon me!
In cunning I must draw my sword upon you:

30 Draw; seem to defend yourself; now quit you° well.   *acquit yourself*
Yield! Come before my father. Light, ho, here!
Fly, brother. Torches, torches! So farewell.   *Exit* EDGAR
Some blood drawn on me would beget opinion°   *produce the impression*
(*wounds his arm*)
Of my more fierce endeavor. I have seen drunkards

35 Do more than this in sport. Father, father!
Stop, stop! No help?

Enter GLOUCESTER, *and servants with torches*

GLOUCESTER Now, Edmund, where's the villain?

EDMUND Here stood he in the dark, his sharp sword out,
Mumbling of wicked charms, conjuring the moon
To stand° auspicious mistress,—   *To act as his*

40 GLOUCESTER   But where is he?

EDMUND Look, sir, I bleed.

---

7. *She . . . shorter:* A girl who would laugh at my leaving would be so foolish that she could not remain a virgin for long; "things" refers both to the unfolding event
and to penises.

2.1 Location: Gloucester's castle.
1. Barely whispered affairs. *bussing:* buzzing.
2. And I have a hazardous and delicate problem.

GLOUCESTER Where is the villain, Edmund?

EDMUND Fled this way, sir. When by no means he could—

GLOUCESTER Pursue him, ho! Go after. *Exeunt some servants*

By no means what?

45 EDMUND Persuade me to the murder of your lordship;

But that° I told him, the revenging gods   *In response to that*

'Gainst parricides did all their thunders bend;

Spoke, with how manifold and strong a bond

The child was bound to the father; sir, in fine,°   *finally*

50 Seeing how loathly opposite° I stood   *opposed*

To his unnatural purpose, in fell° motion,   *deadly*

With his prepared sword, he charges home°   *strikes to the heart of*

My unprovided° body, lanched° mine arm: *unprotected / struck*

But when he saw my best alarumed spirits,

55 Bold in the quarrel's right,[3] roused to the encounter,

Or whether gasted° by the noise I made,   *frightened*

Full suddenly he fled.

GLOUCESTER   Let him fly far.

Not in this land shall he remain uncaught;

And found—dispatch.° The noble duke my master,   *And once found—killed*

60 My worthy arch° and patron, comes to-night: *lord*

By his authority I will proclaim it,

That he which finds him shall deserve our thanks,

Bringing the murderous caitiff° to the stake;[4]   *wretch*

He that conceals him, death.

65 EDMUND When I dissuaded him from his intent,

And found him pight° to do it, with curst° speech   *resolved / bitter*

I threatened to discover° him. He replied,   *expose*

"Thou unpossessing bastard! dost thou think

If I would stand against thee, would the reposal°   *placing*

70 Of any trust, virtue, or worth in thee

Make thy words faithed?° No. What I should deny—   *credible*

As this I would; ay, though thou didst produce

My very character[5]—I'd turn it all

To[6] thy suggestion, plot, and damned practice:°   *scheming*

75 And thou must make a dullard of the world,

If they not thought the profits of my death

Were very pregnant and potential spurs

To make thee seek it."[7]

GLOUCESTER   Strong° and fast'ned° villain!   *Flagrant / incorrigible*

Would he deny his letter? I never got° him.   *begot*

Tucket° within   *Flourish of trumpets*

80 Hark, the Duke's trumpets! I know not why he comes.

All ports° I'll bar; the villain shall not 'scape;   *seaports; exits*

The duke must grant me that. Besides, his picture[8]

I will send far and near, that all the kingdom

May have due note of him; and of my land,

85 Loyal and natural° boy, I'll work the means   *loving; illegitimate*

To make thee capable.°   *legally able to inherit*

---

3. *my best . . . right*: that I was fully roused to action, made brave by righteousness.

4. Treachery and rebellion were crimes for which one could be burned.

5. Handwriting; but also, a true summary of my character.

6. *I'd . . . / To*: I'd blame it all on.

7. *And thou . . . it*: And do you think the world so stupid that it could not see the benefit you would get from my death (and thus a motive for plotting to kill me)? *pregnant*: full. *potential spurs*: powerful temptations.

8. Likenesses of outlaws were drawn up, printed, and publicly displayed, sometimes with an offer of reward as in "Wanted" posters.

Enter CORNWALL, REGAN, *and attendants*

CORNWALL   How now, my noble friend! Since I came hither,
(Which I can call but now) I have heard strange news.

REGAN   If it be true, all vengeance comes too short

90   Which can pursue the offender. How dost, my lord?

GLOUCESTER   O, madam, my old heart is cracked, is cracked!

REGAN   What, did my father's godson seek your life?
He whom my father named? Your Edgar?

GLOUCESTER   O, lady, lady, shame would have it hid!

95   REGAN   Was he not companion with the riotous knights
That tend° upon my father?   *attend*

GLOUCESTER   I know not, madam. 'Tis too bad, too bad!

EDMUND   Yes, madam, he was of that consòrt.°   *company*

REGAN   No marvel, then, though° he were ill affected.°   *that / ill disposed*

100   'Tis they have put him on° the old man's death,   *have urged him to seek*
To have th' expense° and waste of his revènues.   *use*
I have this present evening from my sister
Been well informed of them; and with such cautions
That if they come to sojourn at my house,
I'll not be there.

105   CORNWALL   Nor I, assure thee, Regan.
Edmund, I hear that you have shown your father
A child-like office.°   *filial service*

EDMUND   'Twas my duty, sir.

GLOUCESTER   He did bewray his practice,° and received   *uncover his (Edgar's) plot*
This hurt you see, striving to apprehend him.

CORNWALL   Is he pursued?

110   GLOUCESTER   Ay, my good lord.

CORNWALL   If he be taken, he shall never more
Be feared of doing harm. Make your own purpose,
How in my strength you please.⁹ For you, Edmund,
Whose virtue and obedience doth this instant

115   So much commend itself, you shall be ours.
Natures of such deep trust we shall much need;
You we first seize on.

EDMUND   I shall serve you, sir,
Truly, however else.°   *if nothing else*

GLOUCESTER   For him I thank your grace.

CORNWALL   You know not why we came to visit you—

120   REGAN   Thus out of season, threading dark-eyed night.
Occasions, noble Gloucester, of some poise,°   *weight*
Wherein we must have use of your advice:
Our father he hath writ, so hath our sister,
Of differences,° which I least thought of fit   *quarrels*

125   To answer from our home. The several° messengers   *various*
From hence attend° dispatch. Our good old friend,   *await*
Lay comforts to your bosom, and bestow
Your needful° counsel to our business,   *badly needed*
Which craves the instant use.¹

GLOUCESTER   I serve you, madam.

130   Your graces are right welcome.   *Exeunt*

9. *Make . . . please:* Devise your plots making use of my   1. Which requires immediate attention.
forces and authority as you see fit.

2.2

Enter KENT *and* OSWALD, *severally*°   *separately*

OSWALD   Good dawning to thee, friend. Art° of this house?   *Are you a servant*

KENT   Ay.

OSWALD   Where may we set our horses?

KENT   I' the mire.

5   OSWALD   Prithee, if thou lovest me,° tell me.   *if you will be so kind*

KENT   I love thee not.

OSWALD   Why, then, I care not for thee.

KENT   If I had thee in Lipsbury pinfold,[1] I would make thee care
     for me.

10   OSWALD   Why dost thou use° me thus? I know thee not.   *treat*

KENT   Fellow, I know thee.

OSWALD   What dost thou know me for?

KENT   A knave; a rascal; an eater of broken meats;° a base, proud,   *scraps*
     shallow, beggarly, three-suited, hundred-pound, filthy, worsted-

15   stocking knave;[2] a lily-livered, action-taking knave; a whoreson,
     glass-gazing, superserviceable, finical rogue; one-trunk-inher-
     iting slave;[3] one that wouldst be a bawd in way of good service,[4]
     and art nothing but the composition° of a knave, beggar, cow-   *combination*
     ard, pandar, and the son and heir of a mongrel bitch; one

20   whom I will beat into clamorous whining, if thou deniest the
     least syllable of thy addition.[5]

OSWALD   Why, what a monstrous fellow art thou, thus to rail on
     one that is neither known of° thee nor knows thee!   *by*

KENT   What a brazen-faced varlet° art thou, to deny thou   *rascal*
25   knowest me! Is it two days ago since I tripped up thy heels, and
     beat thee before the king? Draw, you rogue! For, though it be
     night, yet the moon shines. I'll make a sop of the moonshine[6]
     of you. Draw, you whoreson cullionly barber-monger,[7] draw!
        Drawing his sword

OSWALD   Away! I have nothing to do with thee.

30   KENT   Draw, you rascal! You come with letters against the king,
     and take Vanity the puppet's part against the royalty of her
     father.[8] Draw, you rogue, or I'll so carbonado[9] your shanks!
     Draw, you rascal! Come your ways!°   *Come forward*

OSWALD   Help, ho! murther! help!

35   KENT   Strike, you slave! Stand, rogue! Stand, you neat° slave!   *elegant; foppish*
     Strike! [*Beating him*]

OSWALD   Help, ho! muther! murther!

        Enter EDMUND *with his rapier drawn,* CORNWALL,
        REGAN, GLOUCESTER, *and servants*

2.2 Location: Before Gloucester's house.

1. If I had you in the enclosure of my mouth (gripped in my teeth). Lipsbury is probably an invented place-name. *pinfold:* pen, animal enclosure.

2. *three-suited . . . knave:* Oswald is being called a poor imitation of a gentleman. Servants were permitted three suits a year; one hundred pounds was the minimum qualification for the purchase of one of King James's knighthoods; a gentleman would wear silk, not "worsted" (of thick woolen material), stockings.

3. *lily-livered:* cowardly. *action-taking:* litigious, one who would rather use the law than his fists. *glass-gazing:* mirror-gazing. *superserviceable:* overly officious, or too ready to serve. *finical:* finicky, fastidious. *one-trunk-inheriting:* owning only what would fill one trunk.

4. *one that . . . service:* one who would even be a pimp if called upon.

5. Of the descriptions Kent has just applied to him. *addition:* title (used ironically).

6. Kent proposes so to skewer and pierce Oswald that his body might soak up moonlight. *sop:* piece of bread to be steeped or dunked in soup.

7. *cullionly barber-monger:* despicable frequenter of hairdressers. *cullion:* testicle.

8. *and take . . . father:* and support Goneril, here depicted as a dressed-up doll whose pride is contrasted with Lear's kingliness.

9. Slash or score as one would the surface of meat in preparation for broiling.

EDMUND   How now! What's the matter?

Parts them

KENT   With you, goodman boy, an° you please! Come, I'll flesh   *if*
40 ye!¹ Come, on, young master!

GLOUCESTER   Weapons! arms! What's the matter here?

CORNWALL   Keep peace, upon your lives!
He dies that strikes again. What is the matter?

REGAN   The messengers from our sister and the king.

45 CORNWALL   What is your difference?° Speak.   *quarrel*

OSWALD   I am scarce in breath, my lord.

KENT   No marvel, you have so bestirred your valor. You cowardly
rascal, nature disclaims° in thee; a tailor made thee.   *disowns her part*

CORNWALL   Thou art a strange fellow. A tailor² make a man?

50 KENT   Ay, a tailor, sir. A stone-cutter or a painter could not have
made him so ill,° though he had been but two hours at the   *so badly*
trade.

CORNWALL   Speak yet, how grew your quarrel?

OSWALD   This ancient ruffian, sir, whose life I have spared at suit
55 of° his gray beard—   *on account of*

KENT   Thou whoreson zed!³ thou unnecessary letter! My lord, if
you will give me leave, I will tread this unbolted° villain into   *unsifted; coarse*
mortar, and daub the walls of a jakes° with him. Spare my gray   *privy; toilet*
beard, you wagtail!⁴

60 CORNWALL   Peace, sirrah!
You beastly knave, know you no reverence?°   *respect*

KENT   Yes, sir, but anger hath a privilege.

CORNWALL   Why art thou angry?

KENT   That such a slave as this should wear a sword,
65 Who wears no honesty. Such smiling rogues as these,
Like rats, oft bite the holy cords⁵ a-twain
Which are too intrinse° t' unloose; smooth° every passion   *intricate / flatter*
That in natures of their lords rebel;
Bring oil to fire, snow to their colder moods;
70 Renege,° affirm, and turn their halcyon beaks⁶   *Deny*
With every gale and vary° of their masters,   *mood*
Knowing nought, like dogs, but following.
A plague upon your epileptic° visage!   *distorted; grimacing*
Smile you° my speeches, as° I were a fool?   *Do you smile at / as if*
75 Goose, if I had you upon Sarum plain
I'ld drive ye cackling home to Camelot.⁷

CORNWALL   What, art thou mad, old fellow?

GLOUCESTER   How fell you out? say that.

KENT   No contraries° hold more antipathy   *opposites*
80 Than I and such a knave.

CORNWALL   Why dost thou call him knave? What's his offense?

KENT   His countenance likes° me not.   *pleases*

CORNWALL   No more, perchance, does mine, nor his, nor hers.

---

1. I'll initiate you into fighting, as a hunting dog is given the taste of blood to rouse it for the chase.
2. Tailors, considered effeminate, were stock objects of mockery.
3. The letter Z (zed) was considered superfluous and omitted from many dictionaries.
4. A common English bird that takes its name from the up-and-down flicking of its tail; this, and its characteristic hopping from foot to foot, causes it to appear nervous.

5. Bonds of kinship, affection, marriage, or rank.
6. It was believed that the kingfisher (in Greek, *halcyon*) could be used as a weather vane when dead: suspended by a fine thread, its beak would turn whatever way the wind blew.
7. *Goose . . . Camelot:* Comparing him to a cackling goose, Kent tells Oswald that if he had him on Salisbury Plain, he would drive him all the way to Camelot, legendary home of King Arthur.

KENT   Sir, 'tis my occupation to be plain.
85   I have seen better faces in my time
        Than stands on any shoulder that I see
        Before me at this instant.
CORNWALL   This is some fellow,
        Who, having been praised for bluntness, doth affect
        A saucy roughness, and constrains the garb
90   Quite from his nature.⁸ He cannot flatter, he,
        An honest mind and plain, he must speak truth!
        An they will take it, so; if not, he's plain.⁹
        These kind of knaves I know, which in this plainness
        Harbor more craft and more corrupter ends
95   Than twenty silly ducking observants
        That stretch their duties nicely.¹
KENT   Sir, in good sooth, in sincere verity,
        Under the allowance of your great aspect,²
        Whose influence, like the wreath of radiant fire
        On flickering Phoebus' front,°   *the sun god's forehead*
100 CORNWALL   What mean'st by this?
KENT   To go out of my dialect,° which you discommend so   *normal mode of speech*
        much. I know, sir, I am no flatterer. He that beguiled you in a
        plain accent was a plain knave; which for my part I will not be,
        though I should win your displeasure to entreat me to 't.³
105 CORNWALL   What was the offense you gave him?
OSWALD   I never gave him any:
        It pleased the king his master very late°   *lately*
        To strike at me, upon his misconstruction,°   *misunderstanding (me)*
        When he, conjunct,° and flattering his displeasure,   *in league with*
110   Tripped me behind; being down, insulted,° railed,   *I being down, he insulted*
        And put upon him such a deal of man,
        That worthied him,⁴ got praises of the king
        For him attempting who was self-subdued;⁵
        And, in the fleshment° of this dread exploit,   *excitement; flush*
        Drew on me here again.
115 KENT   None of these rogues and cowards
        But Ajax is their fool.⁶
CORNWALL   Fetch forth the stocks!
        You stubborn miscreant knave, you reverent° braggart, *old; revered*
        We'll teach you—
KENT   Sir, I am too old to learn.
120   Call not your stocks for me. I serve the king;
        On whose employment I was sent to you:
        You shall do small respect, show too bold malice
        Against the grace° and person° of my master,   *majesty / personal honor*

---

8. *and constrains . . . nature:* and assumes the appearance though it is untrue to his real self. Alternatively (with "his" meaning "its"), and distorts the true shape of plainness from what it naturally is (by turning it into disrespect).
9. If they will accept (Kent's attitude), well and good; if not, he is a plainspoken man (and does not care).
1. *Than . . . nicely:* Than twenty obsequious attendants who constantly bow idiotically, and who perform their functions with excessive diligence ("nicely").
2. With the permission of your great countenance. "Aspect" also refers to the astrological position of a planet; Kent's bombastic language here raises Cornwall

to the mock-heroic proportions of a heavenly body.
3. *He that . . . to 't:* The person who tried to hoodwink you with plain speaking was, indeed, a pure knave—something I won't be, even if you were to beg me to be one (a plain knave, or flatterer).
4. *And put . . . him:* And put on such a show of manliness that he was thought a worthy fellow.
5. For attacking a man who had already surrendered (Kent attacking Oswald).
6. *None . . . fool:* Such rogues and cowards as these talk as if they were greater warriors (and blusterers) than Ajax; such rogues always make even mighty Ajax out to be a fool.

Stocking° his messenger. *By stocking*

125 CORNWALL   Fetch forth the stocks! As I have life and honor.
There shall he sit till noon.

REGAN   Till noon? Till night, my lord, and all night too!

KENT   Why, madam, if I were your father's dog,
You should not use me so.

REGAN   Sir, being° his knave, I will. *since you are*

130 CORNWALL   This is a fellow of the self-same color° *character*
Our sister° speaks of. Come, bring away the stocks! *sister-in-law*

Stocks brought out

GLOUCESTER   Let me beseech your grace not to do so.
His fault is much, and the good king his master
Will check° him for't. Your purposed° low correction *reprimand / intended*

135 Is such as basest and contemned'st wretches
For pilferings and most common trespasses
Are punished with: the king must take it ill,
That he, so slightly valued in his messenger,
Should have him thus restrained.

CORNWALL   I'll answer° that. *be responsible for*

140 REGAN   My sister may receive it much more worse,
To have her gentleman abused, assaulted,
For following° her affairs. Put in his legs. *carrying out*

KENT *is put in the stocks*
Come, my good lord, away.

Exeunt all but GLOUCESTER *and* KENT

GLOUCESTER   I am sorry for thee, friend: 'tis the duke's pleasure,

145 Whose disposition, all the world well knows,
Will not be rubbed° nor stopped: I'll entreat for thee. *obstructed*

KENT   Pray, do not sir. I have watched° and traveled hard; *gone without sleep*
Some time I shall sleep out, the rest I'll whistle.
A good man's fortune may grow out at heels:[7]

150 Give° you good morrow! *God give*

GLOUCESTER   The duke's to blame in this; 't will be ill-taken.

Exit

KENT   Good king, that must approve° the common saw,° *prove / saying*
Thou out of heaven's benediction comest
To the warm sun![8]

155 Approach, thou beacon[9] to this under globe,
That by thy comfortable beams I may
Peruse this letter! Nothing almost sees miracles
But misery.[1] I know 'tis from Cordelia,
Who hath most fortunately been informed

160 Of my obscurèd° course; (*reads*) "and shall find time *hidden; disguised*
From this enormous state,° seeking to give *awful state of affairs*
Losses their remedies." All weary and o'er-watched,° *too long awake*
Take vantage,° heavy eyes, not to behold *the opportunity*
This shameful lodging.

165 Fortune, good night; smile once more; turn thy wheel![2]

Sleeps

---

7. The fortunes of even good men sometimes wear thin.
8. *Thou . . . sun:* You come from the blessing of heaven into the heat of the sun (go from good to bad).
9. It is arguable whether Kent here refers to the sun or the moon.
1. *Nothing . . . misery:* Only those suffering misery are granted miracles; any comfort seems miraculous to those who are miserable.
2. The goddess Fortune was traditionally depicted with a wheel to signify her mutability and caprice. She was believed to take pleasure in arbitrarily lowering those at the top of her wheel and raising those at the bottom.

2.3

Enter EDGAR

EDGAR   I heard myself proclaimed;°   *declared an outlaw*
And by the happy° hollow of a tree   *opportune*
Escaped the hunt. No port° is free; no place,   *seaport; exit*
That guard, and most unusual vigilance,
5   Does not attend my taking.° Whiles° I may 'scape,   *await my capture / Until*
I will preserve myself; and am bethought°   *resolved*
To take the basest and most poorest shape
That ever penury, in contempt of° man,   *for*
Brought near to beast. My face I'll grime with filth,
10   Blanket my loins, elf[1] all my hair in knots,
And with presented° nakedness out-face   *exposed*
The winds and persecutions of the sky.
The country gives me proof and precedent
Of Bedlam beggars, who, with roaring voices,
15   Strike° in their numbed and mortified° bare arms   *Stick / deadened*
Pins, wooden pricks, nails, sprigs of rosemary;
And with this horrible object,° from low farms,   *spectacle*
Poor pelting° villages, sheep-cotes, and mills,   *paltry; contemptible*
Sometime with lunatic bans,° sometime with prayers,   *curses*
20   Enforce their charity. Poor Turlygod![2] poor Tom!
That's something yet! Edgar I nothing am.[3]   *Exit*

2.4

Enter LEAR, FOOL, *and* GENTLEMAN

LEAR   'Tis strange that they should so depart from home,
And not send back my messenger.
GENTLEMAN   As I learned,
The night before there was no purpose in them°   *they had no intention*
Of this remove.°   *change of residence*
KENT   Hail to thee, noble master!
5   LEAR   Ha!
Makest thou this shame thy pastime?
KENT   No, my lord.
FOOL   Ha, ha! he wears cruel garters.[1] Horses are tied by the
heads, dogs and bears by the neck, monkeys by the loins, and
men by the legs. When a man's over-lusty at legs,[2] then he
10   wears wooden nether-stocks.°   *knee socks*
LEAR   What's° he that hath so much thy place° mistook   *Who's / position*
To set thee here?
KENT   It is both he and she;
Your son° and daughter.   *son-in-law*
LEAR   No.
15   KENT   Yes.
LEAR   No, I say.
KENT   I say, yea.
LEAR   No, no, they would not!
KENT   Yes, yes, they have!

2.3 Location: As before.
1. Tangle the hair into "elf locks," supposed to be a favorite trick of malicious elves.
2. A word of unknown origin.
3. Edgar, I am nothing; I am no longer Edgar.

2.4 Location: As before.
1. Worsted garters, punning on "crewel," a thin yarn. The Fool is actually referring to the stocks in which Kent's feet are held.
2. When a man's liable to run away.

20	LEAR	By Jupiter, I swear, no!	
	KENT	By Juno,[3] I swear, aye!	
	LEAR	They durst not do 't;	

They would not, could not do 't. 'Tis worse than murder,
To do upon respect[4] such violent outrage.
Resolve° me, with all modest° haste, which way   *Inform / reasonable*
25 Thou mightst deserve, or they impose, this usage,
Coming from us.

KENT   My lord, when at their home
I did commend° your highness' letters to them,   *deliver*
Ere I was risen from the place that showed
My duty kneeling, came there a reeking° post,°   *steaming / messenger*
30 Stewed in his haste, half breathless, panting forth
From Goneril his mistress, salutations;
Delivered letters, spite of intermission,[5]
Which presently° they read; on whose contènts,   *immediately*
They summoned up their meiny,° straight° took horse;   *retinue / straightaway*
35 Commanded me to follow, and attend
The leisure of their answer, gave me cold looks,
And meeting here the other messenger,
Whose welcome, I perceived, had poisoned mine—
Being the very° fellow that of late   *same*
40 Displayed so saucily° against your highness—   *Acted so insolently*
Having more man° than wit° about me, drew.   *courage / sense*
He raised the house with loud and coward cries.
Your son and daughter found this trespass worth°   *deserving of*
The shame which here it suffers.

45 FOOL   Winter's not gone yet, if the wild-geese fly that way.[6]
        Fathers that wear rags
           Do make their children blind;[7]
        But fathers that bear bags
           Shall see their children kind.
50   Fortune, that arrant whore,
           Ne'er turns the key° to the poor.   *opens the door*
But, for all this, thou shalt have as many dolors[8] for thy daughters as thou canst tell° in a year.   *count*

LEAR   O, how this mother° swells up toward my heart!   *hysteria*
55 *Hysterica passio*, down, thou climbing sorrow,[9]
Thy element's° below! Where is this daughter?   *natural place is*
KENT   With the earl, sir, here within.
LEAR   Follow me not; stay here.
                               Exit

GENTLEMAN   Made you no more offenses but what you speak of?
KENT   None. How chance the king comes with so small a train?
60 FOOL   An° thou hadst been set i' the stocks for that question,   *If*
thou hadst well deserved it.
KENT   Why, fool?
FOOL   We'll set thee to school to an ant, to teach thee there's no

---

3. Queen of the Roman gods and wife of Jupiter, with whom she constantly quarreled.
4. To do to one who deserves respect.
5. Regardless of interrupting me; despite the interruptions in his account (as he gasped for breath).
6. That is, things will get worse before they get better.
7. Blind to their father's needs.
8. Pains, sorrows; punning on "dollar," the English term for the German "thaler," a large silver coin.
9. Hysterica . . . *sorrow: Hysterica passio* (a Latin expression originating in the Greek *steiros*, "suffering in the womb") was an inflammation of the senses. In Renaissance medicine, vapors from the abdomen were thought to rise up through the body, and in women, the uterus itself to wander around.

laboring i' the winter.[1] All that follow their noses are led by
65 their eyes but blind men, and there's not a nose among twenty
but can smell him that's stinking.° Let go thy hold when a great   *(as his fortunes decay)*
wheel runs down a hill,[2] lest it break thy neck with following
it; but the great one that goes up the hill, let him draw thee
after. When a wise man gives thee better counsel, give me
70 mine again. I would have none but knaves follow it, since a
fool gives it.

> That sir which serves and seeks for gain,
>   And follows but for form,
> Will pack° when it begins to rain,   *pack up and go*
75   And leave thee in the storm.
> But I will tarry; the fool will stay,
>   And let the wise man fly.
> The knave turns fool that runs away;[3]
>   The fool no knave, perdy.°   *by God (pardieu)*

80 KENT   Where learned you this, fool?

FOOL   Not i' the stocks, fool.

   Re-enter LEAR, *with* GLOUCESTER

LEAR   Deny to speak with me? They are sick? they are weary?
They have traveled all the night? Mere fetches;°   *ruses; pretexts*
The images of revolt and flying off.[4]
Fetch me a better answer.

85 GLOUCESTER   My dear lord,
You know the fiery quality° of the duke;   *disposition*
How unremoveable and fixed he is
In his own course.

LEAR   Vengeance! plague! death! confusion!°   *destruction*
90 Fiery? what quality? Why, Gloucester, Gloucester,
I'd speak with the Duke of Cornwall and his wife.

GLOUCESTER   Well, my good lord, I have informed them so.

LEAR   Informed them! Dost thou understand me, man?

GLOUCESTER   Ay, my good lord.

95 LEAR   The king would speak with Cornwall; the dear father
Would with his daughter speak, commands her service.
Are they informed of this? My breath and blood!
Fiery? the fiery duke? Tell the hot duke that—
No, but not yet. May be he is not well.
100 Infirmity doth still° neglect all office°   *always / obligation*
Whereto our health is bound; we are not ourselves
When nature, being oppressed, commands the mind
To suffer with the body. I'll forbear;
And am fallen out with my more headier will,[5]
105 To take° the indisposed and sickly fit   *mistake*
For the sound man. Death on my state![6] Wherefore°   *Why*
   looking on KENT
Should he sit here? This act persuades me
That this remotion° of the duke and her   *remoteness, aloofness*
Is practice° only. Give me my servant forth.   *trickery*

---

1. Ants, proverbially prudent, do not work in winter.
Implicitly, a wise person should know better than to look
for sustenance to an old man who has fallen on wintry
times.
2. A great wheel is a figure for Lear and of Fortune's
wheel itself, which has swung downward.

3. The scoundrel who runs away is the real fool.
4. *images of*: signs of. *flying off*: desertion; insurrection.
5. And disagree with my (earlier) more rash intention.
6. May my royal authority end (an oath). Ironically, this
has already happened.

110   Go tell the duke and 's wife I'd speak with them,

Now, presently!° Bid them come forth and hear me,   *at once*

Or at their chamber-door I'll beat the drum

Till it cry sleep to death.[7]

GLOUCESTER   I would have all well betwixt you.   *Exit*

115   LEAR   O me, my heart, my rising heart! but, down!

FOOL   Cry to it, nuncle, as the cockney° did to the eels when she   *Londoner (city woman)*

put 'em i' the paste° alive; she knapped 'em o' the coxcombs°   *pie; pastry / heads*

with a stick, and cried "Down, wantons,° down!" 'Twas her   *rogues*

brother that, in pure kindness to his horse, buttered his hay.[8]

     Enter CORNWALL, REGAN, GLOUCESTER, *and servants*

LEAR   Good morrow to you both.

120   CORNWALL   Hail to your grace!

     KENT *is set at liberty*

REGAN   I am glad to see your highness.

LEAR   Regan, I think you are; I know what reason

I have to think so. If thou shouldst not be glad,

I would divorce me from thy mother's tomb,

125   Sepulchring° an adultress. (*To* KENT) O, are you free?   *Because it entombed*

Some other time for that. Belovèd Regan,

Thy sister's naught.° O Regan, she hath tied   *wicked; nothing*

Sharp-toothed unkindness, like a vulture, here!

     Points to his heart

I can scarce speak to thee; thou'lt not believe

130   With how depraved a quality—O Regan!

REGAN   I pray you, sir, take patience. I have hope

You less know how to value her desert

Than she to scant her duty.[9]

LEAR   Say, how is that?

REGAN   I cannot think my sister in the least

135   Would fail her obligation. If, sir, perchance

She have restrained the riots of your followers,

'Tis on such ground, and to such wholesome end,

As clears her from all blame.

LEAR   My curses on her!

REGAN   O, sir, you are old;

140   Nature° in you stands on the very verge   *Life*

Of her confine.° You should be ruled and led   *Of its limit*

By some discretion,° that discerns your state   *discreet person*

Better than you yourself. Therefore, I pray you,

That to our sister you do make return;

Say you have wronged her, sir.

145   LEAR   Ask her forgiveness?

Do you but mark how this becomes the house:[1]

"Dear daughter, I confess that I am old; (*kneeling*)

Age° is unnecessary. On my knees I beg   *An old man*

That you'll vouchsafe me raiment,° bed, and food."   *promise me clothing*

150   REGAN   Good sir, no more! These are unsightly tricks.

Return you to my sister.

---

7. Till the noise kills sleep.

8. Like that of his sister (who wanted to make eel pie without killing the eels), his kindness was misplaced: horses will not eat buttered hay.

9. *I have . . . duty:* I expect that you are worse at valuing her deservings than she is at neglecting her duty. The double negative here ("less," "scant") is acceptable Jacobean usage.

1. Do you see how appropriate this is among members of a family (spoken ironically)?

LEAR (*rising*)   Never, Regan!
  She hath abated° me of half my train;   *deprived*
  Looked black upon me; struck me with her tongue
  Most serpent-like, upon the very heart.
155 All° the stored vengeances of heaven fall   *Let all*
  On her ingrateful top!° Strike her young bones,   *head*
  You taking° airs, with lameness!   *infectious; malignant*
CORNWALL   Fie, sir, fie!
LEAR   You nimble lightnings, dart your blinding flames
  Into her scornful eyes! Infect her beauty,
160 You fen-sucked fogs, drawn by the powerful sun,[2]
  To fall and blast her pride!
REGAN   O the blest gods! so will you wish on me,
  When the rash mood is on.
LEAR   No, Regan, thou shalt never have my curse.
165 Thy tender-hefted[3] nature shall not give
  Thee o'er to harshness. Her eyes are fierce; but thine
  Do comfort and not burn. 'Tis not in thee
  To grudge my pleasures, to cut off my train,
  To bandy hasty words, to scant my sizes,°   *reduce my allowances*
170 And in conclusion to oppose the bolt°   *to lock the door*
  Against my coming in. Thou better know'st
  The offices° of nature, bond of childhood,   *duties*
  Effects° of courtesy, dues of gratitude;   *Actions*
  Thy half o' the kingdom hast thou not forgot,
  Wherein I thee endowed.
175 REGAN   Good sir, to the purpose.°   *get to the point*
LEAR   Who put my man i' the stocks?
                Tucket within
CORNWALL   What trumpet's that?
REGAN   I know't, my sister's. This approves° her letter,   *confirms*
  That she would soon be here.
                Enter OSWALD
                              Is your lady come?
LEAR   This is a slave, whose easy-borrowed pride[4]
180 Dwells in the fickle grace of her he follows.
  Out varlet,° from my sight!   *wretch*
CORNWALL   What means your grace?
LEAR   Who stocked my servant? Regan, I have good hope
  Thou didst not know on 't.°   *of it*
                Enter GONERIL
  Who comes here? O heavens,
185 If you do love old men, if your sweet sway
  Allow obedience, if yourselves are old,
  Make it your cause! Send down, and take my part!
  (*To* GONERIL) Art not ashamed to look upon this beard?
  O Regan, wilt thou take her by the hand?
190 GONERIL   Why not by the hand, sir? How have I offended?
  All's not offense that indiscretion finds
  And dotage terms so.
LEAR   O sides,[5] you are too tough!

2. The sun was thought to suck poisonous vapors from
marshy ground.
3. Tenderly placed; firmly set in a tender disposition (as
a knife blade into its haft).
4. Unmerited and unpaid-for arrogance; "pride" may
also refer to Oswald's fine clothing received for his services to Goneril.
5. Chest, where Lear's heart is swelling with emotion.

Will you yet hold? How came my man i' the stocks?

CORNWALL   I set him there, sir; but his own disorders°   *disorderly behavior*
Deserved much less advancement.[6]

195 **LEAR**   You! did you?

REGAN   I pray you, father, being weak, seem so.°   *behave so*
If, till the expiration of your month,
You will return and sojourn with my sister,
Dismissing half your train, come then to me.
200 I am now from home, and out of that provision
Which shall be needful for your entertainment.

LEAR   Return to her, and fifty men dismissed?
No, rather I abjure all roofs, and choose
To wage against the enmity o' the air;
205 To be a comrade with the wolf and owl—
Necessity's sharp pinch![7] Return with her?
Why, the hot-blooded France, that dowerless took
Our youngest born, I could as well be brought
To knee° his throne, and, squire-like, pension beg   *kneel to*
210 To keep base life afoot. Return with her?
Persuade me rather to be slave and sumpter°   *packhorse*
To this detested groom. (*Pointing at* OSWALD)

GONERIL   At your choice, sir.

LEAR   I prithee, daughter, do not make me mad.
I will not trouble thee, my child; farewell.
215 We'll no more meet, no more see one another.
But yet thou art my flesh, my blood, my daughter;
Or rather a disease that's in my flesh,
Which I must needs call mine. Thou art a boil,
A plague-sore, an embossed° carbuncle,   *a swollen*
220 In my corrupted blood. But I'll not chide thee;
Let shame come when it will, I do not call° it.   *call upon*
I do not bid the Thunder-bearer° shoot,   *(Jove)*
Nor tell tales of thee to high-judging Jove.
Mend° when thou canst; be better at thy leisure.   *Make amends*
225 I can be patient, I can stay with Regan,
I and my hundred knights.

REGAN   Not altogether so.
I looked not for° you yet, nor am provided   *I did not expect*
For your fit welcome. Give ear, sir, to my sister;
For those that mingle reason with your passion[8]
230 Must be content to think you old, and so—
But she knows what she does.

LEAR   Is this well° spoken?   *earnestly*

REGAN   I dare avouch° it, sir. What, fifty followers?   *vouch for*
Is it not well? What should you need of more?
Yea, or so many, sith° that both charge° and danger   *since / expense*
235 Speak 'gainst so great a number? How, in one house,
Should many people, under two commands,
Hold amity? 'T is hard; almost impossible.

GONERIL   Why might not you, my lord, receive attendance
From those that she calls servants, or from mine?

---

6. Deserved far worse treatment.
7. *To wage . . . pinch:* To counter, like predators, the harshness of the elements with the hardness brought on by necessity. *pinch:* stress, pressure.
8. For those who temper your passionate argument with their own calm reasoning.

240 REGAN   Why not, my lord? If then they chanced to slack° you,   *neglect*
We could control them. If you will come to me—
For now I spy a danger—I entreat you
To bring but five-and-twenty. To no more
Will I give place or notice.°   *acknowledgment*
LEAR   I gave you all—
245 REGAN   And in good time° you gave it.   *it was about time*
LEAR   Made you my guardians, my depositaries;°   *trustees*
But kept a reservation° to be followed   *reserved a right*
With such a number. What, must I come to you
With five-and-twenty, Regan? Said you so?
250 REGAN   And speak't again, my lord; no more with me.
LEAR   Those wicked creatures yet do look well-favored,°   *attractive*
When others are more wicked; not being the worst
Stands in some rank of praise.[9] (*To* GONERIL) I'll go with thee:
Thy fifty yet doth double five-and-twenty,
And thou art twice her love.
255 GONERIL   Hear me, my lord.
What need you five-and-twenty, ten, or five,
To follow in a house where twice so many
Have a command to tend you?
REGAN   What need one?
LEAR   O, reason not the need! Our basest beggars
260 Are in the poorest thing superfluous.[1]
Allow not° nature more than nature needs,   *If you don't allow*
Man's life's as cheap as beast's. Thou art a lady;
If only to go warm were gorgeous,
Why, nature needs not what thou gorgeous wear'st,
265 Which scarcely keeps thee warm.[2] But, for true need—
You heavens, give me that patience,° patience I need!   *endurance*
You see me here, you gods, a poor old man,
As full of grief as age; wretched in both!
If it be you that stirs these daughters' hearts
270 Against their father, fool me not so much
To bear it tamely;[3] touch me with noble anger,
And let not women's weapons, water-drops,
Stain my man's cheeks! No, you unnatural hags,
I will have such revenges on you both,
275 That all the world shall—I will do such things—
What they are, yet I know not; but they shall be
The terrors of the earth! You think I'll weep;
No, I'll not weep.
I have full cause of weeping, but this heart
280 Shall break into a hundred thousand flaws°   *fragments*
Or ere° I'll weep. O fool, I shall go mad!   *Before*
       Exeunt LEAR, GLOUCESTER, KENT, *and* FOOL.
        Storm and tempest
CORNWALL   Let us withdraw; 't will be a storm.
REGAN   This house is little; the old man and his people
Cannot be well bestowed.°   *lodged*

---

9. Deserves some degree ("rank") of praise.
1. *Our . . . superfluous:* Even the lowliest beggars have
something more than the barest minimum.
2. *If . . . thee warm:* If gorgeousness in clothes is mea-

sured by the warmth they provide, your elaborate clothes
are superfluous, for they barely cover your body.
3. *fool . . . tamely:* do not make me so foolish as to accept
it meekly.

285 GONERIL 'Tis his own blame; hath put himself from° rest,   *deprived himself of*
    And must needs taste his folly.

REGAN For his particular,° I'll receive him gladly,   *single self*
    But not one follower.

GONERIL   So am I purposed.
    Where is my lord of Gloucester?

290 CORNWALL Followed the old man forth. He is returned.

      Re-enter GLOUCESTER

GLOUCESTER The king is in high rage.

CORNWALL   Whither is he going?

GLOUCESTER He calls to horse, but will° I know not whither.   *will go*

CORNWALL 'Tis best to give him way; he leads himself.

GONERIL My lord, entreat him by no means to stay.

295 GLOUCESTER Alack, the night comes on, and the bleak winds
    Do sorely ruffle.° For many miles about   *bluster*
    There's scarce a bush.

REGAN   O, sir, to willful men,
    The injuries that they themselves procure
    Must be their schoolmasters. Shut up your doors.

300   He is attended with a desperate° train;   *violent*
    And what they may incense° him to, being apt   *incite*
    To have his ear abused,° wisdom bids fear.   *deceived*

CORNWALL Shut up your doors, my lord; 'tis a wild night.
    My Regan counsels well. Come out o' the storm.   *Exeunt*

3.1

    Storm still. Enter KENT *and a* GENTLEMAN, *at several*°   *separate*
    doors

KENT Who's there, besides foul weather?

GENTLEMAN One minded like the weather, most unquietly.

KENT I know you. Where's the king?

GENTLEMAN Contending with the fretful elements;
5   Bids the wind blow the earth into the sea,
    Or swell the curlèd waters 'bove the main,°   *mainland*
    That things might change or cease; tears his white hair,
    Which the impetuous blasts, with eyeless rage,
    Catch in their fury, and make nothing of;
10   Strives in his little world of man to out-scorn
    The to-and-fro-conflicting wind and rain.
    This night, wherein the cub-drawn bear would couch,[1]
    The lion and the belly-pinchèd wolf
    Keep their fur dry, unbonneted° he runs,   *hatless; uncrowned*
    And bids what will take all.

15 KENT   But who is with him?

GENTLEMAN None but the fool, who labors to out-jest
    His heart-struck injuries.[2]

KENT   Sir, I do know you;
    And dare, upon the warrant of my note,[3]
    Commend a dear° thing to you. There is division,   *Entrust a crucial*
20   Although as yet the face of it be covered

3.1 Location: Bare, open country.
1. In which even the bear, though starving, having been sucked dry ("drawn") by its cub, would not go out to forage.

2. *to out-jest*: to relieve with laughter; to exorcise through ridicule. *heart-struck injuries*: injuries (from the betrayal of his paternal love) that penetrated to the heart.
3. On the basis of my skill (at judging people).

With mutual cunning, 'twixt Albany and Cornwall;
Who have—as who have not, that their great stars
Throned and set high?⁴—servants, who seem no less,°   *who appear as such*
Which are to France the spies and speculations°   *observers*
25   Intelligent of⁵ our state. What hath been seen,
Either in snuffs and packings° of the dukes,   *quarrels and plots*
Or the hard rein° which both of them have borne   *treatment*
Against the old kind king; or something deeper,
Whereof perchance these are but furnishings;°   *pretexts*
30   But, true it is, from France there comes a power
Into this scattered kingdom; who already,
Wise in° our negligence, have secret feet   *Aware of*
In some of our best ports, and are at point°   *ready*
To show their open banner. Now to you:
35   If on my credit you dare build° so far   *If you trust me*
To make your speed to Dover, you shall find
Some that will thank you, making just° report   *accurate*
Of how unnatural and bemadding° sorrow   *maddening*
The king hath cause to plain.°   *complain*
40   I am a gentleman of blood and breeding;
And, from some knowledge and assurance, offer
This office° to you.   *role; duty*
GENTLEMAN   I will talk further with you.
KENT   No, do not.
For confirmation that I am much more
45   Than my out-wall,° open this purse, and take   *outward appearance*
What it contains. If you shall see Cordelia—
As fear not but you shall—show her this ring,
And she will tell you who your fellow° is   *(Kent himself)*
That yet you do not know. Fie on this storm!
50   I will go seek the king.
GENTLEMAN   Give me your hand. Have you no more to say?
KENT   Few words, but, to effect,° more than all yet;   *in importance*
That, when we have found the king—in which your pain
That way, I'll this⁶—he that first lights on him
55   Holla the other.   *Exeunt severally*

3.2

Enter LEAR *and* FOOL. *Storm still*

LEAR   Blow, winds, and crack your cheeks! rage! blow!
You cataracts and hurricanoes,¹ spout
Till you have drenched our steeples, drowned the cocks!°   *weather vanes*
You sulphurous and thought-executing fires,²
5   Vaunt-couriers° to oak-cleaving thunderbolts,   *Forerunners*
Singe my white head! And thou, all-shaking thunder,
Smite flat the thick rotundity o' the world!
Crack Nature's molds, all germens° spill at once,   *seeds*
That make ingrateful man!

---

4. *as . . . high:* as has everybody who has been favored by destiny.
5. Supplying intelligence about; too well informed of.
6. *in which . . . this:* in which effort you will go that way and I this way.

3.2 Location: As before.
1. *cataracts:* floodgates of the heavens. *hurricanoes:* waterspouts (water from both sky and sea).
2. *thought-executing fires:* lightning that strikes as swiftly as thought.

10 FOOL   O nuncle, court holy-water[3] in a dry house is better than
  this rain-water out o' door. Good nuncle, in, and ask thy daughters' blessing! Here's a night pities neither wise man nor fool.

LEAR   Rumble thy bellyful! Spit, fire! spout, rain!
  Nor rain, wind, thunder, fire, are my daughters:
15 I tax° not you, you elements, with unkindness;   blame
  I never gave you kingdom, called you children,
  You owe me no subscription.° Then let fall   obedience; allegiance
  Your horrible pleasure. Here I stand, your slave,
  A poor, infirm, weak, and despised old man.
20 But yet I call you servile ministers,°   agents
  That have with two pernicious daughters joined
  Your high engendered battles° 'gainst a head   heaven-bred forces
  So old and white as this. O! O! 't is foul!

FOOL   He that has a house to put 's head in has a good head-
25 piece.°   hat; brain
        The cod-piece that will house
          Before the head has any,
        The head and he shall louse;
          So beggars marry many.[4]
30   The man that makes his toe
          What he his heart should make
        Shall of a corn cry woe,
          And turn his sleep to wake.[5]
  For there was never yet fair woman but she made mouths in a
35 glass.[6]

LEAR   No, I will be the pattern of all patience; I will say nothing.

        Enter KENT

KENT   Who's there?

FOOL   Marry, here's grace and a cod-piece; that's a wise man and
  a fool.[7]

40 KENT   Alas, sir, are you here? things that love night
  Love not such nights as these; the wrathful skies
  Gallow° the very wanderers of the dark,   Frighten
  And make them keep° their caves. Since I was man,   keep inside
  Such sheets of fire, such bursts of horrid thunder,
45 Such groans of roaring wind and rain, I never
  Remember to have heard. Man's nature cannot carry°   bear
  The affliction nor the fear.

LEAR   Let the great gods,
  That keep this dreadful pother° o'er our heads,   commotion
  Find out their enemies now. Tremble, thou wretch,
50 That hast within thee undivulgèd crimes,
  Unwhipped of° justice. Hide thee, thou bloody hand;   Unpunished by
  Thou perjured, and thou simular° of virtue   simulator; pretender

---

3. Sprinkled blessings of a courtier; flattery.
4. *The cod-piece . . . many:* Whoever finds his penis a
lodging before providing shelter for his head will end up
in lice-infested poverty and live in married beggary. *codpiece:* a pouchlike covering for the male genitals, often
conspicuous, particularly in the costume of a fool.
  5. *The man . . . wake:* The man who values an inferior
part of his body over the part that is truly valuable will
suffer from and lose sleep over that inferior part.

6. She practiced making pretty faces in a mirror. The
Fool probably refers to Regan's and Goneril's vanity, or
the line may be thrown in to soften the harshness of his
satire.
7. The supposedly wise King is symbolized by royal
grace, the Fool by his codpiece (here, slang for "penis").
The Fool speaks ironically: the King, as he has pointed
out, is now the foolish one. *Marry:* By the Virgin Mary (a
mild oath).

That are incestuous. Caitiff,° to pieces shake, *Wretch*
That under covert and convenient seeming° *fitting hypocrisy*
55 Hast practiced on° man's life. Close° pent-up guilts *against / Secret*
Rive° your concealing continents,° and cry *Split open / coverings*
These dreadful summoners grace.[8] I am a man
More sinned against than sinning.

KENT   Alack, bare-headed?
Gracious my lord, hard by here is a hovel;
60 Some friendship will it lend you 'gainst the tempest.
Repose you there, while I to this hard house°— *household*
More harder than the stones whereof 'tis raised,
Which° even but now, demanding° after you, *Who / I demanding*
Denied me to come in—return, and force
Their scanted° courtesy. *niggardly*

65 LEAR   My wits begin to turn.
Come on, my boy. How dost, my boy? Art cold?
I am cold myself. Where is this straw, my fellow?
The art° of our necessities is strange, *skill; alchemy*
That can make vile things precious. Come, your hovel.
70 Poor fool and knave, I have one part in my heart
That's sorry yet for thee.

FOOL (*singing*)[9]
            He that has and° a little tiny wit°— *even / sense*
            With hey, ho, the wind and the rain—
            Must make content with his fortunes fit,
75   Though the rain it raineth every day.

LEAR   True, boy. Come, bring us to this hovel.

                    Exeunt LEAR *and* KENT

FOOL   This is a brave night to cool a courtesan.[1]
I'll speak a prophecy ere I go:[2]
            When priests are more in word than matter;° *real virtue*
80   When brewers mar their malt with water;
            When nobles are their tailors' tutors;[3]
            No heretics burned, but wenches' suitors;[4]
            When every case in law is right;° *just*
            No squire in debt, nor no poor knight;
85   When slanders do not live in tongues,
            Nor cutpurses° come not to throngs; *pickpockets*
            When usurers tell their gold i' the field,[5]
            And bawds and whores do churches build;
            Then shall the realm of Albion° *Britain*
90   Come to great confusion.° *decay*
Then comes the time, who lives to see 't,
That going° shall be used° with feet. *walking / practiced*
This prophecy Merlin shall make; for I live before his time.[6]

                                        Exit

---

8. *and cry . . . grace:* and pray for mercy from these
elements that bring you to justice.
9. The following song is an adaptation of one sung by
Feste at the end of *Twelfth Night.*
1. To cool even the hot lusts of a prostitute.
2. What follows is a parody of the pseudo-Chaucerian
"Merlin's Prophecy" from *The Arte of English Poesie.*
3. When noblemen follow fashion more closely than

their tailors do.
4. When the only heretics burned are faithless lovers,
who burn from venereal disease.
5. When usurers can count their profits openly (because
they have no shady dealings to hide).
6. Merlin was the great wizard at the legendary court of
King Arthur. Lear's Britain is set in an even more distant
past.

3.3

Enter GLOUCESTER *and* EDMUND

GLOUCESTER Alack, alack, Edmund, I like not this unnatural
dealing. When I desired their leave that I might pity° him, they *relieve*
took from me the use of mine own house; charged me, on pain
of their perpetual displeasure, neither to speak of him, entreat
5 for him, nor any way sustain him.

EDMUND Most savage and unnatural!

GLOUCESTER Go to;° say you nothing. There's a division betwixt *(an expletive)*
the dukes, and a worse matter than that. I have received a letter
this night; 'tis dangerous to be spoken; I have locked the letter
10 in my closet.° These injuries the king now bears will be *private chamber*
revenged home;° there's part of a power already footed;[1] we *to the hilt*
must incline to[2] the king. I will seek him, and privily° relieve *secretly; privately*
him. Go you and maintain talk with the duke, that my charity
be not of him perceived if he ask for me, I am ill, and gone to
15 bed. Though I die for it, as no less is threatened me, the king
my old master must be relieved. There is some strange thing
toward,° Edmund; pray you, be careful. *Exit* *coming*

EDMUND This courtesy,° forbid° thee, shall the duke *act of kindness / forbidden*
Instantly know, and of that letter too.

20 This seems a fair deserving,[3] and must draw me
That which my father loses—no less than all.
The younger rises when the old doth fall. *Exit*

3.4

Enter LEAR, KENT, *and* FOOL

KENT Here is the place, my lord; good my lord, enter:
The tyranny of the open night's too rough
For nature° to endure. *human weakness*
  Storm still

LEAR Let me alone.

KENT Good my lord, enter here.

5 LEAR   Wilt break my heart?

KENT I had rather break mine own. Good my lord, enter.

LEAR Thou think'st 'tis much that this contentious storm
Invades us to the skin. So 'tis to thee;
But where the greater malady is fixed,° *rooted*
10 The lesser is scarce felt. Thou'dst shun a bear;
But if thy flight lay toward the raging sea,
Thou'dst meet the bear i' the mouth. When the mind's free,° *unburdened*
The body's delicate.° The tempest in my mind *sensitive*
Doth from my senses take all feeling else
15 Save° what beats there. Filial ingratitude! *Except*
Is it not as° this mouth should tear this hand *as if*
For lifting food to 't? But I will punish home.° *thoroughly*
No, I will weep no more. In such a night
To shut me out! Pour on; I will endure.
20 In such a night as this! O Regan, Goneril!
Your old kind father, whose frank heart gave all—
O, that way madness lies; let me shun that;
No more of that.

3.3 Location: At Gloucester's castle. 3. This seems an action that deserves to be rewarded.
1. Part of an army already landed. 3.4 Location: Open country, before a cattle shed.
2. We must take the side of.

KENT   Good my lord, enter here.

LEAR   Prithee, go in thyself; seek thine own ease:

25 This tempest will not give me leave to° ponder   *allow me to*
On things would hurt me more. But I'll go in.
(*To the* FOOL) In, boy; go first. You houseless poverty°——   *poor*
Nay, get thee in. I'll pray, and then I'll sleep.

        FOOL *goes in*

Poor naked wretches, whereso'er you are,
30 That bide° the pelting of this pitiless storm,   *endure; dwell in*
How shall your houseless heads and unfed sides,°   *starved ribs*
Your looped and windowed[1] raggedness, defend you
From seasons such as these? O, I have ta'en
Too little care of this! Take physic, pomp;[2]
35 Expose thyself to feel what wretches feel,
That thou mayst shake the superflux[3] to them,
And show the heavens more just.

EDGAR (*within*)   Fathom and half,[4] fathom and half!
Poor Tom!

        The FOOL *runs out from the hovel*

40 FOOL   Come not in here, nuncle, here's a spirit.
Help me, help me!

KENT   Give me thy hand. Who's there?

FOOL   A spirit, a spirit! He says his name's poor Tom.

KENT   What art thou that dost grumble there i' the straw? Come
45 forth.

        Enter EDGAR *disguised as a madman*

EDGAR   Away! the foul fiend follows me!
Through the sharp hawthorn blows the cold wind.[5]
Humh! go to thy cold bed, and warm thee.[6]

LEAR   Hast thou given all to thy two daughters? And art thou
50 come to this?

EDGAR   Who gives any thing to poor Tom? whom the foul fiend
hath led through fire and through flame, through ford and
whirlpool, o'er bog and quagmire; that hath laid knives under
his pillow and halters in his pew; set ratsbane by his porridge;[7]
55 made him proud of heart, to ride on a bay trotting-horse over
four-inched bridges,[8] to course° his own shadow for° a traitor.   *hunt / as*
Bless thy five wits![9] Tom's a-cold—O, do, de, do de, do de.
Bless thee from whirlwinds, star-blasting, and taking![1] Do poor
Tom some charity, whom the foul fiend vexes: there could I
60 have him now—and there—and there again, and there.[2]

        Storm still

LEAR   What, has his daughters brought him to this pass?
Couldst thou save nothing? Didst thou give them all?

---

1. *looped and windowed:* full of holes and vents; "windowed" could also refer to cloth worn through to semi-transparency, like the oilcloth window "panes" of the poor.
2. Cure yourself, pompous person.
3. Superfluity; bodily discharge, suggested by "physic" (which also has the meaning of "purgative") in line 34. Excess here is also excess of wealth.
4. "Nine feet," a sailor's cry when taking soundings to gauge the depth of water.
5. *Through . . . wind:* Perhaps a fragment from a ballad.
6. *go . . . thee:* this expression is also used by the drunken beggar Christopher Sly in *The Taming of the Shrew*, Induction 1.

7. *laid knives . . . porridge:* these are all means by which the foul fiend tempts Tom to commit suicide. *halters:* nooses. *ratsbane:* rat poison.
8. Impossibly narrow, and probably suicidal to attempt without diabolical help.
9. The five wits were common wit, imagination, fantasy, estimation, and memory (from medieval and Renaissance cognitive theory).
1. *whirlwinds, star-blasting:* malign astrological influences capable of causing sickness or death. *taking:* infection; bewitchment.
2. As Edgar speaks this sentence, he might kill vermin on his body as if they were devils.

FOOL   Nay, he reserved a blanket, else we had been all shamed.

LEAR   Now, all the plagues that in the pendulous° air   *overhanging; portentous*
65   Hang fated o'er men's faults light on thy daughters!

KENT   He hath no daughters, sir.

LEAR   Death, traitor! nothing could have subdued nature
        To such a lowness but his unkind daughters.
        Is it the fashion that discarded fathers
70   Should have thus little mercy on their flesh?
        Judicious punishment! 't was this flesh begot
        Those pelican[3] daughters.

EDGAR   Pillicock sat on Pillicock-hill.
        Halloo, halloo, loo, loo![4]

75 FOOL   This cold night will turn us all to fools and madmen.

EDGAR   Take heed o' the foul fiend; obey thy parents; keep thy
        word justly; swear not; commit not with man's sworn spouse;
        set not thy sweet heart on proud array.[5] Tom's a-cold.

LEAR   What hast thou been?

80 EDGAR   A serving-man, proud in heart and mind; that curled my
        hair; wore gloves in my cap;[6] served the lust of my mistress'
        heart, and did the act of darkness with her; swore as many oaths
        as I spake words, and broke them in the sweet face of heaven:
        one that slept in the contriving of lust, and waked to do it. Wine
85   loved I deeply, dice dearly; and in woman out-paramoured the
        Turk.[7] False of heart, light of ear,° bloody of hand; hog in sloth,   *rumor-hungry*
        fox in stealth, wolf in greediness, dog in madness, lion in prey.
        Let not the creaking of shoes[8] nor the rustling of silks betray
        thy poor heart to woman. Keep thy foot[9] out of brothels, thy
90   hand out of plackets,[1] thy pen from lenders' books, and defy
        the foul fiend. Still through the hawthorn blows the cold wind:
        Says suum, mun, ha, no, nonny. Dolphin my boy, my boy,
        sessa! let him trot by.[2]
                Storm still

LEAR   Why, thou wert better in thy grave than to answer° with thy   *encounter*
95   uncovered body this extremity of the skies.° Is man no more than   *violent weather*
        this? Consider him well. Thou owest the worm no silk, the beast
        no hide, the sheep no wool, that cat[3] no perfume. Ha! here's
        three on's° are sophisticated! Thou art the thing itself; unac-   *of us*
        commodated[4] man is no more but such a poor, bare, forked°   *two-legged*
100   animal as thou art. Off, off, you lendings!° come unbutton   *borrowed clothes*
        here.
                Tearing off his clothes

FOOL   Prithee, nuncle, be contented; 'tis a naughty° night to   *foul*
        swim in. Now a little fire in a wild° field were like an old lech-   *barren; lustful*
        er's heart; a small spark, all the rest on's° body cold. Look, here *of his*
105   comes a walking fire.
                Enter GLOUCESTER, with a torch

---

3. Greedy. Young pelicans were reputed to feed on blood
from the wounds they made in their mother's breast; in
some versions, they first killed their father.
4. A fragment of an old rhyme, followed by hunting cries
or a ballad refrain; "Pillicock" was both a term of endearment and a euphemism for "penis."
5. obey . . . array: these are fragments from the Ten Commandments.
6. Favors from his mistress. In Petrarchan poetry, wooers
are "servants" to their ladies.
7. And had more women than the sultan had in his royal

harem.
8. Creaking shoes were a fashionable affectation.
9. Punning on the French *foutre* ("fuck").
1. Slits in skirts or petticoats.
2. These phrases are probably snatches from songs and
proverbs. "Dolphin" is an imagined animal or devil or the
heir to the French throne ("dauphin," which Shakespeare
usually Anglicizes), or all three.
3. Civet cat, in Shakespeare's time the major source of
musk for perfume.
4. Naked; without the trappings of civilization.

EDGAR This is the foul fiend Flibbertigibbet.[5] He begins at cur-
few,° and walks till the first cock.° He gives the web and the   *9:00 P.M. / midnight*
pin,[6] squinies[7] the eye, and makes the hare-lip; mildews the
white° wheat, and hurts the poor creature of earth.   *near-ripe*

110   St. Withold footed thrice the old;[8]
He met the night-mare and her nine-fold;[9]
Bid her alight,
And her troth plight,°   *And gave her word*
And, aroint thee,° witch, aroint thee!   *begone*

115 KENT How fares your grace?

LEAR What's° he?   *Who's*

KENT Who's there? What is't you seek?

GLOUCESTER What are you there? Your names?

EDGAR Poor Tom, that eats the swimming frog, the toad, the

120 tadpole, the wall-newt and the water;° that in the fury of his   *water newt*
heart, when the foul fiend rages, eats cow-dung for sallets;°   *savories*
swallows the old rat and the ditch-dog;[1] drinks the green man-
tle° of the standing-pool; who is whipped from tithing to tith-   *scum*
ing,° and stock-punished,° and imprisoned; who hath had three   *parish / put in stocks*

125 suits to his back, six shirts to his body, horse to ride, and weapon
to wear;
             But mice and rats, and such small deer,[2]
             Have been Tom's food for seven long year.
       Beware my follower. Peace, Smulkin;° peace, thou fiend!   *a Harsnett devil*

130 GLOUCESTER What, hath your grace no better company?

EDGAR The prince of darkness is a gentleman. Modo he's call'd,
and Mahu.[3]

GLOUCESTER Our flesh and blood is grown so vile, my lord,
That it doth hate what gets° it.   *begets*

135 EDGAR Poor Tom's a-cold.

GLOUCESTER Go in with me. My duty cannot suffer°   *permit me*
To obey in all your daughters' hard commands:
Though their injunction be to bar my doors,
And let this tyrannous night take hold upon you

140 Yet have I ventured to come seek you out.
And bring you where both fire and food is ready.

LEAR First let me talk with this philosopher.
What is the cause of thunder?

KENT Good my lord, take his offer; go into the house.

145 LEAR I'll take a word with this same learned Theban.°   *Greek sage*
What is your study?°   *field of expertise*

EDGAR How to prevent the fiend, and to kill vermin.

LEAR Let me ask you one word in private.

KENT Importune him once more to go, my lord;
His wits begin to unsettle.

150 GLOUCESTER   Canst thou blame him?
     Storm still

---

5. A devil drawn from folk beliefs but famous for his prominent place in Samuel Harsnett's *Declaration of Egregious Popish Impostures* (1603); the frequent borrowings from Harsnett in *King Lear* set the earliest possible composition date for the play.
6. *web and the pin:* cataract.
7. Causes squints in.
8. St. Withold traversed the hilly countryside three times. *old:* wold, uplands.

9. *night-mare:* a demon that is not necessarily in the shape of a horse. *fold:* familiar, demon.
1. A dog found dead in a ditch.
2. *deer:* animals. These verses are adapted from a romance popular in Shakespeare's time, *Bevis of Hampton.*
3. Modo and Mahu, more Harsnett devils, were commanding generals of the hellish troops.

His daughters seek his death; ah, that good Kent!
He said it would be thus, poor banished man!
Thou say'st the king grows mad; I'll tell thee, friend,
I am almost mad myself. I had a son,
155   Now outlawed° from my blood. He sought my life.   *disowned*
But lately, very late.° I loved him, friend;   *recently*
No father his son dearer. True to tell thee,
The grief hath crazed my wits. What a night's this!
I do beseech your grace—

LEAR   O, cry you mercy,° sir.   *beg your pardon*
160   Noble philosopher, your company.
KENT   Tom's a-cold.

EDGAR   Tom's a-cold.
GLOUCESTER   In, fellow, there, into the hovel; keep thee warm.
LEAR   Come, let's in all.

                This way, my lord.

KENT   With him!
LEAR   I will keep still with my philosopher.
165   KENT   Good my lord, soothe° him; let him take the fellow.   *humor*
GLOUCESTER   Take him you on.°   *on ahead*
KENT   Sirrah, come on; go along with us.
LEAR   Come, good Athenian.°   *Greek philosopher*
GLOUCESTER   No words, no words: hush.
170   EDGAR   Child Rowland⁴ to the dark tower came,
His word° was still°—Fie, foh, and fum,   *motto / always*
I smell the blood of a British⁵ man.   *Exeunt*

3.5

Enter CORNWALL *and* EDMUND

CORNWALL   I will have my revenge ere I depart his house.
EDMUND   How, my lord, I may be censured,° that nature° thus   *judged / kinship*
gives way to loyalty, something fears me° to think of.   *I am somewhat afraid*
CORNWALL   I now perceive, it was not altogether your brother's
5   evil disposition made him seek his° death; but a provoking   *(Gloucester's)*
merit, set a-work by a reproveable badness in himself.¹
EDMUND   How malicious is my fortune, that I must repent to
be just! This is the letter he spoke of, which approves him an
intelligent party to the advantages of France.² O heavens! that
10   this treason were not, or not I the detector!
CORNWALL   Go with me to the duchess.
EDMUND   If the matter of this paper be certain, you have mighty
business in hand.
CORNWALL   True or false, it hath made thee Earl of Gloucester.
15   Seek out where thy father is, that he may be ready for our
apprehension.°   *arrest*
EDMUND *(aside)*   If I find him comforting the king, it will stuff
his° suspicion more fully.—I will persèver in my course of loy-   *(Cornwall's)*
alty, though the conflict be sore between that and my blood.°   *filial duty*
20   CORNWALL   I will lay trust upon thee, and thou shalt find a
dearer father in my love.   *Exeunt*

---

4. *Child*: an aspirant to knighthood. Roland is the famous hero of the Charlemagne legends.
5. "An Englishman" usually appears in this rhyme from the cycle of tales of which "Jack and the Beanstalk" is the best known. The alteration befits Lear's ancient Britain.
3.5 Location: At Gloucester's castle.

1. *a provoking . . . himself*: Gloucester's own wickedness deservedly triggered the blameworthy evil in Edgar.
2. *which . . . France*: which proves him a spy and informer in the aid of France; "party," or faction, was usually a term of opprobrium in the Renaissance.

3.6

Enter GLOUCESTER, LEAR, KENT, FOOL, *and* EDGAR

GLOUCESTER   Here is better than the open air; take it thankfully.
I will piece out° the comfort with what addition I can; I will   *augment*
not be long from you.

KENT   All the power of his wits have given sway to his impa-
5   tience:[1] the gods° reward your kindness!   *Exit* GLOUCESTER   *may the gods*

EDGAR   Frateretto° calls me; and tells me Nero is an angler in the   *a Harsnett devil*
lake of darkness.[2] Pray, innocent, and beware the foul fiend.

FOOL   Prithee, nuncle, tell me whether a madman be a gentleman or a yeoman?[3]

10   LEAR   A king, a king!

FOOL   No, he's a yeoman that has a gentleman to° his son; for   *for*
he's a mad yeoman that sees his son a gentleman before him.

LEAR   To have a thousand with red burning spits
Come hissing in upon 'em—

15   EDGAR   The foul fiend bites my back.

FOOL   He's mad that trusts in the tameness of a wolf, a horse's
health, a boy's love, or a whore's oath.

LEAR   It shall be done; I will arraign° them straight.°   *prosecute / immediately*
(*To* EDGAR) Come, sit thou here, most learned justicer;

20   (*to the* FOOL) Thou, sapient sir, sit here. Now, you she foxes!

EDGAR   Look, where he stands and glares! Wantest thou eyes° at   *observers*
trial, madam?

FOOL   Come o'er the bourn, Bessy, to me[4]—
Her boat hath a leak,[5]

25   And she must not speak
Why she dares not come over to thee.

EDGAR   The foul fiend haunts poor Tom in the voice of a night-
ingale. Hopdance° cries in Tom's belly for two white° herring.   *a demon / fresh*
Croak° not, black angel; I have no food for thee.   *Growl*

30   KENT   How do you, sir? Stand you not so amazed:
Will you lie down and rest upon the cushions?

LEAR   I'll see their trial first. Bring in the evidence.
(*To* EDGAR) Thou robed man of justice, take thy place;
(*to the* FOOL) And thou, his yoke-fellow of equity,°   *partner of law*

35   Bench° by his side. (*To* KENT) You are o' the commission,°   *Sit / judiciary*
Sit you too.

EDGAR   Let us deal justly.
Sleepest or wakest thou, jolly shepherd?
Thy sheep be in the corn;°   *grain*

40   And for one blast of thy minikin° mouth,   *dainty*
Thy sheep shall take no harm.
Pur! the cat[6] is gray.

LEAR   Arraign her first; 'tis Goneril. I here take my oath before
this honorable assembly, she kicked the poor king her father.

45   FOOL   Come hither, mistress. Is your name Goneril?

LEAR   She cannot deny it.

3.6 Location: Within an outbuilding of Gloucester's.
1. Rage; inability to bear more suffering.
2. In Chaucer's *Monk's Tale*, the infamously cruel Roman Emperor Nero is found fishing in hell (lines 485–86).
3. A free landowner but not a member of the gentry, lacking official family arms and the distinctions they confer.

Shakespeare seems to have procured a coat of arms for his father in 1596.
4. From an old song. *bourn*: a small stream.
5. She has venereal disease; punning on "boat" as body and "burn" as genital discomfort.
6. Pur the cat is another devil; such devils in the shape of cats were the familiars of witches.

FOOL   Cry you mercy, I took you for a joint-stool.[7]

LEAR   And here's another, whose warped looks proclaim
What store° her heart is made on.° Stop her there!   *material / of*

50   Arms, arms, sword, fire! Corruption in the place!
False justicer, why hast thou let her 'scape?

EDGAR   Bless thy five wits!

KENT   O pity! Sir, where is the patience now,
That you so oft have boasted to retain?

55   EDGAR *(aside)*   My tears begin to take his part so much,
They'll mar my counterfeiting.

LEAR   The little dogs and all,°   *Even the little dogs*
Tray, Blanch, and Sweet-heart, see, they bark at me.

EDGAR   Tom will throw his head at° them. Avaunt,° you curs!   *will threaten? / Begone*

60   Be thy mouth or° black or white,   *either*
Tooth that poisons° if it bite;   *gives rabies*
Mastiff, greyhound, mongrel grim,
Hound or spaniel, brach° or him,   *bitch*
Or bobtail tike or trundle-tail.[8]

65   Tom will make them weep and wail:
For, with throwing thus my head,
Dogs leap the hatch,[9] and all are fled.
Do de, de, de. Sessa![1] Come, march to wakes° and fairs and   *parish festivals*
market-towns. Poor Tom, thy horn is dry.[2]

70   LEAR   Then let them anatomize° Regan; see what breeds about   *dissect*
her heart. Is there any cause in nature that makes these hard
hearts? *(To* EDGAR*)* You, sir, I entertain° for one of my hundred;   *retain*
I do not like the fashion of your garments. You will say they are
Persian;° but let them be changed.   *oriental; splendid*

75   KENT   Now, good my lord, lie there and rest awhile.

LEAR   Make no noise, make no noise; draw the curtains.° So, so,   *bed curtains*
so. We'll go to supper i' the morning.

FOOL   And I'll go to bed at noon.

[Re-enter GLOUCESTER*]*

GLOUCESTER   Come hither, friend. Where is the king my master?

80   KENT   Here, sir; but trouble him not; his wits are gone.

GLOUCESTER   Good friend, I prithee, take him in thy arms;
I have o'erheard a plot of death upon° him: *against*
There is a litter ready; lay him in 't
And drive towards Dover, friend, where thou shalt meet

85   Both welcome and protection. Take up thy master.
If thou shouldst dally half an hour, his life,
With thine, and all that offer to defend him,
Stand in assured loss.° Take up, take up!   *Are certainly doomed*
And follow me, that will to some provision
Give thee quick conduct.[3]

90   KENT   Oppressèd nature sleeps:
This rest might yet have balmed° thy broken sinews,°   *soothed / nerves*
Which, if convenience will not allow,

---

7. I beg your pardon, I mistook you for a stool. An idiom
of the day expressing annoyance at being slighted. Here
the part of Goneril is actually being played by a stool.
8. Short-tailed mongrel or long-tailed.
9. Dogs leap over the lower half of a divided door.
1. Apparently nonsense, although "Sessa" may be a ver-

sion of the French *cessez* ("stop" or "hush").
2. A begging formula that refers to the horn vessel that
vagabonds carried for drink; the covert sense is that Edgar
has run out of Bedlamite inspiration.
3. *that . . . conduct*: who will quickly guide you to some
supplies.

Stand in hard cure.° (*To the* FOOL) Come, help to bear thy   *Will be hard to cure*
   master:
Thou must not stay behind.

GLOUCESTER   Come come, away.
                              Exeunt all but EDGAR

95   EDGAR   When we our betters see bearing our° woes,   *our same*
         We scarcely think our miseries our foes.
         Who alone suffers suffers most i' the mind,
         Leaving free° things and happy shows° behind: *carefree / scenes*
         But then the mind much sufferance doth o'erskip
100   When grief hath mates, and bearing° fellowship.   *pain; suffering*
         How light and portable my pain seems now,
         When that which makes me bend makes the king bow;
         He° childed as I fathered! Tom, away!   *He is*
         Mark the high noises,° and thyself bewray°   *important rumors / reveal*
105   When false opinion, whose wrong thought defiles thee,
         In thy just proof repeals and reconciles thee.[4]
         What° will hap° more tonight, safe 'scape the king!   *Whatever / chance*
         Lurk, lurk.   *Exit*

3.7

         Enter CORNWALL, REGAN, GONERIL, EDMUND, *and ser-*
            vants

     CORNWALL (*to* GONERIL)   Post° speedily to my lord your hus-   *Ride*
         band; show him this letter. The army of France is landed. Seek
         out the villain Gloucester.   *Exeunt some of the servants*
     REGAN   Hang him instantly.
5   GONERIL   Pluck out his eyes.
     CORNWALL   Leave him to my displeasure. Edmund, keep you
         our sister° company. The revenges we are bound[1] to take   *sister-in-law*
         upon your traitorous father are not fit for your beholding.
         Advise the duke, where you are going, to a most festinate prep-
10   aration.[2] We are bound° to the like. Our posts° shall be swift and   *committed / messengers*
         intelligent° betwixt us. Farewell, dear sister: farewell, my lord of   *well informed*
         Gloucester.
                          Enter OSWALD
         How now! Where's the king?
     OSWALD   My lord of Gloucester hath conveyed him hence.
15   Some five or six and thirty of his° knights,   *(Lear's)*
         Hot questrists° after him, met him at gate;   *searchers*
         Who, with some other of the lords° dependants,   *(Gloucester's)*
         Are gone with him towards Dover; where they boast
         To have well-armed friends.
     CORNWALL   Get horses for your mistress.
20   GONERIL   Farewell, sweet lord, and sister.
     CORNWALL   Edmund, farewell.
                  Exeunt GONERIL, EDMUND, *and* OSWALD
         Go seek the traitor Gloucester,
         Pinion him° like a thief, bring him before us.   *Tie his arms*
                          Exeunt other servants
         Though well we may not pass° upon his life   *pass sentence*

---

4. *In . . . thee*: When true evidence pardons you and
reconciles you (with your father).
3.7 Location: At Gloucester's castle.

1. Bound by duty; expected by destiny.
2. *Advise . . . preparation*: When you reach Albany, tell
the Duke to prepare quickly.

25 Without the form° of justice, yet our power   *official proceedings*
    Shall do a courtesy[3] to our wrath, which men
    May blame, but not control. Who's there? the traitor?

       Enter GLOUCESTER, *brought in by two or three*

REGAN   Ingrateful fox! 'tis he.
CORNWALL   Bind fast his corky° arms.   *withered*
30 GLOUCESTER   What mean your graces? Good my friends, consider
    You are my guests. Do me no foul play, friends.
CORNWALL   Bind him, I say.

       Servants bind him

REGAN   Hard, hard. O filthy traitor!
GLOUCESTER   Unmerciful lady as you are, I'm none.
CORNWALL   To this chair bind him. Villain, thou shalt find—
              REGAN *plucks his beard*°   *(an extreme insult)*
35 GLOUCESTER   By the kind gods, 'tis most ignobly done
    To pluck me by the beard.
REGAN   So white,° and such a traitor!   *white-haired; venerable*
GLOUCESTER   Naughty° lady,   *Wicked*
    These hairs, which thou dost ravish from my chin,
    Will quicken,° and accuse thee. I am your host.   *come alive*
40 With robbers' hands my hospitable favors°   *features*
    You should not ruffle° thus. What will you do?   *snatch at*
CORNWALL   Come, sir, what letters had you late° from France?   *lately*
REGAN   Be simple° answered, for we know the truth.   *straightforwardly*
CORNWALL   And what confederacy have you with the traitors
45 Late footed° in the kingdom?   *landed*
REGAN   To whose hands have you sent the lunatic king? Speak.
GLOUCESTER   I have a letter guessingly set down,[4]
    Which came from one that's of a neutral heart,
    And not from one opposed.
CORNWALL   Cunning.
REGAN   And false.
50 CORNWALL   Where hast thou sent the king?
GLOUCESTER   To Dover.
REGAN   Wherefore° to Dover? Wast thou not charged° at peril—   *Why / commanded*
CORNWALL   Wherefore to Dover? Let him first answer that.
GLOUCESTER   I am tied to the stake, and I must stand the
55 course.[5]
REGAN   Wherefore to Dover?
GLOUCESTER   Because I would not see thy cruel nails
    Pluck out his poor old eyes; nor thy fierce sister
    In his anointed[6] flesh stick boarish fangs.
60 The sea, with such a storm as his bare head
    In hell-black night endured, would have buoyed° up   *risen*
    And quenched the stellèd° fires.   *stars'*
    Yet, poor old heart, he holp° the heavens to rage.   *helped*
    If wolves had at thy gate howled that dern° time,   *dreary; dreadful*
65 Thou shouldst have said "Good porter, turn the key."°   *(to open the door)*
    All cruels else subscribed.[7] But I shall see
    The wingèd vengeance[8] overtake such children.

3. Shall allow a courtesy or indulgence; shall bow to.
4. Written without confirmation; speculative.
5. An image from bearbaiting, in which a bear on a short
tether had to fight off the assault of dogs.
6. Consecrated with holy oils (as part of a King's coronation).
7. All other cruel creatures yielded to compassion.
8. Swift or heaven-sent revenge; either an angel of God
or the Furies, who were flying executors of divine vengeance in classical mythology.

CORNWALL   See 't shalt thou never. Fellows,° hold the chair.   *Servants*
Upon these eyes of thine I'll set my foot.
70   GLOUCESTER   He that will think° to live till he be old,   *Whoever hopes*
Give me some help! O cruel! O ye gods! [CORNWALL *pulls out*
one of GLOUCESTER's *eyes and stamps on it*]
REGAN   One side will mock another. The other too!
CORNWALL   If you see vengeance—
FIRST SERVANT   Hold your hand, my lord:
I have served you ever since I was a child;
75   But better service have I never done you
Than now to bid you hold.
REGAN   How now, you dog!
FIRST SERVANT   If you did wear a beard upon your chin,
I'd shake it on this quarrel.⁹
80   REGAN   What do you mean?°   *intend*
CORNWALL   My villain!°   *servant; villain*
FIRST SERVANT   Why, then, come on, and take the chance of anger.¹
REGAN   Give me thy sword. A peasant stand up thus!
CORNWALL *is wounded.*
Takes a sword, and runs at him behind
FIRST SERVANT   O, I am slain! My lord, you have one eye left
85   To see some mischief° on him. O!   *Dies*   *injury*
CORNWALL   Lest it see more, prevent it. Out, vile jelly! [*He pulls*
out GLOUCESTER's *other eye*]
Where is thy luster now?
GLOUCESTER   All dark and comfortless. Where's my son Edmund?
Edmund, enkindle all the sparks of nature,²
To quit° this horrid act.   *requite; avenge*
90   REGAN   Out, treacherous villain!
Thou call'st on him that hates thee. It was he
That made the overture° of thy treasons to us;   *revelation*
Who is too good to pity thee.
GLOUCESTER   O my follies! Then Edgar was abused.°   *slandered*
95   Kind gods, forgive me that, and prosper him!
REGAN   Go thrust him out at gates, and let him smell
His way to Dover.   *Exit one with* GLOUCESTER
How is't, my lord? how look you?°   *how do you feel*
CORNWALL   I have received a hurt. Follow me, lady;
100 Turn out that eyeless villain. Throw this slave
Upon the dunghill. Regan, I bleed apace.
Untimely comes this hurt. Give me your arm.
Exit CORNWALL *led by* REGAN
SECOND SERVANT   I'll never care what wickedness I do,
If this man come to good.³
THIRD SERVANT   If she live long,
105 And in the end meet the old° course of death,   *usual*
Woman will all turn monsters.
SECOND SERVANT   Let's follow the old earl, and get the Bedlam°   *madman*
To lead him where he would. His roguish madness
Allows itself to any thing.
110 THIRD SERVANT   Go thou; I'll fetch some flax and whites of eggs

9. I'd pluck it over this point; I'd issue a challenge.
1. Take the risk of fighting when angry; take the fortune
of one who is governed by his anger.
2. All the warmth of filial love; all the anger that your

father has received such treatment.
3. *I'll . . . good:* because this may be a sign that evil goes
unpunished. *this man:* Cornwall.

To apply to his bleeding face. Now, heaven help him!

Exeunt severally

4.1

Enter EDGAR

EDGAR   Yet better thus, and known to be contemned°   despised
 Than still° contemned and flattered. To be worst,   always
 The lowest and most dejected thing of fortune,
 Stands still in esperance, lives not in fear.[1]
5 The lamentable change is from the best;
 The worst returns to laughter.[2] Welcome, then,
 Thou unsubstantial air that I embrace!
 The wretch that thou hast blown unto the worst
 Owes nothing° to thy blasts. But who comes here?   (because he can't pay)

Enter GLOUCESTER, *led by an* OLD MAN

10 My father, parti-eyed?[3] World, world, O world!
 But that thy strange mutrations make us hate thee,
 Life would not yield to age.[4]

OLD MAN   O, my good lord, I have been your tenant, and your
 father's tenant, these fourscore years.

15 GLOUCESTER   Away, get thee away! Good friend, be gone.
 Thy comforts° can do me no good at all;   assistance
 Thee they may hurt.

OLD MAN   Alack, sir, you cannot see your way.

GLOUCESTER   I have no way, and therefore want no eyes;
20 I stumbled when I saw. Full oft 'tis seen,
 Our means secure us, and our mere defects
 Prove our commodities.[5] O dear son Edgar,
 The food° of thy abusèd° father's wrath!   fuel; prey / despised
 Might I but live to see thee in° my touch,   through
 I'd say I had eyes again!

25 OLD MAN   How now! Who's there?

EDGAR *(aside)*   O gods! Who is't can say "I am at the worst"?
 I am worse than e'er I was.

OLD MAN   'Tis poor mad Tom.

EDGAR *(aside)*   And worse I may be yet: the worst is not
 So long as we can say "This is the worst."

OLD MAN   Fellow, where goest?

30 GLOUCESTER   Is it a beggar-man?

OLD MAN   Madman and beggar too.

GLOUCESTER   He has some reason, else he could not beg.
 I' the last night's storm I such a fellow saw;
 Which made me think a man a worm. My son
35 Came then into my mind, and yet my mind
 Was then scarce friends with him. I have heard more since.
 As flies to wanton° boys are we to the gods;   playful; careless
 They kill us for their sport.

EDGAR *(aside)*   How should this be?
 Bad is the trade that must play fool to sorrow,[6]

---

40   Angering itself and others.—Bless thee, master!
     GLOUCESTER   Is that the naked fellow?
     OLD MAN   Ay, my lord.
     GLOUCESTER   Then, prithee, get thee gone. If, for my sake,
       Thou wilt o'ertake us, hence a mile or twain,
       I' the way toward Dover, do it for ancient love;[7]
45   And bring some covering for this naked soul,
       Who I'll entreat to lead me.
     OLD MAN   Alack, sir, he is mad.
     GLOUCESTER   'Tis the times' plague, when[8] madmen lead the blind.
       Do as I bid thee, or rather do thy pleasure;
       Above the rest, be gone.
50   OLD MAN   I'll bring him the best 'parel° that I have,   *apparel; clothing*
       Come on 't what will.   *Exit*
     GLOUCESTER   Sirrah, naked fellow—
     EDGAR   Poor Tom's a-cold. (*Aside*) I cannot daub it further.[9]
     GLOUCESTER   Come hither, fellow.
55   EDGAR (*aside*)   And yet I must.—Bless thy sweet eyes, they bleed.
     GLOUCESTER   Know'st thou the way to Dover?
     EDGAR   Both stile and gate, horse-way and foot-path. Poor Tom
       hath been scared out of his good wits. Bless thee, good man's
       son, from the foul fiend! Five fiends have been in Poor Tom at
60   once; of lust, as Obidicut; Hobbididance, prince of dumbness;
       Mahu, of stealing; Modo, of murder; Flibbertigibbet, of mop-
       ping and mowing,° who since possesses chambermaids and   *making faces*
       waiting-women. So, bless thee, master!
     GLOUCESTER   Here, take this purse, thou whom the heavens' plagues
65   Have humbled to all strokes.° That I am wretched   *to accept all blows*
       Makes thee the happier. Heavens, deal so still!°   *always*
       Let the superfluous and lust-dieted man,[1]
       That slaves° your ordinance,° that will not see   *defers to / authority*
       Because he doth not feel, feel your power quickly;
70   So distribution should undo excess,
       And each man have enough. Dost thou know Dover?
     EDGAR   Ay, master.
     GLOUCESTER   There is a cliff, whose high and bending° head   *overhanging*
       Looks fearfully in the confinèd deep.[2]
75   Bring me but to the very brim of it,
       And I'll repair the misery thou dost bear
       With something rich about me. From that place
       I shall no leading need.
     EDGAR   Give me thy arm.
       Poor Tom shall lead thee.   *Exeunt*

4.2

Enter GONERIL *and* EDMUND
     GONERIL   Welcome, my lord. I marvel our mild husband
       Not° met us on the way.   *Has not*
       Enter OSWALD
               Now where's your master?
     OSWALD   Madam, within, but never man so changed.
       I told him of the army that was landed;

---

7. For the sake of our long and loyal relationship (as master and servant).
8. The time is truly sick when.
9. I cannot continue the charade. *daub*: mask, plaster.

1. Let the overprosperous man who indulges his appetite.
2. Looks fearsomely into the straits below.
4.2 Location: Before Albany's castle.

5 He smiled at it. I told him you were coming;
His answer was "The worse." Of Gloucester's treachery,
And of the loyal service of his son,
When I informed him, then he called me sot,°   *fool*
And told me I had turned the wrong side out.[1]
10 What most he should dislike seems pleasant to him;
What like, offensive.

GONERIL (*to* EDMUND)   Then shall you go no further.
It is the cowish° terror of his spirit,   *cowardly*
That dares not undertake. He'll not feel wrongs
Which tie him to an answer.[2] Our wishes on the way
15 May prove effects.[3] Back, Edmund, to my brother;°   *brother-in-law*
Hasten his musters° and conduct his powers.°   *call-up of troops / armies*
I must change arms at home, and give the distaff[4]
Into my husband's hands. This trusty servant
Shall pass between us. Ere long you are like° to hear,   *likely*
20 If you dare venture in your own behalf,
A mistress's° command. Wear this; spare speech;   *(playing on "lover's")*
    (*giving a favor*)
Decline your head. This kiss, if it durst speak,
Would stretch thy spirits up into the air.
Conceive,° and fare thee well.   *Understand my meaning*
EDMUND   Yours in° the ranks of death.   *even in*
25 GONERIL   My most dear Gloucester!

                         Exit EDMUND

O, the difference of man and man!
To thee a woman's services are due:
My fool usurps my body.[5]
OSWALD   Madam, here comes my lord.   *Exit*
    Enter ALBANY
GONERIL   I have been worth the whistling.[6]
30 ALBANY   O Goneril!
You are not worth the dust which the rude wind
Blows in your face. I fear your disposition.
That nature, which contemns it° origin,   *despises its*
Cannot be bordered certain° in itself.   *be defended securely*
35 She that herself will sliver and disbranch°   *split*
From her material sap, perforce must wither
And come to deadly use.[7]
GONERIL   No more; the text is foolish.
ALBANY   Wisdom and goodness to the vile seem vile;
40 Filths savor but themselves. What have you done?
Tigers, not daughters, what have you performed?
A father, and a gracious aged man,
Whose reverence even the head-lugged° bear would lick,   *dragged by the head*
Most barbarous, most degenerate, have you madded°   *driven mad*
45 Could my good brother° suffer you to do it?   *brother-in-law*
A man, a prince, by him so benefited!

---

1. I had reversed things (by mistaking loyalty for treachery).
2. *He'll . . . answer:* He'll ignore insults that would provoke him to retaliate.
3. May be put into action.
4. A device used in spinning and so emblematic of the female role. To "change arms," therefore, is to swap the insignia of male and female identity.
5. My idiot husband presumes to possess me.

6. At one time, you would have come to welcome me home; referring to the proverb "It is a poor dog that is not worth the whistling."
7. *She . . . use:* The allusion is probably biblical: "But that which beareth thorns and briers is reproved, and is near unto cursing; whose end is to be burned" (Hebrews 6:8). *come to deadly use:* be destroyed; be used for burning.

If that the heavens do not their visible spirits
Send quickly down to tame these vild° offenses,   *wild; vile*
It will come,
50   Humanity must perforce° prey on itself,   *inevitably*
Like monsters of the deep.
GONERIL   Milk-livered° man!   *Cowardly*
That bear'st a cheek for blows, a head for wrongs:[8]
Who hast not in thy brows an eye discerning
Thine honor from thy suffering;[9] that not know'st
55   Fools do those villains pity who are punished
Ere they have done their mischief. Where's thy drum?°   *(to muster troops)*
France spreads his banners in our noiseless° land,   *peaceful*
With plumèd helm thy state begins to threat;
Whiles thou, a moral° fool, sit'st still, and criest   *moralizing*
"Alack, why does he so?"
60   ALBANY   See thyself, devil!
Proper deformity shows not in the fiend
So horrid as in woman.[1]
GONERIL   O vain° fool!   *useless*
ALBANY   Thou changèd and self-covered[2] thing, for shame,
Be-monster not thy feature. Were't my fitness°   *If it were appropriate*
65   To let these hands obey my blood,
They are apt enough to dislocate and tear
Thy flesh and bones. Howe'er° thou art a fiend,   *Although*
A woman's shape doth shield thee.
GONERIL   Marry, your manhood! mew![3]
        Enter a MESSENGER
70   ALBANY   What news?
MESSENGER   O, my good lord, the Duke of Cornwall's dead;
Slain by his servant, going to put out
The other eye of Gloucester.
ALBANY   Gloucester's eyes?
MESSENGER   A servant that he bred, thrilled with remorse,°   *shaken with pity*
75   Opposed against the act, bending° his sword   *directing*
To° his great master; who, thereat enraged,   *Against*
Flew on him, and amongst them felled him dead;
But not without that harmful stroke, which since
Hath plucked him after.[4]
ALBANY   This shows you are above,
80   You justicers,° that these our nether crimes[5]   *judges*
So speedily can venge! But, O poor Gloucester!
Lost he his other eye?
MESSENGER   Both, both, my lord.
This letter, madam, craves a speedy answer;
'T is from your sister.
85   GONERIL *(aside)*   One way I like this well;[6]
But being° a widow, and my Gloucester with her,   *her being*

---

8. *for wrongs:* fit for abuse; ready for cuckold's horns.
9. *discerning . . . suffering:* that can distinguish between
an insult to your honor and something you should
patiently endure.
1. *Proper . . . woman:* Deformity (of morals) is appropriate in the devil and so less horrid than in woman, from
whom virtue is expected. Albany may hold a mirror in
front of Goneril, since Jacobean women sometimes wore
small mirrors attached to their dresses.

2. Altered and with your true (womanly) self concealed.
3. Some manhood! (spoken derisively). *Marry:* By the
Virgin Mary. *mew:* a derisive catcall.
4. Has sent him to follow his servant into death.
5. Lower crimes, and so committed on earth, but also
suggesting that the deeds smack of the netherworld of
hell.
6. Because a political rival has been eliminated.

May all the building in my fancy pluck
Upon my hateful life.[7] Another way,
The news is not so tart.°—I'll read, and answer.   *Exit*   bitter

90 ALBANY   Where was his son when they did take his eyes?

MESSENGER   Come with my lady hither.

ALBANY   He is not here.

MESSENGER   No, my good lord; I met him back° again.   returning

ALBANY   Knows he the wickedness?

MESSENGER   Ay, my good lord; 'twas he informed against him;

95 And quit the house on purpose, that their punishment
Might have the freer course.

ALBANY   Gloucester, I live
To thank thee for the love thou show'dst the king,
And to revenge thine eyes. Come hither, friend.
Tell me what more thou know'st.   *Exeunt*

4.3

Enter KENT *and a* GENTLEMAN

KENT   Why the King of France is so suddenly gone back know
you the reason?

GENTLEMAN   Something he left imperfect° in the state, which   unsettled
since his coming forth is thought of;° which imports° to the   remembered / portends
5 kingdom so much fear and danger, that his personal return was
most required and necessary.

KENT   Who hath he left behind him general?

GENTLEMAN   The Marshall of France, Monsieur LaFar.

KENT   Did your letters pierce the queen to any demonstration of grief?

10 GENTLEMAN   Ay, sir. She took them, in my presence;
And now and then an ample tear trilled down
Her delicate cheek. It seemed she was a queen
Over her passion, who,° most rebel-like,   which
Sought to be king o'er her.

KENT   O, then it moved her.

15 GENTLEMAN   Not to a rage. Patience and sorrow strove
Who should express her goodliest.[1] You have seen
Sunshine and rain at once: her smiles and tears
Were like a° better way. Those happy smilets,   Were similar in a
That played on her ripe lip, seemed not to know
20 What guests were in her eyes, which parted thence,
As pearls from diamonds dropped. In brief,
Sorrow would be a rarity° most beloved,   gem
If all could so become it.[2]

KENT   Made she no verbal question?

GENTLEMAN   'Faith, once or twice she heaved the name of "father"
25 Pantingly forth, as if it pressed her heart;
Cried "Sisters! sisters! Shame of ladies! sisters!
Kent! father! sisters! What, i' the storm? i' the night?
Let pity not be believed!"[3] There she shook
The holy water from her heavenly eyes,
30 And clamor moistened.[4] Then away she started°   sprang
To deal with grief alone.

7. *May . . . life:* May pull down all of my built-up fantasies and thus make my life hateful.
4.3 Location: Near the French camp at Dover.
1. Which should best express her feelings.

2. If everyone wore it so beautifully.
3. Never believe in pity; compassion cannot exist.
4. And moistened her anguish (with tears).

KENT   It is the stars,
The stars above us, govern our conditions;
Else one self mate and make⁵ could not beget
Such different issues.° You spoke not with her since?   offspring
35   GENTLEMAN   No.
KENT   Was this before the king returned?
GENTLEMAN   No, since.
KENT   Well, sir, the poor distressed Lear's i' the town;
Who sometime, in his better tune,° remembers   state of mind
What we are come about, and by no means
Will yield° to see his daughter.   consent
40   GENTLEMAN   Why, good sir?
KENT   A sovereign shame so elbows° him; his own unkindness,   prods; nudges
That stripped her from his benediction, turned her
To foreign casualties,° gave her dear rights   risks
To his dog-hearted daughters, these things sting
45   His mind so venomously, that burning shame
Detains him from Cordelia.
GENTLEMAN   Alack, poor gentleman!
KENT   Of Albany's and Cornwall's powers you heard not?
GENTLEMAN   'Tis so, they are afoot.
KENT   Well, sir, I'll bring you to our master Lear,
50   And leave you to attend him. Some dear cause°   Some important reason
Will in concealment wrap me up awhile;
When I am known aright, you shall not grieve°   repent
Lending me this acquaintance.° I pray you, go   news
Along with me.   *Exeunt*

4.4

Enter, with drum and colors, CORDELIA, DOCTOR, *and
soldiers*

CORDELIA   Alack, 'tis he! Why, he was met even now
As mad as the vexed sea; singing aloud;
Crowned with rank fumiter and furrow-weeds,¹
With hor-docks, hemlock, nettles, cuckoo-flowers,
5   Darnel, and all the idle° weeds that grow   useless
In our sustaining corn. A century° send forth;   battalion (100 men)
Search every acre in the high-grown field,
And bring him to our eye.   *Exit an officer*
What can man's wisdom
10   In the restoring° his bereaved sense?   Do to restore
He that helps him take all my outward° worth.   material
DOCTOR   There is means, madam.
Our foster-nurse of nature² is repose,
The which he lacks. That to provoke in him,
15   Are many simples operative,³ whose power
Will close the eye of anguish.
CORDELIA   All blest secrets,
All you unpublished virtues° of the earth,   obscure healing plants
Spring with my tears! be aidant and remediate°   healing and remedial

---

5. Or else the same pair of spouses; "mate" and "make"
may describe either partner.
4.4 Location: The French camp at Dover.
1. Fumiter was used against brain sickness. Furrow-
weeds, like the other weeds in the following lines, grow
in the furrows of plowed fields.
2. *Our . . . nature:* That which comforts and nourishes
human nature.
3. *That . . . operative:* To induce that ("repose") in him,
there are many effective medicinal herbs.

In the good man's distress! Seek, seek for him;
20 Lest his ungoverned rage dissolve the life
That wants° the means to lead it.   lacks
      Enter a MESSENGER
MESSENGER   News, madam;
The British powers° are marching hitherward.   armies
CORDELIA   'Tis known before; our preparation stands
In expectation of them. O dear father,
25 It is thy business that I go about;[4]
Therefore great France
My mourning and importuned° tears hath pitied.   importunate; solicitous
No blown° ambition doth our arms incite,   inflated
But love, dear love, and our aged father's right.[5]
30 Soon may I hear and see him!   *Exeunt*

4.5

    Enter REGAN *and* OSWALD
REGAN   But are my brother's powers° set forth?   *(Albany's forces)*
OSWALD   Ay, madam.
REGAN   Himself in person there?
OSWALD   Madam, with much ado.°   trouble
Your sister is the better soldier.
5 REGAN   Lord Edmund spake not with your lord at home?
OSWALD   No, madam.
REGAN   What might import° my sister's letter to him?   mean
OSWALD   I know not, lady.
REGAN   Faith, he is posted° hence on serious matter.   hurried
10 It was great ignorance, Gloucester's eyes being out,
To let him live. Where he arrives he moves
All hearts against us. Edmund, I think, is gone,
In pity of his misery,° to dispatch   *(ironic)*
His nighted° life; moreover, to descry°   darkened / investigate
15 The strength o' the enemy.
OSWALD   I must needs after° him, madam, with my letter.   go after
REGAN   Our troops set forth tomorrow. Stay with us;
The ways are dangerous.
OSWALD   I may not, madam:
My lady charged° my duty in this business.   commanded
20 REGAN   Why should she write to Edmund? Might not you
Transport her purposes by word? Belike,°   *Perhaps*
Something—I know not what. I'll love° thee much,   reward
Let me unseal the letter.
OSWALD   Madam, I had rather—
REGAN   I know your lady does not love her husband;
25 I am sure of that; and at her late° being here   recently
She gave strange oeillades° and most speaking looks   amorous glances
To noble Edmund. I know you are of her bosom.°   in her confidence
OSWALD   I, madam?
REGAN   I speak in understanding;° y'are, I know't.   with certainty
30 Therefore I do advise you, take this note:°   take note of this
My lord is dead; Edmund and I have talked;

---

4. The line echoes Christ's explanation of his mission in
Luke 2:49: "I must go about my father's business."
5. *No . . . right:* 1 Corinthians 13:4–5 in the Bishops'

Bible (1568) says that love "swelleth not, dealeth not
dishonestly, seeketh not her own."
4.5 Location: At Gloucester's castle.

And more convenient° is he for my hand   *appropriate*
Than for your lady's. You may gather° more.   *infer*
If you do find him, pray you, give him this;[1]
35 And when your mistress hears thus much from you,
I pray, desire her call her wisdom to her.[2]
So, fare you well.
If you do chance to hear of that blind traitor,
Preferment falls on him that cuts him off.°   *cuts his life short*
40 OSWALD Would I could meet him, madam! I should show
What party I do follow.
REGAN Fare thee well.   *Exeunt*

4.6

Enter GLOUCESTER, *and* EDGAR *dressed like a peasant*

GLOUCESTER When shall we come to the top of that same° hill? *agreed-upon*
EDGAR You do climb up it now. Look how we labor.
GLOUCESTER Methinks the ground is even.
EDGAR   Horrible steep.
Hark, do you hear the sea?
GLOUCESTER   No, truly.
5 EDGAR Why, then, your other senses grow imperfect
By your eyes' anguish.
GLOUCESTER   So may it be, indeed.
Methinks thy voice is altered, and thou speakest
In better phrase and matter° than thou didst.   *sense*
EDGAR Y'are much deceived. In nothing am I changed
But in my garments.
10 GLOUCESTER   Methinks y'are better spoken.
EDGAR Come on, sir; here's the place. Stand still. How fearful
And dizzy 'tis, to cast one's eyes so low!
The crows and choughs° that wing the midway air[1] *jackdaws*
Show° scarce so gross° as beetles. Halfway down *Appear / big*
15 Hangs one that gathers sampire,° dreadful trade! *seaweed*
Methinks he seems no bigger than his head.
The fishermen, that walk upon the beach,
Appear like mice; and yond tall anchoring bark,°   *ship*
Diminished to her cock;° her cock, a buoy   *dinghy*
20 Almost too small for sight. The murmuring surge,
That on the unnumbered° idle pebble chafes,   *innumerable*
Cannot be heard so high. I'll look no more,
Lest my brain turn, and the° deficient sight   *my*
Topple° down headlong.   *Topple me*
GLOUCESTER   Set me where you stand.
25 EDGAR Give me your hand. You are now within a foot
Of th' extreme verge. For all beneath the moon
Would I not leap upright.[2]
GLOUCESTER   Let go my hand.
Here, friend, 's another purse; in it a jewel
Well worth a poor man's taking. Fairies and gods
30 Prosper it[3] with thee! Go thou farther off;
Bid me farewell, and let me hear thee going.

---

1. This information, but possibly another letter or token.
2. *desire . . . to her:* tell her to come to her senses.
4.6 Location: Near Dover.
1. The air between cliff and sea.

2. I would not jump up and down (for fear of losing my balance).
3. Make it increase. Fairies were sometimes held to hoard and multiply treasure.

EDGAR   Now fare you well, good sir.

GLOUCESTER   With all my heart.

EDGAR (*aside*)   Why I do trifle thus with his despair
    Is done to cure it.

GLOUCESTER (*kneeling*)   O you mighty gods!

35   This world I do renounce, and, in your sights,
    Shake patiently my great affliction off.
    If I could bear it longer, and not fall
    To quarrel° with your great opposeless wills,   *Into conflict*
    My snuff and loathèd part of nature[4] should
40   Burn itself out. If Edgar live, O, bless him!
    Now, fellow, fare thee well.
                        He falls forward and swoons

EDGAR   Gone, sir; farewell.—
    And yet I know not how conceit may rob
    The treasury of life, when life itself
    Yields to the theft.[5] Had he been where he thought,
45   By this° had thought been past. Alive or dead?   *now*
    Ho, you sir! friend! Hear you, sir? speak!
    Thus might he pass° indeed. Yet he revives.   *pass away*
    What are you, sir?

GLOUCESTER   Away, and let me die.

EDGAR   Hadst thou been aught° but gossamer, feathers, air,   *anything*
50   So many fathom down precipitating,°   *plunging*
    Thou'dst shivered° like an egg; but thou dost breathe;   *shattered*
    Hast heavy substance; bleed'st not; speak'st; art sound.
    Ten masts at each° make not the altitude   *end to end*
    Which thou hast perpendicularly fell.
55   Thy life's a miracle. Speak yet again.

GLOUCESTER   But have I fallen, or no?

EDGAR   From the dread summit of this chalky bourn.[6]
    Look up a-height; the shrill-gorged° lark so far   *shrill-throated*
    Cannot be seen or heard. Do but look up.

60   GLOUCESTER   Alack, I have no eyes.
    Is wretchedness deprived° that benefit,   *deprived of*
    To end itself by death? 'Twas yet some comfort,
    When misery could beguile° the tyrant's rage,   *cheat*
    And frustrate his proud will.

EDGAR   Give me your arm.
65   Up—so. How is 't? Feel you your legs? You stand.

GLOUCESTER   Too well, too well.

EDGAR   This is above all strangeness.
    Upon the crown o' the cliff, what thing was that
    Which parted from you?

GLOUCESTER   A poor unfortunate beggar.

EDGAR   As I stood here below, methought his eyes
70   Were two full moons; he had a thousand noses,
    Horns whelked° and waved like the enridgèd sea: *twisted*
    It was some fiend. Therefore, thou happy father,°   *lucky old man*
    Think that the clearest° gods, who make them honors   *purest; most illustrious*
    Of men's impossibilities,[7] have preserved thee.

---

4. The scorched and hateful remnant of my lifetime.
snuff: end of a candlewick.
5. *And yet . . . theft:* Edgar worries that the imagined scenario ("conceit") he has invented may be enough to kill his father, particularly as Gloucester wishes for ("yields to") his own death.
6. The white chalk cliffs of Dover, which make a boundary ("bourn") between land and sea.
7. *who . . . impossibilities:* who attain honor for themselves by performing deeds impossible to men.

75 GLOUCESTER I do remember now. Henceforth I'll bear
      Affliction till it do cry out itself
      "Enough, enough," and die. That thing you speak of,
      I took it for a man; often 't would say
      "The fiend, the fiend"—he led me to that place.
80 EDGAR Bear free and patient thoughts. But who comes here?
          Enter LEAR, *fantastically dressed with wild flowers*
      The safer sense will ne'er accommodate
      His master thus.[8]
    LEAR No, they cannot touch me for coining;[9] I am the king
      himself.
85 EDGAR O thou side-piercing sight!
    LEAR Nature's above art in that respect.[1] There's your press-
      money.[2] That fellow handles his bow like a crow-keeper.[3] Draw
      me a clothier's yard.[4] Look, look, a mouse! Peace, peace; this
      piece of toasted cheese will do 't.° There's my gauntlet; I'll   *(lure the mouse)*
90 prove it on a giant.[5] Bring up the brown bills.[6] O, well flown,
      bird!° i' the clout,° i' the clout. Hewgh! Give the word.°   *arrow / bull's-eye / password*
    EDGAR Sweet marjoram.[7]
    LEAR Pass.
    GLOUCESTER I know that voice.
95 LEAR Ha! Goneril, with a white beard! They flattered me like a
      dog;° and told me I had white hairs in my beard ere the black   *fawningly*
      ones were there.[8] To say "aye" and "no" to everything that I
      said!—"Aye" and "no" too was no good divinity.[9] When the
      rain came to wet me once, and the wind to make me chatter;
100 when the thunder would not peace at my bidding; there I
      found° 'em, there I smelt 'em out. Go to, they are not men o'   *understood*
      their words! They told me I was everything. 'Tis a lie, I am not
      ague-proof.°   *immune to illness*
    GLOUCESTER The trick° of that voice I do well remember.   *peculiarity*
      Is 't not the king?
105 LEAR   Aye, every inch a king!
      When I do stare, see how the subject quakes.
      I pardon that man's life. What was thy cause?°   *crime*
      Adultery?
      Thou shalt not die. Die for adultery? No.
110 The wren goes to 't, and the small gilded fly
      Does lecher in my sight.
      Let copulation thrive; for Gloucester's bastard son
      Was kinder to his father than my daughters
      Got 'tween the lawful sheets. To 't luxury,° pell-mell!   *lechery*
115 For I lack soldiers. Behold yond simpering dame,
      Whose face between her forks presages snow;[1]

8. *The . . . thus:* A sane mind would never allow its possessor to dress up this way.
9. Because minting money was the prerogative of the
King, nobody could overtake or equal ("touch") him.
1. My true feelings will always outvalue others' hypocrisy;
my natural supremacy surpasses any attempt to create a
false new reign. This image may also be based on coining
(see note 9, above).
2. Fee paid to a soldier impressed, or forced, into the
army.
3. A person hired as a scarecrow, and thus unfit for anything else.
4. Draw the bowstring the full length of the arrow (a
standard English arrow was a cloth yard [37 inches]

long).
5. I'll defend my stand even against a giant. To throw
down an armored glove ("gauntlet") was to issue a challenge.
6. Brown painted pikes; the soldiers carrying them.
7. Used medicinally against madness.
8. Told me I had wisdom before age.
9. *no good divinity:* poor theology (because insincere);
from James 5:12, "Let your yea be yea; nay, nay."
1. Whose expression implies cold chastity. "Face" refers
to the area between her legs ("forks"), as well as to her
literal facial expression as framed by the aristocratic
lady's starched headpiece, also called a "fork."

That minces° virtue, and does shake the head   *affects*
To hear of° pleasure's name;   *even of*
The fitchew, nor the soilèd horse,[2] goes to 't
120   With a more riotous appetite.
Down from the waist they are Centaurs,[3]
Though women all above.
But° to the girdle° do the gods inherit.°   *Only / waist / own*
Beneath is all the fiends'; there's hell,[4] there's darkness,
125   There's the sulphurous pit, burning, scalding,
Stench, consumption! Fie, fie, fie! pah! pah!
Give me an ounce of civet,[5] good apothecary,
To sweeten my imagination.
There's money for thee.
130   GLOUCESTER   O, let me kiss that hand!
LEAR   Let me wipe it first; it smells of mortality.
GLOUCESTER   O ruined piece° of nature! This great world   *masterpiece*
Shall so wear out to nought.[6] Dost thou know me?
LEAR   I remember thine eyes well enough. Dost thou squiny° at   *squint*
135   me? No, do thy worst, blind Cupid; I'll not love. Read thou this
challenge; mark but the penning of it.
GLOUCESTER   Were all the letters suns, I could not see one.
EDGAR (*aside*)   I would not take° this from report. It is,   *believe*
And my heart breaks at it.
140   LEAR   Read.
GLOUCESTER   What, with the case° of eyes?   *socket*
LEAR   O, ho, are you there with me?[7] No eyes in your head, nor
no money in your purse? Your eyes are in a heavy case,[8] your
purse in a light. Yet you see how this world goes.
145   GLOUCESTER   I see it feelingly.°   *by touch; painfully*
LEAR   What, art mad? A man may see how this world goes with
no eyes. Look with thine ears. See how yond justice rails upon
yond simple° thief. Hark, in thine ear. Change places and,   *lowly; innocent*
handy-dandy,[9] which is the justice, which is the thief? Thou
150   hast seen a farmer's dog bark at a beggar?
GLOUCESTER   Aye, sir.
LEAR   And the creature° run from the cur? There thou mightst   *wretch*
behold the great image of authority: a dog's obeyed in office.
Thou rascal beadle,[1] hold° thy bloody hand!   *restrain*
155   Why dost thou lash that whore? Strip thine own back;
Thou hotly lusts to use her in that kind°   *way*
For which thou whipp'st her. The usurer hangs the cozener.[2]
Through tattered clothes small vices do appear;
Robes and furred gowns hide all. Plate° sin with gold,   *Armor; gild*
160   And the strong lance of justice hurtless° breaks;   *harmlessly*
Arm it in rags, a pigmy's straw does pierce it.
None does offend, none, I say, none; I'll able° 'em;   *authorize*
Take that of me, my friend, who have the power
To seal the accuser's lips. Get thee glass eyes;

---

2. Neither the polecat nor a horse full of fresh grass.
3. Lecherous mythological creatures that have a human body to the waist and the legs and torso of a horse below.
4. Shakespeare's frequent term for female genitals.
5. Exotic perfume derived from the sex glands of the civet cat.
6. Shall decay to nothing in the same way. In Renaissance philosophy, humans were perfectly analogous to

the cosmos, standing for the whole in miniature and as its masterpiece.
7. Is that what you are telling me?
8. In a sad condition; playing on "case" as "sockets."
9. Pick a hand, as in a child's game.
1. The parish officer responsible for whippings.
2. The ruinous moneylender, prosperous enough to be made a judge, convicts the ordinary cheat.

165 And, like a scurvy politician,[3] seem
To see the things thou dost not. Now, now, now, now!
Pull off my boots. Harder, harder! So.

EDGAR O, matter and impertinency° mixed!   *sense and nonsense*
Reason in madness!

170 LEAR If thou wilt weep my fortunes, take my eyes.
I know thee well enough; thy name is Gloucester:
Thou must be patient. We came crying hither;
Thou knows't, the first time that we smell the air,
We wail and cry. I will preach to thee. Mark.

       LEAR *takes off his crown of weeds and flowers*[4]

175 GLOUCESTER Alack, alack the day!

LEAR When we are born, we cry that we are come
To this great stage of fools. This'° a good block;[5]   *This is*
It were a delicate° stratagem, to shoe   *subtle*
A troop of horse with felt.[6] I'll put 't in proof;°   *to the test*
180 And when I have stol'n upon these sons-in-law,
Then, kill, kill, kill, kill, kill, kill!

       Enter a GENTLEMAN, *with attendants*

GENTLEMAN O, here he is; lay hand upon him. Sir,
Your most dear daughter—

LEAR No rescue? What, a prisoner? I am even
185 The natural fool[7] of fortune. Use° me well;   *Treat*
You shall have ransom. Let me have surgeons;
I am cut to the brains.

GENTLEMAN   You shall have any thing.

LEAR No seconds?° all myself?   *supporters*
Why, this would make a man a man of salt,[8]
190 To use his eyes for garden water-pots,
Aye, and laying° autumn's dust.   *settling*

GENTLEMAN   Good sir—

LEAR I will die bravely,[9] like a smug° bridegroom. What!   *an elegant*
I will be jovial. Come, come; I am a king,
My masters, know you that?

195 GENTLEMAN You are a royal one, and we obey you.

LEAR Then there's life° in't. Nay, if you get it, you shall get it   *hope*
with running. Sa, sa, sa, sa.[1] (*Exit running; attendants follow*)

GENTLEMAN A sight most pitiful in the meanest wretch,
Past speaking of in a king! Thou hast one daughter,
200 Who redeems nature from the general curse
Which twain have brought her to.[2]

EDGAR Hail, gentle° sir.   *noble*

GENTLEMAN   Sir, speed you.° What's your will?   *God speed you*

EDGAR Do you hear aught, sir, of a battle toward?°   *coming*

GENTLEMAN Most sure and vulgar.° Everyone hears that,   *commonly known*
Which° can distinguish sound.   *Who*

---

3. A vile schemer. In early modern England, "politician"
meant an ambitious, even Machiavellian, upstart.
4. Like a preacher, removing his hat in the pulpit.
5. Stage (often called "scaffold" and hence linked to executioner's block); block used to shape a felt hat (such as
the hat removed by a preacher before a sermon); mounting block (such as the stump or stock Lear may have sat
on to remove his boots).
6. Hat material, to muffle the sound of the approaching
cavalry.
7. Born plaything; playing on "natural" as "mentally

deficient."
8. A man reduced to nothing but the salt his tears
deposit.
9. With courage; showily. "Die" plays on the Renaissance sense of "have an orgasm."
1. A cry to encourage dogs in the hunt.
2. *Who . . . to:* Who restores proper meaning and order
to a universe plagued by the crimes of the other two
daughters; alluding to the fall of humankind and the natural world caused by the sin of Adam and Eve and to the
universal redemption brought about by Christ's sacrifice.

205 EDGAR   But, by your favor,
    How near's the other army?
    GENTLEMAN   Near and on speedy foot. The main descry°   *appearance*
    Stands on the hourly thought.°   *Is expected forthwith*
    EDGAR   I thank you, sir. That's all.
210 GENTLEMAN   Though that the queen on° special cause° is here,   *for / reason*
    Her army is moved on.
    EDGAR   I thank you, sir.   *Exit* GENTLEMAN
    GLOUCESTER   You ever-gentle gods, take my breath from me;
    Let not my worser spirit[3] tempt me again
    To die before you please!
    EDGAR   Well pray you, father.[4]
215 GLOUCESTER   Now, good sir, what are you?
    EDGAR   A most poor man, made tame to fortune's blows;
    Who, by the art of known and feeling° sorrows,   *profound*
    Am pregnant to° good pity. Give me your hand,   *disposed to feel*
    I'll lead you to some biding.°   *resting place*
    GLOUCESTER   Hearty thanks.
220 The bounty and the benison of heaven
    To boot, and boot![5]
               Enter OSWALD
    OSWALD   A proclaimed prize![6] Most happy!°   *lucky*
    That eyeless head of thine was first framed° flesh   *made of*
    To raise my fortunes. Thou old unhappy traitor,
225 Briefly thyself remember.[7] The sword is out
    That must destroy thee.
    GLOUCESTER   Now let thy friendly hand
    Put strength enough to 't.
             EDGAR *interposes*
    OSWALD   Wherefore, bold peasant.
    Darest thou support a published° traitor? Hence,   *proclaimed*
    Lest that the infection° of his fortune take   *(deathly) sickness*
230 Like° hold on thee. Let go his arm.   *The same*
    EDGAR   Chill[8] not let go, zir, without vurther 'casion.°   *further occasion*
    OSWALD   Let go, slave, or thou diest!
    EDGAR   Good gentleman, go your gait,° and let poor volk pass.   *walk on*
    An chud ha'° bin zwaggered out of my life, 't would not ha' bin   *If I could have*
235 zo long as 'tis by a vortnight. Nay, come not near th' old man;
    keep out, che vor ye, or ise try whether your costard or my
    ballow be the harder.[9] Chill be plain with you.
    OSWALD   Out, dunghill!
    EDGAR   Chill pick your teeth, zir. Come! No matter vor your
240 foins.°   *sword thrusts*
        They fight, and EDGAR *knocks him down*
    OSWALD   Slave, thou hast slain me. Villain, take my purse.
    If ever thou wilt thrive, bury my body;
    And give the letters which thou find'st about me
    To Edmund earl of Gloucester. Seek him out
245 Upon° the British party. O, untimely death!   *Within*
    Death!   *He dies*

---

3. Wicked inclination; bad angel.
4. A term of respect for an elderly man.
5. In addition to my thanks, and may it bring you some worldly reward.
6. A wanted man, with a bounty on his life.
7. Recollect and pray forgiveness for your sins.

8. I will; dialect from Somerset was a stage convention for peasant dialogue.
9. *che vor ye . . . harder:* I warrant you, or I shall test whether your head or my cudgel is harder. *costard:* a kind of apple.

EDGAR I know thee well: a serviceable° villain;   *an officious*
As duteous to the vices of thy mistress
As badness would desire.

GLOUCESTER   What, is he dead?

250 EDGAR Sit you down, father; rest you.
Let's see his pockets; the letters that he speaks of
May be my friends. He's dead; I am only sorry
He had no other death'sman.° Let us see.   *executioner*
Leave,° gentle wax;[1] and, manners blame us not.   *By your leave*
255 To know our enemies' minds, we'd rip their hearts;
Their° papers, is more lawful.   *To rip their*
(*Reads*) "Let our reciprocal vows be remembered. You have
many opportunities to cut him off. If your will want° not, time   *lacks*
and place will be fruitfully offered. There is nothing done,° if   *accomplished*
260 he return the conqueror. Then am I the prisoner, and his bed my
jail; from the loathed warmth whereof deliver me, and supply°   *fill*
the place for your labor.[2]

                                Your—wife, so I would say—
                                        Affectionate servant,
265   Goneril."

O undistinguished space of woman's will![3]
A plot upon her virtuous husband's life;
And the exchange° my brother! Here, in the sands,   *substitute*
Thee I'll rake up,° the post unsanctified°   *cover up / unholy messenger*
270 Of murderous lechers; and in the mature time°   *when the time is ripe*
With this ungracious° paper strike the sight   *ungodly*
Of the death-practiced duke.[4] For him 'tis well
That of thy death and business I can tell.

GLOUCESTER The king is mad. How stiff is my vile sense,[5]
275 That I stand up, and have ingenious feeling[6]
Of my huge sorrows! Better I were distract;°   *mad*
So should my thoughts be severed from my griefs,
And woes by wrong° imaginations lose   *false*
The knowledge of themselves.
        Drum afar off

EDGAR   Give me your hand.
280 Far off, methinks, I hear the beaten drum.
Come, father, I'll bestow° you with a friend.   *Exeunt*   *lodge*

                              4.7
        Enter CORDELIA, KENT, DOCTOR, *and a* GENTLEMAN

CORDELIA O thou good Kent, how shall I live and work,
To match thy goodness? My life will be too short,
And every measure° fail me.   *attempt*

KENT To be acknowledged, madam, is o'erpaid.°   *is more than enough*
5 All my reports go[1] with the modest truth;
Nor more nor clipped, but so.[2]

CORDELIA   Be better suited.°   *attired*
These weeds° are memories of those worser hours.   *clothes*
I prithee, put them off.

---

1. The wax seal on the letter.
2. *for your labor:* as a reward for your endeavors, and
for further sexual exertion.
3. Limitless extent of woman's willfulness. As with "hell"
in line 124, "will" might also refer to a woman's genitals.
4. Of the Duke whose death is plotted.
5. How obstinate is my unwanted power of reason.

6. That I remain upright and firm in my sanity and
have rational perceptions.
4.7 Location: The French camp at Dover.
1. May all accounts of me agree.
2. Not greater or less, but exactly the modest amount I
deserve.

KENT   Pardon me, dear madam;
         Yet to be known shortens my made intent.³
10   My boon I make it,⁴ that you know° me not   acknowledge
         Till time and I think meet.°   suitable
CORDELIA   Then be 't so, my good lord. (*To the* DOCTOR) How
         does the king?
DOCTOR   Madam, sleeps still.
CORDELIA   O you kind gods,
15   Cure this great breach in his abusèd nature!
         The untuned and jarring senses, O, wind up⁵
         Of this child-changèd⁶ father!
DOCTOR   So please your majesty
         That we may wake the king? He hath slept long.
CORDELIA   Be governed by your knowledge, and proceed
20   I' the sway° of your own will. Is he arrayed?°   By the authority / clothed
                Enter LEAR *in a chair carried by servants*
GENTLEMAN   Aye, madam. In the heaviness of his sleep
         We put fresh garments on him.
DOCTOR   Be by, good madam, when we do awake him;
         I doubt not of his temperance.°   calmness
CORDELIA   Very well.
                Music
25 DOCTOR   Please you, draw near. Louder the music there!
CORDELIA   O my dear father! Restoration hang
         Thy medicine on my lips; and let this kiss
         Repair those violent harms that my two sisters
         Have in thy reverence° made!   aged dignity
KENT   Kind and dear princess!
30 CORDELIA   Had you not⁷ been their father, these white flakes°   locks of hair
         Had challenged° pity of them. Was this a face   Would have provoked
         To be opposed against the warring winds?
         To stand against the deep dread-bolted thunder?
         In the most terrible and nimble stroke
35   Of quick, cross lightning? to watch°—poor perdu!⁸—   to stand guard
         With this thin helm?° Mine enemy's dog,   helmet (of hair)
         Though he had bit me, should have stood that night
         Against my fire; and wast thou fain,° poor father,   glad
         To hovel thee with swine, and rogues forlorn,
40   In short° and musty straw? Alack, alack!   scant; broken
         'Tis wonder that thy life and wits at once
         Had not concluded all.° He wakes; speak to him.   altogether
DOCTOR   Madam, do you; 'tis fittest.
CORDELIA   How does my royal lord? How fares your majesty?
45 LEAR   You do me wrong to take me out o' the grave.
         Thou art a soul in bliss; but I am bound
         Upon a wheel of fire, that mine own tears
         Do scald like molten lead.⁹
CORDELIA   Sir, do you know me?
LEAR   You are a spirit, I know. When did you die?
50 CORDELIA   Still, still, far wide!°   unbalanced

---

3. Revealing myself now would abort my designs.
4. The reward I beg is.
5. *The . . . up:* Reorder his confused and delirious mind. The image is of tightening the strings of a lute.
6. Changed by his children; changed into a child; playing on a musical key change.
7. Even if you had not.
8. Lost one; in military terms, a dangerously exposed sentry.
9. *but I . . . lead:* Lear puts himself in either hell or purgatory, both places of such punishment in medieval accounts.

DOCTOR   He's scarce awake. Let him alone awhile.
LEAR   Where have I been? Where am I? Fair daylight?
       I am mightily abused.° I should e'en die with pity,   *wronged; deceived*
       To see another thus. I know not what to say.
55   I will not swear these are my hands. Let's see.
       I feel this pin prick. Would I were assured
       Of my condition!
CORDELIA   O, look upon me, sir,
       And hold your hands in benediction o'er me:
       No, sir, you must not kneel.
60 LEAR   Pray, do not mock me.
       I am a very foolish fond° old man,   *silly*
       Fourscore and upward, not an hour more nor less;
       And, to deal plainly,
       I fear I am not in my perfect mind.
65   Methinks I should know you, and know this man;
       Yet I am doubtful; for I am mainly° ignorant   *entirely*
       What place this is; and all the skill I have
       Remembers not these garments; nor I know not
       Where I did lodge last night. Do not laugh at me;
70   For, as I am a man, I think this lady
       To be my child Cordelia.
CORDELIA   And so I am, I am.
LEAR   Be your tears wet?[1] Yes, faith. I pray, weep not.
       If you have poison for me, I will drink it.
       I know you do not love me; for your sisters
75   Have, as I do remember, done me wrong.
       You have some cause, they have not.
CORDELIA   No cause, no, cause.
LEAR   Am I in France?
KENT   In your own kingdom, sir.
LEAR   Do not abuse° me.   *deceive; mock*
DOCTOR   Be comforted, good madam. The great rage,
80   You see, is killed in him; and yet it is danger
       To make him even o'er° the time he has lost.   *go over*
       Desire him to go in. Trouble him no more
       Till further settling.°   *Until his mind eases*
CORDELIA   Will't please your highness walk?
LEAR   You must bear with me:
85   Pray you now, forget and forgive. I am old and foolish.
                          Exeunt all but KENT *and* GENTLEMAN
GENTLEMAN   Holds it true, sir, that the Duke of Cornwall was so
       slain?
KENT   Most certain, sir.
GENTLEMAN   Who is conductor° of his people?   *commander*
90 KENT   As 'tis said, the bastard son of Gloucester.
GENTLEMAN   They say Edgar, his banished son, is with the Earl
       of Kent in Germany.
KENT   Report° is changeable. 'Tis time to look about.° The pow- *Rumor/prepare defenses*
       ers of the kingdom approach apace.
95 GENTLEMAN   The arbitrement° is like to be bloody. Fare you   *encounter*
       well, sir.   *Exit*
KENT   My point and period[2] will be throughly wrought,
       Or° well or ill, as this day's battle's fought.   *Exit*   *For*

1. Are your tears real?; is this really happening?   2. The purpose and end of my life; literally, the full stop.

5.1

Enter, with drum and colors,° EDMUND, REGAN, GENTLE-   *regimental flags*
MAN, *and soldiers*

EDMUND   Know° of the duke if his last purpose hold,[1]   *Inquire*
   Or whether since he is advised by aught[2]
   To change the course. He's full of alteration°   *indecision*
   And self-reproving. Bring his constant pleasure.°   *his settled intent*

         To a GENTLEMAN, *who goes out*

5   REGAN   Our sister's man is certainly miscarried.[3]

EDMUND   'Tis to be doubted,° madam.   *feared*

REGAN   Now, sweet lord,
   You know the goodness I intend upon you.
   Tell me—but truly—but then speak the truth,
   Do you not love my sister?

EDMUND   In honored° love.   *honorable*

10   REGAN   But have you never found my brother's way
   To the forfended[4] place?

EDMUND   That thought abuses° you.   *deceives*

REGAN   I am doubtful° that you have been conjunct°   *suspicious / complicit*
   And bosomed with° her, as far as we call hers.[5]   *enamored of*

EDMUND   No, by mine honor, madam.

15   REGAN   I never shall endure her. Dear my lord,
   Be not familiar° with her.

EDMUND   Fear° me not.   *intimate / Doubt*
   She and the duke her husband!

         Enter, with drum and colors, ALBANY, GONERIL, *and*
         soldiers

GONERIL *(aside)*   I had rather lose the battle than that sister
   Should loosen° him and me.   *disunite*

20   ALBANY   Our very loving sister, well be-met.
   Sir, this I hear: the king is come to his daughter,
   With others whom the rigor° of our state°   *harshness / government*
   Forced to cry out. Where I could not be honest,°   *honorable*
   I never yet was valiant. For this business,
25   It toucheth° us, as France invades our land,   *concerns*
   Not bolds the king, with others, whom, I fear,
   Most just and heavy causes make oppose.[6]

EDMUND   Sir, you speak nobly.

REGAN   Why is this reasoned?[7]

GONERIL   Combine together 'gainst the enemy;
30   For these domestic and particular broils°   *minor details*
   Are not the question here.

ALBANY   Let's then determine
   With the ancient° of war on our proceeding.   *experienced officer*

EDMUND   I shall attend you presently° at your tent.   *in a moment*

REGAN   Sister, you'll go with us?[8]

35   GONERIL   No.

REGAN   'Tis most convenient;° pray you, go with us.   *suitable*

GONERIL *(aside)*   O, ho, I know the riddle.°—I will go.   *disguised meaning*

         As they are going out, enter EDGAR *disguised*

5.1 Location: The British camp near Dover.
1. If his previous intention (to wage war) remains firm.
2. Since then anything has persuaded him.
3. Has surely come to grief by some accident.
4. Forbidden (to Edmund, because it is adulterous).
5. In total intimacy; all the way.
6. *It . . . oppose*: This is of concern to us because France

lands on our soil, not because it emboldens the King and others, who, I am afraid, have been provoked for good and solid reasons.
7. What is the point of this kind of speech?
8. Regan wants Goneril to go with Albany and her, rather than with Edmund.

EDGAR   If e'er your grace had speech with man so poor,
Hear me one word.

ALBANY   I'll overtake you. Speak.

Exeunt all but ALBANY *and* EDGAR

40   EDGAR   Before you fight the battle, ope this letter.
If you have victory, let the trumpet sound
For him that brought it. Wretched though I seem,
I can produce a champion that will prove°   defend
What is avouched° there. If you miscarry,°   asserted / perish
45   Your business of the world hath so an end,
And machination° ceases. Fortune love you!   plotting

ALBANY   Stay till I have read the letter.

EDGAR   I was forbid it.
When time shall serve, let but the herald cry,
And I'll appear again.

50   ALBANY   Why, fare thee well. I will o'erlook thy paper.

Exit EDGAR

Re-enter EDMUND

EDMUND   The enemy 's in view; draw up your powers.°   troops
Here is the guess° of their true strength and forces   estimate
By diligent discovery;° but your haste   spying
Is now urged on you.

ALBANY   We will greet the time.[9]   *Exit*

55   EDMUND   To both these sisters have I sworn my love;
Each jealous° of the other, as the stung   suspicious
Are of the adder. Which of them shall I take?
Both? one? or neither? Neither can be enjoyed,
If both remain alive. To take the widow
60   Exasperates, makes mad her sister Goneril;
And hardly° shall I carry out my side,°   with difficulty / plan
Her husband being alive. Now then we'll use
His countenance[1] for the battle; which being done,
Let her who would be rid of him devise
65   His speedy taking off. As for the mercy
Which he intends to Lear and to Cordelia,
The battle done, and they within our power,
Shall° never see his pardon; for my state°   They shall / condition
Stands on° me to defend, not to debate.   *Exit*   Obliges

5.2

Alarum within.[1] *Enter, with drum and colors,* LEAR, COR-
DELIA, *and soldiers, over the stage; and exeunt.*
Enter EDGAR *and* GLOUCESTER

EDGAR   Here, father,[2] take the shadow of this tree
For your good host;° pray that the right may thrive: shelter
If ever I return to you again,
I'll bring you comfort.

GLOUCESTER   Grace go with you, sir!   *Exit* EDGAR

Alarum and retreat° within. *Re-enter* EDGAR   trumpet signal

5   EDGAR   Away, old man! give me thy hand! away!

9. We will be ready to meet the occasion.
1. Authority or backing; also suggesting "face," to be
used like a mask for Edmund's ambition.
5.2 Location: The rest of the play takes place near the

battlefield.
1. Trumpet call to battle (backstage).
2. See note to 4.6.214.

King Lear hath lost, he and his daughter ta'en.
Give me thy hand! come on!

GLOUCESTER   No farther, sir; a man may rot even° here.   right

EDGAR   What, in ill thoughts again? Men must endure
10   Their going hence, even as their coming hither;
Ripeness is all.³ Come on!

GLOUCESTER   And that's true, too.   *Exeunt*

5.3

Enter, in conquest, with drum and colors, EDMUND;
LEAR *and* CORDELIA, *prisoners;* CAPTAIN, SOLDIERS, *etc.*

EDMUND   Some officers take them away. Good guard,
Until their greater pleasures¹ first be known
That are to censure° them.   judge

CORDELIA   We are not the first
Who, with best meaning,° have incurred the worst.   intention
5   For thee, oppressèd king, am I cast down;°   (into unhappiness)
Myself could else out-frown false Fortune's frown.²
Shall we not see these daughters and these sisters?

LEAR   No, no, no, no! Come, let's away to prison.
We two alone will sing like birds i' the cage.
10   When thou dost ask me blessing, I'll kneel down,
And ask of thee forgiveness. So we'll live,
And pray, and sing, and tell old tales, and laugh
At gilded butterflies,³ and hear poor rogues
Talk of court news; and we'll talk with them too,
15   Who loses and who wins; who 's in, and who 's out;
And take upon 's the mystery of things,
As if we were Gods' spies; and we'll wear out,°   outlast
In a walled prison, packs and sects of great ones,
That ebb and flow by the moon.⁴

EDMUND   Take them away.
20   LEAR   Upon such sacrifices,⁵ my Cordelia,
The gods themselves throw incense. Have I caught thee?
He that parts us shall bring a brand from heavens,
And fire us hence like foxes.⁶ Wipe thine eyes;
The good-years shall devour them, flesh and fell,⁷
25   Ere they shall make us weep! We'll see 'em starved first.
Come.   *Exeunt* LEAR *and* CORDELIA, *guarded*

EDMUND   Come hither, captain; hark.
Take thou this note (*giving a paper*). Go follow them to prison:
One step I have advanced° thee. If thou dost   promoted
30   As this instructs thee, thou dost make thy way
To noble fortunes. Know thou this, that men
Are as the time is. To be tender-minded
Does not become a sword.° Thy great employment   befit a swordsman

---

3. To await the destined time is the most important thing, as fruit falls only when ripe (playing on Gloucester's "rot," line 8); readiness for death is our only duty (compare *Hamlet* 5.2.160, "The readiness is all").
5.3
1. *Good . . . pleasures:* Guard them well until the desires of those greater persons.
2. Otherwise, I could be defiant in the face of bad fortune.
3. Gaudy courtiers.

4. *packs . . . moon:* followers and factions of important people whose positions at court vary as the tide.
5. Upon such sacrifices as we are or as you have made.
6. *shall . . . foxes:* must have divine aid to do so. The image is of using a torch to smoke foxes out of their holes, or, in the case of Lear and Cordelia, prison cells.
7. *flesh and fell:* meat and skin; entirely. The precise meaning of "good-years" has not been explained; it may signify simply the passage of time or may suggest some ominous, destructive power.

Will not bear question.° Either say thou'lt do 't,   *discussion*
Or thrive by other means.

35   CAPTAIN   I'll do 't, my lord.

    EDMUND   About it; and write happy when thou hast done.[8]
Mark, I say, instantly; and carry it° so   *carry it out*
As I have set it down.

    CAPTAIN   I cannot draw a cart, nor eat dried oats;°   *(like a horse)*
40   If it be a man's work, I'll do it.   *Exit*

>   *Flourish. Enter* ALBANY, GONERIL, REGAN, *another* CAP-
>   TAIN, *and soldiers*

    ALBANY   Sir, you have showed today your valiant strain,°   *qualities; birth*
And fortune led you well. You have the captives
That were the opposites° of this day's strife.   *opponents*
I do require them of you, so to use° them   *treat*
45   As we shall find their merits and our safety
May equally determine.

    EDMUND   Sir, I thought it fit
To send the old and miserable king
To some retention° and appointed guard;   *confinement*
Whose° age has charms in it, whose title more,   *(Lear's)*
50   To pluck the common bosom[9] on his side,
And turn our impressed lances° in our eyes   *conscripted lancers*
Which[1] do command them. With him I sent the queen;
My reason all the same; and they are ready
Tomorrow, or at further space,° t' appear   *at a future point*
55   Where you shall hold your session.° At this time   *court of judgment*
We sweat and bleed; the friend hath lost his friend;
And the best quarrels, in the heat, are cursed
By those that feel their sharpness.[2]
The question of Cordelia and her father
Requires a fitter place.

60   ALBANY   Sir, by your patience,
I hold you but a subject of° this war,   *in waging*
Not as a brother.

    REGAN   That's as we list° to grace him.   *choose*
Methinks our pleasure might have been demanded,[3]
Ere you had spoken so far. He led our powers;°   *armies*
65   Bore the commission of my place and person;
The which immediacy° may well stand up,   *close connection*
And call itself your brother.

    GONERIL   Not so hot!°   *Not so fast*
In his own grace° he doth exalt himself,   *merit*
More than in your addition.[4]

    REGAN   In my rights,
70   By me invested, he compeers° the best.   *equals*

    GONERIL   That were the most,[5] if he should husband you.

    REGAN   Jesters do oft prove prophets.

    GONERIL   Holla, holla!
That eye that told you so looked but a-squint.[6]

---

8. Go to it, and call yourself happy when you are done.
9. To garner the affection of the populace.
1. *in our eyes / Which:* in the eyes of us who.
2. *And . . . sharpness:* And in the heat of battle, even the most just wars are cursed by those who must suffer the fighting.

3. I think you should have inquired into my wishes.
4. In the honors you confer upon him.
5. That investiture would be complete.
6. Squinting was a proverbial effect of jealousy, because of the tendency to look suspiciously at potential rivals.

REGAN   Lady, I am not well; else I should answer

75 From a full-flowing stomach.° General,   *anger*
Take thou my soldiers, prisoners, patrimony:
Dispose of them, of me; the walls° are thine.   *fortress of my heart*
Witness the world, that I create thee here
My lord and master.

GONERIL   Mean you to enjoy him?

80 ALBANY   The let-alone° lies not in your good will.   *veto*

EDMUND   Nor in thine, lord.

ALBANY   Half-blooded° fellow, yes.   *Bastard*

REGAN (*to* EDMUND)   Let the drum strike,[7] and prove my title thine.

ALBANY   Stay yet; hear reason. Edmund, I arrest thee
On capital treason; and, in thine attaint,[8]
This gilded serpent (*pointing to* GONERIL). For your claim, fair
85   sister,°   *sister-in-law*
I bar it in the interest of my wife;
'Tis she is sub-contracted to this lord,
And I, her husband, contradict your banes.°   *announcement of marriage*
If you will marry, make your loves to me,
My lady is bespoke.

90 GONERIL   An interlude!°   *A farce*

ALBANY   Thou art armed, Gloucester. Let the trumpet sound.
If none appear to prove upon thy head
Thy heinous, manifest, and many treasons,
There is my pledge (*throwing down a glove*); I'll prove it on thy heart,
95 Ere I taste bread, thou art in nothing less°   *in no way less guilty*
Than I have proclaimed thee.

REGAN   Sick, O, sick!

GONERIL (*aside*)   If not, I'll ne'er trust medicine.°   *poison (euphemistic)*

EDMUND   There's my exchange (*throwing down a glove*). What°   *Whoever*
in the world he is
That names me traitor, villain-like he lies.
100 Call by thy trumpet. He that dares approach,
On him, on you, who not? I will maintain
My truth and honor firmly.

ALBANY   A herald, ho!

EDMUND   A herald, ho, a herald!

ALBANY   Trust to thy single virtue;° for thy soldiers,   *your unassisted power*
105 All levied in my name, have in my name
Took their discharge.

REGAN   My sickness grows upon me.

ALBANY   She is not well; convey her to my tent.   *Exit* REGAN, *led*
Enter a HERALD
Come hither, herald—Let the trumpet sound—
And read out this.

CAPTAIN   Sound, trumpet! (*A trumpet sounds*)

110 HERALD [*reads*]   "If any man of quality or degree within the
lists of the army will maintain upon Edmund, supposed Earl of
Gloucester, that he is a manifold traitor, let him appear by the
third sound of the trumpet. He is bold in his defense."

EDMUND   Sound! (*First trumpet*)

115 HERALD   Again! (*Second trumpet*)

---

7. Perhaps to announce the betrothal, or a challenge.
8. And in order to accuse you; and as one who shares your corruption or crime.

HERALD   Again! (*Third trumpet*)
          Trumpet answers within
          Enter EDGAR, *at the third sound, armed, with a trumpet*
          before him
ALBANY   Ask him his purposes, why he appears
          Upon this call o' the trumpet.
HERALD   What° are you?   Who
          Your name, your quality?° and why you answer   degree; rank
          This present summons?
120 EDGAR   Know, my name is lost;
          By treason's tooth bare-gnawn and canker-bit.°   worm-eaten
          Yet am I noble as the adversary
          I come to cope.°   to encounter
ALBANY   Which is that adversary?
EDGAR   What's he that speaks for Edmund Earl of Gloucester?
EDMUND   Himself. What say'st thou to him?
125 EDGAR   Draw thy sword,
          That,° if my speech offend a noble heart,   So that
          Thy arm may do thee justice. Here is mine.
          Behold, it is the privilege of mine honors,
          My oath, and my profession. I protest,
130   Maugre° thy strength, youth, place, and eminence,   Despite
          Despite thy victor sword and fire-new° fortune,   newly minted
          Thy valor and thy heart,° thou art a traitor;   courage
          False to thy gods, thy brother, and thy father;
          Conspirant 'gainst this high-illustrious prince;
135   And, from the extremest upward° of thy head   top
          To the descent° and dust below thy foot,   lowest part; sole
          A most toad-spotted⁹ traitor. Say thou "No,"
          This sword, this arm, and my best spirits, are bent°   ready
          To prove upon thy heart, whereto I speak,
          Thou liest.
140 EDMUND   In wisdom I should ask thy name;
          But, since thy outside looks so fair and warlike
          And that thy tongue some say of breeding breathes,
          What safe and nicely I might well delay
          By rule of knighthood, I disdain and spurn.¹
145   Back do I toss these treasons to thy head;
          With the hell-hated° lie o'erwhelm thy heart; hated as much as hell
          Which, for° they yet glance by and scarcely bruise,   since
          This sword of mine shall give them instant way,°   access
          Where they shall rest for ever. Trumpets, speak!
          Alarums. They fight. EDMUND *falls*
ALBANY   Save° him, save him!   Spare
150 GONERIL   This is practice,° Gloucester: trickery
          By the law of arms thou wast not bound to answer
          An unknown opposite.° Thou art not vanquished,   opponent
          But cozened and beguiled.°   cheated and deceived
ALBANY   Shut your mouth, dame,
          Or with this paper shall I stople° it.   plug
155   Thou worse than any name, read thine own evil.
          No tearing, lady! I perceive you know it.

9. Venomous, like a toad; spotted with disgrace.   rules of knighthood (which do not require a knight to
1. *And . . . spurn:* And since your speech may suggest   fight an unknown opponent) and refuse to fight you.
high birth, I will not stick safely and meticulously to the

Gives the letter to EDMUND

GONERIL Say, if I do, the laws are mine, not thine.
Who can arraign° me for 't?   prosecute

ALBANY   Most monstrous! oh!
Know'st thou this paper?

GONERIL   Ask me not what I know. *Exit*

160 ALBANY Go after her: she's desperate; govern° her.   restrain

EDMUND What you have charged me with, that have I done;
And more, much more; the time will bring it out.
'Tis past, and so am I. But what art thou
That hast this fortune on me?[2] If thou 'rt noble,
I do forgive thee.

165 EDGAR   Let's exchange charity.°   forgiveness
I am no less in blood than thou art, Edmund;
If more, the more thou hast wronged me.
My name is Edgar, and thy father's son.
The gods are just, and of our pleasant vices
170 Make instruments to plague us.
The dark and vicious place where thee he got[3]
Cost him his eyes.

EDMUND   Thou hast spoken right, 'tis true;
The wheel° is come full circle! I am here.[4]   Fortune's wheel

ALBANY Methought thy very gait did prophesy
175 A royal nobleness. I must embrace thee.
Let sorrow split my heart, if ever I
Did hate thee or thy father!

EDGAR   Worthy prince. I know 't.

ALBANY Where have you hid yourself?
How have you known the miseries of your father?

180 EDGAR By nursing them, my lord. List° a brief tale;   Listen to
And when 'tis told, O, that my heart would burst!
The bloody proclamation to escape,[5]
That followed me so near—O, our lives' sweetness!
That we the pain of death would hourly die
185 Rather than die at once![6]—taught me to shift
Into a madman's rags; to assume a semblance
That very° dogs disdained; and in this habit   even
Met I my father with his bleeding rings,°   sockets
Their precious stones° new lost; became his guide,   eyes
190 Led him, begged for him, saved him from despair;
Never—O fault!—revealed myself unto him,
Until some half-hour past, when I was armed:
Not sure, though hoping, of this good success,°   conclusion
I asked his blessing, and from first to last
195 Told him my pilgrimage. But his flawed° heart—   cracked
Alack, too weak the conflict to support!—
'Twixt two extremes of passion, joy and grief,
Burst smilingly.

EDMUND   This speech of yours hath moved me,
And shall perchance do good; but speak you on;
200 You look as you had something more to say.

---

2. Who have this good fortune at my expense.
3. The adulterous bed in which you were born; or, possibly, the vagina. *got:* begot.
4. Back at the lowest point.

5. In order to escape the sentence of death.
6. *our . . . once:* how sweet must life be that we prefer the constant pain of dying to death itself.

ALBANY   If there be more, more woeful, hold it in;
  For I am almost ready to dissolve,°   *melt into tears*
  Hearing of this.
EDGAR   This would have seemed a period°   *conclusion*
  To such as love not sorrow; but another,
205 To amplify° too much would make much more, *enlarge; extend*
  And top extremity.
  Whilst I was big in clamor° came there in a man, *lamenting loudly*
  Who, having seen me in my worst estate,
  Shunned my abhorred society; but then, finding
210 Who 'twas that so endured, with his strong arms
  He fastened on my neck, and bellowed out
  As he'd burst heaven; threw him on my father;
  Told the most piteous tale of Lear and him°   *himself*
  That ever ear received; which in recounting
215 His grief grew puissant,° and the strings of life *powerful*
  Began to crack. Twice then the trumpets sounded,
  And there I left him tranced.
ALBANY   But who was this?
EDGAR   Kent, sir, the banished Kent; who in disguise
  Followed his enemy king,[7] and did him service
220 Improper° for a slave.   *Unfit even*
    Enter a GENTLEMAN, *with a bloody knife*
GENTLEMAN   Help, help, O, help!
EDGAR   What kind of help?
ALBANY   Speak, man.
EDGAR   What means that bloody knife?
GENTLEMAN   'Tis hot, it smokes,
  It came even from the heart of—O, she's dead!
ALBANY   Who dead? speak, man.
225 GENTLEMAN   Your lady, sir, your lady! and her sister
  By her is poisoned; she hath confessed it.
EDMUND   I was contracted to them both. All three
  Now marry° in an instant.   *unite (in death)*
    Enter KENT
EDGAR   Here comes Kent.
ALBANY   Produce their bodies, be they alive or dead:
230 This judgment of the heavens, that makes us tremble,
  Touches us not with pity.   *Exit* GENTLEMAN
       O, is this he?
  The time will not allow the compliment
  Which very manners urges.[8]
KENT   I am come
  To bid my king and master aye° good night. *forever*
  Is he not here?
235 ALBANY   Great thing of° us forgot!   *by*
  Speak, Edmund, where's the king? and where's Cordelia?
  See'st thou this object,° Kent?   *spectacle*
    The bodies of GONERIL *and* REGAN *are brought in*
KENT   Alack, why thus?
EDMUND   Yet° Edmund was beloved. *Despite all*

---

7. Because Lear had previously banished him. *enemy:* hostile.

8. *the compliment . . . urges:* the ceremony that barest custom demands.

The one the other poisoned for my sake,
240 And after slew herself.

ALBANY Even so. Cover their faces.

EDMUND I pant for life. Some good I mean to do,
Despite of mine own nature. Quickly send,
Be brief° in it, to the castle; for my writ⁹   *speedy*
245 Is on the life of Lear and on Cordelia:
Nay, send in time.

ALBANY   Run, run, O, run!

EDGAR To who, my lord? Who hath the office?° send   *commission*
Thy token of reprieve.

EDMUND   Well thought on. Take my sword,
Give it the° captain.   *to the*

250 ALBANY   Haste thee for thy life.   *Exit* EDGAR

EDMUND   He hath commission from thy wife and me
To hang Cordelia in the prison, and
To lay the blame upon her own despair,
That she fordid herself.¹

255 ALBANY The gods defend her! Bear him hence awhile.

                                        EDMUND *is borne off*
                    Re-enter LEAR, *with* CORDELIA *dead in his arms;* EDGAR,
                    CAPTAIN, *and others following*

LEAR   Howl, howl, howl, howl! O, you are men of stones:
Had I your tongues and eyes, I'd use them so
That heaven's vault should crack. She's gone forever!
I know when one is dead, and when one lives;
260 She's dead as earth. Lend me a looking-glass;
If that her breath will mist or stain the stone,²
Why, then she lives.

KENT   Is this the promised end?³

EDGAR   Or image of that horror?

ALBANY   Fall, and cease!⁴

LEAR   This feather stirs; she lives! If it be so,
265 It is a chance which does redeem all sorrows
That ever I have felt.

KENT (*kneeling*)   O my good master!

LEAR   Prithee, away.

EDGAR   'Tis noble Kent, your friend.

LEAR   A plague upon you, murderers, traitors all!
I might have saved her; now she's gone for ever!
270 Cordelia, Cordelia! stay a little. Ha!
What is 't thou say'st? Her voice was ever soft,
Gentle, and low, an excellent thing in woman.
I killed the slave that was a-hanging thee.

GENTLEMAN 'Tis true, my lords, he did.

LEAR   Did I not, fellow?
275 I have seen the day, with my good biting falchion°   *light sword*
I would have made them skip: I am old now,

---

9. Order of execution.
1. Destroyed herself. In most of Shakespeare's source texts for the play, Cordelia does in fact kill herself after reigning for some years.
2. Mica, or stone polished to a mirror finish.

3. Doomsday; expected end of the play. In no version of the story previous to Shakespeare's does Cordelia die at this point.
4. Let the world collapse and end.

And these same crosses spoil me.[5] Who are you?
Mine eyes are not o' the best. I'll tell you straight.°   recognize you soon

KENT If fortune brag of two she loved and hated,
280 One of them we behold.[6]

LEAR This is a dull sight.[7] Are you not Kent?

KENT   The same,
Your servant Kent. Where is your servant Caius?°   (Kent's pseudonym)

LEAR He's a good fellow, I can tell you that;
He'll strike, and quickly too. He's dead and rotten.

285 KENT No, my good lord; I am the very man—

LEAR I'll see that straight.[8]

KENT That, from your first of difference and decay,[9]
Have followed your sad steps.

LEAR   You are welcome hither.

KENT Nor no man else.[1] All's cheerless, dark, and deadly.°   deathly
290 Your eldest daughters have fordone° themselves,   destroyed
And desperately° are dead.   in despair

LEAR   Aye, so I think.

ALBANY He knows not what he says; and vain° it is   in vain
That we present us to him.

EDGAR   Very bootless.°   futile

Enter a CAPTAIN

CAPTAIN Edmund is dead, my lord.

ALBANY   That's but a trifle here.
295 You lords and noble friends, know our intent.
What comfort to this great decay° may come   ruin; destruction
Shall be applied. For us, we will resign,
During the life of this old majesty,
To him our absolute power; (*to* EDGAR *and* KENT) you, to your
          rights;
300 With boot,° and such addition° as your honors   reward / distinction
Have more than merited. All friends shall taste
The wages of their virtue, and all foes
The cup of their deserving. O, see, see!

LEAR And my poor fool[2] is hanged! No, no, no life!
305 Why should a dog, a horse, a rat, have life,
And thou no breath at all? Thou'lt come no more,
Never, never, never, never, never!
Pray you, undo this button. Thank you, sir.
Do you see this? Look on her, look, her lips,
Look there, look there!   *Dies*
310 EDGAR   He faints! My lord, my lord!

KENT Break, heart; I prithee, break!

EDGAR   Look up, my lord.

KENT Vex not his ghost.[3] O, let him pass! He hates him much
That would upon the rack[4] of this tough world
Stretch him out longer.

EDGAR   He is gone, indeed.

5. And these recent adversities have weakened me; and
these parries I could once match would now destroy me.
6. *If . . . behold:* If there were only two supreme examples
in the world of Fortune's ability to raise up and cast down,
Lear would be one; alternatively, we are each of us one
(Lear and Kent are here looking at each other).
7. This is a sad sight; my vision is failing.
8. I'll attend to that shortly; I'll comprehend that in a
moment.

9. Who from the beginning of your alteration and deterioration.
1. No, neither I nor anyone else is welcome. Alternatively, I am that man, not disguised as anyone else.
2. A term of endearment, here used for Cordelia, though
it also recalls the disappearance of Lear's Fool after 3.6.
3. Do not disturb his departing soul.
4. Instrument of torture, used to stretch its victims.

315   KENT   The wonder is, he hath endured so long.
      He but usurped his life.[5]
    ALBANY   Bear them from hence. Our present business
      Is general woe. (*To* KENT *and* EDGAR) Friends of my soul, you twain
      Rule in this realm, and the gored° state sustain.   *wounded; bloody*
320   KENT   I have a journey, sir, shortly to go;
      My master calls me, I must not say no.
    EDGAR   The weight of this sad time we must obey;
      Speak what we feel, not what we ought to say.
      The oldest hath borne most; we that are young
325   Shall never see so much, nor live so long.
                                 Exeunt, with dead march

5. From death, which already had a claim on it.

Macbeth

On May 19, 1603, a scant two months after the death of Queen Elizabeth and the accession to the English throne of the Scottish King James, Shakespeare's company, the Lord Chamberlain's Men, was formally declared to be the King's Men. The players had every reason to be grateful to their new royal master for this lucrative distinction and attentive to his pleasure and interest. It has long been argued that one of the most striking signs of their gratitude is *Macbeth,* based on a story from Scottish history particularly apt for a monarch who traced his line back to Banquo, the noble thane whose murder Macbeth orders after he has killed King Duncan.

In Shakespeare's principal historical source, Raphael Holinshed's *Chronicles of England, Scotland, and Ireland* (1587), Banquo aids Macbeth in the murder of the King. Shakespeare suppresses this complicity. The witches (or "weird sisters") who tell Macbeth that he will be king tell Banquo that he will be the father of kings, but Banquo seems determined not to be drawn into any conspiratorial attempt to realize these prophecies. When, just before Duncan's assassination, Macbeth indirectly asks for his support, Banquo speaks of keeping his "allegiance clear" (2.1.27). Macbeth's only co-conspirator, then, is his wife. Innocent of the crime against Duncan, Banquo is killed because Macbeth fears and envies him and because he wishes to keep the crown he has seized from passing, as the witches had prophesied, to Banquo's heirs. Other significant changes Shakespeare made in his source materials further intensify Macbeth's isolation and his evil: in Holinshed's *Chronicles,* Duncan is a relatively young and feeble ruler, and Macbeth, having dispatched him, goes on to reign brilliantly for ten years. As Shakespeare staged the story, Duncan is a mature and virtuous king, and Scotland under the tyrant Macbeth is in the grip of a nightmare from which it will eventually awaken into the happy rule of Banquo's descendants.

As is so often the case with Shakespeare, we do not have a secure date for either the composition or the first performance of *Macbeth.* The first printed text is in the 1623 First Folio, but the play, usually dated 1606, has always seemed the most topical of Shakespeare's great tragedies, cannily alert at once to King James's personal obsessions and to contemporary events. The most unnerving of those events was the Gunpowder Plot, an attempt by a small group of conspirators, embittered by what they perceived as James's unwillingness to extend toleration to Roman Catholics, to set off a massive explosion that would blow up the King and his family along with most of the government. On the night before the intended attempt, the plot was foiled by the arrest of one of the principal conspirators, Guy Fawkes, who revealed under torture the names of his collaborators.

Among those hunted down, brought to trial, and executed for the Gunpowder Plot was Father Henry Garnet, head of the clandestine Jesuit mission in England. Garnet pleaded innocent, but the government prosecutors made much of the fact that he was the author of *A Treatise of Equivocation,* a book showing how to give misleading or ambiguous answers under oath. At a harrowing moment in *Macbeth,* in the immediate wake of the murder of the sleeping King Duncan, an insistent knocking is heard at the castle gate. (The knocking is a simple device, but in performance it almost always has a thrilling effect, famously characterized by the Romantic critic Thomas De Quincey as the reflux of the human upon the fiendish.) A porter, roused by the hammering on the door but still half drunk from the evening's revelry, appears. As he grumblingly goes to unlock the gate, he imagines that he is the gatekeeper in hell, opening the door to new arrivals. "Here's an equivocator," he says of one of these imaginary sinners, "that could swear in both the scales against either scale, who committed treason enough for God's sake, yet could not equivocate to heaven. O, come in, equivocator" (2.3.8–11). This treasonous equivocator knocking on hell's gate is almost certainly an allusion to the recently executed Henry Garnet.

The Gunpowder Plot was only one of the King's sources of anxiety. Not surprising for someone whose mother and father had both been killed, James had a horror of assassination and was convinced that there were many plots against his life. He also held a powerful conviction that a king was a sacred figure, God's own representative on earth. Regicide, in this view, was close to the ultimate crime, a demonic assault not simply on an individual and a community but on the fundamental order of the universe. James, who had written a learned book on witchcraft, suspected the hand of the devil in any plot against an anointed king, believed that witches had at various points in his own life conspired to harm him or render him impotent, and feared the existence of occult, invisible forces bent on bringing all things to ruin.

In several of his earlier plays, most notably in *Richard II*, Shakespeare's characters give voice to the theory that the King is God's deputy on earth and, consequently, that attacks upon him are evil, but kingship's claim to sacred authority is voiced exceptionally powerfully in *Macbeth* (not in Scotland alone, but also in neighboring England, where, as Malcolm tells Macduff, the touch of the pious King Edward cures disease). Exceptionally powerful, too, in this play is the metaphysical horror of regicide. The murder of Duncan is marked in the natural world with dreadful signs and portents and in the human world with an overpowering sense of devastation ironically given its most eloquent expression by the murderer Macbeth:

Henry IV of France (1553–1610) administers the royal touch, thought to cure scrofula. An etching by Pierre Firens, in André Du Laurens's *De mirabilii strumas sanandi vi solis Galliae regibus . . .* (Paris, 1609). See *Macbeth* 4.3.142–60.

> Renown and grace is dead.
> The wine of life is drawn, and the mere lees
> Is left this vault to brag of.
>
> (2.3.90–92)

Macbeth is speaking hypocritically—"look like the innocent flower," his wife had ear-lier counseled him, "but be the serpent under't" (1.5.63–64)—and yet, at least in one interpretation of the part, he is saying what he himself knows to be the grim truth. Far more than any other of Shakespeare's villains, more than the homicidal Richard III, the treacherous Claudius in *Hamlet,* and the cold-hearted Iago in *Othello,* Macbeth is fully aware of the wickedness of his deeds and is tormented by this awareness. Endowed with a clear-eyed grasp of the difference between good and evil, he chooses evil, even though the choice horrifies and sickens him.

Before he has taken the irrevocable step, Macbeth tries to recover his moral bear-ings. The deed he is contemplating, he begins by telling himself, would work only if he could control all consequences, so that his blow "might be the be-all and the end-all" (1.7.5). But he grasps that there is no possibility of such complete control and there-fore no hope of practical success. His thoughts then turn to the overwhelming ethical arguments against the murder: he is not only the King's kinsman and subject but also his host, "who should against his murderer shut the door, / Not bear the knife myself" (1.7.15–16). And from these considerations, practical and ethical, Macbeth's restless, brooding mind rises higher, imagining that the murdered Duncan's virtues will plead like angels against the "deep damnation of his taking-off,"

> And pity, like a naked new-born babe,
> Striding the blast, or heaven's cherubin, horsed
> Upon the sightless couriers of the air,
> Shall blow the horrid deed in every eye
> That tears shall drown the wind.
>
> (1.7.21–25)

No one else in the play has a moral sensibility so intense or so visionary, no one else imagines so vividly the forces that lie beyond the ordinary and familiar horizon of human experience. Macbeth understands exactly what is at stake and what he must do: "We will," he tells his wife decisively, "proceed no further in this business" (1.7.31).

Why, then, does he change his mind and commit a crime he cannot even contem-plate without horror? A significant part of the answer lies in the instigation of his for-midable wife. When we first glimpse Lady Macbeth, she is reading a letter. (Reading was by no means a universal achievement for women of the early seventeenth century, let alone the eleventh, when the play's events are set, but Shakespeare frequently rep-resents it in his plays in a variety of contexts.) The letter makes her burn with visions of the "golden round" that "fate and metaphysical aid" (1.5.26–27) seem to have con-ferred upon her husband. But even though she speaks of the crown as if it were already on Macbeth's head, she fears that he is too full of the "milk of human kindness" (1.5.15) to seize what has been promised him. She resolves then to "chastise" her hus-band, to urge him, in a phrase taken from archery that has a strong sexual undercur-rent, to screw his courage to the sticking place. Lady Macbeth manipulates him in two principal ways. The first is through sexual taunting:

> Art thou afeard
> To be the same in thine own act and valour
> As thou art in desire?
> . . . .
> When you durst do it, then you were a man
>
> (1.7.39–41, 49)

And the second is through the terrible force of her determination:

> I have given suck, and know
> How tender 'tis to love the babe that milks me.
> I would, while it was smiling in my face,
> Have plucked my nipple from his boneless gums
> And dashed the brains out, had I so sworn
> As you have done to this.
>
> (1.7.54–59)

These words, and the gestures that viscerally intensify them onstage, cannot by themselves account for Macbeth's decision. He counters his wife's sexual taunting with a clear sense of the proper boundaries of his identity as a male and as a human being: "I dare do all that may become a man; / Who dares do more is none" (1.7.46–47). As for Lady Macbeth's fantasy of murdering her infant, its horror might have served rather to deter Macbeth from his unnatural crime than to spur him toward it. Virtually everyone is subject to terrible dreams and lawless fantasies—"Merciful powers," Banquo prays, "restrain in me the cursèd thoughts that nature / Gives way to in repose" (2.1.7–9)—but not everyone crosses the fatal line from criminal desire to criminal act.

That in crossing this line Macbeth murders a man toward whom he should be grateful, loyal, and protective, deepens the mystery of his crime, linking it to a long current of theological and philosophical brooding on the nature of evil. For St. Augustine, the great fourth-century church father, evil in its most radical form is gratuitous—that is, without an explicable rationale or motivation—and this notion of gratuitousness haunts subsequent thinkers, including those far from Christian orthodoxy. Thus the Florentine Niccolò Machiavelli, notorious in the sixteenth century for freethinking, writes in Chapter 37 of his *Discourses* that "when men are no longer obliged to fight from necessity, they fight from ambition, which passion is so powerful in the hearts of men that it never leaves them, no matter to what height they may rise." The reason for this, Machiavelli proposes, is that "nature has created men so that they desire everything, but are unable to attain it; desire being thus always greater than the faculty of acquiring, discontent with what they have and dissatisfaction with themselves result from it."

Macbeth and Lady Macbeth act on ambition, restless desire, and a will to power normally kept in check by the pragmatic, ethical, and religious considerations to which the wavering Macbeth initially gives voice. Lady Macbeth in effect works to liberate that will to power in her husband, freeing him from his "sickly" fears of damnation so that he can act with a ruthless blend of murderous violence and cunning. In her radically disenchanted, coolly skeptical view, the murder of the King can be undertaken without fear of guilty conscience, vengeful ghosts, or divine judgment: "The sleeping and the dead," she tells her shaken husband, "are but as pictures. 'Tis the eye of childhood / That fears a painted devil" (2.2.51–53).

This reassurance, Shakespeare's tragedy shows, is hopelessly shallow. As the spectral dagger, the ghost sitting in Macbeth's chair, and the indelible bloodstains on Lady Macbeth's hands all chillingly demonstrate, the secure distinction between representation and reality, the dead and the living, repeatedly breaks down, not simply for the characters but for the spectators as well. In most productions, the dagger and the blood are visible only to the diseased minds of the murderers, but Banquo's ghost is almost always palpably present onstage, visible to the audience as well as to the unhinged Macbeth, though invisible to everyone around him. Moreover, the dream of a "clean" regicide proves psychologically untenable: the seizure of the crown leads to feverish sleeplessness, brooding anxiety about security, and an overwhelming sense of defilement. Macbeth and Lady Macbeth are equally devastated, but the psychological trajectory in the wake of the crime is not the same for the two conspirators. Initially frozen in moral numbness, Lady Macbeth experiences a gradual decomposition, a growing horror that breaks forth unforgettably in the sleepwalking scene with her compulsive attempts to free herself of the smell and stain of blood: "All the perfumes of Arabia will not sweeten this little hand" (5.1.42–43). Initially gripped by a heightened sensitivity to fear, a dread that threatens inward decomposition, Macbeth experiences a gradual hardening and deadening of the self until he reaches a state of absolute numbness:

> Tomorrow, and tomorrow, and tomorrow
> Creeps in this petty pace from day to day
> To the last syllable of recorded time.
> (5.5.18–20)

The assassination also proves, as Macbeth had foreseen, politically untenable. There is always someone who escapes the murderer's net, someone who poses a threat or seeks to redress an injury or simply remembers what it felt like to be free and unafraid. It is impossible to tie up all the loose ends, to break the chain of action and reaction, to reach a stable resting place. There are no clean murders. One crime leads to another and then to another without bringing the criminal any closer to the security or contentment that each desperate act is meant to achieve. Macbeth cannot stop the bloody acts; instead he must multiply and extend them. Where Lady Macbeth had only fantasized the murder of children, Macbeth actually undertakes that and other crimes until he dreams, in his half-crazed words to the "secret, black, and midnight hags" (4.1.64), of universal destruction.

It is Macbeth's first encounter with these hags—the weird (or, in the original spelling, "weyward" or "weyard") sisters—that seems to initiate his descent toward murder and tyranny. But what kind of power do these malevolent bearded women have over Macbeth? Are they responsible, by magical influence or by planting the idea in his mind, for his decision to kill Duncan? Are they somehow privy to a predestined fate, as if they have seen the script of the tragedy before it is performed? Or, alternatively, are they uncanny emblems of Macbeth's psychological condition, a kind of screen onto which he projects his "horrible imaginings" (1.3.137)? The word "weird," in one of its etymologies, derives from the Old English word for "fate," but do the women Shakespeare depicts, trafficking in ambiguous prophecies, fretting over village squabbles, mumbling charms, actually control destiny (or, what amounts to the same thing, the

Macbeth and Banquo encounter the weird sisters (1.3). From Raphael Holinshed, *The Firste Volume of the Chronicles of England, Scotlande, and Irelande* (1577).

tragedy's plot)? What is the nature of these strange creatures that "look not like th'inhabitants o'th' earth," as Banquo observes, "and yet are on't" (1.3.39–40)?

Actors' responses to these questions have ranged wildly, though virtually all productions have recognized that the witches' scenes are among the most theatrically powerful and compelling in the play and that it matters a great deal whether they are made up to look grotesque or stately, perversely comical or terrifying. Scholarly responses have been complicated by the high probability that not all of the witchcraft scenes are by Shakespeare himself: it appears that 3.5 and part of 4.1, the scenes featuring the goddess Hecate, were added to the play some time after its first performance and incorporate songs derived from Thomas Middleton's play *The Witch*. (The Folio text of *Macbeth* cites only the first words of these songs, which are given in full in this edition.) But even if we set aside the problems raised by these interpolated scenes, the status of the witches in Shakespeare's play remains uncertain and seems to be so by design. "What are you?" asks Macbeth when he first encounters the eerie, sexually ambiguous figures, and he receives in reply his own name: "All hail, Macbeth" (1.3.45–46). Banquo urgently renews the inquiry, asking the creatures before his eyes if they truly exist or are only figments of his imagination; but his question, too, remains unanswered. When Macbeth and Banquo demand to know more, the witches vanish: "what seemed corporal / Melted as breath into the wind" (1.3.79–80). "As breath into the wind"—*Macbeth* is a tragedy of meltings, vanishing boundaries, and liminal states.

Much of the play transpires on the border between fantasy and reality, a sickening betwixt and between where a "horrid image" in the mind has the uncanny power to produce bodily effects "against the use of nature" (1.3.134, 136), where one mind is present to the innermost fantasies of another, where manhood threatens to vanish and murdered men walk and blood cannot be washed off. If these effects could be unequivocally attributed to the agency of the witches, the audience would at least have the security of a defined and focused fear. Alternatively, if the witches could be definitively dismissed as fantasy or fraud, the audience would at least have the clear-eyed certainty of witnessing human causes in an altogether secular world. But instead, Shakespeare achieves the remarkable effect of a nebulous infection, a bleeding of the demonic into the secular and the secular into the demonic.

The most famous instance of this effect is Lady Macbeth's great invocation of the "spirits / That tend on mortal thoughts" (1.5.38–39) to unsex her, fill her with cruelty, make thick her blood, and exchange her milk for gall. The speech appears to be a conjuration of demonic powers, an act of witchcraft in which the "murd'ring ministers" (1.5.46) are directed to bring about a set of changes in her body. She calls these ministers "sightless substances" (1.5.47): though invisible, they are—as she conceives them—not figures of speech or projections of her mind, but objective, substantial beings or forces. (Macbeth similarly seems to imagine invisible but objective forces when he speaks of "the sightless couriers of the air," 1.7.23.) But the fact that the spirits she invokes are "sightless" already moves this passage away from the literal existence of the weird sisters and toward the metaphorical use of "spirits" in her speech of a few moments earlier: "Hie thee hither, / That I may pour my spirits in thine ear" (1.5.23–24). The spirits she speaks of here are manifestly figurative—they refer to the bold words, the undaunted mettle, and the sexual taunts with which she intends to incite Macbeth to murder Duncan—but, like all of her expressions of will and passion, they strain toward bodily realization, even as they convey a psychic and hence invisible inwardness. That is, there is something uncannily literal about Lady Macbeth's influence on her husband, as if marital intimacy were akin to demonic possession, as if she had contrived to inhabit his mind, as if, in other words, she had literally poured her spirits in his ear. Conversely, there is something uncannily figurative about the "sightless substances" she invokes, as if the spirit world, the realm of "fate and metaphysical aid," were only a metaphor for her blind and murderous desires, as if the weird sisters were condensations of her own breath.

Witchcraft in Scotland. From *Newes from Scotland* (1591).

In Shakespeare's plays, as in those of his contemporaries, evildoers may wreak havoc for a time, but in the final restoration of order and justice, they and their principal accomplices are almost inevitably punished. Thus, at the close of *Macbeth,* not only are Macbeth and Lady Macbeth dead, but the victorious Malcolm also speaks of settling scores with "the cruel ministers / Of this dead butcher and his fiend-like queen" (5.11.34–35). Yet though the play has deeply implicated the witches in Macbeth's monstrous assault on the fabric of civilized life, there is no gesture toward punishing them, no sign that the victors are even aware of their existence. This omission is the more striking if we recall that at the time Shakespeare wrote his play, the authorities in England and Scotland were bringing women to trial on charges of witchcraft and executing them. The theatrical power of *Macbeth* seems bound up with its refusal to resolve the questions raised by the witches. At once marginal and central to the play, they are only briefly and intermittently onstage, but they are still suggestively present when we cannot see them, when the threats they embody are absorbed in the ordinary relations of everyday life.

"There's no art / To find the mind's construction in the face" (1.4.11–12), says the baffled Duncan about a man who had betrayed his trust, but Macbeth confronts a deeper perplexity, an appalling mystery within himself:

My thought, whose murder yet is but fantastical,
Shakes so my single state of man that function
Is smothered in surmise, and nothing is
But what is not.

(1.3.138–41)

The witches have something to do with this inner torment, but what that something is remains as elusive as the dagger that Macbeth sees before him, handle toward his hand. Scotland is sick, "almost afraid to know itself" (4.3.166). But the sickness cannot be isolated in a conspiracy of witches. If violence stirs in the hinterlands, where marauding armies struggle, it breeds more murderously still in the inmost circles of the realm, where the ruler feels most secure: "This castle hath a pleasant seat," says Duncan, going unwittingly to his death:

> The air
> Nimbly and sweetly recommends itself
> Unto our gentle senses.
>
> (1.6.1–3)

If the mind is subject to "supernatural soliciting" (1.3.129) from some bizarre place, it is gripped still more terribly and irresistibly by "horrible imaginings" (1.3.137) from within. If there is sexual disturbance out on the heath, where the bearded hags stir the ingredients of their hideous caldron, there is deeper sexual disturbance at home, in the murderous intimacy of the marriage bond: "When you durst do it, then you were a man" (1.7.49). If you are worried about losing your manhood, it is not enough to hunt for witches; look to your wife. If you are anxious about your future, scrutinize your best friends: "He was a gentleman on whom I built / An absolute trust" (1.4.13–14). If you are worried about interior temptation, fear your own dreams:

> Merciful powers,
> Restrain in me the cursèd thoughts that nature
> Gives way to in repose.
>
> (2.1.7–9)

And if you fear spiritual desolation, turn your eyes on the contents not only of the hideous caldron but of your skull: "O, full of scorpions is my mind, dear wife!" (3.2.37).

The men who persecuted witches in Shakespeare's age were determined to compel full confessions, to pass judgment, and to escape from the terror of the inexplicable, the unforeseen, the aimlessly malignant. In *Macbeth,* the audience is given something better than confession, for it has visible proof of the demonic in action, but this visibility turns out to be as maddeningly equivocal or frustrating as the witches' riddling words. The "wayward" witches appear and disappear, their promises and prophecies all tricks, like practical jokes with appalling consequences. The language of the play subverts the illusory certainties of sight, and the forces of renewed order, Malcolm and Macduff, are themselves strangely unstable. Malcolm, who spins an elaborate fantasy of his own viciousness, and Macduff, who abandons his wife and children to their slaughter, are peculiar emblems of a renewed, divinely sanctioned order. Shakespeare may have set out to flatter the King, but it is difficult to see how the King, if he paid any attention to the tragedy that the King's Men offered him, could be reassured. The ambiguities of demonic agency are never resolved, and its horror spreads like a mist through a murky landscape. "What is't you do?" Macbeth asks the weird sisters. "A deed without a name" (4.1.65).

By the play's close, Macbeth has begun "to doubt th'equivocation of the fiend, / That lies like truth" (5.5.41–42). Equivocations are lies with mental reservations, words with double meanings, puns, twists of emphasis, and plays on false interpretations (such as the meaning of the phrase "not of woman born"). Like the witches—and, for that matter, like concepts of gender and authority and social order—language in *Macbeth* is a boundary stalker, neither a trustworthy guide nor a manifest illusion. Words sit dangerously in a middle ground; they must be brought under control, but they always threaten to slide into lies or magic charms or riddles or sheer emptiness. It is this emptiness with which Macbeth seems haunted at the end, with his vision of life as

> a tale
> Told by an idiot, full of sound and fury,
> Signifying nothing.
>
> (5.5.25–27)

If the closing moments of the play invite us to recoil from this black hole—after all, the tyrant is killed—they invite us to recoil from too confident and simple a celebration of the triumph of grace. For somewhere beyond the immediate circle of order restored, the witches are dancing around the caldron, and, the play seems to imply, the caldron is in every one of us.

STEPHEN GREENBLATT

TEXTUAL NOTE

The only authoritative text of *Macbeth* is the First Folio (1623), which consequently serves as the control text in this edition. Scholars generally agree that the Folio version (F) was based on a promptbook, a transcript derived, in all likelihood, from Shakespeare's rough draft of the play. F appears to be a fairly reliable record of its manuscript source, the promptbook.

There are, however, signs that this source was itself an abbreviated version of the play as first written and performed, for the text in F is considerably shorter than that of any of the other major tragedies. Moreover, the Folio's *Macbeth* appears to be a version of the play revised, sometime after Shakespeare had ceased to be active with the King's Men, for a court performance in the presence of King James. Scholars have long suspected that it contains material not by Shakespeare. In particular, the two songs referred to in 3.5 and 4.1 of F only by their opening phrases ("Come away, come away, &c.," "Blacke Spirits, &c.") are very likely by the playwright Thomas Middleton. Songs with the same opening phrases appear in a manuscript of Middleton's unsuccessful play *The Witch* (c. 1613) and are restored in full in this edition of *Macbeth*.

Middleton may have been personally responsible for the revision of *Macbeth* reflected in the Folio text. He could, in addition to the songs, have added all of 3.5 (which seems to diverge stylistically from the rest of the play) as well as parts of 4.1, particularly Hecate's speeches.

SELECTED BIBLIOGRAPHY

Adelman, Janet. "'Born of Woman': Fantasies of Maternal Power in *Macbeth*." *Cannibals, Witches, and Divorce: Estranging the Renaissance*. Ed. Marjorie Garber. Baltimore: Johns Hopkins University Press, 1987. 90–121. *Macbeth* represents dueling fantasies of absolute, destructive female power and of escape from that power; masculine authority is consolidated in the end by eliminating the feminine.

Bradley, A. C. *Shakespearean Tragedy: Lectures on "Hamlet," "Othello," "King Lear," "Macbeth."* London: Macmillan, 1905. The most concentrated, classical, and fast-paced of Shakespeare's great tragedies, *Macbeth* produces unequaled dread with its dark atmosphere and sublime central characters.

Calderwood, James L. *If It Were Done: "Macbeth" and Tragic Action*. Amherst: University of Massachusetts Press, 1986. *Macbeth* subverts the models of *Hamlet* and Aristotelian poetics, interrogating the nature of tragedy and the role of violence as both a threat to and a source of social order.

Greenblatt, Stephen. "Shakespeare Bewitched." *New Historical Literary Study: Essays on Reproducing Texts, Representing History*. Ed. Jeffrey N. Cox and Larry J. Reynolds. Princeton: Princeton University Press, 1993. 108–35. In writing *Macbeth*, Shakespeare drew both upon the King's belief in witchcraft and upon a skeptical critique of such belief by Reginald Scot.

Howard, Jean E. "Shakespeare, Geography, and the Work of Genre on the Early Modern Stage." *Modern Language Quarterly* 64.3 (2003): 299–322. Scotland's mingled contemporary reputation for nobility and savagery allowed Shakespeare to desacralize kingship.

Kastan, David Scott. "Macbeth and the 'Name of the King.'" *Shakespeare After Theory*. New York: Routledge, 1999. 165–82. Insistent doubling, blending the figures of the king and tyrant, undermines the attempt in *Macbeth* to contain violence by restoring moral order.

Mullaney, Steven. "Lying Like Truth: Riddle, Representation, and Treason." *The Place of the Stage: License, Play, and Power in Renaissance England*. Chicago: University of Chicago Press, 1988. 116–34. Like the Jacobean spectacle of a traitor on the scaffold, *Macbeth* reveals the generative power of equivocation, challenging the absolutes of royal authority.

Norbrook, David. "Macbeth and the Politics of Historiography." *Politics of Discourse: The Literature and History of Seventeenth-Century England*. Ed. Kevin Sharpe and Steven N. Zwicker. Berkeley: University of California Press, 1987. 78–116. Embroiled in seventeenth-century debates over writing Scottish history, Shakespeare raised the specter of justified regicide even as he drew on King James's monarchist views.

Orgel, Stephen. "Macbeth and the Antic Round." *The Authentic Shakespeare, and Other Problems of the Early Modern Stage*. New York: Routledge, 2002. 159–72. Revisions to the witches' scenes link theatrical spectacle to psychological inwardness and heighten the paradoxical role of women.

Wells, Robin Headlam. "'Arms and the Man': *Macbeth*." *Shakespeare on Masculinity*. New York: Cambridge University Press, 2000. 117–43. *Macbeth* blurs Gospel and classical epic conceptions of manhood, questioning the terms of King James's rule.

FILMS

Macbeth. 1948. Dir. Orson Welles. USA. 107 min. Expressionist, low-budget production, starring Welles and Jeanette Nolan.

Throne of Blood. 1957. Dir. Akira Kurosawa. Japan. 105 min. Kabuki-influenced production set in feudal Japan stars Toshirô Mifune and Isuzu Yamada.

Macbeth. 1971. Dir. Roman Polanski. UK/USA. 140 min. Bleak, misty, bloody vision, with strikingly young leads Jon Finch and Francesca Annis.

Macbeth. 1979. Dir. Philip Casson. UK. 146 min. Minimalist production for television with doubling actors and simple sets. Ian McKellen and Judi Dench star.

Scotland, PA. 2001. Dir. Billy Morrissette. USA. 104 min. Comic recasting in a 1970s American fast-food joint.

The Tragedy of Macbeth

THE PERSONS OF THE PLAY

KING DUNCAN of Scotland

MALCOLM
DONALBAIN } his sons

A CAPTAIN in Duncan's army

MACBETH, Thane of Glamis, later Thane of Cawdor, then King of Scotland

A PORTER at Macbeth's castle

Three MURDERERS attending on Macbeth

SEYTON, servant of Macbeth

LADY MACBETH, Macbeth's wife

A DOCTOR of Physic
A Waiting-GENTLEWOMAN } attending on Lady Macbeth

BANQUO, a Scottish thane

FLEANCE, his son

MACDUFF, Thane of Fife

LADY MACDUFF, his wife

MACDUFF'S SON

LENNOX
ROSS
ANGUS } Scottish Thanes
CAITHNESS

MENTEITH

SIWARD, Earl of Northumberland

YOUNG SIWARD, his son

An English DOCTOR

HECATE, Queen of the Witches

Six WITCHES

Three APPARITIONS, one an armed head, one a bloody child, one a child crowned

A SPIRIT LIKE A CAT

Other SPIRITS

An OLD MAN

A MESSENGER

MURDERERS

SERVANTS

A show of eight kings; Lords and Thanes, attendants, soldiers, drummers

1.1

Thunder and lightning. Enter three WITCHES

FIRST WITCH   When shall we three meet again?
 In thunder, lightning, or in rain?[1]

SECOND WITCH   When the hurly-burly's° done,   *tumult is*
 When the battle's lost and won.

5 THIRD WITCH   That will be ere the set of sun.

1.1 Location: An open place.

1. Witches were thought to be able to cause bad weather.

FIRST WITCH   Where the place?
SECOND WITCH   Upon the heath.
THIRD WITCH   There to meet with Macbeth.
FIRST WITCH   I come, Grimalkin.
SECOND WITCH   Paddock² calls.
THIRD WITCH   Anon.°   *At once*
10 ALL   Fair is foul, and foul is fair,
      Hover through the fog and filthy air.   *Exeunt*

1.2

Alarum within. Enter KING [DUNCAN], MALCOLM, DON-
ALBAIN, LENNOX, *with attendants, meeting a bleeding*
      CAPTAIN°   *staff officer*

KING DUNCAN   What bloody man is that? He can report,
      As seemeth by his plight, of the revolt
      The newest state.
MALCOLM   This is the sergeant
      Who like a good and hardy soldier fought
5   'Gainst my captivity. Hail, brave friend.
      Say to the King the knowledge of the broil°   *battle*
      As thou didst leave it.
CAPTAIN   Doubtful it stood,
      As two spent° swimmers that do cling together   *exhausted*
      And choke their art.¹ The merciless Macdonald—
10   Worthy to be a rebel, for to that°   *that end*
      The multiplying villainies of nature²
      Do swarm upon him—from the Western Isles°   *Hebrides and Ireland*
      Of kerns and galloglasses³ is supplied,
      And fortune on his damnèd quarry⁴ smiling
15   Showed° like a rebel's whore. But all's too weak,   *Appeared*
      For brave Macbeth—well he deserves that name!°—   *epithet*
      Disdaining fortune, with his brandished steel
      Which smoked with bloody execution,
      Like valour's minion°   *favorite*
20   Carved out his passage till he faced the slave,°   *(Macdonald)*
      Which° ne'er shook hands nor bade farewell to him   *Who*
      Till he unseamed him from the nave to th' chops⁵
      And fixed his head upon our battlements.
KING DUNCAN   O valiant cousin,° worthy gentleman!   *kinsman*
25 CAPTAIN   As whence the sun 'gins his reflection⁶
      Shipwrecking storms and direful thunders break,
      So from that spring° whence comfort seemed to come   *source; (season)*
      Discomfort swells.° Mark, King of Scotland, mark.   *wells up*
      No sooner justice had, with valour armed,
30   Compelled these skipping° kerns to trust their heels   *mobile; fleeing*
      But the Norwegian lord, surveying vantage,°   *seeing his chance*
      With furbished° arms and new supplies of men   *polished*
      Began a fresh assault.
KING DUNCAN   Dismayed not this our captains, Macbeth and Banquo?

---

2. Paddock, a toad, and Grimalkin, a gray cat, are the
witches' familiars, or attendant evil spirits.
1.2 Location: A camp near the battlefield.
1. And confound their skill in swimming.
2. The evil aspects of his own nature; the villainous
progeny of nature (the mercenaries).
3. *kerns:* lightly armed Irish foot soldiers. *galloglasses:*
ax-wielding horsemen.

4. Its condemned victim. Fortune smiled temporarily
on Macdonald, although it had already marked him for
destruction. Many editions emend "quarry" to "quarrel."
5. Ripped him open from the navel to the jaw, as one
would rip open the seam of a garment.
6. Begins its return after the spring equinox, thought to
cause turbulent weather.

35	CAPTAIN Yes, as sparrows eagles, or the hare the lion!	
	If I say sooth I must report they were	
	As cannons overcharged with double cracks,[7]	
	So they doubly redoubled strokes upon the foe.	
	Except° they meant to bathe in reeking wounds	*Unless*
40	Or memorize another Golgotha,[8]	
	I cannot tell—	
	But I am faint. My gashes cry for help.	
	KING DUNCAN So well thy words become thee as thy wounds:	
	They smack of honour both.—Go get him surgeons.	

                          [Exit CAPTAIN *with attendants]*

          Enter ROSS *and* ANGUS

	Who comes here?	
45	MALCOLM The worthy Thane[9] of Ross.	
	LENNOX What haste looks through his eyes! So should he look	
	That seems to° speak things strange.	*seems about to*
	ROSS God save the King.	
	KING DUNCAN Whence cam'st thou, worthy thane?	
	ROSS From Fife, great King,	
	Where the Norwegian banners flout° the sky	*mock*
50	And fan our people cold.°	*cold with fear*
	Norway° himself, with terrible numbers,	*The King of Norway*
	Assisted by that most disloyal traitor	
	The Thane of Cawdor, began a dismal° conflict,	*an ominous*
	Till that° Bellona's bridegroom,[1] lapped in proof,[2]	*Until*
55	Confronted him with self-comparisons,°	*comparable deeds*
	Point° against point, rebellious arm 'gainst arm,	*Swordpoint*
	Curbing his lavish° spirit; and to conclude,	*wild*
	The victory fell on us—	
	KING DUNCAN Great happiness.	
	ROSS	
	Sweno, the Norways'° king, craves composition;°	*Norwegians' / a truce*
60	Nor would we deign him burial of his men	
	Till he disbursèd at Saint Colum's inch[3]	
	Ten thousand dollars[4] to our general use.	
	KING DUNCAN No more that Thane of Cawdor shall deceive	
	Our bosom interest.[5] Go pronounce his present° death,	*immediate*
65	And with his former title greet Macbeth.	
	ROSS I'll see it done.	
	KING DUNCAN What he hath lost, noble Macbeth hath won.	

                          Exeunt severally°   *separately*

1.3

Thunder. Enter the three WITCHES

FIRST WITCH   Where hast thou been, sister?

SECOND WITCH   Killing swine.

THIRD WITCH   Sister, where thou?

FIRST WITCH   A sailor's wife had chestnuts in her lap,

And munched, and munched, and munched. 'Give me,' quoth I.

---

7. Overloaded with double charges of gunpowder.
8. Or make the battlefield as memorable as Golgotha, the "place of skulls" where Jesus was crucified.
9. Title of Scottish nobility.
1. Macbeth, imagined as husband to Bellona, the Roman goddess of war.
2. Clad in tested armor.

3. Incholm, the island of St. Columba in the Firth of Forth.
4. German and Spanish coins (first minted in the sixteenth century, five hundred years before the events of the play).
5. Our closest concerns.
1.3 Location: An open place.

5   'Aroint thee,° witch,' the rump-fed runnion¹ cries.   *Begone*
       Her husband's to Aleppo gone, master o'th' *Tiger*.
       But in a sieve I'll thither sail,
       And like a rat without a tail
       I'll do, I'll do, and I'll do.
10   SECOND WITCH   I'll give thee a wind.
       FIRST WITCH   Thou'rt kind.
       THIRD WITCH   And I another.
       FIRST WITCH   I myself have all the other,°   *others*
       And the very ports they blow,°   *blow from*
15   All the quarters° that they know   *directions*
       I'th' shipman's card.°   *compass card*
       I'll drain him dry as hay.
       Sleep shall neither night nor day
       Hang upon his penthouse lid.²
20   He shall live a man forbid.°   *cursed*
       Weary sennights° nine times nine   *weeks*
       Shall he dwindle, peak,° and pine.   *waste away*
       Though his barque cannot be lost,
       Yet it shall be tempest-tossed.
       Look what I have.
25   SECOND WITCH   Show me, show me.
       FIRST WITCH   Here I have a pilot's thumb,
       Wrecked as homeward he did come.
                 Drum within
       THIRD WITCH   A drum, a drum—
       Macbeth doth come.
30   ALL [*dancing in a ring*]   The weird³ sisters hand in hand,
       Posters° of the sea and land,   *Swift travelers*
       Thus do go about, about,
       Thrice to thine, and thrice to mine,
       And thrice again to make up nine.
35   Peace! The charm's wound up.
                 Enter MACBETH *and* BANQUO
       MACBETH   So foul and fair a day I have not seen.
       BANQUO   How far is't called° to Forres?—What are these,   *said to be*
       So withered, and so wild in their attire,
       That look not like th'inhabitants o'th' earth
40   And yet are on't?—Live you, or are you aught
       That man may question?° You seem to understand me   *converse with*
       By each at once her choppy° finger laying   *chapped*
       Upon her skinny lips. You should be women,
       And yet your beards forbid me to interpret
       That you are so.
45   MACBETH [*to the* WITCHES]   Speak, if you can. What are you?
       FIRST WITCH   All hail, Macbeth! Hail to thee, Thane of Glamis.
       SECOND WITCH   All hail, Macbeth! Hail to thee, Thane of Cawdor.
       THIRD WITCH   All hail, Macbeth, that shalt be king hereafter!
       BANQUO   Good sir, why do you start and seem to fear
50   Things that do sound so fair? [*To the* WITCHES] I'th' name of truth,
       Are ye fantastical° or that indeed   *imaginary*

---

1. The fat-rumped, mangy slut.   3. F: "weyward," from the Old English "wyrd," meaning
2. Eyelid, which projects out over the eye like the slop-   "fate."
ing roof of a penthouse.

Which outwardly ye show? My noble partner
You greet with present grace° and great prediction   *title*
Of noble having° and of royal hope,   *estate*
55 That he seems rapt withal.[4] To me you speak not.
If you can look into the seeds of time
And say which grain will grow and which will not,
Speak then to me, who neither beg nor fear
Your favours nor your hate.
60 FIRST WITCH   Hail!
SECOND WITCH   Hail!
THIRD WITCH   Hail!
FIRST WITCH   Lesser than Macbeth, and greater.
SECOND WITCH   Not so happy,° yet much happier.   *fortunate*
65 THIRD WITCH   Thou shalt get° kings, though thou be none.   *beget*
So all hail, Macbeth and Banquo!
FIRST WITCH   Banquo and Macbeth, all hail!
MACBETH   Stay, you imperfect° speakers, tell me more.   *incomplete*
By Sinel's° death I know I am Thane of Glamis,   *Macbeth's father*
70 But how of Cawdor? The Thane of Cawdor lives,
A prosperous gentleman, and to be king
Stands not within the prospect of belief,
No more than to be Cawdor. Say from whence
You owe° this strange intelligence,° or why   *possess / information*
75 Upon this blasted° heath you stop our way   *blighted*
With such prophetic greeting. Speak, I charge you.
        [*The*] WITCHES *vanish*
BANQUO   The earth hath bubbles, as the water has,
And these are of them. Whither are they vanished?
MACBETH   Into the air, and what seemed corporal°   *corporeal*
80 Melted as breath into the wind. Would they had stayed.
BANQUO   Were such things here as we do speak about,
Or have we eaten on the insane root[5]
That takes the reason prisoner?
MACBETH   Your children shall be kings.
BANQUO   You shall be king.
85 MACBETH   And Thane of Cawdor too. Went it not so?
BANQUO   To th' self-same tune and words. Who's here?
        Enter ROSS *and* ANGUS
ROSS   The King hath happily received, Macbeth,
The news of thy success, and when he reads°   *considers*
Thy personal venture° in the rebels' sight   *exploits*
90 His wonders and his praises do contend
Which should be thine or his; silenced with that,[6]
In viewing o'er the rest o'th' self-same day
He finds thee in the stout Norwegian ranks,
Nothing° afeard of what thyself didst make,   *Not at all*
95 Strange images° of death. As thick as hail   *forms*
Came post° with post, and every one did bear   *messenger*
Thy praises in his kingdom's great defence,
And poured them down before him.
ANGUS [*to* MACBETH]   We are sent

4. He seems entranced by these predictions.
5. Of the root causing insanity, possibly hemlock.
6. *His wonders . . . that*: Duncan does not know whether   to speak of his astonishment or his admiration, and so
                                                                 is silent.

To give thee from our royal master thanks;
100   Only to herald thee into his sight,
Not pay thee.
ROSS   And, for an earnest° of a greater honour,   *a pledge*
He bade me from him call thee Thane of Cawdor,
In which addition,° hail, most worthy thane,   *title*
For it is thine.
105 BANQUO   What, can the devil speak true?
MACBETH   The Thane of Cawdor lives. Why do you dress me
In borrowed robes?
ANGUS   Who was the thane lives yet,
But under heavy judgement bears that life
Which he deserves to lose. Whether he was combined°   *allied*
110 With those of Norway, or did line the rebel°   *support Macdonald*
With hidden help and vantage,° or that with both   *benefit*
He laboured in his country's wrack,[7] I know not;
But treasons capital, confessed, and proved
Have overthrown him.
MACBETH [*aside*]   Glamis, and Thane of Cawdor.
115 The greatest is behind.° [*To* ROSS *and* ANGUS] Thanks for your pains.   *to come*
[*To* BANQUO] Do you not hope your children shall be kings
When those that gave the thane of Cawdor to me
Promised no less to them?
BANQUO   That, trusted home,°   *completely*
Might yet enkindle° you unto the crown,   *encourage*
120 Besides the thane of Cawdor. But 'tis strange,
And oftentimes to win us to our harm
The instruments of darkness tell us truths,
Win us with honest trifles to betray's°   *betray us*
In deepest consequence.
125 [*To* ROSS *and* ANGUS] Cousins, a word, I pray you.
MACBETH [*aside*]   Two truths are told
As happy prologues to the swelling act[8]
Of the imperial theme [*To* ROSS *and* ANGUS] I thank you, gentlemen.
[*Aside*] This supernatural soliciting°   *temptation*
130 Cannot be ill, cannot be good. If ill,
Why hath it given me earnest of success
Commencing in a truth? I am Thane of Cawdor.
If good, why do I yield to that suggestion
Whose horrid image doth unfix my hair
135 And make my seated heart knock at my ribs
Against the use° of nature? Present fears   *custom*
Are less than horrible imaginings.
My thought, whose murder yet is but fantastical,[9]
Shakes so my single state of man[1] that function°   *capacity to act*
140 Is smothered in surmise,° and nothing is   *speculation*
But what is not.
BANQUO [*to* ROSS *and* ANGUS]
       Look how our partner's rapt.
MACBETH [*aside*]   If chance will have me king, why, chance may crown me
Without my stir.°   *effort*

7. He worked to bring about his country's ruin.
8. To the developing action, or climactic dramatic action.
9. In which murder is so far only a fantasy.

1. My undivided self. Macbeth feels that his wholeness is coming apart under the pressure of his criminal thought.

BANQUO [*to* ROSS *and* ANGUS]
              New honours come upon him,
    Like our strange° garments, cleave not to their mould°   *new / wearer's form*
    But with the aid of use.

145 MACBETH [*aside*]   Come what come may,
    Time and the hour runs through the roughest day.²

BANQUO   Worthy Macbeth, we stay° upon your leisure.   *wait; attend*

MACBETH   Give me your favour.° My dull brain was wrought°   *pardon / agitated*
    With things forgotten. [*To* ROSS *and* ANGUS] Kind gentlemen,
      your pains

150   Are registered° where every day I turn   *recorded (in my memory)*
    The leaf to read them. Let us toward the King.
    [*Aside to* BANQUO] Think upon what hath chanced, and at
      more time,
    The interim having weighed it, let us speak
    Our free hearts° each to other.   *unconcealed thoughts*

155 BANQUO   Very gladly.

MACBETH   Till then, enough. [*To* ROSS *and* ANGUS] Come, friends.
                                     Exeunt

1.4

Flourish. Enter KING [DUNCAN], LENNOX, MALCOLM,
    DONALBAIN, *and attendants*

KING DUNCAN   Is execution done on Cawdor? Are not
    Those in commission¹ yet returned?

MALCOLM   My liege,
    They are not yet come back. But I have spoke
    With one that saw him die, who did report

5   That very frankly he confessed his treasons,
    Implored your highness' pardon, and set forth
    A deep repentance. Nothing in his life
    Became him like the leaving it. He died
    As one that had been studied° in his death   *practiced*

10   To throw away the dearest thing he owed°   *owned*
    As 'twere a careless° trifle.   *an uncared-for*

KING DUNCAN   There's no art
    To find the mind's construction in the face.
    He was a gentleman on whom I built
    An absolute trust.
        Enter MACBETH, BANQUO, ROSS, *and* ANGUS
    [*To* MACBETH] O worthiest cousin,

15   The sin of my ingratitude even now
    Was heavy on me! Thou art so far before°   *ahead*
    That swiftest wing of recompense is slow
    To overtake thee. Would thou hadst less deserved,
    That the proportion both of thanks and payment

20   Might have been mine.² Only I have left to say,
    'More is thy due than more than all can pay'.

MACBETH   The service and the loyalty I owe,
    In doing it, pays itself. Your highness' part
    Is to receive our duties, and our duties

---

2. *Come . . . day:* What must happen will happen one
way or another.
1.4 Location: A camp near the battlefield.

1. Those charged to execute Cawdor.
2. *That . . . mine:* That the King's rewards would be generously proportional to Macbeth's dessert.

25   Are to your throne and state children and servants
       Which do but what they should by doing everything
       Safe toward° your love and honour.   *To safeguard*
KING DUNCAN   Welcome hither.
       I have begun to plant thee, and will labour
       To make thee full of growing.—Noble Banquo,
30   That hast no less deserved, nor must be known
       No less to have done so, let me enfold thee
       And hold thee to my heart.
BANQUO   There if I grow
       The harvest is your own.
KING DUNCAN   My plenteous joys,
       Wanton° in fullness, seek to hide themselves   *Unrestrained*
35   In drops of sorrow. Sons, kinsmen, thanes,
       And you whose places are the nearest,° know   *nearest to the throne*
       We will establish our estate³ upon
       Our eldest, Malcolm, whom we name hereafter
       The Prince of Cumberland;⁴ which honour must
40   Not unaccompanied invest him only,⁵
       But signs of nobleness, like stars, shall shine
       On all deservers. [*To* MACBETH] From hence to Inverness,°   *Macbeth's estate*
       And bind us further to you.⁶
MACBETH   The rest is labour which is not used for you.⁷
45   I'll be myself the harbinger,⁸ and make joyful
       The hearing of my wife with your approach;
       So humbly take my leave.
KING DUNCAN   My worthy Cawdor.
MACBETH [*aside*]   The Prince of Cumberland—that is a step
       On which I must fall down or else o'erleap,
50   For in my way it lies. Stars, hide your fires,
       Let not light see my black and deep desires;
       The eye wink at the hand;⁹ yet let that be°   *be done*
       Which the eye fears, when it is done, to see.   *Exit*
KING DUNCAN   True, worthy Banquo, he is full so valiant,¹
55   And in his commendations I am fed.
       It is a banquet to me. Let's after him,
       Whose care is gone before to bid us welcome.
       It is a peerless kinsman.   *Flourish. Exeunt*

1.5

                Enter [LADY MACBETH,] *with a letter*
LADY MACBETH [*reading*]   'They met me in the day of success,
       and I have learned by the perfect'st° report they have more in   *most accurate*
       them than mortal knowledge. When I burned in desire to ques-
       tion them further, they made themselves air, into which they
5   vanished. Whiles I stood rapt in the wonder of it came missives°   *messengers*
       from the King, who all-hailed me "Thane of Cawdor", by
       which title before these weird sisters saluted me, and referred
       me to the coming on of time with "Hail, King that shalt be!"

---

3. We will settle the succession of the kingdom. At the
time, the Scottish crown was not hereditary.
4. Title of the Scottish heir apparent.
5. *which . . . only:* honors will not be bestowed on
Malcolm alone.
6. And make me further indebted to you by your hospitality.

7. Even repose seems wearisome when it is not dedicated to your purposes.
8. Forerunner; messenger sent ahead to arrange royal
lodgings.
9. Let the eye deliberately ignore what the hand does.
1. As valiant as you say.
1.5 Location: Inverness, Macbeth's castle.

This have I thought good to deliver° thee, my dearest partner   *inform*
10 of greatness, that thou mightst not lose the dues of rejoicing
by being ignorant of what greatness is promised thee. Lay it
to thy heart, and farewell.'
Glamis thou art, and Cawdor, and shalt be
What thou art promised. Yet do I fear° thy nature.   *doubt*
15 It is too full o'th' milk of human kindness
To catch the nearest° way. Thou wouldst be great,   *most expedient*
Art not without ambition, but without
The illness° should attend it. What thou wouldst highly,   *wickedness (that)*
That wouldst thou holily; wouldst not play false,
20 And yet wouldst wrongly win. Thou'dst have, great Glamis,
That which cries 'Thus thou must do' if thou have it,
And that which rather thou dost fear to do
Than wishest should be undone. Hie° thee hither,   *Hasten*
That I may pour my spirits in thine ear
25 And chastise with the valour of my tongue
All that impedes thee from the golden round°   *crown*
Which fate and metaphysical° aid doth seem   *supernatural*
To have thee crowned withal.°   *with*
     Enter [a SERVANT*]*
                             What is your tidings?
SERVANT   The King comes here tonight.
LADY MACBETH   Thou'rt mad to say it.
30 Is not thy master with him, who, were't so,
Would have informed for preparation?
SERVANT   So please you, it is true. Our thane is coming,
One of my fellows had the speed of° him,   *outdistanced*
Who, almost dead for breath, had scarcely more
Than would make up his message.
35 LADY MACBETH   Give him tending;
He brings great news.   *Exit [*SERVANT*]*
                 The raven[1] himself is hoarse
That croaks the fatal entrance of Duncan
Under my battlements. Come, you spirits
That tend on mortal° thoughts, unsex me here,   *attend deadly*
40 And fill me from the crown to the toe top-full
Of direst cruelty. Make thick my blood,
Stop up th'access and passage to remorse,°   *pity*
That no compunctious visitings of nature
Shake my fell° purpose, nor keep peace° between   *cruel / intervene*
45 Th'effect and it.[2] Come to my woman's breasts,
And take my milk for° gall, you murd'ring ministers,°   *in exchange for / agents*
Wherever in your sightless° substances   *invisible*
You wait on° nature's mischief. Come, thick night,   *assist*
And pall° thee in the dunnest° smoke of hell,   *envelop / darkest*
50 That my keen knife see not the wound it makes,
Nor heaven peep through the blanket of the dark
To cry 'Hold, hold!'
     Enter MACBETH
          Great Glamis, worthy Cawdor,
Greater than both by the all-hail hereafter,

---

1. The raven was considered a bird of ill omen.   2. My purpose and its accomplishment.

Thy letters have transported me beyond
55 This ignorant present, and I feel now
The future in the instant.
MACBETH   My dearest love,
Duncan comes here tonight.
LADY MACBETH   And when goes hence?
MACBETH   Tomorrow, as he purposes.
LADY MACBETH   O never
Shall sun that morrow see.
60 Your face, my thane, is as a book where men
May read strange matters. To beguile the time,
Look like the time;³ bear welcome in your eye,
Your hand, your tongue; look like the innocent flower,
But be the serpent under't. He that's coming
65 Must be provided for; and you shall put
This night's great business into my dispatch,°   management
Which shall to all our nights and days to come
Give solely sovereign sway and masterdom.
MACBETH   We will speak further.
LADY MACBETH   Only look up clear.°   appear innocent
70 To alter favour⁴ ever is to fear.
Leave all the rest to me.   Exeunt

1.6

Hautboys° *and torches. Enter* KING [DUNCAN], MAL-   Oboes
COLM, DONALBAIN, BANQUO, LENNOX, MACDUFF, ROSS,
ANGUS, *and attendants*
KING DUNCAN   This castle hath a pleasant seat.° The air   location
Nimbly and sweetly recommends itself
Unto our gentle senses.
BANQUO   This guest of summer,
The temple-haunting martlet,¹ does approve°   prove
5 By his loved mansionry° that the heavens' breath   nest building
Smells wooingly here. No jutty,° frieze,   projection
Buttress, nor coign of vantage° but this bird   convenient corner
Hath made his pendant bed and procreant° cradle;   for breeding
Where they most breed and haunt I have observed
The air is delicate.
Enter LADY [MACBETH]
10 KING DUNCAN   See, see, our honoured hostess!
The love that follows us sometime is our trouble,
Which still we thank as love.² Herein I teach you
How you shall bid God 'ield us for your pains,
And thank us for your trouble.³
LADY MACBETH   All our service
15 In every point twice done, and then done double,
Were° poor and single° business to contend   Would be / small
Against those honours deep and broad wherewith
Your majesty loads our house. For those of old,
And the late dignities heaped up to them,

---

3. *To . . . like the time:* To deceive the world, match your
expression to the occasion.
4. To alter your facial expression and thereby arouse
suspicion.
1.6 Location: Outside Macbeth's castle.

1. A bird, the martin, that often built its nest in churches.
2. *The . . . love:* Love bestowed upon us sometimes
causes us inconvenience, but we are still grateful for it.
3. *How . . . trouble:* Ask God to reward ("yield") me for
the trouble I cause you.

We rest your hermits.[4]

20 KING DUNCAN   Where's the Thane of Cawdor?
We coursed him at the heels,° and had a purpose   *followed him closely*
To be his purveyor;[5] but he rides well,
And his great love, sharp as his spur, hath holp° him   *helped*
To his home before us. Fair and noble hostess,
We are your guest tonight.

25 LADY MACBETH   Your servants ever
Have theirs, themselves, and what is theirs in count°   *in trust*
To make their audit at your highness' pleasure,
Still to return your own.[6]

KING DUNCAN   Give me your hand.
Conduct me to mine host. We love him highly,
30 And shall continue our graces towards him.
By your leave,[7] hostess.   *Exeunt*

1.7

Hautboys. Torches. Enter a sewer° and divers servants   *butler*
with dishes and service over the stage. Then enter MACBETH

MACBETH   If it were done when 'tis done, then 'twere well
It were done quickly. If th'assassination
Could trammel up the consequence, and catch
With his surcease success:[1] that but this blow
5 Might be the be-all and the end-all, here,°   *in this world*
But here upon this bank and shoal[2] of time,
We'd jump° the life to come. But in these cases   *risk*
We still have judgement[3] here, that° we but teach   *in that*
Bloody instructions which, being taught, return
10 To plague th'inventor. This even-handed° justice   *impartial*
Commends th'ingredience° of our poisoned chalice   *contents*
To our own lips. He's here in double trust:
First, as I am his kinsman and his subject,
Strong both against the deed; then, as his host,
15 Who should against his murderer shut the door,
Not bear the knife myself. Besides, this Duncan
Hath borne his faculties° so meek, hath been   *authority*
So clear° in his great office, that his virtues   *blameless*
Will plead like angels, trumpet-tongued against
20 The deep damnation of his taking-off,°   *murder*
And pity, like a naked new-born babe,
Striding the blast,[4] or heaven's cherubin, horsed
Upon the sightless couriers[5] of the air,
Shall blow the horrid deed in every eye

25   That tears shall drown the wind.⁶ I have no spur
        To prick the sides of my intent, but only
        Vaulting ambition which o'erleaps itself
        And falls on th'other.⁷
                        Enter LADY [MACBETH]
                        How now? What news?
        LADY MACBETH   He has almost supped. Why have you left the chamber?
        MACBETH   Hath he asked for me?
30   LADY MACBETH   Know you not he has?
        MACBETH   We will proceed no further in this business.
        He hath honoured me of late, and I have bought°   *won*
        Golden opinions from all sorts of people,
        Which would be worn now in their newest gloss,
        Not cast aside so soon.
35   LADY MACBETH   Was the hope drunk
        Wherein you dressed yourself? Hath it slept since?
        And wakes it now to look so green° and pale   *sickly*
        At what it did so freely? From this time
        Such I account thy love. Art thou afeard
40   To be the same in thine own act and valour
        As thou art in desire? Wouldst thou have that°   *(the crown)*
        Which thou esteem'st the ornament of life,
        And live a coward in thine own esteem,
        Letting 'I dare not' wait upon 'I would',
        Like the poor cat i'th' adage?⁸
45   MACBETH   Prithee, peace.
        I dare do all that may become a man;
        Who dares do more is none.
        LADY MACBETH   What beast was't then
        That made you break° this enterprise to me?   *broach*
        When you durst do it, then you were a man;
50   And to be more than what you were, you would
        Be so much more the man. Nor time nor place
        Did then adhere,° and yet you would make both.   *agree*
        They have made themselves, and that their fitness now
        Does unmake you. I have given suck, and know
55   How tender 'tis to love the babe that milks me.
        I would, while it was smiling in my face,
        Have plucked my nipple from his boneless gums
        And dashed the brains out, had I so sworn
        As you have done to this.
        MACBETH   If we should fail?
        LADY MACBETH   We fail!⁹
60   But screw your courage to the sticking-place¹
        And we'll not fail. When Duncan is asleep—
        Whereto the rather shall his day's hard journey
        Soundly invite him—his two chamberlains°   *bedroom attendants*
        Will I with wine and wassail° so convince°   *carousing / overpower*
65   That memory, the warder° of the brain,   *guard*
        Shall be a fume, and the receipt° of reason   *receptacle*

---

6. Tears will fall like heavy rain, which was believed to
still the wind.
7. The other side. The image is of a rider vaulting over
his horse instead of into his saddle, or of a horseman who
clears a high obstacle but falls on the other side.

8. Proverbial: "The cat would eat fish but does not dare
to wet her feet."
9. F: "faile?"
1. The notch on a crossbow that holds the string, which
is cranked or screwed taut.

A limbeck[2] only. When in swinish sleep
Their drenchèd natures lies as in a death,
What cannot you and I perform upon
70 Th'unguarded Duncan? What not put upon
His spongy officers, who shall bear the guilt
Of our great quell?°   *murder*

MACBETH   Bring forth men-children only,
For thy undaunted mettle° should compose   *substance*
Nothing but males. Will it not be received,°   *believed*
75 When we have marked with blood those sleepy two
Of his own chamber and used their very daggers,
That they have done't?

LADY MACBETH   Who dares receive it other,
As we shall make our griefs and clamour roar
Upon his death?

MACBETH   I am settled, and bend up
80 Each corporal° agent to this terrible feat.   *bodily*
Away, and mock° the time with fairest show.   *deceive*
False face must hide what the false heart doth know.

                                              Exeunt

2.1

Enter BANQUO *and* FLEANCE, *with a torch*
before him

BANQUO   How goes the night, boy?[1]
FLEANCE   The moon is down. I have not heard the clock.
BANQUO   And she goes down at twelve.
FLEANCE   I take't 'tis later, sir.
BANQUO [*giving* FLEANCE *his sword*] Hold, take my sword.
There's husbandry° in heaven,   *thrift*
5 Their candles are all out. Take thee that,[2] too.
A heavy summons° lies like lead upon me,   *summons to sleep*
And yet I would not sleep. Merciful powers,[3]
Restrain in me the cursèd thoughts that nature
Gives way to in repose.
                    Enter MACBETH, *and a servant with a torch*
                       Give me my sword. Who's there?
10 MACBETH   A friend.
BANQUO   What, sir, not yet at rest? The King's a-bed.
He hath been in unusual pleasure, and
Sent forth great largesse° to your offices.[4]   *gifts*
This diamond he greets your wife withal
15 By the name of most kind hostess, and shut up°   *concluded*
In measureless content.

MACBETH   Being unprepared
Our will became the servant to defect,
Which else should free have wrought.[5]

BANQUO   All's well.
I dreamt last night of the three weird sisters.
To you they have showed some truth.

2. Alembic, the upper part of a still to which fumes rise.
The wine will make the memory a fume that will fill and
cloud the brain, the "receptacle of reason."
2.1 Location: The courtyard of Macbeth's castle.
1. How much of the night has passed?
2. Some article of clothing or armor.

3. Angels invoked as protection against demons.
4. Household departments.
5. *Being . . . wrought:* Our desire to entertain the King
liberally was constrained by the fact that we were unprepared. *defect:* deficiency. *free:* freely.

20 MACBETH   I think not of them;
      Yet, when we can entreat an hour to serve,
      We would spend it in some words upon that business
      If you would grant the time.
   BANQUO   At your kind'st leisure.
   MACBETH   If you shall cleave to my consent when 'tis,[6]
      It shall make honour for you.
25 BANQUO   So° I lose none   *Provided*
      In seeking to augment it, but still keep
      My bosom franchised° and allegiance clear,°   *guiltless / unstained*
      I shall be counselled.°   *receptive*
   MACBETH   Good repose the while.
30 BANQUO   Thanks, sir. The like to you.
                      Exeunt BANQUO [*and* FLEANCE]
   MACBETH [*to the Servant*]   Go bid thy mistress, when my drink is ready,
      She strike upon the bell. Get thee to bed.   *Exit* [*Servant*]
      Is this a dagger which I see before me,
      The handle toward my hand? Come, let me clutch thee.
35   I have thee not, and yet I see thee still.
      Art thou not, fatal vision, sensible°   *perceptible*
      To feeling as to sight? Or art thou but
      A dagger of the mind, a false creation
      Proceeding from the heat-oppressèd° brain?   *fevered*
40   I see thee yet, in form as palpable
      As this which now I draw.
      Thou marshall'st° me the way that I was going,   *guide*
      And such an instrument I was to use.
      Mine eyes are made the fools o'th' other senses,
45   Or else worth all the rest. I see thee still,
      And on thy blade and dudgeon gouts° of blood,   *and handle drops*
      Which was not so before. There's no such thing.
      It is the bloody business which informs°   *creates shapes*
      Thus to mine eyes. Now o'er the one half-world
50   Nature seems dead, and wicked dreams abuse°   *deceive*
      The curtained sleep. Witchcraft celebrates
      Pale Hecate's offerings,[7] and withered murder,
      Alarumed° by his sentinel the wolf,   *Roused*
      Whose howl's his watch,° thus with his stealthy pace, *watchword*
55   With Tarquin's[8] ravishing strides, towards his design° *prey*
      Moves like a ghost. Thou sure and firm-set earth,
      Hear not my steps which way they walk, for fear
      Thy very stones prate of my whereabout,
      And take the present horror° from the time,   *terrible stillness*
60   Which now suits with it. Whiles I threat, he lives.
      Words to the heat of deeds too cold breath gives.
            A bell rings
      I go, and it is done. The bell invites me.
      Hear it not, Duncan; for it is a knell
      That summons thee to heaven or to hell.   *Exit*

---

6. If you will support my opinion or my cause when the time comes.
7. Sacrificial rites offered to Hecate, Greek goddess of witchcraft and of the moon.
8. A Roman prince who ravished the chaste matron Lucrece. Shakespeare tells the story in *The Rape of Lucrece.*

2.2

Enter LADY [MACBETH]

LADY MACBETH   That which hath made them drunk hath made me bold.
What hath quenched them hath given me fire. Hark, peace!—
It was the owl that shrieked, the fatal bellman°   night watchman
Which gives the stern'st good-night.[1] He is about it.
5   The doors are open, and the surfeited grooms°   attendants
Do mock their charge° with snores. I have drugged their   duty
possets°   mulled milk and wine
That death and nature do contend about them
Whether they live or die.

Enter MACBETH [*above*]

MACBETH   Who's there? What ho?   [*Exit*]
LADY MACBETH   Alack, I am afraid they have awaked,
10   And 'tis not done. Th'attempt and not the deed
Confounds° us. Hark!—I laid their daggers ready;   Ruins
He could not miss 'em. Had he not resembled
My father as he slept, I had done't.

[*Enter* MACBETH *below*]

                              My husband!
MACBETH   I have done the deed. Didst thou not hear a noise?
15   LADY MACBETH   I heard the owl scream and the crickets cry.
Did not you speak?
MACBETH   When?
LADY MACBETH   Now.
MACBETH   As I descended?
LADY MACBETH   Ay.
MACBETH   Hark!—Who lies i'th' second chamber?
LADY MACBETH   Donalbain.
MACBETH [*looking at his hands*]   This is a sorry sight.
LADY MACBETH   A foolish thought, to say a sorry sight.
20   MACBETH   There's one did laugh in's sleep, and one cried 'Murder!'
That they did wake each other. I stood and heard them.
But they did say their prayers and addressed them°   settled themselves
Again to sleep.
LADY MACBETH   There are two lodged together.
MACBETH   One cried 'God bless us' and 'Amen' the other,
25   As° they had seen me with these hangman's[2] hands.   As if
List'ning their fear I could not say 'Amen'
When they did say 'God bless us.'
LADY MACBETH   Consider it not so deeply.
MACBETH   But wherefore could not I pronounce 'Amen'?
30   I had most need of blessing, and 'Amen'
Stuck in my throat.
LADY MACBETH   These deeds must not be thought°   thought on
After these ways. So, it will make us mad.
MACBETH   Methought I heard a voice cry 'Sleep no more,
Macbeth does murder sleep'—the innocent sleep,
35   Sleep that knits up the ravelled sleave° of care,   tangled skein
The death of each day's life, sore labour's bath,

2.2 Location: Scene continues with only a brief pause.
1. A bell was rung outside the cells of condemned prisoners the night before they were to be executed.

2. Bloodstained. The hangman had to disembowel and
quarter his victims.

Balm of hurt minds, great nature's second course,[3]
Chief nourisher in life's feast—
LADY MACBETH   What do you mean?
MACBETH   Still it cried 'Sleep no more' to all the house,
40   'Glamis hath murdered sleep, and therefore Cawdor
Shall sleep no more, Macbeth shall sleep no more.'
LADY MACBETH   Who was it that thus cried? Why, worthy thane,
You do unbend° your noble strength to think   slacken
So brain-sickly of things. Go get some water
45   And wash this filthy witness° from your hand.   evidence
Why did you bring these daggers from the place?
They must lie there. Go, carry them, and smear
The sleepy grooms with blood.
MACBETH   I'll go no more.
I am afraid to think what I have done,
Look on't again I dare not.
50   LADY MACBETH   Infirm of purpose!
Give me the daggers. The sleeping and the dead
Are but as pictures. 'Tis the eye of childhood
That fears a painted devil. If he do bleed
I'll gild[4] the faces of the grooms withal,
For it must seem their guilt.
                    Knock within   *Exit*
55   MACBETH   Whence is that knocking?—
How is't with me when every noise appals me?
What hands are here! Ha, they pluck out mine eyes.
Will all great Neptune's ocean wash this blood
Clean from my hand? No, this my hand will rather
60   The multitudinous seas incarnadine,°   turn red
Making the green one red.[5]
              Enter LADY [MACBETH]
LADY MACBETH   My hands are of your colour, but I shame
To wear a heart so white.
                    Knock [*within*]
                              I hear a knocking
At the south entry. Retire we to our chamber.
65   A little water clears us of this deed.
How easy is it then! Your constancy
Hath left you unattended.[6]
                    Knock [*within*]
                              Hark, more knocking.
Get on your nightgown, lest occasion call us
And show us to be watchers.[7] Be not lost
70   So poorly in your thoughts.
MACBETH   To know my deed 'twere best not know myself.[8]
                    Knock [*within*]
Wake Duncan with thy knocking. I would thou couldst.
                                        Exeunt

3. Second, and most nourishing, course of a meal; second, or alternative, habit or practice.
4. Coat as if with gold leaf. Gold was often called red;
compare 2.3.109.
5. *one red*: entirely red.

6. *Your . . . unattended*: Your resolve has deserted you.
7. Those who have stayed awake.
8. It is better that I lose consciousness altogether than
face my deed.

2.3

Enter a PORTER. *Knocking within*

PORTER Here's a knocking indeed! If a man were porter of hell-
gate he should have old° turning the key.　　　　　　　　　　　　　　*plenty of*

Knock [within]

Knock, knock, knock. Who's there, i'th' name of Beelzebub?°　　*name of a devil*
Here's a farmer that hanged himself on th'expectation of
5　　plenty.[1] Come in time![2] Have napkins° enough about you; here　　*handkerchiefs*
you'll sweat for't.

Knock [within]

Knock, knock. Who's there, in th'other devil's name? Faith,
here's an equivocator[3] that could swear in both the scales
against either scale, who committed treason enough for God's
10　　sake, yet could not equivocate to heaven. O, come in, equivocator.

Knock [within]

Knock, knock, knock. Who's there? 'Faith, here's an English
tailor come hither for stealing out of a French hose.[4] Come in,
tailor. Here you may roast your goose.[5]

Knock [within]

15　　Knock, knock. Never at quiet. What are you?—But this place
is too cold for hell. I'll devil-porter it no further. I had thought
to have let in some of all professions that go the primrose way
to th'everlasting bonfire.

Knock [within]

Anon, anon!

[He opens the gate]

20　　I pray you remember the porter.

Enter MACDUFF *and* LENNOX

MACDUFF Was it so late, friend, ere you went to bed
That you do lie so late?

PORTER Faith, sir, we were carousing till the second cock,° and　　*3:00 A.M.*
drink, sir, is a great provoker of three things.

25　　MACDUFF What three things does drink especially provoke?

PORTER Marry,° sir, nose-painting,[6] sleep, and urine. Lechery,　　*Indeed*
sir, it provokes and unprovokes: it provokes the desire but it
takes away the performance. Therefore much drink may be
said to be an equivocator with lechery: it makes him and it
30　　mars him; it sets him on and it takes him off; it persuades him
and disheartens him, makes him stand to° and not stand to; in　　*maintain an erection*
conclusion, equivocates him in a sleep,[7] and, giving him the
lie,[8] leaves him.

MACDUFF I believe drink gave thee the lie last night.

35　　PORTER That it did, sir, i'the very throat on me;[9] but I requited

---

2.3 Location: Scene continues, perhaps after a short
pause.
1. *Here's . . . plenty:* A farmer had hoarded grain to sell at
high prices but was ruined by a crop surplus that forced
prices down.
2. Good timing.
3. One who speaks ambiguously. An allusion to the Jesuit
doctrine that a seemingly false statement was not a lie
(and therefore not repugnant to God) if the speaker had
in mind a different meaning in which the utterance was
true. Possibly an allusion to the 1606 trial of the Jesuit
Henry Garnet for involvement in the Gunpowder Plot to
blow up the Houses of Parliament; Father Garnet had

written a treatise defending equivocation for Catholics
being persecuted for their beliefs.
4. Tight-fitting breeches, which would easily reveal the
tailor's attempt to skimp on the cloth supplied him for
their manufacture. He had apparently been able to do so
undetected when loose-fitting breeches were in fashion.
5. Heat your smoothing iron.
6. Reddening of the nose through drink.
7. Gives him an erotic experience in dreams only.
8. An elaborate pun: calling him a liar; laying him out
flat; making him urinate ("lye," or urine).
9. *i'the . . . me:* provoking a duel by insulting me with
a deliberate lie.

him for his lie, and, I think, being too strong for him, though
he took up my legs sometime, yet I made a shift to cast him.[1]

MACDUFF   Is thy master stirring?

     Enter MACBETH

Our knocking has awaked him: here he comes.   [*Exit* PORTER]

LENNOX [*to* MACBETH]   Good morrow, noble sir.

40   MACBETH   Good morrow, both.

MACDUFF   Is the King stirring, worthy thane?

MACBETH   Not yet.

MACDUFF   He did command me to call timely° on him.   *early*
I have almost slipped the hour.

MACBETH   I'll bring you to him.

MACDUFF   I know this is a joyful trouble to you,

45   But yet 'tis one.

MACBETH   The labour we delight in physics pain.[2]
This is the door.

MACDUFF   I'll make so bold to call,
For 'tis my limited° service.   *Exit* MACDUFF   *appointed*

LENNOX   Goes the King hence today?

MACBETH   He does; he did appoint so.

50   LENNOX   The night has been unruly. Where we lay
Our chimneys were blown down, and, as they say,
Lamentings heard i'th' air, strange screams of death,
And prophesying with accents terrible
Of dire combustion° and confused events   *tumult*

55   New-hatched to th' woeful time. The obscure bird[3]
Clamoured the livelong night. Some say the earth
Was feverous and did shake.

MACBETH   'Twas a rough night.

LENNOX   My young remembrance cannot parallel
A fellow to it.

     Enter MACDUFF

MACDUFF   O horror, horror, horror!

60   Tongue nor heart cannot conceive nor name thee.

MACBETH *and* LENNOX   What's the matter?

MACDUFF   Confusion° now hath made his masterpiece.   *Ruin*
Most sacrilegious murder hath broke ope
The Lord's anointed temple° and stole thence   *(the King's body)*

65   The life o'th' building.

MACBETH   What is't you say—the life?

LENNOX   Mean you his majesty?

MACDUFF   Approach the chamber and destroy your sight
With a new Gorgon.[4] Do not bid me speak.
See, and then speak yourselves. *Exeunt* MACBETH *and* LENNOX

70   Awake, awake!
Ring the alarum bell. Murder and treason!
Banquo and Donalbain, Malcolm, awake!
Shake off this downy sleep, death's counterfeit,
And look on death itself. Up, up, and see

75   The great doom's image.°   Malcolm, Banquo,   *replica of Doomsday*
As from your graves rise up, and walk like sprites

---

1. *being . . . cast him*: the effects of drunkenness are
described in the language of a wrestling match. *cast*:
throw off; vomit.
2. Pleasure in labor mitigates its laboriousness.

3. The owl, bird of darkness.
4. A mythical monster with a woman's figure and snakes
for hair, the sight of whose face turned beholders to
stone. Medusa was one of the three Gorgons.

To countenance° this horror.   *suit; behold*

       Bell rings. Enter LADY [MACBETH]

LADY MACBETH   What's the business,

That such a hideous trumpet calls to parley

The sleepers of the house? Speak, speak.

MACDUFF   O gentle lady,

80   'Tis not for you to hear what I can speak.

The repetition° in a woman's ear   *report*

Would murder as it fell.

       Enter BANQUO

                 O Banquo, Banquo,

Our royal master's murdered!

LADY MACBETH   Woe, alas—

What, in our house?

BANQUO   Too cruel anywhere.

85   Dear Duff, I prithee contradict thyself,

And say it is not so.

       Enter MACBETH, LENNOX, *and* ROSS

MACBETH   Had I but died an hour before this chance°   *occurrence*

I had lived a blessèd time, for from this instant

There's nothing serious in mortality.°   *worth living for*

90   All is but toys.° Renown and grace is dead.   *trifles*

The wine of life is drawn, and the mere lees

Is left this vault° to brag of.   *wine vault; world*

       Enter MALCOLM *and* DONALBAIN

DONALBAIN   What is amiss?

MACBETH   You are, and do not know't.

95   The spring, the head, the fountain of your blood

Is stopped, the very source of it is stopped.

MACDUFF   Your royal father's murdered.

MALCOLM   O, by whom?

LENNOX   Those of his chamber, as it seemed, had done't.

Their hands and faces were all badged° with blood,   *marked*

100   So were their daggers, which, unwiped, we found

Upon their pillows. They stared and were distracted.

No man's life was to be trusted with them.

MACBETH   O, yet I do repent me of my fury

That I did kill them.

MACDUFF   Wherefore did you so?

105   MACBETH   Who can be wise, amazed, temp'rate and furious,

Loyal and neutral in a moment? No man.

Th'expedition° of my violent love   *haste*

Outran the pauser,° reason. Here lay Duncan,   *delayer*

His silver skin laced with his golden blood,

110   And his gashed stabs looked like a breach in nature

For ruin's wasteful° entrance; there the murderers, *destructive*

Steeped in the colours of their trade, their daggers

Unmannerly breeched[5] with gore. Who could refrain,

That had a heart to love, and in that heart

Courage to make 's love known?

115   LADY MACBETH   Help me hence, ho!

MACDUFF   Look to the lady.

MALCOLM [*aside to* DONALBAIN] Why do we hold our tongues,

---

5. Covered—as if with breeches—with blood.

That most may claim this argument° for ours?   *subject*
DONALBAIN [*aside to* MALCOLM] What should be spoken here,
 where our fate,
 Hid in an auger-hole,° may rush and seize us? *in a cranny; in ambush*
 Let's away. Our tears are not yet brewed.
120 MALCOLM [*aside to* DONALBAIN]   Nor our strong sorrow
 Upon the foot of motion.[6]
  BANQUO   Look to the lady;
      [*Exit* LADY MACBETH, *attended*]
 And when we have our naked frailties hid,° *clothed*
 That suffer in exposure, let us meet
 And question° this most bloody piece of work, *discuss*
125 To know it further. Fears and scruples° shake us. *doubts*
 In the great hand of God I stand, and thence
 Against the undivulged pretence I fight
 Of treasonous malice.[7]
  MACDUFF   And so do I.
  ALL   So all.
  MACBETH Let's briefly° put on manly readiness,° *quickly / clothes; resolve*
 And meet i'th' hall together.
130 ALL   Well contented.
    Exeunt [*all but* MALCOLM *and* DONALBAIN]
 MALCOLM What will you do? Let's not consort with them.
 To show an unfelt sorrow is an office
 Which the false man does easy. I'll to England.
  DONALBAIN To Ireland, I. Our separated fortune
135 Shall keep us both the safer. Where we are
 There's daggers in men's smiles. The nea'er in blood,
 The nearer bloody.[8]
  MALCOLM   This murderous shaft that's shot
 Hath not yet lighted,° and our safest way *fallen*
 Is to avoid the aim. Therefore to horse,
140 And let us not be dainty of° leave-taking, *polite about*
 But shift° away. There's warrant° in that theft *slip / justification*
 Which steals itself[9] when there's no mercy left. *Exeunt*

2.4

Enter ROSS *with an* OLD MAN

 OLD MAN Threescore and ten I can remember well,
 Within the volume of which time I have seen
 Hours dreadful and things strange, but this sore night
 Hath trifled former knowings.[1]
  ROSS   Ha, good father,
5 Thou seest the heavens, as troubled with man's act,
 Threatens his bloody stage. By th' clock 'tis day,
 And yet dark night strangles the travelling lamp.° *sun*
 Is't night's predominance° or the day's shame *ascendancy*
 That darkness does the face of earth entomb
 When living light should kiss it?
10 OLD MAN   'Tis unnatural,

---

6. *Nor . . . motion*: Nor has our strong sorrow yet begun to express itself.
7. *Against . . . malice*: I will fight against the hidden purpose behind this treasonous act.
8. *The nea'er . . . bloody*: The closer the kinship, the nearer the danger of murder.
9. *Which steals itself*: Malcolm alludes to the fact that he and Donalbain intend to "steal" away from the castle.
2.4 Location: Not far from Macbeth's castle.
1. Has made previous experiences seem trifling.

Even like the deed that's done. On Tuesday last
A falcon, tow'ring in her pride of place,[2]
Was by a mousing owl[3] hawked at and killed.

ROSS   And Duncan's horses— a thing most strange and certain—
15   Beauteous and swift, the minions° of their race,   *darlings*
Turned wild in nature, broke their stalls, flung out,
Contending 'gainst obedience, as° they would   *as if*
Make war with mankind.

OLD MAN   'Tis said they ate each other.

ROSS   They did so, to th'amazement of mine eyes
That looked upon't.

        Enter MACDUFF

20   Here comes the good Macduff.
How goes the world, sir, now?

MACDUFF   Why, see you not?

ROSS   Is't known who did this more than bloody deed?

MACDUFF   Those that Macbeth hath slain.

ROSS   Alas the day,
What good could they pretend?[4]

MACDUFF   They were suborned.°   *bribed*
25   Malcolm and Donalbain, the King's two sons,
Are stol'n away and fled, which puts upon them
Suspicion of the deed.

ROSS   'Gainst nature still.
Thriftless ambition, that will raven up°   *devour*
Thine own life's means! Then 'tis most like
30   The sovereignty will fall upon Macbeth.

MACDUFF   He is already named and gone to Scone[5]
To be invested.

ROSS   Where is Duncan's body?

MACDUFF   Carried to Colmekill,[6]
35   The sacred storehouse of his predecessors,
And guardian of their bones.

ROSS   Will you to Scone?

MACDUFF   No, cousin, I'll to Fife.[7]

ROSS   Well, I will thither.

MACDUFF   Well, may you see things well done there. Adieu,
Lest our old robes sit easier than our new.

40   ROSS   Farewell, father.

OLD MAN   God's benison° go with you, and with those   *blessing*
That would make good of bad, and friends of foes.

        Exeunt severally

3.1

    Enter BANQUO

BANQUO   Thou hast it now: King, Cawdor, Glamis, all
As the weird women promised; and I fear
Thou played'st most foully for't. Yet it was said
It should not stand in thy posterity,[1]
5   But that myself should be the root and father

---

2. Mounting to her highest point in the sky before swooping down.
3. An owl that usually feeds on mice.
4. What good could they expect to gain from the murder?
5. Ancient royal city where Scottish Kings were invested

with the ceremonial symbols of authority.
6. Iona, the burial place of Scottish Kings.
7. Macduff is the Thane of Fife.
3.1 Location: The royal palace at Forres.
1. It should not pass to your descendants.

Of many kings. If there come truth from them—
As upon thee, Macbeth, their speeches shine°—   *smile favorably*
Why by the verities on thee made good
May they not be my oracles as well,
And set me up in hope? But hush, no more.   10

     Sennet° sounded. Enter MACBETH *as King,* LADY MAC-   *Trumpet call*
     BETH *as Queen,* LENNOX, ROSS, *lords, and attendants*

MACBETH   Here's our chief guest.
LADY MACBETH   If he had been forgotten
It had been as a gap in our great feast,
And all-thing° unbecoming.   *entirely*
MACBETH [*to* BANQUO]   Tonight we hold a solemn° supper, sir,   *formal*
And I'll request your presence.
BANQUO   Let your highness   15
Command upon me, to the which my duties
Are with a most indissoluble tie
For ever knit.
MACBETH   Ride you this afternoon?
BANQUO   Ay, my good lord.   20
MACBETH   We should have else desired your good advice,
Which still° hath been both grave° and prosperous,   *always / weighty*
In this day's council; but we'll talk tomorrow.
Is't far you ride?
BANQUO   As far, my lord, as will fill up the time   25
'Twixt this and supper. Go not my horse the better,²
I must become a borrower of the night
For a dark hour or twain.
MACBETH   Fail not our feast.
BANQUO   My lord, I will not.   30
MACBETH   We hear our bloody cousins are bestowed°   *lodged*
In England and in Ireland, not confessing
Their cruel parricide, filling their hearers
With strange invention.° But of that tomorrow,   *falsehood*
When therewithal we shall have cause of state   35
Craving us jointly.³ Hie you to horse. Adieu,
Till you return at night. Goes Fleance with you?
BANQUO   Ay, my good lord. Our time does call upon 's.
MACBETH   I wish your horses swift and sure of foot,
And so I do commend° you to their backs.   *entrust*   40
Farewell.   *Exit* BANQUO
Let every man be master of his time
Till seven at night. To make society
The sweeter welcome, we will keep ourself
Till supper-time alone. While° then, God be with you.   *Till*   45

     Exeunt [*all but* MACBETH *and a* SERVANT]

Sirrah, a word with you. Attend those men
Our pleasure?
SERVANT   They are, my lord, without° the palace gate.   *outside*
MACBETH   Bring them before us.   *Exit* SERVANT
     To be thus is nothing
But to be safely thus.⁴ Our fears in° Banquo   *of*   50

---

2. If my horse does not go faster than I expect.
3. *cause . . . jointly:* state business demanding our joint attention.
4. *To be thus . . . thus:* To be a King is no good unless one can reign in safety ("thus" refers to "King").

Stick° deep, and in his royalty of nature°   *Prick / natural nobility*
Reigns that which would be feared. 'Tis much he dares,
And to° that dauntless temper of his mind   *added to*
He hath a wisdom that doth guide his valour

55   To act in safety. There is none but he
Whose being I do fear, and under him
My genius° is rebuked as, it is said,[5]   *tutelary spirit*
Mark Antony's was by Caesar.° He chid the sisters   *Octavius Caesar*
When first they put the name of king upon me,

60   And bade them speak to him. Then, prophet-like,
They hailed him father to a line of kings.
Upon my head they placed a fruitless crown,
And put a barren sceptre in my grip,
Thence to be wrenched with° an unlineal hand,   *by*

65   No son of mine succeeding. If't be so,
For Banquo's issue have I filed° my mind,   *defiled*
For them the gracious° Duncan have I murdered,   *full of grace*
Put rancours° in the vessel of my peace   *bitterness*
Only for them, and mine eternal jewel°   *soul*

70   Given to the common enemy of man°   *(the devil)*
To make them kings, the seeds of Banquo kings.
Rather than so, come fate into the list°   *arena*
And champion me to th'utterance.[6] Who's there?
            Enter Servant and two MURDERERS
[*To the Servant*] Now go to the door, and stay there till we call.
                                                            Exit Servant

75   Was it not yesterday we spoke together?
MURDERERS   It was, so please your highness.
MACBETH   Well then, now
Have you considered of my speeches? Know
That it was he in the times past which held you
So under° fortune, which you thought had been   *out of favor with*

80   Our innocent self. This I made good to you
In our last conference, passed in probation° with you   *reviewed the proof*
How you were borne in hand,° how crossed,° the instruments,[7]   *deceived / thwarted*
Who wrought with them, and all things else that might
To half a soul, and to a notion crazed,[8]
Say 'Thus did Banquo'.

85   FIRST MURDERER   You made it known to us.
MACBETH   I did so, and went further, which is now
Our point of second meeting. Do you find
Your patience so predominant in your nature
That you can let this go? Are you so gospelled[9]

90   To pray for this good man and for his issue,
Whose heavy hand hath bowed you to the grave
And beggared yours° for ever?   *your family*
FIRST MURDERER   We are men, my liege.
MACBETH   Ay, in the catalogue ye go for men,
As hounds and greyhounds, mongrels, spaniels, curs,

95   Shoughs, water-rugs, and demi-wolves[1] are clept°   *called*

---

5. Said by Plutarch. Shakespeare paraphrases him in   8. Even to a half-wit or to a crazed mind.
Antony and Cleopatra (2.3).   9. Imbued with the gospel spirit.
6. And fight with me in single combat to the death.   1. Shaggy lapdogs, water dogs (for fowling), and cross-
7. Agents.   breeds between wolf and dog.

All by the name of dogs. The valued file[2]
Distinguishes the swift, the slow, the subtle,
The housekeeper,° the hunter, every one   watchdog
According to the gift which bounteous nature
100   Hath in him closed;° whereby he does receive   enclosed
Particular addition from the bill
That writes them all alike.[3] And so of men.
Now, if you have a station° in the file,   position
Not i'th' worst rank of manhood, say't,
105   And I will put that business in your bosoms
Whose execution takes your enemy off,
Grapples you to the heart and love of us,
Who wear our health but sickly in his life,
Which in his death were perfect.
SECOND MURDERER   I am one, my liege,
110   Whom the vile blows and buffets of the world
Hath so incensed that I am reckless what
I do to spite the world.
FIRST MURDERER   And I another,
So weary with disasters, tugged with° fortune,   mauled by
That I would set° my life on any chance   risk
To mend it or be rid on't.
115   MACBETH   Both of you
Know Banquo was your enemy.
MURDERERS   True, my lord.
MACBETH   So is he mine, and in such bloody distance°   enmity
That every minute of his being thrusts
Against my near'st of life;[4] and though I could
120   With barefaced power sweep him from my sight
And bid my will avouch° it, yet I must not,   warrant
For° certain friends that are both his and mine,   Because of
Whose loves I may not drop, but wail° his fall   must bewail
Who I myself struck down. And thence it is
125   That I to your assistance do make love,°   I crave your aid
Masking the business from the common eye
For sundry weighty reasons.
SECOND MURDERER   We shall, my lord,
Perform what you command us.
FIRST MURDERER   Though our lives—
MACBETH   Your spirits shine through you. Within this hour at most
130   I will advise you where to plant yourselves,
Acquaint you with the perfect spy o'th' time,
The moment on't;[5] for't must be done tonight,
And something° from the palace; always thought°   at some distance / remember
That I require a clearness;[6] and with him,
135   To leave no rubs° nor botches in the work,   flaws
Fleance, his son, that keeps him company—
Whose absence is no less material to me
Than is his father's—must embrace the fate
Of that dark hour. Resolve yourselves apart.[7]
I'll come to you anon.

2. List specifying the value of the cataloged items.
3. *Particular . . . alike*: Distinction apart from a catalog
that lists them indiscriminately.
4. My most vital part, the heart.

5. *Acquaint . . . on't*: I will give you full and precise
instructions as to when it is to be done.
6. A clearance (from suspicion).
7. Make up your minds privately.

140 MURDERERS   We are resolved, my lord.

MACBETH   I'll call upon you straight. Abide within.

[*Exeunt* MURDERERS]

It is concluded. Banquo, thy soul's flight,

If it find heaven, must find it out tonight.   *Exit*

3.2

Enter LADY [MACBETH] *and a* SERVANT

LADY MACBETH   Is Banquo gone from court?

SERVANT   Ay, madam, but returns again tonight.

LADY MACBETH   Say to the King I would attend his leisure

For a few words.

5 SERVANT   Madam, I will.   *Exit*

LADY MACBETH   Naught's had, all's spent,

Where our desire is got without content.°   *happiness*

'Tis safer to be that which we destroy

Than by destruction dwell in doubtful joy.

Enter MACBETH

10 How now, my lord, why do you keep alone,

Of sorriest° fancies your companions making,   *most wretched*

Using° those thoughts which should indeed have died   *Entertaining*

With them they think on? Things without all remedy

Should be without regard.° What's done is done.   *not considered*

15 MACBETH   We have scorched° the snake, not killed it.   *slashed*

She'll close° and be herself, whilst our poor malice   *heal*

Remains in danger of her former tooth.[1]

But let the frame of things disjoint, both the worlds suffer,[2]

Ere we will eat our meal in fear, and sleep

20 In the affliction of these terrible dreams

That shake us nightly. Better be with the dead,

Whom we to gain our peace have sent to peace,

Than on the torture° of the mind to lie   *rack*

In restless ecstasy.° Duncan is in his grave.   *frenzy*

25 After life's fitful fever he sleeps well.

Treason has done his worst. Nor steel nor poison,

Malice domestic, foreign levy,[3] nothing

Can touch him further.

LADY MACBETH   Come on, gentle my lord,

Sleek o'er your rugged looks, be bright and jovial

Among your guests tonight.

30 MACBETH   So shall I, love,

And so I pray be you. Let your remembrance

Apply° to Banquo. Present him eminence°   *Be given / favor*

Both with eye and tongue; unsafe the while that we

Must lave our honours in these flattering streams[4]

35 And make our faces visors° to our hearts,   *masks*

Disguising what they are.

LADY MACBETH   You must leave this.

MACBETH   O, full of scorpions is my mind, dear wife!

Thou know'st that Banquo and his Fleance lives.

3.2 Location: The palace.

1. *our . . . tooth*: we remain in danger of her fangs, which are as dangerous as they were before she was slashed. *poor malice*: weak enmity.

2. Let the universe fall apart, and heaven and earth suffer destruction.

3. An army levied abroad against Scotland.

4. *unsafe . . . streams*: we are unsafe at present, so we must make our reputations look clean by flattering others; we are unsafe as long as we must flatter.

LADY MACBETH   But in them nature's copy's[5] not eterne.°   *everlasting*
40 MACBETH   There's comfort yet, they are assailable.
Then be thou jocund. Ere the bat hath flown
His cloistered° flight, ere to black Hecate's summons   *restricted*
The shard-borne[6] beetle with his drowsy hums
Hath rung night's yawning peal,[7] there shall be done
45 A deed of dreadful note.
LADY MACBETH   What's to be done?
MACBETH   Be innocent of the knowledge, dearest chuck,[8]
Till thou applaud the deed.—Come, seeling[9] night,
Scarf up° the tender eye of pitiful day,   *Blindfold*
And with thy bloody and invisible hand
50 Cancel and tear to pieces that great bond°   *(Banquo's lease on life)*
Which keeps me pale. Light thickens, and the crow
Makes wing to th' rooky° wood.   *full of rooks*
Good things of day begin to droop and drowse,
Whiles night's black agents to their preys do rouse.
55 Thou marvell'st at my words; but hold thee still.
Things bad begun make strong themselves by ill.
So prithee go with me.   *Exeunt*

3.3

Enter three MURDERERS
FIRST MURDERER [*to* THIRD MURDERER]   But who did bid thee
join with us?
THIRD MURDERER   Macbeth.
SECOND MURDERER [*to* FIRST MURDERER]   He needs not our mis-
trust, since he delivers
Our offices and what we have to do
To the direction just.[1]
FIRST MURDERER [*to* THIRD MURDERER]   Then stand with us.
5 The west yet glimmers with some streaks of day.
Now spurs the lated° traveller apace   *belated*
To gain the timely inn, and near approaches
The subject of our watch.
THIRD MURDERER   Hark, I hear horses.
BANQUO [*within*]   Give us a light there, ho!
SECOND MURDERER   Then 'tis he. The rest
10 That are within the note of expectation°   *list of expected guests*
Already are i'th' court.
FIRST MURDERER   His horses go about.[2]
THIRD MURDERER   Almost a mile; but he does usually,
So all men do, from hence to th' palace gate
Make it their walk.
Enter BANQUO *and* FLEANCE *with a torch*
SECOND MURDERER [*aside*]   A light, a light.
THIRD MURDERER [*aside*]   'Tis he.
15 FIRST MURDERER [*aside*]   Stand to't.

---

5. Lease on life (a copyhold lease was subject to cancellation and therefore "not eterne"); the individual human cast from nature's mold.
6. Carried on scaly wings; born in dung ("shards").
7. Macbeth likens the beetle's humming to a bell, signaling the time for sleep.
8. Chick (term of endearment).

9. Eye-closing. Falcons' eyelids were sewn shut ("seeled") as part of their training.
3.3 Location: Near the palace.
1. *He . . . just:* We need not mistrust this man, since he knows perfectly Macbeth's instructions to us.
2. Are led (by servants) to the stables.

BANQUO　It will be rain tonight.
FIRST MURDERER　　　　　　　Let it come down.
　　　[FIRST MURDERER *strikes out the torch. The others attack*
　　　BANQUO]
BANQUO　O, treachery! Fly, good Fleance, fly, fly, fly!
　Thou mayst revenge.—O slave!　　　[*He dies. Exit* FLEANCE]
THIRD MURDERER　Who did strike out the light?
20　FIRST MURDERER　Was't not the way?°　　　　　　　　　　*proper thing*
THIRD MURDERER　There's but one down. The son is fled.
SECOND MURDERER　We have lost best half of our affair.
FIRST MURDERER　Well, let's away and say how much is done.
　　　　　　　　　　　Exeunt [*with Banquo's body*]

3.4

Banquet prepared. Enter MACBETH [*as King*], LADY [MAC-
BETH *as Queen*], ROSS, LENNOX, *Lords, and attendants.*
[LADY MACBETH *sits*]
MACBETH　You know your own degrees;° sit down. At first and last[1]　　*ranks; places*
　The hearty welcome.
LORDS　　　　　　　　　Thanks to your majesty.
　　　[*They sit*]
MACBETH　Ourself will mingle with society
　And play the humble host. Our hostess keeps her state,°　　*chair of state*
5　But in best time we will require° her welcome.　　　　　　*request*
LADY MACBETH　Pronounce it for me, sir, to all our friends,
　For my heart speaks they are welcome.
　　　Enter FIRST MURDERER [*to the door*]
MACBETH　See, they encounter° thee with their hearts' thanks.　　*answer*
　Both sides are even. Here I'll sit, i'th' midst.
10　Be large° in mirth. Anon we'll drink a measure　　　　　*unrestrained*
　The table round. [*To* FIRST MURDERER]　There's blood upon thy face.
FIRST MURDERER　[*aside to* MACBETH]　'Tis Banquo's, then.
MACBETH　'Tis better thee without than he within.[2]
　Is he dispatched?
15　FIRST MURDERER　My lord, his throat is cut. That I did for him.
MACBETH　Thou art the best o'th' cut-throats. Yet he's good
　That did the like for Fleance. If thou didst it,
　Thou art the nonpareil.°　　　　　　　　　　　*paragon (without equal)*
FIRST MURDERER　　　　　　　Most royal sir,
　Fleance is scaped.
20　MACBETH　Then comes my fit again; I had else been perfect,
　Whole as the marble, founded° as the rock,　　　　　　*immovable*
　As broad and general° as the casing° air,　　*unconstrained / surrounding*
　But now I am cabined, cribbed,° confined, bound in　　*penned up*
　To saucy° doubts and fears. But Banquo's safe?　　*importunate*
25　FIRST MURDERER　Ay, my good lord. Safe in a ditch he bides,
　With twenty trenchèd gashes on his head,
　The least a death to nature.
MACBETH　　　　　　　Thanks for that.
　There the grown serpent lies. The worm° that's fled　　*young serpent*
　Hath nature that in time will venom breed,

3.4 Location: The palace.　　　　　　　2. Better on you than inside him.
1. To one and all.

30 No teeth for th' present. Get thee gone. Tomorrow
We'll hear ourselves° again.   *Exit* [FIRST] MURDERER   confer
LADY MACBETH   My royal lord,
You do not give the cheer.° The feast is sold   entertain
That is not often vouched, while 'tis a-making,
'Tis given with welcome.³ To feed° were best at home.   Mere eating
35 From thence° the sauce to meat is ceremony,   Away from home
Meeting were° bare without it.   Company would be
          Enter the Ghost of Banquo, and sits in Macbeth's place
MACBETH   Sweet remembrancer.°   reminder
Now good digestion wait on appetite,
And health on both.
LENNOX   May't please your highness sit?
MACBETH   Here had we now our country's honour roofed⁴
40 Were the graced person of our Banquo present,
Who may I rather challenge for° unkindness   accuse of
Than pity for mischance.
          ROSS   His absence, sir,
Lays blame upon his promise. Please't your highness
To grace us with your royal company?
MACBETH   The table's full.
45 LENNOX   Here is a place reserved, sir.
MACBETH   Where?
LENNOX   Here, my good lord. What is't that moves your highness?
MACBETH   Which of you have done this?
LORDS   What, my good lord?
MACBETH   [*to the Ghost*]   Thou canst not say I did it. Never shake
50 Thy gory locks at me.
ROSS   [*rising*]   Gentlemen, rise. His highness is not well.
LADY MACBETH   [*rising*]   Sit, worthy friends. My lord is often thus,
And hath been from his youth. Pray you, keep seat.
The fit is momentary. Upon a thought°   In a moment
55 He will again be well. If much you note him
You shall offend him, and extend his passion.°   prolong his suffering
Feed, and regard him not.
          [*She speaks apart with* MACBETH]
                    Are you a man?
MACBETH   Ay, and a bold one, that dare look on that
Which might appal the devil.
LADY MACBETH   O proper stuff!°   mere nonsense
60 This is the very painting of your fear;
This is the air-drawn dagger⁵ which you said
Led you to Duncan. O, these flaws° and starts,   outbursts
Impostors to° true fear, would well become   compared with
A woman's story at a winter's fire
65 Authorized by her grandam. Shame itself,
Why do you make such faces? When all's done
You look but on a stool.
MACBETH   Prithee see there. Behold, look, lo—how say you?
Why, what care I? If thou canst nod, speak, too!
70 If charnel-houses and our graves must send

---

3. *The . . . welcome:* A feast is like a purchased meal if
the guests are not assured often that they are welcome.

4. All the Scottish nobility under one roof.
5. The dagger made of, or carried on, the air.

Those that we bury back, our monuments
Shall be the maws of kites.[6]   [*Exit Ghost*]

LADY MACBETH   What, quite unmanned in folly?

MACBETH   If I stand here, I saw him.

LADY MACBETH   Fie, for shame!

MACBETH   Blood hath been shed ere now, i'th' olden time,
75   Ere human statute purged the gentle weal;[7]
      Ay, and since, too, murders have been performed
      Too terrible for the ear. The time has been
      That, when the brains were out, the man would die,
      And there an end. But now they rise again
80   With twenty mortal murders° on their crowns,°   deadly wounds / heads
      And push us from our stools. This is more strange
      Than such a murder is.

LADY MACBETH [*aloud*]   My worthy lord,
      Your noble friends do lack you.

MACBETH   I do forget.
      Do not muse° at me, my most worthy friends.   wonder
85   I have a strange infirmity which is nothing
      To those that know me. Come, love and health to all,
      Then I'll sit down.
To an [*attendant*]   Give me some wine. Fill full.
            Enter Ghost
      I drink to th' general joy of th'whole table,
      And to our dear friend Banquo, whom we miss.
90   Would he were here. To all and him we thirst,°   drink
      And all to all.[8]

LORDS   Our duties, and the pledge.°   toast
            [*They drink*]

MACBETH [*seeing the Ghost*]   Avaunt, and quit my sight! Let the
      earth hide thee.
      Thy bones are marrowless, thy blood is cold.
      Thou hast no speculation° in those eyes   sight
      Which thou dost glare with.

95   LADY MACBETH   Think of this, good peers,
      But as a thing of custom. 'Tis no other;
      Only it spoils the pleasure of the time.

MACBETH   What man dare, I dare.
      Approach thou like the ruggèd Russian bear,
100   The armed° rhinoceros, or th'Hyrcan[9] tiger;   armored
      Take any shape but that,° and my firm nerves°   (Banquo's) / sinews
      Shall never tremble. Or be alive again,
      And dare me to the desert° with thy sword.   deserted place
      If trembling I inhabit then,[1] protest me
105   The baby of a girl.[2] Hence, horrible shadow,
      Unreal mock'ry, hence!   [*Exit Ghost*]
                  Why so, being gone,
      I am a man again. Pray you sit still.

LADY MACBETH   You have displaced the mirth, broke the good meeting
      With most admired° disorder.   wondered at

---

6. *If . . . kites*: If the dead return from their graves, nothing will prevent them from being consumed by birds of
prey.
7. Before human or humane (Elizabethans did not spell
the two words differently) law cleansed the common-

wealth and made it peaceable.
8. All good wishes to everyone.
9. From Hyrcania, a region near the Caspian Sea.
1. If then I tremble; if, trembling, I stay indoors.
2. A baby girl; a girl's doll.

MACBETH   Can such things be
110   And overcome° us like a summer's cloud,   *pass over*
      Without our special wonder? You make me strange
      Even to the disposition that I owe,³
      When now I think you can behold such sights
      And keep the natural ruby of your cheeks
115   When mine is blanched with fear.
ROSS   What sights, my lord?
      LADY MACBETH   I pray you, speak not. He grows worse and worse.
      Question enrages° him. At once, good night.   *Talk aggravates*
      Stand not upon the order of your going,
      But go at once.⁴
      LENNOX   Good night, and better health
      Attend his majesty.
120   LADY MACBETH   A kind good-night to all.   *Exeunt Lords*
      MACBETH   It will have blood, they say. Blood will have blood.
      Stones have been known to move, and trees to speak,
      Augurs° and understood relations⁵ have   *Auguries*
      By maggot-pies and choughs and rooks⁶ brought forth°   *revealed*
125   The secret'st man of blood.° What is the night?⁷   *murderer*
      LADY MACBETH   Almost at odds with morning, which is which.
      MACBETH   How sayst thou⁸ that Macduff denies his person
      At our great bidding?
      LADY MACBETH   Did you send to him, sir?
      MACBETH   I hear it by the way,° but I will send.   *indirectly*
130   There's not a one of them but in his house
      I keep a servant fee'd.° I will° tomorrow,   *paid to spy / will go*
      And betimes° I will, to the weird sisters.   *early*
      More shall they speak, for now I am bent° to know   *determined*
      By the worst means the worst. For mine own good
135   All causes° shall give way. I am in blood   *other concerns*
      Stepped in so far that, should I° wade no more,°   *were I to / no farther*
      Returning were° as tedious as go° o'er.   *would be / going*
      Strange things I have in head that will to hand,
      Which must be acted ere they may be scanned.⁹
140   LADY MACBETH   You lack the season° of all natures, sleep.   *preservative*
      MACBETH   Come, we'll to sleep. My strange and self-abuse°   *self-delusion*
      Is the initiate fear that wants hard use.¹
      We are yet but young in deed.°   *Exeunt*   *crime*

3.5

Thunder. Enter the three WITCHES *meeting* HECATE

      FIRST WITCH   Why, how now, Hecate? You look angerly.
      HECATE   Have I not reason, beldams° as you are?   *hags*
      Saucy and over-bold, how did you dare
      To trade and traffic with Macbeth
5   In riddles and affairs of death,
      And I, the mistress of your charms,
      The close° contriver of all harms,   *secret*

---

3. *You . . . owe:* You make me a stranger to my own
nature, which I had supposed brave.
4. *Stand . . . once:* Do not follow the order of precedence
in departing, but all go at once.
5. Formerly hidden, now revealed relationships between
causes and effects.
6. Magpies, traditionally sacrificed by augurers, and
birds (choughs and rooks) of the crow family.

7. What time of night is it?
8. What do you think of the fact that.
9. *ere . . . scanned:* at once, before they can be considered.
1. Is the fear of a novice who lacks toughening experience.
3.5 Location: An open place.

Was never called to bear my part
Or show the glory of our art?—
10 And, which is worse, all you have done
Hath been but for a wayward son,
Spiteful and wrathful, who, as others do,
Loves for his own ends, not for you.
But make amends now. Get you gone,
15 And at the pit of Acheron°   river in hell
Meet me i'th' morning. Thither he
Will come to know his destiny.
Your vessels and your spells provide,
Your charms and everything beside.
20 I am for th'air. This night I'll spend
Unto a dismal and a fatal end.[1]
Great business must be wrought ere noon.
Upon the corner of the moon
There hangs a vap'rous drop profound.[2]
25 I'll catch it ere it come to ground,
And that, distilled by magic sleights,
Shall raise such artificial sprites[3]
As by the strength of their illusion
Shall draw him on to his confusion.
30 He shall spurn fate, scorn death, and bear
His hopes 'bove wisdom, grace, and fear;
And you all know security°   overconfidence
Is mortals' chiefest enemy.
SPIRITS [singing dispersedly within]°   Come away, come away.   offstage
35 Hecate, Hecate, come away.
HECATE   Hark, I am called! My little spirit, see,
Sits in a foggy cloud and stays for me.
[The Song]
SPIRITS [within]   Come away, come away,[4]
Hecate, Hecate, come away.
40 HECATE   I come, I come, I come, I come,
With all the speed I may,
With all the speed I may.
Where's Stadlin?
SPIRIT [within]   Here.
HECATE   Where's Puckle?
ANOTHER SPIRIT [within]   Here.
OTHER SPIRITS [within]   And Hoppo, too, and Hellwain, too,
45 We lack but you, we lack but you.
Come away, make up the count.
HECATE   I will but 'noint,[5] and then I mount.
[Spirits appear above. A SPIRIT LIKE A CAT descends]
SPIRITS [above]   There's one comes down to fetch his dues,
A kiss, a coll,° a sip of blood,   an embrace
50 And why thou stay'st so long I muse,° I muse,   wonder
Since the air's so sweet and good.
HECATE   O, art thou come? What news, what news?

---

1. Working toward a disastrous and fateful end.
2. Of deep or hidden significance; ready to fall.
3. Spirits produced by magic art.
4. The Folio only includes the first line of this song: the remaining lines, supplied here, come from a song with the same opening words from Thomas Middleton's play *The Witch* (c. 1613). See Textual Note.
5. Anoint myself, perhaps with an ointment to enable flying.

SPIRIT LIKE A CAT   All goes still to our delight.
            Either come, or else refuse, refuse.
55 HECATE   Now I am furnished° for the flight.   *provided*
            [*She ascends with the* SPIRIT *and sings*]
            Now I go, now I fly,
            Malkin my sweet spirit and I.
    SPIRITS *and* HECATE   O what a dainty pleasure 'tis
            To ride in the air
60   When the moon shines fair,
            And sing, and dance, and toy,° and kiss.   *play amorously*
            Over woods, high rocks and mountains,
            Over seas and misty fountains,
            Over steeples, towers and turrets,
65   We fly by night 'mongst troops of spirits.
            No ring of bells to our ears sounds,
            No howls of wolves, no yelps of hounds.
            No, not the noise of waters-breach°   *breaking waves*
            Or cannons' throat our height can reach.
70 SPIRITS [*above*]   No ring of bells to our ears sounds,
            No howls of wolves, no yelps of hounds.
            No, not the noise of waters-breach
            Or cannons' throat our height can reach.
            [*Exeunt into the heavens the*
            SPIRIT LIKE A CAT *and* HECATE]
    FIRST WITCH   Come, let's make haste. She'll soon be back again.
                                    Exeunt

3.6

Enter LENNOX *and another* LORD
    LENNOX   My former speeches have but hit your thoughts,
            Which can interpret farther.¹ Only I say
            Things have been strangely borne.° The gracious Duncan   *carried on*
            Was pitied of Macbeth: marry, he was dead;²
5   And the right valiant Banquo walked too late,
            Whom you may say, if't please you, Fleance killed,
            For Fleance fled: men must not walk too late.
            Who cannot want the thought° how monstrous   *can help thinking*
            It was for Malcolm and for Donalbain
10   To kill their gracious father? Damnèd fact,°   *deed*
            How it did grieve Macbeth! Did he not straight
            In pious° rage the two delinquents tear,   *loyal*
            That were the slaves of drink, and thralls° of sleep?   *slaves*
            Was not that nobly done? Ay, and wisely too,
15   For 'twould have angered any heart alive
            To hear the men deny't. So that I say
            He has borne all things well, and I do think
            That had he Duncan's sons under his key—
            As, an't° please heaven, he shall not—they should find   *if it*
20   What 'twere to kill a father. So should Fleance.
            But peace, for from broad words,³ and 'cause he failed
            His presence at the tyrant's feast, I hear

3.6 Location: Somewhere in Scotland.
1. *My . . . farther:* What I have said has coincided with
your thoughts. I need not say more; you can draw your
own further conclusions.

2. *The . . . dead:* Macbeth pitied Duncan after he was
dead, but not before. *of:* by.
3. As a result of his plain speaking.

Macduff lives in disgrace. Sir, can you tell
Where he bestows himself?°   *lodges*
LORD   The son of Duncan
25 From whom this tyrant holds° the due of birth°   *withholds / birthright*
Lives in the English court, and is received
Of the most pious Edward[4] with such grace
That the malevolence of fortune nothing
Takes from his high respect.[5] Thither Macduff
30 Is gone to pray the holy King upon his aid°   *in aid of Malcolm*
To wake Northumberland and warlike Siward,
That by the help of these—with Him above
To ratify the work—we may again
Give to our tables meat,° sleep to our nights,   *food*
35 Free from our feasts and banquets bloody knives,[6]
Do faithful homage, and receive free[7] honours,
All which we pine for now. And this report
Hath so exasperate their king° that he   *exasperated (Macbeth)*
Prepares for some attempt of war.
40 LENNOX   Sent he to Macduff?
LORD   He did, and with° an absolute 'Sir, not I,'   *on receiving*
The cloudy messenger turns me his back
And hums, as who should say 'You'll rue the time
That clogs me with this answer.'[8]
LENNOX   And that well might
45 Advise him to a caution t'hold what distance
His wisdom can provide.[9] Some holy angel
Fly to the court of England and unfold
His message ere he come, that a swift blessing
May soon return to this our suffering country
Under a hand accursed.[1]
50 LORD   I'll send my prayers with him.
                                    Exeunt

4.1

[A Cauldron.] Thunder. Enter the three WITCHES
FIRST WITCH   Thrice the brinded° cat hath mewed.   *brindled; streaked*
SECOND WITCH   Thrice, and once the hedge-pig° whined.   *hedgehog*
THIRD WITCH   Harpier° cries ''Tis time, 'tis time.'   *(her familiar)*
FIRST WITCH   Round about the cauldron go,
5 In the poisoned entrails throw.
Toad that under cold stone
Days and nights has thirty-one
Sweltered venom sleeping got,[1]
Boil thou first i'th' charmèd pot.
10 ALL   Double, double, toil and trouble,
Fire burn, and cauldron bubble.

4. *received . . . Edward:* received by the saintly King Edward (Edward the Confessor, reigned 1042–1066).
5. Does not deprive Malcolm of respect.
6. Free our feasts from bloody knives.
7. Freely given; enjoyed in freedom.
8. *He did . . . answer:* Macbeth says, "Sir, not I." The scowling ("cloudy") messenger from Macbeth turns his back and hums. His rudeness seems to say ominously, "You'll rue the time that burdens ('clogs') me with this answer."
9. *And . . . provide:* Warn Macduff to keep as far from Macbeth as he can.
1. *country . . . accursed:* country suffering under an accursed hand.
4.1 Location: A cave with a boiling caldron.
1. *has . . . got:* has for thirty-one days and nights exuded poison formed during sleep.

SECOND WITCH   Fillet° of a fenny° snake,   *Slice / from the swamps*
In the cauldron boil and bake.
Eye of newt and toe of frog,
15   Wool of bat and tongue of dog,
Adder's fork° and blind-worm's sting,   *forked tongue*
Lizard's leg and owlet's wing,
For a charm of powerful trouble,
Like a hell-broth boil and bubble.
20   ALL   Double, double, toil and trouble,
Fire burn, and cauldron bubble.
THIRD WITCH   Scale of dragon, tooth of wolf,
Witches' mummy,° maw and gulf²   *mummified flesh*
Of the ravined° salt-sea shark,   *ravenous; glutted*
25   Root of hemlock digged i'th' dark,
Liver of blaspheming Jew,
Gall of goat, and slips of yew
Slivered° in the moon's eclipse,   *Cut off*
Nose of Turk, and Tartar's³ lips,
30   Finger of birth-strangled babe
Ditch-delivered by a drab,°   *whore*
Make the gruel thick and slab.°   *viscous*
Add thereto a tiger's chaudron°   *entrails*
For th'ingredience of our cauldron.
35   ALL   Double, double, toil and trouble,
Fire burn, and cauldron bubble.
SECOND WITCH   Cool it with a baboon's blood,
Then the charm is firm and good.
        Enter HECATE *and the other three* WITCHES
HECATE   O, well done! I commend your pains,
40   And everyone shall share i'th' gains.
And now about the cauldron sing
Like elves and fairies in a ring,
Enchanting all that you put in.
        Music and a song
HECATE   Black spirits and white, red spirits and grey,⁴
45   Mingle, mingle, mingle, you that mingle may.
FOURTH WITCH   Titty,⁵ Tiffin, keep it stiff in;
        Firedrake, Puckey, make it lucky;
        Liard, Robin, you must bob in.
ALL   Round, around, around, about, about,
50   All ill come running in, all good keep out.
FOURTH WITCH   Here's the blood of a bat.
HECATE   Put in that, O put in that!
FIFTH WITCH   Here's leopard's bane.
HECATE   Put in a grain.
55   FOURTH WITCH   The juice of toad, the oil of adder.
FIFTH WITCH   Those will make the younker° madder.   *fashionable young man*
HECATE   Put in, there's all, and rid the stench.
A WITCH   Nay, here's three ounces of a red-haired wench.
ALL   Round, around, around, about, about,
60   All ill come running in, all good keep out.

---

2. Stomach and gullet.   song; see Textual Note.
3. Both thought of as cruel pagans.   5. The proper names are the names of spirits.
4. As in 3.5, the Folio only includes the first line of this

SECOND WITCH   By the pricking of my thumbs,
    Something wicked this way comes.
    [*Knock within*]
    Open, locks, whoever knocks.
    Enter MACBETH

MACBETH   How now, you secret, black, and midnight hags,
    What is't you do?

65 ALL THE WITCHES   A deed without a name.

MACBETH   I conjure you by that which you profess,°   *the black arts*
    Howe'er you come to know it, answer me.
    Though you untie the winds and let them fight
    Against the churches, though the yeasty° waves   *foamy*
70   Confound° and swallow navigation up,   *Defeat*
    Though bladed corn° be lodged° and trees blown down,   *ripe wheat / beaten down*
    Though castles topple on their warders' heads,
    Though palaces and pyramids do slope°   *bend*
    Their heads to their foundations, though the treasure
75   Of nature's germens[6] tumble all together
    Even till destruction sicken,° answer me   *be surfeited*
    To what I ask you.

FIRST WITCH   Speak.

SECOND WITCH   Demand.

THIRD WITCH   We'll answer.

FIRST WITCH   Say if thou'dst rather hear it from our mouths
    Or from our masters.

MACBETH   Call 'em, let me see 'em.

80 FIRST WITCH   Pour in sow's blood that hath eaten
    Her nine farrow;° grease that's sweaten°   *litter of nine / sweated*
    From the murderer's gibbet° throw   *gallows*
    Into the flame.

ALL THE WITCHES   Come high or low,
    Thyself and office° deftly show.   *function*
    Thunder. FIRST APPARITION: *an armed° head*   *armored*

MACBETH   Tell me, thou unknown power—

85 FIRST WITCH   He knows thy thought.
    Hear his speech, but say thou naught.

FIRST APPARITION   Macbeth, Macbeth, Macbeth, beware Macduff,
    Beware the Thane of Fife. Dismiss me. Enough.
    [APPARITION] *descends*

MACBETH   Whate'er thou art, for thy good caution thanks.
90   Thou hast harped° my fear aright. But one word more—   *guessed*

FIRST WITCH   He will not be commanded. Here's another,
    More potent than the first.
    Thunder. SECOND APPARITION: *a bloody child*

SECOND APPARITION   Macbeth, Macbeth, Macbeth.

MACBETH   Had I three ears I'd hear thee.

95 SECOND APPARITION   Be bloody, bold, and resolute. Laugh to scorn
    The power of man, for none of woman born
    Shall harm Macbeth.
    [APPARITION] *descends*

MACBETH   Then live, Macduff—what need I fear of thee?
    But yet I'll make assurance double sure,

---

6. Seeds from which all nature grows. According to Renaissance theories of biology, if they were tumbled together, they would become barren or produce only monsters.

100 And take a bond of fate thou shalt not live,[7]
That I may tell pale-hearted fear it lies,
And sleep in spite of thunder.
        Thunder. THIRD APPARITION: *a child crowned, with a*
        tree in his hand[8]
                        What is this
That rises like the issue of a king,
And wears upon his baby-brow the round
And top° of sovereignty?   *crown*
105 ALL THE WITCHES   Listen, but speak not to't.
THIRD APPARITION   Be lion-mettled, proud, and take no care
Who chafes, who frets, or where conspirers are.
Macbeth shall never vanquished be until
Great Birnam Wood to high Dunsinane Hill
Shall come against him.
            [APPARITION] *descends*
110 MACBETH   That will never be.
Who can impress° the forest, bid the tree   *force into service*
Unfix his earth-bound root? Sweet bodements,° good!   *omens*
Rebellious dead,[9] rise never till the wood
Of Birnam rise, and on's high place Macbeth
115 Shall live the lease of nature,° pay his breath   *natural life span*
To time and mortal custom.[1] Yet my heart
Throbs to know one thing. Tell me, if your art
Can tell so much, shall Banquo's issue ever
Reign in this kingdom?
ALL THE WITCHES   Seek to know no more.
120 MACBETH   I will be satisfied. Deny me this,
And an eternal curse fall on you! Let me know.
           [*The cauldron sinks.*] *Hautboys*
Why sinks that cauldron? And what noise° is this?   *music*
FIRST WITCH   Show.
SECOND WITCH   Show.
125 THIRD WITCH   Show.
ALL THE WITCHES   Show his eyes and grieve his heart,
Come like shadows, so depart.
        A show of eight kings, [the] last with a glass° *in his*   *mirror*
        hand; and BANQUO
MACBETH   Thou art too like the spirit of Banquo. Down!
Thy crown does sear mine eyeballs. And thy hair,
130 Thou other gold-bound brow, is like the first.
A third is like the former. Filthy hags,
Why do you show me this?—A fourth? Start,° eyes!   *Bulge out*
What, will the line stretch out to th' crack of doom?
Another yet? A seventh? I'll see no more—
135 And yet the eighth appears, who bears a glass
Which shows me many more; and some I see
That twofold balls and treble sceptres[2] carry.

---

7. By killing Macduff, Macbeth hopes to bind fate to its
promise that no man of woman born shall harm Macbeth.
8. Signifying Malcolm. The tree anticipates 5.5.31ff.
9. Perhaps Banquo. Some editors emend to "Rebellious
head" or "Rebellion's head," where "head" means
"army."

1. The custom of mortality; natural death.
2. James I was crowned twice, once as King of Scotland
and later as King of England. He carried one orb at each
coronation. "Treble sceptres" refers to the fact that he
held two scepters in the English coronation and one in
the Scottish, or perhaps to his claim to be King of
Britain, France, and Ireland.

Horrible sight! Now I see 'tis true,
For the blood-baltered[3] Banquo smiles upon me,
And points at them for his.[4]

[*Exeunt kings and* BANQUO]

140   What, is this so?

HECATE   Ay, sir, all this is so. But why
Stands Macbeth thus amazedly?°   *entranced*
Come, sisters, cheer we up his sprites,°   *spirits*
And show the best of our delights.

145   I'll charm the air to give a sound
While you perform your antic round,°   *fantastic dance*
That this great king may kindly say
Our duties did his welcome pay.[5]

          Music. The WITCHES *dance, and vanish*

MACBETH   Where are they? Gone? Let this pernicious hour
150   Stand aye° accursèd in the calendar.   *ever*
Come in, without there.

           Enter LENNOX

LENNOX   What's your grace's will?

MACBETH   Saw you the weird sisters?

LENNOX   No, my lord.

MACBETH   Came they not by you?

LENNOX   No, indeed, my lord.

MACBETH   Infected be the air whereon they ride,
155   And damned all those that trust them. I did hear
The galloping of horse. Who was't came by?

LENNOX   'Tis two or three, my lord, that bring you word
Macduff is fled to England.

MACBETH   Fled to England?

LENNOX   Ay, my good lord.

160   MACBETH [*aside*]   Time, thou anticipat'st° my dread exploits.   *forestall*
The flighty purpose never is o'ertook
Unless the deed go with it.[6] From this moment
The very firstlings° of my heart shall be   *first notions*
The firstlings° of my hand. And even now,   *first acts*
165   To crown my thoughts with acts, be it thought and done:
The castle of Macduff I will surprise,
Seize upon Fife, give to th'edge o'th' sword
His wife, his babes, and all unfortunate souls
That trace him in his line. No boasting like a fool;
170   This deed I'll do before this purpose cool.
But no more sights! [*To* LENNOX] where are these gentlemen?
come bring me where they are.   *Exeunt*

4.2

      Enter MACDUFF'S WIFE, *her* SON, *and* ROSS

LADY MACDUFF   What had he done to make him fly the land?

ROSS   You must have patience, madam.

LADY MACDUFF   He had none.

---

3. Having hair matted with blood.
4. Banquo was the legendary founder of the Stuart dynasty.
5. Our service repaid the welcome he gave us.

6. *The flighty . . . it:* The fleeting intention is never realized unless the deed is done immediately.
4.2 Location: Macduff's castle in Fife.

His flight was madness. When our actions do not,
Our fears do make us traitors.[1]

ROSS   You know not
5   Whether it was his wisdom or his fear.

LADY MACDUFF   Wisdom—to leave his wife, to leave his babes,
His mansion, and his titles° in a place   *estates*
From whence himself does fly? He loves us not,
He wants° the natural touch,° for the poor wren,   *lacks / affection*
10   The most diminutive of birds, will fight,
Her young ones in her nest, against the owl.
All is the fear and nothing is the love;
As little is the wisdom, where the flight
So runs against all reason.

ROSS   My dearest coz,°   *kinswoman*
15   I pray you school° yourself. But for your husband,   *control*
He is noble, wise, judicious, and best knows
The fits o'th' season.[2] I dare not speak much further,
But cruel are the times when we are traitors
And do not know ourselves;[3] when we hold rumour
20   From what we fear, yet know not what we fear,[4]
But float upon a wild and violent sea
Each way and none.[5] I take my leave of you;
Shall° not be long but° I'll be here again.   *It shall / before*
Things at the worst will cease, or else climb upward
25   To what they were before. My pretty cousin,°   *(Macduff's son)*
Blessing upon you!

LADY MACDUFF   Fathered he is, and yet he's fatherless.

ROSS   I am so much a fool, should I stay longer
It would be my disgrace and your discomfort.[6]
I take my leave at once.   *Exit*

30   LADY MACDUFF   Sirrah, your father's dead,
And what will you do now? How will you live?

MACDUFF'S SON   As birds do, mother.

LADY MACDUFF   What, with worms and flies?

MACDUFF'S SON   With what I get, I mean, and so do they.

LADY MACDUFF   Poor° bird, thou'dst never fear the net nor lime,[7]   *Pitiful*
35   The pitfall nor the gin.°   *snare*

MACDUFF'S SON   Why should I, mother? Poor° birds they are not   *Worthless*
set for.
My father is not dead, for all your saying.

LADY MACDUFF   Yes, he is dead. How wilt thou do for a father?

MACDUFF'S SON   Nay, how will you do for a husband?

40   LADY MACDUFF   Why, I can buy me twenty at any market.

MACDUFF'S SON   Then you'll buy 'em to sell again.

LADY MACDUFF   Thou speak'st with all thy wit, and yet, i'faith,
with wit enough for thee.

MACDUFF'S SON   Was my father a traitor, mother?

45   LADY MACDUFF   Ay, that he was.

---

1. *When . . . traitors:* Even when we have committed no
treason, our fear of suspicion makes us behave as though
we are guilty.
2. The violent convulsions of the present time; what
befits the time.
3. *we . . . ourselves:* we are denounced as traitors but do
not know why; we have no self-knowledge.

4. *when . . . fear:* when we believe rumors inspired by our
fears, but those fears are themselves vague.
5. In every direction, and so finally in none.
6. I would disgrace myself and embarrass you by
weeping (or perhaps by lingering).
7. Birdlime, a sticky substance smeared on twigs to catch
small birds.

MACDUFF'S SON   What is a traitor?

LADY MACDUFF   Why, one that swears and lies.[8]

MACDUFF'S SON   And be all traitors that do so?

LADY MACDUFF   Everyone that does so is a traitor, and must be
50   hanged.

MACDUFF'S SON   And must they all be hanged that swear° and   *speak profanely*
lie?

LADY MACDUFF   Every one.

MACDUFF'S SON   Who must hang them?

55   LADY MACDUFF   Why, the honest men.

MACDUFF'S SON   Then the liars and swearers are fools, for there
are liars and swearers enough to beat the honest men and hang
up them.

LADY MACDUFF   Now God help thee, poor monkey! But how wilt
60   thou do for a father?

MACDUFF'S SON   If he were dead you'd weep for him. If you
would not, it were a good sign that I should quickly have a
new father.

LADY MACDUFF   Poor prattler, how thou talk'st!

Enter a MESSENGER

65   MESSENGER   Bless you, fair dame. I am not to you known,
Though in your state of honour I am perfect.[9]
I doubt° some danger does approach you nearly.   *fear*
If you will take a homely° man's advice,   *plain*
Be not found here. Hence with your little ones!
70   To fright you thus methinks I am too savage,
To do worse to you were fell cruelty,[1]
Which is too nigh your person.[2] Heaven preserve you.
I dare abide no longer.   *Exit* MESSENGER

LADY MACDUFF   Whither should I fly?
I have done no harm. But I remember now
75   I am in this earthly world, where to do harm
Is often laudable, to do good sometime
Accounted dangerous folly. Why then, alas,
Do I put up that womanly defence
To say I have done no harm?

Enter MURDERERS

                               What are these faces?

80   A MURDERER   Where is your husband?

LADY MACDUFF   I hope in no place so unsanctified
Where such as thou mayst find him.

A MURDERER   He's a traitor.

MACDUFF'S SON   Thou liest, thou shag-haired villain.

A MURDERER [*stabbing him*]   What, you egg!
Young fry° of treachery!   *spawn*

MACDUFF'S SON   He has killed me, mother.
85   Run away, I pray you.

       [*He dies.*] *Exit* [MACDUFF'S WIFE] *crying 'Murder!'*
       [*followed by* MURDERERS *with the Son's body*]

---

8. Takes an oath and breaks it.
9. Though I know perfectly well your high rank (an
apology for bursting in).
1. *To fright . . . cruelty:* Even to frighten you by speaking

of such danger is savage; actually to harm you would be
brutal ("fell") cruelty.
2. Such cruelty is already too near you.

4.3

Enter MALCOLM *and* MACDUFF

MALCOLM   Let us seek out some desolate shade, and there
Weep our sad bosoms empty.

MACDUFF   Let us rather
Hold fast the mortal° sword, and like good men   *deadly*
Bestride our downfall birthdom.¹ Each new morn
5   New widows howl, new orphans cry, new sorrows
Strike heaven on the face that° it resounds   *so that*
As if it felt with Scotland and yelled out
Like syllable of dolour.°   *A similar cry of pain*

MALCOLM   What I believe I'll wail,
What know believe; and what I can redress,
10   As I shall find the time to friend,° I will.   *favorable*
What you have spoke it may be so, perchance.
This tyrant, whose sole° name blisters our tongues,   *mere*
Was once thought honest. You have loved him well.
He hath not touched° you yet. I am young, but something   *injured*
15   You may discern of him through me:² and wisdom°   *it's prudent*
To offer up a weak poor innocent lamb
T'appease an angry god.

MACDUFF   I am not treacherous.

MALCOLM   But Macbeth is.
20   A good and virtuous nature may recoil
In an imperial charge.³ But I shall crave your pardon.
That which you are my thoughts cannot transpose.°   *transform*
Angels are bright still, though the brightest° fell.   *(Lucifer)*
Though all things foul would wear the brows of grace,
Yet grace must still look so.⁴
25   MACDUFF   I have lost my hopes.⁵

MALCOLM   Perchance even there where I did find my doubts.⁶
Why in that rawness° left you wife and child,   *unprotected condition*
Those precious motives,° those strong knots of love,   *inducements to devotion*
Without leave-taking? I pray you,
30   Let not my jealousies° be your dishonours,   *suspicions*
But mine own safeties.° You may be rightly just,   *safeguards*
Whatever I shall think.

MACDUFF   Bleed, bleed, poor country!
Great tyranny, lay thou thy basis° sure,   *foundation*
For goodness dare not check thee. Wear thou thy wrongs;°   *wrongful gains*
35   The title is affeered.° Fare thee well, lord.   *confirmed*
I would not be the villain that thou think'st
For the whole space that's in the tyrant's grasp,
And the rich east to boot.°   *as well*

MALCOLM   Be not offended.
I speak not as in absolute fear° of you.   *complete distrust*
40   I think our country sinks beneath the yoke.
It weeps, it bleeds, and each new day a gash
Is added to her wounds. I think withal°   *nonetheless*

4.3 Location: England, before King Edward's palace.
1. Stand in defense over our downtrodden native land.
2. *I . . . me:* I am inexperienced, but you might gain favor
with Macbeth by betraying me. Many editions emend
"discern" to "deserve."
3. *recoil . . . charge:* give way to a royal command.

4. *Though . . . so:* Though everything evil disguises itself
as virtue, virtue still looks like itself.
5. Hopes of Malcolm's help in a campaign against Macbeth.
6. Doubts of Macduff's loyalty, because he has left his
wife and children.

There would be hands uplifted in my right,
And here from gracious England° have I offer   the King of England
45   Of goodly thousands. But for all this,
When I shall tread upon the tyrant's head,
Or wear it on my sword, yet my poor country
Shall have more vices than it had before,
More suffer, and more sundry° ways, than ever,   in more various
By him that shall succeed.
50   MACDUFF   What° should he be?   Who
MALCOLM   It is myself I mean, in whom I know
All the particulars° of vice so grafted   varieties
That when they shall be opened° black Macbeth   disclosed
Will seem as pure as snow, and the poor state
55   Esteem him as a lamb, being compared
With my confineless° harms.   infinite
MACDUFF   Not in the legions
Of horrid hell can come a devil more damned
In evils to top Macbeth.
MALCOLM   I grant him bloody,
Luxurious,° avaricious, false, deceitful,   Lecherous
60   Sudden,° malicious, smacking of every sin   Violent
That has a name. But there's no bottom, none,
In my voluptuousness. Your wives, your daughters,
Your matrons, and your maids could not fill up
The cistern of my lust, and my desire
65   All continent° impediments would o'erbear   restraining; chaste
That did oppose my will. Better Macbeth
Than such an one to reign.
MACDUFF   Boundless intemperance
In nature° is a tyranny. It hath been   human nature
Th'untimely emptying of the happy throne,
70   And fall of many kings. But fear not yet°   nevertheless
To take upon you what is yours. You may
Convey° your pleasures in a spacious plenty   Manage secretly
And yet seem cold.° The time° you may so hoodwink.°   indifferent / age / deceive
We have willing dames enough. There cannot be
75   That vulture in you to devour so many
As will to greatness dedicate themselves,
Finding it so inclined.
MALCOLM   With this there grows
In my most ill-composed affection° such   character
A staunchless° avarice that were I king   An insatiable
80   I should cut off the nobles for their lands,
Desire his jewels and this other's house,
And my more having would be as a sauce
To make me hunger more, that I should forge
Quarrels unjust against the good and loyal,
Destroying them for wealth.
85   MACDUFF   This avarice
Sticks deeper, grows with more pernicious root
Than summer-seeming⁷ lust, and it hath been
The sword° of our slain kings. Yet do not fear.   undoing
Scotland hath foisons° to fill up your will   plenty

---

7. Appropriate to youth ("summer") but passing with age, unlike avarice; summerlike.

90   Of your mere own.[8] All these are portable,°   *bearable*
         With other graces weighed.
      MALCOLM   But I have none. The king-becoming graces,
         As justice, verity, temp'rance, stableness,
         Bounty, perseverance, mercy, lowliness,°   *humility*
95   Devotion, patience, courage, fortitude,
         I have no relish° of them, but abound   *trace*
         In the division° of each several° crime,   *variations / separate*
         Acting it many ways. Nay, had I power I should
         Pour the sweet milk of concord into hell,
100   Uproar the universal peace, confound
         All unity on earth.
      MACDUFF   O Scotland, Scotland!
      MALCOLM   If such a one be fit to govern, speak.
         I am as I have spoken.
      MACDUFF   Fit to govern?
         No, not to live. O nation miserable,
105   With an untitled° tyrant bloody-sceptered,   *a usurping*
         When shalt thou see thy wholesome days again,
         Since that the truest issue of thy throne
         By his own interdiction° stands accursed   *declaration of unfitness*
         And does blaspheme his breed?° Thy royal father   *disgrace his heritage*
110   Was a most sainted king. The Queen that bore thee,
         Oft'ner upon her knees than on her feet,
         Died[9] every day she lived. Fare thee well.
         These evils thou repeat'st upon thyself
         Hath banished me from Scotland. O, my breast—
         Thy hope ends here!
115   MALCOLM   Macduff, this noble passion,
         Child of integrity, hath from my soul
         Wiped the black scruples,° reconciled my thoughts   *dark suspicions*
         To thy good truth and honour. Devilish Macbeth
         By many of these trains° hath sought to win me   *stratagems*
120   Into his power, and modest wisdom° plucks me   *prudent moderation*
         From over-credulous haste; but God above
         Deal between thee and me, for even now
         I put myself to thy direction and
         Unspeak° mine own detraction, here abjure   *Retract*
125   The taints and blames I laid upon myself
         For° strangers to my nature. I am yet   *As*
         Unknown to woman, never was forsworn,
         Scarcely have coveted what was mine own,
         At no time broke my faith, would not betray
130   The devil to his fellow, and delight
         No less in truth than life. My first false-speaking
         Was this upon myself. What I am truly
         Is thine and my poor country's to command,
         Whither indeed, before thy here-approach,
135   Old Siward with ten thousand warlike men,
         Already at a point,° was setting forth.   *prepared*
         Now we'll together; and the chance of goodness

---

8. *Scotland . . . own:* Scotland is bountiful enough to satisfy your greed with your own royal property alone.

9. Dead to the world. ("By your rejoicing which I have in Christ Jesus our Lord, I die daily," 1 Corinthians 15:31).

Be like our warranted quarrel!¹—Why are you silent?

MACDUFF   Such welcome and unwelcome things at once

140   'Tis hard to reconcile.

         Enter a DOCTOR

MALCOLM   Well, more anon. [*To the* DOCTOR] Comes the King

    forth, I pray you?

DOCTOR   Ay, sir. There are a crew of wretched souls

    That stay° his cure. Their malady convinces   *await*

    The great essay of art,² but at his touch,

145   Such sanctity hath Heaven given his hand,

    They presently amend.°   *heal*

MALCOLM   I thank you, doctor.   *Exit* [DOCTOR]

MACDUFF   What's the disease he means?

MALCOLM   'Tis called the evil³—

    A most miraculous work in this good King,

    Which often since my here-remain in England

150   I have seen him do. How he solicits° heaven   *moves by entreaty*

    Himself best knows, but strangely visited° people,   *afflicted*

    All swoll'n and ulcerous, pitiful to the eye,

    The mere° despair of surgery, he cures,   *utter*

    Hanging a golden stamp° about their necks,   *coin*

155   Put on with holy prayers; and 'tis spoken,

    To the succeeding royalty he leaves

    The healing benediction. With this strange virtue°   *power*

    He hath a heavenly gift of prophecy,

    And sundry blessings hang about his throne

    That speak him full of grace.°   *divine grace*

         Enter ROSS

160 MACDUFF   See who comes here.

MALCOLM   My countryman, but yet I know° him not.   *recognize*

MACDUFF   My ever gentle cousin, welcome hither.

MALCOLM   I know him now. Good God betimes° remove   *quickly*

    The means that makes us strangers!

ROSS   Sir, amen.

MACDUFF   Stands Scotland where it did?

165 ROSS   Alas, poor country,

    Almost afraid to know itself. It cannot

    Be called our mother, but our grave, where nothing

    But who knows nothing is once seen to smile;⁴

    Where sighs and groans and shrieks that rend the air

170   Are made, not marked;° where violent sorrow seems   *noticed*

    A modern ecstasy.° The dead man's knell   *commonplace emotion*

    Is there scarce asked for who,⁵ and good men's lives

    Expire before the flowers in their caps,

    Dying or ere° they sicken.   *before*

MACDUFF   O relation°   *report*

    Too nice° and yet too true!   *detailed*

175 MALCOLM   What's the newest grief?

ROSS   That of an hour's age doth hiss the speaker;⁶

    Each minute teems° a new one.   *yields*

---

1. *the . . . quarrel:* may the chance of success be equal to the justice of our cause.
2. *convinces . . . art:* defeats the best efforts of medical skill.
3. "The king's evil," scrofula, thought to be cured by the royal touch.
4. No one smiles except he who knows nothing.
5. Scarcely anyone asks for whom it is rung.
6. Cause the speaker to be hissed for telling old news.

MACDUFF   How does my wife?
ROSS   Why, well.
MACDUFF   And all my children?
ROSS   Well, too.
MACDUFF   The tyrant has not battered at their peace?
180 ROSS   No, they were well at peace when I did leave 'em.
MACDUFF   Be not a niggard of your speech. How goes't?
ROSS   When I came hither to transport the tidings
Which I have heavily° borne, there ran a rumour   *gravely*
Of many worthy fellows that were out,°   *in arms*
185 Which was to my belief witnessed the rather°   *made more credible*
For that I saw the tyrant's power° afoot.   *army*
Now is the time of° help. [*To* MALCOLM] Your eye in scotland   *moment for*
Would create soldiers, make our women fight
To doff° their dire distresses.   *remove*
MALCOLM   Be't their comfort
190 We are coming thither. Gracious England hath
Lent us good Siward and ten thousand men;
An older and a better soldier none°   *there is none*
That Christendom gives out.°   *proclaims; provides*
ROSS   Would I could answer
This comfort with the like. But I have words
195 That would be howled out in the desert air
Where hearing should not latch° them.   *catch*
MACDUFF   What concern they—
The general cause, or is it a fee-grief°   *private woe*
Due to° some single breast?   *Owned by*
ROSS   No mind that's honest
But in it shares some woe, though the main part
Pertains to you alone.
200 MACDUFF   If it be mine,
Keep it not from me; quickly let me have it.
ROSS   Let not your ears despise my tongue for ever,
Which shall possess them with the heaviest sound
That ever yet they heard.
MACDUFF   H'm, I guess at it.
205 ROSS   Your castle is surprised, your wife and babes
Savagely slaughtered. To relate the manner
Were on the quarry of these murdered deer
To add the death of you.[7]
MALCOLM   Merciful heaven!
[*To* MACDUFF] What, man, ne'er pull your hat upon your
      brows.°   *conceal your grief*
210 Give sorrow words. The grief that does not speak
Whispers the o'erfraught° heart and bids it break.   *overburdened*
MACDUFF   My children too?
ROSS   Wife, children, servants, all
That could be found.
MACDUFF   And I must be° from thence!   *had to be*
My wife killed too?
ROSS   I have said.
MALCOLM   Be comforted.

---

7. To tell how they were murdered would be to add your death to the heap of slaughtered game ("quarry").

215   Let's make us medicines of our great revenge
       To cure this deadly grief.

MACDUFF   He has no children. All my pretty ones?
       Did you say all? O hell-kite! All?
       What, all my pretty chickens and their dam
220   At one fell swoop?

MALCOLM   Dispute° it like a man.   *Fight*

MACDUFF   I shall do so,
       But I must also feel it as a man.
       I cannot but remember such things were
225   That were most precious to me. Did heaven look on
       And would not take their part? Sinful Macduff,
       They were all struck for° thee. Naught° that I am,   *on account of / Wicked*
       Not for their own demerits but for mine
       Fell slaughter on their souls. Heaven rest them now.
230 MALCOLM   Be this the whetstone of your sword. Let grief
       Convert° to anger: blunt not the heart, enrage it.   *Be changed*

MACDUFF   O, I could play the woman with mine eyes
       And braggart with my tongue! But gentle heavens
       Cut short all intermission.° Front to front°   *delay / Face-to-face*
235   Bring thou this fiend of Scotland and myself.
       Within my sword's length set him. If he scape,
       Heaven forgive him too.

MALCOLM   This tune goes manly.
       Come, go we to the King. Our power° is ready;   *army*
       Our lack is nothing but our leave.[8] Macbeth
240   Is ripe for shaking, and the powers above
       Put on their instruments.[9] Receive what cheer you may:
       The night is long that never finds the day.   *Exeunt*

5.1

Enter a DOCTOR *of Physic*° *and a Waiting-*   *Physician*
GENTLEWOMAN

DOCTOR   I have two nights watched with you, but can perceive
    no truth in your report. When was it she last walked?

GENTLEWOMAN   Since his majesty went into the field° I have   *battlefield*
    seen her rise from her bed, throw her nightgown upon her,
5   unlock her closet,° take forth paper, fold it, write upon't, read   *chest*
    it, afterwards seal it, and again return to bed, yet all this while
    in a most fast sleep.

DOCTOR   A great perturbation in nature, to receive at once the
    benefit of sleep and do the effects of watching°. In this slum-   *act as if awake*
10   bery agitation° besides her walking and other actual° perfor-   *movement / active*
    mances, what at any time have you heard her say?

GENTLEWOMAN   That, sir, which I will not report after her.

DOCTOR   You may to me; and 'tis most meet° you should.   *proper*

GENTLEWOMAN   Neither to you nor anyone, having no witness to
15   confirm my speech.

        Enter LADY [MACBETH] *with a taper*
    Lo you, here she comes. This is her very guise,° and, upon my   *exact habit*
    life, fast asleep. Observe her. Stand close.°   *concealed*

---

8. We have only to take leave of the King.   5.1 Location: Macbeth's castle in Dunsinane.
9. Arm themselves; set us to work as their agents.

DOCTOR   How came she by that light?

GENTLEWOMAN   Why, it stood by her. She has light by her con-
20   tinually. 'Tis her command.

DOCTOR   You see her eyes are open.

GENTLEWOMAN   Ay, but their sense are shut.

DOCTOR   What is it she does now? Look how she rubs her hands.

GENTLEWOMAN   It is an accustomed action with her, to seem
25   thus washing her hands. I have known her continue in this a
quarter of an hour.

LADY MACBETH   Yet here's a spot.

DOCTOR   Hark, she speaks. I will set down what comes from her
to satisfy° my remembrance the more strongly.   *support*

30   LADY MACBETH   Out, damned spot; out, I say. One, two,—why,
then 'tis time to do't. Hell is murky. Fie, my lord, fie, a soldier
and afeard? What need we fear who knows it when none can
call our power to account? Yet who would have thought the
old man to have had so much blood in him?

35   DOCTOR   Do you mark that?

LADY MACBETH   The Thane of Fife had a wife. Where is she
now? What, will these hands ne'er be clean? No more o' that,
my lord, no more o' that. You mar all with this starting.°   *startled movement*

DOCTOR   Go to, go to.° You have known what you should not.   *(expression of reproof)*

40   GENTLEWOMAN   She has spoke what she should not, I am sure of
that. Heaven knows what she has known.

LADY MACBETH   Here's the smell of the blood still. All the perfumes of Arabia will not sweeten this little hand. O, O, O!

DOCTOR   What a sigh is there! The heart is sorely charged.°   *burdened*

45   GENTLEWOMAN   I would not have such a heart in my bosom for
the dignity° of the whole body.   *worth*

DOCTOR   Well, well, well.

GENTLEWOMAN   Pray God it be, sir.

DOCTOR   This disease is beyond my practice.° Yet I have known   *skill*
50   those which have walked in their sleep who have died holily in
their beds.

LADY MACBETH   Wash your hands, put on your nightgown, look
not so pale. I tell you yet again, Banquo's buried. He cannot
come out on's° grave.   *of his*

55   DOCTOR   Even so?

LADY MACBETH   To bed, to bed. There's knocking at the gate.
Come, come, come, come, give me your hand. What's done
cannot be undone. To bed, to bed, to bed.   *Exit*

DOCTOR   Will she go now to bed?

60   GENTLEWOMAN   Directly.

DOCTOR   Foul whisp'rings are abroad. Unnatural deeds
Do breed unnatural troubles; infected minds
To their deaf pillows will discharge their secrets.
More needs she the divine° than the physician.   *priest*
65   God, God forgive us all! Look after her.
Remove from her the means of all annoyance,°   *self-injury*
And still keep eyes upon her. So, good night.
My mind she has mated,° and amazed my sight.   *bewildered*
I think, but dare not speak.

GENTLEWOMAN   Good night, good doctor.   *Exeunt*

5.2

Enter MENTEITH, CAITHNESS, ANGUS, LENNOX, *soldiers,*
[*with a drummer*] *and colours*

MENTEITH   The English power is near, led on by Malcolm,
　His uncle Siward, and the good Macduff.
　Revenges burn in them, for their dear causes
　Would to the bleeding° and the grim alarm°　　　　　　　*bloody / call to battle*
　Excite° the mortified° man.　　　　　　　　　　*Rouse / insensible; dead*

5　ANGUS　　　　　　　　　　Near Birnam Wood
　Shall we well° meet them. That way are they coming.　　　　*doubtless*

CAITHNESS   Who knows if Donalbain be with his brother?

LENNOX   For certain, sir, he is not. I have a file°　　　　　*roster*
　Of all the gentry. There is Siward's son,

10　And many unrough° youths that even now　　　　　　　　*beardless*
　Protest their first of manhood.[1]

MENTEITH　　　　　　　　　　What does the tyrant?

CAITHNESS   Great Dunsinane he strongly fortifies.
　Some say he's mad, others that lesser hate him
　Do call it valiant fury; but for certain

15　He cannot buckle his distempered° cause　　　　　　　*disease-swollen*
　Within the belt of rule.°　　　　　　　　　　　　　*restraint*

ANGUS　　　　　　　　　　Now does he feel
　His secret murders sticking on his hands.
　Now minutely° revolts upbraid his faith-breach.　　　　　*every minute*
　Those he commands move only in command,°　　　　　*under constraint*

20　Nothing in love. Now does he feel his title
　Hang loose about him, like a giant's robe
　Upon a dwarfish thief.

MENTEITH　　　　　　　　　Who then shall blame
　His pestered° senses to recoil and start　　　　　　　*tormented*
　When all that is within him does condemn
　Itself for being there?

25　CAITHNESS　　　　　　　Well, march we on
　To give obedience where 'tis truly owed.
　Meet we the medicine° of the sickly weal,°　　　　*(Malcolm) / state*
　And with him pour we in our country's purge,
　Each drop of us.

LENNOX　　　　　　　Or so much as it needs

30　To dew° the sovereign° flower and drown the weeds.　　*bedew / royal; curative*
　Make we our march towards Birnam.　　*Exeunt, marching*

5.3

Enter MACBETH, [*the*] DOCTOR [*of Physic*], *and attendants*

MACBETH   Bring me no more reports. Let them fly all.°　　*Let all thanes desert*
　Till Birnam Wood remove to Dunsinane
　I cannot taint° with fear. What's the boy Malcolm?　　　*be infected*
　Was he not born of woman? The spirits that know

5　All mortal consequences° have pronounced me thus:　　*human destinies*
　'Fear not, Macbeth. No man that's born of woman
　Shall e'er have power upon thee.' Then fly, false thanes,
　And mingle with the English epicures.[1]
　The mind I sway° by and the heart I bear　　　　　　　*rule myself*

5.2 Location: The country near Dunsinane.　　　5.3 Location: Macbeth's castle in Dunsinane.
1. Declare for the first time that they are men.　　1. Lovers of easy, luxurious living.

10　Shall never sag with doubt nor shake with fear.
　　　　　Enter SERVANT.
　　The devil damn thee black, thou cream-faced loon!° 　　　　　　*rogue*
　　Where gott'st thou that goose look?
SERVANT　There is ten thousand—
MACBETH　Geese, villain?
SERVANT　　　　　　　　　Soldiers, sir.
15　MACBETH　Go prick thy face and over-red thy fear,[2]
　　Thou lily-livered[3] boy. What soldiers, patch?° 　　　　　　　　*fool*
　　Death of° thy soul, those linen cheeks of thine 　　　　　　　　*on*
　　Are counsellors to fear.° What soldiers, whey-face? 　　*Teach others to fear*
SERVANT　The English force, so please you.
MACBETH　Take thy face hence.　　　　　　　[*Exit* SERVANT]
20　　　　　　　　　Seyton!—I am sick at heart
　　When I behold—Seyton, I say!—This push° 　　　　　　　　*crisis*
　　Will cheer[4] me ever or disseat° me now. 　　　　　　　　*dethrone*
　　I have lived long enough. My way of life
　　Is fall'n into the sere,° the yellow leaf, 　　　　　　　　*withered state*
25　And that which should accompany old age,
　　As° honour, love, obedience, troops of friends, 　　　　　　　　*Such as*
　　I must not look to have, but in their stead
　　Curses, not loud but deep, mouth-honour,° breath 　　　　　　　　*lip service*
　　Which the poor heart would fain deny and dare not.
30　Seyton!
　　　　　　　Enter SEYTON
SEYTON　What's your gracious pleasure?
MACBETH　　　　　　　　　　　What news more?
SEYTON　All is confirmed, my lord, which was reported.
MACBETH　I'll fight till from my bones my flesh be hacked.
　　Give me my armour.
35　SEYTON　'Tis not needed yet.
MACBETH　I'll put it on.
　　Send out more horses. Skirr° the country round. 　　　　　　　　*Scour*
　　Hang those that talk of fear. Give me mine armour.
　　How does your patient, doctor?
DOCTOR　　　　　　　　　　Not so sick, my lord,
40　As she is troubled with thick-coming fancies
　　That keep her from her rest.
MACBETH　　　　　　　　　Cure her of that.
　　Canst thou not minister to a mind diseased,
　　Pluck from the memory a rooted sorrow,
　　Raze out the written troubles of[5] the brain,
45　And with some sweet oblivious° antidote 　　　　*causing forgetfulness*
　　Cleanse the fraught bosom of that perilous stuff
　　Which weighs upon the heart?
DOCTOR　　　　　　　　　Therein the patient
　　Must minister to himself.
MACBETH　Throw physic° to the dogs; I'll none of it. 　　　　　　　　*medicine*
50　[*To an attendant*] Come, put mine armour on. Give me my staff.° 　　*lance*
　　Seyton, send out. Doctor, the thanes fly from me.

---

2. Redden your fearful pallor.
3. Lacking blood in your liver (thought to be the seat of courage); cowardly.
4. Comfort; enthrone or establish (punning on "cheer/chair").
5. Erase the troubles engraved in.

[*To an attendant*] Come, sir, dispatch.°—If thou couldst, doctor, cast   *hurry*
The water⁶ of my land, find her disease,
And purge it to a sound and pristine health,
55   I would applaud thee to the very echo,
That should applaud again.   [*To an attendant*] Pull't off, I say.⁷
[*To the* DOCTOR] what rhubarb, cyme,° or what purgative drug   *senna (medicinal plant)*
Would scour° these English hence? Hear'st thou of them?   *purge*

DOCTOR   Ay, my good lord. Your royal preparation
Makes us hear something.

60   MACBETH [*to an attendant*]   Bring it⁸ after me.
I will not be afraid of death and bane°   *destruction*
Till Birnam Forest come to Dunsinane.

DOCTOR [*aside*]   Were I from Dunsinane away and clear,
Profit again should hardly draw me here.⁹   *Exeunt*

5.4

Enter MALCOLM, SIWARD, MACDUFF, SIWARD'S SON, MEN-
TEITH, CAITHNESS, ANGUS, *and* SOLDIERS, *marching,*
[*with a drummer*] *and colours*

MALCOLM   Cousins, I hope the days are near at hand
That chambers° will be safe.   *bedrooms*

MENTEITH   We doubt it nothing.°   *not at all*

SIWARD   What wood is this before us?

MENTEITH   The wood of Birnam.

MALCOLM   Let every soldier hew him down a bough
5   And bear't before him. Thereby shall we shadow°   *conceal*
The numbers of our host, and make discovery°   *reconnaissance*
Err in report of us.

A SOLDIER   It shall be done.

SIWARD   We learn no other but the confident tyrant
Keeps still in Dunsinane, and will endure
Our setting down before°'t.   *laying siege to*

10   MALCOLM   'Tis his main hope,
For where there is advantage° to be gone,   *opportunity*
Both more and less° have given him the revolt,   *great and lowly*
And none serve with him but constrainèd things,
Whose hearts are absent too.

MACDUFF   Let our just censures
15   Attend the true event,¹ and put we on
Industrious soldiership.

SIWARD   The time approaches
That will with due decision make us know
What we shall say we have, and what we owe.
Thoughts speculative their unsure hopes relate,
20   But certain issue strokes must arbitrate;²
Towards which, advance the war.   *Exeunt, marching*

---

6. *cast / The water:* analyze the urine as a method of
diagnosis.
7. A piece of armor is not properly fitted; Macbeth
orders the attendant to take it off.
8. The armor not yet on Macbeth.
9. No large fees could lure me back.

5.4 Location: The country near Birnam Wood.
1. *Let . . . event:* Let our judgments await the actual
outcome.
2. *Thoughts . . . arbitrate:* Speculation produces hopes
and unconfirmed optimism, but the issue will only be
decided by action.

5.5

Enter MACBETH, SEYTON, *and soldiers, with [a drummer]*
and colours

MACBETH   Hang out our banners on the outward walls.
The cry is still 'They come.' Our castle's strength
Will laugh a siege to scorn. Here let them lie
Till famine and the ague eat them up.
5   Were they not forced° with those that should be ours   reinforced
We might have met them dareful,° beard to beard,   boldly
And beat them backward home.

A cry within of women

What is that noise?

SEYTON   It is the cry of women, my good lord.   [*Exit*]

MACBETH   I have almost forgot the taste of fears.
10   The time has been my senses would have cooled°   been chilled with terror
To hear a night-shriek, and my fell of hair°   hair on my skin
Would at a dismal treatise° rouse and stir   story
As life were in't. I have supped full with horrors.
Direness, familiar to my slaughterous thoughts,
Cannot once start° me.   startle

[*Enter* SEYTON]

15   Wherefore was that cry?

SEYTON   The Queen, my lord, is dead.

MACBETH   She should have died hereafter.[1]
There would have been a time for such a word.
Tomorrow, and tomorrow, and tomorrow
Creeps in this petty pace from day to day
20   To the last syllable of recorded time,
And all our yesterdays have lighted fools
The way to dusty death. Out, out, brief candle.
Life's but a walking shadow, a poor player
That struts and frets his hour upon the stage,
25   And then is heard no more. It is a tale
Told by an idiot, full of sound and fury,
Signifying nothing.

Enter a MESSENGER

Thou com'st to use
Thy tongue: thy story quickly.

MESSENGER   Gracious my lord,
I should report that which I say I saw,
But know not how to do't.

30   MACBETH   Well, say, sir.

MESSENGER   As I did stand my watch upon the hill
I looked toward Birnam, and anon methought
The wood began to move.

MACBETH   Liar and slave!

MESSENGER   Let me endure your wrath if't be not so.
35   Within this three mile may you see it coming.
I say, a moving grove.

MACBETH   If thou speak'st false
Upon the next tree shalt thou hang alive
Till famine cling° thee. If thy speech be sooth,°   wither / truth

---

5.5 Location: Macbeth's castle.
1. She would certainly have died someday; she should have died at another, more peaceful time.

I care not if thou dost for me as much.

40 I pall° in resolution, and begin   *fail*

To doubt th'equivocation of the fiend,

That lies like truth. 'Fear not till Birnam Wood

Do come to Dunsinane'—and now a wood

Comes toward Dunsinane. Arm, arm, and out.

45 If this which he avouches does appear

There is nor flying hence nor tarrying here.

I 'gin to be aweary of the sun,

And wish th'estate° o'th' world were now undone.   *ordered structure*

Ring the alarum bell. [*Alarums*] Blow wind, come wrack,°   *ruin*

50 At least we'll die with harness° on our back.   *Exeunt*   *armor*

5.6

Enter MALCOLM, SIWARD, MACDUFF, *and their army with*
boughs, [with a drummer] and colours

MALCOLM   Now near enough. Your leafy screens throw down,

And show° like those you are.   *appear*

    [*They throw down the boughs*]

                You, worthy uncle,

Shall with my cousin, your right noble son,

Lead our first battle.° Worthy Macduff and we   *battalion*

5 Shall take upon's what else remains to do

According to our order.°   *battle plan*

SIWARD   Fare you well.

Do we but find the tyrant's power° tonight,   *army*

Let us be beaten if we cannot fight.

MACDUFF   Make all our trumpets speak, give them all breath,

10 Those clamorous harbingers of blood and death.

                      Exeunt. Alarums continued

5.7

Enter MACBETH

MACBETH   They have tied me to a stake. I cannot fly,

But bear-like I must fight the course.[1] What's he

That was not born of woman? Such a one

Am I to fear, or none.

    Enter YOUNG SIWARD

5 YOUNG SIWARD   What is thy name?

MACBETH   Thou'lt be afraid to hear it.

YOUNG SIWARD   No, though thou call'st thyself a hotter name

Than any is in hell.

MACBETH   My name's Macbeth.

YOUNG SIWARD   The devil himself could not pronounce a title

More hateful to mine ear.

MACBETH   No, nor more fearful.

10 YOUNG SIWARD   Thou liest, abhorrèd tyrant. With my sword

I'll prove the lie thou speak'st.

    [*They*] *fight, and* YOUNG SIWARD [*is*] *slain*

MACBETH   Thou wast born of woman,

5.6 Location: As before.
5.7 Location: As before.
1. Referring to the practice of bearbaiting, in which a

bear was tied to a stake and set upon by dogs. *course:*
round of bearbaiting.

But swords I smile at, weapons laugh to scorn,
Brandished by man that's of a woman born.

Exit [with the body]

5.8

Alarums. Enter MACDUFF

MACDUFF That way the noise is. Tyrant, show thy face!
If thou beest slain and with° no stroke of mine,   *by*
My wife and children's ghosts will haunt me still.°   *always*
I cannot strike at wretched kerns,° whose arms   *Irish foot soldiers*
⁵ Are hired to bear their staves.° Either thou, Macbeth,   *spears*
Or else my sword with an unbattered edge
I sheathe again undeeded.¹ There thou shouldst be;
By this great clatter one of greatest note
Seems bruited.° Let me find him, fortune,   *announced*
¹⁰ And more I beg not.   *Exit. Alarums*

5.9

Enter MALCOLM *and* SIWARD

SIWARD This way, my lord. The castle's gently rendered.°   *surrendered*
The tyrant's people on both sides do fight.
The noble thanes do bravely in the war.
The day almost itself professes yours,
And little is to do.
⁵ MALCOLM   We have met with foes
That strike beside us.¹
SIWARD   Enter, sir, the castle. *Exeunt. Alarum*

5.10

Enter MACBETH

MACBETH Why should I play the Roman fool,° and die   *the suicide*
On mine own sword? Whiles I see lives, the gashes
Do better upon them.
         Enter MACDUFF
MACDUFF   Turn, hell-hound, turn.
MACBETH Of all men else I have avoided thee.
⁵ But get thee back. My soul is too much charged
With blood of thine already.
MACDUFF   I have no words;
My voice is in my sword, thou bloodier villain
Than terms can give thee out.°   *words can describe*
         [*They*] *fight; alarum*
MACBETH   Thou losest labour.°   *waste effort*
As easy mayst thou the intrenchant° air   *incapable of being cut*
¹⁰ With thy keen sword impress° as make me bleed.   *mark*
Let fall thy blade on vulnerable crests;
I bear a charmèd life, which must not yield
To one of woman born.
MACDUFF   Despair° thy charm,   *Despair of*
And let the angel° whom thou still hast served   *(evil) spirit*

5.8 Location: Before Macbeth's castle; the battle
continues.
1. Having accomplished no deeds.

5.9 Location: Before Macbeth's castle.
1. Fight on our side; deliberately miss us.
5.10 Location: Scene continues.

15   Tell thee Macduff was from his mother's womb
    Untimely° ripped.   *Prematurely*
  MACBETH   Accursèd be that tongue that tells me so,
    For it hath cowed° my better part of man;   *intimidated*
    And be these juggling fiends no more believed,
20   That palter° with us in a double sense,   *equivocate*
    That keep the word of promise to our ear
    And break it to our hope. I'll not fight with thee.
  MACDUFF   Then yield thee, coward,
    And live to be the show and gaze° o'th' time.   *spectacle*
25   We'll have thee as our rarer monsters° are,   *prodigies*
    Painted upon a pole,[1] and underwrit
    'Here may you see the tyrant.'
  MACBETH   I will not yield
    To kiss the ground before young Malcolm's feet,
    And to be baited° with the rabble's curse.   *harassed*
30   Though Birnam Wood be come to Dunsinane,
    And thou opposed being of no woman born,
    Yet I will try the last.° Before my body   *the last resort*
    I throw my warlike shield. Lay on, Macduff,
    And damned be him that first cries 'Hold, enough!'
                          Exeunt fighting. Alarums
          [They] enter fighting, and MACBETH *[is] slain. [Exit* MAC-
          DUFF *with Macbeth's body]*

5.11

Retreat[1] *and flourish. Enter with [a drummer] and col-*
ours MALCOLM, SIWARD, ROSS, *thanes, and soldiers*
  MALCOLM   I would° the friends we miss were safe arrived.   *wish*
  SIWARD   Some must go off;° and yet by these[2] I see   *die*
    So great a day as this is cheaply bought.
  MALCOLM   Macduff is missing, and your noble son.
5   ROSS *[to* SIWARD]   Your son, my lord, has paid a soldier's debt.
    He only lived but till he was a man,
    The which no sooner had his prowess confirmed
    In the unshrinking station[3] where he fought,
    But like a man he died.
  SIWARD   Then he is dead?
10   ROSS   Ay, and brought off the field. Your cause of sorrow
    Must not be measured by his worth, for then
    It hath no end.
  SIWARD   Had he his hurts before?°   *on his front*
  ROSS   Ay, on the front.
  SIWARD   Why then, God's soldier be he.
    Had I as many sons as I have hairs
15   I would not wish them to a fairer death;
    And so his knell is knolled.
  MALCOLM   He's worth more sorrow,
    And that I'll spend for him.
  SIWARD   He's worth no more.

---

1. Painted on a cloth or board supported by a pole as a form of advertisement.
5.11 Location: Within the castle.

1. A trumpet call signaling the end of the battle.
2. To judge from those who are present.
3. Post from which he did not shrink.

They say he parted° well and paid his score,   *departed*
And so God be with him. Here comes newer comfort.

Enter MACDUFF *with Macbeth's head*

20   MACDUFF [*to* MALCOLM]   Hail, King, for so thou art. Behold where stands⁴
Th'usurper's cursèd head. The time is free.°   *free from tyranny*
I see thee compassed with thy kingdom's pearl,⁵
That speak my salutation in their minds,
Whose voices I desire aloud with mine:
Hail, King of Scotland!

25   ALL BUT MALCOLM   Hail, King of Scotland!
      Flourish

   MALCOLM   We shall not spend a large expense of time
Before we reckon with° your several loves   *make an accounting of*
And make us even with you.° My thanes and kinsmen,   *reward your loyalty*
Henceforth be earls, the first that ever Scotland
30   In such an honour named. What's more to do
Which would be planted newly with the time,⁶
As calling home our exiled friends abroad,
That fled the snares of watchful tyranny,
Producing forth⁷ the cruel ministers°   *agents*
35   Of this dead butcher and his fiend-like queen—
Who, as 'tis thought, by self and violent hands°   *her own violent hands*
Took off her life—this and what needful else
That calls upon us, by the grace of grace
We will perform in measure, time, and place.⁸
40   So thanks to all at once, and to each one,
Whom we invite to see us crowned at Scone.

Flourish. Exeunt Omnes°   *all*

---

4. Presumably upon a pole or lance.
5. I see you surrounded by your nobles, here called the "pearl" of the kingdom.
6. Which should be performed at the beginning of this new era.
7. Bringing forward for trial.
8. In due order, at the proper time and place.

Antony and Cleopatra

What if Shakespeare had had second thoughts about *Romeo and Juliet*? He might have tried something a little different. In this version, the lovers, neither youthful nor married to each other, are involved in a long-standing, adulterous relationship. Romeo, thinking Juliet dead because she has sent a messenger with that lie, kills himself—though with a sword rather than poison. He partly bungles the job, however, and hence takes a while to die. Juliet resolves to follow him, but she delays for the entire fifth act before killing herself—though with poison rather than a sword. And when they are both finally dead, the audience may be less likely to lament the loss of "star-crossed lovers" than celebrate the fulfillment of a heroic passion.

In the event Shakespeare did have second thoughts about *Romeo and Juliet;* he called these second thoughts *Antony and Cleopatra* (late 1606–early 1607). The last of Shakespeare's three love tragedies, the play also rewrites *Othello,* the middle work of this group, converting its threat from the East, there represented by the Turks, into both a threat and an opportunity from the East, here represented by the Egyptians. All three tragedies set their domestic concerns thematically against the backdrop of bloody political conflict, but formally against the expectations of romantic comedy. All three seem like comedies that somehow get derailed. But *Antony and Cleopatra* replaces the emphasis on youth of romantic comedy, of *Romeo and Juliet,* and even of Desdemona in *Othello* with the most sustained, complex portrayal of mature love in Shakespeare's dramatic career.

In Shakespeare's romantic comedies, problem plays, and romances, the female protagonist often dominates the scene. But in the tragedies that Shakespeare composed from roughly 1599 to 1608, *Antony and Cleopatra* is the only such candidate. Moreover, following a series of tragedies—*Hamlet, Othello, King Lear,* and *Macbeth*—in which the protagonist's psychology is consistently probed, *Antony and Cleopatra* almost completely avoids soliloquy. Antony's and Cleopatra's motives often remain opaque—arguably, even to themselves. We never definitively learn why Antony thinks marriage to Octavia will solve his political problems, why Cleopatra flees at Actium, why she negotiates with Caesar in the last act. Instead of self-revelation, the play offers contradictory framing commentary by minor figures. These external perspectives help impart an epic feel, as do the geographical and scenic shifts, which also produce a loose, fragmentary, and capacious structure alien to classically inspired notions of proper dramatic form. *Antony and Cleopatra* is thus a new, transitional kind of tragedy. Its restlessness is of a piece with that of *Pericles,* perhaps the next play Shakespeare wrote and the first of his late romances. And the intimations of transcendence with which *Antony and Cleopatra* ends point toward the magical or supernatural resolutions of the romances more generally.

The play may also be compared to Shakespeare's other Roman tragedies, *Julius Caesar* and *Coriolanus.* All are based on Thomas North's translation of *Plutarch's Lives of the Noble Grecians and Romanes* (1579)—Shakespeare's favorite source, with the exception of Raphael Holinshed's *Chronicles of England, Scotland, and Ireland,* and one that he follows closely here. All three plays rely heavily on blank verse while almost entirely avoiding rhyme. Here Shakespeare may have followed the Earl of Surrey's sixteenth-century blank-verse translation of part of the *Aeneid* (19 B.C.E.), Virgil's epic of the legendary founding of Rome, itself understood as an allegory of the city-state's bloody transition from republic (rule by senatorial aristocracy) to empire (monarchical power) in the poet's own day.

Octavius Caesar, later known as Augustus, as on this medal. From Guillaume Du Choul, *Discours de la Religion des Anciens Romains* (1567 ed.).

It is this transition that Shakespeare dramatizes in *Julius Caesar* and *Antony and Cleopatra*. Chronologically, *Antony* picks up where *Julius Caesar* leaves off. That earlier play focuses on Caesar's assassination by republicans, led by Brutus and Cassius, and the assassins' subsequent defeat at the hands of Mark Antony (Caesar's lieutenant) and Octavius Caesar (Caesar's young grandnephew and adoptive son). *Antony and Cleopatra*, which covers the period from 40 to 30 B.C.E., completes the narrative of Roman civil war and the final destruction of the Republic. The dominant military power throughout the Mediterranean and beyond, Rome is ruled by the triumvirate of Lepidus, Octavius Caesar, and Mark Antony, who govern, respectively, the Mediterranean portions of Africa, Europe, and Asia. Accordingly, *Antony and Cleopatra* partly turns away from *Julius Caesar*'s emphasis on the struggle over Rome's internal political system, looking instead to Rome's external imperial domains. Correspondingly, the stylistic restraint fitted to Brutus's republican restraint gives way to an extravagant, hyperbolic verse in accord with the empire's expansive grandeur. This would thus seem the theater for heroic, legendary, even mythic performance: Antony is associated with Hercules, and Antony and Cleopatra are repeatedly compared to Mars and Venus.

Yet *Antony and Cleopatra* actually investigates the possibility of such performance in a postheroic world. It offers an epic view of the political arena but deprives that arena of heroic significance. Mark Antony and Octavius Caesar contend for political supremacy, but the love between Antony and Cleopatra increasingly occupies center stage. The work then asks whether heroic meaning can be transplanted to the ostensibly private terrain of love. Much of the play's fascination arises from this intertwining of empire and sexuality. Plutarch and other classical writers were preoccupied with what for them was the opposition between the political and moral virtue of the conquering West, and the luxurious, feminized sexuality of the older civilizations of the subjugated East. This understanding of empire reemerged in the Renaissance during a new era of Western expansion, marked by an increasingly racialized and still sexualized view of non-European peoples. Just months before the probable first performance of the play, King James authorized the establishment of an English colony in North America—an undertaking that resulted in the founding of Jamestown the following year. As in other western European countries at the time, Rome was the central model of imperial greatness. The view of Egypt was more mixed, however: it was both the preeminent source of ancient wisdom and a land that, even though Rome had defeated it, threatened to transmit its decadence to the victors.

Accordingly, *Antony and Cleopatra* itself seems designed to elicit complicated judgments. This has often proven difficult in performance. Long supplanted on the stage by John Dryden's *All for Love* (1678), which recasts Shakespeare's story as a tragedy of private life, the play came into its own only after 1800 in the heyday of the British Empire, with Cleopatra routinely embodying Oriental sexual vice. The text initially seems to justify this interpretation: Rome is contrasted to Egypt, West to East, the conquerors to the conquered. Rapid shifts of scene across enormous distances accentuate this division. A sober, masculine military ethos opposes a frivolous, feminized, and sexualized court. Political opportunism drives Antony's marriage to Octavia, love and sexual desire his relationship with Cleopatra; he chooses between fidelity to a chaste, white wife and adultery with a promiscuous, "tawny," "black" seductress (1.1.6, 1.5.28). That seductress has a smaller political role than in Plutarch—a change which accentuates the basic conflict. Where Caesar employs rational self-interest (he is the "universal landlord," 3.13.72), Antony revels in extravagant generosity and challenges Caesar to one-on-one combat. Young Caesar is a bureaucrat of the future, old Antony a warrior of the past. Caesar's concerns are public, Antony's private. Antony is guilty by association with his brother and his previous wife, Fulvia, who attack Caesar. By contrast, Caesar promises that "the time of universal peace is near" (4.6.4), an assertion that anticipates the *Pax Romana* (Roman peace) he instituted throughout the Empire and the birth of Christ in a Roman province during his long rule.

Yet the play seems to create such dichotomies only to undermine them. Antony boasts of his valor at Philippi, while Caesar "alone / Dealt on lieutenantry" (battled exclusively through his officers; 3.11.38–39). Earlier, however, Antony's "officer" Ventidius remarks, "Caesar and Antony have ever won / More in their officer than person" (3.1.16–17). Caesar's promise of "universal peace" is anticipated in a version of Christ's Last Supper that Antony shares with his followers.

> Tend me tonight.
> Maybe it is the period of your duty.
> Haply you shall not see me more; or if,
> A mangled shadow. Perchance tomorrow
> You'll serve another master.
> (4.2.24–28)

Enobarbus, who functions like a skeptical chorus, criticizes Antony for moving his friends to tears. But that skepticism is itself challenged. It leads Enobarbus to become a Judas figure who betrays his master by defecting to Caesar and who dies shortly thereafter, his heart broken by Antony's generosity.

Even the geographical contrast of the play partly dissolves into parallelisms: Roman war is eroticized, Egyptian love is militarized. The external representation of the lovers' relationship, the absence of scenes of them alone, and their pride in exhibiting their affair intensify the feeling that love and war influence each other, that there is no distinction between public and private. Furthermore, love is on both sides of the divide. Late in the play, Antony, focused exclusively on Cleopatra, is heroically preceded in suicide by his aptly named servant Eros (love), a figure from Plutarch. But when the work opens, Antony's neglect of military command is criticized as "this dotage of our General's" by Philo (again, "love"; 1.1.1), a figure invented by Shakespeare.

The eroticization of Rome also takes the form of powerful feelings directed toward Antony. Octavius Caesar at times acts almost as if he were the son—rather than grandnephew and adopted son—of Cleopatra's former lover, Julius Caesar, whose paternal role Antony has usurped. Octavius Caesar is disgusted by Antony and Cleopatra's theatrical coronation:

> At the feet sat
> Caesarion, whom they call my father's son,
> And all the unlawful issue that their lust
> Since then hath made between them.
> (3.6.5–8)

Here, there is a possible confusion between Antony and the older Caesar and a definite one between Caesarion and the younger Caesar, both of whom are "my father's son." At Antony's death, Caesar movingly recalls his foe:

> . . . thou, my brother, my competitor
> In top of all design, my mate in empire,
> Friend and companion in the front of war,

> The arm of mine own body, and the heart
> Where mine his thoughts did kindle.
>
> (5.1.42–46)

This outpouring of emotion leads in contradictory directions. By calling Antony his "brother" and "mate," and by invoking a meeting of "heart" and mind, Caesar on the one hand suggests an intimacy between the two men that recalls Renaissance celebrations of close male friendship but that also borders on the erotic. On the other hand, he neutralizes any filial anxiety he may feel by describing Antony first as "my brother" and then as a subordinate, "the arm of mine own body."

Most important, this strategy of undermining apparent distinctions has the effect of draining the political world of meaning. *Julius Caesar*'s struggle between republic and empire arises only peripherally in *Antony and Cleopatra*, where it is voiced by Pompey (2.6.15–19), who is bought off, attacked, and finally murdered by the triumvirs. The Republic is thus all but dead when *Antony and Cleopatra* opens. Egypt's independence is at stake, although this occurs only to Cleopatra—belatedly and perhaps duplicitously. That leaves only the conflict between Antony and Caesar, a conflict, however, that simply concerns the desires of two ambitious men. The end of the Roman civil war is also important, but it is hard either to celebrate the victory of Caesar or lament the defeat of Antony. The disabused view of political power that emerges could be construed as an implicit critique of the centralizing monarchs of Shakespeare's own time.

On the other hand, the political symbolism of the two men is certainly antithetical. Caesar astutely adopts republican style, whereas Antony offends Roman sensibilities by taking on monarchical trappings (3.6.1–19). Antony's antagonist does not emulate the older Caesar, whose sexual and military conquests were intertwined (3.13.82–85). Hence the younger Caesar represents not the preservation but the diminution of traditional Roman values, a constriction of a heroic culture of which Antony is the last survivor. The play insists that politics and sex (or any kind of grandeur) are irrevocably sundered, that one can no longer have it both ways.

Certainly, Antony and Cleopatra cannot. The play characterizes Antony and Cleopatra through a language of greatness, shared by the protagonists and minor figures alike, only to subvert that rhetoric through still other commentary and, even more, through the behavior of Antony and Cleopatra themselves. Although Shakespeare makes them more sympathetic than they are in Plutarch, they remain maddeningly self-absorbed and self-destructive—lying, ignoring urgent business, acting impulsively, bullying underlings, reveling in vulgarity, apparently betraying each other. They are also militarily peripheral, as the fighting scenes, except for the first Battle of Alexandria, testify. Shakespeare's uncharacteristic decision to follow the practice of classical theater and keep all combat offstage leaves only a feeling of being let down, as helpless observers report on the debacle. Thus, Enobarbus laments at Actium:

> Naught, naught, all naught! I can behold no longer.
> Th'*Antoniad*, the Egyptian admiral,
> With all their sixty, fly and turn the rudder.
>
> (3.10.1–3)

At the last battle of the play, it is Antony's turn:

> All is lost.
> This foul Egyptian hath betrayèd me.
> My fleet hath yielded to the foe, and yonder
> They cast their caps up, and carouse together
> Like friends long lost.
>
> (4.13.9–13)

But this is not the whole story or even, in the end, most of it. Antony and Cleopatra are great not despite their failings but because of them. Inability to fit into Caesar's narrowed world of self-discipline sets them apart. Their outsized grandeur can be described only through paradoxical hyperbole. Antony's heart "is become the bellows and the fan / To cool a gipsy's lust": his heart is a fan that cools Cleopatra's lust by satisfying it, but in so doing he rekindles her passion, as if his heart were also a bellows (1.1.9–10). Similarly, when Cleopatra meets Antony, "pretty dimpled boys" (2.2.208) attend her

> With divers-coloured fans whose wind did seem
> To glow the delicate cheeks which they did cool,
> And what they undid did.
>
> (2.2.209–11)

And when told that marriage to Octavia will force Antony to abandon Cleopatra, Enobarbus demurs in the play's most famous lines:

> Never. He will not.
> Age cannot wither her, nor custom stale
> Her infinite variety. Other women cloy
> The appetites they feed, but she makes hungry
> Where most she satisfies.
>
> (2.2.239–43)

These passages might be considered accounts of insatiable middle-aged lust. The trick of the play is to convince the audience that they are really about love. Antony's feelings may seem easier to believe than Cleopatra's: he is the one who gives up an empire. By contrast, Cleopatra's combination of teasing frivolity, comic jealousy, and cold calculation have rendered her motives suspect. Yet Shakespeare gives her passages of extraordinary dignity early in the play, when Antony decides to leave her upon hearing of his wife Fulvia's death.

> Courteous lord, one word.
> Sir, you and I must part; but that's not it.
> Sir, you and I have loved; but there's not it;
> That you know well. Something it is I would—
> O, my oblivion is a very Antony,
> And I am all forgotten.
>
> (1.3.87–92)

Cleopatra experiences something more than she can express. Its articulation, therefore, initially takes the form of a failure to articulate. There is an echo of this later, when Enobarbus attempts to describe her to his fellow Romans: "her own person . . . beggared all description" (2.2.203–04). Here, however, Cleopatra tries to convey her meaning through a witticism: her forgetfulness makes her like Antony, who is forgetful of her. She forgets and is forgotten. But when Antony misses the point, thinking he has merely witnessed idle wordplay, she corrects him.

> 'Tis sweating labour
> To bear such idleness so near the heart
> As Cleopatra this. But sir, forgive me,
> . . . .
> . . . be deaf to my unpitied folly,
> And all the gods go with you.
>
> (1.3.94–100)

In short, Cleopatra's playfulness is the mere surface of her essential depth, a depth that involves a "sweating labour" like that of childbirth.

The last two acts put that depth to the test, ultimately making Cleopatra the play's central character. *Antony and Cleopatra*'s geographical restlessness diminishes as the protagonists' sphere of activity is reduced to Alexandria. Cleopatra sends Antony a fabricated, manipulative report of her death, he botches his suicide in response, and she then refuses to leave her monument to attend him as he lies dying. Instead, she hoists him up to her with the comment, "Here's sport indeed. How heavy weighs my lord!" (4.16.33), where "sport" is both playful and bitter, where "weighs" carries both physical and psychological meaning, and, hence, where the scene as a whole combines grotesque comedy with genuine pathos. Structurally, Antony's presumably climactic death becomes a mere false ending that shifts the burden of significance to the final act. Egypt and Cleopatra are what matter. Egypt has been associated throughout with the overflowing that Antony is faulted for at the outset. Antony declares his love for Cleopatra by rejecting the state he rules: "Let Rome in Tiber melt, and the wide arch / Of the ranged empire fall" (1.1.35–36). Upon hearing of Antony's marriage to Octavia, Cleopatra prays, "Melt Egypt into Nile, and kindly creatures / Turn all to serpents!" (2.5.78–79). This apocalyptic imagery, which dissolves all distinction, anticipates Antony's loss of self when he thinks Cleopatra has betrayed him. His body seems to him as "indistinct / As water is in water" (4.15.10–11). The language of liquefaction is also connected to the confusion of gender identity. Antony

> is not more manlike
> Than Cleopatra, nor the queen of Ptolemy
> More womanly than he.
>
> (1.4.5–7)

And Cleopatra reports, "I . . . put my tires and mantles on him whilst / I wore his sword Philippan" (2.5.21–23). Depending on one's perspective, this behavior either dangerously confuses gender roles, thereby leading to Antony's ignominious flight at Actium, or overcomes a destructive opposition.

Cleopatra herself, who metaphorically overflows boundaries, is literally linked to Egypt throughout the play. In particular, she is specifically identified with the Egyptian goddess Isis (3.6.17), who is invoked several times in the play, probably on the basis of Plutarch's *On Isis and Osiris*. Isis is the sister-wife of Osiris, whom she restores after he is pursued to his death by his brother-rival, Typhon. The conclusion thus seeks the regenerative powers of the Nile in Cleopatra. It asks whether she really is the equivalent of Isis, whether she really is the wife of Antony (Osiris), whether she really does restore him after he is pursued to his death by his brother (Caesar).

This is the work of Cleopatra's suicide, which makes good on these imagistic patterns, retrospectively justifying Antony's decision to die for her. We may desire the protagonists' deaths in Shakespeare's earlier tragedies, perhaps because life no longer has any meaning for these characters. But *Antony and Cleopatra* goes further: it convinces us that the suicides of the two lovers is a heroic achievement, that anything less would constitute abject failure. The ending also evokes the synthesis precluded by the play's dichotomies but implied by its more subtle patterns. Cleopatra dies the death of a Roman man:

> My resolution's placed, and I have nothing
> Of woman in me. Now from head to foot
> I am marble-constant. Now the fleeting moon
> No planet is of mine.
>
> (5.2.234–37)

She also dies the death of a faithful Roman wife:

> . . . methinks I hear
> Antony call. I see him rouse himself
> To praise my noble act. . . .
> . . . .
> . . . Husband, I come.
> Now to that name my courage prove my title.
>
> (5.2.274–79)

The Nile delta, showing the northern end of the river as it flows into the Mediterranean Sea. Alexandria is visible near the upper left-hand corner. From a map in Sebastian Münster's *Cosmographiae universalis* (1550).

And in taking the poisonous asp to her breast, she may become a Roman mother as well, in a passage that recalls her earlier representation of intense feeling in the language of childbirth:

> Peace, peace.
> Dost thou not see my baby at my breast,
> That sucks the nurse asleep?
> . . . .
> As sweet as balm, as soft as air, as gentle.

> O Antony!
> [*She puts another aspic to her arm*]
> Nay, I will take thee too.
> (5.2.299–303)

Since the Folio lacks the stage direction included here, perhaps the final line can mean that she takes Antony to her breast, like a mother comforting her infant son.

The Clown wishes Cleopatra "joy o'th' worm" (5.2.270) as she prepares to commit suicide. From Edward Topsell's *Historie of Serpents* (1608).

But "O Antony" is also a cry of orgasm that looks back to Cleopatra's earlier sexual assertions, "I am again for Cydnus / To meet Mark Antony" (5.2.224–25) and "Husband, I come" (5.2.278), and forward to Charmian's sexually ecstatic dying words, which Shakespeare added to his source: "Ah, soldier!" (5.2.319). Furthermore, Cleopatra's manner of death is clearly Egyptian. The asp recalls Antony's description of her as "my serpent of old Nile" (1.5.25). Thus, Rome and Egypt, Antony and Cleopatra, martial valor and sexual ecstasy are united in death as they cannot be in life. "Dido and her Aeneas" (4.15.53), in Antony's vision soon to be eclipsed by himself and Cleopatra, wander together through the afterlife of the play. But Dido and Aeneas remain bitterly unreconciled in the *Aeneid*, Shakespeare's source for the characters. There Aeneas abandons Dido, whom Virgil modeled on the historical Cleopatra and thus associated with Eastern sensuality. The abandonment is justified in the name of a higher cause, Rome. Thus, Aeneas, despite his extramarital affair, functions as a fictional forerunner not of the historical Antony but of the historical Octavius Caesar. Insofar as *Antony and Cleopatra* leads the audience to believe that its protagonists really will end up together, then, it answers the *Aeneid*, distancing itself from Roman and, by extension, Renaissance imperialism. It seems to be saying that you *can* have it both ways. East and West, conquered and conqueror are affirmed in a final synthesis.

Yet countercurrents trouble Cleopatra's "immortal longings" (5.2.272). She resolves on suicide not when she learns that Antony killed himself for her but when she becomes certain that Caesar plans to lead her in a humiliating triumph in Rome. Recognizing that her suicide will ruin Caesar's plans, she takes pleasure in imagining that Antony will "mock / The luck of Caesar," that the asp will "call great Caesar ass / Unpolicied" (5.2.276–77, 298–99). The concluding triumphant rhetoric thus cleans up earlier dubious behavior and puts the best face on defeat. Heroic aristocratic individualism can act in the world only by leaving it. Moreover, the domestic Cleopatra of the conclusion might seem the reduction to a conventional gender role of a woman who challenged sexual hierarchy. At her death, Cleopatra "lies / A lass unparalleled" (5.2.305–06). This alliterative eulogy juxtaposes the Latinate "unparalleled," typical of the extravagant rhetoric of the play, with the homespun "lass." Both stylistically and semantically, that humble word also matches Cleopatra's own rhetoric—"Husband," "baby," and "nurse." Moreover, in echoing her contempt for "Caesar [the] ass / Unpolicied," the phrase praises her at his expense. Alternatively, however, has *Antony and Cleopatra* instead presented "lies alas unparalleled?"

The answer depends on the relationship between the ending and the partly incompatible material that has preceded it. Most, though not all, critics have found the conclusion affirmative. But the work registers ambivalence to the last. This duality is captured in Cleopatra's account of the response she expects in Rome:

> The quick comedians
> Extemporally will stage us, and present
> Our Alexandrian revels. Antony
> Shall be brought drunken forth, and I shall see
> Some squeaking Cleopatra boy my greatness
> I'th' posture of a whore.
>
> (5.2.212–17)

Cleopatra shudders at the absurdity of a boy actor badly impersonating her, yet the part of Cleopatra in *Antony and Cleopatra* was originally performed by a boy. This reminder punctures the dramatic illusion just when it seems most essential. It looks back to Cleopatra's deliberate blurring of gender division. And it emphasizes the artifice of Cleopatra herself, a veteran actress in her final performance. Shakespeare here flaunts the power of his medium. But if it is impossible to "boy" Cleopatra's "greatness," to represent her adequately, perhaps that is an invitation, as she has earlier suggested, to look beyond what can be shown, to take seriously her "immortal longings."

WALTER COHEN

TEXTUAL NOTE

The Tragedie of Anthonie, and Cleopatra was published in the First Folio of 1623 (F), which also gives the forms *Anthony and Cleopater* in other references to the title of the play. "Anthony & Cleopatra" was entered on May 20, 1608, in the Stationers' Register, a listing of books intended for legal publication. As it happened, the play went unpublished; this entry may have been designed to prevent someone else from printing it. Both stylistic tests and probable verbal echoes in other plays suggest a date of late 1606 or possibly early 1607. The Folio version is ultimately based on an authorial manuscript but perhaps by way of a transcript. There is no evidence of the revisions necessary for theatrical performance. Thus, the stage directions list characters who have no role in the scene or even the entire play (characters excluded from the present edition); are insufficient at various points, especially in the closing scenes at Cleopatra's monument; and (like the speech prefixes) contain some authorial errors.

The play presents problems in modernizing proper names and in verse lineation. In addition, but less problematically, it has no act or scene divisions after an initial "Actus Primus. Scoena Prima." The ones supplied here follow editorial practice standard since the eighteenth century, except in starting a new scene after 4.7.3 (because the stage is cleared). This decision, of course, changes the scene numbering for the remainder of the act.

SELECTED BIBLIOGRAPHY

Archer, John Michael. "Antiquity and Degeneration in *Antony and Cleopatra*." *Race, Ethnicity, and Power in the Renaissance*. Ed. Joyce Green MacDonald. Madison, N.J.: Fairleigh Dickinson University Press, 1997. 145–64. The ambivalent image of

Egypt in the Renaissance, combining reverence for its antique wisdom with anxiety about contagious decadence.

Bloom, Harold, ed. *William Shakespeare's "Antony and Cleopatra."* New York: Chelsea House, 1988. Eight heterogeneous essays by important critics from the 1970s and 1980s.

Deats, Sara Munson, ed. *Antony and Cleopatra: New Critical Essays.* New York: Routledge, 2005. Fourteen new essays, including a long opening survey of criticism and performance by the editor.

Drakakis, John, ed. *"Antony and Cleopatra," William Shakespeare.* New York: St. Martin's, 1994. Twelve heterogeneous essays by leading critics, mainly from the 1970s and 1980s.

Holderness, Graham, Bryan Loughrey, and Andrew Murphy, eds. *Shakespeare: The Roman Plays.* London: Longman, 1996. Three essays on *Antony and Cleopatra* from the 1980s and 1990s, focusing on psychoanalytical and political issues.

Loomba, Ania. *Shakespeare, Race, and Colonialism.* Oxford: Oxford University Press, 2002. 112–34. Links of empire, gender ambiguity, skin color, gypsies, and role playing.

Madeleine, Richard, ed. *Antony and Cleopatra.* Cambridge: Cambridge University Press, 1998. Book-length history of productions of *Antony and Cleopatra*, combined with an edition of the play annotated with accounts of various performance decisions.

Rose, Mark, ed. *Twentieth Century Interpretations of "Antony and Cleopatra": A Collection of Critical Essays.* Englewood Cliffs, N.J.: Prentice-Hall, 1977. A dozen statements and essays from major critics, from 1945 to 1975, mostly formalist in character, with some attention to historical background.

Wofford, Susanne L. *Shakespeare's Late Tragedies: A Collection of Critical Essays.* Upper Saddle River, N.J.: Prentice Hall, 1996. Five essays on *Antony and Cleopatra* from the 1980s and 1990s, plus substantial discussion of the play in three other more general pieces; primarily issues of subjectivity, race, gender, empire, and performance.

Wood, Nigel, ed. *Antony and Cleopatra.* Buckingham, Eng.: Open University Press, 1996. Four essays connecting theory to interpretation, from the perspectives of mimetic rivalry, postcolonialism, polysemous gynocentrism, and genre.

FILM

Antony and Cleopatra. 1974. Dir. Jon Scoffield. UK. 161 min. Based on the 1972 Royal Shakespeare Company performance, starring Janet Suzman as an intelligent, tawny, feminist Cleopatra. Focuses on love at the expense of politics.

The Tragedy of Antony and Cleopatra

THE PERSONS OF THE PLAY

MARK ANTONY (Marcus Antonius), triumvir of Rome

DEMETRIUS
PHILO
Domitius ENOBARBUS
VENTIDIUS
SILIUS } friends and followers of Antony
EROS
CAMIDIUS
SCARUS
DECRETAS

Octavius CAESAR, triumvir of Rome
OCTAVIA, his sister

MAECENAS
AGRIPPA
TAURUS
DOLABELLA } friends and followers of Caesar
THIDIAS
GALLUS
PROCULEIUS

LEPIDUS, triumvir of Rome
Sextus POMPEY (Pompeius)

MENECRATES
MENAS } friends of Pompey
VARRIUS

CLEOPATRA, Queen of Egypt

CHARMIAN
IRAS
ALEXAS
MARDIAN, a eunuch } attending on Cleopatra
DIOMED
SELEUCUS

A SOOTHSAYER
An AMBASSADOR
MESSENGERS
A BOY who sings
A SENTRY and men of his WATCH
Men of the GUARD
An EGYPTIAN
A CLOWN
SERVANTS
SOLDIERS
Eunuchs, attendants, captains, soldiers, servants

1.1

Enter DEMETRIUS *and* PHILO

PHILO Nay, but this dotage° of our General's   *absurd infatuation*
   O'erflows the measure.¹ Those his goodly eyes,
   That o'er the files and musters°of the war   *lines of troops*
   Have glowed like plated° Mars, now bend, now turn   *armored*
5 The office° and devotion of their view   *duty*
   Upon a tawny front.² His captain's heart,
   Which in the scuffles of great fights hath burst
   The buckles on his breast, reneges all temper,³
   And is become the bellows and the fan
   To cool a gipsy's° lust.   *Egyptian's; hussy's*
     Flourish.° Enter ANTONY, CLEOPATRA, *her ladies, the*   *Trumpet fanfare*
     train,° with eunuchs fanning her   *retinue*
10   Look where they come.
   Take but good note, and you shall see in him
   The triple pillar of the world⁴ transformed
   Into a strumpet's fool. Behold and see.
CLEOPATRA [*to* ANTONY] If it be love indeed, tell me how much.
15 ANTONY There's beggary° in the love that can be reckoned.   *little value*
CLEOPATRA I'll set a bourn° how far to be beloved.   *boundary*
ANTONY Then must thou needs find out new heaven, new earth.⁵
     Enter a MESSENGER
MESSENGER News, my good lord, from Rome.
ANTONY Grates° me: the sum.°   *Irks / summary*
20 CLEOPATRA Nay, hear them, Antony.
   Fulvia° perchance is angry; or who knows   *Antony's wife*
   If the scarce-bearded Caesar⁶ have not sent
   His powerful mandate to you: 'Do this, or this,
   Take in° that kingdom and enfranchise° that.   *Annex / liberate*
25 Perform't, or else we damn thee.'
ANTONY How,° my love?   *What*
CLEOPATRA Perchance? Nay, and most like.⁷
   You must not stay here longer. Your dismission°   *marching orders*
   Is come from Caesar, therefore hear it, Antony.
30 Where's Fulvia's process°—Caesar's, I would say—both?   *summons*
   Call in the messengers. As I am Egypt's queen,
   Thou blushest, Antony, and that blood of thine
   Is Caesar's homager;° else so thy cheek pays shame   *Pays Caesar homage*
   When shrill-tongued Fulvia scolds. The messengers!
35 ANTONY Let Rome in Tiber melt, and the wide arch
   Of the ranged° empire fall. Here is my space.   *orderly; extensive*
   Kingdoms are clay. Our dungy° earth alike   *made of manure*
   Feeds beast as man. The nobleness of life
   Is to do thus;° when such a mutual pair   *act as we do; embrace*
40 And such a twain can do't—in which I bind

1.1 Location: Cleopatra's palace, Alexandria.
1. Goes beyond suitable bounds.
2. A face or forehead of dark complexion (referring to Cleopatra; see the Introduction); military "front," or battle line.
3. Abandons all temperance ("temper" is also the hardness of tempered steel).
4. Antony, Octavius Caesar, and Lepidus were the three triumvirs ruling the Roman Empire (most of the known world, for Romans).

5. Alluding anachronistically to Revelation 21:1 ("I saw a new heaven, and a new earth") and to the discovery of the New World. This second meaning may connect to the imperial theme of the play—its sense of geographical expansiveness and European geographical expansion.
6. The opening of the play is set in 40 B.C.E., when Octavius Caesar was twenty-three; Antony was almost twenty years his senior.
7. It is most likely, rather than merely possible, that Fulvia is angry.

On pain of punishment the world to weet°—   *recognize*
We stand up peerless.
CLEOPATRA [*aside*]   Excellent falsehood!
Why did he marry Fulvia and not love her?
I'll seem the fool I am not. [*To* ANTONY] Antony
Will be himself.[8]
45 ANTONY   But stirred[9] by Cleopatra.
Now, for the love of Love and her soft hours
Let's not confound° the time with conference° harsh.   *ruin / conversation*
There's not a minute of our lives should stretch
Without some pleasure now. What sport° tonight?   *entertainment*
CLEOPATRA   Hear the ambassadors.
50 ANTONY   Fie, wrangling queen,
Whom everything becomes—to chide, to laugh,
To weep; how every passion fully strives
To make itself, in thee, fair and admired!
No messenger but thine;[1] and all alone
55 Tonight we'll wander through the streets and note
The qualities of people. Come, my queen.
Last night you did desire it. [*To the* MESSENGER] Speak not to us.
                    Exeunt [ANTONY *and* CLEOPATRA] *with the train*
                        [*and by another door the* MESSENGER]
DEMETRIUS   Is Caesar with° Antonius prized° so slight?   *by / esteemed*
PHILO   Sir, sometimes when he is not Antony
60 He comes too short of that great property°   *unique characteristic*
Which still° should go with Antony.   *always*
DEMETRIUS   I am full sorry
That he approves° the common liar who   *proves correct*
Thus speaks of him at Rome; but I will hope
Of better deeds tomorrow. Rest you happy.   *Exeunt*

1.2

Enter ENOBARBUS, *a* SOOTHSAYER, CHARMIAN, IRAS, MAR-
DIAN *the eunuch,* ALEXAS [*and attendants*]
CHARMIAN   Lord Alexas, sweet Alexas, most anything Alexas,
almost most absolute° Alexas, where's the soothsayer that you   *perfect*
praised so to th' Queen?
O that I knew this husband, which you say
Must charge his horns[1] with garlands!
5 ALEXAS   Soothsayer!
SOOTHSAYER   Your will?
CHARMIAN   Is this the man? Is't you, sir, that know things?
SOOTHSAYER   In nature's infinite book of secrecy
A little I can read.
10 ALEXAS [*to* CHARMIAN]   Show him your hand.
ENOBARBUS [*calling*]   Bring in the banquet° quickly,   *light meal; dessert*
Wine enough Cleopatra's health to drink.
        [*Enter servants with food and wine, and exeunt*]
CHARMIAN [*to* SOOTHSAYER]   Good sir, give me good fortune.
SOOTHSAYER   I make not, but foresee.

---

8. *I'll . . . himself*: I'll appear to believe Antony's falsehood, although I am really not so credulous; he will continue in his folly. (But Antony construes the words he
hears as a compliment. It is also possible that Antony
hears Cleopatra's entire speech.)

9. Aroused; motivated; disturbed.
1. I will hear only what you have to say.
1.2 Location: Scene continues.
1. Must adorn his (proverbial) cuckold's horns.

	CHARMIAN Pray then, foresee me one.	
15	SOOTHSAYER You shall be yet	
	Far fairer than you are.	
	CHARMIAN He means in flesh.°	*(by getting fatter)*
	IRAS No, you shall paint° when you are old.	*use cosmetics*
	CHARMIAN Wrinkles forbid!	
	ALEXAS Vex not his prescience. Be attentive.	
	CHARMIAN Hush!	
	SOOTHSAYER You shall be more beloving than beloved.	
20	CHARMIAN I had rather heat my liver with drinking.²	
	ALEXAS Nay, hear him.	
	CHARMIAN Good now,° some excellent fortune! Let me be mar-	*Please; fine; begin*
	ried to three kings in a forenoon and widow them all. Let me	
	have a child at fifty to whom Herod of Jewry³ may do homage.	
25	Find° me to marry me with Octavius Caesar, and companion	*Find in my palm*
	me° with my mistress.	*make me equal*
	SOOTHSAYER You shall outlive the lady whom you serve.	
	CHARMIAN O, excellent! I love long life better than figs.⁴	
	SOOTHSAYER You have seen and proved° a fairer former fortune	*undergone*
30	Than that which is to approach.	
	CHARMIAN Then belike° my children shall have no names.°	*likely / be bastards*
	Prithee, how many boys and wenches must I have?	
	SOOTHSAYER If every of your wishes had a womb,	
	And fertile every wish, a million.	
35	CHARMIAN Out, fool—I forgive thee for a witch.⁵	
	ALEXAS You think none but your sheets are privy to your wishes.	
	CHARMIAN [*to the* SOOTHSAYER] Nay, come, tell Iras hers.	
	ALEXAS We'll know all our fortunes.	
	ENOBARBUS Mine, and most of our fortunes, tonight shall be	
40	drunk to bed.	
	IRAS [*showing her hand to the* SOOTHSAYER] There's a palm	
	presages chastity,° if nothing else.	*(a dry palm)*
	CHARMIAN E'en as the o'erflowing Nilus presageth famine.⁶	
	IRAS Go, you wild° bedfellow, you cannot soothsay.	*licentious*
45	CHARMIAN Nay, if an oily palm° be not a fruitful prognostica-	*(sign of sensuality)*
	tion,° I cannot scratch mine ear. [*To the* SOOTHSAYER] Prithee,	*sign of fertility*
	tell her but a workaday° fortune.	*an everyday*
	SOOTHSAYER Your fortunes are alike.	
	IRAS But how, but how? Give me particulars.	
50	SOOTHSAYER I have said.	
	IRAS Am I not an inch of fortune better than she?	
	CHARMIAN Well, if you were but an inch of fortune better than	
	I, where would you choose it?	
	IRAS Not in my husband's nose.°	*(sexual innuendo)*
55	CHARMIAN Our worser° thoughts heavens mend! Alexas—come,	*lascivious*
	his fortune, his fortune. O, let him marry a woman that cannot	
	go, sweet Isis,⁷ I beseech thee, and let her die too, and give him	

2. Both falling in love and excessive drinking were thought to inflame the liver, the seat of the passions.
3. Anachronistic: Charmian wants homage to her child even from Herod, Cleopatra's enemy, who was to become proverbial for his brutality to children when he slaughtered the Holy Innocents in an effort to kill the infant Jesus.
4. Genitalia (possibly proverbial); lines 27–28 also foreshadow 5.2.229–319.

5. Since you are a soothsayer, I will let you speak freely and will not persecute you as a witch; I will forgive your outlandish prognostications because they are unlikely to come true.
6. Ironic: the silt brought down by the flooding Nile each year gave Egypt its fertile soil.
7. Egyptian goddess of fertility, as well as of the earth and moon. For the comparison of Cleopatra to Isis, see the Introduction. *go:* come (sexual); bear children.

a worse, and let worse follow worse till the worst of all follow
him laughing to his grave, fiftyfold a cuckold. Good Isis, hear
60 me this prayer, though thou deny me a matter of more weight;
good Isis, I beseech thee.

IRAS   Amen, dear goddess, hear that prayer of the people. For as
it is a heart-breaking to see a handsome man loose-wived,° so it   ° *wedded to an adulteress*
is a deadly sorrow to behold a foul knave uncuckolded. There-
65 fore, dear Isis, keep decorum,° and fortune him accordingly.   ° *do the right thing*

CHARMIAN   Amen.

ALEXAS   Lo now, if it lay in their hands to make me a cuckold,
they would make themselves whores but they'd do't.[8]

Enter CLEOPATRA

ENOBARBUS   Hush, here comes Antony.

CHARMIAN   Not he, the Queen.

CLEOPATRA   Saw you my lord?

ENOBARBUS   No, lady.

70 CLEOPATRA   Was he not here?

CHARMIAN   No, madam.

CLEOPATRA   He was disposed to mirth, but on the sudden
A Roman° thought hath struck him. Enobarbus!   ° *of Rome; serious*

ENOBARBUS   Madam?

75 CLEOPATRA   Seek him, and bring him hither. Where's Alexas?

ALEXAS   Here at your service. My lord approaches.

Enter ANTONY *with a* MESSENGER

CLEOPATRA   We will not look upon him. Go with us.

Exeunt [all but ANTONY *and the* MESSENGER]

MESSENGER   Fulvia thy wife first came into the field.°   ° *battlefield*

ANTONY   Against my brother Lucius?[9]

80 MESSENGER   Ay, but soon that war had end, and the time's state°   ° *situation at the time*
Made friends of them, jointing their force 'gainst Caesar,
Whose better issue° in the war from Italy   ° *greater success*
Upon the first encounter drave them.°   ° *drove them out*

ANTONY   Well, what worst?

MESSENGER   The nature of bad news infects the teller.[1]

85 ANTONY   When it concerns the fool or coward. On.
Things that are past are done. With me 'tis thus:
Who tells me true, though in his tale lie death,
I hear him as° he flattered.   ° *as if*

MESSENGER   Labienus[2]—
This is stiff news—hath with his Parthian force

90 Extended° Asia; from Euphrates   ° *Seized*
His conquering banner shook, from Syria
To Lydia and to Ionia,
Whilst—

ANTONY   Antony, thou wouldst say—

MESSENGER   O, my lord!

ANTONY   Speak to me home.° Mince not the general tongue.[3]   ° *plainly*
95 Name Cleopatra as she is called in Rome.

8. *but they'd do't:* in order to do so.
9. Lucius Antonius, Roman consul.
1. Makes the teller hated by the hearer. For examples,
see 2.5 and 3.1.
2. Quintus Labienus, who was sent by Brutus and Cassius following their killing of Julius Caesar (see *Julius
Caesar*) to garner support from the Parthians, an Asian
people whose empire came to include much of Mesopotamia (Iraq) and Persia (Iran) and who regularly warred
with Rome. After Brutus's and Cassius's defeat at Philippi
by Antony, Octavius Caesar, and Lepidus, Labienus
defected to take command of the Parthian army and
began a war against the Romans, conquering some of
their provinces in the Middle East (lines 90–92)—provinces Antony was supposed to protect.
3. Do not play down common opinion.

Rail thou in Fulvia's phrase,° and taunt my faults   *words*
With such full licence as both truth and malice
Have power to utter. O, then we bring forth weeds
When our quick° winds lie still, and our ills told us   *living; fertile*
100 Is as our earing.[4] Fare thee well a while.
MESSENGER   At your noble pleasure.   *Exit* MESSENGER
          Enter another MESSENGER
ANTONY   From Sicyon,[5] ho, the news? Speak there.
SECOND MESSENGER   The man from Sicyon—
ANTONY   Is there such a one?
SECOND MESSENGER   He stays upon° your will.   *He attends*
ANTONY   Let him appear.
          [*Exit* SECOND MESSENGER]
105 These strong Egyptian fetters I must break,
Or lose myself in dotage.
          Enter another MESSENGER *with a letter*
                    What are you?
THIRD MESSENGER   Fulvia thy wife is dead.
ANTONY   Where died she?
THIRD MESSENGER   In Sicyon.
Her length of sickness, with what else more serious
Importeth thee° to know, this bears.   *Is important for you*
          [*He gives* ANTONY *the letter*]
110 ANTONY   Forbear° me.   *Leave*
          [*Exit* THIRD MESSENGER]
There's a great spirit gone. Thus did I desire it.
What our contempts doth often hurl from us
We wish it ours again. The present pleasure,
By revolution low'ring,[6] does become
115 The opposite of itself. She's° good being gone;   *Fulvia is*
The hand could° pluck her back that shoved her on.   *would wish to*
I must from this enchanting° queen break off.   *spellbinding*
Ten thousand harms more than the ills I know
My idleness doth hatch. How now, Enobarbus!
          Enter ENOBARBUS
ENOBARBUS   What's your pleasure, sir?
120 ANTONY   I must with haste from hence.
ENOBARBUS   Why, then we kill[7] all our women. We see how
mortal an unkindness is to them; if they suffer our departure,
death's the word.
ANTONY   I must be gone.
125 ENOBARBUS   Under a compelling occasion let women die. It
were pity to cast them away for nothing, though between them
and a great cause they should be esteemed nothing. Cleopatra
catching but the least noise of this dies instantly. I have seen
her die twenty times upon far poorer moment.° I do think there   *for far less reason*
130 is mettle° in death, which commits some loving act upon her,   *(sexual) potency; courage*
she hath such a celerity° in dying.   *speed*
ANTONY   She is cunning past man's thought.

ENOBARBUS   Alack, sir, no. Her passions are made of nothing but
the finest part of pure love. We cannot call her winds and
135   waters sighs and tears; they are greater storms and tempests than
almanacs can report. This cannot be cunning in her; if it be,
she makes a shower of rain as well as Jove.[8]

ANTONY   Would I had never seen her!

ENOBARBUS   O, sir, you had then left unseen a wonderful piece
140   of work,° which not to have been blessed withal° would have   °masterpiece / with
discredited your travel.[9]

ANTONY   Fulvia is dead.

ENOBARBUS   Sir.

ANTONY   Fulvia is dead.

145   ENOBARBUS   Fulvia?

ANTONY   Dead.

ENOBARBUS   Why, sir, give the gods a thankful sacrifice. When it
pleaseth their deities to take the wife of a man from him, it
shows to man the tailors of the earth; comforting therein that
150   when old robes° are worn out there are members[1] to make new.   °clothes; women
If there were no more women but Fulvia, then had you indeed
a cut, and the case to be lamented. This grief is crowned with
consolation; your old smock brings forth a new petticoat, and
indeed the tears live in an onion that should water this sorrow.[2]

155   ANTONY   The business she hath brochèd in the state
Cannot endure my absence.

ENOBARBUS   And the business you have broached here cannot
be without you, especially that of Cleopatra's, which wholly
depends on your abode.°   °staying on here
160   ANTONY   No more light answers. Let our officers
Have notice what we purpose. I shall break
The cause of our expedience° to the Queen,   °haste
And get her leave to part; for not alone
The death of Fulvia, with more urgent touches,°   °concerns
165   Do strongly speak to us, but the letters too
Of many our contriving friends[3] in Rome
Petition us at home.° Sextus Pompeius   °to go home
Hath given the dare to Caesar and commands
The empire of the sea.[4] Our slippery° people,   °inconstant
170   Whose love is never linked to the deserver
Till his deserts are past, begin to throw°   °ascribe (the title of)
Pompey the Great and all his dignities
Upon his son, who—high in name and power,
Higher than both in blood and life°—stands up   °vitality and energy
175   For the main soldier;[5] whose quality, going on,
The sides o'th' world may danger.[6] Much is breeding
Which, like the courser's hair, hath yet but life,
And not a serpent's poison.[7] Say our pleasure,

8. Jupiter; ruler of the gods: one of his duties was governing rain.
9. Would have cast doubt on your success as a traveler.
Travel also suggests travail, or work, as in "piece of work"
(lines 139–40).
1. Limbs; sexual organs. The sexual innuendo is continued in "cut" (line 152: severe blow; slash in a garment;
vagina, "case" (line 152: situation; set of clothes; vagina),
and "broachèd" (line 155, 157: opened or pricked).
2. the tears . . . sorrow: real tears are not called for.
3. Of many friends acting on our behalf.

4. Sextus Pompey was the younger son of Pompey the
Great, who was a foe of Julius Caesar (see *Julius Caesar*
1.1). Previously an outlaw, the Pompey of the play had
gained control of the shipping routes around Sicily.
5. *stands . . . soldier:* acts like the leading soldier.
6. *whose . . . danger:* whose accomplishments and character, should they continue to succeed, might endanger the
entire arrangement of the world.
7. A horse's ("courser's," line 177) hair was believed to
become a live snake if put in water.

To such whose place° is under us, requires   *rank*
Our quick remove from hence.

180 ENOBARBUS   I shall do't. [*Exeunt severally*]

1.3

Enter CLEOPATRA, CHARMIAN, ALEXAS, *and* IRAS

CLEOPATRA   Where is he?

CHARMIAN   I did not see him since.°   *recently*

CLEOPATRA [*to* ALEXAS]   See where he is, who's with him, what he does.
I did not send you.¹ If you find him sad,°   *serious*
Say I am dancing; if in mirth, report

5   That I am sudden sick. Quick, and return.   [*Exit* ALEXAS]

CHARMIAN   Madam, methinks, if you did love him dearly,
You do not hold the method° to enforce   *act appropriately*
The like from him.

CLEOPATRA   What should I do I do not?°   *What else should I do*

CHARMIAN   In each thing give him way; cross him in nothing.

10 CLEOPATRA   Thou teachest like a fool, the way to lose him.

CHARMIAN   Tempt° him not so too far. Iwis,° forbear.   *Test / Indeed*
In time we hate that which we often fear.

       Enter ANTONY

But here comes Antony.

CLEOPATRA   I am sick and sullen.°   *dispirited*

ANTONY   I am sorry to give breathing° to my purpose.   *voice*

15 CLEOPATRA   Help me away, dear Charmian, I shall fall.
It cannot be thus long—the sides of nature²
Will not sustain it.

ANTONY   Now, my dearest queen.

CLEOPATRA   Pray you, stand farther from me.

ANTONY   What's the matter?

CLEOPATRA   I know by that same eye there's some good news.

20   What says the married woman°—you may go?   *(Fulvia)*
Would she had never given you leave to come.
Let her not say 'tis I that keep you here.
I have no power upon you; hers you are.

ANTONY   The gods best know—

CLEOPATRA   O, never was there queen

25   So mightily betrayed! Yet at the first
I saw the treasons planted.

ANTONY   Cleopatra—

CLEOPATRA   Why should I think you can be mine and true—
Though you in swearing shake the thronèd gods³—
Who have been false to Fulvia? Riotous madness,

30   To be entangled with those mouth-made° vows   *hypocritical*
Which break themselves in swearing.°   *as they are made*

ANTONY   Most sweet queen—

CLEOPATRA   Nay, pray you, seek no colour° for your going,   *excuse*
But bid farewell and go. When you sued staying,°   *entreated to remain*
Then was the time for words; no going then.

35   Eternity was in our⁴ lips and eyes,
Bliss in our brow's bent;° none our parts so poor   *curve*

1.3 Location: Scene continues.
1. Do not say I sent you.
2. This cannot go on much longer—the bodily frame.
3. When Jupiter swore an oath, Olympus was supposed

to shake.
4. My (royal plural); possibly also the conventional first
person plural.

But was a race of heaven.[5] They are so still,
Or thou, the greatest soldier of the world,
Art turned the greatest liar.

ANTONY   How now, lady!

40   CLEOPATRA   I would I had thy inches.° Thou shouldst know   size (phallic)
There were a heart in Egypt.[6]

ANTONY   Hear me, Queen.
The strong necessity of time commands
Our services a while, but my full heart
Remains in use° with you. Our Italy   in trust
45   Shines o'er with civil swords.° Sextus Pompeius   swords of civil war
Makes his approaches to the port of Rome.[7]
Equality of two domestic powers
Breed scrupulous faction.° The hated, grown to strength,   distrustful dissent
Are newly grown to love.° The condemned° Pompey,   popularity / banished
50   Rich in his father's honour, creeps° apace   insinuates himself
Into the hearts of such as have not thrived
Upon the present state,° whose numbers threaten;   government
And quietness, grown sick of rest, would purge
By any desperate change.[8] My more particular,°   personal motivation
55   And that which most with you should safe° my going,   sanction
Is Fulvia's death.

CLEOPATRA   Though age from folly could not give me freedom,
It does from childishness. Can Fulvia die?

ANTONY   She's dead, my queen.
[He offers letters]
60   Look here, and at thy sovereign leisure read
The garboils° she awaked. At the last, best,[9]   upheavals
See when and where she died.

CLEOPATRA   O most false love!
Where be the sacred vials[1] thou shouldst fill
With sorrowful water? Now I see, I see,
65   In Fulvia's death how mine received shall be.

ANTONY   Quarrel no more, but be prepared to know
The purposes I bear, which are° or cease   continue
As you shall give th'advice. By the fire°   sun
That quickens Nilus' slime,[2] I go from hence
70   Thy soldier-servant, making peace or war
As thou affects.°   choose

CLEOPATRA   Cut my lace,[3] Charmian, come.
But let it be. I am quickly ill and well;
So[4] Antony loves.

ANTONY   My precious queen, forbear,
And give true evidence° to his love, which stands   be an honest witness
An honourable trial.

75   CLEOPATRA   So Fulvia told me.

---

5. *none . . . heaven:* Even my poorest attributes were
heavenly.
6. There were courage (to respond to such insults) in the
country (Queen) of Egypt.
7. Ostia (16 miles from Rome).
8. *And . . . change:* And peace, made ill by inactivity,
wishes to purge itself of impurities by a violently acting
remedy.
9. The best news last; Fulvia was at her best at the end of
her life.

1. Renaissance writers thought that the Romans filled
small bottles with tears to place in graves; also, where are
your sad and watery eyes ("vials")?
2. That causes plants to grow in the silt that the Nile
deposits.
3. Cutting the strings would be quicker than untying the
lace on her bodice to relieve her from her feigned fainting spell.
4. Thus (falsely); as long as.

I prithee turn aside and weep for her,
Then bid adieu to me, and say the tears
Belong to Egypt.° Good now, play one scene   Cleopatra
Of excellent dissembling, and let it look
Like perfect honour.
80   ANTONY   You'll heat my blood.° No more.   make me angry
      CLEOPATRA   You can do better yet; but this is meetly.°   fairly good (acting)
      ANTONY   Now by my sword—
      CLEOPATRA   And target.⁵ Still he mends.°   improves
      But this is not the best. Look, prithee, Charmian,
      How this Herculean Roman does become
85   The carriage of his chafe.⁶
      ANTONY   I'll leave you, lady.
      CLEOPATRA   Courteous lord, one word.
      Sir, you and I must part; but that's not it.
      Sir, you and I have loved; but there's not it;
90   That you know well. Something it is I would—
      O, my oblivion is a very Antony,
      And I am all forgotten.⁷
      ANTONY   But that your royalty
      Holds idleness your subject, I should take you
      For idleness itself.⁸
      CLEOPATRA   'Tis sweating labour°   work; birth pains
95   To bear such idleness° so near the heart   flippancy; laziness
      As Cleopatra this. But sir, forgive me,
      Since my becomings° kill me when they do not   transformations; graces
      Eye° well to you. Your honour calls you hence,   Look
      Therefore be deaf to my unpitied folly,
100   And all the gods go with you. Upon your sword
      Sit laurel victory,⁹ and smooth success
      Be strewed before your feet.
      ANTONY   Let us go.
      Come. Our separation so abides and flies¹
      That thou residing here goes yet with me,
105   And I hence fleeting, here remain with thee.
      Away.   Exeunt [severally]

1.4

Enter Octavius CAESAR *reading a letter,* LEPIDUS, *and
their train*

      CAESAR   You may see, Lepidus, and henceforth know,
      It is not Caesar's natural vice to hate
      Our great competitor.° From Alexandria   ally; rival
      This is the news: he fishes, drinks, and wastes
5   The lamps of night in revel; is not more manlike
      Than Cleopatra, nor the queen of Ptolemy¹

5. Shield. Cleopatra parodies the blustering oaths of
heroic drama.
6. *does . . . chafe:* emulates Hercules, his heroic ancestor,
with his posture of rage.
7. *my . . . forgotten:* my memory has deserted me as you
are doing, and I have forgotten everything (am totally forgotten—by Antony).
8. *But . . . itself:* If you were not queen over your flippancy and hence in full control of it, I would think that
you were flippancy itself.

9. *Upon . . . victory:* May your military exploits receive
the laurel wreath as the reward for victory.
1. Consists so much of both remaining together and
being separated (in that we are united by the shared experience of it).
1.4 Location: Rome.
1. Julius Caesar had commanded Cleopatra to marry her
half brother Ptolemy XIV (acceptable within the Egyptian royal family); she was said to have had Ptolemy poisoned.

More womanly than he; hardly gave audience[2]
Or vouchsafed to think he had partners. You shall find there°   *(the letter); (Egypt)*
A man who is the abstract° of all faults   *paradigm*
That all men follow.

10 LEPIDUS   I must not think there are
Evils enough to darken all his goodness.
His faults in him seem as the spots of heaven,°   *stars*
More fiery by night's blackness; hereditary
Rather than purchased;° what he cannot change   *acquired*
15 Than° what he chooses.   *Rather than*
CAESAR   You are too indulgent. Let's grant it is not
Amiss to tumble on the bed of Ptolemy,
To give a kingdom for a mirth,° to sit   *joke*
And keep the turn of° tippling with a slave,   *take turns at*
20 To reel the streets at noon, and stand the buffet°   *come to blows*
With knaves that smells of sweat. Say° this becomes him—   *Even if*
As his composure° must be rare indeed   *And his character*
Whom these things cannot blemish—yet must Antony
No way excuse his foils° when we do bear   *faults*
25 So great weight in° his lightness. If he filled   *as a result of*
His vacancy° with his voluptuousness,   *leisure*
Full surfeits and the dryness of his bones[3]
Call on° him for't. But to confound° such time   *Afflict / waste*
That drums° him from his sport, and speaks as loud   *summons*
30 As his own state° and ours— 'tis to be chid   *public responsibility*
As we rate° boys who, being mature in knowledge,   *upbraid*
Pawn their experience to their present pleasure,
And so rebel to judgement.[4]
        Enter a MESSENGER
LEPIDUS   Here's more news.
MESSENGER   Thy biddings have been done, and every hour,
35 Most noble Caesar, shalt thou have report
How 'tis abroad. Pompey is strong at sea,
And it appears he is beloved of those
That only have feared Caesar.[5] To the ports
The discontents° repair, and men's reports   *discontented people*
Give him° much wronged.   *Say he is*
40 CAESAR   I should have known no less.
It hath been taught us from the primal state[6]
That he which is was wished until he were,[7]
And the ebbed° man, ne'er loved till ne'er worth love,   *fallen*
Comes deared° by being lacked. This common body,°   *Is loved / The people*
45 Like to a vagabond flag° upon the stream,   *drifting reed*
Goes to, and back, lackeying° the varying tide,   *following slavishly*
To rot itself with motion.
      [*Enter a* SECOND MESSENGER]
SECOND MESSENGER   Caesar, I bring thee word
Menecrates and Menas, famous pirates,°   *(allied with Pompey)*
Makes the sea serve them, which they ear° and wound   *plow*
50 With keels of every kind. Many hot inroads

---

2. Hardly listened (to Octavius's messengers, in 1.1).
3. *Full . . . bones:* Ill health caused by overeating and venereal disease.
4. *being . . . judgement:* old enough to know better, abandon their wisdom in favor of momentary pleasure, and

thus act against their better judgment.
5. That obeyed Caesar only out of fear.
6. Since the first society was organized.
7. That man who rules was supported until he began to rule.

They make in Italy. The borders maritime°   *coastal territories*
Lack blood° to think on't, and flush° youth revolt.   *Go pallid / spirited*
No vessel can peep forth but 'tis as soon
Taken as seen; for Pompey's name strikes more
Than could his war resisted.[8]   [*Exit*]

55 CAESAR   Antony,
Leave thy lascivious wassails.° When thou once   *drunken revels*
Was beaten from Modena,[9] where thou slew'st
Hirtius and Pansa, consuls, at thy heel
Did famine follow, whom thou fought'st against—
60 Though daintily brought up—with patience more
Than savages could suffer. Thou didst drink
The stale° of horses, and the gilded° puddle   *urine / slime-covered*
Which beasts would cough at.° Thy palate then did deign°   *refuse (to drink) / accept*
The roughest berry on the rudest hedge.
65 Yea, like the stag when snow the pasture sheets,°   *covers*
The barks of trees thou browsed.° On the Alps   *fed upon*
It is reported thou didst eat strange flesh,
Which some did die to look on; and all this—
It wounds thine honour that I speak it now—
70 Was borne so like a soldier that thy cheek
So much as lanked° not.   *grew thin*
LEPIDUS 'Tis pity of him.
CAESAR   Let his shames quickly
Drive him to Rome. 'Tis time we twain
75 Did show ourselves i'th' field; and to that end
Assemble we immediate council. Pompey
Thrives in our idleness.
LEPIDUS   Tomorrow, Caesar,
I shall be furnished to inform you rightly
Both what° by sea and land I can be able°   *what forces / assemble*
To front° this present time.   *To confront the enemy at*
80 CAESAR   Till which encounter
It is my business, too. Farewell.
LEPIDUS   Farewell, my lord. What you shall know meantime
Of stirs° abroad I shall beseech you, sir,   *incidents*
To let me be partaker.
85 CAESAR   Doubt not, sir. I knew it for my bond.°   *Exeunt*   *responsibility*

1.5

Enter CLEOPATRA, CHARMIAN, IRAS, *and* MARDIAN
CLEOPATRA   Charmian!
CHARMIAN   Madam?
CLEOPATRA [*yawning*] Ha, ha. Give me to drink mandragora.[1]
CHARMIAN   Why, madam?
5 CLEOPATRA   That I might sleep out this great gap of time
My Antony is away.
CHARMIAN   You think of him too much.
CLEOPATRA   O, 'tis treason!
CHARMIAN   Madam, I trust not so.
CLEOPATRA   Thou, eunuch Mardian!

---

8. *Pompey's . . . resisted:* Pompey's name alone is more
powerful than his forces would be if confronted in battle.
9. Site of a battle in which Antony was defeated by the
combined armies of Octavius Caesar and the Roman Senate, at the instigation of Cicero.
1.5 Location: Alexandria.
1. A narcotic, made from the mandrake plant.

MARDIAN   What's your highness' pleasure?

CLEOPATRA   Not now to hear thee sing.[2] I take no pleasure

10   In aught[3] an eunuch has. 'Tis well for thee

That, being unseminared,° thy freer thoughts   *castrated*

May not fly forth of Egypt. Hast thou affections?°   *desires*

MARDIAN   Yes, gracious madam.

CLEOPATRA   Indeed?

15   MARDIAN   Not in deed, madam, for I can do° nothing   *(sexually)*

But what indeed is honest° to be done.   *chaste; moral*

Yet have I fierce affections, and think

What Venus did with Mars.[4]

CLEOPATRA   O, Charmian,

Where think'st thou he is now? Stands he or sits he?

20   Or does he walk? Or is he on his horse?

O happy horse, to bear the weight of Antony!

Do bravely, horse, for wot'st° thou whom thou mov'st?—   *know*

The demi-Atlas[5] of this earth, the arm°   *champion*

And burgonet° of men. He's speaking now,   *helmet; guardian*

25   Or murmuring 'Where's my serpent of old Nile?'[6]—

For so he calls me. Now I feed myself

With most delicious poison. Think on me,

That am with Phoebus'° amorous pinches black,   *the sun god*

And wrinkled deep in time. Broad-fronted° Caesar,°   *Broad-browed / (Julius)*

30   When thou wast here above the ground I was

A morsel for a monarch, and great Pompey[7]

Would stand and make his eyes grow in my brow.

There would he anchor his aspect,° and die°   *gaze / (sexual)*

With looking on his life.

Enter ALEXAS

ALEXAS   Sovereign of Egypt, hail!

35   CLEOPATRA   How much unlike art thou Mark Antony!

Yet, coming from him, that great medicine[8] hath

With his tinct° gilded thee. How goes it   *power; color*

With my brave° Mark Antony?   *magnificent*

ALEXAS   Last thing he did, dear Queen,

He kissed—the last of many doubled kisses—

40   This orient[9] pearl. His speech sticks in my heart.

CLEOPATRA   Mine ear must pluck it thence.

ALEXAS   'Good friend,' quoth he,

'Say the firm° Roman to great Egypt° sends   *loyal; resolute / Cleopatra*

This treasure of an oyster; at whose foot,

To mend° the petty present, I will piece°   *improve / add to*

45   Her opulent throne with kingdoms. All the East,

Say thou, shall call her mistress.' So he nodded,

And soberly did mount an arm-jaunced steed,[1]

---

2. Castrati were used in Italian music from the end of
the sixteenth century, and Shakespeare associates singing
eunuchs with the eastern Mediterranean in *Twelfth Night*
and *A Midsummer Night's Dream;* they are not thought to
have been used as singers in ancient Rome.
3. In anything; in the nothing. The eunuch has nothing
instead of testicles.
4. Venus, goddess of love (married to Vulcan), and Mars,
god of war, were lovers.
5. Octavius and Antony between them rule the world—
Lepidus having conveniently been forgotten—as Atlas
bore it on his shoulders.

6. See 2.7.25–26 for the superstition that snakes formed
spontaneously in the Nile mud; the asp in particular was
associated with Isis, with whom Cleopatra identifies herself.
7. Gnaeus Pompey, older brother of Sextus Pompey (the
character in this play) and son of Pompey the Great.
But Cleopatra's phrasing makes him sound like the father.
8. Elixir of life: sought by alchemists, it was thought to
be able to turn base metals to gold and cure all disease.
9. From India (more lustrous than European pearls).
1. Steed jolted by one in armor (or by its own armor).

Who neighed so high that what I would have spoke
Was beastly dumbed° by him.   drowned out
CLEOPATRA   What, was he sad or merry?
50 ALEXAS   Like to the time o'th' year between the extremes
Of hot and cold, he was nor° sad nor merry.   neither
CLEOPATRA   O well divided° disposition! Note him,   balanced
Note him, good Charmian, 'tis the man; but note him.
He was not sad, for he would shine on those
55 That make their looks by his;² he was not merry,
Which seemed to tell them his remembrance lay
In Egypt with his joy; but between both.
O heavenly mingle! Be'st thou sad or merry,
The violence of either thee becomes,
60 So does it no man else. Met'st thou my posts?°   messengers
ALEXAS   Ay, madam, twenty several° messengers.   separate
Why do you send so thick?
CLEOPATRA   Who's° born that day   Whoever is
When I forget to send to Antony
Shall die a beggar. Ink and paper, Charmian!
65 Welcome, my good Alexas. Did I, Charmian,
Ever love Caesar so?
CHARMIAN   O, that brave Caesar!
CLEOPATRA   Be choked with such another emphasis!
Say 'the brave Antony'.
CHARMIAN   The valiant Caesar.
CLEOPATRA   By Isis, I will give thee bloody teeth
70 If thou with Caesar paragon° again   compare
My man of men.
CHARMIAN   By your most gracious pardon,
I sing but after you.
CLEOPATRA   My salad days,
When I was green° in judgement, cold in blood,°   immature / feeling
To say as I said then. But come, away,
75 Get me ink and paper.
He shall have every day a several greeting,
Or I'll unpeople Egypt.³
                                                    Exeunt

                                   2.1
Enter POMPEY, MENECRATES, *and* MENAS, *in warlike
manner*
POMPEY   If the great gods be just, they shall assist
The deeds of justest men.
MENECRATES   Know, worthy Pompey,
That what they do delay they not deny.
POMPEY   Whiles we are suitors to their throne, decays
The thing we sue for.¹
5 MENECRATES   We, ignorant of ourselves,
Beg often our own harms, which the wise powers
Deny us for our° good; so find we profit   our own
By losing of our prayers.
POMPEY   I shall do well.

2. Who are dependent on his mood; who reflect his
appearance in their own.
3. If not, it will be only because I have run out of Egyptians to act as messengers (or, because I have killed all
Egyptians).
2.1 Location: Pompey's headquarters (in Sicily).
1. *Whiles . . . for:* While we are beseeching the gods, what
we request is losing its value.

The people love me, and the sea is mine.
10 My powers are crescent,° and my auguring° hope   *growing / prophesying*
Says it° will come to th' full.[2] Mark Antony   *(my military power)*
In Egypt sits at dinner, and will make
No wars without doors.[3] Caesar gets money where
He loses hearts. Lepidus flatters both,
15 Of° both is flattered; but he neither loves,°   *By / loves neither*
Nor either cares for him.

MENAS   Caesar and Lepidus
Are in the field; a mighty strength they carry.

POMPEY   Where have you this? 'Tis false.

MENAS   From Silvius, sir.

POMPEY   He dreams. I know they are in Rome together,
20 Looking° for Antony. But all the charms° of love,   *Waiting / incantations*
Salt° Cleopatra, soften thy waned[4] lip.   *Lecherous*
Let witchcraft join with beauty, lust with both
Tie up the libertine, in a field of feasts
Keep his brain fuming;° Epicurean[5] cooks   *drunk*
25 Sharpen with cloyless sauce[6] his appetite,
That sleep and feeding may prorogue° his honour   *postpone*
Even till a Lethe'd dullness[7]—

      Enter VARRIUS

                   How now, Varrius?

VARRIUS   This is most certain that I shall deliver:
Mark Antony is every hour in Rome
30 Expected. Since he went from Egypt, 'tis
A space for farther travel.[8]

POMPEY   I could have given less° matter   *less crucial*
A better ear. Menas, I did not think
This amorous surfeiter would have donned his helm°   *helmet*
For such a petty war. His soldiership
35 Is twice the other twain. But let us rear°   *elevate*
The higher our opinion,° that our stirring   *(of ourselves)*
Can from the lap of Egypt's widow[9] pluck
The ne'er lust-wearied Antony.

MENAS   I cannot hope°   *suppose*
Caesar and Antony shall well greet together.
40 His wife that's dead did trespasses to° Caesar,   *offended against*
His brother warred upon him, although, I think,
Not moved° by Antony.   *prompted*

POMPEY   I know not, Menas,
How lesser enmities may give way to greater.
Were't not that we stand up against them all,
45 'Twere pregnant° they should square° between themselves,   *evident / argue*
For they have entertainèd° cause enough   *sustained*
To draw their swords. But how the fear of us
May cement their divisions,° and bind up   *unite them*

---

2. Like the "crescent" moon.

3. Outside doors. Antony is concerned only with the wars of love, conducted indoors.

4. Withered; decreased, like the moon, perhaps in implicit contrast to the "crescent" and potentially "full" moon of Pompey's "powers" (lines 10–11).

5. The philosopher Epicurus and his followers believed that the gods took no interest in men's actions and that the only aim of life was to seek pleasure.

6. Sauce that never wearies or disgusts.

7. Drinking the water of Lethe, one of the rivers bounding Hades, caused total loss of memory.

8. Sufficient time to have traveled even farther (than between Egypt and Rome).

9. Cleopatra had married one of her brothers, Ptolemy XIV, whom she later seems to have had murdered. See note to 1.4.6.

The petty difference, we yet not know.
50 Be't as our gods will have't; it only stands
Our lives upon to use¹ our strongest hands.
Come, Menas.   *Exeunt*

2.2

Enter ENOBARBUS *and* LEPIDUS

LEPIDUS   Good Enobarbus, 'tis a worthy deed,
     And shall become you well, to entreat your captain
     To soft and gentle speech.
ENOBARBUS   I shall entreat him
     To answer like himself.¹ If Caesar move° him,   angers
5   Let Antony look over Caesar's head
     And speak as loud as Mars. By Jupiter,
     Were I the wearer of Antonio's beard
     I would not shave't today.²
LEPIDUS   'Tis not a time
     For private stomaching.°   quarrels
ENOBARBUS   Every time
10 Serves for the matter that is then born in't.
LEPIDUS   But small to greater matters must give way.
ENOBARBUS   Not if the small come first.
LEPIDUS   Your speech is passion.°   not reasoned
     But pray you, stir no embers° up. Here comes   old resentments
     The noble Antony.
     Enter [at one door] ANTONY *and* VENTIDIUS
ENOBARBUS   And yonder Caesar.
     Enter [at another door] CAESAR, MAECENAS, *and* AGRIPPA
15 ANTONY [*to* VENTIDIUS]   If we compose° well here, to Parthia. reach agreement
     Hark, Ventidius.
CAESAR   I do not know,
     Maecenas; ask Agrippa.
LEPIDUS[*to* CAESAR *and* ANTONY]   Noble friends,
     That which combined us was most great; and let not
     A leaner° action rend us. What's amiss,   less important
20 May it be gently heard. When we debate
     Our trivial difference loud,° we do commit   loudly; violently
     Murder in° healing wounds. Then, noble partners,   in the process of
     The rather for° I earnestly beseech,   Especially because
     Touch you the sourest points with sweetest terms,
     Nor curstness grow° to th' matter.   Do not let ill temper add
25 ANTONY   'Tis spoken well.
     Were we° before our armies, and to° fight,   If we were / about to
     I should do thus.³
     [ANTONY *and* CAESAR *embrace.*] *Flourish*
CAESAR   Welcome to Rome.
ANTONY   Thank you.
30 CAESAR   Sit.
ANTONY   Sit, sir.
CAESAR   Nay then.

[*They sit*]

ANTONY I learn you take things ill which are not so,
Or being,° concern you not.   being ill

CAESAR   I must be laughed at

35 If or° for nothing or a little I   either
Should say myself offended, and with you
Chiefly i'th'° world; more laughed at that I should   Of all the
Once name you derogately,° when to sound your name   censoriously
It not concernèd me.

40 ANTONY My being in Egypt, Caesar, what was't to you?

CAESAR No more than my residing here at Rome
Might be to you in Egypt. Yet if you there
Did practise on° my state, your being in Egypt   scheme against
Might be my question.°   concern

ANTONY   How intend you 'practised'?

45 CAESAR You may be pleased to catch at° mine intent   grasp
By what did here befall me. Your wife and brother
Made wars upon me, and their contestation
Was theme for you. You were the word of war.[4]

ANTONY You do mistake the business. My brother never

50 Did urge me in his act.[5] I did enquire° it,   inquire into
And have my learning from some true reports°   reliable sources
That drew their swords with you. Did he not rather
Discredit my authority with yours,
And make the wars alike against my stomach,°   wish

55 Having alike° your cause? Of this, my letters   Since I shared
Before did satisfy you. If you'll patch a quarrel,
As matter whole you have to make it with,[6]
It must not be with this.

CAESAR   You praise yourself
By laying defects of judgement to me, but
You patched up your excuses.

60 ANTONY   Not so, not so.
I know you could not lack, I am certain on't,
Very necessity of this thought,[7] that I,
Your partner in the cause 'gainst which he fought,
Could not with graceful eyes attend[8] those wars

65 Which fronted° mine own peace. As for my wife,   opposed
I would you had her spirit in such another.
The third o'th' world is yours, which with a snaffle[9]
You may pace° easy, but not such a wife.   train to walk

ENOBARBUS Would we had all such wives, that the men might

70 go to wars with the women.

ANTONY So much uncurbable,° her garboils,° Caesar,   uncontrollable / tumults
Made out of her impatience—which not wanted°   did not lack
Shrewdness of policy too—I grieving grant
Did you too much disquiet, for that you must

75 But° say I could not help it.   Only

CAESAR   I wrote to you

---

4. *contestation . . . war*: war was meant as an example for
you to follow (had you as its theme); Your name was the
war cry (war was waged in your name).
5. Claimed to be acting as my proxy.
6. *If . . . with*: If you'll patch together an old quarrel with
trivia, when you have enough material to make a new one

(or, possibly, as if you had enough material to make one).
7. *I know . . . thought*: I'm confident that you must have
been aware.
8. Could not look with approval on.
9. Bridle (one without a curb, for good-tempered horses).

When, rioting in Alexandria, you
Did pocket up my letters, and with taunts
Did gibe my missive out of audience.¹

ANTONY   Sir, he fell upon° me ere admitted, then.   *broke in on*
80   Three kings I had newly feasted, and did want
Of what I was² i'th' morning; but next day
I told him of myself,° which was as much   *my situation*
As to have asked him pardon. Let this fellow
Be nothing° of our strife. If we contend,   *Be no part*
Out of our question° wipe him.   *dispute*

85 CAESAR   You have broken
The article° of your oath, which you shall never   *terms*
Have tongue to charge me with.

LEPIDUS   Soft, Caesar.

ANTONY   No, Lepidus, let him speak.
90   The honour is sacred which he talks on now,
Supposing that I lacked it.³ But on, Caesar:
The article of my oath—

CAESAR   To lend me arms and aid when I required them,
The which you both denied.

ANTONY   Neglected, rather,
95   And then when poisoned hours had bound me up
From mine own knowledge.⁴ As nearly as I may
I'll play the penitent to you, but mine honesty
Shall not make poor my greatness, nor my power
Work without it.⁵ Truth is that Fulvia,
100   To have me out of Egypt, made wars here,
For which myself, the ignorant motive, do
So far ask pardon as befits mine honour°   *dignity*
To stoop in such a case.

LEPIDUS   'Tis noble spoken.

MAECENAS   If it might please you to enforce no further
105   The griefs° between ye; to forget them quite   *grievances*
Were to remember that the present need
Speaks to atone you.°   *Is to reconcile you*

LEPIDUS   Worthily spoken, Maecenas.

ENOBARBUS   Or if you borrow one another's love for the instant,
you may, when you hear no more words of Pompey, return it
110   again. You shall have time to wrangle in when you have nothing else to do.

ANTONY   Thou art a soldier only. Speak no more.

ENOBARBUS   That truth should be silent I had almost forgot.

ANTONY   You wrong this presence,° therefore speak no more.   *(noble) company*
115 ENOBARBUS   Go to, then; your considerate stone.⁶

CAESAR   I do not much dislike the matter,° but   *content*
The manner of his speech, for't cannot be
We shall remain in friendship, our conditions°   *dispositions*
So diff'ring in their acts. Yet if I knew
120   What hoop should hold us staunch,° from edge to edge   *watertight; bound*

---

1. Scoffed my messenger out of your (public) hearing (referring to 1.1).
2. *did . . . was:* was not myself.
3. *The honour . . . it:* What Caesar speaks of now is my sacred honor, which he assumes I lack (even assuming I lack it).
4. *bound . . . knowledge:* prevented me from realizing what I was doing.
5. *mine . . . it:* my honorable behavior (in admitting a fault) will not diminish my power, nor shall my power operate without honor.
6. Very well, then; still and silent, but capable of thought.

O'th' world I would pursue it.

AGRIPPA   Give me leave, Caesar.

CAESAR   Speak, Agrippa.

AGRIPPA   Thou hast a sister by the mother's side,

125 Admired Octavia. Great Mark Antony
Is now a widower.

CAESAR   Say not so, Agrippa.
If Cleopatra heard you, your reproof
Were well deserved of rashness.[7]

ANTONY   I am not married, Caesar. Let me hear

130 Agrippa further speak.

AGRIPPA   To hold you in perpetual amity,
To make you brothers, and to knit your hearts
With an unslipping knot, take Antony°   *let Antony take*
Octavia to° his wife; whose beauty claims   *for*

135 No worse a husband than the best of men;
Whose virtue and whose general graces speak
That which none else can utter.[8] By this marriage
All little jealousies° which now seem great,   *mistrusts*
And all great fears which now import° their dangers,   *bring along*

140 Would then be nothing. Truths would be tales
Where now half-tales be truths.[9] Her love to both
Would each to other and all loves to both
Draw after her. Pardon what I have spoke,
For 'tis a studied, not a present° thought,   *sudden*
By duty ruminated.

145 ANTONY   Will Caesar speak?

CAESAR   Not till he hears how Antony is touched°   *reacts*
With° what is spoke already.   *To*

ANTONY   What power is in Agrippa,
If I would say 'Agrippa, be it so',
To make this good?

150 CAESAR   The power of Caesar,
And his power unto Octavia.

ANTONY   May I never
To this good purpose, that so fairly shows,
Dream of impediment![1] Let me have thy hand.
Further this act of grace, and from this hour

155 The heart of brothers govern in our loves
And sway our great designs.

CAESAR   There's my hand.

[ANTONY *and* CAESAR *clasp hands*]

A sister I bequeath° you whom no brother   *hand over to*
Did ever love so dearly. Let her live
To join our kingdoms and our hearts; and never
Fly off our loves again.[2]

160 LEPIDUS   Happily, amen.

ANTONY   I did not think to draw my sword 'gainst Pompey,
For he hath laid strange° courtesies and great   *uncommon*

---

7. *your . . . rashness:* the reproof you would receive would
befit your rashness.
8. *speak . . . utter:* speak for themselves; speak more
powerfully than in any other woman.
9. *Truths . . . truths:* True reports, even if they were disturbing, could be passed over, regarded as hearsay, where
now incomplete rumors are accepted as truth.

1. *May . . . impediment:* alluding to the Anglican marriage service, as does sonnet 116: "Let me not to the marriage of true minds / Admit impediments." *so fairly shows:*
appears so attractive.
2. *never . . . again:* may our love for each other never
again desert us.

Of late upon me. I must thank him only,°   *at least*
Lest my remembrance° suffer ill report;   *gratitude*
At heel of° that, defy him.   *Right after*

165   **LEPIDUS**   Time calls upon's.
Of° us must Pompey presently° be sought,   *By / immediately*
Or else he seeks out us.

ANTONY   Where lies he?

CAESAR   About the Mount Misena.³

ANTONY   What is his strength
By land?

CAESAR   Great and increasing, but by sea
He is an absolute master.

170   **ANTONY**   So is the fame.°   *report*
Would we had spoke together.° Haste we for it;   *(earlier)*
Yet ere we put ourselves in arms, dispatch we
The business we have talked of.

CAESAR   With most gladness,
And do° invite you to my sister's view,   *I do*
Whither straight I'll lead you.

175   **ANTONY**   Let us, Lepidus,
Not lack your company.

LEPIDUS   Noble Antony,
Not sickness should detain me.

Flourish. Exeunt. Manent ENOBARBUS, AGRIPPA,
                    and MAECENAS

MAECENAS [*to* ENOBARBUS]   Welcome from Egypt, sir.

ENOBARBUS   Half the heart° of Caesar, worthy Maecenas! My   *Beloved friend*
180   honourable friend, Agrippa!

AGRIPPA   Good Enobarbus!

MAECENAS   We have cause to be glad that matters are so well
digested.° You stayed well by't⁴ in Egypt.   *settled*

ENOBARBUS   Ay, sir, we did sleep day out of countenance,⁵ and
185   made the night light° with drinking.   *bright; merry*

MAECENAS   Eight wild boars roasted whole at a breakfast and but
twelve persons there—is this true?

ENOBARBUS   This was but as a fly by° an eagle. We had much   *compared with*
more monstrous matter of feast, which worthily deserved noting.

190   **MAECENAS**   She's a most triumphant° lady, if report be square° to   *magnificent / fair*
her.

ENOBARBUS   When she first met Mark Antony, she pursed up
his heart upon the river of Cydnus.⁶

AGRIPPA   There she appeared indeed, or my reporter devised° well   *imagined*
195   for her.

ENOBARBUS   I will tell you.
The barge° she sat in, like a burnished throne   *oar-driven ship*
Burned on the water. The poop° was beaten gold;   *upper deck*
Purple° the sails, and so perfumèd that   *(royal dye)*
200   The winds were love-sick with them. The oars were silver,
Which to the tune of flutes kept stroke, and made
The water which they beat to follow faster,
As° amorous of their strokes. For° her own person,   *As if / As for*

---

3. Misenum, a hilly outcropping at the north end of the
Bay of Naples.
4. You hung in there; you had a high old time.
5. We disconcerted day by sleeping through it, and did

not see what it looked like.
6. She took possession of his heart on the Cydnus River
in Cilicia, Asia Minor (Turkey), on which the city of Tarsus stood.

It beggared all description. She did lie
205 In her pavilion—cloth of gold, of tissue[7]—
O'er-picturing that Venus where we see
The fancy outwork nature.[8] On each side her
Stood pretty dimpled boys, like smiling Cupids,
With divers-coloured fans whose wind did seem
210 To glow° the delicate cheeks which they did cool,   *make glow*
And what they undid did.

AGRIPPA   O, rare for Antony!

ENOBARBUS   Her gentlewomen, like the Nereides,°   *sea nymphs*
So many mermaids, tended her i'th' eyes,°   *under her watchful eyes*
And made their bends adornings.[9] At the helm
215 A seeming mermaid steers. The silken tackle°   *sails and ropes*
Swell with the touches of those flower-soft hands
That yarely frame° the office. From the barge   *artfully carry out*
A strange invisible perfume hits the sense
Of the adjacent wharfs.° The city cast   *banks*
220 Her people out upon° her, and Antony,   *toward*
Enthroned i'th' market-place, did sit alone,
Whistling to th'air, which but for vacancy[1]
Had° gone to gaze on Cleopatra too,   *Would have*
And made a gap in nature.

AGRIPPA   Rare Egyptian!

225 ENOBARBUS   Upon her landing Antony sent to her,
Invited her to supper. She replied
It should be better he became her guest,
Which she entreated. Our courteous Antony,
Whom ne'er the word of 'No' woman heard speak,
230 Being barbered ten times o'er, goes to the feast,
And for his ordinary° pays his heart   *public meal at an inn*
For what his eyes eat only.

AGRIPPA   Royal wench!
She made great Caesar° lay his sword to bed.   *(Julius)*
He ploughed her, and she cropped.[2]

ENOBARBUS   I saw her once
235 Hop forty paces through the public street,
And having lost her breath, she spoke and panted,
That° she did make defect° perfection,   *So that / her panting*
And breathless, pour breath forth.

MAECENAS   Now Antony
Must leave her utterly.

ENOBARBUS   Never. He will not.
240 Age cannot wither her, nor custom stale°   *familiarity diminish*
Her infinite variety. Other women cloy
The appetites they feed, but she makes hungry
Where most she satisfies. For vilest things
Become themselves° in her, that° the holy priests   *Are becoming / so that*
245 Bless her when she is riggish.°   *acts like a slut*

---

7. Fabric interwoven with gold thread.
8. *O'er-picturing . . . nature:* Outdoing even the picture of Venus in which the artist outdid nature.
9. Made their curtsies additions to the decoration.
1. Which if not for the fact that its absence would have left a vacuum (already in Shakespeare's time proverbially impossible in nature).
2. She bore Caesarion. After the assassination of Julius

Caesar in 44 B.C.E., Cleopatra returned from Rome, where she had accompanied him, to Egypt. There she reigned with their son, who became Ptolemy XV, after she ordered the death of her half brother and previous co-ruler Ptolemy XIV. On Ptolemy XIV, see 1.4.6 with note and 2.1.37 with note. On Antony and Cleopatra's plans for Ptolemy XV, see 3.6.1–16. On Ptolemy XV's fate, see note to 5.2.352.

MAECENAS   If beauty, wisdom, modesty can settle
　　The heart of Antony, Octavia is
　　A blessèd lottery° to him.　　　　　　　　　　　　　　　　　*prize*
AGRIPPA　　　　　　　　　　　Let us go.
　　Good Enobarbus, make yourself my guest
　　Whilst you abide here.
250 ENOBARBUS　　　　　　　Humbly, sir, I thank you.　　*Exeunt*

2.3

Enter ANTONY [*and*] CAESAR; OCTAVIA *between them*
ANTONY   The world and my great office will sometimes
　　Divide me from your bosom.
OCTAVIA　　　　　　　　　All which time,
　　Before the gods my knee shall bow my prayers
　　To them for you.
ANTONY　　　　　　　Good night, sir. My Octavia,
5　　Read not my blemishes in the world's report.
　　I have not kept my square,° but that° to come　　*stayed in line / what's*
　　Shall all be done by th' rule.¹ Good night, dear lady.
　　Good night, sir.
CAESAR   Good night.　　　　　*Exeunt* [CAESAR *and* OCTAVIA]
　　　　　Enter SOOTHSAYER
10 ANTONY   Now, sirrah.² You do wish yourself in Egypt?
SOOTHSAYER   Would I had never come from thence, nor you
　　Gone thither.
ANTONY　　　　　If you can, your reason?
SOOTHSAYER   I see it in my motion,° have it not in my tongue.　　*intuition*
　　But yet hie° you to Egypt again.　　　　　　　　　　　　　*hurry*
ANTONY　　　　　　　　　　Say to me
15　　Whose fortunes shall rise higher: Caesar's or mine?
SOOTHSAYER   Caesar's. Therefore, O Antony, stay not by his side.
　　Thy daemon, that thy spirit³ which keeps thee, is
　　Noble, courageous, high, unmatchable,
　　Where Caesar's is not. But near him thy angel
20　　Becomes afeard, as° being o'erpowered. Therefore　　*as if*
　　Make space enough between you.
ANTONY　　　　　　　　Speak this no more.
SOOTHSAYER   To none but thee; no more but when⁴ to thee.
　　If thou dost play with him at any game
　　Thou art sure to lose; and of° that natural luck　　　　　*by*
25　　He beats thee 'gainst the odds. Thy lustre thickens°　　*Your brightness dims*
　　When he shines by. I say again, thy spirit
　　Is all afraid to govern thee near him;
　　But he away, 'tis noble.
ANTONY　　　　　　　Get thee gone.
　　Say to Ventidius I would speak with him.　　*Exit* [SOOTHSAYER]
30　　He shall to Parthia; be it art or hap,°　　　　　　　　*talent or luck*
　　He° hath spoken true. The very dice obey him,°　　*(the soothsayer) / (Caesar)*
　　And in our sports my better cunning° faints　　　　　　*capability*
　　Under his chance.° If we draw lots, he speeds.°　　　*luck / succeeds*

2.3 Location: Rome.
1. Regulation; ruler, as unit of measure (picking up
"square," line 6, a measuring tool).
2. Term by which a subordinate or social inferior is

addressed.
3. *Thy daemon . . . spirit:* Your guardian angel, which is
the spirit.
4. *no more but when:* only.

His cocks do win the battle still of° mine   *always against*
35 When it is all to nought, and his quails ever
Beat mine, inhooped, at odds.⁵ I will to Egypt;
And though I make this marriage for my peace,
I'th' East my pleasure lies.

     Enter VENTIDIUS

                     O, come, Ventidius.
You must to Parthia, your commission's ready.
40 Follow me, and receive't.   *Exeunt*

2.4

     Enter LEPIDUS, MAECENAS, *and* AGRIPPA

LEPIDUS   Trouble yourselves no further. Pray you, hasten
Your generals after.¹
AGRIPPA   Sir, Mark Antony
Will e'en but° kiss Octavia, and we'll follow.   *merely*
LEPIDUS   Till I shall see you in your soldier's dress,
Which will become you both, farewell.
5 MAECENAS   We shall,
As I conceive the journey, be at the Mount°   *Mount Misenum*
Before you, Lepidus.
LEPIDUS   Your way is shorter.
My purposes do draw me° much about.   *force me to go*
You'll win two days upon me.
MAECENAS *and* AGRIPPA   Sir, good success.
10 LEPIDUS   Farewell.   *Exeunt* [MAECENAS *and* AGRIPPA *at one*
                           door, LEPIDUS *at another*]

2.5

     Enter CLEOPATRA, CHARMIAN, IRAS, *and* ALEXAS

CLEOPATRA   Give me some music—music, moody° food   *melancholy*
Of us that trade in love.
CHARMIAN, IRAS, *and* ALEXAS   The music, ho!

     Enter MARDIAN, *the eunuch*

CLEOPATRA   Let it alone. Let's to billiards. Come, Charmian.
CHARMIAN   My arm is sore. Best play with Mardian.
5 CLEOPATRA   As well a woman with an eunuch played
As with a woman. Come, you'll play with me, sir?
MARDIAN   As well as I can, madam.
CLEOPATRA   And when good will is showed, though't come too short¹
The actor may plead pardon. I'll none now.°   *I won't play now*
10 Give me mine angle.° We'll to th' river. There,   *fishing rod*
My music playing far off, I will betray°   *catch*
Tawny-finned fishes. My bended hook shall pierce
Their slimy jaws, and as I draw them up
I'll think them every one an Antony,
And say 'Ah ha, you're caught!'
15 CHARMIAN   'Twas merry when
You wagered on your angling, when your diver

---

5. *When . . . odds:* When the odds completely favor me, and when our quails are placed in a round enclosure to make them fight, his always beat mine, against all odds.
2.4 Location: Rome.

1. *hasten . . . after:* follow your leaders.
2.5 Location: Alexandria.
1. Referring to Mardian's sexual incapacity.

Did hang a salt° fish on his hook, which he   preserved
With fervency drew up.

CLEOPATRA   That time—O times!—
I laughed him out of patience, and that night
20   I laughed him into patience, and next morn,
Ere the ninth hour, I drunk him to his bed,
Then put my tires and mantles° on him whilst   headdresses and robes
I wore his sword Philippan.²

        Enter a MESSENGER

                    O, from Italy.
Ram thou thy fruitful tidings in mine ears,
That long time have been barren.
25   MESSENGER   Madam, madam!
CLEOPATRA   Antonio's dead. If thou say so, villain,
Thou kill'st thy mistress; but well and free,
If thou so yield° him, there is gold, and here   report
My bluest veins to kiss—a hand that kings
Have lipped, and trembled kissing.
30   MESSENGER   First, madam, he is well.
CLEOPATRA   Why, there's more gold. But, sirrah, mark: we use
To say the dead are well. Bring it to that,
The gold I give thee will I melt and pour
Down thy ill-uttering throat.
35   MESSENGER   Good madam, hear me.
CLEOPATRA   Well, go to, I will.
But there's no goodness in thy face. If Antony
Be free and healthful, so tart a favour°   so sour an expression
To trumpet such good tidings! If not well,
40   Thou shouldst come like a Fury³ crowned with snakes,
Not like a formal° man.   Not in the shape of a
MESSENGER   Will't please you hear me?
CLEOPATRA   I have a mind to strike thee ere thou speak'st.
Yet if thou say Antony lives, is well,
Or friends with Caesar, or not captive to him,
45   I'll set thee in a shower of gold, and hail
Rich pearls upon thee.
MESSENGER   Madam, he's well.
CLEOPATRA   Well said.
MESSENGER   And friends with Caesar.
CLEOPATRA   Thou'rt an honest man.
MESSENGER   Caesar and he are greater friends than ever.
CLEOPATRA   Make thee a fortune from me.
MESSENGER   But yet, madam—
50   CLEOPATRA   I do not like 'But yet'; it does allay°   dissipate
The good precedence.° Fie upon 'But yet'.   preceding good news
'But yet' is as a jailer to bring forth
Some monstrous malefactor. Prithee, friend,
Pour out the pack of matter to mine ear,°   Give me all the news
55   The good and bad together. He's friends with Caesar,
In state of health, thou sayst; and, thou sayst, free.
MESSENGER   Free, madam? No, I made no such report.
He's bound unto Octavia.

2. The sword with which Antony had beaten Brutus   3. In Greek mythology, a female avenging spirit.
and Cassius at Philippi.

CLEOPATRA	For what good turn?°	*good deed*
MESSENGER	For the best turn i'th' bed.	
CLEOPATRA	I am pale, Charmian.	
60 MESSENGER	Madam, he's married to Octavia.	
CLEOPATRA	The most infectious pestilence upon thee!	

[*She*] *strikes him down*

MESSENGER	Good madam, patience!	
CLEOPATRA	What say you?	

[*She*] *strikes him*

Hence, horrible villain, or I'll spurn° thine eyes   *kick*
Like balls before me. I'll unhair thy head,

She hales° *him up and down*   *drags*

65   Thou shalt be whipped with wire and stewed in brine,
Smarting in ling'ring pickle.°   *salt water*

MESSENGER	Gracious madam,	

I that do bring the news made not the match.

CLEOPATRA	Say 'tis not so, a province I will give thee,	

And make thy fortunes proud. The blow thou hadst
70   Shall make thy peace for moving me to rage,
And I will boot° thee with what° gift beside   *compensate / whatever*
Thy modesty can beg.

MESSENGER	He's married, madam.	
CLEOPATRA	Rogue, thou hast lived too long.	

[*She*] *draw[s] a knife*

MESSENGER	Nay then, I'll run.	

What mean you, madam? I have made no fault.   *Exit*

75   CHARMIAN   Good madam, keep yourself within yourself.°   *restrain yourself*
The man is innocent.

CLEOPATRA	Some innocents 'scape not the thunderbolt.	

Melt Egypt into Nile, and kindly° creatures   *harmless*
Turn all to serpents! Call the slave again.
80   Though I am mad I will not bite him. Call!

CHARMIAN   He is afeard to come.

CLEOPATRA	I will not hurt him.	

[*Exit* CHARMIAN]

These hands do lack nobility that they strike
A meaner° than myself, since I myself   *One of lower rank*
Have given myself the cause.°   *(by loving Antony)*

Enter the MESSENGER *again* [*with* CHARMIAN]

Come hither, sir.
85   Though it be honest, it is never good
To bring bad news. Give to a gracious message
An host° of tongues, but let ill tidings tell   *A multitude*
Themselves when they be felt.[4]

MESSENGER   I have done my duty.

90   CLEOPATRA   Is he married?
I cannot hate thee worser than I do
If thou again say 'Yes'.

MESSENGER	He's married, madam.	
CLEOPATRA	The gods confound° thee! Dost thou hold there still?	*destroy*
MESSENGER	Should I lie, madam?	
CLEOPATRA	O, I would thou didst,	

95   So° half my Egypt were submerged and made   *Even if*
A cistern° for scaled snakes. Go, get thee hence.   *reservoir; chamber pot*

---

4. *let . . . felt:* bad news is best revealed by letting the victim feel the effects.

Hadst thou Narcissus[5] in thy face, to me
Thou wouldst appear most ugly. He is married?
MESSENGER   I crave your highness' pardon.
CLEOPATRA   He is married?
100   MESSENGER   Take no offence that I would not° offend you.   do not want to
To punish me for what you make me do
Seems much unequal.° He's married to Octavia.   most unfair
CLEOPATRA   O that his fault should make a knave° of thee,   villain
That act not what thou'rt sure of!^[6] Get thee hence.
105   The merchandise which thou hast brought from Rome
Are all too dear for me. Lie they upon thy hand,[7]
And be undone° by 'em.   [*Exit* MESSENGER]   ruined (financially)
CHARMIAN   Good your highness, patience.
CLEOPATRA   In praising Antony I have dispraised Caesar.
CHARMIAN   Many times, madam.
110   CLEOPATRA   I am paid for't now. Lead me from hence.
I faint. O Iras, Charmian—'tis no matter.
Go to the fellow, good Alexas, bid him
Report the feature° of Octavia: her years,   appearance
Her inclination;° let him not leave out   disposition
115   The colour of her hair. Bring me word quickly.   [*Exit* ALEXAS]
Let him for ever go—let him not, Charmian;
Though he be painted one way like a Gorgon,
The other way's a Mars.[8] [*To* MARDIAN] Bid you Alexas
Bring me word how tall she is. Pity me, Charmian,
120   But do not speak to me. Lead me to my chamber.   *Exeunt*

2.6

Flourish. Enter POMPEY [*and*] MENAS *at one door, with*
[*a*] *drum*[*mer*] *and* [*a*] *trumpet*[*er*]; *at another,* CAESAR,
LEPIDUS, ANTONY, ENOBARBUS, MAECENAS, AGRIPPA, *with*
soldiers marching

POMPEY   Your hostages I have, so have you mine,
And we shall talk before we fight.
CAESAR   Most meet°   fitting
That first we come to words, and therefore have we
Our written purposes° before us sent,   offers
5   Which if thou hast considered, let us know
If 'twill tie up° thy discontented sword   lead you to put aside
And carry back to Sicily much tall° youth   courageous
That else must perish here.
POMPEY   To you all three,
The senators alone° of this great world,   sole governors
10   Chief factors° for the gods: I do not know   agents
Wherefore° my father[1] should revengers want,°   why / lack

5. In Greek mythology, a surprisingly beautiful young
man.
6. Who do not commit the offense you know about;
who do not report the information you know.
7. Leave with your goods unsold.
8. Cleopatra imagines Antony as a figure in a perspective
painting: popular in Shakespeare's time, they showed different images according to the angle from which they
were viewed. In classical mythology, a Gorgon was one of
three female monsters with snakes for hair whose horrific
appearance could turn others to stone.
2.6 Location: Near Misenum, Italy.
1. Pompey the Great. The allusion in the following lines

is primarily to the events dramatized by Shakespeare in
Julius Caesar. After being defeated by Julius Caesar at
Pharsalia, Pompey the Great fled to Egypt and was there
assassinated by agents of Ptolemy, Cleopatra's half brother
(prior to the events in *Julius Caesar*). Julius Caesar was
then himself assassinated by the Roman republican conspirators, who included Cassius and Brutus. The triumvirs Antony, Octavius, and Lepidus defeated and killed
Brutus and Cassius at Philippi in revenge (see note to
1.2.88). The younger Pompey thus believes that by making war on the triumvirate, he avenges his father's death
and the deaths of Brutus and Cassius (and, therefore, he
fights for the Republic).

Having a son and friends, since Julius Caesar,
Who at Philippi the good Brutus ghosted,[2]
There saw you labouring for him.° What was't   *on his behalf*
15 That moved pale Cassius to conspire? And what
Made the all-honoured, honest° Roman Brutus,   *honorable*
With the armed rest, courtiers° of beauteous freedom, *seekers*
To drench° the Capitol but that they would   *(in blood)*
Have one man but a man?° And that is it   *(and not a king)*
20 Hath made me rig° my navy, at whose burden   *equip*
The angered ocean foams; with which I meant
To scourge th'ingratitude that despiteful Rome
Cast on my noble father.

CAESAR   Take your time.

ANTONY Thou canst not fear° us, Pompey, with thy sails. *intimidate*
25 We'll speak with° thee at sea. At land thou know'st *engage*
How much we do o'ercount° thee.   *outnumber*

POMPEY   At land indeed
Thou dost o'ercount me of my father's house,[3]
But since the cuckoo builds not for himself,[4]
Remain in't as thou mayst.°   *as long as you can*

LEPIDUS   Be pleased to tell us—
30 For this is from the present°—how you take *beside the point*
The offers we have sent you.

CAESAR   There's the point.

ANTONY Which do not be entreated to,° but weigh *convinced unfairly of*
What it is worth, embraced.°   *if you consent*

CAESAR   And what may follow,
To try a larger fortune?[5]

POMPEY   You have made me offer
35 Of Sicily, Sardinia; and I must
Rid all the sea of pirates; then to send
Measures of wheat to Rome; this 'greed upon,
To part with unhacked edges,° and bear back *unused swords*
Our targes undinted.°   *shields untouched*

CAESAR, ANTONY, *and* LEPIDUS That's our offer.

POMPEY   Know, then,
40 I came before you here a man prepared
To take this offer. But Mark Antony
Put me to some impatience. Though I lose
The praise of it by telling, you must know,
When Caesar and your brother were at blows,
45 Your mother came to Sicily, and did find
Her welcome friendly.

ANTONY   I have heard it, Pompey,
And am well studied for° a liberal thanks *intend to offer*
Which I do owe you.

POMPEY   Let me have your hand.
    [POMPEY *and* ANTONY *shake hands*]
I did not think, sir, to have met you here.

---

2. Caesar appeared as a ghost to Brutus at the Battle of Philippi.
3. Plutarch records that Antony agreed to buy the elder Pompey's house but ultimately refused to pay for it.
4. The cuckoo lays eggs in the nests of other birds, rather than building a nest of its own.
5. If you try (by fighting us) for a still larger fortune than we have offered.

50 ANTONY   The beds i'th' East are soft; and thanks to you,
        That called me timelier° than my purpose° hither;   *earlier / intention*
        For I have gained by't.
    CAESAR [*to* POMPEY]   Since I saw you last
        There is a change upon you.
    POMPEY   Well, I know not
        What counts harsh fortune casts upon my face,[6]
55   But in my bosom shall she never come
        To make my heart her vassal.
    LEPIDUS   Well met here.
    POMPEY   I hope so, Lepidus. Thus we are agreed.
        I crave our composition° may be written   *pact*
        And sealed between us.
    CAESAR   That's the next to do.
60 POMPEY   We'll feast each other ere we part, and let's
        Draw lots who shall begin.°   *act as host*
    ANTONY   That will I, Pompey.
    POMPEY   No, Antony, take the lot.
        But, first or last, your fine Egyptian cookery
65   Shall have the fame. I have heard that Julius Caesar
        Grew fat with feasting there.
    ANTONY   You have heard much.
    POMPEY   I have fair° meanings, sir.   *amicable*
    ANTONY   And fair° words to them.   *(ironic)*
    POMPEY   Then so much have I heard,
70   And I have heard Apollodorus carried[7]—
    ENOBARBUS   No more o' that, he did so.
    POMPEY   What, I pray you?
    ENOBARBUS   A certain queen to Caesar in a mattress.
    POMPEY   I know thee now. How far'st thou, soldier?
    ENOBARBUS   Well, and well am like to do, for I perceive
        Four feasts are toward.°   *to come*
75 POMPEY   Let me shake thy hand.
            [POMPEY *and* ENOBARBUS *shake hands*]
        I never hated thee. I have seen thee fight
        When I have envied thy behaviour.
    ENOBARBUS   Sir, I never loved you much, but I ha' praised ye
        When you have well deserved ten times as much
80   As I have said you did.
    POMPEY   Enjoy thy plainness.° It nothing ill becomes thee. *matter-of-fact speech*
        Aboard my galley I invite you all.
        Will you lead, lords?
    CAESAR, ANTONY, *and* LEPIDUS   Show's the way, sir.
    POMPEY   Come.
            Exeunt. Manent ENOBARBUS *and* MENAS
    MENAS [*aside*]   Thy father, Pompey, would ne'er have made this treaty.
85   [*To* ENOBARBUS] You and I have known,° sir.   *met each other*
    ENOBARBUS   At sea, I think.
    MENAS   We have, sir.
    ENOBARBUS   You have done well by water.

---

6. What accounts cruel fortune calculates (by marking   her lover, Julius Caesar, by having herself rolled up in a
notches, like wrinkles).   sleeping mat (told in Plutarch).
7. Alluding to the story that Cleopatra gained access to

MENAS   And you by land.

90   ENOBARBUS   I will praise any man that will praise me, though it
cannot be denied what I have done by land.

MENAS   Nor what I have done by water.

ENOBARBUS   Yes, something you can deny for your own safety.
You have been a great thief by sea.

95   MENAS   And you by land.

ENOBARBUS   There I deny my land service; but give me your
hand, Menas. If our eyes had authority,° here they might take   (to make an arrest)
two thieves kissing.[8]

    [*They shake hands*]

MENAS   All men's faces are true,° whatsome'er their hands are.   honest

100   ENOBARBUS   But there is never a fair woman has a true° face.   (without makeup)

MENAS   No slander;° they steal hearts.   That's true

ENOBARBUS   We came hither to fight with you.

MENAS   For my part, I am sorry it is turned to a drinking. Pompey
doth this day laugh away his fortune.

105   ENOBARBUS   If he do, sure he cannot weep't back again.

MENAS   You've said,° sir. We looked not for Mark Antony here.   spoken truly
Pray you, is he married to Cleopatra?

ENOBARBUS   Caesar's sister is called Octavia.

MENAS   True, sir. She was the wife of Caius Marcellus.

110   ENOBARBUS   But she is now the wife of Marcus Antonius.

MENAS   Pray ye, sir?

ENOBARBUS   'Tis true.

MENAS   Then is Caesar and he for ever knit together.

ENOBARBUS   If I were bound to divine° of this unity I would not   make predictions

115   prophesy so.

MENAS   I think the policy of that purpose made more[9] in the
marriage than the love of the parties.

ENOBARBUS   I think so, too. But you shall find the band that
seems to tie their friendship together will be the very strangler

120   of their amity. Octavia is of a holy, cold, and still conversation.°   disposition

MENAS   Who would not have his wife so?

ENOBARBUS   Not he that himself is not so, which is Mark Antony.
He will to his Egyptian dish again; then shall the sighs of
Octavia blow the fire up in Caesar, and, as I said before, that

125   which is the strength of their amity shall prove the immediate
author° of their variance.° Antony will use his affection where   cause / enmity
it is. He married but his occasion here.[1]

MENAS   And thus it may be. Come, sir, will you aboard? I have a
health for you.

130   ENOBARBUS   I shall take it, sir. We have used our throats in
Egypt.

MENAS   Come, let's away.   *Exeunt*

---

8. Arrest two thieves embracing; catch two thieving
hands in a handshake, plotting together.

9. I think the politics of that "unity" weighed more
heavily.

1. *Antony . . . here:* Antony will act on his desire where it
really is located (Egypt). He married out of self-interest
here.

2.7

Music plays. Enter two or three SERVANTS *with a ban-*
quet[1]

FIRST SERVANT   Here they'll be, man. Some o' their plants are ill
rooted[2] already; the least wind i'th' world will blow them down.

SECOND SERVANT   Lepidus is high-coloured.

FIRST SERVANT   They have made him drink alms-drink.[3]

5　SECOND SERVANT   As they pinch one another by the disposition,[4]
he cries out 'No more!'—reconciles them to his entreaty° and　　(*to stop arguing*)
himself to th' drink.

FIRST SERVANT   But it raises the greater war between him and his
discretion.

10　SECOND SERVANT   Why, this it is to have a name° in great men's　　*only a nominal place*
fellowship. I had as lief° have a reed that will do me no service　　*just as soon*
as a partisan I could not heave.[5]

FIRST SERVANT   To be called into a huge sphere and not to be
seen to move in't, are the holes where eyes should be which
15　pitifully disaster the cheeks.[6]

A sennet° sounded. Enter CAESAR, ANTONY, POMPEY,　　*flourish of trumpets*
LEPIDUS, AGRIPPA, MAECENAS, ENOBARBUS, [*and*]
MENAS, *with other captains* [*and a boy*]

ANTONY [*to* CAESAR]   Thus do they, sir: they take the flow° o'th'　　*measure the depth*
Nile
By certain scales i'th'° pyramid. They know　　*marks on the*
By th' height, the lowness, or the mean,° if dearth　　*middle position*
Or foison° follow. The higher Nilus swells　　*abundance*
20　The more it promises; as it ebbs, the seedsman
Upon the slime and ooze scatters his grain,
And shortly comes to harvest.

LEPIDUS   You've strange serpents there?

ANTONY   Ay, Lepidus.

25　LEPIDUS   Your serpent of Egypt is bred now of your mud by the
operation of your sun; so is your crocodile.

ANTONY   They are so.

POMPEY   Sit, and some wine. A health to Lepidus!
[ANTONY, POMPEY, *and* LEPIDUS *sit*]

LEPIDUS   I am not so well as I should be, but I'll ne'er out.°　　*leave; miss a round*

30　ENOBARBUS   Not till you have slept—I fear me you'll be in° till　　*remain; be drunk*
then.

LEPIDUS   Nay, certainly, I have heard the Ptolemies' pyramises[7]
are very goodly things: without contradiction I have heard that.

MENAS [*aside to* POMPEY]   Pompey, a word.

POMPEY [*aside to* MENAS]　　Say in mine ear; what is't?

35　MENAS [*aside to* POMPEY]   Forsake thy seat, I do beseech thee, captain,
And hear me speak a word.

POMPEY [*aside to* MENAS]　　Forbear° me till anon.　　*Wait for*
[*Aloud*] This wine for Lepidus!

2.7 Location: Pompey's galley, off Misenum.
1. One of the courses of the feast, possibly dessert.
2. *their . . . rooted:* the soles of the feet of the (drunken)
leaders are unsteady; the alliance between Antony and
Caesar is shaky.
3. Drink given out of charity; in this case, extra rounds
given to reconcile the parties each time they quarrel; one
too many.
4. As they irritate one another according to their natures.

5. As a spear I could not lift (position without power).
6. *To be . . . cheeks:* To be placed in high circles in which
one is incapable of moving is like having, instead of eyes,
empty eye sockets that disfigure one's face. (In Ptolemaic
astronomy, a planet "moves" within its "sphere," one of a
series of concentric circles of which the universe is
formed, with the earth at the center. A planet's ill influence causes "disaster," which literally means "bad star.")
7. Pyramids (drunken speech).

[Handwritten top margin: amity—friendship origin]

[Handwritten left margin: settle feud.]

[MENAS] *whispers in* [POMPEY'S] *ear*

LEPIDUS   What manner o' thing is your crocodile?

ANTONY   It is shaped, sir, like itself, and it is as broad as it hath
40   breadth. It is just so high as it is, and moves with it° own organs.   its
It lives by that which nourisheth it, and the elements once out
of it, it transmigrates.[8]

LEPIDUS   What colour is it of?

ANTONY   Of it own colour, too.

45   LEPIDUS   'Tis a strange serpent.

ANTONY   'Tis so, and the tears of it are wet.[9]

CAESAR [*to* ANTONY]   Will this description satisfy him?

ANTONY   With the health that Pompey gives him; else he is a
very epicure.°   an insatiable glutton

50   POMPEY [*aside to* MENAS]   Go hang, sir, hang! Tell me of that? Away,
Do as I bid you. [*Aloud*] Where's this cup I called for?

MENAS [*aside to* POMPEY]   If for the sake of merit° thou wilt hear me,   past deeds
Rise from thy stool.

POMPEY [*rising*]   I think thou'rt mad. The matter?

[MENAS *and* POMPEY *stand apart*]

MENAS   I have ever held my cap off to° thy fortunes.   ever served

55   POMPEY   Thou hast served me with much faith. What's else to say?
Be jolly, lords.

ANTONY   These quicksands, Lepidus,
Keep off them, for you sink.

MENAS   Wilt thou be lord of all the world?

POMPEY   What sayst thou?

MENAS   Wilt thou be lord of the whole world? That's twice.

POMPEY   How should that be?

60   MENAS   But entertain° it   consider
And, though thou think me poor, I am the man
Will give thee all the world.

POMPEY   Hast thou drunk well?

MENAS   No, Pompey, I have kept me from the cup.
Thou art, if thou dar'st be, the earthly Jove.

65   Whate'er the ocean pales° or sky inclips°   encloses / embraces
Is thine, if thou wilt ha't.

POMPEY   Show me which way!

MENAS   These three world-sharers, these competitors,°   allies
Are in thy vessel. Let me cut the cable;
And when we are put off,° fall to their throats.   (from shore)
All there is thine.

70   POMPEY   Ah, this thou shouldst have done
And not have spoke on't. In me 'tis villainy,
In thee 't had been good service. Thou must know
'Tis not my profit that does lead mine honour;
Mine honour, it.[1] Repent that e'er thy tongue
75   Hath so betrayed thine act.[2] Being done unknown,
I should have found it afterwards well done,
But must condemn it now. Desist, and drink.

[Handwritten right margin, top: They get Pompey drunk]

[Handwritten right margin: Menas makes offer to Pompey, to kill all three. + 3min Control]

[Handwritten right margin: Egypt vs. Rome]

[Handwritten right margin, bottom: If Menas did it, tell Pompey and killed the 3, he would have accepted it.]

8. Passes into other forms of life: referring to Pythagoras's
theory, apparently of Egyptian origin, that at death the
soul moves into another newborn living thing.
9. Continuing the pattern of comically uninformative
self-identity, this line may also refer to hypocritical crocodile tears and hence to Pompey, as his ensuing exchange
with Menas suggests. See also 3.2.54–60 and 5.1.26–49.
1. *'Tis . . . it:* It is my honor that precedes or is the basis
of my profit.
2. Treacherously disclosed your intentions and so made
it impossible to carry them out.

[*He returns to the others*]

MENAS [*aside*]   For this, I'll never follow thy palled° fortunes more.   diminished
　　　Who seeks and will not take when once 'tis offered,
　　　Shall never find it more.
80 POMPEY   This health to Lepidus!
ANTONY   Bear him ashore.—I'll pledge it° for him, Pompey.   drink the toast
ENOBARBUS   Here's to thee, Menas!
MENAS   Enobarbus, welcome.
POMPEY   Fill till the cup be hid.
　　　[*One lifts* LEPIDUS, *drunk, and carries him off*]
ENOBARBUS   There's a strong fellow, Menas.
MENAS   Why?
85 ENOBARBUS   A° bears the third part of the world, man; seest not?   He
MENAS   The third part then is drunk. Would it were all,
　　　That it might go on wheels.°   easily; out of control
ENOBARBUS   Drink thou, increase the reels.°   revels; spinning
MENAS   Come.
POMPEY   This is not yet an Alexandrian feast.
90 ANTONY   It ripens towards it. Strike the vessels,° ho!   Open more casks
　　　Here's to Caesar!
CAESAR   I could well forbear't.
　　　It's monstrous° labour when I wash my brain,   unnatural
　　　An° it grow fouler.   If as a result
ANTONY   Be a child o'th' time.
95 CAESAR   Possess it, I'll make answer.³
　　　But I had rather fast from all, four days,
　　　Than drink so much in one.
ENOBARBUS [*to* ANTONY]   Ha, my brave Emperor,
　　　Shall we dance now the Egyptian bacchanals,⁴
　　　And celebrate our drink?
100 POMPEY   Let's ha't, good soldier.
ANTONY   Come, let's all take hands
　　　Till that the conquering wine hath steeped our sense
　　　In soft and delicate Lethe.°   oblivion
ENOBARBUS   All take hands.
　　　Make battery to° our ears with the loud music.   Besiege
105 The while I'll place you, then the boy shall sing.
　　　The holding° every man shall beat° as loud   refrain / beat out
　　　As his strong sides can volley.°   fire off
　　　Music plays. ENOBARBUS *places them hand in hand*
BOY [*sings*]   Come, thou monarch of the vine,
　　　　　Plumpy Bacchus, with pink⁵ eyne!
110 　　　In thy vats our cares be drowned,
　　　　　With thy grapes our hairs be crowned!
　　　　　Cup us till the world go round,
　　　　　Cup us till the world go round!
CAESAR   What would you more? Pompey, good night.
　　　[*To* ANTONY]   Good-brother,°   Brother-in-law
115 Let me request you off.° Our graver business   to come ashore
　　　Frowns at this levity. Gentle lords, let's part.
　　　You see we have burnt° our cheeks. Strong Enobarb   flushed

---

3. Take it, and I'll drink, too; be in command of the time,   and revelry.
I say.   5. Half-closed and red from drinking.
4. Wild, drunken revels in honor of Bacchus, god of wine

Is weaker than the wine, and mine own tongue
Splits° what it speaks. The wild disguise° hath almost   *Deforms / drunkenness*
120   Anticked us° all. What needs more words? Good night.   *Made us clowns*
Good Antony, your hand.

POMPEY   I'll try you° on the shore.   *test your drinking*

ANTONY   And shall, sir. Give's your hand.

POMPEY   O Antony,
You have my father's house. But what, we are friends!
Come down into the boat.

             [Exeunt all but ENOBARBUS *and* MENAS*]*

ENOBARBUS   Take heed you fall not, Menas.

125 MENAS   I'll not° on shore.   *not go*
No, to my cabin. These drums, these trumpets, flutes, what!
Let Neptune hear we bid a loud farewell
To these great fellows. Sound and be hanged, sound out!

           Sound a flourish, with drums

ENOBARBUS *[throwing his cap in the air]*   Hoo, says a!° There's   *he*
my cap.

MENAS   Ho, noble captain, come!   *Exeunt*

3.1

Enter VENTIDIUS *[with* SILIUS *and other Roman soldiers]*
as it were in triumph; the dead body of Pacorus borne
before him

VENTIDIUS   Now, darting Parthia,[1] art thou struck; and now
Pleased fortune does of Marcus Crassus'[2] death
Make me revenger. Bear the King's son's body
Before our army. Thy° Pacorus, Orodes,   *Your son*
Pays this for Marcus Crassus.

5 SILIUS   Noble Ventidius,
Whilst yet with Parthian blood thy sword is warm,
The fugitive Parthians follow.[3] Spur through Media,[4]
Mesopotamia, and the shelters whither
The routed fly. So thy grand captain, Antony,
10   Shall set thee on triumphant° chariots and   *triumphal*
Put garlands on thy head.

VENTIDIUS   O Silius, Silius,
I have done enough. A lower place,° note well,   *man of low rank*
May make too great an act. For learn this, Silius:
Better to leave undone than by our deed
15   Acquire too high a fame when him we serve's away.
Caesar and Antony have ever won
More in their officer than person.[5] Sossius,
One of my place in Syria, his° lieutenant,   *(Antony's)*
For quick accumulation of renown,
20   Which he achieved by th' minute,° lost his favour.   *more every minute*
Who does i'th' wars more than his captain can
Becomes his captain's captain; and ambition,

3.1 Location: Syria.
1. Parthian cavalry advanced flinging darts, then retreated shooting arrows. "Parthia" here refers to both the
nation and its King, Orodes.
2. A member, with Pompey the Great and Julius Caesar,
of the first triumvirate, treacherously and cruelly killed in

defeat by Orodes in 53 B.C.E.
3. Chase the fleeing Parthians.
4. The land between Persia and Armenia, east of
Mesopotamia—part of the Parthian Empire.
5. Owing more to the skill of their officers than to their
own skill.

The soldier's virtue, rather makes choice of loss
Than gain which darkens him.°   *eclipses his renown*
25 I could do more to do Antonius good,
But 'twould offend him, and in his offence
Should my performance perish.°   *lose its value*
SILIUS   Thou hast, Ventidius, that°   *(discretion)*
Without the which a soldier and his sword
Grants scarce° distinction. Thou wilt write to Antony?   *Scarcely admits of*
30 VENTIDIUS   I'll humbly signify what in his name,
That magical word of war, we have effected;
How, with his banners and his well-paid ranks,
The ne'er-yet-beaten horse° of Parthia   *cavalry*
We have jaded° out o'th' field.   *chased like tired nags*
SILIUS   Where is he now?
35 VENTIDIUS   He purposeth to Athens; whither, with what haste
The weight we must convey with's will permit,
We shall appear before him.—On there; pass along.   *Exeunt*

3.2

Enter AGRIPPA *at one door,* ENOBARBUS *at another*
AGRIPPA   What, are the brothers parted?°   *brothers-in-law gone*
ENOBARBUS   They have dispatched° with Pompey; he is gone.   *finished the business*
The other three are sealing.° Octavia weeps   *signing their pact*
To part from Rome, Caesar is sad, and Lepidus
5   Since Pompey's feast, as Menas says, is troubled
With the green-sickness.[1]
AGRIPPA   'Tis a noble Lepidus.
ENOBARBUS   A very fine one. O, how he loves Caesar!
AGRIPPA   Nay, but how dearly he adores Mark Antony!
ENOBARBUS   Caesar? Why, he's the Jupiter of men.
10 AGRIPPA   What's Antony—the god of Jupiter?
ENOBARBUS   Spake you of Caesar? How, the nonpareil?°   *incomparable*
AGRIPPA   O Antony, O thou Arabian bird![2]
ENOBARBUS   Would you praise Caesar, say 'Caesar'; go no further.
AGRIPPA   Indeed, he plied them both with excellent praises.
15 ENOBARBUS   But he loves Caesar best; yet he loves Antony—
Hoo! Hearts, tongues, figures,° scribes, bards, poets, cannot   *(of speech); numbers*
Think, speak, cast,° write, sing, number°—hoo!—   *calculate / make verses*
His love to Antony. But as for Caesar—
Kneel down, kneel down, and wonder.
AGRIPPA   Both he loves.
ENOBARBUS   They are his shards,[3] and he their beetle.
[*Trumpet within*]
20   So,
This is° to horse. Adieu, noble Agrippa.   *calls us*
AGRIPPA   Good fortune, worthy soldier, and farewell.
Enter CAESAR, ANTONY, LEPIDUS, *and* OCTAVIA
ANTONY [*to* CAESAR]   No further, sir.

3.2 Location: Rome.
1. Anemia in adolescent, lovesick girls (hence, a feminizing attribute): here, used humorously for Lepidus's hangover and its effect, as well as ironically for his overblown affection for Caesar and Antony.
2. The phoenix, a legendary, self-resurrecting bird, only one of which existed at a time. It was believed to live for several centuries, to die in flames, and to be reborn from its own ashes.
3. Dung patches (between which the beetle crawls to feed and breed); perhaps, wing cases (with which the beetle flies).

CAESAR   You take from me a great part of myself.
25 Use me well in't. Sister, prove such a wife
As my thoughts make thee, and as my farthest bond
Shall pass on thy approof.⁴ Most noble Antony,
Let not the piece° of virtue which is set   *paragon*
Betwixt us as the cement of our love
30 To keep it builded, be the ram to batter
The fortress of it; for better might we
Have loved without this mean° if on both parts   *intermediary*
This be not cherished.
ANTONY   Make me not offended
In° your distrust.   *By*
CAESAR   I have said.
ANTONY   You shall not find,
35 Though you be therein curious,° the least cause   *overly probing*
For what you seem to fear. So, the gods keep you,
And make the hearts of Romans serve your ends.
We will here part.
CAESAR   Farewell, my dearest sister, fare thee well.
40 The elements be kind to thee, and make
Thy spirits all of comfort. Fare thee well.
OCTAVIA [*weeping*]   My noble brother!
ANTONY   The April's in her eyes;° it is love's spring,   *She weeps*
And these the showers to bring it on. Be cheerful.
45 OCTAVIA   Sir, look well to my husband's° house, and—   *(Antony's)*
CAESAR   What, Octavia?
OCTAVIA   I'll tell you in your ear.
    [*She whispers to* CAESAR]
ANTONY   Her tongue will not obey her heart, nor can
Her heart inform her tongue—the swan's-down feather,
That stands upon the swell at full of tide,
50 And neither way inclines.⁵
ENOBARBUS [*aside to* AGRIPPA]   Will Caesar weep?
AGRIPPA [*aside to* ENOBARBUS]   He has a cloud in's face.
ENOBARBUS [*aside to* AGRIPPA]   He were the worse for that were he a horse;⁶
So is he, being a man.
AGRIPPA [*aside to* ENOBARBUS]   Why, Enobarbus,
55 When Antony found Julius Caesar dead
He cried almost to roaring, and he wept
When at Philippi he found Brutus slain.
ENOBARBUS [*aside to* AGRIPPA]   That year indeed he was trou-
bled with a rheum.°   *flu; watery eyes*
What willingly he did confound° he wailed,°   *destroy / mourned*
Believe't, till I wept too.
60 CAESAR   No, sweet Octavia,
You shall hear from me still.° The time shall not   *constantly*
Outgo⁷ my thinking on° you.   *of*
ANTONY   Come, sir, come,
I'll wrestle with you in my strength of love.

---

4. *and as . . . approof*: and (such a wife) as to make my largest contractual commitment (also, my closest tie of affection: here, Caesar's to Octavia) approved on the basis of what you will prove to be.
5. *the swan's-down . . . inclines*: (she is like) the feather of a swan's down that floats in still water, unmoving (just as

she can't speak) when the tide is about to turn. Octavia's emotions, balanced between brother and husband, are too strong to allow speech.
6. A horse with a cloud—a dark rather than a white star on its face—was supposedly ill tempered.
7. *The . . . / Outgo*: Even time will not endure beyond.

Look, here I have you [*embracing* CAESAR]; thus I let you go,
And give you to the gods.

65 CAESAR   Adieu, be happy.
LEPIDUS   Let all the number of the stars give light
To thy fair way.
CAESAR   Farewell, farewell.
          [*He*] *kisses* OCTAVIA
ANTONY   Farewell.
          Trumpets sound. Exeunt [ANTONY, OCTAVIA, *and*
                    ENOBARBUS *at one door,* CAESAR, LEPIDUS, *and*
                              AGRIPPA *at another*]

                    3.3
          Enter CLEOPATRA, CHARMIAN, IRAS, *and* ALEXAS
CLEOPATRA   Where is the fellow?
ALEXAS   Half afeard to come.
CLEOPATRA   Go to, go to.
          Enter the MESSENGER *as before*
                              Come hither, sir.
ALEXAS   Good majesty,
Herod of Jewry[1] dare not look upon you
But when you are well pleased.
CLEOPATRA   That Herod's head
5   I'll have; but how, when Antony is gone,
Through whom I might command it?
          [*To the* MESSENGER]   Come thou near.
MESSENGER   Most gracious majesty!
CLEOPATRA   Didst thou behold
Octavia?
MESSENGER   Ay, dread Queen.
CLEOPATRA   Where?
MESSENGER   Madam, in Rome.
I looked her in the face, and saw her led
10   Between her brother and Mark Antony.
CLEOPATRA   Is she as tall as me?
MESSENGER   She is not, madam.
CLEOPATRA   Didst hear her speak? Is she shrill-tongued or low?
MESSENGER   Madam, I heard her speak. She is low-voiced.
CLEOPATRA   That's not so good.° He cannot like her long.   favorable to Octavia
15   CHARMIAN   Like her? O Isis, 'tis impossible!
CLEOPATRA   I think so, Charmian. Dull of tongue, and dwarfish.
What majesty is in her gait? Remember
If e'er thou looked'st on majesty.
MESSENGER   She creeps.
Her motion and her station° are as one.   standing still
20   She shows° a body rather than a life,   seems to be
A statue than° a breather.   rather than
CLEOPATRA   Is this certain?
MESSENGER   Or I have no observance.°   powers of observation
CHARMIAN   Three in Egypt
Cannot make better note.[2]
CLEOPATRA   He's very knowing,

────────────────────────────

3.3 Location: Alexandria.   2. *Three . . . note:* There are not three better witnesses in
1. Renowned for his irrational cruelty. See note to 1.2.24.   all Egypt.

I do perceive't. There's nothing in her yet.
The fellow has good judgement.

25 CHARMIAN   Excellent.

CLEOPATRA [*to the* MESSENGER]   Guess at her years, I prithee.

MESSENGER   Madam,
She was a widow—

CLEOPATRA   Widow? Charmian, hark.

MESSENGER   And I do think she's thirty.°   (*Cleopatra was 38*)

CLEOPATRA   Bear'st thou her face in mind? Is't long or round?

30 MESSENGER   Round, even to faultiness.

CLEOPATRA   For the most part, too, they are foolish that are so.
Her hair—what colour?

MESSENGER   Brown, madam; and her forehead
As low as she would wish it.[3]

CLEOPATRA [*giving money*]   There's gold for thee.
Thou must not take my former sharpness ill.

35 I will employ thee back° again. I find thee   *to go back to Rome*
Most fit for business. Go, make thee ready.
Our letters are prepared.   [*Exit* MESSENGER]

CHARMIAN   A proper° man.   *An admirable*

CLEOPATRA   Indeed he is so. I repent me much
That so I harried him. Why, methinks, by him,°   *by his account*
This creature's no such thing.°   *nothing special*

40 CHARMIAN   Nothing, madam.

CLEOPATRA   The man hath seen some majesty, and should know.

CHARMIAN   Hath he seen majesty? Isis else defend,
And serving you so long![4]

CLEOPATRA   I have one thing more to ask him yet, good Charmian.

45 But 'tis no matter. Thou shalt bring him to me
Where I will write. All may be well enough.

CHARMIAN   I warrant you, madam.   *Exeunt*

3.4

Enter ANTONY *and* OCTAVIA

ANTONY   Nay, nay, Octavia, not only that,
That were excusable, that and thousands more
Of semblable° import; but he hath waged   *like*
New wars 'gainst Pompey, made his will and read it

5 To public ear,[1] spoke scantly° of me;   *meanly*
When perforce he could not
But pay me terms of honour, cold and sickly
He vented them, most narrow measure° lent me.   *little credit*
When the best hint° was given him, he not took't,   *opportunity*
Or did it from his teeth.°   *insincerely*

10 OCTAVIA   O my good lord,
Believe not all, or if you must believe,
Stomach° not all. A more unhappy lady,   *Resent*
If this division chance, ne'er stood between,
Praying for both parts.

15 The good gods will mock me presently,°   *at once*

---

3. So that she would wish it no lower: high foreheads
were admired.
4. *Isis . . . long:* He surely has, considering how long he's
served you. *else defend:* prohibit that it not be so. There
may be a double irony in the lines, with Charmian appar-

ently denying that anyone who has long served Cleopatra
could recognize true majesty but not really meaning it.
3.4 Location: Athens.
1. Caesar's act implies promises to the public.

When I shall pray 'O, bless my lord and husband!',
Undo that prayer by crying out as loud
'O, bless my brother!' Husband win, win brother
Prays and destroys the prayer; no midway
'Twixt these extremes at all.

20 ANTONY   Gentle Octavia,
Let your best love draw to that point which seeks
Best to preserve it.[2] If I lose mine honour,
I lose myself. Better I were not yours
Than yours so branchless.° But, as you requested,   *amputated*
25 Yourself shall go between's. The meantime, lady,
I'll raise the preparation of a war
Shall stain your brother.° Make your soonest haste;   *hurt his reputation*
So° your desires are yours.   *In this way*
OCTAVIA   Thanks to my lord.
The Jove of power make me most weak, most weak,
30 Your reconciler! Wars 'twixt you twain would be
As if the world should cleave, and that slain men
Should solder° up the rift.   *close*
ANTONY   When it appears to you where this begins,°   *who started this*
Turn your displeasure that way, for our faults
35 Can never be so equal that your love
Can equally move with° them. Provide° your going,   *judge / Prepare for*
Choose your own company, and command what cost
Your heart has mind to.   *Exeunt*

3.5
Enter ENOBARBUS *and* EROS [*meeting*]

ENOBARBUS   How now, friend Eros?
EROS   There's strange news come, sir.
ENOBARBUS   What, man?
EROS   Caesar and Lepidus have made wars upon Pompey.
5 ENOBARBUS   This is old. What is the success?°   *outcome*
EROS   Caesar, having made use of him° in the wars 'gainst Pom-   *(Lepidus)*
pey, presently denied him rivality,° would not let him partake   *equal partnership*
in the glory of the action, and, not resting° here, accuses him   *stopping*
of letters he had formerly wrote to Pompey; upon his° own   *(Caesar's)*
10 appeal° seizes him; so the poor third is up,° till death enlarge   *accusation / imprisoned*
his confine.
ENOBARBUS   Then, world, thou hast a pair of chops,° no more,°   *jaws / (than two)*
And throw° between them all the food thou hast,   *if you should throw*
They'll grind the one the other. Where's Antony?
15 EROS   He's walking in the garden, thus, and spurns°   *kicks*
The rush° that lies before him, cries 'Fool Lepidus!'   *rushes*
And threats the throat of that his officer°   *that officer of his*
That murdered Pompey.[1]
ENOBARBUS   Our great navy's rigged.°   *prepared*
EROS   For Italy and Caesar. More,° Domitius: *There's more (to say)*
20 My lord desires you presently. My news
I might have told hereafter.

---

2. *Let . . . it*: Choose the one of us (Antony or Caesar)
who best strives to preserve your love.
3.5 Location: Athens.
1. Historically, though Shakespeare leaves Antony's re-

sponsibility for the killing unclear, Pompey was said to
have been murdered at the command of Antony, who
here regrets the death because Pompey might have been
a useful ally against Caesar.

ENOBARBUS   'Twill be naught.[2]
    But let it be; bring me to Antony.
EROS   Come, sir.   *Exeunt*

3.6

Enter AGRIPPA, MAECENAS, *and* CAESAR

CAESAR   Contemning° Rome, he has done all this and more   *Despising*
    In Alexandria. Here's the manner of 't:
    I'th' market place on a tribunal° silvered,   *platform*
    Cleopatra and himself in chairs of gold
5   Were publicly enthroned. At the feet sat
    Caesarion, whom they call my father's[1] son,
    And all the unlawful issue that their lust
    Since then hath made between them. Unto her
    He gave the stablishment° of Egypt; made her   *full possession*
10   Of lower Syria, Cyprus, Lydia,[2]
    Absolute queen.
MAECENAS   This in the public eye?
CAESAR   I'th' common showplace, where they exercise.[3]
    His sons he there proclaimed the kings of kings;
    Great Media, Parthia, and Armenia
15   He gave to Alexander. To Ptolemy he assigned
    Syria, Cilicia, and Phoenicia. She
    In th'habiliments° of the goddess Isis   *costume*
    That day appeared, and oft before gave audience,
    As 'tis reported, so.°   *in this costume*
MAECENAS   Let Rome be thus informed.
20 AGRIPPA   Who, queasy with° his insolence already,   *sick of*
    Will their good thoughts call° from him.   *remove*
CAESAR   The people knows it,
    And have now received his accusations.
AGRIPPA   Who does he accuse?
CAESAR   Caesar, and that having in Sicily
25 Sextus Pompeius spoiled,° we had not rated° him *ransacked / allotted*
    His part o'th' isle.° Then does he say he lent me   *Sicily*
    Some shipping, unrestored.° Lastly, he frets   *not returned (by me)*
    That Lepidus of the triumvirate
    Should be deposed; and being,° that we detain   *being deposed*
    All his revenue.
30 AGRIPPA   Sir, this should be answered.
CAESAR   'Tis done already, and the messenger gone.
    I have told him Lepidus was grown too cruel,
    That he his high authority abused
    And did deserve his change. For° what I have conquered, *As for*
35 I grant him part; but then in his Armenia,
    And other of his conquered kingdoms,
    I demand the like.
MAECENAS   He'll never yield to that.
CAESAR   Nor must not then be yielded to in this.

Enter OCTAVIA *with her train*

---

2. Of no consequence; extremely harmful.
3.6 Location: Rome.
1. Julius Caesar (who adopted his grandnephew Octavius
as his son). See 2.2.233–34 with note and note to
5.2.352.

2. District on the west coast of Asia Minor. Shakespeare
took the name from North's translation of Plutarch, but
the original has Libya.
3. In the arena (theater), where they engage in sports
(perform).

OCTAVIA   Hail, Caesar, and my lord; hail, most dear Caesar!

40   CAESAR   That ever I should call thee castaway!

OCTAVIA   You have not called me so, nor have you cause.

CAESAR   Why have you stol'n upon us thus? You come not
    Like Caesar's sister. The wife of Antony
    Should have an army for an usher, and

45   The neighs of horse to tell of her approach
    Long ere she did appear. The trees by th' way
    Should have borne men, and expectation fainted,
    Longing for what it had not. Nay, the dust
    Should have ascended to the roof of heaven,

50   Raised by your populous troops. But you are come
    A market maid to Rome, and have prevented°   *(by coming too early)*
    The ostentation° of our love; which, left unshown,   *public display*
    Is often left unloved.[4] We should have met you
    By sea and land, supplying every stage°   *(of the voyage)*
    With an augmented greeting.

55   OCTAVIA   Good my lord,
    To come thus was I not constrained, but did it
    On my free will. My lord, Mark Antony,
    Hearing that you prepared for war, acquainted
    My grievèd ear withal, whereon I begged
    His pardon for° return.   *permission to*

60   CAESAR   Which soon he granted,
    Being an obstruct 'tween his lust and him.

OCTAVIA   Do not say so, my lord.

CAESAR   I have eyes upon him,
    And his affairs come to me on the wind.
    Where is he now?

OCTAVIA   My lord, in Athens.

65   CAESAR   No, my most wrongèd sister. Cleopatra
    Hath nodded him to her. He hath given his empire
    Up to a whore; who° now are levying   *both of them*
    The kings o'th' earth for war. He hath assembled
    Bocchus, the King of Libya; Archelaus

70   Of Cappadocia; Philadelphos, King
    Of Paphlagonia; the Thracian King Adallas;
    King Malchus of Arabia; King of Pont;
    Herod of Jewry; Mithridates, King
    Of Comagene; Polemon and Amyntas,

75   The Kings of Mede and Lycaonia;[5]
    With a more larger° list of sceptres.   *yet longer*

OCTAVIA   Ay me most wretched,
    That have my heart parted betwixt two friends
    That does afflict each other!

CAESAR   Welcome hither.
    Your letters did withhold our° breaking forth   *restrain me from*

80   Till we perceived both how you were wrong° led   *wrongly*
    And we in negligent danger.° Cheer your heart.   *danger from negligence*
    Be you not troubled with the time,° which drives   *present business*
    O'er your content° these strong necessities;   *contentment*

---

4. Is often thought not to be love at all. Or, *which . . .*   leads to its actual decline.
unloved: lack of opportunity to demonstrate love often   5. All kings from the East.

But let determined things to destiny
85 Hold unbewailed their way.⁶ Welcome to Rome;
Nothing more dear to me. You are abused
Beyond the mark° of thought, and the high gods,   limits
To do you justice, makes their ministers°   agents
Of us and those that love you. Best of comfort,
And ever welcome to us.
90 AGRIPPA   Welcome, lady.
MAECENAS   Welcome, dear madam.
Each heart in Rome does love and pity you.
Only th'adulterous Antony, most large°   unlimited
In his abominations, turns you off,
95 And gives his potent regiment° to a trull°   powerful rule / whore
That noises it° against us.   cries out
OCTAVIA   Is it so, sir?
CAESAR   Most certain. Sister, welcome. Pray you
Be ever known to patience. My dear'st sister!   *Exeunt*

                    3.7
        Enter CLEOPATRA *and* ENOBARBUS
CLEOPATRA   I will be even with thee, doubt it not.
ENOBARBUS   But why, why, why?
CLEOPATRA   Thou hast forspoke° my being in these wars,   opposed
And sayst it is not fit.
ENOBARBUS   Well, is it, is it?
5 CLEOPATRA   Is't not denounced° against us? Why should not we   *Isn't war declared*
Be there in person?
ENOBARBUS [*aside*]   Well, I could reply
If we should serve with horse and mares together,
The horse were merely lost;¹ the mares would bear°   seduce; carry
A soldier and his horse.
CLEOPATRA   What is't you say?
10 ENOBARBUS   Your presence needs must puzzle° Antony,   distract
Take from his heart, take from his brain, from's time
What should not then be spared. He is already
Traduced° for levity; and 'tis said in Rome   Slandered
That Photinus, an eunuch, and your maids
Manage this war.
15 CLEOPATRA   Sink Rome,° and their tongues rot   *To hell with Rome*
That speak against us! A charge° we bear i'th' war,   *An expense; duty*
And as the president of my kingdom will
Appear there for° a man. Speak not against it.   *as if I were*
I will not stay behind.
        Enter ANTONY *and* CAMIDIUS
ENOBARBUS   Nay, I have done.
Here comes the Emperor.
20 ANTONY   Is it not strange, Camidius,
That from Tarentum and Brundisium²
He could so quickly cut° the Ionian° Sea   *Cut across / Adriatic*
And take in° Toryne?°—You have heard on't, sweet?   *overrun / (near Actium)*

---

6. *let . . . way:* let predetermined events go to their destined conclusions without complaint.
3.7 Location: Antony's camp, near Actium, Greece.
1. *If . . . lost:* If we take both male and female horses

(whores) to the wars, the males would have no hope of
triumphing, because of the females ("merely" equals
"mare-ly").
2. Ports in southeast Italy.

CLEOPATRA   Celerity is never more admired°   *wondered at*
    Than by the negligent.
25 ANTONY   A good rebuke,
    Which might have well becomed the best of men
    To taunt at slackness. Camidius, we
    Will fight with him by sea.
CLEOPATRA   By sea—what else?
CAMIDIUS   Why will my lord do so?
ANTONY   For that he dares us to't.
30 ENOBARBUS   So hath my lord dared him to single fight.
CAMIDIUS   Ay, and to wage this battle at Pharsalia,°   *(near Actium)*
    Where Caesar fought with Pompey. But these offers
    Which serve not for his vantage, he shakes off,
    And so should you.
ENOBARBUS   Your ships are not well manned,
35   Your mariners are muleters,° reapers, people   *mule drivers*
    Engrossed° by swift impress.° In Caesar's fleet   *Amassed / conscription*
    Are those that often have 'gainst Pompey fought.
    Their ships are yare,° yours heavy. No disgrace   *smooth running*
    Shall fall° you for refusing him at sea,   *befall*
    Being prepared for land.
40 ANTONY   By sea, by sea.
ENOBARBUS   Most worthy sir, you therein throw away
    The absolute soldiership you have by land;
    Distract° your army, which doth most consist   *Divert*
    Of war-marked footmen; leave unexecuted°   *untapped*
45   Your own renownèd knowledge; quite forgo
    The way which promises assurance,° and   *victory*
    Give up yourself merely° to chance and hazard   *completely*
    From firm security.
ANTONY   I'll fight at sea.
CLEOPATRA   I have sixty sails, Caesar none better.
50 ANTONY   Our overplus of shipping will we burn,[3]
    And with the rest full-manned, from th'head° of Actium   *promontory*
    Beat th'approaching Caesar. But if we fail,
    We then can do't at land.
        Enter a MESSENGER
            Thy business?
MESSENGER   The news is true, my lord. He is descried.°   *He has been seen*
55   Caesar has taken Toryne.
ANTONY   Can he be there in person? 'Tis impossible;
    Strange that his power° should be. Camidius,   *his entire army*
    Our nineteen legions thou shalt hold by land,
    And our twelve thousand horse. We'll to our ship.
    Away, my Thetis![4]
        Enter a SOLDIER
60   How now, worthy soldier?
SOLDIER   O noble Emperor, do not fight by sea.
    Trust not to rotten planks. Do you misdoubt
    This sword and these my wounds? Let th'Egyptians

---

3. Antony seems to have burned his excess ("overplus")   taken by Octavius Caesar.
ships because he did not have enough sailors to man   4. Sea goddess, mother of the Greek hero Achilles.
them adequately and feared that they could easily be

And the Phoenicians go a-ducking;° we   *to sea*
65   Have used to conquer standing on the earth,
      And fighting foot to foot.
ANTONY   Well, well; away!

Exeunt ANTONY, CLEOPATRA, *and* ENOBARBUS

SOLDIER   By Hercules, I think I am i'th' right.
CAMIDIUS   Soldier, thou art; but his whole action grows
      Not in the power on't.⁵ So our leader's led,
      And we are women's men.
70   SOLDIER   You keep by land
      The legions and the horse whole, do you not?
      CAMIDIUS   Marcus Octavius, Marcus Justeius,
      Publicola and Caelius are for sea,
      But we keep whole° by land. This speed of Caesar's   *stay undivided*
      Carries beyond° belief.   *Exceeds*
75   SOLDIER   While he was yet in Rome
      His power went out in such distractions°   *separate detachments*
      As beguiled all spies.
      CAMIDIUS   Who's his lieutenant, hear you?
      SOLDIER   They say, one Taurus.
      CAMIDIUS   Well I know the man.

Enter a MESSENGER

MESSENGER   The Emperor calls Camidius.
80   CAMIDIUS   With news the time's in labour, and throws forth
      Each minute some.⁶   *Exeunt*

3.8

Enter CAESAR *with his army, marching* [*and* TAURUS]

CAESAR   Taurus!
TAURUS   My lord?
CAESAR   Strike not by land. Keep whole.° Provoke not battle   *Stay in reserve*
      Till we have done at sea. [*Giving a scroll*] Do not exceed
5   The prescript° of this scroll. Our fortune lies   *written orders*
      Upon this jump.°   *ploy*

Exit [CAESAR *and his army at one door,* TAURUS *at another*]

3.9

Enter ANTONY *and* ENOBARBUS

ANTONY   Set we our squadrons on yon side o'th' hill
      In eye° of Caesar's battle,° from which place   *view / battle line*
      We may the number of the ships behold,
      And so proceed accordingly.   *Exeunt*

3.10

CAMIDIUS *marcheth with his land army one way over the*
stage, and TAURUS, *the lieutenant of Caesar,* [*with his*
army] *the other way. After their going in is heard the*
noise of a sea-fight. Alarum. Enter ENOBARBUS

ENOBARBUS   Naught, naught, all naught!° I can behold no longer.   *lost; ruined*
      Th'*Antoniad,* the Egyptian admiral,°   *flagship*
      With all their sixty, fly and turn the rudder.

---

5. His entire plan is made without taking into account   3.8 Location: Near Actium.
his resources.   3.9 Location: Scene continues.
6. *throws . . . some:* each minute, more news is born.   3.10 Location: Scene continues.

To see't mine eyes are blasted.°   (*as if by lightning*)
    Enter SCARUS

SCARUS   Gods and goddesses—
All the whole synod° of them!   *assembly*

5 ENOBARBUS   What's° thy passion?   *What provokes*

SCARUS   The greater cantle° of the world is lost   *corner; portion*
With° very ignorance;° we have kissed away   *Through / idiocy*
Kingdoms and provinces.

ENOBARBUS   How appears the fight?

SCARUS   On our side like the tokened pestilence,[1]
10 Where death is sure. Yon riband-red[2] nag of Egypt—
Whom leprosy o'ertake!—i'th' midst o'th' fight—
When vantage like a pair of twins appeared,[3]
Both as the same, or rather ours the elder°—   *ours likely the stronger*
The breese upon her,[4] like a cow in June,
Hoists sails and flies.

15 ENOBARBUS   That I beheld.
Mine eyes did sicken at the sight, and could not
Endure a further view.

SCARUS   She once being luffed,[5]
The noble ruin° of her magic, Antony,   *casualty*
Claps on his sea-wing° and, like a doting mallard,°   *sails / male duck*
20 Leaving the fight in° height, flies after her.   *at its*
I never saw an action of such shame.
Experience, manhood, honour, ne'er before
Did violate so itself.

ENOBARBUS   Alack, alack!
    Enter CAMIDIUS

CAMIDIUS   Our fortune on the sea is out of breath,
25 And sinks most lamentably. Had our general
Been what he knew himself,° it had gone well.   *(to be)*
O, he has given example for our flight
Most grossly by his own.

ENOBARBUS   Ay, are you thereabouts?° Why then, good night   *of the same mind*
indeed!

30 CAMIDIUS   Toward Peloponnesus are they fled.

SCARUS   'Tis easy to't,° and there I will attend   *to reach that place*
What further comes.

CAMIDIUS   To Caesar will I render
My legions and my horse. Six kings already
Show me the way of yielding.

ENOBARBUS   I'll yet follow
35 The wounded chance° of Antony, though my reason   *fortune*
Sits in the wind against me.°   [*Exeunt severally*]   *Opposes*

3.11

Enter ANTONY *with Attendants*

ANTONY   Hark, the land bids me tread no more upon't,
It is ashamed to bear me. Friends, come hither.

---

1. Plague manifested in tokens (red spots presaging death).
2. Decked in red ribbons. This emendation of F's "ribau-dred"—a word of unclear meaning, if any—juxtaposes the image of Cleopatra bedecked like a horse or a whore with the red tokens of the plague.

3. When the fight could have gone either way.
4. Bitten by a gadfly; driven by a breeze.
5. Having prepared the ship's head to sail close to the wind (ready to leave).
3.11 Location: Alexandria.

I am so lated° in the world that I   *lost in the dark*
Have lost my way for ever. I have a ship
5 Laden with gold. Take that; divide it, fly,
And make your peace with Caesar.
ATTENDANTS   Fly? Not we.
ANTONY I have fled myself, and have instructed cowards
To run and show their shoulders.° Friends, be gone.   *backs*
I have myself resolved upon a course
10 Which has no need of you. Be gone.
My treasure's in the harbour. Take it. O,
I followed that° I blush to look upon.   *that which*
My very hairs do mutiny, for the white
Reprove the brown for rashness, and they them°   *they the others*
15 For fear and doting. Friends, be gone. You shall
Have letters from me to some friends that will
Sweep° your way for you. Pray you, look not sad,   *Clear*
Nor make replies of loathness.° Take the hint°   *reluctance / chance*
Which my despair proclaims. Let that be left
20 Which leaves° itself. To the seaside straightway!   *ceases to be*
I will possess you of that ship and treasure.
Leave me, I pray, a little.° Pray you now,   *for a brief time*
Nay, do so; for indeed I have lost command.°   *authority*
Therefore I pray you; I'll see you by and by.

                               [*Exeunt attendants*]

        [*He*] *sits down.*
       Enter CLEOPATRA *led by* CHARMIAN, [IRAS,] *and* EROS
25 EROS Nay, gentle madam, to him. Comfort him.
IRAS Do, most dear Queen.
CHARMIAN Do. Why, what else?
CLEOPATRA Let me sit down. O Juno!
       [*She sits down*]
ANTONY No, no, no, no, no.
30 EROS [*to* ANTONY] See you here, sir?
ANTONY O fie, fie, fie!
CHARMIAN Madam.
IRAS Madam. O good Empress!
EROS Sir, sir.
35 ANTONY Yes, my lord, yes. He° at Philippi kept   *(Octavius)*
His sword e'en like a dancer,° while I struck   *(for decoration only)*
The lean and wrinkled Cassius; and 'twas I
That the mad Brutus ended.° He alone   *defeated*
Dealt on lieutenantry,° and no practice had   *Fought through others*
40 In the brave squares° of war. Yet now—no matter.   *fine formations*
CLEOPATRA [*rising, to* CHARMIAN *and* IRAS] Ah, stand by.
EROS The Queen, my lord, the Queen.
IRAS Go to him, madam.
Speak to him. He's unqualitied°   *lost his sense of self*
With very shame.
45 CLEOPATRA   Well then, sustain me. O!
EROS Most noble sir, arise. The Queen approaches.
Her head's declined, and death will seize her but°   *unless*
Your comfort makes the rescue.
ANTONY I have offended reputation;
A most unnoble swerving.°   *slippage*
50 EROS   Sir, the Queen.

ANTONY [*rising*]   O, whither hast thou led me, Egypt? See
How I convey° my shame out of thine eyes°   *steal back / sight*
By looking back° what I have left behind   *back on*
'Stroyed° in dishonour.   *Destroyed*

CLEOPATRA   O, my lord, my lord,
55   Forgive my fearful sails! I little thought
You would have followed.

ANTONY   Egypt, thou knew'st too well
My heart was to thy rudder tied by th' strings,
And thou shouldst tow me after. O'er my spirit
Thy full supremacy thou knew'st, and that
60   Thy beck° might from the bidding of the gods   *call*
Command me.

CLEOPATRA   O, my pardon!

ANTONY   Now I must
To the young man[1] send humble treaties,° dodge   *appeals*
And palter in the shifts of lowness,[2] who
With half the bulk o'th' world played as I pleased,
65   Making and marring fortunes. You did know
How much you were my conqueror, and that
My sword, made weak by my affection,° would   *desire*
Obey it on all cause.°   *for any reason*

CLEOPATRA   Pardon, pardon!

ANTONY   Fall° not a tear, I say. One of them rates°   *Weep / is worth*
70   All that is won and lost. Give me a kiss.
        [*He kisses her*]
Even this repays me. [*To an Attendant*] We sent our school-
master;°   *tutor to our children*
Is a° come back? [*To* CLEOPATRA] Love, I am full of lead. *he*
        [*Calling*] Some wine
Within there, and our viands!° Fortune knows   *food*
We scorn her most when most she offers blows.   *Exeunt*

3.12

Enter CAESAR, AGRIPPA, THIDIAS, *and* DOLABELLA, *with others*

CAESAR   Let him appear that's come from Antony.
Know you him?

DOLABELLA   Caesar, 'tis his schoolmaster;
An argument° that he is plucked, when hither   *A proof*
He sends so poor a pinion° of his wing,   *an outer feather*
5   Which° had superfluous kings for messengers   *He who*
Not many moons gone by.

        Enter AMBASSADOR *from Antony*

CAESAR   Approach and speak.

AMBASSADOR   Such as I am, I come from Antony.
I was of late as petty° to his ends   *inconsequential*
As is the morn-dew on the myrtle leaf
To his grand sea.[1]

10   CAESAR   Be't so. Declare thine office.°   *business*

AMBASSADOR   Lord of his fortunes he salutes thee, and

---

1. Octavius Caesar at this time (31 B.C.E.) was thirty-two, Antony fifty-one.
2. *dodge . . . lowness:* shuffle and play fast and loose in the shifty ways of a man brought low.

3.12 Location: Caesar's camp, Egypt.
1. In relation to the great sea, ultimate source of dew, that is Antony.

Requires° to live in Egypt; which not granted,   *Asks*
He lessens his requests, and to thee sues
To let him breathe between the heavens and earth,
15   A private man in Athens. This for him.
Next, Cleopatra does confess thy greatness,
Submits her to thy might, and of thee craves
The circle° of the Ptolemies for her heirs,   *crown*
Now hazarded to thy grace.°   *placed at your mercy*

CAESAR   For Antony,
20   I have no ears to his request. The Queen
Of audience nor desire shall fail, so² she
From Egypt drive her all-disgracèd friend,
Or take his life there. This if she perform
She shall not sue unheard. So to them both.

AMBASSADOR   Fortune pursue thee!

25   CAESAR   Bring° him through the bands.°   *Escort / ranks*
                         [*Exit* AMBASSADOR, *attended*]
[*To* THIDIAS] To try thy eloquence now 'tis time. Dispatch.
From Antony win Cleopatra. Promise,
And in our name, what she requires. Add more
As thine invention° offers. Women are not   *imagination*
30   In° their best fortunes strong, but want will perjure   *While in*
The ne'er-touched vestal.³ Try thy cunning, Thidias.
Make thine own edict° for thy pains, which we   *Command your reward*
Will answer as a law.

THIDIAS   Caesar, I go.

CAESAR   Observe how Antony becomes his flaw,°   *reacts to his fall*
35   And what thou think'st his very action speaks
In every power that moves.⁴

THIDIAS   Caesar, I shall.
         Exeunt [CAESAR *and his train at one door, and*
                      THIDIAS *at another*]

3.13

Enter CLEOPATRA, ENOBARBUS, CHARMIAN, AND IRAS
CLEOPATRA   What shall we do, Enobarbus?
ENOBARBUS   Think,° and die.   *(about our misery)*
CLEOPATRA   Is Antony or we in fault for this?
ENOBARBUS   Antony only, that would make his will°   *lust*
Lord of his reason. What though° you fled   *What if*
5   From that great face of war, whose several ranges°   *battle lines*
Frighted each other? Why should he follow?
The itch of his affection should not then
Have nicked° his captainship, at such a point,   *bettered (gambling term)*
When half to half the world opposed, he being
10   The mooted° question. 'Twas a shame no less   *disputed*
Than was his loss, to course° your flying flags   *chase*
And leave his navy gazing.
CLEOPATRA   Prithee, peace.
       Enter the AMBASSADOR *with* ANTONY

---

2. Shall not fail to receive either a hearing or fulfillment of her wishes, as long as.
3. *want . . . vestal:* need will make the purest virgin break her vows.

4. *his very . . . moves:* his actions themselves reveal in every move he makes.
3.13 Location: Alexandria.

ANTONY   Is that his answer?

AMBASSADOR   Ay, my lord.

ANTONY   The Queen shall then have courtesy, so° she   *as long as*
  Will yield us up.

AMBASSADOR   He says so.

15 ANTONY   Let her know't.
  [*To* CLEOPATRA] To the boy Caesar send this grizzled head,
  And he will fill thy wishes to the brim
  With principalities.

CLEOPATRA   That head, my lord?

ANTONY [*to the* AMBASSADOR]   To him again. Tell him he wears the rose
20 Of youth upon him, from which the world should note
  Something particular.° His coin, ships, legions,   *A success of his own*
  May be a coward's, whose ministers° would prevail   *aides; underlings*
  Under the service of a child as soon°   *as well*
  As i'th' command of Caesar. I dare him therefore
25 To lay his gay caparisons° apart   *showy adornments*
  And answer me declined,[1] sword against sword,
  Ourselves alone. I'll write it. Follow me.
                    [*Exeunt* ANTONY *and* AMBASSADOR]

ENOBARBUS [*aside*]   Yes, like enough, high-battled° Caesar will   *with many troops*
  Unstate° his happiness and be staged to th' show[2]   *Overthrow*
30 Against a sworder! I see men's judgements are
  A parcel of° their fortunes, and things outward   *Consistent with*
  Do draw the inward quality after them
  To suffer all alike.° That he should dream,   *To decay together*
  Knowing all measures,[3] the full Caesar will
35 Answer° his emptiness! Caesar, thou hast subdued   *Fight; reply to*
  His judgement, too.
              Enter a SERVANT

SERVANT   A messenger from Caesar.

CLEOPATRA   What, no more ceremony? See, my women:
  Against the blown° rose may they stop their nose,   *decaying*
  That° kneeled unto the buds. Admit him, sir. [*Exit* SERVANT]   *Who once*

40 ENOBARBUS [*aside*]   Mine honesty° and I begin to square.°   *honor / square off; argue*
  The loyalty well held° to fools does make   *given*
  Our faith mere° folly; yet he that can endure   *complete*
  To follow with allegiance a fall'n lord
  Does conquer him that did his master conquer,
  And earns a place i'th' story.
              Enter THIDIAS

45 CLEOPATRA   Caesar's will?

THIDIAS   Hear it apart.

CLEOPATRA   None but friends; say boldly.

THIDIAS   So haply° are they friends to Antony.   *possibly*

ENOBARBUS   He needs as many, sir, as Caesar has,
  Or needs not us.[4] If Caesar please, our master
50 Will leap to be his friend. For us, you know,
  Whose he is, we are: and that is Caesar's.

---

1. And meet me past my prime, in my misfortune.
2. Be displayed to the public gaze (as in the London theater or Roman gladiatorial combat).
3. Having known the best and worst of times ("all measures" of fortune, both "full[ness]" and "emptiness," line
35).
4. *Or needs not us:* If the situation is truly hopeless, he
doesn't even need our friendship.

THIDIAS So. [*To* CLEOPATRA] Thus, then, thou most renowned:
　　Caesar entreats
　　Not to consider° in what case thou stand'st　　　　　　*be concerned*
　　Further than he is Caesar.[5]

CLEOPATRA　　　　　　Go on; right royal.°　　　　　　*most generous*

55　THIDIAS　He knows that you embraced not Antony
　　As you did love, but as you fearèd him.

CLEOPATRA　O.

THIDIAS　The scars upon your honour therefore he
　　Does pity as constrainèd° blemishes,　　　　　　*involuntary*
　　Not as deserved.

60　CLEOPATRA　　　　　He is a god, and knows
　　What is most right. Mine honour was not yielded,
　　But conquered merely.

ENOBARBUS [*aside*]　　　To be sure of that
　　I will ask Antony. Sir, sir, thou art so leaky
　　That we must leave thee to thy sinking, for
　　Thy dearest quit thee.　　　　　　　　　　　*Exit*

65　THIDIAS　　　　　　Shall I say to Caesar
　　What you require° of him?—For he partly begs　　　*request*
　　To be desired to give. It much would please him
　　That of his fortunes you should make a staff
　　To lean upon. But it would warm his spirits
70　To hear from me you had left Antony,
　　And put your self under his shroud,°　　　　*protection; burial sheet*
　　The universal landlord.

CLEOPATRA　　　　　What's your name?

THIDIAS　My name is Thidias.

CLEOPATRA　　　　　　Most kind messenger,
　　Say to great Caesar this in deputation:°　　　*as my representative*
75　I kiss his conqu'ring hand. Tell him I am prompt
　　To lay my crown at's feet, and there to kneel
　　Till from his all-obeying° breath I hear　　　*which all obey*
　　The doom of Egypt.[6]

THIDIAS　　　　　'Tis your noblest course.
　　Wisdom and fortune combating together,
80　If that the former dare but what it can,[7]
　　No chance may shake it. Give me grace to lay
　　My duty on your hand.
　　　　[*He kisses Cleopatra's hand*]

CLEOPATRA　　　　　Your Caesar's father oft,
　　When he hath mused of taking kingdoms in,°　　*subduing kingdoms*
　　Bestowed his lips on that unworthy place,
　　As° it rained kisses.　　　　　　　　　　　　*As if*
　　　　Enter ANTONY *and* ENOBARBUS

85　ANTONY　　　　　Favours, by Jove that thunders!
　　What art thou, fellow?

THIDIAS　　　　　One that but performs
　　The bidding of the fullest[8] man, and worthiest
　　To have command obeyed.

ENOBARBUS　　　　You will be whipped.

---

5. Beyond remembering that he is Caesar—and hence nobly generous in forgiving insult and injury (but with a more sinister undertone as well).

6. What he destines for Egypt and its Queen.

7. If the wise man confines his daring to what is possible.

8. Most complete; most successful.

ANTONY [*calling*]   Approach, there!—Ah, you kite![9] Now, gods and devils,
90   Authority melts from me of late. When I cried 'Ho!',
Like boys unto a muss[1] kings would start forth,
And cry 'Your will?'—Have you no ears? I am
Antony yet.
           Enter servant[s]
           Take hence this jack,° and whip him.   *knave*
ENOBARBUS [*aside to* THIDIAS]   'Tis better playing with a lion's whelp°   *cub*
Than with an old one dying.
95   ANTONY   Moon and stars!
Whip him! Were't twenty of the greatest tributaries
That do acknowledge Caesar, should I find them
So saucy with the hand of she here—what's her name
Since she was Cleopatra?[2] Whip him, fellows,
100   Till like a boy you see him cringe° his face,   *distort*
And whine aloud for mercy. Take him hence.
THIDIAS   Mark Antony—
ANTONY   Tug him away. Being whipped,
Bring him again. This jack of Caesar's shall
Bear us an errand to him.   *Exeunt [servants] with* THIDIAS
105   You were half blasted° ere I knew you. Ha,   *decayed*
Have I my pillow left unpressed in Rome,
Forborne the getting° of a lawful race,   *begetting*
And by a gem of women, to be abused
By one that looks on feeders?°   *parasites; servants*
110   CLEOPATRA   Good my lord—
ANTONY   You have been a boggler° ever.   *fickle one*
But when we in our viciousness grow hard—
O misery on't!—the wise gods seel[3] our eyes,
In our own filth drop our clear judgements, make us
115   Adore our errors, laugh at's while we strut
To our confusion.
CLEOPATRA   O, is't come to this?
ANTONY   I found you as a morsel cold upon
Dead Caesar's trencher;° nay, you were a fragment°   *plate / leftover*
Of Gnaeus Pompey's,[4] besides what hotter hours
120   Unregistered in vulgar fame° you have   *base gossip*
Luxuriously° picked out. For I am sure,   *Wantonly*
Though you can guess what temperance should be,
You know not what it is.
CLEOPATRA   Wherefore is this?
ANTONY   To let a fellow that will take rewards
125   And say 'God quit° you' be familiar with   *repay*
My playfellow your hand, this kingly seal
And plighter° of high hearts! O that I were   *pledger*
Upon the hill of Basan to outroar
The hornèd herd![5] For I have savage cause,
130   And to proclaim it civilly were like
A haltered° neck which does the hangman thank   *in the noose*

---

9. Predator or whore, addressed to either Cleopatra or
Thidias.
1. Game in which small items were tossed to the ground
for children to snatch and grab.
2. Antony's question suggests that since Cleopatra's behavior has changed, her name must have changed as well.
3. Blind: hawks' eyes were sealed (sewn up) to tame

them.
4. Older brother of the Pompey of the play and son of
Pompey the Great. See note to 1.5.31.
5. Alluding to the bulls of the hill of Basan (Bashan) in
Psalms 68:15 and 22:12; Antony sees himself as a cuckold (a man whose wife has committed adultery), conventionally imagined with horns.

   For being yare° about him.   *swift*
    Enter a SERVANT *with* THIDIAS
        Is he whipped?
  SERVANT Soundly, my lord.
  ANTONY Cried he, and begged a° pardon?   *he*
135 SERVANT He did ask favour.
  ANTONY [*to* THIDIAS] If that thy father live, let him repent
   Thou wast not made his daughter; and be thou sorry
   To follow Caesar in his triumph, since
   Thou hast been whipped for following him. Henceforth
140 The white hand of a lady fever thee,[6]
   Shake thou to look on't. Get thee back to Caesar;
   Tell him thy entertainment.° Look° thou say   *treatment / See that*
   He makes me angry with him, for he seems
   Proud and disdainful, harping on what I am,
145 Not what he knew I was. He makes me angry,
   And at this time most easy 'tis to do't,
   When my good stars that were my former guides
   Have empty left their orbs,° and shot their fires   *spheres*
   Into th'abyss of hell. If he mislike
150 My speech and what is done, tell him he has
   Hipparchus, my enfranchèd° bondman, whom   *emancipated*
   He may at pleasure whip, or hang, or torture,
   As he shall like, to quit° me. Urge it thou.   *requite*
   Hence, with thy stripes,° be gone! *Exit* [SERVANT *with*] THIDIAS *wounds*
155 CLEOPATRA Have you done yet?
  ANTONY Alack, our terrene moon[7]
   Is now eclipsed, and it portends alone
   The fall of Antony.
  CLEOPATRA [*aside*] I must stay his time.[8]
  ANTONY To flatter Caesar would you mingle eyes
   With one that ties his points?[9]
160 CLEOPATRA   Not know me yet?
  ANTONY Cold-hearted toward me?
  CLEOPATRA   Ah, dear, if I be so,
   From my cold heart let heaven engender hail,
   And poison it in the source, and the first stone
   Drop in my neck: as it determines,° so   *turns to liquid*
165 Dissolve my life! The next Caesarion smite,
   Till by degrees the memory of my womb,°   *my children*
   Together with my brave Egyptians all,
   By the discandying° of this pelleted storm   *dissolving*
   Lie graveless till the flies and gnats of Nile
   Have buried them for prey!
170 ANTONY   I am satisfied.
   Caesar sits down in° Alexandria, where   *besieges*
   I will oppose his fate.[1] Our force by land
   Hath nobly held; our severed navy too
   Have knit again, and fleet,° threat'ning most sea-like. *are afloat*
175 Where hast thou been, my heart?° Dost thou hear, lady? *bravery*
   If from the field I shall return once more

---

6. May the white hand of a lady make you feverish.
7. Terrestrial moon goddess—Cleopatra.
8. I must hold my tongue until he is over his rage.

9. *would . . . points:* would you flirt with one of his servants? *points:* laces (attaching stockings to other clothing).
1. I will resist his apparently destined victory.

To kiss these lips, I will appear in blood.°   *bloody; vigorous*
I and my sword will earn our chronicle.°   *historical reputation*
There's hope in't yet.
CLEOPATRA   That's my brave lord.
180 ANTONY   I will be treble-sinewed, hearted, breathed,
And fight maliciously;° for when mine hours   *furiously*
Were nice[2] and lucky, men did ransom° lives   *buy their*
Of° me for jests;° but now I'll set my teeth,   *From / trinkets*
And send to darkness all that stop me. Come,
185 Let's have one other gaudy° night. Call to me   *merry*
All my sad captains. Fill our bowls once more.
Let's mock the midnight bell.[3]
CLEOPATRA   It is my birthday.
I had thought to've held it poor,° but since my lord   *modestly commemorated it*
Is Antony again, I will be Cleopatra.
190 ANTONY   We will yet do well.
CLEOPATRA   Call all his noble captains to my lord!
ANTONY   Do so. We'll speak to them, and tonight I'll force
The wine peep through their scars. Come on, my queen,
There's sap in't° yet. The next time I do fight   *vigor in (our cause)*
195 I'll make death love me, for I will contend°   *do battle*
Even with his pestilent° scythe.   *Exeunt [all but* ENOBARBUS]   *plague-dealing*
ENOBARBUS   Now he'll outstare° the lightning. To be furious   *stare down*
Is to be frighted out of fear, and in that mood
The dove will peck the estridge;° and I see still°   *a kind of hawk / always*
200 A diminution in our captain's brain
Restores his heart. When valour preys on reason,
It eats the sword it fights with. I will seek
Some way to leave him.   *Exit*

4.1

Enter CAESAR, *reading a letter, with* AGRIPPA, MAECENAS,
and his army
CAESAR   He calls me boy, and chides as° he had power   *as though*
To beat me out of Egypt. My messenger
He hath whipped with rods, dares me to personal combat,
Caesar to Antony. Let the old ruffian know
5 I have many other ways to die; meantime,
Laugh at° his challenge.   *Mock*
MAECENAS   Caesar must think,
When one so great begins to rage, he's hunted
Even to falling. Give him no breath,° but now   *time to catch breath*
Make boot° of his distraction.° Never anger   *Take advantage / fury*
Made good guard for itself.
10 CAESAR   Let our best heads°   *officers*
Know that tomorrow the last of many battles
We mean to fight. Within our files° there are,   *troops*
Of those that served Mark Antony but late,
Enough to fetch him in.° See it done,   *capture him*
15 And feast the army. We have store to do't,
And they have earned the waste.° Poor Antony!   *Exeunt*   *expense*

---

2. *Were nice:* Permitted me to pick and choose, to act
with noble generosity; were lascivious; were pampered.
3. Let's make a mockery of the hour by revelry; let's mock
the death knell that fate seems to ring for us.
4.1 Location: Caesar's camp, before Alexandria.

4.2

Enter ANTONY, CLEOPATRA, ENOBARBUS, CHARMIAN,
    IRAS, ALEXAS, *with others*

ANTONY   He will not fight with me, Domitius?

ENOBARBUS   No.

ANTONY   Why should he not?

ENOBARBUS   He thinks, being twenty times of better fortune,

   He is twenty men to one.

ANTONY   Tomorrow, soldier,

5   By sea and land I'll fight. Or° I will live   *Either*

   Or bathe my dying honour in the blood

   Shall make it live again. Woot thou° fight well?   *Will you*

ENOBARBUS   I'll strike, and cry 'Take all!'°   *Winner take all*

ANTONY   Well said. Come on!

   Call forth my household servants. Let's tonight

   Be bounteous at our meal.

       Enter SERVITORS

10   Give me thy hand.

   Thou hast been rightly honest; so hast thou,

   Thou, and thou, and thou; you have served me well,

   And kings have been your fellows.°   *companions*

CLEOPATRA [*to* ENOBARBUS]   What means this?

ENOBARBUS [*to* CLEOPATRA]   'Tis one of those odd tricks which

      sorrow shoots

   Out of the mind.

15 ANTONY [*to a* SERVITOR]   And thou art honest too.

   I wish I could be made° so many men,   *split up into*

   And all of you clapped up together in

   An Antony, that I might do you service

   So good as you have done.

SERVITORS   The gods forbid!

20 ANTONY   Well, my good fellows, wait on me tonight.

   Scant not my cups, and make as much of me

   As when mine empire was your fellow° too,   *fellow servant*

   And suffered° my command.   *obeyed*

CLEOPATRA [*aside to* ENOBARBUS]   What does he mean?

ENOBARBUS [*aside to* CLEOPATRA]

   To make his followers weep.

ANTONY   Tend me tonight.

25   Maybe it is the period° of your duty.   *end*

   Haply° you shall not see me more; or if,°   *Maybe / if you do*

   A mangled shadow.° Perchance tomorrow   *phantom*

   You'll serve another master. I look on you

   As one that takes his leave. Mine honest friends,

30   I turn you not away, but, like a master

   Married to your good service, stay till death.

   Tend me tonight two hours. I ask no more;

   And the gods yield° you for't!   *reward*

ENOBARBUS   What mean you, sir,

   To give them this discomfort? Look, they weep,

35   And I, an ass, am onion-eyed.° For shame,   *weepy*

   Transform us not to women.

4.2 Location: Alexandria.

ANTONY   Ho, ho, ho,
Now the witch take° me if I meant it thus!   bewitch
Grace grow where those drops fall. My hearty friends,
You take me in too dolorous a sense;
40   For I spake to you for your comfort, did desire you
To burn this night with torches. Know, my hearts,
I hope well of tomorrow, and will lead you
Where rather I'll expect victorious life
Than death and honour. Let's to supper, come,
45   And drown consideration.°   *Exeunt*   serious thoughts

                              4.3

                    Enter a company of SOLDIERS
FIRST SOLDIER   Brother, good night. Tomorrow is the day.
SECOND SOLDIER   It will determine one way. Fare you well.°   Good luck
Heard you of nothing strange about° the streets?   in
FIRST SOLDIER   Nothing. What news?
5   SECOND SOLDIER   Belike° 'tis but a rumour. Good night to you.   Most likely
FIRST SOLDIER   Well, sir, good night.
            [*Enter*] *other* SOLDIERS, *meet*[*ing them*]
SECOND SOLDIER   Soldiers, have careful watch.
THIRD SOLDIER   And you. Good night, good night.
            They place themselves in every corner of the stage
SECOND SOLDIER   Here we;¹ an if° tomorrow   *an if* = if
Our navy thrive, I have an absolute hope
Our landmen will stand up.°   make a stand
FIRST SOLDIER   'Tis a brave army,
And full of purpose.
            Music of the hautboys° is under the stage   oboes
SECOND SOLDIER   Peace, what noise?
10   FIRST SOLDIER   List, list!
SECOND SOLDIER   Hark!
FIRST SOLDIER   Music i'th' air.
THIRD SOLDIER   Under the earth.
FOURTH SOLDIER   It signs° well, does it not?   bodes
THIRD SOLDIER   No.
FIRST SOLDIER   Peace, I say!
What should this mean?
SECOND SOLDIER   'Tis the god Hercules, whom Antony loved,
Now leaves him.
15   FIRST SOLDIER   Walk. Let's see if other watchmen
Do hear what we do.
SECOND SOLDIER   How now, masters?°   good sirs
ALL (*speak*[*ing*] *together*)²   How now?
How now? Do you hear this?
FIRST SOLDIER   Ay. Is't not strange?
THIRD SOLDIER   Do you hear, masters? Do you hear?
FIRST SOLDIER   Follow the noise so far as we have quarter.³
Let's see how it will give off.°   end
20   ALL   Content. 'Tis strange.   *Exeunt*

4.3 Location: Outside Cleopatra's palace, Alexandria.
1. Here are our positions.
2. Individual soldiers probably address different questions

and comments to one another rather than speaking in
chorus.
3. As far as the limit of our watch.

4.4

Enter ANTONY *and* CLEOPATRA, *with* [CHARMIAN *and*]
others

ANTONY [*calling*]   Eros, mine armour, Eros!

CLEOPATRA   Sleep a little.

ANTONY   No, my chuck.° Eros, come, mine armour, Eros!   *my dear*
    Enter EROS [*with armour*]
    Come, good fellow, put thine iron on.¹
    If fortune be not ours today, it is
    Because we brave° her. Come.   *dare*

5 CLEOPATRA   Nay, I'll help, too.
    What's this for?

ANTONY   Ah, let be, let be! Thou art
    The armourer of my heart. False, false!° This, this!   *wrong*

CLEOPATRA   Sooth, la, I'll help. Thus it must be.
    [*She helps* ANTONY *to arm*]

ANTONY   Well, well,
    We shall thrive now. Seest thou, my good fellow?
    Go put on thy defences.°   *armor*

10 EROS   Briefly,° sir.   *Soon*

CLEOPATRA   Is not this buckled well?

ANTONY   Rarely, rarely.
    He that unbuckles this, till we do please
    To doff 't° for our repose, shall hear a storm.   *remove it*
    Thou fumblest, Eros, and my queen's a squire°   *an attendant to a knight*
15 More tight° at this than thou. Dispatch.° O love,   *able / Finish*
    That thou couldst see my wars today, and knew'st
    The royal occupation! Thou shouldst see
    A workman° in't.   *An expert*
        Enter an armed SOLDIER
                        Good morrow to thee. Welcome.
    Thou look'st like him that knows a warlike charge.°   *purpose*
20 To business that we love we rise betime,°   *early*
    And go to't with delight.

SOLDIER   A thousand, sir,
    Early though't be, have on their riveted trim,°   *armor*
    And at the port expect you.
        Shout [*within*]. *Trumpets flourish. Enter* CAPTAINS *and*
        SOLDIERS

CAPTAIN   The morn is fair. Good morrow, General.

SOLDIERS   Good morrow, General.

25 ANTONY   'Tis well blown,² lads.
    This morning, like the spirit of a youth
    That means to be of note, begins betimes.
    So, so. Come, give me that. This way. Well said.°   *Well done*
    Fare thee well, dame. Whate'er becomes of me,
    This is a soldier's kiss.
        [*He kisses* CLEOPATRA]
30   Rebukable
    And worthy shameful check° it were to stand   *reprimand*
    On more mechanic° compliment. I'll leave thee   *coarse*
    Now like a man of steel. You that will fight,

4.4 Location: Cleopatra's palace.   2. Well sounded (of the trumpet); well started (of the
1. Clad me in that piece of armor of mine that you have.   morning).

Follow me close. I'll bring you to't. Adieu.

Exeunt [all but CLEOPATRA *and* CHARMIAN]

CHARMIAN   Please you retire to your chamber?

35 CLEOPATRA   Lead me.
He goes forth gallantly. That he and Caesar might
Determine this great war in single fight!
Then, Antony—but now! Well, on.   *Exeunt*

4.5

Trumpets sound. Enter ANTONY *and* EROS [*meeting a*
SOLDIER]

SOLDIER   The gods make this a happy° day to Antony!   fortunate
ANTONY   Would thou and those thy scars had once° prevailed   earlier
To make me fight at land!
SOLDIER   Hadst thou done so,
The kings that have revolted,° and the soldier   deserted
5   That has this morning left thee, would have still
Followed thy heels.
ANTONY   Who's gone this morning?
SOLDIER   Who? One ever near thee. Call for Enobarbus,
He shall not hear thee, or from Caesar's camp
Say 'I am none of thine'.
ANTONY   What sayest thou?
SOLDIER   Sir, he is with Caesar.
10 EROS [*to* ANTONY]   Sir, his chests and treasure
He has not with him.
ANTONY   Is he gone?
SOLDIER   Most certain.
ANTONY   Go, Eros, send his treasure after. Do it.
Detain no jot, I charge thee. Write to him—
I will subscribe°—gentle adieus and greetings.   sign my name
15 Say that I wish he never find more cause
To change a master. O, my fortunes have
Corrupted honest men! Dispatch. Enobarbus!   *Exeunt*

4.6

Flourish. Enter AGRIPPA, CAESAR, *with* ENOBARBUS *and*
DOLABELLA

CAESAR   Go forth, Agrippa, and begin the fight.
Our will is Antony be took alive.
Make it so known.
AGRIPPA   Caesar, I shall.   [*Exit*]
CAESAR   The time of universal peace is near.[1]
5   Prove this° a prosp'rous day, the three-nooked world[2]   If this proves
Shall bear the olive° freely.   sign of peace
Enter a MESSENGER
MESSENGER   Antony
Is come into the field.
CAESAR   Go charge Agrippa

4.5 Location: Antony's camp, Alexandria.
4.6 Location: Caesar's camp, Alexandria.
1. Octavius Caesar, later the Emperor Augustus, was known for the *Pax Romana*—Roman peace—of his reign; the phrase also alludes to the birth of Christ, which occurred while Augustus was emperor. See the Introduction.

2. Three-cornered world. Referring (in descending order of probability) to Europe, Asia, Africa (the triumvirate's holdings); the three races descended from Noah's sons (Japhet, Shem, Ham); earth, sea, sky. The three races of Noah can to an extent be superimposed on the three continents and may connect with the later religious connotations of the Roman Empire. See the previous note.

Plant those that have revolted in the van,°   *front lines*
That Antony may seem to spend his fury
10   Upon himself.°   *On his former troops*
        Exeunt [MESSENGER *at one door,* CAESAR *and*
                         DOLABELLA *at another*]
ENOBARBUS   Alexas did revolt, and went to Jewry on
    Affairs of Antony; there did dissuade°   *persuade*
    Great Herod to incline himself to Caesar
    And leave his master, Antony. For this pains,
15   Caesar hath hanged him. Camidius and the rest
    That fell away have entertainment° but   *employment*
    No honourable trust. I have done ill,
    Of which I do accuse myself so sorely
    That I will joy no more.
        Enter a SOLDIER *of Caesar's*
SOLDIER   Enobarbus, Antony
20   Hath after thee sent all thy treasure, with
    His bounty overplus. The messenger
    Came on my guard,° and at thy tent is now   *on my watch*
    Unloading of his mules.
ENOBARBUS   I give it you.
25 SOLDIER   Mock not, Enobarbus,
    I tell you true. Best you safed the bringer
    Out of the host.[3] I must attend mine office,°   *look after my duties*
    Or would have done't myself. Your Emperor
    Continues still a Jove.   *Exit*
30 ENOBARBUS   I am alone the° villain of the earth,   *the single greatest*
    And feel I am so most.° O Antony,   *I feel it most*
    Thou mine of bounty, how wouldst thou have paid
    My better service, when my turpitude
    Thou dost so crown with gold! This blows° my heart.   *swells; bursts*
35   If swift thought° break it not, a swifter mean°   *regret / means (suicide)*
    Shall outstrike thought; but thought will do't, I feel.
    I fight against thee? No, I will go seek
    Some ditch wherein to die. The foul'st best fits
    My latter part of life.   *Exit*

4.7

    Alarum. Enter AGRIPPA [*with*] *drum*[*mer*]*s and trum-*
    pet[*er*]*s*
AGRIPPA   Retire!° We have engaged our selves too far.   *Sound the retreat*
    Caesar himself has work,° and our oppression   *is sorely challenged*
    Exceeds what we expected.   *Exeunt*

4.8

    Alarums. Enter ANTONY, *and* SCARUS *wounded*
SCARUS   O my brave Emperor, this is fought indeed!
    Had we done so at first, we had droven them home
    With clouts° about their heads.   *bandages; blows*
ANTONY   Thou bleed'st apace.

---

3. *Best . . . host*: It would be best if you ensured safe con-   4.7 Location: The battlefield, Alexandria.
duct through the lines for the messenger who brought   4.8 Location: Scene continues.
the treasure.

SCARUS   I had a wound here that was like a T,
But now 'tis made an H.[1]
   [*Retreat sounded*] *far off*

5   ANTONY   They do retire.

SCARUS   We'll beat 'em into bench-holes.° I have yet   *latrine holes*
Room for six scotches° more.   *gashes*
   Enter EROS

EROS   They are beaten, sir, and our advantage serves
For a fair victory.

SCARUS   Let us score° their backs   *slash*
10   And snatch 'em up as° we take hares, behind.   *in the same way as*
'Tis sport to maul a runner.°   *coward*

ANTONY [*to* EROS]   I will reward thee
Once for thy sprightly° comfort, and tenfold   *cheerful*
For thy good valour. Come thee on.

SCARUS   I'll halt° after.   *Exeunt*   *limp*

4.9

Alarum. Enter ANTONY *again in a march;* [*drummers
and trumpeters;*] SCARUS, *with others*

ANTONY   We have beat him to his camp. Run one before,
And let the Queen know of our gests.°   [*Exit a soldier*]   *deeds*
          Tomorrow,
Before the sun shall see's, we'll spill the blood
That has today escaped. I thank you all,
5   For doughty-handed° are you, and have fought   *brave*
Not as° you served the cause, but as't had been   *as though*
Each man's like mine. You have shown all Hectors.[1]
Enter the city, clip° your wives, your friends,   *embrace*
Tell them your feats whilst they with joyful tears
10   Wash the congealment from your wounds, and kiss
The honoured gashes whole.
    Enter CLEOPATRA
[*To* SCARUS]   Give me thy hand.
To this great fairy° I'll commend thy acts,   *enchantress*
Make her thanks bless thee.
[*To* CLEOPATRA, *embracing her*]   O thou day° o'th' world,   *light*
Chain mine armed neck; leap thou, attire and all,
15   Through proof of harness° to my heart, and there   *impenetrable armor*
Ride on the pants° triumphing.   *heartbeats*

CLEOPATRA   Lord of lords!
O infinite virtue,° com'st thou smiling from   *valor*
The world's great snare uncaught?

ANTONY   My nightingale,
We have beat them to their beds. What, girl, though grey
20   Do something° mingle with our younger brown, yet ha' we   *somewhat*
A brain that nourishes our nerves,° and can   *muscles*
Get goal for goal of youth.[2] Behold this man.
Commend unto his lips thy favouring hand;
Kiss it, my warrior.

---

1. *wound . . . H:* the wound was originally shaped like a
T, but another gash across its bottom has made it look like
an H turned sideways (punning on "ache," pronounced
"aitch").
4.9 Location: Scene continues.

1. You have all fought like Hector (the greatest of the
Trojan warriors).
2. Compete with any youth. Antony is clearly referring
here to the "boy" Caesar, but also, possibly, to his own
boyhood.

[SCARUS *kisses Cleopatra's hand*]
He hath fought today

25 As if a god, in hate of mankind, had
Destroyed in such a shape.

CLEOPATRA   I'll give thee, friend,
An armour all of gold. It was a king's.

ANTONY   He has deserved it, were it carbuncled°   *bejeweled*
Like holy Phoebus' car.° Give me thy hand.   *the sun god's chariot*

30 Through Alexandria make a jolly march.
Bear our hacked targets like° the men that owe° them.   *shields as befits / own*
Had our great palace the capacity
To camp° this host, we all would sup together   *put up*
And drink carouses to the next day's fate,

35 Which promises royal° peril. Trumpeters,   *great*
With brazen din blast you the city's ear;
Make mingle with our rattling taborins,°   *small drums*
That heaven and earth may strike their sounds together,
Applauding our approach.   [*Trumpets sound.*] *Exeunt*

4.10

Enter a SENTRY *and his company;* ENOBARBUS *follows*

SENTRY   If we be not relieved within this hour
We must return to th' court of guard.° The night   *guardroom*
Is shiny,° and they say we shall embattle°   *bright / go to battle*
By th' second hour i'th' morn.

FIRST WATCH   This last day was
A shrewd° one to's.   *bad*

5 ENOBARBUS   O bear me witness, night—

SECOND WATCH   What man is this?

FIRST WATCH   Stand close,° and list° him.   *hidden / listen to*

ENOBARBUS   Be witness to me, O thou blessèd moon,
When men revolted° shall upon record   *deserters*
Bear hateful memory, poor Enobarbus did
Before thy face repent.

SENTRY   Enobarbus?

10 SECOND WATCH   Peace; hark further.

ENOBARBUS   O sovereign mistress of true melancholy,°   *(the moon)*
The poisonous damp of night disponge° upon me,   *pour down*
That life, a very rebel to my will,
May hang no longer on me. Throw my heart

15 Against the flint and hardness of my fault,
Which,° being dried with grief, will break to powder,   *(his heart)*
And finish all foul thoughts. O Antony,
Nobler than my revolt is infamous,
Forgive me in thine own particular,[1]

20 But let the world rank me in register°   *its records*
A master-leaver and a fugitive.°   *deserter*
O Antony! O Antony!   [*He dies*][2]

FIRST WATCH   Let's speak to him.

4.10 Location: Caesar's camp.
1. In whatever aspects of this business concern only you.
2. Depending on how this moment is played, Enobarbus's death may not be obvious either to those onstage
or to the audience.

SENTRY   Let's hear him, for the things he speaks
      May concern Caesar.
25 SECOND WATCH   Let's do so. But he sleeps.
SENTRY   Swoons, rather; for so bad a prayer as his
      Was never yet for° sleep.   *in preparation for*
FIRST WATCH   Go we to him.
SECOND WATCH   Awake, sir, awake; speak to us.
FIRST WATCH   Hear you, sir?
SENTRY   The hand of death hath raught° him.   *taken*
      Drums afar off
                                  Hark, the drums
30 Demurely° wake the sleepers. Let us bear him   *With subdued sound*
      To th' court of guard; he is of note. Our hour
      Is fully out.°   *expired*
SECOND WATCH   Come on, then. He may recover yet.
                      Exeunt [with the body]

                          4.11
      Enter ANTONY *and* SCARUS *with their army*
ANTONY   Their preparation is today by sea;
      We please them not by land.
SCARUS   For both, my lord.
ANTONY   I would they'd fight i'th' fire or i'th' air;
      We'd fight there too.[1] But this it is: our foot°   *foot soldiers*
5   Upon the hills adjoining to the city
      Shall stay with us. Order for sea is given.
      They have put forth° the haven—   *departed from*
      Where their appointment° we may best discover,   *purpose; battle plan*
      And look on their endeavour.   *Exeunt*

                          4.12
      Enter CAESAR *and his army*
CAESAR   But being° charged, we will be still° by land—   *unless we're / inactive*
      Which, as I take't, we shall, for his best force
      Is forth to man his galleys. To the vales,°   *valleys*
      And hold our best advantage.°   *Exeunt*   *take the best position*

                          4.13
      Alarum afar off, as at a sea fight.
      Enter ANTONY *and* SCARUS
ANTONY   Yet they are not joined.° Where yon pine does stand   *(in battle)*
      I shall discover all. I'll bring thee word
      Straight° how 'tis like° to go.   *Exit*   *Promptly / likely*
SCARUS   Swallows have built
      In Cleopatra's sails their nests. The augurs°   *soothsayers*
5   Say they know not, they cannot tell, look grimly,
      And dare not speak their knowledge. Antony
      Is valiant, and dejected, and by starts
      His fretted° fortunes give him hope and fear   *diminished*
      Of what he has and has not.
                  Enter ANTONY

4.11 Location: This and the next two scenes take place
on the battlefield.   1. As well as in the other elements, earth and water.
                                          4.12
                                          4.13

ANTONY   All is lost.

10   This foul Egyptian hath betrayèd me.
     My fleet hath yielded to the foe, and yonder
     They cast their caps up, and carouse together
     Like friends long lost. Triple-turned whore![1] 'Tis thou
     Hast sold me to this novice, and my heart
15   Makes only wars on thee. Bid them all fly;
     For when I am revenged upon my charm,°   *sorceress*
     I have done all. Bid them all fly. Be gone.   [*Exit* SCARUS]
     O sun, thy uprise shall I see no more.
     Fortune and Antony part here; even here
20   Do we shake hands.° All come to this? The hearts   *(before parting)*
     That spanieled° me at heels, to whom I gave   *fawned upon*
     Their wishes, do discandy,° melt their sweets   *melt*
     On blossoming Caesar; and this pine° is barked[2]   *(Antony)*
     That overtopped them all. Betrayed I am.
25   O this false soul of Egypt! This grave° charm,   *deadly*
     Whose eye becked° forth my wars and called them home,   *beckoned*
     Whose bosom was my crownet,° my chief end,°   *coronet / reward*
     Like a right° gipsy hath at fast and loose[3]   *true*
     Beguiled° me to the very heart of loss.°   *cheated / ruin*
     What, Eros, Eros!

           Enter CLEOPATRA

30   Ah, thou spell! Avaunt.°   *Leave me*
CLEOPATRA   Why is my lord enraged against his love?
ANTONY   Vanish, or I shall give thee thy deserving
     And blemish Caesar's triumph.° Let him take thee   *triumphal procession*
     And hoist thee up to the shouting plebeians;
35   Follow his chariot, like the greatest spot°   *taint*
     Of all thy sex; most monster-like be shown
     For poor'st diminutives,[4] for dolts, and let
     Patient Octavia plough thy visage up
     With her preparèd° nails.   *Exit* CLEOPATRA   *specially sharpened*
                     'Tis well thou'rt gone,
40   If it be well to live. But better 'twere
     Thou fell'st into° my fury, for one death   *a victim to*
     Might have prevented many. Eros, ho!
     The shirt of Nessus[5] is upon me. Teach me,
     Alcides, thou mine ancestor, thy rage.
45   Let me lodge Lichas on the horns o'th' moon,
     And with those hands that grasped the heaviest club
     Subdue my worthiest self. The witch shall die.
     To the young Roman boy she hath sold me, and I fall
     Under this plot. She dies for't. Eros, ho!   *Exit*

1. Cleopatra is "triple-turned" because disloyal to three (Julius Caesar, Pompey, and Antony); alluding to her changing political allegiances.
2. Stripped of its bark (and so killed).
3. *fast and loose:* a cheating game played by gypsies.
4. For the benefit of (in place of) the lowest people (dwarfs).
5. Hercules, also known as Alcides (line 44), with whom Antony is repeatedly compared, fatally wounded the centaur Nessus for trying to rape his wife, Deianira. Nessus gave her some of his blood, falsely claiming that it would act as a love potion. Years later, she smeared some of the deadly blood on a shirt and sent it to Hercules. Blaming Lichas (line 45), who had brought the shirt, Hercules cast him into the sea. When she realized what she had done, Deianira killed herself.

4.14

Enter CLEOPATRA, CHARMIAN, IRAS, MARDIAN

CLEOPATRA   Help me, my women! O, he's more mad
Than Telamon for his shield;[1] the boar of Thessaly[2]
Was never so embossed.[3]

CHARMIAN   To th' monument![4]
There lock yourself, and send him word you are dead.
5   The soul and body rive° not more in parting   separate
Than greatness going off.°   leaving someone

CLEOPATRA   To th' monument!
Mardian, go tell him I have slain myself.
Say that the last I spoke was 'Antony',
And word it, prithee, piteously. Hence, Mardian,
10   And bring me° how he takes my death. To th' monument!   bring me word
                                                          Exeunt

4.15

Enter ANTONY *and* EROS

ANTONY   Eros, thou yet behold'st me?

EROS   Ay, noble lord.

ANTONY   Sometime we see a cloud that's dragonish,°   in a dragon's shape
A vapour sometime like a bear or lion,
A towered citadel, a pendent° rock,   hanging
5   A forkèd mountain, or blue promontory
With trees upon't that nod unto the world
And mock our eyes with air. Thou hast seen these signs;
They are black vesper's pageants.[1]

EROS   Ay, my lord.

ANTONY   That which is now a horse even with a thought
10   The rack distains,° and makes it indistinct   cloud dims
As water is in water.

EROS   It does, my lord.

ANTONY   My good knave° Eros, now thy captain is   boy
Even such a body. Here I am Antony,
Yet cannot hold this visible shape, my knave.
15   I made these wars for Egypt, and the Queen—
Whose heart I thought I had, for she had mine,
Which whilst it was mine had annexed unto't
A million more, now lost—she, Eros, has
Packed cards° with Caesar, and false-played my glory   Stacked the deck
20   Unto an enemy's triumph.°   victory; trump card
Nay, weep not, gentle Eros. There is left us
Ourselves to end ourselves.

              Enter MARDIAN

                            O thy vile lady,
She has robbed me of my sword!°   valor; manhood

MARDIAN   No, Antony,

4.14 Location: Alexandria.
1. Ajax, also known as Telemon, went mad and killed
himself after the capture of Troy when he was not
awarded Achilles' shield.
2. Sent by Diana to lay waste Calydon (killed by Meleager).
3. Was never so exhaustedly foaming at the mouth—that
is, was never driven to such extremity (a hunting term).

4. The tomb that Cleopatra, forseeing her death, had
built.
4.15 Location: Alexandria.
1. Illusory spectacles heralding the approach of night—
with a probable allusion to funerals and death. (Pageants
were originally moving stages on which miracle plays
were presented.)

My mistress loved thee, and her fortunes mingled
With thine entirely.

25 ANTONY   Hence, saucy° eunuch, peace!   *disrespectful*
She hath betrayed me, and shall die the death.

MARDIAN   Death of one person can be paid but once,
And that she has discharged. What thou wouldst do
Is done unto thy hand.° The last she spake   *for you*
30 Was 'Antony, most noble Antony!'
Then in the midst a tearing groan did break
The name of Antony. It was divided
Between her heart and lips.[2] She rendered° life,   *gave up*
Thy name so buried in her.

ANTONY   Dead, then?

MARDIAN   Dead.

35 ANTONY   Unarm, Eros.[3] The long day's task is done,
And we must sleep. [*To* MARDIAN] That thou depart'st hence safe
Does pay thy labour richly. Go.   *Exit* MARDIAN
                       Off, pluck off.
        [EROS *helps* ANTONY *to unarm*]
The seven-fold shield[4] of Ajax cannot keep
The battery° from my heart. O, cleave, my sides!   *onslaught*
40 Heart, once be stronger than thy continent;°   *container*
Crack thy frail case. Apace,° Eros, apace.   *Quickly*
No more a soldier. Bruisèd pieces,° do;   *of armor*
You have been nobly borne.—From me a while.   *Exit* EROS
I will o'ertake thee, Cleopatra, and
45 Weep for my pardon. So it must be, for now
All length° is torture. Since the torch° is out,   *longer life / (Cleopatra)*
Lie down, and stray no farther. Now all labour
Mars what it does; yea, very force entangles
Itself with strength.[5] Seal,° then, and all is done.   *Finish the deed*
50 Eros!—I come, my queen.—Eros!—Stay for me.
Where souls do couch on flowers[6] we'll hand in hand,
And with our sprightly port° make the ghosts gaze.   *cheerful stance*
Dido and her Aeneas shall want troops,[7]
And all the haunt° be ours. Come, Eros, Eros!   *place; ghosts*
        Enter EROS

EROS   What would my lord?

55 ANTONY   Since Cleopatra died
I have lived in such dishonour that the gods
Detest my baseness. I, that with my sword
Quartered the world, and o'er green Neptune's back°   *on the sea*
With ships made cities,[8] condemn myself to lack°   *for lacking*
60 The courage of a woman; less noble mind
Than she which by her death our Caesar tells
'I am conqueror of myself.' Thou art sworn, Eros,

2. *It . . . lips*: It was half-uttered.
3. Here and in the following lines, the symbolic appropriateness of this historical figure's name ("Eros" means "love") is stressed.
4. A shield made of brass lined with six thicknesses of oxhide.
5. *very . . . strength*: strength defeats itself by its own exertions.
6. Lie ("couch") in the Elysian Fields of the blessed dead in the mythological underworld.

7. Shall lack followers. Dido, Queen of Carthage, commits suicide after being abandoned by her lover Aeneas, legendary Trojan founder of Rome, in Virgil's *Aeneid*; they are not reconciled in the underworld. Dido, who originally hailed from Phoenicia, is meant to recall Cleopatra. In leaving her, Aeneas places public responsibility above personal desire—unlike Antony but very much like Octavius Caesar, whom Virgil intended him to resemble.
8. Put so many ships to sea that the fleet resembled a city.

That when the exigent° should come, which now · ***urgent need***
Is come indeed—when I should see behind me
65   Th'inevitable prosecution° of · ***pursuit***
Disgrace and horror—that on my command
Thou then wouldst kill me. Do't. The time is come.
Thou strik'st not me; 'tis Caesar thou defeat'st.
Put colour in thy cheek.

EROS   The gods withhold me!° · · · · · · · · · · · · · · · · · · ***God forbid***
70   Shall I do that which all the Parthian darts,
Though enemy, lost aim and could not?

ANTONY   Eros,
Wouldst thou be windowed° in great Rome and see · · · · · · · · · · · ***looking from a window***
Thy master thus with pleached° arms, bending down · · · · · · · · · · · · · · · · · · ***tied***
His corrigible° neck, his face subdued · ***submissive***
75   To penetrative° shame, whilst the wheeled seat° · · · · · · · · · · · ***piercing / chariot***
Of fortunate Caesar, drawn before him, branded
His baseness that ensued?⁹

EROS   I would not see't.

ANTONY   Come then; for with a wound I must be cured.
Draw that thy honest° sword, which thou hast worn · · · · · · · · · · · · · ***honorable***
Most useful for thy country.

80   EROS   O sir, pardon me!

ANTONY   When I did make thee free, swor'st thou not then
To do this when I bade thee? Do it at once,
Or thy precedent° services are all · ***earlier***
But accidents unpurposed.° Draw, and come. · · · · · · · · · · · · · · ***But pointless events***

85   EROS   Turn from me then that noble countenance
Wherein the worship° of the whole world lies. · · · · · · · · · · · · · · · ***esteem; worth***

ANTONY [*turning away*]   Lo thee!

EROS   My sword is drawn.

ANTONY   Then let it do at once
The thing why thou hast drawn it.

EROS   My dear master,
90   My captain, and my Emperor: let me say,
Before I strike this bloody stroke, farewell.

ANTONY   'Tis said, man; and farewell.

EROS   Farewell, great chief. Shall I strike now?

ANTONY   Now, Eros.

[EROS *stabs himself*]

EROS   Why, there then, thus I do escape the sorrow
Of Antony's death.   [*He dies*]
95   ANTONY   Thrice nobler than myself,
Thou teachest me, O valiant Eros, what
I should and thou couldst not. My queen and Eros
Have by their brave instruction got upon° me · · · · · · · · · · · · · · ***gained ahead of***
A nobleness in record.° But I will be · ***history***
100   A bridegroom in my death, and run into't
As to a lover's bed.¹ Come then, and, Eros,
Thy master dies thy scholar. To do thus
I learned of thee.

---

9. **branded . . . ensued**: indicated, as if by a criminal's brand, the humiliation of the man who followed.
1. *But . . . bed*: Death is here treated as a form of erotic union or climax, with Antony as the bridegroom and death (and Cleopatra) the bride.

[He stabs] himself

How, not dead? Not dead?

The guard, ho! O, dispatch° me!   *finish*

Enter a GUARD *[and* DECRETAS*]*

FIRST GUARD   What's the noise?

105   ANTONY   I have done my work ill, friends. O, make an end

Of what I have begun!

SECOND GUARD   The star is fall'n.

FIRST GUARD   And time is at his period.°   *its end*

ALL THE GUARDS   Alas

And woe!

ANTONY   Let him that loves me strike me dead.

FIRST GUARD   Not I.

SECOND GUARD   Nor I.

THIRD GUARD   Nor anyone.   *Exeunt [the* GUARD*]*

110   DECRETAS   Thy death and fortunes bid thy followers fly.

[He takes Antony's sword]

This sword but shown to Caesar, with this tidings,

Shall enter me° with him.   *gain me favor*

Enter DIOMEDES

DIOMEDES   Where's Antony?

DECRETAS   There, Diomed, there.

DIOMEDES   Lives he? Wilt thou not answer, man?

[Exit DECRETAS*]*

ANTONY   Art thou there, Diomed? Draw thy sword, and give me

Sufficing° strokes for death.   *Enough*

115   DIOMEDES   Most absolute lord,

My mistress Cleopatra sent me to thee.

ANTONY   When did she send thee?

DIOMEDES   Now, my lord.

ANTONY   Where is she?

DIOMEDES   Locked in her monument. She had a prophesying fear

Of what hath come to pass; for when she saw—

120   Which never shall be found°—you did suspect   *(to be true)*

She had disposed° with Caesar, and that your rage   *made an alliance*

Would not be purged, she sent word she was dead;

But fearing since how it might work, hath sent

Me to proclaim the truth; and I am come,

125   I dread, too late.

ANTONY   Too late, good Diomed. Call my guard, I prithee.

DIOMEDES   What ho, the Emperor's guard! The guard, what ho!

Come, your lord calls.

Enter four or five of the GUARD *of Antony*

ANTONY   Bear me, good friends, where Cleopatra bides.°   *waits; dwells*

130   'Tis the last service that I shall command you.

FIRST GUARD   Woe, woe are we, sir, you may not live to wear

All your true followers out.°   *outlive them*

ALL THE GUARDS   Most heavy day!

ANTONY   Nay, good my fellows, do not please sharp fate

To grace° it with your sorrows. Bid that welcome   *By gracing*

135   Which comes to punish us, and we punish it,

Seeming to bear it lightly. Take me up.

I have led you oft; carry me now, good friends,

And have my thanks for all.   *Exeunt bearing* ANTONY *[and* EROS*]*

4.16

Enter CLEOPATRA *and her maids aloft, with*
    CHARMIAN *and* IRAS

CLEOPATRA   O Charmian, I will never go from hence.

CHARMIAN   Be comforted, dear madam.

CLEOPATRA   No, I will not.
  All strange and terrible events are welcome,
  But comforts we despise. Our size of sorrow,
5 Proportioned to our cause, must be as great
  As that which makes it.

        Enter DIOMEDES [*below*]

                   How now? Is he dead?

DIOMEDES   His death's upon him, but not dead.
  Look out o'th' other side your monument.
  His guard have brought him thither.

        Enter [*below*] ANTONY, [*borne by*] *the guard*

CLEOPATRA   O sun,
10 Burn the great sphere thou mov'st in; darkling¹ stand
  The varying shore o'th' world! O Antony,
  Antony, Antony! Help, Charmian,
  Help, Iras, help, help, friends below!
  Let's draw him hither.

ANTONY   Peace. Not Caesar's valour
15 Hath o'erthrown Antony, but Antony's
  Hath triumphed on itself.

CLEOPATRA   So it should be,
  That none but Antony should conquer Antony.
  But woe 'tis so!

ANTONY   I am dying, Egypt, dying. Only
20 I here importune death° awhile until   *ask death to wait*
  Of many thousand kisses the poor last
  I lay upon thy lips.

CLEOPATRA   I dare not,° dear,   *dare not come down*
  Dear, my lord, pardon. I dare not,
  Lest I be taken. Nor th'imperious show°   *triumphal procession*
25 Of the full-fortuned Caesar ever shall
  Be brooched° with me, if knife, drugs, serpents, have   *decorated*
  Edge, sting, or operation.° I am safe.   *power*
  Your wife, Octavia, with her modest eyes
  And still conclusion,° shall acquire no honour   *silent judgment*
30 Demuring° upon me. But come, come, Antony.—   *Gazing solemnly*
  Help me, my women.—We must draw thee up.
  Assist, good friends.

ANTONY   O quick, or I am gone!

CLEOPATRA   Here's sport indeed. How heavy weighs my lord!
  Our strength is all gone into heaviness,°   *sadness; weight*
35 That makes the weight. Had I great Juno's power
  The strong-winged Mercury should fetch thee up
  And set thee by Jove's side. Yet come a little.
  Wishers were ever fools. O come, come, come!

4.16 Location: Cleopatra's monument, Alexandria.
1. O . . . *darkling:* For the spheres in which the sun, like
the planets and stars, was thought to move around the
earth, see note to 2.7.15. If the sun burned its sphere,
presumably it would move out of orbit, thus leaving the
earth in darkness ("darkling").

They heave ANTONY *aloft to* CLEOPATRA
And welcome, welcome! Die when thou hast lived,°   *lived again*
40   Quicken° with kissing. Had my lips that power,   *Revive*
Thus would I wear them out.
      [*They kiss*]
ALL THE LOOKERS-ON   A heavy sight.
ANTONY   I am dying, Egypt, dying.
Give me some wine, and let me speak a little.
45 CLEOPATRA   No, let me speak, and let me rail so high
That the false hussy Fortune break her wheel,
Provoked by my offence.°   *insults*
ANTONY   One word, sweet queen.
Of Caesar seek your honour, with your safety. O!
CLEOPATRA   They do not go together.
ANTONY   Gentle, hear me.
50 None about Caesar trust but Proculeius.
CLEOPATRA   My resolution and my hands I'll trust,
None about Caesar.
ANTONY   The miserable change now at my end
Lament° nor sorrow at, but please your thoughts   *Neither lament*
55 In feeding them with those my former fortunes,
Wherein I lived the greatest prince o'th' world,
The noblest; and do now not basely die,
Not cowardly put off my helmet to
My countryman; a Roman by a Roman
60 Valiantly vanquished. Now my spirit is going;
I can no more.
CLEOPATRA   Noblest of men, woot die?°   *will you*
Hast thou no care of me? Shall I abide
In this dull world, which in thy absence is
No better than a sty?
      [ANTONY *dies*]
               O see, my women,
65 The crown o'th' earth doth melt. My lord!
O, withered is the garland° of the war.   *crowning glory*
The soldier's pole[2] is fall'n. Young boys and girls
Are level now with men. The odds° is gone,   *distinction among humans*
And there is nothing left remarkable
70 Beneath the visiting moon.
      [*She falls*]
CHARMIAN   O, quietness, lady!
IRAS   She's dead, too, our sovereign.
CHARMIAN   Lady!
IRAS   Madam!
CHARMIAN   O, madam, madam, madam!
IRAS   Royal Egypt, Empress!
CHARMIAN   Peace, peace, Iras!
CLEOPATRA [*recovering*]   No more but e'en° a woman, and   *just (no longer Queen)*
75   commanded
By such poor passion as the maid that milks
And does the meanest chores. It were for° me   *would befit*
To throw my sceptre at the injurious gods,

2. Polestar; military standard; phallus.

To tell them that this world did equal theirs
80   Till they had stol'n our jewel. All's but naught.
     Patience is sottish,° and impatience does   *foolish*
     Become a dog that's mad. Then is it sin
     To rush into the secret house of death
     Ere death dare come to us? How do you, women?
85   What, what, good cheer! Why, how now, Charmian?
     My noble girls! Ah, women, women! Look,
     Our lamp is spent, it's out. Good sirs,° take heart;   *(to the women)*
     We'll bury him, and then what's brave,° what's noble,   *fine*
     Let's do it after the high Roman fashion,
90   And make death proud to take us. Come, away.
     This case of that huge spirit now is cold.
     Ah, women, women! Come. We have no friend
     But resolution, and the briefest° end.   *fastest*

                 Exeunt [those above] bearing off Antony's body

                                5.1

           Enter CAESAR *with his council of war:* AGRIPPA, DOLA-
           BELLA, [MAECENAS, GALLUS, PROCULEIUS]
     CAESAR   Go to him, Dolabella, bid him yield.
     Being so frustrate, tell him, he but mocks
     The pauses that he makes.[1]
     DOLABELLA   Caesar, I shall.   *[Exit]*
           Enter DECRETAS *with the sword of Antony*
     CAESAR   Wherefore is that? And what art thou that dar'st
     Appear thus° to us?   *with a drawn weapon*
5   DECRETAS   I am called Decretas.
     Mark Antony I served, who best was worthy
     Best to be served. Whilst he stood up and spoke
     He was my master, and I wore my life
     To spend° upon his haters. If thou please   *expend*
10   To take me to thee, as I was to him
     I'll be to Caesar; if thou pleasest not,
     I yield thee up my life.
     CAESAR   What is't thou sayst?
     DECRETAS   I say, O Caesar, Antony is dead.
     CAESAR   The breaking° of so great a thing should make   *end; telling*
15   A greater crack.° The rivèd° world   *noise; fracture / split*
     Should have shook lions into civil° streets,   *city*
     And citizens to their° dens. The death of Antony   *(the lions')*
     Is not a single doom; in that name lay
     A moiety° of the world.   *half*
     DECRETAS   He is dead, Caesar,
20   Not by a public minister of justice,
     Nor by a hirèd knife; but that self° hand   *same*
     Which writ his honour in the acts it did
     Hath, with the courage which the heart did lend it,
     Splitted the heart. This is his sword;
25   I robbed his wound of it. Behold it stained
     With his most noble blood.
     CAESAR [*weeping*]   Look you, sad friends,

─────────────────────────────

5.1 Location: Caesar's camp.   1. *he but . . . makes:* his delays are a mere mockery.

The gods rebuke me;° but it is a tidings   *(for his tears)*
To wash the eyes of kings.

AGRIPPA   And strange it is
That nature must compel us to lament
Our most persisted deeds.°   *What we persevered in*

30 **MAECENAS**   His taints and honours
Waged° equal with° him.   *Fought as if / in*

AGRIPPA   A rarer spirit never
Did steer humanity;° but you gods will give us   *govern (any) man*
Some faults to make us men. Caesar is touched.

MAECENAS   When such a spacious mirror's set before him
He needs must see himself.

35 **CAESAR**   O Antony,
I have followed° thee to this. But we do lance°   *pursued / wound to cure*
Diseases in our bodies. I must perforce
Have shown to thee such a declining day,[2]
Or look on thine. We could not stall° together   *live in peace*
40 In the whole world. But yet let me lament,
With tears as sovereign[3] as the blood of hearts,
That thou, my brother, my competitor°   *comrade; foe*
In top of all design,° my mate in empire,   *In the greatest ventures*
Friend and companion in the front of war,
45 The arm of mine own body, and the heart
Where mine his° thoughts did kindle—that our stars,   *its*
Unreconciliable, should divide
Our equalness° to this. Hear me, good friends—   *partnership*
     Enter an EGYPTIAN
But I will tell you at some meeter season.°   *fitter time*
50 The business of this man looks out of him;
We'll hear him what he says.—Whence are you?

EGYPTIAN   A poor Egyptian, yet the Queen my mistress,
Confined in all she has, her monument,
Of thy intents desires instruction,
55 That she preparèdly may frame herself
To th' way she's forced to.

CAESAR   Bid her have good heart.
She soon shall know of us, by some of ours,
How honourable and how kindly we
Determine for her. For Caesar cannot live
To be ungentle.

60 **EGYPTIAN**   So; the gods preserve thee!   *Exit*

CAESAR   Come hither, Proculeius. Go, and say
We purpose her no shame. Give her what comforts
The quality° of her passion° shall require,   *strength / grief*
Lest in her greatness, by some mortal stroke,
65 She do defeat us; for her life in Rome
Would be eternal in our triumph.[4] Go,
And with your speediest bring us what she says
And how you find of her.

PROCULEIUS   Caesar, I shall.   *Exit*

---

2. *I must . . . day:* I would have had to exhibit my demise
to you. *perforce:* necessarily.
3. As efficacious (weeping seems to be paralleled with

bloodletting).
4. *her life . . . triumph:* her presence alive in Rome would
bring eternal renown to my triumphal procession.

CAESAR Gallus, go you along. [*Exit* GALLUS]
                          Where's Dolabella,
    To second Proculeius?
70 ALL BUT CAESAR   Dolabella!
    CAESAR Let him alone; for I remember now
      How he's employed. He shall in time be ready.
      Go with me to my tent, where you shall see
      How hardly° I was drawn into this war,   unwillingly
75   How calm and gentle I proceeded still
      In all my writings.° Go with me, and see   letters to Antony
      What I can show in this.   *Exeunt*

                          5.2

        Enter CLEOPATRA, CHARMIAN, IRAS, *and* MARDIAN
    CLEOPATRA My desolation does begin to make
      A better life. 'Tis paltry to be Caesar.
      Not being Fortune, he's but Fortune's knave,°   servant
      A minister of her will. And it is great
5   To do that thing° that ends all other deeds,   (suicide)
      Which shackles accidents and bolts up change,
      Which sleeps and never palates more the dung,
      The beggar's nurse, and Caesar's.[1]
              Enter PROCULEIUS[2]
    PROCULEIUS Caesar sends greeting to the Queen of Egypt,
10   And bids thee study on° what fair demands   give thought to
      Thou mean'st to have him grant thee.
    CLEOPATRA   What's thy name?
    PROCULEIUS My name is Proculeius.
    CLEOPATRA   Antony
      Did tell me of you, bade me trust you; but
      I do not greatly care to be deceived,
15   That° have no use for trusting.[3] If your master   Because I
      Would have a queen his beggar, you must tell him
      That majesty, to keep decorum, must
      No less beg than a kingdom. If he please
      To give me conquered Egypt for my son,
20   He gives me so much of mine own as° I   that
      Will kneel to him with thanks.
    PROCULEIUS   Be of good cheer.
      You're fall'n into a princely hand; fear nothing.
      Make your full reference° freely to my lord,   case
      Who is so full of grace that it flows over
25   On all that need. Let me report to him
      Your sweet dependency,° and you shall find   meek obeisance
      A conqueror that will pray in aid for kindness,[4]
      Where he for grace is kneeled to.
    CLEOPATRA   Pray you, tell him
      I am his fortune's vassal, and I send him
30   The greatness he has got.[5] I hourly learn

5.2 Location: Cleopatra's monument.
1. *Which sleeps . . . Caesar's:* Which brings a sleep in
which we no longer taste the produce of the earth (dung),
nourisher of all from beggar to emperor.
2. Cleopatra and her women are inside the monument,
the others outside it.
3. Cleopatra claims not to care whether she is deceived,
in the hope that Proculeius will relax his guard and reveal

Caesar's intentions. But she may also mean that she
doesn't like being deceived, knowing as she does the perils of misplaced trust.
4. Who will beg help in finding new ways to be kind.
5. *I am . . . got:* I do homage to his good fortune, and
acknowledge the great position he has won. "Send him"
may suggest Cleopatra's sense of superiority in conferring
greatness upon Caesar.

A doctrine of obedience, and would gladly
Look him i'th' face.

PROCULEIUS   This I'll report, dear lady;
Have comfort, for I know your plight is pitied
Of° him that caused it.   *By*

       [*Enter Roman soldiers from behind*]

35   PROCULEIUS [*to the soldiers*]   You see how easily she may be surprised.
Guard her till Caesar come.

IRAS   Royal Queen—

CHARMIAN   O Cleopatra, thou art taken, Queen!

CLEOPATRA [*drawing a dagger*]   Quick, quick, good hands!

PROCULEIUS [*disarming* CLEOPATRA]   Hold,
worthy lady, hold!
Do not yourself such wrong, who are in this
Relieved° but not betrayed.   *Rescued*

40   CLEOPATRA   What, of° death too,   *deprived of*
That rids our dogs of languish?[6]

PROCULEIUS   Cleopatra,
Do not abuse my master's bounty by
Th'undoing of yourself. Let the world see
His nobleness well acted, which your death
Will never let come forth.°   *allow to be displayed*

45   CLEOPATRA   Where art thou, death?
Come hither, come. Come, come, and take a queen
Worth many babes and beggars.[7]

PROCULEIUS   O temperance, lady!

CLEOPATRA   Sir, I will eat no meat.° I'll not drink, sir.   *food*
If idle talk will once be necessary,[8]

50   I'll not sleep, neither. This mortal house° I'll ruin,   *My body*
Do Caesar what he can. Know, sir, that I
Will not wait pinioned[9] at your master's court,
Nor once be chastised with the sober eye
Of dull Octavia. Shall they hoist me up

55   And show me to the shouting varletry°   *rabble*
Of censuring Rome? Rather a ditch in Egypt
Be gentle grave unto me; rather on Nilus' mud
Lay me stark naked, and let the waterflies
Blow me into abhorring;[1] rather make

60   My country's high pyramides my gibbet,°   *gallows*
And hang me up in chains.

PROCULEIUS   You do extend
These thoughts of horror further than you shall
Find cause in Caesar.

       Enter DOLABELLA

DOLABELLA   Proculeius,
What thou hast done thy master Caesar knows,

65   And he hath sent for thee. For the Queen,
I'll take her to my guard.

PROCULEIUS   So, Dolabella,
It shall content me best. Be gentle to her.

---

6. Which rids even our dogs of protracted demise.
7. *babes and beggars:* death's cheapest victims; those most
often "relieved" (line 39) by the great.
8. (Even) if useless words are at times needed (to keep
me awake); if I am forced to engage in pointless chatter.

9. Will not serve shackled (or, will not wait like a bird
with clipped wings).
1. Lay their eggs on me (thereby breeding maggots) so
that I become disgusting, abhorrent.

[*To* CLEOPATRA] To Caesar I will speak what° you shall please,　　　　　whatever
If you'll employ me to him.

CLEOPATRA　　　　　　　　Say I would die. *Exit* PROCULEIUS

70　DOLABELLA　Most noble Empress, you have heard of me.

CLEOPATRA　I cannot tell.

DOLABELLA　　　　　　　Assurèdly you know me.

CLEOPATRA　No matter, sir, what I have heard or known.
You laugh when boys or women tell their dreams;
Is't not your trick?°　　　　　　　　　　　　　　　　　　custom

DOLABELLA　　　　　　I understand not, madam.

75　CLEOPATRA　I dreamt there was an Emperor Antony.
O, such another sleep, that I might see
But such another man!

DOLABELLA　　　　　　If it might please ye—

CLEOPATRA　His face was as the heav'ns, and therein stuck°　　　were stuck
A sun and moon, which kept their course and lighted
The little O o'th' earth.

80　DOLABELLA　　　　　　Most sovereign creature—

CLEOPATRA　His legs bestrid° the ocean; his reared arm　　　straddled
Crested[2] the world. His voice was propertied
As all the tunèd spheres,[3] and that to friends;
But when he meant to quail° and shake the orb,°　　awe / globe
85　He was as rattling thunder. For his bounty,
There was no winter in't; an autumn 'twas,
That grew the more by reaping. His delights
Were dolphin-like; they showed his back above°　　they rose above
The element they lived in. In his livery°　　　　　　　service
90　Walked crowns and crownets.° Realms and islands were　kings and princes
As plates° dropped from his pocket.　　　　　　　　silver coins

DOLABELLA　　　　　　　　　Cleopatra—

CLEOPATRA　Think you there was, or might be, such a man
As this I dreamt of?

DOLABELLA　　　　　Gentle madam, no.

CLEOPATRA　You lie, up to the hearing of the gods.
95　But if there be, or ever were one such,
It's past the size of dreaming.[4] Nature wants stuff
To vie strange forms with fancy; yet t'imagine
An Antony were nature's piece 'gainst fancy,
Condemning shadows quite.[5]

DOLABELLA　　　　　　Hear me, good madam:
100　Your loss is as yourself, great, and you bear it
As answering to[6] the weight. Would I might never
O'ertake° pursued success but° I do feel,　　　Achieve / unless
By the rebound° of yours, a grief that smites　　reflection
My very heart at root.

CLEOPATRA　　　　　I thank you, sir.
105　Know you what Caesar means to do with me?

DOLABELLA　I am loath to tell you what I would you knew.

CLEOPATRA　Nay, pray you, sir.

2. Formed a crest over (as in heraldry).
3. *was . . . spheres:* sounded like the music of the spheres, supposedly produced by the harmonious structure of the universe. See note to 2.7.15.
4. My vision of him surpasses what can be dreamed.
5. *Nature . . . quite:* Nature lacks material to compete with the remarkable visions of the imagination in creating fantastic forms; but by imaging and creating Antony, nature has produced a masterpiece that outstrips even fancy and thus discredits imaginary conceptions.
6. *you . . . to:* you do justice to.

DOLABELLA Though he be honourable—

CLEOPATRA He'll lead me then in triumph.

DOLABELLA Madam, he will, I know't.

Flourish. Enter CAESAR, [*with*] PROCULEIUS, GALLUS,
MAECENAS, *and others of his train*

ALL° Make way, there! Caesar! (*Caesar's train*)

CAESAR Which is the Queen of Egypt?

DOLABELLA [*to* CLEOPATRA]
It is the Emperor, madam.

CLEOPATRA *kneels*

110 CAESAR Arise! You shall not kneel.
I pray you rise, rise, Egypt.

CLEOPATRA [*rising*] Sir, the gods
Will have it thus.° My master and my lord   *that I obey you*
I must obey.

CAESAR Take to you no hard thoughts.
The record of what injuries you did us,

115 Though written in our flesh, we shall remember
As things but done by chance.

CLEOPATRA Sole sir° o'th' world,   *lord*
I cannot project° mine own cause so well   *lay out*
To make it clear,° but do confess I have   *innocent seeming*
Been laden with like frailties which before
Have often shamed our sex.

120 CAESAR Cleopatra, know
We will extenuate rather than enforce.°   *emphasize (faults)*
If you apply yourself° to our intents,   *conform*
Which towards you are most gentle, you shall find
A benefit in this change; but if you seek

125 To lay on me a cruelty° by taking   *charge of cruelty*
Antony's course, you shall bereave yourself
Of my good purposes and put your children
To that destruction which I'll guard them from,
If thereon you rely. I'll take my leave.

130 CLEOPATRA And may through all the world![7] 'Tis yours, and we,
Your scutcheons° and your signs of conquest, shall   *captured shields*
Hang in what place you please. [*Giving a paper*] Here, my good lord.

CAESAR You shall advise me in all for° Cleopatra.   *concerning*

CLEOPATRA This is the brief° of money, plate, and jewels   *summary*

135 I am possessed of. 'Tis exactly valued,
Not petty things admitted.° Where's Seleucus?   *Except trivial things*
[*Enter* SELEUCUS]

SELEUCUS Here, madam.

CLEOPATRA [*to* CAESAR] This is my treasurer. Let him speak, my lord,
Upon his peril, that I have reserved

140 To myself nothing. Speak the truth, Seleucus.

SELEUCUS Madam, I had rather seal° my lips   *sew up*
Than to my peril speak that which is not.

CLEOPATRA What have I kept back?

SELEUCUS Enough to purchase what you have made known.

145 CAESAR Nay, blush not, Cleopatra. I approve
Your wisdom in the deed.

CLEOPATRA See, Caesar! O, behold

---

7. As you may (take your leave and go) anywhere (as ruler of the world).

How pomp is followed!⁸ Mine° will now be yours,　　　　　*My followers*

And should we shift estates,° yours would be mine.　　　*change positions*

The ingratitude of this Seleucus does

150　Even make me wild.—O slave, of no more trust

Than love that's hired! What, goest thou back? Thou shalt

Go back, I warrant thee; but I'll catch thine eyes

Though° they had wings. Slave, soulless villain, dog!　　*Even if*

O rarely° base!　　　　　　　　　　　　　　　　　　　*exceptionally*

CAESAR　　　　　　Good Queen, let us entreat you.

155　CLEOPATRA　O Caesar, what a wounding shame is this,

That thou vouchsafing° here to visit me,　　　　　　　*stooping to come*

Doing the honour of thy lordliness

To one so meek—that mine own servant should

Parcel° the sum of my disgraces by　　　　　　　　　*Particularize; add to*

160　Addition of his envy.° Say, good Caesar,　　　　　　　*spite*

That I some lady° trifles have reserved,　　　　　　　*ladylike*

Immoment toys,° things of such dignity　　　　　　　　*Worthless trinkets*

As we greet modern° friends withal;° and say　　　　　*everday / with*

Some nobler token I have kept apart

165　For Livia° and Octavia, to induce　　　　　　　　　　*Caesar's wife*

Their mediation—must I be unfolded

With° one that I have bred? The gods! It smites me　　*Turned in by*

Beneath the fall I have. [*To* SELEUCUS] Prithee, go hence,

Or I shall show the cinders° of my spirits　　　　　　*smoldering coals*

170　Through th'ashes of my chance.° Wert thou a man°　　*fortune / (not a eunuch)*

Thou wouldst have mercy on me.

CAESAR　　　　　　　　　　　Forbear, Seleucus.

　　　　　　　　　　　　[*Exit* SELEUCUS]

CLEOPATRA　Be it known that we, the greatest, are misthought°　*misjudged*

For things that others do; and when we fall

We answer others' merits in our name,⁹

Are therefore to be pitied.

175　CAESAR　　　　　　　　　　Cleopatra,

Not what you have reserved nor what acknowledged

Put we i'th' roll of conquest. Still be't yours.

Bestow° it at your pleasure, and believe　　　　　　　*Dispense*

Caesar's no merchant, to make prize° with you　　　　*haggle*

180　Of things that merchants sold. Therefore be cheered.

Make not your thoughts your prisons.¹ No, dear Queen;

For we intend so to dispose you as

Yourself shall give us counsel. Feed and sleep.

Our care and pity is so much upon you

185　That we remain your friend; and so adieu.

CLEOPATRA　My master and my lord!

CAESAR　　　　　　　　　　　　　Not so. Adieu.

　　　　　　Flourish. Exeunt CAESAR *and his train*

CLEOPATRA　He words me, girls, he words me, that I should not

Be noble to myself.² But hark thee, Charmian.

　　　　[*She whispers to* CHARMIAN]

---

8. How the great are served.　　　　　　　　　　　by (or in) your thoughts.

9. We are responsible for the deeds committed by others　2. *He words . . . myself:* He puts me off from committing

in our names (an effort to shift the blame to Seleucus).　suicide with mere words.

1. Don't think yourself a prisoner; don't be imprisoned

IRAS   Finish, good lady. The bright day is done,
        And we are for the dark.
190 CLEOPATRA [to CHARMIAN]   Hie thee again.°   *Hurry back*
        I have spoke already, and it is provided.
        Go put it to the haste.°   *Do it quickly*
    CHARMIAN   Madam, I will.
                Enter DOLABELLA
    DOLABELLA   Where's the Queen?
    CHARMIAN   Behold, sir.   [*Exit*]
    CLEOPATRA   Dolabella!
    DOLABELLA   Madam, as thereto sworn by your command—
195   Which my love makes religion° to obey—   *compels me*
        I tell you this: Caesar through Syria
        Intends his journey, and within three days
        You with your children will he send before.
        Make your best use of this. I have performed
        Your pleasure, and my promise.
200 CLEOPATRA   Dolabella,
        I shall remain your debtor.
    DOLABELLA   I your servant.
        Adieu, good Queen. I must attend on Caesar.
    CLEOPATRA   Farewell, and thanks.   *Exit* [DOLABELLA]
                        Now, Iras, what think'st thou?
        Thou, an Egyptian puppet shall be shown
205   In Rome, as well as I. Mechanic slaves°   *Laborers*
        With greasy aprons, rules,° and hammers shall   *measuring sticks*
        Uplift us to the view. In their thick° breaths,   *foul*
        Rank° of gross diet,° shall we be enclouded,   *Stinking / coarse food*
        And forced to drink° their vapour.   *inhale*
    IRAS   The gods forbid!
210 CLEOPATRA   Nay, 'tis most certain, Iras. Saucy lictors°   *Insolent law officers*
        Will catch at us like strumpets, and scald° rhymers   *scurvy*
        Ballad us out o' tune. The quick comedians
        Extemporally° will stage us, and present   *In improvised manner*
        Our Alexandrian revels. Antony
215   Shall be brought drunken forth, and I shall see
        Some squeaking Cleopatra boy[3] my greatness
        I'th' posture of a whore.
    IRAS   O, the good gods!
    CLEOPATRA   Nay, that's certain.
    IRAS   I'll never see't! For I am sure my nails
        Are stronger than mine eyes.
220 CLEOPATRA   Why, that's the way
        To fool their preparation and to conquer
        Their most absurd intents.
                Enter CHARMIAN
                        Now, Charmian!
        Show° me, my women, like a queen. Go fetch   *Dress*
        My best attires. I am again for Cydnus
225   To meet Mark Antony.[4] Sirrah Iras, go.
        Now, noble Charmian, we'll dispatch° indeed,   *hurry; finish*

---

3. Cleopatra's part will be played by a boy (as it was in   4. See 2.2.192–232.
Shakespeare's day).

And when thou hast done this chore I'll give thee leave
To play till doomsday.—Bring our crown and all.   [*Exit* IRAS]
　　　　A noise within
Wherefore's this noise?
　　　　Enter a GUARDSMAN

GUARDSMAN　　　　　　　　Here is a rural fellow
230　That will not be denied your highness' presence.
He brings you figs.
CLEOPATRA　Let him come in.　　　　　　　　*Exit* GUARDSMAN
　　　　　　　　What° poor an instrument　　　　　*How*
May do a noble deed! He brings me liberty.
My resolution's placed,° and I have nothing　　　　*unwavering*
235　Of woman in me. Now from head to foot
I am marble-constant. Now the fleeting° moon　　　*changeable*
No planet is of mine.
　　　　Enter GUARDSMAN, *and* CLOWN° [*with a basket*]　　*rustic*
GUARDSMAN　　　　　　　This is the man.
CLEOPATRA　Avoid,° and leave him.　　　　*Exit* GUARDSMAN　　*Withdraw*
　　　　　　　　Hast thou the pretty worm[5]
Of Nilus there, that kills and pains not?
240　CLOWN　Truly, I have him; but I would not be the party that
　should desire you to touch him, for his biting is immortal;[6]
　those that do die of it do seldom or never recover.
CLEOPATRA　Remember'st thou any that have died on't?
CLOWN　Very many, men, and women too. I heard of one of
245　them no longer than yesterday, a very honest° woman, but　　*truthful; chaste*
　something given to lie,° as a woman should not do but in the　　*fib; lie with men*
　way of honesty, how she died° of the biting of it, what pain she　　*perished; had an orgasm*
　felt. Truly, she makes a very good report o'th' worm; but he
　that will believe all that they say shall never be saved by half
250　that they do;[7] but this is most falliable:° the worm's an odd　　*(error for "infallible")*
　worm.
CLEOPATRA　Get thee hence, farewell.
CLOWN　I wish you all joy of the worm.
CLEOPATRA　Farewell.
255　CLOWN　You must think this, look you, that the worm will do his
　kind.°　　　　　　　　　　　　　　　　　　*what's in its nature*
CLEOPATRA　Ay, ay; farewell.
CLOWN　Look you, the worm is not to be trusted but in the keep-
　ing of wise people; for indeed there is no goodness in the worm.
260　CLEOPATRA　Take thou no care; it shall be heeded.
CLOWN　Very good. Give it nothing, I pray you, for it is not worth
　the feeding.
CLEOPATRA　Will it eat me?
CLOWN　You must not think I am so simple but I know the devil
265　himself will not eat a woman; I know that a woman is a dish
　for the gods, if the devil dress° her not. But truly, these same　　*prepare (food); clothe*
　whoreson° devils do the gods great harm in their women; for in　　*accursed*
　every ten that they make, the devils mar five.

5. Snake or serpent. In the Clown's description (lines 244–51), the "worm" also suggests the penis.
6. Comic error: the Clown means the opposite, but as so often with such malapropisms in Shakespeare, the mistake reveals an unintended truth. See Cleopatra's "Immortal longings" (line 272).
7. Perhaps the point is that a woman "given to lie" (line 246) is not to be believed. If Cleopatra acts on this "good report o'th' worm," she will "never be saved" (lines 248–49): she will die and, in Christian terms, will lose hope of salvation by committing suicide.

CLEOPATRA Well, get thee gone, farewell.

270 CLOWN Yes, forsooth. I wish you joy o'th' worm.

Exit [leaving the basket]

[Enter IRAS with a robe, crown, and other jewels]

CLEOPATRA Give me my robe. Put on my crown. I have
Immortal longings in me. Now no more
The juice of Egypt's grape shall moist this lip.

[CHARMIAN and IRAS help her to dress]

Yare,° yare, good Iras, quick—methinks I hear   Briskly
275 Antony call. I see him rouse himself
To praise my noble act. I hear him mock
The luck of Caesar, which the gods give men
To excuse their° after wrath. Husband, I come.   (the gods')
Now to that name my courage prove my title.
280 I am fire and air; my other elements
I give to baser life.⁸ So, have you done?
Come then, and take the last warmth of my lips.

[She kisses them]

Farewell, kind Charmian. Iras, long farewell.

[IRAS falls and dies]

Have I the aspic° in my lips? Dost fall?   asp
285 If thou and nature can so gently part,
The stroke of death is as a lover's pinch,
Which hurts and is desired. Dost thou lie still?
If thus thou vanishest, thou tell'st the world
It is not worth leave-taking.

290 CHARMIAN   Dissolve, thick cloud, and rain, that I may say
The gods themselves do weep.

CLEOPATRA   This proves me base.°   ignoble
If she first meet the curlèd° Antony   curly-haired
He'll make demand of° her, and spend that kiss   question; (sexual)
Which is my heaven to have.

*[She takes an aspic from the basket and puts it to her
breast]*

Come, thou mortal wretch,°   deadly creature
295 With thy sharp teeth this knot intrinsicate°   intricate
Of life at once untie. Poor venomous fool,
Be angry, and dispatch. O, couldst thou speak,
That I might hear thee call great Caesar ass
Unpolicied!°   Outsmarted

CHARMIAN   O eastern star!°   Venus; Cleopatra

CLEOPATRA   Peace, peace.
300 Dost thou not see my baby at my breast,
That sucks the nurse asleep?

CHARMIAN   O, break! O, break!

CLEOPATRA As sweet as balm, as soft as air, as gentle.
O Antony!

[She puts another aspic to her arm]

Nay, I will take thee too.
What° should I stay—   *[She] dies*   Why

---

8. *I am . . . life*: The "other elements" (line 280) are earth and water, the lower and heavier elements traditionally linked
to women and thought to explain their fickleness. Cleopatra is particularly associated with these elements through her
equation with (the mud of) Egypt. By asserting that she is only "fire and air," she is claiming to be manly (as in lines
234–35) and is also referring to the separation of the soul from the body at death.

CHARMIAN   In this vile world? So, fare thee well.
305   Now boast thee, death, in thy possession lies
      A lass unparalleled. Downy windows,° close,   *eyelids*
      And golden Phoebus never be beheld
      Of eyes again so royal. Your crown's awry.
      I'll mend it,° and then play—   *set it right*
            Enter the GUARD, *rustling*° *in*   *clattering*
310   FIRST GUARD   Where's the Queen?
      CHARMIAN   Speak softly. Wake her not.
      FIRST GUARD   Caesar hath sent—
      CHARMIAN   Too slow a messenger.
            [*She applies an aspic*]
      O come apace, dispatch! I partly feel thee.
      FIRST GUARD   Approach, ho! All's not well. Caesar's beguiled.°   *deceived*
315   SECOND GUARD   There's Dolabella sent from Caesar. Call him.
                                                  [*Exit a* GUARDSMAN]
      FIRST GUARD   What work is here, Charmian? Is this well done?
      CHARMIAN   It is well done, and fitting for a princess
      Descended of so many royal kings.
      Ah, soldier!   CHARMIAN *dies*
            Enter DOLABELLA
      DOLABELLA   How goes it here?
      SECOND GUARD   All dead.
320   DOLABELLA   Caesar, thy thoughts
      Touch their effects° in this. Thyself art coming   *Are realized*
      To see performed the dreaded act which thou
      So sought'st to hinder.
      ALL   A way there, a way for Caesar!
            Enter CAESAR *and all his train, marching*
      DOLABELLA [*to* CAESAR]   O sir, you are too sure an augurer.
      That° you did fear is done.   *What*
325   CAESAR   Bravest at the last,
      She levelled at° our purposes, and, being royal,   *discerned rightly*
      Took her own way. The manner of their deaths?
      I do not see them bleed.
      DOLABELLA [*to a* GUARDSMAN]   Who was last with them?
      FIRST GUARD   A simple countryman that brought her figs.
      This was his basket.
      CAESAR   Poisoned, then.
330   FIRST GUARD   O Caesar,
      This Charmian lived but now; she stood and spake.
      I found her trimming up the diadem
      On her dead mistress; tremblingly she stood,
      And on the sudden dropped.
      CAESAR   O, noble weakness!
335   If they had swallowed poison, 'twould appear
      By external swelling; but she looks like sleep,
      As° she would catch another Antony   *As if*
      In her strong toil° of grace.   *snare*
      DOLABELLA   Here on her breast
      There is a vent of blood, and something blown.°   *emitted; swollen*
      The like is on her arm.
340   FIRST GUARD   This is an aspic's trail,
      And these fig-leaves have slime upon them such
      As th'aspic leaves upon the caves of Nile.

CAESAR   Most probable
That so she died; for her physician tells me
345   She hath pursued conclusions° infinite   *trial outcomes*
Of easy ways to die. Take up her bed,
And bear her women from the monument.
She shall be buried by her Antony.
No grave upon the earth shall clip° in it   *embrace*
350   A pair so famous. High events as these
Strike° those that make° them, and their story is   *Afflict / cause*
No less in pity than his glory⁹ which
Brought them to be lamented. Our army shall
In solemn show attend this funeral,
355   And then to Rome. Come, Dolabella, see
High order in this great solemnity.
                    Exeunt all [soldiers bearing CLEOPATRA *on her*
                                bed, CHARMIAN, *and* IRAS]

---

9. *their . . . glory:* there is no less pity in their story than there is glory in the exploits of Caesar. The immodesty of these lines, in the guise of praise, recalls Caesar's ambiguous grief, his combination of calculation and sentiment, at the news of Antony's death in 5.1. The historical Octavius Caesar went on to order the murder of Ptolemy XV (Caesarion), Cleopatra's son with Julius Caesar. Since Julius Caesar was Octavius's great-uncle and adoptive father, this act, which ended the Ptolemaic dynasty, might be seen as fraticide. See 2.1.37 with note, 2.2.233–34 with note, and 3.6.1–16 with note to line 6. By contrast, after Antony and Cleopatra's deaths, the historical Octavia, over her brother Octavius's objections, raised Anthony's children by Fulvia and Cleopatra, as well as her own five children with Antony and a previous husband.

Pericles, Prince of Tyre:
A Reconstructed Text

Pericles, Prince of Tyre (1607–08) was one of the most popular plays of its time and has proven effective in modern productions as well. Coherent and innovative, it brought a new dramatic genre—romance—into Shakespeare's work and, arguably, onto the English stage in general. As a text to be read, however, *Pericles* has sometimes proven more problematic. It is not clear whether the difficulty is intrinsic to the play or results from an almost irresistible but partly mistaken tendency to interpret it in light of Shakespeare's earlier works and thus to make unwarranted assumptions about plot, characterization, morality, dramaturgy, and style. Does the romance pattern fully succeed in mastering the messiness of the play's materials? Does the play raise but not resolve a series of social, political, and sexual anxieties, despite its considerable structural and thematic unity? Are these even the right questions to ask?

Shakespeare's younger contemporary Ben Jonson spoke for many subsequent critics in disparaging *Pericles* as "a mouldy tale . . . and stale," and in attributing its success on the stage to its use of "scraps out of every dish." It is easy to see what Jonson is talking about. In *Pericles*, a King adorns his palace walls with the skulls of his victims. A princess commits incest with her father. Another princess is kidnapped by pirates and sold to a brothel. Famine brings a city to its knees. An entire crew is lost in a tumultuous storm. Two royal families are sent to fiery destruction. And Pericles is almost deposed by his restless nobility.

From the perspective of genre, *Pericles* seems to enact a transition from one kind of romance to another. Pericles first looks like a knight-errant willing to risk death in his quest to win the beautiful maiden. But this standard mode of medieval romance quickly gives way to the manner of late antique Greek romance, in which the faithful and virtuous lovers must suffer separation and all manner of misfortune before their ultimate, triumphant reunion. Characteristically, then, Pericles does not act; he is acted upon. Bad things (as well as good) just keep happening to him. Every member of his family narrowly escapes death: two evade assassins sent by murderous monarchs, and the third survives burial at sea. Each is reported dead, only to experience apparently miraculous rebirth. The play seems consciously to eschew the complex probing of the protagonist's psyche that marks Shakespeare's immediately preceding tragic period in favor of clear-cut moral oppositions and an emphatic poetic justice. By the end of *Pericles,* the good have been rewarded and the bad annihilated, but, for the most part, not as a result of the protagonist's own efforts.

Indeed, Pericles does not even get to act out significant portions of his own destiny before the audience. Much of the story is told by Gower, the onstage presence of the fourteenth-century writer John Gower, whose major work, *Confessio Amantis,* is the most important direct source of *Pericles.* The eighth book of this verse narrative is devoted primarily to the tale of Apollonius of Tyre, which, via medieval intermediaries dating back to a fifth- or sixth-century Latin text, derives from a now-lost late classical Latin or, more probably, Greek romance influenced by *The Odyssey.* A different route through the medieval sources, this time incorporating the lives of early Christian saints who suffered persecution in brothels, leads to the other proximate source of the play, Laurence Twine's *Patterne of Painefull Adventures* (written by 1576; published 1594?). *Pericles* is the first dramatization of these lengthy traditions. The shift in the protagonist's name from "Apollonius" to "Pericles" may derive from still other strains in the Apollonius tradition; from

The true History of the Play of *Pericles*, as it was lately presented by the worthy and ancient Poet *John Gower*.

John Gower.

Woodcut of John Gower, from the title page of *The Painfull Adventures of Pericles Prince of Tyre,* by George Wilkins (1608).

Sir Philip Sidney's *Arcadia* (1590), one of whose protagonists is named Pyrocles; or from one of Shakespeare's favorite sources, Plutarch's *Lives,* which perhaps provides still other characters' names. In addition to praising the renowned fifth-century-B.C.E. Athenian statesman Pericles, it harshly judges his rival and successor Cleon as well as the fourth-century general Lysimachus—all names of characters in the play.

Pericles follows its sources more faithfully than do many of Shakespeare's works. One sign of this fidelity is the retention of an episodic plot. More striking still is the appearance of Gower himself as a character. His role as chorus finds its predecessor in *Henry V* (1599), but Gower has the more specific function of giving a (pseudo-) medieval feel to the action. Although he eventually reverts to standard pentameter lines, he starts out primarily in the rhymed tetrameter couplets in which *Confessio Amantis* is written: "To sing a song that old was sung / From ashes ancient Gower is come" (1.1–2). In addition, the theatrical Gower's diction often echoes the medieval poet's, extending even to the use of deliberately antiquated language ("iwis" for "certainly," for example, at 5.2). His moralizing speeches are frequently graced by an unrealistic theatrical device—the dumb show. Further, Gower recounts much of the action in his eight monologues, as if to emphasize that poet's authorship of what sometimes feels like narrative, as opposed to dramatic, material. These strategies are all metatheatrical: they undermine the naturalistic illusion of the play, encouraging the audience to view events from a certain distance, to attend to the larger pattern that unfolds rather than becoming emotionally engaged. Part of the genius of *Pericles,* however, is ultimately to elicit that emotional engagement as well.

Gower's monologues also structure the play more effectively than does the division into five acts introduced by later editors (but not followed here). The scene often shifts within each of the seven main groupings, but there is always a central focus. Gower introduces Antioch and incest (Scene 1), Pentapolis and Pericles' wooing of Thaisa (5), Ephesus and the saving of Thaisa (10), Tarsus and the attempted murder of Marina (15), Mytilene and Marina's virtuous life in the brothel (18), Mytilene again and Marina's reunion with Pericles (20), and Ephesus and the reunion with Thaisa (22), before providing the brief epilogue with which the play concludes.

The actual authorship of *Pericles* is beset by unresolved questions, which are treated at length in the Textual Note. Here it is worth mentioning only that George Wilkins probably wrote most of the first nine scenes and Shakespeare most of the remaining thirteen. Acknowledgment of dual authorship is tied to the long-standing recognition of stylistic differences between the two parts of the play. Wilkins's section of the dialogue is closer to Gower's language than is Shakespeare's. Although both playwrights regularly compose verse in iambic pentameter, Wilkins uses far more end-stopped rhyming couplets than does Shakespeare. By contrast, Shakespeare's predilection for blank-verse enjambment, in which the phrase or idea does not conclude at the end of the line, produces a tension between syntax and verse form.

Thus Wilkins's Pericles decorously repudiates the incestuous Daughter of Antiochus:

> Fair glass of light, I loved you, and could still,
> Were not this glorious casket stored with ill.
> ·
> For he's no man on whom perfections wait
> That, knowing sin within, will touch the gate.
> ·
> But, being played upon before your time,
> Hell only danceth at so harsh a chime.
>   (1.119–28)

Shakespeare's Pericles reacts to a storm in imagistically more complex but also more colloquial verse:

>   . . . O still
> Thy deaf'ning dreadful thunders, gently quench
> Thy nimble sulph'rous flashes. . . .
> ·
>   . . . The seaman's whistle
> Is as a whisper in the ears of death,
> Unheard.—Lychorida!—Lucina, O!
> Divinest patroness, and midwife gentle
> To those that cry by night, convey thy deity
> Aboard our dancing boat, make swift the pangs
> Of my queen's travails!—Now, Lychorida.
>   (11.4–14)

As a result, Shakespeare's section of the play is theatrically livelier, the contrast with the increasingly frequent monologues by Gower correspondingly sharper. Pericles' meeting with the fishermen is the only episode by Wilkins that seems of a piece with such later parts of the play as the second tempest (quoted from above); the revival of Pericles' wife, Thaisa; the two brothel scenes; and the first recognition scene. And structurally, *Pericles* breaks neatly in two: in the first nine scenes, Pericles moves from felicity to misfortune and back to felicity; in the remaining thirteen, he simply repeats this pattern but with greater intensity.

Yet such distinctions are misleading. Many Renaissance plays were written by more than one dramatist; Shakespeare collaborated on about a quarter of his plays, mostly near the beginning and end of his career. Especially in performance, such works do not necessarily seem any less unified than single-author pieces. Even though its "feel" shifts, *Pericles* remains consistent throughout in motif—Pericles as a noble tree, his jewel-like family, destructive eating, providential storms, divine music.

Its episodes also echo one another, within and across the two parts of the play. The deadly skulls at Antiochus's palace are answered by the harmless jousting at Simonides' court, and the bad potential marriage to Antiochus's Daughter is echoed by the good real one to Simonides'. The incestuous relationship between Antiochus and his Daughter is contrasted with the lovingly innocent one between Pericles and Marina. Thaliart's foiled attempt to assassinate Pericles at Antiochus's behest anticipates Leonine's failed effort to murder Marina at Dionyza's. Cleon calls down the "curse of heav'n and men" (4.103) should his family ever prove ungrateful to Pericles, and when his family does so prove, "him and his they [his subjects] in his palace burn" (22.121). The storm that costs Pericles his men but leads him to Thaisa is paralleled by the later tempest that apparently disposes of Thaisa. The vigorous popular culture of the fishermen is set against the degraded popular culture of the brothel. The vow of chastity Simonides attributes to Thaisa to get rid of all her suitors except Pericles is fulfilled both in her genuine vow of chastity when she thinks Pericles gone forever and in Marina's successful defense of her chastity in the brothel. The apparent burial of Thaisa is duplicated in the apparent interment of her daughter. And, more broadly, the excessive love of Antiochus for his daughter and, in a different way, of Dionyza for hers are contrasted with the defective love of Cleon for his daughter and, arguably, of Pericles for Marina—until the end of the play, when Pericles demonstrates the appropriate love of father for daughter: neither too much nor too little.

Throughout, the play insists that the concatenation of miseries inflicted on Pericles and his family ultimately leads to a higher felicity. As noted earlier, this is the structure of tragicomic romance, the genre of nearly all of Shakespeare's final plays. Typically, *Pericles* recapitulates Shakespeare's previous work while reversing its chronology: the tragic mood of the early seventeenth century precedes the comic tone of the 1590s. The play echoes *King Lear* both in its storm scenes and in its reunion of ravaged father and redemptive daughter, who gives "another life / To Pericles thy father" (21.194–95); it then duplicates *The Comedy of Errors*, which draws on the same sources as *Pericles* in its concluding retrieval of the missing wife-turned-priestess from the temple of Diana at Ephesus.

Gower reassuringly emphasizes this larger pattern—"I'll show you those in trouble's reign, / Losing a mite, a mountain gain" (5.7–8)—which becomes especially prominent in Shakespeare's scenes due to the presiding benevolence of Diana. She is first mentioned when, according to Simonides, Thaisa opts for continued virginity (9.9). Then Thaisa invokes her upon awakening in an opened coffin, as does Pericles when he vows not to cut his hair until his baby, Marina, is married (12.102, 13.28). Thaisa becomes her priestess, and Marina places her virginity in the goddess's protection (14.12, 15.4, 16.131). Finally, after Pericles is reunited with Marina, Diana appears to him in a dream, promising him happiness only if he goes to her temple in Ephesus and publicly recounts his loss of Thaisa (21.224–34). This supernatural moment recalls Thaisa's quasi-magical preservation by Cerimon (of whom Pericles says, "The gods can have no mortal officer / More like a god than you," 22.85–86), anticipates Pericles' actual meeting with Thaisa in the final scene (where Diana is repeatedly mentioned), and follows hard upon Pericles' perhaps unique ability to hear "the music of the spheres" (21.214)—the sound of a heavenly harmony that extends to human affairs below. A

Scenic view of the temple of Diana, designed by Inigo Jones for the pastoral *Florentine* (1635).

special sensitivity to music has marked Pericles' family throughout. Pericles is "music's master," Thaisa awakens to "still and woeful music," and, most tellingly, Marina "sings like one immortal" (9.28, 12.86, 20.3).

Although these visual and auditory signs of a divine providence guiding the destiny of Pericles' family are pagan in form, they are Christian in content. Tragicomedy's movement from tribulation to triumph is modeled on the *felix culpa*, the fortunate fall of Adam and Eve that led to the redemptive coming of Christ. Antioch recalls the sinister side of Eden: Pericles will "taste the fruit of yon celestial tree / Or die in the adventure"; Antiochus praises the "golden fruit, but dang'rous to be touched" and later warns, "Touch not, upon thy life" (1.64–65, 71, 130). The eastern Mediterranean of late Greek antiquity in which *Pericles* is set also carries connotations of Judaism and early Christianity. Tyre is connected with the reigns of David and Solomon, and was captured by the Christian forces in the First Crusade. Antioch recalls the rebellion of the Maccabees; in addition, Peter and Paul preached there. Paul was born in Tarsus and had a lengthy ministry in Ephesus. The fishermen on the shore of Pentapolis are literally, like St. Peter, fishers of men. Amid talk of devouring whales (5.63–80), they fish out Pericles, whom "the sea hath cast upon [their] coast" (5.92) in a manner that recalls the biblical Jonah, understood in Christian allegory to prefigure Christ's resurrection. Thaisa later undergoes a similar resurrection; and at Mytilene, the Pander laments, "Neither is our profession any mystery, it's no calling" (16.32–33)—where both "mystery" and "calling" have religious reverberations.

In a final, typically moralistic speech, Gower tells the audience,

> In Pericles, his queen, and daughter seen,
> Although assailed with fortune fierce and keen,
> Virtue preserved from fell destruction's blast,
> Led on by heav'n, and crowned with joy at last.
> (22.110–13)

Although there is no ambiguity here, the play as a whole leaves room for doubts on structural, social and political, and sexual grounds. First, despite the overarching pattern of the triumph over a pagan "fortune" by an implicitly Christian "heav'n," Pericles' sufferings feel arbitrary. It is hard to understand, except according to fairy-tale logic, why his predecessors cannot solve Antiochus's obvious riddle or why the King advertises the very secret he wants to preserve. Similarly, the play does not explain why Pericles leaves his daughter at Tarsus or why Dionyza, eager to be rid of Marina, does not consider sending her home instead of murdering her. More important, the misfortunes in *Pericles* seem unrelenting, unconnected, and unrelated to the character or behavior of their victims. Yet this disjunction fails to inspire any Job-like reflections on injustice. In short, the triumph of divine providence is not fully integrated with the secular saga of misfortune. Perhaps, then, the play reveals a contingent relationship between human vicissitude and redemptive transcendence, thereby raising questions about its own ostensible program.

Second, *Pericles* bears a complicated relationship to its own social and political material. The representation of popular culture provides some of the play's most engaging scenes without, however, always linking up to the larger movement of the plot. The initial storm leaves Pericles "bereft / Unfortunately both of ships and men" (7.79–80). The fishermen who then help him repeatedly receive his praise:

> MASTER   . . . I can compare our rich misers to nothing so fitly as to a whale: a plays and tumbles, driving the poor fry before him, and at last devours them all at a mouthful. . . .
>
> PERICLES [*aside*]   A pretty moral.
>
> (5.68–73)

This disabused account, which may echo the language of the 1607 Midlands Uprising against landlord enclosures of the common lands, leads to a rebuke of the monarch: "If the good King Simonides were of my mind . . . we would purge the land of these drones that rob the bee of her honey" (5.80–84). But the complaint quickly disappears, leaving only the positive image of Pericles' future father-in-law. Similarly, although Pericles promises the fishermen "if that ever my low fortune's better, / I'll pay your bounties, till then rest your debtor" (5.177–78), the debt, which is usually honored in previous tales of Apollonius (including Twine's), is not recalled when Pericles' fortunes quickly improve.

The anticommercial outlook implicit in the Master's denunciation of "rich misers" also informs the brothel scenes, which, like Pericles' encounter with the fishermen, replaces the predominantly Greek Mediterranean setting of the plot with recognizably English characters. Prostitution is the only market-driven activity depicted in the play, although Gower later reports that Marina graduates to an honest livelihood. Earlier, the Bawd advises her in economic terms: "You have fortunes coming upon you. Mark me, you must seem to do that fearfully which you commit willingly, to despise profit where you have most gain. To weep that you live as ye do makes pity in your lovers. Seldom but that pity begets you a good opinion, and that opinion a mere profit" (16.101–06). Marina is thus urged to perform like an actor at one of London's professional theaters. With commerce almost reduced to the oldest profession, a profession widely practiced in the neighborhoods around the theaters, the play implicitly links itself to the very activity that it simultaneously depicts Marina nobly resisting.

Thus, despite successfully exploiting popular culture for theatrical effect, *Pericles* fails to incorporate that culture into the final reconciliation: the play concludes with a purely aristocratic and royal circle. This ending is tacitly anticipated by the linguistic class divisions of the popular scenes: the fishermen and the brothelkeepers speak prose, whereas Pericles and Marina favor blank verse. Nevertheless, *Pericles* is the only one of Shakespeare's romances written before the King's Men began performing during the winter at Blackfriars, a "private," elite, commercial theater. It was acted at the Globe, the preeminent "public" theater, and its success in the early seventeenth century attests to the enduring, at least partly popular appeal of its traditional romance plot.

Furthermore, *Pericles* seems to take its distance from absolute monarchy—in the fishermen's insistence on their rights and in popular political assertiveness at Tarsus. This is important because the political value of aristocratic leadership is questionable. Antioch has been ruled by an incestuous murderer, and there is no indication of his successor. The Governor of Tarsus lets his city slip into famine; his wife is an attempted murderer. Although the inhabitants eventually kill the couple, their own earlier behavior does not inspire confidence: "All poverty was scorned, and pride so great / The name of help grew odious to repeat" (4.30–31). Under duress they are even worse:

> Those mothers who to nuzzle up their babes
> Thought naught too curious are ready now
> To eat those little darlings whom they loved.
> (4.42–44)

The passage echoes in reverse the riddle's equation of cannibalism with incest—"I feed / On mother's flesh" (1.107–08)—while also recalling numerous other moments where "to eat" is to devour. Ephesus's future remains unspecified: Lord Cerimon acts as a private figure. The Governor of Mytilene frequents a brothel until Marina converts him; at the end of the play, the brothel remains, while the Governor, betrothed to Marina, leaves Mytilene in uncertain hands and goes off to rule Tyre.

Earlier, Pericles' departure from Tyre inspires aristocratic "mutiny" (10.29) and begins the practice of absentee landlordism that reaches its climax near the end of the play when his deputy, Helicanus, appoints Aeschines as *his* deputy and sets out with Pericles. Shortly thereafter, Pericles and Thaisa accede to the throne of Pentapolis, a society whose virtues and defects the fishermen have earlier dissected. The death of Thaisa's father, "the good Simonides," is treated not as an occasion for grief but as an opportunity to dole out kingdoms and break up a family that has only just been reunited.

This outcome may parallel the isolation of the various members of James I's family, an isolation emblematized by James's failure to come to the deathbeds of two of his children. Pericles' absenteeism may also reflect on James's style of governing. Alternatively, it may simply recognize the necessity of intergenerational separation for dynastic continuity, just as the redemptive role of Marina may reflect upon Shakespeare's relationship to his own daughter.

Yet *Pericles* also raises sexual doubts. Although the play subjects its protagonists to debased sexuality only to demonstrate their Diana-like purity, they perhaps do not escape unpolluted. In Gower's *Confessio Amantis*, Pericles' daughter is not Marina but Thaisa. From an extradramatic and extratextual perspective, then, sexual relations with Thaisa, which in Gower would have been incest, are here converted into perfectly appropriate marital intimacy. It is almost as if the name change allows Pericles to have the very experience castigated in Antioch under the protection of the marriage bond. When the nearly catatonic Pericles arrives in Mytilene, Lysimachus agrees that Marina might be the cure:

> She questionless, with her sweet harmony
> And other choice attractions, would alarum [Quarto has "allure"]
> And make a batt'ry through his deafened ports.
>
> (21.34–36)

"Alarum" in the second line works better with the last line, but the Quarto's reading goes well with "choice attractions"; thus, "allure" may be correct. If so, Lysimachus, ignorant of Marina's parentage, is suggesting a potentially unfamilial relationship between father and daughter. So, too, does Pericles. He addresses Marina as "thou that begett'st him that did thee beget" (21.182), a line that may simply express gratitude for bringing him back to life. These words recall the generational reversals of Antiochus's incestuous riddle: "He's father, son, and husband mild; / I mother, wife, and yet his child" (1.111–12).

Tragicomic romance often provides a nontragic resolution to the tale of Oedipus, Pericles' predecessor in solving murderous riddles. Do Pericles' words to Marina reverse or repeat Antiochus's riddle? Ambiguities such as this one trouble the providential pattern. By name Pericles recalls an Athenian virtue at odds with the quasi-allegorical landscape through which he travels, a landscape of Asiatic luxury and decadence, of an incest associated with tyranny whose primary alternative seems to be anarchy. In other words, the various social, political, and sexual ambiguities of *Pericles* bear less on the psychology or morality of the protagonist than on the overall import of the play.

Modern performances of *Pericles* have increasingly embraced the challenge posed by this pattern. Although some productions attempt to create naturalistic settings and complex characters, most respect *Pericles*'s relative indifference to such matters by exploiting what's unrealistic about the play and about Renaissance theater generally. First, the doubling of parts has led to the same actress playing Antiochus's Daughter and Marina, Marina and Thaisa, or Thaisa and Dionyza. This procedure can accentuate the differences between the paired characters; more often, however, it has generated an overtone of incest. Relatedly, when one actor plays all the Mediterranean kings, the stage is able to capture the underlying similarity, the repetitiousness, of Pericles' adventures and, hence, the formal, ritualistic quality of the work. Second, although the figure of Gower can establish intimacy between audience and action, the tendency has been to follow the German dramatist Bertolt Brecht in resisting empathy and identification. Gower's role is thus made to underscore the play's theatricality: it has at various times been sung, treated as a voice-over, and played by a street performer. The dramatized action itself has been represented as street theater, as the work of a traveling troupe, as Chinese opera, as an African-American boatswain's sea chantey to his fellow sailors aboard ship, as a child's picture book, as events in an asylum, as the floor show in a gay brothel. One consequence of these techniques has sometimes been an ironic, farcical approach to the absurdities of the plot. The price, however, is the failure of the climactic recognition scenes, which thrive on psychological nuance. Similar problems may arise with overtly political interpretations, though a feminist or multi-ethnic perspective can be a highly suggestive response to the text. Perhaps the solution, in reading as well as performance, is to refuse to level the unevenness of the play, remaining faithful to its various and complex registers.

WALTER COHEN

TEXTUAL NOTE

Pericles, Prince of Tyre poses insuperable textual problems. At some point between 1606 and 1608, most likely in late 1607 or early 1608, Shakespeare probably collaborated on a draft of *Pericles* with George Wilkins, a freelance playwright whose *Miseries of Inforst Mariage* had been successfully staged around 1606 by Shakespeare's company, the King's Men. The exact mechanism of the collaboration is unknown, but Wilkins seems to have composed most of Scenes 1–9 (Acts 1–2 in other modern editions) and Shakespeare most of Scenes 10–22 (Acts 3–5). Each dramatist may also have had a small share in the other's part: for instance, Wilkins seems to have been involved with Gower throughout, writing all of his fifth monologue (Scene 18) and his epilogue (end of Scene 22).

The central evidence for dual authorship and for the attribution to Wilkins is the stylistic disparity between the two sections of the play. The style of the first nine scenes shares a prosaic manner, end-stopped versification, and rhyming couplets with Wilkins's other works during these years. It does not resemble Shakespeare's style at any time (or that of anyone else besides Wilkins proposed so far). By contrast, the final thirteen scenes are in Shakespeare's characteristically idiosyncratic late style, marked by complex imagery and, even more notably, by a radical use of enjambment. At various times, scholars have offered alternative explanations—that Shakespeare wrote the first part of *Pericles* early in his career and came back to it years later; that he wrote it all at once but that the two parts were differently mangled on the path from his manuscript to the printed page; that he deliberately shifted styles midway through the play for aesthetic effect; or that he did collaborate, but with someone other than Wilkins. None of these claims is nearly as plausible as the assumption of joint authorship by Wilkins and Shakespeare.

The play was probably first performed between December 1607 and May 1608, and was apparently a commercial success at the Globe. The King's Men seem to have submitted the company's official promptbook of *Pericles* to the Stationers' Register May 20, 1608, ostensibly with intent to print. Since ownership of the play rested not with the playwright but with the company, however, their real purpose may have been to block Wilkins from illegally exploiting *Pericles*'s popularity by selling it to a publisher himself—something he seems to have done the previous year with *The Miseries of Inforst Mariage*. In the event, the play was not printed in 1608; nonetheless, if the King's Men were trying to stop publication, their strategy failed in at least two respects.

First, Wilkins published a prose rendering of the story entitled *The Painfull Adventures of Pericles Prince of Tyre* sometime in 1608. Its title page advertises its indebtedness to the theatrical version, which for the most part, primarily in Scenes 1–9, it resembles. Yet even in these early scenes, Wilkins's narrative is not as close to the play as might be expected. One purely speculative theory is that he was following not Shakespeare's *Pericles* but an earlier play. It is far more likely, however, that as a collaborating dramatist unattached to an acting company, he would not necessarily have retained a manuscript of the part he wrote and might never have had a personal copy of the entire, jointly authored piece. Indeed, given Wilkins's previous behavior, the King's Men may have made a point of keeping the text out of his hands. *The Painfull Adventures* thus seems to record Wilkins's memory of the play that he recently had helped to write. That memory is less accurate, of course, in the parts he did not compose.

Perhaps the King's Men were unable to prevent publication in another way as well. In 1609, one or more actors who had performed in *Pericles* may have sold it for publication. If so, he or they had to reassemble the text from memory, since an actor routinely possessed a written version of little more than his own part. Since the unauthorized publication of the manuscript would have hurt the interests of the company's actor-shareholders such as Shakespeare, the actors most likely to have gone to press are thus to be found elsewhere. Arguably (although this is disputed), the text was the work of the boy actor who played Lychorida and Marina, as well as some minor other parts, and of a hired man who may have been one of the fishermen and the Pander, again among other small roles. For this claim to hold, these two actors would also had to have acquired a copy of Gower's speeches: perhaps the boy was apprenticed to the actor-shareholder who played Gower.

Almost inevitably, an actor's report significantly differs not only from what Shakespeare wrote but also from what was actually performed. Evidence for this divergence in *Pericles* is to be found especially in the large number of errors in meter, but perhaps also in the repeated confusion of verse and prose (although this may be a product of printing) and in the high degree of verbal repetition. The conjectural identification of the actors who reconstructed the text is based on the relative absence of these defects from the speeches of the characters they presumably played and from the scenes in which they appear. Certainly, the process of reporting cannot account for the stylistic differences between the two parts of the play. The First Quarto (Q1) of *Pericles* was typeset in two printing houses: probably one compositor worked in the first shop, two in the second. But here, again, the division between shops and among compositors does not correspond to the stylistic shift beginning in Scene 10. Neither can compositorial error explain most of the defects in the text. And although the title page names Shakespeare as the author, four other plays published in Quarto before 1623 and attributed to William Shakespeare as well as three more assigned to "W.S." were clearly written by others.

As noted in the Introduction, *Pericles* remained extremely popular in the early seventeenth century. It was revived several times through 1631—at the Globe, on tour in the countryside, and before a more elite audience. The print record is similarly extensive: the Second Quarto (Q2) appeared in the same year as the first, 1609, with subsequent quartos in 1611, 1619, 1630, and 1635. Each was based on the previous Quarto, although Q6 also drew on Q4. But *Pericles* was excluded from the First Folio (F) in 1623, perhaps because the editors thought of it as a collaborative piece. It was published in the second issue of the Third Folio (1664), which relied on Q6; again in the Fourth Folio (1685), which used the Third Folio; and in some major early eighteenth-century editions. But the play then largely dropped out of Shakespeare's works until 1780, when Edmund Malone successfully reintroduced it and provided it with the act and scene divisions—both lacking in Q1—subsequent editors have usually accepted. The play has been routinely included in Shakespeare's canon since then.

Because all editions ultimately derive from Q1, *Pericles* occupies a unique status. For every other Shakespearean play with the ambiguous exception of *Richard III*, at least one early printed version apparently draws directly on either an authorial manuscript or a scribal transcript of it, such as a promptbook. (*Sir Thomas More* remained unpublished during the Renaissance and survives in an authorial manuscript.) Since no reasonably authoritative text of *Pericles* exists, even the claim that Q1 is a report of a performance cannot depend on comparison with a presumably more accurate version but must rely on internal evidence alone. Various unsatisfactory alternatives thus confront an editor. The most commonly adopted strategy in the last fifty years has been to emend the text only conservatively to increase its intelligibility. This approach has the obvious advantage of avoiding the introduction of many new deviations from the original play. On the other hand, it is unlikely to preserve the early printed version, the early performed version, or the authors' original version.

The Oxford editors have taken a different tack. In their original-spelling edition, they reprint Q1. In their modern-spelling edition, followed here, they take advantage of the probable dual authorship of the play and the survival of Wilkins's *Painfull Adventures*, which they treat as a reported text, like Q1. Primarily in Wilkins's share of the play (Scenes 1–9) and in the brothel scenes, this edition draws on *The Painfull Adventures (PA)* when the reporting in Q1 seems to be poor and when Wilkins's prose version seems superior in logic, language, or meter and is not invalidated as a report of the play by dependence on another printed source (Laurence Twine's *The Patterne of Painefull Adventures,* 1594?). Although the rationale for this procedure is clearly strengthened by the assumption that Wilkins wrote the first nine scenes, it is not completely dependent on it.

Wilkins's prose is often metrical, as if he were remembering verse drama. Emendation based on *PA* regularly involves the conversion of prose into verse, as well as a wide variety of discretionary decisions. This policy improves the sense in many places (especially Scene 2). Further, Q1 lacks but apparently refers to a short passage displaying Pericles' musical talent that is reconstructed here (Scene 8a). In addition, by following Wilkins's prose, the rationale for Pericles' marriage to Thaisa is shifted from the nobility of his birth to the nobility of his soul (Scene 9). The same strategy of borrowing, in this instance inspired by the suspicion—disputed by other editors—that Q1 reports a politically censored version of the dialogue between Marina and Lysimachus, initially places Lysimachus in a harsher light (Scene 19). Finally, because this edition's scene divisions often differ from those in other modern editions, the play is divided into scenes but not acts.

Although previous scholars and editors have drawn on *PA* and even engaged in conjectural reconstruction of long passages, this version of *Pericles* pursues such an approach more radically and is bound to remain controversial. It can be criticized not only if some of its underlying assumptions are faulty but even if all of them prove correct. The chance is nil that so many emendations, many of them major, will accurately reproduce what was originally written or performed. Yet this is to say no more than that the Oxford edition takes bigger risks than do its predecessors, but on a play where risk taking makes sense. As already noted, if Q1 is a reported text, other modern editions cannot possibly reproduce the original play at all accurately. This edition may deviate more widely than they do from the original version of *Pericles;* then, again, it may well approximate that version more closely.

So that readers can form their own judgments on this question, for each scene the notes provide the act and scene equivalents in most modern texts of *Pericles.* Where scene division departs from the editorial norm, the deviation is explained. More important, the notes also record every emendation drawn from *PA* that significantly alters the meaning, and every emendation that is one line or longer. Rationales for most of these changes are supplied as well. To avoid overloading the notes to the point of unreadability, less substantial changes appear only in the Textual Variants, which provide selected examples of the conversion in this edition of Q1's prose into verse and a complete record of the verbal borrowings from *PA,* with full quotation except where Wilkins's prose is exactly followed.

SELECTED BIBLIOGRAPHY

Archibald, Elizabeth. *Apollonius of Tyre: Medieval and Renaissance Themes and Variations, Including the Text of the "Historia Apollonii Regis Tyri" with an English Translation.* Cambridge, Eng.: Brewer, 1991. A study of the literary tradition that provided the source material for *Pericles.*

Frye, Susan. "Incest and Authority in *Pericles, Prince of Tyre.*" *Incest and the Literary Imagination.* Ed. Elizabeth Barnes. Gainesville: University Press of Florida, 2002. 39–58. Focuses on three key scenes (incest, tournament, reunion) to argue that incest—understood physically, politically, and psychologically—is tied to questions of the royal family's legitimacy.

Gossett, Suzanne. "'You not your child well loving': Text and Family Structure in *Pericles.*" *A Companion to Shakespeare's Works.* IV: *Poems, Problem Comedies, Late*

Plays. Ed. Richard Dutton and Jean E. Howard. Malden, Mass.: Blackwell, 2003. 348–64. The play as exploration of the proper love between parent and daughter (neither excessive nor deficient), perhaps rooted in Shakespeare's own family experience.

Halpern, Richard. *Shakespeare Among the Moderns.* Ithaca, N.Y.: Cornell University Press, 1997. 140–58. Weak internal causal logic of the plot combined with transcendent romance plan as symptomatic response to decaying older social order.

Jordan, Constance. *Shakespeare's Monarchies: Ruler and Subject in the Romances.* Ithaca, N.Y.: Cornell University Press, 1997. 35–67. A political reading of the play in light of humanist theory; the work espouses mixed or limited monarchy against divine right of kings.

Nevo, Ruth. *Shakespeare's Other Language.* New York: Methuen, 1987. 33–61. Antiochus as Pericles' double, revealing the incest fear the protagonist must flee in a journey through other doubles to an ambiguous resolution.

Orkin, Martin. *Local Shakespeares: Proximations and Power.* London: Routledge, 2005. 63–81. *Pericles* as meditation on male unruliness, in this way providing a partial critique of its own patriarchal romance resolution.

Palfrey, Simon. *Late Shakespeare: A New World of Words.* Oxford: Clarendon, 1997. 57–78. *Pericles* as a skeptical reworking of romance; Pericles as post-heroic protagonist, dependent on popular support.

Skeele, David. *Thwarting the Wayward Seas: A Critical and Theatrical History of Shakespeare's "Pericles" in the Nineteenth and Twentieth Centuries.* Newark: University of Delaware Press, 1998. Charts the shifts from nineteenth-century negative critical views combined with occasional spectacle-based productions, through modernist emphasis on the play's unity, to contemporary celebrations of its disunity.

———, ed. *"Pericles": Critical Essays.* New York: Garland, 2000. A collection of criticism beginning with Ben Jonson in the early seventeenth century and of theatrical reviews beginning in the mid-nineteenth. Modern critics include Knight, Felperin, Barber and Wheeler, Kahn, Mullaney, Adelman, and Novy, among others.

Film

Pericles, Prince of Tyre. 1984. Dir. David Hugh Jones. UK. 177 min. Generally praised BBC production, naturalistic by TV-studio standards but not by those of big-budget movies.

Pericles, Prince of Tyre:
A Reconstructed Text

THE PERSONS OF THE PLAY

John GOWER, the Presenter
ANTIOCHUS, King of Antioch
His DAUGHTER
THALIART, a villain
PERICLES, Prince of Tyre
HELICANUS }
AESCHINES } two grave counsellors of Tyre
MARINA, Pericles' daughter
CLEON, Governor of Tarsus
DIONYZA, his wife
LEONINE, a murderer
KING SIMONIDES, of Pentapolis
THAISA, his daughter
Three FISHERMEN, his subjects
Five PRINCES, suitors of Thaisa
A MARSHAL
LYCHORIDA, Thaisa's nurse
A ship MASTER
CERIMON, a physician of Ephesus
PHILEMON, his servant
LYSIMACHUS, Governor of Mytilene
A BAWD
A PANDER
BOULT, servant to Bawd and Pander
DIANA, goddess of chastity
Lords, ladies, pages, messengers, sailors, pirates, knights,
    gentlemen

Scene 1

Enter GOWER[1] [as Prologue]

GOWER To sing a song that old° was sung[2]   *of old*
    From ashes ancient Gower is come,
    Assuming man's infirmities°   *Donning mortal flesh*
    To glad your ear and please your eyes.
5   It hath been sung at festivals,
    On ember-eves and holy-ales,[3]
    And lords and ladies in their lives
    Have read it for restoratives.°   *as a medicine*

Scene 1 (Q1 lacks act and scene divisions; the present edition numbers scenes consecutively throughout, omitting act divisions [see the Textual Note]. Other modern versions treat Gower's monologue as a prologue and start Act 1, Scene 1, at line 43. This edition, however, assumes that the row of heads referred to by Gower and Antiochus ["yon," lines 40, 77] is seen from roughly the same position both times and is first revealed after line 39. But the heads could be visible from the start.)

Location: The palace at Antioch.
1. Fourteenth-century English poet, whose story of Apollonius of Tyre in the eighth book of his *Confessio Amantis* is an important source of the play. See the Introduction.
2. Like most of Gower's choruses in the play, this one is mainly in rhyming tetrameter couplets.
3. *ember-eves*: evenings before periods of religious fasting. *holy-ales*: country festivals.

The purchase° is to make men glorious,   *benefit*
10 *Et bonum quo antiquius eo melius.*[4]
If you, born in these latter times
When wit's more ripe,° accept my rhymes,   *poetry's more advanced*
And that° to hear an old man sing   *And if*
May to your wishes pleasure bring,
15 I life would wish, and that I might
Waste° it for you like taper°-light.   *Use it up / candle*
This'° Antioch, then; Antiochus the Great[5]   *This is*
Built up this city for his chiefest seat,°   *capital*
The fairest in all Syria.
20 I tell you what mine authors° say.   *sources*
This king unto him took a fere°   *mate*
Who died, and left a female heir
So buxom,° blithe, and full of face°   *lively / attractive?*
As° heav'n had lent her all his° grace,   *As if / its*
25 With whom the father liking took,
And her to incest did provoke.
Bad child, worse father, to entice his own
To evil should° be done by none.   *that should*
By custom what they did begin
30 Was with long use account' no sin.[6]
The beauty of this sinful dame
Made many princes thither frame°   *go*
To seek her as a bedfellow,
In marriage pleasures playfellow,
35 Which to prevent he made a law
To keep her still,° and men in awe,   *always*
That whoso asked her for his wife,
His riddle told not,[7] lost his life.
So for her many a wight° did die,   *fellow*
[*A row of heads is revealed*]
40 As yon grim looks do testify.
What now ensues, to th' judgement of your eye
I give, my cause who best can justify.[8]   *Exit*
[*Sennet.*]° Enter [*King*] ANTIOCHUS, *Prince* PERICLES,[9]   *Trumpet*
and [*lords and peers in their richest ornaments*]

ANTIOCHUS   Young Prince of Tyre,[1] you have at large received°   *fully understood*
The danger of the task you undertake.
45 PERICLES   I have, Antiochus, and with a soul
Emboldened with the glory of her praise
Think death no hazard in this enterprise.
ANTIOCHUS   Music!
[*Music sounds*]
Bring in our daughter, clothèd like a bride
50 Fit for th'embracements ev'n of Jove himself,
At whose conception, till Lucina reigned,
Nature this dowry gave to glad her presence:[2]

4. And the older something good is, the better (Latin).
5. *Antioch . . . Antiochus*: Recalling the Maccabee rebellion and the missions of Peter and Paul.
6. *By . . . sin*: When what they started (incest) became a habit, they no longer experienced it as a sin.
7. If he failed to explain Antiochus's riddle.
8. *my . . . justify*: which (your eye's "judgement") will best perceive the truth of my story.
9. *Pericles*: Named after Pericles, the fifth-century

B.C.E. Athenian leader, from Plutarch's *Lives*, or Pyrocles, a protagonist in Sidney's *Arcadia* (1590).
1. *Tyre*: Associated with David and Solomon; captured by a Christian army in the First Crusade.
2. *At . . . presence*: During pregnancy, until my daughter was born (Lucina was the Roman goddess of childbirth, often equated with Diana), nature gave her this dowry to make her presence welcome (or to make her happy).

The senate-house of planets all did sit,
In her their best perfections to knit.[3]

Enter Antiochus' DAUGHTER

55 PERICLES See where she comes, apparelled like the spring,
    Graces her subjects,[4] and her thoughts the king
    Of ev'ry virtue gives° renown to men;   *that gives*
    Her face the book of praises,[5] where is read
    Nothing but curious° pleasures, as° from thence   *delicate / as if*
60 Sorrow were ever razed and testy wrath
    Could never be her mild° companion.   *(modifies "her")*
    You gods that made me man, and sway° in love,   *hold sway*
    That have inflamed desire in my breast
    To taste the fruit of yon celestial tree
65 Or die in the adventure, be my helps,
    As I am son and servant to your will,
    To compass° such a boundless happiness.   *attain*
    ANTIOCHUS Prince Pericles—
    PERICLES That would be son to great Antiochus.
70 ANTIOCHUS Before thee stands this fair Hesperides,
    With golden fruit, but dang'rous to be touched,
        [*He gestures towards the heads*]
    For death-like dragons here affright thee hard.[6]
        [*He gestures towards his* DAUGHTER]
    Her heav'n-like face enticeth thee to view
    Her countless° glory, which desert must gain;   *(like the stars)*
75 And which without desert, because thine eye
    Presumes to reach, all the whole heap° must die.   *your whole body*
    Yon sometimes° famous princes, like thyself   *at one time*
    Drawn by report, advent'rous by° desire,   *taking a risk out of*
    Tell thee with speechless tongues and semblants° bloodless   *appearances*
80 That without covering save yon field of stars
    Here they stand, martyrs slain in Cupid's wars,
    And with dead cheeks advise thee to desist
    From going on° death's net, whom none resist.   *into*
    PERICLES Antiochus, I thank thee, who hath taught
85 My frail mortality to know itself,
    And by those fearful objects to prepare
    This body, like to them, to what I must;[7]
    For death remembered should be like a mirror
    Who tells us life's but breath, to trust it error.
90 I'll make my will then, and, as sick men do,
    Who know the world, see heav'n, but feeling woe
    Grip not at earthly joys as erst° they did,   *previously*
    So I bequeath a happy peace to you
    And all good men, as ev'ry prince should do;
95 My riches to the earth from whence they came,
    [*To the* DAUGHTER] But my unspotted fire of love to you.
    [*To* ANTIOCHUS] Thus ready for the way of life or death,
    I wait the sharpest blow, Antiochus.

---

3. *The . . . knit*: Astrological forces arranged to give her every perfection.
4. With mastery of all human graces.
5. The anthology of all that is commendable.
6. *Before . . . hard*: The Hesperides (here representing Antiochus's Daughter) were daughters of Hesperus inhab-
iting a garden where golden apples grew, whose entrance was patrolled by a dragon. The "golden fruit, but dang'rous to be touched," like "the fruit of yon celestial tree" (line 64), also evokes Eden.
7. *to what I must*: for death.

ANTIOCHUS   Scorning advice, read the conclusion° then,   *riddle*
　　　　[*He angrily throws down the riddle*]
100   Which read and not expounded, 'tis decreed,
　　　　As these before thee, thou thyself shalt bleed.
DAUGHTER [*to* PERICLES]   Of all 'sayed° yet, mayst thou prove   *who have tried (assayed)*
　　　　prosperous;
　　　　Of all 'sayed yet, I wish thee happiness.
PERICLES   Like a bold champion I assume the lists,°   *enter combat*
105   Nor ask advice of any other thought
　　　　But faithfulness and courage.
　　　　　　　[*He takes up and reads aloud*] *the riddle*
　　　　　　I am no viper, yet I feed
　　　　　　On mother's flesh which did me breed.[8]
　　　　　　I sought a husband, in which labour
110　　　　I found that kindness° in a father.   *kinship; affection*
　　　　　　He's father, son, and husband mild;
　　　　　　I mother, wife, and yet his child.
　　　　　　How this may be and yet in two,°   *only two people*
　　　　　　As you will live resolve it you.
115   Sharp physic is the last.[9] [*Aside*] But O, you powers
　　　　That gives heav'n countless eyes° to view men's acts,   *(the stars)*
　　　　Why cloud they not their sights perpetually
　　　　If this be true which makes me pale to read it?
　　　　　　　[*He gazes on the* DAUGHTER]
　　　　Fair glass° of light, I loved you, and could still,   *image*
120   Were not this glorious casket stored with ill.[1]
　　　　But I must tell you now my thoughts revolt,
　　　　For he's no man on whom perfections wait°   *(as servants)*
　　　　That, knowing sin within, will touch the gate.
　　　　You're a fair viol,[2] and your sense° the strings   *senses*
125   Who, fingered to make man his lawful music,
　　　　Would draw heav'n down and all the gods to hearken,
　　　　But, being played upon before your time,
　　　　Hell only danceth at so harsh a chime.
　　　　Good sooth,° I care not for you.   *Truly*
130 ANTIOCHUS   Prince Pericles, touch not,[3] upon thy life,
　　　　For that's an article within our law
　　　　As dang'rous as the rest. Your time's expired.
　　　　Either expound now, or receive your sentence.
PERICLES   Great King,
135   Few love to hear the sins they love to act.
　　　　'Twould braid° yourself too near° for me to tell it.   *upbraid / plainly*
　　　　Who° has a book of all that monarchs do,   *Whoever*
　　　　He's more secure to keep it shut than shown,
　　　　For vice repeated, like the wand'ring wind,
140   Blows dust in others' eyes to spread itself;
　　　　And yet the end of all is bought thus dear,
　　　　The breath is gone, and the sore eyes see clear
　　　　To stop the air would hurt them.[4] The blind mole casts

---

8. Vipers were thought to eat their way out of their mother's body at birth.
9. This final threat is harsh medicine.
1. If your body weren't so sinful.
2. Stringed instrument; vial.
3. Perhaps Pericles makes some movement that Anti-

ochus misinterprets (further Edenic overtones).
4. *For vice . . . them:* For with the breath used to speak word of others' sins, one blows irritating dust in the eyes of the offenders. But the consequence is merely the speaker's death, since the offenders nevertheless see well enough to stop the news-spreading breath.

Copped° hills towards heav'n to tell° the earth is thronged   Peaked / tell that
145 By man's oppression, and the poor worm doth die for't.[5]
Kings are earth's gods; in vice their law's their will,
And if Jove stray, who dares say Jove doth ill?
It is enough you know,° and it is fit,   (that I know)
What being more known grows worse,[6] to smother° it.   conceal
150 All love the womb that their first being bred;[7]
Then give my tongue like leave to love my head.
    ANTIOCHUS [aside]   Heav'n, that I had thy head! He's found the
        meaning.
But I will gloze° with him. —Young Prince of Tyre,   dissemble
Though by the tenor of our strict edict,
155 Your exposition misinterpreting,
We might proceed to cancel° of your days,   to the termination
Yet hope, succeeding from so fair a tree[8]
As your fair self, doth tune° us otherwise.   move
Forty days longer we do respite you,
160 If by which time our secret be undone,
This mercy shows we'll joy in such a son.
And until then your entertain° shall be   entertainment
As doth befit your worth and our degree.
        [Flourish. Exeunt.] Manet PERICLES solus°   Pericles remains alone
    PERICLES   How courtesy would seem° to cover sin   lie
165 When what is done is like an hypocrite,
The which is good in nothing but in sight.°   appearance
If it be true that I interpret false,
Then were it certain you were not so bad
As with foul incest to abuse your soul,
170 Where now you're both a father and a son
By your uncomely claspings with your child—
Which pleasures fits a husband, not a father—
And she, an eater of her mother's flesh,
By the defiling of her parents' bed,
175 And both like serpents are, who though they feed
On sweetest flowers, yet they poison breed.
Antioch, farewell, for wisdom sees those men°   men who
Blush not in actions blacker than the night
Will 'schew no course° to keep them from the light.   eschew no means
180 One sin, I know, another doth provoke.
Murder's as near to lust as flame to smoke.
Poison and treason are the hands of sin,
Ay, and the targets° to put off the shame.   shields
Then, lest my life be cropped to keep you clear,°   (of blame)
185 By flight I'll shun the danger which I fear.   Exit
        Enter ANTIOCHUS
    ANTIOCHUS   He hath found the meaning, for the which we mean
To have his head. He must not live
To trumpet forth my infamy, nor tell the world
Antiochus doth sin in such a loathèd manner,

---

5. *The blind . . . for't:* When we blindly protest against the injustice of our superiors, we die (with "mole" meaning "worm"), or, less likely, innocent creatures suffer (here, the "mole" is different from the "worm" and may even destroy it).
6. Since bad deeds become worse for being known.
7. All love the daughter they raised when young (hence,

hinting at incest). The obvious meaning—all love their mother's womb—either is nonincestuous or gets the incest backward.
8. Hope of a correct answer (an heir), with the successful answer (succession) coming from such a fine specimen (Pericles' regal lineage).

190 And therefore instantly this prince must die,
For by his fall my honour must keep high.
Who attends us there?
　　　　　　Enter THALIART

THALIART　　　　　　Doth your highness call?
ANTIOCHUS　Thaliart, you are of our chamber,° Thaliart,　　*my chamberlain*
And to your secrecy our mind partakes°　　　　　　　*imparts*
195 Her° private actions. For your faithfulness　　　　　　*Its*
We will advance you, Thaliart. Behold,
Here's poison, and here's gold.
We hate the Prince of Tyre, and thou must kill him.
It fits° thee not to ask the reason. Why?　　　　　　*befits*
200 Because we bid it. Say, is it done?
THALIART　My lord, 'tis done.
ANTIOCHUS　Enough.
　　　　　　Enter a MESSENGER [*hastily*]
Let your breath cool yourself, telling your haste.[9]
MESSENGER　Your majesty, Prince Pericles is fled.　　　*[Exit]*
ANTIOCHUS [*to* THALIART]　As thou wilt live, fly after; like an
205 　　arrow
Shot from a well-experienced archer hits
The mark his eye doth level° at, so thou　　　　　　*aim*
Never return unless it be to say
'Your majesty, Prince Pericles is dead.'
210 THALIART　If I can get him in my pistol's° length°　(*anachronism*) / *range*
I'll make him sure° enough. Farewell, your highness.　*unthreatening (dead)*
ANTIOCHUS　Thaliart, adieu.　　　　　　*[Exit* THALIART*]*
　　　　　Till Pericles be dead
My heart can lend no succour to my head.
　　　　　[Exit. The heads are concealed]

Scene 2

Enter PERICLES [*distempered*] *with his lords*
PERICLES　Let none disturb us.　　　　　*[Exeunt lords]*
　　　　　Why should this change of thoughts,°　*changed state of mind*
The sad companion, dull-eyed melancholy,
Be my so used° a guest as not an hour　　　　　*accustomed*
In the day's glorious walk or peaceful night,
5 The tomb where grief should sleep, can breed me quiet?
Here pleasures court mine eyes, and mine eyes shun them,
And danger, which I feared, 's° at Antioch,　　　　　*is*
Whose arm seems far too short to hit me here.
Yet neither pleasure's art can joy my spirits,
10 Nor yet care's author's distance comfort me.
Then it is thus: the passions of the mind,°　　　　*obsessions*
That have their first conception by misdread,°　　　*fear*
Have after-nourishment and life by care,°　　　　*worry*
And what was first but fear what might be done
15 Grows elder now, and cares it be not done.[1]
And so with me. The great Antiochus,

---

9. Use your rapid breathing to cool yourself by explaining the reason for your haste.
Scene 2 (Act 1, Scene 2, in other modern editions)
Location: The palace at Tyre.

1. *And what . . . done:* And what starts out as simple fear matures into a more rational concern for safety.

'Gainst whom I am too little to contend,
Since he's so great can° make his will his act, *that he can*
Will think me speaking though I swear to silence,
20 Nor boots it° me to say I honour him *does it help*
If he suspect I may dishonour him.
And what may make him blush in being known,
He'll stop the course by which it might be known.
With hostile forces he'll o'erspread the land,
25 And with th'ostent° of war will look so huge *display*
Amazement° shall drive courage from the state, *Terror*
Our men be vanquished ere they do resist,
And subjects punished that ne'er thought offence,
Which care of them, not pity of myself,
30 Who am no more but as the tops of trees
Which fence° the roots they grow by and defend them, *shield*
Makes both my body pine and soul to languish,
And punish that° before that he would punish.² *(myself)*
  Enter all the LORDS, [*among them old* HELICANUS,] *to*
  PERICLES
FIRST LORD Joy and all comfort in your sacred breast!
35 SECOND LORD And keep your mind peaceful³ and comfortable.
HELICANUS Peace, peace, and give experience tongue.
 [*To* PERICLES] You⁴ do not well so to abuse yourself,
To waste your body here with pining sorrow,
Upon whose safety doth depend the lives
40 And the prosperity of a whole kingdom.
'Tis ill in you to do it, and no less
Ill in your council not to contradict it.
They do abuse the King that flatter him,
For flatt'ry is the bellows blows° up sin; *that blows*
45 The thing the which is flattered, but a spark,
To which that wind gives heat and stronger glowing;
Whereas reproof, obedient and in order,
Fits kings as they are men, for they may err.
When Signor Sooth⁵ here does proclaim a peace
50 He flatters you, makes war upon your life.
  [*He kneels*]
Prince, pardon me, or strike me if you please.
I cannot be much lower than my knees.
PERICLES All leave us else;° but let your cares o'erlook *except Helicanus*
What shipping and what lading's⁶ in our haven,
And then return to us.   [*Exeunt* LORDS]
55   Helicane, thou
Hast movèd us. What seest thou in our looks?
HELICANUS An angry brow, dread lord.
PERICLES If there be such a dart° in princes' frowns, *danger*
How durst thy tongue move anger to our brows?
HELICANUS How dares the plants look up to heav'n from
60 whence

---

2. *before . . . punish:* before he punishes me ("that").
3. Q1 has "And keep your mind till you return to us peaceful," a phrase that anticipates Pericles' "return to us" (line 55). The omission here eliminates the speaker's clairvoyance about a trip that no one else contemplates until line 111.

4. Lines 37–42 are not in Q1 but are adapted from Wilkins's *Painfull Adventures* (*PA*). They explain why Helicanus thinks Pericles has been, but should not be, flattered.
5. Mock name for a flatterer, a soother of egos.
6. *let . . . lading's:* look carefully to find out what vessels are coming and going and what cargo is.

They have their nourishment?

PERICLES   Thou knowest I have pow'r to take thy life from thee.

HELICANUS   I have ground the axe myself; do you but strike the
blow.

PERICLES [*lifting him up*]   Rise, prithee, rise. Sit down. Thou art
no flatterer,
65   I thank thee for it, and the heav'ns forbid
That kings should let their ears hear their faults hid.
Fit counsellor and servant for a prince,
Who by thy wisdom mak'st a prince thy servant,
What wouldst thou have me do?

HELICANUS   To bear with patience
70   Such griefs as you do lay upon yourself.

PERICLES   Thou speak'st like a physician, Helicanus,
That ministers a potion unto me
That thou wouldst tremble to receive thyself.
Attend me,° then. I went to Antioch,   Listen to me
75   Where, as thou know'st, against the face of death
I sought the purchase° of a glorious beauty   acquisition
From whence an issue I might propagate,
As children are heav'n's blessings: to parents, objects;[7]
Are arms° to princes, and bring joys to subjects.   weapons
80   Her face was to mine eye beyond all wonder,
The rest—hark in thine ear—as black as incest,
Which by my knowledge found, the sinful father
Seemed not to strike, but smooth.° But thou know'st this,   smooth over
'Tis time to fear when tyrants seems to kiss;
85   Which fear so grew in me I hither fled
Under the covering of careful night,
Who seemed my good protector, and being here
Bethought me what was past, what might succeed.°   happen next
I knew him tyrannous, and tyrants' fears
90   Decrease not, but grow faster than the years.
And should he doubt°—as doubt no° doubt he doth—   suspect / as no
That I should open° to the list'ning air   declare
How many worthy princes' bloods were shed
To keep his bed of blackness unlaid ope,
95   To lop that doubt he'll fill this land with arms,
And make pretence of wrong that I have done him,
When all for mine—if I may call—offence
Must feel war's blow, who° spares not innocence;   which
Which love to all, of which thyself art one,
Who now reproved'st me for't—
100   HELICANUS   Alas, sir.

PERICLES   Drew sleep out of mine eyes, blood from my cheeks,
Musings into my mind, with thousand doubts,
How I might stop this tempest ere it came,
And, finding little comfort to relieve them,°   (his subjects)
105   I thought it princely charity to grieve them.°   (by my sorrow)

HELICANUS   Well, my lord, since you have giv'n me leave to
speak,
Freely will I speak. Antiochus you fear,

---

7. Objects of affection. This line, composed by the Oxford editors, fills a long-recognized gap in Q1 between lines
77 and 79.

And justly too, I think, you fear the tyrant,
Who either by public war or private treason
110 Will take away your life.
Therefore, my lord, go travel for a while,
Till that his rage and anger be forgot,
Or destinies do cut his thread of life.[8]
Your rule direct° to any; if to me,   assign
115 Day serves not light more faithful than I'll be.
PERICLES   I do not doubt thy faith,
But should he in my absence wrong thy liberties?°   jurisdictions
HELICANUS   We'll mingle our bloods together in the earth
From whence we had our being and our birth.
120 PERICLES   Tyre, I now look from thee then, and to Tarsus°   (St. Paul's birthplace)
Intend° my travel, where I'll hear from thee,   Direct
And by whose letters I'll dispose myself.
The care I had and have of subjects' good
On thee I lay, whose wisdom's strength can bear it.
125 I'll take thy word for faith, not ask thine oath;
Who° shuns not to break one will sure crack both.   He who
But in our orbs° we'll live so round° and safe   places / prudently
That time of both this truth shall ne'er convince:°   refute
Thou showed'st a subject's shine, I a true prince.°   prince's
                                                                                    Exeunt

Scene 3

Enter THALIART

THALIART   So this is Tyre, and this the court. Here must I kill
King Pericles, and if I do it and am caught I am like to be
hanged abroad, but[1] if I do it not, I am sure to be hanged at
home. 'Tis dangerous. Well, I perceive he was a wise fellow
5 and had good discretion that, being bid to ask what he would
of the King, desired he might know none of his secrets.[2] Now
do I see he had some reason for't, for if a king bid a man be a
villain, he's bound by the indenture° of his oath to be one.   servant's contract
Hush, here comes the lords of Tyre.

Enter HELICANUS [*and*] AESCHINES, *with
other lords*

10 HELICANUS   You shall not need, my fellow peers of Tyre,
Further to question of your King's departure.
His sealed° commission left in trust with me   (with royal wax)
Does speak sufficiently he's gone to travel.
THALIART [*aside*]   How? The King gone?
15 HELICANUS   If further yet you will be satisfied
Why, as it were unlicensed of your loves,°   without your approval
He would depart, I'll give some light unto you.
Being at Antioch—
THALIART [*aside*]   What from Antioch?
HELICANUS   Royal Antiochus, on what cause I know not,
20 Took some displeasure at him—at least he judged so—
And doubting lest° that he had erred or sinned,   And fearing
To show his sorrow he'd correct° himself;   he wished to punish

8. In Greek mythology, a person died when the three
Fates "cut his thread of life."
Scene 3 (Act 1, Scene 3)
Location: The palace at Tyre.
1. *if . . . but*: this is a conjectural editorial addition that

semantically balances Thaliart's reflection on the consequences of failure. *like*: likely. *abroad*: in Tyre.
2. According to Plutarch's *Lives* and Barnabe Riche in
Souldiers Wishe to Britons Welfare (1604), the poet Philip-
pides made this request of King Lysimachus of Thrace.

So puts himself unto the ship-man's toil,
With whom each minute threatens life or death.

25 THALIART [*aside*]   Well, I perceive I shall not be hanged now,
Although I would.³
But since he's gone, the King's ears it must please
He scaped° the land to perish on the seas.   °escaped
I'll present myself.—Peace to the lords of Tyre.

30 Lord Thaliart am I, of Antioch.⁴
HELICANUS   Lord Thaliart of Antioch is welcome.
THALIART   From King Antiochus I come
With message unto princely Pericles,
But since my landing I have understood
35 Your lord's betook himself to unknown travels.
Now my message must return from whence it came.
HELICANUS   We have no reason to enquire it,
Commended° to our master, not to us.   °Directed
Yet ere you shall depart, this we desire:
40 As friends to Antioch, we may feast° in Tyre.   *Exeunt*   °prepare a feast for you

Scene 4

Enter CLEON, *the Governor of Tarsus, with* [DIONYZA]
his wife, and others

CLEON   My Dionyza, shall we rest us here
And, by relating tales of others' griefs,
See if 'twill teach us to forget our own?
DIONYZA   That were to blow at fire in hope to quench it,
5 For who digs° hills because they do aspire   °whoever digs up
Throws down one mountain to cast up a higher.
O my distressèd lord, e'en such our griefs are;
Here they're but felt and seen with midges' eyes,°   °as small matters
But like to groves, being topped° they higher rise.   °pruned
10 CLEON   O Dionyza,
Who wanteth food and will not say he wants it,
Or can conceal his hunger till he famish?
Our tongues our sorrows dictate to sound° deep   °proclaim; plumb
Our woes into the air, our eyes to weep
15 Till lungs fetch breath that may proclaim them louder,
That, if heav'n slumber while their° creatures want,   °(heaven's)
They° may awake their° helps to comfort them.   °(creatures) / °(heaven's)
I'll then discourse our woes, felt sev'ral years,
And, wanting° breath to speak, help me with tears.   °when I'm out of
20 DIONYZA   As you think best, sir.
CLEON   This Tarsus o'er which I have the government,
A city o'er whom plenty held full hand,°   °generously presided
For riches strewed herself ev'n in the streets,
Whose tow'rs bore heads so high they kissed the clouds,
25 And strangers ne'er beheld but wondered at,°   °without admiring
Whose men and dames so jetted° and adorned°   °strutted / °(themselves)
Like one another's glass to trim them¹ by;
Their tables were stored full to glad the sight,
And not so much to feed on as delight.

---

3. Even if I return home (?); even if that's what I wanted.
4. This line is added by the Oxford editors to explain how Helicanus knows who Thaliart is. Alternatively, Helicanus might simply recognize a leading lord of the dominant regional power.

Scene 4 (Act 1, Scene 4)
Location: Tarsus.
1. Mirror to dress themselves. (Everyone was a model of fashion.)

30   All poverty was scorned, and pride so great
    The name of help grew odious to repeat.
  DIONYZA   O, 'tis too true.
  CLEON   But see what heav'n can do by this our change.
    Those mouths who but of late° earth, sea, and air   *just recently*
35   Were all too little to content and please,
    Although they gave their creatures in abundance,
    As houses are defiled for want° of use,   *by lack*
    They are now starved for want of exercise.
    Those palates who, not yet two summers younger,
40   Must have inventions° to delight the taste   *Demanded novel foods*
    Would now be glad of bread and beg for it.
    Those mothers who to nuzzle up° their babes   *raise*
    Thought naught too curious° are ready now   *exquisite*
    To eat those little darlings whom they loved.
45   So sharp are hunger's teeth that man and wife
    Draw lots who first shall die to lengthen life.°   *(of the other)*
    Here weeping stands a lord, there lies a lady dying,
    Here many sink, yet those which see them fall
    Have scarce strength left to give them burial.
50   Is not this true?
  DIONYZA   Our cheeks and hollow eyes do witness it.
  CLEON   O, let those cities that of plenty's cup
    And her prosperities so largely taste
    With their superfluous riots,° heed these tears!   *excessive indulgence*
55   The misery of Tarsus may be theirs.
        Enter a [fainting] LORD *[of Tarsus slowly]*
  LORD   Where's the Lord Governor?
  CLEON   Here. Speak out thy sorrows which thou bring'st in
    haste,
    For comfort is too far for us t'expect.
  LORD   We have descried upon our neighbouring shore
60   A portly sail° of ships make hitherward.   *stately fleet*
  CLEON   I thought as much.
    One sorrow never comes but brings an heir
    That may succeed as his inheritor,
    And so in ours. Some neighbour nation,
65   Taking advantage of our misery,
    Hath stuffed these hollow vessels with their power°   *soldiers*
    To beat us down, the which are down already,
    And make a conquest of unhappy men,°   *(me: Q1)*
    Whereas no glory's got to overcome.[2]
70   LORD   That's the least fear,° for by the semblance   *not to be feared*
    Of their white flags displayed they bring us peace,
    And come to us as favourers, not foes.
  CLEON   Thou speak'st like him's untutored to repeat;[3]
    Who makes the fairest show means most deceit.
75   But bring they° what they will and what they can,   *let them bring*
    What need we fear?
    Our grave's the low'st,° and we are half-way there.   *lowest we can go*
    Go tell their gen'ral we attend° him here   *await*
    To know for what he comes, and whence he comes.

---

2. Where there's no glory in winning.
3. Like him who hasn't learned (the following lesson) by heart.

80   LORD   I go, my lord.   [*Exit*]

CLEON   Welcome is peace, if he on peace consist;°   *resolve*

   If wars, we are unable to resist.

        Enter [*the* LORD *again conducting*] PERICLES *with atten-
        dants*

PERICLES [*to* CLEON]   Lord Governor, for so we hear you are,

   Let not our ships and number of our men

85   Be like a beacon fixed t'amaze° your eyes.   *to terrify*

   We have heard your miseries as far as Tyre,

   Since entering your unshut gates have witnessed

   The widowed[4] desolation of your streets;

   Nor come we to add sorrow to your hearts,

90   But to relieve them of their heavy load;

   And these our ships, you happily° may think   *perhaps*

   Are like the Trojan horse was fraught within

   With bloody veins importing overthrow,[5]

   Are stored with corn to make your needy bread,

95   And give them life whom hunger starved half dead.

ALL OF TARSUS [*falling on their knees and weeping*]   The gods of

      Greece protect you, and we'll pray for you!

PERICLES   Arise, I pray you, rise.

   We do not look for reverence but for love,

   And harbourage for me, my ships and men.

100   CLEON   The which when any shall not gratify,

   Or pay you with unthankfulness in thought,

   Be it our wives, our children, or ourselves,

   The curse of heav'n and men succeed° their evils!   *follow from*

   Till when—the which I hope shall ne'er be seen—

105   Your grace is welcome to our town and us.

PERICLES   Which welcome we'll accept, feast here a while,

   Until our stars that frown lend us a smile.   *Exeunt*

Scene 5

Enter GOWER

GOWER   Here have you seen a mighty king

   His child, iwis,° to incest bring;   *certainly*

   A better prince° and benign lord   *(Pericles)*

   Prove awe-full° both in deed and word.   *worthy of respect*

5   Be quiet then, as men should be,

   Till he hath passed necessity.[1]

   I'll show you those° in trouble's reign,   *those who*

   Losing a mite, a mountain gain.

   The good in conversation,[2]

10   To whom I give my benison,°   *blessing*

   Is still at Tarsus where each man

   Thinks all is writ he speken can,[3]

   And to remember what he does

---

4. *Since . . . widowed:* This line, adapted from *PA*, replaces Q1's "And seene the"; the substitution prevents the inference that Pericles has "seen" Tarsus's "desolation" "as far as Tyre."

5. *was . . . overthrow:* was laden ("fraught") with Greek soldiers ("bloody veins") who sacked the city.

Scene 5 (Other editions treat Gower's monologue as a prologue to Act 2 and start Act 2, Scene 1, at line 41. The present edition, however, interprets "here he comes" [line

39] as evidence that the scene does not change.) Location: The seashore at Pentapolis, which was the coastal area of Cyrenaica, in the northeast corner of what is now Libya. This scene locates it in Greece, however (line 100).

1. *necessity:* the suffering that is his lot.

2. The good man (Pericles) in conduct.

3. Archaic (as is often the case in Gower's speeches): Thinks all Pericles says is holy scripture ("writ").

His statue build to make him glorious.
15 But tidings to the contrary
Are brought your eyes. What need speak I?
Dumb show.[4]
Enter at one door PERICLES *talking with* CLEON, *all the
train with them. Enter at another door a gentleman with
a letter to* PERICLES. PERICLES *shows the letter to* CLEON.
PERICLES *gives the messenger a reward, and knights him.
Exeunt [with their trains]* PERICLES *at one door and*
CLEON *at another*
Good Helicane that stayed at home,
Not to eat honey like a drone
From others' labours, for that he strive
20 To killen bad, keep good alive,
And to fulfil his prince' desire
Sent word of all that haps in Tyre;
How Thaliart came full bent with° sin   intent on
And hid intent to murdren him,
25 And that in Tarsus was not best
Longer for him to make his rest.
He deeming so put forth to seas,
Where when men been° there's seldom ease,   are
For now the wind begins to blow;
30 Thunder above and deeps below
Makes such unquiet that the ship
Should° house him safe is wrecked and split,   Which should
And he, good prince, having all lost,
By waves from coast to coast is tossed.
35 All perishen of man, of pelf,°   goods
Ne aught escapend° but himself,   Nothing escaping
Till fortune, tired with doing bad,
Threw him ashore to give him glad.°   joy
Enter PERICLES *wet [and half-naked]*
And here he comes. What shall be next
40 Pardon old Gower; this 'longs[5] the text.   [*Exit*]
[*Thunder and lightning*]
PERICLES   Yet cease your ire, you angry stars of heaven!
Wind, rain, and thunder, remember earthly man
Is but a substance that must yield to you,
And I, as fits my nature, do obey you.
45 Alas, the seas hath cast me on the rocks,
Washed me from shore to shore, and left my breath
Nothing to think on but ensuing death.
Let it suffice the greatness of your powers
To have bereft a prince of all his fortunes,
50 And, having thrown him from your wat'ry grave,
Here to have death in peace is all he'll crave.
[*He sits.*]
Enter [two poor] FISHERMEN *[one the* MASTER, *the other
his man]*
MASTER [*calling*]   What ho, Pilch![6]

4. In Renaissance drama, a brief pantomime performance used to advance the plot.
5. Continuing would lengthen Gower's speech too
much; or, *'longs:* belongs to.

6. Nickname derived from a rustic leather garment. The
nicknames, homely references, and social critiques in this
scene have a distinctively English feel.

SECOND FISHERMAN [*calling*]   Ha, come and bring away the nets.

MASTER [*calling*]   What, Patchbreech,° I say!   *(another nickname)*
  [*Enter a* THIRD FISHERMAN *with a hood upon his head*
  and a filthy leathern pelt upon his back, unseemly clad,
  and homely to behold. He brings nets to dry and repair]

55   THIRD FISHERMAN   What say you, master?

MASTER   Look how thou stirrest now. Come away, or I'll fetch
  th' with a wanion.[7]

THIRD FISHERMAN   Faith, master, I am thinking of the poor men
  that were cast away before us° even now.   *in our sight*

60   MASTER   Alas, poor souls, it grieved my heart to hear what pitiful
  cries they made to us to help them when, well-a-day,° we could   *alas*
  scarce help ourselves.

THIRD FISHERMAN   Nay, master, said not I as much when I saw
  the porpoise how he bounced and tumbled?° They say they're   *(predictive of storms)*

65   half fish, half flesh. A plague on them, they ne'er come but I look
  to be washed.° Master, I marvel how the fishes live in the sea. *(by a storm)*

MASTER   Why, as men do a-land°—the great ones eat up the   *on land*
  little ones. I can compare our rich misers to nothing so fitly as
  to a whale: a° plays and tumbles, driving the poor fry before   *he*

70   him, and at last devours them all at a mouthful. Such whales
  have I heard on° o'th' land, who never leave gaping° till they   *of / close their mouths*
  swallowed the whole parish: church, steeple, bells, and all.

PERICLES [*aside*]   A pretty moral.

THIRD FISHERMAN   But, master, if I had been the sexton, I would

75   have been that day in the belfry.

SECOND FISHERMAN   Why, man?

THIRD FISHERMAN   Because he should have swallowed me, too,
  and when I had been in his belly I would have kept such a
  jangling of the bells that he should never have left till he cast° *vomited*

80   bells, steeple, church, and parish up again. But if the good
  King Simonides were of my mind—

PERICLES [*aside*]   Simonides?

THIRD FISHERMAN   We would purge the land of these drones that
  rob the bee of her honey.

85   PERICLES [*aside*]   How from the finny subject° of the sea[8]   *citizens*
  These fishers tell th'infirmities of men,
  And from their wat'ry empire recollect°   *gather*
  All that may men approve or men detect!°   *expose*
  [*Coming forward*] Peace be at your labour, honest fishermen.

90   SECOND FISHERMAN   Honest, good fellow? What's that? If it be a day
  fits you, scratch't out of the calendar, and nobody look after it.[9]

PERICLES   May° see the sea hath cast upon your coast—   *You may*

SECOND FISHERMAN   What a drunken knave was the sea to cast
  thee in our way![1]

95   PERICLES   A man, whom both the waters and the wind
  In that vast tennis-court hath made the ball
  For them to play upon,° entreats you pity him.   *with*
  He asks of you that never used to beg.

7. *Look . . . wanion:* Look how quick you are (ironic).
Hurry along, or I'll beat you with a vengeance.
8. Although the Fishermen speak in prose, Pericles
uses verse.
9. *Honest . . . after it:* If "honest" were a day in the calendar that suited someone in your sorry state, you could
remove it without anyone noticing; honesty is so rare

already, no one would notice its departure. (Perhaps a
line is missing before line 89, in which Pericles wishes
the Fishermen good day.)
1. Like St. Peter, the Fishermen are literally fishers of
men, who help save Pericles from the sea. Their discussion of whales also evokes the tale of Jonah. The scene is
full of biblical echoes.

MASTER No, friend, cannot you beg? Here's them° in our coun- °*There are those*
100   try of Greece gets° more with begging than we can do with °*who get*
    working.

SECOND FISHERMAN Canst thou catch any fishes, then?

PERICLES I never practised it.

SECOND FISHERMAN Nay, then thou wilt starve, sure; for here's
105   nothing to be got nowadays unless thou canst fish for't.° °*get it by deception*

PERICLES What I have been, I have forgot to know,
    But what I am, want teaches me to think on:
    A man thronged up° with cold; my veins are chill, °*overwhelmed*
    And have no more of life than may suffice
110   To give my tongue that heat to crave your help,
    Which if you shall refuse, when I am dead,
    For that° I am a man, pray see me burièd. °*Because*
    [*He falls down*]

MASTER Die, quotha?° Now, gods forbid't an° I have a gown °*says he / if*
    here! [*To* PERICLES, *lifting him up from the ground*] Come, put
115   it on, keep thee warm. Now, afore me,° a handsome fellow! °*on my word*
    Come, thou shalt go home, and we'll have flesh for holidays,
    fish for fasting-days, and moreo'er puddings° and flapjacks, and °*sausages*
    thou shalt be welcome.

PERICLES I thank you, sir.

120 SECOND FISHERMAN Hark you, my friend, you said you could
    not beg?

PERICLES I did but crave.

SECOND FISHERMAN But crave? Then I'll turn craver too, an so I
    shall scape whipping.° °*(for begging)*

125 PERICLES Why, are all your beggars whipped, then?

SECOND FISHERMAN O, not all, my friend, not all; for if all your° °*the*
    beggars were whipped I would wish no better office than to be
    beadle.[2]

MASTER[3] Thine office, knave—

130 SECOND FISHERMAN Is to draw up the other nets. I'll go.
                    [*Exit with* THIRD FISHERMAN]

PERICLES [*aside*] How well this honest mirth becomes their
    labour!

MASTER [*seating himself by* PERICLES] Hark you, sir, do you
    know where ye are?

135 PERICLES Not well.

MASTER Why, I'll tell you. This is called Pentapolis, and our
    king the good Simonides.

PERICLES 'The good Simonides' do you call him?

MASTER Ay, sir, and he deserves so to be called for his peaceable
140   reign and good government.

PERICLES He is a happy king, since from his subjects
    He gains the name of good by his government.
    How far is his court distant from this shore?

MASTER Marry,° sir, some half a day's journey. And I'll tell you, °*To be sure*
145   he hath a fair daughter, and tomorrow is her birthday, and
    there are princes and knights come from all parts of the world
    to joust and tourney for her love.

---

2. Minor parish official who administered corporal punishment.
3. To improve the motivation of the Second Fisherman's

exit, this edition substitutes "MASTER . . . I'll go" for Q1's
continuation of the Second Fisherman's speech: "But
Master, I'll go draw up the net."

PERICLES   Were but my fortunes answerable
  To my desires I could wish to make one° there.   *be one of the princes*
150 MASTER   O, sir, things must be as they may, and what a man
  cannot get himself, he may lawfully deal for with his wife's soul.[4]
    Enter the [other] two FISHERMEN drawing up a net
SECOND FISHERMAN   Help, master, help! Here's a fish hangs in
  the net like a poor man's right in the law; 'twill hardly come out.
    [Before help comes, up comes their prize]
  Ha, bots on't,° 'tis come at last, and 'tis turned to a rusty armour.   *a pox (plague) on it*
155 PERICLES   An armour, friends? I pray you let me see it.
  [*Aside*] Thanks, fortune, yet that after all thy crosses°   *hardships*
  Thou giv'st me somewhat to repair my losses,
  And though° it was mine own, part of my heritage   *Even though*
  Which my dead father did bequeath to me
160 With this strict charge ev'n as he left his life:
  'Keep it, my Pericles; it hath been a shield
  'Twixt me and death,' and pointed to this brace,°   *arm armor*
  'For that° it saved me, keep it. In like necessity,   *Because*
  The which the Gods forfend,° the same may defend thee.'   *forbid*
165 It kept° where I kept, I so dearly loved it,   *remained*
  Till the rough seas that spares not any man
  Took it in rage, though calmed have giv'n't again.
  I thank thee for't. My shipwreck now's no ill,
  Since I have here my° father gave in 's° will.   *what my / his*
170 MASTER   What mean you, sir?
PERICLES   To beg of you, kind friends, this coat of worth,
  For it was sometime target° to a king.   *once a shield*
  I know it by this mark. He loved me dearly,
  And for his sake I wish the having of it,
175 And that you'd guide me to your sov'reign's court,
  Where with't I may appear a gentleman.
  And if that ever my low fortune's better,
  I'll pay your bounties,° till then rest your debtor.   *repay your generosity*
MASTER   Why, wilt thou tourney for the lady?
180 PERICLES   I'll show the virtue I have learned in arms.
MASTER   Why, d'ye take it, and the gods give thee good on't!
SECOND FISHERMAN   Ay, but hark you, my friend, 'twas we that
  made° up this garment through the rough seams of the waters.   *raised*
  There are certain condolements,[5] certain vails.° I hope, sir, if   *tips*
185 you thrive, you'll remember from whence you had this.
PERICLES   Believe't, I will.
  By your furtherance I'm clothed in steel,
  And spite of all the rapture° of the sea   *plundering*
  This jewel holds his building° on my arm.   *its place*
190 Unto thy° value I will mount myself   *(the jewel's)*
  Upon a courser° whose delightsome steps   *a horse*
  Shall make the gazer joy to see him tread.
  Only, my friends, I yet am unprovided
  Of a pair of bases.[6]
195 SECOND FISHERMAN   We'll sure provide. Thou shalt have my

---

4. *what . . . soul:* probably ironic: when a man can no
longer "get" (make a living; have children), he can legitimately do so by persuading his "wife's soul" (her conscience; also, "his wife's hole") to trade (prostitute)
herself (with men who will "get"—beget—children with
her). The additions of "himself" and "with" (line 151) in
this edition make the meaning more accessible.
5. Blunder for "dole."
6. Skirts for armored knights on horseback.

best gown to make thee a pair, and I'll bring thee to the court
myself.

PERICLES   Then honour be but equal to my will,
This day I'll rise, or else add ill to ill.

[*Exeunt with nets and armour*]

Scene 6

[*Sennet.*] *Enter* KING SIMONIDES *and* THAISA *with*
[LORDS *in*] *attendance* [*and sit on two thrones*]

KING SIMONIDES   Are the knights ready to begin the triumph?°   *tournament*
FIRST LORD   They are, my liege,
And stay° your coming to present themselves.   *await*
KING SIMONIDES   Return° them we are ready; and our daughter,   *Answer*
5 In honour of whose birth these triumphs are,
Sits here like beauty's child, whom nature gat°   *conceived*
For men to see and, seeing, wonder at.

[*Exit one*]

THAISA   It pleaseth you, my father, to express
My commendations great, whose merit's less.
10 KING SIMONIDES   It's fit it should be so, for princes° are   *rulers*
A model which heav'n makes like to itself.
As jewels lose their glory if neglected,
So princes their renown, if not respected.
'Tis now your office, daughter, to entertain°   *review*
15 The labour of each knight in his device.[1]
THAISA   Which, to preserve mine honour, I'll perform.

[*Flourish.*] *The first knight passes by* [*richly armed, and
his page before him, bearing his device on his shield,
delivers it to the Lady* THAISA]

KING SIMONIDES   Who is the first that doth prefer° himself?   *present*
THAISA   A knight of Sparta, my renownèd father,
And the device he bears upon his shield
20 Is a black Ethiop reaching at the sun.
The word, *Lux tua vita mihi.*[2]

[*She presents it to the* KING]

KING SIMONIDES   He loves you well that holds his life of° you.   *receives his life from*
[*He returns it to the page, who exits with the first
knight.*]
[*Flourish.*] *The second knight* [*passes by richly armed,
and his page before him, bearing his device on his
shield, delivers it to the Lady* THAISA]
Who is the second that presents himself?
THAISA   A prince of Macedon, my royal father,
25 And the device he bears upon his shield
An armèd knight that's conquered by a lady.
The motto thus: *Piùe per dolcezza che per forza.*[3]

[*She presents it to the* KING]

KING SIMONIDES   You win him more by lenity than force.[4]

Scene 6 (Act 2, Scene 2)
Location: Pentapolis, area near the tournament arena,
including a reviewing stand.
1. The ingenuity of each knight's emblem on his shield.
2. Your light is my life (Latin).

3. More by gentleness than by force (Italian). Q1 precedes this phrase with the words "in Spanish"—probably
an error by the reporter. (See the Textual Note.)
4. Not in Q1; adapted from *PA*. Simonides comments
on three of the other five mottoes.

[*He returns it to the page, who exits with the second knight.*]

[*Flourish. The*] third knight [*passes by richly armed, and his page before him, bearing his device on his shield, delivers it to the Lady* THAISA]

And what's the third?

THAISA   The third of Antioch,

30   And his device a wreath of chivalry.[5]
        The word, *Me pompae provexit apex.*[6]
        [*She presents it to the* KING]

KING SIMONIDES   Desire of renown he doth devise,
        The which hath drawn him to this enterprise.[7]
        [*He returns it to the page, who exits with the third knight.*]

        [*Flourish. The*] fourth knight [*passes by richly armed, and his page before him, bearing his device on his shield, delivers it to the Lady* THAISA]

        What is the fourth?

THAISA   A knight of Athens bearing[8]

35   A burning torch that's turnèd upside down.
        The word, *Qui me alit me extinguit.*[9]
        [*She presents it to the* KING]

KING SIMONIDES   Which shows that beauty hath this power and will,
        Which can as well inflame as it can kill.
        [*He returns it to the page, who exits with the fourth knight.*]

        [*Flourish. The*] fifth knight [*passes by richly armed, and his page before him, bearing his device on his shield, delivers it to the Lady* THAISA]

        And who the fifth?

THAISA   The fifth, a prince of Corinth,

40   Presents[1] an hand environèd with clouds,
        Holding out gold that's by the touchstone[2] tried.
        The motto thus: *Sic spectanda fides.*[3]
        [*She presents it to the* KING]

KING SIMONIDES   So faith is to be looked into.[4]
        [*He returns it to the page, who exits with the fifth knight.*]

        [*Flourish. The*] sixth knight [PERICLES, *in a rusty armour, who, having neither page to deliver his shield nor shield to deliver, presents his device unto the Lady* THAISA]

        And what's the sixth and last, the which the knight himself

45   With such a graceful courtesy° delivereth?   bow

THAISA   He seems to be a stranger, but his present° is   presented object
        A withered branch that's only green at top.
        The motto, *In hac spe vivo.*°   I live in this hope

KING SIMONIDES   From the dejected state wherein he is

50   He hopes by you his fortunes yet may flourish.

---

5. (Heraldic term): twisted band that joins the crest and the knight's helmet.
6. The summit of glory has led me on (Latin).
7. Lines 32–33 are not in Q1; adapted from *PA*.
8. Not in Q1; adapted from *PA*.
9. Who nourishes me extinguishes me.
1. Lines 39–40, adapted from *PA*, replace Q1's "The fift";

the substitution produces symmetry with the other knights' introductions.
2. Black stone used to check the purity of gold and silver; symbol of fidelity.
3. Thus is faith to be examined.
4. Not in Q1; adapted from *PA*.

FIRST LORD   He had need mean° better than his outward show   *must intend something*
Can any way speak in his just commend,°   *on his behalf*
For by his rusty outside he appears
T'have practised more the whipstock than the lance.⁵
55   SECOND LORD   He well may be a stranger,° for he comes   *foreigner*
Unto an honoured triumph strangely furnished.°   *bizarrely equipped*
THIRD LORD   And on set purpose let his armour rust
Until this day, to scour it in the dust.⁶
KING SIMONIDES   Opinion's but a fool, that makes us scan
60   The outward habit° for the inward man.   *costume*
[*Cornetts*]°   *Ceremonial trumpets*
But stay, the knights are coming. We will withdraw
Into the gallery.   [*Exeunt*]
[*Cornetts and*] *great shouts* [*within*], *and all cry 'The*
mean° *knight!*'   *impoverished*

Scene 7

[*A stately banquet is brought in.*] *Enter* KING [SIMON-
IDES, THAISA *and their train at one door, and at another*
door a MARSHAL *conducting* PERICLES] *and* [*the other*]
KNIGHTS *from tilting*

KING SIMONIDES [*to the* KNIGHTS]   To say you're welcome were
superfluous.
To place upon the volume of your deeds
As in a title page¹ your worth in arms
Were more than you expect, or more than's fit,
5   Since every worth in show° commends itself.   *in practice*
Prepare for mirth, for mirth becomes a feast.
You're princes, and my guests.
THAISA [*to* PERICLES]   But you, my knight and guest;
To whom this wreath of victory I give,
And crown you king of this day's happiness.
10   PERICLES   'Tis more by fortune, lady, than my merit.
KING SIMONIDES   Call it by what you will, the day is yours,
And here I hope is none that envies it.
In framing° artists art hath thus decreed,   *making*
To make some good, but others to exceed.
You are her laboured scholar.² [*To* THAISA] Come, queen
15   o'th' feast—
For, daughter, so you are—here take your place.
[*To* MARSHAL]   Marshal the rest as they deserve their grace.³
KNIGHTS   We are honoured much by good Simonides.
KING SIMONIDES   Your presence glads our days; honour we love,
20   For who hates honour hates the gods above.
MARSHAL [*to* PERICLES]   Sir, yonder is your place.
PERICLES   Some other is more fit.
FIRST KNIGHT   Contend not, sir, for we are gentlemen
Have° neither in our hearts nor outward eyes   *Who've*
Envied the great, nor shall the low despise.

5. *he appears . . . lance:* he looks more like a manual laborer (a "whipstock" was the handle of a whip used to drive workhorses) than a knight.
6. To polish it in the dust (when he loses).
Scene 7 (Act 2, Scene 3)
Location: The palace at Pentapolis.

1. Renaissance publishers often advertised the contents on the title page of a book ("volume").
2. Art (creative power) worked hard to make you.
3. Arrange the others according to the honor they deserve.

PERICLES   You are right courteous knights.

25   KING SIMONIDES   Sit, sir, sit.

[PERICLES *sits directly over against° the* KING *and*   °across from
THAISA. *The guests feed apace.* PERICLES *sits still and*
eats nothing]

[*Aside*] By Jove I wonder, that is king of thoughts,
These cates distaste me, he but thought upon.[4]

THAISA [*aside*]   By Juno, that is queen of marriage,
I am amazed all viands that I eat

30   Do seem unsavoury, wishing him my meat.
[*To the* KING]   Sure he's a gallant gentleman.

KING SIMONIDES   He's but a country gentleman.
He's done no more than other knights have done.
He's broke a staff° or so, so let it pass.   °*an opponent's lance*

35   THAISA [*aside*]   To me he seems like diamond to glass.

PERICLES [*aside*]   Yon king's to me like to my father's picture,
Which tells me in what glory once he was—
Had princes sit like stars about his throne,
And he the sun for them to reverence.

40   None that beheld him but like lesser lights
Did vail° their crowns to his supremacy;   °*lower*
Where now his son's a glow-worm in the night,
The which hath fire in darkness, none in light;
Whereby I see that time's the king of men;

45   He's both their parent and he is their grave,
And gives them what he will, not what they crave.

KING SIMONIDES   What, are you merry, knights?

THE OTHER KNIGHTS   Who can be other in this royal presence?

KING SIMONIDES   Here with a cup that's stored unto the brim,

50   As you do love, full[5] to your mistress' lips,
We drink this health to you.

THE OTHER KNIGHTS   We thank your grace.

KING SIMONIDES   Yet pause a while. Yon knight doth sit too melancholy,
As if the entertainment in our court
Had not a show might countervail° his worth.   °*that might equal*
Note it not you, Thaisa?

55   THAISA   What is't to me, my father?

KING SIMONIDES   O, attend, my daughter. Princes in this
Should live like gods above, who freely give
To everyone that come to honour them.
And princes not so doing are like gnats

60   Which make a sound but, killed, are wondered at.[6]
Therefore to make his entertain° more sweet,   °*entertainment*
Here bear this standing-bowl° of wine to him.   °*bowl on a pedestal*

THAISA   Alas, my father, it befits not me
Unto a stranger knight to be so bold.

65   He may my proffer take for an offence,
Since men take women's gifts for impudence.

KING SIMONIDES   How? Do as I bid you, or you'll move° me else.   °*anger*

THAISA [*aside*]   Now, by the gods, he could not please me better.

---

4. *These . . . upon:* (I'm so taken with him that, merely)
thinking of him, I lose my appetite for delicacies.
5. Just as you love, fully (all the way).

6. Which, when dead, appear surprisingly small for all
the noise they made alive.

KING SIMONIDES   Furthermore, tell him we desire to know
70   Of whence he is, his name and parentage.
        [THAISA *bears the cup to* PERICLES]
THAISA   The King my father, sir, has drunk to you,
        Wishing it so much blood unto your life.
PERICLES   I thank both him and you, and pledge° him freely.   *drink to*
        [*He pledges the* KING]
THAISA   And further he desires to know of you
75   Of whence you are, your name and parentage.
PERICLES   A gentleman of Tyre, my name Pericles,
        My education been in arts° and arms,   *liberal arts*
        Who, looking for adventures in the world,
        Was by the rough unconstant seas bereft
80   Unfortunately both of ships and men,
        And after shipwreck driven upon this shore.
        [THAISA *returns to the* KING]
THAISA   He thanks your grace, names himself Pericles,
        A gentleman of Tyre, who, seeking adventures,
        Was solely by misfortune of the seas
85   Bereft of ships and men, cast on this shore.
KING SIMONIDES   Now by the gods I pity his mishaps,
        And will awake him from his melancholy.
        [SIMONIDES, *rising from his state, goes forthwith and*
            embraces PERICLES]
        Be[7] cheered, for what misfortune hath impaired° you of,   *deprived*
        Fortune by my help can repair° to you.   *restore*
90   My self and country both shall be your friends,
        And presently° a goodly milk-white steed   *directly*
        And golden spurs I first bestow upon you,
        The prizes due your merit, and ordained
        For this day's enterprise.
95   PERICLES   Your kingly courtesy I thankfully accept.
KING SIMONIDES   Come, gentlemen, we sit° too long on trifles,   *dwell*
        And waste the time which looks for other revels.
        Ev'n in your armours, as you are addressed,°   *dressed*
        Your limbs will well become a soldier's dance.
100 I will not have excuse with saying this,
        'Loud music° is too harsh for ladies' heads',   *The sound of armor*
        Since they love men in arms as well as beds.
        [*The* KNIGHTS] *dance*
        So° this was well asked, 'twas so well performed.   *Just as*
        Come, here's a lady that wants breathing° too.   *exercise*
105 [*To* PERICLES] And I have heard, sir, that the knights of Tyre
        Are excellent in making ladies trip,°   *dance; go astray*
        And that their measures° are as excellent.   *dances; means*
PERICLES   In those that practise them they are, my lord.
KING SIMONIDES   O, that's as much as you would be denied
110 Of your fair courtesy.[8] Unclasp, unclasp.[9]
        They dance
        Thanks, gentlemen, to all. All have done well,
        [*To* PERICLES] But you the best.—Lights, pages, to conduct

---

7. Lines 88–95 are not in Q1; they are adapted from *PA*
to improve the transition between lines 87 and 96.
8. *that's . . . courtesy:* that's just what your modesty dic-
tates you should say.

9. Remove (your armor); if the stage direction "*They
dance*" is misplaced in Q and really should follow
"unclasp," Simonides is presumably ordering Pericles and
Thaisa not to dance so intimately.

These knights unto their sev'ral° lodgings.—Yours, sir,   *separate*
We have giv'n order should be next our own.
115 PERICLES   I am at your grace's pleasure.
KING SIMONIDES   Princes, it is too late to talk of love,
  And that's the mark I know you level° at.   *aim*
  Therefore each one betake him to his rest;
  Tomorrow all for speeding do their best.[1] [*Exeunt severally*]°   *separately*

Scene 8

Enter HELICANUS *and* AESCHINES

HELICANUS   No, Aeschines, know this of me:
  Antiochus from incest lived not free,
  For which the most high gods, not minding° longer   *wishing*
  To hold the vengeance that they had in store
5 Due to this heinous capital offence,
  Even in the height and pride of all his glory,
  When he was seated in a chariot
  Of an inestimable value, and
  His daughter with him, both apparelled all in jewels,[1]
10 A fire from heaven came and shrivelled up
  Their bodies e'en to loathing, for they so stunk
  That all those eyes adored° them ere their fall   *that adored*
  Scorn now their° hands should give them burial.   *that their*
AESCHINES   'Twas very strange.
HELICANUS   And yet but justice, for though
15 This king were great, his greatness was no guard
  To bar heav'n's shaft, but sin had his° reward.   *its*
AESCHINES   'Tis very true.

Enter three LORDS [*and stand aside*]

FIRST LORD   See, not a man in private conference
  Or council has respect° with him but he.°   *influence / (Aeschines)*
20 SECOND LORD   It shall no longer grieve° without reproof.   *cause us grief*
THIRD LORD   And cursed be he that will not second it.
FIRST LORD   Follow me, then.—Lord Helicane, a word.
HELICANUS   With me? And welcome. Happy day, my lords.
FIRST LORD   Know that our griefs° are risen to the top,   *grievances*
25 And now at length they overflow their banks.
HELICANUS   Your griefs? For what? Wrong not your prince you love.
FIRST LORD   Wrong not yourself, then, noble Helicane,
  But if the prince do live, let us salute him
  Or know what ground's made happy by his step,
30 And be resolved° he lives to govern us,   *reassured*
  Or dead, give 's° cause to mourn his funeral   *us*
  And leave us to our free election.
SECOND LORD   Whose death indeed's the strongest° in our   *(likelihood)*
    censure,°   *judgment*
  And knowing this—kingdoms without a head,
35 Like goodly buildings left without a roof,
  Soon fall to utter ruin—your noble self,
  That best know how to rule and how to reign,
  We thus submit unto as sovereign.

---

1. Each one do his best to succeed (in wooing the   **Scene 8** (Act 2, Scene 4)
Princess).   Location: Tyre, the Governor's house.
                                                         1. *both . . . jewels*: not in Q1; taken from PA.

ALL [*kneeling*]   Live, noble Helicane!
40 HELICANUS   By honour's cause, forbear your suffrages.°   *voting (for me)*
    If that you love Prince Pericles, forbear.
        [*The* LORDS *rise*]
    Take I° your wish I leap into the seas   *If I accept*
    Where's° hourly trouble for a minute's ease,   *Where there is*
    But if I cannot win you to this love,[2]
45 A twelvemonth longer then let me entreat you
    Further to bear the absence of your king;
    If in which time expired he not return,
    I shall with agèd patience bear your yoke.
    Go, seek your noble prince like noble subjects,
50 And in your search spend your adventurous worth,
    Whom if you find and win unto° return,   *persuade to*
    You shall like diamonds sit about his crown.
    FIRST LORD   To wisdom he's a fool that will not yield,
    And since Lord Helicane enjoineth us,
55 We with our travels will endeavour us.
    If in the world he live we'll seek him out;
    If in his grave he rest, we'll find him there.[3]
    HELICANUS   Then you love us, we you, and we'll clasp hands.
    When peers thus knit, a kingdom ever stands.   *Exeunt*

Scene 8a
[*Enter* PERICLES *with* GENTLEMEN *with lights*]

FIRST GENTLEMAN   Here is your lodging, sir.
PERICLES   Pray leave me private.
    Only for instant solace pleasure me
    With[1] some delightful instrument, with which,
    And with my former practice,° I intend   *(of music)*
5   To pass away the tediousness of night,
    Though slumbers were more fitting.
FIRST GENTLEMAN   Presently.°   *At once*
                                    [*Exit* FIRST GENTLEMAN]
SECOND GENTLEMAN   Your will's obeyed in all things, for our
        master
    Commanded you be disobeyed in nothing.
        [*Enter* FIRST GENTLEMAN *with a stringed instrument*]
PERICLES   I thank you. Now betake you to your pillows,
10 And to the nourishment of quiet sleep.   [*Exeunt* GENTLEMEN]
        [PERICLES *plays and sings*]
    Day—that hath still that sovereignty to draw back
    The empire of the night, though for a while
    In darkness she usurp—brings morning on.
    I will go give his grace that salutation
15 Morning requires of me.   [*Exit with instrument*]

2. Love of Pericles (line 41). This line appears in Q1 after line 48, thereby rendering incomprehensible the First Lord's willingness to "yield" (line 53) to the suggestion of searching for Pericles.
3. Lines 56–57 appear after line 29 in Q1. There, they make lines 30–32 problematic and, as in note 2, undermine the First Lord's agreement to travel.

Scene 8a (This scene is not in Q1 or other modern editions. It was adapted from *PA* and provides a reference point for Simonides' compliments in Scene 9, lines 23–28. See the Textual Note.)
Location: The palace at Pentapolis.
1. *pleasure me / With*: grant me.

Scene 9

Enter KING [SIMONIDES] *at one door reading of a letter,*
the KNIGHTS [*enter at another door and*] *meet him*

FIRST KNIGHT   Good morrow to the good Simonides.

KING SIMONIDES   Knights, from my daughter this I let you know:
That for this twelvemonth she'll not undertake
A married life. Her reason to herself
5   Is only known, which from her none can get.

SECOND KNIGHT   May we not have access to her, my lord?

KING SIMONIDES   Faith, by no means. It is impossible,
She hath so strictly tied her to her chamber.
One twelve moons more she'll wear Diana's liv'ry.[1]
10   This by the eye of Cynthia[2] hath she vowed,
And on her virgin honour will not break it.

THIRD KNIGHT   Loath to bid farewell, we take our leaves.

[*Exeunt* KNIGHTS]

KING SIMONIDES   So, they are well dispatched. Now to my
  daughter's letter.
She tells me here she'll wed the stranger knight,
15   Or never more to view nor° day nor light.[3]   *neither*
I like that well. Nay, how absolute she's in't,
Not minding whether I dislike or no!
Mistress, t'is well, I do commend your choice,
And will no longer have it be delayed.

Enter PERICLES

20   Soft, here he comes. I must dissemble that
In show, I have determined on in heart.[4]

PERICLES   All fortune to the good Simonides.

KING SIMONIDES   To you as much, sir. I am beholden to you
For your sweet music this last night. My ears,
25   I do protest, were never better fed
With such delightful pleasing harmony.

PERICLES   It is your grace's pleasure to commend,
Not my desert.

KING SIMONIDES   Sir, you are music's master.

PERICLES   The worst of all her scholars, my good lord.

KING SIMONIDES   Let me ask you one thing. What think you of
30   my daughter?

PERICLES   A most virtuous princess.

KING SIMONIDES   And fair, too, is she not?

PERICLES   As a fair day in summer; wondrous fair.

KING SIMONIDES   My daughter, sir, thinks very well of you;
So well indeed that you must be her master
35   And she will be your scholar;° therefore look to it.°   *student* *be prepared*

PERICLES   I am unworthy for her schoolmaster.

KING SIMONIDES   She thinks not so. Peruse this writing else.°   *if you doubt me*

[*He gives the letter to* PERICLES, *who reads*]

PERICLES [*aside*]   What's here?—a letter that she loves the knight
of Tyre?
'Tis the King's subtlety to have my life.

Scene 9 (Act 2, Scene 5)
Location: The palace at Pentapolis.
1. She'll serve Diana, goddess of chastity.
2. Diana, also goddess of the moon.
3. After this line, Q1 has " 'Tis well Mistress, your choice

agrees with mine," which is omitted in this edition
because the same thoughts are expressed in lines 16 and
18.
4. *that . . . heart:* replace Q1's "it" (adapted from *PA*).
that / In show: outwardly what.

[*He prostrates himself at the King's feet*]

40 O, seek not to entrap me, gracious lord,
A stranger and distressèd gentleman
That never aimed so high to° love your daughter, | *as to*
But bent all offices to honour her.[5]
Never did thought of mine levy° offence, | *give*
45 Nor never did my actions yet commence
A deed might° gain her love or your displeasure. | *that might*

KING SIMONIDES Thou liest like a traitor.

PERICLES Traitor?

KING SIMONIDES Ay, traitor,
That thus disguised art stol'n into my court
With witchcraft of thy actions to bewitch
50 The yielding spirit of my tender child.

PERICLES [*rising*] Who calls me traitor, unless it be the King,
Ev'n in his bosom I will write the lie.° | *(with my sword)*

KING SIMONIDES [*aside*] Now, by the gods, I do applaud his
courage.

PERICLES My actions are as noble as my blood,
55 That never relished of° a base descent. | *gave a hint of*
I came unto your court in search of honour,
And not to be a rebel to your state;
And he that otherwise accounts of me,
This sword shall prove he's honour's enemy.

60 KING SIMONIDES I shall prove otherwise, since both your practice° | *actions*
And her consent therein is evident
There, by my daughter's hand, as she can witness.[6]

Enter THAISA

PERICLES [*to* THAISA] Then as you are as virtuous as fair,
By what you hope of heaven or desire
65 By your best wishes here i'th' world fulfilled,[7]
Resolve° your angry father if my tongue | *Inform*
Did e'er solicit, or my hand subscribe
To any syllable made° love to you. | *that made*

THAISA Why, sir, say if you had,
70 Who takes offence at that° would make me glad? | *what*

KING SIMONIDES How, minion, are you so peremptory?° | *determined*
[*Aside*] I am glad on't.—Is[8] this a fit match for you?
A straggling Theseus, born we know not where,[9]
One that hath neither blood nor merit
75 For thee to hope for, or himself to challenge° | *claim for himself*
Of thy perfections e'en the least allowance.° | *share*

THAISA [*kneeling*] Suppose his birth were base, when that° his life | *even though*
Shows that he is not so, yet he hath virtue,
The very ground of all nobility,
80 Enough to make him noble. I entreat you
To remember that I am in love,

---

5. After this line, Q1 has

KING Thou hast bewitched my daughter,
 And thou art a villain.
PERICLES By the Gods I have not.

This passage breaks up what is a single speech in *PA*. It is omitted here and replaced by Simonides' speech at lines 47–50, which is adapted from *PA* and is more powerful. *bent all offices:* performed all services.
6. Except for "she can witness," lines 60–62 are adapted

from *PA*; they replace Q1's "No? here comes my daughter, she can witness it," which echoes *Othello* 1.3.169. The reporter of this passage may have played Desdemona.
7. *By what . . . fulfilled:* not in Q1; adapted from *PA*.
8. Lines 72–96, adapted from *PA*, replace Q1's "with all my heart"; inclusion of this passage shifts the emphasis from nobility of birth to nobility of soul.
9. Theseus was an Athenian hero of ambiguous parentage who sometimes mistreated women.

The power of which love cannot be confined
By th' power of your will. Most royal father,
What with my pen I have in secret written
85 With my tongue now I openly confirm,
Which is I have no life but in his love,
Nor any being but in joying of his worth.
KING SIMONIDES   Equals to equals, good to good is joined.
This not being so, the bavin° of your mind   firewood
90 In rashness kindled must again be quenched,
Or purchase° our displeasure.—And for you, sir,   provoke
First learn to know I banish you my court,
And yet I scorn our rage should stoop so low.
For your ambition, sir, I'll have your life.
95 THAISA [to PERICLES]   For every drop of blood he sheds of yours
He'll draw another from his only child.
KING SIMONIDES   I'll tame you, yea, I'll bring you in subjection.
Will you not having my consent
Bestow your love and your affections
100 Upon a stranger?—[aside] who for aught I know
May be, nor can I think the contrary,
As great in blood as I myself.
      [He catches THAISA rashly by the hand]
Therefore hear you, mistress: either frame° your will to mine—   mold
      [He catches PERICLES rashly by the hand]
And you, sir, hear you: either be ruled by me—
Or I shall make you
      [He claps their hands together]
105   man and wife.
Nay, come, your hands and lips must seal it too,
      [PERICLES and THAISA kiss]
And being joined, I'll thus your hopes destroy,
      [He parts them]
And for your further grief, God give you joy.
What, are you pleased?
THAISA   Yes, [to PERICLES] if you love me, sir.
110 PERICLES   Ev'n as my life° my blood that fosters it.   as my life loves
KING SIMONIDES   What, are you both agreed?
PERICLES and THAISA   Yes, if't please your majesty.
KING SIMONIDES   It pleaseth me so well that I will see you wed,
Then with what haste you can, get you to bed.   Exeunt

Scene 10

Enter GOWER
GOWER   Now sleep y-slackèd hath the rout,[1]
No din but snores the house about,
Made louder by the o'erfed breast
Of this most pompous° marriage feast.   lavish
5 The cat with eyne° of burning coal   eyes
Now couches fore the mouse's hole,
And crickets sing at th'oven's mouth
As the blither for their drouth.[2]
Hymen° hath brought the bride to bed,   god of marriage

Scene 10 (Act 3, Chorus)   2. As if happier for being dry.
1. Sleep has rendered everyone inactive.

10 Where by the loss of maidenhead
A babe is moulded. Be attent,°   *attentive*
And time that is so briefly spent°   *spent onstage*
With your fine fancies quaintly eche.°   *skillfully fill out*
What's dumb in show, I'll plain° with speech.   *clarify*

[*Dumb show.*]

Enter PERICLES *and* SIMONIDES *at one door with atten-*
dants. A messenger [comes hastily in to] them, kneels,
and gives PERICLES *a letter.* PERICLES *shows it* SIMON-
IDES; the lords kneel to him. Then enter THAISA *with*
child, with LYCHORIDA, *a nurse. The* KING *shows her the*
letter. She rejoices. She and PERICLES *take leave of her*
father and depart [with LYCHORIDA *at one door;* SIMON-
IDES and attendants depart at another]

15 By many a dern° and painful perch°   *wild / patch of land*
Of Pericles the care-full search,
By the four opposing coigns°   *corners*
Which the world together joins,
Is made with all due diligence
20 That horse and sail and high expense
Can stead° the quest. At last from Tyre   *sustain in*
Fame° answering the most strange enquire,°   *Rumor / distant queries*
To th' court of King Simonides
Are letters brought, the tenor these:
25 Antiochus and his daughter dead,
The men of Tyrus on the head
Of Helicanus would set on
The crown of Tyre, but he will° none.   *desires*
The mutiny there he hastes t'appease,
30 Says to 'em if King Pericles
Come not home in twice six moons
He, obedient to their dooms,°   *judgments*
Will take the crown. The sum of this
Brought hither to Pentapolis
35 Y-ravishèd° the regions round,   *Enraptured*
And everyone with claps can° sound   *started to*
'Our heir-apparent is a king!
Who dreamt, who thought of such a thing?'
Brief° he must hence depart to Tyre;   *In short; quickly*
40 His queen with child makes her desire—
Which who shall cross?—along to go.
Omit we all their dole and woe.
Lychorida her nurse she takes,
And so to sea. Their vessel shakes
45 On Neptune's billow. Half the flood°   *sea*
Hath their keel cut, but fortune's mood
Varies again. The grizzled° north   *grisly*
Disgorges such a tempest forth
That as a duck for life that dives,
50 So up and down the poor ship drives.
The lady shrieks, and well-a-near°   *alas*
Does fall in travail° with her fear,   *Goes into labor*
And what ensues in this fell° storm   *cruel*
Shall for itself itself perform;
55 I nill° relate; action may   *will not*

Conveniently the rest convey,
Which might not what by me is told.[3]
In your imagination hold°   *think*
This stage the ship, upon whose deck
60 The sea-tossed Pericles appears to speke.   [*Exit*]

Scene 11

[*Thunder and lightning.*] *Enter* PERICLES *a-shipboard*

PERICLES   The god of this great vast° rebuke these surges   *vast sea*
Which wash both heav'n and hell; and thou that hast
Upon the winds command, bind them in brass,
Having called them from the deep. O still°   *quiet*
5 Thy deaf'ning dreadful thunders, gently quench
Thy nimble sulph'rous flashes.—O, ho, Lychorida!
How does my queen?—Thou stormest venomously.
Wilt thou spit all thyself? The seaman's whistle
Is as a whisper in the ears of death,°   *of a dead person*
10 Unheard.—Lychorida!—Lucina,° O!   *goddess of childbirth*
Divinest patroness, and midwife gentle
To those that cry by night, convey thy deity
Aboard our dancing boat, make swift the pangs
Of my queen's travails!—Now, Lychorida.

Enter LYCHORIDA [*with an infant*]

15 LYCHORIDA   Here is a thing too young for such a place,
Who, if it had conceit,° would die, as I   *understanding*
Am like° to do. Take in your arms this piece   *likely*
Of your dead queen.
PERICLES   How, how, Lychorida?
LYCHORIDA   Patience, good sir, do not assist the storm.°   *(by ranting and tears)*
20 Here's all that is left living of your queen,
A little daughter. For the sake of it
Be manly, and take comfort.
PERICLES   O you gods!
Why do you make us love your goodly gifts,
And snatch them straight away? We here below
25 Recall° not what we give, and therein may   *Demand back*
Use honour with you.[1]
LYCHORIDA   Patience, good sir,
E'en for this charge.[2]

[*She gives him the infant.* PERICLES, *looking mournfully
upon it, shakes his head, and weeps*]

PERICLES   Now mild may be thy life,
For a more blust'rous birth had never babe;
Quiet and gentle thy conditions,° for   *circumstances*
30 Thou art the rudeliest welcome to this world
That e'er was prince's child; happy° what follows.   *let be happy*
Thou hast as chiding° a nativity   *upsetting*
As fire, air, water, earth, and heav'n can make
To herald thee from th' womb. Poor inch of nature,
35 Ev'n at the first thy loss is more than can

---

3. Which could not easily "convey" what I've related so
far.
Scene 11 (Act 3, Scene 1)
Location: At sea.

1. *therein . . . you*: so we can criticize you by this standard
of honor.
2. For the sake of this child.

Thy partage quit with all thou canst find here.[3]
Now the good gods throw their best eyes° upon't.   *look favorably*
     Enter [the MASTER *and a]* SAILOR
MASTER   What, courage, sir! God save you.
PERICLES   Courage enough, I do not fear the flaw;°   *squall*
40   It hath done to me its worst. Yet for the love
    Of this poor infant, this fresh new seafarer,
    I would it would be quiet.
MASTER *[calling]*   Slack the bow-lines, there.—Thou° wilt not,   *(the storm)*
    wilt thou? Blow, and split thyself.
45 SAILOR   But searoom,[4] an° the brine and cloudy billow kiss the   *if*
    moon, I care not.
MASTER *[to* PERICLES*]*   Sir, your queen must overboard. The sea
    works° high, the wind is loud, and will not lie° till the ship be   *surges / lie still*
    cleared of the dead.
50 PERICLES   That's but your superstition.
MASTER   Pardon us, sir; with us at sea it hath been still° observed,   *always*
    and we are strong in custom. Therefore briefly° yield 'er, for   *quickly*
    she must overboard straight.
PERICLES   As you think meet. Most wretched queen!
LYCHORIDA   Here she lies, sir.
    [She draws the curtains and discovers the body of Thaisa
    in a bed. PERICLES *gives* LYCHORIDA *the infant]*
55 PERICLES *[to* THAISA*]*   A terrible childbed hast thou had, my dear,
    No light, no fire. Th'unfriendly elements
    Forgot thee utterly, nor have I time
    To give thee hallowed to thy grave, but straight
    Must cast thee, scarcely coffined, in the ooze,°   *seabed*
60   Where, for° a monument upon thy bones   *in place of*
    And aye-remaining° lamps, the belching whale   *ever-burning*
    And humming water must o'erwhelm thy corpse,
    Lying with simple shells.—O Lychorida,
    Bid Nestor bring me spices, ink, and paper,
65   My casket and my jewels, and bid Nicander
    Bring me the satin coffer. Lay the babe
    Upon the pillow. Hie° thee whiles I say   *Hurry*
    A priestly farewell to her. Suddenly,° woman.   *Immediately*
                                [Exit LYCHORIDA*]*
SAILOR   Sir, we have a chest beneath the hatches caulked and
70   bitumed[5] ready.
PERICLES   I thank thee. *[To the* MASTER*]* Mariner, say, what coast is this?
MASTER   We are near Tarsus.
PERICLES   Thither, gentle mariner,
    Alter thy course from Tyre. When canst thou reach it?
MASTER   By break of day, if the wind cease.
PERICLES   Make for Tarsus.
75   There will I visit Cleon, for the babe
    Cannot hold out to Tyrus. There I'll leave it
    At careful nursing. Go thy ways,° good mariner.   *Get to it*
    I'll bring the body presently.
             *Exit [*MASTER *at one door and* SAILOR *beneath*
                 the hatches. Exit PERICLES *to* THAISA,
                     closing the curtains]

---

3. *than . . . here:* than your share of anything you find in this life can make up for.

4. As long as we're at sea (safe from the rocks).

5. *bitumed:* caulked with pitch.

Scene 12

Enter Lord CERIMON *with a [poor man and a] servant*

CERIMON Philemon, ho!

Enter PHILEMON

PHILEMON   Doth my lord call?

CERIMON Get fire and meat for those poor men.[1]

[*Exit* PHILEMON]

'T'as been a turbulent and stormy night.

SERVANT I have seen many, but such a night as this
5   Till now I ne'er endured.

CERIMON Your master will be dead ere you return.
      There's nothing can be ministered in nature
      That can recover him. [*To poor man*] Give this to th' pothecary°   *druggist*
      And tell me how it works.

[*Exeunt poor man and servant*]

Enter two GENTLEMEN

FIRST GENTLEMAN   Good morrow.

SECOND GENTLEMAN   Good morrow to your lordship.
10   CERIMON   Gentlemen,
      Why do you stir so early?

FIRST GENTLEMAN   Sir,
      Our lodgings, standing bleak upon° the sea,   *exposed to*
      Shook as° the earth did quake.   *as if*
      The very principals° did seem to rend   *principal rafters*
15   And all to topple. Pure surprise and fear
      Made me to quit the house.

SECOND GENTLEMAN   That is the cause we trouble you so early;
      'Tis not our husbandry.°   *good work habits*

CERIMON   O, you say well.

FIRST GENTLEMAN But I much marvel that your lordship should,
20   Having rich tire° about you, at this hour   *bed furniture*
      Shake off the golden slumber of repose. 'Tis most strange,
      Nature to be so conversant with pain,[2]
      Being thereto not compelled.

CERIMON   I held it ever;°   *always believed*
      Virtue and cunning° were endowments greater   *knowledge*
25   Than nobleness and riches. Careless heirs
      May the two latter darken and dispend,°   *expend*
      But immortality attends the former,
      Making a man a god. 'Tis known I ever°   *always*
      Have studied physic,° through which secret art,   *medicine*
30   By turning o'er authorities,° I have,   *reading learned texts*
      Together with my practice, made familiar
      To me and to my aid° the blest infusions   *assistant*
      That dwells in vegetives,[3] in metals, stones,
      And so can speak of the disturbances
35   That nature works, and of her cures, which doth give me
      A more content° and cause of true delight   *greater happiness*
      Than to be thirsty after tott'ring° honour,   *unstable*
      Or tie my pleasure up in silken bags°   *(of money)*
      To glad the fool and death.[4]

Scene 12 (Act 3, Scene 2)
Location: Cerimon's house in Ephesus.
1. Offstage supplicants. Qls "these poor men" might refer to characters onstage.

2. That your nature should be so accustomed to labor.
3. Beneficial substances in plants.
4. To gladden the fool who trusts in wealth, which death inherits.

SECOND GENTLEMAN   Your honour has
40   Through Ephesus poured forth your charity,
        And hundreds call themselves your creatures[5] who by you
        Have been restored. And not alone your knowledge,
        Your personal pain,° but e'en your purse still° open   labor / always
        Hath built Lord Cerimon such strong renown
45   As time shall never—
                Enter [PHILEMON *and one*] *or two[6] with a chest*
PHILEMON   So, lift there.
CERIMON   What's that?
PHILEMON   Sir, even now
        The sea tossed up upon our shore this chest.
        'Tis off some wreck.
50 CERIMON   Set't down. Let's look upon't.
SECOND GENTLEMAN   'Tis like a coffin, sir.
CERIMON   Whate'er it be,
        'Tis wondrous heavy.—Did the sea cast it up?
PHILEMON   I never saw so huge a billow, sir,
        Or a more eager.[7]
CERIMON   Wrench it open straight.
                [The others start to work]
55   If the sea's stomach be o'ercharged with gold
        'Tis by a good constraint of queasy fortune[8]
        It belches upon us.
SECOND GENTLEMAN   'Tis so, my lord.
CERIMON   How close° 'tis caulked and bitumed!   tightly
                [They force the lid]
                                        Soft,° it smells   But wait
        Most sweetly in my sense.
SECOND GENTLEMAN   A delicate odour.
60 CERIMON   As ever hit my nostril. So, up with it.
                [They take the lid off]
        O you most potent gods! What's here—a corpse?
SECOND GENTLEMAN
        Most strange.
CERIMON   Shrouded in cloth of state,° and crowned,   royal fabric
        Balmed and entreasured with full bags of spices.
        A passport,° too!   An identification paper
                [He takes a paper from the chest]
65   Apollo perfect me i'th' characters.[9]
        'Here I give to understand,
        If e'er this coffin drives a-land,
        I, King Pericles, have lost
        This queen worth all our mundane cost.°   earthly wealth
70   Who° finds her, give her burying;   Whoever
        She was the daughter of a king.
        Besides this treasure for a fee,
        The° gods requite his charity.'   May the

5. *call . . . creatures:* owe their lives to you.
6. "Philemon" replaces Q1's "two or three" here, "Servant" in the speech prefixes to lines 46–53, and "one" in the stage direction to line 84, in accord with the emphasis on one of Cerimon's assistants in Twine's *Patterne of Painefull Adventures* and in order to make sense of Philemon's appearance at the beginning of the scene.
7. *Did . . . eager:* In Q1, these lines appear after "bitumed" (line 58), where the question seems inappro-

priate. The passage is then followed by "Wrench it open," which repeats line 54. Here, "Or a more eager," adapted from *PA*, replaces Q1's "as tossed it upon shore" (which repeats Q1's "toss up upon our shore," line 49). These changes seek to remedy the possibly faulty memory of the reporters.
8. By the force of uncertain fortune that.
9. Apollo (patron of both scholars and physicians) help me read the writing correctly.

If thou liv'st, Pericles, thou hast a heart

75   That even cracks for woe. This chanced tonight.°   occurred last night
SECOND GENTLEMAN   Most likely, sir.
CERIMON   Nay, certainly tonight,
    For look how fresh she looks. They were too rash
    That threw her in the sea. Make a fire within.
    Fetch hither all my boxes in my closet.   [*Exit* PHILEMON]
80 Death may usurp on nature many hours,
    And yet the fire of life kindle again
    The o'erpressed° spirits. I have heard   overcome
    Of an Egyptian nine hours dead
    Who was by good appliances° recovered.   medical treatments
        Enter [PHILEMON] *with napkins and fire*
85 Well said, well said, the fire and cloths.
    The still° and woeful music that we have,   soft
    Cause it to sound, beseech you.
        [*Music*]
                        The vial° once more.   (of medicine)
    How thou stirr'st,[1] thou block! The music there!
    I pray you give her air.° Gentlemen,   (pun on "heir")
90 This queen will live. Nature awakes, a warmth
    Breathes out of her. She hath not been entranced°   unconscious
    Above five hours. See how she 'gins to blow°   bloom
    Into life's flow'r again.
FIRST GENTLEMAN   The heavens
    Through you increase our wonder, and set up
    Your fame for ever.
95 CERIMON   She is alive. Behold,
    Her eyelids, cases to those heav'nly jewels
    Which Pericles hath lost,
    Begin to part their fringes of bright gold.
    The diamonds of a most praisèd water°   luster
100 Doth appear to make the world twice rich.[2]—Live,
    And make us weep to hear your fate, fair creature,
    Rare° as you seem to be.   Exquisite
        She moves
THAISA   O dear Diana,
    Where am I? Where's my lord? What world is this?
SECOND GENTLEMAN
    Is not this strange?
FIRST GENTLEMAN   Most rare.
CERIMON   Hush, gentle neighbours.
105 Lend me your hands. To the next chamber bear her.
    Get linen. Now this matter must be looked to,
    For her relapse is mortal.° Come, come,   would be fatal
    And Aesculapius° guide us.   *They carry her away. Exeunt*   god of healing

Scene 13

Enter PERICLES *at Tarsus, with* CLEON *and* DIONYZA
[*and* LYCHORIDA *with a babe*]
PERICLES   Most honoured Cleon, I must needs be gone.
    My twelve months are expired, and Tyrus stands

---

1. How lively you are (ironic).
2. Once by the precious gold of her eyelids and again by the jewels they conceal.

Scene 13 (Act 3, Scene 3)
Location: The Governor's house in Tarsus.

In a litigious° peace. You and your lady   *conflict-ridden*
Take from my heart all thankfulness. The gods
Make up the rest upon you![1]

5   CLEON   Your strokes of fortune,
Though they hurt you mortally, yet glance
Full woundingly on us.
DIONYZA   O your sweet queen!
That the strict fates had pleased you'd brought her hither
T'have blessed mine eyes with her!
PERICLES   We cannot but obey
10   The pow'rs above us. Should° I rage and roar   *Even if*
As doth the sea she lies in, yet the end
Must be as 'tis. My gentle babe Marina,
Whom for° she was born at sea I have named so,   *because*
Here I charge° your charity withal,° and leave her   *saddle / with*
15   The infant of your care, beseeching you
To give her princely training, that she may be
Mannered° as she is born.   *Instructed in manners*
CLEON   Fear not, my lord, but think
Your grace, that fed my country with your corn—
For which the people's pray'rs still fall upon you—
20   Must in your child be thought on. If neglection
Should therein make me vile, the common body°   *the people*
By you relieved would force me to my duty.
But if to that° my nature need a spur,   *that duty*
The gods revenge it upon me and mine
To th' end of generation.
25   PERICLES   I believe you.
Your honour and your goodness teach me to't°   *to do so*
Without your vows.—Till she be married, madam,
By bright Diana, whom we honour all,
Unscissored shall this hair of mine remain,
30   Though I show ill° in't. So I take my leave.   *look bad*
Good madam, make me blessèd in your care
In bringing up my child.
DIONYZA   I have one myself,
Who shall not be more dear to my respect°   *attention*
Than yours, my lord.
PERICLES   Madam, my thanks and prayers.
35   CLEON   We'll bring your grace e'en to the edge o'th' shore,
Then give you up to th' masted Neptune° and   *ship-conveying sea*
The gentlest winds of heaven.
PERICLES   I will embrace your offer.—Come, dear'st madam.—
O, no tears, Lychorida, no tears.
40   Look to your little mistress, on whose grace°   *favor*
You may depend hereafter.—Come, my lord.   [*Exeunt*]

Scene 14

Enter CERIMON *and* THAISA
CERIMON   Madam, this letter and some certain jewels
Lay with you in your coffer, which are all
At your command. Know you the character?°   *handwriting*

---

1. Give you the rest of what you deserve.   **Scene 14** (Act 3, Scene 4)
                                                         Location: Cerimon's house in Ephesus.

THAISA   It is my lord's. That I was shipped° at sea   *on a ship*
5   I well remember, ev'n on my eaning° time,   *birthing*
       But whether there delivered, by th' holy gods
       I cannot rightly say. But since King Pericles,
       My wedded lord, I ne'er shall see again,
       A vestal liv'ry[1] will I take me to,
10   And never more have joy.

CERIMON   Madam, if this you purpose° as ye speak,   *intend*
       Diana's temple is not distant far,
       Where till your date° expire you may abide.   *time of life*
       Moreover, if you please a niece of mine
15   Shall there attend you.

THAISA   My recompense is thanks, that's all,
       Yet my good will is great, though the gift small.   *Exeunt*

Scene 15

       Enter GOWER

GOWER   Imagine Pericles arrived at Tyre,
       Welcomed and settled to his own desire.
       His woeful queen we leave at Ephesus,
       Unto Diana there 's a votaress.°   *as a devotee*
5   Now to Marina bend your mind,
       Whom our fast-growing scene must find
       At Tarsus, and by Cleon trained
       In music, letters; who hath gained
       Of education all the grace,
10   Which makes her both the heart and place°   *focal point*
       Of gen'ral wonder. But, alack,
       That monster envy, oft the wrack°   *ruin*
       Of earnèd praise, Marina's life
       Seeks to take off by treason's knife,
15   And in this kind° our Cleon has   *connection*
       One daughter, and a full-grown lass
       E'en ripe for marriage-rite. This maid
       Hight° Philoten, and it is said   *Is called*
       For certain in our story she
20   Would ever° with Marina be,   *always*
       Be't when they weaved the sleided° silk   *divided into filaments*
       With fingers long, small, white as milk;
       Or when she would with sharp nee'le° wound   *needle*
       The cambric° which she made more sound   *fine linen*
25   By hurting it, or when to th' lute
       She sung, and made the night bird° mute,   *nightingale*
       That still records° with moan; or when   *always sings*
       She would with rich and constant pen
       Vail° to her mistress Dian. Still   *Inscribe praises*
30   This Philoten contends in skill
       With absolute° Marina; so   *perfect*
       With dove of Paphos might the crow

---

1. Vestal virgin's uniform of religious chastity.
Scene 15 (Other modern editions treat Gower's monologue as a prologue to Act 4 and start Act 4, Scene 1, at
line 53. This edition assumes that the grave Marina goes
"to strew" [line 66] "is revealed" during Gower's speech
[stage direction after line 42], that Dionyza and Leonine
enter here, rather than [as in Q1] at the end of that
speech, and hence that the scene does not change.)
Location: Tarsus, near the seashore.

Vie feathers white.[1] Marina gets
All praises which are paid as debts,
35　And not as given.[2] This so darks°　　　　　　　　　　(by comparison)
In Philoten all graceful marks
That Cleon's wife with envy rare°　　　　　　　　　　　　　extreme
A present murder does prepare
For good Marina, that her daughter
40　Might stand peerless by° this slaughter.　　　　　　　by means of
The sooner her vile thoughts to stead°　　　　　　　　　　help
Lychorida, our nurse, is dead,
　　　　[A tomb is revealed]
And cursèd Dionyza hath
The pregnant instrument of wrath
45　Pressed for this blow.[3] Th'unborn event°　　　　　　　outcome
I do commend to your content,°　　　　　　　　　(viewing) pleasure
Only I carry wingèd Time
Post° on the lame feet of my rhyme,　　　　　　　　　　Quickly
Which never could I so convey
50　Unless your thoughts went on my way.
　　　　Enter DIONYZA with LEONINE
Dionyza does appear,
With Leonine, a murderer.　　　　　　　　　　　　　　Exit
DIONYZA　Thy oath remember. Thou hast sworn to do't.
'Tis but a blow, which never shall be known.
55　Thou canst not do a thing i'th' world so soon°　　　　quickly
To yield thee so much profit. Let not conscience,
Which is but cold, or fanning love thy bosom
Unflame[4] too nicely,° nor let pity, which　　　　scrupulously
E'en women have cast off, melt thee; but be
A soldier to thy purpose.
60　LEONINE　　　　　　　　　　I will do't;
But yet she is a goodly creature.
DIONYZA　The fitter then the gods should have her.
　　　　Enter MARINA [to the tomb] with a basket of flowers
Here she comes, weeping her only nurse's death.
Thou art resolved.
LEONINE　　　　　　　I am resolved.
65　MARINA　No, I will rob Tellus of her weed°　　earth of its garment
To strew thy grave with flow'rs. The yellows, blues,
The purple violets and marigolds
Shall as a carpet hang upon thy tomb
While summer days doth last. Ay me, poor maid,
70　Born in a tempest when my mother died,
This world to me is but a ceaseless storm
Whirring° me from my friends.　　　　　　　　　　　Hurrying
DIONYZA　How now, Marina, why do you keep alone?
How chance° my daughter is not with you?　　　　　Why is it
75　Do not consume your blood with sorrowing.[5]
Have you a nurse of me.[6] Lord, how your favour°　　appearance
Is changed with this unprofitable woe!

---

1. so . . . white: so might the crow try to be whiter than
the dove. Paphos was a city sacred to Venus.
2. Marina . . . given: Marina's virtues compel praise,
whether or not one wants to.
3. Has prepared a ready means for the murder.

4. or . . . / Unflame: or cooling love blow out the murderous flame in your bosom. Editors variously emend Q1's
"in flaming, thy love bosom, enslave."
5. Sighs were thought to consume one's blood.
6. Let me be your nurse.

Give me your flowers. Come, o'er the sea margin°   *seashore*
Walk with Leonine. The air is piercing there,
80 And quick;° it sharps the stomach.° Come, Leonine,   *refreshing / appetite*
Take her by th' arm. Walk with her.

MARINA   No, I pray you,
I'll not bereave you of your servant.

DIONYZA   Come, come,
I love the King your father and yourself
With more than foreign heart.° We ev'ry day   *As if we were kin*
85 Expect him here. When he shall come and find
Our paragon to all reports thus blasted,[7]
He will repent the breadth of his great voyage,
Blame both my lord and me, that we have taken
No care to your best courses.° Go, I pray you,   *courses of action*
90 Walk and be cheerful once again; resume
That excellent complexion which did steal
The eyes of young and old. Care not for me.
I can go home alone.

MARINA   Well, I will go,
But truly I have no desire to it.

95 DIONYZA   Nay, I know 'tis good for you. Walk half an hour,
Leonine, at the least; remember
What I have said.

LEONINE   I warr'nt° you, madam.   *guarantee*

DIONYZA [*to* MARINA]   I'll leave you, my sweet lady, for a while.
Pray you walk softly, do not heat your blood.
What, I must have care of you!

100 MARINA   My thanks, sweet madam.

                                                        [*Exit* DIONYZA]

Is this wind westerly that blows?

LEONINE   South-west.

MARINA   When I was born the wind was north.

LEONINE   Was't so?

MARINA   My father, as nurse says, did never fear,
But cried 'Good seamen' to the mariners,
105 Galling° his kingly hands with haling° ropes,   *Irritating / pulling*
And, clasping to the mast, endured a sea
That almost burst the deck.

LEONINE   When was this?

MARINA   When I was born.
110 Never was waves nor wind more violent.
Once from the ladder tackle washes off
A canvas-climber.° 'Ha!' says one, 'wolt out?'[8]   *sailor in the rigging*
And with a dropping° industry they skip   *dripping-wet*
From stem to stern. The boatswain whistles, and
115 The master calls and trebles their confusion.

LEONINE   Come, say your prayers.

MARINA   What mean you?

LEONINE   If you require a little space for prayer
I grant it. Pray, but be not tedious.°   *drawn out*
120 The gods are quick of ear, and I am sworn
To do my work with haste.

---

7. Our universally admired paragon of beauty so   8. So you want to get off ship? (a cruel joke).
blighted.

MARINA   Why would you kill me?

LEONINE   To satisfy my lady.

MARINA   Why would she have me killed?
Now, as I can remember, by my troth°   faith
I never did her hurt in all my life.
125 I never spake bad word, nor did ill turn
To any living creature. Believe me, la.°   (exclamation)
I never killed a mouse nor hurt a fly.
I trod once on a worm against my will,
But I wept for it. How have I offended
130 Wherein my death might yield her any profit
Or my life imply her danger?

LEONINE   My commission
Is not to reason of the deed, but do't.

MARINA   You will not do't for all the world, I hope.
You are well favoured, and your looks foreshow
135 You have a gentle heart. I saw you lately
When you caught° hurt in parting two that fought.   got
Good sooth,° it showed well in you. Do so now.   Truly
Your lady seeks my life. Come you between,
And save poor me, the weaker.

LEONINE [drawing out his sword] I am sworn,
140 And will dispatch.

        Enter PIRATES [running]

FIRST PIRATE   Hold, villain.

        [LEONINE runs away and hides behind the tomb]

SECOND PIRATE   A prize,° a prize.   Booty (Marina)

THIRD PIRATE   Half-part,° mates, half-part. Come, let's have her   To be shared
aboard suddenly.°   quickly

        Exeunt [PIRATES carrying MARINA]

        LEONINE [steals back]

145 LEONINE   These roguing° thieves serve the great pirate Valdes.[9]   law-breaking
An° they have seized Marina, let her go.   If
There's no hope she'll return. I'll swear she's dead
And thrown into the sea; but I'll see further.
Perhaps they will but please themselves upon her,°   will only rape her
150 Not carry her aboard. If she remain,
Whom they have ravished must by me be slain.

        Exit. [The tomb is concealed]

Scene 16

[A brothel sign.] Enter [the PANDER, his wife] the BAWD
[and their man BOULT][1]

PANDER   Boult.

BOULT   Sir.

PANDER   Search the market narrowly.° Mytilene is full of gal-   carefully
lants. We lose too much money this mart° by being wenchless.   market time
5 BAWD   We were never so much out of creatures.° We have but   prostitutes
poor three, and they can do no more than they can do, and
they with continual action are even as good as rotten.°   have venereal disease
PANDER   Therefore let's have fresh ones, whate'er we pay for

---

9. Probably named after an admiral in the Spanish
Armada.
Scene 16 (Act 4, Scene 2)
Location: Mytilene, on the island of Lesbos; before a

brothel.
1. *Pander*: sexual go-between, after Pandarus in *Troilus
and Cressida*. *Bawd*: supplier of prostitutes. The name
"Boult" may have phallic connotations.

them. If there be not a conscience to be used[2] in every trade,
10   we shall never prosper.

BAWD   Thou sayst true. 'Tis not our bringing up of poor bas-
tards°—as I think I have brought up some eleven—   *that enriches us*

BOULT   Ay, to eleven, and brought them down again.[3] But shall
I search the market?

15 BAWD   What else, man? The stuff we have, a strong wind will
blow it to pieces, they are so pitifully sodden.[4]

PANDER   Thou sayst true. They're too unwholesome, o' con-
science.° The poor Transylvanian is dead that lay with the little   *on my conscience*
baggage.°   *prostitute*

20 BOULT   Ay, she quickly pooped° him, she made him roast meat   *overcame (by disease)*
for worms. But I'll go search the market.   *Exit*

PANDER   Three or four thousand chequins° were as pretty a pro-   *gold coins*
portion° to live quietly, and so give over.°   *sum / retire*

BAWD   Why to give over, I pray you? Is it a shame to get° when   *earn*
25   we are old?

PANDER   O, our credit comes not in like the commodity, nor the
commodity wages not with the danger.[5] Therefore if in our
youths we could pick up some pretty estate, 'twere not amiss to
keep our door hatched.° Besides, the sore terms we stand upon   *closed for business*
30   with the gods[6] will be strong° with us for giving o'er.   *a strong argument*

BAWD   Come, other sorts offend as well as we.

PANDER   As well as we? Ay, and better too; we offend worse. Nei-
ther is our profession any mystery,[7] it's no calling.° But here   *(religious) vocation*
comes Boult.

         Enter BOULT *with the* PIRATES *and* MARINA

35 BOULT [*to the* PIRATES]   Come your ways,° my masters,° you say   *Come along / gentlemen*
she's a virgin?

A PIRATE   O sir, we doubt it not.

BOULT [*to* PANDER]   Master, I have gone through° for this piece°   *bargained / (of flesh)*
you see. If you like her, so;° if not, I have lost my earnest.°   *fine / deposit*

40 BAWD   Boult, has she any qualities?°   *accomplishments*

BOULT   She has a good face, speaks well, and has excellent good
clothes. There's no farther necessity of qualities can° make her   *whose absence can*
be refused.

BAWD   What's her price, Boult?

45 BOULT   I cannot be bated one doit of[8] a hundred sesterces.

PANDER [*to* PIRATES]   Well, follow me, my masters. You shall
have your money presently.° [*To* BAWD] Wife, take her in,   *immediately*
instruct her what she has to do, that she may not be raw in her
entertainment.[9]   [*Exeunt* PANDER *and* PIRATES]

50 BAWD   Boult, take you the marks of her, the colour of her hair,
complexion, height, her age, with warrant of her virginity, and
cry 'He that will give most shall have her first.' Such a maidenhead were no cheap thing if men were as they have been. Get
this done as I command you.

---

2. If we don't proceed diligently; if conscience can't be
economically exploited; perhaps a comic blunder for "if
conscience is involved."

3. And brought them to prostitution when they turned
eleven.

4. Overboiled in the sweating tub as treatment for venereal disease.

5. Our reputation doesn't accumulate like our profit, nor

does the profit justify the danger (with extended economic wordplay: "credit," "commodity," "wages").

6. This out-of-character admission is part of the religious
undercurrent of the scene.

7. Any secret; any (holy) trade.

8. I cannot get the price reduced a penny (*doit:* small
coin) from.

9. May not be unprepared to entertain customers.

55 BOULT Performance shall follow.   *Exit*

MARINA Alack that Leonine was so slack, so slow.
He should have struck, not spoke; or that° these pirates,   *if only*
Not enough barbarous, had but o'erboard thrown me
To seek my mother.

60 BAWD Why lament you, pretty one?

MARINA That I am pretty.

BAWD Come, the gods have done their part in you.

MARINA I accuse them not.

BAWD You are light° into my hands, where you are like° to live.   *arrived / likely*

65 MARINA The more my fault°   *misfortune*
To scape his hands where I was like to die.

BAWD Ay, and you shall live in pleasure.

MARINA No.

BAWD Yes, indeed shall you, and taste gentlemen of all fashions.
70 You shall fare well. You shall have the difference of all complexions.[1] What, do you stop your ears?

MARINA Are you a woman?

BAWD What would you have me be an I be not a woman?

MARINA An honest° woman, or not a woman.   *A chaste*

75 BAWD Marry, whip the gosling! I think I shall have something to
do° with you. Come, you're a young foolish sapling, and must   *some trouble*
be bowed as I would have you.

MARINA The gods defend me!

80 BAWD If it please the gods to defend you by men, then men
must comfort you, men must feed you, men must stir you up.
          Enter BOULT
Now, sir, hast thou cried° her through the market?   *advertised*

BOULT I have cried her almost to° the number of her hairs. I   *down to*
have drawn her picture with my voice.

BAWD And I prithee tell me, how dost thou find the inclination
85 of the people, especially of the younger sort?

BOULT Faith, they listened to me as they would have hearkened
to their fathers' testament.° There was a Spaniard's mouth   *will*
watered as he went to bed to her very description.

BAWD We shall have him here tomorrow with his best ruff° on.   *collar*

90 BOULT Tonight, tonight. But mistress, do you know the French
knight that cowers i' the hams?[2]

BAWD Who, Monsieur Veroles?

BOULT Ay, he. He offered to cut a caper[3] at the proclamation,
but he made a groan at it, and swore he would see her
95 tomorrow.

BAWD Well, well, as for him, he brought his disease hither.[4]
Here he does but repair° it. I know he will come in our shadow   *renew*
to scatter his crowns of the sun.[5]

BOULT Well, if we had of every nation a traveller, we should
100 lodge them all with this sign.[6]

BAWD [*to* MARINA] Pray you, come hither a while. You have fortunes coming upon you.[7] Mark me, you must seem to do that

---

1. The variety of appearances (temperaments; ethnici-
ties).
2. Who crouches (from venereal disease).
3. He prepared to leap up and clap his heels together.
4. Englishmen called syphilis "the French disease." This
allusion is one indication of the distinctively English feel
of the scene; see also Scene 5.
5. He will come inside our house to spend his French

crowns; to lose hair from syphilis; to spend his money on
Marina ("sun," if Q1's "in the sun" is retained). With a
play on "shadow" and "sun."
6. We would draw them all here by my pictorial description of Marina.
7. You have prosperity (wealthy men) about to come to
(have an orgasm on top of) you.

fearfully which you commit willingly, to despise profit where
you have most gain. To weep that you live as ye do° makes pity   *(by prostitution)*
105 in your lovers. Seldom but that pity begets you a good opinion,
and that opinion a mere° profit.   *clear*

MARINA   I understand you not.

BOULT [*to* BAWD]   O, take her home,° mistress, take her home.   *inside; to task*
These blushes of hers must be quenched with some present
110 practice.

BAWD   Thou sayst true, i'faith, so they must, for your bride goes
to that with shame which is her way to go with warrant.°   *legitimately*

BOULT   Faith, some do and some do not. But mistress, if I have
bargained for the joint°—   *cut of meat*
115 BAWD   Thou mayst cut a morsel off the spit.°   *deflower her*

BOULT   I may so.

BAWD   Who should deny it? [*To* MARINA] Come, young one, I
like the manner of your garments well.

BOULT   Ay, by my faith, they shall not be changed yet.[8]
120 BAWD [*giving him money*]   Boult, spend thou that in the town.
Report what a sojourner we have. You'll lose nothing by cus-
tom.[9] When nature framed this piece° she meant thee a good   *(of work); (of flesh)*
turn. Therefore say what a paragon she is, and thou reapest the
harvest out of thine own setting forth.
125 BOULT   I warrant you, mistress, thunder shall not so awake the
beds of eels[1] as my giving out her beauty stirs up the lewdly
inclined. I'll bring home some tonight.   [*Exit*]

BAWD   Come your ways, follow me.

MARINA   If fires be hot, knives sharp, or waters deep,
130 Untied I still my virgin knot will keep.[2]
Diana° aid my purpose.   *goddess of chastity*

BAWD   What have we to do with Diana? Pray you, will you go
with me?   *Exeunt.* [*The sign is removed*]

Scene 17

Enter [in mourning garments] CLEON *and* DIONYZA

DIONYZA   Why, are you foolish? Can it be undone?

CLEON   O Dionyza, such a piece of slaughter
The sun and moon ne'er looked upon.

DIONYZA   I think you'll turn a child again.
5 CLEON   Were I chief lord of all this spacious world
I'd give it to undo the deed. A lady°   *(Marina)*
Much less in blood than virtue, yet a princess
To equal any single crown o'th' earth
I'th' justice of compare.° O villain Leonine,   *In a fair comparison*
10 Whom thou hast poisoned too,
If thou hadst drunk to him 't'ad been a kindness
Becoming well thy fact.[1] What canst thou say
When noble Pericles demands his child?

DIONYZA   That she is dead. Nurses are not the fates.

---

8. Exchanged or sold (for a prostitute's wardrobe), since they proclaim her virginity and social status.
9. You'll profit from the resulting increase in our customers; (perhaps) you'll get your turn with Marina.
1. Eels were supposedly roused by thunder.
2. An "Untied . . . virgin knot" presumably means loss of virginity—not what Marina wants. Perhaps her intent is

suggested by the pun of "knot" and "not"—hence, not untied.
Scene 17 (Act 4, Scene 3)
Location: The Governor's house in Tarsus.
1. *If . . . fact:* If you had drunk his health (from the same poison), the self-punishment would have fit the crime.

15   To foster is not ever° to preserve.   *always*
       She died at night. I'll say so. Who can cross° it,   *deny*
       Unless you play the pious innocent
       And, for an honest attribute,° cry out   *reputation*
       'She died by foul play.'
   CLEON   O, go to.° Well, well,   *(contemptuous)*
20   Of all the faults beneath the heav'ns the gods
       Do like this worst.
   DIONYZA   Be one of those that thinks
       The petty wrens of Tarsus will fly hence
       And open° this to Pericles. I do shame   *disclose*
       To think of what a noble strain° you are,   *bloodline*
       And of how cowed a spirit.
25   CLEON   To such proceeding
       Whoever but his approbation added,
       Though not his prime° consent, he did not flow   *prior*
       From honourable sources.
   DIONYZA   Be it so, then.
       Yet none does know but you how she came dead,
30   Nor none can know, Leonine being gone.
       She did distain° my child, and stood between   *stain (by comparison)*
       Her and her fortunes. None would look on her,
       But cast their gazes on Marina's face
       Whilst ours was blurted at,° and held a malkin°   *scorned / dirty peasant*
35   Not worth the time of day. It pierced me through,
       And though you call my course unnatural,
       You not your child well loving, yet I find
       It greets° me as an enterprise of kindness   *strikes*
       Performed to your sole daughter.
40   CLEON   Heavens forgive it.
   DIONYZA   And as for Pericles,
       What should he say? We wept after her hearse,
       And yet° we mourn. Her monument   *still*
       Is almost finished, and her epitaphs
45   In glitt'ring golden characters express
       A gen'ral praise to her and care in us,
       At whose expense 'tis done.
   CLEON   Thou art like the harpy,[2]
       Which, to betray, dost, with thine angel face,
       Seize in thine eagle talons.
50   DIONYZA   Ye're like one that superstitiously
       Do swear to th' gods that winter kills the flies,[3]
       But yet I know you'll do as I advise.   *Exeunt*

Scene 18

   Enter GOWER
   GOWER   Thus time we waste,° and long leagues make we short,[1]   *pass quickly*
       Sail seas in cockles,° have and wish but for't,[2]   *seashells*
       Making to take° imagination   *Proceeding by*
       From bourn° to bourn, region to region.   *border*

---

2. Monstrous creature with a woman's face and an eagle's talons.
3. *Ye're . . . flies:* perhaps, You're so afraid of the gods that you'd feel it necessary to tell them insignificant and unalterable things they already know (that winter killed the flies).

Scene 18 Scene 18 (Act, Scene 4)
Location: Before Marina's tomb in Tarsus.
1. Here Gower speaks in pentameter couplets.
2. Get something merely by wishing for it.

5   By you being pardoned, we commit no crime
    To use one language in each sev'ral clime°   *separate region*
    Where our scene seems to live. I do beseech you
    To learn of me, who stand i'th' gaps° to teach you   *(between scenes)*
    The stages of our story: Pericles
10 Is now again thwarting° the wayward seas,   *crossing*
    Attended on by many a lord and knight,
    To see his daughter, all his life's delight.
    Old Helicanus goes along. Behind
    Is left to govern, if you bear in mind,
15 Old Aeschines, whom Helicanus late°   *recently*
    Advanced in Tyre to great and high estate.°   *rank*
    Well sailing ships and bounteous winds have brought
    This king to Tarsus—think his pilot thought;[3]
    So with his steerage shall your thoughts go on—
20 To fetch his daughter home, who first° is gone.   *already*
    Like motes and shadows[4] see them move a while;
    Your ears unto your eyes I'll reconcile.

                              [*Dumb show.*]
            Enter PERICLES *at one door with all his train,* CLEON
            and DIONYZA [*in mourning garments*] *at the other.*
            CLEON [*draws the curtain and*] *shows* PERICLES *the*
            tomb, whereat PERICLES *makes lamentation, puts on*
            sack-cloth, and in a mighty passion° departs [*followed by*   *sorrow*
            his train. CLEON *and* DIONYZA *depart at the other door*]

    See how belief may suffer by foul show.°   *false appearances*
    This borrowed passion stands for true-owed woe,[5]
25 And Pericles, in sorrow all devoured,
    With sighs shot through, and biggest tears o'ershow'red,
    Leaves Tarsus, and again embarks. He swears
    Never to wash his face nor cut his hairs.
    He puts on sack-cloth, and to sea. He bears
30 A tempest which his mortal vessel tears,[6]
    And yet he rides it out. Now please you wit°   *know*
    The epitaph is° for Marina writ   *that is*
    By wicked Dionyza.

                    [*He reads Marina's epitaph*[7] *on the tomb*]
    'The fairest, sweetest, best lies here,
35 Who withered in her spring of year.°   *early in life*
    In nature's garden, though by growth a bud,
    She was the chiefest flower: she was good.'
    No visor does become black villainy
    So well as soft and tender flattery.
40 Let Pericles believe his daughter's dead
    And bear his courses to be orderèd[8]
    By Lady Fortune, while our scene must play
    His daughter's woe and heavy well-a-day°   *lamentation*
    In her unholy service. Patience then,
45 And think you now are all in Mytilene.

                                                            Exit

3. Think that his pilot is swiftly traveling thought.
4. Like specks of dust in a sunbeam and like (theatrical)
illusions.
5. Cleon and Dionyza's "woe" is "borrowed," not "true-
owed" (owned); perhaps also a self-referential comment
on the sorrow simulated by the actor playing Pericles.
6. *He bears . . . tears:* His suffering assaults his body.

(Note the internalization of the earlier storms.)
7. The four-line epitaph is from *PA*, which may preserve
the author's revised version of this passage. Q1's ten-line
version (see the Additional Passage at the end of the play)
includes the first two lines here.
8. And allow his fate to be arranged.

Scene 19

[*A brothel sign.*] *Enter two* GENTLEMEN

FIRST GENTLEMAN Did you ever hear the like?

SECOND GENTLEMAN No, nor never shall do in such a place as
this, she being once gone.

FIRST GENTLEMAN But to have divinity preached there—did you
5   ever dream of such a thing?

SECOND GENTLEMAN No, no. Come, I am for no more bawdy
houses. Shall 's go hear the vestals sing?[1]

FIRST GENTLEMAN I'll do anything now that is virtuous, but I am
out of the road of rutting° for ever.   *Exeunt*   fornication

Enter [PANDER,] BAWD [*and* BOULT]

10   PANDER Well, I had rather than twice the worth of her she had
ne'er come here.

BAWD Fie, fie upon her, she's able to freeze the god Priapus and
undo the whole of generation.[2] We must either get her ravished
or be rid of her. When she should do for clients her fitment°   duty
15   and do me the kindness of our profession,[3] she has° me her   gives
quirks, her reasons, her master reasons, her prayers, her knees,°   (kneeling to plead)
that she would make a puritan of the devil if he should
cheapen° a kiss of her.   bargain for

BOULT Faith, I must ravish her, or she'll disfurnish us of all our
20   cavalleria° and make our swearers[4] priests.   gentlemen customers

PANDER Now, the pox upon her green-sickness[5] for me.

BAWD Faith, there's no way to be rid on't but by the way to the pox.°   venereal disease

Enter LYSIMACHUS [*disguised*]

Here comes the Lord Lysimachus, disguised.

BOULT We should have both lord and loon° if the peevish bag-   lowborn
25   gage° would but give way to custom.[6]   worthless woman

LYSIMACHUS How now, how° a dozen of virginities?   how much for

BAWD Now, the gods to-bless your honour!

BOULT I am glad to see your honour in good health.

LYSIMACHUS You may so. 'Tis the better for you that your resort-
30   ers stand upon sound legs.[7] How now, wholesome iniquity°   healthy whore
have you, that a man may deal withal° and defy the surgeon?°   with / avoid the doctor

BAWD We have here one, sir, if she would—but there never
came her like in Mytilene.

LYSIMACHUS If she'd do the deed of darkness, thou wouldst say.

35   BAWD Your honour knows what 'tis to say° well enough.   what I mean

LYSIMACHUS Well, call forth, call forth.   [*Exit* PANDER]

BOULT For flesh and blood, sir, white and red, you shall see a
rose. And she were a rose indeed, if she had but—[8]

LYSIMACHUS What, prithee?

40   BOULT O sir, I can be modest.

Scene 19 (Other modern editions divide this scene in
two: Act 4, Scene 5 [lines 1–9] and Scene 6 [lines 10–
211]. But the location remains in or around the brothel
throughout. This edition assumes both that there is no
gap in time between the two parts and that the modest
shifts in locale within the scene do not violate the relatively unspecific notion of place on the early seventeenth-
century stage.)
Location: The brothel in Mytilene.
1. Shall we go hear the vestal virgins (religious devotees)
sing?
2. Able to stop the "whole" (hole) work of breeding.

Priapus was the god of procreation, especially of male
virility and lechery. "The whole of" emends Q1's "a
whole."
3. Enable me to profit from her profession of prostitution;
perhaps also homoerotic: have sex with me.
4. Loyal (blasphemous) customers.
5. Moody stubbornness, supposedly caused by anemia in
young women; queasiness from lack of experience.
6. Customers; customary behavior. Q1 has "customers."
7. Rather than upon legs bent from venereal disease.
8. If she had but a thorn; if she were sexually experienced.

LYSIMACHUS   That dignifies the renown of a bawd no less than
    it gives a good report to a noble to be chaste.[9]
                Enter [PANDER *with*] MARINA

BAWD   Here comes that which grows to° the stalk, never plucked   *affixed to*
    yet, I can assure you. Is she not a fair creature?

45 LYSIMACHUS   Faith, she would serve after a long voyage at sea.
    Well, there's for you. Leave us.
            [*He pays the* BAWD]

BAWD   I beseech your honour give me leave: a word, and I'll
    have done presently.°   *be done soon*

LYSIMACHUS   I beseech you, do.

50 BAWD [*aside to* MARINA]   First, I would have you note this is an
    honourable man.

MARINA   I desire to find him so, that I may honourably know him.

BAWD   Next, he's the governor of this country, and a man whom
    I am bound to.

55 MARINA   If he govern the country you are bound to him indeed,
    but how honourable he is in that, I know not.

BAWD   Pray you, without any more virginal fencing, will you use
    him kindly? He will line your apron with gold.

MARINA   What he will do graciously I will thankfully receive.

60 LYSIMACHUS [*to* BAWD]   Ha' you done?

BAWD   My lord, she's not paced° yet. You must take some pains   *trained (like a horse)*
    to work her to your manège.[1] [*To* BOULT *and* PANDER] Come,
    we will leave his honour and hers together. Go thy ways.°   *Come along*
             Exeunt [PANDER,] BAWD [*and* BOULT]

LYSIMACHUS   Fair one, how long have you been at this trade?

65 MARINA   What trade, sir?

LYSIMACHUS   I cannot name it but I shall offend.

MARINA   I cannot be offended with my trade.
    Please you to name it.

LYSIMACHUS   How long have you been
Of this profession?

MARINA   E'er since I can remember.

70 LYSIMACHUS   Did you go to't° so young? Were you a gamester°   *copulate / loose woman*
    At five, or seven?

MARINA   Earlier too, sir,
If now I be one.

LYSIMACHUS   Why, the house you dwell in
Proclaimeth you a creature of sale.

MARINA   And do you know this house to be a place
75 Of such resort° and will come into it?   *purpose*
I hear say you're of honourable blood,
And are the governor of this whole province.

LYSIMACHUS   What, hath your principal° informed you who I am?   *employer*

MARINA   Who is my principal?

LYSIMACHUS   Why, your herb-woman;
80 She that sets seeds of shame, roots of iniquity.
        [MARINA *weeps*]
O, you've heard something of my pow'r, and so
Stand off aloof for a more serious wooing.

---

9. Than it gives a noble(wo)man a (falsely) good reputation for being chaste. Q1 has "number" for "noble."

1. To bring her under your control (from horsemanship).

But I protest to thee,
Pretty one, my authority can wink
85   At blemishes,[2] or can on faults look friendly;
Or my displeasure punish at my pleasure,
From which displeasure, not thy beauty shall
Privilege thee, nor my affection,° which   *lust*
Hath drawn me here, abate with further ling'ring.
90   Come bring me to some private place. Come, come.
MARINA   Let not authority, which teaches you
To govern others, be the means to make you
Misgovern much yourself.[3]
If you were born to honour,° show it now;   *high status; virtue*
95   If put upon you,[4] make the judgement good
That thought you worthy of it. What[5] reason's in
Your justice, who hath power over all,
To undo any? If you take from me
Mine honour, you're like him that makes a gap
100   Into forbidden ground, whom after
Too many enter, and of all their evils
Yourself are guilty. My life is yet unspotted;°   *still free of sin*
My chastity unstainèd ev'n in thought.
Then if your violence deface this building,°   *body*
105   The workmanship of heav'n, you do kill your honour,
Abuse your justice, and impoverish me.
My yet good lord, if there be fire before me,
Must I straight fly° and burn myself? Suppose this house—   *go immediately*
Which too too many feel such houses are—
110   Should be the doctor's patrimony, and
The surgeon's feeding;° follows it, that I   *livelihood*
Must needs infect myself to give them maint'nance?
LYSIMACHUS   How's this, how's this? Some more. Be sage.
MARINA [*kneeling*]   For me
That am a maid, though most ungentle fortune
115   Have franked° me in this sty, where since I came   *shut*
Diseases have been sold dearer than physic—[6]
That the gods would set me free from this unhallowed place,
Though they did change me to the meanest° bird   *humblest*
That flies i'th' purer air!
LYSIMACHUS [*moved*]   I did not think
120   Thou couldst have spoke so well, ne'er dreamt thou couldst.
[*He lifts her up with his hands*]
Though I brought hither a corrupted mind,
Thy speech hath altered it,
[*He wipes the wet from her eyes*]
                                    and my foul thoughts
Thy tears so well hath laved° that they're now white.   *cleansed*
I came here meaning but to pay the price,

2. *can wink / At blemishes:* can refuse to see moral shortcomings. Lines 84–89 are adapted from *PA* and replace
Q1's "my authority shall not see thee, or else look friendly
upon thee," which doesn't reflect as badly on Lysimachus. Here and in subsequent passages in this scene,
PA may preserve Shakespeare's original words.
3. *Let . . . yourself:* not in Q1 adapted from *PA*.

4. If you were granted rank not by birth but by merit.
5. Lines 96–112 are not in Q1 but were adapted from
PA. Q1's lines 94–96 ("If . . . it") and 113–19 ("For . . .
air") seem inadequate to produce Lysimachus's response
at line 113 and dramatic conversion at lines 119–20.
6. Sold at a higher price than medical treatment.

125 A piece of gold for thy virginity;
Here's twenty to relieve thine honesty.[7]
Persever still° in that clear way thou goest,   *always*
And the gods strengthen thee.

MARINA   The good gods preserve you!

LYSIMACHUS   The[8] very doors and windows savour vilely.

130 Fare thee well. Thou art a piece of virtue,
The best wrought up° that ever nature made,[9]   *created*
And I doubt not thy training hath been noble.
A curse upon him, die he° like a thief,   *may he die*
That robs thee of thy honour. Hold, here's more gold.

135 If thou dost hear from me, it shall be for thy good.
[*Enter* BOULT *standing ready at the door, making his
obeisance unto him as* LYSIMACHUS *should go out*]

BOULT   I beseech your honour, one piece for me.

LYSIMACHUS   Avaunt,° thou damnèd door-keeper!   *Begone*
Your house, but for this virgin that doth prop it,
Would sink and overwhelm you. Away.   [*Exit*]

140 BOULT   How's this? We must take another course with you. If
your peevish chastity, which is not worth a breakfast in the
cheapest country under the cope,° shall undo a whole house-   *sky*
hold, let me be gelded like a spaniel. Come your ways.

MARINA   Whither would you have me?

145 BOULT   I must have your maidenhead taken off, or the common
executioner shall do it.[1] We'll have no more gentlemen driven
away. Come your ways, I say.
Enter BAWD [*and* PANDER]

BAWD   How now, what's the matter?

BOULT   Worse and worse, mistress, she has here spoken holy
150 words to the Lord Lysimachus.

BAWD   O, abominable!

BOULT   She makes our profession as it were to stink afore the
face of the gods.

BAWD   Marry° hang her up for ever!   *(expresses irritation)*

155 BOULT   The nobleman would have dealt with her like a nobleman,[2] and she sent him away as cold as a snowball, saying his
prayers, too.

PANDER   Boult, take her away. Use her at thy pleasure. Crack the
ice of her virginity, and make the rest malleable.

160 BOULT   An if° she were a thornier piece of ground than she is,   *Even if*
she shall be ploughed.

MARINA   Hark, hark, you gods!

BAWD   She conjures.° Away with her! Would she had never   *calls on the gods*
come within my doors.—Marry, hang you!—She's born to
165 undo us.—Will you not go the way of womenkind? Marry,
come up, my dish of chastity with rosemary and bays.[3]
Exeunt [BAWD *and* PANDER]

BOULT [*catching her rashly by the hand*]   Come, mistress, come
your way with me.

---

7. To assist your chastity. Lines 124–26, adapted from
PA, replace Q1's "Hold here's gold for thee."
8. Q1 precedes these lines with "For me be you
thoughten [understand], that I came with no ill intent,
for to me."
9. Line 131 not in Q1; adapted from *PA*.

1. "Executioner shall do" replaces Q1's "hāg-man shall
execute," producing wordplay on "maidenhead" and
"executioner" (one who chops off heads).
2. Would have used her and rewarded her well.
3. The Bawd chides Marina for thinking herself too exquisite a dish (for making too much of her chastity).

MARINA   Whither wilt thou have me?

170 BOULT   To take from you the jewel you hold so dear.

MARINA   Prithee, tell me one thing first.

BOULT   Come, now, your one thing.

MARINA   What canst thou wish thine enemy to be?[4]

BOULT   Why, I could wish him to be° my master, or rather my   (as bad as)

175   mistress.

MARINA   Neither of these can be so bad as thou art,
    Since they do better thee in their command.[5]
    Thou hold'st a place the painèd'st° fiend of hell   most tortured
    Would not in reputation change with thee,

180 Thou damnèd doorkeeper to ev'ry coistrel°   base fellow
    That comes enquiring for his Tib.°   loose woman
    To th' choleric fisting of ev'ry rogue
    Thy ear is liable.[6] Thy food is such
    As hath been belched on by infected lungs.

185 BOULT   What would you have me do? Go to the wars, would
    you, where a man may serve seven years for the loss of° a leg,   only to lose
    and have not money enough in the end to buy him a wooden one?

MARINA   Do anything but this thou dost. Empty
    Old receptacles or common sew'rs of filth,

190   Serve by indenture° to the public hangman—   as apprentice
    Any of these are yet better than this.
    For what thou professest a baboon, could he speak,
    Would own a name too dear.[7] Here's gold for thee.
    If that thy master would make gain by me,

195   Proclaim that I can sing, weave, sew, and dance,
    With other virtues° which I'll keep from boast,   accomplishments
    And I will undertake all these to teach.
    I doubt not but this populous city will
    Yield many scholars.°   pupils

200 BOULT   But can you teach all this you speak of?

MARINA   Prove° that I cannot, take me home again   If you prove
    And prostitute me to the basest groom°   lowest servant
    That doth frequent your house.

BOULT   Well, I will see what I can do for thee. If I can place

205   thee, I will.

MARINA   But amongst honest women.

BOULT   Faith, my acquaintance lies little amongst them; but
    since my master and mistress hath bought you, there's no going
    but by their consent. Therefore I will make them acquainted

210   with your purpose, and I doubt not but I shall find them tracta-
    ble enough. Come, I'll do for thee what I can. Come your ways.
                              Exeunt. [The sign is removed]

Scene 20

Enter GOWER

GOWER   Marina thus the brothel scapes, and chances[1]
    Into an honest house, our story says.

---

4. What is the worst thing you could wish on your
enemy?
5. Since they can command you to do what even they
wouldn't do themselves.
6. *To . . . liable:* Even the lowest rogue would box your
ear if angry.
7. Would consider beneath him. Q1 follows this sen-

tence with "That the gods would safely deliver me from
this place: here"—a repetition of line 117 that is out of
place here.
Scene 20 (Act 5, Chorus)
1. Unlike Gower's other prologues, which are in tetrameter or, less often, pentameter rhyming couplets, this one
rhymes alternate pentameter lines.

She sings like one immortal, and she dances
    As goddess-like to her admirèd lays.°   *songs*
5 Deep clerks she dumbs,[2] and with her nee'le° composes   *needle*
    Nature's own shape, of bud, bird, branch, or berry,
That e'en her art sisters° the natural roses.   *equals*
Her inkle,° silk, twin with the rubied cherry;   *linen thread*
That° pupils lacks she none of noble race,   *So that*
10 Who pour their bounty on her, and her gain
She gives the cursèd Bawd. Here we her place,
    And to her father turn our thoughts again.
We left him on the sea. Waves there him tossed,
    Whence, driven tofore° the winds, he is arrived   *before*
15 Here where his daughter dwells, and on this coast
    Suppose him now at anchor. The city strived°   *surpassed itself*
God Neptune's annual feast to keep, from whence
Lysimachus our Tyrian ship espies,
    His° banners sable,° trimmed with rich expense;   *Its / black*
20 And to him° in his barge with fervour hies.   *it*
In your supposing° once more put your sight;   *imagination*
    Of heavy° Pericles think this the barque,°   *sad / ship*
Where what is done in action, more if might,
    Shall be discovered.[3] Please you sit and hark.   *Exit*

Scene 21

Enter HELICANUS [*above; below, enter*] *to him* [*at the first door*] *two* SAILORS [*one* OF TYRE, *the other* OF MYTI-LENE]

SAILOR OF TYRE [*to* SAILOR OF MYTILENE] Lord Helicanus can
    resolve[1] you, sir.
    [*To* HELICANUS] There is a barge put off from Mytilene.
    In it, Lysimachus, the governor,
    Who craves to come aboard. What is your will?
HELICANUS That he have his.
          [*Exit* SAILOR OF MYTILENE *at first door*]
5   Call up some gentlemen.
                    [*Exit* HELICANUS *above*]
SAILOR OF TYRE Ho, my lord calls!
    Enter [*from below the stage*] *two or three*
    GENTLEMEN[; *to them, enter* HELICANUS]
FIRST GENTLEMAN   What is your lordship's pleasure?
HELICANUS Gentlemen, some of worth° would come aboard.   *some noble visitor*
    I pray you, greet him fairly.
    Enter LYSIMACHUS [*at first door, with the* SAILOR *and*
    LORDS OF MYTILENE]
SAILOR OF MYTILENE [*to* LYSIMACHUS] This is the man that can
    in aught resolve° you.   *answer anything for*
10 LYSIMACHUS [*to* HELICANUS] Hail, reverend sir; the gods preserve you!
HELICANUS And you, sir, to outlive the age I am,
    And die as I would do.

---

2. Her wisdom reduces learned men to silence.
3. *Where . . . discovered:* Where the stage action, which
would show more if it could, will reveal what happens.

Scene 21 (Act 5, Scene 1)
Location: Pericles' ship, off Mytilene.
1. Answer. This line replaces Q1's "Where is Lord Heli-canus? He can resolve you, / O here he is sir."

LYSIMACHUS   You wish me well.
    I am the governor of Mytilene;[2]
    Being on shore, honouring of Neptune's triumphs,[3]
15 Seeing this goodly vessel ride before us,
    I made to it to know of whence you are.
HELICANUS   Our vessel is of Tyre, in it our king,
    A man who for this three months hath not spoken
    To anyone, nor taken sustenance
20 But to prorogue° his grief.   ° extend
LYSIMACHUS   Upon what ground grew his distemp'rature?°   ° emotional disturbance
HELICANUS   'Twould be too tedious to tell it over,
    But the main grief springs from the precious loss
    Of a belovèd daughter and a wife.
LYSIMACHUS   May we not see him?
25 HELICANUS   See him, sir, you may,
    But bootless° is your sight. He will not speak   ° pointless
    To any.
LYSIMACHUS   Let me yet obtain my wish.
HELICANUS   Behold him.
        [HELICANUS *draws a curtain, revealing* PERICLES *lying*
        upon a couch with a long overgrown beard, diffused°   ° disorderly
        hair, undecent nails on his fingers, and attired in sack-
        cloth]
                This was a goodly person
    Till the disaster of one mortal° night   ° fatal
    Drove him to this.
30 LYSIMACHUS [*to* PERICLES]   Sir, King, all hail. Hail, royal sir.
        [PERICLES *shrinks himself down upon his pillow*]
HELICANUS   It is in vain. He will not speak to you.
LORD OF MYTILENE   Sir, we have a maid in Mytilene I durst wager
    Would win some words of him.
LYSIMACHUS   'Tis well bethought.
    She questionless, with her sweet harmony
35 And other choice attractions, would alarum[4]
    And make a batt'ry through his deafened ports,
    Which now are midway stopped.° She in all happy,°   ° half closed / skillful
    As the fair'st of all, among her fellow maids
    Dwells now i'th' leafy shelter that abuts
40 Against the island's side. Go fetch her hither.   [*Exit* LORD]
HELICANUS   Sure, all effectless; yet nothing we'll omit
    That bears recov'ry's name.° But since your kindness   ° *That might cure him*
    We have stretched thus far, let us beseech you
    That for our gold we may provision have,
45 Wherein we are not destitute for want,
    But weary for the staleness.
LYSIMACHUS   O sir, a courtesy
    Which if we should deny, the most just gods
    For every graft° would send a caterpillar,   ° cultivated plant
    And so inflict° our province. Yet once more   ° afflict (with famine)

---

2. This line replaces Q1's
    HELICANUS   First what is your place?
    LYSIMACHUS   I am the Governor of this place you lie
        before,
which appears after line 16, where it interrupts the dialogue and attributes to Helicanus a rudeness that seems

gratuitous, since he already knows who Lysimachus is
(see line 3).
3. Observing Neptune's festival.
4. Awaken (as a trumpet). Q1 has "allure," which
introduces a sexual innuendo (see the Introduction).

50 Let me entreat to know at large° the cause   *in detail*
  Of your king's sorrow.
  HELICANUS   Sit, sir. I will recount it.
        [*Enter* LORD *with* MARINA *and another* MAID]
  But see, I am prevented.
  LYSIMACHUS   O, here's the lady that I sent for.—
  Welcome, fair one.—Is't not a goodly presence?°   *Isn't she attractive*
55 HELICANUS   She's a gallant° lady.   *fine*
  LYSIMACHUS   She's such a one that, were I well assured
  Came of gentle kind° or noble stock, I'd wish   *a gentry family*
  No better choice to think me rarely° wed.—   *superbly*
  Fair one, all goodness that consists in bounty
60 Expect e'en here, where is a kingly patient;
  If that thy prosperous and artificial feat°   *artful skill*
  Can draw him but to answer thee in aught,
  Thy sacred physic° shall receive such pay   *treatment*
  As thy desires can wish.
  MARINA   Sir, I will use
65 My utmost skill in his recure,° provided   *cure*
  That none but I and my companion maid
  Be suffered° to come near him.   *permitted*
  LYSIMACHUS [*to the others*]   Let us leave her,
  And the gods prosper her.   [*The men stand aside*]
      The Song⁵
  LYSIMACHUS [*coming forward*]   Marked° he your music?   *Noticed*
  MAID   No, nor looked on us.
  LYSIMACHUS [*to the others*]   See, she will speak to him.
70 MARINA [*to* PERICLES]   Hail, sir; my lord, lend ear.
  PERICLES   Hmh, ha!
       [*He roughly repulses her*]
  MARINA   I am a maid,
  My lord, that ne'er before invited eyes,
  But have been gazed on like a comet.° She speaks,   *in awe*
75 My lord, that maybe hath endured a grief
  Might° equal yours, if both were justly weighed.   *That might*
  Though wayward fortune did malign my state,°   *reduce my status*
  My derivation was from ancestors
  Who stood equivalent with mighty kings,
80 But time hath rooted out⁶ my parentage,
  And to the world and awkward casualties°   *adverse events*
  Bound me in servitude. [*Aside*] I will desist.
  But there is something glows upon my cheek,
  And whispers in mine ear 'Stay till he speak.'
85 PERICLES   My fortunes, parentage, good parentage,
  To equal mine? Was it not thus? What say you?
  MARINA   I said if you did know my parentage,
  My lord, you would not do me violence.
  PERICLES   I do think so. Pray you, turn your eyes upon me.
90 You're like something that—what countrywoman?°   *what nationality*
  Here of these shores?
  MARINA   No, nor of any shores,

5. The song is given in *PA*, which takes it from Twine's   one in particular.
Patterne of Painefull Adventures. The early texts of   6. Uprooted me from; obscured; killed.
Shakespeare often call for a song without specifying any

Yet I was mortally[7] brought forth, and am
No other than I seem.

PERICLES [aside]   I am great° with woe, and shall deliver   pregnant
   weeping.
95   My dearest wife was like this maid, and such
   My daughter might have been. My queen's square brows,
   Her stature to an inch, as wand-like straight,
   As silver-voiced, her eyes as jewel-like,
   And cased as richly, in pace° another Juno,   stride
100   Who starves the ears she feeds, and makes them hungry
   The more she gives them speech.—Where do you live?

MARINA   Where I am but a stranger.° From the deck   foreigner
   You may discern the place.

PERICLES   Where were you bred,
   And how achieved you these endowments which
   You make more rich to owe?°   by your owning them

105   MARINA   If I should tell
   My history, it would seem like lies
   Disdained in the reporting.°   as soon as told

PERICLES   Prithee speak.
   Falseness cannot come from thee, for thou look'st
   Modest as justice, and thou seem'st a palace
110   For the crowned truth to dwell in. I will believe thee,
   And make my senses credit thy relation°   trust your story
   To° points that seem impossible. Thou show'st   Even to
   Like one I loved indeed. What were thy friends?°   kin
   Didst thou not say, when I did push thee back—
115   Which was when I perceived thee—that thou cam'st
   From good descending?

MARINA   So indeed I did.

PERICLES   Report thy parentage. I think thou said'st
   Thou hadst been tossed from wrong to injury,
   And that thou thought'st thy griefs might equal mine,
   If both were opened.°   revealed

120   MARINA   Some such thing I said,
   And said no more but what my circumstance
   Did warrant° me was likely.   assure

PERICLES   Tell thy story.
   If thine considered prove the thousandth part
   Of my endurance,° thou art a man, and I   suffering
125   Have suffered like a girl. Yet thou dost look
   Like patience gazing on kings' graves, and smiling
   Extremity out of act.[8] What were thy friends?
   How lost thou them? Thy name, my most kind[9] virgin?
   Recount, I do beseech thee. Come, sit by me.
      [She sits]

MARINA   My name, sir, is Marina.

130   PERICLES   O, I am mocked,
   And thou by some incensèd god sent hither
   To make the world to laugh at me.

7. "Normally," not supernaturally, despite not being born
on "any shores"; perhaps also "fatally"—to her mother.
8. Yet . . . act: Yet you seem able to bear even the deaths
of Kings (like statues of Patience personified, perhaps

on royal tombs) and to face down the worst extremities
(especially suicidal despair) with a smile.
9. Sympathetic; related by blood ("kind" also meant
"kin").

MARINA   Patience, good sir,
Or here I'll cease.

PERICLES   Nay, I'll be patient.
Thou little know'st how thou dost startle me
To call thyself Marina.

135 MARINA   The name
Was given me by one that had some power:
My father, and a king.

PERICLES   How, a king's daughter,
And called Marina?

MARINA   You said you would believe me,
But not to be a troubler of your peace
I will end here.

140 PERICLES   But are you flesh and blood?
Have you a working pulse and are no fairy?
Motion° as well? Speak on. Where were you born,   (of life)
And wherefore called Marina?

MARINA   Called Marina
For I was born at sea.

PERICLES   At sea? What mother?

145 MARINA   My mother was the daughter of a king,
Who died when I was born, as my good nurse
Lychorida hath oft recounted weeping.

PERICLES   O, stop there a little! [*Aside*] This is the rarest dream
That e'er dulled sleep did mock sad fools withal.°   with
150 This cannot be my daughter, buried. Well.
[*To* MARINA] Where were you bred? I'll hear you more to th'
    bottom°   the end
Of your story, and never interrupt you.

MARINA   You will scarce believe me. 'Twere best I did give o'er.°   stop

PERICLES   I will believe you by the syllable
155 Of what you shall deliver. Yet give me leave.°   (to ask)
How came you in these parts? Where were you bred?

MARINA   The King my father did in Tarsus leave me,
Till cruel Cleon, with his wicked wife,
Did seek to murder me, and wooed a villain
160 To attempt the deed; who having drawn to do't,
A crew of pirates came and rescued me.
To Mytilene they brought me. But, good sir,
What will you° of me? Why do you weep? It may be   What do you want
You think me an impostor. No, good faith,
165 I am the daughter to King Pericles,
If good King Pericles be.°   live

PERICLES [*rising*]   Ho, Helicanus!

HELICANUS [*coming forward*]   Calls my lord?

PERICLES   Thou art a grave and noble counsellor,
170 Most wise in gen'ral. Tell me if thou canst
What this maid is, or what is like° to be,   likely
That thus hath made me weep.

HELICANUS   I know not.
But here's the regent, sir, of Mytilene
Speaks° nobly of her.   Who speaks

LYSIMACHUS   She would never tell
175 Her parentage. Being demanded that,
She would sit still and weep.

PERICLES O Helicanus, strike me, honoured sir,
    Give me a gash, put me to present° pain,   *immediate*
    Lest this great sea of joys rushing upon me
180   O'erbear° the shores of my mortality   *Overflow*
    And drown me with their sweetness! [*To* MARINA] O, come hither,
        [MARINA *stands*]
    Thou that begett'st him that did thee beget,[1]
    Thou that wast born at sea, buried at Tarsus,
    And found at sea again!—O Helicanus,
185   Down on thy knees, thank the holy gods as loud
    As thunder threatens us, this is Marina!
    [*To* MARINA] What was thy mother's name? Tell me but that,
    For truth can never be confirmed enough,
    Though doubts did ever sleep.[2]
MARINA   First, sir, I pray,
    What is your title?
190 PERICLES   I am Pericles
    Of Tyre. But tell me now my drowned queen's name.
    As in the rest thou hast been godlike perfect,°   *have been omniscient*
    So prove but true in that, thou art my daughter,[3]
    The heir of kingdoms, and another life
    To Pericles thy father.
195 MARINA [*kneeling*]   Is it no more
    To be your daughter than to say my mother's name?
    Thaisa was my mother, who did end
    The minute I began.
PERICLES   Now blessing on thee! Rise. Thou art my child.
        [MARINA *stands. He kisses her*]
200   [*To attendants*] Give me fresh garments.—Mine own, Helicanus!
    Not dead at Tarsus, as she should have been[4]
    By savage Cleon. She shall tell thee all,
    When thou shalt kneel and justify in knowledge°   *satisfy yourself that*
    She is thy very princess. Who is this?
205 HELICANUS   Sir, 'tis the governor of Mytilene,
    Who, hearing of your melancholy state,
    Did come to see you.
PERICLES [*to* LYSIMACHUS] I embrace you, sir.—
    Give me my robes.
        [*He is attired in fresh robes*]
             I am wild in my beholding.[5]
    O heavens, bless my girl!
        [*Celestial music*]
             But hark, what music?
210   Tell Helicanus, my Marina, tell him
    O'er point by point, for yet he seems to doubt,
    How sure you are my daughter. But what music?
HELICANUS   My lord, I hear none.
PERICLES   None? The music of the spheres![6] List,° my Marina.   *Listen*
LYSIMACHUS [*aside to the others*] It is not good to cross him. Give

---

1. The possible sexual complications here, including incest, can be highlighted in performance by doubling the part of Marina with that of Thaisa or Antiochus's Daughter. (For the possible relevance of doubling the part of Marina to the transmission of the text, see the Textual Note.)
2. Even in the absence of doubts.
3. Line is not in Q1; it was added to fill a suspected gap.
4. As she was believed (intended) to be.
5. Unkempt in my appearance, ecstatic at what I see.
6. A sign of celestial harmony, brought about by the proper movement of the heavenly bodies around earth (hence a sign of divine order).

215   him way.

PERICLES Rar'st sounds. Do ye not hear?

LYSIMACHUS Music, my lord?

PERICLES I hear most heav'nly music.

 It raps° me unto list'ning, and thick slumber   *compels*

220 Hangs upon mine eyelids. Let me rest.

    [*He sleeps*]

LYSIMACHUS A pillow for his head.

   [*To* MARINA *and others*]   Companion friends,

 If this but answer to my just belief

 I'll well remember° you. So leave him all.   *reward; recall*

       [*Exeunt all but* PERICLES]

    DIANA [*descends from the heavens*]

DIANA My temple stands in Ephesus. Hie thee thither,

225 And do upon mine altar sacrifice.

 There when my maiden priests are met together,

  At large discourse thy fortunes in this wise:

 With a full voice[7] before the people all,

  Reveal how thou at sea didst lose thy wife.

230 To mourn thy crosses,° with thy daughter's, call   *losses*

  And give them repetition to the life.[8]

 Perform my bidding, or thou liv'st in woe;

 Do't, and rest happy, by my silver bow.[9]

 Awake, and tell thy dream. [DIANA *ascends into the heavens*]

235 PERICLES Celestial Dian, goddess argentine,°   *silver (like the moon)*

 I will obey thee. [*Calling*] Helicanus!

   [*Enter* HELICANUS, LYSIMACHUS, *and* MARINA]

HELICANUS   Sir?

PERICLES My purpose was for Tarsus, there to strike

 Th'inhospitable Cleon, but I am

 For other service first. Toward Ephesus

240 Turn our blown° sails. Eftsoons° I'll tell thee why. *inflated / Later*

        [*Exit* HELICANUS]

 Shall we refresh us, sir, upon your shore,

 And give you gold for such provision

 As our intents will need?

LYSIMACHUS   With all my heart, sir,

 And when you come ashore I have a suit.

245 PERICLES You shall prevail, were it to woo my daughter,

 For it seems you have been noble towards her.

LYSIMACHUS Sir, lend me your arm.

PERICLES   Come, my Marina.

   Exit [PERICLES *with* LYSIMACHUS *at one arm,*

      MARINA *at the other*]

Scene 22

    Enter GOWER

GOWER Now our sands are almost run;

 More a little, and then dumb.°   *silent*

 This my last boon give me,

---

7. *At . . . voice:* Not in Q1; added to fill a suspected gap. *At large discourse:* Tell in detail (in public). *wise:* way.
8. *call . . . life:* speak loudly and repeat exactly what happened.
9. A crescent moon. Diana was goddess of the moon and a renowned hunter.

Scene 22 Scene 22 (Other modern editions divide this scene in two: Act 5, Scene 2 [Gower's monologue, lines 1–20] and Scene 3 [lines 21–125]. But they anomalously keep Thaisa and the temple of Diana onstage across the scene break. Even Gower may remain.) Location: The temple of Diana in Ephesus.

For such kindness must relieve me,
5 That you aptly will suppose°   *readily will imagine*
What pageantry, what feats, what shows,
What minstrelsy and pretty din
The regent° made in Mytilene   *Lysimachus*
To greet the King. So well he° thrived   *(Lysimachus)*
10 That he is promised to be wived
To fair Marina, but in no wise°   *way*
Till he° had done his sacrifice   *(Pericles)*
As Dian bade, whereto being bound
The int'rim, pray you, all confound.°   *skip*
15 In feathered° briefness sails are filled,   *winged*
And wishes fall out as they're willed.
At Ephesus the temple see:
        [*An altar,* THAISA *and other vestals are revealed*]
Our king, and all his company.
        Enter PERICLES, MARINA, LYSIMACHUS, HELICANUS[, CER-
        IMON, *with attendants*]
That he can hither come so soon
20 Is by your fancies' thankful doom.[1]
        [GOWER *stands aside*]
PERICLES   Hail, Dian. To perform thy just° command   *precise*
I here confess myself the King of Tyre,
Who, frighted from my country, did espouse
The fair Thaisa
        [THAISA *starts*]
            at Pentapolis.
25 At sea in childbed died she, but brought forth
A maid° child called Marina, who, O goddess,   *girl*
Wears yet thy silver liv'ry.[2] She at Tarsus
Was nursed with° Cleon, whom at fourteen years   *by*
He sought to murder, but her better stars
30 Bore her to Mytilene, 'gainst whose shore riding[3]
Her fortunes brought the maid aboard our barque,
Where, by her own most clear remembrance, she
Made known herself my daughter.
THAISA   Voice and favour°—   *appearance*
You are, you are—O royal Pericles!
        [*She falls*]
35 PERICLES   What means the nun? She dies. Help, gentlemen!
CERIMON   Noble sir,
If you have told Diana's altar true,
This is your wife.
PERICLES   Reverend appearer,° no.   *reverend-looking man*
I threw her overboard with these same arms.
CERIMON   Upon this coast, I warr'nt you.
40 PERICLES   'Tis most certain.
CERIMON   Look to the lady. O, she's but o'erjoyed.
Early one blustering morn this lady
Was thrown upon this shore. I oped the coffin,
Found there rich jewels, recovered° her, and placed her   *revived*

---

1. Thanks to your imaginations' agreement.
2. Still wears your uniform (remains a virgin).

3. *'gainst . . . riding:* where, as we rode at anchor.

Here in Diana's temple.

45 PERICLES   May we see them?

CERIMON   Great sir, they shall be brought you to° my house,   at
Whither I invite you. Look, Thaisa is
Recoverèd.

THAISA   O, let me look upon him!
If he be none of mine, my sanctity
50 Will to my sense bend no licentious ear,
But curb it, spite of seeing.[4] O, my lord,
Are you not Pericles? Like him you spake,
Like him you are. Did you not name a tempest,
A birth and death?

55 PERICLES   The voice of dead Thaisa!

THAISA   That Thaisa
Am I, supposèd dead and drowned.

PERICLES [*taking Thaisa's hand*]   Immortal Dian!

THAISA   Now I know you better.
60 When we with tears parted° Pentapolis,   *departed*
The King my father gave you such a ring.

PERICLES   This, this! No more, you gods. Your present kindness
Makes my past miseries sports;° you shall do well   *trifles*
That° on the touching of her lips I may   *If*
65 Melt, and no more be seen.—O come, be buried
A second time within these arms.
          [*They embrace and kiss*]

MARINA [*kneeling to* THAISA]   My heart
Leaps to be gone into my mother's bosom.

PERICLES   Look who kneels here: flesh of thy flesh, Thaisa,
Thy burden at the sea, and called Marina
For she was yielded° there.   *Because she was born*

70 THAISA [*embracing* MARINA]   Blessed, and mine own!

HELICANUS [*kneeling to* THAISA]
Hail, madam, and my queen.

THAISA   I know you not.

PERICLES   You have heard me say, when I did fly from Tyre,
I left behind an ancient substitute.
Can you remember what I called the man?
75 I have named him oft.

THAISA   'Twas Helicanus then.

PERICLES   Still confirmation.
Embrace him, dear Thaisa; this is he.
Now do I long to hear how you were found,
80 How possibly preserved, and who to thank—
Besides the gods—for this great miracle.

THAISA   Lord Cerimon, my lord. This is the man
Through whom the gods have shown their pow'r, that can
From first to last resolve° you.   *answer everything for*

PERICLES [*to* CERIMON]   Reverend sir,
85 The gods can have no mortal officer
More like a god than you. Will you deliver°   *explain*
How this dead queen re-lives?

CERIMON   I will, my lord.
Beseech you, first go with me to my house,

4. *my sanctity . . . seeing*: my religious vows will forbid my sense to feel desire, in spite of what I see.

Where shall be shown you all was° found with her,   *that was*
90   And told how in this temple she came° placed,   *came to be*
      No needful thing omitted.
      PERICLES   Pure Diana,
      I bless thee for thy vision,° and will offer   *(in Scene 21)*
      Nightly oblations° to thee.—Beloved Thaisa,   *offerings*
      This prince, the fair betrothèd of your daughter,
95   At Pentapolis shall marry her.
      [*To* MARINA] And now this ornament°   *this hair that*
      Makes me look dismal will I clip to form,
      And what this fourteen years no razor touched,
      To grace thy marriage day I'll beautify.
100   THAISA   Lord Cerimon hath letters of good credit,°   *trustworthiness*
      Sir, from Pentapolis: my father's dead.
      PERICLES   Heav'n make a star of him! Yet there, my queen,
      We'll celebrate their nuptials, and ourselves
      Will in that kingdom spend our following days.
105   Our son and daughter shall in Tyrus reign.—
      Lord Cerimon, we do our longing stay°   *delay our desire*
      To hear the rest untold. Sir, lead 's the way.

                                    Exeunt [*all but*] GOWER

      GOWER   In Antiochus and his daughter you have heard[5]
      Of monstrous lust the due and just reward;
110   In Pericles, his queen, and daughter seen,°   *you have seen*
      Although assailed with fortune fierce and keen,
      Virtue preserved from fell° destruction's blast,   *cruel*
      Led on by heav'n, and crowned with joy at last.
      In Helicanus may you well descry
115   A figure of truth, of faith, of loyalty.
      In reverend Cerimon there well appears
      The worth that learnèd charity aye° wears.   *always*
      For wicked Cleon and his wife, when fame°   *rumor*
      Had spread their cursèd deed to° th' honoured name   *against*
120   Of Pericles, to rage the city turn,°   *turned*
      That° him and his they in his palace burn.   *So that*
      The gods for murder seemèd so content
      To punish that, although not done, but meant.
      So on your patience evermore attending,
125   New joy wait on you. Here our play has ending.   [*Exit*]

                          ## Additional Passage

Q gives this more expansive version of Marina's Epitaph (18.34–37):

      'The fairest, sweetest, best lies here,
      Who withered in her spring of year.
      She was of Tyrus the King's° daughter,   *the King of Tyre's*
      On whom foul death hath made this slaughter.
5   Marina was she called, and at her birth
      Thetis,[1] being proud, swallowed° some part o'th' earth;   *flooded*

---

5. The second of Gower's speeches in pentameter couplets.
Additional Passage
1. A sea nymph here confused with Tethys, wife of Oceanus (in Greek mythology, the ruler of a river that encircled the earth). The image in this passage is of the ocean (because of Thetis/Tethys) surging happily in response to Marina's birth and angrily in response to her death.

Therefore the earth, fearing to be o'erflowed,
Hath Thetis' birth-child on the heav'ns bestowed,
Wherefore she° does, and swears she'll never stint,   *(Thetis)*
10 Make raging batt'ry upon shores of flint.'°   *rocky shores*

Coriolanus

Hērōs, the Greek word for "hero," originally meant "warrior." By Homer's time, eight centuries before the birth of Christ, the term was already beginning to be applied by extension to other kinds of praiseworthy people, but even today the military connotations of the word remain strong. The Latin word for "virtue" has a similar history, as the ancient historian Plutarch remarks in his biography of Coriolanus, Shakespeare's principal source for his play. "Now in those days valiantness was honored in Rome above all other virtues: which they call *virtūs*, by the name of virtue itself, as including in that general name, all other special virtues besides. So that *virtūs* in the Latin, was as much as valiantness."

Writing *Coriolanus* in 1608, Shakespeare considers the extent to which excellence in battle translates into other forms of meritoriousness. He works in an ageless tradition, still vital in the twenty-first century, of exalting great warriors: the mythically dauntless Hercules and Theseus, the fierce battle chieftains of classical epic, the indomitable knights of medieval chivalric romance, the superheroes of modern films and comic books. Yet Shakespeare also deviates from that tradition. Caius Martius Coriolanus performs astonishing, almost superhuman, acts of strength and bravery in battle, fighting on behalf of a society that seems to venerate war. His aggressiveness ought to mesh perfectly, one would think, with the needs of the community. If successful belligerence is the highest, or only, form of excellence, then Coriolanus, the preeminent soldier, is a natural candidate for Rome's top leadership positions.

In fact, however, Coriolanus's career is disastrous. Despite his phenomenal military successes and despite Rome's esteem for warriors, Coriolanus not only fails to win election as consul (leader) of Rome but barely escapes the death penalty. He is banished from the city and eventually killed while in the employ of Rome's enemies. The relationship between the supposedly exemplary individual and the culture from which he springs seems anything but straightforward; so does the connection between "valiantness" and other forms of virtue.

What goes wrong in *Coriolanus*? Shakespeare suggests that his hero brings many of his problems upon his own head. Coriolanus succeeds as a warrior by channeling overpowering anger into feats of extraordinary strength, by refusing to calculate possible harm to himself or to others, and by preferring action to words. In the political domain, by contrast, relative goods are often more important than absolutes, negotiated compromises preferable to flat conquest. The ability to control oneself in the interests of manipulating others is crucial; so, too, is the capacity to predict the effects of one's own and other people's words and actions. Coriolanus's phenomenal forcefulness, such a superb advantage on the battlefield, cripples his effectiveness for other enterprises. His initial lack of political ambitions together with his hopeless awkwardness as a candidate suggest that his military prowess is not merely irrelevant to peacetime employment but indeed renders him politically incompetent or even dangerous.

Like most of Shakespeare's tragic heroes after Richard II, then, Coriolanus is betrayed not so much by his vices or shortcomings as by what, in different circumstances, would be his best traits. Shakespeare alters his source material in order to make this pattern more distinct. For instance, Shakespeare entirely omits Plutarch's account of the historical Coriolanus's considerable political savvy. Plutarch's Coriolanus had already played several influential political roles before he made his bid for the consulship. He underwent without apparent compunction the traditional rituals required of all seekers after office; the plebeians later repudiated him on the grounds of a long political record that, in Shakespeare, does not exist. After his exile, Plutarch's Coriolanus cleverly exacerbated class strife in Rome by selectively refraining from burning patrician estates as he approached the city with his Volscian army. Shakespeare's relentless but hotheaded character would hardly be capable of such a calculated act.

The effect of Shakespeare's changes is to open up a chasm that does not exist in his sources between military and civic values. The general Cominius, praising Coriolanus in the senate house, seems superficially to be echoing Plutarch's comment that "*virtūs* in the Latin, was as much as valiantness":

> It is held
> That valour is the chiefest virtue, and
> Most dignifies the haver. If it be,
> The man I speak of cannot in the world
> Be singly counterpoised.
>
> (2.2.79–83)

But even in the process of making his argument, Cominius appears, in his evasive passive constructions and his conditional "if," to be partly disowning it.

Coriolanus's tragedy is not, however, merely a matter of personal idiosyncrasy and self-destructiveness. His career is inseparable from the society that both exalts and repudiates him. During Coriolanus's lifetime in the late fifth century B.C.E., Rome had already embarked on the expansionist course that would culminate in its domination of Europe, North Africa, and the Middle East four hundred years later, in the time of Julius Caesar, Marcus Brutus, and Mark Antony. But in these early years, dreams of world rule were far in the future: Coriolanus's Rome was still battling the nearby Volscians. Roman bellicosity was a cultural tendency, not yet a clear pathway to empire. At home, Rome struggled to devise a new form of government. In Coriolanus's youth, Lucius Junius Brutus and his allies had driven out King Tarquin and his family on the grounds that they had been abusing their power (an episode upon which Shakespeare based his narrative poem *The Rape of Lucrece*). In place of the monarchy, Brutus instituted a republic: government not by a King but by a senate composed of patricians (aristocrats). For military and civic matters requiring executive authority, the senate elected consuls for short terms. Soon, however, this system proved inadequate, as the large plebeian, or working, class clamored for a say in the city's rule. In the aftermath of the uprising depicted in *Coriolanus* 1.1, the plebeians were granted the right to elect their own representatives, called tribunes.

In its eventual form, therefore, the Roman Republic was a "mixed" form of government that attempted to distribute rather than to concentrate power, as well as to balance the rights and privileges of various constituencies. Inventing republican institutions entailed addressing important questions about the nature of the polity and of citizenship. Is the Roman state, as Menenius suggests, an impersonal force "whose course will on / The way it takes" (1.1.60–61) no matter what the majority of the city's residents desire? Or does the state merely express collective opinion, as the plebeians insist when they cry, "The people are the city" (3.1.200)? Ought the Roman state to concern itself mainly with managing affairs within the city walls, or should its military undertakings outside the city take political precedence? Who has a voice in the government of the city, and on what basis is suffrage granted: class status? personal merit? place of residence? Does citizenship, as Coriolanus argues, primarily entail duties such as military service? Or is citizenship, as the tribunes assume, an entitlement, giving everyone a voice in political and judicial affairs?

For Shakespeare and his contemporaries, these were not questions of merely antiquarian interest. Most premodern states, including classical republics and Shakespeare's England, consisted of a relatively small, property-owning, politically empowered class and a large subpolitical population that was supposed to submit to the laws but that had no voting rights. But how small ought to be the privileged group, how large the disempowered group, and how distinct the differences between the two?

These were matters of hot debate in Jacobean England. King James I and his son Charles, who liked to associate themselves with the imagery of imperial Rome, were attracted by absolutist models of government in which the monarch exercised virtually unlimited sway. By contrast, their opponents in Parliament often invoked the Roman Republic, which dispersed power over consuls, senate, and tribunes, as an analogue to the English commonwealth with its monarch, House of Lords, and House of Commons.

Given the contemporary resonances of his story, Shakespeare's extensive alterations of Plutarch's account are fascinating. *Coriolanus* opens, as already mentioned, with an uprising among Rome's common people. According to Plutarch, the plebeians revolted because the moneyed patricians had promised easier terms on loans if the plebeians would agree to fight the nearby Sabines. After the plebeians acquitted themselves bravely in battle, the patricians reneged on the agreement and sold into slavery those debtors—many of them war veterans—who were bankrupted by high interest rates. Shakespeare's plebeians, by contrast, make only fleeting references to usury. Their main complaint is simple hunger: a familiar grievance to an English audience in 1608. Barely a year before *Coriolanus*'s first performance, food shortages precipitated serious rioting by the rural poor in the Midland counties west of London, where Stratford-upon-Avon was located. The rioters accused the rich of hoarding foodstuffs in hopes of higher prices and of having created a dearth by replacing the traditional cultivation of cereal grains with lucrative sheep farming. The rich countered that bad weather was to blame.

In updating the motives of his lower-class characters, Shakespeare translates Roman class conflicts into terms more immediate for his contemporaries. But his revision has other consequences, too: it minimizes the plebeians' political sophistication, their military indispensability, and much of the justification for their outrage. The famine might well be a natural rather than a political calamity: there is no hint of any prior betrayed agreement and no suggestion of unrewarded plebeian military service. Unlike Plutarch's plebeians, Shakespeare's are mediocre soldiers or worse: in *Coriolanus*, Shakespeare's Rome fails to appreciate Coriolanus's *virtūs* simply because the society is not, as Plutarch had claimed it to be, fully a warrior culture at all.

In Shakespeare's rendering, valor in battle seems less a "Roman" than a distinctively aristocratic trait, exercised and uniquely cherished by the patrician class. The difficulties Coriolanus experiences in trying to translate that valor into a civilian context reflect a persistent problem in defining the male aristocrat's proper role. Just as the equation of "valiantness" and "virtue" could fail in early republican Rome, it could also be seen to be failing in early modern England. In medieval times, noblemen had been feudally obliged to serve as battle captains over troops of their own vassals; the aristocrat's military function was his raison d'être, although proficiency in war was supposed to carry over into the management of civic affairs. In Shakespeare's time, the aristocrat's function was theoretically unchanged, but altered social circumstances placed it under increasing pressure. Throughout the late sixteenth and early seventeenth centuries, bureaucrats and policy makers like William Cecil, Robert Cecil, and Francis Bacon were sharply at odds with swashbuckling militarists like Walter Ralegh, King James's son Prince Henry, and Shakespeare's erstwhile patron the Earl of Essex. In these conflicts, the bureaucrats almost always had the advantage. Their skill at such tasks as overhauling the taxation system was hardly glamorous but proved indispensable for the newly powerful nation-state. By the early seventeenth century, the notion that the aristocrat rendered his most important service to his King on the battlefield seemed a remnant of a simpler age.

Coriolanus then, like Hotspur in Shakespeare's *1 Henry IV*, seems to embody a conception of aristocratic excellence whose historical moment, for better or worse, has already passed. Interestingly, a sense of the archaic quality of mighty warriors seems almost universal. Homer's epic heroes were already beginning to specialize their functions during the siege of Troy. For Plutarch, writing in the time of the Roman Empire, the original identification of aristocrat and warrior seems to have shattered in the long-ago days of the Roman Republic. Medieval writers locate both the flowering of knightly service and the beginning of its breakdown in the legendary fourth-century Arthurian court. Many Hollywood Westerns look back to a time in the nineteenth century when the older, rougher codes of the Indian fighter or nomadic frontiersman were being displaced by the values of permanent white settlers, including women and professional-caste men. From time immemorial, glorifying warriors has been tied up with nostalgia—not merely for the mighty soldier himself, but for a simpler, "manly" alternative to civilized complexities, an alternative always already lost.

In the tense dramatic milieu of *Coriolanus,* compounded from Shakespeare's own experience and what his sources provided him, the nature of his protagonist's heroism thus seems more intelligible and its failure less surprising. Since the heterogeneous Roman population has difficulty coming to any consensus about what it values, no single individual could possibly exemplify its ideals. Rather, Coriolanus possesses a narrow subset of traits more appealing to some groups (the patricians) than others (the plebeians) and more useful in some situations (war) than in others (peace). Coriolanus's mother, Volumnia, describing her son's education, suggests how his "heroism" has been developed by rigorously selecting for desired traits and just as sternly suppressing others.

> When yet he was but tenderbodied and the only son of my womb, when youth with comeliness plucked all gaze his way, when for a day of kings' entreaties a mother should not sell him an hour from her beholding, I, considering how honour would become such a person . . . was pleased to let him seek danger where he was like to find fame. To a cruel war I sent him, from whence he returned his brows bound with oak. I tell thee, daughter, I sprang not more in joy at first hearing he was a man-child than now in first seeing he had proved himself a man. (1.3.5–15)

Volumnia's own shrewdness and ferocity seems to belie the "naturalness" of a system that excludes women from politics and combat. Unlike Coriolanus's wife, Virgilia, Volumnia hardly seems content to stay home and do the sewing. But the incongruity between her personality and her prescribed social role does not render her skeptical of that role. Instead, she embraces her gendered destiny with characteristic zeal. In maternity she finds an improbable outlet for her own aggressiveness.

> The breasts of Hecuba
> When she did suckle Hector looked not lovelier
> Than Hector's forehead when it spit forth blood
> At Grecian sword, contemning.
>
> (1.3.37–40)

Symbolically equating milk and blood, the lactating mother with her wounded son, Volumnia both identifies vicariously with her war hero and wishes suffering upon him, delighting not merely in his triumphs but in his pain. Virgilia's conventionally feminine recoil from Volumnia's gory fantasies makes their aberrancy clear for the audience. In Volumnia, the discipline required to submit to rules of Roman womanliness seems to have generated a complicated sadomasochistic adaptation. She displaces her own forbidden bellicosity onto a dream of exaggerated masculinity and then attempts to realize that dream in her son.

Volumnia's ruthless mothering produces a man whose characteristic gesture is violently to resist whatever he perceives to be outside himself. Battle is Coriolanus's model for identity formation, and his ideal self is like an impermeably walled city. Overstated *differences*—between patrician and plebeian, between Roman and Volsce, between male and female, between man and boy—are the principles upon which Coriolanus has established his own sense of identity. Contempt and anger, like aggression, reinforce and clarify the boundaries of the self, marking it vividly off from those whom one hates, despises, or conquers. Coriolanus does not merely happen to be inflexible and narrow-minded; too much tolerance, too much sensitivity, would endanger him to the core. So would introspection, which might reveal an unwelcome complexity within. Coriolanus is hardly a taciturn character, but he is perhaps Shakespeare's most opaque tragic protagonist, for he is not inclined to reflect upon his own motives either in conversation or alone (indeed, he has only a single short soliloquy in the entire play). The great moments of Coriolanus's life are moments of embattled solitude: fighting by himself inside Corioles, standing alone for consul or separated from the Roman people after his exile, reflecting in an unaccompanied moment in Aufidius's hall, isolated in Corioles again at the end of the play, shouting at his old (and new) enemy: "Alone I did it" (5.6.117). He is thrilled by fantasies of absolute independence: "As if a man were author of himself / And knew no other kin" (5.3.36–37). With some justice, the hostile tribunes accuse him of wanting to be the only man left in Rome and of considering himself a god superior to ordinary mortals.

In his defiant self-sufficiency, however, Coriolanus is far needier than he acknowledges. When he allies himself with Aufidius, his former enemy, Aufidius's elated speech of welcome clarifies their shared dilemma.

> I loved the maid I married; never man
> Sighed truer breath. But that I see thee here,
> Thou noble thing, more dances my rapt heart
> Than when I first my wedded mistress saw
> Bestride my threshold. . . .
> . . . .
> Thou hast beat me out
> Twelve several times, and I have nightly since
> Dreamt of encounters 'twixt thyself and me—
> We have been down together in my sleep,
> Unbuckling helms, fisting each other's throat—
> And waked half dead with nothing.
> (4.5.113–25)

Coriolanus and the attack on Corioli. Jost Amman, from *Icones Livianae* (1572).

The combination of pain and pleasure to which Aufidius bears witness is strikingly reminiscent of Volumnia's maternal feelings, in which aggressiveness toward the beloved
seems to loom so large. It is impossible here to distinguish hostility from attraction,
competition from dependency, combat from homosexual embrace. The warrior loves
his adversary because he needs a manly competitor against whom to establish his own
identity. The striving for autonomy depends on the existence of something set off
against, beside, or below it.

To distinguish oneself from other people, then, one must rely on them. "Thy valiantness was mine, thou suck'st it from me," Volumnia informs her son (3.2.129). Coriolanus wants to imagine his courage and honor as intrinsically his own, rather than
conferred by others. But "our virtues," as Aufidius claims, "lie in th'interpretation of the
time" (4.7.49–50). Roman merit, inextricable from social goals and needs, demands an
admiring audience. Even while he professes to despise flattery, Coriolanus takes pride
in such apparently trivial honorific gestures as the surname or the oaken garland conferred upon him by those who value his services. Insignificant in themselves, such symbols acquire meaning from the way in which they are regarded by the group. The exiled
Coriolanus defiantly insists that "there is a world elsewhere" (3.3.139), but it is impossible for him to retire to a quiet corner of Italy and live out his life in obscurity. He needs
to prove himself against an enemy, but now that enemy, Rome, is the place from which
his life has drawn its meaning. Threatening to annihilate the community that bore him,
he puts himself in a painfully contradictory position.

Thus the superior is always dependent on the inferior, the inside on the outside, the
civilized on the barbarian, the patrician on the plebeian, the performer on the audience,
the man on the woman and on the boy, even while the "upper" term prides itself on its
difference from its subordinate. Moreover, just as important, the dependency works in
both directions, as the action of *Coriolanus* shows. If Coriolanus depends on the
Roman populace in ways he refuses to recognize, so does the populace depend on him.
By imagining it can dispense with him and what he represents, it comes close to bringing destruction on its head.

Since we hear an unusual amount about Coriolanus's boyhood, it is easy to see his
self-contradictory desire for autonomy in terms of his simultaneous flight from and
dependence on Volumnia. But that is an oversimplification: Coriolanus is not merely
the product of a uniquely bad upbringing. His anxieties about autonomy and dependence, competitiveness and cooperation, are shared, in some form, by almost everyone
in the play: they are aspects of social and political dilemmas, not merely individual neu-
roses. Early in the first scene, the First Citizen notes—perhaps enviously but also
accurately—that the patricians enjoy seeing the lower classes suffer, because that suffering enhances their sense of comparative privilege. Who depends on whom, how far
ought that dependency to extend, what forms ought it to take?

These concerns are powerfully evoked in the imagery of *Coriolanus*. It was a cliché
already old in Plutarch's time, and still current in Shakespeare's, that human communities were modeled on individual bodies. In the optimistic version of this analogy, the
state is a collection of harmoniously interrelated organs, each selflessly performing its
own distinctive function in the service of the whole. Interconnectedness is the apparent moral of Menenius's "pretty tale" (1.1.80) of the belly in the opening scene. But
even in Menenius's version, the analogy veers toward grotesquerie, the body-state
becoming an apparently headless entity equipped with an unnaturally smiling belly.
Elsewhere in *Coriolanus*, the body is less a marvel of smooth interaction than a site of
disintegration: Coriolanus imagines the plebeians as "fragments" and as "voices"
(1.1.212, 2.3.115–20); Menenius rebukes a malcontent he calls "the great toe of this
assembly" (1.1.144). The mutilations of the battlefield begin to seem corporeal equivalents for a profound crisis of the body politic. The shared needs of embodied, vulnerable human beings for food, shelter, and defense provide an obvious material basis for
societies. But individual bodies tend to be selfish, unwilling to forgo their own urgent
requirements in the interests of a collective good, reluctant to admit their reliance on

one another lest that reliance be made a pretext for exploitation. Once again, dependence and autonomy seem simultaneously antithetical and inextricable.

Because the body in *Coriolanus* is so often imagined in negative terms—as starving, wounded, or cut to pieces—attempts to escape corporeal limitation seem understandable, even laudable. In fact, Coriolanus's battlefield heroism seems largely a matter of refusing to acknowledge physical constraints: he is inexhaustible, undaunted by wounds or by danger. Late in the play, Menenius describes him as a kind of robot: "When he walks, he moves like an engine, and the ground shrinks before his treading" (5.4.15–16). But within a few lines, Menenius is proven wrong: blood relationships, the ties of the body, prove impossible for Coriolanus to disown. Volumnia, Virgilia, and young Martius come to the Volscian camp to plead for their city and their people; and in a capitulation he knows to be virtually suicidal, Coriolanus grasps his mother's hand.

Coriolanus is not only the last of Shakespeare's tragedies but the last of a series of plays about ancient Rome. It seems to look back upon, and to anatomize, social and individual pathologies that in *Julius Caesar* and even *Antony and Cleopatra* were merely hinted at: the way "Roman" valor on the battlefield, for instance, becomes both a flight from and a replacement for heterosexuality; the way aggression and repression undergird the psyches of Roman men and women; the way both sexes deform their personalities in order to conform to highly restrictive patterns of masculinity or femininity. While in *Julius Caesar* class tensions serve mainly to exalt the patrician class, here the plebeians' grievances, and their different priorities, are understandable. Coriolanus's inability to comprehend the plebeians is a telling sign of both his personal rigidity and the alienation of rich from poor. *Coriolanus* has seemed to many audiences a relentlessly bleak play, and no wonder. Subjecting both its formidable but unpleasant hero and his society to intense critical scrutiny, *Coriolanus*

Volumnia entreating Coriolanus. Jost Amman, from *Icones Livianae* (1572).

implies that no political arrangement could possibly satisfy human needs, portrayed here as incorrigibly self-contradictory.

KATHARINE EISAMAN MAUS

TEXTUAL NOTE

The 1623 First Folio is the only authority for *Coriolanus*. Some believe that the compositors set the Folio text of this play directly from Shakespeare's manuscript, but the Oxford editors argue that the immediate source for F was more likely to have been a promptbook. Stage directions are unusually elaborate and give important performance clues: for instance, the act divisions were clearly marked (since intermissions were observed at "private" theaters like the Blackfriars), and the specifications for small musical instruments like cornets also suggest a more intimate performance space. The F compositors may have had trouble reading the handwriting in the manuscript (whether it was Shakespeare's or a member of the theater company's). There are some obvious errors requiring emendation and some confusion in setting verse lines. On the whole, however, *Coriolanus* is not one of the more textually vexing of Shakespeare's plays.

SELECTED BIBLIOGRAPHY

Adelman, Janet. "'Anger's My Meat': Feeding, Dependency, and Aggression in *Coriolanus.*" *Representing Shakespeare: New Psychoanalytic Essays.* Ed. Murray M. Schwartz and Coppélia Kahn. Baltimore: Johns Hopkins University Press, 1980. 129–49. Argues that the play's political and psychological anxieties crystallize around the figure of the mother who does not feed her children.

Barton, Anne. "Livy, Machiavelli, and Shakespeare's *Coriolanus.*" *Shakespeare Survey* 38 (1985): 115–29. The Roman historian Livy and Machiavelli's commentary upon Livy as sources of inspiration for *Coriolanus.*

Bloom, Harold, ed. *William Shakespeare's "Coriolanus."* New York: Chelsea House, 1988. Anthology of critical essays.

Calderwood, James. "*Coriolanus:* Wordless Meanings and Meaningless Words." *Studies in English Literature* 6 (1966): 211–24. Problems of language in the play as they corollate with its psychological and political dilemmas.

Cantor, Paul A. "Part One: *Coriolanus.*" *Shakespeare's Rome: Republic and Empire.* Ithaca, N.Y.: Cornell University Press, 1976. 55–124. Strengths and weaknesses of the Roman Republic as Shakespeare contrasts them with the later imperial system.

Cavell, Stanley. "Who Does the Wolf Love?" *Disowning Knowledge in Six Plays by Shakespeare.* Cambridge, Mass.: Cambridge University Press, 1987. 143–78. *Coriolanus*'s affinity with sacrificial feasts, especially the Christian ritual of Communion.

Fish, Stanley. "How to Do Things with Austin and Searle: Speech-Act Theory and Literary Criticism." *Is There a Text in This Class?: The Authority of Interpretive Communities.* Cambridge, Mass.: Harvard University Press, 1980. 197–245. Coriolanus's problems with speech-acts.

Goldberg, Jonathan. "The Anus in *Coriolanus.*" *Historicism, Psychoanalysis, and Early Modern Culture.* Ed. Carla Mazzio and Doug Trevor. New York: Routledge, 2000. 260–271. Anal imagery and homoeroticism in the play.

Jorgensen, Paul. "Shakespeare's Coriolanus: Elizabethan Soldier." *PMLA* 64 (1949): 221–35. *Coriolanus* reflects the military problems of Shakespeare's era.

Patterson, Annabel. "Speak, Speak! The Popular Voice and the Jacobean State." *Shakespeare and the Popular Voice*. Cambridge, Mass.: Blackwood, 1989. *Coriolanus* and disenfranchised groups in Shakespeare's England.

Wheeler, David, ed. *"Coriolanus": Critical Essays*. New York: Garland, 1995. An anthology of essays and reviews of theatrical productions.

FILMS

Coriolanus. 1951. Dir. Paul Nickell. USA. This Westinghouse Studio One black-and-white abridged television version, interspersed with occasional ads for refrigerators and laundry appliances, is performed in modern dress and strongly marked by the recent traumas of fascism and World War II. Richard Greene is handsome but inexpressive in the role of Coriolanus.

Coriolanus. 1984. Dir. Elijah Moshinsky. UK. BBC-TV's spare, gripping production featuring Alan Howard as a tightly-wound Coriolanus, Mike Gwilym as a canny Aufidius, and Irene Worth as a terrifying Volumnia.

The Tragedy of Coriolanus

THE PERSONS OF THE PLAY

CAIUS MARTIUS, later surnamed CORIOLANUS ⎫
MENENIUS Agrippa   ⎬ patricians of
Titus LARTIUS ⎱ generals   ⎭ Rome
COMINIUS ⎰
VOLUMNIA, Coriolanus' mother
VIRGILIA, his wife
YOUNG MARTIUS, his son
VALERIA, a chaste lady of Rome
SICINIUS Velutus ⎱ tribunes of the Roman people
Junius BRUTUS ⎰
CITIZENS of Rome
SOLDIERS in the Roman army
Tullus AUFIDIUS, general of the Volscian army
His LIEUTENANT
His SERVINGMEN
CONSPIRATORS with Aufidius
Volscian LORDS
Volscian CITIZENS
SOLDIERS in the Volscian army
ADRIAN, a Volscian
NICANOR, a Roman
A Roman HERALD
MESSENGERS
AEDILES
A gentlewoman, an usher, Roman and Volscian senators and
    nobles, captains in the Roman army, officers, lictors

1.1

Enter a Company of mutinous CITIZENS *with staves,*
clubs, and other weapons

FIRST CITIZEN   Before we proceed any further, hear me speak.

ALL   Speak, speak.

FIRST CITIZEN   You are all resolved rather to die than to famish?

ALL   Resolved, resolved.

5   FIRST CITIZEN   First, you know Caius Martius is chief enemy to
    the people.

ALL   We know't, we know't.

FIRST CITIZEN   Let us kill him, and we'll have corn° at our own   *grain*
    price. Is't a verdict?°   *Do we agree*

10   ALL   No more talking on't, let it be done. Away, away.

SECOND CITIZEN   One word, good citizens.

FIRST CITIZEN   We are accounted poor citizens, the patricians
    good.° What authority[1] surfeits on would relieve us. If they   *noble; well off*
    would yield us but the superfluity° while it were wholesome°   *excess / still edible*
15   we might guess they relieved us humanely, but they think we

---

1.1 Location: A street in Rome.   1. The nobility.

are too dear.² The leanness that afflicts us, the object° of our   *visible fact*
misery, is as an inventory to particularize their abundance;³ our
sufferance° is a gain to them. Let us revenge this with our pikes°   *distress / spears; pitch*
ere we become rakes;⁴ for the gods know I speak this in hunger   *forks*
20   for bread, not in thirst for revenge.

SECOND CITIZEN   Would you proceed especially against Caius
    Martius?

THIRD CITIZEN   Against him first.

FOURTH CITIZEN   He's a very dog to° the commonalty.⁵   *persecutor of*

25 SECOND CITIZEN   Consider you what services he has done for his
    country?

FIRST CITIZEN   Very well, and could be content to give him good
    report for't, but that he pays himself with being proud.

FIFTH CITIZEN   Nay, but speak not maliciously.

30 FIRST CITIZEN   I say unto you, what he hath done famously,° he   *that has won fame*
    did it to that end°—though soft-conscienced men can be con- *(to advance his pride)*
    tent to say 'it was for his country', 'he did it to please his mother,
    and to be partly proud'°—which he is even to the altitude of   *partly out of pride*
    his virtue.⁶

35 SECOND CITIZEN   What he cannot help in his nature you ac-
    count a vice in him. You must in no way say he is covetous.

FIRST CITIZEN   If I must not, I need not be barren of accusations.
    He hath faults, with surplus, to tire in repetition.
         Shouts within
    What shouts are these? The other side o'th' city is risen. Why
40   stay we prating° here? To th' Capitol!   *chattering*

ALL   Come, come.
         Enter MENENIUS

FIRST CITIZEN   Soft,° who comes here?   *Wait*

SECOND CITIZEN   Worthy Menenius Agrippa, one that hath
    always loved the people.

45 FIRST CITIZEN   He's one honest enough. Would all the rest were
    so!

MENENIUS   What work's, my countrymen, in hand? Where go you
    With bats° and clubs? The matter. Speak, I pray you.   *cudgels*

FIRST CITIZEN   Our business is not unknown to th' senate. They
50   have had inkling this fortnight what we intend to do, which now
    we'll show 'em in deeds. They say poor suitors° have strong⁷   *petitioners*
    breaths; they shall know we have strong arms, too.

MENENIUS   Why, masters,° my good friends, mine honest neigh-   *(artisans' title)*
    bours,
    Will you undo° yourselves?   *destroy*

55 FIRST CITIZEN   We cannot, sir. We are undone already.

MENENIUS   I tell you, friends, most charitable care
    Have the patricians of you. For° your wants,   *As for*
    Your suffering in this dearth,° you may as well   *famine*
    Strike at the heaven with your staves as lift them
60   Against the Roman state, whose course will on
    The way it takes, cracking ten thousand curbs⁸
    Of more strong link asunder than can ever

---

2. We cost too much to preserve; we are too rich.
3. To make their prosperity stand out by comparison.
4. Rakes are proverbially thin; playing on "pikes."
5. Common people.

6. That is, his pride is equal to his valor.
7. Strong-smelling, from eating onions, the food of the poor.
8. Chain bits used to restrain unruly horses.

Appear in your impediment.[9] For the dearth,
The gods, not the patricians, make it, and
65 Your knees to them, not arms, must help. Alack,
You are transported by calamity
Thither where more attends° you, and you slander   *awaits*
The helms° o'th' state, who care for you like fathers,   *helmsmen*
When you curse them as enemies.

70 FIRST CITIZEN   Care for us? True, indeed! They ne'er cared for
us yet: suffer us to famish, and their storehouses crammed with
grain; make edicts for usury[1] to support usurers; repeal daily
any wholesome act established against the rich; and provide
more piercing° statutes daily to chain up and restrain the poor.   *severe*
75 If the wars eat us not up, they will; and there's all the love they
bear us.

MENENIUS   Either you must
Confess yourselves wondrous malicious
Or be accused of folly. I shall tell you
80 A pretty tale. It may be you have heard it,
But since it serves my purpose, I will venture
To stale't a little more.°   *To make it more familiar*

FIRST CITIZEN   Well, I'll hear it, sir. Yet you must not think to
fob off our disgrace[2] with a tale. But an't° please you, deliver.   *if it*

85 MENENIUS   There was a time when all the body's members,
Rebelled against the belly, thus accused it:
That only like a gulf° it did remain   *abyss*
I'th' midst o'th' body, idle and unactive,
Still cupboarding the viand,[3] never bearing
90 Like° labour with the rest; where th'other instruments°   *Equal / organs*
Did see and hear, devise, instruct, walk, feel,
And, mutually participate,° did minister   *participating*
Unto the appetite and affection° common   *desire*
Of the whole body. The belly answered—

95 FIRST CITIZEN   Well, sir, what answer made the belly?

MENENIUS   Sir, I shall tell you. With a kind of smile,
Which ne'er came from the lungs,° but even thus—   *(organs of laughter)*
For look you, I may make the belly smile
As well as speak—it tauntingly replied
100 To th' discontented members, the mutinous parts
That envied his receipt;° even so most fitly[4]   *what it received*
As you malign our senators for that°   *because*
They are not such as you.

FIRST CITIZEN   Your belly's answer—what?
The kingly crownèd head, the vigilant eye,
105 The counsellor heart, the arm our soldier,
Our steed the leg, the tongue our trumpeter,
With other muniments° and petty helps   *supports*
In this our fabric,° if that they—   *body*

MENENIUS   What then?
Fore me,° this fellow speaks! What then? What then?   *(an oath)*

110 FIRST CITIZEN   Should by the cormorant° belly be restrained,   *rapacious*
Who is the sink° o'th' body—   *cesspool*

---

9. *than . . . impediment*: than you can ever offer in
opposition.
1. Permitting the lending of money at interest (widely
considered immoral, because it enriched wealthy lenders

at the expense of poor borrowers).
2. Dismiss our hardship.
3. Always hoarding the food.
4. In just the way.

MENENIUS   Well, what then?

FIRST CITIZEN   The former agents, if they did complain,
    What could the belly answer?

MENENIUS   I will tell you,
    If you'll bestow a small° of what you have little—   *small amount*
115   Patience—a while, you'st hear the belly's answer.

FIRST CITIZEN   You're long about it.

MENENIUS   Note me this, good friend:
    Your° most grave belly was deliberate,   *This*
    Not rash like his accusers, and thus answered:
    'True is it, my incorporate° friends,' quoth he,   *united in one body*
120   'That I receive the general food at first
    Which you do live upon, and fit it is,
    Because I am the storehouse and the shop
    Of the whole body. But, if you do remember,
    I send it through the rivers of your blood
125   Even to the court, the heart, to th' seat° o'th' brain;   *throne*
    And through the cranks and offices[5] of man
    The strongest nerves° and small inferior veins   *muscles*
    From me receive that natural competency°   *sustenance*
    Whereby they live. And though that all at once'—
130   You my good friends, this says the belly, mark me—

FIRST CITIZEN   Ay, sir, well, well.

MENENIUS   'Though all at once cannot
    See what I do deliver out to each,
    Yet I can make my audit up[6] that all
    From me do back receive the flour[7] of all
135   And leave me but the bran.' What say you to't?

FIRST CITIZEN   It was an answer. How apply you this?

MENENIUS   The senators of Rome are this good belly,
    And you the mutinous members. For examine
    Their counsels and their cares, digest[8] things rightly
140   Touching the weal o'th' common,[9] you shall find
    No public benefit which you receive
    But it proceeds or comes from them to you,
    And no way from yourselves. What do you think,
    You, the great toe of this assembly?

145   FIRST CITIZEN   I the great toe? Why the great toe?

MENENIUS   For that, being one o'th' lowest, basest, poorest
    Of this most wise rebellion, thou goest foremost.
    Thou rascal, that art worst in blood[1] to run,
    Lead'st first to win some vantage.°   *benefit*
150   But make you ready your stiff bats and clubs.
    Rome and her rats are at the point of battle.
    The one side must have bale.°   *injury*

       Enter MARTIUS   Hail, noble Martius!

MARTIUS   Thanks.—What's the matter, you dissentious° rogues,   *rebelling*
    That, rubbing the poor itch of your opinion,
    Make yourselves scabs?

155   FIRST CITIZEN   We have ever your good word.

MARTIUS   He that will give good words to thee will flatter

---

5. Through the winding passages and workrooms.
6. Show on my balance sheet.
7. Nourishment (punning on "flower," or choicest part).
8. Interpret (playing on the belly's function).
9. Concerning the public good.
1. Most desperate; lowest born. *rascal*: wretch; inferior deer or dog.

Beneath abhorring. What would you have, you curs
That like nor° peace nor war? The one affrights you,   *neither*
The other makes you proud.° He that trusts to you,   *rebellious*
160 Where he should find you lions finds you hares,
Where foxes, geese. You are no surer, no,
Than is the coal of fire upon the ice,
Or hailstone in the sun. Your virtue° is   *characteristic skill*
To make him worthy whose offence subdues him,²
165 And curse that justice did it. Who deserves greatness
Deserves° your hate, and your affections° are   *Incurs / propensities*
A sick man's appetite, who desires most that
Which would increase his evil.° He that depends   *illness*
Upon your favours swims with fins of lead,
170 And hews down oaks with rushes. Hang ye! Trust ye?
With every minute you do change a mind,
And call him noble that was now° your hate,   *just now*
Him vile that was your garland.³ What's the matter,
That in these several° places of the city   *various*
175 You cry against the noble senate, who,
Under the gods, keep you in awe, which else°   *who otherwise*
Would feed on one another?
[*To* MENENIUS]   What's their seeking?
MENENIUS   For corn at their own rates,° whereof they say   *prices*
The city is well stored.
MARTIUS   Hang 'em! They say?
180 They'll sit by th' fire and presume to know
What's done i'th' Capitol,⁴ who's like to rise,
Who thrives and who declines; side° factions and give out°   *side with / announce*
Conjectural marriages, making parties strong
And feebling such as stand not in their liking
185 Below their cobbled° shoes. They say there's grain enough!   *patched*
Would the nobility lay aside their ruth°   *compassion*
And let me use my sword, I'd make a quarry⁵
With thousands of these quartered⁶ slaves as high
As I could pitch my lance.
190 MENENIUS   Nay, these are all most thoroughly persuaded,°   *appeased*
For though abundantly they lack discretion,
Yet are they passing° cowardly. But I beseech you,   *exceedingly*
What says the other troop?
MARTIUS   They are dissolved. Hang 'em.
They said they were an-hungry,° sighed forth proverbs—   *very hungry*
195 That hunger broke stone walls, that dogs° must eat,   *(even dogs)*
That meat was made for mouths, that the gods sent not
Corn for the rich men only. With these shreds
They vented° their complainings, which being answered,   *spoke; excreted*
And a petition granted them—a strange one,
200 To break the heart of generosity°   *the nobility*
And make bold power look pale—they threw their caps
As they would hang them on the horns o'th' moon,
Shouting their emulation.⁷

---

2. To extol the man whose wrongdoing makes him liable to punishment.
3. Hero (traditionally wreathed with laurel or oak leaves).
4. The temple of Jupiter and hub of the Roman state.

5. A pile of animals killed in hunting.
6. Hacked to pieces (a punishment for treason).
7. Rivalry (either to shout loudest, or to defy the nobility).

MENENIUS   What is granted them?

MARTIUS   Five tribunes° to defend their vulgar wisdoms,   *representatives*

205   Of their own choice. One's Junius Brutus,

Sicinius Velutus, and I know not. 'Sdeath,°   *God's death (an oath)*

The rabble should have first unroofed the city

Ere so prevailed with me! It will in time

Win upon power° and throw forth greater themes   *Prevail upon authority*

210   For insurrection's arguing.

MENENIUS   This is strange.

MARTIUS *[to the* CITIZENS*]*   Go get you home, you fragments.°   *scraps of uneaten food*

           Enter a MESSENGER *hastily*

MESSENGER   Where's Caius Martius?

MARTIUS   Here. What's the matter?

215   MESSENGER   The news is, sir, the Volsces are in arms.

MARTIUS   I am glad on't. Then we shall ha' means to vent

Our musty superfluity.°   *moldy excess*

           Enter SICINIUS, BRUTUS, COMINIUS, LARTIUS, *with other*
           SENATORS

                         See, our best elders.

FIRST SENATOR   Martius, 'tis true that you have lately told us.

The Volsces are in arms.

MARTIUS   They have a leader,

220   Tullus Aufidius, that will put you to't.°   *to the test*

I sin in envying his nobility,

And were I anything but what I am,

I would wish me only he.

COMINIUS   You have fought together!

MARTIUS   Were half to half the world by th' ears[8] and he

225   Upon my party,° I'd revolt to make   *side*

Only my wars with him. He is a lion

That I am proud to hunt.

FIRST SENATOR   Then, worthy Martius,

Attend upon° Cominius to these wars.   *Serve under*

COMINIUS *[to* MARTIUS*]*   It is your former promise.

MARTIUS   Sir, it is,

230   And I am constant. Titus Lartius, thou

Shalt see me once more strike at Tullus' face.

What, art thou stiff?[9] Stand'st out?

LARTIUS   No, Caius Martius.

I'll lean upon one crutch and fight with th'other

Ere stay behind this business.

MENENIUS   O true bred!

235   FIRST SENATOR   Your company to th' Capitol, where I know

Our greatest friends attend us.

LARTIUS *[to* COMINIUS*]*   Lead you on.

    [To MARTIUS*]* Follow Cominius. We must follow you,

Right worthy° your priority.   *Who well deserve*

COMINIUS   Noble Martius.

FIRST SENATOR *[to the* CITIZENS*]*   Hence to your homes, be
           gone.

MARTIUS   Nay, let them follow.

240   The Volsces have much corn. Take these rats thither

---

8. If one-half of the world were fighting the other.   9. Obstinate (but Lartius understands "stiff with age").

To gnaw their garners.°   CITIZENS *steal away*   °*storehouses*
                   Worshipful mutineers,
   Your valour puts well forth.[1] [*To the* SENATORS] Pray follow.
           Exeunt. Manent° SICINIUS *and* BRUTUS   °*Remain onstage*

   SICINIUS   Was ever man so proud as is this Martius?
   BRUTUS   He has no equal.
245   SICINIUS   When we were chosen tribunes for the people—
   BRUTUS   Marked you his lip and eyes?
   SICINIUS   Nay, but his taunts.
   BRUTUS   Being moved,° he will not spare to gird[2] the gods.   °*angry*
   SICINIUS   Bemock the modest moon.
   BRUTUS   The present wars devour him! He is grown
      Too proud to be so valiant.
250   SICINIUS   Such a nature,
      Tickled° with good success, disdains the shadow   °*Excited; flattered*
      Which he treads on at noon. But I do wonder
      His insolence can brook° to be commanded   °*endure*
      Under Cominius.
   BRUTUS   Fame, at the which he aims—
255   In whom already he's well graced—cannot
      Better be held nor more attained than by
      A place below the first; for what miscarries
      Shall be the general's fault, though he perform
      To th' utmost of a man, and giddy censure°   °*rash opinion*
260   Will then cry out of Martius 'O, if he
      Had borne the business!'
   SICINIUS   Besides, if things go well,
      Opinion, that so sticks on° Martius, shall   °*clings to*
      Of his demerits° rob Cominius.   °*Of Cominius's deserts*
   BRUTUS   Come,
      Half all Cominius' honours are to Martius,
265   Though Martius earned them not; and all his faults
      To Martius shall be honours, though indeed
      In aught he merit not.
   SICINIUS   Let's hence and hear
      How the dispatch is made,° and in what fashion,   °*business is executed*
      More than his singularity,[3] he goes
      Upon this present action.
270   BRUTUS   Let's along.   *Exeunt*

1.2

Enter AUFIDIUS, *with* SENATORS *of Corioles*

   FIRST SENATOR   So, your opinion is, Aufidius,
      That they of Rome are entered° in our counsels   °*instructed*
      And know how we proceed.
   AUFIDIUS   Is it not yours?
      What ever have been thought on in this state
5   That could be brought to bodily act ere Rome
      Had circumvention?° 'Tis not four days gone   °*means to circumvent it*
      Since I heard thence.° These are the words. I think   °*from there*
      I have the letter here—yes, here it is.
           [*He reads the letter*]

---

1. Promises well, like a budding plant (ironic).
2. He will not refrain from sneering at.
3. Apart from his idiosyncrasies.
1.2 Location: Corioles, chief city of the Volscians.

'They have pressed a power,° but it is not known   *conscripted an army*

10   Whether for east or west. The dearth is great,
The people mutinous, and it is rumoured
Cominius, Martius your old enemy,
Who is of Rome worse hated than of you,
And Titus Lartius, a most valiant Roman,

15   These three lead on this preparation
Whither 'tis bent.° Most likely 'tis for you.   *Wherever it is bound*
Consider of it.'

FIRST SENATOR   Our army's in the field.
We never yet made doubt but Rome was ready
To answer us.

AUFIDIUS   Nor did you think it folly

20   To keep your great pretences° veiled till when   *aims*
They needs must show themselves, which in the hatching,
It seemed, appeared° to Rome. By the discovery   *became known*
We shall be shortened in our aim,° which was   *have to lower our sights*
To take in° many towns ere, almost, Rome   *seize*
Should know we were afoot.

25 SECOND SENATOR   Noble Aufidius,
Take your commission, hie° you to your bands.°   *haste / troops*
Let us alone to guard Corioles.
If they set down° before's, for the remove°   *encamp / to raise the siege*
Bring up your army, but I think you'll find
They've not prepared for us.

30 AUFIDIUS   O, doubt not that.
I speak from certainties. Nay, more,
Some parcels° of their power are forth already,   *parts*
And only hitherward.° I leave your honours.   *marching toward us*
If we and Caius Martius chance to meet,

35 'Tis sworn between us we shall ever strike°   *keep fighting*
Till one can do no more.

ALL THE SENATORS   The gods assist you!

AUFIDIUS   And keep your honours safe.

FIRST SENATOR   Farewell.

SECOND SENATOR   Farewell.

ALL   Farewell.

Exeunt [AUFIDIUS *at one door,*
SENATORS *at another door*]

1.3

Enter VOLUMNIA *and* VIRGILIA, *mother and wife to Mar-*
tius. They set them down on two low stools and sew

VOLUMNIA   I pray you, daughter, sing, or express yourself in a
more comfortable sort.° If my son were my husband, I should   *cheerful manner*
freelier rejoice in that absence wherein he won honour than in
the embracements of his bed where he would show most love.

5   When yet he was but tenderbodied and the only son of my
womb, when youth with comeliness plucked all gaze his way,
when for a day of kings' entreaties a mother should not sell him
an hour from her beholding, I, considering how honour would
become such a person°—that it was no better than, picture-   *handsome figure*

10 like, to hang by th' wall if renown made it not stir[1]—was

---

1.3 Location: Caius Martius's house, in Rome.   1. If desire for fame did not move it to action.

pleased to let him seek danger where he was like to find fame.
To a cruel war I sent him, from whence he returned his brows
bound with oak.[2] I tell thee, daughter, I sprang not more in joy
at first hearing he was a man-child than now in first seeing he
15   had proved himself a man.

VIRGILIA   But had he died in the business, madam, how then?

VOLUMNIA   Then his good report should have been my son. I
therein would have found issue. Hear me profess sincerely: had
I a dozen sons, each in my love alike, and none less dear than
20   thine and my good Martius', I had rather had eleven die nobly
for their country than one voluptuously surfeit out of action.[3]

        Enter a GENTLEWOMAN

GENTLEWOMAN   Madam, the Lady Valeria is come to visit you.

VIRGILIA [*to* VOLUMNIA]   Beseech you give me leave to retire
myself.°   ° *to go in*

25 VOLUMNIA   Indeed you shall not.
Methinks I hear hither your husband's drum,
See him pluck Aufidius down by th' hair;
As children from a bear, the Volsces shunning° him.   ° *fleeing*
Methinks I see him stamp thus, and call thus:

30   'Come on, you cowards, you were got° in fear   ° *begotten*
Though you were born in Rome!' His bloody brow
With his mailed° hand then wiping, forth he goes,   ° *armored*
Like to a harvest-man that's tasked° to mow   ° *ordered*
Or° all or lose his hire.°   ° *Either* / *pay*

35 VIRGILIA   His bloody brow? O Jupiter, no blood!

VOLUMNIA   Away, you fool! It more becomes a man
Than gilt° his trophy. The breasts of Hecuba[4]   ° *gold leaf*
When she did suckle Hector[5] looked not lovelier
Than Hector's forehead when it spit forth blood
At Grecian sword, contemning.°   ° *expressing contempt*

40   [*To the* GENTLEWOMAN]   Tell Valeria
We are fit° to bid her welcome.   *Exit* GENTLEWOMAN   ° *ready*

VIRGILIA   Heavens bless my lord from fell° Aufidius!   ° *fierce*

VOLUMNIA   He'll beat Aufidius' head below his knee
And tread upon his neck.

        Enter VALERIA, *with an usher and the* GENTLEWOMAN

45 VALERIA   My ladies both, good day to you.

VOLUMNIA   Sweet madam.

VIRGILIA   I am glad to see your ladyship.

VALERIA   How do you both? You are manifest housekeepers.[6]
What are you sewing here? A fine spot,° in good faith. How   ° *embroidered design*
50   does your little son?

VIRGILIA   I thank your ladyship; well, good madam.

VOLUMNIA   He had rather see the swords and hear a drum
than look upon his schoolmaster.

VALERIA   O' my word, the father's son! I'll swear 'tis a very pretty
55   boy. O' my troth, I looked upon him o' Wednesday half an
hour together. He's such a confirmed° countenance! I saw him   ° *determined*
run after a gilded butterfly, and when he caught it he let it go
again, and after it again, and over and over° he comes, and up   ° *head over heels*

---

2. A garland of oak leaves (awarded to one who saved
the life of a Roman citizen in battle).
3. Indulge himself to excess away from the battlefield.
4. Trojan queen, mother of many sons.

5. The greatest Trojan warrior, killed by the Greek
Achilles (*see Troilus and Cressida*).
6. You are clearly being stay-at-homes.

again, catched it again. Or whether his fall enraged him, or
60 how 'twas, he did so set° his teeth and tear it! O, I warrant, how
he mammocked° it!

VOLUMNIA   One on's° father's moods.

VALERIA   Indeed, la, 'tis a noble child.

VIRGILIA   A crack,° madam.

65 VALERIA   Come, lay aside your stitchery. I must have you play
the idle housewife° with me this afternoon.

VIRGILIA   No, good madam, I will not out of doors.

VALERIA   Not out of doors?

VOLUMNIA   She shall, she shall.

70 VIRGILIA   Indeed, no, by your patience. I'll not over the threshold till my lord return from the wars.

VALERIA   Fie, you confine yourself most unreasonably. Come,
you must go visit the good lady that lies in.°

VIRGILIA   I will wish her speedy strength, and visit her with my
75 prayers, but I cannot go thither.

VOLUMNIA   Why, I pray you?

VIRGILIA   'Tis not to save labour, nor that I want love.°

VALERIA   You would be another Penelope.[7] Yet they say all the
yarn she spun in Ulysses' absence did but fill Ithaca full of
80 moths. Come, I would your cambric° were sensible° as your
finger, that you might leave pricking it for pity. Come, you
shall go with us.

VIRGILIA   No, good madam, pardon me, indeed I will not forth.

VALERIA   In truth, la, go with me, and I'll tell you excellent news
85 of your husband.

VIRGILIA   O, good madam, there can be none yet.

VALERIA   Verily, I do not jest with you: there came news from
him last night.

VIRGILIA   Indeed, madam?

90 VALERIA   In earnest, it's true. I heard a senator speak it. Thus it
is: the Volsces have an army forth, against whom Cominius the
general is gone with one part of our Roman power. Your lord
and Titus Lartius are set down before their city Corioles. They
nothing doubt prevailing,[8] and to make it brief wars. This is
95 true, on mine honour; and so, I pray, go with us.

VIRGILIA   Give me excuse,° good madam, I will obey you in
everything hereafter.

VOLUMNIA [to VALERIA]   Let her alone, lady. As she is now she
will but disease° our better mirth.

100 VALERIA   In truth, I think she would. Fare you well, then. Come,
good sweet lady. Prithee, Virgilia, turn thy solemness out o'
door and go along with us.

VIRGILIA   No, at a word, madam. Indeed, I must not. I wish you
much mirth.

105 VALERIA   Well then, farewell.

Exeunt [VALERIA, VOLUMNIA, and usher at one door,
VIRGILIA and GENTLEWOMAN at another door]

clench
shredded
of his

lively lad

hussy

is confined with child

lack affection for her

fine white linen / sensitive

Pardon me

trouble

---

7. In Homer's *Odyssey*, Ulysses' wife, Penelope, pretends during his protracted absence that she cannot
remarry until she finishes her weaving, which she
secretly unravels each night.
8. They don't at all doubt that they will prevail.

1.4

Enter MARTIUS, LARTIUS *with [a trumpeter and] drum*
and colors,° with captains and soldiers [carrying scaling   *drummer and flag bearer*
ladders], as before the city Corioles;[1] to them a MES-
SENGER

MARTIUS   Yonder comes news. A wager they have met.
LARTIUS   My horse to yours, no.
MARTIUS   'Tis done.
LARTIUS   Agreed.
MARTIUS *[to the* MESSENGER*]*   Say, has our general met the enemy?
MESSENGER   They lie in view, but have not spoke° as yet.   *encountered*
LARTIUS   So, the good horse is mine.
5   MARTIUS   I'll buy him of you.
LARTIUS   No, I'll nor° sell nor give him. Lend you him I will,   *neither*
For half a hundred years.
     [To the trumpeter]   Summon the town.
MARTIUS *[to the* MESSENGER*]*   How far off lie these armies?
MESSENGER   Within
     this mile and half.
MARTIUS   Then shall we hear their 'larum,° and they ours.   *call to arms*
10   Now Mars,° I prithee, make us quick in work,   *Roman god of war*
That we with smoking° swords may march from hence   *steaming (with blood)*
To help our fielded friends.[2]
     [To the trumpeter]   Come, blow thy blast.
          They sound a parley.[3] Enter two SENATORS, *with others,*
          on the walls of Corioles
     [To the SENATORS*]* Tullus Aufidius, is he within your walls?
FIRST SENATOR   No, nor a man that fears you less than he:
That's lesser than a little.
          Drum afar off
15   *[To the Volscians]*   Hark, our drums
Are bringing forth our youth. We'll break our walls
Rather than they shall pound us up.° Our gates,   *confine us*
Which yet seem shut, we have but pinned with rushes.°   *hollow reeds*
They'll open of themselves.
          Alarum far off
     [To the Romans]   Hark you, far off
20   There is Aufidius. List what work he makes
Amongst your cloven° army.   *divided; cut to pieces*
          [Exeunt Volscians from the walls]
MARTIUS   O, they are at it!
LARTIUS   Their noise be our instruction. Ladders, ho!
          [They prepare to assault the walls.]
          Enter the army of the Volsces [from the gates]
MARTIUS   They fear us not, but issue° forth their city.   *rush from*
Now put your shields before your hearts, and fight
25   With hearts more proof ° than shields. Advance, brave Titus.   *impenetrable*
They do disdain us much beyond our thoughts,[4]
Which makes me sweat with wrath. Come on, my fellows.

1.4 Location: Before the walls of Corioles.   2. Our comrades in the battlefield.
1. The rear of the stage represented the city walls, the   3. Trumpet call for conference with the enemy.
tiring-house door the gate, and the balcony the ramparts.   4. More than we had imagined.

He that retires, I'll take him for a Volsce,
And he shall feel mine edge.°   *(sword edge)*

Alarum. The Romans are beat back [and exeunt]
to their trenches[, the Volsces following]

1.5

Enter [Roman SOLDIERS, *in retreat, followed by]* MAR-
TIUS, *cursing*

MARTIUS   All the contagion of the south[1] light on you,
You shames of Rome! You herd of—boils and plagues
Plaster you o'er, that you may be abhorred°   *(by your smell)*
Farther than seen, and one infect another
5   Against the wind a mile!° You souls of geese   *Even a mile upwind*
That bear the shapes of men, how have you run
From slaves that apes would beat! Pluto° and hell: *god of the underworld*
All hurt behind![2] Backs red, and faces pale
With flight and agued° fear! Mend and charge home,[3]   *shivering*
10   Or by the fires of heaven° I'll leave the foe   *the stars*
And make my wars on you. Look to't. Come on.
If you'll stand fast, we'll beat them to their wives,
As they us to our trenches. Follow.

[The Romans come forward towards the walls.]
Another alarum, and [enter the army of the Volsces.]
MARTIUS *[beats them back through] the gates*

So, now the gates are ope. Now prove good seconds.°   *supporters*
15   'Tis for the followers fortune widens° them,   *opens*
Not for the fliers. Mark me, and do the like.

[He] enters the gates

FIRST SOLDIER   Foolhardiness! Not I.
SECOND SOLDIER   Nor I.

*Alarum continues. [The gates close,] and [*MARTIUS*] is*
shut in

FIRST SOLDIER   See, they have shut him in.
THIRD SOLDIER   To th' pot,° I warrant him.   *cooking pot*

Enter LARTIUS

LARTIUS   What is become of Martius?
FOURTH SOLDIER   Slain, sir, doubtless.
20   FIRST SOLDIER   Following the fliers at the very heels,
With them he enters, who upon the sudden
Clapped-to° their gates. He is himself alone   *Shut*
To answer° all the city.   *confront*
LARTIUS   O noble fellow,
Who sensibly° outdares his senseless sword   *though having sensation*
25   And, when it bows, stand'st up! Thou art lost, Martius.
A carbuncle entire,° as big as thou art,   *flawless ruby*
Were not so rich a jewel. Thou wast a soldier
Even to Cato's[4] wish, not fierce and terrible
Only in strokes, but with thy grim looks and
30   The thunder-like percussion of thy sounds
Thou mad'st thine enemies shake as if the world
Were feverous and did tremble.

1.5   Scene continues.
1. South wind (thought to carry disease).
2. An injury taken in flight was a disgrace.

3. Charge to the heart of their defenses.
4. Cato the Censor, Roman general and moralist.

Enter MARTIUS, *bleeding, assaulted by the enemy*

FIRST SOLDIER   Look, sir.

LARTIUS   O, 'tis Martius!

Let's fetch him off, or make remain alike.[5]

They fight, and all [exeunt] into the city

1.6

Enter certain ROMANS *with spoils*

FIRST ROMAN   This will I carry to Rome.

SECOND ROMAN   And I this.

THIRD ROMAN   A murrain° on't, I took this for silver.   plague

[*He throws it away.*]

Alarum continues still afar off. Enter MARTIUS, [*bleeding,*] *and* [LARTIUS] *with a trumpet[er]. Exeunt* [ROMANS
with spoils]

MARTIUS   See here these movers[1] that do prize their honours

5   At a cracked drachma!° Cushions, leaden spoons,   *Greek coin*
    Irons of a doit,[2] doublets that hangmen would
    Bury with those that wore them,[3] these base slaves,
    Ere yet the fight be done, pack up. Down with them!
    And hark what noise the general makes. To him.

10   There is the man of my soul's hate, Aufidius,
    Piercing our Romans. Then, valiant Titus, take
    Convenient numbers to make good° the city,   *secure*
    Whilst I, with those that have the spirit, will haste
    To help Cominius.

LARTIUS   Worthy sir, thou bleed'st.

15   Thy exercise hath been too violent
    For a second course° of fight.   *bout*

MARTIUS   Sir, praise me not.
    My work hath yet not warmed me. Fare you well.
    The blood I drop is rather physical[4]
    Than dangerous to me. To Aufidius thus
    I will appear and fight.

20   LARTIUS   Now the fair goddess fortune
    Fall deep in love with thee, and her great charms
    Misguide thy opposers' swords! Bold gentleman,
    Prosperity be thy page.°   *Success attend you*

MARTIUS   Thy friend° no less   *(Prosperity)*
    Than those she placeth highest. So farewell.

25   LARTIUS   Thou worthiest Martius!   [*Exit* MARTIUS]
    Go sound thy trumpet in the market-place.
    Call thither all the officers o'th' town,
    Where they shall know our mind. Away.   *Exeunt [severally]*

1.7

Enter COMINIUS, *as it were in retire, with soldiers*

COMINIUS   Breathe you,° my friends. Well fought. We are come   *Get your breath back*
    off[1]
    Like Romans, neither foolish in our stands

---

5. Let's rescue him, or share his fate.
1.6 Location: Corioles.
1. Active persons (ironic); plunderers.
2. Worthless swords (a "doit" was a very small coin).
doublets: close-fitting jackets (common male attire in
Jacobean England).

3. That is, even a hangman, whose wage is his victim's
clothing, would spurn these garments.
4. Curative (bloodletting was a common medical practice).
1.7 Location: The battlefield.
1. We have retreated.

Nor cowardly in retire. Believe me, sirs,
We shall be charged again. Whiles we have struck,°   *we were fighting*
5   By interims and conveying gusts² we have heard
The charges of our friends. The Roman gods
Lead their successes as we wish our own,
That both our powers, with smiling fronts° encount'ring,   *faces; front ranks*
May give you° thankful sacrifice!   *(the gods)*
        Enter a MESSENGER
                     Thy news?
10   MESSENGER   The citizens of Corioles have issued,°   *(from the gates)*
And given to Lartius and to Martius battle.
I saw our party to their trenches driven,
And then I came away.
COMINIUS   Though thou speak'st truth,
Methinks thou speak'st not well. How long is't since?
15   MESSENGER   Above an hour, my lord.
COMINIUS   'Tis not a mile; briefly° we heard their drums.   *a short time ago*
How couldst thou in a mile confound° an hour,   *waste*
And bring thy news so late?
MESSENGER   Spies of the Volsces
Held me in chase, that I was forced to wheel°   *detour*
20   Three or four miles about; else had I, sir,
Half an hour since brought my report.   [*Exit*]
        Enter MARTIUS [*bloody*]
COMINIUS   Who's yonder,
That does appear as he were flayed? O gods!
He has the stamp° of Martius, and I have   *form*
Before-time° seen him thus.   *Previously*
MARTIUS   Come I too late?
25   COMINIUS   The shepherd knows not thunder from a tabor°   *small drum*
More than I know the sound of Martius' tongue
From every meaner° man.   *lesser*
MARTIUS   Come I too late?
COMINIUS   Ay, if you come not in the blood of others,
But mantled in your own.
MARTIUS   O, let me clip° ye   *clasp*
30   In arms as sound as when I wooed, in heart
As merry as when our nuptial day was done,
And tapers burnt to bedward!
        [*They embrace*]
COMINIUS   Flower of warriors! How is't with Titus Lartius?
MARTIUS   As with a man busied about decrees,
35   Condemning some to death and some to exile,
Ransoming him or pitying, threat'ning th'other;
Holding Corioles in the name of Rome
Even like a fawning greyhound in the leash,
To let him slip° at will.   *off the leash*
COMINIUS   Where is that slave
40   Which told me they had beat you to your trenches?
Where is he? Call him hither.
MARTIUS   Let him alone.
He did inform° the truth. But for our gentlemen,°   *report / (sarcastic)*
The common file°—a plague—tribunes for them?—   *sort*

---

2. At intervals, conveyed by the wind.

The mouse ne'er shunned the cat as they did budge°   *flinch*
From rascals worse than they.
45   COMINIUS   But how prevailed you?
MARTIUS   Will the time serve to tell? I do not think.
Where is the enemy? Are you lords o'th' field?
If not, why cease you till you are so?
COMINIUS   Martius, we have at disadvantage fought,
50   And did retire to win our purpose.°   *for tactical reasons*
MARTIUS   How lies their battle?° Know you on which side   *army*
They have placed their men of trust?
COMINIUS   As I guess, Martius,
Their bands i'th' vanguard are the Antiates,
Of their best trust; o'er them Aufidius,
Their very heart of hope.
55   MARTIUS   I do beseech you
By all the battles wherein we have fought,
By th' blood we have shed together, by th' vows we have made
To endure° friends, that you directly set me   *remain*
Against Aufidius and his Antiates,
60   And that you not delay the present,° but,   *matter at hand*
Filling the air with swords advanced and darts,
We prove° this very hour.   *try*
COMINIUS   Though I could wish
You were conducted to a gentle bath
And balms applied to you, yet dare I never
65   Deny your asking. Take your choice of those
That best can aid your action.
MARTIUS   Those are they
That most are willing. If any such be here—
As it were sin to doubt—that love this painting°   *(blood)*
Wherein you see me smeared; if any fear
70   Lesser his person than an ill report[3]
If any think brave death outweighs bad life,
And that his country's dearer than himself,
Let him alone, or so many so minded,
        [*He waves his sword*]
Wave thus to express his disposition,
75   And follow Martius.
        They all shout and wave their swords, [then some] take
        him up in their arms and [they] cast up their caps
O' me alone, make you a sword of me?
If these shows be not outward,° which of you   *superficial*
But is four Volsces? None of you but is
Able to bear against the great Aufidius
80   A shield as hard as his. A certain number—
Though thanks to all—must I select from all.
The rest shall bear the business in some other fight
As cause will be obeyed.° Please you to march,   *the situation requires*
And I shall quickly draw out my command,[4]
Which men are best inclined.
85   COMINIUS   March on, my fellows.
Make good this ostentation,° and you shall   *show of enthusiasm*
Divide in all[5] with us.   *Exeunt [marching]*

3. Less for his body than for his reputation.   5. Share the honor and winnings.
4. Select those I will command.

1.8

Enter LARTIUS [*through the gates of*] *Corioles, with
drum and trumpet, a* LIEUTENANT, *other soldiers, and a
scout*

LARTIUS [*to the* LIEUTENANT]   So, let the ports° be guarded. Keep your duties   gates
As I have set them down. If I do send, dispatch
Those centuries[1] to our aid. The rest will serve
For a short holding.° If we lose the field   brief occupation
5   We cannot keep the town.
LIEUTENANT   Fear not our care, sir.
LARTIUS   Hence, and shut your gates upon's.   [*Exit* LIEUTENANT]
[*To the scout*] Our guider, come; to th' Roman camp conduct us.
                    Exeunt toward COMINIUS *and* MARTIUS

1.9

Alarum, as in battle. Enter MARTIUS, [*bloody,*] *and*
AUFIDIUS *at several*° *doors*   separate
MARTIUS   I'll fight with none but thee, for I do hate thee
Worse than a promise-breaker.
AUFIDIUS   We hate alike.
Not Afric owns° a serpent I abhor   Africa doesn't contain
More than thy fame and envy.° Fix thy foot.   enviable reputation
5 MARTIUS   Let the first budger die the other's slave,
And the gods doom him after.
AUFIDIUS   If I fly, Martius,
Holla° me like a hare.   Shout in pursuit of
MARTIUS   Within these three hours, Tullus,
Alone I fought in your Corioles' walls,
And made what work I pleased. 'Tis not my blood
10   Wherein thou seest me masked. For thy revenge,
Wrench up thy power to th' highest.
AUFIDIUS   Wert thou the Hector
That was the whip of your bragged progeny,[1]
Thou shouldst not scape me here.
                    Here they fight, and certain Volsces come in the aid of
                    AUFIDIUS. MARTIUS *fights till* [*the Volsces*] *be driven in*
                    breathless[, MARTIUS *following*]
Officious° and not valiant, you have shamed me   Meddling
15   In your condemnèd seconds.[2]
                                        Exit

1.10

Alarum. A retreat is sounded. Flourish.[1] *Enter at one
door* COMINIUS *with the Romans, at another door* MAR-
TIUS *with his arm in a scarf*°   sling
COMINIUS [*to* MARTIUS]   If I should tell thee o'er this thy day's work
Thou'lt not believe thy deeds. But I'll report it
Where senators shall mingle tears with smiles,
Where great patricians shall attend and shrug,°   (with incredulity)
5   I'th' end admire;° where ladies shall be frighted   marvel

---

1.8 Location: The gates of Corioles.
1. Companies of a hundred men.
1.9 Location: The battlefield.
1. Romans claimed descent from the Trojans; Hector, the finest Trojan soldier, was the scourge ("whip") of the

Greeks.
2. Contemptible assistance.
1.10 Location: The battlefield.
1. Trumpet call for the entry of the victorious Romans. *retreat:* signal to cease pursuit.

And, gladly quaked,° hear more; where the dull° tribunes,   *made to tremble / sullen*
That with the fusty° plebeians hate thine honours,   *moldy; stinking*
Shall say against their hearts° 'We thank the gods   *despite themselves*
Our Rome hath such a soldier.'
10   Yet cam'st thou to a morsel of this feast,
Having fully dined before.[2]

       Enter [LARTIUS,] with his power,° from the pursuit   *troops*

LARTIUS   O general,
Here is the steed, we the caparison.[3]
Hadst thou beheld—

MARTIUS   Pray now, no more. My mother,
Who has a charter° to extol her blood,°   *right / offspring*
15   When she does praise me grieves me. I have done
As you have done, that's what I can; induced
As you have been, that's for my country.
He that has but effected his good will[4]
Hath overta'en mine act.

COMINIUS   You shall not be
20   The grave of your deserving. Rome must know
The value of her own. 'Twere a concealment
Worse than a theft, no less than a traducement,°   *slander*
To hide your doings and to silence that
Which, to the spire and top of praises vouched,°   *declared*
25   Would seem but modest.° Therefore, I beseech you—   *inadequate*
In sign° of what you are, not to reward   *As a token*
What you have done—before our army hear me.

MARTIUS   I have some wounds upon me, and they smart
To hear themselves remembered.

COMINIUS   Should they not,
30   Well might they fester 'gainst ingratitude,
And tent[5] themselves with death. Of all the horses—
Whereof we have ta'en good, and good store[6]—of all
The treasure in this field achieved and city,
We render you the° tenth, to be ta'en forth   *one*
35   Before the common distribution
At your only° choice.   *sole*

MARTIUS   I thank you, general,
But cannot make my heart consent to take
A bribe to pay my sword. I do refuse it,
And stand° upon my common part with those   *insist*
40   That have upheld the doing.

       A long flourish. They all cry 'Martius, Martius!' [and]
       cast up their caps and lances. COMINIUS *and* LARTIUS
       stand bare

May these same instruments which you profane
Never sound more. When drums and trumpets shall
I'th' field prove flatterers, let courts and cities be
Made all of false-faced soothing.[7] When steel grows
45   Soft as the parasite's° silk, let him be made   *flatterer's*

---

2. *Yet . . . before:* either "The feast of description is a morsel compared with the full dinner of your deeds," or "Your final onslaught was a mere morsel in addition to your earlier fighting."
3. That is, here is he who really did the work (Coriolanus, the horse); we are only the horse's trappings ("caparison").
4. Carried out his resolution.
5. Heal (a "tent" was a probe that cleansed a wound).
6. We have captured good quality and quantity.
7. Hypocritical compliments.

An overture for th' wars.[8] No more, I say.
For that I have not washed my nose that bled,
Or foiled some debile° wretch, which without note   *feeble*
Here's many else° have done, you shout me forth   *others*
50   In acclamations hyperbolical,°   *In exaggerated praise*
As if I loved my little[9] should be dieted°   *fattened*
In praises sauced with lies.

COMINIUS   Too modest are you,
More cruel to your good report than grateful
To us that give° you truly. By your patience,   *describe*
55   If 'gainst yourself you be incensed we'll put you,
Like one that means his proper harm,° in manacles,   *harm to himself*
Then reason safely with you. Therefore be it known,
As to us, to all the world, that Caius Martius
Wears this war's garland, in token of the which
60   My noble steed, known to the camp, I give him,
With all his trim belonging;° and from this time,   *fine trappings*
For what he did before Corioles, call him,
With all th'applause and clamour of the host,
Martius Caius Coriolanus. Bear th'addition°   *title*
65   Nobly ever!
                Flourish. Trumpets sound, and drums
ALL   Martius Caius Coriolanus!
CORIOLANUS [*to* COMINIUS]   I will go wash,
And when my face is fair° you shall perceive   *clean*
Whether I blush or no. Howbeit, I thank you.
70   I mean to stride° your steed, and at all times   *bestride; ride on*
To undercrest° your good addition   *uphold*
To th' fairness° of my power.   *best*

COMINIUS   So, to our tent,
Where, ere we do repose us, we will write
To Rome of our success. You, Titus Lartius,
75   Must to Corioles back. Send us to Rome
The best,[1] with whom we may articulate°   *make terms*
For their own good and ours.

LARTIUS   I shall, my lord.
CORIOLANUS   The gods begin to mock me. I, that now
Refused most princely gifts, am bound to beg
Of my lord general.

80   COMINIUS   Take't, 'tis yours. What is't?
CORIOLANUS   I sometime lay here in Corioles,
And at a poor man's house. He used° me kindly.   *treated*
He cried° to me; I saw him prisoner;   *appealed*
But then Aufidius was within my view,
85   And wrath o'erwhelmed my pity. I request you
To give my poor host freedom.

COMINIUS   O, well begged!
Were he the butcher of my son he should
Be free as is the wind. Deliver° him, Titus.   *Free*

LARTIUS   Martius, his name?
CORIOLANUS   By Jupiter, forgot!
90   I am weary, yea, my memory is tired.
Have we no wine here?

---

8. *let . . . wars*: a debated and perhaps corrupt passage: 9. Small achievement.
perhaps "let the parasite call soldiers to war."   1. The most noble Volscians.

COMINIUS   Go we to our tent.
The blood upon your visage dries; 'tis time
It should be looked to. Come.   *Exeunt. A flourish [of] cornetts*

1.11

Enter AUFIDIUS, *bloody, with two or three* SOLDIERS

AUFIDIUS   The town is ta'en.
A SOLDIER   'Twill be delivered back on good condition.[1]
AUFIDIUS   Condition?
    I would I were a Roman, for I cannot,
5   Being a Volsce, be that I am.° Condition?   *what I am (proud)*
    What good condition can a treaty find
    I'th' part that is at mercy?° Five times, Martius,   *For the conquered side*
    I have fought with thee; so often hast thou beat me,
    And wouldst do so, I think, should we encounter
10 As often as we eat. By th' elements,
    If e'er again I meet him beard to beard,
    He's mine, or I am his! Mine emulation°   *rivalry*
    Hath not that honour in't it had, for where°   *whereas*
    I thought to crush him in an equal force,
15 True sword to sword, I'll potch° at him some way   *thrust*
    Or° wrath or craft may get him.   *Either*
A SOLDIER   He's the devil.
AUFIDIUS   Bolder, though not so subtle. My valour, poisoned
    With only suff'ring stain° by him, for him   *disgrace*
    Shall fly out of itself. Nor sleep nor sanctuary,[2]
20 Being naked, sick, nor fane° nor Capitol,   *temple*
    The prayers of priests nor times of sacrifice—
    Embargements° all of fury—shall lift up   *Impediments*
    Their rotten° privilege and custom 'gainst   *worn-out*
    My hate to Martius. Where I find him, were it
25 At home upon° my brother's guard,° even there,   *under / protection*
    Against the hospitable canon,° would I   *rule of hospitality*
    Wash my fierce hand in's heart. Go you to th' city.
    Learn how 'tis held, and what they are that must
    Be hostages for Rome.
A SOLDIER   Will not you go?
30 AUFIDIUS   I am attended° at the cypress grove. I pray you— *expected*
    'Tis south the city mills—bring me word thither
    How the world goes, that to the pace of it[3]
    I may spur on my journey.
A SOLDIER   I shall, sir.
                    *Exeunt [*AUFIDIUS *at one door,* SOLDIERS
                              at another door]

2.1

Enter MENENIUS *with the two tribunes of the people,*
                SICINIUS *and* BRUTUS

MENENIUS   The augurer[1] tells me we shall have news tonight.
BRUTUS   Good or bad?
MENENIUS   Not according to the prayer of the people, for they
    love not Martius.

1.11 Location: Outside Corioles.
1. Terms (Aufidius takes the meaning "state of being").
2. In early modern England, those who sought sanctuary in a church were protected from attack or legal prosecution. *fly out of itself*: deviate from its nature.
3. In accordance with the situation.
2.1 Location: Rome.
1. Religious official who interpreted omens.

5 SICINIUS Nature teaches beasts to know their friends.

 MENENIUS Pray you, who does the wolf love?

 SICINIUS The lamb.

 MENENIUS Ay, to devour him, as the hungry plebeians would
  the noble Martius.

10 BRUTUS He's a lamb indeed that baas like a bear.

 MENENIUS He's a bear indeed that lives like a lamb.[2] You two
  are old men. Tell me one thing that I shall ask you.

 SICINIUS *and* BRUTUS Well, sir?

 MENENIUS In what enormity is Martius poor in that you two
15 have not in abundance?

 BRUTUS He's poor in no one fault, but stored° with all.   *well stocked*

 SICINIUS Especially in pride.

 BRUTUS And topping all others in boasting.

 MENENIUS This is strange now. Do you two know how you are
20 censured° here in the city—I mean of us o'th' right-hand file.[3] *judged*
  Do you?

 SICINIUS *and* BRUTUS Why, how are we censured?

 MENENIUS Because—you talk of pride now—will you not be
  angry?

25 SICINIUS *and* BRUTUS Well, well, sir, well?

 MENENIUS Why, 'tis no great matter, for a very little thief of
  occasion will rob you of a great deal of patience.[4] Give your
  dispositions the reins, and be angry at your pleasures—at the
  least, if you take it as a pleasure to you in being so. You blame
30 Martius for being proud?

 BRUTUS We do it not alone, sir.

 MENENIUS I know you can do very little alone, for your helps
  are many, or else your actions would grow wondrous single.° *solitary; trivial*
  Your abilities are too infant-like for doing much alone. You talk
35 of pride. O that you could turn your eyes toward the napes of
  your necks, and make but an interior survey of your good
  selves! O that you could!

 SICINIUS *and* BRUTUS What then, sir?

 MENENIUS Why, then you should discover a brace° of unmer- *pair*
40 iting, proud, violent, testy magistrates, alias fools, as any in
  Rome.

 SICINIUS Menenius, you are known well enough too.

 MENENIUS I am known to be a humorous° patrician, and one *whimsical*
  that loves a cup of hot wine with not a drop of allaying Tiber° *water*
45 in't; said to be something imperfect in favouring the first complaint,[5] hasty and tinder-like upon too trivial motion;° one that *provocation*
  converses more with the buttock of the night than with the
  forehead of the morning.[6] What I think, I utter, and spend my
  malice in my breath. Meeting two such wealsmen° as you *statesmen*
50 are—I cannot call you Lycurguses[7]—if the drink you give me
  touch my palate adversely, I make a crooked face at it. I cannot
  say your worships have delivered the matter well, when I find
  the ass in compound with the major part of your syllables.[8] And

---

2. That is, how can you accuse him of being a bear when he lives an innocent life?

3. Patrician class (who made up the right-hand "file," or line, in battle).

4. The least pretext will make you lose your temper.

5. *favouring the first complaint*: accepting the first ver-

sion of a dispute I hear before considering the other side.

6. That experiences more late nights than early mornings.

7. Lycurgus was a famous Spartan lawgiver of the ninth century B.C.E.

8. I find stupidity mixed in most of what you say.

though I must be content to bear with those that say you are
55 reverend grave men, yet they lie deadly° that tell you have good   extremely
faces. If you see this in the map of my microcosm,⁹ follows it
that I am known well enough too? What harm can your bisson
conspectuities° glean out of this character,¹ if I be known well   dim vision
enough too?

60 BRUTUS   Come, sir, come, we know you well enough.

MENENIUS   You know neither me, yourselves, nor anything. You
are ambitious for poor knaves' caps and legs.² You wear out a
good wholesome forenoon in hearing a cause between an
orange-wife and a faucet-seller,³ and then rejourn° the contro-   adjourn
65 versy of threepence to a second day of audience.° When you   hearing
are hearing a matter between party and party, if you chance to
be pinched with the colic,° you make faces like mummers,⁴ set   intestinal gas
up the bloody flag° against all patience, and in roaring for a   declare war
chamber-pot, dismiss the controversy bleeding,° the more   unhealed
70 entangled by your hearing. All the peace you make in their
cause is calling both the parties knaves. You are a pair of
strange ones.

BRUTUS   Come, come, you are well understood to be a perfecter
giber for the table than a necessary bencher in the Capitol.⁵

75 MENENIUS   Our very priests must become mockers if they shall
encounter such ridiculous subjects° as you are. When you   objects; citizens
speak best unto the purpose it is not worth the wagging of your
beards, and your beards deserve not so honourable a grave as
to stuff a botcher's° cushion or to be entombed in an ass's pack-   clothes mender
80 saddle.⁶ Yet you must be saying 'Martius is proud', who, in a
cheap estimation,° is worth all your predecessors since Deuca-   low estimate
lion,⁷ though peradventure some of the best of 'em were heredi-
tary hangmen.⁸ Good e'en to your worships. More of your con-
versation would infect my brain, being° the herdsmen of   you two being
85 the beastly plebeians. I will be bold to take my leave of you.

[He leaves] BRUTUS and SICINIUS, [who stand] aside.
Enter [in haste] VOLUMNIA, VIRGILIA, and VALERIA

How now, my as fair as noble ladies—and the moon,⁹ were she
earthly, no nobler—whither do you follow your eyes so fast?

VOLUMNIA   Honourable Menenius, my boy Martius approaches.
For the love of Juno, let's go.

90 MENENIUS   Ha, Martius coming home?

VOLUMNIA   Ay, worthy Menenius, and with most prosperous
approbation.¹

MENENIUS [throwing up his cap]   Take my cap, Jupiter, and I
thank thee! Hoo, Martius coming home?

95 VIRGILIA and VALERIA   Nay, 'tis true.

VOLUMNIA   Look, here's a letter from him. The state hath another, his wife another, and I think there's one at home for
you.

---

9. My face (thought to map the "little world" of the
human body).
1. Verbal description.
2. For deferentially doffed caps and bent legs.
3. Between a woman fruit vendor and someone who
sells taps for liquor barrels.
4. Dumb-show actors (who use exaggerated facial
expressions).

5. perfecter giber . . . Capitol: better at dinner jests
than at serving in the senate.
6. Hair from cut beards was used as stuffing.
7. Deucalion and his wife were sole survivors of a great
flood; their son was the ancestor of the Greeks.
8. A very base occupation.
9. Diana, goddess of chastity.
1. Rich praise; happy success.

MENENIUS   I will make my very house reel tonight. A letter for
100   me?
VIRGILIA   Yes, certain, there's a letter for you; I saw't.
MENENIUS   A letter for me? It gives me an estate° of seven years'   *endowment; condition*
       health, in which time I will make a lip° at the physician. The   *sneer*
       most sovereign° prescription in Galen² is but empiricutic° and,   *effective / quackish*
105   to° this preservative, of no better report than a horse-drench.³   *compared with*
       Is he not wounded? He was wont° to come home wounded.   *accustomed*
VIRGILIA   O, no, no, no!
VOLUMNIA   O, he is wounded, I thank the gods for't!
MENENIUS   So do I, too, if it be not too much. Brings a° victory   *If he brings*
110   in his pocket, the wounds become him.
VOLUMNIA   On's brows, Menenius. He comes the third time
       home with the oaken garland.
MENENIUS   Has he disciplined Aufidius soundly?
VOLUMNIA   Titus Lartius writes they fought together, but Aufid-
115   ius got off.
MENENIUS   And 'twas time for him too, I'll warrant him that. An°   *If*
       he had stayed by him, I would not have been so fidiussed⁴ for
       all the chests in Corioles and the gold that's in them. Is the
       senate possessed° of this?   *informed*
120   VOLUMNIA   Good ladies, let's go. Yes, yes, yes. The senate has
       letters from the general, wherein he gives my son the whole
       name° of the war. He hath in this action outdone his former   *credit*
       deeds doubly.
VALERIA   In truth, there's wondrous things spoke of him.
125   MENENIUS   Wondrous, ay, I warrant you; and not without his
       true purchasing.°   *truly earning it*
VIRGILIA   The gods grant them true.
VOLUMNIA   True? Pooh-whoo!
MENENIUS   True? I'll be sworn they are true. Where is he
130   wounded? [*To the tribunes*] God save your good worships. Mar-
       tius is coming home. He has more cause to be proud. [*To
       VOLUMNIA*] Where is he wounded?
VOLUMNIA   I'th' shoulder and i'th' left arm. There will be large
       cicatrices° to show the people when he shall stand for his   *scars*
135   place.⁵ He received in the repulse of Tarquin⁶ seven hurts
       i'th' body.
MENENIUS   One i'th' neck and two i'th' thigh—there's nine that
       I know.
VOLUMNIA   He had before this last expedition twenty-five wounds
140   upon him.
MENENIUS   Now it's twenty-seven. Every gash was an enemy's
       grave.

       A shout and flourish

       Hark, the trumpets.
VOLUMNIA   These are the ushers of Martius. Before him he car-
145   ries noise, and behind him he leaves tears.
       Death, that dark spirit, in's nervy° arm doth lie,   *muscular*
       Which being advanced, declines;° and then men die.   *being raised, descends*

---

2. Ancient medical authority still standard in the Renaissance (Galen actually lived six centuries after Coriolanus).
3. Horse medicine.
4. "Aufidiussed." Menenius's coinage for "beaten."

5. Will offer himself as a candidate for consul, republican Rome's highest office.
6. Martius's first military experience was in the war
against the former King Tarquin.

Trumpets sound a sennet.° Enter [in state] COMINIUS *the*   *ceremonial flourish*
general and LARTIUS, *between them* CORIOLANUS,
crowned with an oaken garland, with captains and sol-
diers and a HERALD

HERALD   Know, Rome, that all alone Martius did fight
   Within Corioles' gates, where he hath won

150   With fame a name to° 'Martius Caius'; these   *in addition to*
   In honour follows 'Coriolanus'.
   Welcome to Rome, renownèd Coriolanus!
      A flourish sound[s]

ALL   Welcome to Rome, renownèd Coriolanus!

CORIOLANUS   No more of this, it does offend my heart.
   Pray now, no more.

COMINIUS   Look, sir, your mother.

155 CORIOLANUS [*to* VOLUMNIA]   O,
   You have, I know, petitioned all the gods
   For my prosperity!°   *success*
      [*He*] *kneels*

VOLUMNIA   Nay, my good soldier, up,
   My gentle Martius, worthy Caius,
      [*He rises*]
   And, by deed-achieving honour newly named—

160   What is it?—'Coriolanus' must I call thee?
   But O, thy wife!

CORIOLANUS [*to* VIRGILIA]   My gracious silence, hail.
   Wouldst thou have laughed had I come coffined home,
   That weep'st to see me triumph? Ah, my dear,
   Such eyes the widows in Corioles wear,
   And mothers that lack sons.

165 MENENIUS   Now the gods crown thee!

CORIOLANUS [*to* VALERIA]   And live you yet? O my sweet lady, pardon.

VOLUMNIA   I know not where to turn. O, welcome home!
   And welcome, general, and you're welcome all!

MENENIUS   A hundred thousand welcomes! I could weep

170   And I could laugh, I am light and heavy.° Welcome!   *(of heart)*
   A curse begnaw at very root on's heart
   That is not glad to see thee. You are three
   That Rome should dote on. Yet, by the faith of men,
   We have some old crab-trees° here at home that will not   *(gnarled, sour men)*

175   Be grafted to your relish.° Yet welcome, warriors!   *liking*
   We call a nettle but a nettle, and
   The faults of fools but folly.

COMINIUS   Ever right.

CORIOLANUS   Menenius, ever, ever.

HERALD   Give way there, and go on.

180 CORIOLANUS [*to* VOLUMNIA *and* VIRGILIA]   Your hand, and yours.
   Ere in our own house I do shade my head
   The good patricians must be visited,
   From whom I have received not only greetings,
   But with them change of honours.°   *a new set of honors*

VOLUMNIA   I have lived

185   To see inherited° my very wishes,   *realized*
   And the buildings of my fancy. Only
   There's one thing wanting, which I doubt not but
   Our Rome will cast upon thee.

CORIOLANUS   Know, good mother,
  I had rather be their servant in my way
  Than sway[7] with them in theirs.

190 COMINIUS   On, to the Capitol.

    Flourish [of] cornetts. Exeunt in state, as before, [all
    but] BRUTUS *and* SICINIUS[, *who come forward*]

BRUTUS   All tongues speak of him, and the blearèd sights°   *dim-sighted people*
  Are spectacled to see him. Your prattling nurse
  Into a rapture° lets her baby cry   *fit*
  While she chats him;[8] the kitchen malkin° pins   *wench*
195 Her richest lockram° 'bout her reechy° neck,   *linen / filthy*
  Clamb'ring the walls to eye him. Stalls, bulks,[9] windows
  Are smothered up, leads filled and ridges horsed
  With variable complexions,[1] all agreeing
  In earnestness to see him. Seld-shown flamens°   *Seldom-seen priests*
200 Do press among the popular° throngs, and puff°   *plebeian / pant*
  To win a vulgar station.° Our veiled dames   *a place in the crowd*
  Commit the war of white and damask[2] in
  Their nicely[3] guarded cheeks to th' wanton spoil
  Of Phoebus'° burning kisses. Such a pother°   *the sun's / commotion*
205 As if that whatsoever god who leads him°   *(Coriolanus)*
  Were slily crept into his human powers
  And gave him graceful posture.

SICINIUS   On the sudden°   *At once*
  I warrant him consul.

BRUTUS   Then our office may
  During his power° go sleep.   *term of authority*

210 SICINIUS   He cannot temp'rately transport° his honours   *convey*
  From where he should begin and end,° but will   *to where he should end*
  Lose those he hath won.

BRUTUS   In that there's comfort.

SICINIUS   Doubt not
  The commoners, for whom we stand, but they
  Upon their ancient malice[4] will forget
215 With the least cause these his new honours, which°   *(which cause)*
  That he will give them make I as little question
  As[5] he is proud to do't.

BRUTUS   I heard him swear,
  Were he to stand for consul, never would he
  Appear i'th' market-place nor on him put
220 The napless vesture° of humility,   *threadbare garment*
  Nor, showing, as the manner is, his wounds
  To th' people, beg their stinking breaths.°   *votes*

SICINIUS   'Tis right.

BRUTUS   It was his word. O, he would miss it° rather   *forgo the consulship*
  Than carry° it, but by the suit of the gentry to him,   *go through with it*
  And the desire of the nobles.

225 SICINIUS   I wish no better
  Than have him hold that purpose, and to put it
  In execution.

---

7. Rule; prevail; deviate from a straight course.
8. Discusses Coriolanus.
9. Framework projecting from shopfronts ("stalls").
1. *leads . . . complexions:* lead roofs filled and rooftops
bestridden by all types of people.

2. The conflict between white and pink in delicate skin
("damask" refers to the dark-pink damask rose).
3. Fastidiously (by the veils they usually wear).
4. Because of their long-standing hostility.
5. *I as . . . as:* I have as little doubt as that.

BRUTUS   'Tis most like he will.

SICINIUS   It shall be to him then, as our good wills,°   as our benefit requires
A sure destruction.

BRUTUS   So it must fall out
230   To him, or our authority's for an end.
      We must suggest° the people in what hatred   insinuate to
      He still° hath held them; that to's power he would   always
      Have made them mules, silenced their pleaders,°   representatives
      And dispropertied° their freedoms, holding them   taken away
235   In human action and capacity,
      Of no more soul nor fitness for the world
      Than camels in their war, who have their provand°   food
      Only for bearing burdens, and sore blows
      For sinking under them.

SICINIUS   This, as you say, suggested
240   At some time when his soaring insolence
      Shall touch° the people—which time shall not want°   kindle / be lacking
      If he be put upon't, and that's as easy
      As to set dogs on sheep—will be his fire
      To kindle their dry stubble,⁶ and their blaze
      Shall darken him for ever.
                    Enter a MESSENGER
245   BRUTUS   What's the matter?

MESSENGER   You are sent for to the Capitol. 'Tis thought
      That Martius shall be consul. I have seen
      The dumb men throng to see him, and the blind
      To hear him speak. Matrons flung gloves,
250   Ladies and maids their scarves and handkerchiefs,
      Upon him as he passed. The nobles bended
      As to Jove's statue, and the commons made
      A shower and thunder with their caps and shouts.
      I never saw the like.

BRUTUS   Let's to the Capitol,
255   And carry with us ears and eyes for th' time,°   present occasion
      But hearts for the event.°   outcome

SICINIUS   Have with you.°   *Exeunt*   Let's go; I'm with you.

2.2

Enter two OFFICERS, *to lay cushions, as it were
in the Capitol*

FIRST OFFICER   Come, come, they are almost here. How many
      stand for consulships?

SECOND OFFICER   Three, they say, but 'tis thought of everyone
      Coriolanus will carry it.

5   FIRST OFFICER   That's a brave fellow, but he's vengeance° proud   intensely
      and loves not the common people.

SECOND OFFICER   Faith, there hath been many great men that
      have flattered the people who ne'er loved them; and there be
      many that they° have loved they know not wherefore,° so that   (the people) / why
10   if they love they know not why, they hate upon no better a
      ground. Therefore for Coriolanus neither to care whether they
      love or hate him manifests the true knowledge he has in° their   of

6. That is, Coriolanus's fiery insolence will kindle the   **2.2 Location:** The Capitol, Rome.
dry fuel of the plebeians' resentment.

disposition, and out of his noble carelessness lets them plainly
see't.

15   FIRST OFFICER   If he did not care whether he had their love or
no he waved indifferently[1] 'twixt doing them neither good nor
harm; but he seeks their hate with greater devotion than they
can render it him, and leaves nothing undone that may fully
discover° him their opposite.° Now to seem to affect° the mal-   *reveal / adversary / desire*
20   ice and displeasure of the people is as bad as that which he
dislikes, to flatter them for their love.

  SECOND OFFICER   He hath deserved worthily of his country, and
his ascent is not by such easy degrees as those who, having been
supple and courteous to the people, bonneted,[2] without any
25   further deed to have them at all into their estimation and
report.° But he hath so planted his honours in their eyes   *good opinion*
and his actions in their hearts that for their tongues to be silent
and not confess so much were a kind of ingrateful injury. To
report otherwise were a malice that, giving itself the lie,[3] would
30   pluck reproof and rebuke from every ear that heard it.

  FIRST OFFICER   No more of him. He's a worthy man. Make way,
they are coming.

> *A sennet. Enter the Patricians, and* [SICINIUS *and* BRU-
> TUS], *the tribunes of the people, lictors*[4] *before them;*
> CORIOLANUS, MENENIUS, COMINIUS *the consul.* [*The
> Patricians take their places and sit.*] SICINIUS *and* BRU-
> TUS *take their places by themselves.* CORIOLANUS *stands*

  MENENIUS   Having determined of° the Volsces, and   *made a decision about*
To send for Titus Lartius, it remains
35   As the main point of this our after-meeting
To gratify° his noble service that   *reward*
Hath thus stood for his country. Therefore please you,
Most reverend and grave elders, to desire
The present consul and last° general   *recent*
40   In our well-found° successes to report   *happily encountered*
A little of that worthy work performed
By Martius Caius Coriolanus, whom
We met here both to thank and to remember
With honours like° himself.   *befitting*
    [CORIOLANUS *sits*]

  FIRST SENATOR   Speak, good Cominius.
45   Leave nothing out for° length, and make us think   *on account of*
Rather our state's defective for requital
Than we to stretch it out.[5]
  [*To the tribunes*]   Masters o'th' people,
We do request your kindest ears and, after,
Your loving motion toward° the common body   *persuasion of*
To yield° what passes here.   *agree to*
50   SICINIUS   We are convented°   *met together*
Upon a pleasing treaty,° and have hearts   *subject for discussion*
Inclinable to honour and advance
The theme of our assembly.

  BRUTUS   Which the rather

1. He would waver without caring.
2. Put their bonnets back on (after doffing them as a gesture of respect).
3. Showing itself to be false.
4. Officers who attended upon magistrates.
5. *Rather our . . . out:* We lack resources for adequate reward, rather than the will to reward him to the utmost.

	We shall be blessed° to do if he remember	*happy*
55	A kinder value of the people than	
	He hath hereto prized them at.	
	MENENIUS That's off, that's off.°	*irrelevant*
	I would you rather had been silent. Please you	
	To hear Cominius speak?	
	BRUTUS Most willingly,	
	But yet my caution was more pertinent	
	Than the rebuke you give it.	
60	MENENIUS He loves your people,	
	But tie him not to be their bedfellow.	
	Worthy Cominius, speak.	
	CORIOLANUS *rises and offers° to go away*	*begins*
	[*To* CORIOLANUS] Nay, keep your place.	
	FIRST SENATOR Sit, Coriolanus. Never shame to hear	
	What you have nobly done.	
	CORIOLANUS Your honours' pardon,	
65	I had rather have my wounds to heal again	
	Than hear say how I got them.	
	BRUTUS Sir, I hope	
	My words disbenched° you not?	*unseated*
	CORIOLANUS No, sir, yet oft	
	When blows have made me stay I fled from words.	
	You soothed° not, therefore hurt not; but your people,	*flattered*
	I love them as they weigh°—	*deserve*
70	MENENIUS Pray now, sit down.	
	CORIOLANUS I had rather have one scratch my head i'th' sun	
	When the alarum° were struck than idly sit	*battle summons*
	To hear my nothings monstered.⁶ *Exit*	
	MENENIUS Masters of the people,	
	Your multiplying spawn° how can he flatter—	*fast-breeding plebeians*
75	That's thousand to one good one—when you now see	
	He had rather venture all his limbs for honour	
	Than one on's° ears to hear it? Proceed, Cominius.	*of his*
	COMINIUS I shall lack voice; the deeds of Coriolanus	
	Should not be uttered feebly. It is held	
80	That valour is the chiefest virtue, and	
	Most dignifies the haver. If it be,	
	The man I speak of cannot in the world	
	Be singly counterpoised.° At sixteen years,	*equaled by anyone*
	When Tarquin made a head for° Rome, he fought	*raised an army against*
85	Beyond the mark° of others. Our then dictator,⁷	*reach*
	Whom with all praise I point at, saw him fight	
	When with his Amazonian⁸ chin he drove	
	The bristled lips° before him. He bestrid	*bearded soldiers*
	An o'erpressed° Roman, and, i'th' consul's view,	*overwhelmed*
90	Slew three opposers. Tarquin's self he met,	
	And struck him on his knee. In that day's feats,	
	When he might act the woman in the scene,⁹	
	He proved best man i'th' field, and for his meed°	*reward*
	Was brow-bound with the oak. His pupil age	

6. My trivial actions treated as marvels.
7. Roman magistrate with absolute authority, elected during emergencies.

8. Beardless (like a female Amazon warrior).
9. Might be expected to be cowardly (with an allusion to boys acting women's parts in the theater).

95   Man-entered thus, he waxèd like a sea,
      And in the brunt° of seventeen battles since   *violence*
      He lurched° all swords of the garland. For this last   *cheated*
      Before and in Corioles, let me say
      I cannot speak him home.° He stopped the fliers,   *praise him enough*
100   And by his rare example made the coward
      Turn terror into sport. As weeds before
      A vessel under sail, so men obeyed
      And fell below his stem.° His sword, death's stamp,   *prow*
      Where it did mark, it took.¹ From face to foot
105   He was a thing of blood, whose every motion
      Was timed² with dying cries. Alone he entered
      The mortal° gate of th' city, which he, painted   *fatal*
      With shunless destiny,³ aidless came off,
      And with a sudden reinforcement struck
110   Corioles like a planet.⁴ Now all's his.
      When by and by the din of war gan° pierce   *began to*
      His ready° sense, then straight his doubled spirit   *alert*
      Requickened° what in flesh was fatigate,°   *Reanimated / exhausted*
      And to the battle came he, where he did
115   Run reeking⁵ o'er the lives of men as if
      'Twere a perpetual spoil;° and till we called   *slaughter*
      Both field and city ours he never stood
      To ease his breast with panting.
      MENENIUS   Worthy man.
      FIRST SENATOR   He cannot but with measure° fit the honours   *exactly*
      Which we devise him.
120   COMINIUS   Our spoils he kicked at,°   *spurned*
      And looked upon things precious as° they were   *as if*
      The common muck of the world. He covets less
      Than misery° itself would give, rewards   *poverty*
      His deeds with doing them, and is content
      To spend the time to° end it.   *merely in order to*
125   MENENIUS   He's right noble.
      Let him be called for.
      FIRST SENATOR   Call Coriolanus.
      OFFICER   He doth appear.
               Enter CORIOLANUS
      MENENIUS   The senate, Coriolanus, are well pleased
      To make thee consul.
130   CORIOLANUS   I do owe them still°   *always*
      My life and services.
      MENENIUS   It then remains
      That you do speak to the people.
      CORIOLANUS   I do beseech you,
      Let me o'erleap that custom, for I cannot
      Put on the gown, stand naked,° and entreat them   *exposed*
135   For my wounds' sake to give their suffrage.
      Please you that I may pass this doing.
      SICINIUS   Sir, the people
      Must have their voices,° neither will they bate°   *votes / forgo*

---

1. It made a clear imprint (of death).
2. Rhythmically accompanied.
3. *painted . . . destiny*: covered with the blood of his victims, unable to avoid their fate.

4. Planets were believed to have the power to afflict, or blast, people and places.
5. Steaming (with blood and sweat).

One jot of ceremony.

MENENIUS [to CORIOLANUS]   Put them not to't.°   *Do not defy them*
Pray you, go fit you° to the custom and   *adapt yourself*
140   Take to you, as your predecessors have,
Your honour with your form.°   *the custom prescribed you*

CORIOLANUS   It is a part
That I shall blush in acting, and might well
Be taken from the people.

BRUTUS [to SICINIUS]   Mark you that?

CORIOLANUS   To brag unto them 'Thus I did, and thus',
145   Show them th'unaching scars, which I should hide,
As if I had received them for the hire
Of their breath° only!   *voice*

MENENIUS   Do not stand° upon't.—   *insist*
We recommend° to you, tribunes of the people,   *commit*
Our purpose° to them; and to our noble consul   *proposal*
150   Wish we all joy and honour.

SENATORS   To Coriolanus come all joy and honour!

Flourish [of] cornetts, then exeunt. Manent
SICINIUS *and* BRUTUS

BRUTUS   You see how he intends to use the people.

SICINIUS   May they perceive's intent! He will require° them   *ask from*
As if he did contemn° what he requested   *scorn that*
Should be in them to give.

155   BRUTUS   Come, we'll inform them
Of our proceedings here. On th' market-place
I know they do attend° us.   [*Exeunt*]   *await*

2.3

Enter seven or eight CITIZENS

FIRST CITIZEN   Once,° if he do require our voices we ought not   *In short*
to deny him.

SECOND CITIZEN   We may, sir, if we will.

THIRD CITIZEN   We have power in ourselves to do it, but it is a
5   power that we have no power to do.° For if he show us his   *no justification to use*
wounds and tell us his deeds, we are to put our tongues into
those wounds[1] and speak for them; so if he tell us his noble
deeds we must also tell him our noble acceptance of them.
Ingratitude is monstrous, and for the multitude to be ingrateful
10   were to make a monster of the multitude, of the which we,
being members, should bring ourselves to be monstrous members.

FIRST CITIZEN   And to make us no better thought of, a little help
will serve;° for once we stood up about the corn, he himself   *it won't take much*
15   stuck° not to call us the many-headed multitude.   *hesitated*

THIRD CITIZEN   We have been called so of many, not that our
heads are some brown, some black, some abram,° some bald,   *auburn*
but that our wits are so diversely coloured; and truly I think if
all our wits were to issue out of one skull, they would fly east,
20   west, north, south, and their consent of° one direct way should   *agreement to go*
be at once to all the points o'th' compass.

SECOND CITIZEN   Think you so? Which way do you judge my
wit would fly?

2.3 Location: The marketplace in Rome.   1. That is, let those wounds inspire our voices.

THIRD CITIZEN Nay, your wit will not so soon out as another
25 man's will, 'tis strongly wedged up in a blockhead. But if it
were at liberty, 'twould sure southward.[2]

SECOND CITIZEN Why that way?

THIRD CITIZEN To lose itself in a fog where, being three parts
melted away with rotten° dews, the fourth would return for con-   °unwholesome
30 science' sake, to help to get thee a wife.

SECOND CITIZEN You are never without your tricks. You may,
you may.°   °(have your joke)

THIRD CITIZEN Are you all resolved to give your voices? But
that's no matter, the greater part carries it.° I say, if he would   °majority decides
35 incline to° the people there was never a worthier man.   °support

Enter CORIOLANUS *in a gown of humility, with* MENENIUS
Here he comes, and in the gown of humility. Mark his behaviour. We are not to stay all together, but to come by him where
he stands by ones, by twos, and by threes. He's to make his
requests by particulars,° wherein every one of us has a single   °to individuals
40 honour in giving him our own voices with our own tongues.
Therefore follow me, and I'll direct you how you shall go by
him.

ALL THE CITIZENS Content, content.   [*Exeunt* CITIZENS]

MENENIUS O sir, you are not right. Have you not known
The worthiest men have done 't?

45 CORIOLANUS   What must I say?
'I pray, sir'? Plague upon 't, I cannot bring
My tongue to such a pace. 'Look, sir, my wounds.
I got them in my country's service, when
Some certain of your brethren roared and ran
From th' noise of our own drums'?

50 MENENIUS   O me, the gods!
You must not speak of that, you must desire them
To think upon you.

CORIOLANUS   Think upon me? Hang 'em.
I would they would forget me like the virtues
Which our divines lose by 'em.[3]

MENENIUS   You'll mar all.
55 I'll leave you. Pray you, speak to 'em, I pray you,
In wholesome[4] manner.

CORIOLANUS   Bid them wash their faces
And keep their teeth clean.   *Exit* [MENENIUS]
Enter three of the CITIZENS
    So, here comes a brace.
You know the cause, sir, of my standing here.

THIRD CITIZEN We do, sir. Tell us what hath brought you to 't.

60 CORIOLANUS Mine own desert.

SECOND CITIZEN Your own desert?

CORIOLANUS Ay, but not mine own desire.

THIRD CITIZEN How not your own desire?

CORIOLANUS No, sir, 'twas never my desire yet to trouble the
65 poor with begging.

THIRD CITIZEN You must think if we give you anything we hope
to gain by you.

---

2. The south is associated with plague.   4. Proper (but Coriolanus takes it as "healthy").
3. Our priests vainly try to instill in them.

CORIOLANUS Well then, I pray, your price o'th' consulship?

FIRST CITIZEN The price is to ask it kindly.

70 CORIOLANUS Kindly, sir, I pray let me ha't. I have wounds to
show you which shall be yours° in private. [*To* SECOND CITIZEN]   yours to see
Your good voice, sir. What say you?

SECOND CITIZEN You shall ha't, worthy sir.

CORIOLANUS A match,° sir. There's in all two worthy voices   agreement

75 begged. I have your alms. Adieu.

THIRD CITIZEN [*to the other* CITIZENS]   But this is something odd.

SECOND CITIZEN An° 'twere to give again—but 'tis no matter.   If

Exeunt [CITIZENS]

Enter two other CITIZENS

CORIOLANUS Pray you now, if it may stand° with the tune of your   accord
voices that I may be consul, I have here the customary gown.

80 FOURTH CITIZEN You have deserved nobly of your country, and
you have not deserved nobly.

CORIOLANUS Your enigma?

FOURTH CITIZEN You have been a scourge to her enemies, you
have been a rod to her friends. You have not, indeed, loved the

85 common people.

CORIOLANUS You should account me the more virtuous that I
have not been common° in my love. I will, sir, flatter my sworn   indiscriminate
brother the people to earn a dearer estimation of them. 'Tis° a   (Flattery) is
condition they account gentle.° And since the wisdom of their   noble

90 choice is rather to have my hat than my heart, I will practise
the insinuating nod and be off° to them most counterfeitly; that   bareheaded
is, sir, I will counterfeit the bewitchment° of some popular   charisma
man,° and give it bountiful to the desirers. Therefore, beseech   demagogue
you I may be consul.

95 FIFTH CITIZEN We hope to find you our friend, and therefore
give you our voices heartily.

FOURTH CITIZEN You have received many wounds for your
country.

CORIOLANUS I will not seal° your knowledge with showing them.   confirm

100 I will make much of your voices, and so trouble you no farther.

BOTH CITIZENS The gods give you joy, sir, heartily.

CORIOLANUS Most sweet voices.   [*Exeunt* CITIZENS]
Better it is to die, better to starve,
Than crave the hire which first we do deserve.[5]

105 Why in this womanish toge[6] should I stand here
To beg of Hob and Dick[7] that does appear
Their needless vouches?° Custom calls me to't.   votes
What custom wills, in all things should we do't,
The dust on antique time would lie unswept,

110 And mountainous error be too highly heaped
For truth to o'erpeer.[8] Rather than fool it° so,   act the fool
Let the high office and the honour go
To one that would do thus. I am half through.
The one part suffered, the other will I do.

Enter three CITIZENS *more*

115 Here come more voices.

---

5. Than beg for the wages we have already earned.
6. F has "woolvish toge"; some editors read "wolvish" or
"wool-less." The "toge" is the toga (gown of humility).

7. Any Tom, Dick, or Harry.
8. To look over the top.

Your voices! For your voices I have fought,
Watched° for your voices, for your voices bear   *Gone sleepless*
Of wounds two dozen odd; battles thrice six
I have seen and heard of for your voices, have
120   Done many things, some less, some more. Your voices!
Indeed I would be consul.
SIXTH CITIZEN   He has done nobly, and cannot go without any
    honest man's voice.
SEVENTH CITIZEN   Therefore let him be consul. The gods give
125   him joy and make him good friend to the people!
ALL THE CITIZENS   Amen, amen. God save thee, noble consul!
CORIOLANUS   Worthy voices.   [*Exeunt* CITIZENS]
            Enter MENENIUS *with* BRUTUS *and* SICINIUS
MENENIUS   You have stood your limitation,° and the tribunes   *allotted time*
    Endue° you with the people's voice. Remains   *Invest*
130   That in th' official marks° invested, you   *insignia*
    Anon° do meet the senate.   *Immediately*
CORIOLANUS   Is this done?
SICINIUS   The custom of request° you have discharged.   *requesting votes*
    The people do admit you, and are summoned
    To meet anon upon your approbation.⁹
CORIOLANUS   Where, at the senate-house?
135   SICINIUS   There, Coriolanus.
CORIOLANUS   May I change these garments?
SICINIUS   You may, sir.
CORIOLANUS   That I'll straight do, and, knowing myself again,
    Repair to th' senate-house.
MENENIUS   I'll keep you company. [*To the tribunes*] Will you along?
BRUTUS   We stay here for the people.
140   SICINIUS   Fare you well.
            Exeunt CORIOLANUS *and* MENENIUS
He has it now, and by his looks methinks
'Tis warm at's heart.¹
BRUTUS   With a proud heart he wore
    His humble weeds.° Will you dismiss the people?   *garments*
            Enter the Plebeians
SICINIUS   How now, my masters, have you chose this man?
145   FIRST CITIZEN   He has our voices, sir.
BRUTUS   We pray the gods he may deserve your loves.
SECOND CITIZEN   Amen, sir. To my poor unworthy notice
    He mocked us when he begged our voices.
THIRD CITIZEN   Certainly. He flouted us downright.
150   FIRST CITIZEN   No, 'tis his kind of speech. He did not mock us.
SECOND CITIZEN   Not one amongst us save yourself but says
    He used us scornfully. He should have showed us
    His marks of merit, wounds received for's country.
SICINIUS   Why, so he did, I am sure.
ALL THE CITIZENS   No, no; no man saw 'em.
155   THIRD CITIZEN   He said he had wounds which he could show in private,
    And with his hat, thus waving it in scorn,
    'I would be consul,' says he. 'Agèd custom
    But by your voices will not so permit me.
    Your voices therefore.' When we granted that,

9. For your ratification as consul.   1. That is, he's well pleased.

160   Here was 'I thank you for your voices, thank you.
           Your most sweet voices. Now you have left your voices
           I have no further° with you.' Was not this mockery?   *(to do)*
           SICINIUS   Why either were you ignorant° to see't,   *were you either unable*
           Or, seeing it, of such childish friendliness
           To yield your voices?
165   BRUTUS [*to the* CITIZENS]   Could you not have told him
           As you were lessoned: when he had no power
           But was a petty servant to the state,
           He was your enemy, ever spake against
           Your liberties and the charters that you bear
170   I'th' body of the weal;° and now arriving°   *state / reaching*
           A place of potency and sway o'th' state,
           If he should still malignantly remain
           Fast foe to th' plebeii, your voices might
           Be curses to yourselves. You should have said
175   That as his worthy deeds did claim no less
           Than what he stood for,° so his gracious nature   *the office he sought*
           Would think upon you for your voices and
           Translate° his malice towards you into love,   *Change*
           Standing your friendly lord.
           SICINIUS [*to the* CITIZENS]   Thus to have said
180   As you were fore-advised had touched° his spirit   *tested*
           And tried his inclination, from him plucked
           Either his gracious promise which you might,
           As cause had called you up, have held him to,
           Or else it would have galled his surly nature,
185   Which easily endures not article°   *stipulation*
           Tying him to aught. So putting him to rage,
           You should have ta'en th'advantage of his choler°   *wrath*
           And passed him unelected.
           BRUTUS [*to the* CITIZENS]   Did you perceive
           He did solicit you in free contempt
190   When he did need your loves, and do you think
           That his contempt shall not be bruising to you
           When he hath power to crush? Why, had your bodies
           No heart among you? Or had you tongues to cry
           Against the rectorship of judgement?°   *rule of common sense*
           SICINIUS [*to the* CITIZENS]   Have you
195   Ere now denied the asker, and now again,
           Of him that did not ask but mock, bestow
           Your sued-for tongues?
           THIRD CITIZEN   He's not confirmed, we may deny him yet.
           SECOND CITIZEN   And will deny him.
200   I'll have five hundred voices of that sound.
           FIRST CITIZEN   I twice five hundred, and their friends to piece° 'em.   *add to*
           BRUTUS   Get you hence instantly, and tell those friends
           They have chose a consul that will from them take
           Their liberties, make them of no more voice
205   Than dogs that are as often beat for barking,
           As therefor kept to do so.
           SICINIUS [*to the* CITIZENS]   Let them assemble,
           And on a safer° judgement all revoke   *sounder*
           Your ignorant election. Enforce° his pride   *Emphasize*
           And his old hate unto you. Besides, forget not

210 With what contempt he wore the humble weed,
How in his suit° he scorned you; but your loves,   *petition; apparel*
Thinking upon his services, took from you
Th'apprehension° of his present portance,°   *perception / demeanor*
Which most gibingly, ungravely he did fashion
After the inveterate hate he bears you.

215 BRUTUS [*to the* CITIZENS]   Lay
A fault on us your tribunes, that we laboured
No impediment between,² but that you must
Cast your election on him.

SICINIUS [*to the* CITIZENS]   Say you chose him
More after our commandment than as guided

220 By your own true affections, and that your minds,
Preoccupied with what you rather must do
Than what you should, made you against the grain
To voice him consul. Lay the fault on us.

BRUTUS [*to the* CITIZENS]   Ay, spare us not. Say we read lectures to you,

225 How youngly he began to serve his country,
How long continued, and what stock he springs of,
The noble house o'th' Martians, from whence came
That Ancus Martius, Numa's daughter's son,
Who after great Hostilius here was king;

230 Of the same house Publius and Quintus were,
That our best water brought by conduits hither;
And Censorinus that was so surnamed,³
And nobly named so, twice being censor,⁴
Was his great ancestor.

SICINIUS [*to the* CITIZENS]   One thus descended,

235 That hath beside well in his person wrought
To be set high in place, we did commend
To your remembrances, but you have found,
Scaling° his present bearing with his past,   *Weighing*
That he's your fixèd enemy, and revoke
Your sudden° approbation.   *hasty*

240 BRUTUS [*to the* CITIZENS]   Say you ne'er had done't—
Harp on that still—but by our putting on;°   *instigation*
And presently when you have drawn° your number,   *gathered*
Repair to th' Capitol.

A CITIZEN   We will so.

ANOTHER CITIZEN   Almost all
Repent in their election.   *Exeunt* [CITIZENS]

BRUTUS   Let them go on.

245 This mutiny were better put in hazard°   *risked*
Than stay,° past doubt, for greater.   *await*
If, as his nature is, he fall in rage
With their refusal, both observe and answer
The vantage of ⁵ his anger.

SICINIUS   To th' Capitol, come.

250 We will be there before the stream o'th' people,
And this shall seem, as partly 'tis, their own,
Which we have goaded onward.   *Exeunt*

---

2. *we . . . between:* we refused to allow anything to stand in the way.
3. Line missing in F; reconstructed from Plutarch.
4. Roman magistrate who supervised public morals and drew up the census.
5. *answer the vantage of:* seize the opportunity provided by.

3.1

Cornetts. Enter CORIOLANUS, MENENIUS, *all the gentry;*°   patricians
    COMINIUS, LARTIUS, *and other* SENATORS

CORIOLANUS Tullus Aufidius then had made new head?°   *raised a new army*
LARTIUS He had, my lord, and that it was which caused
 Our swifter composition.[1]
CORIOLANUS So then the Volsces stand but as at first,
5 Ready when time shall prompt them to make raid
 Upon's again.
COMINIUS   They are worn,° lord consul, so   *exhausted*
 That we shall hardly in our ages see
 Their banners wave again.
CORIOLANUS [*to* LARTIUS]   Saw you Aufidius?
LARTIUS On safeguard° he came to me, and did curse *Under safe-conduct*
10 Against the Volsces for they had so vilely
 Yielded the town. He is retired to Antium.
CORIOLANUS Spoke he of me?
LARTIUS   He did, my lord.
CORIOLANUS   How? What?
LARTIUS How often he had met you sword to sword;
 That of all things upon the earth he hated
15 Your person most; that he would pawn his fortunes
 To hopeless restitution,[2] so he might
 Be called your vanquisher.
CORIOLANUS At Antium lives he?
LARTIUS At Antium.
20 CORIOLANUS I wish I had a cause to seek him there,
 To oppose his hatred fully. Welcome home.
    Enter SICINIUS *and* BRUTUS
 Behold, these are the tribunes of the people,
 The tongues o'th' common mouth. I do despise them,
 For they do prank them° in authority   *adorn themselves*
25 Against all noble sufferance.[3]
SICINIUS Pass no further.
CORIOLANUS Ha, what is that?
BRUTUS It will be dangerous to go on. No further.
CORIOLANUS What makes this change?
30 MENENIUS The matter?
COMINIUS Hath he not passed° the noble and the common? *been accepted by*
BRUTUS Cominius, no.
CORIOLANUS   Have I had children's voices?
FIRST SENATOR Tribunes, give way. He shall to th' market-place.
BRUTUS The people are incensed against him.
SICINIUS   Stop,
 Or all will fall in broil.°   *turmoil*
35 CORIOLANUS   Are these your herd?
 Must these have voices, that can yield them now
 And straight° disclaim their tongues? What are your offices? *immediately*
 You being their mouths, why rule you not their teeth?
 Have you not set them on?
MENENIUS   Be calm, be calm.
40 CORIOLANUS It is a purposed° thing, and grows by plot *deliberate*

3.1 Location: A street in Rome.
1. Agreement (about returning Corioles to the Volscians).
2. Without hope of recovery.
3. Beyond what the nobility can endure.

To curb the will of the nobility.
Suffer't, and live with such as cannot rule
Nor ever will be ruled.

BRUTUS   Call't not a plot.
The people cry you mocked them, and of late
45 When corn was given them gratis, you repined,
Scandalled° the suppliants for the people, called them   *Defamed*
Time-pleasers, flatterers, foes to nobleness.

CORIOLANUS   Why, this was known before.

BRUTUS   Not to them all.

CORIOLANUS   Have you informed them sithence?°   *since*

BRUTUS   How, I inform them?

50 CORIOLANUS   You are like to do such business.

BRUTUS   Not unlike
Each way to better yours.[4]

CORIOLANUS   Why then should I be consul? By yon clouds,
Let me deserve so ill as you, and make me
Your fellow tribune.

55 SICINIUS   You show too much of that°   *(quality)*
For which the people stir.° If you will pass   *are aroused*
To where you are bound,[5] you must enquire your way,
Which you are out of,° with a gentler spirit,   *strayed from*
Or never be so noble as a consul,
Nor yoke with him° for tribune.   *(Brutus)*

60 MENENIUS   Let's be calm.

COMINIUS   The people are abused, set on. This palt'ring°   *trifling*
Becomes not Rome, nor has Coriolanus
Deserved this so dishonoured rub,° laid falsely   *shameful obstruction*
I'th' plain way of his merit.

CORIOLANUS   Tell me of corn?
65 This was my speech, and I will speak't again.

MENENIUS   Not now, not now.

FIRST SENATOR   Not in this heat, sir, now.

CORIOLANUS   Now as I live,
I will. My nobler friends, I crave their pardons.
70 For the mutable rank-scented meinie,°   *multitude*
Let them regard me, as I do not flatter,
And therein behold themselves. I say again,
In soothing them we nourish 'gainst our Senate
The cockle° of rebellion, insolence, sedition,   *weed*
75 Which we ourselves have ploughed for, sowed, and scattered
By mingling them with us, the honoured number
Who lack not virtue, no, nor power, but that
Which they have given to beggars.

MENENIUS   Well, no more.

FIRST SENATOR   No more words, we beseech you.

CORIOLANUS   How, no more?
80 As for my country I have shed my blood,
Not fearing outward force, so shall my lungs
Coin words till their decay against those measles°   *skin eruptions*
Which we disdain should tetter° us, yet sought   *infect*
The very way to catch them.

4. *Not unlike . . . yours:* Not unlikely in every respect to   5. That is, the marketplace; the consulship.
do better than you.

85 BRUTUS You speak o'th' people as if you were a god
　　　To punish, not a man of their infirmity.° 　　　　　*with the same frailty*
　SICINIUS 　'Twere well we let the people know't.
　MENENIUS 　　　　　　　　　　　What, what, his choler?
　CORIOLANUS 　Choler? Were I as patient as the midnight sleep,
　　　By Jove, 'twould be my mind.° 　　　　　　　　*opinion*
　SICINIUS 　　　　　　　　　　　It is a mind
90 　That shall remain a poison where it is,
　　　Not poison any further.
　CORIOLANUS 　　　　　　　'Shall remain'?
　　　Hear you this Triton[6] of the minnows? Mark you
　　　His absolute 'shall'?
　COMINIUS 　　　　　　　'Twas from the canon.° 　　　*out of order*
　CORIOLANUS 　　　　　　　　　　　　　'Shall'?
　　　O good but most unwise patricians, why,
95 　You grave but reckless senators, have you thus
　　　Given Hydra[7] here to choose an officer
　　　That, with his peremptory 'shall', being but
　　　The horn and noise° o'th' monster's, wants not spirit 　*noisy horn*
　　　To say he'll turn your current° in a ditch 　　　*stream of power*
100 　And make your channel his? If he have power,
　　　Then vail° your impotence; if none, awake° 　*bow down / awake from*
　　　Your dangerous lenity.° If you are learned, 　　　*forbearance*
　　　Be not as common fools; if you are not,
　　　Let them have cushions by° you. You are plebeians 　*senate seats beside*
105 　If they be senators, and they are no less
　　　When, both your voices blended, the great'st taste
　　　Most palates theirs.[8] They choose their magistrate,
　　　And such a one as he, who puts his 'shall',
　　　His popular° 'shall', against a graver bench[9] 　　　*plebeian*
110 　Than ever frowned in Greece. By Jove himself,
　　　It makes the consuls base, and my soul aches
　　　To know, when two authorities are up,° 　　　*established*
　　　Neither supreme, how soon confusion° 　　　　*chaos*
　　　May enter 'twixt the gap of both and take° 　　*overthrow*
　　　The one by th' other.
115 COMINIUS 　　　　　　　Well, on to th' market-place.
　CORIOLANUS 　Whoever gave that counsel to give forth
　　　The corn o'th' storehouse gratis, as 'twas used
　　　Sometime in Greece—
　MENENIUS 　　　　　　　Well, well, no more of that.
　CORIOLANUS 　Though there the people had more absolute power—
120 　I say they nourished disobedience, fed
　　　The ruin of the state.
　BRUTUS 　　　　　　　Why shall the people give
　　　One that speaks thus their voice?
　CORIOLANUS 　　　　　　　　　　I'll give my reasons,
　　　More worthier than their voices. They know the corn
　　　Was not our recompense,° resting well assured 　*a payment from us*
125 　They ne'er did service for't. Being pressed° to th' war, 　*conscripted*
　　　Even when the navel° of the state was touched,° 　*center / threatened*

---

6. Neptune's trumpeter, a minor sea god.
7. Mythical many-headed snake, a common figure for
the multitude.

8. *the great'st . . . theirs:* the result tastes more like (or appeals more to) them than you.
9. A more respected body.

They would not thread° the gates. This kind of service   *go through*
Did not deserve corn gratis. Being i'th' war,
Their mutinies and revolts, wherein they showed
130 Most valour, spoke not° for them. Th'accusation   *did not speak well*
Which they have often made against the senate,
All cause unborn,° could never be the native°   *Without any cause / source*
Of our so frank° donation. Well, what then?   *liberal*
How shall this bosom multiplied[1] digest
135 The senate's courtesy? Let deeds express
What's like to be their words: 'We did request it,
We are the greater poll,° and in true fear   *number*
They gave us our demands.' Thus we debase
The nature of our seats,° and make the rabble   *senatorial positions*
140 Call our cares fears, which will in time
Break ope the locks o'th' senate and bring in
The crows to peck the eagles.[2]

MENENIUS   Come, enough.
BRUTUS   Enough with over-measure.
CORIOLANUS   No, take more.
What may be sworn by, both divine and human,
145 Seal° what I end withal!° This double worship,[3]   *Authorize / with*
Where one part does disdain with cause, the other
Insult° without all reason, where gentry, title, wisdom   *Behave insolently*
Cannot conclude but by the yea and no
Of general ignorance, it must omit°   *neglect*
150 Real necessities, and give way the while
To unstable slightness.° Purpose° so barred, it follows   *trifling / Purposefulness*
Nothing is done to purpose.° Therefore beseech you—   *any effect*
You that will be less fearful than discreet,°   *judicious*
That love the fundamental part of state
155 More than you doubt the change on't,[4] that prefer
A noble life before a long, and wish
To jump° a body with a dangerous physic°   *risk / medicine*
That's sure of death without it—at once pluck out
The multitudinous tongue;[5] let them not lick
160 The sweet which is their poison. Your dishonour
Mangles true judgement, and bereaves the state
Of that integrity which should become't,
Not having the power to do the good it would
For° th'ill which doth control't.[6]   *Because of*
BRUTUS   He's said enough.
165 SICINIUS   He's spoken like a traitor, and shall answer
As traitors do.
CORIOLANUS   Thou wretch, despite° o'erwhelm thee!   *contempt*
What should the people do with these bald° tribunes,   *paltry*
On whom depending, their obedience fails
To th' greater bench?° In a rebellion,   *(of the senate)*
170 When what's not meet but what must be was law,[7]
Then were they chosen. In a better hour

---

1. Multifarious belly (of the many-headed multitude).
2. The eagle not only is associated with courage and nobility but is the symbol of Roman power.
3. Divided magistracy.
4. You fear changing it (by repudiating the tribunes).
5. The tongue of the multitude, as represented by the
tribunes.
6. Overpower it.
7. *When . . . law*: When necessity rather than propriety
prevailed. *meet*: proper.

Let what is meet be said it must be meet,[8]
And throw their power i'th' dust.

BRUTUS   Manifest treason.

SICINIUS   This a consul? No.

BRUTUS   The aediles,° ho!   *tribune's officers*

Enter an AEDILE

175   Let him be apprehended.

SICINIUS   Go call the people,   [*Exit* AEDILE]
    [*To* CORIOLANUS]   in whose name myself
    Attach° thee as a traitorous innovator,°   *Arrest / revolutionary*
    A foe to th' public weal. Obey, I charge thee,
    And follow to thine answer.°   *trial*

CORIOLANUS   Hence, old goat!

ALL THE PATRICIANS   We'll surety him.°   *ensure his compliance*

180 COMINIUS [*to* SICINIUS]   Aged sir, hands off.

CORIOLANUS [*to* SICINIUS]   Hence, rotten thing, or I shall shake thy bones
    Out of thy garments.

SICINIUS   Help, ye citizens!

Enter a rabble of Plebeians, with the AEDILES

MENENIUS   On both sides more respect.

SICINIUS   Here's he
    That would take from you all your power.

BRUTUS   Seize him, aediles.

ALL THE CITIZENS   Down with him, down with him!

185 SECOND SENATOR   Weapons, weapons, weapons!

They all bustle about CORIOLANUS

CITIZENS *and* PATRICIANS [*in dispersed cries*]   Tribunes! Patricians!
    Citizens! What ho!
    Sicinius! Brutus! Coriolanus! Citizens!

SOME CITIZENS *and* PATRICIANS   Peace, peace, peace! Stay! Hold! Peace!

MENENIUS   What is about to be? I am out of breath.

190 Confusion's° near; I cannot speak. You tribunes   *Chaos is*
    To th' people, Coriolanus, patience!
    Speak, good Sicinius.

SICINIUS   Hear me, people, peace.

ALL THE CITIZENS   Let's hear our tribune! Peace! Speak, speak, speak!

SICINIUS   You are at point° to lose your liberties.   *about*

195 Martius would have all from you—Martius
    Whom late you have named for consul.

MENENIUS   Fie, fie, fie,
    This is the way to kindle, not to quench.

FIRST SENATOR   To unbuild the city, and to lay all flat.

SICINIUS   What is the city but the people?

ALL THE CITIZENS   True,
    The people are the city.

200 BRUTUS   By the consent of all
    We were established the people's magistrates.

ALL THE CITIZENS   You so remain.

MENENIUS   And so are like to do.

CORIOLANUS   That is the way to lay the city flat,
    To bring the roof to the foundation,

205 And bury all which yet distinctly ranges[9]
    In heaps and piles of ruin.

8. Let what is proper be declared necessary.   9. Extends in orderly ranks.

SICINIUS   This deserves death.

BRUTUS   Or° let us stand to our authority,   *Either*
Or let us lose it. We do here pronounce,
Upon the part o'th' people in whose power

210   We were elected theirs, Martius is worthy
Of present° death.   *immediate*

SICINIUS   Therefore lay hold of him,
Bear him to th' rock Tarpeian;[1] and from thence
Into destruction cast him.

BRUTUS   Aediles, seize him.

ALL THE CITIZENS   Yield, Martius, yield.

MENENIUS   Hear me one word.

215   Beseech you, tribunes, hear me but a word.

AEDILES   Peace, peace!

MENENIUS [*to the tribunes*]   Be that you seem, truly your country's friend,
And temp'rately proceed to what you would
Thus violently redress.

BRUTUS   Sir, those cold ways

220   That seem like prudent helps are very poisons
Where the disease is violent. Lay hands upon him,
And bear him to the rock.

           CORIOLANUS *draws his sword*

CORIOLANUS   No, I'll die here.
There's some among you have beheld me fighting.
Come, try upon yourselves what you have seen me.

225 MENENIUS   Down with that sword. Tribunes, withdraw a while.

BRUTUS   Lay hands upon him.

MENENIUS   Help Martius, help!
You that be noble, help him, young and old.

ALL THE CITIZENS   Down with him, down with him!

      In this mutiny the tribunes, the AEDILES, *and the*
      people are beat in

MENENIUS [*to* CORIOLANUS]   Go get you to your house. Be gone, away!
All will be naught else.

230 SECOND SENATOR [*to* CORIOLANUS]   Get you gone.

CORIOLANUS   Stand fast; we have as many friends as enemies.

MENENIUS   Shall it be put to that?

FIRST SENATOR   The gods forbid!
[*To* CORIOLANUS]   I prithee, noble friend, home to thy house.
Leave us to cure this cause.°   *disease*

MENENIUS   For 'tis a sore upon us

235   You cannot tent° yourself. Be gone, beseech you.   *treat*

COMINIUS   Come, sir, along with us.

CORIOLANUS   I would they were barbarians, as they are,
Though in Rome littered;° not Romans, as they are not,   *born (like animals)*
Though calved i'th' porch o'th' Capitol.

MENENIUS   Be gone.

240   Put not your worthy° rage into your tongue.   *justifiable*
One time will owe° another.   *occasion will compensate*

CORIOLANUS   On fair ground
I could beat forty of them.

MENENIUS   I could myself
Take up a brace o'th' best of them, yea, the two tribunes.

---

1. The cliff from which murderers and traitors were hurled to their deaths.

COMINIUS   But now 'tis odds beyond arithmetic,°   calculation
245   And manhood° is called foolery when it stands   courage
       Against a falling fabric.°   building
       [*To* CORIOLANUS]   Will you hence
       Before the tag° return, whose rage doth rend   rabble
       Like interrupted° waters, and o'erbear   overflowing
       What they are used to bear?²

MENENIUS [*to* CORIOLANUS]   Pray you be gone.
250   I'll try whether my old wit be in request
       With those that have but little. This must be patched
       With cloth of any colour.³

COMINIUS   Nay, come away. *Exeunt* CORIOLANUS *and* COMINIUS

A PATRICIAN   This man has marred his fortune.

255   MENENIUS   His nature is too noble for the world.
       He would not flatter Neptune for his trident
       Or Jove for's power to thunder. His heart's his mouth.
       What his breast forges, that his tongue must vent,
       And, being angry, does forget that ever
       He heard the name of death.
                    A noise within
260   Here's goodly work.

A PATRICIAN   I would they were abed.

MENENIUS   I would they were in Tiber.
       What the vengeance, could he not speak 'em fair?°   speak to them politely
       Enter BRUTUS *and* SICINIUS, *with the rabble again*

SICINIUS   Where is this viper
       That would depopulate the city and
       Be every man himself?

265   MENENIUS   You worthy tribunes—

SICINIUS   He shall be thrown down the Tarpeian rock
       With rigorous hands. He hath resisted law,
       And therefore law shall scorn° him further trial   deny
       Than the severity of the public° power,   commoners'
       Which he so sets at naught.

270   FIRST CITIZEN   He shall well know
       The noble tribunes are the people's mouths,
       And we their hands.

ALL THE CITIZENS   He shall, sure on't.

MENENIUS   Sir, sir.

SICINIUS   Peace!

MENENIUS   Do not cry havoc⁴ where you should but hunt
       With modest warrant.

275   SICINIUS   Sir, how comes't that you
       Have help to make this rescue?⁵

MENENIUS   Hear me speak.
       As I do know the consul's worthiness,
       So can I name his faults.

SICINIUS   Consul? What consul?

280   MENENIUS   The consul Coriolanus.

BRUTUS   He consul?

ALL THE CITIZENS   No, no, no, no, no!

---

2. *o'erbear . . . bear:* overpower that to which they ordinarily submit.
3. *patched . . . colour:* mended by whatever means possible.

4. "Havoc" was the signal to an army to pillage.
5. Have helped to remove this prisoner from custody
("make rescue" is a legal term).

MENENIUS   If, by the tribunes' leave and yours, good people,
I may be heard, I would crave a word or two,
285 The which shall turn° you to no further harm   bring
Than so much loss of time.

SICINIUS   Speak briefly, then,
For we are peremptory to dispatch
This viperous traitor. To eject him hence
Were but our danger, and to keep him here
290 Our certain death. Therefore it is decreed
He dies tonight.

MENENIUS   Now the good gods forbid
That our renownèd Rome, whose gratitude
Towards her deservèd° children is enrolled   deserving
In Jove's own book, like an unnatural dam°   mother
295 Should now eat up her own!

SICINIUS   He's a disease that must be cut away.

MENENIUS   O, he's a limb that has but a disease—
Mortal to cut it off, to cure it easy.
What has he done to Rome that's worthy death?
300 Killing our enemies, the blood he hath lost—
Which I dare vouch is more than that he hath
By many an ounce—he dropped it for his country;
And what is left, to lose it by his country
Were to us all that do't and suffer° it   allow
A brand° to th' end o'th' world.   stigma

305 SICINIUS   This is clean cam.°   completely perverse
BRUTUS   Merely° awry. When he did love his country   Absolutely
It honoured him.

SICINIUS   The service of the foot,
Being once gangrened, is not then respected
For what before it was.

BRUTUS   We'll hear no more.
310 Pursue him to his house and pluck him thence,
Lest his infection, being of catching nature,
Spread further.

MENENIUS   One word more, one word!
This tiger-footed rage, when it shall find
The harm of unscanned° swiftness, will too late   heedless
315 Tie leaden pounds° to's heels. Proceed by process,° weights / due process
Lest parties°—as he is beloved—break out   factions
And sack great Rome with Romans.

BRUTUS   If it were so?

SICINIUS [to MENENIUS]   What do ye talk?
320 Have we not had a taste of his obedience:
Our aediles smote, ourselves resisted? Come.

MENENIUS Consider this: he has been bred i'th' wars
Since a could draw a sword, and is ill-schooled
In bolted[6] language. Meal and bran° together   Flour and husks
325 He throws without distinction. Give me leave,
I'll go to him and undertake to bring him
Where he shall answer by a lawful form,
In peace, to his utmost peril.[7]

FIRST SENATOR   Noble tribunes,

---

6. Sifted; that is, carefully considered.   7. Even at peril of his life.

It is the humane way. The other course
330   Will prove too bloody, and the end of it
Unknown to the beginning.

SICINIUS   Noble Menenius,
Be you then as the people's officer.
[*To the* CITIZENS] Masters, lay down your weapons.

BRUTUS   Go not home.

SICINIUS   Meet on the market-place. [*To* MENENIUS] We'll attend° you there,   *await*
335   Where if you bring not Martius, we'll proceed
In our first way.

MENENIUS   I'll bring him to you.
[*To the* SENATORS] Let me desire your company. He must come,
Or what is worst will follow.

FIRST SENATOR   Pray you, let's to him.

                    Exeunt [tribunes and CITIZENS *at one door,*
                              PATRICIANS *at another door]*

                                        3.2
                    Enter CORIOLANUS, *with Nobles*

CORIOLANUS   Let them pull all about mine ears, present me
Death on the wheel or at wild horses' heels,
Or pile ten hills on the Tarpeian rock,
That the precipitation° might down stretch   *steepness*
5   Below the beam of sight, yet will I still
Be thus to them.

                    Enter VOLUMNIA

A PATRICIAN   You do the nobler.

CORIOLANUS   I muse° my mother   *wonder that*
Does not approve me further, who was wont
To call them woollen° vassals, things created   *coarsely clad*
To buy and sell with groats,° to show bare heads   *fourpenny pieces*
10   In congregations, to yawn, be still, and wonder,
When one but of my ordinance° stood up   *rank*
To speak of peace or war. [*To* VOLUMNIA] I talk of you.
Why did you wish me milder? Would you have me
False to my nature? Rather say I play
The man I am.

15   VOLUMNIA   O, sir, sir, sir,
I would have had you put your power well on
Before you had worn it out.

CORIOLANUS   Let go.°   *Stop*

VOLUMNIA   You might have been enough the man you are
With striving less to be so. Lesser had been
20   The taxings° of your dispositions if   *challenging*
You had not showed them how ye were disposed
Ere they lacked° power to cross you.   *Before they lost*

CORIOLANUS   Let them hang.

VOLUMNIA   Ay, and burn too.

                    Enter MENENIUS *with the* SENATORS

MENENIUS [*to* CORIOLANUS]   Come, come, you have been too rough,
           something too rough.
You must return and mend it.

25   FIRST SENATOR   There's no remedy

3.2 Location: Coriolanus's house.

Unless, by not so doing, our good city
Cleave in the midst and perish.

VOLUMNIA [*to* CORIOLANUS]   Pray be counselled.
I have a heart as little apt as yours,
But yet a brain that leads my use of anger
To better vantage.

30   MENENIUS   Well said, noble woman.
Before he should thus stoop to th' herd, but that
The violent fit o'th' time craves it as physic°   *medicine*
For the whole state, I would put mine armour on,
Which I can scarcely bear.

35   CORIOLANUS   What must I do?
MENENIUS   Return to th' tribunes.
CORIOLANUS   Well, what then, what then?
MENENIUS   Repent what you have spoke.
CORIOLANUS   For them? I cannot do it to the gods.
Must I then do't to them?

40   VOLUMNIA   You are too absolute,°   *inflexible*
Though therein you can never be too noble,
But when extremities° speak. I have heard you say,   *extreme situations*
Honour and policy,° like unsevered friends,   *tactical shrewdness*
I'th' war do grow together. Grant that, and tell me

45   In peace what each of them by th' other lose
That they combine not there.

CORIOLANUS   Tush, tush!
MENENIUS   A good demand.
VOLUMNIA   If it be honour in your wars to seem
The same° you are not, which for your best ends   *That which*
You adopt your policy, how is it less or worse

50   That it° shall hold companionship in peace   *(dissimulation)*
With honour, as in war, since that to both
It stands in like request?°   *need*

CORIOLANUS   Why force° you this?   *urge*
VOLUMNIA   Because that now it lies you on to speak to th' people,
Not by your own instruction,° nor by th' matter   *conviction*

55   Which your heart prompts you, but with such words
That are but roted° in your tongue, though but   *memorized*
Bastards and syllables of no allowance
To[1] your bosom's truth. Now this no more
Dishonours you at all than to take in°   *capture*

60   A town with gentle words, which else would put you
To your fortune[2] and the hazard of much blood.
I would dissemble with my nature where
My fortunes and my friends at stake required
I should do so in honour. I am in this°   *I speak in this for*

65   Your wife, your son, these senators, the nobles;
And you will rather show our general° louts   *common*
How you can frown than spend a fawn° upon 'em   *cringing courtesy*
For the inheritance° of their loves and safeguard   *acquisition*
Of what that want° might ruin.   *lack (of their loves)*

MENENIUS   Noble lady!

70   [*To* CORIOLANUS] Come, go with us, speak fair. You may salve° so,   *smooth over*

---

1. *Bastards . . . / To:* Illegitimate words not acknowledged
by.

2. *put . . . fortune:* force you to take your chances (in
battle).

Not what is dangerous present, but the loss
Of what is past.[3]

VOLUMNIA   I prithee now, my son,
[*She takes his bonnet*]
Go to them with this bonnet° in thy hand,   hat
And thus far having stretched it—here be with them—
75 Thy knee bussing° the stones—for in such business   kissing
Action is eloquence, and the eyes of th' ignorant
More learnèd than the ears—waving° thy head,   repeatedly bowing
With often, thus, correcting thy stout heart,
Now humble[4] as the ripest mulberry
80 That will not hold the handling; or say to them
Thou art their soldier and, being bred in broils,°   tumults
Hast not the soft way which, thou dost confess,
Were fit for thee to use as they to claim,°   for them to expect
In asking their good loves; but thou wilt frame
85 Thyself, forsooth, hereafter theirs so far
As thou hast power and person.°   ability and authority
MENENIUS [*to* CORIOLANUS]   This but done
Even as she speaks, why, their hearts were yours;
For they have pardons, being asked, as free
As words to little purpose.
VOLUMNIA [*to* CORIOLANUS]   Prithee now,
90 Go, and be ruled, although I know thou hadst rather
Follow thine enemy in a fiery gulf
Than flatter him in a bower.°   arbor
    Enter COMINIUS
              Here is Cominius.
COMINIUS   I have been i'th' market-place; and, sir, 'tis fit
You make strong party,° or defend yourself   gather strong support
95 By calmness or by absence. All's in anger.
MENENIUS   Only fair speech.
COMINIUS   I think 'twill serve, if he
Can thereto frame his spirit.
VOLUMNIA   He must, and will.
Prithee now, say you will, and go about it.
CORIOLANUS   Must I go show them my unbarbèd sconce?°   unhelmeted head
100 Must I with my base tongue give to my noble heart
A lie that it must bear? Well, I will do't.
Yet were there but this single plot° to lose,   (Coriolanus's body)
This mould° of Martius they to dust should grind it   form; earth
And throw't against the wind. To th' market-place.
105 You have put me now to such a part which never
I shall discharge to th' life.°   perform convincingly
COMINIUS   Come, come, we'll prompt you.
VOLUMNIA   I prithee now, sweet son, as thou hast said
My praises made thee first a soldier, so,
To have my praise for this, perform a part
Thou hast not done before.
110 CORIOLANUS   Well, I must do't.
Away, my disposition; and possess me
Some harlot's[5] spirit! My throat of war be turned,

---

3. *Not . . . past:* Not only the present danger, but what was   4. Malleable (or possibly a verb, "let droop").
lost before.   5. Vagabond; buffoon; prostitute.

Which choired° with my drum, into a pipe   *harmonized*
Small as an eunuch or the virgin voice
115 That babies lull asleep! The smiles of knaves
Tent° in my cheeks, and schoolboys' tears take up   *Encamp*
The glasses° of my sight! A beggar's tongue   *windows*
Make motion through my lips, and my armed knees,
Who bowed but in my stirrup, bend like his
120 That hath received an alms! I will not do't,
Lest I surcease° to honour mine own truth,   *cease*
And by my body's action teach my mind
A most inherent° baseness.   *fixed*
VOLUMNIA   At thy choice, then.
To beg of thee it is my more dishonour
125 Than thou of them. Come all to ruin. Let
Thy mother rather feel° thy pride than fear   *suffer*
Thy dangerous stoutness,° for I mock at death   *stubbornness*
With as big heart as thou. Do as thou list.°   *wish*
Thy valiantness was mine, thou sucked'st it from me,
But owe° thy pride thyself.   *own*
130 CORIOLANUS   Pray be content.
Mother, I am going to the market-place.
Chide me no more. I'll mountebank⁶ their loves,
Cog° their hearts from them, and come home beloved   *Wheedle*
Of all the trades in Rome. Look, I am going.
135 Commend me to my wife. I'll return consul,
Or never trust to what my tongue can do
I'th' way of flattery further.
VOLUMNIA   Do your will.   *Exit* VOLUMNIA
COMINIUS   Away! The tribunes do attend you. Arm yourself
To answer mildly, for they are prepared
140 With accusations, as I hear, more strong
Than are upon you yet.
CORIOLANUS   The word is 'mildly'. Pray you let us go.
Let them accuse me by invention,° I   *with invented charges*
Will answer in mine honour.
145 MENENIUS   Ay, but mildly.
CORIOLANUS   Well, mildly be it, then—mildly.   *Exeunt*

3.3

Enter SICINIUS *and* BRUTUS

BRUTUS   In this point charge him home:¹ that he affects°   *desires*
Tyrannical power. If he evade us there,
Enforce° him with his envy° to the people,   *Urge against / malice*
And that the spoil got on° the Antiats   *booty taken from*
Was ne'er distributed.
Enter an AEDILE
5   What, will he come?
AEDILE   He's coming.
BRUTUS   How accompanied?
AEDILE   With old Menenius, and those senators
That always favoured him.
SICINIUS   Have you a catalogue

---

6. Cajole (a mountebank was an itinerant quack who   3.3 Location: The marketplace.
sold his cures from an improvised platform).   1. Press charges against him forcefully.

Of all the voices° that we have procured,   *votes*
Set down by th' poll?°   *individually*

10   AEDILE   I have, 'tis ready.

    SICINIUS   Have you collected them by tribes?[2]

    AEDILE   I have.

    SICINIUS   Assemble presently the people hither,
And when they hear me say 'It shall be so
I'th' right and strength o'th' commons', be it either
15   For death, for fine, or banishment, then let them,
If I say 'Fine', cry 'Fine!', if 'Death', cry 'Death!',
Insisting on the old prerogative
And power i'th' truth o'th' cause.[3]

    AEDILE   I shall inform them.

    BRUTUS   And when such time they have begun to cry,
20   Let them not cease, but with a din confused
Enforce the present execution[4]
Of what we chance to sentence.

    AEDILE   Very well.

    SICINIUS   Make them be strong, and ready for this hint
When we shall hap° to give't them.   *chance*

    BRUTUS [*to the* AEDILE]   Go about it. [*Exit* AEDILE]
25   Put him to choler° straight. He hath been used   *anger at once*
Ever to conquer and to have his worth[5]
Of contradiction. Being once chafed,° he cannot   *excited*
Be reined again to temperance. Then he speaks
What's in his heart, and that is there which looks
30   With us[6] to break his neck.

           Enter CORIOLANUS, MENENIUS, *and* COMINIUS, *with*
           other [SENATORS *and* PATRICIANS]

    SICINIUS   Well, here he comes.

    MENENIUS [*to* CORIOLANUS]   Calmly, I do beseech you.

    CORIOLANUS   Ay, as an hostler° that for th' poorest piece°   *stable keeper / coin*
Will bear the knave by th' volume.[7]—Th' honoured gods
35   Keep Rome in safety and the chairs of justice
Supplied with worthy men, plant love among's,
Throng our large temples with the shows° of peace,   *ceremonies*
And not our streets with war!

    FIRST SENATOR   Amen, amen.

40   MENENIUS   A noble wish.

           Enter the AEDILE *with the* CITIZENS

    SICINIUS   Draw near, ye people.

    AEDILE   List to your tribunes. Audience!
Peace, I say.

    CORIOLANUS   First, hear me speak.

    SICINIUS and BRUTUS   Well, say.—Peace ho!

    CORIOLANUS   Shall I be charged no further than this present?°   *at this present time*
Must all determine° here?   *be determined*

    SICINIUS   I do demand
45   If you submit you to the people's voices,
Allow° their officers, and are content   *Acknowledge*

---

2. Romans voted by tribes (districts) or by social class; the former method favored the plebeians.
3. *old prerogative . . . cause:* traditional right to determine the truth of the case.

4. Insist upon the immediate performance.
5. Enjoy his fill; establish his reputation from.
6. *looks / With us:* promises with our help.
7. Will endure being called knave any number of times.

To suffer lawful censure for such faults
As shall be proved upon you.

CORIOLANUS   I am content.

MENENIUS   Lo, citizens, he says he is content.
50   The warlike service he has done, consider. Think
Upon the wounds his body bears, which show
Like graves i'th' holy churchyard.

CORIOLANUS   Scratches with briers,
Scars to move laughter only.

MENENIUS   Consider further
That when he speaks not like a citizen,
55   You find him like a soldier. Do not take
His rougher accents for malicious sounds,
But, as I say, such as become a soldier
Rather than envy° you.   *show hatred to*

COMINIUS   Well, well, no more.

60   CORIOLANUS   What is the matter
That, being passed for consul with full voice,
I am so dishonoured that the very hour
You take it off again?

SICINIUS   Answer to us.

65   CORIOLANUS   Say, then. 'Tis true I ought so.

SICINIUS   We charge you that you have contrived to take
From Rome all seasoned° office, and to wind°   *time-honored / insinuate*
Yourself into a power tyrannical,
For which you are a traitor to the people.

CORIOLANUS   How, traitor?

70   MENENIUS   Nay, temperately—your promise.

CORIOLANUS   The fires i'th' lowest hell fold in° the people!   *enfold*
Call me their traitor, thou injurious° tribune?   *insulting*
Within thine eyes sat twenty thousand deaths,
In thy hands clutched as many millions, in
75   Thy lying tongue both numbers, I would say
'Thou liest' unto thee with a voice as free
As I do pray the gods.

SICINIUS   Mark you this, people?

ALL THE CITIZENS   To th' rock, to th' rock with him!

80   SICINIUS   Peace!
We need not put new matter to his charge.
What you have seen him do and heard him speak,
Beating your officers, cursing yourselves,
Opposing laws with strokes, and here defying
85   Those whose great power must try him—
Even this, so criminal and in such capital kind,[8]
Deserves th'extremest death.

BRUTUS   But since he hath
Served well for Rome—

CORIOLANUS   What do you prate° of service?   *babble*

BRUTUS   I talk of that that know it.

CORIOLANUS   You?

90   MENENIUS   Is this the promise that you made your mother?

COMINIUS   Know, I pray you—

8. Important; deserving death.

CORIOLANUS   I'll know no further.
Let them pronounce the steep Tarpeian death,
Vagabond exile, flaying, pent° to linger   imprisoned
But with a grain a day, I would not buy
95   Their mercy at the price of one fair word,
Nor check my courage° for what they can give   restrain my spirit
To have't with saying 'Good morrow'.
SICINIUS   For that he has,
As much as in him lies, from time to time
Inveighed against the people, seeking means
100   To pluck away their power, as now at last
Given hostile strokes, and that not in the presence
Of dreaded justice, but on the ministers
That doth distribute it, in the name o'th' people,
And in the power of us the tribunes, we
105   E'en from this instant banish him our city
In peril of precipitation
From off the rock Tarpeian, never more
To enter our Rome gates. I'th' people's name
I say it shall be so.
ALL THE CITIZENS   It shall be so,
110   It shall be so. Let him away. He's banished,
And it shall be so.
COMINIUS   Hear me, my masters and my common friends.
SICINIUS   He's sentenced. No more hearing.
COMINIUS   Let me speak.
I have been consul, and can show for Rome
115   Her enemies' marks upon me. I do love
My country's good with a respect more tender,
More holy and profound, than mine own life,
My dear wife's estimate,° her womb's increase,   reputation
And treasure of my loins.° Then if I would   (that is, children)
Speak that—
120   SICINIUS   We know your drift. Speak what?
BRUTUS   There's no more to be said, but he is banished,
As enemy to the people and his country.
It shall be so.
ALL THE CITIZENS   It shall be so, it shall be so.
CORIOLANUS   You common cry° of curs, whose breath I hate   yelping pack
125   As reek° o'th' rotten fens,° whose loves I prize   vapor / swamps
As the dead carcasses of unburied men
That do corrupt my air: I banish you.
And here remain with your uncertainty.
Let every feeble rumour shake your hearts;
130   Your enemies, with nodding of their plumes,°   (helmet plumes)
Fan you into despair! Have the power still
To banish your defenders, till at length
Your ignorance—which finds not till it feels⁹—
Making but reservation of° yourselves,   Seeking only to preserve
135   Still your own foes, deliver you
As most abated° captives to some nation   debased
That won you without blows! Despising

9. Which does not learn until it undergoes.

For° you the city, thus I turn my back.   *On account of*
There is a world elsewhere.

Exeunt CORIOLANUS, COMINIUS, *and* [MENENIUS],
with [*the rest of the Patricians. The* CITIZENS] *all shout,
and throw up their caps*

140   AEDILE   The people's enemy is gone, is gone.

ALL THE CITIZENS   Our enemy is banished, he is gone. Hoo-oo!

SICINIUS   Go see him out at gates, and follow him
As he hath followed you, with all despite.°   *contempt*
Give him deserved vexation. Let a guard
145   Attend us through the city.

ALL THE CITIZENS   Come, come, let's see him out at gates. Come.
The gods preserve our noble tribunes! Come.   *Exeunt*

4.1

Enter CORIOLANUS, VOLUMNIA, VIRGILIA, MENENIUS,
[*and*] COMINIUS, *with the young nobility of Rome*

CORIOLANUS   Come, leave your tears. A brief farewell. The beast
With many heads butts me away. Nay, mother,
Where is your ancient° courage? You were used   *former*
To say extremities was the trier of spirits,
5   That common chances common men could bear,
That when the sea was calm all boats alike
Showed mastership in floating; fortune's blows
When most struck home, being gentle wounded craves
A noble cunning.[1] You were used to load me
10   With precepts that would make invincible
The heart that conned° them.   *learned*

VIRGILIA   O heavens, O heavens!

CORIOLANUS   Nay, I prithee, woman—

VOLUMNIA   Now the red pestilence[2] strike all trades in Rome,
And occupations° perish!   *handicrafts*

15   CORIOLANUS   What, what, what?
I shall be loved when I am lacked. Nay, mother,
Resume that spirit when you were wont to say,
If you had been the wife of Hercules[3]
Six of his labours you'd have done, and saved
20   Your husband so much sweat. Cominius,
Droop not. Adieu. Farewell, my wife, my mother.
I'll do well yet. Thou old and true Menenius,
Thy tears are salter than a younger man's,
And venomous to thine eyes. My sometime[4] general,
25   I have seen thee stern, and thou hast oft beheld
Heart-hard'ning spectacles. Tell these sad women
'Tis fond° to wail inevitable strokes   *as foolish*
As 'tis to laugh at 'em. My mother, you wot° well   *know*
My hazards still° have been your solace, and—   *always*
30   Believe't not lightly—though I go alone,
Like to a lonely dragon that his fen
Makes feared° and talked of more than seen, your son   *fearful*

4.1 Location: Near the city gates of Rome.
1. *being . . . cunning*: to suffer nobly requires a gentle-man's skill.
2. Bubonic plague or typhoid.

3. Mythical hero of great strength who was assigned twelve near-impossible labors.
4. Former (addressing Cominius).

Will or° exceed the common° or be caught   *either/usual standard*
With cautelous° baits and practice.   *deceitful*

VOLUMNIA   My first son,
35 Whither will thou go? Take good Cominius
With thee a while. Determine on some course
More than a wild exposure to each chance
That starts° i'th' way before thee.   *leaps up*

VIRGILIA   O the gods!

COMINIUS   I'll follow thee a month, devise with thee
40 Where thou shalt rest, that thou mayst hear of us
And we of thee. So, if the time thrust forth
A cause for thy repeal,° we shall not send   *recall from banishment*
O'er the vast world to seek a single man,
And lose advantage,° which doth ever cool   *favorable occasion*
45 I'th' absence of the needer.

CORIOLANUS   Fare ye well.
Thou hast years upon thee, and thou art too full
Of the wars' surfeits to go rove with one
That's yet unbruised. Bring me but out at gate.
Come, my sweet wife, my dearest mother, and
50 My friends of noble touch.° When I am forth,   *proven nobility*
Bid me farewell, and smile. I pray you come.
While I remain above the ground you shall
Hear from me still, and never of me aught
But what is like me formerly.

MENENIUS   That's worthily
55 As any ear can hear. Come, let's not weep.
If I could shake off but one seven years
From these old arms and legs, by the good gods,
I'd with thee every foot.

CORIOLANUS   Give me thy hand. Come.   *Exeunt*

4.2

Enter the two tribunes, SICINIUS *and* BRUTUS, *with the*
AEDILE

SICINIUS [*to the* AEDILE]   Bid them all home. He's gone, and we'll no further.
The nobility are vexed, whom we see have sided
In his behalf.

BRUTUS   Now we have shown our power,
Let us seem humbler after it is done
Than when it was a-doing.

5 SICINIUS [*to the* AEDILE]   Bid them home.
Say their great enemy is gone, and they
Stand in their ancient strength.

BRUTUS   Dismiss them home.
                                        Exit AEDILE

Enter VOLUMNIA, VIRGILIA [*weeping*], *and* MENENIUS
Here comes his mother.

SICINIUS   Let's not meet her.

10 BRUTUS   Why?

SICINIUS   They say she's mad.

BRUTUS   They have ta'en note of us. Keep on your way.

4.2 Location: Near the city gates of Rome.

VOLUMNIA   O, you're well met! Th'hoarded plague o'th' gods
    Requite° your love!   *Repay*
MENENIUS   Peace, peace, be not so loud.

15 VOLUMNIA [*to the tribunes*]   If that I could for weeping, you should hear—
    Nay, and you shall hear some. Will you be gone?
VIRGILIA [*to the tribunes*]   You shall stay, too. I would I had the power
    To say so to my husband.
SICINIUS [*to* VOLUMNIA]   Are you mankind?¹
VOLUMNIA   Ay, fool. Is that a shame? Note but this, fool:

20 Was not a man my father? Hadst thou foxship°   *slyness*
    To banish him that struck more blows for Rome
    Than thou hast spoken words?
SICINIUS   O blessèd heavens!
VOLUMNIA   More noble blows than ever thou wise words,
    And for Rome's good. I'll tell thee what—yet go.

25 Nay, but thou shalt stay too. I would my son
    Were in Arabia,² and thy tribe before him,
    His good sword in his hand.
SICINIUS   What then?
VIRGILIA   What then?
    He'd make an end of thy posterity.
VOLUMNIA   Bastards and all.

30 Good man, the wounds that he does bear for Rome!
MENENIUS   Come, come, peace.
SICINIUS   I would he had continued to his country
    As he began, and not unknit° himself   *untied*
    The noble knot he made.
BRUTUS   I would he had.

35 VOLUMNIA   'I would he had'! 'Twas you incensed the rabble—
    Cats that can judge as fitly of his worth
    As I can of those mysteries which heaven
    Will not have earth to know.
BRUTUS [*to* SICINIUS]   Pray, let's go.

40 VOLUMNIA   Now pray, sir, get you gone.
    You have done a brave deed. Ere you go, hear this:
    As far as doth the Capitol exceed
    The meanest house in Rome, so far my son—
    This lady's husband here, this, do you see?—

45 Whom you have banished does exceed you all.
BRUTUS   Well, well, we'll leave you.
SICINIUS   Why stay we to be baited
    With one that wants° her wits?   *Exeunt tribunes*   *lacks*
VOLUMNIA   Take my prayers with you.
    I would the gods had nothing else to do
    But to confirm my curses. Could I meet 'em

50 But once a day, it would unclog° my heart   *unburden*
    Of what lies heavy to't.
MENENIUS   You have told them home³
    And, by my troth, you have cause. You'll sup° with me?   *dine*
VOLUMNIA   Anger's my meat, I sup upon myself,
    And so shall starve with feeding.

---

1. Male (thus to speak in public); Volumnia takes the   places to hide.
word to mean "human."   3. Scolded them thoroughly.
2. That is, in a desert without political institutions or

[*To* VIRGILIA]   Come, let's go.
55 Leave this faint puling and lament as I do,
In anger, Juno-like.[4] Come, come, come.

                              Exeunt VOLUMNIA *and* VIRGILIA

MENENIUS   Fie, fie, fie.   *Exit*

                                   4.3

Enter [NICANOR,] *a Roman, and* [ADRIAN,] *a Volsce* ▪

NICANOR   I know you well, sir, and you know me. Your name, I
think, is Adrian.

ADRIAN   It is so, sir. Truly, I have forgot you.

NICANOR   I am a Roman, and my services are, as you are, against
5   'em.° Know you me yet?   *(the Romans)*

ADRIAN   Nicanor, no?

NICANOR   The same, sir.

ADRIAN   You had more beard when I last saw you, but your
favour° is well approved° by your tongue. What's the news in   *face / attested*
10 Rome? I have a note° from the Volscian state to find you out   *instruction*
there. You have well saved me a day's journey.

NICANOR   There hath been in Rome strange insurrections, the
people against the senators, patricians, and nobles.

ADRIAN   Hath been?—is it ended then? Our state thinks not so.
15 They are in a most warlike preparation, and hope to come
upon them in the heat of their division.

NICANOR   The main blaze of it is past, but a small thing would
make it flame again, for the nobles receive so to heart the banishment of that worthy Coriolanus that they are in a ripe apt-
20 ness to take all power from the people, and to pluck from them
their tribunes for ever. This lies glowing,° I can tell you, and is   *smoldering*
almost mature for the violent breaking out.

ADRIAN   Coriolanus banished?

NICANOR   Banished, sir.

25 ADRIAN   You will be welcome with this intelligence, Nicanor.

NICANOR   The day° serves well for them° now. I have heard it   *moment / (the Volscians)*
said the fittest time to corrupt a man's wife is when she's fallen
out with her husband. Your noble Tullus Aufidius will appear
well in these wars, his great opposer Coriolanus being now in
30 no request of° his country.   *unvalued by*

ADRIAN   He cannot choose.° I am most fortunate thus acciden-   *He is bound to*
tally to encounter you. You have ended my business, and I will
merrily accompany you home.

NICANOR   I shall between this and supper tell you most strange
35 things from Rome, all tending to the good of their adversaries.
Have you an army ready, say you?

ADRIAN   A most royal one—the centurions and their charges distinctly billeted already in th'entertainment,[1] and to be on foot
at an hour's warning.

40 NICANOR   I am joyful to hear of their readiness, and am the man,
I think, that shall set them in present° action. So, sir, heartily   *immediate*
well met, and most glad of your company.

---

4. Goddess of marriage and childbirth (and frequently
infuriated by the infidelities of her husband, Jupiter, king
of the gods).

4.3 Location: A road between Rome and Antium.
1. *their . . . entertainment:* the men under their command
already listed unit by unit on the payroll.

ADRIAN You take my part° from me, sir. I have the most cause to   *lines*
be glad of yours.

45   NICANOR   Well, let us go together.   *Exeunt*

4.4

Enter CORIOLANUS *in mean apparel, disguised*
and muffled

CORIOLANUS   A goodly city is this Antium. City,
'Tis I that made thy widows. Many an heir
Of these fair edifices fore my wars°   *before my onslaught*
Have I heard groan and drop. Then know me not,
5   Lest that thy wives with spits and boys with stones
In puny battle slay me.
    Enter a CITIZEN
                    Save° you, sir.   *God save*
CITIZEN   And you.
CORIOLANUS   Direct me, if it be your will,
Where great Aufidius lies. Is he in Antium?
CITIZEN   He is, and feasts the nobles of the state
At his house this night.
10   CORIOLANUS   Which is his house, beseech you?
CITIZEN   This here before you.
CORIOLANUS   Thank you, sir. Farewell.
                            Exit CITIZEN
O world, thy slippery turns! Friends now fast sworn,
Whose double bosoms seem to wear one heart,
Whose hours, whose bed, whose meal and exercise
15   Are still together, who twin as 'twere in love
Unseparable, shall within this hour,
On a dissension of a doit,° break out   *trivial quarrel*
To bitterest enmity. So fellest foes,
Whose passions and whose plots have broke their sleep
20   To take the one the other,[1] by some chance,
Some trick° not worth an egg, shall grow dear friends   *trifle*
And interjoin their issues.[2] So with me.
My birthplace hate I, and my love's upon
This enemy town. I'll enter. If he slay me,
25   He does fair justice; if he give me way,°   *allows me to proceed*
I'll do his country service.   *Exit*

4.5

Music plays. Enter a SERVINGMAN
FIRST SERVINGMAN   Wine, wine, wine! What service is here?
I think our fellows° are asleep.   [*Exit*]   *fellow servants*
    Enter [*a* SECOND] SERVINGMAN
SECOND SERVINGMAN   Where's Cotus? My master calls for him.
Cotus!   *Exit*
    Enter CORIOLANUS [*as before*]
5   CORIOLANUS   A goodly house. The feast
Smells well, but I appear not like a guest.
    Enter the FIRST SERVINGMAN

4.4 Location: Before Aufidius's house in Antium.   2. Unite their causes; marry their children to one another.
1. Whose plots to capture one another have kept them   **4.5** Location: Inside Aufidius's house.
awake.

FIRST SERVINGMAN   What would you have, friend? Whence are
   you? Here's no place for you. Pray go to the door.   *Exit*
CORIOLANUS   I have deserved no better entertainment
10   In being Coriolanus.
          Enter SECOND [SERVINGMAN]
SECOND SERVINGMAN   Whence are you, sir? Has the porter his
   eyes in his head, that he gives entrance to such companions?°   low persons
   Pray get you out.
CORIOLANUS   Away!
15 SECOND SERVINGMAN   Away? Get you away.
CORIOLANUS   Now thou'rt troublesome.
SECOND SERVINGMAN   Are you so brave?° I'll have you talked   insolent
   with anon.°   right away
          Enter THIRD SERVINGMAN. *The* FIRST *meets him*
THIRD SERVINGMAN   What fellow's this?
20 FIRST SERVINGMAN   A strange one as ever I looked on. I cannot
   get him out o'th' house. Prithee, call my master to him.
THIRD SERVINGMAN [*to* CORIOLANUS]   What have you to do° here,   are you doing
   fellow? Pray you, avoid° the house.   leave
CORIOLANUS   Let me but stand. I will not hurt your hearth.
25 THIRD SERVINGMAN   What are you?
CORIOLANUS   A gentleman.
THIRD SERVINGMAN   A marvellous poor one.
CORIOLANUS   True, so I am.
THIRD SERVINGMAN   Pray you, poor gentleman, take up some other
30   station.¹ Here's no place for you. Pray you, avoid. Come.
CORIOLANUS   Follow your function.² Go and batten° on cold   gorge
   bits.
          [*He*] *pushes him away from him*
THIRD SERVINGMAN   What, you will not?—Prithee tell my master
   what a strange guest he has here.
35 SECOND SERVINGMAN   And I shall.   *Exit* SECOND SERVINGMAN
THIRD SERVINGMAN   Where dwell'st thou?
CORIOLANUS   Under the canopy.°   (of the sky)
THIRD SERVINGMAN   Under the canopy?
CORIOLANUS   Ay.
40 THIRD SERVINGMAN   Where's that?
CORIOLANUS   I'th' city of kites and crows.°   (carrion birds)
THIRD SERVINGMAN   I'th' city of kites and crows? What an ass it
   is! Then thou dwell'st with daws,³ too?
CORIOLANUS   No, I serve not thy master.
45 THIRD SERVINGMAN   How, sir? Do you meddle⁴ with my master?
CORIOLANUS   Ay, 'tis an honester service than to meddle with
   thy mistress. Thou prat'st and prat'st. Serve with thy trencher.°   wooden plate
   Hence!
          [*He*] *beats him away.*
          Enter AUFIDIUS, *with the* [SECOND] SERVINGMAN
AUFIDIUS   Where is this fellow?
50 SECOND SERVINGMAN   Here, sir. I'd have beaten him like a dog
   but for disturbing the lords within.
          [*The* SERVINGMEN *stand aside*]

1. Place to stand (punning on "social rank").
2. Perform your servant's tasks.
3. Jackdaws (proverbially foolish).

4. Busy yourself; but Coriolanus plays on the sense "have sexual intercourse."

AUFIDIUS Whence com'st thou? What wouldst thou? Thy name?
　　　Why speak'st not? Speak, man. What's thy name?
CORIOLANUS [*unmuffling his head*]　　　　　　If, Tullus,
　　　Not yet thou know'st me, and seeing me dost not
55　Think me for the man I am, necessity
　　　Commands me name myself.
AUFIDIUS　　　　　　　　What is thy name?
CORIOLANUS A name unmusical to the Volscians' ears
　　　And harsh in sound to thine.
AUFIDIUS　　　　　　　　Say, what's thy name?
　　　Thou hast a grim appearance, and thy face
60　Bears a command in't. Though thy tackle's torn,
　　　Thou show'st° a noble vessel. What's thy name?　　　　　*appear to be*
CORIOLANUS Prepare thy brow to frown. Know'st thou me yet?
AUFIDIUS I know thee not. Thy name?
CORIOLANUS My name is Caius Martius, who hath done
65　To thee particularly, and to all the Volsces,
　　　Great hurt and mischief. Thereto witness may
　　　My surname Coriolanus. The painful service,
　　　The extreme dangers, and the drops of blood
　　　Shed for my thankless country, are requited
70　But with that surname—a good memory°　　　　　*reminder*
　　　And witness of the malice and displeasure
　　　Which thou shouldst bear me. Only that name remains.
　　　The cruelty and envy of the people,
　　　Permitted by our dastard nobles, who
75　Have all forsook me, hath devoured the rest,
　　　And suffered me by th' voice of slaves to be
　　　Whooped out of Rome. Now this extremity
　　　Hath brought me to thy hearth. Not out of hope—
　　　Mistake me not—to save my life, for if
80　I had feared death, of all the men i'th' world
　　　I would have 'voided thee, but in mere° spite　　　　　*utter*
　　　To be full quit of° those my banishers　　　　　*revenged upon; rid of*
　　　Stand I before thee here. Then if thou hast
　　　A heart of wreak° in thee, that wilt revenge　　　　　*vengeance*
85　Thine own particular wrongs and stop those maims
　　　Of shame seen through thy country, speed° thee straight,　　　　　*hasten*
　　　And make my misery serve thy turn. So use it
　　　That my revengeful services may prove
　　　As benefits to thee; for I will fight
90　Against my cankered° country with the spleen°　　　　　*infected / wrath*
　　　Of all the under-fiends.° But if so be　　　　　*underworld fiends*
　　　Thou dar'st not this, and that to prove° more fortunes　　　　　*try*
　　　Thou'rt tired, then, in a word, I also am
　　　Longer to live most weary, and present
95　My throat to thee and to thy ancient° malice,　　　　　*long-standing*
　　　Which not to cut would show thee but a fool,
　　　Since I have ever followed thee with hate,
　　　Drawn tuns° of blood out of thy country's breast,　　　　　*huge casks*
　　　And cannot live but to thy shame unless
　　　It be to do thee service.
100　AUFIDIUS　　　　　　　　O Martius, Martius!
　　　Each word thou hast spoke hath weeded from my heart
　　　A root of ancient envy. If Jupiter

Should from yon cloud speak divine things
And say ''Tis true', I'd not believe them more
105 Than thee, all-noble Martius. Let me twine
Mine arms about that body whereagainst
My grainèd ash⁵ an hundred times hath broke,
And scarred the moon with splinters.
                          [*He embraces* CORIOLANUS]
                          Here I clip°   embrace
The anvil⁶ of my sword, and do contest
110 As hotly and as nobly with thy love
As ever in ambitious strength I did
Contend against thy valour. Know thou first,
I loved the maid I married; never man
Sighed truer breath. But that I see thee here,
115 Thou noble thing, more dances my rapt heart
Than when I first my wedded mistress saw
Bestride my threshold. Why, thou Mars, I tell thee
We have a power on foot,° and I had purpose   army in the field
Once more to hew thy target° from thy brawn,°   shield / arm
120 Or lose mine arm for't. Thou hast beat me out°   outright
Twelve several° times, and I have nightly since   separate
Dreamt of encounters 'twixt thyself and me—
We have been down° together in my sleep,   (on the ground)
Unbuckling helms, fisting° each other's throat—   clutching
125 And waked half dead with nothing. Worthy Martius,
Had we no other quarrel else to Rome but that
Thou art thence banished, we would muster all°   enlist everyone
From twelve to seventy,° and, pouring war   (years old)
Into the bowels of ungrateful Rome,
130 Like a bold flood o'erbear't. O, come, go in,
And take our friendly senators by th' hands
Who now are here taking their leaves of me,
Who am prepared against your territories,
Though not for Rome itself.
CORIOLANUS   You bless me, gods.
135 AUFIDIUS   Therefore, most absolute° sir, if thou wilt have   perfect
The leading of thine own revenges, take
Th'one half of my commission° and set down°—   force / determine
As best thou art experienced, since thou know'st
Thy country's strength and weakness—thine own ways:
140 Whether to knock against the gates of Rome,
Or rudely visit° them in parts remote   afflict
To fright them ere destroy. But come in.
Let me commend thee first to those that shall
Say yea to thy desires. A thousand welcomes!
145 And more a friend than ere an enemy;
Yet, Martius, that was much. Your hand. Most welcome!
                                                  Exeunt
              [*The*] *two* SERVINGMEN [*come forward*]
FIRST SERVINGMAN   Here's a strange alteration!
SECOND SERVINGMAN   By my hand, I had thought to have strucken

---

5. Close-grained ashwood spear.
6. Coriolanus's body, on which Aufidius has beaten his sword.

him with a cudgel, and yet my mind gave° me his clothes made   *suggested to*
150   a false report of him.

FIRST SERVINGMAN   What an arm he has! He turned me about with his finger and his thumb as one would set up a top.

SECOND SERVINGMAN   Nay, I knew by his face that there was something in him. He had, sir, a kind of face, methought—I
155   cannot tell how to term it.

FIRST SERVINGMAN   He had so, looking, as it were—would I were hanged but I thought there was more in him than I could think.

SECOND SERVINGMAN   So did I, I'll be sworn. He is simply the
160   rarest man i'th' world.

FIRST SERVINGMAN   I think he is yet a greater soldier than he you wot on.°   *know of*

SECOND SERVINGMAN   Who, my master?

FIRST SERVINGMAN   Nay, it's no matter for° that.   *no doubt about*

165   SECOND SERVINGMAN   Worth six on him.

FIRST SERVINGMAN   Nay, not so, neither; but I take him to be the greater soldier.

SECOND SERVINGMAN   Faith, look you, one cannot tell how to say[7] that. For the defence of a town our general is excellent.

170   FIRST SERVINGMAN   Ay, and for an assault too.

Enter the THIRD SERVINGMAN

THIRD SERVINGMAN   O, slaves, I can tell you news—news, you rascals!

FIRST *and* SECOND SERVINGMEN   What, what, what? Let's partake.

THIRD SERVINGMAN   I would not be a Roman of all nations. I had
175   as lief° be a condemned man.   *gladly*

FIRST *and* SECOND SERVINGMEN   Wherefore? Wherefore?

THIRD SERVINGMAN   Why, here's he that was wont to thwack our general, Caius Martius.

FIRST SERVINGMAN   Why do you say 'thwack our general'?

180   THIRD SERVINGMAN   I do not say 'thwack our general'; but he was always good enough for him.

SECOND SERVINGMAN   Come, we are fellows and friends. He was ever too hard for him. I have heard him say so himself.

FIRST SERVINGMAN   He was too hard for him directly.° To say the   *simply*
185   truth on't, before Corioles he scotched° him and notched him   *scored*
like a carbonado.[8]

SECOND SERVINGMAN   An° he had been cannibally given, he   *If*
might have broiled and eaten him too.

FIRST SERVINGMAN   But more of thy news!

190   THIRD SERVINGMAN   Why, he is so made on° here within as if he   *made so much of*
were son and heir to Mars; set at upper end o'th' table, no
question asked him by any of the senators but they stand bald°   *hatless*
before him. Our general himself makes a mistress of° him,   *woos*
sanctifies himself with's hand,[9] and turns up the white o'th'
195   eye° to his discourse. But the bottom° of the news is, our gen-   *(in pious devotion) / gist*
eral is cut i'th' middle, and but one half of what he was yester-
day, for the other° has half by the entreaty and grant of the   *(Coriolanus)*
whole table. He'll go, he says, and sowl° the porter of Rome   *drag*

---

7. There's no basis for saying.
8. Piece of meat for broiling.

9. Treats the touch of his hand as holy.

gates by th' ears. He will mow all down before him, and leave
his passage polled.°   *stripped*

SECOND SERVINGMAN   And he's as like to do't as any man I can
imagine.

THIRD SERVINGMAN   Do't? He will do't; for look you, sir, he has
as many friends as enemies; which friends, sir, as it were durst
not—look you, sir—show themselves, as we term it, his friends
whilst he's in dejectitude.°   *disgraced*

FIRST SERVINGMAN   Dejectitude? What's that?

THIRD SERVINGMAN   But when they shall see, sir, his crest up
again and the man in blood,¹ they will out of their burrows like
conies° after rain, and revel all with him.   *rabbits*

FIRST SERVINGMAN   But when goes this forward?

THIRD SERVINGMAN   Tomorrow, today, presently.° You shall have   *at once*
the drum struck up this afternoon. 'Tis as it were a parcel° of   *part*
their feast, and to be executed ere they wipe their lips.

SECOND SERVINGMAN   Why, then we shall have a stirring° world   *busy*
again. This peace is nothing but to rust iron, increase tailors,
and breed ballad-makers.²

FIRST SERVINGMAN   Let me have war, say I. It exceeds peace as
far as day does night. It's sprightly walking, audible and full of
vent.³ Peace is a very apoplexy, lethargy; mulled,° deaf, sleepy,   *stupefied*
insensible; a getter of more bastard children than war's a
destroyer of men.

SECOND SERVINGMAN   'Tis so, and as war in some sort may be
said to be a ravisher, so it cannot be denied but peace is a great
maker of cuckolds.

FIRST SERVINGMAN   Ay, and it makes men hate one another.

THIRD SERVINGMAN   Reason; because they then less need one another. The wars for my money. I hope to see Romans as cheap
as Volscians.

     [*A sound within*]

They are rising, they are rising.°   *(from dinner)*

FIRST *and* SECOND SERVINGMEN   In, in, in, in.   *Exeunt*

4.6

Enter the two tribunes, SICINIUS *and* BRUTUS

SICINIUS   We hear not of him, neither need we fear him.
His remedies are tame¹—the present peace
And quietness of the people, which before
Were in wild hurry.° Here do we make his friends   *tumult*
Blush that the world goes well, who rather had,
Though they themselves did suffer by't, behold
Dissentious numbers pest'ring° streets than see   *obstructing*
Our tradesmen singing in their shops and going
About their functions friendly.

     Enter MENENIUS

BRUTUS   We stood to't° in good time. Is this Menenius?   *acted resolutely*

SICINIUS   'Tis he, 'tis he. O, he is grown most kind of late.
Hail, sir.

---

1. In full vigor (usually refers to hounds).
2. Fashionable dress and idle songs flourish in
peacetime.
3. *audible . . . vent:* either loud and full of action, or quick
of hearing and scent (like a hunting dog).

4.6 Location: A public place in Rome.
1. Those who favor him are unable to act; curing ourselves of him is without violent effects.

MENENIUS   Hail to you both.

SICINIUS   Your Coriolanus is not much missed

15   But with° his friends. The commonwealth doth stand,   by
    And so would do were he more angry at it.

MENENIUS   All's well, and might have been much better if
    He could have temporized.

SICINIUS   Where is he, hear you?

20   MENENIUS   Nay, I hear nothing.
    His mother and his wife hear nothing from him.

Enter three or four CITIZENS

ALL THE CITIZENS [*to the tribunes*]   The gods preserve you both.

SICINIUS   Good e'en, our
    neighbours.

BRUTUS   Good e'en to you all, good e'en to you all.

FIRST CITIZEN   Ourselves, our wives and children, on our knees
    Are bound to pray for you both.

25   SICINIUS   Live and thrive.

BRUTUS   Farewell, kind neighbours.
    We wished Coriolanus had loved you as we did.

ALL THE CITIZENS   Now the gods keep you!

SICINIUS *and* BRUTUS   Farewell, farewell.

Exeunt CITIZENS

SICINIUS   This is a happier and more comely time

30   Than when these fellows ran about the streets
    Crying confusion.

BRUTUS   Caius Martius was
    A worthy officer i'th' war, but insolent,
    O'ercome with pride, ambitious past all thinking,°   *beyond imagination*
    Self-loving—

SICINIUS   And affecting one sole throne°   *aspiring to rule alone*
    Without assistance.

35   MENENIUS   I think not so.

SICINIUS   We should by this,° to all our lamentation,   *now*
    If he had gone forth consul found it so.

BRUTUS   The gods have well prevented it, and Rome
    Sits safe and still without him.

Enter an AEDILE

AEDILE   Worthy tribunes,

40   There is a slave whom we have put in prison
    Reports the Volsces, with two several powers,°   *separate armies*
    Are entered in the Roman territories,
    And with the deepest malice of the war
    Destroy what lies before 'em.

MENENIUS   'Tis Aufidius,

45   Who, hearing of our Martius' banishment,
    Thrusts forth his horns again into the world,
    Which were inshelled when Martius stood for Rome,
    And durst not once peep out.

SICINIUS   Come, what talk you of Martius?

BRUTUS [*to the* AEDILE]   Go see this rumourer whipped. It cannot be
    The Volsces dare break° with us.   *(their treaty)*

50   MENENIUS   Cannot be?
    We have record that very well it can,
    And three examples of the like hath been
    Within my age. But reason° with the fellow,   *discuss*

Before you punish him, where he heard this,
55 Lest you shall chance to whip your information
And beat the messenger who bids beware
Of what is to be dreaded.

SICINIUS   Tell not me.
I know this cannot be.

BRUTUS   Not possible.

Enter a MESSENGER

MESSENGER   The nobles in great earnestness are going
60 All to the senate-house. Some news is come
That turns° their countenances.   changes

SICINIUS   'Tis this slave.
[*To the* AEDILE] Go whip him fore the people's eyes.—His raising,°   incitement
Nothing but his report.   *Exit* AEDILE

MESSENGER   Yes, worthy sir,
The slave's report is seconded, and more,
More fearful, is delivered.

65 SICINIUS   What more fearful?

MESSENGER   It is spoke freely out of many mouths—
How probable I do not know—that Martius,
Joined with Aufidius, leads a power 'gainst Rome,
And vows revenge as spacious as between
The young'st and oldest thing.

70 SICINIUS   This is most likely!°   (sarcastic)

BRUTUS   Raised only that the weaker sort may wish
Good Martius home again.

SICINIUS   The very trick on't.°   Exactly

MENENIUS   This is unlikely.
75 He and Aufidius can no more atone°   reconcile
Than violent'st contrariety.

Enter [another] MESSENGER

SECOND MESSENGER   You are sent for to the senate.
A fearful army, led by Caius Martius
Associated with Aufidius, rages
80 Upon our territories, and have already
O'erborne their way, consumed with fire and took
What lay before them.

Enter COMINIUS

COMINIUS   O, you have made good work!

MENENIUS   What news? What news?

85 COMINIUS   You have holp° to ravish your own daughters and   helped
To melt the city leads° upon your pates,°   roof lead / heads
To see your wives dishonoured to° your noses.   in front of

MENENIUS   What's the news? What's the news?

COMINIUS   Your temples burnèd in their cement,° and   to their foundations
90 Your franchises,° whereon you stood,° confined   freedoms / insisted
Into an auger's bore.[2]

MENENIUS   Pray now, your news?
[*To the tribunes*] You have made fair work, I fear me.
[*To* COMINIUS]   Pray, your news.
If Martius should be joined wi'th' Volscians—

COMINIUS   If? He is their god. He leads them like a thing
95 Made by some other deity than nature,

2. A drill hole (that is, a narrow space).

That shapes man better, and they follow him
Against us brats° with no less confidence   *mere children*
Than boys pursuing summer butterflies,
Or butchers killing flies.

MENENIUS [*to the tribunes*]   You have made good work,
100   You and your apron-men,° you that stood so much   *(artisans wore aprons)*
Upon the voice of occupation° and   *opinion of tradesmen*
The breath of garlic-eaters!

COMINIUS [*to the tribunes*]   He'll shake your Rome about your ears.

MENENIUS   As Hercules did shake down mellow fruit.[3]
105   [*To the tribunes*] You have made fair work.

BRUTUS   But is this true, sir?

COMINIUS   Ay, and you'll look pale
Before you find it other.° All the regions   *otherwise*
Do smilingly° revolt, and who resists   *gladly*
110   Are mocked for valiant° ignorance,   *steadfast*
And perish constant° fools. Who is't can blame him?   *obstinate*
Your enemies° and his[4] find something in him.   *(the patricians)*

MENENIUS   We are all undone unless
The noble man have mercy.

COMINIUS   Who shall ask it?
115   The tribunes cannot do't, for shame; the people
Deserve such pity of° him as the wolf   *from*
Does of the shepherds. For his best friends, if they
Should say 'Be good to Rome', they charged° him even   *would direct*
As those should do that had deserved his hate,
And therein showed° like enemies.   *would behave*
120 MENENIUS   'Tis true.
If he were putting to my house the brand°   *fire*
That should consume it, I have not the face°   *shamelessness*
To say 'Beseech you, cease.'
[*To the tribunes*]   You have made fair hands,°   *done well*
You and your crafts! You have crafted fair!

COMINIUS [*to the tribunes*]   You have brought
125   A trembling upon Rome such as was never
S'incapable of help.

SICINIUS *and* BRUTUS   Say not we brought it.

MENENIUS   How? Was't we?
We loved him, but like beasts and cowardly nobles
130   Gave way unto your clusters,° who did hoot   *crowds*
Him out o'th' city.

COMINIUS   But I fear
They'll roar° him in again. Tullus Aufidius,   *(in fear)*
The second name of men,[5] obeys his points°   *directions*
As if he were his officer. Desperation
135   Is all the policy, strength, and defence
That Rome can make against them.

Enter a troop of CITIZENS

MENENIUS   Here come the clusters.
[*To the* CITIZENS] And is Aufidius with him? You are they
That made the air unwholesome when you cast

---

3. Hercules' twelfth labor was to gather the apples of
the Hesperides.

4. The Volscians.

5. The second in reputation only to Coriolanus.

Your stinking greasy caps in hooting at
140 Coriolanus' exile. Now he's coming,
And not a hair upon a soldier's head
Which will not prove a whip. As many coxcombs°   fools
As you threw caps up will he tumble down,
And pay you for your voices. 'Tis no matter.
145 If he could burn us all into one coal,
We have deserved it.

ALL THE CITIZENS   Faith, we hear fearful news.

FIRST CITIZEN   For mine own part,
When I said 'banish him' I said 'twas pity.

150 SECOND CITIZEN   And so did I.

THIRD CITIZEN   And so did I, and to say the truth so did very
many of us. That° we did, we did for the best, and though we   What
willingly consented to his banishment, yet it was against our
will.

COMINIUS   You're goodly things, you voices.

155 MENENIUS   You have made good work,
You and your cry. Shall's to the Capitol?

COMINIUS   O, ay, what else? Exeunt [MENENIUS and COMINIUS]

SICINIUS   Go, masters, get you home. Be not dismayed.
These are a side° that would be glad to have   faction
160 This true which they so seem to fear. Go home,
And show no sign of fear.

FIRST CITIZEN   The gods be good to us! Come, masters, let's home.
I ever said we were i'th' wrong when we banished him.

SECOND CITIZEN   So did we all. But come, let's home.

                                        Exeunt CITIZENS

BRUTUS   I do not like this news.

165 SICINIUS   Nor I.

BRUTUS   Let's to the Capitol. Would half my wealth
Would buy this for a lie.

SICINIUS   Pray let's go.   Exeunt

4.7

Enter AUFIDIUS *with his* LIEUTENANT

AUFIDIUS   Do they still fly to th' Roman?

LIEUTENANT   I do not know what witchcraft's in him, but
Your soldiers use him as the grace fore meat,
Their talk at table, and their thanks at end,
5 And you are darkened° in this action, sir,   overshadowed
Even by your own.°   (followers)

AUFIDIUS   I cannot help it now,
Unless by using means° I lame the foot   stratagems
Of our design. He bears himself more proudlier,
Even to my person, than I thought he would
10 When first I did embrace him. Yet his nature
In that's no changeling,° and I must excuse   waverer
What cannot be amended.

LIEUTENANT   Yet I wish, sir—
I mean for your particular°—you had not   own sake
Joined in commission° with him, but either   command
15 Have borne the action of yourself or else
To him had left it solely.

4.7 Location: The Volscian camp near Rome.

AUFIDIUS   I understand thee well, and be thou sure,
    When he shall come to his account,[1] he knows not
    What I can urge against him. Although it seems—
20   And so he thinks, and is no less apparent
    To th' vulgar eye—that he bears all things fairly
    And shows good husbandry for the Volscian state,
    Fights dragon-like, and does achieve as soon
    As draw his sword, yet he hath left undone
25   That which shall break his neck or hazard mine
    Whene'er we come to our account.
LIEUTENANT   Sir, I beseech you, think you he'll carry° Rome?   *defeat*
AUFIDIUS   All places yields to him ere he sits down,°   *lays siege*
    And the nobility of Rome are his.
30   The senators and patricians love him too.
    The tribunes are no soldiers, and their people
    Will be as rash in the repeal° as hasty   *recall from exile*
    To expel him thence. I think he'll be to Rome
    As is the osprey to the fish, who takes it
35   By sovereignty of nature.[2] First he was
    A noble servant to them, but he could not
    Carry his honours even.° Whether 'twas pride,   *equably*
    Which out of daily fortune[3] ever taints
    The happy° man; whether defect of judgement,   *fortunate*
40   To fail in the disposing of those chances
    Which he was lord of; or whether nature,
    Not to be other than one thing, not moving
    From th' casque° to th' cushion,° but commanding peace   *helmet / senate seat*
    Even with the same austerity and garb°   *stern demeanor*
45   As he controlled the war: but one of these—
    As he hath spices° of them all—not all,   *touches*
    For I dare so far free him—made him feared,
    So hated, and so banished. But he has a merit
    To choke it in the utt'rance.[4] So our virtues
50   Lie in th'interpretation of the time,°   *contemporary observers*
    And power, unto itself most commendable,
    Hath not a tomb so evident as a chair
    T'extol what it hath done.[5]
    One fire drives out one fire, one nail one nail;
55   Rights by rights falter, strengths by strengths do fail.
    Come, let's away. When, Caius, Rome is thine,
    Thou art poor'st of all; then shortly art thou mine.   *Exeunt*

5.1

Enter MENENIUS, COMINIUS, SICINIUS, BRUTUS, *the two*
tribunes, with others

MENENIUS   No, I'll not go. You hear what he hath said
    Which was sometime his general,° who loved him   *(Cominius)*
    In a most dear particular.° He called me father,   *affectionate regard*
    But what o' that? [*To the tribunes*] Go, you that banished him.
5   A mile before his tent fall down, and knee°   *crawl*

---

1. That is, with the Volscian state.
2. Fish were imagined to surrender to ospreys without a struggle.
3. As a result of repeated successes.
4. *he has . . . utt'rance*: his merit is so great that it overwhelms the recital of his faults; alternatively, his merit is of a kind that impedes attempts to praise it.

5. *Hath not . . . done*: a confusing passage, perhaps meaning, Will fall into certain oblivion unless it receives praise from the public rostrum; alternatively, is clearly ruined by public praise. In the first case, power requires reputation; in the second, reputation threatens power.
5.1 Location: A public place in Rome.

The way into his mercy. Nay, if he coyed°   *was reluctant*
To hear Cominius speak, I'll keep at home.
COMINIUS   He would not seem° to know me.   *pretended not*
MENENIUS [*to the tribunes*]   Do you hear?
COMINIUS   Yet one time he did call me by my name.
10   I urged our old acquaintance and the drops
That we have bled together. 'Coriolanus'
He would not answer to, forbade all names.
He was a kind of nothing, titleless,
Till he had forged himself a name o'th' fire
Of burning Rome.
MENENIUS [*to the tribunes*]
15   Why, so! You have made good work.
A pair of tribunes that have wracked° fair Rome   *destroyed*
To make coals cheap—a noble memory!°   *memorial*
COMINIUS   I minded him how royal 'twas to pardon
When it was less expected. He replied
20   It was a bare° petition of a state   *worthless; barefaced*
To one whom they had punished.
MENENIUS   Very well.
Could he say less?
COMINIUS   I offered° to awaken his regard   *tried*
For's private friends. His answer to me was
25   He could not stay to pick them in° a pile   *pick them out from*
Of noisome, musty chaff. He said 'twas folly,
For one poor grain or two, to leave unburnt
And still to nose° th'offence.   *smell*
MENENIUS   For one poor grain or two?
I am one of those. His mother, wife, his child,
30   And this brave fellow too—we are the grains.
[*To the tribunes*] You are the musty chaff, and you are smelt
Above the moon. We must be burnt for you.
SICINIUS   Nay, pray be patient. If you refuse your aid
In this so never-needed help, yet do not
35   Upbraid's with our distress. But sure, if you
Would be your country's pleader, your good tongue,
More than the instant army we can make,[1]
Might stop our countryman.
MENENIUS   No, I'll not meddle.
SICINIUS   Pray you go to him.
MENENIUS   What should I do?
40   BRUTUS   Only make trial what your love can do
For Rome towards Martius.
MENENIUS   Well, and say that Martius return me,
As Cominius is returned, unheard—what then?
But as a discontented friend, grief-shot°   *grief-stricken*
With his unkindness? Say't be so?
45   SICINIUS   Yet your good will
Must have that thanks from Rome after the measure
As° you intended well.   *To the extent that*
MENENIUS   I'll undertake't.
I think he'll hear me. Yet to bite his lip°   *(in anger)*
And 'hmh' at good Cominius much unhearts me.

---

1. The army we can raise right now.

50 He was not taken well,[2] he had not dined.
The veins unfilled, our blood is cold, and then
We pout upon the morning, are unapt
To give or to forgive; but when we have stuffed
These pipes and these conveyances° of our blood   *channels*
55 With wine and feeding, we have suppler souls
Than in our priest-like fasts. Therefore I'll watch him
Till he be dieted° to my request,   *made amenable by food*
And then I'll set upon him.
BRUTUS   You know the very road into his kindness,
And cannot lose your way.
60 MENENIUS   Good faith, I'll prove° him.   *try*
Speed° how it will, I shall ere long have knowledge   *Turn out*
Of my success.°   *Exit*   *whether I succeed*
COMINIUS   He'll never hear him.
SICINIUS   Not?
COMINIUS   I tell you, he does sit in gold, his eye
Red as 'twould burn Rome, and his injury[3]
65 The jailer to his pity. I kneeled before him;
'Twas very faintly he said 'Rise', dismissed me
Thus with his speechless hand. What he would do
He sent in writing after me, what he would not,
Bound with an oath to hold to his conditions.
70 So that all hope is vain unless his noble mother
And his wife, who as I hear mean to solicit him
For mercy to his country. Therefore let's hence,
And with our fair entreaties haste them on.   *Exeunt*

5.2

Enter MENENIUS *to the Watch or guard*

FIRST WATCHMAN   Stay. Whence are you?
SECOND WATCHMAN   Stand, and go back.
MENENIUS   You guard like men; 'tis well.
But, by your leave, I am an officer
5 Of state, and come to speak with Coriolanus.
FIRST WATCHMAN   From whence?
MENENIUS   From Rome.
FIRST WATCHMAN   You may not pass, you must return.
Our general will no more hear from thence.
SECOND WATCHMAN   You'll see your Rome embraced with fire before
You'll speak with Coriolanus.
10 MENENIUS   Good my friends,
If you have heard your general talk of Rome
And of his friends there, it is lots to blanks°   *the odds are*
My name hath touched your ears. It is Menenius.
FIRST WATCHMAN   Be it so; go back. The virtue° of your name   *power*
Is not here passable.[1]
15 MENENIUS   I tell thee, fellow,
Thy general is my lover.° I have been   *friend*
The book° of his good acts, whence men have read   *recorder*
His fame unparalleled happily amplified;

---

2. Not tackled at the right time.
3. The wrong inflicted on him.

5.2 Location: The Volscian camp near Rome.
1. Current (like a coin); effective (as a password).

For I have ever verified² my friends,

20 Of whom he's chief, with all the size° that verity   amplitude
Would without lapsing suffer.° Nay, sometimes,   erring allow
Like to a bowl upon a subtle° ground,   misleading
I have tumbled past the throw,³ and in his praise
Have almost stamped the leasing.⁴ Therefore, fellow,

25 I must have leave to pass.

FIRST WATCHMAN   Faith, sir, if you had told as many lies in his
behalf as you have uttered words in your own, you should not
pass here, no, though it were as virtuous to lie as to live
chastely.⁵ Therefore go back.

30 MENENIUS   Prithee, fellow, remember my name is Menenius,
always factionary on° the party of your general.   adherent to

SECOND WATCHMAN   Howsoever you have been his liar, as you
say you have, I am one that, telling true under him, must say
you cannot pass. Therefore go back.

35 MENENIUS   Has he dined, canst thou tell? For I would not speak
with him till after dinner.

FIRST WATCHMAN   You are a Roman, are you?

MENENIUS   I am as thy general is.

FIRST WATCHMAN   Then you should hate Rome as he does. Can

40 you, when you have pushed out your gates the very defender of
them, and in a violent popular ignorance given your enemy
your shield, think to front° his revenges with the easy⁶ groans   confront
of old women, the virginal palms of your daughters, or with the
palsied intercession of such a decayed dotant° as you seem to   old fool

45 be? Can you think to blow out the intended fire your city is
ready to flame in with such weak breath as this? No, you are
deceived, therefore back to Rome, and prepare for your execution. You are condemned, our general has sworn you out of
reprieve and pardon.

50 MENENIUS   Sirrah, if thy captain knew I were here, he would
use me with estimation.°   esteem

FIRST WATCHMAN   Come, my captain knows you not.

MENENIUS   I mean thy general.

FIRST WATCHMAN   My general cares not for you. Back, I say, go,

55 lest I let forth your half pint of blood. Back. That's the utmost
of your having.° Back.   the most you'll get

MENENIUS   Nay, but fellow, fellow—

Enter CORIOLANUS *with* AUFIDIUS

CORIOLANUS   What's the matter?

MENENIUS [*to* FIRST WATCHMAN]   Now, you companion,° I'll say   knave

60 an errand° for you. You shall know now that I am in estimation.   deliver a message
You shall perceive that a jack guardant° cannot office⁷ me from   uncouth guard
my son Coriolanus. Guess but by my entertainment with him
if thou stand'st not i'th' state of hanging, or of some death more
long in spectatorship and crueller in suffering. Behold now

65 presently, and swoon for what's to come upon thee. [*To* CORIO-
LANUS] The glorious gods sit in hourly synod° about thy particu-   council
lar prosperity, and love thee no worse than thy old father
Menenius does! [*Weeping*] O, my son, my son, thou art prepar-

---

2. Testified to the character of.
3. Overshot the mark (from the game of bowls).
4. Authenticated falsehood.

5. Honestly (but playing on "lies with a sexual partner").
6. Easily obtained; insignificant.
7. Officiously keep.

ing fire for us. Look thee, here's water to quench it. I was
70 hardly° moved to come to thee, but being assured none but   *with difficulty*
myself could move thee, I have been blown out of our gates
with sighs, and conjure thee to pardon Rome and thy petition-
ary° countrymen. The good gods assuage thy wrath and turn   *suppliant*
the dregs of it upon this varlet here, this, who like a block° hath   *blockhead; obstruction*
75 denied my access to thee!
    CORIOLANUS Away!
    MENENIUS How? Away?
    CORIOLANUS Wife, mother, child, I know not. My affairs
Are servanted° to others. Though I owe   *subjected*
80 My revenge properly,[8] my remission° lies   *forgiveness*
In Volscian breasts. That we have been familiar,
Ingrate forgetfulness shall poison rather
Than pity note how much.[9] Therefore be gone.
Mine ears against your suits are stronger than
85 Your gates against my force. Yet, for° I loved thee,   *because*
    [*He gives him a letter*]
Take this along. I writ it for thy sake,
And would have sent it. Another word, Menenius,
I will not hear thee speak.—This man, Aufidius,
Was my beloved in Rome; yet thou behold'st.
90 AUFIDIUS You keep a constant temper.
    Exeunt [CORIOLANUS *and* AUFIDIUS]
    FIRST WATCHMAN Now, sir, is your name Menenius?
    SECOND WATCHMAN 'Tis a spell, you see, of much power. You
know the way home again.
    FIRST WATCHMAN Do you hear how we are shent° for keeping   *scolded*
95 your greatness back?
    SECOND WATCHMAN What cause do you think I have to swoon?
    MENENIUS I neither care for th' world nor your general. For
such things as you, I can scarce think there's any, you're so
slight. He that hath a will to die by himself° fears it not from   *at his own hand*
100 another. Let your general do his worst. For you, be that you are
long, and your misery increase with your age. I say to you as I
was said to, 'Away!'   *Exit*
    FIRST WATCHMAN A noble fellow, I warrant him.
    SECOND WATCHMAN The worthy fellow is our general. He's the
105 rock, the oak, not to be wind-shaken.   *Exeunt*

5.3

Enter CORIOLANUS *and* AUFIDIUS [*with Volscian soldiers.*
    CORIOLANUS *and* AUFIDIUS *sit*]
    CORIOLANUS We will before the walls of Rome tomorrow
Set down our host.° My partner in this action,   *Lay siege with our forces*
You must report to th' Volscian lords how plainly
I have borne this business.
    AUFIDIUS   Only their ends
5 You have respected, stopped your ears against
The general suit of Rome, never admitted

8. *owe . . . properly:* possess my own power of revenge.
9. *That we . . . much:* The memory of our friendship shall
be poisoned by Rome's (alternatively, my own) ungrateful
forgetfulness, rather than compassion be awakened by my
awareness of how intimate we were.
5.3 Location: The Volscian camp.

A private whisper, no, not with such friends
That thought them sure of you.
CORIOLANUS   This last old man,
  Whom with a cracked heart I have sent to Rome,
10 Loved me above the measure of a father,
  Nay, godded° me indeed. Their latest refuge°   deified/last hope
  Was to send him, for whose old love I have—
  Though I showed sourly to him—once more offered
  The first conditions, which they did refuse
15 And cannot now accept, to grace him only
  That thought he could do more. A very little
  I have yielded to. Fresh embassies and suits,
  Nor from the state nor private friends, hereafter
  Will I lend ear to.
                       Shout within
                              Ha, what shout is this?
20 Shall I be tempted to infringe my vow
  In the same time 'tis made? I will not.
              Enter VIRGILIA, VOLUMNIA, VALERIA, YOUNG MARTIUS,
              with attendants
  My wife comes foremost, then the honoured mould
  Wherein this trunk° was framed, and in her hand   body
  The grandchild to her blood. But out, affection!
25 All bond and privilege of nature break;
  Let it be virtuous to be obstinate.
              [VIRGILIA *curtsies*]
  What is that curtsy worth? Or those dove's eyes
  Which can make gods forsworn? I melt, and am not
  Of stronger earth than others.
              [VOLUMNIA *bows*]
                              My mother bows,
30 As if Olympus to a molehill should
  In supplication nod; and my young boy
  Hath an aspect of intercession° which   pleading look
  Great nature cries 'Deny not'.—Let the Volsces
  Plough Rome and harrow Italy! I'll never
35 Be such a gosling° to obey instinct, but stand   (foolish) baby goose
  As if a man were author of himself
  And knew no other kin.
VIRGILIA   My lord and husband.
CORIOLANUS   These eyes are not the same I wore in Rome.
VIRGILIA   The sorrow that delivers° us thus changed   presents
  Makes you think so.
40 CORIOLANUS   Like a dull actor now
  I have forgot my part, and I am out°   at a loss
  Even to a full disgrace. [*Rising*] Best of my flesh,
  Forgive my tyranny, but do not say
  For that 'Forgive our Romans'.
              [VIRGILIA *kisses him*]
                              O, a kiss
45 Long as my exile, sweet as my revenge!
  Now, by the jealous queen of heaven,[1] that kiss
  I carried from thee, dear, and my true lip

---

1. Juno, queen of the gods and guardian of marriage.

Hath virgined it e'er since. You gods, I prate,
And the most noble mother of the world
50 Leave unsaluted! Sink, my knee, i'th' earth.
    [*He*] *kneels*
Of thy deep duty more impression° show   *indentation; effect*
Than that of common sons.
VOLUMNIA   O, stand up blest,
    [CORIOLANUS *rises*]
Whilst with no softer cushion than the flint
I kneel before thee, and unproperly°   *against propriety*
55 Show duty as mistaken all this while
Between the child and parent.
    [*She kneels*]
CORIOLANUS   What's this?
Your knees to me? To your corrected² son?
    [*He raises her*]
Then let the pebbles on the hungry beach
Fillip° the stars; then let the mutinous winds   *Strike against*
60 Strike the proud cedars 'gainst the fiery sun,
Murd'ring³ impossibility to make
What cannot be slight work.⁴
VOLUMNIA   Thou art my warrior.
I holp to frame° thee. Do you know this lady?   *helped to make*
CORIOLANUS   The noble sister of Publicola,
65 The moon° of Rome, chaste as the icicle   *(emblem of chastity)*
That's candied° by the frost from purest snow   *crystallized*
And hangs on Dian's⁵ temple—dear Valeria!
VOLUMNIA [*showing* CORIOLANUS *his son*]   This is a poor epitome°   *abridgment*
    of yours,
Which by th' interpretation of full time⁶
May show like all yourself.
70 CORIOLANUS [*to* YOUNG MARTIUS]   The god of soldiers,
With the consent of supreme Jove, inform
Thy thoughts with nobleness, that thou mayst prove
To shame unvulnerable, and stick° i'th' wars   *stand firm*
Like a great sea-mark standing every flaw⁷
75 And saving those that eye thee!
VOLUMNIA [*to* YOUNG MARTIUS]   Your knee, sirrah.
    [YOUNG MARTIUS *kneels*]
CORIOLANUS   That's my brave boy.
VOLUMNIA   Even he, your wife, this lady, and myself
Are suitors to you.
CORIOLANUS   I beseech you, peace.
80 Or if you'd ask, remember this before:
The things I have forsworn to grant may never
Be held by you denials.⁸ Do not bid me
Dismiss my soldiers, or capitulate°   *come to terms*
Again with Rome's mechanics.° Tell me not   *workmen*
85 Wherein I seem unnatural. Desire not t'allay
My rages and revenges with your colder reasons.
VOLUMNIA   O, no more, no more!

---

2. Rebuked (by Volumnia's irony).
3. Putting an end to the idea of.
4. An easy task of what cannot be.
5. Goddess of the moon and of chastity.

6. When time has clarified its full meaning.
7. Like a landmark at sea, withstanding every gust.
8. Be regarded by you as refusals.

You have said you will not grant us anything—
For we have nothing else to ask but that
90 Which you deny already. Yet we will ask,
That, if you fail in our request, the blame
May hang upon your hardness. Therefore hear us.
CORIOLANUS Aufidius and you Volsces, mark, for we'll
Hear naught from Rome in private.
          [*He sits*]

                                    Your request?
95 VOLUMNIA Should we be silent and not speak, our raiment
And state of bodies would bewray° what life   divulge
We have led since thy exile. Think with thyself
How more unfortunate than all living women
Are we come hither, since that thy sight, which should
100 Make our eyes flow with joy, hearts dance with comforts,
Constrains them weep and shake with fear and sorrow,
Making the mother, wife, and child to see
The son, the husband, and the father tearing
His country's bowels out; and to poor we
105 Thine enmity's most capital.° Thou barr'st us   fatal
Our prayers to the gods, which is a comfort
That all but we enjoy. For how can we,
Alas, how can we for our country pray,
Whereto we are bound, together with thy victory,
110 Whereto we are bound? Alack, or° we must lose   either
The country, our dear nurse, or else thy person,
Our comfort in the country. We must find
An evident° calamity, though we had   A certain
Our wish which side should win. For either thou
115 Must as a foreign recreant° be led   traitor
With manacles thorough our streets, or else
Triumphantly tread on thy country's ruin,
And bear the palm for having bravely shed
Thy wife and children's blood. For myself, son,
120 I purpose not to wait on fortune till
These wars determine.° If I cannot persuade thee   conclude
Rather to show a noble grace to both parts°   sides
Than seek the end of one, thou shalt no sooner
March to assault thy country than to tread—
125 Trust to't, thou shalt not—on thy mother's womb
That brought thee to this world.
VIRGILIA   Ay, and mine,
That brought you forth this boy to keep your name
Living to time.
YOUNG MARTIUS A° shall not tread on me.   He
I'll run away till I am bigger, but then I'll fight.
130 CORIOLANUS Not of a woman's tenderness to be
Requires nor child nor woman's face to see.[9]
I have sat too long.
          [*He rises and turns away*]
VOLUMNIA   Nay, go not from us thus.
If it were so that our request did tend
To save the Romans, thereby to destroy

9. *Not . . . see:* To avoid having a woman's tenderness, a man must not see a child's or woman's face.

135 The Volsces whom you serve, you might condemn us
As poisonous of your honour. No, our suit
Is that you reconcile them: while the Volsces
May say 'This mercy we have showed', the Romans
'This we received', and each in either side
140 Give the all-hail to thee and cry 'Be blest
For making up this peace!' Thou know'st, great son,
The end of war's uncertain; but this certain,
That if thou conquer Rome, the benefit
Which thou shalt thereby reap is such a name
145 Whose repetition will be dogged with curses,
Whose chronicle thus writ:[1] 'The man was noble,
But with his last attempt he wiped it out,
Destroyed his country, and his name remains
To th' ensuing age abhorred.' Speak to me, son.
150 Thou hast affected° the fine strains° of honour,   cherished / qualities
To imitate the graces of the gods,
To tear with thunder the wide cheeks o'th' air,
And yet to charge thy sulphur[2] with a bolt
That should but rive[3] an oak. Why dost not speak?
155 Think'st thou it honourable for a noble man
Still° to remember wrongs? Daughter, speak you,   Perpetually
He cares not for your weeping. Speak thou, boy.
Perhaps thy childishness will move him more
Than can our reasons. There's no man in the world
160 More bound to's mother, yet here he lets me prate
Like one i'th' stocks.[4] Thou hast never in thy life
Showed thy dear mother any courtesy,
When she, poor hen, fond of° no second brood,   desiring
Has clucked thee to the wars and safely home,
165 Loaden with honour. Say my request's unjust,
And spurn me back. But if it be not so,
Thou art not honest, and the gods will plague thee
That thou restrain'st° from me the duty which   withhold'st
To a mother's part belongs.—He turns away.
170 Down, ladies. Let us shame him with our knees.
To his surname 'Coriolanus' 'longs° more pride   belongs
Than pity to our prayers.[5] Down! An end.
This is the last.
         [*The ladies and* YOUNG MARTIUS *kneel*]
                    So we will home to Rome,
And die among our neighbours.—Nay, behold's.
175 This boy, that cannot tell what he would have,
But kneels and holds up hands for fellowship,
Does reason our petition with more strength
Than thou hast to deny't.—Come, let us go.
This fellow had a Volscian to his mother.
180 His wife is in Corioles, and this child
Like him by chance.—Yet give us our dispatch.[6]

---

1. Whose biography will thus be written.
2. To discharge thy thunder (like Jove, king of the gods, whose tree was the oak).
3. Tear (destroy a tree, not human beings).
4. *prate . . . stocks:* rail pointlessly like a prisoner sen-

tenced to public humiliation in the stocks.
5. Volumnia reinterprets the name as a sign of allegiance to Corioles.
6. Dismissal (with wordplay on "deathblow").

I am hushed until our city be afire,
And then I'll speak a little.

        [*He*] *holds her by the hand, silent*

CORIOLANUS   O mother, mother!
What have you done? Behold, the heavens do ope,
185   The gods look down, and this unnatural scene
They laugh at. O my mother, mother, O!
You have won a happy victory to Rome;
But for your son, believe it, O believe it,
Most dangerously you have with him prevailed,
190   If not most mortal to him. But let it come.

        [*The ladies and* YOUNG MARTIUS *rise*]

Aufidius, though I cannot make true° wars,   *(as I vowed)*
I'll frame convenient° peace. Now, good Aufidius,   *suitable*
Were you in my stead would you have heard
A mother less, or granted less, Aufidius?
AUFIDIUS   I was moved withal.°   *as well*
195   CORIOLANUS   I dare be sworn you were.
And, sir, it is no little thing to make
Mine eyes to sweat compassion. But, good sir,
What peace you'll make, advise me. For my part,
I'll not to Rome; I'll back with you, and pray you
200   Stand to° me in this cause.—O mother! Wife!   *by*
AUFIDIUS [*aside*]   I am glad thou hast set thy mercy and thy honour
At difference in thee. Out of that I'll work
Myself a former fortune.[7]
CORIOLANUS [*to* VOLUMNIA *and* VIRGILIA]   Ay, by and by.
But we will drink together, and you shall bear
205   A better witness back than words, which we
On like conditions will have counter-sealed.
Come, enter with us. Ladies, you deserve
To have a temple built you. All the swords
In Italy, and her confederate arms,
210   Could not have made this peace.   *Exeunt*

5.4

   Enter MENENIUS *and* SICINIUS

MENENIUS   See you yon coign° o'th' Capitol, yon cornerstone?   *corner*
SICINIUS   Why, what of that?
MENENIUS   If it be possible for you to displace it with your little
   finger, there is some hope the ladies of Rome, especially his
5   mother, may prevail with him. But I say there is no hope in't,
   our throats are sentenced and stay upon° execution.   *wait for*
SICINIUS   Is't possible that so short a time can alter the condition°   *character*
   of a man?
MENENIUS   There is difference between a grub and a butterfly,
10   yet your butterfly was a grub. This Martius is grown from man
   to dragon. He has wings, he's more than a creeping thing.
SICINIUS   He loved his mother dearly.
MENENIUS   So did he me, and he no more remembers his
   mother now than° an eight-year old horse. The tartness of his   *than does*
15   face sours ripe grapes. When he walks, he moves like an
   engine,° and the ground shrinks before his treading. He is able   *war machine*

---

7. *work . . . fortune:* regain my former preeminence.   **5.4** Location: A public place in Rome.

to pierce a corslet° with his eye, talks like a knell, and his 'hmh!'   *armored shirt*
is a battery.° He sits in his state as a thing made for Alexander.¹   *bombardment*
What he bids be done is finished with his bidding. He wants°   *lacks*
20   nothing of a god but eternity and a heaven to throne in.

SICINIUS   Yes: mercy, if you report him truly.

MENENIUS   I paint him in the character.° Mark what mercy his   *as he is*
mother shall bring from him. There is no more mercy in him
than there is milk in a male tiger. That shall our poor city find;
25   and all this is 'long° of you.   *on account*

SICINIUS   The gods be good unto us!

MENENIUS   No, in such a case the gods will not be good unto
us. When we banished him we respected not them, and, he
returning to break our necks, they respect not us.

Enter a MESSENGER

30   MESSENGER [*to* SICINIUS]   Sir, if you'd save your life, fly to your house.
The plebeians have got your fellow tribune
And hale° him up and down, all swearing if   *drag*
The Roman ladies bring not comfort home
They'll give him death by inches.°   *little by little*

Enter another MESSENGER

SICINIUS   What's the news?

35   SECOND MESSENGER   Good news, good news. The ladies have prevailed,
The Volscians are dislodged,° and Martius gone.   *broken*
A merrier day did never yet greet Rome,
No, not th'expulsion of the Tarquins.

SICINIUS   Friend,
Art thou certain this is true? Is't most certain?

40   SECOND MESSENGER   As certain as I know the sun is fire.
Where have you lurked that you make doubt of it?
Ne'er through an arch so hurried the blown° tide   *swollen*
As the recomforted° through th' gates.   *reinvigorated*

Trumpets, hautboys,° drums, beat all together   *oboes*
                          Why, hark you,
The trumpets, sackbuts, psalteries,° and fifes,   *trombones, zithers*
45   Tabors° and cymbals and the shouting Romans   *Drums*
Make the sun dance.

A shout within

                  Hark you!

MENENIUS   This is good news.
I will go meet the ladies. This Volumnia
Is worth of consuls, senators, patricians,
A city full; of tribunes such as you,
50   A sea and land full. You have prayed well today.
This morning for ten thousand of your throats
I'd not have given a doit.°   *small coin*

[*Music*] *sound*[*s*] *still with the shouts*
              Hark how they joy!

SICINIUS [*to the* MESSENGER]   First, the gods bless you for your tidings. Next,
[*Giving money*] Accept my thankfulness.

55   SECOND MESSENGER   Sir, we have all great cause to give great thanks.

SICINIUS   They are near the city.

---

1. Sits on his throne like a statue of Alexander the Great (who actually postdated Coriolanus).

SECOND MESSENGER   Almost at point to enter.

SICINIUS We'll meet them, and help the joy.   *Exeunt*

5.5

Enter [at one door] Lords [and CITIZENS; *at another*
door] two SENATORS *with [the] ladies [*VOLUMNIA, VIR-
GILIA, *and* VALERIA,*] passing over the stage*

A SENATOR Behold our patroness, the life of Rome!
  Call all your tribes together, praise the gods,
  And make triumphant fires.° Strew flowers before them.   *(of sacrifice)*
  Unshout the noise that banished Martius,
5 Repeal[1] him with the welcome of his mother.
  Cry 'Welcome, ladies, welcome!'

ALL   Welcome, ladies, welcome!

A flourish with drums and trumpets. Exeunt

5.6

Enter Tullus AUFIDIUS *with attendants*

AUFIDIUS Go tell the lords o'th' city I am here.
  Deliver them this paper. Having read it,
  Bid them repair to th' market-place, where I,
  Even in theirs and in the commons' ears,
5 Will vouch the truth of it. Him I accuse
  The city ports° by this° hath entered, and   *gates / this time*
  Intends t'appear before the people, hoping
  To purge himself with words. Dispatch.   [*Exeunt attendants*]

Enter three or four CONSPIRATORS *of Aufidius' faction*

                                  Most welcome.

FIRST CONSPIRATOR How is it with our general?

AUFIDIUS   Even so
10 As with a man by his own alms impoisoned,
  And with his charity slain.

SECOND CONSPIRATOR   Most noble sir,
  If you do hold the same intent wherein
  You wished us parties,° we'll deliver you   *allies*
  Of° your great danger.   *From*

AUFIDIUS   Sir, I cannot tell.
15 We must proceed as we do find the people.

THIRD CONSPIRATOR The people will remain uncertain whilst
  'Twixt you there's difference,° but the fall of either   *disagreement*
  Makes the survivor heir of all.

AUFIDIUS   I know it,
  And my pretext to strike at him admits
20 A good construction.° I raised him, and I pawned   *interpretation*
  Mine honour for his truth; who being so heightened,
  He watered his new plants[1] with dews of flattery,
  Seducing so my friends; and to this end
  He bowed his nature, never known before
25 But to be rough, unswayable, and free.

THIRD CONSPIRATOR Sir, his stoutness°   *stubbornness*
  When he did stand for consul, which he lost
  By lack of stooping—

5.5 Location: Near the city gates of Rome.   **5.6** Location: Corioles.
1. Recall him from banishment.   1. Followers (formerly Aufidius's adherents).

AUFIDIUS   That I would have spoke of.
    Being banished for't, he came unto my hearth,
30   Presented to my knife his throat. I took him,
    Made him joint-servant° with me, gave him way   *partner*
    In all his own desires; nay, let him choose
    Out of my files,° his projects to accomplish,   *troops*
    My best and freshest men; served his designments°   *plans*
35   In mine own person, holp to reap the fame
    Which he did end all his,[2] and took some pride
    To do myself this wrong, till at the last
    I seemed his follower, not partner, and
    He waged° me with his countenance° as if   *paid / appearance*
    I had been mercenary.
40 FIRST CONSPIRATOR   So he did, my lord.
    The army marvelled at it, and in the last,
    When he had carried° Rome and that we looked   *was about to vanquish*
    For no less spoil than glory—
AUFIDIUS   There was it,
    For which my sinews shall be stretched upon him.
45   At a few drops of women's rheum,° which are   *tears*
    As cheap as lies, he sold the blood and labour
    Of our great action; therefore shall he die,
    And I'll renew me in his fall.
         Drums and trumpets sound, with great shouts of the
         people
              But hark.
FIRST CONSPIRATOR   Your native town you entered like a post,[3]
50   And had no welcomes home; but he returns
    Splitting the air with noise.
SECOND CONSPIRATOR   And patient fools,
    Whose children he hath slain, their base throats tear
    With giving him glory.
THIRD CONSPIRATOR   Therefore, at your vantage,°   *best opportunity*
    Ere he express himself or move the people
55   With what he would say, let him feel your sword,
    Which we will second. When he lies along,°   *prostrate*
    After your way° his tale pronounced shall bury   *In your version*
    His reasons with his body.
      Enter the LORDS *of the city*
AUFIDIUS   Say no more.
    Here come the lords.
60 ALL THE LORDS   You are most welcome home.
AUFIDIUS   I have not deserved it.
    But, worthy lords, have you with heed perused
    What I have written to you?
ALL THE LORDS   We have.
FIRST LORD   And grieve to hear't.
    What faults he made before the last, I think
65   Might have found easy fines.° But there to end   *light penalties*
    Where he was to begin, and give away
    The benefit of our levies,° answering us   *levied troops*

---

2. Which he did conclude was (or did finally make)   3. Messenger (bearing news of Coriolanus).
entirely his own.

With our own charge,[4] making a treaty where
There was a yielding—this admits no excuse.

70 AUFIDIUS   He approaches. You shall hear him.

Enter CORIOLANUS *marching with drum and colors, the*
Commoners being with him

CORIOLANUS   Hail, lords! I am returned your soldier,
No more infected with my country's love
Than when I parted hence, but still subsisting
Under your great command. You are to know
75 That prosperously[5] I have attempted, and
With bloody passage led your wars even to
The gates of Rome. Our spoils we have brought home
Doth more than counterpoise a full third part[6]
The charges of the action. We have made peace
80 With no less honour to the Antiates
Than shame to th' Romans. And we here deliver,
Subscribed by th' consuls and patricians,
Together with the seal o'th' senate, what
We have compounded° on.   agreed

He gives the LORDS *a paper*

AUFIDIUS   Read it not, noble lords,
85 But tell the traitor in the highest degree
He hath abused your powers.

CORIOLANUS   Traitor? How now?

AUFIDIUS   Ay, traitor, Martius.

CORIOLANUS   Martius?

90 AUFIDIUS   Ay, Martius, Caius Martius. Dost thou think
I'll grace thee with that robbery, thy stol'n name,
'Coriolanus', in Corioles?
You lords and heads o'th' state, perfidiously
He has betrayed your business, and given up,
95 For certain drops of salt,° your city, Rome—   (tears)
I say your city—to his wife and mother,
Breaking his oath and resolution like
A twist° of rotten silk, never admitting   thread
Counsel o'th' war.[7] But at his nurse's tears
100 He whined and roared away your victory,
That pages[8] blushed at him, and men of heart°   courage
Looked wond'ring each at others.

CORIOLANUS   Hear'st thou, Mars?

AUFIDIUS   Name not the god, thou boy of tears.

CORIOLANUS   Ha?

AUFIDIUS   No more.

CORIOLANUS   Measureless liar, thou hast made my heart
105 Too great for what contains it. 'Boy'? O slave!—
Pardon me, lords, 'tis the first time that ever
I was forced to scold. Your judgements, my grave lords,
Must give this cur the lie, and his own notion°—   awareness of the truth
Who wears my stripes° impressed upon him, that   wounds

4. *answering . . . charge*: rewarding us with our own costs
(of mounting the campaign); answering accusations by
saying that he acted on our authority.
5. Successfully; with gain of wealth.

6. Outweighs by more than a third.
7. *admitting . . . war*: taking any advice about the war.
8. Youthful servants.

110 Must bear my beating to his grave—shall join
To thrust° the lie unto him.   *turn the accusation of*
FIRST LORD   Peace both, and hear me speak.
CORIOLANUS   Cut me to pieces, Volsces. Men and lads,
Stain all your edges° on me. 'Boy'! False hound,   *sword blades*
If you have writ your annals true, 'tis there
115 That, like an eagle in a dove-cote,° I   *pigeon house*
Fluttered your Volscians in Corioles.
Alone I did it. 'Boy'!
AUFIDIUS   Why, noble lords,
Will you be put in mind of his blind⁹ fortune,
Which was your shame, by this unholy braggart,
Fore your own eyes and ears?
120 ALL THE CONSPIRATORS   Let him die for't.
ALL THE PEOPLE [*shouting dispersedly*]   Tear him to pieces! Do
         it presently!°   *immediately*
He killed my son! My daughter! He killed my cousin
Marcus! He killed my father!
SECOND LORD   Peace, ho! No outrage,° peace.   *violence*
The man is noble, and his fame folds in°   *envelops*
125 This orb o'th' earth. His last offences to us
Shall have judicious hearing. Stand,° Aufidius,   *Hold off*
And trouble not the peace.
CORIOLANUS [*drawing his sword*]   O that I had him with six Aufidiuses,
Or more, his tribe, to use my lawful sword!
AUFIDIUS [*drawing his sword*]   Insolent villain!
130 ALL THE CONSPIRATORS   Kill, kill, kill, kill, kill him!
         [*Two*] CONSPIRATORS *draw and kill* MARTIUS, *who falls.*
         AUFIDIUS [*and* CONSPIRATORS] *stand on him*
LORDS   Hold, hold, hold, hold!
AUFIDIUS   My noble masters, hear me speak.
FIRST LORD   O Tullus!
SECOND LORD [*to* AUFIDIUS]   Thou hast done a deed whereat
Valour will weep.
THIRD LORD [*to* AUFIDIUS *and the* CONSPIRATORS]
                         Tread not upon him, masters.
All be quiet. Put up your swords.
135 AUFIDIUS   My lords,
When you shall know—as in this rage
Provoked by him you cannot—the great danger
Which this man's life did owe° you, you'll rejoice   *hold in store for*
That he is thus cut off. Please it your honours
140 To call me to your senate, I'll deliver°   *show*
Myself your loyal servant, or endure
Your heaviest censure.
FIRST LORD   Bear from hence his body,
And mourn you for him. Let him be regarded
As the most noble corpse that ever herald
Did follow to his urn.
145 SECOND LORD   His own impatience
Takes from Aufidius a great part of blame.
Let's make the best of it.
AUFIDIUS   My rage is gone,

9. Random (fortune was commonly personified as blind).

And I am struck with sorrow. Take him up.
Help three o'th' chiefest soldiers; I'll be one.
150 Beat thou the drum, that it speak mournfully.
Trail your steel pikes. Though in this city he
Hath widowed and unchilded many a one,
Which to this hour bewail the injury,
Yet he shall have a noble memory.° Assist.   memorial
                    A dead march sounded. Exeunt
                    bearing the body of Martius

The Winter's Tale

In his induction to *Bartholomew Fair* (1614), Ben Jonson complained of plays that "make Nature afraid" and "beget Tales, Tempests, and such like Drolleries." His remarks seem aimed directly at his contemporary William Shakespeare, who, in the last years of his theatrical career, had written a number of plays, including *The Winter's Tale* (1609–11) and *The Tempest* (1611), that by some accounts might be said to "make Nature afraid." Jonson implies that such plays, eschewing realism, present fantastic or impossible events that defy the laws of nature. While Jonson found such concoctions unpalatable, most of Shakespeare's contemporaries did not. In prose romances popular throughout the period, characters regularly undertake impossible quests, encounter marvels, and are unexpectedly reunited with lost children. Shakespeare's late plays participate fully in this taste for the marvelous, reveling in, rather than being embarrassed by, the strange and the improbable. In the case of *The Winter's Tale*, we possess a rather full description of the play by Simon Forman, a London astrologer and doctor, who saw it performed on May 15, 1611, and described its complicated plot with no hint that he found either its events absurd or the play defective. On the contrary, Forman's detailed description suggests him to have been fully absorbed by what he saw. Concluding with an account of the deceptive tricks of the play's rogue, Autolycus, Forman moralized: "Beware trusting feigned beggars or fawning fellows."

Modern editors often group *Pericles*, *The Winter's Tale*, *Cymbeline*, and *The Tempest* together under the label "romances," although this is not a category used in the Folio (1623). There Shakespeare's plays are divided into comedies, tragedies, and histories. *Pericles* is not included in the Folio; *Cymbeline* is placed at the end of the tragedies; *The Tempest* appears as the first of the comedies and *The Winter's Tale* as the last. These placements are suggestive of the mixed tragicomic nature of these particular dramas. Like Shakespeare's earlier comedies, they all end happily, with families reunited and marriages in prospect; but the late plays also engage with the tragic dimensions of human life to a degree not customary for the early comedies. Before the characters in these plays reach safe harbor, they encounter tyranny, incest, the loss of wives and children, and the treachery of brothers. The protagonists suffer intensely, both because of fortune's blows and because of their own folly. Only by what is experienced as miracle does tragedy turn to mirth and suffering cease. While the miraculous quality of these reversals binds these plays together as a group, it is also at the heart of Jonson's objections. Improbable occurrences and unexpected transformations of sorrow into joy can affront sober common sense, but they also make romance emotionally and theatrically appealing. In defiance of probability, these plays construct a world in which (at least for some fortunate characters) second chances are possible.

By its very title *The Winter's Tale* signals its affiliations with popular storytelling. Within the play, Mamillius, the King of Sicilia's young son, informs his mother that "a sad tale's best for winter" (2.1.27) and offers to tell her one "of sprites and goblins" (2.1.28). The only sprites and goblins in Shakespeare's play turn out to be the internal demons of jealousy and suspicion that erupt in the mind of its protagonist, King Leontes, but *The Winter's Tale* is permeated by sadness, even during its festive conclusion, and its plot is full of wonders. Its starting point is King Leontes' sudden certainty that his wife, Hermione, is pregnant not with his own child, but with that of his childhood friend, King Polixenes of Bohemia, a visitor at Leontes' Sicilian court. Warned of Leontes' jealousy, Polixenes flees back to Bohemia, leaving the King to vent his wrath on Hermione. Imprisoned, she gives birth to a daughter, Perdita, whom Leontes orders

In the early seventeenth century, popular pamphlet literature circulated sensational stories of parents, especially unmarried women, who murdered or abandoned their children. In this title page from *The Bloudy Mother* (1609), a serving woman and her master bury the illegitimate child she has killed. On the right, for his part in begetting and disposing of the child, the master is consumed by lice and worms.

to be abandoned in the countryside far from Sicilia. Even when the oracle of Apollo subsequently declares Hermione innocent, Leontes continues to insist on her guilt. As he does, the death of his only son, Mamillius, is announced, and Hermione appears to die of grief. The first three acts of *The Winter's Tale* thus enact a miniature tragedy (not unlike Shakespeare's tragedy of the jealous Othello) in which Leontes' actions result in the loss of wife, daughter, and son. His personal tragedy also affects his kingdom. The oracle proclaims: "the King shall live without an heir if that which is lost be not found" (3.2.133–34). A kingdom without an heir to the throne is a kingdom in danger.

But then something extraordinary happens. The character Time appears onstage, informing the audience that sixteen years have passed and that Perdita, abandoned on the seacoast of Bohemia, has survived. Suddenly, instead of the wintry world of Leontes' Sicilian court, the play bursts with the energies of a Bohemian summer. The

Old Shepherd who rescued Perdita is about to hold a sheepshearing festival, and Florizel, King Polixenes' son, has fallen in love with Perdita. A series of extraordinary events returns the young couple to Leontes' court, where Perdita's true status as his child and heir is revealed. More wonders follow. Taken to see what they believe to be a statue of the long-dead Hermione, the King and his newly recovered daughter witness the seeming miracle of the statue's transformation into flesh and blood.

Shakespeare's chief source for this tale was Robert Greene's popular prose romance *Pandosto,* first published in 1588. Greene provided Shakespeare with the story of a jealous King who loses Queen and daughter but eventually has his daughter restored to him. But the differences between Shakespeare's play and Greene's prose tale are as striking as the similarities. For example, Shakespeare carefully changed the names of most of the characters he borrowed from Greene. In *Pandosto,* the King's lost daughter is Fawnia, but Shakespeare names her Perdita, a word that in Latin means "that which is lost." In Shakespeare's hands, Perdita's lover ceases to be Dorastus and becomes, instead, Florizel, which suggests the young prince's connection with the flowers of spring. Greene's protagonist, Pandosto, is transformed into Leontes, evoking the leonine or lionlike nature of his wrath. Shakespeare also reversed the kingdoms ruled by Greene's Kings. In *Pandosto,* the protagonist is King of Bohemia and his childhood friend rules Sicilia. In *The Winter's Tale,* the reverse is true, and one reason may be the association of Sicilia with the myth of Proserpina, the beautiful daughter of Ceres abducted by Dis, the god of the underworld, as she was picking flowers. Her mother attempted to free Proserpina, but she was allowed to return to the upper world only six months of each year. During that period, spring and summer came to the earth, but winter reigned when Proserpina returned to Dis's kingdom. The sixteen years of mourning Leontes undergoes in Perdita's absence provide a counterpart to aspects of this myth.

Shakespeare, however, made much larger changes in Greene's romance. For example, he enhanced the role of Leontes' son, who is barely mentioned by Greene; he added the characters of Paulina, Emilia, Antigonus, Autolycus, Clown, Time, and rustics such as Dorcas and Mopsa (in *Pandosto,* Mopsa was the name of the Old Shepherd's wife; in *The Winter's Tale,* that wife is long dead). The magnificent sheepshearing festival is Shakespeare's invention; nothing like it exists in *Pandosto.* Most importantly, Greene's romance ends on a tragic note. Although the King and his daughter are finally reunited, Pandosto's wife is never restored to him, and overcome with desire for his grown daughter, he attempts incest and later takes his own life.

Shakespeare clearly saw in Greene's grim tale the basis for a much more resonant narrative of loss and redemption. The play is a diptych of winter and summer, hinged by the appearance of Time. It is probably a mistake to account for this structure by using only one interpretive framework, for the play's elegant simplicity resonates with many narratives of renewal. Some have read the play in Christian terms, seeing Leontes as a sinner who, after a period of suffering and repentance, receives the gift of God's grace through the return of his daughter and the Christlike resurrection of his wife. The play loosely traces the liturgical calendar, moving from the hospitality associated with Christmas to the Lenten period of deprivation and repentance to the joyous celebration of Easter and the Maying festivals associated with Whitsuntide, which occurs seven weeks after Easter. Other critics have stressed the mythic qualities of the play, its resemblance, for example, to the myth of Proserpina, or to fertility rites in which the coming of spring and sexual fulfillment depend on the sacrifice of a figure, usually an old King, associated with winter. In *The Winter's Tale,* Leontes does not die, but he does mourn for sixteen years; and his servant Antigonus, who takes the babe to Bohemia and there names her Perdita, becomes Leontes' sacrificial substitute. Once he has deposited Perdita, Antigonus is mauled and eaten by a bear. As the Old Shepherd who rescues Perdita says to his son, who has witnessed this death, "Thou metst with things dying, I with things new-born" (3.3.104–05), the latter event seemingly dependent on the former. Other critics stress the pattern of generational renewal informing the play as the sins of the father, Leontes, give way to the innocent goodness of Florizel and Perdita. In some productions, the actress playing Hermione also plays Perdita (although a double for one of them usually has to be employed in the statue scene when they are both on stage together), deepening the sense that it is through their children that parents have a second life. Resonating with all these interpretive paradigms, *The Winter's Tale* draws richly on the many narratives and structures of belief through which Western culture has produced and sustained its desire for transcendence and renewal.

In modern productions, the symbolic power of the play's diptych structure is often highlighted by contrasts in the costumes and sets used to distinguish Sicilia and Bohemia. Sicilia, for example, is often a snow kingdom, dominated by white clothing and metallic props; Bohemia is a summer kingdom, the stage carpeted in green, the characters at the sheepshearing festival a riot of variegated colors. When the Bohemian party comes to Sicilia, the winter landscape is literally overwritten with the colorful clothes associated with Whitsuntide.

The play, however, is not simply about the triumph of the young, the rebirth of a world of possibility. *The Winter's Tale*, as befits a tragicomedy, moves from sorrow to joy, but that joy is bittersweet. However important the younger generation is to this old tale, the focus in this and the other romances stays resolutely on the older generation. It is Leontes who sins and must repent, Leontes whose family is reconstituted. Crucially, that reconstitution is only partial and imperfect. Mamillius, the young son, dies, the ultimate sacrifice to Leontes' tyrannous actions; and in the play's last scene, the playwright is at pains to stress that the "statue" of Hermione has wrinkles, the mark of time on her body. Traduced while a fertile wife and mother, Hermione returns as a woman past childbearing. Time, whose appearance marks the hinge of the play, may heal old sorrows and bring new births to pass, but it also shuts down possibilities and destroys youth and strength. The ending of Shakespeare's old tale induces wonder and joy, but it cannot make an old man young or erase all the consequences of rash deeds. Shakespeare's late plays achieve their rich emotional effects from the deep strains of melancholia that underwrite their measured celebrations of the return of love and hope to a chastened social order.

Nor, despite the archaic quality that permeates these plays, are they simple enactments of timeless patterns and narratives. The precipitating event of the play—the eruption of Leontes' jealousy—is a symptom of the faultlines in a particular patriarchal culture. Often said to be "irrational," this jealousy in actuality has its roots in the cultural practices that in Jacobean England made men the heads of families, lineages, and kingdoms, but at the same time made them crucially dependent on women's reproductive powers to generate legitimate heirs. As *The Winter's Tale* opens, Leontes asks Polixenes to extend his stay in Sicilia. Polixenes refuses, but when Hermione entreats him, he agrees. This event, and the sight of his pregnant wife conversing with his friend and holding him by the hand, triggers in Leontes so deep a suspicion of his wife's fidelity that he plans to have Polixenes killed and doubts the legitimacy of his son as well. In part, what disturbs Leontes is the unknowability of the biological origins of his children. Men theoretically had dominion over their wives, but as Leontes says, "No barricado for a belly" (1.2.205)—that is, no absolute defense of a woman's chastity but her own honor, and that lies in her control, not her husband's.

A deep ambivalence toward women and sexuality, moreover, surfaces earlier in the same scene when, reminiscing about his boyhood friendship with Leontes, Polixenes describes the two of them as twinned lambs who experienced a fall from paradise only when they felt sexual passion and had their first encounters with women. In this conversation, the two men echo a strand of early modern thought that viewed men's friendships with men as of greater worth than what were seen as men's more dangerous and unpredictable relations with women, an idea examined as early in Shakespeare's work as *The Two Gentlemen of Verona*. Construed as physically imperfect and as intellectually inferior to men, women were supposedly ruled by their passions and could in turn evoke dangerous and degrading emotions in men. Yet men were enjoined to marry these irrational creatures to procreate and to continue family lineage. Leontes' rage at Hermione seems to stem in part from his dependence on her to give him legitimate heirs.

Other tensions permeate the opening scenes. If in their younger days Polixenes and Leontes were like twinned lambs, in adulthood their friendship is tinged with competitiveness, with Hermione gradually becoming the focus of their rivalry. Polixenes' attendant Archidamus opens the play expressing uneasiness about repaying the generous hospitality provided by Leontes and suggesting rivalry as well as friendship between the two kingdoms; in 1.2 Leontes asks Polixenes if he loves *his* son as dearly as Leontes loves Mamillius, again suggesting competitiveness between the two Kings at the level of paternal affection for their sons. In this general context of subterranean rivalry, Leontes' command that Hermione entreat Polixenes to stay not only expresses his ostentatious generosity (he will even share his wife's attentions with his friend), but also calls forth his rivalrous jealousy (perhaps his friend has taken advantage of his generosity and assumed Leontes' place in Hermione's bed).

Once his jealousy has been triggered, Leontes gives the rein to a deadly rage that finds its chief object in Hermione's pregnant body. This anger is played out in part through Leontes' increasing identification with his young son, Mamillius. In Mamillius, Leontes sees himself as he once was, a young boy not yet wearing either the breeches or the sharp phallic dagger associated with adult manhood (1.2.157–58). It is an image of innocence but also of vulnerability. The name Mamillius, another of Shakespeare's brilliant inventions, suggests one source of that vulnerability. *Mamilla* is the word for the nipple on a breast or a diminutive form of *mamma,* the Latin word for the breast itself. His name thus connects Mamillius to the lactating breast and to the world of women, who in early modern culture presided over childbirth and the early years of children's lives. In a culture in which baby formula did not exist, infants depended utterly on women, either wet nurses or mothers, to provide the crucial sustenance, breast milk. As was often true of women from the upper class, Hermione does not herself seem to have nursed Mamillius. As Leontes bitterly exclaims: "I am glad you did not nurse him" (2.1.58). Nonetheless, the young boy's name and his appearance in 2.1 with his pregnant mother and her waiting women clearly associate him with the feminine sphere of birth, lactation, and early childhood. In identifying with Mamillius, a boy so young his nurse's milk is scarcely out of him, Leontes seems to feel both the vulnerability of the infant dependent on the lactating body of woman and the vulnerability of the adult husband dependent on the pregnant body and the chastity of his wife for legitimate offspring. As if to deny these dependencies, Leontes banishes Mamillius from his mother's presence, and he banishes Hermione to prison. Mamillius dies; Leontes appears to lose all that would link him to the future: wife, son, daughter.

The Winter's Tale makes Leontes a dangerous tyrant in Acts 1 to 3 and portrays his anger and paranoia as forces that torture his speech and profoundly isolate him. In the first three acts, Leontes' most characteristic action is to turn away from those who love or attempt to help him. He sends his wife to prison; casts out his infant daughter; refuses the good counsel of his courtiers; rages in misogynistic fury at Paulina, who brings Perdita to him from prison; and finally defies the oracle of Apollo. Lacking trust in his wife and in all those around him, Leontes condemns himself to deathlike isolation. As in Shakespeare's other late plays, much of the language of *The Winter's Tale* is difficult and dense. Normal word order is inverted; speeches begin and end in the middle of a line; figurative language is given elliptical expression. During his period of intense jealousy, Leontes' language becomes even more dense and compressed than is typical of the rest of the play. Looking at his son, he exclaims:

> Can thy dam—may't be?—
> Affection, thy intention stabs the centre.
> Thou dost make possible things not so held,
> Communicat'st with dreams—how can this be?—

With what's unreal thou coactive art,
And fellow'st nothing. Then 'tis very credent
Thou mayst co-join with something, and thou dost—
And that beyond commission; and I find it—
And that to the infection of my brains
And hard'ning of my brows.

(1.2.139–48)

In this difficult passage, Leontes wrestles with the knowledge that his "affection" (the passions of rage, jealousy, and suspicion released in him) wounds him and perhaps leads him to imagine things to be true that are not. On the other hand, his suspicions *may* be justified; he may already be a cuckold. In this horrible state of uncertainty, Leontes' speech verges on incoherence. He interrupts the flow of his own thoughts with questions and ejaculations; his mind darts from boy to mother to his own pain; he realizes he may be wrong, but returns, obsessively, to the coarse and shameful image of his forehead disfigured with the horns of a cuckold.

The inner disorder suggested by this language finds its outward manifestation in Leontes' increasingly tyrannical actions. In the early modern period, the ruler of a king-

In the early modern period, childbirth was largely the affair of women. In this picture from Jakob Rüff's *De conceptu et generatione hominis* (Concerning the conception and birth of man) (1580), several women attend to a woman in labor while, in the background, two men cast the child's horoscope.

dom was often compared to the head of a family. Good order in the commonwealth had its foundation in a well-ordered domestic realm. In *The Winter's Tale*, Leontes oversteps his just authority in both domains, refusing to take counsel from his courtiers, defying the gods, and condemning his wife for adultery with no evidence but his own suspicions. Nowhere, however, does he more certainly exceed his patriarchal authority than when he orders Hermione to stand trial before the proper period of her lying-in has passed. In the Renaissance, childbirth was recognized as an event both important and dangerous. Women gave birth surrounded by other women, usually a hired midwife, as well as by neighbors and female family members. The laboring female body, opened to let the child pass into the world, was considered to be in a particularly vulnerable state, needing to be protected from the unhealthful air that might enter the open womb. Consequently, birthing took place in a closed chamber, and after birth had occurred, women lay in their chambers for an extended period, recovering strength and purging their bodies of the blood and other fluids associated with pregnancy. At the end of this period, often lasting a month but sometimes longer, the woman came out of her house and returned to her normal routines. This occasion was marked by a "churching" ceremony, a rite of purification and celebration in which thanks were given for the safe delivery of a child and the woman's body declared cleansed of the impurities of pregnancy and birth.

When Hermione is made to stand trial, the pathos of her dignified defense of herself is heightened by her weakened state. In many productions, she appears on stage unattended, almost unable to stand. Among the wrongs done her, she accuses Leontes of having "with immodest hatred / The childbed privilege denied, which 'longs / To women of all fashion; lastly, hurried / Here, to this place, i'th' open air, before / I have got strength of limit" (3.2.100–04). Leontes' fury against the maternal body extends to denying that body the privileges of the lying-in period and exposing it to the dangers of the open air of a public place. This is domestic tyranny of a hideous sort.

After such cruelty, what recovery? Bohemia seems to be the place of hope in the play, and that feeling is conveyed in part by the vast expansion of character and event in that pastoral locale. After the claustrophobic focus on Leontes, the action unfolds to encompass the tricks of a wily rogue, Autolycus (whose name links him to the Autolycus of classical mythology, a crafty thief and grandfather of Ulysses; Autolycus's own father, Mercury, was the god of thieves); the sports of a sheepshearing festival; the courtship of Florizel and Perdita; and the intrigues that take many of these players back to Sicilia. The scene depicting the festival at the Old Shepherd's farm, 4.4, is one of the longest in Shakespeare's canon (810 lines), is entirely his own invention, and is a great feast of languages and events. It includes the singing of ballads, a dance of twelve satyrs, Perdita's lyrical catalog of the flowers appropriate to each stage of life, and the painful moment when Polixenes forbids his son's marriage.

As this last moment shows, although Bohemia is a place of healing, it is not a paradise. In Bohemia, "great creating nature" for a time replaces Apollo as the deity who presides over the action. The fertility of the earth and, by extension, the fertility of woman may here seem to be redeemed from the curse laid upon them by Leontes' suspicion of his wife; and Florizel's staunch commitment to Perdita in the face of mounting obstacles to their love augers well. But Polixenes just as staunchly opposes their union, threatening to use his patriarchal power in a way that, as with Leontes, would separate him from his son and from the possibility of future lineage. Bohemia also contains the rogue Autolycus, picking the pockets of country bumpkins and hiding his identity by a series of disguises. Further, Bohemian life is marked by enormous disparities of wealth. The Old Shepherd is rich, in part because of the money he found with Perdita. For the sheepshearing feast, Perdita can afford ingredients—raisins, rice, and spices, for example—that were exotic luxury goods, foodstuffs in excess of the subsistence diet of bread, beer, and cheese that was still the staple for many. It also possible that some of the Old Shepherd's wealth comes from the new profitability of raising sheep. Throughout the sixteenth and seventeenth centuries, land was increasingly enclosed—that is,

In this late seventeenth-century woodcut from the Pepysian collection of early modern ballads, a peddler carries a huge pack and holds several rabbits, or conies, which suggests that he is also a cony-catcher—that is, a con man (like Autolycus), whose victims were popularly called conies.

fenced off for grazing sheep rather than available for communal use in raising food and feeding cattle. These enclosures were popularly blamed for perceived increases in rural poverty and for the creation of masterless men, poor folk who roamed the countryside without fixed places of residence and who were believed to feign sickness or deformity in order to enforce charity from those they met. Autolycus, pretending to have lost his c'othes to a highwayman, is a comic version of such a masterless man, yet his presence in the play, juxtaposed to that of the rich shepherd, is a reminder of the social tensions and economic stratifications that permeate the rural landscape with widespread enclosures and other changes in rural life.

Bohemia is also the locale of one of the great set pieces of the play—the debate between Polixenes and Perdita concerning the relative values of art and nature and the relationship between them. This was an ancient debate and one that could give off a decidedly musty odor, even though it was dusted off by a number of Shakespeare's contemporaries. At the heart of this debate lay the question of artifice. Was it a good thing? Did it distort or enhance nature? Given the imperfections of the fallen world and humankind's weaknesses, could art be instrumental in calling into being a better world, or was it merely a temptation to pride or to competition with the divine creator? The refreshing thing about the handling of these issues in *The Winter's Tale* is that the play comes to no abstract resolution concerning them. Rather, it encases the actual debate between Polixenes and Perdita in multiple ironies, and it complexly connects this debate to the actions of characters who seemingly have no involvement with it. For Perdita, product of the pastoral landscape, art is a bad thing. She wants no grafted or hybrid flowers in her garden. Yet even as she speaks her condemnation of art, Perdita is reluctantly dressed as Queen of the sheepshearing feast, a bit of artifice that reveals a truth she herself cannot know: namely, that she is a Queen's daughter. Polixenes, for his part, champions art, declaring that the practice of mixing wild and cultivated plants produces sturdy hybrids and that the art of grafting is itself a gift of nature. Yet when his son wishes to graft himself to a shepherd's daughter, Polixenes finds such a practice abhorrent.

Besides making the obvious point that people don't always act on their stated beliefs, this exchange shows the extreme pressure the play puts on the art-nature dichotomy. In Perdita's case, her "natural" condition as princess is revealed only by means of two kinds of artifice: her dress as Queen of the feast and the role Camillo creates for her as Florizel's Libyan Princess when he devises a way for the two young lovers to return to Leontes' court. Camillo even goes so far as to provide lines for the two to speak. His goal is ameliorative: to satisfy the desires of the young (as well as his own deep longings to again see his homeland) and to heal the breach between the two dissevered kingdoms. The point seems to be not whether in some abstract sense "art" violates "nature," but how artfulness, defined broadly as the representation of the world through painting, statuary, plays, and song, can open new possibilities for imagining what nature is or could be.

This is not an inconsequential point, for in the badly flawed world depicted in *The Winter's Tale* art gradually emerges as one of the resources people can use, either badly

or well, to affect the world around them: to correct old mistakes and to forge new realities. Its effects are determined and limited, of course, by the skill and intentions of the
artist and by the receptiveness of the audience. Autolycus is a subversive con man who
uses disguises and deceptions to fleece money from gulls. By contrast, in the play's final
movement, Paulina emerges as the chief representative of the ameliorative artist who
uses her skills to make better the world around her. Once reviled by Leontes as a witch,
Paulina becomes the King's spiritual guide in the last half of the play (her name linking
her to the New Testament evangelist, St. Paul). This strikingly outspoken woman spends
sixteen years preparing Leontes to be a fit spectator to the tableau of resurrection and
renewal enacted in the last scene. When she had first brought the infant to Leontes from
prison, Paulina had seemed to believe in the self-evident nature of truth. Laying the babe
at Leontes' feet, she proclaimed that the "good goddess Nature" (2.3.104) had made it
an exact copy of the father. Leontes had only to read what nature had written in the face
of his child. But distorting jealousy and rage at his wife had bleared the King's vision.
He would not or could not see himself in the female child he had fathered. So for sixteen years Paulina worked another way, fueling Leontes' remorse and artfully withholding both from him and from the theater audience the knowledge that Hermione lived.
When the disguised Princess returns to Sicilia, Leontes gets a second chance. Looking
at Perdita, he is finally able to see—not so much himself as the unslandered image of
his wife in the young girl before him. Having admired Perdita, Leontes says to Paulina,
"I thought of her [Hermione] / Even in these looks I made" (5.1.226–27). When he can
believe in the potential goodness of women, and specifically in the chastity of the young
woman who is the simulacrum of his wife, then Leontes can help to create the reality
in which Perdita is truly a Princess and his wife a living being rather than the corpse into
which his rage and distrust had transformed her.

   The statue scene itself is one of the most moving dramatic moments in any of
Shakespeare's plays. Like Leontes, the untutored audience does not know that
Hermione lives. Consequently, under Paulina's careful guidance, the spectators both
onstage and off seem to participate in willing the statue into life. When Hermione
descends from her pedestal, the audience can feel itself present at the miraculous resurrection of the dead. In theological terms, this scene touches on controversial matters. Protestants repudiated what they characterized as Catholic idolatry, which
involved the veneration of images, including statues of the Virgin Mary. Protestants, by
contrast, typically stressed the ear over the eye, words over images, faith over works. In
the wake of the Reformation, more radical Protestants went so far as to smash stained-
glass windows and the statues of saints that had for many centuries adorned Catholic
churches. The final moments of *The Winter's Tale* gesture toward this repudiated world
of images and their veneration. While Paulina insists that the audience awaken its faith,
she does so in a scene that is visually organized to focus all eyes on a statue that in its
chapel setting might well evoke memories of prior Catholic practices. In his characteristic way, Shakespeare seems to have things two ways: drawing on the emotional
power of Catholic rituals centered on the image, he simultaneously suggests that there
is no statue on the stage at all, only a living woman roused to new vigor by the recovery of a long-lost daughter.

   However ambiguous the theological implications of the final scene, ultimately the
old tale ends happily, or mostly so. At the end of the play, patriarchy has been reformed,
but its potential for abuses has hardly been eradicated. In the final scene, the highly
charged image of the pregnant female body is nowhere to be seen. Perdita is not yet a
wife; both Paulina and Hermione are probably too old for childbearing. For Perdita and
Florizel perhaps the greatest tests of faith and mutuality lie ahead, when Perdita's transformation from maid into wife and mother will present new occasions for jealousy and
distrust. Moreover, in *The Winter's Tale* the remembrance of things that were lost and
can never be regained intrudes even on the celebration of the return of Perdita and of
Hermione. Paulina pointedly recalls her husband, Antigonus, lost in carrying Perdita to
Bohemia; Hermione speaks to Perdita of the sixteen long years of their separation; her

wrinkles attest to other losses; Mamillius is gone forever. The point of *The Winter's Tale* hardly seems to be that folly has no consequences or that earthly paradise is possible. Those claims would indeed make nature afraid. Rather, the play celebrates the true miracle of partial restorations, of moments of exquisite joy wrested by work, art, and good fortune from the pains of the imperfect world that men and women have made.

JEAN E. HOWARD

TEXTUAL NOTE

The Winter's Tale was first printed in the Folio of 1623 at the end of the group of comedies. Simon Forman, a London doctor, saw a performance at the Globe on May 15, 1611, and it was performed at court on November 11 of that year. Its exact date of composition, however, is unknown. Largely on stylistic evidence and because *The Winter's Tale* is at several points indebted to Plutarch, a principal source for Shakespeare's classical tragedies such as *Coriolanus* (1608), the Oxford editors place the date of composition in 1609, before *Cymbeline*. Other editors believe the play was written late in 1610 or early in 1611 before the May performance witnessed by Forman. In Act 4, Scene 4, working men at the sheepshearing festival perform a satyr dance that resembles a dance in Ben Jonson's *Masque of Oberon*, which was performed at court on January 1, 1611. In Shakespeare's play, the Old Shepherd remarks that three of the performers had "danced before the King" (4.4.324). This reference has been used to suggest that Shakespeare either was writing *The Winter's Tale* in January of 1611 and so incorporated a contemporary court event into his play, or that he composed the bulk of the play after that date. It is also possible that Shakespeare—or someone else—added this dance to *The Winter's Tale* after the play had already been written and was in performance in order to capitalize on the glamour attached to court occasions, especially if, as the Old Shepherd indicates, members of Shakespeare's company performed in Jonson's masque. If so, the dance would have been recorded in the promptbook but not necessarily in Shakespeare's original manuscript.

The Folio text of the play was probably set from a transcript prepared by Ralph Crane, a scrivener who transcribed a number of plays associated with the King's Men. In many of the manuscripts prepared by Crane, and this is true for *The Winter's Tale*, all the characters who appear in certain scenes, regardless of when they actually come on stage, are listed in the opening stage direction. Crane sometimes modified stage directions in the interest of clarity and imposed his own punctuation and spelling on the playscripts, showing a decided preference for the heavy use of parentheses, hyphens, and apostrophes. The changes Crane made while copying the plays make it difficult to recognize what kind of manuscript lay behind his transcriptions: promptbook or foul papers. As with other plays set from Crane's transcriptions, the Folio *Winter's Tale* is a relatively clean text. Act and scene divisions are carefully and consistently noted, although stage directions are sparse. There are only forty-three in the Folio, and they are regularly supplemented in modern editions.

SELECTED BIBLIOGRAPHY

Adelman, Janet. "Masculine Authority and the Maternal Body: The Return to Origins in the Romances." *Suffocating Mothers: Fantasies of Maternal Origin in Shakespeare's Plays, "Hamlet" to "The Tempest."* New York: Routledge, 1992. 193–238. Argues that the romances attempt to redress the loss of the idealized parents enacted in *Hamlet* and that *The Winter's Tale* dramatizes the positive restoration of the sexualized mother in the person of Hermione.

Dolan, Frances. "Finding What Has Been 'Lost': Representations of Infanticide and *The Winter's Tale.*" *Dangerous Familiars: Representations of Domestic Crime in England, 1550–1700.* Ithaca, N.Y.: Cornell University Press, 1994. 121–70. Connects *The Winter's Tale* to early modern stories of child abandonment and murder, arguing that the play ultimately forgives the tyrannous father, Leontes, for the exposure of Perdita.

Egan, Robert. "'The Art Itself Is Nature': *The Winter's Tale.*" *Drama Within Drama: Shakespeare's Sense of His Art in "King Lear," "The Winter's Tale," and "The Tempest."* New York: Columbia University Press, 1975. 56–89. Discusses the role of art in rectifying the disordered world of *The Winter's Tale.*

Frye, Northrop. "The Triumph of Time." *A Natural Perspective: The Development of Shakespearean Comedy and Romance.* New York: Columbia University Press, 1965. 72–117. Discusses structures of action and conventions common across Shakespeare's comedies and romances.

Hunt, Maurice. "'Bearing Hence' Shakespeare's *The Winter's Tale.*" *Studies in English Literature 1500–1900* 44 (2004): 333–46. Explores Shakespeare's creative play with the words "bear" and "bear away" in a play in which a bear appears on stage and is often associated with the tyrannous King Leontes.

Mowat, Barbara A. "Rogues, Shepherds, and the Counterfeit Distressed: Texts and Infracontexts of *The Winter's Tale* 4.3." *Shakespeare Studies* 22 (1994): 58–76. Examines the cultural contexts that help make sense of the figure of Autolycus, rogue and con man, in *The Winter's Tale.*

Newcomb, Lori H. "'If That Which Is Lost Be Not Found': Monumental Bodies, Spectacular Bodies in *The Winter's Tale.*" *Ovid and the Renaissance Body.* Ed. Goran V. Stanivukovic. Toronto: University of Toronto Press, 2001. Analyzes the tension between the monumental (stasis and constraint) and the spectacular (metamorphosis and performative freedom) in both the text of *The Winter's Tale* and in its material history as book and as theater piece.

O'Connor, Marion. "'Imagine Me, Gentle Spectators': Iconomachy and *The Winter's Tale.*" *A Companion to Shakespeare's Works. IV: The Poems, Problem Comedies, Late Plays.* Ed. Richard Dutton and Jean E. Howard. Malden, Mass.: Blackwell, 2003. 365–88. Discusses the Renaissance theological debate about the value and truth of images as it bears on a number of early modern plays, including *The Winter's Tale*, in which statues are staged. Argues that Shakespeare insists on the collaboration of word and image, eschewing a total embrace of Reformation logocentrism or Catholic image-worship.

Paster, Gail Kern. "Quarreling with the Dug, or 'I Am Glad You Did Not Nurse Him'." *The Body Embarrassed: Drama and the Disciplines of Shame in Early Modern England.* Ithaca, N.Y.: Cornell University Press, 1993. 215–80. Sets *The Winter's Tale* in an array of Shakespearean texts that anxiously explore early modern cultural practices surrounding reproduction and infant care, especially the practice of wet-nursing.

Wilson, Richard. "The Statue of Our Queen: Shakespeare's Open Secret." *Secret Shakespeare: Studies in Theatre, Religion and Resistance.* Manchester: Manchester University Press, 2004. 246–70. Argues for *The Winter's Tale*'s connection to recusant culture, especially the play's emphasis on the importance of secret spaces dominated by women.

FILM

The Winter's Tale. 1999. Dir. Robin Lough. UK. 170 min. A dark and moving Royal Shakespeare Company production with Anthony Sher as a Leontes truly made mad by jealousy and an impressively dignified Alexandra Gilbreath as Hermione. Imaginative staging of the bear and riveting statue scene as Hermione very slowly comes to life.

The Winter's Tale

THE PERSONS OF THE PLAY

LEONTES, King of Sicilia
HERMIONE, his wife
MAMILLIUS, his son
PERDITA, his daughter
CAMILLO ⎫
ANTIGONUS ⎪
CLEOMENES ⎬ Lords at Leontes' court
DION ⎭
PAULINA, Antigonus's wife
EMILIA, a lady attending on Hermione
A JAILER
A MARINER
Other Lords and Gentlemen, Ladies, Officers, and Servants at
   Leontes' court
POLIXENES, King of Bohemia
FLORIZEL, his son, in love with Perdita; known as Doricles
ARCHIDAMUS, a Bohemian lord
AUTOLYCUS, a rogue, once in the service of Florizel
OLD SHEPHERD
CLOWN, his son
MOPSA ⎫
DORCAS ⎬ shepherdesses
SERVANT of the Old Shepherd
Other Shepherds and Shepherdesses
Twelve countrymen disguised as satyrs
TIME, as chorus

1.1

Enter CAMILLO *and* ARCHIDAMUS

ARCHIDAMUS   If you shall chance, Camillo, to visit Bohemia on
   the like occasion whereon my services are now on foot,[1] you
   shall see, as I have said, great difference betwixt our Bohemia
   and your Sicilia.
5   CAMILLO   I think this coming summer the King of Sicilia means
   to pay Bohemia the visitation which he justly owes him.
ARCHIDAMUS   Wherein our entertainment shall shame us, we
   will be justified in our loves;[2] for indeed—
CAMILLO   Beseech you—
10   ARCHIDAMUS   Verily, I speak it in the freedom of my knowledge.
   We cannot with such magnificence—in so rare— I know not
   what to say.—We will give you sleepy drinks,° that your senses, *drinks to make you drowsy*
   unintelligent of our insufficience,[3] may, though they cannot
   praise us, as little accuse us.
15   CAMILLO   You pay a great deal too dear for what's given freely.

1.1 Location: Sicilia. The palace of Leontes.
1. On an occasion similar to the one in which I am now
engaged (that is, as attendant lord to a visiting King).

2. Insofar as our less elaborate hospitality will put us to
shame, we will compensate by (the depth of) our love.
3. Unaware of our inadequacy.

ARCHIDAMUS   Believe me, I speak as my understanding instructs
me, and as mine honesty puts it to utterance.

CAMILLO   Sicilia cannot show himself over-kind to Bohemia.
They were trained together in their childhoods, and there
20 rooted betwixt them then such an affection which cannot
choose but branch[4] now. Since their more mature dignities
and royal necessities made separation of their society,° their   *forced them apart*
encounters—though not personal— hath been royally attor-
neyed[5] with interchange of gifts, letters, loving embassies, that°   *so that*
25 they have seemed to be together, though absent; shook hands
as over a vast;° and embraced as it were from the ends of   *wide expanse*
opposed winds.[6] The heavens continue their loves.

ARCHIDAMUS   I think there is not in the world either malice or
matter to alter it. You have an unspeakable° comfort of° your   *inexpressible / in*
30 young prince, Mamillius. It° is a gentleman of the greatest   *(He)*
promise that ever came into my note.

CAMILLO   I very well agree with you in the hopes of him. It is a
gallant child; one that, indeed, physics the subject,[7] makes old
hearts fresh. They that went on crutches ere he was born desire
35 yet their life° to see him a man.   *hope to live long enough*

ARCHIDAMUS   Would they else be content to die?

CAMILLO   Yes—if there were no other excuse why they should
desire to live.

ARCHIDAMUS   If the King had no son they would desire to live on
40 crutches till he had one.   *Exeunt*

1.2

Enter LEONTES, HERMIONE, MAMILLIUS, POLIXENES, *and*
CAMILLO[1]

POLIXENES   Nine changes of the wat'ry star hath been
The shepherd's note[2] since we[3] have left our throne
Without a burden.° Time as long again   *an occupant*
Would be filled up, my brother, with our thanks,
5 And yet we should for perpetuity
Go hence in debt.[4] And therefore, like a cipher,
Yet standing in rich place,[5] I multiply
With one 'We thank you' many thousands more
That go before it.

LEONTES   Stay° your thanks a while,   *Postpone*
And pay them when you part.

10 POLIXENES   Sir, that's tomorrow.
I am questioned by my fears° of what may chance[6]   *I am afraid*
Or breed upon° our absence, that may blow   *develop because of*
No sneaping winds at home to make us say

<hr />

4. Flourish and spread (as a tree does when it puts forth branches); divide.
5. Performed by deputies.
6. From opposite ends of the earth. Early modern atlases often showed the four "corners" of the earth as the source of the winds.
7. Restores the health of the King's subjects.
1.2 Location: Sicilia. The palace of Leontes.
1. Though listed in the stage direction in F, Camillo has no part in this scene until line 210, when Leontes says, "What, Camillo there!" Camillo may be a silent observer

for the first 210 lines, or, as some editors believe, his first entrance may be marked by Leontes' exclamation.
2. The shepherd has observed nine changes of the moon (that is, nine months). The moon is "the wat'ry star" because it governs the tides.
3. Both Kings employ the royal "we," speaking of themselves in the plural.
4. And even then we would depart forever in your debt.
5. Like a zero ("cipher"), which is worthless in itself, but valuable when it follows another number.
6. Happen by chance.

'This is put forth too truly.'[7] Besides, I have stayed
To tire your royalty.

LEONTES   We are tougher, brother,
Than you can put us to't.[8]

POLIXENES   No longer stay.

LEONTES   One sennight° longer.   *week*

POLIXENES   Very sooth,° tomorrow.   *In truth (a mild oath)*

LEONTES   We'll part the time° between's, then; and in that   *split the difference*
I'll no gainsaying.°   *allow no contradiction*

POLIXENES   Press me not, beseech you, so.
There is no tongue that moves, none, none i'th' world
So soon as yours, could win me. So it should now,
Were there necessity in your request, although
'Twere needful I denied it. My affairs
Do even drag me homeward; which to hinder
Were, in your love, a whip to me;[9] my stay
To you a charge and trouble. To save both,
Farewell, our brother.

LEONTES   Tongue-tied, our queen? Speak you.

HERMIONE   I had thought, sir, to have held my peace until
You had drawn oaths from him not to stay. You, sir,
Charge him too coldly. Tell him you are sure
All in Bohemia's well. This satisfaction
The bygone day proclaimed.[1] Say this to him,
He's beat from his best ward.[2]

LEONTES   Well said, Hermione!

HERMIONE   To tell° he longs to see his son were strong.   *assert*
But let him say so then, and let him go.
But let him swear so and he shall not stay,
We'll thwack him hence with distaffs.[3]
[*To* POLIXENES] Yet of your royal presence I'll adventure°   *risk*
The borrow° of a week. When at Bohemia   *loan*
You take my lord, I'll give him my commission°   *permission*
To let him there a month behind the gest
Prefixed for's parting.[4]—Yet, good deed,° Leontes,   *indeed*
I love thee not a jar° o'th' clock behind   *tick*
What lady she her lord.[5]—You'll stay?

POLIXENES   No, madam.

HERMIONE   Nay, but you will?

POLIXENES   I may not, verily.

HERMIONE   Verily?
You put me off with limber° vows. But I,   *weak*
Though you would seek t'unsphere the stars[6] with oaths,
Should yet say 'Sir, no going.' Verily
You shall not go. A lady's 'verily''s
As potent as a lord's. Will you go yet?

Force me to keep you as a prisoner,
Not like a guest: so you shall pay your fees
55   When you depart,[7] and save your thanks. How say you?
My prisoner? or my guest? By your dread 'verily',
One of them you shall be.

POLIXENES   Your guest then, madam.
To be your prisoner should import offending,°   *mean I have offended you*
Which is for me less easy to commit
Than you to punish.

60 HERMIONE   Not your jailer then,
But your kind hostess. Come, I'll question you
Of my lord's tricks and yours when you were boys.
You were pretty lordings° then?   *young lords*

POLIXENES   We were, fair Queen,
Two lads that thought there was no more behind°   *(in the future)*
65   But such a day tomorrow as today,
And to be boy eternal.

HERMIONE   Was not my lord
The verier wag° o'th' two?   *greater mischief-maker*

POLIXENES   We were as twinned° lambs that did frisk i'th' sun,   *identical*
70   And bleat the one at th'other. What we changed°   *exchanged*
Was innocence for innocence. We knew not
The doctrine of ill-doing, nor dreamed
That any did. Had we pursued that life,
And our weak spirits ne'er been higher reared
75 With stronger blood,° we should have answered heaven   *With more mature passions*
Boldly, 'Not guilty', the imposition cleared
Hereditary ours.[8]

HERMIONE   By this we gather
You have tripped° since.   *sinned*

POLIXENES   O my most sacred lady,
Temptations have since then been born to's; for
80 In those unfledged[9] days was my wife a girl.
Your precious self had then not crossed the eyes
Of my young playfellow.

HERMIONE   Grace to boot!°   *Heaven help me!*
Of this make no conclusion,[1] lest you say
Your queen and I are devils. Yet go on.
85 Th'offences we have made you do we'll answer,°   *answer for*
If you first sinned with us, and that with us
You did continue fault, and that you slipped not
With any but with us.

LEONTES   Is he won yet?

HERMIONE   He'll stay, my lord.

LEONTES   At my request he would not.
90 Hermione, my dearest, thou never spok'st
To better purpose.

HERMIONE   Never?

LEONTES   Never but once.

HERMIONE   What, have I twice said well? When was't before?

---

7. In early modern England, prisoners were required to pay fees to jailers both for provisions and upon their release.
8. Freed even of the charge of original sin. The doctrine of original sin held that everyone at birth was tainted by sin because the first humans, Adam and Eve, disobeyed God in the Garden of Eden. Here original sin is linked to the sexual desires that come with maturity.
9. Youthful. An unfledged, or young, bird is one as yet lacking the feathers necessary for flight.
1. Do not follow out this line of reasoning.

I prithee tell me. Cram's° with praise, and make's   *Stuff us; overfeed us*
As fat as tame things. One good deed dying tongueless
95   Slaughters a thousand waiting upon that.[2]
Our praises are our wages. You may ride's
With one soft kiss a thousand furlongs ere
With spur we heat° an acre.[3] But to th' goal.°   *race over / purpose*
My last good deed was to entreat his stay.
100 What was my first? It has an elder sister,
Or I mistake you. O, would her name were Grace![4]
But once before I spoke to th' purpose? When?
Nay, let me have't. I long.

LEONTES   Why, that was when
Three crabbèd° months had soured themselves to death   *bitter*
105 Ere I could make thee open thy white hand
And clap° thyself my love. Then didst thou utter,   *pledge*
'I am yours for ever.'

HERMIONE   'Tis grace indeed.
Why lo you now; I have spoke to th' purpose twice.
The one for ever earned a royal husband;
Th'other, for some while a friend.[5]
      [*She gives her hand to* POLIXENES.[6]
      They stand aside]

110 LEONTES [*aside*]   Too hot, too hot:
To mingle friendship farre is mingling bloods.[7]
I have *tremor cordis*[8] on me. My heart dances,
But not for joy, not joy. This entertainment°   *hospitality*
May a free° face put on, derive a liberty   *innocent*
115 From heartiness, from bounty, fertile bosom,°   *generous affection*
And well become the agent.[9] 'T may, I grant.
But to be paddling° palms and pinching fingers,[1]   *caressing*
As now they are, and making practised smiles
As in a looking-glass; and then to sigh, as 'twere
120 The mort o'th' deer[2]—O, that is entertainment
My bosom likes not, nor my brows.[3]—Mamillius,
Art thou my boy?

MAMILLIUS   Ay, my good lord.

LEONTES   I'fecks,°   *In faith (a mild oath)*
Why, that's my bawcock.° What? Hast smutched° thy nose?   *fine fellow / dirtied*
They say it is a copy out of mine. Come, captain,
125 We must be neat—not neat,[4] but cleanly, captain.
And yet the steer, the heifer, and the calf

2. If one virtuous act goes unremarked, then the thousand more that might have been inspired by it will not come to be.
3. That is, "You'll go much farther with us if you will treat us kindly," with a pun on "ride" as meaning "enjoy us sexually."
4. Would that my first good act were virtuous (full of God's Grace). Hermione may be countering Polixenes' earlier suggestion that she first caused Leontes to sin. With a possible allusion to the Three Graces (Aglaia, Euphrosyne, and Thalia) of classical mythology. Usually depicted nude and dancing in a circle, the three women represented the epitome of earthly beauty and harmony.
5. "Friend" could also mean "lover," a meaning that Leontes takes up in his next speech.
6. It is not certain when Hermione and Polixenes join hands, but by line 117 Leontes remarks that they are

"paddling palms and pinching fingers." Joined hands—or hands separated from one another—are an important and recurring visual motif in the play, culminating at 5.3.107, when Paulina commands Leontes to "present your hand" to Hermione as she ceases to appear a statue.
7. Uniting in passion; having sexual intercourse.
8. A malady marked by an erratic heart rate.
9. And makes the actor of these deeds (Hermione) appear attractive.
1. Early modern texts often represent hands as erotic body parts. Moist palms were believed to be signs of sexual arousal; finger games may suggest sexual penetration.
2. To sigh as loudly as the horn blast that proclaims the death of a hunted deer.
3. Alluding to the proverbial notion that a cuckold sprouted horns from his brow.
4. Punning on neat as meaning both "clean" and "cattle with horns."

Are all called neat.—Still virginalling
Upon his palm?[5]—How now, you wanton° calf— *playful*
Art thou my calf?

MAMILLIUS   Yes, if you will, my lord.

130 LEONTES   Thou want'st a rough pash° and the shoots° that I have, *shaggy head / horns*
To be full° like me. Yet they say we are *entirely; fully*
Almost as like as eggs. Women say so,
That will say anything. But were they false
As o'er-dyed blacks,[6] as wind, as waters, false
135 As dice are to be wished by one that fixes
No bourn° 'twixt his and mine, yet were it true *boundary; limit*
To say this boy were like me. Come, sir page,
Look on me with your welkin° eye. Sweet villain, *sky blue*
Most dear'st, my collop![7] Can thy dam°—may't be?— *mother*
140 Affection, thy intention stabs the centre.[8]
Thou dost make possible things not so held,° *things held as impossible*
Communicat'st with dreams—how can this be?—
With what's unreal thou coactive art,° *you collaborate*
And fellow'st° nothing. Then 'tis very credent° *are companion to / believable*
145 Thou mayst co-join with something, and thou dost—
And that beyond commission;° and I find it— *what is permitted*
And that to the infection of my brains
And hard'ning of my brows.° *(with cuckold's horns)*

POLIXENES   What means Sicilia?

HERMIONE   He something seems° unsettled. *seems somewhat*

POLIXENES   How, my lord!

LEONTES   What cheer? How is't with you, best brother?

150 HERMIONE   You look
As if you held a brow of much distraction.
Are you moved,° my lord? *angry*

LEONTES   No, in good earnest.
How sometimes nature will betray its folly,
Its tenderness, and make itself a pastime° *source of amusement*
155 To harder bosoms! Looking on the lines
Of my boy's face, methoughts I did recoil° *go back*
Twenty-three years, and saw myself unbreeched,[9]
In my green velvet coat; my dagger muzzled,° *in its sheath; blunted*
Lest it should bite its master, and so prove,
160 As ornament oft does, too dangerous.
How like, methought, I then was to this kernel,
This squash,° this gentleman.—Mine honest friend, *unripe peapod*
Will you take eggs for money?[1]

MAMILLIUS   No, my lord, I'll fight.

LEONTES   You will? Why, happy man be's dole![2]—My brother,

---

5. Still caressing his hand as if playing the virginal, a legless keyboard instrument played on the lap; still acting chastely (like a virgin).
6. Referring to textiles dyed black. Such black cloth was made "false" or weakened by the harsh chemicals in the dye. With a possible reference to Africans, whose dark skin was said to result from overexposure to the sun. It was a commonplace that Africans were prone to licentiousness and were thus sexually "false."
7. That is, "my own flesh." A "collop" is a portion of meat.
8. Passion (probably the passion of jealousy), your

intensity ("intention") pierces my heart or to the core of my being.
9. Not yet old enough to wear men's clothing ("breeches"). Before about the age of six, both girls and boys in early modern England wore a dresslike garment. Giving a boy breeches was a sign of his passage out of childhood and out of the care of women into the world of men.
1. A proverbial expression meaning "Will you accept a trifle in place of something valuable?"
2. Proverbial for "May you have good luck!"

165 Are you so fond of your young prince as we
Do seem to be of ours?

POLIXENES   If at home, sir,
He's all my exercise, my mirth, my matter;°   concern
Now my sworn friend, and then mine enemy;
My parasite, my soldier, statesman, all.
170 He makes a July's day short as December,
And with his varying childness° cures in me   youthful ways
Thoughts that would thick my blood.[3]

LEONTES   So stands this squire
Officed with me.[4] We two will walk, my lord,
And leave you to your graver steps. Hermione,
175 How thou lov'st us show in our brother's welcome.
Let what is dear in Sicily be cheap.
Next to thyself and my young rover, he's
Apparent° to my heart.   Heir apparent

HERMIONE   If you would seek us,
We are yours i'th' garden. Shall's attend you there?
180 LEONTES   To your own bents° dispose you. You'll be found,   inclinations
Be you beneath the sky. [Aside] I am angling° now,   fishing; scheming
Though you perceive me not how I give line.
Go to, go to!
How she holds up the neb, the bill to him,[5]
185 And arms her° with the boldness of a wife   herself
To her allowing° husband!   approving

[Exeunt POLIXENES and HERMIONE]
Gone already.
Inch-thick, knee-deep, o'er head and ears a forked° one!—   horned
Go play, boy, play. Thy mother plays,° and I   dallies sexually
Play° too; but so disgraced a part, whose issue[6]   Play a role
190 Will hiss me to my grave. Contempt and clamour
Will be my knell. Go play, boy, play. There have been,
Or I am much deceived, cuckolds ere now,
And many a man there is, even at this present,
Now, while I speak this, holds his wife by th'arm,
195 That little thinks she has been sluiced[7] in's absence,
And his pond[8] fished by his next neighbour, by
Sir Smile, his neighbour.[9] Nay, there's comfort in't,
Whiles other men have gates,[1] and those gates opened,
As mine, against their will. Should all despair
200 That have revolted° wives, the tenth of mankind   rebellious; unfaithful
Would hang themselves. Physic° for't there's none.   Medicine
It is a bawdy planet, that will strike
Where 'tis predominant;[2] and 'tis powerful. Think it:

3. Ideas that would make me melancholy, a physical and emotional malady connected with a supposed excess of "thick blood."
4. So this young man performs the same duty for me.
5. How she holds up her face, her mouth to him (to be kissed).
6. Outcome, with puns on "issue" as also meaning "offspring" and "the exit an actor makes from a stage." Leontes' words imply that in playing the part of a cuckold, the result of his role will be disgrace; the illegitimate offspring produced by his wife will bring him disgrace; and his exit from the stage (at death) will be a disgraceful one.
7. Little thinks she has had sexual relations. A sluice

was a trough or channel through which water could be directed. To be sluiced was to have water poured down one's "channel," here probably referring to the vagina where sperm entered.
8. Slang term for the sexual organs of his wife.
9. It is possible that "Sir Smile" is a reference to Polixenes, who may be laughing or smiling in his conversation with Hermione.
1. Another slang term for female genitalia. Leontes imagines the vulva as a gateway that ought to be entered only by a husband.
2. Alluding to the notion that planets control human actions and may exercise malign influences ("strike") when they are in certain "predominant" positions.

From east, west, north, and south, be it concluded,
205　No barricado for a belly.³ Know't,
　　It will let in and out the enemy
　　With bag and baggage.⁴ Many thousand on's° — — — — — — — — — — *of us*
　　Have the disease and feel't not.—How now, boy?
　　MAMILLIUS　I am like you, they say.
　　LEONTES　　　　　　　　　　Why, that's some comfort.
　　What, Camillo there!
210　CAMILLO [coming forward]　Ay, my good lord.
　　LEONTES　Go play, Mamillius, thou'rt an honest man.
　　　　　　　　　　　　　　　　[Exit MAMILLIUS]
　　Camillo, this great sir will yet stay longer.
　　CAMILLO　You had much ado to make his anchor hold.
　　When you cast out, it still came home.° — — — — — — — — — *always failed to hold*
　　LEONTES　　　　　　　　　Didst note it?
215　CAMILLO　He would not stay at your petitions, made
　　His business more material.° — — — — — — — — — — — — — — — *important*
　　LEONTES　　　　　　　Didst perceive it?
　　[Aside] They're here with me⁵ already, whisp'ring, rounding,° — — *murmuring*
　　'Sicilia is a so-forth'. 'Tis far gone
　　When I shall gust° it last.—How came't, Camillo, — — — — — *perceive; taste*
　　That he did stay?
220　CAMILLO　　　　　At the good Queen's entreaty.
　　LEONTES　'At the Queen's' be't. 'Good' should be pertinent,
　　But so° it is, it is not. Was this taken° — — — — — — — — — *as / perceived*
　　By any understanding pate but thine?
　　For thy conceit is soaking,° will draw in — — — — — — — — *your wit is quick*
225　More than the common blocks.° Not noted, is't, — — — — — — *dimwits*
　　But of° the finer natures? By some severals° — — — — — — *by / individuals*
　　Of head-piece° extraordinary? Lower messes⁶ — — — — — — *intellect*
　　Perchance are to this business purblind?° Say. — — — — — — *blind*
　　CAMILLO　Business, my lord? I think most understand
230　Bohemia stays here longer.
　　LEONTES　Ha?
　　CAMILLO　Stays here longer.
　　LEONTES　Ay, but why?
　　CAMILLO　To satisfy your highness, and the entreaties
　　Of our most gracious mistress.
235　LEONTES　　　　　　　　Satisfy?⁷
　　Th'entreaties of your mistress? Satisfy?
　　Let that suffice. I have trusted thee, Camillo,
　　With all the near'st things to my heart, as well
　　My chamber-counsels,° wherein, priest-like, thou — — — — — *secret matters*
240　Hast cleansed my bosom, I from thee departed
　　Thy penitent reformed. But we have been
　　Deceived in thy integrity, deceived
　　In that which seems so.
　　CAMILLO　　　　　Be it forbid, my lord.
　　LEONTES　To bide° upon't: thou art not honest; or — — — — — *dwell*
245　If thou inclin'st that way, thou art a coward,

3. No means of defending a womb.
4. With full military (or sexual) equipment.
5. They know my secret.
6. Those of lower social status at the dining table. A

"mess" refers to a group of four people who share meals together.
7. Punning on "satisfy" as meaning both "appease" and "give sexual pleasure to."

Which hoxes honesty behind,[8] restraining
From course required.[9] Or else thou must be counted
A servant grafted in my serious trust[1]
And therein negligent, or else a fool
250   That seest a game played home,° the rich stake drawn,°   *in earnest / won*
And tak'st it all for jest.
CAMILLO   My gracious lord,
I may be negligent, foolish, and fearful.
In every one of these no man is free,°   *guiltless*
But that his negligence, his folly, fear,
255   Among the infinite doings of the world
Sometime puts forth.° In your affairs, my lord,   *reveals itself*
If ever I were wilful-negligent,
It was my folly. If industriously°   *deliberately*
I played the fool, it was my negligence,
260   Not weighing well the end. If ever fearful
To do a thing where I the issue° doubted,   *outcome*
Whereof the execution did cry out
Against the non-performance,[2] 'twas a fear
Which oft infects the wisest. These, my lord,
265   Are such allowed infirmities that honesty
Is never free of. But beseech your grace
Be plainer with me, let me know my trespass
By its own visage. If I then deny it,
'Tis none of mine.
LEONTES   Ha' not you seen, Camillo—
270   But that's past doubt; you have, or your eye-glass°   *the lens of your eye*
Is thicker than a cuckold's horn—or heard—
For, to a vision° so apparent, rumour   *sight*
Cannot be mute—or thought—for cogitation
Resides not in that man that does not think—
275   My wife is slippery? If thou wilt confess—
Or else be impudently negative°   *shamelessly deny*
To have nor eyes, nor ears, nor thought—then say
My wife's a hobby-horse,[3] deserves a name
As rank° as any flax-wench[4] that puts to°   *indecent / has sexual relations*
280   Before her troth-plight.° Say't, and justify't.   *betrothal*
CAMILLO   I would not be a stander-by to hear
My sovereign mistress clouded so without
My present° vengeance taken. 'Shrew° my heart,   *immediate / Curse*
You never spoke what did become you less
285   Than this, which to reiterate° were sin   *repeat*
As deep as that, though true.[5]
LEONTES   Is whispering nothing?
Is leaning cheek to cheek? Is meeting noses?
Kissing with inside lip? Stopping the career°   *full gallop*
Of laughter with a sigh?—a note° infallible   *sign*

---

8. Which ensures that frankness is shackled.
9. Keeping (honesty) from the path it must take (to find out truth).
1. A servant who has grown into my confidence as a cutting is grafted onto a plant.
2. Even when the need to do the deed protested against its nonperformance.
3. Whore. The image is of a woman, who, like a horse, can be mounted. F has "Holy-Horse," an obscure phrase nearly all modern editors emend to "hobbyhorse."
4. A girl or woman, usually of low social status, who worked with flax, a fibrous plant used to make candlewicks, clothing, and linen.
5. That is, "As grave as is the sin that you accuse your wife of, even if it were true (which it is not)."

290 Of breaking honesty.° Horsing foot on foot?[6] *violating chastity*
    Skulking in corners? Wishing clocks more swift,
    Hours minutes, noon midnight? And all eyes
    Blind with the pin and web° but theirs, theirs only, *cataract disease*
    That would unseen be wicked? Is this nothing?
295 Why then the world and all that's in't is nothing,
    The covering sky is nothing, Bohemia nothing,
    My wife is nothing, nor nothing have these nothings[7]
    If this be nothing.

CAMILLO   Good my lord, be cured
    Of this diseased opinion, and betimes,° *quickly*
    For 'tis most dangerous.

300 LEONTES   Say it be, 'tis true.

CAMILLO   No, no, my lord.

LEONTES   It is. You lie, you lie.
    I say thou liest, Camillo, and I hate thee,
    Pronounce thee a gross lout, a mindless slave,
    Or else a hovering° temporizer, that *irresolute*
305 Canst with thine eyes at once see good and evil,
    Inclining to them both. Were my wife's liver
    Infected as her life, she would not live
    The running of one glass.° *hourglass*

CAMILLO   Who does infect her?

LEONTES   Why, he that wears her like her medal,[8] hanging
310 About his neck, Bohemia, who, if I
    Had servants true about me, that bare° eyes *possessed*
    To see alike mine honour as their profits,
    Their own particular thrifts,° they would do that *personal gain*
    Which should undo° more doing.° Ay, and thou *stop / sexual acts*
315 His cupbearer,[9] whom I from meaner form° *lower rank or place*
    Have benched, and reared to worship,[1] who mayst see
    Plainly as heaven sees earth and earth sees heaven,
    How I am galled,° mightst bespice a cup *sorely vexed*
    To give mine enemy a lasting wink,[2]
    Which draught to me were cordial.[3]

320 CAMILLO   Sir, my lord,
    I could do this, and that with no rash° potion, *quick-acting*
    But with a ling'ring° dram, that should not work *slow-working*
    Maliciously,° like poison. But I cannot *Violently*
    Believe this crack° to be in my dread mistress, *flaw*
325 So sovereignly being honourable.
    I have loved thee—

LEONTES   Make that thy question,° and go rot! *concern*
    Dost think I am so muddy, so unsettled,
    To appoint° myself in this vexation? *put*
    Sully the purity and whiteness of my sheets—
330 Which to preserve is sleep, which being spotted
    Is goads, thorns, nettles, tails of wasps—

---

6. Mounting or rubbing one foot on another. A sexually
titillating pastime.
7. Alluding to the proverbial notion that nothing can
come of nothing.
8. As though she were a miniature portrait of herself.
Ornate lockets containing miniature portraits were
popular love tokens among courtiers.
9. In a noble household a male servant whose responsibilities included serving wine to his master.
1. Given authority and elevated to a dignified position.
Referring to his "bench" or place at the dining table as
a sign of his high rank.
2. To close my enemy's eyes forever.
3. Which drink would be medicinal to me; which drink
would cure my heartsickness (perhaps the *"tremor
cordis"* to which Leontes referred at 1.2.112).

Give scandal to the blood o'th' prince, my son—
Who I do think is mine, and love as mine—
Without ripe moving° to't? Would I do this?   *good reason*
Could man so blench?°   *stray (from sense)*
335   CAMILLO   I must believe you, sir.
I do, and will fetch off° Bohemia for't,   *kill; rescue*
Provided that when he's removed your highness
Will take again your queen as yours at first,
Even for your son's sake, and thereby for sealing°   *silencing*
340   The injury of tongues in courts and kingdoms
Known and allied to yours.
LEONTES   Thou dost advise me
Even so as I mine own course have set down.
I'll give no blemish to her honour, none.
CAMILLO   My lord, go then, and with a countenance as clear
345   As friendship wears at feasts, keep° with Bohemia   *associate*
And with your queen. I am his cupbearer.
If from me he have wholesome beverage,
Account me not your servant.
LEONTES   This is all.
Do't, and thou hast the one half of my heart;
Do't not, thou splitt'st thine own.
350   CAMILLO   I'll do't, my lord.
LEONTES   I will seem friendly, as thou hast advised me.   *Exit*
CAMILLO   O miserable lady. But for me,
What case stand I in? I must be the poisoner
Of good Polixenes, and my ground to do't
355   Is the obedience to a master—one
Who in rebellion with himself, will have
All that are his so too. To do this deed,
Promotion follows. If I could find example
Of thousands that had struck anointed kings
360   And flourished after, I'd not do't. But since
Nor° brass, nor stone, nor parchment⁴ bears not one,   *Neither*
Let villainy itself forswear't.° I must   *swear not to do it*
Forsake the court. To do't, or no, is certain
To me a break-neck.°   *(death)*
          Enter POLIXENES
                   Happy° star reign now!   *Lucky*
Here comes Bohemia.
365   POLIXENES [*aside*]   This is strange. Methinks
My favour here begins to warp. Not speak?—
Good day, Camillo.
CAMILLO   Hail, most royal sir.
POLIXENES   What is the news i'th' court?
CAMILLO   None rare,° my lord.   *noteworthy*
POLIXENES   The King hath on him such a countenance
370   As° he had lost some province, and a region   *As if*
Loved as he loves himself. Even now I met him
With customary compliment, when he,
Wafting his eyes to th' contrary,° and falling   *Shifting his gaze away*
A lip of much contempt,° speeds from me, and   *sneering*

---

4. That is, since no form of historical record (brass monuments, stone markers, or paper manuscripts) shows an example of a man who flourished after killing a King.

375   So leaves me to consider what is breeding
     That changes thus his manners.

CAMILLO   I dare not know, my lord.

POLIXENES   How, 'dare not'? Do not? Do you know, and dare not?
     Be intelligent° to me. 'Tis thereabouts.[5]   *informative*
     For to yourself what you do know you must,°   *(know)*
380   And cannot say you 'dare not'. Good Camillo,
     Your changed complexions are to me a mirror
     Which shows me mine changed, too; for I must be
     A party in this alteration,° finding   *(of Leontes' manner)*
     Myself thus altered with't.

CAMILLO   There is a sickness
385   Which puts some of us in distemper, but
     I cannot name th' disease, and it is caught
     Of you that yet are well.

POLIXENES   How caught of me?
     Make me not sighted like the basilisk.[6]
     I have looked on thousands who have sped° the better   *fared*
390   By my regard, but killed none so. Camillo,
     As you are certainly a gentleman, thereto
     Clerk-like experienced,[7] which no less adorns
     Our gentry° than our parents' noble names,   *status as gentlemen*
     In whose success we are gentle:[8] I beseech you,
395   If you know aught which does behove my knowledge
     Thereof to be informed,[9] imprison't not
     In ignorant concealment.[1]

CAMILLO   I may not answer.

POLIXENES   A sickness caught of me, and yet I well?
     I must be answered. Dost thou hear, Camillo,
400   I conjure thee, by all the parts° of man   *duties*
     Which honour does acknowledge, whereof the least
     Is not this suit of mine, that thou declare
     What incidency° thou dost guess of harm   *event*
     Is creeping toward me; how far off, how near,
405   Which way to be prevented, if to be;
     If not, how best to bear it.

CAMILLO   Sir, I will tell you,
     Since I am charged in honour, and by him
     That I think honourable. Therefore mark my counsel,
     Which must be e'en as swiftly followed as
410   I mean to utter it; or both yourself and me
     Cry lost, and so good night!°   *good-bye forever*

POLIXENES   On, good Camillo.

CAMILLO   I am appointed him to murder you.

POLIXENES   By whom, Camillo?

CAMILLO   By the King.

POLIXENES   For what?

CAMILLO   He thinks, nay, with all confidence he swears
415   As he had seen't, or been an instrument
     To vice° you to't, that you have touched his queen   *force*
     Forbiddenly.

---

5. That is, "I'm more or less right (that you are afraid to tell me)."
6. A mythical serpent whose glance was said to be fatal.
7. Also having the experience of an educated man.

8. By succession from whom we are made noble.
9. Which it is necessary for me to know.
1. In concealment that keeps me ignorant; in concealment on the pretense that you are ignorant.

POLIXENES   O, then my best blood turn
          To an infected jelly, and my name
          Be yoked with his° that did betray the Best!°   *(Judas's) name / Christ*
420   Turn then my freshest reputation to
          A savour° that may strike the dullest nostril   *foul odor*
          Where I arrive, and my approach be shunned,
          Nay hated, too, worse than the great'st infection
          That e'er was heard or read.
CAMILLO   Swear his thought over²
425   By each particular star in heaven, and
          By all their influences,³ you may as well
          Forbid the sea for to obey the moon
          As or° by oath remove or counsel shake   *either*
          The fabric of his folly, whose foundation
430   Is piled upon his faith, and will continue
          The standing of his body.°   *As long as he lives*
POLIXENES   How should this grow?°   *come to be*
CAMILLO   I know not, but I am sure 'tis safer to
          Avoid what's grown than question how 'tis born.
          If therefore you dare trust my honesty,
435   That lies enclosèd in this trunk° which you   *body*
          Shall bear along impawned,⁴ away tonight!
          Your followers I will whisper to the business,
          And will by twos and threes at several posterns°   *city gates*
          Clear them o'th' city. For myself, I'll put
440   My fortunes to your service, which are here
          By this discovery° lost. Be not uncertain,   *revelation*
          For by the honour of my parents, I
          Have uttered truth; which if you seek to prove,
          I dare not stand by; nor shall you be safer
445   Than one condemnèd by the King's own mouth,
          Thereon his execution sworn.
POLIXENES   I do believe thee,
          I saw his heart in's face. Give me thy hand.
          Be pilot to me, and thy places° shall   *your position*
          Still neighbour° mine. My ships are ready, and   *Always be near*
450   My people did expect my hence departure
          Two days ago. This jealousy
          Is for a precious creature. As she's rare
          Must it be great; and as his person's mighty
          Must it be violent; and as he does conceive
455   He is dishonoured by a man which ever
          Professed° to him, why, his revenges must   *Professed love*
          In that be made more bitter. Fear o'ershades me.
          Good expedition° be my friend and comfort   *Let speed (in leaving)*
          The gracious Queen, part of his theme, but nothing
460   Of his ill-ta'en suspicion.⁵ Come, Camillo,
          I will respect thee as a father if
          Thou bear'st my life off hence. Let us avoid.°   *be gone*

---

2. You may swear that his allegations are false.
3. Substances that, according to contemporary astrological theories, were emitted by stars and helped to
shape human destiny.

4. Shall carry with you as a pledge (of my faith).
5. And make easier the situation of the virtuous Queen,
who is a part of Leontes' accusation, but who is not
guilty of his unjustified suspicion.

CAMILLO   It is in mine authority to command
    The keys of all the posterns. Please your highness
465   To take the urgent hour.° Come, sir, away.   *Exeunt*   *seize the moment*

2.1

Enter HERMIONE, MAMILLIUS, [*and*] LADIES

HERMIONE   Take the boy to you. He so troubles me
    'Tis past enduring.
FIRST LADY   Come, my gracious lord,
    Shall I be your play-fellow?
MAMILLIUS   No, I'll none of you.
5   FIRST LADY   Why, my sweet lord?
MAMILLIUS   You'll kiss me hard, and speak to me as if
    I were a baby still. [*To* SECOND LADY] I love you better.
SECOND LADY   And why so, my lord?
MAMILLIUS   Not for because
    Your brows° are blacker—yet black brows they say   *eyebrows*
10 Become some women best, so that there be not
    Too much hair there, but in a semicircle,
    Or a half-moon made with a pen.
SECOND LADY   Who taught° 'this?   *taught you*
MAMILLIUS   I learned it out of women's faces. Pray now,
    What colour are your eyebrows?
FIRST LADY   Blue, my lord.
15 MAMILLIUS   Nay, that's a mock. I have seen a lady's nose
    That has been blue,[1] but not her eyebrows.
FIRST LADY   Hark ye,
    The Queen your mother rounds apace.° We shall   *grows round quickly*
    Present our services to a fine new prince
    One of these days, and then you'd wanton° with us,   *play*
    If we would have you.
20 SECOND LADY   She is spread of late
    Into a goodly bulk, good time encounter her.°   *good fortune be with her*
HERMIONE   What wisdom stirs amongst you? Come sir, now
    I am for you again. Pray you sit by us,
    And tell's a tale.
25 MAMILLIUS   Merry or sad shall't be?
HERMIONE   As merry as you will.
MAMILLIUS   A sad tale's best for winter. I have one
    Of sprites and goblins.
HERMIONE   Let's have that, good sir.
    Come on, sit down, come on, and do your best
30 To fright me with your sprites. You're powerful at it.
MAMILLIUS   There was a man—
HERMIONE   Nay, come sit down, then on.
MAMILLIUS [*sitting*]   Dwelt by a churchyard.—I will tell it softly,
    Yon crickets° shall not hear it.   (*the other women*)
HERMIONE   Come on then, and give't me in mine ear.
    [*Enter apart* LEONTES, ANTIGONUS, *and* LORDS][2]

2.1 Location: Sicilia. The palace of Leontes.
1. It is unclear whether Mamillius is making a joke here or possibly referring to noses made "blue" by the cold or disfigured by venereal disease.
2. As with many scenes in this play, Ralph Crane, the scrivener who probably prepared the manuscript for the

printer, massed all the entrances for 2.1 in the initial stage direction, regardless of when individual characters actually appeared on stage. Though it is clear that Leontes, Antigonus, and the other Lords enter only at 2.1.34, in F no entrance is marked for them here, and their names are included in the direction preceding 2.1.1.

35   LEONTES   Was he met there? His train?° Camillo with him?   *retinue*
    A LORD   Behind the tuft of pines I met them. Never
      Saw I men scour° so on their way. I eyed them   *hurry*
      Even to their ships.
    LEONTES   How blest am I
      In my just censure,° in my true opinion!   *judgment*
40   Alack, for lesser knowledge°—how accursed   *Would I knew less*
      In being so blest! There may be in the cup
      A spider steeped, and one may drink, depart,
      And yet partake no venom, for his knowledge
      Is not infected;³ but if one present
45   Th'abhorred ingredient to his eye, make known
      How he hath drunk, he cracks his gorge,° his sides,   *throat*
      With violent hefts.° I have drunk, and seen the spider.   *retching*
      Camillo was his help in this, his pander.
      There is a plot against my life, my crown.
50   All's true that is mistrusted.° That false villain   *suspected*
      Whom I employed was pre-employed by him.
      He has discovered° my design, and I   *revealed*
      Remain a pinched° thing, yea, a very trick   *tormented*
      For them to play at will. How came the posterns
      So easily open?
55   A LORD   By his great authority,
      Which often hath no less prevailed than so
      On your command.
    LEONTES   I know't too well.
      [*To* HERMIONE] Give me the boy. I am glad you did not nurse him.⁴
      Though he does bear some signs of me, yet you
      Have too much blood in him.
60   HERMIONE   What is this? Sport?
    LEONTES [*to a* LORD]   Bear the boy hence. He shall not come about her.
      Away with him, and let her sport herself
      With that she's big with, [*to* HERMIONE] for 'tis Polixenes
      Has made thee swell thus.   [*Exit one with* MAMILLIUS]
    HERMIONE   But I'd say he had not,
65   And I'll be sworn you would believe my saying,
      Howe'er you lean to th' nayward.°   *the contrary*
    LEONTES   You, my lords,
      Look on her, mark her well. Be but about
      To say she is a goodly lady, and
      The justice of your hearts will thereto add
70   ' 'Tis pity she's not honest,° honourable.'   *chaste*
      Praise her but for this her without-door° form—   *external*
      Which on my faith deserves high speech—and straight°   *immediately*
      The shrug, the 'hum' or 'ha', these petty brands°   *expressions; stigmas*
      That calumny° doth use—O, I am out,°   *slander / wrong*
75   That mercy does, for calumny will sear°   *stigmatize*
      Virtue itself⁵—these shrugs, these 'hum's and 'ha's',
      When you have said she's goodly, come between
      Ere you can say she's honest. But be't known

---

3. Alluding to the belief that a spider consumed with food or drink would be poisonous only if its presence were known to the consumer.
4. Women who breast-fed infants were believed to shape an infant's character by substances transmitted in their milk.
5. Leontes seems to mean that calumny (slander) will openly attack virtue, and since Hermione is not virtuous, it is not calumny to attack her. Rather, it is mercy who speaks in indirect "hum's" and "ha's" about her behavior.

From him that has most cause to grieve it should be,
She's an adultress.

80 HERMIONE   Should a villain say so,
The most replenished° villain in the world,   *complete*
He were as much more° villain. You, my lord,   *by so much more a*
Do but mistake.

LEONTES   You have mistook,° my lady—   *erred; improperly taken*
Polixenes for Leontes. O, thou thing,
85 Which I'll not call a creature of thy place[6]
Lest barbarism,° making me the precedent,   *uncivilized rudeness*
Should a like° language use to all degrees,°   *the same / all ranks*
And mannerly distinguishment° leave out   *proper distinction*
Betwixt the prince and beggar. I have said
90 She's an adultress, I have said with whom.
More, she's a traitor, and Camillo is
A federary° with her, and one that knows   *confederate*
What she should shame to know herself,
But with her most vile principal:° that she's   *partner*
95 A bed-swerver,° even as bad as those   *adultress*
That vulgars give bold'st titles;[7] ay, and privy
To this their late° escape.   *recent*

HERMIONE   No, by my life,
Privy to none of this. How will this grieve you
When you shall come to clearer knowledge, that
100 You thus have published° me? Gentle my° lord,   *proclaimed / My noble*
You scarce can right me throughly° then to say   *fully do me justice*
You did mistake.

LEONTES   No. If I mistake
In those foundations which I build upon,
The centre° is not big enough to bear   *earth*
105 A schoolboy's top.—Away with her to prison!
He who shall speak for her is afar-off° guilty,   *indirectly*
But that he speaks.°   *Merely for speaking*

HERMIONE   There's some ill planet reigns.[8]
I must be patient till the heavens look
With an aspect more favourable.[8] Good my° lords,   *My good*
110 I am not prone to weeping, as our sex
Commonly are; the want of which vain dew
Perchance shall dry your pities. But I have
That honourable grief lodged here which burns
Worse than tears drown. Beseech you all, my lords,
115 With thoughts so qualified° as your charities   *tempered*
Shall best instruct you, measure me; and so
The King's will be performed.

LEONTES   Shall I be heard?

HERMIONE   Who is't that goes with me? Beseech your highness
My women may be with me, for you see
120 My plight requires it.—Do not weep, good fools,°   *dear ones*
There is no cause. When you shall know your mistress
Has deserved prison, then abound in tears
As I come out. This action I now go on

---

6. To whom I'll not give the title of your (high) social position.
7. That common people call by the coarsest names.

8. Another allusion to the belief that planets can have an evil effect or "aspect" when situated in certain positions.

Is for my better grace.[9]—Adieu, my lord.
125 I never wished to see you sorry; now
I trust I shall. My women, come, you have leave.°   *permission*

LEONTES   Go, do our bidding. Hence!

[*Exit* HERMIONE, *guarded, with* LADIES]

A LORD   Beseech your highness, call the Queen again.

ANTIGONUS [*to Leontes*]   Be certain what you do, sir, lest your justice
130 Prove violence, in the which three great ones suffer—
Yourself, your queen, your son.

A LORD [*to* LEONTES]   For her, my lord,
I dare my life lay down, and will do't, sir,
Please you t'accept it, that the Queen is spotless
I'th' eyes of heaven and to you—I mean
In this which you accuse her.

135 ANTIGONUS [*to* LEONTES]   If it prove
She's otherwise, I'll keep my stables where
I lodge my wife,[1] I'll go in couples with her;[2]
Than when I feel and see her, no farther trust her.
For every inch of woman in the world,
140 Ay, every dram° of woman's flesh is false   *smallest piece*
If she be.

LEONTES   Hold your peaces.

A LORD   Good my lord—

ANTIGONUS [*to* LEONTES]   It is for you we speak, not for ourselves.
You are abused, and by some putter-on°   *instigator*
That will be damned for't. Would I knew the villain—
145 I would land-damn him.[3] Be she honour-flawed—
I have three daughters: the eldest is eleven;
The second and the third nine and some five;
If this prove true, they'll pay for't. By mine honour,
I'll geld 'em all.[4] Fourteen they shall not see,
150 To bring false generations.° They are co-heirs,   *illegitimate children*
And I had rather glib° myself than they   *castrate*
Should not produce fair issue.°   *legitimate offspring*

LEONTES   Cease, no more!
You smell this business with a sense as cold
As is a dead man's nose. But I do see't and feel't
155 As you feel doing thus;[5] and see withal
The instruments that feel.[6]

ANTIGONUS   If it be so,
We need no grave to bury honesty;°   *chastity*
There's not a grain of it the face to sweeten°   *to sweeten the face*
Of the whole dungy° earth.   *foul*

LEONTES   What? Lack I credit?

160 A LORD   I had rather you did lack than I, my lord,
Upon this ground;° and more it would content me   *In this affair*

---

9. This trial I am enduring is for my greater honor
(when vindicated); *or* This suffering I am enduring is to
refine and purge me, leading to greater virtue.
1. An obscure passage, meaning that he'll guard his
wife's lodgings as vigilantly as he guards his horses *or*
that he will treat his wife's lodgings as he does his
stables, where mares are separated from stallions.
2. Have her tied to me (as hounds were leashed
together for the hunt).
3. A term of abuse whose exact meaning is unclear. It

may be a dialect form of "lamback" or "lambaste,"
which means "thrash."
4. I'll make them all barren. Literally, I'll cut out their
organs of generation.
5. Leontes here probably does some action (touching a
courtier or rubbing his hands together) that shows the
immediacy of his sensory reactions.
6. I see the fingers ("instruments") with which I touch
things; I see the sinners, Hermione and Polixenes, who
touch one another.

To have her honour true than your suspicion,
Be blamed for't how you might.

LEONTES   Why, what need we

Commune with you of this, but rather follow
165 Our forceful instigation?° Our prerogative   *Our own powerful impulse*
Calls not your counsels,[7] but our natural goodness
Imparts this;° which, if you—or° stupefied   *this information / either*
Or seeming so in skill°—cannot or will not   *cunningly*
Relish° a truth like us, inform yourselves   *Appreciate*
170 We need no more of your advice. The matter,
The loss, the gain, the ord'ring on't,° is all   *of it*
Properly ours.

ANTIGONUS   And I wish, my liege,
You had only in your silent judgement tried it
Without more overture.°   *public disclosure*
To see her women? Any of th

LEONTES   How could that be?

175 Either thou art most ignorant by age
Or thou wert born a fool. Camillo's flight
Added to their familiarity,
Which was as gross as ever touched conjecture
That lacked sight only, naught for approbation
180 But only seeing,[8] all other circumstances
Made up to th' deed°—doth push on this proceeding.[9]   *Pointed to the deed*
Yet for a greater confirmation—
For in an act of this importance 'twere
Most piteous to be wild°—I have dispatched in post°   *rash / haste*
185 To sacred Delphos,[1] to Apollo's temple,
Cleomenes and Dion, whom you know
Of stuffed sufficiency.° Now from the oracle   *ample competence*
They will bring all, whose spiritual counsel had°   *obtained*
Shall stop or spur me. Have I done well?

190 A LORD   Well done, my lord.

LEONTES   Though I am satisfied, and need no more
Than what I know, yet shall the oracle
Give rest to th' minds of others such as he,
Whose ignorant credulity will not
195 Come up to th' truth. So have we thought it good
From our free° person she should be confined,   *openly accessible*
Lest that the treachery of the two fled hence
Be left her to perform. Come, follow us.
We are to speak in public; for this business
Will raise° us all.   *rouse (to action)*

200 ANTIGONUS [*aside*]   To laughter, as I take it,
If the good truth were known.   *Exeunt*

2.2

Enter PAULINA, *a Gentleman*[, *and attendants*]

PAULINA   The keeper of the prison, call to him.
Let him have knowledge who I am.   [*Exit Gentleman*]

---

7. My privileges as King do not require that I seek your
advice.
8. As obvious ("gross") as any suspicion ("conjecture")
ever was that only lacked eyewitnesses ("sight" and
"seeing") to confirm its truth.
9. Does urge on this course of action.

1. Delos, often called Delphos by Renaissance writers,
was the island where Apollo, the sun god, was supposedly buried. It is here conflated with Delphi, the Greek
mainland town where the oracle of Apollo could be consulted.
2.2 Location: Sicilia. A prison.

                                        Good lady,
No court in Europe is too good for thee.
What dost thou then in prison?
        [*Enter* JAILER *and Gentleman*]
                                Now, good sir,
You know me, do you not?
5   JAILER   For a worthy lady,
And one who much I honour.
    PAULINA   Pray you then,
Conduct me to the Queen.
    JAILER   I may not, madam. To the contrary
I have express commandment.
10 PAULINA   Here's ado,°   *Here's such a fuss*
To lock up honesty and honour from
Th'access of gentle° visitors. Is't lawful, pray you,   *noble; kind*
To see her women? Any of them? Emilia?
    JAILER   So please you, madam,
15 To put apart these your attendants, I
Shall bring Emilia forth.
    PAULINA   I pray now call her.—
Withdraw yourselves.   [*Exeunt Gentleman and attendants*]
    JAILER   And, madam,
20 I must be present at your conference.
    PAULINA   Well, be't so, prithee.   [*Exit* JAILER]
Here's such ado, to make no stain a stain
As passes colouring.[1]
        [*Enter* JAILER *and* EMILIA]
                        Dear gentlewoman,
How fares our gracious lady?
25 EMILIA   As well as one so great and so forlorn
May hold together. On° her frights and griefs,   *Because of*
Which never tender lady hath borne greater,
She is, something° before her time, delivered.   *somewhat*
    PAULINA   A boy?
    EMILIA   A daughter, and a goodly babe,
30 Lusty,° and like° to live. The Queen receives   *Vigorous / likely*
Much comfort in't; says, 'My poor prisoner,
I am innocent as you.'
    PAULINA   I dare be sworn.
These dangerous, unsafe lunes° i'th' King, beshrew them!   *fits of lunacy*
He must be told on't, and he shall. The office°   *job*
35 Becomes a woman best. I'll take't upon me.
If I prove honey-mouthed, let my tongue blister,[2]
And never to my red-looked° anger be   *red-faced*
The trumpet[3] any more. Pray you, Emilia,
Commend° my best obedience to the Queen.   *Send*
40 If she dares trust me with her little babe
I'll show't the King, and undertake to be
Her advocate to th' loud'st. We do not know
How he may soften at the sight o'th' child.

---

1. To make from no stain at all a stain that exceeds what the art of dyeing can do; to make of no sin a sin that surpasses all attempts to justify it.
2. Alluding to the proverb that deceitfulness causes blisters on the tongue.

3. In early modern warfare, a "trumpet" was a soldier who, bearing a trumpet, went before the red-coated herald who carried messages, often angry ones, to the enemy camp.

The silence often of pure innocence
Persuades when speaking fails.

45 EMILIA   Most worthy madam,
Your honour and your goodness is so evident
That your free° undertaking cannot miss   *generous*
A thriving issue.[4] There is no lady living
So meet° for this great errand. Please your ladyship   *suitable*
50 To visit the next room, I'll presently
Acquaint the Queen of your most noble offer,
Who but today hammered of° this design   *mused upon*
But durst not tempt a minister of honour[5]
Lest she should be denied.

PAULINA   Tell her, Emilia,
55 I'll use that tongue I have. If wit flow from't
As boldness from my bosom, let't not be doubted
I shall do good.

EMILIA   Now be you blest for it!
I'll to the Queen. Please you come something° nearer.   *somewhat*

JAILER   Madam, if't please the Queen to send the babe
60 I know not what° I shall incur to pass it,[6]   *what (risk)*
Having no warrant.

PAULINA   You need not fear it, sir.
This child was prisoner to the womb, and is
By law and process of great nature thence
Freed and enfranchised, not a party to
65 The anger of the King, nor guilty of—
If any be—the trespass of the Queen.

JAILER   I do believe it.

PAULINA   Do not you fear. Upon mine honour,
I will stand twixt you and danger.   *Exeunt*

2.3

Enter LEONTES

LEONTES   Nor° night nor day, no rest! It is but weakness   *Neither*
To bear the matter thus, mere weakness. If
The cause were not in being°—part o'th' cause,   *alive*
She, th'adultress; for the harlot° King   *lewd*
5 Is quite beyond mine arm, out of the blank°   *target*
And level° of my brain, plot-proof; but she   *aim*
I can hook to me. Say that she were gone,
Given to the fire,[1] a moiety° of my rest   *portion*
Might come to me again. Who's there?

[*Enter a* SERVANT]

SERVANT   My lord.

LEONTES   How does the boy?

10 SERVANT   He took good rest tonight.
'Tis hoped his sickness is discharged.

LEONTES   To see his nobleness!
Conceiving° the dishonour of his mother   *Realizing*
He straight° declined, drooped, took it deeply,   *immediately*
15 Fastened and fixed the shame on't° in himself;   *of it*

---

4. A successful outcome, with a pun on "issue" as "offspring."
5. But dared not risk asking a person of higher rank.
6. To let it pass (out of the prison).
2.3 Location: Sicilia. The palace of Leontes.
1. Burned at the stake (for treason against the King).

Threw off his spirit, his appetite, his sleep,
And downright languished. Leave me solely.° Go,   *alone*
See how he fares.   [*Exit* SERVANT]
             Fie, fie, no thought of him.°
                                     (Polixenes)
The very thought of my revenges that way
20   Recoil upon me. In himself too mighty,
And in his parties,° his alliance.° Let him be   *supporters / allies*
Until a time may serve. For present vengeance,
Take it on her. Camillo and Polixenes
Laugh at me, make their pastime at my sorrow.
25   They should not laugh if I could reach them, nor
Shall she, within my power.
          Enter PAULINA [*carrying a babe, with* ANTIGONUS,
          LORDS, *and the* SERVANT, *trying to restrain her*]
A LORD   You must not enter.
PAULINA   Nay rather, good my lords, be second to me.°   *help me*
Fear you his tyrannous passion more, alas,
Than the Queen's life?—a gracious, innocent soul,
More free° than he is jealous.   *innocent*
30 ANTIGONUS   That's enough.
SERVANT   Madam, he hath not slept tonight, commanded
None should come at him.
PAULINA   Not so hot, good sir.
I come to bring him sleep. 'Tis such as you,
That creep like shadows by him, and do sigh
35   At each his needless heavings, such as you
Nourish the cause of his awaking.° I   *wakefulness*
Do come with words as medicinal as true,
Honest as either, to purge him of that humour°   *mental disorder*
That presses him from sleep.
LEONTES   What noise there, ho?
40 PAULINA   No noise, my lord, but needful conference
About some gossips² for your highness.
LEONTES   How?
Away with that audacious lady! Antigonus,
I charged thee that she should not come about me.
I knew she would.
ANTIGONUS   I told her so, my lord,
45   On your displeasure's peril° and on mine,   *At the risk of your anger*
She should not visit you.
LEONTES   What, canst not rule her?
PAULINA   From all dishonesty he can. In this,
Unless he take the course that you have done—
Commit° me for committing honour—trust it,   *Imprison*
He shall not rule me.
50 ANTIGONUS   La you now, you hear.
When she will take the rein I let her run,
But she'll not stumble.
PAULINA [*to* LEONTES]   Good my liege, I come—
And I beseech you hear me, who professes
Myself your loyal servant, your physician,
55   Your most obedient counsellor; yet that dares
Less appear so in comforting° your evils   *condoning*

---

2. Godparents or sponsors at a child's baptism.

Than such as most seem yours³—I say, I come
From your good queen.

LEONTES   Good queen?

60 **PAULINA** Good queen, my lord, good queen, I say good queen,
And would by combat make her good,⁴ so were I
A man, the worst about° you.   *lowest in rank of*

LEONTES [*to* LORDS]   Force her hence.

PAULINA Let him that makes but trifles of his eyes
First hand° me. On mine own accord, I'll off.   *touch*

65 But first I'll do my errand. The good Queen—
For she is good—hath brought you forth a daughter—
Here 'tis—commends it to your blessing.
          [*She lays down the babe*]

LEONTES   Out!
A mankind° witch! Hence with her, out o'door—   *manlike*
A most intelligencing bawd.°   *spying go-between*

PAULINA   Not so.

70 I am as ignorant in that as you
In so entitling me,° and no less honest   *In calling me that*
Than you are mad, which is enough, I'll warrant,
As this world goes, to pass for honest.

LEONTES [*to* LORDS]   Traitors,
Will you not push her out?
[*To* ANTIGONUS]   Give her the bastard.

75 Thou dotard, thou art woman-tired,⁵ unroosted
By thy Dame Partlet here.⁶ Take up the bastard,
Take't up, I say. Give't to thy crone.°   *old woman*

PAULINA [*to* ANTIGONUS]   For ever
Unvenerable° be thy hands if thou   *Unworthy of respect*
Tak'st up the princess by that forcèd baseness⁷
Which he has put upon't.

80 **LEONTES**   He dreads° his wife.   *fears*

PAULINA So I would you did. Then 'twere past all doubt
You'd call your children yours.

LEONTES   A nest of traitors.

ANTIGONUS I am none, by this good light.

PAULINA   Nor I, nor any
But one that's here, and that's himself, for he

85 The sacred honour of himself, his queen's,
His hopeful son's, his babe's, betrays to slander,
Whose sting is sharper than the sword's; and will not—
For as the case now stands, it is a curse
He cannot be compelled to't—once remove

90 The root of his opinion, which is rotten
As ever oak or stone was sound.

LEONTES [*to* LORDS]   A callat°   *scold; harlot*
Of boundless tongue, who late° hath beat her husband,   *recently*
And now baits° me! This brat is none of mine.   *provokes*
It is the issue° of Polixenes.   *offspring*

---

3. Than those who (wrongly) seem most loyal.
4. Prove her to be innocent. Alluding to the chivalric trials by combat in which knights would establish innocence or guilt by means of duels.
5. You are pecked at by women. A metaphor from fal-

conry referring to tearing of flesh with the beak.
6. Expelled from your "roost" or "perch," the position of domestic authority assigned to men. In medieval tales, "Partlett" is a traditional name for a hen.
7. Under that wrongful name of bastard.

95   Hence with it, and together with the dam
        Commit them to the fire.
        PAULINA   It is yours,
        And might we lay th'old proverb to your charge,°   *apply the proverb to you*
        So like you 'tis the worse. Behold, my lords,
        Although the print° be little, the whole matter   *copy*
100   And copy of the father: eye, nose, lip,
        The trick° of's frown, his forehead, nay, the valley,[8]   *distinctive character*
        The pretty dimples of his chin and cheek, his smiles,
        The very mould and frame of hand, nail, finger.
        And thou good goddess Nature, which hast made it
105   So like to him that got° it, if thou hast   *begot*
        The ordering of the mind too, 'mongst all colours
        No yellow[9] in't, lest she suspect, as he does,
        Her children not her husband's.
        LEONTES [*to* ANTIGONUS]   A gross hag!—
        And lozel,° thou art worthy to be hanged,   *scoundrel*
        That wilt not stay her tongue.
110   ANTIGONUS   Hang all the husbands
        That cannot do that feat, you'll leave yourself
        Hardly one subject.
        LEONTES   Once more, take her hence.
        PAULINA   A most unworthy and unnatural lord
        Can do no more.
        LEONTES   I'll ha' thee burnt.
        PAULINA   I care not.
115   It is an heretic that makes the fire,
        Not she which burns in't.[1] I'll not call you tyrant;
        But this most cruel usage of your queen—
        Not able to produce more accusation
        Than your own weak-hinged fancy—something savours
120   Of tyranny, and will ignoble make you,
        Yea, scandalous to the world.
        LEONTES [*to* ANTIGONUS]   On your allegiance,
        Out of the chamber with her! Were I a tyrant,
        Where were her life? She durst not call me so
        If she did know me one. Away with her!
125   PAULINA   I pray you do not push me, I'll be gone.
        Look to your babe, my lord; 'tis yours. Jove°   *(King of the gods)*
        A better guiding spirit. What needs these hands?[2]
        You that are thus so tender o'er° his follies   *gentle with*
        Will never do him good, not one of you.
130   So, so. Farewell, we are gone.   *Exit*
        LEONTES [*to* ANTIGONUS]   Thou, traitor, hast set on thy wife to this.
        My child? Away with't! Even thou, that hast
        A heart so tender o'er it, take it hence
        And see it instantly consumed with fire.
135   Even thou, and none but thou. Take it up straight.°   *at once*
        Within this hour bring me word 'tis done,
        And by good testimony,° or I'll seize thy life,   *with good evidence*

---

8. Referring to an indentation in the lip or a cleft in the chin.
9. Proverbially, the color of jealousy.
1. The heretic is the one who unjustly makes the fire

(Leontes), not the woman who burns in it (Hermione).
2. Why is it necessary for you to push me out? (spoken to Leontes' attendant lords).

With what thou else call'st thine. If thou refuse
And wilt encounter with my wrath, say so.
140 The bastard brains with these my proper° hands   own
Shall I dash out. Go, take it to the fire;
For thou set'st on thy wife.

ANTIGONUS   I did not, sir.
These lords, my noble fellows, if they please
Can clear me in't.

LORDS   We can. My royal liege,
145 He is not guilty of her coming hither.

LEONTES   You're liars all.

A LORD   Beseech your highness, give us better credit.°   think us more honorable
We have always truly served you, and beseech
So to esteem of us. And on our knees we beg,
150 As recompense of our dear services
Past and to come, that you do change this purpose
Which, being so horrible, so bloody, must
Lead on to some foul issue. We all kneel.

LEONTES   I am a feather for each wind that blows.
155 Shall I live on, to see this bastard kneel
And call me father? Better burn it now
Than curse it then. But be it. Let it live.
It shall not neither.
[To ANTIGONUS]   You, sir, come you hither,
You that have been so tenderly officious
160 With Lady Margery³ your midwife there,
To save this bastard's life—for 'tis a bastard,
So sure as this beard's grey. What will you adventure°   risk
To save this brat's life?

ANTIGONUS   Anything, my lord,
That my ability may undergo,
165 And nobleness impose. At least thus much,
I'll pawn the little blood which I have left⁴
To save the innocent; anything possible.

LEONTES   It shall be possible. Swear by this sword
Thou wilt perform my bidding.

ANTIGONUS   I will, my lord.

170 LEONTES   Mark, and perform it. Seest thou? For the fail°   failure
Of any point in't shall not only be
Death to thyself but to thy lewd-tongued wife,
Whom for this time we pardon. We enjoin thee,
As thou art liegeman° to us, that thou carry   loyal servant
175 This female bastard hence, and that thou bear it
To some remote and desert place, quite out
Of our dominions; and that there thou leave it,
Without more mercy, to it° own protection   its
And favour of the climate. As by strange fortune⁵
180 It came to us, I do in justice charge thee,
On thy soul's peril and thy body's torture,
That thou commend it strangely to some place⁶
Where chance may nurse° or end it. Take it up.   nurture; help

---

3. A contemptuous name (like "Dame Partlett") for a
disorderly woman. "Margery-prater" is a slang term for
"hen."
4. Aging was thought to reduce the amount of blood in
the body.
5. Since by some unusual chance; since by the act of a
foreigner (Polixenes).
6. That you take it to some foreign land.

ANTIGONUS   I swear to do this, though a present death

185 Had been more merciful. Come on, poor babe,
Some powerful spirit instruct the kites° and ravens   *birds of prey*
To be thy nurses. Wolves and bears, they say,
Casting their savageness aside, have done
Like° offices of pity. Sir, be prosperous   *Similar*

190 In more than this deed does require;⁷ [*to the babe*] and blessing
Against° this cruelty, fight on thy side,   *To counteract*
Poor thing, condemned to loss.°   *Exit [with the babe]*   *ruin*

LEONTES   No, I'll not rear
Another's issue.

Enter a SERVANT

SERVANT   Please your highness, posts°   *messengers*
From those you sent to th'oracle are come

195 An hour since. Cleomenes and Dion,
Being well arrived from Delphos, are both landed,
Hasting to th' court.

A LORD [*to* LEONTES]   So please you, sir, their speed
Hath been beyond account.°   *without precedent*

LEONTES   Twenty-three days
They have been absent. 'Tis good speed, foretells

200 The great Apollo suddenly° will have   *at once*
The truth of this appear. Prepare you, lords.
Summon a session,° that we may arraign   *trial*
Our most disloyal lady; for as she hath
Been publicly accused, so shall she have

205 A just and open trial. While she lives
My heart will be a burden to me. Leave me,
And think upon my bidding.   *Exeunt [severally]*°   *separately*

3.1

Enter CLEOMENES *and* DION

CLEOMENES   The climate's delicate, the air most sweet;
Fertile the isle,¹ the temple much surpassing
The common praise it bears.

DION   I shall report,
For most it caught° me, the celestial habits—°   *charmed / garments*

5   Methinks I so should term them—and the reverence
Of the grave wearers. O, the sacrifice—
How ceremonious, solemn, and unearthly
It was i'th' off'ring!

CLEOMENES   But of all, the burst°   *blast (of thunder)*
And the ear-deaf'ning voice o'th' oracle,

10   Kin to Jove's thunder, so surprised my sense
That I was nothing.

DION   If th'event° o'th' journey   *outcome*
Prove as successful to the Queen—O, be't so!—
As it hath been to us rare, pleasant, speedy,
The time is worth the use on't.²

CLEOMENES   Great Apollo

---

7. To a greater extent or in more ways than this action deserves.
3.1 Location: A road in Sicilia.
1. The island of Delphos (Delos), Apollo's birthplace,

here conflated with Delphi, where Apollo's oracle was located. See note to 2.1.185.
2. The time will have been well spent.

15   Turn all to th' best! These proclamations,
           So forcing faults upon Hermione,
           I little like.

DION   The violent carriage° of it   *rash handling*
           Will clear or end the business. When the oracle,
           Thus by Apollo's great divine° sealed up,   *priest*
20   Shall the contents discover,° something rare   *reveal*
           Even then will rush to knowledge. Go. Fresh horses!
           And gracious be the issue.°   *Exeunt*   *result; the child*

3.2

Enter LEONTES, LORDS, [*and*] OFFICERS

LEONTES   This sessions, to our great grief we pronounce,
           Even pushes 'gainst our heart: the party tried
           The daughter of a king, our wife, and one
           Of us° too much beloved. Let us be cleared   *By us*
5   Of being tyrannous since we so openly
           Proceed in justice, which shall have due course
           Even to the guilt or the purgation.°   *acquittal*
           Produce the prisoner.

OFFICER   It is his highness' pleasure
           That the Queen appear in person here in court.

[*Enter* HERMIONE *guarded, with* PAULINA *and Ladies*]

10   Silence.[1]

LEONTES   Read the indictment.

OFFICER [*reads*]   Hermione, queen to the worthy Leontes, King
           of Sicilia, thou art here accused and arraigned of high treason
           in committing adultery with Polixenes, King of Bohemia, and
15   conspiring with Camillo to take away the life of our sovereign
           lord the King, thy royal husband; the pretence° whereof being   *purpose*
           by circumstances partly laid open, thou, Hermione, contrary to
           the faith and allegiance of a true subject, didst counsel and aid
           them for their better safety to fly away by night.

20 HERMIONE   Since what I am to say must be but° that   *only*
           Which contradicts my accusation, and
           The testimony on my part no other
           But what comes from myself, it shall scarce boot° me   *profit*
           To say 'Not guilty'. Mine integrity
25   Being counted falsehood shall, as I express it,
           Be so received. But thus: if powers divine
           Behold our human actions—as they do—
           I doubt not then but innocence shall make
           False accusation blush, and tyranny
30   Tremble at patience. You, my lord, best know—
           Who least will seem to do so—my past life
           Hath been as continent, as chaste, as true
           As I am now unhappy; which° is more   *which unhappiness*
           Than history can pattern,[2] though devised
35   And played to take° spectators. For behold me,   *captivate*
           A fellow of the royal bed, which owe°   *who owns*
           A moiety° of the throne; a great king's daughter,   *A portion*

3.2 Location: Sicilia. A court of justice.
1. In F, the word "Silence" is printed in italics and set as a stage direction. Here it is treated as an imperative and assigned to the Officer who announces the Queen's entrance.
2. Than story or drama can show a precedent for.

The mother to a hopeful prince, here standing
To prate and talk for life and honour, fore°   *before*
40 Who please to come and hear. For° life, I prize° it   *As for / value*
As I weigh° grief, which I would spare.° For honour,   *value / do without*
'Tis a derivative³ from me to mine,°   *(my children)*
And only that I stand° for. I appeal   *fight*
To your own conscience, sir, before Polixenes
45 Came to your court how I was in your grace,
How merited to be so; since he came,
With what encounter so uncurrent° I   *conduct so unacceptable*
Have strained° t'appear thus.° If one jot beyond   *transgressed / (on trial)*
The bound of honour, or in act or will
50 That way inclining, hardened be the hearts
Of all that hear me, and my near'st of kin
Cry 'Fie' upon my grave.
LEONTES   I ne'er heard yet
That any of these bolder vices wanted
Less° impudence to gainsay° what they did   *Were more lacking in / deny*
Than to perform it first.
55 HERMIONE   That's true enough,
Though 'tis a saying, sir, not due° to me.   *relevant*
LEONTES   You will not own it.
HERMIONE   More than mistress of
Which comes to me in name of fault, I must not
At all acknowledge.⁴ For Polixenes,
60 With whom I am accused, I do confess
I loved him as in honour he required;°   *was his due*
With such a kind of love as might become
A lady like me; with a love, even such,
So, and no other, as yourself commanded;
65 Which not to have done I think had been in me
Both disobedience and ingratitude
To you and toward your friend, whose love had spoke
Even since it could speak, from an infant, freely
That it was yours. Now for conspiracy,
70 I know not how it tastes, though it be dished°   *served*
For me to try how. All I know of it
Is that Camillo was an honest man;
And why he left your court, the gods themselves,
Wotting° no more than I, are ignorant.   *If they know*
75 LEONTES   You knew of his departure, as you know
What you have underta'en to do in's absence.
HERMIONE   Sir,
You speak a language that I understand not.
My life stands in the level of your dreams,⁵
Which I'll lay down.
80 LEONTES   Your actions are my 'dreams'.
You had a bastard by Polixenes,
And I but° dreamed it. As you were past all shame—   *merely*
Those of your fact° are so—so past all truth;   *(guilty) of your crime*

---

3. Something handed on.
4. I must not answer for ("acknowledge") more than
those faults that I actually possess (am "mistress of").
Hermione is denying she possesses the "bolder vices" of

which Leontes accuses her in line 53.
5. As the target ("level") of your delusions. A metaphor
from archery.

Which to deny concerns more than avails;⁶ for as

85 Thy brat hath been cast out, like to itself,°   *as it should be*
No father owning it—which is indeed
More criminal in thee than it—so thou
Shalt feel our justice, in whose easiest passage
Look for no less than death.⁷

HERMIONE   Sir, spare your threats.

90 The bug° which you would fright me with, I seek.   *horrible object*
To me can life be no commodity.°   *profit; comfort*
The crown and comfort of my life, your favour,
I do give° lost, for I do feel it gone   *reckon*
But know not how it went. My second joy,°   *(Mamillius)*

95 And first fruits of my body, from his presence
I am barred, like one infectious. My third comfort,
Starred most unluckily,⁸ is from my breast,
The innocent milk in it° most innocent mouth,   *its*
Haled° out to murder; myself on every post⁹   *Dragged*

100 Proclaimed a strumpet, with immodest° hatred   *excessive*
The childbed privilege¹ denied, which 'longs°   *belongs*
To women of all fashion;° lastly, hurried   *ranks*
Here, to this place, i'th' open air,² before
I have got strength of limit.³ Now, my liege,

105 Tell me what blessings I have here alive,
That I should fear to die. Therefore proceed.
But yet hear this—mistake me not—no life,
I prize it not a straw; but for mine honour,
Which I would free:° if I shall be condemned   *vindicate*

110 Upon surmises, all proofs sleeping else°   *except*
But what your jealousies awake, I tell you
'Tis rigour, and not law.⁴ Your honours all,
I do refer me° to the oracle.   *appeal*
Apollo be my judge.

A LORD   This your request

115 Is altogether just. Therefore bring forth,
And in Apollo's name, his oracle.   [*Exeunt certain Officers*]

HERMIONE   The Emperor of Russia⁵ was my father.
O that he were alive, and here beholding
His daughter's trial; that he did but see

120 The flatness° of my misery—yet with eyes   *boundlessness*
Of pity, not revenge.

              [*Enter* OFFICERS *with* CLEOMENES *and* DION]

OFFICER   You here shall swear upon this sword of justice
That you, Cleomenes and Dion, have
Been both at Delphos, and from thence have brought

125 This sealed-up oracle, by the hand delivered

---

6. Your denial of the truth costs you more effort than it's worth.
7. In the mildest course of justice, you can expect death. The implication is that death may well be preceded by torture.
8. Born under most unlucky stars.
9. Alluding to the early modern practice of nailing proclamations to posts in public places.
1. The right to enjoy a period of bedrest and seclusion after childbirth.
2. Exposure to air outside the domestic space was con-

sidered unsafe for women weakened by childbirth.
3. Before I have the strength that follows the customary period of confinement.
4. Playing on the expression "the rigor of the law," Hermione implies that judgment against her would be mere tyranny ("rigor") and not law.
5. Possibly a reference to the legendary Czar Ivan the Terrible, who died in 1584. Many London merchants were interested in trade with Russia, especially after the formation of the Muscovy Company in 1553.

Of great Apollo's priest; and that since then
You have not dared to break the holy seal,
Nor read the secrets in't.

CLEOMENES *and* DION   All this we swear.

130 LEONTES   Break up the seals, and read.

OFFICER [*reads*]   Hermione is chaste, Polixenes blameless, Camillo a true subject, Leontes a jealous tyrant, his innocent babe
truly begotten, and the King shall live without an heir if that
which is lost be not found.

LORDS   Now blessèd be the great Apollo!

135 HERMIONE   Praised!

LEONTES   Hast thou read truth?

OFFICER   Ay, my lord, even so as it is here set down.

LEONTES   There is no truth at all i'th' oracle.
The sessions shall proceed. This is mere falsehood.

[*Enter a* SERVANT]

SERVANT   My lord the King! The King!

140 LEONTES   What is the business?

SERVANT   O sir, I shall be hated to report it.
The prince your son, with mere conceit° and fear   thought
Of the Queen's speed,° is gone.   fortune

LEONTES   How, 'gone'?

SERVANT   Is dead.

LEONTES   Apollo's angry, and the heavens themselves
Do strike at my injustice.

[HERMIONE *falls to the ground*]

145   How now there?

PAULINA   This news is mortal to the Queen. Look down
And see what death is doing.

LEONTES   Take her hence.
Her heart is but o'ercharged.° She will recover.   overburdened (by emotion)
I have too much believed mine own suspicion.

150 Beseech you, tenderly apply to her
Some remedies for life.

[*Exeunt* PAULINA *and Ladies, carrying* HERMIONE]

                    Apollo, pardon
My great profaneness 'gainst thine oracle.
I'll reconcile me to Polixenes,
New woo my queen, recall the good Camillo,

155 Whom I proclaim a man of truth, of mercy;
For being transported by my jealousies
To bloody thoughts and to revenge, I chose
Camillo for the minister to poison
My friend Polixenes, which had° been done,   would have

160 But that the good mind of Camillo tardied°   delayed
My swift command. Though I with death and with
Reward did threaten and encourage him,
Not doing it, and being done,[6] he, most humane
And filled with honour, to my kingly guest

165 Unclasped my practice,° quit his fortunes here—   Revealed my plot
Which you knew great—and to the certain hazard
Of all incertainties himself commended,°   consigned himself

6. That is, "Though I threatened him with death if he did not do it and encouraged him with the promise of reward
if he did do it."

No richer than his honour.[7] How he glisters
Through my rust![8] And how his piety
Does my deeds make the blacker!

[*Enter* PAULINA]

170 PAULINA   Woe the while!
O cut my lace,[9] lest my heart, cracking it,
Break too.

A LORD   What fit is this, good lady?

PAULINA [*to* LEONTES] What studied° torments, tyrant, hast for me?   *expertly devised*
What wheels, racks, fires? What flaying, boiling
175 In leads or oils?[1] What old or newer torture
Must I receive, whose every word deserves
To taste of thy most worst? Thy tyranny,
Together working with thy jealousies—
Fancies too weak for boys, too green and idle°   *immature and foolish*
180 For girls of nine—O think what they have done,
And then run mad indeed, stark mad, for all
Thy bygone fooleries were but spices° of it.   *slight tastes*
That thou betrayed'st Polixenes, 'twas nothing.
That did but show thee, of° a fool, inconstant,   *for*
185 And damnable° ingrateful. Nor was't much   *damnably; cursedly*
Thou wouldst have poisoned good Camillo's honour
To have him kill a king—poor° trespasses,   *minor*
More monstrous standing by,[2] whereof I reckon
The casting forth to crows thy baby daughter
190 To be or° none or little, though a devil   *either*
Would have shed water out of fire ere done't.[3]
Nor is't directly laid to thee the death
Of the young prince, whose honourable thoughts—
Thoughts high for one so tender°—cleft the heart   *young*
195 That could conceive a gross° and foolish sire   *stupid*
Blemished his gracious dam.° This is not, no,   *mother*
Laid to thy answer.[4] But the last—O lords,
When I have said,° cry woe! The Queen, the Queen,   *finished speaking*
The sweet'st, dear'st creature's dead, and vengeance for't
Not dropped down yet.

200 A LORD   The higher powers forbid!

PAULINA I say she's dead. I'll swear't. If word nor oath
Prevail not, go and see. If you can bring
Tincture° or lustre in her lip, her eye,   *Color*
Heat outwardly or breath within, I'll serve you
205 As I would do the gods. But O thou tyrant,
Do not repent these things, for they are heavier
Than all thy woes° can stir.° Therefore betake thee   *grief / remove*
To nothing but despair. A thousand knees,
Ten thousand years together, naked, fasting,
210 Upon a barren mountain, and still° winter   *always*

---

7. Possessing no fortune but his honor.
8. How he shines ("glisters") in comparison with my rust. The image alludes to polished and rusty armor.
9. It was believed that fainting might be prevented by cutting the stays on the tight bodices characteristic of female dress in this period.
1. A list of early modern forms of torture. The wheel was a device to which a person was tied and his or her limbs broken, usually by beating. The rack typically consisted of a frame with a roller at each end; a person was attached to this frame and his or her limbs stretched by turning the rollers. To "flay" was to strip off someone's skin while he or she was still alive.
2. In comparison with more monstrous ones near at hand.
3. A devil would have shed tears from his fiery eyes (or from hellfires) before he had done it.
4. Presented as a charge you must answer.

In storm perpetual, could not move the gods
To look that way thou wert.°   *in your direction*

LEONTES   Go on, go on.
Thou canst not speak too much. I have deserved
All tongues to talk their bitt'rest.

A LORD [*to* PAULINA]   Say no more.
215 Howe'er the business goes, you have made fault
I'th' boldness of your speech.

PAULINA   I am sorry for't.
All faults I make, when I shall come to know them
I do repent. Alas, I have showed too much
The rashness of a woman. He is touched
220 To th' noble heart. What's gone and what's past help
Should be past grief.
    [*To* LEONTES]   Do not receive affliction
At my petition.° I beseech you, rather   *Because of my injunction*
Let me be punished, that have minded° you   *reminded*
Of what you should forget. Now, good my liege,
225 Sir, royal sir, forgive a foolish woman.
The love I bore your queen—lo, fool again!
I'll speak of her no more, nor of your children.
I'll not remember you of my own lord,
Who is lost too. Take your patience to you,°   *Be patient*
And I'll say nothing.

230 LEONTES   Thou didst speak but well
When most the truth, which I receive much better
Than to be pitied of° thee. Prithee bring me   *by*
To the dead bodies of my queen and son.
One grave shall be for both. Upon them shall
235 The causes of their death appear, unto
Our shame perpetual. Once a day I'll visit
The chapel where they lie, and tears shed there
Shall be my recreation.[5] So long as nature°   *my bodily being*
Will bear up with this exercise, so long
240 I daily vow to use it. Come, and lead me
To these sorrows.
                                              Exeunt

3.3

Enter ANTIGONUS, [*carrying the*] *babe,* [*with*] *a* MARINER

ANTIGONUS   Thou art perfect° then our ship hath touched upon   *certain*
The deserts of Bohemia?

MARINER   Ay, my lord, and fear
We have landed in ill time. The skies look grimly
And threaten present blusters.° In my conscience,°   *impending storms / opinion*
5 The heavens with that we have in hand are angry,
And frown upon's.

ANTIGONUS   Their sacred wills be done. Go get aboard.
Look to thy barque.° I'll not be long before   *ship*
I call upon thee.

MARINER   Make your best haste, and go not
10 Too far i'th' land. 'Tis like to be loud° weather.   *stormy*

---

5. My only diversion; my spiritual renewal or recreation.
3.3 Location: Bohemia. The seacoast. This play, as
does Greene's *Pandosto,* credits Bohemia with a coast.

Only for two brief periods in the late Middle Ages may
Bohemia have controlled a small piece of territory on
the Adriatic Sea, but it was otherwise landlocked.

Besides, this place is famous for the creatures
Of prey that keep° upon't.   °live
ANTIGONUS   Go thou away.
   I'll follow instantly.
MARINER   I am glad at heart
   To be so rid o'th' business.   *Exit*
ANTIGONUS   Come, poor babe.
15   I have heard, but not believed, the spirits o'th' dead
   May walk again. If such thing be, thy mother
   Appeared to me last night, for ne'er was dream
   So like a waking. To me comes a creature,
   Sometimes her head on one side, some another.
20   I never saw a vessel° of like sorrow,   °person; receptacle
   So filled and so becoming.[1] In pure white robes
   Like very sanctity she did approach
   My cabin where I lay, thrice bowed before me,
   And, gasping to begin some speech, her eyes
25   Became two spouts. The fury spent, anon°   °soon
   Did this break from her: 'Good Antigonus,
   Since fate, against thy better disposition,
   Hath made thy person for the thrower-out
   Of my poor babe according to thine oath,
30   Places remote enough are in Bohemia.
   There weep, and leave it crying; and for° the babe   °because
   Is counted lost for ever, Perdita[2]
   I prithee call't. For this ungentle° business   °unkind; ignoble
   Put on thee by my lord, thou ne'er shalt see
35   Thy wife Paulina more.' And so with shrieks
   She melted into air. Affrighted much,
   I did in time collect myself, and thought
   This was so, and no slumber. Dreams are toys,°   °trifles
   Yet for this once, yea superstitiously,
40   I will be squared° by this. I do believe   °ruled
   Hermione hath suffered death, and that
   Apollo would—this being indeed the issue°   °child
   Of King Polixenes—it should here be laid,
   Either for life or death, upon the earth
45   Of its right father. Blossom, speed° thee well!   °fare
   [*He lays down the babe and a scroll*]
   There lie, and there thy character.[3]
   [*He lays down a box*]
                      There these,[4]
   Which may, if fortune please, both breed thee, pretty,
   And still rest thine.[5]
   [*Thunder*]
             The storm begins. Poor wretch,
   That for thy mother's fault art thus exposed
50   To loss and what may follow! Weep I cannot,
   But my heart bleeds, and most accursed am I
   To be by oath enjoined to this. Farewell.

---

1. So filled with sorrow and so beautiful.
2. Latin for "lost one."
3. The written account of your history and parentage.
4. The gold and jewels with which the Old Shepherd grows rich and which are later used to identify the

Princess. See 5.2.29–36.
5. Which may, if you are lucky, be sufficient to pay for your upbringing, pretty child, and still leave you with something besides.

The day frowns more and more. Thou'rt like to have
A lullaby too rough. I never saw
55   The heavens so dim by day. A savage clamour!
Well may I get aboard. This is the chase.°   *hunt*
I am gone for ever!   *Exit, pursued by a bear*[6]
       [*Enter an* OLD SHEPHERD]
OLD SHEPHERD   I would there were no age between ten and
three-and-twenty, or that youth would sleep out the rest; for
60   there is nothing in the between but getting wenches with child,
wronging the ancientry,° stealing, fighting—hark you now,   *elderly people*
would any but these boiled-brains° of nineteen and two-and-   *lunatics*
twenty hunt this weather? They have scared away two of my
best sheep, which I fear the wolf will sooner find than the mas-
65   ter. If anywhere I have them, 'tis by the seaside, browsing of°   *on*
ivy. Good luck, an't° be thy will!   *if it*
       [*He sees the babe*]
What have we here? Mercy on's, a bairn!° A very pretty bairn.   *child*
A boy or a child,° I wonder? A pretty one, a very pretty one.   *girl*
Sure some scape.[7] Though I am not bookish,° yet I can read   *not familiar with books*
70   'waiting-gentlewoman' in the scape. This has been some stair-
work, some trunk-work, some behind-door-work.[8] They were
warmer that got° this than the poor thing is here. I'll take it up   *begot*
for pity; yet I'll tarry till my son come. He hallooed but even
now. Whoa-ho-hoa!
       Enter CLOWN°   *Bumpkin*
75   CLOWN   Hilloa, loa!
OLD SHEPHERD   What, art so near? If thou'lt see a thing to talk
on° when thou art dead and rotten, come hither. What ail'st   *about*
thou, man?
CLOWN   I have seen two such sights, by sea and by land! But I
80   am not to say it is a sea, for it is now the sky. Betwixt the firmament and it you cannot thrust a bodkin's° point.   *needle's*
OLD SHEPHERD   Why, boy, how is it?
CLOWN   I would you did but see how it chafes, how it rages, how
it takes up the shore. But that's not to the point. O, the most
85   piteous cry of the poor souls! Sometimes to see 'em, and not to
see 'em; now the ship boring° the moon with her mainmast,   *piercing*
and anon swallowed with yeast° and froth, as you'd thrust a cork   *foam*
into a hogshead.° And then for the land-service,[9] to see how the *cask of liquor*
bear tore out his shoulder-bone, how he cried to me for help,
90   and said his name was Antigonus, a nobleman! But to make an
end of the ship—to see how the sea flap-dragoned it![1] But first,
how the poor souls roared, and the sea mocked them, and how

---

6. One of the most famous stage directions in English drama. A real bear, rather than a man in a bear suit, might have been used in this scene, perhaps discreetly led on a rope by the fleeing Antigonus. There were reports of tame bears in Shakespeare's London, and bearbaiting (setting dogs on chained bears) was a popular Elizabethan sport, sometimes occurring in the same amphitheaters used at other times for stage plays. It is more likely, however, that the bear was impersonated by an actor in a bear costume. Modern productions vary significantly in their representation of the bear. Some strive for realism, having a bearskin-clad actor or a mechanical likeness of a bear pass across a darkened stage illuminated only by the occasional

lightning bolt. Others productions are more stylized, suggesting a bear by the obvious artifice of a mask or symbol.
7. Sexual transgression. English ballads and other popular literature of the period offer numerous accounts of female servants who abandon or kill children born out of wedlock.
8. Some secret sexual affair conducted on back stairs, in chests, or behind doors.
9. Punning on the military and culinary meanings of "service" to suggest both "combat on land" and "food to be served up on land."
1. Devoured it as if it were a flapdragon, a raisin floating on flaming brandy.

the poor gentleman roared, and the bear mocked him, both
roaring louder than the sea or weather.

95 OLD SHEPHERD   Name of mercy, when was this, boy?

CLOWN   Now, now. I have not winked° since I saw these sights.   blinked an eye
The men are not yet cold under water, nor the bear half dined
on the gentleman. He's at it now.

OLD SHEPHERD   Would I had been by to have helped the old
100 man!

CLOWN   I would you had been by the ship side, to have helped
her. There your charity would have lacked footing.²

OLD SHEPHERD   Heavy° matters, heavy matters. But look thee   Sad
here, boy. Now bless thyself. Thou metst with things dying, I
105 with things new-born. Here's a sight for thee. Look thee, a bear-
ing-cloth³ for a squire's child.

[He points to the box]

Look thee here, take up, take up, boy. Open't. So, let's see. It
was told me I should be rich by the fairies. This is some
changeling.⁴ Open't. What's within, boy?

110 CLOWN [opening the box]   You're a made° old man. If the sins of   prosperous
your youth are forgiven you, you're well to live.° Gold, all gold!   well off; virtuous

OLD SHEPHERD   This is fairy gold,⁵ boy, and 'twill prove so. Up
with't, keep it close.° Home, home, the next° way. We are   secret / nearest
lucky, boy, and to be so still° requires nothing but secrecy. Let   always
115 my sheep go. Come, good boy, the next way home.

CLOWN   Go you the next way with your findings. I'll go see if the
bear be gone from the gentleman, and how much he hath
eaten. They are never curst° but when they are hungry. If there   vicious
be any of him left, I'll bury it.

120 OLD SHEPHERD   That's a good deed. If thou mayst discern by that
which is left of him what he is,° fetch me to th' sight of him.   his identity or rank

CLOWN   Marry⁶ will I; and you shall help to put him i'th' ground.

OLD SHEPHERD   'Tis a lucky day, boy, and we'll do good deeds
on't.   Exeunt

4.1

Enter TIME,¹ the Chorus

TIME   I that please some, try° all; both joy and terror   test
Of good and bad; that makes and unfolds error,
Now take upon me in the name° of Time   with the authority
To use my wings. Impute it not a crime
5 To me or my swift passage that I slide
O'er sixteen years and leave the growth untried°   development unexamined
Of that wide gap, since it is in my power
To o'erthrow law, and in one self-born° hour   selfsame
To plant and o'erwhelm° custom. Let me pass   establish and overthrow
10 The same I am ere ancient'st order was

2. There you would not have had a secure place to
stand, with a pun on "footing" as meaning "a foundation" (upon which a charity might be founded).
3. The blanket used to wrap an infant in preparation
for baptism. A squire's child, being of a fairly high
social position, would have a rich bearing-cloth.
4. A child secretly substituted for another by fairies. The
term could apply to the abducted child (usually beautiful)
or to the one (often ugly or deformed) left in its place.
5. Riches left by fairies were unreliable. If not kept
secret, they brought bad luck.

6. A mild oath derived from the name of the Virgin
Mary.
4.1 Location: Scene continues.
1. In early modern texts, Time was conventionally represented as an old bald man with wings, signifying how
swiftly time passes. He often carried an hourglass and
a scythe, symbol of the power of time to destroy life. A
common saying was that Time was the revealer of
Truth, or that Truth was the daughter of Time. Robert
Greene's Pandosto, Shakespeare's chief source for The
Winter's Tale, was subtitled The Triumph of Time.

Or what is now received.[2] I witness to
The times that brought them in; so shall I do
To th' freshest things now reigning, and make stale
The glistering° of this present as my tale   *glittering shine*
15 Now seems to it.[3] Your patience this allowing,
I turn my glass,° and give my scene such growing   *hourglass*
As° you had slept between. Leontes leaving   *As if*
Th'effects of his fond° jealousies, so grieving   *foolish*
That he shuts up himself, imagine me,
20 Gentle spectators, that I now may be
In fair Bohemia, and remember well
I mentionèd a son o'th' King's, which Florizel
I now name to you; and with speed so pace°   *proceed*
To speak of Perdita, now grown in grace
25 Equal with wond'ring.[4] What of her ensues
I list not° prophesy, but let Time's news   *do not wish to*
Be known when 'tis brought forth. A shepherd's daughter
And what to her adheres,° which follows after,   *pertains*
Is th'argument° of Time. Of this allow,   *subject matter*
30 If ever you have spent time worse ere now.
If never, yet that Time himself doth say
He wishes earnestly you never may.   *Exit*

4.2

Enter POLIXENES *and* CAMILLO

POLIXENES   I pray thee, good Camillo, be no more importunate.
'Tis a sickness denying° thee anything, a death to grant this.   *to deny*
CAMILLO   It is sixteen[1] years since I saw my country. Though I
have for the most part been aired abroad,° I desire to lay my   *breathed foreign air*
5 bones there. Besides, the penitent King, my master, hath sent
for me, to whose feeling° sorrows I might be some allay°—or I   *deeply felt / relief*
o'erween° to think so—which is another spur to my departure.   *am bold enough*
POLIXENES   As thou lov'st me, Camillo, wipe not out the rest of
thy services by leaving me now. The need I have of thee thine
10 own goodness hath made. Better not to have had thee than thus
to want° thee. Thou, having made me businesses[2] which none   *be without*
without thee can sufficiently manage, must either stay to execute them thyself or take away with thee the very services thou
hast done; which if I have not enough considered°—as too   *rewarded*
15 much I cannot—to be more thankful to thee shall be my study,
and my profit therein, the heaping friendships.[3] Of that fatal°   *deadly*
country Sicilia, prithee speak no more, whose very naming
punishes me with the remembrance of that penitent—as thou
callest him—and reconciled King my brother, whose loss of his
20 most precious queen and children are even now to be afresh°   *newly*
lamented. Say to me, when sawest thou the Prince Florizel,
my son? Kings are no less unhappy, their issue° not being gra-   *children*
cious,° than they are in losing them when they have ap-   *not proving virtuous*
proved° their virtues.   *demonstrated*

---

2. Let me remain as I have been from before the beginnings of civilization even to the time of present customs.
3. As my tale now seems stale in comparison with the
present.
4. Now grown so gracious as to inspire admiration.
4.2 Location: Bohemia. The palace of Polixenes.

1. F reads "fifteene." At 4.1.6, Time says that sixteen
years have passed. This apparent error may be due to
carelessness on Shakespeare's part or to a misreading of
a Roman numeral by a compositor or scribe.
2. Performed services for me.
3. The accumulation of your kindnesses.

25 CAMILLO   Sir, it is three days since I saw the Prince. What his
      happier affairs may be are to me unknown; but I have missingly
      noted° he is of late much retired from court, and is less fre-   *noted by his absence*
      quent to° his princely exercises than formerly he hath   *less often engaged in*
      appeared.
30 POLIXENES   I have considered so much, Camillo, and with some
      care, so far that I have eyes under my service° which look upon   *spies in my employ*
      his removedness,° from whom I have this intelligence: that he   *retirement (from court)*
      is seldom from the house of a most homely° shepherd, a man,   *simple*
      they say, that from very nothing, and beyond the imagination
35   of his neighbours, is grown into an unspeakable estate.°   *untold wealth*
    CAMILLO   I have heard, sir, of such a man, who hath a daughter
      of most rare note.° The report of her is extended more than can   *quality*
      be thought to begin° from such a cottage.   *originate*
    POLIXENES   That's likewise part of my intelligence; but, I fear,
40   the angle° that plucks our son thither. Thou shalt accompany   *fishhook*
      us to the place, where we will, not appearing what we are, have
      some question with the shepherd; from whose simplicity I
      think it not uneasy° to get the cause of my son's resort thither.   *difficult*
      Prithee, be my present partner in this business, and lay aside
45   the thoughts of Sicilia.
    CAMILLO   I willingly obey your command.
    POLIXENES   My best Camillo! We must disguise ourselves.
                                                 Exeunt

4.3

Enter AUTOLYCUS *singing*

AUTOLYCUS
        When daffodils begin to peer,
          With heigh, the doxy° over the dale,   *beggar's wench*
        Why then comes in the sweet° o'the year,   *sweetest part*
          For the red blood reigns in the winter's pale.°   *skin made pale by winter*

5   The white sheet bleaching on the hedge,[1]
          With heigh, the sweet birds, O how they sing!
        Doth set my pugging° tooth on edge,   *thieving*
          For a quart of ale is a dish for a king.

        The lark, that tirra-lirra chants,
10   With heigh, with heigh, the thrush and the jay,
        Are summer songs for me and my aunts[2]
          While we lie tumbling in the hay.

    I have served Prince Florizel, and in my time wore three-pile,[3]
    but now I am out of service.

15   But shall I go mourn for that, my dear?
          The pale moon shines by night,
        And when I wander here and there
          I then do most go right.

        If tinkers[4] may have leave° to live,   *permission*
20   And bear the sow-skin budget,[5]

4.3 Location: Bohemia. Near the cottage where the
Old Shepherd, the Clown, and Perdita live.
1. It was common practice to set clothes out to dry on
hedges.
2. Another slang term for women who take beggars or
vagabonds for lovers.

3. A rich velvet cloth with a thick nap or "pile."
4. Menders of metal pots and kettles. The term was
also applied to itinerant beggars and thieves.
5. Pigskin bag. Bag in which a tinker carried his tools;
hence, a sign of his trade.

Then my account I well may give,
And in the stocks avouch it.°   *acknowledge (my crime)*
My traffic° is sheets. When the kite builds, look to lesser linen.[6]   *trade*
My father named me Autolycus,[7] who being, as I am, littered
25   under Mercury,[8] was likewise a snapper-up of unconsidered
trifles. With die and drab° I purchased this caparison, and my   *dice and whores*
revenue is the silly cheat.[9] Gallows and knock° are too power-   *beatings*
ful on the highway.[1] Beating and hanging are terrors to me. For°   *As for*
the life to come, I sleep out the thought of it. A prize, a prize!

            Enter CLOWN

30   CLOWN   Let me see. Every 'leven wether tods,[2] every tod yields
pound and odd° shilling. Fifteen hundred shorn, what comes   *one*
the wool to?
AUTOLYCUS   [*aside*]   If the springe° hold, the cock's[3] mine.   *trap*
CLOWN   I cannot do't without counters.[4] Let me see, what am I
35   to buy for our sheep-shearing feast?[5] Three pound of sugar, five
pound of currants, rice—what will this sister of mine do with
rice? But my father hath made her mistress of the feast, and she
lays it on. She hath made me four-and-twenty nosegays for the
shearers—three-man-song-men,[6] all, and very good ones—but
40   they are most of them means° and basses, but one Puritan   *tenors*
amongst them, and he sings psalms to hornpipes.[7] I must have
saffron to colour the warden° pies; mace; dates, none—that's   *winter pear*
out of my note;° nutmegs, seven; a race° or two of ginger—but   *not on my list / root*
that I may beg; four pound of prunes, and as many of raisins
45   o'th' sun.°   *sun-dried*
AUTOLYCUS   [*grovelling on the ground*] O, that ever I was born!
CLOWN   I'th' name of me!
AUTOLYCUS   O help me, help me! Pluck but off these rags, and
then death, death!
50   CLOWN   Alack, poor soul, thou hast need of more rags to lay on
thee rather than have these off.
AUTOLYCUS   O sir, the loathsomeness of them offend me more
than the stripes° I have received, which are mighty ones and   *blows*
millions.
55   CLOWN   Alas, poor man, a million of beating may come to a
great matter.[8]
AUTOLYCUS   I am robbed, sir, and beaten; my money and apparel
ta'en from me, and these detestable things put upon me.
CLOWN   What, by a horseman, or a footman?°   *man on foot*
60   AUTOLYCUS   A footman, sweet sir, a footman.
CLOWN   Indeed, he should be a footman, by the garments he has
left with thee. If this be a horseman's coat it hath seen very hot

---

6. The kite, a small bird of prey, supposedly stole small pieces of linen to make its nest. Autolycus steals sheets, larger pieces of linen, probably those left to dry on hedges.
7. In classical mythology, a crafty thief and grandfather of Ulysses; Autolycus's own father, Mercury, was the god of thieves.
8. Fathered by Mercury; born when the planet Mercury was ascendant.
9. I was reduced to wearing this garb, and my income derives from petty swindles.
1. Autolycus fears the penalties meted out to highwaymen. He would rather be a petty thief.
2. Every eleven rams will yield 28 pounds (a "tod") of wool. The Clown and his father could expect to earn a substantial amount of money (almost 150 pounds) for

their wool.
3. Woodcock, a bird easily caught and hence proverbial for its stupidity.
4. Disks used in calculating sums.
5. In rural England, a traditional summer event in which people of different ranks took part in feasting and revelry.
6. Men who sing three-part songs.
7. Shrill-sounding musical instruments often played at country dances and hardly appropriate to accompany the singing of psalms. Shakespeare may here be satirizing Puritans, who were notorious for their opposition to music and dancing.
8. A million blows can be a serious affair, with a pun on "matter" as "pus," the sign of an infection caused by open wounds.

service. Lend me thy hand, I'll help thee. Come, lend me thy hand.

[*He helps* AUTOLYCUS *up*]

65 AUTOLYCUS O, good sir, tenderly. O!

CLOWN Alas, poor soul!

AUTOLYCUS O, good sir, softly,° good sir! I fear, sir, my shoulder-   *gently*
blade is out.

CLOWN How now? Canst stand?

70 AUTOLYCUS Softly, dear sir. Good sir, softly.

[*He picks the* CLOWN's *pocket*]⁹

You ha' done me a charitable office.°   *service*

CLOWN [*reaching for his purse*] Dost lack any money? I have a
little money for thee.

AUTOLYCUS No, good sweet sir, no, I beseech you, sir.¹ I have a
75 kinsman not past three-quarters of a mile hence, unto whom I
was going. I shall there have money, or anything I want. Offer
me no money, I pray you. That kills° my heart.   *touches*

CLOWN What manner of fellow was he that robbed you?

AUTOLYCUS A fellow, sir, that I have known to go about with
80 troll-madams.° I knew him once a servant of the Prince. I can-   *whores*
not tell, good sir, for which of his virtues it was, but he was
certainly whipped out of the court.

CLOWN His vices, you would say. There's no virtue whipped out
of the court. They cherish it to make it stay there; and yet it
85 will no more but abide.°   *stay there only briefly*

AUTOLYCUS Vices, I would say, sir. I know this man well. He
hath been since an ape-bearer,² then a process-server—a bai-
liff—then he compassed a motion° of the Prodigal Son,³ and   *devised a puppet show*
married a tinker's wife within a mile where my land and living°   *property*
90 lies, and having flown over many knavish professions, he settled
only in rogue. Some call him Autolycus.

CLOWN Out upon him! Prig,° for my life, prig! He haunts   *Thief*
wakes,° fairs, and bear-baitings.   *festivals*

AUTOLYCUS Very true, sir. He, sir, he. That's the rogue that put
95 me into this apparel.

CLOWN Not a more cowardly rogue in all Bohemia. If you had
but looked big and spit at him, he'd have run.

AUTOLYCUS I must confess to you, sir, I am no fighter. I am false
of heart° that way, and that he knew, I warrant him.   *without courage*

100 CLOWN How do you now?

AUTOLYCUS Sweet sir, much better than I was. I can stand, and
walk. I will even take my leave of you, and pace softly towards
my kinsman's.

CLOWN Shall I bring thee° on the way?   *escort you*

105 AUTOLYCUS No, good-faced sir, no, sweet sir.

CLOWN Then fare thee well. I must go buy spices for our sheep-
shearing.

AUTOLYCUS Prosper you, sweet sir.   *Exit* [*the* CLOWN]

9. It is uncertain when Autolycus actually picks the
Clown's pocket, but it adds to the humor if Autolycus's
next line, "You ha' done me a charitable office," can
refer both to the kindness the Clown has knowingly
shown Autolycus *and* to the kindness the Clown has
unwittingly done him in making available a purse for
the wily rogue to steal.
1. Autolycus does not want the Clown to find out he

has picked his pocket and so left him with no money.
He may here restrain the Clown from putting his hand
into his pocket.
2. One who carried about a trained monkey.
3. Alluding to the New Testament story of a spendthrift
son who squandered his money only to be forgiven by
his father.

Your purse is not hot° enough to purchase your spice. I'll be   full
110   with you at your sheep-shearing, too. If I make not this cheat°   deception
bring out° another, and the shearers prove sheep, let me be   lead to
unrolled[4] and my name put in the book of virtue.
       [Sings]   Jog on, jog on, the footpath way,
                    And merrily hent° the stile[5]-a.   grab (to leap over)
115   A merry heart goes all the day,
                    Your sad tires in a mile-a.   Exit

4.4

Enter FLORIZEL [*dressed as Doricles a countryman*],
[*and*] PERDITA [*as Queen of the Feast*][1]

FLORIZEL   These your unusual weeds° to each part of you   garments
Does give a life; no shepherdess, but Flora°   goddess of flowers
Peering in April's front.[2] This your sheep-shearing
Is as a meeting of the petty gods,
And you the queen on't.°   of it
5   PERDITA   Sir, my gracious lord,
To chide at your extremes° it not becomes me—   extravagances
O, pardon that I name them! Your high self,
The gracious mark o'th' land,[3] you have obscured
With a swain's wearing,° and me, poor lowly maid,   shepherd's costume
10   Most goddess-like pranked up.° But that our feasts   adorned
In every mess[4] have folly, and the feeders°   those who eat
Digest it with a custom,[5] I should blush
To see you so attired; swoon, I think,
To show myself a glass.°   mirror
FLORIZEL   I bless the time
15   When my good falcon made her flight across
Thy father's ground.
PERDITA   Now Jove afford you cause!
To me the difference° forges dread; your greatness   (in rank)
Hath not been used to fear. Even now I tremble
To think your father by some accident
20   Should pass this way, as you did. O, the fates!
How would he look to see his work,° so noble,   offspring; writings
Vilely bound up?[6] What would he say? Or how
Should I, in these my borrowed flaunts,° behold   rich garments
The sternness of his presence?
FLORIZEL   Apprehend
25   Nothing but jollity. The gods themselves,
Humbling their deities to love, have taken
The shapes of beasts upon them. Jupiter
Became a bull, and bellowed; the green Neptune
A ram, and bleated; and the fire-robed god,
30   Golden Apollo, a poor humble swain,

---

4. Let my name be taken off the list (of thieves and
vagabonds).
5. Steps by which people pass over a fence or hedge.
4.4 Location: Bohemia. In front of the cottage where
the Old Shepherd, the Clown, and Perdita live.
1. Again, F lists in the initial stage direction all the
major characters who appear in this very long scene.
Florizel and Perdita seem, however, to have a private
conversation before the Old Shepherd, Polixenes, and

others enter to them at line 54.
2. Peeping out in early April.
3. The one whose graces make him admired by all.
4. A group of four served at table together. See note to
1.2.227.
5. Tolerate it because they have grown used to it.
6. Outfitted in such an inferior way. A bookbinding
metaphor.

As I seem now.[7] Their transformations
Were never for a piece° of beauty rarer,   *person*
Nor in a way so chaste,[8] since my desires
Run not before mine honour, nor my lusts
Burn hotter than my faith.

35 PERDITA   O, but sir,
Your resolution cannot hold when 'tis
Opposed, as it must be, by th' power of the King.
One of these two must be necessities,
Which then will speak that you must change this purpose,
Or I my life.[9]

40 FLORIZEL   Thou dearest Perdita,
With these forced° thoughts I prithee darken not   *unnatural; farfetched*
The mirth o'th' feast. Or° I'll be thine, my fair,   *Either*
Or not my father's. For I cannot be
Mine own, nor anything to any, if
45 I be not thine. To this I am most constant,
Though destiny say no. Be merry, gentle;
Strangle such thoughts as these with anything
That you behold the while. Your guests are coming.
Lift up your countenance as° it were the day   *as if*
50 Of celebration of that nuptial which
We two have sworn shall come.

PERDITA   O Lady Fortune,[1]
Stand you auspicious!

FLORIZEL   See, your guests approach.
Address° yourself to entertain them sprightly,   *Prepare*
And let's be red with mirth.

[*Enter the* OLD SHEPHERD, *with* POLIXENES *and* CA-
MILLO, *disguised, the* CLOWN, MOPSA, DORCAS, *and
others*]

55 OLD SHEPHERD [*to* PERDITA]   Fie, daughter, when my old wife lived, upon
This day she was both pantler,° butler, cook,   *pantry maid*
Both dame° and servant, welcomed all, served all,   *mistress of the house*
Would sing her song and dance her turn, now here
At upper end o'th' table, now i'th' middle,
60 On his° shoulder, and his,° her face afire   *one person's / another's*
With labour, and the thing she took to quench it
She would to each one sip. You are retired
As if you were a feasted one° and not   *a guest*
The hostess of the meeting. Pray you bid
65 These unknown friends to's welcome, for it is
A way to make us better friends, more known.
Come, quench your blushes, and present yourself
That which you are, mistress o'th' feast. Come on,
And bid us welcome to your sheep-shearing,
As your good flock shall prosper.

70 PERDITA [*to* POLIXENES]   Sir, welcome.
It is my father's will I should take on me

---

7. In classical mythology, Jupiter transformed himself
into a bull and abducted Europa; Neptune took on the
shape of a ram to carry off Theopane; and the sun god
Apollo disguised himself as a shepherd to court Alcestis.
8. Nor ever conducted with so chaste a purpose.

9. One of two things will become necessary: either you
must change your plans, or I must change my life (that
is, risk death).
1. In classical and Renaissance mythology, a woman of
fickle disposition whose favors cannot be relied upon.

The hostess-ship o'th' day.

[*To* CAMILLO]   You're welcome, sir.

Give me those flowers there, Dorcas. Reverend sirs,

For you there's rosemary and rue. These keep°   *retain*

75   Seeming° and savour° all the winter long.   *Color / scent*

Grace and remembrance[2] be to you both,

And welcome to our shearing.

POLIXENES   Shepherdess,

A fair one are you. Well you fit our ages

With flowers of winter.

PERDITA   Sir, the year growing ancient,

80   Not yet on summer's death, nor on the birth

Of trembling winter, the fairest flowers o'th' season

Are our carnations and streaked gillyvors,[3]

Which some call nature's bastards. Of that kind

Our rustic garden's barren, and I care not

To get slips of them.

85   POLIXENES   Wherefore, gentle maiden,

Do you neglect them?

PERDITA   For I have heard it said

There is an art[4] which in their piedness° shares   *streaked color*

With great creating nature.

POLIXENES   Say there be,

Yet nature is made better by no mean°   *means*

90   But nature makes that mean. So over that art

Which you say adds to nature is an art

That nature makes. You see, sweet maid, we marry

A gentler scion to the wildest stock,

And make conceive a bark of baser kind

95   By bud of nobler race.[5] This is an art

Which does mend nature—change it rather; but

The art itself is nature.

PERDITA   So it is.

POLIXENES   Then make your garden rich in gillyvors,

And do not call them bastards.

PERDITA   I'll not put

100   The dibble° in earth to set° one slip of them,   *trowel / plant*

No more than, were I painted,° I would wish   *wearing cosmetics*

This youth should say 'twere well, and only therefore

Desire to breed by me. Here's flowers for you:

Hot[6] lavender, mints, savory, marjoram,

105   The marigold, that goes to bed wi'th' sun,

And with him rises, weeping.[7] These are flowers

Of middle summer, and I think they are given

To men of middle age. You're very welcome.

[*She gives them flowers*]

2. Grace ("repentance") and remembrance are qualities associated with rue and rosemary, respectively.
3. Gillyflowers or multicolored carnations. Their variations in color were thought to result from crossbreeding with other flowers, which may be why Perdita calls them "nature's bastards." They were proverbially associated with sexual license.
4. The art of crossbreeding or grafting.
5. We unite a cutting from a highly cultivated plant to the stem of a lesser one and cause the lesser plant to

bring forth a highly cultivated flower, that puns on "gentler scion," "wildest stock," "baser kind," and "nobler race" to suggest a successful union between a highborn heir and a member of the lower social orders.
6. Herbs were divided into "hot" and "cold" varieties based on their supposed temperatures.
7. The marigold, sometimes called "the spouse of the sun," supposedly closed at sunset and opened, filled with dew, in the morning when the sun came up.

CAMILLO I should leave grazing were I of your flock,
And only live by gazing.

110 PERDITA   Out, alas,
You'd be so lean that blasts of January
Would blow you through and through.
[*To* FLORIZEL]   Now, my fair'st friend,
I would I had some flowers o'th' spring that might
Become your time of day; [*to* MOPSA *and* DORCAS] and yours, and yours,
115 That wear upon your virgin branches yet
Your maidenheads growing. O Proserpina,[8]
For the flowers now that, frighted, thou letst fall
From Dis's wagon!°—daffodils,   *chariot*
That come before the swallow dares, and take°   *charm*
120 The winds of March with beauty; violets, dim,°   *with hanging head*
But sweeter than the lids of Juno's eyes
Or Cytherea's breath;[9] pale primroses,
That die unmarried ere they can behold
Bright Phoebus° in his strength—a malady   *the sun god*
125 Most incident to maids;[1] bold oxlips, and
The crown imperial;[2] lilies of all kinds,
The flower-de-luce[3] being one. O, these I lack,
To make you garlands of, and my sweet friend,
To strew him o'er and o'er.

FLORIZEL   What, like a corpse?
130 PERDITA No, like a bank, for love to lie and play on,
Not like a corpse—or if, not to be buried,
But quick° and in mine arms. Come, take your flowers.   *living*
Methinks I play as I have seen them do
In Whitsun pastorals.[4] Sure this robe of mine
Does change my disposition.

135 FLORIZEL   What you do
Still° betters what is done. When you speak, sweet,   *Always*
I'd have you do it ever; when you sing,
I'd have you buy and sell so, so give alms,
Pray so; and for the ord'ring° your affairs,   *arranging for*
140 To sing them too. When you do dance, I wish you
A wave o'th' sea, that you might ever do
Nothing but that, move still, still so,
And own° no other function. Each your doing,°   *have / Each thing you do*
So singular° in each particular,   *distinctive*
145 Crowns what you are doing in the present deeds,
That all your acts are queens.

PERDITA   O Doricles,[5]
Your praises are too large. But that your youth
And the true blood which peeps so fairly through't

---

8. In Ovid's *Metamorphoses*, Proserpina, the daughter of Ceres, is abducted by Dis, or Pluto, as she gathers flowers and is taken in his chariot ("wagon") to his underworld kingdom. Sought out by Ceres, Proserpina is allowed to return to earth for six months each year. Her sojourn on earth coincides with spring and summer, her return to the underworld with fall and winter.
9. Juno was queen of the gods; "Cytherea" was another name for Venus, the goddess of love.
1. Alluding to the superstition that women who died of a kind of anemia known as green sickness would be transformed into primroses. Green sickness was espe-

cially associated with young virginal women; vigorous sexual activity was sometimes advocated as a cure.
2. A lily first imported into England from Turkey in the late sixteenth century.
3. Fleur-de-lis, the national flower of France.
4. English rural festivities traditionally held at Whitsuntide, a religious festival occurring in the spring, seven weeks after Easter. The festivities, often organized under a festival King and Queen, included morris dances and Robin Hood plays.
5. The name Florizel has assumed.

Do plainly give you out an unstained shepherd,
150   With wisdom I might fear, my Doricles,
You wooed me the false way.

FLORIZEL   I think you have
As little skill° to fear as I have purpose   reason
To put you to't. But come, our dance, I pray;
Your hand, my Perdita. So turtles⁶ pair,
That never mean to part.

155 PERDITA   I'll swear for 'em.

POLIXENES [to CAMILLO]   This is the prettiest low-born lass that ever
Ran on the greensward.° Nothing she does or seems   grassy turf
But smacks of something greater than herself,
Too noble for this place.

CAMILLO   He tells her something
160 That makes her blood look out.° Good sooth, she is   makes her blush
The queen of curds and cream.⁷

CLOWN   Come on, strike up!

DORCAS   Mopsa must be your mistress. Marry, garlic to mend
her kissing with!⁸

MOPSA   Now, in good time!

165 CLOWN   Not a word, a word, we stand upon our manners. Come,
strike up!
        [Music.] Here a dance of shepherds and shepherdesses

POLIXENES   Pray, good shepherd, what fair swain is this
Which dances with your daughter?

OLD SHEPHERD   They call him Doricles, and boasts himself°   he boasts
170 To have a worthy feeding;° but I have it   good pasture land
Upon his own report, and I believe it.
He looks like sooth.° He says he loves my daughter.   appears to be honest
I think so, too, for never gazed the moon
Upon the water as he'll stand and read,
175 As 'twere, my daughter's eyes; and to be plain,
I think there is not half a kiss to choose
Who loves another° best.   the other

POLIXENES   She dances featly.°   nimbly

OLD SHEPHERD   So she does anything, though I report it
That° should be silent. If young Doricles   Who
180 Do light upon her, she shall bring him that
Which he not dreams of.
        Enter [a] SERVANT

SERVANT   O, master, if you did but hear the pedlar at the door,
you would never dance again after a tabor and pipe.⁹ No, the
bagpipe could not move you. He sings several° tunes faster than   different
185 you'll tell° money. He utters them as he had eaten ballads,¹   count
and all men's ears grew° to his tunes.   listened intently

CLOWN   He could never come better.° He shall come in. I love   at a better time
a ballad but even too well, if it be doleful matter merrily set
down, or a very pleasant thing indeed, and sung lamentably.

190 SERVANT   He hath songs for man or woman, of all sizes. No milli-
ner² can so fit his customers with gloves. He has the prettiest

6. Turtledoves, which proverbially mate for life.
7. Referring perhaps to a cream custard known as
"white pot." In some May games, a woman was chosen
as Queen of white-pot cream.
8. To make her breath sweet (said ironically).
9. A small drum and fife used for morris dancing.

1. Alluding to the broadside ballads that were sung
and sold by peddlers who traveled throughout the
country.
2. One who sells fashionable articles of clothing such
as hats and gloves. Originally, the word meant one who
sells items imported from Milan.

love songs for maids, so without bawdry, which is strange, with
such delicate burdens° of dildos and fadings, 'Jump her, and   *refrains*
thump her';³ and where some stretch-mouthed° rascal would,   *obscene*
195   as it were, mean mischief and break a foul gap into the matter,⁴
he makes the maid to answer, 'Whoop, do me no harm, good
man'; puts him off, slights him, with 'Whoop, do me no harm,
good man!'

POLIXENES   This is a brave° fellow.   *fine*

200 CLOWN   Believe me, thou talkest of an admirable conceited° fel-   *very witty*
low. Has he any unbraided° wares?   *new; not shopworn*

SERVANT   He hath ribbons of all the colours i'th' rainbow; points⁵
more than all the lawyers in Bohemia can learnedly handle,
though they come to him by th' gross; inkles, caddises, cam-
205   brics, lawns⁶—why, he sings 'em over as they were gods or goddesses. You would think a smock° were a she-angel, he so   *a woman's undergarment*
chants to the sleeve-hand° and the work about the square on't.⁷   *wristband*

CLOWN   Prithee bring him in, and let him approach singing.

PERDITA   Forewarn him that he use no scurrilous words in's
210 tunes.   *[Exit* SERVANT*]*

CLOWN   You have of these° pedlars that have more in them than   *There are some*
you'd think, sister.

PERDITA   Ay, good brother, or go about° to think.   *intend*

Enter AUTOLYCUS *[wearing a false beard, carrying his
pack, and] singing*

AUTOLYCUS   Lawn as white as driven snow,
215   Cypress⁸ black as e'er was crow,
Gloves as sweet° as damask roses,   *perfumed*
Masks for faces, and for noses;⁹
Bugle-bracelet,¹ necklace amber,
Perfume for a lady's chamber;
220   Golden coifs,° and stomachers²   *caps*
For my lads to give their dears;
Pins and poking-sticks of steel,³
What maids lack from head to heel
Come buy of me, come, come buy, come buy,
225   Buy, lads, or else your lasses cry. Come buy!

CLOWN   If I were not in love with Mopsa thou shouldst take no
money of me, but being enthralled as I am, it will also be the
bondage of certain ribbons and gloves.⁴

MOPSA   I was promised them against° the feast, but they come   *in time for*
230 not too late now.

DORCAS   He hath promised you more than that,⁵ or there be
liars.

---

3. Though the servant claims that the songs are without bawdiness, the refrains are in fact full of sexual
puns that the servant may not understand. "Dildos" are
artificial penises; "fadings" can mean "orgasms"; and
"jump her and thump her" denotes sexual relations with
a woman.
4. Would interrupt the song with an indecent insertion.
5. Laces for fastening garments, with a pun on "points"
as meaning "legal arguments."
6. "Inkles" were linen tapes; "caddises" were worsted
tapes used for garters; "cambrics" and "lawns" were
heavy and sheer linens.
7. The stitching about the yoke of the garment.
8. A crepe material imported from Cyprus and used for

mourning clothes.
9. Many upper-class English women wore masks to
protect their skin from exposure to the sun. Some
women's noses were eaten away by syphilis, and masks
would also cover this deformity.
1. A bracelet of shiny black beads.
2. Embroidered bodices for dresses.
3. Metal rods used to iron the ruffs or stiff collars worn
by both men and women. The term is also slang for
"penis."
4. Because I am the prisoner of love, certain ribbons
and gloves must also be put in bondage (bound up in a
parcel).
5. (Perhaps he has promised marriage.)

MOPSA   He hath paid° you all he promised you. Maybe he has ⟶ *given; had sex with*
  paid you more, which will shame you to give him again.⁶

235 CLOWN   Is there no manners left among maids? Will they wear
  their plackets where they should bear their faces?⁷ Is there not
  milking-time, when you are going to bed, or kiln-hole,° to whis- ⟶ *fireplace*
  tle of these secrets, but you must be tittle-tattling before all our
  guests? 'Tis well they are whispering. Clammer your tongues,⁸

240   and not a word more.

MOPSA   I have done. Come, you promised me a tawdry-lace⁹ and
  a pair of sweet gloves.

CLOWN   Have I not told thee how I was cozened by the way,° ⟶ *cheated on the road*
  and lost all my money?

245 AUTOLYCUS   And indeed, sir, there are cozeners abroad, therefore
  it behoves men to be wary.

CLOWN   Fear not thou, man, thou shalt lose nothing here.

AUTOLYCUS   I hope so, sir, for I have about me many parcels of
  charge.° ⟶ *valuable goods*

250 CLOWN   What hast here? Ballads?

MOPSA   Pray now, buy some. I love a ballad in print, alife,° for ⟶ *on my life*
  then we are sure they are true.

AUTOLYCUS   Here's one to a very doleful tune, how a usurer's
  wife was brought to bed of twenty money-bags at a burden,° and ⟶ *in one childbirth*

255   how she longed to eat adders' heads and toads carbonadoed.° ⟶ *cut and grilled*

MOPSA   Is it true, think you?

AUTOLYCUS   Very true, and but a month old.

DORCAS   Bless me from marrying a usurer!

AUTOLYCUS   Here's the midwife's name to't, one Mistress Tail-

260   Porter,¹ and five or six honest° wives' that were present. Why ⟶ *truthful; chaste*
  should I carry lies abroad?

MOPSA [*to* CLOWN]   Pray you now, buy it.

CLOWN   Come on, lay it by, and let's first see more ballads. We'll
  buy the other things anon.

265 AUTOLYCUS   Here's another ballad, of a fish that appeared upon
  the coast on Wednesday the fourscore° of April, forty thousand ⟶ *eightieth day*
  fathom° above water, and sung this ballad against the hard ⟶ *measurement of six feet*
  hearts of maids. It was thought she was a woman, and was
  turned into a cold fish for she would not exchange flesh° with ⟶ *have sex*

270   one that loved her. The ballad is very pitiful, and as true.

DORCAS   Is it true too, think you?

AUTOLYCUS   Five justices' hands at it,° and witnesses more than ⟶ *signatures on it*
  my pack will hold.

CLOWN   Lay it by, too. Another.

275 AUTOLYCUS   This is a merry ballad, but a very pretty one.

MOPSA   Let's have some merry ones.

AUTOLYCUS   Why, this is a passing° merry one, and goes to the ⟶ *very*
  tune of 'Two Maids Wooing a Man'. There's scarce a maid
  westward° but she sings it. 'Tis in request, I can tell you. ⟶ *in the west*

---

6. "More" may allude to a pregnancy that will result in
an illegitimate child that she will give to the Clown.
7. That is, "Will they reveal their most private affairs in
public?" There is a pun on "placket," which refers to
both an opening in a petticoat and female genitals.
8. An obscure phrase. The Clown clearly means they
are to be quiet. "To clammer" is a term from bell ringing that means to make the jangling sound characteristic of bells before they grow silent. In F, the phrase is

printed as "clamor your tongues." Many emendations
have been proposed.
9. A cheap, brightly colored scarf associated with St.
Audrey's Fair. St. Audrey was the founder of Ely Cathedral; she died of a throat tumor that she believed was a
punishment for wearing gay neckerchiefs in her youth.
1. The name punningly suggests one who reports gossip ("tales") as well as one who handles genitalia (slang
meaning of "tail").

280 MOPSA We can both sing it. If thou'lt bear a part² thou shalt
      hear; 'tis in three parts.

DORCAS We had the tune on't° a month ago.   *of it*

AUTOLYCUS I can bear my part, you must know, 'tis my occu-
      pation.° Have at it with you.   *job; act of copulation*

      [*They sing*]

285 AUTOLYCUS Get you hence, for I must go³
                Where it fits not you to know.

DORCAS   Whither?

MOPSA   O whither?

DORCAS   Whither?

MOPSA It becomes thy oath full well
       Thou to me thy secrets tell.

290 DORCAS Me too. Let me go thither.

MOPSA Or thou go'st to th' grange° or mill,   *farm*

DORCAS If to either, thou dost ill.

AUTOLYCUS Neither.

DORCAS   What neither.

AUTOLYCUS   Neither.

DORCAS Thou hast sworn my love to be.

295 MOPSA Thou hast sworn it more to me.
            Then whither goest? Say, whither?

CLOWN We'll have this song out anon by ourselves. My father
      and the gentlemen are in sad° talk, and we'll not trouble them.   *serious*
      Come, bring away thy pack after me. Wenches, I'll buy for you
300 both. Pedlar, let's have the first choice. Follow me, girls.

            [*Exit with* DORCAS *and* MOPSA]

AUTOLYCUS And you shall pay well for 'em.

      [*Sings*]   Will you buy any tape,
                   Or lace for your cape,
                My dainty duck, my dear-a?
305   Any silk, any thread,
                Any toys° for your head,   *small ornaments*
             Of the new'st and fin'st, fin'st wear-a?
                Come to the pedlar,
                Money's a meddler,
310   That doth utter° all men's ware-a.   *Exit*   *put on sale*

      [*Enter* SERVANT]

SERVANT Master, there is three carters,° three shepherds, three   *drivers of carts*
      neatherds,° three swineherds that have made themselves all   *keepers of cows*
      men of hair.⁴ They call themselves saultiers,° and they have a   *jumpers*
      dance which the wenches say is a gallimaufry of gambols,°   *jumble of jumps*
315 because they are not in't. But they themselves are o'th' mind,
      if it be not too rough for some that know little but bowling,° it   *(a more sedate sport)*
      will please plentifully.

OLD SHEPHERD Away. We'll none on't. Here has been too much
      homely° foolery already. [*To* POLIXENES] I know, sir, we weary   *rough*
320 you.

POLIXENES You weary those that° refresh us. Pray, let's see these   *who*
      four threes° of herdsmen.   *trios*

SERVANT One three of them, by their own report, sir, hath

---

2. Sing a part in the song; play a role (in a sexual
encounter with the two women).
3. F prints "Song" before this line and "Autolycus"
before the next.

4. Probably they have disguised themselves in animal
skins in order to resemble satyrs—mythical woodland
figures, part man, part beast, having the pointed ears,
legs, and short horns of a goat.

danced before the King,[5] and not the worst of the three but
325   jumps twelve foot and a half by th' square.°   *exactly*
    OLD SHEPHERD   Leave your prating. Since these good men are
    pleased, let them come in—but quickly, now.
    SERVANT   Why, they stay at door, sir.
        Here a dance of twelve satyrs
    POLIXENES [*to the* OLD SHEPHERD]   O, father, you'll know more of that hereafter.
330   [*To* CAMILLO] Is it not too far gone? 'Tis time to part them.
    He's simple, and tells much.
    [*To* FLORIZEL]   How now, fair shepherd,
    Your heart is full of something that does take
    Your mind from feasting. Sooth, when I was young
    And handed love° as you do, I was wont   *pledged love*
335   To load my she with knacks.° I would have ransacked   *small gifts; trifles*
    The pedlar's silken treasury, and have poured it
    To her acceptance.° You have let him go,   *For her to choose*
    And nothing marted° with him. If your lass   *bought from*
    Interpretation should abuse,° and call this   *Should misinterpret*
340   Your lack of love or bounty, you were straited°   *hard-pressed*
    For a reply, at least if you make a care
    Of happy holding her.°   *Of keeping her happy*
    FLORIZEL   Old sir, I know
    She prizes not such trifles as these are.
    The gifts she looks° from me are packed and locked   *expects*
345   Up in my heart, which I have given already,
    But not delivered.
    [*To* PERDITA]   O, hear me breathe my life°   *make vows of eternal love*
    Before this ancient sir, who, it should seem,
    Hath sometime loved. I take thy hand, this hand
    As soft as dove's down, and as white as it,
350   Or Ethiopian's tooth, or the fanned snow that's bolted°   *sifted*
    By th' northern blasts twice o'er.
    POLIXENES   What follows this?
    How prettily the young swain seems to wash
    The hand was° fair before! I have put you out.°   *that was / interrupted you*
    But to your protestation. Let me hear
    What you profess.
355   FLORIZEL   Do, and be witness to't.
    POLIXENES   And this my neighbour too?
    FLORIZEL   And he, and more
    Than he; and men, the earth, the heavens, and all,
    That were I crowned the most imperial monarch,
    Thereof most worthy, were I the fairest youth
360   That ever made eye swerve,° had force and knowledge   *commanded attention*
    More than was ever man's, I would not prize them
    Without her love; for her employ them all,
    Commend them and condemn them to her service
    Or to their own perdition.[6]
    POLIXENES   Fairly offered.
    CAMILLO   This shows a sound affection.

---

5. This may be a reference to a court performance of
Ben Jonson's *Masque of Oberon*, which included a dance
of twelve satyrs. It was first put on in January of 1611.

6. Either dedicate my attributes to her service or sentence them to destruction, with a pun on "perdition"
and "Perdita."

365   OLD SHEPHERD   But, my daughter,
      Say you the like to him?
    PERDITA   I cannot speak
      So well, nothing so well, no, nor mean better.
      By th' pattern of mine own thoughts I cut out
      The purity of his.[7]
    OLD SHEPHERD   Take hands, a bargain;
370   And, friends unknown, you shall bear witness to't.
      I give my daughter to him, and will make
      Her portion° equal his.   *dowry*
    FLORIZEL   O, that must be
      I'th' virtue of your daughter. One° being dead,   *Someone*
      I shall have more than you can dream of yet,
375   Enough then for your wonder. But come on,
      Contract us fore these witnesses.[8]
    OLD SHEPHERD   Come, your hand;
      And, daughter, yours.
    POLIXENES   Soft,° swain, a while, beseech you.   *Go slowly*
      Have you a father?
    FLORIZEL   I have. But what of him?
380   POLIXENES   Knows he of this?
    FLORIZEL   He neither does nor shall.
    POLIXENES   Methinks a father
      Is at the nuptial of his son a guest
      That best becomes the table. Pray you once more,
385   Is not your father grown incapable
      Of reasonable affairs?[9] Is he not stupid
      With age and alt'ring rheums?° Can he speak, hear,   *debilitating disease*
      Know man from man? Dispute° his own estate?°   *Discuss / condition*
      Lies he not bed-rid, and again does nothing
      But what he did being childish?
390   FLORIZEL   No, good sir.
      He has his health, and ampler strength indeed
      Than most have of his age.
    POLIXENES   By my white beard,
      You offer him, if this be so, a wrong
      Something unfilial.° Reason my son[1]   *Somewhat unbecoming a son*
395   Should choose himself a wife, but as good reason
      The father, all whose joy is nothing else
      But fair posterity, should hold some counsel
      In such a business.
    FLORIZEL   I yield° all this;   *grant*
      But for some other reasons, my grave sir,
400   Which 'tis not fit you know, I not acquaint
      My father of this business.
    POLIXENES   Let him know't.
    FLORIZEL   He shall not.
    POLIXENES   Prithee let him.
    FLORIZEL   No, he must not.
    OLD SHEPHERD   Let him, my son. He shall not need to grieve
      At knowing of thy choice.

---

7. By my pure thoughts I recognize the purity of his. A dressmaking metaphor.
8. A pledge of marriage spoken before two witnesses was legally binding.

9. Unfit to handle matters requiring reason and good sense.
1. It is reasonable that my son.

FLORIZEL   Come, come, he must not.
Mark our contract.

405   POLIXENES [*removing his disguise*]   Mark your divorce, young sir,
Whom son I dare not call. Thou art too base
To be acknowledged. Thou a sceptre's heir,
That thus affects° a sheep-hook?   *desires*
[*To the* OLD SHEPHERD]   Thou, old traitor,
I am sorry that by hanging thee I can but
Shorten thy life one week.

410   [*To* PERDITA]   And thou, fresh piece
Of excellent witchcraft,[2] who of force° must know   *of necessity*
The royal fool thou cop'st° with—   *you deal; you have sex*
OLD SHEPHERD   O, my heart!
POLIXENES   I'll have thy beauty scratched with briers and made
More homely than thy state.
[*To* FLORIZEL]   For thee, fond° boy,   *foolish*

415   If I may ever know thou dost but sigh
That thou no more shalt see this knack,° as never   *worthless thing*
I mean thou shalt, we'll bar thee from succession,
Not hold thee of our blood, no, not our kin,
Farre than Deucalion off.[3] Mark thou my words.
Follow us to the court.

420   [*To the* OLD SHEPHERD]   Thou churl, for this time,
Though full of our displeasure, yet we free thee
From the dead° blow of it.   *deadly*
[*To* PERDITA]   And you, enchantment,
Worthy enough a herdsman—yea, him° too,   *(Florizel)*
That makes himself, but for our honour therein,

425   Unworthy thee[4]—if ever henceforth thou
These rural latches to his entrance open,
Or hoop° his body more with thy embraces,   *encircle*
I will devise a death as cruel for thee
As thou art tender to't.   *Exit*

PERDITA   Even here undone.

430   I was not much afeard, for once or twice
I was about to speak, and tell him plainly
The selfsame sun that shines upon his court
Hides not his visage from our cottage, but
Looks on alike.° Will't please you, sir, be gone?   *both alike*

435   I told you what would come of this. Beseech you,
Of your own state take care. This dream of mine
Being now awake, I'll queen it no inch farther,°   *play the queen no further*
But milk my ewes and weep.
CAMILLO [*to the* OLD SHEPHERD]   Why, how now, father?
Speak ere thou diest.
OLD SHEPHERD   I cannot speak, nor think,
Nor dare to know that which I know.

440   [*To* FLORIZEL]   O sir,
You have undone a man of fourscore-three,°   *eighty-three*

2. You beautiful young woman skilled in witchcraft.
Some people believed that witches could induce love by
potions.
3. Less linked in kinship than Deucalion, who according to classical mythology was, along with his wife, the
only person to escape a flood sent by Zeus. He thus was
the ancestor of humankind and the most distant relation one might have.
4. A difficult passage. Polixenes seems to mean that
Florizel, by his actions, has made himself unworthy of
even a shepherd's daughter were it not for the fact that
he is a King's son and so would harm his father's honor
by such a marriage.

That thought to fill his grave in quiet, yea,
To die upon the bed my father died,
To lie close by his honest bones. But now
445 Some hangman must put on my shroud, and lay me
Where no priest shovels in dust.⁵
[*To* PERDITA]   O cursed wretch,
That knew'st this was the Prince, and wouldst adventure
To mingle faith° with him. Undone, undone!   *exchange vows*
If I might die within this hour, I have lived
To die when I desire.   *Exit*

450 FLORIZEL [*to* PERDITA]   Why look you so upon me?
I am but sorry, not afeard; delayed,
But nothing altered. What I was, I am,
More straining on for plucking back,⁶ not following
My leash unwillingly.⁷
CAMILLO   Gracious my lord,
455 You know your father's temper. At this time
He will allow no speech—which I do guess
You do not purpose° to him; and as hardly°   *intend / unwillingly*
Will he endure your sight as yet, I fear.
Then till the fury of his highness settle,
Come not before him.
460 FLORIZEL   I not purpose it.
I think, Camillo?⁸
CAMILLO   Even he, my lord.
PERDITA [*to* FLORIZEL]   How often have I told you 'twould be thus?
How often said my dignity would last
But° till 'twere known?   *Only*
FLORIZEL   It cannot fail but by
465 The violation of my faith, and then
Let nature crush the sides o'th' earth together
And mar the seeds° within. Lift up thy looks.   *sources of life*
From my succession wipe me, father! I
Am heir to my affection.
CAMILLO   Be advised.°   *prudent*
470 FLORIZEL   I am, and by my fancy.° If my reason   *love*
Will thereto be obedient, I have reason.⁹
If not, my senses, better pleased with madness,
Do bid it° welcome.   *(madness)*
CAMILLO   This is desperate, sir.
FLORIZEL   So call it. But it does fulfil my vow.
475 I needs must think it honesty. Camillo,
Not for Bohemia, nor the pomp that may
Be thereat gleaned; for all the sun sees, or
The close° earth wombs,° or the profound seas hides   *secret / holds in her womb*
In unknown fathoms, will I break my oath
480 To this my fair beloved. Therefore, I pray you,
As you have ever been my father's honoured friend,
When he shall miss me—as, in faith, I mean not
To see him any more—cast your good counsels

---

5. As a criminal, he would be buried without ritual under the gallows. In regular funeral rites, the priest customarily placed the first shovelful of dirt on the grave.
6. More eager to go forward because of being pulled back.

7. Not following this course of action unwillingly (like a dog dragged by its leash).
8. Camillo may here have taken off his disguise or been recognized by Florizel even with it on.
9. If my reason will obey love, I will embrace reason.

Upon his passion.° Let myself and fortune · *anger*
485 Tug° for the time to come. This you may know, · *Contend*
And so deliver:° I am put to sea · *report*
With her who here I cannot hold on shore;
And most opportune to her need, I have
A vessel rides fast by,° but not prepared · *anchored nearby*
490 For this design. What course I mean to hold
Shall nothing benefit your knowledge, nor
Concern me the reporting.[1]

CAMILLO   O my lord,
I would your spirit were easier for advice,° · *to advise*
Or stronger for your need.

FLORIZEL   Hark, Perdita—
   [*To* CAMILLO] I'll hear you by and by.

495 CAMILLO [*aside*]   He's irremovable,° · · · · · · · · · · · · · · · · *unyielding*
Resolved for flight. Now were I happy if
His going I could frame to serve my turn,
Save him from danger, do him love and honour,
Purchase the sight again of dear Sicilia
500 And that unhappy king, my master, whom
I so much thirst to see.

FLORIZEL   Now, good Camillo,
I am so fraught with curious business° that · · · · · · · · · · · · · · · · *matters requiring care*
I leave out ceremony.

CAMILLO   Sir, I think
You have heard of my poor services i'th' love
That I have borne your father?

505 FLORIZEL   Very nobly
Have you deserved. It is my father's music
To speak your deeds, not little of his care
To have them recompensed as thought on.[2]

CAMILLO   Well, my lord,
If you may please to think I love the King,
510 And through him what's nearest to him, which is
Your gracious self, embrace but my direction,° · · · · · · · · · · · · *simply follow my advice*
If your more ponderous° and settled project · *weighty*
May suffer° alteration. On mine honour, · *permit*
I'll point you where you shall have such receiving
515 As shall become your highness, where you may
Enjoy your mistress—from the whom I see
There's no disjunction° to be made but by, · *separation*
As heavens forfend,° your ruin—marry her, · *forbid*
And with my best endeavours in your absence
520 Your discontenting° father strive to qualify° · · · · · · · · · · · · *discontented / appease*
And bring him up to liking.° · *to giving approval*

FLORIZEL   How, Camillo,
May this, almost a miracle, be done?—
That I may call thee something more than man,
And after that trust to thee.

CAMILLO   Have you thought on° · *of*
A place whereto you'll go?

525 FLORIZEL   Not any yet.

---

1. Would not benefit you to know nor me to report.
2. And no small matter among his affairs to reward your deeds as fully as he values them.

But as th'unthought-on accident is guilty
To what we wildly do,[3] so we profess
Ourselves to be the slaves of chance, and flies
Of every wind that blows.[4]

CAMILLO   Then list to me.
530   This follows, if you will not change your purpose
But undergo this flight: make for Sicilia,
And there present yourself and your fair princess,
For so I see she must be, fore Leontes.
She shall be habited° as it becomes   *dressed*
535   The partner of your bed. Methinks I see
Leontes opening his free° arms and weeping   *generous*
His welcomes forth; asks thee there 'Son, forgiveness!'
As 'twere i'th' father's person,[5] kisses the hands
Of your fresh princess; o'er and o'er divides him
540   'Twixt his unkindness and his kindness.[6] Th'one
He chides° to hell, and bids the other grow   *rebukes*
Faster than thought or time.

FLORIZEL   Worthy Camillo,
What colour° for my visitation shall I   *pretext*
Hold up before him?

CAMILLO   Sent by the King your father
545   To greet him, and to give him comforts. Sir,
The manner of your bearing towards him, with
What you, as from your father, shall deliver—°   *say*
Things known betwixt us three—I'll write you down,
The which shall point you forth° at every sitting   *direct you*
550   What you must say, that he shall not perceive
But that you have your father's bosom° there,   *trust*
And speak his very heart.

FLORIZEL   I am bound to you.
There is some sap° in this.   *life*

CAMILLO   A course more promising
Than a wild dedication of yourselves
555   To unpathed waters, undreamed shores; most certain,
To miseries enough—no hope to help you,
But as you shake off one, to take another;
Nothing so certain° as your anchors, who   *certain (to detain you)*
Do their best office if they can but stay° you   *keep*
560   Where you'll be loath to be. Besides, you know,
Prosperity's the very bond of love,
Whose fresh complexion and whose heart together
Affliction alters.°   *changes for the worse*

PERDITA   One of these is true.
I think affliction may subdue the cheek°   *make one pale*
But not take in° the mind.   *conquer*

565   CAMILLO   Yea, say you so?
There shall not at your father's house these seven years[7]
Be born another such.

FLORIZEL   My good Camillo,

---

3. But as the unexpected event (Polixenes' discovery of
our love) is responsible for our rash behavior now.
4. And like flies blown about by the winds.
5. As if he were your father; *or* as if you were your father.

6. That is, he divides his speech between his past
unkindness to your father and the kindness he is eager
to perform now.
7. Proverbial expression meaning "for a long time."

She's as forward of her breeding as
She is i'th' rear our birth.[8]

CAMILLO   I cannot say 'tis pity
570   She lacks instructions,° for she seems a mistress°   *schooling / teacher*
To most that teach.

PERDITA   Your pardon, sir. For this
I'll blush you thanks.

FLORIZEL   My prettiest Perdita!
But O, the thorns we stand upon! Camillo,
Preserver of my father, now of me,
575   The medicine of our house, how shall we do?
We are not furnished° like Bohemia's son,   *dressed; equipped*
Nor shall appear so in Sicilia.

CAMILLO   My lord,
Fear none of this. I think you know my fortunes
580   Do all lie there. It shall be so my care
To have you royally appointed° as if   *outfitted*
The scene you play were mine.° For instance, sir,   *written by me*
That you may know you shall not want—one word.

        [They speak apart.]
        Enter AUTOLYCUS

AUTOLYCUS   Ha, ha! What a fool honesty is, and trust—his sworn
585   brother—a very simple gentleman! I have sold all my trumpery;
not a counterfeit stone, not a ribbon, glass, pomander,[9] brooch,
table-book,° ballad, knife, tape, glove, shoe-tie, bracelet, horn-   *notebook*
ring[1] to keep my pack from fasting.° They throng who should   *from going empty*
buy first, as if my trinkets had been hallowed,° and brought a   *blessed; made sacred*
590   benediction to the buyer; by which means I saw whose purse
was best in picture;° and what I saw, to my good use I remem-   *looked best (to steal)*
bered. My clown, who wants but something° to be a reasonable   *lacks only one thing*
man, grew so in love with the wenches' song that he would not
stir his pettitoes° till he had both tune and words, which so   *feet (pigs' toes)*
595   drew the rest of the herd to me that all their other senses stuck
in ears.° You might have pinched a placket, it was sense-   *were devoted to hearing*
less.° 'Twas nothing to geld a codpiece of a purse.[2] I could have   *felt nothing*
filed keys off that hung in chains. No hearing, no feeling but
my sir's song, and admiring the nothing of it.[3] So that in this
600   time of lethargy I picked and cut most of their festival purses,
and had not the old man come in with a hubbub against his
daughter and the King's son, and scared my choughs° from the   *jackdaws (silly birds)*
chaff, I had not left a purse alive in the whole army.

        *[*CAMILLO, FLORIZEL, *and* PERDITA *come forward]*

CAMILLO   Nay, but my letters by this means being there
605   So soon as you arrive shall clear that doubt.

FLORIZEL   And those that you'll procure from King Leontes—

CAMILLO   Shall satisfy your father.

PERDITA   Happy be you!
All that you speak shows fair.

CAMILLO *[seeing* AUTOLYCUS*]*   Who have we here?

---

8. That is, "She is as superior to her lowly upbringing
as she is inferior to our noble birth."
9. A mixture of sweet-smelling substances made into a
ball and carried about for ornament or to prevent infection.
1. A ring made from horn, which was said to possess

magical qualities.
2. It was easy to cut a purse loose from a codpiece, the
baglike article of dress attached to the front of a man's
hose and covering his genitals.
3. The silliness of it, with a pun on "nothing" and "noting" (meaning "tune"), which were similarly pronounced.

We'll make an instrument of this, omit

610 Nothing° may give us aid.   *Nothing that*

AUTOLYCUS [*aside*] If they have overheard me now—why,
hanging!

CAMILLO How now, good fellow? Why shakest thou so? Fear
not, man. Here's no harm intended to thee.

615 AUTOLYCUS I am a poor fellow, sir.

CAMILLO Why, be so still.° Here's nobody will steal that from   *always*
thee. Yet for the outside of thy poverty,° we must make an   *your ragged clothes*
exchange. Therefore disease° thee instantly— thou must think   *undress*
there's a necessity in't—and change garments with this gentle-
620 man. Though the pennyworth° on his side be the worst, yet   *bargain*
hold thee, [*giving him money*] there's some boot.°   *something more*

AUTOLYCUS I am a poor fellow, sir. [*Aside*] I know ye well
enough.

CAMILLO Nay prithee, dispatch°—the gentleman is half flayed[4] *hurry*
625 already.

AUTOLYCUS Are you in earnest,[5] sir? [*Aside*] I smell the trick on't.

FLORIZEL Dispatch, I prithee.

AUTOLYCUS Indeed, I have had earnest, but I cannot with conscience take it.

630 CAMILLO Unbuckle, unbuckle.
[FLORIZEL *and* AUTOLYCUS *exchange clothes*]
[*To* PERDITA] Fortunate mistress—let my prophecy
Come home to ye![6]—you must retire yourself
Into some covert,° take your sweetheart's hat   *hiding place*
And pluck it o'er your brows, muffle your face,
635 Dismantle you,° and, as you can, disliken°   *Take off your cloak / disguise*
The truth of your own seeming,° that you may—   *appearance*
For I do fear eyes°—over to shipboard   *spies*
Get undescried.

PERDITA   I see the play so lies
That I must bear a part.

CAMILLO   No remedy.
[*To* FLORIZEL] Have you done there?

640 FLORIZEL   Should I now meet my father
He would not call me son.

CAMILLO   Nay, you shall have no hat.
[*He gives the hat to* PERDITA]
Come, lady, come. Farewell, my friend.

AUTOLYCUS   Adieu, sir.

FLORIZEL O Perdita, what have we twain forgot!
Pray you, a word.
[*They speak aside*]

645 CAMILLO [*aside*] What I do next shall be to tell the King
Of this escape, and whither they are bound;
Wherein my hope is I shall so prevail
To force him after, in whose company
I shall re-view Sicilia, for whose sight
I have a woman's longing.[7]

---

4. Half undressed (skinned).
5. "Serious," with a pun on "earnest" as meaning both "sincere" and "an advance payment." See line 628.
6. Let my prophecy (that she be fortunate) be fulfilled.
7. Women, especially pregnant women, were said to be vulnerable to irrational and very intense cravings.

650 FLORIZEL   Fortune speed us!
Thus we set on, Camillo, to th' seaside.
CAMILLO   The swifter speed the better.

                    Exeunt [FLORIZEL, PERDITA, *and* CAMILLO][8]

AUTOLYCUS   I understand the business, I hear it. To have an open
ear, a quick eye, and a nimble hand is necessary for a cutpurse.
655   A good nose is requisite also, to smell out work for th'other
senses. I see this is the time that the unjust man doth thrive.
What an exchange had this been without boot!° What a boot[9]   even without payment
is here with this exchange! Sure the gods do this year connive
at° us, and we may do anything extempore.° The Prince him-   indulge / spontaneously
660   self is about a piece of iniquity, stealing away from his father
with his clog° at his heels. If I thought it were a piece of honesty   encumbrance (Perdita)
to acquaint the King withal,° I would not do't. I hold it the   with it
more knavery to conceal it, and therein am I constant° to my   faithful
profession.

                    Enter [*the*] CLOWN *and* [*the* OLD] SHEPHERD[, *carrying a*
                    fardel° *and a box*]   bundle

665   Aside, aside! Here is more matter for a hot brain. Every lane's
end, every shop, church, session,° hanging, yields a careful   court session
man work.
CLOWN   See, see, what a man you are now! There is no other
way but to tell the King she's a changeling,[1] and none of your
670   flesh and blood.
OLD SHEPHERD   Nay, but hear me.
CLOWN   Nay, but hear *me*.
OLD SHEPHERD   Go to,° then.   Go ahead
CLOWN   She being none of your flesh and blood, your flesh and
675   blood has not offended the King, and so your flesh and blood
is not to be punished by him. Show those things you found
about her, those secret things, all but what she has with her.
This being done, let the law go whistle, I warrant you.
OLD SHEPHERD   I will tell the King all, every word, yea, and his
680   son's pranks, too, who, I may say, is no honest man, neither to
his father nor to me, to go about to make me the King's brother-
in-law.
CLOWN   Indeed, brother-in-law was the farthest off° you could   most remote relation
have been to him, and then your blood had been the dearer by
685   I know not how much an ounce.
AUTOLYCUS [*aside*]   Very wisely, puppies.
OLD SHEPHERD   Well, let us to the King. There is that in this
fardel will make him scratch his beard.
AUTOLYCUS [*aside*]   I know not what impediment this complaint
690   may be to the flight of my master.°   (Florizel)
CLOWN   Pray heartily he be at'° palace.   at the
AUTOLYCUS [*aside*]   Though I am not naturally honest, I am so
sometimes by chance. Let me pocket up my pedlar's excre-
ment.°   hair
                    [*He removes his false beard*]
695   —How now, rustics, whither are you bound?
OLD SHEPHERD   To th' palace, an° it like your worship.   if

---

8. F marks a single *"Exit"* here for Camillo, but Florizel   9. Benefit; shoe.
and Perdita undoubtedly exit also, leaving Autolycus   1. A child left or abducted by fairies. See note to
alone on stage to comment on what he has witnessed.   3.3.109.

AUTOLYCUS   Your affairs there? What? With whom? The condi-
tion of that fardel?° The place of your dwelling? Your names?   *nature of that bundle*
Your ages? Of what having,° breeding,° and anything that is   *property / upbringing*
700   fitting to be known, discover.°   *reveal*

CLOWN   We are but plain° fellows, sir.   *simple; smooth*

AUTOLYCUS   A lie, you are rough and hairy. Let me have no
lying. It becomes none but tradesmen, and they often give us
soldiers the lie,[2] but we pay them for it with stamped coin, not
705   stabbing steel, therefore they do not *give* us the lie.[3]

CLOWN   Your worship had like to have given us one° if you had   *(the lie)*
not taken yourself with the manner.[4]

OLD SHEPHERD   Are you a courtier, an't like you, sir?

AUTOLYCUS   Whether it like me or no, I am a courtier. Seest thou
710   not the air of the court in these enfoldings?° Hath not my gait   *garments*
in it the measure° of the court? Receives not thy nose court   *stately walk*
odour from me? Reflect I not on thy baseness court-contempt?
Thinkest thou, for that I insinuate° to toze° from thee thy busi-   *subtly work / tease out*
ness, I am therefore no courtier? I am courtier cap-à-pie,° and   *from head to foot*
715   one that will either push on or pluck back thy business there.
Whereupon I command thee to open° thy affair.   *reveal*

OLD SHEPHERD   My business, sir, is to the King.

AUTOLYCUS   What advocate hast thou to him?

OLD SHEPHERD   I know not, an't like you.

720   CLOWN [*aside to the* OLD SHEPHERD]   'Advocate' 's the court
word for a pheasant.[5] Say you have none.

OLD SHEPHERD   None, sir. I have no pheasant, cock nor hen.

AUTOLYCUS [*aside*]   How blessed are we that are not simple men!
Yet nature might have made me as these are,
725   Therefore I will not disdain.

CLOWN   This cannot be but° a great courtier.   *anyone but*

OLD SHEPHERD   His garments are rich, but he wears them not
handsomely.

CLOWN   He seems to be the more noble in being fantastical.° A   *eccentric*
730   great man, I'll warrant. I know by the picking on's teeth.[6]

AUTOLYCUS   The fardel there, what's i'th' fardel? Wherefore that
box?

OLD SHEPHERD   Sir, there lies such secrets in this fardel and box
which none must know but the King, and which he shall know
735   within this hour, if I may come to th' speech of him.

AUTOLYCUS   Age,° thou hast lost thy labour.   *Old man*

OLD SHEPHERD   Why, sir?

AUTOLYCUS   The King is not at the palace, he is gone aboard a
new ship to purge° melancholy and air himself; for if thou   *rid himself of*
740   beest capable of° things serious, thou must know the King is   *can understand*
full of grief.

OLD SHEPHERD   So 'tis said, sir; about his son, that should have
married a shepherd's daughter.

AUTOLYCUS   If that shepherd be not in handfast,° let him fly. The   *arrested*

---

2. They call us soldiers liars; they cheat us soldiers.
3. Punning on "give the lie" as meaning both "cheat"
and "insult me in a way that requires a challenge to a
duel." The point seems to be that since soldiers pay
with good currency rather than by stabbing (the appropriate response to an insult), vendors can't claim to
have given anything—including the lie—to anyone, and
a duel can be successfully avoided.

4. If you had not stopped yourself in the middle.
5. The Clown thinks "advocate" means "bribe" or
"gift," of which a pheasant would be an example. He is
confusing the King's court with a law court in which
game birds were supposedly given as bribes to local
magistrates.
6. Ornate toothpicks were considered fashionable
accessories.

745 curses he shall have, the tortures he shall feel, will break the
back of man, the heart of monster.

CLOWN   Think you so, sir?

AUTOLYCUS   Not he alone shall suffer what wit can make heavy
and vengeance bitter, but those that are germane° to him,   *related*
750 though removed fifty times, shall all come under the hangman,
which, though it be great pity, yet it is necessary. An old sheep-
whistling rogue,[7] a ram-tender, to offer to have his daughter
come into grace!° Some say he shall be stoned; but that death   *favor (at court)*
is too soft for him, say I. Draw our throne into a sheepcote?°   *pen for sheep*
755 All deaths are too few, the sharpest too easy.

CLOWN   Has the old man e'er a son, sir, do you hear, an't like
you, sir?

AUTOLYCUS   He has a son, who shall be flayed alive, then
'nointed over with honey, set on the head of a wasps' nest, then
760 stand till he be three-quarters-and-a-dram° dead, then recov-   *a tiny bit*
ered again with aqua-vitae,° or some other hot infusion, then,   *brandy*
raw as he is, and in the hottest day prognostication° proclaims,   *almanac prediction*
shall he be set against a brick wall, the sun looking with a
southward eye upon him, where he is to behold him with flies
765 blown° to death. But what talk we of these traitorly rascals,   *swollen*
whose miseries are to be smiled at, their offences being so
capital? Tell me, for you seem to be honest plain men, what
you have° to the King. Being something gently considered,[8] I'll   *have to say*
bring you where he is aboard, tender° your persons to his pres-   *deliver*
770 ence, whisper him in your behalfs, and if it be in man, besides
the King, to effect your suits, here is man shall do it.

CLOWN [to the OLD SHEPHERD]   He seems to be of great author-
ity. Close° with him, give him gold; and though authority be a   *Make a deal*
stubborn bear, yet he is oft led by the nose with gold. Show the
775 inside of your purse to the outside of his hand, and no more
ado. Remember—'stoned', and 'flayed alive'.

OLD SHEPHERD   An't please you, sir, to undertake the business
for us, here is that° gold I have. I'll make it as much more, and   *what*
leave this young man in pawn° till I bring it you.   *as security*
780 AUTOLYCUS   After I have done what I promised?

OLD SHEPHERD   Ay, sir.

AUTOLYCUS   Well, give me the moiety.° [To the CLOWN] Are you   *half*
a party in this business?

CLOWN   In some sort, sir. But though my case° be a pitiful one,   *condition; skin*
785 I hope I shall not be flayed out of it.

AUTOLYCUS   O, that's the case of the shepherd's son. Hang him,
he'll be made an example.

CLOWN [to the OLD SHEPHERD]   Comfort, good comfort. We
must to the King, and show our strange sights. He must
790 know 'tis none of your daughter, nor my sister. We are gone°   *lost (dead)*
else.° [To AUTOLYCUS] Sir, I will give you as much as this old   *otherwise*
man does when the business is performed, and remain, as he
says, your pawn till it be brought you.

AUTOLYCUS   I will trust you. Walk before° toward the seaside. Go   *ahead of me*
795 on the right hand. I will but look upon the hedge,[9] and follow
you.

7. An old rascal who whistles while he tends sheep.   will give me a bribe worthy of my high rank.
8. As I am a highly regarded gentleman at court; if you   9. Slang for "relieve myself."

CLOWN [*to the* OLD SHEPHERD]   We are blessed in this man, as I
may say, even blessed.

OLD SHEPHERD   Let's before, as he bids us. He was provided to
800   do us good.   [*Exit with the* CLOWN]

AUTOLYCUS   If I had a mind to be honest, I see fortune would
not suffer° me. She drops booties° in my mouth. I am courted   permit / prizes
now with a double occasion:° gold, and a means to do the   opportunity
Prince my master good, which who knows how that may turn
805   back to my advancement? I will bring these two moles, these
blind ones, aboard him.° If he think it fit to shore them[1] again,   (his ship)
and that the complaint they have to the King concerns him
nothing, let him call me rogue for being so far officious, for I
am proof against° that title, and what shame else belongs to't.   impervious to
810   To him will I present them. There may be matter in it.   *Exit*

5.1
Enter LEONTES, CLEOMENES, DION, [*and*] PAULINA

CLEOMENES [*to* LEONTES]   Sir, you have done enough, and have performed
A saint-like sorrow. No fault could you make
Which you have not redeemed, indeed, paid down
More penitence than done trespass.[1] At the last
5   Do as the heavens have done, forget your evil.
With them, forgive yourself.

LEONTES   Whilst I remember
Her and her virtues I cannot forget
My blemishes in them,° and so still think of   in relation to them
The wrong I did myself, which was so much
10   That heirless it hath made my kingdom, and
Destroyed the sweet'st companion that e'er man
Bred his hopes out of. True?

PAULINA   Too true, my lord.
If one by one you wedded all the world,
Or from the all that are took something good
15   To make a perfect woman, she you killed
Would be unparalleled.

LEONTES   I think so. Killed?
She I killed? I did so. But thou strik'st me
Sorely to say I did; it is as bitter
Upon thy tongue as in my thought. Now, good now,°   if you would
Say so but seldom.

20   CLEOMENES   Not at all,° good lady.   Never (say these things)
You might have spoke a thousand things that would
Have done the time more benefit,[2] and graced°   showed
Your kindness better.

PAULINA   You are one of those
Would have him wed again.

DION   If you would not so
25   You pity not the state,° nor the remembrance   kingdom
Of his most sovereign name,[3] consider little
What dangers, by his highness' fail of issue,°   lack of offspring
May drop upon his kingdom and devour

---

1. Put them ashore.
5.1 Location: Sicilia. The palace of Leontes.
1. Performed more penance than your sin warranted.

2. That would have been more useful in these times.
3. Nor the perpetuation of his royal lineage (through a new child).

    Incertain lookers-on.[4] What were more holy
30   Than to rejoice the former queen is well?°   *(in heaven)*
    What holier, than for royalty's repair,
    For present comfort and for future good,
    To bless the bed of majesty again
    With a sweet fellow to't?
PAULINA   There is none worthy
35   Respecting° her that's gone. Besides, the gods   *In comparison to*
    Will have fulfilled their secret purposes.[5]
    For has not the divine Apollo said?
    Is't not the tenor of his oracle
    That King Leontes shall not have an heir
40   Till his lost child be found? Which that it shall
    Is all as monstrous° to our human reason   *incredible*
    As my Antigonus to break his grave
    And come again to me, who, on my life,
    Did perish with the infant. 'Tis your counsel
45   My lord should to the heavens be contrary,
    Oppose against their wills.
    [*To* LEONTES]   Care not for issue.
    The crown will find an heir. Great Alexander
    Left his to th' worthiest,[6] so his successor
    Was like to be the best.
LEONTES   Good Paulina,
50   Who hast the memory of Hermione,
    I know, in honour—O, that ever I
    Had squared me° to thy counsel! Then even now   *conformed my actions*
    I might have looked upon my queen's full eyes,
    Have taken treasure from her lips.
PAULINA   And left them
    More rich for what they yielded.
55 LEONTES   Thou speak'st truth.
    No more such wives, therefore no wife. One worse,
    And better used,° would make her sainted spirit   *treated*
    Again possess her° corpse, and on this stage,   *(Hermione's)*
    Where we offenders mourn, appear soul-vexed,°   *with troubled soul*
    And begin, 'Why° to me?'   *Why offer this insult*
60 PAULINA   Had she such power
    She had just cause.
LEONTES   She had, and would incense me
    To murder her I married.
PAULINA   I should so.
    Were I the ghost that walked I'd bid you mark
    Her eye, and tell me for what dull part in't
65   You chose her. Then I'd shriek that even your ears
    Should rift° to hear me, and the words that followed   *split*
    Should be, 'Remember mine'.°   *(my eyes)*
LEONTES   Stars, stars,
    And all eyes else,° dead coals! Fear thou no wife.   *all other eyes*
    I'll have no wife, Paulina.

---

4. And destroy those subjects who are bewildered (by
the matter of his successor).
5. Will ensure that their secret purposes are fulfilled.
6. Alexander the Great (356–323 B.C.E.), conqueror of
Greece, Persia, and Egypt, died before his own son was
born and reportedly urged his followers simply to
choose the worthiest man as his successor.

PAULINA   Will you swear
70   Never to marry but by my free leave?

LEONTES   Never, Paulina, so be blest my spirit.

PAULINA   Then, good my lords, bear witness to his oath.

CLEOMENES   You tempt him over-much.

PAULINA   Unless another
      As like Hermione as is her picture
      Affront° his eye—   *Confront*

75   CLEOMENES   Good madam, I have done.[7]

PAULINA   Yet if my lord will marry—if you will, sir;
      No remedy but you will—give me the office
      To choose your queen. She shall not be so young
      As was your former, but she shall be such
80   As, walked your first queen's ghost,[8] it should take joy
      To see her in your arms.

LEONTES   My true Paulina,
      We shall not marry till thou bidd'st us.

PAULINA   That
      Shall be when your first queen's again in breath.°   *alive*
      Never till then.

            Enter a SERVANT

85   SERVANT   One that gives out himself° Prince Florizel,   *claims to be*
      Son of Polixenes, with his princess—she
      The fairest I have yet beheld—desires access
      To your high presence.

LEONTES   What° with him? He comes not   *Who comes*
      Like to° his father's greatness. His approach,   *As befits*
90   So out of circumstance° and sudden, tells us   *informal*
      'Tis not a visitation framed,° but forced   *planned*
      By need and accident. What train?°   *retinue*

SERVANT   But few,
      And those but mean.°   *of low rank*

LEONTES   His princess, say you, with him?

SERVANT   Ay, the most peerless piece of earth, I think,
      That e'er the sun shone bright on.

95   PAULINA   O, Hermione,
      As every present time doth boast itself
      Above a better, gone, so must thy grave
      Give way to what's seen now![9]
      [*To the* SERVANT]   Sir, you yourself
      Have said and writ so; but your writing now
100   Is colder than that theme. She had not been
      Nor was not to be equalled—thus your verse
      Flowed with her beauty once. 'Tis shrewdly° ebbed   *grievously*
      To say you have seen a better.

SERVANT   Pardon, madam.
      The one° I have almost forgot—your pardon!   *(Hermione)*
105   The other, when she has obtained your eye,
      Will have your tongue too. This is a creature,

Would she begin a sect, might quench the zeal
Of all professors else;[1] make proselytes°   converts
Of who° she but bid follow.   Of those who

PAULINA   How? Not women!

110 SERVANT   Women will love her that she is a woman
More worth° than any man; men, that she is   worthy
The rarest of all women.

LEONTES   Go, Cleomenes.
Yourself, assisted with your honoured friends,
Bring them to our embracement.   *Exit* [CLEOMENES]
                                      Still 'tis strange
He thus should steal upon us.

115 PAULINA   Had our prince,
Jewel of children, seen this hour, he had paired
Well with this lord. There was not full a month°   a full month
Between their births.

LEONTES   Prithee no more, cease. Thou know'st
He dies to me again when talked of. Sure,
120 When I shall see this gentleman thy speeches
Will bring me to consider that which may
Unfurnish me of reason.° They are come.   Make me go mad

       Enter FLORIZEL, PERDITA, CLEOMENES, *and others*
Your mother was most true to wedlock, Prince,
For she did print your royal father off,[2]
125 Conceiving you. Were I but twenty-one,
Your father's image is so hit° in you,   exact
His very air, that I should call you brother,
As I did him, and speak of something wildly
By us performed before. Most dearly welcome,
130 And your fair princess—goddess! O, alas,
I lost a couple that 'twixt heaven and earth
Might thus have stood, begetting wonder, as
You, gracious couple, do; and then I lost—
All mine own folly—the society,
135 Amity too, of your brave° father, whom,   stouthearted
Though bearing misery, I desire my life[3]
Once more to look on him.

FLORIZEL   By his command
Have I here touched Sicilia, and from him
Give you all greetings that a king at friend°   in friendship
140 Can send his brother; and but° infirmity,   were it not that
Which waits upon worn times,° hath something seized   accompanies old age
His wished ability,[4] he had himself
The lands and waters 'twixt your throne and his
Measured° to look upon you, whom he loves—   Journeyed across
145 He bade me say so—more than all the sceptres,
And those that bear them, living.

LEONTES   O, my brother!
Good gentleman, the wrongs I have done thee stir
Afresh within me, and these thy offices,°   greetings
So rarely° kind, are as interpreters   extraordinarily

1. Of all those who professed other religions.   3. Whom, though I am suffering, I wish to live long
2. Made an exact copy of Polixenes, as a printer pro-   enough.
duces a book.   4. Has somewhat deprived him of his desired strength.

150 Of my behindhand slackness.[5] Welcome hither,
As is the spring to th'earth! And hath he too
Exposed this paragon to th' fearful usage—
At least ungentle—of the dreadful Neptune°   *god of the sea*
To greet a man not worth her pains, much less
Th'adventure° of her person?   *risk*

155 FLORIZEL   Good my lord,
She came from Libya.

LEONTES   Where the warlike Smalus,[6]
That noble honoured lord, is feared and loved?

FLORIZEL   Most royal sir, from thence; from him whose daughter
His tears proclaimed his, parting with her. Thence,

160 A prosperous south wind friendly, we have crossed,
To execute the charge my father gave me
For visiting your highness. My best train
I have from your Sicilian shores dismissed;
Who for Bohemia bend,° to signify   *make their way*

165 Not only my success in Libya, sir,
But my arrival, and my wife's, in safety
Here where we are.

LEONTES   The blessèd gods
Purge all infection from our air whilst you
Do climate° here! You have a holy father,   *reside*

170 A graceful gentleman, against whose person,
So sacred as it is, I have done sin,
For which the heavens, taking angry note,
Have left me issueless; and your father's blessed,
As he from heaven merits it, with you,

175 Worthy his goodness. What might I have been,
Might I a son and daughter now have looked on,
Such goodly things as you?

Enter a LORD

LORD   Most noble sir,
That which I shall report will bear no credit
Were not the proof so nigh. Please you, great sir,

180 Bohemia greets you from himself by me;
Desires you to attach° his son, who has,   *arrest*
His dignity and duty[7] both cast off,
Fled from his father, from his hopes, and with
A shepherd's daughter.

LEONTES   Where's Bohemia? Speak.

185 LORD   Here in your city. I now came from him.
I speak amazedly,° and it becomes°   *confusedly / befits*
My marvel° and my message. To your court   *astonishment*
Whiles he was hast'ning—in the chase, it seems,
Of this fair couple—meets he on the way

190 The father of this seeming° lady and   *apparent; false*
Her brother, having both their country quitted
With this young prince.

FLORIZEL   Camillo has betrayed me,

---

5. Are reminders of my slowness (in greeting you).
6. An obscure allusion. The name may be a misprint for "Synalus," a soldier from Carthage mentioned by
Plutarch.
7. His royal status and his duty to his father.

Whose honour and whose honesty till now
Endured all weathers.

LORD   Lay't so to his charge.°   *Accuse him directly*
He's with the King your father.

195 LEONTES   Who, Camillo?

LORD   Camillo, sir. I spake with him, who now
Has these poor men in question. Never saw I
Wretches so quake. They kneel, they kiss the earth,
Forswear° themselves as often as they speak.   *Perjure*

200 Bohemia stops his ears, and threatens them
With divers deaths in death.°   *With diverse tortures*

PERDITA   O, my poor father!
The heaven sets spies upon us, will not have
Our contract celebrated.

LEONTES   You are married?

FLORIZEL   We are not, sir, nor are we like to be.

205 The stars, I see, will kiss the valleys first.
The odds for high and low's alike.[8]

LEONTES   My lord,
Is this the daughter of a king?

FLORIZEL   She is,
When once she is my wife.

LEONTES   That 'once', I see, by your good father's speed
210 Will come on very slowly. I am sorry,
Most sorry, you have broken from his liking
Where you were tied in duty; and as sorry
Your choice is not so rich in worth° as beauty,   *rank*
That you might well enjoy her.

FLORIZEL [*to* PERDITA]   Dear, look up.
215 Though fortune, visible an enemy,
Should chase us with my father, power no jot
Hath she to change our loves.[9]—Beseech you, sir,
Remember since you owed no more to time
Than I do now.° With thought of such affections,   *when you were my age*
220 Step forth mine advocate. At your request
My father will grant precious things as trifles.

LEONTES   Would he do so, I'd beg your precious mistress,
Which he counts but a trifle.

PAULINA   Sir, my liege,
Your eye hath too much youth in't. Not a month
225 Fore your queen died she was more worth such gazes
Than what you look on now.

LEONTES   I thought of her
Even in these looks I made.
[*To* FLORIZEL]   But your petition
Is yet unanswered. I will to your father.
Your honour not o'erthrown by your desires,[1]
230 I am friend to them and you. Upon which errand
I now go toward him. Therefore follow me,
And mark what way I make. Come, good my lord.   *Exeunt*

---

8. That is, "Chance treats those of high and low rank identically."
9. Even if Lady Fortune were to make herself apparent as our enemy and join my father in pursuit, she would remain powerless to change our love.
1. So long as you have not allowed passion to destroy your virtue.

5.2

Enter AUTOLYCUS *and a* GENTLEMAN

AUTOLYCUS Beseech you, sir, were you present at this relation?° *when this was told*

FIRST GENTLEMAN I was by at the opening of the fardel, heard
the old shepherd deliver the manner how he found it; whereupon, after a little amazedness, we were all commanded out of
5 the chamber. Only this, methought I heard the shepherd say
he found the child.

AUTOLYCUS I would most gladly know the issue° of it. *outcome*

FIRST GENTLEMAN I make a broken delivery° of the business, but *confused report*
the changes I perceived in the King and Camillo were very
10 notes of admiration.[1] They seemed almost, with staring on one
another, to tear the cases° of their eyes. There was speech in *burst the sockets*
their dumbness, language in their very gesture. They looked as° *as if*
they had heard of a world ransomed, or one destroyed. A
notable passion of wonder appeared in them, but the wisest
15 beholder, that knew no more but seeing, could not say if
th'importance were joy or sorrow. But in the extremity of the
one,° it must needs be. *of the one or the other*

Enter another GENTLEMAN

Here comes a gentleman that happily° knows more. The news, *perhaps*
Ruggiero!

20 SECOND GENTLEMAN Nothing but bonfires. The oracle is fulfilled. The King's daughter is found. Such a deal° of wonder is *a great quantity*
broken out within this hour, that ballad-makers cannot be able
to express it.[2]

Enter another GENTLEMAN

Here comes the Lady Paulina's steward. He can deliver you
25 more.—How goes it now, sir? This news which is called true is
so like an old tale that the verity of it is in strong suspicion. Has
the King found his heir?

THIRD GENTLEMAN Most true, if ever truth were pregnant by circumstance.° That which you hear you'll swear you see, there is *proven by evidence*
30 such unity in the proofs. The mantle of Queen Hermione's,
her jewel about the neck of it, the letters of Antigonus found
with it, which they know to be his character;° the majesty of *handwriting*
the creature, in resemblance of the mother; the affection of° *instinct toward*
nobleness which nature shows above° her breeding,° and many *in excess of / upbringing*
35 other evidences proclaim her with all certainty to be the King's
daughter. Did you see the meeting of the two kings?

SECOND GENTLEMAN No.

THIRD GENTLEMAN Then have you lost a sight which was to be
seen, cannot be spoken of. There might you have beheld one
40 joy crown another, so and in such manner that it seemed sorrow wept to take leave of them, for their joy waded in tears.
There was casting up of eyes, holding up of hands, with counte-
nance° of such distraction[3] that they were to be known by gar- *face*
ment, not by favour.° Our king being ready to leap out of *features*
45 himself for joy of his found daughter, as if that joy were now
become a loss cries, 'O, thy mother, thy mother!', then asks
Bohemia forgiveness, then embraces his son-in-law, then again

---

5.2 Location: Sicilia. The palace of Leontes.
1. Were the very marks of wonder.
2. Ballads often provided accounts of contemporary

scandals and sensations.
3. So altered by emotion.

worries he° his daughter with clipping° her. Now he thanks the   *he agitates / embracing*
old shepherd, which stands by like a weather-bitten conduit of
50   many kings' reigns.[4] I never heard of such another encounter,
which lames report to follow it,[5] and undoes° description to do°   *defies / express*
it.

SECOND GENTLEMAN   What, pray you, became of Antigonus, that
carried hence the child?

55   THIRD GENTLEMAN   Like an old tale still, which will have matter
to rehearse° though credit° be asleep and not an ear open. He   *relate / belief*
was torn to pieces with a bear. This avouches° the shepherd's   *vows*
son, who has not only his innocence,° which seems much, to   *simplemindedness*
justify him, but a handkerchief and rings of his,° that Paulina   *(of Antigonus)*
60   knows.

FIRST GENTLEMAN   What became of his barque° and his fol-   *ship*
lowers?

THIRD GENTLEMAN   Wrecked the same instant of their master's
death, and in the view of the shepherd; so that all the instru-
65   ments which aided to expose the child were even then lost
when it was found. But O, the noble combat that 'twixt joy and
sorrow was fought in Paulina! She had one eye declined for
the loss of her husband, another elevated[6] that the oracle was
fulfilled. She lifted the Princess from the earth, and so locks
70   her in embracing as if she would pin her to her heart, that she
might no more be in danger of losing.°   *of being lost*

FIRST GENTLEMAN   The dignity of this act was worth the audience of kings and princes, for by such was it acted.

THIRD GENTLEMAN   One of the prettiest touches of all, and that
75   which angled for mine eyes—caught the water,° though not   *(my tears)*
the fish—was when at the relation of the Queen's death, with
the manner how she came to't bravely confessed and lamented
by the King, how attentiveness° wounded his daughter till from   *intent listening*
one sign of dolour° to another she did, with an 'Alas', I would   *grief*
80   fain say bleed tears; for I am sure my heart wept blood. Who
was most marble° there changed colour. Some swooned, all   *unfeeling*
sorrowed. If all the world could have seen't, the woe had been
universal.

FIRST GENTLEMAN   Are they returned to the court?

85   THIRD GENTLEMAN   No. The Princess, hearing of her mother's
statue, which is in the keeping of Paulina, a piece many years
in doing, and now newly performed° by that rare Italian master   *completed*
Giulio Romano,[7] who, had he himself eternity and could put
breath into his work, would beguile° nature of her custom,° so   *cheat / business*
90   perfectly he is her ape.° He so near to Hermione hath done   *imitator*
Hermione that they say one would speak to her and stand in
hope of answer. Thither with all greediness of affection are
they gone, and there they intend to sup.

SECOND GENTLEMAN   I thought she had some great matter there
95   in hand, for she hath privately twice or thrice a day, ever since
the death of Hermione, visited that removed° house. Shall we   *distant; hidden*
thither, and with our company piece° the rejoicing?   *join*

---

4. Who stands by weeping like a waterspout that has
been around for the reigns of many Kings. Some large
buildings had "conduits" or waterpipes in the form of
gargoyles or gnarled human faces.
5. Which makes any account of it seem deficient.
6. That is, Paulina simultaneously cried and laughed.

7. An Italian painter, a follower of Raphael, who died in
1546 and was most famous for a series of erotic draw-
ings illustrating sexual positions, or "postures." It is not
clear whether Shakespeare, in fact, had ever seen any of
his work.

FIRST GENTLEMAN   Who would be thence, that has the benefit
of access? Every wink of an eye some new grace will be born.
100   Our absence makes us unthrifty to our knowledge.[8] Let's
along.   *Exeunt* [GENTLEMEN]

AUTOLYCUS   Now, had I not the dash° of my former life in me,   *stain; touch*
would preferment° drop on my head. I brought the old man   *royal favor*
and his son aboard the° Prince; told him I heard them talk of a   *aboard the ship of the*
105   fardel, and I know not what. But he at that time over-fond of
the shepherd's daughter—so he then took her to be—who
began to be much sea-sick, and himself little better, extremity
of weather continuing, this mystery remained undiscovered.
But 'tis all one to me, for had I been the finder-out of this secret
110   it would not have relished° among my other discredits.   *appeared well*

        Enter [*the* OLD] SHEPHERD *and* [*the*] CLOWN [*dressed as*
        gentlemen]

Here come those I have done good to against my will, and
already appearing in the blossoms of their fortune.

OLD SHEPHERD   Come, boy; I am past more children, but thy
sons and daughters will be all gentlemen born.
115 CLOWN [*to* AUTOLYCUS]   You are well met, sir. You denied to
fight with me this other° day because I was no gentleman born.   *the other*
See you these clothes? Say you see them not, and think me
still no gentleman born. You were best say these robes are not
gentlemen born. Give me the lie,[9] do, and try whether I am
120   not now a gentleman born.

AUTOLYCUS   I know you are now, sir, a gentleman born.

CLOWN   Ay, and have been so any time these four hours.

OLD SHEPHERD   And so have I, boy.

CLOWN   So you have; but I was a gentleman born before my
125   father, for the King's son took me by the hand and called me
brother; and then the two kings called my father brother; and
then the Prince my brother and the Princess my sister called
my father father; and so we wept; and there was the first gentleman-like tears that ever we shed.
130 OLD SHEPHERD   We may live, son, to shed many more.

CLOWN   Ay, or else 'twere hard luck, being in so preposterous
estate[1] as we are.

AUTOLYCUS   I humbly beseech you, sir, to pardon me all the
faults I have committed to your worship, and to give me your
135   good report to the Prince my master.

OLD SHEPHERD   Prithee, son, do, for we must be gentle° now we   *act nobly*
are gentlemen.

CLOWN   Thou wilt amend thy life?

AUTOLYCUS   Ay, an it like your good worship.
140 CLOWN   Give me thy hand. I will swear to the Prince thou art as
honest a true fellow as any is in Bohemia.

OLD SHEPHERD   You may say it, but not swear it.

CLOWN   Not swear it now I am a gentleman? Let boors° and   *peasants*
franklins° say it; I'll swear it.   *small farmers*
145 OLD SHEPHERD   How if it be false, son?

CLOWN   If it be ne'er so false,° a true gentleman may swear it in   *Even if it is false*

---

8. Makes us squander an opportunity to add to our
knowledge.
9. Insult me so that I must respond with the challenge
of a duel.
1. The Clown probably means "prosperous," but "pre-

posterous" is a nice blunder for it suggests that their
new status as gentlemen is preposterous in the sense of
(1) contrary to nature or (2) putting last what should be
first—that is, inverting the social order by putting "real"
gentlemen behind "false" gentlemen like themselves.

the behalf of his friend, [*to* AUTOLYCUS] and I'll swear to the
Prince thou art a tall fellow of thy hands° and that thou wilt not   *a brave man of action*
be drunk; but I know thou art no tall fellow of thy hands and
150   that thou wilt be drunk; but I'll swear it, and I would thou
wouldst be a tall fellow of thy hands.

AUTOLYCUS   I will prove so, sir, to my power.°   *as well as I can*

CLOWN   Ay, by any means prove a tall fellow. If I do not wonder
how thou dar'st venture to be drunk, not being a tall fellow,
155   trust me not.
     [*Flourish within*]
Hark, the kings and princes, our kindred, are going to see the
Queen's picture.° Come, follow us. We'll be thy good masters.   *likeness*
                                        Exeunt

5.3

Enter LEONTES, POLIXENES, FLORIZEL, PERDITA, CA-
MILLO, PAULINA, LORDS [*and attendants*][1]

LEONTES   O grave and good Paulina, the great comfort
That I have had of thee!

PAULINA   What,° sovereign sir,   *Whatever*
I did not well, I meant well. All my services
You have paid home,° but that you have vouchsafed°   *fully rewarded / vowed*
5   With your crowned brother and these young contracted
Heirs of your kingdoms my poor house to visit,
It is a surplus° of your grace which never   *an additional sign*
My life may last to answer.

LEONTES   O Paulina,
We honour you with trouble.[2] But we came
10   To see the statue of our queen. Your gallery
Have we passed through, not without much content
In many singularities;° but we saw not   *In seeing many rarities*
That which my daughter came to look upon,
The statue of her mother.

PAULINA   As she lived peerless,
15   So her dead likeness I do well believe
Excels what ever yet you looked upon,
Or hand of man hath done. Therefore I keep it
Lonely,° apart. But here it is. Prepare   *Alone*
To see the life as lively mocked° as ever   *realistically imitated*
20   Still° sleep mocked death. Behold, and say 'tis well.   *Quiet*
     [*She draws a curtain and reveals the figure of* HERMI-
     ONE, *standing like a statue*]
I like your silence; it the more shows off
Your wonder. But yet speak; first you, my liege.
Comes it not something° near?   *somewhat*

LEONTES   Her natural posture.
Chide me, dear stone, that I may say indeed
25   Thou art Hermione; or rather, thou art she
In thy not chiding, for she was as tender

5.3 Location: Sicilia. Paulina's house.
1. In F, the stage direction reads: "*Enter Leontes, Polix-*
enes, Florizell, Perdita, Camillo, Paulina: Hermione (like
a Statue:) Lords, etc." For a reader of the play, this direction suggests that Hermione is a living character pretending to be a statue. For a theatergoer unacquainted

with the play, by contrast, the immobile female figure
seen on stage is probably first assumed to be an actual
statue of the dead Queen.
2. The honor we pay to you demands much of you (by
way of hospitality).

    As infancy and grace. But yet, Paulina,
    Hermione was not so much wrinkled, nothing°   *not at all*
    So agèd as this seems.
    POLIXENES   O, not by much.
30   PAULINA   So much the more our carver's excellence,
    Which lets go by some sixteen years, and makes her
    As° she lived now.   *As if*
    LEONTES   As now she might have done,
    So much to my good comfort as it is
    Now piercing to my soul. O, thus she stood,
35   Even with such life of majesty—warm life,
    As now it coldly stands—when first I wooed her.
    I am ashamed. Does not the stone rebuke me
    For being more stone° than it? O royal piece!°   *hard-hearted / work of art*
    There's magic in thy majesty, which has
40   My evils conjured° to remembrance, and   *summoned*
    From thy admiring° daughter took the spirits,   *wondering*
    Standing like stone with thee.
    PERDITA   And give me leave,
    And do not say 'tis superstition, that
    I kneel and then implore her blessing.[3] Lady,
45   Dear Queen, that ended when I but began,
    Give me that hand of yours to kiss.
    PAULINA   O, patience!
    The statue is but newly fixed;° the colour's   *painted*
    Not dry.
    CAMILLO [*to* LEONTES]   My lord, your sorrow was too sore° laid on,   *painfully*
50   Which sixteen winters cannot blow away,
    So many summers dry.[4] Scarce any joy
    Did ever so long live; no sorrow
    But killed itself much sooner.
    POLIXENES [*to* LEONTES]   Dear my brother,
    Let him that was the cause of this have power
55   To take off so much grief from you as he
    Will piece up in himself.[5]
    PAULINA [*to* LEONTES]   Indeed, my lord,
    If I had thought the sight of my poor image
    Would thus have wrought you°—for the stone is mine—   *made you distraught*
    I'd not have showed it.
          [*She makes to draw the curtain*]
    LEONTES   Do not draw the curtain.
60   PAULINA   No longer shall you gaze on't, lest your fancy
    May think anon it moves.
    LEONTES   Let be, let be!
    Would I were dead but that methinks already.[6]
    What was he that did make it? See, my lord,
    Would you not deem it breathed, and that those veins
    Did verily bear blood?
65   POLIXENES   Masterly done.
    The very life seems warm upon her lip.
    LEONTES   The fixture of her eye has motion in't,[7]

---

3. A possible reference to the Protestant attack on the Catholic practice of kneeling before images of the Virgin Mary.
4. And an equal number of summers cannot dry up.
5. Will make a part of himself.
6. May I die if I do not think it already moves.
7. The setting ("fixture") of her eye gives the appearance of motion.

As° we are mocked with art.   *In such a way that*

PAULINA   I'll draw the curtain.
My lord's almost so far transported that
He'll think anon it lives.

70   LEONTES   O sweet Paulina,
Make me to think so twenty years together.
No settled senses° of the world can match   *calm state of mind*
The pleasure of that madness. Let't alone.

PAULINA   I am sorry, sir, I have thus far stirred you; but
I could afflict you farther.

75   LEONTES   Do, Paulina,
For this affliction has a taste as sweet
As any cordial° comfort. Still methinks   *restorative*
There is an air comes from her.° What fine chisel   *she seems to breathe*
Could ever yet cut breath? Let no man mock me,
For I will kiss her.

80   PAULINA   Good my lord, forbear.
The ruddiness upon her lip is wet.
You'll mar it if you kiss it, stain your own
With oily painting.° Shall I draw the curtain?   *paint*

LEONTES   No, not these twenty years.

PERDITA   So long could I
Stand by, a looker-on.

85   PAULINA   Either forbear,
Quit presently° the chapel, or resolve you   *immediately*
For more amazement. If you can behold it,
I'll make the statue move indeed, descend,
And take you by the hand. But then you'll think—

90   Which I protest against—I am assisted
By wicked powers.

LEONTES   What you can make her do
I am content to look on; what to speak,
I am content to hear; for 'tis as easy
To make her speak as move.

PAULINA   It is required

95   You do awake your faith. Then, all stand still.
Or those that think it is unlawful business
I am about, let them depart.

LEONTES   Proceed.
No foot shall stir.

PAULINA   Music; awake her; strike!°   *strike up!*
[*Music*]
[*To* HERMIONE] 'Tis time. Descend. Be stone no more. Approach.

100 Strike all that look upon with marvel. Come,
I'll fill your grave up. Stir. Nay, come away.
Bequeath to death your numbness, for from him°   *(death)*
Dear life redeems you.
[*To* LEONTES]   You perceive she stirs.
[HERMIONE *slowly descends*]
Start not. Her actions shall be holy as

105 You hear my spell is lawful. Do not shun her
Until you see her die again, for then
You kill her double.[8] Nay, present your hand.
When she was young, you wooed her. Now, in age,

---

8. That is, "If you were to shun her in this new life, you would kill her again."

Is she become the suitor?

LEONTES   O, she's warm!
110 If this be magic, let it be an art
Lawful as eating.
POLIXENES   She embraces him.
CAMILLO   She hangs about his neck.
If she pertain to life,° let her speak too.   be truly alive
115 POLIXENES   Ay, and make it manifest where she has lived,
Or how stol'n from the dead.
PAULINA   That she is living,
Were it but told you, should be hooted at
Like an old tale. But it appears she lives,
Though yet she speak not. Mark a little while.
120 [To PERDITA] Please you to interpose, fair madam. Kneel,
And pray your mother's blessing.—Turn, good lady,
Our Perdita is found.
HERMIONE   You gods, look down,
And from your sacred vials pour your graces
Upon my daughter's head.—Tell me, mine own,
125 Where hast thou been preserved? Where lived? How found
Thy father's court? For thou shalt hear that I,
Knowing by Paulina that the oracle
Gave hope thou wast in being,° have preserved   alive
Myself to see the issue.°   the outcome; the child
PAULINA   There's time enough for that,
130 Lest they desire upon this push to trouble
Your joys with like relation.⁹ Go together,
You precious winners all; your exultation
Partake° to everyone. I, an old turtle,¹   Spread your happiness
Will wing me to some withered bough, and there
135 My mate, that's never to be found again,
Lament till I am lost.°   dead
LEONTES   O peace, Paulina!
Thou shouldst a husband take by my consent,
As I by thine a wife. This is a match,
And made between's by vows. Thou hast found mine,
140 But how is to be questioned, for I saw her,
As I thought, dead, and have in vain said many
A prayer upon her grave. I'll not seek far—
For him, I partly know his mind—to find thee
An honourable husband. Come, Camillo,
145 And take her by the hand, whose worth and honesty
Is richly noted, and here justified°   testified to
By us, a pair of kings. Let's from this place.
[To HERMIONE] What, look upon my brother. Both your pardons,
That e'er I put between your holy looks
150 My ill suspicion. This'° your son-in-law   This is
And son unto the King, whom heavens directing
Is troth-plight° to your daughter. Good Paulina,   betrothed
Lead us from hence, where we may leisurely
Each one demand and answer to his part
155 Performed in this wide gap of time since first
We were dissevered. Hastily lead away.   *Exeunt*

9. Lest they (bystanders?) desire at this crucial moment to trouble your happiness with similar stories.
1. I.e., turtledove, a symbol of faithful love.

Cymbeline

Toward the end of *Cymbeline,* one of the chief characters, Posthumus Leonatus, awakens from a dream vision to find a tablet on his chest, left there by Jupiter, king of the gods. In the dream, Jupiter had promised that the tablet would explain Posthumus's future fortunes. But when Posthumus reads the writing on the tablet, it is incomprehensible to him:

> 'Tis still a dream, or else such stuff as madmen
> Tongue, . . .
> Or senseless speaking, or a speaking such
> As sense cannot untie.

Yet he concludes: "Be what it is, / The action of my life is like it" (5.5.238–42). By his own estimation, Posthumus's life is a senseless riddle. His immediate circumstances perhaps warrant such a conclusion. When Jupiter appears to him, Posthumus, a Briton crucial to his country's recent defeat of Rome, has subsequently disguised himself as a Roman and been put in a British prison. Posthumus deliberately sought his own capture and death because of the guilt he felt for having wrongly commanded the death of his virtuous wife, Innogen, the British King's daughter, falsely accused of sexual infidelity. Unbeknownst to him, however, Innogen, not dead but also disguised as a Roman boy named Fidele, is likewise among those held captive by the Britons.

Such plot complexities are typical of *Cymbeline,* leading not only Posthumus, but also theatergoers, to find it a baffling muddle. In this play, an inordinate number of characters assume disguises, have more than one name, don't know who their "real" parents are, or find themselves unable to decipher the complicated events around them. In one of the play's most famous (or infamous) scenes, Innogen, traveling in a page's disguise to find Posthumus, wakes up from a drug-induced sleep to find herself lying beside the body of a headless man dressed in her husband's clothing. The man is really Cloten, Posthumus's rival for Innogen's hand and the wicked son of Innogen's evil stepmother. Seeing the headless body, Innogen breaks into a lament for the man she believes to be her husband. Her grief is genuine and affecting, but it is prompted by a profound misreading of the object before her.

The improbabilities and complexities of *Cymbeline*'s plot have given some critics pause, as has the freedom with which times and places are handled. Ostensibly set in Roman Britain at the time of Christ's birth (which, according to the chronicles, occurred during the reign of Cymbeline), the play also contains scenes that appear to take place in contemporary sixteenth-century Italy. It is in this modern Italy, for example, that Posthumus is tricked into believing that Innogen is sexually unfaithful to him. Reacting to the play's unusual features, the eighteenth-century critic Samuel Johnson complained:

> This play has many just sentiments, some natural dialogues, and some pleasing scenes, but they are obtained at the expense of much incongruity. To remark the folly of the fiction, the absurdity of the conduct, the confusion of the names, and manners of different times, and the impossibility of the events in any system of life, were to waste criticism upon unresisting imbecility, upon faults too evident for detection, and too gross for aggravation.

This response, however, may say more about Johnson's neoclassical tastes than about the ultimate value of Shakespeare's play. In *Cymbeline,* the complexity of the action seems deliberate rather than inadvertent or unskillful. It creates in the audience both a longing for clarity and control and an anxiety that the play may afford neither. The pleasure of the final act, therefore, stems from the relief experienced when—after a dizzying whirl of events, reversals, revelations, and disguises—peace descends, all identities revealed and all riddles expounded. The sense of wonder produced by this miraculous untangling of complicated events is one of the signal effects of Shakespeare's late plays: amazement that after astonishing suffering can come new hope, after labyrinthine confusions the solace of questions answered.

This feature of the play is one of the reasons why in modern criticism *Cymbeline* is usually called a romance or sometimes a tragicomedy, even though in the First Folio of 1623 it was grouped with the tragedies, probably because it dramatizes serious historical matter taken from the reign of an early Briton King. Like other plays written late in Shakespeare's career, however, such as *The Winter's Tale, Pericles,* and *The Tempest, Cymbeline* does not end tragically. Rather, it ultimately emphasizes the transformation of suffering into joy. While verging on tragedy, each of these plays wins through to a bittersweet conclusion in which shattered families are reconstituted and plot complexities untangled—but always at a cost. Mistakes have consequences in these plays. Sons die; years are lost in exile and wandering; women suffer from unjust slander. If, in the end, good fortune returns to the sufferers, it does not cancel their former pain but provides a miraculous contrast to it.

The date of *Cymbeline* is uncertain, although it is usually given as 1609 or 1610. Scholars differ as to whether it preceded or followed *The Winter's Tale.* We know that it was in performance by 1611, because Simon Forman, a London doctor and astrologer, wrote about seeing it, probably between April 20 and April 30 of that year. It is not clear whether he saw the play at the Globe, the outdoor theater that Shakespeare's company used after 1599, or at Blackfriars, the indoor theater that they also began to use in 1608. The spectacular scenic effects possible in staging this play, such as the descent of Jupiter on the back of an eagle in Act 5, may have been designed with the more elaborate technical capacities of the Blackfriars venue in mind. Some critics have tried to date the play by relating it to the investiture of Henry, King James's oldest son, as Prince of Wales in 1610, since a number of the key scenes of the play take place in Wales. We have no record of a court performance of the play until 1634, however, when it was played before King Charles, who liked it. Other critics have tried to determine the play's relationship to Beaumont and Fletcher's popular tragicomedy *Philaster,* usually dated 1609, to which *Cymbeline* bears some resemblance. But even though the two plays are related, it is not clear which influenced the other.

Whatever its exact date, *Cymbeline* belongs to Shakespeare's late period, and because of its setting it allowed Shakespeare simultaneously to address his longstanding interests both in British and in Roman history. The play intertwines three plot lines and draws on a variety of source materials. The main plot involves Innogen, the daughter and apparently the only living heir of Cymbeline, King of Britain, and her thwarted attempts to live with her chosen husband, Posthumus. Angry that Innogen loves a man of lesser social rank than herself and that she has not married Cloten, his second wife's son, Cymbeline banishes Posthumus from Britain. Posthumus goes to Italy, where he wagers on his wife's chastity with the villain Giacomo, who ultimately makes Posthumus believe Innogen unfaithful. Whether the love of Innogen and Posthumus can be restored is one of the key questions of this plot. This wager story draws on two sources: Boccacio's *Decameron,* a series of prose tales first translated into English in 1620 but available in a French translation in the sixteenth century, and *Frederick of Jennen,* an English translation of a German version of the same story.

A second plot strand deals with Britain's relationship with Rome, especially Rome's demand that the Britons pay the tribute pledged to Julius Caesar upon his conquest of the isle. For this part of the story, Shakespeare drew primarily on the brief account of Cymbeline's reign in Raphael Holinshed's *Chronicles of England, Scotland, and Ireland* (second edition, 1587). Cymbeline was King when the Roman Emperor Augustus Caesar ushered in the famous time of peace known as the *Pax Romana.* In most of the sources, it was Cymbeline's son Guiderius who refused to pay Rome tribute. Shakespeare modified the story, however, so that Cymbeline, urged on by his Queen and her son, is the one who withholds the tribute and provokes a Roman invasion.

The third plotline has to do with two sons of Cymbeline, stolen from their nursery by a wrongly defamed courtier, Belarius, who raises them in the mountains of Wales. By chance, their sister Innogen, disguised as a boy, stumbles upon their mountain cave on her flight from her father's court in pursuit of Posthumus. Near this cave, Cloten, wearing Posthumus's clothes, is killed by one of these sons; also near this cave, Innogen awakes from her sleep to find herself beside his headless body. For the play to reach its resolution, Cymbeline's sons must be reunited with their father. This reunion occurs, but only after the sons play a decisive role in the final battle against the Roman invaders. Their heroic actions in this battle are modeled on quite another part of Holinshed, *The History of Scotland*, which recounts the story of a farmer named Hay and his two sons, who routed Danish invaders at the Battle of Luncarty in about 976 C.E.

From these complex and diverse materials, Shakespeare wove a play whose rich allusiveness has invited many kinds of topical interpretations. One line of criticism has focused on *Cymbeline*'s relationship to events and ideas connected to the reign of King James I. James was interested in linking imperial Rome and the Roman Emperors to modern Britain and to his own kingship. He had himself painted crowned with laurel leaves, in the Roman manner, and had coins stamped with his laurel-crowned profile. Like Augustus Caesar, James presented himself as the great peacemaker after Elizabeth's

Qui regis imperio divisas orbe Britannos,
Rex tot virorum fortium;
Qui terrore tui solius nominis SoStes
Premis, quietis appetens;

Qui pace ecclesiam, jus
Forum, scholas doctoribus;
Atq; inter vates pangis pia carmina, sceptro
Jungis decenter lauream.

James I liked to present himself as heir to Roman greatness. In this 1613 engraving, Crispin van de Passe portrays him crowned with the laurel wreath worn by Roman emperors.

reluctant involvement in wars in Ireland and in defending the Protestant countries of the Continent against Catholic powers, especially Spain. Moreover, just as Augustus ruled over a vast empire, James aspired to unite Scotland and England (along with the already incorporated Wales) into a single entity with one church and one set of laws. His project failed, but he exerted much effort in promoting this union during the first years of his reign. *Cymbeline* uncannily echoes some of James's preoccupations. Sometimes called Shakespeare's last Roman play, *Cymbeline* dramatizes ancient Britain's attempts to come to terms with imperial Rome. Names of Roman gods—particularly Diana, Apollo, and Jupiter—abound (Jupiter alone is mentioned over thirty times); and figures from Roman mythology and history, such as Tarquin, Philomela, and Aeneas, are often evoked. The play's title character, like James, is a British monarch respectful of Rome, even when asserting his independence in the matter of the tribute. The final word of the play, spoken by the King, is "peace." The analogies between the play and the Stuart court, however, have their limits. Cymbeline is also a King duped by his wicked Queen and her doltish son—hardly a compliment to James and the royal family if events in the play are seen literally to mirror their circumstances.

Other allusions expand the play's possible range of meanings. Much is made, for example, of Milford Haven, the port in southern Wales where the Romans come ashore for their invasion of England. This port was famous to Shakespeare's audience as the place where Henry Richmond landed in 1485 to begin his assault on the forces of Richard III. Having defeated Richard, Richmond was crowned Henry VII, first of the Tudor Kings; Henry's daughter Margaret married James IV of Scotland, grandfather to the James who assumed the English throne in 1603. When the Romans land at Milford Haven, they in effect precipitate a transformation of the kingdom, much as Henry Richmond was to do 1,500 years later. At the time of their arrival, Cymbeline believes his two sons dead, and his daughter and Cloten have both fled the court. Britain is without an heir. But through the battle with the Romans, the lost sons of Cymbeline are discovered and the kingdom renewed. So, too, James fancied himself an agent of renewal, a second Henry VII arriving from Scotland to unite the whole island under his rule.

Wales itself is an important symbolic location in this play. Although officially incorporated into England in the 1530s, Wales remained distinct, often stigmatized as rude and uncivilized. The Welsh language, banned from use in public contexts, was taken to symbolize the barbarity of this borderland region. On the other hand, in some narratives, Wales was also the place from which the legitimate rulers of England sprang. The stories surrounding the mythical King Arthur give him a Welsh origin, and traditionally the eldest son of the British monarch was (and still is) given the title Prince of Wales. In *Cymbeline,* Wales is imagined as a harsh pastoral landscape in which Belarius and the King's sons live in a cave, hunt the food they eat, and have little contact with other human beings. These sons, Guiderius and Arviragus, frequently complain that they know nothing of the world and its customs and manners. But Wales shelters these sons as they grow to manhood and protects them from the vices of court life. In fact, as is traditional in pastoral literature, the Welsh scenes contain a good deal of anticourt satire. In the play's spatial and symbolic economies, Wales is the place where true British manhood is preserved. In part, the Welsh material can be seen as a compliment to Prince Henry, who was a staunch champion of the Protestant cause in Europe and showed every promise of being a more martial figure than his peace-loving father.

There can be little doubt that *Cymbeline* works with material imbued with a new kind of significance under the reign of James. Yet it may be a mistake to tie the play too closely to the royal family or to particular events. The play doesn't just reflect the world around it; it transforms the materials from that world into a powerful imaginative and ideological structure. In the largest sense, *Cymbeline* works to define both Britain and proper British manhood by constructing a complex narrative about national origins. The wager plot, with its story of sexual slander and threatened rape, is central to that narrative, not only because Innogen often seems to stand for Britain itself (she is several times addressed as "Britain," and she bears the name of the wife of Brute, the legendary ancient King of Britain), but also because the realignment of gender relations plays a crucial role in the "renewal" of Britain and in the play's turn from tragedy to comedy.

Strikingly, this play about Britain's past never mentions the word "England." In the history plays written in the 1590s, the reverse tends to be true: "Britain" is seldom employed, "England" is invoked with great frequency. There are several reasons for Shakespeare's choice in this later play. He is, of course, deliberately evoking the world of the ancient Britons, the early inhabitants of the island who provide the starting point for his creation of a fictive national past. At the same time, he is to some extent reflecting, and helping to create, the Stuart monarch's sense of the entity over which he ruled. James, after all, was not an "Englander" in the same way Elizabeth had been. He was a Scotsman who spoke with an accent and aspired to bring the entire island into a new political alignment.

Setting the play in the reign of Cymbeline allowed Shakespeare to imagine a primitive Britain that was also the cosmopolitan heir to the westward movement of empire. The treatment of Rome is particularly interesting in *Cymbeline*. Partly, the Romans are figured as an invading force, threatening the island. Yet the British characters most eager to repel the Romans and to treat them as an enemy are the evil Queen and her evil son. Cymbeline himself, while defending Britain's right to live free and under its own laws, is more disposed to come to terms with his great opponents and invariably treats them with respect. There is, in fact, a pronounced tension in the play between Britain's desires to defeat the Romans and to emulate them. This tension is managed in part through the splitting of the Romans into the noble figure of Lucius and the devilish figure of Giacomo, who in his deceit and misogyny embodies sixteenth-century stereotypes concerning the villainous Italian.

When Giacomo comes to Britain to test Innogen's fidelity, he fails in his initial attempt to portray Posthumus as a philanderer upon whom Innogen should seek sexual revenge. He then proceeds more secretly; he has himself conveyed in a trunk into her bedroom, from which he issues in the dead of night to survey her sleeping body and the contents of her room. His stealthy act is framed by references to infamous acts of rape. As he steps from the trunk, Giacomo compares himself to Tarquin, the Roman tyrant who raped Lucrece (a story told in Shakespeare's lengthy poem *The Rape of Lucrece,* written in the 1590s). Furthermore, the book that Innogen had been reading when she fell asleep is opened to the story of Tereus, who raped Philomela and cut out her tongue. Although

Tarquin's Rape of Lucrece. Sixteenth-century copy of an engraving by Agostino Veneziano.

Giacomo does not literally rape Innogen, he violates the privacy of her body with his peering eyes and rapes her honor by lying successfully to Posthumus about her infidelity. At one level, this incident is about the unjust sufferings of a slandered woman. At another level, Innogen is Britain, threatened by a skillful invader. Giacomo penetrates Innogen's bedchamber, and later he penetrates the ear of Posthumus with his poisonous slander.

In the play's denouement, the threat of foreign penetration is graphically repelled when Belarius and the sons of Cymbeline come from the Welsh mountains, joined by Posthumus disguised as a British peasant, and take a stand "in a narrow lane," putting the Romans to flight and instilling courage in the British. The vulnerable narrow lane is thus barricaded against outsiders by the sons of Cymbeline crying, "Stand, stand" (5.5.28). The moment has gendered and sexual overtones. A vulnerable and feminized Britain is protected from invasion by the swords of virile young men whose cry, "Stand," means both to "hold one's ground" and to "have an erection." This event proves pivotal, lending itself equally well to aphorism and to Posthumus's mocking rhyme: "Two boys, an old man twice a boy, a lane, / Preserved the Britons, was the Romans' bane" (5.5.57–58). In the play's symbolic economy, the threat of penetration initiated by Giacomo is thus repulsed by Innogen's long-lost brothers, and in the final scene Giacomo kneels to Posthumus, asking his forgiveness—the Italian subdued by the Briton.

Something quite different occurs with Lucius, the Roman military leader, who embodies the laudable virtues of ancient Rome rather than the hideous vices of sixteenth-century Italy. Even though the Roman army is defeated, Cymbeline decides to resume paying tribute, and in his final speech the King says: "let / A Roman and a British ensign wave / Friendly together" (5.6.479–81). This rapprochment of warring powers is ratified by one of the play's several mysterious visions. Before the battle, a Roman soothsayer told Lucius what the gods had revealed to him:

> I saw Jove's bird, the Roman eagle, winged
> From the spongy south to this part of the west,
> There vanished in the sunbeams; which portends,
> Unless my sins abuse my divination,
> Success to th' Roman host.
>
> (4.2.350–54)

In this play, not even soothsayers have perfect interpretive skills. The outcome of the battle requires some revisions in the exegesis of the vision. After the battle, the soothsayer says:

> For the Roman eagle,
> From south to west on wing soaring aloft,
> Lessened herself, and in the beams o'th' sun
> So vanished; which foreshowed our princely eagle
> Th'imperial Caesar should again unite
> His favour with the radiant Cymbeline,
> Which shines here in the west.
>
> (5.6.470–76)

Conquest has been transformed into concord as the Roman eagle and the British sun merge and as Cymbeline celebrates this peace within the temple of Jupiter.

In stressing the final union of Britain and Rome, the play's conclusion makes Britain the heir of Rome's imperial legacy even as Britain proclaims the integrity of her own land, laws, and customs. In the early modern period, the course of empire was thought to move westward. When Troy fell, the Trojan hero Aeneas bore his father on his back from the fires of the burning city and eventually fulfilled his destiny by establishing a new kingdom in Italy in what was to become the center of the Roman Empire. In the soothsayer's vision, the Roman eagle journeys even farther west, renewing itself, as eagles were believed to do, by enduring the burning fires of Britain's sun to purge away old feathers in preparation for the growth of new.

The eagle, king of birds and emblem of the Roman god Jupiter; according to myth, it could stare at the sun without blinking and fly into the sun in order to burn off its old feathers. From Joachim Camerarius, *Symbolorum et Emblematum* (1605 ed.).

The play's culminating vision of a Britain separate unto itself but also the cosmopolitan heir of an imperial tradition is anticipated in the actions of Innogen and Posthumus. In the final act, both are partly Roman in their dress and sympathies. Posthumus Leonatus comes to Britain in the company of the Italian gentry, but then dresses as a British peasant and fights with Belarius in the narrow lane before reassuming his Italian garb. Innogen is present at the battle as page to Lucius, the Roman general who had found her weeping over the headless corpse of Cloten. In the final moments of reconciliation, Cymbeline's daughter and her husband stand before the British King in foreign clothes. Innogen, moreover, earlier makes a telling speech about Britain's place in the world when discussing with a trusted servant where she would live after Posthumus had come to believe her unchaste. Her father's court, with Cloten present, she finds unthinkable. She then asks:

> Hath Britain all the sun that shines? Day, night,
> Are they not but in Britain? I'th' world's volume
> Our Britain seems as of it but not in't,
> In a great pool a swan's nest.

(3.4.136–39)

Innogen nicely captures the play's most complex view of Britain. Eschewing an insular patriotism associated with Cloten and the Queen, she recognizes a vast world beyond the shores of Britain. Punning on the double meaning of "volume" as "expanse" or "book," Innogen suggests Britain's partial separation from a larger entity. Britain is a little part of a bigger expanse, a page detached from a large book, or a swan's nest in a great pool. As the image of the swan's nest suggests, Britain remains the special seat of grace and beauty. But it is also connected to something larger than itself. There are other pages in the volume to which, even if detached, Britain belongs.

The play, then, seems to be negotiating a new vision of the nation suited for the Stuart moment, a vision resulting from the richly suggestive concatenation of discursive traditions that Shakespeare brought together in this play. Reaching back into the chronicle materials of ancient Britain, he provides a genealogy for modern Britain that (1) insists on the integrity and freedom of the island kingdom but (2) presents it as purged—largely through the efforts of the King's "Welsh" sons—of the corruptions of modern court life as embodied in figures such as Giacomo or Cloten, and (3) aligns Britain with the cosmopolitan values of Rome, positioning the island kingdom as the appropriate heir of Roman greatness: both warlike and peace-loving.

The renewed Britain has a fourth striking characteristic, and that is its decidedly masculine coloration. The wager plot makes plain the role of gender in configuring British national identity. Consider first the changing fortunes of Innogen. At the beginning of the play, she is a beloved and important figure in her father's court. Cymbeline's only living heir, the Princess is also strong-willed and decisive. She chooses Posthumus for her husband even though he has little money and is not of royal birth. By the end of the play, Innogen has been displaced from the succession by her two rediscovered brothers; she has also been ordered killed by her husband, threatened with rape, knocked unconscious by a drug she believes to be medicine, and struck by her husband when, in her page's attire, she steps forward to reveal her identity to him in the last scene. Though cross-dressed for much of the second half of the play, she does not, like Portia in *The Merchant of Venice* and Rosalind in *As You Like It*, use that disguise aggressively to shape her own destiny. Rather, burdened by the knowledge that her husband unjustly and inexplicably desires her death, Innogen grows less powerful and more passive as the play progresses. Her decline can be summarized in the pun on "heir" and "air." Innogen begins as the former and ends as the latter. The mysterious tablet laid on Posthumus's breast contained a riddling prophecy: "Whenas a lion's whelp shall, to himself unknown, without seeking find, and be embraced by a piece of tender air; and when from a stately cedar shall be lopped branches which, being dead many years, shall after revive, be jointed to the old stock, and freshly grow; then shall Posthumus end his miseries, Britain be fortunate and flourish in peace and plenty" (5.5.232–37). When the soothsayer finally untangles this riddle, he declares Posthumus Leonatus to be the lion's offspring; Cymbeline the cedar tree; his lost sons the lopped branches; and Innogen the tender air, because "tender air" in Latin translates as *mollis aer,* which (by a stretch of the imagination) derives from *mulier,* Latin for "wife." When Posthumus is embraced by the "tender air" (no longer an "heir"), his miseries will cease. Apparently because she is now less important to the succession, Innogen is allowed to live with her chosen husband, his masculinity affirmed by his pivotal role in the British victory over the Roman forces.

Victorian critics loved Innogen, idealizing her as a paragon of selfless and long-suffering womanhood. For example, the Princess never protests her demotion from the position of heir apparent; in fact, she says that she considers finding her brothers worth the loss of the kingdom. To many contemporary critics, however, her role in the play's narrative of nation is a troubling one. Britain renews itself as women are disempowered or disappear. Cymbeline's Queen is an embodiment of hypocritical viciousness (Shakespeare does not even bother to give her a name), and her son, a figure whose father is never mentioned or seen, bears her taint. The play's happy resolution occurs only after all traces of this Queen and her offspring have been erased. When finally united with his children, Cymbeline articulates the fantasy of having himself given birth to all three: "O, what am I? / A mother to the birth of three? Ne'er mother / Rejoiced deliverance more" (5.6.369–71). This is the dream of androgenesis, reproduction without union with women.

Much earlier in the play, Posthumus, believing himself cuckolded by Innogen, voices a similar wish: "Is there no way for men to be, but women / Must be half-workers?" (2.5.1–2). In one of the most deeply misogynist speeches in the Shakespeare canon, Posthumus then blames all the vices of the world on "the woman's part" (line 20)—on woman herself and on that part of woman lodged in man, Eve's mark upon the human race. This mistaken projection onto woman of responsibility for evil may partly explain Cymbeline's fantasy of androgenesis and also why, in the last scene, no persons appareled as women are to be seen (Innogen is still dressed as a page). The happy union of Britain and Rome and Wales is overwhelmingly a union of men.

The play's own counterpoint to its exclusion of women from public power is its demonization of the slanderous Giacomo and its depiction of Posthumus's gradual recovery of faith in Innogen. When Posthumus receives a bloody cloth signifying (falsely) that his order to murder Innogen has been fulfilled, he is overcome with remorse and berates husbands like himself for murdering wives "for wrying but a little" (5.1.5). At this point, Posthumus still believes his wife to have been sexually unfaithful to him, yet he castigates himself for having ordered her punished. His words form a remarkable exception to the more usual patriarchal assumption that female chastity is the primary marker of a woman's value and virtue and that loss of chastity is an unforgivable crime. Critics differ as to how much weight to assign this speech. Posthumus makes it when he believes Innogen to be dead; and generally it is easier to forgive the dead than the living. By the time he is finally reconciled to the living, breathing woman, Giacomo's lies have been exposed and Posthumus takes to himself a wife whose chastity is not in question.

The play, however, overtly punishes violence against women when the evil Cloten, who had fantasized raping Innogen, is beheaded, and it punishes misogynous lies when Giacomo must submit to Posthumus in the final scene. Posthumus, who had formerly himself believed slander against Innogen and had attempted to have her killed, repents and becomes the play's image of the proper husband. After Posthumus's performance in battle and when Innogen is no longer heir apparent, Cymbeline withdraws his objections to Posthumus's union with her. Nevertheless, Innogen's formerly dominant position in that marriage now seems to belong to Posthumus, with Jupiter himself providing the warrant for this reversal. In prison, Posthumus has a dream that not only reconnects him to his familial origins but also provides an image of his own future family. As he sleeps, Posthumus's two warlike brothers and his warlike father appear to him. The father is described as "leading in his hand an ancient matron, his wife, and mother to Posthumus" (stage direction following 5.5.123). After this dream, sent by Jupiter, Posthumus recovers his "true" identity as Innogen's husband and Britain's warrior hero. As he assumes his position in the honored line of Leonati men, the place marked for Innogen is that of Roman / British wife, "led in his hand." In its narratives of nation, Cymbeline seems able to reprove the most virulent forms of misogyny only when it simultaneously removes women from public power, transforms them into chaste, domesticated wives, and reaffirms the dominance of husbands.

Samuel Johnson was right when he said that Cymbeline is a play with many incongruities of time, place, and circumstance. And yet it is not an incoherent play but rather one that richly interweaves the history of the nation with the stories of the figures who take up their positions in that nation. What is eerie about Cymbeline is that its characters often understand so little about what is happening to them, and yet each appears to play out the part assigned to him or her by some higher power: Jupiter, destiny, time. In this regard, Cymbeline is of a piece with Shakespeare's other romances, plays in which a higher power often seems to steer all boats to shore and reunite long-severed families. But fictions of inevitability can be deceiving. One should remember that the soothsayer had to revise his interpretation of his vision of the eagle and the sun to make his narrative square with events as they actually happened. And to decipher Posthumus's tablet, he could make the prophecy tally with the facts only by means of a tortuous transformation of "tender air" into "wife." This might suggest that in this play, at least, the higher powers determine less than they appear to do; rather, the forms taken by family, nation, and empire are in some measure the result of human efforts, interventions, and narratives. Shakespeare's play is one such narrative. The resolution of its complex plot may invite relieved assent to its culminating vision, but the very artifice of that resolution also reveals its contingency, suggesting that there is nothing either natural or inevitable about the familial and political arrangements that are repeatedly contested and reordered in this tragicomic play.

JEAN E. HOWARD

TEXTUAL NOTE

Cymbeline was first printed in the First Folio (F) of 1623. Its heavy punctuation suggests that it was prepared for printing by a professional scribe—perhaps by Ralph Crane, who is believed to have prepared five of Shakespeare's other plays for the print shop. While not every feature associated with a Crane manuscript is displayed, the use of parentheses, hyphens, and apostrophes in the Folio text of *Cymbeline* is consistent with Crane's practice. Because the scribe regularized the manuscript he copied, it is hard to determine the exact nature of that manuscript. It may or may not have been a promptbook. Although the Folio text contains almost no stage directions relating to sounds, such as trumpet flourishes to mark ceremonial entrances and exits or the noises associated with battle or with hunting parties, this elision of clues to performance practice is characteristic of "literary" transcripts of the sort associated with Crane.

In this edition, several names have been changed from the versions that appear in F. F's "Iachimo" has been modernized to "Giacomo," the Italian name for "James," on the grounds that a modernized text of Shakespeare should also give personal names in modernized forms. Other editors have proposed "Jackimo" as an alternative modernization. F's "Philario" has also been modernized to "Filario." In this instance, F itself uses the form "Filario" at 1.1.98, though elsewhere it employs "Philario." Finally, the heroine's name, given as "Imogen" in F, is here changed to "Innogen." There are several reasons for this alteration. In Holinshed's *Chronicles,* one of Shakespeare's sources for the play, the wife of Brute (an early King of England) was named Innogen. Many scholars assume that this was Shakespeare's source for the name. In addition, Simon Forman, one of Shakespeare's contemporaries, who described a performance of the play in 1611, gave the name of the Princess as Innogen. Forman could have gotten the name wrong, but he might have been accurately recording a fact of performance lost in the printed text. Finally, in *Much Ado About Nothing,* Leonato has a wife called Innogen (who never makes a stage appearance); that couple might thus anticipate the Innogen and Leonatus of *Cymbeline.* The Oxford editors surmise that the compositors who set type for F misread the word "Innogen," mistaking "nn" for "m" and so printing "Imogen." Other scholars disagree, arguing that Shakespeare might well have changed a name he found in his sources and that Forman may have misheard what he observed on the stage or may have remembered the name from his own reading and mistakenly attributed it to the production.

Act and scene divisions in this text follow those employed in most editions since the eighteenth century, with several exceptions, all in Act 5. In most texts, the culminating battle between the Romans and Britons occurs in 5.2. The Oxford editors divide this battle sequence into three scenes—5.2, 5.3, and 5.4—because at two points the stage is momentarily cleared. On the other hand, most editions separate the action that immediately follows the battle into two scenes: Posthumus's arrest by the Britons after this battle, then the actual depiction of his captivity and the appearance of his family to him in a dream. This edition makes these events into one continuous scene, 5.5, since there is no evidence that Posthumus and his jailers ever leave the stage between these two actions.

SELECTED BIBLIOGRAPHY

Adelman, Janet. "Masculine Authority and the Maternal Body: The Return to Origins in the Romances." *Suffocating Mothers: Fantasies of Maternal Origins in Shakespeare's Plays, "Hamlet" to "The Tempest."* New York: Routledge, 1992. 193–238. Argues that *Cymbeline* recovers the idealized father lost in *Hamlet*, but does so by denigrating maternal authority and the sexualized female body.

Floyd-Wilson, Mary. "'Delving to the root': *Cymbeline*, Scotland, and the English Race," *British Identities and English Renaissance Literature.* Ed. David J. Baker and Willy Maley. Cambridge, Eng.: Cambridge University Press, 2002. 101–15. Partly by associating Cymbeline's evil Queen with Scoto-Britons, Floyd-Wilson argues that *Cymbeline* repudiates the Scottish role in British history, thereby contributing to an Anglocentric historiography.

Hunt, Maurice. "Dismemberment, Corporal Reconstitution, and the Body Politic in *Cymbeline.*" *Studies in Philology* 99.4 (Fall 2002): 404–31. Examines the idea of the body politic—its destruction and reconstitution—in *Cymbeline.*

Jones, Emrys. "Stuart *Cymbeline.*" *Essays in Criticism* 11 (1961): 84–99. Takes an historical approach to the play emphasizing its links to James I's dedication to peace and the role of Milford Haven in Tudor national mythology.

Kahn, Coppélia. "Postscript: *Cymbeline*: Paying Tribute to Rome." *Roman Shakespeare: Warriors, Wounds, and Women.* London: Routledge, 1997. 160–70. Argues that *Cymbeline* shares much with Shakespeare's other Roman plays, including a preoccupation with Roman *virtu* as the root of masculine identity, but an identity constantly made precarious by the woman's part in its formation.

Knight, G. Wilson. "Cymbeline." *The Crown of Life: Essays in Interpretation of Shakespeare's Final Plays.* London: Oxford University Press, 1947. 129–202. Explores national and religious themes in *Cymbeline,* culminating with a sustained analysis of Posthumus's vision of Jupiter.

Mikalachki, Jodi. "Cymbeline and the Masculine Romance of Roman Britain," *The Legacy of Boadicea: Gender and Nation in Early Modern England.* London: Routledge, 1998. 96–114. From a feminist perspective, explores the respective roles of ancient British savagery and Roman civility in the forging of an all-male national community in *Cymbeline.*

Parker, Patricia. "Romance and Empire: Anachronistic *Cymbeline,*" *Unfolded Tales: Essays on Renaissance Romance.* Ed. George M. Logan and Gordon Teskey. Ithaca, N.Y.: Cornell University Press, 1989. 189–207. Examines the pervasive allusions to *The Aeneid* in *Cymbeline,* arguing that the play intimates the passing of Rome's imperial greatness westward to Britain.

Warren, Roger. *Cymbeline.* Shakespeare in Performance series. Manchester: Manchester University Press, 1989. Focuses on performances of the play, especially on striking stage and television versions from the second half of the twentieth century.

Wayne, Valerie. "The Woman's Parts of *Cymbeline.*" *Staged Properties in Early Modern English Drama.* Ed. Jonathan Gil Harris and Natasha Korda. Cambridge, Eng.: Cambridge University Press, 2002. 288–315. Traces the history of three stage properties—manacle, ring, and bloody cloth—as they represent Innogen, and woman more generally, in *Cymbeline.*

FILM

Cymbeline. 1982. Dir. Elijah Moshinsky. UK. 175 min. Boasts such cast luminaries as Richard Johnson (the King), Claire Bloom (the Queen), and Helen Mirren (Innogen), among others.

Cymbeline, King of Britain

THE PERSONS OF THE PLAY

CYMBELINE, King of Britain
Princess INNOGEN, his daughter, later disguised as a man
    named Fidele
GUIDERIUS, known as Polydore ⎫
ARVIRAGUS, known as Cadwal ⎭ Cymbeline's sons, stolen by Belarius
QUEEN, Cymbeline's wife, Innogen's stepmother
Lord CLOTEN, her son
BELARIUS, a banished lord, calling himself Morgan
CORNELIUS, a physician
HELEN, a lady attending on Innogen
Two LORDS attending on Cloten
Two GENTLEMEN
Two British CAPTAINS
Two JAILERS
POSTHUMUS Leonatus, a poor gentleman, Innogen's husband
PISANIO, his servant
FILARIO, a friend of Posthumus
GIACOMO, an Italian ⎫
A FRENCHMAN ⎪
A DUTCHMAN ⎬ Filario's friends
A SPANIARD ⎭
Caius LUCIUS, ambassador from Rome, later General of the
    Roman forces
Two Roman SENATORS
Roman TRIBUNES
A Roman CAPTAIN
Philharmonus, a SOOTHSAYER
JUPITER
Ghost of SICILIUS Leonatus, father of Posthumus
Ghost of the MOTHER of Posthumus
Ghosts of the BROTHERS of Posthumus
Lords attending on Cymbeline, ladies attending on the Queen,
    musicians attending on Cloten, messengers, soldiers

1.1

Enter two GENTLEMEN

FIRST GENTLEMAN   You do not meet a man but frowns. Our bloods
    No more obey the heavens than our courtiers
    Still seem as does the King.[1]
SECOND GENTLEMAN   But what's the matter?
FIRST GENTLEMAN   His daughter, and the heir of 's kingdom, whom
5   He purposed to° his wife's sole son—a widow   *intended for*
    That late° he married—hath referred° herself   *recently / given*
    Unto a poor but worthy gentleman. She's wedded,

1.1 Location: Cymbeline's court, Britain.
1. *Our . . . King:* Our dispositions ("bloods") are not
more subject to planetary influences than our courtiers'
moods are determined by the King's. (The planets were
believed to affect human actions and emotions.)

Her husband banished, she imprisoned. All
Is outward sorrow, though I think the King
Be touched at very heart.

10 SECOND GENTLEMAN   None but the King?

FIRST GENTLEMAN   He° that hath lost her, too. So is the Queen,   *(the Queen's son)*
That most desired the match. But not a courtier—
Although they wear their faces to the bent
Of° the King's looks—hath a heart that is not   *In accordance with*
Glad of the thing they scowl at.

15 SECOND GENTLEMAN   And why so?

FIRST GENTLEMAN   He that hath missed the Princess is a thing
Too bad for bad report, and he that hath her—
I mean that married her—alack, good man,
And therefore banished!—is a creature such
20 As, to seek through the regions of the earth
For one his like, there would be something failing°   *lacking*
In him that should compare.² I do not think
So fair an outward and such stuff° within   *substance; fabric*
Endows a man but he.

SECOND GENTLEMAN   You speak him far.°   *praise him greatly*

25 FIRST GENTLEMAN   I do extend him, sir, within himself;³
Crush him together rather than unfold
His measure duly.⁴

SECOND GENTLEMAN   What's his name and birth?

FIRST GENTLEMAN   I cannot delve him to the root.⁵ His father
Was called Sicilius, who did join his honour°   *prowess (as a soldier)*
30 Against the Romans with Cassibelan
But had his titles by Tenantius,⁶ whom
He served with glory and admired success,
So gained the sur-addition 'Leonatus';⁷
And had, besides this gentleman in question,
35 Two other sons who in the wars o'th' time
Died with their swords in hand; for which their father,
Then old and fond of issue,° took such sorrow   *of his offspring*
That he quit being, and his gentle lady,
Big of° this gentleman, our theme, deceased   *Pregnant with*
40 As he was born. The King, he takes the babe
To his protection, calls him Posthumus⁸ Leonatus,
Breeds him,° and makes him of his bedchamber;⁹   *Brings him up*
Puts to him° all the learnings that his time   *Offers him*
Could make him the receiver of, which he took
45 As we do air, fast as 'twas ministered,
And in 's spring became a harvest; lived in court—
Which rare it is to do—most praised, most loved;
A sample° to the youngest, to th' more mature   *An example*
A glass that feated them,¹ and to the graver
50 A child that guided dotards.° To his mistress,   *foolish old men*

---

2. In any man selected for comparison.
3. I set forth his virtues, sir, within the boundaries of his own merit.
4. *rather . . . duly*: rather than reveal what he is really worth. The metaphor picks up on the sense of "stuff" as "fabric" in line 23. Fabric can be crushed together or unfolded and accurately measured.
5. I cannot completely account for his lineage.
6. Tenantius was Cymbeline's father and the brother of

Cassibelan, who in 3.1.5 is described as Cymbeline's uncle.
7. The additional name "Leonatus" (born of a lion).
8. In Latin, the word means "after death." As applied to a child, it means "one born after his or her father's death."
9. Makes him a personal servant.
1. A mirror that furnished ("feated") them with images of virtue or elegance.

For whom he now is banished, her own price
Proclaims how she esteemed him and his virtue.[2]
By her election° may be truly read   *choice (of him)*
What kind of man he is.

SECOND GENTLEMAN   I honour him
55 Even out° of your report. But pray you tell me,   *Even beyond the limits*
Is she sole child to th' King?

FIRST GENTLEMAN   His only child.
He had two sons—if this be worth your hearing,
Mark it: the eld'st of them at three years old,
I'th' swathing° clothes the other, from their nursery   *swaddling*
60 Were stol'n, and to this hour no guess in knowledge°   *no informed conjecture*
Which way they went.

SECOND GENTLEMAN   How long is this ago?

FIRST GENTLEMAN   Some twenty years.

SECOND GENTLEMAN   That a king's children should be so conveyed,
65 So slackly guarded, and the search so slow
That could not trace them!

FIRST GENTLEMAN   Howsoe'er 'tis strange,
Or that the negligence may well be laughed at,
Yet is it true, sir.

SECOND GENTLEMAN   I do well believe you.

Enter the QUEEN, POSTHUMUS, *and* INNOGEN[3]

FIRST GENTLEMAN   We must forbear.° Here comes the gentleman,   *withdraw*
70 The Queen and Princess.   *Exeunt [the two* GENTLEMEN]*[4]

QUEEN   No, be assured you shall not find me, daughter,
After the slander of[5] most stepmothers,
Evil-eyed unto you. You're my prisoner, but
Your jailer shall deliver you the keys
75 That lock up your restraint. For you, Posthumus,
So soon as I can win th'offended King
I will be known your advocate. Marry,[6] yet
The fire of rage is in him, and 'twere good
You leaned unto° his sentence with what patience   *You obeyed*
Your wisdom may inform° you.   *instill in*

80 POSTHUMUS   Please your highness,
I will from hence today.

QUEEN   You know the peril.
I'll fetch a turn about the garden, pitying
The pangs of barred affections, though the King
Hath charged you should not speak together.   *Exit*

85 INNOGEN   O dissembling courtesy! How fine this tyrant
Can tickle° where she wounds! My dearest husband,   *flatter*
I something° fear my father's wrath, but nothing—   *somewhat*
Always reserved my holy duty—what

2. *her . . . virtue*: the price she paid (for loving him) demonstrates how much she valued him and his virtue; her own worth ("price") shows the high esteem in which she held him and his virtues.
3. In F, the name of the Princess is Imogen; but in Holinshed's *Chronicles*, the wife of the ancient English King Brute is called Innogen. A number of scholars have concluded that Shakespeare took the name from Holinshed. For a fuller discussion of the Innogen/Imo-

gen debate, see the Textual Note.
4. F marks *Scena Secunda* (second scene) after the gentlemen exit. Then the Queen, Posthumus, and Innogen enter. There is, however, no change of time or place, and the Queen and the lovers are probably in view at line 69 when the First Gentleman announces their entrance. Most previous editors do not indicate a new scene here.
5. In accordance with the slanderous things said about.
6. A mild oath, from the name of the Virgin Mary.

His rage can do on me.⁷ You must be gone,
90 And I shall here abide the hourly shot
Of angry eyes, not comforted to live
But that there is this jewel in the world
That I may see again.

POSTHUMUS   My queen, my mistress!
O lady, weep no more, lest I give cause
95 To be suspected of more tenderness
Than doth become a man. I will remain
The loyal'st husband that did e'er plight troth;°   pledge marriage
My residence in Rome at one Filario's,
Who to my father was a friend, to me
100 Known but by letter; thither write, my queen,
And with mine eyes I'll drink the words you send
Though ink be made of gall.°   bile; bitter liquid

Enter QUEEN

QUEEN   Be brief, I pray you.
If the King come, I shall incur I know not
How much of his displeasure. [*Aside*] Yet I'll move him
105 To walk this way. I never do him wrong
But he does buy my injuries, to be friends,⁸
Pays dear for my offences.   [*Exit*]

POSTHUMUS   Should we be taking leave
As long a term° as yet we have to live,   time
The loathness° to depart would grow. Adieu.   unwillingness
110 INNOGEN   Nay, stay a little.
Were you but riding forth to air yourself
Such parting were too petty. Look here, love:
This diamond was my mother's. Take it, heart;
    [*She gives him a ring*]
But keep it till you woo another wife
When Innogen is dead.

115 POSTHUMUS   How, how? Another?
You gentle gods, give me but this I have,
And cere up⁹ my embracements from a next°   another wife
With bonds of death! Remain, remain thou here
    [*He puts on the ring*]
While sense° can keep it on; and, sweetest, fairest,   the ability to feel
120 As I my poor self did exchange for you
To your so infinite loss, so in our trifles°   love tokens
I still win of you.¹ For my sake wear this.
    [*He gives her a bracelet*]
It is a manacle of love. I'll place it
Upon this fairest prisoner.

INNOGEN   O the gods!
When shall we see again?

Enter CYMBELINE *and lords*
125 POSTHUMUS   Alack, the King!
CYMBELINE   Thou basest° thing, avoid hence,° from my sight!   most lowborn / be off

---

7. **but . . . me:** an ambiguous phrase. My holy duty of obedience to my father excepted (a bond put in jeopardy by Cymbeline's act), I do not at all ("nothing") fear what Cymbeline's rage can do to me. Or: My holy duty to my husband excepted (which Cymbeline could disrupt by interfering with the marriage), I do not at all fear what Cymbeline's rage may do to me.

8. But he does endure the consequences of ("buy") my injuries in order to be friends.
9. And wrap up (in the cerecloth, or waxed linen, used in burial shrouds).
1. I still am enriched by you. Posthumus suggests that he is unequal in rank and wealth to Innogen. Correspondingly, his love token is of less value than hers.

If after this command thou fraught° the court   burden
With thy unworthiness, thou diest. Away.
Thou'rt poison to my blood.
POSTHUMUS   The gods protect you,
130 And bless the good remainders of° the court!   people remaining at
I am gone.   *Exit*
INNOGEN   There cannot be a pinch° in death   pain
More sharp than this is.
CYMBELINE   O disloyal thing,
That shouldst repair° my youth, thou heap'st   restore
A year's age on me.
INNOGEN   I beseech you, sir,
135 Harm not yourself with your vexation.
I am senseless of° your wrath. A touch° more rare   unable to feel / An emotion
Subdues all pangs, all fears.
CYMBELINE   Past grace,° obedience—   all sense of duty
INNOGEN   Past hope and in despair: that way past grace.[2]
CYMBELINE   That mightst have had the sole son of my queen!
140 INNOGEN   O blessèd that I might not! I chose an eagle
And did avoid a puttock.[3]
CYMBELINE   Thou took'st a beggar, wouldst have made my throne
A seat for baseness.
INNOGEN   No, I rather added
A lustre to it.
CYMBELINE   O thou vile one!
INNOGEN   Sir,
145 It is your fault that I have loved Posthumus.
You bred him as my playfellow, and he is
A man worth any woman, over-buys me
Almost the sum he pays.[4]
CYMBELINE   What, art thou mad?
INNOGEN   Almost, sir. Heaven restore me! Would I were
150 A neatherd's° daughter, and my Leonatus   cowherd's
Our neighbour shepherd's son.
        Enter QUEEN
CYMBELINE   Thou foolish thing.
[*To* QUEEN] They were again together; you have done
Not after° our command. [*To lords*] Away with her,   according to
And pen her up.
QUEEN   Beseech° your patience, peace,   I beseech
155 Dear lady daughter, peace. Sweet sovereign,
Leave us to ourselves, and make yourself some comfort
Out of your best advice.
CYMBELINE   Nay, let her languish
A drop of blood a day,[5] and, being aged,
Die of this folly.   *Exit [with lords]*
QUEEN   Fie, you must give way.
        Enter PISANIO
160 Here is your servant. How now, sir? What news?

---

2. Redemption. Alluding to the Christian belief that those who despair distrust God and are beyond the reach of grace.
3. A kite, or common predatory bird.
4. *over-buys . . . pays:* pays too much for me by almost the amount he gives for me. (Posthumus both gives himself to Innogen in marriage and also pays the price of banishment.) Innogen insists that Posthumus's worth equals her own and that their marriage consequently does not degrade her.
5. Referring to the popular belief that one lost a drop of blood with each sigh.

PISANIO   My lord your son drew° on my master.   *drew a sword*

QUEEN   Ha!

No harm, I trust, is done?

PISANIO   There might have been,

But that my master rather played than fought,

And had no help of anger. They were parted

By gentlemen at hand.

165   QUEEN   I am very glad on't.

INNOGEN   Your son's my father's friend; he takes his part

To draw upon an exile°—O brave sir!   *(Posthumus)*

I would they were in Afric° both together,   *Africa*

Myself by with a needle, that I might prick°   *urge on*

The goer-back.° [*To* PISANIO] Why came you from your   *swordsman who retreated*

170   master?

PISANIO   On his command. He would not suffer° me   *allow*

To bring him to the haven, left these notes

Of what commands I should be subject to

When't pleased you to employ me.

QUEEN   This hath been

175   Your faithful servant. I dare lay mine honour

He will remain so.

PISANIO   I humbly thank your highness.

QUEEN   Pray walk a while.   [*Exit*]⁶

INNOGEN   About some half hour hence, pray you speak with me.

180   You shall at least go see my lord aboard.

For this time leave me.   *Exeunt* [*severally*]°   *separately*

1.2

Enter CLOTEN *and two* LORDS

FIRST LORD   Sir, I would advise you to shift° a shirt. The violence   *change*

of action hath made you reek° as a sacrifice. Where air comes   *emit vapors; stink*

out, air comes in. There's none abroad so wholesome as that

you vent.¹

5   CLOTEN   If my shirt were bloody, then to shift it.° Have I hurt   *then I would change it*

him?

SECOND LORD [*aside*]   No, faith, not so much as his patience.

FIRST LORD   Hurt him? His body's a passable° carcass if he be   *pretty good; penetrable*

not hurt. It is a thoroughfare for steel if he be not hurt.

10   SECOND LORD [*aside*]   His steel was in debt—it went o'th' back-

side the town.²

CLOTEN   The villain would not stand° me.   *confront; stay still for*

SECOND LORD [*aside*]   No, but he fled forward still,° toward your   *always*

face.

15   FIRST LORD   Stand you? You have land enough of your own, but

he added to your having, gave you some ground.°   *fell back before you*

SECOND LORD [*aside*]   As many inches as you have oceans.° Pup-   *(i.e., no inches)*

pies!

CLOTEN   I would they had not come between us.

---

6. F does not mark a separate exit for the Queen here, but Innogen appears to be speaking privately to Pisanio, and only Pisanio, in the following three lines.
1.2 Location: Cymbeline's court.
1. The First Lord flatters Cloten by saying that the odorous vapors he is giving off are more healthful than

the outside ("abroad") air that is being exchanged for them.
2. Cloten's sword, like a debtor avoiding creditors, kept to the backstreets—that is, avoided the thoroughfare or main street of Posthumus's body (with a possible allusion to anal penetration).

20 SECOND LORD [*aside*]   So would I, till you had measured how
    long a fool you were upon the ground.
  CLOTEN   And that she should love this fellow and refuse me!
  SECOND LORD [*aside*]   If it be a sin to make a true election,[3] she
    is damned.
25 FIRST LORD   Sir, as I told you always, her beauty and her brain
    go not together. She's a good sign,° but I have seen small   °*she has a good appearance*
    reflection of her wit.
  SECOND LORD [*aside*]   She shines not upon fools lest the reflec-
    tion should hurt her.
30 CLOTEN   Come, I'll to my chamber. Would there had been some
    hurt done.
  SECOND LORD [*aside*]   I wish not so, unless it had been the fall
    of an ass, which is no great hurt.
  CLOTEN [*to* SECOND LORD]   You'll go with us?
35 FIRST LORD   I'll attend your lordship.
  CLOTEN   Nay, come, let's go together.
  SECOND LORD   Well, my lord.   *Exeunt*

1.3
Enter INNOGEN *and* PISANIO

  INNOGEN   I would thou grew'st unto the shores o'th' haven
    And questionedst every sail. If he should write
    And I not have it, 'twere a paper lost
    As offered mercy is.[1] What was the last
    That he spake to thee?
5 PISANIO   It was his queen, his queen.
  INNOGEN   Then waved his handkerchief?
  PISANIO   And kissed it, madam.
  INNOGEN   Senseless° linen, happier therein than I!   °*Unfeeling*
    And that was all?
  PISANIO   No, madam. For so long
    As he could make me with this eye or ear
10 Distinguish him from others he did keep
    The deck, with glove or hat or handkerchief
    Still waving, as the fits and stirs of 's mind
    Could best express how slow his soul sailed on,
    How swift his ship.
  INNOGEN   Thou shouldst have made him
15 As little as a crow, or less, ere left
    To after-eye him.[2]
  PISANIO   Madam, so I did.
  INNOGEN   I would have broke mine eye-strings,[3] cracked them, but
    To look upon him till the diminution
    Of space had pointed him sharp as my needle;[4]
20 Nay, followed him till he had melted from
    The smallness of a gnat to air, and then
    Have turned mine eye and wept. But, good Pisanio,
    When shall we hear from him?

3. A proper choice; with a pun on the Christian doctrine that certain souls are "elected," or predestined for
salvation.
1.3 Location: Cymbeline's palace.
1. *'twere . . . is*: the lost letter would be a document written in vain, like an offer of mercy that is not accepted or
received (for example, a judge's reprieve that comes too

late or God's mercy to an unrepentant sinner).
2. *ere . . . him*: before ceasing to gaze after him.
3. The muscles of the eye, which were supposed to
break at death or from overuse.
4. *till . . . needle*: until the distance between us had
made him seem as small as the point on my needle.

PISANIO Be assured, madam,

25   With his next vantage.°   *his first opportunity*

INNOGEN I did not take my leave of him, but had
      Most pretty things to say. Ere I could tell him
      How I would think on him at certain hours,
      Such thoughts and such, or I could make him swear

30   The shes° of Italy should not betray   *women*
      Mine interest° and his honour, or have charged him   *My entitlement (to him)*
      At the sixth hour of morn, at noon, at midnight
      T'encounter me with orisons⁵—for then
      I am in heaven for him—or ere I could

35   Give him that parting kiss which I had set
      Betwixt two charming words,⁶ comes in my father,
      And, like the tyrannous breathing of the north,°   *north wind*
      Shakes all our buds from growing.

                     Enter a LADY

LADY   The Queen, madam,
      Desires your highness' company.

40 INNOGEN [*to* PISANIO] Those things I bid you do, get them dispatched.
      I will attend the Queen.

PISANIO   Madam, I shall.

      Exeunt [INNOGEN *and* LADY *at one door,* PISANIO *at another*]

                              1.4

      [*A table brought out, with a banquet upon it.*]¹ *Enter*
      FILARIO, GIACOMO, *a* FRENCHMAN, *a* DUTCHMAN, *and a*
      SPANIARD

GIACOMO Believe it, sir, I have seen him in Britain. He was then
      of a crescent note,° expected to prove so worthy as since he   *growing reputation*
      hath been allowed the name of. But I could then have looked
      on him without the help of admiration,° though the catalogue   *wonder*
5   of his endowments had been tabled° by his side and I to peruse   *listed*
      him by items.°   *part by part*

FILARIO You speak of him when he was less furnished than now
      he is with that which makes° him both without and within.   *constitutes*

FRENCHMAN I have seen him in France. We had very many

10   there could behold the sun with as firm eyes as he.²

GIACOMO This matter of marrying his king's daughter, wherein
      he must be weighed rather by her value than his own, words
      him, I doubt not, a great deal from the matter.³

FRENCHMAN And then his banishment.

15 GIACOMO Ay, and the approbation of those that weep this
      lamentable divorce under her colours⁴ are wonderfully to
      extend him,° be it but to fortify her judgement, which else an   *exaggerate his worth*
      easy battery° might lay flat for taking a beggar without less qual-   *a slight assault*

---

5. To join me in prayers ("orisons"); to assail me (as an
object of devotion) with prayers.
6. Between two words carrying a charm to ward off
danger.
1.4 Location: Filario's house, Rome.
1. No banquet—a light meal of fruit, sweetmeats, and
wine following the main meal—is specified in F, but in
other texts, such as Boccacio's *Decameron*, parallel
wager scenes occur during a meal; and at 5.6.155, Gia-

como, retelling the tale of the wager, says it occurred "at
a feast."
2. Alluding to the popular belief that only eagles could
gaze directly on the sun. At 1.1.140, Innogen described
Posthumus as an eagle.
3. *words . . . matter:* causes his reputation, I am sure,
to be amplified beyond what is true.
4. That is, on Innogen's side (with a pun on "colours"
as meaning both "a military banner" and "pretexts").

ity.° But how comes it he is to sojourn with you? How creeps   *of no rank or merit*
20 acquaintance?⁵

FILARIO   His father and I were soldiers together, to whom I have
been often bound for no less than my life.

     Enter POSTHUMUS

Here comes the Briton. Let him be so entertained amongst you
as suits with gentlemen of your knowing° to a stranger of his   *knowledge*
25 quality.° I beseech you all, be better known to this gentleman,   *foreigner of his rank*
whom I commend to you as a noble friend of mine. How wor-
thy he is I will leave to appear hereafter rather than story° him   *give an account of*
in his own hearing.

FRENCHMAN [*to* POSTHUMUS]   Sir, we have known together° in   *been acquainted*
30 Orléans.

POSTHUMUS   Since when I have been debtor to you for courtesies
which I will be ever to pay, and yet pay still.

FRENCHMAN   Sir, you o'er-rate my poor kindness. I was glad I did
atone° my countryman and you. It had been pity you should   *reconcile*
35 have been put together° with so mortal° a purpose as then each   *(in a duel) / deadly*
bore, upon importance° of so slight and trivial a nature.   *matters*

POSTHUMUS   By your pardon, sir, I was then a young traveller,
rather shunned to go even° with what I heard than⁶ in my every   *refused to agree*
action to be guided by others' experiences; but upon my
40 mended° judgement—if I offend not to say it is mended—my   *improved*
quarrel was not altogether slight.

FRENCHMAN   Faith, yes, to be put to the arbitrement of swords,°   *settlement by duel*
and by such two that would by all likelihood have confounded°   *destroyed*
one the other, or have fallen both.

45 GIACOMO   Can we with manners ask what was the difference?

FRENCHMAN   Safely, I think. 'Twas a contention in public, which
may without contradiction suffer° the report. It was much like   *permit*
an argument that fell out last night, where each of us fell in
praise of our country mistresses,⁷ this gentleman at that time
50 vouching—and upon warrant of bloody affirmation°—his to be   *affirming it with blood*
more fair, virtuous, wise, chaste, constant, qualified,° and less   *having notable qualities*
attemptable° than any the rarest of our ladies in France.   *open to seduction*

GIACOMO   That lady is not now living, or this gentleman's opinion by this° worn out.   *by now*
55 POSTHUMUS   She holds her virtue still, and I my mind.

GIACOMO   You must not so far prefer her fore ours of Italy.

POSTHUMUS   Being so far provoked as I was in France I would
abate her nothing,⁸ though I profess myself her adorer, not her
friend.°   *lover; spouse*
60 GIACOMO   As fair and as good—a kind of hand-in-hand compari-
son⁹—had been something too fair and too good for any lady
in Britain. If she went before° others I have seen—as that dia-   *she surpassed*
mond of yours outlustres many I have beheld—I could not but
believe she excelled many; but I have not seen the most pre-
65 cious diamond that is, nor you the lady.

POSTHUMUS   I praised her as I rated° her; so do I my stone.   *valued*

GIACOMO   What do you esteem it at?

---

5. How does he claim a connection to you? Giacomo implies that Posthumus cunningly insinuated himself into Filario's friendship.
6. Than to appear.
7. The women of our country.

8. I would subtract nothing from my estimation of her.
9. A comparison claiming equality (not superiority); with a possible pun on the "handfast" by which couples pledged their duty to one another at their betrothal.

POSTHUMUS   More than the world enjoys.°   *possesses*

GIACOMO   Either your unparagoned mistress is dead, or she's

70   outprized° by a trifle.   *exceeded in value*

POSTHUMUS   You are mistaken. The one° may be sold or given,   *(the ring)*

or if° there were wealth enough for the purchase or merit for   *if either*

the gift. The other° is not a thing for sale, and only the gift of   *(his mistress)*

the gods.

75   GIACOMO   Which the gods have given you?

POSTHUMUS   Which, by their graces, I will keep.

GIACOMO   You may wear her in title yours;[1] but, you know,

strange fowl light upon neighbouring ponds.[2] Your ring[3] may

be stolen too; so your brace of unprizable estimations,[4] the one

80   is but frail, and the other casual.[5] A cunning thief or a that-way

accomplished courtier[6] would hazard° the winning both of first   *venture*

and last.

POSTHUMUS   Your Italy contains none so accomplished a court-

ier to convince° the honour of my mistress if in the holding or   *overcome*

85   loss of that you term her frail. I do nothing doubt you have

store° of thieves; notwithstanding, I fear not[7] my ring.   *an abundance*

FILARIO   Let us leave° here, gentlemen.   *stop the conversation*

POSTHUMUS   Sir, with all my heart. This worthy signor, I thank

him, makes no stranger of me. We are familiar at first.

90   GIACOMO   With five times so much conversation I should get

ground of[8] your fair mistress, make her go back° even to the   *relent*

yielding, had I admittance and opportunity to friend.°   *to assist me*

POSTHUMUS   No, no.

GIACOMO   I dare thereupon pawn the moiety° of my estate to   *one half*

95   your ring, which in my opinion o'ervalues it something. But I

make my wager rather against your confidence than her repu-

tation, and, to bar your offence[9] herein too, I durst attempt it

against any lady in the world.

POSTHUMUS   You are a great deal abused in too bold a persua-

100   sion,[1] and I doubt not you sustain° what you're worthy of by   *will receive*

your attempt.

GIACOMO   What's that?

POSTHUMUS   A repulse; though your attempt, as you call it,

deserve more—a punishment, too.

105   FILARIO   Gentlemen, enough of this. It came in too suddenly.

Let it die as it was born; and, I pray you, be better acquainted.

GIACOMO   Would I had put my estate and my neighbour's on

th'approbation° of what I have spoke.   *the proof*

POSTHUMUS   What lady would you choose to assail?

110   GIACOMO   Yours, whom in constancy you think stands so safe. I

will lay° you ten thousand ducats to your ring that, commend   *wager*

me to the court where your lady is, with no more advantage

than the opportunity of a second conference, and I will bring

from thence that honour of hers which you imagine so

115   reserved.

---

1. You may claim her as your legal possession (with a
pun on "wear" as meaning "enjoy her sexually").
2. *strange . . . ponds:* strangers may come upon your
property (with a pun on "pond" as referring to female
genitals).
3. Punning on "ring" as another slang term for "female
genitals."
4. So of the two ("brace of") objects you deem invaluable.

5. And the other subject to accident (referring to the
ring).
6. A courtier skilled in that way (in the arts of seduction and theft).
7. Am not anxious about.
8. Get the advantage of.
9. To prevent you from feeling personally affronted.
1. A great deal deceived in your too bold belief.

POSTHUMUS   I will wage against your gold, gold to it;° my ring I   *gold equal to it*
hold dear as my finger, 'tis part of it.

GIACOMO   You are a friend, and therein the wiser.[2] If you buy
ladies' flesh at a million a dram,[3] you cannot preserve it from
120   tainting. But I see you have some religion in you, that° you   *since*
fear.

POSTHUMUS   This is but a custom in your tongue.[4] You bear a
graver purpose, I hope.

GIACOMO   I am the master of my speeches, and would undergo°   *undertake*
125   what's spoken, I swear.

POSTHUMUS   Will you? I shall but lend my diamond till your
return. Let there be covenants° drawn between 's. My mistress   *agreements*
exceeds in goodness the hugeness of your unworthy thinking. I
dare you to this match. Here's my ring.

130 FILARIO   I will have it no lay.°   *wager*

GIACOMO   By the gods, it is one. If I bring you no sufficient testimony that I have enjoyed the dearest bodily part of your mistress, my ten thousand ducats are yours; so is your diamond too.
If I come off and leave her in such honour as you have trust in,
135   she your jewel, this your jewel, and my gold are yours, provided
I have your commendation for my more free entertainment.[5]

POSTHUMUS   I embrace these conditions; let us have articles
betwixt us. Only thus far you shall answer: if you make your
voyage upon her and give me directly° to understand you have   *plainly*
140   prevailed, I am no further your enemy; she is not worth our
debate. If she remain unseduced, you not making it appear
otherwise, for your ill opinion and th'assault you have made to
her chastity you shall answer me with your sword.

GIACOMO   Your hand, a covenant. We will have these things set
145   down by lawful counsel, and straight away° for Britain, lest the   *depart at once*
bargain should catch cold and starve.° I will fetch my gold and   *die*
have our two wagers recorded.

POSTHUMUS   Agreed.   [*Exit with* GIACOMO]

FRENCHMAN   Will this hold, think you?

150 FILARIO   Signor Giacomo will not from it. Pray let us follow 'em.
                               Exeunt. [*Table is removed*]

1.5

Enter QUEEN, LADIES, *and* CORNELIUS [*a doctor*]

QUEEN   Whiles yet the dew's on ground, gather those flowers.
Make haste. Who has the note° of them?   *list*

A LADY   I, madam.

QUEEN   Dispatch.°   *Exeunt* LADIES   *Make haste*
Now, Master Doctor, have you brought those drugs?

5 CORNELIUS   Pleaseth° your highness, ay. Here they are, madam.   *If it please*
                   [*He gives her a box*]
But I beseech your grace, without offence—
My conscience bids me ask—wherefore° you have   *why*
Commanded of me these most poisonous compounds,

---

2. Implying that Posthumus's intimacy with Innogen
("friend" means "lover" or "husband") makes him wise
enough not to risk his ring in a wager on her chastity or
wise enough to know the danger of this wager.
3. Even if you pay a large amount of money for a very

small amount (a "dram") of female flesh.
4. This is merely a conventional way for you to speak.
5. Provided I have your introduction (to Innogen) to
ensure a generous reception.
1.5 Location: Cymbeline's court, Britain.

Which are the movers of a languishing death,
But though slow, deadly.

10 QUEEN   I wonder, doctor,
Thou ask'st me such a question. Have I not been
Thy pupil long? Hast thou not learned° me how   *taught*
To make perfumes, distil, preserve—yea, so
That our great King himself doth woo me oft
15 For my confections?° Having thus far proceeded,   *medical compounds*
Unless thou think'st me devilish, is't not meet°   *fitting*
That I did amplify my judgement in
Other conclusions?° I will try° the forces   *experiments / test*
Of these thy compounds on such creatures as
20 We count not worth the hanging, but none human,
To try the vigour of them, and apply
Allayments to their act,[1] and by them° gather   *(these experiments)*
Their several virtues[2] and effects.
CORNELIUS   Your highness
Shall from this practice but make hard your heart.
25 Besides, the seeing these effects will be
Both noisome° and infectious.   *offensive*
QUEEN   O, content thee.

Enter PISANIO

[*Aside*] Here comes a flattering rascal; upon him
Will I first work. He's factor° for his master,   *an agent*
And enemy to my son. [*Aloud*] How now, Pisanio?—
30 Doctor, your service for this time is ended.
Take your own way.
CORNELIUS [*aside*]   I do suspect you, madam.
But you shall do no harm.
QUEEN [*to* PISANIO]   Hark thee, a word.
CORNELIUS [*aside*]   I do not like her. She doth think she has
Strange ling'ring poisons. I do know her spirit,
35 And will not trust one of her malice with
A drug of such damned nature. Those she has
Will stupefy and dull the sense a while,
Which first, perchance, she'll prove° on cats and dogs,   *test*
Then afterward up higher; but there is
40 No danger in what show of death it makes
More than the locking up the spirits a time,[3]
To be more fresh, reviving. She is fooled
With a most false effect, and I the truer
So to be false with her.
QUEEN   No further service, doctor,
Until I send for thee.
45 CORNELIUS   I humbly take my leave.   *Exit*
QUEEN [*to* PISANIO]   Weeps she still, sayst thou? Dost thou think in time
She will not quench,° and let instructions° enter   *grow cool / good advice*
Where folly now possesses? Do thou work.
When thou shalt bring me word she loves my son
50 I'll tell thee on the instant thou art then
As great as is thy master—greater, for
His fortunes all lie speechless, and his name°   *reputation*

---

1. *apply . . . act*: apply antidotes to their operation.
2. Their (the compounds') individual powers.
3. Other than the temporary suspension of the vital functions.

Is at last gasp. Return he cannot, nor
Continue where he is. To shift his being°   *change his abode*
55   Is to exchange one misery with another,
And every day that comes comes to decay°   *destroy*
A day's work in him. What shalt thou expect
To be depender on a thing that leans,[4]
Who cannot be new built nor has no friends
So much as but to prop him?

    [*She drops her box. He takes it up*]

60   Thou tak'st up
Thou know'st not what; but take it for thy labour.
It is a thing I made which hath the King
Five times redeemed from death. I do not know
What is more cordial.° Nay, I prithee take it.   *restorative*
65   It is an earnest° of a farther good   *initial payment*
That I mean to thee. Tell thy mistress how
The case stands with her; do't as from thyself.
Think what a chance thou changest on,[5] but think
Thou hast thy mistress still; to boot,° my son,   *in addition*
70   Who shall take notice of thee.° I'll move the King   *give attention to you*
To any shape of thy preferment,° such   *any kind of advancement*
As thou'lt desire; and then myself, I chiefly,
That set thee on to this desert,° am bound   *action deserving reward*
To load thy merit richly. Call my women.
Think on my words.   *Exit* PISANIO
75   A sly and constant knave,
Not to be shaked; the agent for his master,
And the remembrancer of her° to hold   *the one who reminds her*
The hand-fast° to her lord. I have given him that[6]   *marriage contract*
Which, if he take, shall quite unpeople her
80   Of liegers for her sweet,[7] and which she after,
Except she bend her humour,[8] shall be assured
To taste of too.

    Enter PISANIO *and* LADIES
               So, so; well done, well done.
The violets, cowslips, and the primroses
Bear to my closet.° Fare thee well, Pisanio.   *private chamber*
Think on my words, Pisanio.
85 PISANIO   And shall do.

    Exeunt QUEEN *and* LADIES
But when to my good lord I prove untrue,
I'll choke myself—there's all I'll do for you.   *Exit*

1.6

    Enter INNOGEN
INNOGEN A father cruel and a stepdame false,
A foolish suitor to a wedded lady
That hath her husband banished.[1] O, that husband,
My supreme crown of grief, and those repeated[2]
5   Vexations of it! Had I been thief-stol'n,

---

4. To be dependent on a thing that is about to fall.
5. Consider what opportunity you have to change your
service (and become my servant).
6. The box supposedly containing poison.
7. Of ambassadors for her sweetheart.

8. Unless she changes her disposition.
1.6 Location: Cymbeline's court.
1. Who has a banished husband.
2. Those already enumerated. Innogen has already
complained of her father, stepmother, and foolish suitor.

As my two brothers, happy;[3] but most miserable
Is the desire that's glorious.[4] Blest be those,
How mean soe'er,[5] that have their honest wills,°   *simple desires*
Which seasons comfort.[6]

   Enter PISANIO *and* GIACOMO
      Who may this be? Fie!

10 PISANIO Madam, a noble gentleman of Rome
  Comes from my lord with letters.

GIACOMO   Change you,° madam?   *Do you turn pale*
  The worthy Leonatus is in safety,
  And greets your highness dearly.
   [*He gives her the letters*]

INNOGEN   Thanks, good sir.
  You're kindly welcome.
   [*She reads the letters*]

15 GIACOMO [*aside*] All of her that is out of door° most rich!   *is visible*
  If she be furnished with a mind so rare
  She is alone, th'Arabian bird,[7] and I
  Have lost the wager. Boldness be my friend;
  Arm me audacity from head to foot,
20 Or, like the Parthian, I shall flying fight;[8]
  Rather, directly fly.

INNOGEN *reads* [*aloud*] 'He is one of the noblest note,° to whose   *reputation*
  kindnesses I am most infinitely tied. Reflect° upon him accord-   *Bestow attention*
  ingly, as you value
25   Your truest
          Leonatus.'
  [*To Giacomo*] So far I read aloud,
  But even the very middle of my heart
  Is warmed by th' rest, and takes it thankfully.
30 You are as welcome, worthy sir, as I
  Have words to bid you, and shall find it so
  In all that I can do.

GIACOMO   Thanks, fairest lady.
  What, are men mad? Hath nature given them eyes
  To see this vaulted arch° and the rich crop°   *the sky / harvest*
35 Of sea and land, which can distinguish 'twixt
  The fiery orbs above and the twinned° stones   *identical*
  Upon th'unnumbered beach,[9] and can we not
  Partition make with spectacles[1] so precious
  'Twixt fair and foul?

INNOGEN   What makes your admiration?°   *causes you wonder*

40 GIACOMO It cannot be i'th' eye—for apes and monkeys,
  'Twixt two such shes,° would chatter this way[2] and   *women*
  Contemn with mows° the other; nor i'th' judgement,   *Scorn with grimaces*
  For idiots in this case of favour° would   *question of preference*
  Be wisely definite; nor i'th' appetite—
45 Sluttery,° to such neat° excellence opposed,   *Sluttishness / elegant*

---

3. *happy:* I would have been glad or fortunate.
4. But most wretched is the longing for what is exalted (in her case, a longing for Posthumus).
5. However low in status.
6. Which adds spice to their comfort.
7. The phoenix, only one of which existed at any given time. This mythical bird consumed itself in fire every

five hundred years but then rose from its own ashes.
8. The mounted archers of Parthia were famous for their tactics in warfare, which included shooting arrows behind them as they retreated.
9. Upon the beach whose grains of sand are uncounted.
1. Make distinction with organs of sight.
2. Would make their preference (for Innogen) clear.

Should make desire vomit emptiness,
Not so allured to feed.³

INNOGEN   What is the matter, trow?°   *in truth*

GIACOMO   The cloyèd will,°   *sated sexual desire*

50   That satiate° yet unsatisfied desire, that tub   *glutted*
Both filled and running,° ravening° first the lamb,   *emptying itself / devouring*
Longs after for the garbage.

INNOGEN   What, dear sir,
Thus raps° you? Are you well?   *transports*

GIACOMO   Thanks, madam, well. [*To* PISANIO] Beseech° you, sir,   *I ask*

55   Desire° my man's abode where I did leave him.   *Seek out*
He's strange° and peevish.°   *a foreigner / irritable*

PISANIO   I was going, sir,
To give him welcome.   *Exit*

INNOGEN   Continues well my lord?
His health, beseech you?

GIACOMO   Well, madam.

INNOGEN   Is he disposed to mirth? I hope he is.

60   GIACOMO   Exceeding pleasant, none a stranger° there   *none of the foreigners*
So merry and so gamesome.⁴ He is called
The Briton Reveller.

INNOGEN   When he was here
He did incline to sadness,° and oft-times   *seriousness*
Not knowing why.

GIACOMO   I never saw him sad.

65   There is a Frenchman his companion, one
An eminent monsieur that, it seems, much loves
A Gallian° girl at home. He furnaces⁵   *French*
The thick sighs from him, whiles the jolly° Briton—   *lively; lustful*
Your lord, I mean—laughs from 's free° lungs, cries 'O,   *unconstrained*

70   Can my sides hold, to think that man, who knows
By history, report or his own proof
What woman is, yea, what she cannot choose
But must be, will 's free hours languish°   *pine away*
For assurèd bondage?'

INNOGEN   Will my lord say so?

75   GIACOMO   Ay, madam, with his eyes in flood with laughter.
It is a recreation to be by
And hear him mock the Frenchman. But heavens know
Some men are much to blame.

INNOGEN   Not he, I hope.

GIACOMO   Not he; but yet heaven's bounty towards him might

80   Be used more thankfully. In himself 'tis much;
In you, which I count his, beyond all talents.⁶
Whilst I am bound to wonder, I am bound
To pity too.

INNOGEN   What do you pity, sir?

GIACOMO   Two creatures heartily.

INNOGEN   Am I one, sir?

---

3. *Should . . . feed:* Should destroy sexual desire, not
arouse it (literally, should make desire vomit until it is
empty, not tempt it to eat).
4. Sportive; sexually playful.
5. He exhales like a furnace.

6. *In himself . . . talents:* As regards his own qualities,
heaven's generosity is considerable. In giving him you,
whom I consider his, heaven's generosity surpasses all
abundance.

85   You look on me; what wreck° discern you in me   *downfall*
    Deserves your pity?
GIACOMO   Lamentable! What,
    To hide me from the radiant sun, and solace°   *take comfort*
    I'th' dungeon by a snuff?°   *candle end*
INNOGEN   I pray you, sir,
    Deliver with more openness your answers
90   To my demands. Why do you pity me?
GIACOMO   That others do—
    I was about to say enjoy your—but
    It is an office° of the gods to venge° it,   *a duty / revenge*
    Not mine to speak on't.°   *of it*
INNOGEN   You do seem to know
95   Something of me, or what concerns me. Pray you,
    Since doubting° things go ill often hurts more   *suspecting*
    Than to be sure they do—for certainties
    Either are past remedies, or, timely knowing,
    The remedy then born[7]—discover° to me   *reveal*
    What both you spur and stop.[8]
100 GIACOMO   Had I this cheek
    To bathe my lips upon; this hand whose touch,
    Whose every touch, would force the feeler's soul
    To th'oath of loyalty; this object which
    Takes prisoner the wild motion of mine eye,
105   Firing° it only here: should I, damned then,   *Enflaming*
    Slaver with lips as common as the stairs
    That mount the Capitol;[9] join grips with hands
    Made hard with hourly falsehood—falsehood as
    With labour;[1] then by-peeping° in an eye   *glancing coyly*
110   Base and illustrous° as the smoky light   *lacking luster*
    That's fed with stinking tallow—it were fit
    That all the plagues of hell should at one time
    Encounter° such revolt.°   *Confront / infidelity*
INNOGEN   My lord, I fear,
    Has forgot Britain.
GIACOMO   And himself. Not I
115   Inclined to this intelligence pronounce
    The beggary of his change,[2] but 'tis your graces
    That from my mutest conscience° to my tongue   *most quiet inner being*
    Charms this report out.
INNOGEN   Let me hear no more.
GIACOMO   O dearest soul, your cause doth strike my heart
120   With pity that doth make me sick. A lady
    So fair, and fastened to an empery°   *empire*
    Would make the great'st king double,° to be partnered   *twice as great*
    With tomboys hired with that self exhibition[3]
    Which your own coffers yield; with diseased ventures°   *prostitutes; vendors*
125   That play with all infirmities for gold

---

7. *or . . . born*: or, they being known about in time, the remedy is then brought about.
8. What you both urge on and restrain (as one commands a horse).
9. *Slaver . . . Capitol*: Offer drooling kisses to whores who, like the stairs to the Roman Capitol building, are available to everyone.
1. *join . . . labour*: clasp hands made as hard with

hourly lies or sexual infidelities as they might have been made hard with work.
2. *Not . . . change*: It is not because I am disposed to give this information that I report the contemptible nature of his change.
3. With whores ("tomboys") hired with that same payment.

Which rottenness can lend to nature; such boiled stuff[4]
As well might poison poison! Be revenged,
Or she that bore you was no queen, and you
Recoil° from your great stock.   *Degenerate*

INNOGEN   Revenged?
130 How should I be revenged? If this be true—
As I have such a heart that both mine ears
Must not in haste abuse[5]—if it be true,
How should I be revenged?

GIACOMO   Should he make me
Live like Diana's priest[6] betwixt cold sheets
135 Whiles he is vaulting variable ramps,[7]
In your despite, upon your purse[8]—revenge it.
I dedicate myself to your sweet pleasure,
More noble than that runagate° to your bed,   *renegade*
And will continue fast° to your affection,   *constant*
Still close as sure.[9]

140 INNOGEN   What ho, Pisanio!

GIACOMO   Let me my service tender on your lips.

INNOGEN   Away, I do condemn mine ears that have
So long attended thee. If thou wert honourable
Thou wouldst have told this tale for virtue, not
145 For such an end thou seek'st, as base as strange.
Thou wrong'st a gentleman who is as far
From thy report as thou from honour, and
Solicit'st here a lady that disdains
Thee and the devil alike. What ho, Pisanio!
150 The King my father shall be made acquainted
Of thy assault. If he shall think it fit
A saucy stranger in his court to mart°   *do business*
As in a Romish stew,° and to expound   *Roman brothel*
His beastly mind to us, he hath a court
155 He little cares for, and a daughter who
He not respects at all. What ho, Pisanio!

GIACOMO   O happy Leonatus! I may say
The credit° that thy lady hath of° thee   *trust / in*
Deserves thy trust, and thy most perfect goodness
160 Her assured credit.[1] Blessèd live you long,
A lady to the worthiest sir that ever
Country called his;° and you his mistress, only   *its own*
For the most worthiest fit. Give me your pardon.
I have spoke this to know if your affiance°   *faith*
165 Were deeply rooted, and shall make your lord
That which he is new o'er;[2] and he is one
The truest mannered,[3] such a holy witch°   *a charming person*
That he enchants societies into° him;   *crowds of people to*
Half all men's hearts are his.

4. Such diseased prostitutes. Sweating, usually
induced by the steam from boiling water, was a common treatment for syphilis.
5. *a heart . . . abuse:* a heart that my ears must not
abuse by too hastily accepting what they hear.
6. That is, live chastely. Diana was the Roman goddess
of the hunt known for her chastity and her circle of virgin followers.
7. While he is having sexual intercourse with whores
("ramps") of all kinds.

8. In contempt of you, with your money.
9. Always as secret as I am true.
1. *and . . . credit:* and your most perfect goodness
deserves her absolute trust.
2. *and . . . o'er:* and I (by this news of your fidelity) shall
make your lord feel afresh what he already is (that is,
your lord).
3. *he . . . mannered:* he is above all others the most perfect in conduct.

INNOGEN   You make amends.
170   GIACOMO   He sits 'mongst men like a descended god.
       He hath a kind of honour sets him off
       More than a mortal seeming.⁴ Be not angry,
       Most mighty princess, that I have adventured°   dared
       To try° your taking of a false report, which hath   test
175   Honoured with confirmation your great judgement
       In the election of a sir so rare
       Which° you know cannot err. The love I bear him   Whom
       Made me to fan⁵ you thus, but the gods made you,
       Unlike all others, chaffless.° Pray, your pardon.   without chaff; perfect
180   INNOGEN   All's well, sir. Take my power i'th' court for yours.
       GIACOMO   My humble thanks. I had almost forgot
       T'entreat your grace but in a small request,
       And yet of moment° too, for it concerns   importance
       Your lord; myself and other noble friends
       Are partners in the business.
185   INNOGEN   Pray what is't?
       GIACOMO   Some dozen Romans of us, and your lord—
       Best feather of our wing—have mingled sums
       To buy a present for the Emperor,
       Which I, the factor° for the rest, have done   agent
190   In France. 'Tis plate⁶ of rare device, and jewels
       Of rich and exquisite form; their value's great,
       And I am something curious,° being strange,°   somewhat anxious / foreign
       To have them in safe stowage. May it please you
       To take them in protection?
       INNOGEN   Willingly,
195   And pawn mine honour for their safety; since
       My lord hath interest° in them, I will keep them   a stake
       In my bedchamber.
       GIACOMO   They are in a trunk
       Attended by my men. I will make bold
       To send them to you, only for this night.
       I must aboard tomorrow.
200   INNOGEN   O, no, no!
       GIACOMO   Yes, I beseech, or I shall short° my word   break
       By length'ning my return. From Gallia°   France
       I crossed the seas on purpose and on promise
       To see your grace.
       INNOGEN   I thank you for your pains;
       But not away tomorrow!
205   GIACOMO   O, I must, madam.
       Therefore I shall beseech you, if you please
       To greet your lord with writing, do't tonight.
       I have outstood° my time, which is material   overstayed
       To th' tender° of our present.   the offering
       INNOGEN   I will write.
210   Send your trunk to me, it shall safe be kept,
       And truly yielded° you. You're very welcome.   faithfully returned to
                                         Exeunt [severally]

---

4. So that he appears more than mortal.   winnowed from the bad.
5. Winnow. When grain was harvested, wheat was win-   6. Objects, often tableware, either made of precious
nowed from the chaff; metaphorically, the good was   metals or covered ("plated") with them.

2.1

Enter CLOTEN *and the two* LORDS

CLOTEN   Was there ever man had such luck? When I kissed the jack[1] upon an upcast,° to be hit away! I had a hundred pound on't, and then a whoreson jackanapes° must take me up[2] for swearing, as if I borrowed mine oaths of him, and might not spend them at my pleasure.

on a final throw
an idiotic bastard

FIRST LORD   What got he by that? You have broke his pate with your bowl.

SECOND LORD [*aside*]   If his wit had been like him that broke it, it would have run all out.

CLOTEN   When a gentleman is disposed to swear it is not for any standers-by to curtail[3] his oaths, ha?

SECOND LORD   No, my lord [*aside*]—nor crop the ears of them.

CLOTEN   Whoreson dog! I give him satisfaction? Would he had been one of my rank.[4]

SECOND LORD [*aside*]   To have smelled like a fool.

CLOTEN   I am not vexed more at anything in th'earth. A pox on't,[5] I had rather not be so noble as I am. They dare not fight with me because of the Queen, my mother. Every jack-slave° hath his bellyful of fighting, and I must go up and down like a cock that nobody can match.°

lowborn fellow

equal; fight with

SECOND LORD [*aside*]   You are cock and capon too an you crow cock with your comb on.[6]

CLOTEN   Sayst thou?

SECOND LORD   It is not fit your lordship should undertake° every companion° that you give offence to.

take on
fellow

CLOTEN   No, I know that, but it is fit I should commit offence to[7] my inferiors.

SECOND LORD   Ay, it is fit for your lordship only.

CLOTEN   Why, so I say.

FIRST LORD   Did you hear of a stranger° that's come to court tonight?

foreigner

CLOTEN   A stranger, and I not know on't?°

of it

SECOND LORD [*aside*]   He's a strange fellow himself and knows it not.

FIRST LORD   There's an Italian come, and, 'tis thought, one of Leonatus' friends.

CLOTEN   Leonatus? A banished rascal; and he's another, whatsoever he be. Who told you of this stranger?

FIRST LORD   One of your lordship's pages.

CLOTEN   Is it fit I went to look upon him? Is there no derogation° in't?

loss of dignity

SECOND LORD   You cannot derogate,[8] my lord.

CLOTEN   Not easily, I think.

2.1 Location: Cymbeline's court, Britain.
1. In the game of bowls, the jack is the target ball. To "kiss the jack" is to roll one's ball so that it touches the jack.
2. Challenge me; rebuke me.
3. Shorten, as one bobbed the tails (and sometimes the ears) of certain dogs. This leads the Second Lord to talk of cropping the ears of oaths in line 12.
4. Social position. Gentlemen were only supposed to fight ("give satisfaction" to) men of their own rank. The

Second Lord puns on "rank" as meaning "strong smell."
5. A mild oath meaning "a plague on it."
6. And a castrated cock too if you brag ("crow") that you are a cock while wearing a fool's cap (coxcomb). There are puns here on "capon" and "cap on," on "cock's comb" and "coxcomb."
7. I should assault, with the perhaps unintended secondary meaning of "to defecate upon."
8. You cannot forfeit your dignity; you have no dignity to lose.

SECOND LORD [*aside*]   You are a fool granted,° therefore your   *an acknowledged fool*
45   issues,° being foolish, do not derogate.   *deeds*
CLOTEN   Come, I'll go see this Italian. What I have lost today at
bowls I'll win tonight of him. Come, go.
SECOND LORD   I'll attend your lordship.
Exeunt [CLOTEN *and* FIRST LORD]
That such a crafty devil as is his mother
50   Should yield the world this ass!—a woman that
Bears all down° with her brain, and this her son   *Overcomes everyone*
Cannot take two from twenty, for his heart,°   *for the life of him*
And leave eighteen. Alas, poor princess,
Thou divine Innogen, what thou endur'st,
55   Betwixt a father by thy stepdame governed,
A mother hourly coining plots, a wooer
More hateful than the foul expulsion is
Of thy dear husband, than that horrid act
Of the divorce he'd make! The heavens hold firm
60   The walls of thy dear honour, keep unshaked
That temple, thy fair mind, that thou mayst stand
T'enjoy thy banished lord and this great land!   *Exit*

2.2

[*A trunk and arras.*[1] *A*] *bed* [*is thrust forth with*] INNO-
GEN [*in it, reading a book. Enter to her* HELEN], *a lady*[2]
INNOGEN   Who's there? My woman Helen?
HELEN   Please you, madam.
INNOGEN   What hour is it?
HELEN   Almost midnight, madam.
INNOGEN   I have read three hours then. Mine eyes are weak.
Fold down the leaf where I have left. To bed.
5   Take not away the taper; leave it burning,
And if thou canst awake by four o'th' clock,
I prithee call me. Sleep hath seized me wholly.   [*Exit* HELEN]
To your protection I commend me, gods.
From fairies° and the tempters of the night   *evil beings*
10   Guard me, beseech ye.°   *I entreat you*
[*She*] *sleeps.*
GIACOMO [*comes*] *from the trunk*
GIACOMO   The crickets sing, and man's o'er-laboured sense
Repairs itself by rest. Our Tarquin[3] thus
Did softly press the rushes[4] ere he wakened
The chastity he wounded. Cytherea,[5]
15   How bravely° thou becom'st thy bed! Fresh lily,   *splendidly*
And whiter than the sheets! That I might touch,
But kiss, one kiss! Rubies unparagoned,
How dearly they do't![6] 'Tis her breathing that
Perfumes the chamber thus. The flame o'th' taper

2.2 Location: Innogen's chambers.
1. Tapestry wall covering.
2. F's stage direction reads "Enter Imogen, in her Bed,
and a Lady." The trunk in which Giacomo is concealed
is probably brought onstage as the scene opens, either
carried on or raised up through the trapdoor in the stage
floor. Beds typically were "thrust forth" from a door at the
back of the stage. Giacomo mentions an arras in his
ensuing description of Innogen's bedroom. One may

have been hung up at the back of the stage for this scene.
3. The ancient Roman Sextus Tarquinius, whose rape
of Lucrece (Lucretia) was the subject of a poem by
Shakespeare.
4. Reeds commonly used as a floor covering.
5. A name for Aphrodite, or Venus, the goddess of
beauty and love, who first set foot on the island of
Cytherea after her birth from sea-foam.
6. How dearly do they (her ruby lips) kiss one another.

20 Bows toward her, and would underpeep her lids,
To see th'enclosèd lights, now canopied
Under these windows,° white and azure-laced   *eyelids*
With blue of heaven's own tinct.° But my design—   *hue*
To note the chamber. I will write all down.
   [*He writes in his tables*]°   *writing tablets*
25 Such and such pictures, there the window, such
Th'adornment of her bed, the arras, figures,
Why, such and such; and the contents o'th' story.[7]
Ah, but some natural notes° about her body   *marks*
Above ten thousand meaner movables[8]
30 Would testify t'enrich mine inventory.
O sleep, thou ape° of death, lie dull° upon her,   *mimic / heavy*
And be her sense but as a monument[9]
Thus in a chapel lying. Come off, come off;
As slippery as the Gordian knot was hard.[1]
   [*He takes the bracelet from her arm*]
35 'Tis mine, and this will witness outwardly,
As strongly as the conscience does within,[2]
To th' madding° of her lord. On her left breast   *maddening*
A mole, cinque-spotted,° like the crimson drops   *with five spots*
I'th' bottom of a cowslip. Here's a voucher°   *piece of evidence*
40 Stronger than ever law could make. This secret
Will force him think I have picked the lock and ta'en
The treasure of her honour.[3] No more. To what end?
Why should I write this down that's riveted,
Screwed to my memory? She hath been reading late,
45 The tale of Tereus.[4] Here the leaf's turned down
Where Philomel gave up. I have enough.
To th' trunk again, and shut the spring of it.
Swift, swift, you dragons of the night, that dawning
May bare the raven's eye![5] I lodge in fear.
50 Though this' a heavenly angel, hell is here.
   Clock strikes
One, two, three. Time, time!
   Exit [*into the trunk. The bed and trunk are removed*]

2.3

Enter CLOTEN *and* [*the two*] LORDS
FIRST LORD   Your lordship is the most patient man in loss, the
   most coldest° that ever turned up ace.[1]   *least passionate*
CLOTEN   It would make any man cold to lose.

---

7. The design on the tapestry (?). In 2.4.66–91, Giacomo describes in more detail what he saw in Innogen's bedchamber: a tapestry depicting the story of Antony and Cleopatra and a chimneypiece carving of Diana bathing. He could here be referring to the "figures" and "contents" of either the tapestry or chimneypiece.
8. Less important pieces of property, especially furniture or furnishings.
9. And let her senses be like those of an effigy on a tomb.
1. As easy to open as the Gordian knot was difficult to untie. Alluding to the myth of Gordius, King of Phrygia, who tied an impossibly intricate knot and declared that whoever untied it would reign over Asia; with a single thrust of his sword, Alexander the Great cut through it. Giacomo's unclasping of the bracelet has sexual implications. He is metaphorically violating Innogen's

chastity and, by stealing Posthumus's love token, is interfering in the marriage bond that links Posthumus and Innogen.
2. As powerfully as does his inward consciousness.
3. Giacomo means his knowledge of the mole will make Posthumus believe he has slept with Innogen. To "pick the lock" is a euphemism for "to have sex."
4. In Greek mythology, Tereus, King of Thrace, raped his wife's sister Philomela and cut out her tongue so she could not reveal what had happened. Philomela later wove the story into a tapestry.
5. May cause the raven to wake. The bird supposedly slept facing east and awakened at dawn.
2.3 Location: A room near Innogen's chambers.
1. *that . . . ace:* who ever threw the lowest score in a game of dice, with a pun on "ass."

FIRST LORD   But not every man patient after° the noble temper   *according to*
of your lordship. You are most hot and furious when you win.

CLOTEN   Winning will put any man into courage. If I could get
this foolish Innogen I should have gold enough. It's almost
morning, is't not?

FIRST LORD   Day, my lord.

CLOTEN   I would this music would come. I am advised to give
her music o' mornings; they say it will penetrate.[2]

    Enter MUSICIANS

Come on, tune. If you can penetrate her with your fingering,
so; we'll try with tongue too.[3] If none will do,° let her remain;   *suffice*
but I'll never give o'er. First, a very excellent good-conceited°   *ingenious*
thing; after, a wonderful sweet air with admirable rich words
to it; and then let her consider.

    [*Music*]

MUSICIAN [*sings*][4]   Hark, hark, the lark at heaven gate sings,
  And Phoebus gins° arise,[5]   *Apollo (sun god) begins*
  His steeds to water at those springs
    On chaliced flowers[6] that lies,
  And winking Mary-buds° begin to ope their golden eyes;   *closed marigold buds*
  With everything that pretty is, my lady sweet, arise,
    Arise, arise!

CLOTEN   So, get you gone. If this penetrate I will consider° your   *value*
music the better; if it do not, it is a vice° in her ears which   *defect*
horse hairs and calves' guts[7] nor the voice of unpaved[8] eunuch
to boot can never amend.   [*Exeunt* MUSICIANS]

    Enter CYMBELINE *and* [*the*] QUEEN

SECOND LORD   Here comes the King.

CLOTEN   I am glad I was up so late, for that's the reason I was up
so early. He cannot choose but take this service I have done
fatherly. Good morrow to your majesty, and to my gracious
mother.

CYMBELINE   Attend you here the door of our stern daughter?
Will she not forth?

CLOTEN   I have assailed her with musics, but she vouchsafes no
notice.

CYMBELINE   The exile of her minion° is too new.   *darling*
She hath not yet forgot him. Some more time
Must wear the print° of his remembrance out,   *imprint*
And then she's yours.

QUEEN [*to* CLOTEN]   You are most bound to th' King,
Who lets go by no vantages° that may   *opportunities*
Prefer° you to his daughter. Frame° yourself   *Recommend / Prepare*
To° orderly solicits,° and be friended   *With / solicitations*
With aptness of the season.[9] Make denials
Increase your services; so seem as if
You were inspired to do those duties which
You tender to her; that you in all obey her,

2. Affect her emotions; arouse her sexually.
3. If your instrumental music can move her, that's good. We'll try to move her with song as well. These lines also carry an explicitly sexual secondary meaning: If you can insert your fingers inside her, that's good. We'll try oral sex as well. It is unclear if Cloten understands the bawdy import of his own words.
4. F does not attribute this song to a particular singer but simply introduces it as "SONG." It also appears in a
seventeenth-century manuscript located in the Bodleian Library at Oxford.
5. These lines also echo Shakespeare's sonnet 29, lines 10–12: "my state / Like to the lark at break of day arising / From sullen earth, sings hymns at heaven's gate."
6. Flowers with cuplike blossoms.
7. Both were used as strings for musical instruments.
8. Castrated (lacking stones).
9. And be assisted by appropriate timing.

Save when command to your dismission tends,
And therein you are senseless.[1]

CLOTEN   Senseless? Not so.

[*Enter a* MESSENGER]

50 MESSENGER [*to* CYMBELINE]   So like you,° sir, ambassadors from Rome;   *If you please*
The one is Caius Lucius.

CYMBELINE   A worthy fellow,
Albeit he comes on angry purpose now:
But that's no fault of his. We must receive him
According to the honour of his sender,
55 And towards himself, his goodness forespent on us,[2]
We must extend our notice. Our dear son,
When you have given good morning to your mistress,
Attend the Queen and us. We shall have need
T'employ you towards this Roman. Come, our queen.

Exeunt [*all but* CLOTEN]

60 CLOTEN   If she be up, I'll speak with her; if not,
Let her lie still and dream.

[*He knocks*]

By your leave, ho!—
I know her women are about her; what
If I do line° one of their hands? 'Tis gold   *fill (with gold)*
Which buys admittance—oft it doth—yea, and makes
65 Diana's rangers false° themselves, yield up   *gamekeepers turn false*
Their deer to th' stand o'th' stealer;[3] and 'tis gold
Which makes the true man killed and saves the thief,
Nay, sometime hangs both thief and true man. What
Can it not do and undo? I will make
70 One of her women lawyer to° me, for   *advocate for*
I yet not understand the case[4] myself.—
By your leave.

Knocks. Enter a LADY

LADY   Who's there that knocks?

CLOTEN   A gentleman.

LADY   No more?

CLOTEN   Yes, and a gentlewoman's son.

LADY   That's more
75 [*Aside*][5] Than some whose tailors are as dear° as yours   *expensive*
Can justly boast of. [*To him*] What's your lordship's pleasure?

CLOTEN   Your lady's person. Is she ready?°   *dressed; prepared*

LADY   Ay.

[*Aside*] To keep her chamber.

CLOTEN   There is gold for you.
Sell me your good report.

80 LADY   How, my good name?°—or to report of you   *reputation*
What I shall think is good?

Enter INNOGEN

The Princess.   [*Exit*]

---

1. *Save . . . senseless:* Except what pertains to your dismissal ("dismission"), which you are incapable of understanding. Cloten, however, takes "senseless" to mean "stupid."
2. *his . . . us:* in view of the virtue he has shown in previous dealings with us.
3. *yield . . . stealer:* surrender their deer to the place where the thief stands to shoot; surrender what is most dear or valuable (their chastity) to the thief's erect

penis ("th' stand").
4. *for . . . case:* for I still do not know how to manage the matter (with wordplay on "stand under" as slang for "sexually penetrate" and on "case" as slang for "vagina").
5. The Lady's speaking all or part of this and her next speech in asides explains the outspokenness of her comments; it also follows the pattern of 2.1 and of later scenes in which Cloten's words are slyly subjected to derogatory commentary by those with whom he converses.

CLOTEN   Good morrow, fairest. Sister, your sweet hand.

INNOGEN   Good morrow, sir. You lay out too much pains
   For purchasing but trouble. The thanks I give
85 Is telling you that I am poor of thanks,
   And scarce can spare them.

CLOTEN   Still I swear I love you.

INNOGEN   If you but said so, 'twere as deep° with me.   *solemn; binding*
   If you swear still,° your recompense is still   *always*
   That I regard it not.

CLOTEN   This is no answer.

90 INNOGEN   But° that you shall not say I yield being silent,   *Except*
   I would not speak. I pray you, spare me. Faith,
   I shall unfold equal discourtesy[6]
   To your best kindness. One of your great knowing°   *knowledge*
   Should learn, being taught, forbearance.

95 CLOTEN   To leave you in your madness, 'twere my sin.
   I will not.

INNOGEN   Fools cure not mad folks.

CLOTEN   Do you call me fool?

INNOGEN   As I am mad, I do.
   If you'll be patient, I'll no more be mad;
   That cures us both. I am much sorry, sir,
100 You put me to forget a lady's manners
   By being so verbal;[7] and learn now for all
   That I, which know my heart, do here pronounce
   By th' very truth of it: I care not for you,
   And am so near the lack of charity
105 To accuse myself I hate you,[8] which I had rather
   You felt than make't my boast.°   *than I had to say it*

CLOTEN   You sin against
   Obedience which you owe your father. For°   *As for*
   The contract you pretend° with that base wretch,   *claim*
   One bred of alms and fostered with cold dishes,
110 With scraps o'th' court, it is no contract, none.
   And though it be allowed in meaner° parties—   *socially inferior*
   Yet who than he more mean?—to knit their souls,
   On whom there is no more dependency
   But brats and beggary,[9] in self-figured° knot,   *self-contracted*
115 Yet you are curbed from that enlargement° by   *freedom*
   The consequence o'th' crown,[1] and must not foil°   *defile*
   The precious note° of it with a base slave,   *reputation*
   A hilding for a livery,[2] a squire's cloth,°   *uniform*
   A pantler°—not so eminent.   *pantry servant*

INNOGEN   Profane fellow,
120 Wert thou the son of Jupiter,° and no more   *king of the gods*
   But what thou art besides, thou wert too base
   To be his° groom; thou wert dignified enough,[3]   *(Posthumus's)*
   Even to the point of envy, if 'twere made
   Comparative for your virtues to be styled

---

6. I shall display discourtesy equal.

7. "Verbal" (talkative; plainspoken) may refer either to Cloten or to Innogen.

8. *And . . . you:* And I am so near uncharitableness that I can charge myself with hating you.

9. *On . . . beggary:* Upon whose marriage nothing depends but worthless children and extreme poverty.

1. *by . . . crown:* by the importance of the crown; by the consequences that flow from your inheritance of the crown.

2. A worthless person fit only to wear the uniform ("livery") of his master's household.

3. You were raised in status sufficiently.

125   The under-hangman[4] of his kingdom, and hated
    For being preferred° so well.   *advanced*
CLOTEN   The south-fog[5] rot him!
INNOGEN   He never can meet more mischance than come
    To be but named of° thee. His meanest garment   *by*
    That ever hath but clipped° his body is dearer   *encircled*
130   In my respect than all the hairs above thee,°   *on your head*
    Were they all made such men. How now, Pisanio!
        Enter PISANIO
CLOTEN   His garment? Now the devil—
INNOGEN [*to* PISANIO]   To Dorothy, my woman, hie thee presently.°   *at once*
CLOTEN   His garment?
INNOGEN [*to* PISANIO]   I am sprited with° a fool,   *am haunted by*
135   Frighted, and angered worse. Go bid my woman
    Search for a jewel that too casually
    Hath left mine arm. It was thy master's. 'Shrew me°   *Beshrew me (plague on me)*
    If I would lose it for a revenue
    Of any king's in Europe! I do think
140   I saw't this morning; confident I am
    Last night 'twas on mine arm; I kissed it.
    I hope it be not gone to tell my lord
    That I kiss aught but he.
PISANIO   'Twill not be lost.
INNOGEN   I hope so. Go and search.   [*Exit* PISANIO]
CLOTEN   You have abused me.
    'His meanest garment'?
145 INNOGEN   Ay, I said so, sir.
    If you will make't an action,° call witness to't.   *a lawsuit*
CLOTEN   I will inform your father.
INNOGEN   Your mother too.
    She's my good lady, and will conceive,° I hope,°   *think / expect*
    But the worst of me. So I leave you, sir,
    To th' worst of discontent.   *Exit*
150 CLOTEN   I'll be revenged.
    'His meanest garment'? Well!   *Exit*

2.4

       Enter POSTHUMUS *and* FILARIO
POSTHUMUS   Fear it not, sir. I would I were so sure
    To win the King as I am bold her honour
    Will remain hers.
FILARIO   What means° do you make to him?   *intercessions*
POSTHUMUS   Not any; but abide the change of time,
5   Quake in the present winter's state, and wish
    That warmer days would come. In these seared° hopes   *withered*
    I barely gratify° your love; they failing,   *repay*
    I must die much your debtor.
FILARIO   Your very goodness and your company
10   O'erpays all I can do. By this,° your king   *By now*
    Hath heard of great Augustus. Caius Lucius
    Will do 's commission throughly.° And I think   *thoroughly*

---

4. *if 'twere . . . under-hangman*: if a comparison were made between your virtues and those of Posthumus and you were given the job of assistant hangman; if, in accordance with your virtues, you were given the job of assistant hangman.
5. A damp fog brought by the south wind and supposed to breed infections.
2.4 Location: Filario's house, Rome.

He'll grant the tribute, send th'arrearages,° | *overdue payments*
Ere look upon our Romans, whose remembrance° | *the memory of whom*
Is yet fresh in their grief.[1]

15 POSTHUMUS   I do believe,
Statist° though I am none, nor like to be, | *Statesman*
That this will prove a war, and you shall hear
The legions now in Gallia sooner landed
In our not-fearing Britain than have tidings
20 Of any penny tribute paid. Our countrymen
Are men more ordered° than when Julius Caesar | *better disciplined*
Smiled at their lack of skill but found their courage
Worthy his frowning at. Their discipline,
Now wing-led[2] with their courage, will make known
25 To their approvers° they are people such | *those who would test them*
That mend upon the world.[3]

       Enter GIACOMO

FILARIO   See, Giacomo.
POSTHUMUS [*to* GIACOMO]   The swiftest harts° have posted° you | *deer / conveyed*
    by land,
And winds of° all the corners° kissed your sails | *from / (of the globe)*
To make your vessel nimble.
FILARIO [*to* GIACOMO]   Welcome, sir.
30 POSTHUMUS [*to* GIACOMO]   I hope the briefness of your answer made° | *caused*
The speediness of your return.
GIACOMO   Your lady is
One of the fair'st that I have looked upon—
POSTHUMUS   And therewithal the best, or let her beauty
Look through a casement[4] to allure false hearts,
And be false with them.
35 GIACOMO   Here are letters for you.
POSTHUMUS   Their tenor good, I trust.
GIACOMO   'Tis very like.

      [POSTHUMUS *reads the letters*]

FILARIO   Was Caius Lucius in the Briton court
When you were there?
GIACOMO   He was expected then,
But not° approached. | *had not*
POSTHUMUS   All is well yet.
40 Sparkles this stone as it was wont, or is't not
Too dull for your good wearing?
GIACOMO   If I had lost it
I should have lost the worth of it in gold.
I'll make a journey twice as far t'enjoy
A second night of such sweet shortness which
45 Was mine in Britain; for the ring is won.
POSTHUMUS   The stone's too hard to come by.
GIACOMO   Not a whit,
Your lady being so easy.
POSTHUMUS   Make not, sir,
Your loss your sport. I hope you know that we
Must not continue friends.

---

1. The Britons' grief; the grief inflicted by the Romans.
2. Carried aloft (as if on wings); led on each flank (each "wing"). The Second Folio (F2, printed in 1632) has "mingled," an emendation adopted by some editors.
3. *such . . . world*: who improve in the world's estimation.
4. Look out through a window (alluding to the manner in which prostitutes solicited customers).

GIACOMO   Good sir, we must,
50 If you keep covenant. Had I not brought
The knowledge° of your mistress home I grant   *A sexual account*
We were to question° farther, but I now   *dispute*
Profess myself the winner of her honour,
Together with your ring, and not the wronger
55 Of her or you, having proceeded but
By both your wills.
POSTHUMUS   If you can make't apparent
That you have tasted her in bed, my hand
And ring is yours. If not, the foul opinion
You had of her pure honour gains or loses
60 Your sword or mine,[5] or masterless leaves both°   *both swords*
To who shall find them.
GIACOMO   Sir, my circumstances,°   *detailed evidence*
Being so near the truth as I will make them,
Must first induce you to believe; whose strength
I will confirm with oath, which I doubt not
65 You'll give me leave to spare° when you shall find   *omit*
You need it not.
POSTHUMUS   Proceed.
GIACOMO   First, her bedchamber—
Where I confess I slept not, but profess
Had that was well worth watching°—it was hanged   *staying awake for*
With tapestry of silk and silver; the story
70 Proud Cleopatra when she met her Roman,[6]
And Cydnus[7] swelled above the banks, or for°   *either because of*
The press of boats or pride: a piece of work
So bravely° done, so rich, that it did strive   *splendidly*
In workmanship and value;[8] which I wondered
75 Could be so rarely and exactly wrought,
Such the true life on't was.
POSTHUMUS   This is true,
And this you might have heard of here, by me
Or by some other.
GIACOMO   More particulars
Must justify° my knowledge.   *confirm*
POSTHUMUS   So they must,
Or do your honour injury.
80 GIACOMO   The chimney°   *fireplace*
Is south the chamber, and the chimney-piece[9]
Chaste Dian[1] bathing. Never saw I figures
So likely to report themselves;[2] the cutter
Was as another nature; dumb, outwent her,
Motion and breath left out.[3]
85 POSTHUMUS   This is a thing
Which you might from relation° likewise reap,   *report*

5. *gains . . . mine:* makes one of us the winner, the
other the loser, of his sword in a duel.
6. Alluding to a meeting, described also in Shakespeare's play *Antony and Cleopatra*, between the Egyptian Queen Cleopatra and Mark Antony, a Roman
general who was her lover.
7. A river in Cilicia (now Turkey).
8. *that . . . value:* that craftsmanship and monetary
worth both competed for preeminence.

9. Ornament above the fireplace.
1. Another reference to the goddess associated in classical mythology with hunting, childbirth, and chastity.
2. So lifelike that they could give an account of themselves.
3. *the cutter . . . out:* the sculptor ("cutter") was like a
second nature in creative power. Speechless, the sculp-
ture surpassed nature, apart from its lack of movement
and breathing.

Being, as it is, much spoke of.

GIACOMO   The roof o'th' chamber

With golden cherubins is fretted.° Her andirons—   *carved*

I had forgot them—were two winking Cupids[4]

90   Of silver, each on one foot standing, nicely°   *ingeniously*

Depending° on their brands.°   *Leaning / torches*

POSTHUMUS   This is her honour!

Let it be granted you have seen all this—and praise

Be given to your remembrance—the description

Of what is in her chamber nothing saves

The wager you have laid.

95   GIACOMO   Then, if you can

Be pale,° I beg but leave to air this jewel. See!   *Be unmoved*

[*He shows the bracelet*]

And now 'tis up° again; it must be married   *put away*

To that your diamond. I'll keep them.

POSTHUMUS   Jove!°   *king of the gods*

Once more let me behold it. Is it that

Which I left with her?

100 GIACOMO   Sir, I thank her, that.

She stripped it from her arm. I see her yet.

Her pretty action did outsell° her gift,   *exceed in value*

And yet enriched it too. She gave it me,

And said she prized it once.

POSTHUMUS   Maybe she plucked it off

To send it me.

105 GIACOMO   She writes so to you, doth she?

POSTHUMUS   O, no, no, no—'tis true! Here, take this too.

[*He gives* GIACOMO *his ring*]

It is a basilisk[5] unto mine eye,

Kills me to look on't. Let there be no honour

Where there is beauty, truth where semblance,° love   *the mere appearance of it*

110 Where there's another man. The vows° of women   *Let the vows*

Of no more bondage be to where they are made

Than they are° to their virtues, which is nothing!   *Than women are bound*

O, above measure false!

FILARIO   Have patience, sir,

And take your ring again; 'tis not yet won.

115 It may be probable she lost it, or

Who knows if one° her woman, being corrupted,   *one of*

Hath stol'n it from her?

POSTHUMUS   Very true,

And so I hope he came by't. Back my ring.

[*He takes his ring again*]

Render to me some corporal sign about her

120 More evident° than this; for this was stol'n.   *conclusive*

GIACOMO   By Jupiter,[6] I had it from her arm.

POSTHUMUS   Hark you, he swears, by Jupiter he swears.

'Tis true, nay, keep the ring, 'tis true. I am sure

She would not lose it. Her attendants are

125 All sworn° and honourable. They induced to steal it?   *bound by oaths*

---

4. Two statues of Cupid, the god of love, with eyes
shut. Cupid was often depicted as a beautiful boy with
wings and a torch and wearing a blindfold to signify the
blindness of love.

5. A mythical reptile able with a glance to kill those it
gazed upon.

6. Another reference to the king of the gods. Only the
most solemn vows would be made in his name.

And by a stranger? No, he hath enjoyed her.
The cognizance° of her incontinency   token
Is this. She hath bought the name of whore thus dearly.
    [*He gives* GIACOMO *his ring*]
There, take thy hire,° and all the fiends of hell   fee
Divide themselves between you!
130 FILARIO   Sir, be patient.
This is not strong enough to be believed
Of one persuaded° well of.   thought
POSTHUMUS   Never talk on't.
She hath been colted° by him.   sexually enjoyed
GIACOMO   If you seek
For further satisfying, under her breast—
135 Worthy the pressing—lies a mole, right proud
Of that most delicate lodging. By my life,
I kissed it, and it gave me present° hunger   immediate
To feed again, though full. You do remember
This stain° upon her?   mark
POSTHUMUS   Ay, and it doth confirm
140 Another stain as big as hell can hold,
Were there no more but it.
GIACOMO   Will you hear more?
POSTHUMUS   Spare your arithmetic, never count the turns.°   sexual acts
Once, and a million!⁷
GIACOMO   I'll be sworn.
POSTHUMUS   No swearing.
If you will swear you have not done't, you lie,
145 And I will kill thee if thou dost deny
Thou'st made me cuckold.
GIACOMO   I'll deny nothing.
POSTHUMUS   O that I had her here to tear her limb-meal!°   limb from limb
I will go there and do't i'th' court, before
Her father. I'll do something.   *Exit*
FILARIO   Quite besides°   beyond
150 The government° of patience! You have won.   control
Let's follow and pervert° the present wrath   turn aside
He hath against himself.
GIACOMO   With all my heart.   *Exeunt*

2.5

Enter POSTHUMUS¹
POSTHUMUS   Is there no way for men to be,° but women   to exist
Must be half-workers?° We are bastards all,   be partners
And that most venerable man which I
Did call my father was I know not where
5 When I was stamped.² Some coiner with his tools³
Made me a counterfeit; yet my mother seemed
The Dian of that time: so doth my wife
The nonpareil° of this. O vengeance, vengeance!   one who has no equal

---

7. That is, there is no difference between having been unfaithful once and having done it a million times.
2.5 Location: Scene continues.
1. In F, Posthumus's soliloquy is part of 2.4. He is making a reentry, however, after his departure at line 149,

and most modern editions mark the soliloquy as a separate scene.
2. Conceived, as coins are stamped with images when they are made.
3. With pun on "tool" as meaning "penis."

Me of my lawful pleasure⁴ she restrained,
10   And prayed me oft forbearance;⁵ did it with
     A pudency° so rosy the sweet view on't°   *modesty / of it*
     Might well have warmed old Saturn;⁶ that I thought her
     As chaste as unsunned snow. O all the devils!
     This yellow° Giacomo in an hour—was't not?—   *sallow*
15   Or less—at first?° Perchance he spoke not, but   *instantly*
     Like a full-acorned boar,⁷ a German one,
     Cried 'O!' and mounted; found no opposition
     But what he looked for should oppose⁸ and she
     Should from encounter guard. Could I find out
20   The woman's part in me—for there's no motion°   *impulse*
     That tends to vice in man but I affirm
     It is the woman's part; be it lying, note it,
     The woman's; flattering, hers; deceiving, hers;
     Lust and rank thoughts, hers, hers; revenges, hers;
25   Ambitions, covetings, change of prides,° disdain,   *varying extravagances*
     Nice° longing, slanders, mutability,   *Lustful*
     All faults that man can name, nay, that hell knows,
     Why, hers in part or all, but rather all—
     For even to vice
30   They are not constant, but are changing still
     One vice but of a minute old for one
     Not half so old as that. I'll write against them,
     Detest them, curse them, yet 'tis greater skill°   *cleverness*
     In a true hate to pray they have their will.°   *desire*
35   The very devils cannot plague them better.   *Exit*

3.1

[*Flourish.*] *Enter in state* CYMBELINE, [*the*] QUEEN,
   CLOTEN, *and lords at one door, and at another, Caius*
   LUCIUS *and attendants*

CYMBELINE   Now say, what would Augustus Caesar with us?
LUCIUS   When Julius Caesar—whose remembrance yet
     Lives in men's eyes, and will to ears and tongues
     Be theme and hearing ever—was in this Britain
5   And conquered it, Cassibelan, thine uncle,
     Famous in Caesar's praises no whit less
     Than in his feats deserving it, for him
     And his succession° granted Rome a tribute,   *heirs*
     Yearly three thousand pounds, which by thee lately
     Is left untendered.
10   QUEEN   And, to kill the marvel,¹
     Shall be so ever.
CLOTEN   There will be many Caesars
     Ere such another Julius. Britain's a world
     By itself, and we will nothing pay
     For wearing our own noses.²

---

4. The sexual pleasure to which marriage entitled him.
5. And often begged me to defer sexual pleasures.
6. The Roman god of agriculture, usually characterized
as cold and melancholy.
7. A boar fed full of acorns (with a pun on "boor" as
meaning "a German or Dutch peasant").
8. *found . . . oppose:* found no opposition except the
body parts he expected to encounter.

3.1 Location: Cymbeline's court, Britain.
1. And, to put a stop to the amazement (which our
nonpayment has caused).
2. Perhaps referring to contemporary theories of physiognomy that identified specific physical features, such
as noses, with racial types. Roman noses were notoriously prominent.

QUEEN   That opportunity
15   Which then they had to take from 's, to resume°   take back
      We have again. Remember, sir, my liege,°   sovereign
      The kings your ancestors, together with
      The natural bravery° of your isle, which stands   splendor
      As Neptune's park,³ ribbed and paled in°   enclosed and fenced in
20   With banks unscalable and roaring waters,
      With sands that will not bear your enemies' boats,
      But suck them up to th' topmast. A kind of conquest
      Caesar made here, but made not here his brag
      Of 'came and saw and overcame'.⁴ With shame—
25   The first that ever touched him—he was carried
      From off our coast, twice beaten; and his shipping,°   ships
      Poor ignorant° baubles, on our terrible seas   silly
      Like eggshells moved upon their surges, cracked
      As easily 'gainst our rocks; for joy whereof
30   The famed Cassibelan, who was once at point°—   ready
      O giglot° fortune!—to master Caesar's sword,   fickle; whorish
      Made Lud's town⁵ with rejoicing fires bright,
      And Britons strut with courage.
CLOTEN   Come, there's no more tribute to be paid. Our king-
35   dom is stronger than it was at that time, and, as I said, there is
      no more such Caesars. Other of them may have crooked noses,
      but to owe° such straight° arms, none.   possess / powerful
CYMBELINE   Son, let your mother end.
CLOTEN   We have yet many among us can grip as hard as Cassi-
40   belan. I do not say I am one, but I have a hand. Why tribute?
      Why should we pay tribute? If Caesar can hide the sun from us
      with a blanket, or put the moon in his pocket, we will pay him
      tribute for light; else, sir, no more tribute, pray you now.
CYMBELINE [to LUCIUS]   You must know,
45   Till the injurious° Romans did extort   insulting
      This tribute from us we were free. Caesar's ambition,
      Which swelled so much that it did almost stretch
      The sides o'th' world, against all colour⁶ here
      Did put the yoke upon 's, which to shake off
50   Becomes a warlike people, whom we reckon
      Ourselves to be. We do say then to Caesar,
      Our ancestor was that Mulmutius⁷ which
      Ordained our laws, whose use the sword of Caesar
      Hath too much mangled, whose repair and franchise°   free exercise
55   Shall by the power we hold be our good deed,
      Though Rome be therefore angry. Mulmutius made our laws,
      Who was the first of Britain which did put
      His brows within a golden crown and called
      Himself a king.
LUCIUS   I am sorry, Cymbeline,
60   That I am to pronounce Augustus Caesar—

3. As grounds owned by Neptune, Roman god of the sea.
4. When Julius Caesar, leading an army into Asia, defeated King Pharnaces and his allies, Plutarch reports that Caesar wrote three words to his friend Anitius in Rome: *veni, vidi, vici* ("I came, I saw, I overcame"). See Plutarch's *Life of Julius Caesar* in his *Lives of the Noble Grecians and Romanes* as translated by Thomas North

(1579).
5. London. Contemporary texts such as Holinshed's *Chronicles* erroneously asserted that "London" was derived from "Lud," the name of the mythological British King who was Cymbeline's grandfather.
6. Without any pretense of justice.
7. According to Holinshed, the first King of Britain.

Caesar, that hath more kings his servants than
Thyself domestic officers—thine enemy.
Receive it from me, then: war and confusion°   *destruction*
In Caesar's name pronounce I 'gainst thee. Look
65 For fury not to be resisted. Thus defied,
I thank thee for myself.

CYMBELINE   Thou art welcome, Caius.
Thy Caesar knighted me; my youth I spent
Much under him; of him I gathered honour,
Which he to seek of me again perforce
70 Behoves me keep at utterance.[8] I am perfect°   *fully aware*
That the Pannonians and Dalmatians[9] for
Their liberties are now in arms, a precedent
Which not to read would show the Britons cold;°   *lacking in spirit*
So Caesar shall not find them.

LUCIUS   Let proof° speak.   *the result*
75 CLOTEN His majesty bids you welcome. Make pastime with us a
day or two or longer. If you seek us afterwards in other terms,
you shall find us in our salt-water girdle.[1] If you beat us out of
it, it is yours; if you fall in the adventure, our crows shall fare
the better for you; and there's an end.
80 LUCIUS So, sir.

CYMBELINE I know your master's pleasure, and he mine.
All the remain° is 'Welcome'.   [*Flourish.*] *Exeunt*   *All that is left to say*

3.2

Enter PISANIO, *reading of a letter*

PISANIO How? Of adultery? Wherefore write you not
What monster's her accuser? Leonatus,
O master, what a strange infection
Is fall'n into thy ear! What false Italian,
5 As poisonous tongued as handed,[1] hath prevailed
On thy too ready hearing? Disloyal? No.
She's punished for her truth,° and undergoes,   *faithfulness*
More goddess-like than wife-like, such assaults
As would take in° some virtue. O my master,   *overcome*
10 Thy mind to° hers is now as low as were   *compared to*
Thy fortunes. How? That I should murder her,
Upon the love and truth and vows which I
Have made to thy command? I her? Her blood?
If it be so to do good service, never
15 Let me be counted serviceable. How look I,
That I should seem to lack humanity
So much as this fact° comes to? [*Reads*] 'Do't. The letter   *action*
That I have sent her, by her own command
Shall give thee opportunity.' O damned paper,[2]
20 Black as the ink that's on thee! Senseless bauble,°   *toy; worthless object*

---

8. *Which . . . utterance:* His seeking that honor of me
again makes it necessary for me to defend ("keep") it to
the death.
9. Inhabitants of Hungary and Dalmatia, a region on
the Adriatic Sea.
1. In the sea that encircles us (as a girdle does the

body).
3.2 Location: Cymbeline's court.
1. Having as many poisons (lies) in his tongue as in his
hands. Contemporary texts depicted Italians as infinitely skilled in making and administering poisons.
2. O hellish object (referring to the letter).

Art thou a fedary° for this act, and look'st   *an accomplice*
So virgin-like without?°   *on the outside*
    Enter INNOGEN
                     Lo, here she comes.
I am ignorant in° what I am commanded.   *will pretend ignorance of*
  INNOGEN   How now, Pisanio?
25 PISANIO   Madam, here is a letter from my lord.
  INNOGEN   Who, thy lord that is my lord, Leonatus?
O learned indeed were that astronomer°   *astrologer*
That knew the stars as I his characters°—   *handwriting*
He'd lay the future open. You good gods,
30 Let what is here contained relish° of love,   *taste*
Of my lord's health, of his content—yet not
That we two are asunder; let that grieve him.
Some griefs are med'cinable;° that is one of them,   *beneficial*
For it doth physic love³—of his content
35 All but in that. Good wax,° thy leave. Blest be   *sealing wax*
You bees that make these locks of counsel!° Lovers   *for private matters*
And men in dangerous bonds⁴ pray not alike;
Though forfeiters you cast in prison,⁵ yet
You clasp° young Cupid's tables.° Good news, gods!   *lovingly embrace / tablets*
    [*She opens and reads the letter*]
40 'Justice and your father's wrath, should he take me in his
dominion, could not be so cruel to me as° you, O the dearest   *but that*
of creatures, would even renew me° with your eyes. Take   *would revive me*
notice that I am in Cambria,° at Milford Haven.⁶ What your   *Wales*
own love will out of this advise you, follow. So he wishes you
45 all happiness, that remains loyal to his vow, and your increasing
in love,
                     Leonatus Posthumus.'
O for a horse with wings! Hear'st thou, Pisanio?
He is at Milford Haven. Read, and tell me
50 How far 'tis thither. If one of mean affairs°   *with unimportant business*
May plod it in a week, why may not I
Glide thither in a day? Then, true Pisanio,
Who long'st like me to see thy lord, who long'st—
O let me bate°—but not like me—yet long'st   *moderate my speech*
55 But in a fainter kind—O, not like me,
For mine's beyond beyond; say, and speak thick°—   *speak quickly*
Love's counsellor should fill the bores of hearing,°   *the ears*
To th' smothering of the sense⁷—how far it is
To this same blessèd Milford. And by° th' way   *on*
60 Tell me how Wales was made so happy as
T'inherit such a haven. But first of all,
How we may steal from hence; and for the gap
That we shall make in time from our hence-going
Till our return, to excuse; but first, how get hence.
65 Why should excuse be born or ere begot?⁸

---

3. For it nurtures love; for it keeps love in good health.
4. Men bound by agreements imposing penalties (which are sealed with wax). Innogen is contrasting the fear with which men in legal trouble greet sealed documents to the joy with which lovers receive a sealed love letter.
5. Although you cast those who default on agreements in prison (because sealed bonds lead to indictments).
6. A port in southern Wales that became important in

later British history when Henry Tudor landed there in 1485. Defeating the army of Richard III, he was crowned Henry VII, bringing to an end the civil strife known as the Wars of the Roses.
7. Until the sense of hearing is overwhelmed.
8. Why should an excuse be born even before it is conceived—that is, be manufactured before it is needed?

We'll talk of that hereafter. Prithee speak,
How many score of° miles may we well ride   *set of twenty*
'Twixt hour and hour?°   *In an hour*
PISANIO   One score 'twixt sun and sun,
Madam, 's enough for you, and too much too.
70 INNOGEN   Why, one that rode to 's execution, man,
Could never go so slow. I have heard of riding wagers
Where horses have been nimbler than the sands
That run i'th' clock's behalf.[9] But this is fool'ry.
Go bid my woman feign a sickness, say
75 She'll home to her father; and provide me presently°   *at once*
A riding-suit no costlier than would fit°   *suit*
A franklin's housewife.[1]
PISANIO   Madam, you're best° consider.   *you'd better*
INNOGEN   I see before° me, man. Nor here, nor here,   *straight ahead of*
Nor what ensues,[2] but have a fog in them
80 That I cannot look through. Away, I prithee,
Do as I bid thee. There's no more to say:
Accessible is none but Milford way.   *Exeunt*

3.3

Enter BELARIUS, [*followed by*] GUIDERIUS *and* ARVIRA-
GUS [*from a cave in the woods*][1]

BELARIUS   A goodly day not to keep house° with such   *stay home*
Whose roof 's as low as ours. Stoop, boys; this gate
Instructs you how t'adore the heavens, and bows you° *makes you bow down*
To a morning's holy office.° The gates of monarchs   *a morning prayer*
5 Are arched so high that giants may jet° through   *swagger*
And keep their impious turbans[2] on without
Good morrow to the sun. Hail, thou fair heaven!
We house i'th' rock, yet use thee not so hardly°   *badly*
As prouder livers° do.   *those living more grandly*
GUIDERIUS   Hail, heaven!
ARVIRAGUS   Hail, heaven!
10 BELARIUS   Now for our mountain sport. Up to yon hill,
Your legs are young; I'll tread these flats.° Consider,   *this plain*
When you above perceive me like a crow,
That it is place° which lessens and sets off,°   *position / enhances*
And you may then revolve° what tales I have told you   *consider*
15 Of courts, of princes, of the tricks in war;
That service is not service, so being done,
But being so allowed.[3] To apprehend thus
Draws us a profit from all things we see,
And often to our comfort shall we find
20 The sharded beetle[4] in a safer hold°   *refuge*

9. *than . . . behalf:* than the sands that run through the
hourglass.
1. The wife of a landowning farmer whose social status
was lower than that of the gentry. Early modern English
sumptuary codes prescribed specific fabrics and styles
of dress for people of different ranks.
2. *Nor here . . . ensues:* Neither (what is) on this side,
nor on that, nor what will happen (after Milford Haven
is reached).
3.3 Location: The cave of Belarius, Wales.
1. In his account of a performance of the play in 1611,
Simon Forman wrote of "the Cave in the woods" and of
the "woods" where Innogen's supposedly dead body
was laid. It is possible that some form of stage foliage

surrounded the entrance to Belarius's cave.
2. The idea of giants wearing turbans may come from
romances in which giants were often equated with
Saracens, or followers of Islam, who wore turbans and
were seen as impious enemies of Christians. See, for
example, the Giant Disdain in Edmund Spenser's *Faerie
Queene,* who "on his head a roll of linnen plight, / Like
to the Mores of Malabar" (6.7.43.5–6).
3. *That service . . . allowed:* That acts of service are not
acts of service simply by being done, but rather by being
acknowledged as such (by superiors).
4. The beetle who lives in dung. "Shard" means "patch
of dung."

Than is the full-winged eagle. O, this life
Is nobler than attending for a check,[5]
Richer than doing nothing for a bauble,
Prouder than rustling in unpaid-for silk;
25 Such gain the cap of him that makes 'em fine,
Yet keeps his book uncrossed.[6] No life to ours.

GUIDERIUS Out of your proof° you speak. We, poor unfledged,[7]   experience
Have never winged from view o'th' nest, nor know not
What air's from° home. Haply° this life is best,   away from / Perhaps
30 If quiet life be best; sweeter to you
That have a sharper known; well corresponding
With your stiff age, but unto us it is
A cell of ignorance, travelling abed,°   only while dreaming
A prison for a debtor, that not dares
To stride a limit.[8]

35 ARVIRAGUS [to BELARIUS] What should we speak of
When we are old as you? When we shall hear
The rain and wind beat dark December, how,
In this our pinching cave,[9] shall we discourse
The freezing hours away? We have seen nothing.
40 We are beastly:° subtle as the fox for prey,   like beasts
Like° warlike as the wolf for what we eat.   As
Our valour is to chase what flies; our cage
We make a choir, as doth the prisoned bird,
And sing our bondage freely.

BELARIUS   How you speak!
45 Did you but know the city's usuries,[1]
And felt them knowingly; the art o'th' court,
As hard to leave as keep,° whose top to climb   dwell in
Is certain falling, or so slipp'ry that
The fear's as bad as falling; the toil o'th' war,
50 A pain° that only seems to seek out danger   labor
I'th' name of fame and honour, which dies i'th' search
And hath as oft a sland'rous epitaph
As record of fair act; nay, many times
Doth ill deserve° by doing well; what's worse,   earn ill treatment
55 Must curtsy at the censure.[2] O boys, this story
The world may read in me. My body's marked
With Roman swords, and my report° was once   reputation
First with the best of note.° Cymbeline loved me,   the most renowned
And when a soldier was the theme my name
60 Was not far off. Then was I as a tree
Whose boughs did bend with fruit; but in one night
A storm or robbery, call it what you will,
Shook down my mellow hangings,° nay, my leaves,   ripe fruit
And left me bare to weather.

GUIDERIUS   Uncertain favour!
65 BELARIUS My fault being nothing, as I have told you oft,
But that two villains, whose false oaths prevailed

---

5. Than acting as a servant only to be rebuked.
6. *Such . . . uncrossed*: Such men win the deference
(shown by removing "the cap") of the tailor who is the
source of their grandeur, yet continue to have their debts
standing ("uncrossed") in the tailor's account book.
7. Lacking the feathers necessary for flight (spoken of
a young bird).

8. *that . . . limit*: who does not dare to leave a place of
sanctuary (for fear of being arrested).
9. Our confining cave; our cave that pinches us with
cold.
1. Financial practices whereby money was lent at
excessive or illegal rates of interest.
2. Must defer to the person who finds fault.

Before my perfect honour, swore to Cymbeline
I was confederate with the Romans. So
Followed my banishment, and this twenty years
70 This rock and these demesnes° have been my world,   *regions*
Where I have lived at honest freedom, paid
More pious debts to heaven than in all
The fore-end° of my time. But up to th' mountains!   *early days*
This is not hunter's language. He that strikes
75 The venison first shall be the lord o'th' feast,
To him the other two shall minister,
And we will fear no poison which attends°   *is always present*
In place of greater state. I'll meet you in the valleys.
                 Exeunt [GUIDERIUS *and* ARVIRAGUS]
How hard it is to hide the sparks of nature!
80 These boys know little they are sons to th' King,
Nor Cymbeline dreams that they are alive.
They think they are mine, and though trained up thus meanly°   *in a humble style*
I'th' cave wherein they bow, their thoughts do hit
The roofs of palaces, and nature prompts them
85 In simple and low things to prince it° much   *to act like princes*
Beyond the trick° of others. This Polydore,   *custom*
The heir of Cymbeline and Britain, who
The King his father called Guiderius—Jove,
When on my three-foot stool I sit and tell
90 The warlike feats I have done, his spirits fly out
Into my story: say 'Thus mine enemy fell,
And thus I set my foot on 's neck', even then
The princely blood flows in his cheek, he sweats,
Strains his young nerves,° and puts himself in posture   *sinews*
95 That acts my words. The younger brother, Cadwal,
Once Arviragus, in as like a figure°   *acting the part as aptly*
Strikes life into my speech, and shows much more
His own conceiving.°   *imagination*
     [*A hunting-horn sounds*]
                       Hark, the game is roused!
O Cymbeline, heaven and my conscience knows[3]
100 Thou didst unjustly banish me, whereon
At three and two years old I stole these babes,
Thinking to bar thee of succession as
Thou reft'st° me of my lands. Euriphile,   *deprived*
Thou wast their nurse; they took thee for their mother,
105 And every day do honour to her grave.
Myself, Belarius, that am Morgan called,
They take for natural father.
     [*A hunting-horn sounds*]
                    The game is up.°   *Exit*   *roused*

3.4

Enter PISANIO, *and* INNOGEN [*in a riding-suit*]
INNOGEN Thou told'st me when we came from horse° the place   *we dismounted*
Was near at hand. Ne'er longed my mother so

---

3. Editors have conjectured that lines 99–107 are either a non-Shakespearean addition or a section he added in revision. They stand apart from the rest of the speech, providing a hurried summary of information. Moreover, "the game is roused" (line 98) is repeated in "The game is up" (line 107). 3.4 Location: Wales, near Milford Haven.

To see me first as I have° now. Pisanio, man,   *do*
Where is Posthumus? What is in thy mind
5   That makes thee stare thus? Wherefore breaks that sigh
From th'inward of thee? One but painted thus
Would be interpreted a thing perplexed°   *bewildered*
Beyond self-explication. Put thyself
Into a haviour of less fear,[1] ere wildness°   *madness*
10 Vanquish my staider senses. What's the matter?
         [PISANIO *gives her a letter*]
Why tender'st thou that paper to me with
A look untender? If 't be summer news,
Smile to't before; if winterly, thou need'st
But keep that count'nance still. My husband's hand?
15 That drug-damned Italy[2] hath out-craftied° him,   *outwitted*
And he's at some hard point.° Speak, man. Thy tongue   *in some crisis*
May take off some extremity° which to read   *reduce the horror*
Would be even mortal° to me.   *fatal*
PISANIO   Please you read,
And you shall find me, wretched man, a thing
20 The most disdained of fortune.
INNOGEN *reads*   'Thy mistress, Pisanio, hath played the strumpet
in my bed, the testimonies whereof lies bleeding in me. I speak
not out of weak surmises but from proof as strong as my grief
and as certain as I expect my revenge. That part thou, Pisanio,
25 must act for me, if thy faith be not tainted with the breach of
hers. Let thine own hands take away her life. I shall give thee
opportunity at Milford Haven. She hath my letter for the purpose, where if thou fear to strike and to make me certain it is
done, thou art the pander to her dishonour and equally to me
30 disloyal.'
PISANIO [*aside*]   What shall I need to draw my sword? The paper
Hath cut her throat already. No, 'tis slander,
Whose edge is sharper than the sword, whose tongue
Outvenoms all the worms of Nile,[3] whose breath
35 Rides on the posting° winds and doth belie°   *speeding / deceive*
All corners of the world. Kings, queens, and states,
Maids, matrons, nay, the secrets of the grave
This viperous slander enters. [*To* INNOGEN] What cheer, madam?
INNOGEN   False to his bed? What is it to be false?
40 To lie in watch° there and to think on him?   *wakefulness*
To weep 'twixt clock and clock?° If sleep charge° nature,   *continually / overcome*
To break it with a fearful dream of° him   *a dream fearful for*
And cry myself awake? That's false to 's bed, is it?
PISANIO   Alas, good lady.
45 INNOGEN   I false? Thy conscience witness, Giacomo,
Thou didst accuse him of incontinency.
Thou then lookedst like a villain; now, methinks,
Thy favour's° good enough. Some jay° of Italy,   *appearance is / strumpet*
Whose mother was her painting,[4] hath betrayed him.

1. *Put . . . fear:* Adopt a less fearsome manner.
2. That country notorious for its poisons.
3. Alluding to the poisonous serpents associated with
Egypt's Nile River. Slander was often personified as a
woman with snakes issuing from her mouth. In early
modern England, women frequently brought cases in
the ecclesiastical courts against those who defamed or
slandered them; overwhelmingly, they were defending
their reputations against claims that they had committed a sexual offense and were unchaste. Pisanio rightly
assumes that Innogen is the victim of just such slanderous accusations.
4. Whose mother was entirely the product of her
cosmetics—i.e., who was false.

50 Poor I am stale,° a garment out of fashion,   *out of date; not new*
    And for I am richer than to hang by th' walls
    I must be ripped.[5] To pieces with me! O,
    Men's vows are women's traitors. All good seeming,°   *appearance*
    By thy revolt, O husband, shall be thought
55 Put on for villainy; not born where't grows,
    But worn a bait for ladies.
PISANIO   Good madam, hear me.
INNOGEN   True honest men being heard like false Aeneas[6]
    Were in his time thought false, and Sinon's[7] weeping
    Did scandal° many a holy tear, took pity   *discredit*
60 From most true wretchedness. So thou, Posthumus,
    Wilt lay the leaven on all proper men.[8]
    Goodly° and gallant shall be false and perjured   *Admirable*
    From thy great fail.° [*To* PISANIO] Come, fellow, be thou honest, *failure*
    Do thou thy master's bidding. When thou seest him,
65 A little witness° my obedience. Look,   *Briefly attest to*
    I draw the sword myself. Take it, and hit
    The innocent mansion of my love, my heart.
    Fear not, 'tis empty of all things but grief.
    Thy master is not there, who was indeed
70 The riches of it. Do his bidding; strike.
    Thou mayst be valiant in a better cause,
    But now thou seem'st a coward.
PISANIO   Hence, vile instrument,
    Thou shalt not damn my hand!
INNOGEN   Why, I must die,
    And if I do not by thy hand thou art
75 No servant of thy master's. Against self-slaughter
    There is a prohibition so divine
    That cravens° my weak hand. Come, here's my heart.   *makes cowardly*
    Something's afore't. Soft,° soft, we'll no defence;   *Gently*
    Obedient as the scabbard. What is here?
    [*She takes letters from her bosom*]
80 The scriptures° of the loyal Leonatus,   *writing; sacred texts*
    All turned to heresy? Away, away,
    Corrupters of my faith, you shall no more
    Be stomachers[9] to my heart. Thus may poor fools
    Believe false teachers. Though those that are betrayed
85 Do feel the treason sharply, yet the traitor
    Stands in worse case of woe. And thou, Posthumus,
    That didst set up° my disobedience 'gainst the King   *instigate*
    My father, and make me put into contempt the suits
    Of princely fellows,° shalt hereafter find   *those equal to my rank*
90 It is no act of common passage but
    A strain of rareness;[1] and I grieve myself
    To think, when thou shalt be disedged° by her   *surfeited*

5. *And . . . ripped:* And because I am too valuable to be discarded (by being hung up and forgotten about), I must be torn apart (so that the material may be reused).
6. Being heard as though they were as false as the hero of Virgil's *Aeneid,* Aeneas, who deserted his love, Dido, the Queen of Carthage.
7. Another deceitful character from the *Aeneid.* Sinon betrayed Troy to the Greeks by inducing the Trojans to let into the city a wooden horse in which Greek warriors were concealed.
8. Will corrupt the reputations of all faithful men (as a portion of inferior dough spoils the rest).
9. Ornamented chest coverings worn by women under their bodices.
1. *It . . . rareness:* My choice was no commonplace action but the sign of exceptional qualities.

That now thou tirest on,² how thy memory
Will then be panged by° me. [*To* PISANIO] Prithee, dispatch.   *pierced by thoughts of*
95 The lamb entreats the butcher. Where's thy knife?
Thou art too slow to do thy master's bidding
When I desire it too.
PISANIO   O gracious lady,
Since I received command to do this business
I have not slept one wink.
INNOGEN   Do't, and to bed, then.
PISANIO   I'll wake mine eyeballs out first.³
100 INNOGEN   Wherefore then
Didst undertake it? Why hast thou abused
So many miles with a pretence?—this place,
Mine action, and thine own? Our horses' labour,
The time inviting thee? The perturbed court,
105 For my being absent, whereunto I never
Purpose° return? Why hast thou gone so far   *Intend*
To be unbent⁴ when thou hast ta'en thy stand,°   *shooting position*
Th'elected° deer before thee?   *The chosen*
PISANIO   But to win time
To lose so bad employment, in the which
110 I have considered of a course. Good lady,
Hear me with patience.
INNOGEN   Talk thy tongue weary. Speak.
I have heard I am a strumpet, and mine ear,
Therein false struck, can take no greater wound,
Nor tent to bottom that.⁵ But speak.
PISANIO   Then, madam,
I thought you would not back° again.   *go back (to court)*
115 INNOGEN   Most like,
Bringing me here to kill me.
PISANIO   Not so, neither.
But if I were as wise as honest, then
My purpose would prove well. It cannot be
But that my master is abused.° Some villain,   *deceived*
120 Ay, and singular° in his art, hath done you both   *unmatched*
This cursèd injury.
INNOGEN   Some Roman courtesan.
PISANIO   No, on my life.
I'll give but notice you are dead, and send him
125 Some bloody sign of it, for 'tis commanded
I should do so. You shall be missed at court,
And that will well confirm it.
INNOGEN   Why, good fellow,
What shall I do the while, where bide, how live,
Or in my life what comfort when I am
Dead to my husband?
130 PISANIO   If you'll back° to th' court—   *return*
INNOGEN   No court, no father, nor no more ado
With that harsh, churlish, noble, simple nothing,

---

2. Whom now you feed on (in the manner of a bird of   4. To be with bow unready.
prey).   5. Nor probe ("tent") the depths of that wound.
3. I'll stay awake until my eyes drop out before I'll do it.

That Cloten, whose love suit hath been to me
As fearful as a siege.

PISANIO   If not at court,
Then not in Britain must you bide.

135 INNOGEN   Where then?
Hath Britain all the sun that shines? Day, night,
Are they not but° in Britain? I'th' world's volume   *Do they exist only*
Our Britain seems as of it but not in't,[6]
In a great pool a swan's nest. Prithee, think
There's livers out of Britain.[7]

140 PISANIO   I am most glad
You think of other place. Th'ambassador,
Lucius the Roman, comes to Milford Haven
Tomorrow. Now if you could wear a mind
Dark° as your fortune is, and but disguise   *Secret; dismal*
145 That which t'appear itself must not yet be
But by self-danger,[8] you should tread a course
Pretty and full of view;[9] yea, haply° near   *perhaps*
The residence of Posthumus; so nigh, at least,
That though his actions were not visible, yet
150 Report should render° him hourly to your ear   *describe*
As truly as he moves.

INNOGEN   O, for such means,°   *a method of access*
Though peril° to my modesty, not death on't,°   *a danger / of it*
I would adventure.°   *take the risk*

PISANIO   Well then, here's the point:
You must forget to be a woman; change
155 Command[1] into obedience, fear and niceness°—   *daintiness*
The handmaids of all women, or more truly
Woman it pretty self[2]—into a waggish° courage,   *mischievous*
Ready in gibes, quick-answered, saucy and
As quarrelous° as the weasel. Nay, you must   *quarrelsome*
160 Forget that rarest treasure of your cheek,
Exposing it[3]—but O, the harder heart![4]—
Alack, no remedy—to the greedy touch
Of common-kissing Titan,[5] and forget
Your laboursome and dainty trims° wherein   *apparel*
Your made great Juno° angry.   *queen of the gods*

165 INNOGEN   Nay, be brief.
I see into thy end,° and am almost   *purpose*
A man already.

PISANIO   First, make yourself but like one.
Forethinking° this, I have already fit°—   *Anticipating / at hand*
'Tis in my cloak-bag—doublet, hat, hose, all
170 That answer to° them. Would you in their serving,[6]   *go with*
And with what imitation you can borrow

---

6. Seems part of the world, yet distinct. The metaphor is of the world as a book in which Britain is a page, but one not bound into the volume.
7. *Prithee . . . Britain:* I pray you, believe that there are people living outside Britain.
8. *and but . . . self-danger:* and simply disguise your appearance, which if it were now to show itself for what it is would put you in danger.
9. Advantageous and with good prospects.
1. The commanding ways of a princess.
2. *or . . . self:* or, more accurately, womanhood itself.

3. In early modern England, English women of the upper classes shielded themselves from the sun and cultivated pale complexions, the "treasure" of their cheeks.
4. The "harder heart" probably refers to Innogen, who must harden her heart even as she tans her skin. It may refer to Posthumus's cruelty to Innogen or to Pisanio's cruelty in forcing these harsh facts upon Innogen.
5. The sun god who shines on ("kisses") everyone alike.
6. If you would with their help.

From youth of such a season,° fore° noble Lucius   *an age / before*
Present yourself, desire his service,° tell him   *to serve him*
Wherein you're happy[7]—which will make him know°   *convince him*
175 If that his head have ear in music—doubtless
With joy he will embrace you, for he's honourable,
And, doubling that, most holy. Your means° abroad—   *As for means of support*
You have me, rich, and I will never fail
Beginning nor supplyment.[8]

INNOGEN   Thou art all the comfort
180 The gods will diet° me with. Prithee away.   *feed*
There's more to be considered, but we'll even°   *keep pace with*
All that good time will give us. This attempt
I am soldier to,° and will abide it with   *committed to*
A prince's courage. Away, I prithee.

185 PISANIO   Well, madam, we must take a short farewell
Lest, being missed, I be suspected of
Your carriage° from the court. My noble mistress,   *removal*
Here is a box. I had it from the Queen.
What's in't is precious. If you are sick at sea
190 Or stomach-qualmed° at land, a dram° of this   *nauseous / tiny portion*
Will drive away distemper. To some shade,
And fit you to your manhood.[9] May the gods
Direct you to the best.

INNOGEN   Amen. I thank thee. *Exeunt* [*severally*]

3.5

[*Flourish.*] *Enter* CYMBELINE, [*the*] QUEEN, CLOTEN,
    LUCIUS, *and lords*
CYMBELINE [*to* LUCIUS]   Thus far, and so farewell.
LUCIUS   Thanks, royal sir.
My emperor hath wrote I must from hence;
And am right sorry that I must report ye
My master's enemy.
CYMBELINE   Our subjects, sir,
5 Will not endure his yoke, and for ourself
To show less sovereignty than they must needs
Appear unkinglike.
LUCIUS   So, sir, I desire of you
A conduct° over land to Milford Haven.   *An escort*
[*To the* QUEEN] Madam, all joy befall your grace, [*to* CLOTEN] and you.
10 CYMBELINE   My lords, you are appointed for that office.°   *duty*
The due of honour in no point omit.
So farewell, noble Lucius.
LUCIUS   Your hand, my lord.
CLOTEN   Receive it friendly, but from this time forth
I wear it as your enemy.
LUCIUS   Sir, the event°   *outcome*
15 Is yet to name the winner. Fare you well.
CYMBELINE   Leave not the worthy Lucius, good my lords,
Till he have crossed the Severn.[1] Happiness.
                        Exeunt LUCIUS [*and lords*]

7. In which things you are skilled.
8. In providing the initial amount nor in supplement-
ing it.
9. Dress yourself in accordance with your (pretended)
manhood.
3.5 Location: Cymbeline's court, Britain.
1. River flowing between Wales and England.

QUEEN   He goes hence frowning, but it honours us
That we have given him cause.

CLOTEN   'Tis all the better.

20 Your valiant Britons have their wishes in it.

CYMBELINE   Lucius hath wrote already to the Emperor
How it goes here. It fits° us therefore ripely°   *befits / quickly*
Our chariots and our horsemen be in readiness.
The powers° that he already hath in Gallia   *military forces*

25 Will soon be drawn to head,[2] from whence he moves
His war for Britain.

QUEEN   'Tis not sleepy business,
But must be looked to speedily and strongly.

CYMBELINE   Our expectation that it would be thus
Hath made us forward.° But, my gentle queen,   *well prepared*

30 Where is our daughter? She hath not appeared
Before the Roman, nor to us hath tendered
The duty of the day. She looks us° like   *seems to us*
A thing more made of malice than of duty.
We have noted it. Call her before us, for
We have been too slight in sufferance.°   [*Exit one or more*]   *mild in our tolerance*

35 QUEEN   Royal sir,
Since the exile of Posthumus most retired
Hath her life been, the cure whereof, my lord,
'Tis time must do. Beseech your majesty
Forbear sharp speeches to her. She's a lady

40 So tender of° rebukes that words are strokes,   *sensitive to*
And strokes death to her.

Enter a MESSENGER

CYMBELINE   Where is she, sir? How
Can her contempt be answered?

MESSENGER   Please you, sir,
Her chambers are all locked, and there's no answer
That will be given to th' loud'st of noise we make.

45 QUEEN   My lord, when last I went to visit her
She prayed me to excuse her keeping close,°   *staying confined*
Whereto constrained by her infirmity,
She should that duty leave unpaid to you
Which daily she was bound to proffer. This

50 She wished me to make known, but our great court°   *court business*
Made me to blame° in memory.   *at fault*

CYMBELINE   Her doors locked?
Not seen of late? Grant heavens that which I
Fear prove false.   *Exit*

QUEEN   Son, I say, follow the King.

CLOTEN   That man of hers, Pisanio, her old servant,
I have not seen these two days.

55 QUEEN   Go, look after. *Exit* [CLOTEN]
Pisanio, thou that stand'st so for° Posthumus!   *so much takes the part of*
He hath a drug of mine. I pray his absence
Proceed by° swallowing that, for he believes   *Results from*
It is a thing most precious. But for her,

60 Where is she gone? Haply° despair hath seized her,   *Perhaps*
Or, winged with fervour of her love, she's flown

2. Be gathered to their full strength.

To her desired Posthumus. Gone she is
To death or to dishonour, and my end
Can make good use of either. She being down,
65   I have the placing of the British crown.
          Enter CLOTEN
How now, my son?
CLOTEN   'Tis certain she is fled.
Go in and cheer the King. He rages, none
Dare come about him.
QUEEN   All the better. May
This night forestall him of the coming day.[3]   *Exit*
70 CLOTEN   I love and hate her. For° she's fair and royal,   *Because*
And that she hath all courtly parts° more exquisite   *features*
Than lady, ladies, woman—from every one
The best she hath, and she, of all compounded,
Outsells° them all—I love her therefore; but   *Exceeds in value*
75 Disdaining me, and throwing favours on
The low Posthumus, slanders° so her judgement   *discredits*
That what's else° rare is choked; and in that point   *otherwise*
I will conclude to hate her, nay, indeed,
To be revenged upon her. For when fools
Shall—
          Enter PISANIO
80   Who is here? What, are you packing,° sirrah?[4]   *scheming*
Come hither. Ah, you precious pander! Villain,
Where is thy lady? In a word, or else
Thou art straightway with the fiends.
PISANIO   O good my lord!
CLOTEN   Where is thy lady?—or, by Jupiter,
85 I will not ask again. Close° villain,   *Secretive*
I'll have this secret from thy tongue or rip
Thy heart to find it. Is she with Posthumus,
From whose so many weights° of baseness cannot   *measures*
A dram of worth be drawn?
PISANIO   Alas, my lord,
90 How can she be with him? When was she missed?
He is in Rome.
CLOTEN   Where is she, sir? Come nearer.°   *Be more precise*
No farther halting. Satisfy me home°   *completely*
What is become of her.
PISANIO   O my all-worthy lord!
95 CLOTEN   All-worthy villain,
Discover° where thy mistress is at once,   *Reveal*
At the next word. No more of 'worthy lord'.
Speak, or thy silence on the instant is
Thy condemnation and thy death.
PISANIO   Then, sir,
100 This paper is the history of my knowledge
Touching her flight.
       [*He gives* CLOTEN *a letter*]
CLOTEN   Let's see't. I will pursue her
Even to Augustus' throne.
PISANIO [*aside*]   Or° this or perish.   *Either*

---

3. That is, kill him. *forestall:* deprive.   4. Fellow (a common form of address to a social inferior).

She's far enough, and what he learns by this
May prove his travel,[5] not her danger.

CLOTEN   Hum!

105 PISANIO [aside]   I'll write to my lord she's dead. O Innogen,
Safe mayst thou wander, safe return again!

CLOTEN   Sirrah, is this letter true?

PISANIO   Sir, as I think.

CLOTEN   It is Posthumus' hand; I know't. Sirrah, if thou wouldst
not be a villain but do me true service, undergo° those employ-   undertake
110 ments wherein I should have cause to use thee with a serious
industry—that is, what villainy soe'er I bid thee do, to perform
it directly and truly—I would think thee an honest man. Thou
shouldst neither want° my means for thy relief nor my voice for   find lacking
thy preferment.°   advancement

115 PISANIO   Well, my good lord.

CLOTEN   Wilt thou serve me? For since patiently and constantly
thou hast stuck to the bare fortune of that beggar Posthumus,
thou canst not in the course of gratitude but be a diligent follower of mine. Wilt thou serve me?

120 PISANIO   Sir, I will.

CLOTEN   Give me thy hand. Here's my purse. Hast any of thy
late° master's garments in thy possession?   former

PISANIO   I have, my lord, at my lodging the same suit he wore
when he took leave of my lady and mistress.

125 CLOTEN   The first service thou dost me, fetch that suit hither.
Let it be thy first service. Go.

PISANIO   I shall, my lord.   Exit

CLOTEN   Meet thee at Milford Haven! I forgot to ask him one
thing;[6] I'll remember't anon. Even there, thou villain Posthu-
130 mus, will I kill thee. I would these garments were come. She
said upon a time—the bitterness of it I now belch from my
heart—that she held the very garment of Posthumus in more
respect than my noble and natural person, together with the
adornment of my qualities. With that suit upon my back will I
135 ravish her—first kill him, and in her eyes; there shall she see
my valour, which will then be a torment to her contempt. He
on the ground, my speech of insultment° ended on his dead   contemptuous triumph
body, and when my lust hath dined—which, as I say, to vex her
I will execute in the clothes that she so praised—to the court
140 I'll knock° her back, foot° her home again. She hath despised   beat / kick
me rejoicingly, and I'll be merry in my revenge.

                Enter PISANIO [with Posthumus' suit]
Be those the garments?

PISANIO   Ay, my noble lord.

CLOTEN   How long is't since she went to Milford Haven?

PISANIO   She can scarce be there yet.

145 CLOTEN   Bring this apparel to my chamber. That is the second
thing that I have commanded thee. The third is that thou wilt
be a voluntary mute to° my design. Be but duteous, and true   be quiet about
preferment shall tender itself to thee. My revenge is now at
Milford. Would I had wings to follow it. Come, and be true.
                                                                        Exit

---

5. May turn out to be merely a long journey for him.
6. The "one thing" may be how long a time has passed

since Innogen set out for Milford Haven (see Cloten's
question at line 143).

150 PISANIO   Thou bidd'st me to my loss,° for true to thee   *perdition*
       Were to prove false, which I will never be
       To him that is most true. To Milford go,
       And find not her whom thou pursuest. Flow, flow,
       You heavenly blessings, on her. This fool's speed
155   Be crossed° with slowness; labour be his meed.°   *Exit*   *thwarted / reward*

3.6

Enter INNOGEN [*dressed as a man, before the cave*]

INNOGEN   I see a man's life is a tedious one.
       I have tired myself, and for two nights together
       Have made the ground my bed. I should be sick,
       But that my resolution helps me. Milford,
5   When from the mountain-top Pisanio showed thee,
       Thou wast within a ken.° O Jove, I think   *within sight*
       Foundations¹ fly the wretched—such, I mean,
       Where they should be relieved.² Two beggars told me
       I could not miss my way. Will poor folks lie,
10   That have afflictions on them, knowing 'tis
       A punishment or trial?³ Yes. No wonder,
       When rich ones scarce tell true. To lapse in fullness°   *To do wrong when rich*
       Is sorer° than to lie for need, and falsehood   *worse*
       Is worse in kings than beggars. My dear lord,
15   Thou art one o'th' false ones. Now I think on thee
       My hunger's gone, but even before° I was   *just a moment ago*
       At point° to sink for° food. But what is this?   *Ready / for want of*
       Here is a path to't. 'Tis some savage hold.°   *refuge*
       I were best not call; I dare not call; yet famine,
20   Ere clean° it o'erthrow nature, makes it valiant.   *completely*
       Plenty and peace breeds cowards, hardness° ever   *hardship*
       Of hardiness is mother. Ho! Who's here?
       If anything that's civil, speak; if savage,
       Take or lend.⁴ Ho! No answer? Then I'll enter.
25   Best draw my sword, and if mine enemy
       But fear the sword like me he'll scarcely look on't.
       Such a foe, good heavens!⁵   *Exit* [*into the cave*]

Enter BELARIUS, GUIDERIUS, *and* ARVIRAGUS⁶

BELARIUS   You, Polydore, have proved best woodman° and   *hunter*
       Are master of the feast. Cadwal and I
30   Will play the cook and servant; 'tis our match.°   *bargain*
       The sweat of industry would dry and die
       But for the end it works to. Come, our stomachs
       Will make what's homely° savoury. Weariness   *plain*
       Can snore upon the flint when resty° sloth   *lazy*
35   Finds the down pillow hard. Now peace be here,
       Poor house, that keep'st thyself.°   *goes untended*

GUIDERIUS   I am throughly weary.

ARVIRAGUS   I am weak with toil yet strong in appetite.

3.6 Location: Before the cave of Belarius, Wales.
1. Certainties; charitable institutions.
2. *such . . . relieved:* such certainties, I mean, as should give mental relief to the wretched; such charitable institutions as should give physical relief (food and rest) to the wretched.

3. *knowing . . . trial:* knowing that poverty is a punishment or a test of one's virtue.
4. Take everything I have, or help me.
5. May it please heaven I meet such a timid foe.
6. F marks a new scene at this point, but the action is continuous.

GUIDERIUS   There is cold meat i'th' cave. We'll browse° on that   nibble
    Whilst what we have killed be cooked.
BELARIUS [*looking into the cave*]   Stay, come not in.
40   But° that it eats our victuals I should think   *But for the fact*
    Here were a fairy.
GUIDERIUS   What's the matter, sir?
BELARIUS   By Jupiter, an angel—or, if not,
    An earthly paragon. Behold divineness
    No elder than a boy.
        Enter INNOGEN [*from the cave, dressed as a man*]
INNOGEN   Good masters, harm me not.
45   Before I entered here I called, and thought°   *intended*
    To have begged or bought what I have took. Good truth,
    I have stol'n naught, nor would not, though I had found
    Gold strewed i'th' floor. Here's money for my meat.
    I would have left it on the board so° soon   *as*
50   As I had made my meal, and parted
    With prayers for the provider.
GUIDERIUS   Money, youth?
ARVIRAGUS   All gold and silver rather turn to dirt,
    As 'tis no better reckoned but of° those   *better thought of but by*
    Who worship dirty gods.
INNOGEN   I see you're angry.
55   Know, if you kill me for my fault, I should
    Have died had I not made it.
BELARIUS   Whither bound?
INNOGEN   To Milford Haven.
BELARIUS   What's your name?
INNOGEN   Fidele,[7] sir. I have a kinsman who
    Is bound for Italy. He embarked at Milford,
60   To whom being going, almost spent with hunger,
    I am fall'n in° this offence.   *into*
BELARIUS   Prithee, fair youth,
    Think us no churls,° nor measure our good minds   *base fellows*
    By this rude° place we live in. Well encountered.   *wild*
    'Tis almost night. You shall have better cheer°   *provisions*
65   Ere you depart, and thanks to° stay and eat it.   *our gratitude if you*
    Boys, bid him welcome.
GUIDERIUS   Were you a woman, youth,
    I should woo hard but be° your groom in honesty,   *rather than fail to be*
    Ay, bid for you as I'd buy.[8]
ARVIRAGUS   I'll make't my comfort
    He is a man, I'll love him as my brother.
70   [*To* INNOGEN] And such a welcome as I'd give to him
    After long absence, such is yours. Most welcome.
    Be sprightly,° for you fall 'mongst friends.   *cheerful*
INNOGEN   'Mongst friends
    If brothers.[9] [*Aside*] Would it had been so that they
    Had been my father's sons. Then had my price°   *worth*

---

7. In French and Italian, the name means "faithful one."
8. Yes, make an offer for you with every intent to buy
(that is, to marry you).
9. *'Mongst . . . brothers:* Yes, certainly I am among
friends, if you claim me as a brother.

75   Been less, and so more equal ballasting°   *equal in weight*
         To thee, Posthumus.
                [The three men speak apart]
BELARIUS   He wrings° at some distress.   *twists in pain*
GUIDERIUS   Would I could free't.°   *remove it*
ARVIRAGUS   Or I, whate'er it be,
         What° pain it cost, what danger. Gods!   *Whatever*
BELARIUS   Hark, boys.
                [They whisper]
INNOGEN *[aside]*   Great men
80   That had a court no bigger than this cave,
         That did attend° themselves and had the virtue   *wait on*
         Which their own conscience sealed° them, laying by°   *assured / disregarding*
         That nothing-gift of differing multitudes,[1]
         Could not outpeer° these twain. Pardon me, gods,   *surpass*
85   I'd change my sex to be companion with them,
         Since Leonatus' false.
BELARIUS   It shall be so.
         Boys, we'll go dress our hunt.° Fair youth, come in.   *game*
         Discourse is heavy, fasting.[2] When we have supped
         We'll mannerly demand thee of thy story,
         So far as thou wilt speak it.
90 GUIDERIUS   Pray draw near.
ARVIRAGUS   The night to th' owl and morn to th' lark less welcome.
INNOGEN   Thanks, sir.
ARVIRAGUS   I pray draw near.   *Exeunt [into the cave]*

                            3.7
            Enter two Roman SENATORS, *and* TRIBUNES
FIRST SENATOR   This is the tenor of the Emperor's writ:
         That since the common men are now in action
         'Gainst the Pannonians and Dalmatians,
         And that the legions now in Gallia are
5   Full weak° to undertake our wars against   *Too weak*
         The fall'n-off° Britons, that we do incite   *rebelling*
         The gentry to this business. He creates
         Lucius pro-consul,[1] and to you the tribunes,
         For this immediate levy, he commends°   *entrusts*
10   His absolute commission.° Long live Caesar!   *authority*
A TRIBUNE   Is Lucius general of the forces?
SECOND SENATOR   Ay.
A TRIBUNE   Remaining now in Gallia?
FIRST SENATOR   With those legions
         Which I have spoke of, whereunto your levy
         Must be supplyant.° The words of your commission   *auxiliary*
15   Will tie you to° the numbers and the time   *indicate to you*
         Of their dispatch.
A TRIBUNE   We will discharge our duty.   *Exeunt*

---

1. That worthless gift offered by a public that cannot   3.7 Location: A public place, Rome.
agree on anything.   1. One who acted as governor or military commander
2. Conversation is difficult when one is without food.   in a Roman province.

4.1

Enter CLOTEN [*in Posthumus' suit*]

CLOTEN   I am near to th' place where they should meet, if
Pisanio have mapped it truly. How fit° his garments serve me!   *aptly*
Why should his mistress, who was made by him that made the
tailor, not be fit° too?—the rather—saving reverence of the   *apt; sexually compatible*
5   word[1]—for 'tis said a woman's fitness comes by fits.[2] Therein I
must play the workman. I dare speak it to myself, for it is not
vainglory for a man and his glass° to confer in his own cham-   *mirror*
ber. I mean the lines of my body are as well drawn as his: no
less young, more strong, not beneath him in fortunes, beyond
10   him in the advantage of the time,[3] above him in birth, alike
conversant in general services, and more remarkable in single
oppositions.[4] Yet this imperceiverant° thing loves him in my   *stupid*
despite.° What mortality[5] is! Posthumus, thy head which now   *to spite me*
is growing upon thy shoulders shall within this hour be off, thy
15   mistress enforced,° thy garments cut to pieces before thy face;   *raped*
and all this done, spurn her home to her father, who may haply
be a little angry for my so rough usage; but my mother, having
power of° his testiness, shall turn all into my commendations.   *over*
My horse is tied up safe. Out, sword, and to a sore purpose!
20   Fortune, put them into my hand. This is the very description
of their meeting-place, and the fellow dares not deceive me.
                                                                    Exit

4.2

Enter BELARIUS, GUIDERIUS, ARVIRAGUS, *and* INNOGEN
[*dressed as a man,*] *from the cave*

BELARIUS [*to* INNOGEN]   You are not well. Remain here in the cave.
We'll come to you from hunting.
ARVIRAGUS [*to* INNOGEN]   Brother, stay here.
Are we not brothers?
INNOGEN   So man and man should be,
But clay and clay[1] differs in dignity,°   *social position*
5   Whose dust[2] is both alike. I am very sick.
GUIDERIUS [*to* BELARIUS *and* ARVIRAGUS]   Go you to hunting.
I'll abide with him.
INNOGEN   So sick I am not, yet I am not well;
But not so citizen a wanton as
To seem to die ere sick.[3] So please you, leave me.
10   Stick to your journal course.° The breach of custom   *daily routine*
Is breach of all. I am ill, but your being by me
Cannot amend me. Society is no comfort
To one not sociable. I am not very sick,
Since I can reason of° it. Pray you, trust me here.   *talk about*
15   I'll rob none but myself; and let me die,
Stealing so poorly.[4]

GUIDERIUS   I love thee: I have spoke it;
How much the quantity,° the weight as much,   *As greatly*
As I do love my father.
BELARIUS   What, how, how?
ARVIRAGUS   If it be sin to say so, sir, I yoke me°   *I share*
20 In my good brother's fault. I know not why
I love this youth, and I have heard you say
Love's reason's without reason. The bier⁵ at door
And a demand who is't shall die, I'd say
'My father, not this youth'.
BELARIUS [*aside*]   O noble strain!°   *inherited character*
25 O worthiness of nature, breed of greatness!
Cowards father cowards, and base things sire base.
Nature hath meal and bran,° contempt and grace.   *flour and husks*
I'm not their father, yet who this should be
Doth miracle itself, loved before me.⁶
[*Aloud*] 'Tis the ninth hour o'th' morn.
30 ARVIRAGUS [*to* INNOGEN]   Brother, farewell.
INNOGEN   I wish ye sport.
ARVIRAGUS   You health.—So please you, sir.
INNOGEN [*aside*]   These are kind creatures. Gods, what lies I have heard!
Our courtiers say all's savage but at court.
Experience, O thou disprov'st report!
35 Th'imperious° seas breeds monsters; for the dish   *imperial*
Poor tributary rivers as sweet fish.⁷
I am sick still, heart-sick. Pisanio,
I'll now taste of thy drug.
[*She swallows the drug. The men speak apart*]
GUIDERIUS   I could not stir him.
He said he was gentle° but unfortunate,   *a gentleman by birth*
40 Dishonestly afflicted but yet honest.
ARVIRAGUS   Thus did he answer me, yet said hereafter
I might know more.
BELARIUS   To th' field, to th' field!
[*To* INNOGEN] We'll leave you for this time. Go in and rest.
ARVIRAGUS [*to* INNOGEN]   We'll not be long away.
BELARIUS [*to* INNOGEN]   Pray be not sick,
For you must be our housewife.
45 INNOGEN   Well or ill,
I am bound° to you.   *Exit*   *indebted*
BELARIUS   And shalt be ever.
This youth, howe'er distressed, appears° hath had   *apparently*
Good ancestors.
ARVIRAGUS   How angel-like he sings!
50 GUIDERIUS   But his neat° cookery!   *dainty*
BELARIUS⁸   He cut our roots in characters,°   *alphabet shapes*
And sauced our broths as° Juno had been sick   *as if*
And he her dieter.°   *cook*
ARVIRAGUS   Nobly he yokes

5. The litter, or platform, on which a corpse was carried to the grave.
6. *yet . . . me*: yet who this may be who is loved more than me is a source of great wonder.
7. *for . . . fish*: but when it comes to eating, small tributaries breed fish as sweet as does the sea.
8. F assigns this speech to Arviragus, but he has the next one as well. One editorial solution has been to assign the lines to Guiderius as an extension of his prior speech. Another, as here, is to give the lines to Belarius, who thus joins his adopted sons in praising Innogen/Fidele.

A smiling with a sigh, as if the sigh
55 Was that° it was for not being such a smile;   *Was what*
The smile mocking the sigh that° it would fly   *because*
From so divine a temple to commix°   *join*
With winds that sailors rail at.
GUIDERIUS   I do note
That grief and patience, rooted in him both,
Mingle their spurs° together.   *roots*
60 ARVIRAGUS   Grow patience,
And let the stinking elder,⁹ grief, untwine
His perishing° root with° the increasing vine.   *deadly / from*
BELARIUS   It is great morning.° Come away. Who's there?   *full daylight*

Enter CLOTEN [*in Posthumus' suit*]

CLOTEN   I cannot find those runagates.° That villain   *runaways; fugitives*
Hath mocked me. I am faint.
65 BELARIUS [*aside to* ARVIRAGUS *and* GUIDERIUS]   'Those runagates'?
Means he not us? I partly know him; 'tis
Cloten, the son o'th' Queen. I fear some ambush.
I saw him not these many years, and yet
I know 'tis he. We are held as outlaws. Hence!
GUIDERIUS [*aside to* ARVIRAGUS *and* BELARIUS]   He is but one.
70 You and my brother search
What companies° are near. Pray you, away.   *companions*
Let me alone with him.   [*Exeunt* ARVIRAGUS *and* BELARIUS]
CLOTEN   Soft, what are you
That fly me thus? Some villain mountaineers?°   *lowborn mountain people*
I have heard of such. What slave art thou?
GUIDERIUS   A thing
75 More slavish did I ne'er than answering
A slave without a knock.°   *without striking him*
CLOTEN   Thou art a robber,
A law-breaker, a villain. Yield thee, thief.
GUIDERIUS   To who? To thee? What art thou? Have not I
An arm as big as thine, a heart as big?
80 Thy words, I grant, are bigger, for I wear not
My dagger in my mouth.¹ Say what thou art,
Why I should yield to thee.
CLOTEN   Thou villain base,
Know'st me not by my clothes?
GUIDERIUS   No, nor thy tailor, rascal,
Who is thy grandfather. He made those clothes,
Which, as it seems, make thee.²
85 CLOTEN   Thou precious varlet,°   *absolute scoundrel*
My tailor made them not.
GUIDERIUS   Hence, then, and thank
The man that gave them thee. Thou art some fool.
I am loath to beat thee.
CLOTEN   Thou injurious° thief,   *insulting*
Hear but my name and tremble.
GUIDERIUS   What's thy name?

---

9. A tree with strong-smelling leaves and flowers on
which Judas, the disciple who betrayed Jesus, is said to
have hanged himself.

1. *for . . . mouth:* for I don't let words substitute for
weapons.
2. Alluding to the proverb "The tailor makes the man."

90 CLOTEN Cloten, thou villain.

GUIDERIUS Cloten, thou double villain, be thy name,
I cannot tremble at it. Were it toad or adder, spider,
'Twould move me sooner.

CLOTEN   To thy further fear,
Nay, to thy mere confusion,° thou shalt know   *absolute destruction*
I am son to th' Queen.

95 GUIDERIUS   I am sorry for't, not seeming
So worthy as thy birth.

CLOTEN   Art not afeard?

GUIDERIUS Those that I reverence, those I fear, the wise.
At fools I laugh, not fear them.

CLOTEN   Die the death.
When I have slain thee with my proper° hand   *own*
100 I'll follow those that even now fled hence,
And on the gates of Lud's town° set your heads.[3]   *London*
Yield, rustic mountaineer.   *Fight and exeunt*

          Enter BELARIUS *and* ARVIRAGUS

BELARIUS   No company's abroad?°   *about*

ARVIRAGUS None in the world. You did mistake him, sure.

BELARIUS I cannot tell. Long is it since I saw him,
105 But time hath nothing blurred those lines of favour°   *facial features*
Which then he wore. The snatches° in his voice   *hesitations*
And burst° of speaking were as his. I am absolute°   *sudden rush / sure*
'Twas very Cloten.°   *Cloten himself*

ARVIRAGUS   In this place we left them.
I wish my brother make good time with him,[4]
You say he is so fell.°   *fierce*

110 BELARIUS   Being scarce made up,°   *barely full-grown*
I mean to man, he had not apprehension°   *had no consciousness*
Of roaring terrors; for defect of judgement
Is oft the cause of fear.[5]

          Enter GUIDERIUS [*with Cloten's head*]
                    But see, thy brother.

GUIDERIUS This Cloten was a fool, an empty purse,
115 There was no money in't. Not Hercules[6]
Could have knocked out his brains, for he had none.
Yet I not doing this,° the fool had borne   *had I not done this*
My head as I do his.

BELARIUS   What hast thou done?

GUIDERIUS I am perfect° what: cut off one Cloten's head,   *certain*
120 Son to the Queen after his own report,
Who called me traitor, mountaineer, and swore
With his own single hand he'd take us in,°   *capture us*
Displace our heads where—thanks, ye gods—they grow,
And set them on Lud's town.

BELARIUS   We are all undone.

125 GUIDERIUS Why, worthy father, what have we to lose
But that° he swore to take, our lives? The law   *what*

---

3. The heads of criminals were frequently displayed on poles on London Bridge and other places throughout the city.
4. I hope my brother is successful with him.
5. *for . . . fear*: an obscure passage. It may mean that Cloten's faulty judgment, which led him to know no fear, caused fear in others. A less likely meaning is that while defects in judgment cause fear, Cloten knew no fear because he had absolutely no judgment, being utterly witless.
6. Mythical hero of enormous strength.

Protects not us: then why should we be tender
To let⁷ an arrogant piece of flesh threat us,
Play judge and executioner all himself,
130 For° we do fear the law? What company   *Because*
Discover you abroad?⁸

BELARIUS   No single soul
Can we set eye on, but in all safe reason
He must have some attendants. Though his humour°   *disposition*
Was nothing but mutation,° ay, and that   *changeableness*
135 From one bad thing to worse, not° frenzy,   *neither*
Not° absolute madness, could so far have raved°   *Nor / made him mad enough*
To bring him here alone. Although perhaps
It may be heard at court that such as we
Cave° here, hunt here, are outlaws, and in time   *Live in a cave*
140 May make some stronger head,° the which he hearing—   *raise a stronger force*
As it is like him—might break out, and swear
He'd fetch us in, yet is't not probable
To come° alone, either he so undertaking,   *That he would come*
Or they so suffering.⁹ Then on good ground we fear
145 If we do fear this body hath a tail°   *rear end; followers*
More perilous than the head.

ARVIRAGUS   Let ord'nance°   *destiny*
Come as the gods foresay° it; howsoe'er,   *predict*
My brother hath done well.

BELARIUS   I had no mind
To hunt this day. The boy Fidele's sickness
Did make my way long forth.°   *my journey tedious*
150 GUIDERIUS   With his own sword,
Which he did wave against my throat, I have ta'en
His head from him. I'll throw't into the creek
Behind our rock, and let it to the sea
And tell the fishes he's the Queen's son, Cloten.
That's all I reck.°   *Exit [with Cloten's head]*   *care*
155 BELARIUS   I fear 'twill be revenged.
Would, Polydore, thou hadst not done't, though valour
Becomes thee well enough.

ARVIRAGUS   Would I had done't,
So the revenge alone pursued me.° Polydore,   *only pursued me*
I love thee brotherly, but envy much
160 Thou hast robbed me of this deed. I would revenges
That possible strength might meet would seek us through
And put us to our answer.¹

BELARIUS   Well, 'tis done.
We'll hunt no more today, nor seek for danger
Where there's no profit. I prithee, to our rock.
165 You and Fidele play the cooks. I'll stay
Till hasty Polydore return, and bring him
To dinner presently.

ARVIRAGUS   Poor sick Fidele!
I'll willingly to him. To gain° his colour   *restore*

---

7. *be tender / To let:* be so meek as to allow.
8. What companions (of Cloten) did you find hereabouts?
9. *either . . . suffering:* either that he would undertake

it or that they would allow it.
1. *I would . . . answer:* I wish that revenges equal to all
the power that we might muster would find us out and
test our mettle.

I'd let a parish of such Clotens blood,[2]
And praise myself for charity.   *Exit [into the cave]*

170 BELARIUS   O thou goddess,
Thou divine Nature, how thyself thou blazon'st[3]
In these two princely boys! They are as gentle
As zephyrs° blowing below the violet,   *breezes from the west*
Not wagging his sweet head; and yet as rough,°   *violent*
175 Their royal blood enchafed,° as the rud'st wind   *enflamed*
That by the top doth take the mountain pine
And make him stoop to th' vale. 'Tis wonder
That an invisible instinct should frame° them   *shape*
To royalty unlearned, honour untaught,
180 Civility not seen from other,° valour   *not witnessed in others*
That wildly° grows in them, but yields a crop   *without cultivation*
As if it had been sowed. Yet still it's strange
What Cloten's being here to us portends,
Or what his death will bring us.

Enter GUIDERIUS

GUIDERIUS   Where's my brother?
185 I have sent Cloten's clotpoll° down the stream   *blockhead*
In embassy to his mother. His body's hostage
For his return.[4]

      Solemn music

BELARIUS   My ingenious° instrument!—   *artfully crafted*
Hark, Polydore, it sounds. But what occasion
Hath Cadwal now to give it motion? Hark!
GUIDERIUS   Is he at home?
190 BELARIUS   He went hence even now.
GUIDERIUS   What does he mean? Since death of my dear'st mother
It did not speak before. All solemn things
Should answer° solemn accidents. The matter?   *correspond to*
Triumphs for nothing and lamenting toys
195 Is jollity for apes and grief for boys.[5]
Is Cadwal mad?

Enter [from the cave] ARVIRAGUS *with* INNOGEN, *dead,*
bearing her in his arms

BELARIUS   Look, here he comes,
And brings the dire occasion in his arms
Of what we blame him for.
ARVIRAGUS   The bird is dead
That we have made so much on.° I had rather   *of*
200 Have skipped from sixteen years of age to sixty,
To have turned my leaping time° into a crutch,°   *youth / (old age)*
Than have seen this.
GUIDERIUS *[to* INNOGEN*]*   O sweetest, fairest lily!
My brother wears thee not one half so well
As when thou grew'st thyself.
BELARIUS   O melancholy,
205 Who ever yet could sound thy bottom,° find   *measure your depths*
The ooze to show what coast thy sluggish crare°   *small ship*
Might easiliest harbour in? Thou blessèd thing,

---

2. I'd draw blood from a whole parish full of fools like Cloten.
3. How you proclaim yourself (as in a coat of arms).
4. *His body's . . . return:* I will hold his body hostage until his head returns (which will be never).
5. *Triumphs . . . boys:* Public celebrations for no reason and showing great grief for trivial matters are foolish and unmanly.

Jove knows what man thou mightst have made; but I,°   *I know*
Thou diedst a most rare boy, of melancholy.
[*To* ARVIRAGUS] How found you him?

210 ARVIRAGUS   Stark,° as you see,   *stiff*
Thus smiling as° some fly had tickled slumber,   *as if*
Not as death's dart being laughed at;[6] his right cheek
Reposing on a cushion.

GUIDERIUS   Where?

ARVIRAGUS   O'th' floor,
His arms thus leagued.° I thought he slept, and put   *linked together*

215 My clouted brogues° from off my feet, whose rudeness   *hobnailed boots*
Answered° my steps too loud.   *Rendered*

GUIDERIUS   Why, he but sleeps.
If he be gone he'll make his grave a bed.
With female fairies will his tomb be haunted,
[*To* INNOGEN] And worms will not come to thee.

ARVIRAGUS [*to* INNOGEN]   With fairest flowers

220 Whilst summer lasts and I live here, Fidele,
I'll sweeten thy sad grave. Thou shalt not lack
The flower that's like thy face, pale primrose, nor
The azured harebell,° like thy veins; no, nor   *blue hyacinth*
The leaf of eglantine,° whom not to slander   *honeysuckle*

225 Outsweetened not thy breath. The ruddock would
With charitable bill—O bill sore shaming
Those rich-left heirs that let their fathers lie
Without a monument!—bring thee all this,
Yea, and furred moss besides, when flowers are none,
To winter-gown thy corpse.[7]

230 GUIDERIUS   Prithee, have done,
And do not play in wench-like words[8] with that
Which is so serious. Let us bury him,
And not protract with admiration° what   *wonder*
Is now due debt. To th' grave.

ARVIRAGUS   Say, where shall 's° lay him?   *ought we to*

GUIDERIUS   By good Euriphile, our mother.

235 ARVIRAGUS   Be't so,
And let us, Polydore, though now our voices
Have got the mannish crack, sing him to th' ground
As once our mother; use like note° and words,   *a similar tune*
Save that 'Euriphile' must be 'Fidele'.

240 GUIDERIUS   Cadwal,
I cannot sing. I'll weep, and word° it with thee,   *speak*
For notes of sorrow out of tune are worse
Than priests and fanes° that lie.   *temples*

ARVIRAGUS   We'll speak it then.

BELARIUS   Great griefs, I see, medicine° the less, for Cloten   *cure*

245 Is quite forgot. He was a queen's son, boys,
And though he came our enemy, remember
He was paid° for that. Though mean° and mighty rotting   *punished / lowborn*
Together have one dust, yet reverence,

---

6. Not as if laughing at the approach of death. Death was often depicted carrying a spear ("dart").
7. *The ruddock . . . corpse*: referring to the belief that the robins ("ruddocks") covered dead bodies with flowers and moss. *winter-gown*: clothe for winter.

8. Words appropriate to women. In Shakespeare's plays, speeches about flowers are often delivered by female characters, perhaps most notably in *Hamlet* 4.5.173–82 and *The Winter's Tale* 4.4.73–134.

That angel of the world,[9] doth make distinction
250 Of place 'tween high and low. Our foe was princely,
And though you took his life as being our foe,
Yet bury him as a prince.

GUIDERIUS   Pray you, fetch him hither.
Thersites' body is as good as Ajax'[1]
When neither are alive.

ARVIRAGUS [to BELARIUS]   If you'll go fetch him,
We'll say our song the whilst.   [Exit BELARIUS]
255   Brother, begin.

GUIDERIUS Nay, Cadwal, we must lay his head to th'east.[2]
My father hath a reason for't.

ARVIRAGUS   'Tis true.

GUIDERIUS Come on, then, and remove him.

ARVIRAGUS   So, begin.[3]

GUIDERIUS Fear no more the heat o'th' sun,
260   Nor the furious winter's rages.
      Thou thy worldly task hast done,
            Home art gone and ta'en thy wages.
      Golden lads and girls all must,
            As° chimney-sweepers, come to dust.   Like

265 ARVIRAGUS Fear no more the frown o'th' great,
            Thou art past the tyrant's stroke.
      Care no more to clothe and eat,
            To thee the reed is as the oak.[4]
      The sceptre, learning, physic,° must   medical knowledge
270   All follow this and come to dust.

GUIDERIUS Fear no more the lightning flash,
ARVIRAGUS   Nor th'all-dreaded thunder-stone.°   thunderbolt
GUIDERIUS Fear not slander, censure rash.
ARVIRAGUS   Thou hast finished joy and moan.
275 GUIDERIUS and ARVIRAGUS   All lovers young, all lovers must
                        Consign to thee[5] and come to dust.

GUIDERIUS No exorcisor° harm thee,   conjurer of spirits
ARVIRAGUS Nor no witchcraft charm thee.
GUIDERIUS Ghost unlaid forbear thee.[6]
280 ARVIRAGUS Nothing ill come near thee.
GUIDERIUS and ARVIRAGUS   Quiet consummation° have,   ending
                        And renownèd be thy grave.

            Enter BELARIUS with the body of Cloten [in Posthumus'
            suit]

GUIDERIUS We have done our obsequies. Come, lay him down.
BELARIUS   Here's a few flowers, but 'bout midnight more;
285 The herbs that have on them cold dew o'th' night°   of the night
Are strewings fitt'st for graves upon th'earth's face.
You were as flowers, now withered; even so

These herblets shall,° which we upon you strow.   *shall wither*
Come on, away; apart upon our knees⁷
290   [   ]
The ground that gave them° first has them again.   *gave them life*
Their pleasures here are past, so is their pain.
            Exeunt [BELARIUS, ARVIRAGUS, *and* GUIDERIUS]
INNOGEN *awakes*   Yes, sir, to Milford Haven. Which is the way?
I thank you. By yon bush? Pray, how far thither?
295   'Od's pitykins,° can it be six mile yet?   *By God's pity (mild oath)*
I have gone° all night. 'Faith, I'll lie down and sleep.   *walked*
            [*She sees* CLOTEN]
But soft,° no bedfellow! O gods and goddesses!   *wait*
These flowers are like the pleasures of the world,
This bloody man the care on't.⁸ I hope I dream,
300   For so° I thought I was a cavekeeper,   *For then*
And cook to honest creatures. But 'tis not so.
'Twas but a bolt° of nothing, shot of° nothing,   *an arrow / from*
Which the brain makes of fumes.⁹ Our very eyes
Are sometimes like our judgements, blind. Good faith,
305   I tremble still with fear; but if there be
Yet left in heaven as small a drop of pity
As a wren's eye, feared gods, a part of it!
The dream's here still. Even when I wake it is
Without me as within me; not imagined, felt.
310   A headless man? The garments of Posthumus?
I know the shape of 's leg; this is his hand,
His foot Mercurial, his Martial¹ thigh,
The brawns° of Hercules; but his Jovial² face—   *muscles*
Murder in heaven! How? 'Tis gone. Pisanio,
315   All curses madded Hecuba³ gave the Greeks,
And mine to boot, be darted on thee! Thou,
Conspired° with that irregulous° devil Cloten,   *Conspiring / lawless*
Hath here cut off my lord. To write and read
Be henceforth treacherous! Damned Pisanio
320   Hath with his forgèd letters—damned Pisanio—
From this most bravest° vessel of the world   *splendid*
Struck the main-top!° O Posthumus, alas,   *top of the mast; his head*
Where is thy head? Where's that? Ay me, where's that?
Pisanio might have killed thee at the heart
325   And left thy head on. How should this be? Pisanio?
'Tis he and Cloten. Malice and lucre° in them   *greed*
Have laid this woe here. O, 'tis pregnant,° pregnant!   *clear*
The drug he gave me, which he said was precious
And cordial° to me, have I not found it   *restorative*
330   Murd'rous to th' senses? That confirms it home.°   *completely*
This is Pisanio's deed, and Cloten—O,
Give colour to my pale cheek with thy blood,
That we the horrider° may seem to those   *more terrifying*
Which chance to find us!

7. Some other place ("apart"), let us pray (be "upon our knees"). Because the previous two lines rhyme, as do the next two lines, it is probable that a line is missing here. The sense of "apart upon our knees" also seems obscure, probably because the thought is truncated.
8. This bloody man is like the sorrow of the world.
9. "Fumes" (vapors) were thought to rise from the stom-

ach and cause dreams and distortions of the imagination.
1. Fashioned for battle, like that of Mars, the god of war. *Mercurial:* Like that of Mercury, the fleet-footed messenger of the gods.
2. Majestic like the face of Jove, king of the gods.
3. The Queen of Troy, Priam's wife, whose desire for revenge against the Greeks made her insane ("madded").

[*She smears her face with blood*]
　　　　　　　　O my lord, my lord!
[*She faints.*]
　　Enter LUCIUS, [*Roman*] *Captains, and a* SOOTHSAYER
A ROMAN CAPTAIN [*to* LUCIUS]　To them° the legions garrisoned　　　*In addition to them*
335　　in Gallia
　　After your will⁴ have crossed the sea, attending°　　　　　　　*waiting for*
　　You here at Milford Haven with your ships.
　　They are hence in readiness.
LUCIUS　　　　　　　　　　　But what from Rome?
A ROMAN CAPTAIN　The senate hath stirred up the confiners°　　*inhabitants*
340　　And gentlemen of Italy, most willing spirits
　　That promise noble service, and they come
　　Under the conduct of bold Giacomo,
　　Siena's° brother.　　　　　　　　　　　　　　　*The Duke of Siena's*
LUCIUS　　　　　　　When expect you them?
A ROMAN CAPTAIN　With the next benefit o'th' wind.
LUCIUS　　　　　　　　　　　　This forwardness°　　　*readiness*
345　　Makes our hopes fair. Command our present numbers
　　Be mustered; bid the captains look to't.　　[*Exit one or more*]
　　[*To* SOOTHSAYER]　　　　　　　　Now, sir,
　　What have you dreamed of late of this war's purpose?°　　*outcome*
SOOTHSAYER　Last night the very gods showed me a vision—
　　I fast,° and prayed for their intelligence°—thus:　*fasted / information*
350　　I saw Jove's bird, the Roman eagle, winged
　　From the spongy° south to this part of the west,　　　　*damp*
　　There vanished in the sunbeams; which portends,
　　Unless my sins abuse° my divination,　　　　　　　　　*falsify*
　　Success to th' Roman host.
LUCIUS　　　　　　　　　Dream often so,
　　And never false.°　　　　　　　　　　　　　　　*dream falsely*
　　[*He sees Cloten's body*]
355　　　　　　　Soft, ho, what trunk is here
　　Without his top? The ruin speaks that sometime°　　　　*once*
　　It was a worthy building. How, a page?
　　Or° dead or sleeping on him? But dead rather,　　　　　*Either*
　　For nature doth abhor to make his bed
360　　With the defunct, or sleep upon the dead.
　　Let's see the boy's face.
A ROMAN CAPTAIN　　　　　He's alive, my lord.
LUCIUS　He'll then instruct us of this body. Young one,
　　Inform us of thy fortunes, for it seems
　　They crave to be demanded. Who is this
365　　Thou mak'st thy bloody pillow? Or who was he
　　That, otherwise than noble nature did,⁵
　　Hath altered that good picture? What's thy interest
　　In this sad wreck?° How came't? Who is't?　　　　　　*ruin*
　　What art thou?
INNOGEN　　　　　　I am nothing; or if not,
370　　Nothing to be were better.⁶ This was my master,
　　A very valiant Briton, and a good,
　　That here by mountaineers lies slain. Alas,

4. According to your command.　　　　　6. It were better to be nothing.
5. Who, in a manner different from nature's workings.

There is no more such masters. I may wander
From east to occident, cry out for service,
375 Try many, all good; serve truly, never
Find such another master.
LUCIUS   'Lack,° good youth,   *Alack*
Thou mov'st no less with thy complaining than
Thy master in bleeding. Say his name, good friend.
INNOGEN   Richard du Champ.[7] [*Aside*] If I do lie and do
380 No harm by it, though the gods hear I hope
They'll pardon it. [*Aloud*] Say you, sir?
LUCIUS   Thy name?
INNOGEN   Fidele, sir.
LUCIUS   Thou dost approve° thyself the very same.   *show*
Thy name well fits thy faith,° thy faith thy name.   *fidelity*
Wilt take thy chance with me? I will not say
385 Thou shalt be so well mastered, but be sure,
No less beloved. The Roman Emperor's letters
Sent by a consul to me should not sooner
Than thine own worth prefer° thee. Go with me.   *recommend*
INNOGEN   I'll follow, sir. But first, an't° please the gods,   *if it*
390 I'll hide my master from the flies as deep
As these poor pickaxes° can dig; and when   *(her hands)*
With wild-wood leaves and weeds I ha' strewed his grave
And on it said a century of° prayers,   *a hundred*
Such as I can, twice o'er I'll weep and sigh,
395 And leaving so his service, follow you,
So please you entertain° me.   *employ*
LUCIUS   Ay, good youth,
And rather father thee than master thee. My friends,
The boy hath taught us manly duties. Let us
Find out the prettiest daisied plot we can,
400 And make him with our pikes and partisans[8]
A grave. Come, arm° him. Boy, he is preferred°   *lift / recommended*
By thee to us, and he shall be interred
As soldiers can. Be cheerful. Wipe thine eyes.
Some falls are means the happier to arise.[9]

Exeunt [*with Cloten's body*]

4.3

Enter CYMBELINE, LORDS, *and* PISANIO

CYMBELINE   Again, and bring me word how 'tis with her.

Exit one or more

A fever with° the absence of her son,   *on account of*
A madness of which her life's in danger—heavens,
How deeply you at once do touch° me! Innogen,   *afflict*
5 The great part of my comfort, gone; my queen
Upon a desperate bed,° and in a time   *Extremely ill in bed*
When fearful wars point at me; her son gone,
So needful for this present!° It strikes me past   *So needed now*
The hope of comfort. [*To* PISANIO] But for thee, fellow,

---

7. This French name translates as "Richard of the
Field," perhaps an allusion to a well-known London
printer named Richard Field, who was born in
Stratford-upon-Avon and printed Shakespeare's *Rape of
Lucrece* and *Venus and Adonis* in the 1590s.

8. With our spears and our halberds (long-handled
weapons with axlike blades).
9. Some falls are means by which good fortune arises.
4.3 Location: Cymbeline's court, Britain.

10 Who needs must know of her departure and
Dost seem so ignorant, we'll enforce it from thee
By a sharp torture.

PISANIO   Sir, my life is yours.
I humbly set it at your will. But for my mistress,
I nothing know° where she remains, why gone,   *know nothing about*
15 Nor when she purposes° return. Beseech° your highness,   *intends to / I beseech*
Hold me° your loyal servant.   *Regard me as*

A LORD   Good my liege,
The day that she was missing he was here.
I dare be bound he's true, and shall perform
All parts of his subjection° loyally. For Cloten,   *duty as a subject*
20 There wants° no diligence in seeking him,   *is lacking*
And will° no doubt be found.   *he will*

CYMBELINE   The time is troublesome.°   *dire*
[*To* PISANIO] We'll slip you° for a season, but our jealousy *let you go*
Does yet depend.[1]

A LORD   So please your majesty,
The Roman legions, all from Gallia drawn,
25 Are landed on your coast with a supply
Of Roman gentlemen by the senate sent.

CYMBELINE   Now for° the counsel of my son and queen!   *If only I now had*
I am amazed° with matter.°   *overwhelmed / business*

A LORD   Good my liege,
Your preparation can affront no less
30 Than what you hear of.[2] Come more, for more you're ready.
The want° is but to put those powers in motion   *The only thing needed*
That long to move.

CYMBELINE   I thank you. Let's withdraw,
And meet the time as it seeks us. We fear not
What can from Italy annoy° us, but   *harm*
35 We grieve at chances° here. Away.   *events*

                    Exeunt [CYMBELINE *and* LORDS]

PISANIO   I heard no letter from my master since
I wrote him Innogen was slain. 'Tis strange.
Nor hear I from my mistress, who did promise
To yield me often tidings. Neither know I
40 What is betid° to Cloten, but remain   *has happened*
Perplexed in all. The heavens still must work.
Wherein I am false I am honest; not true, to be true.
These present wars shall find I love my country
Even to the note° o'th' King, or I'll fall in them.   *notice*
45 All other doubts, by time let them be cleared:
Fortune brings in some boats that are not steered.   *Exit*

                    ## 4.4
          Enter BELARIUS, GUIDERIUS, *and* ARVIRAGUS

GUIDERIUS   The noise is round about us.
BELARIUS   Let us from it.
ARVIRAGUS   What pleasure, sir, find we in life to lock it°   *shut it off*
From action and adventure?
GUIDERIUS   Nay, what hope

---

1. *but . . . depend:* but our suspicions still hold.
2. *Your . . . of:* Your forces can confront all those you
have heard of.
4.4 Location: Before the cave of Belarius, Wales.

Have we in hiding us? This way° the Romans — *By this course of action*

5 Must or° for Britains slay us, or receive us — *either*

For barbarous and unnatural revolts° — *rebels*

During their use,[1] and slay us after.

BELARIUS Sons,

We'll higher to the mountains; there secure us.

To the King's party there's no going. Newness

10 Of Cloten's death—we being not known, not mustered

Among the bands°—may drive us to a render° — *troops / an account*

Where we have lived, and so extort from 's that

Which we have done, whose answer would be death

Drawn on° with torture. *Prolonged*

GUIDERIUS This is, sir, a doubt

15 In such a time nothing becoming you

Nor satisfying us.

ARVIRAGUS It is not likely

That when they hear the Roman horses neigh,

Behold their quartered files,° have both their eyes — *orderly troops*

And ears so cloyed importantly[2] as now,

20 That they will waste their time upon our note,° — *in observing us*

To know from whence we are.

BELARIUS O, I am known

Of° many in the army. Many years, *By*

Though Cloten then° but young, you see, not wore° him — *was then / did not wear*

From my remembrance. And besides, the King

25 Hath not deserved my service nor your loves,

Who find in my exile the want of breeding,

The certainty of this hard life;[3] aye hopeless

To have the courtesy your cradle promised,[4]

But to be still° hot summer's tanlings,[5] and *always*

The shrinking slaves of winter.

30 GUIDERIUS Than be so,

Better to cease to be. Pray, sir, to th'army.

I and my brother are not known; yourself

So out of thought, and thereto° so o'ergrown,[6] — *in addition*

Cannot be questioned.

ARVIRAGUS By this sun that shines,

35 I'll thither. What thing is't[7] that I never

Did see man die, scarce ever looked on blood

But that of coward hares, hot° goats, and venison, *lecherous*

Never bestrid a horse save one that had

A rider like myself, who ne'er wore rowel[8]

40 Nor iron on his heel! I am ashamed

To look upon the holy sun, to have

The benefit of his blest beams, remaining

So long a poor unknown.

GUIDERIUS By heavens, I'll go.

If you will bless me, sir, and give me leave,

45 I'll take the better care;° but if you will not, *be the more careful*

1. While they have need of us.
2. So completely taken up with important matters.
3. *Who . . . life:* (You) who experience as a result of my exile a lack of proper education, the enduring fact of this hard life.
4. *aye . . . promised:* yes, without hope to have the cultivated existence your noble birth promised.
5. People exposed to the sun. In England at this time, tanned skin denoted low social status.
6. So overgrown with hair or beard; so grown in years; so grown out of memory.
7. What a bad state of affairs it is.
8. Small rotating disk at the end of a spur. Wearing spurs was the privilege of gentlemen.

The hazard therefore due[9] fall on me by
The hands of Romans.

ARVIRAGUS   So say I, amen.

BELARIUS   No reason I, since of your lives you set
So slight a valuation, should reserve
50 My cracked° one to more care. Have with you,° boys!   weakened / Come then
If in your country° wars you chance to die,   country's
That is my bed, too, lads, and there I'll lie.
Lead, lead. [Aside] The time seems long. Their blood thinks scorn°   disdains itself
Till it fly out and show them princes born.   Exeunt

5.1

Enter POSTHUMUS [dressed as an Italian
gentleman, carrying a bloody cloth]

POSTHUMUS   Yea, bloody cloth, I'll keep thee, for I once wished
Thou shouldst be coloured thus. You married ones,
If each of you should take this course, how many
Must murder wives much better than themselves
5 For wrying° but a little! O Pisanio,   erring
Every good servant does not all commands,
No bond but° to do just ones. Gods, if you   No obligation except
Should have ta'en vengeance on my faults, I never
Had lived to put on this;° so had you saved   to undertake this deed
10 The noble Innogen to repent, and struck
Me, wretch, more worth your vengeance. But alack,
You snatch some hence for little faults; that's love,
To have them fall no more.[1] You some permit
To second° ills with ills, each elder° worse,   reinforce / later fault
15 And make them dread ill, to the doer's thrift.[2]
But Innogen is your own. Do your blest wills,
And make me blest to obey. I am brought hither
Among th'Italian gentry, and to fight
Against my lady's kingdom. 'Tis enough
20 That, Britain, I have killed thy mistress-piece;[3]
I'll give no wound to thee. Therefore, good heavens,
Hear patiently my purpose. I'll disrobe me
Of these Italian weeds, and suit° myself   dress
As does a Briton peasant.
[He disrobes himself]
So I'll fight
25 Against the part° I come with; so I'll die   side
For thee, O Innogen, even for whom my life
Is every breath a death; and, thus unknown,
Pitied° nor hated, to the face of peril   Neither pitied
Myself I'll dedicate. Let me make men know
30 More valour in me than my habits° show.   garments
Gods, put the strength o'th' Leonati in me.
To shame the guise° o'th' world, I will begin   customs; dress
The fashion—less without and more within.   Exit

---

9. May the danger due to me (as a result of my disobedience).
5.1 Location: The Roman camp, Britain.
1. that's . . . more: that is a sign of love, to have them no
longer sin.
2. And make them fear punishment, to their own benefit.
3. Punning on "masterpiece." Most editions, following

F, read: "'Tis enough / That, Britain, I have killed thy
mistress; peace." "Mistress-piece," which can be found
in other texts from the period, suggests the extraordinary excellence of Innogen. "Piece" could be spelled
"peace" in the early modern period, and the unfamiliar
compound might have been misread by the person setting type for the play.

5.2

[*A march.*] *Enter* LUCIUS, GIACOMO, *and the Roman
army at one door, and the Briton army at another, Leonatus* POSTHUMUS *following like a poor soldier. They
march over and go out.* [*Alarums.*] *Then enter again in
skirmish* GIACOMO *and* POSTHUMUS: *he vanquisheth and
disarmeth* GIACOMO, *and then leaves him*

GIACOMO   The heaviness and guilt within my bosom
  Takes off° my manhood. I have belied° a lady,   *Destroys / slandered*
  The princess of this country, and the air on't°   *of it*
  Revengingly enfeebles me; or° could this carl,°   *otherwise / peasant*
5 A very drudge° of nature's, have subdued me   *slave*
  In my profession? Knighthoods and honours borne
  As I wear mine are titles but° of scorn.   *merely*
  If that thy gentry, Britain, go before°   *surpass*
  This lout as he exceeds our lords, the odds
10 Is that we scarce are men and you are gods.   *Exit*

5.3[1]

The battle continues. [*Alarums. Excursions. The trumpets sound a retreat.*] *The Britons fly,* CYMBELINE *is
taken. Then enter to his rescue* BELARIUS, GUIDERIUS,
and ARVIRAGUS

BELARIUS   Stand, stand, we have th'advantage of the ground.
  The lane is guarded. Nothing routs us but
  The villainy of our fears.
GUIDERIUS *and* ARVIRAGUS   Stand, stand, and fight.
  Enter POSTHUMUS [*like a poor soldier*], *and seconds the
  Britons. They rescue* CYMBELINE *and exeunt*

5.4

[*The trumpets sound a retreat,*] *then enter* LUCIUS, GIA-
COMO, *and* INNOGEN

LUCIUS [*to* INNOGEN]   Away, boy, from the troops, and save thyself;
  For friends kill friends, and the disorder's such
  As war were hoodwinked.[1]
GIACOMO   'Tis their fresh supplies.
LUCIUS   It is a day turned strangely. Or betimes
5 Let's reinforce, or fly.[2]   *Exeunt*

5.5

Enter POSTHUMUS [*like a poor soldier*], *and a Briton*
  LORD
LORD   Cam'st thou from where they made the stand?
POSTHUMUS   I did,
  Though you, it seems, come from the fliers.
LORD   Ay.
POSTHUMUS   No blame be to you, sir, for all was lost,
  But° that the heavens fought. The King himself   *Had it not been*

5.2 Location: A field between the British and Roman
camps, Britain.
5.3 Location: Scene continues.
1. In F and most modern editions, there is no new
scene marked here or at 5.4, since 5.2, 5.3, and 5.4
form one continuous battle sequence. However, the
stage is temporarily cleared where the Oxford editors

have marked 5.3 and 5.4, and a cleared stage is the
usual signal of a new scene on the Renaissance stage.
5.4 Location: Scene continues.
1. As if war were blindfolded.
2. *Or betimes . . . fly:* Let us either promptly reinforce
our troops or flee.
5.5 Location: Scene continues.

5   Of his wings destitute,[1] the army broken,
And but° the backs of Britons seen, all flying   *only*
Through a strait° lane; the enemy full-hearted,°   *narrow / bold*
Lolling the tongue with slaught'ring,[2] having work
More plentiful than tools to do't, struck down
10   Some mortally, some slightly touched,° some falling   *wounded*
Merely through fear, that the strait pass was dammed°   *clogged*
With dead men hurt behind,[3] and cowards living
To die with lengthened shame.[4]

LORD   Where was this lane?

POSTHUMUS   Close by the battle, ditched, and walled with turf;
15   Which gave advantage to an ancient soldier,
An honest one, I warrant, who deserved
So long a breeding as his white beard came to,[5]
In doing this for 's country. Athwart° the lane   *Across*
He with two striplings—lads more like° to run   *likely*
20   The country base[6] than to commit such slaughter;
With faces fit for masks,[7] or rather fairer
Than those for preservation cased, or shame[8]—
Made good° the passage, cried to those that fled   *Secured*
'Our Britain's harts die flying, not her men.
25   To darkness fleet° souls that fly backwards. Stand,   *rush*
Or we are Romans,[9] and will give you that°   *(death)*
Like beasts which you shun beastly,° and may save   *in cowardly fashion*
But to look back in frown.[1] Stand, stand.' These three,
Three thousand confident,[2] in act as many—
30   For three performers are the file° when all   *entire force*
The rest do nothing—with this word 'Stand, stand',
Accommodated° by the place, more charming[3]   *Assisted*
With their own nobleness, which could have turned
A distaff to a lance,[4] gilded° pale looks;   *brought color to*
35   Part shame, part spirit renewed,[5] that some, turned coward
But by example[6]—O, a sin in war,
Damned in the first beginners![7]—gan° to look   *began*
The way that they° did and to grin[8] like lions   *(the three)*
Upon the pikes o'th' hunters. Then began
40   A stop° i'th' chaser, a retire. Anon°   *halt / Soon*
A rout, confusion thick; forthwith they fly
Chickens the way which they stooped eagles;[9] slaves,
The strides they victors made;[1] and now our cowards,
Like fragments° in hard voyages, became   *scraps of food*

---

1. Deprived of his wings (that is, the troops to either side of the main division of the army).
2. With their tongues hanging out either from the labor of slaughter or from eagerness to commit the slaughter.
3. Hurt on their backs (as they were fleeing).
4. To die later after a life of prolonged shame.
5. *who . . . to:* who deserved to live so long again as his white beard indicated he had already lived.
6. *to run . . . base:* to play a children's game (prisoner's house) that involves running between two bases.
7. Gentlewomen wore masks to protect their complexions from the elements.
8. *fairer . . . shame:* more delicate than those covered with masks for protection ("preservation") or out of modesty.
9. Or we will behave like Romans.
1. *and may . . . frown:* and may prevent only by turning

back upon the enemy with threatening face.
2. As confident as if they were three thousand.
3. *more charming:* casting a spell on others.
4. *could . . . lance:* that is, could have made women fight. The distaff, an instrument used in spinning wool, was a proverbial symbol of womanhood.
5. Shame inspired some, courage others.
6. Because of the example set by others.
7. In those who first set the example (of cowardly behavior).
8. To bare their teeth.
9. *forthwith . . . eagles:* straightway they (the Romans) fled like chickens along the passage down which they had just swooped like eagles.
1. *slaves . . . made:* like slaves, they retrace the steps they had made as victors.

45 The life o'th' need.[2] Having found the back door open
Of the unguarded hearts,[3] heavens, how they wound!
Some slain before,[4] some dying, some their friends
O'erborne° i'th' former wave, ten chased by one,   *Overwhelmed*
Are now each one the slaughterman of twenty.
50 Those that would die or ere° resist are grown   *before they would*
The mortal bugs° o'th' field.   *deadly terrors*

LORD   This was strange chance:
A narrow lane, an old man, and two boys.

POSTHUMUS   Nay, do not wonder at it. Yet you are made
Rather to wonder at the things you hear
55 Than to work° any. Will you rhyme upon't,   *perform*
And vent it[5] for a mock'ry? Here is one:
'Two boys, an old man twice a boy,° a lane,   *in his second childhood*
Preserved the Britons, was the Romans' bane.'

LORD   Nay, be not angry, sir.

POSTHUMUS   'Lack,° to what end?   *Alas*
60 Who dares not stand° his foe, I'll be his friend,   *confront*
For if he'll do as he is made° to do,   *inclined*
I know he'll quickly fly my friendship too.
You have put° me into rhyme.   *forced*

LORD   Farewell; you're angry.   *Exit*

POSTHUMUS   Still going?° This a lord? O noble misery,[6]   *Still running away*
65 To be i'th' field and ask 'What news?' of me!
Today how many would have given their honours
To have saved their carcasses—took heel to do't,
And yet died too!° I, in mine own woe charmed,[7]   *anyway*
Could not find death where I did hear him groan,
70 Nor feel him where he struck. Being an ugly monster,
'Tis strange he hides him in fresh cups, soft beds,
Sweet words, or hath more ministers° than we   *other agents*
That draw his knives i'th' war. Well, I will find him;
For being now a favourer to the Briton,[8]
75 No more° a Briton, I have resumed again   *I am no more*
The part° I came in. Fight I will no more,   *role*
But yield me to the veriest hind° that shall   *peasant*
Once touch my shoulder.° Great the slaughter is   *try to arrest me*
Here made by th' Roman; great the answer be°   *great the retaliation*
80 Britons must take. For me, my ransom's death,
On either side I come to spend my breath,°   *give up my life*
Which neither here I'll keep nor bear° again,   *carry away*
But end it by some means for Innogen.
     Enter two [Briton] CAPTAINS, *and soldiers*

FIRST CAPTAIN   Great Jupiter be praised, Lucius is taken.
85 'Tis thought the old man and his sons were angels.

SECOND CAPTAIN   There was a fourth man, in a seely habit,°   *rustic garments*
That gave th'affront with them.

FIRST CAPTAIN   So 'tis reported,
But none of 'em can be found. Stand, who's there?

POSTHUMUS   A Roman,

---

2. Vital in the time of crisis.
3. *Having . . . hearts*: Having found unprotected the weak
spot of these undefended souls (that is, the Romans).
4. Some that earlier were as good as dead.
5. And circulate ("vent") your rhymes.
6. What noble wretchedness.
7. In my despair preserved, as if by a charm.
8. Since death is now looking kindly upon Britons.

90   Who had not now been drooping here if seconds°   *supporters*
     Had answered him.°   *followed him*
   SECOND CAPTAIN [*to soldiers*]   Lay hands on him, a dog!
     A leg of Rome shall not return to tell
     What crows have pecked them here. He brags his service
     As if he were of note.° Bring him to th' King.   *high rank*
         [*Flourish.*] *Enter* CYMBELINE [*and his train*], BELARIUS,
           GUIDERIUS, ARVIRAGUS, PISANIO, *and Roman captives.*
         The CAPTAINS *present* POSTHUMUS *to* CYMBELINE, *who*
         delivers him over to a JAILER. [*Exeunt all but* POSTHU-
         MUS *and two* JAILERS *who lock gyves*° *on his legs*]⁹   *fetters*
95 FIRST JAILER   You shall not now be stol'n. You have locks upon you,
     So graze as you find pasture.
   SECOND JAILER   Ay, or a stomach.   [*Exeunt* JAILERS]
   POSTHUMUS   Most welcome, bondage, for thou art a way,
     I think, to liberty. Yet am I better
     Than one that's sick o' th' gout, since he had rather
100 Groan so in perpetuity than be cured
     By th' sure physician, death, who is the key
     T'unbar these locks. My conscience, thou art fettered
     More than my shanks° and wrists. You good gods give me   *legs*
     The penitent instrument to pick that bolt,
105 Then free for ever.¹ Is't enough I am sorry?
     So children temporal fathers do appease;
     Gods are more full of mercy. Must I repent,
     I cannot do it better than in gyves
     Desired more than constrained.° To satisfy,°   *forced (upon me)* / *atone*
110 If of my freedom 'tis the main part,² take
     No stricter render° of me than my all.   *repayment*
     I know you are more clement° than vile men   *merciful*
     Who of their broken° debtors take a third,   *bankrupt*
     A sixth, a tenth, letting them thrive again
115 On their abatement.° That's not my desire.   *reduced amount*
     For Innogen's dear life take mine, and though
     'Tis not so dear,° yet 'tis a life; you coined it.   *valuable*
     'Tween man and man they weigh not every stamp;
     Though light, take pieces for the figure's sake;³
120 You rather mine, being yours.⁴ And so, great powers,
     If you will make this audit,° take this life,   *settle this account*
     And cancel these cold bonds.⁵ O Innogen,
     I'll speak to thee in silence!

9. F and most modern editions mark a new scene here.
Confusion arises because in F, no exit is marked for any
character after Posthumus is handed over to a Jailer.
Either everyone exits and Posthumus then reenters with
two Jailers, indicating a new scene, or, as here, Posthumus and Jailers stay onstage continuously. The latter
option means that Posthumus is fettered in the open
fields, giving new point to the First Jailer's injunction to
"graze as you find pasture" (5.5.96). Usually, Posthumus
is assumed to be fettered inside a British prison.
1. *The . . . ever:* Give me penitence, the instrument to
pick that lock (the lock on his conscience, which is fettered by guilt). Then (I am) free forever; then free me

(by death).
2. If it is the most important element in freeing me
from guilt.
3. *Tween . . . sake:* In business dealings between men,
they do not weigh every coin ("stamp"). Even though
some coins are deficient in weight ("light"), they accept
them because of the image (of the King) stamped on them.
4. You should be more inclined to accept my coin (me),
since your image is stamped on me. This line refers to
the Christian belief that humans are made in the image
of God.
5. These old legal agreements; these cruel links with
life; these harsh fetters.

[*He sleeps.*] *Solemn music. Enter, as in an apparition,*
SICILIUS *Leonatus (father to Posthumus, an old man),*
attired like a warrior, leading in his hand an ancient
matron, his wife, and MOTHER *to Posthumus, with music*
before them. Then, after other music, follows the two
young Leonati, BROTHERS *to Posthumus, with wounds as*
they died in the wars. They circle POSTHUMUS *round as*
he lies sleeping

SICILIUS   No more, thou thunder-master,[6] show
125   Thy spite on mortal flies.°   *frail creatures*
With Mars° fall out, with Juno° chide,   *god of war / Jove's wife*
That° thy adulteries   *Who*
Rates° and revenges.   *Berates*
Hath my poor boy done aught but well,
130   Whose face I never saw?
I died whilst in the womb he stayed,
Attending nature's law,[7]
Whose father then—as men report
Thou orphans' father art—
135   Thou shouldst have been, and shielded him
From this earth-vexing smart.[8]

MOTHER   Lucina° lent not me her aid,   *goddess of childbirth*
But took me in my throes,
That from me was Posthumus ripped,
140   Came crying 'mongst his foes,
A thing of pity.

SICILIUS   Great nature like his ancestry
Moulded the stuff° so fair   *substance*
That he deserved the praise o'th' world
145   As great Sicilius' heir.

FIRST BROTHER   When once he was mature for man,°   *had matured into manhood*
In Britain where was he
That could stand up his parallel,
Or fruitful° object be   *life-giving*
150   In eye of Innogen, that best
Could deem° his dignity?°   *judge / worth*

MOTHER   With marriage wherefore° was he mocked,   *why*
To be exiled, and thrown
From Leonati seat and cast
155   From her his dearest one,
Sweet Innogen?

SICILIUS   Why did you suffer Giacomo,
Slight° thing of Italy,   *Worthless*
To taint his nobler heart and brain
160   With needless jealousy,
And to become the geck° and scorn   *dupe*
O'th' other's villainy?

SECOND BROTHER   For this from stiller seats[9] we come,
Our parents and us twain,
165   That striking in our country's cause
Fell bravely and were slain,

---

6. Jupiter, or Jove, the king of the gods, often made himself known to humans through thunder and lightning.
7. Awaiting the decree of nature (for his birth).
8. From this suffering that afflicts all humans.
9. From calmer regions (alluding to the Elysian Fields—in classical mythology the abode of the blessed after death).

Our fealty and Tenantius'° right   (*Cymbeline's father*)
With honour to maintain.
FIRST BROTHER   Like hardiment° Posthumus hath   *Similar bold deeds*
170   To Cymbeline performed.
Then, Jupiter, thou king of gods,
Why hast thou thus adjourned°   *deferred*
The graces for his merits due,
Being all to dolours° turned?   *sorrows*
175 **SICILIUS**   Thy crystal window ope;° look out;   *open*
No longer exercise
Upon a valiant race thy harsh
And potent injuries.
MOTHER   Since, Jupiter, our son is good,
180   Take off his miseries.
SICILIUS   Peep through thy marble mansion. Help,
Or we poor ghosts will cry
To th' shining synod° of the rest°   *assembly / rest of the gods*
Against thy deity.°   *godhead*
185 **BROTHERS**   Help, Jupiter, or we appeal,
And from thy justice fly.
    JUPITER *descends in thunder and lightning, sitting upon*
    an eagle. He throws a thunderbolt. The ghosts fall on
    their knees
JUPITER   No more, you petty spirits of region low,
Offend our hearing. Hush! How dare you ghosts
Accuse the thunderer, whose bolt, you know,
190   Sky-planted,° batters all rebelling coasts?   *Rooted in the heavens*
Poor shadows of Elysium, hence, and rest
Upon your never-withering banks of flowers.
Be not with mortal accidents° oppressed;   *events*
No care of yours it is; you know 'tis ours.
195   Whom best I love, I cross,° to make my gift,   *thwart*
The more delayed, delighted.° Be content.   *the more pleasing*
Your low-laid son our godhead will uplift.
His comforts thrive, his trials well are spent.°   *ended*
Our Jovial star° reigned at his birth, and in   *The planet Jupiter*
200   Our temple was he married. Rise, and fade.
He shall be lord of Lady Innogen,
And happier much by his affliction made.
This tablet lay upon his breast, wherein
Our pleasure his full fortune doth confine.[1]
    [*He gives the ghosts a tablet which they lay upon Posthu-*
    mus' breast]
205 And so away. No farther with your din
Express impatience, lest you stir up mine.
Mount, eagle, to my palace crystalline.   [*He*] *ascends* [*into the heavens*]
SICILIUS   He came in thunder. His celestial breath
Was sulphurous to smell.[2] The holy eagle
210   Stooped, as to foot us.[3] His ascension is
More sweet than our blest fields. His royal bird

---

1. *wherein . . . confine:* wherein it is our pleasure his
great fortune precisely to set forth.
2. Sulfur was popularly associated with thunder and
lightning. As a constituent of gunpowder, its smell may
have been detectable in the theater when gunpowder
was used.
3. Swooped as if to seize us in its talons.

Preens the immortal wing and claws his beak
As when his god is pleased.

ALL THE GHOSTS   Thanks, Jupiter.

SICILIUS   The marble pavement⁴ closes, he is entered
215   His radiant roof. Away, and, to be blest,
Let us with care perform his great behest.   [*The ghosts*] *vanish*
                    [POSTHUMUS *awakes*]

POSTHUMUS   Sleep, thou hast been a grandsire, and begot
A father to me; and thou hast created
A mother and two brothers. But, O scorn,°   bitter mockery
220   Gone! They went hence so soon as they were born,
And so I am awake. Poor wretches that depend
On greatness' favour dream as I have done,
Wake and find nothing. But, alas, I swerve.°   go astray
Many dream not to find, neither deserve,
225   And yet are steeped in favours; so am I,
That have this golden chance and know not why.
What fairies haunt this ground? A book? O rare one,
Be not, as is our fangled world,⁵ a garment
Nobler than that it covers. Let thy effects
230   So follow to° be most unlike our courtiers,   that they
As good as promise.
                [*He*] *reads*
'Whenas° a lion's whelp shall, to himself unknown, without   When
seeking find, and be embraced by a piece of tender air; and
when from a stately cedar shall be lopped branches which,
235   being dead many years, shall after revive, be jointed to the old
stock, and freshly grow; then shall Posthumus end his miseries,
Britain be fortunate and flourish in peace and plenty.'
'Tis still a dream, or else such stuff as madmen
Tongue,° and brain° not; either both, or nothing,   Speak / understand
240   Or senseless speaking,° or a speaking such   Either meaningless speech
As sense° cannot untie. Be what it is,   reason
The action of my life is like it, which I'll keep,
If but for sympathy.⁶
                Enter JAILER

JAILER   Come, sir, are you ready for death?
245   POSTHUMUS   Over-roasted rather; ready long ago.

JAILER   Hanging⁷ is the word, sir. If you be ready for that, you
are well cooked.

POSTHUMUS   So, if I prove a good repast to the spectators, the
dish pays the shot.⁸

250   JAILER   A heavy reckoning for you, sir. But the comfort is, you
shall be called to no more payments, fear no more tavern bills,
which are as often the sadness of parting as the procuring of
mirth. You come in faint for want of meat, depart reeling with
too much drink, sorry that you have paid too much and sorry
255   that you are paid too much;⁹ purse and brain both empty: the
brain the heavier for being too light,° the purse too light, being   foolish

----

4. Referring to the closing of the trapdoor in the ceiling above the stage, which represents the floor ("pavement") of the heavens.
5. Our world so obsessed with fashions.
6. If only because of the similarity.

7. Death by hanging, with a pun on "hanging" as referring
to the practice of hanging up raw meat before cooking.
8. The food pays the reckoning; I am worth what it
costs to hang me.
9. Subdued by too much drink.

drawn of heaviness.[1] Of this contradiction you shall now be
quit. O, the charity of a penny cord! It sums up thousands in a
trice.° You have no true debitor and creditor[2] but it: of what's | *an instant*
past, is, and to come the discharge.° Your neck, sir, is pen, | *release from debt*
book, and counters;[3] so the acquittance° follows. | *deliverance*

POSTHUMUS I am merrier to die than thou art to live.

JAILER Indeed, sir, he that sleeps feels not the toothache; but a
man that were to° sleep your sleep, and a hangman to help him | *were about to*
to bed, I think he would change places with his officer;° for | *(the hangman)*
look you, sir, you know not which way you shall go.

POSTHUMUS Yes, indeed do I, fellow.

JAILER Your death has eyes in 's head, then. I have not seen him
so pictured.[4] You must either be directed by some that take
upon them° to know, or take upon yourself that which I am | *some who profess*
sure you do not know, or jump° the after-enquiry on your own | *risk*
peril; and how you shall speed° in your journey's end I think | *succeed*
you'll never return to tell on.° | *of*

POSTHUMUS I tell thee, fellow, there are none want° eyes to | *lacking*
direct them the way I am going but such as wink° and will not | *shut their eyes*
use them.

JAILER What an infinite mock is this, that a man should have
the best use of eyes to see the way of blindness!° I am sure | *the way to death*
hanging's the way of winking.

Enter a MESSENGER

MESSENGER Knock off his manacles, bring your prisoner to the
King.

POSTHUMUS Thou bring'st good news, I am called to be made
free.[5]

JAILER I'll be hanged then.

POSTHUMUS Thou shalt be then freer than a jailer; no bolts for
the dead.[6]

JAILER [*aside*] Unless a man would marry a gallows and beget
young gibbets, I never saw one so prone.° Yet, on my con- | *eager*
science, there are verier knaves desire to live, for all° he be a | *even though*
Roman; and there be some of them, too, that die against their
wills; so should I if I were one. I would we were all of one
mind, and one mind good. O, there were desolation° of jailers | *the ruin*
and gallowses! I speak against my present profit, but my wish
hath a preferment[7] in't. *Exeunt*

5.6

[*Flourish.*] *Enter* CYMBELINE, BELARIUS, GUIDERIUS,
ARVIRAGUS, PISANIO, *and lords*

CYMBELINE [*to* BELARIUS, GUIDERIUS, *and* ARVIRAGUS] Stand by
my side, you whom the gods have made
Preservers of my throne. Woe is my heart

---

1. Being emptied of the money that makes it heavy.
2. Account book.
3. Metal tokens used for making calculations.
4. So depicted (referring to visual representations of death as a skeleton or skull with no eyes).
5. Posthumus means "set free by death." The Jailer thinks he means "set free from prison."
6. Most editions, following F2, have everyone leave the stage here except the Jailer. However, the Jailer himself

has been ordered to bring the prisoner to the King, which would mean that he must not be separated from Posthumus. Rather than being a monologue, the ensuing speech may be largely spoken in asides to the audience as the Jailer unlocks Posthumus's fetters and prepares to take him to Cymbeline.
7. Had a promotion in it (implying that a world without the need for jailers could offer him better employment).
5.6 Location: The camp of Cymbeline, Britain.

That the poor soldier that so richly fought,
Whose rags shamed gilded arms, whose naked breast
5   Stepped before targs of proof,[1] cannot be found.
He shall be happy that can find him, if
Our grace can make him so.

BELARIUS   I never saw
Such noble fury in so poor a thing,
Such precious deeds in one that promised naught
But beggary and poor looks.

10 CYMBELINE   No tidings of him?

PISANIO   He hath been searched° among the dead and living,   sought
But no trace of him.

CYMBELINE   To my grief I am
The heir of his reward, which I will add
[*To* BELARIUS, GUIDERIUS, *and* ARVIRAGUS] To you, the liver,
        heart, and brain of Britain,
15   By whom I grant she lives. 'Tis now the time
To ask of whence you are. Report it.

BELARIUS   Sir,
In Cambria° are we born, and gentlemen.   Wales
Further to boast were neither true nor modest,
Unless I add we are honest.

CYMBELINE   Bow your knees.
        [*They kneel. He knights them*]
20   Arise, my knights o'th' battle.[2] I create you
Companions to our person, and will fit° you   supply
With dignities becoming your estates.°   (new) rank
        [BELARIUS, GUIDERIUS, *and* ARVIRAGUS *rise.*]
        Enter CORNELIUS *and* LADIES
There's business in these faces. Why so sadly
Greet you our victory? You look like Romans,
And not o'th' court of Britain.

25 CORNELIUS   Hail, great King!
To sour your happiness I must report
The Queen is dead.

CYMBELINE   Who worse than a physician
Would this report become? But I consider
By medicine life may be prolonged, yet death
30   Will seize the doctor too. How ended she?

CORNELIUS   With horror, madly dying, like her life,
Which being cruel to the world, concluded
Most cruel to herself. What she confessed
I will report, so please you. These her women
35   Can trip me° if I err, who with wet cheeks   point out my mistakes
Were present when she finished.

CYMBELINE   Prithee, say.

CORNELIUS   First, she confessed she never loved you, only
Affected° greatness got by you, not you;   Desired
Married your royalty, was wife to your place,°   position
Abhorred your person.

40 CYMBELINE   She alone knew this,
And but° she spoke it dying, I would not   except that

1. *targs of proof*: shields whose strength had been tested.
2. A special group of knights who won their titles for extraordinary bravery on the battlefield.

Believe her lips in opening it. Proceed.

CORNELIUS   Your daughter, whom she bore in hand° to love   she pretended
With such integrity, she did confess
45 Was as a scorpion to her sight, whose life,
But that her flight prevented it, she had
Ta'en off° by poison.   Ended

CYMBELINE   O most delicate° fiend!   subtle
Who is't can read a woman? Is there more?

CORNELIUS   More, sir, and worse. She did confess she had
50 For you a mortal mineral° which, being took,   a deadly poison
Should by the minute feed on life, and, ling'ring,
By inches waste you. In which time she purposed
By watching,° weeping, tendance,³ kissing, to   staying awake
O'ercome you with her show;° and in fine,°   performance / finally
55 When she had fit you with° her craft, to work   shaped you by
Her son into th'adoption of the crown;⁴
But failing of her end by his strange absence,
Grew shameless-desperate, opened° in despite   revealed
Of heaven and men her purposes, repented
60 The evils she hatched were not effected; so
Despairing died.

CYMBELINE   Heard you all this, her women?

LADIES   We did, so please your highness.

CYMBELINE   Mine eyes
Were not in fault, for she was beautiful;
Mine ears that heard her flattery, nor my heart
65 That thought her like her seeming.° It had been vicious°   appearance / wrong
To have mistrusted her. Yet, O my daughter,
That it was folly in me thou mayst say,
And prove it in thy feeling.⁵ Heaven mend all!

                    Enter LUCIUS, GIACOMO, SOOTHSAYER, *and other Roman*
                    prisoners, POSTHUMUS *behind, and* INNOGEN [*dressed as*
                    a man, all guarded by Briton soldiers]

Thou com'st not, Caius, now for tribute. That
70 The Britons have razed out,° though with the loss   erased
Of many a bold one; whose kinsmen have made suit
That their good souls° may be appeased with slaughter   (of the dead Britons)
Of you, their captives, which ourself have granted.
So think of your estate.°   condition

75 LUCIUS   Consider, sir, the chance of war. The day
Was yours by accident. Had it gone with us,
We should not, when the blood was cool, have threatened
Our prisoners with the sword. But since the gods
Will have it thus, that nothing but our lives
80 May be called ransom, let it come. Sufficeth
A Roman with a Roman's heart can suffer.
Augustus lives to think on't;⁶ and so much
For my peculiar care.° This one thing only   concern for myself
I will entreat:

                    [*He presents* INNOGEN *to* CYMBELINE]
                    my boy, a Briton born,

---

3. Showing attention to you.
4. *to work . . . crown:* to work her son into the position
of heir to the crown.
5. And find it true by your experience.
6. Augustus lives and can consider what to do.

85	Let him be ransomed. Never master had	
	A page so kind, so duteous, diligent,	
	So tender over his occasions,° true,	*thoughtful of his needs*
	So feat,° so nurse-like; let his virtue join	*graceful*
	With my request, which I'll make bold your highness	
90	Cannot deny. He hath done no Briton harm,	
	Though he have served a Roman. Save him, sir,	
	And spare no blood beside.°	*no one else*

CYMBELINE   I have surely seen him.
    His favour° is familiar to me. Boy,   *face*
    Thou hast looked thyself into my grace,[7]
95   And art mine own. I know not why, wherefore,
    To say 'Live, boy'. Ne'er thank thy master. Live,
    And ask of Cymbeline what boon° thou wilt   *reward*
    Fitting my bounty and thy state,° I'll give it,   *rank*
    Yea, though thou do demand a prisoner
    The noblest ta'en.

100 INNOGEN   I humbly thank your highness.
   LUCIUS I do not bid thee beg my life, good lad,
    And yet I know thou wilt.
   INNOGEN   No, no. Alack,
    There's other work in hand. I see a thing[8]
    Bitter to me as death. Your life, good master,
    Must shuffle° for itself.   *shift*
105 LUCIUS   The boy disdains me.
    He leaves me, scorns me. Briefly die their joys
    That place them on the truth of girls and boys.[9]
    Why stands he so perplexed?
   CYMBELINE [*to* INNOGEN]   What wouldst thou, boy?
    I love thee more and more; think more and more
110   What's best to ask. Know'st him thou look'st on? Speak,
    Wilt have him live? Is he thy kin, thy friend?
   INNOGEN He is a Roman, no more kin to me
    Than I to your highness, who, being born your vassal,
    Am something nearer.
   CYMBELINE   Wherefore ey'st him so?
115 INNOGEN I'll tell you, sir, in private, if you please
    To give me hearing.
   CYMBELINE   Ay, with all my heart,
    And lend my best attention. What's thy name?
   INNOGEN Fidele, sir.
   CYMBELINE   Thou'rt my good youth, my page.
    I'll be thy master. Walk with me, speak freely.
           [CYMBELINE *and* INNOGEN *speak apart*]
   BELARIUS [*aside to* GUIDERIUS *and* ARVIRAGUS] Is not this boy
    revived from death?
120 ARVIRAGUS   One sand° another   *One grain of sand*
    Not more resembles that° sweet rosy lad   *than he resembles that*
    Who died, and was Fidele. What think you?
   GUIDERIUS The same dead thing alive.
   BELARIUS Peace, peace, see further. He eyes us not. Forbear.

---

7. You have by your appearance gained my favor.
8. Referring to the ring that she gave to Posthumus and that is now on Giacomo's finger.

9. *Briefly . . . boys:* Quickly dies the happiness of those who depend on the fidelity of girls and boys.

125 Creatures may be alike. Were't he, I am sure
He would have spoke to us.
GUIDERIUS   But we see° him dead.   *saw*
BELARIUS   Be silent; let's see further.
PISANIO [*aside*]   It is my mistress.
Since she is living, let the time run on
To good or bad.
CYMBELINE [*to* INNOGEN]   Come, stand thou by our side,
130 Make thy demand aloud. [*To* GIACOMO]   Sir, step you forth.
Give answer to this boy, and do it freely,
Or, by our greatness and the grace of it,
Which is our honour, bitter torture shall
Winnow° the truth from falsehood.   *Separate*
[*To* INNOGEN]   On, speak to him.
135 INNOGEN   My boon is that this gentleman may render°   *declare*
Of whom he had this ring.
POSTHUMUS [*aside*]   What's that to him?
CYMBELINE [*to* GIACOMO]   That diamond upon your finger, say,
How came it yours?
GIACOMO   Thou'lt torture me to leave° unspoken that   *for leaving*
Which to be spoke would torture thee.
140 CYMBELINE   How, me?
GIACOMO   I am glad to be constrained to utter that°   *what*
Torments me to conceal. By villainy
I got this ring; 'twas Leonatus' jewel,
Whom thou didst banish; and, which more may grieve thee,
145 As it doth me, a nobler sir ne'er lived
'Twixt sky and ground. Wilt thou hear more, my lord?
CYMBELINE   All that belongs to this.
GIACOMO   That paragon thy daughter,
For whom my heart drops blood, and my false spirits
Quail to remember—give me leave, I faint.
150 CYMBELINE   My daughter? What of her? Renew thy strength.
I had rather thou shouldst live while nature will°   *as long as nature allows*
Than die ere I hear more. Strive, man, and speak.
GIACOMO   Upon a time—unhappy was the clock
That struck the hour—it was in Rome—accursed
155 The mansion where—'twas at a feast—O, would
Our viands had been poisoned, or at least
Those which I heaved to head!°—the good Posthumus—   *raised to my mouth*
What should I say?—he was too good to be
Where ill men were, and was the best of all
160 Amongst the rar'st of good ones—sitting sadly,
Hearing us praise our loves of Italy
For beauty that made barren the swelled boast[1]
Of him that best could speak; for feature laming
The shrine of Venus or straight-pitched Minerva,[2]
165 Postures beyond brief nature;[3] for condition,°   *character*
A shop of all the qualities that man
Loves woman for; besides that hook of wiving,°   *bait for marriage*
Fairness which strikes the eye—

1. For beauty so great that it rendered hollow even the exaggerated boasts.
2. for . . . Minerva: for looks rendering deficient even the body (shrine) of the goddess of love (Venus) or the magisterial goddess of the arts (Minerva). *straight-pitched*: with erect posture.
3. Forms surpassing those of mere mortals.

CYMBELINE   I stand on fire.
    Come to the matter.

GIACOMO   All too soon I shall,

170   Unless thou wouldst grieve quickly. This Posthumus,
    Most like a noble lord in love and one
    That had a royal lover, took his hint,
    And not dispraising whom we praised—therein
    He was as calm as virtue—he began

175   His mistress' picture, which by his tongue being made,
    And then a mind put in't, either our brags
    Were cracked° of kitchen-trulls, or his description   *uttered in defense*
    Proved us unspeaking sots.°   *fools incapable of speech*

CYMBELINE   Nay, nay, to th' purpose.

GIACOMO   Your daughter's chastity—there it begins.

180   He spake of her as° Dian had hot° dreams   *as if / lustful*
    And she alone were cold,° whereat I, wretch,   *chaste*
    Made scruple of° his praise, and wagered with him   *Disputed*
    Pieces of gold 'gainst this which then he wore
    Upon his honoured finger, to attain

185   In suit° the place of 's bed and win this ring   *By urging my suit*
    By hers and mine adultery. He, true knight,
    No lesser of her honour confident
    Than I did truly find her, stakes this ring—
    And would so had it been a carbuncle

190   Of Phoebus' wheel,[4] and might so safely had it
    Been all the worth of 's car.° Away to Britain   *worth the entire chariot*
    Post° I in this design. Well may you, sir,   *Hasten*
    Remember me at court, where I was taught
    Of° your chaste daughter the wide difference   *By*

195   'Twixt amorous and villainous. Being thus quenched
    Of hope, not longing,° mine Italian brain   *though not of desire*
    Gan° in your duller Britain[5] operate   *Began*
    Most vilely; for my vantage,° excellent.   *profit*
    And, to be brief, my practice° so prevailed   *deceit*

200   That I returned with simular° proof enough   *pretended; specious*
    To make the noble Leonatus mad
    By wounding his belief in her renown°   *reputation*
    With tokens thus and thus; averring° notes   *confirming*
    Of chamber-hanging, pictures, this her bracelet—

205   O cunning, how I got it!—nay, some marks
    Of secret on her person, that he could not
    But think her bond of chastity quite cracked,
    I having ta'en the forfeit.[6] Whereupon—
    Methinks I see him now—

POSTHUMUS [*coming forward*]   Ay, so thou dost,

210   Italian fiend! Ay me, most credulous fool,
    Egregious murderer, thief, anything
    That's due[7] to all the villains past, in being,
    To come! O, give me cord, or knife, or poison,
    Some upright justicer!° Thou, King, send out   *judge*

215   For torturers ingenious. It is I

---

4. *had . . . wheel:* even if it had been a precious stone
from the wheel of the sun god's chariot.
5. Alluding to the belief that England's northern climate
made its inhabitants sluggish and slow of wit.
6. Believing I had taken what she gave up (her chastity).
7. *anything / That's due:* any name that's owed.

That all th'abhorrèd things o'th' earth amend[8]
By being worse than they. I am Posthumus,
That killed thy daughter—villain-like, I lie:
That caused a lesser villain than myself,

220 A sacrilegious thief, to do't. The temple
Of virtue was she; yea, and she herself.°   *she was virtue herself*
Spit and throw stones, cast mire upon me, set
The dogs o'th' street to bay me. Every villain
Be called Posthumus Leonatus, and

225 Be 'villain' less than 'twas![9] O Innogen!
My queen, my life, my wife, O Innogen,
Innogen, Innogen!

INNOGEN [*approaching him*]   Peace, my lord. Hear, hear.
POSTHUMUS   Shall 's have a play of this? Thou scornful page,
There lie thy part.°   *Your role is to lie there*
     [*He strikes her down*]

PISANIO [*coming forward*]   O gentlemen, help!
230 Mine and your mistress! O my lord Posthumus,
You ne'er killed Innogen till now. Help, help!
[*To* INNOGEN] Mine honoured lady.

CYMBELINE   Does the world go round?

POSTHUMUS   How comes these staggers[1] on me?

PISANIO [*to* INNOGEN]   Wake, my mistress.

CYMBELINE   If this be so, the gods do mean to strike me
235 To death with mortal° joy.   *death-causing*

PISANIO [*to* INNOGEN]   How fares my mistress?

INNOGEN   O, get thee from my sight!
Thou gav'st me poison. Dangerous fellow, hence.
Breathe not where princes are.

CYMBELINE   The tune of Innogen.

240 PISANIO   Lady, the gods throw stones of sulphur° on me if   *thunderbolts*
That box I gave you was not thought by me
A precious thing. I had it from the Queen.

CYMBELINE   New matter still.

INNOGEN   It poisoned me.

CORNELIUS   O gods!
I left out one thing which the Queen confessed
245 [*To* PISANIO] Which must approve° thee honest. 'If Pisanio   *prove*
Have', said she, 'given his mistress that confection°   *compound*
Which I gave him for cordial, she is served
As I would serve a rat.'

CYMBELINE   What's this, Cornelius?

CORNELIUS   The Queen, sir, very oft importuned me
250 To temper° poisons for her, still° pretending   *mix / always*
The satisfaction of her knowledge only
In killing creatures vile, as cats and dogs
Of no esteem.° I, dreading that her purpose   *value*
Was of more danger, did compound for her
255 A certain stuff which, being ta'en, would cease
The present power of life, but in short time

---

8. Who makes all loathsome things seem better.
9. *Every . . . 'twas:* May the word "villain" be less abhorrent than it was, since "Posthumus Leonatus" has replaced it.

1. A disease, usually of horses, that causes an unsteady walk; dizziness.

All offices of nature° should again   *All natural faculties*
Do their due functions. [*To* INNOGEN] Have you ta'en of it?

INNOGEN   Most like° I did, for I was dead.   *likely*

BELARIUS [*aside to* GUIDERIUS *and* ARVIRAGUS]   My boys,
There was our error.

260 GUIDERIUS   This is sure Fidele.

INNOGEN [*to* POSTHUMUS]   Why did you throw your wedded
    lady from you?
Think that you are upon a lock,[2] and now
Throw me again.
        [*She throws her arms about his neck*]

POSTHUMUS   Hang there like fruit, my soul,
Till the tree die.

CYMBELINE [*to* INNOGEN]   How now, my flesh, my child?

265 What, mak'st thou me a dullard° in this act?   *sluggish performer*
Wilt thou not speak to me?

INNOGEN [*kneeling*]   Your blessing, sir.

BELARIUS [*aside to* GUIDERIUS *and* ARVIRAGUS]   Though you did
    love this youth, I blame ye not.
You had a motive° for't.   *reason*

CYMBELINE   My tears that fall
Prove holy water on thee!
        [*He raises her*]
                        Innogen,
Thy mother's dead.

270 INNOGEN   I am sorry for't, my lord.

CYMBELINE   O, she was naught,° and 'long° of her it was   *worthless / because*
That we meet here so strangely.° But her son   *like strangers*
Is gone, we know not how nor where.

PISANIO   My lord,
Now fear is from me I'll speak truth. Lord Cloten,

275 Upon my lady's missing,° came to me   *absence*
With his sword drawn, foamed at the mouth, and swore
If I discovered° not which way she was gone   *revealed*
It was my instant death. By accident°   *chance*
I had a feignèd letter of my master's[3]

280 Then in my pocket, which directed him
To seek her on the mountains near to Milford,
Where in a frenzy, in my master's garments,
Which he enforced from me, away he posts°   *hastens*
With unchaste purpose, and with oath to violate

285 My lady's honour. What became of him
I further know not.

GUIDERIUS   Let me end the story.
I slew him there.

CYMBELINE   Marry, the gods forfend!
I would not thy good deeds° should from my lips   *(on the battlefield)*
Pluck a hard sentence. Prithee, valiant youth,

290 Deny't again.°   *Take it back*

GUIDERIUS   I have spoke it, and I did it.

CYMBELINE   He was a prince.

GUIDERIUS   A most incivil° one. The wrongs he did me   *barbarous*

---

2. You are in a wrestling hold. This is a disputed pas-   3. Referring to the letter written by Posthumus to mis-
sage; F here reads "rock."   lead Innogen.

Were nothing prince-like, for he did provoke me
295 With language that would make me spurn the sea
If it could so roar to me. I cut off 's head,
And am right glad he is not standing here
To tell this tale of mine.[4]
CYMBELINE   I am sorrow for thee.
By thine own tongue thou art condemned, and must
Endure our law. Thou'rt dead.
300 INNOGEN   That headless man
I thought had been my lord.
CYMBELINE [*to soldiers*]   Bind the offender,
And take him from our presence.
BELARIUS   Stay, sir King.
This boy is better than the man he slew,
As well descended as thyself, and hath
305 More of thee merited than a band of Clotens
Had ever scar for.[5] Let his arms alone;
They were not born for bondage.
CYMBELINE   Why, old soldier,
Wilt thou undo the worth thou art unpaid for[6]
By tasting of our wrath? How of descent
As good as we?
310 ARVIRAGUS   In that he spake too far.
CYMBELINE [*to* BELARIUS][7]   And thou shalt die for't.
BELARIUS   We will die all three
But I will prove° that two on 's° are as good   *Unless I prove / of us*
As I have given out him. My sons, I must
For mine own part unfold a dangerous speech,
Though haply° well for you.   *perhaps*
315 ARVIRAGUS   Your danger's ours.
GUIDERIUS   And our good his.
BELARIUS   Have at it then. By leave,[8]
Thou hadst, great King, a subject who
Was called Belarius.
CYMBELINE   What of him? He is
A banished traitor.
BELARIUS   He it is that hath
320 Assumed° this age. Indeed, a banished man;   *Reached*
I know not how a traitor.
CYMBELINE [*to soldiers*]   Take him hence.
The whole world shall not save him.
BELARIUS   Not too hot.°   *fast*
First pay me for the nursing of thy sons,
And let it° be confiscate all so soon   *(the payment)*
As I have received it.
325 CYMBELINE   Nursing of my sons?
BELARIUS   I am too blunt and saucy. [*Kneeling*] Here's my knee.
Ere I arise I will prefer° my sons,   *advance*
Then spare not the old father. Mighty sir,

---

4. To tell a tale of cutting off my head.
5. *than . . . for*: than an army of Clotens ever earned by their battle scars.
6. The merit you are not yet rewarded for.
7. It is unclear to whom—Arviragus or Belarius—Cymbeline speaks the next line. Arviragus has just

addressed Cymbeline, and one might expect the King's reply to be directed to him. Belarius, however, made the offending remark about Guiderius being of as good birth as Cloten, and the threat of death probably applies to him.
8. Let's begin, then. With your permission.

These two young gentlemen that call me father
330 And think they are my sons are none of mine.
They are the issue° of your loins, my liege,   *offspring*
And blood of your begetting.

CYMBELINE   How, my issue?

BELARIUS   So sure as you your father's. I, old Morgan,[9]
Am that Belarius whom you sometime° banished.   *once*
335 Your pleasure was my mere offence,[1] my punishment
Itself, and all my treason. That I suffered
Was all the harm I did. These gentle princes—
For such and so they are—these twenty years
Have I trained up. Those arts° they have as I   *accomplishments*
340 Could put into them. My breeding was, sir,
As your highness knows. Their nurse Euriphile,
Whom for the theft I wedded, stole these children
Upon my banishment. I moved° her to't,   *persuaded*
Having received the punishment before
345 For that which I did then. Beaten° for loyalty   *Having been beaten*
Excited me to treason. Their dear loss,
The more of you 'twas felt, the more it shaped°   *suited*
Unto° my end° of stealing them. But, gracious sir,   *With / purpose*
Here are your sons again, and I must lose
350 Two of the sweet'st companions in the world.
The benediction of these covering heavens
Fall on their heads like dew, for they are worthy
To inlay heaven with stars.°   *To become constellations*

CYMBELINE   Thou weep'st, and speak'st.
The service that you three have done is more
355 Unlike° than this thou tell'st. I lost my children.   *Improbable*
If these be they, I know not how to wish
A pair of worthier sons.

BELARIUS [*rising*]   Be pleased a while.
This gentleman, whom I call Polydore,
Most worthy prince, as yours, is true Guiderius.
     [GUIDERIUS *kneels*]
360 This gentleman, my Cadwal, Arviragus,
Your younger princely son.
     [ARVIRAGUS *kneels*]
              He, sir, was lapped°   *wrapped*
In a most curious° mantle wrought by th' hand   *delicately fashioned*
Of his queen mother, which for more probation°   *proof*
I can with ease produce.

CYMBELINE   Guiderius had
365 Upon his neck a mole, a sanguine° star.   *blood-red*
It was a mark of wonder.

BELARIUS   This is he,
Who hath upon him still that natural stamp.
It was wise nature's end in the donation°   *purpose in giving it*
To be his evidence now.

CYMBELINE   O, what am I?
370 A mother to the birth of three? Ne'er mother

---

9. Morgan was the Welsh name Belarius assumed during the years he spent in Wales.   1. What you pleased (to accuse me of) was my entire offense.

Rejoiced deliverance more.[2] Blest pray you be,
That, after this strange starting from your orbs,[3]
You may reign in them now!
      [GUIDERIUS *and* ARVIRAGUS *rise*]
                   O Innogen,
Thou hast lost by this a kingdom.

INNOGEN   No, my lord,

375   I have got two worlds by't. O my gentle brothers,
Have we thus met? O, never say hereafter
But I am truest speaker. You called me brother
When I was but your sister; I you brothers
When ye were so indeed.

CYMBELINE   Did you e'er meet?

ARVIRAGUS   Ay, my good lord.

380   GUIDERIUS   And at first meeting loved,
Continued so until we thought he died.

CORNELIUS   By the Queen's dram she swallowed.

CYMBELINE   O rare instinct!
When shall I hear all through? This fierce° abridgement   *drastic*
Hath to it circumstantial branches which

385   Distinction should be rich in.[4] Where? How lived you?
And when came you to serve our Roman captive?
How parted with your brothers? How first met them?
Why fled you from the court? And whither? These,
And your three motives° to the battle, with   *the motives of you three*

390   I know not how much more, should be demanded,
And all the other by-dependences,°   *circumstances*
From chance° to chance. But nor° the time nor place   *occurrence / neither*
Will serve our long inter'gatories.° See,   *lengthy questioning*
Posthumus anchors upon Innogen,

395   And she, like harmless lightning, throws her eye
On him, her brothers, me, her master, hitting
Each object with a joy. The counterchange
Is severally in all.[5] Let's quit this ground,
And smoke° the temple with our sacrifices.   *fill with smoke*

400   [*To* BELARIUS] Thou art my brother; so we'll hold thee ever.

INNOGEN [*to* BELARIUS]   You are my father too, and did relieve° me   *save*
To see this gracious season.

CYMBELINE   All o'erjoyed,
Save these in bonds. Let them be joyful too,
For they shall taste our comfort.

INNOGEN [*to* LUCIUS]   My good master,
I will yet do you service.

405   LUCIUS   Happy be you!

CYMBELINE   The forlorn° soldier that so nobly fought,   *wretched*
He would have well becomed this place, and graced
The thankings of a king.

POSTHUMUS   I am, sir,
The soldier that did company these three

---

2. Never did giving birth cause a mother to rejoice more.
3. After this unnatural displacement from your rightful positions. Referring to astrological theories that each heavenly body moved in its proper orb, or circle, around the earth. For a planet to move outside its orb caused

disturbances in the heavens.
4. *circumstantial . . . in:* many ramifications that will provide particulars in rich abundance.
5. *The . . . all:* The exchange (of glances) passes from each to each.

410 In poor beseeming.° 'Twas a fitment⁶ for   *appearance*
The purpose I then followed. That I was he,
Speak, Giacomo; I had you down, and might
Have made you finish.°   *die*

GIACOMO [*kneeling*]   I am down again,
But now my heavy conscience sinks my knee
415 As then your force did. Take that life, beseech you,
Which I so often owe;° but your ring first,   *owe so many times over*
And here the bracelet of the truest princess
That ever swore her faith.

POSTHUMUS [*raising him*]   Kneel not to me.
The power that I have on you is to spare you,
420 The malice towards you to forgive you. Live,
And deal with others better.

CYMBELINE   Nobly doomed!°   *sentenced*
We'll learn our freeness of a son-in-law.
Pardon's the word to all.

ARVIRAGUS [*to* POSTHUMUS]   You holp° us, sir,   *helped*
As° you did mean indeed to be our brother.   *As if*
425 Joyed are we that you are.

POSTHUMUS   Your servant, princes. [*To* LUCIUS] Good my lord of Rome,
Call forth your soothsayer. As I slept, methought
Great Jupiter, upon his eagle backed,°   *riding on his eagle*
Appeared to me with other spritely° shows   *ghostly*
430 Of mine own kindred. When I waked I found
This label° on my bosom, whose containing°   *tablet / contents*
Is so from sense in hardness that I can
Make no collection of it.⁷ Let him show
His skill in the construction.°   *interpretation*

LUCIUS   Philharmonus.

SOOTHSAYER   Here, my good lord.

435 LUCIUS   Read, and declare the meaning.

SOOTHSAYER *reads* [*the tablet*] 'Whenas a lion's whelp shall, to
himself unknown, without seeking find, and be embraced by a
piece of tender air; and when from a stately cedar shall be
lopped branches which, being dead many years, shall after
440 revive, be jointed to the old stock, and freshly grow: then shall
Posthumus end his miseries, Britain be fortunate and flourish
in peace and plenty.'
Thou, Leonatus, art the lion's whelp.
The fit and apt construction of thy name,
445 Being *leo-natus*,° doth import so much.   *lion-born*
[*To* CYMBELINE] The piece of tender air thy virtuous daughter,
Which we call '*mollis aer*';⁸ and '*mollis aer*'
We term it '*mulier*', [*to* POSTHUMUS] which '*mulier*' I divine
Is this most constant wife, who even now,
450 Answering the letter of the oracle,⁹
Unknown to you, unsought, were clipped about°   *embraced*
With this most tender air.

CYMBELINE   This hath some seeming.

SOOTHSAYER   The lofty cedar, royal Cymbeline,

---

6. A suitable disguise.
7. *Is . . . it:* Is so difficult to make sense of that I can
draw no conclusion from it.

8. Latin for "gentle air." An ancient (and erroneous)
etymology for *mulier,* Latin for "woman" or "wife."
9. Fulfilling the exact terms of the oracle.

Personates° thee, and thy lopped branches point *Stands for*
455 Thy two sons forth, who, by Belarius stol'n,
For many years thought dead, are now revived,
To the majestic cedar joined, whose issue
Promises Britain peace and plenty.

CYMBELINE   Well,
My peace we will begin; and, Caius Lucius,
460 Although the victor, we submit to Caesar
And to the Roman empire, promising
To pay our wonted tribute, from the which
We were dissuaded by our wicked queen,
Whom° heavens in justice both on her and hers *On whom*
465 Have laid most heavy hand.

SOOTHSAYER The fingers of the powers above do tune
The harmony of this peace. The vision,
Which I made known to Lucius ere the stroke
Of this yet scarce-cold battle,[1] at this instant
470 Is full° accomplished. For the Roman eagle, *entirely*
From south to west on wing soaring aloft,
Lessened herself,[2] and in the beams o'th' sun
So vanished; which foreshowed our princely eagle
Th'imperial Caesar should again unite
475 His favour with the radiant Cymbeline,
Which shines here in the west.

CYMBELINE   Laud we the gods,
And let our crookèd° smokes climb to their nostrils *curling*
From our blest altars. Publish° we this peace *Proclaim*
To all our subjects. Set we forward,° let *Let us go forth*
480 A Roman and a British ensign° wave *banner*
Friendly together. So through Lud's town march,
And in the temple of great Jupiter
Our peace we'll ratify, seal it with feasts.
Set on there.° Never was a war did cease, *March forth*
485 Ere bloody hands were washed, with such a peace.

[Flourish.] Exeunt [in triumph]

---

1. *ere . . . battle:* before the action of this battle, which 2. Made herself small (by flying into the distance).
has only just ceased.

The Tempest

Near the close of *King Lear,* the ruined old king, stripped of the last vestiges of his power, dreams of being locked away happily in prison with his beloved Cordelia. Father and daughter have a more tragic fate in store for them, but Shakespeare returns to the dream in *The Tempest.* The play opens on a remote island of exile where Prospero, deposed from power and thrust out of Milan by his wicked brother, has found shelter with his only daughter, Miranda. Unlike many of Shakespeare's plays, *The Tempest* does not appear to have a single dominant source for its plot, but it is a kind of echo chamber of Shakespearean motifs. Its story of loss and recovery and its air of wonder link it closely to the group of late plays that modern editors generally call "romances" (*Pericles, The Winter's Tale, Cymbeline*), but it resonates as well with issues that haunted Shakespeare's imagination throughout his career: the painful necessity for a father to let his daughter go (*Othello, King Lear*); the treacherous betrayal of a legitimate ruler (*Richard II, Julius Caesar, Hamlet, Macbeth*); the murderous hatred of one brother for another (*Richard III, As You Like It, Hamlet, King Lear*); the passage from court society to the wilderness and the promise of a return (*A Midsummer Night's Dream, As You Like It*); the young heiress, torn from her place in the social hierarchy (*Twelfth Night, Pericles, The Winter's Tale*); the dream of manipulating others by means of art, especially by staging miniature plays within plays (*1 Henry IV, Much Ado About Nothing, Hamlet*); the threat of a radical loss of identity (*The Comedy of Errors, Richard II, King Lear*); the relationship between nature and nurture (*Pericles, The Winter's Tale*); the harnessing of magical powers (*The First Part of the Contention* [*2 Henry VI*], *A Midsummer Night's Dream, Macbeth*).

Though it is the first play printed in the First Folio (1623), *The Tempest* is probably one of the last that Shakespeare wrote. It can be dated fairly precisely: it uses material that was not available until late 1610, and there is a record of a performance before the king on Hallowmas Night, 1611. Since Shakespeare retired soon after to Stratford, *The Tempest* has seemed to many to be his valedictory to the theater. In this view, Prospero's strangely anxious and moving epilogue—"Now my charms are all o'erthrown, / And what strength I have's mine own"—is the expression of Shakespeare's own professional leave-taking. There are reasons to be skeptical: after finishing *The Tempest,* he collaborated on at least two other plays, *All Is True* (*Henry VIII*) and *The Two Noble Kinsmen,* and it is perilous to identify Shakespeare too closely with any of his characters, let alone an exiled, embittered, manipulative princely wizard. Yet the echo-chamber effect is striking, and when Prospero and others speak of his powerful "art," it is difficult not to associate the skill of the great magician with the skill of the great playwright. Near the end of the play, the association is made explicit when Prospero uses his magic powers to produce what he terms "some vanity of mine art" (4.1.41), a betrothal masque performed by spirits whom he calls forth "to enact / My present fancies" (4.1.121–22). The masque, typically a lavish courtly performance with music and dancing, may have seemed particularly appropriate on the occasion of another early performance: *The Tempest* was one of fourteen plays provided as part of the elaborate festivities in honor of the betrothal and marriage of King James's daughter Elizabeth to Frederick, the elector palatine. As Prospero's gift of the beautiful spectacle displays his magnificence and authority, so *The Tempest* and the other plays commanded by the king for his daughter's wedding would have enhanced his own prestige.

The Tempest opens with a spectacular storm that recalls *King Lear* not only in its violence but in its indifference to the ruler's authority: "What cares these roarers for

Magical storm. From Olaus Magnus, *Historia de Gentibus Septentrionalibus* (1555 ed.).

the name of king?" (1.1.15–16), shouts the exasperated Boatswain at the aristocrats who are standing in his way. The Boatswain's outburst seems unanswerable: like the implacable thunder in *King Lear,* the tempest marks the point at which exalted titles are revealed to be absurd pretensions, substanceless in the face of the elemental forces of nature and the desperate struggle for survival. But we soon learn that this tempest is not in fact natural and that it emphatically does hear and respond to human power, a power that is terrifying but, at least by its own account, benign: "The direful spectacle of the wreck," Prospero tells his daughter, "I have with such provision in mine art / So safely ordered" (1.2.26, 28–29) that no one on board has been harmed.

Shakespeare's contemporaries were fascinated by the figure of the magus, the great magician who by dint of deep learning, ascetic discipline, and patient skill could command the secret forces of the natural and supernatural world. Distinct from the village witch and "cunning man," figures engaged in local acts of healing and malice, and distinct, too, from alchemical experimenters bent on turning base metal into gold, the magus, cloaked in a robe covered with mysterious symbols, pronounced his occult charms, called forth spirits, and ranged in his imagination through the heavens and the earth, conjoining contemplative wisdom with virtuous action in order to confer great benefits upon his age. But there was a shiver of fear mingled with the popular admiration: when the person in Shakespeare's time most widely identified as a magus, the wizard John Dee, was away from his house, his library, one of the greatest private collections of books in England, was set on fire and burned to the ground.

Book, costume, powerful language, the ability to enact the fancies of the brain: these are key elements of both magic and theater. "I have bedimmed / The noontide sun," Prospero declares (5.1.41–42), beginning an enumeration of extraordinary accomplishments that culminates with the revelation that

> graves at my command
> Have waked their sleepers, oped, and let 'em forth
> By my so potent art.
>
> (5.1.48–50)

For the playwright who conjured up the ghosts of Caesar and old Hamlet, the claim does not seem extravagant, but for a magician it amounts to an extremely dangerous confession. Necromancy—communing with the spirits of the dead—was the very essence of black magic, the hated practice from which Prospero is careful to distinguish himself throughout the play. Before his exile, the island had been the realm of the "damned witch Sycorax," who was banished there "for mischiefs manifold and sorceries terrible" (1.2.265–66). The legitimacy of Prospero's power, including power over his slave Caliban, Sycorax's son, depends on his claims to moral authority, but for one disturbing moment it is difficult to see the difference between "foul witch" and princely magician. Small wonder that as soon as he has disclosed that he has trafficked with the dead, Prospero declares that he abjures his "rough magic" (5.1.50).

Prospero does not give an explicit reason for this abjuration, but it appears to be a key stage in the complex process that has led, before the time of the play, to his overthrow and will lead, after the play's events are over, to his return to power. This process in its entirety requires years to unfold, but the play depicts only a small, though crucially important, fragment of it. Together with his early *Comedy of Errors, The Tempest* is unusual among Shakespeare's plays in observing what literary critics of the age called the unities of time and place; unlike *Antony and Cleopatra,* for example, which ranges over a huge territory, or *The Winter's Tale,* which covers a huge span of time, the actions of *The Tempest* all take place in a single locale, the island, during the course of a single day. In a long scene of exposition just after the spectacular opening storm, Prospero tells Miranda that he is at a critical moment; everything depends on his seizing the opportunity that fortune has granted him. The whole play, then, is the spectacle of his timing, timing that might be cynically termed political opportunism or theatrical cunning but that Prospero himself associates with the working out of "providence divine" (1.2.160). The opportunity he seizes has its tangled roots in what he calls "the dark backward and abyss of time" (1.2.50). Many years before, when he was Duke of Milan, Prospero's preoccupation with "secret studies" gave his ambitious and unscrupulous brother Antonio the opportunity to topple him from power. Now those same studies, perfected during his long exile, have enabled Prospero to cause

The conjurer. Engraving by Theodore de Bry after a drawing by John White. From Thomas Hariot, *A Briefe and True Report of the New Found Land of Virginia* (1590).

Antonio and his shipmates, sailing back to Italy from Tunis, to be shipwrecked on his island, where they have fallen unwittingly under his control. His magic makes it possible not only to wrest back his dukedom but to avenge himself for the terrible wrong that his brother and his brother's principal ally, Alonso, the King of Naples, have done him: "They now are in my power" (3.3.90). Audiences in Shakespeare's time would have had an all too clear image of how horrendous the vengeance of enraged princes usually was. That Prospero restrains himself from the full exercise of his power to harm his enemies, that he breaks his magic staff and drowns his book, is his highest moral achievement, a triumphant display of self-mastery: "The rarer action is / In virtue than in vengeance" (5.1.27–28).

All of those who are shipwrecked on the island undergo the same shock of terror and unexpected survival, but their experiences, as they cross the yellow sands and make their way toward the interior of the island, differ markedly. The least affected are the mariners, including the feisty Boatswain; after their exhausting labors in the storm, they have sunk into a strange, uneasy sleep, only to be awakened in time to sail the miraculously restored ship back to Italy. The others are put through more complex trials; exposed to varying degrees of anxiety, temptation, grief, fear, and penitence, they are in effect subjects in a psychological experiment carefully conducted by Prospero, who attempts to instill in them moral self-control and work-discipline. The most generously treated is Ferdinand, the only son of the King of Naples, whom Prospero, in what is essentially a carefully planned dynastic alliance, has secretly chosen to be his son-in-law. As Ferdinand bewails what he assumes is his father's death by drowning, he hears strange, haunting music, including the remarkable song of death and metamorphosis, "Full fathom five thy father lies" (1.2.400). Ferdinand is the only one of the shipwrecked company, until the play's final scene, to encounter Prospero directly; the magician makes the experience menacing, humiliating, and frustrating, but this is the modest, salutary price the young man must pay to win the hand of the beautiful Miranda, who seems to him a goddess and who, for her part, has fallen in love with him at first sight.

Prospero directs the experience of the rest as well, but not in person; instead they principally encounter his diligent servant, Ariel. Ariel is not human, although at a crucial moment he is able to imagine what he would feel "were I human" (5.1.20). He is, as the cast of characters describes him, an "airy spirit," capable of moving at immense speed, altering the weather, and producing vivid illusions. We learn that Ariel possesses an inherent moral "delicacy," a delicacy that in the past (that is, before the time depicted in the play) has brought him pain. For, as Prospero reminds him, he had been Sycorax's servant and was, for refusing "to act her earthy and abhorred commands" (1.2.275), imprisoned by the witch for many years in a cloven pine. Prospero freed him from confinement and now demands in return a fixed term of service, which Ariel provides with a mixture of brilliant alacrity and grumbling. Prospero responds in turn with mingled affection and anger, alternating warm praises and dire threats. Although Prospero's "art," through which he commands Ariel and the lesser spirits, seems to foresee and control everything, this control is purchased by constant discipline.

And, for all his godlike powers, there are limits to what Prospero can do. He can make the loathed Antonio and the others know something of the bitterness of loss and isolation; he can produce in them irresistible drowsiness and startled awakenings; he can command Ariel to lay before them a splendid banquet and then make it suddenly vanish; he can drive them to desperation and madness. But in the case of his own brother and Alonso's similarly wicked brother Sebastian, Prospero cannot reshape their inner lives and effect a moral transformation. The most he can do with these men without conscience is to limit through continual vigilance any further harm they might do and to take back what is rightfully his. When, with an obvious effort, Prospero declares that he forgives his brother's "rankest fault" (5.1.134), Antonio is conspicuously silent.

But the higher moral purpose of Prospero's art is not all a failure. With Alonso, the project of provoking repentance by generating intense grief and fear succeeds admirably: Alonso not only gives up his power over the dukedom of Milan but begs Prospero's pardon for the wrong he committed in conspiring to overthrow him. (Both rulers, Alonso and Prospero, can look forward to a unification of their states in the next generation, through the marriage of Ferdinand and Miranda.) Moreover, Prospero's carefully contrived scenarios succeed in confirming the decency, loyalty, and goodness of Alonso's counselor, Gonzalo, who had years before provided the exiled Duke and his daughter with the means necessary for their survival.

It is Gonzalo's goodness that at the end of the play enables him to grasp the dynastic providence in the bewildering tangle of events—"Was Milan thrust from Milan, that his issue / Should become kings of Naples?" (5.1.208–09)—and that earlier inspires him to sense the miraculous nature of their survival. Indifferent to the contemptuous mockery of the cynical Antonio and Sebastian, Gonzalo responds to shipwreck on the strange island by speculating on how he would govern it were he responsible for its "plantation":

> I'th' commonwealth I would by contraries
> Execute all things. For no kind of traffic
> Would I admit, no name of magistrate;
> Letters should not be known; riches, poverty,
> And use of service, none; contract, succession,
> Bourn, bound of land, tilth, vineyard, none;
> No use of metal, corn, or wine, or oil;
> No occupation, all men idle, all.
>
> (2.1.147–54)

Shakespeare adapted Gonzalo's utopian speculations from a passage in "Of Cannibals" (1580), a remarkably free-spirited essay by the French humanist Michel de Montaigne. The Brazilian Indians, Montaigne admiringly writes (in John Florio's 1603 translation), have "no kind of traffic, no knowledge of letters, no intelligence of numbers, no name

America. Engraving by Theodor Galle after a drawing by Jan van der Straet (c. 1580).

of magistrate nor of politic superiority, no use of service, of riches or of poverty, no con-tracts, no successions . . . no occupation but idle, no respect of kindred but common, no apparel but natural, no manuring of lands, no use of wine, corn, or metal." For Montaigne, the European adventurers and colonists, confident in their cultural superiority, are the real barbarians, while the American natives, with their cannibalism and free love, live in accordance with nature.

The issues raised by Montaigne, and more generally by New World voyages, may have been particularly interesting to *The Tempest*'s early audiences as news reached London of the extraordinary adventures of the Virginia Company's colony at Jamestown. Shakespeare seems to have read a detailed account of these adventures in a letter written by the colony's secretary, William Strachey; although the letter was not printed until 1625, it was evidently circulating in manuscript in 1610. In 1609, a fleet carrying more than four hundred persons sent out to reinforce the colony was struck by a hurricane near the Virginia coast. Two of the vessels reached their destination, but the third, the ship carrying the governor, Sir Thomas Gates, ran aground on an uninhabited island in the Bermudas. Remarkably enough, all of the passengers and crew survived; but their tribulations were not over. By forcing everyone to labor side by side in order to survive, the violence of the storm had weakened the governor's authority, and both the natural abundance and the isolation of the island where they were shipwrecked weakened it further. Gates ordered the company to build new ships in order to sail to Jamestown, but his command met with ominous grumblings and threats of mutiny. According to Strachey's letter, the main troublemaker directly challenged Gates's authority: "therefore let the Governour (said he) kiss, etc." In response, Gates had the troublemaker shot to death. New ships were built, and in an impressive feat of navigation, the entire company reached Jamestown. The group found the settlement deeply demoralized: illness was rampant, food was scarce, and relations with the neighboring Indians, once amicable, had completely broken down. Only harsh military discipline kept the English colony from falling apart.

With the possible exception of some phrases from Strachey's description of the storm and a few scattered details, *The Tempest* does not directly use any of this vivid narrative. Prospero's island is evidently in the Mediterranean, and the New World is only mentioned as a far-off place, "the still-vexed Bermudas" (1.2.230), where the swift Ariel flies to fetch dew. Yet Shakespeare's play seems constantly to echo precisely the issues raised by the Bermuda shipwreck and its aftermath. What does it take to survive? How do men of different classes and moral character react during a state of emergency? What is the proper relation between theoretical understanding and practical experience or between knowledge and power? Is obedience to authority willing or forced? How can those in power protect themselves from the conspiracies of malcontents? Is it possible to detect a providential design in what looks at first like a succession of accidents? If there are natives to contend with, how should colonists establish friendly and profitable relations with them? What is to be done if relations turn sour? How can those who rule prevent an alliance between hostile natives and the poorer colonists, often disgruntled and themselves exploited? And—Montaigne's more radical questions—what is the justification of one person's rule over another? Who is the civilized man, and who is the barbarian?

The unregenerate nastiness of Antonio and Sebastian, conjoined with the goodness of Gonzalo, might seem indirectly to endorse Montaigne's critique of the Europeans and his praise of the cannibals, were it not for the disturbing presence in *The Tempest* of the character whose name is almost an anagram for "cannibal," Caliban. Caliban, whose god Setebos is mentioned in accounts of Magellan's voyages as a Patagonian deity, is anything but a noble savage. Shakespeare does not shrink from the darkest European fantasies about the Wild Man. Indeed, he exaggerates them: Caliban is deformed, lecherous, evil-smelling, treacherous, naive, drunken, lazy, rebellious, violent, and devil-worshipping. According to Prospero, he is not even human: "A devil, a born devil, on whose nature / Nurture can never stick" (4.1.188–89). When he first came to the island, Prospero recalls, he treated Caliban "with human care" (1.2.349), lodging him in his own cell until the savage tried to rape Miranda. The arrival of the other Europeans brings out still worse qualities. Encountering the basest of the company, Alonso's jester, Trinculo, and drunken butler, Stefano, Caliban falls at their feet in brutish worship and then devises a conspiracy to murder Prospero in his sleep. Were the conspiracy to succeed, Caliban would get neither the girl for whom he lusts nor the freedom for which he shouts—he would become "King" Stefano's "foot-licker" (4.1.218)—but he would satisfy the enormous hatred he feels for Prospero.

Prospero's power, Caliban reasons, derives from his superior knowledge. "Remember / First to possess his books," he urges the louts, "for without them / He's but a sot as I am. . . . Burn but his books" (3.2.86–90). The strategy is a canny one, in recognizing an underlying link between literacy and authority, but the problem is not only that Stefano and Trinculo are hopeless fools but also that Prospero, like all Renaissance princes, has a diligent spy network: the invisible Ariel overhears the conspirators and warns his master of the approaching danger. Prospero's sudden recollection of the warning leads him to break off the betrothal masque with one of the most famous speeches in all of Shakespeare, "Our revels now are ended" (4.1.148ff.). This brooding meditation on the theatrical insubstantiality of the entire world and the dreamlike nature of human existence has seemed to many the pinnacle of the play's visionary wisdom. But it does not subsume in its rich cadences the other voices in *The Tempest*; specifically, it does not silence the surprising power of Caliban's voice.

That voice has been amplified in the centuries that followed the first performances of *The Tempest*, as European colonialism saw its grand political, moral, and economic claims disputed and, after violent struggles, dismantled. During these struggles, many anticolonial writers and critics rewrote Shakespeare's play, casting Prospero as a smugly racist, sexist oppressor, Ariel as a native coopted and corrupted by his colonial master, and Caliban as a victimized hero. "Prospero invaded the islands," declared the Cuban writer Roberto Fernández Retamar, "killed our ancestors, enslaved Caliban, and taught him his language to make himself understood. What else can Caliban do but use that same language—today he has no other—to curse him, to wish that the 'red plague' would fall on him?"

Shakespeare, who wrote when the colonialist project was still in its early stages, could not have anticipated this afterlife, and some scholars have argued that the relevance to *The Tempest* of the New World voyages has been greatly exaggerated. But, as the Barbadian writer George Lamming puts it, "Caliban keeps answering back." Caliban enters the play cursing, grumbling, and, above all, disputing Prospero's authority: "This island's mine, by Sycorax my mother, / Which thou tak'st from me" (1.2.334–35). By the close, his attempt to kill Prospero foiled and his body racked with cramps and bruises, Caliban declares that he will "be wise hereafter, / And seek for grace" (5.1.298–99). Yet it is not his mumbled reformation but his vehement protests that leave an indelible mark on *The Tempest*. The play may depict Caliban, in Prospero's ugly term, as "filth," but it gives him a remarkable, unforgettable eloquence. To Miranda's taunting reminder that she taught him to speak, Caliban retorts, "You taught me language, and my profit on't / Is I know how to curse" (1.2.366–67). It is not only in cursing, however, that Caliban is gifted: in richly sensuous poetry, he speaks of the island's natural resources and of his dreams. Caliban can be beaten into submission, but the master cannot eradicate his slave's desires, his pleasures, and his inconsolable pain. And across the vast gulf that divides the triumphant prince and the defeated savage, there is a momentary, enigmatic glimpse of a hidden bond: "This thing of darkness," Prospero says of Caliban, "I / Acknowledge mine" (5.1.278–79). The words need only be a claim of ownership, but they seem to hint at a deeper, more disturbing link between father and monster, legitimate ruler and savage, judge and criminal. Perhaps the link is only an illusion, a trick of the imagination on a strange island, but as Prospero leaves the island, it is he who begs for pardon.

STEPHEN GREENBLATT

TEXTUAL NOTE

The only authoritative printed text of *The Tempest* is in the First Folio of 1623 (F), where it appears as the first play, at the head of the comedies. The text seems to have been prepared with care. It includes a list of characters (*"Names of the Actors"*) printed at the end of the play and supplies act and scene divisions that this edition follows. There are also unusually full stage directions, although scholars have argued about whether these were written entirely by Shakespeare or were supplied or elaborated by the person who transcribed the author's manuscript for the compositors. Certain features of this transcription have led scholars to the conclusion that it was done by Ralph Crane, an experienced scribe who was responsible for the preparation of at least four other Shakespeare plays.

Most of the songs in *The Tempest* are preserved in early to mid-seventeenth-century manuscripts. These manuscripts indicate repeats and refrains, which have accordingly been accepted in the text of this edition.

SELECTED BIBLIOGRAPHY

Albanese, Denise. "Admiring Miranda and Enslaving Nature." *New Science, New World*. Durham, N.C.: Duke University Press, 1996. 59–91. Miranda as the feminine locus of the play's exploration of nature and culture.

Barker, Francis, and Peter Hulme. "Nymphs and Reapers Heavily Vanish: The Discursive Con-texts of *The Tempest*." *Alternative Shakespeares*. Vol. I. Ed. John Drakakis. London: Methuen, 1985. 191–205. English colonialism as a discursive context for the play's interest in the usurpation of power.

Brotton, Jerry. " 'This Tunis, sir, was Carthage': Contesting Colonialism in *The Tempest*." *Post-Colonial Shakespeares*. Ed. Ania Loomba and Martin Orkin. London: Routledge, 1998. 23–42. The play's Mediterranean geography exposes a bifurcated interest in both the Old and the New Worlds.

Brown, Paul. " 'This Thing of Darkness I Acknowledge Mine': *The Tempest* and the Discourse of Colonialism." *Political Shakespeare: New Essays in Cultural Materialism*. Ed. Jonathan Dollimore and Alan Sinfield. Ithaca, N.Y.: Cornell University Press, 1985. 48–71. Shakespeare's ambivalent depictions of political, social, and sexual authority read in relation to contemporary colonial practice.

Callaghan, Dympna. "Irish Memories in *The Tempest*." *Shakespeare Without Women: Representing Gender and Race on the Renaissance Stage*. London: Routledge, 2000. 97–138. Using the play's Irish echoes, considers how selective colonial recollection suppresses the cultural memory of the colonized.

Cartelli, Thomas. "Prospero in Africa: *The Tempest* as Colonialist Text and Pretext." *Repositioning Shakespeare: National Formations, Postcolonial Appropriations*. London: Routledge, 1999. 87–104. *The Tempest* can be made to operate both for and against the interests of modern Western ideology.

Greenblatt, Stephen. "Martial Law in the Land of Cockaigne." *Shakespearean Negotiations: The Circulation of Social Energy in Renaissance England*. Berkeley: University of California Press, 1988. 129–63. The play apparently celebrates the restoration of patriarchal order yet also ironically scrutinizes the political manipulation of anxiety.

Hulme, Peter, and William H. Sherman, eds. *"The Tempest" and Its Travels*. Philadelphia: University of Pennsylvania Press, 2000. A range of critical and creative materials, situating the play amid the local and global contexts of its time and beyond.

Orgel, Stephen. *The Illusion of Power: Political Theater in the English Renaissance*. Berkeley: University of California Press, 1975. Compares public and court theater practice, highlighting the masque's role in the allegorized expression of sovereign power.

Vaughan, Virginia Mason, and Alden T. Vaughan. *Critical Essays on Shakespeare's "The Tempest."* New York: Hall, 1998. Eleven essays illustrating the breadth and diversity of critical and cultural engagement with the play.

Films

Forbidden Planet. 1956. Dir. Fred M. Wilcox. USA. 98 min. A science-fiction cult classic in which Ariel is a robot and Caliban a monster of the id.

The Tempest. 1960. Dir. George Schaefer. USA. 76 min. A made-for-TV, one-camera film of a solid, though short stage rendition, with Richard Burton standing out as Caliban.

The Tempest. 1979. Dir. Derek Jarman. UK. 95 min. Part Gothic, part punk. Renders Juno's masque as a Broadway musical number.

Tempest. 1982. Dir. Paul Mazursky. USA. 140 min. Disenchanted New York architect escapes to a Greek island to reexamine his life.

Prospero's Books. 1991. Dir. Peter Greenaway. UK. 129 min. Surreal and baroque, focusing on the imagined contents of Prospero's library. John Gielgud stars.

The Tempest

THE PERSONS OF THE PLAY

PROSPERO, the rightful Duke of Milan
MIRANDA, his daughter
ANTONIO, his brother, the usurping Duke of Milan
ALONSO, King of Naples
SEBASTIAN, his brother
FERDINAND, Alonso's son
GONZALO, an honest old counsellor of Naples
ADRIAN
FRANCISCO } lords
ARIEL, an airy spirit attendant upon Prospero
CALIBAN, a savage and deformed native of the island, Prospero's slave
TRINCULO, Alonso's jester
STEFANO, Alonso's drunken butler
The MASTER of a ship
BOATSWAIN
MARINERS
SPIRITS
    The Masque
Spirits appearing as:
IRIS
CERES
JUNO
Nymphs, reapers

1.1

A tempestuous noise of thunder and lightning heard.
Enter a SHIPMASTER *and a* BOATSWAIN[1] [*at separate*
doors]

MASTER   Boatswain!
BOATSWAIN   Here, Master. What cheer?
MASTER   Good,[2] speak to th' mariners. Fall to't yarely,° or we run   *promptly*
   ourselves aground. Bestir, bestir!   *Exit*
   Enter MARINERS
5 BOATSWAIN   Heigh, my hearts!° Cheerly, cheerly, my hearts!   *hearties*
   Yare, yare! Take in the topsail![3] Tend° to th' Master's whistle!—   *Attend*
   Blow till thou burst thy wind, if room enough.[4]
       Enter ALONSO, SEBASTIAN, ANTONIO, FERDINAND, GON-
       ZALO, *and others*
ALONSO   Good Boatswain, have care. Where's the Master?
   [*To the* MARINERS] Play the men!°   *Act like men*
10 BOATSWAIN   I pray now, keep below.
ANTONIO   Where is the Master, Boatswain?

1.1 Location: A ship at sea.
1. The Boatswain probably enters after the shipmaster calls him; the latter is perhaps on the upper stage.
2. Acknowledging the Boatswain's presence; or perhaps short for "good man."

3. To reduce the surface area of the sail, and thereby lessen the force of the wind pushing the ship toward the island.
4. The wind may blow until it splits itself, provided there is enough sea room to maneuver in.

BOATSWAIN   Do you not hear him? You mar our labour. Keep
your cabins; you do assist the storm.

GONZALO   Nay, good,° be patient.   *good man*

15   BOATSWAIN   When the sea is. Hence! What cares these roarers
for the name of king?[5] To cabin! Silence; trouble us not.

GONZALO   Good, yet remember whom thou hast aboard.

BOATSWAIN   None that I more love than myself. You are a councillor;[6] if you can command these elements to silence and work

20   peace of the present,[7] we will not hand° a rope more. Use your   *handle*
authority. If you cannot, give thanks you have lived so long and
make yourself ready in your cabin for the mischance of the
hour, if it so hap.° [*To the* MARINERS] Cheerly, good hearts! [*To*   *happen*
GONZALO] Out of our way, I say!   *Exit*

25   GONZALO   I have great comfort from this fellow. Methinks he
hath no drowning mark[8] upon him; his complexion is perfect
gallows.[9] Stand fast, good Fate, to his hanging. Make the rope
of his destiny our cable,[1] for our own doth little advantage.° If   *use*
he be not born to be hanged, our case is miserable.

                                              Exit [*Courtiers*]

                      Enter BOATSWAIN

30   BOATSWAIN   Down with the topmast![2] Yare! Lower, lower! Bring
her to try wi'th' main-course![3]

                      A cry within

A plague upon this howling! They are louder than the weather,
or our office.[4]

                      Enter SEBASTIAN, ANTONIO, *and* GONZALO

Yet again? What do you here? Shall we give o'er° and drown?   *up*

35   Have you a mind to sink?

SEBASTIAN   A pox o'your throat, you bawling, blasphemous,
incharitable dog!

BOATSWAIN   Work you, then.

ANTONIO   Hang, cur, hang, you whoreson insolent noisemaker.

40   We are less afraid to be drowned than thou art.

                                              [*Exeunt* MARINERS]

GONZALO   I'll warrant him for drowning,[5] though° the ship were   *even if*
no stronger than a nutshell and as leaky as an unstanched°   *a freely menstruating*
wench.

BOATSWAIN   Lay her a-hold, a-hold! Set her two courses![6] Off to

45   sea again! Lay her off!

                      Enter MARINERS, *wet*

MARINERS   All lost! To prayers, to prayers! All lost!

                                              [*Exeunt* MARINERS]

BOATSWAIN   What, must our mouths be cold?[7]

GONZALO   The King and Prince at prayers! Let's assist them,
For our case is as theirs.

---

5. "Roarers," referring here to the waves, was also a
term for riotous people.
6. Member of the King's council; also an adviser or per-
suader.
7. Of the present circumstances.
8. Birthmark whose position was held to portend death
by drowning. "He that was born to be hanged will never
be drowned" was proverbial.
9. His physiognomy, appearance, shows that he will
certainly be hanged.
1. Anchor cable (an anchor is actually useless in a storm).

2. To reduce the top weight of the ship and make it
more stable.
3. Bring the ship close to the wind sailing only with the
mainsail.
4. Duties (in shouting orders).
5. I'll guarantee him against drowning.
6. Set the foresail in addition to the mainsail.
7. To be cold in the mouth—to be dead—was proverbial; may also suggest that the mariners warm their
mouths with liquor (line 50).

SEBASTIAN   I'm out of patience.

50   ANTONIO   We are merely° cheated of our lives by drunkards.   utterly
     This wide-chopped° rascal—would thou mightst lie drowning   large-mouthed
     The washing of ten tides.[8]

     GONZALO   He'll be hanged yet,
     Though every drop of water swear against it
     And gape at wid'st to glut° him.   its widest to swallow

     A confused noise within

     MARINERS [*within*]   Mercy on us!

55   We split, we split! Farewell, my wife and children!
     Farewell, brother! We split, we split, we split!

                                        [*Exit* BOATSWAIN]

     ANTONIO   Let's all sink wi'th' King.

     SEBASTIAN   Let's take leave of him.

                                Exit [ANTONIO *and* SEBASTIAN]

     GONZALO   Now would I give a thousand furlongs of sea for an
     acre of barren ground: long heath, broom, furze,[9] anything.
60   The wills above be done, but I would fain die a dry death.

                                                            Exit

                              1.2

     Enter PROSPERO [*in his magic cloak, with a staff*], *and*
          MIRANDA

     MIRANDA[1]   If by your art,[2] my dearest father, you have
     Put the wild waters in this roar, allay them.
     The sky, it seems, would pour down stinking pitch,
     But that the sea, mounting to th' welkin's° cheek,   sky's
5   Dashes the fire out. O, I have sufferèd
     With those that I saw suffer! A brave° vessel,   splendid
     Who had, no doubt, some noble creature in her,
     Dashed all to pieces! O, the cry did knock
     Against my very heart! Poor souls, they perished.
10   Had I been any god of power, I would
     Have sunk the sea within the earth, or ere°   before
     It should the good ship so have swallowed and
     The fraughting souls[3] within her.

     PROSPERO   Be collected.
     No more amazement.° Tell your piteous° heart   consternation / pitying
     There's no harm done.

     MIRANDA   O woe the day!

15   PROSPERO   No harm.
     I have done nothing but in care of thee,
     Of thee, my dear one, thee, my daughter, who
     Art ignorant of what thou art, naught knowing
     Of whence I am, nor that I am more better°   higher in rank

---

8. Pirates were hanged on the shore at low-water mark
and left there for the ebbing and flowing of three tides.
9. Heather, yellow shrubs, and gorse—all shrubs that
grow in poor soil.
1.2 Location: The rest of the play is set in various parts
of Prospero's island.
1. *Miranda* in Latin means "admirable" or "wonder-

ing." Miranda uses the formal "you," contrasting with
Prospero's more familiar "thou."
2. Skill; magic; learning; science.
3. Souls constituting the freight; perhaps also suggesting "burdened."
4. *Prospero* in Italian and Spanish means "fortunate" or
"prosperous."

20 Than Prospero, master of a full poor cell[5]
And thy no greater father.

MIRANDA   More to know
Did never meddle with° my thoughts.   *intrude upon*

PROSPERO   'Tis time
I should inform thee farther. Lend thy hand,
And pluck my magic garment from me.

[MIRANDA *removes Prospero's cloak, and he lays it on the*
ground]
                                        So.

25 Lie there, my art.—Wipe thou thine eyes; have comfort.
The direful spectacle of the wreck, which touched
The very virtue of compassion in thee,
I have with such provision° in mine art   *foresight*
So safely ordered that there is no soul—

30 No, not so much perdition° as an hair   *loss*
Betid° to any creature in the vessel,   *Happened*
Which° thou heard'st cry, which thou saw'st sink. Sit down,   *Whom*
For thou must now know farther.

[MIRANDA *sits*]

MIRANDA   You have often
Begun to tell me what I am, but stopped

35 And left me to a bootless inquisition,°   *profitless inquiry*
Concluding 'Stay; not yet'.

PROSPERO   The hour's now come.
The very minute bids thee ope° thine ear,   *open*
Obey, and be attentive. Canst thou remember
A time before we came unto this cell?

40 I do not think thou canst, for then thou wast not
Out° three years old.   *Fully*

MIRANDA   Certainly, sir, I can.

PROSPERO   By° what? By any other house or person?   *About*
Of anything the image tell me that
Hath kept with thy remembrance.

MIRANDA   'Tis far off,

45 And rather like a dream than an assurance°   *a certainty*
That my remembrance warrants.° Had I not   *guarantees is true*
Four or five women once that tended me?

PROSPERO   Thou hadst, and more, Miranda. But how is it
That this lives in thy mind? What seest thou else

50 In the dark backward° and abyss of time?   *past*
If thou rememb'rest aught° ere thou cam'st here,   *anything*
How thou cam'st here thou mayst.

MIRANDA   But that I do not.

PROSPERO   Twelve year since, Miranda, twelve year since,
Thy father was the Duke of Milan,[6] and
A prince of power—

55 MIRANDA   Sir, are not you my father?

PROSPERO   Thy mother was a piece° of virtue,° and   *perfect example / chastity*
She said thou wast my daughter; and thy father
Was Duke of Milan, and his only heir
And princess no worse issued.°   *no less nobly born*

---

5. Suggesting a hermit's or a poor man's dwelling. *full:*   6. Pronounced with stress on the first syllable.
very.

MIRANDA   O the heavens!
60   What foul play had we that we came from thence?
      Or blessèd° was't we did?   providential
PROSPERO   Both, both, my girl.
      By foul play, as thou sayst, were we heaved thence,
      But blessedly holp° hither.   helped
MIRANDA   O, my heart bleeds
      To think o'th' teen° that I have turned you to,   sorrow; trouble
65   Which is from° my remembrance. Please you, farther.   out of
PROSPERO   My brother and thy uncle called Antonio—
      I pray thee mark me, that a brother should
      Be so perfidious—he whom next° thyself   after
      Of all the world I loved, and to him put
70   The manage° of my state—as at that time   control
      Through all the signories° it was the first,   lordships
      And Prospero the prime° duke—being so reputed   foremost
      In dignity, and for the liberal arts[7]
      Without a parallel—those being all my study,
75   The government I cast upon my brother,
      And to my state grew stranger, being transported[8]
      And rapt in secret studies. Thy false uncle—
      Dost thou attend me?
MIRANDA   Sir, most heedfully.
PROSPERO   Being once perfected how to grant suits,[9]
80   How to deny them, who t'advance and who
      To trash for over-topping,[1] new created
      The creatures° that were mine, I say—or changed 'em   dependents
      Or else new formed 'em;[2] having both the key°   control
      Of officer and office, set all hearts i'th' state
85   To what tune pleased his ear, that° now he was   so that
      The ivy which had hid my princely trunk
      And sucked my verdure° out on't. Thou attend'st not!   vitality; power
MIRANDA   O good sir, I do.
PROSPERO   I pray thee mark me.
      I, thus neglecting worldly ends, all dedicated
90   To closeness° and the bettering of my mind   seclusion
      With that which but° by being so retired   merely
      O'er-priced all popular rate,[3] in my false brother
      Awaked an evil nature; and my trust,
      Like a good parent,[4] did beget of him
95   A falsehood, in its contrary° as great   inverse qualities
      As my trust was, which had indeed no limit,
      A confidence sans° bound. He being thus lorded   without
      Not only with what my revenue yielded
      But what my power might else exact, like one
100   Who having into° truth, by telling oft,   unto
      Made such a sinner of his memory
      To credit his own lie,[5] he did believe

---

7. As opposed to the "mechanical arts," the "liberal arts" encompassed the trivium (grammar, logic, and rhetoric) and the quadrivium (arithmetic, geometry, music, and astronomy).

8. Enraptured, with suggestions of "conveyed to another place." *grew stranger:* grew alienated from; became a foreigner to.

9. Having mastered handling formal requests.

1. For rising too high. *trash:* restrain, hold back (as by a leash).

2. *changed . . . 'em:* changed the duties and allegiance of existing officials, or created new ones.

3. Became too precious for the people to value, or understand.

4. From the colloquial "Good parents breed bad children."

5. *like one . . . lie:* like someone who comes to believe his own repeatedly stated lie. *To:* So as to.

He was indeed the Duke. Out o'th'° substitution,   *As a consequence of the*
And executing° th'outward face° of royalty   *portraying / image*
105   With all prerogative, hence his ambition growing—
Dost thou hear?

MIRANDA   Your tale, sir, would cure deafness.

PROSPERO   To have no screen between this part he played
And him he played it for, he needs will be
Absolute Milan.⁶ Me,° poor man—my library   *As for me*
110   Was dukedom large enough—of temporal royalties°   *rule*
He thinks me now incapable; confederates,°   *(he) plots*
So dry° he was for sway,° wi'th' King of Naples   *thirsty / power*
To give him annual tribute, do him homage,
Subject his coronet to his crown,⁷ and bend
115   The dukedom, yet unbowed—alas, poor Milan—
To most ignoble stooping.⁸

MIRANDA   O the heavens!

PROSPERO   Mark his condition° and th'event,° then tell me   *treaty / outcome*
If this might be a brother.

MIRANDA   I should sin
To think but° nobly of my grandmother.   *anything but*
Good wombs have borne bad sons.⁹

120 PROSPERO   Now the condition.
This King of Naples, being an enemy
To me inveterate, hearkens my brother's suit;
Which was that he, in lieu o'th' premises¹
Of homage and I know not how much tribute,
125   Should presently extirpate me and mine
Out of the dukedom, and confer fair Milan,
With all the honours, on my brother. Whereon,
A treacherous army levied, one midnight
Fated to th' purpose did Antonio open
130   The gates of Milan; and, i'th' dead of darkness,
The ministers° for th' purpose hurried thence   *agents*
Me and thy crying self.

MIRANDA   Alack, for pity!
I, not remem'bring how I cried out then,
Will cry it o'er again; it is a hint°   *an occasion*
That wrings mine eyes to't.

135 PROSPERO [*sitting*]   Hear a little further,
And then I'll bring thee to the present business
Which now's upon's, without the which this story
Were most impertinent.°   *irrelevant*

MIRANDA   Wherefore did they not
That hour destroy us?

PROSPERO   Well demanded, wench;²
140   My tale provokes that question. Dear, they durst not,
So dear the love my people bore me; nor set
A mark so bloody on the business, but
With colours fairer painted their foul ends.
In few,° they hurried us aboard a barque,°   *short / ship*

---

6. *To have . . . Milan:* He wanted to be the Duke of
Milan in actual fact, rather than merely exercising power
as the Duke's proxy. *screen:* partition, barrier.
7. Subject Antonio's coronet to Alonso's crown. *coronet:*
a lesser crown indicating the wearer's inferiority to the
sovereign.
8. *and bend . . . stooping:* by making Milan, previously

free, a tributary subject of Naples.
9. Antonio's character need not imply that his mother
was a bad parent (see line 94).
1. In return for the conditions agreed upon.
2. A young woman; also term of endearment to wife,
daughter, or sweetheart.

145   Bore us some leagues to sea, where they prepared
      A rotten carcass of a butt,³ not rigged,
      Nor tackle, sail, nor mast—the very rats
      Instinctively have quit it. There they hoist us,
      To cry to th' sea that roared to us, to sigh
150   To th' winds, whose pity, sighing back again,
      Did us but loving wrong.⁴

MIRANDA   Alack, what trouble
      Was I then to you!

PROSPERO   O, a cherubin
      Thou wast that did preserve me. Thou didst smile,
      Infusèd with a fortitude from heaven,
155   When I have decked° the sea with drops° full salt,   *covered; adorned / tears*
      Under my burden groaned;⁵ which° raised in me   *(Miranda's smile)*
      An undergoing stomach,° to bear up   *A courage to endure*
      Against what should ensue.

MIRANDA   How came we ashore?

160 PROSPERO   By providence divine.
      Some food we had, and some fresh water, that
      A noble Neapolitan, Gonzalo,
      Out of his charity—who being then appointed
      Master of this design—did give us; with
165   Rich garments, linens, stuffs, and necessaries
      Which since have steaded° much. So, of his gentleness,⁶   *been useful*
      Knowing I loved my books, he furnished me
      From mine own library with volumes that
      I prize above my dukedom.

MIRANDA   Would I might
      But ever see that man!

170 PROSPERO   Now I arise.⁷
      *[He stands and puts on his cloak]*⁸
      Sit still,° and hear the last of our sea-sorrow.   *Continue to sit*
      Here in this island we arrived, and here
      Have I thy schoolmaster made thee more profit°   *profit more*
      Than other princes⁹ can, that have more time
175   For vainer hours and tutors not so careful.°   *caring*

MIRANDA   Heavens thank you for't. And now I pray you, sir—
      For still 'tis beating in my mind—your reason
      For raising this sea-storm.

PROSPERO   Know thus far forth.
      By accident most strange, bountiful Fortune,
180   Now my dear lady,¹ hath mine enemies
      Brought to this shore; and by my prescience
      I find my zenith² doth depend upon
      A most auspicious star,³ whose influence
      If now I court not, but omit,° my fortunes   *disregard*

3. Cask or tub: here, deprecatory for "boat."
4. The winds, responding sympathetically to our sighs, only blew us farther out to sea.
5. The secondary sense provides an image of giving birth.
6. Nobility; kindness.
7. Referring to the action of standing; or to Prospero's rising fortunes (as in lines 179–85). The former might visually reinforce the latter, especially if Prospero also resumes his magical powers by putting on his cloak.

8. This direction, necessary before Prospero can charm Miranda to sleep, follows naturally from the reference to Prospero's books, his other source of power.
9. *princes:* a generic plural for "princes and princesses."
1. Traditional characterization of Fortune as a woman changeable in her affections.
2. Highest point, as of a star in the sky.
3. Referring to the belief that celestial bodies had astrological influence on people and events.

185   Will ever after droop. Here cease more questions.
        Thou art inclined to sleep; 'tis a good dullness,°   *drowsiness*
        And give it way. I know thou canst not choose.
        [MIRANDA *sleeps*]
        Come away,° servant, come! I am ready now.   *Come here*
        Approach, my Ariel,[4] come!
            Enter ARIEL
190 ARIEL   All hail, great master, grave sir, hail. I come
        To answer thy best pleasure. Be't to fly,
        To swim, to dive into the fire, to ride
        On the curled clouds, to thy strong bidding task
        Ariel and all his quality.°   *cohorts; faculties*
    PROSPERO   Hast thou, spirit,
195   Performed to point° the tempest that I bade thee?   *in detail*
    ARIEL   To every article.
        I boarded the King's ship. Now on the beak,°   *prow*
        Now in the waste,° the deck,° in every cabin,   *midship / poop*
        I flamed amazement.[5] Sometime I'd divide,
200   And burn in many places;[6] on the top-mast,
        The yards, and bowsprit, would I flame distinctly;
        Then meet and join. Jove's lightning, the precursors
        O'th' dreadful thunderclaps, more momentary
        And sight-outrunning° were not. The fire and cracks   *quicker than the eye*
205   Of sulphurous[7] roaring the most mighty Neptune
        Seem to besiege, and make his bold waves tremble,
        Yea, his dread trident shake.
    PROSPERO   My brave spirit!
        Who was so firm, so constant, that this coil°   *turmoil*
        Would not infect his reason?
    ARIEL   Not a soul
210   But felt a fever of the mad,° and played   *such as madmen feel*
        Some tricks of desperation. All but mariners
        Plunged in the foaming brine and quit the vessel,
        Then all afire with me. The King's son Ferdinand,
        With hair upstaring°—then like reeds, not hair—   *standing on end*
215   Was the first man that leaped; cried 'Hell is empty,
        And all the devils are here'.
    PROSPERO   Why, that's my spirit!
        But was not this nigh shore?
    ARIEL   Close by, my master.
    PROSPERO   But are they, Ariel, safe?
    ARIEL   Not a hair perished.
        On their sustaining[8] garments not a blemish,
220   But fresher than before. And, as thou bad'st° me,   *commanded*
        In troops° I have dispersed them 'bout the isle.   *groups*
        The King's son have I landed by himself,
        Whom I left cooling of ° the air with sighs   *cooling*
        In an odd angle° of the isle, and sitting,   *corner*
        His arms in this sad knot.[9]

---

4. Ariel's name, along with sounding like "airy," also means in Hebrew "lion of God." The name appears as a magical spirit in various occult texts.
5. I appeared as flames, causing terror.
6. The phosphorescent effect of St. Elmo's fire, caused in a thunderstorm by the charge of static electricity that builds up particularly around metal projections.
7. Sulphur was popularly associated with thunder and lightning.
8. Buoying up, and thus suggesting "life-giving."
9. Folded sadly, like this (folded arms implied sorrow).

225   **PROSPERO**   Of the King's ship,
         The mariners, say how thou hast disposed,
         And all the rest o'th' fleet.

     ARIEL   Safely in harbour
         Is the King's ship, in the deep nook where once
         Thou called'st me up at midnight to fetch dew

230   From the still-vexed° Bermudas, there she's hid;   *ever-stormy*
         The mariners all under hatches stowed,
         Who, with° a charm joined to° their suffered labour,   *by virtue of / with*
         I have left asleep. And for the rest o'th' fleet,
         Which I dispersed, they all have met again,

235   And are upon the Mediterranean float°   *billow; sea*
         Bound sadly home for Naples,
         Supposing that they saw the King's ship wrecked,
         And his great person perish.

  PROSPERO   Ariel, thy charge
         Exactly is performed; but there's more work.
         What is the time o'th' day?

240   **ARIEL**   Past the mid season.°   *noon*

  PROSPERO   At least two glasses.° The time 'twixt six and now   *hourglasses*
         Must by us both be spent most preciously.

     ARIEL   Is there more toil? Since thou dost give me pains,°   *tasks*
         Let me remember° thee what thou hast promised   *remind*
         Which is not yet performed me.

245   **PROSPERO**   How now? Moody?
         What is't thou canst demand?

     ARIEL   My liberty.

  PROSPERO   Before the time be out? No more!

     ARIEL   I prithee,
         Remember I have done thee worthy service,
         Told thee no lies, made thee no mistakings, served

250   Without or° grudge or grumblings. Thou did promise   *either*
         To bate° me a full year.   *remit; excuse*

  PROSPERO   Dost thou forget
         From what a torment I did free thee?

     ARIEL   No.

  PROSPERO   Thou dost, and think'st it much to tread the ooze
         Of the salt deep,

255   To run upon the sharp wind of the north,
         To do me business in the veins[1] o'th' earth
         When it is baked° with frost.   *dried and hardened*

     ARIEL   I do not, sir.

  PROSPERO   Thou liest, malignant thing. Hast thou forgot
         The foul witch Sycorax, who with age and envy

260   Was grown into a hoop?° Hast thou forgot her?   *bent over with age*

     ARIEL   No, sir.

  PROSPERO   Thou hast. Where was she born? Speak, tell me!

     ARIEL   Sir, in Algiers.

  PROSPERO   O, was she so! I must
         Once in a month recount what thou hast been,

265   Which thou forget'st. This damned witch Sycorax,
         For mischiefs manifold and sorceries terrible
         To enter human hearing, from Algiers

---

1. Mineral veins or subterranean rivers.

Thou know'st was banished. For one thing she did
They would not take her life.[2] Is not this true?

270 ARIEL   Ay, sir.

PROSPERO   This blue-eyed[3] hag was hither brought with child,
And here was left by th' sailors. Thou, my slave,
As thou report'st thyself, was then her servant;
And for° thou wast a spirit too delicate   *because*
275 To act her earthy[4] and abhorred commands,
Refusing her grand hests,° she did confine thee   *commands*
By help of her more potent ministers,°   *agents; slaves*
And in her most unmitigable rage,
Into a cloven pine; within which rift
280 Imprisoned thou didst painfully remain
A dozen years, within which space she died
And left thee there, where thou didst vent thy groans
As fast as mill-wheels strike.° Then was this island—   *hit the water*
Save for the son that she did litter° here,   *give birth to*
285 A freckled whelp, hag-born—not honoured with
A human shape.

ARIEL   Yes, Caliban her son.

PROSPERO   Dull thing, I say so:[5] he, that Caliban
Whom now I keep in service. Thou best know'st
What torment I did find thee in. Thy groans
290 Did make wolves howl, and penetrate° the breasts   *arouse sympathy in*
Of ever-angry bears; it was a torment
To lay upon the damned, which Sycorax
Could not again undo. It was mine art,
When I arrived and heard thee, that made gape
The pine and let thee out.

295 ARIEL   I thank thee, master.

PROSPERO   If thou more murmur'st, I will rend an oak,
And peg thee in his° knotty entrails till   *its*
Thou hast howled away twelve winters.

ARIEL   Pardon, master.
I will be correspondent° to command,   *compliant*
300 And do my spriting gently.°   *graciously*

PROSPERO   Do so, and after two days
I will discharge thee.[6]

ARIEL   That's my noble master!
What shall I do? Say what, what shall I do?

PROSPERO   Go make thyself like to a nymph o'th' sea. Be subject
305 To no sight but thine and mine, invisible
To every eyeball else.[7] Go take this shape,°   *appearance; disguise*
And hither come in't. Go; hence with diligence!   *Exit* [ARIEL]
Awake, dear heart, awake! Thou hast slept well;
Awake.

MIRANDA [*awaking*] The strangeness of your story put
Heaviness° in me.   *Sleepiness*

310 PROSPERO   Shake it off. Come on;

---

2. *For . . . life:* Only because she got pregnant. Capital
sentences were commuted for pregnant women; ordinarily, condemned witches were either hanged or burned
at the stake.
3. Blue eyelids were thought to be a sign of pregnancy.
4. Difficult for Ariel, whose element is air; also, grossly

material, coarse.
5. You dullard, that's just what I said.
6. Prospero reduces this to within two days at line 425
and actually releases Ariel in about four hours' time.
7. *Be . . . else:* Ariel may wear a conventional costume,
indicating his invisibility to other characters onstage.

We'll visit Caliban my slave, who never
Yields us kind answer.

MIRANDA   'Tis a villain, sir,
I do not love to look on.

PROSPERO   But as 'tis,
We cannot miss° him. He does make our fire,   avoid; do without
315   Fetch in our wood, and serves in offices°   capacities; duties
That profit us.—What ho! Slave, Caliban!
Thou earth, thou, speak!

CALIBAN (within)   There's wood enough within.

PROSPERO   Come forth, I say! There's other business for thee.
Come, thou tortoise! When?

                    Enter ARIEL, like a water-nymph

320   Fine apparition! My quaint[8] Ariel,
Hark in thine ear.

                    [He whispers]

ARIEL   My lord, it shall be done.   Exit

PROSPERO   Thou poisonous slave, got° by the devil[9] himself   begot
Upon thy wicked dam,° come forth!   harmful, foul mother

                    Enter CALIBAN

CALIBAN   As wicked dew as e'er my mother brushed[1]
325   With raven's feather from unwholesome fen°   bog
Drop on you both! A southwest[2] blow on ye,
And blister you all o'er!

PROSPERO   For this be sure tonight thou shalt have cramps,
Side-stitches that shall pen thy breath up. Urchins[3]
330   Shall forth at vast of° night, that they may work   during the boundless
All exercise on thee.[4] Thou shalt be pinched
As thick as honeycomb,[5] each pinch more stinging
Than bees that made 'em.°   (honeycomb cells)

CALIBAN   I must eat my dinner.
This island's mine, by Sycorax my mother,
335   Which thou tak'st from me. When thou cam'st first,
Thou strok'st me and made much of me, wouldst give me
Water with berries in't, and teach me how
To name the bigger light, and how the less,[6]
That burn by day and night; and then I loved thee,
340   And showed thee all the qualities o'th' isle,
The fresh springs, brine-pits, barren place and fertile—
Cursed be I that did so! All the charms°   spells
Of Sycorax, toads, beetles, bats, light on you;
For I am all the subjects that you have,
345   Which first was mine own king, and here you sty me°   pen me up
In this hard rock, whiles you do keep from me
The rest o'th' island.

PROSPERO   Thou most lying slave,
Whom stripes° may move, not kindness! I have used° thee,   lashes / treated

8. The term could simultaneously mean "ingenious,"
"curious in appearance," and "elegant."
9. Not merely an insult, but also an allusion to Caliban's
birth from the devil (incubus) and witch.
1. Brushed up, collected. Dew was a common ingredient
of magical potions.
2. A southerly wind was considered plague-bearing.
3. Hedgehogs; but here indicates spirits disguised as
hedgehogs.

4. that . . . thee: in order that they may perform their
habitual activity.
5. Thou . . . honeycomb: The pinch marks will be as
closely packed as, and of similar texture to, the cells of a
honeycomb.
6. Recalls Genesis 1:16: "God then made two great
lights: the greater light to rule the day, and the less light
to rule the night."

Filth as thou art, with human care, and lodged thee
350 In mine own cell, till thou didst seek to violate
The honour of my child.

CALIBAN   O ho, O ho! Would't had been done!
Thou didst prevent me; I had peopled else
This isle with Calibans.

MIRANDA[7]   Abhorrèd slave,
355 Which any print° of goodness wilt not take,   impression
Being capable of° all ill! I pitied thee,   susceptible to
Took pains to make thee speak, taught thee each hour
One thing or other. When thou didst not, savage,
Know thine own meaning, but wouldst gabble like
360 A thing most brutish, I endowed thy purposes
With words that made them known. But thy vile race,°   hereditary nature
Though thou didst learn, had that in't which good natures
Could not abide to be with; therefore wast thou
Deservedly confined into this rock,
365 Who hadst deserved more than a prison.

CALIBAN   You taught me language, and my profit on't
Is I know how to curse. The red plague rid you[8]
For learning me your language!

PROSPERO   Hag-seed,° hence!   Offspring of a hag
Fetch us in fuel. And be quick, thou'rt best,
370 To answer other business.°—Shrug'st thou, malice?   perform other tasks
If thou neglect'st or dost unwillingly
What I command, I'll rack thee with old[9] cramps,
Fill all thy bones with aches,[1] make thee roar,
That beasts shall tremble at thy din.

CALIBAN   No, pray thee.
375 [Aside] I must obey. His art is of such power
It would control my dam's god Setebos,[2]
And make a vassal of him.

PROSPERO   So, slave, hence!   Exit CALIBAN
Enter FERDINAND and ARIEL, invisible, playing and
singing.[3] [PROSPERO and MIRANDA stand aside]

                         Song

ARIEL   Come unto these yellow sands,
              And then take hands;
380   Curtsied when you have and kissed—
              The wild waves whist[4]—
           Foot it featly° here and there,   Dance nimbly
              And, sweet sprites, bear°   sing
           The burden.° Hark, hark.   refrain
385 SPIRITS (dispersedly [within]) Bow-wow!
ARIEL   The watch-dogs bark.
SPIRITS [within] Bow-wow!

---

7. Many editors assign this speech to Prospero, believing
it to be out of character for Miranda.
8. The plague that gives red sores destroy, kill you.
9. As of aged people; long-accustomed.
1. As a noun, this was probably pronounced "aitches."
2. A name found in travel narratives as a god of the Pata-
gonians.

3. This probably does not imply that Ferdinand enters
first, even though such a staging is possible if Ferdinand
is bewildered as to where this music is coming from. Ariel
is invisible to all but Prospero and the audience. He is
probably still dressed as a water nymph.
4. Become hushed and attentive.

ARIEL	Hark, hark, I hear
	The strain of strutting Chanticleer
390	Cry 'cock-a-diddle-dow'.
FERDINAND	Where should this music be? I'th' air or th'earth?

It sounds no more; and sure it waits° upon   *attends*
Some god o'th' island. Sitting on a bank,
Weeping again the King my father's wreck,
395   This music crept by me upon the waters,
Allaying both their fury and my passion°   *grief*
With its sweet air.° Thence I have followed it—   *melody*
Or it hath drawn me rather. But 'tis gone.
No, it begins again.

Song

400 ARIEL	Full fathom five thy father lies.
	Of his bones are coral made;
	Those are pearls that were his eyes;
	Nothing of him that doth fade
	But doth suffer a sea-change
405	Into something rich and strange.
	Sea-nymphs hourly ring his knell:
SPIRITS [*within*]	Ding dong.
ARIEL	Hark, now I hear them.
SPIRITS [*within*]	Ding-dong bell. [*etc.*]
FERDINAND	The ditty does remember⁵ my drowned father.

410   This is no mortal° business, nor no sound   *human; of death*
That the earth owes.°   *owns*
         [*Music*]
                    I hear it now above me.
PROSPERO [*to* MIRANDA]   The fringèd curtains of thine eye advance,°   *raise*
And say what thou seest yon.

MIRANDA	What is't? A spirit?

Lord, how it looks about! Believe me, sir,
415   It carries a brave° form. But 'tis a spirit.   *splendid; gallant*
PROSPERO   No, wench, it eats and sleeps, and hath such senses
As we have, such. This gallant° which thou seest   *fine gentleman*
Was in the wreck, and but° he's something° stained   *except that / somewhat*
With grief, that's beauty's canker,⁶ thou mightst call him
420   A goodly person. He hath lost his fellows,
And strays about to find 'em.

MIRANDA	I might call him

A thing divine, for nothing natural
I ever saw so noble.
PROSPERO [*aside*]⁷   It° goes on, I see,   *(My plan)*
As my soul prompts it. [*To* ARIEL] Spirit, fine spirit, I'll free thee
Within two days for this.

425 FERDINAND [*aside*]	Most sure the goddess

On whom these airs attend.⁸ [*To* MIRANDA] Vouchsafe° my prayer   *Grant*
May know if you remain° upon this island,   *dwell*

---

5. Commemorate. *ditty*: the words of the song.
6. Cankerworm; caterpillar ("beauty" being seen as a flower); spreading sore.
7. Prospero's asides here and at lines 442, 454, and 497 may be either private utterances or addressed to Ariel. If the former, Ariel may nevertheless hear them; Prospero

speaks to Ariel after all these instances. Their import may well be purposefully enigmatic.
8. *Most . . . attend*: Probably spoken aside, but possibly an invocation. *Most sure the goddess*: Echoes Aeneas's reaction to seeing Venus after his shipwreck, "o dea certe" (*Aeneid* I.328). *airs*: Ariel's melodies.

And that you will some good instruction give
How I may bear me° here. My prime request,   *conduct myself*

430   Which I do last pronounce, is—O you wonder⁹—
If you be maid¹ or no?

MIRANDA   No wonder, sir,
But certainly a maid.

FERDINAND   My language! Heavens!
I am the best² of them that speak this speech,
Were I but where 'tis spoken.

PROSPERO   How, the best?

435   What wert thou if the King of Naples heard thee?

FERDINAND   A single³ thing, as I am now that wonders
To hear thee speak of Naples. He does hear me,⁴
And that he does I weep. Myself am Naples,°   *King of Naples*
Who with mine eyes, never since at ebb,° beheld   *ceasing to flow*
The King my father wrecked.

440   MIRANDA   Alack, for mercy!

FERDINAND   Yes, faith, and all his lords, the Duke of Milan
And his brave son⁵ being twain.

PROSPERO [*aside*]   The Duke of Milan
And his more braver daughter could control⁶ thee,
If now 'twere fit to do't. At the first sight

445   They have changed eyes.⁷—Delicate° Ariel,   *Graceful; artful*
I'll set thee free for this. [*To* FERDINAND] A word, good sir.
I fear you have done yourself some wrong.⁸ A word.

MIRANDA [*aside*]   Why speaks my father so ungently?° This   *discourteously*
Is the third man that e'er I saw, the first

450   That e'er I sighed for. Pity move my father
To be inclined my way.

FERDINAND   O, if a virgin,
And your affection not gone forth,⁹ I'll make you
The Queen of Naples.

PROSPERO   Soft, sir! One word more.
[*Aside*] They are both in either's powers. But this swift business

455   I must uneasy° make, lest too light¹ winning   *difficult*
Make the prize light. [*To* FERDINAND] One word more. I charge thee
That thou attend me. Thou dost here usurp
The name thou ow'st° not; and hast put thyself   *own*
Upon this island as a spy, to win it
From me the lord on't.°   *of it*

460   FERDINAND   No, as I am a man.

MIRANDA   There's nothing ill can dwell in such a temple.²
If the ill spirit have so fair a house,
Good things will strive to dwell with't.

PROSPERO [*to* FERDINAND]   Follow me.
[*To* MIRANDA] Speak not you for him; he's a traitor. [*To* FERDINAND] Come!

---

9. Miracle, punning on the meaning of Miranda's name.
1. Unmarried virgin; made (human).
2. Highest in rank, assuming he has succeeded his father.
3. Weak and helpless; solitary; one and the same.
4. "He" and "me" both refer to Ferdinand. Presuming his father to be dead, Ferdinand takes himself to be the new King of Naples (and as such, he hears himself speaking). Alternatively, Ferdinand thinks his father's spirit hears him.
5. The only instance in which Antonio is mentioned as

having a son.
6. Challenge; take to task; exercise power over.
7. Exchanged loving glances; fallen in love at first sight.
8. Euphemistic for "told a lie about yourself."
9. Given over to someone else.
1. Easy; playing on the meanings of "little valued" and also "promiscuous" in line 456.
2. A common metaphor for the body; also a conventional Renaissance notion that moral qualities were physically manifest.

465   I'll manacle thy neck and feet together.
       Sea-water shalt thou drink; thy food shall be
       The fresh-brook mussels,³ withered roots, and husks
       Wherein the acorn cradled. Follow!

FERDINAND   No.
       I will resist such entertainment° till   *treatment*
       Mine enemy has more power.
            He draws, and is charmed from moving

470   **MIRANDA**   O dear father,
       Make not too rash a trial of him, for
       He's gentle, and not fearful.⁴

PROSPERO   What, I say,
       My foot° my tutor? Put thy sword up, traitor,   *inferior*
       Who mak'st a show but dar'st not strike, thy conscience
475   Is so possessed with guilt. Come from thy ward,°   *defensive stance*
       For I can here disarm thee with this stick°   *magician's wand*
       And make thy weapon drop.

MIRANDA   Beseech you, father!

PROSPERO   Hence! Hang not on my garments.

MIRANDA   Sir, have pity.
       I'll be his surety.

PROSPERO   Silence! One word more
480   Shall make me chide thee, if not hate thee. What,
       An advocate for an impostor? Hush!
       Thou think'st there is no more such shapes° as he,   *forms; men*
       Having seen but him and Caliban. Foolish wench!
       To° th' most of men this is a Caliban,   *Compared to*
       And they to him are angels.

485   **MIRANDA**   My affections
       Are then most humble. I have no ambition
       To see a goodlier man.

PROSPERO [*to* FERDINAND]   Come on; obey.
       Thy nerves° are in their infancy again,   *sinews*
       And have no vigour in them.

FERDINAND   So they are.
490   My spirits,° as in a dream, are all bound up.   *mental powers*
       My father's loss, the weakness which I feel,
       The wreck of all my friends, nor this man's threats
       To whom I am subdued, are but light to me,
       Might I but through my prison once a day
495   Behold this maid. All corners else o'th' earth
       Let liberty make use of; space enough
       Have I in such a prison.

PROSPERO [*aside*]   It works. [*To* ARIEL] Come on.—
       Thou hast done well, fine Ariel. [*To* FERDINAND] Follow me.
       [*To* ARIEL] Hark what thou else shalt do me.

MIRANDA [*to* FERDINAND]   Be of comfort.
500   My father's of a better nature, sir,
       Than he appears by speech. This is unwonted°   *unusual*
       Which now came from him.

PROSPERO [*to* ARIEL]   Thou shalt be as free
       As mountain winds; but then° exactly do   *until then*
       All points of my command.

---

3. Freshwater mussels are inedible.   4. He's noble and, therefore, not cowardly. Alternatively, not fearsome.

505 ARIEL   To th' syllable.

PROSPERO [*to* FERDINAND]   Come, follow. [*To* MIRANDA] Speak
    not for him.   *Exeunt*

2.1

Enter ALONSO, SEBASTIAN, ANTONIO, GONZALO, ADRIAN,
    and FRANCISCO

GONZALO [*to* ALONSO]   Beseech you, sir, be merry. You have cause,
    So have we all, of joy; for our escape
    Is much beyond our loss. Our hint° of woe   occasion
    Is common; every day some sailor's wife,
5   The masters of some merchant, and the merchant,[1]
    Have just° our theme of woe. But for the miracle,   exactly
    I mean our preservation, few in millions
    Can speak like us. Then wisely, good sir, weigh
    Our sorrow with° our comfort.   against
ALONSO   Prithee, peace.[2]
10 SEBASTIAN [*to* ANTONIO]   He receives comfort like cold porridge.° broth
ANTONIO   The visitor[3] will not give him o'er so.°   leave him alone
SEBASTIAN   Look, he's winding up the watch of his wit. By and
    by it will strike.
GONZALO [*to* ALONSO]   Sir—
15 SEBASTIAN [*to* ANTONIO]   One: tell.°   keep count
GONZALO [*to* ALONSO]   When every grief is entertained° that's harbored
        offered,
    Comes to th'entertainer[4]—
SEBASTIAN   A dollar.[5]
GONZALO   Dolour° comes to him indeed. You have spoken truer   Sorrow
20   than you purposed.
SEBASTIAN   You have taken it wiselier than I meant you should.
GONZALO [*to* ALONSO]   Therefore my lord—
ANTONIO [*to* SEBASTIAN]   Fie, what a spendthrift is he of his
        tongue!
25 ALONSO [*to* GONZALO]   I prithee, spare.°   spare your words
GONZALO   Well, I have done. But yet—
SEBASTIAN [*to* ANTONIO]   He will be talking.
ANTONIO   Which of he or Adrian, for a good wager, first begins
        to crow?[6]
30 SEBASTIAN   The old cock.
ANTONIO   The cockerel.[7]
SEBASTIAN   Done. The wager?
ANTONIO   A laughter.[8]
SEBASTIAN   A match!
35 ADRIAN [*to* GONZALO]   Though this island seem to be desert°— uninhabited
ANTONIO [*to* SEBASTIAN]   Ha, ha, ha!
SEBASTIAN   So, you're paid.[9]
ADRIAN   Uninhabitable, and almost inaccessible—
SEBASTIAN [*to* ANTONIO]   Yet—
40 ADRIAN   Yet—

2.1
1. The chief officers of some merchant ship and its
owner.
2. Sebastian takes this as "pease," as in "pease porridge."
3. Antonio compares Gonzalo with one who visits and
comforts the sick and distressed.
4. There comes to the person who accepts that grief.

5. *dollar:* English name for the German thaler.
6. Which of the two will first begin to speak ("crow")?
7. "The young cock crows as the old hears" was proverbial. "Old cock" refers to Gonzalo and "cockerel" to
Adrian.
8. From the proverb "He laughs that wins."
9. Antonio's laugh is his prize.

ANTONIO [*to* SEBASTIAN]   He could not miss't.

ADRIAN   It must needs be of subtle, tender, and delicate[1]
  temperance.°   *climate*

ANTONIO [*to* SEBASTIAN]   Temperance was a delicate wench.[2]

45   SEBASTIAN   Ay, and a subtle, as he most learnedly delivered.[3]

ADRIAN [*to* GONZALO]   The air breathes upon us here most
  sweetly.

SEBASTIAN [*to* ANTONIO]   As if it had lungs, and rotten ones.

ANTONIO   Or as 'twere perfumed by a fen.°   *bog*

50   GONZALO [*to* ADRIAN]   Here is everything advantageous to life.

ANTONIO [*to* SEBASTIAN]   True, save° means to live.   *except*

SEBASTIAN   Of that there's none, or little.

GONZALO [*to* ADRIAN]   How lush and lusty° the grass looks!   *tender and luxuriant*
  How green!

55   ANTONIO   The ground indeed is tawny.

SEBASTIAN   With an eye[4] of green in't.

ANTONIO   He misses not much.

SEBASTIAN   No, he doth but mistake the truth totally.

GONZALO [*to* ADRIAN]   But the rarity[5] of it is, which is indeed
60   almost beyond credit—

SEBASTIAN [*to* ANTONIO]   As many vouched° rarities are.   *alleged, accepted*

GONZALO [*to* ADRIAN]   That our garments being, as they were,
  drenched in the sea, hold notwithstanding their freshness and
  glosses, being rather new-dyed than stained with salt water.

65   ANTONIO [*to* SEBASTIAN]   If but one of his pockets[6] could speak,
  would it not say he lies?

SEBASTIAN   Ay, or very falsely pocket up his report.[7]

GONZALO [*to* ADRIAN]   Methinks our garments are now as fresh
  as when we put them on first in Afric, at the marriage of the
70   King's fair daughter Claribel to the King of Tunis.

SEBASTIAN   'Twas a sweet marriage, and we prosper well in our
  return.

ADRIAN   Tunis was never graced before with such a paragon to°   *for*
  their queen.

75   GONZALO   Not since widow Dido's[8] time.

ANTONIO [*to* SEBASTIAN]   Widow?[9] A pox o'that! How came that
  'widow' in? Widow Dido!

SEBASTIAN   What if he had said 'widower Aeneas' too? Good
  Lord, how you take° it!   *fuss about*

80   ADRIAN [*to* GONZALO]   'Widow Dido' said you? You make me
  study of ° that: she was of Carthage, not of Tunis.   *examine*

GONZALO   This Tunis, sir, was Carthage.[1]

ADRIAN   Carthage?

GONZALO   I assure you, Carthage.

---

1. Exquisite, but in Antonio's usage (line 44), "given to
pleasure." *subtle:* fine, but in Sebastian's usage (line 45),
"sexually expert" or "crafty."
2. Antonio takes "Temperance" to be the name of a girl.
delicate: voluptuous, given to pleasure.
3. "Learnedly delivered" was a popular phrase among
Puritans who wanted to appear pious.
4. A tinge. In Antonio's reply, an "eye of green" refers to
Gonzalo's optimistic capacity to see green.
5. Exceptional quality; but in Sebastian's usage (line 61),
"uncommon thing."
6. Seen as the garments' "mouth"; also implying that

Gonzalo's pockets are stained.
7. The evidence of stained pockets would confute Gonzalo's words and reputation for honesty. *pocket up:* suppress, or keep silent; also, receive unprotestingly.
8. Queen of ancient Carthage, whose tragic love affair
with Aeneas is related in Virgil's *Aeneid.*
9. Antonio picks on this designation for a woman abandoned by her lover as being either irrelevant or conspicuously prudish. Dido, however, was in fact a widow when
she met Aeneas.
1. The city of Tunis was actually built 10 miles from the
site of Carthage.

85 ANTONIO [*to* SEBASTIAN]   His word is more than the miraculous harp.²

SEBASTIAN   He hath raised the wall, and houses too.

ANTONIO   What impossible matter will he make easy next?

SEBASTIAN   I think he will carry this island home in his pocket,

90 and give it his son for an apple.

ANTONIO   And sowing the kernels° of it in the sea, bring forth   *seeds*
more islands.

GONZALO [*to* ADRIAN]   Ay.³

ANTONIO [*to* SEBASTIAN]   Why, in good time.

95 GONZALO [*to* ALONSO]   Sir, we were talking that our garments
seem now as fresh as when we were at Tunis, at the marriage
of your daughter, who is now queen.

ANTONIO   And the rarest that e'er came there.

SEBASTIAN   Bate,⁴ I beseech you, widow Dido.

100 ANTONIO   O, widow Dido? Ay, widow Dido.

GONZALO [*to* ALONSO]   Is not, sir, my doublet as fresh as the first
day I wore it? I mean in a sort.⁵

ANTONIO [*to* SEBASTIAN]   That 'sort' was well fished for.

GONZALO [*to* ALONSO]   When I wore it at your daughter's
105 marriage.

ALONSO   You cram these words into mine ears against
The stomach of my sense.⁶ Would I had never
Married my daughter there! For, coming thence,
My son is lost; and, in my rate,° she too,   *consideration*
110 Who is so far from Italy removed
I ne'er again shall see her. O thou mine heir
Of Naples and of Milan, what strange fish
Hath made his meal on thee?

FRANCISCO   Sir, he may live.
I saw him beat the surges under him
115 And ride upon their backs. He trod the water,
Whose enmity he flung aside, and breasted
The surge, most swoll'n, that met him. His bold head
'Bove the contentious waves he kept, and oared
Himself with his good arms in lusty° stroke   *vigorous*
120 To th' shore, that o'er his wave-worn basis bowed,⁷
As° stooping to relieve him. I not° doubt   *As if / do not*
He came alive to land.

ALONSO   No, no; he's gone.

SEBASTIAN [*to* ALONSO]   Sir, you may thank yourself for this great loss,
That would not bless our Europe with your daughter,
125 But rather loose° her to an African,   *lose; release*
Where she, at least, is banished from your eye,
Who° hath cause to wet the grief° on't.   *(Claribel) / weep*

ALONSO   Prithee, peace.

SEBASTIAN   You were kneeled to and importuned otherwise⁸
By all of us, and the fair soul herself
130 Weighed between loathness and obedience at

2. Referring to Amphion's harp, to the music of which the walls (but not the houses) of Thebes arose.
3. Affirming his belief that Tunis was Carthage; Antonio mocks the length of time this took.
4. Except (as a verb); don't mention.
5. Comparatively speaking; Antonio plays on "drawing lots."
6. *You . . . sense:* The image is of one being force-fed words against the appetite ("stomach") for hearing them.
7. *that . . . bowed:* that extended out and drooped over the foot of the cliff, which had been eroded by waves.
8. *otherwise:* to act differently.

Which end o'th' beam should bow.[9] We have lost your son,
I fear, for ever. Milan and Naples have
More widows in them of this business' making
Than we bring men to comfort them. The fault's your own.

ALONSO   So is the dear'st o'th' loss.[1]

135   GONZALO   My lord Sebastian,
The truth you speak doth lack some gentleness
And time to speak it in. You rub the sore[2]
When you should bring the plaster.

SEBASTIAN [*to* ANTONIO]   Very well.

140   ANTONIO   And most chirurgeonly.°   surgeonlike

GONZALO [*to* ALONSO]   It is foul weather in us all, good sir,
When you are cloudy.

SEBASTIAN [*to* ANTONIO]   Fowl weather?[3]

ANTONIO   Very foul.

GONZALO [*to* ALONSO]   Had I plantation[4] of this isle, my lord—

ANTONIO [*to* SEBASTIAN]   He'd sow't with nettle-seed.

SEBASTIAN   Or docks,
or mallows.[5]

145   GONZALO   And were the king on't, what would I do?

SEBASTIAN [*to* ANTONIO]   Scape being drunk, for want of wine.

GONZALO   I'th' commonwealth I would by contraries
Execute all things.[6] For no kind of traffic°   commerce
Would I admit, no name of magistrate;

150   Letters° should not be known; riches, poverty,   Writing; erudition
And use of service,° none; contract, succession,[7]   servants
Bourn,° bound of land, tilth,° vineyard, none;   Boundary / tillage
No use of metal, corn,° or wine, or oil;   grain
No occupation, all men idle, all;

155   And women too—but innocent and pure;[8]
No sovereignty—

SEBASTIAN [*to* ANTONIO]   Yet he would be king on't.

ANTONIO   The latter end of his commonwealth forgets the
beginning.

GONZALO [*to* ALONSO]   All things in common° nature should   for communal use
produce

160   Without sweat or endeavour. Treason, felony,
Sword, pike, knife, gun, or need of any engine,°   weapon
Would I not have; but nature should bring forth
Of it° own kind all foison,° all abundance,   its / plenty
To feed my innocent people.

165   SEBASTIAN [*to* ANTONIO]   No marrying[9] 'mong his subjects?

ANTONIO   None, man, all idle: whores and knaves.

GONZALO [*to* ALONSO]   I would with such perfection govern, sir,
T'excel the Golden Age.[1]

---

9. *Weighed . . . bow*: Weighed loathness to marry against
obedience to her father to find out which end of the
scales' beam would sink.
1. That is, the most grievous, or costliest, part of the loss
is also my own.
2. "To rub the sore" was proverbial. *plaster* (line 138): a
soothing remedy.
3. Perhaps recalling lines 28–31.
4. Had I responsibility for colonization of the island, but
also interpreted as "planting" by Antonio and Sebastian.
5. Cited as wild plants prone to grow on uncultivated
land; but dock is a traditional soother of nettle stings, and

mallow roots were used to make soothing ointment.
6. *I would . . . things*: I would advance the opposite to
what would be usual. This speech is based on a passage
in John Florio's translation of Montaigne's essay "Of the
Cannibals."
7. Inheritance of property.
8. Idleness proverbially begets lust.
9. Seen as irrelevant to sexually innocent people; also a
form of contract (line 151).
1. In classical mythology, the earliest of the ages—a time
without strife, labor, or injustice, when abundant food
grew without cultivation.

SEBASTIAN   Save° his majesty!   *God save*

ANTONIO   Long live Gonzalo!

GONZALO [*to* ALONSO]   And—do you mark me, sir?

170   ALONSO   Prithee, no more. Thou dost talk nothing to me.

GONZALO   I do well believe your highness, and did it to minister
    occasion² to these gentlemen, who are of such sensible° and   *sensitive*
    nimble lungs that they always use° to laugh at nothing.   *are accustomed*

ANTONIO   'Twas you we laughed at.

175   GONZALO   Who, in this kind of merry fooling, am nothing to
    you. So you may continue, and laugh at nothing still.

ANTONIO   What a blow was there given!

SEBASTIAN   An it had not fallen flat-long.³

GONZALO   You are gentlemen of brave mettle.⁴ You would lift
180   the moon out of her sphere, if she would continue in it five
    weeks without changing.⁵

               Enter ARIEL, [*invisible,*] *playing solemn music*

SEBASTIAN   We would so, and then go a-bat-fowling.⁶

ANTONIO [*to* GONZALO]   Nay, good my lord, be not angry.

GONZALO   No, I warrant you, I will not adventure my discretion
185   so weakly.⁷ Will you laugh me asleep? For I am very heavy.°   *tired; serious*

ANTONIO   Go sleep, and hear us.

        [GONZALO, ADRIAN, *and* FRANCISCO *sleep*]

ALONSO   What, all so soon asleep? I wish mine eyes
    Would, with themselves, shut up my thoughts.—I find
    They are inclined to do so.

SEBASTIAN   Please you, sir,
190   Do not omit° the heavy offer° of it.   *neglect / opportunity*
    It seldom visits sorrow; when it doth,
    It is a comforter.

ANTONIO   We two, my lord,
    Will guard your person while you take your rest,
    And watch your safety.

ALONSO   Thank you. Wondrous heavy.

        [*He sleeps. Exit* ARIEL]

195   SEBASTIAN   What a strange drowsiness possesses them!

ANTONIO   It is the quality o'th' climate.

SEBASTIAN   Why
    Doth it not then our eyelids sink? I find
    Not myself disposed to sleep.

ANTONIO   Nor I; my spirits are nimble.
    They fell together all, as by consent;°   *consensus*
200   They dropped as by a thunderstroke. What might,
    Worthy Sebastian, O, what might—? No more!—
    And yet methinks I see it in thy face.
    What thou shouldst be th'occasion speaks° thee, and   *opportunity reveals to*
    My strong imagination sees a crown
    Dropping upon thy head.

205   SEBASTIAN   What, art thou waking?°   *awake*

ANTONIO   Do you not hear me speak?

---

2. *minister occasion:* afford opportunity.
3. If it had not fallen on the flat, harmless side of the
sword.
4. Courage; punning on "metal," as of a sword blade.
5. *You would . . . changing:* If the moon were to remain
in her orbit ("sphere") one week longer than usual (five

weeks), you would steal her from her place.
6. Trapping birds by using light to attract them and bats
to strike them down; may also mean swindling and vic-
timizing the simple.
7. I will not put my sound judgment at risk so foolishly.

SEBASTIAN   I do, and surely
It is a sleepy language, and thou speak'st
Out of thy sleep. What is it thou didst say?
This is a strange repose, to be asleep
210   With eyes wide open; standing, speaking, moving,
And yet so fast asleep.
ANTONIO   Noble Sebastian,
Thou letst thy fortune sleep, die rather; wink'st°   *shut your eyes*
Whiles thou art waking.
SEBASTIAN   Thou dost snore distinctly;°   *meaningfully*
There's meaning in thy snores.
215   ANTONIO   I am more serious than my custom. You
Must be so too if heed° me, which to do   *if you heed*
Trebles thee o'er.
SEBASTIAN   Well, I am standing water.[8]
ANTONIO   I'll teach you how to flow.
SEBASTIAN   Do so; to ebb
Hereditary sloth[9] instructs me.
ANTONIO   O,
220   If you but knew how you the purpose cherish
Whiles thus you mock it;[1] how in stripping it
You more invest° it! Ebbing° men, indeed,   *clothe / Declining*
Most often do so near the bottom run
By their own fear or sloth.
SEBASTIAN   Prithee, say on.
225   The setting° of thine eye and cheek proclaim   *fixed look*
A matter° from thee, and a birth, indeed,   *Something important*
Which throes[2] thee much to yield.
ANTONIO   Thus, sir.
Although this lord° of weak remembrance,° this,   *(Gonzalo) / memory*
Who shall be of as little memory°   *remembered*
230   When he is earthed,° hath here almost persuaded—   *buried*
For he's a spirit of persuasion, only
Professes[3] to persuade—the King his son's alive,
'Tis as impossible that he's undrowned
As he that sleeps here swims.
SEBASTIAN   I have no hope
That he's undrowned.
235   ANTONIO   O, out of that 'no hope'
What great hope have you! No hope that way° is   *(that he's not drowned)*
Another way so high a hope that even
Ambition cannot pierce a wink° beyond,   *catch a glimpse*
But doubt discovery there.[4] Will you grant with me
That Ferdinand is drowned?
SEBASTIAN   He's gone.
240   ANTONIO   Then tell me,
Who's the next heir of Naples?
SEBASTIAN   Claribel.

8. Between tides, and thus open to suggestion; also associated with being slothful. *Trebles thee o'er:* Makes you three times as great.
9. Inherited laziness, or the slowness to attain prosperity arising from being born a younger brother.
1. *If . . . it:* If you only understood that your mockery reveals how great your aspirations really are; also, the

hereditary position you mock is actually to your advantage. *cherish:* hold dear; cultivate.
2. Which puts in agony, as in childbirth.
3. *only / Professes:* his sole vocation is.
4. Doubt that there is anything to achieve beyond the high hope of the crown.

ANTONIO   She that is Queen of Tunis; she that dwells
    Ten leagues beyond man's life;° she that from Naples   *lifetime journey*
    Can have no note°—unless the sun were post°—   *information / messenger*
245   The man i'th' moon's too slow—till new-born chins
    Be rough and razorable; she that from° whom   *returning from*
    We all were sea-swallowed, though some cast again⁵—
    And by that destiny, to perform an act
    Whereof what's past is prologue, what to come
    In yours and my discharge.°   *performance*
250 SEBASTIAN   What stuff is this? How say you?
    'Tis true my brother's daughter's Queen of Tunis;
    So is she heir of Naples; 'twixt which regions
    There is some space.
ANTONIO   A space whose every cubit°   *about 18 to 22 inches*
    Seems to cry out 'How shall that Claribel
255   Measure us° back to Naples? Keep° in Tunis,   *(the cubits) / Stay*
    And let Sebastian wake.'° Say this were death   *(to his opportunity)*
    That now hath seized them; why, they were no worse
    Than now they are. There be that° can rule Naples   *those that*
    As well as he that sleeps, lords that can prate
260   As amply and unnecessarily
    As this Gonzalo; I myself could make
    A chough of as deep chat.⁶ O, that you bore
    The mind that I do, what a sleep were this
    For your advancement! Do you understand me?
SEBASTIAN   Methinks I do.
265 ANTONIO   And how does your content
    Tender° your own good fortune?   *Regard; care for*
SEBASTIAN   I remember
    You did supplant your brother Prospero.
ANTONIO   True;
    And look how well my garments sit upon me,
    Much feater° than before. My brother's servants   *more trimly*
270   Were then my fellows; now they are my men.
SEBASTIAN   But for your conscience.
ANTONIO   Ay, sir, where lies that? If 'twere a kibe⁷
    'Twould put me to° my slipper; but I feel not   *make me wear*
    This deity in my bosom. Twenty consciences
275   That stand 'twixt me and Milan, candied⁸ be they,
    And melt ere they molest. Here lies your brother,
    No better than the earth he lies upon
    If he were that which now he's like—that's dead;
    Whom I with this obedient steel,° three inches of it,   *sword*
280   Can lay to bed for ever; whiles you, doing thus,
    To the perpetual wink for aye° might put   *sleep forever*
    This ancient morsel, this Sir Prudence, who
    Should not upbraid our course. For all the rest,
    They'll take suggestion° as a cat laps milk;   *prompting to evil*
285   They'll tell the clock° to any business that   *chime; agree*
    We say befits the hour.
SEBASTIAN   Thy case, dear friend,

---

5. Regurgitated, cast ashore; also, possibly, theatrical role-playing.
6. *I . . . chat:* I could train a jackdaw (known for imitating speech) to speak as profoundly.
7. Chilblain; sore on the heel.
8. Turned to sugar; crystallized in sugar.

Shall be my precedent. As thou got'st Milan,
I'll come by Naples. Draw thy sword. One stroke
Shall free thee from the tribute which thou payest,
And I the King shall love thee.

290 ANTONIO   Draw together,
And when I rear my hand, do you the like
To fall it on Gonzalo.

[*They draw*]

SEBASTIAN   O, but one word.

Enter ARIEL, [*invisible,*] *with music and song*

ARIEL [*to* GONZALO]   My master through his art foresees the danger
That you his friend are in—and sends me forth,
295 For else° his project dies, to keep them⁹ living.   otherwise

[*He*] *sings in Gonzalo's ear*

        While you here do snoring lie,
        Open-eyed conspiracy
        His time° doth take.   opportunity
        If of life you keep a care,
300   Shake off slumber, and beware.
        Awake, awake!

ANTONIO [*to* SEBASTIAN]   Then let us both be sudden.
GONZALO [*awaking*]   Now good angels
Preserve the King!

ALONSO [*awaking*]   Why, how now? Ho, awake!

[*The others awake*]

[*To* ANTONIO *and* SEBASTIAN]   Why are you° drawn?   your weapons
[*To* GONZALO] Wherefore this ghastly° looking?   fearful

305 GONZALO   What's the matter?
SEBASTIAN   Whiles we stood here securing° your repose,   guarding
Even now we heard a hollow burst of bellowing,
Like bulls, or rather lions. Did't not wake you?
It struck mine ear most terribly.

ALONSO   I heard nothing.

310 ANTONIO   O, 'twas a din to fright a monster's ear,
To make an earthquake! Sure it was the roar
Of a whole herd of lions.

ALONSO   Heard you this, Gonzalo?

GONZALO   Upon mine honour, sir, I heard a humming,
And that a strange one too, which did awake me.
315 I shaked you, sir, and cried.° As mine eyes opened   called out
I saw their weapons drawn. There was a noise,
That's verily.° 'Tis best we stand upon our guard,   the truth
Or that we quit this place. Let's draw our weapons.

ALONSO   Lead off this ground, and let's make further search
For my poor son.

320 GONZALO   Heavens keep him from these beasts!
For he is sure i'th' island.

ALONSO   Lead away.   [*Exeunt all but* ARIEL]¹

ARIEL   Prospero my lord shall know what I have done.
So, King, go safely on to seek thy son.   *Exit*

---

9. Gonzalo and Alonso.
1. Ariel's following lines are spoken as the other characters depart; he probably exits in another direction.

2.2

Enter CALIBAN, [*wearing a gaberdine,*[1] *and*] *with a bur-*
den of wood

CALIBAN [*throwing down his burden*]   All the infections that the
     sun sucks up
From bogs, fens, flats,° on Prosper fall, and make him   marshes
By inch-meal° a disease!   inch by inch
     [*A noise of thunder heard*][2]
                                 His spirits hear me,
And yet I needs must curse. But they'll nor pinch,
5   Fright me with urchin-shows,[3] pitch me i'th' mire,
Nor lead me like a fire-brand in the dark
Out of my way, unless he bid 'em. But
For every trifle are they set upon me;
Sometime like apes, that mow° and chatter at me   grimace
10 And after bite me; then like hedgehogs, which
Lie tumbling in my barefoot way and mount
Their pricks at my footfall; sometime am I
All wound with° adders, who with cloven tongues   entwined by
Do hiss me into madness.
     Enter TRINCULO[4]
                          Lo now, lo!
15 Here comes a spirit of his, and to torment me
For bringing wood in slowly. I'll fall flat.
Perchance he will not mind° me.   notice
     [*He lies down*]

TRINCULO   Here's neither bush nor shrub to bear off° any   ward off
     weather at all, and another storm brewing. I hear it sing i'th'
20   wind. Yon same black cloud, yon huge one, looks like a foul
     bombard[5] that would shed his liquor. If it should thunder as it
     did before, I know not where to hide my head. Yon same cloud
     cannot choose but fall by pailfuls. [*Seeing* CALIBAN] What have
     we here, a man or a fish? Dead or alive?—A fish, he smells
25   like a fish; a very ancient and fish-like smell; a kind of not-of-
     the-newest poor-john.[6] A strange fish! Were I in England now,
     as once I was, and had but this fish painted,[7] not a holiday-fool
     there but would give a piece of silver. There would this mon-
     ster make a man.[8] Any strange beast there makes a man. When
30   they will not give a doit° to relieve a lame beggar, they will lay   small coin
     out ten to see a dead Indian.[9] Legged like a man, and his fins
     like arms! Warm, o'my troth! I do now let loose my opinion,
     hold it no longer. This is no fish, but an islander that hath
     lately suffered by a thunderbolt.
     [*Thunder*]
35   Alas, the storm is come again. My best way is to creep under
     his gaberdine; there is no other shelter hereabout. Misery
     acquaints a man with strange bedfellows. I will here shroud°   take cover
     till the dregs[1] of the storm be past.

2.2
1. A loose smock made of coarse material.
2. Caliban takes this as a response to his curse; in F, the
direction comes before Caliban speaks.
3. With the sight of hedgehoglike spirits.
4. Trinculo is probably dressed in traditional fool's motley (many-colored garment).
5. Large leather drinking vessel; stone-throwing military

engine.
6. Dried hake, a poor person's staple.
7. On a sign to attract spectators.
8. Make a fortune for a man; become a man.
9. An allusion to exhibitions of American Indians in
London.
1. Drinks, as from a "bombard" of wine.

[*He hides under Caliban's gaberdine.*]
Enter STEFANO, *singing* [*with a wooden bottle in his hand*]

STEFANO   I shall no more to sea, to sea,
40   Here shall I die ashore—
This is a very scurvy tune to sing at a man's funeral.
Well, here's my comfort.
    [*He*] *drinks,* [*then*] *sings*
        The master, the swabber, the boatswain, and I,
          The gunner and his mate,
45   Loved Mall, Meg, and Marian, and Margery,
          But none of us cared for Kate.
            For she had a tongue with a tang,°   *sting*
            Would cry to a sailor 'Go hang!'
        She loved not the savour of tar nor of pitch,
50   Yet a tailor might scratch her where'er she did itch.[2]
            Then to sea, boys, and let her go hang!
            Then to sea [*etc.*].
This is a scurvy tune, too. But here's my comfort.
    [*He*] *drinks*
CALIBAN [*to* TRINCULO]   Do not torment me! O!
55 STEFANO   What's the matter?° Have we devils here? Do you put   *What's going on?*
tricks upon's with savages and men of Ind,° ha? I have not   *India*
scaped drowning to be afeard now of your four legs. For it hath
been said: 'As proper a man as ever went on four legs[3] cannot
make him give ground.' And it shall be said so again, while
60 Stefano breathes at'° nostrils.   *at the*
CALIBAN   The spirit torments me. O!
STEFANO   This is some monster of the isle with four legs, who
hath got, as I take it, an ague.° Where the devil should he learn   *a fit of fever*
our language? I will give him some relief, if it be but for that.
65 If I can recover° him and keep him tame and get to Naples   *cure*
with him, he's a present for any emperor that ever trod on neat's
leather.°   *cowhide; shoes*
CALIBAN [*to* TRINCULO]   Do not torment me, prithee! I'll bring
my wood home faster.
70 STEFANO   He's in his fit now, and does not talk after° the wisest.   *in the manner of*
He shall taste of my bottle. If he have never drunk wine afore,
it will go near to° remove his fit. If I can recover him and keep   *almost*
him tame, I will not take too much for him.[4] He shall pay for
him that hath° him, and that soundly.   *gets*
75 CALIBAN [*to* TRINCULO]   Thou dost me yet but little hurt. Thou
wilt anon, I know it by thy trembling. Now Prosper works upon
thee.
STEFANO   Come on your ways.° Open your mouth. Here is that   *Come on*
which will give language to you, cat.[5] Open your mouth. This
80 will shake° your shaking, I can tell you, and that soundly. You   *dislodge*
cannot tell who's your friend. Open your chaps again.
    [CALIBAN *drinks*]

---

2. Implying sexual desire and gratification. Tailors were often mocked for supposed lack of virility.
3. Comically varying "on two legs" (upright); also sug-
gesting "on crutches."
4. No sum can be too high for him.
5. "Ale will make a cat speak" was proverbial.

TRINCULO   I should know that voice. It should be—but he is drowned, and these are devils. O, defend me!

STEFANO   Four legs and two voices—a most delicate° monster!   *exquisitely made*
His forward voice now is to speak well of his friend; his backward voice is to utter foul speeches and to detract. If all the wine in my bottle will recover him,[6] I will help his ague. Come.

   [CALIBAN *drinks*]
Amen.° I will pour some in thy other mouth.   *Enough*

TRINCULO   Stefano!

STEFANO   Doth thy other mouth call me? Mercy, mercy! This is a devil, and no monster. I will leave him. I have no long spoon.[7]

TRINCULO   Stefano! If thou beest Stefano, touch me and speak to me, for I am Trinculo. Be not afeard. Thy good friend Trinculo.

STEFANO   If thou beest Trinculo, come forth. I'll pull thee by the lesser legs. If any be Trinculo's legs, these are they.

   [*He pulls out* TRINCULO *by the legs*]
Thou art very° Trinculo indeed! How cam'st thou to be the   *actual*
siege° of this moon-calf?[8] Can he vent° Trinculos?   *excrement / defecate*

TRINCULO [*rising*]   I took him to be killed with a thunderstroke. But art thou not drowned, Stefano? I hope now thou art not drowned. Is the storm overblown? I hid me under the dead moon-calf's gaberdine for fear of the storm. And art thou living, Stefano? O Stefano, two Neapolitans scaped!

   [*He dances* STEFANO *round*]

STEFANO   Prithee, do not turn me about. My stomach is not constant.

CALIBAN   These be fine things, an if ° they be not spirits.   *an if = if*
That's a brave° god, and bears celestial liquor.   *an excellent; a fine*
I will kneel to him.

   [*He kneels*]

STEFANO [*to* TRINCULO]   How didst thou scape? How cam'st thou hither? Swear by this bottle how thou cam'st hither. I escaped upon a butt of sack[9] which the sailors heaved o'erboard, by this bottle—which I made of the bark of a tree with mine own hands since I was cast ashore.

CALIBAN   I'll swear upon that bottle to be thy true subject, for the liquor is not earthly.

STEFANO [*offering* TRINCULO *the bottle*]   Here. Swear then how thou escapedst.

TRINCULO   Swum ashore, man, like a duck. I can swim like a duck, I'll be sworn.

STEFANO   Here, kiss the book.[1]

   [TRINCULO *drinks*]
Though thou canst swim like a duck, thou art made like a goose.[2]

---

6. If it takes all the wine in my bottle to cure him.
7. From the proverbial "He should have a long spoon that sups with the devil."
8. Deformed creature; miscarriage, owing to the supposed detrimental influence of the moon.
9. Cask of Spanish or Canary wine.

1. Confirming an oath by kissing the Bible; or the proverbial "Kiss the cup" ("Drink").
2. Probably alluding to Trinculo's outstretched neck with the bottle as a beak; also a byword for giddiness and unsteadiness on the feet.

125   TRINCULO   O Stefano, hast any more of this?
     STEFANO   The whole butt, man. My cellar is in a rock by th' sea-
     side, where my wine is hid.
           [CALIBAN *rises*]
     How now, moon-calf? How does thine ague?
     CALIBAN   Hast thou not dropped from heaven?
130   STEFANO   Out o'th' moon, I do assure thee. I was the man i'th'
     moon when time was.°   *once upon a time*
     CALIBAN   I have seen thee in her, and I do adore thee.
     My mistress° showed me thee, and thy dog and thy bush.[3]   *(Miranda)*
     STEFANO   Come, swear to that. Kiss the book. I will furnish it
135   anon with new contents. Swear.
           [CALIBAN *drinks*]
     TRINCULO   By this good light,° this is a very shallow monster! I   *sun*
     afeard of him? A very weak monster! The man i'th' moon? A
     most poor, credulous monster! Well drawn,° monster, in good   *drunk*
     sooth!
140   CALIBAN [*to* STEFANO]   I'll show thee every fertile inch o'th' island,
     And I will kiss thy foot. I prithee, be my god.
     TRINCULO   By this light, a most perfidious and drunken monster!
     When's god's asleep, he'll rob his bottle.
     CALIBAN [*to* STEFANO]   I'll kiss thy foot. I'll swear myself thy subject.
145   STEFANO   Come on then; down, and swear.
           [CALIBAN *kneels*]
     TRINCULO   I shall laugh myself to death at this puppy-headed
     monster. A most scurvy monster! I could find in my heart to
     beat him—
     STEFANO [*to* CALIBAN]   Come, kiss.
           [CALIBAN *kisses his foot*]
150   TRINCULO   But that the poor monster's in drink.° An abominable   *drunk*
     monster!
     CALIBAN   I'll show thee the best springs; I'll pluck thee berries;
     I'll fish for thee, and get thee wood enough.
     A plague upon the tyrant that I serve!
155   I'll bear him no more sticks, but follow thee,
     Thou wondrous man.
     TRINCULO   A most ridiculous monster, to make a wonder of a
     poor drunkard!
     CALIBAN [*to* STEFANO]   I prithee, let me bring thee where crabs°   *crab apples*
     grow,
160   And I with my long nails will dig thee pig-nuts,°   *edible tubers*
     Show thee a jay's nest, and instruct thee how
     To snare the nimble marmoset. I'll bring thee
     To clust'ring filberts, and sometimes I'll get thee
     Young seamews° from the rock. Wilt thou go with me?   *seagulls*
165   STEFANO   I prithee now, lead the way without any more talk-
     ing.—Trinculo, the King and all our company else being
     drowned, we will inherit here.—Here, bear my bottle.[4]—Fel-
     low Trinculo, we'll fill him° by and by again.   *it*
     CALIBAN (*sings drunkenly*)[5]   Farewell, master, farewell, farewell!
170   TRINCULO   A howling monster, a drunken monster!

---

3. A dog and a thornbush were traditional attributes of
the man in the moon; cf. *A Midsummer Night's Dream*
5.1.248–49.

4. Probably spoken to Caliban.
5. This stage direction may be misplaced and may actually refer to the following song, "No more dams."

CALIBAN [*sings*]   No more dams I'll make for° fish,   *to trap*
                  Nor fetch in firing°   *firewood*
                  At requiring,
                  Nor scrape trenchering,[6] nor wash dish.
175   'Ban, 'ban, Cacaliban
                  Has a new master.—Get a new man!
     Freedom, high-day!° High-day, freedom! Freedom, high-day,   *holiday*
     freedom!
STEFANO   O brave° monster! Lead the way.   *Exeunt*   *excellent; fine*

3.1

Enter FERDINAND, *bearing a log*

FERDINAND   There be some sports are painful, and their labour
     Delight in them sets off.[1] Some kinds of baseness
     Are nobly undergone, and most poor matters
     Point to rich ends. This my mean° task   *lowly*
5   Would be as heavy to me as odious, but°   *except that*
     The mistress which I serve quickens° what's dead,   *enlivens*
     And makes my labours pleasures. O, she is
     Ten times more gentle than her father's crabbed,
     And he's composed of harshness. I must remove
10   Some thousands of these logs and pile them up,
     Upon a sore° injunction. My sweet mistress   *harsh*
     Weeps when she sees me work, and says such baseness
     Had never like executor. I forget,
     But these sweet thoughts do even refresh my labours,
     Most busil'est[2] when I do it.°   *(labor)*

Enter MIRANDA, *and* PROSPERO [*following at a distance*]

15 MIRANDA   Alas now, pray you
     Work not so hard. I would the lightning had
     Burnt up those logs that you are enjoined to pile.
     Pray set it down, and rest you. When this burns
     'Twill weep[3] for having wearied you. My father
20   Is hard at study. Pray now, rest yourself.
     He's safe° for these three hours.   *We are safe from him*
FERDINAND   O most dear mistress,
     The sun will set before I shall discharge
     What I must strive to do.
MIRANDA   If you'll sit down
     I'll bear your logs the while. Pray give me that;
     I'll carry it to the pile.
25 FERDINAND   No, precious creature.
     I had rather crack my sinews, break my back,
     Than you should such dishonour undergo
     While I sit lazy by.
MIRANDA   It would become me
     As well as it does you; and I should do it
30   With much more ease, for my good will is to it,
     And yours it is against.

6. Trenchers, or wooden plates.
7. Addressed to the old master, Prospero.
3.1
1. *their . . . off*: the greater effort invested amounts to

more pleasure; the labor of painful activities ("sports") is offset by whatever delight we take in them.
2. Most busily (giving a double superlative).
3. By exuding drops of resin.

PROSPERO [*aside*]   Poor worm, thou art infected.[4]
 This visitation[5] shows it.

MIRANDA [*to* FERDINAND]   You look wearily.

FERDINAND   No, noble mistress, 'tis fresh morning with me
  When you are by at night. I do beseech you,
35 Chiefly that I might set it in my prayers,
  What is your name?

MIRANDA   Miranda. O my father,
  I have broke your hest° to say so!   °disobeyed your command

FERDINAND   Admired[6] Miranda!
  Indeed the top of admiration, worth
  What's dearest to the world. Full many a lady
40 I have eyed with best regard, and many a time
  Th'harmony of their tongues hath into bondage
  Brought my too diligent° ear. For several virtues   °attentive
  Have I liked several° women; never any   °various
  With so full soul but some defect in her
45 Did quarrel with the noblest grace she owed°   °owned
  And put it to the foil.[7] But you, O you,
  So perfect and so peerless, are created
  Of every creature's best.

MIRANDA   I do not know
  One of my sex, no woman's face remember
50 Save from my glass° mine own; nor have I seen   °mirror
  More that I may call men than you, good friend,
  And my dear father. How features are abroad[8]
  I am skilless° of ; but, by my modesty,°   °ignorant / virginity
  The jewel in my dower,° I would not wish   °dowry
55 Any companion in the world but you;
  Nor can imagination form a shape
  Besides° yourself to like of. But I prattle   °Other than
  Something° too wildly, and my father's precepts   °Somewhat
  I therein do forget.

FERDINAND   I am in my condition°   °rank
60 A prince, Miranda, I do think a king—
  I would° not so—and would no more endure   °wish it were
  This wooden slavery[9] than to suffer
  The flesh-fly[1] blow my mouth. Hear my soul speak.
  The very instant that I saw you did
65 My heart fly to your service; there resides
  To make me slave to it. And for your sake
  Am I this patient log-man.

MIRANDA   Do you love me?

FERDINAND   O heaven, O earth, bear witness to this sound,
  And crown what I profess with kind event°   °favorable outcome
70 If I speak true! If hollowly,° invert   °falsely
  What best is boded° me to mischief !° I,   °foretold to / misfortune
  Beyond all limit of what° else i'th' world,   °whatsoever
  Do love, prize, honour you.

---

4. Inflicted with lovesickness. *worm*: an expression of
tenderness; but a worm was often thought to carry disease.
5. Suggesting a pastoral or charitable visit to the sick; or
may indicate a visit by the plague, here lovesickness.
6. Playing on the meaning of Miranda's name.

7. Foiled it, or made it ineffectual; challenged it, as in a
fencing match (compare "quarrel" in line 45).
8. What people look like elsewhere.
9. The log as a symbol of Prospero's oppression.
1. Species of fly that deposits its eggs ("blows") in dead
flesh.

MIRANDA [*weeping*] I am a fool
　　To weep at what I am glad of.
PROSPERO [*aside*] Fair encounter
75　　Of two most rare affections! Heavens rain grace
　　On that which breeds between 'em.
FERDINAND [*to* MIRANDA] Wherefore weep you?
MIRANDA　At mine unworthiness, that dare not offer
　　What I desire to give, and much less take
　　What I shall die to want.[2] But this is trifling,
80　　And all the more it seeks to hide itself
　　The bigger bulk it shows.[3] Hence, bashful cunning,° *artful shyness*
　　And prompt me, plain and holy innocence.
　　I am your wife, if you will marry me.
　　If not, I'll die your maid.° To be your fellow° *virgin; servant / equal*
85　　You may deny me, but I'll be your servant
　　Whether you will or no.
FERDINAND [*kneeling*] My mistress,° dearest; *sweetheart*
　　And I thus humble ever.
MIRANDA　My husband then?
FERDINAND　Ay, with a heart as willing° *desirous*
90　　As bondage e'er of freedom. Here's my hand.[4]
MIRANDA　And mine, with my heart in't. And now farewell
　　Till half an hour hence.
FERDINAND　A thousand thousand.° *(farewells)*
　　Exeunt [*severally*° MIRANDA *and* FERDINAND] *separately*
PROSPERO　So glad of this as they I cannot be,
　　Who are surprised with all;° but my rejoicing *overwhelmed by all*
95　　At nothing can be more. I'll to my book,° *book of magic*
　　For yet ere supper-time must I perform
　　Much business appertaining.　　*Exit*

3.2

Enter CALIBAN, STEFANO, *and* TRINCULO

STEFANO [*to* CALIBAN] Tell not me. When the butt is out we will
　　drink water, not a drop before. Therefore bear up and board
　　'em.[1] Servant monster, drink to me.
TRINCULO　Servant monster? The folly° of this island! They say *absurdity*
5　　there's but five upon this isle. We are three of them; if th'other
　　two be brained° like us, the state totters. *have brains*
STEFANO　Drink, servant monster, when I bid thee. Thy eyes are
　　almost set° in thy head. *fixed by drunkenness*
TRINCULO　Where should they be set° else? He were a brave *placed*
10　　monster indeed if they were set in his tail.
STEFANO　My man-monster hath drowned his tongue in sack.
　　For my part, the sea cannot drown me. I swam, ere I could
　　recover the shore, five and thirty leagues,° off and on.[2] By this *about 100 miles*

---

2. *At . . . want:* Miranda is not at liberty to bestow her
virginity nor to obtain the consummation that she desires
and lacs.
3. *all . . . shows:* an image of secret pregnancy.
4. *I am your wife . . . hand:* Such an exchange could
actually have constituted a marriage ceremony. In
Shakespeare's time, weddings did not need to be witnessed and performed in a church to be valid (compare
4.1.14–19).
3.2
1. Force a way aboard, continuing the naval-warfare
terminology; take onboard (drink). *bear up:* sail to the
attack.
2. Tacking away from and toward the shore.

light, thou shalt be my lieutenant, monster, or my standard.[3]

15 TRINCULO   Your lieutenant if you list;° he's no standard.   *wish*
STEFANO   We'll not run, Monsieur Monster.
TRINCULO   Nor go° neither; but you'll lie[4] like dogs, and yet say   *walk*
nothing neither.
STEFANO   Moon-calf, speak once in thy life, if thou beest a good
20   moon-calf.
CALIBAN   How does thy honour? Let me lick thy shoe.
I'll not serve him; he is not valiant.
TRINCULO   Thou liest, most ignorant monster! I am in case° to   *prepared*
jostle a constable. Why, thou debauched fish, thou, was there
25   ever man a coward that hath drunk so much sack as I today?
Wilt thou tell a monstrous lie, being but half a fish and half a
monster?
CALIBAN [*to* STEFANO]   Lo, how he mocks me! Wilt thou let him,
my lord?
30 TRINCULO   'Lord' quoth he? That a monster should be such a
natural![5]
CALIBAN [*to* STEFANO]   Lo, lo, again! Bite him to death, I prithee.
STEFANO   Trinculo, keep a good tongue in your head. If you
prove a mutineer, the next tree.° The poor monster's my sub-   *(for a gallows)*
35   ject, and he shall not suffer indignity.
CALIBAN   I thank my noble lord. Wilt thou be pleased
To hearken once again to the suit I made to thee?
STEFANO   Marry, will I. Kneel and repeat it. I will stand, and so
shall Trinculo.
[CALIBAN *kneels*.]
Enter ARIEL, *invisible*
40 CALIBAN   As I told thee before, I am subject to a tyrant, a sor-
cerer, that by his cunning hath cheated me of the island.
ARIEL   Thou liest.
CALIBAN [*to* TRINCULO]   Thou liest, thou jesting monkey, thou.
I would my valiant master would destroy thee.
45   I do not lie.
STEFANO   Trinculo, if you trouble him any more in's tale, by this
hand, I will supplant° some of your teeth.   *uproot*
TRINCULO   Why, I said nothing.
STEFANO   Mum, then, and no more. [*To* CALIBAN] Proceed.
50 CALIBAN   I say by sorcery he got this isle;
From me he got it. If thy greatness will
Revenge it on him—for I know thou dar'st,
But this thing[6] dare not—
STEFANO   That's most certain.
55 CALIBAN   Thou shalt be lord of it, and I'll serve thee.
STEFANO   How now shall this be compassed?° Canst thou bring   *accomplished*
me to the party?°   *person concerned*
CALIBAN   Yea, yea, my lord. I'll yield him thee asleep
Where thou mayst knock a nail into his head.[7]
60 ARIEL   Thou liest, thou canst not.

---

3. Standard-bearer, but in Trinculo's reply "one who can
stand up."
4. Lie (down); tell lies; excrete.
5. An idiot, punning on the idea that monsters were

unnatural.
6. Trinculo; or perhaps Caliban himself.
7. As Jael murdered sleeping Sisera in Judges 4:21 and
5:26.

CALIBAN   What a pied ninny's° this! [*To* TRINCULO] Thou scurvy   *fool in motley*
    patch!°   *jester; idiot*
  [*To* STEFANO] I do beseech thy greatness give him blows,
  And take his bottle from him. When that's gone
  He shall drink naught but brine, for I'll not show him
65 Where the quick freshes° are.   *fast-flowing springs*
  STEFANO   Trinculo, run into no further danger. Interrupt the
  monster one word further, and, by this hand, I'll turn my mercy
  out o'doors and make a stockfish of thee.[8]
  TRINCULO   Why, what did I? I did nothing. I'll go farther off.
70 STEFANO   Didst thou not say he lied?
  ARIEL   Thou liest.
  STEFANO   Do I so? [*Striking* TRINCULO] Take thou that. As you   *call me a liar*
  like this, give me the lie° another time.
  TRINCULO   I did not give the lie. Out o'your wits and hearing
75 too? A pox o'your bottle! This can sack and drinking do. A
  murrain° on your monster, and the devil take your fingers.   *plague*
  CALIBAN   Ha, ha, ha!
  STEFANO   Now forward with your tale. [*To* TRINCULO] Prithee,
  stand further off.
80 CALIBAN   Beat him enough; after a little time
  I'll beat him too.
  STEFANO [*to* TRINCULO]
          Stand farther. [*To* CALIBAN] Come, proceed.
  CALIBAN   Why, as I told thee, 'tis a custom with him
  I'th' afternoon to sleep. There° thou mayst brain him,   *Then*
  Having first seized his books; or with a log
85 Batter his skull, or paunch° him with a stake,   *disembowel*
  Or cut his weasand° with thy knife. Remember   *windpipe*
  First to possess his books, for without them
  He's but a sot° as I am, nor hath not   *stupid fool*
  One spirit to command—they all do hate him
90 As rootedly as I. Burn but his books.
  He has brave utensils,[9] for so he calls them,
  Which when he has a house he'll deck withal.
  And that most deeply to consider is
  The beauty of his daughter. He himself
95 Calls her a nonpareil.° I never saw a woman   *one without equal*
  But only Sycorax my dam and she,
  But she as far surpasseth Sycorax
  As great'st does least.
  STEFANO   Is it so brave° a lass?   *excellent; fine*
  CALIBAN   Ay, lord. She will become thy bed, I warrant,
100 And bring thee forth brave brood.
  STEFANO   Monster, I will kill this man. His daughter and I will
  be king and queen—save° our graces!—and Trinculo and thy-   *God save*
  self shall be viceroys. Dost thou like the plot, Trinculo?
  TRINCULO   Excellent.
105 STEFANO   Give me thy hand. I am sorry I beat thee. But while
  thou liv'st, keep a good tongue in thy head.

8. Proverbial allusion to the beating of dried fish before cooking it.   9. Perhaps confusing implements for magic and household goods.

CALIBAN   Within this half hour will he be asleep.
  Wilt thou destroy him then?
STEFANO   Ay, on mine honour.
110 ARIEL [*aside*]   This will I tell my master.
CALIBAN   Thou mak'st me merry; I am full of pleasure.
  Let us be jocund. Will you troll° the catch°   *sing / round; song*
  You taught me but while-ere?°   *a short time ago*
STEFANO   At thy request, monster, I will do reason, any rea-
115 son.°—Come on, Trinculo, let us sing.   *anything reasonable*
  (*Sings*)   Flout 'em and cout[1] 'em,
                    And scout° 'em and flout 'em.   *mock*
                    Thought is free.
CALIBAN   That's not the tune.
  ARIEL *plays the tune on a tabor and pipe*[2]
120 STEFANO   What is this same?
TRINCULO   This is the tune of our catch, played by the picture
  of Nobody.[3]
STEFANO [*calls towards* ARIEL]   If thou beest a man, show thyself
  in thy likeness. If thou beest a devil, take't as thou list.°   *wish*
125 TRINCULO   O, forgive me my sins!
STEFANO   He that dies pays all debts.[4] [*Calls*] I defy thee.—
  Mercy upon us![5]
CALIBAN   Art thou afeard?
STEFANO   No, monster, not I.
130 CALIBAN   Be not afeard. The isle is full of noises,
  Sounds, and sweet airs,° that give delight and hurt not.   *tunes*
  Sometimes a thousand twangling instruments
  Will hum about mine ears, and sometime voices
  That if I then had waked after long sleep
135 Will make me sleep again; and then in dreaming
  The clouds methought would open and show riches
  Ready to drop upon me, that when I waked
  I cried to dream again.
STEFANO   This will prove a brave kingdom to me, where I shall
140 have my music for nothing.[6]
CALIBAN   When Prospero is destroyed.
STEFANO   That shall be by and by.° I remember the story.   *very soon*
                              [*Exit* ARIEL, *playing music*]
TRINCULO   The sound is going away. Let's follow it, and after do
  our work.
145 STEFANO   Lead, monster; we'll follow.—I would I could see this
  taborer. He lays it on.[7]
TRINCULO [*to* CALIBAN]   Wilt come? I'll follow Stefano.   *Exeunt*

1. Probably a dialectal form of "colt" (cheat). The stage direction ("Sings") suggests that the others cannot manage the catch and remain in bewildered silence. But Trinculo, and perhaps Caliban, may attempt to join in.
2. The tabor was a small drum slung on the left-hand side of the body; the tabor pipe was a long narrow pipe played with the left hand. The combination was associated with rustic dances and merrymaking.
3. "Nobody" was a character in a comedy who was depicted on the title page of the printed text. Large breeches up to his neck made him appear to have no trunk.
4. Varying the proverbial "Death pays all debts."
5. Stefano's defiance comically collapses.
6. James I spent large sums on court music, but not typically of the popular kind Ariel now plays.
7. He sets himself to his music vigorously. Stefano deserts Caliban in order to follow the music. Trinculo and Caliban in turn follow Stefano (line 147).

3.3

Enter ALONSO, SEBASTIAN, ANTONIO, GONZALO, ADRIAN, *and* FRANCISCO

GONZALO [*to* ALONSO]   By'r la'kin,[1] I can go no further, sir.
My old bones ache. Here's a maze trod indeed
Through forthrights and meanders.° By your patience,   direct and winding paths
I needs must rest me.

ALONSO   Old lord, I cannot blame thee,
5   Who am myself attached° with weariness   seized
To th' dulling of my spirits. Sit down and rest.
Even° here I will put off my hope, and keep it   Exactly
No longer for° my flatterer. He is drowned   as
Whom thus we stray to find, and the sea mocks
10 Our frustrate° search on land. Well, let him go.   vain
     [*They sit*]

ANTONIO [*aside to* SEBASTIAN]   I am right glad that he's so out of hope.
Do not for° one repulse forgo the purpose   on account of
That you resolved t'effect.

SEBASTIAN [*aside to* ANTONIO] The next advantage
Will we take throughly.°   thoroughly

ANTONIO [*aside to* SEBASTIAN] Let it be tonight,
15 For now they are oppressed with travel.° They   journey; travail
Will not nor cannot use such vigilance
As when they are fresh.

SEBASTIAN [*aside to* ANTONIO] I say tonight. No more.
     Solemn and strange music. [*Enter*] PROSPERO *on the
     top,[2] invisible*

ALONSO   What harmony is this? My good friends, hark.

GONZALO   Marvellous sweet music.
     Enter [*spirits, in*] *several strange shapes, bringing in* [*a
     table and*] *a banquet, and dance about it with gentle
     actions of salutations, and, inviting the King and* [*his
     companions*] *to eat, they depart*

20 ALONSO   Give us kind keepers,° heavens! What were these?   guardian angels

SEBASTIAN   A living drollery.[3] Now I will believe
That there are unicorns; that in Arabia
There is one tree, the phoenix' throne, one phoenix[4]
At this hour reigning there.

ANTONIO   I'll believe both;
25 And what does else want credit° come to me,   lack belief
And I'll be sworn 'tis true. Travellers ne'er did lie,[5]
Though fools at home condemn 'em.

GONZALO   If in Naples
I should report this now, would they believe me—
If I should say I saw such islanders?
30 For certes° these are people of the island,   certainly
Who though they are of monstrous shape, yet note
Their manners are more gentle-kind than of
Our human generation you shall find
Many, nay, almost any.

3.3
1. Ladykin: a colloquial form of reference to the Virgin Mary.
2. A small acting area above the upper stage.
3. A puppet show with live actors.

4. The unicorn and phoenix, a bird, were two mythological creatures that sometimes figured in travelers' tales. Only one pheonix was said to exist in the world at any one time.
5. Proverbially, "A traveler may lie with authority."

PROSPERO [*aside*]   Honest lord,
35   Thou hast said well, for some of you there present
    Are worse than devils.
ALONSO   I cannot too much muse.°   *marvel*
    Such shapes, such gesture, and such sound, expressing—
    Although they want the use of tongue°—a kind   *language*
    Of excellent dumb discourse.
PROSPERO [*aside*]   Praise in departing.[6]
FRANCISCO   They vanished strangely.
40   SEBASTIAN   No matter, since
    They have left their viands° behind, for we have stomachs.° *food / good appetites*
    Will't please you taste of what is here?
ALONSO   Not I.
GONZALO   Faith, sir, you need not fear. When we were boys,
    Who would believe that there were mountaineers°   *mountain dwellers*
45   Dewlapped like bulls, whose throats had hanging at 'em
    Wallets° of flesh? Or that there were such men   *Pouches*
    Whose heads stood in their breasts? Which now we find
    Each putter-out of five for one[7] will bring us
    Good warrant of.
ALONSO [*rising*]   I will stand to and feed,°   *begin eating*
50   Although my last—no matter, since I feel
    The best is past. Brother, my lord the Duke,
    Stand to, and do as we.
        [ALONSO, SEBASTIAN, *and* ANTONIO *approach the table.*]
        Thunder and lightning. Enter ARIEL [*descending*] *like a*
        harpy,[8] *claps his wings upon the table, and, with a*
        quaint device,° the banquet vanishes[9]   *an ingenious mechanism*
ARIEL   You are three men of sin, whom destiny—
    That hath to° instrument this lower world   *as its*
55   And what is in't—the never-surfeited sea
    Hath caused to belch up you, and on this island
    Where man doth not inhabit, you 'mongst men
    Being most unfit to live. I have made you mad,
    And even with suchlike valour[1] men hang and drown
    Their proper selves.°   *Themselves*
        [ALONSO, SEBASTIAN, *and* ANTONIO *draw*][2]
60   You fools! I and my fellows
    Are ministers of fate. The elements
    Of whom your swords are tempered[3] may as well
    Wound the loud winds, or with bemocked-at stabs
    Kill the still-closing[4] waters, as diminish
65   One dowl° that's in my plume.° My fellow ministers   *featherlet / plumage*
    Are like° invulnerable. If you could hurt,   *similarly*

---

6. Reserve your praise until the end of the event.
7. A traveler could profit from a voyage by laying down a sum with a broker before departing and undertaking to bring back evidence of having reached his destination; if successful, he was repaid fivefold.
8. A mythological monster with a vulture's wings and claws and a woman's face. Aeneas and his companions encountered these harpies, who stole their meals and threatened to punish them with slow starvation. *Thunder and lightning*: Both spectacular and functional for disguising the mechanics of the "quaint device."
9. The simplest effective staging is by means of a rotating tabletop with the vessels of the banquet fixed to its surface. Leg-to-leg planks supporting the tabletop or a hang-

ing cloth would conceal the vanished banquet. The harpy's wings would hide the mechanics from the audience, and clapping them would provide a visual distraction.
1. *suchlike valour*: fearlessness that comes from madness.
2. Ariel perhaps ascends beyond their reach here. Aeneas's companions, like Alonso here, similarly attempted to kill the harpies with swords.
3. Compounded and hardened. Metal was sometimes thought of as being compounded of earth and fire, here contrasted with winds and waters.
4. Self-healing, since they close immediately once parted.

Your swords are now too massy° for your strengths   *heavy*
And will not be uplifted.
    [ALONSO, SEBASTIAN, *and* ANTONIO *stand amazed°*]   *crazed; bewildered*
         —   But remember,
For that's my business to you, that you three

70   From Milan did supplant good Prospero;
Exposed unto the sea, which hath requit it,
Him and his innocent child; for which foul deed,
The powers, delaying not forgetting,[5] have
Incensed the seas and shores, yea, all the creatures,[6]

75   Against your peace. Thee of thy son, Alonso,
They have bereft, and do pronounce by me
Ling'ring perdition[7]—worse than any death
Can be at once—shall step by step attend
You and your ways; whose[8] wraths to guard you from—

80   Which here in this most desolate[9] isle else falls
Upon your heads—is nothing° but heart's sorrow   *there is no alternative*
And a clear life° ensuing.   *a life innocent of sin*
        He [ascends and] vanishes[1] in thunder. Then, to soft
        music, enter the [spirits] again, and dance with mocks
        and mows,° and [they depart,] carrying out the table   *grimaces*
PROSPERO   Bravely the figure of this harpy hast thou
Performed, my Ariel; a grace it had devouring.[2]

85   Of my instruction hast thou nothing bated°   *omitted*
In what thou hadst to say. So with good life[3]
And observation strange[4] my meaner ministers°   *lesser spirits*
Their several kinds° have done.° My high charms work,   *various roles / performed*
And these mine enemies are all knit up

90   In their distractions. They now are in my power;
And in these fits I leave them, while I visit
Young Ferdinand, whom they suppose is drowned,
And his and mine loved darling.   [*Exit*]
    [GONZALO, ADRIAN, *and* FRANCISCO *go towards the*
    others]
GONZALO   I'th' name of something holy, sir, why stand you
In this strange stare?

95 ALONSO   O, it is monstrous, monstrous!
Methought the billows spoke and told me of it,
The winds did sing it to me, and the thunder,
That deep and dreadful organ-pipe, pronounced
The name of Prosper. It did bass my trespass.[5]

100 Therefor° my son i'th' ooze is bedded, and   *For that*
I'll seek him deeper than e'er plummet sounded,
And with him there lie mudded.   *Exit*
SEBASTIAN   But one fiend at a time,
I'll fight their legions o'er.°   *from beginning to end*

---

5. Related to the proverb "God stays long but strikes at last."
6. Compare Genesis 1:21: "Then God created . . . everything living and moving."
7. Slow starvation; hell on earth of spiritual suffering. The phrase is first the object of "pronounce" and then the subject of "shall . . . attend."
8. Refers to "the powers" in line 73.
9. Joyless; wretched; barren, deserted.

1. Ariel is raised out of sight into the canopy.
2. In clapping his wings, Ariel has created the illusion of having devoured the banquet.
3. Convincingly; with vitality. So: In the same way.
4. Remarkable attention to the requirements of their parts, or instructions.
5. The thunder proclaimed my sin ("trespass") in a bass voice, or with a bass background; perhaps wordplay on the "utter baseness" of trespass.

ANTONIO   I'll be thy second.
                    Exeunt [SEBASTIAN *and* ANTONIO]
    GONZALO   All three of them are desperate.° Their great guilt,   *in despair; reckless*
105   Like poison given to work° a great time after,   *take effect*
        Now 'gins to bite the spirits. I do beseech you
        That are of suppler joints, follow them swiftly,
        And hinder them from what this ecstasy°   *madness*
        May now provoke them to.
    ADRIAN   Follow, I pray you.   *Exeunt*

4.1

Enter PROSPERO, FERDINAND, *and* MIRANDA

    PROSPERO [*to* FERDINAND]   If I have too austerely punished you,
        Your compensation makes amends, for I
        Have given you here a third¹ of mine own life—
        Or that for which I live—who° once again   *whom*
5   I tender° to thy hand. All thy vexations   *offer*
        Were but my trials of thy love, and thou
        Hast strangely° stood the test. Here, afore heaven,   *wonderfully*
        I ratify this my rich gift. O Ferdinand,
        Do not smile at me that I boast of her,
10   For thou shalt find she will outstrip all praise,
        And make it halt° behind her.   *limp*
    FERDINAND   I do believe it
        Against an oracle.²
    PROSPERO   Then, as my gift and thine own acquisition
        Worthily purchased,° take my daughter. But   *Gained by effort*
15   If thou dost break her virgin-knot° before   *virginity*
        All sanctimonious° ceremonies may   *holy*
        With full and holy rite be ministered,
        No sweet aspersion° shall the heavens let fall   *shower of grace*
        To make this contract grow; but barren hate,
20   Sour-eyed disdain, and discord, shall bestrew
        The union of your bed with weeds³ so loathly
        That you shall hate it both. Therefore take heed,
        As Hymen's⁴ lamps shall light you.
    FERDINAND   As I hope
        For quiet days, fair issue,° and long life   *children*
25   With such love as 'tis now, the murkiest den,°   *cave*
        The most opportune place, the strong'st suggestion°   *temptation*
        Our worser genius can,⁵ shall never melt
        Mine honour into lust to take away
        The edge° of that day's celebration;   *unblunted desire*
30   When I shall think or° Phoebus' steeds are foundered⁶   *either*
        Or night kept chained below.
    PROSPERO   Fairly spoke.

4.1
1. Miranda. The usual poetic conceit was a half; commentators variously conjecture the other third to be his dukedom, his books, or his late wife.
2. *I . . . oracle:* I would believe it even if an oracle said otherwise.
3. Weeds in place of the flowers traditionally strewn on the marriage bed; wordplay on both "marriage bed" and

"seed-bed."
4. Classical god of marriage.
5. Is capable of. *worser genius:* evil spirit corresponding to a guardian angel.
6. Collapsed and made lame. *Phoebus' steeds:* the mythological horses that drew the chariot of the sun. Ferdinand anticipates that on his wedding day he will in his impatience think that the night will never come.

Sit, then, and talk with her. She is thine own.

[FERDINAND *and* MIRANDA *sit and talk together*]

What,° Ariel, my industrious servant Ariel!   *Now, then*

Enter ARIEL

ARIEL What would my potent master? Here I am.

35 PROSPERO Thou and thy meaner° fellows your last service *lesser*
Did worthily perform, and I must use you
In such another trick. Go bring the rabble,⁷
O'er whom I give thee power, here to this place.
Incite them to quick motion, for I must
40 Bestow upon the eyes of this young couple
Some vanity⁸ of mine art. It is my promise,
And they expect it from me.

ARIEL   Presently?°   *At once*

PROSPERO Ay, with a twink.⁹

ARIEL   Before you can say 'Come' and 'Go',
45   And breathe twice, and cry 'So, so',
Each one tripping on his toe
Will be here with mop and mow.¹
Do you love me, master? No?

PROSPERO Dearly, my delicate Ariel. Do not approach
Till thou dost hear me call.

50 ARIEL   Well; I conceive.°   *Exit* *understand*

PROSPERO [*to* FERDINAND] Look thou be true.² Do not give dalliance
Too much the rein.³ The strongest oaths are straw
To th' fire i'th' blood. Be more abstemious,
Or else, good night your vow.

FERDINAND   I warrant you, sir,
55 The white cold virgin snow upon my heart
Abates the ardour of my liver.⁴

PROSPERO   Well.—
Now come, my Ariel! Bring a corollary°   *surplus*
Rather than want° a spirit. Appear, and pertly.° *lack / briskly*
Soft music

[*To* FERDINAND *and* MIRANDA] No tongue, all eyes! Be silent.

Enter IRIS⁵

60 IRIS Ceres, most bounteous lady, thy rich leas⁶
Of wheat, rye, barley, vetches,⁷ oats, and peas;
Thy turfy mountains where live nibbling sheep,
And flat meads° thatched with stover,⁸ them to keep; *meadows*
Thy banks with peonied and twillèd⁹ brims
65 Which spongy° April at thy hest betrims¹   *wet*
To make cold nymphs chaste crowns; and thy broom-groves,²
Whose shadow the dismissèd bachelor° loves, *rejected suitor*

---

7. Troupe of lesser spirits: *trick:* theatrical device, or clever artifice.
8. Trifle; conceit; illusion; display.
9. In the twinkling of an eye.
1. With derisive and grimacing gestures.
2. Take care that you remain faithful to your promise. Prospero may have caught the lovers just indulging in dalliance.
3. To "give the rein" is to make a horse gallop.
4. *The . . . liver:* Virgin snow lies on his heart because he has remained chaste, never having given in to his ardent liver. The liver was held to be the seat of passion.

5. Goddess of the rainbow and messenger of Juno; her apparel is in the colors of the rainbow, and she wears "saffron wings" (line 78).
6. Arable land. Ceres was the Roman goddess of agriculture and generative nature.
7. Pealike plants grown for fodder.
8. Hay for winter fodder.
9. Reinforced with entwined branches to prevent riverbank erosion. *peonied:* covered with peonies.
1. Adorns with flowers; recalls the colloquial "April showers bring forth May flowers."
2. Thickets of gorse, yellow-flowered shrubs. *cold:* chaste.

Being lass-lorn; thy pole-clipped vineyard,[3]
And thy sea-marge,° sterile and rocky-hard,   *seashore*
70   Where thou thyself dost air:° the Queen o'th' Sky,°   *take fresh air / Juno*
Whose wat'ry arch° and messenger am I,   *rainbow*
Bids thee leave these, and with her sovereign grace

       JUNO [*appears in the air*][4]

Here on this grass-plot,[5] in this very place,
To come and sport.—Her peacocks fly amain.[6]
75   Approach, rich Ceres, her to entertain.

       Enter [ARIEL *as*] CERES[7]

CERES   Hail, many-coloured messenger, that ne'er
Dost disobey the wife of Jupiter;°
Who with thy saffron wings upon my flowers   *Juno*
Diffusest honey-drops, refreshing showers,
80   And with each end of thy blue bow dost crown
My bosky[8] acres and my unshrubbed down,
Rich scarf[9] to my proud earth. Why hath thy queen
Summoned me hither to this short-grassed green?

IRIS   A contract of true love to celebrate,
85   And some donation freely to estate°   *bestow*
On the blest lovers.

CERES   Tell me, heavenly bow,°   *rainbow*
If Venus or her son,[1] as° thou dost know,   *as far as*
Do now attend the Queen. Since they did plot
The means that dusky Dis[2] my daughter got,
90   Her and her blind boy's scandalled° company   *scandalous; notorious*
I have forsworn.

IRIS   Of her society
Be not afraid. I met her deity
Cutting the clouds towards Paphos,[3] and her son
Dove-drawn[4] with her. Here thought they to have done
95   Some wanton charm upon[5] this man and maid,
Whose vows are that no bed-right[6] shall be paid
Till Hymen's torch be lighted[7]—but in vain.
Mars's hot minion° is returned again.   *lover; Venus*
Her waspish-headed[8] son has broke his arrows,
100   Swears he will shoot no more, but play with sparrows,[9]
And be a boy right out.°   *an ordinary boy*

       [*Music.* JUNO *descends to the stage*][1]

CERES   Highest queen of state,
Great Juno, comes; I know her by her gait.°   *majestic bearing*

---

3. Vineyard with vines embracing, twined around, their
supporting poles; pruned vineyard. "Vineyard" was pronounced as three syllables. *lass-lorn:* abandoned by the
girl he wooed.
4. Juno was queen of the heavens and goddess of women,
held to protect marriages and preside over childbirth. Her
chair is ornamented with a peacock motif. She descends
by a "flight" mechanism to a position suspended in the
air above the stage. Music may be played. Juno remains
in view aloft until line 101. If, however, F's direction here
is misplaced, she may not appear until line 101.
5. Compare "this short-grassed green" (line 83) and "this
green land" (line 130): a green carpet on the acting area
is indicated.
6. In haste. Peacocks, sacred to Juno, drew her chariot.
7. Her part is probably played by Ariel (see line 167).
8. Covered with bushes and thickets.
9. Ornamental and hung across the body rather than

around the neck.
1. Cupid, proverbially blind.
2. King of the underworld in classical mythology. Venus
and her son Cupid made him fall in love with Ceres'
daughter Proserpine, whom he abducted (Ovid, *Metamorphoses* 5.395ff.).
3. City in Cyprus: associated with Venus.
4. Doves were sacred to Venus and drew her chariot.
5. *done . . . upon:* cast a lustful spell upon.
6. Right to consummate the marriage; also suggesting a
rite, as in line 17.
7. Until the wedding ceremony is performed.
8. Peevish, irritable, and with arrows like the wasp's sting.
9. Sparrows were associated with Venus because they
were proverbially lustful.
1. This completes Juno's flight to the stage; again, music
may be played.

JUNO   How does my bounteous sister? Go with me
    To bless this twain, that they may prosperous be,
105   And honoured in their issue.
              [CERES *joins* JUNO, *and*] *they sing*[2]

JUNO   Honour, riches, marriage-blessing,
    Long continuance and increasing,
    Hourly joys be still° upon you!   *always*
    Juno sings her blessings on you.
110 CERES   Earth's increase, and foison° plenty,   *abundance*
    Barns and garners° never empty,   *granaries*
    Vines with clust'ring bunches growing,
    Plants with goodly burden bowing;
    Spring come to you at the farthest,
115   In the very end of harvest.[3]
    Scarcity and want shall shun you,
    Ceres' blessing so is on you.
FERDINAND   This is a most majestic vision, and
    Harmonious charmingly.[4] May I be bold°   *Would I be right*
    To think these spirits?
120 PROSPERO   Spirits, which by mine art
    I have from their confines[5] called to enact
    My present fancies.
FERDINAND   Let me live here ever!
    So rare a wondered° father and a wise   *endowed with wonders*
    Makes this place paradise.
          JUNO *and* CERES *whisper, and send* IRIS *on employment*
PROSPERO   Sweet° now, silence.   *Softly*
125   Juno and Ceres whisper seriously.
    There's something else to do. Hush, and be mute,
    Or else our spell is marred.
IRIS   You nymphs called naiads of the wind'ring[6] brooks,
    With your sedged crowns° and ever-harmless looks,   *garlands of reeds*
130   Leave your crisp channels, and on this green land
    Answer your summons; Juno does command.
    Come, temperate nymphs, and help to celebrate
    A contract of true love. Be not too late.
          Enter certain nymphs
    You sunburned sicklemen,° of August weary,   *harvesters*
135   Come hither from the furrow and be merry;
    Make holiday, your rye-straw hats put on,
    And these fresh nymphs encounter every one
    In country footing.
          Enter certain reapers, properly habited.[7] *They join with*
          the nymphs in a graceful dance; towards the end whereof
          PROSPERO *starts suddenly, and speaks*
PROSPERO [*aside*]   I had forgot that foul conspiracy
140   Of the beast Caliban and his confederates
    Against my life. The minute of their plot

---

2. Ceres and Juno might be raised together in the flight apparatus and sing suspended above the stage. They would then vanish (line 142 stage direction) by being raised into the heavens.

3. Let spring return immediately after harvest, without any intervening winter. (In Greek mythology, winter was originally caused by Ceres abandoning the earth in search of Proserpine.)

4. Delightfully; magically; harmoniously.

5. Regions of dwelling. Word is accented on the second syllable.

6. Perhaps a conflation of "wandering" and "winding." The naiads were mythical river nymphs.

7. Either properly or finely dressed.

Is almost come. [*To the spirits*] Well done! Avoid;° no more!   *Begone*
To a strange, hollow, and confused noise, the [*spirits in*
the pageant] heavily vanish.[8]
      [FERDINAND *and* MIRANDA *rise*]

FERDINAND [*to* MIRANDA]   This is strange. Your father's in some passion
That works° him strongly.   *agitates*

MIRANDA   Never till this day

145   Saw I him touched with anger so distempered.°   *troubled; distracted*

PROSPERO   You do look, my son, in a moved sort,°   *disturbed manner*
As if you were dismayed. Be cheerful, sir.
Our revels[9] now are ended. These our actors,
As I foretold you,° were all spirits, and   *told you before*
150   Are melted into air, into thin air;
And like the baseless fabric[1] of this vision,
The cloud-capped towers, the gorgeous palaces,
The solemn temples, the great globe[2] itself,
Yea, all which it inherit,[3] shall dissolve;
155   And, like this insubstantial pageant faded,
Leave not a rack° behind. We are such stuff   *wisp of cloud*
As dreams are made on,° and our little life   *of*
Is rounded[4] with a sleep. Sir, I am vexed.
Bear with my weakness. My old brain is troubled.
160   Be not disturbed with my infirmity.
If you be pleased, retire into my cell,
And there repose. A turn or two I'll walk
To still my beating mind.

FERDINAND *and* MIRANDA   We wish your peace.
                  Exeunt [FERDINAND *and* MIRANDA]

PROSPERO   Come with a thought![5] I thank thee, Ariel. Come!
      Enter ARIEL

ARIEL   Thy thoughts I cleave to. What's thy pleasure?
165 PROSPERO   Spirit,
We must prepare to meet with Caliban.

ARIEL   Ay, my commander. When I presented[6] Ceres
I thought to have told thee of it, but I feared
Lest I might anger thee.
170 PROSPERO   Say again: where didst thou leave these varlets?°   *ruffians*

ARIEL   I told you, sir, they were red-hot with drinking;
So full of valour that they smote the air
For breathing in their faces, beat the ground
For kissing of their feet; yet always bending°   *aiming*
175   Towards their project. Then I beat my tabor,°   *side drum*
At which like unbacked° colts they pricked their ears,   *never-ridden*
Advanced° their eyelids, lifted up their noses   *Opened*
As° they smelt music. So I charmed their ears   *As if*
That calf-like they my lowing° followed, through   *mooing*
180   Toothed briars, sharp furzes, pricking gorse,° and thorns, *prickly shrubs*
Which entered their frail shins. At last I left them
I'th' filthy-mantled[7] pool beyond your cell,

---

8. Sorrowfully depart (probably not implying a trick of
staging).
9. Entertainment, in both festive and theatrical senses.
1. An edifice or substance without foundations; insubstantial, alluding to buildings in masque scenery.
2. World; also with a passing allusion to the Globe Theatre.

3. All who come into possession of it.
4. Rounded off; surrounded; or, possibly, crowned.
5. Come as fast as thought, a colloquial simile.
6. Acted; produced the masque of; introduced while
playing Iris.
7. Covered with filthy scum.

There dancing up to th' chins, that° the foul lake so that
O'er-stunk[8] their feet.

PROSPERO This was well done, my bird.° chick; dear
185 Thy shape invisible retain thou still.
The trumpery° in my house, go bring it hither cheap goods
For stale° to catch these thieves. decoy; bait

ARIEL I go, I go. Exit

PROSPERO   A devil, a born devil, on whose nature
Nurture can never stick; on whom my pains,
190 Humanely taken, all, all lost, quite lost,
And, as with age his body uglier grows,
So his mind cankers.° I will plague them all, festers
Even to roaring.

Enter ARIEL, *laden with glistening apparel, etc.*

Come, hang them on this lime.[9]

[ARIEL *hangs up the apparel. Exeunt* PROSPERO *and*
ARIEL]

Enter CALIBAN, STEFANO, *and* TRINCULO, *all wet*

CALIBAN   Pray you, tread softly, that the blind mole may
195 Not hear a foot fall. We now are near his cell.

STEFANO   Monster, your fairy, which you say is a harmless fairy,
has done little better than played the Jack° with us. knave; will-o'-the-wisp

TRINCULO   Monster, I do smell° all horse-piss, at which my smell of
nose is in great indignation.

200 STEFANO   So is mine. Do you hear, monster? If I should take a
displeasure against you, look you—

TRINCULO   Thou wert but a lost monster.

CALIBAN   Good my lord, give me thy favour still.
Be patient, for the prize I'll bring thee to
205 Shall hoodwink[1] this mischance. Therefore speak softly.
All's hushed as midnight yet.

TRINCULO   Ay, but to lose our bottles in the pool!

STEFANO   There is not only disgrace and dishonour in that,
monster, but an infinite loss.

210 TRINCULO   That's more to me than my wetting. Yet this is your
harmless fairy, monster.

STEFANO   I will fetch off[2] my bottle, though I be o'er ears° for drowned
my labour.

CALIBAN   Prithee, my king, be quiet. Seest thou here;
215 This is the mouth o'th' cell. No noise, and enter.
Do that good mischief which may make this island
Thine own for ever, and I thy Caliban
For aye° thy foot-licker. ever

STEFANO Give me thy hand.
I do begin to have bloody thoughts.

220 TRINCULO [*seeing the apparel*]   O King Stefano, O peer! O worthy Stefano, look what a wardrobe here is for thee![3]

CALIBAN   Let it alone, thou fool, it is but trash.

TRINCULO [*putting on a gown*]   O ho, monster, we know what
belongs to a frippery!° O King Stefano! old-clothes shop

---

8. Made smelly; smelled worse than.
9. Lime tree, indicating a stage property.
1. Blind with a hood, as was done to pacify a hawk—
hence, make harmless; also, put out of sight.

2. Recover; rescue; drink off.
3. Recalling "King Stephen was and a worthy peer, / His
breeches cost him but a crown," a popular ballad about
King Stephen, sung in part in *Othello* 2.3.77ff.

225   STEFANO   Put off that gown, Trinculo. By this hand, I'll have that
gown.

TRINCULO   Thy grace shall have it.

CALIBAN   The dropsy[4] drown this fool! What do you mean
To dote thus on such luggage?° Let't alone,   encumbrances
230   And do the murder first. If he awake,
From toe to crown he'll fill our skins with pinches,
Make us° strange stuff.   Turn us into

STEFANO   Be you quiet, monster.—Mistress lime, is not this my
jerkin?° Now is the jerkin under the line.[5] Now, jerkin, you are   leather jacket
235   like to lose your hair and prove a bald jerkin.[6]

          [STEFANO and TRINCULO take garments]

TRINCULO   Do, do! We steal by line and level,[7] an't like° your   if it please
grace.

STEFANO   I thank thee for that jest. Here's a garment for't. Wit
shall not go unrewarded while I am king of this country. 'Steal
240   by line and level' is an excellent pass of pate.[8] There's another
garment for't.

TRINCULO   Monster, come, put some lime upon your fingers,[9]
and away with the rest.

CALIBAN   I will have none on't. We shall lose our time,
245   And all be turned to barnacles,[1] or to apes
With foreheads villainous° low.   wretchedly

STEFANO   Monster, lay to° your fingers. Help to bear this away   apply
where my hogshead of wine is, or I'll turn you out of my kingdom. Go to, carry this.

250   TRINCULO   And this.

STEFANO   Ay, and this.

          [They load CALIBAN with apparel.]
          A noise of hunters heard. Enter divers° spirits in shape of   various
          dogs and hounds, hunting them about; PROSPERO and
          ARIEL setting them on

PROSPERO   Hey, Mountain, hey!

ARIEL   Silver! There it goes, Silver!

PROSPERO   Fury, Fury! There, Tyrant, there! Hark, hark!

          [Exeunt STEFANO, TRINCULO, and CALIBAN, pursued by spirits]
          [To ARIEL] Go, charge my goblins that they grind their joints
255   With dry convulsions,[2] shorten up their sinews
With agèd cramps, and more pinch-spotted[3] make them
Than pard or cat o'mountain.[4]

          [Cries within]

ARIEL   Hark, they roar!

PROSPERO   Let them be hunted soundly.° At this hour   thoroughly
Lies at my mercy all mine enemies.

---

4. A disease characterized by the accumulation of fluid
in connective tissue.
5. Below the lime tree; south of the equator; below the
waist. Also a possible allusion to the proverb "Thou hast
stricken the ball under the line," meaning "You have
cheated." Stefano has taken the jerkin from the lime tree.
6. Baldness caused either through tropical disease or by
sailors who customarily shaved the heads of passengers
when they crossed the line of the equator for the first
time. "Under the [waist]line" (line 234) could also be an
allusion to baldness from syphilis.
7. An idiomatic expression for "properly, by the rules"—
literally, "by plumb line and carpenter's level"; also pun-

ning on "lime." Do, do: an expression of approval.
8. Thrust of wit (fencing term).
9. Be "lime-fingered," sticky-fingered (alluding to birdlime, a gluey substance used to catch birds).
1. Barnacle geese, also known as "tree geese" and supposed to begin life as barnacle shells.
2. Afflicting "sapless," or old, people.
3. Spotted with bruises from pinches. agèd cramps: the
convulsions of old age.
4. Both terms are synonymous with "leopard"; the second
is from Jeremiah 13:23: "May a man of Ind change his
skin, and the cat of the mountain her spots?" (Bishops'
Bible).

260   Shortly shall all my labours end, and thou
      Shalt have the air at freedom. For a little,
      Follow, and do me service.   *Exeunt*

5.1

Enter PROSPERO, *in his magic robes, and* ARIEL

PROSPERO   Now does my project gather to a head.[1]
      My charms crack not, my spirits obey, and time
      Goes upright with his carriage.[2] How's the day?
   ARIEL   On the sixth hour; at which time, my lord,
      You said our work should cease.
5   PROSPERO   I did say so
      When first I raised the tempest. Say, my spirit,
      How fares the King and's° followers?   *and his*
   ARIEL   Confined together
      In the same fashion as you gave in charge,
      Just as you left them; all prisoners, sir,
10   In the lime-grove which weather-fends[3] your cell.
      They cannot budge till your release.° The King,   *you release them*
      His brother, and yours, abide all three distracted,°   *out of their wits*
      And the remainder mourning over them,
      Brimful of sorrow and dismay; but chiefly
15   Him that you termed, sir, the good old lord Gonzalo:
      His tears run down his beard like winter's drops
      From eaves of reeds.° Your charm so strongly works 'em   *thatched roofs*
      That if you now beheld them your affections°   *feelings*
      Would become tender.
   PROSPERO   Dost thou think so, spirit?
   ARIEL   Mine would, sir, were I human.
20   PROSPERO   And mine shall.
      Hast thou, which art but air, a touch,° a feeling   *sense*
      Of their afflictions, and shall not myself,
      One of their kind, that relish all as sharply
      Passion as they,[4] be kindlier[5] moved than thou art?
25   Though with their high° wrongs I am struck to th' quick,   *great*
      Yet with my nobler reason 'gainst my fury
      Do I take part.° The rarer action is   *side*
      In virtue than in vengeance. They being penitent,
      The sole drift of my purpose doth extend
30   Not a frown further. Go release them, Ariel.
      My charms I'll break, their senses I'll restore,
      And they shall be themselves.
   ARIEL   I'll fetch them, sir.   *Exit*
      [PROSPERO *draws a circle with his staff*][6]
   PROSPERO[7]   Ye elves of hills, brooks, standing lakes and groves,
      And ye that on the sands with printless foot
35   Do chase the ebbing Neptune, and do fly him
      When he comes back; you demi-puppets[8] that

5.1

1. Draw to its fulfillment. "Project" suggests an alchemical projection or "experiment."
2. Because his carriage, or burden, is now light.
3. Which protects from the weather.
4. *that . . . they:* who feel as much strong emotion as they do.
5. More tenderly; more naturally.
6. The original text does not indicate when the circle is

drawn. Other possibilities are at the beginning of the scene or before the entry at line 57.
7. Prospero's speech closely follows Ovid's *Metamorphoses* 7.265–77, in Arthur Golding's translation (1567); the speaker in Ovid is the sorceress Medea, who uses her witchcraft to vengeful ends.
8. Puppets; elves; quasi puppets.

By moonshine do the green sour ringlets⁹ make
Whereof the ewe not bites; and you whose pastime
Is to make midnight° mushrooms, that rejoice   *springing up overnight*
40 To hear the solemn curfew;¹ by whose aid,
Weak masters² though ye be, I have bedimmed
The noontide sun, called forth the mutinous winds,
And 'twixt the green sea and the azured vault°   *the sky*
Set roaring war—to the dread rattling thunder
45 Have I given fire, and rifted° Jove's stout oak   *split*
With his own bolt;° the strong-based promontory   *lightning bolt*
Have I made shake, and by the spurs° plucked up   *roots*
The pine and cedar; graves at my command
Have waked their sleepers, oped, and let 'em forth
50 By my so potent art. But this rough³ magic
I here abjure. And when I have required°   *summoned*
Some heavenly music—which even now I do—
To work mine end upon their senses that°   *the senses of whom*
This airy⁴ charm is for, I'll break my staff,
55 Bury it certain° fathoms in the earth,   *several*
And deeper than did ever plummet sound
I'll drown my book.

> *Solemn music. Here enters [first]* ARIEL *[invisible]; then*
> ALONSO, *with a frantic gesture, attended by* GONZALO;
> SEBASTIAN *and* ANTONIO, *in like manner, attended by*
> ADRIAN *and* FRANCISCO. *They all enter the circle which*
> PROSPERO *had made, and there stand charmed; which*
> PROSPERO *observing, speaks*

[*To* ALONSO]⁵ A solemn air,° and° the best comforter   *song / which is*
To an unsettled fancy,° cure thy brains,   *imagination*
Now useless, boiled within thy skull.
60 [*To* SEBASTIAN *and* ANTONIO]⁶   There stand,
For you are spell-stopped.—
Holy Gonzalo, honourable man,
Mine eyes, ev'n sociable° to the show° of thine,   *sympathetic / appearance*
Fall fellowly drops. [*Aside*] The charm dissolves apace,
65 And as the morning steals upon the night,
Melting the darkness, so their rising senses
Begin to chase the ignorant fumes⁷ that mantle°   *envelop*
Their clearer° reason.—O good Gonzalo,   *growing clearer*
My true preserver, and a loyal sir°   *gentleman*
70 To him thou follow'st, I will pay° thy graces   *requite*
Home° both in word and deed.—Most cruelly   *Fully*
Didst thou, Alonso, use me and my daughter.
Thy brother was a furtherer° in the act.—   *an accomplice*
Thou art pinched° for't now, Sebastian.   *tortured; afflicted*
[*To* ANTONIO]   Flesh and blood,
75 You, brother mine, that entertained ambition,
Expelled remorse and nature,⁸ whom,° with Sebastian—   *who*

---

9. Fairy rings: distinctive circles of grass supposed to be caused by dancing fairies but actually caused by mushrooms.
1. The bell rung at nightfall, indicating the time when spirits are abroad.
2. Ineffectual when acting independently; without supernatural power; subordinate spirits.
3. Violent; discordant; crudely approximate.

4. Wrought by spirits of the air.
5. Prospero remains invisible and inaudible to Alonso and his party until he greets Alonso at line 108.
6. Or perhaps to all the shipwrecked lords.
7. Fogs of ignorance; the image is of the sun ("rising senses") dissipating morning mist.
8. Pity and brotherly affection.

Whose inward pinches therefore are most strong,—
Would here have killed your king, I do forgive thee,
Unnatural though thou art. [*Aside*] Their understanding
80 Begins to swell,° and the approaching tide   *(as does a tide)*
Will shortly fill the reasonable shores
That now lie foul and muddy. Not° one of them   *There is not*
That yet looks on me, or would know me.—Ariel,
Fetch me the hat and rapier⁹ in my cell.
85 I will discase° me, and myself present   *undress*
As I was sometime Milan.¹ Quickly, spirit!
Thou shalt ere long be free.

       ARIEL *sings and helps to attire him* [*as Duke of Milan*]

ARIEL   Where the bee sucks, there suck I:
        In a cowslip's bell I lie;
90   There I couch when owls do cry.
        On the bat's back I do fly
        After summer merrily.
        Merrily, merrily shall I live now
        Under the blossom that hangs on the bough.
95   Merrily, merrily shall I live now
        Under the blossom that hangs on the bough.

PROSPERO   Why, that's my dainty Ariel! I shall miss thee,
But yet thou shalt have freedom.—So, so, so.²—
To the King's ship, invisible as thou art!
100 There shalt thou find the mariners asleep
Under the hatches. The Master and the Boatswain
Being awake, enforce them to this place,
And presently,° I prithee.   *immediately*

ARIEL   I drink the air before me, and return
105 Or ere° your pulse twice beat.   *Exit*   *Before*

GONZALO   All torment, trouble, wonder, and amazement°   *bewilderment*
Inhabits here. Some heavenly power guide us
Out of this fearful° country!   *fearsome*

PROSPERO   Behold, sir King,
The wrongèd Duke of Milan, Prospero.
110 For more assurance that a living prince
Does now speak to thee, I embrace thy body;
And to thee and thy company I bid
A hearty welcome.

       [*He embraces* ALONSO]

ALONSO   Whe'er° thou beest he or no,   *Whether*
Or some enchanted trifle³ to abuse° me,   *delude; maltreat*
115 As late I have been, I not know. Thy pulse
Beats as of flesh and blood; and since I saw thee
Th'affliction of my mind amends, with which
I fear a madness held me. This must crave°—   *requires, as explanation*
An if this be at all⁴—a most strange story.
120 Thy dukedom⁵ I resign, and do entreat

---

9. Elements of normal aristocratic dress.
1. Formerly, when Duke of Milan.
2. Prospero arranges his attire approvingly.
3. With a suggestion of the old sense of "trifle" as "deception."
4. If this is really happening.
5. Alonso's rights of homage and tribute from it.

Thou pardon me my wrongs. But how should Prospero
Be living and be here?
PROSPERO [to GONZALO]   First, noble friend,
    Let me embrace thine age,° whose honour cannot   *old body*
    Be measured or confined.
            [*He embraces* GONZALO]
GONZALO   Whether this be
    Or be not, I'll not swear.
125 PROSPERO   You do yet taste
    Some subtleties⁶ o'th' isle that will not let you
    Believe things certain.—Welcome, my friends all.
            [*Aside to* SEBASTIAN *and* ANTONIO]
    But you, my brace° of lords, were I so minded,   *pair*
    I here could pluck his highness' frown upon you
130 And justify° you traitors. At this time   *prove*
    I will tell no tales.
SEBASTIAN [*to* ANTONIO] The devil speaks in him.
PROSPERO   No.
    [*To* ANTONIO]   For you, most wicked sir, whom° to call brother   *who*
    Would even infect my mouth, I do forgive
    Thy rankest fault, all of them, and require
135 My dukedom of thee, which perforce° I know   *necessarily*
    Thou must restore.
ALONSO   If thou beest Prospero,
    Give us particulars of thy preservation,
    How thou hast met us here, whom three hours since
    Were wrecked upon this shore, where I have lost—
140 How sharp the point of this remembrance is!—
    My dear son Ferdinand.
PROSPERO   I am woe° for't, sir.   *I grieve*
ALONSO   Irreparable is the loss, and patience
    Says it is past her cure.
PROSPERO   I rather think
    You have not sought her help, of° whose soft grace°   *by / mercy*
145 For the like loss I have her sovereign aid,
    And rest myself content.
ALONSO   You the like loss?
PROSPERO   As great to me as late;° and supportable   *recent*
    To make the dear loss⁷ have I means much weaker
    Than you may call to comfort you, for I
    Have lost my daughter.⁸
150 ALONSO   A daughter?
    O heavens, that they were living both in Naples,
    The king and queen there! That they were, I wish
    Myself were mudded in that oozy bed
    Where my son lies. When did you lose your daughter?
155 PROSPERO   In this last tempest. I perceive these lords
    At this encounter do so much admire°   *wonder*
    That they devour their reason,⁹ and scarce think
    Their eyes do offices of truth,° these words   *function accurately*

---

6. *You . . . subtleties:* You still experience some of the illusions. "Subtleties" were also sweet confections shaped like castles, temples, beasts, allegorical figures, etc., and arranged like a pageant.

7. *supportable . . . loss:* in order to make the heartfelt loss bearable.

8. Prospero apparently means that Alonso still has a child, his daughter Claribel, to comfort him.

9. "Reason" has the additional sense of "discourse"; hence the phrase is an extension of "swallow their words."

Are natural breath. But howsoe'er you have
160 Been jostled from your senses, know for certain
That I am Prospero, and that very Duke
Which was thrust forth of Milan, who most strangely,
Upon this shore where you were wrecked, was landed
To be the lord on't. No more yet of this,
165 For 'tis a chronicle of day by day,
Not a relation for a breakfast, nor
Befitting this first meeting. Welcome, sir.
This cell's my court. Here have I few attendants,
And subjects none abroad.[1] Pray you, look in.
170 My dukedom since you have given me again,
I will requite you with as good a thing;
At least bring forth a wonder to content ye
As much as me my dukedom.

> *Here* PROSPERO *discovers*[2] FERDINAND *and* MIRANDA,
> *playing at chess*

MIRANDA   Sweet lord, you play me false.°   *trick me*
175 FERDINAND   No, my dearest love,
I would not for the world.
MIRANDA   Yes, for a score of kingdoms you should wrangle,
An I would call it fair play.[3]
ALONSO   If this prove
A vision of the island, one dear son
Shall I twice lose.
180 SEBASTIAN   A most high miracle.
FERDINAND [*coming forward*]   Though the seas threaten, they are merciful.
I have cursed them without cause.
    [*He kneels*]
ALONSO   Now all the blessings
Of a glad father compass thee about.°   *surround you*
Arise and say how thou cam'st here.
    [FERDINAND *rises*]
MIRANDA [*coming forward*]   O wonder!
185 How many goodly creatures are there here!
How beauteous mankind is! O brave new world
That has such people in't!
PROSPERO   'Tis new to thee.
ALONSO [*to* FERDINAND]   What is this maid with whom thou
        wast at play?
Your eld'st° acquaintance cannot be three hours.   *longest*
190 Is she the goddess that hath severed us,
And brought us thus together?
FERDINAND   Sir, she is mortal;
But by immortal providence she's mine.
I chose her when I could not ask my father
For his advice, nor thought I had one. She
195 Is daughter to this famous Duke of Milan,
Of whom so often I have heard renown,
But never saw before; of whom I have

---

1. Elsewhere about the island; beyond the cell.
2. Reveals by drawing back a curtain hanging in front of the discovery space.
3. *for . . . play*: if I would not accuse you of cheating, you would quarrel for twenty kingdoms. Other editions read "And" for "An" (i.e., you could quarrel for twenty kingdoms, and I would still call it fair play.)

Received a second life; and second father
This lady makes him to me.

ALONSO   I am hers.[4]
200   But O, how oddly will it sound, that I
      Must ask my child° forgiveness!   *(Miranda)*

PROSPERO   There, sir, stop.
      Let us not burden our remembrance with
      A heaviness° that's gone.   *sorrow*

GONZALO   I have inly wept,
      Or should have spoke ere this. Look down, you gods,
205   And on this couple drop a blessèd crown,
      For it is you that have chalked forth° the way   *marked out*
      Which brought us hither.

ALONSO   I say amen, Gonzalo.

GONZALO   Was Milan° thrust from Milan, that his issue   *the Duke of Milan*
      Should become kings of Naples? O rejoice
210   Beyond a common joy! And set it down
      With gold on lasting pillars:[5] in one voyage
      Did Claribel her husband find at Tunis,
      And Ferdinand her brother found a wife
      Where he himself was lost; Prospero his dukedom
215   In a poor isle; and all of us ourselves,
      When no man was his own.[6]

ALONSO [*to* FERDINAND *and* MIRANDA] Give me your hands.
      Let grief and sorrow still° embrace his heart   *always*
      That° doth not wish you joy.   *Who*

GONZALO   Be it so! Amen!
      Enter ARIEL, *with the* MASTER *and* BOATSWAIN *amazedly*
      following
      O look, sir, look, sir, here is more of us!
220   I prophesied if a gallows were on land
      This fellow could not drown. [*To the* BOATSWAIN] Now,
          blasphemy,°   *blasphemer*
      That swear'st grace o'erboard: not an oath on shore?
      Hast thou no mouth by land? What is the news?

BOATSWAIN   The best news is that we have safely found
225   Our King and company. The next, our ship,
      Which but three glasses° since we gave out° split,   *hourglasses / declared*
      Is tight and yare[7] and bravely rigged, as when
      We first put out to sea.

ARIEL [*aside to* PROSPERO] Sir, all this service
      Have I done since I went.

PROSPERO [*aside to* ARIEL]   My tricksy° spirit!   *capricious; neat*
230 ALONSO   These are not natural events; they strengthen°   *increase*
      From strange to stranger. Say, how came you hither?

BOATSWAIN   If I did think, sir, I were well awake
      I'd strive to tell you. We were dead of° sleep,   *with*
      And—how we know not—all clapped° under hatches,   *shut up*
235   Where but even now, with strange and several° noises   *various*
      Of roaring, shrieking, howling, jingling chains,
      And more diversity of sounds, all horrible,

4. I will be her second father, Alonso's assent to the betrothal.
5. Suggesting, perhaps, the triumphal arches commissioned to celebrate notable occasions.
6. When we all had lost our senses.
7. Is sound and ready to sail.

We were awaked; straightway at liberty;
Where we in all her trim freshly beheld
240 Our royal, good, and gallant ship, our Master
Cap'ring to eye° her. On° a trice, so please you,   *Dancing to see / In*
Even in a dream, were we divided from them,
And were brought moping° hither.   *dazed*

ARIEL [*aside to* PROSPERO]   Was't well done?
PROSPERO [*aside to* ARIEL]   Bravely, my diligence. Thou shalt be free.

245 ALONSO   This is as strange a maze as e'er men trod,
And there is in this business more than nature
Was ever conduct° of. Some oracle   *conductor*
Must rectify our knowledge.

PROSPERO   Sir, my liege,
Do not infest° your mind with beating on[8]   *trouble*
250 The strangeness of this business. At picked leisure,
Which shall be shortly, single° I'll resolve you,   *in private*
Which to you shall seem probable,° of every   *plausible*
These happened accidents;° till when be cheerful,   *occurrences*
And think of each thing well. [*Aside to* ARIEL] Come hither, spirit.
255 Set Caliban and his companions free.
Untie the spell.   [*Exit* ARIEL]
[*To* ALONSO]   How fares my gracious sir?
There are yet missing of your company
Some few odd lads that you remember not.

          Enter ARIEL, *driving in* CALIBAN, STEFANO, *and* TRIN-
          CULO, *in their stolen apparel*

STEFANO   Every man shift for all the rest, and let no man take
260 care for himself,[9] for all is but fortune. Coragio, bully-monster,[1]
coragio!

TRINCULO   If these° be true spies which I wear in my head, here's   *these eyes*
a goodly sight.

CALIBAN   O Setebos, these be brave spirits indeed!
265 How fine° my master is! I am afraid   *splendidly dressed*
He will chastise me.

SEBASTIAN   Ha, ha! What things are these, my lord Antonio?
Will money buy 'em?

ANTONIO   Very like;° one of them   *likely*
Is a plain° fish, and no doubt marketable.   *mere*

270 PROSPERO   Mark but the badges[2] of these men, my lords,
Then say if they° be true. This misshapen knave,   *(the men); (the badges)*
His mother was a witch, and one so strong
That could control the moon, make flows and ebbs,
And deal in her command without her power.[3]
275 These three have robbed me, and this demi-devil,[4]
For he's a bastard one, had plotted with them
To take my life. Two of these fellows you
Must know and own.[5] This thing of darkness I
Acknowledge mine.

CALIBAN   I shall be pinched to death.

280 ALONSO   Is not this Stefano, my drunken butler?

---

8. With repeatedly worrying about.
9. Stefano drunkenly confuses the saying "Every man for himself."
1. Gallant monster. *Coragio:* Take courage (Italian).
2. Livery. Servants often wore their master's emblem,

but Prospero probably refers to the stolen apparel.
3. And wield her (the moon's) power without her authority, or beyond the reach of her might.
4. Being the offspring of Sycorax and the devil.
5. And acknowledge to be yours.

SEBASTIAN   He is drunk now. Where had he wine?

ALONSO   And Trinculo is reeling ripe.° Where should they   *drunk*
    Find this grand liquor that hath gilded⁶ 'em?
    [*To* TRINCULO] How cam'st thou in this pickle?⁷

285   TRINCULO   I have been in such a pickle since I saw you last that,
    I fear me, will never out of my bones. I shall not fear flyblowing.⁸

SEBASTIAN   Why, how now, Stefano?

STEFANO   O, touch me not! I am not Stefano, but a cramp.

290   PROSPERO   You'd be king o'the isle, sirrah?

STEFANO   I should have been a sore° one, then.   *an inept; severe; pained*

ALONSO [*pointing to* CALIBAN]   This is a strange thing as e'er I
    looked on.

PROSPERO   He is as disproportioned in his manners⁹
295   As in his shape. [*To* CALIBAN] Go, sirrah, to my cell.
    Take with you your companions. As you look
    To have my pardon, trim° it handsomely.   *tidy; decorate*

CALIBAN   Ay, that I will; and I'll be wise hereafter,
    And seek for grace. What a thrice-double ass
300   Was I to take this drunkard for a god,
    And worship this dull fool!

PROSPERO   Go to, away!   [*Exit* CALIBAN]¹

ALONSO [*to* STEFANO *and* TRINCULO]
    Hence, and bestow your luggage where you found it.

SEBASTIAN   Or stole it, rather.   [*Exeunt* STEFANO *and* TRINCULO]

PROSPERO [*to* ALONSO]   Sir, I invite your highness and your train
305   To my poor cell, where you shall take your rest
    For this one night; which part of it° I'll waste°   *part of which / spend*
    With such discourse as I not doubt shall make it
    Go quick away: the story of my life,
    And the particular accidents° gone by   *events*
310   Since I came to this isle. And in the morn
    I'll bring you to your ship, and so to Naples,
    Where I have hope to see the nuptial
    Of these our dear-belovèd solemnized;
    And thence retire me to my Milan, where
    Every third thought shall be my grave.

315   ALONSO   I long
    To hear the story of your life, which must
    Take° the ear strangely.   *Captivate*

PROSPERO   I'll deliver° all,   *relate*
    And promise you calm seas, auspicious gales,
    And sail so expeditious that shall° catch   *it will*
320   Your royal fleet far off. [*Aside to* ARIEL] My Ariel, chick,
    That is thy charge. Then to the elements
    Be free, and fare thou well.   [*Exit* ARIEL]
                    Please you, draw near.°   *go in*
                 Exeunt [*all but* PROSPERO]²

---

6. Probably alluding to the alchemical elixir ("liquor") known as *aurum potabile* (drinkable gold); hence "gilded" (flushed).

7. Sorry plight; Trinculo takes up the literal sense of "preserving liquid," recalling both his drunkenness and his drenching in the lake.

8. Not fear being infested with flies, since he has been "pickled" (preserved).

9. Behavior; moral character.

1. The Folio does not explicitly say that Caliban leaves the stage in response to Prospero's command.

2. The general exeunt is through Prospero's cell; Ariel departs in another direction.

Epilogue

PROSPERO   Now my charms are all o'erthrown,
And what strength I have's mine own,
Which is most faint. Now 'tis true
I must be here confined by you
5   Or sent to Naples. Let me not,
Since I have my dukedom got,
And pardoned the deceiver, dwell
In this bare island° by your spell;   *(the stage)*
But release me from my bands°   *fetters*
10   With the help of your good hands.°   *(applause)*
Gentle breath° of yours my sails   *Favorable comment*
Must fill, or else my project fails,
Which was to please. Now I want°   *lack*
Spirits to enforce, art to enchant;
15   And my ending[1] is despair
Unless I be relieved by prayer,
Which pierces so, that it assaults
Mercy itself, and frees all faults.
As you from crimes would pardoned be,
20   Let your indulgence[2] set me free.
                    [*He awaits applause, then*] *exit*

Epilogue
1. Punning on the sense "death."   2. Approval; appeasement; remission for sin.

Cardenio

Many plays acted in Shakespeare's time have failed to survive; they may easily include some that he wrote. The mystery of *Love's Labour's Won* is discussed above. Certain manuscript records of the seventeenth century suggest that at least one other play in which he had a hand may have disappeared. On 9 September 1653 the London publisher Humphrey Moseley entered in the Stationers' Register a batch of plays including 'The History of Cardenio, by Mr Fletcher and Shakespeare'. Cardenio is a character in Part One of Cervantes' *Don Quixote*, published in English translation in 1612. Two earlier allusions suggest that the King's Men owned a play on this subject at the time that Shakespeare was collaborating with John Fletcher (1579–1625). On 20 May 1613 the Privy Council authorized payment of £20 to John Heminges, as leader of the King's Men, for the presentation at court of six plays, one listed as 'Cardenno'. On 9 July of the same year Heminges received £6 13s. 4d. for his company's performance of a play 'called Cardenna' before the ambassador of the Duke of Savoy.

No more information about this play survives from the seventeenth century, but in 1728 Lewis Theobald published a play based on the story of Cardenio called *Double Falsehood, or The Distrest Lovers,* which he claimed to have 'revised and adapted' from one 'written originally by W. Shakespeare'. It had been successfully produced at Drury Lane on 13 December 1727, and was given thirteen times up to 1 May 1728. Other performances are recorded in 1740, 1741, 1767 (when it was reprinted), 1770, and 1847. In 1770 a newspaper stated that 'the original manuscript' was 'treasured up in the Museum of Covent Garden Playhouse'; fire destroyed the theatre, including its library, in 1808.

Theobald claimed to own several manuscripts of an original play by Shakespeare, and remarked that some of his contemporaries thought the style was Fletcher's, not Shakespeare's. When he himself came to edit Shakespeare's plays he did not include either *Double Falsehood* or the play on which he claimed to have based it; he simply edited the plays of the First Folio, not adding either *Pericles* or *The Two Noble Kinsmen*, though he believed they were partly by Shakespeare. It is quite possible that *Double Falsehood* is based (however distantly) on a play of Shakespeare's time; if so, the play is likely to have been the one performed by the King's Men and ascribed by Moseley in 1653 to Fletcher and Shakespeare.

Double Falsehood is a tragicomedy; the characters' names differ from those in *Don Quixote*; and the story is varied. Henriquez rapes Violante, then falls in love with Leonora, loved by his friend Julio. Her parents agree to the marriage, but Julio interrupts the ceremony. Leonora (who had intended to kill herself) swoons and later takes sanctuary in a nunnery. Julio goes mad with desire for vengeance on his false friend; and the wronged Violante, disguised as a boy, joins a group of shepherds, and is almost raped by one of them. Henriquez's virtuous brother, Roderick, ignorant of his villainy, helps him to abduct Leonora. Leonora and Violante both denounce Henriquez to Roderick. Finally Henriquez repents and marries Violante, while Julio (now sane) marries Leonora.

Some of the motifs of *Double Falsehood*, such as the disguised heroine wronged by her lover, the hero's descent into madness, and the ultimate restoration of sundered relationships, recall Shakespeare's late plays. But most of the dialogue seems un-Shakespearean. Theobald's play stands as a tantalizing reminder of what has been lost.

THE OXFORD EDITORS
Revised by Stephen Greenblatt

All Is True (Henry VIII)

All Is True (*Henry VIII*; 1613) is the Shakespearean play that brought down the house. During a performance on June 29, 1613, when it "had beene acted not passing 2 or 3 times before," "certain Chambers" (small cannons) were shot off. The thatch of the Globe Theatre ignited, and the building burned down. Contemporary accounts disagree about whether the accident occurred early in the play, when King Henry participates in "a Masque at the Cardinal Wolsey's house" and the stage direction reads "Chambers discharged" (1.4.50), or, more improbably, when it "was almost ended." Apparently there was only one injury, to a man who "was scalded with the fire by adventuring in to save a child which otherwise had been burnt." Another version claims that the injured man "had his breeches set on fire, that would perhaps have broyled him, if he had not by the benefit of a provident wit put it out with bottle Ale." (See the Henry Wotton letter, page 3120.)

All Is True does indeed show "a provident wit" and "save a child," though perhaps not in the fashion the two commentators had in mind. In reviewing some of the important events of the reign of Henry VIII, and in parading many of its central historical figures before the audience, the play ultimately reveals the workings of a divine providence that watches over England and assures the birth of the future Queen Elizabeth. It achieves this effect through the mixing of dramatic genres: in *All Is True*, the national history play meets the tragicomic romance. Known as *Henry VIII* at least since 1623, the text is a collaborative effort of Shakespeare and John Fletcher—with Shakespeare apparently the senior partner. It draws on narratives of relatively recent English history—primarily Raphael Holinshed's *Chronicles of England, Scotland, and Ireland* (1587 ed.), Shakespeare's main source for his earlier English history plays, and, for much of Act 5, John Foxe's epic of Protestant propaganda, *Book of Martyrs*. In so doing, the playwrights returned to a genre that Shakespeare had dominated during its heyday in the 1590s. By contrast, tragicomic romance, influenced by late Renaissance elite Italian theater, was very much in vogue in 1613, thanks largely to the recent works of Shakespeare, Francis Beaumont, and Fletcher.

The Shakespearean history play focuses on dynastic instabilities and civil conflicts of the late fourteenth and fifteenth centuries, and especially on the national implications of struggles between aristocratic factions. Shakespearean romance characteristically deploys a fictional plot in which long suffering and separation (often across the sea) are transcended through the virtuous daughter, who redeems her father, and through magical interventions that produce providential outcomes. The synthesis of romance and history in *All Is True* thus emphasizes a providential interpretation of English history. The resulting implication—that the antagonisms of earlier history are justified by the felicity of the present reign—risks chauvinistic sycophancy. Yet *All Is True* also challenges this celebratory interpretation: it is in the tension between these two tendencies that the play's interest lies.

The historical narrative, which combines close reliance on the sources with chronological compression and rearrangement, spans more than fifteen years. Its principal structural unit, first alluded to in the Prologue (lines 25–30), is *de casibus* tragedy, which recounts the fall of illustrious figures and resembles the morality play's abstractly allegorical focus on virtue and vice. The wheel of fortune is the form's dominant, cyclical image: what goes up must come down. Providential romance, however, is more linear and unidirectional: you start in one place and end somewhere else. Moreover, it ends in felicity rather than disaster. *All Is True* reconciles these apparently incompatible movements through an elegant structural trick: it makes a series of local *de casibus* tragedies serve a single overarching providential purpose that does not emerge until the very end. Much of the play accordingly seems to have nothing to do with a transcendently ordered pattern. It does not even concern the ups and downs of monarchs and their rivals, as in Shakespeare's earlier histories. Instead, we witness the successive falls of people close to Henry VIII—Buckingham, Katherine, and Cardinal Wolsey—and the near fall of Cranmer, Archbishop of Canterbury. Each gets a day in court—his or her fifteen minutes of fame—before passing from the scene. These downfalls, like other events in the play, are rendered through stirring speeches and pageantry that recall the spectacle of the contemporary court theatrical form known as the "masque" (see 1.4), which for centuries made the work a success on the stage and which left their mark on film versions of Henry's reign, even those not based on *All Is True* (see the list of films).

Initially, the repetitive *de casibus* structure doesn't seem to be heading anywhere. Yet the linguistic patterning suggests a larger purpose. Beginning with the Prologue's invocation of tears and pity (lines 5–6), the play emphasizes suffering, the burden of life, acquiescence in defeat, forgiveness of one's foes, patience, religious serenity, and an understanding of the fall from power as part of a natural pattern like life itself. Cardinal Wolsey's undoing offers a striking instance of the transformation of conflict into reconciliation. Surrey correctly blames Wolsey for the execution of Buckingham, Surrey's father-in-law. Taunting the Cardinal at the moment of his ruin, he is finally rebuked:

> LORD CHAMBERLAIN   O, my lord,
> Press not a falling man too far. 'Tis virtue.
> His faults lie open to the laws. Let them,
> Not you, correct him. My heart weeps to see him
> So little of his great self.
>   SURREY   I forgive him.
>   (3.2.333–37)

Once the lords have left, Wolsey, in a deviation from Holinshed, gets a moving repentance. Discovering his religious vocation only following the collapse of his secular

Now, to let matters of State sleep, I will entertain you at the present with what hath happened this week at the banks side. The Kings Players had a new Play, called *All is true*, representing some principall pieces of the raign of *Henry* 8. which was set forth with many extraordinary circumstances of Pomp and Majesty, even to the matting of the stage; the Knights of the Order, with their Georges and Garter, the Guards with their embroidered Coats, and the like: sufficient in truth within a while to make greatness very familiar, if not ridiculous. Now, King *Henry* making a Masque at the Cardinal *Wolsey's* house, and certain Chambers being shot off at his entry, some of the paper, or other stuff wherewith one of them was stopped, did light on the thatch, where being thought at first but an idle smoak, and their eyes more attentive to the show, it kindled inwardly, and ran round like a train, consuming within less then an hour the whole house to the very grounds.

This was the fatal period of that vertuous fabrique, wherein yet nothing did perish, but wood and straw, and a few forsaken cloaks; only one man had his breeches set on fire, that would perhaps have broyled him, if he had not by the benefit of a provident wit put it out with bottle Ale. The rest when we meet: till when, I protest every minute is the siege of Troy. Gods dear blessings till then and ever be with you.

Your poor Uncle and
faithful servant,

HENRY WOTTON.

One of several accounts of the burning of the Globe Theatre. From a letter of July 2, 1613, in *Letters of Sir Henry Wotton to Sir Edmund Bacon* (1661).

career, the hitherto villainous Cardinal experiences a shift in outlook that aligns him
with his victims, Buckingham and Katherine. Asked how he feels, Wolsey replies:

> Why, well—
> Never so truly happy, my good Cromwell.
> I know myself now, and I feel within me
> A peace above all earthly dignities,
> A still and quiet conscience.
>
> (3.2.377–81)

Thus, like Buckingham's and Katherine's precipitous descents, but also like Adam and
Eve's, Wolsey's fall is a fortunate one.

The Cardinal considers his former responsibilities "a burden / Too heavy for a man
that hopes for heaven" (3.2.385–86). But not too heavy for a woman: the burden is
delivered at the end of the play when Queen Anne gives birth to the future Queen
Elizabeth—the moment toward which all previous events have been tending. The
critic Northrop Frye noted in the play "an invisible but omnipotent and ruthless providence who is ready to tear the whole social and religious structure of England to
pieces in order to get Queen Elizabeth born." Buckingham has a serious claim to the
crown, so he must be removed. Katherine's defect is that she is not the queen who will
bear Elizabeth. Wolsey, who favors a diplomatically useful French alliance for Henry
and hence opposes the king's marriage to Anne, unwittingly brings them together at a
party he hosts (1.4). The individual tragedies are thus both personally and politically
fortunate. Elizabeth's birth promises not only her own reign but also that of her successor, King James I, England's sovereign at the time of *All Is True*. Praise of these two
monarchs is accompanied by compliments to James's daughter Elizabeth, who was
married in February 1613. Archbishop Cranmer's concluding prophecy makes the link
explicit:

> when
> The bird of wonder dies—the maiden phoenix—
> Her ashes new create another heir
> As great in admiration as herself.
>
> (5.4.39–42)

Although Queen Elizabeth is the "maiden phoenix" and James the heir, James's daughter was also compared to the phoenix at the time of her marriage.

This connection also lays to rest Henry's persistent desire for a male heir. That
absent royal son earlier justifies Henry's divorce of Katherine:

> methought
> I stood not in the smile of heaven. . . .
> . . . .
> I weighed the danger which my realms stood in
> By this my issue's fail, and that gave to me
> Many a groaning throe.
>
> (2.4.183–96)

Henry assumes the burden himself, experiencing "many a groaning throe" as if he could
deliver the son that Katherine cannot. When Anne takes on the burden, Henry reveals
his ongoing anxiety:

> KING HENRY   Is the Queen delivered?
> Say, 'Ay, and of a boy.'
> OLD LADY   Ay, ay, my liege,
> And of a lovely boy. The God of heaven
> Both now and ever bless her! 'Tis a girl
> Promises boys hereafter.
>
> (5.1.163–67)

Cardinal Wolsey is forced "to render up the great seal" to Norfolk and Suffolk (3.2.230). From George Cavendish, *The Life and Death of Cardinal Wolsey* (1557).

The Old Lady's flattery reveals the truth: Elizabeth *is* "a girl / Promises boys hereafter." In having James succeed her, she fulfills the properly self-effacing function of women in this patriarchal fantasy and delivers to Henry what Anne could not—a male heir.

Providence also enters the play through the standard sea journeys of Shakespearean romance, journeys that typically bring separation, suffering, and a transformation whose association with water links it to baptism. Set entirely in England, *All Is True* seems remote from such concerns. Yet the aquatic and nautical imagery of destruction pervades the play. The "hideous storm" immediately following the conclusion of the Anglo-French treaty is a "tempest" that prophesies the dissolution of the alliance (1.1.90–92). Buckingham metaphorically warns against false friends, who,

> when they once perceive
> The least rub in your fortunes, fall away
> Like water from ye, never found again
> But where they mean to sink ye.
> (2.1.129–32)

Henry finds himself "hulling in / The wild sea of my conscience" over his marriage to Katherine (2.4.196–97), who worries about her "shipwrecked" ladies-in-waiting. Wolsey's foes are "rav'nous fishes" who ineffectually attack his "new trimmed" "vessel" (1.2.80–81). Wolsey himself is a "rock" that threatens Buckingham and will protect Henry "against the chiding flood" of danger and rebellion (1.1.113; 3.2.198). He is a boat that "coasts / And hedges" but will "founder" (3.2.38–39, 40). He has swum "far beyond my depth" and is at "the mercy / Of a rude stream that must for ever hide me" (3.2.362, 364–65). He has borne "a load would sink a navy" (3.2.384), but he tells Cromwell that he, who "sounded all the depths and shoals of honour, / Found thee a way, out of his wreck, to rise in" (3.2.437–38). Approaching death, Wolsey is "broken with the storms of state" (4.2.21).

Positive associations with water and the sea are often connected with colonialism, important in the London of 1613 because of western Europe's unprecedented global expansion beginning in the fifteenth century and, in particular, because of the very recent establishment of England's first permanent settlement in the New World. The English nobility in France were so opulently attired that they "made Britain India"

(1.1.21)—an image of fabulous wealth that evokes both the West and East Indies, both the Caribbean and the vast region extending from India to Southeast Asia. "Our King has all the Indies in his arms" (4.1.45) when he embraces Anne, "a very fresh fish" at court (2.3.87). At her public appearance, "such a noise arose / As the shrouds make at sea in a stiff tempest" (4.1.73–74). The perilous journeys and shipwrecks are redeemed by Elizabeth's watery baptism, which has the crowd appeal of "some strange Indian with the great tool" (5.3.32)—a phrase that unites ethnic exoticism and sexual titillation. Speaking of James, Cranmer predicts,

> Wherever the bright sun of heaven shall shine,
> His honour and the greatness of his name
> Shall be, and make new nations.
>
> (5.4.50–52)

The capital of the "new nation" is Jamestown and the nation itself Virginia, named for "the maiden phoenix" who died "yet a virgin" (5.4.40, 60)—James's predecessor, the infant Elizabeth.

Although the providential logic that leads first Elizabeth and then James to the throne often works against human intentions, Henry takes an increasingly active role in securing the destined end. The crucial moment is Cranmer's trial. Just before it begins, the stage direction reads *Enter* KING [HENRY] . . . *at a window, above*" (5.2.18). There, seeing but unseen, he is quasi-divine, as he himself suggests in angrily observing the council's humiliation of Cranmer: "Is this the honour they do one another? / 'Tis well there's one above 'em yet" (5.2.25–26). The "one above 'em" can be either God or the King, a distinction the scene blurs. This elevated perspective presumably pleased James, who held an absolutist, divine-right view of monarchy. Henry's intervention later in the scene to protect Cranmer preserves the man who later established the doctrinal basis of the English Reformation. As suggested by Cranmer's prophetic promise about Elizabeth's reign—"God shall be truly known" (5.4.36)—this religious outcome is also part of the providential pattern. Yet except in Cranmer's conflict with the Catholic Gardiner, who accuses him of being "a sectary" and Cromwell of being "a favourer / Of this new sect" (5.2.104, 114–15), and in Wolsey's dismissive description of Anne as "a spleeny Lutheran" (3.2.100), little is made of the central event of Henry's reign: the break with Rome. The characters are judged not by their religious sympathies but by their integrity. Accordingly, the outstanding figures are an English Protestant, Cranmer, and a Spanish Catholic, Katherine. The notion of conscience, which is far more prominent here than in Holinshed's *Chronicles* and which Protestants used against the papacy to repudiate blind adherence to any human doctrinal authority, is deployed by the playwrights to judge Catholics and Protestants alike. This impartiality may be more the work of Shakespeare than of Fletcher (see the Textual Note); in any case, the overall result is the characteristic national reconciliation of Shakespeare's history plays.

National reconciliation also transcends class antagonism, an issue largely absent from the sources. Like the other lords, the Duke of Buckingham resents the usurpation of the nobility's traditional power by the proud "beggar" Wolsey, a "butcher's cur" (1.1.122, 120): the Cardinal's father was supposedly a butcher. Despite these humble origins, Wolsey adopts the aristocratic outlook of the position he has risen to. He opposes Henry's marriage to Anne, who came from the gentry rather than the nobility and who had been one of Katherine's ladies-in-waiting: "A knight's daughter / To be her mistress' mistress? The Queen's queen?" (3.2.95–96). But the play also posits a harmony between upper class and lower that can be disturbed only by self-serving intermediaries who mistreat humble folk. Buckingham is betrayed to Wolsey by his surveyor, whom he fired for oppressing his tenants. Katherine gets Henry to repeal a tax levied by Wolsey that is so onerous it drives the poor to rebellion. Interclass unity is affirmed in the popular excitement about the baby Elizabeth, which the play refracts through the lower-class prose of the exasperated Porter (5.3)—a prose noteworthy in a play composed overwhelmingly in blank verse. Similarly, at Anne's earlier coronation, one of the gentlemen, who play the role of a chorus absent from the sources, remarks,

> The citizens,
> I am sure, have shown at full their royal minds—
> As, let 'em have their rights, they are ever forward.
>   (4.1.7–9)

And, in slightly different fashion, Cranmer renders hereditary class hierarchy a thing of the past. "Those about" Elizabeth "from her shall read the perfect ways of honour, / And by those claim their greatness, not by blood" (5.4.36–38).

Yet as recent productions have emphasized, *All Is True* offers a critical account of Henry's reign. In particular, the play implicitly suggests the costs of the Elizabethan Protestant succession. Even though only Buckingham is executed, *All Is True* makes that execution resonate. The innocent and virtuous Katherine is given a strength of character, consequent impressiveness, and spiritual coronation absent both from Holinshed's portrayal and from her successor, Anne. Yet Henry's "princely commendations" to the dying Katherine are "like a pardon after execution" (4.2.119, 122). As Katherine is succeeded by Anne, so Wolsey is replaced by Sir Thomas More, Cromwell, and Cranmer (3.2.392–460). All four of these successors were later executed, as the audience well knew. Wolsey hopes that More will "do justice / For truth's sake and his conscience" (lines 397–98)—principles that were to cost the Catholic More his life. Anne actually predicts her own fate in lamenting Katherine's mistreatment:

> Much better
> She ne'er had known pomp; though't be temporal,
> Yet if that quarrel, fortune, do divorce
> It from the bearer, 'tis a sufferance panging
> As soul and bodies severing.
>   (2.3.12–16)

Wolsey advises Cromwell:

> Be just, and fear not.
> Let all the ends thou aim'st at be thy country's,
> Thy God's, and truth's. Then if thou fall'st, O Cromwell,
> Thou fall'st a blessèd martyr.
>   (3.2.447–50)

Gardiner's anti-Protestant attacks on Cranmer and Cromwell foreshadow his later success in sending both men to their death. Even Elizabeth's christening evokes execution: "Belong to th' gallows, and be hanged" (5.3.5).

Ambivalence extends as well to the centrally providential characters. No man utters anything but praise for the "beauty and honour" of that "angel" Anne Boleyn (2.3.76, 4.1.44). Skepticism about her "honour" is instead voiced by a woman. When Anne denies any desire for political advancement, the Old Lady calls this position "hypocrisy," ridicules Anne's pliant "conscience," and finds her claim "strange" (2.3.26, 32, 36). Yet Anne does become queen, without an explanation of her supposed change of heart but with a suggestive pun on "quean" (whore) characteristic of the entire sexualized exchange and of Anne's earlier banter (1.4.46–49). The scene with the Old Lady, apparently invented by Shakespeare, thus sullies Anne before she becomes a purely ceremonial figure reduced to bearing royal children. Moreover, Elizabeth's conception before Henry and Anne's marriage may be alluded to in the "great-bellied women" at Anne's coronation and the "fry of fornication" at Elizabeth's christening (4.1.78, 5.3.33–34).

As for Henry himself, although he is repeatedly praised by his victims (2.1.87–95, 3.2.381–93, 4.2.161–65), his increasing attention to government raises retrospective questions about his earlier behavior. The Henry of the play, more troubling than Holinshed's, seems oddly abstracted, either culpably unaware or disingenuously disavowing knowledge of foreign affairs, taxation, and treason. He often seems the Teflon king, to whom no blame sticks. The self-destructive zigzags in foreign policy—alliance with

Henry VIII, age fifty-two, in the posthumous
portrait engraved by Cornelis Metsys in 1548.
Gardiner's unsuccessful attack on Cranmer probably occurred around this time.

France, alliance with Spain, attempted alliance with France—are Wolsey's doings, not his: the buck stops elsewhere. Moreover, his interventions are not fully reassuring. His charges against Wolsey ignore major issues to focus on personal, peripheral concerns. Even his protection of Cranmer is necessary only because Henry allows his biased council to proceed in the first place. Indeed, the play suggests that the law serves the man with power, whether Wolsey or the King.

Explicit skepticism about Henry is produced by his divorce proceedings. *All Is True* shows a man "afflicted" by a "wounded conscience," by "conscience, conscience," by "my conscience" (2.2.62, 74, 142; 2.4.167, 179, 200). But earlier, at Wolsey's banquet, it shows a man attracted to Anne Boleyn: "The fairest hand I ever touched. O beauty, / Till now I never knew thee" (1.4.76–77). This meeting is the play's invention. A disabused view is openly voiced later:

LORD CHAMBERLAIN It seems the marriage with his brother's wife
    Has crept too near his conscience.
SUFFOLK   No, his conscience
    Has crept too near another lady.
                                                                    (2.2.15–17)

Even apologists for Henry's behavior suspect his motives. Overwhelmed by the sight of Anne, the Second Gentleman remarks, "I cannot blame his conscience" (4.1.47). It is hard to determine whether such criticism undermines the providential pattern or renders the pattern's transcendence of such formidable obstacles all the more miraculous. Like many Shakespearean plays, *All Is True* opposes means and ends, showing and telling, dramatized plot and asserted conclusion, pity and jubilation.

The critique of Henry may have been targeted at James as well, despite the play's closing compliment to him. The satire on French fashion (1.3) ridicules behavior at James's court in which the King participated. Like Henry, James neglected affairs of state, to the dismay of his subjects. His court was riven by factionalism; his absolutist view of monarchy at times resulted in a subordination of law to royal desire. Yet the crucial contemporary parallels lie elsewhere. In urging punishment of Cranmer's Protestantism, Gardiner warns that laxity leads to falling dominoes:

    Commotions, uproars—with a general taint
    Of the whole state, as of late days our neighbours,
    The upper Germany, can dearly witness.
                                                                    (5.2.62–64)

The reference is to the Peasants' War in Germany (1524–26), in which the German aristocracy massacred perhaps 100,000 peasants. The danger of popular unrest in England is suggested by the court's fear of "loud rebellion" and the unruly "rabble" (1.2.30,

5.3.65). Similarly, the rowdies at Elizabeth's christening are "your faithful friends o'th' suburbs" (5.3.66). The suburbs were the location of the outdoor "public" theaters, such as the Globe, where *All Is True* was performed. The Porter remarks, "These are the youths that thunder at a playhouse, and fight for bitten apples, that no audience but the tribulation of Tower Hill or the limbs of Limehouse, their dear brothers, are able to endure" (5.3.55–58). The comparison is between the unruly apprentices who come to the theater and the rough crowds who attend public executions or frequent the dockyards. A christening recalls an execution; an ostensibly orthodox play in a suburban theater emphasizes the criminal character of suburb and audience alike.

It is thus the interaction between *All Is True* and its audience that undermines orthodoxy. This interaction is self-reflexive, or metadramatic, in character. That is, while providing a plausibly realistic dramatization of events, the play simultaneously indicates that it is merely a play, just a dramatization, by calling attention to the venue of performance—the "suburbs," the "playhouse," the "audience." As we have seen, however, this self-referentiality is the very opposite of apolitical aesthetic detachment. Furthermore, the Globe, which is surely the playhouse referred to in this scene, is not the only commercial theater that acquires thematic resonance in *All Is True*. By the time of the composition of the play, Shakespeare's acting company, the King's Men, divided its time—in the summer working at the Globe, in the winter at the Blackfriars, a more elite indoor, "private" theater in London itself rather than the suburbs. When Henry decides upon a judicial proceeding to determine whether or not his marriage to Katherine should be annulled, he also specifies a location for the event:

> The most convenient place I can think of
> For such receipt of learning is Blackfriars.
> (2.2.137–38)

Two scenes later, that is where the hearing is held, with the result that the audience of the play sits in judgment in the very place where the decision was actually rendered almost a century earlier, in 1529.

By placing the affluent audience of the Blackfriars in a position where it evaluates the conduct of a king, did *All Is True* undermine aristocratic and royal authority? Perhaps not as much as when the play was performed in the outdoor theater. According to Sir Henry Wotton, a spectator at the fateful performance when the Globe burned down, the work represented "some principall pieces of the raign of *Henry* 8 which was set forth with many extraordinary circumstances of Pomp and Majesty . . . sufficient in truth within a while to make greatness very familiar, if not ridiculous." Rather than dazzling into awestruck submission, the play's pageantry reduced the mystique of monarchy, turning the politically disenfranchised popular audience into moral arbiters of royal power. James's favorite, the Duke of Buckingham, may have felt as much when, in 1628, he commissioned a performance of *All Is True*, only to walk out after his namesake's beheading. In 1649, a Parliament driven by popular pressure emulated the play by staging an execution of its own. This time, however, the victim was James I's own son: the man on the scaffold was the King.

WALTER COHEN

TEXTUAL NOTE

Although the play was initially printed in the First Folio of 1623 (F) under the title *The Famous History of the Life of Henry the Eight* and today is generally known as *Henry VIII*, comments on early performances suggest that it was originally called *All Is True*. Perhaps the compilers of the Folio changed its title to make it conform to the pattern of using monarchs' names for the English history plays: it is placed at the end of this group of plays. Or perhaps John Fletcher, Shakespeare's collaborator on the play, is responsible for the switch (see below). The text is based not on an authorial manuscript but on a scribal copy; either the authorial or the scribal version may have been slightly revised for theatrical performance. F's division into acts and scenes is followed in the present edition; some editors, however, introduce a scene division after 5.2.34.

All Is True probably has links to the marriage on February 14, 1613, of Princess Elizabeth, King James's daughter, to the German Prince Frederick, the Elector Palatine. If so, it might have been written in late 1612. Unlike other plays by Shakespeare, it was not performed at court as part of the wedding festivities, but the text's reference to Blackfriars suggests that it could have been staged during the same period at that theater. But the accidental burning of the Globe Theatre at one of the first performances of the play on June 29, 1613, makes composition following the marriage, with the initial performance at the Globe in June 1613, equally likely. (See the Introduction.)

F attributes the play to Shakespeare. But beginning in the eighteenth century and especially since 1850, many critics have concluded that John Fletcher, who succeeded Shakespeare as the principal dramatist of the King's Men, collaborated on *All Is True*. External evidence for this position is inferential and inconclusive. Toward the end of his career, as perhaps at the beginning, Shakespeare seems to have turned to collaboration— in *Pericles,* the lost *Cardenio,* and *The Two Noble Kinsmen.* In the last two plays, dating from 1612–14, he apparently worked with Fletcher. On the other hand, these plays were all excluded from F by the editors, who were Shakespeare's fellow actors in the King's Men. Even though a minority of scholars continues to believe that Shakespeare was the sole author of *All Is True,* the internal stylistic and linguistic evidence strongly suggests that Fletcher wrote at least one-quarter of the piece—primarily 1.3–4, 3.1, and 5.2–4. (He seems to have written a little more than half of *The Two Noble Kinsmen.*) Yet the problem of attribution is not that simple. Shakespeare may have had some role in 3.1 and especially 5.2–4. Fletcher is likely to have played a part in 2.1–2 and 4.1–2. The unusually full stage directions may also be his work. Fletcher's sections of the play arguably have a more pro-Protestant outlook than Shakespeare's relatively balanced and uncommitted treatment of religious controversy. Finally, scholarly skepticism about the attribution of certain scenes (notably 2.1 and 4.1) to either Shakespeare or Fletcher has led to speculation about a third author. Francis Beaumont, who regularly collaborated with Fletcher, has been proposed, but the suggestion remains conjectural.

In short, both the broad conception of the play and most of the "big" scenes appear to be Shakespeare's.

SELECTED BIBLIOGRAPHY

Bergeron, David M. *Shakespeare's Romances and the Royal Family.* Lawrence: University Press of Kansas, 1985. 203–22. Links the play politically to James I and his family, and generically more to the late romances than to the earlier English history plays.

Frye, Susan. "Queens and the Structure of History in *Henry VIII.*" *A Companion to Shakespeare's Works,* Vol. 4: *Poems, Problem Comedies, Late Plays.* Ed. Richard Dutton and Jean E. Howard. Malden, Mass.: Blackwell, 2003. 427–44. Parallels between the courts of Henry VIII and James I, centered on Queens struggling with a succession of male favorites.

Healy, Thomas. "History and Judgement in *Henry VIII.*" *Shakespeare's Late Plays: New Readings.* Ed. Jennifer Richards and James Knowles. Edinburgh: Edinburgh University Press, 1999. 158–75. Argues that the play is structured to encourage the audience to respond with judgment rather than emotion to the conflicting possible interpretations of history.

Hodgdon, Barbara. *The End Crowns All: Closure and Contradiction in Shakespeare's History.* Princeton: Princeton University Press, 1991. 212–34. Focuses on Elizabeth as the concluding figure of the play, uniting masquelike and anti-masquelike (or carnivalesque) elements.

Kermode, Frank. "What Is Shakespeare's *Henry VIII* About?" *Shakespeare, The Histories: A Collection of Critical Essays.* Ed. Eugene M. Waith. Englewood Cliffs, N.J.: Prentice-Hall, 1965. 168–79. Henry as God's deputy and the agent of England's future felicity, by means of a morality structure involving the successive falls of the other leading figures.

Knight, G. Wilson. *The Crown of Life: Essays in Interpretation of Shakespeare's Final Plays.* London: Oxford University Press, 1947. 256–336. Sees the play as Shakespeare's culminating work, moving from order through tragic falls to concluding ritual.

McMullan, Gordon, ed. *King Henry VIII (All Is True).* London: Arden Shakespeare, 2000. Outstanding scholarly edition with a book-length critical introduction.

Noling, Kim H. "Grubbing Up the Stock: Dramatizing Queens in *Henry VIII.*" *Shakespeare Quarterly* 39 (1988): 291–306. Katherine's strong stage positions contrasted with Anne's relatively weak role, including dissociation from her daughter, Elizabeth—all in the service of flattering male monarchs, Henry and James.

Shirley, Frances A., ed. *"King John" and "Henry VIII": Critical Essays.* New York: Garland, 1988. Twelve essays on the play from nineteenth- and twentieth-century theatrical and literary criticism.

Wegemer, Gerard. "Henry VIII on Trial: Confronting Malice and Conscience in Shakespeare's *All Is True.*" *Renascence* 52 (2000): 111–30. Argues that, in addition to the public trials structuring the play, covert trials of Thomas More and of Henry himself produce a critical view of the monarch.

FILMS

The Private Life of Henry VIII. 1933. Dir. Alexander Korda. UK. 97 min. Unrelated to *All Is True.* Starring Charles Laughton.

A Man for All Seasons. 1966. Dir. Fred Zinnemann. UK. 120 min. Unrelated to *All Is True.* Based on Robert Bolt's play about Sir Thomas More's religious conflict over Henry's decision to divorce Katherine and wed Anne. Stellar cast, including Paul Scofield in the title role; Oscars for Best Actor, Director, Picture.

Anne of the Thousand Days. 1969. Dir. Charles Jarrott. UK. 145 min. Unrelated to *All Is True.* On Anne Boleyn's rise and fall. Distinguished cast, including Geneviève Bujold as Anne and Richard Burton as Henry.

Henry VIII. 1979. Dir. Kevin Billington. UK. 166 min. Highly praised BBC production minimizing the pomp and ceremony in plays or films on Henry and his age, in favor of a contrast between public political life and inwardness and morality, focused on Katherine, played by Claire Bloom.

All Is True

THE PERSONS OF THE PLAY

PROLOGUE
KING HENRY the Eighth
Duke of BUCKINGHAM
Lord ABERGAVENNY }
Earl of SURREY } his sons-in-law
Duke of NORFOLK
Duke of SUFFOLK
LORD CHAMBERLAIN
LORD CHANCELLOR
Lord SANDS (also called Sir William SANDS)
Sir Thomas LOVELL
Sir Anthony DENNY
Sir Henry GUILDFORD
CARDINAL WOLSEY
Two SECRETARIES
BUCKINGHAM'S SURVEYOR
CARDINAL CAMPEIUS
GARDINER, the King's new secretary, later Bishop of Winchester
His PAGE
Thomas CROMWELL
CRANMER, Archbishop of Canterbury
QUEEN KATHERINE, later KATHERINE, Princess Dowager
GRIFFITH, her gentleman usher
PATIENCE, her waiting-woman
Other WOMEN
Six spirits, who dance before Katherine in a vision
A MESSENGER
Lord CAPUTIUS
ANNE Boleyn
An OLD LADY
BRANDON }
SERJEANT-at-arms } who arrest Buckingham and Abergavenny
Sir Nicholas VAUX }
Tipstaves }
Halberdiers } after Buckingham's arraignment
Common people }
Two vergers }
Two SCRIBES }
Archbishop of Canterbury }
Bishop of LINCOLN }
Bishop of Ely }
Bishop of Rochester } appearing at the Legatine Court
Bishop of Saint Asaph }
Two priests }
Serjeant-at-arms }
Two noblemen }
A CRIER }

3129

Three GENTLEMEN
Two judges
Choristers
Lord Mayor of London
Garter King-of-Arms
Marquis Dorset } appearing in the Coronation
Four Barons of the Cinque Ports
Stokesley, Bishop of London
Old Duchess of Norfolk
Countesses

A DOORKEEPER
Doctor BUTTS, the King's physician } At Cranmer's trial
Pursuivants, pages, footboys, grooms

A PORTER
His MAN
Two aldermen
Lord Mayor of London
GARTER King-of-Arms } at the Christening
Six noblemen
Old Duchess of Norfolk, godmother
The child, Princess Elizabeth
Marchioness Dorset, godmother

EPILOGUE
Ladies, gentlemen, a SERVANT, guards, attendants, trumpeters

Prologue

[*Enter* PROLOGUE]

PROLOGUE   I come no more to make you laugh. Things now
That bear a weighty and a serious brow,
Sad, high, and working,° full of state° and woe—   *full of pathos / grandeur*
Such noble scenes as draw the eye to flow
5   We now present. Those that can pity here
May, if they think it well, let fall a tear.
The subject will deserve it. Such as give
Their money out of hope they may believe,
May here find truth, too. Those that come to see
10   Only a show or two, and so agree
The play may pass, if they be still, and willing,
I'll undertake may see away their shilling
Richly in two short hours.[1] Only they
That come to hear a merry bawdy play,
15   A noise of targets,° or to see a fellow   *shields*
In a long motley coat guarded[2] with yellow,
Will be deceived. For, gentle hearers, know
To rank our chosen truth with such a show
As fool and fight is, beside forfeiting
20   Our own brains, and the opinion that we bring
To make that only true we now intend,[3]

Prologue
1. *Those . . . hours:* If those who come only for a spectacle ("show") and approve the play on those terms are quiet and willing, I promise they'll get their shilling's worth (the price of more expensive, genteel seating) in two hours (plays ran two to three hours).
2. Ornamented on its border. The fool's "motley," or patchwork, coat may refer to other plays about Henry's life, including Samuel Rowley's *When You See Me, You Know Me* (1605), which featured Henry's fool, Will Summers, and was reprinted and perhaps revived in 1613.
3. *beside . . . intend:* in addition to wasting our mental labor, and our intention of presenting an entirely truthful representation.

Will leave us never an understanding[4] friend.
Therefore, for goodness' sake, and as you are known
The first and happiest hearers° of the town,   *finest audience*
25 Be sad° as we would make ye. Think ye see   *grave*
The very persons of our noble story
As they were living; think you see them great,°   *of high rank*
And followed with the general throng and sweat
Of thousand friends; then, in a moment, see
30 How soon this mightiness meets misery.
And if you can be merry then, I'll say
A man may weep upon his wedding day.   [*Exit*]

1.1

[*A cloth of state throughout the play.*][1] *Enter the Duke
of* NORFOLK *at one door; at the other* [*door enter*] *the
Duke of* BUCKINGHAM *and the Lord* ABERGAVENNY

BUCKINGHAM [*to* NORFOLK]   Good morrow, and well met. How have ye done
    Since last we saw° in France?   *met*
NORFOLK   I thank your grace,
    Healthful, and ever since a fresh° admirer   *an eager*
    Of what I saw there.[2]
BUCKINGHAM   An untimely ague
5   Stayed me a prisoner in my chamber[3] when
    Those suns of glory, those two lights of men,
    Met in the vale of Ardres.
NORFOLK   'Twixt Guisnes and Ardres.[4]
    I was then present, saw them salute on horseback,
    Beheld them when they lighted,° how they clung   *got off*
10 In their embracement as° they grew together,   *as if*
    Which had they,° what four throned ones could have weighed[5]   *if they had*
    Such a compounded one?
BUCKINGHAM   All the whole time
    I was my chamber's prisoner.
NORFOLK   Then you lost
    The view of earthly glory. Men might say
15 Till this time pomp was single, but now married
    To one above itself.[6] Each following day
    Became the next day's master, till the last
    Made former wonders its.[7] Today the French,
    All clinquant° all in gold, like heathen gods   *glittering*
20 Shone down the English; and tomorrow they
    Made Britain India.[8] Every man that stood
    Showed like a mine. Their dwarfish pages were

4. Punning reference to the lower-class groundlings, who are literally "understanding" in the sense of "standing under" the raised stage.
1.1. Location: The court at London.
1. A seat under a canopy for the King or Cardinal Wolsey, perhaps onstage throughout the play. The original Globe performances also had "matting" (a woven straw floor-covering) on the stage.
2. The reference is to the rendezvous of Henry VIII and Francis I of France near Calais in June 1520, at the Field of the Cloth of Gold, named for the sumptuous displays by the two Kings.
3. Actually, Buckingham was present, if reluctantly (because of the expense), at the Field of the Cloth of

Gold. The fictional "ague," or fever, allows the dramatist to show Buckingham responding to Norfolk's detailed description.
4. Guisnes belonged to England, Ardres to France.
5. Been as heavy as.
6. *Till . . . itself:* The pomp of each King now joins ("marries") that of the other, making a greater pomp than either alone could display.
7. *Each . . . its:* Each day learned wonders from the previous one, making the last day the most wonderful of all. *master:* standard.
8. *they . . . India:* the English made Britain look as (fabulously) rich as India or the West Indies.

As cherubim, all gilt;[9] the *mesdames*,° too,   *ladies*
Not used to toil, did almost sweat to bear
25 The pride° upon them, that° their very labour   *fancy adornment / so that*
Was to them as a painting.[1] Now this masque
Was cried° incomparable, and th'ensuing night   *said to be*
Made it a fool and beggar. The two kings
Equal in lustre, were now best, now worst,
30 As presence did present them.[2] Him in eye
Still him in praise,[3] and being present both,
'Twas said they saw but one, and no discerner
Durst wag his tongue in censure.[4] When these suns—
For so they phrase 'em—by their heralds challenged
35 The noble spirits to arms, they did perform
Beyond thought's compass, that former fabulous story
Being now seen possible enough, got credit
That *Bevis* was believed.[5]
BUCKINGHAM   O, you go far!
NORFOLK   As I belong to worship,° and affect   *the aristocracy*
40 In honour honesty,[6] the tract of ev'rything
Would by a good discourser lose some life
Which action's self was tongue to.[7] All was royal.
To the disposing° of it naught rebelled.   *arrangement*
Order gave each thing view. The office did
Distinctly his full function.[8]
45 BUCKINGHAM   Who did guide—
I mean, who set the body and the limbs
Of this great sport° together, as you guess?   *show*
NORFOLK   One, certes, that promises no element[9]
In such a business.
BUCKINGHAM   I pray you who, my lord?
50 NORFOLK   All this was ordered by the good discretion
Of the right reverend Cardinal of York.°   *(Wolsey)*
BUCKINGHAM   The devil speed° him! No man's pie is freed   *ruin*
From his ambitious finger. What had he
To do in these fierce° vanities? I wonder   *excessive*
55 That such a keech[1] can, with his very bulk,
Take up the rays o'th' beneficial sun,°   *(Henry)*
And keep it from the earth.
NORFOLK   Surely, sir,
There's in him stuff that puts° him to these ends.   *spurs*
For being not propped by ancestry, whose grace
60 Chalks successors their way,[2] nor called upon
For high feats done to th' crown, neither allied
To eminent assistants,° but spider-like,   *ministers of state*
Out of his self-drawing° web, a° gives us note   *spun from himself / he*

---

9. Gold-plated statues of cherubim, often found in churches.
1. Made them rosy, as if with makeup.
2. According to who was present.
3. *Him . . . praise*: To the King on display at the time went all the acclaim.
4. *no . . . censure*: no one watching dared say one outshone the other.
5. *they did . . . believed*: their performance was such that stories formerly deemed mere fables, now looking possible, gained plausibility. Even *Sir Bevis of Hampton* (Southampton), a popular medieval romance, was

believed.
6. *and . . . honesty*: and honorably love truth.
7. *the tract . . . to*: the events surpass their telling.
8. *Order . . . Distinctly*: Careful organization made everything appropriately visible. Each responsible person properly fulfilled his role.
9. One, without doubt, who seems out of place.
1. Hunk of fat from a slaughtered animal. Wolsey was said to be a butcher's son.
2. *ancestry . . . way*: noble ancestors, whose honorable qualities mark the way for future generations.

65 The force of his own merit makes his way—
A gift that heaven gives for him which buys
A place next to the King.

ABERGAVENNY   I cannot tell
What heaven hath given him—let some graver eye
Pierce into that; but I can see his pride
Peep through each part of him. Whence has he that?°   *(such pride)*
70 If not from hell, the devil is a niggard°   *selfish*
Or has given all before,° and he° begins   *already / (Wolsey)*
A new hell in himself.

BUCKINGHAM   Why the devil,
Upon this French going out,° took he upon him   *journey*
Without the privity° o'th' King t'appoint   *private sanction*
75 Who should attend on him? He makes up the file°   *roll*
Of all the gentry, for the most part such
To whom as great a charge as little honour
He meant to lay upon;³ and his own letter,
The honourable board of council out,
Must fetch him in, he papers.⁴
80 ABERGAVENNY   I do know
Kinsmen of mine—three at the least—that have
By this so sickened° their estates that never   *wasted*
They shall abound as formerly.

BUCKINGHAM   O, many
Have broke their backs with laying manors on 'em⁵
85 For this great journey. What did this vanity
But minister communication of
A most poor issue?⁶

NORFOLK   Grievingly I think
The peace between the French and us not values°   *does not merit*
The cost that did conclude it.

BUCKINGHAM   Every man,
90 After the hideous storm that followed, was
A thing inspired, and, not consulting,° broke   *without conferring*
Into a general° prophecy—that this tempest,   *collective*
Dashing the garment of this peace, aboded°   *prophesied*
The sudden breach on't.°   *of it*

NORFOLK   Which is budded out°—   *has occurred*
95 For France hath flawed° the league, and hath attached°   *betrayed / seized*
Our merchants' goods at Bordeaux.

ABERGAVENNY   Is it therefore°   *on this account*
Th'ambassador is silenced?

NORFOLK   Marry is't.°   *Of course it is*

ABERGAVENNY   A proper title of a° peace, and purchased   *A fine thing to call*
At a superfluous rate.°   *too high a cost*

BUCKINGHAM   Why, all this business
Our reverend Cardinal carried.°   *oversaw*

100 NORFOLK   Like it° your grace,   *May it please*
The state takes notice of the private difference

---

3. *To whom . . . upon:* (Wolsey gave) places of little honor to the noblemen on whom he laid the greatest expense for the display.

4. *and . . . papers:* and with the council ignored ("out"), his own summons ("letter") forces every person he lists ("papers") to comply.

5. *many . . . 'em:* many have sold off their estates—and

thus bankrupted themselves—to pay for a costly wardrobe; with a pun on "manners."

6. *What . . . issue:* What did such wasteful expense do but bankrupt their own children ("poor issue"); or encourage talk for a trivial outcome ("poor issue")?

Betwixt you and the Cardinal. I advise you—
And take it from a heart that wishes towards you
Honour and plenteous safety—that you read°   *assess*
105 The Cardinal's malice and his potency
Together; to consider further that
What his high hatred would effect wants° not   *lacks*
A minister° in his power. You know his nature,   *An agent*
That he's revengeful; and I know his sword
110 Hath a sharp edge—it's long, and't may be said
It reaches far; and where 'twill not extend
Thither he darts it. Bosom up° my counsel,   *Keep secret; take to heart*
You'll find it wholesome. Lo, where comes that rock
That I advise your shunning.

Enter CARDINAL WOLSEY, *the purse*[7] *[containing the*
great seal] borne before him. [Enter with him] certain
of the guard, and two SECRETARIES *with papers. The*
CARDINAL *in his passage fixeth his eye on* BUCKINGHAM
and BUCKINGHAM *on him, both full of disdain*

CARDINAL WOLSEY [*To a* SECRETARY]   The Duke of Buckingham's
115   surveyor,° ha?   *overseer of an estate*
Where's his examination?°   *testimony*
SECRETARY   Here, so please you.
CARDINAL WOLSEY   Is he in person ready?
SECRETARY   Ay, please your grace.
CARDINAL WOLSEY   Well, we shall then know more, and Buckingham
Shall lessen this big° look.   *pompous*

Exeunt CARDINAL [WOLSEY] *and his train*

120 BUCKINGHAM   This butcher's cur is venom-mouthed, and I
Have not the power to muzzle him; therefore best
Not wake him in his slumber. A beggar's book°   *learning*
Outworths a noble's blood.°   *inherited privilege*
NORFOLK   What, are you chafed?°   *annoyed*
Ask God for temp'rance; that's th'appliance only° *the only medicine*
Which your disease requires.
125 BUCKINGHAM   I read in's looks
Matter against me, and his eye reviled
Me as his abject° object. At this instant   *discarded*
He bores° me with some trick. He's gone to th' King— *pierces; defrauds*
I'll follow, and outstare him.
NORFOLK   Stay, my lord,
130 And let your reason with your choler° question°   *anger/dispute*
What 'tis you go about. To climb steep hills
Requires slow pace at first. Anger is like
A full hot° horse who, being allowed his way,   *feisty*
Self-mettle° tires him. Not a man in England   *His own disposition*
135 Can advise me like you. Be to yourself
As you would to your friend.[8]
BUCKINGHAM   I'll to the King,
And from a mouth of honour[9] quite cry down
This Ipswich° fellow's insolence, or proclaim   *(Wolsey's birthplace)*
There's difference in no persons.°   *Rank no longer matters*

---

7. A special bag that held the "great seal," part of the
Lord Chancellor's insignia of office.
8. *Be . . . friend*: Don't do anything you wouldn't advise

a friend to do.
9. An aristocratic, virtuous mouth.

NORFOLK   Be advised.°   *Be careful*
140   Heat not a furnace for your foe so hot
      That it do singe yourself. We may outrun
      By violent swiftness that which we run at,°   *toward*
      And lose by over-running. Know you not
      The fire that mounts° the liquor till't run o'er   *swells (by boiling)*
145   In seeming to augment it wastes it? Be advised.
      I say again there is no English soul
      More stronger to direct you than yourself,
      If with the sap of reason you would quench
      Or but allay° the fire of passion.   *abate*

BUCKINGHAM   Sir,
150   I am thankful to you, and I'll go along
      By your prescription; but this top-proud° fellow—   *proudest of all*
      Whom from the flow of gall I name not, but
      From sincere motions¹—by intelligence,°   *covert information*
      And proofs as clear as founts° in July when   *springs*
155   We see each grain of gravel, I do know
      To be corrupt and treasonous.

NORFOLK   Say not 'treasonous'.

BUCKINGHAM   To th' King I'll say't, and make my vouch° as strong   *case*
      As shore of rock. Attend: this holy fox,
      Or wolf, or both—for he is equal° rav'nous   *as*
160   As he is subtle, and as prone to mischief
      As able to perform't, his mind and place°   *high position*
      Infecting one another, yea, reciprocally—
      Only to show his pomp as well in France
      As here at home, suggests° the King our master   *tempts*
165   To this last° costly treaty, th'interview°   *latest / the meeting*
      That swallowed so much treasure and, like a glass,
      Did break i'th' rinsing.

NORFOLK   Faith, and so it did.

BUCKINGHAM   Pray give me favour,° sir. This cunning Cardinal,   *let me continue*
      The articles o'th' combination° drew   *terms of the treaty*
170   As himself pleased, and they were ratified
      As he cried 'Thus let be', to as much end°   *effect*
      As give a crutch to th' dead. But our count-Cardinal²
      Has done this, and 'tis well for worthy Wolsey,
      Who cannot err, he did it. Now this follows—
175   Which, as I take it, is a kind of puppy
      To th'old dam,° treason—Charles the Emperor,³   *bitch; mother*
      Under pretence to see the Queen his aunt°—   *(Katherine)*
      For 'twas indeed his colour,° but he came   *alibi*
      To whisper° Wolsey—here makes visitation.   *meet covertly with*
180   His fears were that the interview betwixt
      England and France might through their amity
      Breed him some prejudice, for from this league
      Peeped harms that menaced him. Privily° he   *Clandestinely*
      Deals with our Cardinal and, as I trow°—   *believe*
185   Which I do well, for I am sure the Emperor
      Paid ere he promised, whereby his suit was granted

---

1. *Whom . . . motions:* Whom I name not from a rancorous impulse but from pure motives.
2. Church leader assuming secular, aristocratic rank
(compare "King-Cardinal," 2.2.18).
3. Charles V, Holy Roman Emperor and King of Spain.

Ere it was asked—but when the way was made,
And paved with gold, the Emperor thus desired
That he° would please to alter the King's course   *(Wolsey)*
190   And break the foresaid peace. Let the King know,
As soon he shall by me, that thus the Cardinal
Does buy and sell his° honour as he° pleases,   *(Henry's) / (Wolsey)*
And for his own advantage.
    NORFOLK   I am sorry
To hear this of him, and could wish he were
Something mistaken° in't.   *Partly misrepresented*
195   BUCKINGHAM   No, not a syllable.
I do pronounce him in that very shape
He shall appear in proof.°   *in practice*
        Enter BRANDON, *a* SERJEANT-*at-arms before him, and*
            two or three of the guard
    BRANDON   Your office, serjeant, execute it.
    SERJEANT   Sir.
        [*To* BUCKINGHAM] My lord the Duke of Buckingham and Earl
200   Of Hereford, Stafford, and Northampton, I
Arrest thee of high treason in the name
Of our most sovereign King.
    BUCKINGHAM [*to* NORFOLK]   Lo° you, my lord,   *Look*
The net has fall'n upon me. I shall perish
Under device and practice.°   *trickery and schemes*
    BRANDON   I am sorry
205   To see you ta'en from liberty to look on[4]
The business present. 'Tis his highness' pleasure
You shall to th' Tower.
    BUCKINGHAM   It will help me nothing
To plead mine innocence, for that dye is on me
Which makes my whit'st part black. The will of heav'n
210   Be done in this and all things. I obey.
O, my lord Abergavenny, fare you well.
    BRANDON   Nay, he must bear you company.
        [*To* ABERGAVENNY]   The King
Is pleased you shall to th' Tower till you know
How he determines further.
    ABERGAVENNY   As the Duke said,
215   The will of heaven be done and the King's pleasure
By me obeyed.
    BRANDON   Here is a warrant from
The King t'attach° Lord Montague and the bodies   *to seize*
Of the duke's confessor, John de la Car,
One Gilbert Perk, his chancellor—
    BUCKINGHAM   So, so;
220   These are the limbs o'th' plot. No more, I hope.
    BRANDON   A monk o'th' Chartreux.°   *Carthusian*
    BUCKINGHAM   O, Nicholas Hopkins?
    BRANDON   He.
    BUCKINGHAM   My surveyor is false. The o'er-great Cardinal
Hath showed him gold. My life is spanned° already.   *marked out*
225   I am the shadow of poor Buckingham,

---

4. *to look on:* and (sorry) to behold.

Whose figure even this instant cloud puts on
By dark'ning my clear sun.[5] [*To* NORFOLK] My lord, farewell.

Exeunt [NORFOLK *at one door,* BUCKINGHAM *and*
ABERGAVENNY *under guard at another*]

1.2

Cornetts. Enter KING HENRY *leaning on Cardinal*
[*Wolsey*]'*s shoulder.* [*Enter with them Wolsey's two* SEC-
RETARIES,] *the nobles, and Sir Thomas* LOVELL. [*The*
KING *ascends to his seat under the cloth of state;*] CAR-
DINAL [WOLSEY] *places himself under the King's feet°*   below the throne
on his right side

KING HENRY [*to* WOLSEY]   My life itself and the best heart° of it   essential core
Thanks you for this great care. I stood i'th' level°   line of fire
Of a full-charged confederacy,° and give thanks   loaded conspiracy
To you that choked it. Let be called before us

5   That gentleman of Buckingham's.° In person   (the surveyor)
I'll hear him his confessions justify,°   verify
And point by point the treasons of his master
He shall again relate.

CRIER (*within*)   Room for the Queen, ushered by the Duke of Norfolk.

Enter QUEEN [KATHERINE, *the Duke of*] NORFOLK, *and*
[*the Duke of*] SUFFOLK. *She kneels.* KING [HENRY]
riseth from his state,° takes her up, and kisses her   throne

10   QUEEN KATHERINE   Nay, we must longer kneel. I am a suitor.

KING HENRY   Arise, and take place by us.

[*He*] *placeth* [*her*] *by him*

Half your suit
Never name to us. You have half our power,
The other moiety° ere you ask is given.   half
Repeat your will° and take it.   State your wish

QUEEN KATHERINE   Thank your majesty.

15   That you would love yourself, and in that love
Not unconsidered leave your honour nor
The dignity of your office, is the point
Of my petition.

KING HENRY   Lady mine, proceed.

QUEEN KATHERINE   I am solicited,° not by a few,   apprised
20   And those of true condition,° that your subjects   loyal character
Are in great grievance. There have been commissions
Sent down among 'em[1] which hath flawed° the heart   broken
Of all their loyalties; wherein, although,
My good lord Cardinal, they vent reproaches
25   Most bitterly on you, as putter-on
Of these exactions,° yet the King our master—   taxes
Whose honour heaven shield from soil°—even he escapes not   blemish
Language unmannerly, yea, such which breaks
The sides[2] of loyalty, and almost appears
In loud rebellion.

30   NORFOLK   Not 'almost appears'—
It doth appear; for upon these taxations

---

5. A cloud having overshadowed my former glory and
come between me and my king ("sun" may refer to
either Buckingham or Henry).
1.2 Location: A council chamber at court.

1. There . . . 'em: They have received writs authorizing
the collection of taxes.
2. which . . . sides: which oversteps the limits.

The clothiers all, not able to maintain
The many to them 'longing,° have put off°   *they employ / let go*
The spinsters, carders, fullers,[3] weavers, who,
35   Unfit for other life, compelled by hunger
And lack of other means, in desperate manner
Daring th'event to th' teeth,[4] are all in uproar,
And danger serves among them.
KING HENRY   Taxation?
Wherein, and what taxation? My lord Cardinal,
40   You that are blamed for it alike with us,
Know you of this taxation?
CARDINAL WOLSEY   Please you, sir,
I know but of a single° part in aught°   *(his own) / anything*
Pertains to th' state, and front but in that file
Where others tell steps with me.[5]
QUEEN KATHERINE   No, my lord?
45   You know no more than others? But you frame
Things that are known alike, which are not wholesome
To those which would not know them, and yet must
Perforce be their acquaintance.[6] These exactions
Whereof my sovereign would have note,° they are   *knowledge*
50   Most pestilent to th' hearing, and to bear 'em
The back is sacrifice to° th' load. They say   *broken by*
They are devised by you, or else you suffer
Too hard an exclamation.°   *a complaint*
KING HENRY   Still exaction!
The nature of it? In what kind, let's know,
Is this exaction?
55   QUEEN KATHERINE   I am much too venturous
In tempting of your patience, but am boldened
Under your promised pardon. The subjects' grief °   *grievance*
Comes through commissions which compels from each
The sixth part of his substance° to be levied   *wealth*
60   Without delay, and the pretence for this
Is named your wars in France. This makes bold mouths.
Tongues spit their duties out, and cold hearts freeze
Allegiance in them. Their curses now
Live where their prayers did, and it's come to pass
65   This tractable obedience is a slave
To each incensèd will.[7] I would your highness
Would give it quick consideration, for
There is no primer° business.   *more pressing*
KING HENRY   By my life,
This is against our pleasure.
CARDINAL WOLSEY   And for me,
70   I have no further gone in this than by
A single voice,[8] and that not passed me but
By learnèd approbation° of the judges. If I am   *approval*
Traduced° by ignorant tongues, which neither know   *Slandered*

3. All involved in wool production: "spinsters" spun the
wool; "carders" combed through, extracting impurities;
and "fullers" beat the wool to thicken and cleanse it.
4. Refusing adamantly to comply with the result.
5. *front . . . me:* I walk at the front of a line only of those
who have power equal to my own (literally, who march in
step behind me). Wolsey is denying that he is responsible.

6. *But . . . acquaintance:* But you originate measures
that all know, that harm even those who would rather
not accept them yet must.
7. *This . . . will:* Each subject's formerly compliant
obedience is dominated by his anger.
8. *I . . . voice:* I have only cast my single vote; I have
concurred with a unanimous vote.

My faculties° nor person yet will be   *abilities*
75 The chronicles of my doing, let me say
'Tis but the fate of place,° and the rough brake°   *rank / thicket*
That virtue must go through. We must not stint°   *halt*
Our necessary actions in the fear
To cope° malicious censurers, which ever,   *Of facing*
80 As rav'nous fishes, do a vessel follow
That is new trimmed,° but benefit no further   *newly rigged*
Than vainly longing. What we oft do best,
By sick interpreters, once weak ones, is
Not ours or not allowed;[9] what° worst, as oft,   *what we do*
85 Hitting a grosser quality,° is cried up   *Appealing to the base*
For our best act. If we shall stand still,
In fear our motion[1] will be mocked or carped at,
We should take root here where we sit,
Or sit state-statues only.[2]
KING HENRY   Things done well,
90 And with a care, exempt themselves from fear;
Things done without example,° in their issue°   *precedent / effects*
Are to be feared. Have you a precedent
Of this commission? I believe not any.
We must not rend our subjects from our laws
95 And stick them in our will.° Sixth part of each?   *use them at our whim*
A trembling contribution! Why, we take
From every tree lop,° bark, and part o' th' timber,   *branches*
And though we leave it with a root, thus hacked
The air will drink the sap. To every county
100 Where this is questioned° send our letters with   *challenged*
Free pardon to each man that has denied°   *refused*
The force of this commission. Pray look to 't—
I put it to your care.
CARDINAL WOLSEY [*to a* SECRETARY]   A word with you.
Let there be letters writ to every shire
Of the King's grace° and pardon.   *mercy*
105 [*Aside to the* SECRETARY]   The grievèd commons
Hardly° conceive of me. Let it be noised°   *Severely / rumored*
That through our intercession this revokement
And pardon comes. I shall anon advise you
Further in the proceeding.   *Exit* SECRETARY
Enter [BUCKINGHAM'S] SURVEYOR
110 QUEEN KATHERINE [*to the* KING]   I am sorry that the Duke of Buckingham
Is run in° your displeasure.   *Has provoked*
KING HENRY   It grieves many.
The gentleman is learnèd, and a most rare speaker,
To nature none more bound;[3] his training such
That he may furnish and instruct great teachers
115 And never seek for aid out of ° himself. Yet see,   *outside of*
When these so noble benefits shall prove
Not well disposed,° the mind growing once corrupt,   *employed*
They turn to vicious forms ten times more ugly
Than ever they were fair. This man so complete,°   *accomplished*

9. *What . . . allowed:* Formerly foolish, now corrupt   2. Or become nothing but decorative statues of leaders.
("sick") observers never attribute to us or approve in us   3. No man has been given greater gifts by nature.
what we do best.
1. For fear our proposal (or action).

120   Who was enrolled 'mongst wonders—and when we
        Almost with ravished° list'ning could not find   *spellbound*
        His hour of speech a minute—he, my lady,
        Hath into monstrous habits° put the graces   *shapes; behavior; clothes*
        That once were his, and is become as black
125   As if besmeared in hell. Sit by us. You shall hear—
        This was his gentleman in trust of him—
        Things to strike honour sad.
        [*To* WOLSEY]   Bid him recount
        The fore-recited practices° whereof   *schemes*
        We cannot feel too little, hear too much.
     CARDINAL WOLSEY [*to the* SURVEYOR]   Stand forth, and with bold
130   spirit relate what you
        Most like a careful subject have collected°   *gathered as evidence*
        Out of° the Duke of Buckingham.   *(by observing)*
     KING HENRY [*to the* SURVEYOR]   Speak freely.
     BUCKINGHAM'S SURVEYOR   First, it was usual with him, every day
        It would infect his speech, that if the King
135   Should without issue die, he'll carry it so°   *arrange so as*
        To make the sceptre his. These very words
        I've heard him utter to his son-in-law,
        Lord Abergavenny, to whom by oath he menaced
        Revenge upon the Cardinal.
     CARDINAL WOLSEY [*to the* KING]   Please your highness note
140   His dangerous conception in this point,
        Not friended by his wish to your high person.[4]
        His will is most malignant, and it stretches
        Beyond you to your friends.
     QUEEN KATHERINE   My learned Lord Cardinal,
        Deliver all with charity.
     KING HENRY [*to the* SURVEYOR]   Speak on.
145   How grounded he his title to the crown
        Upon our fail?° To this point hast thou heard him   *childlessness; death*
        At any time speak aught?
     BUCKINGHAM'S SURVEYOR   He was brought to this
        By a vain prophecy of Nicholas Hopkins.
     KING HENRY   What was that Hopkins?
     BUCKINGHAM'S SURVEYOR   Sir, a Chartreux friar,
150   His confessor, who fed him every minute
        With words of sovereignty.
     KING HENRY   How know'st thou this?
     BUCKINGHAM'S SURVEYOR   Not long before your highness sped to France,
        The Duke being at the Rose,[5] within the parish
        Saint Lawrence Poutney, did of me demand
155   What was the speech° among the Londoners   *gossip*
        Concerning the French journey. I replied
        Men feared the French would prove perfidious,
        To the King's danger; presently° the Duke   *at once*
        Said 'twas the fear indeed, and that he doubted°   *suspected*
160   'Twould prove the verity of certain words
        Spoke by a holy monk that oft, says he,
        'Hath sent to me, wishing me to permit

---

4. Since he has not been granted ("friended by") his   5. Manor owned by Buckingham just outside London.
wish that the King die without an heir.

John de la Car, my chaplain, a choice hour°   *a suitable time*
To hear from him a matter of some moment;
165   Whom after under the confession's seal
He solemnly had sworn, that what he spoke
My chaplain to no creature living but
To me should utter, with demure° confidence   *grave*
This pausingly ensued: "neither the King nor's heirs",
170   Tell you the Duke, "shall prosper. Bid him strive
To win the love o'th' commonalty.° The Duke   *common people*
Shall govern England."'

QUEEN KATHERINE   If I know you well,
You were the Duke's surveyor, and lost your office
On the complaint o'th' tenants. Take good heed
175   You charge not in your spleen° a noble person   *spite*
And spoil° your nobler soul. I say, take heed;   *ruin*
Yes, heartily beseech you.

KING HENRY   Let him on.°   *continue*
[*To the* SURVEYOR] Go forward.

BUCKINGHAM'S SURVEYOR   On my soul I'll speak but truth.
I told my lord the Duke, by th' devil's illusions
180   The monk might be deceived, and that 'twas dangerous
To ruminate on this so far until
It forged him some design which, being believed,
It was much like to do.⁶ He answered, 'Tush,
It can do me no damage', adding further
185   That had the King in his last sickness failed,°   *died*
The Cardinal's and Sir Thomas Lovell's heads
Should have gone off.

KING HENRY   Ha? What, so rank?° Ah, ha!   *rotten*
There's mischief in this man. Canst thou say further?

BUCKINGHAM'S SURVEYOR   I can, my liege.

KING HENRY   Proceed.

BUCKINGHAM'S SURVEYOR   Being at Greenwich,
190   After your highness had reproved the Duke
About Sir William Bulmer—

KING HENRY   I remember
Such a time, being my sworn servant,
The Duke retained him his.° But on—what hence?   *for his own*

BUCKINGHAM'S SURVEYOR   'If', quoth he, 'I for this had been committed'—
195   As to the Tower, I thought—'I would have played
The part my father⁷ meant to act upon
Th'usurper Richard who, being at Salisbury,
Made suit to come in's presence; which if granted,
As he made semblance of his duty,° would   *seemed to kneel*
Have put his knife into him.'
200   KING HENRY   A giant traitor!

CARDINAL WOLSEY [*to the* QUEEN]   Now, madam, may° his highness   *can*
live in freedom,
And this man out of prison?

QUEEN KATHERINE   God mend all.

---

6. *until . . . do*: until the Duke's ruminations made him imagine ("forged him") some scheme that, if he believed in it (and hence in the Monk's prophecy), he would probably undertake.
7. The Duke of Buckingham during Richard III's reign.

KING HENRY [*to the* SURVEYOR]   There's something more would
         out of thee—what sayst?
BUCKINGHAM'S SURVEYOR   After 'the Duke his father', with 'the knife',
205   He stretched him,° and with one hand on his dagger,   *stood up straight*
    Another spread on's breast, mounting° his eyes,   *raising up*
    He did discharge a horrible oath whose tenor
    Was, were he evil used,° he would outgo   *poorly treated*
    His father by as much as a performance°   *true performance*
    Does an irresolute purpose.
210   KING HENRY   There's his period°—   *ultimate goal*
    To sheathe his knife in us. He is attached.°   *arrested*
    Call him to present° trial. If he may   *immediate*
    Find mercy in the law, 'tis his; if none,
    Let him not seek't of us. By day and night,
215   He's traitor to th' height.°   [*Flourish.*] *Exeunt*   *to the greatest degree*

1.3

Enter [*the*] LORD CHAMBERLAIN *and Lord* SANDS

LORD CHAMBERLAIN   Is't possible the spells of France should juggle°   *enchant*
    Men into such strange mysteries?°   *outlandish conduct*
SANDS   New customs,
    Though they be never so ridiculous—
    Nay, let 'em be unmanly°—yet are followed.   *effeminate*
5   LORD CHAMBERLAIN   As far as I see, all the good our English
    Have got by the late voyage° is but merely   *(to France)*
    A fit or two o'th' face.° But they are shrewd ones,   *Odd new expressions*
    For when they hold 'em° you would swear directly   *maintain these looks*
    Their very noses had been counsellors
10   To Pépin or Clotharius, they keep state so.[1]
SANDS   They have all new legs,° and lame ones; one would take it,   *new walks and bows*
    That never see 'em pace° before, the spavin   *saw them walk*
    Or spring-halt reigned among 'em.[2]
LORD CHAMBERLAIN   Death,° my lord,   *By God's death*
    Their clothes are after such a pagan cut to't
    That sure they've worn out Christendom.[3]
Enter Sir Thomas LOVELL
15   How now—
    What news, Sir Thomas Lovell?
LOVELL   Faith, my lord,
    I hear of none but the new proclamation
    That's clapped upon the court gate.
LORD CHAMBERLAIN   What is't for?
LOVELL   The reformation of our travelled gallants
20   That fill the court with quarrels, talk, and tailors.
LORD CHAMBERLAIN   I'm glad 'tis there. Now I would pray our '*messieurs*'
    To think an English courtier may be wise
    And never see the Louvre.°   *French king's palace*
LOVELL   They must either,
    For so run the conditions, leave those remnants

1.3 Location: The court.
1. *To . . . so:* To sixth- and seventh-century kings of France, their noses ("they") have such dignified (but convoluted) postures.
2. *the spavin . . . 'em:* they seem to be lame. *spavin:* swelling in horses' legs. *spring-halt:* spasms in horses'
legs.
3. *Their . . . Christendom:* They have run out of the fashions of Christendom and have moved on to pagan habits. This mockery reflects contemporary anxieties about the "effeminacy" of imported Continental fashions. *are after:* have.

25 Of fool and feather° that they got in France,   *folly and adornment*
With all their honourable points of ignorance[4]
Pertaining thereunto—as fights and fireworks,°   *whoring*
Abusing better men than they can be
Out of a foreign wisdom, renouncing clean
30 The faith they have in tennis and tall stockings,
Short blistered breeches, and those types of travel[5]—
And understand again like honest men,
Or pack° to their old playfellows. There, I take it,   *return*
They may, *cum privilegio, 'oui'* away
35 The lag end of their lewdness[6] and be laughed at.

SANDS   'Tis time to give 'em physic,° their diseases   *medicine*
Are grown so catching.

LORD CHAMBERLAIN   What a loss our ladies
Will have of these trim vanities!°   *well-dressed fops*

LOVELL   Ay, marry,°   *indeed*
There will be woe indeed, lords. The sly whoresons
40 Have got a speeding° trick to lay down° ladies.   *an expeditious / seduce*
A French song and a fiddle has no fellow.°   *equal*

SANDS   The devil fiddle 'em! I am glad they are going,
For sure there's no converting of 'em.° Now   *changing their ways*
An honest country lord, as I am, beaten
45 A long time out of play,° may bring his plainsong°   *love / unadorned tune*
And have an hour of hearing, and, by'r Lady,
Held current° music, too.   *modern; stylish*

LORD CHAMBERLAIN   Well said, Lord Sands.
Your colt's tooth is not cast yet?[7]

SANDS   No, my lord,
Nor shall not while I have a stump.°   *(of a tooth—sexual)*

LORD CHAMBERLAIN [*to* LOVELL]   Sir Thomas,
Whither were you a-going?

50 LOVELL   To the Cardinal's.
Your lordship is a guest too.

LORD CHAMBERLAIN   O, 'tis true.
This night he makes° a supper, and a great one,   *holds*
To many lords and ladies. There will be
The beauty of this kingdom, I'll assure you.
55 LOVELL   That churchman bears a bounteous mind indeed,
A hand as fruitful° as the land that feeds us.   *benevolent*
His dews° fall everywhere.   *(pun on "dues," taxes)*

LORD CHAMBERLAIN   No doubt he's noble.
He had a black mouth that said other of him.[8]

SANDS   He may, my lord; he's wherewithal.° In him   *he can afford to*
60 Sparing° would show a worse sin than ill doctrine.°   *Stinginess / heresy*
Men of his way° should be most liberal.   *profession*
They are set here for examples.

LORD CHAMBERLAIN   True, they are so,
But few now give so great ones.° My barge stays.°   *examples / waits*
Your lordship shall along.° [*To* LOVELL] Come, good Sir Thomas,   *join me*

4. Which, in their ignorance, they consider honorable.
5. *Abusing . . . travel:* They must stop "abusing" their betters out of a misplaced faith in French wisdom, and start "renouncing" French habits like tennis, tall stockings, puffed breeches, and such marks of travel (which were affected by Henry VIII and James I, as well as James's courtiers).

6. *They . . . lewdness:* They may, with immunity ("*cum privilegio*"), indulge their remaining decadence by copying the French. *oui:* yes.
7. You haven't abandoned your youthful lasciviousness ("colt's tooth") yet?
8. Anyone who denies this generosity must have an evil mouth.

65 We shall be late else, which I would not be,
For I was spoke to,° with Sir Henry Guildford,   *invited*
This night to be comptrollers.°   *stewards*

SANDS   I am your lordship's. *Exeunt*

1.4

Hautboys.[1] [*Enter servants with*] *a small table for* CAR-
DINAL [WOLSEY *which they place*] *under the* [*cloth of*]
state, [*and*] *a longer table for the guests. Then enter at
one door* ANNE *Boleyn and divers other ladies and gentlemen as guests,* [*and*] *at another door enter Sir Henry*
GUILDFORD

GUILDFORD   Ladies, a general welcome from his grace
Salutes ye all. This night he dedicates
To fair content and you. None here, he hopes,
In all this noble bevy,° has brought with her   *company*
5   One care abroad. He would have all as merry
As feast, good company, good wine, good welcome
Can make good people.
            Enter [*the*] LORD CHAMBERLAIN, *Lord* SANDS, *and* [*Sir
            Thomas*] LOVELL
[*To the* LORD CHAMBERLAIN] O, my lord, you're tardy.
The very thought of this fair company
Clapped wings to me.

LORD CHAMBERLAIN   You are young, Sir Harry Guildford.

10 SANDS   Sir Thomas Lovell, had the Cardinal
But half my lay° thoughts in him, some of these   *secular*
Should find a running banquet,[2] ere they rested,
I think would better please 'em. By my life,
They are a sweet society of fair ones.

15 LOVELL   O, that your lordship were but now confessor
To one or two of these.

SANDS   I would I were.
They should find easy penance.

LOVELL   Faith, how easy?

SANDS   As easy as a down bed would afford it.

LORD CHAMBERLAIN   Sweet ladies, will it please you sit?
[*To* GUILDFORD]   Sir Harry,
20 Place you° that side, I'll take the charge of this.   *Arrange seating on*
            [*They sit about the longer table. A noise within*]
His grace is ent'ring. Nay, you must not freeze—
Two women placed together makes cold weather.
My lord Sands, you are one will keep 'em waking.°   *spirited*
Pray sit between these ladies.

SANDS   By my faith,
And thank your lordship.
            [*He sits between* ANNE *and another*]
25   By your leave, sweet ladies.
If I chance to talk a little wild, forgive me.
I had it from my father.

ANNE   Was he mad, sir?

1.4 Location: Westminster, a hall in York Place.   2. Light refreshments; furtive, stolen pleasures.
1. Early reeded wind instrument, ancestor of the oboe.

SANDS O, very mad; exceeding mad—in love, too.
　　But he would bite° none. Just as I do now,　　　　　　　　*(sign of madness)*
　　He would kiss you twenty with a breath.[3]
　　　　　[*He kisses her*]

30　LORD CHAMBERLAIN　　　　　　　　Well said,° my lord.　　　　　*done*
　　So now you're fairly seated. Gentlemen,
　　The penance lies on you if these fair ladies
　　Pass away frowning.

SANDS　For my little cure,°　　　　　　　　　　　　　　*duty; (of souls)*
35　Let me alone.
　　　　　Hautboys. Enter CARDINAL WOLSEY [*who*] *takes his*
　　　　　[*seat at the small table under the*] state°　　　　*chair of state*

CARDINAL WOLSEY　You're welcome, my fair guests. That noble lady
　　Or gentleman that is not freely merry
　　Is not my friend. This, to confirm my welcome,
　　And to you all, good health!
　　　　　[*He drinks*]

SANDS　　　　　　　　　　Your grace is noble.
40　Let me have such a bowl may° hold my thanks,　　　　　*as may*
　　And save me so much talking.

CARDINAL WOLSEY　　　　　　　My lord Sands,
　　I am beholden to you. Cheer° your neighbours.　　　　　*Amuse*
　　Ladies, you are not merry! Gentlemen,
　　Whose fault is this?

SANDS　　　　　　　The red wine first must rise
45　In their fair cheeks, my lord, then we shall have 'em
　　Talk us to silence.

ANNE　　　　　　　You are a merry gamester,°　　　　　*fellow; gambler*
　　My lord Sands.

SANDS　　　　　Yes, if I make my play.[4]
　　Here's to your ladyship; and pledge it,° madam,　　　　　*drink to it*
　　For 'tis to such a thing—

ANNE　　　　　　　You cannot show me.°　　　　　　　*(sexual)*

SANDS [*to* WOLSEY]　I told your grace they would talk anon.
　　　　　Drum and trumpet. Chambers discharged[5]

50　CARDINAL WOLSEY　　　　　　　　　　　What's that?

LORD CHAMBERLAIN [*to the* SERVANTS]
　　Look out there, some of ye.　　　　　[*Exit a* SERVANT]

CARDINAL WOLSEY　　　　　What warlike voice,
　　And to what end is this? Nay, ladies, fear not.
　　By all the laws of war you're privileged.°　　　　　*safe from harm*
　　　　　Enter [*the*] SERVANT

LORD CHAMBERLAIN　How now—what is't?

SERVANT　　　　　　　　A noble troop of strangers,
55　For so they seem. They've left their barge and landed,
　　And hither make as° great ambassadors　　　　　　*come like*
　　From foreign princes.

CARDINAL WOLSEY　　　Good Lord Chamberlain,
　　Go give 'em welcome—you can speak the French tongue.
　　And pray receive 'em nobly, and conduct 'em

---

3. He would kiss you twenty times with a single breath.
4. If I win my hand (at cards or love).
5. Small cannon fired. The firing of this cannon in a

June 29, 1613, performance of the play probably
caused the fire that destroyed the Globe Theatre. See
the Introduction.

60   Into our presence where this heaven of beauty
      Shall shine at full upon them. Some attend him.
                  [*Exit* CHAMBERLAIN, *attended*]
         All rise, and [*some servants*] *remove* [*the*] *tables*
      You have now a broken banquet, but we'll mend it.
      A good digestion to you all, and once more
      I shower a welcome on ye—welcome all.
        Hautboys. Enter, ushered by the LORD CHAMBERLAIN,
        King [HENRY] *and others as masquers habited like shep-*
        herds. They pass directly before CARDINAL [WOLSEY]
        and gracefully salute him
65   A noble company. What are their pleasures?
    LORD CHAMBERLAIN   Because they speak no English, thus they prayed
      To tell your grace, that, having heard by fame°   *rumor*
      Of this so noble and so fair assembly
      This night to meet here, they could do no less,
70   Out of the great respect they bear to beauty,
      But leave their flocks, and, under your fair conduct,°   *if you'll permit me*
      Crave leave to view these ladies, and entreat
      An hour of revels[6] with 'em.
    CARDINAL WOLSEY   Say, Lord Chamberlain,
      They have done my poor house grace, for which I pay 'em
75   A thousand thanks, and pray 'em take their pleasures.
        [*The masquers*] *choose ladies.* [*The*] KING [*chooses*]
        ANNE *Boleyn*
    KING HENRY [*to* ANNE]   The fairest hand I ever touched. O beauty,
      Till now I never knew thee.
      Music. [*They*] *dance*
    CARDINAL WOLSEY [*to the* LORD CHAMBERLAIN]   My lord.
    LORD CHAMBERLAIN   Your grace.
80   CARDINAL WOLSEY   Pray tell 'em thus much from me.
      There should be one amongst 'em by his person
      More worthy this place° than myself, to whom,   *chair of state*
      If I but knew him, with my love and duty
      I would surrender it.
    LORD CHAMBERLAIN   I will, my lord.
        [*He*] *whisper*[*s with the masquers*]
    CARDINAL WOLSEY   What say they?
85   LORD CHAMBERLAIN   Such a one they all confess
      There is indeed, which they would have your grace
      Find out, and he will take it.°   *(the place of honor)*
    CARDINAL WOLSEY [*standing*]   Let me see then.
      By all your good leaves, gentlemen, here I'll make
      My royal choice.
        [*He bows before the* KING]
    KING HENRY [*unmasking*]   Ye have found him, Cardinal.
90   You hold a fair assembly. You do well, lord.
      You are a churchman, or I'll tell you, Cardinal,
      I should judge now unhappily.[7]
    CARDINAL WOLSEY   I am glad
      Your grace is grown so pleasant.°   *merry*
    KING HENRY   My Lord Chamberlain,
      Prithee come hither.

---

6. Entertainment; perhaps, more specifically, the danc-   7. I would judge such ostentatiousness unfavorably.
ing with the audience of the actors in a court masque.

[*Gesturing towards* ANNE] What fair lady's that?

LORD CHAMBERLAIN   An't° please your grace, Sir Thomas   *If it*
95   Boleyn's daughter—
    The Viscount Rochford—one of her highness' women.

KING HENRY   By heaven, she is a dainty one. [*To* ANNE] Sweetheart,
    I were unmannerly to take you out°   *(to dance)*
    And not to kiss you [*kisses her*]. A health,° gentlemen;   *toast*
    [*He drinks*]
100   Let it go round.

CARDINAL WOLSEY   Sir Thomas Lovell, is the banquet ready
    I'th' privy chamber?

LOVELL   Yes, my lord.

CARDINAL WOLSEY [*to the* KING]   Your grace
    I fear with dancing is a little heated.

KING HENRY   I fear too much.

105   CARDINAL WOLSEY   There's fresher air, my lord,
    In the next chamber.

KING HENRY   Lead in your ladies, every one. [*To* ANNE] Sweet partner,
    I must not yet forsake you. [*To* WOLSEY] Let's be merry,
    Good my lord Cardinal. I have half a dozen healths
110   To drink to these fair ladies, and a measure°   *majestic dance*
    To lead 'em once again, and then let's dream
    Who's best in favour.[8] Let the music knock it.°   *strike it up*

                    Exeunt with trumpets

2.1

    Enter two GENTLEMEN, *at several° doors*   *separate*

FIRST GENTLEMAN   Whither away so fast?

SECOND GENTLEMAN   O, God save ye.
    Ev'n to the hall° to hear what shall become   *Westminster Hall*
    Of the great Duke of Buckingham.

FIRST GENTLEMAN   I'll save you
    That labour, sir. All's now done but the ceremony
    Of bringing back the prisoner.

5   SECOND GENTLEMAN   Were you there?

FIRST GENTLEMAN   Yes, indeed was I.

SECOND GENTLEMAN   Pray speak what has happened.

FIRST GENTLEMAN   You may guess quickly what.

SECOND GENTLEMAN   Is he found guilty?

FIRST GENTLEMAN   Yes, truly is he, and condemned upon't.

SECOND GENTLEMAN   I am sorry for't.

10   FIRST GENTLEMAN   So are a number more.

SECOND GENTLEMAN   But pray, how passed it?°   *how did the trial go*

FIRST GENTLEMAN   I'll tell you in a little.° The great Duke   *concisely*
    Came to the bar, where to his accusations
    He pleaded still not guilty, and allegèd°   *offered up*
15   Many sharp reasons to defeat the law.°   *the crown's case*
    The King's attorney, on the contrary,
    Urged on the examinations,° proofs,° confessions,   *depositions / statements*
    Of divers witnesses, which the Duke desired
    To him brought *viva voce*° to his face—   *in person*
20   At which appeared against him his surveyor,
    Sir Gilbert Perk his chancellor, and John Car,

---

8. Who's most popular with the ladies; who's best   2.1 Location: A street in Westminster.
looking.

Confessor to him, with that devil-monk,
Hopkins, that made this mischief.

SECOND GENTLEMAN   That was he
That fed him with his prophecies.

FIRST GENTLEMAN   The same.
25   All these accused him strongly, which he fain[1]
Would have flung from him, but indeed he could not.
And so his peers, upon this evidence,
Have found him guilty of high treason. Much
He spoke, and learnèdly, for life, but all
30   Was either pitied in him or forgotten.[2]

SECOND GENTLEMAN   After all this, how did he bear himself?

FIRST GENTLEMAN   When he was brought again to th' bar to hear
His knell rung out, his judgement,° he was stirred   sentence
With such an agony he sweat extremely,
35   And something spoke in choler,° ill and hasty;   anger
But he fell to° himself again, and sweetly   got control of
In all the rest showed a most noble patience.

SECOND GENTLEMAN   I do not think he fears death.

FIRST GENTLEMAN   Sure he does not.
He never was so womanish. The cause
He may a little grieve at.

40   SECOND GENTLEMAN   Certainly
The Cardinal is the end° of this.   source

FIRST GENTLEMAN   'Tis likely
By all conjectures: first, Kildare's attainder,
Then deputy of Ireland,[3] who, removed,
Earl Surrey was sent thither—and in haste, too,
Lest he should help his father.°   father-in-law

45   SECOND GENTLEMAN   That trick of state
Was a deep envious° one.   deeply spiteful

FIRST GENTLEMAN   At his return
No doubt he will requite it. This is noted,
And generally:° whoever the King favours,   by all
The Card'nal instantly will find employment—
And far enough from court, too.

50   SECOND GENTLEMAN   All the commons
Hate him perniciously° and, o' my conscience,   want him dead
Wish him ten fathom deep. This Duke as much
They love and dote on, call him 'bounteous Buckingham,
The mirror° of all courtesy[4]—   exemplar

Enter [the Duke of] BUCKINGHAM *from his arraignment, tipstaves before him, the axe with the edge
towards him, halberd[ier]s on each side, accompanied
with Sir Thomas* LOVELL, *Sir Nicholas* VAUX, *Sir
[William]* SANDS,[5] *and common people*

FIRST GENTLEMAN   Stay there, sir,
55   And see the noble ruined man you speak of.

1. Which accusations he gladly.
2. *all . . . forgotten:* (Buckingham's defense) either was
fruitless or brought only pity.
3. Thomas Fitzgerald, Earl of Kildare, Lord Lieutenant
of Ireland, lost his estates and position ("attainder")
and was sentenced to death by Wolsey.
4. Polished manners, but also courtliness more
generally.
5. *tipstaves:* court-appointed officers who carried

tipstaves, staffs tipped with metal. *halberdiers:* guards
who carried halberds, long-handled weapons with both
spear tips and battle-ax blades. "Sir William Sands" is
called "Lord Sands" in the stage directions at the beginning of 1.3 and at 1.4.7. The discrepancy occurs
because the play violates chronology here: Henry and
Anne actually met years after Buckingham's trial, and
Sands became a baron in the interim.

SECOND GENTLEMAN   Let's stand close° and behold him.   *aside; silent*
        [*They stand apart*]
    BUCKINGHAM [*to the common people*]   All good people,
        You that thus far have come to pity me,
        Hear what I say, and then go home and lose° me.   *forget*
        I have this day received a traitor's judgement,°   *sentence*
60   And by that name must die. Yet, heaven bear witness,
        And if I have a conscience let it sink° me,   *destroy*
        Even as the axe falls, if I be not faithful.
        The law I bear no malice for my death.
        'T has done, upon the premises,° but justice.   *evidence*
65   But those that sought it I could wish more° Christians.   *truer*
        Be what they will, I heartily forgive 'em.
        Yet let 'em look° they glory not in mischief,   *beware*
        Nor build their evils on the graves of great men,[6]
        For then my guiltless blood must cry against 'em.
70   For further life in this world I ne'er hope,
        Nor will I sue, although the King have mercies
        More than I dare make faults.° You few that loved me,   *commit misdeeds*
        And dare be bold to weep for Buckingham,
        His noble friends and fellows, whom to leave
75   Is only bitter to him, only dying,[7]
        Go with me like good angels to my end,
        And, as the long divorce° of steel falls on me,   *(of body and soul)*
        Make of your prayers one sweet sacrifice,°   *offering*
        And lift my soul to heaven. [*To the guard*] Lead on, i' God's name.
80 LOVELL   I do beseech your grace, for charity,
        If ever any malice in your heart
        Were hid against me, now to forgive me frankly.
    BUCKINGHAM   Sir Thomas Lovell, I as free forgive you
        As I would be forgiven. I forgive all.
85   There cannot be those numberless offences
        'Gainst me that I cannot take° peace with. No black envy°   *make / spite*
        Shall mark my grave. Commend me to his grace,
        And if he speak of Buckingham, pray tell him
        You met him half in heaven. My vows and prayers
90   Yet are the King's, and, till my soul forsake,°   *depart (my body)*
        Shall cry for blessings on him. May he live
        Longer than I have time to tell° his years;   *count*
        Ever beloved and loving may his rule be;
        And, when old time° shall lead him to his end,   *old age*
95   Goodness and he fill up one monument.°   *share one tomb*
    LOVELL   To th' waterside I must conduct your grace,
        Then give my charge up to Sir Nicholas Vaux,
        Who undertakes° you to your end.   *leads*
    VAUX [*to an attendant*]   Prepare there—
        The Duke is coming. See the barge be ready,
100   And fit it with such furniture° as suits   *trappings*
        The greatness of his person.
    BUCKINGHAM   Nay, Sir Nicholas,
        Let it alone. My state[8] now will but mock me.
        When I came hither I was Lord High Constable

---

6. Nor advance their evil designs through plotting the downfall of noblemen.
7. *His . . . dying*: Leaving his friends is the only bitter part of Buckingham's sentence, the only death.
8. status; "furniture" (line 100).

And Duke of Buckingham; now, poor Edward Bohun.[9]
105   Yet I am richer than my base accusers,
That never knew what truth meant. I now seal it,°   *attest to truth*
And with that blood will make 'em one day groan for't.
My noble father, Henry of Buckingham,
Who first raised head° against usurping Richard,   *an army*
110   Flying for succour to his servant Banister,
Being distressed, was by that wretch betrayed,
And without trial fell. God's peace be with him.
Henry the Seventh succeeding, truly pitying
My father's loss, like a most royal prince,
115   Restored me to my honours, and out of ruins
Made my name once more noble. Now his son,
Henry the Eighth, life, honour, name, and all
That made me happy, at one stroke has taken
For ever from the world. I had my trial,
120   And must needs say a noble one; which makes me
A little happier than my wretched father.
Yet thus far we are one in fortunes: both
Fell by our servants, by those men we loved most—
A most unnatural and faithless service.
125   Heaven has an end° in all. Yet, you that hear me,   *a purpose*
This from a dying man receive as certain—
Where you are liberal of your loves and counsels,
Be sure you be not loose;° for those you make friends   *unrestrained*
And give your hearts to, when they once perceive
130   The least rub° in your fortunes, fall away   *obstacle*
Like water from ye, never found again
But where they mean to sink° ye. All good people   *destroy*
Pray for me. I must now forsake ye. The last hour
Of my long weary life is come upon me.
135   Farewell, and when you would say something that is sad,
Speak how I fell. I have done, and God forgive me.
         Exeunt [the] Duke [of BUCKINGHAM] *and train*
         [*The two* GENTLEMEN *come forward*]
FIRST GENTLEMAN   O, this is full of pity, sir; it calls,
I fear, too many curses on their heads
That were the authors.
SECOND GENTLEMAN   If the Duke be guiltless,
140   'Tis full of woe. Yet I can give you inkling°   *forewarning*
Of an ensuing evil, if it fall,°   *should occur*
Greater than this.
FIRST GENTLEMAN   Good angels keep it from us.
What may it be? You do not doubt my faith,[1] sir?
SECOND GENTLEMAN   This secret is so weighty, 'twill require
A strong faith to conceal it.
145 FIRST GENTLEMAN   Let me have it—
I do not talk much.
SECOND GENTLEMAN   I am confident;°   *I trust you*
You shall, sir. Did you not of late days hear
A buzzing° of a separation   *gossip*
Between the King and Katherine?
FIRST GENTLEMAN   Yes, but it held not.°   *did not persist*

---

9. Actually Edward Stafford; Shakespeare copies Holinshed's mistake.
1. "Faith" (here and in line 145) picks up the religious language of "curses" (line 138) and "angels" (line 142), while suggesting fidelity, loyalty, trustworthiness, and, as line 146 suggests, discretion.

150 For when the King once heard it, out of anger
He sent command to the Lord Mayor straight
To stop the rumour and allay° those tongues   *suppress*
That durst disperse it.
SECOND GENTLEMAN   But that slander, sir,
Is found a truth now, for it grows again
155 Fresher than e'er it was, and held° for certain   *believed*
The King will venture at it. Either the Cardinal
Or some about him near° have, out of malice   *his confidants*
To the good Queen, possessed him with a scruple°   *doubt*
That will undo her. To confirm this, too,
160 Cardinal Campeius² is arrived, and lately,
As all think, for this business.
FIRST GENTLEMAN   'Tis the Cardinal;
And merely to revenge him on the Emperor³
For not bestowing on him at his asking
The Archbishopric of Toledo this is purposed.
SECOND GENTLEMAN   I think you have hit the mark.° But is't not   *guessed correctly*
165   cruel
That she should feel the smart° of this? The Cardinal   *pain*
Will have his will, and she must fall.
FIRST GENTLEMAN   'Tis woeful.
We are too open° here to argue this.   *exposed*
Let's think in private more.   *Exeunt*

2.2

Enter [the] LORD CHAMBERLAIN *[with a] letter*

LORD CHAMBERLAIN *[reads]* 'My lord, the horses your lordship
sent for, with all the care I had, I saw well chosen, ridden, and
furnished.° They were young and handsome, and of the best   *trained and equipped*
breed in the north. When they were ready to set out for Lon-
5   don, a man of my lord Cardinal's, by commission and main
power,¹ took 'em from me with this reason—his master would be
served before a subject, if not before the King; which stopped
our mouths, sir.'
I fear he will indeed. Well, let him have them.
10 He will have all, I think.

Enter to the LORD CHAMBERLAIN *the Dukes of* NORFOLK
and SUFFOLK

NORFOLK   Well met, my Lord Chamberlain.
LORD CHAMBERLAIN   Good day to both your graces.
SUFFOLK   How is the King employed?
LORD CHAMBERLAIN   I left him private,°   *alone*
Full of sad° thoughts and troubles.   *grave*
NORFOLK   What's the cause?
15 LORD CHAMBERLAIN   It seems the marriage with his brother's wife
Has crept too near his conscience.
SUFFOLK   No, his conscience
Has crept too near another lady.

---

2. Henry had to get a special dispensation from the
Pope before marrying Katherine, because her previous
husband was Prince Arthur, Henry's brother, who died
a year after the marriage took place. Wolsey had Cardinal Laurence Campeius (Lorenzo Campeggio) come to
London as a papal legate in 1528 to reopen debate
about the marriage and to aid his plot to have it
annulled.
3. Charles V, Holy Roman Emperor and King of Spain,
was Katherine's nephew.
2.2 Location: The court at London.
1. By warrant and superior strength.

NORFOLK   'Tis so.
This is the Cardinal's doing. The King-Cardinal,
That blind priest, like the eldest son of fortune,
20   Turns what he list.[2] The King will know him° one day.   *(for what he is)*
SUFFOLK   Pray God he do. He'll never know himself else.
NORFOLK   How holily he° works in all his business,   *(Wolsey)*
And with what zeal! For now he has cracked the league
Between us and the Emperor, the Queen's great-nephew,[3]
25   He dives into the King's soul and there scatters
Dangers, doubts, wringing° of the conscience,   *affliction*
Fears, and despairs—and all these for his marriage.
And out of all these, to restore the King,
He counsels a divorce—a loss of her
30   That like a jewel has hung twenty years
About his neck, yet never lost her lustre;
Of her that loves him with that excellence°   *great virtue*
That angels love good men with; even of her
That, when the greatest stroke° of fortune falls,   *severest blow*
35   Will bless the King[4]—and is not this course° pious?°   *(of action)* / *(ironic)*
LORD CHAMBERLAIN   Heaven keep me from such counsel! 'Tis most true—
These news are everywhere, every tongue speaks 'em,
And every true heart weeps for't. All that dare
Look into these affairs see this main end°—   *ultimate aim*
40   The French king's sister.[5] Heaven will one day open
The King's eyes, that so long have slept, upon
This bold bad man.
SUFFOLK   And free us from his slavery.
NORFOLK   We had need pray,
45   And heartily, for our deliverance,
Or this imperious man will work us all
From princes into pages. All men's honours
Lie like one lump° before him, to be fashioned   *(of clay)*
Into what pitch° he please.   *stature*
SUFFOLK   For me, my lords,
50   I love him not, nor fear him—there's my creed.
As I am made without him, so I'll stand,[6]
If the King please. His curses and his blessings
Touch me alike; they're breath I° not believe in.   *I do*
I knew him, and I know him; so I leave him
To him that made him proud—the Pope.
55   NORFOLK   Let's in,
And with some other business put the King
From these sad thoughts that work too much upon him.
[*To the* LORD CHAMBERLAIN] My lord, you'll bear us company?
LORD CHAMBERLAIN   Excuse me,
The King has sent me otherwhere. Besides,
60   You'll find a most unfit time to disturb him.
Health to your lordships.

---

2. *The King-Cardinal . . . list:* Like Fortune, his
mother, Wolsey blindly turns the wheel of fortune as he
likes ("list").
3. Wolsey has now broken the alliance between Henry
and Charles V to get additional revenge on Charles: see
2.1.161–64. Previously (1.1.176–93), to gain favor
with Charles, he engineered the breaking of the treaty
with France sealed at the Field of the Cloth of Gold.

4. Prophetic: Katherine does later "bless the King"
who has repudiated her (4.2.164).
5. Henry's marriage to the Duchess of Alençon will reunite the English and French Kings, thus still further
injuring Charles V. See 3.2.86–87.
6. Since not Wolsey but the King granted my nobility
of rank, I'll remain firm in my position.

NORFOLK   Thanks, my good Lord Chamberlain.

                         Exit [the] LORD CHAMBERLAIN

              KING [HENRY] *draws the curtain,*[7] *and sits reading pen-*
              sively

SUFFOLK   How sad° he looks! Sure he is much afflicted.°   *grave / distressed*

KING HENRY   Who's there? Ha?

NORFOLK   Pray God he be not angry.

KING HENRY   Who's there, I say? How dare you thrust yourselves

65   Into my private meditations!

    Who am I? Ha?

NORFOLK   A gracious king that pardons all offences

    Malice ne'er meant. Our breach of duty this way°   *in this respect*

    Is business of estate,° in which we come   *state*

    To know your royal pleasure.

70   KING HENRY   Ye are too bold.

    Go to, I'll make ye know your times of business.

    Is this an hour for temporal affairs? Ha?

        Enter [CARDINAL] WOLSEY *and* [CARDINAL] CAMPEIUS,
        [*the latter*] *with a commission*

    Who's there? My good lord Cardinal? O, my Wolsey,

    The quiet° of my wounded conscience,   *ease*

    Thou art a cure° fit for a king.   *balm; curate (priest)*

75   [*To* CAMPEIUS]   You're welcome,

    Most learnèd reverend sir, into our kingdom.

    Use us, and it. [*To* WOLSEY] My good lord, have great care

    I be not found a talker.[8]

CARDINAL WOLSEY   Sir, you cannot.

    I would your grace would give us but an hour

    Of private conference.

80   KING HENRY [*to* NORFOLK *and* SUFFOLK]   We are busy; go.

    [NORFOLK *and* SUFFOLK *speak privately to one another*
    as they depart]

NORFOLK   This priest has no pride in him!°   *(more irony)*

SUFFOLK   Not to speak of.

    I would not be so sick, though, for his place[9]—

    But this cannot continue.

NORFOLK   If it do

    I'll venture one have-at-him.°   *thrust (in fencing)*

SUFFOLK   I another.

        Exeunt NORFOLK *and* SUFFOLK

CARDINAL WOLSEY [*to the* KING]   Your grace has given a precedent°   *model*

85   of wisdom

    Above all princes in committing freely

    Your scruple to the voice of Christendom.[1]

    Who can be angry now? What envy reach you?

    The Spaniard,° tied by blood and favour to her,   *Charles V*

90   Must now confess, if they have any goodness,

    The trial just and noble. All the clerks°—   *clerics*

    I mean the learnèd ones in Christian kingdoms—

    Have their free voices.° Rome, the nurse of judgement,   *may vote freely*

---

7. Almost certainly drawn by an attendant. The King's chamber is upstage in the discovery space, a curtained-off, perhaps recessed area at the back of the stage.
8. *have . . . talker:* make sure my offer of hospitality counts for more than mere words.

9. I would not want to be afflicted with such pride, even for his exalted position.
1. *voice of Christendom:* the papal legate Campeius and the representatives of the great European universities who have come to England to hear the case.

Invited by your noble self, hath sent
95 One general tongue° unto us: this good man,   *representative voice*
This just and learnèd priest, Card'nal Campeius,
Whom once more I present unto your highness.
KING HENRY [*embracing* CAMPEIUS]   And once more in mine
        arms I bid him welcome,
And thank the holy conclave° for their loves.   *College of Cardinals*
100 They have sent me such a man I would have wished for.
CARDINAL CAMPEIUS   Your grace must needs deserve all strangers'° loves,   *foreigners'*
You are so noble. To your highness' hand
I tender my commission,
        [*He gives the commission to the* KING]
[*to* WOLSEY]   by whose virtue,
The Court of Rome commanding, you, my lord
105 Cardinal of York, are joined with me their servant
In the unpartial° judging of this business.   *impartial*
KING HENRY   Two equal° men. The Queen shall be acquainted°   *fair / apprised*
Forthwith for what you come. Where's Gardiner?
CARDINAL WOLSEY   I know your majesty has always loved her
110 So dear in heart not to deny her that°   *that which*
A woman of less place° might ask by law—   *rank*
Scholars allowed freely to argue for her.
KING HENRY   Ay, and the best she shall have, and my favour
To him that does best, God forbid else. Cardinal,
115 Prithee call Gardiner to me, my new secretary.[2]
        [CARDINAL WOLSEY *goes to the door and calls* GARDINER]
I find him a fit fellow.
        Enter GARDINER
CARDINAL WOLSEY [*aside to* GARDINER]   Give me your hand. Much joy
        and favour to you.
You are the King's now.
GARDINER [*aside to* WOLSEY]   But to be commanded
For ever by your grace, whose hand has raised me.
120 KING HENRY   Come hither, Gardiner.
        [*The* KING] *walks* [*with* GARDINER] *and whispers* [*with
        him*]
CARDINAL CAMPEIUS [*to* WOLSEY]   My lord of York, was not one
        Doctor Pace[3]
In this man's place before him?
CARDINAL WOLSEY   Yes, he was.
CARDINAL CAMPEIUS   Was he not held a learnèd man?
CARDINAL WOLSEY   Yes, surely.
CARDINAL CAMPEIUS   Believe me, there's an ill opinion spread then,
        Even of yourself, lord Cardinal.
125 CARDINAL WOLSEY   How? Of me?
CARDINAL CAMPEIUS   They will not stick° to say you envied him,   *scruple*
And fearing he would rise, he was so virtuous,
Kept him a foreign man still,° which so grieved him   *always abroad*
That he ran mad and died.
CARDINAL WOLSEY   Heav'n's peace be with him—
130 That's Christian care enough. For living murmurers°   *malcontents*

---

2. Stephen Gardiner, former secretary to Wolsey, became Henry's secretary in July 1529 through Wolsey's preferment, and Bishop of Winchester in 1531.
3. Richard Pace, the King's former secretary, was now sent frequently abroad by Wolsey on diplomatic business, apparently as punishment for becoming too close to the King.

There's places of rebuke. He was a fool,
For he would needs be virtuous.
[*Gesturing towards* GARDINER]   That good fellow,
If I command him, follows my appointment.°   *orders*
I will have none so near⁴ else. Learn this, brother:
135   We live not to be griped° by meaner persons.   *grasped; brought down*
KING HENRY [*to* GARDINER]   Deliver this with modesty° to th'   *Announce this mildly*
        Queen.   *Exit* GARDINER
The most convenient place that I can think of
For such receipt of⁵ learning is Blackfriars;
There ye shall meet about this weighty business.
140   My Wolsey, see it furnished.° O, my lord,   *fitted out properly*
Would it not grieve an able° man to leave   *a (sexually) vigorous*
So sweet a bedfellow? But conscience, conscience—
O, 'tis a tender place,° and I must leave her.   *Exeunt*   *(conscience); (sexual)*

2.3

Enter ANNE *Boleyn and an* OLD LADY

ANNE   Not for that neither. Here's the pang that pinches°—   *pain that torments*
His highness having lived so long with her, and she
So good a lady that no tongue could ever
Pronounce dishonour of her—by my life,
5   She never knew harm-doing—O now, after
So many courses of the sun° enthronèd,   *years*
Still° growing in a majesty and pomp the which   *Ever*
To leave a thousandfold more bitter than
'Tis sweet at first t'acquire—after this process,
10   To give her the avaunt,° it is a pity   *boot*
Would move a monster.
OLD LADY   Hearts of most hard temper°   *constitution*
Melt and lament for her.
ANNE   O, God's will! Much better
She ne'er had known pomp; though't be temporal,°   *only of this world*
Yet if that quarrel,° fortune, do divorce   *quarreler*
15   It from the bearer, 'tis a sufferance panging°   *as painful*
As soul and bodies severing.
OLD LADY   Alas, poor lady!
She's a stranger° now again.   *foreigner*
ANNE   So much the more
Must pity drop upon her. Verily,
I swear, 'tis better to be lowly born
20   And range with humble livers in content
Than to be perked up in a glist'ring grief¹
And wear a golden sorrow.
OLD LADY   Our content
Is our best having.°   *possession*
ANNE   By my troth° and maidenhead,   *faith*
I would not be a queen.
OLD LADY   Beshrew me,° I would—   *Devil take me*
25   And venture maidenhead for't; and so would you,
For all this spice° of your hypocrisy.   *sample*
You, that have so fair parts° of woman on you,   *qualities; beauty*

4. I want no one else on such intimate terms with the King.
5. For hearing such scholarly disputation, or such scholars.

2.3 Location: The Queen's apartments at court.
1. *'tis . . . grief*: it's better to be born poor and to occupy a lowly rank happily than to be unhappy despite one's riches (literally, to be dressed up in a glittering sadness).

Have, too, a woman's heart which ever yet
Affected° eminence, wealth, sovereignty;   *Craved*
30 Which, to say sooth,° are blessings; and which gifts,   *truth*
Saving your mincing,° the capacity   *Despite your affectation*
Of your soft cheveril° conscience would receive   *kid leather (pliant)*
If you might please to stretch it.
ANNE   Nay, good troth.[2]
OLD LADY   Yes, troth and troth. You would not be a queen?
35 ANNE   No, not for all the riches under heaven.
OLD LADY   'Tis strange. A threepence bowed would hire me,
    Old as I am, to queen it.[3] But I pray you,
    What think you of a duchess? Have you limbs
    To bear that load of title?
ANNE   No, in truth.
40 OLD LADY   Then you are weakly made. Pluck off[4] a little;
    I would not be a young count in your way
    For more than blushing comes to.[5] If your back
    Cannot vouchsafe this burden,[6] 'tis too weak
    Ever to get a boy.
ANNE   How you do talk!
45 I swear again, I would not be a queen
For all the world.
OLD LADY   In faith, for little England
    You'd venture an emballing;[7] I myself
    Would for Caernarfonshire,[8] although there 'longed°   *belonged*
    No more to th' crown but that. Lo, who comes here?
          Enter [the] LORD CHAMBERLAIN
50 LORD CHAMBERLAIN   Good morrow, ladies. What were't worth to know
    The secret of your conference?°   *conversation*
ANNE   My good lord,
    Not your demand; it values not° your asking.   *does not merit*
    Our mistress' sorrows we were pitying.
LORD CHAMBERLAIN   It was a gentle business, and becoming
55 The action of good women. There is hope
All will be well.
ANNE   Now I pray God, amen.
LORD CHAMBERLAIN   You bear a gentle mind, and heav'nly blessings
    Follow such creatures. That you may, fair lady,
    Perceive I speak sincerely, and high note's
60 Ta'en of your many virtues, the King's majesty
Commends his good opinion of you,° and   *Sends his compliments*
Does purpose° honour to you no less flowing°   *intend / copious*
Than Marchioness of Pembroke; to which title
A thousand pound a year annual support
Out of his grace he adds.
65 ANNE   I do not know
    What kind of my obedience I should tender.

---

2. Faith (exclamatory); perhaps a pun on "trot," a demeaning term for an old woman.
3. *A threepence . . . it:* A bent ("bowed") and hence worthless coin would convince me to be a Queen. Sexual puns ("queen"—"quean," or whore; "bowed"— bawd) continue through the scene.
4. Come lower in rank; undress.
5. *I . . . to:* Perhaps: If you persist in this "way" (path; being unable to bear the load of being duchess; condi-

tion of virginity), a "count" (an earl, the rank below duke) will get no more from you than blushes. Also: I would give up being a young virginal cunt ("count") like you with no more than a blush.
6. Cannot bear these honors. "Burden," like "bear" (line 39), suggests both intercourse and childbearing.
7. *for . . . emballing:* for England you'd accept investiture with the royal emblem of ball and scepter (you'd get laid).
8. Particularly poor Welsh county.

More than my all is nothing; nor my prayers
Are not° words duly hallowed, nor my wishes   *no more than*
More worth than empty vanities; yet prayers and wishes
70   Are all I can return. Beseech your lordship,
Vouchsafe° to speak my thanks and my obedience,   *Condescend*
As from a blushing handmaid to his highness,
Whose health and royalty I pray for.
LORD CHAMBERLAIN   Lady,
I shall not fail t'approve° the fair conceit°   *endorse / opinion*
75   The King hath of you. [*Aside*] I have perused her well.
Beauty and honour in her are so mingled
That they have caught the King, and who knows yet
But from this lady may proceed a gem
To lighten⁹ all this isle. [*To* ANNE] I'll to the King
80   And say I spoke with you.
ANNE   My honoured lord.

                              Exit [*the*] LORD CHAMBERLAIN

OLD LADY   Why, this it is—see, see!
I have been begging sixteen years in court,
Am yet a courtier beggarly,° nor could   *still begging*
85   Come pat betwixt too early and too late
For any suit of pounds;¹ and you—O, fate!—
A very fresh fish here—fie, fie upon
This compelled° fortune!—have your mouth filled up   *forced upon you*
Before you open it.
ANNE   This is strange to me.
90   OLD LADY   How tastes it? Is it bitter? Forty pence, no.²
There was a lady once—'tis an old story—
That would not be a queen, that would she not,
For all the mud in Egypt.³ Have you heard it?
ANNE   Come, you are pleasant.°   *merry; joking*
OLD LADY   With your theme I could
95   O'ermount the lark. The Marchioness of Pembroke?
A thousand pounds a year, for pure° respect?   *mere*
No other obligation? By my life,
That promises more thousands. Honour's train
Is longer than his foreskirt.⁴ By this time
100   I know your back will bear a duchess. Say,
Are you not stronger than you were?
ANNE   Good lady,
Make yourself mirth with your particular fancy,°   *private fantasies*
And leave me out on't. Would I had no being,
If this salute° my blood a jot. It faints me°   *agitates / I faint*
105   To think what follows.⁵
The Queen is comfortless, and we forgetful
In our long absence. Pray do not deliver
What here you've heard to her.
OLD LADY   What do you think me—

                                             Exeunt

---

9. To bring light to (alluding to Elizabeth), with religious connotations. Gems were believed to emit light.
1. *nor . . . pounds:* nor could I arrive at just the right moment to succeed in any petition for money.
2. I'll bet a small sum (conventionally, 40 pence) that it isn't.
3. For all the wealth (in this case, the fertile land, or

"mud") of Egypt.
4. *That . . . foreskirt:* Future rewards will exceed present ones, just as a noblewoman's dress is longer in back than in front.
5. "What follows," ultimately, is Anne's execution at Henry's order in 1536, on the charge of adultery.

2.4

Trumpets: sennet.° [Then] cornetts. Enter two vergers[1]   fanfare
with short silver wands; next them two SCRIBES *in the*
habit of doctors;[2] after them the [Arch]bishop of Can-
terbury alone; after him the Bishops of LINCOLN, *Ely,*
Rochester, and Saint Asaph; next them, with some small
distance, follows a gentleman bearing [both] the purse
[containing] the great seal and a cardinal's hat; then
two priests bearing each a silver cross; then a gentleman
usher, bare-headed, accompanied with a serjeant-at-
arms bearing a silver mace;° then two gentlemen bear-   ceremonial staff
ing two great silver pillars; after them, side by side, the
*two cardinals, [*WOLSEY *and* CAMPEIUS; *then] two noble-*
men with the sword and mace. The KING *[ascends to his*
seat] under the cloth of state; the two cardinals sit
under him as judges; the QUEEN *[attended by* GRIFFITH
her gentleman usher] takes place some distance from
the KING; *the Bishops place themselves on each side the*
court in [the] manner of a consistory,° below them,   church court
the SCRIBES. *The lords sit next the Bishops. The rest of*
the attendants stand in convenient order about the stage

CARDINAL WOLSEY   Whilst our commission from Rome is read
  Let silence be commanded.
KING HENRY   What's the need?
  It hath already publicly been read,
  And on all sides th'authority allowed.°   accepted
  You may then spare that time.
5 CARDINAL WOLSEY   Be't so. Proceed.
SCRIBE [*to the* CRIER]   Say, 'Henry, King of England, come into the court'.
CRIER   Henry, King of England, come into the court.
KING HENRY   Here.
SCRIBE [*to the* CRIER]   Say, 'Katherine, Queen of England, come
  into the court'.
10 CRIER   Katherine, Queen of England, come into the court.
    The QUEEN *makes no answer, [but] rises out of her chair,*
    goes about the court, comes to the KING, *and kneels at*
    his feet. Then [she] speaks
QUEEN KATHERINE   Sir, I desire you do me right and justice,
  And to bestow your pity on me; for
  I am a most poor woman, and a stranger,°   foreigner
  Born out of your dominions, having here
15 No judge indifferent,° nor no more assurance   impartial
  Of equal° friendship and proceeding.° Alas, sir,   just / legal order
  In what have I offended you? What cause
  Hath my behaviour given to your displeasure
  That thus you should proceed to put me off,°   abandon me
20 And take your good grace° from me? Heaven witness   good will; yourself
  I have been to you a true and humble wife,
  At all times to your will conformable,

2.4 Location: A hall in Blackfriars.
1. Officials who carry the verge (a staff symbolizing the
authority of office) before a bishop or other dignitary.
2. Furred black gown and flat caps of doctors of law.

Ever in fear to kindle your dislike,
Yea, subject to your countenance, glad or sorry
25 As I saw it inclined. When was the hour
I ever contradicted your desire,
Or made it not mine too? Or which of your friends
Have I not strove to love, although I knew
He were mine enemy? What friend of mine
30 That had to him derived° your anger did I   *incurred*
Continue in my liking? Nay, gave notice
He was from thence discharged? Sir, call to mind
That I have been your wife in this obedience
Upward of twenty years, and have been blessed
35 With many children by you.[3] If, in the course
And process of this time, you can report—
And prove it, too—against mine honour aught,°   *anything*
My bond to wedlock, or my love and duty
Against° your sacred person, in God's name   *Toward*
40 Turn me away, and let the foul'st contempt
Shut door upon me, and so give me up
To the sharp'st kind of justice. Please you, sir,
The King your father was reputed for
A prince most prudent, of an excellent
45 And unmatched wit° and judgement. Ferdinand   *wisdom*
My father, King of Spain, was reckoned one
The wisest[4] prince that there had reigned by many
A year before. It is not to be questioned
That they had gathered a wise council to them
50 Of every realm, that did debate this business,
Who deemed our marriage lawful. Wherefore I humbly
Beseech you, sir, to spare me till I may
Be by my friends in Spain advised, whose counsel
I will implore. If not, i'th' name of God,
Your pleasure be fulfilled.
55 CARDINAL WOLSEY   You have here, lady,
And of your choice, these reverend fathers, men
Of singular integrity and learning,
Yea, the elect o'th' land, who are assembled
To plead your cause. It shall be therefore bootless°   *pointless*
60 That longer you desire° the court, as well   *beg (for a delay)*
For your own quiet,° as to rectify   *peace of mind*
What is unsettled in the King.
CARDINAL CAMPEIUS   His grace
Hath spoken well and justly. Therefore, madam,
It's fit this royal session do proceed,
65 And that without delay their arguments
Be now produced and heard.
QUEEN KATHERINE [*to* WOLSEY]   Lord Cardinal,
To you I speak.
CARDINAL WOLSEY   Your pleasure, madam.
QUEEN KATHERINE   Sir,
I am about to weep, but thinking that
We are a queen, or long have dreamed so, certain°   *without doubt*

---

3. Queen Katherine bore five of Henry's children. All   4. *was ... wisest:* was judged the very wisest.
but one, later Queen Mary, died at birth or in infancy.

70 The daughter of a king, my drops of tears
    I'll turn to sparks of fire.

CARDINAL WOLSEY   Be patient yet.

QUEEN KATHERINE   I will when you are humble! Nay, before,
    Or God will punish me. I do believe,
    Induced° by potent circumstances, that   *Convinced*
75 You are mine enemy, and make my challenge°   *legal objection that*
    You shall not be my judge. For it is you
    Have blown this coal betwixt my lord and me,
    Which God's dew quench. Therefore I say again,
    I utterly abhor,° yea, from my soul,   *loathe; reject*
80 Refuse you for my judge, whom yet once more
    I hold my most malicious foe, and think not
    At all a friend to truth.

CARDINAL WOLSEY   I do profess°   *declare*
    You speak not like yourself, who ever yet°   *always*
    Have stood to° charity, and displayed th'effects   *upheld*
85 Of disposition gentle and of wisdom
    O'er-topping woman's power. Madam, you do me wrong.
    I have no spleen° against you, nor injustice   *malevolence*
    For you or any. How far I have proceeded,
    Or how far further shall, is warranted
90 By a commission from the consistory,°   *College of Cardinals*
    Yea, the whole consistory of Rome. You charge me
    That I 'have blown this coal'. I do deny it.
    The King is present. If it be known to him
    That I gainsay my deed,° how may he wound,   *deny what took place*
95 And worthily,° my falsehood—yea, as much   *justly*
    As you have done my truth. If he know
    That I am free of your report, he knows
    I am not of your wrong.[5] Therefore in him
    It lies to cure° me, and the cure is to   *absolve*
100 Remove these thoughts from you. The which before
    His highness shall speak in,° I do beseech   *about*
    You, gracious madam, to unthink your speaking,
    And to say so no more.

QUEEN KATHERINE   My lord, my lord—
    I am a simple woman, much too weak
105 T'oppose your cunning. You're meek and humble-mouthed;
    You sign your place and calling, in full seeming,
    With meekness and humility[6]—but your heart
    Is crammed with arrogancy, spleen,° and pride.   *malice*
    You have by fortune and his highness' favours
110 Gone slightly° o'er low steps, and now are mounted   *effortlessly*
    Where powers are your retainers, and your words,
    Domestics to you, serve your will as't please
    Yourself pronounce their office.[7] I must tell you,
    You tender more° your person's honour than   *have more regard for*
115 Your high profession spiritual, that again
    I do refuse you for my judge, and here,

---

5. *If . . . wrong*: If he agrees that I am innocent ("free") of your accusation, then he knows that I have done you no wrong; and that I have no part in the wrong you do me by thus accusing me.

6. *You . . . humility*: You mark your office and role with great outward display of meekness and humility.

7. *and now . . . office*: and now have attained a place where men of authority ("powers") serve you, and your words are like attendants ("domestics"), which transform into deeds anything you pronounce as your will.

Before you all, appeal unto the Pope,
To bring my whole cause 'fore his holiness,
And to be judged by him.

She curtsies to the KING *and [begins] to depart*

CARDINAL CAMPEIUS   The Queen is obstinate,
120 Stubborn° to justice, apt to accuse it, and   Impervious
Disdainful to be tried by't. 'Tis not well.
She's going away.

KING HENRY [*to the* CRIER]   Call her again.

CRIER   Katherine, Queen of England, come into the court.

GRIFFITH [*to the* QUEEN]   Madam, you are called back.

QUEEN KATHERINE   What° need you note it? Pray you keep your   Why
125   way.°   keep going
When *you* are called, return. Now the Lord help.
They vex me past my patience. Pray you, pass on.
I will not tarry; no, nor ever more
Upon this business my appearance make
In any of their courts.

Exeunt QUEEN [KATHERINE] *and her attendants*

130 KING HENRY   Go thy ways, Kate.
That man i'th' world who shall report he has
A better wife, let him in naught be trusted
For speaking false in that. Thou art alone—
If thy rare qualities, sweet gentleness,
135 Thy meekness saint-like, wife-like government,°   restraint
Obeying in commanding,[8] and thy parts°   qualities
Sovereign and pious else° could speak thee out°—   besides / describe you
The queen of earthly queens. She's noble born,
And like her true nobility she has
Carried° herself towards me.   Conducted

140 CARDINAL WOLSEY   Most gracious sir,
In humblest manner I require° your highness   entreat
That it shall please you to declare in hearing
Of all these ears—for where I am robbed and bound,
There must I be unloosed, although not there
145 At once and fully satisfied°—whether ever I   given recompense
Did broach this business to your highness, or
Laid any scruple in your way which might
Induce you to the question on't,° or ever   of it
Have to you, but with thanks to God for such
150 A royal lady, spake one the least° word that might   the very least
Be to the prejudice of her present state,
Or touch° of her good person?   censure

KING HENRY   My lord Cardinal,
I do excuse you;° yea, upon mine honour,   forgive you fully
I free you from't. You are not° to be taught   do not require
155 That you have many enemies that know not
Why they are so, but, like to village curs,
Bark when their fellows do. By some of these
The Queen is put in anger. You're excused.
But will you be more justified?° You ever   vindicated
160 Have wished the sleeping of this business, never desired
It to be stirred, but oft have hindered, oft,

8. Acting like an obedient wife even as you rule like a Queen.

The passages° made toward it. On my honour   *proceedings*
I speak my good lord Card'nal to this point,
And thus far clear him.⁹ Now, what moved me to't,°   *convinced me of it*
165   I will be bold with time and your attention.
Then mark th'inducement.° Thus it came—give heed to't.   *what influenced me*
My conscience first received a tenderness,°   *sensitivity*
Scruple, and prick, on° certain speeches uttered   *from*
By th' Bishop of Bayonne, then French Ambassador,
170   Who had been hither sent on the debating
A marriage 'twixt the Duke of Orléans¹ and
Our daughter Mary. I'th' progress of this business,
Ere a determinate resolution,° he—   *decisive settlement*
I mean the Bishop—did require a respite
175   Wherein he might the King his lord advertise°   *make aware*
Whether our daughter were legitimate,
Respecting this our marriage with the dowager,
Sometimes° our brother's wife. This respite shook   *Formerly*
The bosom of my conscience, entered me,
180   Yea, with a spitting° power, and made to tremble   *piercing*
The region of my breast; which forced such way
That many mazed considerings did throng
And prest in with this caution.² First, methought
I stood not in the smile of heaven, who had
185   Commanded nature that my lady's womb,
If it conceived a male child by me, should
Do no more offices of life to't than
The grave does yield to th' dead. For her male issue
Or° died where they were made, or shortly after   *Either*
190   This world had aired them.° Hence I took a thought   *given life to; shown*
This was a judgement on me that my kingdom,
Well worthy the best heir³ o'th' world, should not
Be gladded° in't by me. Then follows that   *made joyful*
I weighed the danger which my realms stood in
195   By this my issue's fail,° and that gave to me   *lack; death*
Many a groaning throe.° Thus hulling in⁴   *pang (of pregnancy)*
The wild sea of my conscience, I did steer
Toward this remedy, whereupon we are
Now present here together—that's to say
200   I meant to rectify my conscience, which
I then did feel full sick, and yet° not well,   *still*
By all the reverend fathers of the land
And doctors learned. First I began in private
With you, my lord of Lincoln.⁵ You remember
205   How under my oppression I did reek°   *sweat*
When I first moved° you.   *appealed to*
LINCOLN   Very well, my liege.
KING HENRY   I have spoke long. Be pleased yourself to say
How far you satisfied me.

---

9. *I speak . . . Him*: Here the King speaks to the court as a whole, announcing that up to this point he exonerates the Cardinal of any wrongdoing.
1. Second son of King Francis I of France, he later became Henry II of France.
2. *many . . . caution*: many confused thoughts crowded

in at this warning.
3. Pun on "aired" (line 190).
4. Floating aimlessly, like a ship adrift in the current that is not making use of its sails.
5. The Bishop of Lincoln, according to Holinshed, was the King's confessor.

LINCOLN   So please your highness,
The question did at first so stagger me,
210 Bearing a state of mighty moment° in't   *so weighty, urgent a matter*
And consequence of dread,° that I committed   *dire consequences*
The daring'st counsel which I had to doubt,[6]
And did entreat your highness to this course
Which you are running here.
KING HENRY [*to Canterbury*]   I then moved you,
215 My lord of Canterbury, and got your leave
To make this present summons. Unsolicited
I left no reverend person in this court,
But by particular consent proceeded
Under your hands and seals.[7] Therefore, go on,
220 For no dislike i'th' world against the person
Of the good Queen, but the sharp thorny points
Of my allegèd° reasons, drives this forward.   *advanced by me*
Prove but our marriage lawful, by my life
And kingly dignity, we are contented
225 To wear our mortal state to come with her,
Katherine, our queen, before the primest° creature   *most perfect*
That's paragoned o'°th' world.   *considered a model by*
CARDINAL CAMPEIUS   So please your highness,
The Queen being absent, 'tis a needful fitness°   *only appropriate*
That we adjourn this court till further° day.   *a later*
230 Meanwhile must be an earnest motion°   *plea*
Made to the Queen to call back her appeal
She intends unto his holiness.
KING HENRY [*aside*]   I may perceive
These cardinals trifle with me. I abhor
This dilatory sloth and tricks of Rome.
235 My learnèd and well-belovèd servant, Cranmer,
Prithee return.[8] With thy approach I know
My comfort comes along. [*Aloud*] Break up the court.
I say, set on.°   *Exeunt in manner as they entered*   *proceed*

3.1

Enter QUEEN [KATHERINE] *and her women, as at work*
QUEEN KATHERINE   Take thy lute, wench. My soul grows sad with troubles.
Sing, and disperse 'em if thou canst. Leave° working.   *Cease*
GENTLEWOMAN [*sings*]   Orpheus[1] with his lute made trees,
And the mountain tops that freeze,
5   Bow themselves when he did sing.
To his music plants and flowers
Ever sprung, as° sun and showers   *as if*
There had made a lasting spring.
Everything that heard him play,
10   Even the billows of the sea,
Hung their heads, and then lay by.°   *were still*

---

6. *I committed . . . doubt:* I distrusted even the boldest
advice I myself could offer.
7. With your written agreement.
8. The King here apostrophizes Thomas Cranmer, who
is not present but is traveling on the Continent collecting opinions on the status of Henry and Katherine's

marriage. See 3.2.401–02 for mention of his return and
his elevation to the position of Archbishop of Canterbury.
3.1 Location: The Queen's apartments at court.
1. In Greek mythology, he was famous for the power of
his music.

In sweet music is such art,
Killing care and grief of heart
Fall asleep, or hearing, die.

Enter [GRIFFITH,] *a gentleman*

15 QUEEN KATHERINE   How now?

GRIFFITH   An't please your grace, the two great cardinals
Wait in the presence.°   reception chamber

QUEEN KATHERINE   Would they speak with me?

GRIFFITH   They willed me say so, madam.

QUEEN KATHERINE   Pray their graces
To come near.   [*Exit* GRIFFITH]
               What can be their business
20 With me, a poor weak woman, fall'n from favour?
I do not like their coming, now I think on't;
They should be good men, their affairs as righteous—
But all hoods make not monks.²

Enter the two cardinals, WOLSEY *and* CAMPEIUS [*ushered*
by GRIFFITH]

CARDINAL WOLSEY   Peace to your highness.

QUEEN KATHERINE   Your graces find me here part of a housewife—
25 I would be all,³ against° the worst may happen.   in case
What are your pleasures with me, reverend lords?

CARDINAL WOLSEY   May it please you, noble madam, to withdraw
Into your private chamber, we shall give you
The full cause of our coming.

QUEEN KATHERINE   Speak it here.
30 There's nothing I have done yet, o' my conscience,
Deserves a corner.° Would all other women   subterfuge
Could speak this with as free° a soul as I do.   innocent
My lords, I care not—so much I am happy°   favored
Above a number°—if my actions   many
35 Were tried by ev'ry tongue, ev'ry eye saw 'em,
Envy and base opinion° set against 'em,   Spite and base gossip
I know my life so even.° If your business   uniformly virtuous
Seek me out and that way I am wife in,⁴
Out with it boldly. Truth loves open dealing.

40 CARDINAL WOLSEY   *Tanta est erga te mentis integritas, Regina serenissima*⁵—

QUEEN KATHERINE   O, good my lord, no Latin.
I am not such a truant° since my coming°   so idle / (to England)
As not to know the language I have lived in.
A strange° tongue makes my cause more strange° suspicious—   foreign / unusually
45 Pray, speak in English. Here are some will thank you,
If you speak truth, for their poor mistress' sake.
Believe me, she has had much wrong. Lord Cardinal,
The willing'st° sin I ever yet committed   most premeditated
May be absolved in English.

CARDINAL WOLSEY   Noble lady,
50 I am sorry my integrity should breed—
And service to his majesty and you—
So deep suspicion, where all faith° was meant.   loyalty
We come not by the way° of accusation,   for the sake

2. Proverbial: religious trappings do not ensure piety.   behavior as wife.
3. I would like to be not just partly but completely a   5. So great is the integrity of (my) mind toward you,
housewife.   most serene Queen (Latin).
4. *If . . . in:* If your business concerns me and my

To taint that honour every good tongue blesses,

55 Nor to betray you any way° to sorrow—   *by any means*
You have too much, good lady—but to know
How you stand minded° in the weighty difference   *Your deliberation*
Between the King and you, and to deliver,°   *recount*
Like free° and honest men, our just opinions   *unprejudiced*
And comforts to your cause.

60 CARDINAL CAMPEIUS   Most honoured madam,
My lord of York, out of his noble nature,
Zeal, and obedience he still bore° your grace,   *has always borne*
Forgetting, like a good man, your late censure
Both of his truth and him—which was° too far—   *went*
65 Offers, as I do, in a sign of peace,
His service and his counsel.

QUEEN KATHERINE [*aside*]   To betray me.
[*Aloud*] My lords, I thank you both for your good wills.
Ye speak like honest men—pray God ye prove so.
But how to make ye suddenly° an answer   *without deliberation*
70 In such a point of weight, so near° mine honour—   *bound up with*
More near my life, I fear—with my weak wit,°   *comprehension*
And to such men of gravity and learning,
In truth I know not. I was set° at work   *sitting*
Among my maids, full little—God knows—looking
75 Either for such men or such business.
For her sake that I have been[6]—for I feel
The last fit° of my greatness—good your graces,   *spell*
Let me have time and counsel for my cause.
Alas, I am a woman friendless, hopeless.

80 CARDINAL WOLSEY   Madam, you wrong the King's love with these fears.
Your hopes and friends are infinite.

QUEEN KATHERINE   In England
But little for my profit.° Can you think, lords,   *of little use to me*
That any Englishman dare give me counsel,
Or be a known friend 'gainst his highness' pleasure—
85 Though he be grown so desperate° to be honest—   *rash enough*
And live a subject?° Nay, forsooth, my friends,   *survive in this land*
They that must weigh out° my afflictions,   *offset*
They that my trust must grow to, live not here.
They are, as all my other comforts, far hence,
In mine own country, lords.

90 CARDINAL CAMPEIUS   I would your grace
Would leave your griefs and take my counsel.

QUEEN KATHERINE   How, sir?

CARDINAL CAMPEIUS   Put your main cause into the King's protection.
He's loving and most gracious. 'Twill be much
Both for your honour better and your cause,
95 For if the trial of the law o'ertake ye
You'll part away° disgraced.   *leave*

CARDINAL WOLSEY [*to the* QUEEN]   He tells you rightly.

QUEEN KATHERINE   Ye tell me what ye wish for both—my ruin.
Is this your Christian counsel? Out upon ye!
Heaven is above all yet—there sits a judge
That no king can corrupt.

6. For the sake of the woman—the Queen—I once was.

100	CARDINAL CAMPEIUS Your rage mistakes° us.	*misrepresents*
	QUEEN KATHERINE The more shame for ye! Holy men I thought ye,	
	Upon my soul, two reverend cardinal virtues⁷—	
	But cardinal sins and hollow hearts I fear ye.	
	Mend° 'em, for shame, my lords! Is this your comfort?	*Reform*
105	The cordial° that ye bring a wretched lady,	*restoring medicine*
	A woman lost° among ye, laughed at, scorned?	*ruined*
	I will not wish ye half my miseries—	
	I have more charity. But say I warned ye.	
	Take heed, for heaven's sake take heed, lest at once°	*all at once*
110	The burden of my sorrows fall upon ye.	
	CARDINAL WOLSEY Madam, this is a mere distraction.°	*utter madness; evasion*
	You turn the good we offer into envy.°	*malevolence*
	QUEEN KATHERINE Ye turn me into nothing. Woe upon ye,	
	And all such false professors.° Would you have me—	*(of religion)*
115	If you have any justice, any pity,	
	If ye be anything but churchmen's habits°—	*vestments*
	Put my sick cause into his hands that hates me?	
	Alas, he's banished me his bed already—	
	His love, too, long ago. I am old, my lords,	
120	And all the fellowship I hold now with him	
	Is only my obedience. What can happen	
	To me above° this wretchedness? All your studies	*beyond*
	Make me accursed like this.⁸	*immediate*
	CARDINAL CAMPEIUS Your fears are worse.°	*(than reality)*
	QUEEN KATHERINE Have I lived thus long—let me speak° myself,	*represent*
125	Since virtue finds no friends—a wife, a true one?	
	A woman, I dare say, without vainglory,°	*conceit*
	Never yet branded with suspicion?	
	Have I with all my full affections	
	Still° met the King, loved him next° heav'n, obeyed him,	*Always / next to*
130	Been out of fondness superstitious° to him,	*overly devoted*
	Almost forgot my prayers to content him?	
	And am I thus rewarded? 'Tis not well, lords.	
	Bring me a constant woman to her husband,	
	One that ne'er dreamed a joy beyond his pleasure,	
135	And to that woman when she has done most,	
	Yet will I add an° honour, a great patience.	*another*
	CARDINAL WOLSEY Madam, you wander from° the good we aim at.	*misinterpret*
	QUEEN KATHERINE My lord, I dare not make myself so guilty	
	To give up willingly that noble title	
140	Your master wed me to. Nothing but death	
	Shall e'er divorce my dignities.	
	CARDINAL WOLSEY Pray, hear me.	
	QUEEN KATHERINE Would I had never trod this English earth,	
	Or felt the flatteries that grow upon it.	
	Ye have angels' faces, but heaven knows your hearts.	
145	What will become of me now, wretched lady?	
	I am the most unhappy woman living.	
	[*To her women*] Alas, poor wenches, where are now your forturnes?	

---

7. The cardinal virtues (justice, temperance, prudence, and fortitude, with a play on their rank), which, along with the three theological virtues (faith, hope, and charity), constitute the seven virtues. These oppose the seven deadly ("cardinal," punning on "carnal") sins

referred to in the next line.
8. *All . . . this:* All your endeavors (and inquiries) bring me only these miseries; I defy you, with all your clerical learning, to imagine a more terrible fate than this.

Shipwrecked upon a kingdom where no pity,
No friends, no hope, no kindred weep for me?
150 Almost no grave allowed me? Like the lily,
That once was mistress of the field and flourished,
I'll hang my head and perish.

CARDINAL WOLSEY   If your grace
Could but be brought to know our ends° are honest,   *intentions*
You'd feel more comfort. Why should we, good lady,
155 Upon what cause, wrong you? Alas, our places,°   *official duties*
The way of our profession, is against it.
We are to cure such sorrows, not to sow 'em.
For goodness' sake, consider what you do,
How you may hurt yourself, ay, utterly
160 Grow from the King's acquaintance by this carriage.°   *behavior*
The hearts of princes kiss obedience,
So much they love it, but to stubborn spirits
They swell and grow as terrible as storms.
I know you have a gentle noble temper,°   *temperament*
165 A soul as even° as a calm. Pray, think us   *unwavering*
Those we profess—peacemakers, friends, and servants.

CARDINAL CAMPEIUS   Madam, you'll find it so. You wrong your virtues
With these weak women's fears. A noble spirit,
As yours was put° into you, ever casts   *given*
170 Such doubts as false coin from it. The King loves you.
Beware you lose it not. For° us, if you please   *As for*
To trust us in your business, we are ready
To use our utmost studies in your service.

QUEEN KATHERINE   Do what ye will, my lords, and pray forgive me.
175 If I have used° myself unmannerly,   *behaved*
You know I am a woman, lacking wit°   *understanding*
To make a seemly answer to such persons.
Pray do my service° to his majesty.   *give my respects*
He has my heart yet, and shall have my prayers
180 While I shall have my life. Come, reverend fathers,
Bestow your counsels on me. She now begs
That° little thought, when she set footing here,°   *Who / (in England)*
She should have bought her dignities so dear.   *Exeunt*

3.2

Enter the Duke of NORFOLK, *[the] Duke of* SUFFOLK,
Lord SURREY, *and [the]* LORD CHAMBERLAIN

NORFOLK   If you will now unite in your complaints,
And force them with a constancy,° the Cardinal   *persevere in them*
Cannot stand under them. If you omit°   *neglect*
The offer of this time,° I cannot promise   *This opportunity*
5 But that you shall sustain more new disgraces
With these you bear already.

SURREY   I am joyful
To meet the least occasion that may give me
Remembrance of my father-in-law the Duke,°   *(of Buckingham)*
To be revenged on him.°   *(Wolsey)*

SUFFOLK   Which of the peers
10 Have uncontemned gone° by him, or at least   *not been disdained*
Strangely neglected?° When did he regard   *snubbed as a stranger*

3.2 Location: The court.

The stamp of nobleness in any person
Out of° himself?   *Aside from*
LORD CHAMBERLAIN My lords, you speak your pleasures.
What he deserves of you and me I know;
15 What we can do to him—though now the time
Gives way to° us—I much fear. If you cannot   *Favors*
Bar his access to th' King, never attempt
Anything on° him, for he hath a witchcraft   *against*
Over the King in's tongue.
NORFOLK   O, fear him not.
20 His spell in that is out.° The King hath found   *past*
Matter against him that for ever mars
The honey of his language. No, he's settled,
Not to come off, in his displeasure.[1]
SURREY   Sir,
I should be glad to hear such news as this
Once every hour.
25 NORFOLK   Believe it, this is true.
In the divorce his contrary proceedings°   *double-dealing*
Are all unfolded,° wherein he appears   *exposed*
As I would wish mine enemy.
SURREY   How came
His practices° to light?   *schemes*
SUFFOLK   Most strangely.
SURREY   O, how, how?
30 SUFFOLK The Cardinal's letters to the Pope miscarried,° *went astray; got diverted*
And came to th' eye o'th' King, wherein was read
How that the Cardinal did entreat his holiness
To stay° the judgement o'th' divorce, for if   *delay*
It did take place, 'I do', quoth he, 'perceive
35 My king is tangled in affection to
A creature° of the Queen's, Lady Anne Boleyn'.   *servant*
SURREY Has the King this?
SUFFOLK   Believe it.
SURREY   Will this work?
LORD CHAMBERLAIN The King in this perceives him how he coasts° *sails indirectly*
And hedges° his own way. But in this point   *moves secretly*
40 All his tricks founder, and he brings his physic°   *medicine*
After his patient's death. The King already
Hath married the fair lady.
SURREY   Would he had.
SUFFOLK May you be happy in your wish, my lord,
For I profess you have it.
SURREY   Now all my joy
Trace the conjunction.°   *Follow the union*
SUFFOLK   My amen to't.
45 NORFOLK   All men's.
SUFFOLK There's order given for her coronation.
Marry, this is yet but young,° and may be left   *recent*
To some ears unrecounted. But, my lords,
She is a gallant° creature, and complete°   *an excellent / perfect*
50 In mind and feature. I persuade me,° from her   *am sure*
Will fall some blessing to this land which shall
In it be memorized.[2]

1. No, Wolsey is stuck, with no way out, in Henry's displeasure. Or: No, Henry is firm, with no possibility of

changing, in his displeasure toward Wolsey.
2. Be made memorable (alluding to Elizabeth).

SURREY But will the King
Digest° this letter of the Cardinal's?   *Tolerate*
The Lord forbid!

NORFOLK   Marry, amen.

SUFFOLK   No, no—

55 There be more wasps that buzz about his nose
Will make this sting the sooner. Cardinal Campeius
Is stol'n away to Rome; hath ta'en no leave;
Has left the cause o'th' King unhandled,° and   *unsettled*
Is posted° as the agent of our Cardinal   *Has rushed*
60 To second all his plot. I do assure you
The King cried 'Ha!'³ at this.

LORD CHAMBERLAIN   Now God incense him,
And let him cry 'Ha!' louder.

NORFOLK   But, my lord,
When returns Cranmer?

SUFFOLK He is returned in his opinions, which
65 Have satisfied the King for his divorce,
Together with all famous colleges,
Almost, in Christendom.⁴ Shortly, I believe,
His second marriage shall be published,° and   *announced publicly*
Her coronation. Katherine no more
70 Shall be called 'Queen', but 'Princess Dowager',
And 'widow to Prince Arthur'.

NORFOLK   This same Cranmer's
A worthy fellow, and hath ta'en much pain°   *great pains*
In the King's business.

SUFFOLK   He has, and we shall see him
For it an archbishop.

NORFOLK   So I hear.

SUFFOLK   'Tis so.

Enter [CARDINAL] WOLSEY *and* CROMWELL
The Cardinal.

75 NORFOLK   Observe, observe—he's moody.

[*They stand apart and observe* WOLSEY *and* CROMWELL]

CARDINAL WOLSEY [*to* CROMWELL] The packet,° Cromwell—   *parcel of letters*
gave't you the King?

CROMWELL To his own hand, in's bedchamber.

CARDINAL WOLSEY   Looked he
O'th' inside of the paper?°   *wrapper*

CROMWELL   Presently°   *Immediately*
He did unseal them, and the first he viewed
80 He did it with a serious mind; a heed°   *concerned look*
Was in his countenance. You he bade
Attend him here this morning.

CARDINAL WOLSEY   Is he ready
To come abroad?

CROMWELL I think by this° he is.   *by this time*

85 CARDINAL WOLSEY Leave me a while.   *Exit* CROMWELL
[*Aside*] It shall be to the Duchess of Alençon,
The French King's sister—he shall marry her.

---

3. Henry's characteristic expression of impatience and part of his legend in the Renaissance. See, for instance, 1.2.187 and 2.2.63, 66.
4. *He . . . Christendom:* Cranmer has sent ahead the opinions concerning the King's marriage that he collected on the Continent, and the results have satisfied both the King and most learned clerics.

Anne Boleyn? No, I'll no Anne Boleyns for him.
There's more in't than fair visage. Boleyn?
90 No, we'll no Boleyns. Speedily I wish
To hear from Rome. The Marchioness of Pembroke?
    [*The nobles speak among themselves*]
NORFOLK   He's discontented.
SUFFOLK   Maybe he hears the King
Does whet his anger to° him.   *against*
SURREY   Sharp enough,
Lord, for thy justice.
CARDINAL WOLSEY [*aside*]   The late° Queen's gentlewoman? A   *former*
95   knight's daughter
To be her mistress' mistress? The Queen's queen?
This candle burns not clear;° 'tis I must snuff it,   *bright*
Then out it goes. What though I know her virtuous
And well deserving? Yet I know her for
100 A spleeny Lutheran,⁵ and not wholesome° to   *beneficial*
Our cause, that she should lie i'th' bosom of
Our hard-ruled° King. Again, there is sprung up   *hard-to-advise*
An heretic, an arch-one, Cranmer, one°   *one who*
Hath crawled into the favour of the King
And is his oracle.⁶
    [*The nobles speak among themselves*]
105 NORFOLK   He is vexed at something.
    Enter KING [HENRY] *reading a schedule*° [*and* LOVELL   *scroll*
    with him]
SURREY   I would 'twere something that would fret the string,
The master-cord on's heart!⁷
SUFFOLK   The King, the King!
KING HENRY [*aside*]   What piles of wealth hath he accumulated
To his own portion?° And what expense by th' hour   *share*
110 Seems to flow from him? How i'th' name of thrift
Does he rake this together? [*To the nobles*] Now, my lords,
Saw you the Cardinal?
NORFOLK   My lord, we have
Stood here observing him. Some strange commotion°   *rebellion*
Is in his brain. He bites his lip, and starts,
115 Stops on a sudden, looks upon the ground,
Then lays his finger on his temple, straight°   *immediately*
Springs out into fast gait, then stops again,
Strikes his breast hard, and anon he casts
His eye against the moon. In most strange postures
We have seen him set himself.
120 KING HENRY   It may well be
There is a mutiny in's mind. This morning
Papers of state he sent me to peruse
As I required, and wot° you what I found   *know*
There, on my conscience put unwittingly?
125 Forsooth, an inventory thus importing°   *delineating*
The several parcels of his plate,⁸ his treasure,

---

5. Passionate Lutheran. It is possible that Wolsey objected to Henry's marriage to Anne on religious grounds, as well as on the class grounds that he outlines in this speech.
6. *is his oracle*: is considered by Henry to be divinely inspired.

7. *would . . . heart*: would eat through ("fret") the heart-strings (tying Henry to Wolsey), with a musical allusion: "fret" (fingering bar), "string," and "cord" (chord).
8. *plate*: gold and silver functional household equipment that also stored and displayed wealth.

Rich stuffs, and ornaments of household which
I find at such proud rate° that it outspeaks   *high value*
Possession of a subject.⁹

NORFOLK   It's heaven's will.

130 Some spirit put this paper in the packet
To bless your eye withal.°   *with*

KING HENRY   If we did think
His contemplation were above the earth
And fixed on spiritual object, he should still
Dwell in his musings. But I am afraid

135 His thinkings are below the moon,° not worth   *mundane*
His serious considering.

                   [*The*] KING *takes his seat* [*and*] *whispers* [*with*] LOVELL,
                   who [*then*] *goes to the* CARDINAL

CARDINAL WOLSEY   Heaven forgive me!
[*To the* KING] Ever God bless your highness!

KING HENRY   Good my lord,
You are full of heavenly stuff,¹ and bear the inventory
Of your best graces in your mind, the which

140 You were now running o'er. You have scarce time
To steal from spiritual leisure a brief span
To keep your earthly audit. Sure, in that,
I deem you an ill husband, and am glad
To have you therein my companion.²

CARDINAL WOLSEY   Sir,

145 For holy offices I have a time; a time
To think upon the part of business which
I bear i'th' state; and nature does require
Her times of preservation which, perforce,
I, her frail son, amongst my brethren mortal,
Must give my tendance to.°   *take care of*

150 KING HENRY   You have said well.

CARDINAL WOLSEY   And ever may your highness yoke together,
As I will lend you cause, my doing well
With my well-saying.

KING HENRY   'Tis well said again,
And 'tis a kind of good deed to say well—

155 And yet words are no deeds. My father loved you.
He said he did, and with his deed did crown°   *make good*
His word upon you. Since I had my office,
I have kept you next° my heart, have not alone   *nearest to*
Employed you where high profits might come home,

160 But pared my present havings° to bestow   *given up possessions*
My bounties upon you.

CARDINAL WOLSEY [*aside*]   What should this mean?

SURREY [*aside*]   The Lord increase this business!

KING HENRY   Have I not made you
The prime° man of the state? I pray you tell me   *principal*
If what I now pronounce you have found true,

---

9. *a . . . subject:* it inventories more wealth than is fit
for a subject.
1. Godly qualities, but Henry's ironic language ("stuff,"
"steal," "audit") refers to both worldly and spiritual
matters.
2. Henry jokes that both he and Wolsey are "ill husbands," Wolsey because he cannot manage ("husband")

his household resources (ostensibly, he is otherworldly,
but really he is a greedy spendthrift) and because he
now opposes Henry's remarriage, and perhaps Henry
because he has literally been a poor husband to Katherine. Henry is being ironic, however, and may merely
mean that he has husbanded his resources badly in
trusting them to Wolsey.

165 And, if you may confess it, say withal
If you are bound to us or no. What say you?
CARDINAL WOLSEY   My sovereign, I confess your royal graces°   *favors*
Showered on me daily have been more than could
My studied purposes requite,° which went   *conscious efforts repay*
170 Beyond all man's endeavours. My endeavours
Have ever come too short of my desires,°   *aspirations*
Yet filed° with my abilities. Mine own ends°   *matched / aims*
Have been mine so that° evermore they pointed   *only insofar as*
To th' good of your most sacred person and
175 The profit of the state. For your great graces
Heaped upon me, poor undeserver, I
Can nothing render but allegiant° thanks,   *loyal*
My prayers to heaven for you, my loyalty,
Which ever has and ever shall be growing,
Till death, that winter, kill it.
180 KING HENRY   Fairly answered.
A loyal and obedient subject is
Therein illustrated. The honour of it
Does pay the act of it, as, i'th' contrary,
The foulness is the punishment.³ I presume
185 That as my hand has opened° bounty to you,   *freely offered*
My heart dropped love, my power rained honour, more
On you than any, so your hand and heart,
Your brain, and every function of your power,
Should, notwithstanding that° your bond of duty,°   *despite / (to Rome)*
190 As 'twere in love's particular,° be more   *peculiar intimacy*
To me, your friend, than any.
CARDINAL WOLSEY   I do profess
That for your highness' good I ever laboured
More than mine own; that am, have,° and will be—   *have been*
Though all the world should crack° their duty to you,   *forswear*
195 And throw it from their soul, though perils did
Abound, as thick as thought could make 'em, and
Appear in forms more horrid—yet, my duty,
As doth a rock against the chiding° flood,   *roaring*
Should the approach of this wild river break,°   *check*
And stand unshaken yours.
200 KING HENRY   'Tis nobly spoken.
Take notice, lords, he has a loyal breast,
For you have seen him open't. [*To* WOLSEY] Read o'er this,
        [*He gives him a paper*]
And after this [*giving him another paper*], and then to breakfast with
What appetite you have.
                    Exit KING [HENRY], *frowning upon the*
                    CARDINAL. *The nobles throng after*
                    [*the* KING], *smiling and whispering*
CARDINAL WOLSEY   What should this mean?
205 What sudden anger's this? How have I reaped° it?   *acquired*
He parted frowning from me, as if ruin
Leaped from his eyes. So looks the chafèd° lion   *angry*
Upon the daring huntsman that has galled° him,   *wounded*

---

3. **The honour . . . punishment:** The reward for loyalty and obedience is the honor they bring. Similarly, disloyalty and corruption are their own punishment, causing the subject dishonor.

Then makes him nothing.° I must read this paper—   *slaughters the hunter*
I fear, the story of his anger.
    [*He reads one of the papers*]
210   'Tis so.
This paper has undone° me. 'Tis th'account   *ruined*
Of all that world° of wealth I have drawn together   *vast quantity*
For mine own ends—indeed, to gain the popedom,
And fee° my friends in Rome. O negligence,   *pay off*
215 Fit for a fool to fall by! What cross° devil   *perverse*
Made me put this main° secret in the packet   *most important*
I sent the King? Is there no way to cure this?
No new device to beat this from his brains?
I know 'twill stir him strongly. Yet I know
220 A way, if it take right,° in spite of fortune   *if it succeed*
Will bring me off° again. What's this?   *save me*
    [*He reads the other paper*]
                      'To th' Pope'?
The letter, as I live, with all the business
I writ to's holiness. Nay then, farewell.
I have touched the highest point of all my greatness,
225 And from that full meridian° of my glory   *a star's highest point*
I haste now to my setting. I shall fall
Like a bright exhalation° in the evening,   *shooting star*
And no man see me more.
    Enter to [CARDINAL] WOLSEY *the Dukes of* NORFOLK
    and SUFFOLK, *the Earl of* SURREY, *and the* LORD CHAM-
    BERLAIN
NORFOLK   Hear the King's pleasure, Cardinal, who commands you
230 To render up the great seal presently°   *immediately*
Into our hands, and to confine yourself
To Asher House, my lord of Winchester's,
Till you hear further from his highness.
CARDINAL WOLSEY   Stay—
Where's your commission,° lords? Words cannot carry   *written warrant*
Authority so weighty.
235 SUFFOLK   Who dare cross° 'em   *challenge*
Bearing the King's will from his mouth expressly?
CARDINAL WOLSEY   Till I find more than will or words to do it—
I mean your malice—know, officious lords,
I dare and must deny it. Now I feel
240 Of what coarse metal° ye are moulded—envy.°[4]   *(also) mettle*
How eagerly ye follow my disgraces
As if it fed ye, and how sleek° and wanton°   *obsequious / impetuous*
Ye appear in everything may bring my ruin!
Follow your envious courses, men of malice.
245 You have Christian warrant for 'em, and no doubt
In time will find their fit rewards.[5] That seal
You ask with such a violence,° the King,   *vehemence*
Mine and your master, with his own hand gave me,
Bade me enjoy it, with the place° and honours,   *position*
250 During my life; and, to confirm his goodness,
Tied it by letters patents.° Now, who'll take it?   *open letters*
SURREY   The King that gave it.

4. Malice; jealousy.
5. *You . . . rewards:* You emulate other, equally unjust Christians and will reap their "rewards" (punishments).

CARDINAL WOLSEY   It must be himself then.

SURREY   Thou art a proud traitor, priest.

CARDINAL WOLSEY   Proud lord, thou liest.
Within these forty hours Surrey durst better
Have burnt that tongue than said so.

255   SURREY   Thy ambition,
Thou scarlet sin,⁶ robbed this bewailing land
Of noble Buckingham, my father-in-law.
The heads of all thy brother cardinals
With thee and all thy best parts° bound together   attributes
260   Weighed° not a hair of his. Plague of° your policy,°   Equaled / on / scheming
You sent me deputy for Ireland,
Far from his succour, from the King, from all
That might have mercy on the fault thou gav'st him;°   charged him wtih
Whilst your great goodness, out of holy pity,
Absolved him with an axe.

265   CARDINAL WOLSEY   This, and all else
This talking lord can lay upon my credit,°   good reputation
I answer is most false. The Duke by law
Found his deserts. How innocent I was
From° any private malice in his end,   Of
270   His noble jury and foul cause can witness.
If I loved many words, lord, I should tell you
You have as little honesty as honour,
That° in the way of loyalty and truth   I who
Toward the King, my ever royal master,
275   Dare mate° a sounder man than Surrey can be,   rival
And all that love his follies.

SURREY   By my soul,
Your long coat, priest, protects you; thou shouldst feel
My sword i'th' life-blood of thee else. My lords,
Can ye endure to hear this arrogance,
280   And from this fellow?° If we live thus tamely,   (contemptuous)
To be thus jaded° by a piece of scarlet,   cowed
Farewell nobility. Let his grace go forward
And dare us with his cap, like larks.⁷

CARDINAL WOLSEY   All goodness
Is poison to thy stomach.

SURREY   Yes, that goodness
285   Of gleaning all the land's wealth into one,
Into your own hands, Card'nal, by extortion;
The goodness of your intercepted packets
You writ to th' Pope against the King; your goodness—
Since you provoke me—shall be most notorious.
290   My lord of Norfolk, as you are truly noble,
As you respect the common good, the state
Of our despised nobility, our issues°—   sons
Whom if he° live will scarce be gentlemen—   (Wolsey)
Produce the grand sum of his sins, the articles°   charges against him
295   Collected from his life. [To WOLSEY] I'll startle you

---

6. *scarlet*: referring to the cardinal's robes; see line 281 and 3.1.103. *scarlet sin*: egregious sin in the Bible; see Isaiah 1:18.

7. And befuddle us with his scarlet cap, as larks are caught by dazzling them with scarlet cloth.

Worse than the sacring-bell when the brown wench
Lay kissing in your arms,[8] lord Cardinal.

CARDINAL WOLSEY [*aside*]   How much, methinks, I could despise this man,
But that I am bound in charity against it.

300   NORFOLK [*to* SURREY]   Those articles, my lord, are in the King's hand;°   possession
But thus° much—they are foul ones.   I'll tell you this

CARDINAL WOLSEY   So much fairer
And spotless shall mine innocence arise
When the King knows my truth.°   loyalty

SURREY   This cannot save you.
I thank my memory I yet remember
305   Some of these articles, and out they shall.
Now, if you can blush and cry 'Guilty', Cardinal,
You'll show a little honesty.

CARDINAL WOLSEY   Speak on, sir;
I dare your worst objections.° If I blush,   accusations
It is to see a nobleman want° manners.   lack

310   SURREY   I had rather want those than my head. Have at you!°   (a challenge)
First, that without the King's assent or knowledge
You wrought to be a legate,[9] by which power
You maimed the jurisdiction of all bishops.

NORFOLK [*to* WOLSEY]   Then, that in all you writ to Rome, or else
315   To foreign princes, '*Ego et Rex meus*'[1]
Was still° inscribed—in which you brought the King   always
To be your servant.

SUFFOLK [*to* WOLSEY]   Then, that without the knowledge
Either of King or Council, when you went
Ambassador to the Emperor,° you made bold   Charles V
320   To carry into Flanders the great seal.

SURREY [*to* WOLSEY]   Item,° you sent a large commission°   Next / delegation
To Gregory de Cassado, to conclude,
Without the King's will or the state's allowance,°   consent
A league between his highness and Ferrara.

325   SUFFOLK [*to* WOLSEY]   That out of mere° ambition you have caused   pure
Your holy hat to be stamped on the King's coin.[2]

SURREY [*to* WOLSEY]   Then, that you have sent innumerable substance°—   untold riches
By what means got, I leave to your own conscience—
To furnish° Rome, and to prepare the ways   supply; bribe
330   You have for dignities to the mere undoing°   complete destruction
Of all the kingdom. Many more there are,
Which since they are of you, and odious,
I will not taint my mouth with.

LORD CHAMBERLAIN   O, my lord,
Press° not a falling man too far. 'Tis virtue.°   Oppress / (not to)
335   His faults lie open to° the laws. Let them,   exposed before
Not you, correct him. My heart weeps to see him
So little of his great self.

SURREY   I forgive him.

---

8. *I'll . . . arms:* The small "sacring bell" was rung at Mass when the priest elevated the consecrated Host. Surrey imagines Wolsey surprised with a country girl ("brown" because tanned or dirty from working, or perhaps ugly or promiscuous) when he should have been at Mass.
9. You schemed to be a papal representative.
1. I and my King. Norfolk accuses Wolsey of putting him-self before the King and of making the King his depen-dent. Technically, however, the Latin word order is correct and means "my King and I," thus making it less offensive.
2. Allowed to produce half groats and half pennies with his insignia in his home diocese of York, Wolsey had his cardinal's hat stamped on a groat, thereby usurping the King's monopoly on coins of larger denominations.

SUFFOLK   Lord Cardinal, the King's further pleasure is—
        Because all those things you have done of late,
340   By your power legantine within this kingdom,
        Fall into th' compass of a praemunire[3]—
        That therefore such a writ be sued° against you,   *served*
        To forfeit all your goods, lands, tenements,
        Chattels,° and whatsoever, and to be   *Personal property*
345   Out of the King's protection. This is my charge.
NORFOLK [*to* WOLSEY]   And so we'll leave you to your meditations
        How to live better. For your stubborn answer
        About the giving back the great seal to us,
        The King shall know it and, no doubt, shall thank you.
350   So fare you well, my little good lord Cardinal. *Exeunt all but* WOLSEY
CARDINAL WOLSEY   So farewell—to the little good you bear me.
        Farewell, a long farewell, to all my greatness!
        This is the state of man. Today he puts forth
        The tender leaves of hopes; tomorrow blossoms,
355   And bears his blushing° honours thick upon him;   *resplendent*
        The third day comes a frost, a killing frost,
        And when he thinks, good easy° man, full surely   *trusting*
        His greatness is a-ripening, nips his root,
        And then he falls, as I do. I have ventured,
360   Like little wanton boys that swim on bladders,[4]
        This many summers in a sea of glory,
        But far beyond my depth; my high-blown pride
        At length broke under me, and now has left me
        Weary, and old with service, to the mercy
365   Of a rude stream° that must for ever hide me.   *turbulent current*
        Vain pomp and glory of this world, I hate ye!
        I feel my heart new opened. O, how wretched
        Is that poor man that hangs on princes' favours!
        There is betwixt that smile we would aspire to,
370   That sweet aspect of princes, and their ruin,[5]
        More pangs and fears than wars or women have,
        And when he falls, he falls like Lucifer,°   *(from heaven to hell)*
        Never to hope again.
                Enter CROMWELL, [*who then*] *stand*[*s*] *amazed*
                                Why, how now, Cromwell?
CROMWELL   I have no power to speak, sir.
CARDINAL WOLSEY   What, amazed
375   At my misfortunes? Can thy spirit wonder
        A great man should decline?°   *fall from power*
                [CROMWELL *begins to weep*]
                                Nay, an° you weep   *if*
        I am fall'n indeed.
CROMWELL   How does your grace?
CARDINAL WOLSEY   Why, well—
        Never so truly happy, my good Cromwell.
        I know myself now, and I feel within me

---

3. Having made himself a papal legate, Wolsey is subject to punishment because he has broken the law of
praemunire—that is, he has appealed to an outside
(here, papal) court when the offense fell under the
jurisdiction of English courts. Wolsey is thus charged

with elevating the Pope's authority over his sovereign's.
4. Like frolicsome little boys who stay afloat (only by)
using inflated membranes from an animal's body.
5. *their ruin*: the destruction they cause.

380 A peace above all earthly dignities,
A still and quiet conscience. The King has cured me.
I humbly thank his grace, and from these shoulders,
These ruined pillars,[6] out of pity, taken
A load would sink a navy—too much honour.
385 O, 'tis a burden, Cromwell, 'tis a burden
Too heavy for a man that hopes for heaven.

CROMWELL   I am glad your grace has made that right use of it.

CARDINAL WOLSEY   I hope I have. I am able now, methinks,
Out of a fortitude of soul I feel,
390 To endure more miseries and greater far
Than my weak-hearted enemies dare offer.
What news abroad?

CROMWELL   The heaviest and the worst
Is your displeasure° with the King.   *disgrace*

CARDINAL WOLSEY   God bless him.

CROMWELL   The next is that Sir Thomas More is chosen
Lord Chancellor in your place.

395 CARDINAL WOLSEY   That's somewhat sudden.
But he's a learnèd man. May he continue
Long in his highness' favour, and do justice
For truth's sake and his conscience, that his bones,
When he has run his course and sleeps in blessings,
400 May have a tomb of orphans' tears wept on him.[7]
What more?

CROMWELL   That Cranmer is returned° with welcome,   *(from the Continent)*
Installed lord Archbishop of Canterbury.[8]

CARDINAL WOLSEY   That's news indeed.

CROMWELL   Last, that the Lady Anne,
Whom the King hath in secrecy long married,
405 This day was viewed in open as his queen,
Going to chapel, and the voice° is now   *gossip*
Only about her coronation.

CARDINAL WOLSEY   There was the weight that pulled me down.
    O, Cromwell,
The King has gone beyond° me. All my glories   *overreached*
410 In° that one woman I have lost for ever.   *Due to*
No sun shall ever usher forth mine honours,
Or gild again the noble troops° that waited   *retainers*
Upon my smiles. Go, get thee from me, Cromwell.
I am a poor fall'n man, unworthy now
415 To be thy lord and master. Seek the King—
That sun I pray may never set—I have told him
What and how true thou art. He will advance thee.
Some little memory of me will stir him.
I know his noble nature not to let
420 Thy hopeful service perish too. Good Cromwell,
Neglect him not. Make use° now, and provide   *Seize your chance*
For thine own future safety.

CROMWELL [*weeping*]   O, my lord,
Must I then leave you? Must I needs forgo°   *renounce*

---

6. Perhaps the pillars carried during Wolsey's triumphal entrance in 2.4.
7. The Lord Chancellor's duties included guardianship of all children under twenty-one, particularly

orphans. Henry had More beheaded in 1535 for his
Catholicism.
8. In 1533; Cranmer was beheaded by Henry's oldest
daughter, Queen Mary, in 1556 for his Protestantism.

So good, so noble, and so true a master?
425 Bear witness, all that have not hearts of iron,
With what a sorrow Cromwell leaves his lord.
The King shall have my service, but my prayers
For ever and for ever shall be yours.

CARDINAL WOLSEY [*weeping*]   Cromwell, I did not think to shed a tear
430 In all my miseries, but thou hast forced me,
Out of thy honest truth, to play the woman.°   ° to weep
Let's dry our eyes, and thus far hear me, Cromwell,
And when I am forgotten, as I shall be,
And sleep in dull cold marble, where no mention
435 Of me more must be heard of, say I taught thee—
Say Wolsey, that once trod the ways of glory,
And sounded° all the depths and shoals of honour,   ° fathomed
Found thee a way, out of his wreck,° to rise in,   ° shipwreck
A sure and safe one, though thy master missed it.
440 Mark but my fall, and that that ruined me.
Cromwell, I charge thee, fling away ambition.⁹
By that sin fell the angels. How can man, then,
The image of his maker, hope to win° by it?   ° profit
Love thyself last. Cherish those hearts that hate thee.
445 Corruption wins not more than honesty.
Still° in thy right hand carry gentle peace   ° Ever
To silence envious tongues. Be just, and fear not.
Let all the ends thou aim'st at be thy country's,
Thy God's, and truth's. Then if thou fall'st, O Cromwell,
450 Thou fall'st a blessèd martyr.¹
Serve the King. And prithee, lead me in—
There take an inventory of all I have:
To the last penny 'tis the King's. My robe,
And my integrity to heaven, is all
455 I dare now call mine own. O Cromwell, Cromwell,
Had I but served my God with half the zeal
I served my King, He would not in mine age
Have left me naked° to mine enemies.   ° utterly exposed

CROMWELL   Good sir, have patience.

CARDINAL WOLSEY   So I have. Farewell
460 The hopes of court; my hopes in heaven do dwell.   *Exeunt*

4.1

Enter [the] two GENTLEMEN *meeting one another. [The
first holds a paper]*

FIRST GENTLEMAN   You're well met once again.¹

SECOND GENTLEMAN   So are you.

FIRST GENTLEMAN   You come to take your stand here and behold
The Lady Anne pass from her coronation?

SECOND GENTLEMAN   'Tis all my business. At our last encounter
5   The Duke of Buckingham came from his trial.

FIRST GENTLEMAN   'Tis very true. But that time offered sorrow,
This, general joy.

SECOND GENTLEMAN   'Tis well. The citizens,

---

9. Cromwell did not take Wolsey's advice; Henry had   Shakespeare's time.
him beheaded in 1540 for treason and heresy after an   4.1 Location: A street in Westminster.
even more rapid rise and fall than Wolsey's.   1. See 2.1.
1. As Cromwell was sometimes thought to be in

I am sure, have shown at full their royal minds°— royalist allegiance
As, let 'em have their rights, they are ever forward²—
10 In celebration of this day with shows,
Pageants, and sights of honour.

FIRST GENTLEMAN   Never greater,
Nor, I'll assure you, better taken,° sir. received

SECOND GENTLEMAN   May I be bold to ask what that contains,
That paper in your hand?

FIRST GENTLEMAN   Yes, 'tis the list
15 Of those that claim their offices this day
By custom of the coronation.
The Duke of Suffolk is the first, and claims
To be High Steward; next, the Duke of Norfolk,
He to be Earl Marshal. You may read the rest.
        [He gives him the paper]
20 SECOND GENTLEMAN   I thank you, sir. Had I not known those customs,
I should have been beholden to your paper.
But I beseech you, what's become of Katherine,
The Princess Dowager? How goes her business?

FIRST GENTLEMAN   That I can tell you too. The Archbishop
25 Of Canterbury, accompanied with other
Learnèd and reverend fathers of his order,
Held a late° court at Dunstable, six miles off Recently held a
From Ampthill, where the Princess lay;° to which resided
She was often cited° by them, but appeared not. summoned
30 And, to be short, for not appearance, and
The King's late scruple, by the main assent° consensus
Of all these learnèd men, she was divorced,
And the late marriage made of none effect,° null
Since which she was removed to Kimbolton,
Where she remains now sick.

35 SECOND GENTLEMAN   Alas, good lady!
        [Flourish of trumpets within]
The trumpets sound. Stand close.° The Queen is coming. aside
        [Enter the coronation procession, which] pass[es] over
        the stage in order and state. Hautboys [within,
        play during the procession]

        THE ORDER OF THE CORONATION

        1. [First, enter] trumpet[ers, who play] a lively flourish.
        2. Then, [enter] two judges.
        3. [Then, enter the] LORD CHANCELLOR, with [both the]
        purse [containing the great seal] and [the] mace [borne]
        before him.
        4. [Then, enter] choristers singing; [with them,]
        music[ians playing.]
        5. [Then, enter the Lord] Mayor of London bearing the
        mace, [followed by] Garter [King-of-Arms° wearing] his chief herald
        coat of arms and a gilt copper crown.
        6. [Then, enter] Marquis Dorset bearing a sceptre of
        gold, [and wearing,] on his head, a demi-coronal of
        gold [and, about his neck, a collar of esses].³ With him

2. As, to give them their due, they are always eager to demonstrate.

3. Heavy gold chain made of S-shaped links worn around the neck by men of high office.

[enter] the Earl of SURREY bearing the rod of silver with
the dove, crowned with an earl's coronet, [and also wearing a] collar of esses.
7. [Next, enter the] Duke of SUFFOLK as High Steward,
in his robe of estate, [with] his coronet on his head,
[and] bearing a long white wand. With him, [enter] the
Duke of NORFOLK with the rod of marshalship [and] a
coronet on his head. [Each wears a] collar of esses.
8. [Then,] under a canopy borne by four [barons] of
the Cinque Ports,⁴ [enter] ANNE, the [new] Queen, in
her robe. Her hair, [which hangs loose,° is] richly   (a bridal custom)
adorned with pearl. [She wears a] crown. [Accompany-
ing] her on [either] side [are] the Bishops of London
and Winchester.
9. [Next, enter] the old Duchess of Norfolk, in a coronal
of gold wrought with flowers, bearing the Queen's train.
10. [Finally, enter] certain ladies or countesses, with
plain circlets of gold without flowers.
[The two GENTLEMEN comment on the procession as it
passes over the stage]

SECOND GENTLEMAN   A royal train,° believe me. These I know.   procession
  Who's that that bears the sceptre?
FIRST GENTLEMAN   Marquis Dorset.
  And that, the Earl of Surrey with the rod.
40 SECOND GENTLEMAN   A bold brave gentleman. That should be
  The Duke of Suffolk?
FIRST GENTLEMAN   'Tis the same: High Steward.
SECOND GENTLEMAN   And that, my lord of Norfolk?
FIRST GENTLEMAN   Yes.
SECOND GENTLEMAN [seeing ANNE]   Heaven bless thee!
  Thou hast the sweetest face I ever looked on.
  Sir, as I have a soul, she is an angel.
45 Our King has all the Indies⁵ in his arms,
  And more, and richer, when he strains° that lady.   embraces
  I cannot blame his conscience.
FIRST GENTLEMAN   They that bear
  The cloth of honour° over her are four barons   canopy
  Of the Cinque Ports.
50 SECOND GENTLEMAN   Those men are happy,
  And so are all° are near her.   all who
  I take it she that carries up the train
  Is that old noble lady, Duchess of Norfolk.
FIRST GENTLEMAN   It is. And all the rest are countesses.
55 SECOND GENTLEMAN   Their coronets say so. These are stars indeed—
FIRST GENTLEMAN   And sometimes falling ones.°   meteors; (sexual)
SECOND GENTLEMAN   No more of that.
            Exit [the last of the procession,] and then
                  a great flourish of trumpets [within]
        Enter a third GENTLEMAN [in a sweat]
FIRST GENTLEMAN   God save you, sir. Where have you been broiling?°   overheating
THIRD GENTLEMAN   Among the crowd i'th'Abbey, where a finger

4. By traditional prerogative, the barons of the Cinque   over the sovereign at state occasions.
Ports (Hastings, Sandwich, Dover, Romney, and Hythe   5. The East and West Indies were considered sources
on the southeast coast of England) carried a canopy   of great wealth. See 1.1.21.

Could not be wedged in more. I am stifled
60   With the mere rankness° of their joy.   *exuberance; odor*
SECOND GENTLEMAN   You saw the ceremony?
THIRD GENTLEMAN   That I did.
FIRST GENTLEMAN   How was it?
THIRD GENTLEMAN   Well worth the seeing.
SECOND GENTLEMAN   Good sir, speak° it to us.   *describe*
THIRD GENTLEMAN   As well as I am able. The rich stream
65   Of lords and ladies, having brought the Queen
To a prepared place in the choir,° fell off°   *company / drew back*
A distance from her, while her grace sat down
To rest a while—some half an hour or so—
In a rich chair of state, opposing° freely   *displaying*
70   The beauty of her person to the people.
Believe me, sir, she is the goodliest° woman   *fairest*
That ever lay by man; which when the people
Had the full view of, such a noise arose
As the shrouds° make at sea in a stiff tempest,   *ship's rigging*
75   As loud and to as many tunes. Hats, cloaks—
Doublets,° I think—flew up, and had their faces   *Short jackets*
Been loose, this day they had been lost. Such joy
I never saw before. Great-bellied women,
That had not half a week to go, like rams°   *battering rams*
80   In the old time of war, would shake the press,°   *crowd*
And make 'em reel before 'em. No man living
Could say 'This is my wife' there, all were woven
So strangely in one piece.
SECOND GENTLEMAN   But what followed?
THIRD GENTLEMAN   At length her grace rose, and with modest paces
85   Came to the altar, where she kneeled, and saint-like
Cast her fair eyes to heaven, and prayed devoutly,
Then rose again, and bowed her to the people,
When by the Archbishop of Canterbury
She had all the royal makings° of a queen,   *essential trappings*
90   As holy oil, Edward Confessor's crown,
The rod and bird of peace, and all such emblems
Laid nobly on her. Which performed, the choir,
With all the choicest music° of the kingdom,   *musicians*
Together sung *Te Deum.*[6] So she parted,°   *departed*
95   And with the same full state° paced back again   *ceremony*
To York Place, where the feast is held.
FIRST GENTLEMAN   Sir,
You must no more call it York Place—that's past,
For since the Cardinal fell, that title's lost.
'Tis now the King's, and called Whitehall.
THIRD GENTLEMAN   I know it,
100   But 'tis so lately altered that the old name
Is fresh about me.
SECOND GENTLEMAN   What two reverend bishops
Were those that went on each side of the Queen?
THIRD GENTLEMAN   Stokesley and Gardiner, the one of Winchester—

---

6. Hymn of praise and thanksgiving beginning *"Te Deum laudamus,"* "We praise thee, O Lord."

Newly preferred° from the King's secretary—   *promoted*
The other London.[7]

105 SECOND GENTLEMAN   He of Winchester
Is held no great good lover of the Archbishop's,
The virtuous Cranmer.

THIRD GENTLEMAN   All the land knows that.
However, yet there is no great breach. When it comes,
Cranmer will find a friend will not° shrink from him.   *who will not*

SECOND GENTLEMAN   Who may that be, I pray you?

110 THIRD GENTLEMAN   Thomas Cromwell,
A man in much esteem with th' King, and truly
A worthy friend. The King has made him
Master o'th' Jewel House,
And one already of the Privy Council.

SECOND GENTLEMAN   He will deserve more.

115 THIRD GENTLEMAN   Yes, without all doubt.
Come, gentlemen, ye shall go my way,
Which is to th' court, and there ye shall be my guests.
Something° I can command. As I walk thither   *Some influence*
I'll tell ye more.

FIRST *and* SECOND GENTLEMEN   You may command us, sir.

Exeunt

4.2

[*Three chairs.*] *Enter* KATHERINE *Dowager, sick, led
between* GRIFFITH *her gentleman usher, and* PATIENCE
her woman

GRIFFITH   How does your grace?

KATHERINE   O Griffith, sick to death.
My legs, like loaden° branches, bow to th' earth,   *heavily laden*
Willing to leave their burden. Reach a chair.
[*A chair is brought to her. She sits*]
So now, methinks, I feel a little ease.

5   Didst thou not tell me, Griffith, as thou led'st me,
That the great child of honour,° Cardinal Wolsey,   *(ironic)*
Was dead?

GRIFFITH   Yes, madam, but I think your grace,
Out of the pain you suffered, gave no ear to't.

KATHERINE   Prithee, good Griffith, tell me how he died.

10   If well, he stepped before me happily°   *aptly*
For my example.

GRIFFITH   Well, the voice° goes, madam.   *talk*
For after the stout Earl Northumberland
Arrested him at York, and brought him forward,
As a man sorely tainted,° to his answer,°   *disgraced / hearing*

15   He fell sick, suddenly, and grew so ill
He could not sit his mule.

KATHERINE   Alas, poor man.

GRIFFITH   At last, with easy roads,° he came to Leicester,   *stages of a journey*
Lodged in the abbey, where the reverend abbot,
With all his convent,° honourably received him,   *monastery*

7. John Stokesley was Bishop of London; already secretary to the King, Gardiner also became Bishop of
Winchester following Wolsey's demise.
4.2 Location: Katherine's apartments in Kimbolton.

20   To whom he gave these words: 'O father abbot,
      An old man broken with the storms of state
      Is come to lay his weary bones among ye.
      Give him a little earth,° for charity.'   *a resting place*
      So went to bed, where eagerly his sickness
25   Pursued him still, and three nights after this,
      About the hour of eight, which he himself
      Foretold should be his last, full of repentance,
      Continual meditations, tears, and sorrows,
      He gave his honours to the world again,
30   His blessèd part° to heaven, and slept in peace.   *soul*

KATHERINE   So may he rest, his faults lie gently on him.
      Yet thus far, Griffith, give me leave to speak° him,   *describe*
      And yet with charity. He was a man
      Of an unbounded stomach,° ever ranking   *ambition*
35   Himself with princes; one that by suggestion°   *underhanded dealing*
      Tied° all the kingdom. Simony[1] was fair play.   *Shackled*
      His own opinion was his law. I'th' presence°   *King's chamber*
      He would say untruths, and be ever double°   *duplicitous*
      Both in his words and meaning. He was never,
40   But where he meant to ruin, pitiful.°   *merciful*
      His promises were, as he then was, mighty;
      But his performance, as he is now, nothing.
      Of his own body he was ill,° and gave   *sexually immoral*
      The clergy ill example.

GRIFFITH   Noble madam,
45   Men's evil manners live in brass, their virtues
      We write in water.[2] May it please your highness
      To hear me speak his good now?

KATHERINE   Yes, good Griffith,
      I were malicious else.

GRIFFITH   This cardinal,
      Though from an humble stock, undoubtedly
50   Was fashioned to much honour. From his cradle
      He was a scholar, and a ripe and good one,
      Exceeding wise, fair-spoken, and persuading;°   *persuasive*
      Lofty and sour to them that loved him not,
      But to those men that sought him,° sweet as summer.   *befriended him*
55   And though he were unsatisfied° in getting°—   *insatiable / (riches)*
      Which was a sin—yet in bestowing, madam,
      He was most princely: ever witness for him
      Those twins of learning that he raised° in you,   *set up*
      Ipswich and Oxford[3]—one of which fell with him,
60   Unwilling to outlive the good that did it;
      The other, though unfinished, yet so famous,
      So excellent in art,° and still so rising,   *scholarship*
      That Christendom shall ever speak his virtue.
      His overthrow heaped happiness upon him,
65   For then, and not till then, he felt° himself,   *recognized*
      And found the blessèdness of being little.°   *humble*

---

1. Trading, for money or favors, in ecclesiastical offices.
2. *Men's . . . water:* Evil deeds are long remembered, good ones soon forgotten (proverbial).
3. Wolsey founded colleges at Ipswich and Oxford; the latter survives as Christ Church.

And to add greater honours to his age
Than man could give him, he died fearing God.

KATHERINE After my death I wish no other herald,
70 No other speaker of my living actions
To keep mine honour from corruption
But such an honest chronicler as Griffith.
Whom I most hated living,° thou hast made me,   *while alive*
With thy religious truth and modesty,°   *equanimity*
75 Now in his ashes honour. Peace be with him.
[*To her woman*] Patience, be near me still, and set me lower.
I have not long to trouble thee. Good Griffith,
Cause the musicians play me that sad note°   *melody*
I named my knell, whilst I sit meditating
80 On that celestial harmony I go to.[4]

Sad and solemn music. [KATHERINE *sleeps*]

GRIFFITH [*to the woman*] She is asleep. Good wench, let's sit down quiet
For fear we wake her. Softly, gentle Patience.
[*They sit*]

THE VISION

*Enter, solemnly tripping one after another, six person-
ages clad in white robes, wearing on their heads garlands of bays, and golden visors on their faces.*[5] [*They*]
carry] *branches of bays or palm in their hands. They first
congé° unto* [KATHERINE], *then dance; and, at certain*   *bow*
changes,° the first two hold a spare garland over her   *dance movements*
*head at which the other four make reverent curtsies.
Then the two that held the garland deliver the same to
the other next two, who observe the same order in their
changes and holding the garland over her head. Which
done, they deliver the same garland to the last two who
likewise observe the same order. At which, as it were by
inspiration, she makes in her sleep signs of rejoicing, and
holdeth up her hands to heaven. And so in their dancing
vanish, carrying the garland with them. The music continues*

KATHERINE [*waking*] Spirits of peace, where are ye? Are ye all gone,
And leave me here in wretchedness behind ye?
[GRIFFITH *and* PATIENCE *rise and come forward*]

GRIFFITH Madam, we are here.
85 KATHERINE   It is not you I call for.
Saw ye none enter since I slept?

GRIFFITH   None, madam.

KATHERINE No? Saw you not even now a blessèd troop
Invite me to a banquet, whose bright faces
Cast thousand beams upon me, like the sun?
90 They promised me eternal happiness,
And brought me garlands, Griffith, which I feel
I am not worthy yet to wear. I shall,
Assuredly.

4. After death, the soul supposedly could hear the
music of the spheres (the heavenly bodies) as they
revolved around the earth.

5. White to signify purity; bay leaves ("bays") to indicate triumph or joy; golden masks ("visors") perhaps to
suggest they are spirits.

GRIFFITH   I am most joyful, madam, such good dreams
  Possess your fancy.°   *Fill your imagination*

95   KATHERINE   Bid the music° leave.   *musicians*
  They are harsh and heavy° to me.   *tiresome*
    Music ceases

PATIENCE [*to* GRIFFITH]   Do you note
  How much her grace is altered on the sudden?
  How long her face is drawn? How pale she looks,
  And of an earthy colour? Mark her eyes?

GRIFFITH   She is going, wench. Pray, pray.

100   PATIENCE   Heaven comfort her.
    Enter a MESSENGER

MESSENGER [*to* KATHERINE]
  An't like° your grace—   *If it please*

KATHERINE   You are a saucy fellow—
  Deserve we no more reverence?

GRIFFITH [*to the* MESSENGER]   You are to blame,
  Knowing she will not lose her wonted° greatness,   *forgo her usual*
  To use so rude behaviour. Go to, kneel.

MESSENGER [*kneeling before* KATHERINE]   I humbly do entreat
105   your highness' pardon.
  My haste made me unmannerly. There is staying°   *waiting*
  A gentleman sent from the King to see you.

KATHERINE   Admit him entrance, Griffith. But this fellow
  Let me ne'er see again.   *Exit* MESSENGER
    Enter Lord CAPUTIUS [*ushered by* GRIFFITH]
          If my sight fail not,

110   You should be lord ambassador from the Emperor,°   *Charles V*
  My royal nephew, and your name Caputius.

CAPUTIUS   Madam, the same, [*bowing*] your servant.

KATHERINE   O, my lord,
  The times and titles now are altered strangely
  With me since first you knew me. But I pray you,
  What is your pleasure with me?

115   CAPUTIUS   Noble lady,
  First mine own service to your grace; the next,
  The King's request that I would visit you,
  Who grieves much for your weakness, and by me
  Sends you his princely commendations,°   *compliments*
120   And heartily entreats you take good comfort.

KATHERINE   O, my good lord, that comfort comes too late,
  'Tis like a pardon after execution.
  That gentle physic,° given in time, had cured me;   *medicine*
  But now I am past all comforts here but prayers.
  How does his highness?

125   CAPUTIUS   Madam, in good health.

KATHERINE   So may he ever do, and ever flourish
  When I shall dwell with worms, and my poor name
  Banished the kingdom. [*To her woman*] Patience, is that letter
  I caused you write yet sent away?

PATIENCE   No, madam.

130   KATHERINE [*to* CAPUTIUS]   Sir, I most humbly pray you to deliver
  This to my lord the King.
    [*The letter is given to* CAPUTIUS]

CAPUTIUS   Most willing,° madam.   *willingly*

KATHERINE   In which I have commended to his goodness
           The model° of our chaste loves, his young daughter[6]—   *image*
           The dews of heaven fall thick in blessings on her—
135   Beseeching him to give her virtuous breeding.°   *raise her virtuously*
           She is young, and of a noble modest nature.
           I hope she will deserve well—and a little
           To love her for her mother's sake, that loved him,
           Heaven knows how dearly. My next poor petition
140   Is that his noble grace would have some pity
           Upon my wretched women, that so long
           Have followed both my fortunes° faithfully;   *(good and bad)*
           Of which there is not one, I dare avow—
           And now I should not lie[7]—but will deserve,
145   For virtue and true beauty of the soul,
           For honesty° and decent carriage,°   *chastity / conduct*
           A right good husband. Let him be a noble,
           And sure those men are happy that shall have 'em.
           The last is for my men—they are the poorest,
150   But poverty could never draw 'em from me—
           That they may have their wages duly paid 'em,
           And something over to remember me by.
           If heaven had pleased to have given me longer life,
           And able° means, we had not parted thus.   *sufficient*
155   These are the whole contents; and, good my lord,
           By that you love the dearest in this world,
           As you wish Christian peace to souls departed,
           Stand these poor people's friend and urge the King
           To do me this last rite.°   *(also) right*
CAPUTIUS   By heaven I will,
160   Or let me lose the fashion of a man.°   *forfeit my humanity*
KATHERINE   I thank you, honest lord. Remember me
           In all humility unto his highness.
           Say his long trouble now is passing
           Out of this world. Tell him, in death I blessed him,
165   For so I will. Mine eyes grow dim. Farewell,
           My lord. Griffith, farewell.
           [*To her woman*]   Nay, Patience,
           You must not leave me yet. I must to bed.
           Call in more women. When I am dead, good wench,
           Let me be used° with honour. Strew me over   *treated*
170   With maiden° flowers, that all the world may know   *(signifying chastity)*
           I was a chaste wife to my grave. Embalm me,
           Then lay me forth.° Although unqueened, yet like   *prepare me for burial*
           A queen and daughter to a king inter me.
           I can° no more.   *can say or do*
               Exeunt [CAPUTIUS *and* GRIFFITH *at one door;*
               PATIENCE] *leading* KATHERINE [*at another*]

---

6. Mary was Katherine and Henry's only child who survived infancy (see 2.4.35 and note). She was Queen for
five years (1553–58) before Elizabeth, her half sister.

7. Now, on the point of death, I would not (ought not
to) lie. It was generally thought that people spoke truth
on their deathbeds.

5.1

Enter [at one door] GARDINER, *Bishop of Winchester;*
before him, a PAGE *with a torch*

GARDINER   It's one o'clock, boy, is't not?

PAGE   It hath struck.

GARDINER   These should be hours for necessities,
Not for delights; times to repair° our nature   restore
With comforting repose, and not for us
To waste these times.

[Enter at another door] Sir Thomas LOVELL *[meeting*
them]

5   Good hour of night, Sir Thomas!
Whither so late?

LOVELL   Came you from the King, my lord?

GARDINER   I did, Sir Thomas, and left him at primero°   a card game
With the Duke of Suffolk.

LOVELL   I must to him too,
Before he go to bed. I'll take my leave.

10 GARDINER   Not yet, Sir Thomas Lovell—what's the matter?
It seems you are in haste. An if there be
No great offence° belongs to't, give your friend   inappropriateness
Some touch° of your late business. Affairs that walk,   hint
As they say spirits do, at midnight, have
15 In them a wilder nature than the business
That seeks dispatch° by day.   to be done

LOVELL   My lord, I love you,
And durst commend° a secret to your ear   entrust
Much weightier than this work.° The Queen's in labour—   my affairs
They say in great extremity—and feared°   it is feared that
She'll with the labour end.

20 GARDINER   The fruit she goes with
I pray for heartily, that it may find
Good time,° and live. But, for the stock,° Sir Thomas,   Fortune / trunk (Anne)
I wish it grubbed up° now.   rooted out

LOVELL   Methinks I could
Cry the amen,° and yet my conscience says   Agree
25 She's a good creature and, sweet lady, does
Deserve our better wishes.

GARDINER   But sir, sir,
Hear me, Sir Thomas. You're a gentleman
Of mine own way.[1] I know you wise, religious.
And let me tell you, it will ne'er be well—
30 'Twill not, Sir Thomas Lovell, take't of me—
Till Cranmer, Cromwell—her two hands—and she,
Sleep in their graves.

LOVELL   Now, sir, you speak of two
The most remarked° i'th' kingdom. As for Cromwell,   regarded
Beside that of the Jewel House is made Master
35 O'th' Rolls and the King's secretary. Further, sir,
Stands in the gap and trade° of more preferments   open road
With which the time will load him. Th'Archbishop

5.1 Location: London, a gallery at court.
1. Of my religious persuasion (Catholicism, as opposed to Anne's Lutheranism).

Is the King's hand and tongue, and who dare speak
One syllable against him?

GARDINER   Yes, yes, Sir Thomas—
40 There are that dare, and I myself have ventured
To speak my mind of him, and, indeed, this day,
Sir—I may tell it you, I think—I have
Incensed° the lords o'th' Council that he is—   °*Angered*
For so I know he is, they know he is—
45 A most arch heretic, a pestilence
That does infect the land; with which they, moved,°   °*angered*
Have broken with° the King, who hath so far   °*revealed to*
Given ear to our complaint, of his great grace
And princely care, foreseeing those fell mischiefs
50 Our reasons laid before him, hath° commanded   °*that he has*
Tomorrow morning to the Council board
He be convented.° He's a rank° weed, Sir Thomas,   °*summoned / rotten*
And we must root him out. From your affairs
I hinder you too long. Good night, Sir Thomas.
55 LOVELL   Many good nights, my lord; I rest° your servant.   °*remain*

Exeunt GARDINER *and* PAGE [*at one door*]
Enter KING [HENRY] *and* SUFFOLK [*at another door*]

KING HENRY [*to* SUFFOLK]   Charles, I will play no more tonight.
My mind's not on't. You are too hard° for me.   °*skillful*
SUFFOLK   Sir, I did never win of you before.
KING HENRY   But little, Charles,
60 Nor shall not when my fancy's° on my play.   °*attention is*
Now, Lovell, from the Queen what is the news?
LOVELL   I could not personally deliver to her
What you commanded me, but by her woman
I sent your message, who returned her thanks
65 In the great'st humbleness, and desired your highness
Most heartily to pray for her.
KING HENRY   What sayst thou? Ha?
To pray for her? What, is she crying out?
LOVELL   So said her woman, and that her suffrance° made   °*suffering*
Almost each pang a death.
KING HENRY   Alas, good lady.
70 SUFFOLK   God safely quit° her of her burden, and   °*release*
With gentle travail,° to the gladding° of   °*labor / making joyful*
Your highness with an heir.
KING HENRY   'Tis midnight, Charles.
Prithee to bed, and in thy prayers remember
Th'estate° of my poor queen. Leave me alone,   °*condition*
75 For I must think of that which company
Would not be friendly to.²
SUFFOLK   I wish your highness
A quiet night, and my good mistress will°   °*I will*
Remember in my prayers.
KING HENRY   Charles, good night. *Exit* SUFFOLK

Enter Sir Anthony DENNY
Well, sir, what follows?
80 DENNY   Sir, I have brought my lord the Archbishop,
As you commanded me.

---

2. *which . . . to:* which requires privacy.

KING HENRY   Ha, Canterbury?

DENNY Ay, my good lord.

KING HENRY   'Tis true—where is he, Denny?

DENNY He attends your highness' pleasure.

KING HENRY   Bring him to us.

                                  [*Exit* DENNY]

LOVELL [*aside*] This is about that which the Bishop° spake.   *Gardiner*

85   I am happily° come hither.   *fortunately*

        Enter CRANMER [*the Archbishop, ushered by*] DENNY

KING HENRY [*to* LOVELL *and* DENNY] Avoid° the gallery.   *Quit*

    [DENNY *begins to depart.*] LOVELL *seems to stay*

    Ha? I have said. Be gone.

    What?   *Exeunt* LOVELL *and* DENNY

CRANMER [*aside*] I am fearful. Wherefore° frowns he thus?   *Why*

    'Tis his aspect° of terror. All's not well.   *countenance*

90   KING HENRY How now, my lord? You do desire to know

    Wherefore I sent for you.

CRANMER [*kneeling*]   It is my duty

    T'attend your highness' pleasure.

KING HENRY   Pray you, arise,

    My good and gracious Lord of Canterbury.

    Come, you and I must walk a turn together.

95   I have news to tell you. Come, come—give me your hand.

        [CRANMER *rises. They walk*]

    Ah, my good lord, I grieve at what I speak,

    And am right sorry to repeat what follows.

    I have, and most unwillingly, of late

    Heard many grievous°—I do say, my lord,   *serious*

100 Grievous—complaints of you, which, being considered,

    Have moved us and our Council that you shall

    This morning come before us, where I know

    You cannot with such freedom purge° yourself   *with ease clear*

    But that, till further trial in those charges

105 Which will require your answer, you must take

    Your patience to you,³ and be well contented

    To make your house our Tower. You a brother of us,°   *a fellow councillor*

    It fits we thus proceed, or else no witness

    Would come against you.

CRANMER [*kneeling*]   I humbly thank your highness,

110 And am right glad to catch this good occasion

    Most throughly to be winnowed, where my chaff

    And corn shall fly asunder.⁴ For I know

    There's none stands under° more calumnious tongues   *is subject to*

    Than I myself, poor man.

KING HENRY   Stand up, good Canterbury.

115 Thy truth and thy integrity is rooted

    In us, thy friend. Give me thy hand. Stand up.

    Prithee, let's walk.

        [CRANMER *rises. They walk*]

          Now, by my halidom,°   *by our Lady*

    What manner of man are you? My lord, I looked°   *predicted*

---

3. *must . . . you:* must be patient.

4. *And am . . . asunder:* And I am glad to have the occasion thoroughly to see the bad ("chaff") separated from the good ("corn," or wheat) in my character. See Matthew 3:12 and Luke 3:17.

	You would have given me your petition that	
120	I should have ta'en some pains to bring together	
	Yourself and your accusers, and to have heard you	
	Without indurance° further.	*imprisonment*

CRANMER   Most dread liege,
    The good° I stand on is my truth and honesty.   *virtue*
    If they shall fail, I with mine enemies
125 Will triumph o'er my person, which I weigh not,
    Being of those virtues vacant.⁵ I fear nothing°   *not at all*
    What can be said against me.

KING HENRY   Know you not
    How your state stands i'th' world, with the whole world?
    Your enemies are many, and not small;° their practices   *insignificant*
130 Must bear the same proportion, and not ever
    The justice and the truth o'th' question carries
    The dew o'th' verdict with it.⁶ At what ease°   *How easily*
    Might corrupt minds procure knaves as corrupt
    To swear against you? Such things have been done.
135 You are potently° opposed, and with a malice   *powerfully*
    Of as great size. Ween you of ° better luck,   *Do you anticipate*
    I mean in perjured witness,° than your master,°   *evidence / Christ*
    Whose minister you are, whiles here he lived
    Upon this naughty° earth? Go to, go to.   *wicked*
140 You take a precipice for no leap of danger,
    And woo your own destruction.

CRANMER   God and your majesty
    Protect mine innocence, or I fall into
    The trap is° laid for me.   *that is*

KING HENRY   Be of good cheer.
    They shall no more prevail than we give way to.°   *let them*
145 Keep comfort to you, and this morning see
    You do appear before them. If they shall chance,
    In charging you with matters, to commit° you,   *imprison*
    The best persuasions to the contrary
    Fail not to use, and with what vehemency
150 Th'occasion shall instruct you. If entreaties
    Will render you no remedy, [*giving his ring*] this ring
    Deliver them, and your appeal to us
    There make before them.
          [CRANMER *weeps*]
                 Look, the good man weeps.
    He's honest, on mine honour. God's blest mother,
155 I swear he is true-hearted, and a soul
    None better in my kingdom. Get you gone,
    And do as I have bid you.   *Exit* CRANMER
                 He has strangled
    His language in his tears.
         Enter [*the*] OLD LADY

LOVELL (*within*)   Come back! What mean you?
        [*Enter* LOVELL, *following her*]

OLD LADY   I'll not come back. The tidings that I bring

---

5. *If . . . vacant*: If I lack truth and honesty, I will agree
with my enemies in condemning myself, whom I do not
value in the absence of truth and honesty.
6. *their . . . it*: their schemes are equally numerous and

powerful, and justice and truth do not always prevail.
"Dew" suggests fecundity or generosity; there may also
be a sense of "due," implying justness.

160 Will make my boldness manners.° [*To the* KING] Now good angels   *into manners*
   Fly o'er thy royal head, and shade thy person
   Under their blessèd wings.

KING HENRY   Now by thy looks
   I guess thy message. Is the Queen delivered?
   Say, 'Ay, and of a boy.'

OLD LADY   Ay, ay, my liege,
165 And of a lovely boy. The God of heaven
   Both now and ever bless her! 'Tis a girl°   *Anne; Elizabeth*
   Promises boys hereafter. Sir, your queen
   Desires your visitation, and° to be   *and for you*
   Acquainted with this stranger. 'Tis as like you
   As cherry is to cherry.

KING HENRY   Lovell—

170 LOVELL   Sir?

KING HENRY   Give her an hundred marks.° I'll to the Queen.   *roughly 65 pounds*

                                                    Exit

OLD LADY   An hundred marks? By this light, I'll ha' more.
   An ordinary groom is for° such payment.   *deserves*
   I will have more, or scold it out of him.
175 Said I for this the girl was like to him? I'll
   Have more, or else unsay't; and now, while 'tis hot,
   I'll put it to the issue.   *Exeunt*

5.2

Enter [pursuivants,° pages, footboys, and grooms. Then   *messengers*
   enter] CRANMER, *Archbishop of Canterbury*

CRANMER   I hope I am not too late, and yet the gentleman
   That was sent to me from the council prayed me
   To make great haste. All fast?° What means this? [*Calling at*   *The doors closed*
   the door] Ho!
   Who waits there?
                    Enter [a DOOR]KEEPER
                    Sure you know me?

DOORKEEPER   Yes, my lord,
   But yet I cannot help you.

5 CRANMER   Why?
                    Enter Doctor BUTTS [*passing over the stage*]

DOORKEEPER   Your grace must wait till you be called for.

CRANMER   So.

BUTTS [*aside*]   This is a piece of malice. I am glad
   I came this way so happily.° The King   *fortunately*
   Shall understand it presently.°   *Exit*   *immediately*

CRANMER [*aside*]   'Tis Butts,
10 The King's physician. As he passed along
   How earnestly he cast his eyes upon me!
   Pray heaven he sound° not my disgrace. For certain   *fathom; publicize*
   This is of purpose laid° by some that hate me—   *carried out*
   God turn their hearts, I never sought their malice—
15 To quench° mine honour. They would shame to make me   *destroy*
   Wait else at door, a fellow Councillor,
   'Mong boys, grooms, and lackeys. But their pleasures
   Must be fulfilled, and I attend with patience.

5.2 Location: Anteroom and council chamber at court.

Enter KING [HENRY] *and* [*Doctor*] BUTTS *at a window,*
above

BUTTS   I'll show your grace the strangest sight—

KING HENRY   What's that, Butts?

20 BUTTS   I think your highness saw this many a day.

KING HENRY   Body o'me, where is it?

BUTTS [*pointing at* CRANMER, *below*]   There, my lord.

    The high promotion of his grace of Canterbury,

    Who holds his state° at door, 'mongst pursuivants,   *waits with dignity*

    Pages, and footboys.

KING HENRY   Ha? 'Tis he indeed.

25 Is this the honour they do one another?

    'Tis well there's one above 'em[1] yet. I had thought

    They had parted° so much honesty among 'em—   *shared*

    At least good manners—as not thus to suffer

    A man of his place° and so near our favour   *rank*

30 To dance attendance on their lordships' pleasures,

    And at the door, too, like a post with packets!°   *courier with letters*

    By holy Mary, Butts, there's knavery!

    Let 'em alone, and draw the curtain close.

    We shall hear more anon.

        [CRANMER *and the* DOORKEEPER *stand to one side.*
                                    Exeunt the lackeys]
        [*Above,* BUTTS *partly draws the curtain close. Below,*][2] *a*
        council table [*is*] *brought in* [*along*] *with chairs and*
        stools, and placed under the [*cloth of*] *state. Enter* [*the*]
        LORD CHANCELLOR, [*who*] *places himself at the upper*
        end of the table, on the left hand, [*leaving*] *a seat void*
        above him [*at the table's head*] *as*° *for Canterbury's seat.*   *as if*
        [*The*] *Duke of* SUFFOLK, [*the*] *Duke of* NORFOLK, [*the*
        Earl of] SURREY, [*the*] LORD CHAMBERLAIN, [*and*] GARDI-
        NER, [*the Bishop of Winchester,*] *seat themselves in order*
        on each side [*of the table*]. CROMWELL [*sits*] *at* [*the*]
        lower end, [*and acts*] *as secretary*

35 LORD CHANCELLOR [*to* CROMWELL]   Speak to the business, master secretary.

    Why are we met in council?

CROMWELL   Please your honours,

    The chief cause concerns his grace of Canterbury.

GARDINER   Has he had° knowledge of it?   *been given*

CROMWELL   Yes.

NORFOLK [*to the* DOORKEEPER]   Who waits there?

DOORKEEPER [*coming forward*]

    Without,° my noble lords?   *Outside*

GARDINER   Yes.

DOORKEEPER   My lord Archbishop;

40 And has done half an hour, to know your pleasures.

LORD CHANCELLOR   Let him come in.

DOORKEEPER [*to* CRANMER]   Your grace may enter now.

        CRANMER *approaches the Council table*

LORD CHANCELLOR   My good lord Archbishop, I'm very sorry

    To sit here at this present° and behold   *moment*

---

1. Both God and King, here implicitly linked.
2. Some editions begin a new scene here. But Cranmer
should be visible throughout, and the King and Butts

stay sequestered in the gallery above the stage until the
King's abrupt entrance.

That chair stand empty, but we all are men

45 In our own natures frail, and capable°   *prone to failings*
Of our flesh; few are angels; out of which frailty
And want° of wisdom, you, that best should teach us,   *lack*
Have misdemeaned yourself,° and not a little,   *behaved badly*
Toward the King first, then his laws, in filling

50 The whole realm, by your teaching and your chaplains'—
For so we are informed—with new opinions,
Diverse and dangerous, which are heresies,
And, not reformed, may prove pernicious.°   *lethal*

GARDINER   Which reformation must be sudden too,

55 My noble lords; for those that tame wild horses
Pace 'em not in their hands to make 'em gentle,[3]
But stop their mouths with stubborn bits and spur 'em
Till they obey the manège.° If we suffer,°   *training / allow*
Out of our easiness° and childish pity   *leniency*

60 To one man's honour, this contagious sickness,
Farewell all physic°—and what follows then?   *remedies*
Commotions, uproars—with a general taint
Of the whole state, as of late days our neighbours,
The upper Germany, can dearly witness,[4]

65 Yet freshly pitied in our memories.

CRANMER   My good lords, hitherto in all the progress
Both of my life and office, I have laboured,
And with no little study,° that my teaching   *effort*
And the strong course of my authority

70 Might go one way, and safely; and the end
Was ever to do well. Nor is there living—
I speak it with a single° heart, my lords—   *pure*
A man that more detests, more stirs against,°   *actively resists*
Both in his private conscience and his place,°   *office*

75 Defacers° of a public peace than I do.   *Destroyers*
Pray heaven the King may never find a heart
With less allegiance in it. Men that make
Envy and crooked malice nourishment
Dare bite the best. I do beseech your lordships

80 That, in this case of justice, my accusers,
Be what they will,° may stand forth face to face,   *Whoever they are*
And freely urge against° me.   *openly accuse*

SUFFOLK   Nay, my lord,
That cannot be. You are a Councillor,
And by that virtue° no man dare accuse you.   *by virtue of that*

GARDINER [*to* CRANMER]   My lord, because we have business of

85   more moment,°   *import*
We will be short° with you. 'Tis his highness' pleasure   *brief*
And our consent, for better trial of you,
From hence you be committed to the Tower
Where, being but a private man again,

90 You shall know many dare accuse you boldly,
More than, I fear, you are provided for.°   *ready for*

CRANMER   Ah, my good lord of Winchester, I thank you.
You are always my good friend. If your will pass,°   *is approved*

---

3. Do not put them through their paces with only a hand for restraint.
4. Alluding to Protestant sects in Germany who fomented uprisings in urban centers in the 1520s and 1530s (the Peasants' War, 1524–26, and perhaps the killing of the Münster Anabaptists in 1535).

I shall both find your lordship judge and juror,[5]
95   You are so merciful. I see your end°—   *aim*
'Tis my undoing. Love and meekness, lord,
Become a churchman better than ambition.
Win straying souls with modesty again;
Cast none away. That I shall clear myself,
100 Lay all the weight ye can upon my patience,
I make as little doubt as you do conscience[6]
In doing daily wrongs. I could say more,
But reverence to your calling makes me modest.°   *temperate*
GARDINER   My lord, my lord—you are a sectary,°   *Protestant*
105 That's the plain truth. Your painted gloss discovers,
To men that understand you, words and weakness.[7]
CROMWELL [*to* GARDINER]   My lord of Winchester, you're a little,
By your good favour,° too sharp. Men so noble,   *If you'll excuse me*
However faulty, yet should find° respect   *be offered*
110 For what they have been. 'Tis a cruelty
To load° a falling man.   *burden further*
GARDINER   Good master secretary,
I cry your honour mercy.[8] You may worst°   *least justifiably*
Of all this table say so.
CROMWELL   Why, my lord?
GARDINER   Do not I know you for a favourer
Of this new sect? Ye are not sound.°   *loyal; orthodox*
115 CROMWELL   Not sound?
GARDINER   Not sound, I say.
CROMWELL   Would you were half so honest!
Men's prayers then would seek you, not their fears.
GARDINER   I shall remember this bold language.
CROMWELL   Do.
Remember your bold life, too.
LORD CHANCELLOR   This is too much.
Forbear, for shame, my lords.
GARDINER   I have done.
120 CROMWELL   And I.
LORD CHANCELLOR [*to* CRANMER]   Then thus for you, my lord. It
    stands agreed,
I take it, by all voices,° that forthwith   *votes*
You be conveyed to th' Tower a prisoner,
There to remain till the King's further pleasure
125 Be known unto us. Are you all agreed, lords?
ALL THE COUNCIL   We are.
CRANMER   Is there no other way of mercy,
But I must needs to° th' Tower, my lords?   *must go to*
GARDINER   What other
Would you expect? You are strangely° troublesome.   *extraordinarily*
Let some o'th' guard be ready there.
       Enter the guard
CRANMER   For me?
Must I go like a traitor thither?
130 GARDINER [*to the guard*]   Receive° him,   *Take*
And see him safe i'th' Tower.

---

5. Gardiner would both try (as "judge") and pass judgment (as "juror")—to Cranmer, an injustice.
6. I doubt no more than you act ethically.
7. *Your . . . weakness:* Your false exterior (or, perhaps,

your specious language) exposes, to men who can see
through you, empty words and human frailty.
8. I beg your pardon.

CRANMER   Stay, good my lords.
I have a little yet to say. Look there, my lords—
        [*He shows the King's ring*]
By virtue of that ring I take my cause
Out of the grips° of cruel men, and give it   clutches
135   To a most noble judge, the King my master.
LORD CHAMBERLAIN   This is the King's ring.
SURREY   'Tis no counterfeit.
SUFFOLK   'Tis the right ring, by heav'n. I told ye all
When we first put this dangerous stone a-rolling
'Twould fall upon ourselves.
NORFOLK   Do you think, my lords,
140   The King will suffer but the little finger
Of this man to be vexed?
LORD CHAMBERLAIN   'Tis now too certain.
How much more is his life in value with him!°   esteemed by the King
Would I were fairly out on't.°   out of (the plot)
                    [*Exit* KING *with* BUTTS *above*]
CROMWELL   My mind gave me,°   I suspected
In seeking tales and informations
145   Against this man, whose honesty the devil
And his disciples only envy at,°   covet; despise
Ye blew the fire that burns ye. Now have at ye!°   be on guard
            Enter [*below,*] KING [HENRY] *frowning on them.*
            [*He*] *takes his seat*
GARDINER   Dread sovereign, how much are we bound to heaven
In daily thanks, that gave us such a prince,
150   Not only good and wise, but most religious.
One that in all obedience makes the church
The chief aim of his honour, and, to strengthen
That holy duty, out of dear respect,°   sincere piety
His royal self in judgement comes to hear
155   The cause betwixt her° and this great offender.   (the Church)
KING HENRY   You were ever good at sudden commendations,°   extempore flattery
Bishop of Winchester. But know I come not
To hear such flattery now; and in my presence
They are too thin and base to hide offences.
160   To me you cannot reach. You play the spaniel,
And think with wagging of your tongue to win me.
But whatsoe'er thou tak'st me for, I'm sure
Thou hast a cruel nature and a bloody.
[*To* CRANMER] Good man, sit down.
            [CRANMER *takes his seat at the head of the Council
            table*]
                          Now let me see the proudest,
165   He° that dares most, but wag his finger at thee.   The man
By all that's holy, he had better starve°   die
Than but once think this place becomes thee not.
SURREY   May it please your grace—
KING HENRY   No, sir, it does not please me!
I had thought I had had men of some understanding
170   And wisdom of° my Council, but I find none.   in
Was it discretion, lords, to let this man,
This good man—few of you deserve that title—
This honest man, wait like a lousy footboy

At chamber door? And one as great as you are?
175 Why, what a shame° was this! Did my commission   shameful act
Bid ye so far forget yourselves? I gave ye
Power as he was a Councillor to try him,
Not as a groom. There's some of ye, I see,
More out of malice than integrity,
180 Would try him to the utmost, had ye mean;°   the means
Which ye shall never have while I live.

LORD CHANCELLOR   Thus far,
My most dread sovereign, may it like° your grace   please
To let my tongue excuse all. What was purposed°   intended
Concerning his imprisonment was rather—
185 If there be faith in men—meant for his trial
And fair purgation° to the world than malice,   acquittal of suspicion
I'm sure, in me.

KING HENRY   Well, well, my lords—respect him.
Take him and use him well, he's worthy of it.
I will say thus much for him—if a prince
190 May be beholden to a subject, I
Am for his love and service so to him.
Make me no more ado, but all embrace him.
Be friends, for shame, my lords. (To CRANMER) My lord of Canterbury,
I have a suit which you must not deny me:
195 That is a fair young maid that yet wants baptism—
You must be godfather, and answer for her.

CRANMER   The greatest monarch now alive may glory
In such an honour; how may I deserve it,
That am a poor and humble subject to you?

200 KING HENRY   Come, come, my lord—you'd spare your spoons.⁹
You shall have two noble partners with you—the old Duchess
of Norfolk and Lady Marquis Dorset. Will these please you?
[To GARDINER] Once more, my lord of Winchester, I charge you
Embrace and love this man.

GARDINER   With a true heart
And brother-love I do it.
        [GARDINER and CRANMER embrace]
205 CRANMER [weeping]   And let heaven
Witness how dear I hold this confirmation.

KING HENRY   Good man, those joyful tears show thy true heart.
The common voice,° I see, is verified   opinion
Of thee which says thus, 'Do my lord of Canterbury
210 A shrewd turn,° and he's your friend for ever.'   An act of malice
Come, lords, we trifle time away. I long
To have this young one made a Christian.
As I have made ye one, lords, one remain—
So I grow stronger, you more honour gain.   Exeunt

5.3
Noise and tumult within.° Enter PORTER [with rushes]   offstage
and his MAN [with a broken cudgel]
PORTER [to those within]   You'll leave° your noise anon, ye rascals.   stop
Do you take

___

9. The King teases Cranmer that he hesitates only because   spoons, the customary gift from a godparent to a child.
he wants to spare himself the expense of christening   5.3 Location: The palace yard.

The court for Paris Garden,[1] ye rude slaves?
Leave your gaping.°   *yelling*
ONE (*within*)   Good master porter, I belong to th' larder.°   *serve in the pantry*
5   PORTER   Belong to th' gallows, and be hanged, ye rogue!
Is this a place to roar in?
[*To his* MAN] Fetch me a dozen crab-tree staves, and strong ones,
[*Raising his rushes*] These are but switches to 'em.
[*To those within*]   I'll scratch your heads.
You must be seeing christenings? Do you look
10   For ale and cakes here, you rude rascals?
MAN   Pray, sir, be patient. 'Tis as much impossible,
Unless we sweep 'em from the door with cannons,
To scatter 'em as 'tis to make 'em sleep
On May-day morning[2]—which will never be.
15   We may as well push against Paul's° as stir 'em.   *St. Paul's Cathedral*
PORTER   How got they in, and be hanged?°   *(a curse or expletive)*
MAN   Alas, I know not. How gets the tide in?
As much as one sound cudgel° of four foot—   *club*
[*He raises his cudgel*]
You see the poor remainder°—could distribute,   *what's left of it*
I made no spare,° sir.   *spared no one*
20   PORTER   You did nothing, sir.
MAN   I am not Samson, nor Sir Guy, nor Colbrand,[3]
To mow 'em down before me; but if I spared any
That had a head to hit, either young or old,
He or she, cuckold or cuckold-maker,
25   Let me ne'er hope to see a chine° again—   *cut of beef*
And that I would not for a cow,° God save her!   *for anything*
ONE (*within*)   Do you hear, master porter?
PORTER   I shall be with you presently,
Good master puppy. [*To his* MAN] Keep the door close, sirrah.
MAN   What would you have me do?
30   PORTER   What should you do,
but knock 'em down by th' dozens? Is this Moorfields[4] to muster in? Or have we some strange Indian with the great tool
come to court,[5] the women so besiege us? Bless me, what a fry
of fornication[6] is at door! On my Christian conscience, this one
35   christening will beget a thousand. Here will be father, godfather, and all together.
MAN   The spoons° will be the bigger, sir. There is a fellow some-   *(for christening)*
what near the door, he should be a brazier° by his face, for o'   *brass worker*
my conscience twenty of the dog-days° now reign in's nose. All   *hottest summer days*
40   that stand about him are under the line[7]—they need no other
penance. That fire-drake° did I hit three times on the head, and   *fiery dragon*
three times was his nose discharged against me. He stands there
like a mortar-piece, to blow us.[8] There was a haberdasher's wife
of small wit near him, that railed upon me till her pinked por-

1. A park for bear- and bullbaiting located in Southwark, a London suburb, where the Globe Theatre also stood.
2. On May Day, revelers rose before dawn for festivities to greet spring.
3. Figures of legendary physical powers. In the Bible, Samson is renowned for his strength; in the romance tradition, Sir Guy of Warwick, who killed the Danish giant Colebrand, was also known for his prowess.
4. Parkland outside London's walls where citizen militias may have trained.
5. Indians brought to England and exhibited at court excited popular fascination, here about their genitalia.
6. Crowd of would-be fornicators or bastards.
7. All those near him seem to be standing at the equator, his face is so red.
8. Like a cannon, ready to blow us up; ready to blow his nose at us.

45 ringer⁹ fell off her head, for kindling such a combustion° in the   *tumult*
state. I missed the meteor° once, and hit that woman, who cried   *brazier*
out 'Clubs!',¹ when I might see from far some forty truncheon-
ers° draw to her succour, which were the hope o'th' Strand,²   *men with cudgels*
where she was quartered.° They fell on.° I made good my place.   *lived / attacked*
50 At length they came to th' broomstaff to° me. I defied 'em still,   *right next to*
when suddenly a file of boys behind 'em, loose shot,³ delivered
such a shower of pebbles that I was fain° to draw mine honour   *obliged*
in and let 'em win the work.° The devil was amongst 'em, I   *fort*
think, surely.

55 PORTER   These are the youths° that thunder at a playhouse, and   *apprentices*
fight for bitten apples, that no audience but the tribulation of
Tower Hill or the limbs of Limehouse,⁴ their dear brothers, are
able to endure. I have some of 'em in *limbo patrum*,⁵ and there
they are like to dance these three days, besides the running
60 banquet of two beadles that is to come.⁶
                    Enter [the] LORD CHAMBERLAIN

LORD CHAMBERLAIN   Mercy o' me, what a multitude are here!
They grow still, too—from all parts they are coming,
As if we kept a fair here! Where are these porters,
These lazy knaves? [*To the* PORTER *and his* MAN] You've made
        a fine hand,° fellows!   *nice work (ironic)*
65 There's a trim° rabble let in—are all these   *an elegant (ironic)*
Your faithful friends o'th' suburbs?⁷ we shall have
Great store of room, no doubt, left for the ladies
When they pass back from the christening!

PORTER   An't° please your honour,   *If it*
We are but men, and what so many may do,
70 Not being torn a-pieces, we have done.
An army cannot rule 'em.°   *keep them in order*

LORD CHAMBERLAIN   As I live,
If the King blame me for't, I'll lay ye all
By th' heels,° and suddenly—and on your heads   *In the stocks*
Clap round° fines for neglect. You're lazy knaves,   *large*
75 And here ye lie baiting of bombards° when   *you lie drinking*
Ye should do service.
                    [*Flourish of trumpets within*]
                    Hark, the trumpets sound.
They're come, already, from the christening.
Go break among the press,° and find a way out   *crowd*
To let the troop pass fairly,° or I'll find   *fittingly*
80 A Marshalsea shall hold ye play⁸ these two months.
                    [*As they leave, the* PORTER *and his* MAN *call within*]
PORTER   Make way there for the Princess!

---

9. Perforated small cap.
1. London apprentices would shout this when about to begin or end a street fight.
2. Fashionable shopping and residential part of London.
3. Marksmen (here, throwers) unattached to a company.
4. The tough crowds at the Tower for executions; or further east in Limehouse, a rough part of London near the docks.
5. In prison (literally, limbo of the fathers). Jewish patriarchs, because they predated Christ, at death went not to Christian heaven but to limbo, near hell, where

they remained until Judgment Day. With echoes of "limbs of Limehouse" (line 57).
6. *dance . . . come*: festive celebration ("dance") with dessert ("running banquet"); public whipping of prisoners (like a "running banquet," or dessert) after imprisonment (the main course) by minor law-enforcement officials ("beadles").
7. From the suburbs, areas outside London's city walls, beyond the city's legal jurisdiction, and hence considered lawless.
8. *I'll . . . play*: I'll shut you in the Marshalsea, a prison in Southwark.

MAN   You great fellow,[9]
    Stand close up,° or I'll make your head ache.   *Move aside*
PORTER   You i'th' camlet,° get up o'th' rail—   *rough cloth*
    I'll peck you o'er the pales else.[1]   *Exeunt*

5.4

Enter trumpet[er]s, sounding. Then [enter] two alder-
men, [the] Lord Mayor [of London], GARTER *[King-of-*
Arms], CRANMER *[the Archbishop of Canterbury, the]*
Duke of NORFOLK *with his marshal's staff, [the] Duke of*
SUFFOLK, two noblemen bearing great standing bowls for
the christening gifts; then [enter] four noblemen bearing
a canopy, under which [is] the Duchess of Norfolk, god-
mother, bearing the child [Elizabeth] richly habited in a
mantle, [whose] train [is] borne by a lady. Then follows
the Marchioness Dorset, the other godmother, and
ladies. The troop pass once about the stage and GARTER
speaks

GARTER   Heaven, from thy endless goodness send prosperous
    life, long, and ever happy, to the high and mighty Princess of
    England, Elizabeth.[1]
        Flourish. Enter KING [HENRY] *and guard*
CRANMER [*kneeling*]   And to your royal grace, and the good Queen!
5   My noble partners° and myself thus pray   *fellow godparents*
    All comfort, joy, in this most gracious lady,
    Heaven ever laid up to make parents happy,
    May hourly fall upon ye.
KING HENRY   Thank you, good lord Archbishop.
    What is her name?
CRANMER   Elizabeth.
KING HENRY   Stand up, lord.
        [CRANMER *rises*]
    [*To the child*] With this kiss take my blessing—
    [*He kisses the child*]
10   God protect thee,
    Into whose hand I give thy life.
CRANMER   Amen.
KING HENRY [*to* CRANMER, *old duchess, and Marchioness*]
    My noble gossips,° you've been too prodigal.°   *godparents / generous*
    I thank ye heartily. So shall this lady,
    When she has so much English.
CRANMER   Let me speak, sir,
15 For heaven now bids me, and the words I utter
    Let none think flattery, for they'll find 'em truth.
    This royal infant—heaven still° move about her—   *always*
    Though in her cradle, yet now promises
    Upon this land a thousand thousand blessings
20 Which time shall bring to ripeness. She shall be—
    But few now living can behold that goodness—
    A pattern to all princes living with her,

9. Addressed to someone either onstage or in the audience.
1. *get . . . else:* get off the rail (the railing running
around the edge of the stage), or I'll throw you off.
5.4 Location: The court.
1. This formulaic speech is similar to one given at the 1613

wedding of King James I's daughter Elizabeth to Prince
Frederick, the Elector Palatine. This scene parallels the
christening celebration of one Princess Elizabeth, in
the play, to the wedding celebration of another, at the
time of the play's first production.

And all that shall succeed. Saba² was never
More covetous° of wisdom and fair virtue   *desirous*
25   Than this pure soul shall be. All princely graces
That mould up° such a mighty piece° as this is,   *produce / masterpiece*
With all the virtues that attend the good,
Shall still be doubled on her. Truth shall nurse her,
Holy and heavenly thoughts still counsel her.
30   She shall be loved and feared. Her own° shall bless her;   *own people*
Her foes shake like a field of beaten° corn,   *windswept*
And hang their heads with sorrow. Good grows with her.
In her days every man shall eat in safety
Under his own vine what he plants, and sing
35   The merry songs of peace to all his neighbours.
God shall be truly known,° and those about her   *(via Protestantism)*
From her shall read° the perfect ways of honour,   *learn*
And by those claim their greatness, not by blood.
Nor shall this peace sleep with her, but, as when
40   The bird of wonder dies—the maiden phoenix³—
Her ashes new create another heir
As great in admiration° as herself,   *deserving of wonder*
So shall she leave her blessèdness to one,°   *(James I)*
When heaven shall call her from this cloud of darkness,°   *earthly state*
45   Who from the sacred ashes of her honour
Shall star-like rise as great in fame as she was,
And so stand fixed. Peace, plenty, love, truth, terror,
That were the servants to this chosen infant,
Shall then be his, and, like a vine, grow to him.
50   Wherever the bright sun of heaven shall shine,
His honour and the greatness of his name
Shall be, and make new nations.⁴ He shall flourish,
And like a mountain cedar reach his branches
To all the plains about him. Our children's children
Shall see this, and bless heaven.
55   **KING HENRY**   Thou speakest wonders.
CRANMER   She shall be, to the happiness of England,
An agèd princess. Many days shall see her,
And yet no day without a deed° to crown it.   *an accomplishment*
Would I had known no more. But she must die—
60   She must, the saints must have her—yet a virgin,
A most unspotted lily shall she pass
To th' ground, and all the world shall mourn her.
KING HENRY   O lord Archbishop,
Thou hast made me now a man. Never before
65   This happy child did I get° anything.   *beget; achieve*
This oracle of comfort has so pleased me
That when I am in heaven I shall desire
To see what this child does, and praise my maker.
I thank ye all. To you, my good Lord Mayor,

2. The Queen of Sheba visited Solomon in Jerusalem in order to benefit from his wisdom, and thus became a model for wise (but presumably deferential) women. See 1 Kings 10:1–10.
3. Mythical Arabian bird, the only one of its kind, who, when it dies after a long life, regenerates itself from its own ashes. James I inherits the spirit of the phoenix, Queen Elizabeth—a spirit now, perhaps, being passed on to his daughter Princess Elizabeth.
4. See Genesis 17:4: "A father of many nations have I made thee." The passage was frequently invoked in relation to Princess Elizabeth's marriage. The play here also compliments James on the "new nation" he has established in America, appropriately named Virginia after the "virgin" Queen Elizabeth (line 60).

70 And your good brethren, I am much beholden.
I have received much honour by your presence,
And ye shall find me thankful. Lead the way, lords.
Ye must all see the Queen, and she must thank ye.
She will be sick° else. This day, no man think   *unhappy*
75 He's business at his house, for all shall stay°—   *stop work*
This little one shall make it holiday.   [*Flourish.*] *Exeunt*

Epilogue

[*Enter* EPILOGUE]
EPILOGUE   'Tis ten to one this play can never please
All that are here. Some come to take their ease,
And sleep an act or two; but those, we fear,
We've frighted with our trumpets; so, 'tis clear,
5 They'll say 'tis naught.° Others to hear the city   *worth nothing*
Abused extremely, and to cry 'That's witty!'[1]—
Which we have not done neither; that,° I fear,   *such that*
All the expected good° we're like to hear   *anticipated praise*
For this play at this time is only in
10 The merciful construction of ° good women,   *interpretation by*
For such a one we showed 'em. If they smile,
And say "Twill do', I know within a while
All the best men are ours—for 'tis ill hap°   *luck*
If they hold° when their ladies bid 'em clap.   [*Exit*]   *refrain*

Epilogue
1. "The city," both London and its citizens, was sati-
rized in "city comedies" at the private theaters (as
opposed to public playhouses like the Globe, whose
leading dramatist here retaliates).

The Two Noble Kinsmen

When Prospero proclaims near the end of *The Tempest* (1611), "But this rough magic / I here abjure" (5.1.50–51), audiences often think they are hearing Shakespeare's farewell to the theater. But the final passage Shakespeare wrote for the stage is more likely to be found at the conclusion of *The Two Noble Kinsmen* (1613–14). Theseus, Duke of Athens, the play's highest-ranking character, attempts to grasp the ironic, paradoxical twists of fate he has witnessed:

> Never fortune
> Did play a subtler game—the conquered triumphs,
> The victor has the loss. Yet in the passage
> The gods have been most equal.
> . . . .
> Let us be thankful
> For that which is, and with you [the gods] leave dispute
> That are above our question. Let's go off
> And bear us like the time.
>
> (5.6.112–37)

It is thus tempting to interpret Theseus's resigned disillusionment as Shakespeare's last word—perhaps on life, certainly on *The Two Noble Kinsmen*. The message of the play is not that easy to determine, however. Theseus's emphasis on the gods, his confidence in their justice (they "have been most equal"), and his counsel of an ambivalent mixture of joy and sorrow ("bear us like the time") underestimate the grim cynicism that accompanies the undeniable pathos of the play. Chivalric military and sexual norms give a touching nobility to the action; but, arguably, they also generate the misery and destruction to which the bewildered Theseus attempts to respond.

The problem of determining the work's tone is related to the question of authorship. Shakespeare probably wrote *The Two Noble Kinsmen* with John Fletcher, a younger contemporary who succeeded him as the leading dramatist of Shakespeare's acting company, the King's Men. Several of Shakespeare's very early and very late plays may have involved collaboration. In his final years, he worked with Fletcher—on the lost *Cardenio* (1612–13; probably based on an episode of Part One of Cervantes's *Don Quixote*, 1605; translated 1612), on *All Is True* (*Henry VIII*; 1613), and on *The Two Noble Kinsmen*. For this last play, Shakespeare seems to have written most of the first and last acts plus a few other scenes, while his colleague composed the rest and, hence, slightly more than half of the work as a whole. (There may also be a third hand involved; see the Textual Note). The two main dramatists differ in style, presentation, and outlook. The rhetorically knotty, ritualistic, near-tragic grandeur in Shakespeare's share contrasts with the syntactically simpler, dramatically more dynamic, near-absurd deflation in Fletcher's. The play as a whole is, therefore, neither simply Shakespearean nor simply Fletcherian. It is the product of their collaboration and is accordingly marked by dissonance as well as unity.

Broadly speaking, *The Two Noble Kinsmen* represents a moment of transition from the more popular theater of Shakespeare's time to the more elite drama of Fletcher's. In many respects, it is typical of the very last phase of Shakespeare's career, and it offers a particularly illuminating comparison to other tragicomic romances written separately by Shakespeare and Fletcher in the preceding six or seven years. Among Shakespeare's leading works in this genre—*Pericles, The Winter's Tale, Cymbeline,* and *The Tempest*—one finds parallels to *The Two Noble Kinsmen's* medieval source, pseudo-historical ancient Greek setting, emphasis on spectacle and ceremony, defense of innocence in the midst of corruption, striving for self-mastery, and transcendence of self-interest. There are further similarities in the insistence on death as a necessary price of the survivors' happiness, successful supplication to the gods for aid, and consequent sense of a controlling metaphysical presence that orders events in a way that is beyond human control. Although *The Two Noble Kinsmen* occurs exclusively on dry land, the work replicates even the trademark maritime imagery of Shakespearean romance, with its focus on peril and destruction: the dying Arcite "such a vessel 'tis that floats but for / The surge that next approaches" (5.6.83–84).

Yet *The Two Noble Kinsmen* has a very different feel from other romances of the time. As the Prologue explains, "Chaucer, of all admired, the story gives" (line 13). The main plot is taken—with greater freedom by Shakespeare than by Fletcher—from *The Knight's Tale,* which immediately follows *The General Prologue* in *The Canterbury Tales* (late fourteenth century). Its subject is the mortal rivalry between Palamon and Arcite, the two cousins referred to in the title, for the hand of Emilia. But the play's atypicality stems only partly from its resulting stylized chivalric ethos and accompanying acts of courtesy, acts that go beyond even what is found in Chaucer. What sets *The Two Noble Kinsmen* apart is its unusually somber resolution to the impossible dilemmas of the plot. Despite Theseus's assertions, the behavior of the gods does not restore confidence in a benevolent Providence. Indeed, Mars, whose intercession Arcite requests, and Venus, to whom Palamon prays, emblematize the chaos reigning in human affairs. The play is also structurally distinctive. Shakespearean romance reveals the passage from suffering to serenity, the redemption of the older generation by the younger (and particularly by the virtuous daughter). But Shakespeare and Fletcher's play has no interest in the restorative workings of time. All relationships occur within a single generation, and the young woman (Emilia) incites violence rather than reconciliation.

For these reasons, *The Two Noble Kinsmen* is sometimes viewed as an antiromance. As such, it bears comparison both to Shakespeare's other collaborations with Fletcher, noted earlier, and to a number of Shakespeare's earlier plays, which are pervasively echoed particularly in Fletcher's scenes. Palamon and Arcite's initial resignation in prison recalls *Richard II*; their conflict over Emilia, *The Two Gentlemen of Verona*; Emilia's comparison of pictures, *Hamlet.* When Arcite asks for a sign before his decisive battle with Palamon, he correctly takes Mars's answering thunder as a promise of victory. But this reassurance is no less duplicitous than the guarantee that "none of woman born / Shall harm Macbeth" (*Macbeth,* 4.1.96–97), with the important difference that Macbeth is a usurping mass murderer whereas Arcite is guilty only of desiring a woman his cousin saw first. The divine poetic justice often thought to be operating, however deviously, in *Macbeth* seems like little more than a dirty trick in *The Two Noble Kinsmen.*

A similar indebtedness to previous Shakespearean plays marks the subplot, which has no known source and which dramatizes the unrequited love of the Jailer's Daughter for Palamon. It is mainly the work of Fletcher, who borrowed the morris dance before Theseus and Hippolyta in 3.5 not from Shakespeare but from a masque (an aristocratic theatrical event emphasizing song, dance, and spectacle) that Francis Beaumont had composed for court performance in February 1613. (The morris dance itself is a rural folk form often performed on May Day by dancers in outlandish costumes who employ stock characters to partly mime traditional stories.) Otherwise, the Shakespearean legacy is pronounced. The Daughter's fall into madness when ignored by Palamon is modeled on Ophelia's in *Hamlet,* complete with an attempted suicide. Her willow song (4.1.79–80) was earlier sung by Desdemona in *Othello*. The Doctor who prescribes her cure previously ministered to King Lear and rather more unsuccessfully to Lady Macbeth. When the Daughter joins the people whom "ruder tongues distinguish 'villager' " (3.5.106) in the morris dance, the allusion is to another play indebted to *The Knight's Tale*: in *A Midsummer Night's Dream*, "rude mechanicals" (artisans, 3.2.9) also perform before Theseus and Hippolyta on the occasion of their wedding, and unrequited lovers wander through the forest.

But *The Two Noble Kinsmen* is *A Midsummer Night's Dream* with a difference. One of Shakespeare's previous romances, *The Winter's Tale*, might be understood as the tragic jealousy of *Othello* lightened and redeemed by the pastoral experience of a romantic comedy, *As You Like It*. By contrast, in *The Two Noble Kinsmen*, the comic tone of *A Midsummer Night's Dream* is darkened by the intervening experience of *Measure for Measure*, *All's Well That Ends Well*, and especially *Troilus and Cressida*, a work also drawing on Chaucerian narrative to depict a combination of chivalry and sensuality that leads to self-destructive violence and an indifference to the desires of the idealized woman. Indeed, Theseus's final words, quoted earlier, have been likened to Gloucester's metaphysical despair in *King Lear*:

> As flies to wanton boys are we to th' gods;
> They kill us for their sport.
>
> (Folio, 4.1.37–38)

A geographical and legendary legacy lies behind this outlook. Although the opening scene and the vast majority of the remainder of the play are set in and around Athens, the darker influence of Thebes is immediately felt. In an episode greatly expanded from the source, three widowed queens beg Theseus to come to their aid against Thebes, thus introducing the military dimension of chivalric conduct. Theseus reluctantly yields to Hippolyta's and Emilia's entreaties to defer his own pleasure (marriage to Hippolyta) to help dowagers in distress. His intervention pits him against Palamon and Arcite, who conclude that they must fight for their home city despite their hatred of its ruler, Creon. This initial sequence implicitly invokes Thebes' history of intrafamilial violence. According to ancient Greek narratives, Cadmus sows the soil with serpent's teeth, from which armed men grow; these men slaughter each other and, together with Cadmus, the few survivors found Thebes. Later, Oedipus unwittingly murders his father, and as the play opens, his two sons have killed each other in a battle for the throne that has also widowed the three queens.

The two cousins, imprisoned following Theseus's victory over Thebes, are compelled to repeat this history. When Theseus catches them fighting each other over Emilia, he orders their death, only to reverse his decision at Hippolyta's and Emilia's request. He ultimately proposes a chivalric combat in which each cousin is to be aided by three knights and all members of the losing side are to be executed. This plan increases the expected death toll beyond what is necessary and, indeed, beyond what is found in Chaucer. It is thwarted by the accidental death of Arcite, a death that is hard to see as providential but that undeniably makes Theseus's strategy look bad by comparison. Earlier, Palamon laments "Mars's so-scorned altar" and yearns for war "to get the soldier work, that peace might purge / For her repletion" (1.2.20, 23–24). This image of war as the virtuous means of purging the excesses of peace is echoed in Arcite's prayer to Mars, who

> heal'st with blood
> The earth when it is sick, and cur'st the world
> O'th' plurisy of people.
>
> (5.1.63–65)

Yet *The Two Noble Kinsmen* sees in war and chivalric combat less a cure for society than a loss of life.

A compulsive sexuality bears much of the blame for the havoc that is wreaked. As Theseus says, "Being sensually subdued / We lose our human title" (1.1.231–32). Arcite and especially Palamon are willing to kill and die for a woman about whom they know nothing except her appearance, and even that only at a distance. Arcite seems partly motivated by competitive emulation, by a desire to spite Palamon. He tells his cousin that when he sees Emilia, he will "pitch between her arms to anger thee" (2.2.221). The kinsmen claim rights to Emilia while serving life sentences in prison and without her being aware of their existence, much less expressing any interest in them. Her feelings don't matter to them. From this perspective, chivalric combat seems an appropriate mechanism for determining which cousin deserves her. In the event, this stance is validated by their society through the intervention of Theseus. Emilia really doesn't have the choice of rejecting them both. When, bowing to the inevitable, she temporarily is attracted to them, she is unable to decide between "two such young handsome men" (4.2.3). She, too, looks only to looks.

Palamon's prayer to Venus unwittingly reveals a simultaneous approval and denigration of sexuality:

> I knew a man
> Of eighty winters, this I told them, who
> A lass of fourteen brided—'twas thy power
> To put life into dust. The agèd cramp
> Had screwed his square foot round,
> The gout had knit his fingers into knots,
> Torturing convulsions from his globy eyes
> Had almost drawn their spheres, that what was life
> In him seemed torture. This anatomy
> Had by his young fair fere a boy, and I
> Believed it was his, for she swore it was,
> And who would not believe her?
>
> (5.2.39–50)

The power of love is thus exalted through deliberately repellent description. The reference to the "boy" anticipates imagery of sexuality and reproduction at the conclusion—

The beginning of *The Knight's Tale*, from *The Workes of Our Ancient and Learned English Poet, Geffrey Chaucer* (1602 ed.).

"consummation," "miscarry," "conceives," "deliver" (5.5.94, 101, 137, 138)—that is unremittingly associated with loss. And the account ends with an apparently rhetorical but actually open question that undermines both Venus's sovereignty and female chastity. The very celebration of love has the effect of raising anxieties about women's fidelity and childbirth.

Heterosexual desire is rendered even more unappealing in *The Two Noble Kinsmen* by the extended representation of what it destroys. This positive alternative is same-sex attachment, whether understood as the Renaissance ideal of male friendship, as girlish intimacy, or as homoerotic attraction. In a romantic comedy such as *Much Ado About Nothing*, the rejection of heterosexual bonding is seen as an immature

The imprisoned Palamon and Arcite gazing at Emilia in the garden below. From a French translation of about 1455 of Giovanni Boccaccio's *Teseida* (the source of Chaucer's *Knight's Tale*), by René of Anjou.

foible to be overcome. Here, however, the movement from same-sex innocence to heterosexual experience is figured primarily as loss—comically in the Prologue, with its comparison of "new plays and maidenheads" (line 1), more grimly thereafter. Although in no other respect an Amazon, Emilia emphatically does prefer virginity and the company of females to the prospect of marriage. She tells Theseus that if he does not grant her petition, she will not "be so hardy / Ever to take a husband" (1.1.203–4). In her sexual joking with her Woman, she says that "men are mad things" (2.2.126) and praises the rose above all other flowers because "it is the very emblem of a maid" (2.2.137). Even after coming to admire the cousins, she still prays to Diana either that the more loving and deserving win her or that she be allowed to continue a virgin "in thy band" (5.3.26). When Theseus tells her, "If you can love, end this difference" by choosing one of the kinsmen, she evasively replies, "I cannot, sir. They are both too excellent" (3.6.277, 285).

This stance is explained by Emilia's earlier touching recollection of her intimacy with Flavina, who died when each was eleven. Her account of two girls who "loved for [simply because] we did" (1.3.61) culminates in this exchange:

> EMILIA . . . the true love 'tween maid and maid may be
> More than in sex dividual.
> HIPPOLYTA You're out of breath,
> And this high-speeded pace is but to say
> That you shall never, like the maid Flavina,
> Love any that's called man.
> EMILIA I am sure I shall not.
>
> (1.3.81–86)

Female friendship thus stands against the absolute monarch's commitment to enforced marriage. Neither she nor the play repudiates this position.

Palamon and Arcite do so, however, choosing to kill and die—and hence to ruin the most precious thing in their lives, their love for each other—out of desire for Emilia. This resolution of the standard Renaissance debate over the respective claims of love and friendship has a paradoxical effect. The very depreciation of the cousins' attachment, which is not emphasized in Chaucer, only highlights its value. When they are first imprisoned, though they regret that life imprisonment precludes marriage and family, their thoughts quickly turn to each other. Arcite recommends "the enjoying of our griefs together" (2.2.60) and misogynistically notes the danger of freedom, which "might, like women / Woo us to wander from" "the ways of honour" (lines 75–76, 73). "Were we at liberty / A wife might part us lawfully," but in prison "we are one another's wife, ever begetting / New births of love" (lines 88–89, 80–81).

As they boast of their loving friendship, Palamon's first sight of Emilia undermines their resolution. She is talking to her Woman about the narcissus flower. This leads her to reflect upon the myth of Narcissus, who fell in love with his own beautiful reflection in a pool and died pining for it: "That was a fair boy, certain, but a fool / To love himself. Were there not maids enough?" (2.2.120–21). This implicit connection between Palamon and Narcissus is made explicit when Emilia remarks that Palamon shows

> not a smile.
> Yet these that we count errors may become him:
> Narcissus was a sad boy, but a heavenly.
> (4.2.30–32)

Palamon's suggested autoeroticism and preference for males over females is anticipated in Emilia's immediately preceding, unequivocally homosexual description of Arcite:

> Just such another wanton Ganymede
> Set Jove afire once, and enforced the god
> Snatch up the goodly boy and set him by him.
> (4.2.15–17)

Similarly, as the cousins prepare to arm and then battle each other, Arcite admiringly remarks, "Defy me in these fair terms, and you show / More than a mistress to me" (3.6.25–26). And most strikingly of all, when Arcite is released from prison, Palamon imagines what would happen if the roles were reversed:

> Were I at liberty I would do things
> Of such a virtuous greatness that this lady,
> This blushing virgin, should take manhood to her
> And seek to ravish me.
> (2.2.260–63)

Even the thought of the woman he loves becomes a fantasy of homosexual rape.

If the play anywhere offers an ideal balance between same-sex and other-sex bonding, it is in Theseus, whose friendship with Pirithous coexists comfortably with his impending marriage to Hippolyta. As suggested earlier, however, Theseus's conduct is open to question. Moreover, it is at least suggested that marriage to Hippolyta will never measure up to friendship with Pirithous. Most important, the catastrophic experience of Emilia and the kinsmen carries far more weight than Theseus's greater success in negotiating potentially antagonistic emotional and sexual attachments. Nonetheless, the figure of Theseus may be crucial to an extended allusion to the Jacobean court in *The Two Noble Kinsmen*. Theseus is perhaps an idealized image of King James, who combined marriage with homosexual behavior. In this interpretation, Arcite's death corresponds to the death of James's oldest son, Prince Henry, in the fall of 1612. The concluding, bittersweet union of Emilia with Palamon similarly parallels the marriage a few months later of James's daughter Elizabeth with the Elector Palatine. The probable revivals of 1619–20 and 1625–26, as well as the publication of the First Quarto in 1634, may also have resonated with court life. On the other hand, the evidence is not overwhelming for a direct connection of the play to the Jacobean court, whose members in any case might not have been flattered by the comparison. Such questions could not much matter to subsequent audiences, however, and with the exception of an adaptation in the late 1660s, *The Two Noble Kinsmen* seems to have remained unstaged until 1928. Since then, performances have tended to be effective when they have eschewed realism for ritual. But an interesting alternative is provided by a 1979 production, where the decision to employ an all-male cast emphasized the work's homoerotic motifs.

A joust celebrating the marriage of Henry IV of England to Joan of Navarre. From the Beauchamp Pageant (1485–90).

In general, however, beginning with the late seventeenth-century adaptation, the most consistently successful feature of the staging has been the Jailer's Daughter, who, though isolated and powerless, often emerges as the drama's central figure. Her four successive soliloquies in the middle of the play (2.4, 2.6, 3.2, 3.4), three of them probably—and the fourth perhaps—by Fletcher, are marked by exclamations, questions, and a consequent intimacy with the audience are denied the other characters. The Daughter's special stage position thus helps win sympathy for her. In Shakespeare's plays, this position is characteristically reserved for a lower-class male character, especially the clown or fool, with whom the groundlings might identify. Here, however, we see a meshing of Shakespeare's interest in the folk with Fletcher's in strong women.

The Daughter stands at the center of a subplot that interacts with and critically reflects on the main action. Immediately following some frank sexual talk by the morris dancers in 2.3, she delivers her first soliloquy and then frees Palamon from prison in the hope that he will satisfy her sexual desire for him. Even though the genders are reversed, the situation is the same as in the main plot: the person in love knows little of the beloved, who, in turn, is almost completely oblivious of the lover. When the Daughter later joins the morris dance, she is appropriately cast as the "She-fool" (3.5.138 stage direction). In a dramaturgical sense, she *is* the female equivalent of the fool, for by this time Palamon's indifference has driven her mad. Her illness is cured pragmatically and amorally. On the advice of the Doctor and over the principled objections of her father (the Jailer), the Wooer pretends to be Palamon and makes love with her. Tricked into losing a virginity she was not trying to preserve, "she's well restored / And to be married shortly" (5.6.27–28) to the man who is socially and emotionally right for her. (Earlier, he foils her attempted suicide.) This outcome makes perfect sense in light of Renaissance medicine, which believed hysteria was caused by a wandering womb that could be returned to its proper place by intercourse. More cynically, however, one might conclude that the only thing women really need is sex and that any man will do.

The Daughter thinks she is marrying one man only to end up with another. Similarly, as Emilia settles into her fate, fate forces her to resettle her affections. Neither woman is given a choice—which is just as well, since neither is capable of making distinctions. The generic names in the subplot—Daughter, Jailer, Wooer, Doctor, Brother, Friends—highlight lack of individuality while pointing toward a similar absence in the main plot. The critical effort to discriminate between Palamon and Arcite inadvertently reaffirms what it seeks to deny: that it takes an effort to tell the cousins apart.

Even the Daughter's madness is arguably no more deviant and certainly much less destructive than the suicidal and homicidal behavior of Palamon and Arcite. Yet the two noble kinsmen are taken seriously in a way that she is not. Either because she is a woman or because she is from the lower class or both, she has no right to expect her feelings to be reciprocated, even though she has done more for Palamon than either of the cousins has for Emilia. It is unclear, however, whether the play aims to call attention to this obvious double standard. Ironically, her service to Palamon leads to Arcite's death after earlier bringing Palamon within a hair's breadth of the executioner's ax. Palamon meets the Jailer on his way to the block, graciously acknowledges his gratitude to "your gentle daughter" (5.6.24), and "gives his purse" (5.6.32 stage direction) as part of the dowry for her impending marriage. His generosity infects the other knights slated to die with him:

FIRST KNIGHT	Nay, let's be offerers all.
SECOND KNIGHT	Is it a maid?
PALAMON	Verily, I think so—
	(5.6.32–33)

Thus, with the play's characteristic irony, "they give their purses" (5.6.35 stage direction) on a doubly false assumption—that they are doomed and that they are contributing to a virgin's dowry. But in another sense, the Daughter is bought off. Palamon speaks with greater accuracy than he knows in saying she is "more to me deserving / Than I can quit [requite] or speak of " (5.6.34–35).

Long before this, the Daughter's sequence of soliloquies has come to an end. In the second half of the play, having moved from one form of folly to another, she appears only in dialogue scenes and hence partly loses her unique contact with the audience. Yet even here, her vigorous language and stage presence produce an immediacy that effectively combines with the pathos of her predicament. It is, finally, a pathos she shares with the characters in the main plot, who watch in bewildered incomprehension as their most cherished ideals fail them when it matters most.

WALTER COHEN

TEXTUAL NOTE

The Two Noble Kinsmen dates from between February 20, 1613, and October 31, 1614. The mention of "our losses" in the Prologue (line 32) has sometimes been taken as a reference to the burning of the Globe Theatre on June 29, 1613. If so, this is Shakespeare's final play, perhaps performed at Blackfriars, the King's Men's indoor theater, in the fall of 1613 or winter of 1614, or at the opening of the rebuilt Globe, their outdoor theater, a year after the fire. Both the only substantive text, the Quarto of 1634 (Q), and an entry from earlier the same year in the Stationers' Register (a listing of books approved for publication), which calls the play a "TragiComedy," attribute it to John Fletcher and Shakespeare. The exclusion of *The Two Noble Kinsmen* from the First Folio of 1623 (F) has sometimes led to doubts about Shakespeare's authorship, but most scholars accept the attribution, which is supported by other internal and external evidence.

Although the exact division of labor between the two playwrights cannot be determined with certainty, Shakespeare probably wrote a little less than half the play: 1.1–2.1 (although some scholars give Fletcher 1.4–1.5), perhaps 2.3, 3.1, perhaps 3.2, perhaps 4.3, 5.1.34–5.3 (although 5.2 is sometimes attributed to Fletcher), and 5.5–5.6. These attributions are necessarily tentative, given the likelihood that the plan of the play changed a bit in the course of composition and that Fletcher undertook some revision to bring the play to its final form—perhaps of Shakespeare's text, perhaps of his own in light of Shakespeare's sections. A further complication is the possible presence of a third, less central, author—either Francis Beaumont, a major collaborator with Fletcher, or, more likely, Nathan Field, who also collaborated with Fletcher at this time and might have been one of the leading actors in the performance of the play.

Q is based either on the authors' manuscript or on a scribal transcript. The latter is the more likely alternative. The manuscript apparently underwent some revision, possibly by an author, perhaps in the Prologue, more probably in 4.2, and especially in 4.3. Whether authorial or scribal, it was annotated with stage directions and other indications (for instance, about props) in preparation for performance, perhaps more than once—for the original production and again for a revival in 1625–26 by Edward Knight, who worked for the King's Men at the time.

Two compositors probably set the type for Q, alternating work quite frequently. The printed text is a good one, but it contains two scenes headed 2.4 (followed by 2.6); editors routinely convert the second 2.4 to 2.5. Q also follows 3.4 with 3.6 and 3.7, perhaps a sign of an original 3.5 that was cut without the subsequent scenes being renumbered, as they are here (as 3.5 and 3.6). In addition, it missets verse as prose and, more often (2.1, 4.3), prose as verse. Some editors have ignored Q's scene break between 2.1 and 2.2 on the grounds that the scene is continuous. As the notes explain, the present edition proposes a staging for the two scenes that justifies the scene division. On the other hand, though again for reasons of staging, this edition expands Q's

5.1 into three scenes: the final three scenes in the play are, therefore, converted from 5.2–4 to 5.4–6.

SELECTED BIBLIOGRAPHY

Berggren, Paula S. "'For what we lack / We laugh': Incompletion and *The Two Noble Kinsmen*." *Modern Language Studies* 14.4 (1984): 3–17. Sees the play as an anti-romance marked by frustrated attempts at action, intensified through the imagery, and by lack of either divine justice or redemptive reconciliation.

Briggs, Julia. "Tears at the Wedding: Shakespeare's Last Phase." *Shakespeare's Late Plays: New Readings*. Ed. Jennifer Richards and James Knowles. Edinburgh: Edinburgh University Press, 1999. 210–27. *The Two Noble Kinsmen* as typical of Shakespeare's late collaborations with Fletcher in its grim posing of irreconcilable choices in the absence of metaphysical consolation.

Bruster, Douglas. "The Jailer's Daughter and the Politics of Madwomen's Language." *Shakespeare Quarterly* 46 (1995): 277–300. Sees the Daughter as powerless and isolated but nonetheless central to the play, her unique language marked by class and gender, her madness constituting a form of resistance; more generally, her depiction understood as the intersection of Shakespeare's interest in the folk and Fletcher's in strong women characters, and also as indicative of a transition to a less popular drama.

Finkelpearl, Philip J. "Two Distincts, Division None: Shakespeare's and Fletcher's *The Two Noble Kinsmen* of 1613." *Elizabethan Theater: Essays in Honor of S. Schoenbaum*. Ed. R. B. Parker and S. P. Zitner. Newark: University of Delaware Press, 1996. 184–99. Shakespearean cosmological concerns versus Fletcher's more worldly and irreverent approach, united by a critical independence from views of honor and chivalry associated with the royal family.

Frey, Charles, ed. *Shakespeare, Fletcher, and "The Two Noble Kinsmen."* Columbia: University of Missouri Press, 1989. A collection of modern criticism together with a review of scholarship on the play.

Herman, Peter C. "'Is This Winning?': Prince Henry's Death and the Problem of Chivalry in *The Two Noble Kinsmen*." *South Atlantic Review* 62 (1997): 1–31. The death of King James's son and heir as a blow to chivalry, generating in the play a skepticism about its martial and erotic implications.

Potter, Lois, ed. *The Two Noble Kinsmen*. 3rd ed. Walton-on-Thames, Surrey: Thomas Nelson, 1997. Outstanding scholarly edition with a lengthy critical introduction.

Shannon, Laurie J. "Emilia's Argument: Friendship and 'Human Title' in *The Two Noble Kinsmen*." *English Literary Renaissance* 64 (1997): 657–682. Emilia as Amazonian rational advocate of female friendship (understood as chastity, homoeroticism, and conscience) against irrational absolute power (understood as imposing the obligation to marry).

Spencer, Theodore. "*The Two Noble Kinsmen*." *Modern Philology* 36 (1939): 255–76. Contrasts the ritualistic action and convoluted rhetoric of Shakespeare's scenes with the greater emotional intensity but slighter thematic depth of Fletcher's.

Stewart, Alan. "'Near Akin': The Trials of Friendship in *The Two Noble Kinsmen*." *Shakespeare's Late Plays: New Readings*. Ed. Jennifer Richards and James Knowles. Edinburgh: Edinburgh University Press, 1999. 57–71. The main plot as the failure of idealized male friendship and especially kinship, showing the incompatibility of classical and chivalric ideals with Jacobean social reality.

The Two Noble Kinsmen

THE PERSONS OF THE PLAY

PROLOGUE
THESEUS, Duke of Athens
HIPPOLYTA, Queen of the Amazons, later wife of Theseus
EMILIA, her sister
PIRITHOUS, friend of Theseus
PALAMON ⎱ the two noble kinsmen, cousins, nephews of
ARCITE ⎰ Creon, the King of Thebes
Hymen, god of marriage
A BOY, who sings
ARTESIUS, an Athenian soldier
Three QUEENS, widows of kings killed in the siege of Thebes
VALERIUS, a Theban
A HERALD
WOMAN, attending Emilia
An Athenian GENTLEMAN
MESSENGERS
Six KNIGHTS, three attending Arcite and three Palamon
A SERVANT
A JAILER in charge of Theseus' prison
The JAILER'S DAUGHTER
The JAILER'S BROTHER
The WOOER of the Jailer's daughter
Two FRIENDS of the Jailer
A DOCTOR
Six COUNTRYMEN, one dressed as a babion, or baboon
Gerald, a SCHOOLMASTER
NELL, a country wench
Four other country wenches: Friz, Madeline, Luce, and
    Barbara
Timothy, a TABORER
EPILOGUE
Nymphs, attendants, maids, executioner, guard

Prologue

Flourish.° [*Enter* PROLOGUE]   *Trumpet call*
PROLOGUE   New plays and maidenheads are near akin:
    Much followed both, for both much money giv'n
    If they stand sound and well.[1] And a good play,
5   Whose modest scenes blush on his marriage day
    And shake to lose his honour,[2] is like her
    That after holy tie° and first night's stir   *marriage*
    Yet still is modesty, and still retains

Prologue
1. *stand sound and well:* sexual wordplay about virility and lack of venereal disease.
2. *Whose . . . honour:* Whose previously unwatched scenes are "modest" and shy (they "blush") on opening night and "shake" with fear at the thought of being viewed (losing their virginity).

More of the maid to sight than husband's pains.³

We pray our play may be so,° for I am sure   *(modest)*

10   It has a noble breeder° and a pure,   *begetter*

  A learnèd, and a poet never went

  More famous yet 'twixt Po and silver Trent.⁴

  Chaucer, of° all admired, the story gives: *by*

  There° constant to eternity it lives.   *In his words*

15   If we let fall° the nobleness of this°   *demean / (the poem)*

  And the first sound this child° hear be a hiss,   *play*

  How will it shake the bones of that good man,°   *(Chaucer)*

  And make him cry from under ground, 'O fan

  From me the witless chaff of such a writer,

20   That blasts my bays and my famed works makes lighter

  Than Robin Hood'?⁵ This is the fear we bring,

  For to say truth, it were an endless° thing   *never-ending; pointless*

  And too ambitious to aspire to him,°   *(Chaucer)*

  Weak as we are, and almost breathless swim

25   In this deep water. Do but you hold out

  Your helping hands and we shall tack about

  And something do to save us.⁶ You shall hear

  Scenes, though below his art, may yet appear

  Worth two hours' travail.⁷ To his bones, sweet sleep;

30   Content to you. If this play do not keep

  A little dull time from us,⁸ we perceive

  Our losses fall so thick we must needs leave.⁹   *Flourish.* [*Exit*]

1.1

Music. Enter Hymen° *with a torch burning, a* BOY *in a*   *god of marriage*
white robe before, singing and strewing flowers. After
Hymen, a nymph encompassed in her tresses, bearing a
wheaten garland.¹ Then THESEUS *between two other*
nymphs with wheaten chaplets° on their heads. Then   *wreaths*
HIPPOLYTA,² *the bride, led by* [PIRITHOUS] *and another*
holding a garland over her head, her tresses likewise
hanging. After her, EMILIA *holding up her train.* [*Then*
ARTESIUS *and other attendants*]

BOY [*sings during procession*]

    Roses, their sharp spines being gone,

    Not royal in their smells alone,

    But in their hue;

---

3. *still . . . pains:* still looks more like a virgin ("maid") than like a married woman who has experienced her husband's sexual exertions.

4. *a poet . . . Trent:* there has never been a more famous poet from Italy to England. The Po is a river in Italy, the Trent an English waterway.

5. *That . . . Hood:* Who disgraces my fame as a poet (garlands of bay or laurel were awarded to great poets, hence the name "poet laureate") and makes my renowned creations seem more trivial than a popular tale or ballad (such as Robin Hood).

6. *Do but . . . us:* Help us by applauding, and we will turn like a sailboat in the breeze produced by your clapping hands, thereby saving our reputation.

7. *two hours' travail:* the actors' labor ("travail") for two hours in performing the play (standard length was two to three hours); also, since Q reads "travel," the audience will take part in a two-hour imaginative journey

while watching the play. "Travail" continues the metaphor of childbirth and rearing begun in line 10, which itself develops from the image of the loss of virginity on the marriage night.

8. *keep . . . us:* keep us amused.

9. Our losses will be so great that we will need to quit the theater. The "losses" refer to the decline in reputation from a poorly received play and perhaps also to the burning of the Globe Theatre on June 29, 1613, during a performance of *All Is True* (*Henry VIII*).

1.1 Location: Athens, near the temple where Hippolyta and Theseus are to be married.

1. The young woman's hair hangs loose, indicating virginity; her garland signifies fertility.

2. According to legend, Hippolyta was Queen of the Amazons before Theseus conquered her race of women warriors and brought her to Thebes as his captive and bride.

Maiden pinks, of odour faint,
5   Daisies smell-less, yet most quaint,°   *fine*
      And sweet thyme true;

Primrose, first-born child of Ver,°   *spring*
Merry springtime's harbinger,
      With harebells dim;°   *dark hyacinths*
10   Oxlips,° in their cradles growing,   *Flowering herbs*
Marigolds, on deathbeds blowing,°   *flowering on graves*
      Lark's-heels trim;°   *Fine larkspur*
All dear nature's children sweet,
Lie fore bride and bridegroom's feet,
15 [*He*] *strew*[*s*] *flowers*
      Blessing their sense.
Not an angel of the air,°   *bird*
Bird melodious, or bird fair,
      Is absent hence.

20 The crow, the sland'rous³ cuckoo, nor
The boding° raven, nor chough hoar,⁴   *ominous*
      Nor chatt'ring pie,°   *magpie*
May on our bridehouse° perch or sing,   *wedding venue*
Or with them any discord bring,
      But from it fly.

Enter three QUEENS *in black, with veils stained,° with*   *dyed black*
imperial crowns. The FIRST QUEEN *falls down at the*
foot of THESEUS; *the* SECOND *falls down at the foot of*
25   HIPPOLYTA; *the* THIRD, *before* EMILIA

FIRST QUEEN [*to* THESEUS]   For pity's sake and true gentility's,
      Hear and respect° me.   *attend to*
SECOND QUEEN [*to* HIPPOLYTA]   For your mother's sake,
And as you wish your womb may thrive with fair ones,
      Hear and respect me.
THIRD QUEEN [*to* EMILIA]   Now for the love of him whom Jove
30   hath marked°   *singled out for*
The honour of your bed, and for the sake
Of clear° virginity, be advocate   *unspotted*
For us and our distresses. This good deed
Shall raze you out o'th' Book of Trespasses
All you are set down there.⁵
THESEUS [*to* FIRST QUEEN]   Sad lady, rise.
35 HIPPOLYTA [*to* SECOND QUEEN]   Stand up.
EMILIA [*to* THIRD QUEEN]   No knees to me.
What woman I may stead° that is distressed   *assist*
Does bind me to her.
THESEUS [*to* FIRST QUEEN]   What's your request? Deliver° you   *Speak*
      for all.
FIRST QUEEN [*kneeling still*]   We are three queens whose sovereigns
      fell before
40 The wrath of cruel Creon;⁶ who° endured   *(the sovereigns)*

3. Because it yelled out "cuckold" (husband of an adulterous wife), impugning faithful wives.
4. A jackdaw—a small, rare, gray-headed ("hoar"), red-
beaked, cliff-dwelling member of the crow family.
5. *Shall . . . there:* Will expunge your sins from the
divine ledger.
6. Brother to Jocasta and, hence, both brother-in-law

and uncle to Oedipus, Creon succeeded Oedipus's son
Eteocles as King of Thebes following the siege known
as the "Seven Against Thebes," in which both Eteocles
and all the attackers, led by Eteocles' brother Polynices,
were killed. Creon refused to bury any of the seven,
including the husbands of the Three Queens.

The beaks of ravens, talons of the kites,
And pecks of crows in the foul fields° of Thebes.   *battlefields*
He will not suffer us to burn their bones,
To urn their ashes, nor to take th'offence

45 Of mortal loathsomeness from the blest eye
Of holy Phoebus,° but infects the winds   *the sun*
With stench of our slain lords. O pity, Duke!
Thou purger of the earth,[7] draw thy feared sword
That does good turns to'th' world; give us the bones

50 Of our dead kings that we may chapel° them;   *entomb*
And of° thy boundless goodness take some note   *in*
That for our crownèd heads we have no roof,
Save this,° which is the lion's and the bear's,   *(the sky)*
And vault° to everything.   *ceiling*

THESEUS   Pray you, kneel not:
55 I was transported with° your speech, and suffered   *moved by*
Your knees to wrong themselves.° I have heard the fortunes   *(by kneeling)*
Of your dead lords, which gives me such lamenting
As wakes my vengeance and revenge for 'em.
King Capaneus was your lord: the day

60 That he should° marry you—at such a season   *was about to*
As now it is with me—I met your groom
By Mars's altar. You were that time fair,
Not Juno's mantle fairer than your tresses,
Nor in more bounty spread her.[8] Your wheaten wreath

65 Was then nor° threshed nor blasted;° fortune at you   *neither / withered*
Dimpled her cheek with smiles; Hercules our kinsman—
Then weaker than° your eyes—laid by his club.   *overwhelmed by*
He tumbled down upon his Nemean hide
And swore his sinews thawed.[9] O grief and time,

70 Fearful° consumers, you will all devour.   *Terrifying*
FIRST QUEEN [*kneeling still*]   O, I hope some god,
Some god hath put his mercy in your manhood,
Whereto he'll infuse power and press you forth
Our undertaker.°   *champion*

THESEUS   O no knees, none, widow:
    [*The* FIRST QUEEN *rises*]
75 Unto the helmeted Bellona° use them   *Roman goddess of war*
And pray for me, your soldier. Troubled I am.
    [*He*] *turns away*
SECOND QUEEN [*kneeling still*]   Honoured Hippolyta,
Most dreaded Amazonian, that hast slain
The scythe-tusked boar,[1] that with thy arm, as strong

80 As it is white, wast near to° make the male   *almost managed to*
To thy sex captive, but that this, thy lord—
Born to uphold creation in that honour
First nature styled it in[2]—shrunk thee into

---

7. Like his cousin Hercules (see 1.1.66, 3.6.175), Theseus was known for ridding the world of monsters and
evildoers.
8. Nor is Juno (goddess of marriage) more luxuriantly
wrapped in her mantle than you were in your hanging
tresses.
9. *He . . . thawed:* He (Hercules) flopped down on the
hide of the Nemean lion (which he wore after killing it
as one of his twelve labors) and swore his muscles were
turned to water by your beauty. Most powerful of Greek

mythological heroes, performer of "twelve strong
labours" set for him by his cousin (3.6.175), Hercules
was typically portrayed armed with a club.
1. *Honored . . . boar:* Hippolyta is here confused with
Atalanta, another Amazon, who participated with
Meleager in the hunt for the Calydonian boar. See note
to 3.5.18.
2. *Born . . . in:* Born to sustain the natural order of
creation—the order of man over woman.

85 The bound thou wast o'erflowing,[3] at once subduing
    Thy force and thy affection; soldieress,
    That equally canst poise° sternness with pity,   balance
    Whom now I know hast much more power on° him   over
    Than ever he had on thee, who ow'st° his strength,   owns
    And his love too, who is a servant for
90 The tenor of thy speech;[4] dear glass of° ladies,   mirror for
    Bid him that we, whom flaming war doth scorch,
    Under the shadow of his sword may cool us.
    Require him he° advance it o'er our heads.   Ask him to
    Speak't in a woman's key, like such a woman
95 As any of us three. Weep ere you fail.
    Lend us a knee:[5]
    But touch the ground for us no longer time
    Than a dove's motion when the head's plucked off.
    Tell him, if i'th' blood-sized° field lay swoll'n,   blood-soaked
100 Showing the sun his teeth, grinning at the moon,
    What you would do.

HIPPOLYTA   Poor lady, say no more.
    I had as lief trace[6] this good action with you
    As that° whereto I am going, and never yet   (marriage)
    Went I so willing way. My lord is taken°   affected
105 Heart-deep with your distress. Let him consider.
    I'll speak anon.°   soon
        [*The* SECOND QUEEN *rises*]
THIRD QUEEN (*kneel[ing still] to* EMILIA)   O, my petition was
    Set down in ice,[7] which by hot grief uncandied°   thawed
    Melts into drops; so sorrow, wanting form,
    Is pressed with deeper matter.[8]
EMILIA   Pray stand up:
    Your grief is written in your cheek.
110 THIRD QUEEN   O woe,
    You cannot read it there; there,° through my tears,   in my eye
    Like wrinkled pebbles in a glassy stream,
    You may behold 'em.°   (my sorrows)
        [*The* THIRD QUEEN *rises*]
                          Lady, lady, alack—
    He that will all the treasure know o'th' earth
115 Must know° the centre too; he that will fish   dig deep throughout
    For my least minnow, let him lead° his line   weight with lead
    To catch one at my heart. O, pardon me:
    Extremity, that sharpens sundry wits,
    Makes me a fool.[9]
EMILIA   Pray you, say nothing, pray you.
120 Who cannot feel nor see the rain, being in't,
    Knows neither wet nor dry. If that you were
    The ground-piece of some painter,[1] I would buy you
    T'instruct me 'gainst a capital° grief, indeed   deadly

---

3. *shrunk . . . o'erflowing*: returned you to the limits of your sex, which you had previously exceeded.
4. *who is . . . speech*: who, like a good lover, obeys your every spoken desire.
5. *Speak't . . . knee*: Don't speak like an Amazon. Use tears to avoid defeat. Join us in kneeling.
6. I would as willingly follow through.
7. *my . . . ice*: my former speech was cold and formal.

8. *so . . . matter*: so sorrow, lacking a way to express itself, is made yet more oppressive by its inarticulateness; or, perhaps, receives the stamp of "deeper" impulses.
9. *Extremity . . . fool*: Extreme suffering, which makes some minds more clear, has made me speak inappropriately.
1. *If . . . painter*: If you were merely the subject (model; preliminary sketch?) of a painting.

Such heart-pierced° demonstration; but, alas,   *heartrending*
125 Being a natural sister of our sex,[2]
Your sorrow beats so ardently° upon me   *burningly*
That it shall make a counter-reflect 'gainst[3]
My brother's° heart, and warm it to some pity,   *brother-in-law's*
Though it were made of stone. Pray have good comfort.

130 THESEUS   Forward to th' temple.° Leave not out a jot   *(for the wedding)*
O'th' sacred ceremony.

FIRST QUEEN   O, this celebration
Will longer last and be more costly than
Your suppliants' war. Remember that your fame
Knolls° in the ear o'th' world: what you do quickly   *Tolls like a bell*
135 Is not done rashly; your first thought is more
Than others' laboured meditance;° your premeditating   *careful meditation*
More than their actions. But, O Jove, your actions,
Soon as they move, as ospreys do the fish,[4]
Subdue before they touch. Think, dear Duke, think
What beds our slain kings have.

140 SECOND QUEEN   What griefs our beds,
That our dear lords have none.

THIRD QUEEN   None fit for th' dead.
Those that with cords, knives, drams,° precipitance,°   *poisons / leaps*
Weary of this world's light, have to themselves
Been death's most horrid agents, human grace°   *mercy*
Affords them dust and shadow.

145 FIRST QUEEN   But our lords
Lie blist'ring fore the visitating° sun,   *inspecting*
And were good kings, when living.

THESEUS   It is true,
And I will give you comfort to give° your dead lords graves,   *by giving*
The which to do must make some work with Creon.

150 FIRST QUEEN   And that work presents itself to th' doing.[5]
Now 'twill take form, the heats are gone tomorrow.[6]
Then, bootless° toil must recompense itself   *fruitless*
With its own sweat; now he's secure,°   *unaware of danger*
Not dreams we stand before your puissance°   *power*
155 Rinsing our holy begging in our eyes
To make petition clear.°   *pure; manifest*

SECOND QUEEN   Now you may take him,
Drunk with his victory.

THIRD QUEEN   And his army full
Of bread and sloth.

THESEUS   Artesius, that best knowest
How to draw out,° fit to this enterprise   *select*
160 The prim'st° for this proceeding and the number   *best soldiers*
To carry° such a business: forth and levy   *conduct; win*
Our worthiest instruments, whilst we dispatch
This grand act of our life, this daring deed
Of fate[7] in wedlock.

---

2. Since you are actually a live woman (rather than a
representation of a grieving wife).
3. That, like a mirror, I'll reflect your (sunlike) sorrow
back toward.
4. According to popular legend, ospreys had the power
to compel fish to rise to the surface and turn over, making themselves available for capture.

5. And that work needs to be done as soon as possible.
6. While the plan, like molten metal, is still hot, it can
be transformed into something—once it grows cold, it
can no longer be shaped.
7. *this daring deed / Of fate*: this act (marriage) that
challenges fate.

FIRST QUEEN [*to the other two* QUEENS]   Dowagers,° take hands;   *Widows*
165   Let us be widows to our woes; delay
      Commends us to a famishing hope.[8]
ALL THREE QUEENS   Farewell.
SECOND QUEEN   We come unseasonably,° but when could grief   *at a bad time*
      Cull forth,° as unpanged° judgement can, fitt'st time   *Choose / untormented*
      For best solicitation?
THESEUS   Why, good ladies,
170   This is a service whereto I am going
      Greater than any war—it more imports me°   *means more to me*
      Than all the actions that I have foregone,°   *done to date*
      Or futurely can cope.°   *achieve*
FIRST QUEEN   The more proclaiming°   *Clearly showing that*
      Our suit shall be neglected when her arms,
175   Able to lock Jove from a synod,[9] shall
      By warranting° moonlight corslet thee![1] O when   *authorizing*
      Her twinning cherries° shall their sweetness fall°   *lips / let fall*
      Upon thy tasteful° lips, what wilt thou think   *tasting*
      Of rotten kings or blubbered° queens? What care   *tear-soaked*
180   For what thou feel'st not, what thou feel'st being able
      To make Mars spurn his drum?° O, if thou couch   *(battle signal)*
      But one night with her, every hour in't will
      Take hostage of thee° for a hundred,° and   *Commit you / (more)*
      Thou shalt remember nothing more than what
      That banquet bids° thee to.   *appetizer invites*
185   HIPPOLYTA [*to* THESEUS]   Though much unlike
      You should be so transported, as much sorry
      I should be such a suitor[2]—yet I think
      Did I not by th'abstaining of my joy,
      Which breeds a deeper longing, cure their surfeit°   *excess of grief*
190   That craves a present medicine,° I should pluck   *an immediate relief*
      All ladies' scandal° on me. [*Kneels*] Therefore, sir,   *reproach*
      As I shall here make trial of my prayers,
      Either presuming them to have some force,
      Or sentencing for aye their vigour dumb,[3]
195   Prorogue° this business we are going about, and hang   *Delay*
      Your shield afore your heart—about that neck
      Which is my fee,° and which I freely lend   *property*
      To do these poor queens service.
ALL THREE QUEENS [*to* EMILIA]   O, help now,
      Our cause cries for your knee.
EMILIA [*kneels to* THESEUS]   If you grant not
200   My sister her petition in that force°   *with that energy*
      With that celerity and nature° which   *spontaneous speed*
      She makes it in, from henceforth I'll not dare
      To ask you anything, nor be so hardy°   *bold*
      Ever to take a husband.
THESEUS   Pray stand up.

---

8. *Let . . . hope*: Let us mourn our misfortunes as we
mourned our husbands (or, let us, widowlike, part from
our woes), since by delaying the battle until his marriage is completed, Theseus consigns us to failure.
9. Able to keep Jupiter from a meeting of the gods.
1. Encircle you like a "corslet," close-fitting defensive
armor. Theseus has traded arms (armor) for arms
(embraces).

2. *Though . . . suitor*: Although it's highly unlikely
you'd be so carried away, and just as unlikely I'd now
request you to postpone the wedding.
3. Or forever "sentencing" my prayers to silence, than
which they are no more effectual.

[*They rise*]

205 I am entreating of myself to do
That which you kneel to have me.°—Pirithous,   *have me do*
Lead on the bride: get you° and pray the gods   *go*
For success and return; omit not anything
In the pretended° celebration.—Queens,   *intended*
210 Follow your soldier.° [*To* ARTESIUS] As before, hence you,   *Theseus*
And at the banks of Aulis⁴ meet us with
The forces you can raise, where we shall find
The moiety of a number for a business
More bigger looked.⁵   [*Exit* ARTESIUS]
[*To* HIPPOLYTA]   Since that our theme is haste,
215 I stamp this kiss upon thy current lip—
Sweet, keep it as my token.⁶ [*To the wedding party*] Set you
    forward,
For I will see you gone.
[*To* EMILIA] Farewell, my beauteous sister.—Pirithous,
Keep the feast full:° bate° not an hour on't.°   *fully / abate / of it*
PIRITHOUS   Sir,
220 I'll follow you at heels. The feast's solemnity°   *ceremonial splendor*
Shall want° till your return.   *be lacking*
THESEUS   Cousin,° I charge you   *Friend*
Budge not from Athens. We shall be returning
Ere you can end this feast, of which, I pray you,
Make no abatement.°—Once more, farewell all.   *reduction*
          Exeunt [HIPPOLYTA, EMILIA, PIRITHOUS, *and train*]
                                    towards the temple
FIRST QUEEN   Thus dost thou still make good the tongue o'th'
225   world.⁷
SECOND QUEEN   And earn'st a deity equal with Mars—
THIRD QUEEN   If not above him, for
Thou being but mortal mak'st affections° bend   *sexual urges*
To godlike honours;⁸ they themselves, some say,
Groan under such a mast'ry.⁹
230 THESEUS   As we are men,
Thus should we do; being sensually subdued°   *overcome by appetites*
We lose our human title.° Good cheer, ladies.   *claim to humanity*
Now turn we towards your comforts.   *Flourish. Exeunt*

1.2
Enter PALAMON *and* ARCITE
ARCITE   Dear Palamon, dearer in love than blood,
And our prime cousin,° yet unhardened in   *nearest kin*
The crimes of nature,¹ let us leave the city,

4. Port where the Greek troops assembled before sailing for Troy.
5. *where . . . looked:* where we shall find part of an army
already assembled for a larger campaign than this one.
6. *I . . . token:* puns on coining and engraving. *stamp:*
press (a kiss); make a coin by impressing an image on
metal. *current:* flowing away (like a stream); red (cur-
rant); genuine, not counterfeit. *token:* memento (often
of love); metal stamped and used as a coin.
7. In this way, you (Theseus) prove true everything the
world says of you.
8. *mak'st . . . honours:* subordinate your human passions to godlike deeds.

9. *they . . . mast'ry:* the gods themselves complain of
such self-restraint; suffer because their passions master them.
1.2 Location: Thebes.
1. *unhardened . . . nature:* inexperienced in the natural
vices of man. In this scene, a number of the most
important themes of the play are introduced: that
maturity and experience necessitate a loss of innocence; that friendship constitutes a stronger tie than
either marriage / love relations or blood; and that duty
to the knightly virtue of honor is stronger than duty to
human laws and sovereigns (except in times of war).

Thebes, and the temptings° in't, before we further · *temptations*
5   Sully our gloss of° youth. · *Tarnish our pristine*
And here to keep in abstinence we shame
As in incontinence;[2] for not to swim
I'th' aid o'th' current° were almost to sink— · *With the flow*
At least to frustrate striving;[3] and to follow
10   The common stream 'twould bring us to an eddy
Where we should turn° or drown; if labour through, · *spin endlessly*
Our gain but life and weakness.[4]

PALAMON   Your advice
Is cried up with example.[5] What strange ruins° · *ruined men*
Since first we went to school may we perceive
15   Walking in Thebes? Scars and bare weeds° · *tattered clothes*
The gain o'th' martialist° who did propound · *soldier*
To his bold ends[6] honour and golden ingots,
Which though he won, he had not;[7] and now flirted° · *(is) mocked*
By peace for whom he fought. Who then shall offer
20   To Mars's so-scorned altar? I do bleed
When such I meet, and wish great Juno[8] would
Resume her ancient° fit of jealousy · *former*
To get the soldier work, that peace might purge
For her repletion[9] and retain° anew · *take into service*
25   Her° charitable heart, now hard and harsher · *(Juno's); (peace's)*
Than strife or war could be.

ARCITE   Are you not out?° · *off the point*
Meet you no ruin but the soldier in
The cranks and turns° of Thebes? You did begin · *winding streets*
As if you met decays of many kinds.
30   Perceive you none that do arouse your pity
But th'unconsidered° soldier? · *neglected*

PALAMON   Yes, I pity
Decays where'er I find them, but such most
That, sweating in an honourable toil,
Are paid with ice° to cool 'em. · *treated coldly*

ARCITE   'Tis not this
35   I did begin to speak of. This is virtue,
Of no respect in Thebes. I spake of Thebes,
How dangerous, if we will keep our honours,
It is for our residing where every evil
Hath a good colour,° where every seeming good's · *appearance*
40   A certain evil, where not to be ev'n jump
As they are here were to be strangers, and
Such things to be, mere monsters.[1]

PALAMON   'Tis in our power,
Unless we fear that apes can tutor's,° to · *that we're mere mimics*
Be masters of our manners. What need I
45   Affect another's gait, which is not catching° · *infectious; attractive*

---

2. *here . . . incontinence:* we incur as much shame here (in a corrupt city) by remaining innocent as we would elsewhere by debauching ourselves.
3. And at least renders our exertions (on behalf of goodness) pointless.
4. *if . . . weakness:* if we were to pass through such a whirlpool ("eddy"), we would gain only our lives in a weakened state.
5. Is borne out by numerous examples.
6. *propound . . . ends:* propose as recompense for his

courage.
7. Which, though victorious in battle, he didn't receive.
8. Juno's jealousy led to the Trojan War and other conflicts.
9. *purge / For her repletion:* take medicine to alleviate her (peace's) overeating (the indulgent life of peacetime).
1. *where . . . monsters:* where failure to conform exactly ("jump") makes you a foreigner and perfect conformity makes you a monster.

Where there is faith?[2] Or to be fond° upon   *to dote*
Another's way of speech, when by mine own
I may be reasonably conceived°—saved, too—   *understood*
Speaking it° truly? Why am I bound   *If I speak*
50   By any generous° bond to follow him   *noble*
Follows° his tailor, haply° so long until   *Who heeds / at least*
The followed make pursuit?° Or let me know   *(for unpaid bills)*
Why mine own barber is unblest—with him
My poor chin, too—for 'tis not scissored just
55   To such a favourite's glass?° What canon° is there   *image / law*
That does command my rapier from my hip
To dangle't in my hand? Or to go tiptoe
Before the street be foul?[3] Either I am
The fore-horse in the team or I am none
60   That draw i'th' sequent trace.[4] These poor slight sores
Need not a plantain.[5] That which rips my bosom
Almost to th' heart's—

ARCITE   Our uncle Creon.

PALAMON   He,
A most unbounded° tyrant, whose successes   *unrestrained*
Makes heaven unfeared and villainy assured°   *assured that*
65   Beyond its power there's nothing; almost puts
Faith in a fever,[6] and deifies alone
Voluble chance;° who only attributes   *Variable fortune*
The faculties of other instruments
To his own nerves and act;[7] commands men's service,
70   And what they win in't, boot° and glory; one   *booty; gain*
That fears not to do harm, good dares not.° Let   *dares not do good*
The blood of mine that's sib° to him be sucked   *related*
From me with leeches. Let them break° and fall   *burst*
Off me with that° corruption.   *(Creon's)*

ARCITE   Clear-spirited° cousin,   *Noble-spirited*
75   Let's leave his court that we may nothing share
Of his loud° infamy: for our milk   *well-known*
Will relish of the pasture,[8] and we must
Be vile or disobedient; not his kinsmen
In blood unless in quality.[9]

PALAMON   Nothing truer.
80   I think the echoes of his shames have deafed
The ears of heav'nly justice. Widows' cries
Descend again into their throats and have not

Enter VALERIUS

Due audience of° the gods—Valerius.   *Proper notice from*

VALERIUS   The King calls for you; yet be leaden-footed°   *go slowly*
85   Till his great rage be off him. Phoebus, when
He broke his whipstock and exclaimed against
The horses of the sun,[1] but whispered to°   *compared to*

---

2. Self-reliance. Palamon's speech echoes familiar criticisms of the contrived, "effeminate" manners of
courtiers and men of fashion, here contrasted with
implicit religious norms ("faith"; "saved," line 48;
"canon," line 55).
3. *go . . . foul:* tiptoe on a clean street.
4. *Either . . . trace:* I will not pull behind the lead
("fore-") horse (follow fashion).
5. Herb used for treating wounds.
6. *puts . . . fever:* undermines religion.

7. *attributes . . . act:* takes credit for others' successes.
8. Like cows whose milk absorbs the taste of whatever
they eat.
9. *not . . . quality:* we ought not to act like his kinsmen
unless we're willing to act like him; we're not his kinsmen unless we act like him.
1. After his son Phaeton died driving the horses of the
sun, Phoebus (the sun) vented his grief at the horses—
hence the broken whip handle ("whipstock").

The loudness of his fury.

PALAMON   Small winds shake him.
But what's the matter?

90 VALERIUS   Theseus, who where he threats, appals, hath sent
Deadly defiance to him° and pronounces   (Creon)
Ruin to Thebes, who° is at hand to seal   (Theseus)
The promise of his wrath.[2]

ARCITE   Let him approach.
But that we fear the gods in him,° he brings not   justness of his cause
95 A jot of terror to us. Yet what man
Thirds his own worth—the case is each of ours—
When that his action's dregged with mind assured
'Tis bad he goes about.[3]

PALAMON   Leave that unreasoned.°   Forget that
Our services stand now for Thebes, not Creon,
100 Yet to be neutral to him were dishonour,
Rebellious° to oppose. Therefore we must   Treasonable
With him stand to the mercy of° our fate,   submit to
Who hath bounded our last minute.[4]

ARCITE   So we must.
Is't said this war's afoot? Or it shall be
On fail of° some condition?   If Thebes rejects

105 VALERIUS   'Tis in motion,
The intelligence of state° came in the instant   official announcement
With the defier.°   herald of Theseus

PALAMON   Let's to the King, who, were he
A quarter carrier of that honour which
His enemy come in, the blood we venture
110 Should be as for our health,[5] which were not spent,°   wasted
Rather laid out for purchase.° But, alas,   invested for profit
Our hands advanced before° our hearts, what will   beyond
The fall o'th' stroke do damage?[6]

ARCITE   Let th'event°—   outcome
That never-erring arbitrator—tell us
115 When we know all ourselves,[7] and let us follow
The becking° of our chance.   *Exeunt*   calling

                              1.3
          Enter PIRITHOUS, HIPPOLYTA, *and* EMILIA

PIRITHOUS   No further.

HIPPOLYTA   Sir, farewell. Repeat my wishes
To our great lord, of whose success I dare not
Make any timorous question; yet I wish him
Excess and overflow of power, an't might be,°   if possible
5 To dure° ill-dealing fortune. Speed to him;   endure
Store[1] never hurts good governors.

PIRITHOUS   Though I know
His ocean needs not my poor drops, yet they
Must yield their tribute there. [*To* EMILIA] My precious maid,

---

2. *seal . . . wrath:* turn anger to action.
3. *Yet . . . about:* Yet any man reduces his worth by two-thirds—as we do—when he knows the action he undertakes is unworthy.
4. *Who . . . minute:* Which has determined when we die.
5. *the blood . . . health:* our loss of blood in combat

would be equivalent to a therapeutic bloodletting.
6. *what . . . damage:* what harm will "the fall o'th' stroke" do?
7. *tell . . . ourselves:* speak for itself.
1.3 Location: The outskirts of Athens.
1. Abundant resources (here, good men like Pirithous).

Those best affections° that the heavens infuse   *inclinations*
10   In their best-tempered pieces° keep enthroned   *greatest creations*
In your dear heart.

EMILIA   Thanks, sir. Remember me
To our all-royal brother, for whose speed°   *success*
The great Bellona I'll solicit; and
Since in our terrene state° petitions are not   *earthly condition*
15   Without gifts understood, I'll offer to her
What I shall be advised she likes. Our hearts
Are in his army, in his tent.

HIPPOLYTA   In's bosom.
We have been soldiers,° and we cannot weep   *(as Amazons)*
When our friends don their helms,° or put to sea,   *helmets*
20   Or tell of babes broached° on the lance, or women   *speared*
That have sod° their infants in—and after eat them—   *boiled*
The brine they wept at killing 'em:[2] then if
You stay to see of us such spinsters, we
Should hold you here forever.[3]

PIRITHOUS   Peace be to you
25   As I pursue this war, which° shall be then   *(peace)*
Beyond further requiring.°   *Exit* PIRITHOUS   *In no need of prayer*

EMILIA   How his longing
Follows his friend! Since his depart,° his sports,   *Theseus's departure*
Though craving° seriousness and skill, passed slightly   *requiring*
His careless execution,[4] where nor° gain   *neither*
30   Made him regard or loss consider, but
Playing one business in his hand, another
Directing in his head, his mind nurse equal
To these so diff'ring twins.[5] Have you observed him
Since our great lord departed?

HIPPOLYTA   With much labour;°   *diligence*
35   And I did love him for't. They two have cabined°   *shared quarters*
In many as dangerous as poor a corner,
Peril and want contending;[6] they have skiffed°   *sailed across*
Torrents whose roaring tyranny and power
I'th' least of these° was dreadful, and they have   *At the weakest point*
40   Fought out together where death's self was lodged;[7]
Yet fate hath brought them off. Their knot of love,
Tied, weaved, entangled with so true, so long,
And with a finger of so deep a cunning,°   *skill*
May be outworn,° never undone. I think   *worn out (in death)*
45   Theseus cannot be umpire to himself,
Cleaving his conscience into twain and doing
Each side like° justice, which[8] he loves best.   *equal*

EMILIA   Doubtless
There is a best, and reason has no manners
To say it is not you. I was acquainted
50   Once with a time when I enjoyed a playfellow;
You were at wars when she the grave enriched,

---

2. Miriam killed, cooked, and ate her son during the Roman siege of Jerusalem, adding her own tears for sauce.
3. *then if . . . forever:* if you wait long enough for us to turn into spinners (housewives), you'll wait forever.
4. *passed . . . execution:* were pursued carelessly.

5. *his . . . twins:* his attention divided equally between sports and Theseus.
6. Contending for which was the greater hardship.
7. *where . . . lodged:* the underworld, to rescue Proserpina.
8. Pirithous or Hippolyta.

Who made too proud the bed;° took leave o'th' moon⁹—   *grave*
Which then looked pale at parting—when our count°   *age*
Was each eleven.

HIPPOLYTA   'Twas Flavina.

EMILIA   Yes.

55 You talk of Pirithous' and Theseus' love:
Theirs has more ground,° is more maturely seasoned,   *a stronger base*
More buckled° with strong judgement, and their needs   *joined together*
The one of th'other may be said to water
Their intertangled roots of love; but I
60 And she I sigh and spoke of were things innocent,
Loved for° we did, and like the elements,¹   *simply because*
That know not what, nor why, yet do effect°   *create*
Rare issues° by their operance, our souls   *Amazing results*
Did so to one another. What she liked
65 Was then of° me approved; what not, condemned—   *by*
No more arraignment.° The flower that I would pluck   *inquiry*
And put between my breasts—O then but beginning
To swell about the blossom—she would long°   *desire*
Till she had such another, and commit it
70 To the like innocent cradle, where, phoenix-like,
They died in perfume.² On my head no toy°   *trifle*
But was her pattern.° Her affections—pretty,   *model*
Though happily her careless wear—I followed
For my most serious decking.³ Had mine ear
75 Stol'n some new air,° or at adventure° hummed one,   *tune / by chance*
From musical coinage,° why, it was a note   *improvisation*
Whereon her spirits would sojourn—rather dwell on—
And sing it in her slumbers. This rehearsal—
Which, seely innocence wots well, comes in
80 Like old emportment's bastard⁴—has this end:
That the true love 'tween maid and maid may be
More than in sex dividual.⁵

HIPPOLYTA   You're out of breath,
And this high-speeded pace is but to say
That you shall never, like the maid Flavina,
85 Love any that's called man.

EMILIA   I am sure I shall not.

HIPPOLYTA   Now alack, weak sister,
I must no more believe thee in this point—
Though in't I know thou dost believe thyself—
90 Than I will trust a sickly appetite
That loathes even as it longs. But sure, my sister,
If I were ripe for your persuasion,° you   *open to your views*
Have said enough to shake me from the arm

---

9. Diana (the moon goddess), who watched over virgins and Amazons; hence Emilia's (equivocal) patron.
1. Air, fire, earth, and water—constituents of all matter.
2. The phoenix died by being burned on aromatic
wood, only to be reborn from its own ashes.
3. *Her affections . . . decking*: Whatever she wore—
even though she wasn't aware of how appealing it
was—I'd imitate with utmost seriousness. For "happily"
Q has "happely," which could also mean "haply" (by
chance).

4. *This . . . bastard*: This narrative, which, as any happy
innocent well knows, is an illegitimate descendant
(poor likeness) of my former passion (or, the former significance of the relationship). For "seely innocence" Q
has "fury-innocent" (innocent passionate love), which
may be correct.
5. *in sex dividual*: between two sexes. Q has "individuall," which in the seventeenth century could mean the
indivisible unity of male and female, and hence may be
correct.

95 Of the all-noble Theseus, for whose fortunes
I will now in and kneel, with great assurance
That we more than his Pirithous possess
The high throne in his heart.

EMILIA   I am not
Against your faith, yet I continue mine.   *Exeunt*

1.4

Cornetts. A battle struck within. Then a retreat.
Flourish.[1] Then enter THESEUS, *victor. The three* QUEENS
meet him and fall on their faces before him. [Also enter
a HERALD, *and attendants bearing]* PALAMON *and*
ARCITE [*on*] *two hearses°*   biers

FIRST QUEEN [*to* THESEUS]   To thee no star be dark.°   unfavorable
SECOND QUEEN [*to* THESEUS]   Both heaven and earth
Friend thee for ever.

THIRD QUEEN [to THESEUS]   All the good that may
Be wished upon thy head, I cry 'Amen' to't.

THESEUS   Th'impartial gods, who from the mounted° heavens   high
5 View us their mortal herd, behold who err
And in their time chastise. Go and find out
The bones of your dead lords and honour them
With treble ceremony: rather than a gap
Should be in their dear° rites we would supply't.   valued
10 But those we will depute which shall invest°   clothe
You in your dignities, and even° each thing   rectify
Our haste does leave imperfect. So adieu,
And heaven's good eyes look on you.   *Exeunt* [*the*] QUEENS
                                   What are those?

HERALD   Men of great quality,° as may be judged   rank
15 By their appointment.° Some of Thebes have told's   armor and weapons
They are sisters' children, nephews to the King.

THESEUS   By th' helm° of Mars I saw them in the war,   helmet
Like to a pair of lions smeared with prey,
Make lanes in troops aghast. I fixed my note°   attention
20 Constantly on them, for they were a mark°   striking sight
Worth a god's view. What prisoner was't that told me
When I enquired their names?

HERALD   Wi' leave, they're called
Arcite and Palamon.

THESEUS   'Tis right: those, those.
They are not dead?

25 HERALD   Nor in a state of life. Had they been taken
When their last hurts were given, 'twas possible
They might have been recovered.° Yet they breathe,   healed
And have the name of men.

THESEUS   Then like men use 'em.
The very lees of such, millions of rates
30 Exceed the wine of others.[2] All our surgeons
Convent° in their behoof;° our richest balms,   Assemble / behalf
Rather than niggard,° waste. Their lives concern us   use stingily

---

1.4 Location: On the outskirts of Thebes.
1. Small horns sound offstage, signaling the start of
battle, a retreat, and then a triumphal entrance.

2. *The very . . . others*: The dregs of such men far
exceed the best that others can offer.

Much more than Thebes is worth. Rather than have 'em
Freed of this plight and in their morning° state—   *former (healthy)*
35   Sound and at liberty—I would 'em dead;
But forty-thousandfold we had rather have 'em
Prisoners to us, than death. Bear 'em speedily
From our kind air, to them unkind,[3] and minister
What man to man may do—for our sake, more,
40   Since I have known frights, fury, friends' behests,
Love's provocations, zeal, a mistress' task,
Desire of liberty, a fever, madness,
Hath set a mark which nature could not reach to
Without some imposition, sickness in will
45   O'er-wrestling strength in reason.[4] For our love
And great Apollo's° mercy, all our best   *god of healing*
Their best skill tender.—Lead into the city
Where, having bound things scattered,° we will post°   *reimposed order / hurry*
To Athens fore our army.   *Flourish. Exeunt*

1.5

Music. Enter the [three] QUEENS *with the hearses of*
their [lords] in a funeral solemnity [with attendants]
      Song
      Urns and odours, bring away,
      Vapours, sighs, darken the day;
            Our dole° more deadly looks than dying.   *mourning*
      Balms and gums[1] and heavy cheers,°   *sad countenances*
5   Sacred vials filled with tears,
            And clamours through the wild air flying:

      Come all sad and solemn shows,
      That are quick-eyed pleasure's foes.
      We convent naught else but woes,
10   We convent naught else but woes.
THIRD QUEEN   This funeral path brings° to your household's   *leads*
      grave—
      Joy seize on you again, peace sleep with him.
SECOND QUEEN   And this to yours.
FIRST QUEEN   Yours this way. Heavens lend
      A thousand differing ways to one sure end.°   *death*
15   THIRD QUEEN   This world's a city full of straying streets,
      And death's the market-place where each one meets.
                  Exeunt severally°   *separately*

2.1

Enter [the] JAILER *and [the]* WOOER
JAILER   I may depart with° little, while I live; something I may   *may spare*
   cast° to you, not much. Alas, the prison I keep, though it be for   *give (as a dowry)*
   great ones, yet they seldom come; before one salmon you shall
   take a number of minnows. I am given out to be better lined°   *said to be richer*
5   than it can appear to me report° is a true speaker. I would I   *rumor*

---

3. Fresh air was thought dangerous to wounds.
4. *Since . . . reason:* Since compelling incentives can
impel men to perform beyond their normal abilities,
whereas otherwise weak will triumphs over strong reason. *mark:* target. *imposition:* command.
1.5 Scene continues.

1. Aromatic substances used in mourning rituals.
2.1 Location: The palace garden in Athens, perhaps
with the second, or higher, gallery above representing
the window of the cell where Palamon and Arcite are
being held.

were really that° I am delivered° to be. Marry¹, what I have—   *what / reported*
be it what it will—I will assure upon° my daughter at the day   *bequeath to*
of my death.

10 WOOER   Sir, I demand no more than your own offer, and I will
estate° your daughter in what I have promised.   *settle*

JAILER   Well, we will talk more of this when the solemnity² is
past. But have you a full promise of° her?   *from*

    Enter [the JAILER'S] DAUGHTER [*with rushes*]°   (*as floor coverings*)
When that shall be seen, I tender my consent.

WOOER   I have, sir. Here she comes.

15 JAILER [*to* DAUGHTER]   Your friend and I have chanced to name
you here, upon the old business—but no more of that now. So
soon as the court hurry is over we will have an end of it. I'th'
mean time, look tenderly° to the two prisoners. I can tell you   *carefully*
they are princes.

20 JAILER'S DAUGHTER   These strewings° are for their chamber. 'Tis   *rushes*
pity they are in prison, and 'twere pity they should be out. I do
think they have patience to make any adversity ashamed; the
prison itself is proud of 'em, and they have all the world in
their chamber.³

25 JAILER   They are famed° to be a pair of absolute° men.   *reputed / perfect*

JAILER'S DAUGHTER   By my troth, I think fame but stammers°   *underrates*
'em—they stand a grece° above the reach of report.   *step*

JAILER   I heard them reported in the battle to be the only doers.°   *supreme achievers*

JAILER'S DAUGHTER   Nay, most likely, for they are noble sufferers.⁴
30 I marvel how they would have looked had they been victors, that
with such a constant nobility enforce a freedom out of bondage,
making misery their mirth, and affliction a toy° to jest at.   *trifle*

JAILER   Do they so?

JAILER'S DAUGHTER   It seems to me they have no more sense of
35 their captivity than I of ruling Athens. They eat well, look merrily, discourse of many things, but° nothing of their own   *but say*
restraint° and disasters. Yet sometime a divided° sigh—martyred   *captivity / half-audible*
as 'twere i'th' deliverance—will break from one of them, when
the other presently° gives it so sweet a rebuke that I could wish   *immediately*
40 myself a sigh to be so chid, or at least a sigher to be comforted.

WOOER   I never saw 'em.

JAILER   The Duke himself came privately in the night,

    PALAMON *and* ARCITE [*appear at a window*] *above*
and so did they.⁵ What the reason of it is I know not. Look,
yonder they are. That's Arcite looks out.

45 JAILER'S DAUGHTER   No, sir, no—that's Palamon. Arcite is the
lower° of the twain—[*pointing at* ARCITE] you may perceive a   *shorter*
part of him.

JAILER   Go to,° leave your pointing. They would not make us   *Come now*
their object.⁶ Out of their sight.

50 JAILER'S DAUGHTER   It is a holiday to look on them. Lord, the difference of ° men!   *Exeunt*   *between*

---

1. To be sure (originally, by the Virgin Mary).
2. Theseus and Hippolyta's wedding.
3. They have everything they need in their prison cell, because they have each other. See 2.2.60.
4. For they endure nobly what others do to them. To do

and to suffer are antithetical.
5. Theseus brought them secretly at night.
6. They would not be so rude as to point at us; they don't want to look at us.

2.2

Enter PALAMON *and* ARCITE *in prison* [*in shackles,*
  above]

PALAMON   How do you, noble cousin?

ARCITE   How do you, sir?

PALAMON   Why, strong enough to laugh at misery
  And bear the chance° of war. Yet we are prisoners,   uncertainties
  I fear, for ever, cousin.

ARCITE   I believe it,
  And to that destiny have patiently
5 Laid up my hour to come.°   Consigned my future

PALAMON   O, cousin Arcite,
  Where is Thebes now?[1] Where is our noble country?
  Where are our friends and kindreds? Never more
  Must we behold those comforts, never see
  The hardy youths strive for° the games of honour,   in
10 Hung with the painted favours° of their ladies,   love tokens
  Like tall ships under sail; then start amongst 'em
  And, as an east wind, leave 'em all behind us,
  Like lazy clouds, whilst Palamon and Arcite,
  Even in the wagging of a wanton leg,[2]
15 Outstripped the people's praises, won the garlands
  Ere they have time to wish 'em ours. O never
  Shall we two exercise, like twins of honour,
  Our arms again and feel our fiery horses
  Like proud seas under us. Our good swords, now—
20 Better° the red-eyed god of war ne'er wore—   Better swords
  Ravished° our sides, like age must run to rust   Torn from
  And deck the temples of those gods that hate us.
  These hands shall never draw 'em out like lightning
  To blast° whole armies more.   annihilate

ARCITE   No, Palamon,
25 Those hopes are prisoners with us. Here we are,
  And here the graces of our youths must wither,
  Like a too-timely° spring. Here age must find us   buds in a premature
  And, which is heaviest,° Palamon, unmarried—   what is saddest
  The sweet embraces of a loving wife
30 Loaden with kisses, armed with thousand Cupids,
  Shall never clasp our necks; no issue° know us;   offspring
  No figures° of ourselves shall we e'er see   images
  To glad our age, and, like young eagles, teach 'em
  Boldly to gaze against bright arms[3] and say,
35 'Remember what your fathers were, and conquer.'
  The fair-eyed maids shall weep our banishments,
  And in their songs curse ever-blinded fortune,
  Till she for shame see what a wrong she has done
  To youth and nature. This is all our world.
40 We shall know nothing here but one another,

2.2 Location: The prison in Athens, perhaps represented by the principal upper stage, located on the first,
or lower, gallery; as in 2.1, the garden is located on the
main stage. The shift of Palamon and Arcite from the
higher to the lower gallery is implied by the stage directions and start of a new scene here in Q.

1. The kinsmen's view of Thebes in 1.2 is very different, perhaps because Shakespeare probably wrote the
earlier scene and Fletcher this one.
2. *Even . . . leg:* Effortlessly.
3. Eagles supposedly could gaze at the sun without
being blinded.

Hear nothing but the clock that tells° our woes.   *counts*
The vine shall grow, but we shall never see it;
Summer shall come, and with her all delights,
45 But dead-cold winter must inhabit here still.
   PALAMON   'Tis too true, Arcite. To our Theban hounds
That shook the agèd forest with their echoes,
No more now must we holler; no more shake
Our pointed javelins whilst the angry swine°   *the wild boar*
50 Flies like a Parthian quiver⁴ from our rages,
Struck with our well-steeled darts. All valiant uses°—   *activities*
The food and nourishment of noble minds—
In us two here shall perish; we shall die—
Which is the curse of honour—lastly,°   *at last*
Children of grief and ignorance.°   *Sad and unknown*
55 ARCITE   Yet, cousin,
Even from the bottom of these miseries,
From all that fortune can inflict upon us,
I see two comforts rising—two mere° blessings,   *pure*
If the gods please, to hold here a brave patience
60 And the enjoying of our griefs together.
Whilst Palamon is with me, let me perish
If I think this our prison.
   PALMON   Certainly
'Tis a main° goodness, cousin, that our fortunes   *the greatest*
Were twined together. 'Tis most true, two souls
65 Put in two noble bodies, let 'em suffer
The gall of hazard,° so° they grow together,   *bitterest luck / if*
Will never sink;° they must not, say° they could.   *succumb / even if*
A willing man dies sleeping⁵ and all's done.
   ARCITE   Shall we make worthy uses of this place
70 That all men hate so much?
   PALAMON   How, gentle cousin?
   ARCITE   Let's think this prison holy sanctuary,
To keep us from corruption of worse men.
We are young, and yet desire the ways of honour
That liberty and common conversation,°   *worldly acquaintances*
75 The poison of pure spirits, might, like women,
Woo us to wander from. What worthy blessing
Can be, but our imaginations
May make it ours? And here being thus together,
We are an endless mine° to one another: *resource*
80 We are one another's wife, ever begetting
New births of love; we are father, friends, acquaintance;
We are in one another, families—
I am your heir, and you are mine; this place
Is our inheritance: no hard oppressor
85 Dare take this from us. Here, with a little patience,
We shall live long and loving. No surfeits° seek us—   *diseases from excess*
The hand of war hurts none here, nor the seas
Swallow their youth. Were we at liberty

---

4. During the era of ancient Rome's supremacy, the Parthians were renowned archers, famous for shooting behind them at their enemies as they pretended to flee.

5. A man resigned to his fate dies in peace, as if merely falling asleep.

A wife might part us lawfully, or business;
90 Quarrels consume us; envy of ill men
Crave our acquaintance.⁶ I might sicken, cousin,
Where you should never know it, and so perish
Without your noble hand to close mine eyes,
Or prayers to the gods. A thousand chances,
Were we from hence, would sever us.

95 PALAMON   You have made me—
I thank you, cousin Arcite—almost wanton°   *frolicsome*
With my captivity. What a misery
It is to live abroad,° and everywhere!   *out of captivity*
'Tis like a beast, methinks. I find the court here;
100 I am sure, a more content;° and all those pleasures   *greater happiness*
That woo the wills of men to vanity
I see through now, and am sufficient
To tell the world 'tis but a gaudy shadow,
That old Time, as he passes by, takes with him.
105 What had we been, old° in the court of Creon,   *grown old*
Where sin is justice, lust and ignorance
The virtues of the great ones? Cousin Arcite,
Had not the loving gods found this place for us,
We had died as they do, ill° old men, unwept,   *wicked*
110 And had° their epitaphs, the people's curses.   *had for*
Shall I say more?

ARCITE   I would hear you still.°   *forever*

PALAMON   Ye shall.
Is there record of any two that loved
Better than we do, Arcite?

ARCITE   Sure there cannot.

PALAMON   I do not think it possible our friendship
Should ever leave us.

115 ARCITE   Till our deaths it cannot,

Enter EMILIA *and her* WOMAN [*below.*° PALAMON *sees*   (*in the garden*)
EMILIA *and is silent*]

And after death our spirits shall be led
To those that love eternally.° Speak on, sir.   (*in Elysium*)

EMILIA [*to her* WOMAN]   This garden has a world of pleasure in't.
What flower is this?

WOMAN   'Tis called narcissus, madam.

120 EMILIA   That was a fair boy, certain, but a fool
To love himself.⁷ Were there not maids enough?

ARCITE [*to* PALAMON]   Pray forward.°   *go on speaking*

PALAMON   Yes.

EMILIA [*to her* WOMAN]   Or were they all hard-hearted?

WOMAN   They could not be to one so fair.

EMILIA   Thou wouldst not.

WOMAN   I think I should not, madam.

EMILIA   That's a good wench—
But take heed to your kindness, though.

125 WOMAN   Why, madam?

EMILIA   Men are mad things.

---

6. *envy . . . acquaintance*: the malice (or, our envy) of
evil men might infect us.
7. Narcissus fell in love with his own reflection in a

pool and drowned trying to embrace it. After his death,
he was turned into a flower.

ARCITE [*to* PALAMON]   Will ye go forward, cousin?

EMILIA [*to her* WOMAN]   Canst not thou work° such flowers in   *embroider*
   silk, wench?

WOMAN   Yes.

EMILIA   I'll have a gown full of 'em, and of these.
   This is a pretty colour—will't not do
   Rarely° upon a skirt, wench?   *Beautifully*

130 WOMAN   Dainty,° madam.   *Very nicely*

ARCITE [*to* PALAMON]   Cousin, cousin, how do you, sir? Why,
   Palamon!

PALAMON   Never till now was I in prison, Arcite.

ARCITE   Why, what's the matter, man?

PALAMON   Behold and wonder!
   [ARCITE *sees* EMILIA]
   By heaven, she is a goddess!

ARCITE   Ha!

PALAMON   Do reverence.
   She is a goddess, Arcite.

135 EMILIA [*to her* WOMAN]   Of all flowers
   Methinks a rose is best.

WOMAN   Why, gentle madam?

EMILIA   It is the very emblem of a maid—
   For when the west wind courts her gently,
   How modestly she blows,° and paints the sun[8]   *blooms*

140   With her chaste blushes! When the north° comes near her,   *north wind*
   Rude and impatient, then, like chastity,
   She locks her beauties in her bud again,
   And leaves him to base briers.°   *thorns*

WOMAN   Yet, good madam,
   Sometimes her modesty will blow° so far   *open*

145   She falls for't°—a maid,   *because of it*
   If she have any honour, would be loath
   To take example by her.

EMILIA   Thou art wanton.

ARCITE [*to* PALAMON]   She is wondrous fair.

PALAMON   She is all the beauty extant.

EMILIA [*to her* WOMAN]   The sun grows high—let's walk in.
   Keep these flowers.

150   We'll see how close art can come near their colours.
   I am wondrous merry-hearted—I could laugh now.

WOMAN   I could lie down, I am sure.[9]

EMILIA   And take one° with you?   *(a rose); (a lover)*

WOMAN   That's as we bargain, madam.

EMILIA   Well, agree° then.   *let's bargain*
   Exeunt EMILIA *and* [*her*] WOMAN

PALAMON   What think you of this beauty?

ARCITE   'Tis a rare one.

PALAMON   Is't but a rare one?

155 ARCITE   Yes, a matchless beauty.

PALAMON   Might not a man well lose himself and love her?

ARCITE   I cannot tell what you have done; I have,
   Beshrew mine eyes° for't. Now I feel my shackles.   *Curse me (an oath)*

---

8. Tints the sunlight pink; the inside of a rose looks like an image of the sun.

9. "Laugh and lie down" was an Elizabethan card game; sexual allusion.

PALAMON   You love her then?

160 ARCITE   Who would not?

PALAMON   And desire her?

ARCITE   Before my liberty.

PALAMON   I saw her first.

ARCITE   That's nothing.

PALAMON   But it shall be.

ARCITE   I saw her too.

PALAMON   Yes, but you must not love her.

165 ARCITE   I will not, as you do, to worship her
        As she is heavenly and a blessèd goddess!
        I love her as a woman, to enjoy her—
        So both may love.

PALAMON   You shall not love at all.

ARCITE   Not love at all—who shall deny me?

170 PALAMON   I that first saw her, I that took possession
        First with mine eye of all those beauties
        In her revealed to mankind. If thou¹ lov'st her,
        Or entertain'st a hope to blast my wishes,
        Thou art a traitor, Arcite, and a fellow°   *(contemptuous)*

175   False as thy title to° her. Friendship, blood,   *claim to possess*
        And all the ties between us I disclaim,
        If thou once think upon her.

ARCITE   Yes, I love her—
        And if the lives of all my name lay° on it,   *my family depended*
        I must do so. I love her with my soul—

180   If that will lose ye, farewell, Palamon!
        I say again,
        I love her, and in loving her maintain
        I am as worthy and as free° a lover,   *noble*
        And have as just a title to her beauty,

185   As any Palamon, or any living
        That is a man's son.

PALAMON   Have I called thee friend?

ARCITE   Yes, and have found me so. Why are you moved° thus?   *incensed*
        Let me deal coldly° with you. Am not I   *dispassionately*
        Part of your blood, part of your soul? You have told me
        That I was Palamon and you were Arcite.

190 PALAMON   Yes.

ARCITE   Am not I liable to those affections,°   *passions*
        Those joys, griefs, angers, fears, my friend shall suffer?

PALAMON   Ye may be.

ARCITE   Why then would you deal so cunningly,
        So strangely, so unlike a noble kinsman,

195   To love alone? Speak truly. Do you think me
        Unworthy of her sight?

PALAMON   No, but unjust
        If thou pursue that sight.

ARCITE   Because another
        First sees the enemy, shall I stand still,
        And let mine honour down, and never charge?

PALAMON   Yes, if he be but one.°   *be alone*

---

1. The contemptuous "thou" replaces the more polite "you." Arcite follows suit at line 218.

200 ARCITE   But say that one
        Had rather combat me?
     PALAMON   Let that one say so,
        And use thy freedom; else, if thou pursuest her,
        Be as that cursèd man that hates his country,
        A branded villain.
     ARCITE   You are mad.
     PALAMON   I must be.
205   Till thou art worthy, Arcite, it concerns me;
        And in this madness if I hazard° thee   *endanger*
        And take thy life, I deal but truly.°   *fairly*
     ARCITE   Fie, sir.
        You play the child extremely. I will love her,
        I must, I ought to do so, and I dare—
        And all this justly.
210 PALAMON   O, that now, that now
        Thy false self and thy friend had but this fortune—
        To be one hour at liberty and grasp
        Our good swords in our hands! I would quickly teach thee
        What 'twere to filch affection from another.
215   Thou art baser in it than a cutpurse.°   *thief*
        Put but thy head out of this window more
        And, as I have a soul, I'll nail thy life to't.°   *to the window frame*
     ARCITE   Thou dar'st not, fool; thou canst not; thou art feeble.
        Put my head out? I'll throw my body out
220   And leap° the garden when I see her next,   *jump down to*
                Enter [the JAILER above]
        And pitch° between her arms to anger thee.   *hurl myself*
     PALAMON   No more—the keeper's coming. I shall live
        To knock thy brains out with my shackles.
     ARCITE   Do.
     JAILER   By your leave, gentlemen.
     PALAMON   Now, honest keeper?
225 JAILER   Lord Arcite, you must presently to th' Duke.
        The cause I know not yet.
     ARCITE   I am ready, keeper.
     JAILER   Prince Palamon, I must a while bereave you
        Of your fair cousin's company.
                        Exeunt ARCITE and [the JAILER]
     PALAMON   And me, too,
        Even when you please, of life. Why is he sent for?
230   It may be he shall marry her—he's goodly,°   *handsome*
        And like enough the Duke hath taken notice
        Both of his blood° and body. But his falsehood!   *noble family*
        Why should a friend be treacherous? If that
        Get him a wife so noble and so fair,
235   Let honest men ne'er love again. Once more
        I would but see this fair one. Blessèd garden,
        And fruit and flowers more blessèd, that still° blossom   *perpetually*
        As her bright eyes shine on ye! Would I were,
        For all the fortune of my life hereafter,
240   Yon little tree, yon blooming apricot—
        How I would spread and fling my wanton arms
        In at her window! I would bring her fruit
        Fit for the gods to feed on; youth and pleasure

Still as° she tasted should be doubled on her;   *Whenever*
245 And if she be not heavenly, I would make her
So near the gods in nature they should fear her—
       Enter [the JAILER *above*]
And then I am sure she would love me. How now, keeper,
Where's Arcite?
JAILER   Banished—Prince Pirithous
Obtained his liberty;² but never more,
250 Upon his oath and life, must he set foot
Upon this kingdom.
PALAMON [*aside*]   He's a blessèd man.
He shall see Thebes again, and call to arms
The bold young men that, when he bids 'em charge,
Fall on like fire. Arcite shall have a fortune,°   *chance*
255 If he dare make himself a worthy lover,
Yet in the field to strike a battle for her;
And if he lose her then, he's a cold coward.
How bravely may he bear himself to win her
If he be noble Arcite; thousand ways!
260 Were I at liberty I would do things
Of such a virtuous greatness that this lady,
This blushing virgin, should take manhood to her
And seek to ravish me.
JAILER   My lord, for you
I have this charge° to—   *order*
PALAMON   To discharge my life.
265 JAILER   No, but from this place to remove your lordship—
The windows are too open.
PALAMON   Devils take 'em
That are so envious° to me—prithee kill me.   *spiteful*
JAILER   And hang for't afterward?
PALAMON   By this good light,
Had I a sword I would kill thee.
JAILER   Why, my lord?
270 PALAMON   Thou bring'st such pelting° scurvy news continually,   *paltry*
Thou art not worthy life. I will not go.
JAILER   Indeed you must, my lord.
PALAMON   May I° see the garden?   *Will I be able to*
JAILER   No.
PALAMON   Then I am resolved—I will not go.
JAILER   I must constrain you, then; and for° you are dangerous,   *because*
I'll clap more irons on you.
275 PALAMON   Do, good keeper.
I'll shake 'em so ye shall not sleep:
I'll make ye a new morris.³ Must I go?
JAILER   There is no remedy.
PALAMON   Farewell, kind window.
May rude wind never hurt thee. O, my lady,
280 If ever thou hast felt what sorrow was,
Dream how I suffer. Come, now bury me.⁴
       Exeunt PALAMON *and* [*the* JAILER]

---

2. The motives behind Pirithous's intercession are not explained.
3. Morris dancers wore bells on their clothes.

4. Palamon's new cell will be like a grave because he will be banished from Emilia.

2.3

Exeunt ARCITE

ARCITE Banished the kingdom? 'Tis a benefit,
  A mercy I must thank 'em for; but banished
  The free enjoying of that face I die for—
  O, 'twas a studied° punishment, a death   *deliberate*
5 Beyond imagination; such a vengeance
  That, were I old and wicked, all my sins
  Could never pluck upon me. Palamon,
  Thou hast the start° now—thou shalt stay and see   *advantage*
  Her bright eyes break° each morning 'gainst thy window,   *(like dawn)*
10 And let in life into thee. Thou shalt feed
  Upon the sweetness of a noble beauty
  That nature ne'er exceeded, nor ne'er shall.
  Good gods! What happiness has Palamon!
  Twenty to one he'll come to speak to her,
15 And if she be as gentle as she's fair,
  I know she's his—he has a tongue will tame
  Tempests and make the wild rocks wanton.°   *full of joy*
  Come what can come,
  The worst is death. I will not leave the kingdom.
20 I know mine own° is but a heap of ruins,   *(Thebes)*
  And no redress there. If I go he has her.
  I am resolved another shape° shall make me,   *a disguise*
  Or end my fortunes. Either way I am happy—
  I'll see her and be near her, or no more.°   *or die*

Enter four COUNTRY [MEN], *one [of whom carries] a
garland before them.* [ARCITE *stands apart*]

25 FIRST COUNTRYMAN My masters, I'll be there—that's certain.
SECOND COUNTRYMAN And I'll be there.
THIRD COUNTRYMAN And I.
FOURTH COUNTRYMAN Why then, have with ye,° boys! 'Tis but *I'll come too*
  a chiding[1]—
  Let the plough play° today, I'll tickle't out   *be idle*
  Of the jades' tails tomorrow.[2]
30 FIRST COUNTRYMAN   I am sure
  To have my wife as jealous as a turkey[3]—
  But that's all one. I'll go through, let her mumble.°   *grumble*
SECOND COUNTRYMAN Clap her aboard tomorrow night and
  stow her,[4]
  And all's made up again.
THIRD COUNTRYMAN   Ay, do but put
35 A fescue° in her fist and you shall see her   *teacher's pointer*
  Take a new lesson out° and be a good wench.   *Learn a new lesson*
  Do we all hold against the maying?[5]
FOURTH COUNTRYMAN Hold? What should ail us?°   *prevent us*
THIRD COUNTRYMAN   Arcas will be there.
SECOND COUNTRYMAN And Sennois, and Rycas, and three bet-
40 ter lads ne'er danced under green tree; and ye know what
  wenches, ha? But will the dainty dominie,° the schoolmaster, *fussy teacher*

2.3 Location: The countryside outside Athens.
1. The worst punishment I'll get (for not working) is a scolding.
2. *I'll . . . tomorrow:* I'll whip extra work out of the horses ("jades") tomorrow.

3. Thought to be jealously territorial.
4. Sexual metaphor: board her (like a ship) and fill up her cargo hold.
5. Are we still going to participate in the May Day celebrations (of fertility and the coming of spring)?

keep touch,° do you think? For he does all,⁶ ye know.   *keep this promise*

THIRD COUNTRYMAN He'll eat a hornbook⁷ ere he fail. Go to, the
matter's too far driven° between him and the tanner's daughter   *affair's gone too far*
45 to let slip now, and she must see the Duke, and she must dance too.

FOURTH COUNTRYMAN Shall we be lusty?°   *lively*

SECOND COUNTRYMAN All the boys in Athens blow wind i'th'
breech on's!⁸ And here I'll be and there I'll be, for our town,
and here again and there again—ha, boys, hey for the weavers!⁹

50 FIRST COUNTRYMAN This must be done i'th' woods.

FOURTH COUNTRYMAN O, pardon me.

SECOND COUNTRYMAN By any° means, our thing of learning°   *all / our teacher*
said so; where he himself will edify the Duke most parlously°   *cleverly*
in our behalfs— he's excellent i'th' woods, bring him to th'
55 plains, his learning makes no cry.°   *falls silent*

THIRD COUNTRYMAN We'll see the sports, then every man to's
tackle°—and, sweet companions, let's rehearse, by any means,   *morris-dancing gear*
before the ladies see us, and do sweetly, and God knows what
may come on't.

60 FOURTH COUNTRYMAN Content—the sports once ended, we'll
perform. Away boys, and hold.°   *keep your word*

ARCITE [*coming forward*] By your leaves, honest friends, pray
you whither go you?

FOURTH COUNTRYMAN Whither? Why, what a° question's that?   *what sort of a*

ARCITE Yet 'tis a question
To me that know not.

65 THIRD COUNTRYMAN To the games, my friend.

SECOND COUNTRYMAN Where were you bred, you know it not?

ARCITE   Not far, sir—
Are there such games today?

FIRST COUNTRYMAN   Yes, marry, are there,
And such as you never saw. The Duke himself
Will be in person there.

ARCITE   What pastimes are they?

SECOND COUNTRYMAN Wrestling and running. [*To the others*]
70   'Tis a pretty fellow.

THIRD COUNTRYMAN [*to* ARCITE]
Thou wilt not go along?

ARCITE   Not yet, sir.

FOURTH COUNTRYMAN   Well, sir,
Take your own time. [*To the others*] Come, boys.

FIRST COUNTRYMAN   My mind misgives me—
This fellow has a vengeance trick o'th' hip:¹
Mark how his body's made for't.

SECOND COUNTRYMAN   I'll be hanged though
75 If he dare venture; hang him, plum porridge!²
He wrestle? He roast eggs!³ Come, let's be gone, lads.

                    Exeunt [*the*] *four* [COUNTRYMEN]

ARCITE This is an offered° opportunity   *unsought*
I durst not° wish for. Well I could have wrestled⁴—   *would not have dared*

---

6. For he arranges everything.
7. A primer or tablet, protected by a translucent plate
of horn, inscribed with the alphabet.
8. Will try—and fail—to keep up with us.
9. Hooray for the weavers (the profession to which the
speaker apparently belongs).
1. *My . . . hip*: I fear that this man may be a skillful

wrestler.
2. Contemptuous, suggesting that Arcite is out of
shape. Plum porridge was a heavy dessert of stewed
dried fruits eaten at Christmas.
3. He'd be a better cook than wrestler (?); he probably
can't cook an egg (?).
4. I knew how to wrestle.

	The best men called it excellent—and run	
80	Swifter than wind upon a field of corn,°	*wheat*
	Curling the wealthy° ears, never° flew. I'll venture,	*abundant / ever*
	And in some poor disguise be there. Who knows	
	Whether my brows may not be girt with garlands,	
	And happiness prefer° me to a place	*good fortune promote*
85	Where I may ever dwell in sight of her?	*Exit*

2.4

Enter [the] JAILER'S DAUGHTER

	JAILER'S DAUGHTER Why should I love this gentleman? 'Tis	
	odds°	*Chances are*
	He never will affect° me. I am base,	*love*
	My father the mean° keeper of his prison,	*lowly*
	And he a prince. To marry him is hopeless,	
5	To be his whore¹ is witless. Out upon't,°	*(Expressing abhorrence)*
	What pushes° are we wenches driven to	*extremities*
	When fifteen° once has found us? First, I saw him;	*(the age)*
	I, seeing, thought he was a goodly man;	
	He has as much to please a woman in him—	
10	If he please to bestow it so—as ever	
	These eyes yet looked on. Next, I pitied him,	
	And so would any young wench, o'my conscience,	
	That ever dreamed or vowed her maidenhead	
	To a young handsome man. Then, I loved him,	
15	Extremely loved him, infinitely loved him—	
	And yet he had a cousin fair as he, too.	
	But in my heart was Palamon, and there,	
	Lord, what a coil he keeps!° To hear him	*turmoil he makes*
	Sing in an evening, what a heaven it is!	
20	And yet his songs are sad ones. Fairer spoken	
	Was never gentleman. When I come in	
	To bring him water in a morning, first	
	He bows his noble body, then salutes° me, thus:	*greets*
	'Fair, gentle maid, good morrow. May thy goodness	
25	Get thee a happy husband.' Once he kissed me—	
	I loved my lips the better ten days after.	
	Would he would do so every day! He grieves much,	
	And me as much to see his misery.	
	What should I do to make him know I love him?	
30	For I would fain° enjoy him. Say I ventured	*eagerly*
	To set him free? What says the law then? Thus much	
	For law or kindred! I will do it,	
	And this night; ere tomorrow he shall love me.	*Exit*

2.5

Short flourish of cornetts and shouts within. Enter THE-
SEUS, HIPPOLYTA, PIRITHOUS, EMILIA, ARCITE *[disguised]*
with a garland [and attendants]

	THESEUS You have done worthily. I have not seen	
	Since Hercules a man of tougher sinews.°	*muscles*
	Whate'er you are, you run the best and wrestle°	*wrestle the best*
	That these times can allow.°	*show*

2.4 Location: The prison in Athens.
1. Premarital sex, not prostitution.

2.5 Location: Athens, near the site of the athletic
games.

ARCITE   I am proud to please you.

THESEUS   What country bred you?

5   ARCITE   This—but far off, prince.

THESEUS   Are you a gentleman?

ARCITE   My father said so,
And to those gentle uses gave me life.¹

THESEUS   Are you his heir?

ARCITE   His youngest, sir.

THESEUS   Your father
Sure is a happy sire, then. What proves you?°   *(a gentleman)*

10   ARCITE   A little of all noble qualities.°   *accomplishments*
I could have kept° a hawk and well have hollered   *I knew how to keep*
To a deep° cry of dogs; I dare not praise   *loud*
My feat in horsemanship, yet they that knew me
Would say it was my best piece;° last and greatest,   *attribute*
I would° be thought a soldier.   *used to*

15   THESEUS   You are perfect.

PIRITHOUS   Upon my soul, a proper° man.   *handsome*

EMILIA   He is so.

PIRITHOUS [*to* HIPPOLYTA]   How do you like him, lady?

HIPPOLYTA   I admire° him.   *am amazed at*
I have not seen so young a man so noble—
If he say true—of his sort.°   *rank*

EMILIA   Believe°   *Be sure*

20   His mother was a wondrous handsome woman—
His face methinks goes that way.°   *demonstrates that*

HIPPOLYTA   But his body
And fiery mind illustrate° a brave father.   *indicate; copy*

PIRITHOUS   Mark how his virtue,° like a hidden sun,   *excellence*
Breaks through his baser garments.

HIPPOLYTA   He's well got,° sure.   *wellborn*

THESEUS [*to* ARCITE]   What made you seek this place, sir?

25   ARCITE   Noble Theseus,
To purchase name° and do my ablest service   *get a reputation*
To such a well-found° wonder as thy worth,   *well-deserved*
For only in thy court of all the world
Dwells fair-eyed honour.

PIRITHOUS   All his words are worthy.

30   THESEUS [*to* ARCITE]   Sir, we are much indebted to your travel,°   *journey; effort*
Nor shall you lose your wish.—Pirithous,
Dispose of° this fair gentleman.   *Place*

PIRITHOUS   Thanks, Theseus.
[*To* ARCITE] Whate'er you are, you're mine, and I shall give you
To a most noble service, to this lady,

35   This bright young virgin; pray observe° her goodness.   *respect*
You have honoured her fair birthday with your virtues,
And as your due you're hers. Kiss her fair hand, sir.

ARCITE   Sir, you're a noble giver. [*To* EMILIA] Dearest beauty,
Thus let me seal my vowed faith.
                         [*He kisses her hand*]
                                    When your servant,
Your most unworthy creature, but offends you,
Command him die, he shall.

40

---

1. And raised me for those genteel pursuits.

EMILIA   That were too cruel.
    If you deserve well, sir, I shall soon see't.
    You're mine, and somewhat better than your rank° I'll use you.   *position*

PIRITHOUS [*to* ARCITE]   I'll see you furnished,° and, because you   *equipped*
    say
45   You are a horseman, I must needs entreat you
    This afternoon to ride—but 'tis a rough one.°   *(horse)*

ARCITE   I like him better, prince—I shall not then
    Freeze in my saddle.

THESEUS [*to* HIPPOLYTA]   Sweet, you must be ready—
    And you, Emilia, [*to* PIRITHOUS] and you, friend—and all,
50   Tomorrow by the sun,° to do observance   *by sunrise*
    To flow'ry May in Dian's wood. [*To* ARCITE] Wait well, sir,
    Upon your mistress.—Emily, I hope
    He shall not go afoot.

EMILIA   That were a shame, sir,
    While I have horses. [*To* ARCITE] Take your choice, and what
55   You want,° at any time, let me but know it.   *lack*
    If you serve faithfully, I dare assure you,
    You'll find a loving mistress.

ARCITE   If I do not,
    Let me find that° my father ever hated—   *that which*
    Disgrace and blows.

THESEUS   Go, lead the way—you have won it.[2]
60   It shall be so: you shall receive all dues
    Fit for the honour you have won. 'Twere wrong else.
    [*To* EMILIA] Sister, beshrew my heart, you have a servant
    That, if I were a woman, would be master.
    But you are wise.

EMILIA   I hope too wise for that, sir. *Flourish. Exeunt*

2.6

Enter [*the*] JAILER'S DAUGHTER

JAILER'S DAUGHTER   Let all the dukes and all the devils roar—
    He is at liberty! I have ventured° for him,   *taken a risk*
    And out I have brought him. To a little wood
    A mile hence I have sent him, where a cedar
    Higher than all the rest spreads like a plane,°   *plane tree*
    Fast° by a brook—and there he shall keep close°   *Close / shall hide*
5   Till I provide him files and food, for yet
    His iron bracelets° are not off. O Love,°   *shackles / Cupid*
    What a stout-hearted child thou art! My father
    Durst better have endured cold iron than done it.[1]
    I love him beyond love and beyond reason
10   Or wit° or safety. I have made him know it—   *sense*
    I care not, I am desperate. If the law
    Find me and then condemn me for't, some wenches,
    Some honest-hearted maids, will sing my dirge
    And tell to memory my death was noble,
15   Dying almost a martyr. That way he takes,
    I purpose, is my way too. Sure, he cannot

---

2. Won the honor of leading the procession.
2.6 Location: Near the prison in Athens.

1. *My . . . it*: My father would sooner have been run
through than have freed a prisoner.

Be so unmanly as to leave me here.
20   If he do, maids will not so easily
Trust men again. And yet, he has not thanked me
For what I have done—no, not so much as kissed me—
And that, methinks, is not so well. Nor scarcely
Could I persuade him to become a free man,
25   He made such scruples of the wrong he did
To me and to my father. Yet, I hope
When he considers more, this love of mine
Will take more root within him. Let him do
What he will with me—so he use me kindly.[2]
30   For use me,° so he shall, or I'll proclaim him,   *(sexually)*
And to his face, no man.° I'll presently   *(sexually)*
Provide him necessaries and pack my clothes up,
And where there is a patch of ground I'll venture,
So he be with me. By him, like a shadow,
35   I'll ever dwell. Within this hour the hubbub
Will be all o'er the prison—I am then
Kissing the man they look for. Farewell, father:
Get° many more such prisoners and such daughters,   *Catch; beget*
And shortly you may keep yourself.[3] Now to him.   [*Exit*]

3.1

[*A bush in place.*] *Cornetts in sundry*° *places. Noise and*   *various (offstage)*
hollering as [*of*] *people a-Maying.*[1]
    Enter ARCITE

ARCITE   The Duke has lost Hippolyta—each took°   *went to*
A several laund.° This is a solemn rite   *A different clearing*
They owe bloomed May, and the Athenians pay° it   *observe*
To th' heart of° ceremony. O, Queen Emilia,   *With the utmost*
5   Fresher than May, sweeter
Than her gold buttons° on the boughs, or all   *buds*
Th'enamelled knacks° o'th' mead° or garden—yea,   *flowers / meadow*
We challenge too the bank of any nymph
That makes the stream seem flowers;[2] thou, O jewel
10   O'th' wood, o'th' world, hast likewise blessed a pace°   *path through the woods*
With thy sole presence in thy [
                       ][3] rumination
That I, poor man, might eftsoons come between
And chop on some cold thought.[4] Thrice blessèd chance
15   To drop on° such a mistress, expectation   *run into*
Most guiltless on't!° Tell me, O Lady Fortune,   *unexpectedly*
Next after Emily my sovereign, how far
I may be proud. She takes strong note of me,
Hath made me near her, and this beauteous morn,

2. Provided that he treat me gently; naturally; nobly, in a manner befitting a man of his kind.
3. You yourself may use the jail, since everyone else will either have escaped or been freed.
3.1 Location: All of Act 3 takes place in a forest near Athens.
1. May Day celebrations included feasts, hunting, music, entertainments (such as the morris dance of 3.5.139), and dancing around the maypole. See note to 2.3.37.

2. *We . . . flowers*: Emilia surpasses in beauty even a nymph's flowered riverbank, whose reflection makes the river itself seem covered with flowers.
3. Q has a comma after "presence" and lacks this gap. Editors often strengthen the punctuation by starting a new sentence with "In thy rumination." It is unclear how Arcite could "come between" (line 13) a "rumination," however—hence the hypothesis of a missing line.
4. *might . . . thought*: might suddenly come upon you and seize some chaste thought.

20	The prim'st° of all the year, presents me with	*best*
	A brace° of horses—two such steeds might well	*pair*
	Be by a pair of kings backed,° in a field	*ridden*
	That their crowns' titles tried.⁵ Alas, alas,	
	Poor cousin Palamon, poor prisoner—thou	
25	So little dream'st upon my fortune that	
	Thou think'st thyself the happier thing to be	
	So near Emilia. Me thou deem'st at Thebes,	
	And therein wretched, although free. But if	
	Thou knew'st my mistress breathed on me, and that	
30	I eared her language,° lived in her eye—O, coz,	*listened to her*
	What passion would enclose° thee!	*rage would possess*

Enter PALAMON *as out of a bush with his shackles.* [*He*]
bends° his fist at ARCITE   *shakes*

PALAMON   Traitor kinsman,
Thou shouldst perceive my passion if these signs
Of prisonment⁶ were off me, and this hand
But owner of a sword. By all oaths in one,
35 I and the justice of my love would make thee
A confessed traitor. O thou most perfidious
That ever gently looked,° the void'st of honour   *seemed gentlemanly*
That e'er bore gentle token,° falsest cousin   *wore noble emblems*
That ever blood made kin—call'st thou her thine?
40 I'll prove it in my shackles, with these hands,
Void of appointment,° that thou liest and art   *Devoid of weapons*
A very thief in love, a chaffy° lord   *worthless*
Not worth the name of villain. Had I a sword
And these house-clogs° away—   *fetters*

ARCITE   Dear cousin Palamon—
45 PALAMON   Cozener° Arcite, give me language such   *Cheater (punning)*
As thou hast showed me feat.⁷

ARCITE   Not finding in
The circuit of my breast any gross stuff
To form me like your blazon holds me to
This gentleness of answer⁸—'tis your passion
50 That thus mistakes, the which, to you being enemy,
Cannot to me be kind.⁹ Honour and honesty
I cherish and depend on, howsoe'er
You skip° them in me, and with them, fair coz,   *ignore*
I'll maintain my proceedings. Pray be pleased
55 To show in generous° terms your griefs,° since that   *genteel / grievances*
Your question's° with your equal, who professes   *dispute is*
To clear his own way¹ with the mind and sword
Of a true gentleman.

PALAMON   That thou durst,° Arcite!   *You wouldn't dare*

ARCITE   My coz, my coz, you have been well advertised°   *informed*
60 How much I dare; you've seen me use my sword
Against th'advice° of fear. Sure, of° another   *warning / by*

5. *in . . . tried:* on a battlefield where they were fighting for each other's kingdoms.
6. *signs / Of prisonment:* shackles.
7. *give . . . feat:* use words that accord better with your (perfidious) actions.
8. *Not . . . answer:* Since I find nothing in me that fits your description of me, I answer gently. *blazon:* (description of a) coat of arms.
9. *'tis . . . kind:* your anger ("passion") is your enemy (distorts your judgment) and thus to me cannot be kind (because you are my kinsman—"kind" also means "kin"—and friend, and hence we share all enemies).
1. To justify; to make his own way.

You would not hear me doubted, but your silence
Should break out, though i'th' sanctuary.[2]

PALAMON   Sir,
I have seen you move in such a place° which well   *battle; tournament*
65 Might justify your manhood; you were called
A good knight and a bold. But the whole week's not fair
If any day it rain: their valiant temper°   *attitude*
Men lose when they incline to treachery,
And then they fight like compelled bears³—would fly
Were they not tied.

70 ARCITE   Kinsman, you might as well
Speak this and act it in your glass° as to   *mirror*
His ear which now disdains you.

PALAMON   Come up to me,
Quit° me of these cold gyves,° give me a sword,   *Free / chains*
Though it be rusty, and the charity
75 Of one meal lend me. Come before me then,
A good sword in thy hand, and do but say
That Emily is thine—I will forgive
The trespass° thou hast done me, yea, my life,   *wrong*
If then thou carry't;° and brave souls in shades°   *beat me / Hades*
80 That have died manly, which will seek of me
Some news from earth, they shall get none but this—
That thou art brave and noble.

ARCITE   Be content,
Again betake you to° your hawthorn house.   *go back into*
With counsel of the night⁴ I will be here
85 With wholesome viands.° These impediments°   *food / shackles*
Will I file off. You shall have garments and
Perfumes to kill the smell o'th' prison. After,
When you shall stretch yourself and say but 'Arcite,
I am in plight',° there shall be at your choice   *I am ready*
Both sword and armour.

90 PALAMON   O, you heavens, dares any
So noble bear a guilty business!° None   *act shamefully*
But only Arcite, therefore none but Arcite
In this kind is so bold.

ARCITE   Sweet Palamon.

PALAMON   I do embrace you and your offer—for
95 Your offer do't I only, sir; your person,
Without hypocrisy, I may not wish
        Wind° horns [within]   *Sound*
More than my sword's edge on't.

ARCITE   You hear the horns—
Enter your muset° lest this match between's   *gap in a thicket*
Be crossed ere met.° Give me your hand, farewell.   *prevented before begun*
100 I'll bring you every needful thing—I pray you,
Take comfort and be strong.

PALAMON   Pray hold your promise,
And do the deed with a bent brow.° Most certain   *stern countenance*
You love me not—be rough with me and pour

---

2. *your . . . sanctuary:* you would speak to defend me
even if you were hiding in a safe place (or in a church).
3. In bearbaiting competitions (a popular pastime with
connections to the theater), bears were tied to a stake.
4. With darkness to assist (and hide) me.

This oil° out of your language. By this air,   *smoothness; flattery*
105   I could for each word give a cuff, my stomach°   *anger*
    Not reconciled by reason.

ARCITE   Plainly spoken,
    Yet—pardon me—hard language: when I spur
    Wind horns [*within*]
    My horse I chide him not. Content and anger
    In me have but one face.° Hark, sir, they call   *the same expression*
110   The scattered to the banquet. You must guess
    I have an office° there.   *assigned duty*

PALAMON   Sir, your attendance
    Cannot please heaven, and I know your office
    Unjustly is achieved.°   *Was earned unfairly*

ARCITE   'Tis a good title.°   *It was won justly*
115   I am persuaded this question, sick between's,
    By bleeding must be cured.⁵ I am a suitor°   *I beg*
    That to your sword you will bequeath this plea°   *lawsuit*
    And talk of it no more.

PALAMON   But this one word:
    You are going now to gaze upon my mistress—
    For note you, mine she is—

ARCITE   Nay then—

PALAMON   Nay, pray you—
120   You talk of feeding me to breed me strength—
    You are going now to look upon a sun
    That strengthens what it looks on. There you have
    A vantage° o'er me, but enjoy it till   *advantage*
    I may enforce my remedy. Farewell.
    Exeunt [*severally,* PALAMON *as into the bush*]

3.2

Enter [*the*] JAILER'S DAUGHTER [*with a file*]

JAILER'S DAUGHTER   He has mistook the brake° I meant, is gone   *thicket*
    After¹ his fancy. 'Tis now wellnigh morning.
    No matter—would it were perpetual night,
    And darkness lord o'th' world. Hark, 'tis a wolf!
5   In me hath grief slain fear, and, but for one thing,
    I care for nothing—and that's Palamon.
    I reck° not if the wolves would jaw° me, so°   *care / gnaw / if*
    He had this file. What if I hollered for him?
    I cannot holler. If I whooped, what then?
10   If he not answered, I should call a wolf
    And do him but that service.² I have heard
    Strange howls this livelong night—why may't not be
    They have made prey of him? He has no weapons;
    He cannot run; the jangling of his gyves°   *fetters*
15   Might call fell° things to listen, who have in them   *wild*
    A sense to know a man unarmed, and can
    Smell where resistance is. I'll set it down°   *take it as fact*
    He's torn to pieces: they howled many together

---

5. *I am . . . cured:* I am convinced that the dispute
between us (here, imagined as a sick person) can only
be settled (cured) by a bloodletting.

3.2
1. *is gone / After:* is led by (only).
2. I would at least serve him by calling a wolf to attack
him (ironic).

And then they fed on him. So much for that.

20 Be bold to ring the bell.° How stand I then?   *ring his death knell*

All's chared° when he is gone. No, no, I lie: *My work is all done*

My father's to be hanged for his escape,

Myself to beg, if I prized life so much

As to deny my act—but that I would not,

25 Should I try death by dozens.³ I am moped°—   *dazed*

Food took I none these two days,

Sipped some water. I have not closed mine eyes

Save when my lids scoured off their brine.⁴ Alas,

Dissolve, my life; let not my sense unsettle,°   *reason come unhinged*

30 Lest I should drown or stab or hang myself.

O state of nature,° fail together° in me,   *life / entirely*

Since thy best props° are warped. So which way now?   *supports*

The best way is the next° way to a grave,   *nearest*

Each errant step beside⁵ is torment. Lo,

35 The moon is down, the crickets chirp, the screech-owl

Calls in the dawn. All offices are done

Save what I fail in:⁶ but the point is this,

An end,° and that is all.   *Exit*   *A death*

3.3

Enter ARCITE *with [a bundle containing] meat, wine,*
and files

ARCITE   I should be near the place. Ho, cousin Palamon!

Enter PALAMON [*as from the bush*]

PALAMON   Arcite.

ARCITE   The same. I have brought you food and files.

Come forth and fear not, here's no Theseus.

PALAMON   Nor none so honest, Arcite.

ARCITE   That's no matter—

5 We'll argue that hereafter. Come, take courage—

You shall not die thus beastly.° Here, sir, drink;   *like an animal*

I know you are faint. Then I'll talk further with you.

PALAMON   Arcite, thou mightst now poison me.

ARCITE   I might—

But I must° fear you first. Sit down and, good now,   *should need to*

10 No more of these vain parleys.° Let us not,   *pointless comments*

Having our ancient¹ reputation with us,

Make talk for² fools and cowards. To your health, sir.

PALAMON   Do.°   *You drink first*

[ARCITE *drinks*]

ARCITE   Pray sit down, then, and let me entreat you,

By all the honesty and honour in you,

15 No mention of this woman—'twill disturb us.

We shall have time enough.

PALAMON   Well, sir, I'll pledge you.°   *drink your health*

[PALAMON *drinks*]

ARCITE   Drink a good hearty draught; it breeds good blood,° man.   *makes you strong*

---

3. Even if I had to die dozens of times (ways).
4. Except when I blinked to clear my eyes of tears.
5. Each step that wanders from the direct path to the grave.
6. *All . . . in:* All tasks are done, except the one I've failed to complete (either giving the file to Palamon or

killing herself).

3.3
1. Of long standing; former (now reestablished through escape).
2. Talk as though we were; make ourselves the talk of.

Do not you feel it thaw you?

PALAMON   Stay, I'll tell you
After a draught or two more.
                    [PALAMON *drinks*]
ARCITE   Spare it not—
The Duke has more, coz. Eat now.
PALAMON   Yes.
                    [PALAMON *eats*]
20   ARCITE   I am glad
You have so good a stomach.°   *an appetite; an anger*
PALAMON   I am gladder
I have so good meat° to't.   *(to feed my anger)*
ARCITE   Is't not mad,° lodging   *strange; maddening*
Here in the wild woods,³ cousin?
PALAMON   Yes, for them
That have wild° consciences.   *uncivilized*
ARCITE   How tastes your victuals?
Your hunger needs no sauce, I see.
25   PALAMON   Not much.
But if it did, yours is too tart,⁴ sweet cousin.
What is this?
ARCITE   Venison.
PALAMON   'Tis a lusty° meat—   *hearty*
Give me more wine. Here, Arcite, to the wenches
We have known in our days. [*Drinking*] The lord steward's
   daughter.
Do you remember her?
30   ARCITE   After you,⁵ coz.
PALAMON   She loved a black-haired man.
ARCITE   She did so; well, sir.
PALAMON   And I have heard some call him Arcite, and—
ARCITE   Out with't, faith.
PALAMON   She met him in an arbour—
What did she there, coz? Play o'th' virginals?⁶
ARCITE   Something° she did, sir—   *To some extent*
35   PALAMON   Made her groan a month for't—
Or two, or three, or ten.°   *(in pregnancy)*
ARCITE   The marshal's sister
Had her share too, as I remember, cousin,
Else there be tales° abroad. You'll pledge her?   *false rumors*
PALAMON   Yes.
                    [*They drink*]
ARCITE   A pretty brown° wench 'tis. There was a time   *brunette*
40   When young men went a-hunting, and a wood,
And a broad beech, and thereby hangs a tale—
Heigh-ho!°   *(a sigh)*
PALAMON   For Emily, upon my life! Fool,
Away with this strained mirth. I say again,
That sigh was breathed for Emily. Base cousin,
Dar'st thou break⁷ first?
ARCITE   You are wide.°   *wide of the mark*

---

3. *woods:* Pun on "wode" (mad).
4. Your insolence ("sauce," line 25) is too bitter ("tart").
5. Finish your toast first, before I propose mine.
6. Small keyboard instrument; (sexual).
7. Break our agreement (not to refer to Emilia).

45   PALAMON   By heaven and earth,
      There's nothing in thee honest.
    ARCITE   Then I'll leave you—
      You are a beast° now.   *behaving savagely*
    PALAMON   As thou mak'st me, traitor.
    ARCITE [*pointing to the bundle*]   There's all things needful: files
          and shirts and perfumes—
      I'll come again some two hours hence and bring
      That that shall quiet° all.   *silence*
50   PALAMON   A sword and armour.
    ARCITE   Fear° me not. You are now too foul.° Farewell.   *Doubt / beastly*
      Get off your trinkets:° you shall want naught.   *shackles*
    PALAMON   Sirrah°—   *(an insult)*
    ARCITE   I'll hear no more.   *Exit*
    PALAMON   If he keep touch°, he dies for't.   *keeps his promise*
                             Exit [as into the bush]

3.4

Enter [the] JAILER'S DAUGHTER

  JAILER'S DAUGHTER   I am very cold, and all the stars are out too,
    The little stars and all, that look like aglets°—   *shiny ornaments*
    The sun has seen my folly. Palamon!
    Alas, no, he's in heaven. Where am I now?
5   Yonder's the sea and there's a ship—how't tumbles!
    And there's a rock lies watching under water—
    Now, now, it° beats upon it—now, now, now,   *(the ship)*
    There's a leak sprung, a sound° one—how they cry!   *large*
    Open her[1] before the wind—you'll lose all else.
10   Up with a course° or two and tack° about, boys.   *lower sail / turn*
    Good night, good night, you're gone. I am very hungry.
    Would I could find a fine frog—he would tell me
    News from all parts o'th' world, then would I make
    A carrack° of a cockle-shell, and sail   *cargo ship*
15   By east and north-east to the King of Pygmies,
    For he tells fortunes rarely.° Now my father,   *wonderfully*
    Twenty to one, is trussed up in a trice°   *to be hanged quickly*
    Tomorrow morning. I'll say never a word.
    [*She*] *sing[s]*
    For I'll cut my green coat, a foot above my knee,
20   And I'll clip my yellow locks, an inch below mine eye,
      Hey nonny, nonny, nonny,
    He s'buy° me a white cut,[2] forth for to ride,   *He shall buy*
    And I'll go seek him, through the world that is so wide,
      Hey nonny, nonny, nonny.
25   O for a prick now, like a nightingale,
    To put my breast against.[3] I shall sleep like a top° else.   *Exit*   *soundly*

3.4
1. Open her sails (so she can run).
2. Horse (called a "cut" because it was a gelding or had a cropped tail).

3. O . . . *against*: nightingales supposedly pricked themselves to stay awake at night. "Prick" also carries a sexual meaning; compare the sexual punning here with that in Ophelia's "mad" speeches in *Hamlet*.

3.5

Enter [Gerald] a SCHOOLMASTER, *[five]* COUNTRYMEN,
[one of whom is dressed as a] BABION, *[five]* Wenches,
[and Timothy,] a TABORER. *[All are attired as morris
dancers]*[1]

SCHOOLMASTER Fie, fie,
What tediosity and disinsanity[2]
Is here among ye! Have my rudiments°   *lessons; rehearsals*
Been laboured so long with ye, milked unto ye,
5   And, by a figure,° even the very plum-broth   *figure of speech*
And marrow[3] of my understanding laid upon ye?
And do you still cry 'where?' and 'how?' and 'wherefore?'
You most coarse frieze capacities, ye jean judgements,[4]
Have I said, 'thus let be', and 'there let be',
10 And 'then let be', and no man understand me?
Proh deum, medius fidius[5]—ye are all dunces.
Forwhy, here stand I. Here the Duke comes. There are you,
Close° in the thicket. The Duke appears. I meet him,   *Hidden*
And unto him I utter learnèd things
15 And many figures. He hears, and nods, and hums,°   *murmurs approval*
And then cries, 'Rare!', and I go forward.° At length   *continue*
I fling my cap up—mark there—then do you,
As once did Meleager and the boar,[6]
Break comely out° before him, like true lovers,[7]   *Appear decorously*
20 Cast yourselves in a body decently,[8]
And sweetly, by a figure, trace° and turn, boys.   *follow the steps*
FIRST COUNTRYMAN And sweetly we will do it, master Gerald.
SECOND COUNTRYMAN Draw up the company. Where's the
    taborer?
THIRD COUNTRYMAN Why, Timothy!
TABORER   Here, my mad boys, have at ye!° *go ahead; I'm ready*
SCHOOLMASTER But I say, where's these women?
25 FOURTH COUNTRYMAN   Here's Friz and Madeline.
SECOND COUNTRYMAN And little Luce with the white legs, and
    bouncing° Barbara.   *robust*
FIRST COUNTRYMAN And freckled Nell, that never failed her
    master.°   *(with sexual overtone)*
SCHOOLMASTER Where be your ribbons,[9] maids? Swim° with *Dance gracefully*
    your bodies
And carry it° sweetly and deliverly,°   *move / nimbly*
30 And now and then a favour° and a frisk.°   *kiss; bow / leap*
NELL Let us alone,° sir.   *Leave it to us*
SCHOOLMASTER   Where's the rest o'th' music?°   *musicians*
THIRD COUNTRYMAN Dispersed° as you commanded.   *Placed here and there*
SCHOOLMASTER   Couple,° then,   *Pair up*
And see what's wanting.° Where's the babion?   *who's missing*

3.5
1. The morris dance was a rural folk dance of north
English origin, performed in costume. *babion*: one morris dancer, who took the part of the fool, always wore
the costume of an ape or a baboon. *taborer*: drummer.
2. What tedium and folly (pedantic).
3. "Plum-broth" (hearty stew of dried fruits and suet)
and "marrow" both suggest essence or fortifying sustenance.
4. *You . . . judgements*: You people of rudimentary
intellects. "Frieze" and "jean" were coarse fabrics worn

by laborers.
5. O God, heaven help me (Latin).
6. Meleager was a Greek warrior who killed the great
Calydonian boar and brought its head to the Amazon
warrior Atalanta.
7. Like loving subjects of Theseus; in couples, as lovers
do.
8. Position yourselves appropriately for the dance.
9. Morris dancers carried ribbons or streamers as
props.

[*To the* BABION] My friend, carry your tail without offence°   *sexual offense*
35 Or scandal to the ladies; and be sure
You tumble with audacity and manhood,°   *bravery*
And when you bark,[1] do it with judgement.

BABION   Yes, sir.

SCHOOLMASTER *Quousque tandem?*[2] Here is a woman wanting!

FOURTH COUNTRYMAN We may go whistle—all the fat's i'th'
    fire.[3]

40 SCHOOLMASTER We have,
As learnèd authors utter, washed a tile;°   *worked in vain*
We have been *fatuus*,° and laboured vainly.   *foolish*

SECOND COUNTRYMAN This is that scornful piece, that scurvy
    hilding°   *worthless woman*
That gave her promise faithfully she would be here—
45 Cicely, the seamstress' daughter.
The next gloves that I give her shall be dogskin.°   *cheap leather*
Nay, an° she fail me once—you can tell, Arcas,   *if*
She swore by wine and bread she would not break.°   *(her solemn oath)*

SCHOOLMASTER An eel and woman,
50 A learnèd poet says, unless by th' tail
And with thy teeth thou hold, will either° fail—   *both*
In manners this was false position.[4]

FIRST COUNTRYMAN A fire-ill take her!° Does she flinch now?   *A pox infect her*

THIRD COUNTRYMAN   What
    Shall we determine,° sir?   *decide to do*

SCHOOLMASTER   Nothing;
55 Our business is become a nullity,
Yea, and a woeful and a piteous nullity.

FOURTH COUNTRYMAN Now, when the credit of our town lay on it,
Now to be frampold, now to piss o'th' nettle![5]
Go thy ways—I'll remember thee, I'll fit thee!°   *get even with you*

Enter [the] JAILER'S DAUGHTER

JAILER'S DAUGHTER [*sings*]
60   The *George Alow*[6] came from the south,
      From the coast of Barbary-a;
    And there he met with brave gallants of war,°   *warships*
      By one, by two, by three-a.
    'Well hailed, well hailed, you jolly gallants,
65   And whither now are you bound-a?
    O let me have your company
      Till I come to the sound-a.'

There was three fools fell out about an owlet—

    The one he said it was an owl,
70   The other he said nay,
    The third he said it was a hawk,
      And her bells were cut away.[7]

---

1. Baboons were considered half man, half dog.
2. How much longer (must I wait)? (Latin, as throughout the scene.) Expression of impatience that opens the ancient Roman writer Cicero's first oration against Catiline but here indicates the Schoolmaster's pomposity.
3. We may as well give up, since all our work has produced nothing. Both phrases were proverbial, although the second has a different meaning today.

4. A false (pro)position is a logical fallacy. The Schoolmaster compares Cicely's flawed manners to faulty logic.
5. Now to be temperamental, to lose her temper.
6. Probably taken from "The George Aloe and the Sweepstake," a ballad published in 1611. The *George Aloe* was a ship.
7. Hawks used for falconry wore bells in order to make them easier to catch.

THIRD COUNTRYMAN   There's a dainty° madwoman, master,   *fine*
Comes i'th' nick,° as mad as a March hare.   *nick (of time)*
75 If we can get her dance, we are made again.°   *all will be well*
I warrant her, she'll do the rarest gambols.°   *finest capers*
FIRST COUNTRYMAN   A madwoman? We are made, boys.
SCHOOLMASTER [*to the* JAILER'S DAUGHTER]   And are you mad,
    good woman?
JAILER'S DAUGHTER   I would be sorry else.
    Give me your hand.
SCHOOLMASTER   Why?
JAILER'S DAUGHTER   I can tell your fortune.
    [*She examines his hand*]
80 You are a fool. Tell ten—I have posed him.[8] Buzz!°   *Silence*
Friend, you must eat no white bread—if you do,
Your teeth will bleed extremely. Shall we dance, ho?
I know you—you're a tinker.° Sirrah tinker,   *mender of kettles*
Stop no more holes but what you should.°   *(sexual)*
SCHOOLMASTER   Dii boni°—   *Good gods*
    A tinker, damsel?
85 JAILER'S DAUGHTER   Or a conjurer°—   *magician*
Raise me a devil now and let him play
Qui passa o'th' bells and bones.[9]
SCHOOLMASTER   Go, take her,
And fluently persuade her to a peace.°   *to do what we want*
Et opus exegi, quod nec Iovis ira, nec ignis[1]—
Strike up, and lead her in.
90 SECOND COUNTRYMAN   Come, lass, let's trip it.°   *let's dance*
JAILER'S DAUGHTER   I'll lead.
THIRD COUNTRYMAN   Do, do.
SCHOOLMASTER   Persuasively and cunningly°—   *skillfully*
    Wind horns [*within*]   away, boys,
I hear the horns. Give me some meditation,°   *time to think*
And mark° your cue.   *don't forget*
    Exeunt all but [Gerald the] SCHOOLMASTER
95   Pallas° inspire me.   *goddess of wisdom*
    Enter THESEUS, PIRITHOUS, HIPPOLYTA, EMILIA, ARCITE,
    and train
THESEUS   This way the stag took.
SCHOOLMASTER   Stay and edify.°   *be edified*
THESEUS   What have we here?
PIRITHOUS   Some country sport, upon my life, sir.
THESEUS [*to the* SCHOOLMASTER]   Well, sir, go forward—we will
100   edify.
Ladies, sit down—we'll stay it.°   *stay to watch*
    [*They sit:* THESEUS *in a chair, the others on stools*]
SCHOOLMASTER   Thou doughty Duke, all hail! All hail, sweet
    ladies.
THESEUS   This is a cold° beginning.   *(punning on "hail")*

---

8. *Tell . . . him:* Count to ten (a common test for insanity or idiocy)—I have stumped ("posed") him. The
Jailer's Daughter tests the Schoolmaster for idiocy and
fails him.
9. *Chi passa* (Italian: who passes) were the first words
of a common dance tune. Bones were used as percussion instruments, along with bells.
1. "And I have created a work which neither Jove's
anger nor fire [can destroy]." Slightly misquoted from
Ovid's *Metamorphoses* 15.871.

SCHOOLMASTER   If you but favour,[2] our country pastime made is.

105 We are a few of those collected here,
     That ruder tongues distinguish° 'villager';   call
     And to say verity, and not to fable,
     We are a merry rout, or else a rabble,
     Or company, or, by a figure,° chorus,   figure of speech
110 That fore thy dignity will dance a morris.
     And I, that am the rectifier° of all,   director; connector
     By title *pedagogus*,° that let fall   teacher
     The birch upon the breeches of the small ones,
     And humble with a ferula° the tall ones,   cane
115 Do here present this machine, or this frame;[3]
     And dainty Duke, whose doughty dismal° fame   awe-inspiring
     From Dis to Daedalus,[4] from post to pillar,
     Is blown abroad, help me, thy poor well-willer,°   well-wisher
     And with thy twinkling eyes, look right and straight
120 Upon this mighty 'Moor'—of mickle° weight—   much
     'Ice' now comes in,[5] which, being glued together,
     Makes 'morris', and the cause that we came hither.
     The body of our sport, of no small study,[6]
     I first appear, though rude, and raw, and muddy,
125 To speak, before thy noble grace, this tenor[7]
     At whose great feet I offer up my penner.°   pen case
     The next,° the Lord of May and Lady bright;   next to appear
     The Chambermaid and Servingman, by night
     That seek out silent hanging;[8] then mine Host
130 And his fat Spouse, that welcomes, to their cost,
     The gallèd° traveller, and with a beck'ning   tired
     Informs the tapster° to inflame the reck'ning;°   bartender / overcharge
     Then the beest-eating Clown;[9] and next, the Fool;
     The babion with long tail and eke long tool,°   penis
135 *Cum multis aliis*° that make a dance—   With many others
     Say 'ay', and all shall presently° advance.   at once

THESEUS   Ay, ay, by any means, dear dominie.°   teacher

PIRITHOUS   Produce.°   Put on (your show)

SCHOOLMASTER   (knock[s] for the dance)
     Intrate filii,[1] come forth and foot it.
     [He flings up his cap.] Music.
     [The SCHOOLMASTER ushers in
     May Lord,   May Lady.
     Servingman,   Chambermaid.
     A Country Clown,
     or Shepherd,   Country Wench.

---

2. Approve. Compare Quince's speech to Theseus in A *Midsummer Night's Dream* 5.1.126–50.
3. Both "machine" and "frame" mean "structure" or "production."
4. Dis was god of the underworld; Daedalus was creator of the Cretan labyrinth and inventor of wings for human flight. Theseus triumphed over both the underworld and the labyrinth. Daedalus is invoked for the sake of alliteration and, because of his association with flight and hence the heavens, for contrast to Dis.
5. The Schoolmaster displays the word "morris" from two placards, possibly held by the dancers. In Q, the word is split into two syllables, "Morr" and "Is" (here emended to "Moor" and "Ice"). They may have been

spelled out, or perhaps pictograms were used, with the first placard depicting a Moor and the second the allegorical figure Winter.
6. The main part in our entertainment, carefully prepared.
7. Argument; tenner (ten-syllable line).
8. Curtain behind which they can make love.
9. Clown or country shepherd (see stage direction at line 138) who likes "beest," the thick milk produced by a cow for the first few days after calving.
1. Come in, my sons (children). The masculine *filii* is especially appropriate, since the women's parts were played by boy actors.

An Host,	Hostess.
A He-babion,	She-babion.
A He-fool,	The JAILER'S DAUGHTER as
	She-fool.

All these persons apparelled to the life,° the men issuing   *in lifelike costume*
out of one door and the wenches from the other. They
dance a morris]

Ladies, if we have been merry,
140 And have pleased ye with a derry,
And a derry, and a down,°   *(song refrain words)*
Say the schoolmaster's no clown.
Duke, if we have pleased thee too,
And have done as good boys should do,
145 Give us but a tree or twain
For a maypole, and again,
Ere another year run out,
We'll make thee laugh, and all this rout.°   *company*

THESEUS   Take twenty, dominie. [*To* HIPPOLYTA] How does my
sweetheart?

HIPPOLYTA   Never so pleased, sir.

150 EMILIA   'Twas an excellent dance,
And for a preface,° I never heard a better.   *as for the prologue*

THESEUS   Schoolmaster, I thank you. One see 'em all rewarded.

PIRITHOUS   And here's something to paint your pole withal.
[*He gives them money*]

THESEUS   Now to our sports again.

SCHOOLMASTER
155 May the stag thou hunt'st stand long,°   *give a good chase*
And thy dogs be swift and strong;
May they kill him without lets,°   *obstacles*
And the ladies eat his dowsets.°   *testicles (a delicacy)*
[*Exeunt* THESEUS *and train.*] *Wind horns* [*within*]
Come, we are all made. *Dii deaeque omnes,*°   *Gods and goddesses all*
160 Ye have danced rarely, wenches.   *Exeunt*

3.6

Enter PALAMON *from the bush*

PALAMON   About this hour my cousin gave his faith°   *word*
To visit me again, and with him bring
Two swords and two good armours;° if he fail,   *suits of armor*
He's neither man nor soldier. When he left me,
5 I did not think a week could have restored
My lost strength to me, I was grown so low
And crest-fall'n with my wants. I thank thee, Arcite,
Thou art yet a fair foe, and I feel myself,
With this refreshing, able once again
10 To out-dure° danger. To delay it longer   *endure; outlast*
Would make the world think, when it comes to hearing,°   *when word gets out*
That I lay fatting, like a swine, to fight,
And not a soldier.¹ Therefore this blest morning

3.6
1. *fatting . . . soldier*: being fattened like a swine for the slaughter, rather than preparing myself like a warrior for
the fight.

Shall be the last; and that sword he refuses,°   *(in choosing first)*

15   If it but hold,° I kill him with; 'tis justice.   *Unless it breaks*

So, love and fortune for me!

Enter ARCITE *with [two] armours and [two] swords*

O, good morrow.

ARCITE   Good morrow, noble kinsman.

PALAMON   I have put you

To too much pains, sir.

ARCITE   That too much, fair cousin,

Is but a debt to honour, and my duty.

20   PALAMON   Would you were so in all, sir—I could wish ye

As kind a kinsman, as you force me find

A beneficial foe, that my embraces

Might thank ye, not my blows.

ARCITE   I shall think either,

Well done, a noble recompense.

PALAMON   Then I shall quit° you.   *repay*

25   ARCITE   Defy me in these fair terms, and you show°   *show youself to be*

More than a mistress to me—no more anger,

As you love anything that's honourable.

We were not bred to talk, man. When we are armed

And both upon our guards, then let our fury,

30   Like meeting of two tides, fly strongly from us;

And then to whom the birthright° of this beauty   *rightful possession*

Truly pertains°—without upbraidings, scorns,   *belongs*

Despisings of our persons, and such poutings

Fitter for girls and schoolboys—will be seen,

35   And quickly, yours or mine. Will't please you arm, sir?

Or, if you feel yourself not fitting° yet,   *ready*

And furnished with your old strength, I'll stay,° cousin,   *wait*

And every day discourse you into health,

As I am spared.° Your person I am friends with,   *In my spare time*

40   And I could wish I had not said I loved her,

Though I had died;[2] but loving such a lady,

And justifying° my love, I must not fly from't.   *affirming*

PALAMON   Arcite, thou art so brave an enemy

That no man but thy cousin's fit to kill thee.

I am well and lusty°—choose your arms.   *eager to do battle*

45   ARCITE   Choose you, sir.

PALAMON   Wilt thou exceed in all,[3] or dost thou do it

To make me spare thee?

ARCITE   If you think so, cousin,

You are deceived, for as I am a soldier,

I will not spare you.

PALAMON   That's well said.

ARCITE   You'll find it.°   *find it so*

50   PALAMON   Then as I am an honest man, and love

With all the justice of affection,[4]

I'll pay thee soundly.°   *punish you properly*

[He chooses one armour]

This I'll take.

---

2. Although it would have killed me to keep silent.
3. Will you always outdo me in courtesy (as here, by letting me choose my arms first)?

4. Palamon's love of Emilia is just; Palamon will deal justly (honorably) with Arcite because he loves him.

ARCITE [*indicating the remaining armour*]   That's mine, then.
    I'll arm you first.
PALAMON   Do.
                [ARCITE *arms* PALAMON]
                        Pray thee tell me, cousin,
    Where gott'st thou this good armour?
ARCITE   'Tis the Duke's,
    And to say true, I stole it. Do I pinch you?
55 PALAMON   No.
ARCITE   Is't not too heavy?
PALAMON   I have worn a lighter—
    But I shall make it serve.
ARCITE   I'll buckle't close.°   *tightly*
PALAMON   By any means.
ARCITE   You care not for a grand guard?[5]
PALAMON   No, no, we'll use no horses. I perceive
    You would fain be at that fight.°   *rather fight mounted*
60 ARCITE   I am indifferent.
PALAMON   Faith, so am I. Good cousin, thrust the buckle
    Through far enough.
ARCITE   I warrant you.°   *Trust me*
PALAMON   My casque° now.   *helmet*
ARCITE   Will you fight bare-armed?
PALAMON   We shall be the nimbler.
ARCITE   But use your gauntlets, though—those are o'th' least.°   *too small*
    Prithee take mine, good cousin.
65 PALAMON   Thank you, Arcite.
    How do I look? Am I fall'n much away?°   *much thinner*
ARCITE   Faith, very little—love has used you kindly.
PALAMON   I'll warrant thee, I'll strike home.
ARCITE   Do, and spare not—
    I'll give you cause, sweet cousin.
PALAMON   Now to you, sir.
                [PALAMON *arms* ARCITE]
70 Methinks this armour's very like that, Arcite,
    Thou wor'st that day the three kings fell, but lighter.
ARCITE   That was a very good one, and that day,
    I well remember, you outdid me, cousin.
    I never saw such valour. When you charged
75 Upon the left wing of the enemy,
    I spurred hard to come up,° and under me   *keep up with you*
    I had a right good horse.
PALAMON   You had indeed—
    A bright bay, I remember.
ARCITE   Yes. But all
    Was vainly laboured in me—you outwent me,
80 Nor could my wishes reach you.[6] Yet a little
    I did by imitation.
PALAMON   More by virtue°—   *valor*
    You are modest, cousin.
ARCITE   When I saw you charge first,
    Methought I heard a dreadful clap of thunder
    Break from the troop.

---

5. Chest plate for fighting on horseback.   6. My wishes to keep up with you were not answered.

PALAMON   But still before that flew
85   The lightning of your valour. Stay a little,
   Is not this piece too strait?°   *tight*
ARCITE   No, no, 'tis well.
PALAMON   I would have nothing hurt thee but my sword—
   A bruise would be dishonour.
ARCITE   Now I am perfect°.   *ready*
PALAMON   Stand off,° then.   *Step back*
ARCITE   Take my sword; I hold° it better.   *consider*
90 PALAMON   I thank ye. No, keep it—your life lies° on it.   *depends*
   Here's one—if it but hold,° I ask no more   *holds together*
   For all my hopes. My cause and honour guard me.
ARCITE   And me, my love.
    They bow several ways,[7] *then advance and stand*
                  Is there aught else to say?
PALAMON   This only, and no more. Thou art mine aunt's son,
95   And that blood we desire to shed is mutual:
   In me, thine, and in thee, mine. My sword
   Is in my hand, and if thou kill'st me,
   The gods and I forgive thee. If there be
   A place prepared for those that sleep in honour,
100   I wish his weary soul that falls may win it.
   Fight bravely, cousin. Give me thy noble hand.
ARCITE   Here, Palamon. This hand shall never more
   Come near thee with such friendship.
PALAMON   I commend thee.°   *(to God)*
ARCITE   If I fall, curse me, and say I was a coward—
105   For none but such dare die in these just trials.
   Once more farewell, my cousin.
PALAMON   Farewell, Arcite.
    Fight. Horns within; they stand
ARCITE   Lo, cousin, lo, our folly has undone us.
PALAMON   Why?
ARCITE   This is the Duke a-hunting, as I told you.
   If we be found, we are wretched. O, retire,
110   For honour's sake, and safely, presently,
   Into your bush again. Sir, we shall find
   Too many° hours to die. In, gentle cousin—   *More than enough*
   If you be seen, you perish instantly
   For breaking prison, and I, if you reveal me,
115   For my contempt.[8] Then all the world will scorn us,
   And say we had a noble difference,
   But base disposers of it.°   *settled it ignobly*
PALAMON   No, no, cousin,
   I will no more be hidden, nor put off
   This great adventure° to a second trial.   *undertaking*
120   I know your cunning and I know your cause°—   *motive (for delay)*
   He that faints° now, shame take him! Put thyself   *is fainthearted*
   Upon thy present guard°—   *At once on guard*
ARCITE   You are not mad?
PALAMON   Or° I will make th'advantage of this hour   *Either I'm mad or*

---

7. They make ceremonial bows in various directions, as if they were jousting in a tournament.

8. For my disobedience to Theseus's order that I be banished.

Mine own, and what to come shall threaten me
125   I fear less than my fortune.° Know, weak cousin,   (in this fight)
I love Emilia, and in that I'll bury
Thee and all crosses else.°   all other obstacles

ARCITE   Then come what can come,
Thou shalt know, Palamon, I dare as well
Die as discourse or sleep. Only this fears° me,   frightens
130   The law will have the honour of our ends.⁹
Have at thy life!

PALAMON   Look to thine own well, Arcite!

[They] fight again.
Horns. Enter THESEUS, HIPPOLYTA, EMILIA, PIRITHOUS,
and train. [THESEUS separates PALAMON and ARCITE]

THESEUS   What ignorant and mad malicious° traitors   evil-minded
Are you, that 'gainst the tenor° of my laws   purport
Are making battle, thus like knights appointed,°   armed
135   Without my leave and officers of arms?¹
By Castor,² both shall die.

PALAMON   Hold° thy word, Theseus.   Keep
We are certainly both traitors, both despisers°   disobedient
Of thee and of thy goodness. I am Palamon,
That cannot love thee, he that broke thy prison—
140   Think well what that deserves. And this is Arcite;
A bolder traitor never trod thy ground,
A falser ne'er seemed friend. This is the man
Was begged° and banished; this is he contemns thee,   petitioned for
And what thou dar'st do; and in this disguise,
145   Against thine own edict, follows thy sister,°   sister-in-law
That fortunate bright° star, the fair Emilia,   luck-bringing
Whose servant°—if there be a right in seeing   courtly lover
And first bequeathing of the soul to—justly
I am; and, which is more, dares think her his.
150   This treachery, like a most trusty lover,
I called him now to answer. If thou be'st
As thou art spoken,° great and virtuous,   reported to be
The true decider of all injuries,
Say, 'Fight again', and thou shalt see me, Theseus,
155   Do such a justice thou thyself wilt envy.
Then take my life—I'll woo thee to't.

PIRITHOUS   O heaven,
What more than man is this!

THESEUS   I have sworn.

ARCITE   We seek not
Thy breath of mercy, Theseus. 'Tis to me
A thing as soon to die as thee to say it,
160   And no more moved. Where this man calls me traitor
Let me say thus much—if in love be treason,
In service of so excellent a beauty,
As I love most, and in that faith will perish,
As I have brought my life here to confirm it,
165   As I have served her truest, worthiest,
As I dare kill this cousin that denies it,

---

9. We will die by execution rather than combat.   2. Common Roman oath. Castor and Pollux, twins,
1. Overseers of chivalric combat.   were sons of Jupiter.

So let me be most traitor and ye please me.
For° scorning thy edict, Duke, ask that lady   *As for*
Why she is fair, and why her eyes command me
170   Stay here to love her, and if she say, 'Traitor',
I am a villain fit to lie unburied.
      PALAMON   Thou shalt have pity of° us both, O Theseus,   *on*
If unto neither thou show mercy. Stop,
As thou art just, thy noble ear against us;
175   As thou art valiant, for thy cousin's° soul,   *(Hercules')*
Whose twelve strong labours crown his memory,
Let's die together, at one instant, Duke.
Only a little let him fall before me,
That I may tell my soul he shall not have her.
180   THESEUS   I grant your wish; for to say true, your cousin
Has ten times more offended, for I gave him
More mercy than you found, sir, your offences
Being no more than his. None here speak for 'em,
For ere the sun set both shall sleep for ever.
185   HIPPOLYTA [*to* EMILIA]   Alas, the pity! Now or never, sister,
Speak, not to be denied. That face of yours
Will bear the curses else of after ages
For these lost cousins.
      EMILIA   In my face, dear sister,
I find no anger to 'em, nor no ruin.
190   The misadventure of their own eyes kill° 'em.   *kills*
Yet that° I will be woman and have pity,   *to show that*
      [*She kneels*]
My knees shall grow to th' ground, but° I'll get mercy.   *unless*
Help me, dear sister—in a deed so virtuous
The powers of all women will be with us.
      [HIPPOLYTA *kneels*]
Most royal brother—
      HIPPOLYTA   Sir, by our tie of marriage—
      EMILIA   By your own spotless honour—
195   HIPPOLYTA   By that faith,
That fair hand, and that honest heart you gave me—
      EMILIA   By that you would have pity in another,[3]
By your own virtues infinite—
      HIPPOLYTA   By valour,
By all the chaste° nights I have ever pleased you—   *faithful only to you*
      THESEUS   These are strange conjurings.°   *incantations*
200   PIRITHOUS   Nay, then, I'll in too.
      [*He kneels*]
By all our friendship, sir, by all our dangers,
By all you love most: wars, and this sweet lady—
      EMILIA   By that° you would have trembled to deny   *(chivalric aid)*
A blushing maid—
      HIPPOLYTA   By your own eyes, by strength—
In which you swore I went beyond° all women,   *I excelled*
205   Almost all men—and yet I yielded, Theseus—
      PIRITHOUS   To crown all this, by your most noble soul,
Which cannot want° due mercy, I beg first—   *lack*

3. By whatever you would expect someone else to pity.

HIPPOLYTA   Next hear my prayers—

210 EMILIA   Last let me entreat, sir—

PIRITHOUS   For mercy.

HIPPOLYTA   Mercy.

EMILIA   Mercy on these princes.

THESEUS   Ye make my faith reel.[4] Say I felt
　　　　Compassion to 'em both, how would you place° it?　　　　　　　*have me bestow*
　　　　[*They rise*]

EMILIA   Upon their lives—but with their banishments.

215 THESEUS   You are a right° woman, sister: you have pity,　　　　　　*typical*
　　　　But want the understanding where to use it.
　　　　If you desire their lives, invent a way
　　　　Safer than banishment. Can these two live,
　　　　And have the agony of love about 'em,
220　　And not kill one another? Every day
　　　　They'd fight about you, hourly bring your honour
　　　　In public question with their swords.[5] Be wise, then,
　　　　And here forget 'em. It concerns your credit°　　　　　　　　　*reputation*
　　　　And my oath equally. I have said—they die.
225　　Better they fall by th' law than one another.
　　　　Bow not my honour.[6]

EMILIA   O my noble brother,
　　　　That oath was rashly° made, and in your anger.　　　　　　　*impulsively*
　　　　Your reason will not hold° it. If such vows　　　　　　　　　*sustain*
　　　　Stand for express will,° all the world must perish.　　　　　*steadfast resolve*
230　　Beside, I have another oath 'gainst yours,
　　　　Of more authority, I am sure more love—
　　　　Not made in passion, neither, but good heed.°　　　　　　　　*thoughtfulness*

THESEUS   What is it, sister?

PIRITHOUS [*to* EMILIA]   Urge it home, brave lady.

EMILIA   That you would ne'er deny me anything
235　　Fit for my modest suit and your free granting.
　　　　I tie you to your word now; if ye fail in't,
　　　　Think how you maim your honour—
　　　　For now I am set a-begging, sir. I am deaf
　　　　To all but your compassion—how their lives
240　　Might breed the ruin of my name, opinion.°　　　　　　　　　　*my reputation*
　　　　Shall anything that loves me perish for° me?　　　　　　　　　*because of*
　　　　That were a cruel wisdom: do men prune
　　　　The straight young boughs that blush with thousand blossoms
　　　　Because they may be° rotten? O, Duke Theseus,　　　　　　　　*become*
245　　The goodly mothers that have groaned for these,°　　　　　　　*(in childbirth)*
　　　　And all the longing maids that ever loved,
　　　　If your vow stand,° shall curse me and my beauty,　　　　　　*holds*
　　　　And in their funeral songs for these two cousins
　　　　Despise my cruelty and cry woe worth° me,　　　　　　　　　　*befall*
250　　Till I am nothing but the scorn of women.
　　　　For heaven's sake, save their lives and banish 'em.

THESEUS   On what conditions?

EMILIA   Swear 'em° never more　　　　　　　*Have them swear*
　　　　To make me their contention, or to know me,°　　　　　　　　*think of me*

---

4. You make my constancy to my own oath (to kill the
kinsmen) waver.
5. *They'd . . . swords:* They'd fight publicly over you,
thus compromising your honor.
6. Don't force me to lower (bend) my standards of
honor.

To tread upon thy dukedom; and to be,
255 Wherever they shall travel, ever strangers
To one another.

PALAMON   I'll be cut a-pieces
Before I take this oath—forget I love her?
O all ye gods, despise me, then. Thy banishment
I not mislike, so we may fairly carry
260 Our swords and cause along—else, never trifle,
But take our lives, Duke. I must love, and will;
And for that love must and dare kill this cousin
On any piece° the earth has.   *spot of ground*

THESEUS   Will you, Arcite,
Take these conditions?

PALAMON   He's a villain then.

PIRITHOUS   These are men!
265 ARCITE No, never, Duke. 'Tis worse to me than begging,
To take° my life so basely. Though I think   *value*
I never shall enjoy her, yet I'll preserve
The honour of affection and die for her,
Make death a devil.°   *Even horribly*

270 THESEUS What may be done? For now I feel compassion.

PIRITHOUS Let it not fall° again, sir.   *diminish*

THESEUS   Say, Emilia,
If one of them were dead—as one must—are you
Content to take the other to your husband?
They cannot both enjoy you. They are princes
275 As goodly as your own eyes, and as noble
As ever fame yet spoke of. Look upon 'em,
And if you can love, end this difference.
I give consent. [*To* PALAMON *and* ARCITE] Are you content too,
princes?

PALAMON *and* ARCITE With all our souls.

THESEUS   He that she refuses
Must die, then.

280 PALAMON *and* ARCITE Any death thou canst invent, Duke.

PALAMON If I fall from that mouth,° I fall with favour,   *(because of her decision)*
And lovers yet unborn shall bless my ashes.

ARCITE If she refuse me, yet my grave will wed me,
And soldiers sing my epitaph.

THESEUS [*to* EMILIA]   Make choice, then.

285 EMILIA I cannot, sir. They are both too excellent.
For° me, a hair shall never fall of these men.   *On account of*

HIPPOLYTA [*to* THESEUS] What will become of 'em?

THESEUS   Thus I ordain it,
And by mine honour once again it stands,
Or both shall die. [*To* PALAMON *and* ARCITE] You shall both to your country,
290 And each within this month, accompanied
With three fair knights, appear again in this place,
In which I'll plant° a pyramid; and whether,°   *fix / whichever*
Before us that are here, can force his cousin,
By fair and knightly strength, to touch the pillar,
295 He shall enjoy her; the other lose his head,
And all his friends; nor shall he grudge to fall,[7]

---

7. And all his friends will die with him; nor should he consider his execution unjust.

Nor think he dies with interest in° this lady.   *a rightful claim to*
Will this content ye?

PALAMON   Yes. Here, cousin Arcite,
I am friends again till that hour.

ARCITE   I embrace ye.

THESEUS [*to* EMILIA]   Are you content, sister?

300 EMILIA   Yes, I must, sir,
Else both miscarry.°   *perish*

THESEUS [*to* PALAMON *and* ARCITE]
           Come, shake hands again, then,
And take heed, as you are gentlemen, this quarrel
Sleep till the hour prefixed, and hold your course.°   *keep your resolve*

PALAMON   We dare not fail thee, Theseus.

THESEUS   Come, I'll give ye
305 Now usage like to princes and to friends.
When ye return, who wins I'll settle here,°   *set up in Athens*
Who loses, yet I'll weep upon his bier.

         Exeunt. [*In the act-time the bush is removed*]

4.1

Enter [*the*] JAILER *and his* FRIEND

JAILER   Hear you no more? Was nothing said of me
Concerning the escape of Palamon?
Good sir, remember.

FRIEND   Nothing that I heard,
For I came home before the business
5 Was fully ended. Yet I might perceive,
Ere I departed, a great likelihood
Of both their pardons: for Hippolyta
And fair-eyed Emily upon their knees
Begged with such handsome pity that the Duke,
10 Methought, stood staggering° whether he should follow   *wavering as to*
His rash oath or the sweet compassion
Of those two ladies; and to second them
That truly noble prince, Pirithous—
Half his own heart[1]—set in too, that° I hope   *so that*
15 All shall be well. Neither heard I one question
Of your name or his scape.

         Enter [*the*] SECOND FRIEND

JAILER   Pray heaven it hold° so.   *continue*

SECOND FRIEND   Be of good comfort, man. I bring you news,
Good news.

JAILER   They are welcome.

SECOND FRIEND   Palamon has cleared you,
And got your pardon, and discovered° how   *exposed*
20 And by whose means he scaped—which was your daughter's,
Whose pardon is procured too; and the prisoner,
Not to be held ungrateful to her goodness,
Has given a sum of money to her marriage—
A large one, I'll assure you.

JAILER   Ye are a good man,
And ever bring good news.

25 FIRST FRIEND   How was it ended?

4.1 Location: The prison   1. Hippolyta is (has) the other half.

SECOND FRIEND   Why, as it should be: they that ne'er begged,
But° they prevailed, had their suits fairly granted—   *Still*
The prisoners have their lives.

FIRST FRIEND   I knew 'twould be so.

SECOND FRIEND   But there be new conditions which you'll hear of
At better time.

JAILER   I hope they are good.

30   SECOND FRIEND   They are honourable—
How good they'll prove I know not.

         Enter [the] WOOER

FIRST FRIEND   'Twill be known.

WOOER   Alas, sir, where's your daughter?

JAILER   Why do you ask?

WOOER   O, sir, when did you see her?

SECOND FRIEND   How he looks!

JAILER   This morning.

WOOER   Was she well? Was she in health?
Sir, when did she sleep?

35   FIRST FRIEND   These are strange questions.

JAILER   I do not think she was very well: for now
You make me mind° her, but this very day   *remind me of*
I asked her questions and she answered me
So far from what she was,° so childishly,   *her usual manner*
40   So sillily, as if she were a fool,
An innocent—and I was very angry.
But what of her, sir?

WOOER   Nothing, but my pity²—
But you must know it, and as good by me
As by another that less loves her—

JAILER   Well, sir?

FIRST FRIEND   Not right?°   *in her right mind*

WOOER   No, sir, not well.

45   SECOND FRIEND   Not well?

WOOER   'Tis too true—she is mad.

FIRST FRIEND   It cannot be.

WOOER   Believe, you'll find it so.

JAILER   I half suspected
What you told me—the gods comfort her!
Either this was her love to Palamon,
50   Or fear of my miscarrying on³ his scape,
Or both.

WOOER   'Tis likely.

JAILER   But why all this haste, sir?

WOOER   I'll tell you quickly. As I late was angling°   *fishing*
In the great lake that lies behind the palace,
From the far shore, thick set with reeds and sedges,
55   As patiently I was attending sport,°   *awaiting a fish*
I heard a voice—a shrill one—and attentive
I gave my ear, when I might well perceive
'Twas one that sung, and by the smallness° of it   *high pitch*
A boy or woman. I then left my angle°   *fishing rod*
60   To his own skill,° came near, but yet perceived not   *To fish by itself*
Who made the sound, the rushes and the reeds

---

2. My pity for you and her makes me speak.   3. My being punished because of.

Had so encompassed it.° I laid me down   *overgrown the place*
And listened to the words she sung, for then,
Through a small glade cut by the fishermen,
I saw it was your daughter.

65   JAILER   Pray go on, sir.

     WOOER   She sung much, but no sense; only I heard her
Repeat this often—'Palamon is gone,
Is gone to th' wood to gather mulberries;
I'll find him out tomorrow.'

     FIRST FRIEND   Pretty soul!

70   WOOER   'His shackles will betray him—he'll be taken,
And what shall I do then? I'll bring a bevy,°   *company*
A hundred black-eyed maids that love as I do,
With chaplets° on their heads of daffodillies,   *wreaths*
With cherry lips and cheeks of damask roses,
75   And all we'll dance an antic° fore the Duke   *a grotesque dance*
And beg his pardon.'⁴ Then she talked of you, sir—
That you must lose your head tomorrow morning,
And she must gather flowers to bury you,
And see the house made handsome.° Then she sung   *neat*
80   Nothing but 'willow, willow, willow',⁵ and between
Ever was 'Palamon, fair Palamon',
And 'Palamon was a tall° young man'. The place   *valiant*
Was knee-deep° where she sat; her careless tresses   *(in rushes)*
A wreath of bull-rush rounded;° about her stuck   *encircled*
85   Thousand freshwater flowers of several° colours—   *various*
That° she appeared, methought, like the fair nymph   *Such that*
That feeds the lake with waters, or as Iris⁶
Newly dropped down from heaven. Rings she made
Of rushes that grew by,⁷ and to 'em spoke
90   The prettiest posies⁸—'Thus our true love's tied',
'This you may lose, not me', and many a one.
And then she wept, and sung again, and sighed—
And with the same breath smiled and kissed her hand.

     SECOND FRIEND   Alas, what pity it is!

     WOOER   I made in to° her: *approached*
95   She saw me and straight sought the flood°—I saved her,   *at once jumped in*
And set her safe to land, when presently
She slipped away and to the city made,
With such a cry and swiftness that, believe me,
She left me far behind her. Three or four
100   I saw from far off cross° her—one of 'em   *intercept*
I knew to be your brother, where she stayed°   *stopped*
And fell, scarce to be got away. I left them with her,

Enter [the JAILER'S] BROTHER, [*the* JAILER'S] DAUGHTER,
and others

And hither came to tell you—here they are.

     JAILER'S DAUGHTER [*sings*]   'May you never more enjoy the
             light . . .'°   *(unknown song)*
Is not this a fine song?

105   JAILER'S BROTHER   O, a very fine one.

---

4. Beg Duke Theseus to pardon Palamon.
5. Refrain of a popular song, also sung by Desdemona in *Othello* 4.3.
6. Goddess of the rainbow and Juno's messenger.
7. *Rings . . . by*: sometimes used as wedding rings in rural (or mock) wedding ceremonies.
8. Mottoes and aphorisms, sometimes engraved on the inside of rings.

JAILER'S DAUGHTER I can sing twenty more.

JAILER'S BROTHER   I think you can.

JAILER'S DAUGHTER Yes, truly can I—I can sing 'The Broom'
And 'Bonny Robin'⁹—are not you a tailor?

JAILER'S BROTHER Yes.

JAILER'S DAUGHTER Where's my wedding gown?

JAILER'S BROTHER   I'll bring it tomorrow.

110 JAILER'S DAUGHTER Do, very rarely°—I must be abroad else,°   *early / or I'll be out*
　　To call the maids and pay the minstrels,
　　For I must lose my maidenhead by cocklight,°   *before dawn*
　　'Twill never thrive else.¹ (*Sings*) 'O fair, O sweet . . .'²

JAILER'S BROTHER [*to the* JAILER] You must e'en take it
　　patiently.

JAILER   'Tis true.

JAILER'S DAUGHTER Good ev'n, good men. Pray, did you ever
115 hear
　　Of one young Palamon?

JAILER   Yes, wench, we know him.

JAILER'S DAUGHTER Is't not a fine young gentleman?

JAILER   'Tis, love.

JAILER'S BROTHER By no mean cross her, she is then distempered
　　Far worse than now she shows.³

FIRST FRIEND [*to the* JAILER'S DAUGHTER] Yes, he's a fine man.

JAILER'S DAUGHTER O, is he so? You have a sister.

120 FIRST FRIEND   Yes.

JAILER'S DAUGHTER But she shall never have him, tell her so,
　　For° a trick that I know. You'd best look to her,   *Because of*
　　For if she see him once, she's gone—she's done
　　And undone in an hour. All the young maids
125 Of our town are in love with him, but I laugh at 'em
　　And let 'em all alone. Is't not a wise course?

FIRST FRIEND   Yes.

JAILER'S DAUGHTER There is at least two hundred now with
　　child by him,
　　There must be four;° yet I keep close⁴ for all this,   *four hundred*
　　Close as a cockle;° and all these° must be boys—   *clam / (the offspring)*
130 He has the trick on't°—and at ten years old   *of producing boys*
　　They must be all gelt for musicians⁵
　　And sing the wars of Theseus.

SECOND FRIEND   This is strange.

JAILER'S BROTHER As ever you heard, but say nothing.

FIRST FRIEND   No.

JAILER'S DAUGHTER They come from all parts of the dukedom
135 　　to him.
　　I'll warrant ye, he had not so few last night
　　As twenty to dispatch. He'll tickle't up°   *do the (sexual) job*
　　In two hours, if his hand be in.°   *if he's in good shape*

JAILER   She's lost
　　Past all cure.

---

9. "The Broom" and "Bonny Robin" were popular
songs (Ophelia sings a line of the latter in *Hamlet* 4.5).
"Robin" could mean "penis."
1. Otherwise things (or possibly the marriage) won't
prosper for me.
2. A song adapted from the seventh of Sir Philip Sid-

ney's *Certain Sonnets* (1598).
3. *By . . . shows*: Don't contradict her in any way, or
she'll become far more deranged than she is now.
4. Keep my mouth (and thighs) closed.
5. They must all be castrated so that their voices do not
break and they can become singers.

JAILER'S BROTHER Heaven forbid, man!

JAILER'S DAUGHTER [*to the* JAILER] Come hither—you are a
    wise man.

FIRST FRIEND Does she know him?°   *recognize her father*

SECOND FRIEND No—would she did.

140 JAILER'S DAUGHTER   You are master of a ship?

JAILER Yes.

JAILER'S DAUGHTER Where's your compass?

JAILER   Here.

JAILER'S DAUGHTER   Set it to th' north.
    And now direct your course to th' wood where Palamon
    Lies longing for me. For the tackling,°   *rigging*
    Let me alone.° Come, weigh,° my hearts, cheerly all. *I'll do it / (anchor)*

145   Uff, uff, uff !⁶ 'Tis up.° The wind's fair. Top° the bowline. *(the anchor) / Tighten*
    Out with the mainsail. Where's your whistle, master?

JAILER'S BROTHER Let's get her in.°   *inside (an aside)*

JAILER Up to the top,° boy!   *top of the mast*

JAILER'S BROTHER   Where's the pilot?

FIRST FRIEND   Here.

JAILER'S DAUGHTER What kenn'st thou?°   *What do you see*

SECOND FRIEND   A fair wood.

JAILER'S DAUGHTER   Bear for° it, master. *Steer toward*

150 Tack about!
    (*Sings*) 'When Cynthia° with her borrowed light . . .'⁷ *the moon*
                                     Exeunt

4.2

Enter EMILIA, *with two pictures*°   *(Palamon and Arcite)*

EMILIA Yet I may bind those wounds up that must open
    And bleed to death for my sake else—I'll choose,
    And end their strife. Two such young handsome men
    Shall never fall for° me; their weeping mothers   *die because of*

5   Following the dead cold ashes of their sons,
    Shall never curse my cruelty. Good heaven,
    What a sweet face has Arcite! If wise nature,
    With all her best endowments, all those beauties
    She sows into the births of noble bodies,

10   Were here a mortal woman and had in her
    The coy° denials of young maids, yet doubtless   *modest*
    She would run mad for this man. What an eye,
    Of what a fiery sparkle and quick° sweetness   *lively*
    Has this young prince! Here° love himself sits smiling! *In his eye*

15   Just such another wanton Ganymede
    Set Jove afire once, and enforced the god
    Snatch up the goodly boy and set him by him,
    A shining constellation.¹ What a brow,
    Of what a spacious majesty, he carries!

20   Arched like the great-eyed Juno's, but far sweeter,
    Smoother than Pelops' shoulder!° Fame and honour, *(made of ivory)*

---

6. Grunts of exertion; possibly the sound of the wind in
the sails.
7. Line from an unknown song.

4.2 Location: Theseus's palace in Athens.
1. Ganymede was a beautiful youth whom Jupiter
became enamored of and carried off to be his cupbearer
on Mt. Olympus. In the end, Ganymede was transformed into the constellation Aquarius.

Methinks, from hence,° as from a promontory   *his brow*
Pointed° in heaven, should clap their wings and sing   *Reaching its peak*
To all the under world° the loves and fights   *the earth*
25   Of gods, and such men near 'em.° Palamon   *men most like gods*
Is but his foil;[2] to him a mere dull shadow;
He's swart and meagre,° of an eye as heavy°   *dark and thin / sad*
As if he had lost his mother; a still temper,°   *lethargic disposition*
No stirring in him, no alacrity,
30   Of all this° sprightly sharpness, not a smile.°   *(Arcite's) / trace*
Yet these° that we count errors may become him: *these qualities*
Narcissus was a sad° boy, but a heavenly.°   *serious / beautiful*
O, who can find the bent of woman's fancy?[3]
I am a fool, my reason is lost in me,
35   I have no choice,[4] and I have lied so lewdly°   *wickedly*
That women ought to beat me. On my knees
I ask thy pardon, Palamon, thou art alone°   *uniquely*
And only beautiful, and these the eyes,
These the bright lamps of beauty, that command
40   And threaten love—and what young maid dare cross° 'em?   *oppose*
What a bold gravity, and yet inviting,
Has this brown manly face? O, love, this only
From this hour is complexion.[5] Lie there, Arcite,
Thou art a changeling to him, a mere gypsy,[6]
45   And this the noble body. I am sotted,°   *made stupid*
Utterly lost—my virgin's faith[7] has fled me.
For if my brother, but even now, had asked me
Whether I loved, I had run mad for Arcite;
Now if my sister, more for Palamon.
50   Stand both together.° Now come ask me, brother—   *(comparing portraits)*
Alas, I know not; ask me now, sweet sister—
I may go look.° What a mere child is fancy,   *seek further*
That having two fair gauds° of equal sweetness,   *toys*
Cannot distinguish,° but must cry for both!   *choose*

    Enter [a] GENTLEMAN

How now, sir?
55 GENTLEMAN   From the noble Duke your brother,
Madam, I bring you news. The knights are come.
EMILIA   To end the quarrel?
GENTLEMAN   Yes.
EMILIA   Would I might end first!
What sins have I committed, chaste Diana,[8]
That my unspotted youth must now be soiled°   *defiled*
60   With blood of princes, and my chastity
Be made the altar where the lives of lovers—
Two greater and two better never yet
Made mothers joy—must be the sacrifice
To my unhappy beauty?

---

2. Piece of thin, reflective metal in which a jewel was set, enhancing the jewel's brilliance (setting it off by contrast).
3. Who can discern which way a woman's affections will tend?
4. I am incapable of choosing.
5. *this only . . . complexion:* the only "complexion" I'll appreciate from now on is a dark one.
6. A changeling was an ugly or deformed child left by fairies in exchange for one they stole. Gypsies were also thought to steal children; otherwise the meaning is unclear, since the word generally referred to a swarthy person and Palamon has the dark complexion. Perhaps if a dark complexion is "fair," Arcite's fair skin will be considered the "gypsy" one.
7. My prior oath (1.3.86ff.) to remain a virgin.
8. Virgin goddess of the moon and of the Amazons. See 1.3.52 and note.

Enter THESEUS, HIPPOLYTA, PIRITHOUS, *and attendants*

THESEUS   Bring 'em in

65   Quickly, by any means, I long to see 'em.   [*Exit one or more*]

     [*To* EMILIA] Your two contending lovers are returned,

     And with them their fair knights. Now, my fair sister,

     You must love one of them.

EMILIA   I had rather both,

     So° neither for my sake should fall untimely.°   *So that / prematurely*

         Enter [*a*] MESSENGER

THESEUS   Who saw 'em?

PIRITHOUS   I a while.

70   GENTLEMAN   And I.

THESEUS [*to the* MESSENGER]

     From whence come you, sir?

MESSENGER   From the knights.

THESEUS   Pray speak,

     You that have seen them, what they are.

MESSENGER   I will, sir,

     And truly what I think. Six braver spirits

     Than these they have brought, if we judge by the outside,

75   I never saw nor read of.⁹ He that stands

     In the first place with Arcite, by his seeming,°   *appearance*

     Should be a stout° man; by his face, a prince.   *brave*

     His very looks so say° him: his complexion,   *declare*

     Nearer a brown than black, stern and yet noble,

80   Which shows him hardy, fearless, proud° of dangers.   *scornful*

     The circles of his eyes show fire within him,

     And, as a heated° lion, so he looks.   *an angry*

     His hair hangs long behind him, black and shining,

     Like ravens' wings. His shoulders, broad and strong;

85   Armed long and round;¹ and on his thigh a sword

     Hung by a curious baldric, when he frowns

     To seal his will with.² Better,° o' my conscience,   *A better sword*

     Was never soldier's friend.

THESEUS   Thou hast well described him.

90   PIRITHOUS   Yet a great deal short,

     Methinks, of him that's first with Palamon.

THESEUS   Pray speak° him, friend.   *describe*

PIRITHOUS   I guess he is a prince too,

     And, if it may be, greater—for his show°   *appearance*

     Has all the ornament of honour in't.

95   He's somewhat bigger than the knight he° spoke of,   *(the messenger)*

     But of a face far sweeter. His complexion

     Is as a ripe grape, ruddy. He has felt,

     Without doubt, what he fights for,° and so apter   *(love)*

     To make this cause his own. In's face appears

100   All the fair hopes of ° what he undertakes,   *confidence about*

     And when he's angry, then a settled° valour,   *steady*

     Not tainted with extremes, runs through his body

     And guides his arm to brave things. Fear he cannot—

---

9. *nor read of:* possibly a joke on the playwright's part; the following descriptions closely follow Chaucer's *Knight's Tale* 2129–78.
1. With long, well-muscled arms.

2. *Hung . . . with:* Hung from an artfully crafted ("curious") sword belt ("baldric"), which he uses to carry out his will when he is angry.

105	He shows no such soft temper. His head's yellow,	
	Hard-haired³ and curled, thick twined: like ivy tods,°	bushes
	Not to undo with° thunder. In his face	Not destroyed by
	The livery of the warlike maid⁴ appears,	
	Pure red and white—for yet no beard has blessed him—	
	And in his rolling° eyes sits victory,	passionate
110	As if she ever° meant to court his valour.	(victory) always
	His nose stands high, a character° of honour;	distinguishing mark
	His red lips, after fights, are fit for ladies.	

EMILIA   Must these men die too?

PIRITHOUS   When he speaks, his tongue

	Sounds like a trumpet. All his lineaments°	body parts
115	Are as a man would wish 'em—strong and clean.°	perfectly shaped
	He wears a well-steeled° axe, the staff ° of gold.	well-honed / handle
	His age, some five-and-twenty.	

MESSENGER   There's another—

	A little man, but of a tough soul, seeming	
	As great° as any. Fairer promises	noble
120	In such a body yet I never looked on.	

PIRITHOUS   O, he that's freckle-faced?

MESSENGER   The same, my lord.

	Are they° not sweet ones?	(the freckles)

PIRITHOUS   Yes, they are well.

MESSENGER   Methinks,

	Being so few and well disposed,° they show	arranged
	Great and fine art in nature. He's white-haired°—	blond
125	Not wanton white,° but such a manly colour	effeminately fair
	Next to an auburn, tough and nimble set,°	and lithe
	Which shows an active soul. His arms are brawny,	
	Lined with strong sinews—to the shoulder piece	
	Gently they swell, like women new-conceived,°	starting pregnancy
130	Which speaks him prone to labour, never fainting	
	Under the weight of arms; stout-hearted, still,°	when motionless
	But when he stirs, a tiger. He's grey-eyed,⁵	
	Which yields compassion where he conquers; sharp	
	To spy advantages, and where he finds 'em,	
135	He's swift to make 'em his. He does no wrongs,	
	Nor takes none.° He's round-faced, and when he smiles	tolerates any
	He shows° a lover; when he frowns, a soldier.	looks like
	About his head he wears the winner's oak,⁶	
	And in it stuck the favour of his lady.	
140	His age, some six-and-thirty. In his hand	
	He bears a charging staff ° embossed with silver.	lance

THESEUS   Are they all thus?

PIRITHOUS   They are all the sons of honour.

THESEUS   Now as I have a soul, I long to see 'em.

[To HIPPOLYTA] Lady, you shall see men fight now.

HIPPOLYTA   I wish it,

145	But not the cause, my lord. They would show

---

3. Perhaps influenced by Thomas Speght's 1602 edition of Chaucer's *Knight's Tale*, where King Emetrius's hair "was of yron" (was made of iron) instead of "yronne" (curled).
4. *The . . . maid*: His allegiance to Bellona, goddess of war (or possibly to Athena, also associated with warlike

powers).
5. With eyes of blue or blue-gray. Eyes of this color supposedly implied compassion.
6. Valiant soldiers received a wreath of oak leaves, particularly if they saved their friends in battle.

Bravely about the titles of two kingdoms[7]—
'Tis pity love should be so tyrannous.
[*To* EMILIA] O my soft-hearted sister, what think you?
Weep not till they weep blood. Wench, it must be.

THESEUS [*to* EMILIA]
You have steeled 'em° with your beauty.   *made them determined*
150   [*To* PIRITHOUS]   Honoured friend,
To you I give the field:° pray order it   *charge of the combat*
Fitting the persons that must use it.

PIRITHOUS   Yes, sir.

THESEUS   Come, I'll go visit 'em—I cannot stay,°   *wait*
Their fame° has fired me so. Till they appear,   *This account of them*
Good friend, be royal.°   *treat them royally*
155 PIRITHOUS   There shall want no bravery.°   *splendor*

EMILIA [*aside*]   Poor wench, go weep—for whosoever wins
Loses a noble cousin for thy sins.   *Exeunt*

4.3

Enter [*the*] JAILER, [*the*] WOOER, [*and the*] DOCTOR

DOCTOR   Her distraction is more at some time of the moon than
at other some,° is it not?   *at others*

JAILER   She is continually in a harmless distemper:° sleeps little;   *state of confusion*
altogether without appetite, save often drinking; dreaming of
5   another world, and a better; and what broken piece of matter
soe'er she's about, the name 'Palamon' lards it,[1] that she
farces° every business   *stuffs*

Enter [*the* JAILER'S] DAUGHTER

withal,° fits it to every question. Look where she comes—you   *with it*
shall perceive her behaviour.

[*They stand apart*]

10 JAILER'S DAUGHTER   I have forgot it quite—the burden on't° was   *refrain of the song*
'Down-a, down-a', and penned by no worse man than Giraldo,
Emilia's schoolmaster. He's as fantastical,° too, as ever he may   *fanciful*
go upon's legs°— for in the next world will Dido see Palamon,   *as any man*
and then will she be out of love with Aeneas.[2]

15 DOCTOR   What stuff 's here? Poor soul.

JAILER   E'en thus all day long.

JAILER'S DAUGHTER   Now for this charm that I told you of—you
must bring a piece of silver on the tip of your tongue, or no
ferry:[3] then, if it be your chance to come where the blessed
20   spirits are—there's a sight now! We maids that have our livers
perished,[4] cracked to pieces with love, we shall come there and
do nothing all day long but pick flowers with Proserpine.[5] Then
will I make Palamon a nosegay, then let him mark me,° then—   *notice me*

DOCTOR   How prettily she's amiss! Note her a little further.

25 JAILER'S DAUGHTER   Faith, I'll tell you: sometime we go to barley-

---

7. *They . . . kingdoms:* It would be more appropriate if
they were fighting for each other's kingdoms.
4.3 Location: The prison.
1. Whatever disjointed piece of business she tries to
do (or discuss), Palamon's name is inserted into it (like
a piece of fat into lean meat in order to make it cook
better).
2. Presumably the Schoolmaster has written a song
about Dido and her lover, Aeneas, who abandons her in
Virgil's *Aeneid*. The Jailer's Daughter imagines a new
ending in which Dido falls in love with Palamon rather

than Aeneas in the afterworld.
3. Charon demanded payment for ferrying dead souls
across the river Styx to the underworld. Hence the custom of placing a coin on the tongues of the dead.
4. Shrivel up from unrequited love. The liver was supposed to be the seat of the passions.
5. One day while she was picking flowers, Proserpine
was spotted by Pluto, who carried her off to the underworld to be his queen. Her mother, Demeter, got Zeus
to allow her to spend six months on earth each year.

break,[6] we of the blessed. Alas, 'tis a sore life they have i'th' other place—such burning, frying, boiling, hissing, howling, chattering, cursing—O they have shrewd measure°—take heed! If one be mad or hang or drown themselves, thither they
30 go, Jupiter bless us, and there shall we be put in a cauldron of lead and usurers' grease,[7] amongst a whole million of cutpurses, and there boil there like a gammon° of bacon that will never be enough.°

harsh retribution

side
cooked enough

DOCTOR How her brain coins!°

invents

35 JAILER'S DAUGHTER Lords and courtiers that have got maids with child—they are in this place. They shall stand in fire up to the navel and in ice up to th' heart, and there th'offending part burns, and the deceiving part freezes—in truth a very grievous punishment as one would think for such a trifle. Believe me,
40 one would marry a leprous witch to be rid on't, I'll assure you.

DOCTOR How she continues this fancy! 'Tis not an engrafted madness, but a most thick and profound melancholy.[8]

JAILER'S DAUGHTER To hear there a proud° lady and a proud city wife° howl together! I were a beast an° I'd call it good sport.
45 One cries, 'O this smoke!', th'other, 'This fire!'; one cries, 'O that ever I did it behind the arras!',° and then howls—th'other curses a suing fellow and her garden-house.[9]
(*Sings*) 'I will be true, my stars, my fate . . .'° *Exit* DAUGHTER

an aristocratic merchant's wife / if

wall hanging

(unknown song)

JAILER [*to the* DOCTOR] What think you of her, sir?
50 DOCTOR I think she has a perturbed mind, which I cannot minister to.

JAILER Alas, what then?

DOCTOR Understand you she ever affected° any man ere she beheld Palamon?

loved

55 JAILER I was once, sir, in great hope she had fixed her liking on this gentleman, my friend.

WOOER I did think so too, and would account I had a great penn'orth° on't to give half my state° that both she and I, at this present, stood unfeignedly on the same terms.

bargain / property

60 DOCTOR That intemperate surfeit of her eye hath distempered the other senses.[1] They may return and settle again to execute their preordained faculties, but they are now in a most extravagant vagary.° This you must do: confine her to a place where the light may rather seem to steal in than be permitted; take
65 upon you, young sir her friend, the name of Palamon; say you come to eat with her and to commune of love. This will catch her attention, for this her mind beats upon°—other objects that are inserted 'tween her mind and eye become the pranks and friskins° of her madness. Sing to her such green songs[2] of love
70 as she says Palamon hath sung in prison; come to her stuck in° as sweet flowers as the season is mistress of, and thereto make an addition of some other compounded odours° which are

errant wandering

is obsessed with

tricks and frolics
decorated with

blended perfumes

---

6. A game played with male-female couples: one couple assigned to a place in the field called "hell" attempted to entrap the other couples.
7. The traditional punishment for avarice was boiling in oil (here, imagined as the sweat, "grease," given off by usurers).
8. It is not a rooted ("an engrafted"), true madness, but a deep depression (what today might be called love

sickness).
9. *a suing . . . garden-house:* the persuasive Wooer who lured her into a garden house, a site notorious for amorous trysts.
1. Her excessive gazing at Palamon has thrown her other senses off.
2. Songs typical of youth.

grateful° to the sense. All this shall become° Palamon, for · · · · · · · · *pleasant / befit*
Palamon can sing, and Palamon is sweet and every good thing.
75 Desire to eat with her, carve° her, drink to her, and still among³ · · · *carve for*
intermingle your petition of grace and acceptance into her
favour. Learn what maids have been her companions and play
feres,° and let them repair to her, with Palamon in their mouths, · · · *playmates*
and appear with tokens as if they suggested° for him. It is a · · · *interceded*
80 falsehood° she is in, which is with falsehoods to be combated. · · · *delusion*
This may bring° her to eat, to sleep, and reduce what's now out · · · *induce*
of square° in her into their former law and regiment.° I have · · · *disordered / rule*
seen it approved,⁴ how many times I know not, but to make the
number more I have great hope in this. I will between the
85 passages° of this project come in with my appliance.⁵ Let us · · · *stages*
put it in execution, and hasten the success,° which doubt not · · · *outcome*
will bring forth comfort. *Exeunt*

5.1

[*An altar prepared.*] *Flourish. Enter* THESEUS, PIRI-
THOUS, HIPPOLYTA, *attendants*

THESEUS   Now let 'em enter and before the gods
Tender their holy prayers. Let the temples
Burn bright with sacred fires, and the altars
In hallowed clouds commend° their swelling incense · · · *deliver*
5 To those above us. Let no due° be wanting. · · · *proper ritual*
Flourish of cornetts
They have a noble work in hand, will° honour · · · *which will*
The very powers that love 'em.
Enter PALAMON [*with his three*] *Knights* [*at one door*],
and ARCITE [*with his three Knights at the other door*]
PIRITHOUS   Sir, they enter.
THESEUS   You valiant and strong-hearted enemies,
You royal german° foes that this day come · · · *closely related*
10 To blow that nearness° out that flames between ye, · · · *close kinship*
Lay by your anger for an hour and, dove-like,
Before the holy altars of your helpers,
The all-feared gods, bow down your stubborn bodies.
Your ire° is more than mortal—so° your help be; · · · *anger / so may*
15 And as the gods regard° ye, fight with justice. · · · *are watching*
I'll leave you to your prayers, and betwixt ye
I part my wishes.° · · · *divide my hopes*
PIRITHOUS   Honour crown the worthiest.
Exit THESEUS *and his train*
PALAMON [*to* ARCITE]   The glass° is running now that cannot · · · *hourglass*
finish
Till one of us expire. Think you but thus,
20 That were there aught in me which strove to show° · · · *to expose itself as*
Mine enemy in this business, were't one eye
Against another, arm oppressed by arm,
I would destroy th'offender—coz, I would,

---

3. Among these pastimes.
4. I have seen this type of treatment successfully carried out.
5. My final mode of treatment (see 5.4).
5.1 Location: The forest. A single altar is probably visible upstage, perhaps on the inner stage, for this scene

(at least from line 34) and the next two. Here, it is dedicated to Mars. Q treats these first three scenes as a
single one. This makes sense if there are three altars
onstage, rather than, as assumed here, only one, which
successively represents three different altars, presumably in different locations.

Though parcel° of myself. Then from this gather   *it were a piece*
How I should tender° you.   *treat*

25 ARCITE   I am in labour
To push your name, your ancient love, our kindred,°   *kinship*
Out of my memory, and i'th' selfsame place
To seat something I would confound.° So hoist we   *destroy*
The sails that must these vessels port even where°   *carry wherever*
The heavenly limiter° pleases.   *(of life)*

30 PALAMON   You speak well.
Before I turn,° let me embrace thee, cousin—   *turn away*
This I shall never do again.

ARCITE   One farewell.

PALAMON   Why, let it be so—farewell, coz.

ARCITE   Farewell, sir.

Exeunt PALAMON *and his [three] Knights*

Knights, kinsmen, lovers—yea, my sacrifices,[1]
35 True worshippers of Mars, whose spirit in you
Expels the seeds of fear and th'apprehension
Which still is father of it,[2] go with me
Before the god of our profession.° There   *god we worship*
Require° of him the hearts of lions and   *Request*
40 The breath° of tigers, yea, the fierceness too,   *endurance*
Yea, the speed also—to go on,° I mean,   *go forward*
Else° wish we to be snails. You know my prize   *Otherwise (in retreat)*
Must be dragged out of blood—force and great feat
Must put my garland on me, where she sticks,
45 The queen of flowers.[3] Our intercession, then,
Must be to him° that makes the camp a cistern   *(Mars)*
Brimmed with the blood of men—give me your aid,
And bend your spirits towards him.

They kneel [before the altar, fall on their faces, then on
their knees again]

[Praying to Mars]   Thou mighty one,
That with thy power hast turned green Neptune° into purple;[4]   *god of the sea*
50 Whose havoc in vast field comets prewarn,°   *forecast*
Unearthèd° skulls proclaim; whose breath blows down   *As yet unburied*
The teeming Ceres' foison;[5] who dost pluck°   *pull down*
With hand armipotent° from forth blue clouds   *powerful in arms*
The masoned° turrets, that both mak'st and break'st   *stone*
55 The stony girths° of cities; me thy pupil,   *walls*
Youngest follower of thy drum, instruct this day
With military skill, that to thy laud°   *praise*
I may advance my streamer,° and by thee   *banner*
Be styled° the lord o'th' day. Give me, great Mars,   *named*
60 Some token of thy pleasure.

Here they fall on their faces, as formerly, and there is
heard clanging of armour, with a short thunder, as the
burst of a battle, whereupon they all rise and bow to
the altar

---

1. The three knights may literally become human sacrifices from Arcite to Mars if Arcite loses the battle.
2. *th'apprehension . . . it:* the anticipation of a daunting situation, which always breeds fear.
3. *Must put . . . flowers:* Will win for my head (where Emilia already resides) the victor's laurels, of which she, as the most beautiful of flowers, is part.
4. Red with blood.
5. *whose breath . . . foison:* whose breath (wind) destroys the plenty of the fields produced by Ceres, goddess of agriculture.

O great corrector of enormous° times,   *disordered*
Shaker of o'er-rank° states, thou grand decider   *overripe*
Of dusty and old titles, that heal'st with blood°   *through bloodletting*
The earth when it is sick, and cur'st the world
65 O'th' plurisy° of people, I do take   *excess*
Thy signs auspiciously, and in thy name,
To my design, march boldly. [*To his Knights*] Let us go.

Exeunt

5.2

Enter PALAMON *and his Knights with the former*
observance

PALAMON [*to his Knights*] Our stars must glister° with new fire,   *fortunes must glisten*
  or be
Today extinct.° Our argument is love,   *extinguished*
Which if the goddess of it grant, she gives
Victory too. Then blend your spirits with mine,
5 You whose free nobleness° do make my cause   *generous nobility*
Your personal hazard. To the goddess Venus
Commend° we our proceeding, and implore   *Commit*
Her power unto our party.
    Here they kneel [before the altar, fall on their faces then
    on their knees again]
[*Praying to Venus*] Hail, sovereign queen of secrets,¹ who hast
  power
10 To call the fiercest tyrant from his rage
And weep unto a girl;² that hast the might,
Even with an eye-glance, to choke° Mars's drum   *silence*
And turn th'alarum° to whispers; that canst make   *call to arms*
A cripple flourish with° his crutch, and cure him   *brandish*
15 Before Apollo;³ that mayst force the king
To be his subject's vassal, and induce
Stale gravity° to dance; the polled° bachelor   *old men / bald*
Whose youth, like wanton boys through bonfires,
Have skipped° thy flame, at seventy thou canst catch   *Has escaped*
20 And make him to the scorn° of his hoarse throat   *(by listeners)*
Abuse young lays of love.⁴ What godlike power
Hast thou not power upon? To Phoebus° thou   *the sun*
Add'st flames hotter than his—the heavenly fires
Did scorch his mortal son,⁵ thine him. The huntress,
25 All moist and cold, some say, began to throw
Her bow away and sigh.⁶ Take to thy grace
Me, thy vowed soldier, who do bear thy yoke
As 'twere a wreath of roses, yet is° heavier   *though the yoke is*
Than lead itself, stings more than nettles.
30 I have never been foul-mouthed against thy law;
Ne'er revealed secret, for I knew none; would not,
Had I kenned° all that were. I never practised   *known*
Upon⁷ man's wife, nor would the libels° read   *(against love)*

5.2 Location: The altar, here dedicated to Venus.
1. As the rest of the speech (lines 31ff.) indicates,
secrecy and discretion were essential components of
the chivalric love code.
2. Make him weep for a girl (or, weep so much that he
becomes like a girl).
3. Even more quickly than Apollo, the god of medicine.

4. Botch young lovers' love songs.
5. See note to 1.2.85–87.
6. *The huntress . . . sigh*: Diana, notwithstanding her
vow of chastity, fell in love with the shepherd
Endymion. *cold*: chaste.
7. *practised / Upon*: wooed.

Of liberal° wits. I never at great feasts   *licentious*
35   Sought to betray° a beauty, but have blushed   *expose the affairs of*
At simp'ring sirs that did. I have been harsh
To large confessors,[8] and have hotly asked them
If they had mothers—I had one, a woman,
And women 'twere they wronged. I knew a man
40   Of eighty winters, this I told them, who
A lass of fourteen brided°—'twas thy° power   *wedded / Venus's*
To put life into dust. The agèd cramp°   *cramp of old age*
Had screwed° his square foot round,   *twisted*
The gout had knit his fingers into knots,
45   Torturing convulsions from his globy eyes°   *swollen sockets*
Had almost drawn their spheres,° that° what was life   *eyeballs / so that*
In him seemed torture. This anatomy°   *skeleton*
Had by his young fair fere° a boy, and I   *mate*
Believed it was his, for she swore it was,
50   And who would not believe her? Brief °—I am   *In short*
To those that prate and have done,[9] no companion;
To those that boast and have not,° a defier;   *have done nothing*
To those that would and cannot, a rejoicer.
Yea, him I do not love that tells close offices°   *secret matters*
55   The foulest way, nor names concealments[1] in
The boldest language. Such a one I am,
And vow that lover never yet made sigh
Truer than I. O, then, most soft sweet goddess,
Give me the victory of this question,° which   *conflict*
60   Is true love's merit,° and bless me with a sign   *just deserts*
Of thy great pleasure.
       Here music is heard, doves° are seen to flutter. They fall   (*sacred to Venus*)
          again upon their faces, then on their knees
O thou that from eleven to ninety reign'st
In mortal bosoms, whose chase° is this world   *hunting ground*
And we in herds thy game, I give thee thanks
65   For this fair token, which, being laid unto°   *added to*
Mine innocent true heart, arms in assurance
My body to this business. [*To his Knights*] Let us rise
And bow before the goddess.
          They [rise and] bow
                    Time comes on.   *Exeunt*

                              5.3
          Still° music of record[er]s. Enter EMILIA in white, her   *Soft*
          hair about her shoulders, [with] a wheaten wreath; one
          in white holding up her train, her hair stuck with flow-
          ers; one before her carrying a silver hind° in which is   (*sacred to Diana*)
          conveyed incense and sweet odours, which being set
          upon the altar, her maids standing [apart], she sets fire
          to it. Then they curtsy and kneel
EMILIA [*praying to Diana*]   O sacred, shadowy, cold,[1] and con-
          stant queen,
       Abandoner of revels, mute contemplative,

---

8. To those who boast of their love conquests.
9. To those who talk of deeds they have actually done.
1. Nor exposes what should remain hidden.
5.3 Location: The altar, here dedicated to Diana.

1. *shadowy*: a goddess of the moon, Diana was associated with the night. *cold*: chaste. See 1.3.52, 4.2.58,
and notes to these lines.

Sweet, solitary, white as chaste, and pure
As wind-fanned° snow, who to thy female knights   *windblown*
5 Allow'st no more blood° than will make a blush,   *sexual desire*
Which is their order's robe: I here, thy priest,
Am humbled fore thine altar. O, vouchsafe
With that thy rare green eye, which never yet
Beheld thing maculate,° look on thy virgin;   *tainted*
10 And, sacred silver mistress, lend thine ear—
Which ne'er heard scurril° term, into whose port°   *scurrilous / opening*
Ne'er entered wanton° sound—to my petition,   *lewd*
Seasoned with holy fear.° This is my last   *pious awe*
Of vestal office.² I am bride-habited,°   *dressed as a bride*
15 But maiden-hearted. A husband I have 'pointed,°   *have been assigned*
But do not know him. Out of two, I should
Choose one and pray for his success, but I
Am guiltless of election.³ Of mine eyes
Were I to lose one, they are equal precious—
20 I could doom neither: that which perished should
Go to't unsentenced. Therefore, most modest queen,
He of the two pretenders° that best loves me   *suitors*
And has the truest title in't,° let him   *claim to me*
Take off my wheaten garland,° or else grant   *Take my virginity*
25 The file and quality I hold I may
Continue in thy band.⁴
        Here the hind vanishes under the altar and in the place
        ascends a rose tree having one rose° upon it   *(symbol of virginity)*
[*To her women*] See what our general of ebbs and flows⁵
Out from the bowels of her holy altar,
With sacred act, advances—but one rose!
30 If well inspired,⁶ this battle shall confound°   *destroy*
Both these brave knights, and I a virgin flower
Must grow alone, unplucked.
        Here is heard a sudden twang of instruments and the
        rose falls from the tree
The flower is fall'n, the tree descends. [*To Diana*] O mistress,
Thou here dischargest me—I shall be gathered.⁷
35 I think so, but I know not thine own will.
Unclasp thy mystery.° [*To her women*] I hope she's pleased;   *Reveal your meaning*
Her signs were gracious.   *They curtsy and exeunt*

5.4

Enter [the] DOCTOR, [the] JAILER, and [the] WOOER in
[the] habit of° Palamon   *dressed as*
DOCTOR   Has this advice I told you done any good upon her?
WOOER   O, very much. The maids that kept her company have
half persuaded her that I am Palamon. Within this half-hour
she came smiling to me, and asked me what I would eat, and
5 when I would kiss her. I told her presently,° and kissed her   *at once*
twice.

---

2. *my . . . office*: my last duty as your virginal devotee.
3. Am not guilty of having made a choice (and hence
of having betrayed my vows).
4. *grant . . . band*: grant that I may continue to hold the
rank and condition (of virginity) as one of your devotees.

5. Our ruler of the moon and, hence, of tides.
6. If this is a true omen.
7. I shall be married; I shall lose my virginity.
5.4 Location: The prison.

DOCTOR 'Twas well done—twenty times had been far better,
For there° the cure lies mainly.   *(in kissing)*

WOOER   Then she told me
She would watch° with me tonight, for well she knew   *stay up*
What hour my fit° would take me.   *urgent inclination*

10 DOCTOR   Let her do so,
And when your fit comes, fit her home,[1]
And presently.

WOOER   She would have me sing.

DOCTOR You did so?

WOOER   No.

DOCTOR   'Twas very ill done, then.
You should observe° her every way.   *accommodate*

WOOER   Alas,
15 I have no voice, sir, to confirm° her that way.   *assure*

DOCTOR That's all one,° if ye make a noise.   *That doesn't matter*
If she entreat° again, do anything—   *beg*
Lie with her if she ask you.

JAILER   Ho there, Doctor.

DOCTOR Yes, in the way of cure.

JAILER   But first, by your leave,
I'th' way of honesty.°   *(after marriage)*

20 DOCTOR   That's but a niceness°—   *an excessive scruple*
Ne'er cast your child away for honesty.[2]
Cure her first this way, then if she will° be honest,   *wants to*
She has the path° before her.   *(of marriage)*

JAILER   Thank ye, Doctor.

DOCTOR Pray bring her in and let's see how she is.

25 JAILER I will, and tell her her Palamon stays° for her.   *waits*
But, Doctor, methinks you are i'th' wrong still.   *Exit* JAILER

DOCTOR Go, go. You fathers are fine fools—her honesty?
An we should give her physic till we find that[3]—

WOOER Why, do you think she is not honest, sir?

DOCTOR How old is she?

WOOER   She's eighteen.

30 DOCTOR   She may be—
But that's all one. 'Tis nothing to our purpose.°   *It makes no difference*
Whate'er her father says, if you perceive
Her mood inclining that way that I spoke of,
Videlicet,° the way of flesh—you have me?   *Namely*

WOOER Yes, very well, sir.

35 DOCTOR   Please her appetite,
And do it home°—it cures her, *ipso facto,*[4]   *completely*
The melancholy humour° that infects her.   *mood (medical)*

WOOER I am of your mind, Doctor.

Enter [the] JAILER *and [his]* DAUGHTER *[mad]*

DOCTOR You'll find it so—she comes: pray humour her.
[The DOCTOR *and the* WOOER *stand apart]*

JAILER *[to his* DAUGHTER*]* Come, your love Palamon stays for
40 you, child,

---

1. Fully serve her needs (have sex with her).
2. A paradox: don't lose your daughter (to her madness) in order to keep her (honest).
3. If we were to treat her until we could be sure of her virginity (the obvious continuation of the unfinished thought being, we'd be treating her forever).
4. By the very act (*ipso facto*) of having sex, she'll be cured. The Doctor assumes, correctly in the event, that the Daughter suffers from hysteria, thought to be caused by a wandering womb and cured by intercourse.

And has done this long hour, to visit you.

JAILER'S DAUGHTER I thank him for his gentle patience.
He's a kind gentleman, and I am much bound° to him.   obliged
Did you ne'er see the horse he gave me?

JAILER   Yes.

JAILER'S DAUGHTER How do you like him?

45 JAILER   He's a very fair° one.   beautiful

JAILER'S DAUGHTER You never saw him dance?

JAILER   No.

JAILER'S DAUGHTER   I have, often.
He dances very finely, very comely,
And, for a jig, come cut and long-tail to him,[5]
He turns ye like a top.

JAILER   That's fine, indeed.

50 JAILER'S DAUGHTER He'll dance the morris twenty mile an hour,
And that will founder the best hobbyhorse,[6]
If I have any skill,° in all the parish—   judgment
And gallops to the tune of 'Light o' love'.[7]
What think you of this horse?

JAILER   Having these virtues
55 I think he might be brought° to play at tennis.   taught

JAILER'S DAUGHTER Alas, that's nothing.

JAILER   Can he write and read too?

JAILER'S DAUGHTER A very fair hand, and casts himself th'accounts[8]
Of all his hay and provender. That ostler
Must rise betime that cozens° him. You know   get up early to cheat
The chestnut mare the Duke has?

60 JAILER   Very well.

JAILER'S DAUGHTER She is horribly in love with him, poor beast,
But he is like his master—coy° and scornful.   aloof

JAILER What dowry has she?

JAILER'S DAUGHTER   Some two hundred bottles°   bales of hay
And twenty strike° of oats, but he'll ne'er have her.   bushels
65 He lisps in's neighing, able to entice
A miller's mare.[9] He'll be the death of her.

DOCTOR What stuff she utters!

JAILER Make curtsy—here your love comes.

WOOER [coming forward] Pretty soul,
How do ye?
          [She curtsies]
70   That's a fine maid, there's a curtsy.

JAILER'S DAUGHTER Yours to command, i'th' way of honesty—
How far is't now to th' end o'th' world, my masters?

DOCTOR Why, a day's journey, wench.

JAILER'S DAUGHTER [to WOOER]   Will you go with me?

WOOER What shall we do there, wench?

---

5. *He . . . him:* He dances finely no matter what horse
he is compared with. *cut:* a horse with a docked tail (see
note to 3.4.22). There is sexual wordplay throughout
this scene.
6. That will lame ("founder") the best morris dancer.
hobbyhorse: one extremely agile morris dancer was
dressed as a horse and imitated its movements.
7. Popular ballad, also referred to in *Much Ado About*

Nothing 3.4.39 and *The Two Gentlemen of Verona*
1.2.83. The title means "inconstant in love."
8. He has beautiful penmanship and reckons his own
expenses.
9. *He . . . mare:* He's such a smooth talker he could
seduce even a miller's mare—a workhorse renowned for
its steadfast, circular plodding and, hence, least likely
to be distracted.

JAILER'S DAUGHTER   Why, play at stool-ball[1]—
What is there else to do?

75 WOOER   I am content
If we shall keep our wedding° there.   *As long as we marry*

JAILER'S DAUGHTER   'Tis true—
For there, I will assure you, we shall find
Some blind priest for the purpose that will venture
To marry us, for here they are nice,° and foolish.   *too scrupulous*

80 Besides, my father must be hanged tomorrow,
And that would be a blot i'th' business.
Are not you Palamon?

WOOER   Do not you know me?

JAILER'S DAUGHTER   Yes, but you care not for me. I have nothing
But this poor petticoat and two coarse smocks.°   *undergarments*

WOOER   That's all one—I will have you.

85 JAILER'S DAUGHTER   Will you surely?

WOOER   Yes, by this fair hand, will I.

JAILER'S DAUGHTER   We'll to bed then.

WOOER   E'en when you will.°   *Whenever you like*
[*He kisses her*]

JAILER'S DAUGHTER [*rubbing off the kiss*]
        O, sir, you would fain be nibbling.

WOOER   Why do you rub my kiss off?

JAILER'S DAUGHTER   'Tis a sweet one,
And will perfume me finely against° the wedding.   *in preparation for*
[*Indicating the* DOCTOR] Is not this your cousin Arcite?

90 DOCTOR   Yes, sweetheart,
And I am glad my cousin Palamon
Has made so fair a choice.

JAILER'S DAUGHTER   Do you think he'll have me?

DOCTOR   Yes, without doubt.

JAILER'S DAUGHTER [*to the* JAILER]   Do you think so too?

JAILER   Yes.

JAILER'S DAUGHTER   We shall have many children. [*To the* DOCTOR]
     Lord, how you're grown!

95 My Palamon, I hope, will grow too,[2] finely,
Now he's at liberty. Alas, poor chicken,
He was kept down with hard meat° and ill lodging,   *coarse food*
But I'll kiss him up again.

Enter a MESSENGER

MESSENGER   What do you here? You'll lose the noblest sight
That e'er was seen.

JAILER   Are they i'th' field?

100 MESSENGER   They are—
You bear a charge° there too.   *have a duty*

JAILER   I'll away straight.
[*To the others*] I must e'en leave you here.

DOCTOR   Nay, we'll go with you—
I will not lose the sight.

JAILER   How did you like her?

DOCTOR   I'll warrant you, within these three or four days

---

1. A game, somewhat like cricket, played with ball and   2. Get fat; have an erection.
bat by women or by men and women together.

I'll make her right again.

                    [Exit the JAILER *with the* MESSENGER]

105   *[To the* WOOER]   You must not from her,
But still preserve° her in this way.   *keep treating*

WOOER   I will.

DOCTOR   Let's get her in.

WOOER   *[to the* JAILER'S DAUGHTER]
                  Come, sweet, we'll go to dinner,
And then we'll play at cards.

JAILER'S DAUGHTER   And shall we kiss too?

WOOER   A hundred times.

JAILER'S DAUGHTER   And twenty.

WOOER   Ay, and twenty.

JAILER'S DAUGHTER   And then we'll sleep together.

110 DOCTOR   *[to the* WOOER]   Take her offer.

WOOER   *[to the* JAILER'S DAUGHTER]
Yes, marry, will we.

JAILER'S DAUGHTER   But you shall not hurt me.

WOOER   I will not, sweet.

JAILER'S DAUGHTER   If you do, love, I'll cry.   *Exeunt*

5.5

Flourish. Enter THESEUS, HIPPOLYTA, EMILIA,
PIRITHOUS, *and some attendants*

EMILIA   I'll no step further.

PIRITHOUS   Will you lose this sight?

EMILIA   I had rather see a wren hawk at° a fly   *attack in midair*
Than this decision. Every blow that falls
Threats a brave life; each stroke laments
5   The place whereon it falls, and sounds more like
A bell° than blade. I will stay here.   *death knell*
It is enough my hearing shall be punished
With what shall happen, 'gainst the which there is
No deafing, but to hear;[1] not taint mine eye
With dread sights it may shun.

10 PIRITHOUS   *[to* THESEUS]   Sir, my good lord,
Your sister will no further.

THESEUS   O, she must.
She shall see deeds of honour in their kind,°   *true nature*
Which sometime show well pencilled.° Nature now   *even when just drawn*
Shall make and act° the story, the belief   *invent and perform*
Both sealed with eye and ear.[2] *[To* EMILIA] You must be
15   present—
You are the victor's meed,° the price and garland   *reward*
To crown the question's title.[3]

EMILIA   Pardon me,
If I were there I'd wink.°   *keep my eyes closed*

THESEUS   You must be there—
This trial is, as 'twere, i'th' night, and you
The only star to shine.

20 EMILIA   I am extinct.°   *extinguished*

5.5 Location: The forest, near the tournament field.   by all that is seen and heard.
1. *there . . . hear:* there is no way to block out the noise   3. To crown the rightful victor in the dispute.
in order not to hear.
2. *the belief . . . ear:* the story will be rendered credible

There is but envy° in that light which shows   *malice*
The one the other. Darkness, which ever was
The dam° of horror, who does stand accursed   *mother*
Of many mortal millions, may even now,
25 By casting her black mantle over both,
That° neither could find other, get herself   *So that*
Some part of a good name, and many a murder
Set off whereto° she's guilty.   *Atone for of which*
HIPPOLYTA   You must go.
EMILIA   In faith, I will not.
THESEUS   Why, the knights must kindle
30 Their valour at your eye. Know, of this war
You are the treasure, and must needs be by°   *nearby*
To give the service pay.°   *reward the winner*
EMILIA   Sir, pardon me—
The title of a kingdom may be tried
Out of itself.°   *Outside the kingdom*
THESEUS   Well, well—then at your pleasure.
35 Those that remain with you could wish their office
To any of their enemies.
HIPPOLYTA   Farewell, sister.
I am like to know your husband fore yourself,
By some small start of time. He whom the gods
Do of the two know° best, I pray them he   *know to be*
40 Be made your lot.   *Exeunt [all but* EMILIA]
    [EMILIA *takes out two pictures, one from her right side,*
    and one from her left]
EMILIA   Arcite is gently visaged,° yet his eye   *has a gentle expression*
Is like an engine bent[4] or a sharp weapon
In a soft sheath. Mercy and manly courage
Are bedfellows in his visage. Palamon
45 Has a most menacing aspect. His brow
Is graved° and seems to bury what it frowns on,   *frowned*
Yet sometime 'tis not so, but alters to°   *according to*
The quality° of his thoughts. Long time his eye   *nature*
Will dwell upon his object. Melancholy
50 Becomes° him nobly—so does Arcite's mirth.   *Suits*
But Palamon's sadness is a kind of mirth,
So mingled as if mirth did make him sad
And sadness merry. Those darker humours° that   *moods*
Stick misbecomingly° on others, on them   *Seem misplaced*
55 Live in fair dwelling.[5]
    Cornetts. Trumpets sound as to a charge
Hark, how yon spurs to spirit° do incite   *bravery*
The princes to their proof.° Arcite may win me,   *to prove themselves*
And yet may Palamon wound Arcite to
The spoiling of his figure.° O, what pity   *(so as to disfigure him)*
60 Enough for such a chance![6] If I were by°   *near*
I might do hurt, for they would glance their eyes
Toward my seat, and in that motion might
Omit a ward or forfeit an offence

---

4. Is like a weapon, such as a bow, ready to be released.   6. Would be sufficient for such a (sad) turn of events.
5. *on them . . . dwelling:* suit them well.

Which craved that very time.[7] It is much better
    Cornetts. A great cry and noise within, crying,
    'A Palamon'
65 I am not there. O better never born,
Than minister to such harm.
    Enter SERVANT
                        What is the chance?°   *Who won*
SERVANT   The cry's 'A Palamon'.
EMILIA   Then he has won. 'Twas ever likely—
He looked all grace and success, and he is
70 Doubtless the prim'st° of men. I prithee run   *most perfect*
And tell me how it goes.
    Shout and cornetts, crying, 'A Palamon'
SERVANT   Still 'Palamon'.
EMILIA   Run and enquire.   *[Exit* SERVANT]
    [She speaks to the picture in her right hand]
               Poor servant,° thou hast lost.   *lover (Arcite)*
Upon my right side still I° wore thy picture,   *I always*
Palamon's on the left. Why so, I know not.
75 I had no end° in't, else chance would have it so.   *purpose*
    Another cry and shout within and cornetts
On the sinister side the heart lies—Palamon
Had the best-boding chance.[8] This burst of clamour
Is sure the end o'th' combat.
    Enter SERVANT
SERVANT   They said that Palamon had Arcite's body
80 Within an inch o'th' pyramid—that the cry
Was general 'A Palamon'. But anon
Th'assistants° made a brave redemption,° and   *knights / rescue*
The two bold titlers° at this instant are   *fighters for the title*
Hand to hand at it.
EMILIA   Were they° metamorphosed   *I wish they were*
85 Both into one! O why? There were no woman
Worth so composed a man:[9] their single share,
Their nobleness peculiar to them, gives
The prejudice of disparity, value's shortness,
To any lady breathing[1]—
    Cornetts. Cry within, 'Arcite, Arcite'
               More exulting?
'Palamon' still?
90 SERVANT   Nay, now the sound is 'Arcite'.
EMILIA   I prithee, lay attention to the cry.
    Cornetts. A great shout and cry, 'Arcite, victory!'
Set both thine ears to th' business.
SERVANT   The cry is
'Arcite' and 'Victory'—hark, 'Arcite, victory!'
The combat's consummation° is proclaimed   *conclusion*
By the wind instruments.
95 EMILIA   Half sights saw°   *Mere glimpses showed*
That Arcite was no babe. God's lid,° his richness   *By God's eyelid*

---

7. *might . . . time:* might miss the perfect moment for
a defensive parry or an offensive move.
8. *On . . . chance:* The location of Palamon's picture—
on Emilia's left ("sinister") side, where her heart is—
portended victory, since the contest is about love.

9. *There . . . man:* No woman could be worthy of this
composite man made up of both Palamon and Arcite.
1. *their single . . . breathing:* no woman could have as
much nobility as either one of them. *their single share:*
each one's value.

And costliness of spirit looked through him—it could
No more be hid in him than fire in flax,°   *straw*
Than humble banks can go to law with° waters   *can battle*
100   That drift° winds force to raging. I did think   *driving*
Good Palamon would miscarry, yet I knew not
Why I did think so. Our reasons are not prophets
When oft our fancies are. They are coming off°—   *leaving the field*
Alas, poor Palamon.
       [*She puts away the pictures.*]
       Cornetts. Enter THESEUS, HIPPOLYTA, PIRITHOUS, ARCITE
       as victor, and attendants
105   THESEUS   Lo, where our sister is in expectation,
Yet quaking and unsettled. Fairest Emily,
The gods by their divine arbitrament
Have given you this knight. He is a good one
As ever struck at head. [*To* ARCITE *and* EMILIA] Give me your
       hands.
[*To* ARCITE] Receive you her, [*to* EMILIA] you him: [*to both*]
110   be plighted with
A love that grows as you decay.
    ARCITE   Emilia,
To buy you I have lost what's dearest to me
Save what is bought,° and yet I purchase cheaply   *(Emilia)*
As I do rate your value.
    THESEUS [*to* EMILIA]   O lovèd sister,
115   He speaks now of as brave a knight as e'er
Did spur a noble steed. Surely the gods
Would have him die a bachelor lest his race
Should show i'th' world too godlike. His behaviour
So charmed me that, methought, Alcides° was   *Hercules*
120   To him a sow[2] of lead. If I could praise
Each part of him to th'all I have spoke,[3] your Arcite
Did° not lose by't; for he that was thus good,   *Would*
Encountered yet his better. I have heard
Two emulous Philomels[4] beat the ear o'th' night
125   With their contentious throats, now one the higher,
Anon the other, then again the first,
And by and by out-breasted, that the sense[5]
Could not be judge between 'em—so it fared
Good space° between these kinsmen, till heavens did   *For a good while*
130   Make hardly° one the winner. [*To* ARCITE] Wear the garland   *Barely make*
With joy that you have won.—For the subdued,°   *losers*
Give them our present° justice, since I know   *immediate*
Their lives but pinch° 'em. Let it here be done.   *torment*
The scene's not for our seeing; go we hence
135   Right joyful, with some sorrow. [*To* ARCITE] Arm° your prize;   *Give your arm to*
I know you will not lose her. Hippolyta,
I see one eye of yours conceives a tear,
The which it will deliver.
       Flourish

---

2. Smelted metal taken from a furnace.
3. *to . . . spoke:* in the same way I have praised Palamon as a whole.
4. Two rival nightingales. In Greek mythology,
Philomela was raped by her sister's husband, who cut

out her tongue so she couldn't accuse him. By weaving
the story into cloth, she nonetheless informed her sister, who fed her husband their son. The gods turned the
sister into a nightingale and Philomela into a swallow.
5. And by and by outsung, so that the sense of hearing.

EMILIA   Is this winning?
  O all you heavenly powers, where is your mercy?
140 But that your wills have said it must be so,
  And charge me live to comfort this unfriended,°   *deprived of his friend*
  This miserable prince, that cuts away
  A life more worthy from him than all women,
  I should and would die too.

HIPPOLYTA   Infinite pity
145 That four such eyes should be so fixed on one°   *one woman*
  That two must needs be blind for't.[6]

THESEUS   So it is.   Exeunt

5.6

Enter [guarded] PALAMON *and his [three]* KNIGHTS *pinioned; [enter with them the]* JAILER *[and an]* executioner *[with block and axe]*

PALAMON   There's many a man alive that hath outlived
  The love o'th' people; yea, i'th' selfsame state
  Stands many a father with his child: some comfort
  We have by so considering. We expire,
5   And not without men's pity; to live still,
  Have their good wishes.[1] We prevent°   *avoid*
  The loathsome misery of age, beguile°   *cheat*
  The gout and rheum° that in lag° hours attend   *coughing / final*
  For grey approachers;° we come towards the gods   *(to death)*
10 Young and unwappered,° not halting° under crimes   *untired / limping morally*
  Many and stale°—that sure shall please the gods   *long gone*
  Sooner than such,° to give us nectar with 'em,   *(sinful old men)*
  For we are more clear° spirits. My dear kinsmen,   *innocent*
  Whose lives for this poor comfort are laid down,
  You have sold 'em° too too cheap.   *(your lives)*

15 FIRST KNIGHT   What ending could be
  Of more content? O'er us the victors have
  Fortune, whose title° is as momentary   *claim*
  As to us death is certain—a grain of honour
  They not o'erweigh us.[2]

SECOND KNIGHT   Let us bid farewell,
20 And with our patience anger tott'ring° fortune,   *unstable*
  Who at her certain'st reels.[3]

THIRD KNIGHT   Come, who begins?

PALAMON   E'en he that led you to this banquet shall
  Taste to you all.[4] *[To the* JAILER*]* Aha, my friend, my friend,
  Your gentle daughter gave me freedom once;
25 You'll see't done° now for ever. Pray, how does she?   *see me set free*
  I heard she was not well; her kind of ill°   *illness*
  Gave me some sorrow.

JAILER   Sir, she's well restored
  And to be married shortly.

PALAMON   By my short life,

---

6. That two eyes must be blinded (in death); that two
men could be so blind as to fight to the death for one
woman.
5.6 Location: Scene continues.
1. *We expire . . . wishes:* Even though we are to die, we
have men's good wishes that we might go on living.

2. *a grain . . . us:* they have no more honor than we do.
3. Who, when she seems most certain, suddenly
changes direction.
4. Taste (death) first, like the servant at a state banquet
who was required to taste the food before the king and
guests to make sure it wasn't poisoned.

I am most glad on't. 'Tis the latest° thing   *last*
30   I shall be glad of. Prithee, tell her so;
    Commend me to her, and to piece her portion°   *increase her dowry*
    Tender her this.
       [*He gives his purse*]
FIRST KNIGHT   Nay, let's be offerers all.
SECOND KNIGHT   Is it a maid?°   *virgin*
PALAMON   Verily, I think so—
    A right good creature more to me° deserving   *from me*
    Than I can quit° or speak of.   *requite*
35 ALL THREE KNIGHTS   Commend us to her.
       They give their purses
JAILER   The gods requite you all, and make her thankful.
PALAMON   Adieu, and let my life be now as short
    As my leave-taking.
       [*He*] *lies on the block*
FIRST KNIGHT   Lead, courageous cousin.
SECOND AND THIRD KNIGHTS   We'll follow cheerfully.
       A great noise within: crying, 'Run! Save! Hold!'
       Enter in haste a MESSENGER
40 MESSENGER   Hold! Hold! O, hold! Hold! Hold!
       Enter PIRITHOUS *in haste*
PIRITHOUS   Hold, ho! It is a cursèd haste you made
    If you have done° so quickly! Noble Palamon,   *finished*
    The gods will show their glory in a life
    That thou art yet to lead.
PALAMON   Can that be,
45   When Venus, I have said, is false? How do things fare?
PIRITHOUS   Arise, great sir, and give the tidings ear
    That are most rarely sweet and bitter.
PALAMON   What
    Hath waked us from our dream?
PIRITHOUS   List,° then: your cousin,   *Listen*
    Mounted upon a steed that Emily
50   Did first bestow on him, a black one owing°   *owning*
    Not a hair-worth of white—which some will say
    Weakens his price[5] and many will not buy
    His goodness with this note;° which superstition   *distinctive mark*
    Here finds allowance°—on this horse is Arcite   *gains support*
55   Trotting the stones of Athens, which the calkins
    Did rather tell than trample;[6] for the horse
    Would make his length° a mile, if 't pleased his rider   *length of stride*
    To put pride in him. As he thus went counting
    The flinty pavement, dancing, as 'twere, to th' music
60   His own hooves made—for, as they say, from iron
    Came music's origin[7]—what envious flint,°   *cobblestone*
    Cold as old Saturn[8] and like him possessed
    With fire malevolent, darted a spark,

---

5. Makes him less valuable, because dark horses were considered vicious or ill omened.
6. *which . . . trample*: the horse's gait was so long and light that its feet seemed more to count ("tell") the cobbles one by one than to trample them. *calkins*: turned-down edges of a horseshoe.
7. Pythagoras is supposed to have discovered music

when walking through a blacksmith's forge.
8. According to Chaucer's *Knight's Tale,* Saturn, father of Jupiter, was responsible for the reversal of fortune described here, because he had promised Venus that Palamon would win Emilia. Shakespeare and Fletcher limit Saturn's responsibility to a simile.

Or what fierce sulphur else, to this end made,[9]
65 I comment not—the hot horse, hot as fire,
Took toy° at this and fell to what disorder   *a capricious dislike*
His power could give his will; bounds; comes on end;
Forgets school-doing,° being therein trained   *school training*
And of kind manège;° pig-like he whines   *well disciplined*
70 At the sharp rowel,° which he frets at rather   *spur*
Than any jot obeys; seeks all foul means
Of boist'rous and rough jad'ry° to disseat   *behavior like a nag*
His lord, that kept it° bravely. When naught served,   *who kept his seat*
When neither curb would crack, girth break, nor diff'ring°   *various*
     plunges
75 Disroot his rider whence he grew,° but that   *was fixed*
He kept him 'tween his legs, on his hind hooves—
On end he stands—
That Arcite's legs, being higher than his head,
Seemed with strange art to hang. His victor's wreath
80 Even then fell off his head; and presently
Backward the jade comes o'er and his full poise°   *weight*
Becomes the rider's load. Yet is he living;
But such a vessel 'tis that floats but for
The surge that next approaches.[1] He much desires
85 To have some speech with you—lo, he appears.

     Enter THESEUS, HIPPOLYTA, EMILIA, [*and*] ARCITE *in a*
     chair [*borne by attendants*]

PALAMON   O miserable end of our alliance!
The gods are mighty. Arcite, if thy heart,
Thy worthy manly heart, be yet unbroken,
Give me thy last words. I am Palamon,
One that yet loves thee dying.
90 ARCITE   Take Emilia,
And with her all the world's joy. Reach° thy hand—   *Give me*
Farewell—I have told° my last hour. I was false,   *counted*
Yet never treacherous.[2] Forgive me, cousin—
One kiss from fair Emilia—[*they kiss*] 'tis done.
Take her; I die.   [*He dies*]
95 PALAMON   Thy brave soul seek Elysium.
EMILIA [*to Arcite's body*]   I'll close thine eyes, Prince. Blessèd
     souls be with thee.
Thou art a right good man, and, while I live,
This day I give to tears.
PALAMON   And I to honour.
THESEUS   In this place first you fought, e'en very here
100 I sundered you.° Acknowledge to the gods   *separated your fight*
Our thanks that you are living.
His part is played, and, though it were too short,
He did it well. Your day is lengthened and
The blissful dew of heaven does arrouse° you.   *sprinkle*
105 The powerful Venus well hath graced her altar,
And given you your love; our master, Mars,

9. Or some spark of hellfire made for this purpose.
1. *But such . . . approaches:* But he can live only until
the next onslaught (like a boat that can stay afloat only
until the next wave hits).

2. *I was . . . treacherous:* I was "false" to our friendship
(because Palamon did see Emilia first) but "never
treacherous" in vying for Emilia's love.

Hath vouched° his oracle, and to Arcite gave   *made good on*
The grace of the contention.° So the deities   *victory in the battle*
Have showed due justice.—Bear this hence.

[*Exeunt attendants with Arcite's body*]

PALAMON   O cousin,
110 That we should things desire which do cost us
     The loss of our desire! That naught could buy
     Dear love, but loss of dear love!

THESEUS   Never fortune
     Did play a subtler game—the conquered triumphs,
     The victor has the loss. Yet in the passage°   *proceedings*
115 The gods have been most equal.° Palamon,   *impartial*
     Your kinsman hath confessed the right o'th' lady°   *the right to Emilia*
     Did lie in you,° for you first saw her and   *Was yours*
     Even then proclaimed your fancy. He restored her
     As your stol'n jewel, and desired your spirit
120 To send him hence forgiven. The gods my justice
     Take from my hand, and they themselves become
     The executioners.° Lead your lady off,   *executors of justice*
     And call your lovers from the stage of death,°   *friends from the scaffold*
     Whom I adopt my friends. A day or two
125 Let us look sadly and give grace unto
     The funeral of Arcite, in whose end°   *after which*
     The visages of bridegrooms we'll put on
     And smile with Palamon, for whom an hour,
     But one hour since, I was as dearly sorry
130 As glad of Arcite, and am now as glad
     As for him sorry. O you heavenly charmers,°   *gods who enchant us*
     What things you make of us! For what we lack
     We laugh, for what we have, are sorry; still
     Are children in some kind. Let us be thankful
135 For that which is, and with you leave dispute
     That are above our question.³ Let's go off
     And bear us like° the time.   *Flourish. Exeunt*   *act in accordance with*

Epilogue

[*Enter* EPILOGUE]

EPILOGUE   I would now ask ye how ye like the play,
     But, as it is with schoolboys, cannot say.°   *speak*
     I am cruel fearful.° Pray yet stay awhile,¹   *horribly afraid*
     And let me look upon ye. No man smile?
5   Then it goes hard, I see. He that has
     Loved a young handsome wench, then, show his face—
     'Tis strange if none be here—and, if he will,
     Against his conscience let him hiss and kill
     Our market.° 'Tis in vain, I see, to stay ye.   *Our chance of success*
10   Have at the worst can come,° then! Now, what say ye?   *Do your worst*
     And yet mistake me not—I am not bold—
     We have no such cause.° If the tale we have told—   *purpose*
     For 'tis no other—any way content° ye,   *please*
     For to that honest purpose it was meant ye,°   *intended for you*

3. *with . . . question:* cease to dispute with you, who   **Epilogue**
are beyond our questioning.   1. Don't hiss or applaud yet.

15   We have our end;° and ye shall have ere long,   *achieved our aim*
      I dare say, many a better to prolong
      Your old loves to us. We and all our might°   *all we can do*
      Rest at your service. Gentlemen, good night.   *Flourish.* [*Exit*]

APPENDICES

APPENDICES

Early Modern Map Culture

In the early modern period, maps were often considered rare and precious objects, and seeing a map could be an important and life-changing event. This was so for Richard Hakluyt, whose book *The Principal Navigations, Voiages, Traffiques and Discoveries of the English Nation* (1598–1600) was the first major collection of narratives describing England's overseas trading ventures. Hakluyt tells how, as a boy still at school in London, he visited his uncle's law chambers and saw a book of cosmography lying open there. Perceiving his nephew's interest in the maps it contained, the uncle turned to a modern map and "pointed with his wand to all the knowen Seas, Gulfs, Bayes, Straights, Capes, Rivers, Empires, Kingdomes, Dukedomes, and Territories of ech part, with declaration also of their speciall commodities and particular wants, which by the benefit of traffike, and entercourse of merchants, are plentifully supplied. From the Mappe he brought me to the Bible, and turning to the 107 Psalme, directed mee to the 23 and 24 verses, where I read, that they which go downe to the sea in ships, and occupy [work] by the great waters, they see the works of the Lord, and his woonders in the deepe." This event, Hakluyt records, made so deep an impression upon him, that he vowed he would devote his life to the study of this kind of knowledge. *The Principal Navigations* was the result, a book that mixes a concern with the profit to be made from trade and from geographical knowledge with praise for the Christian god who made the "great waters" and, in Hakluyt's view, looked with special favor on the English merchants and sailors who voyaged over them.

In the early modern period, access to maps was far less easy than it is today. Before the advent of printing in the late fifteenth century, maps were drawn and decorated by hand. Because they were rare and expensive, these medieval maps were for the most part owned by the wealthy and the powerful. Sometimes adorned with pictures of fabulous sea monsters and exotic creatures, maps often revealed the Christian worldview of those who composed them. Jerusalem appeared squarely in the middle of many maps (called T and O maps), with Asia, Africa, and Europe, representing the rest of the known world, arranged symmetrically around the Holy City. Because they had not yet been discovered by Europeans, North and South America were not depicted.

Mapping practices changed markedly during the late fifteenth and sixteenth centuries both because of the advent of print and also because European nations such as Portugal and Spain began sending ships on long sea voyages to open new trade routes to the East and, eventually, to the Americas. During this period, monarchs competed to have the best cartographers supply them with accurate maps of their realms and especially of lands in Africa, Asia, or the Americas, where they hoped to trade or plant settlements. Such knowledge was precious and jealously guarded. The value of such maps and the secrecy that surrounded them are indicated by a story published in Hakluyt's *The Principal Navigations*. An English ship had captured a Portuguese vessel in the Azores, and a map was discovered among the ship's valuable cargo, which included spices, silks, carpets, porcelain, and other exotic commercial objects. The map was "inclosed in a case of sweete Cedar wood, and lapped up almost an hundred fold in fine calicut-cloth, as though it had been some incomparable jewell." The value of the map and what explains the careful way in which it was packed lay in the particular information it afforded the English about Portuguese trading routes. More than beautiful objects, maps like this one were crucial to the international race to find safe sea routes to the most profitable trading centers in the East.

In the sixteenth century, books of maps began to be printed, making them more affordable for ordinary people, though some of these books, published as big folio volumes, remained too dear for any but wealthy patrons to buy. Yet maps were increasingly a part of daily life, and printing made many of them more accessible. Playgoers in Shakespeare's audiences must have understood in general the value and uses of maps, for they appear as props in a number of his plays. Most famously, at the beginning of *King Lear*, the old king has a map brought onstage showing the extent of his kingdom. He then points on the map to the three separate parts into which he is dividing his realm to share among his daughters. The map, often unfurled with a flourish on a table or held up for view by members of Lear's retinue, signals the crucial relationship of the land to the monarch. He is his domains, and the map signifies his possession of them. To divide the kingdom, in essence to tear apart the map, would have been judged foolish and destructive by early modern political theorists. Similarly, in *1 Henry IV*, when rebels against the sitting monarch, Henry IV, plot to overthrow him, they bring a map onstage in order to decide what part of the kingdom will be given to each rebel leader. Their proposed dismemberment of the realm signifies the danger they pose. Treasonously, they would rend in pieces the body of the commonwealth.

Maps, of course, had other uses besides signifying royal domains. In some instances, they were used pragmatically to help people find their way from one place to another. A very common kind of map, a portolan chart, depicted in minute detail the coastline of a particular body of water. Used by sailors, these maps frequently were made by people native to the region they described. Many world or regional maps, because they were beautifully decorated and embellished with vivid colors, were used for decorative purposes. John Dee, a learned adviser to Queen Elizabeth and a great book collector, wrote that some people used maps "to beautifie their Halls, Parlers, Chambers, Galeries, Studies, or Libraries." He also spoke of more scholarly uses for these objects. They could, for example, be useful aids in the study of history or geography, enabling people to locate "thinges past, as battels fought, earthquakes, heavenly fyringes, and such occurents in histories mentioned." Today we make similar use of maps, like those included in this volume, when, in reading Shakespeare's plays, we resort to a map to find out where the Battle of Agincourt took place or where Othello sailed when he left Venice for Cyprus.

This edition of the *Norton Shakespeare* includes six maps. Three of them are modern maps drawn specifically to show the location of places important to Shakespeare's plays. They depict London, the British Isles and France, and the eastern Mediterranean. This edition also includes three early modern maps that indicate some of the different kinds of printed maps that people might have seen in Shakespeare's lifetime. The earliest is a map of London that appeared in a 1574 edition of a famous German atlas, *Civitates Orbis Terrarum (Cities of the World)*, compiled by George Braun with engravings by Franz Hogenberg. This remarkable atlas includes maps and information on cities throughout Europe, Asia, and North Africa; the first of its six volumes appeared in 1572, the last in 1617. Being included in the volume indicated a city's status as a recognized metropolitan center. In a charming touch, Braun added to his city maps pictures of figures in local dress. At the bottom of the map of London, for example, there are four figures who appear to represent the city's prosperous citizens. In the center, a man in a long robe holds the hand of soberly dressed matron. On either side of them are younger and more ornately dressed figures. The young man sports a long sword and a short cloak, the woman a dress with elaborate skirts. In the atlas, the map is colored, and the clothes of the two young people echo one another in shades of green and red.

At the time the map was made, London was a rapidly expanding metropolis. In 1550, it contained about 55,000 people; by 1600, it would contain nearly 200,000. The map shows the densely populated old walled city north of the Thames River, in the middle of which was Eastcheap, the commercial district where, in Shakespeare's plays about the reign of Henry IV, Falstaff holds court in a tavern. The map also shows that by 1570 London was spreading westward beyond the wall toward Westminster Palace. This medieval structure, which appears on the extreme left side of the map, was where English monarchs resided when in London and where, at the end of *2 Henry IV*, the king dies in the fabled Jerusalem Chamber of the Westminster complex. On the far right of the map, one can see the Tower of London, where Edward IV's young sons were imprisoned by Richard III, an event depicted in Shakespeare's *The Tragedy of King Richard the Third*. The map also indicates the centrality of the Thames to London's commercial life. It shows the river full of boats, some of those on the east side of London Bridge large oceangoing vessels with several masts. South of the river, where many of the most famous London theaters, including Shakespeare's Globe, were to be constructed in the 1590s, there are relatively few buildings. By 1600, this would change, as Southwark, as it was known, came to be an increasingly busy entertainment, residential, and commercial district.

The map of the Christian Holy Lands at the eastern tip of the Mediterranean Sea had extremely wide distribution because it was included in the many editions of the Geneva Bible, an English translation of the Scriptures put together by a group of Puritan scholars working in Geneva in the 1550s. Moderately sized and priced, the Geneva Bible became the most popular Bible in English until the King James version was produced in 1611. Even after that date, many ordinary Protestant readers continued to use the popular Geneva Bible, which underwent refinements, changes, and additions throughout the second half of the sixteenth century, including in 1576 a new translation of the New Testament heavily indebted to the scholarship of the French theologian Théodore de Bèze.

The map included here is from a 1592 edition of this Bible, printed in London by Christopher Barker. The map was placed before Matthew, the first book of the New Testament, and it shows places mentioned in the first four Gospels (Matthew, Mark, Luke, and John), which collectively tell of the life and deeds of Jesus. It indicates, for example, the location of Bethlehem, where he was born; Nazareth, where he spent his youth; and Cana of Galilee, where he turned water into wine at a marriage. It suggests that, to the English reader, this particular territory was overwritten by and completely intertwined with Christian history. Yet in the Mediterranean Sea, on the left of the map, several large ships are visible, and they are reminders of another fact about this region: it was a vigorous trading arena where European Christian merchants did business with local merchants—Christian, Jew, and Muslim—and with traders bringing luxury goods by overland routes from the East. A number of Shakespeare's plays are set in this complex eastern Mediterranean region where several religious traditions laid claim to its territories and many commercial powers competed for preeminence. *Pericles,* for example, has a hero who is the ruler of Tyre, a city on the upper right side of the map. In the course of his wanderings, Pericles visits many cities along the eastern coasts of the Mediterranean. The conclusion of the play, in which the hero is reunited both with his long-lost daughter and the wife he believes dead, has seemed to many critics to share in a sense of Christian miracle, despite the fact of its ostensibly pagan setting. *The Comedy of Errors* and parts of *Othello* and of *Antony and Cleopatra* are also set in the eastern Mediterranean. One of Shakespeare's earliest plays, *The Comedy of Errors,* is an urban comedy in which the protagonists are merchants deeply involved in commercial transactions. It is also the first play in which Shakespeare mentions the Americas in an extended joke in which he compares parts of a serving woman's body to the countries on a map including Ireland, France, and the Americas. In *Othello,* the eastern Mediterranean island of Cyprus is represented as a tense Christian outpost defending Venetian interests against the Muslim Turks. In *Antony and Cleopatra,* Egypt figures as the site of Eastern luxury and also of imperial conquest, an extension of the Roman Empire. Clearly, this region was to Shakespeare and his audiences one of the most complex and most highly charged areas of the world: a site of religious, commercial, and imperial significance.

The map of Great Britain and Ireland comes from a 1612 edition of John Speed's *The Theatre of the Empire of Great Britaine,* an innovative atlas containing individual maps of counties and towns in England and Wales, as well as larger maps that include Scotland and Ireland. Speed was by trade a tailor who increasingly devoted his time to the study of history and cartography. Befriended by the antiquarian scholar William Camden, he eventually won patronage from Sir Fulke Greville, who gave him a pension that allowed him to devote full time to his scholarly endeavors. *The Theatre* was one product of this newfound freedom. The map included here is one of his most ambitious. It shows the entire British Isles, nominated by Speed as "The Kingdome of Great Britaine and Ireland," though at this time Ireland was far from under the control of the English crown and Scotland was still an independent kingdom, despite the fact that James I, a Scot by birth, had tried hard to forge a formal union between England and Scotland. This problem of the relationship of the parts of the British Isles to one another, and England's assertion of power over the others, is treated in *Henry V*, in which officers from Wales, Ireland, and Scotland are sharply delineated yet all depicted as loyal subjects of the English king.

One striking aspect of Speed's map is the balance it strikes between the two capital cities, London on the left, prominently featuring the Thames and London Bridge, and Edinburgh on the right. This would have pleased James, whose interest in his native country Shakespeare played to in his writing of *Macbeth*, based on material from Scottish history. Speed's map acknowledges the claims of the monarch to the territory it depicts. In the upper left corner, the British lion and the Scottish unicorn support a roundel topped with a crown. When James became king of England in 1603, he created this merged symbol of Scottish-English unity. The motto of the Royal Order of the Garter, "Honi soit qui mal y pense" (Shamed be he who thinks ill of it), is inscribed around the circumference. In the bottom left corner of the map, another locus of authority is established. Two cherubs, one holding a compass, the other a globe, sit beneath a banner on which is inscribed the words: "Performed by John Speede." If the territory is the monarch's, the craft that depicts it belongs to the tailor turned cartographer.

Today, maps are readily available from any gasoline station or on the Internet, but in early modern England they were still rare and valuable objects that could generate great excitement in those who owned or beheld them. Along with other precious items, maps were sometimes put on display in libraries and sitting rooms, but they had functions beyond the ornamental. They helped to explain and order the world, indicating who claimed certain domains, showing where the familiar stories of the Bible or of English history occurred, helping merchants find their way to distant markets. As John Dee, the early modern map enthusiast concluded, "Some, for one purpose: and some, for an other, liketh, loveth, getteth, and useth, Mappes, Chartes, and Geographicall Globes."

JEAN E. HOWARD

Ireland, Scotland, Wales, England, and Western France: Places Important to Shake-speare's Plays.

London: Places Important to Shakespeare's Plays and London Playgoing.

The Mediterranean World: Places Important to Shakespeare's Plays.

Map of the "Kingdome of Great Britaine and Ireland," from John Speed's 1612 edition of *The Theatre of the Empire of Great Britaine.*

Printed map of London, 1574, taken from a German atlas of European cities by George Braun and Franz Hogenberg.

Map of the Holy Land, from the Théodore de Bèze Bible, printed in London, 1592.

Documents

This selection of documents provides a range of contemporary testimony about Shakespeare's character, his work, and the social and institutional conditions under which it was produced. In the absence of newspapers and reviewers, few references to the theater survive. The availability of such hints and fragments as are presented here serves as a mark of Shakespeare's distinction, for the theater was perceived by much of the literate population as ephemeral popular entertainment. The reports of spectators whose accounts we have are more like reviews than any other texts the period has to offer; hence the importance even of brief notes such as Nashe's or Platter's, and the particular value of extended accounts such as those of Simon Forman. The government documents included here offer a vivid glimpse of the institutional procedures by which the theater was regulated. The legal documents—a contract for the construction of a theater modeled on the Globe, and Shakespeare's will—provide the most detailed account available of the material conditions of his life and work. The extracts from criticism and other literary texts show the diversity of contemporary response to his art.

The source for each text is given at the end of the introductory headnote. Additional documents can be found at wwnorton.com/shakespeare.

WS: E. K. Chambers, *William Shakespeare: A Study of Facts and Problems*, 2 vols. (Oxford: Clarendon Press, 1930).
ES: E. K. Chambers, *The Elizabethan Stage*, 4 vols. (Oxford: Clarendon Press, 1923).

Robert Greene on Shakespeare (1592)

[Robert Greene (1560–1592), a prolific author of plays, romances, and pamphlets, attacked Shakespeare in his *Greenes, Groats-worth of Witte, bought with a million of Repentance*. Greene had studied at Cambridge, and his "M.A." was prominently displayed on his title pages. Shakespeare's lack of a university education is clearly one motive for the professional resentment of the following excerpt. Another is probably that Greene was poor and very ill and felt forsaken while writing the *Groats-worth of Witte*; the preface refers to it as his "Swanne-like song," and the narrative is framed as the repentance of a dying man. (Some scholars have held that the posthumously published work contains fabrications by a publisher attempting to capitalize on Greene's name.) The three colleagues Greene addresses are likely to be Christopher Marlowe, Thomas Nashe, and George Peele. The text is that of 1596, as printed in Alexander B. Grosart's *Life and Complete Works in Prose and Verse of Robert Greene*, vol. 12 (New York: Russell and Russell).]

> *To those Gentlemen his Quondam acquaintance,*
> *that spend their wits in making Plaies, R. G.*
> *wisheth a better exercise, and wisdome*
> *to prevent his extremities. . . .*

Base minded men al three of you, if by my miserie ye be not warned: for unto none of you (like me) fought those burres to cleave: those Puppits (I meane) that speake from our mouthes, those Anticks garnisht in our colours. Is it not strange that I, to whom they al have beene beholding: is it not like that you, to whome they all have beene beholding, shall (were ye in that case that I am now) be both at once of them forsaken? Yes trust them not: for there is an upstart Crow, beautified with our feathers, that with his *Tygers heart wrapt in a Players hide*,[1] *supposes he is as well able to bumbast out a blanke verse as the best of you: and being an absolute Johannes fac totum*,[2] is in his owne conceit the onely Shake-scene in a countrie. O that I might intreate your rare wits to be imployed in more profitable courses: & let those Apes imitate your past excellence, and never more acquaint them with your admired inventions. I know the best husband[3] of you all will never prove an Usurer, and the kindest of them / all will never proove a kinde nurse: yet whilst you may, seeke you better Maisters; for it is pittie men of such rare wits, should be subject to the pleasures of such rude groomes.

Thomas Nashe on *1 Henry VI* (1592)

[Thomas Nashe (1567–1601), Greene's fellow playwright and pamphleteer, protests the attribution to himself of the *Groats-worth of Witte* in the preface to the 1592 edition of a pamphlet of his own, *Pierce Penilisse; His Supplication to the Devil.* The satire of *Pierce Penilisse* is more general and political than that of the *Groats-worth*, attacking the manners of the middle class. The allusion to the Talbot scenes of *1 Henry VI* (4.2–7) comes in a section subtitled "The defence of Playes." Talbot is supposed to have been played by Richard Burbage, later the leading actor of the Lord Chamberlain's and King's Men. The text is from Ronald B. McKerrow's 1904 edition of Nashe's *Works*, vol. 1 (London: Bullen).]

How would it have joyed brave *Talbot* (the terror of the French) to thinke that after he had lyne two hundred yeares in his Tombe, hee should triumphe againe on the Stage, and have his bones newe embalmed with the teares of ten thousand spectators at least (at severall times), who, in the Tragedian that represents his person, imagine they behold him fresh bleeding.

Francis Meres on Shakespeare (1598)

[Francis Meres (1565–1647) was educated at Cambridge and was active in London literary circles in 1597–98, after which he became a rector and schoolmaster in the country. The descriptions of Shakespeare are taken from a section on poetry in *Palladis Tamia, Wits Treasury*, a work largely consisting of translated classical quotations and exempla. Unlike the main body of the work, the subsections on poetry, painting, and music include comparisons of English artists to figures of antiquity. Meres goes on after the extract below to list Shakespeare among the best English writers for lyric, tragedy, comedy, elegy, and love poetry. The text is from Don Cameron Allen's 1933 edition of the section "Poetrie" (Urbana: University of Illinois).]

From XI

As the Greeke tongue is made famous and eloquent by *Homer, Hesiod, Euripedes, Aeschilus, Sophocles, Pindarus, Phocylides* and *Aristophanes*; and the Latine tongue by *Virgill, Ovid, Horace, Silius Italicus, Lucanus, Lucretius, Ausonius* and *Claudianus:* so the English tongue is mightily enriched, and gorgeouslie invested

---

1. A parody of *Richard Duke of York* (3 *Henry VI*) 1.4.138: "O tiger's heart wrapped in a woman's hide!" This obvious allusion and the following pun on Shakespeare's name make it certain that Shakespeare is the   "crow" described here.
2. Jack-of-all-trades. *conceit:* imagination.
3. Steward.

in rare ornaments and resplendent abiliments by Sir *Philip Sidney, Spencer, Daniel, Drayton, Warner, Shakespeare, Marlow* and *Chapman*.

From XIV

As the soule of *Euphorbus* was thought to live in *Pythagoras*: so the sweete wittie soule of Ovid lives in mellifluous & honytongued *Shakespeare*, witnes his *Venus and Adonis*, his *Lucrece*, his sugred Sonnets.

From XV

As *Plautus* and *Seneca* are accounted the best for Comedy and Tragedy among the Latines: so *Shakespeare* among ye English is the most excellent in both kinds for the stage; for Comedy, witnes his *Gētlemē of Verona*, his *Errors*, his *Love labors lost*, his *Love labours wonne*,[1] his *Midsummers night dreame*, & his *Merchant of Venice*: for Tragedy his *Richard the 2. Richard the 3. Henry the 4. King John, Titus Andronicus* and his *Romeo* and *Juliet*.

As *Epius Stolo* said, that the Muses would speake with *Plautus* tongue, if they would speak Latin: so I say that the Muses would speak with *Shakespeares* fine filed phrase, if they would speake English.

Thomas Platter on *Julius Caesar* (September 21, 1599)

[Thomas Platter (b. 1574), a Swiss traveler, recorded his experience at the Globe playhouse in an account of his travels. The German text is printed in *WS* 2:322.]

Den 21 Septembris nach dem Imbissessen, etwan umb zwey vhren, bin ich mitt meiner geselschaft v̄ber daz wasser gefahren, haben in dem streüwinen Dachhaus die Tragedy vom ersten Keyser Julio Caesare mitt ohngefahr 15 personen sehen gar artlich agieren; zu endt der Comedien dantzeten sie ihrem gebraucht nach gar v̄berausz zierlich, ye zwen in mannes vndt 2 in weiber kleideren angethan, wunderbahrlich mitt einanderen.

On the 21st of September after lunch, about two o'clock, I crossed the water [the Thames] with my party, and we saw the tragedy of the first emperor Julius Caesar acted very prettily in the house with the thatched roof, with about fifteen characters; at the end of the comedy, according to their custom, they danced with exceeding elegance, two each in men's and two in women's clothes, wonderfully together.

[Translated by Noah Heringman]

Gabriel Harvey on *Hamlet, Venus and Adonis,* and *The Rape of Lucrece* (1598–1603)

[Gabriel Harvey (c. 1550–1631), a scholar perhaps best remembered as the particular friend of Spenser, gave the following account of Shakespeare and other contemporaries in a long manuscript note in his copy of Speght's 1598 edition of Chaucer. The date of the note is uncertain, but internal evidence makes it highly unlikely to be later than 1603. The references to Shakespeare are brief but suggestive, and the note is useful both in providing a context for the appreciation of Shakespeare and for its characteris-

---

1. The play—or at least the title—has not survived; a bookseller's record of the title does survive, however.

tically keen assessment of the state of modern literature. The text is from G. C. Moore Smith's edition of *Gabriel Harvey's Marginalia* (Stratford-upon-Avon: Shakespeare Head Press, 1913).]

And now translated Petrarch, Ariosto, Tasso, & Bartas himself deserve curious comparison with Chaucer, Lidgate, & owre best Inglish, auncient & moderne. Amongst which, the Countesse of Pembrokes Arcadia, & the Faerie Queene ar now freshest in request: & Astrophil, & Amyntas ar none of the idlest pastimes of sum fine humanists. The Earle of Essex much commendes Albions England:[1] and not unworthily for diverse notable pageants, before, & in the Chronicle. Sum Inglish, & other Histories nowhere more sensibly described, or more inwardly discovered. The Lord Mountjoy makes the like account of Daniels peece of the Chronicle,[2] touching the Usurpation of Henrie of Bullingbrooke, which in deede is a fine, sententious, & politique peece of Poetrie: as proffitable, as pleasurable. The younger sort takes much delight in Shakespeares Venus, & Adonis: but his Lucrece, & his tragedie of Hamlet, Prince of Denmarke, have it in them, to please the wiser sort. Or such poets: or better: or none.

> Vilia miretur vulgus: mihi flavus Apollo
> Pocula Castaliæ plena ministret aquæ:[3]

quoth Sir Edward Dier, betwene jest, & earnest. Whose written devises farr excell most of the sonets, and cantos in print. His Amaryllis, & Sir Walter Raleighs Cynthia, how fine & sweet inventions? Excellent matter of emulation for Spencer, Constable, France, Watson, Daniel, Warner, Chapman, Silvester, Shakespeare, & the rest of owr florishing metricians. I looke for much, aswell in verse, as in prose, from mie two Oxford frends, Doctor Gager, & M. Hackluit: both rarely furnished for the purpose: & I have a phansie to Owens new Epigrams, as pithie as elegant, as plesant as sharp, & sumtime as weightie as breife: & amongst so manie gentle, noble, & royall spirits meethinkes I see sum heroical thing in the clowdes: mie soveraine hope. Axiophilus[4] shall forgett himself, or will remember to leave sum memorials behinde him: & to make an use of so manie rhapsodies, cantos, hymnes, odes, epigrams, sonets, & discourses, as at idle howers, or at flowing fitts he hath compiled. God knowes what is good for the world, & fitting for this age.

Contract for the Building of the Fortune Theatre (1600)

[This contract was drawn up between Philip Henslowe and Edward Alleyn, partners in the venture, and Peter Street, the carpenter (or general contractor) in charge of the construction. In fact, Alleyn seems to have put up all the money, £440 for the work specified in the contract in addition to £80 for decoration and considerable sums to acquire the lot and surrounding properties. Alleyn faced opposition from residents of the neighborhood, but he had secured the favor of key supporters, so that he was able to proceed with the construction. As the new home of the Lord Admiral's Men, the Fortune did in fact become a center of disturbances, with complaints coming to the Middlesex Bench of assaults, petty thefts, and riotous behavior. Alleyn had been the leading actor of the Lord Admiral's Men, chief competitors of the Lord Chamberlain's Men, and the Fortune was conceived to compete with the Globe, meanwhile replacing the decaying and poorly situated Rose Theatre. The contract's

---

1. By William Warner (1586).
2. *The Ciuile Wars Between the Two Houses of Lancaster and Yorke* (1595).
3. "Let what is cheap excite the marvel of the crowd; for me may golden Apollo minister full cups from the

Castalian fount" (Ovid, *Amores* 1.15.35–36, Loeb translation). These lines also appear on the title page of Shakespeare's *Venus and Adonis* (1592–93).
4. Probably Harvey himself.

descriptions and frequent references to the Globe, given this background, can be seen as providing some of our best evidence on the nature of the Globe itself. The text is reprinted in *ES*, vol. 2.]

'This Indenture made the Eighte daie of Januarye 1599,[1] and in the Twoe and Fortyth yeare of the Reigne of our sovereigne Ladie Elizabeth, by the grace of god Queene of Englande, Fraunce and Irelande, defender of the Faythe, &c. betwene Phillipp Henslowe and Edwarde Allen of the parishe of Ste Saviours in Southwark in the Countie of Surrey, gentlemen, on thone parte, and Peeter Streete, Cittizen and Carpenter of London, on thother parte witnesseth That whereas the saide Phillipp Henslowe & Edward Allen, the daie of the date hereof, have bargayned, compounded & agreed with the saide Peter Streete ffor the erectinge, buildinge & settinge upp of a new howse and Stadge for a Plaiehouse in and uppon a certeine plott or parcell of grounde appoynted oute for that purpose, scytuate and beinge nere Goldinge lane in the parishe of Ste Giles withoute Cripplegate of London,[2] to be by him the saide Peeter Streete or somme other sufficyent woorkmen of his provideinge and appoyntemente and att his propper costes & chardges, for the consideracion hereafter in theis pres- entes expressed, made, erected, builded and sett upp in manner & forme followinge (that is to saie); The frame of the saide howse to be sett square[3] and to conteine ffow- erscore foote of lawfull assize everye waie square withoutt and fiftie five foote of like assize square everye waie within, with a good suer and stronge foundacion of pyles, brick, lyme and sand bothe without & within, to be wroughte one foote of assize att the leiste above the grounde; And the saide fframe to conteine three Stories in heighth, the first or lower Storie to conteine Twelve foote of lawfull assize in heighth, the second Storie Eleaven foote of lawfull assize in heigth, and the third or upper Sto- rie to conteine Nyne foote of lawfull assize in heigth; All which Stories shall conteine Twelve foote and a halfe of lawfull assize in breadth througheoute, besides a juttey forwardes in either of the saide twoe upper Stories of Tenne ynches of lawfull assize, with ffower convenient divisions for gentlemens roomes,[4] and other sufficient and convenient divisions for Twoe pennie roomes, with necessarie seates to be placed and sett, aswell in those roomes as througheoute all the rest of the galleries of the saide howse, and with suchelike steares, conveyances & divisions withoute & within, as are made & contryved in and to the late erected Plaiehowse on the Banck in the saide parishe of Ste Saviours called the Globe; With a Stadge and Tyreinge howse[5] to be made, erected & settupp within the saide fframe, with a shadowe or cover[6] over the saide Stadge, which Stadge shalbe placed & sett, as alsoe the stearecases of the saide fframe, in suche sorte as is prefigured in a plott[7] thereof drawen, and which Stadge shall conteine in length Fortie and Three foote of lawfull assize and in breadth to extende to the middle of the yarde[8] of the saide howse; The same Stadge to be paled in belowe with good, stronge and sufficyent newe oken bourdes, and likewise the lower Storie of the saide fframe withinside, and the same lower storie to be alsoe laide over and fenced with stronge yron pykes; And the saide Stadge to be in all other pro- porcions contryved and fashioned like unto the Stadge of the saide Plaie howse called the Globe; With convenient windowes and lightes glazed to the saide Tyreinge howse; And the saide fframe, Stadge and Stearecases to be covered with Tyle, and to have a sufficient gutter of lead to carrie & convey the water frome the coveringe of the saide Stadge to fall backwardes; And also all the saide fframe and the Stairecases thereof

1. 1600 (New Style).
2. *nere . . . London:* an area then in the northwest suburbs, literally outside Cripplegate and, like the Globe across the water, outside the jurisdiction of a City Council often inimical to the theater.
3. This square shape was unusual; the outlines of comparable theaters of the period were round or polygonal (with more than four sides).
4. Something like the VIP boxes of the present day.

5. "Attiring house," a dressing room and backstage area extending onto the rear of the stage.
6. A roof (known as "the heavens") partially covering the stage, supported by the pillars that also served as versatile pieces of scenery.
7. Plan.
8. *in breadth . . . yarde:* the stage would then extend about 27 feet into the yard, specified earlier as 55 feet square.

to be sufficyently enclosed withoute with lathe, lyme & haire, and the gentlemens roomes and Twoe pennie roomes to be seeled[9] with lathe, lyme & haire, and all the fflowers of the saide Galleries, Stories and Stadge to be bourded with good & sufficyent newe deale bourdes of the whole thicknes, wheare need shalbe; And the saide howse and other thinges beforemencioned to be made & doen to be in all other contrivitions, conveyances, fashions, thinge and thinges effected, finished and doen accordinge to the manner and fashion of the saide howse called the Globe, saveinge only that all the princypall and maine postes of the saide fframe and Stadge forwarde shalbe square and wroughte palasterwise,[1] with carved proporcions called Satiers[2] to be placed & sett on the topp of every of the same postes, and saveinge alsoe that the said Peeter Streete shall not be chardged with anie manner of pay[ntin]ge in or aboute the saide fframe howse or Stadge or anie parte thereof, nor rendringe[3] the walls within, nor seeling anie more or other roomes then the gentlemens roomes, Twoe pennie roomes and Stadge before remembred. Nowe theiruppon the saide Peeter Streete dothe covenant, promise and graunte ffor himself, his executours and administratours, to and with the saide Phillipp Henslowe and Edward Allen and either of them, and thexecutours and administratours of them and either of them, by theis presentes in manner & forme followeinge (that is to saie); That he the saide Peeter Streete, his executours or assignes, shall & will att his or their owne propper costes & chardges well, woorkmanlike & substancyallie make, erect, sett upp and fully finishe in and by all thinges, accordinge to the true meaninge of theis presentes, with good, stronge and substancyall newe tymber and other necessarie stuff, all the saide fframe and other woorkes whatsoever in and uppon the saide plott or parcell of grounde (beinge not by anie aucthoretie restrayned, and haveinge ingres, egres & regres to doe the same) before the ffyve & twentith daie of Julie next commeinge after the date hereof; And shall alsoe at his or theire like costes and chardges provide and finde all manner of woorkmen, tymber, joystes, rafters, boordes, dores, boltes, hinges, brick, tyle, lathe, lyme, haire, sande, nailes, lade, iron, glasse, woorkmanshipp and other thinges whatsoever, which shalbe needefull, convenyent & necessarie for the saide fframe & woorkes & everie parte thereof; And shall alsoe make all the saide fframe in every poynte for Scantlinges[4] lardger and bigger in assize then the Scantlinges of the timber of the saide newe erected howse called the Globe; And alsoe that he the saide Peeter Streete shall furthwith, aswell by himself as by suche other and soemanie woorkmen as shalbe convenient & necessarie, enter into and upon the saide buildinges and woorkes, and shall in reasonable manner proceede therein withoute anie wilfull detraccion untill the same shalbe fully effected and finished. In consideracion of all which buildinges and of all stuff & woorkemanshipp thereto belonginge, the saide Phillipp Henslowe & Edward Allen and either of them, ffor themselves, theire, and either of theire executours & administratours, doe joynctlie & severallie covenante & graunte to & with the saide Peeter Streete, his executours & administratours by theis presentes, that they the saide Phillipp Henslowe & Edward Allen or one of them, or the executours administratours or assignes of them or one of them, shall & will well & truelie paie or cawse to be paide unto the saide Peeter Streete, his executours or assignes, att the place aforesaid appoynted for the erectinge of the saide fframe, the full somme of Fower hundred & Fortie Poundes of lawfull money of Englande in manner & forme followeinge (that is to saie), att suche tyme and when as the Tymberwoork of the saide fframe shalbe rayzed & sett upp by the saide Peeter Streete his executours or assignes, or within seaven daies then next followeinge, Twoe hundred & Twentie poundes, and att suche time and when as the saide fframe & woorkes shalbe fullie effected & ffynished as is aforesaide, or within seaven daies then next followeinge, thother Twoe hundred and Twentie poundes,

9. Coated both on the "ceiling" (a related word) and the walls.
1. Finished in the form of pilasters, ornamental columns in the classical style.

2. Satyrs. *proporcions*: figures.
3. Plastering.
4. Prescribed dimensions of the beams.

withoute fraude or coven.[5] Provided allwaies, and it is agreed betwene the saide parties, that whatsoever somme or sommes of money the saide Phillipp Henslowe & Edward Allen or either of them, or thexecutours or assignes of them or either of them, shall lend or deliver unto the saide Peter Streete his executours or assignes, or anie other by his appoyntemente or consent, ffor or concerninge the saide woorkes or anie parte thereof or anie stuff thereto belonginge, before the raizeinge & settinge upp of the saide fframe, shalbe reputed, accepted, taken & accoumpted in parte of the firste paymente aforesaid of the saide some of Fower hundred & Fortie poundes, and all suche somme & sommes of money, as they or anie of them shall as aforesaid lend or deliver betwene the razeinge of the saide fframe & finishinge thereof and of all the rest of the saide woorkes, shalbe reputed, accepted, taken & accoumpted in parte of the laste pamente aforesaid of the same somme of Fower hundred & Fortie poundes, anie thinge abovesaid to the contrary notwithstandinge. In witnes whereof the parties abovesaid to theis presente Indentures Interchaungeably have sett theire handes and seales. Geoven[6] the daie and yeare ffirste abovewritten.

P S

Sealed and delivered by the saide Peter Streete in the presence of me William Harris Pub[lic] Scr[ivener] And me Frauncis Smyth appr[entice] to the said Scr[ivener]
    [Endorsed:] Peater Street ffor The Building of the Fortune.

Augustine Phillips, Francis Bacon, et al. on Richard II (1601)

[These extracts from testimony submitted at the Earl of Essex's trial for treason, and related documents, show that some of Essex's supporters had contracted with the Lord Chamberlain's Men to revive *Richard II*, apparently in order to provide a model for the justified deposition of a monarch and thus propitiate the coup in which Essex planned to depose Elizabeth. The play was performed on February 7, and "it was on the same day," according to E. K. Chambers, "that Essex received a summons to appear before the Privy Council. This interrupted his plans for securing possession of the Queen's person and arresting her ministers, and precipitated his futile outbreak of February 8." Augustine Phillips was one of Shakespeare's colleagues in the Lord Chamberlain's Men. Sir Edward Coke was, for a time, chief justice under King James. The last excerpt is a contemporary record of a conversation between the queen and her archivist several months after Essex was executed. The texts are from *WS*, vol. 2.]

From the Abstract of Evidence

The Erle of Essex is charged with high Treason, namely, That he plotted and practised with the Pope and king of Spaine for the disposing and settling to himself Aswell the Crowne of England, as of the kingdom of Ireland.

From the Examination of Augustine Phillips, February 18, 1601

The Examination of Augustyne Phillypps servant unto the L Chamberlyne and one of hys players taken the xviij[th] of Februarij 1600 upon hys oth

He sayeth that on Fryday last was sennyght or Thursday S[r] Charles Percy S[r] Josclyne Percy and the L. Montegle with some thre more spak to some of the play-

---

ers in the presans of thys examinate to have the play of the deposyng and kyllyng of Kyng Rychard the second to be played the Saterday next promysyng to gete them xls. more then their ordynary to play yt. Wher thys Examinate and hys fellowes were determyned to have played some other play, holdyng that play of Kyng Richard to be so old & so long out of use as that they shold have small or no Company at yt. But at their request this Examinate and his fellowes were Content to play yt the Saterday and had their xls. more then their ordynary for yt and so played yt accordyngly

Augustine Phillipps

From the speech of Sir Edward Coke at Essex's trial, February 19

I protest upon my soul and conscience I doe beleeve she should not have long lived after she had been in your power. Note but the precedents of former ages, how long lived Richard the Second after he was surprised in the same manner? The pretence was alike for the removing of certain counsellors, but yet shortly after it cost him his life.

From [Francis Bacon's] "A Declaration of the . . . Treasons . . . by Robert late Earle of Essex"

The afternoone before the rebellion, Merricke,[1] with a great company of others, that afterwards were all in the action, had procured to bee played before them, the play of deposing King Richard the second. Neither was it casuall, but a play bespoken by Merrick. And not so onely, but when it was told him by one of the players, that the play was olde, and they should have losse in playing it, because fewe would come to it: there was fourty shillings extraordinarie given to play it, and so thereupon playd it was. So earnest hee was to satisfie his eyes with the sight of that tragedie which hee thought soone after his lord should bring from the stage to the state, but that God turned it upon their owne heads.

From a Memorandum in the Lambard family manuscript, August 4

. . . so her Majestie fell upon[2] the reign of King Richard II. saying, 'I am Richard II. know ye not that?'

W.L. 'Such a wicked imagination was determined and attempted by a most unkind Gent. the most adorned creature that ever your Majestie made.'

Her Majestie. 'He that will forget God, will also forget his benefactors; this tragedy was played 40[tie] times in open streets and houses.'

John Manningham on Twelfth Night and Richard III (1602)

[John Manningham (d. 1622) kept a diary during his time as a law student at the Middle Temple, recording the witticisms of his colleagues and a rich variety of anecdotes. The vibrant and boisterous life of the Inns of Court is also illustrated by the Gesta Grayorum (see above). The February entry describes the festivities organized for Candlemas Day at the Middle Temple, while the second recounts an anecdote related to Manningham by one Mr. Touse (this name is difficult to read in the manuscript). As with all the documents in this section, any date before March 25 is assigned to the following year according to our calendar, so that 1601 here becomes 1602 (New Style).

---

1. Sir Gilly Merrick, one of Essex's supporters, was later tried separately for treason.
2. Came across (in reading). The memorandum

describes a scene in which the queen is reading over the archives that have been in the keeping of her interlocutor, William Lambard.

The text is from the 1976 edition of Robert Sorlien (Hanover, N.H.: University Press of New England).]

Febr. 1601

2. At our feast wee had a play called "Twelve night, or what you will"; much like the commedy of errores, or Menechmi[1] in Plautus, but most like and neere to that in Italian called Inganni.[2] A good practise in it to make the steward beleeve his Lady widdowe[3] was in Love with him, by counterfayting a letter, as from his Lady, in generall termes, telling him what shee liked best in him, and prescribing his gesture in smiling, his apparraile, &c., and then when he came to practise, making him beleeve they tooke him to be mad.

Marche. 1601

13. . . . Upon a tyme when Burbidge played Rich[ard] 3. there was a Citizen grewe soe farr in liking with him, that before shee went from the play shee appointed him to come that night unto hir by the name of Ri[chard] the 3. Shakespeare, overhearing their conclusion, went before, was intertained, and at his game ere Burbidge came. Then message being brought that Richard the 3d. was at the dore, Shakespeare caused returne to be made that William the Conquerour was before Rich[ard] the 3. Shakespeare's name William. (Mr. Touse.)

Letters Patent Formalizing the Adoption of the Lord Chamberlain's Men as the King's Men (May 19, 1603)

[James I issued the warrant ordering this patent shortly after his coronation, enhancing the status of Shakespeare's company. As retainers of the royal household with the title of Grooms of the Chamber, they performed at the court with increasing frequency (177 times between 1603 and 1616) and assisted occasionally with other court functions; but, more important, they acted throughout the kingdom under the authority of the royal patent, whose scope the forceful wording below makes clear. The patent, bearing the Great Seal, was issued May 19 as ordered in the warrant of May 17. There is some evidence to suggest that James was particularly taken with Shakespeare's poetry, and the playwright's valorization of James's ancestry (as originating with Banquo) in *Macbeth* certainly suggests that Shakespeare cultivated his esteem. The text is from *ES*, vol. 2.]

Commissio specialis pro Laurencio Fletcher & Willelmo Shakespeare et aliis[2]

James by the grace of god &c. To all Justices, Maiors, Sheriffes, Constables, hedborowes,[1] and other our Officers and lovinge Subjectes greeting. Knowe yee that Wee of our speciall grace, certeine knowledge, & mere motion[3] have licenced and aucthorized and by theise presentes[4] doe licence and aucthorize theise our Servauntes Lawrence Fletcher, William Shakespeare, Richard Burbage, Augustyne Phillippes, John Heninges, Henrie Condell, William Sly, Robert Armyn, Richard Cowly, and the rest of theire Assosiates freely to use and exercise the Arte and faculty of playinge

---

1. Source for *The Comedy of Errors*.
2. The two plays with this exact title (1562 and 1592) seem less likely to be "most like" *Twelfth Night* than another Italian play, *Ingannati* (1537), which has characters named Fabio and Malevolti and makes reference to Twelfth Night (Epiphany).
3. Olivia is not a widow in the version of Shakespeare's play that has come down to us, though she is

so described in one of Shakespeare's principal sources for the play.
1. A parish officer similar to a petty constable.
2. *Commissio . . . aliis:* By special commission on behalf of . . . and others.
3. Inclination, desire.
4. The present document.

Comedies, Tragedies, histories, Enterludes, moralls,[5] pastoralls, Stageplaies, and Suche others like as theie have alreadie studied or hereafter shall use or studie, aswell for the recreation of our lovinge Subjectes, as for our Solace and pleasure when wee shall thincke good to see them, duringe our pleasure. And the said Commedies, tragedies, histories, Enterludes, Morralles, Pastoralls, Stageplayes, and suche like to shewe and exercise publiquely to theire best Commoditie,[6] when the infection of the plague shall decrease, aswell within theire nowe usual howse called the Globe within our County of Surrey, as alsoe within anie towne halls or Moute halls[7] or other conveniente places within the liberties and freedome of anie other Cittie, universitie, towne, or Boroughe whatsoever within our said Realmes and domynions. Willinge and Commaundinge you and everie of you, as you tender our pleasure, not onelie to permitt and suffer them herein without anie your lettes hindrances or molestacions during our said pleasure, but alsoe to be aidinge and assistinge to them, yf anie wronge be to them offered, And to allowe them such former Curtesies as hath bene given to men of theire place and quallitie,[8] and alsoe what further favour you shall shewe to theise our Servauntes for our sake wee shall take kindlie at your handes. In wytnesse whereof &c. witnesse our selfe at Westminster the nyntenth day of May

per breve de privato sigillo[9] &c.

Master of the Wardrobe's Account (March 1604)

[This entry offers us a rare glimpse of the players in the entourage of King James, sporting festive regalia in their capacity as Grooms of the Chamber. The royal procession took place March 15, 1604. The text is from *WS*, vol. 2.]

Red Clothe bought of sondrie persons and given by his Majestie to diverse persons against[1] his Majesties sayd royall proceeding through the Citie of London, viz.:— . . .

The Chamber . . .	
Fawkeners[2] &c. &c.	Red cloth
William Shakespeare	iiii yardes di.
Augustine Phillipps	"
Lawrence Fletcher	"
John Hemminges	"
Richard Burbidge	"
William Slye	"
Robert Armyn	"
Henry Cundell	"
Richard Cowley	"

Simon Forman on *Macbeth, Cymbeline,* and *The Winter's Tale* (1611)

[Simon Forman (1552–1611) was a largely self-educated physician and astrologer who rose from humble beginnings to establish a successful London practice. A large parcel of his manuscripts, including scientific and autobiographical material as well as the diary from which this account of the plays is taken, has survived, making his life one of the best-documented Elizabethan lives. These manuscripts provide

---

5. Morality plays.
6. Advantage.
7. Council chambers.
8. Profession.
9. In sum, from the privy seal.

1. For.
2. Obsolete form of "falconers," very likely the men who trained the falcons used for James's fowl-hunting expeditions. The falconers might owe their place in the retinue to James's well-known passion for hunting.

detailed information about Forman's many sidelines, such as the manufacture of talismans, alchemy, and necromancy, as well about his sex life. The text is from *WS*, vol. 2.]

The Bocke of Plaies and Notes therof per formane for Common Pollicie[1]

In Mackbeth at the Glob, 1610 ⟨1611⟩, the 20 of Aprill ♄ (Saturday), ther was to be observed, firste, howe Mackbeth and Bancko, 2 noble men of Scotland, Ridinge thorowe a wod, the ⟨r⟩ stode before them 3 women feiries or Nimphes, And saluted Mackbeth, sayinge, 3 tyms unto him, haille Mackbeth, king of Codon;[2] for thou shalt be a kinge, but shalt beget No kinges, &c. Then said Bancko, What all to Mackbeth And nothing to me. Yes, said the nimphes, haille to thee Bancko, thou shalt beget kinges, yet be no kinge. And so they departed & cam to the Courte of Scotland to Dunkin king of Scotes, and yt was in the dais of Edward the Confessor. And Dunkin bad them both kindly wellcome, And made Mackbeth forth with Prince of Northumberland,[3] and sent him hom to his own castell, and appointed Mackbeth to provid for him, for he would sup with him the next dai at night, & did soe. And Mackebeth contrived to kill Dunkin, & thorowe the persuasion of his wife did that night Murder the kinge in his own Castell, beinge his guest. And ther were many prodigies seen that night & the dai before. And when Mack Beth had murdred the kinge, the blod on his handes could not be washed of by Any meanes, nor from his wives handes, which handled the bloddi daggers in hiding them, By which means they became both moch amazed & Affronted. The murder being knowen, Dunkins 2 sonns fled, the on to England, the ⟨other to⟩ Walles, to save them selves, they being fled, they were supposed guilty of the murder of their father, which was nothinge so. Then was Mackbeth crowned kinge, and then he for feare of Banko, his old companion, that he should beget kinges but be no kinge him selfe, he contrived the death of Banko, and caused him to be Murdred on the way as he Rode. The next night, beinge at supper with his noble men whom he had bid to a feaste to the which also Banco should have com, he began to speake of Noble Banco, and to wish that he wer ther. And as he thus did, standing up to drincke a Carouse to him, the ghoste of Banco came and sate down in his cheier behind him. And he turninge About to sit down Again sawe the goste of Banco, which fronted him so, that he fell into a great passion of fear and fury, Utterynge many wordes about his murder, by which, when they hard that Banco was Murdred they Suspected Mackbet.

Then MackDove fled to England to the kinges sonn, And soe they Raised an Army, And cam into Scotland, and at Dunston Anyse overthrue Mackbet. In the meantyme whille Macdovee was in England, Mackbet slewe Mackdoves wife & children, and after in the battelle Mackdove slewe Mackbet.

Observe Also howe Mackbetes quen did Rise in the night in her slepe, & walke and talked and confessed all, & the docter noted her wordes.

Of Cimbalin king of England.

Remember also the storri of Cymbalin king of England, in Lucius tyme, howe Lucius Cam from Octavus Cesar for Tribut, and being denied, after sent Lucius with a greate Arme of Souldiars who landed at Milford haven, and Affter wer vanquished by Cimbalin, and Lucius taken prisoner, and all by means of 3 outlawes, of the which 2 of them were the sonns of Cimbalim, stolen from him when they were but 2 yers old by an old man whom Cymbalin banished, and he kept them as his own sonns 20 yers with him in A cave. And howe ⟨one⟩ of them slewe Clotan, that was the quens sonn, goinge to Milford haven to sek the love of Innogen the

---

1. *Common Pollicie*: practical use. Forman's title for his notes on plays is not printed in Chambers, but interpolated here from G. Blakemore Evans's transcription in the *Riverside Shakespeare*.

2. Cawdor.

3. Probably Forman's error; Duncan gives Macbeth the title Thane of Cawdor. Duncan's son Malcolm is the Prince of Northumberland.

kinges daughter, whom he had banished also for lovinge his daughter,[4] and howe the Italian that cam from her love conveied him selfe into A Cheste, and said yt was a chest of plate sent from her love & others, to be presented to the kinge. And in the depest of the night, she being aslepe, he opened the cheste, & cam forth of yt, And vewed her in her bed, and the markes of her body, & toke awai her braslet, & after Accused her of adultery to her love, &c. And in thend howe he came with the Romains into England & was taken prisoner, and after Reveled to Innogen, Who had turned her self into mans apparrell & fled to mete her love at Milford haven, & chanchsed to fall on the Cave in the wodes wher her 2 brothers were, & howe by eating a sleping Dram they thought she had bin deed, & laid her in the wodes, & the body of Cloten by her, in her loves apparrell that he left behind him, & howe she was found by Lucius, &c.

In the Winters Talle at the glob 1611 the 15 of maye ☿ ⟨Wednesday⟩.

Observe ther howe Lyontes the kinge of Cicillia was overcom with Jelosy of his wife with the kinge of Bohemia his frind that came to see him, and howe he contrived his death and wold have had his cup berer to have poisoned, who gave the king of Bohemia warning therof & fled with him to Bohemia.

Remember also howe he sent to the Orakell of Appollo & the Annswer of Apollo, that she was giltles and that the king was jelouse &c. and howe Except the child was found Again that was loste the kinge should die without yssue, for the child was caried into Bohemia & ther laid in a forrest & brought up by a sheppard And the kinge of Bohemia his sonn maried that wentch & howe they fled into Cicillia to Leontes, and the sheppard having showed the letter of the nobleman by whom Leontes sent a was ⟨away?⟩ that child and the jewells found about her, she was knowen to be Leontes daughter and was then 16 yers old.

Remember also the Rog[5] that cam in all tottered like coll pixci[6] and howe he feyned him sicke & to have bin Robbed of all that he had and howe he cosened the por man of all his money, and after cam to the shep sher[7] with a pedlers packe & ther cosened them Again of all their money And howe he changed apparrell with the kinge of Bomia his sonn, and then howe he turned Courtier &c. Beware of trustinge feined beggars or fawninge fellouss.

Sir Henry Wotton on *All Is True (Henry VIII)* and the Burning of the Globe (1613)

[Sir Henry Wotton (1568–1639), a highly educated poet and essayist, distinguished diplomat, and finally provost of Eton College, wrote to his nephew Sir Edmund Bacon shortly after the burning of the Globe. Chambers includes several other accounts of this incident in *The Elizabethan Stage,* vol. 2, pp. 419ff. The event is also recorded in John Stow's chronicles and was lamented by poets, including (several years later) Ben Jonson, and held up by Puritan divines like Prynne as an intimation of God's wrath. The excerpt below is from the earliest extant text, *Letters of Sir Henry Wotton to Sir Edmund Bacon* (London, 1661), p. 29.]

Now, to let matters of State sleep, I will entertain you at the present with what hath happened this week at the banks side. The Kings Players had a new Play, called *All is true,* representing some principall pieces of the raign of *Henry* 8, which was set forth with many extraordinary circumstances of Pomp and Majesty, even to the matting of the stage; the Knights of the Order, with their Georges and Garter, the Guards with their embroidered Coats, and the like: sufficient in truth within a while to make

---

4. Morgan/Belarius is not banished in the version of the play that comes down to us.
5. Rogue (Autolycus).

6. Probably "colt-pixie," a mischievous sprite or fairy.
7. Sheep shearing.

greatness very familiar, if not ridiculous. Now, King *Henry* making a Masque at the Cardinal, *Wolsey*'s house, and certain Chambers[1] being shot off at his entry, some of the paper, or other stuff wherewith one of them was stopped, did light on the thatch, where being thought at first but an idle smoak, and their eyes more attentive to the show, it kindled inwardly, and ran round like a train, consuming within less then an hour the whole house to the very grounds.

This was the fatal period of that vertuous fabrique, wherein yet nothing did perish, but wood and straw, and a few forsaken cloaks; only one man had his breeches set on fire, that would perhaps have broyled him, if he had not by the benefit of a provident wit put it out with bottle Ale. The rest when we meet.

Ben Jonson on *The Tempest* (and *Titus Andronicus*) (1614)

[This extract from *Bartholomew Fair* contains one of several allusions to Shakespeare in the plays of his associate and sometime rival. The first paragraph alludes to the fashion for revenge plays such as Shakespeare's *Titus Andronicus* and Kyd's *Spanish Tragedy*, at its height roughly twenty-five years before *Bartholomew Fair* was written. The second paragraph refers disapprovingly to *The Tempest* (1613), first produced shortly before *Bartholomew Fair*. The text is that reprinted in *WS*, vol. 2, from the 1631 edition of Jonson's play (from the play's Induction).]

Hee that will sweare, *Jeronimo,* or *Andronicus* are the best playes, yet, shall passe unexcepted at,[1] heere, as a man whose Judgement shewes it is constant, and hath stood still, these five and twentie, or thirtie yeeres. . . .

If there bee never a *Servant-monster* i' the Fayre; who can helpe it? he[2] sayes; nor a nest of Antiques?[3] Hee is loth to make Nature afraid[4] in his *Playes,* like those that beget *Tales, Tempests,* and such like *Drolleries,* to mix his head with other mens heeles; let the concupisence of *Jigges* and *Dances,* raigne as strong as it will amongst you.[5]

Shakespeare's Will (March 25, 1616)

[Shakespeare probably dictated this will sometime around January 1616. The first draft seems to have been dated in January, and 1616 is the most likely inference for the year (see note 1). The final revision was certainly made on the date given, but no clean copy was prepared, so the manuscript contains a substantial number of insertions and deletions. The text here has been silently emended to assist in ease of reading. Deleted passages have been eliminated; the most significant of these is reproduced in the notes, where significant interlineations are also identified. Most of the altered passages, as Chambers writes, simply "correct slips, make the legal terminology more precise, or incorporate afterthoughts." The revision of the will was occasioned chiefly by the February marriage of Shakespeare's daughter Judith. Our text is adapted from E. A. J. Honigmann and Susan Brock, eds., *Playhouse Wills, 1558–1642* (Manchester: Manchester University Press, 1993). For a facsimile and thorough discussion of the will, see *WS* 2:169–80.]

1. Small pieces of artillery, used for firing salutes.
1. Uncriticized.
2. The author.
3. Variant spelling of "antics," grotesque or ludicrous representations, or the actors (such as the clowns in *The Tempest*) playing such parts.
4. Make nature afraid by inexact imitation or too much

fantasy.
5. *concupisence . . . you:* a reference to the dance generally incorporated into theatrical performance (see, for example, Platter's account above). Jonson suggests he is refusing to cater to the vulgar taste for more dancing in plays.

Testamentum willelmij Shackspeare
Vicesimo Quinto die martij Anno Regni Domini nostri Jacobi nunc Regis Anglie &c
decimo quarto & Scotie xlixo Annoque domini 1616[1]
In the name of god Amen I William Shackspeare of Stratford upon Avon in the countie of warrwick gentleman in perfect health & memorie god be praysed doe make &
Ordayne this my last will & testament in manner & forme followeing That ys to saye
ffirst I Comend my Soule into the handes of god my Creator hoping & assuredlie
beleeving through thonelie merittes of Jesus Christe my Saviour to be made partaker
of lyfe everlastinge And my bodye to the Earth whereof yt ys made Item I Gyve &
bequeath unto my Daughter Judyth One Hundred & ffyftie poundes of lawfull English money to be paied unto her in manner & forme followeing That ys to saye One
Hundred Poundes in discharge of her marriage porcion[2] within one yeare after my
Deceas with consideracion[3] after the Rate of twoe shillinges in the pound for soe
long tyme as the same shalbe unpaied unto her after my deceas & the ffyftie poundes
Residewe thereof upon her Surrendring of or gyving of such sufficient securitie as
the overseers of this my Will shall like of to Surrender or graunnte All her[4] estate &
Right that shall discend or come unto her after my deceas or that shee nowe hath of
in or to one Copiehold tenemente with thappurtenaunces lyeing & being in Stratford upon Avon aforesaied in the saied countie of warrwick being parcell or holden
of the mannour of Rowington unto my Daughter Susanna Hall & her heires for ever
Item I Gyve & bequeath unto my saied Daughter Judith One Hundred & ffyftie
Poundes more if shee or Anie issue of her bodie be Lyvinge att thend of three Yeares
next ensueing the daie of the Date of this my Will during which tyme my executours
to paie her consideracion from my deceas according to the Rate afore saied And if
she dye within the saied terme without issue of her bodye then my will ys & I doe
gyve & bequeath One Hundred Poundes thereof to my Neece Elizabeth Hall & the
ffiftie Poundes to be sett fourth by my executours during the lief of my Sister Johane
Harte & the use & proffitt thereof Cominge shalbe payed to my saied Sister Jone &
after her deceas the saied l li[5] shall Remaine Amongst the children of my saied Sister Equallie to be Devided Amongst them But if my saied Daughter Judith be lyving
att thend of the saied three Yeares or anie yssue of her bodye then my Will ys & soe
I devise & bequeath the saied Hundred & ffyftie poundes to be sett out by my executours & overseers for the best benefitt of her & her issue & the stock[6] not to be paied
unto her soe long as she shalbe marryed & Covert Baron[7] but my will ys that she shall
have the consideracon yearelie paied unto her during her lief & after her deceas the
saied stock and consideracion to bee paied to her children if she have Anie & if not
to her executours or assignes she lyving the saied terme after my deceas Provided that
if such husbond as she shall att thend of the saied three Yeares be marryed unto
or attaine after doe sufficientle Assure unto her & thissue of her bodie landes
Awnswereable to the porcion by this my will gyven unto her & to be adjudged soe by
my executours & overseers then my will ys that the saied Cl li[8] shalbe paied to such
husbond as shall make such assurance to his owne use Item I gyve & bequeath unto
my saied sister Jone xx li & all my wearing Apparrell to be paied & Delivered within
one yeare after my deceas And I doe Will & devise unto her the house with thappurtenaunces in Stratford wherein she dwelleth for her naturall lief under the yearelie Rent of xii d. Itm I gyve & bequeath unto her three sonns William Harte[9]

1. *Testamentum . . . 1616:* The Will of William
Shakespeare (marginal heading). On the twenty-fifth
day of March, in the fourteenth year of the reign of
our lord James now King of England, etc., and of Scotland the forty-ninth, in the year of our Lord 1616.
(The abbreviation for "January" is crossed out in the
manuscript, "March" having been substituted at the
time the will was revised.)
2. The phrase "in discharge of her marriage porcion"
was inserted during the course of revision.

3. Compensation, or interest.
4. Susanna Hall's. (The preceding "All" marks the
beginning of a new sentence.)
5. *l li:* £50.
6. Principal.
7. *Covert Baron:* under the protection of a husband.
8. *Cl li:* £150.
9. A blank in the manuscript. Shakespeare appears to
have forgotten the name of one of his nephews,
Thomas.

hart & Michaell Harte ffyve poundes A peece to be payed within one Yeare after my deceas[1] Item I gyve & bequeath unto her the saied Elizabeth Hall All my Plate (except my brod silver & gilt bole)[2] that I nowe have att the Date of this my Will Itm I gyve & bequeath unto the Poore of Stratford aforesaied tenn poundes to mr Thomas Combe my Sword to Thomas Russell Esquier ffyve poundes & to ffrauncis Collins of the Borough of Warrwick in the countie of Warrwick gentleman thirteene poundes Six shillinges & Eight pence to be paied within one Yeare after my Deceas Itm I gyve & bequeath to Hamlett Sadler xxvi s viii d[3] to buy him A Ringe to William Raynoldes gentleman xxvi s viii d to buy him A Ringe to my godson William Walker xx s in gold to Anthonye Nashe gentleman xxvi s viii d & to mr John Nashe xx vi s viii d & to my fellows John Hemynnges Richard Burbage & Henry Cundell xxvi s viii d A peece to buy them Ringes[4] Item I Gyve Will bequeath & Devise unto my Daughter Susanna Hall for better enabling of her to performe this my will & towardes the performans thereof All that Capitall messuage or tenemente[5] with thappurtenaunces in Stratford aforesaied Called the newe place Wherein I nowe Dwell & twoe messuages or tenementes with thappurtenaunces scituat lyeing & being in Henley streete within the borough of Stratford aforesaied And all my barnes stables Orchardes gardens landes tenementes & hereditamentes[6] Whatsoever scituat lyeing & being or to be had Receyved perceyved or taken within the townes Hamlettes villages ffieldes & groundes of Stratford upon Avon Oldstratford Bushopton & Welcombe or in anie of them in the saied countie of warrwick And alsoe All that Messuage or tenemente with thappurtenaunces wherein one John Robinson dwelleth scituat lyeing & being in the blackfriers in London nere the Wardrobe & all other my landes tenementes & hereditamentes Whatsoever To Have & to hold All & singuler the saied premisses with their Appurtenaunces unto the saied Susanna Hall for & During the terme of her naturall lief & after her Deceas to the first sonne of her bodie lawfullie Issueing & to the heires males of the bodie of the saied first Sonne lawfullie Issueinge & for defalt of such issue to the second Sonne of her bodie lawfullie issueinge & to the heires males of the bodie of the saied Second Sonne lawfullie issueinge & for defalt of such heires to the third Sonne of the bodie of the saied Susanna Lawfullie issueing & of the heries males of the bodie of the saied third sonne lawfullie issueing And for defalt of such issue the same soe to be & Remaine to the ffourth ffyfth sixte & Seaventh sonnes of her bodie lawfullie issueing one after Another & to the heires[7] Males of the bodies of the saied ffourth fifth Sixte & Seaventh sonnes lawfullie issueing in such manner as yt ys before Lymitted to be & Remaine to the first second & third Sonns of her bodie & to their heires males And for defalt of such issue the saied premisses to be & Remaine to my sayed Neece Hall[8] & the heires Males of her bodie Lawfullie yssueing for Defalt of such issue to my Daughter Judith & the heires Males of her bodie lawfullie issueinge And for Defalt of such issue to the Right heires of me the saied William

1. *unto . . . deceas:* this passage was inserted at the top of the second page, probably when the will was revised. The following lines, with which the page originally began, are crossed out in the original: "to be sett out for her within one Yeare after my Deceas by my executours with thadvise & direccions of my overseers for her best proffitt untill her Marriage & then the same with the increase thereof to be paied unto her." These lines evidently referred to Judith Shakespeare as unmarried.
2. This parenthetical clause is an insertion, and has sparked some debate about Shakespeare's opinion of Judith's marriage.
3. The "s" stands for "shillings," the "d" for "pence."
4. *to my fellows . . . Ringes:* Shakespeare's "fellows," or colleagues, Heminges, Burbage, and Condell, had worked with him in the Lord Chamberlain's Men and

King's Men for many years. Many other wills and documents of the period provide evidence of the practice of wearing mourning rings alluded to here.
5. Residence. *messuage:* dwelling house with its outbuildings or adjoining lands.
6. Heritable property.
7. In addition to the signature near the end, Shakespeare signed the will here, in the bottom right-hand corner of the second page.
8. Susanna Hall's daughter Elizabeth, actually Shakespeare's granddaughter (the sense of "niece" is less restricted in early modern usage). Elizabeth proved to be Susanna's only surviving child, and since Susanna was already thirty-three in 1616, the hypothetical series of seven sons preceding this mention of Elizabeth is doubly remarkable.

Shackspere for ever Itm I gyve unto my wief my second best bed[9] with the furniture Item I gyve & bequeath to my saied Daughter Judith my broad silver gilt bole
All the Rest of my goodes Chattelles Leases plate Jewels & household stuffe
Whatsoever after my dettes and Legasies paied & my funerall expences discharged
I gyve Devise & bequeath to my Sonne in Lawe John Hall gentleman & my Daughter Susanna his wief Whom I ordaine & make executours of this my Last Will &
testament And I doe intreat & Appoint the saied Thomas Russell Esquier &
ffrauncis Collins gentleman to be overseers hereof And doe Revoke All former
wills & publishe this to be my last Will & testament In Witnes Whereof I have here
unto put my hand the Daie & Yeare first above Written. /   By me
William Shakespeare witnes to the publishing hereof Fra: Collyns Julyus Shawe
John Robinson Hamnet Sadler Robert Whattcott[1]

Front Matter from the First Folio of Shakespeare's Plays (1623)

[John Heminges and Henry Condell, friends and colleagues of Shakespeare, organized
this first publication of his collected (thirty-six) plays. Eighteen of the plays had not
appeared in print before, and for these the First Folio is the sole surviving source. Only
Pericles, The Two Noble Kinsmen, and *Sir Thomas More* are not included in the volume.
Four of the first twelve (printed) pages of the Folio are reproduced below in reduced facsimile. They include Jonson's brief address "To the Reader," Droeshout's portrait of
Shakespeare, a table of contents, and a list of actors.]

---

9. This bequest to Shakespeare's wife, Anne, was
inserted in the course of his revision of the will. She
is not mentioned elsewhere in the will at least partly
because, as Shakespeare's widow, she would be guaranteed a certain portion of the estate by law. The
appearance of this inserted bequest is nevertheless

strange enough to have evoked much speculation.
1. After Shakespeare's death, the will was endorsed
here at the bottom of the third page with a Latin
inscription indicating that the will had gone to pro-
bate before a magistrate on June 22, 1616.

To the Reader.

This Figure, that thou here seeſt put,
 It was for gentle Shakeſpeare cut;
Wherein the Grauer had a ſtrife
 with Nature, to out-doo the life :
O, could he but haue drawne his wit
 As well in braſſe, as he hath hit
His face ; the Print would then ſurpaſſe
 All, that vvas euer vvrit in braſſe.
But, ſince he cannot, Reader, looke
 Not on his Picture, but his Booke.

         B. I.

Mr. WILLIAM

SHAKESPEARES

COMEDIES,
HISTORIES, &
TRAGEDIES.

Published according to the True Originall Copies.

Martin Droeshout sculpsit London.

LONDON

Printed by Isaac Iaggard, and Ed. Blount. 1623.

A CATALOGVE

of the seuerall Comedies, Histories, and Tragedies contained in this Volume.

The Workes of William Shakespeare,

containing all his Comedies, Histories, and
Tragedies: Truely set forth, according to their first
ORIGINALL.

The Names of the Principall Actors
in all these Playes.

William Shakespeare.	Samuel Gilburne.
Richard Burbadge.	Robert Armin.
John Hemmings.	William Ostler.
Augustine Phillips.	Nathan Field.
William Kempt.	John Underwood.
Thomas Poope.	Nicholas Tooley.
George Bryan.	William Ecclestone.
Henry Condell.	Joseph Taylor.
William Slye.	Robert Benfield.
Richard Cowly.	Robert Goughe.
John Lowine.	Richard Robinson.
Samuell Crosse.	Iohn Shancke.
Alexander Cooke.	Iohn Rice.

John Milton on Shakespeare (1630)

[John Milton (1608–1674) was born in London and as a boy might conceivably have seen Shakespeare's company act. This poem first appeared prefixed to the Second Folio of Shakespeare's works in 1632 and again in the 1640 *Poems* of Shakespeare. The text is from the 1645 edition of Milton's *Poems*, as reprinted in *WS*, vol. 2, but the title given is from the Second Folio version.]

An Epitaph on the admirable Dramaticke Poet, W. Shakespeare

What needs my *Shakespear* for his honour'd Bones,
The labour of an age in piled Stones,
Or that his hallow'd reliques should be hid
Under a star-ypointing[1] *Pyramid?*
Dear son of memory, great heir of Fame,
What need'st thou such weak witnes of thy name?
Thou in our wonder and astonishment
Hast built thy self a live-long Monument.
For whilst toth' shame of slow-endeavouring art,
They easie numbers flow, and that each heart
Hath from the leaves of thy unvalu'd[2] Book,
Those Delphick[3] lines with deep impression took,
Then thou our fancy of itself bereaving,[4]
Dost make us Marble with too much conceaving;
And so Sepulcher'd in such pomp dost lie,
That Kings for such a Tomb would wish to die.

Ben Jonson on Shakespeare (1623–37)

[In addition to numerous allusions to Shakespeare in his plays, Ben Jonson (1573–1637) writes explicitly about his friend, colleague, and rival in a number of places, most significantly in the two commendatory poems prefixed to the First Folio (see above) and in the published extracts from his notebooks entitled *Timber: or, Discoveries; Made upon Men and Matter,* first published in his *Works* of 1640. It is impossible to date the original entries precisely; Chambers's conjecture is that the following entry on Shakespeare was made after 1630. The text is from the authoritative edition by C. H. Herford and Percy Simpson, vol. 8 (Oxford: Clarendon Press, 1952).]

Indeed, the multitude commend Writers, as they doe Fencers, or Wrastlers; who if they come in robustiously, and put for it, with a deale of violence, are received for the *braver-fellowes:* when many times their owne rudenesse is a cause of their disgrace; and a slight touch of their Adversary, gives all that boisterous force the foyle. But in these things, the unskilfull are naturally deceiv'd, and judging wholly by the bulke, thinke rude things greater then polish'd; and scatter'd more numerous, then compos'd: Nor thinke this only to be true in the sordid multitude, but the neater sort of our *Gallants:* for all are the multitude; only they differ in cloaths, not in judgement or understanding.

I remember, the Players have often mentioned it as an honour to *Shakespeare,*

---

1. Pointing to the stars.
2. Invaluable.
3. Reference to Apollo, god of poetry, whose most famous shrine was at Delphi.

4. *our . . . bereaving:* "our imaginations are rapt 'out of ourselves,' leaving behind our soulless bodies like statues"—Isabel MacCaffrey.

that in his writing, (whatsoever he penn'd) hee never blotted out line.[1] My answer hath beene, Would he had blotted a thousand. Which they thought a malevolent speech. [I had not told posterity this,] but for their ignorance, who choose that circumstance to commend their friend by, wherein he most faulted. And to justifie mine owne candor, (for I lov'd the man, and doe honour his memory (on this side Idolatry) as much as any.) Hee was (indeed) honest, and of an open, and free nature: had an excellent *Phantsie*[2]; brave notions, and gentle expressions: wherein hee flow'd with that facility, that sometime it was necessary he should be stop'd: *Sufflaminandus erat;*[3] as *Augustus* said of *Haterius*.[4] His wit was in his owne power; would the rule of it had beene so too. Many times hee fell into those things, could not escape laughter: As when hee said in the person of *Cæsar*, one speaking to him; *Cæsar, thou dost me wrong*. Hee replyed: *Cæsar did never wrong, but with just cause*[5]: and such like; which were ridiculous. But hee redeemed his vices, with his vertues. There was ever more in him to be praysed, then to be pardoned.

John Aubrey on Shakespeare (1681)

[What Chambers calls "the Shakespeare-mythos" was already well under way by the time John Aubrey (1626–1697) collected these anecdotes for the biographies in his *Brief Lives*, first anthologized in 1692. Aubrey's chief sources were prominent figures of the Restoration stage, which had seen increasingly popular revivals and adaptations of *Hamlet, The Tempest,* and many other plays of Shakespeare. Numerous actors and critics in the latter part of the seventeenth century helped to "rehabilitate" Shakespeare; if at the time of the Restoration his plays had seemed terribly musty and old-fashioned, by the 1680s his reputation as an author of lasting value was well established, thanks to the enthusiasm of Restoration playgoers. Aubrey's first source, Christopher Beeston, was the son of a one-time member of Shakespeare's company. William Davenant was a formidable entrepreneur as well as a dramatist, and Thomas Shadwell a prolific playwright perhaps best remembered as Dryden's King of Dullness. The text is from Chambers's transcription (*WS*, vol. 2), with a few silent emendations for ease of reading. Some of the material is from the published version of *Brief Lives*, and some of it from manuscript notes apparently used in writing the *Lives*.]

> the more to be admired q[uia][1] he was not a company keeper[2]
> lived in Shoreditch, wouldnt be debauched, & if invited to
> writ; he was in paine.[3]
>
> W. Shakespeare.

M[r]. William Shakespear. [*bay-wreath in margin*] was borne at Stratford upon Avon, in the County of Warwick; his father was a Butcher, & I have been told heretofore by some of the neighbours, that when he was a boy he exercised his father's Trade, but when he kill'd a Calfe, he would doe it in a *high style,* & make a Speech. There was at that time another Butcher's son in this Towne, that was held not at all inferior to him for a naturall witt, his acquaintance & coetanean,[4] but dyed young. This Wm. being inclined naturally to Poetry and acting, came to London I guesse about 18. and was an Actor at one of the Play-houses and did act

---

1. Compare Heminges and Condell's address to the reader in the First Folio: "And what he thought, he uttered with that easinesse, that wee have scarse received from him a blot in his papers."
2. Imagination.
3. "He needed the drag-chain" (adapted from Marcus Seneca's *Controversiae* 4, Preface).
4. Quintus Haterius, Roman rhetorician (d. 26 C.E.).
5. See *Julius Caesar* 3.1.47.

1. Because.
2. "Company keeper" can mean "libertine" or "reveler"; the general sense of the passage is that Shakespeare is "the more to be admired" for his temperance and modesty.
3. The embarrassment ("paine") at being asked to write is presumably due to the same alleged modesty.
4. Contemporary.

exceedingly well: now B. Johnson was never a good Actor, but an excellent Instructor. He began early to make essayes at Dramatique Poetry, which at that time was very lowe; and his Playes tooke well: He was a handsome well shap't man: very good company, and of a very readie and pleasant smooth Witt. The Humour[5] of . . . the Constable in a Midsomersnight's Dreame, he happened to take at Grendon [*In margin*, 'I thinke it was Midsomer night that he happened to lye there'.] in Bucks[6] which is the roade from London to Stratford, and there was living that Constable about 1642 when I first came to Oxon.[7] M[r]. Jos. Howe is of that parish and knew him. Ben Johnson and he did gather Humours of men dayly where ever they came. One time as he was at the Tavern at Stratford super[8] Avon, one Combes an old rich Usurer was to be buryed, he makes there this extemporary[9] Epitaph

> Ten in the Hundred[1] the Devill allowes
> But *Combes* will have twelve, he sweares & vowes:
> If any one askes who lies in this Tombe:
> Hoh! quoth the Devill, 'Tis my John o' Combe.

He was wont to goe to his native Country once a yeare. I thinke I have been told that he left 2 or 300[li] per annum[2] there and therabout: to a sister. [*In margin*, 'V.[3] his Epitaph in Dugdales Warwickshire'.] I have heard S[r] Wm. Davenant and M[r]. Thomas Shadwell (who is counted the best Comœdian we have now) say, that he had a most prodigious Witt, and did admire his naturall parts beyond all other Dramaticall writers. He was wont to say, That he never blotted out a line in his life: sayd Ben: Johnson, I wish he had blotted out a thousand. [*In margin*, 'B. Johnsons Underwoods'.] His Comœdies will remaine witt, as long as the English tongue is understood; for that he handles mores hominum;[4] now our present writers reflect so much upon particular persons, and coxcombeities, that 20 yeares hence, they will not be understood. Though as Ben: Johnson sayes of him, that he had but little Latine and lesse Greek, He understood Latine pretty well: for he had been in his younger yeares a Schoolmaster in the Countrey. [*In margin*, 'from M[r] —— Beeston'.]

S[r] William Davenant Knight Poet Laureate was borne in _____ street in the City of Oxford, at the Crowne Tavern. His father was John Davenant a Vintner there, a very grave and discreet Citizen: his mother was a very beautifull woman, & of a very good witt and of conversation extremely agreable. . . . M[r] William Shakespeare was wont to goe into Warwickshire once a yeare, and did commonly in his journey lye at this house in Oxon: where he was exceedingly respected. I have heard parson Robert D[avenant] say that here M[r] W. Shakespeare here gave him a hundred kisses. Now S[r] Wm. would sometimes when he was pleasant over a glasse of wine with his most intimate friends e.g. Sam: Butler (author of Hudibras) &c. say, that it seemed to him that he writt with the very spirit that Shakespeare,[5] and seemed contented enough to be thought his Son: he would tell them the story as above. in which way his mother had a very light report, whereby she was called a whore.

5. Character, personality.
6. Buckinghamshire.
7. Oxford.
8. Upon.
9. Extemporaneous.
1. 10-percent interest. (Combe is damned because he charges 12 percent on his loans, 2 percent above the maximum allowed for usury not to be a mortal sin.)
2. £300 a year.
3. See.
4. *for that . . . hominum*: because he treats of (general) human manners or customs.
5. A word such as "had" seems to be missing.

TIMELINE

TEXT	CONTEXT
	1558 Queen Mary I, a Roman Catholic, dies; her sister Elizabeth, raised Protestant, is proclaimed queen.
	1559 Church of England is reestablished under the authority of the sovereign with the passage of the Act of Uniformity and the Act of Supremacy.
1562 *The Tragedy of Gorboduc*, by Thomas Norton and Thomas Sackville, is performed; it is the first English play in blank verse.	**1563** The Church of England adopts the Thirty-nine Articles of Religion, detailing its points of doctrine and clarifying its differences both from Roman Catholicism and from more extreme forms of Protestantism.
	1564 William Shakespeare is born in Stratford to John and Mary Arden Shakespeare; he is christened a few days later, on April 23.
	1565 John Shakespeare is made an alderman of Stratford.
	1567 Mary Queen of Scots is imprisoned on suspicion of the murder of her husband, Lord Darnley. Their infant son, Charles James, is crowned James VI of Scotland.
	1568 John Shakespeare is elected Bailiff of Stratford, the town's highest office. Performances in Stratford by the Queen's Players and the Earl of Worcester's men.
	1572 An act is passed that severely punishes vagrants and wanderers, including actors not affiliated with a patron. Performances in Stratford by the Earl of Leicester's men.
	1574 The Earl of Warwick's and Earl of Worcester's men perform in Stratford.
	1576 James Burbage, father of Richard, later the leading actor in Shakespeare's company, builds the Theatre in Shoreditch, a suburb of London.
	1577 The Curtain Theatre opens in Shoreditch.

TEXT	CONTEXT
	1577–1580 Sir Francis Drake circumnavigates the globe.
	1578 Mary Shakespeare pawns her lands, suggesting that the family is in financial distress. Lord Strange's Men and Lord Essex's Men perform at Stratford.
	1580 A Jesuit mission is established in England with the aim of reconverting the nation to Roman Catholicism.
	1582 Shakespeare marries Anne Hathaway.
	1583 The birth of Shakespeare's older daughter, Susanna.
	1584 Sir Walter Ralegh establishes the first English colony in the New World at Roanoke Island in modern North Carolina; the colony fails.
	1585 The birth of Shakespeare's twin son and daughter, Hamnet and Judith. John Shakespeare is fined for not going to church.
	1586 Sir Philip Sidney dies from battle wounds.
1587 Thomas Kyd's *The Spanish Tragedy* (pub. c. 1592) and Christopher Marlowe's *Tamburlaine* (pub. 1590) are performed.	1587 Mary Queen of Scots is executed for treason against Elizabeth I. Francis Drake defeats the Spanish fleet at Cádiz. John Shakespeare loses his position as an alderman. Philip Henslowe builds the Rose theater at Bankside, on the Thames.
	1588 The Spanish Armada attempts an invasion of England but is defeated.
1589 Robert Greene, *Friar Bacon and Friar Bungay*. Thomas Kyd, *Hamlet* (not extant; perhaps a source for Shakespeare's *Hamlet*). Christopher Marlowe, *The Jew of Malta*.	1589 Shakespeare is probably affiliated with the amalgamated Lord Strange's and Lord Admiral's Men from about this time until 1594.
1590 Anonymous, *The True Chronicle History of King Leir, and his Three Daughters*.	1590 James VI of Scotland marries Anne of Denmark, but believes himself to be bewitched on his honeymoon when he cannot consummate the marriage. Witch trials in Scotland.
1591 Shakespeare's *1, 2*, and *3 Henry VI* performed.	1592 The theatrical manager of the Admiral's Men, Philip Henslowe, begins his diary, continued until 1604, recording his business

TEXT	CONTEXT
	transactions, an important source for theater historians.
1592–1593 *Richard III.* *Venus and Adonis.* *The Comedy of Errors.* *Titus Andronicus.* *The Taming of the Shrew.*	From June 1592 to June 1594, London theaters are shut down because of the plague; acting companies tour the provinces.
1594 Shakespeare dedicates *The Rape of Lucrece* to Henry Wriothesley, Earl of Southampton.	**1594** Roderigo Lopez, Portuguese physician and a Jewish convert to Christianity, is executed on slight evidence for having plotted to poison Elizabeth I.
1594–1596 *A Midsummer Night's Dream.* *Richard II.* *Romeo and Juliet.*	The birth of James VI's first son, Henry.
	1595 Shakespeare lives in St. Helen's Parish, Bishopsgate, London. Shakespeare apparently becomes a sharer in (provides capital for) the newly re-formed Lord Chamberlain's Men. The Swan Theatre is built in Bankside. Hugh O'Neill, Earl of Tyrone, rebels against English rule in Ireland. Walter Ralegh explores Guiana, on the north coast of South America.
1596 *King John.* *The Merchant of Venice.* *1 Henry IV.*	**1596** John Shakespeare is granted a coat of arms; hence the title of "gentleman." William Shakespeare's son Hamnet dies.
1597 *The Merry Wives of Windsor.*	**1597** James Burbage builds the second Blackfriars Theatre. But the Lord Chamberlain's Men are not permitted to play in it, so they rent it to boys' companies for a number of years. The landlord refuses to renew the lease on the land under the Theatre in Shoreditch.
1598 *2 Henry IV.* *Much Ado About Nothing.* Ben Jonson, *Every Man in His Humor,* which lists Shakespeare as one of the actors.	**1598** The Edict of Nantes ends the French civil wars, granting toleration to Protestants. Materials from the demolished Theatre in Shoreditch are transported across the Thames to be used in building the Globe Theatre.
1599 *Henry V.* *Julius Caesar.* *As You Like it.*	**1599** The queen's favorite, Robert Devereux, Earl of Essex, leads an expedition to Ireland in March but returns home without permission in October and is imprisoned. Satires and other offensive books are prohibited by ecclesiastical order. Extant copies are gathered and burned. Two notorious satirists, Thomas Nashe and Gabriel Harvey, are forbidden to publish.

TEXT	CONTEXT
1600 *Hamlet.* Michael Drayton and several collaborators, who object to Shakespeare's depiction of Oldcastle-Falstaff in the *Henry IV* plays, write *The First Part of the True and Honorable History of the Life of Sir John Oldcastle, the Good Lord Cobham.*	**1600** The Earl of Essex is suspended from some of his offices and confined to house arrest. The birth of James VI's second son, Charles. The founding of the East India Company. Edward Alleyn and Philip Henslowe build the Fortune Theatre for the Lord Admiral's Men, competing with the Lord Chamberlain's Men at the Globe.
1601 "The Phoenix and the Turtle" published in Robert Chester's *Love's Martyr.* *Twelfth Night.* In the "War of the Theaters," Ben Jonson, John Marston, and Thomas Dekker write a series of satiric plays mocking one another.	**1601** The Earl of Essex leads some gentlemen against Elizabeth I, but the rising is quickly quelled. A few of the rebels, including Shakespeare's patron, the Earl of Southampton, arrange a staging of *Richard II* at the Globe, apparently to incite rebellion. Essex is convicted of treason and beheaded. Shakespeare's father dies.
1602 *Troilus and Cressida.*	**1602** Shakespeare makes substantial real-estate purchases in Stratford. The opening of the Bodleian Library in Oxford.
	1603 Queen Elizabeth dies; she is succeeded by her cousin, James VI of Scotland (now James I of England). Shakespeare's name appears for the last time in Ben Jonson's lists of actors, as a "principal tragedian" in *Sejanus.* Plague closes the London theaters from mid-1603 to April 1604. Hugh O'Neill surrenders in Ireland.
1604 *Measure for Measure.* *Othello.*	**1604** The conclusion of a peace with Spain makes travel across the Atlantic safer, encouraging plans for English colonies in the Americas.
1605 *All's Well That Ends Well.* *King Lear.*	**1605** The discovery of the Gunpowder Plot by some radical Catholics to blow up the Houses of Parliament during its opening ceremonies, when the royal family, Lords, and Commons are assembled in one place. The Red Bull Theatre built.
1606 *Macbeth.* *Antony and Cleopatra.* Ben Jonson, *Volpone.* Anonymous, *The Revenger's Tragedy.*	**1606** The London and Plymouth Companies receive charters to colonize Virginia. Parliament passes "An Act to Restrain Abuses of Players," prohibiting oaths or blasphemy onstage.
1607 *Timon of Athens.* *Pericles.*	**1607** An English colony is established in Jamestown, Virginia. Shakespeare's daughter Susanna marries John Hall. Shakespeare's brother Edmund (described as a player) dies.

TEXT	CONTEXT
1608 *Coriolanus.*	1608 The King's Men obtain permission to play at the second Blackfriars Theatre, a smaller indoor venue.
1609 *Cymbeline.* Unauthorized publication of the sonnets.	
1610 *The Winter's Tale.* Ben Jonson, *The Alchemist.*	1610 Henry is made Prince of Wales. Shakespeare probably returns to Stratford and settles there.
1611 *The Tempest.* Francis Beaumont and John Fletcher, *A King and No King.* Publication of the Authorized (King James) Bible.	1611 Plantation of Ulster in Ireland, a colony of English and Scottish Protestants settled on land confiscated from Irish rebels.
1612 *All Is True (Henry VIII),* with John Fletcher. John Webster, *The White Devil.*	1612 Prince Henry dies.
1613 *The Two Noble Kinsmen,* with John Fletcher.	1613 Princess Elizabeth marries Frederick V, Elector Palatine. The Globe Theatre burns down during a performance of *All Is True.*
1614 Ben Jonson, *Bartholomew Fair.* John Webster, *The Duchess of Malfi.*	1614 Philip Henslowe and Jacob Meade build the Hope Theatre, used both for play performances and as a bearbaiting arena. The Globe Theatre reopens.
1616 Ben Jonson publishes *The Works of Benjamin Jonson,* the first collection of plays by an English author.	1616 William Harvey describes the circulation of the blood. Shakespeare's daughter Judith marries. Shakespeare dies on April 23.
1623 Members of the King's Men publish the First Folio of Shakespeare's plays.	

Textual Variants

THE TWO GENTLEMEN OF VERONA

CONTROL TEXT: F

F: The Folio of 1623
Fa, Fb: Successive states of F incorporating various print-shop corrections and changes

s.p. PANTHINO [F sometimes refers to Antonio's servant as *Panthino* and sometimes as *Panthion*. Standardized as *Panthino* throughout.]

1.1.26 **swam** swom **43 doting** eating **65 leave** loue **66 metamorphosed** metamorphis'd **76 a sheep** Sheepe **133 testerned** cestern'd **136 wreck** wrack

1.2.83 **o' love** O'Loue **97 your** you **99 bauble** babble

1.3.50 **O** Pro⟨*teus*⟩. Oh **88 father** Fathers

2.1.100 **stead** steed

2.3.24 **moved woman** would-woman

2.4.101 **worthy** worthy a **157 braggartism** Bragadisme **159 makes** make **189 Is it** It is **189 mine eye, or** mine, or

2.5.1 **Milan** *Padua* **35 that** that that

3.1.81 **of Verona** in *Verona* **269 catalogue** Cate-log **269 conditions** Condition **289 Try** [Fb] thy [Fa] **297 sew** sowe **311 follows** [Fa] follow [Fb] **313 be broken with** be **320 talk** [Fb] take [Fa] **322 villain** [Fb] villanie [Fa] **329 love** [Fb] lone [Fa] **339 hair** [Fb] haires [Fa] **342 last** [Fb; not in Fa]

3.2.14 **grievously** [Fb] heauily [Fa]

4.1.34 **I had been often** I often had beene often **44 aweful** awfull **47 An heir, and near** And heire and Neece,

4.2.107 **his** her

4.3.17 **abhors** abhor'd

4.4.48 **hangman boys** Hangmans boyes **54 on end** an end **62 thou** thee **66 to** not **165 beholden** beholding

5.2.7 s.p. JULIA Pro⟨*teus*⟩. **13** s.p. JULIA Thu⟨*rio*⟩. **18 your** you

5.3.7 **Moses** Moyses

5.4.150 **endowed** endu'd

THE TAMING OF THE SHREW

CONTROL TEXT: F

s.p. KATHERINE [F's use of *Katerina, Katherina, Katerine, Kate,* and *Katherine* has been standardized throughout.]

s.p. PETRUCCIO [F's use of *Petruchio* has been changed throughout.]

s.p. SLY [F's use of *Beggar* has been changed throughout.]

s.p. BARTHOLOMEW [F's use of *Lady* when Bartholomew is dressed as a woman has been changed throughout.]

Induction 1.13 **Breathe** Brach **78** s.p. A PLAYER **2.** *Player* **86** s.p. ANOTHER PLAYER *Sincklo*

Induction 2.2 **lordship** Lord **51 wi'th'** with **91 Greet** Greece

1.1.3 **fore** for **13 Vincentio** Vincentio's **25** *Mi perdonate* Me Pardonato **156 captum** captam **232 faith** 'faith **237 your** you

1.2.18 **masters** mistris **23** *Con tutto il cuore ben trovato* Contutti le core bene trobatto **24** *ben* bene **24** *molto onorato* multo honorata **31 pip** peepe **43 this'** this **70 as** is as **115 me and other more,** me. Other more **167 help me** helpe one **185** Antonio's *Butonios* **186 his fortune** my fortune **209 ours** yours **263 feat** seeke **278** *ben* Been

2.1.8 **thee** [not in F] **60 Licio** Litio [*Licio* is four times referred to as *Lisio* and three times as *Litio* in F. Standardized to "Licio" throughout.] **75–76 wooing. Neighbour** wooing neighbors **78 unto you** vnto **240 askance** asconce **322 in me** **343 cypress** Cypres **367 Marseilles** Marcellus

3.1.4 **this Bianca is,** this **is 28, 32, 41** *Sigeia . . . Sigeia . . . Sigeia* sigeria . . . Sigeria . . . sigeria **46–48** s.p. HORTENSIO **How . . . yet.** [assigned to Lucentio in F] **49** s.p. BIANCA *Lucentio* **50** s.p. LUCENTIO Bian⟨*ca*⟩. **52** s.p. BIANCA Hort⟨*ensio*⟩. **79 change** charge **odd** old **80** s.p. MESSENGER *Nicke.*

3.2.16 **them** [not in F] **29 thy** [not in F] **30 old news** [not in F] **33 hear** heard **51 weighed** Waid **52 half-cheeked** halfe-chekt **84 not** [not in F]

3.3.1 **sir, to love** sir, Loue **3 I** [not in F] **39 vicar** wench

4.1.22 s.p. CURTIS Gru⟨*mio*⟩. **75 sleekly** slickely **99** s.p. GRUMIO Gre⟨*mio*⟩.

4.2.4 s.p. HORTENSIO Luc⟨*entio*⟩. **6** s.p. LUCENTIO Hor⟨*tensio*⟩. **8** s.p. LUCENTIO Hor⟨*tensio*⟩. **13 none** me **31 her** them **72** [ascribed to "*Par.*"] **in** me

4.3.63 s.p. HABERDASHER *Fel.* **81 a** [not in F] **88 like** a like **93 nor cap** neither cap **175 account'st** accountedst

4.4.1 **Sir** Sirs
4.5.5 **he's** has **16 except** expect **26 t'attend**
to come
4.6.19 **is** in **23 so it shall be still** so it shall be
so **39 where is** whether is **79 be** [not in F]
5.1.5 **master's** mistris **43 master's** Mistris **56**
copintank copataine
5.2.2 **done** come **38 thee, lad** the lad **46 two**
too **110 wonders** a wonder **132 a fiue 136**
you're your

The First Part of the Contention of the Two Famous Houses of York and Lancaster (The Second Part of Henry VI)

CONTROL TEXT: F, primarily, and Q1 for some
passages: 1.1.54–70; 2.1.70 s.d.; 2.1.116–53
s.d.; 4.5 initial s.d.–4.6 initial s.d.; and most
of 2.3, from s.d. following line 58 to initial
s.d. in 2.4. In these five passages, readings
taken from F are treated as variants of Q1
and marked as such. In addition, this edition
prints some material from Q not in F but
that derives, the Oxford editors believe, from
a revised version of the Folio text. These passages are also marked in the variants
because they are alterations to the control
text. For discussion of the status of this text,
see the Textual Note; for a much fuller collation and discussion of Quarto and Folio
variants, see Oxford's *William Shakespeare:*
A Textual Companion.

F: The Folio of 1623
Q1: The Quarto of 1594
Q2: The Quarto of 1600
Q3: The Quarto of 1619

s.p. KING HENRY [F's use of *King* has been
changed throughout.]
s.p. QUEEN MARGARET [F's use of *Queen* has
been changed throughout.]
s.p. CARDINAL BEAUFORT [F's use of *Cardinal*
and *Winchester* has been standardized
throughout.]
s.p. GLOUCESTER [F's use of *Gloucester* and
Humphrey has been standardized
throughout.]
s.p. DUCHESS [F's use of *Elianor* and *Duchess*
has been standardized throughout.]
s.p. HORNER [F's use of *Armorer* has been
changed throughout.]
s.p. BOLINGBROKE [F's spelling, *Bulling-*
brooke, has been changed throughout.]
s.p. ASNATH [F's use of *Spirit* (in 1.4) has
been changed.]
s.p. SIMPCOX'S WIFE [F's use of *Wife* (in 2.1)
has been changed.]

s.p. CAPTAIN [F's use of *Lieutenant* (in 4.1)
has been changed to Q's *Captain*.]
s.p. WHITMORE [F's use of *Whitmore* and *Wal-*
ter (in 4.1) has been standardized.]
s.p. FIRST REBEL [F's use of *Bevis* has been
changed throughout.]
s.p. SECOND REBEL [F's use of *Holland* has
been changed throughout.]
s.p. MESSENGER [F's use of *Michael* (in 4.2)
has been changed.]
s.p. STAFFORD'S BROTHER [F's use of *Brother*
(in 4.2) has been changed.]
s.p. WEAVER [F's use of *Smith* and *Weaver* has
been standardized throughout.]
s.p. BUTCHER [F's use of *Dicke* and *Butcher*
has been standardized throughout.]
s.p. REBEL [Q's use of *Robin* has been
changed at 4.7.116 (Q is control text for
this section).]
s.p. CLIFFORD [F's use of *Clifford* and *Old*
Clifford has been standardized
throughout.]
s.p. YOUNG CLIFFORD [F's use of *Clifford* and
Young Clifford has been standardized
throughout.]

Title: *The first part of the contention of the two*
famous / Houses, of Yorke and Lancaster [Q
running title] THE / First part of the Con- /
tention betwixt the two famous Houses of
Yorke / and Lancaster, with the death of the
good / Duke Humphrey: / And the banishment
and death of the Duke of / Suffolke, and the
Tragicall end of the proud Cardinall / of *Win-*
chester, with the notable Rebellion / of *Jacke*
Cade: / And the Duke of Yorkes first claime
unto / the Crowne [Q title page] The second
Part of Henry the Sixt, / with the death of the
Good Duke / HUMFREY [F head title]

1.1.24–29 Th' ... **King** [Q, not in F; for F's
version of this speech, see inset passage in
text.] **24 excess of** excessive **28 naught**
nothing **35 s.p. LORDS** kneel[ing] *All kneel.*
44 René Raynard [Q] Reignier [F] **47 it**
is further agreed between them
[Q; not in F] **49 fa–** [Q] *father* **54–70** [Q is
control text for these lines.] **55 duchy of**
Anjou and the county of Duches of *Anioy*
and of **56 delivered** delivered over
63 I'th [F] in the **89 had** hath **141 But**
I'll . . . speak. [Q; not in F] **166 hoist**
hoyse **175 Protector** [Q] Protectors **189**
thee [Q] the **196–97 The reverence . . .**
command. [Q; not in F] **207 Then let's**
away Then lets make hast away **250 surfeit**
in the surfetting in **255 in** [Q] in in
1.2.19 hour thought **22 dream** dreames **38**
are [Q] wer **75 Jordan** *Jordane* **cunning**
witch of Eye cunning witch [F]

1.3.6 s.p. FIRST PETITIONER *Peter* **33 master** Mistresse **34–36 usurer . . . usurper** [Q] Usurper **45 s.p.** ALL PETITIONERS *All* **72 haught** haughtie **94 their** the **104 helm** [Q] Helme. *Exit.* **146 I'd** [Q] I could [F] **149 pamper** hamper **154 fury** Fume **208 judge by case** judge **215 s.p.** KING HENRY Then . . . of Somerset [Q; not in F] **216–17 We make . . . foes.** We make your grace Regent over the French, / And to defend our rights gainst forraine foes, / And so do good unto the Realme of *France* [Q; not in F] **226 be shall** be

1.4.23 Asnath Asmath **31 Tell me what fate awaits** [Q2, Q3] what fates await **33 betide** [Q] befall **37–38** [For Q's version of these lines, see inset passage in text.] **42 deep** deeply **56–57 What have . . . posse.** [In F, York reads the prophecies aloud at this point; Q transposes this reading to the next scene and assigns it to King Henry at 2.1.177–87]. **56 s.d.** [*He*] *reads* [*the writings*] *Reades.* / *The Duke yet lives, that* Henry *shall depose:* / *But him out-live, and dye a violent death.* **57 Aeacidam** AEacida **posse** posso. / Well, to the rest: / Tell me what fate awaits the Duke of Suffolke? / *By Water shall he dye, and take his end.* / What shall betide the Duke of Somerset? / *Let him shunne Castles, Safer shall he be upon the sandie Plaines,* / *Then where Castles mounted stand* **58–59 These oracles are hardily attained** / **And hardly understood. Come, come, my lord,** Come, come, my Lords, These oracles are hardly attained / And hardly understood.

2.1.26 some such **37–43 s.p.** GLOUCESTER . . . **words.** [Q; not in F] **46 an if** And if **53 s.p.** CARDINAL BEAUFORT [F makes the line a continuation of Gloucester's prior speech.] **65 tell** and tell **74 sight** his sight **109 Alban** Albones **114 And . . . sir;** [Q] What Coulour is my Gowne of? / *Simpc*⟨*oxe*⟩. Black forsooth, **116–53** [Q is control text for this section.] **117 before** [F] ere a **many** [F] many, a one **118 s.p.** SIMPCOX'S WIFE . . . **life.** [F; not in Q] **119 Tell** [F] But tell **128 Simon** Sander **Simpcox** [F; not in Q] **129 Simon** Sander **thou** [not in Q] **131 our** all our **133 distinguish** distinguish of **135 Saint** My Lords, Saint **Alban** [F] Albones **136 Would** and would **138 that** [F] I would **141 We have, my lord, an if it please your grace.** Yes, my Lord, if it please your Grace. **144 Bring** Now fetch **stool** stoole hither by and by **145 o'er** over **147 am not able even to** am not able to **149 sirrah** Sir **150 Whip** Sirrah Beadle, whip **177–87** [Following Q, the Oxford editors move the reading of the prophecies from 1.4.56 to this location.] **176 And here's . . . them.** [Q; not in F] **177 s.p.** KING HENRY [Q] *Yorke.* **First . . . of him become?** become of

him? [Q; not in F] **178–79 The Duke . . . death.** [after Q; not in F here] **180 God's will be done in all.** [Q; not in F] **Well, to the rest** [after F] **181–82 Tell . . . end.** [after Q; not in F here] **183–184 s.p.** SUFFOLK . . . lie. [Q; not in F] **185 s.p.** KING HENRY [Q; F assigns to York] **185–87 What . . . stand.** [after Q; not in F here]

2.2.6 out at full **at full** 26 well all **28 Duke of York** Duke **41 Owain Glyndŵr** *Owen Glendour* **45 was son** was **46 son** Sonnes Sonne **56 John's** his **77 off** we off

2.3.3 sins sinne **19 grave** ground **30 helm** Realme **34 erst** [Q1, Q2] ere **35 willing** [Q] willingly **2.3.58–2.4.0** [In these lines, Q is control text for 2.3.58–75, 2.3.83–88, and 2.3.101–2.4.0] **78 an if** and if **88 well** [F; not in Q] **98 wame** way **99 enemy** Enemies **2.4.18 sheriffs** [Q] Sherife **77, 103 s.p.** FIRST SHERIFF Sh⟨*erife*⟩, Sherife

3.1.78 wolf Wolves **98 Suffolk's Duke** [Q] *Suffolke* **137 my good** [Q] my **211 strains** strayes **264 conceit** deceit **319–30** [For the Q version of these lines, see inset passage in the text.] **330.2 'gainst** against **348 nurse** nourish **363 porcupine** Porpentine **381 coistrel** [Q] rascall [F]

3.2.14 Then draw the curtains close; away, be gone! Away, be gone **26 Meg** Nell **75 leper** Leaper **79 Queen Margaret** Dame *Elianor* **ne'er** neere **82 wrecked** wrack'd **83, 85 winds** [Q] winde **100 Margaret** Elianor **107 heart** Hart **116 witch** watch **120 Margaret** Elinor **223 born** borne **236 s.p.** COMMONS . . . **Suffolk! Down with Suffolk!** [Q; not in F; F s.d. reads *A noyse within.*] **243 s.p.** COMMONS . . . **the commons** [after Q; not in F] **272 s.p.** COMMONS ⟨*within*⟩ (*Commons within.*) **280 s.p.** COMMONS ⟨*within*⟩ *Within.* **310 enemies** [Q] enemy **312 Could** [Q] Would **320 My** mine **on an distraught** distract **334 turn** turnes **336 this** [Q] the **346 upon these** lips upon these **395 his** [Q] it's **402 By thee to die** [Q] To dye by thee

3.3.10 whe'er where

4.1.6 Clip Cleape **20 s.p.** WHITMORE Cut Cut **22** [line assumed missing] **33 thee** death **49 Jove sometime went disguised, and why not I?** [Q; not in F] **51 s.p.** SUFFOLK (*Suf.*) [Q; not in F] **52 The** [Q] *Suf*⟨*folke*⟩. The **53 jady** [Q] iaded **71 s.p.** CAPTAIN . . . *Ay Lieu. Poole,* Sir *Poole?* Lord, / *I* **77 shalt** [Q] shall **85 mother's bleeding** Mother-bleeding **93 are** and **113 s.p.** CAPTAIN . . . **rage.** [not in F] **114 s.p.** SUFFOLK [not in F] **116 s.p.** CAPTAIN Walter– **s.p.** WHITMORE Come Lieu⟨*tenant*⟩. Water: W. Come **118** *Paene Pine* **121 daunted** danted **134 s.p.** SUFFOLK Come Come **135 That** *Suf*⟨*folke*⟩. That

4.2.30 fall fail **75 Chatham** [Q] Chartam **80 He's** Ha's **87 that** [Q] it **90 an** a **132 an** [Q] if **135 testify** [Q1, Q2] testifie it **147 maimed** main'd

4.3.6 Thou [Q1, Q2] and thou **6 licence** a License

4.4.20 lamenting and mourning lamenting and mourning for **38 Kenilworth** Killingworth **42 trait'rous rabble hateth** Traitors hateth **48 almost** [Q; not in F] **57 be betrayed** betraid

4.5–4.6.0 [Q is control text for these lines.] **2 lord Scales** Lord **2–3 he and his men** they **3–4 did withstand** withstand **8 essayed** [F] attempted **9 Get you to Smithfield, there to gather head** But get you to Smythfield, and gather head **10 will I** I will

4.6.5 otherwise [Q] other **7 Zounds** [Q; not in F] **10 My** *Dicke.* My **11 go on** [Q] go **12 afire** [Q1, Q3] on fire

4.7.21 serge Surge **24 Dauphin** Dolphine **39 on** [Q] in **43 their shirts** their shirt **48–51 *Bonum* . . . well enough.** [Q] Away with him, away with him, he speaks Latine. **63 But** Kent **81 caudle** Candle **81–82 the health o'** the help of **100 to the Standard in Cheapside** [Q; not in F] **101 go to Mile End Green** [Q; not in F] **113 Married men** [Q] Men **115 s.d.–131 s.d.** *Enter . . . Sergeant* [Q; not in F] **117 quench** [Q3] squench **124 went and** went and and **proper** paper **131 brain** Brave **134–36 He that . . . smock.** [Q; not in F] **147 What noise is this?** What noise is this heare? **156 rebel** rabble

4.8.27 stout Irish stout **34 calmed** calme

4.9.6 oe'r on **18 waning** warning **22 Zounds** Sounes [Q; not in F] **52 Stand you all aside.** [Q; not in F] **56 God** [Q] love **74 bore** bare

5.1.10 sword soule **72 Iwis** I was **83 wi'th'** with th' **109 Sirrah** Wold'st have me kneele? First let me ask of thee, / If they can brooke I bow a knee to man: / Sirrah **sons** [Q] sonne **111 for** of **147 bearheard** Berard **192 or** and **195 you** [Q] thee **199 household** [Q] housed **205 to** [Q] io [or possibly "so"]

5.2.0–6 *Alarums . . . Somerset's body.* [After F; F places this passage following 5.3.65.]

5.3.8 s.d. CLIFFORD Warwick . . . come. [Q; not in F] **20–30 s.d.** YORK Clifford . . . York. [Q; not in F. For the F version of this encounter, see inset passage in the text.] **20 Clifford** Now Clifford **22 know** now **25 not** never **30.10 oeuvres** *eumenes*

5.5.1–4 How now, . . . rights. [Q; not in F] **5.5.17 s.d.–19 Enter . . . York** [Q] But Noble as he is, looke where he comes. / s.d. Enter Salisbury **37 drums** Drumme

RICHARD DUKE OF YORK (3 HENRY VI)

CONTROL TEXT: F

F: The Folio of 1623
O: The Octavo of 1595
Q2: The Quarto of 1600
Q3: The Quarto of 1619
Fa, Fb: Successive states of F incorporating various print-shop corrections and changes

s.p. YORK [F's *Plantagenet* and *York* have been standardized throughout.]

s.p. KING HENRY [F's *Henry* has been changed throughout.]

s.p. QUEEN MARGARET [F's *Queen* and *Margaret* have been changed throughout.]

s.p. PRINCE EDWARD [F's *Prince* and *Prince Edward* have been standardized throughout.]

s.p. GEORGE/GEORGE OF CLARENCE [F's *Clarence* has been changed to "George" (1.1–3.1) and to "George of Clarence" once he is granted the title Duke of Clarence.]

s.p. RICHARD OF GLOUCESTER [F's *Richard* has been changed after 3.1 once he is granted the title Duke of Gloucester.]

s.p. KING EDWARD [F's *King* and *King Edward* have been standardized from 3.2 to the end of the play.]

s.p. LADY GRAY [F's *Widow, Lady Gray,* and *Gray* have been standardized throughout.]

s.p. KING LOUIS [F's *Lewis* has been changed throughout.]

s.p. LADY BONA [F's *Bona* has been changed throughout.]

s.p. MESSENGER [F's *Gabriel* has been changed at 1.2.49.]

s.p. SOLDIER [F's *Son* has been changed throughout 2.5.]

s.p. SECOND SOLDIER [F's *Father* has been changed throughout 2.5.]

s.p. FIRST GAMEKEEPER [F's *Sinklo* has been changed throughout 3.1]

s.p. SECOND GAMEKEEPER [F's *Humfrey* has been changed throughout 3.1.]

Title: The true Tragedie of Richard Duke / *of Yorke, and the good King* / Henry the Sixt [O head title] The true Tragedie of Richard / *Duke of Yorke, and the death of* / good King Henrie the Sixt, / *with the whole contention betweene* / the two Houses Lancaster / and Yorke, as it was sundrie times / acted by the Right Honoura- / ble the Earle of Pem- / brooke his servants. [O title page] The third Part of Henry the Sixt, / with the death of the Duke of / YORKE [F]

1.1.19 hap hope 69 s.p. EXETER [O]
Westm⟨orland⟩ 78 mine [O, Q2] my 83 and
that's [Q3] that's 105 Thy [O] My 120–24
s.p. NORTHUMBERLAND . . . king [O; for F,
see inset passage in text.] 121 York *Plantagenet* 122 both both both 138 An And
171 me [O; not in F] 197 thine [O, Q2] an
200 nor neyther 255 the utter ruin vtter
ruine 260 with [O; not in F] 262 from [O]
to 269 coast cost

1.2.40 to Edmund Brook [O] vnto my 65 s.p.
SIR JOHN *John* 72 uncles Vnckle

1.4.51 buckle [O] buckler 82 thy [O] the
138 tiger's Tygres 151 passions move [O]
passions moues

2.1.113 And, very well appointed as I
thought, [O; not in F] 127 captains [O]
Captiues 131 an idle [O] a lazie 144 his
[O] the

2.2.92 our brother out [O] out me 133 s.p.
RICHARD [O] *War⟨wicke⟩* 172 deniest [O]
denied'st

2.5.38 weeks [not in F] 119 E'en Men

2.6.6 commixture [O] Commixtures 8 The
common people swarm like summer flies,
[O; not in F] 42 s.p. EDWARD [O] *Rich⟨ard⟩*
43 s.p. RICHARD A [O] A 44 s.p. EDWARD . . .
See [O] See 44 And [O] *Ed⟨ward⟩* And 60
his [O] is 80 buy but [O] buy

3.1.17 wast was 24 thee the sour adversity
sower Aduesaries 30 Is I: 55 thou that [O]
thou 96 in the the

3.2.3 lands [O] Land 28 whip me then [O]
then whip me 30 an [O, Q2] if 32 them
[O] then 119 as [O] your 123 honourably
[O] honourable

3.3.11 state Seat 33 An And 124 eternal [O]
externall 156 Warwick, peace Warwicke
202 ay I 228 I'll [O] I

4.1.17 you [not in F] 28 my [O, Q2] mine 91
thy [O] the 133 near'st [O, Q2] neere

4.2.2 sort people 12 come welcome 15
towns Towne

4.6.4 stands stand 8 Comes Come

4.7.11 prisonment imprisonment 55 be confiscate confiscate

4.8.67–74 Ay . . . fight. [O omits line 4.8.70
and the following stage direction and assigns
the remainder of these lines to Montgomery.
F divides them among Montgomery, Hastings, and a soldier.] 71 s.p. MONTGOMERY
[O] *Soul⟨dier⟩* 72 Ireland [O] *Ireland, & c.*
73 And [O] *Mount⟨gomerie⟩* And

4.9.12 stir stirre vp

5.1.68 bye buy 75 an [O, Q2] if 78 an in
80–83 s.p. GEORGE OF CLARENCE . . . WAR-
WICKE [O; not in F] 94 Jephthah Iephah
102 brothers [O] Brother

5.4.27 raggèd raged 35 York [not in F] 82
s.d.–5.5.17 *Alarum . . . ambitious York.*

[For the O version, see inset passage in the
text.]

5.5.17.1 s.p. ALL THE LANCASTER PARTY *All*
17.2 Now [F] Lo 17.5 Go, bear thence
hence [F] Awaie 17.8 Edward [F] Now
Edward 49 The [O; not in F] 76–77
butcher, / Hard-favoured Richard? [O]
butcher *Richard?*

5.6.46 tempests [O] Tempest 80 I had no
father, I am like no father; [O; not in F]
85 kept'st keept'st 90–91 Henry . . . the
rest, [O, Q2] King *Henry,* and the
Prince his Son are gone, / *Clarence* thy
turne is next, and then the rest 90 art [F;
not in O]

5.7.5 renowned [O] Renowne 21 an [O, Q2]
if 25 and [Fb] add [Fa] thou [O] that 27
kiss [Fb] 'tis [Fa] 30 s.p. LADY GRAY
Cla⟨rence⟩ Thanks [O] Thanke 42 rests
[Fb] tests [Fa]

TITUS ANDRONICUS

CONTROL TEXT: Q1; ADDITIONAL MATERIAL FROM
F

F: The Folio of 1623
Q1: The Quarto of 1594
Q2: The Quarto of 1600
Q3: The Quarto of 1611

s.p. SATURNINUS [Q1's use of *Saturnine, King,*
and *Emperour* has been standardized
throughout.]

s.p. AARON [Q1's use of *Moore* and *Aron* has
been standardized throughout.]

s.p. YOUNG LUCIUS [*Puer* in Q1; standardized
throughout.]

1.1.18 s.p. MARCUS [not in Q1] 35 field; [Four
lines follow in Q1, indented in this edition.]
35.2 the that 40 succeeded succeede 64
s.p. Captain [not in Q1] 98 *manes manus*
141 quit her quit the 157 s.p. LAVINIA [not
in Q1] 226 Titan's [Q2] Tytus 242 Pantheon Pathan 264 chance [Q2] change
280 *cuique* cuiqum 283 guard? [Q1 and F
have four lines following, indented in this
edition.] 295 Follow . . . back [In Q1, this
line follows 1.1.285.] 313 Phoebe Thebe
355 s.p. QUINTUS and MARTIUS Titus two
sonnes speakes. 357 s.p. QUINTUS Titus
sonne speakes. 365 s.p. MARTIUS 3. Sonne.
366 s.p. QUINTUS 2. Sonne. 395 s.p. MAR-
CUS Yes . . . remunerate [The line does not
occur in Q1; it does appear in F, but without
the attribution to Marcus.] 471 s.p. LUCIUS
[not in Q1] All. [Q3] Son. [F]

2.1.110 than this

2.2.1 morn [Q3] Moone 24 run runs
2.3.33 and ann 72 swart [F] swartie 85 note notice 88 have I I have 115 henceforward hence forth 126 quaint painted 131 ye desire we desire 153 Some [Q2] So me 192 s.p. AARON [not in Q1] 210 unhallowed [F] vnhollow 222 berayed bereaud 231 Pyramus Priamus 236 Cocytus Ocitus 260 gripped griude 268 s.p. SATURNINUS [s.p. "King." printed after the text of the letter, at line 276.]
2.4.11 s.p. MARCUS [not in Q1] 27 him them 30 three their 38 Philomel Philomela
3.1.12 two [not in Q1] 35 must must, / and bootlesse vnto them 146 with his with her 215 sorrows sorrow 224 blow flow 280–81 And Lavinia, thou shalt be employed. / Bear thou my hand, sweet wench, between thine arms. And *Lauinia* thou shalt be imployde in these Armes, / Beare thou my hand sweet wench betweene thy teethe:
3.2 [This scene appears first in F. There is no Q1 counterpart.] 13 with outrageous without ragious 39 complainer complaynet 52 thy [not in F] 53 fly Flys 55 are [not in F] 60 father, brother? father and mother? 62 dirges doings 72 myself my selfes
4.1.10 s.p. MARCUS [In Q1, speech continued to Titus.] 69 here [not in Q1] 77 s.p. TITUS [not in Q1] 90 sware sweare
4.2.15 that [not in Q1] 123 that [Q3] your 135 do join joine 177 fat feede
4.3.32 But [Catchword in Q1 but not reproduced on the following page, presumably because a line was accidentally omitted.] 40 now so 54 Apollinem Apollonem 57 'To Saturn', Caius To Saturnine, to Caius 77 [Speech continued to Titus in Q2 is attributed to the Clown in Q1.] 92 [After this line, Q1 and F print a short exchange, indented in this edition.]
4.4.5 as know [not in Q1] 92 feed [Q3] seede 104 on in 112 incessantly sucessantly
5.1.17 s.p. GOTHS [not in Q1] 46 What, deaf? What, not a word? what deafe, not a word? 53 Get me a ladder [attributed to Aaron in Q1] 133 haystacks haystalks 165 come. Away! come, march away
5.2.18 it action F that accord 49 globe Globes 50 two thee two 52 murderers murder 52 caves cares 56 Hyperion's Epeons 61 they thy them thy
5.3.26 gracious [Q2–3, F, not in Q1] 42 effectual and effectuall 124 cause course 140 s.p. ROMANS Marcus. 141 s.p. MARCUS [not in Q1] 143 adjudged [Q3] adiudge 145 s.p. ROMANS [not on Q1] 153 bloodstained blood slaine

THE FIRST PART OF HENRY THE SIXTH

CONTROL TEXT: F

F: The Folio of 1623

s.p. KING HENRY [F's use of *King* has been changed throughout.]
s.p. JOAN [F's use of *Joan, Pucelle,* and *Puzzel* (see note 4 to 1.6.85) has been standardized throughout.]
s.p. CHARLES [F's use of *Dolphin (Dauphin)* and *Charles* has been standardized throughout.]
s.p. RICHARD PLANTAGENET / RICHARD DUKE OF YORK [F's use of *York* and *Richard* has been standardized to "Richard Plantagenet" until 3.1.175–77, when he regains his title; thereafter, "Richard Duke of York" is used.]
s.p. WINCHESTER [F's use of *Winchester* and *Cardinal* has been standardized throughout.]
s.p. FASTOLF [F's use of *Falstaff* has been changed throughout (see note to 1.1.131).]
s.p. RENÉ [F's use of *Reigneir* and *Reignier* has been changed throughout.]
s.p. GLASDALE [F's spelling, *Glansdale,* has been changed throughout.]
s.p. ALENÇON [F's spelling, *Alanson,* has been changed throughout.]

1.1.50 marish Nourish 60 Rouen, Rheims, Rheimes, 62 corpse Coarse 89 s.p. SECOND MESSENGER Mess. 94 René Reynold 103 s.p. THIRD MESSENGER Mes. 131 Fastolf Falstaffe 132 vanguard Vauward 157 Fore Orléans for Orleance is 176 steal send
1.2.21 flee fly
1.3.9 bred breed 78 five fine 92 rites rights 110 halcyon's Halcyons
1.4.5 knocketh knocks 19 My lord The Cardinall 29 vizier Vmphier 36 If Ile canuas thee in thy broad Cardinalls Hat, If 41 purple Scarlet 48 I'll I bishop's mitre Cardinalls Hat 55 cloakèd Scarlet 72 s.p. OFFICER [not in F] 77 Bishop Cardinall 82 bishop is Cardinall's
1.5.8 Prince's spials Princes espyals 10 Wont Went
1.6.5 Duke Earle 11 pilled pil'd 41 Glasdale Glansdale 44 Lou Lords 67 Bear . . . bury it [F places after 1.6.64] 73 like thee, Nero, like thee, 79 la Pucelle *de Puzel* 85 *Pucelle* or pucelle Puzel or Pussel Dauphin Dolphin
1.7.3 men them 29 style Soyle
1.8.3 la Pucelle *de Puzel* 21 pyramid Pyramis 22 of or 29 la Pucelle *de Puzel*
2.1.5 s.p. A SENTINEL Sent. 29 all together altogether 38 s.p. SENTINELS Sent.

2.2.6 centre Centure **20 Arc** Acre

2.3.21 seely silly

2.4.41 from the tree are cropped are cropt from the Tree **57 law** you **117 wiped** whipt **132 gentles** gentle

2.5.3 rack Wrack **6–7 Argue . . . Mortimer, / Nestor-like . . . care.** Nestor-like . . . Care, / Argue . . . Mortimer. **44 dis-ease** Disease **71 King** [not in F] **75 the third** third **76 the King** hee **129 mine ill** my will

3.1.52 s.p. GLOUCESTER Warw⟨icke⟩. **53 s.p. WARWICK** [not in F, where this line and the prior three words, here assigned to Glouces-ter, are given to Warwick] **54 so** see **64 intertalk** enter talke **83 pebble** peeble **167 alone** all alone **175 gird** gyrt **203 should lose** loose

3.2.13 *Qui* Che

3.5.32 Goodbye God b'uy

4.1.14 thee the **19 Patay** *Poictiers* **48 my** [not in F] **180 I wist** I wish

4.2.3 captain Captaines **calls** call **15 s.p. GENERAL** *Cap.* **29 fire** ryue **34 due** dew

4.3.17 s.p. LUCY 2. *Mes.* **30 s.p. LUCY** *Mes.* **34 s.p. LUCY** *Mes.* **47 s.p. LUCY** *Mes.*

4.4.16 legions Regions **19 unadvantaged** in aduantage **26 and** [not in F] **27 René Reignard** 31 horse hoast

4.5.39 shamed shame

4.7.70 *Maréchal* Marshall **89 have them** haue him **94 with them** with him

5.1.59 nor neither

5.2.17–18 s.p. JOAN Now . . . fear. / Of Now . . . feare. / *Pucel.* Of

5.3.8 speed and quick speedy and quicke

5.4.15 comest comst

5.5.4–5 And . . . side. / I . . . peace, I . . . peace, / And . . . side. 12 his her **18 stream** streames **24 here to hear** heere **41 ran-dom** randon **92 Assent** Consent **110 coun-tries** Country **135 modestly** modestie

5.6.10 an't and **37 one** me, **49 Arc** Aire **68 ingling** iugling **70 we will** we'll

5.7.60 That [not in F]

THE TRAGEDY OF KING RICHARD THE THIRD

CONTROL TEXT: F (EXCEPT FOR 3.1.0–148 AND 5.5.4—END, FOR WHICH THE COPY TEXT IS Q1)

F: The Folio of 1623
Q1: The Quarto of 1597
Q2: The Quarto of 1598
Q3: The Quarto of 1602
Q4: The Quarto of 1605
Q5: The Quarto of 1612
Q6: The Quarto of 1622

1.1–3.1 and 3.1.148–5.5.4

s.p. RICHARD GLOUCESTER [F's use of *Richard* and *Gloucester* has been standardized until 4.2.]

s.p. KING RICHARD [F's use of *King* and *Rich-ard* has been standardized after 4.2.]

s.p. BRACKENBURY [F's use of *Brackenbury* and *Lieutenant* has been standardized throughout.]

s.p. LORD HASTINGS [F's use of *Hastings* has been changed throughout.]

s.p. LADY ANNE [F's use of *Anne* has been changed throughout.]

s.p. HALBERDIER [F uses *Gentleman.*]

s.p. QUEEN ELIZABETH [F's use of *Queen* has been standardized throughout.]

s.p. STANLEY [F's use of *Stanley* and *Derby* has been standardized throughout.]

s.p. QUEEN MARGARET [F's use of *Queen Mar-garet* and *Margaret* has been standardized throughout.]

s.p. A MURDERER, MURDERERS [F's use of *Vil-lain* has been standardized throughout.]

s.p. FIRST MURDERER [F's use of *1 Murderer* and *1* has been standardized through-out.]

s.p. SECOND MURDERER [F's use of *2 Mur-derer* and *2* has been standardized throughout.]

s.p. KING EDWARD [F's use of *King* has been standardized throughout.]

s.p. BOY [F's use of *Boy* and *Edward* has been standardized until 3.1.]

s.p. DUCHESS OF YORK [F's use of *Duchess of York* and *Duchess* has been standardized throughout.]

s.p. GIRL [F's use of *Daughter* has been stan-dardized throughout.]

s.p. FIRST CITIZEN [F's use of *1 Citizen* and *1* has been standardized throughout.]

s.p. SECOND CITIZEN [F's use of *2 Citizen* and *2* has been standardized throughout.]

s.p. THIRD CITIZEN [F's use of *3* has been standardized throughout.]

s.p. CARDINAL [F's use of *Archbishop* and *Cardinal* has been standardized throughout.]

s.p. MAYOR [F's use of *Lord Mayor* and *Mayor* has been standardized throughout.]

s.p. BISHOP OF ELY [F's use of *Ely* has been standardized throughout.]

s.p. ALL BUT RICHARD [F's use of *All* has been standardized throughout.]

s.p. SECOND MESSENGER, THIRD MESSENGER, FOURTH MESSENGER [F only uses *Messenger.*]

s.p. SIR CHRISTOPHER [F's use of *Christopher* has been standardized throughout.]

s.p. HENRY EARL OF RICHMOND [F's use of *Richmond* has been standardized throughout.]

3.1.0–148 and 5.5.4–end

s.p. KING RICHARD [Q's use of *King Richard* and *Richard* has been standardized throughout.]

s.p. PRINCE EDWARD [Q's use of *Prince* has been standardized throughout.]

s.p. GHOST OF PRINCE EDWARD, GHOST OF KING HENRY, GHOST OF CLARENCE, GHOSTS OF THE PRINCES, GHOST OF HASTINGS [Q's use of *Ghost* has been standardized throughout.]

s.p. GHOST OF GRAY [Q's use of *Gray* has been standardized throughout.]

s.p. GHOST OF VAUGHAN [Q's use of *Vaughan* has been standardized throughout.]

Title: *The Tragedy of King Richard the Third*] THE TRAGEDY OF / King Richard the third. / Containing, / His treacherous Plots against his brother Clarence: / the pittiefull murther of his innocent nephewes: / his tyrannicall vsurpation: with the whole course / of his detested life, and most deserued death. [Q title page] The Tragedy of Richard the Third: / with the Landing of Earle Richmond, and the / Battell at Bosworth Field. [F head title]

1.1.26 spy [Q] see **49 Belike** O belike **52 for** [Q] but **67 Woodeville** *Woodeulle* **73 Mrs** Mistresse **74 ye** [Q] you **75 for his** for her **88 An't** and **92 jealous** [Q] iealious **96 kin** kindred **104 I** [Q] I do **do withal** withal **113 dearer** deeper **116 or** [Q] or else **125 the** [Q1] this **134 prey** [Q] play **139 Paul** [Q] Iohn **146 haste** horse

1.2.15 Cursèd . . . hence, [F places the line after 1.2.16.] **39 stand** [Q] Stand'st **56 Ope** Open **60 deed** Deeds **61 supernatural** most vnnaturall **70 no** [Q] nor **78 a** [Q; not in F] **80 t'accuse** to curse **92 hand** [Q] hands **101 ye** [Q1] yee **120 of that accursed effect** and most accurst effect **126 rend** [Q] rent **127 sweet** [Q] y^t **154 drops.** [Q; F here adds twelve lines; see indented passage.] **Shamed** [Q, F (text)] For [F (catchword)] **189 s.p. RICHARD GLOUCESTER** [Q; not in F] **190 s.p. LADY ANNE . . . give.** [Q; not in F] **213 s.p. RICHARD GLOUCESTER . . . corpse.** [Q; not in F] **214 Blackfriars** white Friers **238 denier** denier

1.3.6 If . . . me? [Q; F gives the line twice, spanning a page break.] **7 s.p. RIVERS** [Q] If he were dead, what would betide me on / Gray. [F (text)] Gray. [F (catchword)] **17 come** [Q1] comes **Lords** [Q] Lord **30 s.p. RIVERS** [Q] Qu⟨een Elizabeth⟩. **33 With** [Q1] What **43 are they** [Q] is it **complain** complaines **54 s.p. RIVERS** [Q] Gray. whom [Q1] who **68–69 that . . . it** that he may

learne the ground **114 Tell . . . said,** [Q; not in F] **118 remember** [Q] do remember **153 may you** [Q] you may **155 Ah** A **160 of** [Q] off **166 go.** [Q; F here adds three lines; see indented passage.] **197 my** [Q] our **270 was** [Q] is **271 s.p. RICHARD GLOUCESTER** *Buc⟨kingham⟩.* **290 naught** not **302 s.p. HASTINGS** [Q] *Buc⟨kingham⟩.* **307 s.p. QUEEN ELIZABETH** [Q] *Mar⟨garet⟩.* **319 you my gracious lords** yours my gracious Lord **325 whom** [Q] who

1.4.19 sought thought **22 waters** [Q1] water **22–23 my . . . my** [Q1] mine . . . mine **25 Ten** [Q] A **26 ouches** anchors **29 those** [Q] the **32 Which** [Q] That **50 cried** [Q] spake **58 methoughts** [Q1] me thought **66 Brackenbury** [Q] Keeper, Keeper **68 me.** [Q; F here adds four lines; see indented passage.] **69 Keeper, I pray thee** Keeper, I prythee **90 of** [Q] from **96 I** [Q1] we **112 pray thee** [Q] prythee **119 'Swounds** [Q] Come **136 'Swounds** [Q; not in F] **177 to have redemption** [Q] for any goodnesse **178 By . . . sins,** [Q; not in F] **201 ye** [Q] you **225 And . . . other,** [Q; not in F] **227 of** [Q1] on **230 As** Right as **251–55 Which distress—** [F places the lines after 1.4.244.] **257 serve** [Q] do **261 guilty murder done** [Q] murther

2.1.5 in [Q] to **7 Hastings and Rivers** *Dorset* and *Riuers* **19 your** [Q] you **50 Brother** [Q] Gloster **57 unwittingly** [Q] vnwillingly **59 By** [Q] To **67 Of you . . . of you** [Q] Of you and you, Lord *Riuers* and of *Dorset* **68 me.—** [Q] me: / Of you Lord *Wooduill* and Lord *Scales,* of you, **70 Englishman** [Q] Englishmen **82 s.p. RIVERS** [Q] *King* **85 one** [Q] man **93 but** [Q] and **97 pray thee** [Q] prethee **105 slew** [Q] kill'd **108 at** [Q] and **131 once** [Q] onee

2.2.3 you [Q; not in F] **13 this** [Q] it **26 his** [Q] a **27 shapes** [Q] shape **39 mark** make **47 I** [Q; not in F] **83 weep** [Q] weepes **84–85 and . . . weep** [Q; not in F] **88 lamentation.** [F here adds twelve lines; see indented passage.] **105 hearts** [Q] hates **106 splinted** [Q, F] splinterd **110 king.** [Q; F here adds eighteen lines; see indented passage.] **112 Ludlow** [Q] London **114 weighty** [Q; not in F] **115 s.p. QUEEN . . . YORK** [not in F] **With . . . hearts.** [Q; not in F] **117 God's sake** [Q] God sake **124 Ludlow** [Q] London

2.3.35 make [Q] makes **43 Ensuing** [Q, F (catchword)] Pursuing [F (text)]

2.4.1 hear [Q1] heard **them** [not in F] **1–2 Northampton. / at Stony Stratford** [Q] Stony Stratford, / And at Northampton **9 young** [Q] good **12 nuncle** Vnkle **13 gross** great **21 s.p. CARDINAL Why** [Q] *Yor⟨k⟩.* And **26 pray thee** [Q] prythee **36 s.p. CARDINAL**

[Q] *Dut.* (Duchess of York) **37 your son, Lord Dorset** a Messenger **38 Lord Marquis** [Q; not in F] **s.p. DORSET** [Q; throughout scene] *Mes⟨senger⟩.* **40 then** [Q; not in F] **42 And with them** and with them, / Sir **48 our** [Q] my **50 jet** [Q] Iutt **64 death** [Q] earth

3.1.0 [Right after this stage direction, F loses its independent authority until c. 3.1.148. Q1 is the control text in this interim; F is here a direct reprint of Q3, which contains errors that need to be corrected by reference to Q1.] **22 hastes** comes **24 In happy time** And in good time **39 Anon expect him** Anone expect him here **41 sacred** holy **46 not** but **52 my mind, he** mine opinion **53 'longs** is **54 You . . . charter** You breake no priuiledge nor charter there **59 I come** I go **74 liege.** Lo: **85 t'enrich** enrich **87 made** makes **88 yet** now **90 good** gratious **101 noble cousin** Cosen noble **102 uncle, well** Vnckle **107 He . . . you then** Then he . . . you **109 as** as in **110 render** giue **111 With all** [Q3–6, F] withall **113–14 give, / It being but** giue, / And being but **121 I'd** I **132 sharp, prodigal** sharpe, prouided **136 My . . . along** [Q, F; none of the many attempts to pad out this line carries any conviction.] **143 there** [not in Q] **148 and** [F, not in Q] **149 we** I **153 parlous** perillous **161 Lord William** William Lo: **166 Will not** [F; F regains its full authority at this line.] Will **170 purpose.** [Q; for F, see indented passage.] **174 your** [Q] the **188 My** Now my

3.2.1 from Lord from the lo: **3 my Lord Stanley** Stanley **17 councils** [Q] Councell **74 you do** [Q; not in F] **87 talked** [Q1] talke **91 follow presently** [Q] talke with this good fellow **92 Well met, Hastings** [Q] How now, Sirrha? **95 I met thee** [Q] thou met'st me **102 Hastings** [Q] fellow **103 God save your lordship** [Q] I thanke your

3.3.14 heads, [Q] Heads / When shee exclaim'd on *Hastings,* you, and I **16–17 Hastings . . . Richard** [Q] *Richard . . . Hastings*

3.4.4 that [Q] the **solemn** royall **9 methinks** [Q] we thinke **26 not you** [Q] you not **39 worshipful** [Q] worshipfully **55 likelihood** [Q] liuelyhood **58 s.p. STANLEY I . . . not.** [not in F] **65 whatsoe'er** [Q] whosoe're **68 See** [Q] Looke **78 Some see it done** [Q] *Louell* and *Ratcliffe,* looke that it be done **82 raze** [Q] rowse **83 But** [Q] And **94 s.p. CATESBY** *Ra⟨tcliffe⟩.* **98 th'air** aire **102 s.p. CATESBY** *Lou⟨ell⟩.*

3.5.4 wert [Q] were **6 Tremble . . . straw,** [F places the line after 3.5.7.] **12 s.p. RICHARD GLOUCESTER . . . Mayor** [Q] But what, is *Catesby* gone? / *Rich⟨ard⟩.* He is, and see he

brings the Maior along **13 Let . . . him.** [Q; not in F] **19 innocence** [Q1] innocencie **20 O . . . Catesby** [Q] Be patient, they are friends: *Ratcliffe,* and *Louell.* **21 s.p. CATESBY** *Louell.* **31 attainder** attainder **32 The** Well, well, he was the **48 I** [Q] *Buck⟨ingham⟩. I* **50 s.p. RICHARD GLOUCESTER** [Q4; not in F] **54 we** [Q] I **hear** heard **56 treason** [Q] Treasons **60 word** [Q] words **64 cause** [Q1] case **82 listed** [Q] lusted **101 Now** [Q; for F, see indented passage.] **in** [Q] goe **103 notice** [Q] order

3.6.13 naught [Q1] nought

3.7.7 insatiate [Q] vnsatiate **14 face** forme **20 mine** [Q1] my **40 wisdoms** [Q] wisdome **43–44 s.p. BUCKINGHAM No . . . lord. / s.p. RICHARD GLOUCESTER** [Q; not in F] **49 build** [Q] make **50 request** [Q] requests **54 we'll** [Q] we **72 lolling** [Q, F] lulling **day-bed** [Q] Loue-Bed **101 request** [Q] requests **125 her** [Q] his **126 Her** [Q] His **127 Her** His **143 condition.** [Q; F here adds ten lines; see indented passage.] **160 no doubt, us** [Q] no doubt vs **203 equally** [Q, F] egallie **209 'Swounds, I'll** [Q] we will **210 s.p. RICHARD GLOUCESTER O . . . Buckingham.** [Q; not in F] **212 s.p. ANOTHER** [Q; not in F] **214 stone** stones **215 entreats** [Q] entreaties **230 kind** King **237 cousin** [Q] Cousins

4.1.46 counted England's Englands counted **57 in** [Q] with **75 made** [not in F] **96 racked** [Q, F] wrackt **teen.** [Q; F here adds seven lines; see indented passage.]

4.2.14 liege [Q] Lord **20 immediately** suddenlie **50 those parts beyond the seas** [Q] the parts **55 born** [Q] poore **73 there** [Q] then **81 'Tis** [Q] There is **84–85 s.p. KING RICHARD Shall . . . lord.** [Q; not in F] **90 to** [Q] vnto **101 perhaps.** [Q; not in F] **101–19 s.p. BUCKINGHAM . . . today.** [Q; not in F] **120 Why . . . no?** [Q] May it please you to resolue me in my suit.

4.3.4 whom [Q] who **5 ruthless** [Q1] ruthfull **8 two** [Q] to **15 once** [Q] one **31 at** [Q] and **39 goodnight** [Q] good night **40 Breton** [Q, F] Brittaine **42 o'er** [Q] on **45 Good news or bad** [Q] Good or bad newes **46 Ely** [Q] *Mourton* **53 leads** [Q] leds **55 an** and

4.4.10 unblown [Q] vnblowed **30 innocents'** [Q] innocent **36 seniory** [Q] signeurie **39 Tell . . . mine.** [Q; not in F] **45 holpst** hop'st **56 charnel** [Q, F] carnal **64 Thy** [Q] The **quite** [Q6] quit **77 plead** pray **93 are** [Q1] be **100 For queen . . . care** [Q; F places the line after 4.4.101.] **107 wert** [Q1] wast **112 weary** [Q1] wearied **118 nights . . . days** [Q1] night . . . day **127 client** [Q1] Clients **128 recorders** succeeders **intestate** [Q] intestine **141 Where** [Q]

Where't **175 in** [Q] with **176 Hewer** *Hower* **180 pray thee** prythee **188 heavy** [Q] greeuous **216 births** [Q] Birth **221 life.** [Q; F here adds fourteen lines; see indented passage.] **225 or** [Q1–5] and **243 that it 254 would I** [Q1] I would **260 sometimes** [Q1] sometime **270 is** [Q; not in F] **273 this.** [Q; F here adds fifty-five lines; see indented passage.] **286 love** [Q] low **295 s.p. KING RICHARD . . . past.** [Q1; F places the line after 4.4.296.] **296 s.p. QUEEN ELIZABETH** [Q1; not in F] **297 s.p. KING RICHARD** [Q; not in F] **300 holy** [Q] Lordly **301 lordly** knightlie **307 that** [Q] it **308 God . . . God's** [Q] Heauen . . . Heavens **323 in** [Q1] with **327 o'erpast** [Q] repast **343 good** [Q] deare **348 peevish-fond** [Q] peeuish found **356 recomfiture** [Q] recomforture **375 Ratcliffe** *Catesby* **391 mile** [Q] miles **395 renegade** [Q, F] runnagate **398 Ely** [Q] *Morton* **421 Ay, ay** [Q] I **431 Courtenay** [Q, F] Courtney **434 Guildfords** [Q, F] Guilfords **441 flood . . . water** [Q] Floods . . . Waters **445 Ratcliffe . . . gave him** [Q] There is my Purse, to cure that Blow of thine **452 Breton** [Q, F] Brittaine **458 Bretagne** [Q, F] Brittaine **465 tidings,** [Q1] Newes, but **4.5.2 this** [Q] the **5 aid** [Q] ayde. / So get thee gone: commend me to thy Lord **17–18 Tell . . . daughter.** [Q; F places the lines after 4.5.5.] **17 Tell him** [Q] Withall say, that **5.2.8 spoils** spoild **11 Lies** [Q] Is **12 Near** [Q] Ne're **17 swords** [Q] men **5.3.2 Why, how now, Catesby** [Q] My Lord of Surrey **3 s.p. CATESBY** [Q] Sur⟨rey⟩. **5.4.4 standard.** [Q; F places 5.4.21–24 here and adds, "My Lord of Oxford, you Sir *William Brandon*, / And your Sir *Walter Herbert* stay with me."] **21–24 Give . . . power.** [Q, F places the lines after 5.4.4.] **5.5.3** [Q1 is the control text for the remainder of the play, although a handful of Folio variants are considered or adopted, as derived from the damaged final leaves of the manuscript.] **8 sentinels** [F] centinell **10 s.p. KING RICHARD Stir** [F, Q (text)] Sturr [Q (catchword)] **11 s.p. CATESBY** Rat⟨cliffe⟩. **19 Ratcliffe** [Q6, F (italic)] Ratliffe **25 some** a boule of **29 Leave me. Bid my guard watch.** Bid my guard watch, leaue me. **30–31 About . . . tent, / Ratcliffe, and** Ratliffe about . . . tent / And **32 sit** [Q2] set **43 mortal-sharing** mortal staring **53 sundered** [Q3] sundried **72 tomorrow, / Prince . . . Sixth.** to morrow. **84 Comforts** Doth comfort **85 sit** [Q2] set **on** [Q5] in **93 s.p. GHOST OF RIVERS** [Q3] *King* **on** [Q5] in **97 pointless** [not in Q] **99 Will** [Q2] Wel **100 s.p. GHOSTS OF THE PRINCES** [F] *Ghost.*

110 Hastings, then Hastings **137 am** [Q2] and **140 Myself** What my selfe **156 Nay** [F] And **163 My** Ratcliffe, my **167 all our friends prove** our friends proue all **168 Ratcliffe** O Ratcliffe **177 s.p. LORDS** [Q3–6] Lo⟨rds⟩. **180 s.p. A LORD** [Q] Lo⟨rd⟩. **189 s.p. A LORD** [Q] Lo⟨rd⟩. **191 Much that I could say** More than I haue said **193 on** vpon **196 forces** faces **199 friends** gentlemen **212 foison** fat **pays** shall paie **219–20 this . . . my** my . . . this **221 to the 223 bold and** boldlie, and

5.6.12 not [Q2] nor **25 placed strongly** shall be placed **27 multitude** foote and horse **28 ourself** [not in Q] **29 both sides** either side **31 boot!** [Q3] bootes **32 s.p. NORFOLK A good** [F, Q (text)] A good [Q (catchword)] **33 paper** [not in Q] **34 Jackie** [Q, F] Iockie too so **37 each** euery **47 Bretons** [Q, F] Brittains **49 ventures** aduentures **52 distain** restraine **54 Bretagne** [Q, F] Brittaine **55 milksop** [Q6, F] milkesopt **74 young** his sonne

5.8.8–9 s.p. KING . . . But [F, Q (text)] But [Q (catchword)] **9 young George Stanley, is he** is yong George Stanley **13 s.p. STANLEY** [F] Der⟨by⟩. [not in Q] **14 Ferrers** Ferris **15 becomes** become **27 that** this **28 United** Deuided **32 his** thy **37 forth** in

VENUS AND ADONIS

CONTROL TEXT: Q1

Q1: The Quarto of 1593
Q2, Q3, Q7: Successive printings of Q1 that incorporate various corrections.

466 loss loue
680 overshoot ouer-shut [The Oxford editors point out that "shut" is a spelling variant of "shoot" in the early modern period.]
748 th'impartial [Q2] the th'impartiall
1031 as [Q3] are
1054 was [Q7] had

THE RAPE OF LUCRECE

CONTROL TEXT: Q1

Q1: The Quarto of 1594

The poem is called "LUCRECE" on the title page but "*The Rape of Lucrece*" in the head title and running titles.

550 blows blow
950 blemish cherish

1316 **stain's** stain'd
1475 **Thine** Thy
1544 **armèd, too** armed to
1662 **wreathèd** wretched
1713 **in it** it in

THE COMEDY OF ERRORS

CONTROL TEXT: F

F: The Folio of 1623
F2: Later printing of F (1632) that incorporates various corrections

s.p. EGEON [F's use of *Merchant* and *Father* has been standardized throughout.]

s.p. NELL [F also uses *Luce*. Standardized throughout.]

s.p. ANGELO [F uses both *Angelo* and *Goldsmith* but generally prefers the latter. Standardized throughout.]

1.1.17 **seen at** seene at any **22 ransom** to ransome **38 me happy** me; me too [F2] **42 the** he **54 mean-born** meane **102 upon** vp **116 barque** backe **123 thee** they **143–44 Which . . . disanul, / Against . . . dignity,** Against . . . dignity, / Which . . . disanull **151 health** helpe
1.2.4 **arrival** a riuall **40 unhappy** vnhappie a **66 clock** cooke
2.1.8 **mistress** Master **12 ill** thus **60 thousand** hundred **63 come home** come **67 thy mistress not** not thy mistresse **106 o'** a **109 her** his **110–11 will / Wear gold,** will, / Where gold **111 yet** [not in F]
2.2.12 **didst** did didst **80 men them** 98 **tiring** trying **148 unstained** distain'd **175 stronger** stranger **186 offered** free'd **191 oafs** Owles **194 drone** Dromio **195 not I** I not
3.1.47 **pate** face **aim** a name **75 you, sir** your sir **89, 91 her** your **106 once** [not in F] **116 Porcupine** Porpentine
3.2.1 **s.p. LUCIANA** Iulia. **4 building** buildings **ruinous** ruinate **16 attaint** attaine **21 but** not **26 wife** wise **46 sister's** sister **49 bed** bud **them** thee **57 where** when **109 and** is **120 her hand** the hand
4.1.17 **her** their **87 she** sir she
4.2.6 **Of** Oh, **30 How?** How **47–48 at, / That** at / Thus **60 a be** I be
4.3.13 **redemption from** [not in F] **55 you do** do **56 and** or **60 thou** then
4.4.38 **to prophesy** the prophesie **99 those** these **108 his** this
5.1.46 **much, much** much **49 at** of **119 point's** points **122 death** depth **169 s.p. MESSENGER** [not in F] **321 bay** boy **350 his** her **404 ne'er** are **407 joy** go

LOVE'S LABOUR'S LOST

CONTROL TEXT: Q

F: The Folio of 1623
Q: The Quarto of 1598
Qa, Qb: Successive states of Q incorporating various print-shop corrections and changes

s.p. KING [Q's use of *King, Navarre,* and *Ferdinand* has been standardized throughout.]

s.p. BIRON, LONGUEVILLE, DUMAINE [Q's *Berowne* and *Longauill* (and other spellings) are transliterations of the French, here restored and modernized. "Dumaine" transliterates "Duc de Mayenne," not quite correctly. Rhyme and meter require two syllables.]

s.p. ARMADO [Q's use of *Armado* and *Braggart* has been standardized throughout.]

s.p. MOTE [Q uses either *Boy* or *Page,* which have been replaced throughout. In dialogue and s.d.'s, the name appears as "Moth," meaning "moth" or "mote" (speck). It is pronounced like the latter word, and that sense may be primary; hence the spelling adopted here.]

s.p. PRINCESS [Q more frequently uses *Queene,* but this edition uses "Princess" until she becomes a queen and is addressed as one, at 5.2.708.]

s.p. MARIA, CATHERINE, ROSALINE [In 2.1, they are referred to variously as *Lady,* 2 *Lady* (or *Lady* 2), and 3 *Lady* (or *Lady* 3). For details, see the variants list below and the notes to the text. For interpretation, see the Textual Note and the Introduction.]

s.p. COSTARD [Q generally prefers *Clown* over *Costard;* standardized throughout.]

s.p. JAQUENETTA [Q uses *Maid* more often than *Jaquenetta;* standardized throughout.]

s.p. NATHANIEL [Q's use of *Curate, Nathaniel,* and *Curate Nathaniel* has been standardized throughout.]

s.p. HOLOFERNES [Q uses *Pedant* more often than *Holofernes;* standardized throughout.]

s.p. DULL [Q's use of *Dull, Constable,* and *Anthony* has been standardized throughout.]

1.1.24 **three** [F] thee **31 pomp** [F] pome **62 feast** fast **127 s.p. BIRON** [In Q, Longueville speaks lines 126–30; Biron's s.p. appears at line 131.] **184 Señor** Signeour **192 laughing** hearing **211 simplicity** [F] sinplicitie **224–48** [Q prints the King's speech continuously, with Costard's interruptions bracketed.] **247 with, with** *Which* **with 275 s.p. KING** Fer⟨dinand⟩. [F] Ber⟨owne⟩.

1.2.9, 10, 15 Señor Signeor **91 blushing** blush-in **130 s.p. DULL** Clo⟨wn⟩. **145 Master** [F] M.

2.1.32 Importunes [F] Importuous **34 visaged** [F] visage **39 Lord Longueville** Longauill. **40 s.p. MARIA** 1. Lady. **44 parts** [F] peerelsse **53 s.p. MARIA** Lad⟨y⟩. **56 s.p. CATHERINE** 2 Lad⟨y⟩. **64 s.p. ROSALINE** [F] 3 Lad⟨y⟩. **88 unpeopled** [F] vnpeeled **113–25 s.p. ROSALINE** [F] Kath⟨erine⟩. **129 of** [F] of, of **189 Non point** No poynt **194 Catherine** Rosalin⟨e⟩ **209 Rosaline** Katherin⟨e⟩ **220–23 s.p. CATHERINE** La⟨dy⟩. **253 s.p. ROSALINE** [F] Lad⟨y⟩. **254 s.p. MARIA** [F] Lad⟨y⟩. **2 255 s.p. CATHERINE** Lad⟨y⟩. **3 256 s.p. MARIA** Lad⟨y⟩. **257 s.p. CATHERINE** Lad⟨y⟩.

3.1.11 throat as if throate, if **12 through the nose** through: nose **14 thin-belly** [F] thinbellies **22 penny** penne **63 salve in the mail** salue, in thee male **131, 134, 136, 138, 142, 144, 159** [Each line in Q starts with "O"; probably a misreading of the s.p. "Bero" as "Ber. O . . ."] **155 guerdon** gardon **165 Junior** Iunios **175 clock** Cloake

4.1.3 s.p. BOYET [F] Forr⟨ester⟩. **50 fit** [Qb] fir [Qa] **64 set's** [Qa] set [Qb] **65 penurious** pernicious **65 was** [Qb] is was [Qa] **72 King's** King **104 suitor** shooter **126 did hit it** did hit [Qb] hid hit [Qa] **132 pin** is in **140 o'th' t'other** ath toothen **144 a** [not in Q] **144.1 s.d. Shout within** Shoot within

4.2.11 a 'auld grey doe' a haud credo **26 of** [not in Q] **33 Dictynna . . . Dictynna** Dictisima . . . dictisima **44 'twas** [Qb] was [Qa] **47–48 call I** cald **57 sore 'l'** sorell: **61–96 s.p. HOLOFERNES** Nath⟨aniel⟩. The s.p.'s of Holofernes (lines 61, 71, 76, 80, 86, 96) and Nathaniel (lines 67, 95) are reversed in Q.] **64 pia mater** prima-/ter **66 in whom** [F] whom **71 ingenious** ingenous **73 sapit** sapis **76 'pierce one'** Person **89–90 Venezia . . . prezia** vemchie, vencha, que non te vnde, que non te perreche **96–98 s.p. HOLOFERNES . . . NATHANIEL** Nath⟨aniel⟩. [In Q, Nathaniel speaks lines 96–111; here, Holofernes delivers lines 96–97, Nathaniel lines 98–111.] **111 singeth** singes **112 apostrophus** apostraphas **113 canzonet** cangenct **113 Here are** Nath⟨aniel⟩. Here are. [Q assigns lines 112–13 to Holofernes and, beginning with "Here are," lines 113–19 to Nathaniel. This edition assigns Holofernes all of lines 112–19.] **118–19 domicella—virgin** Damosella virgin **120 sir** sir from one mounsier Berowne, one of the strange Queenes Lordes. **121 s.p. HOLOFERNES** Nath⟨aniel⟩. [Q assigns lines 121–25 to Nathaniel, beginning Holofernes' speech at line 125 with "Sir." This edition assigns the entire speech, lines 121–31, to Holofernes.] **124 writing** written

125 Sir Nathaniel Ped⟨ant⟩. Sir Holofernes [See line 121 above.] **144 ben** bien

4.3.34 wilt [F] will **44 s.p. KING** Long⟨ueville⟩. **54 slop** Shop **70 idolatry** [F] ydolatrie **89 I** [not in Q] **104 Wished** [Passionate Pilgrim] Wish. [Dumaine's poem also appears in a poetic collection attributed to Shakespeare, The Passionate Pilgrim (c. 1599).] **108 thorn** [England's Helicon] throne [Dumaine's poem also appears in the collection England's Helicon (1600).] **113 great** [not in Q] **118 true love's** trueloues **142 Faith so** Fayth **151 coaches. In your tears** couches in your teares **172 to . . . by** by . . . to **176 like you** like **178 Joan** [Qb] Loue [Qa] **192 Where** King. Where [Q repeats s.p. "King." (here omitted) after the s.d. "reads the letter."] **204 e'en** and **251 style** Schoole **255 and** [not in Q] **279 Nothing** O nothing **291** [Q follows this line with the twenty-three lines printed here, indented, probably an unrevised version of 4.3.285–91, 292–339.] **333 authors** authour **335 Let** Lets **341 standards** standars **357 Allons, allons!** Alone alone

5.1.18 sine 'b' fine **23 insanire** in-/famie **25 bone** bene **26 Bone? Bon, fort bon** Bome boon for boon **31 Quare** Quari **51 wave** [F] wane **59 circum** circa vnu cita **79 choice** chose **88 mustachio** [F] mustachie **100 Nathaniel** Holofernes **101 rendered** [F] rended **102 assistance** assistants **107–08 myself, Judas Maccabeus; and this gallant gentleman, Hector** my selfe, and this Gallant Gentle-/man Iudas Machabeus **129 Allons** Alone

5.2.17 been a [F] bin **43 ho!** How? **46 jest; I beshrew** iest, and I beshrow **53, 57 s.p. MARIA** [F] Marg⟨aret⟩. **53 pearls** [F] Pearle **65 hests** deuice **67 pursuivant-like** perttaunt like **74 wantonness** wantons be **80 stabbed** [F] stable [Q] **89 sycamore** [F] Siccamone **96 they** [F] thy **124 love-suit** Louefeat **130** [Q follows this line with the two lines printed here, indented, probably an unrevised version of 5.2.131–32.] **133 too** [F] two **147 her** his **151 ne'er** ere **162 ever** [F] euen **217 s.p. ROSALINE** [Before line 216 in Q, which gives Rosaline both lines.] **242–55 s.p. CATHERINE** Maria. **273 Ah, they** They **277 Non point** No poynt **309 run over** runs ore **407 affectation** affection **463 zany** [F] saine **482 manège** nuage **500 they** [F] thy **513 least** [F] best **516 There** Their **551 s.p. PRINCESS** Lady. **559 this** [F] his **589 proved** [F] proud **633 gilt** [F] gift **657 The party is gone.** [Q centers, italicizes, and fails to attribute this line to Armado or any other character.] **673–74 on, stir** or stir **696 s.p. MOTE** [Q's prefix, "Boy.," could refer to Mote or Boyet.] **719 nimble** humble **745**

strange straying **752 them** [not in Q] **760 the** [F; not in Q] **764 in** [not in Q] **798 hermit** herrite **798** [Both Q and F follow this line with the six lines printed here, indented, probably an unrevised version of parts of 5.2.814–31.] **798.2 rank** rackt **800 A wife?** [In Q, this begins Catherine's answer to Dumaine (also line 800).] **868 Ver, begin** [In F, as here, this is part of Armado's speech. In Q, it is separated from Armado's words by a blank line and preceded by "B."] **869 s.p. / s.d. Spring** [sings] *The Song.* [centered in Q] **870, 871** [Lines in reverse order in Q.] **891 foul** [F] full **903 s.p. ARMADO** [F; not in Q] **904 You that way, we this way** [F; not in Q]

A MIDSUMMER NIGHT'S DREAM

CONTROL TEXT: Q1

F: The Folio of 1623
Q1: The Quarto of 1600
Q2: The Quarto of 1619

Title: A Midsummer Night's Dream [Q1 title page, head title] A mydsomer nighte dreame [Stationers' Register] A Midsommer nightes dream [Q1 running titles]

s.p. THESEUS [Q's use of *Theseus* and *Duke* has been standardized throughout.]
s.p. HIPPOLYTA [Q's use of *Hippolyta* and *Duchess* has been standardized throughout.]
s.p. BOTTOM [Q's use of *Bottom, Pyramus,* and *Clown* has been standardized throughout.]
s.p. FLUTE [Q's use of *Flute* and *Thisbe* has been standardized throughout.]
s.p. ROBIN [Q's use of *Robin* and *Puck* has been standardized throughout.]
s.p. QUINCE [Q's use of *Quince* and *Prologue* has been standardized throughout.]
s.p. SNOUT [Q's use of *Snout* and *Wall* has been standardized throughout.]
s.p. SNUG [Q's use of *Snug* and *Lion* has been standardized throughout.]
s.p. TITANIA [Q's use of *Titania* and *Queen* has been standardized throughout.]
s.p. STARVELING [Q's use of *Starveling* and *Moonshine* has been standardized throughout.]

1.1.4 wanes [Q2, F] waues **10 New** Now **24 Stand forth Demetrius.** [Q italicizes and centers on a separate line.] **26 Stand forth Lysander.** [Q italicizes and centers on a separate line.] **27 This** This man **136 low** loue **139 merit** else, it **159–60 And . . . son. / From . . . leagues.** From . . . leagues? /

And . . . sonne: **191 I'd** ile **200 Helen** Helena **212 sleights** flights **219 stranger companies** strange companions

1.2.20 stones stormes **64 s.p. ALL THE REST** All.

2.1.7 moonës Moons **58 make room** roome **61 Fairies** Fairy **78 Perigouna** Perigenia **79 Aegles** Eagles **101 cheer** heere **109 thin** chinne **158 the** [not in Q] **190 slay . . . slayeth** stay . . . stayeth **201 nor** [F] not **206 lose** loose

2.2.9 s.p. FIRST FAIRY [not in Q] **13 s.p. CHORUS** [not in Q] **25–30 Sing . . . with lullaby.** &c. **31–32 Hence . . . sentinel** [indented as part of the song] **44–45 comfort . . . Be it** [Q2, F] comfor . . . Bet it **49 good** [Q2, F] god **53 is** [Q2, F] it

3.1.44 s.p. SNOUT *Sn.* **59 and** or **71 Odours, odours.** [F] Odours, odorous **76 s.p. ROBIN** *Puck.* [F] *Quin⟨ce⟩.* **82 bristly** brisky **133 own** [Q2, F] owe **144 Mote** Moth **145 s.p. A FAIRY . . . ANOTHER . . . ANOTHER . . . ANOTHER . . .** All Four *Fairies* **148 apricots** Apricocks **157 s.p. A FAIRY** I. *Fai.* **157–58 mortal. / ANOTHER Hail.** mortall, haile **159–60 s.p. ANOTHER . . . ANOTHER** 2. *Fai . . .* 3. *Fai.* **170 you** of you **182 love's** louers

3.2.19 mimic [F] Minnick **80 so** [not in Q] **85 sleep** slippe **137 s.p. HELENA** [not in Q] **165 here** heare **202 is all quite forgot** is all forgot **214 like** life **221 passionate** [F; not in Q] **251 prayers** praise **258 No, no, sir** [F] No, no **yield** heele **280 doubt** of doubt **300 gentlemen** [Q2, F] gentleman **327 but** [Q2, F] hut **387 exiled** exile

3.3.14 shalt [Q2, F] shat **37 to** [not in Q]

4.1.19 courtesy curtsie **21–22 Pease- / Blossom** Cobwebbe **33 thee off** thee **38 all ways** alwaies **52 flow'rets** flouriets **70 o'er** or **79 these five** these, fine **93 nightës** nights **102 vanguard** vaward **114 Seemed** Seeme **125 this is** [Q2, F] this **170 in sickness a** sicknesse **188 found** [Q2, F] fonnd **189 It** [F] Are you sure / That we are awake? It **195 let us** [Q2, F] lets **201 t'expound** expound **203–4 a patched fool** [F] patcht a foole **208 ballad** Ballet

4.2.3 s.p. STARVELING [F] *Flut⟨e⟩.* **26 no** [F] not

5.1.34 our [F] Or **38 Egeus** [F] Philostrate **38, 42, 61, 72, 76, 106 s.p. EGEUS** [F] *Philostrate* **44 s.p. LYSANDER** [F] *The⟨seus⟩.* **46, 50, 54, 58 s.p. THESEUS** [F; not in Q] **48, 52, 56 s.p. LYSANDER** [F; not in Q] **59 strange** black strange **189 up in thee** [F] now againe **204 wall Moon** down [F] used **263 gleams** beames **299 prove** [Q2, F] yet prooue **306 mote** moth **307 warrant** warnd **337 s.p. BOTTOM** [F] *Lyon.*

5.2.1 lion Lyons **2 behowls** beholds **13 we** wee **49–50 And . . . blessed** / **Ever . . . rest.** Euer . . . rest, / And . . . blest.

THE MOST EXCELLENT AND LAMENTABLE TRAGEDY OF ROMEO AND JULIET

CONTROL TEXT: Q2 (Q1 FOR 1.2.51–1.3.36)

F: The Folio of 1623
Q1: The Quarto of 1597
Q2: The Quarto of 1599
Q3: The Quarto of 1609
Q4: The Quarto of 1623

Title: The . . . Iuliet [Q2 (title-page and head title above 1.1.)] *The most lamentable Tragedie of Romeo and Iuliet.* [Q2 (running title)]

s.p. CITIZENS OF THE WATCH [Q2's use of *Officer(s)* has been standardized throughout.]

s.p. CAPULET'S WIFE [Q2's use of *Capulet's Wife, Old Lady, Wife, Lady,* and *Mother* has been standardized throughout.]

s.p. MONTAGUE'S WIFE [Q2's use of *Wife* and *Wife. 2.* has been standardized throughout.]

s.p. CAPULET [Q2's use of *Capulet, I. Capulet,* and *Father* has been standardized throughout.]

s.p. PETER [Q2's use of *Peter* and *Servingman* has been standardized throughout.]

s.p. CAPULET'S COUSIN [Q2's use of *2. Capulet* has been standardized throughout.]

s.p. FRIAR LAURENCE [Q2's use of *Friar* and *Lawrence* has been standardized throughout.]

s.p. FIRST SERVINGMAN [Q2's use of *1., 3.,* and *Fellow* has been standardized throughout.]

s.p. SECOND SERVINGMAN [Q2's use of *2.* has been standardized throughout.]

s.p. FIRST MUSICIAN [Q2's use of *Musician, Fiddler,* and *Minstrel* has been standardized throughout.]

s.p. SECOND MUSICIAN [Q2's use of *2. Musician, Fiddler,* and *2. Minstrel* has been standardized throughout.]

s.p. THIRD MUSICIAN [Q2's use of *3. Musician, 3. Fiddler,* and *3. Minstrel* has been standardized throughout.]

s.p. BALTHASAR [Q2's use of *Man* and *Balthasar* has been standardized throughout.]

1.1.24 in [Q1; not in Q2] **34 side** [Q1] sides **140 his** [Q3] is **146 sun** same **170 create** [Q1] created **172 well-seeming** [Q4] welseeing **185 lovers'** louing **195 Bid a . . . make** [Q1] A . . . make **204 unharmed** [Q1] vncharmed **211 makes** [Q4] make

1.2.13 made [Q1; Q2 continues: "Earth hath swallowed all my hopes but she, / Shees the hopefull Lady of my earth"] **27 female** [Q1] femme **65 Vitruvio** Vtruuio **89 fires** fire

1.3.4 where is Wher's **68 honour** [Q1] houre **69 honour** [Q1] *houre* **101 it** [Q1; not in Q2]

1.4.6–8 crowkeeper . . . entrance. [Q1] Crowkeeper. **23 s.p. MERCUTIO** [Q4] *Horatio.* **31 deformity** [Q1] deformities **39 done** [Q3] dum **42 save your reverence** [F] saue you reuerence **45 like lights** lights lights **47 five** fine **54 s.p. BENVOLIO Queen . . . she?** [Q1; not in Q2] **55–91 She . . . bodes.** [Q2 omits 1.4.68–70 and prints "She . . . bodes" as prose.] **55 s.p. MERCUTIO** [not in Q2] **59 Athwart** [Q1] Ouer **62–64 Her . . . bone** her traces of the smallest spider web / her collors of the moonshines watry beams, her whip of Crickets bone **64 film** Philome **67 maid** [Q1] man **73 O'er** [Q1] On **straight;** [Q2 continues: "ore Lawyerrs fingers who strait dreame on fees"] **76 breaths** [Q1] breath **77 lawyer's** [Q1] Courtiers **lip** nose **81 dreams he** [Q1] he dreams **90 elf-locks** [Q1] Elklocks **92 face** [Q1] side **113 sail** [Q1] sute

1.5.6 marzipan March-pane **13 longest** longer **15 a bout** about **16 Aha** [Q1] Ah **91 gentler** gentle **92 ready** [Q1] did readie

2.0.4 matched [Q3] match

2.1.10 Pronounce [Q1] prouaunt **dove** [Q1] day **12 heir** [Q1] her **13 Adam** Abraham **trim** [Q1] true **38 open-arse** an open, or **58 do** [Q1] to **73 passing** [Q1] puffing **83–84 nor any . . . name** o be some other name / Belonging to a man. **87 were** [Q1] wene **107 kinsmen** [Q1] kismen **125 washed** [Q1] washeth **141 'haviour** [Q1] behauior **143 more cunning** [Q1] coying **152 circled** [Q1] circle **190 lord** L. **191 s.p. NURSE** [not in Q2] **193–95 thee . . . come.—** thee (by and by I come) Madam. **207 mine** [Q1; not in Q2] **108 Romeo's name. Romeo!** [Q1] *Romeo.* **212 My nyas** My Neece **225 silk** [Q1] silken **229–32 Parting . . . s.p. ROMEO Sleep . . . Would** Parting . . . *Iu⟨liet⟩.* Sleep . . . *Ro⟨meo⟩.* Would **232 rest.** [Q1; Q2 continues: "The grey eyde morne smiles on the frowning night, / checkring the Easterne Clouds with streaks of light / And darknesse fleckted like a drunkard reeles, / From forth daies pathway, made by *Tytans* wheeles."] **233 sire's close** Friers close

2.2.4 **path and Titan's fiery** [Q1] path, and *Titans* burning [Q2 (Version B)] pathway, made by Tytans [Q2 (Version A)] **22 sometime's** [Q1] sometime **26 slays** [Q1] staies **74 yet ring** [Q4] yet ringing

2.3.6 **kinsman** [Q1] kisman **16 s.p. BENVOLIO** [Q1] *Ro⟨meo⟩.* **23 hai** Hay **25–26 phantasims** phantacies **29 pardon-me's** [Q1] pardons mees **60 Switch . . . switch** Swits . . . swits **84 s.p. BENVOLIO** [not in Q2] **102 for** [Q1; not in Q2] **181–91 Well . . . letter** [prose in Q2] **179 I warrant** Warrant **192 Ah** A **dog's** [Q3] dog

2.4.11 **three** [Q3] there **15–19 And . . . away** M. And [Q2's M. is indented as a speech prefix]

2.5.27 **music's** [Q4] musicke **34 sum up some** sum up sum

3.1.2 **Capels are** [Q1] *Capels* **63 injured** [F] iniuried **69** *stoccado* stucatho **70 come . . . walk** will you walke **85 s.p. PETRUCCIO Away, Tybalt!** Away Tybalt. [as stage direction] **87 both your** both **117 He gad** He gan **119 fire-eyed** [Q1] end **140 kinsman** [Q1] kisman **145 fray** [Q1, F] bloudie fray **160 agent** aged **170 kinsman** [Q3] kisman **178 s.p. MONTAGUE** [Q4] *Capu⟨let⟩.* **182 hate's** [Q1] hearts **186 I** [Q1] It

3.2.1 **s.p. JULIET** [Q1, F; not in Q2] **9 By** [Q4] And by **15 grown** grow **19 on** vpon **73 s.p. JULIET O . . . face** [Q1; assigned to *Nur⟨se⟩.* in Q2] **76 Dove-feathered** Rauenous douefeatherd **79 damned** [Q4] dimme **87 dissemblers all** all dissemblers **128 corpse** course

3.3.15 **Hence** [Q1] Here **19 banished** [Q1] blanisht **40–43 But . . . death?** This may flyes do, when I from this must flie, / And sayest thou yet, that exile is not death? / But *Romeo* may not, he is banished. / Flies may do this, but I from this must flie: / They are freemen, but I am banished.

3.3.52 **Thou** [Q1] Then **62 men** [Q1] man **82 Where is** [Q1] Wheres **109 denote** [Q1] deuote **116 lives** lies **143 pout'st upon** [Q4] puts vp **167 disguised** [Q3] disguise

3.4.13 **be** [Q1] me **23 We'll** [Q1] Well

3.5.13 **sun exhaled** Sun exhale **19 the** [Q1] the the **31 changed** change **43 my** [Q1] ay **82 him** [Q4; not in Q2] **106 I** [Q4; not in Q2] **139 gives** [Q3] giue **176 work, play;** houre, tide, time, worke, play **180 lined** liand **225 hence** here

4.1.45 **cure** [Q1] care **72 slay** [Q1] stay **83 chapless** [Q1] chapels **85 tomb** [not in Q2] **98 breath** [Q1] breast **100 wanny** many **110 In** [Q3] Is **bier** [Q2 continues: "Be borne to buriall in thy kindreds graue"] **111 shalt** [Q3] shall **116 waking** [Q3] walking

4.2.14 **self-willed harlotry** [Q1] selfewield harlottry **26 becoming** becomd

4.3.48 **wake** [Q4] walke

4.4.20 **faith** [Q4] father **63 See** [not in Q2] **68 long** [Q1] loue **70–73 Beguiled . . . death** [follows Nurse's speech 4.4.80–85] **82 behold** [Q3] bedold **92 cure** care **108 All in** And in **109 fond** some **126 by my** [Q1] my my **131 full of woe** [Q4] full **132 s.p. FIRST MUSICIAN** [Q1] *Minstrels.* **146 s.p. PETER Then . . . I** [Q4] Then . . . *Peter.* **I. 148 grief** [Q1] griefes **149 And . . . oppress** [Q1; not in Q2] **152 Matthew Minikin** Simon Catling **157 Simon** [Q1] *Iames*

5.1.3 **lord** L. **15 fares my Juliet** [Q1] doth my Lady *Iuliet* **24 defy** [Q1] denie **77 pay** [Q1] pray

5.3.3. **yew trees** [Q1] young tree **20 rite** right **40, 43 s.p. BALTHASAR** [Q1] *Pet⟨er⟩.* **68 conjuration** commiration **71 s.p. PAGE** [Q1; line not assigned to anyone in Q2] **102–3 Shall I believe / That I will beleeue, /** Shall I beleeue that **108 Depart again.** [Q4] Depart again, come lye thou in my arme. / Here's to thy health, where ere thou tumblest in. / O true Appothecarie! / Thy drugs are quicke. Thus with a kisse I die. / Depart againe **137 yew** yong **186 too** [F] too too **189 is so shrieked** is so shrike **193 our** your **198 slaughtered** [Q4, F] slaughter **208 more early** [Q1] now earling **231 that** [Q4] thats **298 raise** [Q4, F] raie

THE TRAGEDY OF KING RICHARD THE SECOND

CONTROL TEXT: Q1; ADDITIONAL MATTER FROM F

F: The Folio of 1623
Q1: The Quarto of 1597
Q2, Q3: Quartos of 1598
Q4: The Quarto of 1608
Q5: The Quarto of 1615
Q6: The Quarto of 1634

Title: The Tragedie of Richard II [Q] The life and death of King Richard the Second [F]

s.p. KING RICHARD King [to 5.1]

1.1.118 **by my** [F] by **152 gentlemen** [F] gentleman **157 time** [F] month **162–63 Harry, when? / Obedience bids** *Harrie,* when? Obedience bids, / Obedience bids [F] Harry? when obedience bids, / Obedience bids **186 down** [F] vp

1.2.1 **Gloucester's** [F]; Woodstockes **58 it** [Q2, F] is

1.3.33 **comest** [Q5] comes [Q1] com'st [F] **55 just** [F] right **127 swords** [F] sword

127–28 swords, / Which [F; Q1 has a five-line passage after line 127 omitted in F, indented in this edition. See Textual Note.] 166 then [F; not in Q] 174 you owe [F] y'owe 215 night [Q4, F] nightes 220 sudden [F] sullen 231–32 father. / Alas [F; Q has a four-line passage omitted in F, indented in this edition after line 235.] 251 travel trauaile 256–57 return. / s.p. BOLINGBROKE [F; Q has twenty-six lines omitted from F, indented in this edition after line 256.] 256.2 remember remember me

1.4.7 grew [F] blew 19 cousin, cousin [F] Coosens Coosin 22 Bushy, Bagot here, and Green [Q6] Bushie, [Q1] Bushy: heere Bagot and Greene [F] 51–52 Enter Bushy / Bushy, what news? [F] Enter Bushie with newes. [Q1] 58 in his [F] in the [Q1] into the [Q2] 63 late! [F] late, / Amen [indented]

2.1.18 whose taste the wise are feared whose taste the wise are found [Q1] Whose state the wise are found [Q2] his state: then there are sound [F] 48 as a [Q4, F] as 70 reined ragde 102 encagèd [F] inraged 113 now, now not, 115–16 And— / s.p. KING RICHARD And thou, a [F] And thou—/ King. A 125 brother [Q2] brothers 178 the [F] a 233 that thou wouldst thou wouldst [Q1] thou'dst [F] 255 his [F] his noble 258 King's grown [Q3, F] King growen 278 Port le [F] le Port 281 Thomas . . . Arundel [not in Q1, F; a line is missing, probably a result of censorship.] 284 Thomas Ramston John Ramston 286 Coint [F] Coines

2.2.12 At . . . With With . . . at 16 eye [F] eyes 31 As thought— As thought [Q1] As though [Q2, F] 59 broke [Q2, F] broken 119 Castle [F; not in Q1] 138 commoners commons 148–49 s.p. BAGOT Farewell . . . / BUSHY Well [continued to Green] Farewell . . . / Bush⟨ie⟩ Well [Q1] Bush⟨y⟩. Farewell . . . Well [F]

2.3.36 Hereford, [Q3] Herefords 98 the [F; not in Q1] 124 kinsman [F] cousin 157 to [Q2, F] vnto

3.1.32 England. [F] England, Lords farewell.

3.2.1 Harlechly Barkloughly 28–29 all. / s.p. AUMERLE [F; Q1 has four lines omitted in F, indented in this edition after line 28.] 31 friends [F] power 36 bloody [Q2, F] bouldy 51 from [F] off from 80 sluggard [F] coward 81 forty [F] twenty 98 loss, [F] and 130 offence [F; not in Q1] 174 wail their present woes [F] sit and wail theyr woes 199 faction [F] partie

3.3.13 with you [F; not in Q1] 35 Upon [F] on both 58–59 rain / My waters [F] raigne. / My water's 90 is [F] standes 118 a prince and princesse [Q1] a Prince [Q3] a Prince, is [F] 126 We [Q4, F] King. We 126 ourself [F] our selues 170 mock [F] laugh

3.4.11 joy grief 35 too [F] two 58 garden! We at garden at [Q1] garden, at [Q3, F] 68 then [not in Q1, F] 81 Cam'st [Q2, F] them

4.1.21 him [Q3, F] them 50–51 foe. / s.p. SURREY [F; Q1 has an eight-line passage omitted from F, indented in this edition after line 50.] 50.3 may it may 50.4 sun to sun sinne to sinne 67 my [Q3, F; not in Q1] the [Q2] 92 Bishop of Carlisle Bishop [Q3, F] B. [Q1] 103 of that name the fourth [F] fourth of that name 136 you [Q2, F] yon 136 rear [F] raise 139 Prevent Preuent it 145–308 May . . . fall [F (and similarly Q4); not in Q1. Only departures from F are noted for these lines.] 227 upon [Q4] vpon me 241 and [Q4] a 245 Nor [Q4] No, nor 309–10 On . . . yourselves [Q4, F] Let it be so, and loe on wednesday next, / We solemnly proclaime our Coronation, / Lords be ready all [Q1] 322 I will Ile

5.1.25 stricken [F] throwne 44 fall [F] tale 66 friends [F] men 78 queen [F] wife 84 s.p. NORTHUMBERLAND [F] King.

5.2.52 Hold these jousts and triumphs Hold those Iusts & Triumphs [F] do these iusts & triumphs hold 55 prevent it preuent 78 by my life, my by my life, by my [Q1] my life, my [Q2, F] 82 son [F] Aumerle

5.3.1 tell [F] tell me 14 these [F] those 21 days [F] yeares 30 the my 35 I may [Q2, F] May 55 lest lest thy 73 voiced [Q3, F] voice 91 kneel [F] walke 100 mouth [Q2, F] month 109 s.p. KING HENRY [Q2, F] yorke 142 so [not in Q1, F] too [Q6]

5.4.3, 6 s.p. FIRST, SECOND [not in Q1, F] 3 Those [F] These

5.5.13–14 faith . . . faith [F] word . . . word 33 treason makes [F] treasons make 55 sounds that tell sound that tells 56 that [F] which 58 hours, and times [F] times, and houres 65 a sign [Q2, F] asigne 94 spur-galled [F] Spurrde, galld

5.6.8 Salisbury, Spencer, Blunt [F] Oxford, Salisbury, Blunt [Q1] Oxford, Salisbury [Q2] 17 not [Q2, F1] nor 43 through the [F] through

THE LIFE AND DEATH OF KING JOHN

CONTROL TEXT: F

F: The Folio of 1623

s.p. KING JOHN [F's use of King John, John, and England has been standardized throughout.]

s.p. QUEEN ELEANOR [F most often uses Eleanor, but also Queen, Queen Mother, and Old Queen. The choice of speech prefix often corresponds to the immediate context; they have been standardized throughout.]

s.p. BASTARD [F uses *Philip* until line 138 and *Bastard* almost exclusively thereafter: standardized throughout.]

s.p. FALCONBRIDGE [F's use of *Robert* has been altered throughout.]

s.p. KING PHILIP [In many places, noted individually below, F confuses the King with the Dauphin (*Lewis*). Otherwise, F's use of *King*, *Philip*, and *France* has been standardized throughout.]

s.p. LOUIS THE DAUPHIN [F uses *Dauphin* (*Dolphin*) alone: expanded throughout.]

1.1.11 Poitou *Poyctiers* **161 arise** rise **188 'Tis too** 'Tis two **208 smack** smoake **237 Could a** Could **257 Thou** That

2.1.1, 18 s.p. KING PHILIP *Lewis* **63 Ate** Ace **113 breast** beast **144 shows** shooes **149 King Philip** King *Lewis* **150** s.p. KING PHILIP *Lew⟨is⟩* **152 Anjou** *Angiers* **169 Draw** Drawes **215 Confront your** Comfort yours **325** s.p. CITIZEN *Hubert.* **327 your** yonr **335 run** rome **362 who's** whose **368** s.p. CITIZEN *Fra⟨nce⟩* **371 Kinged** Kings **425 niece** neece **435 complete, O** compleat of **488 Anjou** *Angiers* **489 side** fide **501 sun** sonne **524 shall** still **540 rites** rights **572 lose** loose

3.1.34 God heauens **36 day** daies **62 God** heauen **74 task** tast **81 God** heauen **122 it** that **162 God** Heauen **185 crazèd** cased **208 troth** truth **210 swear'st** sweares **224 Wilt** Wil't

3.3.8–10 Of . . . liberty. Of hoording Abbots: imprisoned angells / Set at libertie: the fat ribs of peace / Must by the hungry now be fed vpon: **52 broad-eyed** brooded

3.4.44 art not art **48 God** heauen **64 Friends** fiends **110 world's** words **149 vilely born** euilly borne **182 make** makes

4.1.23 God heauen **63 his** this **77 God's** heauen **91 God** heauen **114 eyes** eye **131 God** heauen

4.2.1 again against **31 worser** worse **42 when** then **73 Does** Do **117 ear** care

4.3.16 Who's Whose **17 'Tis Is 33 man** mans **147 scramble** scamble **156 cincture** center

5.1.54 glisten glister

5.2.36 gripple cripple **43 thou** [not in F] **133 unhaired** vn-heard **135 these** this **145 his** this

5.3.8 Swineshead *Swinsted*

5.4.34 cresset Crest

5.5.3 measured measure **7 tatt'ring** tott'ring

5.6.13 eyeless endles

5.7.16 invincible inuisible **17 mind** winde **21 cygnet** Symet **42 strait** straight **60 God** heauen **88 our own** our **108 kind of** kinde

THE COMICAL HISTORY OF THE MERCHANT OF VENICE, OR OTHERWISE CALLED THE JEW OF VENICE

CONTROL TEXT: Q1

F: The Folio of 1623
Q1: The Quarto of 1600
Q2: The Quarto of 1619

s.p. SHYLOCK [Q1's use of *Iew⟨e⟩* has been standardized throughout.]

s.p. LAUNCELOT [Q1's use of *Clo⟨wne⟩* has been standardized throughout.]

s.p. SALERIO [Q1's use of *Salarino* in some s.d.'s and s.p.'s has been standardized throughout.]

Title: The Comical History of the Merchant of Venice, or Otherwise Called the Jew of Venice [after Q half title and Stationers' Register entry] The comicall History of the Mer / *chant of Venice* [Q half title and running title] The most excellent / Historie of the *Merchant / of Venice*. With the extreame crueltie of *Shylocke* the Iewe / towards the sayd Merchant, in cutting a iust pound / of his flesh: and the obtayning of *Portia* / by the choyse of three / chests. *As it hath been diuers times acted by the Lord / Chamberlaine his Seruants.* / Written by William Shakespeare. [Q title page] The Merchant of Venice [F]

1.1.27 Andrew, decks *Andrew* docks **113 Yet is** It is

1.2.51 throstle Trassell

1.3.108 spit spet **121 spat** spet

2.2.3–7 Gobbo Iobbe **87 last** [Q2] lost **159 a suit** [Q2, F] sute

2.4.5 as us

2.5.41 Jew's Iewes

2.6.14 younker younger **24 therein** then **58 gentlemen** [Q2, F] gentleman

2.7.69 tombs *timber*

2.8.39 Slubber [Q2, F] slumber

2.9.47 chaff [F] chaft

3.1.62 s.p. MAN [not in Q, F] **89 heard** [F] heere

3.2.63 s.p. ONE FROM PORTIA'S TRAIN [not in Q, F] **66 ALL** [not in Q, F] **67 eyes** [F] eye **71 I'll begin it** [in Q and F, printed in Roman rather than italic (as the rest of the song), as if not part of the song] **81 vice** voyce **93 makes** [F] maketh **101 Therefore, thou** [Q2] Therefore then thou [Q1, F] **301 thorough** through

3.4.23 Hear other things: heere other things **49 Padua** Mantua **50 cousin's hands** [Q2] cosin hand [Q1] cosins hand [F] **53 traject** Tranect **82 my** [F] my my

3.5.67 merit it meane it, it **74 for** a [F] for **4.1.29 his** [Q2, F] this **30 flint** [Q2] flints [Q1, F] **50 Mistress** Maisters **73 bleat** [F] bleake [Q] **74 pines** [F] of Pines **99 'Tis** [Q2, F] as **121 forfeit** forfaiture **127 inexorable** inexcrable **225 No, not** [Q2, F] Not **392 not** [Q2] not to [Q1, F] **395 s.p. GRAZIANO** [Q2, F] Shy⟨locke⟩. [Q1]
5.1.42 Master Lorenzo! Sola M. *Lorenzo* sola [Q2] & M. *Lorenzo* sola [Q1, F] **47–48 morning.** / LORENZO . . . Sweet soul, let's morning sweet soule / *Loren⟨zo⟩.* Let's **86 Erebus** Erobus [F] Terebus [Q] **152 it** [Q2, F; not in Q1] **232 my bedfellow** [Q2, F] mine bedfellow

THE HISTORY OF HENRY THE FOURTH (1 HENRY IV)

CONTROL TEXT: Q1 FOR 1.3.199–2.3.19, Q2 ELSEWHERE

F: THE FOLIO OF 1623
Q1: Remaining fragment of the Quarto of 1598
Q2: The complete Quarto of 1598
Q3: The Quarto of 1599
Q4: The Quarto of 1604
Q5: The Quarto of 1608
Q6: The Quarto of 1613
Q5b, Q6b: Successive states of Q5 and Q6 incorporating various print-shop corrections and changes
Q7: The Quarto of 1622

Title: THE / HISTORY OF / HENRIE THE / FOURTH; / With the battell at Shrewsburie, / *betweene the King and Lord* / Henry Percy, surnamed / Henrie Hotspur of / the North. / *With the humorous conceits of Sir* / John Falstalffe [Q2 title page] The First Part of Henry the Fourth, / with the Life and Death of HENRY / Sirnamed HOT-SPURRE. [F head title]

s.p. KING HENRY [Q's use of *King* has been changed throughout.]
s.p. PRINCE HARRY [Q's use of *Prince* has been changed throughout.]
s.p. POINS [Q's use of *Poines / Poynes* has been standardized throughout.]
s.p. HOTSPUR [Q's use of *Hotspur / Percy* has been standardized throughout.]
s.p. FIRST TRAVELLER and **SECOND TRAVELLER** [Q's *Traveler* of 2.2 has been differentiated into two persons.]
s.p. LADY PERCY [Q's use of *Lady* has been changed throughout.]
s.p. BARDOLPH [Q's use of *Russell / Bardoll* has been standardized throughout.]
s.p. GLYNDŴR [Q's use of *Glendower* has been changed throughout.]

s.p. SIR MICHAEL [Q's use of *Sir M⟨ighell⟩* in 4.4 has been modernized.]
s.p. JOHN OF LANCASTER [Q's use of *Prince John / John / John of Lancaster* has been standardized throughout.]

1.1.39 Herefordshire [Q7, F] Herdforshire **40 Glyndŵr** Glendower [similarly throughout] **62 a dear** [Q5b, F] deere **71 the Earl** Earle **73 Moray** Murrey **75–76 not? / s.p. WESTMORLAND In faith, it is a** not? In faith it is. / *West⟨merland⟩.* A
1.2.70 similes [Q6]; smiles **71 sweet** [Q3, F]; sweer **100 John,** sack-and-sugar **Jack?** John Sacke, and Sugar Jacke? **114 visors** vizards **144 Peto, Bardolph** Harvey, Rossill **148 But how** [F] How **154 Ay** [F] Yea **158 visors** vizards **161 But** [F] Yea, but
1.3.12 too [F] to **25 was** [F] is **26 Who either through** envy [F] Either envie therefore **27 Was** [F] Is **52 or** [F] or he **65 Made me to answer** [F] I answered **83 the** [Q3, F] that **115 Owain** Owen [similarly throughout] **122 you'll** [F] you wil **126 Although it be with** [F] Albeit I make a **131 In his behalf** [F] Yea on his part **133 downfall** [F] down-trod **199 s.p. HOTSPUR** [Q6, F; no s.p. in Q1] **209–10 a while . . . me.** [F] a while. **237 whipped** [Q2, F] whip **240 d'ye** [F] do you **241 upon't** [F] upon it **253 to't** [F] to it **254 We'll** [F] We wil **264 is't** [F] is it **265 Bristol** Bristow **Scrope** Scroop **289 Lord** Lo: **292 our** [Q2, F] out
2.1.1 An't [F] An it **23 races** razes **38 quoth** a [F] quoth he **51 Weald** wild **64 he's** [F] he is **68 foot-landrakers** [Q4, F] footland rakers **71 'oyez'-ers** Oneyres **80 recipe** receyte
2.2.16 two-and-twenty [F] xxii: **25 upon't** [F] upon it **45–46 Gadshill, what news? / s.p. GADSHILL Bardoll, what newes.** / *Bar⟨doll⟩.* **46 visors** vizards **70, 78 s.p. FIRST TRAVELLER** [unnumbered in Q] **71 their** our **74 s.p. SECOND TRAVELLER** [unnumbered in Q]
2.4.2 respect [Q7, F] the respect **42 thee** the **48 ransomed** ransome **63 A roan** [Q4, F] Roane **70 to** unto **83 maumets** mammets
2.5.29 precedent [F] present **32 s.p. POINS** [Q5, F] *Prin⟨ce⟩.* **61 o'** a **110 sun's** sonnes **159 s.p. PRINCE HARRY** [F] *Gad⟨shill⟩.* **160, 162, 166 s.p. GADSHILL** [F] *Ross⟨ill⟩.* **230 to't** [F] to it **303 talon** talent **311 Owain** O **346 joint-stool** joynd stoole **358 Father** [F] father **359 tristful** trustfull **366 yet** [Q4, F] so **431 lean** [Q3, F] lane **478, 479 Good . . . good** God . . . god **487 s.p. PETO** [F; not in Q] **492 s.p. PRINCE HARRY** [F; not in Q]
3.1.48 speaketh speakes **67 here's** [F] here is **97 cantle** [F] scantle **126 metre** miter **129**

on an **152 the least** least **182 nobleman** [F] noble man **197 thou down pourest** thou powrest downe **228 he's** [F] he is

3.2.59 won wan **84 gorged** [Q3, F] gordge **96 then** [F] than **112 swaddling-clothes** swathling cloaths **156 intemperature** [F] intemperance **157 bonds** bands

3.3.30 that's [Q4] that **49 tithe** tight **65 four-and-twenty** [F] xxiiii. **107 no thing** [F] nothing **122 owed** ought **158 guests** [F] ghesse **173–4 two-and-twenty** [F] xxii. **184 o'clock** of clocke

4.1.18 jostling justling **20 my lord** my mind **31 sickness stays him** sicknesse **50 sole** soule **55 is** [F] tis **98 ostriches** Estridges **98–100 that with the wind** / [. . .] / **Baiting** that with the wind / Baited **106 cuishes** cushes **109 dropped** [Q3, F] drop **117 altar** [Q5, F] altars **124 corpse** coarse **127 cannot** [Q6b, F] can **128 yet** [Q6, F] it **135 merrily** [F] merely

4.2.3 Coldfield cop- / hill **14–15 yeomen's** Yeomans **22 ensigns** Ancients **28 feazed ensign** fazd ancient **31 tattered** tottered

4.3.23 horse [Q5, F] horses **26 the half** the halfe of **84 country's** [Q6b, F] Countrey

4.4.30 more mo

5.1.42, 58 Doncaster [F] Dancaster **83 our** [F] your **135 o' a 136 will it** [Q3, F] wil

5.2.3 undone [Q6, F] under one **10 ne'er** [F] never

5.3.1 in the in **22 A fool** Ah foole **35 ragamuffins** rag of Muffins **39 stand'st** [F] stands **42 as yet** are yet **50 gett'st** [F] gets

5.4.57 Sir S. 67 Nor [F] Now **91 thee** the **97 rites** [F] rights **108 Embowelled** Inbowelled **110 Embowelled** Inboweld **110 embowel** inbowel **144 take't on** [F] take it upon **147 e'er** [F] ever

THE MERRY WIVES OF WINDSOR

CONTROL TEXT: F

F: The Folio of 1623
Q: The Quarto of 1602

s.p. MASTER/MISTRESS [F uses *M.* to abbreviate both words. Except at 4.4.24 and 5.5.196, *M.* occurs in speech prefixes when the reference is clear because either the wife or husband is not onstage, or as an abbreviation for "Mistress" when the husband has an immediately adjacent speech. Standardized throughout.]

s.p. JOHN [F's *Ser⟨vant⟩* and *1 Ser⟨vant⟩* have been replaced throughout.]

s.p. ROBERT [F's *2 Ser⟨vant⟩* has been replaced.]

s.p. FALSTAFF [F's use of *Falstaff* and *Sir John* has been standardized throughout.]

Title: A / Most pleasaunt and / excellent conceited Co- / medie, of Syr *Iohn Falstaffe*, and the / merrie Wiues of *Windsor*. / Entermixed with sundrie / variable and pleasing humors, of *Syr Hugh* / the Welch Knight, Iustice *Shallow*, and his / wise Cousin M. *Slender*. With the swaggering vaine of Auncient *Pistoll*, and Corporall *Nym*. [Q title page] A pleasant conceited Co- / medie, of Syr *Iohn Falstaffe*, and the / merry Wiues of *Windsor*. [Q head title] A *pleasaunt Comedie, of the merry Wiues of Windsor* [Q running title] An excellent & pleasant conceited cōmedie of S^r *Io Faulstof* and the merry *Wyves of Windesor* [Stationers' Register entry]

1.1.16 coad coat **19 cod** coate **24 py'r Lady** per-lady **28 compromises** compremises **39 George** *Thomas*. [Perhaps "Geo." in Shakespeare's handwriting could be misread "Tho."] **42 fery** ferry **51** s.p. SHALLOW *Slen⟨der⟩*. **73 Cotswold** *Cotsall* **87 Master M.** ["M." in dialogue is similarly interpreted throughout unless separately noted, or unless the character in question is obviously female (e.g., "M. Anne").] **117 Garter** Gater **119 Fery** Ferry **210 contempt** content **212 faul'** fall

1.2.3 'oman woman [Q] Nurse

1.3.13 lime lyme [Q] liue **19 his mind is not heroic.** [not in F] **42 studied her well** [Q] Studied her will **46 legion** legend **72 o'th'** ith' **73 humour** [Q] honor **80 stars** star **88 this** the

1.4.19 whey face wee-face **32 for God's sake** [Q; not in F] **39 un boîtier vert** vnboyteene verd **44–45 Ma foi, il fait fort chaud! Je m'en vais à la cour. La grande affaire.** mai foy, il fait for ehando, Ie man voi a le Court la grand affaires. **47 Mets-le à ma pochette. Dépêche** mette le au mon pocket, de-peech **52 and** aad **54 qu'ai-j'** que ay ie **60 larron** La-roone **77 baile** ballow **82 your** yoe your **106 goodyear** good-ier **110–11 Anne—** / *Exeunt Doctor* [CAIUS *and* RUGBY] / —**asshead** *An*-fooles head. [In this edition, "Anne" ("an") serves the double function of proper name and indefinite article.] **139 that I will** that wee will

2.1.1 have I haue **21 i'th'** with / The **26 O God, that I knew how to** [Q] how shall I **28 By my faith** Trust me **30 by my faith** trust me **51 praised** praise **54–55 hundred and fifty psalms** hundred Psalms **90 goodman** good man **127 Cathayan** *Cataian* **169 God bless you, bully rook, God bless you!** How now Bully-Rooke **185–86 guest cavaliero** guest-Caualeire **187** s.p. FORD *Shal⟨low⟩*. **188 Brooke** [Q] *Broome* **192 mijn'-heers** An-heires **201 than** then

2.2.2–3 I will retort . . . penny. [not in F] **21 Ay, ay,** I I, I, I **22 God** [Q] heauen **23–24 you, you** you **27 wouldst** [Q] would **50 God bless** [Q] heauen-blesse **63 rustling** rushling **101 O God no, sir** [Q; not in F] **139 God bless** 'Blesse **155 half, or all** all, or halfe **207 exchange** enchange **232 spokesmate** [Q] assistant **270 God** [Q] Heauen **274 God's my life** [Q] fie, fie, fie

2.3.16 God bless [Q] 'Blesse **17 God save** [Q] 'Saue **25 Galen** Galien **49 word** [Q; not in F] **Monsieur** Mounseur **70 s.p. PAGE, SHALLOW, and SLENDER** All. **79 patiences** patinces [Q] patients [F]

3.1.4 Petty pittie **8 Jeshu pless me** [Q] 'Plesse my soule **25 God** Heauen **35 God save** [Q] 'Saue **36 God pless** [Q] 'Plesse **54 pottage** porredge **75 By Jeshu** [Q; not in F] **88 Give . . . terrestrial—so.** [Q; not in F] **93 lads** [Q] Lad **95 Afore God** [Q] Trust me

3.2.43 By my faith [Q] Trust me **78 s.p. PAGE, CAIUS, and EVANS** All.

3.3.3 Robert Robin **33–34 pumpkin** Pumpion **51 By the Lord** [Q; not in F] **54–55 were, with nature,** were not nature **57–58 thee there's** [Q] thee. ther's **66 kiln** kill **129 s.p. JOHN** Ser⟨vant(s)⟩. **139 uncoop** vncape **152 what** who **163 foolish** foolish-ion **172 Ay,** I I, I **173 me** you **176 Ay, ay,** I I, I: I **192 heartily** hartly

3.4.12 s.p. FENTON [not in F] **44 by God** be God [Q; not in F] **55 God** [Q] Heauen **56 God** Heauen **64 Fenton** Fenter

3.5.7 'Sblood, the [Q] The **14 By the Lord** [Q] I should haue beene **53 By the mass** [Q] Oh he [Q] be **54 God bless** God save [Q] Blesse **73 God** [Q] good lucke **74 by** [Q] in **78 By the Lord** [Q] Yes **104 surge** serge

4.1.52 Genitivo Genitiue **53 Jenny's** Ginyes **57–58 hick . . . hack . . . 'whorum'** hic . . . hac . . . horum **59 lunatics** Lunaties

4.2.4 accoutrement accustrement **46 s.p. MISTRESS PAGE** [not in F] **53 s.p. MISTRESS PAGE** Mist⟨ress⟩ Ford. **61 Brentford** Brainford **84 direct** direct direct **87 him** [not in F] **97 as lief** liefe as **100 villains** villaine **102 gang** gin **113 this is** thi is **114 God be** Heauen be **125 s.p. PAGE** M⟨istress⟩ Ford. **157 not strike** strike **167 Jeshu** [Q] yea, and no **174 By my troth** [Q] Trust me

4.3.1 Germans desire Germane desires **7 them** [Q] him **9 house** [Q] houses

4.4.6 cold gold **24 s.p. MISTRESS FORD** M⟨istress⟩ Ford. **30 trees** tree **31 makes** make **41 Disguised . . . head** [Q; not in F] **59 s.p. MISTRESS FORD** Ford. **67 vizors** vizards **70 tire** tyre [Q] time **77 fery** ferry

4.5.35 s.p. SIMPLE Fal⟨staff⟩. **43 Ay, Sir** Tike I Sir: like **46 Thou art** [Q] Thou are **51 O Lord** [Q] Out alas **62–63 cozen Gar-**

mombles [Q] Cozen-Iermans **64 Colnbrook** Cole-brooke **91 O Lord, sir, and** [Q] And **97 Brentford** Braineford

4.6.26 ever euen **38 denote** deuote **39 visored** vizarded

5.1.20 Goliath Goliah

5.2.2 my daughter my **9 struck** strooke **10 lights** light **11 God** Heauen

5.3.11 Hugh Herne

5.5.1 struck stroke **9 foul fault** fowle-fault **28 God** [Q] Heauen **39, 80, 85 s.p. HOB-GOBLIN** Pist⟨ol⟩. **46 Bead** Bede **65 More** Mote **78 God** [Q] Heauens **113 mate** meete **117 By the Lord** [not in F] **180 white** greene **184 green** white **187 un garçon** oon Garsoon **un paysan** oon pesant **189 green** white **196 s.p. MISTRESS PAGE** M⟨istress⟩ Page.

THE SECOND PART OF HENRY THE FOURTH

CONTROL TEXT: Q; ADDITIONAL PASSAGES FROM F

F: The Folio of 1623
Q: The Quarto of 1600
QA: First issue of 1600 Q, lacking 3.1
QB: Second issue of 1600, containing 3.1

Title: THE / Second part of Henrie / the fourth, continuing to his death, / and coronation of Henrie / the fift. / With the humours of Sir John Fal- / staffe, and swaggering / Pistoll. [Q title page] **The Second part of Henry the Fourth, / Containing his Death: and the Coronation / of King Henry the Fift.** [F head title]

s.p. LORD BARDOLPH [Q's use of Bardolph (for the nobleman) has been changed throughout.]

s.p. NORTHUMBERLAND [Q's use of Earl / Northumberland has been standardized throughout.]

s.p. FALSTAFF [Q's use of Oldcastle / John / Sir John / Falstaff has been standardized throughout.]

s.p. PAGE [Q's use of Boy / Page has been standardized throughout.]

s.p. LORD CHIEF JUSTICE [Q's use of Lord / Justice has been standardized throughout.]

s.p. ARCHBISHOP OF YORK [Q's use of Bishop has been changed throughout.]

s.p. MOWBRAY [Q's use of Marshall / Mowbray has been standardized throughout.]

s.p. MISTRESS QUICKLY [Q's use of Hostess / Quickly has been standardized throughout.]

s.p. GOWER [Q's use of Gower / Messenger has been standardized throughout.]

s.p. PRINCE HARRY [Q's use of *Prince* / *Harry* has been standardized throughout.]

s.p. LADY NORTHUMBERLAND [Q's use of *Wife* has been changed throughout.]

s.p. LADY PERCY [Q's use of *Kate* has been changed throughout.]

s.p. FIRST DRAWER and SECOND DRAWER [Q's use of *Francis* and *Drawer* has been changed throughout (with some speeches redistributed).]

s.p. DOLL TEARSHEET [Q's use of *Tere-sheet* / *Doll* / *Dorothy* / *Whoore* has been standardized throughout.]

s.p. PRINCE JOHN [Q's use of *John* / *Prince* / *Lancaster* has been standardized throughout.]

s.p. KING HENRY [Q's use of *King* has been changed throughout.]

s.p. GLOUCESTER [Q's use of *Humphrey* / *Gloucester* has been standardized throughout.]

s.p. FIRST and SECOND GROOM [Q's use of *Strewers of Rushes 1, 2,* and *3* has been changed throughout (with some speeches redistributed).]

s.p. FIRST BEADLE [Q's use of *Sinklo* has been changed throughout.]

The following variants record only where the Norton text departs from Q, the control text. 3.1, missing in QA, is based on QB, but where material in QA was reset in QB, QA remains the authoritative text. F, however, contains eight lengthy passages (and some shorter ones) that do not appear in Q (1.1.165–78, 1.1.188–208, 1.3.21–24, 1.3.36–55, 1.3.85–108, 2.3.23–45, 4.1.55–79, 4.1.101–37). These are marked in the variants and are based on F Material originally in Q but absent in F (and in the Oxford text) is printed in the variants or in inset passages within this text. For a much fuller collation of Q and F, see Oxford's *William Shakespeare: A Textual Companion.*

Induction [F; heading not in Q] **s.p. RUMOUR** [not in Q] **13 griefs** [F] griefe **21 anatomize** anothomize **35 hold** hole **36 Where** [F] When

1.1.34 Lord Bardolph Sir John Umfreuile **41 ill** [F] bad **55 should the** [F] should that **59 a venture** a venter **96 say so** [F; not in Q] **103 knolling** [F] tolling **126 Too** [F] So **161 s.p. LORD BARDOLPH** [F] *Umfr⟨euile⟩.* This strained passion doth you wrong my lord. / *Bard⟨olfe⟩.* **163 Lean on your** [F] Leave on you **165–78 You . . . be?** [F; not in Q] **177 doth** hath **181 was** [F] twas **188–208 The . . . him.** [F; not in Q]

1.2.3 more moe **6 clay, man** clay-man **7 tends** [F] intends **10 o'erwhelmed** [F] overwhelmd **14 set** [F] in-set **25 Dumbleton**

Dommelton [Q] *Dombledon* [F] **26 slops** [F] my sloppes **31 rascally** [F] rascall **33 smooth-pates** [F] smoothy-pates **41 it;** [F] it: wheres Bardolf, **42 him. Where's Bardolph?** [F] him. **45 An** and **67 want** [F] need **88 age** [F] an ague **93 An't** andt **101 is, as I take it, a** [F] as I take it? is a **110 s.p. FALSTAFF** [F] Old⟨castle⟩. **131 waist** waste **slenderer** [F] slender **156 bearherd** Berod **158 this** [F] his **them, are** [F] the one **161 vanguard** vaward **176 th'ear** [F] the yeere **185–86 and Prince Harry** [not in Q] **192 my bottle, would** [F] a bottle. I would

1.3.21–24 Till . . . admitted. [F; not in Q] **26 case** [F] cause **28 on** [F] and **29 with** [F] in **36–55 Yes . . . else** [F; not in Q] **58 one** on **66 a** [F] so **71 Are** [F] And **78 not** [F] not to **79 He . . . Welsh** [F] French and Welch he leaves his back unarmde, they **84 'gainst** [F] against **85–108 s.p. ARCHBISHOP OF YORK . . . worst.** [F; not in Q] **109 s.p. MOWBRAY** [F] *Bish⟨op⟩.*

2.1.18 An I and **I an a** and a **19 vice** [F] view **22–23 continuantly** [F] continually **25 Lombard** [F] Lumbert **29 fobbed** fubd **38 Sir John** [F; not in Q] **44 Ah** a **45 Ah** a **48 s.p. FANG** [F] *Offic⟨er⟩.* **52 s.p. PAGE** [F] *Boy* **66–67 all, all** [F] al **73 Fie, what** [F] what **95 mad** made **134 tapestries** [F] tapestrie **134–35 ten pound** [F] X £. **138 Come** [F] come, come **152 good** [F; not in Q] **154 Basingstoke** [F] Billingsgate

2.2.14 hast—videlicet these [F] hast with these **15 ones** [F] once **19 thy** [F] the **20 made a shift to** [F; not in Q] holland. [F; Q here prints additional lines, and these are included as an inset passage after 2.2.20 of the text.] **23 lying** [F] being **yours** [F] yours at this time **28 you'll** [F] you will **49 engrafted** engraffed **65 A calls me e'en now** A calls me enow **68 red petticoat** peticote **70 rabbit** [F] rabble **72 Althea** [F] Althear **78 good** [F; not in Q] **81 An** And **82 be wronged** [F] have wrong **84 my good** [F] my **98 borrower's** borowed **106 Sure he** [F] He sure **112 familiars** [F] family **115 My lord . . .** [F; no speech prefix before this line] *Poynes* My lord . . . **144 road** rode **150 like** [F] as **151 declension** [F] descension **152 prince** [F] pince **153 everything** [F] enery thing

2.3.11 endeared [F] endeere **23–45 He . . . grave** [F; not in Q]

2.4.1 s.p. FIRST DRAWER [F] *Fran⟨cis⟩.* **3 s.p. SECOND DRAWER** [F] *Draw⟨er⟩.* **8 s.p. FIRST DRAWER** [F] *Fran⟨cis⟩.* **11 s.p. SECOND DRAWER** [F] Francis. **14 s.p. FIRST DRAWER** [F] *Dra⟨wer⟩.* **16 s.p. SECOND DRAWER** [F] *Francis.* **20 in good truth,** la in good truth, law **22 we** [F] one **32 an** and **38 them; I** [F] I **42 Yea, Jesu** Yea, joy **46 bravely.** [F] bravely. / *Doll* Hang your selfe, you muddie Cunger, hang your selfe. **48–49 i'good truth** ygood truth **59 Ensign** Antient [similarly elsewhere] **71 your** [F] & your **113 this.** [F] this. / *Sir John* No more Pistol, I would not have you go off here, discharge your selfe of our company, Pistoll. **117 An** and **123 'captain' odious** [F] as odious as the word occupy, which was an excellent good worde before it was il sorted **133 Where** [F] with **135 Fates** [F] faters **144 Trojan** troiant **150 Die men** [F] Men **152 O' A** **168 an a** and a **189 o' a 198 A** [F] Ah **207 o'...o'** a...a **213 ha'** chipped a chipt **223 boot** [F] bootes **228 the scales** [F] scales **240 master's** [F] master **248 o'Thursday** a thursday **251 By my troth, thou'lt** By my troth **thou't an** and **286 o' a 293 him** [F] thee **306 outbids** [F] blinds **356 good Doll.** [F] good Doll, come, shee comes blubberd, yea? wil you come Doll?

3.1.1–103 [QB; not in QA] **18 mast** [F] masse **22 billows** [F] pillowes **26 thy** [F] them **27 sea-boy** [F] season **52 liquors!** [F; Q here contains additional lines printed in this text as an inset passage after this word.] **80 beginnings** [F] beginning

3.2.11 o' a 19 o' a 20 bona-robas [F] bona robes **35 Stamford** [F] Samforth **41 o' Gaunt** a Gaunt **42 i'th'** ith **50 s.p. SHALLOW** [F] *Bardolfe* [QA] **61 accommodated** [F] accommodate **75 your** [F] your good **79 Surecard** [F] Soccard **90 so. Yea** so (so, so) yea **94 an't** and't **98 an't** and't **103 s.p. FALSTAFF** Prick him. [F] *John prickes him.* [Q s.d. is indented from right-hand margin on same type line as "well said."] **104 an** and **122 not** [F] much **133 for his** [F] for **143 he'd ha'** hee'd a **165 thou'rt** [F] thou art **168 caught** [F] cought **174 There** [F] Here **181–82 good Master Shallow, no more of that** [F] master Shallow. **199 in** [F] that we have, in **200 Hem boys** [F] Hemboies **205 lief** [F] live **217 I'll ne'er** ile nere **217–18 An't...an't** and't...and't **252 chapped** chopt **263 will** wooll **268 As you** [F] at your **my house** [F] our house **274 On** [F] *Shal⟨low⟩.* On **285 invisible** invincible **famine.** [Q here contains additional lines printed in this text as an inset passage after this word.] **285.2 ever** [F] over **291 trussed** [F] thrust

4.1.34 rags rage **36 appeared** appeare **55–79 And...wrong.** [F; not in Q] **71 shore** there **80 days** [F] daie's **101–37 O...King.** [F; not in Q. The s.p. "West." is set before 4.1.138 in Q.] **114 force** forc'd **137 indeed** and did **173 to our** [F] our **consigned** confinde **178 And At 234 Than** [F] That **man** [F] man talking **245 th'imagined** th'imagine **250 Employ** Imply **274**

this [F] his **292–93 redresses. s.p. / PRINCE JOHN I** [F] redresses, / I **295 s.p. HASTINGS** [F] *Prince* **327 Our...dispersed** [F] My lord, our army is disperst already **343 rebellion...yours.** [F] rebellion: **348 these** this **traitors** [F] traitour

4.2.2 I pray [F; not in Q] **37 Rome** [F] Rome, there cosin **62 gav'st away** [F] gavest away gratis **63 Have** [F] Now, have **75 pray** [F; not in Q] **78 but** [F; not in Q] **96 illuminateth** [F] illumineth **100 his** [F] this

4.3.32 melting [F] meeting **39 line** [F] time **52 accompanied? Canst thou tell that?** [F] accompanied **94 heaven** [F] heavens **104 write...letters** [F] wet...termes **120 and will break out** [F; not in Q] **132 chamber; softly, pray** [F] chamber **179 How fares your grace?** [F; not in Q] **183 him.** [F] him: he is not here. **203 Culling** [F] tolling **203–4 the virtuous sweets, / Our thighs** [F] Our thigh **209 have** hands **275 true and inward** [F] inward true and **288 worst of** [F] worse then **289 fine in carat, is** [F] fine, in karrat **292 my** [F] my most **305 O my son** [F; not in Q] **306 put it** [F] put **348 My gracious leige** [F; not in Q]

5.1.1 pie [F] pie sir **8 Davy, Davy, Davy** [F] Davy, Davy, Davy, Davy **8–9 see. William** [F] see Davy, let me see, yea mary William **12 headland** [F] hade land **19 Sir** [F] Now sir **21 Hinkley** [F] Hunkly **29–30 marvellous** [F] marvailes **33 o'th'** a'th' **40 An** and **46 Come,** [F] come, come, come **49 all** [F; not in Q]

5.2.21 s.p. GLOUCESTER *and* CLARENCE [F] *Princ. ambo* **46 mix** [F] mixt **62 s.p. PRINCE...CLARENCE** *Bro.* other [F] otherwise

5.3.3 grafting graffing **5 here a...and a** [F] here...and **24 Good Master Bardolph!** [F] Give master Bardolfe **46 thee** the **52–53 to th'** too'th **57 cavalieros** [F] cabileros **59 An** And **64 'tis** a tis **75 An't** And't **84 By'r Lady** Birlady **86 in thy** [F] ith thy **95 Cophetua** Covetua **117 knighthood** [F] Knight

5.4.8 an and **11 He** [F] I **22 o'ercome** overcom

5.5.1–3 s.p. FIRST GROOM, SECOND GROOM, FIRST GROOM [Q opens with s.d. *Enter strewers of rushes.* The first three speeches are assigned to *1, 2,* and *3,* each presumably a strewer.] **3 o' a 3–4 coronation.** *Exeunt / Enter* coronation, dispatch, dispatch. / *Trumpets sound, and the King, and his traine passe over the Stage; after them enter* **5 Robert** [F; not in Q] **14 s.p. SHALLOW** [F] *Pist⟨ol⟩.* **21–22 most certain.** / s.p. FALSTAFF But [F] best certaine: but **23 affairs** [F] affaires else **26 absque** obsque all [F; not in Q] **49 awake** [F] awakt **53 fool-born**

fool-borne **69 our** [F] my **82 I fear that** [F] that I feare

Epilogue 9 did mean [F; in F, the Epilogue is set in italics] meant **13–14 infinitely.** [F] infinitely: and so I kneele downe before you; but indeed, to pray for the Queene. **21 before** [F; not in Q] **27 died a** [F] died **29–30 and . . . Queen** [F; in Q, these lines follow Epilogue 15] **29 kneel** [F] I kneele

MUCH ADO ABOUT NOTHING

CONTROL TEXT: Q

Q: The Quarto of 1600
F: The Folio of 1623
F2: The Folio of 1632

s.p. DON JOHN [Q's use of *John* and *Bastard* has been standardized throughout.]

s.p. DON PEDRO [Q's use of *Pedro* and *Prince* has been standardized throughout.]

s.p. ANTONIO [Q's use of *Old*, *Antonio*, and *Brother* has been standardized throughout.]

s.p. DOGBERRY [Q's use of *Dogberry* and *Constable* has been standardized throughout.]

s.p. VERGES [Q uses both *Verges* and *Headborough*, but generally prefers the former, standardized throughout.]

1.1.8 Pedro Peter **34–35 bird-bolt** Burbolt
1.2.6 event [F2] euents
1.3.3 it [not in Q] **39 brothers** [F] bothers **44 on** on
2.1.33 bearherd Berrord **39 Peter fore** Peter: for . . . heavens **71 a bout** about **83, 86, 88 s.p. BALTHASAR** *Benedicke*
2.3.22 an [F] and **37 hid-fox** kid-foxe **56 s.p. BALTHASAR** [not in Q] **124 us of** [F] of vs
3.2.24 can cannot **45 s.p. DON PEDRO** [F] *Benedicke*
3.3.10, 15 s.p. SECOND WATCHMAN . . . FIRST WATCHMAN [reversed in Q] **24 s.p. FIRST WATCHMAN** *Watch 2* **34, 41, 45, 50, 61, 94, 110 s.p. A WATCHMAN** *Watch* **78, 85 s.p. FIRST WATCHMAN** *Watch* **145, 151 s.p. A WATCHMAN** *Watch 2* **154–55 A WATCHMAN** Never . . . us. [The speech is assigned to *Conrade* in Q.]
3.4.16 in [F] it
3.5.8 off of
4.1.201 princes left for dead princess (left for dead,)
4.2.1 s.p. DOGBERRY *Keeper* **2, 5 s.p. VERGES** *Couley* **4 s.p. DOGBERRY** *Andrew* **8, 11, 14, 17, 23, 27, 31, 36, 39, 44, 50, 63, 67 s.p. DOGBERRY** *Kemp* **45 s.p. VERGES** *Constable* **60 s.p. DOGBERRY** *Constable* **61–62 s.p. VERGES** Let them be, in the hands— / CON-

RAD Off, coxcomb! *Couley* Let them be in the hands of Coxcombe.
5.1.16 Bid And **97 an** [not in Q]
5.2.41 for [not in Q] **53 maintain** maintaind **73 myself. So** my self so
5.3.4–11 s.p. CLAUDIO Done . . . dumb [These lines follow the Lord's in Q with no distinct speech prefix] **11 dumb** [F] dead **23 s.p. CLAUDIO** *Lo.*
5.4.54 s.p. ANTONIO *Leonato* **96 s.p. BENEDICK** *Leonato*

THE LIFE OF HENRY THE FIFTH

CONTROL TEXT: F; ADDITIONAL MATTER FROM Q1

F: The Folio of 1623
Q1: The Quarto of 1600
Q3: The Quarto of 1619

s.p. KING HARRY [F's use of *King* has been standardized throughout.]

s.p. KING CHARLES [F's use of *King* has been standardized throughout.]

1.2.38 succedant succedual **50 there** [Q] then **72 fine** [Q] find **74 heir** [Q] th'Heire **77 Ninth** Tenth **99 son** man **115 those** these **131 blood** Bloods **147 unmasked his power** [Q] went with his forces **unto** into **154 the bruit thereof** the brute hereof [Q] th'ill neighborhood **163 your** [Q] their **166 A LORD** [Q] Bish⟨op of⟩ Ely. **183 True.** [Q; not in F] **197 majesty** [Q] Maiesties **208 Fly** [Q] Come **212 end** [Q] And **213 defect** [Q] defeat **276 have I** I haue [F] haue we [Q1] we haue [Q3] **284 from** [Q] with **287 Ay,** [Q] And
2.0.32 —perforce— [not in F]
2.1.21 mare [Q] name **23 Good morrow, Ensign Pistol** [Q; not in F] **25 NIM** [Q; not in F] **26 Gad's lugs** [Q] this hand **65 thee defy** [Q] defie thee **72 enough.** [Q] enough to **73 you** your **95 s.p. NIM I shall have my eight shillings?** *Nim.* I shal haue my eight shillings I woon of you at beating? [Q; not in F] **105 that's** that
2.2.1 s.p. GLOUCESTER [Q; throughout scene] Bed⟨ford⟩. [F; throughout scene] **35 their** [Q] the **84 him** [Q; not in F] **85 vile** [Q; not in F] **95 ha'** [Q1] haue **104 a** an **136 mark** make the thee **144 Henry** [Q] *Thomas* **154 heartily in sufferance** in sufferance heartily **163 and fixed** [Q; not in F] **172 have** [Q; not in F] **173 ye** [Q1] you
2.3.15 babbled Table **22 up'ard and up'ard** vpward and vpward [Q] up-peer'd and upward **29 s.p. HOSTESS** *Woman.* **35 hell-fire** [Q1] Hell **41 word** [Q1] world

2.4.4 **Bourbon** [Q] Britaine 33 **agèd** [Q] Noble 57 **mountant** Mountaine 75 **England** [Q1] of England 106 **Turns he** [Q] Turning 107 **pining** [Q] priuy 123 **for** [Q] of

3.0.6 **fanning** fayning

3.1.7 **conjure** commune 17 **noblest** Noblish 24 **men** me 32 **Straining** Straying

3.2.19 **God's plud** [Q; not in F] 19 **breaches** [Q] breach 26 **runs** wins

3.3 s.p. **FLUELLEN** [Q; throughout scene] Welch. [F; throughout scene] s.p. **JAMY** [Q; throughout scene] Scot. [F; throughout scene] s.p. **MACMORRIS** [Q; throughout scene] Irish. [F; throughout scene] 55–56 **Aye owe Got** a aye, or goe to 109 **heady** headly 112 **Defile** Desire 124 **dread** [Q] great

3.4.3 **Un** En 4 **j'apprenne** ie apprend 5 **parler** parlen **Comment** Comient 6 **La main?** Elle est appelée Le main il & appelle 7 **Et les doigts** [continued to Catherine] Alice. E le doyts. 8 s.p. **ALICE** Kat⟨herine⟩ 8–9 **souviendrai** souemeray 9 **sont** ont **fingers. Oui** fingres, ou 11 s.p. **CATHERINE** Alice. 12 **la bonne écolière; j'ai** le bon escholier. / Kat⟨herine⟩. I'ay 13 **les** le 14 **Les** Le 15 **De nails.** Ecoutez— De Nayles escoute: 19 **arma** Arme 20 **le** de 22 **la répétition** le repeticio 39 **Non, et** Nome 43 **Sauf** Sans **honneur** honeus 44 **dis** de 45 **pieds** pied **la robe** [Q] de roba 46 **De foot** Le foot 46, 47, 51, 53 **cown** con [Q] Count 47 **De foot et de Le Foot,** & **le Ils** Il 51 **De foot et de Le Foot** & **le Néanmoins** neant moys 53 **foot, de foote,** e de [Q] Foot, le

3.5.10, 32 s.p. **BOURBON** [Q] Brit⟨ain⟩. 11 **de** du 26 **'Poor' may** we Poore we 45 **Foix** Loys 46 **knights** Kings

3.6.23 **Of** and of 27 **her** [Q] his 49 **executions** [Q] execution 58 **is this the ensign you told me of** [Q] this is an arrant counterfeit Rascall 82 **com'st** cam'st 99 **here** [Q; not in F] 102 **lenity** [Q] Leuitie

3.7.7 s.p. **BOURBON** [Q; throughout scene] Dolph⟨in⟩. [F; throughout scene] 12 **Ah ha** Ch'ha 14 **qui a** ches 60 **vomissement** vemissement et est 61 **truie** leuye 83 **Duke of Bourbon** [Q] Dolphin

4.0.16 **name** nam'd

4.1.92 **Thomas** Iohn 148 **deaths** [Q] death **propose** purpose 173 s.p. **BATES** 3. Lord. [Q] Will⟨iams⟩. 227 **adoration** odoration 267 **or** of 280 **have I** [Q] I haue 286 **ill** all

4.2 s.p. **BOURBON** [Q; throughout scene] Dolph⟨in⟩. [F; throughout scene] 5 **plus?** puis 6 **Cieux** Cein 11 **dout** doubt 25 **'gainst** against 35 **sonance** Sonuance 46 **hands** hand 47 **drooping** dropping 49 **palled** pale 60 **guidon** Guard: on

4.3.2 s.p. **CLARENCE** Bed⟨ford⟩. 3 s.p. **WARWICK** [Q; throughout scene] West⟨merland⟩. [F; throughout scene] 8 **Clarence** [Q] Bedford

11, 15 s.p. **CLARENCE** Bed⟨ford⟩. [F; speeches not in Q] 44 **t'old** old 48 **And . . . day.'** [Q; not in F] 106 **grazing** crasing 118 **as** or 119 **your** [Q] the 129 **come** come againe

4.4.4 **Qualité 'Calin** o **Qualtitie** calmie 12 **miséricorde** miserecordie **pitié** pité 14 **Or** for 46 **prisonnier** prisonner **néanmoins** neant-mons 47 **lui ci** layt a **promettez** promets 48 **je se** 49 **remerciements** remercious 49–50 **j'ai tombé** le intombe 50 **mains** main. **comme** [not in F] **pense** peuse 51 **treis-distingué** tres distinie 59 **Suivez** Saaue

4.5 [Both Bourbon and the Dauphin appear in this scene in F. Whereas in most instances the textual differences between Q and F merely involve speech prefixes, here they are more substantial. See Additional Passages, pp. 1520–21, for F and Q versions of this scene.] 2 **Seigneur** sigueur **perdu . . . perdu** perdia . . . perdie 3 s.p. **BOURBON** [Q] Dol⟨phin⟩. **Mort de** Mor **Dieu** 7–9 **We are . . . upon** [Q; F places after 4.5.17] 10 **order** [Q] Order **now** 12 **home** [Q] hence 13 **leno** [Q] Pander 14 **by a slave** [Q] a base slaue

4.6.14–15 **face,** / **And** [Q] face. / **He** 15 **dear** [Q] my 39 s.p. **PISTOL** Coup' la gorge. [Q; not in F]

4.7.18 **e'en** in 19 **world** Orld 36 **made an end** [Q] made 83 **Crispian** Crispianus 102 **countryman** [Q] Countrymen 115 **a live** aliue 118 **a lived** aliue 150 **that I would see** that I might see

4.8.9 **God's plood, and his** Gode plut, and his [Q1] 'Sblud 23 **what is** [Q1] what's 94 **Vaudemont** Vandemont 98 **Keighley** Ketly 107 **we** me 118 **in** [Q; no in F]

5.0.10 **maids** [not in F] 29 **high-loving** by loving

5.1.13 **a** [Q1] hee 36 **By Jesu** [Q1] I say 37 **and four nights** [Q; not in F] 80 **swear** [Q] swore

5.2.50 **scythe, all** Sythe, withall 169 **vat** wat 172–73 **suis le possesseur** sur le possession 236 **grandeur** grandeus 237 **de votre seigneurie** nostre Seigneur **indigne** indignie 244 **vat** wat 246 **entend** entendre 291 **before that it** before it 297 **never** [not in F] 305 s.p. **WARWICK** West⟨merland⟩. 306 **so** [not in F] 328 **ALL** Lords. 337 **paction** Pation

The Tragedy of Julius Caesar

CONTROL TEXT: F

F: The Folio of 1623

1.2.104 **Said Caesar** Caesar saide 140 **were** are 156 **walls** Walkes

1.3.128 **In favour's** Is Fauors

2.1.40 ides first **67 of** of a **83 put** path **96 Cinna,** this; this, *Cinna;* **266 his** hit **312, 315, 319 s.p.** LIGARIUS *Cai⟨us⟩.*

2.2.46 are heare **81 Of** And **108 Cassius** *Publius* **109 s.p.** CASSIUS *Pub⟨lius⟩.* **Cassius** *Publius*

3.1.39 law lane **47 but** with just cause [not in F; line is quoted by Ben Jonson in *Timber, or Discoveries.*] **116 lies** lye **175 unstrung** in strength **286 for** from

3.2.50 s.p. FOURTH PLEBEIAN **2. 63 s.p.** FIFTH PLEBEIAN **4. 101 art** are **107 he** not hee **196–97 revenged. /** ALL THE PLEBEIANS **Revenge!** reueng'd: Reuenge **213 wit** writ

4.1.44 meinies meanes

4.2.2 s.p. SOLDIER *Lucil⟨lius⟩.* **34–36 s.p.'s** FIRST SOLDIER, SECOND SOLDIER, THIRD SOLDIER [not in F] **80 bay** baite **170 ill-tempered** too. ill remper'd too.s **204 Impatience** Impatient **269 to** ro **301 will** will it

5.1.42 teeth teethes **55 swords** Sword **79 ensigns** Ensigne **88 give** giue up **95 rest** rests

5.3.103 Thasos *Tharsus*

5.4.7 s.p. LUCILLIUS [not in F] **17 the** thee

5.5.76 With all Withall

As You Like It

CONTROL TEXT: F

F: The Folio of 1623

s.p. TOUCHSTONE [F's use of *Clowne* has been changed throughout.]

s.p. DUKE FREDERICK [F's use of *Duke* has been changed throughout.]

s.p. SIR OLIVER MARTEXT [F's use of *Oliver* has been changed in 3.3.]

s.p. JAQUES DE BOIS [F's use of *Second Brother* in 5.4 has been changed at lines 140 and 172.]

1.1.10 manège mannage **48, 50 villein . . . villeins** villaine . . . villaines **49 Bois** Boys **75 Denis** Dennis **94 she** hee **99 Ardenne** *Arden* [similarly throughout] **138 s.p.** OLIVER [not in F]

1.2.3 I [not in F] **69 s.p.** CELIA *Ros⟨alind⟩.* **76 Le** the **239 shorter** taller **256 Rosalind** *Rosaline*

1.3.1 Rosalind *Rosaline* **51 likelihood** likelihoods **84 Rosalind** *Rosaline* **90 Rosalind, lack'st thou then** *Rosaline* lacks then **131 we in** in we

2.1.49 much must **56 should** doe **59 the** [not in F]

2.3.16 s.p. ORLANDO [not in F] **30 s.p.** ORLANDO *Ad⟨am⟩.* **72 seventeen** seauentie

2.4.1 weary merry **39 thy** they **wound** would **43–44 batlet** batler **44 chapped** chopt

64 you your **69 travel** trauaile **78 cot** Coate [similarly throughout]

2.5.1 s.p. AMIENS [F has the heading "Song" and no speech prefix.] **32 s.p.** ALL [F has no prefix, but the heading *"Song."* and the phrase *"Altogether heere."*] **37–39 see . . . weather** *see. &c.* **43 s.p.** JAQUES *Amy⟨ens⟩.*

2.7.55 aught but [not in F] **87 comes** come **174 s.p.** AMIENS [There is no speech prefix in F, but the heading "Song."] **182 Then** The **190–93 sing . . . jolly** *sing, &c.* **201 master** masters

3.2.106 graft graffe **113 a** [not in F] **133 her** his **216 such** [not in F] **222 thy** the **328 deifying** defying **336 are** art

3.3.17 it [not in F] **79 s.p.** TOUCHSTONE *Ol⟨iuer⟩.*

3.4.27 a [not in F] **37 puny** puisny

3.5.129 I [not in F]

4.1.1 be [not in F] **17 my** by **53 beholden** beholding **66 warr'nt** warne **132 hyena** Hyen **180 it** in

4.2.2 s.p. FIRST LORD *Lord.* **7 s.p.** SECOND LORD *Lord.* **10 s.p.** LORDS [not in F, which has the heading "Musicke, Song."]

4.3.96 handkerchief handkercher **141 I'** I **154 his** this

5.2.6 her [not in F] **24 handkerchief** handkercher **28 overcame** ouercome **88 obedience** obseruance **106 I satisfy** I satisfi'd

5.3.14 s.p. BOTH PAGES [not in F, which has the heading "Song."] **17 In** In the **ring** rang **32–37** [F places these lines after 5.3.19.]

5.4.21 your you your **75 to** the to **103 her** *his* **153 them** him **186 so** [not in F]

The Tragedy of Hamlet, Prince of Denmark

CONTROL TEXT: F

F: The Folio of 1623
Fa, Fb: Successive states of F incorporating various print-shop corrections and changes
Q1: The Quarto of 1603 ("bad")
Q2: The Quarto of 1604 ("good")
Q2a, Q2b: Successive states of Q2 incorporating various print-shop corrections and changes
Q3: The Quarto of 1611

s.p. KING CLAUDIUS [F's use of *King* has been standardized throughout.]

s.p. QUEEN GERTRUDE [F's use of *Queen* has been standardized throughout.]

s.p. PLAYER KING [F's use of *King* has been standardized throughout.]

s.p. PLAYER QUEEN [F's use of *Baptista* and *Queen* has been standardized throughout.]

s.p. FIRST CLOWN [F's use of *Clown* has been standardized throughout.]
s.p. SECOND CLOWN [F's use of *Other* has been changed throughout.]

Title: *The Tragedie of Hamlet Prince of Denmarke* [Q2 (head title, running titles), F (head title), Q1 (running titles)] THE Tragicall Historie of HAMLET, *Prince of Denmarke* [Q2 (title page)] *The Tragedie of Hamlet* [F (running titles, table of contents)] THE Tragicall Historie of HAMLET *Prince of Denmarke* [Q1 (title page, head title)]

1.1.60 he [Q1, Q2; not in F] **62 Polacks** Pollax **93 designed** designe **106.8 tenantless** tennatlesse [Q2] **106.10 At** As [Q2] **106.14 feared** feare [Q2] **106.18 climature** climatures [Q2] **131 morn** [Q2] day **139 say** [Q1, Q2] sayes **144 takes** [Q1, Q2] talkes **155 Let's** [Q1, Q2] Let
1.2.8 sometime [Q2] sometimes **21 Coleaguèd** Coleagued [Q2] Colleagued **34 Valtemand** [Q2] *Voltemond* **35 bearers** [Q1, Q2] bearing **58–60 wrung . . . consent** [Q2; not in F] wrung from me a forced graunt [Q1; Oxford editor G. R. Hibbard argues that the "forced graunt" recollected by the Q1 reporter suggests that he was aware of Laertes' "laboursome petition" as it appears in Q2. The omission is therefore most likely an accident, not an authorial cut.] **77 good-mother** good Mother **119 pray thee** [Q2] prythee **132 canon** cannon **134 Seem** [Q2] Seemes **135 ah** [Q2] Oh **141 beteem** [Q2] beteene **150 God** [Q1, Q2] Heauen **164 Marcellus.** [Q2; F (text) indents, like a speech prefix; F (c.w.) is "*Mar-*."] **167 Wittenberg** [Q2] *Wittemberge* **176 prithee** [Q2] pray thee **186 A** [Q2] He **195 God's** [Q1, Q2] Heauens **204 distilled** [Q1, Q2] bestil'd **209 Where, as** [Q1] Whereas **237 s.p. BARNARDO** *and* MARCELLUS *Both.* [Q2] *All.* [F] **242 walk** [Q1, Q2] wake
1.3.1 inbarqued [Q1, Q2] imbark't **5 favour** [Q2] fauours **8 Forward** [Q2] Froward **9 perfume and** [Q2; not in F] **16 will** [Q2] feare **21 sanity and** sanctity and **whole** [Q2] weole **40 their** [Q2] the **46 watchman** [Q2] watchmen **57 thee** [Q1, Q2] you **65 new-hatched** [Q2] vnhatch't **74 all** a **109 Running** Roaming **117 Lends** [Q1, Q2] Giues **120 From** [Q2] For **128 dye** [Q2] eye **129 imploratators** implorators **130 bawds** bonds
1.4.1 it is [Q2] is it **10 wassail** [Q1, Q2] wassels **18.1 revel** [Q3] reueale [Q2] **18.11 the** their [Q2] **18.20 evil** eale [Q2] **18.21 over** of a [Q2] **daub** doubt [Q2] **23 intents** [Q1, Q2] euents **26 O** [Q1] Oh, oh **37 the**

[Q1, Q2] thee **51 summit** [Q2] Sonnet **53 assume** [Q1, Q2] assumes **59 artere** Artire
1.5.1 Whither [Q1, Q2] Where **19 on** [Q1] an **20 porcupine** Porpentine **22 List, Hamlet, list, O list!** list *Hamlet,* oh list **24 God** [Q1, Q2] Heauen **35 'Tis** [Q1, Q2] It's **43 wit** wits **with traitorous gifts—** [Q2] hath Traitorous guifts. **45 to his** [Q1, Q2] to to this **69 eager** Aygre **71 barked** bak'd **75 of queen** [Q1, Q2] and Queene **93 Hold, hold** [Q2] hold **117 s.p. HAMLET** *Marcellus* **120 is't** [Q1, Q2] ist't **137 whirling** [Q1, Q2] hurling **140 Horatio** [Q1, Q2] my Lord **158 our** [Q1, Q2] for **164 earth** [Q1, Q2] ground **175 this headshake** [Q1, Q2] thus, head shake **178 they** [Q1, Q2] there
2.1.1 this [Q1, Q2] his **3 marv'lous** maruels **4 to** [Q2] you **enquire** [Q2] inquiry **14 As** [Q2] And **47 and the addition** Addition **49 does a this—a does—** [Q2] he this? / He does: **50 By the mass** [Q2; not in F] **58 a** [Q2] he **62 carp** [Q2] Cape **69 b'wi'** [Q2] buy **69 Fare ye** [Q2] fare you **77 i'th' name of God** [Q2] in the name of Heauen **92 a** [Q2] he **98 shoulder** [Q1, Q2] shoulders **102 Come,** [Q2; not in F] **113 feared** [Q2] feare **115 By heaven** [Q1, Q2] It seemes
2.2.17 Whether . . . thus [Q2; not in F] **20 is** [Q2] are **29 But we** [Q2] We **31 service** [Q2] Seruices **39 Ay** [Q2; not in F] **45 and** [Q1, Q2] one **48 it hath** [Q2] I haue **52 fruit** [Q2] Newes **58 my** [Q2; not in F] **59 Valtemand** [Q2] *Voltumand* **99 'tis 'tis** [Q2] it is **126 solicitings** [Q2] soliciting **150 wherein** [Q2] whereon **162 does** [Q2] ha's **168 But** [Q2] And **180 ten** [Q1, Q2] two **188 a said** [Q2] he said **189 A is** [Q2] he is **195 read** [Q2] meane **199 lack** [Q2] locke **200 most** [Q2; not in F] **210–11 My Lord, I will take** [Q1, Q2] My Honourable Lord, I will most humbly / Take **213 except my life, my life, my life** except my life, my life **216 the** [Q2] my **221 Ah** [Q2] Oh **272 of** [Q1, Q2; not in F] **286 discovery, and** [Q2] discovery of **289 heavily** [Q2] heauenly **302 then, when** [Q1, Q2] when **328 berattle** be-ratled **334 like most will** like most **350 'Sblood** [Q2; not in F] **367 Haply** [Q2] Happily **373 was** [Q1, Q2; not in F] **378 came** [Q2] can **382 individable** [Q2] indiuible **403 pious chanson** [Q2] *Pons Chanson* **407 valanced** [Q2] valiant **415 good** [Q1, Q2; not in F] **418 caviare** [Q1, Q2] *Cauiarie* **419 judgements** [Q1, Q2] iudgement **425–26 as wholesome as sweet, and . . . fine** [Q2; not in F] **426 One** [Q2] One cheefe **437 total** [Q1, Q2] to take **445 So, proceed you** [Q2; not in F] so goe on [Q1; probably an accidental omission. See

variant at 1.2.58–60.] **449 antique** anticke [probably punning on "antic"] **470 armour** [Q2] Armours **479 to the** [Q1, Q2] to'th **482 mobbled** [Q1, Q2] inobled **484 mobbled** [Q1] Inobled **485 flames** [Q2] flame **499 whe'er** [Q2] whether **500 Prithee** [Q2] Pray you **506 live** [Q1, Q2] liued **508 much** [Q2; not in F] **516 s.p. PLAYERS** Play⟨ers⟩. **526 b'wi'** [F, Q2] buy **531 wanned** [Q2] warm'd **553 'Swounds** [Q2] Why **556 'a'** [Q1, Q2] haue **557 offal. Bloody, bawdy** [Q2] Offall, bloudy: a Bawdy **560 Why,** [Q2] Who? **561 the dear murderèd** Deere **574 a** [Q2] he

3.1.32 here [Q2] there **45 please you** [Q2] please ye **50 sugar** [Q2] surge **51 too true** [Q2] true **73 Th'** [Q2] The **proud** [Q2] poore **76 th'** [Q2] the **89 awry** [Q2] away **99 you know** [Q1, Q2] I know **101 Their perfume** lost then perfume left **112 with** [Q1, Q2] your **133 nowhere** [Q1, Q2] no way **142 paintings, too** [Q1] pratlings too **143 hath** [Q1, Q2] has **face** [Q1, Q2] pace **selves** [Q1, Q2] selfe **154 And** [Q2] Haue

3.2.4 with [Q1, Q2; not in F] **6 your** [Q2; not in F] **8 hear** [Q1, Q2] see **11 would** [Q1, Q2] could **17 o'erstep** [Q2] ore-stop **28–29 nor no man** or Norman **53 tongue lick** [Q2] tongue, like **55 feigning** faining **56 her** [Q2] my **72 thy** [Q2] my **77 stithy** [Q2] Stythe **heedful** [Q2] needfull **81 a** [Q2] he **89 mine now. My Lord, you** mine. Now my Lord, you **120 a must** [Q2] he must **121 a suffer** [Q2] he suffer **124** *malhecho* Malicho **127 this fellow** [Q1, Q2] these Fellowes **129 a** [Q2] they **148 former** [Q2] forme **156 their** [Q2] my **178 either** [Q2] other **179 enactures** [Q2] enactors **186 favourite** [Q2] fauourites **198 me give** [Q2] giue me **199.2 An** And [Q2] **221 wince** [Q2] winch **222 unwrung** [Q2] vnrung **224 as good as a** [Q1, Q2] a good **228 mine** [Q2] my **230 mis-take** [Q2] mistake **your** [Q1, Q2; not in F] **239 A** [Q2] He **248 s.p. COURTIERS** All. **249 stricken** [F] strucken **268 Ah ha!** [Q2] Oh, ha? **296 as you** [Q2] you **298 struck** stroke **330 fingers** [Q2] finger **339 it speak.** [Q2] it **S'blood** [Q2] Why I [Q1, Q2] that I **345 yonder** [Q1, Q2] that of [Q1, Q2] like **347 mass** [Q2] Misse **and 'tis,** [Q2] and it's

3.3.14 weal [Q2] spirit **18 summit** Somnet **73 a** [Q2] he **74 a** [Q2] he **77 sole** [Q2] soule **80 A** [Q2] He **81 flush** [Q2] fresh **88 hint** hent

3.4.1 A [Q2] He **12 a wicked** [Q2] an idle **31 better** [Q2] Betters **36 brassed** braz'd **41 off** [Q2] of **43 sets** [Q2] makes **54 this** [Q2] his **64 brother** [Q2] breath **78 And** [Q2] As **108 you do** [Q2] you **109 th'in-**

corporal [Q2] their corporall **122 whom** [Q2] who **142 o'er** or **143 ranker** [Q2] ranke **144 these** this **151.1–2 eat, / Of habits devilish** eate / Of habits deuill [Q2] **151.5 Refrain tonight** [F] to refraine night [Q2] **151.9 either in** either [Q2] **166 bloat** [Q2] blunt **172 mad** [Q2] made **185.6 and't** an't [Q2]

4.1.1 matter [Q2] matters **6 sea** [Q1, Q2] Seas **11 O** [Q2] On **21 let** [Q2] let's **26 a** [Q2] He **34 mother's closet** [Q2] Mother Clossets **39.1 So envious slander** [not in Q2]

4.2.16 like an ape an apple like an Ape

4.3.7 never [Q2] neerer **20 a** [Q2] he **21 politic** [Q1, Q2; not in F] **23 ourselves** [Q2] our selfe **26–28 s.p. KING CLAUDIUS** Alas . . . that worm [Q2; not in F] **38 A will** [Q2] He will **44 is** [Q2] at **50 them** [Q2] him

4.4.9.16 now [not in Q2]

4.5.12 might [Q2] would **41 God'ield** God dil'd **65 thus** [Q2] this **74 sorrows come** [Q2] sorrowes comes **75 battalions** [Q2] Battaliaes **85 Feeds** [Q2] Keepes **this** [Q2] his **88 Wherein** [Q2] Where in **93 is** [Q2] are **96 impetuous** impittious **115 that's calm** [Q2] that calmes **124 Where is** [Q2] Where's **138 is't** [Q2] if **139 sweepstake** Soop-stake **144 pelican** [Q2] Politician **148 sensibly** [Q2] sensible **151 s.p. VOICES** [not in F] **165 rained** [Q2] *raines* **166 Fare you well, my dove.** [F italicizes as part of the song.] **174 pansies** [Q2] Paconcies **181 a made** [Q2] he made **185–86 a . . . a** [Q2] *he . . . he* **194 God 'a' mercy** [Q1, Q2] *Gramercy* **196 O God** [Q2] you Gods **197 commune** common **212 call't** [Q2] call

4.6.8 A [Q2] Hee **9 ambassador** [Q2] Ambassadours **11 Horatio** [Q2; not in F] **21 thine** [Q2] *your*

4.7.11 they're [Q2] they are **21 guilts** Gyues **24 aimed** [Q2] arm'd **27 Who has** Who was **48 abuse, and** [Q2] abuse? Or **66 since** [Q2] hence **69 can** [Q2] ran **77 Lamord** [Q2] *Lamound* **79 the** [Q2] our **made** [Q2] mad **84.1 Th'escrimers** the Scrimures [Q2] **84 Sir, this** [Q2] Sir. This **88 What** [Q2] Why **97 in deed** indeed **114 that, but dip** [Q2] I but dipt **127 cunnings** [Q2] commings **129 that** [Q2] the **133 How now, sweet Queen?** how sweet Queene. **135 they** [Q2] they'l **139 Therewith** [Q2] There with **make** [Q2] come **143 crownet** Coronet **152 their** [Q1, Q2] her **153 lay** [Q2] buy

5.1.4 coroner [Q2] Crowner **11 to act** [Q2] an Act **23 o'** [Q2] of **31 A** [Q2] He **60 there-a-was nothing-a** [Q2] *there was nothing* **61 a** [Q2] he **71 'twere** [Q2] it / were **72 This** [Q2] It **73 would** [Q2] could **78 a**

[Q2] he 83 an [Q2] if 90 of [Q1] of of 101–2 th'inheritor [Q2] the Inheritor 108 sirrah [Q2] Sir 129 heel [Q1, Q2] heeles 129–30 the courtier [Q1, Q2] our Courtier 139–40 a . . . A . . . a . . . [Q2] he . . . hee . . . he 140 'tis [Q2] it's 142 him there. There [Q2] him, there 149 sexton [Q2] sixteene 152 a . . . a [Q2] he . . . he 154 a will [Q2] he will 166 This same skull, sir [Q2] This same Scull Sir, this same Scull sir 173 now, how [Q1, Q2] how 177 Not [Q2] No grinning [Q2] Ieering 185 Pah puh 188 a [Q2] he 202 rites rights 204 of [Q2; not in F] 212 prayers [Q2] praier 230 treble woe [Q2] terrible woer 237 To o'ertop [Q2] To o'retop 238 grief [Q2] griefes 240 Conjures [Q2] Conuire 246 For [Q1, Q2] Sir 250 ALL THE LORDS Gentlemen! [not in F] s.p. HORATIO [Q2] Gen. 259 'Swounds [Q2] Come 260 woot fast [Q2; not in F] 272 couplets [Q2] Cuplet 279 your [Q2] you

5.2.7 praised [Q2] praise 8 sometime [Q2] sometimes 9 pall paule 21 reasons [Q2] reason 30 villainies villaines 38 Th' [Q2] The effect [Q2] effects 41 like [Q2] as 49 ordinant [Q2] ordinate 52 the form of th' forme of the 55 sequent [Q2] sement 59 defeat [Q2] debate 79 court count 88 chuff Chowgh 89 say [Q2] saw 92 sir [Q2; not in F] 100 a [Q2] he 102 Nay, good my Lord [Q2] Nay, in good faith, 102.2 gentleman gentlemen [Q2] 102.4 feelingly [Q3] sellingly [Q2a] fellingly [Q2b] 102.8 dizzy [Q3] dazzie [Q2] 102.9 yaw [Q2a] raw [Q2b] 102.20 to't [Q2a] doo't [Q2b] rarely really [Q2] 102.34 his this [Q2] 108 King, sir [Q2] sir King hath wagered [Q2] ha's wag'd 110 hanger [Q2] Hangers 120 bet [Q2] but 122 laid, sir [Q2] laid 124 on't one nine [Q2] mine it [Q2] that 132 and [Q2] if 138 turn [Q2] tongue 140 A [Q2] He a [Q2] hee 141 has [Q2] had many [Q2] mine 144 fanned fond 145 trial [Q2] tryalls 150 it [Q2; not in F] 181 brother [Q1, Q2] Mother 187 ungored [Q2] vngorg'd 213 trumpet speak [Q2] Trumpets speake 219 my lord [Q2] on sir 227 Set it [Q1, Q2] set 231 Here, Hamlet, take my Heere's a 249 mine own [Q2] mine 254 Ho! [Q2] How? 265 s.p. ALL THE COURTIERS [Q2] All. 281 cause aright [Q2] causes right 285 ha't [Q2] haue't 286 God [Q2] good 299 th'occurrents [Q2] the occurents 302 cracks [Q2] cracke 308 This [Q2] His 310 shot [Q2] shoote 329 th'inventors' [Q2] the Inuentors 333 rights [Q1, Q2] Rites 334 now [Q1, Q2] are 335 also [Q2] alwayes

TWELFTH NIGHT, OR WHAT YOU WILL

CONTROL TEXT: F

F: The Folio of 1623

s.p. ORSINO [F's use of *Duke* and *Du⟨ke⟩* has been changed throughout.]
s.p. SIR TOBY [F's use of *Sir To⟨by⟩*, *To⟨by⟩*, and *Tob⟨y⟩* has been standardized throughout.]
s.p. SIR ANDREW [F's use of *And⟨rew⟩* and *An⟨drew⟩* has been standardized throughout.]
s.p. FESTE [F's use of *Clo⟨wne⟩*, *Clow⟨ne⟩*, and *Cl⟨owne⟩* has been changed throughout.]

1.1.25 years' heat yeares heate
1.2.14 Arion *Orion* 48 pray thee prethee
1.3.44 s.p. SIR ANDREW *Ma⟨lvolio⟩*. 46 Mary Accost *Mary,* accost 83 curl by coole my 84 me we 86 housewife huswife 109 cinquepace Sinke-a-pace 114 diverscoloured dam'd colour'd 117 That's That
1.5.156 'countable comptible 271 County's Countes
2.2.18 straight [not in F] 29 our O 30 made of, made, if
2.3.68 Cathayan *Catayan* 121 a nayword an ayword
2.4.50 s.p. FESTE[*sings*] [not in F] 86 I it
2.5.103 staniel stallion 109 ay I 126 born become achieve atcheeues 154 dear *deero*
3.1.7 king Kings 61 wise men wisemens 116 grece grize
3.2.7 thee the the 57 nine mine
3.3.36 latchèd lapsed
3.4.23 s.p. OLIVIA *Ma⟨lvolio⟩*. 65 tang langer with 153 If s.p. *To⟨by⟩*. If 154 You Yon 179 out on't 244 virago firago
4.2.5 in in in 63 to the the 77 Master M.
5.1.73 wreck wracke 110 hath haue 193 pavan panyn 393 With [not in F]

TROILUS AND CRESSIDA

CONTROL TEXT: F; OCCASIONALLY, AS NOTED BELOW, Q

F: The Folio of 1623

Q: The Quarto of 1609
Qa, Qb, Fa, Fb: The "b" texts of both Q and F are corrected versions. The change from Qa to Qb is significant: Qb adds a prefatory epistle not found in Qa or in either state of F. See the Introduction and the Textual Note.

Title: *Troilus and Cressida* [F most running titles] The booke of Troilus and Cresseda [Stationers' Register, 1603], THE history of

Troylus and Cressida [Stationers' Register, 1609], THE Historie of Troylus and Cresseida [Qa title page], THE Famous Historie of Troylus *and* Cresseid [Qb title page], The history of *Troylus* and *Cresseida* [Q head title; running titles, all italic], THE TRAGEDIE OF Troylus and Cressida [F title page; initial running titles, all italic]

s.p. PROLOGUE [It is unclear whether the lines of the Prologue in F are actually attributed to a character called "Prologue," as they are in this edition.]

s.p. BASTARD [As in F, Margareton is referred to in the s.p.'s and s.d.'s of 5.8 as *Bastard*. In F, he is mistakenly referred to in dialogue (at 5.5.7) as *Margarelon*.]

s.p. PANDARUS [F's occasional use of *Pandar* in s.p.'s and s.d.'s may be deliberate, but it has been standardized to "Pandarus" throughout.]

s.p. ALEXANDER [F refers to Cressida's servant in 1.2 as *Her Man* or simply as *Man,* while Pandarus refers to him in dialogue as *Alexander*. His name has been standardized to "Alexander" throughout that scene.]

s.p. MAN [Reserved in this edition for the servant of Troilus, who is referred to in the s.p.'s of 3.2 (in this edition as in F) as "Man."]

s.p. SERVANT [Reserved in 3.1 for the servant of Paris and in 5.5 for the servant of Diomedes, both of whom are also referred to in F as *Servant*]

Pro. **12 barques** *Barke* **13 freightage** *frautage* **17 Antenorides** Antenonidus **18 full-filling** fulfilling **19 Spar** *Stirre*

1.1.0–1.2.215 Enter . . . Hector's, and how he [F in these lines simply reprints Q with a few errors; therefore its readings and press variants are here treated as without substantive authority. Q is taken as control text; thus variants from Q rather than from F will be noted for these lines. Rejected Q readings are labeled "[Q]" to avoid confusion. See below also 2.2.103–209, 3.3.1–95, and 4.6.0–64.] **29 So, traitor! 'When she comes'? When is she thence?** so traitor then she comes when she is thence [Q] **35 askance** a' scorne [Q] **68 on of you** [F] of you [Q] **72 not kin** [Fb] kin [Q] **73 care I** [F] I [Q] **97 resides** [F] reides [Q]

1.2.17 they [F] the [Q] **22 farced** sauced [Q] **108 lift** [F] liste [Q] **120 the** thee [Q] **136 pot** [F] por [Q] **137 or** [not in Q] **176 a man** [F] man [Q] **188 man's** [F] mans man [Q] **215 looks and how** [At this point, F regains its independent authority and becomes the control text again.] **220 an eye**

[Q] money 221 comes [Q] come **234 season** [Q] seasons **237 date is** [Q] dates **243 lie at a** [Q] lye at, at a **267 price** [Q] prize **272 Then** [Q] That

1.3.7 Infects [Q] Infect **18 shames** [Q] shame **50 flee** fled **53 Retorts** Retires **58 th'** [Q] the **62 As, Agamemnon, every hand** As *Agamemnon* and the hand **66 On** [Q] In **83 masque** Maske **84 [ ]** [The conjectured missing line is not in Q or F. Some contrast with "Th'unworthiest" (line 83) seems required.] **87 Infixture** Insisture **101 fixture** fixure **106 primogenity** [Q] primogenitiue **117 resides** recides **118 their** [Q] her **127 it is** [Q] is it **156 scaffoldage** Scaffolage **159 a-mending** a mending **161 seem** [Q] seemes **202 calls** [Q] call **207 swinge** [Q] swing **209 finesse** [Q] finenesse **221 heart** head **236 great** [Q; not in F] **acorn** accord **240 that the** [Q] that he **241 what, repining, the** what the repining **260 resty** [Q] rusty **262 among** [Q] among'st **298 prove** [Q] pawne **348 e'en** in

2.1.6 then [Q; not in F] **13 thou** [Q] you **unsifted** whinid'st **18 o' thy** ath thy **27 foot.** An foot, and **42–43 in thy skull** [not in F] **45 thrash** [Q] thresh **53 ye thus** you this **87 bade the** [Q] bad the bad thee **96 an** [Q] and if **97 a knock** he knocke **A were** [Q] he were **101 your** their **106 wit** [not in F] **109 peace** [Q; not in F] **brach** Brooch

2.2.9 toucheth [Q] touches **34 reason** [Q] reasons **44–45 And . . . reason** [Q; lines transposed in F] **47 hare** [Q] hard **49 Make** [Q] Makes **55 mad** [Q] madde made **70 sewer** same **89 never fortune** [Q] Fortune neuer **103–209 old . . . shriek** [F shows no sign of access to manuscript copy in these lines; Q therefore again becomes the control text for this passage.] **110 Ah . . . ah** a . . . a [Q] **119 the** [not in Q] **163 But** and [Q] **209** [After "shriek," F again becomes the control text.]

2.3.10 ye [Q] thou **14 their** [Q] the **16 Neapolitan** [Q; not in F] **21 could ha'** [Q] could haue **30 prayer** [Q] a prayer **32 s.p. PATROCLUS** Amen [Q; not in F] **41 Thersites** [Q] thy selfe **65 whore and a cuckold** [Q] Cuckold and a Whore **66 emulous** [Q] emulations **72 faced** sent **74 so, lest** so, least [Q] of, so [F] **80 you will** [Q] will 'tis it is **97–98 his legs . . . flexure** [Q] his legge . . . flight **110 on** [Q] of **112 unwholesome** [Q] vnholdsome **114 come** [Q] came **118 tend** [Q] tends **122 lunes** lines **128 Bring** [Fb] ring [Fa] **132 second** [Fb]; fecond [Fa] **161 worth** [Q] wroth **165 himself** [Q] it selfe **208 s.p. AJAX** Ulis⟨ses⟩. **209 s.p. ULYSSES** Aia⟨x⟩. **211 Farce** Force **216 does** [Q] do's doth **228 Famed** [Q]

Fame **230 thine** [Q] thy **245 great** [Q; not in F] **247 today to Troy** to *Troy* **252 sail . . . hulks** [Q] may saile . . . bulkes

3.1.6 notable [Q] noble **16 titles** [Q] title **27 thou** [Q] thou art **31 visible inuisible 33 not you** [Q] you not **36 Cressid** [Q] *Cressida* **39 s.d.** HELEN [Q] *Helena* **52 Will you** well, you **66 Ay, faith** I faith **77 sweet** [Q] sweere **80 I'll lay my life** [Q; not in F] **80, 82 dispenser** disposer **83 make 's** makes [Q] make [F] **85 dispenser's** disposer's **104–05 s.p.** PANDARUS In . . . so. [*Sings*] Love [Fb] In . . . so. Pan⟨darus⟩: *Love* [Fa] [In Fa, Paris continues to speak until the beginning of the song. The song itself is then attributed to Pandarus.] **105 still love, still more** [Q] *still more* **111, 113 O! O!** oh ho **115, 116 O! O!** *O ho* **118 ay, faith** [Q] I faith yfaith **141 these** [Q] this **148 s.p.** PARIS [not in F. The line is attributed to Helen.]

3.2.12 Pandar [Q] *Pandarus* **20 repurèd** [Q] reputed **22 tuned** [Q] and **30 spirit** [Q] spirite sprite **31 as short** [Q] so short **64 fears** teares **66 safer** [Q] safe **71 Nor** [Q] Not **109 till now not** [Q] not till now **111 grown** [Q] grone grow **121 Cunning . . . in my** Comming . . . from my **139 speak so** [Q] speakes so **157 truth** [Q] truths **179 wind or** [Q] as Wind, as **180 or** [Q] as **186 pain** [Q] paines **193–94 with a bed** [not in F] **197 pander** [Q] and Pander

3.3.1–95 Now . . . virtues [F shows no clear evidence of manuscript authority until "shining" (3.3.95). Q thus becomes the control text in the interim.] **1 you** [F; not in Q] **3 your** [F; not in Q] **4 come** loue [Q] **5 profession** possession [Q] **67 use** us'd [Q] **95 shining** [F] ayming [Q; here F regains its status as control text, though (as elsewhere) some of the variants it retrieved from the manuscript were themselves errors.] **97 givers** [Q] giuer **100–101 To . . . behold itself** [Q; not in F] **105 mirrored** married **107 at** [Q] it at **110 man** [Q] may **111 be** [Q] is **115 they're** th'are [Q] they are [F] **132 fasting** [Q] feasting **156 abject rear** abiect, neere **162 Welcome** the welcome **163 Farewell** [Q] farewels **172 give** goe **177 sooner** [Q] begin to **178 once** [Q] out **192 aught** thought **193 infant** [not in F] **203 his island** her Iland **218 air** [Q] ayre ayrie ayre **237 as** [not in F] **244 a** [Q] he **247 this** [Q] his **260 his presence** [Q] hit presence **make** [Q] make his **286 ye** [Q] you **290 am feared** am sure

4.1.9 wherein [Q] within **10 e'en** in **17 meet** [Q] meetes **37 'twas** [Q] it was **45 wherefore** [Q] whereof **67 nor less** [Q] no lesse **80 but** not

4.2.4 lull kill **6 As to** As **12 joys** [Q] eyes **26 Here** [Q] heere Heare **33 Ah . . . capoc-**

chia a *Chipochia* **53 It's** [Q] 'tis **56 Whoa** Who **57 you are** [Q] y'are **67 Diomedes'** [Q] *Diomeds* **68 so concluded** [Q] concluded so **74 secrecies** secrets

4.3.5 Ah, ah [Q] Ah, ha **26 force** orce **30 I'll** [Q] Ile I will

4.4.3 us [not in F] **9 own** [Q; not in F]

4.5.4 violenteth [Q] no lesse **9 dross** [Q] crosse **11 Ah** a **ducks** [Q] ducke **14 you** [not in F] **23 strained** [Q] strange **40 one** [Q] our **47 Distasted** [Q] Distasting **48 s.p.** AENEAS *Aeneas within* **56 When** [Q] *Troy⟨lus⟩*. When [F attributes the line to Troilus rather than, as here, to Cressida.] **77 gifts . . . flowing** guift . . . Flawing **79 novelty** [Q] nouelties **82 afeard** [Q] affraid **119 usage** vsage [Q] visage [F] **122 zeal seale thee** [Q; not in F] **123 In** [Q] I **132 you** [Q] my **144 s.p.** DEIPHOBUS *Dio⟨medes⟩*.

4.6.0–64 Enter . . . game. [F in this passage shows no sign of manuscript influence and repeats several suspicious or erroneous Q readings. F is therefore here regarded as a mere reprint, and Q is taken as control text.] **38 s.p.** MENELAUS *Patr⟨oclus⟩*. [Q] **44 not** [F] nor [Q] **49 too** then [Q] **60 accosting** a coasting [Q] **64 Exeunt** Exennt [F; not in Q. F here regains its access to manuscript authority and hence its status as control text.] **71 they** [Q; not in F] **75 s.p.** ACHILLES *Aga⟨memnon⟩*. **94 breath** [Q] breach

4.7.28 could [Q] could'st **72 th'advancèd** thy aduanced **147 have** [Q; not in F] **168 you** [Q] thee

5.1.5 botch batch **24 cur, no** [Q] curre **58 sprites** [Q] spirits **68 sewer** sure **84 it: that** it, that it

5.2.3 your [Q] you **10 sing** [Q] finde **11 clef** [Q] Cliff life **13 s.p.** CRESSIDA *Cal⟨chas⟩*. **22 forsworn** [Q] a forsworne **27 do** [Q] doe not **40 prithee** [Q] pray thee **41 all hell's** [Q] hell **57 la lo 72 ha't** [Q] haue't **83–84 s.p.** DIOMEDES As . . . thee. CRESSIDA Nay . . . withal As . . . thee. *Dio⟨medes⟩*: Nay . . . me. *Cres⟨sida⟩*: He . . . withal [F makes "As I kiss thee" the end of Cressida's preceding speech and attributes "Nay . . . me" to Diomedes and "He . . . withal" to Cressida. Here, "As I kiss thee" is attributed to Diomedes, and both "Nay . . . me" and the succeeding line, "He . . . withal," to Cressida.] **84 doth take** [Q] rakes **90 one's** [Q] on's one **103 s.p.** TROILUS *Ther⟨sites⟩*: you [Q] me **114 said** [Q] say **122 th'attest** [Q] that test **136 a** [Q] he **139 be sanctimonies** [Q] are sanctimonie **144 Bifold** [Q] By foule **161 e'en** be be **167 as I** I **Cressid** [Q] *Cressida* **173 sun** [Q] Fenne

5.3.4 in [Q] gone 5 all [Q; not in F] 21 give much, to use count giue much to as 47 mother [Q] Mothers 75 sire sir 85 do [Q] doth 87 dolours [Q] dolour 92 Yet [Q] yes 106 o' these o'th's

5.4.8 stale [Q] stole 10 proved not not proou'd

5.5.6 Polydamas [Q] Polidamus 7 Margare-ton Margarelon 11 Cedius Cedus 12 Thoas Thous 17 Go [Q] Coe 24 strawy [Q] straying 47 brave [not in F]

5.6.7 the thy 13 Ha [Q; not in F]

5.7.6 arms [Q] arme

5.8.3 horned Spartan hen'd sparrow 8–9 am bastard begot [Q] am a Bastard begot

5.9.7 dark'ning [Q] darking 13 and [Q; not in F] 15 retire [Q] retreat 16 sound [Q] sounds 20 bait [Q] bed

5.11.7 smite smile 12 fear of [Q] feare, of 17 their [Q] there 20 Cold Coole

THE SONNETS AND "A LOVER'S COMPLAINT"

CONTROL TEXT: Q

Q: The Quarto of 1609

Qa, Qb: Qa is the uncorrected version, Qb the corrected version

Other texts cited:

B1—British Library Add. MS 10309, fol. 143 (c. 1630; Margaret Bellasys)

B2—British Library Add. MS 21433, fol. 114ᵛ (c. 1630; Inns of Court)

B3—British Library Add. MS 25303, fol. 119ᵛ (c. 1620s–30s; Inns of Court)

M—Pierpont Morgan MA 1057, p. 96 (c. 1630s)

MS—St. John's, Cambridge, MS S. 23 (James 416), fols. 38ʳ–38ᵛ (c. 1630s–40s)

Passionate Pilgrim, c. 1599

R—Rosenbach MS 1083 / 16, p. 256 (c. 1630)

W—Westminster Abbey, MS 41, fol. 49 (1619–30s; George Morley)

Sonnets

1 [number not in Q]

2 [For another version of this sonnet, present in eleven manuscripts, see the Alternative Versions.] 4 tattered [MS] totter'd

5.14 Lose Leese

12.4 ensilvered o'er or siluer'd ore

13.7 Yourself You selfe

20.7 hues Hews

23.14 with . . . wit wit . . . wiht

25.9 might worth

26.12 thy their

27.10 thy their

28.12 gild'st the even guil'st th'eauen 14 strength length

31.8 thee there

34.12 cross losse

35.8 thy . . . thy their . . . their

37.7 thy their

39.12 doth dost

41.12 troth truth

43.11 thy their

44.13 naught naughts

45.12 thy their

46.3, 8, 13, 14 thy their 9 'cide side

47.10 art are 11 no nor

50.6 dully duly

51.10 perfect'st perfects 11 rein naigh

54.14 fade vade

55.11 monuments monument

56.13 Or As

61.8 tenor tenure

62.10 chapped chopt

63.5 travelled trauaild

65.12 of or

67.6 seeming seeing

69.3 due end 5 Thy Their 14 soil solye

70.6 Thy their

71.4 vilest vildest

73.4 ruined choirs rn'wd quiers

76.7 tell fel

77.10 blanks blacks

82.8 these the

85.3 thy their

86.13 filled fild

89.11 profane prophane [Qb]; proface [Qa]

90.11 shall stall

91.9 better bitter

99.9 One Our 13 ate eate

100.14 prevene'st preuenst

102.8 her his

106 [For another version of this sonnet, present in two manuscripts, see the Alternative Versions.] 12 skill [MSS] still

111.1 with wish

112.14 they're dead y'are dead

113.6 latch lack 14 makes mine eye maketh mine

116 119 [all but one extant copy of Q]

126.2 sickle-hour sickle, hower 8 minutes mynuit 12 [After this line, Q prints parentheses for each line of an imagined couplet.]

127.10 brow eyes

128.11, 14 thy their

129.9 Mad Made 11 proved proud a and

132.6 the east th'East 9 mourning morning

135.1, 2, 11, 12, 14 Will Will

136.2, 5, 14 Will Will 6 Ay I

138 [For another version of this sonnet, see the Alternative Versions.] 12 to have [Passionate Pilgrim] t'haue

140.13 belied be lyde

143.13 Will Will

144 [For another version of this sonnet, see the Alternative Versions.] 6 side [Passionate Pilgrim] sight 9 fiend finde

146.2 [   ] My sinfull earth
153.8 **strange** strang **14 eyes** eye

"A Lover's Complaint"
7 **sorrow's** sorrowes,
37 **beaded** bedded
51 **'gan** gaue
112 **manège** mannad'g
118 **Came** Can
131 **Consents** Consent's
139 **labour** labouring
161 **wills** wits
182 **woo** vovv
198 **pallid** palyd [sometimes interpreted as "palèd," which properly means "having grown pale"]
204 **hair** heir
208 **th'annexations** th'annexions
228 **Hallowed** Hollowed
233 **A** Or
241 **Planing** Playing
251 **immured** enur'd
252 **procured** procure
260 **nun** Sunne
261 **ay** I
270 **kindred,** kindred
293 **O** Or

Alternative Versions

Spes Altera
Control text: W
Spes Altera [B1, B2, B3] To one yᵗ would dye a Mayd
3 **liv'ry** [B1] liuery
5 **lies** lye [cropped control-text ms.]
8 **praise** prays [cropped control-text ms.]

On his Mistress' Beauty
Control text: M
2 **descriptions** [R] discription
3 **rhyme** [R] mine [but with "rime" written in the margin as a correction]
6 **hand** [R] hands
8 **E'en** Ev'n [M] Euen [R]
10 **these** [R] those
12 **your** thy

Various Poems

Title variants are not included in the lists below.

A Song
Control text: B
B: Bodleian MS Rawlinson poet. 160, fols. 108ʳ–109ᵛ
Y: Yale Osborn b. 197
5 **sue** shewe **10 joining** [Y] Ioying **13 conceiving** breeding **19 Fie** [Y] Fly **29 will** [Y]

wit **30** stanza number 4 [Y] [no number in B] **38 pleasure** [Y] our pleasure **49 You** [Y] Then **52 neat** next **68 their culled** thats cald **commendations** [B may instead read "commendatious."] **71 Pretty** [Y] A pretty **77 mis-shape** mishap **82 From** For **83 plenty** [Y] in plenty

Upon a pair of gloves
Control text: Shakespeare Birthplace Trust Record Office (MS ER.93)

Poems from *The Passionate Pilgrim*
Control text, poems 4, 17, 18: O1; remaining poems: O2
O1: The First Octavo of 1599
O2: The Second Octavo of 1599
Fo2: Folger Library MS V.a.339, fol. 203
Madrigals: Thomas Weelkes, *Madrigals* (1597)
Helicon: *England's Helicon* (1600)
4.5 **ear** [Fo2] eares **10 her** [O2] his
10.1, 2 **faded** vaded **8, 9 left'st** leftts
12.12 **stay'st** staies
13.2, 6, 8 **fadeth . . . faded . . . faded** vadeth . . . vaded . . . vaded
14.17 **Philomela sings** Philomela sits and sings **19 dite** ditte **20 daylight** [not in O2] **24 sighed** sight **27 a moon** an houre
17.3 **faith's** Faithes **4 Heart's** harts **16 freighted** fraughted **27 Herd** Heards **28 back** [*Madrigals*] blacke **33 lass** [*Madrigals*] loue **34 moan** [*Helicon*] woe
18.45 **be** [Fo2] by

The Phoenix and Turtle
Control text: Robert Chester, *Loves Martyr: or Rosalins Complaint. Allegorically shadowing the truth of Loue, in the constant Fate of the Phoenix and Turtle* (1601), sigs. Z3ᵛ–Z4ᵛ

Verses upon the Stanley Tomb at Tong
Control text: Inscription on the Stanley tomb at Tong

On Ben Jonson
Control text: Bodleian MS Ashmole 38, p. 181 (c. 1650), a transcript, probably in the hand of Nicholas Burgh

An Epitaph on Elias James
Control text: John Stow, *Survey of London* (1633), p. 825
B: Bodleian MS Rawlinson poet. 160, fol. 41
3 **reposeth** [B] reposes

An extemporary epitaph on John Combe, a noted usurer
Control text: Fo1

Fo1: Folger MS V.a. 147, fol. 72ʳ (1673), a transcript, probably in the hand of Robert Dobyns

Fo2: Folger MS V.a. 345, p. 232

1 here lies here lyeth **2 not** now **3 lies** [Fo2] lyeth

Another Epitaph on John Combe

Control text: Bodleian MS Ashmole 38, p. 180 (c. 1650), a transcript, probably in the hand of Nicholas Burgh

William Shakespeare hee [The epitaph is attributed at the end to "W. Shak."]

Upon the King

Control text: King James I, *Works* (1616), beneath the engraving of the King on the frontispiece

Epitaph on Himself

Control text: Shakespeare's grave at Stratford

SIR THOMAS MORE

CONTROL TEXT: BRITISH LIBRARY MS HARLEY 7368: ADD.II.D. (FOLS. 8ᴿ— 9ᴿ); ADD.III (FOL. 11*ᵛ)

Add.II.D s.d. [John . . . aloof] *Enter Lincoln. Doll. Clown. Georg betts williamson others And a sergaunt at armes* **27 now? Prentices 'simple'?** now prenty prentisses symple **34 s.p. SHERWIN** [Hand D, crossed out] williamson [Hand C] **42 s.p. SOME** all **43 s.p. OTHERS** [Hand D, crossed out] **54 s.p. SOME** all **55 s.p. OTHERS** all **89 order** orderd (?) **153 s.p. ONE** all

Add.III 18 stings state

MEASURE FOR MEASURE

CONTROL TEXT: F

F: The Folio of 1623

s.p. MISTRESS OVERDONE [F's use of *Bawd* has been changed throughout.]

s.p. POMPEY [F's use of *Clown* has been changed throughout.]

1.1.8 But this But that **51 leavened** a leauen'd **1.2.17 wast** was't **31 pil'd . . . pilled** pil'd . . . pil'd **75 you?** [In F, a short exchange follows between Pompey and Mistress Overdone, which the preceding dialogue apparently was meant to replace: printed in this edition as Additional Passage A.] **102 bonds** words **113 morality** mortality **145 fourteen** nineteene **166 thy** the

1.3.10 a witless witlesse **27 More mocked becomes** More mock'd **43 T'allow in** To do in

1.4.5. sisterhood Sisterstood

2.1.12 your our **21–23 What . . . on thieves?/What's . . . seizes.** what's . . . ceizes./What . . . on theeves? **21 law** Lawes **34 execute** executed **39 vice** Ice **205 spay** splay

2.2.25 God save 'Save **98 raw** now **101 ere** here **119 Split'st** splits **164 prayer is crossed** prayers crosse **166 God save** 'Save

2.3.42 law Loue

2.4.4 God heauen **9 seared** feard **12 in** for **17 now the** not the **45 God's heauens 48 moulds** meanes **53 or** and **75 craftily** crafty **76 me be** be **94 all-binding law** all-building-Law **112 Ignominy** Ignomie

3.1.29 sire fire **38 in** yet in **51 me . . . them** them . . . me **67 Though** Through **89 enew** emmew **92, 95 precise** prenzie **121 dilated** delighted **130 penury** perjury **169 falsify** satisfie **265 on** and **280 eat, array** eate away **294 Free from** From **or as 356 ungenerative** generatiue **413 not** now **450 it** as it **451 inconstant** constant **494 Make my** Making

4.1.1 s.p. BOY Song. **6 though** but **51 and so** and **58 their** these **72 tilth's** Tithes **93–94 s.p. PROVOST** *Duke.*

4.2.81 unlisting vnsisting **100 s.p. DUKE** Pro⟨vost⟩. **111 s.p. PROVOST** The letter [centered on a separate line]

4.3.13 Forthright Forthlight **81 yonder** yond

4.4.4 redeliver reliver

4.5.6 Flavio's Flavia's **8 Valentinus** Valencius

5.1.13 me your we your **167 her face** your face **237 even to** to **367 wast** was't **415 confiscation** confutation **532 that's meet** that meete

Additional Passage Very well met Very well met, and well come

THE TRAGEDY OF OTHELLO, THE MOOR OF VENICE

CONTROL TEXT: F

F: The Folio of 1623

Q: The Quarto of 1622

Fa, Fb, Qc, Qd: Successive states of F or Q incorporating various print-shop corrections and changes

Title: *The Tragedy of* Othello *the Moore of Venice* [Q] *Tragoedy* [Q title page] THE TRAGEDIE OF Othello, the Moore of Venice [F, Stationers' Register entry]

1.1.1 Tush [Q; not in F] **4 'Sblood** [Q; not in F] **24 togaed** [Q] Tongued **28 other** [Q]

others **32 God** [Q; not in F] **53 'em** [Q] them **66 full** [Q] fall **79 thieves, thieves thieves** [Q] Theeues, Theeues **86 'Swounds, sir** [Q] Sir **101 bravery** [Q] knauerie **110 'Swounds, sir** [Q] Sir **118 now** [Q; not in F] **183 night** [Q] might

1.2.34 Duke [Q] Dukes **46 sent** [Q] hath sent **55 comes another** [Q] come another [Fa] come sanother [Fb] **59 Roderigo? Come** [Q, Fa] *Rodorigoc? Cme* [Fb] **60 'em** [Q] them **69 darlings** [Q] Deareling **88 I** [Q; not in F]

1.3.1 There is [Q] There's **these** [Q] this **53 nor** [Q] hor **73 s.p. SENATORS** *All.* **90 tale** [Q] u Tale **106 upon** [Q] vp on **s.p. DUKE** [Q *(Du⟨ke⟩);* not in F] **107 overt** [Q] over **129 battles** [Q] Battaile **fortunes** [Q] Fortune **139 antres** [Q *(Antrees)]* Antars **140 and hills whose heads** [Q] Hills, whose head **142 other** [Q] others **143 Anthropophagi** [Q] *Antropophague* **144 Do grow** [Q] Grew **146 thence** [Q] hence **154 intentively** [Q] instinctiuely **188 b'wi'you** [Q *(bu'y)]* be with you **197 'em** [Q] them **200 Into your favour** [Q; not in F] **218 ear** [Q] eares **228 couch** [Q] Coach **247 I did** [Q] I **263 me** my **269 instruments** [Q] Instrument **277 DESDEMONA . . . This night** [Q; not in F] **299 the** [Q] the the **309 ha'** [Q] haue **322 beam** braine **326 our unbitted** [Q] or vnbitted **343 error** [Q] errors **347 a super-subtle** [Q] super-subtle **349 pox o'** [Q] pox of **367 a** [Q; not in F] **370 He has** She ha's **385 ha't** [Q] haue't

2.1.7 ha' [Q] hath **13 mane** [Q *(mayne)]* Maine **27 Veronessa** [Q] *Verennessa* **34 prays** [Q] praye **41 s.p. THIRD GENTLEMAN** [Q *(3 Gent.)]* *Gent.* **43 arrivance** [Q] Arriuancie **44 this** [Q] the **52 s.p. / s.d. VOICES** *(within) Within* [s.p.] **83 And bring all** Cyprus comfort [Q; not in F] **89 me** [Q; not in F] **95 VOICES** *(within)* A sail, a sail! *Within.,* A Saile, a Saile. [after line 96] **97 their** [Q] this **108 ha'** [Q] haue **111 ha'** [Q] haue **115 hussies** Huswiues **123 essay** assay **174 an** [Q] and **211 hither** [Q] thither **222 again** [Q] a game **235 has** [Q] he's **251 mutualities** [Q] mutabilities **293 rank** [Q] right

2.2.5 addiction addition **9 Heaven bless** [Q] Blesse

2.3.33 ha' [Q] haue **53 to put** [Q] put to **57 God** [Q] heauen **66 God** [Q] Heauen **70 Englishman** [Q] Englishmen **84 Then** [Q] *And* **86 Fore God** [Q] Why **89 God's** [Q] heau'ns **96 ha'** [Q] haue **97 God forgive** [Q] Forgiue **124 engraffed** ingraft **129 VOICES** *(within)* Help, help! [Q *(Helpe, helpe, within.);* not in F] **130 'Swounds, you** [Q] You **141 God's will** [Q] Alas **142 Sir! Montano! Sir!** [Q] *Sir Montano:* **145 God's**

will [Q] Fie, fie **hold** [Q; not in F] **147 'Swounds** [Q; not in F] **151 Hold, hold** [Q] hold **173 be** [Q] to be **190 'Swounds, if I** [Q] If I once **201 leagued** [Q] league **204 ha'** [Q] haue **216 the** [Q] then **236 now** [Q; not in F] **245 God** [Q] Heauen **246 ha'** [Q] haue **247 ha'** [Q] haue **249 thought** [Q] had thought **269 O God** [Q] Oh **291 I'll** [Q] I **294 denotement** deuotement **306 here** [Q; not in F] **317 were't** [Q] were **339 ha'** [Q] haue **343 ha'** [Q] haue **348 hast** [Q] hath **351 By the mass** [Q] Introth

3.1.3 ha' [Q] haue **8–9 tail . . . tale** tale . . . tale **17 ha'** [Q] haue **20 my** [Q] me, mine **23 general's wife** Cenerals wife [Q] Generall **28 CASSIO Do, good my friend** [Q; not in F] **29 ha'** [Q] haue **30 ha'** [Q] haue **47 To take the saf'st occasion by the front** [Q; not in F]

3.3.16 circumstance [Q] Circumstances **53 Yes, faith** [Q] I sooth **61 or** [Q] on **75 By'r Lady** [Q] Trust me **96 you** [Q] he **110 By heaven** [Q] Alas **116 In** [Q] Of **140 free to** [Q] free **144 But some** [Q] Wherein **152 oft** [Q] of **153 that your wisdom then I** intreate you then [Q] that your wisedome **166 By heaven** [Q; not in F] **174 fondly soundly** [Q] God [Q] Heauen **184 once** [Q; not in F] **189 well** [Q; not in F] **206 God** [Q] Heauen **208 keep't** kept **219 I'faith** [Q] Trust me **221 my** [Q] your **253 hold** [Q; not in F] **263 qualities** [Q] Quantities **277 of** [Q] to **282 O then heaven mocks** [Q] Heauen mock'd **289 Faith** [Q] Why **300 ha'** [Q] haue **316 faith** [Q] but **319 with it** [Q] with't **343 of** [Q] in **396 sir** [Q; not in F] **400 supervisor** [Q] supervision **413 ha't** [Q] haue't **428 lay** laid **434 s.p. IAGO** [Q *(Iag⟨o⟩.).* Prefixed to line 435 *(Iago.):* in other words, F gives line 434 to Othello.] **445 that was it** was **458 knows** keepes **463 s.d.** *He kneels* [Q; not in F]

3.4.53 faith [Q] indeed **73 I'faith** [Q] Indeed? **75 God** [Q] Heauen seen it [Q] seene't **79 Heaven bless** [Q] Blesse **84 sir** [Q; not in F] **89–90 DESDEMONA I pray, talk me of Cassio. / OTHELLO The handkerchief.** [Q; not in F] **94 I'faith** [Q] Insooth **95 'Swounds** [Q] Away **166 I'faith** [Q] Indeed **182 by my faith** [Q] in good troth

4.1.32 Faith [Q] Why **35 'Swounds,** [Q; not in F] **49 No, forbear** [Q; not in F] **75 unsuiting** [Qd] vnfitting [Qc] resulting **77 'scuse** [Q] scuses **92 hussy** huswife **99 conster** [Q] conserue **101 now** [Q; not in F] **105 power** [Q] dowre **109 a woman** [Q] woman **110 i'faith** [Q] indeed **120 Faith** [Q] Why **123 Ha'** [Q] Haue **127 beckons** [Q] becomes **129 the sea-** [Fb] the the Sea- [Fa] **145 whole** [Q; not in F] **153 An . . .**

An [Q] If . . . if 156 Faith [Q; not in F] 158 Faith [Q] Yes 179 so [Fb] fo [Fa] 207 God save the [Q] Save you 227 the letter [Q] thle etter [Fa] thLetter [Fb] 230 By my troth [Q] Trust me 243 an [Q; not in F] 276 denote [Q] deonte [Fa] deuote [Fb]

4.2.5 'em [Q] them 16 ha' [Q] haue 24 ha' [Q] haue 32 nay [Q] May 33 knees [Q] knee 35 But not the words [Q; not in F] 49 God Heauen 50 He [Q] they 71 ne'er [Q] neuer 97 ha' [Q] haue 105 ha' [Q] haue 116 ha' [Q] haue 120 hearts [Fb] heart [Fa] 145 heaven [Q] Heauens 152 O God O Good [Q] Alas 159 them in them: or 171 And he does chide with you [Q; not in F] 186 Faith [Q; not in F] I have heard too much, for your words, and [Q] And hell gnaw his bones, [Fa] I haue heard too much: and your words and [Fb] 192 'em [Q] them 224 takes [Q] taketh 228 of [Q; not in F]

4.3.12 He [Q] And 20 in them [Q; not in F] 22 faith [Q] Father 23 thee [Q; not in F] 37 nether [Fb] neither [Fa] 38 soul sat [Fb] Sonle set [Fa] sighing sining [Fa] singing [Fb] 73 Ud's pity [Q] why 102 God [Q] Heauen

5.1.1 bulk [Q] Barke 22 hear [Q] heard 34 dear [Q] deere 36 Forth [Q] For 51 heaven's heauen 62 'em [Q] them 91 O heaven [Q] yes, 'tis 106 out [Q; not in F] 109 an [Q] if 116 dead [Q] quite dead 125 Fough [Q; not in F]

5.2.37 so [Q; not in F] 62 Then Lord [Q] O Heauen 82 'em [Q] them 88 an [Q] if 93 DESDEMONA O Lord, Lord, Lord! [Q; not in F] 96 that am [Fb] am that [Fa] 106 ha' [Q] haue 110 Should [Q] Did 127 O Lord, [Q] Alas! 136 heard [Q] heare 166 worst [Q] wotst 224 God! O heavenly God! [Q] Heauen! oh heauenly Powres! 225 'Swounds [Q] come 227 'em [Q] them 247 here [Q; not in F] 260 ice-brook's Ise-brookes [Q] Ice brookes 356 Indian [Q] Iudean

ALL'S WELL THAT ENDS WELL

COPY TEXT: F

F: The Folio of 1623

s.p. COUNTESS [also called Mother, Lady, Old Lady]

s.p. HELEN [occasionally called Hellena in F, although Hellen is the more common form]

s.p. LAVATCH [changed from Clowne]

s.p. REYNALDO [changed from Steward]

s.p. LAFEU [occasionally called old Lafew]

s.p. BERTRAM [standardized from Bertram, Count, and Rossillion]

s.p. FIRST and SECOND LORD DUMAINE [standardized from F's French E. and French G., Captaine E. and Captaine G., Lord E., and 1 Lord E]

1.1.50 not [not in F] 63 Farewell. Farwell 121 got goe

1.2.18 Roussillon Rosignoll

1.3.37 madam— Madam 46 Poisson Poysam 78 ere ore 100 Dian no [not in F] 155 loneliness louelinesse 161 to th'other tooth to th'other 186 intenable intemible 200 to find not not to finde

2.1.3 gain all, gaine, all: 41 with his cicatrice his sicatrice, with 60 fee see 61 bought brought 139–40 denied [. . .] denied. 143 fits shifts 154 impostor Impostrue 161 coacher torcher 172 nay ne 191 heaven helpe

2.2.26 beyond below 35 I pray you La⟨dy⟩. I pray you 53 An end, sir! To And end sir to

2.3.59 these those 62 s.p. ALL [but HELEN] All. 89 her heere 92 s.p. HELEN La⟨dy⟩. 121 when whence 126 it is is is 133 word's a slave words, a slaue 134 grave graue: 276 detested detected

2.4.14 fortunes fortune 31 s.p. PAROLES In myself, knave. [not in F]

2.5.25 End And 43 wit [not in F] 46 not [not in F]

3.1.17 nation nature 23 to the to'th the

3.2.8 sold hold 19 s.p. COUNTESS [reads the letter aloud] A Letter. 41 heard heare 110 cleave moue still-piecing still-peering

3.4.4 s.p. REYNALDO [not in F, which has "Letter."] 18 s.p. COUNTESS [not in F]

3.5.5 greatest great'st 17 their these 30 you [not in F] 63 warr'nt write 82 those places these places

3.6.32 his this 33 ore ours 98 s.p. SECOND LORD DUMAINE Cap⟨tain⟩. G. 101, 108 s.p. FIRST LORD DUMAINE Cap⟨tain⟩. E.

3.7.19 Resolved Resolue 46 wicked act lawfull act

4.1.1 s.p. SECOND LORD DUMAINE 1. Lord E. 38 mute Mule 59 SOLDIERS [severally] All. 83 art [not in F]

4.2.39 toys e'en such a surance rope's in such a scarre

4.3.80 FIRST LORD DUMAINE Ber⟨tram⟩. 84 apiece; a peece, 114 s.p. FIRST LORD DUMAINE [not in F] 115 s.p. SECOND LORD DUMAINE Cap⟨tain⟩. G. 122 s.p. SECOND LORD DUMAINE Cap⟨tain⟩. G. 134 s.p. FIRST LORD DUMAINE [not in F] 155 die liue 157 Guillaume Guiltan 188 lordship Lord 242–43 bedclothes; but they about him bed-cloathes about him: but they 262 quart d'écu Cardceue

4.4.16 you, mistress your Mistris 31 that the

4.5.3 Else [not in F] **7 a** I **16 grass** hearbes **33 name** maine **41 since** sure **42 the nobility** his Nobilitie
5.2.21 similes smiles **27 under her** vnder **34 one** [not in F]
5.3.27 s.p. ATTENDANT Gent⟨leman⟩. **51 Stained** Scorn'd **60 grace-sender** great sender, **72 s.p.** COUNTESS [not in F] **102 Plutus** Platus **115 conjectural** connecturall **141 s.p.** KING [not in F] **156 since** sir, **184 them.** Fairer them fairer: **198 gem; lemme 218 inf'nite cunning** insuite comming **220 my** any **310 are** is

THE LIFE OF TIMON OF ATHENS

CONTROL TEXT: F

F: The Folio of 1623

s.p. ISIDORE' S SERVANT [F's use of Isid. has been changed throughout.]
s.p. VARRO' S SERVANT [F's use of Var. has been changed throughout.]
s.p. VARRO' S SECOND SERVANT [F's use of 2. Var. has been changed throughout.]
s.p. LUCIUS' SERVANT [F's use of Luci. has been changed throughout.]
s.p. FIRST LORD, SECOND LORD [F's use of 1, 2 has been changed throughout.]
s.p. FIRST STRANGER, SECOND STRANGER, THIRD STRANGER [F's use of 1, 2, 3 has been changed throughout.]
s.p. FIRST THIEF [F's use of 1 has been changed throughout.]

1.1.21 gum which oozes Gowne, which vses **25 chafes** chases **40 man** men **47 tax** wax **56 service** services **88 hands** hand **fall** sit **212 cost** cast **235 augury but** angry wit **250 'mongst** amongest **272 Come** Comes **273 taste** raste **283 s.p.** FIRST LORD [not in F]
1.2.28 ever verie **79 thou** then thou **119 smell, all** all **123 s.p.** FIRST LORD Luc. **144 s.p.** LADY Lord. **147 'tends** attends **165 Accept** Accept it
2.1.33 Take I go sir? / Take **34 in count** in. Come
2.2.4 resumes resume **37 broken** debt, broken **59, 61, 65, 88, 92 s.p.** ALL SERVANTS Al., All. **69 mistress'** Masters **123 proposed** propose **130 summed** sound **181 s.p.** ALL SERVANTS Ser. **199 treasure** Treature
3.1.51 this hour his Honor
3.2.19 not mistook mistooke **23 s.p.** LUCIUS Lucil⟨ius⟩. **43 before** a before for a **44 I,** I I **59 spirit** sport
3.3.21 I 'mongst lords 'mong'st Lords

3.4.59 If If't **77 an answer** answer **85 s.p.** HORTENSIUS' SERVANT 1 Var⟨ro⟩. **86 s.p.** VARRO'S FIRST and SECOND SERVANTS 2. Var⟨ro⟩.
3.5.8 Sempronius—all luxors, Sempronius Ullorxa: **11 There is** There's
3.6.1 lords Lord **17 An** And **22 behave his** behoove his **49 felon** fellow **61 Why, I** Why **65 'em** him **100 your** our
3.7.73 foes Fees **74 tag** legge **83 with your flattery** you with Flatteries **99 the rhe 104 s.p.** THIRD 2 **105 s.p.** SECOND 3
4.1.6 steads steeds **13 Son** Some **21 let** yet
4.2.41 does do
4.3.9–10, 11–13 It . . . lean. / Raise . . . honour. Raise . . . Honor. / It . . . leaue: **11 demit** deny't **12 senator** Senators **15 say** fay **39 wappered** wappen'd **41 at, this** at. This **73–75 If thou wilt promise . . . If thou dost not perform** If thou wilt not promise . . . if thou do'st performe **87 tub-fast** Fubfast **116 bars** Barne **121 thy** the **132, 148, 166 s.p.** PHYRNIA and TIMANDRA Both. **134 wholesomeness** Whores **143 pain-sick paines** six **155 scolds** scold'st **185 thy** the **204 fortune** future **223 mossed** moyst **255 command** command'st **285 my** thy **375 son and sire** Sunne and fire **391 them** then **402 s.p.** OTHER THIEVES All. **427 villainy** villaine **441 Steal no** Steal **446 us,** vs **467 grant'st thou'rt man,** grunt'st, th'art a man. **484 mild** wilde **501 A** If not a
5.1.5 Phrynia Phrinica **Timandra** Timandylo **50 worship** worship **68 men** man **105 apart** a part
5.2.1 is in is **11 chance** chanc'd **32 sense** since
5.3.1 s.p. THIRD SENATOR 1 **4 s.p.** FOURTH SENATOR 2 **14 s.p.** FIRST SENATOR 3
5.4.2 this? this? / Tymon is dead, who hath out-stretcht his span, / Some beast read this; There do's not liue a Man.
5.5.37 revenges Reuenge **55 Descend** Defend **66 s.p.** SOLDIER Mes⟨senger⟩.

THE HISTORY OF KING LEAR

CONTROL TEXT: Q1

F: The Folio of 1623
F2: The Folio of 1632
Q1: The Quarto of 1608
Q2: The Quarto of 1619
Qa, Qb: Successive printings of Q1 incorporating various printshop corrections and changes
Title: The Historie of King Lear [Q running title] M. William Shak-speare / HIS / Historie, of King Lear. [Q head title, Stationers' Register] M. William Shak-speare: /

HIS / True Chronicle Historie of the life and / death of King LEAR and his three / Daughters. / *With the vnfortunate life of* Edgar, *sonne* / and heire to the Earle of Gloster, and his / sullen and assumed humor of / TOM of Bedlam: [Q title page]

s.p. EDMUND [Q's use of *Bastard* has been standardized throughout.]

s.p. OSWALD [Q's use of *Oswald, Gentleman,* and *Steward* has been standardized throughout.]

s.p. ALBANY [Q's use of *Duke* and *Albany* has been standardized throughout.]

s.p. CORNWALL [Q's use of *Duke* and *Cornwall* has been standardized throughout.]

s.p. FIRST GENTLEMAN, SECOND GENTLEMAN [Q only uses *Gentleman*.]

s.p. SECOND CAPTAIN, THIRD CAPTAIN [Q only uses *Captain*.]

1.37 off of 51 as [F] a 100 mysteries [F2] mistresse night [F] might 117 dowers [F] dower 128 crownet Coronet 135 mad [Q2, F] man 163 next tenth 208 your [F] you 215 acknow may know 219 the for 230 a [F] and 244 my [F] thy 255 Ye The 267 the worst the worth

2.13 dull-eyed dull lyed 14 creating [F] creating of 15 then [F] the 35 s.p. EDMUND Ba⟨stard⟩. [Qb; not in Qa] 73 ay I 103 honesty [F] honest 109 spherical [F] spirituall 119 on's cue out out 120 sigh sithe

4.2 diffuse defuse 60 these this 79 if you have you haue 94 my any 95 off of 98 Lady the brach Ladie oth'e brach 99 gall [F] gull 136 ladies [Qb] lodes [Qa] 159 learn to [Qb] learne [Qa] 171 Now [Qb] thou [Qa] 186 it [F; not in Q] 207 lethargied [F] lethergie 223 more like to more like 237 my any 241 are [F] and 260 thwart thourt disnatured [F] disueutr'd 262 cadent [F] accent 277 And [not in Q] 278 Untented [Qb] vntender [Qa] 279 Pierce [Qb] peruse [Qa] thee! the 281 cast you [F] you cast 294 thee [F; not in Q] 308 And after [Qa] & hasten [Qb] retinue returne 309 milky [Qb] mildie [Qa] 311 ataxed alapt [Qa] attaskt [Qb] for want [Qb] want [Qa] 312 praised [F] praise

5.6 were [Q2] where 16 stands [Q2] stande

6.18 Wit [not in Q] 27 you your 29 cunning [F] crauing 36 Ho no 47 fine [F] a fine 51 lanced lancht 54 ghasted gasted 55 Or . . . I know not [not in Q] 65 pitched pight 95 tend tends 100 the spoil and waste these—and wast [Qa, Q2] his [Qb] this his [Qa] 118 This Thus 119 poise [Qb] prise [Qa] 122 differences [Qb] defences [Qa] least [Qb] best [Qa] 123 home [Qb, F] hand [Qa]

7.58 Z Zedd 62 have you you haue 69 entrenched intrench unloose, [F] inloose 71 fire [F] stir 74 dogs [F] dayes 76 Smile Smoile 78 Camelot [F] Camulet 87 Than [Q2, F] That 90 roughness [F] ruffines 101 flickering flitkering 102 dialect [F] dialogue 114 fleshment [F] flechuent 117 ancient [F] ausrent [Qa] miscreant [Qb] 123 Stocking [F] Stobing [Qa] Stopping [Qb] 129 speaks [Q2, F] speake 133 contemnèd temnest [Qa] 146 out [Q2, F] ont 150 say [Qa] saw [Qb] 155 miracles [F] my rackles [Qa] my wracke [Qb] 157 now not [Qa] most [Qb] 159 For From 160 their [Qb] and [Qa] overwatched [Q2, F] ouerwatch 161 Take [Qb] Late [Qa] 163 heard [F] heare 167 Does [F] Dost 172 elf [F] else 177 and [Qb; not in Qa] 178 Pins [Qb] Pies [Qa] 179 farms [F] seruice 182 Tuelygod [Qa] *Turlygod* [Qb] 184 home [F] hence 189 cruel [F] crewell 190 heads [F] heeles 201 propose purpose 210 meiny [F] men 222 *Histerica Historica* 246 pardie perdy 250 insolence Iustice 259 father [Qb] fate [Qa] 260 his [Qb] the [Qa] commands [Qb] come and [Qa] tends [Qa] her [Qb] 261 'Fiery'? The The fierie [Qa] Fierie [Qb] 265 commands [Q2] Cōmand 287 divorce [Qb] deuose [Qa] shrine, tombe 293 deplored deptoued [Qa] depriued [Qb] 294 you [F; not in Q] 299 in [F] on 317 s.p. LEAR [Q2; not in Q1, which does indent the line as though it were the beginning of a speech] 323 Thy [F] The 342 your [F] you 361–62 To be . . . air [In Q, the lines appear in the opposite order: "To be . . . owle" after "To wage . . . Ayre."] 366 beg [Q2, F] bag 375 boil bile 417 need [F] deed 420 life is [F] life as 428 so [F] to 429 tamely [F] lamely 438 into [F] in flaws [F] flowes

8.9 outstorm outscorne 36 am [F; not in Q] 45 In which endeavor [not in Q]

9.2 cataracts [F] caterickes hurricanoes [F] Hicanios 8 germens Germains 15 tax [F] taske 34 but [Qb] hut [Qa] 43 wanderers [F] wanderer 59 than [F] their 65 you [F] me 71 your [F] you 74 tiny tine

10.3 took [Q2, F] tooke me 23 The [F] then

11.2 The [Qb] the/the [Qa] 4 here [F; not in Q] 6 contentious [F] crulentious [Qa] tempestious [Qb] 10 roaring [Qb, F] raging [Qa] 12 This [Qb] the [Qa] 14 beats [Qb, F] beares [Qa] 22 own one 51 starblasting [F] starre-blusting 53 there, and [Q2] there, and / and 54 has his [F2] his 69 word words 84 no nonny [F] no on ny 92 lendings [Qb] leadings [Qa] on, be true [Qa] on [Qb] 95 on 's [F] in 97 Flibberti-gibbet [F] fliberdegibek 98 gives [Qb] gins [Qa] and the [Qb] the [Qa] 99 pin,

squinies pin- / queues [Qa] pin, / squemes [Qb] **hare** [Qb] harte [Qa] **101 Swithin** Swithald **wold** old **102 A** [Qa] he [Qb] **met the** [Qb] nellthu [Qa] **mare** [Qb] more [Qa] **foal** fold **103 her alight** [F] her, O light **105 witch** [Qb] with [Qa] **110 tadpole** tod pole **wall-newt** [Qb] wall-wort [Qa] **119 Smolking** snulbug **122 Mahu** [F] ma hu **158 tower** [F] towne
12.10 were not [F] were
13.5 discern deserue **6 Frateretto** [F] *Fretereto* **16 justicer** Iustice **19 troll** tral **20 burn** broome **28 cushions** cushings **29 the** their **30 robèd** robbed **41 she** [Q2; not in Q1] **44 join-stool** ioyne stoole **46 on** an **58 mongrel** mungril **58–59 grim,** / **Hound** [F] grim-hound **84 Take up, take up** [F] Take vp to keepe [Qa] take vp the King [Qb]
14.5 revenges [F] reuenge **8 festinate** [F2] festuent **posts** [F] post **14 questants** questrits **55 anointed** [Qb] aurynted [Qa] **56 as** [F] of [Qa] on [Qb] **bowed** lou'd [Qa] lowd [Qb] **57 bouyed** [F] layd [Qa] bod [Qb] **58 stellèd** [Qb, F] steeled [Qa] **60 howled** [F] heard **62 I'll subscribe** else subscrib'd **70 you** [Q2, F; not in Q1] **83 enkindle** [F] vnbridle **84 quite** quit **96 s.p. SECOND** [not in Q] **97 s.p. THIRD** 2 **100 s.p. SECOND I 101 roguish** [Qa; not in Qb]
15.4 esperance [F] experience **7 parti-eyed** [Qb] poorlie, leed [Qa] **35 to** [F] are toth' **36 kill** [F] bitt **37 play fool** [F] play the / foole **41 hence** [F] here **55 thee** the **57 as . . . lust,** Of lust, as *Obidicut, Stiberdigebit* mocking Mobing, **59 mowing** *Mohing* **67 undo** [F] vnder **71 saucily** firmly
16.10 defy desire **12 terror** [Qb, F] curre [Qa, Q2] **15 Edmund** [Q2, F] *Edgar* **21 command** [Qb, F] coward [Qa, Q2] **27 a** [Qb; not in Qa] **28 My foot usurps my body** [Qa] A Foole vsurps my bed [Qb] **29 whistling** [Qb] whistle [Qa] **44 benefacted** beniflicted [Qa] benifited [Qb] **46 these** [Qb] the [Qa] **48 Humanity** [Qb] Humanly [Qa] **51 discerning** [F] deseruing **55 noiseless** [Qb] noystles [Qa] **56 flaxen biggin threats** thy flayer begin threats [Qa] thy state begins thereat [Qb] **59 shows** [Qb] seemes [Qa] **64 dislocate** dislecate **67 mew** [Qb] now [Qa] **77 You** [Qb] your [Qa] **justicers** [Qb] Iustices [Qa]
17.9 Maréchal Marshall **12 sir** say **17 strove** streme **21 seemed** seeme **30 Let piety not be believed** Let pitie not be beleeft **32 mastered** moystened her
18.2 racked vent **3 fumitor** femiter **4 burdocks** hor-docks **6 The centuries** a centurie is **send** [F] sent **28 incite** [Q2] in sight
19.4 Lord [F] Lady **11 Edmund** [F] and now **15 after** after him **letters, madam.** letters **27 I, madam?** [F] I Madam.

20.2 up it now [F] it vpnow **39 snuff** [Q2] snurff **40 bless him** [F] blesse **42 may** [Q2, F] my **53 a-length** at each **57 summit** [F] sommons **65 how now** how **68 beggar** [Q2, F] bagger **81 ne'er** neare **91 Ha!** hagh **102 ague-proof** [F] argue-proofe **104 every** [Q2, F] euer **109 Does** [F] doe **115 does** [F] do **116 To** [F; not in Q] **117 The** [F] to **129 Shall** [F] should **133 of 't** oft **149 An** And **150 dog's obeyed** [F] dogge, so bade **153 Thy blood as** thy bloud **155 tattered** tottered **158 No tears, now** no now **170 shoe** [F] shoot **171 felt** [F] fell **181 a man a man** [F] a man **183 s.p. FIRST GENTLEMAN** Good Sir— [not in Q1] **191 speaking** speaking of **201 speedy foot** [F] speed fort **descriers** descryes **202 Stands** [F] Standst **214 bounty** [Qb, Q2, F] bornet [Qa] **the benison** [Qb, Q2, F] beniz [Qa] **215 send thee** saue thee [Qa; not in Qb] **boot to boot** [Qb, Q2; not in Qa] **216 first** [Qb, Q2, F; not in Qa] **228 vortnight** [Qb, Q2, F] fortnight [Qa] **229 costard** [Qb, Q2, F] coster [Qa] **230 baton** bat- / tero [Qa] bat [Qb] **257 venture** *Venter*
21.19–21 s.p. FIRST GENTLEMAN . . . DOCTOR Doct⟨or⟩. . . . Gent⟨leman⟩. **33 perdu** Per du **34 injurer's** iniurious **mean'st** [not in Q]
22.3 abdication [Qa] alteration [Qb] **28 Yet** Not **bold's** bolds **32 poor** dore **56 Here** [F] Hard **59 sisters** [Q2, F] sister **60 stung** [F] sting
24.24 goodyear good **45 send** [Qb, Q2, F] saue [Qa] **46 and appointed guard,** [Qb, Q2; not in Q1] **48 common coren?** bosom [Qa] bossome [Qb] **on** [F] of [Qa] **54 We** [Qb] mee **56 sharpness** [Qb] sharpes **83 bar** bare **85 banns** banes **119 ere** are **128 fortune** [F] fortun'd **131 Conspirant** [F] Conspicuate **135 are** [F] As **139 tongue** [F] being **140 My** by **142 hated lie** [F] hatedly **o'erturn** oreturnd **146 s.p. ALL** Alb⟨any⟩. **163 ignobly** [not in Q] **165 vices** [F] vertues, **209 him** me **264 you** [Q2, F] your **278 you** [F; not in Q] **282 from your first** [F] from your life **285 fordone** [F] foredoome **291 great** [F; not in Q] **295 honours** [Q2, F] honor **300 have** [Q2, F] of

THE TRAGEDY OF KING LEAR

CONTROL TEXT: F

F1: The Folio of 1623
F2: The Folio of 1632
Q1: The Quarto of 1608
Q2: The Quarto of 1619
Qa, Qb, Fa, Fb: Successive printings of Q1 and F incorporating various printshop corrections and changes

s.p. EDMOND [F's use of *Edmond* and *Bastard* are standardized throughout.]
s.p. OSWALD [F only uses *Steward*.]
s.p. FIRST GENTLEMAN [F uses only *Gentleman*.]
s.p. LEAR [F uses *Kear* once.]
s.p. KENT [F uses *Lent* once.]

1.1.53 words [Q] word **72 possesses** [Q] professes **98 Haply** Happily **108 mysteries** [F2] miseries **137 crownet** Coronet **153 a** [Q, F2; not in F1] **154 ne'er feared** nere feare **159 s.p. ALBANY** *and* **CORDELIA** *Alb⟨any⟩. Cor⟨delia⟩.* **167 sentence** [Q] sentences **173 seventh** tenth **213 best** [Q; not in F] **dear'st** deerest **223 well** [Q] will **228 the** for **265 Ye** The **278 pleated** plighted **279 covert** couers
1.2.119 Fut! [Q; not in F]
1.4.1 well [Q] will **2 diffuse** defuse **18 thou'rt** [Q1] thou art **28 canst** [Q1] canst thou **44 Daughter** [Q] daughters **48 A** [Q1] he **61 these** this **96 off** of **122 know** [Q1] thou know **129 crown** [Q] crownes **130 o'th'** [Q1] on thy **144 fools** [Q] foole **145 Prithee** [Q] Pry'thy **163 nor crumb,** [Q] not crum **249–50 that she may feel—** / **That she may feel** That she may feele, **306 You** [F1] your [F2] **attasked** [Qb] at task
1.5.21 a may [Q1] he may
2.1.2 you [Q] your **36 Ho** no **39 stand 's** [Q1] stand **54 ghasted** gasted **69 I should** [Q] should I **70 ay,** [Q; not in F] **78 why** [Q] wher **86 strange news** [Q] strangenesse **94 tend** tended **99 spoil** [Qb] wast **120 poise** [Qb] prize **123 least** [Qb] best **thought** [Q] though
2.2.20 clamorous [Q] clamours **59 you'll** [Q1] you will **68 holy** [Fb] holly [Fa] **72 Renege** [Q] Reuenge **77 an** [Q1] if **93 take't** [Q1] take it **101 flick'ring** flicking **114 dread** [Q] dead **121 respect** [Q] respects **136 good** [Q1; not in F] **137 Duke's** [Q] Duke **144 to** [Q1] too **145 say** [Qa] saw **152 now** most **154 For** From **161 unusual** [Q1] vnusall **175 sheep-cotes** [Q] sheeps-coates **176 Sometime** [Q] sometimes **177 Tuelygod** [Qa] *Turlygod* **180 messenger** [Q] Messengers **186 man's** [Q] man **204 whose** [Q] those **216 wild** wil'd **226 *Histerica*** *Historica* **231 the** [Q] the the **242 gives** [Q, Fb] giue [Fa] **have** [Q] hause **246 begin** [Q1] begins **293 you** [Q] your **295 mother's** [Q] Mother **shrine** tombe **336 tender-hafted** tenderhefted **351 sickly** fickly a [Q1] he **374–75 To be a comrade with the wolf and owl, / To wage against the enmity o'th' air** To wage against the enmity oth'ayre, / To be a Comrade with the Wolfe, and Owle, **377 hot-blooded** [Fa] hot-bloodied [Fb] **451 mad** [Q, Fb] mads [Fa] **471 to** [Q1] too **472 wild** [Q] wil'd

3.1.2 s.p. FIRST GENTLEMAN *Gen⟨tleman⟩.* [The stage direction calls for "a Gentleman," and F uses this combination to mean this specific character who reappears in 5.3.196–249.]
3.2.3 drowned [Q] drown **49 pother** pudder **84–85 Then . . . confusion.** [in F, after 3.2.91]
3.3.15 for't [Q1] for it
3.4.10 thy [Q] they **12 This** [Qb] the **31 looped** lop'd **44 Thorough** [Q1] through **45 cold** [Q; not in F] **47 two** [Q; not in F] **50 led through** [Q] led though **ford** [Q] Sword **55 Bless** Blisse **82 deeply** [Q2] deerely **89 Dauphin** Dolphin *cessez Sesey* **103 fiend** [Q; not in F] **104 till the** [Q] at **107 Swithin** *Swithold* wold old **108 A** [Qa] he **nine foal,** nine-fold **120 had** [Q; not in F] **150 a** [Q1] he **156 in t'** [Q1] into th'
3.5.22 dearer [Q] deere
3.6.25 Bobtail [Q] Or Bobtaile **tyke** [Q] tight **trundle** [Q2] Troudle **32 makes** [Q] make
3.7.8 festinate festiuate **63 cruels I'll subscribe** Cruels else subscribe
4.1.10 parti-eyed [Qb] poorly led **32 A** [Q1] He
4.2.30 whistling [Qb] whistle **36 shows** [Qb] seemes **43 threat enraged** [Q, F2] threat-enrag'd **47 justicers** [Qb] Iustices
4.3.3 fumitor [Q] Fenitar **4 burdocks** Hardokes **18 distress** [Q] desires **good man's** [Q] Goodmans
4.4.6 letters [Q1] Letter **15 after, madam** after him, Madam **39 him** [Q, F2; not in F1]
4.5.7 speak'st [Q2] speakest **17 walk** [Q] walk'd **53 a-length** at each **69 methoughts** [Q1] me thought **119 They're** [Q1] they are **154 Through** [Q] Tho- / rough [F's unmetrical substitution straddles a page break in a passage set as justified prose; "Through" could not be split, and the compositor almost certainly added the "o" for reasons of page makeup.] **155 Plate sin** Place sinnes **178 s.p. FIRST GENTLEMAN** *Gent. ⟨leman⟩.* **195 speaking** speaking of **201–2 hears that /** **That** [Q] heares that, which **206 in** on **225 Durst** [Q1] Dar'st **228 'cagion** [Q] 'casion **231 swaggered** [Q1] zwaggerd **232 so** [Q1] zo **234 baton** Ballow **I'll** [Q1] chill **236 sir** [Q1] zir **249 sorrow** [Q1] sorry **261 and for you her own for venture,** [Q1; not in F]

THE TRAGEDY OF MACBETH

CONTROL TEXT: F

F: The Folio of 1623
Fa, Fb: Successive states of F incorporating various print-shop corrections and changes

s.p. FIRST WITCH, SECOND WITCH, THIRD WITCH [F's use of *1*, *2*, and *3* has been standardized throughout.]

s.p. KING DUNCAN [F's use of *King* has been standardized throughout.]

s.p. LADY MACBETH [F's use of *Lady* has been standardized throughout.]

s.p. FIRST MURDERER [F's use of *1 Murderer, 1,* and *Murderer* has been standardized throughout.]

s.p. SECOND MURDERER [F's use of *2 Murderer* and *2* has been standardized throughout.]

s.p. THIRD MURDERER [F's use of *3* has been standardized throughout.]

s.p. ALL THE WITCHES [F's use of *All.* has been standardized throughout.]

s.p. FIRST APPARITION, SECOND APPARITION, THIRD APPARITION [F's use of *1 Apparition, 2 Apparition,* and *3 Apparition* has been standardized throughout.]

s.p. LADY MACDUFF [F's use of *Wife* has been standardized throughout.]

s.p. MACDUFF'S SON [F's use of *Son* has been standardized throughout.]

s.p. A MURDERER [F's use of *Murderer* has been standardized throughout.]

s.p. A SOLDIER [F's use of *Soldier* has been standardized throughout.]

1.1.9–11 s.p. SECOND WITCH **Paddock calls.** / THIRD WITCH **Anon.** / ALL **Fair . . . air.** *All. Padock calls anon: faire . . . ayre.*
1.2.13 **galloglasses** Gallowgrosses **26 break** [not in F] **31 Norwegian** Norweyan **46 haste** a haste **61 Colum's** Colmes
1.3.30 **weird** weyward **37 Forres** Soris **95 hail** Tale **96 Came** Can
1.4.1 **Are** Or
1.5.21 **'Thus . . . do'** [not in F] **29, 32 s.p. SERVANT** Mess. **63 the innocent** th'innocent
1.6.4 **martlet** Barlet **9 most** must
1.7.6 **shoal** Schoole **47 do** no
2.1.55 **strides** sides **56 sure** sowre **57 way they** they may
2.3.77 **horror.** horror. **Ring the Bell. 108 Outran** Out-run
3.1.2, 3.4.132, 4.1.152 **weird** weyard **23 talk** take **76 s.p. MURDERERS** [F uses *Murth.* three times in 3.1, and each time it would be appropriate for both to speak. See also 3.1.116 and 3.1.140.]
3.3.7 **and** end
3.4.77 **time** times **88 of** o' **143 in deed** indeed
3.5.34–35 s.p. SPIRITS . . . **away.** [not in F; see Textual Note] **38–73 s.p. SPIRITS . . . reach.** [not in F; see Textual Note]
3.6.24 **son** Sonnes
4.1.44–60 s.p. HECATE . . . **out.** [not in F; see Textual Note] **75 germens** Germaine **109 Dunsinane** Dunsmane **114 on's high place** our high plac'd
4.2.22 **none** moue **83 shag-haired** shagge-ear'd

4.3.134 **thy** they **155 with** [Fb] my with [Fa] **161 not** nor **237 tune** time
5.3.41 **Cure her** Cure **46 fraught** stufft
5.4.11 **gone** giuen
5.5.40 **pall** pull
5.11.25 s.p. ALL BUT MALCOLM *All.*

The Tragedy of Antony and Cleopatra

Control text: F

F: The Folio of 1623
Fa, Fb: Fa is the uncorrected version, Fb the corrected version of F

Title: Anthony & Cleopatra [Stationers' Register entry] *Anthony and Cleopater* [F table of contents] *The Tragedie of Anthonie, and Cleopatra* [F head title] *The Tragedie of Anthony and Cleopatra* [F running title]

s.p. SILIUS [F's use of *Romaine* in 3.1 (where Silius is referred to by name in dialogue) is standardized throughout.]

s.p. BOY [Not in F's speech prefixes or stage directions, although Enobarbus refers to the boy in dialogue. See 2.7.]

s.p. WATCH, GUARD, SERVANTS, SOLDIERS [F refers to these characters either by category (*Soldier, 3. Watch,* etc.) or by number (*1, 2,* etc.). This edition never uses numbers alone, preferring prefixes such as "First Servant," "Third Soldier," etc.]

1.1.52 **how** who
1.2.0 s.d. *Enter . . . attendants Enter Enobarbus, Lamprius, a Southsayer, Rannius, Lucillius, Charmian, Iras, Mardian the Eunuch, and Alexas.* [Rannius and Lucillius are ghost characters; so is Lamprius, unless he is the soothsayer. As these three are not mentioned again, their names are irrelevant and hence omitted.] **5 charge** change **34 fertile** fore- / tell **55 Alexas—come** *Alexas.* Come [F attributes the rest of the speech, beginning with "Come," to Alexas, taking the name as a speech prefix rather than an address.] **70 Saw you** Saue you **102 ho** how **103 s.p. SECOND MESSENGER** The . . . Sicyon— / s.p. ANTHONY **Is . . . one?** *1. Mes.* (First Messenger) The *Scicion,* / Is . . . one? [The First Messenger speaks the entire line in F.] **125 occasion** an occasion **163 leave** loue **168 Hath** Haue **177 hair** heire **179 place is under us, requires** places under us, require
1.3.11 **Iwis** I wish **82 my** [not in F]
1.4.3 **Our** One **8 vouchsafed** vouchsafe **9 the abstract** th'abstracts **44 deared** fear'd **46**

lackeying lacking 56 wassails Vassailes 57 Modena *Medena* 58 Pansa Pausa 76 we me 76 council counsell

1.5.3 mandragora *Mandragoru* 47 armjaunced Arme-gaunt 49 dumbed dumbe 60 man mans

2.1.2, 5, 16, 18, 38 s.p. MENECRATES . . . MENECRATES . . . MENAS . . . MENAS . . . MENAS *Mene⟨crates⟩*. [Menecrates throughout in F] 21 waned wand 38 ne'er neere 41 warred wan'd

2.2.49 the your 126 not so, Agrippa not, say *Agrippa* 127 reproof proofe 210 glow gloue 212 gentlewoman Gentlewoman 238 breathless, pour breath breathlesse powre breath

2.3.12 Gone thither thither 20 afeard a feare 28 away, alway

2.4.6 at the at 9 s.p. MAECENAS *and* AGRIPPA *Both.*

2.5.2 s.p. CHARMIAN, IRAS, *and* ALEXAS *Omnes.* 12 finned fine 43 is 'tis 52 But Bur 104 act art

2.6.16 the [not in F] 19 is his 39 s.p. CAESAR, ANTONY, *and* LEPIDUS *Omnes.* 53 There is ther's 67 meanings meaning 71 o' [not in F] 83 s.p. CAESAR, ANTONY, *and* LEPIDUS *All.*

2.7.1–13 s.p. FIRST SERVANT . . . SECOND SERVANT . . . FIRST SERVANT *I* . . . *2* . . . *I* 86 part then is part, then he is 108 s.p. BOY [*sings*] The Song. 110 vats Fattes 115 off of 119 speaks. The [Fa] speakest: he [Fb] 123 father's Father 125 s.p. MENAS [Not in F; Enobarbus continues speaking until the second half of 1.129, which is spoken by Menas in F, as in this edition.] 127 hear [Fb] heare a [Fa] a loud aloud

3.1.5, 27, 34 s.p. SILIUS *Romaine.* [variously spelled] 14 to [Fa] too [Fb] 37 there [Fa] their [Fb]

3.2.3 are [Fb] art [Fa] 10 s.p. AGRIPPA *Ant⟨ony⟩.* 16 figures Figure 26 bond Band 49 at at the full of [Fa]; of full [Fb] 60 wept weepe

3.3.17 gait? gate, 18 looked'st look'st

3.4.8 them, then 9 took't look't 24 yours your 30 Your You 38 has he's

3.5.12 world, thou hast a pair of chops, would thou hadst a pair of chaps 14 one the [not in F]

3.6.13 he there . . . kings of kings hither . . . King of Kings 61 obstruct abstract 72 Malchus *Mauchus* 74 Comagene; Polemon Comageat, *Polemen* 75 Lycaonia Licoania 88 their his

3.7.4 it is it it 5 Is't not If not, 21 Brundisium Brandusium 23 Toryne Troine 51 Actium Action 69 leader's led Leaders leade 72 s.p. CAMIDIUS *Ven⟨tidius⟩.* 78 Taurus *Towrus* 80 in with

3.10.10 riband-red ribaudred 14 June Inne 27 he his

3.11.6 s.p. ATTENDANTS *Omnes.* 19 that them 47 seize cease 58 tow stowe 59 Thy The

3.12.0 s.d. DOLABELLA *Dollabello* 13 lessens Lessons 29 As From

3.13.10 mooted meered 25 caparisons Comparisons 54 Caesar *Caesars* 55 embraced embrace 74 deputation disputation 76–77 kneel / Till kneele. / Tell him, 103 This the 149 abyss Abisme 165 smite smile 168 discandying discandering 171 sits sets 201 on in

4.2.1 Domitius *Domitian* 19 s.p. SERVITORS *Omnes.*

4.3.7 s.p. THIRD SOLDIER *I.*

4.4.5–6 too. / . . . for? s.p. ANTONY too, *Antony.* / . . . for? [In F, Cleopatra's speech includes lines 6–7 and thus continues uninterrupted from line 5 to line 8.] 13 doff't daft 24 s.p. CAPTAIN *Alex⟨as⟩.* 25 s.p. SOLDIERS *All.*

4.5.1, 3, 7 s.p. SOLDIER *Eros.*

4.6.15 Camidius *Caminidus* 19 more mote

4.8 [Most editions continue 4.7, even though the stage is cleared. The new scene affects the numbering of the remaining scenes in the act.]

4.9.2 gests guests 18 My Mine

4.13.4 augurs Auguries 21 spanieled pannelled

4.15.4 towered toward 10 distains dislimes 19 Caesar *Caesars* 107, 132 s.p. ALL THE GUARDS *All.* 110 s.p. DECRETAS *Dercetus.* 122 sent word sent you word

4.16.42 s.p. ALL THE LOOKERS-ON *All.* 46 hussy huswife 75 e'en in 77 chores chares 89 do it doo't

5.1.0 s.d. MAECENAS *Menas* 2 but [not in F] 15 rivèd round 18 that the 27 a [not in F] 28, 31 s.p. AGRIPPA *Dola⟨bella⟩.* 36 lance launch 59 live leaue 70 s.p. ALL BUT CAESAR *All.*

5.2.80 O [not in F] 86 autumn 'twas *Anthony* it was 95 or nor 103 smites suites 212 Ballad Ballads o' a 219 my mine 224 Cydnus *Cidrus* 304 vile wilde 308 awry away

PERICLES, PRINCE OF TYRE

CONTROL TEXT: Q1

Q1: The Quarto of 1609
Q2: The Quarto of 1609
Q3: The Quarto of 1611
Q4: The Quarto of 1619
Q5: The Quarto of 1630
Q6: The Quarto of 1635
Qa, Qb: Successive states of Q1 incorporating various print-shop corrections and changes

PA: George Wilkins, THE Painfull Aduentures of *Pericles* Prince of Tyre. *Being* The true History of the Play of *Pericles,* as it was lately presented by the worthy and ancient Poet *Iohn Gower*

Title: Pericles, Prynce of Tyre [Stationers' Register entry] THE LATE, / And much admired Play, / Called / Pericles, Prince of Tyre. / With the true Relation of the whole Historie, / aduentures, and fortunes of the said Prince: / As also, / The no lesse strange, and worthy accidents, / in the Birth and Life, of his Daughter / *MARIANA.* [Q1 title page] The Play of Pericles / Prince of Tyre. &c. [Q1 head title] *The Play of Pericles Prince of Tyre* [Q1 running titles]

Scene 1 [not in Q1; see note to Scene 1] 6 holy-ales Holydayes 11 these [Q2] those 17 This' This 21 fere Peere 29 By But 30 account' account'd 39 a wight of wight 42 s.d. *lords and peers in their richest ornaments* [PA] *fellowers* 50 Fit for th' For 54 In her their best perfections to knit To knit in her, their best perfections 60 razed racte 67 boundless bondlesse 73 heav'n-like face face like Heauen 79 semblants semblance bloodless pale 83 From For 99 s.p. ANTIOCHUS [not in Q1] s.d. *He ... riddle* [not in Q1] which the tyrant receiuing with an angry brow, threw downe the Riddle [PA] 102 'sayed sayd 107 s.d. *He ... riddle* [not in Q1] which the Prince taking vp, read aloude [PA] 113 this [PA] they 139 like is like 152 He's he ha's 154 our your 156 cancel counsell 163 your worth and our degree our honour and your worth 170 you're you 171 uncomely vntimely 179 'schew shew 186 the which which 194–95 And ... your And our minde pertakes her priuat actions, / To your secrecie; and for your 202 s.d. *hastily* [PA; not in Q1] 204 Your majesty My Lord 205 after; like after, and like 208 it be to say thou say 209 Your majesty [not in Q1] 210–11 If ... highness My Lord, if I can get him within my Pistols length, Ile make him sure enough, so farewell to your highnesse. [prose] 212 s.p. ANTIOCHUS [Q4; not in Q1]

Scene 2 [not in Q1] s.d. *distempered* [not in Q1] Princes distemperature [PA] 3 Be my By me 7 feared, 's fearde is 10 care's author's the others 20 honour him honour 25 th'ostent the stint 30 am once 33 s.d. *among them old* HELICANUS [not in Q1] olde [PA, describing Helicanus] 37–42 You ... contradict it [not in Q1] he did not wel so to abuse himselfe, to waste his body there with pyning sorrow, vpon whose safety depended the liues and proserity of a whole kingdome, that it was ill in him to doe it, and

no lesse in his counsell to suffer him, without contradicting it [PA; Helicanus to Pericles] 46 wind sparke 49 a [not in Q1] 55 Helicane *Hellicans* 59 brows face 63 you but [Q4] but you 64 s.d. *lifting him up* [PA; not in Q1] 65 for it [Q4] fort the heav'ns heauē 68 mak'st makes 70 you you your selfe 75 Where, as [Q2] Whereas 78 As children are heav'n's blessings: to parents, objects [not in Q1] 86 of of a 88 me [not in Q1] 89 fears feare 91 doubt—as doubt no doubt doo't, as no doubt 105 grieve griue for 113 Or or til the 117 in my absence wrong thy liberties wrong my liberties in my absence 120 Tarsus *Tharsus* 126 sure crack cracke 127 we'll will

Scene 3 [not in Q1] 2–3 and am caught ... but if I do it [not in Q1] 10–40 You ... Tyre [prose in Q1] 11 question question mee 21 lest that he lest hee 27 King's ears it Kings seas 28 on the seas at the Sea 30 Lord Thaliart am I, of Antioch [not in Q1] 31 s.p. HELICANUS [Q4; not in Q1] of Antioch from *Antiochus* 32 King Antiochus him 35 lord's Lord has betoke [Q2] betake 36 Now my now 37 enquire desire

Scene 4 [not in Q1] 8 they're they are midges' mischiefs 13 our sorrows and sorrowes 15 lungs toungs 17 helps helpers 20 As you think best Ile doe my best 22 o'er on 23 the [Q3] her 34 Those These 36 they [Q2] thy 39 two summers [PA] too sauers 47 Here weeping stands a lord, there lies a lady dying Heere stands a Lord, and there a Ladie weeping; heere standes one weeping, and there lies another dying [PA] 54 heed heare 55 s.d. *fainting ... slowly* a fainting messenger came slowly into them [PA] 57 thou [Q4] thee 58 t'expect to expect 64 neighbour [PA] neighbouring 66 Hath That these the 68 men mee 72 not not as 73 him's himnes 77 grave's grounds 79 whence he comes. whence he comes, and what he craues? 82 s.d. the LORD *again conducting* [not in Q1] he demaunded of the fellow where the Gouernour was, and foorthwith to be conducted to him [PA] 87–88 Since entering your unshut gates have witnessed / The widowed desolation And seene the desolation; Pericles ... no sooner entred into their unshut gates, but his princely eies were partaking witnesses of their widowed desolation [PA] 89 hearts teares 92 fraught stuft; fraughted [PA] 93 importing expecting 96 s.p. ALL OF TARSUS Omnes. s.d. *falling ... weeping* [not in Q1] the feeble soules ... fell on their knees, and wept [PA] 99 me, my selfe, our 104 ne'er neare

Scene 5 [not in Q1] 4 Prove That Will prove 11 Tarsus *Tharstill* 12 speken spoken 14

His statue build Build his Statue **17 Helicane** [Q3] *Helicon* **19 for that** for though **22 Sent word** Sau'd one **24 hid intent to murden** hid in Tent to murdred [Qa] had intent to murder [Qb] **25 Tarsus** *Tharsis* **27 deeming** doing **36 aught** ought **51 s.d.** *two poor* three; pore Fishermen [*PA*; in this edition, the Third Fisherman enters after the first two.] **52 s.p.** MASTER I.; the maister Fisherman [*PA*; changed throughout, except at line 80, where "I." is changed to "THIRD FISHERMAN"] **What ho, Pilch** What, to pelch **54 s.d.** *He . . . repair* [not in Q1] certayne *Fishermen . . .* were come out from their homely cottages to dry and repaire their nettes [*PA*] **56–72, 74–75, 77–81, 83–84, 90–92, 93–94, 99–101, 123, 136–37, 139–40, 144–47, 152–54, 195–97** [verse in Q1] **70 devours** deuowre **77 s.p.** THIRD FISHERMAN [Q4] 3. FISHER-MAN I. **110 crave** aske **112 pray** [Q4] pray you **113 quotha** ke-tha **an** and **114 s.d.** *To . . . ground* the chiefe of these fishermen . . . lifting him vp from the ground [*PA*] **116 holidays** all day **117 moreo'er** more; or **123 an** and **124 all your** you **128–30 beadle.** MASTER **Thine office, knave—** SECOND FISHERMAN **Is to draw up the other nets. I'll go** Beadle: But Maister, Ile goe draw vp the Net; goe dragge vp some other nettes [*PA*; the Master commanding his servants—hence, this edition introduces an interjection by the Master into the Second Fisherman's speech.] **133 s.d.** *seating . . . Pericles* [not in Q1] the maister . . . seated himselfe by him [*PA*] **136 is** [Q2] I **141–42 from his subjects / He gains** from / His subjects **144 some half** [*PA*] halfe **148 Were but** [*PA*] Were **answerable** [*PA*] equall **151 get himself** get **for with** for **153 s.d.** *Before . . . prize* [not in Q1] before helpe came, vp came the Fish expected, but prooued indeede to be a rusty armour. [*PA*] **155 pray** [Qb] pary [Qa] **156 thy** [not in Q1] all her crosses [*PA*] **157 losses** selfe **164 forfend, the same may** protect thee, Fame may **169 in 's** [Q4] in his **176 with't** with it **180 learned** [*PA*] borne **185 this** them **187 I'm** I am **188 rapture** rupture **191 delightsome** delight **193 friends** friend **198 equal** a Goale

Scene 6 [not in Q1] **s.d.** *and sit on two thrones* [not in Q1] They thus seated [*PA*] **4 daughter** daughter heere **8 my** my royall **13 renown** Renownes **14 office** honour **16 s.d.** *richly . . .* THAISA [not in Q1] richly armed, their Pages before them bearing their Deuices on their shields being by the knights Page deliuered to the Lady [*PA*; repeated for each knight in this edition] **21 s.d.** *She . . .* KING [not in Q1] from her presented to the King her father [*PA*; repeated for each knight

in this edition] **22 s.d.** [See note to 6.16.] **26 An armèd** Is an Armed **27 thus** thus in Spanish **Piùe per dolcezza che per forza** *Pue Per doleera kee per forsa* **s.d.** [See note to 6.21.] **28 You . . . force** [not in Q1] more by lenitie than by force [*PA*] **s.d.** [See note to 6.16.] **29 what's** [Q4] with **31 pompae** *Pompey; pompa* [*PA*] **s.d.** [See note to 6.21.] **32–33 Desire . . . enterprise** [not in Q1] desire of renowne drew him to this enterprise [*PA*] **33 s.d.** [See note to 6.16.] **34 A knight of Athens bearing** [not in Q1] The fift of *Athens,* and his Deuice was [*PA*] **36 s.d.** [See note to 6.21.] **37 this** his **38 s.d.** [See note to 6.16.] **39 And who the fifth?** [not in Q1] **39–40 a prince of Corinth / Presents** [not in Q1] a prince of *Corinth* [*PA*] **43 So . . . into** [*PA*; not in Q1] **s.d.** PERICLES . . . THAISA [not in Q1] The sixt and last was *Pericles,* Prince of *Tyre,* who hauing neither Page to deliuer his shield, nor shield to deliuer . . . Himselfe with a most gracefull curtesie presented it vnto her . . . being himselfe in a rusty Armour [*PA*] **45 delivereth** deliuered **49 From** A pretty morrall frõ **54 T'have** To haue **56 Unto** To **60 for** by

Scene 7 [not in Q1] **s.d.** *A stately banquet is brought in* [not in Q1] a most stately banquet [*PA*] *a* MARSHAL *conducting* [not in Q1] by the Kings Marshall conducted [*PA*] **1 to the** KNIGHTS To say Knights, to say **2 To I 7 You're** You are **11 yours** [Q4] your **13 artists** an Artist **15 You are** And you are **24 Envied** Enuies **25 s.d.** PERICLES . . . THAISA placed directly ouer-against where the king and his daughter sate [*PA* (said of Pericles)] **27 distaste** resist **but** not **29 I am amazed** [not in Q1] **34 broke** broken **36 Yon** [Q2] You **37 me** [Q4; not in Q1] **what** that **42 son's** sonne a **like a 48 s.p.** THE OTHER KNIGHTS *Knights* **49 stored** stur'd **50 you do** [Q4] do you **full** fill **51 s.p.** THE OTHER KNIGHTS *Knight.* **59 so doing** doing so **like** like to **61 entertain** entraunce **62 bear** say wee drinke **69 Furthermore** And furthermore **know** know of him **71–72** THAISA The King . . . Wishing *Tha.* The king my father (sir) has drunke to you / *Peri.* I thanke him / *Tha.* Wishing **79 unconstant** [not in Q1] and vnconstant [*PA*] **79–80 bereft / Unfortunately both** reft [Q1] most vnfortunately bereft both [*PA*] **83–84 seeking adventures / Was** [not in Q1] **83–84 A gentleman . . . seas** A Gentleman of *Tyre:* who onely by misfortune of the seas **84 solely** onely **86 mishaps** misfortune **87 s.d.–95** SIMONIDES . . . *accept* [not in Q1] Which mishaps of his the king vnderstanding of, hee was strucke with present pitty to him, and rising from his state, he came foorthwith and imbraced him, bade him be cheered, and tolde him, that whatsoeuer misfortune had impayred him of, fortune, by his helpe, could repayre to him, for both himselfe and Countrey should be his friendes, and presently calling for a goodly milke white Steede, and a payre of golden spurres, them first hee bestowed vppon him, telling him, they were the prises due to his merite, and ordained for that dayes enterprise: which kingly curtesie Pericles as thankefully accepting. Much time beeing spent in dauncing and other reuells [PA] **99 Your limbs will** Will **104 Come** Come sir **105 sir, that the** you **112 Lights, pages, to** Pages and lights to **114 should** [not in Q1] **116 s.p. KING SIMONIDES** [Q3; not in Q1, where the speech continues as Pericles']

Scene 8 [not in Q1] **4 hold** with-hold **9 both apparelled all in jewels** [PA; not in Q1] **11 Their** those **13 hands** hand **29 step** breath **33 death indeed's** death in deed, **34 this—kingdoms** this Kingdome is **36 utter** [not in Q1] **38 unto** as vnto our **40 By** Try **44 But . . . love** [follows line 48 in Q1] **45 longer then let me** longer, let me **46 Further to bear** To forbeare **49 seek your noble prince** search like nobles, **55 us** [not in Q1] **56–57 If . . . out / If . . . there** [after line 29 in Q1]

Scene 8a [not in Q1] Prince *Pericles* hauing had (as before is mentioned) his lodging directed next adioyning to the kings bedchamber, whereas all the other Princes vppon their comming to their lodgings betooke themselues to their pillowes, and to the nourishment of a quiet sleepe, he of the Gentlemen that attended him, (for it is to be noted, that vpon the grace that the king had bestowed on him, there was of his Officers toward him no attendance wanting) hee desired that hee might be left priuate, onely that for his instant solace they would pleasure him with some delightfull Instrument, with which, and his former practise hee intended to passe away the tediousnesse of the night insteade of more fitting slumbers. His wil was presently obeyed in all things since their master had commaunded he should be disobeyed in nothing: the Instrument is brought him, and as hee had formerly wished, the Chamber is disfurnished of any other company but himselfe [PA, from which this scene is reconstructed] **8 s.d.** *a stringed instrument* [implied by PA, which refers to the "fingering" of the instrument and describes Pericles singing as he plays] **9–10 Now . . . sleep** all the other Princes . . . betooke themselues to their pillowes [PA] **10 s.d. PERICLES** *plays and sings* [PA elaborately describes the performance.] **11–13 Day . . . on.** But day that hath still that soueraigntie to drawe backe the empire of the night, though a while shee in darkenesse vsurpe, brought the morning on [PA] **14–15 I . . . me** euen in the instant came in *Pericles,* to giue his Grace that salutation which the morning required of him [PA]

Scene 9 [not in Q1] **5 none can** by no meanes can I **6 have** get **7–8 It . . . chamber** she hath so strictly / Tyed her to her Chamber, that t'is impossible **15 light** light / T'is well Mistris, your choyce agrees with mine **18 Mistress, 'tis well** Well, **your** her **20–21 that / In show, I have determined on in heart** it; the king intending to dissemble that in shew, which hee had determined on in heart [PA] **24–25 night. My ears, / I do protest** night: / I do protest, my eares **30 think you of my daughter** do you thinke of my Daughter, sir **31 And** And she is **33 My daughter, sir** Sir, my Daughter **34 So well indeed** I so well **39 s.d. He . . . feet** [not in Q1] foorthwith prostrating himselfe at the kings feete [PA] **43 her** her. / *king.* Thou has bewicht my daughter, / And thou art a villaine. / *Peri.* By the Gods I haue not **47 Thou liest like a traitor** Traytor, thou lyest **48–50 That . . . child** [not in Q1] I, traytour, quoth the king, that thus disguised, art stolne into my Court, with the witchcraft of thy actions to bewitch, the yeelding spirit of my tender Childe [PA] **51–52 Who calls me traitor, unless it be the King, / Ev'n in his bosom I will write the lie** Even in his throat, vnlesse it be the King, / That cals me Traytor, I returne the lye [Q1] were it any in his Court, except himselfe, durst call him traytor, even in his bosome he would write the lie [PA] **54 blood** thoughts **56 in search of honour** [PA] for Honours cause **57 your state** her state [Q1] his State [PA] **60–62 I . . . witness** No? heere comes my Daughter, she can witnesse it [Q1] answered, he should prooue it otherwise, since by his daughters hand, it there was euident, both his practise and her consent therein [PA] **64–65 By what . . . fulfilled** [not in Q1] demaunded of her by the hope she had of heauen, or the desire she had to haue her best wished fulfilled heere in the worlde [PA] **68 made** that made **71 How, minion** [PA] Yea Mistris **72–96 I am glad on't . . . only child** I am glad on't with all my heart [Q1] How minion, quoth her Father (taking her off at the very word, who dare be displeased withalle) Is this a fit match for you? a stragling *Theseus* borne we knowe not where, one that hath neither bloud nor merite for thee to hope for, or himselfe to challenge euen the least allowaunce of thy perfections, when she humbling her princely knees before her Father, besought him to consider, that suppose his birth were base (when his life shewed him not to be so) yet hee had vertue, which is the very ground of all nobilitie, enough to make him noble: she intreated him to remember that she was in loue, the power of which loue was not to be confined by the power of his will. And my most royall Father, quoth shee, what with my penne I haue in secret written vnto you, with my tongue now I openly confirme, which is, that I haue no life but his loue, neither any being but in the enioying of his worth. But daughter (quoth *Symonides*) equalles to equalls, good to good is ioyned, this not being so, the bauine of your minde in rashnesse kindled, must againe be quenched, or purchase our displeasure, And for you sir (speaking to prince *Pericles*) first learne to know, I banish you my Court, and yet scorning that our kingly inragement should stoope so lowe, for that your ambition sir, Ile haue your life. Be constant quoth *Thaysa*, for euerie droppe of blood hee sheades of yours, he shall draw an other from his onely childe [PA] **97 yea** [not in Q1] **102 s.d.** *He . . . hand* [not in Q1] catching them both rashly by the handes [PA] **103 s.d.** *He . . . hand* [not in Q1; see note to line 102 s.d.] **105 I shall** Ile **s.d.** *He . . . together* [not in Q1] heclapt them hand in hand [PA] **106 s.d.** PERICLES *and* THAISA *kiss* [not in Q1] while they as louingly ioyned lip to lip [PA] **108 your further** further you you both **112 s.p.** PERICLES *and* THAISA *Ambo.* **113 Then** And then

Scene 10 [not in Q1] **2 the house about** about the house **6 fore** from **7 crickets** Cricket **8 As** Are **10 Where** by [Q2] Whereby **13 eche** each **14 s.d.** *comes hastily in to meetes;* came hastily in to them [PA] **17 coigns** Crignes **21 stead** steed **29 mutiny there he** mutanie, hee there **t'appease** t'oppresse **46 fortune's mood** fortune mou'd **60 sea-tossed** seas tost **speke** speake

Scene 11 [not in Q1] **7 Thou stormest** then storme **8 spit** speat **11 patroness** [Q4] patrioness **midwife** my wife **27 s.d.** *She . . . infant* [not in Q1] vp comes *Lycorida* the Nurse . . . and into his armies deliuers his Sea-borne Babe [PA] **s.d.** PERICLES . . . *weeps* [not in Q1] *Pericles* looking mournfully vpon it, shooke his head, and wept [PA] **34 Poor inch of nature** [PA; not in Q1] **36 partage** portage **37 s.d.** *the* MASTER *and a* SAILOR *two* Saylers **38, 43, 47, 51 s.p.** MASTER 1. *Sayl.* **40 its worst** the worst **43–53** [verse in Q1] **43 Slack** Slacke [Qb] Slake [Qa] **bow-lines** bolins **45 s.p.** SAILOR 2.

Sayl. **an** and **50 but** [not in Q1] **52 custom** easterne **52–54 yield 'er . . . queen!** yeeld'er, / *Per.* As you thinke meet; for she must ouer board straight: / Most wretched Queene. **59 ooze** oare **61 And** The **aye-remaining** ayre remayning **64 paper** [Q2] Taper **66 coffer** coffin **69 s.p.** SAILOR 2. **72, 74 s.p.** MASTER 2. **73 from** for **74 Make** O make

Scene 12 [not in Q1] **s.d.** *poor man and a* some that came to him both for helpe for themselues, and reliefe for others [PA] **2 those** these **4 seen** been in **5 ne'er** neare **7 in** to **8 to th'** to the **19–20 lordship should, / Having . . . you, at** Lordship, / Hauing . . . you, should at **20 this hour** these early howers **22 to** should **23 held** hold **26 dispend** [PA] expend **34 so** [not in Q1] **36 and cause** in course **39 glad** please **42 alone** [not in Q1] **46 48, 53 s.p.** PHILEMON *Seru⟨ant⟩* [variously abbreviated] **49 The sea tossed up** did the sea tosse vp **52–53 Did . . . sir** [Question and answer occur after "bitumed" at line 58 in Q1.] **54 Or a more eager** as tost it vpon shore **s.p.** CERIMON [not in Q1; see last note to line 58] **56 by** [not in Q1] **queasy** [not in Q1] **58 bitumed** bottomed **soft** *Cer.* Wrench it open soft. **62 and crowned** [not in Q1] crowned [PA] **65 i'th'** in the **75 even** [Q4] euer **77 rash** rough **82 have heard** heard **83 nine hours dead** that had 9. howers lien dead **84 appliances** applyaunce **84 s.d.** PHILEMON *one* **86 still** rough **87 vial** Violl **90–91 warmth / Breathes** warmth breath **94 set** sets **104 gentle** my gentle

Scene 13 [not in Q1] **5 strokes** shakes **6 hurt** hant **7 woundingly** wondringly **8 you'd** you had **9 T'have** to haue **10 Should** Could **14 and leave** leauing **25 th'** the **29 Unscissored** vncisserd [PA] vnsisterd **29 hair** heyre **32 s.p.** DIONYZA I [Q1] *Cler.* I [Q1 catchword] **35 s.p.** CLEON *Cler.* **36 th' masted** the mask'd

Scene 14 [not in Q1] **s.d.** THAISA *Tharsa* **2 are all** are **5 eaning** learning **6 th'** the **11 s.p.** CERIMON *Cler.* **13 till your date expire you may abide** you may abide till your date expire **16 s.p.** THAISA [Q4] *Thin.*

Scene 15 [not in Q1] **8 music** Musicks **10 her** hie **the heart** the art **14 Seeks** Seeke **15 has** hath **16 lass** wench **17 ripe** [Q2] right **rite** sight **26 bird** bed **32 With dove of Paphos might the** The Doue of *Paphos* might with the **38 murder** murderer **42 s.d.** *A tomb is revealed* a monument in remembrance [PA] **47 carry** carried **55 i'th'** in the **57–58 or fanning love thy bosom / Unflame in** flaming, thy loue bosome, enflame **63 weeping** weeping for **nurse's** Mistresse **66 grave** greene **68 tomb** graue

71 but [not in Q1] **ceaseless** lasting **76–77 favour / Is changed** fauours / Changd **78 Give me your flowers. Come** Come giue me your flowers **o'er** ere **margin** marre it **79 is piercing** is quicke **80 And quick; it sharps** And it perces and sharpens **81 th'** the **81–151 No . . . slain** [prose in Q1; many of the following emendations help create metrical verse lines] **90 resume** reserue **94 truly yet 95 Nay** Come, come **99 Pray you** pray **104 mariners** Saylers **105 with** [not in Q1] **111 Once** and **114 stem** stern **120 The** for the **121 would** will **128 once on a worm** vpon a worme **129 for it** [Q4] fort **131 danger** any danger **139 s.d. drawing out his sword** [PA] **140 s.d. running** [PA] **144 s.d. PIRATES carrying MARINA** the pyrates who had thus rescued *Marina*, carried her to their shippes [PA] **LEONINE steals back** Enter Leonine; he secretly stole back [PA] **146 An** and **147 she'll** shee will

Scene 16 [not in Q1] **4 lose** lost **too much** [Q2] too much much **4 wenchless** too wenchlesse **17 They're too** there's two **33 mystery** trade **37 s.p. A PIRATE** Sayler. **45 hundred sesterces** [PA] thousand peeces **58 had but** had not **59 To** for to **66 like** [Q4; not in Q1] **80 must stir** [Q4] stir **88 watered as** watred, and **92 Veroles** Verollus **98 of** in **100 all** [not in Q1] **103 to despise** despise **111 s.p. BAWD** Mari⟨na⟩ **123–24 reapest the harvest out of thine own setting forth** hast the haruest out of thine owne report **133 with me** with vs

Scene 17 [not in Q1] **s.d. in mourning garments** mourning garments [PA] **1 are** ere **5–47 Were . . . done** [prose in Q1] **6 A lady** O Ladie **12 fact** face **13 demands** shall demaund **15 is not** it, not **17 pious** [PA] impious **25 cowed** coward **27 prime** prince **28 sources** courses **31 distain** disdaine **33 Marina's** [Q2] *Marianas* **34 malkin** Mawkin **48 angel** Angells **49 in thine eagle talons** with thine Eagles talents

Scene 18 [not in Q1] **1 make we** make **3 take** take our **7 scene** sceanes **8 i'th'** with **10 the** [Q2] thy **14 govern, if** gouerne it, **16 Tyre** time **18 his** this **19 go on** grone **24 true-owed** true olde **29 puts** put **34 sweetest, best** sweetest, and best **36–37 In . . . good** [PA; not in Q1. For the eight lines from Q1 omitted here, see Additional Passage.] **42 scene** Steare

Scene 19 [not in Q1] **2 s.p. SECOND GENTLEMAN** [Qa, Qb, Qb catchword] Gower. [Qa catchword] **13 the whole of** a whole **24 loon** Lowne **25 custom** customers **27 to-bless** to blesse **34 deed** deedes **41 dignifies** dignities **42 noble** number **52 honourably know** worthilie note **63 hers** her **64–139**

Fair . . . Away [prose in Q1; many of the following emendations help create metrical verse lines] **64 Fair** Now prittie **66 I Why I name it but** name but **71 or** or at **73 Proclaimeth you** proclaimes you to be **74 And** [not in Q1] **75 into it** intoo't **76 blood** parts **77 whole province** place **78 What** Why **informed** made knowne vnto **80 seeds of shame, roots of** seeds and rootes of shame and **s.d. MARINA weeps** [not in Q1] teares [PA] **81 you've** you haue **82 off aloof for a** aloft for **84–89 can . . . ling'ring** shall not see thee, or else looke friendly vpon thee; vrging her, that he was the Gouernour, whose authoritie coulde wincke at those blemishes, her selfe, and that sinnefull house could cast vppon her, or his displeasure punish at his owne pleasure, which displeasure of mine, thy beauty shall not priuiledge thee from, nor my affection, which hath drawen me vnto this place abate, if thou with further lingering withstand me [PA] **85 or can on faults look friendly** or else looke friendly vpon thee [not in PA] **91–93 Let . . . yourself** [not in Q1] If as you say (my Lorde) you are the Gouernour, let not your authoritie, which should teach you to rule others, be the meanes to make you misgouerne your selfe [PA] **96–106 What . . . impoverish me** [not in Q1] What reason is there in your Justice, who hath power ouer all, to vndoe any? If you take from mee mine honour, you are like him, that makes a gappe into forbidden ground, after whome too many enter, and you are guiltie of all their euilles: my life is yet vnspotted, my chastitie vnstained in thought. Then if your violence deface this building, the workemanship of heauen, made vp for good, and not to be the exercise of sinnes intemperaunce, you do kill your owne honour, abuse your owne iustice, and impouerish me. . . . Is there a necessitie (my yet good Lord) if there be fire before me, that I must strait then thither flie and burne my selfe? Or if suppose this house, (which too too many feele such houses are) should be the Doctors patrimony, and Surgeons feeding; folowes it therefore, that I must needs infect my self to giue them maintenaunce? [PA] **114 s.d. kneeling** [not in Q1] which wordes (being spoken vpon her knees) [PA] **115 franked** plac't **119 s.d. moved** [PA; not in Q1] **120 s.d. He . . . hands** [not in Q1] hee lift her vp with his hands [PA] **121 Though** Had **122 hath** had **s.d. He . . . eyes** [not in Q1] in steede of willing her to drie her eyes, he wiped the wet himselfe off [PA] **and my foul thoughts** [not in Q1] I hither came with thoughte intemperate, foule and deformed [PA] **123 Thy . . . white** [not in Q1] the which your paines so well hath laued, that they are now white [*PA*] **124–26 I . . . honesty** holde, heeres golde for thee [Q1] and for my parte, who hither came but to haue payd the price, a peece of golde for your virginitie, now giue you twenty to releeue your honesty [*PA*] **127 Persever still** perseuer **128 The** For me be you thoughten, that I came with no ill intent, for to me the **131 The . . . made** [*PA*; not in Q1] **132 not** not but **noble** noble, hold, heeres more golde for thee **134 honour. Hold, here's more gold. / If** goodnes, if [A shorter version of the words omitted at line 132 is reintroduced here.] **135 s.d. *Enter . . . out*** [not in Q1] the bawde standing ready at the doore, as hee should go out, making his obeysaunce vnto him as hee should returne [*PA*] **146 executioner shall do** hăg-man shal execute **We'll come your way,** weele **152 She** He **158 s.p. PANDER** *Bawd.* **159 ice** glass **167 s.d. *catching . . . hand*** [*PA*; not in Q1] **176–84 Neither . . . lungs** [prose in Q1; many of the following emendations help create metrical verse lines] **176 can be** are **178 place** place for which **179 change with thee** change **180 Thou** Thou art the **182 To th'** To the **ev'ry** euery **190 sew'rs** shores **190 public** common **191 these** these wayes **193 dear** deere, that the gods wold safely deliuer me from this place **Here's** here, heers **194 make gain** gaine **197 I will** will **206 women** [Q4] woman

Scene 20 [not in Q1] **8 twin** Twine **13 We** Where wee **Waves there him tossed** wee there him left **14 Whence** Where **tofore** before **20 fervour** [Qb] former [Qa] **22 the** his

Scene 21 [not in Q1] **1 s.p. SAILOR OF TYRE** 1 *Say.* **1–53 Where . . . prevented** [prose in Q1] **1 Lord Helicanus can resolve you, sir** Where is Lord *Helicanus?* hee can resolue you, O here he is Sir **3 In it** and in it is **6 s.p. SAILOR OF TYRE** 2 *Say.* **6 Ho** Ho Gentlemen **What is your lordship's pleasure** Doeth your Lordship call **7 some** there is some **8 you** [not in Q1] **9 s.p. SAILOR OF MYTILENE** *Hell.* [Qa] 1 *Say* [Qb] **This Sir, this aught** ought you would **11 sir** [not in Q1] **12–16 You wish me well. / I . . . Mytilene; / Being . . . are** *Li⟨simachus⟩* You wish mee well, beeing . . . are. *Hell⟨icanus⟩* First what is your place? *Ly⟨simachus⟩* I . . . this place you lie before [Helicanus's question in Q1 is omitted, and an emended version of Lysimachus's reply ("I . . . before") is moved to an earlier position, after "You wish me well."] **17 Our** Syr our **our king** the King **21 grew is** **22 tell it ouer** repeat **23 precious** [not in Q1] **25 See him, sir, you may** You may **26 sight. He** [Qb] sight see [Qa] **27 any. LYSIMACHUS Let me yet** any, yet let me [speech

continued by Helicanus in Q1, with different word order] **28 s.p. HELICANUS** [Q4] *Lys⟨imachus⟩* **s.d. *lying . . . sack-cloth*** [not in Q1] so attired from the ordinary habite of other men, as with a long ouer-growne beard, diffused hayre, vndecent nayles on his fingers, and himselfe lying vppon his cowch groueling on his face [*PA*; when Pericles first learns of Marina's death, *PA* reports that "hee apparrelles himselfe in sacke-cloth."] **28–29 person, / Till** [Q4] person. / *Hell⟨icanus⟩* Till [In this edition, Helicanus is already speaking.] **29 of** that **night** wight **30 all hail** all haile, the Gods preserue you **s.d. PERICLES . . . *pillow*** hee shruncke himselfe downe vppon his pillow [*PA*] **35 choice** chosen **alarum** allure **36 deafened ports** defend parts **37 in all** is all **38 among** and **39 Dwells now i'th'** now vpon the **40 Go fetch her hither** [not in Q1] **47 gods** God **51 it** it to you **54 presence** present **57 of** of a **or** and **I'd** [Q4] I do **58 to** and **wed** [Q4] to wed **59 one** on **bounty** beautie **60 feat** fate **64–140 Sir . . . end here** [prose in Q1; many of the following emendations help to create metrical verse lines] **65 recure** recouerie **67 Let** Come, let **68 prosper her** make her prosperous **Marked** [Q4] Marke **69 s.p. MAID** *Mar⟨ina⟩* **84 Stay** go not **88 My lord** [after "said," line 87, in Q1] **90–91 what . . . shores?** what Countrey women heare of these shewes? **93 seem** appeare **95 such** sucha one **99 cased** caste **109 palace** *Pallas* **111 make my senses** [Q4] makes senses **112 Thou show'st** for thou lookest **114 say** stay **121 circumstance** thoughts **123 thousandth** thousand **128 lost thou them?** Thy name lost thou thy name **130 sir,** [not in Q1] **142 Motion as well?** Motion well **146 when** the minute **147 recounted** deliuered **153 You will scarce believe me** You scorne, beleeue me **159 wooed** hauing wood **160 the deed** it **162 To Mytilene they brought me** Brought me to *Metaline* **163 What will you of me** whither wil you haue me? **164 impostor** imposture **167 s.p. PERICLES** *Hell⟨icanus⟩* **174 would never** neuer would **192 rest** rest you sayd **193 So prove but true in that, thou art my daughter** [not in Q1] **194 life** like **196 name?** name was *Thaisa* **199 Thou art** [Q4] th'art **s.d. *He kisses her*** he falls on hir necke, and kisses her [*PA*] **201 Not** shee is not **207 sir** [not in Q1] **211 doubt** doat **217–18 LYSIMACHUS Music, my lord? / PERICLES I hear most** *Lys.* Musicke my Lord? I heare. / *Per.* Most **219 raps** nips **220 eyelids** eyes **s.d. *He sleeps*** he fell into a slumber [*PA*] **221 A . . . head. Companion** A Pillow for his head, so leaue him all. / Well my companion **223 So leave** him all [after "head" (line 222) in Q1] 227–28 At large . . . voice [not in Q1] 231 life like 232 Perform or performe 233 rest [not in Q1] 238 Th' The

Scene 22 [not in Q1] 9 well [not in Q1] 23 espouse [PA] wed 24 The fair Thaisa . . . at Pentapolis at Pentapolis, the faire Thaisa s.d. THAISA starts At the naming of whome, she her selfe being by, could not choose but starte [PA] 26 who whom 28 whom who 30 Bore brought 31 our barque vs 35 nun mum 39 same verie 42 one in 48 upon him [not in Q1] 70 s.d. embracing MARINA [not in Q1] giuing his daughter to her armes to embrace her as a child [PA] 72 s.p. PERI-CLES [Q4] Hell⟨icanus⟩ 82 is the [not in Q1] 90 And told how in this temple she came placed How shee came plac'ste heere in the Temple [Q1] for in this Temple was she placed [PA] 91 Diana Dian 92 I [not in Q1] 93 Nightly Night Beloved [not in Q1] 95 At Pentapolis shall marry her shall marrie her at Pentapolis 101 from Pentapolis [not in Q1] 102 Heav'n Heauens [Q1] Heauen [Q1 catchword] 112 preserved preferd 113 Led [Q2] Led 119 their [Q4] his deed to th' deede, the 123 that [not in Q1]

THE TRAGEDY OF CORIOLANUS

CONTROL TEXT: F

F: The Folio of 1623

s.p. NICANOR Roman.
s.p. ADRIAN Vol⟨scian⟩.

1.1.23–24 s.p. THIRD CITIZEN Against . . . first. / s.p. fourth citizen He's . . . com-monalty. All. Against . . . comonality. 29 s.p. FIFTH CITIZEN All. 49 s.p. FIRST CITI-ZEN 2 Cit⟨izen⟩; likewise for the remainder of 1.1. 82 stale't scale't 99 tauntingly taint-ingly 161 geese. You are no Geese you are: No 190 all most almost 205 Junius Annius 207 unroofed vnroo'st 230 Lartius Lucius 232, 236 s.p. LARTIUS Tit⟨us⟩.
1.3.33 that's that 40 Grecian sword, con-temning. Tell Grecian sword. Contenning, tell 77 s.p. VIRGILIA Vlug. 79 Ithaca Athica
1.5.13 trenches. Follow Trenches followes 18 s.p. THIRD SOLDIER All. 19 s.p. LARTIUS Tit⟨us⟩. s.p. FOURTH SOLDIER All. 25 art lost, art left, 28 Cato's Calues
1.6.4 honours hours
1.7.53 Antiates Antients 70 Lesser Lessen 76 O' Oh 84 I foure
1.10.40 upheld beheld 67, 78, 81 s.p. CORI-OLANUS Martius. 82 And at At 89 s.p. CORIOLANUS Martius.

1.11.17 valour, poisoned valors poison'd
2.1.16 with all withall 22 how are ho ware 51 cannot can 95 s.p. VIRGILIA and VALE-RIA 2. Ladies. 151 Coriolanus Martius Caius Coriolanus 166 s.p. CORIOLANUS Com⟨inius⟩. 171 begnaw at begin at 172 You Yon 203 guarded gawded 241 touch teach
2.2.63, 119, 127 s.p. FIRST SENATOR Senat⟨or⟩.
2.3.47 tongue tougne 62 but not but 80, 83 s.p. FOURTH CITIZEN 1. 95 s.p. FIFTH CITI-ZEN 2. 97 s.p. FOURTH CITIZEN 1. 104 hire higher 105 womanish toge Wooluish tongue 108 do't doo't? 122 s.p. SIXTH CIT-IZEN 1. Cit⟨izen⟩. 232 And . . . surnamed [not in F] 243 s.p. A CITIZEN We . . . s.p. ANOTHER CITIZEN Almost All. We . . . almost
3.1.33 s.p. FIRST SENATOR Senat. 50 s.p. CORIOLANUS Com⟨inius⟩. 61 abused, set on. abus': set on, 94 good God! 101 impo-tence Ignorance 146 Where one Whereon 180 s.p. ALL THE PATRICIANS All. 185 s.p. ALL THE CITIZENS All. 186 s.p. CITIZENS AND PATRICIANS [not in F] 193, 199 s.p. ALL THE CITIZENS All. 198 s.p. FIRST SENA-TOR Sena⟨tor⟩. 203 s.p. CORIOLANUS Com⟨inius⟩. 220 poisons poysonous 228 s.p. ALL THE CITIZENS All. 229 your our 231 s.p. CORIOLANUS Com⟨inius⟩. 236 s.p. COMINIUS Corio⟨lanus⟩. 237 s.p. CORI-OLANUS Mene⟨nius⟩. 239 s.p. MENENIUS Be Be 272, 282 s.p. ALL THE CITIZENS All. 289 our one 307 s.p. SICINIUS Menen⟨ius⟩. 326 bring him bring him in peace
3.2.20 taxings things 25 s.p. FIRST SENATOR Sen. 31 herd heart 78 With Which 101 bear? Well beare well? 102 plot to lose, Plot, to loose
3.3.33 for th' fourth 37 Throng Through 56 accents Actions 99 Inveighed Enui'd 114 for from 143 despite. despight
4.1.38 s.p. VIRGILIA Corio⟨lanus⟩.
4.3.9 approved appear'd
4.4.13 seem seems 23 hate haue
4.5.130 o'erbear't o're-beate 161 is yet is: but 188 broiled boyld 206, 207 dejecti-tude Directitude 220 sleepy sleepe 221 war's Warres
4.6.36 lamentation Lamention 60 come comming 145 one oue
4.7.37 'twas 'was 39 defect detect 49 virtues Vertue, 55 falter fouler
5.1.16 fair for 69 hold to his yeeld to his
5.2.62 but by but 71 our your
5.3.48 prate pray 63 holp hope 66 candied curdied 81 things thing 116 thorough through 150 fine fiue 153 charge change 170 him with him with him with 180 this his
5.6.116 Fluttered Flatter'd

THE WINTER'S TALE

CONTROL TEXT: F

F: THE FOLIO OF 1623

s.p. OLD SHEPHERD [F's use of "Shep⟨heard⟩." has been changed throughout.]

s.p. FIRST LADY [F's use of "Lady" has been changed at 2.1.2, 5, 14, 16.]

s.p. A LORD [F's use of "Lord" has been changed throughout 2.1; at 2.3.26, 147, and 197; and at 3.2.114, 172, 200, and 214.]

1.2.106 And A 160 ornament Ornaments 209 they [not in F] 278 hobby-horse Holy-Horse
2.2.56 let't le't 69 twixt betwixt
2.3.39 What Who
3.2.10 Silence. [italicized and set as stage direction in F] 31 Who Whom 166 certain [not in F]
3.3.67 bairn Barne 73 hallooed hallow'd 110 made mad
4.2.3 sixteen fifteene
4.3.10 With heigh, with heigh, With heigh,
4.4.12 it [not in F] 13 swoon sworne 98 your you 148 so [not in F] 160 out on't 237 kiln-hole kill-hole 239 Clammer clamor 298 gentlemen Gent. 347 who whom 407 acknowledged acknowledge 411 who whom 416 see neuer see 427 hoop hope 455 your my 577 so [not in F] 597 could would 685 know not know 713 to at
5.1.21 spoke spoken 58–59 stage, / Where . . . mourn, appear Stage / (Where . . . now appeare) 61 just iust such 78 your you a
5.3.5 young contracted your contracted 18 Lonely Louely 67 fixture fixure 96 Or those On: those 150 This' This

CYMBELINE, KING OF BRITAIN

CONTROL TEXT: F

F: The Folio of 1623
Fa, Fb: Successive states of F incorporating various print-shop corrections and changes

Title: Cymbeline King of Britaine [F table of contents] The Tragedie of Cymbeline [F head title]

s.p. INNOGEN [F's use of Imogen is changed throughout.]
s.p. GIACOMO [F's use of Iachimo is modernized throughout.]
s.p. HELEN [In 2.2, F's use of La. is changed throughout.]

s.p. FILARIO [F's use of Philario is modernized throughout.]
s.p. A ROMAN CAPTAIN [F's Captain is changed at 4.2.335, 339, 344, and 361.]
s.p. A LORD [F's use of Lord is changed at 4.3.16, 23, 28.]
s.p. FIRST JAILER [F's use of Gao is changed at 5.5.95.]

1.1.3 King Kings 15 of at 30 Cassibelan Cassibulan 98 Filario's Filorio's
1.2.9 steel if he Steele if it
1.3.9 this his
1.4.40 not to to 62 Britain Britanie 63 not but not 72 purchase purchases 90 five [Fb] fine [Fa] 111 thousand thousands
1.5.28 factor for for 85 words, Pisanio words
1.6.7 desire desires 25 truest trust. 29 takes take 37 th'unnumbered the number'd 81 count account 126 lend to lend 163 me [Fb] ma [Fa] 169 men's men 170 descended defended 187 Best The best
2.1.21 an and 24 your you 31 tonight night 58 husband, than husband then.
2.2.2 hour houre [Fb] houe [Fa] 43 riveted riueted [Fb] riuete [Fa] 49 bare beare
2.3.6 s.p. CLOTEN [not in text] 17 s.p. MUSICIAN [not in F] heaven Heauens 24 s.p. CLOTEN [not in F] 25 vice voyce 27 amend amed 39 out on't 43 solicits solicity 96 cure are 116 foil foyle 132 garment Garments 149 you your
2.4.6 seared hopes fear'd hope 14 Ere Or 18 legions Legion 24 courage courages 34 through thorough 37 s.p. FILARIO Post. 41 had haue 47 not note 57 you yon 60 leaves leaue 76 Such since 116 her woman her women 135 the her 151 follow follow him
2.5.2 bastards all all Bastards 16 German one Iarmen on 27 man can name name
3.1.5 Cassibelan Cassibulan 11 There will There 20 banks Oakes 30, 39–40 Cassibelan Cassibulan
3.2.2 accuser accuse 10 to hers to her 14 to do good [Fb] to go do od [Fa] 22 here [Fb] her [Fa] 64 Till And 67 score store ride rid 78 Nor here, nor nor heere, not
3.3.2 Stoop Sleepe 15–16 war; / That Warre. / This 23 bauble Babe 25 'em him 28 know knowes 33 travelling abed trauailing a bed 34 prison for Prison, or 83 wherein they bow whereon the Bowe 86 Polydore Poladour 106 Morgan Mergan
3.4.78 afore't a-foot 88 make makes 100 out [not in F] 132 churlish, noble noble
3.5.32 looks looke 40 strokes, stroke; 44 loud'st lowd of 86 tongue heart

3.6.68 Ay I **I'd** I do **74 price** prize
3.7.9 commends commands
4.2.2 from after **47 hath** he hath **51 s.p. BELARIUS** *Arui⟨ragus⟩*. **59 him** them **60 patience** patient **123 thanks,** ye thanks the **133 humour** Honor **171 how** thou **187 ingenious** ingenuous **203 not** not the **206 crare** care **207 Might** Might'st **225 ruddock** Raddocke **230 winter-gown** winterground **238 once** once to **258 begin.** begin. / SONG. **286 th'earth's** face their Faces **288 strow** strew **292 is** are **325 thy** this **338 are** hence are heere **392 wildwood** leaves wild wood-leaues **401 he is** hee's
4.3.40 betid betide
4.4.2 find we we finde **17 the** their **18 files** Fires **27 hard** heard
5.1.1 once wished am wisht **15 dread** ill dread it **16 blest** best **20 mistress-piece** Mistris: Peace
5.5.2 Ay I did **24 harts** hearts **her** our **42 stooped** stopt **43 they** the **53 Yet you** you **64 This** This is **121 make** take **161 geck** geeke **163 come** came **175 look** looke / looke **212 Preens** Prunes **claws** cloyes **252 are** as are **257 Of** Oh, of **260 sir** Sis **270 or take** or to take **273 on** one
5.6.54 and in fine and in time **55 fit** fitted **62 s.p. LADIES** *La.* **64 heard** heare **134 On** One **142 Torments** Which torments **205 got it** got **225 villain** villany **261 from** fro **262 lock** Rocke **303 boy** man **335 mere** neere **352 like** liks **379 you** we **387 brothers** Brother **393 inter'gatories** Interrogatories **406 so** no **469 this yet** yet this

THE TEMPEST

CONTROL TEXT: F

F: The Folio of 1623
Fa, Fb: Successive states of F incorporating various print-shop corrections and changes

1.1.18–19 councillor Councellor **19–20 work peace** worke the peace **31 wi'th'** with **54 s.p. MARINERS** [not in F] **57 wi'th'** with' **59 broom** Browne **furze** firrs
1.2.100 oft of it. **112 wi'th'** with **153 wast** was't **174 princes** Princesse **201 bowsprit** Bore-spritt **230 Bermudas** *Bermoothes* **262 Algiers** *Argier* **284 she** he **304 to** [not in F] **330 forth at** for that **349 human** humane **383 sprites** *Sprights* **385–88 s.p. SPIRITS . . . ARIEL . . . SPIRITS** [Only the last refrain, "Hark, hark, I hear," is assigned to *Ar⟨iel⟩.* in F.] **390 cock-a-diddle-dow** *cockadiddle-dowe* **407 s.p. SPIRITS . . .** *dong* Burthen ding dong **408 s.p. SPIRITS** [*within*] [not in F] **470 power** pow'r

2.1.37 s.p. ANTONIO. . . Sebastian *Seb⟨astian⟩. . . . Ant⟨onío⟩.* **133 More** Mo **140 chirurgeonly** Chirurgeonly **253 every** eu'ry
2.2.52 Then to sea [*etc.*] [not in F] **108 spirits** sprights **120 Swum** Swom **164 seamews** Scamels
3.1.2 sets set **15 busil'est** busie **lest 47 peerless** peetlesse
3.2.24 debauched debosh'd **30 s.p. TRINCULO** [F (text)] *Cal⟨iban⟩.* [F (catchword)]
3.3.2 ache akes **15 travel** trauaile **29 islanders** Islands **33 human** humaine **65 plume** plumbe **99 bass** base
4.1.9 of her her of **13 gift** guest **17 rite** right **52 rein** raigne **53 abstemious** abstenious **61 vetches** Fetches **peas** Pease **64 peonied** pioned **74 Her** here **81 bosky** boskie **83 short-grassed** short gras'd **110 s.p. CERES** [not in F] **and** [not in F] **123 wise** wife **136 holiday** holly day **180 gorse** gosse **193 them on** on them **lime** line **229 Let't alone** let's alone
5.1.10 lime-grove *Line-groue* **16 run** runs **60 boiled** boile **72 Didst** [F (catchword)] Did [F (text)] **75 entertained** entertaine **81 shores** shore **93–96 Merrily . . . bough** [In F, these lines are not repeated.] **113 Whe'er** Where **126 not** nor **158 these** Their **178 An** And **202 remembrance** remembrances **230 events** [Fb] euens [Fa] **237 more** mo **239 her** our **288 Why** [Fb] Who [Fa]

ALL IS TRUE (HENRY VIII)

CONTROL TEXT: F

F: The Folio of 1623

Title: The Famous History of the Life of King **HENRY** the Eight [main Title] *The Life of King Henry the Eight* [running title; see the Introduction]

s.p. PROLOGUE, EPILOGUE [Though treated in this edition as characters, F's THE PROLOGVE and THE EPILOGVE could be either speech prefixes or section headings.]
s.p. KING HENRY [F's *King* has been expanded throughout.]
s.p. LORD CHAMBERLAIN [F uses *Chamberlain* and *Lord Chamberlain*; standardized throughout.]
s.p. LORD CHANCELLOR [F's *Chancellor* has been expanded throughout.]
s.p. SANDS [F uses *Sands* and *Lord Sands*; standardized throughout. See note to 2.1.54 stage direction.]
s.p. GUILDFORD [F's *Sir Henry Guilford* has been shortened throughout.]

s.p.CARDINAL WOLSEY [F uses *Cardinal* and *Wolsey*. The latter occurs primarily when Cardinal Campeius is also onstage, although even then Cardinal Wolsey is usually referred to in the dialogue as "Cardinal"; standardized throughout.]

s.p.BUCKINGHAM'S SURVEYOR [F's *Surveyor* has been expanded throughout.]

s.p.CARDINAL CAMPEIUS [F uses *Campeius*, presumably in part to distinguish him from Cardinal Wolsey; expanded throughout.]

s.p.PAGE [F's *Boy* has been changed throughout.]

Epilogue

s.p.QUEEN KATHERINE, KATHERINE [F uses *Queen* until she becomes the princess dowager (4.2), at which point it switches to *Katherine*. Similarly, this edition switches from "Queen Katherine" to "Katherine" at 4.2.]

s.p.GRIFFITH [F's *Gentleman Usher* (2.4), *Gentleman* (3.1), and *Griffith* have been standardized throughout. See notes below for more information.]

s.p.ANNE Boleyn [F uses *Anne* and *Anne Bullen*; standardized throughout.]

s.p.OLD LADY [F uses *Old Lady* more frequently than *Lady*; standardized throughout.]

s.p.LINCOLN [F uses *Lincoln* and *Bishop of Lincoln*; standardized throughout.]

s.p.GENTLEMEN [F's "1," "2," and "3" have been expanded to "First Gentleman," etc.]

Prologue s.d. / s.p. *Enter* PROLOGUE / PROLOGUE *THE PROLOGVE.* **11 pass,** if *passe:* If

1.1.7 Ardres . . . Guisnes . . . Ardres Andren . . . Guynes . . . Arde **23** *mesdames* Madams **42–48** to. All . . . function. **s.p.** BUCKINGHAM Who . . . together, as you guess? **s.p.** NORFOLK too. / *Buc⟨kingham⟩.* All . . . Function: who . . . together? / *Nor⟨folk⟩.* As you guesse: [In F, Buckingham begins speaking at "All was Royal" (line 42) and continues through "together" (line 47). Norfolk then begins the following speech with the phrase "As you guesse" (line 47).] **63 web,** a Web. O **116, 117 s.p.** SECRETARY *Secr⟨etary⟩.* [We cannot be certain which secretary speaks which lines, since two enter with Wolsey and they are not distinguished by speech prefix.] **120 venom-mouthed** venom'd-mouth'd **154 July** *Inly* **167 rinsing** wrenching **183 Privily he** Priuily **200 Hereford** *Hertford* **211 Abergavenny** *Aburgany* **219 Perk,** his chancellor *Pecke,* his Councellour. [The emendation derives from Holinshed.] **221 Nicholas** *Michaell* [The emendation derives from Holinshed.] **227 lord** Lords

1.2.9 s.p. CRIER (*within*) Room . . . Norfolk. *A noyse within crying roome . . . Duke of Norfolke.* [In F, this entire sentence is a stage direction, and there is no speech prefix.] **68 business** basenesse **140 His** This **148, 149 Hopkins** *Henton.* [The emendation derives from Holinshed. At 1.1.221, the name is presented correctly.] **157 feared** feare **165 confession's** Commissions [The emendation derives from Holinshed.] **171 win** [not in F] **181 To** For this to **191 Bulmer** *Blumer* [The emendation derives from Holinshed.] **191 remember** remember of

1.3.13 Or A **21 'messieurs'** Monsieurs **34 'oui'** wee **59 he's** Ha's

1.4.6 feast first

2.1.21 Perk *Pecke.* **54 s.d. William** *Walter* [The emendation derives from Holinshed.] **79 i'** a **87 mark** make

2.2.1 s.p. LORD CHAMBERLAIN [*reads*] [not in F]

2.3.59 note's notes **61 of you** of you, to you **87 fie, fie** fye, fye, fye

2.4.7, 10 come into the court &c. **11 s.p.** QUEEN KATHERINE [not in F] **124 s.p.** GRIFFITH *Gent⟨leman⟩ Vsh⟨er⟩.* [It seems reasonable to suppose that this gentleman is the same as the *Gentleman* who attends the queen at 3.1.14. s.d. and is referred to as *Gent⟨leman⟩* at 3.1.16, 18 s.p., later identified as *Griffith, her Gentleman Vsher* at 4.2.0 s.d. **171 A** And **188 does yield to th'** does to th' **196 throe** throw

3.1.3 s.p. GENTLEWOMAN [*sings*] SONG. [In F, no speech prefix precedes the song.] **16, 18 s.p.** GRIFFITH *Gent⟨leman⟩.* **60 your** our **118 he's** ha's **123 accursed** a Curse

3.2.58 Has Ha's **143 glad** gald **172 filed** fill'd **340 legantine** Legatiue **344 Chattels** Castles

4.1.20 s.p. SECOND GENTLEMAN I **56 s.p.** FIRST GENTLEMAN [not in F, which gives all of lines 55–56 to "2." Here, FIRST GENTLEMAN speaks the beginning of line 56.] **103 Stokesley** *Stokeley* [The emendation derives from Holinshed.] **119 s.p.** FIRST *and* SECOND GENTLEMEN *Both.*

4.2.5 led'st lead'st **7 think** thanke **99 colour** cold **109 s.d.** CAPUTIUS *Capuchius*

5.1.37 time Lime **140 precipice** Precepit **158 s.p.** LOVELL (*within*) *Gent⟨leman⟩ within.*

5.2.7 piece Peere **119, 121 s.p.** LORD CHANCELLOR ⟨*Lord*⟩ *Cham⟨berlain⟩.* **126 s.p.** ALL THE COUNCIL *All.* **167 this** his **207 heart** hearts

5.3.2 Paris Parish **4, 27 s.p.** ONE (*within*) *Within.* **78** *a way* away

5.4.37 ways way **70 your** you **75 He's** 'Has

Epilogue s.d. / s.p. *Enter* EPILOGUE / EPILOGUE *The Epilogve.*

THE TWO NOBLE KINSMEN

Control text: Q

Q: The Quarto of 1634
Qa, Qb: The uncorrected (Qa) and corrected (Qb) states of Q

Title: *The Two Noble Kinsmen* [Q] a Tragi-Comedy called the two noble kinsmen [Stationers' Register]

s.p. PROLOGUE , EPILOGUE [Q simply titles each section "PROLOGVE" and "EPILOGVE," which could be interpreted either as speech prefixes or as section headings.]
s.p. JAILER [Q alternates between *Jailer* and *Keeper*. Standardized throughout.]
s.p. JAILER'S DAUGHTER [Q's consistent use of *Daughter* is expanded throughout.]
s.p. JAILER'S BROTHER [Q's consistent use of *Brother* is expanded throughout.]
s.p. COUNTRYMEN [Q uses only numbers to refer to the Countrymen, except in 3.5, when one of the Countrymen, who is dressed as a baboon, is referred to as *Baum* or *Bavian* ("babion," old form of "baboon") in Q and "babion" in this edition.]
Prologue s.d. *Enter* PROLOGUE / s.p. PRO-LOGUE PROLOGVE. 26 tack take

1.1. s.d. PIRITHOUS Theseus 1 s.p. BOY The Song. [In Q, the song is not assigned to a particular character. It is clear from the preceding stage direction, however, that it is the boy who sings.] 7 born borne 9 harebells *her bels* 13–14 children sweet, / Lie *children: sweete- / Ly* 20 chough hoar *Clough hee* 68 Nemean Nenuan 90 thy the 112 glassy glasse 132 longer long 138 move mooves 155 Rinsing Wrinching 158 Artesius *Artesuis* 166 s.p. ALL THREE QUEENS *All.* 171 war was 177 twinning twyning. ["Twined" remains a possible alternative modernization. Compare 2.2.64.] 211 Aulis Anly
1.2.55 canon Cannon 69 men's service men service 70 glory; one glory on
1.3.31 one ore 54 eleven a eleven 54 Flavina Flauia 73 happily happely 73 wear were 75 one on 79 seely innocence fury-innocent 82 dividual individuall 82 out ont
1.4.18 smeared [Qb] succard [Qa] 22 Wi'leave We leave 45 O'erwrestling Or wrastling 49 fore for
1.5. s.d. Song [not in Q] 9–10 woes, / We . . . woes. woes. *We convent, &c.*
2.2.21 wore were 22 Ravished Bravishd 64 twined twyn'd 118–19 s.p. EMILIA This . . . in't. / What This . . . in't. / *Emil.* What [In Q, Arcite continues speaking until the end of line 118.] 132 was I I was 150 close neere

182 love her love 189 your blood you blood 264 to too 272 you yon
2.3.6 sins [Qb] fins [Qa] 24 s.d. garland garlond [Qb] *Garlon* [Qa] 40 ye yet 53 said sees 64 Yet Yes
2.4.33 night; ere tomorrow night, or to-morrow
2.5 Scaena 4 28 For Fo
2.6.33 patch path
3.1.2 laund land 11–12 With . . . rumination [Q prints as one line with no lacuna marked.] 37 looked, the void'st lookd the voydes 43 Not Nor 96 s.d. within *of Cornets.* [In Q's *"Winde hornes of Cornets," "Cornets"* may be a playhouse addition; *"of"* could mean "off," or "offstage," here rendered as "within."] 98 muset Musicke 108 not nor 113 'Tis If 123 enjoy it enjoy't
3.2.1 mistook the brake mistooke; the Beake 7 reck wreake 19 fed feed 28 brine bine
3.3.12 sir &c. 23 them then 52 Sirrah— Sir ha:
3.4.9 Open Vpon 10 tack take 19 a foot *afoote*
3.5 Scaena 6 s.d. BABION Baum 8 jean jave 25 these their 33, 134 babion *Bavian* 67 I [not in Q] 68 There . . . owlet— *There . . . howlet* [Q's italics appear to derive from the compositor mistakenly interpreting this line as part of the song.] 69 he [not in Q] 100 s.p. THESEUS *Per.* [Pirithous] 120 'Moor' Morr 121 'Ice' Is 125 tenor tenner 133 beest-eating beast eating 138 s.p. SCHOOLMASTER [not in Q] 139–48 Ladies . . . rout [italics in Q. The compositor possibly misinterpreted this speech as a song.] 140 ye *thee* 143 thee *three* 152 you yon
3.6 Scaena 7 145 thine this 236 fail fall 272 must muff 273 the other th'other 279, 280 s.p. PALAMON *and* ARCITE *Both.*
4.1.11 oath o'th 20 he scaped he escapt 45 WOOER No, Sir, not well. SECOND FRIEND Not well? 2 *Fr.* Not well?—*Wooer,* No Sir not well. 63 sung song 84 wreath wreake 86 she appeared, methought, me thought she appeard 104 light . . .' *light, &c.* [Here and at 4.1.113 and 151 and 4.3.48, Q's "&c." suggests that more than the single line of the song printed in the text was sung.] 113 sweet . . .' *sweete, &c.* 119 Far For 133 s.p. JAILER'S BROTHER *Daugh.* [Jailer's Daughter] 140 s.p. SECOND FRIEND *I. Fr.* [First Friend] 144–45 Cheerly all. / Uff cheerely. / *All.* Owgh [In Q, the "All" pretend to join in.] 150 Tack Take 151 light . . .' *light, &c.*
4.2.16 Jove afire once Loue a fire with 54–55 both! / s.d. *Enter* [a] GENTLEMAN How both. / s.d. *Enter Emil⟨ia⟩ and Gent⟨leman⟩:* s.p. *Emil⟨ia⟩.* How [Q's superfluous refer-

ences to Emilia in the s.d. and s.p. are omitted.] **76 first** fitst **81 fire** faire **105 tods** tops **110 court** corect

4.3.20 spirits are spirits, as **27 i'th' other** i'th / Thother **41 engrafted** engraffed **45 th'other** another **46 behind** [Qb] behold [Qa] **48 fate . . .'** *fate, &c.* **75 carve** crave

5.1.37 father of farther off **44 me** [not in Q] **49–50 purple; / Whose havoc in vast field comets prewarn,** purple. / Comets prewarne, whose havocke in vaste Feild **53 armipotent** armenypotent

5.2, 5.3 [Q continues as part of 5.1]

5.4 Scaena 2 34 Yes, Yet **38 s.d.** *mad Maide* **39 humour** honour **53 tune** turne **103 lose the sight** loose the Fight

5.5 Scaena 3 78 the end th'end **111 Emilia** *Emily* **139 your** you

5.6 Scaena 4 1 s.p. PALAMON [not in Q] **39 s.p.** SECOND *and* THIRD KNIGHTS *1.2. K⟨nights⟩.* **47 rarely** early **79 victor's** [Qb] victoros [Qa] **107 Hath** Hast

Epilogue s.d. *Enter* EPILOGUE / **s.p.** EPILOGUE EPILOGVE.

General Bibliography*

There is a huge and ever-expanding scholarly literature about Shakespeare and his culture. This general list and the lists that accompany the individual plays and the poems in this volume are only a small sampling of the available resources. Journals devoted to Shakespeare studies include *Shakespeare Bulletin, Shakespeare Jahrbuch* (Germany), *Shakespeare Quarterly, Shakespeare Studies,* and *Shakespeare Survey* (England); other journals, such as *English Literary History, English Literary Renaissance, Renaissance Quarterly, Representations,* or *Studies in English Literature,* also frequently publish essays on Shakespeare's works. The categories below are only approximate; many of the texts could properly belong in more than one category.

Guides and Companions to Shakespeare Studies

Callaghan, Dympna, ed. *A Feminist Companion to Shakespeare.* Malden, Mass.: Blackwell, 2000.

De Grazia, Margreta, and Stanley Wells, eds. *The Cambridge Companion to Shakespeare.* Cambridge, Eng.: Cambridge University Press, 2001.

Drakakis, John, ed. *Alternative Shakespeares.* 2nd ed. London: Routledge, 1985.

Dutton, Richard, and Jean E. Howard, eds. *A Companion to Shakespeare's Works,* I: *The Tragedies.* Malden, Mass.: Blackwell, 2003.

———, eds. *A Companion to Shakespeare's Works,* II: *The Histories.* Malden, Mass.: Blackwell, 2003.

———, eds. *A Companion to Shakespeare's Works,* III: *The Comedies.* Malden, Mass.: Blackwell, 2003.

———, eds. *A Companion to Shakespeare's Works,* IV: *Poems, Problem Comedies, Late Plays.* Malden, Mass.: Blackwell, 2003.

Hattaway, Michael, ed. *The Cambridge Companion to Shakespeare's History Plays.* Cambridge, Eng.: Cambridge University Press, 2002.

Hawkes, Terence, ed. *Alternative Shakespeares, Volume* 2. London: Routledge, 1996.

Hodgdon, Barbara, and W. B. Worthen, eds. *A Companion to Shakespeare and Performance.* Malden, Mass.: Blackwell, 2005.

Jackson, Russell, ed. *The Cambridge Companion to Shakespeare on Film.* 2nd ed. Cambridge, Eng.: Cambridge University Press, 2007.

Kasten, David Scott, ed. *A Companion to Shakespeare.* Malden, Mass.: Blackwell, 1999.

Kinney, Arthur F. *Shakespeare by Stages: An Historical Introduction.* Malden, Mass.: Blackwell, 2003.

Leggatt, Alexander, ed. *The Cambridge Companion to Shakespearean Comedy.* Cambridge, Eng.: Cambridge University Press, 2002.

McDonald, Russ, ed. *The Bedford Companion to Shakespeare: An Introduction with Documents.* 2nd ed. Houndmills, Basingstoke: Palgrave Macmillan, 2001.

———, ed. *Shakespeare: An Anthology of Criticism and Theory, 1945–2000.* Malden, Mass.: Blackwell, 2004.

McEachern, Claire, ed. *The Cambridge Companion to Shakespearean Tragedy.* Cambridge, Eng.: Cambridge University Press, 2002.

*Edited by Holger Schott Syme, Department of English, University of Toronto.

Schoenfeldt, Michael. *A Companion to Shakespeare's Sonnets*. Malden, Mass.: Blackwell, 2006.

Smith, Emma, ed. *Shakespeare's Comedies: A Guide to Criticism*. Malden, Mass.: Blackwell, 2003.

———, ed. *Shakespeare's Histories: A Guide to Criticism*. Malden, Mass.: Blackwell, 2003.

———, ed. *Shakespeare's Tragedies: A Guide to Criticism*. Malden, Mass.: Blackwell, 2003.

Wells, Stanley, and Lena Cowen Orlin, eds. *Shakespeare: An Oxford Guide*. Oxford: Oxford University Press, 2003.

Wells, Stanley, and Sarah Stanton, eds. *The Cambridge Companion to Shakespeare on Stage*. New York: Cambridge University Press, 2002.

Shakespeare's World

Social, Political, and Economic History

Amussen, Susan Dwyer. *An Ordered Society: Gender and Class in Early Modern England*. New York: Columbia University Press, 1993.

Archer, Ian W. *The Pursuit of Stability: Social Relations in Elizabethan London*. New York: Cambridge University Press, 1991.

Ariès, Philippe, and Georges Duby, general eds. *A History of Private Life*, Volume III: *Passions of the Renaissance*. Ed. Roger Chartier. Trans. Arthur Goldhammer. Cambridge, Mass.: Belknap Press, 1989.

Armitage, David, and Michael J. Braddick, eds. *The British Atlantic World, 1500–1800*. New York: Palgrave Macmillan, 2002.

Barry, Jonathan, ed. *The Tudor and Stuart Town: A Reader in English Urban History, 1530–1688*. London: Longman, 1990.

Barry, Jonathan, and Christopher Brooks. *The Middling Sort of People: Culture, Society and Politics in England, 1550–1800*. Houndmills, Basingstoke: Palgrave Macmillan, 1994.

Barthelmey, Anthony Gerard. *Black Face, Maligned Race: The Representation of Blacks in English Drama from Shakespeare to Southerne*. Baton Rouge: Louisiana State University Press, 1987.

Beier, A. L. *Masterless Men: The Vagrancy Problem in England, 1560–1640*. New York: Methuen, 1985.

Beier, A. L., and Roger Finlay, eds. *London 1500–1700: The Making of the Metropolis*. New York: Longman, 1986.

Ben-Amos, Ilana Krausman. *Adolescence and Youth in Early Modern England*. New Haven: Yale University Press, 1994.

Bridenbaugh, Carl. *Vexed and Troubled Englishmen, 1590–1642*. New York: Oxford University Press, 1976.

Brigden, Susan. *New Worlds, Lost Worlds: The Rule of the Tudors, 1485–1603*. New York: Viking, 2001.

Burgess, Glenn. *The Politics of the Ancient Constitution: An Introduction to English Political Thought, 1603–1642*. University Park: Pennsylvania State University Press, 1993.

Capp, Bernard S. *When Gossips Meet: Women, Family, and Neighbourhood in Early Modern England*. Oxford: Oxford University Press, 2003.

Clark, Alice. *Working Life of Women in the Seventeenth Century*. Introduction by Amy Louise Erickson. 1968. New York: Routledge, 1992.

Clay, C. G. A. *Economic Expansion and Social Change: England 1500–1700*. 2 vols. New York: Cambridge University Press, 1984.

Cressy, David. *Birth, Marriage, and Death: Ritual, Religion, and the Life-Cycle in Tudor and Stuart England*. Oxford: Oxford University Press, 1997.

Cruickshank, Charles Greig. *Elizabeth's Army.* 2nd ed. Oxford: Clarendon, 1966.

Elliot, John Huxtable. *The Old World and the New, 1492–1650.* New York: Cambridge University Press, 1970.

Ellis, Steven G. *Tudor Ireland: Crown, Community, and the Conflict of Cultures, 1470–1603.* London: Longman, 1985.

Elton, G. R. *England Under the Tudors.* 3rd ed. New York: Routledge, 1991.

———. *The Tudor Revolution in Government: Administrative Changes in the Reign of Henry VIII.* Cambridge, Eng.: Cambridge University Press, 1959.

Emmison, F. G. *Elizabethan Life.* Chelmsford: Essex County Council, 1970.

Erickson, Amy Louise. *Women and Property in Early Modern England.* New York: Routledge, 1993.

Finlay, Roger. *Population and Metropolis: The Demography of London, 1580–1650.* Cambridge, Eng.: Cambridge University Press, 1981.

Fletcher, Anthony. *Gender, Sex, and Subordination in England, 1500–1800.* New Haven: Yale University Press, 1995.

Fletcher, Anthony, and John Stevenson, eds. *Order and Disorder in Early Modern England.* New York: Cambridge University Press, 1985.

Gaskill, Malcolm. *Crime and Mentalities in Early Modern England.* New York: Cambridge University Press, 2000.

Gittings, Clare. *Death, Burial and the Individual in Early Modern England.* London: Croom Helm, 1984.

Gowing, Laura. *Common Bodies: Women, Touch and Power in Seventeenth-Century England.* New Haven: Yale University Press, 2003.

Griffiths, Paul. *Youth and Authority: Formative Experiences in England, 1560–1640.* Oxford: Clarendon, 1996.

Griffiths, Paul, Adam Fox, and Steve Hindle, eds. *The Experience of Authority in Early Modern England.* New York: St. Martin's, 1996.

Guy, John A. *Queen of Scots: The True Life of Mary Stuart.* Boston: Houghton Mifflin, 2004.

———, ed. *The Reign of Elizabeth I: Court and Culture in the Last Decade.* Cambridge, Eng.: Cambridge University Press, 1995.

———. *Tudor England.* New York: Oxford University Press, 1988.

Heal, Felicity, and Clive Holmes. *The Gentry in England and Wales, 1500–1700.* Basingstoke: Macmillan, 1994.

Herrup, Cynthia B. *The Common Peace: Participation and the Criminal Law in Seventeenth-Century England.* New York: Cambridge University Press, 1987.

Hindle, Steve. *The State and Social Change in Early Modern England, c.1550–1640.* New York: St. Martin's, 2000.

Hirst, Derek. *Authority and Conflict: England, 1603–1658.* Cambridge, Mass.: Harvard University Press, 1986.

Ingram, Martin. *Church Courts, Sex, and Marriage in England, 1570–1640.* New York: Cambridge University Press, 1987.

James, Mervyn. *Society, Politics and Culture: Studies in Early Modern England.* New York: Cambridge University Press, 1986.

King, John N. *Tudor Royal Iconography: Literature and Art in an Age of Religious Crisis.* Princeton: Princeton University Press, 1989.

Kishlansky, Mark A. *A Monarchy Transformed: Britain 1603–1714.* New York: Penguin Books, 1996.

Klein, Joan Larsen. *Daughters, Wives, and Widows: Writings by Men about Women and Marriage in England, 1500–1640.* Urbana: University of Illinois Press, 1992.

Lake, Peter, with Michael Questier. *The Anti-Christ's Lewd Hat: Protestants, Papists and Players in Post-Reformation England.* New Haven: Yale University Press, 2002.

Laslett, Peter. *The World We Have Lost: Further Explored.* 3rd ed. New York: Scribner, 1984.

Levin, Carole. *The Heart and Stomach of a King: Elizabeth I and the Politics of Sex and Power.* Philadelphia: University of Pennsylvania Press, 1994.

Lockyer, Roger. *The Early Stuarts: A Political History of England, 1603–1642.* 2nd ed. London: Longman, 1999.

MacCaffrey, Wallace T. *Elizabeth I: War and Politics, 1588–1603.* Princeton: Princeton University Press, 1992.

Manning, Roger B. *Village Revolts: Social Protest and Popular Disturbances in England, 1509–1640.* Oxford: Clarendon, 1988.

Matar, Nabil I. *Islam in Britain, 1558–1685.* New York: Cambridge University Press, 1998.

———. *Turks, Moors, and Englishmen in the Age of Discovery.* New York: Columbia University Press, 1999.

Mendelson, Sara Heller, and Patricia Crawford. *Women in Early Modern England, 1550–1720.* Oxford: Clarendon, 1998.

Moody, T. W., F. X. Martin, and F. J. Byrne, eds. *A New History of Ireland,* Volume 3: *Early Modern Ireland, 1534–1691.* Oxford: Oxford University Press, 2001.

Mukerji, Chandra. *From Graven Images: Patterns of Modern Materialism.* New York: Columbia University Press, 1983.

Neale, J. E. *Elizabeth I and Her Parliaments, 1559–1581.* London: Cape, 1971.

———. *Queen Elizabeth I.* London: Pimlico, 1998.

Nichols, John, ed. *The Progresses and Public Processions of Queen Elizabeth.* 3 vols. London: J. Nichols, 1823.

Palliser, D. M. *The Age of Elizabeth: England under the Later Tudors, 1547–1603.* 2nd ed. New York: Longman, 1992.

Parry, J. H. *The Age of Reconnaissance: Discovery, Exploration, and Settlement, 1450 to 1650.* New York: Praeger, 1969.

Pearson, Lu Emily Hess. *Elizabethans at Home.* Stanford: Stanford University Press, 1967.

Peck, Linda Levy. *Court Patronage and Corruption in Early Stuart England.* Boston: Unwin Hyman, 1990.

Peters, Christine. *Women in Early Modern Britain, 1450–1640.* New York: Palgrave Macmillan, 2004.

Pocock, J. G. A. *The Ancient Constitution and the Feudal Law: Study of English Historical Thought in the Seventeenth Century—A Reissue with a Retrospect.* Rev. ed. New York: Cambridge University Press, 1987.

Rappaport, Steve. *Worlds within Worlds: Structures of Life in Sixteenth-Century London.* New York: Cambridge University Press, 1989.

Sharpe, J. A. *Crime in Early Modern England, 1550–1750.* 2nd ed. New York: Longman, 1999.

———. *Early Modern England: A Social History, 1550–1760.* 2nd ed. London: Arnold, 1997.

Slack, Paul. *The Impact of Plague in Tudor and Stuart England.* Boston: Routledge and Kegan Paul, 1985.

———. *Poverty and Policy in Tudor and Stuart England.* New York: Longman, 1988.

———, ed. *Rebellion, Popular Protest, and the Social Order in Early Modern England.* New York: Cambridge University Press, 1984.

Stone, Lawrence. *The Causes of the English Revolution, 1529–1642.* New York: Routledge, 2002.

———. *The Crisis of the Aristocracy, 1558–1641.* Oxford: Clarendon, 1965.

———. *The Family, Sex and Marriage in England, 1500–1800.* New York: Harper & Row, 1979.

Thirsk, Joan. *Economic Policy and Projects: The Development of a Consumer Society in Early Modern England.* Oxford: Clarendon, 1978.

Thomas, Keith. *Religion and the Decline of Magic: Studies in Popular Beliefs in Sixteenth and Seventeenth Century England.* New York: Scribner, 1971.

Underdown, David. *Fire from Heaven: Life in an English Town in the Seventeenth Century.* London: HarperCollins, 1992.

———. *Revel, Riot, and Rebellion: Popular Politics and Culture in England, 1603–1660.* Oxford: Clarendon, 1985.

Williams, Penry. *The Later Tudors: England, 1547–1603*. New York: Oxford University Press, 1995.

Wrightson, Keith. *Earthly Necessities: Economic Lives in Early Modern Britain*. New Haven: Yale University Press, 2000.

———. *English Society, 1580–1680*. London: Hutchinson, 1982.

Yates, Frances Amelia. *Astraea: The Imperial Theme in the Sixteenth Century*. London: Routledge and Kegan Paul, 1975.

Zagorin, Perez. *Rebels and Rulers, 1500–1660*. 2 vols. New York: Cambridge University Press, 1982.

Intellectual and Religious History

Armitage, David. *The Ideological Origins of the British Empire*. New York: Cambridge University Press, 2000.

Baker, Herschel Clay. *The Race of Time: Three Lectures on Renaissance Historiography*. Toronto: University of Toronto Press, 1967.

Barkan, Leonard. *Nature's Work of Art: The Human Body as Image of the World*. New Haven: Yale University Press, 1975.

Bossy, John. *Christianity in the West, 1400–1700*. New York: Oxford University Press, 1985.

Bouwsma, William James. *John Calvin: A Sixteenth-Century Portrait*. New York: Oxford University Press, 1988.

Cassirer, Ernst. *The Individual and the Cosmos in Renaissance Philosophy*. Trans. Mario Domandi. Philadelphia: University of Pennsylvania Press, 1972.

Clark, Stuart. *Thinking with Demons: The Idea of Witchcraft in Early Modern Europe*. New York: Oxford University Press, 1997.

Collinson, Patrick. *The Birthpangs of Protestant England: Religion and Cultural Change in the Sixteenth and Seventeenth Centuries*. New York: St. Martin's, 1988.

———. *The Elizabethan Puritan Movement*. New York: Oxford University Press, 1990.

———. *The Religion of Protestants: The Church in English Society, 1559–1625*. Oxford: Clarendon, 1982.

Doran, Susan, and Christopher Durston. *Princes, Pastors, and People: The Church and Religion in England, 1500–1700*. Rev. ed. New York: Routledge, 2003.

Duffy, Eamon. *The Stripping of the Altars: Traditional Religion in England, c. 1400–c. 1580*. 2nd ed. New Haven: Yale University Press, 1992.

Gadd, Ian, and Alexandra Gillespie, eds. *John Stow (1525–1605) and the Making of the English Past*. London: British Library, 2004.

Haigh, Christopher. *English Reformations: Religion, Politics, and Society under the Tudors*. New York: Oxford University Press, 1993.

Hill, Christopher. *Society and Puritanism in Pre-Revolutionary England*. New York: Schocken Books, 1964.

Houlbrooke, Ralph A. *Death, Religion, and the Family in England, 1480–1700*. New York: Oxford University Press, 1998.

Kelly, Henry Ansgar. *Divine Providence in the England of Shakespeare's Histories*. Cambridge, Mass.: Harvard University Press, 1970.

Kilroy, Gerard. *Edmund Campion. Memory and Transcription*. Aldershot, Eng.: Ashgate, 2005.

Klaits, Joseph. *Servants of Satan: The Age of the Witch Hunts*. Bloomington: Indiana University Press, 1985.

Kristeller, Paul Oskar. *Renaissance Thought: The Classic, Scholastic, and Humanistic Strains*. New York: Harper & Row, 1961.

Levao, Ronald. *Renaissance Minds and Their Fictions: Cusanus, Sidney, Shakespeare*. Berkeley: University of California Press, 1985.

Levin, Harry. *The Myth of the Golden Age in the Renaissance*. Bloomington: University of Indiana Press, 1969.

Levy, Fred Jacob. *Tudor Historical Thought*. San Marino, Calif.: Huntington Library Press, 1967.

MacCulloch, Diarmaid. *The Later Reformation in England, 1547–1603*. 2nd ed. New York: Palgrave, 2001.

———. *The Reformation*. New York: Viking, 2004.

Mack, Peter, ed. *Renaissance Rhetoric*. New York: St. Martin's, 1994.

Marotti, Arthur F. *Religious Ideology and Cultural Fantasy: Catholic and Anti-Catholic Discourses in Early Modern England*. Notre Dame, Ind.: University of Notre Dame Press, 2005.

Marshall, Peter. *Beliefs and the Dead in Reformation England*. London: Oxford University Press, 2002.

Oldridge, Darren, ed. *The Witchcraft Reader*. London: Routledge, 2001.

Patterson, Annabel M. *Reading Holinshed's Chronicles*. Chicago: University of Chicago Press, 1994.

Popkin, Richard H. *The History of Skepticism from Erasmus to Spinoza*. Berkeley: University of California Press, 1979.

Sharpe, James. *Instruments of Darkness: Witchcraft in England 1550–1750*. New York: Penguin Books, 1996.

Shuger, Debora Kuller. *Habits of Thought in the English Renaissance: Religion, Politics, and the Dominant Culture*. Berkeley: University of California Press, 1990.

Sonnino, Lee A. *A Handbook to Sixteenth-Century Rhetoric*. London: Routledge and Kegan Paul, 1968.

Strong, Roy. *The Cult of Elizabeth: Elizabethan Portraiture and Pageantry*. London: Thames and Hudson, 1977.

———. *The English Icon: Elizabethan & Jacobean Portraiture*. New York: Pantheon Books, 1969.

Walsham, Alexandra. *Providence in Early Modern England*. New York: Oxford University Press, 1999.

Watt, Tessa. *Cheap Print and Popular Piety, 1560–1649*. New York: Cambridge University Press, 1991.

Wind, Edgar. *Pagan Mysteries in the Renaissance*. Rev. and enl. ed. London: Oxford University Press, 1980.

Woolf, D. R. *Reading History in Early Modern England*. New York: Cambridge University Press, 2000.

———. *The Social Circulation of the Past: English Historical Culture, 1500–1730*. New York: Oxford University Press, 2003.

Cultural History and Early Modern Cultural Studies

Aers, David, Bob Hodge, and Gunther Kress. *Literature, Language, and Society in England, 1589–1680*. Totowa, N.J.: Barnes & Noble Books, 1981.

Agnew, Jean-Christophe. *Worlds Apart: The Market and the Theater in Anglo-American Thought, 1550–1750*. New York: Cambridge University Press, 1986.

Andersen, Jennifer, and Elizabeth Sauer, eds. *Books and Readers in Early Modern England: Material Studies*. Philadelphia: University of Pennsylvania Press, 2001.

Bakhtin, Mikhail. *Rabelais and His World*. Trans. Hélène Iswolsky. Rev. ed. Bloomington: Indiana University Press, 1984.

Baldwin, Thomas Whitfield. *William Shakespere's Small Latine & Lesse Greeke*. Urbana: University of Illinois Press, 1944.

Barkan, Leonard. *The Gods Made Flesh: Metamorphosis & the Pursuit of Paganism*. New Haven: Yale University Press, 1986.

Barker, Francis. *The Tremulous Private Body: Essays on Subjection*. New York: Methuen, 1984.

Baron, Sabrina Alcorn, ed. *The Reader Revealed*. Washington, D.C.: Folger Shakespeare Library, 2001.

Bartels, Emily Carroll. *Spectacles of Strangeness: Imperialism, Alienation, and Marlowe*. Philadelphia: University of Pennsylvania Press, 1993.

Beilin, Elaine V. *Redeeming Eve: Women Writers of the English Renaissance*. Princeton: Princeton University Press, 1987.

Blank, Paula. *Broken English: Dialects and the Politics of Language in Renaissance Literature*. New York: Routledge, 1996.

Bloom, Gina. *Voice in Motion: Staging Gender, Shaping Sound in Early Modern England*. Philadelphia: Pennsylvania University Press, 2007.

Bray, Alan. *Homosexuality in Renaissance England*. Rev. ed. New York: Columbia University Press, 1995.

Brayman Hackel, Heidi. *Reading Material in Early Modern England: Print, Gender, and Literacy*. New York: Cambridge University Press, 2005.

Briggs, Julia. *This Stage-Play World: Texts and Contexts, 1580–1625*. 2nd ed. New York: Oxford University Press, 1997.

Bristol, Michael D. *Carnival and Theater: Plebeian Culture and the Structure of Authority in Renaissance England*. New York: Methuen, 1985.

Brotton, Jerry. *Trading Territories: Mapping the Early Modern World*. London: Reaktion Books, 1997.

Brown, Pamela Allen. *Better a Shrew than a Sheep: Women, Drama, and the Culture of Jest in Early Modern England*. Ithaca, N.Y.: Cornell University Press, 2003.

Burke, Peter. *Popular Culture in Early Modern Europe*. New York: New York University Press, 1978.

Burt, Richard, and John Michael Archer, eds. *Enclosure Acts: Sexuality, Property, and Culture in Early Modern England*. Ithaca, N.Y.: Cornell University Press, 1994.

Bushnell, Rebecca W. *A Culture of Teaching: Early Modern Humanism in Theory and Practice*. Ithaca, N.Y.: Cornell University Press, 1996.

Buxton, John. *Elizabethan Taste*. London: Macmillan, 1963.

Caldwell, John. *The Oxford History of English Music*. New York: Oxford University Press, 1991.

Carroll, William C. *Fat King, Lean Beggar: Representations of Poverty in the Age of Shakespeare*. Ithaca, N.Y.: Cornell University Press, 1996.

Clegg, Cyndia Susan. *Press Censorship in Elizabethan England*. New York: Cambridge University Press, 1997.

———. *Press Censorship in Jacobean England*. New York: Cambridge University Press, 2001.

Cox, John D. *The Devil and the Sacred in English Drama, 1350–1642*. New York: Cambridge University Press, 2000.

Crane, Mary Thomas. *Framing Authority: Sayings, Self, and Society in Sixteenth-Century England*. Princeton: Princeton University Press, 1993.

Crawford, Julie. *Marvelous Protestantism: Monstrous Births in Post-Reformation England*. Baltimore: Johns Hopkins University Press, 2005.

Cressy, David. *Literacy and the Social Order: Reading and Writing in Tudor and Stuart England*. New York: Cambridge University Press, 1980.

De Grazia, Margreta, Maureen Quilligan, and Peter Stallybrass, eds. *Subject and Object in Renaissance Culture*. New York: Cambridge University Press, 1996.

Diehl, Huston. *Staging Reform, Reforming the Stage: Protestantism and Popular Theater in Early Modern England*. Ithaca, N.Y.: Cornell University Press, 1997.

Dolan, Frances E. *Dangerous Familiars: Representations of Domestic Crime in England, 1550–1700*. Ithaca, N.Y.: Cornell University Press, 1994.

———. *Whores of Babylon: Catholicism, Gender, and Seventeenth-Century Print Culture*. Ithaca, N.Y.: Cornell University Press, 1999.

Eisenstein, Elizabeth L. *The Printing Press as an Agent of Change: Communications and Cultural Transformations in Early-Modern Europe*. 2 vols. New York: Cambridge University Press, 1979.

Ferguson, Margaret W. *Dido's Daughters: Literacy, Gender, and Empire in Early Modern England and France*. Chicago: University of Chicago Press, 2003.

Ferguson, Margaret W., Maureen Quilligan, and Nancy J. Vickers, eds. *Rewriting the Renaissance: The Discourses of Sexual Difference in Early Modern Europe*. Chicago: University of Chicago Press, 1986.

Fisher, Will. *Materializing Gender in Early Modern English Literature and Culture*. New York: Cambridge University Press, 2006.

Fleming, Juliet. *Graffiti and the Writing Arts of Early Modern England*. Philadelphia: University of Pennsylvania Press, 2001.

Frye, Susan. *Elizabeth I: The Competition for Representation*. New York: Oxford University Press, 1993.

Fumerton, Patricia. *Cultural Aesthetics: Renaissance Literature and the Practice of Social Ornament*. Chicago: University of Chicago Press, 1991.

———. *Unsettled: The Culture of Mobility and the Working Poor in Early Modern England*. Chicago: University of Chicago Press, 2006.

Gillies, John. *Shakespeare and the Geography of Difference*. New York: Cambridge University Press, 1994.

Goldberg, Jonathan. *James I and the Politics of Literature: Jonson, Shakespeare, Donne, and Their Contemporaries*. Baltimore: Johns Hopkins University Press, 1983.

———. *Writing Matter: From the Hands of the English Renaissance*. Stanford: Stanford University Press, 1990.

———, ed. *Queering the Renaissance*. Durham, N.C.: Duke University Press, 1994.

Greenblatt, Stephen. *Learning to Curse: Essays in Early Modern Culture*. New York: Routledge, 1990.

———. *Renaissance Self-Fashioning: From More to Shakespeare*. Chicago: University of Chicago Press, 1980.

———, ed. *New World Encounters*. Berkeley: University of California Press, 1993.

———, ed. *Representing the English Renaissance*. Berkeley: University of California Press, 1988.

Grout, Donald Jay, and Hermine Weigel Williams. *A Short History of Opera*. 4th ed. New York: Columbia University Press, 2003.

Hall, Kim F. *Things of Darkness: Economies of Race and Gender in Early Modern England*. Ithaca, N.Y.: Cornell University Press, 1995.

Harris, Jonathan Gil. *Foreign Bodies and the Body Politic: Discourses of Social Pathology in Early Modern England*. New York: Cambridge University Press, 1998.

Harvey, Elizabeth D., ed. *Sensible Flesh: On Touch in Early Modern Culture*. Philadelphia: University of Pennsylvania Press, 2003.

Haselkorn, Anne M., and Betty S. Travitsky, eds. *The Renaissance Englishwoman in Print: Counterbalancing the Canon*. Amherst: University of Massachusetts Press, 1990.

Helgerson, Richard. *Forms of Nationhood: The Elizabethan Writing of England*. Chicago: University of Chicago Press, 1992.

Henderson, Katherine Usher, and Barbara F. McManus. *Half Humankind: Contexts and Texts of the Controversy About Women in England, 1540–1640*. Urbana: University of Illinois Press, 1985.

Hendricks, Margo, and Patricia Parker, eds. *Women, "Race," and Writing in the Early Modern Period*. New York: Routledge, 1994.

Hillman, David, and Carla Mazzio, eds. *The Body in Parts: Fantasies of Corporeality in Early Modern Europe*. New York: Routledge, 1997.

Hoeniger, F. David. *Medicine and Shakespeare in the English Renaissance*. Newark: University of Delaware Press, 1992.

Huizinga, Johan. *The Autumn of the Middle Ages*. Trans. Rodney J. Payton and Ulrich Mammitzsch. Chicago: University of Chicago Press, 1996.

Hull, Suzanne W. *Chaste, Silent & Obedient: English Books for Women, 1475–1640*. San Marino, Calif.: Huntington Library, 1982.

Hutson, Lorna. *The Usurer's Daughter: Male Friendship and Fictions of Women in Sixteenth-Century England*. New York: Routledge, 1994.

Javitch, Daniel. *Poetry and Courtliness in Renaissance England*. Princeton: Princeton University Press, 1978.

Jones, Ann Rosalind, and Peter Stallybrass. *Renaissance Clothing and the Materials of Memory*. New York: Cambridge University Press, 2000.

Jordan, Constance. *Renaissance Feminism: Literary Texts and Political Models*. Ithaca, N.Y.: Cornell University Press, 1990.

Knapp, Jeffrey. *Shakespeare's Tribe: Church, Nation, and Theater in Renaissance England*. Chicago: University of Chicago Press, 2002.

Laqueur, Thomas Walter. *Making Sex: Body and Gender from the Greeks to Freud*. Cambridge, Mass.: Harvard University Press, 1990.

MacDonald, Joyce Green. *Women and Race in Early Modern Texts*. New York: Cambridge University Press, 2002.

Magnusson, Lynne. *Shakespeare and Social Dialogue: Dramatic Language and Elizabethan Letters*. New York: Cambridge University Press, 1999.

Manley, Lawrence. *Literature and Culture in Early Modern London*. New York: Cambridge University Press, 1995.

Marcus, Leah S. *The Politics of Mirth: Jonson, Herrick, Milton, Marvell, and the Defense of Old Holiday Pastimes*. Chicago: University of Chicago Press, 1986.

McJannet, Linda. *The Sultan Speaks: Dialogue in English Plays and Histories about the Ottoman Turks*. New York: Palgrave Macmillan, 2006.

Meron, Theodor. *Bloody Constraint: War and Chivalry in Shakespeare*. New York: Oxford University Press, 1998.

Miller, David Lee, Sharon O'Dair, and Harold Weber, eds. *The Production of English Renaissance Culture*. Ithaca, N.Y.: Cornell University Press, 1994.

Montrose, Louis. *The Subject of Elizabeth: Authority, Gender, and Representation*. Chicago: University of Chicago Press, 2006.

Neill, Michael. *Issues of Death: Mortality and Identity in English Renaissance Tragedy*. Oxford: Clarendon, 1997.

Netzloff, Mark. *England's Internal Colonies: Class, Capital, and the Literature of Early Modern English Colonialism*. New York: Palgrave Macmillan, 2003.

Orlin, Lena Cowen. *Private Matters and Public Culture in Post-Reformation England*. Ithaca, N.Y.: Cornell University Press, 1994.

———, ed. *Material London, ca. 1600*. Philadelphia: University of Pennsylvania Press, 2000.

Parry, Graham. *The Golden Age Restor'd: The Culture of the Stuart Court, 1603–42*. New York: St. Martin's, 1981.

Paster, Gail Kern. *The Body Embarrassed: Drama and the Disciplines of Shame in Early Modern England*. Ithaca, N.Y.: Cornell University Press, 1993.

———. *Humoring the Body: Emotions and the Shakespearean Stage*. Chicago: University of Chicago Press, 2004.

Paster, Gail Kern, Katherine Rowe, and Mary Floyd-Wilson, eds. *Reading the Early Modern Passions: Essays in the Cultural History of Emotion*. Philadelphia: University of Pennsylvania Press, 2004.

Patterson, Annabel M. *Censorship and Interpretation: The Conditions of Writing and Reading in Early Modern England*. Madison: University of Wisconsin Press, 1984.

Peck, Linda Levy. *Consuming Splendor: Society and Culture in Seventeenth-Century England*. New York: Cambridge University Press, 2005.

Platt, Peter G. *Reason Diminished: Shakespeare and the Marvelous*. Lincoln: University of Nebraska Press, 1997.

Pollard, Tanya. *Drugs and Theater in Early Modern England*. New York: Oxford University Press, 2005.

Sanders, Eve Rachele. *Gender and Literacy on Stage in Early Modern England*. New York: Cambridge University Press, 1998.

Sawday, Jonathan. *The Body Emblazoned: Dissection and the Human Body in Renaissance Culture*. New York: Routledge, 1995.

Schoenfeldt, Michael C. *Bodies and Selves in Early Modern England: Physiology and Inwardness in Spenser, Shakespeare, Herbert, and Milton*. New York: Cambridge University Press, 1999.

Schwyzer, Philip. *Literature, Nationalism, and Memory in Early Modern England and Wales*. New York: Cambridge University Press, 2004.

Shapiro, James. *Shakespeare and the Jews*. New York: Columbia University Press, 1996.

Sharpe, Kevin, and Peter Lake, eds. *Culture and Politics in Early Stuart England*. Stanford: Stanford University Press, 1993.

Sherman, William H. *John Dee: The Politics of Reading and Writing in the English Renaissance*. Amherst: University of Massachusetts Press, 1995.

Shuger, Debora. *Censorship and Cultural Sensibility: The Regulation of Language in Tudor-Stuart England*. Philadelphia: University of Pennsylvania Press, 2006.

Simon, Joan. *Education and Society in Tudor England*. Cambridge, Eng.: Cambridge University Press, 1966.

Singh, Jyotsna G. *Colonial Narratives/Cultural Dialogues: 'Discoveries' of India in the Language of Colonialism*. New York: Routledge, 1996.

Smith, Bruce R. *The Acoustic World of Early Modern England: Attending to the O-Factor*. Chicago: University of Chicago Press, 1999.

———. *Homosexual Desire in Shakespeare's England: A Cultural Poetics*. Chicago: University of Chicago Press, 1994.

Smuts, R. Malcolm. *Court Culture and the Origins of a Royalist Tradition in Early Stuart England*. Philadelphia: University of Pennsylvania Press, 1987.

Stallybrass, Peter, and Allon White. *The Politics and Poetics of Transgression*. Ithaca, N.Y.: Cornell University Press, 1986.

Traub, Valerie, M. Lindsay Kaplan, and Dympna Callaghan, eds. *Feminist Readings of Early Modern Culture: Emerging Subjects*. New York: Cambridge University Press, 1996.

Turner, Henry S. *The English Renaissance Stage: Geometry, Poetics, and the Practical Spatial Arts 1580–1630*. New York: Oxford University Press, 2006.

Turner, James Grantham, ed. *Sexuality and Gender in Early Modern Europe: Institutions, Texts, Images*. New York: Cambridge University Press, 1993.

Wall, Wendy. *Staging Domesticity: Household Work and English Identity in Early Modern Drama*. New York: Cambridge University Press, 2002.

Watson, Robert N. *The Rest Is Silence: Death as Annihilation in the English Renaissance*. Berkeley: University of California Press, 1994.

Whigham, Frank. *Ambition and Privilege: The Social Tropes of Elizabethan Courtesy Theory*. Berkeley: University of California Press, 1984.

Woodbridge, Linda. *Vagrancy, Homelessness, and English Renaissance Literature*. Urbana: University of Illinois Press, 2001.

———. *Women and the English Renaissance: Literature and the Nature of Womankind, 1540 to 1620*. Urbana: University of Illinois Press, 1984.

Shakespeare's Generic, Literary, and Theatrical Contexts

Alpers, Paul. *What Is Pastoral?* Chicago: University of Chicago Press, 1996.

Altman, Joel. *The Tudor Play of Mind: Rhetorical Inquiry and the Development of Elizabethan Drama*. Berkeley: University of California Press, 1978.

Barish, Jonas. *The Antitheatrical Prejudice*. Berkeley: University of California Press, 1981.

Bate, Jonathan. *Shakespeare and Ovid*. Oxford: Clarendon, 1993.

Bates, Catherine. *The Rhetoric of Courtship in Elizabethan Language and Literature*. New York: Cambridge University Press, 1992.

Beckwith, Sarah. *Signifying God: Social Relation and Symbolic Act in the York Corpus Christi Plays*. Chicago: University of Chicago Press, 2001.

Belsey, Catherine. *The Subject of Tragedy: Identity and Difference in Renaissance Drama*. New York: Methuen, 1985.

Bevington, David M. *From "Mankind" to Marlowe: Growth of Structure in the Popular Drama of Tudor England*. Cambridge, Mass.: Harvard University Press, 1962.

———. *Tudor Drama and Politics: A Critical Approach to Topical Meaning*. Cambridge, Mass.: Harvard University Press, 1968.

Bly, Mary. *Queer Virgins and Virgin Queans on the Early Modern Stage*. New York: Oxford University Press, 2000.

Bowers, Fredson Thayer. *Elizabethan Revenge Tragedy, 1587–1642*. Princeton: Princeton University Press, 1940.

Braden, Gordon. *Renaissance Tragedy and the Senecan Tradition: Anger's Privilege*. New Haven: Yale University Press, 1985.

Bruster, Douglas. *Drama and the Market in the Age of Shakespeare*. New York: Cambridge University Press, 1992.

Bullough, Geoffrey, ed. *Narrative and Dramatic Sources of Shakespeare*. 8 vols. New York: Columbia University Press, 1957–75.

Butler, Martin. *Theatre and Crisis, 1632–1642*. New York: Cambridge University Press, 1984.

Carroll, William C. *The Metamorphoses of Shakespearean Comedy*. Princeton: Princeton University Press, 1985.

Cartwright, Kent. *Theatre and Humanism: English Drama in the Sixteenth Century*. New York: Cambridge University Press, 1999.

Clubb, Louise George. *Italian Drama in Shakespeare's Time*. New Haven: Yale University Press, 1989.

Cohen, Walter. *Drama of a Nation: Public Theater in Renaissance England and Spain*. Ithaca, N.Y.: Cornell University Press, 1985.

Crewe, Jonathan. *Trials of Authorship: Anterior Forms and Poetic Reconstruction from Wyatt to Shakespeare*. Berkeley: University of California Press, 1990.

Danson, Lawrence. *Shakespeare's Dramatic Genres*. New York: Oxford University Press, 2000.

Dawson, Anthony B., and Paul Yachnin. *The Culture of Playgoing in Shakespeare's England: A Collaborative Debate*. New York: Cambridge University Press, 2001.

Dillon, Janette. *Language and Stage in Medieval and Renaissance England*. New York: Cambridge University Press, 1998.

Felperin, Howard. *Shakespearean Romance*. Princeton: Princeton University Press, 1972.

Finkelpearl, Philip J. *John Marston of the Middle Temple: An Elizabethan Dramatist in His Social Setting*. Cambridge, Mass.: Harvard University Press, 1969.

Gardiner, Harold C. *Mysteries' End: An Investigation of the Last Days of the Medieval Religious Stage*. New Haven: Yale University Press, 1946.

Halasz, Alexandra. *The Marketplace of Print: Pamphlets and the Public Sphere in Early Modern England*. New York: Cambridge University Press, 1997.

Harbage, Alfred. *Shakespeare and the Rival Traditions*. New York: Macmillan, 1952.

Hardison, O. B. *Christian Rite and Christian Drama in the Middle Ages: Essays in the Origin and Early History of Modern Drama*. Baltimore: Johns Hopkins University Press, 1965.

Heinemann, Margot. *Puritanism and Theatre: Thomas Middleton and Opposition Drama under the Early Stuarts*. New York: Cambridge University Press, 1980.

Honan, Park. *Christopher Marlowe: Poet & Spy*. New York: Oxford University Press, 2005.

Honigmann, E. A. J., ed. *Shakespeare and His Contemporaries: Essays in Comparison*. Manchester: Manchester University Press, 1986.

———, ed. *Shakespeare's Impact on His Contemporaries*. London: Macmillan, 1982.

Howard, Jean E. *Theater of a City: The Places of London Comedy, 1598–1642*. Philadelphia: University of Pennsylvania Press, 2007.

Hunter, G. K. *John Lyly: The Humanist as Courtier*. Cambridge, Mass.: Harvard University Press, 1962.

Jones, Emrys. *The Origins of Shakespeare*. Oxford: Clarendon, 1977.

———. *Scenic Form in Shakespeare*. Oxford: Clarendon, 1971.

Kastan, David Scott, and Peter Stallybrass, eds. *Staging the Renaissance: Reinterpretations of Elizabethan and Jacobean Drama*. New York: Routledge, 1991.

Kermode, Lloyd Edward, Jason Scott-Warren, and Martine van Elk, eds. *Tudor Drama Before Shakespeare, 1485–1590: New Directions for Research, Criticism, and Pedagogy*. New York: Palgrave Macmillan, 2004.

Kolve, V. A. *The Play Called Corpus Christi*. Stanford: Stanford University Press, 1966.

Leggatt, Alexander. *Citizen Comedy in the Age of Shakespeare*. Toronto: University of Toronto Press, 1973.

———. *Introduction to English Renaissance Comedy*. Manchester: Manchester University Press, 1999.

Levin, Harry. *Shakespeare and the Revolution of the Times: Perspectives and Commentaries*. New York: Oxford University Press, 1976.

Levith, Murray J. *Shakespeare's Italian Settings and Plays*. Basingstoke: Macmillan, 1989.

Lomax, Marion. *Stage Images and Traditions: Shakespeare to Ford*. New York: Cambridge University Press, 1987.

Martindale, Charles, and A. B. Taylor, eds. *Shakespeare and the Classics*. New York: Cambridge University Press, 2004.

Masten, Jeffrey. *Textual Intercourse: Collaboration, Authorship, and Sexualities in Renaissance Drama*. New York: Cambridge University Press, 1997.

McLuskie, Kathleen. *Renaissance Dramatists*. New York: Harvester Wheatsheaf, 1989.

McMillin, Scott. *The Elizabethan Theatre and the Book of Sir Thomas More*. Ithaca, N.Y.: Cornell University Press, 1987.

McMillin, Scott, and Sally-Beth MacLean. *The Queen's Men and Their Plays*. New York: Cambridge University Press, 1998.

McMullan, Gordon, and Jonathan Hope, eds. *The Politics of Tragicomedy: Shakespeare and After*. New York: Routledge, 1991.

Miola, Robert S. *Shakespeare's Reading*. New York: Oxford University Press, 2000.

———. *Shakespeare's Rome*. New York: Cambridge University Press, 1983.

Newcomb, Lori Humphrey. *Reading Popular Romance in Early Modern England*. New York: Columbia University Press, 2002.

Norbrook, David. *Poetry and Politics in the English Renaissance*. London: Routledge and Kegan Paul, 1984.

Orgel, Stephen. *The Illusion of Power: Political Theater in the English Renaissance*. Berkeley: University of California Press, 1975.

Peters, Julie Stone. *Theatre of the Book, 1480–1880: Print, Text, and Performance in Europe*. New York: Oxford University Press, 2000.

Riggs, David. *Ben Jonson: A Life*. Cambridge, Mass.: Harvard University Press, 1989.

———. *The World of Christopher Marlowe*. London: Faber and Faber, 2004.

Rose, Mark. *Shakespearean Design*. Cambridge, Mass.: Belknap Press, 1972.

Rose, Mary Beth. *The Expense of Spirit: Love and Sexuality in English Renaissance Drama*. Ithaca, N.Y.: Cornell University Press, 1988.

Salingar, Leo. *Dramatic Form in Shakespeare and the Jacobeans: Essays*. New York: Cambridge University Press, 1986.

———. *Shakespeare and the Traditions of Comedy*. New York: Cambridge University Press, 1974.

Schwyzer, Philip. *Archaeologies of English Renaissance Literature*. New York: Oxford University Press, 2007.

Shapiro, James. *Rival Playwrights: Marlowe, Jonson, Shakespeare*. New York: Columbia University Press, 1991.

Snyder, Susan. *The Comic Matrix of Shakespeare's Tragedies*: Romeo and Juliet, Hamlet, Othello, *and* King Lear. Princeton: Princeton University Press, 1979.

Spivack, Bernard. *Shakespeare and the Allegory of Evil: The History of a Metaphor in Relation to His Major Villains*. New York: Columbia University Press, 1958.

Thomas, Vivian. *The Moral Universe of Shakespeare's Problem Plays*. New York: Routledge, 1991.

Vickers, Brian, ed. *English Renaissance Literary Criticism*. New York: Oxford University Press, 1999.

Vitkus, Daniel. *Turning Turk: English Theater and the Multicultural Mediterranean, 1570–1630*. New York: Palgrave Macmillan, 2003.

Weimann, Robert. *Shakespeare and the Popular Tradition in the Theater: Studies in the Social Dimension of Dramatic Form and Function*. Ed. Robert Schwartz. Baltimore: Johns Hopkins University Press, 1978.

Whitney, Charles. *Early Responses to Renaissance Drama*. New York: Cambridge University Press, 2006.

Woolf, Rosemary. *The English Mystery Plays*. Berkeley: University of California Press, 1972.

The Playing Field: Theaters, Actors, Patrons, and the State

Astington, John H. *English Court Theatre, 1558–1642*. Cambridge, Eng.: Cambridge University Press, 1999.

———, ed. *The Development of Shakespeare's Theater*. New York: AMS Press, 1992.

Barroll, J. Leeds. *Politics, Plague, and Shakespeare's Theater: The Stuart Years*. Ithaca, N.Y.: Cornell University Press, 1991.

Beckerman, Bernard. *Shakespeare at the Globe, 1599–1609*. New York: Macmillan, 1962.

Bentley, Gerald Eades. *The Jacobean and Caroline Stage*. 7 vols. Oxford: Clarendon, 1941–68.

———. *The Profession of Dramatist in Shakespeare's Time, 1590–1642*. Princeton: Princeton University Press, 1971.

———. *The Profession of Player in Shakespeare's Time, 1590–1642*. Princeton: Princeton University Press, 1984.

Berry, Herbert. *Shakespeare's Playhouses*. Illustrated by C. Walter Hodges. New York: AMS Press, 1987.

Bradbrook, M. C. *The Rise of the Common Player: A Study of Actor and Society in Shakespeare's England*. Cambridge, Mass.: Harvard University Press, 1962.

Chambers, E. K. *The Elizabethan Stage*. 4 vols. Oxford: Clarendon, 1923.

———. *The Mediaeval Stage*. 2 vols. Oxford: Clarendon, 1903.

Clare, Janet. *Art Made Tongue-Tied by Authority: Elizabethan and Jacobean Dramatic Censorship*. 2nd ed. Manchester: Manchester University Press, 1999.

Cook, Ann Jennalie. *The Privileged Playgoers of Shakespeare's London: 1576–1642*. Princeton: Princeton University Press, 1981.

Cox, John D., and David Scott Kastan, eds. *A New History of Early English Drama*. New York: Columbia University Press, 1997.

Dessen, Alan C. *Elizabethan Stage Conventions and Modern Interpreters*. Cambridge, Eng.: Cambridge University Press, 1984.

———. *Recovering Shakespeare's Theatrical Vocabulary*. New York: Cambridge University Press, 1995.

Dessen, Alan C., and Leslie Thomson. *A Dictionary of Stage Directions in English Drama, 1580–1642*. New York: Cambridge University Press, 1999.

Dillon, Janette. *The Cambridge Introduction to Early English Theatre*. New York: Cambridge University Press, 2006.

Dutton, Richard. *Licensing, Censorship and Authorship in Early Modern England: Buggeswords*. Houndmills, Basingstoke: Palgrave Macmillan, 2000.

———. *Mastering the Revels: The Regulation and Censorship of English Renaissance Drama*. London: Macmillan, 1991.

Dutton, Richard, Alison Findlay, and Richard Wilson, eds. *Region, Religion, and Patronage: Lancastrian Shakespeare*. Manchester: Manchester University Press, 2003.

Erne, Lukas. *Shakespeare as Literary Dramatist*. New York: Cambridge University Press, 2003.

Foakes, R. A. *Illustrations of the English Stage, 1580–1642*. Stanford: Stanford University Press, 1985.

Gair, W. Reavley. *The Children of Paul's: The Story of a Theatre Company, 1553–1608*. New York: Cambridge University Press, 1982.

Greg, W. W., ed. *Dramatic Documents from the Elizabethan Playhouses: Stage Plots: Actor's Parts: Prompt Books*. 2 vols. Oxford: Clarendon, 1931.

Gurr, Andrew. *Playgoing in Shakespeare's London*. 3rd ed. New York: Cambridge University Press, 2004.

———. *The Shakespeare Company, 1594–1642*. New York: Cambridge University Press, 2004.

———. *The Shakespearian Playing Companies*. Oxford: Clarendon, 1996.

———. *The Shakespearean Stage, 1574–1642*. 3rd ed. New York: Cambridge University Press, 1992.

Gurr, Andrew, and John Orrell. *Rebuilding Shakespeare's Globe*. London: Weidenfeld & Nicolson, 1989.

Harris, Jonathan Gil, and Natasha Korda, eds. *Staged Properties in Early Modern Drama*. New York: Cambridge University Press, 2002.

Hattaway, Michael. *Elizabethan Popular Theatre: Plays in Performance*. London: Routledge and Kegan Paul, 1982.

Henslowe, Philip. *Henslowe's Diary*. Ed. R. A. Foakes. 2nd ed. New York: Cambridge University Press, 2002.

Hodges, C. Walter. *The Globe Restored: A Study of the Elizabethan Theatre*. New York: Norton, 1973.

Holland, Peter, and Stephen Orgel, eds. *From Performance to Print in Shakespeare's England*. New York: Palgrave Macmillan, 2006.

———, eds. *From Script to Stage in Early Modern England*. Houndmills, Basingstoke: Palgrave Macmillan, 2004.

Ingram, William. *The Business of Playing: The Beginnings of Adult Professional Theater in Elizabethan London*. Ithaca, N.Y.: Cornell University Press, 1992.

Kernan, Alvin. *Shakespeare, the King's Playwright: Theater in the Stuart Court, 1603–1613*. New Haven: Yale University Press, 1995.

King, T. J. *Shakespearean Staging, 1599–1642*. Cambridge, Mass.: Harvard University Press, 1971.

Knutson, Roslyn Lander. *Playing Companies and Commerce in Shakespeare's Time*. Cambridge, Eng.: Cambridge University Press, 2001.

———. *The Repertory of Shakespeare's Company, 1594–1613*. Fayetteville: University of Arkansas Press, 1991.

Laroque, François. *Shakespeare's Festive World: Elizabethan Seasonal Entertainment and the Professional Stage*. New York: Cambridge University Press, 1991.

Lopez, Jeremy. *Theatrical Convention and Audience Response in Early Modern Drama*. New York: Cambridge University Press, 2002.

MacIntyre, Jean. *Costumes and Scripts in the Elizabethan Theatres*. Edmonton: University of Alberta Press, 1992.

Milling, Jane, and Peter Thomson, eds. *The Cambridge History of British Theatre*, Vol. 1: *Origins to 1660*. New York: Cambridge University Press, 2004.

Mulryne, J. R., and Margaret Shewring, eds. *Shakespeare's Globe Rebuilt*. New York: Cambridge University Press, 1997.

Munro, Lucy. *Children of the Queen's Revels: A Jacobean Theatre Repertory*. New York: Cambridge University Press, 2005.

Palfrey, Simon, and Tiffany Stern. *Shakespeare in Parts*. Oxford: Oxford University Press, 2007.

Shapiro, Michael. *Children of the Revels: The Boy Companies of Shakespeare's Time and Their Plays*. New York: Columbia University Press, 1977.

Smith, Irwin. *Shakespeare's Blackfriars Playhouse: Its History and Its Design*. New York: New York University Press, 1964.

Stern, Tiffany. *Making Shakespeare: From Stage to Page*. New York: Routledge, 2004.

———. *Rehearsal from Shakespeare to Sheridan*. Oxford: Clarendon, 2000.

White, Paul Whitfield, and Suzanne Westfall, eds. *Shakespeare and Theatrical Patronage in Early Modern England*. New York: Cambridge University Press, 2002.

Wickham, Glynne. *Early English Stages, 1300 to 1660*. 4 vols. New York: Routledge, 2002.

Wickham, Glynne, Herbert Berry, and William Ingram, eds. *English Professional Theatre, 1530–1660*. New York: Cambridge University Press, 2000.

Shakespeare's Life

Alexander, Peter. *Shakespeare's Life and Art*. New ed. New York: New York University Press, 1961.

Bate, Jonathan. *The Genius of Shakespeare*. London: Picador, 1997.

Bradbrook, M. C. *Shakespeare: The Poet in His World*. New York: Columbia University Press, 1978.

Chambers, E. K. *William Shakespeare: A Study of Facts and Problems*. 2 vols. Oxford: Clarendon, 1930.

Duncan-Jones, Katherine. *Ungentle Shakespeare: Scenes from His Life*. London: Arden Shakespeare, 2001.

Eccles, Mark. *Shakespeare in Warwickshire*. Madison: University of Wisconsin Press, 1961.

Edwards, Philip. *Shakespeare: A Writer's Progress*. New York: Oxford University Press, 1986.

Fraser, Russell A. *Shakespeare, The Later Years*. New York: Columbia University Press, 1992.

———. *Young Shakespeare*. New York: Columbia University Press, 1988.

Greenblatt, Stephen. *Will in the World: How Shakespeare Became Shakespeare*. New York: Norton, 2004.

Greer, Germaine. *Shakespeare*. New York: Oxford University Press, 1986.

Honan, Park. *Shakespeare: A Life*. New York: Oxford University Press, 1998.

Honigmann, E. A. J. *Shakespeare: The Lost Years*. 2nd ed. Manchester: Manchester University Press, 1998.

Hotson, Leslie. *Shakespeare Versus Shallow*. Boston: Little, Brown, and Company, 1931.

Levi, Peter. *The Life and Times of William Shakespeare*. New York: Macmillan, 1988.

Matus, Irvin Leigh. *Shakespeare, The Living Record*. Houndmills, Basingstoke: Macmillan, 1991.

Reese, M. M. *Shakespeare: His World and His Work*. Rev. ed. London: Edward Arnold, 1980.

Sams, Eric. *The Real Shakespeare: Retrieving the Early Years, 1564–1594*. New Haven: Yale University Press, 1995.

Schmidgall, Gary. *Shakespeare and the Poet's Life*. Lexington: University Press of Kentucky, 1990.

Schoenbaum, Samuel. *Shakespeare's Lives*. New ed. New York: Oxford University Press, 1991.

———. *William Shakespeare: A Compact Documentary Life*. Rev. ed. New York: Oxford University Press, 1987.

Shapiro, James. *A Year in the Life of William Shakespeare: 1599.* New York: Harper-Collins, 2005.

Taylor, Gary. *Reinventing Shakespeare: A Cultural History, from the Restoration to the Present.* New York: Weidenfeld & Nicolson, 1989.

Thomson, Peter. *Shakespeare's Professional Career.* New York: Cambridge University Press, 1992.

Wells, Stanley. *Shakespeare: A Life in Drama.* New York: Norton, 1995.

———. *Shakespeare: For All Time.* London: Macmillan, 2002.

Wood, Michael. *In Search of Shakespeare.* London: BBC, 2003.

Critical Approaches

Classics of Shakespeare Criticism

Barber, C. L. *Shakespeare's Festive Comedy: A Study of Dramatic Form and Its Relation to Social Custom.* Princeton: Princeton University Press, 1959.

Bradley, A. C. *Shakespearean Tragedy: Lectures on* Hamlet, Othello, King Lear, Macbeth. 3rd ed. New York: St. Martin's Press, 1992.

Coleridge, Samuel Taylor. *Coleridge on Shakespeare: The Text of the Lectures of 1811–12.* Ed. R. A. Foakes. Charlottesville: University Press of Virginia, 1971.

———. *Shakespearean Criticism.* 2 vols. Ed. T. M. Raysor. 2nd ed. New York: Dutton, 1969.

Eliot, T. S. "Shakespeare and the Stoicism of Seneca." *Selected Essays, 1917–1932.* New ed. New York: Harcourt, Brace, 1950.

Empson, William. *The Structure of Complex Words.* 3rd ed. London: Chatto & Windus, 1977.

Frye, Northrop. *Fools of Time: Studies in Shakespearean Tragedy.* Toronto: University of Toronto Press, 1967.

———. *A Natural Perspective: The Development of Shakespearean Comedy and Romance.* New York: Columbia University Press, 1965.

Hazlitt, William. *Characters of Shakespear's Plays.* London, 1817.

Johnson, Samuel. *Samuel Johnson on Shakespeare.* Ed. H. R. Woudhuysen. New York: Penguin, 1989.

Jones, Ernest. *Hamlet and Oedipus.* New York: Norton, 1949.

Kermode, Frank, ed. *Four Centuries of Shakespearian Criticism.* 1965. New York: Avon, 1965.

Knight, G. Wilson. *The Wheel of Fire: Interpretations of Shakespearean Tragedy, with Three New Essays.* 4th ed. New York: Harper & Row, 1977.

Kott, Jan. *Shakespeare Our Contemporary.* Trans. Boleslaw Taborski. Garden City, N.Y.: Anchor Books, 1966.

Morgann, Maurice. *Shakespearean Criticism.* Ed. Daniel A. Fineman. Oxford: Clarendon, 1972.

Spurgeon, Caroline F. E. *Shakespeare's Imagery, and What It Tells Us.* New York: Macmillan, 1935.

Tillyard, E. M. W. *Shakespeare's History Plays.* London: Chatto and Windus, 1944.

Vickers, Brian, ed. *Shakespeare: The Critical Heritage.* 6 vols. London: Routledge and Kegan Paul, 1974–1981.

General Studies

Barton, Anne. *Essays, Mainly Shakespearean.* New York: Cambridge University Press, 1994.

Bloom, Harold. *Shakespeare: The Invention of the Human.* New York: Riverhead Books, 1998.

Burckhardt, Sigurd. *Shakespearean Meanings*. Princeton: Princeton University Press, 1968.

Garber, Marjorie. *Shakespeare After All*. New York: Pantheon, 2004.

Hibbard, G. R. *The Making of Shakespeare's Dramatic Poetry*. Toronto: University of Toronto Press, 1981.

Honigmann, E. A. J. *Myriad-Minded Shakespeare: Essays on the Tragedies, Problem Comedies, and Shakespeare the Man*. 2nd ed. New York: St. Martin's Press, 1998.

Jones, John. *Shakespeare at Work*. New York: Oxford University Press, 1995.

Nuttall, A. D. *Shakespeare the Thinker*. New Haven: Yale University Press, 2007.

Ryan, Kiernan. *Shakespeare*. 3rd ed. New York: Palgrave Macmillan, 2001.

Language and Style

Baxter, John. *Shakespeare's Poetic Styles: Verse into Drama*. London: Routledge and Kegan Paul, 1980.

Blake, N. F. *Shakespeare's Language: An Introduction*. New York: St. Martin's Press, 1983.

Cercignani, Fausto. *Shakespeare's Works and Elizabethan Pronunciation*. New York: Oxford University Press, 1981.

Clemen, Wolfgang. *Shakespeare's Soliloquies*. Trans. Charity Scott Stokes. New York: Methuen, 1987.

———. *The Development of Shakespeare's Imagery*. New York: Hill and Wang, 1962.

Danson, Lawrence. *Tragic Alphabet: Shakespeare's Drama of Language*. New Haven: Yale University Press, 1974.

Donawerth, Jane. *Shakespeare and the Sixteenth-Century Study of Language*. Urbana: University of Illinois Press, 1984.

Edwards, Philip, Inga-Stina Ewbank, and G. K. Hunter, eds. *Shakespeare's Styles: Essays in Honour of Kenneth Muir*. New York: Cambridge University Press, 1980.

Gross, Kenneth. *Shakespeare's Noise*. Chicago: University of Chicago Press, 2001.

Hope, Jonathan. *Shakespeare's Grammar*. London: Arden Shakespeare, 2003.

Houston, John Porter. *Shakespearean Sentences: A Study in Style and Syntax*. Baton Rouge: Louisiana State University Press, 1988.

Hussey, S. S. *The Literary Language of Shakespeare*. 2nd ed. New York: Longman, 1992.

Kökeritz, Helge. *Shakespeare's Pronunciation*. New Haven: Yale University Press, 1953.

Mahood, M. M. *Shakespeare's Wordplay*. London: Methuen, 1957.

McDonald, Russ. *Shakespeare and the Arts of Language*. New York: Oxford University Press, 2001.

———. *Shakespeare's Late Style*. New York: Cambridge University Press, 2006.

Miriam Joseph, Sister. *Shakespeare's Use of the Arts of Language*. New York: Columbia University Press, 1947.

Palfrey, Simon. *Late Shakespeare: A New World of Words*. Oxford: Clarendon, 1997.

Parker, Patricia. *Literary Fat Ladies: Rhetoric, Gender, Property*. New York: Methuen, 1987.

———. *Shakespeare from the Margins: Language, Culture, Context*. Chicago: University of Chicago Press, 1996.

Partridge, Eric. *Shakespeare's Bawdy: A Literary & Psychological Essay and a Comprehensive Glossary*. 3rd ed. New York: Routledge, 1991.

Trousdale, Marion. *Shakespeare and the Rhetoricians*. Chapel Hill: University of North Carolina Press, 1982.

Vickers, Brian. *The Artistry of Shakespeare's Prose*. London: Methuen, 1968.

———. "Shakespeare's Use of Rhetoric." *A New Companion to Shakespeare Studies*. Ed. Kenneth Muir and S. Schoenbaum. Cambridge, Eng.: Cambridge University Press, 1971. 83–98.

Wright, George T. *Shakespeare's Metrical Art*. Berkeley: University of California Press, 1988.

Young, David. *The Action to the Word: Structure and Style in Shakespearean Tragedy*. New Haven: Yale University Press, 1990.

Psychoanalytic Criticism

Adelman, Janet. *Suffocating Mothers: Fantasies of Maternal Origin in Shakespeare's Plays, Hamlet to The Tempest*. New York: Routledge, 1992.

Armstrong, Philip. *Shakespeare in Psychoanalysis*. New York: Routledge, 2001.

Berger, Harry Jr. *Making Trifles of Terrors: Redistributing Complicities in Shakespeare*. Stanford: Stanford University Press, 1997.

Charnes, Linda. *Notorious Identity: Materializing the Subject in Shakespeare*. Cambridge, Mass.: Harvard University Press, 1993.

Enterline, Lynn. *The Rhetoric of the Body from Ovid to Shakespeare*. Cambridge, Eng.: Cambridge University Press, 2000.

Fineman, Joel. *Shakespeare's Perjured Eye: The Invention of Poetic Subjectivity in the Sonnets*. Berkeley: University of California Press, 1986.

Freedman, Barbara. *Staging the Gaze: Postmodernism, Psychoanalysis, and Shakespearean Comedy*. Ithaca, N.Y.: Cornell University Press, 1991.

Garber, Marjorie. *Coming of Age in Shakespeare*. New York: Methuen, 1981.

———. *Shakespeare's Ghost Writers: Literature as Uncanny Causality*. New York: Methuen, 1987.

Girard, René. *A Theater of Envy: William Shakespeare*. New York: Oxford University Press, 1991.

Holland, Norman N. *Psychoanalysis and Shakespeare*. New York: Octagon, 1966.

Lupton, Julia Reinhard, and Kenneth Reinhard. *After Oedipus: Shakespeare in Psychoanalysis*. Ithaca, N.Y.: Cornell University Press, 1993.

Marshall, Cynthia. *The Shattering of the Self: Violence, Subjectivity, and Early Modern Texts*. Baltimore: Johns Hopkins University Press, 2002.

Mazzio, Carla, and Douglas Trevor, eds. *Historicism, Psychoanalysis, and Early Modern Culture*. New York: Routledge, 2000.

Pye, Christopher. *The Regal Phantasm: Shakespeare and the Politics of Spectacle*. New York: Routledge, 1990.

———. *The Vanishing: Shakespeare, the Subject, and Early Modern Culture*. Durham, N.C.: Duke University Press, 2000.

Schwartz, Murray M., and Coppélia Kahn, eds. *Representing Shakespeare: New Psychoanalytic Essays*. Baltimore: Johns Hopkins University Press, 1982.

Skura, Meredith Anne. *The Literary Use of the Psychoanalytic Process*. New Haven: Yale University Press, 1981.

———. *Shakespeare the Actor and the Purposes of Playing*. Chicago: University of Chicago Press, 1993.

Wheeler, Richard P. *Shakespeare's Development and the Problem Comedies: Turn and Counter-Turn*. Berkeley: University of California Press, 1981.

Zimmerman, Susan, ed. *Erotic Politics: Desire on the Renaissance Stage*. New York: Routledge, 1992.

Feminism, Gender Studies, and Queer Studies

Bamber, Linda. *Comic Women, Tragic Men: A Study of Gender and Genre in Shakespeare*. Stanford: Stanford University Press, 1982.

Barker, Deborah, and Ivo Kamps, eds. *Shakespeare and Gender: A History*. New York: Verso, 1995.

Boose, Lynda E. "The Father and the Bride in Shakespeare." *PMLA* 97 (1982): 325–47.

Callaghan, Dympna. *Shakespeare Without Women: Representing Gender and Race on the Renaissance Stage*. New York: Routledge, 2000.

————. *Women and Gender in Renaissance Tragedy: A Study of* King Lear, Othello, The Duchess of Malfi, *and* The White Devil. Atlantic Highlands, N.J.: Humanities Press International, 1989.

Chedgzoy, Kate, ed. *Shakespeare, Feminism and Gender.* Houndmills, Basingstoke: Palgrave Macmillan, 2001.

Dash, Irene G. *Wooing, Wedding, and Power: Women in Shakespeare's Plays.* New York: Columbia University Press, 1981.

DiGangi, Mario. *The Homoerotics of Early Modern Drama.* New York: Cambridge University Press, 1997.

Dusinberre, Juliet. *Shakespeare and the Nature of Women.* 3rd ed. New York: Palgrave Macmillan, 2003.

Erickson, Peter. *Patriarchal Structures in Shakespeare's Drama.* Berkeley: University of California Press, 1985.

French, Marilyn. *Shakespeare's Division of Experience.* New York: Summit Books, 1981.

Garner, Shirley Nelson, and Madelon Sprengnether, eds. *Shakespearean Tragedy and Gender.* Bloomington: Indiana University Press, 1996.

Goldberg, Jonathan. *Sodometries: Renaissance Texts, Modern Sexualities.* Stanford: Stanford University Press, 1992.

Howard, Jean E., and Phyllis Rackin. *Engendering a Nation: A Feminist Account of Shakespeare's English Histories.* New York: Routledge, 1997.

Jardine, Lisa. *Still Harping on Daughters: Women and Drama in the Age of Shakespeare.* 2nd ed. New York: Columbia University Press, 1989.

Kahn, Coppèlia. *Man's Estate: Masculine Identity in Shakespeare.* Berkeley: University of California Press, 1981.

————. *Roman Shakespeare: Warriors, Wounds, and Women.* New York: Routledge, 1997.

Korda, Natasha. *Shakespeare's Domestic Economies: Gender and Property in Early Modern England.* Philadelphia: University of Pennsylvania Press, 2002.

Lenz, Carolyn, Ruth Swift, Gayle Greene, and Carol Thomas Neely, eds. *The Woman's Part: Feminist Criticism of Shakespeare.* Urbana: University of Illinois Press, 1980.

Neely, Carol Thomas. *Broken Nuptials in Shakespeare's Plays.* New Haven: Yale University Press, 1985.

————. *Distracted Subjects: Madness and Gender in Shakespeare and Early Modern Culture.* Ithaca, N.Y.: Cornell University Press, 2004.

Newman, Karen. *Fashioning Femininity and English Renaissance Drama.* Chicago: University of Chicago Press, 1991.

Novy, Marianne. *Love's Argument: Gender Relations in Shakespeare.* Chapel Hill: University of North Carolina Press, 1984.

————, ed. *Women's Re-Visions of Shakespeare: On the Responses of Dickinson, Woolf, Rich, H.D., George Eliot, and Others.* Urbana: University of Illinois Press, 1990.

Orgel, Stephen. *Impersonations: The Performance of Gender in Shakespeare's England.* New York: Cambridge University Press, 1996.

Shapiro, Michael. *Gender in Play on the Shakespearean Stage: Boy Heroines and Female Pages.* Ann Arbor: University of Michigan Press, 1994.

Shepherd, Simon. *Amazons and Warrior Women: Varieties of Feminism in Seventeenth Century Drama.* New York: St. Martin's, 1981.

Traub, Valerie. *Desire and Anxiety: Circulations of Sexuality in Shakespearean Drama.* New York: Routledge, 1992.

————. *The Renaissance of Lesbianism in Eary Modern England.* New York: Cambridge University Press, 2002.

Wayne, Valerie, ed. *The Matter of Difference: Materialist Feminist Criticism of Shakespeare.* Ithaca, N.Y.: Cornell University Press, 1991.

Historical Approaches: Materialism, New Historicism, and Cultural Materialism

Archer, John Michael. *Citizen Shakespeare: Freemen and Aliens in the Language of the Plays*. New York: Palgrave Macmillan, 2005.

Arnold, Oliver. *The Third Citizen: Shakespeare's Theater and the Early Modern House of Commons*. Baltimore: Johns Hopkins University Press, 2007.

Belsey, Catherine. *Shakespeare and the Loss of Eden: The Construction of Family Values in Early Modern Culture*. New Brunswick, N.J.: Rutgers University Press, 1999.

Berry, Ralph. *Shakespeare and Social Class*. Atlantic Highlands, N.J.: Humanities Press International, 1988.

Bristol, Michael D. *Shakespeare's America, America's Shakespeare*. New York: Routledge, 1990.

Bruster, Douglas. *Shakespeare and the Question of Culture: Early Modern Literature and the Cultural Turn*. New York: Palgrave Macmillan, 2003.

Cox, John D. *Shakespeare and the Dramaturgy of Power*. Princeton: Princeton University Press, 1989.

Dollimore, Jonathan. *Radical Tragedy: Religion, Ideology, and Power in the Drama of Shakespeare and His Contemporaries*. 3rd ed. New York: Palgrave Macmillan, 2004.

Dollimore, Jonathan, and Alan Sinfield, eds. *Political Shakespeare: Essays in Cultural Materialism*. 2nd ed. Ithaca, N.Y.: Cornell University Press, 1994.

Dubrow, Heather, and Richard Strier, eds. *The Historical Renaissance: New Essays on Tudor and Stuart Literature and Culture*. Chicago: University of Chicago Press, 1988.

Eagleton, Terry. *William Shakespeare*. Malden, Mass.: Blackwell, 1986.

Greenblatt, Stephen. *Hamlet in Purgatory*. Princeton: Princeton University Press, 2001.

———. *Shakespearean Negotiations: The Circulation of Social Energy in Renaissance England*. Berkeley: University of California Press, 1988.

Hadfield, Andrew. *Shakespeare and Republicanism*. New York: Cambridge University Press, 2005.

Hawkes, Terence. *Meaning by Shakespeare*. New York: Routledge, 1992.

———. *That Shakespeherian Rag: Essays on a Critical Process*. New York: Methuen, 1986.

Holderness, Graham, ed. *The Shakespeare Myth*. Manchester: Manchester University Press, 1988.

———, ed. *Shakespeare's History Plays: Richard II to Henry V*. Houndmills, Basingstoke: Palgrave Macmillan, 1992.

Howard, Jean E. *The Stage and Social Struggle in Early Modern England*. New York: Routledge, 1994.

Howard, Jean E., and Scott Cutler Shershow, eds. *Marxist Shakespeares*. New York: Routledge, 2001.

Howard, Jean E., and Marion F. O'Connor, eds. *Shakespeare Reproduced: The Text in History and Ideology*. New York: Methuen, 1987.

Jardine, Lisa. *Reading Shakespeare Historically*. New York: Routledge, 1996.

Jordan, Constance. *Shakespeare's Monarchies: Ruler and Subject in the Romances*. Ithaca, N.Y.: Cornell University Press, 1997.

Kamps, Ivo, ed. *Materialist Shakespeare: A History*. New York: Verso, 1995.

Kastan, David Scott. *Shakespeare After Theory*. London: Routledge, 1999.

———. *Shakespeare and the Shapes of Time*. Hanover, N.H.: University Press of New England, 1982.

Mallin, Eric S. *Inscribing the Time: Shakespeare and the End of Elizabethan England*. Berkeley: University of California Press, 1995.

Marcus, Leah S. *Puzzling Shakespeare: Local Reading and Its Discontents*. Berkeley: University of California Press, 1988.

Maus, Katharine Eisaman. *Inwardness and Theater in the English Renaissance*. Chicago: University of Chicago Press, 1995.

Montrose, Louis. *The Purpose of Playing: Shakespeare and the Cultural Politics of the Elizabethan Theatre*. Chicago: University of Chicago Press, 1996.

Mullaney, Steven. *The Place of the Stage: License, Play, and Power in Renaissance England*. Chicago: University of Chicago Press, 1988.

Orgel, Stephen. *The Authentic Shakespear: and Other Problems of the Early Modern Stage*. New York: Routledge, 2002.

Patterson, Annabel. *Shakespeare and the Popular Voice*. Malden, Mass.: Blackwell, 1989.

Rackin, Phyllis. *Stages of History: Shakespeare's English Chronicles*. Ithaca, N.Y.: Cornell University Press, 1990.

Siemon, James R. *Word Against Word: Shakespearean Utterance*. Amherst: University of Massachusetts Press, 2002.

Sinfield, Alan. *Shakespeare, Authority, Sexuality: Unfinished Business in Cultural Materialism*. New York: Routledge, 2006.

Tennenhouse, Leonard. *Power on Display: The Politics of Shakespeare's Genres*. New York: Methuen, 1986.

Weimann, Robert. *Author's Pen and Actor's Voice: Playing and Writing in Shakespeare's Theatre*. Ed. Helen Higbee and William West. New York: Cambridge University Press, 2000.

Wells, Robin Headlam. *Shakespeare, Politics, and the State*. Houndmills, Basingstoke: Palgrave Macmillan, 1986.

Wilson, Richard. *Secret Shakespeare: Studies in Theatre, Religion and Resistance*. Manchester: Manchester University Press, 2004.

———. *Will Power: Essays on Shakespearean Authority*. Detroit: Wayne State University Press, 1993.

Postcolonial Criticism, Race, and Ethnicity

Alexander, Catherine M. S., and Stanley Wells, eds. *Shakespeare and Race*. New York: Cambridge University Press, 2000.

Cartelli, Thomas. *Repositioning Shakespeare: National Formations, Postcolonial Appropriations*. New York: Routledge, 1999.

de Sousa, Geraldo U. *Shakespeare's Cross-Cultural Encounters*. Houndmills, Basingstoke: Palgrave Macmillan, 2002.

Floyd-Wilson, Mary. *English Ethnicity and Race in Early Modern Drama*. New York: Cambridge University Press, 2003.

Hendricks, Margo. " 'Obscured by dreams:' Race, Empire, and Shakespeare's A Midsummer Night's Dream." *Shakespeare Quarterly* 47 (1996): 37–60.

Hulme, Peter. *Colonial Encounters: Europe and the Native Caribbean, 1492–1797*. New York: Methuen, 1986.

Knapp, Jeffrey. *An Empire Nowhere: England, America, and Literature from Utopia to The Tempest*. Berkeley: University of California Press, 1992.

Loomba, Ania. *Gender, Race, Renaissance Drama*. Manchester: Manchester University Press, 1989.

Loomba, Ania, and Martin Orkin, eds. *Post-colonial Shakespeares*. New York: Routledge, 1998.

Maley, Willy. *Nation, State, and Empire in English Renaissance Literature: Shakespeare to Milton*. New York: Palgrave Macmillan, 2003.

Vaughan, Virginia Mason. *Performing Blackness on English Stages, 1500–1800*. New York: Cambridge University Press, 2005.

Other Philosophical and Theoretical Approaches

Booth, Stephen. *King Lear, Macbeth, Indefinition, and Tragedy*. New Haven: Yale University Press, 1983.

Cavell, Stanley. *Disowning Knowledge in Seven Plays of Shakespeare*. Updated ed. New York: Cambridge University Press, 2003.

Engle, Lars. *Shakespearean Pragmatism: Market of His Time*. Chicago: University of Chicago Press, 1993.

Evans, Malcolm. *Signifying Nothing: Truth's True Contents in Shakespeare's Text*. Athens: University of Georgia Press, 1986.

Felperin, Howard. *The Uses of the Canon: Elizabethan Literature and Contemporary Theory*. New York: Oxford University Press, 1990.

Goldberg, Jonathan. *Shakespeare's Hand*. Minneapolis: University of Minnesota Press, 2003.

Grady, Hugh. *The Modernist Shakespeare: Critical Texts in a Material World*. Oxford: Clarendon, 1991.

———. *Shakespeare, Machiavelli, and Montaigne: Power and Subjectivity from Richard II to Hamlet*. Oxford: Oxford University Press, 2002.

Grady, Hugh, and Terence Hawkes, eds. *Presentist Shakespeares*. New York: Routledge, 2006.

Hawkes, Terence. *Shakespeare in the Present*. New York: Routledge, 2002.

Knapp, Robert S. *Shakespeare—The Theater and the Book*. Princeton: Princeton University Press, 1989.

Lukacher, Ned. *Daemonic Figures: Shakespeare and the Question of Conscience*. Ithaca, N.Y.: Cornell University Press, 1994.

Lupton, Julia Reinhard. *Citizen-Saints: Shakespeare and Political Theology*. Chicago: University of Chicago Press, 2005.

Parker, Patricia, and Geoffrey Hartman, eds. *Shakespeare and the Question of Theory*. New York: Methuen, 1985.

Pechter, Edward. *What Was Shakespeare?: Renaissance Plays and Changing Critical Practice*. Ithaca, N.Y.: Cornell University Press, 1995.

Rabkin, Norman. *Shakespeare and the Problem of Meaning*. Chicago: University of Chicago Press, 1981.

Schalkwyk, David. *Speech and Performance in Shakespeare's Sonnets and Plays*. Cambridge, Eng.: Cambridge University Press, 2002.

Textual Criticism and Bibliography

Allen, Michael J. B., and Kenneth Muir, eds. *Shakespeare's Plays in Quarto: A Facsimile Edition of Copies Primarily from the Henry E. Huntington Library*. Berkeley: University of California Press, 1981.

Blayney, Peter W. M. *The First Folio of Shakespeare*. Washington, D.C.: Folger Library Publications, 1991.

———. *The Texts of King Lear and Their Origins*. Vol. 1: *Nicholas Okes and the First Quarto*. New York: Cambridge University Press, 1982.

Bowers, Fredson. *On Editing Shakespeare*. Charlottesville: University Press of Virginia, 1966.

Brooks, Douglas A. *From Playhouse to Printing House: Drama and Authorship in Early Modern England*. New York: Cambridge University Press, 2000.

De Grazia, Margreta. "Homonyms Before and After Lexical Standardization." *Deutsche Shakespeare-Gesellschaft West* (Jahrbuch 1990): 143–56.

———. *Shakespeare Verbatim: The Reproduction of Authenticity and the 1790 Apparatus*. New York: Oxford University Press, 1991.

De Grazia, Margreta, and Peter Stallybrass. "The Materiality of the Shakespearean Text." *Shakespeare Quarterly* 44 (1993): 255–83.

Erne, Lukas, and Margaret Jane Kidnie, eds. *Textual Performances: The Modern Reproduction of Shakespeare's Drama*. New York: Cambridge University Press, 2004.

Franklin, Colin. *Shakespeare Domesticated: The Eighteenth-Century Editions*. Brookfield, Vt.: Gower Publishing Company, 1991.

Hinman, Charlton, ed. *The First Folio of Shakespeare*. 2nd ed. New York: Norton, 1996.

———. *The Printing and Proof-Reading of the First Folio of Shakespeare*. 2 vols. Oxford: Clarendon, 1963.

Honigmann, E. A. J. *The Stability of Shakespeare's Text*. London: E. Arnold, 1965.

Ioppolo, Grace. *Dramatists and Their Manuscripts in the Age of Shakespeare, Jonson, Middleton and Heywood: Authorship, Authority and the Playhouse*. New York: Routledge, 2006.

———. *Revising Shakespeare*. Cambridge, Mass.: Harvard University Press, 1991.

Irace, Kathleen O. *Reforming the "Bad" Quartos: Performance and Provenance of Six Shakespearean First Editions*. Newark: University of Delaware Press, 1994.

Jackson, MacDonald P. *Defining Shakespeare: Pericles as Test Case*. New York: Oxford University Press, 2003.

Kastan, David Scott. *Shakespeare and the Book*. New York: Cambridge University Press, 2001.

Lesser, Zachary. *Renaissance Drama and the Politics of Publication: Readings in the English Book Trade*. New York: Cambridge University Press, 2004.

Maguire, Laurie E. *Shakespearean Suspect Texts: The "Bad" Quartos and Their Contexts*. New York: Cambridge University Press, 1996.

Maguire, Laurie E., and Thomas L. Berger, eds. *Textual Formations and Reformations*. Newark: University of Delaware Press, 1998.

Marcus, Leah S. *Unediting the Renaissance: Shakespeare, Marlowe, Milton*. New York: Routledge, 1996.

McKerrow, Ronald B. *Prolegomena for the Oxford Shakespeare: A Study in Editorial Method*. Oxford: Clarendon, 1939.

McLeod, Randall, ed. *Crisis in Editing: Texts of the English Renaissance*. New York: AMS Press, 1994.

———. "UN*Editing* Shak-speare." *SubStance* 33/34 (1982): 26–55.

——— [as Random Cloud]. "The Psychopathology of Everyday Art." *The Elizabethan Theatre IX*. Ed. G. R. Hibbard. Port Credit, Ontario: P. D. Meany, 1986. 100–68.

Murphy, Andrew. *Shakespeare in Print: A History and Chronology of Shakespeare Publishing*. New York: Cambridge University Press, 2003.

———, ed. *The Renaissance Text: Theory, Editing, Textuality*. Manchester: Manchester University Press, 2000.

Pollard, Alfred W. *Shakespeare's Folios and Quartos: A Study in the Bibliography of Shakespeare's Plays, 1594–1685*. London: Methuen, 1909.

Seary, Peter. *Lewis Theobald and the Editing of Shakespeare*. Oxford: Clarendon, 1990.

Taylor, Gary, and Michael Warren, eds. *The Division of the Kingdoms: Shakespeare's Two Versions of King Lear*. Oxford: Clarendon, 1986.

Urkowitz, Steven. *Shakespeare's Revision of King Lear*. Princeton: Princeton University Press, 1980.

Vickers, Brian. *Shakespeare, Co-Author: A Historical Study of Five Collaborative Plays*. New York: Oxford University Press, 2002.

Walker, Alice. *Textual Problems of the First Folio: Richard III, King Lear, Troilus & Cressida, 2 Henry IV, Hamlet, Othello*. Cambridge, Eng.: Cambridge University Press, 1953.

Wells, Stanley. *Re-Editing Shakespeare for the Modern Reader*. New York: Oxford University Press, 1984.

Wells, Stanley, and Gary Taylor. *Modernizing Shakespeare's Spelling*. Oxford: Clarendon, 1979.

———. *William Shakespeare: A Textual Companion*. Oxford: Clarendon, 1987.

Werstine, Paul. "A Century of 'Bad' Shakespeare Quartos." *Shakespeare Quarterly* 50 (1999): 310–33.

———. "Narratives about Printed Shakespeare Texts: 'Foul Papers' and 'Bad' Quartos." *Shakespeare Quarterly* 41 (1990): 65–86.

Williams, George Walton. *The Craft of Printing and the Publication of Shakespeare's Works.* Washington, D.C.: Folger Shakespeare Library, 1985.

Wilson, J. Dover. *The Manuscript of Shakespeare's "Hamlet" and the Problems of Its Transmission: An Essay in Critical Bibliography.* 2 vols. New York: Macmillan, 1934.

Shakespeare and Performance

Aebischer, Pascale. *Shakespeare's Violated Bodies: Stage and Screen Performance.* New York: Cambridge University Press, 2003.

Aebischer, Pascale, Edward J. Esche, and Nigel Wheale, eds. *Remaking Shakespeare: Performance Across Media, Genres, and Cultures.* New York: Palgrave Macmillan, 2003.

Bartholomeusz, Dennis. *"Macbeth" and the Players.* Cambridge, Eng.: Cambridge University Press, 1969.

Barton, John. *Playing Shakespeare.* London: Methuen, 1984.

Bate, Jonathan, and Russell Jackson, eds. *Shakespeare: An Illustrated Stage History.* New York: Oxford University Press, 1996.

Berger, Harry Jr. *Imaginary Audition: Shakespeare on Stage and Page.* Berkeley: University of California Press, 1989.

Berry, Francis. *The Shakespeare Inset: Word and Picture.* London: Routledge and Kegan Paul, 1965.

Berry, Ralph. *Changing Styles in Shakespeare.* Boston: Allen & Unwin, 1981.

Bevington, David M. *Action Is Eloquence: Shakespeare's Language of Gesture.* Cambridge, Mass.: Harvard University Press, 1984.

———. *This Wide and Universal Theater: Shakespeare in Performance, Then and Now.* Chicago: University of Chicago Press, 2007.

Branam, George Curtis. *Eighteenth-Century Adaptations of Shakespearean Tragedy.* Berkeley: University of California Press, 1956.

Bratton, Jacky, and Julie Hankey, gen. eds. The Shakespeare in Production Series. Cambridge, Eng.: Cambridge University Press, 1996–.

Brennan, Anthony. *Onstage and Offstage Worlds in Shakespeare's Plays.* New York: Routledge, 1989.

———. *Shakespeare's Dramatic Structures.* Boston: Routledge and Kegan Paul, 1986.

Brown, Ivor. *Shakespeare and the Actors.* London: Bodley Head, 1970.

Brown, John Russell. *Shakespeare and the Theatrical Event.* Houndmills, Basingstoke: Palgrave Macmillan, 2002.

———. *Shakespeare's Dramatic Style:* Romeo and Juliet, As You Like It, Julius Caesar, Twelfth Night, Macbeth. London: Heinemann, 1970.

Bulman, James C., ed. *Shakespeare, Theory, and Performance.* New York: Routledge, 1996.

Calderwood, James. *Shakespearean Metadrama: The Argument of the Play in* Titus Andronicus, Love's Labour's Lost, Romeo and Juliet, A Midsummer Night's Dream, *and* Richard II. Minneapolis: University of Minnesota Press, 1971.

Carlisle, Carol Jones. *Shakespeare from the Greenroom: Actors' Criticisms of Four Major Tragedies.* Chapel Hill: University of North Carolina Press, 1969.

Cohn, Ruby. *Modern Shakespeare Offshoots.* Princeton: Princeton University Press, 1976.

Dean, Winton. "Shakespeare in the Opera House." *Shakespeare Survey* 18 (1965): 75–93.

Dobson, Michael. *The Making of the National Poet: Shakespeare, Adaptation and Authorship, 1660–1769.* Oxford: Clarendon, 1992.

————, ed. *Performing Shakespeare's Tragedies Today: The Actor's Perspective.* New York: Cambridge University Press, 2006.

Downer, Alan S. *The Eminent Tragedian William Charles Macready.* Cambridge, Mass.: Harvard University Press, 1966.

Duffin, Ross W. *Shakespeare's Songbook.* New York: Norton, 2004.

Foulkes, Richard, ed. *Shakespeare and the Victorian Stage.* New York: Cambridge University Press, 1986.

Goldman, Michael. *Acting and Action in Shakespearean Tragedy.* Princeton: Princeton University Press, 1985.

Hirsch, James E. *The Structure of Shakespearean Scenes.* New Haven: Yale University Press, 1981.

Hogan, Charles Beecher, ed. *Shakespeare in the Theatre, 1701–1800.* 2 vols. Oxford: Clarendon, 1952–57.

Holland, Peter. *English Shakespeares: Shakespeare on the English Stage in the 1990's.* New York: Cambridge University Press, 1997.

Homan, Sidney, ed. *Shakespeare's "More Than Words Can Witness": Essays on Visual and Nonverbal Enactment in the Plays.* Lewisburg, Pa.: Bucknell University Press, 1980.

————, ed. *When the Theater Turns to Itself: The Aesthetic Metaphor in Shakespeare.* Lewiston, Pa.: Bucknell University Press, 1981.

Hoenselaars, Ton, ed. *Shakespeare's History Plays: Performance, Translation and Adaptation in Britain and Abroad.* Cambridge, Eng.: Cambridge University Press, 2004.

Howard, Jean E. *Shakespeare's Art of Orchestration: Stage Technique and Audience Response.* Urbana: University of Illinois Press, 1984.

Jones, Emrys. *Scenic Form in Shakespeare.* Oxford: Clarendon, 1971.

Kennedy, Dennis. *Looking at Shakespeare: A Visual History of Twentieth-Century Performance.* 2nd ed. New York: Cambridge University Press, 2001.

————, ed. *Foreign Shakespeare: Contemporary Performance.* New York: Cambridge University Press, 1993.

Marshall, Gail, and Adrian Poole, eds. *Victorian Shakespeare.* New York: Palgrave Macmillan, 2003.

McGuire, Philip C. *Speechless Dialect: Shakespeare's Open Silences.* Berkeley: University of California Press, 1985.

McGuire, Philip C., and David A. Samuelson. *Shakespeare: The Theatrical Dimension.* New York: AMS Press, 1979.

Mooney, Michael E. *Shakespeare's Dramatic Transactions.* Durham, N.C.: Duke University Press, 1990.

Mowat, Barbara A. *The Dramaturgy of Shakespeare's Romances.* Athens: University of Georgia Press, 1976.

Odell, George Clinton Densmore. *Shakespeare from Betterton to Irving.* 2 vols. New York: Scribner, 1920.

Parsons, Keith, and Pamela Mason, eds. *Shakespeare in Performance.* London: Salamander, 1995.

Poel, William. *Shakespeare in the Theater.* London: Sidgwick and Jackson, 1913.

Rosenberg, Marvin. *The Masks of King Lear.* Berkeley: University of California Press, 1972.

Rosenberg, Marvin, et al. *Clamorous Voices: Shakespeare's Women Today.* London: Women's Press, 1988.

Rutter, Carol, gen. ed. The Shakespeare in Performance Series. Manchester: Manchester University Press, 1982–.

Shattuck, Charles H. *Shakespeare on the American Stage,* vol. 1: *From the Hallams to Edwin Booth.* Washington, D.C.: Folger Shakespeare Library, 1976.

————. *Shakespeare on the American Stage,* vol. 2: *From Booth and Barrett to Sothern and Marlowe.* Washington, D.C.: Folger Shakespeare Library, 1987.

———. *The Shakespeare Promptbooks: A Descriptive Catalogue*. Urbana: University of Illinois Press, 1965.

Slater, Ann. *Shakespeare, the Director*. Totowa, N.J.: Barnes & Noble Books, 1982.

Smallwood, Robert, ed. *Players of Shakespeare*. 6 vols. New York: Cambridge University Press, 1985–2004.

———, gen. ed. The Shakespeare at Stratford series. London: Arden Shakespeare, 2002– .

Speaight, Robert. *Shakespeare on the Stage: An Illustrated History of Shakespearian Performance*. London: Collins, 1973.

———. *William Poel and the Elizabethan Revival*. Cambridge, Mass.: Harvard University Press, 1954.

Spencer, Hazelton. *Shakespeare Improved: The Restoration Versions in Quarto and On the Stage*. Cambridge, Mass.: Harvard University Press, 1927.

Styan, J. L. *The Shakespeare Revolution: Criticism and Performance in the Twentieth Century*. New York: Cambridge University Press, 1977.

———. *Shakespeare's Stagecraft*. Cambridge, Eng.: Cambridge University Press, 1967.

———. "Sight and Space: The Perception of Shakespeare on Stage and Screen." *Shakespeare, Pattern of Excelling Nature: Shakespeare Criticism in Honor of America's Bicentennial*. Ed. David Bevington and Jay L. Halio. Newark: University of Delaware Press, 1978.

Thompson, Marvin and Ruth, eds. *Shakespeare and the Sense of Performance*. Newark: University of Delaware Press, 1989.

Trewin, J. C. *Shakespeare on the English Stage, 1900–1964*. London: Barrie and Rockliff, 1964.

Wells, Stanley. *Royal Shakespeare: Four Major Productions at Stratford-upon-Avon*. Manchester: Manchester University Press, 1977.

———, ed. *Shakespeare in the Theatre: An Anthology of Criticism*. New York: Oxford University Press, 1997.

Worthen, William B. *Shakespeare and the Authority of Performance*. New York: Cambridge University Press, 1997.

———. *Shakespeare and the Force of Modern Performance*. New York: Cambridge University Press, 2003.

Shakespeare on Film

Ball, Robert Hamilton. *Shakespeare on Silent Film: A Strange Eventful History*. London: Allen & Unwin, 1968.

Burt, Richard, and Lynda E. Boose, eds. *Shakespeare the Movie: Popularizing the Plays on Film, TV, and Video*. New York: Routledge, 1997.

———. *Shakespeare the Movie II: Popularizing the Plays on Film, TV, Video, and DVD*. New York: Routledge, 2003.

Bristol, Michael D. *Big-Time Shakespeare*. New York: Routledge, 1996.

Buchanan, Judith. *Shakespeare on Film*. New York: Pearson Longman, 2005.

Buchman, Lorne Michael. *Still in Movement: Shakespeare on Screen*. New York: Oxford University Press, 1991.

Bulman, J. C., and H. R. Coursen, eds. *Shakespeare on Television: An Anthology of Essays and Reviews*. Hanover, N.H.: University Press of New England, 1988.

Burnett, Mark Thornton, and Ramona Wray, eds. *Shakespeare, Film, Fin de Siècle*. New York: St. Martin's, 2000.

Burt, Richard. *Shakespeare After Mass Media*. New York: Palgrave Macmillan, 2002.

Cartelli, Thomas, and Katherine Rowe, eds. *New Wave Shakespeare on Screen*. Malden, Mass.: Polity Press, 2007.

Crowl, Samuel. *Shakespeare at the Cineplex: The Kenneth Branagh Era*. Athens: Ohio University Press, 2003.

————. *Shakespeare and Film*. New York: Norton, 2008.

Davies, Anthony, and Stanley Wells, eds. *Shakespeare and the Moving Image: The Plays on Film and Television*. New York: Cambridge University Press, 1994.

Donaldson, Peter S. *Shakespearean Films/Shakespearean Directors*. Boston: Unwin Hyman, 1990.

Henderson, Diana E. *Collaborations with the Past: Reshaping Shakespeare Across Time and Media*. Ithaca, N.Y.: Cornell University Press, 2006.

————. *A Concise Companion to Shakespeare on Screen*. Malden, Mass.: Blackwell, 2007.

Hindle, Maurice. *Studying Shakespeare on Film*. New York: Palgrave Macmillan, 2007.

Kliman, Bernice W. *Hamlet: Film, Television, and Audio Performance*. Madison, N.J.: Fairleigh Dickinson University Press, 1988.

Lehmann, Courtney. *Shakespeare Remains: Theater to Film, Early Modern to Postmodern*. Ithaca, N.Y.: Cornell, 2002.

Lehmann, Courtney, and Lisa S. Starks, eds. *Spectacular Shakespeare: Critical Theory and Popular Cinema*. Madison, N.J.: Fairleigh Dickinson University Press, 2002.

Rothwell, Kenneth S. *A History of Shakespeare on Screen: A Century of Film and Television*. 2nd ed. Cambridge, Eng.: Cambridge University Press, 2004.

Glossary

STAGE TERMS

"Above"   The gallery on the upper level of the *frons scenae*. In open-air theaters, such as the Globe, this space contained the lords' rooms. The central section of the gallery was sometimes used by the players for short scenes. Indoor theaters such as Blackfriars featured a curtained alcove for musicians above the stage.

"Aloft"   See *"Above."*

Amphitheater   An open-air theater, such as the Globe.

Arras   See *Curtain.*

Cellerage   See *Trap.*

Chorus   In the works of Shakespeare and other Elizabethan playwrights, a single individual (not, as in Greek tragedy, a group) who speaks before the play (and often before each act), describing events not shown on stage as well as commenting on the action witnessed by the audience.

Curtain   Curtains, or arras (hanging tapestries), covered a part of the *frons scenae,* thus concealing the discovery space, and may also have been draped around the edge of the stage to conceal the open area underneath.

Discovery space   A central opening or alcove concealed behind a curtain in the center of the *frons scenae*. The curtain could be drawn aside to "discover" tableaux such as Portia's caskets, the body of Polonius, or the statue of Hermione. Shakespeare appears to have used this stage device only sparingly.

Doubling   The common practice of having one actor play multiple roles, so that a play with a large cast of characters might be performed by a relatively small company.

Dumb shows   Mimed scenes performed before a play (or before each act), summarizing or foreshadowing the plot. Dumb shows were popular in early Elizabethan drama; although they already seemed old-fashioned in Shakespeare's time, they were employed by writers up to the 1640s.

Epilogue   A brief speech or poem addressed to the audience by an actor after the play. In some cases, as in *2 Henry IV,* the epilogue could be combined with, or could merge into, the jig.

Forestage   The front of the stage, closest to the audience.

Frons scenae   The wall at the back of the stage, behind which lay the players' tiring-house. The *frons scenae* of the Globe featured two doors flanking the central discovery space, with a gallery "above."

Gallery   Covered seating areas surrounding the open yard of the public amphitheaters. There were three levels of galleries at the Globe; admission to these seats cost an extra penny (in addition to the basic admission fee of one penny to the yard), and seating in the higher galleries another penny yet. In indoor theaters such as Blackfriars, where there was no standing room, gallery seating was less expensive than seating in the pit; indeed, seats nearest the stage were the most expensive.

Gatherers   Persons employed by the playing company to take money at the entrances to the theater.

Groundlings   Audience members who paid the minimum price of admission (one penny) to stand in the yard of the open-air theaters; also referred to as "understanders."

Heavens   The canopied roof over the stage in the open-air theaters, protecting the players and their costumes from rain. The "heavens" would be brightly decorated with sun, moon, and stars, and perhaps the signs of the zodiac.

Hut   A structure on the top of the cover over the stage, where stagehands produced the effects of thunder and lightning and operated the machinery by which gods, such as Jupiter in *Cymbeline,* descended through the trapdoor in the "heavens."

Jig   A song-and-dance performance by the clown and other members of the company at the conclusion of a play. These performances were frequently bawdy and were officially banned in 1612.

Lords' rooms   Partitioned sections of the gallery "above," where the most prestigious and expensive seats in the public playhouses were located. These rooms were designed not to provide the best view of the action on the stage below, but to make their privileged occupants conspicuous to the rest of the audience.

Open-air theaters   Unroofed public playhouses in the suburbs of London, such as The Theatre, the Rose, and the Globe.

Part   The character played by an actor. In Shakespeare's theater, actors were given a roll of paper called a "part" containing all of the speeches and all of the cues belonging to their character. The term "role," synonymous with "part," is derived from such rolls of paper.

Patrons   Important nobles and members of the royal family under whose protection the theatrical companies of London operated; players not in the service of patrons were punishable as vagabonds. The companies were referred to as their patrons' "Men" or "Servants." Thus the name of the company to which Shakespeare belonged for most of his career was first the Lord Chamberlain's Men, then was changed to the King's Men in 1603, when James I became their patron.

Pillars   The "heavens" were supported by two tall painted pillars or posts near the front of the stage. These occasionally played a role in stage action, allowing a character to "hide" while remaining in full view of the audience.

Pit   The area in front of the stage in indoor theaters such as Blackfriars, where the most expensive and prestigious bench seating was to be had.

Posts   See *Pillars.*

Proscenium   The space of the transparent "fourth wall," which divides the actors from the orchestra and audience in the standard modern theater. The stages on which Shakespeare's plays were first performed had no proscenium.

Rearstage   The back of the stage, farthest from the audience.

Repertory   The stock of plays a company had ready for performance at a given time. Companies generally performed a different play each day, often more than a dozen plays in a month and more than thirty in the course of the season.

Role See *Part*.

Sharers Senior actors holding shares in a joint-stock theatrical company; they paid for costumes, hired hands, and new plays, and they shared profits and losses equally. Shakespeare was not only a longtime "sharer" of the Lord Chamberlain's Men but, from 1599, a "housekeeper," the holder of a one-eighth share in the Globe playhouse.

Tiring-house The players' dressing (attiring) room, a structure located at the back of the stage and connected to the stage by two or more doors in the *frons scenae*.

Trap A trapdoor near the front of the stage that allowed access to the "cellarage" beneath and was frequently associated with hell's mouth. Another trapdoor in the "heavens" opened for the descent of gods to the stage below.

"Within" The tiring-house, from which offstage sound effects such as shouts, drums, and trumpets were produced.

Yard The central space in open-air theaters such as the Globe, into which the stage projected and in which audience members stood. Admission to the yard in the public theaters cost a penny, the cheapest admission available.

TEXTUAL TERMS

Aside See *Stage direction*.

Autograph Text written in the author's own hand. With the possible exception of a few pages of the collaborative play *Sir Thomas More,* no dramatic works or poems written in Shakespeare's hand are known to survive.

Canonical Of an author, the writings generally accepted as authentic. In the case of Shakespeare's dramatic works, only two plays that are not among the thirty-six plays contained in the First Folio, *Pericles* and *The Two Noble Kinsmen,* have won widespread acceptance into the Shakespearean canon. (This sense of "canonical" should not be confused with the use of "the canon" to denote the entire body of literary works, including but not limited to Shakespeare's, that have traditionally been regarded as fit objects of admiration and study.)

Catchword A word printed below the text at the bottom of a page, matching the first word on the following page. The catchword enabled the printer to keep the pages in their proper sequence. Where the catchword fails to match the word at the top of the next page, there is reason to suspect that something has been lost or misplaced.

Compositor A person employed in a print shop to set type. To speed the printing process, most of Shakespeare's plays were set by more than one compositor. Compositors frequently followed their own standards in spelling and punctuation. They inevitably introduced some errors into the text, often by selecting the wrong piece from the type case or by setting the correct letter upside down.

Conflation A version of a play created by combining readings from more than one substantive edition. Since the early eighteenth century, for example, most versions of *King Lear* and of several other plays by Shakespeare have been conflations of quarto and First Folio texts.

Control text   The text upon which a modern edition is based.

Dramatis personae   A list of the characters appearing in the play. In the First Folio such lists were printed at the end of some but not all of the plays. The editor Nicholas Rowe (1709) first provided lists of dramatis personae for all of Shakespeare's dramatic works.

Exeunt / Exit   See *Stage direction*.

Fair copy   A transcript of the "foul papers" made either by a scribe or by the playwright.

Folio   A bookmaking format in which each large sheet of paper is folded once, making two leaves (four pages front and back). This format produced large volumes, generally handsome and expensive. The First Folio of Shakespeare's plays was printed in 1623.

Foul papers   An author's first completed draft of a play, typically full of blotted-out passages and revisions. None of Shakespeare's foul papers is known to survive.

Licensing   By an order of 1581, new plays could not be performed until they had received a license from the Master of the Revels. A separate license, granted by the Court of High Commission, was required for publication, though in practice plays were often printed without license. From 1610, the Master of the Revels had the authority to license plays for publication as well as for performance.

Manent / Manet   See *Stage direction*.

Memorial reconstruction   The conjectured practice of reconstructing the text of a play from memory. Companies touring in the provinces without access to promptbooks may have resorted to memorial reconstruction. This practice also provides a plausible explanation for the existence of the so-called bad Quartos.

Octavo   A bookmaking format in which each large sheet of paper is folded three times, making eight leaves (sixteen pages front and back). Only one of Shakespeare's plays, *Richard Duke of York* (*3 Henry VI*, 1595), was published in octavo format.

Playbook   See *Promptbook*.

Press variants   Minor textual variations among books of the same edition, resulting from corrections made in the course of printing or from damaged or slipped type.

Promptbook   A manuscript of a play (either foul papers or fair copy) annotated and adapted for performance by the theatrical company. The promptbook incorporated stage directions, notes on properties and special effects, and revisions, sometimes including those required by the Master of the Revels. Promptbooks are usually identifiable by the replacement of characters' names with actors' names.

Quarto   A bookmaking format in which each large sheet of paper is folded twice, making four leaves (eight pages front and back). Quarto volumes were smaller and less expensive than books printed in the folio format.

Scribal copy   A transcript of a play produced by a professional scribe (or "scrivener"). Scribes tended to employ their own preferred spellings and abbreviations and could be responsible for introducing a variety of errors.

Speech prefix (s.p.)   The indication of the identity of the speaker of the following line or lines. Early editions of Shakespeare's plays often use different prefixes at different points to designate the same person. On occasion, the name of the actor who was to play the role appears in place of the name of the character.

Stage direction (s.d.) The part of the text that is not spoken by any character but that indicates actions to be performed onstage. Stage directions in the earliest editions of Shakespeare's plays are sparse and are sometimes grouped together at the beginning of a scene rather than next to the spoken lines they should precede, accompany, or follow. By convention, the most basic stage directions were written in Latin. "Exit" indicates the departure of a single actor from the stage, "exeunt" the departure of more than one. "Manet" indicates that a single actor remains onstage, "manent" that more than one remains. Lines accompanied by the stage direction "aside" are spoken so as not to be heard by the others onstage. This stage direction appeared in some early editions of Shakespeare plays, but other means were also used to indicate such speech (such as placing the words within parentheses), and sometimes no indication was provided.

Stationers' Register The account books of the Company of Stationers (of which all printers were legally required to be members), recording the fees paid for permission to print new works as well as the fines exacted for printing without permission. The Stationers' Register thus provides a valuable if incomplete record of publication in England.

Substantive text The text of an edition based upon access to a manuscript, as opposed to a derivative text based only on an earlier edition.

Variorum editions Comprehensive editions of a work or works in which the various views of previous editors and commentators are compiled.

General Introduction Plague death bill: By permission of the Folger Shakespeare Library • Webbe: By permission of the British Library • Amman: Spencer Collection, The New York Public Library, Astor, Lenox and Tilden Foundation • *Swetnam* title page: By permission of The Huntington Library, San Marino, California • Pope as Antichrist: By permission of the Folger Shakespeare Library • de Heere: The National Museum of Wales • Armada portrait: By kind permission of Marquess of Tavistock and Trustees of the Bedford Estate • Boaistuau: By permission of The Huntington Library, San Marino, California • Mandeville: By permission of the Houghton Library, Harvard University • Funeral procession: Additional Ms. 35324, folio 37v. By permission of the British Library • Gheeraerts: By permission of the Trustees of Dulwich Picture Gallery • van den Broek: Fitzwilliam Museum, University of Cambridge • Swimming: Bodleian Library, University of Oxford, 4° G.17.Art • Panorama of London: By permission of the British Library • Tarleton: Harley 3885, folio 19. By permission of the British Library • Hanging: Pepys Library, Magdalene College, Cambridge • Syphilis victim: By permission of The Huntington Library, San Marino, California • *Spanish Tragedy* title page: By permission of the Folger Shakespeare Library • Stratford-upon-Avon: By permission of City of York Libraries • Cholmondeley sisters: Tate Gallery, London • Alleyn: By permission of the Trustees of Dulwich Picture Library • *If You Know Not Me* title page: By permission of The Huntington Library, San Marino, California • van der Straet: By permission of the Folger Shakespeare Library

The Shakespearean Stage Braun and Hogenburg: 8.Tab.c.4. Bk.1.pl.1. By permission of the British Library • Hollar: Guildhall Library, Corporation of London • Interior of the "new" Globe: Courtesy of The International Shakespeare Globe Center Ltd. Photo: John Tramper • Exterior of the "new" Globe: Courtesy of The International Shakespeare Globe Center Ltd. Photo: Richard Kalina • *Frons scenae* of the "new" Globe: Courtesy of The International Shakespeare Globe Center Ltd. Photo: Richard Kalina • Oliver: The Burghley House Collection. Photograph: Courtauld Institute of Art • Peacham: Reproduced by permission of the Marquess of Bath, Longleat House, Warminster, Wiltshire, Great Britain. Photograph: Courtauld Institute of Art • de Witt: University Library, Utrecht, MS 842, f.132r • Middle Temple Hall: The Benchers of the Honorable Society of the Middle Temple, London • Hollar: Guildhall Library, Corporation of London

The Two Gentlemen of Verona Brathwaite: By permission of the Folger Shakespeare Library • Oliver: Powis Castle Estate (National Trust). Photograph: Courtauld Institute • Whitney: By permission of the Folger Shakespeare Library

The Taming of the Shrew Rowlands: C151e6(1). By permission of the British Library • Brushfield: By permission of the Folger Shakespeare Library • Flötner: Bancroft Library, University of California, Berkeley

The First Part of the Contention (2 Henry VI) Child king: Additional Ms. 48976, Figure 50. By permission of the British Library • Kemp: By permission of the Folger Shakespeare Library • Halle: By permission of the Folger Shakespeare Library

Richard Duke of York (3 Henry VI) Halberd: Reproduced by permission of the Trustees of the Wallace Collection • Edward IV: The Royal Collection. © Her Majesty Queen Elizabeth II • Whitney: By permission of the Folger Shakespeare Library

Titus Andronicus Tempesta: © British Museum • van der Noot: Reproduced by permission of The Huntington Library, San Marino, California

1 Henry VI Holinshed: Reproduced by permission of the Huntington Library, San Marino, California • Henry VI: By courtesy of the National Portrait Gallery, London • Joan of Arc: Giraudon/Art Resource, NY

Richard III Richard III: By courtesy of the National Portrait Gallery, London • Sittow: By courtesy of the National Portrait Gallery, London • Vischer: By permission of the Folger Shakespeare Library

Venus and Adonis Tempesta: © British Museum • Wither: By permission of the Houghton Library, Harvard University • Peacham: By permission of the Folger Shakespeare Library

The Rape of Lucrece Raphael: Private collection • Titian: Fitzwilliam Museum, University of Cambridge • Amman: Rare Books and Manuscripts Division, The New York Public Library, Astor, Lenox and Tilden Foundations

The Reign of King Edward the Third Holinshed: Reproduced by permission of the Huntington Library, San Marino, California

The Comedy of Errors Merchant: Reproduced by permission of The Huntington Library, San Marino, California • Terence: Chapin Library of Rare Books, Williams College • Hollar: By permission of the Folger Shakespeare Library

Love's Labour's Lost Hill: Bodleian Library, University of Oxford, Douce M 399 • Turberville: Reproduced by permission of The Huntington Library, San Marino, California • Quarto extract: Reproduced by permission of The Huntington Library, San Marino, California • Folio extract: *The Norton Facsimile of the First Folio of Shakespeare*

A Midsummer Night's Dream Corrozet: By permission of the Houghton Library, Harvard University • Wither: By permission of the Houghton Library, Harvard University • Magnus: Bodleian Library, University of Oxford, H 4 12 Art

Romeo and Juliet Wither: By permission of the Houghton Library, Harvard University • Speed: By permission of the Folger Shakespeare Library

Richard II Rastell: C.15.e.6. By permission of the British Library • Holbein: Reproduced by courtesy of the Trustees, The National Gallery, London • Tempesta: © British Museum

King John Coronation: Eton College Ms. 123. Reproduced by permission of the Provost and Fellows of Eton College • Tomb: Reproduced by permission of The Huntington Library, San Marino, California

The Merchant of Venice Braun and Hogenburg: 8 Tab.c.4, Bk. 1 pl. 43. By permission of the British Library • Amman: Spencer Collection, The New York Public Library, Astor, Lenox and Tilden Foundation. Photo: Robert D. Rubic

1 Henry IV Owain Glydŵr seal: By permission of The National Museum of Wales • William Blake: Photograph © Museum of Fine Arts, Boston • Peacham: By Permission of the Folger Shakespeare Library

The Merry Wives of Windsor Cuckold: By permission of the Floger Shakespeare Library • Elizabeth I: © British Museum • Skimmington: By permission of the Folger Shakespeare Library

2 Henry IV 1600 Quarto page: By permission of the Folger Shakespeare Library • Cartari: By permission of the Folger Shakespeare Library • Rollos: Spencer Collection, The New York Public Library, Astor, Lenox and Tilden Foundations, Photo: Robert D. Rubic

Much Ado About Nothing Peacham: By permission of the Folger Shakespeare Library • Dekker: By permission of the Folger Shakespeare Library • Wither: By permission of the Houghton Library, Harvard University

Henry V Rastell: G6030. By permission of the British Library • Renatus: By permission of the Houghton Library, Harvard University • Comenius: By permission of the Folger Shakespeare Library

Julius Caesar Plutarch (Caesar and Marc Antony): By permission of the Folger Shakespeare Library • Whitney: By permission of the Folger Shakepeare Library

As You Like It Robin Hood: The Trustees of the National Library of Scotland • Bonasone: All rights reserved. The Metropolitan Museum of Art, Gift of Philip Hofer, 1933 (33.77.5) • Weindler: Bancroft Library, University of California, Berkeley

Hamlet Clerke: By permission of the Houghton Library, Harvard University • von Landshut: © British Museum • Saviolo: By permission of the Folger Shakespeare Library

Twelfth Night Stubbes: By permission of the Folger Shakespeare Library • Amman: Spencer Collection, The New York Public Library, Astor, Lenox and Tilden Foundation

Troilus and Cressida Whitney: By permission of the Folger Shakespeare Library • 1609 Quarto: Reproduced by permission of The Huntington Library, San Marino, California • Chapman title page: By permission of the Folger Shakespeare Library

Sonnets Whitney: By permission of the Folger Shakespeare Library

Sir Thomas Moore From *The Booke of Sir Thomas Moore:* Harley 7368, folio 9. By permission of the British Library

Measure for Measure Whitney: By permission of the Folger Shakespeare Library • Amman: Audio-Visual Archives, Special Collections and Archives, University of Kentucky Libraries

Othello Moorish ambassador: Reproduced by permission of the Shakespeare Institute, University of Birmingham, UK • Knight: By permission of the Folger Shakespeare Library

All's Well That Ends Well Whitney: By permission of the Folger Shakespeare Library • Whitney: By permission of the Folger Shakespeare Library • Flötner: Ashmolean Museum, University of Oxford

Timon of Athens Inigo Jones: Devonshire Collection, Chatsworth. Reproduced by permission of the Duke of Devonshire and the Chatsworth Settlement Trustees. Photo credit: The Courtauld Institute of Art • Wither: By permission of the Houghton Library, Harvard University

King Lear Holinshed: By permission of the Houghton Library, Harvard University • Cypriano: By permission of the Houghton Library, Harvard University • Gheeraerts: Tom Durie by Marcus Gheeraerts the Younger, 1614. The Scottish National Portrait Gallery

Macbeth Firens: Bibliothèque Nationale de France • Holinshed: By permission of the Houghton Library, Harvard University • Witchcraft: Courtesy of the Archbishop of Canterbury and the Trustees of Lambeth Palace Library

Antony and Cleopatra du Choul: By permission of the Folger Shakespeare Library • Topsell: By permission of the Folger Shakespeare Library

Pericles Gower title page: C.34.L.8. By permission of the British Library • Inigo Jones: Devonshire Collection, Chatsworth. Reproduced by permission of the Duke of Devonshire and the Chatsworth Settlement Trustees. Photo credit: The Courtauld Institute of Art

Coriolanus Amman (attack on Colioli; Volumnia entreating Coriolanus): Rare Books and Manuscripts Division, The New York Public Library, Astor, Lenox and Tilden Foundations

The Winter's Tale *Bloudy Mother* title page: By permission of the Houghton Library, Harvard University • Rüff: By permission of the Folger Shakespeare Library • Pedlar: Pepys Library, Magdalene College, Cambridge

Cymbeline van de Passe: © British Museum • Enea Vico: By permission of Abaris Books

The Tempest Magnus: Reproduced by permission of the Huntington Library • Galle: The Burndy Library, Norwalk, Connecticut

All Is True (Henry VIII) Wotton/Bacon letter: Bodleian Library, University of Oxford, Vet. A. 3.f.137 • Cavendish: Bodleian Library, University of Oxford, Douce 363 for. 71R • Metsys: © British Museum

The Two Noble Kinsmen "The Knight's Tale" extract: Division of Rare Books and Manuscript Collections, Cornell University Library • René of Anjou: Österreichische Nationalbibliothek, Vienna • Beauchamp Pageant: Cotton Julius E IV art 6, folio 3. By permission of the British Library.

Early Modern Map Culture Speed: © British Library/HIP/Art Resource, NY • Braun and Hogenberg: HIP/Art Resource, NY. Museum of London, London, Great Britain

Contemporary Documents
First Folio front matter: *The Norton Facsimile of the First Folio of Shakespeare,* 2nd ed. (1996)

Index of Poems: Titles
and First Lines

Index of Songs

Index of Plays

THE HOUSE OF LANCASTER

EDWARD III

John of Gaunt, Duke of Lancaster m. Katherine Swynford
m. Blanche of Lancaster

Henry Bollingbroke
(HENRY IV)

Thomas Beaufort,
Duke of Exeter

Henry Beaufort,
Bishop of Winchester

John Beaufort,
Earl of Somerset

Joan Beaufort m. Ralph Neville,
Earl of Westmoreland

Thomas,
Duke of Clarence

John of Lancaster,
Duke of Bedford

Humphrey,
Duke of Gloucester

John Beaufort,
Duke of Somerset

Edmund Beaufort,
Duke of Somerset

Richard Neville,
Earl of Salisbury

Henry of Monmouth
(HENRY V)
m. Catherine of France

Margaret Beaufort
m. Edmund Tudor,
Earl of Richmond

Henry Beaufort,
Duke of Somerset

John Neville,
Marquess of Montague

Richard Neville,
Earl of Warwick

HENRY VI m. Margaret of Anjou

Henry Tudor, Earl of Richmond (HENRY VII) m. Elizabeth of York

Edward, Prince of Wales m. Anne Neville

THE HOUSE OF YORK

EDWARD III

Lionel, Duke of Clarence

Edmund of Langley, Duke of York

Philippa m. Edmund Mortimer

Edward, Duke of Aumerle

Edmund Mortimer, Earl of March

Anne Mortimer m. Richard, Earl of Cambridge

Richard Plantagenet, Duke of York m. Cicely Neville

Edmund, Earl of Rutland

Edward, Earl of March (EDWARD IV)
m. Elizabeth Woodville

George, Duke of Clarence
m. Isabella Neville

Richard, Duke of Gloucester
(RICHARD III) m. Anne Neville

Edward, Prince of Wales
(EDWARD V)

Richard, Duke of York

Elizabeth m. HENRY VII